# The HAMMOND ALMANAC

## THE ONE-VOLUME ENCYCLOPEDIA OF A MILLION FACTS & RECORDS

## 1983

Martin A. Bacheller,
Editor in Chief

**Hammond Almanac, Inc.**

Maplewood, N.J. 07040

---

*Data for the Index of U.S. Colleges and Universities found on pages 738–759 were supplied by Peterson's Guides, P.O. Box 2123, Princeton, N.J. 08540, a communications company specializing in higher educational data.*

---

*The Hammond Almanac is the successor to The New York Times Encyclopedic Almanac.*

---



---

*Published simultaneously in the United States and Canada*
*Printed in the United States of America*
ISSN 0734-9092

ISBN 0-451-82075-4 (Softcover)
ISBN 0-8437-4032-9 (Hardcover)

---

**HAMMOND ALMANAC, INC.**
Maplewood, New Jersey 07040
HUGH JOHNSON, *President*

# CONTENTS

# NEWS PHOTOS

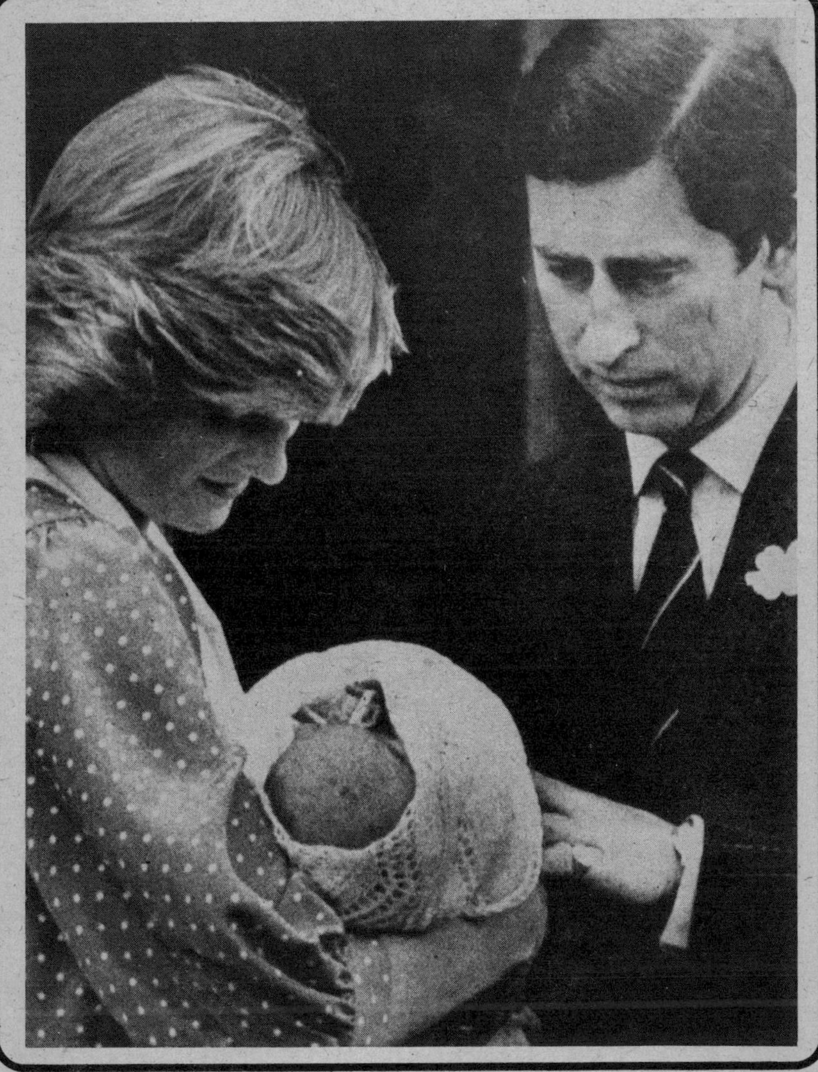

Proud parents-of-the-year, Prince Charles and Princess Diana, leave London Hospital with newborn son, Prince William. (June 22, 1982 – UPI)

Argentine soldiers occupy a Port Stanley building after the April 1982 take-over of the Falkland Islands. The Falklands, 250 miles off Argentina, have been a British colony since 1832.
(April 8, 1982 – UPI)

U.S. Secretary of State Alexander Haig (*left*) meets with Argentine President Leopoldo Galtieri to try to settle the dispute with Great Britain over the Falklands.
(April 10, 1982 – UPI)

The Argentine cruiser, *General Belgrano,* lists heavily before sinking after being attacked by a British submarine. This photo was taken by an Argentine sailor who was rescued from a lifeboat. (May 2, 1982 – UPI)

HMS *Antelope,* a British frigate, explodes in naval action off the East Falklands. A bomb disposal man was killed attempting to defuse an Argentine bomb lodged in the engine room. (May 24, 1982 – UPI)

Captured Argentine soldier is escorted by a British paratrooper after British landings on East Falkland Island. Within 10 days the British forces had recaptured most of the island and were besieging Argentine troops in Port Stanley. (May 23, 1982 – UPI)

Israeli troops lead blindfolded and bound Palestinian guerrillas out of a building after house-to-house fighting near Tyre during operations against the PLO in Lebanon. The Israeli invasion of southern Lebanon began June 6, 1982. (June 10, 1982 – UPI)

Israeli troops on armored personnel carriers move through the Lebanon port city of Sidon after landing by sea. (June 7, 1982 – UPI)

Multiple explosions rock West Beirut as Israeli jet planes strike Palestinian strong points during the fighting in Lebanon. Some of the dark smoke is from exploding caches of ammunition. (July 26, 1982 – Wide World)

Following the assassination of the president of Lebanon, Israel sent [...] West Beirut. Here Israeli troops advance under cover fire from two of their [...]
(Se[...]2 – UPI)

Palestinians mourn for the over 300 men, women and children killed by the Lebanese Christian militiamen in the Shatila and Sabra refugee camps of West Beirut.
(September 23, 1982 – The New York Times/Micha Bar Am)

Pope John Paul II, flanked by Robert Runcie, the Archbishop of Canterbury, and the Archbishop of Sourzeh, of the Russian Orthodox Church, pray at Canterbury Cathedral. This was the first papal visit to Britain.
(May 29, 1982 – UPI)

President François Mitterrand of France addressing the concluding session of the Versailles summit conference. Other Western leaders (*from top left*) are Prime Minister Margaret Thatcher of Britain, President Reagan, Chancellor Helmut Schmidt of Germany and Prime Minister Elliott Trudeau of Canada. (June 5, 1982 – UPI)

Tear gas swirls around demonstrators and police during a street clash in Gdańsk, Poland. The demonstration was part of the continuing protest against the imposition of martial law in Poland. (August 31, 1982 – UPI)

President Hosni Mubarak of Egypt meets with King Fahd, who succeeded to the throne of Saudi Arabia after the death of King Khalid. (June 14, 1982 – UPI)

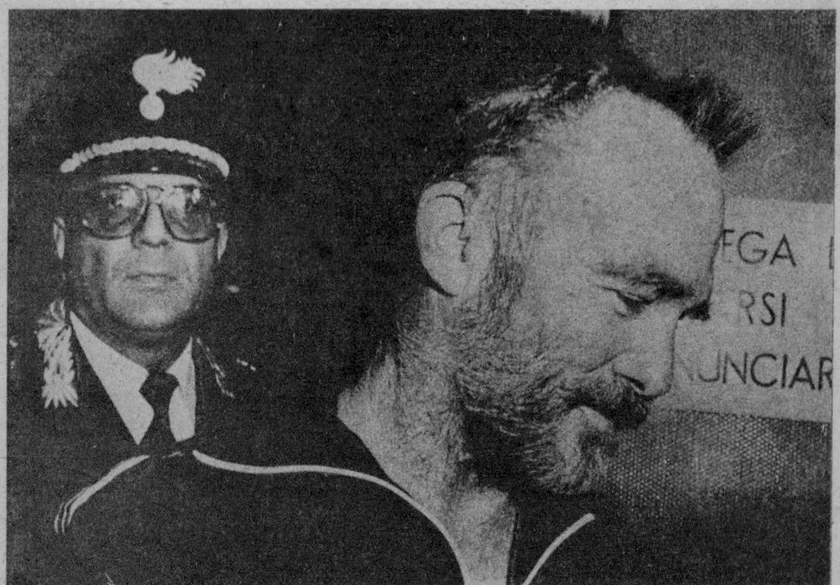

U.S. Brig. General James L. Dozier leaves police headquarters in Padua, Italy, after being rescued from Red Brigades terrorists. (January 28, 1982 – UPI)

Salvadorean soldiers guard a suspect captured crossing fields toward a guerrilla-held zone in northern El Salvador. (January 18, 1982 – UPI)

The new Secretary-General of the United Nations, Javier Pérez de Cuéllar, *center*, holds his first press conference since taking office on the first of the year.
(January 21, 1982 – UN Photo)

Mexicans queuing up for copies of the latest rules on currency exchange; the Mexican peso had to be devalued twice within six months' time. Financially troubled Mexico has an unemployment rate over 50 percent. (August 18, 1982 – UPI)

Anti-nuclear marchers in New York leave the United Nations Plaza for a mammoth rally in Central Park that included close to three-quarters of a million people.
(June 12, 1982 – UPI)

The crowded lines at this Detroit unemployment compensation office reflect the 10 million people in U.S. out of work in 1982 and the particularly high unemployment rates in the automotive industry. (March 12, 1982 – UPI)

Wall Street rewrites its record book in a burst of frenzied trading. In late August 1982 the market surged to a record level; 137.33 million shares were traded and a one-week rise of 81.24 points was set. (August 26, 1982 – NY Stock Exchange)

President Reagan at Camp David, walking with his new Secretary of State, George Shultz. Shultz was selected to succeed Alexander Haig. (June 26, 1982 – UPI)

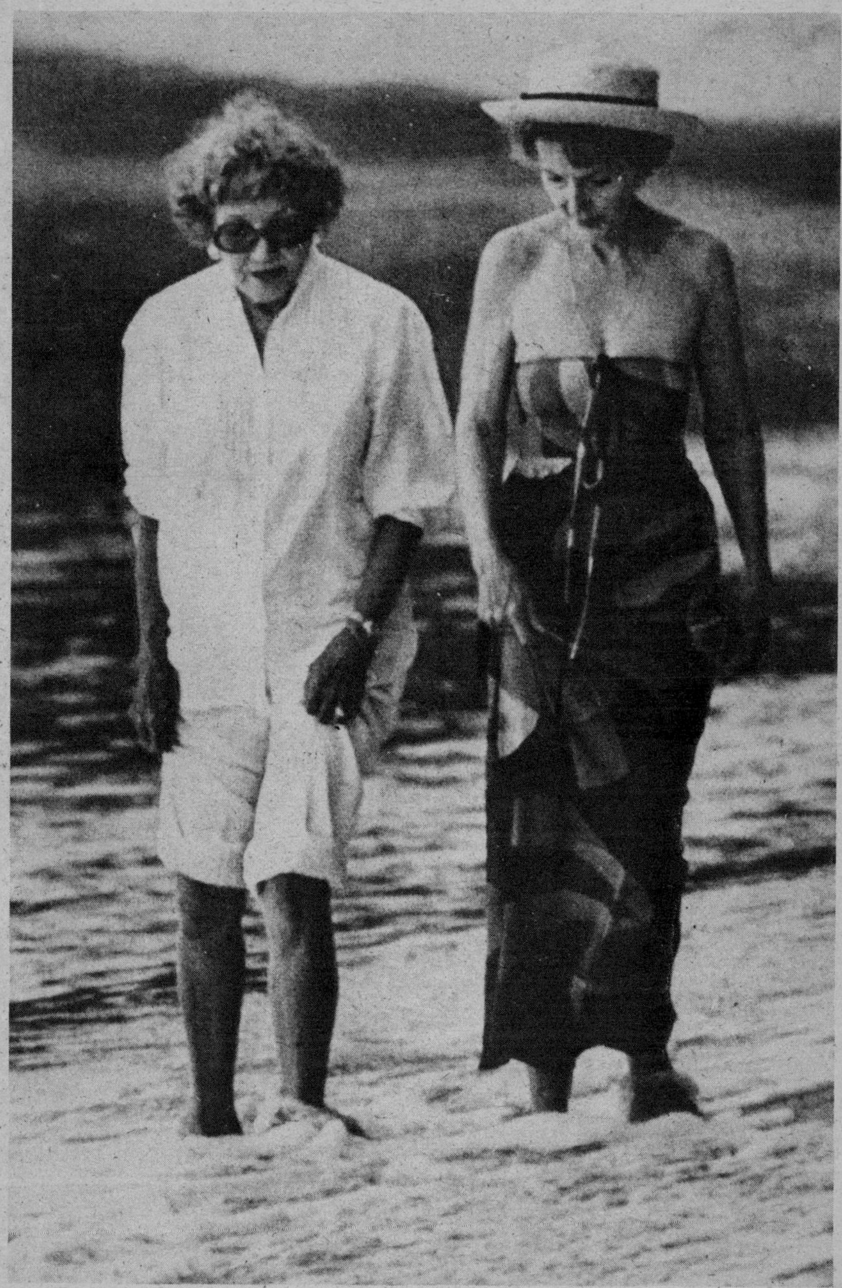

Nancy Reagan, *right*, and actress Claudette Colbert take a walk at surf edge in Barbados where the President and First Lady visited. (April 9, 1982 – UPI)

The USS *Ohio*, America's largest and most powerful nuclear submarine, at commissioning ceremonies in Groton, Connecticut. The *Ohio* is the first of a new class of submarines armed with Trident missiles. (November 12, 1981 – UPI)

Female recruits at Parris Island Marine Base, South Carolina, now receive defensive combat training. The role of women in the military services has increased in recent years.
(March 20, 1981 – UPI)

The U.S. space shuttle, *Columbia*, clears the gantry as the countdown clock ticks off the seconds after ignition. This was the fourth and final test flight of the reusable spacecraft.
(June 27, 1982 – UPI)

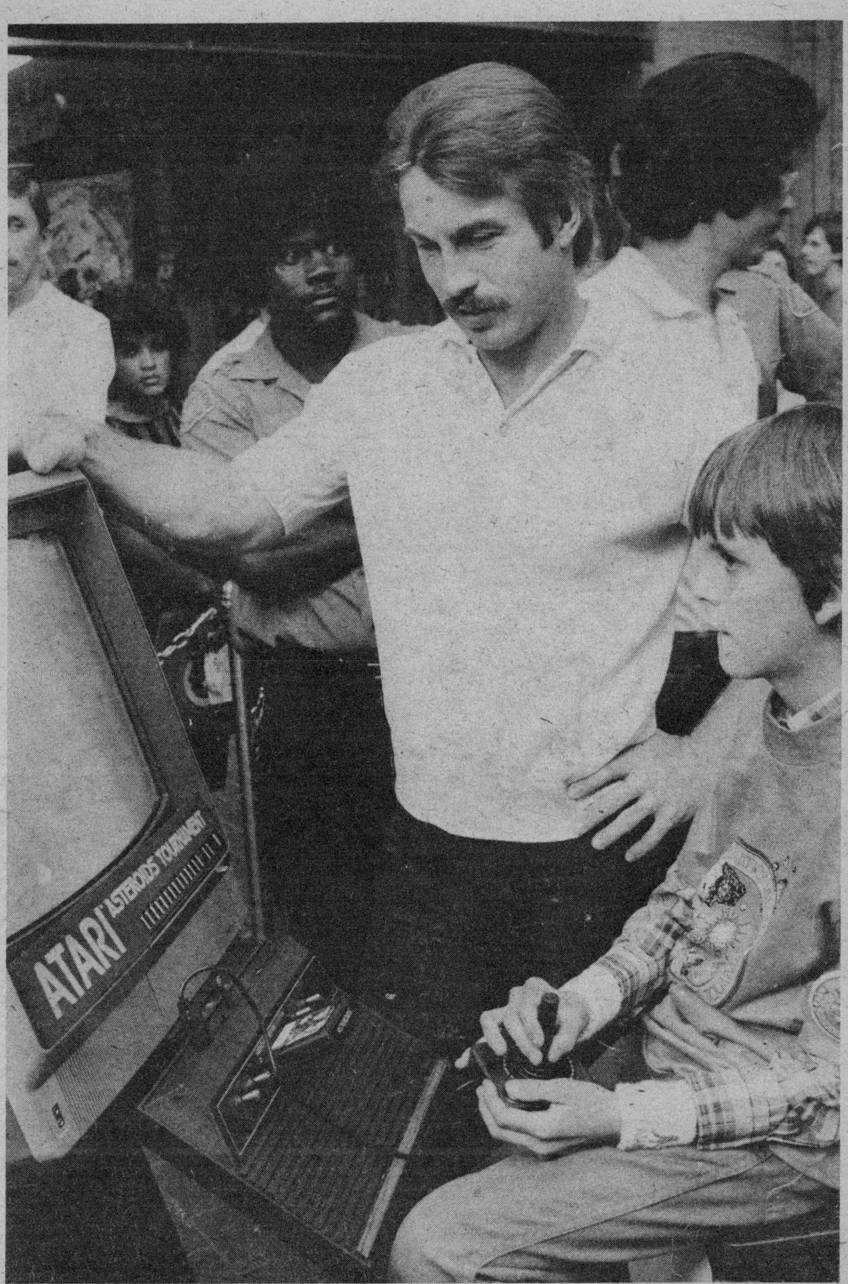


Video games have become a major attraction to old and young Americans. Here, Los Angeles third baseman Ron Cey offers advice to a youngster at a video game tournament in Pasadena. (November 30, 1981 – UPI)

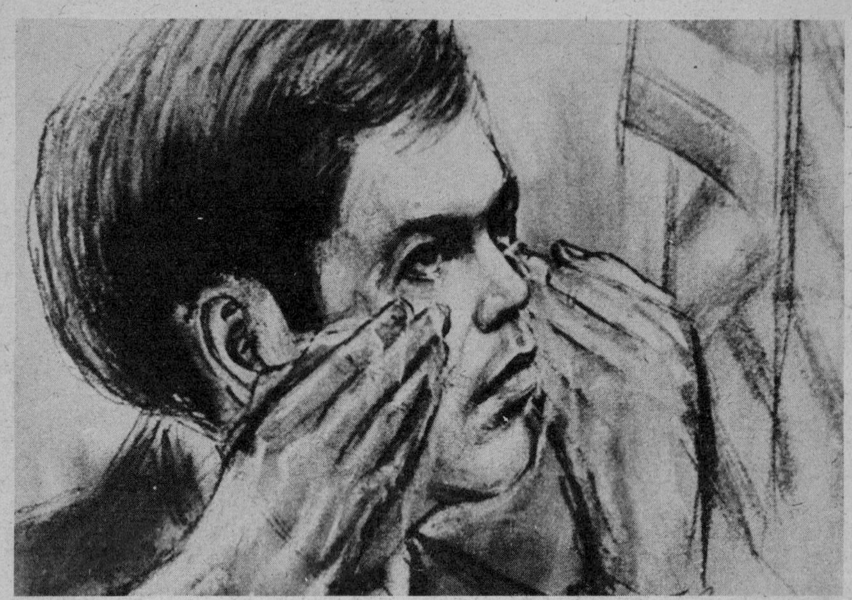

Courtroom drawing shows defendant John W. Hinckley, Jr., wiping tears from his eyes as the jury finds him innocent by reason of insanity in the shooting of President Reagan.
(June 21, 1982 – UPI)

Convicted murderer Frank J. Coppola, shown in this picture taken from a television screen before his execution in Virginia's electric chair, after four years on death row.
(August 10, 1982 – UPI)

Shattered tail section of Air Florida Flight 90 being lifted from the Potomac River after crash which took the lives of 74 of 79 aboard and 4 motorists on a Washington bridge.
(January 14, 1982 – UPI)

Italy's Paolo Rossi raises his hands in jubilation after scoring Italy's first goal in the World Cup final. Italy defeated the top-rated West German team 3-1.

(July 11, 1982 – Wide World)

Heavyweight champion, Larry Holmes, *right*, exchanging blows with challenger, Gerry Cooney. Holmes won the fight in a knockout late in the 13th round.

(June 11, 1982 – Wide World)

Mary Decker Tabb finishes first in the women's mile race at the New York Millrose Games. Mrs. Tabb set three women's distance records in 1982. (February 12, 1982 – UPI)

Tom Watson chips in a birdie 2 at the 17th hole in winning the U.S. Open tournament at Pebble Beach, California. This was Watson's first Open title. (June 20, 1982 – UPI)

Mexico's 5-month-old panda cub and mother make a rare public appearance at the Mexico City Zoo. The panda, named Cancun, is the first panda born outside China.
(January 5, 1982 – UPI)

Film star Sophia Loren gives a press interview in Rome after serving 17 days of a 30-day jail sentence on an old income tax evasion charge.
(July 15, 1982 – UPI)

Henry Fonda with Jane Fonda and Katharine Hepburn in a scene from *On Golden Pond.* Mr. Fonda died of heart disease 4½ months after winning an Oscar for his role.

(August 12, 1982 – UPI)

*Far right:*
Ingrid Bergman, the three-time Academy Award-winning actress, died of cancer in London on her 67th birthday.
(August 29, 1982 – UPI)

*Right:*
Princess Grace of Monaco, the former actress Grace Kelly, died at 52 years from a cerebral hemorrhage after an auto crash on the Riviera.
(September 14, 1982 – UPI)

# NEWS MAPS

NORWEGIAN
SEA
ICELAND
Kare Willoch is appointed Norwegian prime minister following Conservative party gains in Sept. 14, 1981, parliamentary elections.
Mauno Koivisto succeeds Urho Kekkonen as president (Jan. 27, 1982).
SWEDEN
FINLAND
Pope John Paul II visits Britain (May 28 - June 2, 1982).
NORWAY
Helsinki
Oil
Oil
Former Prime Minister Charles Haughey returns to power following elections to the Dail on Feb. 18, 1982.
Stockholm
UNITED KINGDOM
NORTH SEA
No. Ire.
BALTIC SEA
U.S.S.R.
DENMARK
IRELAND
Wojciech Jaruzelski replaces Stanislaw Kania as head of Polish United Workers' party (Oct. 18, 1981). Jaruzelski imposes martial law on Dec. 13, and arrests 5,000 Solidarity members, including Lech Walesa. Pro-Solidarity demonstrations occur during 1982.
Arab terrorists wound Israeli ambassador to Britain (June 3, 1982).
NETHERLANDS
EAST GERMANY
Berlin
London
WEST GERMANY
POLAND
Rhine
A son, William Arthur Philip Louis, is born to Princess Diana and Prince Charles (June 21, 1982).
BELGIUM
LUX.
CZECHOSLOVAKIA
Paris
Versailles
Leaders of seven top industrial nations meet to discuss economic issues (June 4-6, 1982).
SWITZERLAND
AUSTRIA
HUNGARY
FRANCE
ROMANIA
Verona
Padua
Belgrade
Danube
MONACO
YUGOSLAVIA
BLACK SEA
PORTUGAL
BULGARIA
ITALY
Madrid
Lisbon
Rome
ALBANIA
SPAIN
TURKEY
Princess Grace of Monaco dies Sept. 14, 1982, following an auto accident.
GREECE
Athens
MEDITERRANEAN SEA
U.S. Brig. General James L. Dozier is kidnapped in Verona by Red Brigade terrorists (Dec. 17, 1981), and held captive in Padua for 42 days until rescued by crack police force on Jan. 28, 1982.
Spain becomes 16th member of NATO (May 30, 1982).
MALTA
Premier Mehmet Shehu commits suicide (Dec. 1981).
Andreas Papandreou becomes premier following election victory of his PASOK party on Oct. 18, 1981.
MOROCCO
TUNISIA
EGYPT
ALGERIA
LIBYA
EUROPE
European Community members are underlined
© Copyright HAMMOND INCORPORATED, Maplewood, N. J.

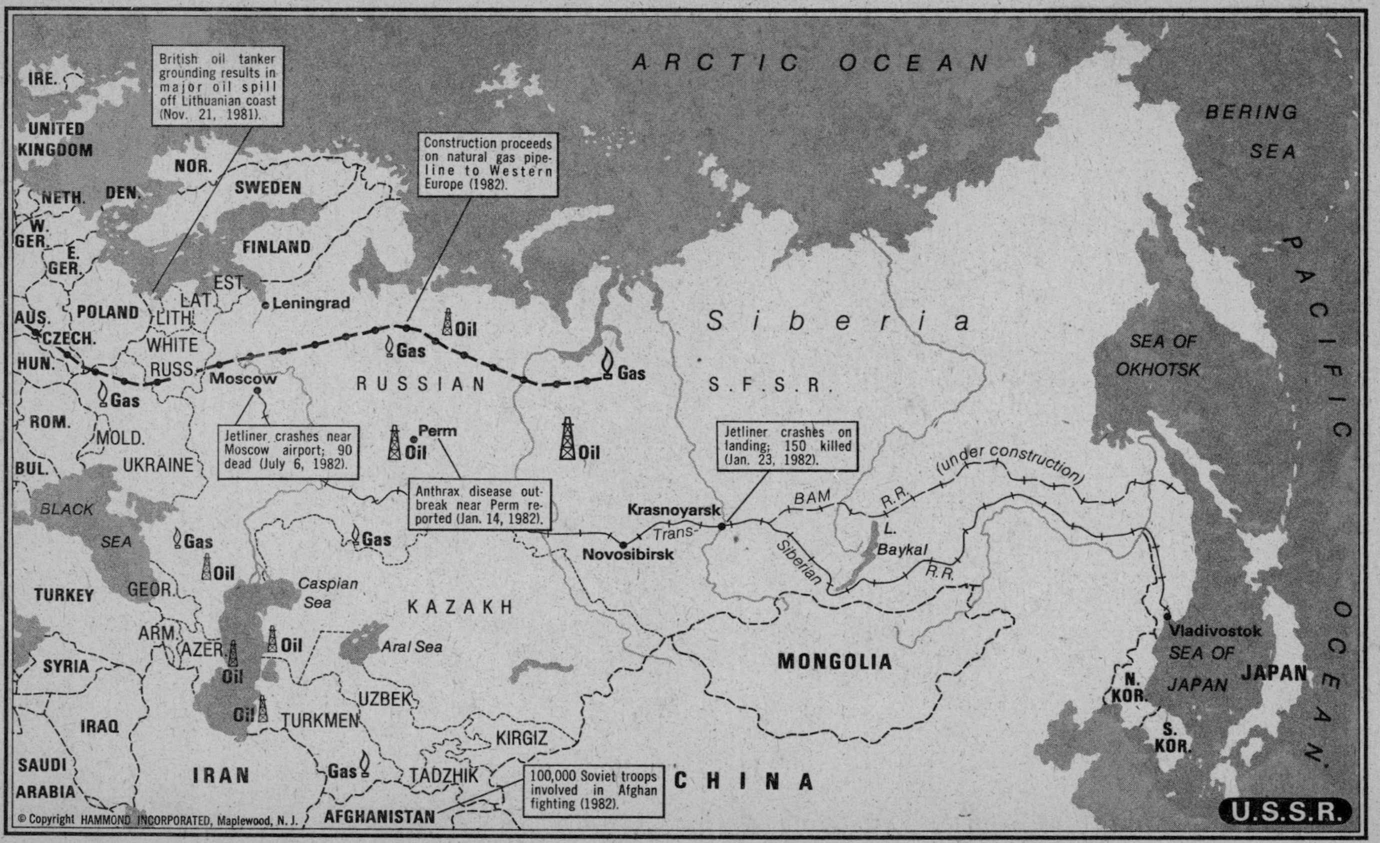
ARCTIC OCEAN
British oil tanker grounding results in major oil spill off Lithuanian coast (Nov. 21, 1981).
Construction proceeds on natural gas pipeline to Western Europe (1982).
BERING SEA
PACIFIC OCEAN
SEA OF OKHOTSK
IRE.
UNITED KINGDOM
NOR.
NETH.
DEN.
SWEDEN
W. GER.
E. GER.
FINLAND
EST.
LAT.
Leningrad
AUS.
POLAND
LITH.
CZECH.
WHITE RUSS.
HUN.
Moscow
Gas
Oil
RUSSIAN
Siberia
S.F.S.R.
ROM.
MOLD.
UKRAINE
BUL.
Jetliner crashes near Moscow airport; 90 dead (July 6, 1982).
Perm
Anthrax disease outbreak near Perm reported (Jan. 14, 1982).
Jetliner crashes on landing; 150 killed (Jan. 23, 1982).
(under construction)
BAM R.R.
Krasnoyarsk
Trans-Siberian R.R.
Novosibirsk
L. Baykal
BLACK SEA
TURKEY
GEOR.
ARM.
AZER.
Caspian Sea
KAZAKH
Aral Sea
SYRIA
IRAQ
UZBEK
TURKMEN
KIRGIZ
TADZHIK
SAUDI ARABIA
IRAN
AFGHANISTAN
100,000 Soviet troops involved in Afghan fighting (1982).
CHINA
MONGOLIA
Vladivostok
SEA OF JAPAN
JAPAN
N. KOR.
S. KOR.
U.S.S.R.

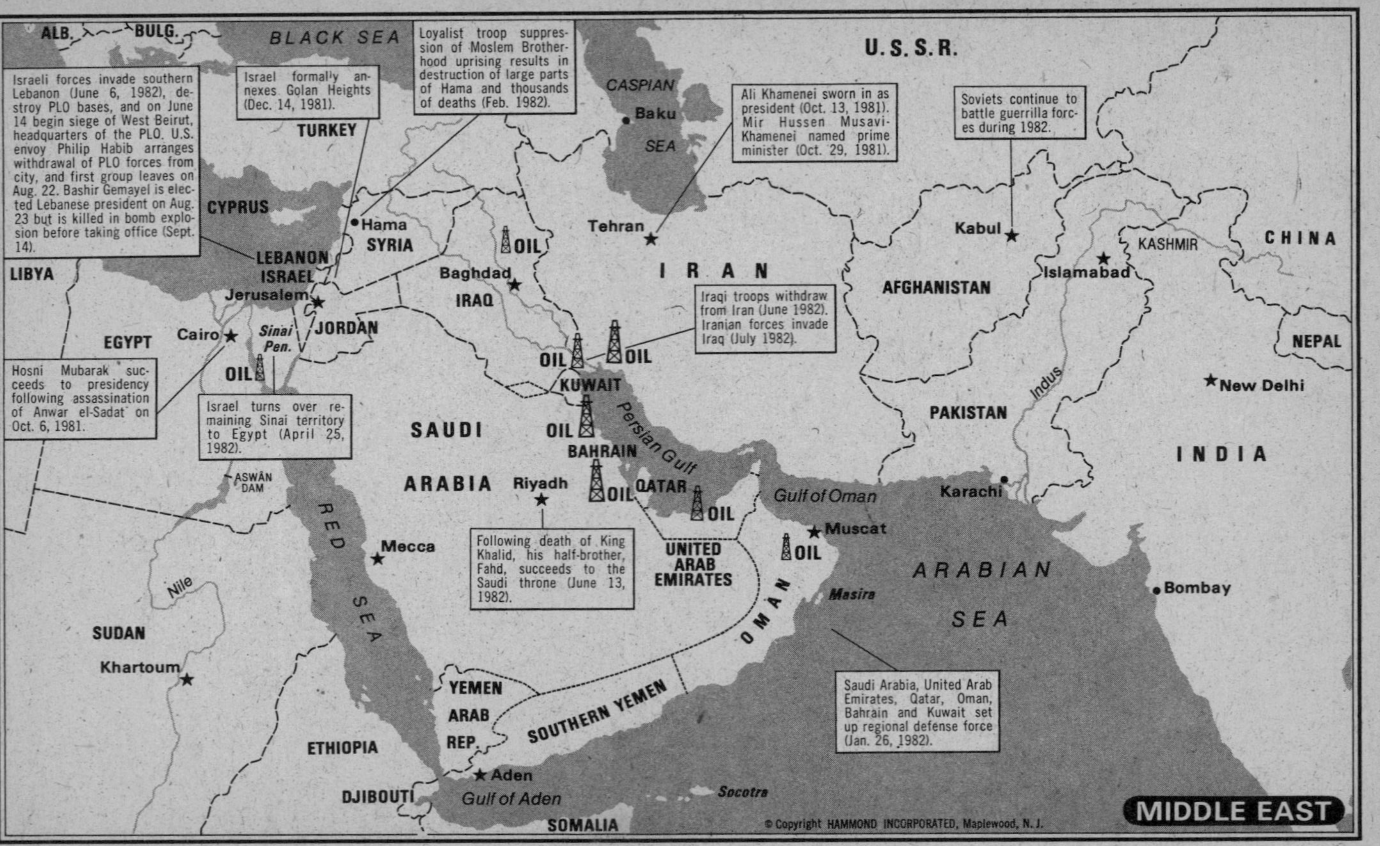
ALB.
BULG.
BLACK SEA
Israeli forces invade southern Lebanon (June 6, 1982), destroy PLO bases, and on June 14 begin siege of West Beirut, headquarters of the PLO. U.S. envoy Philip Habib arranges withdrawal of PLO forces from city, and first group leaves on Aug. 22. Bashir Gemayel is elected Lebanese president on Aug. 23 but is killed in bomb explosion before taking office (Sept. 14).
Israel formally annexes Golan Heights (Dec. 14, 1981).
Loyalist troop suppression of Moslem Brotherhood uprising results in destruction of large parts of Hama and thousands of deaths (Feb. 1982).
CASPIAN
Baku
SEA
U.S.S.R.
Ali Khamenei sworn in as president (Oct. 13, 1981). Mir Hussen Musavi-Khamenei named prime minister (Oct. 29, 1981).
Soviets continue to battle guerrilla forces during 1982.
TURKEY
CYPRUS
Hama
SYRIA
OIL
Tehran
Kabul
CHINA
KASHMIR
LEBANON
ISRAEL
Jerusalem
LIBYA
Baghdad
IRAQ
IRAN
AFGHANISTAN
Islamabad
EGYPT
Cairo
Sinai Pen.
JORDAN
Iraqi troops withdraw from Iran (June 1982). Iranian forces invade Iraq (July 1982).
NEPAL
Hosni Mubarak succeeds to presidency following assassination of Anwar el-Sadat on Oct. 6, 1981.
Israel turns over remaining Sinai territory to Egypt (April 25, 1982).
KUWAIT
Indus
New Delhi
PAKISTAN
SAUDI ARABIA
BAHRAIN
Persian Gulf
INDIA
ASWAN DAM
Riyadh
QATAR
Gulf of Oman
Karachi
Muscat
Mecca
Following death of King Khalid, his half-brother, Fahd, succeeds to the Saudi throne (June 13, 1982).
UNITED ARAB EMIRATES
RED SEA
ARABIAN SEA
Bombay
Nile
Masira
OMAN
SUDAN
Khartoum
YEMEN ARAB REP.
SOUTHERN YEMEN
Saudi Arabia, United Arab Emirates, Qatar, Oman, Bahrain and Kuwait set up regional defense force (Jan. 26, 1982).
ETHIOPIA
Aden
DJIBOUTI
Gulf of Aden
Socotra
SOMALIA
© Copyright HAMMOND INCORPORATED, Maplewood, N.J.
MIDDLE EAST

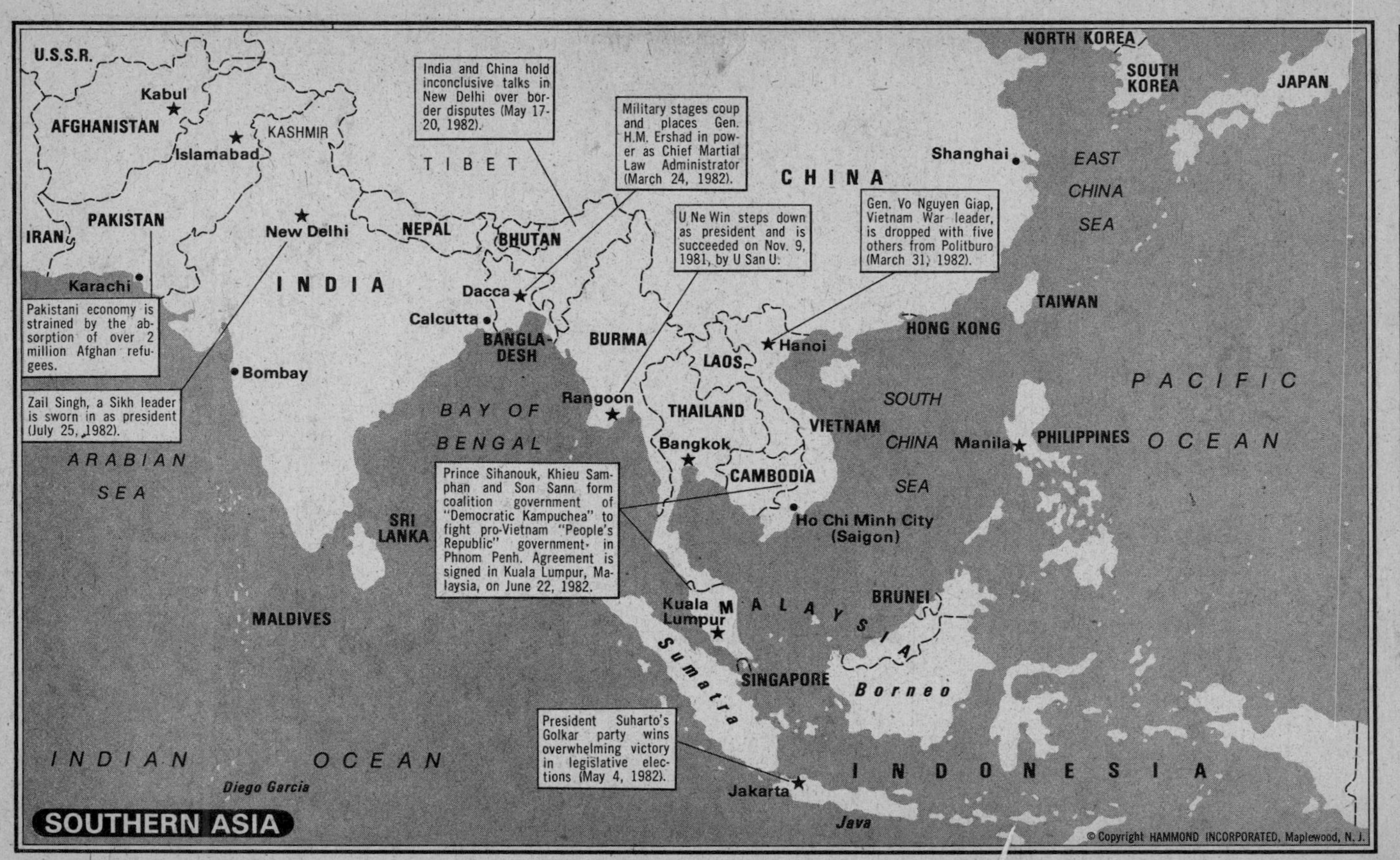
SOUTHERN ASIA
India and China hold inconclusive talks in New Delhi over border disputes (May 17-20, 1982).
Military stages coup and places Gen. H.M. Ershad in power as Chief Martial Law Administrator (March 24, 1982).
U Ne Win steps down as president and is succeeded on Nov. 9, 1981, by U San U.
Gen. Vo Nguyen Giap, Vietnam War leader, is dropped with five others from Politburo (March 31, 1982).
Prince Sihanouk, Khieu Samphan and Son Sann form coalition government of "Democratic Kampuchea" to fight pro-Vietnam "People's Republic" government in Phnom Penh. Agreement is signed in Kuala Lumpur, Malaysia, on June 22, 1982.
President Suharto's Golkar party wins overwhelming victory in legislative elections (May 4, 1982).
Pakistani economy is strained by the absorption of over 2 million Afghan refugees.
Zail Singh, a Sikh leader is sworn in as president (July 25, 1982).
U.S.S.R.
AFGHANISTAN
Kabul
IRAN
PAKISTAN
Islamabad
Karachi
KASHMIR
New Delhi
INDIA
Bombay
NEPAL
BHUTAN
TIBET
CHINA
Shanghai
Dacca
Calcutta
BANGLADESH
BURMA
Rangoon
LAOS
Hanoi
THAILAND
Bangkok
CAMBODIA
VIETNAM
Ho Chi Minh City (Saigon)
HONG KONG
TAIWAN
PHILIPPINES
Manila
NORTH KOREA
SOUTH KOREA
JAPAN
EAST CHINA SEA
SOUTH CHINA SEA
PACIFIC OCEAN
BAY OF BENGAL
ARABIAN SEA
INDIAN OCEAN
SRI LANKA
MALDIVES
Diego Garcia
MALAYSIA
Kuala Lumpur
SINGAPORE
BRUNEI
Borneo
Sumatra
Java
Jakarta
INDONESIA
© Copyright HAMMOND INCORPORATED, Maplewood, N.J.

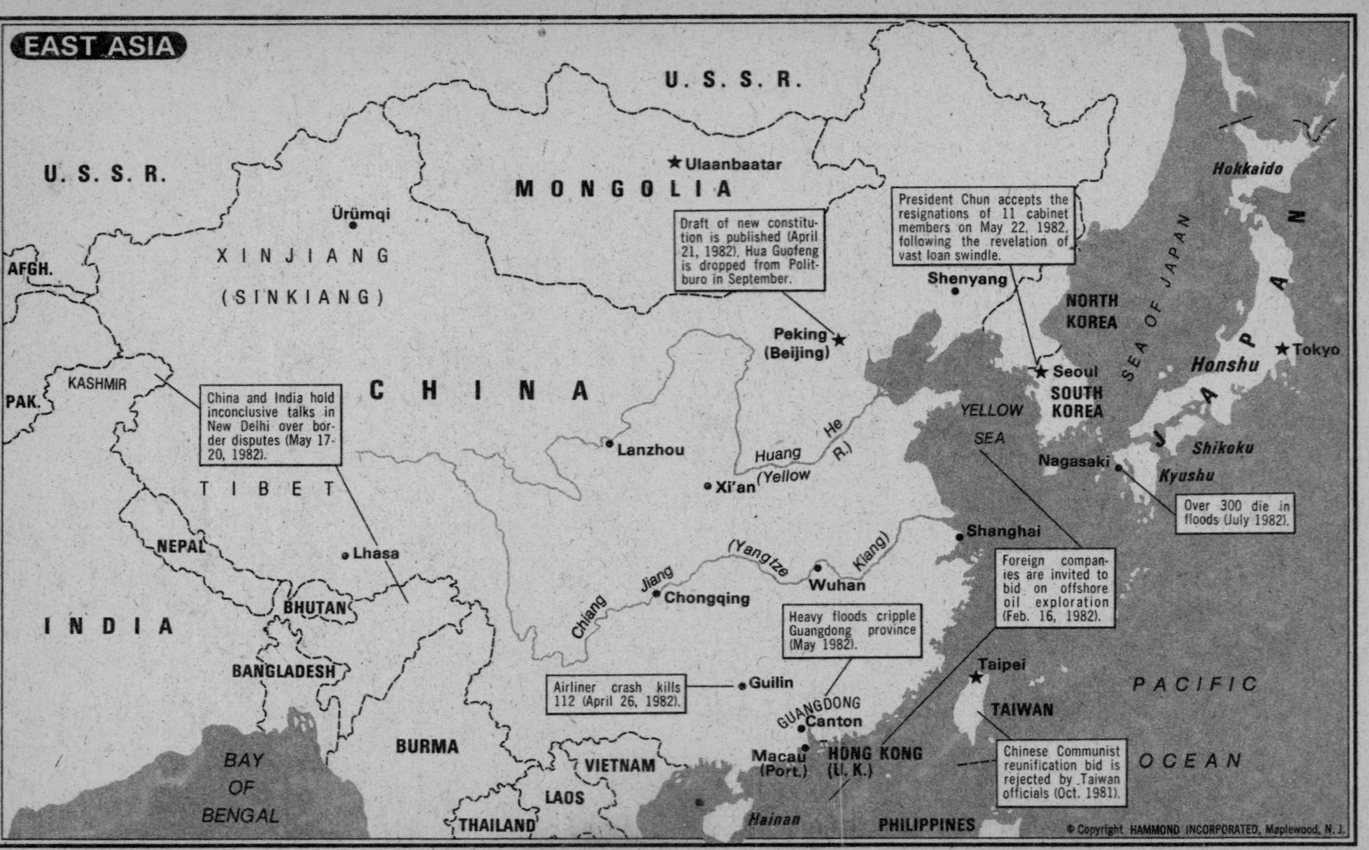
EAST ASIA
U. S. S. R.
U. S. S. R.
MONGOLIA
Ulaanbaatar
CHINA
XINJIANG
(SINKIANG)
Ürümqi
TIBET
Lhasa
Lanzhou
Xi'an
Peking (Beijing)
Shenyang
Shanghai
Wuhan
Chongqing
Guilin
Canton
GUANGDONG
Macau (Port.)
HONG KONG (U.K.)
Hainan
Huang He (Yellow R.)
(Yangtze Kiang)
Chiang Jiang
NORTH KOREA
SOUTH KOREA
Seoul
YELLOW SEA
SEA OF JAPAN
JAPAN
Hokkaido
Honshu
Shikoku
Kyushu
Tokyo
Nagasaki
TAIWAN
Taipei
PHILIPPINES
PACIFIC OCEAN
VIETNAM
LAOS
THAILAND
BURMA
BANGLADESH
BHUTAN
NEPAL
INDIA
KASHMIR
PAK.
AFGH.
BAY OF BENGAL
President Chun accepts the resignations of 11 cabinet members on May 22, 1982, following the revelation of vast loan swindle.
Draft of new constitution is published (April 21, 1982). Hua Guofeng is dropped from Politburo in September.
China and India hold inconclusive talks in New Delhi over border disputes (May 17-20, 1982).
Over 300 die in floods (July 1982).
Foreign companies are invited to bid on offshore oil exploration (Feb. 16, 1982).
Heavy floods cripple Guangdong province (May 1982).
Airliner crash kills 112 (April 26, 1982).
Chinese Communist reunification bid is rejected by Taiwan officials (Oct. 1981).
© Copyright HAMMOND INCORPORATED, Maplewood, N.J.

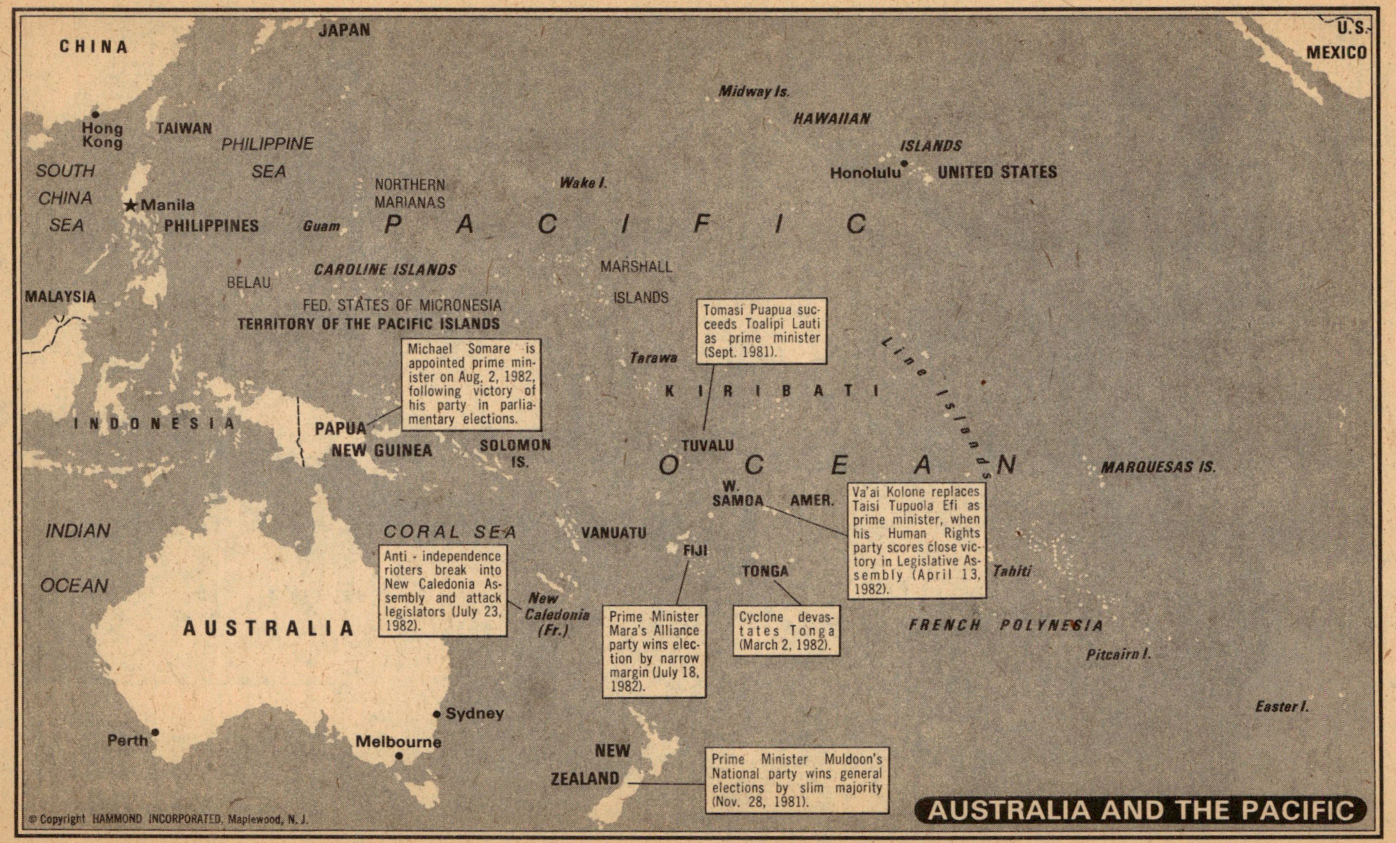
AUSTRALIA AND THE PACIFIC
CHINA
JAPAN
Hong Kong
TAIWAN
PHILIPPINE SEA
SOUTH CHINA SEA
Manila
PHILIPPINES
Guam
NORTHERN MARIANAS
P A C I F I C
O C E A N
Midway Is.
HAWAIIAN ISLANDS
Honolulu
UNITED STATES
Wake I.
U.S.
MEXICO
BELAU
CAROLINE ISLANDS
MARSHALL ISLANDS
MALAYSIA
FED. STATES OF MICRONESIA
TERRITORY OF THE PACIFIC ISLANDS
Michael Somare is appointed prime minister on Aug. 2, 1982, following victory of his party in parliamentary elections.
Tomasi Puapua succeeds Toalipi Lauti as prime minister (Sept. 1981).
Tarawa
K I R I B A T I
Line Islands
INDONESIA
PAPUA NEW GUINEA
SOLOMON IS.
TUVALU
W. SAMOA
AMER.
Va'ai Kolone replaces Taisi Tupuola Efi as prime minister, when his Human Rights party scores close victory in Legislative Assembly (April 13, 1982).
MARQUESAS IS.
INDIAN OCEAN
CORAL SEA
VANUATU
FIJI
TONGA
Tahiti
Anti - independence rioters break into New Caledonia Assembly and attack legislators (July 23, 1982).
New Caledonia (Fr.)
Prime Minister Mara's Alliance party wins election by narrow margin (July 18, 1982).
Cyclone devastates Tonga (March 2, 1982).
FRENCH POLYNESIA
Pitcairn I.
AUSTRALIA
Sydney
Perth
Melbourne
Easter I.
NEW ZEALAND
Prime Minister Muldoon's National party wins general elections by slim majority (Nov. 28, 1981).

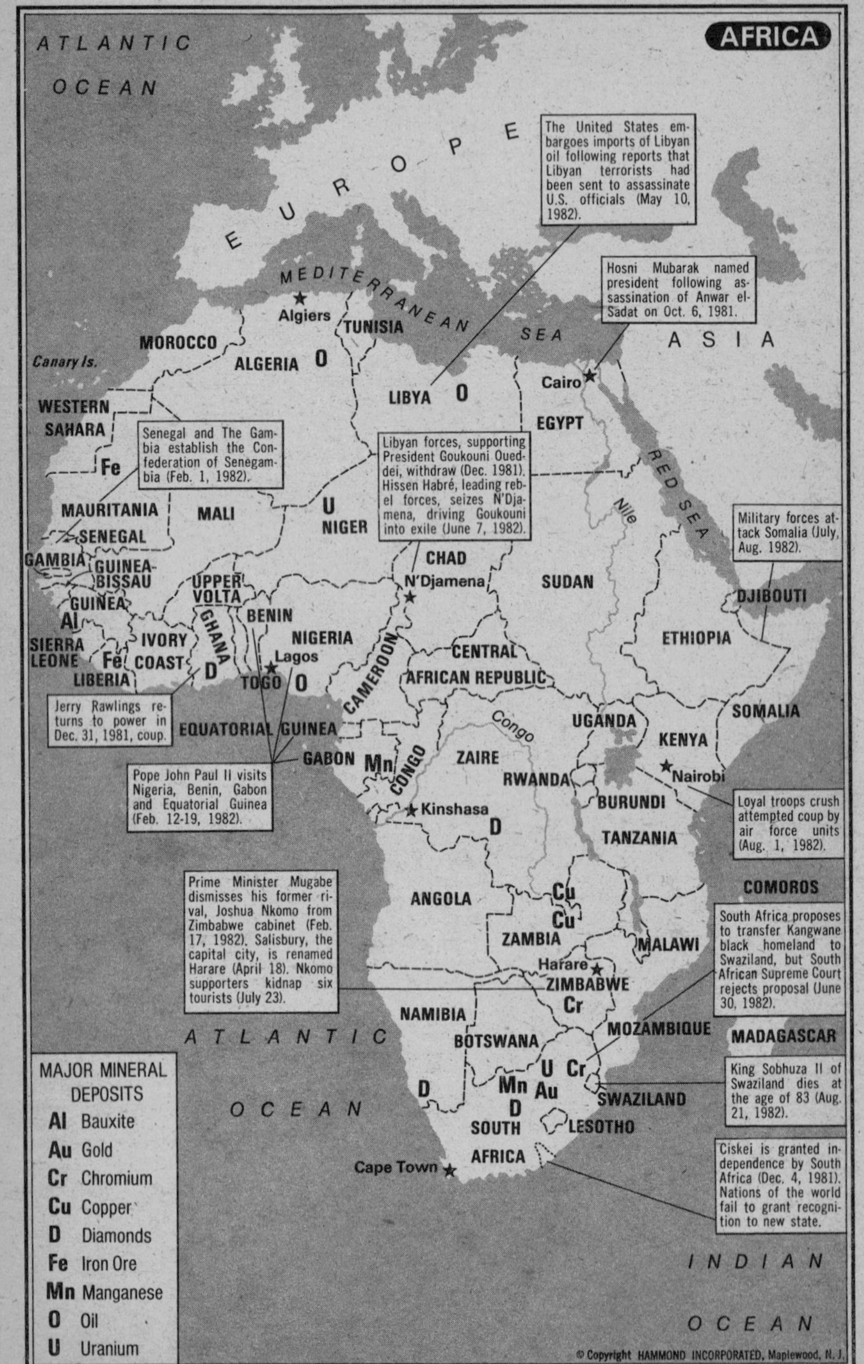
AFRICA
ATLANTIC OCEAN
EUROPE
MEDITERRANEAN SEA
ASIA
RED SEA
Nile
Congo
ATLANTIC OCEAN
INDIAN OCEAN
The United States embargoes imports of Libyan oil following reports that Libyan terrorists had been sent to assassinate U.S. officials (May 10, 1982).
Hosni Mubarak named president following assassination of Anwar el-Sadat on Oct. 6, 1981.
Senegal and The Gambia establish the Confederation of Senegambia (Feb. 1, 1982).
Libyan forces, supporting President Goukouni Oueddei, withdraw (Dec. 1981). Hissen Habré, leading rebel forces, seizes N'Djamena, driving Goukouni into exile (June 7, 1982).
Military forces attack Somalia (July, Aug. 1982).
Jerry Rawlings returns to power in Dec. 31, 1981, coup.
Pope John Paul II visits Nigeria, Benin, Gabon and Equatorial Guinea (Feb. 12-19, 1982).
Loyal troops crush attempted coup by air force units (Aug. 1, 1982).
Prime Minister Mugabe dismisses his former rival, Joshua Nkomo from Zimbabwe cabinet (Feb. 17, 1982). Salisbury, the capital city, is renamed Harare (April 18). Nkomo supporters kidnap six tourists (July 23).
South Africa proposes to transfer Kangwane black homeland to Swaziland, but South African Supreme Court rejects proposal (June 30, 1982).
King Sobhuza II of Swaziland dies at the age of 83 (Aug. 21, 1982).
Ciskei is granted independence by South Africa (Dec. 4, 1981). Nations of the world fail to grant recognition to new state.
Canary Is.
MOROCCO
Algiers
ALGERIA
TUNISIA
LIBYA
Cairo
EGYPT
WESTERN SAHARA
MAURITANIA
MALI
NIGER
CHAD
SUDAN
SENEGAL
GAMBIA
GUINEA-BISSAU
GUINEA
SIERRA LEONE
LIBERIA
IVORY COAST
UPPER VOLTA
GHANA
TOGO
BENIN
NIGERIA
Lagos
N'Djamena
CAMEROON
CENTRAL AFRICAN REPUBLIC
DJIBOUTI
ETHIOPIA
SOMALIA
UGANDA
KENYA
Nairobi
EQUATORIAL GUINEA
GABON
CONGO
ZAIRE
Kinshasa
RWANDA
BURUNDI
TANZANIA
COMOROS
ANGOLA
ZAMBIA
MALAWI
Harare
ZIMBABWE
MOZAMBIQUE
MADAGASCAR
NAMIBIA
BOTSWANA
SWAZILAND
LESOTHO
SOUTH AFRICA
Cape Town
MAJOR MINERAL DEPOSITS
Al Bauxite
Au Gold
Cr Chromium
Cu Copper
D Diamonds
Fe Iron Ore
Mn Manganese
O Oil
U Uranium

UNITED STATES
ALASKA
BEAUFORT SEA
YUKON TERRITORY
Mackenzie R.
NORTHWEST TERRITORIES
Victoria I.
Yellowknife
Baffin Island
GREENLAND
QUEEN ELIZABETH ISLANDS
ARCTIC OCEAN
Ellesmere I.
PACIFIC OCEAN
BRITISH COLUMBIA
ALBERTA
SASKATCH-EWAN
MANITOBA
ONTARIO
QUÉBEC
HUDSON BAY
Labrador
NEWFOUNDLAND
Vancouver
Edmonton
Winnipeg
Montréal
Ottawa
Toronto
NEW BRUNSWICK
P.E.I.
Halifax
NOVA SCOTIA
ST. PIERRE & MIQUELON (Fr.)
ATLANTIC OCEAN
UNITED STATES
Alsands oil sands project canceled (April 30, 1982).
Unemployment reaches postwar high of 11.8% in July 1982.
New Democratic party wins 34 of 57 Assembly seats in November 17, 1981, election.
Final results of April 26, 1982, legislature election show Progressive Conservatives with 55 seats to 9 for the New Democrats.
Queen Elizabeth II proclaims new Canadian constitution in Ottawa on April 17, 1982. Quebec government protests new document.
Strong earthquake rocks western New Brunswick (Jan. 9, 1982).
Progressive Conservatives increase their hold on legislature by winning 44 of 52 seats in April 6, 1982, election.
CANADA
© Copyright HAMMOND INCORPORATED, Maplewood, N. J.

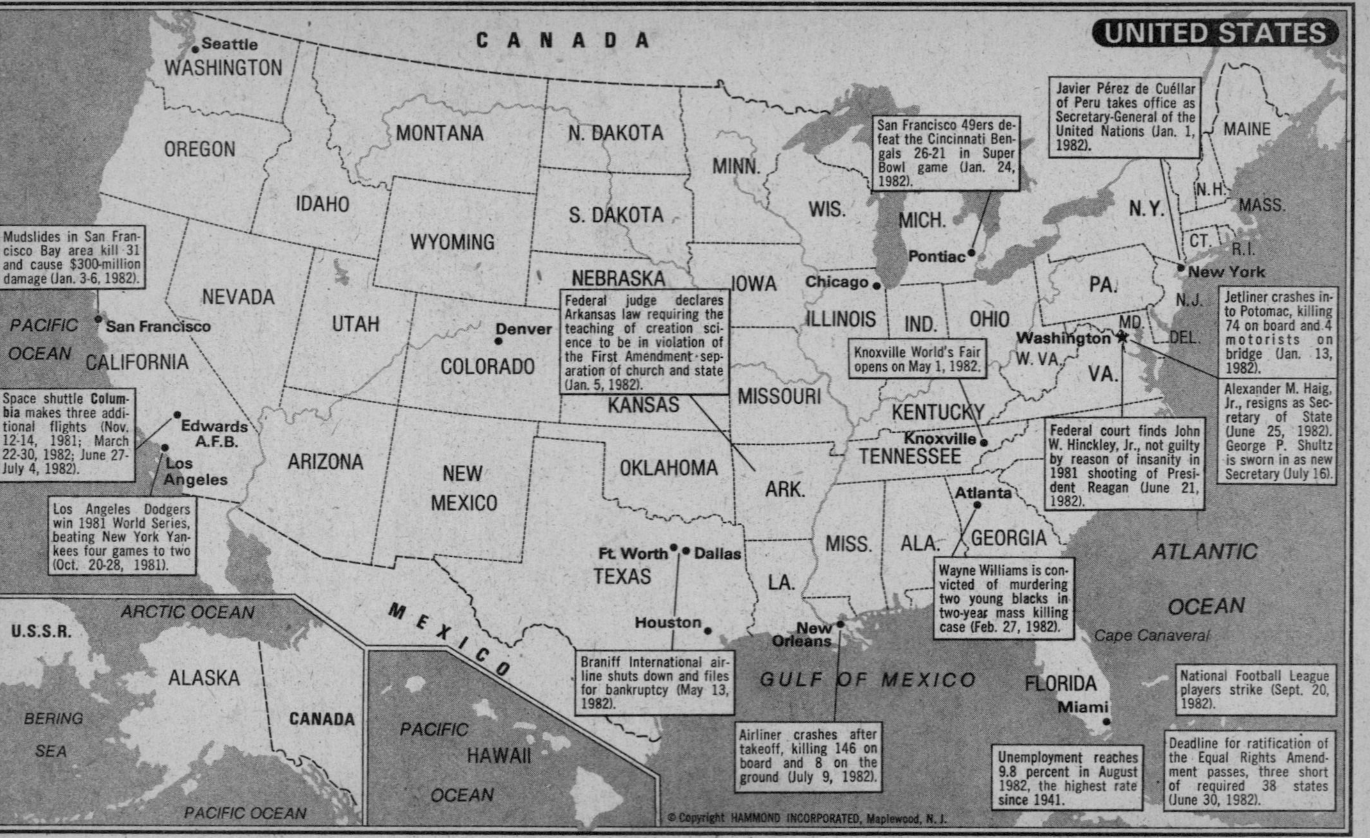
UNITED STATES
CANADA
Javier Pérez de Cuéllar of Peru takes office as Secretary-General of the United Nations (Jan. 1, 1982).
San Francisco 49ers defeat the Cincinnati Bengals 26-21 in Super Bowl game (Jan. 24, 1982).
Mudslides in San Francisco Bay area kill 31 and cause $300-million damage (Jan. 3-6, 1982).
Federal judge declares Arkansas law requiring the teaching of creation science to be in violation of the First Amendment separation of church and state (Jan. 5, 1982).
Jetliner crashes into Potomac, killing 74 on board and 4 motorists on bridge (Jan. 13, 1982).
Alexander M. Haig, Jr., resigns as Secretary of State (June 25, 1982). George P. Shultz is sworn in as new Secretary (July 16).
Knoxville World's Fair opens on May 1, 1982.
Space shuttle Columbia makes three additional flights (Nov. 12-14, 1981; March 22-30, 1982; June 27-July 4, 1982).
Federal court finds John W. Hinckley, Jr., not guilty by reason of insanity in 1981 shooting of President Reagan (June 21, 1982).
Los Angeles Dodgers win 1981 World Series, beating New York Yankees four games to two (Oct. 20-28, 1981).
Wayne Williams is convicted of murdering two young blacks in two-year mass killing case (Feb. 27, 1982).
Braniff International airline shuts down and files for bankruptcy (May 13, 1982).
Airliner crashes after takeoff, killing 146 on board and 8 on the ground (July 9, 1982).
National Football League players strike (Sept. 20, 1982).
Unemployment reaches 9.8 percent in August 1982, the highest rate since 1941.
Deadline for ratification of the Equal Rights Amendment passes, three short of required 38 states (June 30, 1982).
Seattle
WASHINGTON
OREGON
IDAHO
MONTANA
WYOMING
N. DAKOTA
S. DAKOTA
NEBRASKA
MINN.
WIS.
MICH.
Pontiac
IOWA
Chicago
ILLINOIS
IND.
OHIO
PA.
N.Y.
New York
MAINE
N.H.
MASS.
CT.
R.I.
N.J.
MD.
DEL.
Washington
W. VA.
VA.
KENTUCKY
Knoxville
TENNESSEE
MISSOURI
KANSAS
Denver
COLORADO
UTAH
NEVADA
San Francisco
CALIFORNIA
PACIFIC OCEAN
Edwards A.F.B.
Los Angeles
ARIZONA
NEW MEXICO
OKLAHOMA
ARK.
Ft. Worth
Dallas
TEXAS
Houston
LA.
New Orleans
MISS.
ALA.
Atlanta
GEORGIA
FLORIDA
Miami
Cape Canaveral
ATLANTIC OCEAN
GULF OF MEXICO
MEXICO
U.S.S.R.
ARCTIC OCEAN
ALASKA
CANADA
BERING SEA
PACIFIC OCEAN
PACIFIC
HAWAII
OCEAN

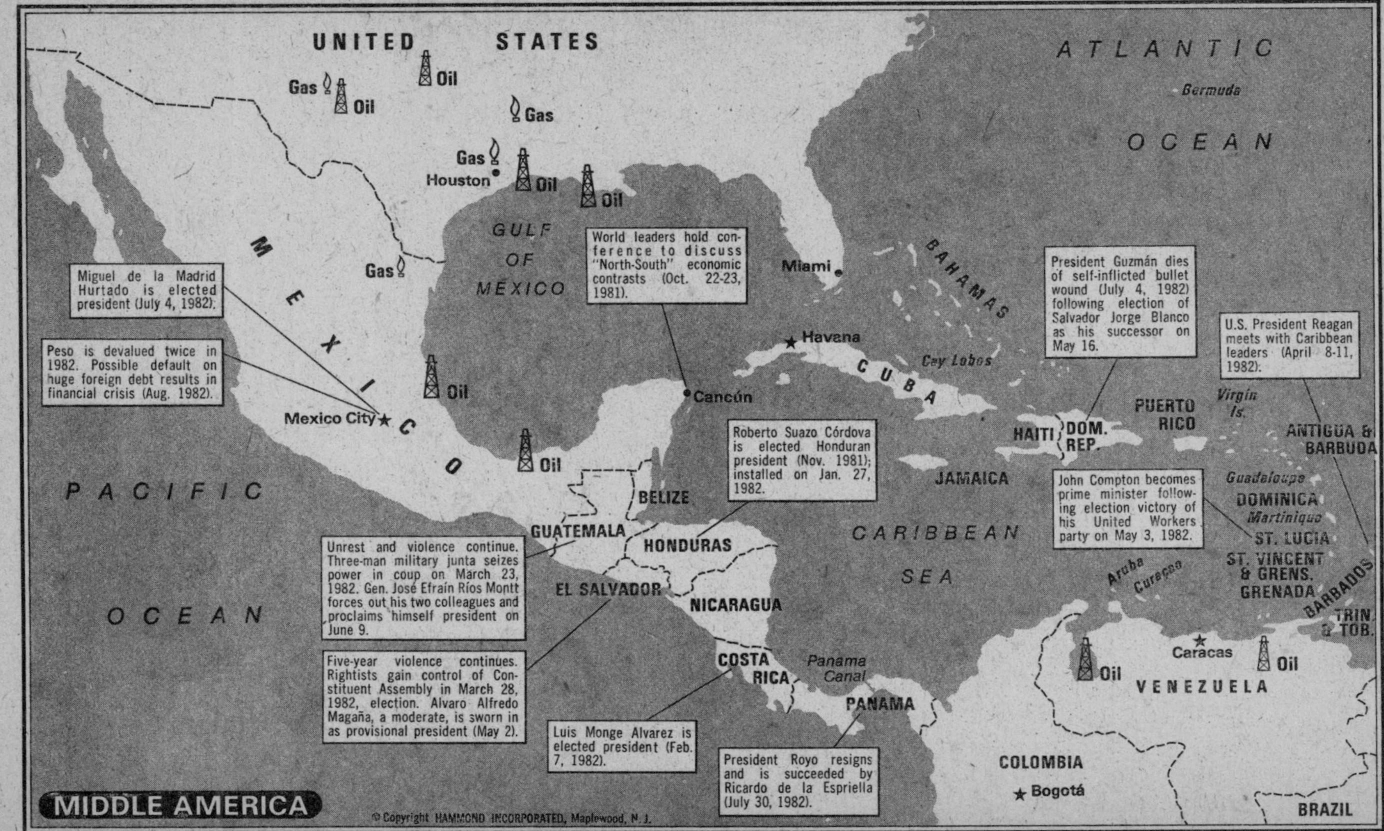
UNITED STATES
Gas
Oil
Houston
GULF OF MEXICO
World leaders hold conference to discuss "North-South" economic contrasts (Oct. 22-23, 1981).
Miami
BAHAMAS
ATLANTIC OCEAN
Bermuda
President Guzmán dies of self-inflicted bullet wound (July 4, 1982) following election of Salvador Jorge Blanco as his successor on May 16.
U.S. President Reagan meets with Caribbean leaders (April 8-11, 1982).
MEXICO
Miguel de la Madrid Hurtado is elected president (July 4, 1982).
Peso is devalued twice in 1982. Possible default on huge foreign debt results in financial crisis (Aug. 1982).
Mexico City
Havana
Cay Lobos
CUBA
Cancún
Virgin Is.
PUERTO RICO
HAITI
DOM. REP.
ANTIGUA & BARBUDA
Roberto Suazo Córdova is elected Honduran president (Nov. 1981); installed on Jan. 27, 1982.
JAMAICA
John Compton becomes prime minister following election victory of his United Workers party on May 3, 1982.
Guadeloupe
DOMINICA
Martinique
ST. LUCIA
ST. VINCENT & GRENS.
GRENADA
BARBADOS
TRIN. & TOB.
PACIFIC OCEAN
BELIZE
GUATEMALA
HONDURAS
CARIBBEAN SEA
Unrest and violence continue. Three-man military junta seizes power in coup on March 23, 1982. Gen. José Efraín Ríos Montt forces out his two colleagues and proclaims himself president on June 9.
EL SALVADOR
NICARAGUA
Aruba
Curaçao
Five-year violence continues. Rightists gain control of Constituent Assembly in March 28, 1982, election. Alvaro Alfredo Magaña, a moderate, is sworn in as provisional president (May 2).
COSTA RICA
Panama Canal
PANAMA
Caracas
VENEZUELA
Luis Monge Alvarez is elected president (Feb. 7, 1982).
President Royo resigns and is succeeded by Ricardo de la Espriella (July 30, 1982).
COLOMBIA
Bogotá
BRAZIL
MIDDLE AMERICA
© Copyright HAMMOND INCORPORATED, Maplewood, N. J.

ATLANTIC OCEAN
CARIBBEAN SEA
WEST INDIES
Belisario Betancur Cuartas, a Conservative, is elected president (May 31, 1982).
Venezuela claims over half of Guyana as 12-year moratorium on claim expires (June 18, 1982).
Prime Minister Henk R. Chin A Sen is deposed by the National Military Council (Feb. 4, 1982). Right-wing coup is put down (March 11-13).
Caracas
VENEZUELA
GUYANA
FRENCH GUIANA
SURINAME
Bogotá
Cali
COLOMBIA
U.S. financier, Daniel K. Ludwig, abandons billion-dollar Jari industrial project in Amazon rain forest area (Jan. 1982).
Seven terrorists release 128 hostages from hijacked plane and are flown to unknown destination (Jan. 27, 1982).
ECUADOR
Amazon
Belém
BRAZIL
PERU
Recife
Lima
Brasília
La Paz
Following the resignation of Celso Torrelio Villa, Gen. Guido Vildoso Calderón succeeds to the presidency (July 21, 1982).
BOLIVIA
PACIFIC OCEAN
PARAGUAY
São Paulo
Rio de Janeiro
CHILE
URUGUAY
Santiago
Buenos Aires
Pope John Paul II visits Argentina (June 11-12, 1982).
ARGENTINA
President Viola is succeeded by Gen. Galtieri (Dec. 11, 1981). Galtieri resigns after Falklands surrender and Gen. Bignone assumes presidency (July 1, 1982).
Argentine armed forces seize the British colony of the Falkland Islands (April 2, 1982). Following fierce naval and air engagements between the contending nations, British army and marine units land on East Falkland (May 22). British retake Stanley, the capital, on June 14 and all Argentine forces surrender.
FALKLAND IS.
ATLANTIC OCEAN
SOUTH AMERICA
© Copyright HAMMOND INCORPORATED, Maplewood, N. J.

# '81/'82 MONTH-BY-MONTH CHRONOLOGY

## OCTOBER 1981

### NATIONAL

1 / On the first day of the new fiscal year, President Ronald W. Reagan vows to adhere to his policy of reducing government expenditures despite a depressed economy.

2 / Pres. Reagan announces that the MX intercontinental missiles will occupy the existing silos now housing Titan and Minuteman missiles. He also plans to proceed with development of the B-1 bomber.

4 / The coffin of Lee Harvey Oswald is exhumed and an autopsy is performed on the remains inside, confirming the body to be that of the man accused of assassinating Pres. John F. Kennedy in 1963.

5 / The House of Representatives approves an open-ended extension of the 1965 Voting Rights Act.

7 / The Federal Reserve Board announces that consumer installment credit in August swelled to a seasonally adjusted $2.86 billion, as compared with $1.95 billion in July.

8 / The Labor Department partially lifts a ban on the manufacture of six classifications of goods in the home, including knitted outerwear, if the worker is elderly, disabled, or forced to care for an invalid in the home.

Pres. Reagan announces the lifting of a 1977 ban on the commercial reprocessing of spent nuclear fuel.

9 / The Bureau of Labor Statistics reports that the government's Producer Price Index for finished goods increased only two-tenths of 1 percent during September, an indication of slowing inflation.

10 / Sources report that the White House and Speaker of the House of Representatives Thomas P. (Tip) O'Neill, Jr., have reached agreement on the composition of a bipartisan panel to study the Social Security System.

11 / Prospects for an expeditious solution to the question of the political future for Micronesia, the U.S.-administered U.N. trust territory, are improved, according to the U.S. negotiator at a series of meetings with the islanders. The possibility of autonomy for the Pacific islands, with military protection from the U.S., appears promising.

12 / Unidentified officials close to the President reveal that the White House fears losing ground for Republicans in Congress if the economic downturn continues into 1982, an election year.

13 / G. William Hoagland, head of the Agriculture Department's Food and Nutrition Service, says Pres. Reagan would like the states to set their own standards for food stamp eligibility rather than abide by uniform regulations set by the federal government.

14 / Invoking executive privilege for the first time, Pres. Reagan refuses to release to the House Energy and Commerce Subcommittee documents relating to the take-over of U.S. energy companies by Canadians.

15 / The Senate approves, in a 95-0 vote, a bill designed to maintain the solvency of the Social Security System through the 1980s and to restore the minimum Social Security benefit that was to be eliminated by legislation passed in July.

16 / Price supports for peanuts and sugar are dropped as a result of the House of Representatives' vote on an amendment to the four-year farm bill now under consideration. The defeat of the continuation measure is seen to reflect the possible end to a firm alliance of farm-state Congress members.

17 / Leaders of the Democratic party, meeting in Baltimore, urge their fellow Democrats to work on alternatives to the Reagan policies rather than wait for the Republican party's programs to fail.

18 / More than 100 labor, political, and social organizations conclude two days of meetings in Detroit and announce plans for demonstrations throughout the country, beginning on April 26, 1982, to protest budget cuts proposed by the Reagan Administration.

19 / The 200th anniversary of the British surrender at Yorktown, Va., is commemorated, with Pres. Reagan and French Pres. François Mitterrand participating in the observance.

21 / The Commerce Department reaffirms the specter of a recession as it announces a 0.6 percent drop in the Gross National Product during the third quarter of the year.

22 / The Federal Labor Relations Authority decertifies the Professional Air Traffic Controllers Organization (PATCO) as the bargaining representatives for the air traffic controllers employed by the federal government.

A loss of $468 million in the third quarter of the fiscal year is reported by General Motors, the largest automaker in the world.

23 / Consumer prices rose 1.2 percent in September, fueled by higher costs for food, medical care, transportation, and borrowing money, it is reported.

26 / Federal Trade Commission chairman James C. Miller 3d tells a news conference that the commission should not be responsible for protecting the public from advertising claims that are unsubstantiated and products that are defective.

28 / The Los Angeles Dodgers defeat the New York Yankees to win the 1981 World Series of baseball, four games to two. It is the California team's first world championship since 1965.

29 / The index of leading economic indicators dropped 2.7 percent in September, according to a Commerce Department report released today.

30 / Treasury Secretary Donald T. Regan says a balanced budget is unlikely in 1984.

31 / Attorney General William French Smith advocates changes in the Voting Rights Act, but favors retaining enforcement provisions, scheduled to expire in August 1982.

### INTERNATIONAL

1 / U.S. President Ronald W. Reagan, in a news conference, pledges to protect Saudi Arabia from any domestic or foreign forces that would cut off oil exports to the West.

2 / Lech Walesa easily wins reelection to the post of chairman of Solidarity, the Polish labor union. It was the first time that an Eastern bloc country was the site of national elections not sponsored by the Communist party.

Hojatolislam Mohammed Ali Khamenei, personal spokesman for the Ayatollah Ruhollah Khomeini, wins the election for the presidency of Iran.

3 / Irish republican prisoners held in the Maze Prison near Belfast, Northern Ireland, call off their seven-month protest. Since the hunger strike began, ten prisoners have died.

4 / In order to relieve the pressure placed by speculators on the foreign exchange market, Western European finance ministers agree to adjust the values of national currencies in France, Italy, the Netherlands, and West Germany.

5 / Santa Fe International Corporation is to be purchased by Kuwait's state-owned oil company, Kuwait Petroleum Corporation. The $2.5-billion transaction, announced today, is the largest amount of Mideast oil funds ever invested in a publicly traded U.S. corporation.

6 / President Anwar el-Sadat of Egypt is assassinated near Cairo while he is reviewing a parade commemorating the 1973 Egyptian war against Israel.

7 / Israeli Prime Minister Menachem Begin reasserts his nation's commitment to its peace treaty with Egypt as long as the post-Sadat Egyptian government upholds the pact.

8 / Quebec's provincial government will expropriate most of the assets of the U.S.-owned Asbestos Corporation Ltd., headquartered in Montreal, according to a provincial government announcement.

9 / Great Britain's newly formed Social Democratic party concludes its first conference. Among its decisions was one to ally itself with the Liberal party in election contests.

10 / An estimated 250,000 demonstrators in Bonn, West Germany, protest plans by the North Atlantic Treaty Organization (N.A.T.O.) to modernize and expand its nuclear capability in Europe.

11 / Former U.S. Presidents Gerald R. Ford and Jimmy Carter assert that the U.S. and the Palestine Liberation Organization (P.L.O.) must hold discussions if a lasting peace is to come to the Middle East.

12 / Twelve Egyptian Army officers reported to be Moslem fanatics lose their posts following the assassination of Pres. Sadat, it is announced.

13 / Japan announces it will not take part in trade talks with the U.S. and the European Communities that had been scheduled for November.

The U.S. government reasserts its pledge to aid the Sudan in its conflict with Libya if the latter attacks Sudanese territory.

Hosni Mubarak, who served as Egypt's vice-president under Anwar el-Sadat, is elected president in a national referendum one week after Sadat's assassination.

14 / The U.S. House of Representatives votes against the sale of $8.5 billion in weapons to Saudi Arabia. The aid package includes five Airborne Warning and Control System (AWACS) radar planes.

Kare Willoch is appointed premier of Norway, following the resignation of the Brundtland government on Oct. 13.

15 / The U.S. Senate Foreign Relations Committee, in a 9 to 8 vote, rejects the Reagan Administration's plan for selling weapons to Saudi Arabia.

16 / Moshe Dayan, Israel's former Chief of Staff, Defense Minister, and Foreign Minister, dies of a heart ailment in Tel Aviv.

Egyptian Pres. Mubarak orders a sweep throughout that nation to arrest Moslem fundamentalists who he says are attempting to disrupt the country.

17 / Pres. Reagan asserts that the U.S. will stand firm in defense of Saudi Arabia to avoid a repeat of the revolution that overthrew the government of the Shah of Iran.

18 / Poland's Communist party removes Stanislaw Kania as its leader and replaces him with Gen. Wojciech Jaruzelski, who, the Central Committee hopes, will present a firmer stand against Solidarity and the more liberal elements within that organization.

Greece's Prime Minister George Rallis's New Democratic party loses its power in parliamentary elections to the so-called PASOK party of Socialists, led by Andreas Papandreou.

19 / Pres. Mubarak of Egypt announces the beginning of arrests among extremist Moslems in connection with the assassination of his predecessor, Anwar el-Sadat.

20 / Pres. Reagan, in a draft letter, urges the U.S. Senate to approve the sale of AWACS planes to Saudi Arabia while promising to cancel the sale if disruptive policies are put forth by that Mideast nation.

21 / Pres. Reagan declares that the United States is not planning to engage in nuclear war with the USSR at the expense of Europe, where anti-nuclear protests are taking place.

22 / A two-day meeting of world leaders opens in Cancún, Mexico, to discuss world economic problems.

24 / Wildcat strikes take place in 36 of Poland's 49 provinces to protest food shortages.

25 / Prime Minister Papandreou asserts that his Greek government will not end its participation in N.A.T.O. nor force the closing of U.S. miltary bases in Greece.

26 / Polish government leaders send small military units throughout the country in anticipation of labor strikes set for Oct. 28.

27 / Urho Kekkonen resigns as president of Finland because of ill health. The Social Democrat has served for more than 25 years.

28 / Intense lobbying by the White House results in a U.S. Senate vote to sell AWACS planes to Saudi Arabia.

An hour-long general strike is staged in Poland to protest food shortages.

29 / The nation-members of the Organization of Petroleum Exporting Countries (O.P.E.C.) agree to freeze oil prices at $34 per barrel through 1982.

30 / Polish leader Gen. Jaruzelski dismisses six ministers, including a deputy prime minister, to bring more nonparty members into the higher eschelons of government. He also issues an appeal to end the strikes that have plagued the nation.

31 / Israel expresses opposition to the U.S. over recent statements by Reagan Administration officials on the Mideast peace plan proposed by Saudi Arabia in August.

## NOVEMBER 1981

### NATIONAL

1 / A delay in tax increases aimed at cutting federal budget deficits should be put off until 1983 and 1984, suggests Secretary of the Treasury Donald T. Regan and Robert Dole (R-Kans.), Chairman of the Senate Finance Committee.

2 / The Census Bureau reports that an increasing number of families are eligible for welfare assistance. It attributes this increase to the decline in real income and the rise in the number of families whose incomes fall below the poverty level.

4 / The Tennessee-Tombigbee Waterway in Alabama and Mississippi and the Clinch River Breeder Reactor in Tennessee survive Senate amendments that would have canceled funding for the two projects.

5 / The National Council of Catholic Bishops announces its support of the Hatch amendment, giving states the right to enact legislation on abortion within their own jurisdictions.

6 / The October unemployment rate reached 8 percent, according to figures released by the Labor Department today.

7 / Richard S. Schweiker, Secretary of Health and Human Services, announces that the Reagan Administration will make changes in Medicaid and Medicare programs. Among them would be increased premium payments and reduced federal outlays for hospital and doctors' fees.

9 / Treasury Secretary Regan says the Reagan Administration has dropped its plan to raise an additional $3 billion in taxes during the 1982 fiscal year.

10 / The Producer Price Index for October rose only six-tenths of 1 percent, according to the Labor Department, indicating a slowing of inflation.

11 / The *Atlantic Monthly* magazine's December issue is released, containing an interview with David A. Stockman, director of the Office of Management and Budget. In it, Stockman says he has always had little faith in the Reagan economic policies.

12 / The space shuttle *Columbia* is launched at Cape Canaveral, Florida, on its second test flight after mechanical delays.

13 / After 63 years in the military, Adm. Hyman G. Rickover, the chief nuclear officer in the Navy, is ordered to retire from the post in January 1982.

14 / *Columbia*, the first reusable spaceship, lands safely at Edwards Air Force Base in California after a test flight abbreviated by fuel-cell problems.

15 / Murray L. Weidenbaum, chairman of the President's Council of Economic Advisers, says unemployment could reach 9 percent before the Reagan Administration's policies begin to work.

16 / Pres. Reagan dismisses the chairman of the U.S. Commission on Civil Rights and an advocate of busing and affirmative action, Arthur S. Flemming, and selects Clarence M. Pendleton, a conservative Republican, to replace him.

17 / A compromise over the amount needed to continue government operations beyond Nov. 20 could be reached between the White House and Congress, Pres. Reagan insists. The funding measure is needed because Congress has passed only one of 13 bills appropriating money to run the government.

18 / The House of Representatives passes a $197.4-billion appropriations bill for the military—an amount that would allow for development of the MX missile and the B-1 bomber.

19 / The license to operate the Diablo Canyon nuclear power plant, near San Luis Obispo, Calif., is suspended by the Nuclear Regulatory Commission until seismic test can be performed following discovery of design errors in the plant.
20 / The House and Senate fail to agree on a stopgap appropriations bill for federal government operations by the midnight deadline. It is believed that government functions can continue for a few days without passage of a bill, however.
21 / Despite a lack of authorization for spending, the federal government's functions continue with little interruption.
22 / Following the passage of a $428-billion spending bill by Congress, Pres. Reagan says he will veto the stopgap funding measure because it is excessive, and he will force the shutdown of nonessential government operations.
23 / Pres. Reagan uses his veto power for the first time, striking down the government finance bill. Congress subsequently extends spending at the present level for three weeks.
25 / The National Association of Independent Insurers files a suit against the Reagan Administration's decision to drop the requirement for air bags or automatic seat belts in automobiles. The ruling was to have taken effect in the fall of 1982.
26 / Reminiscent of protests during the presidency of Herbert Hoover, a tent city named Reaganville sprouts in Washington's Lafayette Park, across the street from the White House. The squatters, attempting to protest social services cuts by the Reagan Administration, are ordered to leave after feeding several hundred of Washington, D.C.'s destitute.
29 / The 1981 White House Conference on Aging opens, with some delegates protesting the ground rule of voting on all committee reports as a unit.
30 / A move by Mobil Corporation to acquire Marathon Oil Company is declared by a Federal District Court to be in violation of antitrust laws.

### INTERNATIONAL

1 / The civil administration of the West Bank, occupied by Israel, is taken over by a civilian, Professor Menachem Milson. Nonmilitary personnel will replace the existing military government.
Antigua and Barbuda, in the Caribbean, attains independence.
2 / King Hussein of Jordan, in Washington, D.C., affirms his support of the Saudi peace plan for the Mideast, but U.S. Pres. Reagan stands by the Camp David accords.
Iran's prime minister, Mir Hussein Musavi-Khamenei, elected on Oct. 29, announces the 21 members of his cabinet. Most had been chosen by the late Pres. Mohammed Ali Rajai during the summer.
3 / Soviet leader Leonid Brezhnev asserts that the USSR does not intend to initiate a nuclear war but wishes only to defend itself.
4 / U.S. Secretary of State Alexander M. Haig, Jr., says the detonation of a nuclear warhead as a deterrence is a part of a contingency plan for the defense of Europe.
5 / The federal government of Canada and those of its nine predominantly English-speaking provinces reach agreement on a new constitution for the country that transfers the British North America Act to Canada along with the power to amend it.
6 / The participation of European forces in the Sinai peacekeeping effort is placed in doubt, U.S. officials say, because of the European Economic Community's desire for an addressing of the Palestinian rights issue.
Sweden releases a Soviet submarine that had run aground inside Swedish waters on Oct. 27.
7 / On the 64th anniversary of the Bolshevik Revolution, Soviet Defense Minister Dmitri F. Ustinov asserts his government's vow to match any military buildup that would place the USSR in an "underdog" position.
8 / In a major speech to his nation's parliament, Pres. Mubarak of Egypt states his support for the Camp David accords and Egypt's commitment to nonalignment.
9 / Israel threatens military moves to destroy Syrian missiles in Lebanon and P.L.O. armaments in southern Lebanon if U.S. attempts at finding a solution to the Palestinian/West Bank problem fail.
Burma's parliament elects U San Yu to succeed the resigned U Ne Win as president.
10 / U.S. Pres. Reagan reaffirms his praise for the Mideast peace plan offered by Saudi Arabia, because, he says, it shows a willingness to negotiate a settlement.
11 / Poland marks the anniversary of its reestablishment as an independent country in 1918. The open celebrations are the first held since 1939.
12 / The Exxon Corporation announces its withdrawal from petroleum and gas operations in Libya without revealing the reasons behind the decision.
13 / The cash payment of $1,000 to National Security Advisor Richard V. Allen by a Japanese magazine in exchange for an interview with Nancy Reagan will be examined by the Justice Department, the White House reveals.
14 / Operation Bright Star, combining U.S., Egyptian, Somali, Omani, and Sudanese troops, begins with desert training in Egypt.
15 / P.L.O. leader Yasir Arafat orders the mobilization of his troops in the face of what he terms imminent attack by Israel.
16 / In a report to the Central Committee of the Communist party in the USSR, Leonid Brezhnev describes food production and distribution to be the greatest problem facing the Soviets today.
18 / Pres. Reagan announces his intention to drop planned deployment of U.S. intermediate-range missiles in Europe if the USSR will dismantle similar installations. The Soviet news agency Tass accuses Reagan of misleading the public by ignoring the U.S.'s submarine-based missiles, weapons carried aboard bombers in Western Europe, and British and French nuclear weapons.
19 / The Foreign Affairs Committee of the U.S. House of Representatives fails to block the proposed sale of 40 F-16 fighter aircraft to Pakistan.
20 / An agreement that could lead to a $10-billion sale for the USSR is signed in Bonn, West Germany. The Soviets will construct a pipeline from their gas fields in Western Siberia to their border with Czechoslovakia.
21 / Twenty-four defendants, all Moslem fundamentalists, begin their trial in Cairo, Egypt, on charges of killing Pres. Anwar el-Sadat.
22 / Greece's Prime Minister, Andreas Papandreou, announces his government's intention to establish a deadline for the removal of U.S. military forces in Greece.
23 / Britain, France, Italy, and the Netherlands agree to assist in peacekeeping efforts in the Sinai following the withdrawal of Israel in April 1982.
Soviet leader Leonid Brezhnev, in talks with West German Chancellor Helmut Schmidt, proposes freezing deployment of medium-range nuclear weapons in Europe until formal talks with the U.S. can bring about forced reductions.
25 / A meeting of Arab League representatives ends shortly after it opened because of Syrian opposition to Saudi Arabia's Mideast peace plan.
26 / The third European Economic Community summit conference opens in London. Funding of the organization is the principal topic.
27 / Poland's military leaders are told by the Communist Party Politburo to secure legislation banning strikes.
29 / At least 64 people are killed when an explosives-loaded car blows up in downtown Damascus, Syria. The government blames the outlawed Moslem Brotherhood for the attack.
30 / Israel and the U.S. sign a memorandum of understanding to cooperate militarily against Soviet or Soviet-backed forces in the Mideast.
U.S. and Soviet representatives hold their first talks on nuclear arms reduction in Geneva, Switzerland.

## DECEMBER 1981

### NATIONAL

1 / The White House Conference on Aging hears Pres. Reagan affirm his commitment to save the financially troubled Social Security System.
2 / The Senate approves an amendment to shift $334

million from funding to place MX missiles in existing silos to research into other methods of storing the weapons.

3 / Republican Congressional leaders and the White House concur on a spending bill to finance the government through September 1982.

4 / The national unemployment rate reached 8.4 percent in November, the Bureau of Labor Statistics reports. The last time the jobless rate surpassed that level was in the 1974-75 recession.

The Senate approves a military spending bill of $208 billion, the largest value ever to be passed in Congress.

Pres. Reagan issues a 17-page executive order widening the surveillance powers of government intelligence agencies in the U.S. The C.I.A. has been forbidden to execute covert actions in the U.S. until this time.

6 / Leaders of the National Governors Association close a weekend of meetings at which it was agreed that austerity in public services is likely for some time to come.

7 / The federal budget deficit is expected to reach $109 billion in the 1982 fiscal year, according to Administration officials.

8 / Detroit's Roman Catholic Archbishop Edmund C. Szoka, addressing the House Ways and Means Committee, says private charities cannot make up for the losses experienced by the drop in government aid to the poor.

9 / A ban on federal employment for dismissed air traffic controllers is ended by Pres. Reagan, but the strikers may not be rehired in their former capacities.

10 / A $413-billion bill to operate the federal government through March 31, 1982, is passed in the House of Representatives.

11 / The Senate Environment and Public Works Committee decides not to act on changing the Clean Air Act until 1982.

12 / The Worldwatch Institute issues a report that says Washington, D.C., has the highest infant mortality rate of any city in the nation.

14 / Congressional conferees agree on a military appropriations bill of $200 billion for fiscal year 1982—less than $1 billion below Pres. Reagan's request.

15 / U.S. automakers petition Congress to relax tailpipe emission standards set by the Clean Air Act so as to ease their financial plight.

16 / Pres. Reagan elects to abolish the cabinet-level Department of Energy and place its functions within the Commerce Department as the semiautonomous Energy Research and Technology Administration.

The House of Representatives approves restoration of the minimum Social Security benefit of $122 per month, as Pres. Reagan announces formation of a 15-member committee to seek a way of bringing fiscal solvency to the Social Security System.

17 / Five national recreation areas are to be opened to mining of minerals and drilling for oil and gas, according to the Department of the Interior, if the request is approved by the Office of Management and Budget.

20 / Idaho's Gov. John V. Evans asks conservationists not to initiate a boycott of Idaho products following two weekends in which an estimated 17,000 jackrabbits were clubbed to death. The animals are reported to have inflicted much damage to crops there.

22 / A four-year, $11-billion farm support bill is signed by Pres. Reagan. One of its provisions calls for distribution to the nation's needy a total of 30 million pounds of cheese made from dairy products purchased from farmers at support prices.

23 / Federal District Judge Marion J. Callister rules that Congress unconstitutionally extended the ratification deadline for the Equal Rights Amendment, which, without the extension, should have been ratified by March 29, 1979.

24 / A federal judge rules that U.S. Steel can legally buy the Marathon Oil Company.

26 / The General Accounting Office recommends a narrowing of scope by the Interior Department in the latter's attempts to open nearly all offshore waters to oil and gas leasing.

28 / The trial of Wayne B. Williams, accused of killing 2 blacks in a string of 29 unsolved murders in Atlanta, Ga., opens in that city.

29 / Attorney Leon Silverman is appointed by a three-judge panel to serve as special prosecutor in an investigation of corruption allegations against Labor Secretary Raymond J. Donovan.

31 / Reagan Administration officials announce that 40 MX missiles will be placed in existing Minuteman missile silos in the northern midwest.

## INTERNATIONAL

1 / Although cleared today of receiving $1,000 from a Japanese magazine in exchange for an interview with Nancy Reagan, National Security Advisor Richard V. Allen will undergo investigation over his acceptance of two watches and inconsistencies in his financial disclosure form, the U.S. Justice Department announces.

3 / Reports surface that Libyan assassination agents are in the U.S. attempting to kill the President and other government officials. The Federal Bureau of Investigation and Secret Service are mobilized to seek out the terrorists.

4 / In an address to the Organization of American States, U.S. Secretary of State Haig asks for a stop in the arms buildup in the Western Hemisphere.

5 / Defense cooperation through a joint defense group of U.S. and Turkish members is confirmed at a conference between U.S. Secretary of Defense Caspar Weinberger and Turkish Defense Minister Haluk Bayulken.

6 / Col. Muammar el-Qaddafi denies initiating an attempt on the lives of the U.S. President and other high government officials.

7 / Using tape-recorded evidence, the Polish government accuses Solidarity union leaders of seeking the overthrow of the government.

8 / Prime Minister Andreas Papandreou announces that his Greek government will begin pulling out of some commitments to N.A.T.O.

10 / Pres. Reagan asks all U.S. citizens to leave Libya immediately and blocks travel to that country by holders of U.S. passports.

11 / The U.N. Security Council nominates Javier Pérez de Cuéllar of Peru to be the United Nations' fifth Secretary-General.

Roberto Eduardo Viola is removed from the presidency of Argentina and replaced by a three-member military junta led by Gen. Leopoldo Galtieri.

12 / East German leader Erich Honecker tells West German Chancellor Helmut Schmidt that improved ties between their countries hinges on the West German plan to place U.S. nuclear weapons in its territory.

13 / A state of emergency is proclaimed in Poland and a military government is imposed.

14 / Israel formally annexes the disputed Golan Heights as a buffer along the Syrian border.

Reports of strikes in defiance of the newly imposed military regime reach Western news sources from within Poland, despite a communications blackout.

15 / The Reagan Administration announces it will train 1,500 Salvadorean soldiers and junior officers to fight off leftist insurgents in that country.

16 / Archbishop Jozef Glemp, Primate of Poland, asks his country's military rulers to end martial law, free political prisoners, and permit union activities in the country.

17 / The U.N. Security Council votes unanimously for a resolution calling Israel's annexation of the Golan Heights illegal.

Brig. Gen. James L. Dozier, a U.S. representative to N.A.T.O., is kidnapped from his Verona, Italy, apartment. The Red Brigades terrorist group claims responsibility.

18 / A shortage of food, attributed by the government to hoarding, is reported by the Polish military government.

The U.S. government suspends a military cooperation agreement with Israel because of the Mideast nation's annexation of the Golan Heights.

19 / The Polish government announces that criminal actions have begun against union leaders who are attempting to organize strikes, illegal under current martial law.

20 / Romauld Spasowski, Poland's Ambassador to the U.S., is granted asylum in Washington, D.C.

21 / Polish coal miners numbering more than 2,800 strike in Silesia, and union activists blockade them-

selves in a Katowice steel mill to protest the military government.

23 / Among sanctions announced by Pres. Reagan against Poland today are a continued suspension of agricultural shipments to that country, the blocking of renewal of Poland's export credit insurance line through the Export-Import Bank, and suspension of Polish civil aviation privileges in the U.S.

24 / U.S. Secretary of State Haig asks the Western allies to apply pressures to force an end to the government repression in Poland.

25 / Despite an announcement by the U.S. that a strategic cooperation agreement had been cancelled following Israeli annexation of the Golan Heights, Israel's Defense Minister Ariel Sharon says he considers the agreement to remain in effect.

26 / The U.S. has adopted the views of Saudi Arabia, says Israel's newly chosen ambassador to Washington, Moshe Arens.

27 / Faced with food shortages, the Polish government announces a reduction in meat rations beginning in January.

29 / For its part in the increased repression in Poland, the USSR will be subject to curtailment of trade with and air travel to the U.S., Pres. Reagan announces.

30 / Allies of the U.S. fail to support its sanctions against the USSR taken in light of the Polish government crisis.

The U.S. State Department accuses the USSR of jamming Voice of America radio signals beamed into Poland.

Recognition of Israel by Saudi Arabia is possible only if Israel recognizes the rights of the Palestinians and agrees to return occupied lands, according to the Saudi Foreign Minister, Prince Saud al-Faisal.

31 / Jerry J. Rawlings, a former Ghanaian Air Force pilot, overthrows the government of Hilla Limann, who had been elected to the presidency in 1979 following Rawlings's overthrow of the Akuffo government.

## JANUARY 1982

### NATIONAL

3 / Government officials say the contents of White House tapes dating from the Nixon Administration will not be available until at least 1987 because of cuts in the staff working on the project.

4 / The formal resignation of Richard V. Allen from the post of national security advisor is accepted by the White House. Under his successor, William P. Clark, the post will be upgraded, with Clark reporting directly to the President.

5 / A federal district judge rules that Arkansas cannot legally require the teaching of "creation science" along with evolution in the classroom, because "creation science" is not a science but a religious doctrine.

6 / Chief Justice Warren E. Burger refuses to ban the purchase of the Marathon Oil Company by the U.S. Steel Corporation.

7 / Pres. Reagan announces that he will continue draft registration of 18-year-old males but anticipates no return to conscription.

8 / In the settlement of an antitrust suit against the American Telephone and Telegraph Company, the telecommunications giant agrees to give up the nation's 22 Bell System companies.

The Justice Department announces that it is dropping antitrust action against the International Business Machines Corporation.

9 / The Lawyers Committee for Civil Rights Under Law announces it will contest in court the legality of an Administration decision to grant tax-exempt status to private schools and colleges that practice racial discrimination.

10 / Robert Nimmo, head of the Veterans Administration, says free medical care to all military veterans over 65 years of age may have to be curtailed because of the large number of World War II veterans reaching 65.

11 / The state of California is sued by 38 of its 58 counties for refusing to pay for enforcement of 23 new laws, as required by the state constitution.

12 / In an about-face, Pres. Reagan says tax-exempt status will not be granted to schools practicing discrimination if Congress passes his suggested legislation to prohibit such an exemption.

United Auto Workers representatives and General Motors agree to wage and benefit concessions if the prices of automobiles will be lowered to reflect the lowered manufacturer's cost.

13 / An Air Florida jet bound for Tampa, Fla., crashes into a bridge shortly after takeoff from National Airport in Washington, D.C., and plunges into the Potomac River. Twelve persons are known dead, and 50 are missing.

15 / The Producer Price Index for finished goods rose only 7 percent in 1981, the Department of Labor announces.

16 / Pres. Reagan's initial announcement concerning tax-exempt status for schools practicing segregation was caused by a communications breakdown in the White House, officials reveal.

17 / An amendment to the Austin, Tex., Fair Housing Ordinance that would have permitted discrimination on the basis of sexual orientation is overwhelmingly defeated.

18 / Four members of the Air Force Thunderbirds flying team die while practicing stunts when their planes crash in the Nevada desert.

19 / Unlimited spending by political action groups is upheld by the Supreme Court.

20 / The Gross National Product fell at an annual rate of 5.2 percent, after adjustment for inflation, during the fourth quarter of 1981, the government announces.

21 / Attorney General William French Smith says that the Federal Bureau of Investigation will take over the government's role in narcotics cases.

22 / The rise of 8.9 percent in consumer prices during 1981 was the lowest in four years, reports the Department of Labor.

24 / The Bureau of Labor Statistics releases data showing that medical care costs rose 12.5 percent over all in 1981, and the cost of a hospital room rose 17 percent. The overall increase was the highest ever reported.

25 / Reagan Administration officials say the President has rejected the advice of his staff and will not seek higher excise taxes on liquor, gasoline, and tobacco for the 1983 and 1984 fiscal years.

26 / Pres. Reagan, in his first State of the Union address, proposes a policy of "New Federalism," which, by 1984, would turn over to state and local governments responsibility for $47 billion in programs such as food stamps and aid to families with dependent children.

27 / Attorney General William French Smith, in testimony before the Senate Judiciary subcommittee, asserts the President's commitment to extend the Voting Rights Act, but supports changes in the measure that would eliminate the need for certain states and counties to submit for approval revisions in election laws.

28 / National Transportation Safety Board investigators reveal that the anti-icing device had been shut off in the engine system of the Air Florida jet that crashed in Washington, D.C., on Jan. 13.

29 / The one-house veto is itself struck down by the Washington, D.C., federal appeals court. The veto prevented the policies of Federal agencies from taking effect when only one house of Congress objected.

The Philadelphia *Bulletin* ends 134 years of publishing an afternoon paper and goes out of business.

31 / Vermont Gov. Richard A. Snelling, chairman of the National Governors Association, announces support for Pres. Reagan's New Federalism program, but he wants a minimum standard of aid set before programs are transferred from federal to state jurisdiction.

### INTERNATIONAL

1 / Pope John Paul II, in his New Year's address, asks Polish officials to permit the existence of the national labor union, Solidarity.

2 / The Polish military government removes 90 city and provincial leaders from office because, it was felt, they could not control unrest in their jurisdictions.

Egyptian Pres. Mubarak dismisses his cabinet and appoints Ahmad Fuad Mohieddin prime minister with the task of forming a new government.

4 / The European Economic Community declines to join the U.S. in its economic sanctions against Poland, but it pledges not to undermine the U.S. sanctions.

6 / The U.S. will not insist on N.A.T.O.'s agreement with U.S.-imposed sanctions against the USSR and Poland at next week's N.A.T.O. meetings, U.S. Secretary of State Haig reveals.

7 / Nicaragua will buy French "nonoffensive" military equipment and have naval officers and pilots trained by France, the French defense minister reports.

8 / Spain announces it will open its border with British-owned Gibraltar on April 30, 12 years after it was closed.

9 / Poland's military leader, Gen. Wojciech Jaruzelski, and its Roman Catholic Primate, Archbishop Jozef Glemp, meet. At the same time censorship of press dispatches leaving Poland is lifted.

10 / The U.S. requests a halt in the shipment of parts from European nations and Japan for use in building the natural gas pipeline from the USSR to Western Europe.

11 / The U.S. State Department announces that Taiwan will be permitted to purchase only F-5E fighter planes, not more sophisticated aircraft, from the U.S.

At a meeting of N.A.T.O. representatives, a declaration is issued condemning Soviet involvement in Poland.

12 / Canada reorganizes its government structure in an effort to increase exports and lessen regional economic disparities.

13 / U.S. Secretary of State Haig announces that Egyptian President Mubarak has agreed to speed up negotiations with Israel over the Palestinian issue.

14 / Daniel K. Ludwig, a U.S. financier, is abandoning his enormous Brazilian development project in the Amazon region, blaming Brazilian government bureaucracy and his inability to obtain Brazilian financing.

15 / U.S. Secretary of State Haig concludes four days of talks with Egyptian and Israeli leaders over the issue of Palestinian self-rule.

16 / Japanese and Western national representatives agree to avoid the imposition of trade barriers in order to constrict imports.

17 / France's nationalization program, aimed at five major industries as well as some investment houses and banks, is set back by a ruling that requires increased compensation to stockholders.

18 / In India, at the end of a second day of nationwide strikes to protest the government's economic policies, 6,000 persons are reported to have been arrested.

19 / The U.S.'s refusal to assist monetarily an international program to improve third-world journalism and communications is criticized at a U.N.E.S.C.O.-sponsored conference in Mexico.

20 / Nikolai A. Tikhonov, Prime Minister of the USSR, says his country seeks meaningful dialogue with the U.S., not confrontation.

The U.S. vetoes a U.N. Security Council resolution calling for punishment of Israel because of its annexation of the Golan Heights.

21 / More than 100 Polish intellectuals and artists petition their government to end martial law.

23 / The economic report for 1981, issued by the Soviet government today, indicates that agriculture suffered severe setbacks but natural gas production exceeded the projected volume.

25 / Egypt's government confirms that it has asked the USSR for 66 technicians to work on major industrial projects.

26 / U.S. Secretary of State Haig and Soviet Foreign Minister Andrei A. Gromyko discuss various issues related to East-West tensions at a meeting in Geneva, Switzerland.

27 / Honduras inaugurates Dr. Roberto Suazo Córdova to the post of president. He becomes the first civilian president of Honduras in ten years.

28 / U.S. Brig. Gen. James L. Dozier is freed from his kidnappers in Padua, Italy, 42 days after Red Brigades terrorists abducted him from his apartment.

29 / Soviet ideologist Mikhail A. Suslov, who died Jan. 25, is buried with full state honors in Moscow.

30 / Less-than-capacity crowds at gatherings across the U.S., Europe, and Japan take part in a worldwide day of protest against military rule in Poland. The observance was called for by U.S. Pres. Reagan.

31 / The Israeli cabinet votes to accept Sinai peacekeeping troops from Britain, France, Italy, and the Netherlands—forces that Israel had earlier rejected because of their countries' positions favoring Palestinian self-rule.

## FEBRUARY 1982

### NATIONAL

1 / The General Motors Corporation, in spite of slow car and truck sales, announces a 1981 profit of $333 million, attributed principally to cost-cutting and the profits earned by its finance and insurance subsidiaries.

2 / The Reagan Administration will ask for almost $260 billion in 1983 military appropriations, according to Secretary of Defense Weinberger.

3 / Senate Majority Leader Howard H. Baker, Jr. (R-Tenn.), announces that Pres. Reagan may accept a joint resolution of Congress, rather than legislation, denying tax-exempt status for schools practicing racial discrimination.

4 / In a vote of 58 to 38, the Senate passes a proposal that would bar federal judges from imposing busing plans requiring trips of more than 5 miles or 15 minutes in duration.

6 / A crowd of more than 300 marchers begins a 140-mile walk from Carrollton to Montgomery, Ala., in support of the federal Voting Rights Act.

8 / Representatives from state gubernatorial and legislative bodies attack the proposed federal budget because of costly transfers of responsibility from the federal to the state level.

9 / Pres. Reagan, in a speech in Indianapolis, Ind., challenge critics of his budget to offer alternatives that would hold down the deficit.

10 / Federal Reserve Board chairman Paul A. Volcker says the board will continue its tight-money policy during the year to slow inflation.

11 / Revising its plan to use silos strengthened with steel, the Reagan Administration announces that 40 MX missiles will be placed in unreinforced Minuteman missile silos.

13 / The Ford Motor Company and the United Auto Workers reach tentative agreement on a national contract. Wage and benefit concessions in exchange for job security highlight the pact.

14 / Federal Reserve Board chairman Volcker blames government budget deficits for the prevailing high interest rates.

15 / At the opening session of its annual meeting, the A.F.L.-C.I.O. executive council calls for a plan by which any increases in military spending by the federal government will be covered by tax surcharges.

16 / Senator Harrison A. Williams, Jr. (D-N.J.), is sentenced to three years in prison and is fined $50,000 after being convicted of bribery and conspiracy by using his office for monetary gain.

18 / Pres. Reagan expresses support for the Federal Reserve Board and its tight-money policy for fighting inflation.

19 / The Reagan Administration issues a rule requiring parental notification when children under 18 years of age seek contraceptives or birth control devices from clinics supported by federal funds.

21 / Reversing his stand of last year, Interior Secretary James G. Watt announces he will seek to ban all mining and drilling until the end of the 1900s in all Federal wilderness areas.

22 / The Consumer Product Safety Commission bars the sale of urea formaldehyde for use as a foam insulation because of potential health hazards.

23 / Predicting inevitable defeat for the Reagan budget, Republican Congressional leaders announce they will work with Democrats for an alternative.

24 / A study by the University of Chicago is released, indicating that low-income families, under the proposed Reagan budget, would be financially better

off if they depended entirely on federal aid rather than worked at low-wage jobs.

25 / A change in the design of walkways over the lobby of the Hyatt Regency Hotel in Kansas City, Mo., caused their collapse on July 17, 1981, according to a report released today by the National Bureau of Standards.

27 / Wayne B. Williams is found guilty of killing two black youths in Atlanta, Ga. Prosecutors suggest he may be responsible for any number of the other 27 unsolved murders in the Atlanta area.

28 / The Ford Motor Company's union workers overwhelmingly accept a new contract that specifies concessions in wages and benefits by the workers in exchange for greater job security.

### INTERNATIONAL

1 / The African nations of Senegal and Gambia form a confederation, Senegambia, but they retain their sovereignties.

2 / In testimony before the Senate Foreign Relations Committee, Secretary of State Haig says that the Reagan Administration had not ruled out the use of U.S. troops in El Salvador.

4 / Pres. Reagan reveals that he has presented to the USSR at arms negotiations talks in Geneva, Switzerland, a draft treaty that calls for eliminating medium-range nuclear missiles from Europe.

5 / Laker Airways, which in 1978 pioneered bargain airfares between the U.S. and England, declares bankruptcy.

In an 86-21 vote, the U.N. General Assembly votes to urge the isolation of Israel from other world nations because of its annexation of the Golan Heights.

6 / Polish officials announce their plan to boycott upcoming meetings in Madrid, Spain, on East-West cooperation in Europe if conferees bring up the issue of martial law in Poland.

7 / China's leader, Deng Xiaoping, has relieved himself of basic operational duties of government to assume the role of advisor, it is learned from a Chinese government official. Deng remains chairman of the Military Affairs Commission and deputy chairman of the Communist party in China.

Luis Alberto Monge Alvarez of the National Liberation party is elected president of Costa Rica.

8 / In response to the oil glut in world markets, Britain lowers the per-barrel price of its crude oil by $1.50 to $35.00.

9 / The U.S. and Western European nations agree to stop East-West cooperation talks until martial law is ended in Poland.

10 / Six Salvadorean soldiers are turned over to civilian authorities to face possible charges in the deaths of four American women—three Roman Catholic nuns and a lay worker—in December 1980.

12 / Reports that U.S. military advisors carried weapons in El Salvador, violating U.S. government policy, will be investigated, Pres. Reagan says.

Morocco and the U.S. announce agreement on a joint military commission and progress toward establishment of transit rights for U.S. forces in Morocco.

13 / U.S. Secretary of Defense Weinberger says he will ask the White House for additional arms sales to Jordan.

15 / The Ocean Ranger, an oil-drilling rig off the coast of Newfoundland, sinks during a severe storm; 84 men are missing and presumed drowned.

16 / Zimbabwe's Prime Minister Robert Mugabe expropriates properties belonging to the opposition Patriotic Front, headed by Joshua Nkomo.

17 / West German Chancellor Schmidt expresses concern over the predicted U.S. budget deficit, fearing that world political destabilization could result.

Joshua Nkomo, minister without portfolio, is removed from the cabinet of Zimbabwe's prime minister, Robert Mugabe.

19 / Pope John Paul II expresses opposition to U.S.-imposed sanctions against Poland.

21 / Mexico's President José Lopez Portillo offers to serve as an intermediary between the U.S. and Central American countries to resolve major differences between the nations.

22 / U.N. officials announce that 1,000 additional soldiers will be sent to southern Lebanon to preserve a ceasefire along the Lebanese-Israeli border.

23 / Poland's government press agency attacks Lech Walesa, leader of Solidarity, as a front for an anti-Communist crusade.

24 / Pres. Reagan proposes a six-point plan to improve the economies of the developing Caribbean countries.

26 / Israel orders the closing of roads leading into the Sinai to prevent an influx of militants opposed to the peninsula's return to Egypt in April.

27 / The D'Oyly Carte Opera Company stages its final performance in London, ending 106 years of presenting operettas.

The Roman Catholic bishops of Poland call for an end to military rule and for participation by Solidarity in national life.

28 / The Israeli cabinet announces that Egypt's President Mubarak will not be invited to Israel unless he agrees to visit Jerusalem. Mubarak has opposed the Israeli's designation of that city as its capital.

## MARCH 1982

### NATIONAL

1 / The International Brotherhood of Teamsters ratifies a contract which freezes wages for truck drivers and warehouse workers for a two-year minimum period.

2 / The Senate passes a bill that would prohibit busing for purposes of racial integration.

3 / The Senate Select Committee on Ethics presents evidence to the entire chamber recommending expulsion of Sen. Harrison Williams (D-N.J.) following his conviction for bribery and conspiracy in connection with the ABSCAM affair.

4 / Pres. Reagan nominates Army Gen. John W. Vessey, Jr., to the post of chairman of the Joint Chiefs of Staff.

5 / The national unemployment rate in February, reported today by the Department of Labor, reached 8.8 percent, or 9,575,000 people.

6 / Revised estimates on the 1983 fiscal year budget for the U.S. are released by the Office of Management and Budget, increasing the projected shortfall to $96.4 billion.

7 / Sen. Pete V. Domenici (R-N. Mex.), chairman of the Senate Budget Committee, says a bipartisan effort will result in an alternative budget to that proposed by Pres. Reagan. The new budget will trim entitlements, cut military spending, and increase taxes.

9 / Pres. Reagan, speaking to Senate Republicans, says he will not accept a budget that was not supported by both parties in the House and Senate.

10 / A proposed constitutional amendment enabling the U.S. Congress or states to pass laws banning abortions is endorsed by the Senate Judiciary Committee.

11 / Harrison Williams resigns his seat in the Senate, the first senator since 1922 to do so over charges of misconduct.

12 / The Producer Price Index fell during February, the Labor Department announces. Although the drop was only one-tenth of 1 percent, it was the first decline in six years, and indicated a lessening of inflation.

14 / The Environmental Protection Agency eliminates a requirement that hazardous waste manufacturers report annually on the disposition of their products.

15 / Murray L. Weidenbaum, chairman of the Council of Economic Advisers, says that high interest rates may hurt chances for economic recovery in the spring.

16 / For the first time since July 1981, industrial output rose 1.6 percent in February, it is reported.

17 / The Environmental Protection Agency reverses its earlier decision and prohibits burying any container holding toxic liquids in visible quantities.

19 / Pentagon officials, in their quarterly report, cite an increase of $114.5 billion in the cost of 44 major weapons programs.

22 / The space shuttle *Columbia* lifts off for its third voyage, scheduled for seven days' duration.

23 / The Supreme Court upholds a Federal Trade Commission ruling that requires the American Medical Association to permit advertising by doctors.

The Senate passes a measure giving Congress the right to veto new rules issued by federal regulatory agencies.

26 / Groundbreaking for a memorial to honor those Americans killed in Vietnam takes place on the Mall in Washington, D.C.

Veterans' organizations are ineligible for tax-exempt status because of their lobbying activities, a federal appellate court rules.

29 / Because of a severe sandstorm in the landing area, the space shuttle *Columbia* is forced to continue in orbit beyond today's scheduled landing.

30 / *Columbia* lands safely at the White Sands Missile Range in New Mexico after eight days in space.

31 / The day after four paratroopers were killed in a training exercise in California, U.S. Army officers report that wind gusts caused the deaths of the men and injuries to 156 others.

## INTERNATIONAL

2 / U.S. Secretary of State Haig claims he has evidence supporting his allegations that El Salvador's rebels are controlled by outsiders.

3 / The U.S. State Department announces that it will attempt to negotiate the use of air bases in Colombia and Honduras for defense purposes.

4 / U.S. Secretary of State Haig reports the capture by the Salvadorean army of a Nicaraguan who claims to be aiding the rebels in El Salvador, thus proving Haig's allegations concerning foreign involvement in El Salvador's civil strife.

6 / Five Moslem fundamentalists are sentenced to die for the assassination of Egypt's Pres. Anwar el-Sadat.

9 / Charles J. Haughey of the Fianna Fail party is returned to the office of prime minister of Ireland after winning the election in the Dail (Parliament) held less than a year after he was defeated by Garret FitzGerald's Fine Gael party.

Gen. Angel Anibal Guevara, a conservative, claims victory in Guatemala's presidential elections, held on March 7.

10 / The U.S. government bans the importation of oil from Libya and exports of high-technology materials to that country.

12 / Orlando José Tardencillas, the Nicaraguan captured in El Salvador, recants his earlier statements regarding his homeland's involvement in the Salvadorean civil strife. The Reagan Administration presented the soldier as evidence of Nicaraguan aid to the Salvadorean rebels.

15 / U.S. Secretary of State Haig releases details of his proposals for normalization of relations with Nicaragua, a major part of which hinges on the withdrawal of Nicaraguan forces from El Salvador.

16 / Soviet leader Leonid Brezhnev announces that the USSR has ceased placement of medium-range nuclear weapons in European Russia.

17 / Pres. Reagan asks Congress to provide $128 million for emergency economic aid to El Salvador.

18 / Four members of a television crew from the Netherlands are killed in El Salvador, reportedly when caught in fighting between government soldiers and rebels.

19 / Nicaragua's leaders ask the U.N. to call the Security Council into session for the purpose of denouncing the U.S.'s "imminent" invasion of that Central American country.

20 / The U.S. State Department charges Cuba with planning to disrupt the elections scheduled in El Salvador for March 28.

O.P.E.C. member-nations agree to lower total oil production by 700,000 barrels a day in an effort to avoid a price drop.

22 / The U.S. government releases a report to the U.S. Congress and the U.N. that contains evidence to show that the USSR and its southeast Asian allies used chemical warfare in Afghanistan, Cambodia, and Laos.

23 / The newly elected government of Guatemala, led by Gen. Angel Anibal Guevara, is overthrown by a group of army officers. They name a military junta to rule the country.

24 / Bangladeshi army officers stage a coup, oust Pres. Abdus Sattar, and impose martial law in the country.

Guatemala's new military government suspends the nation's constitution and bars all activities by political parties.

25 / A White House spokesperson says the U.S. government is willing to engage in talks with Cuba, although he expresses little optimism on the effects that such a meeting would have toward normalizing relations between the two countries.

26 / The U.S. formally joins the U.N. peacekeeping force in the Sinai Peninsula.

27 / U.S. Secretary of Defense Weinberger tells Japanese leaders that the U.S. will withdraw some of its military forces or place import restrictions on Japanese goods if that nation does not increase its military strength.

28 / El Salvador holds nationwide elections; despite threats of attack by rebels, the turnout is heavy.

29 / The early vote tally in El Salvador's election gives the victory to the Christian Democratic party of Pres. José Napoleón Duarte.

30 / Fifty-eight U.S. senators endorse a resolution calling for a freeze on nuclear weapons by the U.S. and USSR at sharply reduced levels.

31 / Pres. Reagan rejects the proposal of a global arms freeze because of Soviet superiority in atomic weapons.

---

## APRIL 1982

---

## NATIONAL

1 / The Senate Armed Services Committee recommends cutting $3.2 billion from the proposed $216-billion military budget for 1983, primarily by trimming funds for interim deployment of the first 40 MX intercontinental missiles and for building of a new Army attack helicopter.

2 / The national unemployment rate for March rose to 9 percent, according to the Labor Department. Almost 9.9 million persons were out of work.

3 / In his first in a series of radio broadcasts, Pres. Reagan asks for patience to permit his economic policies to work toward easing the recession.

5 / Pres. Reagan announces a plan to open federal lands to mineral development as a way to reduce U.S. dependence on foreign sources.

6 / White House officials concede defeat this year in their attempts to legislate the transfer of food stamp and welfare programs to the states from the federal government.

8 / The Fair Budget Action Campaign, an alliance of more than 80 national organizations, announces plans for a grass-roots campaign in opposition to Pres. Reagan's domestic policies, with efforts focused on cuts in social welfare programs.

9 / For the second month in a row, the Producer Price Index is reported to have dropped in March, indicating continued progress against inflation.

10 / In an effort to counter criticism from middle-income families, Pres. Reagan says that his administration's cutbacks on government-funded student loans would be offset by private lenders.

11 / A total of 1,151 U.S. counties and cities have been designated areas of high unemployment, following the addition of one city and five counties to the list. Such designation gives employers in those areas preferences in bidding on Federal contracts.

14 / By including the value of subsidy benefits such as Medicaid and food stamps, a spokesperson reports, the Census Bureau hopes to reduce the number of persons classified by federal standards as "poor."

15 / Addressing a group of educators, Pres. Reagan outlines his plan to give income tax credits to families paying private elementary and secondary school tuition.

17 / In the third in a series of weekly radio broadcasts, Pres. Reagan asserts that nuclear warfare must never take place, and, to ensure that it does not, he asks Americans to support his proposed military buildup as a deterrence.

18 / Ground Zero Week begins, sponsored by an organization that attempts to focus public attention on the consequences of nuclear war.

19 / The U.S. Census Bureau releases its initial summary report on population characteristics compiled from the 1980 census. The statistical sample reveals the U.S. population to be better educated, better housed, and more mobile than the 1970 sample.

21 / A drop in the annual growth rate of the Gross National Product of 3.9 percent occurred in the first quarter of 1982, the Commerce Department reports. The news indicates that the current recession continued through March 1982.

22 / In an appearance before the Senate Defense Appropriations Subcommittee, Richard N. Perle, Assistant Secretary of Defense for International Security Policy, says that "nostalgia" for détente has hurt the West's military rebuilding efforts.

23 / For the first time in almost 17 years, consumer prices declined during March, dipping three-tenths of 1 percent, it was announced. The drop was attributed to falling gasoline prices and a decrease in the costs of food and housing.

24 / Data compiled by the Census Bureau show that nearly all economic gains made by the average U.S. family during the 1970s were erased by inflation.

26 / President Reagan names John N. McMahon to serve as Deputy Director of the Central Intelligence Agency. McMahon succeeds Adm. Bobby R. Inman, who announced his resignation effective July 1, 1982.

27 / Jury selection begins in the trial of John W. Hinckley, Jr., who is accused of shooting Pres. Reagan on March 30, 1981.

28 / An impasse between the White House and Democratic Congressional leaders over controlling the budget deficit cannot be broken, Pres. Reagan concedes. Thus, Congress will have to construct a federal budget on its own—one which the President fears will increase the national debt.

29 / In a television address to the nation, Pres. Reagan expresses his support for a constitutional amendment that would require a balanced federal budget.

### INTERNATIONAL

1 / Britain requests action by the U.N. Security Council and Argentina seeks backing from the O.A.S. in their dispute over the Falkland Islands.

2 / A combined force of more than 4,000 Argentines seize the Falkland Islands, South Georgia, and the South Sandwich Islands—all British possessions in the South Atlantic Ocean. Britain promptly breaks relations with Argentina and activates its navy to regain the dependencies.

3 / British ships prepare to leave port for the South Atlantic to retake the Falkland Islands from Argentina.

The U.N. Security Council demands the withdrawal of Argentine military personnel from the Falklands.

4 / Three Argentine marines die in a battle with British marines at Port Grytviken in the South Georgia Islands.

5 / British Foreign Secretary Lord Carrington resigns over the Argentine seizure of the Falklands, calling the invasion a "humiliating affront." Prime Minister Thatcher replaces him with Francis Pym, leader of the House of Commons.

6 / El Salvador's rightist National Republican Alliance and National Conciliation party agree to exclude centrist Christian Democrats from key positions in the new government.

7 / Britain announces a 200-mile war zone around the Falkland Islands and threatens to sink any Argentine ships in the zone.

8 / U.S. Secretary of State Haig begins shuttle diplomacy with Britain and Argentina to settle the Falkland Islands dispute.

9 / The U.S. State Department offers Nicaragua a nine-point plan of cooperation in an effort to heal the rift between the two nations.

10 / Argentine President Leopoldo Galtieri affirms his nation's willingness to fight if provoked by Britain over the Falklands.

The European Economic Community approves a ban on all imports from Argentina until the Latin American nation pulls out of the Falklands.

11 / A U.S.-born Israeli soldier shoots his way into Jerusalem's Dome of the Rock Islamic shrine, killing two Arabs and wounding at least nine others.

12 / Thirty Arabs are shot by Israeli soldiers during demonstrations protesting the attack on the Dome of the Rock shrine.

The British 200-mile war zone around the Falklands goes into effect.

13 / Taiwan will be sold military spare parts by the U.S., says the Reagan Administration, despite warnings of a setback in relations between the U.S. and China.

The O.A.S. passes a compromise resolution expressing concern over the Falkland Islands crisis and offers to cooperate with the current peace efforts.

14 / Nicaragua agrees to the Reagan Administration's plan for reconciliation between it and the U.S. under the condition that the U.S. desist from threatening Nicaraguan security.

15 / Five Moslem fundamentalists are executed for the assassination of Egypt's President Anwar el-Sadat.

17 / Queen Elizabeth II of England signs Canada's Constitution Act, giving that nation power to amend its constitution without British approval.

19 / The U.S. government announces plans for travel restrictions on U.S. citizens wishing to visit Cuba. After May 15, 1982, only official trips, visits by news reporters and academicians, or travel for purposes of family reunification will be permitted.

20 / Chancellor Helmut Schmidt of West Germany, in a speech to Social Democratic party members, states that a freeze on nuclear weapons by N.A.T.O. members would give the USSR dominance over Europe.

21 / Israeli planes attack Palestinian-controlled villages in southern Lebanon in retaliation for the land-mine death of an Israeli soldier on patrol. The action ends a nine-month-old cease-fire between Israel and the Palestine Liberation Organization.

22 / El Salvador's new Constituent Assembly elects Roberto d'Aubuisson, leader of the extreme right-wing Nationalist Republican Alliance, to the post of Assembly president. All other leadership positions are won by rightists.

24 / The Reagan Administration announces that, after a four-year freeze, the U.S. will resume arms sales to Guatemala following what seemed to be an improvement in human rights conditions there since the military coup in March.

25 / The last Israeli soldiers move out of the Sinai to make way for an Egyptian take-over of the peninsula.

The port of Grytviken on South Georgia, Falkland Islands, is retaken by British troops, three weeks after Argentine forces occupied the island.

26 / British Prime Minister Thatcher tells the British House of Commons that combat appears inevitable in the Falkland Islands despite continuing negotiations.

28 / Argentine leaders rebuff an offer by U.S. Secretary of State Haig to meet with them in Buenos Aires over the Falkland Islands crisis and instead prepare for a British attack on the Falklands.

Poland's ruling military announces the end on May 2 of the nighttime curfew throughout the country and the release of 800 persons from internment camps.

29 / Argentina's leaders announce the immediate imposition of a 200-mile blockade around the Falkland Islands. Britain had earlier declared an identical blockade, effective April 30, at 7 A.M. EDT.

30 / The U.S. government officially backs Great Britain in its dispute with Argentina over the Falklands as the British air and sea blockade around the islands begins.

After eight years of negotiations, the Law of the Sea Treaty is passed in the U.N., by a vote of 130 to 4, with 17 abstentions. The U.S. is among the 4 opposing the treaty.

## MAY 1982

### NATIONAL

1 / Pres. Reagan speaks at opening-day ceremonies of the 1982 World's Fair in Knoxville, Tenn.

2 / The Exxon Corporation announces that it is abandoning its 60-percent share in the Colony shale oil project in Colorado, casting doubt on the future of the synthetic fuel venture.
3 / The Senate Judiciary Committee reaches agreement on a compromise version of the Voting Rights Act. Under the legislation, bias could be proved by examining the effects of discrimination without the need to prove intent to discriminate.
4 / Senate Budget Committee Chairman Pete V. Domenici (R-N. Mex.) proposes a compromise budget that, against Pres. Reagan's wishes, would place a one-year freeze on Social Security benefits and other social programs and impose a three-year tax increase.
5 / National Governors Association officials announce that it and the White House have formulated a plan for reorganizing federal and state jurisdictions over Medicaid and welfare.
6 / The White House endorses an antibusing bill and Pres. Reagan announces he will propose a constitutional amendment allowing voluntary prayer in public schools.
7 / The national unemployment rate, released today by the Labor Department, reached 9.4 percent in April, the highest level in 40 years.
8 / White House officials say Defense Secretary Weinberger will choose to place MX missiles either in continually flying aircraft or in a closely packed land base.
10 / Democratic leaders in the House conclude formulation of a budget proposal that maintains current Social Security benefits and increases taxes 50 percent more than the Republican-proposed budget.

The House passes a bill that increases penalties for counterfeiting and selling motion pictures, records, and tapes protected by copyright laws. Reproduction for home use only is not affected.
11 / An unexpectedly high surplus of $436 million, accumulated since Oct. 1, 1981, is reported by the Postal Service.
12 / The House of Representatives passes a supplemental spending bill of almost $6 billion to the budget, with the funds earmarked for such items as mortgage subsidies and student loans.
13 / Braniff Airlines files for protection under bankruptcy laws and becomes the first major airline to fail.
14 / The bribery conviction of former U.S. Congressman Richard Kelly of Florida, stemming from the ABSCAM inquiry, is overturned, because of the federal government's "outrageous" tactics.
16 / The Census Bureau reports that 90 percent of the population growth in the country since the 1980 census has taken place in the southern and western states.
17 / Pres. Reagan formally proposes a constitutional amendment allowing organized prayer in public schools.
18 / Republican senators decide not to push for saving $40 billion in Social Security outlays over a three-year period, but they announce their intention to find a way of ensuring the system's solvency before the end of the year.

The Rev. Sun Myung Moon, head of the Unification Church, is convicted of conspiring to defraud the U.S. government and of filing false federal income-tax returns.
19 / The Commerce Department reports that corporate profits fell a near-record 17.5 percent and the gross national product dropped at an annual rate of 4.3 percent, after adjustment for inflation, in the first quarter of 1982.
20 / The Senate Judiciary Committtee rejects the Reagan Administration's efforts to alter the Freedom of Information Act by refusing to exclude information on terrorism and foreign counterintelligence from the act.

The third and final stage of a federal income tax cut, effective July 1, 1983, will take place as scheduled following the Senate defeat of a Democratic proposal to repeal or defer the final stage.
21 / The Senate votes approval of a $784-billion budget for the 1983 fiscal year.

The California Board of Prison Terms cancels the parole date of Sirhan B. Sirhan, convicted assassin of Sen. Robert F. Kennedy, because of death threats contained in letters written by Sirhan since his incarceration.
22 / Former presidential candidate and three-term governor George C. Wallace announces his candidacy for a fourth term as Alabama's chief executive.
25 / Reagan Administration spokespersons ask Congress to begin work on raising the federal debt ceiling before the government is unable to pay its obligations.
26 / For the fisrt time ever, Congress vetoes a rule proposed by the Federal Trade Commission. The rule would have required dealers to make known to customers any major defects in used cars.
27 / The House of Representatives votes to retain current Medicare spending levels by shifting to that sector $4.8 billion from the military budget.
30 / Treasury Secretary Regan says the U.S. is close to economic recovery, but that turnaround could be a weak one.

The Marshall Islands and the U.S. sign a pact that, after approval by a Marshallese plebiscite and the U.S. Congress, will grant the U.S. 50 years of military rights on the Pacific island group.

## INTERNATIONAL

1 / Both Argentina and Britain claim victories in open warfare over the Falkland Islands, with each nation scoring hits on the other's ships.

Ignoring the official government celebration of May Day, about 30,000 Poles march to show support for the Solidarity union movement and opposition to martial law.
2 / A British submarine torpedoes the Argentine cruiser *General Belgrano*.

El Salvador's provisional president, Alvaro Alfredo Magana Borja, takes the oath of office. The centrist will serve until the Constituent Assembly schedules presidential elections.
3 / Reversing its earlier denial, the Argentine government concedes that its only cruiser, the *General Belgrano*, was torpedoed and sunk, and only 123 of the 1,042 sailors on board have been rescued so far.

A crowd of about 10,000 protesting martial law in Poland are met by Warsaw police with tear gas and water cannons.
4 / Curfews are reinstated and telephone service is cut in Warsaw, Poland, following demonstrations protesting government policies.
5 / Peru's President Fernando Belaúnde Terry presents to Argentina a simplified version of the U.S. proposal for ending the Falklands crisis.
6 / Efforts by the U.S. and Peru to secure a cease-fire between Argentina and Britain over the Falklands fail as two British Sea Harrier jets are lost in severe weather in the South Atlantic.
7 / Britain widens its blockade around the Falklands to reach within 12 miles of the Argentine coast, but Argentina claims Britain's forces are too meager to enforce the blockade.
8 / The Iraqi government announces that it has pulled back from the Iranian province of Khuzistan, reportedly to aid forces in the area of Khurramshahr.
9 / In an address to the graduating class at Eureka College, his alma mater, Pres. Reagan says he has written to Soviet leader Brezhnev suggesting that both the U.S. and USSR reduce their nuclear arsenals by one third and later agree on an "equal ceiling" on the total payload of all nuclear missiles.

Israeli bombers, breaking a cease-fire in effect since July 23, 1981, attack Palestinian bases in southern Lebanon. Palestinian guerrillas answer the assault by shelling northern Israel.
10 / Argentina's leaders announce that their nation's sovereignty over the Falklands need not be recognized before their troops leave the islands, but later negotiations should eventually lead to Argentine possession of the territory.
11 / British sources report the sinking of an Argentine ship in the waters between East and West Falkland islands by a British frigate.
12 / The Reagan Administration's proposed $60 million in military appropriations for El Salvador is approved by the House Foreign Affairs Committee.

Three French sailors reveal that they witnessed the landing of Argentine commandos on the Falkland Islands' South Georgia under cover of darkness on March 25, one week before the Argentine invasion of the islands.

14 / Vladimir P. Suslov, head of the USSR's foreign ministry section dealing with British affairs, reads a statement from his government to the British Ambassador in Moscow. The Soviets state that the war zones established by Great Britain around the Falklands are unlawful.

A Spanish priest living in France is formally charged with attempting to kill Pope John Paul II while the pontiff was visiting the shrine at Fatima, Portugal.

15 / U.S. Secretary of State Haig reports progress in talks with Greece's Prime Minister Papandreou over issues affecting relations between their nations.

16 / The national parliament of Yugoslavia elects Milka Planinc of Croatia to the post of prime minister, the first woman to serve in that office.

17 / Salvador Jorge Blanco of the Revolutionary party is declared the winner in the Dominican Republic's presidential elections.

18 / A declaration urging worldwide efforts to preserve the earth's resources is adopted at the conclusion of the second U.N. Conference on the Global Environment.

19 / Israeli Prime Minister Begin survives a no-confidence test by one vote.

20 / The U.N. talks resolving the Falkland Islands crisis break down when Great Britain rejects proposals to continue negotiations.

21 / British troops land on East Falkland Island while Argentine and British planes and ships engage in all-out combat.

22 / British forces continue landing on East Falkland Island as efforts to reach a peaceful resolution in the South Atlantic go on at the U.N.

Representatives from Ontario, Quebec, and the eight U.S. states bordering the Great Lakes vote to form an international federation of citizen groups to preserve the Great Lakes.

23 / Iranian troops encircle the city of Khurramshahr and attempt to retake the last Iraqi stronghold in Iran.

24 / Iran claims it has recaptured Khurramshahr and taken prisoner the 30,000 Iraqis who have been holding the port city.

The European Economic Community extends indefinitely its trade sanctions against Argentina as an expression of support for Great Britain in the Falklands crisis.

25 / Argentine Foreign Minister Nicanor Costa Méndez, at the U.N., calls for a negotiated settlement to the Falkland Islands conflict.

26 / Yuri V. Andropov resigns as head of the K.G.B., the USSR's intelligence organization, and is succeeded by Vitali V. Fedorchek. Andropov has been frequently mentioned as a possible successor to Leonid Brezhnev.

27 / At an emergency meeting of foreign ministers of the Organization of American States (O.A.S.), Argentina's Nicanor Costa Méndez attacks the U.S. for supporting Great Britain in the Falkland Islands crisis.

28 / Pope John Paul II arrives in England for a six-day visit. It is the first time a reigning pontiff has journeyed to Great Britain.

29 / In a 17 to 0 vote, the O.A.S. condemns the British attack on the Falkland Islands and urges the U.S. to stop its aid to Britain.

U.S. Department of Defense officials reveal that they have drawn up a strategy for fighting an extended nuclear war with the USSR.

30 / Spain becomes the first country to join N.A.T.O. since 1955. The new member commits 340,000 soldiers to the pact's fighting strength.

31 / British land forces advance to within 15 miles of Stanley, Falkland Islands, in their effort to retake the capital and last stronghold of the Argentines on the islands.

## JUNE 1982

### NATIONAL

1 / The Supreme Court rules that police may search automobiles and the contents of items found inside without a warrant if they have "probable cause."

2 / A three-volume report is issued by the Reagan Administration on the 1981 White House Conference on Aging. The report concludes that problems of the elderly are overemphasized, and that solvency of the Social Security System is of major importance.

3 / The House of Representatives votes approval of a new bill that imposes both imprisonment and fine penalties on persons convicted of revealing the identities of U.S. intelligence agents, sources, and informers.

4 / The Labor Department reports that May's unemployment rate rose one-tenth of 1 percent over the April figure, to 9.5 percent.

7 / The Reagan Administration announces that it will force four million welfare recipients to grant permission for government examination of forms on record with the Internal Revenue Service. The forms would reveal information on unearned income.

8 / The House of Representatives votes to extend for three years the Endangered Species Act.

9 / U.S. Congress members will lose their automatic $75-per-day tax deduction, following a House vote to repeal the measure as part of a supplemental appropriation bill.

11 / The Professional Air Traffic Controllers' Organization loses its union status by the ruling of a federal appeals court.

12 / A gathering estimated at more than 750,000 persons demonstrate their opposition to nuclear arms during a rally in New York City.

14 / In an 8-1 vote, the Supreme Court declares unconstitutional an Alaskan proposal to distribute its oil revenue surplus among the state's residents on the basis of the individuals' lengths of residence in the state.

15 / In Washington, D.C., Federal District Judge Gerhard A. Gesell orders that the Department of Health and Human Services stop requiring welfare recipients to waive the right to privacy so that their tax records could be examined.

17 / Gulf Oil Corporation announces that it will purchase the Cities Service Company, creating the seventh-largest industrial corporation in the U.S.

18 / The Voting Rights Act of 1965 will remain in effect for another 25 years, following the extension of the measure by the Senate today.

19 / Treasury Department officials reveal an ongoing study of monetary policy at the White House, with the possibility of future changes in the Federal Reserve Board.

21 / John W. Hinckley, Jr., is acquitted, by reason of insanity, on charges of shooting Pres. Reagan and three other men in Washington, D.C., on March 30, 1981.

22 / The House of Representatives votes 210-108 for a Republican-sponsored budget with a projected deficit of $103.9 billion.

23 / With three Republicans and three Democrats voting counter to their parties' positions, the Senate approves the compromise Republican-sponsored federal budget for fiscal year 1983.

24 / The Supreme Court rules that the U.S. President is exempt from lawsuits stemming from action undertaken while in office.

25 / Alexander Haig abruptly resigns from his post of secretary of state. He cryptically cites changes in U.S. foreign policy as the reason for his departure. George P. Shultz, a cabinet member during the Nixon Administration, succeeds him.

27 / The space shuttle *Columbia* embarks on its fourth journey into orbit carrying its first payloads of a commercial or military nature.

A three-day national meeting of Democrats closes in Philadelphia after approving a party policy in opposition to the Reagan Administration.

28 / Special prosecutor Leon Silverman releases a report on Labor Secretary Raymond J. Donovan in which he concludes that insufficient evidence exists to link the cabinet member to organized crime figures.

29 / After a federal district judge ordered the release of most Haitian refugees held in U.S. detention facilities, the Justice Department announces it will appeal the court decision.

30 / In a televised news conference, Pres. Reagan reasserts his confidence in his economic policy and

assails those who claim he is trying to cut Social Security benefits.

The proposed Equal Rights Amendment to the U.S. Constitution fails to meet June 30th deadline and expires, three states short of the needed 38.

### INTERNATIONAL

1 / The Revolutionary Cells Terrorist Group takes credit for bombings that damage facilities at four U.S. military bases in West Germany.

2 / Efforts by the Secretary-General of the U.N., Javier Pérez de Cuéllar, to mediate a cease-fire in the Falklands crisis have failed, the leader of the international body admits.

3 / The Soviet Communist party newspaper *Pravda* in an editorial, rejects Pres. Reagan's plan for reduction in strategic arms.

Shlomo Argov, Israeli ambassador to Britain, is shot and critically wounded in London.

4 / Israeli jets bomb Palestinian camps in southern Lebanon in retaliation for the shooting of the Israeli ambassador to Britain.

An economic summit conference attended by the leaders of seven industrial countries, including Pres. Reagan, opens in Versailles, France.

5 / At the economic summit, conferees reject Pres. Reagan's proposal to restrict government-subsidized export credits to the USSR.

6 / Israelis attack southern Lebanon by sea, air and land, passing U.N. peacekeeping forces on their way to destroy P.L.O. bases.

7 / Former defense minister Hissen Habre leads a group of rebels to take over Chad's capital, N'Djamena, and overthrow the government of President Goukouni Oueddei.

Beaufort Castle, a Palestinian guerrilla stronghold in southern Lebanon, is taken by Israeli troops as they push northward. Meanwhile, Syria sends troops to fight off the Israeli incursion.

8 / The U.S. vetoes a U.N. Security Council resolution threatening sanctions against Israel for its refusal to stop military actions against Lebanon.

9 / Israel's ground troops advance to within sight of Beirut while its planes engage in air combat with Syrian MIGs in eastern Lebanon.

10 / N.A.T.O. leaders agree to build up their nations' defenses and to attempt negotiations with the USSR on unilateral arms reductions.

11 / Both Israel and Syria declare cease-fires in the Lebanon conflict. Israel, however, does not consider the truce to extend to the Palestinian guerrillas.

12 / Israeli government officials announce that they are stopping attacks on Palestinians in the Beirut, Lebanon, area.

13 / Warplanes from Israel attack Palestinian areas in Lebanon after Palestinians shoot at Israeli positions, breaking the cease-fire in its first day.

Khalid, king of Sauldi Arabia, dies of a heart attack and is succeeded by his half-brother, Crown Prince Fahd.

14 / Argentine soldiers raise white flags over Stanley, Falkland Islands. Surrender talks begin between Britain and Argentina.

The Egyptian government announces that it is suspending talks with Israel on self-rule for the Palestinians in light of Israel's invasion of Lebanon.

15 / In an address at the U.N. General Assembly's special session on disarmament, Soviet Foreign Minister Andrei A. Gromyko reads a letter from Leonid I. Brezhnev in which the Soviet leader pledges that the USSR will not be the first to use nuclear weapons in a war.

As the Union Jack once again flies over Stanley, Falkland Islands, British troops begin rounding up the Argentine soldiers who surrendered.

Former C.I.A. agent Edmund P. Wilson, charged with aiding the Libyan government by shipping explosives to that country and training Libyan terrorists, is arrested in New York City.

16 / A meeting between Pres. Reagan and Israeli Prime Minister Begin, scheduled for June 18, is assured of taking place after Begin says Israeli troops will not enter and take Beirut, Lebanon.

17 / Domestic events precipitated by the Argentine invasion of the Falklands result in the resignation of Pres. Galtieri of Argentina. He is temporarily replaced by Maj. Gen. Alfredo Oscar St. Jean.

18 / Argentine leaders say that an end to hostilities with Great Britain can come only after British forces are removed from the Falklands, the blockade along the Argentine coast is lifted, and economic sanctions against the Latin American nation are ended.

19 / U.S. Secretary of State Haig announces that the USSR has held extensive strategic weapons tests within the past few days.

20 / Foreign ministers of the E.E.C. agree to lift a trade embargo against Argentina over the objections of Great Britain.

21 / Palestinian camps and residential sections of western Beirut, Lebanon, become the targets of Israeli attack from land and sea. Meanwhile, Israeli and Syrian troops engage in shooting along the route between Beirut and Damascus.

22 / Announcement is made in Malaysia of the creation of a Cambodian government in exile, led by Prince Norodom Sihanouk, Khieu Samphan, and former prime minister Son Sann.

Maj. Gen. Reynaldo Antonio Bignone is named by army leaders to serve as president of Argentina following the forced resignation of Lieut. Gen. Leopoldo Galtieri.

23 / The Japanese computer manufacturer Hitachi Ltd. admits authorizing payment of $540,000 to a consulting firm in the U.S. in order to obtain confidential computer information belonging to the International Business Machines Corporation. The consulting firm is believed to have been a decoy operation of the F.B.I.

24 / Foreign nationals and Lebanese with U.S. immigration documents leave Lebanon aboard a transport ship of the Sixth Fleet after the closing of the U.S. embassy in Beirut.

26 / In the U.N. Security Council, the U.S. vetoes a resolution calling for the limited withdrawal of both Israeli and P.L.O. forces from Beirut.

27 / Israeli warplanes drop leaflets on Beirut urging residents to flee the city for their own safety.

28 / The government of Israel says it will not permit the P.L.O. an extended period of time to leave Beirut under the Israeli offer of safe passage from the surrounded city.

29 / Strategic arms reduction talks between the U.S. and the USSR begin in Geneva in an effort to reach an accord on strategic nuclear weapons manufacture and use.

## JULY 1982

### NATIONAL

1 / A $24-billion, five-year job training program to replace the Comprehensive Employment and Training Act (CETA) is passed by the Senate. A major feature of the bill is increased reliance on private-sector involvement in youth job training.

2 / The Bureau of Labor Statistics releases unemployment figures for June. The 9.5 percent matches the May figure, but increased joblessness was found among adult males and black teenagers.

4 / *Columbia*, the space shuttle, lands at Edwards Air Force Base, Calif., on schedule, successfully completing its fourth and final test flight.

6 / Pres. Reagan expresses interest in a flat-rate income tax, and he suggests the concept be studied further.

7 / A study of the U.S. Postal Service, after 10 years of independent operation, concludes that improvements in services and cost-cutting proposals would enhance the organization's efficiency.

9 / A Pan American World Airways 727 jet crashes into a residential area shortly after taking off from New Orleans International Airport. All 143 aboard are killed, along with an undetermined number of people on the ground.

Federal investigators report that a former Congressional page has failed lie-detector tests conducted in response to the man's allegations concerning homosexual activity among members of Congress and Congressional pages. Leroy Williams's accusations are central to an investigation of drug and sex abuses on Capitol Hill.

Trapeze artist Miguel Vazquez successfully executes the first-ever quadruple somersault during a performance in Tucson, Ariz.

11 / Federal aviation officials reveal that two warnings of "wind shear" conditions were radioed to the jet that crashed after takeoff from New Orleans' Moisant International Airport on July 9. Wind shear is an atmospheric phenomenon characterized by sudden directional changes in surface winds.

12 / The last boxy, roomy Checker taxicab comes off the Kalamazoo, Mich., assembly line of the Checker Motor Corporation, ending 23 years of production for the bulky vehicle.

13 / A report of more than 500 pages is issued by the Environmental Protection Agency detailing federal regulations on the dumping of hazardous wastes in land sites.

14 / The Senate Foreign Relations Committee unanimously approves the nomination of George P. Shultz to the office of Secretary of State.

More than 200 U.S. Congress members reintroduce the Equal Rights Amendment, two weeks after the deadline for ratification by the states of the previous measure.

15 / Taxpayer subsidies for tobacco growers are curtailed by Congressional legislation.

16 / Secretary of Labor Raymond J. Donovan proposes an easing of child labor laws to permit 14- and 15-year-olds to increase the number of working hours and expand the types of jobs they are permitted to hold.

George P. Shultz is sworn in as Secretary of State by Pres. Reagan.

17 / A federal judge in Miami, Fla., reverses his earlier decision and permits a deer hunt in the Everglades. The State Game and Fresh Water Fish Commission called for the elimination of 2,000 deer because high water levels in the area destroyed much of the animals' food supply.

19 / The Census Bureau reports that 14 percent of the U.S. population was officially classified as "poor" in 1981, an increase of 7.4 percent over the previous year. The 1981 figure is the highest since 1967.

20 / Voting begins on amendments to trim the $177-billion military appropriations outlay. If passed, the amendments would lower the total amount by more than $50 billion.

21 / Mitsui & Company (U.S.A.) pleads guilty to fraud and issuing false statements in connection with the sale of Japanese steel at prices low enough to prompt a government investigation.

Attorney General William French Smith's accepting of severance pay from a steel company and investing in two tax shelters will not result in the calling of a special prosecutor, the Justice Department announces.

22 / The Senate approves a proposed 10 percent withholding tax on stock dividends and interest, and votes in favor of increased federal taxes on cigarettes and telephone service.

The House of Representatives votes to block funding for the development of new forms of chemical weapons that, when combined, produce a deadly nerve gas.

The White House announces that Murray L. Weidenbaum, Chairman of the President's Council of Economic Advisers and a leading member of the Reagan Administration, is resigning to return to an academic position.

23 / The Labor Department reports that consumer prices rose 1 percent in June—the same rate as that of May—to keep the annual inflation rate at double-digit levels.

The Senate passes a $99-billion revenue raising bill that includes a provision to halve the business deduction for local meals and entertainment.

24 / Pres. Reagan signs a bill blocking tax subsidies for those holders of tobacco allotments who do not actually grow the crop but lease the allotment to others.

25 / Officials of the Department of Housing and Urban Development say it has eliminated the Division of Environmental Hazards Research, a Unit whose director, Irwin H. Billick, was instrumental in uncovering the effects of lead in gasoline on the health of children.

26 / A federal appeals court rules that federal remedial education aid to states can be distributed according to 1970, rather than 1980, census data.

27 / The Reagan Administration concedes that the large number of males failing to register for the draft raises doubts on the enforcement potential of the law. An estimated 675,000 have thus far not registered as required.

28 / In a televised news conference, Pres. Reagan says economic recovery has been slowed by Democratic Congressional opposition to his requested deficit reductions.

29 / The Reagan Administration's opposition to extending unemployment insurance for jobless workers to one full year is criticized by Senate Finance Committee members of both parties.

30 / The Washington Post Company is assessed $2.05 million in damages by a federal jury in a libel case brought by William P. Tavoulareas, president of Mobil Oil Corp. The plaintiff accused the newspaper of falsely reporting that he had used corporate funds to establish a shipping company for his son and then provided him with Mobil contracts.

## INTERNATIONAL

1 / British Prime Minister Thatcher rebukes the U.S. government for attempting to constrain foreign companies in their effort to honor contracts connected to construction of the natural gas pipeline between the USSR and Western Europe.

2 / Former E.E.C. president Roy Jenkins wins election to the leadership of Britain's new Social Democratic party.

3 / Israeli troops blockade access to West Beirut, cutting off the Palestinians from the rest of Lebanon.

Rioting and strikes by black gold miners in South Africa result in death to eight miners as police and mine guards attempt to end the labor unrest.

4 / The Dominican Republic's president, Antonio Guzman, dies of gunshot wound in the head. Private speculation later suggests that he committed suicide.

5 / West Beirut, Lebanon, is bombed by Israeli forces, who are attempting to force the Palestinians out of Lebanon.

6 / Pres. Reagan announces that he has agreed to send a small force of U.S. troops to act as temporary peacekeepers in Beirut if a settlement is reached in Lebanon.

7 More than 1,000 South African black miners are removed from mining areas after a week of rioting that resulted in the deaths of 10 workers.

8 / The Soviet news agency Tass reports that Leonid Brezhnev wrote Pres. Reagan, warning that the USSR will modify its Mideast policy in response to the stated U.S. intention to send troops to Lebanon.

9 / A spokesman for Syria's government says his country will not accept Palestinian fighters now under siege in Beirut, Lebanon.

10 / O.P.E.C. member nations fail to gain unanimity during a two-day meeting called to plan ways of limiting production and maintaining price levels.

The U.N. special session on disarmament ends without reaching agreement on an overall program to control and reduce arms.

11 / Italy wins the World Cup soccer championship for the first time in 44 years, defeating West Germany by the score of 3-1.

12 / A British government official reports that his nation considers the Falkland Islands war to be ended. The 593 Argentine prisoners are to be returned to their homes as soon as possible.

13 / The Vatican announces that three outside banking experts will investigate relationships between the Vatican bank and Banco Ambrosiano. Italy's largest private bank, Banco Ambrosiano, is currently under investigation over $1.4 billion in unsecured loans made by its Latin American subsidiaries.

14 / Iranian troops move into Iraq and aim for Basra, 14 miles from the Iranian border.

15 / Egypt's Pres. Mubarak calls for an organized effort by Arab leaders to find a solution to the Palestinian issue in the Mideast. He also asks for mutual recognition of Israel and the P.L.O.

16 / In a move interpreted to be an attempt at consolidation of power, Polish leader Jaruzelski reorganizes the Polish Communist party executive hierarchy.

17 / A major breach in security, with resulting release of secret information from Britain's Government Communications Headquarters at Cheltenham, Eng., is under investigation, it is revealed.
18 / Bolivia's President, Brig. Gen. Celso Torrelio, offers to resign in response to pressures stemming from the nation's economic and political crises.
19 / U.S. Secretary of State George P. Shultz, in a meeting with the foreign ministers of Saudi Arabia and Syria, reaffirms the U.S. position regarding the P.L.O. The Reagan Administration is seeking safety for the P.L.O. in an existing Arab state.
20 / Two bombs explode in London, Eng., parks. The first goes off in Hyde Park as the Queen's Household Cavalry is en route to the changing of the guard ceremony; two men and six horses are killed. The second blast in Regent's Park, kills six army musicians performing on the bandstand.
21 / Poland's leader, Gen. Wojciech Jaruzelski, announces that more than 1,200 persons detained by the government are to be released.
22 / Despite a U.S. ban on the use of American licenses in the manufacture of parts for the USSR-Western Europe gas pipeline, the French government announces that French companies will fulfill their contracts. The French firm of Alsthom-Atlantique, which has a license from General Electric to manufacture rotors, is to produce 40 of them for the project.
23 / The International Whaling Commission, meeting in Brighton, Eng., votes 25-7 to ban all commercial whaling by 1986.
24 / A letter sent by Interior Secretary James G. Watt to Israeli Ambassador to the U.S. Moshe Arens is disavowed by the White House. In the correspondence, dated June 17, Watt stated that U.S. support for Israel could be shaken if Jewish liberals in the U.S. oppose the Reagan energy resource development program.
25 / Yasir Arafat, leader of the P.L.O., signs a document accepting U.N. resolutions concerning the Palestinian question, but does not mention specifically Israel's right to exist.
26 / The U.S. Justice Department reveals it has begun an investigation of six Japanese firms charged with fixing prices on semiconductor computer chips.
27 / In an attempt to continue U.S. aid to El Salvador, Pres. Reagan asserts that the Central American nation is making progress on human rights and on changing its economic and political systems.
28 / A request by the Reagan Administration to develop, test and operate nuclear weapons in opposition to the strategic arms limitation agreements with the USSR is blocked by the House of Representatives.
29 / In a White House meeting, Pres. Reagan and Indian Prime Minister Indira Gandhi agree to a plan by which low-enriched uranium fuel from a U.S.-built atomic power plant in Bombay, India, would be supplied to that country by France.
30 / P.L.O. leaders send Philip C. Habib, the U.S. special envoy, a letter detailing their plan for a withdrawal from West Beirut, Lebanon. The strategy, estimated to take one month, would result in the resettlement of the P.L.O. in Syria, Jordan, and Egypt.
31 / U.S. government officials report that the USSR is willing to cut its long-range missile and bomber force if the U.S. will cancel deployment of medium-range missiles in Europe and restrict future cruise missile deployment.

## AUGUST 1982

### NATIONAL

1 / At the opening session of the National Urban League's four-day conference, the organization's president, John E. Jacob, calls for a national program of training and employment for the jobless.
2 / Members of the staff of St. Elizabeth's Hospital in Washington, D.C., issue a report in which they conclude John W. Hinckley, Jr., to be mentally ill and a danger to himself and others. On June 21, Hinckley was acquitted, by reason of insanity, of shooting Pres. Reagan.
3 / Addressing the centennial meeting of the Supreme Council of the Knights of Columbus, Pres. Reagan asks the nation's Roman Catholics to reject the proposed nuclear freeze concept.
4 / In a 69 to 31 vote, the U.S. Senate approves a proposed Constitutional amendment that would require a balanced federal budget be passed by Congress each year.

A federal appeals court, voiding a Reagan Administration decision, rules that all new cars sold after September 1983 must have either air bags or automatic seat belts.
5 / The House of Representatives rejects an arms freeze but passes the Reagan Administration's arms reduction resolution by a two-vote margin.
6 / The Labor Department reports that unemployment in July rose to 9.8 percent—from June's 9.5 percent—and sets a postwar record.
7 / Associate Supreme Court Justice John Paul Stevens, in a speech to the American Judicature Society, suggests that an intermediate federal appellate court be created to select those cases that should be heard by the Supreme Court.
8 / Because of their frustration with the Reagan Administration's "New Federalism," leaders of the National Governors Association, meeting in Afton, Okla., choose to formulate their own plan for changing the division of responsibilities between the federal and state governments.
9 / Lyn Nofziger, former assistant to Pres. Reagan for political affairs, announces that he will return to the White House to serve as a consultant in the Administration's efforts to pass a $98.5-billion tax increase.

John W. Hinckley, Jr., the assailant of Pres. Reagan, is committed to a mental hospital for an indefinite period by a federal judge.
10 / A federal district court judge rules that American Telephone and Telegraph must divest itself of its 22 wholly owned local subsidiaries, as demanded by the Justice Department, but it can keep its research laboratories, long-distance division, and manufacturing subsidiary. The ruling by Judge Harold H. Greene also stipulates that he himself must review all reorganization steps.
12 / In a 340-58 vote, the House passes a measure blocking the sale of oil and gas exploration leases in federal wilderness areas.
13 / Pres. Reagan declares that only 20 percent of his proposed $98.9-billion revenue increase is actually composed of taxes. The other 80 percent, he says, will come from tax reform.
14 / Businesses will be able to continue deducting the cost of certain meals if the provisions of a House-Senate conference committee decision regarding the pending tax increase are passed.
15 / Senate-House negotiators approve Pres. Reagan's $98.3-billion tax bill—the total of which is only $600 million less than the President requested.
16 / *Saturday Review*, a periodical devoted to culture, ends publication after 58 years.
17 / The Senate passes major revisions in U.S. immigration laws. Among the provisions is amnesty for all illegal aliens who arrived in the U.S. before Jan. 1, 1980.

The New York Stock Exchange experiences its second-busiest day on record and its greatest one-day advance in history following a drop in interest rates. The Dow Jones industrial average rises a record 38.81 points.
18 / The New York Stock Exchange sets a new volume record as 132.7 million shares trade hands.

Speaker of the House Thomas P. O'Neill (D-Mass.) joins Pres. Reagan in urging passage of the $98.3-billion tax bill.
19 / By a vote of 226 to 207, the House approves the revenue-raising bill; the Senate follows suit, passing the measure by a vote of 52 to 47.
20 / The New York Stock Exchange finishes its trading week with yet another high volume session, the Dow Jones industrial average rises another 30.72 points, and major banks lower their prime lending rate for the third time in a week.
23 / The stock market continues its frantic pace, and the Dow Jones average hits an eight-month high of 891.17.

24 / The Labor Department reports a rise of six-tenths of 1 percent in consumer prices during July.
25 / Representative Frederick W. Richmond (D-N.Y.) pleads guilty to charges of tax evasion, possession of marijuana, and illegal payments to obtain government contracts for the former Brooklyn Navy Yard. Richmond promptly resigns his House seat.
26 / In a move designed to avoid impending lawsuits brought by victims of asbestosis and lung cancer, the Manville Corporation, world's largest asbestos producer, files for bankruptcy.
27 / A former Congressional page, whose allegations of sexual misconduct on Capitol Hill brought about an investigaton, states that he lied. Leroy Williams tells a news conference that he made up the accusations to draw attention to the lack of supervision for the pages.
28 / Pres. Reagan vetoes a $14.1-billion spending bill designed to see the federal government through to Sept. 30, when the present fiscal year ends.
29 / Senator Robert Dole (R-Kans.), in a television interview, suggests Congress be called back into session after the election to work on solutions to the Social Security System's financial problems.
30 / An award of $13.5 million is ordered to be paid by the U.S. government and Lockheed Aircraft Corp. to 45 children evacuated from Vietnam immediately preceding the fall of Saigon in 1975. The youngsters, since adopted by U.S. citizens, were injured when the plane in which they were escaping lost a rear door, crashed and exploded.
31 / The Commerce Department reports that the government index of leading economic indicators advanced 1.3 percent in July, the fourth successive month of increases. The news is credited, in part, for spurring stock market gains and a Dow Jones industrial average close of 901.31.

## INTERNATIONAL

1 / Kenya's president, Daniel arap Moi, reveals that an attempt by junior air force personnel to overthrow his government has been foiled.
2 / In a meeting at the White House, Pres. Reagan tells Israeli Foreign Minister Yitzhak Shamir that Israel must end its attacks on West Beirut and permit food, water and medical supplies to reach the besieged city.
3 / U.N. Secretary-General Javier Pérez de Cuéllar blames Israel's lack of cooperation for the delay in placing U.N. peacekeeping officials in Lebanon to monitor the latest cease-fire in that Mideast nation.
5 / Despite a direct plea from Pres. Reagan, Israeli leaders refuse to consider a pull-back of their troops in West Beirut.
6 / Banco Ambrosiano, Italy's largest private bank and the subject of an extensive investigation of its Latin American subsidiaries, is liquidated by the Italian government.
7 / Ankara, Turkey, airport is the site of an attack by submachine gun-armed Armenians. Seven people are killed and 69 wounded.

Italy's five-party coalition government collapses following the withdrawal of the Socialist party and the subsequent resignation of Prime Minister Giovanni Spadolini.

Belisario Betancur Cuartas, leader of the Conservative party, is inaugurated president of Colombia.
8 / In response to information received concerning planned strikes and possible violence, Philippine Pres. Ferdinand E. Marcos announces the formation of a 1,000-member secret police force to patrol the city of Manila.
9 / A peace plan for West Beirut, Lebanon, is presented to Israel by the U.S. It would provide for the stationing of a multinational force in West Beirut as the P.L.O.'s military units begin to withdraw from the city.
10 / Israel's leaders agree to the provisions of the U.S. peace plan for Lebanon, but demand that most of the P.L.O. guerrillas leave West Beirut before the arrival of a peacekeeping force. The Syrian government announces that it will permit the P.L.O. evacuees to enter its borders.

In a 22-12 vote, the U.S. House Foreign Affairs Committee approves a bill that would block the Reagan Administration's sanctions against the sale of equipment for construction of the USSR-Western Europe gas pipeline.
11 / As an addition to an appropriations bill, the Senate approves an amendment calling for the prevention of the spread of Cuban influence in the Western Hemisphere. The amendment must be approved by a Senate-House conference committee before inclusion in the final measure.
12 / West Beirut, Lebanon, experiences 11 hours of bombing by Israeli jets; negotiations on the withdrawal of P.L.O. guerrillas from the city break off.
13 / Demonstrations by supporters of the Solidarity labor movement to mark the eighth month of martial law in Poland break up after the militia uses force against marchers in the cities of Warsaw, Cracow, Gdańsk and Wroclaw.
14 / The trial of Iran's former foreign minister, Sadegh Ghotbzadeh, begins in Tehran. The former leader is accused of plotting the overthrow of Ayatollah Khomeini's government.
15 / Israel agrees to the provisions of Philip C. Habib's peace plan for Lebanon put forth on Aug. 9.
16 / Egypt's foreign minister informs the U.S.'s chargé d'affaires in Cairo that Palestinian guerrillas evacuated from Lebanon are not welcome in Egypt if the U.S. will not assist in devising a comprehensive Mideast peace plan that includes a provision for a Palestinian state.
17 / Pres. Reagan, in an address to Taiwan, reassures that nation of his government's support, despite the U.S. intention to reduce arms sales to Taiwan, because he expects China to work toward peaceful reunification with the Taiwanese.
18 / Lebanon's cabinet approves the proposals by Philip C. Habib of the U.S. for ending the crisis in its nation by removing Palestinian guerrillas from West Beirut and installing a multinational peacekeeping force.
19 / Israeli approval of the Lebanon peace plan ends their 10-week siege of West Beirut and ensures the return of two Israeli soldiers captured during the conflict.

Mexico meets with bankers to seek a postponement in its debt repayment to foreign banks. The country owes $80 billion, half of which is due within a year.
20 / The USSR agrees to extend for one year its grain sale agreement with the U.S., purchasing 17.8 million tons of wheat and corn.
22 / Part of the first group of Palestinian guerrillas to leave Lebanon arrives in Jordan and is greeted by King Hussein.
23 / The Lebanese parliament elects Bashir Gemayel, leader of the right-wing Christian militia, to the presidency of that nation.

Italy's 42nd government since World War II is seated; Prime Minister Giovanni Spadolini heads a cabinet composed of the same members as the previous one.
24 / A U.S. company, Dresser Industries, can be penalized for permitting its French subsidiary to supply parts for the USSR-Western Europe gas pipeline, a federal judge rules. The French government had ordered Dresser France to provide three compressors valued at $2 million.
25 / U.S. Marines land in Beirut to take part in multinational peacekeeping efforts in Lebanon.
26 / The U.S. government places trade sanctions on two French companies—Dresser France, a subsidiary of U.S.-headquartered Dresser Industries, and Creusot-Loire—for supplying equipment to build the Soviet pipeline to Western Europe.
27 / Col. Atilla Altikat, Turkish military attaché in Ottawa, Canada, is killed by a gunman later reported to be under orders of the Justice Commandos for Armenian Genocide.
29 / Two Britons successfully complete the first circumnavigation of the world that crossed the North and South Poles. The voyage of Sir Ranulph Twisleton-Wykeham Fiennes and Charles Burton began on Sept. 2, 1979.
30 / P.L.O. leader Yasir Arafat leaves Beirut, Lebanon, aboard a cruise ship destined for Athens, Greece; he is expected to take up residence in Tunisia.
31 / On the second anniversary of the Solidarity union's formation, demonstrations take place in Poland's cities. Two anti-government protestors are reported killed in confrontations between riot police and demonstrators.

## SEPTEMBER 1982

### NATIONAL

2 / In response to the growing popularity of hang gliding and ultralight powered aircraft flying, the Federal Aviation Administration issues the first federal rules for their operation.

3 / National unemployment remained at 9.8 percent in August, according to the U.S. Labor Dept. The percentage figure actually indicates 15,000 more unemployed in August than in July because of an enlarged work force.

Four former Congressmen convicted in the ABSCAM case fail to have their convictions overturned by a three-judge federal panel in New York City.

4 / A Los Angeles, Calif., apartment building is gutted by fire, killing 18 residents and injuring 31, 5 critically.

6 / The U.S. [illegible]tes the 100th Labor Day holiday under the clouds of high unemployment and employee "give-backs" to secure jobs.

The Bendix Corp., in a takeover attempt, reports that 58 percent of Martin Marietta Corp.'s outstanding shares of stock have been tendered to Bendix. Martin Marietta announces that it will proceed with a counteroffer.

7 / The threatened furlough of 19,000 employees of the Internal Revenue Service is averted when the House's Treasury Subcommittee approves the transfer of funds within the Treasury Department.

8 / In voting at three separate conventions, the Lutheran Church in America, the American Lutheran Church, and the Association of Evangelical Lutheran Churches agree to merge by 1987.

9 / Private enterprise's first venture into space, *Conestoga 1,* lifts off Matagorda Island, Tex., and lands 10.5 minutes later 321 miles away. The spacecraft was developed by Space Services Inc. of America, based in Houston, Tex.

10 / The Senate, in a 60-30 vote, overrides Pres. Reagan's veto of a $14.1-billion supplemental security bill—the first override for the Reagan Administration.

12 / Following the issuance of a court order, the Agriculture Dept. announces the re-allocation of $9.8 million to fund a program that provides food to malnourished mothers of small children.

13 / Special Prosecutor Leon Silverman releases the results of his investigation into activities of Labor Sec. Raymond J. Donovan. The report concludes that no evidence exists to prosecute Donovan on his alleged involvement with organized crime.

15 / The Senate, by a 47 to 46 vote defeats a proposal to ban federal funding of abortions.

16 / The House of Representatives passes a $1-billion-plus public works bill intended to create jobs in cities with high unemployment.

17 / In testimony during a trial brought against the U.S. government by 24 cancer victims or their survivors from northern Ariz. and southern Utah, a medical researcher from the Center for Disease Control reports an unexpectedly high incidence of leukemia in the victims' home area. The plaintiffs attribute the occurrence of the disease to atmospheric testing of nuclear weapons conducted upwind of their homes from 1951 to 1962.

18 / All 241 Democratic members of the House put forth a long-term economic policy stressing both public and private investment and public-private cooperation in economic planning.

19 / Locomotive engineers on non-Conrail train lines throughout the nation walk off the job in a pay dispute and cut off commuter service to an estimated 100,000 people.

20 / The National Football League's Players Association calls a strike of its members after bargaining talks with team owners break down. It is the first in-season strike in the 63-year history of the league.

21 / Senate supporters of a bill to permit officially sanctioned prayer in schools fail to end a filibuster for the second day by opponents of the measure.

22 / Emergency legislation is passed by Congress and signed by Pres. Reagan that forces striking locomotive engineers back to work.

23 / The August consumer price index, released today by the Labor Dept., was only three-tenths of 1 percent higher than in July.

24 / The Senate approves a bill designed to provide federal aid for savings institutions by allowing regulatory agencies to issue them government-backed promissory notes.

The Allied Corp. and Bendix Corp. agree to merge, thus ending one of the most complex takeover attempts in the history of Wall Street. The Martin Marietta and United Technologies corporations, one-time participants in the battle of mergers and take-overs, remain independent.

25 / Funds from the Community Development Block Grants program of the Dept. of Housing and Urban Development will no longer be monitored by the federal government, it is announced. Cities will be free to use the money as they see fit.

27 / The possibility of criminal action in the failure of Oklahoma City's Penn Square Bank will be examined by the Justice Department, according to federal bank regulators.

28 / Pres. Reagan, in a prime-time news conference states that his administration's economic policies have rescued the nation from fiscal disaster.

29 / Yielding to Congressional pressure, Secretary of Education T. H. Bell agrees to withdraw some of the regulations proposed to ease requirements on the education of the handicapped.

30 / The McNeil Consumer Products Company of Fort Washington, Pa., orders the recall of its Extra-Strength Tylenol pain relief capsules following the deaths of five persons. The fatalities were attributed to suspected contamination of capsules with cyanide poison.

### INTERNATIONAL

1 / Mexico's Pres. José López Portillo announces the nationalization of private banks in his country. The Bank of Mexico will assume control of the banks when they reopen on Sept. 6.

The contents of a letter to Israel's Prime Minister Begin from Pres. Reagan are made public and denounced by Israeli leaders. Among the proposals were a call for a freeze on Jewish settlement construction in the West Bank and Gaza Strip and the the eventual annexation of the West Bank to Jordan.

2 / Foreseeing the development of a hostile Palestinian state, the Israeli cabinet votes unanimously against Pres. Reagan's proposals on creation of an independent Palestinian homeland in the West Bank occupied territory.

3 / Israel's opposition Labor party intends to open a national debate in that country over the Palestinian self-rule plan proposed by Pres. Reagan, it is revealed.

4 / Ten nations, including the U.S., agree to increase their contributions to the International Monetary Fund to assist financially troubled nations in paying their debts.

Twin giant pandas are born to Shao-Shao, a resident of the Madrid, Spain, zoo; it is the first multiple birth for the species in captivity in the Western world.

5 / The Israeli government allocates funds to construct three new settlements in the occupied West Bank territory; seven others are approved.

6 / The Communist party of China, at its twelfth congress, approved a new party constitution that eliminates honorific references to Mao Zedong, abolishes the post of chairman, and creates a central advisory commission to which older members may retire.

Men claiming to be members of a Polish resistance group seize the Polish Embassy in Berne, Switz., and threaten to blow it up if martial law is not ended in Poland and Solidarity leaders are not released from detention.

7 / U.N. Secretary-General Javier Pérez de Cuéllar, in his first report on the status of the international body, states that the U.N. is being ignored and that steps should be taken to increase the organization's powers.

8 / A Quebec judge rules that the guarantees of education in the Canadian constitution supercede provincial law. Quebec had attempted to restrict the number of students in provincial English-language schools.

9 / At a meeting of the Arab League, members ap-

prove an eight-point peace plan for the Mideast, calling for a Palestinian state and tacitly recognizing Israel.

Swiss police storm the Polish Embassy in Berne, free the five diplomats held hostage and arrest the four men who held the building for three days.

10 / The contingent of 800 U.S. marines sent to Lebanon as part of an international peacekeeping force departs Beirut after serving 16 days during which Palestinian guerrillas withdrew from that city.

11 / All 46 persons aboard a U.S. Army helicopter are killed when the aircraft crashes onto a highway in West Germany. The passengers were part of an international parachute team en route to an air show.

12 / Hua Guofeng, hand-picked successor to Mao Zedong as leader of the Communist party of China, is relieved of party duties. Deng Xiaoping retains party leadership and Hu Yaobang assumes the post of general secretary.

13 / A charter jetliner bound for New York City crashes on takeoff from Malaga, Spain; 46 passengers are known to have died in the fiery crash.

14 / Princess Grace of Monaco dies after suffering injuries in Sept. 13 car accident.

Bashir Gemayel, president-elect of Lebanon, is killed in a bomb explosion that destroys the headquarters of the Lebanese Christian Phalangists.

15 / In the wake of the assassination of Lebanon's president, Israeli troops move toward West Beirut; the action, the Israelis say, is to prevent a combined Palestinian-Moslem attack on Lebanese Christians.

16 / Israeli forces seize West Beirut, Lebanon, and the Israeli government states that its military will remain in place until the Lebanese armed forces assume control.

17 / The 13-year-old coalition government in West Germany collapses in the wake of the withdrawal of the Free Democrats. The action leaves Chancellor Helmut Schmidt with a minority government.

18 / Two Palestinian refugee camps in Lebanon are the scenes of massacres by Lebanese Christian militiamen; more than 300 are reported killed.

19 / Olof Palme's Social Democratic party wins the general elections in Sweden, ending six years of non-Socialist coalition governments.

20 / Pres. Reagan announces that the U.S. Marines who left Beirut, Lebanon, ten days ago will be returned to that city to share peacekeeping duties with French and Italian forces.

21 / Amin Gemayel, brother of the late president-elect Bashir Gemayel, is elected president of Lebanon.

The 37th session of the U.N. General Assembly opens under the presidency of Hungarian Imre Hollai.

22 / Israeli Defense Minister Ariel Sharon says his government had suspicions about the actions of Christian Phalangist militiamen after the Lebanese were permitted, by Israeli Army leaders, to enter the two Palestinian refugee camps where massacres took place last weekend.

Israel announces it will pull its troops out of Beirut by Sunday, Sept. 26.

23 / More than 1,200 residents of El Salvador and Guatemala are known to have died in flooding caused by four days of torrential rains.

24 / In an effort to stem mounting criticism of his policies, Prime Minister Begin of Israel requests a judicial inquiry into the massacre of Palestinians in Beirut.

25 / At a rally in Tel Aviv, Israel, hundreds of thousands of demonstrators call for the resignation of Prime Minister Begin and Defense Minister Ariel Sharon.

26 / The 800 U.S. Marines returned to Beirut, Lebanon, remain offshore because Israeli troops delay their withdrawal from Lebanon until Sept. 29.

27 / In an address to the U.N. General Assembly, Brazilian Pres. João Baptista Figueiredo predicts a worldwide economic depression if international trade and loans are not made more readily accessible to poorer nations.

28 / The Free Democratic party of West Germany decides to cast its votes in parliament on Friday for Helmut Kohl, leader of the Christian Democrats, thus ensuring Kohl's selection as the country's new chancellor.

29 / U.S. Marines take up positions in Beirut and open the city's airport after Israeli troops withdraw from the vicinity.

30 / A U.S. Marine engaged in clean-up operations at Beirut International Airport is killed when an explosive is accidentally detonated. Three others are injured.

## LATE CHANGES (To October 18, 1982)

**Bolivia** The National Congress, reconvened after being suspended for two years, elected Hernán Siles Zuazo, born 1914, as President on October 5, 1982.

**Canada** In Parliamentary by-elections on October 12, 1982, Prime Minister Trudeau's Liberal party lost two seats to the Progressive Conservatives and one seat to the New Democratic party. In the election for members of the New Brunswick Legislative Assembly, the Conservatives captured 39 of 58 seats.

**Equatorial Guinea** It was reported in late September 1982 that voters had approved a new constitution on August 15. The new constitution provides for a National Assembly and extends President Teodoro Obiang Nguema Mbasogo's term of office for seven years.

**Japan** Prime Minister Zenko Suzuki announced on October 12, 1982, that he would resign shortly.

**Lebanon** Shafiq Wazzan was reappointed as Premier by President Amin Gemayel on October 4, 1982.

**Netherlands** Premier Andries van Agt resigned on October 13, 1982.

**Swaziland** It was reported in early October 1982 that executive power resides in the hands of Prince Sozisa who acts on behalf of the royal council and Queen Mother Dzeliwe. A new monarch to succeed the late King Sobhuza II has not been announced as yet.

**Sweden** Olof Palme, born 1927, was sworn in on October 7, 1982, as Prime Minister, following the electoral victory of his Social Democratic party on September 19.

**Western Samoa** In September 1982 it was announced that the Supreme Court had nullified the February election of Prime Minister Va'ai Kolone.

**West Germany** Helmut Kohl, born 1930, was elected Chancellor by Parliament on October 1, 1982.

# THE UNITED STATES

## OUTLINE OF UNITED STATES HISTORY

### 16TH CENTURY

**1564** French Huguenots failed in attempts to establish settlements in present-day South Carolina and Florida.

**1565** Spaniards built fort at St. Augustine, Florida, first permanent white colony in present-day United States.

**1585** Sir Walter Raleigh dispatched expedition to Roanoke Island, Virginia; settlement abandoned (1586).

**1590** No traces found of second Roanoke settlement—the Lost Colony (established 1587)—and birthplace of Virginia Dare, first English child born (1587) in America.

**1598** Juan de Oñate began settlement in New Mexico.

### 17TH CENTURY

**1607** Colony established at Jamestown, Virginia; Captain John Smith elected (1608) head of group.

Pocahontas, daughter of Powhatan, head of an Indian confederacy in that region, rescued John Smith after Indian capture.

**1612** John Rolfe developed effective method of curing tobacco; later (1614) married Pocahontas.

**1614** Dutch established trading post in what is now New York State.

**1619** House of Burgesses, first representative assembly in America, met at Jamestown.

The first 20 blacks arrived in Virginia as indentured servants.

**1620** Pilgrims arrived from England in *Mayflower* and founded colony at Plymouth, Massachusetts; signed Mayflower Compact, first written constitution in colonies.

**1626** Peter Minuit bought Manhattan Island from Indians for the equivalent of $24 and named it New Amsterdam.

**1629** Massachusetts Bay Company formed; John Winthrop elected governor.

**1630** Settlement established at Boston, Massachusetts.

**1630–1640** "Great Migration" of Puritans from England settled Massachusetts and Connecticut.

**1632** Cecilius Calvert, 2d Lord Baltimore, established Roman Catholic colony in Maryland.

**1636** Banished (1635) from Massachusetts Bay colony, Roger Williams founded Providence, Rhode Island, first English colony to grant religious freedom.

Harvard College founded.

**1638** First printing press established in Cambridge, Massachusetts; printed (1640) *Bay Psalm Book.*

**1647** Peter Stuyvesant became head of New Netherlands; his dictatorial rule was resented.

**1655** Stuyvesant seized Swedish forts on Delaware, ending Swedish rule in North America.

**1662** Virginia became the first colony to declare slavery hereditary.

**1664** English took New Amsterdam, changing name to New York.

**1676** Nathaniel Bacon led Virginia frontiersmen against raiding Indians and then against Governor Berkeley; Bacon's death virtually ended rebellion.

**1677** William Penn framed first charter separating church and state at the Quaker colony of West Jersey.

**1680** New Hampshire became separate province.

**1682** La Salle reached mouth of Mississippi and claimed area from Quebec to Gulf Coast—Louisiana—for France.

William Penn founded Philadelphia for Quakers.

**1686** New England made a royal dominion; tyrannical rule of Edmund Andros ended in 1689 when England's "Glorious Revolution" spread to the colonies.

**1689** King William's War between French and English began as part of greater European war; Treaty of Ryswick (1697) restored prewar positions.

**1690** Benjamin Harris published first newspaper, in Boston, that was suppressed after one issue for criticizing conduct of war.

**1692** Witch trials began in Salem, Massachusetts; 20 "witches" executed before hunt ended (1693).

**1693** William and Mary College founded in Williamsburg, Virginia.

**1699** Sieur d'Iberville founded Old Biloxi (now Ocean Springs) on Biloxi Bay, first permanent settlement in Louisiana Territory.

### 18TH CENTURY

**1700** By this date, shipbuilding and whaling industries had developed in New England; plantation system in Virginia, Maryland, and Carolina fully established.

**1704** Boston *News-Letter,* first continuous colonial newspaper, was started.

**1716** First American theater built, in Williamsburg.

**1724** English established Fort Dummer near site of Brattleboro, considered first permanent Vermont settlement.

**1732–1757** Benjamin Franklin annually published *Poor Richard's Almanack.*

**1733** James Oglethorpe founded colony in Savannah, Georgia, last of the original 13 colonies to be settled.

**1734–1735** John Peter Zenger, editor and publisher of *New-York Weekly Journal,* tried for sedition; acquittal was landmark in assuring freedom of press in America.

**1734–1750** Jonathan Edwards, in New England, and George Whitefield, in Georgia, led Great Awakening, a series of religious revivals.

**1741** Captain Vitus Bering discovered Alaska and claimed it for Russia.

**1744** King George's War, extension in America of War of the Austrian Succession in Europe, began; Treaty of Aix-la-Chapelle (1748) restored prewar position.

**1754** French erected Fort Duquesne, on site of Pittsburgh, Pennsylvania.

George Washington's fight with French in Ohio territory became first skirmish of French and Indian War, which spread (1756) to Europe and became known as the Seven Years War.

**1763** Treaty of Paris ended French control east of Mississippi; Spain ceded Florida to England in return for Cuba.

**1764** Parliament passed the Sugar Act, first law to raise money for crown in the colonies, and Currency Act, which forbade all colonies to issue paper money.

James Otis denounced acts in pamphlet, noting British offense of taxation without representation.

**1765** College of Philadelphia (later part of University of Pennsylvania) offered first professional medical training in colonies.

Parliament issued Stamp Act, first direct tax levied by crown on American colonies.

Colonials convoked Stamp Act Congress; organized Sons of Liberty.

**1766** Stamp Act repealed, but Parliament passed Declaratory Act, affirming its right to legislate for colonies.

**1767** Townshend Acts passed by Parliament, imposing import duties; many colonies enacted nonimportation agreements.

**1769–1782** Fray Junípero Serra founded nine Franciscan missions in California.

**1770** In Boston, several colonists were killed by English soldiers in a melee, later known as the Boston Massacre.

Townshend Acts repealed, except for tea tax; colonial merchants worked for conciliation.

**1773** Parliament passed Tea Act granting East India Company full remission of all tea duties.

Boston Tea Party occurred, when patriots dressed

as Indians dumped tea shipment into Boston Harbor.

**1774** First Continental Congress met in Philadelphia, with representatives from all colonies except Georgia.

**1775** Patrick Henry made his "Liberty or Death" speech before Virginia Assembly.

Parliament passed New England Restraining Act, forbidding colonies to trade with any nation except Britain and British West Indies.

Minutemen fought British at Lexington and Concord, signaling start of American Revolution's military phase.

Second Continental Congress met in Philadelphia and appointed Washington chief of Continental forces.

The first abolitionist society in America was established in Philadelphia.

British defeated Americans at Bunker Hill and attacked Boston; city under siege until March 1776.

**1776** Thomas Paine's *Common Sense* published, calling for American independence.

Declaration of Independence adopted by Congress.

Nathan Hale ("I only regret that I have but one life to lose for my country") executed by British as American spy.

Washington, leading troops across Delaware River, made surprise attack on British at Trenton, New Jersey.

**1777** General Burgoyne's defeat at Saratoga was major American victory.

Articles of Confederation adopted by Congress (ratified by all colonies by 1781).

Congress recommended that colonial governments appropriate Loyalist property.

Washington and troops took up winter quarters at Valley Forge, Pennsylvania.

**1778** Americans and French signed Treaty of Alliance.

British took Savannah, Georgia.

**1779** John Paul Jones ("I have not yet begun to fight"), commanding *Bon Homme Richard,* defeated British frigate *Serapis,* off coast of England.

**1780** Washington's troops mutinied at Morristown, New Jersey, because of sparse supplies and delayed salaries.

Benedict Arnold's treason exposed.

**1781** Washington and Rochambeau planned joint Franco-American Yorktown (Va.) campaign, which brought surrender of Cornwallis and virtually ended hostilities.

Congress chartered Bank of North America to supply government with money.

**1782** John Adams, Benjamin Franklin, and John Jay negotiated peace treaty with British in Paris.

**1783** Treaty of Paris acknowledged independence of the United States.

Almost the entire American army disbanded without authority and Congress fled Philadelphia to escape discontented soldiers.

Last of 100,000 Loyalists fled country.

General Washington bade farewell to his officers at Fraunces Tavern, New York City.

**1786** Daniel Shays led discontented Massachusetts farmers in armed rebellion; insurrection crushed (1787) and later Massachusetts enacted more liberal legislation.

**1787** Constitutional Convention held in Philadelphia.

Congress adopted the Northwest Ordinance creating and providing a government for the Northwest Territory; slavery in region was prohibited.

Alexander Hamilton, James Madison, and John Jay began writing *The Federalist Papers,* which urged acceptance of Constitution.

Delaware was first state to ratify Constitution.

**1788** New Hampshire ratified the Constitution, thereby achieving the necessary nine-state acceptance.

**1789** George Washington elected nation's first President and John Adams became Vice-President.

First Congress met in New York, nation's first capital.

Federal Judiciary Act provided for organization of Supreme Court, 13 district courts, and three circuit courts; John Jay became first Chief Justice.

**1790** Hamilton organized national fiscal program.

First census recorded American population as 3,929,214.

Capital temporarily moved to Philadelphia.

**1791** Bill of Rights became part of Constitution.

Bank of the United States established.

**1793** Washington declared American neutrality vis-à-vis France and Britain.

Citizen Genêt, Minister of French Republic to the United States, asked to leave because of his conduct; later became American citizen.

The Fugitive Slave Act was passed, making it illegal to give comfort to or prevent the arrest of a runaway slave.

Eli Whitney invented cotton gin.

**1794** Federal troops put down Whisky Rebellion in western Pennsylvania.

Jay's treaty with Britain concluded; provision included British agreement to withdraw from Northwest posts; ratified (1795).

**1795** 11th Constitutional Amendment is ratified: a state cannot be sued by citizen of another state.

**1796** In his Farewell Address, Washington warned of permanent foreign alliances and encouraged temporary ones in times of emergency.

John Adams (Federalist) elected President; Thomas Jefferson (Democratic-Republican) elected Vice-President.

**1797** Affairs with France deteriorated, especially after the XYZ Affair: Talleyrand's agents tried to extort bribes from American commissioners in Paris.

**1798–1800** Americans fought undeclared naval war with France; Convention of 1800 released United States from alliance with France.

**1798** Alien and Sedition Acts passed by Federalists to repress political opposition.

Kentucky and Virginia Resolutions maintained unconstitutionality of Alien and Sedition Acts; expressed early states rights theory.

**1799** Washington died at Mount Vernon.

## 19TH CENTURY

**1800** Washington, D.C., became nation's capital.

**1801** House of Representatives chose Jefferson for President and Aaron Burr Vice-President after electoral tie; Jefferson was first President inaugurated in new capital.

**1802** Congress established U.S. Military Academy at West Point, New York.

**1803** In *Marbury* v. *Madison,* Chief Justice Marshall established principle of judicial review.

United States purchased Louisiana from France for about $15 million, doubling nation's area.

Meriwether Lewis and William Clark began their westward expedition.

**1804** Hamilton killed in duel with Aaron Burr.

**1807** Congress enacted law prohibiting importation of slaves after January 1, 1808.

Embargo enacted because of British harassment on seas; repealed (1809), but trade with France and Great Britain still prohibited.

**1808** Congress prohibited the admission of any new slaves into the United States.

**1809** James Madison sworn in as President with George Clinton as Vice-President.

**1811** General William Henry Harrison defeated Tecumseh's forces at Battle of Tippecanoe.

**1812** War declared on Great Britain for impressing U.S. seamen, blockading, and violating neutrality; Americans suffered setbacks on land, but naval successes boosted low morale.

**1813** British blockaded coast, but Captain Oliver Hazard Perry's naval victory secured Lake Erie for United States.

**1814** British took offensive, capturing and burning Washington, but suffered losses in attempt to invade New York from Canada.

Francis Scott Key wrote lyrics of "Star-spangled Banner."

At Hartford Convention, New England delegates met to revise Constitution and oppose war.

Treaty of Ghent ended war.

**1815** Andrew Jackson defeated British at New Orleans before news of peace arrived.

Fleet under Stephen Decatur ended Barbary states' imposition of tribute on American merchant vessels.

**1816** James Monroe elected President and Daniel D. Tompkins, Vice-President.

First protective tariff enacted.

**1817** New York State legislature authorized construction of Erie Canal; it opened in 1825.

**1818** U.S.-Canadian boundary to Rockies fixed; United States and Britain agreed to occupy Oregon Territory jointly.

**1819** Financial panic seized nation.
Adams-Onís Treaty, ceding Spain's Florida holding to the United States, signed; Andrew Jackson became (1821) Florida's first governor.

**1820** Missouri Compromise prohibited slavery in Louisiana Territory north of Missouri's southern border; Missouri admitted to Union as slave state and Maine as free state.
First American missionaries arrived in Hawaii.

**1821** Spain granted Moses Austin land in Texas for settlement.

**1822–1826** U.S. government recognized newly independent Latin American republics.

**1823** Monroe Doctrine promulgated: any further European effort to colonize the Americas or interfere in their affairs would be considered a hostile act.

**1824–1825** Presidential election resulted in no candidate having a majority; House chose John Quincy Adams President after much bargaining between candidates.

**1828** Congress passed protectionist "Tariff of Abominations."
Andrew Jackson elected first Democratic President; introduced spoils system on national level; Calhoun reelected Vice-President.

**1829** David Walker, a free black, published his famous "Appeal," one of the most militant antislavery documents.

**1830** Senators Daniel Webster (Mass.) and Robert Y. Hayne (S.C.) engaged in historic states' rights debate.

**1831** William Lloyd Garrison began to publish *The Liberator.*
Nat Turner led major slave insurrection in Virginia.

**1832** President Jackson vetoed renewal of National Bank.
South Carolina nullified U.S. tariff laws; Jackson declared action was rebellion and ordered Forts Moultrie and Sumter reinforced.

**1833** Jackson began second term; ordered public deposits withdrawn from Bank of the United States and put into state banks; Secretary of the Treasury Taney deposited funds in "pet banks."
American Anti-Slavery Society founded at Philadelphia as abolitionist movement grew more vocal.

**1834** Whig party had come into being; Henry Clay led group formed by National Republicans, states' righters, and dissident Democrats.

**1835** Seminoles in Florida resisted forced transportation West; despite capture (1837) of their leader Osceola, resistance continued until 1842.

**1836** Mexican leader Santa Anna captured fort of Alamo at San Antonio, Texas; Sam Houston later led American victory at Battle of San Jacinto.
Texas declared its independence from Mexico; Houston became president of independent republic.

**1837** Martin Van Buren inaugurated as President.
Panic of 1837 depressed economy.

**1840** By this time, Underground Railroad was fully organized to rescue fugitive slaves.

**1841** President William Henry Harrison died a month after inauguration; John Tyler became first Vice-President to succeed to Presidency as a result of incumbent's death.
Horace Greeley founded the New York *Tribune.*

**1842** Webster-Ashburton Treaty with Britain settled northeastern U.S. boundary.

**1843** United States recognized independence of Hawaii.

**1844** James K. Polk elected President; George M. Dallas elected Vice-President.

**1845** Texas agreed to join Union and was annexed.
Mexico broke off diplomatic relations with United States.
U.S. Naval Academy established at Annapolis, Maryland.

**1846** Mexican War broke out after Mexican troops crossed Rio Grande; Zachary Taylor led American victory at Battles of Palo Alto, Resaca de la Palma, Monterrey, and Buena Vista.
Oregon boundary established by treaty with Great Britain.
Wilmot Proviso, banning slavery in territory acquired from Mexican War, failed to pass (1846, 1847) Congress.

**1847** General Winfield Scott captured Mexico City.
Led by Brigham Young, the Mormons settled at Salt Lake City, Utah.

**1848** Treaty of Guadalupe Hidalgo signed by the United States and Mexico; established Rio Grande as boundary; Mexico recognized U.S. claim to Texas and ceded New Mexico and California in return for $15 million.
First Women's Rights Convention, led by Lucretia Mott and Elizabeth Cady Stanton, held at Seneca Falls, New York.
Discovery of gold in California touched off "Gold Rush."

**1849** Zachary Taylor (Whig) was inaugurated.
The first school integration lawsuit was filed by Benjamin Roberts against the City of Boston. The Massachusetts Supreme Court rejected the suit, setting the groundwork for the "separate but equal" doctrine.

**1850** Vice-President Millard Fillmore (Whig) succeeded to the Presidency after Taylor died of cholera.
Congress passed Henry Clay's Compromise of 1850: California admitted as free state; remainder of Mexican territory divided into New Mexico and Utah, without prior decision on slavery; more effective Fugitive Slave Law enacted; slave trade abolished in capital.
Clayton-Bulwer Treaty, concerning freedom of future canal zone, signed with Britain; abrogated (1901).

**1852** Harriet Beecher Stowe's *Uncle Tom's Cabin* published.

**1853** Commodore Matthew C. Perry visited Japan and obtained (1854) trade agreement.
Gadsden Purchase: land now included in New Mexico and Arizona purchased from Mexico.

**1854** Congress enacted Kansas and Nebraska Act, sponsored by Stephen A. Douglas: repealed Missouri Compromise and provided that people in states would decide slavery issue.

**1854–1856** Settlement of Kansas brought bloody fighting; U.S. Senate engaged in violent debates.

**1856** Republican party, formed in large part by Northern Whigs, held its first convention.

**1857** Supreme Court's Dred Scott decision ruled Missouri Compromise unconstitutional, holding that a slave's residence in free territory did not make him free and denying citizenship rights to descendants of slaves.

**1858** Abraham Lincoln debated Senator Douglas on slavery issue and became national figure.

**1859** John Brown, Kansas abolitionist, unsuccessfully tried to seize federal arsenal at Harpers Ferry, Virginia, to start slave insurrection; captured, he was hanged for treason.
First oil well drilled at Titusville, Pa., by Col. Edwin L. Drake.

**1860** Lincoln elected President; South Carolina passed ordinance of secession.

**1861** Mississippi, Florida, Alabama, Georgia, Louisiana, and Texas seceded from Union; Confederate States of America formed with Jefferson Davis (Miss.) as president; constitution based on states' rights doctrine.
South Carolina troops fired on Fort Sumter (April 12), forcing Union troops to evacuate; signaled start of Civil War.
Lincoln proclaimed blockade of Confederate states.
Virginia, Arkansas, Tennessee, and North Carolina joined Confederacy.
Robert E. Lee and Joseph E. Johnston resigned from U.S. Army.
West Virginia broke away from Virginia; admitted to Union in 1863.

**1862** Lincoln issued Emancipation Proclamation to take effect January 1863.
Major Civil War battles of Shiloh, *Monitor* and *Merrimack,* Peninsular Campaign, Second Bull Run, Antietam, and Fredericksburg occurred.

**1863** First national conscription act enacted; draft riots exploded in New York City.
General George Meade's Union forces defeated General Lee's army at Gettysburg; Lincoln delivered famous address at dedication of Gettysburg Cemetery.

1864 General Ulysses S. Grant became commander of Union armies.
General William Tecumseh Sherman marched through Georgia to the sea; captured Atlanta and Savannah.

1865 13th Amendment abolishing slavery was ratified.
Lee surrendered (April 9) at Appomattox (Va.) Courthouse.
Lincoln assassinated (April 14) by John Wilkes Booth at Ford's Theater, Washington, D.C.; Vice-President Andrew Johnson became President.

1866 Ku Klux Klan formed in Tennessee.
Civil Rights Act, bestowing citizenship on blacks passed over Johnson's veto.
Congress adopted the 14th Amendment containing "due process" and "equal protection" clauses guaranteeing civil rights of blacks.

1867 Three Reconstruction Acts passed over Johnson's vetoes; divided South into military districts and abolished qualifications for Confederate States' readmission to Union.
Secretary of State William H. Seward purchased Alaska from Russia for $7.2 million.
Northerners, called "carpetbaggers," participated in Southern Reconstruction; Southern whites allying themselves with Radicals were called "scalawags."

1868 Andrew Johnson was impeached by House and tried by Senate; two-thirds vote required for conviction failed by one vote.
Seven former Confederate states readmitted to Union.
14th Amendment was ratified.
The transcontinental railroad was completed.

1869 15th Amendment, giving blacks right to vote, proposed; ratified (1870).

1870 *New York Times* began exposé of Tammany Hall corruption; led to eventual imprisonment of Boss Tweed.
Joseph H. Rainey of South Carolina became the first black to sit in the House of Representatives after election to the 41st Congress; he subsequently was reelected four times.
General Robert E. Lee died.
The 15th Amendment was adopted, guaranteeing the right to vote to all U.S. citizens.

1871 Civil service reform began with establishment of first Civil Service Commission.
Disastrous fire destroyed most of Chicago.

1872 New York *Sun* charged prominent Republicans with taking bribes in Crédit Mobilier scandal (corruption in building Union Pacific railroad); resulted (1873) in Congressional investigation.

1873 Financial panic developed into five-year depression, worst to date.

1875 Civil Rights Act was passed forbidding discrimination against blacks in public facilities.

1876 General Custer and his troops were massacred by Sitting Bull's Sioux Indians at the Little Bighorn.
Presidential election contest between Samuel Tilden and Rutherford B. Hayes disputed; special electoral commission declared (1877) Hayes President.

1877 Reconstruction Era officially ended.
Federal troops put down a series of railroad strikes.

1878 Bland-Allison Act, passed over Hayes's veto, required government to purchase silver.

1881 President James A. Garfield was shot; succeeded by Chester A. Arthur.

1882 Chinese Exclusion Act barred immigration of Chinese laborers for 10 years; later legislation continued policy until 1943.

1883 Pendleton Act established civil service system.
Supreme Court ruled antidiscrimination portions of 1875 Civil Rights Act invalid, opening the way for repassage of Jim Crow laws.

1886 American Federation of Labor organized with Samuel Gompers as first president.
Statue of Liberty unveiled in New York harbor.
Capture of Apache chief Geronimo ended Southwest Indian warfare.
Anarchists convicted of Haymarket Massacre.

1889 Oklahoma "land rush" opened all but panhandle of Oklahoma Territory for settlement.
U.S.-Latin American conference established (1890) body later called Pan American Union.

1890 Sherman Anti-Trust Act became law.
Highly protective McKinley Tariff adopted.

1891 Populist party formed as part of agrarian protest movement.

1893 Financial panic caused partly by severe gold drain began; thousands of banks and commercial institutions failed before economy recovered (1897).
World's Columbian Exposition held in Chicago.

1894 Unemployment became widespread; "Coxey's Army" of the jobless marched on Washington to demand public works program.
Pullman strike brought federal intervention.

1895 Southern states inaugurated "grandfather" clauses as part of program (including literacy tests and poll taxes) to disfranchise blacks.
U.S. involvement in British-Venezuelan dispute led to broad construction of Monroe Doctrine, stressing right of the United States to intercede in hemispheric disputes.

1896 Supreme Court in *Plessy* v. *Ferguson* upheld Louisiana law requiring segregated railroad facilities, under "separate but equal" doctrine.

1897 Gold rush in Klondike began.

1898 Spanish-American War broke out after battleship *Maine* exploded in harbor of Havana, Cuba; in Treaty of Paris Spain granted Cuba independence, ceded Puerto Rico, Guam, and Philippines to United States in return for payment of $20 million; Cuba came under U.S. military control, headed by General Leonard Wood.
United States annexed Hawaii.

1899 United States participated in first Hague Conference, which established Permanent Court of Arbitration.

## 20TH CENTURY

1900 United States expressed its commitment to Chinese Open Door policy.
U.S. troops helped relieve Peking during Boxer Rebellion.
Samoan Islands were divided between the United States and Germany.

1901 U.S. military rule of Philippines ended and civil government organized; islands became territory (1902).
Platt amendment, which Cubans had to incorporate (1902) in their constitution and recognize (1903) in treaty, made island virtual American protectorate; abrogated (1934).
Second Hay-Pauncefote Treaty gave Americans free hand in Isthmian canal.
President McKinley was shot in Buffalo; Theodore Roosevelt became President.

1902 Roosevelt pledged "Square Deal" for both labor and industry; began "trust-busting" with prosecution of the Northern Securities Company.

1903 Wright brothers flew first successful heavier-than-air machine.

1904 Roosevelt's annual message contained his "Corollary" to the Monroe Doctrine: United States' obligation to maintain order in Latin America.

1905 Russo-Japanese peace treaty signed at Portsmouth, New Hampshire; Roosevelt's role of mediator brought him (1906) Nobel Peace Prize.
Industrial Workers of the World, radical labor organization, founded in Chicago.

1906 Earthquake and fire destroyed San Francisco.
Pure Food and Drug and Meat Inspection Acts signed.

1907 "Gentlemen's Agreement": Japan agreed not to allow laborers to migrate to America.

1908 William Howard Taft elected President.

1909 Payne-Aldrich Tariff set high protective rates.
Robert E. Peary discovered North Pole.

1912 Roosevelt bolted Republican party and was Progressive (Bull Moose) party's candidate for President.
Woodrow Wilson won three-way Presidential race.
U.S. marines landed in Nicaragua to protect American interests during revolt.

1913 The 16th (income tax) and 17th (popular election of U.S. Senators) Amendments ratified.
Federal Reserve System established national banking and currency system.
United States began intervention in Mexican Revolution.

1914 Federal Trade Commission established.
Clayton Anti-Trust Act supplemented and strength-

ened Sherman Anti-Trust Act.
United States proclaimed its neutrality in World War I.
U.S. naval forces bombarded and occupied Vera Cruz, Mexico.
Panama Canal opened.

**1915** *Lusitania* and *Arabic* sinkings brought strong protest notes from Wilson and modification of German submarine warfare.

**1916** General John J. Pershing's troops pursued Pancho Villa 200 miles into Mexico without success.

**1916–1924** U.S. troops occupied Santo Domingo.

**1917** United States severed relations with Germany.
Publication of secret Zimmermann note, proposing German-Mexican alliance, helped Wilson gain House approval for arming merchantmen.
Congress declared war on Germany (April 6); General Pershing appointed head of American Expeditionary Force (AEF).
Congress passed Selective Service Act; Espionage Act; and Trading with the Enemy Act, forbidding commerce with enemy nations.
United States purchased Virgin Islands from Denmark.

**1918** Wilson announced his "Fourteen Points" for peace.
Germany surrendered and armistice signed (November 11); U.S. war deaths, 112,432, many from disease.
Sedition Act passed; many Socialist and pacifist leaders imprisoned during next few years.

**1919** Wilson toured country on behalf of League of Nations; awarded Nobel Peace Prize; suffered stroke.
18th Amendment (Prohibition) ratified.

**1920** 19th Amendment (women's suffrage) ratified.
Socialist Presidential candidate Eugene Debs, in prison, polled almost a million votes.
A. Mitchell Palmer ordered mass arrests of agitators during "Red scare" period.
Senate refused to ratify Versailles Treaty, ending World War I.
Warren G. Harding (Republican) and Calvin Coolidge elected President and Vice-President.

**1922** Leading powers agreed to limit naval forces at Washington Arms Conference.

**1923** Harding died; Coolidge became President.

**1923–1924** Knowledge that Secretary of the Interior Albert B. Fall had secretly leased Teapot Dome oil reserves to Harry F. Sinclair was one of many Harding administration scandals made public.

**1924** Soldiers Bonus Act compensated veterans for overseas duty.

**1925** John Scopes, Tennessee schoolteacher, was defended by Clarence Darrow and prosecuted by William Jennings Bryan; Bryan secured the conviction of Scopes for teaching evolution.

**1926** Richard Byrd and Floyd Bennett became first men to fly over North Pole.
U.S. troops landed in Nicaragua to quell rebellion; troops finally withdrawn in 1933.

**1927** Charles A. Lindbergh made first nonstop solo flight from New York to Paris, becoming an international hero overnight.

**1928** Kellogg-Briand Pact, outlawing war, signed by the United States; ratified by Senate (1929).
Al Smith, a Roman Catholic, ran as Democratic Presidential candidate.
Herbert C. Hoover and Charles Curtis elected President and Vice-President.

**1929** Stock Market crash grew into worldwide Great Depression; low point came 1932–1933.
St. Valentine's Day massacre in Chicago marked peak of gangster wars.

**1930** United States, Great Britain, and Japan agreed to limit navies at London Naval Conference.
Hawley-Smoot Tariff brought duty level to an all-time high.

**1931** Hoover proposed one-year moratorium on inter-allied debts and reparations because of world-wide economic crisis.

**1932** Reconstruction Finance Corporation established.
Lindbergh's son kidnapped and slain.
"Bonus Army," camped in Washington seeking early payment of veterans' benefits, was dispersed by Army troops led by Douglas MacArthur.
Franklin Delano Roosevelt and John Nance Garner were elected President and Vice-President.

**1933** Roosevelt's "New Deal" began with bank holiday to lessen severe economic crisis; later he took nation off gold standard and delivered his radio "fireside chats."
"Hundred Days" session of Congress produced Emergency Banking Relief Act, Agricultural Adjustment Act, Federal Emergency Relief Act, and established Civilian Conservation Corps, Civil Works Administration, and Federal Bank Deposit Insurance Corporation. Supreme Court later declared several New Deal Acts unconstitutional.
Congress created Tennessee Valley Authority and established Commodity Credit Corporation.
21st Amendment repealed Prohibition.
Roosevelt's "Good Neighbor Policy" included opposition to armed intervention in Latin America.

**1933–1936** Severe drought converted Great Plains into "Dust Bowl."

**1934** Export-Import Bank established.
Congress passed Securities Exchange Act and established Federal Communications Commission and Federal Housing Administration.
John Dillinger slain by FBI agents in Chicago.

**1935** Additional New Deal agencies created included Works Progress Administration, with Harry L. Hopkins as head; Resettlement Administration, directed by Rexford G. Tugwell; Rural Electrification Administration; and a new National Labor Relations Board.
Social Security Act created federal-state system of unemployment and old-age compensation.

**1937** Supreme Court upheld New Deal legislation such as N.L.R.A. and Social Security; Roosevelt allowed "Court packing" plan to drop.
Relations with Japan started to deteriorate after sinking of U.S. gunboat *Panay*.

**1938** Congress voted billion-dollar naval building program.
Fair Labor Standards Act (Wages and Hours Law) set up minimum wage and maximum hours for companies connected with interstate commerce.
Mexican expropriation of U.S. oil property caused long controversy.

**1939** American neutrality pledged after war broke out in Europe; but "cash and carry" policy allowed for exports of arms to belligerent powers.
Albert Einstein and other scientists told Roosevelt of possibilities of developing atomic bomb.

**1940** Smith Act (Alien Registration Act) included provisions that made it unlawful to advocate or teach the overthrow or destruction of any government in the United States by force and to be a member of any group dedicated to such a policy.
Selective Training and Service Act (Burke-Wadsworth Bill), nation's first peacetime program of compulsory military service was enacted.

**1941** Roosevelt delivered Four Freedom's speech.
Lend-Lease Act allowed friendly nations to secure arms without cash.
Atlantic Charter, joint statement of postwar aims, issued by Roosevelt and Prime Minister Churchill.
Japanese attacked (December 7) Pearl Harbor; Congress declared war on Japan.
Germany and Italy declared war (December 11) on United States.

**1942** Pacific Coast Japanese-Americans were relocated to Western detention camps; released in 1944; action upheld by Supreme Court.
In Pacific, Bataan and Corregidor fell to Japanese; U.S. Marines won major victory at Guadalcanal; U.S. planes, led by Major General James H. Doolittle, raided Tokyo.
First self-sustaining nuclear reaction achieved at the University of Chicago.
United Nations Pact signed by 26 nations at Washington.

**1943** American forces helped drive Germans from North Africa and invaded Italy, which surrendered to Allies.
U.S. troops in the Pacific began island-hopping operations and combined with ANZAC troops to force retreat of Japanese in New Guinea.
Roosevelt attended conferences in Casablanca, Quebec, Cairo, and Teheran.

**1944** Dwight D. Eisenhower became Supreme Commander of American Expeditionary Forces.
Allies invaded Europe and liberated France, Belgium, and Luxembourg.
Roosevelt defeated Thomas E. Dewey and won fourth term; Harry S. Truman elected Vice-President.

**1945** U.S. troops recaptured Philippines from Japanese.
Churchill, Roosevelt, and Stalin met at Yalta.
Roosevelt died (April 12); succeeded by Truman.
United Nations established in San Francisco.
Germany surrendered (May 7) unconditionally.
United States dropped atomic bombs on Japanese cities of Hiroshima and Nagasaki; Japan surrendered (August 14).
Potsdam Conference, to plan occupation and settlement of Europe, attended by Truman, Churchill (succeeded by Clement Attlee), and Stalin.

**1946** Philippines gained independence from U.S.
United States set up Atomic Energy Commission for civilian control of atomic energy.
United Nations established permanent headquarters in New York City.
Churchill delivered his "Iron Curtain" speech at Fulton, Missouri; marked beginning of Cold War.

**1947** "Truman Doctrine," economic and military assistance, began with aid to Greece and Turkey.
General George C. Marshall proposed plan for European recovery.
Taft-Hartley Act, limiting power of labor, passed over Truman's veto.

**1948** Whittaker Chambers accused Alger Hiss of transmitting documents to Russians; Hiss denied charges, was indicted for perjury, and convicted (1950).
Truman issued Executive Order ending segregation in the armed forces.
U.S. airlift frustrated Soviet blockade of Berlin.
Truman defeated Dewey in upset election.

**1949** Truman outlined his Point Four program of technical assistance to aid world peace.
North Atlantic Treaty Organization approved.

**1950** South Korea invaded by North Korean troops; Truman ordered U.S. forces into area.
Senator Joseph McCarthy charged that the State Department was infiltrated by Communists.

**1951** 22d Amendment, limiting President to two terms, ratified.
Truman recalled General MacArthur from Korea for insubordination.

**1952** Supreme Court declared Truman's seizure of steel mills during strike unconstitutional.
McCarran-Walter Bill restricted immigration.
General Dwight D. Eisenhower became first Republican to win Presidency since 1928.

**1953** Korean armistice signed.

**1954** *Brown* v. *Board of Education of Topeka:* Supreme Court outlawed racial segregation in public schools, as "inherently unequal."
United States commitment in Southeast Asia began with formation of SEATO and financial aid to Indo-China (Vietnam, Laos, and Cambodia).

**1955** Supreme Court ordered school desegregation to proceed "with all deliberate speed."
AFL and CIO merged into one labor organization.

**1956** Arrest of seamstress Rosa Parks for refusing to give her seat to a white man on a bus in Montgomery, Alabama, resulted in a bus boycott led by Martin Luther King, Jr.

**1957** Eisenhower extended Truman Doctrine to Middle East with aid to Jordan.
Governor Orval Faubus called out Arkansas National Guard to prevent integration of Little Rock schools; Eisenhower sent federal troops to protect rights of black students.
Civil Rights Act was passed—the first such legislation since Reconstruction.

**1958** First U.S. Earth satellite was launched.
Eisenhower sent marines to Lebanon during civil insurrection.

**1959** Alaska and Hawaii admitted to Union.
Soviet Premier Khrushchev met with Eisenhower at Camp David, Maryland.

**1960** American U-2 reconnaissance plane shot down over Soviet territory; Francis Gary Powers, pilot, exchanged for Rudolf Abel in 1962.
John F. Kennedy elected President with Lyndon B. Johnson as Vice-President.

**1961** Anti-Castro invasion at Bay of Pigs failed.
Kennedy established Peace Corps and proposed Alliance for Progress.
**Alan B. Shepard, Jr.; first American in space.**

**1962** After bloody campus clashes, James H. Meredith became the first black to enter the University of Mississippi.
**John H. Glenn, Jr.; first American to orbit Earth.**
Kennedy protested presence of Russian missiles on Cuba; danger of nuclear war ended with Soviet dismantling of weapons.

**1963** Racial violence broke out in Birmingham, Ala.
United States, Britain, and Soviet Union signed treaty barring atmospheric nuclear testing.
Washington and Moscow opened "hot line" phone connection to reduce risk of accidental war.
Martin Luther King led "March on Washington."
Kennedy assassinated in Dallas; Lyndon B. Johnson became President.

**1964** Civil Rights Act strengthened voting guarantee, prohibited segregation in public facilities.
24th Amendment, abolishing poll tax, ratified.
Johnson won landslide victory over Barry Goldwater in Presidential election.

**1965** Large-scale antiwar demonstrations developed after Johnson announced Vietnam troop build-up.
Race riot erupted in Watts section of Los Angeles.
Johnson sent troops to Dominican Republic.

**1966** Medicare program went into effect.
Chicago, Cleveland, and other Northern cities experienced major race riots.

**1967** Antiwar, antidraft, and race riots increased.
Johnson and Premier Kosygin met at Glassboro, New Jersey.
25th Amendment, providing continuity in case of Presidential disability, ratified.
Treaty pledging peaceful uses of outer space signed with Soviet Union and Great Britain.

**1968** North Korea seized U.S. Navy intelligence ship *Pueblo;* men released 11 months later.
Reverend Martin Luther King, Jr. and Senator Robert F. Kennedy assassinated.
Delegates from Washington and Hanoi met in Paris for preliminary Vietnam peace talks.
Richard M. Nixon won Presidential election; Spiro Agnew became Vice-President.

**1969** Americans Neil A. Armstrong and Edwin E. Aldrin, Jr., were first men to land on Moon.

**1970** U.S. and South Vietnamese troops enter Cambodia.

**1971** 26th Amendment grants voting rights to 18-year-olds. Nixon froze wages and prices; devalued dollar by 8.57%.

**1972** Nixon visited Russia and China.
"Watergate Burglars" caught inside Democratic party's national headquarters.
Richard M. Nixon and Spiro T. Agnew reelected President and Vice-President.

**1973** "Watergate" dominated American political scene.
Spiro T. Agnew resigned vice-presidency; Gerald R. Ford replaced him.

**1974** **President Nixon resigned and Gerald Ford became the 38th president.**

**1975** The Vietnam war ended.

**1976** Jimmy Carter defeated Ford in Presidential election; Walter F. Mondale elected Vice-President.

**1977** Carter established "human rights" as a key element in U.S. foreign policy.

**1978** U.S. dollar fell in value against Western European and Japanese currencies.

**1979** U.S. recognized the People's Republic of China.
Gasoline and fuel oil prices rose sharply.
Canal Zone ceded to Panama.
U.S. Embassy personnel taken hostage in Iran.

**1980** Over 125,000 refugees fled Cuba for U.S.
Ronald W. Reagan defeated Carter in Presidential election; George H. W. Bush elected Vice-President.

**1981** Iran returned hostages to U.S.
President Reagan shot in Washington, but recovered successfully.
Astronauts Young and Crippen piloted space shuttle *Columbia* around earth in 36 orbits.

**1982** Unemployment reached 9.8% (Aug.).

## In CONGRESS, July 4, 1776

# A DECLARATION

### By the REPRESENTATIVES of the UNITED STATES OF AMERICA,

### In GENERAL CONGRESS assembled.

WHEN in the Course of human Events, it becomes necessary for one People to dissolve the Political Bands which have connected them with another, and to assume among the Powers of the Earth, the separate and equal Station to which the Laws of Nature and of Nature's God entitle them, a decent Respect to the Opinions of Mankind requires that they should declare the causes which impel them to the Separation.

We hold these Truths to be self-evident, that all Men are created equal, that they are endowed by their Creator with certain unalienable Rights, that among these are Life, Liberty, and the Pursuit of Happiness—That to secure these Rights, Governments are instituted among Men, deriving their just Powers from the Consent of the Governed, that whenever any Form of Government becomes destructive of these Ends, it is the Right of the People to alter or to abolish it, and to institute new Government, laying its Foundation on such Principles, and organizing its Powers in such Form, as to them shall seem most likely to effect their Safety and Happiness. Prudence, indeed, will dictate that Governments long established should not be changed for light and transient Causes; and accordingly all Experience hath shewn, that Mankind are more disposed to suffer, while Evils are sufferable, than to right themselves by abolishing the Forms to which they are accustomed. But when a long Train of Abuses and Usurpations, pursuing invariably the same Object, evinces a Design to reduce them under absolute Despotism, it is their Right, it is their Duty, to throw off such Government, and to provide new Guards for their future Security. Such has been the patient Sufferance of these Colonies; and such is now the Necessity which constrains them to alter their former Systems of Government. The History of the present King of Great-Britain is a History of repeated Injuries and Usurpations, all having in direct Object the Establishment of an absolute Tyranny over these States. To prove this, let Facts be submitted to a candid World.

He has refused his Assent to Laws, the most wholesome and necessary for the public Good.

He has forbidden his Governors to pass Laws of immediate and pressing Importance, unless suspended in their Operation till his Assent should be obtained; and when so suspended, he has utterly neglected to attend to them.

He has refused to pass other Laws for the Accommodation of large Districts of People, unless those People would relinquish the Right of Representation in the Legislature, a Right inestimable to them, and formidable to Tyrants only.

He has called together Legislative Bodies at Places unusual, uncomfortable, and distant from the Depository of their public Records, for the sole Purpose of fatiguing them into Compliance with his Measures.

He has dissolved Representative Houses repeatedly, for opposing with manly Firmness his Invasions on the Rights of the People.

He has refused for a long Time, after such Dissolutions, to cause others to be elected; whereby the Legislative Powers, incapable of Annihilation, have returned to the People at large for their exercise; the State remaining in the mean time exposed to all the Dangers of Invasion from without, and Convulsions within.

He has endeavoured to prevent the Population of these States; for that Purpose obstructing the Laws for Naturalization of Foreigners; refusing to pass others to encourage their Migrations hither, and raising the Conditions of new Appropriations of Lands.

He has obstructed the Administration of Justice, by refusing his Assent to Laws for establishing Judiciary Powers.

He has made Judges dependent on his Will alone, for the Tenure of their Offices, and the Amount and Payment of their Salaries.

He has erected a Multitude of new Offices, and sent hither Swarms of Officers to harass our People, and eat out their Substance.

He has kept among us, in Times of Peace, Standing Armies, without the consent of our Legislatures.

He has affected to render the Military independent of and superior to the Civil Power.

He has combined with others to subject us to a Jurisdiction foreign to our Constitution, and unacknowledged by our Laws; giving his Assent to their Acts of pretended Legislation:

For quartering large Bodies of Armed Troops among us:

For protecting them, by a mock Trial, from Punishment for any Murders which they should commit on the Inhabitants of these States:

For cutting off our Trade with all Parts of the World:

For imposing Taxes on us without our Consent:

For depriving us, in many Cases, of the Benefits of Trial by Jury:

For transporting us beyond Seas to be tried for pretended Offences:

For abolishing the free System of English Laws in a neighbouring Province, establishing therein an arbitrary Government, and enlarging its Boundaries, so as to render it at once an Example and fit Instrument for introducing the same absolute Rule into these Colonies:

For taking away our Charters, abolishing our most valuable Laws, and altering fundamentally the Forms of our Governments:

For suspending our own Legislatures, and declaring themselves invested with Power to legislate for us in all Cases whatsoever.

He has abdicated Government here, by declaring us out of his Protection and waging War against us.

He has plundered our Seas, ravaged our Coasts, burnt our Towns, and destroyed the Lives of our People.

He is, at this Time, transporting large Armies of foreign Mercenaries to compleat the Works of Death, Desolation, and Tyranny, already begun with circumstances of Cruelty and Perfidy, scarcely paralleled in the most barbarous Ages, and totally unworthy the Head of a civilized Nation.

He has constrained our fellow Citizens taken Captive on the high Seas to bear Arms against their Country, to become the Executioners of their Friends and Brethren, or to fall themselves by their Hands.

He has excited domestic Insurrections amongst us, and has endeavoured to bring on the Inhabitants of our Frontiers, the merciless Indian Savages, whose known Rule of Warfare, is an undistinguished Destruction of all Ages, Sexes and Conditions.

In every stage of these Oppressions we have Petitioned for Redress in the most humble Terms: Our repeated Petitions have been answered only by repeated Injury. A Prince, whose Character is thus marked by every act which may define a Tyrant, is unfit to be the Ruler of a free People.

Nor have we been wanting in Attentions to our British Brethren. We have warned them from Time to Time of Attempts by their Legislature to extend an unwarrantable Jurisdiction over us. We have reminded them of the Circumstances of our Emigration and Settlement here. We have appealed to their native Justice and Magnanimity, and we have conjured them by the Ties of our common Kindred to disavow these Usurpations, which, would inevitably interrupt our Connections and Correspondence. They too have been deaf to the Voice of Justice and of Consanguinity. We must, therefore, acquiesce in the Necessity, which denounces our Separation, and hold them, as we hold the rest of Mankind, Enemies in War, in Peace, Friends.

We, therefore, the Representatives of the UNITED STATES OF AMERICA, in General Congress, Assembled, appealing to the Supreme Judge of the World for the Rectitude of our Intentions, do, in the Name, and by Authority of the good People of these Colonies, solemnly Publish and Declare, That these United Colonies are, and of Right ought to be, Free and Independent States; that they are absolved from all Allegiance to the British Crown, and that all political Connection between them and the State of Great-Britain, is and ought to be totally dissolved; and that as Free and Independent States, they have full Power to levy War, conclude Peace, contract Alliances, establish Commerce, and to do all other Acts and Things which Independent States may of right do. And for the support of this Declaration, with a firm Reliance on the Protection of divine Providence, we mutually pledge to each other our Lives, our Fortunes, and our sacred Honor.

*Signed by* Order *and in*
Behalf *of the* Congress,
JOHN HANCOCK, President

Attest.
CHARLES THOMSON, Secretary.

## SIGNERS OF THE DECLARATION OF INDEPENDENCE: 1776

| Name | Age | Occupation | Education | Representing | Birthplace | Born | Died |
|---|---|---|---|---|---|---|---|
| **John Adams** | 40 | Lawyer | Harvard | Massachusetts | Braintree, Mass. | 1735 | 1826 |
| **Samuel Adams** | 53 | Politician | Harvard | Massachusetts | Boston, Mass. | 1722 | 1803 |
| **Josiah Bartlett** | 46 | Physician | Private tutors | New Hampshire | Amesbury, Mass. | 1729 | 1795 |
| **Carter Braxton** | 39 | Planter | William & Mary | Virginia | Newington, Va. | 1736 | 1797 |
| **Charles Carroll** | 38 | Planter | Educated in Europe | Maryland | Annapolis, Md. | 1737 | 1832 |
| **Samuel Chase** | 35 | Lawyer | Private tutors | Maryland | Somerset Co., Md. | 1741 | 1811 |
| **Abraham Clark** | 40 | Lawyer-Farmer | Self-educated | New Jersey | Elizabethtown, N.J. | 1726 | 1794 |
| **George Clymer** | 37 | Merchant | Self-educated | Pennsylvania | Philadelphia, Pa. | 1739 | 1813 |
| **William Ellery** | 48 | Lawyer | Harvard | Rhode Island | Newport, R.I. | 1727 | 1820 |
| **William Floyd** | 41 | Farmer | Private tutors | New York | Brookhaven, N.Y. | 1734 | 1821 |
| **Benjamin Franklin** | 71 | Public servant | Grammar school | Pennsylvania | Boston, Mass. | 1706 | 1790 |
| **Elbridge Gerry** | 31 | Merchant | Harvard | Massachusetts | Marblehead, Mass. | 1744 | 1814 |
| **Button Gwinnett** | c. 41 | Planter | Preparatory studies | Georgia | Gloucestershire, England | c. 1735 | 1777 |
| **Lyman Hall** | 52 | Physician | Yale | Georgia | Wallingford, Conn. | 1724 | 1790 |
| **John Hancock** | 39 | Merchant | Harvard | Massachusetts | Braintree, Mass. | 1737 | 1793 |
| **Benjamin Harrison** | c. 50 | Planter | Attended William & Mary | Virginia | Charles City Co., Va. | c. 1726 | 1791 |
| **John Hart** | c. 65 | Farmer | Self-educated | New Jersey | Stonington, Conn. | c. 1711 | 1779 |
| **Joseph Hewes** | 46 | Merchant | Grammar school | North Carolina | Kingston, N.J. | 1730 | 1779 |
| **Thomas Heyward** | 29 | Lawyer | Studied law in England | South Carolina | St. Helena's Parish, S.C. | 1746 | 1809 |
| **William Hooper** | 34 | Lawyer | Harvard | North Carolina | Boston, Mass. | 1742 | 1790 |
| **Stephen Hopkins** | 70 | Public servant | Self-educated | Rhode Island | Providence, R.I. | 1707 | 1785 |
| **Francis Hopkinson** | 38 | Lawyer | College of Philadelphia[1] | New Jersey | Philadelphia, Pa. | 1737 | 1791 |
| **Samuel Huntington** | 45 | Lawyer | Self-educated | Connecticut | Windham, Conn. | 1731 | 1796 |
| **Thomas Jefferson** | 33 | Lawyer-Planter | William & Mary | Virginia | Goochland Co., Va. | 1743 | 1826 |
| **Richard Henry Lee** | 44 | Planter | Private tutors | Virginia | Westmoreland Co., Va. | 1732 | 1794 |
| **Francis Lightfoot Lee** | 41 | Planter | Private tutors | Virginia | Westmoreland Co., Va. | 1734 | 1797 |
| **Francis Lewis** | 63 | Merchant | Grammar school | New York | Llandaff, Wales | 1713 | c. 1802 |
| **Philip Livingston** | 60 | Merchant | Yale | New York | Albany, N.Y. | 1716 | 1778 |
| **Thomas Lynch** | 26 | Planter | Studied law in England | South Carolina | Prince George's Parish, S.C. | 1749 | 1779 |
| **Thomas McKean** | 42 | Lawyer | Preparatory studies | Delaware | New London Township, Pa. | 1734 | 1817 |
| **Arthur Middleton** | 34 | Planter | Studied law in England | South Carolina | near Charlestown, S.C. | 1742 | 1787 |
| **Lewis Morris** | 50 | Landowner | Yale | New York | Morrisania, N.Y. | 1726 | 1798 |
| **Robert Morris** | 42 | Merchant | Self-educated | Pennsylvania | Liverpool, England | 1734 | 1806 |
| **John Morton** | c. 42 | Surveyor | Private tutors | Pennsylvania | Ridely, Pa. | c. 1724 | 1777 |

| Name | Age | Occupation | Education | Representing | Birthplace | Born | Died |
|---|---|---|---|---|---|---|---|
| **Thomas Nelson** | 41 | Planter | Educated in England | Virginia | Yorktown, Va. | 1738 | 1789 |
| **William Paca** | 37 | Lawyer | College of Philadelphia;[1] attended schools in England | Maryland | near Abingdon, Md. | 1740 | 1799 |
| **Robert Treat Paine** | 45 | Lawyer | Harvard | Massachusetts | Boston, Mass. | 1731 | 1814 |
| **John Penn** | c. 36 | Lawyer | Self-educated | North Carolina | Caroline Co., Va. | c. 1740 | 1788 |
| **George Read** | 42 | Lawyer | Preparatory studies | Delaware | near Northeast, Cecil Co., Md. | 1733 | 1798 |
| **Caesar Rodney** | 48 | Landowner | Private tutors | Delaware | near Dover, Del. | 1728 | 1784 |
| **George Ross** | 46 | Lawyer | Preparatory studies | Pennsylvania | New Castle, Del. | 1730 | 1779 |
| **Benjamin Rush** | 30 | Physician | College of New Jersey;[2] medical education, Univ. of Edinburgh | Pennsylvania | Byberry, Pa. | 1745 | 1813 |
| **Edward Rutledge** | 26 | Lawyer | Studied law in England | South Carolina | Charleston, S.C. | 1749 | 1800 |
| **Roger Sherman** | 55 | Merchant | Self-educated | Connecticut | Newton, Mass. | 1721 | 1793 |
| **James Smith** | c. 57 | Lawyer-Iron master | Preparatory studies | Pennsylvania | Ireland | c. 1719 | 1806 |
| **Richard Stockton** | 46 | Lawyer | College of New Jersey[2] | New Jersey | Princeton, N.J. | 1730 | 1781 |
| **Thomas Stone** | c. 33 | Lawyer-Planter | Private tutors | Maryland | Charles Co., Md. | 1743 | 1787 |
| **George Taylor** | c. 60 | Iron master | Preparatory studies | Pennsylvania | Ireland | 1716 | 1781 |
| **Matthew Thornton** | c. 62 | Physician | Preparatory studies | New Hampshire | Ireland | c. 1714 | 1803 |
| **George Walton** | c. 35 | Lawyer | Self-educated | Georgia | Prince Edward Co., Va. | c. 1741 | 1804 |
| **William Whipple** | 46 | Merchant | Grammar school | New Hampshire | Kittery, Me. | 1730 | 1785 |
| **William Williams** | 45 | Public servant-Merchant | Harvard | Connecticut | Lebanon, Conn. | 1731 | 1811 |
| **James Wilson** | 33 | Lawyer | Educated in Scotland | Pennsylvania | near St. Andrews, Scotland | 1742 | 1798 |
| **John Witherspoon** | 53 | College president-Clergyman | Univ. of Edinburgh | New Jersey | Gifford, Haddingtonshire, Scotland | 1723 | 1794 |
| **Oliver Wolcott** | 49 | Lawyer | Yale | Connecticut | Windsor, Conn. | 1726 | 1797 |
| **George Wythe** | c. 50 | Lawyer | Attended William & Mary | Virginia | Elizabeth City Co., Va. | 1726 | 1806 |

[1] now University of Pennsylvania. [2] now Princeton University.

# THE CONSTITUTION

WE, the People of the United States, in order to form a more perfect union, establish justice, insure domestic tranquility, provide for the common defence, promote the general welfare, and secure the blessings of liberty to ourselves and our posterity, do ordain and establish this Constitution for the United States of America.

## ARTICLE I.

*Sect.* 1. ALL legislative powers herein granted shall be vested in a Congress of the United States, which shall consist of a Senate and House of Representatives.

*Sect.* 2. The House of Representatives shall be composed of members chosen every second year by the people of the several states, and the electors in each state shall have the qualifications requisite for electors of the most numerous branch of the state legislature.

No person shall be a representative who shall not have attained to the age of twenty-five years, and been seven years a citizen of the United States, and who shall not, when elected, be an inhabitant of that state in which he shall be chosen.

[1]**[Representatives and direct taxes shall be apportioned among the several states which may be included within this Union, according to their respective numbers, which shall be determined by adding to the whole number of free persons, including those bound to service for a term of years, and excluding Indians not taxed, three-fifths of all other persons.]** The actual enumeration shall be made within three years after the first meeting of the Congress of the United States, and within every subsequent term of ten years, in such manner as they shall by law direct. The number of representatives shall not exceed one for every thirty thousand, but each state shall have at least one representative; and until such enumeration shall be made, the state of New-Hampshire shall be entitled to chuse three, Massachusetts eight, Rhode-Island and Providence Plantations one, Connecticut five, New-York six, New-Jersey four, Pennsylvania eight, Delaware one, Maryland six, Virginia ten, North-Carolina five, South-Carolina five, and Georgia three.

When vacancies happen in the representation from any state, the Executive authority thereof shall issue writs of election to fill such vacancies.

The House of Representatives shall chuse their Speaker and other officers; and shall have the sole power of impeachment.

*Sect.* 3. The Senate of the United States shall be composed of two senators from each state, [2]**[chosen by the legislature thereof,]** for six years; and each senator shall have one vote.

Immediately after they shall be assembled in consequence of the first election, they shall be divided as equally as may be into three classes. The seats of the senators of the first class shall be vacated at the expiration of the second year, of the second class at the expiration of the fourth year, and of the third class at the expiration of the sixth year, so that one-third may be chosen every second year; [3]**[and if vacancies happen by resignation, or otherwise, during the recess of the**

[1] The part enclosed by brackets was changed by section 2 of Amendment XIV. [2] The clause enclosed by brackets was changed by clause 1 of Amendment XVII. [3] The part enclosed by brackets was changed by clause 2 of Amendment XVII.

**Legislature of any state, the Executive thereof may make temporary appointments until the next meeting of the Legislature, which shall then fill such vacancies.]**

No person shall be a senator who shall not have attained to the age of thirty years, and been nine years a citizen of the United States, and who shall not, when elected, be an inhabitant of that state for which he shall be chosen.

The Vice-President of the United States shall be President of the Senate, but shall have no vote, unless they be equally divided.

The Senate shall chuse their other officers, and also a President pro tempore, in the absence of the Vice-President, or when he shall exercise the office of President of the United States.

The Senate shall have the sole power to try all impeachments. When sitting for that purpose, they shall be on oath or affirmation. When the President of the United States is tried, the Chief Justice shall preside: And no person shall be convicted without the concurrence of two-thirds of the members present.

Judgment in cases of impeachment shall not extend further than to removal from office and disqualification to hold and enjoy any office of honor, trust or profit under the United States; but the party convicted shall nevertheless be liable and subject to indictment, trial, judgment and punishment, according to law.

*Sect.* 4. The times, places and manner of holding elections for senators and representatives, shall be prescribed in each state by the legislature thereof; but the Congress may at any time by law make or alter such regulations, except as to the places of chusing Senators.

The Congress shall assemble at least once in every year, and such meeting shall [4]**[be on the first Monday in December,]** unless they shall by law appoint a different day.

*Sect.* 5. Each house shall be the judge of the elections, returns and qualifications of its own members, and a majority of each shall constitute a quorum to do business; but a smaller number may adjourn from day to day, and may be authorized to compel the attendance of absent members, in such manner, and under such penalties as each house may provide.

Each house may determine the rules of its proceedings, punish its members for disorderly behaviour, and, with the concurrence of two-thirds, expel a member.

Each house shall keep a journal of its proceedings, and from time to time publish the same, excepting such parts as may in their judgment require secrecy; and the yeas and nays of the members of either house on any question shall, at the desire of one-fifth of those present, be entered on the journal.

Neither house, during the session of Congress shall, without the consent of the other, adjourn for more than three days, nor to any other place than that in which the two houses shall be sitting.

*Sect.* 6. The senators and representatives shall receive a compensation for their services, to be ascertained by law, and paid out of the treasury of the United States. They shall in all cases, except treason, felony and breach of the peace, be privileged from arrest during their attendance at the session of their respective houses, and in going to and returning from the same; and for any speech or debate in either house, they shall not be questioned in any other place.

No senator or representative shall, during the time for which he was elected, be appointed to any civil office under the authority of the United States, which shall have been created, or the emoluments whereof shall have been encreased during such time; and no person holding any office under the United States, shall be a member of either house during his continuance in office.

*Sect.* 7. All bills for raising revenue shall originate in the house of representatives; but the senate may propose or concur with amendments as on other bills.

Every bill which shall have passed the house of representatives and the senate, shall, before it become a law, be presented to the president of the United States; if he approve he shall sign it, but if not he shall return it, with his objections to that house in which it shall have originated, who shall enter the objections at large on their journal, and proceed to reconsider it. If after such reconsideration two-thirds of that house shall agree to pass the bill, it shall be sent, together with the objections, to the other house, by which it shall likewise be reconsidered, and if approved by two-thirds of that house, it shall become a law. But in all such cases the votes of both houses shall be determined by yeas and nays, and the names of the persons voting for and against the bill shall be entered on the journal of each house respectively. If any bill shall not be returned by the President within ten days (Sundays excepted) after it shall have been presented to him, the same shall be a law, in like manner as if he had signed it, unless the Congress by their adjournment prevent its return, in which case it shall not be a law.

Every order, resolution, or vote to which the concurrence of the Senate and House of Representatives may be necessary (except on a question of adjournment) shall be presented to the President of the United States; and before the same shall take effect, shall be approved by him, or, being disapproved by him, shall be repassed by two-thirds of the Senate and House of Representatives, according to the rules and limitations prescribed in the case of a bill.

*Sect.* 8. The Congress shall have power

To lay and collect taxes, duties, imposts and excises, to pay the debts and provide for the common defence and general welfare of the United States; but all duties, imposts and excises shall be uniform throughout the United States;

To borrow money on the credit of the United States;

To regulate commerce with foreign nations, and among the several states, and with the Indian tribes;

To establish an uniform rule of naturalization, and uniform laws on the subject of bankruptcies throughout the United States;

To coin money, regulate the value thereof, and of foreign coin, and fix the standard of weights and measures;

To provide for the punishment of counterfeiting the securities and current coin of the United States;

To establish post offices and post roads;

To promote the progress of science and useful arts, by securing for limited times to authors and inventors the exclusive right to their respective writings and discoveries;

[4] The clause enclosed by brackets was changed by section 2 of Amendment XX.

To constitute tribunals inferior to the supreme court;

To define and punish piracies and felonies committed on the high seas, and offences against the law of nations;

To declare war, grant letters of marque and reprisal, and make rules concerning captures on land and water;

To raise and support armies, but no appropriation of money to that use shall be for a longer term than two years;

To provide and maintain a navy;

To make rules for the government and regulation of the land and naval forces;

To provide for calling forth the militia to execute the laws of the union, suppress insurrections and repel invasions;

To provide for organizing, arming, and disciplining, the militia, and for governing such part of them as may be employed in the service of the United States, reserving to the States respectively, the appointment of the officers, and the authority of training the militia according to the discipline prescribed by Congress;

To exercise exclusive legislation in all cases whatsoever, over such district (not exceeding ten miles square) as may, by cession of particular States, and the acceptance of Congress, become the seat of the government of the United States, and to exercise like authority over all places purchased by the consent of the legislature of the states in which the same shall be, for the erection of forts, magazines, arsenals, dock-yards, and other needful buildings;—And

To make all laws which shall be necessary and proper for carrying into execution the foregoing powers, and all other powers vested by this constitution in the government of the United States, or in any department or officer thereof.

*Sect.* 9. The migration or importation of such persons as any of the states now existing shall think proper to admit, shall not be prohibited by the Congress prior to the year one thousand eight hundred and eight, but a tax or duty may be imposed on such importation, not exceeding ten dollars for each person.

The privilege of the writ of habeas corpus shall not be suspended, unless when in cases of rebellion or invasion the public safety may require it.

No bill of attainder or ex post facto law shall be passed.

No capitation, or other direct, tax shall be laid, unless in proportion to the census or enumeration herein before directed to be taken.[5]

No tax or duty shall be laid on articles exported from any state. No preference shall be given by any regulation of commerce or revenue to the ports of one state over those of another: nor shall vessels bound to, or from, one state, be obliged to enter, clear, or pay duties in another.

No money shall be drawn from the treasury, but in consequence of appropriations made by law; and a regular statement and account of the receipts and expenditures of all public money shall be published from time to time.

No title of nobility shall be granted by the United States:—And no person holding any office of profit or trust under them, shall, without the consent of the Congress, accept of any present, emolument, office, or title, of any kind whatever, from any king, prince, or foreign state.

*Sect.* 10. No state shall enter into any treaty, alliance, or confederation; grant letters of marque and reprisal; coin money; emit bills of credit; make any thing but gold and silver coin a tender in payment of debts; pass any bill of attainder, ex post facto law, or law impairing the obligation of contracts, or grant any title of nobility.

No state shall, without the consent of the Congress, lay any imposts or duties on imports or exports, except what may be absolutely necessary for executing its inspection laws; and the net produce of all duties and imposts, laid by any state on imports or exports, shall be for the use of the Treasury of the United States; and all such laws shall be subject to the revision and controul of the Congress. No state shall, without the consent of Congress, lay any duty of tonnage, keep troops, or ships of war in time of peace, enter into any agreement or compact with another state, or with a foreign power, or engage in war, unless actually invaded, or in such imminent danger as will not admit of delay.

## II.

*Sect.* 1. The executive power shall be vested in a president of the United States of America. He shall hold his office during the term of four years, and, together with the vice-president, chosen for the same term, be elected as follows.

Each state shall appoint, in such manner as the legislature thereof may direct, a number of electors, equal to the whole number of senators and representatives to which the state may be entitled in the Congress: but no senator or representative, or person holding an office of trust or profit under the United States, shall be appointed an elector.

[6]**[The electors shall meet in their respective states, and vote by ballot for two persons, of whom one at least shall not be an inhabitant of the same state with themselves. And they shall make a list of all the persons voted for, and of the number of votes for each; which list they shall sign and certify, and transmit sealed to the seat of the government of the United States, directed to the president of the senate. The president of the senate shall, in the presence of the senate and house of representatives, open all the certificates, and the votes shall then be counted. The person having the greatest number of votes shall be the president, if such number be a majority of the whole number of electors appointed; and if there be more than one who have such majority, and have an equal number of votes, then the house of representatives shall immediately chuse by ballot one of them for president; and if no person have a majority, then from the five highest on the list the said house shall in like manner chuse the president. But in chusing the president, the votes shall be taken by states, the representation from each state having one vote; a quorum for this purpose shall consist of a member or members from two-thirds of the states, and a majority of all the states shall be necessary to a choice. In every case, after the choice of the president, the person having the greatest number of votes of the electors shall be the vice-president. But if there should remain two or more who have equal votes, the senate shall chuse from them by ballot the vice-president.]**

The Congress may determine the time of chusing the electors, and the day on which they shall give their votes; which day shall be the same throughout the United States.

[5] **See also Amendment XVI.** [6] **This paragraph has been superseded by Amendment XII.**

No person except a natural born citizen, or a citizen of the United States, at the time of the adoption of this constitution, shall be eligible to the office of president; neither shall any person be eligible to that office who shall not have attained to the age of thirty-five years, and been fourteen years a resident within the United States.

[7]In case of the removal of the president from office, or of his death, resignation, or inability to discharge the powers and duties of the said office, the same shall devolve on the vice-president, and the Congress may by law provide for the case of removal, death, resignation or inability, both of the president and vice-president, declaring what officer shall then act as president, and such officer shall act accordingly, until the disability be removed, or a president be elected.

The president shall, at stated times, receive for his services, a compensation, which shall neither be encreased nor diminished during the period for which he shall have been elected, and he shall not receive within that period any other emolument from the United States, or any of them.

Before he enter on the execution of his office, he shall take the following oath or affirmation:

"I do solemnly swear (or affirm) that I will faithfully execute the office of president of the United States, and will to the best of my ability, preserve, protect and defend the constitution of the United States."

*Sect.* 2. The president shall be commander in chief of the army and navy of the United States, and of the militia of the several States, when called into the actual service of the United States; he may require the opinion, in writing, of the principal officer in each of the executive departments, upon any subject relating to the duties of their respective offices, and he shall have power to grant reprieves and pardons for offences against the United States, except in cases of impeachment.

He shall have power, by and with the advice and consent of the senate, to make treaties, provided two-thirds of the senators present concur; and he shall nominate, and by and with the advice and consent of the senate, shall appoint ambassadors, other public ministers and consuls, judges of the supreme court, and all other officers of the United States, whose appointments are not herein otherwise provided for, and which shall be established by law. But the Congress may by law vest the appointment of such inferior officers, as they think proper, in the president alone, in the courts of law, or in the heads of departments.

The president shall have power to fill up all vacancies that may happen during the recess of the senate, by granting commissions which shall expire at the end of their session.

*Sect.* 3. He shall from time to time give to the Congress information of the state of the union, and recommend to their consideration such measures as he shall judge necessary and expedient; he may, on extraordinary occasions, convene both houses, or either of them, and in case of disagreement between them, with respect to the time of adjournment, he may adjourn them to such time as he shall think proper; he shall receive ambassadors and other public ministers; he shall take care that the laws be faithfully executed, and shall commission all the officers of the United States.

*Sect.* 4. The president, vice-president and all civil officers of the United States, shall be removed from office on impeachment for, and conviction of, treason, bribery, or other high crimes and misdemeanors.

## III.

*Sect.* 1. The judicial power of the United States, shall be vested in one supreme court, and in such inferior courts as the Congress may from time to time ordain and establish. The judges, both of the supreme and inferior courts, shall hold their offices during good behaviour, and shall, at stated times, receive for their services, a compensation, which shall not be diminished during their continuance in office.

*Sect.* 2. The judicial power shall extend to all cases, in law and equity, arising under this constitution, the laws of the United States, and treaties made, or which shall be made, under their authority; to all cases of admiralty and maritime jurisdiction; to controversies to which the United States shall be a party; to controversies between two or more States, between a state and citizens of another state,[8] between citizens of different States, between citizens of the same state claiming lands under grants of different States, and between a state, or the citizens thereof, and foreign States, citizens or subjects.

In all cases affecting ambassadors, other public ministers and consuls, and those in which a state shall be party, the supreme court shall have original jurisdiction. In all the other cases before mentioned, the supreme court shall have appellate jurisdiction, both as to law and fact, with such exceptions, and under such regulations as the Congress shall make.

The trial of all crimes, except in cases of impeachment, shall be by jury; and such trial shall be held in the state where the said crimes shall have been committed; but when not committed within any state, the trial shall be at such place or places as the Congress may by law have directed.

*Sect.* 3. Treason against the United States, shall consist only in levying war against them, or in adhering to their enemies, giving them aid and comfort. No person shall be convicted of treason unless on the testimony of two witnesses to the same overt act, or on confession in open court.

The Congress shall have power to declare the punishment of treason, but no attainder of treason shall work corruption of blood, or forfeiture except during the life of the person attainted.

## IV.

*Sect.* 1. Full faith and credit shall be given in each state to the public acts, records, and judicial proceedings of every other state. And the Congress may by general laws prescribe the manner in which such acts, records and proceedings shall be proved, and the effect thereof.

*Sect.* 2. The citizens of each state shall be entitled to all privileges and immunities of citizens in the several states.

A person charged in any state with treason, felony, or other crime, who shall flee from justice, and be found in another state, shall, on demand of the executive authority of the state from which he fled, be delivered up, to be removed to the state having jurisdiction of the crime.

[9]**[No person held to service or labour in one state, under the laws thereof, escaping into another, shall, in consequence of any law or regulation therein, be discharged from such service or labour, but shall be delivered up on claim of**

[7] Affected by Amendment XXV. [8] Affected by Amendment XI. [9] Superseded by Amendment XIII.

the party to whom such service or labour may be due.]

*Sect.* 3. New states may be admitted by the Congress into this union; but no new state shall be formed or erected within the jurisdiction of any other state; nor any state be formed by the junction of two or more states, or parts of states, without the consent of the legislatures of the states concerned as well as of the Congress.

The Congress shall have power to dispose of and make all needful rules and regulations respecting the territory or other property belonging to the United States; and nothing in this Constitution shall be so construed as to prejudice any claims of the United States, or of any particular state.

*Sect.* 4. The United States shall guarantee to every state in this union a Republican form of government, and shall protect each of them against invasion; and on application of the legislature, or of the executive (when the legislature cannot be convened) against domestic violence.

V.

The Congress, whenever two-thirds of both houses shall deem it necessary, shall propose amendments to this constitution, or, on the application of the legislatures of two-thirds of the several states, shall call a convention for proposing amendments, which, in either case, shall be valid to all intents and purposes, as part of this constitution, when ratified by the legislatures of three-fourths of the several states, or by conventions in three-fourths thereof, as the one or the other mode of ratification may be proposed by Congress; Provided, that no amendment which may be made prior to the year one thousand eight hundred and eight shall in any manner affect the first and fourth clauses in the ninth section of the first article; and that no state, without its consent, shall be deprived of its equal suffrage in the senate.

VI.

All debts contracted and engagements entered into, before the adoption of this Constitution, shall be as valid against the United States under this Constitution, as under the confederation.

This constitution, and the laws of the United States which shall be made in pursuance thereof; and all treaties made, or which shall be made, under the authority of the United States, shall be the supreme law of the land; and the judges in every state shall be bound thereby, any thing in the constitution or laws of any state to the contrary notwithstanding.

The senators and representatives beforementioned, and the members of the several state legislatures, and all executive and judicial officers, both of the United States and of the several States, shall be bound by oath or affirmation, to support this constitution; but no religious test shall ever be required as a qualification to any office or public trust under the United States.

VII.

The ratification of the conventions of nine States, shall be sufficient for the establishment of this constitution between the States so ratifying the same.

[*Done in Convention, by the unanimous consent of the States present, the seventeenth day of September, in the year of our Lord one thousand seven hundred and eighty-seven, and of the Independence of the United States of America the twelfth. In witness whereof we have hereunto subscribed our Names.*]

## SIGNERS OF THE CONSTITUTION: 1787

| Name | Age | Occupation | Education | Representing | Birthplace | Born | Died |
|---|---|---|---|---|---|---|---|
| Abraham Baldwin | 32 | Lawyer | Yale | Georgia | Guilford, Conn. | 1754 | 1807 |
| Richard Bassett | 42 | Lawyer | Private tutors | Delaware | Cecil Co., Md. | 1745 | 1815 |
| Gunning Bedford | c. 40 | Lawyer | College of New Jersey[1] | Delaware | Philadelphia, Pa. | 1747 | 1812 |
| John Blair | c. 55 | Jurist | Studied law in England | Virginia | Williamsburg, Va. | 1732 | 1800 |
| William Blount | 38 | Public servant | Private tutors | North Carolina | Bertie Co., N.C. | 1749 | 1800 |
| David Brearley | 42 | Jurist | Private tutors | New Jersey | Spring Grove, N.J. | 1745 | 1790 |
| Jacob Broom | 35 | Businessman | Preparatory studies | Delaware | Wilmington, Del. | 1752 | 1810 |
| Pierce Butler | 43 | Planter | Private tutors | South Carolina | Co. Carlow, Ireland | 1744 | 1822 |
| Daniel Carroll | 57 | Planter-Businessman | Educated at Jesuit schools in Maryland and France | Maryland | Upper Marlboro, Md. | 1730 | 1796 |
| George Clymer | 48 | Merchant | Self-educated | Pennsylvania | Philadelphia, Pa. | 1739 | 1813 |
| Jonathan Dayton | 26 | Lawyer | College of New Jersey[1] | New Jersey | Elizabeth-Town, N.J. | 1760 | 1824 |
| John Dickinson | 55 | Public servant | Studied law in England | Delaware | Talbot Co., Md. | 1732 | 1808 |
| William Few | 39 | Lawyer | Self-educated | Georgia | near Baltimore, Md. | 1748 | 1828 |
| Thomas Fitzsimons | c. 46 | Businessman | Self-educated | Pennsylvania | Ireland | 1741 | 1811 |
| Benjamin Franklin | 81 | Public servant | Grammar school | Pennsylvania | Boston, Mass. | 1706 | 1790 |
| Nicholas Gilman | 32 | Public servant | Grammar school | New Hampshire | Exeter, N.H. | 1755 | 1814 |
| Nathaniel Gorham | 49 | Businessman | Private tutors | Massachusetts | Charlestown, Mass. | 1738 | 1796 |
| Alexander Hamilton | 32 | Lawyer | King's College[2] | New York | West Indies | 1755 | 1804 |
| Jared Ingersoll | 37 | Lawyer | Yale; studied law in England | Pennsylvania | New Haven, Conn. | 1749 | 1822 |
| Daniel of St. Thomas Jenifer | c. 64 | Planter-Public servant | Preparatory studies | Maryland | Charles Co., Md. | 1723 | 1790 |
| William Samuel Johnson | 59 | Lawyer-College president | Yale; A.M., Harvard | Connecticut | Stratford, Conn. | 1727 | 1819 |
| Rufus King | 32 | Lawyer | Harvard | Massachusetts | Scarboro, Mass. | 1755 | 1827 |
| John Langdon | 46 | Businessman | Grammar School | New Hampshire | Portsmouth, N.H. | 1741 | 1819 |
| William Livingston | 53 | Public servant | Yale | New Jersey | Albany, N.Y. | 1723 | 1790 |
| James Madison | 36 | Lawyer | College of New Jersey[1] | Virginia | Port Conway, Va. | 1751 | 1836 |
| James McHenry | c. 34 | Businessman | Educated in Ireland and Delaware; studied medicine under Benjamin Rush | Maryland | Ireland | c. 1753 | 1816 |
| Thomas Mifflin | 33 | Merchant | College of Philadelphia[3] | Pennsylvania | Philadelphia, Pa. | 1744 | 1800 |
| Gouverneur Morris | 35 | Lawyer | King's College[2] | Pennsylvania | Morrisania, N.Y. | 1752 | 1816 |
| Robert Morris | 53 | Merchant | Self-educated | Pennsylvania | Liverpool, England | 1734 | 1806 |
| William Paterson | 31 | Lawyer | College of New Jersey[1] | Maryland | Co. Antrim, Ireland | 1745 | 1806 |

| Name | Age | Occupation | Education | Representing | Birthplace | Born | Died |
|---|---|---|---|---|---|---|---|
| Charles Pinckney | 29 | Lawyer | Preparatory studies | South Carolina | Charleston, S.C. | 1757 | 1824 |
| Charles Cotesworth Pinckney | 41 | Lawyer | Oxford | South Carolina | Charleston, S.C. | 1746 | 1825 |
| George Read | 53 | Lawyer | Preparatory studies | Delaware | near Northeast, Cecil Co., Md. | 1733 | 1798 |
| John Rutledge | c. 58 | Public servant | Studied law in England | South Carolina | Charleston, S.C. | 1739 | 1800 |
| Roger Sherman | 66 | Businessman | Self-educated | Connecticut | Newton, Mass. | 1721 | 1793 |
| Richard Dobbs Spaight | 29 | Planter | Educated in Ireland and Scotland | North Carolina | New Bern, N.C. | 1758 | 1802 |
| George Washington | 55 | Planter | Private tutors | Virginia | Westmoreland Co., Va. | 1732 | 1799 |
| Hugh Williamson | 41 | Businessman-Physician | College of Philadelphia;[3] M.D., Univ. of Utrecht | North Carolina | West Nottingham, Pa. | 1735 | 1819 |
| James Wilson | 44 | Lawyer | Educated in Scotland | Pennsylvania | Scotland | 1742 | 1798 |

[1] now Princeton University. [2] now Columbia University. [3] now University of Pennsylvania.

## THE CONSTITUTIONAL AMENDMENTS

The first ten amendments* to the original Constitution are known as the Bill of Rights.

### AMENDMENT [I]

Congress shall make no law respecting an establishment of religion, or prohibiting the free exercise thereof; or abridging the freedom of speech, or of the press; or the right of the people peaceably to assemble, and to petition the Government for a redress of grievances.

### AMENDMENT [II]

A well regulated Militia, being necessary to the security of a free State, the right of the people to keep and bear Arms, shall not be infringed.

### AMENDMENT [III]

No Soldier shall, in time of peace be quartered in any house, without the consent of the Owner, nor in time of war, but in a manner to be prescribed by law.

### AMENDMENT [IV]

The right of the people to be secure in their persons, houses, papers, and effects, against unreasonable searches and seizures, shall not be violated, and no Warrants shall issue, but upon probable cause, supported by Oath or affirmation, and particularly describing the place to be searched, and the persons or things to be seized.

### AMENDMENT [V]

No person shall be held to answer for a capital, or otherwise infamous crime, unless on a presentment or indictment of a Grand Jury, except in cases arising in the land or naval forces, or in the Militia, when in actual service in time of War or public danger; nor shall any person be subject for the same offence to be twice put in jeopardy of life or limb; nor shall be compelled in any criminal case to be a witness against himself, nor be deprived of life, liberty, or property, without due process of law; nor shall private property be taken for public use, without just compensation.

### AMENDMENT [VI]

In all criminal prosecutions, the accused shall enjoy the right to a speedy and public trial, by an impartial jury of the State and district wherein the crime shall have been committed, which district shall have been previously ascertained by law, and to be informed of the nature and cause of the accusation; to be confronted with the witnesses against him; to have compulsory process for obtaining witnesses in his favor, and to have the Assistance of Counsel for his defence.

### AMENDMENT [VII]

In Suits at common law, where the value in controversy shall exceed twenty dollars, the right of trial by jury shall be preserved, and no fact tried by a jury, shall be otherwise re-examined in any Court of the United States, than according to the rules of the common law.

### AMENDMENT [VIII]

Excessive bail shall not be required, nor excessive fines imposed, nor cruel and unusual punishments inflicted.

### AMENDMENT [IX]

The enumeration in the Constitution, of certain rights, shall not be construed to deny or disparage others retained by the people.

### AMENDMENT [X]

The powers not delegated to the United States by the Constitution, nor prohibited by it to the States, are reserved to the States respectively, or to the people.

### AMENDMENT [XI][1]

The Judicial power of the United States shall not be construed to extend to any suit in law or equity, commenced or prosecuted against one of the United States by Citizens of another State, or by Citizens or Subjects of any Foreign State.

### AMENDMENT [XII][2]

The Electors shall meet in their respective states, and vote by ballot for President and Vice-President, one of whom, at least, shall not be an inhabitant of the same state with themselves; they shall name in their ballots the person voted for as President, and in distinct ballots the person voted for as Vice-President, and they shall make distinct lists of all persons voted for as President, and

* The first 10 amendments, together with 2 others that failed of ratification, were proposed to the several States by resolution of Congress on September 25, 1789. The ratifications were transmitted by the Governors to the President and by him communicated to Congress from time to time. The first 10 amendments were ratified by 11 of the 14 States. Virginia completed the required three fourths by ratification on December 15, 1791, and its action was communicated to Congress by the President on December 30, 1791. The legislatures of Massachusetts, Georgia, and Connecticut ratified them on March 2, 1939, March 18, 1939, and April 19, 1939, respectively.

[1] The Eleventh Amendment was proposed by resolution of Congress on March 4, 1794. It was declared by the President, in a message to Congress dated January 8, 1798, to have been ratified by three fourths of the several States. Records of the National Archives show that the 11th Amendment was ratified by 13 of the 16 States. It was not ratified by New Jersey or Pennsylvania.

[2] The Twelfth Amendment was proposed in lieu of the original third paragraph of section 1 of article II, by resolution of Congress on December 9, 1803. It was declared in a proclamation of the Secretary of State, dated September 25, 1804, to have been ratified by three fourths of the States. Records of the National Archives show that it was ratified by 14 States and rejected by Connecticut and Delaware.

of all persons voted for as Vice-President, and of the number of votes for each, which lists they shall sign and certify, and transmit sealed to the seat of the government of the United States, directed to the President of the Senate;—The President of the Senate shall, in the presence of the Senate and House of Representatives, open all the certificates and the votes shall then be counted;—The person having the greatest number of votes for President, shall be the President, if such number be a majority of the whole number of Electors appointed; and if no person have such majority, then from the persons having the highest numbers not exceeding three on the list of those voted for as President, the House of Representatives shall choose immediately, by ballot, the President. But in choosing the President, the votes shall be taken by states, the representation from each state having one vote; a quorum for this purpose shall consist of a member or members from two-thirds of the states, and a majority of all the states shall be necessary to a choice. [3]**[And if the House of Representatives shall not choose a President whenever the right of choice shall devolve upon them, before the fourth day of March next following, then the Vice-President shall act as President, as in the case of the death or other constitutional disability of the President.]**—The person having the greatest number of votes as Vice-President, shall be the Vice-President, if such number be a majority of the whole number of Electors appointed, and if no person have a majority, then from the two highest numbers on the list, the Senate shall choose the Vice-President; a quorum for the purpose shall consist of two-thirds of the whole number of Senators, and a majority of the whole number shall be necessary to a choice. But no person constitutionally ineligible to the office of President shall be eligible to that of Vice-President of the United States.

### AMENDMENT [XIII][4]

Section 1. Neither slavery nor involuntary servitude, except as a punishment for crime whereof the party shall have been duly convicted, shall exist within the United States, or any place subject to their jurisdiction.

Section 2. Congress shall have power to enforce this article by appropriate legislation.

### AMENDMENT [XIV][5]

Section 1. All persons born or naturalized in the United States, and subject to the jurisdiction thereof, are citizens of the United States and of the State wherein they reside. No State shall make or enforce any law which shall abridge the privileges or immunities of citizens of the United States; nor shall any State deprive any person of life, liberty, or property, without due process of law; nor deny to any person within its jurisdiction the equal protection of the laws.

Section 2. Representatives shall be apportioned among the several States according to their respective numbers, counting the whole number of persons in each State, excluding Indians not taxed. But when the right to vote at any election for the choice of electors for President and Vice President of the United States, Representatives in Congree, the Executive and Judicial officers of a State, or the members of the Legislature thereof, is denied to any of the male inhabitants of such State, being twenty-one years of age, and citizens of the United States, or in any way abridged, except for participation in rebellion, or other crime, the basis of representation therein shall be reduced in the proportion which the number of such male citizens shall bear to the whole number of male citizens twenty-one years of age in such State.

Section 3. No person shall be a Senator or Representative in Congress, or elector of President and Vice President, or hold any office, civil or military, under the United States, or under any State, who, having previously taken an oath, as a member of Congress, or as an officer of the United States, or as a member of any State legislature, or as an executive or judicial officer of any State, to support the Constitution of the United States, shall have engaged in insurrection or rebellion against the same, or given aid or comfort to the enemies thereof. But Congress may by a vote of two-thirds of each House, remove such disability.

Section 4. The validity of the public debt of the United States, authorized by law, including debts incurred for payment of pensions and bounties for services in suppressing insurrection or rebellion, shall not be questioned. But neither the United States nor any State shall assume or pay any debt or obligation incurred in aid of insurrection or rebellion against the United States, or any claim for the loss or emancipation of any slave; but all such debts, obligations and claims shall be held illegal and void.

Section 5. The Congress shall have power to enforce, by appropriate legislation, the provisions of this article.

### AMENDMENT [XV][6]

Section 1. The right of citizens of the United States to vote shall not be denied or abridged by the United States or by any State on account of race, color, or previous condition of servitude.

Section 2. The Congress shall have power to enforce this article by appropriate legislation.

### AMENDMENT [XVI][7]

The Congress shall have power to lay and collect taxes on incomes, from whatever source de-

[3] The part enclosed by brackets has been superseded by section 3 of Amendment XX.

[4] The Thirteenth Amendment was proposed by resolution of Congress on January 31, 1865. It was declared in a proclamation of the Secretary of State, dated December 18, 1865, to have been ratified by 27 States. Subsequent records of the National Archives show that the 13th Amendment was ratified by 7 additional States. It was rejected by Kentucky and Mississippi.

[5] The Fourteenth Amendment was proposed by resolution of Congress on June 13, 1866. By a concurrent resolution of Congress adopted July 21, 1868, it was declared to have been ratified by "three fourths and more of the several States of the Union," and the Secretary of State was required duly to promulgate the amendment as a part of the Constitution. He accordingly issued a proclamation, dated July 28, 1868, declaring the amendment to have been ratified by 30 States, "being more than three fourths." Records of the National Archives show that the 14th Amendment was subsequently ratified by 8 additional States. It was rejected by Kentucky.

[6] The Fifteenth Amendment was proposed by resolution of Congress on February 26, 1869. It was declared in a proclamation of the Secretary of State, dated March 30, 1870, to have been ratified by 29 States, which "constitute three fourths." Records of the National Archives show that the 15th Amendment was subsequently ratified by 6 more of the States. It was rejected by Kentucky, Maryland, and Tennessee.

[7] The Sixteenth Amendment was proposed by resolution of Congress on July 12, 1909. It was declared in a proclamation of the Secretary of State, dated February 25, 1913, to have been ratified by 38 States, which "constitute three fourths." Subsequent records of the National Archives show that the 16th Amendment was ratified by 4 additional States. It was rejected by Connecticut, Florida, Rhode Island, and Utah.

rived, without apportionment among the several States, and without regard to any census or enumeration.

AMENDMENT [XVII][8]

The Senate of the United States shall be composed of two Senators from each State, elected by the people thereof, for six years; and each Senator shall have one vote. The electors in each State shall have the qualifications requisite for electors of the most numerous branch of the State legislatures.

When vacancies happen in the representation of any State in the Senate, the executive authority of such State shall issue writs of election to fill such vacancies: *Provided*, That the legislature of any State may empower the executive thereof to make temporary appointments until the people fill the vacancies by election as the legislature may direct.

This amendment shall not be so construed as to affect the election or term of any Senator chosen before it becomes valid as part of the Constitution.

AMENDMENT [XVIII][9]

[Section 1. After one year from the ratification of this article the manufacture, sale, or transportation of intoxicating liquors within, the importation thereof into, or the exportation thereof from the United States and all territory subject to the jurisdiction thereof for beverage purposes is hereby prohibited.

[Sec. 2. The Congress and the several States shall have concurrent power to enforce this article by appropriate legislation.

[Sec. 3. This article shall be inoperative unless it shall have been ratified as an amendment to the Constitution by the legislatures of the several States, as provided in the Constitution, within seven years from the date of the submission hereof to the States by the Congress.]

AMENDMENT [XIX][10]

The right of citizens of the United States to vote shall not be denied or abridged by the United States or by any State on account of sex.

Congress shall have power to enforce this article by appropriate legislation.

AMENDMENT [XX][11]

Section 1. The terms of the President and Vice President shall end at noon on the 20th day of January, and the terms of Senators and Representatives at noon on the 3d day of January, of the years in which such terms would have ended if this article had not been ratified; and the terms of their successors shall then begin.

Sec. 2. The Congress shall assemble at least once in every year, and such meeting shall begin at noon on the 3d day of January, unless they shall by law appoint a different day.

Sec. 3. If, at the time fixed for the beginning of the term of the President, the President elect shall have died, the Vice President elect shall become President. If a President shall not have been chosen before the time fixed for the beginning of his term, or if the President elect shall have failed to qualify, then the Vice President elect shall act as President until a President shall have qualified; and the Congress may by law provide for the case wherein neither a President elect nor a Vice President elect shall have qualified, declaring who shall then act as President, or the manner in which one who is to act shall be selected, and such person shall act accordingly until a President or Vice President shall have qualified.

Sec. 4. The Congress may by law provide for the case of the death of any of the persons from whom the House of Representatives may choose a President whenever the right of choice shall have devolved upon them, and for the case of the death of any of the persons from whom the Senate may choose a Vice President whenever the right of choice shall have devolved upon them.

Sec. 5. Sections 1 and 2 shall take effect on the 15th day of October following the ratification of this article.

Sec. 6. This article shall be inoperative unless it shall have been ratified as an amendment to the Constitution by the legislatures of three-fourths of the several States within seven years from the date of its submission.

AMENDMENT [XXI][12]

Section 1. The eighteenth article of amendment to the Constitution of the United States is hereby repealed.

Sec. 2. The transportation or importation into any State, Territory, or possession of the United States for delivery or use therein of intoxicating liquors, in violation of the laws thereof, is hereby prohibited.

Sec. 3. This article shall be inoperative unless it shall have been ratified as an amendment to the Constitution by conventions in the several States, as provided in the Constitution, within seven

[8] The Seventeenth Amendment was proposed by resolution of Congress on May 13, 1912. It was declared in a proclamation of the Secretary of State, dated May 31, 1913, to have been ratified by 36 States, which "constitute three fourths." Records of the National Archives show that the 17th Amendment was subsequently ratified by 1 additional State. It was rejected by Utah and Delaware.

[9] The Eighteenth Amendment was proposed by resolution of Congress on December 18, 1917. It was declared in a proclamation of the Acting Secretary of State, dated January 29, 1919, to have been ratified by 36 States, which "constitute three fourths." Subsequent records of the National Archives show that the 18th Amendment was ratified by 10 additional States. It was rejected by Rhode Island. By its own terms the 18th Amendment became effective one year after its ratification, which was consummated on January 16, 1919, and therefore went into effect on January 16, 1920.

Repeal of the 18th Amendment on December 5, 1933, was proclaimed by the President in his proclamation of that date, when the ratification of the 21st Amendment was certified by the Acting Secretary of State.

[10] The Nineteenth Amendment was proposed by resolution of Congress on June 4, 1919. It was declared in a proclamation of the Secretary of State, dated August 26, 1920, to have been ratified by 36 States, which "constitute three fourths." Subsequent records of the National Archives show that the 19th Amendment was ratified by 5 additional States. It was rejected by Georgia, South Carolina, Mississippi, Delaware, and Louisiana.

[11] The Twentieth Amendment was proposed by resolution of Congress on March 2, 1932. It was declared in a proclamation of the Secretary of State, dated February 6, 1933, to have been ratified by 39 States, which "constitute more than the requisite three fourths." Subsequent records of the National Archives show that the 20th Amendment was ratified by all 48 States before sections 1 and 2 became effective on October 15, 1933. The other sections of the amendment became effective on January 23, 1933, when its ratification was consummated by three fourths of the States.

[12] The Twenty-first Amendment was proposed by resolution of Congress on February 20, 1933. It was certified in a proclamation of the Acting Secretary of State dated December 5, 1933, to have been ratified by conventions of 36 States, which "constitute the requisite three fourths of the whole number of States." Subsequent records of the National Archives show that the 21st Amendment was ratified by 2 additional States. It was rejected by the convention of South Carolina. North Carolina voted against holding a convention.

years from the date of the submission hereof to the States by the Congress.

AMENDMENT [XXII][13]

Section 1. No person shall be elected to the office of the President more than twice, and no person who has held the office of President, or acted as President, for more than two years of a term to which some other person was elected President shall be elected to the office of the President more than once. But this Article shall not apply to any person holding the office of President when this Article was proposed by the Congress, and shall not prevent any person who may be holding the office of President, or acting as President, during the term within which this Article becomes operative from holding the office of President or acting as President during the remainder of such term.

Sec. 2. This article shall be inoperative unless it shall have been ratified as an amendment to the Constitution by the legislatures of three-fourths of the several States within seven years from the date of its submission to the States by the Congress.

AMENDMENT [XXIII][14]

Section 1. The District constituting the seat of Government of the United States shall appoint in such manner as the Congress may direct:

A number of electors of President and Vice President equal to the whole number of Senators and Representatives in Congress to which the District would be entitled if it were a State, but in no event more than the least populous State; they shall be in addition to those appointed by the States, but they shall be considered, for the purposes of the election of President and Vice President, to be electors appointed by a State; and they shall meet in the District and perform such duties as provided by the twelfth article of amendment.

Section 2. The Congress shall have power to enforce this article by appropriate legislation.

AMENDMENT [XXIV][15]

Section 1. The right of citizens of the United States to vote in any primary or other election for President or Vice President, for electors for President or Vice President, or for Senator or Representative in Congress, shall not be denied or abridged by the United States or any State by reason of failure to pay any poll tax or other tax.

Section 2. The Congress shall have power to enforce this article by appropriate legislation.

AMENDMENT [XXV][16]

Section 1. In case of removal of the President from office or of his death or resignation, the Vice President shall become President.

Sec. 2. Whenever there is a vacancy in the office of the Vice President, the President shall nominate a Vice President who shall take office upon confirmation by a majority vote of both Houses of Congress.

Sec. 3. Whenever the President transmits to the President pro tempore of the Senate and the Speaker of the House of Representatives his written declaration that he is unable to discharge the powers and duties of his office, and until he transmits to them a written declaration to the contrary, such powers and duties shall be discharged by the Vice President as Acting President.

Sec. 4. Whenever the Vice President and a majority of either the principal officers of the executive departments or of such other body as Congress may by law provide, transmit to the President pro tempore of the Senate and the Speaker of the House of Representatives their written declaration that the President is unable to discharge the powers and duties of his office, the Vice President shall immediately assume the powers and duties of the office as Acting President.

Thereafter, when the President transmits to the President pro tempore of the Senate and the Speaker of the House of Representatives his written declaration that no inability exists, he shall resume the powers and duties of his office unless the Vice President and a majority of either the principal officers of the executive department or of such other body as Congress may by law provide, transmit within four days to the President pro tempore of the Senate and the Speaker of the House of Representatives their written declaration that the President is unable to discharge the powers and duties of his office. Thereupon Congress shall decide the issue, assembling within forty-eight hours for that purpose if not in session. If the Congress, within twenty-one days after receipt of the latter written declaration, or, if Congress is not in session, within twenty-one days after Congress is required to assemble, determines by two-thirds vote of both Houses that the President is unable to discharge the powers and duties of his office, the Vice President shall continue to discharge the same as Acting President; otherwise, the President shall resume the powers and duties of his office.

AMENDMENT [XXVI][17]

Section 1. The right of citizens of the United States, who are eighteen years of age or older, to vote shall not be denied or abridged by the United States or by any State on account of age.

Sec. 2. The Congress shall have power to enforce this article by appropriate legislation.

[13] The Twenty-second Amendment was proposed by resolution of Congress on March 24, 1947. Ratification was completed on February 27, 1951, when the thirty-sixth State (Minnesota) approved the amendment. On March 1, 1951, the Administrator of General Services certified that "the States whose Legislatures have so ratified the said proposed Amendment constitute the requisite three-fourths of the whole number of States in the United States." Records of the National Archives show that the 22d Amendment was subsequently ratified by 5 additional States.

[14] The Twenty-third Amendment was proposed by resolution of Congress on June 16, 1960. The Administrator of General Services certified the ratification and adoption of the amendment by three-fourths of the States on April 3, 1961. It was rejected by Arkansas.

[15] The Twenty-fourth Amendment was proposed by resolution of Congress on August 27, 1962. It was declared in a Proclamation of the Administrator of General Services dated February 4, 1964, to have been ratified by three-fourths of the States. It was rejected by the legislature of Mississippi on December 20, 1962.

[16] The Twenty-fifth Amendment to the Constitution was proposed by the Congress on July 6, 1965. It was declared in a certificate of the Administrator of General Services, dated February 23, 1967, to have been ratified by the legislatures of 39 of the 50 States. Ratification was completed on February 10, 1967.

[17] The Twenty-sixth Amendment was proposed by resolution of Congress on March 23, 1971. On July 5, 1971, the Administrator of General Services certified the ratification and adoption of the amendment by three fourths of the states.

## ADMINISTRATIONS, CABINETS, AND CONGRESSES

SOURCE: *Biographical Directory of the American Congress* and other sources

A cabinet officer is not appointed for a fixed term and does not necessarily go out of office with the President who appointed him; while it is customary to tender his resignation at the time a change of administration takes place, he remains formally at the head of his department until a successor is appointed. Subordinates acting temporarily as heads of departments are not considered cabinet officers; in the earlier period of the nation's history, not all cabinet officers were heads of departments.

The dates immediately following the names of executive officers are those upon which commissions were issued, unless otherwise specifically noted. Where periods of time are indicated by dates as, for instance, March 4, 1793–March 3, 1797, both such dates are included as portions of the time period.

The National Security Act of 1947 (Pub. Law 253, 80th Cong., 1st sess.), approved July 26, 1947, created the office of Secretary of Defense and merged the War and Navy Departments into the National Military Establishment. The act was subsequently amended (Pub. Law 216, 81st Cong., 1st sess.): Section 201. (a) There is hereby established, as an executive department of the Government, the **Department of Defense.**

The Reorganization Plan Number 1 of 1953 (Pub. Law 13, 83d Cong., 1st sess.), approved April 1, 1953, abolished the Federal Security Agency and created the **Department of Health, Education, and Welfare,** which was renamed the **Department of Health and Human Services** in 1979.

**The Department of Housing and Urban Development** was established by the Department of Housing and Urban Development Act of September 9, 1965 (79 Stat. 667; 5 U.S.C. 642).

**The Department of Transportation** was established by the Department of Transportation Act of October 15, 1966 (80 Stat. 931; 49 U.S.C. 1681).

As of July 1, 1971, the Post Office Department became **The U.S. Postal Service,** a quasi-independent nonprofit corporation. The Postmaster General ceased to be a member of the cabinet.

**The Department of Energy** was established by Public Law 95-91, August 4, 1977.

**The Department of Education** was established by Public Law 96-88, October 17, 1979.

Congressional vacancies are not noted below.

### First Administration of GEORGE WASHINGTON

### APRIL 30, 1789, TO MARCH 3, 1793

PRESIDENT—George Washington, of Virginia (No party). VICE-PRESIDENT—John Adams, of Massachusetts. SECRETARY OF STATE—John Jay, of New York, was Secretary for Foreign Affairs under the Confederation, and continued to act, at the request of Washington, until Jefferson took office. Thomas Jefferson, of Virginia, September 26, 1789; entered upon duties March 22, 1790. SECRETARY OF THE TREASURY—Alexander Hamilton, of New York, September 11, 1789. SECRETARY OF WAR—Henry Knox, of Massachusetts, September 12, 1789. ATTORNEY GENERAL—Edmund Randolph, of Virginia, September 26, 1789; entered upon duties February 2, 1790. POSTMASTER GENERAL—Samuel Osgood, of Massachusetts, September 26, 1789. Timothy Pickering, of Pennsylvania, August 12, 1791; entered upon duties August 19, 1791.

**1st Congress**

1st Session: Mar. 4, 1789–Sept. 29, 1789[1]; 2d Session: Jan. 4, 1790–Aug. 12, 1790; 3d Session: Dec. 6, 1790–Mar. 3, 1791.

President pro tempore of the Senate: John Langdon, of New Hampshire (elected Apr. 6, 1789). Speaker of the House: Frederick A. C. Muhlenberg, of Pennsylvania (elected Apr. 1, 1789).
Senate: 17 pro-administration; 9 opposition
House: 38 pro-administration; 26 opposition

**2d Congress**

1st Session: Oct. 24, 1791–May 8, 1792; 2d Session: Nov. 5, 1792–Mar. 2, 1793; Special Session of the Senate: Mar. 4, 1791.

President pro tempore of the Senate: Richard H. Lee, of Virginia (elected Apr. 18, 1792); John Langdon, of New Hampshire (elected Nov. 5, 1792 and Mar. 1, 1793). Speaker of the House: Jonathan Trumbull, of Connecticut (elected Oct. 24, 1791).
Senate: 16 Federalist; 13 Democratic-Republican
House: 37 Federalist; 33 Democratic-Republican

### Second Administration of GEORGE WASHINGTON

### MARCH 4, 1793, TO MARCH 3, 1797

PRESIDENT—George Washington, of Virginia (No party). VICE-PRESIDENT—John Adams, of Massachusetts. SECRETARY OF STATE—Thomas Jefferson, of Virginia, continued from preceding administration. Edmund Randolph, of Virginia, January 2, 1794. Timothy Pickering, of Pennsylvania (Secretary of War), ad interim, August 20, 1795. Timothy Pickering, of Pennsylvania, December 10, 1795. SECRETARY OF THE TREASURY—Alexander Hamilton, of New York, continued from preceding administration. Oliver Wolcott, Jr., of Connecticut, February 2, 1795. SECRETARY OF WAR—Henry Knox, of Massachusetts, continued from preceding administration. Timothy Pickering, of Pennsylvania, January 2, 1795. Timothy Pickering, of Pennsylvania (Secretary of State), ad interim, December 10, 1795, to February 5, 1796. James McHenry, of Maryland, January 27, 1796; entered upon duties February 6, 1796. ATTORNEY GENERAL—Edmund Randolph, of Virginia, continued from preceding administration. William Bradford, of Pennsylvania, January 27, 1794; entered upon duties January 29, 1794. Charles Lee, of Virginia, December 10, 1795. POSTMASTER GENERAL—Timothy Pickering, of Pennsylvania, continued from preceding administration. Timothy Pickering, of Pennsylvania, recommissioned June 1, 1794. Joseph Habersham, of Georgia, February 25, 1795.

**3d Congress**

1st Session: Dec. 2, 1793–June 9, 1794; 2d Session: Nov. 3, 1794–Mar. 3, 1795; Special Session of the Senate: Mar. 4, 1793.

President pro tempore of the Senate: Ralph Izard, of South Carolina (elected May 31, 1794); Henry Tazewell, of Virginia (elected Feb. 20, 1795). Speaker of the House: Frederick A. C. Muhlenberg, of Pennsylvania (elected Dec. 2, 1793).
Senate: 17 Federalist; 13 Democratic-Republican
House: 57 Democratic-Republican; 48 Federalist

**4th Congress**

1st Session: Dec. 7, 1795–June 1, 1796; 2d Session: Dec. 5, 1796–Mar. 3, 1797; Special Session of the Senate: June 8, 1795–June 26, 1795.

President pro tempore of the Senate: Henry Tazewell, of Virginia (elected Dec. 7, 1795), Samuel Livermore, of New Hampshire (elected May 6, 1796), William Bingham, of Pennsylvania (Feb. 16, 1797). Speaker of the House: Jonathan Dayton, of New Jersey (elected Dec. 7, 1795).
Senate: 19 Federalist; 13 Democratic-Republican
House: 54 Federalist; 52 Democratic-Republican

### Administration of JOHN ADAMS

### MARCH 4, 1797, TO MARCH 3, 1801

PRESIDENT—John Adams, of Massachusetts (Federalist). VICE-PRESIDENT—Thomas Jefferson, of Virginia. SECRETARY OF STATE—Timothy Pickering, of Pennsylvania, continued from preceding administration; resignation requested May 10, 1800, but declining to resign, he was dismissed May 12, 1800. Charles Lee, of Virginia (Attorney General), ad interim, May 13, 1800. John Marshall, of Virginia, May 13, 1800; entered upon duties June 6, 1800. John Marshall, of Virginia (Chief Justice of the United States), ad interim, February 4, 1801, to March 3, 1801. SECRETARY OF THE TREASURY—Oliver Wolcott, Jr., of Connecticut, continued from preceding administration. Samuel Dexter, of Massachusetts, January 1. 1801. SECRETARY OF WAR—James McHenry, of Maryland, continued from preceding administration. Benjamin Stoddert, of Maryland (Secretary of the Navy), ad interim, June 1, 1800, to June 12, 1800. Samuel Dexter, of Massachusetts, May 13, 1800; entered upon duties June 12, 1800. Samuel Dexter, of Massachusetts (Secretary of the Treasury), ad interim, January 1, 1801. ATTORNEY GENERAL—Charles Lee, of Virginia, continued from preceding administration. POSTMASTER GENERAL—Joseph Habersham, of Georgia, continued from preceding administration. SECRETARY OF THE NAVY—Benjamin Stoddert, of Maryland, May 21, 1798; entered upon duties June 18, 1798.

**5th Congress**

1st Session: May 15, 1797–July 10, 1797; 2d Session: Nov. 13, 1797–July 16, 1798; 3d Session: Dec. 3, 1798–Mar. 3, 1799; Special Sessions of the Senate: Mar. 4, 1797; July 17, 1798–July 19, 1798.

President pro tempore of the Senate: William Bradford, of Rhode Island (elected July 6, 1797); Jacob Read, of South Carolina (elected Nov. 22, 1797); Theodore Sedgwick, of Massachusetts (elected June 27, 1798); John Laurence, of New York (elected Dec. 6, 1798); James Ross of Pennsylvania (elected Mar. 1, 1799). Speaker of the House: Jonathan Dayton, of New Jersey (reelected May 15, 1797); George Dent, of Maryland served as Speaker pro tempore Apr. 20, 1798, and May 28, 1798.
Senate: 20 Federalist; 12 Democratic-Republican
House: 58 Federalist; 48 Democratic-Republican

[1] Both houses met for the first time on Mar. 4, 1789, but each lacked a quorum. They met from day to day until the House attained a quorum on Apr. 1, 1789, and the Senate on Apr. 6, 1789.

**6th Congress**

1st Session: Dec. 2, 1799–May 14, 1800; 2d Session: Nov. 17, 1800–Mar. 3, 1801.

President pro tempore of the Senate: Samuel Livermore, of New Hampshire (elected Dec. 2, 1799); Uriah Tracy, of Connecticut (elected May 14, 1800); John E. Howard, of Maryland (elected Nov. 21, 1800); James Hillhouse, of Connecticut (elected Feb. 28, 1801). Speaker of the House: Theodore Sedgwick, of Massachusetts (elected Dec. 2, 1799).

Senate: 19 Federalist; 13 Democratic-Republican
House: 64 Federalist; 42 Democratic-Republican

## First Administration of THOMAS JEFFERSON
## MARCH 4, 1801, TO MARCH 3, 1805

PRESIDENT—Thomas Jefferson, of Virginia (Democratic-Republican). VICE-PRESIDENT—Aaron Burr, of New York. SECRETARY OF STATE—John Marshall, of Virginia (Chief Justice of the United States), for one day (March 4, 1801), and for a special purpose. Levi Lincoln, of Massachusetts (Attorney General), ad interim, March 5, 1801. James Madison, of Virginia, March 5, 1801; entered upon duties May 2, 1801. SECRETARY OF THE TREASURY—Samuel Dexter, of Massachusetts, continued from preceding administration to May 6, 1801. Albert Gallatin, of Pennsylvania, May 14, 1801. SECRETARY OF WAR—Henry Dearborn, of Massachusetts, March 5, 1801. ATTORNEY GENERAL—Levi Lincoln, of Massachusetts, March 5, 1801, to December 31, 1804. POSTMASTER GENERAL—Joseph Habersham, of Georgia, continued from preceding administration. Gideon Granger, of Connecticut, November 28, 1801. SECRETARY OF THE NAVY—Benjamin Stoddert, of Maryland, continued from preceding administration. Henry Dearborn, of Massachusetts (Secretary of War), ad interim, April 1, 1801. Robert Smith, of Maryland, July 15, 1801; entered upon duties July 27, 1801.

**7th Congress**

1st Session: Dec. 7, 1801–May 3, 1802; 2d Session: Dec. 6, 1802–March 3, 1803; Special Session of the Senate: Mar. 4, 1801–Mar. 5, 1801.

President pro tempore of the Senate: Abraham Baldwin, of Georgia (elected Dec. 7, 1801; Apr. 17, 1802); Stephen R. Bradley, of Vermont (elected Dec. 14, 1802; Feb. 25, 1803; Mar. 2, 1803). Speaker of the House: Nathaniel Macon, of North Carolina (elected Dec. 7, 1801).

Senate: 18 Democratic-Republican; 14 Federalist
House: 69 Democratic-Republican; 36 Federalist

**8th Congress**

1st Session: Oct. 17, 1803–Mar. 27, 1804; 2d Session: Nov. 5, 1804–Mar. 3, 1805.

President pro tempore of the Senate: John Brown, of Kentucky (elected Oct. 17, 1803; Jan. 23, 1804); Jesse Franklin, of North Carolina (elected Mar. 10, 1804); Joseph Anderson, of Tennessee (elected Jan. 15, 1805; Feb. 28, 1805; Mar. 2, 1805). Speaker of the House: Nathaniel Macon, of North Carolina (reelected Oct. 17, 1803).

Senate: 25 Democratic-Republican; 9 Federalist
House: 102 Democratic-Republican; 39 Federalist

## Second Administration of THOMAS JEFFERSON
## MARCH 4, 1805, TO MARCH 3, 1809

PRESIDENT—Thomas Jefferson, of Virginia (Democratic-Republican). VICE-PRESIDENT—George Clinton, of New York. SECRETARY OF STATE—James Madison, of Virginia, continued from preceding administration. SECRETARY OF THE TREASURY—Albert Gallatin, of Pennsylvania, continued from preceding administration. SECRETARY OF WAR—Henry Dearborn, of Massachusetts, continued from preceding administration. John Smith (chief clerk), ad interim, February 17, 1809. ATTORNEY GENERAL—John Breckinridge, of Kentucky, August 7, 1805 (died December 14, 1806). Caesar A. Rodney, of Delaware, January 20, 1807. POSTMASTER GENERAL—Gideon Granger, of Connecticut, continued from preceding administration. SECRETARY OF THE NAVY—Robert Smith, of Maryland, continued from preceding administration.

**9th Congress**

1st Session: Dec. 2, 1805–Apr. 21, 1806; 2d Session: Dec. 1, 1806–Mar. 3, 1807; Special Session of the Senate: Mar. 4, 1805.

President pro tempore of the Senate: Samuel Smith, of Maryland (elected Dec. 2, 1805; Mar. 18, 1806; Mar. 2, 1807). Speaker of the House: Nathaniel Macon, of North Carolina (reelected Dec. 2, 1805).

Senate: 27 Democratic-Republican; 7 Federalist
House: 116 Democratic-Republican; 25 Federalist

**10th Congress**

1st Session: Oct. 26, 1807–Apr. 25, 1808; 2d Session: Nov. 7, 1808–Mar. 3, 1809.

President pro tempore of the Senate: Samuel Smith, of Maryland (elected Apr. 16, 1808); Stephen R. Bradley, of Vermont (elected Dec. 28, 1808); John Milledge, of Georgia (elected Jan. 30, 1809). Speaker of the House: Joseph B. Varnum, of Massachusetts (elected Oct. 26, 1807).

Senate: 28 Democratic-Republican; 6 Federalist
House: 118 Democratic-Republican; 24 Federalist

## First Administration of JAMES MADISON
## MARCH 4, 1809, TO MARCH 3, 1813

PRESIDENT—James Madison, of Virginia (Democratic-Republican). VICE-PRESIDENT—George Clinton, of New York. (Died April 20, 1812.) SECRETARY OF STATE—Robert Smith, of Maryland, March 6, 1809. James Monroe, of Virginia, April 2, 1811; entered upon duties April 6, 1811. SECRETARY OF THE TREASURY—Albert Gallatin, of Pennsylvania, continued from preceding administration. SECRETARY OF WAR—John Smith (chief clerk), ad interim, continued from preceding administration. William Eustis, of Massachusetts, March 7, 1809; entered upon duties April 8, 1809; served to December 31, 1812. James Monroe, of Virginia (Secretary of State), ad interim, January 1, 1813. John Armstrong, of New York, January 13, 1813; entered upon duties February 5, 1813. ATTORNEY GENERAL—Caesar A. Rodney, of Delaware, continued from preceding administration; resigned December 5, 1811. William Pinkney, of Maryland, December 11, 1811; entered upon duties January 6, 1812. POSTMASTER GENERAL—Gideon Granger, of Connecticut, continued from preceding administration. SECRETARY OF THE NAVY—Robert Smith, of Maryland, continued from preceding administration. Charles W. Goldsborough (chief clerk), ad interim, March 8, 1809. Paul Hamilton, of South Carolina, March 7, 1809; entered upon duties May 15, 1809; served to December 31, 1812. Charles W. Goldsborough (chief clerk), ad interim, January 7, 1813, to January 18, 1813. William Jones, of Pennsylvania, January 12, 1813; entered upon duties January 19, 1813.

**11th Congress**

1st Session: May 22, 1809–June 28, 1809; 2d Session: Nov. 27, 1809–May 1, 1810; 3d Session: Dec. 3, 1810–Mar. 3, 1811; Special Session of the Senate: Mar. 4, 1809–Mar. 7, 1809.

President pro tempore of the Senate: Andrew Gregg, of Pennsylvania (elected June 26, 1809); John Gaillard, of South Carolina (elected Feb. 28, 1810; Apr. 17, 1810); John Pope, of Kentucky (elected Feb. 23, 1811). Speaker of the House: Joseph B. Varnum, of Massachusetts (reelected May 22, 1809).

Senate: 28 Democratic-Republican; 6 Federalist
House: 94 Democratic-Republican; 48 Federalist

**12th Congress**

1st Session: Nov. 4, 1811 to July 6, 1812; 2d Session: Nov. 2, 1812–Mar. 3, 1813.

President pro tempore of the Senate: William H. Crawford, of Georgia (elected Mar. 24, 1812). Speaker of the House: Henry Clay, of Kentucky (elected Nov. 4, 1811).

Senate: 30 Democratic-Republican; 6 Federalist
House: 108 Democratic-Republican; 36 Federalist

## Second Administration of JAMES MADISON
## MARCH 4, 1813, TO MARCH 3, 1817

PRESIDENT—James Madison, of Virginia (Democratic-Republican). VICE-PRESIDENT—Elbridge Gerry, of Massachusetts (died November 23, 1814). SECRETARY OF STATE—James Monroe, of Virginia, continued from preceding administration. James Monroe, of Virginia (Secretary of War), ad interim, October 1, 1814. James Monroe, of Virginia, February 28, 1815. SECRETARY OF THE TREASURY—Albert Gallatin, of Pennsylvania, continued from preceding administration. William Jones, of Pennsylvania (Secretary of the Navy), performed the duties of the Secretary of the Treasury during the absence of Mr. Gallatin in Europe (April 21, 1813, to February 9, 1814). George W. Campbell, of Tennessee, February 9, 1814. Alexander J. Dallas, of Pennsylvania, October 6, 1814; entered upon duties October 14, 1814. William H. Crawford, of Georgia, October 22, 1816. SECRETARY OF WAR—John Armstrong, of New York, continued from preceding administration. James Monroe, of Virginia (Secretary of State), ad interim, August 30, 1814. James Monroe, of Virginia, September 27, 1814; entered upon duties October 1, 1814. James Monroe, of Virginia (Secretary of State), ad interim, March 1, 1815. Alexander J. Dallas, of Pennsylvania (Secretary of the Treasury), ad interim, March 14, 1815, to August 8, 1815. William H. Crawford, of Georgia, August 1, 1815; entered upon duties August 8, 1815. George Graham (chief clerk), ad interim, October 22, 1816, to close of administration. ATTORNEY GENERAL—William Pinkney, of Maryland, continued from preceding administration. Richard Rush, of Pennsylvania, February 10, 1814; entered upon duties the day following. POSTMASTER

GENERAL—Gideon Granger, of Connecticut, continued from preceding administration. Return J. Meigs, Jr., of Ohio, March 17, 1814; entered upon duties April 11, 1814. SECRETARY OF THE NAVY—William Jones, of Pennsylvania, continued from preceding administration. Benjamin Homans (chief clerk), ad interim, December 2, 1814. Benjamin W. Crowninshield, of Massachusetts, December 19, 1814; entered upon duties January 16, 1815.

**13th Congress**

1st Session: May 24, 1813–Aug. 2, 1813; 2d Session: Dec. 6, 1813–Apr. 18, 1814; 3d Session: Sept. 19, 1814–Mar. 3, 1815.

President pro tempore of the Senate: Joseph B. Varnum, of Massachusetts (elected Dec. 6, 1813); John Gaillard, of South Carolina (elected Apr. 18, 1814; Nov. 25, 1814). Speaker of the House: Henry Clay, of Kentucky (reelected May 24, 1813); Langdon Cheves, of South Carolina (elected Jan. 19, 1814).

Senate: 27 Democratic-Republican; 9 Federalist
House: 112 Democratic-Republican; 68 Federalist

**14th Congress**

1st Session: Dec. 4, 1815–Apr. 30, 1816; 2d Session: Dec. 2, 1816–Mar. 3, 1817.

President pro tempore of the Senate: John Gaillard, of South Carolina (continued from preceding Congress). Speaker of the House: Henry Clay, of Kentucky (reelected Dec. 4, 1815).

Senate: 25 Democratic-Republican; 11 Federalist
House: 117 Democratic-Republican; 65 Federalist

---

### First Administration of JAMES MONROE
### MARCH 4, 1817, TO MARCH 3, 1821

PRESIDENT—James Monroe, of Virginia (Democratic-Republican). VICE-PRESIDENT—Daniel D. Tompkins, of New York. SECRETARY OF STATE—John Graham (chief clerk), ad interim, March 4, 1817. Richard Rush, of Pennsylvania (Attorney General), ad interim, March 10, 1817. John Quincy Adams, of Massachusetts, March 5, 1817; entered upon duties September 22, 1817. SECRETARY OF THE TREASURY—William H. Crawford, of Georgia, continued from preceding administration. William H. Crawford, of Georgia, recommissioned March 5, 1817. SECRETARY OF WAR—George Graham (chief clerk), ad interim, March 4, 1817. John C. Calhoun, of South Carolina, October 8, 1817; entered upon duties December 10, 1817. ATTORNEY GENERAL—Richard Rush, of Pennsylvania, continued from preceding administration to October 30, 1817. William Wirt, of Virginia, November 13, 1817; entered upon duties November 15, 1817. POSTMASTER GENERAL—Return J. Meigs, Jr., of Ohio, continued from preceding administration. SECRETARY OF THE NAVY—Benjamin W. Crowninshield, of Massachusetts, continued from preceding administration. John C. Calhoun, of South Carolina (Secretary of War), ad interim, October 1, 1818. Smith Thompson, of New York, November 9, 1818; entered upon duties January 1, 1819.

**15th Congress**

1st Session: Dec. 1, 1817–Apr. 20, 1818; 2d Session: Nov. 16, 1818–Mar. 3, 1819; Special Session of the Senate: Mar. 4, 1817–Mar. 6, 1817.

President pro tempore of the Senate: John Gaillard, of South Carolina (continued from preceding Congress; elected Mar. 6, 1817; Mar. 31, 1818). James Barbour, of Virginia (elected Feb. 15, 1819). Speaker of the House: Henry Clay, of Kentucky (reelected Dec. 1, 1817).

Senate: 34 Democratic-Republican; 10 Federalist
House: 141 Democratic-Republican; 42 Federalist

**16th Congress**

1st Session: Dec. 6, 1819–May 15, 1820; 2d Session: Nov. 13, 1820–Mar. 3, 1821.

President pro tempore of the Senate: James Barbour, of Virginia (continued from preceding Congress); John Gaillard, of South Carolina (elected Jan. 25, 1820). Speaker of the House: Henry Clay, of Kentucky (reelected Dec. 6, 1819), John W. Taylor, of New York (elected Nov. 15, 1820).

Senate: 35 Democratic-Republican; 7 Federalist
House: 156 Democratic-Republican; 27 Federalist

---

### Second Administration of JAMES MONROE
### MARCH 4, 1821, TO MARCH 3, 1825

PRESIDENT—James Monroe, of Virginia (Democratic-Republican). VICE-PRESIDENT—Daniel D. Tompkins, of New York. SECRETARY OF STATE—John Quincy Adams, of Massachusetts, continued from preceding administration. SECRETARY OF THE TREASURY—William H. Crawford, of Georgia, continued from preceding administration. SECRETARY OF WAR—John C. Calhoun, of South Carolina, continued from preceding administration. ATTORNEY GENERAL—William Wirt, of Virginia, continued from preceding administration. POSTMASTER GENERAL—Return J. Meigs, Jr., of Ohio, continued from preceding administration. John McLean, of Ohio, commissioned June 26, 1823, to take effect July 1, 1823. SECRETARY OF THE NAVY—Smith Thompson, of New York, continued from preceding administration. John Rodgers (commodore, United States Navy, and President of the Board of Navy Commissioners), ad interim, September 1, 1823. Samuel L. Southard, of New Jersey, September 16, 1823.

**17th Congress**

1st Session: Dec. 3, 1821–May 8, 1822; 2d Session: Dec. 2, 1822–Mar. 3, 1823.

President pro tempore of the Senate: John Gaillard, of South Carolina (elected Feb. 1, 1822; Feb. 19, 1823). Speaker of the House: Philip P. Barbour, of Virginia (elected Dec. 4, 1821).

Senate: 44 Democratic-Republican; 4 Federalist
House: 158 Democratic-Republican; 25 Federalist

**18th Congress**

1st Session: Dec. 1, 1823–May 27, 1824; 2d Session: Dec. 6, 1824–Mar. 3, 1825.

President pro tempore of the Senate: John Gaillard, of South Carolina (elected May 21, 1824). Speaker of the House: Henry Clay, of Kentucky (elected Dec. 1, 1823).

Senate: 44 Democratic-Republican; 4 Federalist
House: 187 Democratic-Republican; 26 Federalist

---

### Administration of JOHN QUINCY ADAMS
### MARCH 4, 1825, TO MARCH 3, 1829

PRESIDENT—John Quincy Adams, of Massachusetts (Democratic-Republican). VICE-PRESIDENT—John C. Calhoun, of South Carolina. SECRETARY OF STATE—Daniel Brent (chief clerk), ad interim, March 4, 1825. Henry Clay, of Kentucky, March 7, 1825. SECRETARY OF THE TREASURY—Samuel L. Southard, of New Jersey (Secretary of the Navy), ad interim, March 7, 1825. Richard Rush, of Pennsylvania, March 7, 1825; entered upon duties August 1, 1825. SECRETARY OF WAR—James Barbour, of Virginia, March 7, 1825. Samuel L. Southard, of New Jersey (Secretary of the Navy), ad interim, May 26, 1828. Peter B. Porter, of New York, May 26, 1828; entered upon duties June 21, 1828. ATTORNEY GENERAL—William Wirt, of Virginia, continued from preceding administration. POSTMASTER GENERAL—John McLean, of Ohio, continued from preceding administration. SECRETARY OF THE NAVY—Samuel L. Southard, of New Jersey, continued from preceding administration.

**19th Congress**

1st Session: Dec. 5, 1825–May 22, 1826; 2d Session: Dec. 4, 1826–Mar. 3, 1827; Special Session of the Senate: Mar. 4, 1825–Mar. 9, 1825.

President pro tempore of the Senate: John Gaillard, of South Carolina (elected Mar. 9, 1825). Nathaniel Macon, of North Carolina (elected May 20, 1826; Jan. 2, 1827; Mar. 2, 1827). Speaker of the House: John W. Taylor, of New York (elected Dec. 5, 1825).

Senate: 26 pro-administration; 20 opposition
House: 105 pro-administration; 97 opposition

**20th Congress**

1st Session: Dec. 3, 1827–May 26, 1828; 2d Session: Dec. 1, 1828–Mar. 3, 1829.

President pro tempore of the Senate: Samuel Smith, of Maryland (elected May 15, 1828). Speaker of the House: Andrew Stevenson, of Virginia (elected Dec. 3, 1827).

Senate: 20 pro-administration; 26 opposition
House: 94 pro-administration; 119 opposition

---

### First Administration of ANDREW JACKSON
### MARCH 4, 1829, TO MARCH 3, 1833

PRESIDENT—Andrew Jackson, of Tennessee (Democratic). VICE-PRESIDENT—John C. Calhoun, of South Carolina (resigned December 28, 1832). SECRETARY OF STATE—James A. Hamilton, of New York, ad interim, March 4, 1829. Martin Van Buren, of New York, March 6, 1829; entered upon duties March 28, 1829. Edward Livingston, of Louisiana, May 24, 1831. SECRETARY OF THE TREASURY—Samuel D. Ingham, of Pennsylvania, March 6, 1829. Asbury Dickins (chief clerk), ad interim, June 21, 1831. Louis McLane, of Delaware, August 8, 1831. SECRETARY OF WAR—John H. Eaton, of Tennessee, March 9, 1829. Philip G. Randolph (chief clerk), ad interim, June 20, 1831. Roger B. Taney, of Maryland (Attorney General), ad interim, July 21, 1831. Lewis Cass, of Ohio, August 1, 1831; entered upon duties August 8, 1831. ATTORNEY GENERAL—John M. Berrien, of Georgia, March 9, 1829, to June 22, 1831. Roger B. Taney, of Maryland, July 20, 1831. POSTMASTER GENERAL—John McLean, of Ohio, continued from preceding administration. William T. Barry, of Kentucky, March 9, 1829; entered upon duties April 6, 1829. SECRETARY OF THE NAVY—Charles Hay (chief clerk), ad interim, March 4, 1829. John Branch, of North Carolina, March 9, 1829. John Boyle (chief clerk), ad interim, May 12, 1831. Levi Woodbury, of New Hampshire, May 23, 1831.

**21st Congress**

1st Session: Dec. 7, 1829–May 31, 1830; 2d Session: Dec. 6, 1830–Mar. 3, 1831; Special Session of the Senate: Mar. 4, 1829–Mar. 17, 1829.

President pro tempore of the Senate: Samuel Smith, of Maryland (elected Mar. 13, 1829; May 29, 1830; Mar. 1, 1831). Speaker of the House: Andrew Stevenson, of Virginia (reelected Dec. 7, 1829).

Senate: 26 Democratic; 22 National Republican
House: 139 Democratic; 74 National Republican

**22d Congress**

1st Session: Dec. 5, 1831–July 16, 1832; 2d Session: Dec. 3, 1832–Mar. 2, 1833.

President pro tempore of the Senate: Littleton W. Tazewell, of Virginia (elected July 9, 1832); Hugh L. White, of Tennessee (elected Dec. 3, 1832). Speaker of the House: Andrew Stevenson of Virginia (reelected Dec. 5, 1831).

Senate: 25 Democratic; 21 National Republican
House: 141 Democratic; 58 National Republican

## Second Administration of ANDREW JACKSON
## MARCH 4, 1833, TO MARCH 3, 1837

PRESIDENT—Andrew Jackson, of Tennessee (Democratic). VICE-PRESIDENT—Martin Van Buren, of New York. SECRETARY OF STATE—Edward Livingston, of Louisiana, continued from preceding administration. Louis McLane of Delaware, May 29, 1833. John Forsyth, of Georgia, June 27, 1834; entered upon duties July 1, 1834. SECRETARY OF THE TREASURY—Louis McLane, of Delaware, continued from preceding administration. William J. Duane, of Pennsylvania, May 29, 1833; entered upon duties June 1, 1833. Roger B. Taney, of Maryland, September 23, 1833. McClintock Young (chief clerk), ad interim, June 25, 1834. Levi Woodbury, of New Hampshire, June 27, 1834; entered upon duties July 1, 1834. SECRETARY OF WAR—Lewis Cass, of Ohio, continued from preceding administration. Carey A. Harris, of Tennessee (Commissioner of Indian Affairs), ad interim, October 5, 1836. Benjamin F. Butler, of New York (Attorney General), ad interim, October 26, 1836. Benjamin F. Butler, of New York, commissioned March 3, 1837, ad interim, "during the pleasure of the President, until a successor, duly appointed, shall accept such office and enter upon the duties thereof." ATTORNEY GENERAL—Roger B. Taney, of Maryland, continued from preceding administration to September 23, 1833. Benjamin F. Butler, of New York, November 15, 1833; entered upon duties November 18, 1833. POSTMASTER GENERAL—William T. Barry, of Kentucky, continued from preceding administration. Amos Kendall, of Kentucky, May 1, 1835. SECRETARY OF THE NAVY—Levi Woodbury, of New Hampshire, continued from preceding administration. Mahlon Dickerson, of New Jersey, June 30, 1834.

**23d Congress**

1st Session: Dec. 2, 1833–June 30, 1834; 2d Session: Dec. 1, 1834–Mar. 3, 1835.

President pro tempore of the Senate: Hugh L. White, of Tennessee (continued from the previous Congress); George Poindexter, of Mississippi (elected June 28, 1834); John Tyler, of Virginia (elected Mar. 3, 1835). Speaker of the House: Andrew Stevenson, of Virginia (reelected Dec. 2, 1835); John Bell, of Tennessee (elected June 2, 1834); Henry Hubbard, of New Hampshire served as Speaker pro tem May 16, 1834.

Senate: 20 Democratic; 20 National Republican
House: 147 Democratic; 113 various parties

**24th Congress**

1st Session: Dec. 7, 1835–July 4, 1836; 2d Session: Dec. 5, 1836–Mar. 3, 1837.

President pro tempore of the Senate: William R. King, of Alabama (elected July 1, 1836; Jan. 28, 1837). Speaker of the House: James K. Polk, of Tennessee (elected Dec. 7, 1835).

Senate: 27 Democratic; 25 Whig
House: 145 Democratic; 98 Whig

## Administration of MARTIN VAN BUREN
## MARCH 4, 1837, TO MARCH 3, 1841

PRESIDENT—Martin Van Buren, of New York (Democratic). VICE-PRESIDENT—Richard M. Johnson, of Kentucky. SECRETARY OF STATE—John Forsyth, of Georgia, continued from preceding administration. SECRETARY OF THE TREASURY—Levi Woodbury, of New Hampshire, continued from preceding administration. SECRETARY OF WAR—Benjamin F. Butler, of New York, ad interim, continued from preceding administration. Joel R. Poinsett, of South Carolina, March 7, 1837; entered upon duties March 14, 1837. ATTORNEY GENERAL—Benjamin F. Butler, of New York, continued from preceding administration. Felix Grundy, of Tennessee, July 5, 1838, to take effect September 1, 1838. Henry D. Gilpin, of Pennsylvania, January 11, 1840. POSTMASTER GENERAL—Amos Kendall, of Kentucky, continued from preceding administration. John M. Niles, of Connecticut, May 19, 1840, to take effect May 25, 1840; entered upon duties May 26, 1840. SECRETARY OF THE NAVY—Mahlon Dickerson, of New Jersey, continued from preceding administration. James K. Paulding, of New York, June 25, 1838, to take effect "after the 30th instant"; entered upon duties July 1, 1838.

**25th Congress**

1st Session: Sept. 4, 1837–Oct. 16, 1837; 2d Session: Dec. 4, 1837–July 9, 1838; 3d Session: Dec. 3, 1838–Mar. 3, 1839; Special Session of the Senate: Mar. 4, 1837–Mar. 10, 1837.

President pro tempore of the Senate: William R. King, of Alabama (elected Mar. 7, 1837; Oct. 13, 1837; July 2, 1838; Feb. 25, 1839). Speaker of the House: James K. Polk, of Tennessee (reelected Sept. 4, 1837).

Senate: 30 Democratic; 18 Whig; 4 other
House: 108 Democratic; 107 Whig; 24 other

**26th Congress**

1st Session: Dec. 2, 1839–July 21, 1840; 2d Session: Dec. 7, 1840–Mar. 3, 1841.

President pro tempore of the Senate: William R. King, of Alabama (continued from the preceding Congress; reelected July 3, 1840; Mar. 3, 1841). Speaker of the House: Robert M. T. Hunter, of Virginia (elected Dec. 16, 1839).

Senate: 28 Democratic; 22 Whig
House: 124 Democratic; 118 Whig

## Administration of WILLIAM HENRY HARRISON
## MARCH 4, 1841, TO APRIL 4, 1841

PRESIDENT—William Henry Harrison, of Ohio (Whig) (died April 4, 1841). VICE-PRESIDENT—John Tyler, of Virginia. SECRETARY OF STATE—J. L. Martin (chief clerk), ad interim, March 4, 1841. Daniel Webster, of Massachusetts, March 5, 1841. SECRETARY OF THE TREASURY—McClintock Young (chief clerk), ad interim, March 4, 1841. Thomas Ewing, of Ohio, March 5, 1841. SECRETARY OF WAR—John Bell, of Tennessee, March 5, 1841. ATTORNEY GENERAL—John J. Crittenden, of Kentucky, March 5, 1841. POSTMASTER GENERAL—Selah R. Hobbie, of New York (First Assistant Postmaster General), ad interim, March 4, 1841. Francis Granger, of New York, March 6, 1841; entered upon duties March 8, 1841. SECRETARY OF THE NAVY—John D. Simms (chief clerk), ad interim, March 4, 1841. George E. Badger, of North Carolina, March 5, 1841.

## Administration of JOHN TYLER
## APRIL 6, 1841, TO MARCH 3, 1845

PRESIDENT—John Tyler, of Virginia (Whig). SECRETARY OF STATE—Daniel Webster, of Massachusetts, continued from preceding administration. Hugh S. Legaré, of South Carolina (Attorney General), ad interim, May 9, 1843. William S. Derrick (chief clerk), ad interim, June 21, 1843. Abel P. Upshur, of Virginia (Secretary of the Navy), ad interim, June 24, 1843. Abel P. Upshur, of Virginia, July 24, 1843 (killed by the explosion of a gun on the U.S.S. **Princeton** February 28, 1844). John Nelson, of Maryland (Attorney General), ad interim, February 29, 1844. John C. Calhoun, of South Carolina, March 6, 1844; entered upon duties April 1, 1844. SECRETARY OF THE TREASURY—Thomas Ewing, of Ohio, continued from preceding administration. McClintock Young (chief clerk), ad interim, September 13, 1841. Walter Forward, of Pennsylvania, September 13, 1841. McClintock Young (chief clerk), ad interim, March 1, 1843. John C. Spencer, of New York, March 3, 1843; entered upon duties March 8, 1843. McClintock Young (chief clerk), ad interim, May 2, 1844. George M. Bibb, of Kentucky, June 15, 1844; entered upon duties July 4, 1844. SECRETARY OF WAR—John Bell, of Tennessee, continued from preceding administration. Albert M. Lea, of Maryland (chief clerk), ad interim, September 12, 1841. John C. Spencer, of New York, October 12, 1841. James M. Porter, of Pennsylvania, March 8, 1843. William Wilkins, of Pennsylvania, February 15, 1844; entered upon duties February 20, 1844. ATTORNEY GENERAL—John J. Crittenden, of Kentucky, continued from preceding administration. Hugh S. Legaré, of South Carolina, September 13, 1841; entered upon duties September 20, 1841 (died June 20, 1843). John Nelson, of Maryland, July 1, 1843. POSTMASTER GENERAL—Francis Granger, of New York, continued from preceding administration. Selah R. Hobbie, of New York (First Assistant Postmaster General) ad interim, September 14, 1841. Charles A. Wickliffe, of Kentucky, September 13, 1841; entered upon duties October 13, 1841. SECRETARY OF THE NAVY—George E. Badger, of North Carolina, continued from preceding administration. John D. Simms (chief clerk), ad interim, September 11, 1841. Abel P. Upshur, of Virginia, September 13, 1841; entered upon duties October 11, 1841. David Henshaw, of Massachusetts, July 24, 1843. Thomas W. Gilmer, of Virginia, February 15, 1844; entered upon duties February 19, 1844 (killed by the explosion of a gun on the U.S.S. **Princeton** February 28, 1844). Lewis Warrington (captain, United States Navy), ad interim, February 29, 1844. John Y. Mason, of Virginia, March 14, 1844; entered upon duties March 26, 1844.

**27th Congress**

1st Session: May 31, 1841–Sept. 13, 1841; 2d Session: Dec. 6, 1841–Aug. 31, 1842; 3d Session: Dec. 5, 1842–Mar. 3, 1843; Special Session of the Senate: Mar. 4, 1841–Mar. 15, 1841.

President pro tempore of the Senate: William R. King, of Alabama (elected Mar. 4, 1841); Samuel L. Southard, of New Jersey (elected Mar. 11, 1841); Willie P. Mangum, of North Carolina (elected May 31, 1842). Speaker of the House: John White, of Kentucky (elected May 31, 1841).

Senate: 28 Whig; 22 Democratic; 2 other
House: 133 Whig; 102 Democratic; 6 other

**28th Congress**

1st Session: Dec. 4, 1843–June 17, 1844; 2d Session: Dec. 2, 1844–Mar. 3, 1845.

President pro tempore of the Senate: Willie P. Mangum, of North Carolina (continued from the preceding Congress). Speaker of the House: John W. Jones, of Virginia (elected Dec. 4, 1843); George Hopkins acted as Speaker for part of the day Feb. 28, 1845.

Senate: 28 Whig; 25 Democratic; 1 other
House: 115 Whig; 108 Democratic; 4 other

---

## Administration of JAMES K. POLK
## MARCH 4, 1845, TO MARCH 3, 1849

PRESIDENT—James K. Polk, of Tennessee (Democratic). VICE-PRESIDENT—George M. Dallas, of Pennsylvania. SECRETARY OF STATE—John C. Calhoun, of South Carolina, continued from preceding administration. James Buchanan, of Pennsylvania, March 6, 1845; entered upon duties March 10, 1845. SECRETARY OF THE TREASURY—George M. Bibb, of Kentucky, continued from preceding administration. Robert J. Walker, of Mississippi, March 6, 1845; entered upon duties March 8, 1845. SECRETARY OF WAR—William Wilkins, of Pennsylvania, continued from preceding administration. William L. Marcy, of New York, March 6, 1845; entered upon duties March 8, 1845. ATTORNEY GENERAL—John Nelson, of Maryland, continued from preceding administration. John Y. Mason, of Virginia, March 6, 1845; entered upon duties March 11, 1845. Nathan Clifford, of Maine, October 17, 1846, to March 18, 1848, when he resigned. Isaac Toucey, of Connecticut, June 21, 1848; entered upon duties June 29, 1848. POSTMASTER GENERAL—Charles A. Wickliffe, of Kentucky, continued from preceding administration. Cave Johnson, of Tennessee, March 6, 1845. SECRETARY OF THE NAVY—John Y. Mason, of Virginia, continued from preceding administration. George Bancroft, of Massachusetts, March 10, 1845. John Y. Mason, of Virginia, September 9, 1846.

**29th Congress**

1st Session: Dec. 1, 1845–Aug. 10, 1846; 2d Session: Dec. 7, 1846–Mar. 3, 1847; Special Session of the Senate: Mar. 4, 1845–Mar. 20, 1845.

President pro tempore of the Senate: Ambrose H. Sevier, of Arkansas (under designation of the Vice-President served Dec. 27, 1845); David R. Atchison, of Missouri (elected Aug. 8, 1846; Jan. 11, 1847; Mar. 3, 1847). Speaker of the House: John W. Davis, of Indiana (elected Dec. 1, 1845).

Senate: 31 Democratic; 25 Whig
House: 143 Democratic; 77 Whig; 6 other

**30th Congress**

1st Session: Dec. 6, 1847–Aug. 14, 1848; 2d Session: Dec. 4, 1848–Mar. 3, 1849.

President pro tempore of the Senate: David R. Atchison, of Missouri (elected Feb. 2, 1848; June 1, 1848; June 26, 1848; July 29, 1848; Dec. 26, 1848; Mar. 2, 1849). Speaker of the House: Robert C. Winthrop, of Massachusetts (elected Dec. 6, 1847); Armistead Burt served as Speaker pro tem June 19–22, 1848.

Senate: 36 Democratic; 21 Whig; 1 other
House: 115 Whig; 108 Democratic; 4 other

---

## Administration of ZACHARY TAYLOR
## MARCH 4, 1849, TO JULY 9, 1850

PRESIDENT—Zachary Taylor, of Louisiana (Whig). (Oath administered March 5, 1849. Died July 9, 1850.) VICE-PRESIDENT—Millard Fillmore, of New York. SECRETARY OF STATE—James Buchanan, of Pennsylvania, continued from preceding administration. John M. Clayton, of Delaware, March 7, 1849. SECRETARY OF THE TREASURY—Robert J. Walker, of Mississippi, continued from preceding administration. McClintock Young (chief clerk), ad interim, March 6, 1849. William M. Meredith, of Pennsylvania, March 8, 1849. SECRETARY OF WAR—William L. Marcy, of New York, continued from preceding administration. Reverdy Johnson, of Maryland (Attorney General), ad interim, March 8, 1849. George W. Crawford, of Georgia, March 8, 1849; entered upon duties March 14, 1849. ATTORNEY GENERAL—Isaac Toucey, of Connecticut, continued from preceding administration. Reverdy Johnson, of Maryland, March 8, 1849. POSTMASTER GENERAL—Cave Johnson, of Tennessee, continued from preceding administration. Selah R. Hobbie, of New York (First Assistant Postmaster General), ad interim, March 6, 1849. Jacob Collamer, of Vermont, March 8, 1849. SECRETARY OF THE NAVY—John Y. Mason, of Virginia, continued from preceding administration. William B. Preston, of Virginia, March 8, 1849. SECRETARY OF THE INTERIOR—Thomas Ewing, of Ohio, March 8, 1849.

---

## Administration of MILLARD FILLMORE
## JULY 10, 1850, TO MARCH 3, 1853

PRESIDENT—Millard Fillmore, of New York (Whig). SECRETARY OF STATE—John M. Clayton, of Delaware, continued from preceding administration. Daniel Webster, of Massachusetts, July 22, 1850 (died October 24, 1852). Charles M. Conrad, of Louisiana (Secretary of War), ad interim, October 25, 1852. Edward Everett, of Massachusetts, November 6, 1852. SECRETARY OF THE TREASURY—William M. Meredith, of Pennsylvania, continued from preceding administration. Thomas Corwin, of Ohio, July 23, 1850. SECRETARY OF WAR—George W. Crawford, of Georgia, continued from preceding administration. Samuel J. Anderson (chief clerk), ad interim, July 23, 1850. Winfield Scott (major general, U.S. Army), ad interim, July 24, 1850. Charles M. Conrad, of Louisiana, August 15, 1850. ATTORNEY GENERAL—Reverdy Johnson, of Maryland, continued from preceding administration, served to July 22, 1850. John J. Crittenden, of Kentucky, July 22, 1850; entered upon duties August 14, 1850. POSTMASTER GENERAL—Jacob Collamer, of Vermont, continued from preceding administration. Nathan K. Hall, of New York, July 23, 1850. Samuel D. Hubbard, of Connecticut, August 31, 1852; entered upon duties September 14, 1852. SECRETARY OF THE NAVY—William B. Preston, of Virginia, continued from preceding administration. Lewis Warrington (captain, U.S. Navy), ad interim, July 23, 1850. William A. Graham, of North Carolina, July 22, 1850; entered upon duties August 2, 1850. John P. Kennedy, of Maryland, July 22, 1852; entered upon duties July 26, 1852. SECRETARY OF THE INTERIOR—Thomas Ewing, of Ohio, continued from preceding administration. Daniel C. Goddard (chief clerk), ad interim, July 23, 1850. Thomas M. T. McKennan, of Pennsylvania, August 15, 1850. Daniel C. Goddard (chief clerk), ad interim, August 27, 1850. Alexander H. H. Stuart, of Virginia, September 12, 1850; entered upon duties September 16, 1850.

**31st Congress**

1st Session: Dec. 3, 1849–Sept. 30, 1850; 2d Session: Dec. 2, 1850–Mar. 3, 1851; Special Session of the Senate: Mar. 5, 1849–Mar. 23, 1849.

President pro tempore of the Senate: David R. Atchison, of Missouri (elected Mar. 5, 1849; Mar. 16, 1849). William R. King, of Alabama (elected May 6, 1850, July 11, 1850). Speaker of the House: Howell Cobb, of Georgia (elected Dec. 22, 1849), Robert C. Winthrop, of Massachusetts, served as Speaker pro tem April 19, 1850.

Senate: 35 Democratic; 25 Whig; 2 other
House: 112 Democratic; 109 Whig; 9 other

**32d Congress**

1st Session: Dec. 1, 1851–Aug. 31, 1852; 2d Session: Dec. 6, 1852–Mar. 3, 1853; Special Session of the Senate: Mar. 4, 1851–Mar. 13, 1851.

President pro tempore of the Senate: William R. King, of Alabama (continued from preceding Congress); David R. Atchison, of Missouri (elected Dec. 20, 1852). Speaker of the House: Linn Boyd, of Kentucky (elected Dec. 1, 1851).

Senate: 35 Democratic; 24 Whig; 3 other
House: 140 Democratic; 88 Whig; 5 other

---

## Administration of FRANKLIN PIERCE
## MARCH 4, 1853, TO MARCH 3, 1857

PRESIDENT—Franklin Pierce, of New Hampshire (Democratic). VICE-PRESIDENT—William R. King, of Alabama (died April 18, 1853). SECRETARY OF STATE—William Hunter (chief clerk), ad interim, March 4, 1853. William L. Marcy, of New York,

March 7, 1853. SECRETARY OF THE TREASURY—Thomas Corwin, of Ohio, continued from preceding administration. James Guthrie, of Kentucky, March 7, 1853. SECRETARY OF WAR—Charles M. Conrad, of Louisiana, continued from preceding administration. Jefferson Davis, of Mississippi, March 7, 1853. Samuel Cooper (Adjutant General, U.S. Army), ad interim, March 3, 1857. ATTORNEY GENERAL—John J. Crittenden, of Kentucky, continued from preceding administration. Caleb Cushing, of Massachusetts, March 7, 1853. POSTMASTER GENERAL—Samuel D. Hubbard, of Connecticut, continued from preceding administration. James Campbell, of Pennsylvania, March 7, 1853. SECRETARY OF THE NAVY—John P. Kennedy, of Maryland, continued from preceding administration. James C. Dobbin, of North Carolina, March 7, 1853. SECRETARY OF THE INTERIOR—Alexander H. H. Stuart, of Virginia, continued from preceding administration. Robert McClelland, of Michigan, March 7, 1853.

**33d Congress**

1st Session: Dec. 5, 1853–Aug. 7, 1854; 2d Session: Dec. 4, 1854–Mar. 3, 1855; Special Session of the Senate: Mar. 4, 1853–Apr. 11, 1853.

President pro tempore of the Senate: David R. Atchison, of Missouri (elected Mar. 4, 1853); Lewis Cass, of Michigan (elected Dec. 4, 1854); Jesse D. Bright, of Indiana (elected Dec. 5, 1854). Speaker of the House: Linn Boyd, of Kentucky (re-elected Dec. 5, 1853).

Senate: 38 Democratic; 22 Whig; 2 other
House: 159 Democratic; 71 Whig; 4 other

**34th Congress**

1st Session: Dec. 3, 1855–Aug. 18, 1856; 2d Session: Aug. 21, 1856–Aug. 30, 1856; 3d Session: Dec. 1, 1856–Mar. 3, 1857.

President pro tempore of the Senate: Jesse D. Bright, of Indiana (continued from preceding Congress; elected June 11, 1856); Charles E. Stuart, of Michigan (served June 5, 1856; elected June 9, 1856); James M. Mason, of Virginia (served Jan. 5, 1857; elected Jan. 6, 1857). Speaker of the House: Nathaniel P. Banks, of Massachusetts (elected Feb. 2, 1856).

Senate: 40 Democratic; 15 Republican; 5 other
House: 108 Republican; 83 Democratic; 43 other

## Administration of JAMES BUCHANAN

### MARCH 4, 1857, TO MARCH 3, 1861

PRESIDENT—James Buchanan, of Pennsylvania (Democratic). VICE-PRESIDENT—John C. Breckinridge, of Kentucky. SECRETARY OF STATE—William L. Marcy, of New York, continued from preceding administration. Lewis Cass, of Michigan, March 6, 1857. William Hunter (chief clerk), ad interim, December 15, 1860. Jeremiah S. Black, of Pennsylvania, December 17, 1860. SECRETARY OF THE TREASURY—James Guthrie, of Kentucky, continued from preceding administration. Howell Cobb, of Georgia, March 6, 1857. Isaac Toucey, of Connecticut (Secretary of the Navy), ad interim, December 10, 1860. Philip F. Thomas, of Maryland, December 12, 1860. John A. Dix, of New York, January 11, 1861; entered upon duties January 15, 1861. SECRETARY OF WAR—Samuel Cooper (Adjutant General, U.S. Army), ad interim, March 4, 1857. John B. Floyd, of Virginia, March 6, 1857. Joseph Holt, of Kentucky (Postmaster General), ad interim, January 1, 1861. Joseph Holt, of Kentucky, January 18, 1861. ATTORNEY GENERAL—Caleb Cushing, of Massachusetts, continued from preceding administration. Jeremiah S. Black, of Pennsylvania, March 6, 1857; entered upon duties March 11, 1857. Edwin M. Stanton, of Pennsylvania, December 20, 1860; entered upon duties December 22, 1860. POSTMASTER GENERAL—James Campbell, of Pennsylvania, continued from preceding administration. Aaron V. Brown, of Tennessee, March 6, 1857 (died March 8, 1859). Horatio King, of Maine (First Assistant Postmaster General), ad interim, March 9, 1859. Joseph Holt, of Kentucky, March 14, 1859. Horatio King, of Maine (First Assistant Postmaster General), ad interim, January 1, 1861. Horatio King, of Maine, February 12, 1861. SECRETARY OF NAVY—James C. Dobbin, of North Carolina, continued from preceding administration. Isaac Toucey, of Connecticut, March 6, 1857. SECRETARY OF THE INTERIOR—Robert McClelland, of Michigan, continued from preceding administration. Jacob Thompson, of Mississippi, March 6, 1857; entered upon duties March 10, 1857. Moses Kelly (chief clerk), ad interim, January 10, 1861.

**35th Congress**

1st Session: Dec. 7, 1857–June 14, 1858; 2d Session: Dec. 6, 1858–Mar. 3, 1859; Special Sessions of the Senate: Mar. 4, 1857–Mar. 14, 1857; June 15, 1858–June 16, 1858.

President pro tempore of the Senate: James M. Mason, of Virginia (elected Mar. 4, 1857); Thomas J. Rusk, of Texas (elected Mar. 14, 1857); Benjamin Fitzpatrick, of Alabama (elected Dec. 7, 1857; Mar. 29, 1858; June 14, 1858; Jan. 25, 1859). Speaker of the House: James L. Orr, of South Carolina (elected Dec. 7, 1857).

Senate: 36 Democratic; 20 Republican; 8 other
House: 118 Democratic; 92 Republican; 26 other

**36th Congress**

1st Session: Dec. 5, 1859–June 25, 1860; 2d Session: Dec. 3, 1860–Mar. 3, 1861: Special Sessions of the Senate: Mar. 4, 1859–Mar. 10, 1859; June 26, 1860–June 28, 1860.

President pro tempore of the Senate: Benjamin Fitzpatrick, of Alabama (elected Mar. 9, 1859; Dec. 19, 1859; Feb. 20, 1860; June 26, 1860); Jesse D. Bright, of Indiana (June 12, 1860); Solomon Foot, of Vermont (elected Feb. 16, 1861). Speaker of the House: William Pennington, of New Jersey (elected Feb. 1, 1860).

Senate: 36 Democratic; 26 Republican; 4 other
House: 114 Republican; 92 Democratic; 31 other

## First Administration of ABRAHAM LINCOLN

### MARCH 4, 1861, TO MARCH 3, 1865

PRESIDENT—Abraham Lincoln, of Illinois (Republican). VICE-PRESIDENT—Hannibal Hamlin, of Maine. SECRETARY OF STATE—Jeremiah S. Black, of Pennsylvania, continued from preceding administration. William H. Seward, of New York, March 5, 1861. SECRETARY OF THE TREASURY—John A. Dix, of New York, continued from preceding administration. Salmon P. Chase, of Ohio, March 5, 1861; entered upon duties March 7, 1861. George Harrington, of the District of Columbia (Assistant Secretary), ad interim, July 1, 1864. William P. Fessenden, of Maine, July 1, 1864; entered upon duties July 5, 1864. SECRETARY OF WAR—Joseph Holt, of Kentucky, continued from preceding administration. Simon Cameron, of Pennsylvania, March 5, 1861; entered upon duties March 11, 1861. Edwin M. Stanton, of Pennsylvania, January 15, 1862; entered upon duties January 20, 1862. ATTORNEY GENERAL—Edwin M. Stanton, of Pennsylvania, continued from preceding administration. Edward Bates, of Missouri, March 5, 1861. James Speed, of Kentucky, December 2, 1864; entered upon duties December 5, 1864. POSTMASTER GENERAL—Horatio King, of Maine, continued from preceding administration. Montgomery Blair, of the District of Columbia, March 5, 1861; entered upon duties March 9, 1861. William Dennison, of Ohio, September 24, 1864; entered upon duties October 1, 1864. SECRETARY OF THE NAVY—Isaac Toucey, of Connecticut, continued from preceding administration. Gideon Welles, of Connecticut, March 5, 1861; entered upon duties March 7, 1861. SECRETARY OF THE INTERIOR—Moses Kelly (chief clerk), ad interim, March 4, 1861. Caleb B. Smith, of Indiana, March 5, 1861. John P. Usher, of Indiana (Assistant Secretary), ad interim, January 1, 1863. John P. Usher, of Indiana, January 8, 1863.

**37th Congress**

1st Session: July 4, 1861–Aug. 6, 1861; 2d Session: Dec. 2, 1861–July 17, 1862; 3d Session: Dec. 1, 1862–Mar. 3, 1863; Special Session of the Senate: Mar. 4, 1861–Mar. 28, 1861.

President pro tempore of the Senate: Solomon Foot, of Vermont (elected Mar. 23, 1861; July 18, 1861; Jan. 15, 1862; Mar. 31, 1862; June 19, 1862; Feb. 18, 1863). Speaker of the House: Galusha A. Grow, of Pennsylvania (elected July 4, 1861).

Senate: 31 Republican; 10 Democratic; 8 other
House: 105 Republican; 43 Democratic; 30 other

**38th Congress**

1st Session: Dec. 7, 1863–July 4, 1864; 2d Session: Dec. 5, 1864–Mar. 3, 1865; Special Session of the Senate: Mar. 4, 1863–Mar. 14, 1863.

President pro tempore of the Senate: Solomon Foot, of Vermont (elected Mar. 4, 1863; Dec. 18, 1863; Feb. 23, 1864; Mar. 11, 1864; Apr. 11, 1864); Daniel Clark, of New Hampshire (elected Apr. 26, 1864; Feb. 9, 1865). Speaker of the House: Schuyler Colfax, of Indiana (elected Dec. 7, 1863).

Senate: 36 Republican; 9 Democratic; 5 other
House: 102 Republican; 75 Democratic; 9 other

## Second Administration of ABRAHAM LINCOLN

### MARCH 4, 1865, TO APRIL 15, 1865

PRESIDENT—Abraham Lincoln, of Illinois (Republican) (died April 15, 1865). VICE-PRESIDENT—Andrew Johnson, of Tennessee. SECRETARY OF STATE—William H. Seward, of New York, continued from preceding administration. SECRETARY OF THE TREASURY—George Harrington, of the District of Columbia (Assistant Secretary), ad interim, March 4, 1865. Hugh McCulloch, of Indiana, March 7, 1865; entered upon duties March 9, 1865. SECRETARY OF WAR—Edwin M. Stanton, of Pennsylvania, continued from preceding administration. ATTORNEY GENERAL—James Speed, of Kentucky, continued from preceding administration. POSTMASTER GENERAL—William Dennison, of Ohio, continued from preceding administration. SECRETARY OF THE NAVY—Gideon Welles, of Connecticut, continued from preceding administration. SECRETARY OF THE INTERIOR—John P. Usher, of Indiana, continued from preceding administration.

### Administration of ANDREW JOHNSON

**APRIL 15, 1865, TO MARCH 3, 1869**

PRESIDENT—Andrew Johnson, of Tennessee (Republican). SECRETARY OF STATE—William H. Seward, of New York, continued from preceding administration. SECRETARY OF THE TREASURY—Hugh McCulloch, of Indiana, continued from preceding administration. SECRETARY OF WAR—Edwin M. Stanton, of Pennsylvania, continued from preceding administration; suspended August 12, 1867. Ulysses S. Grant (General of the Army), ad interim, August 12, 1867. Edwin M. Stanton, of Pennsylvania, reinstated January 13, 1868, to May 26, 1868. John M. Schofield, of Illinois, May 28, 1868; entered upon duties June 1, 1868. ATTORNEY GENERAL—James Speed, of Kentucky, continued from preceding administration. J. Hubley Ashton, of Pennsylvania (Assistant Attorney General), acting, July 17, 1866. Henry Stanbery, of Ohio, July 23, 1866. Orville H. Browning, of Illinois (Secretary of the Interior), ad interim, March 13, 1868. William M. Evarts, of New York, July 15, 1868; entered upon duties July 20, 1868. POSTMASTER GENERAL—William Dennison, of Ohio, continued from preceding administration. Alexander W. Randall, of Wisconsin (First Assistant Postmaster General), ad interim, July 17, 1866. Alexander W. Randall, of Wisconsin, July 25, 1866. SECRETARY OF THE NAVY—Gideon Welles, of Connecticut, continued from preceding administration. SECRETARY OF THE INTERIOR—John P. Usher, of Indiana, continued from preceding administration. James Harlan, of Iowa, May 15, 1865. Orville H. Browning, of Illinois, July 27, 1866, to take effect September 1, 1866.

**39th Congress**

1st Session: Dec. 4, 1865–July 28, 1866; 2d Session: Dec. 3, 1866–Mar. 3, 1867; Special Session of the Senate: Mar. 4, 1865–Mar. 11, 1865.

President pro tempore of the Senate: Lafayette S. Foster, of Connecticut (elected Mar. 7, 1865); Benjamin F. Wade, of Ohio (elected Mar. 2, 1867). Speaker of the House: Schuyler Colfax, of Indiana (reelected Dec. 4, 1865).

Senate: 42 Union; 10 Democratic
House: 149 Union; 42 Democratic

**40th Congress**

1st Session: Mar. 4, 1867–Mar. 30, 1867; July 3, 1867–July 20, 1867; Nov. 21, 1867–Dec. 1, 1867; 2d Session: Dec. 2, 1867–July 27, 1868; Sept. 21, 1868; Oct. 16, 1868; Nov. 10, 1868; 3d Session: Dec. 7, 1868–Mar. 3, 1869; Special Session of the Senate: Apr. 1, 1867–Apr. 20, 1867.

President pro tempore of the Senate: Benjamin F. Wade, of Ohio (continued from the preceding Congress). Speaker of the House: Schuyler Colfax, of Indiana (reelected Mar. 4, 1867); Theodore M. Pomeroy, of New York (elected Mar. 3, 1869).

Senate: 42 Republican; 11 Democratic
House: 143 Republican; 49 Democratic

---

### First Administration of ULYSSES S. GRANT

**MARCH 4, 1869, TO MARCH 3, 1873**

PRESIDENT—Ulysses S. Grant, of Illinois (Republican). VICE-PRESIDENT—Schuyler Colfax, of Indiana. SECRETARY OF STATE—William H. Seward, of New York, continued from preceding administration. Elihu B. Washburne, of Illinois, March 5, 1869. Hamilton Fish, of New York, March 11, 1869; entered upon duties March 17, 1869. SECRETARY OF THE TREASURY—Hugh McCulloch, of Indiana, continued from preceding administration. John F. Hartley, of Maine (Assistant Secretary), ad interim, March 5, 1869. George S. Boutwell, of Massachusetts, March 11, 1869. SECRETARY OF WAR—John M. Schofield, of Illinois, continued from preceding administration. John A. Rawlins, of Illinois, March 11, 1869. William T. Sherman, of Ohio, September 9, 1869; entered upon duties September 11, 1869. William W. Belknap, of Iowa, October 25, 1869; entered upon duties November 1, 1869. ATTORNEY GENERAL—William M. Evarts, of New York, continued from preceding administration. J. Hubley Ashton, of Pennsylvania (Assistant Attorney General), acting, March 5, 1869. Ebenezer R. Hoar, of Massachusetts, March 5, 1869; entered upon duties March 11, 1869. Amos T. Akerman, of Georgia, June 23, 1870; entered upon duties July 8, 1870. George H. Williams, of Oregon, December 14, 1871, to take effect January 10, 1872. POSTMASTER GENERAL—St. John B. L. Skinner, of New York (First Assistant Postmaster General), ad interim, March 4, 1869. John A. J. Creswell, of Maryland, March 5, 1869. SECRETARY OF THE NAVY—William Faxon, of Connecticut (Assistant Secretary), ad interim, March 4, 1869. Adolph E. Borie, of Pennsylvania, March 5, 1869; entered upon duties March 9, 1869. George M. Robeson, of New Jersey, June 25, 1869. SECRETARY OF THE INTERIOR—William T. Otto, of Indiana (Assistant Secretary), ad interim, March 4, 1869. Jacob D. Cox, of Ohio, March 5, 1869; entered upon duties March 9, 1869. Columbus Delano, of Ohio, November 1, 1870.

**41st Congress**

1st Session: Mar. 4, 1869–Apr. 10, 1869; 2d Session: Dec. 6, 1869–July 15, 1870; 3d Session: Dec. 5, 1870–Mar. 3, 1871; Special Session of the Senate: Apr. 12, 1869–Apr. 22, 1869.

President pro tempore of the Senate: Henry B. Anthony, of Rhode Island (elected Mar. 23, 1869; Apr. 9, 1869; May 28, 1870; July 1, 1870; July 14, 1870). Speaker of the House: James G. Blaine, of Maine (elected Mar. 4, 1869).

Senate: 56 Republican; 11 Democratic
House: 149 Republican; 63 Democratic

**42d Congress**

1st Session: Mar. 4, 1871–Apr. 20, 1871; 2d Session: Dec. 4, 1871–June 10, 1872; 3d Session: Dec. 2, 1872–Mar. 3, 1873; Special Session of the Senate: May 10, 1871–May 27, 1871.

President pro tempore of the Senate: Henry B. Anthony, of Rhode Island (elected Mar. 10, 1871; April 17, 1871; May 23, 1871; Dec. 21, 1871; Feb. 23, 1872; June 8, 1872; Dec. 4, 1872; Dec. 13, 1872; Dec. 20, 1872; Jan. 24, 1873). Speaker of the House: James G. Blaine, of Maine (reelected Mar. 4, 1871).

Senate: 52 Republican; 17 Democratic; 5 other
House: 134 Democratic; 104 Republican; 5 other

---

### Second Administration of ULYSSES S. GRANT

**MARCH 4, 1873, TO MARCH 3, 1877**

PRESIDENT—Ulysses S. Grant, of Illinois (Republican). VICE-PRESIDENT—Henry Wilson, of Massachusetts (died November 22, 1875). SECRETARY OF STATE—Hamilton Fish, of New York, continued from preceding administration. Hamilton Fish, of New York, recommissioned March 17, 1873. SECRETARY OF THE TREASURY—George S. Boutwell, of Massachusetts, continued from preceding administration. William A. Richardson, of Massachusetts, March 17, 1873. Benjamin H. Bristow, of Kentucky, June 2, 1874; entered upon duties June 4, 1874. Charles F. Conant, of New Hampshire (Assistant Secretary), ad interim, June 21, 1876, to June 30, 1876. Lot M. Morrill, of Maine, June 21, 1876; entered upon duties July 7, 1876. SECRETARY OF WAR—William W. Belknap, of Iowa, continued from preceding administration. William W. Belknap, of Iowa, recommissioned March 17, 1873. George M. Robeson, of New Jersey (Secretary of the Navy), ad interim, March 2, 1876. Alphonso Taft, of Ohio, March 8, 1876; entered upon duties March 11, 1876. James D. Cameron, of Pennsylvania, May 22, 1876; entered upon duties June 1, 1876. ATTORNEY GENERAL—George H. Williams, of Oregon, continued from preceding administration. George H. Williams, of Oregon, recommissioned March 17, 1873. Edwards Pierrepont, of New York, April 26, 1875, to take effect May 15, 1875. Alphonso Taft, of Ohio, May 22, 1876; entered upon duties June 1, 1876. POSTMASTER GENERAL—John A. J. Creswell, of Maryland, continued from preceding administration. John A. J. Creswell, of Maryland, recommissioned March 17, 1873. James W. Marshall, of Virginia, July 3, 1874; entered upon duties July 7, 1874. Marshall Jewell, of Connecticut, August 24, 1874; entered upon duties September 1, 1874. James N. Tyner, of Indiana, July 12, 1876. SECRETARY OF THE NAVY—George M. Robeson, of New Jersey, continued from preceding administration. George M. Robeson, of New Jersey, recommissioned March 17, 1873. SECRETARY OF THE INTERIOR—Columbus Delano, of Ohio, continued from preceding administration. Columbus Delano, of Ohio, recommissioned March 17, 1873. Benjamin R. Cowen, of Ohio (Assistant Secretary), ad interim, October 1, 1875. Zachariah Chandler, of Michigan, October 19, 1875.

**43d Congress**

1st Session: Dec. 1, 1873–June 23, 1874; 2d Session: Dec. 7, 1874–Mar. 3, 1875; Special Session of the Senate: Mar. 4, 1873–Mar. 26, 1873.

President pro tempore of the Senate: Mathew H. Carpenter, of Wisconsin (elected Mar. 12, 1873; Mar. 26, 1873; Dec. 11, 1873; Dec. 23, 1874); Henry B. Anthony, of Rhode Island (elected Jan. 25, 1875; Feb. 15, 1875). Speaker of the House: James G. Blaine (reelected Dec. 1, 1873).

Senate: 49 Republican; 19 Democratic; 5 other
House: 194 Republican; 92 Democratic; 14 other

**44th Congress**

1st Session: Dec. 6, 1875–Aug. 15, 1876; 2d Session: Dec. 4, 1876–Mar. 3, 1877; Special Session of the Senate: Mar. 5, 1875–Mar. 24, 1875.

President pro tempore of the Senate: Thomas W. Ferry, of Michigan (elected Mar. 9, 1875; Mar. 19, 1875; Dec. 20, 1875). Speaker of the House: Michael C. Kerr, of Indiana (elected Dec. 6, 1875); Samuel J. Randall, of Pennsylvania (elected Dec. 4, 1876).

Senate: 45 Republican; 29 Democratic; 2 other
House: 169 Democratic; 109 Republican; 14 other

---

### Administration of RUTHERFORD B. HAYES

**MARCH 4, 1877, TO MARCH 3, 1881**

PRESIDENT—Rutherford B. Hayes, of Ohio (Republican) (oath administered March 5, 1877). VICE-PRESIDENT—William A. Wheeler, of New York. SECRETARY OF STATE—Hamilton Fish, of

New York, continued from preceding administration. William M. Evarts, of New York, March 12, 1877. SECRETARY OF THE TREASURY—Lot M. Morrill, of Maine, continued from preceding administration. John Sherman, of Ohio, March 8, 1877; entered upon duties March 10, 1877. SECRETARY OF WAR—James D. Cameron, of Pennsylvania, continued from preceding administration. George W. McCrary, of Iowa, March 12, 1877. Alexander Ramsey, of Minnesota, December 10, 1879; entered upon duties December 12, 1879. ATTORNEY GENERAL—Alphonso Taft, of Ohio, continued from preceding administration. Charles Devens, of Massachusetts, March 12, 1877. POSTMASTER GENERAL—James N. Tyner, of Indiana, continued from preceding administration. David M. Key, of Tennessee, March 12, 1877; resigned June 1, 1880; served to August 24, 1880. Horace Maynard, of Tennessee, June 2, 1880; entered upon duties August 25, 1880. SECRETARY OF THE NAVY—George M. Robeson, of New Jersey, continued from preceding administration. Richard W. Thompson, of Indiana, March 12, 1877. Alexander Ramsey, of Minnesota (Secretary of War), ad interim, December 20, 1880. Nathan Goff, Jr., of West Virginia, January 6, 1881. SECRETARY OF THE INTERIOR—Zachariah Chandler, of Michigan, continued from preceding administration. Carl Schurz, of Missouri, March 12, 1877.

**45th Congress**

1st Session: Oct. 15, 1877–Dec. 3, 1877; 2d Session: Dec. 3, 1877–June 20, 1878; 3d Session: Dec. 2, 1878–Mar. 3, 1879; Special Session of the Senate: Mar. 5, 1877–Mar. 17, 1877.

President pro tempore of the Senate: Thomas W. Ferry of Michigan (elected Mar. 5, 1877; Feb. 26, 1878; Apr. 17, 1878; Mar. 3, 1879). Speaker of the House: Samuel J. Randall, of Pennsylvania (reelected Oct. 15, 1877).

Senate: 39 Republican; 36 Democratic; 1 other
House: 153 Democratic; 140 Republican

**46th Congress**

1st Session: Mar. 18, 1879–July 1, 1879; 2d Session: Dec. 1, 1879–June 16, 1880; 3d Session: Dec. 6, 1880–Mar. 3, 1881.

President pro tempore of the Senate: Allen G. Thurman, of Ohio (elected Apr. 15, 1879; Apr. 7, 1880, May 6, 1880). Speaker of the House: Samuel J. Randall, of Pennsylvania (reelected Mar. 18, 1879).

Senate: 42 Democratic; 33 Republican; 1 other
House: 149 Democratic; 130 Republican; 14 other

## Administration of JAMES A. GARFIELD

## MARCH 4, 1881, TO SEPTEMBER 19, 1881

PRESIDENT—James A. Garfield, of Ohio (Republican) (died September 19, 1881). VICE-PRESIDENT—Chester A. Arthur, of New York. SECRETARY OF STATE—William M. Evarts, of New York, continued from preceding administration. James G. Blaine, of Maine, March 5, 1881; entered upon duties March 7, 1881. SECRETARY OF THE TREASURY—Henry F. French, of Massachusetts (Assistant Secretary), ad interim, March 4, 1881. William Windom, of Minnesota, March 5, 1881; entered upon duties March 8, 1881. SECRETARY OF WAR—Alexander Ramsey, of Minnesota, continued from preceding administration. Robert T. Lincoln, of Illinois, March 5, 1881; entered upon duties March 11, 1881. ATTORNEY GENERAL—Charles Devens, of Massachusetts, continued from preceding administration. Wayne MacVeagh, of Pennsylvania, March 5, 1881; entered upon duties March 7, 1881. POSTMASTER GENERAL—Horace Maynard, of Tennessee, continued from preceding administration. Thomas L. James, of New York, March 5, 1881; entered upon duties March 8, 1881. SECRETARY OF THE NAVY—Nathan Goff, Jr., of West Virginia, continued from preceding administration. William H. Hunt, of Louisiana, March 5, 1881; entered upon duties March 7, 1881. SECRETARY OF THE INTERIOR—Carl Schurz, of Missouri, continued from preceding administration. Samuel J. Kirkwood, of Iowa, March 5, 1881; entered upon duties March 8, 1881.

## Administration of CHESTER A. ARTHUR

## SEPTEMBER 20, 1881, TO MARCH 3, 1885

PRESIDENT—Chester A. Arthur, of New York. SECRETARY OF STATE—James G. Blaine, of Maine, continued from preceding administration. Frederick T. Frelinghuysen, of New Jersey, December 12, 1881; entered upon duties December 19, 1881. SECRETARY OF THE TREASURY—William Windom, of Minnesota, continued from preceding administration. Charles J. Folger, of New York, October 27, 1881; entered upon duties November 14, 1881 (died September 4, 1884). Charles E. Coon, of New York (Assistant Secretary), ad interim, September 4, 1884. Henry F. French, of Massachusetts (Assistant Secretary), ad interim, September 8, 1884. Charles E. Coon, of New York (Assistant Secretary), ad interim, September 15, 1884. Walter Q. Gresham, of Indiana, September 24, 1884. Henry F. French, of Massachusetts (Assistant Secretary), ad interim, October 29, 1884. Hugh McCulloch, of Indiana, October 28, 1884; entered upon duties October 31, 1884. SECRETARY OF WAR—Robert T. Lincoln, of Illinois, continued from preceding administration: ATTORNEY GENERAL—Wayne MacVeagh, of Pennsylvania, continued from preceding administration. Samuel F. Phillips, of North Carolina (Solicitor General), ad interim, November 14, 1881. Benjamin H. Brewster, of Pennsylvania, December 19, 1881; entered upon duties January 3, 1882. POSTMASTER GENERAL—Thomas L. James, of New York, continued from preceding administration. Thomas L. James, of New York, recommissioned October 27, 1881. Timothy O. Howe, of Wisconsin, December 20, 1881; entered upon duties January 5, 1882 (died March 25, 1883). Frank Hatton, of Iowa (First Assistant Postmaster General), ad interim, March 26, 1883. Walter Q. Gresham, of Indiana, April 3, 1883; entered upon duties April 11, 1883. Frank Hatton, of Iowa (First Assistant Postmaster General), ad interim, September 25, 1884. Frank Hatton, of Iowa, October 14, 1884. SECRETARY OF THE NAVY—William H. Hunt, of Louisiana, continued from preceding administration. William E. Chandler, of New Hampshire, April 12, 1882; entered upon duties April 17, 1882. SECRETARY OF THE INTERIOR—Samuel J. Kirkwood, of Iowa, continued from preceding administration. Henry M. Teller, of Colorado, April 6, 1882; entered upon duties April 17, 1882.

**47th Congress**

1st Session: Dec. 5, 1881–Aug. 9, 1882; 2d Session: Dec. 4, 1882–Mar. 3, 1883; Special Sessions of the Senate: Mar. 4, 1881–May 20, 1881; Oct. 10, 1881–Oct. 29, 1881.

President pro tempore of the Senate: Thomas F. Bayard, of Delaware (elected Oct. 10, 1881); David Davis, of Illinois (elected Oct. 13, 1881); George F. Edmunds, of Vermont (elected Mar. 3, 1883). Speaker of the House: J. Warren Keifer, of Ohio (elected Dec. 5, 1881).

Senate: 37 Republican; 37 Democratic; 1 other
House: 147 Republican; 135 Democratic; 11 other

**48th Congress**

1st Session: Dec. 3, 1883–July 7, 1884; 2d Session: Dec. 1, 1884–Mar. 3, 1885.

President pro tempore of the Senate: George F. Edmunds, of Vermont (reelected Jan. 14, 1884). Speaker of the House: John G. Carlisle, of Kentucky (elected Dec. 3, 1883).

Senate: 38 Republican; 36 Democratic; 2 other
House: 197 Democratic; 118 Republican; 10 other

## First Administration of GROVER CLEVELAND

## MARCH 4, 1885, TO MARCH 3, 1889

PRESIDENT—Grover Cleveland, of New York (Democratic). VICE-PRESIDENT—Thomas A. Hendricks, of Indiana (died November 25, 1885). SECRETARY OF STATE—Frederick T. Frelinghuysen, of New Jersey, continued from preceding administration. Thomas F. Bayard, of Delaware, March 6, 1885. SECRETARY OF THE TREASURY—Hugh McCulloch, of Indiana, continued from preceding administration. Daniel Manning, of New York, March 6, 1885; entered upon duties March 8, 1885. Charles S. Fairchild, of New York, April 1, 1887. SECRETARY OF WAR—Robert T. Lincoln, of Illinois, continued from preceding administration. William C. Endicott, of Massachusetts, March 6, 1885. ATTORNEY GENERAL—Benjamin H. Brewster, of Pennsylvania, continued from preceding administration. Augustus H. Garland, of Arkansas, March 6, 1885; entered upon duties March 9, 1885. POSTMASTER GENERAL—Frank Hatton, of Iowa, continued from preceding administration. William F. Vilas, of Wisconsin, March 6, 1885. Don M. Dickinson, of Michigan, January 16, 1888. SECRETARY OF THE NAVY—William E. Chandler, of New Hampshire, continued from preceding administration. William C. Whitney, of New York, March 6, 1885. SECRETARY OF THE INTERIOR—Merritt L. Joslyn, of Illinois (Assistant Secretary), ad interim, March 4, 1885. Lucius Q. C. Lamar, of Mississippi, March 6, 1885. Henry L. Muldrow, of Mississippi (First Assistant Secretary), ad interim, January 11, 1888. William F. Vilas, of Wisconsin, January 16, 1888. SECRETARY OF AGRICULTURE—Norman J. Colman, of Missouri, February 13, 1889.

**49th Congress**

1st Session: Dec. 7, 1885–Aug. 5, 1886; 2d Session: Dec. 6, 1886–Mar 3, 1887; Special Session of the Senate: Mar. 4, 1885–Apr. 2, 1885.

President pro tempore of the Senate: John Sherman, of Ohio (elected Dec. 7, 1885); John J. Ingalls, of Kansas (elected Feb. 25, 1887). Speaker of the House: John G. Carlisle, of Kentucky (reelected Dec. 7, 1885).

Senate: 43 Republican; 34 Democratic
House: 183 Democratic; 140 Republican; 2 other

**50th Congress**

1st Session: Dec. 5, 1887–Oct. 20, 1888; 2d Session: Dec. 3, 1888–Mar. 3, 1889.

President pro tempore of the Senate: John J. Ingalls, of Kansas (continued from the preceding Congress). Speaker of the House: John G. Carlisle, of Kentucky (reelected Dec. 5, 1887).

Senate: 39 Republican; 37 Democratic
House: 169 Democratic; 152 Republican; 4 other

**Administration of BENJAMIN HARRISON**

**MARCH 4, 1889, TO MARCH 3, 1893**

PRESIDENT—Benjamin Harrison, of Indiana (Republican). VICE-PRESIDENT—Levi P. Morton, of New York. SECRETARY OF STATE—Thomas F. Bayard, of Delaware, continued from preceding administration. James G. Blaine, of Maine, March 5, 1889; entered upon duties March 7, 1889. William F. Wharton, of Massachusetts (Assistant Secretary), ad interim, June 4, 1892. John W. Foster, of Indiana, June 29, 1892. William F. Wharton, of Massachusetts (Assistant Secretary), ad interim, February 23, 1893. SECRETARY OF THE TREASURY—Charles S. Fairchild, of New York, continued from preceding administration. William Windom, of Minnesota, March 5, 1889; entered upon duties March 7, 1889 (died January 29, 1891). Allured B. Nettleton, of Minnesota (Assistant Secretary), ad interim, January 30, 1891. Charles Foster, of Ohio, February 24, 1891. SECRETARY OF WAR—William C. Endicott, of Massachusetts, continued from preceding administration. Redfield Proctor, of Vermont, March 5, 1889. Lewis A. Grant, of Minnesota (Assistant Secretary), ad interim, December 6, 1891. Stephen B. Elkins, of West Virginia, December 22, 1891; entered upon duties December 24, 1891. ATTORNEY GENERAL—Augustus H. Garland, of Arkansas, continued from preceding administration. William H. H. Miller, of Indiana, March 5, 1889. POSTMASTER GENERAL—Don M. Dickinson, of Michigan, continued from preceding administration. John Wanamaker, of Pennsylvania, March 5, 1889. SECRETARY OF THE NAVY—William C. Whitney, of New York, continued from preceding administration. Benjamin F. Tracy, of New York, March 5, 1889. SECRETARY OF THE INTERIOR—William F. Vilas, of Wisconsin, continued from preceding administration. John W. Noble, of Missouri, March 5, 1889; entered upon duties March 7, 1889. SECRETARY OF AGRICULTURE—Norman J. Colman, of Missouri, continued from preceding administration, Jeremiah M. Rusk, of Wisconsin, March 5, 1889; entered upon duties March 7, 1889.

**51st Congress**

1st Session: Dec. 2, 1889–Oct. 1, 1890; 2d Session: Dec. 1, 1890–Mar. 2, 1891; Special Session of the Senate: Mar. 4, 1889–Apr. 2, 1889.

President pro tempore of the Senate: John J. Ingalls, of Kansas (reelected Mar. 7, 1889; Apr. 2, 1889; Feb. 28, 1890; Apr. 3, 1890); Charles F. Manderson, of Nebraska (elected Mar. 2, 1891). Speaker of the House: Thomas B. Reed, of Maine (elected Dec. 2, 1889).

Senate: 39 Republican; 37 Democratic
House: 166 Republican; 159 Democratic

**52d Congress**

1st Session: Dec. 7, 1891–Aug. 5, 1892; 2d Session: Dec. 5, 1892–Mar. 3, 1893.

President pro tempore of the Senate: Charles F. Manderson, of Nebraska (continued from preceding Congress). Speaker of the House: Charles F. Crisp, of Georgia (elected Dec. 8, 1891).

Senate: 47 Republican; 39 Democratic; 2 other
House: 235 Democratic; 88 Republican; 9 other

**Second Administration of GROVER CLEVELAND**

**March 4, 1893, TO MARCH 3, 1897**

PRESIDENT—Grover Cleveland, of New York (Democratic). VICE-PRESIDENT—Adlai E. Stevenson, of Illinois. SECRETARY OF STATE—William F. Wharton, of Massachusetts (Assistant Secretary), ad interim, continued from preceding administration. Walter Q. Gresham, of Illinois, March 6, 1893 (died May 28, 1895). Edwin F. Uhl, of Michigan (Assistant Secretary), ad interim, May 28, 1895. Alvey A. Adee, of the District of Columbia (Second Assistant Secretary), ad interim, May 31, 1895. Edwin F. Uhl, of Michigan (Assistant Secretary), ad interim, June 1, 1895. Richard Olney, of Massachusetts, June 8, 1895; entered upon duties June 10, 1895. SECRETARY OF THE TREASURY—Charles Foster, of Ohio, continued from preceding administration. John G. Carlisle, of Kentucky, March 6, 1893. SECRETARY OF WAR—Stephen B. Elkins, of West Virginia, continued from preceding administration. Daniel S. Lamont, of New York, March 6, 1893. ATTORNEY GENERAL—William H. H. Miller, of Indiana, continued from preceding administration. Richard Olney, of Massachusetts, March 6, 1893. Judson Harmon, of Ohio, June 8, 1895; entered upon duties June 11, 1895. POSTMASTER GENERAL—John Wanamaker, of Pennsylvania, continued from preceding administration. Wilson S. Bissell, of New York, March 6, 1893. William L. Wilson, of West Virginia, March 1, 1895; entered upon duties April 4, 1895. SECRETARY OF THE NAVY—Benjamin F. Tracy, of New York, continued from preceding administration. Hilary A. Herbert, of Alabama, March 6, 1893. SECRETARY OF THE INTERIOR—John W. Noble, of Missouri, continued from preceding administration. Hoke Smith, of Georgia, March 6, 1893. John M. Reynolds, of Pennsylvania (Assistant Secretary), ad interim, September 1, 1896. David R. Francis, of Missouri, September 1, 1896; entered upon duties September 4, 1896. SECRETARY OF AGRICULTURE—Jeremiah M. Rusk, of Wisconsin, continued from preceding administration. Julius Sterling Morton, of Nebraska, March 6, 1893.

**53d Congress**

1st Session: Aug. 7, 1893–Nov. 3, 1893; 2d Session: Dec. 4, 1893–Aug. 28, 1894; 3d Session: Dec. 3, 1894–Mar. 3, 1895; Special Session of the Senate: Mar. 4, 1893–Apr. 15, 1893.

President pro tempore of the Senate: Charles F. Manderson, of Nebraska (continued from preceding Congress); Isham G. Harris, of Tennessee (elected Mar. 22, 1893; Jan. 10, 1895); Matt W. Ransom, of North Carolina (elected Jan. 7, 1895). Speaker of the House: Charles F. Crisp, of Georgia (reelected Aug. 7, 1893).

Senate: 44 Democratic; 38 Republican; 3 other
House: 218 Democratic; 127 Republican; 11 other

**54th Congress**

1st Session: Dec. 2, 1895–June 11, 1896; 2d Session: Dec. 7, 1896–Mar. 3, 1897.

President pro tempore of the Senate: William P. Frye, of Maine (elected Feb. 7, 1896). Speaker of the House: Thomas B. Reed, of Maine (elected Dec. 2, 1895).

Senate: 43 Republican; 39 Democratic; 6 other
House: 244 Republican; 105 Democratic; 7 other

**First Administration of WILLIAM McKINLEY**

**MARCH 4, 1897, TO MARCH 3, 1901**

PRESIDENT—William McKinley, of Ohio (Republican). VICE-PRESIDENT—Garret A. Hobart, of New Jersey (died November 21, 1899). SECRETARY OF STATE—Richard Olney, of Massachusetts, continued from preceding administration. John Sherman, of Ohio, March 5, 1897. William R. Day, of Ohio, April 26, 1898; entered upon duties April 28, 1898. Alvey A. Adee (Second Assistant Secretary), ad interim, September 17, 1898. John Hay, of the District of Columbia, September 20, 1898; entered upon duties September 30, 1898. SECRETARY OF THE TREASURY—John G. Carlisle, of Kentucky, continued from preceding administration. Lyman J. Gage, of Illinois, March 5, 1897. SECRETARY OF WAR—Daniel S. Lamont, of New York, continued from preceding administration. Russell A. Alger, of Michigan, March 5, 1897. Elihu Root, of New York, August 1, 1899. ATTORNEY GENERAL—Judson Harmon, of Ohio, continued from preceding administration. Joseph McKenna, of California, March 5, 1897; entered upon duties March 7, 1897. John K. Richards, of Ohio (Solicitor General), ad interim, January 26, 1898. John W. Griggs, of New Jersey, January 25, 1898; entered upon duties February 1, 1898. POSTMASTER GENERAL—William L. Wilson, of West Virginia, continued from preceding administration. James A. Gary, of Maryland, March 5, 1897. Charles Emory Smith, of Pennsylvania, April 21, 1898. SECRETARY OF THE NAVY—Hilary A. Herbert, of Alabama, continued from preceding administration. John D. Long, of Massachusetts, March 5, 1897. SECRETARY OF THE INTERIOR—David R. Francis, of Missouri, continued from preceding administration. Cornelius N. Bliss, of New York, March 5, 1897. Ethan A. Hitchcock, of Missouri, December 21, 1898; entered upon duties February 20, 1899. SECRETARY OF AGRICULTURE—Julius Sterling Morton, of Nebraska, continued from preceding administration. James Wilson, of Iowa, March 5, 1897.

**55th Congress**

1st Session: Mar. 15, 1897–July 24, 1897; 2d Session: Dec. 6, 1897–July 8, 1898; 3d Session: Dec. 5, 1898–Mar. 3, 1899; Special Session of the Senate: Mar. 4, 1897–Mar. 10, 1897.

President pro tempore of the Senate: William P. Frye, of Maine (continued from preceding Congress). Speaker of the House: Thomas B. Reed, of Maine (reelected Mar. 15, 1897).

Senate: 47 Republican; 34 Democratic; 7 other
House: 204 Republican; 113 Democratic; 40 other

**56th Congress**

1st Session: Dec. 4, 1899–June 7, 1900; 2d Session: Dec. 3, 1900–Mar. 3, 1901.

President pro tempore of the Senate: William P. Frye, of Maine (continued from preceding Congress). Speaker of the House: David B. Henderson, of Iowa (elected Dec. 4, 1899).

Senate: 53 Republican; 26 Democratic; 8 other
House: 185 Republican; 163 Democratic; 9 other

**Second Administration of WILLIAM McKINLEY**

**MARCH 4, 1901, TO SEPTEMBER 14, 1901**

PRESIDENT—William McKinley, of Ohio (Republican) (died September 14, 1901). VICE-PRESIDENT—Theodore Roosevelt, of New York. SECRETARY OF STATE—John Hay, of the District of Columbia, continued from preceding administration. John Hay, of the District of Columbia, recommissioned March 5, 1901. SECRETARY OF THE TREASURY—Lyman J. Gage, of Illinois, continued from preceding administration. Lyman J. Gage, of

Illinois, recommissioned March 5, 1901. SECRETARY OF WAR—Elihu Root, of New York, continued from preceding administration. Elihu Root, of New York, recommissioned March 5, 1901. ATTORNEY GENERAL—John W. Griggs, of New Jersey, continued from preceding administration. John W. Griggs, of New Jersey, recommissioned March 5, 1901. John K. Richards, of Ohio (Solicitor General), ad interim, April 1, 1901. Philander C. Knox, of Pennsylvania, April 5, 1901; entered upon duties April 10, 1901. POSTMASTER GENERAL—Charles Emory Smith, of Pennsylvania, continued from preceding administration. Charles Emory Smith, of Pennsylvania, recommissioned March 5, 1901. SECRETARY OF THE NAVY—John D. Long, of Massachusetts, continued from preceding administration. John D. Long, of Massachusetts, recommissioned March 5, 1901. SECRETARY OF THE INTERIOR—Ethan A. Hitchcock, of Missouri, continued from preceding administration. Ethan A. Hitchcock, of Missouri, recommissioned March 5, 1901. SECRETARY OF AGRICULTURE—James Wilson, of Iowa, continued from preceding administration. James Wilson, of Iowa, recommissioned March 5, 1901.

### First Administration of THEODORE ROOSEVELT

### SEPTEMBER 14, 1901, TO MARCH 3, 1905

PRESIDENT—Theodore Roosevelt, of New York (Republican). SECRETARY OF STATE—John Hay, of the District of Columbia, continued from preceding administration. SECRETARY OF THE TREASURY—Lyman J. Gage, of Illinois, continued from preceding administration. Leslie M. Shaw, of Iowa, January 9, 1902; entered upon duties February 1, 1902. SECRETARY OF WAR—Elihu Root, of New York, continued from preceding administration. William H. Taft, of Ohio, January 11, 1904, to take effect February 1, 1904. ATTORNEY GENERAL—Philander C. Knox, of Pennsylvania, continued from preceding administration. Philander C. Knox, of Pennsylvania, recommissioned December 16, 1901. William H. Moody, of Massachusetts, July 1, 1904. POSTMASTER GENERAL—Charles Emory Smith, of Pennsylvania, continued from preceding administration. Henry C. Payne, of Wisconsin, January 9, 1902. Robert J. Wynne, of Pennsylvania, October 10, 1904. SECRETARY OF THE NAVY—John D. Long, of Massachusetts, continued from preceding administration. William H. Moody, of Massachusetts, April 29, 1902; entered upon duties May 1, 1902. Paul Morton, of Illinois, July 1, 1904. SECRETARY OF THE INTERIOR—Ethan A. Hitchcock, of Missouri, continued from preceding administration. SECRETARY OF AGRICULTURE—James Wilson, of Iowa, continued from preceding administration. SECRETARY OF COMMERCE AND LABOR—George B. Cortelyou, of New York, February 16, 1903. Victor H. Metcalf, of California, July 1, 1904.

**57th Congress**

1st Session: Dec. 2, 1901–July 1, 1902; 2d Session: Dec. 1, 1902–Mar. 3, 1903; Special Session of the Senate: Mar. 4, 1901–Mar. 9, 1901.

President pro tempore of the Senate: William P. Frye, of Maine (reelected Mar. 7, 1901). Speaker of the House: David B. Henderson, of Iowa (reelected Dec. 2, 1901).

Senate: 55 Republican; 35 Democratic; 4 other
House: 197 Republican; 151 Democratic; 9 other

**58th Congress**

1st Session: Nov. 9, 1903–Dec. 7, 1903; 2d Session: Dec. 7, 1903–Apr. 28, 1904; 3d Session: Dec. 5, 1904–Mar. 3, 1905; Special Session of the Senate: Mar. 5, 1903–Mar. 19, 1903.

President pro tempore of the Senate: William P. Frye, of Maine (continued from preceding Congress). Speaker of the House: Joseph G. Cannon, of Illinois (elected Nov. 9, 1903).

Senate: 57 Republican; 33 Democratic
House: 208 Republican; 178 Democratic

### Second Administration of THEODORE ROOSEVELT

### MARCH 4, 1905, TO MARCH 3, 1909

PRESIDENT—Theodore Roosevelt, of New York (Republican). VICE-PRESIDENT—Charles Warren Fairbanks, of Indiana. SECRETARY OF STATE—John Hay, of the District of Columbia, continued from preceding administration. John Hay, of the District of Columbia, recommissioned March 6, 1905 (died July 1, 1905). Francis B. Loomis, of Ohio (Assistant Secretary), ad interim, July 1, 1905, to July 18, 1905. Elihu Root, of New York, July 7, 1905; entered upon duties July 19, 1905. Robert Bacon, of New York, January 27, 1909. SECRETARY OF THE TREASURY—Leslie M. Shaw, of Iowa, continued from preceding administration. Leslie M. Shaw, of Iowa, recommissioned March 6, 1905. George B. Cortelyou, of New York, January 15, 1907, to take effect March 4, 1907. SECRETARY OF WAR—William H. Taft, of Ohio, continued from preceding administration. William H. Taft, of Ohio, recommissioned March 6, 1905. Luke E. Wright, of Tennessee, June 29, 1908; entered upon duties July 1, 1908. ATTORNEY GENERAL—William H. Moody, of Massachusetts, continued from preceding administration. William H. Moody, of Massachusetts, recommissioned March 6, 1905. Charles J. Bonaparte, of Maryland, December 12, 1906; entered upon duties December 17, 1906. POSTMASTER GENERAL—Robert J. Wynne, of Pennsylvania, continued from preceding administration. George B. Cortelyou, of New York, March 6, 1905. George von L. Meyer, of Massachusetts, January 15, 1907, to take effect March 4, 1907. SECRETARY OF THE NAVY—Paul Morton, of Illinois, continued from preceding administration. Paul Morton, of Illinois, recommissioned March 6, 1905. Charles J. Bonaparte, of Maryland, July 1, 1905. Victor H. Metcalf, of California, December 12, 1906; entered upon duties December 17, 1906. Truman H. Newberry, of Michigan, December 1, 1908. SECRETARY OF THE INTERIOR—Ethan A. Hitchcock, of Missouri, continued from preceding administration. Ethan A. Hitchcock, of Missouri, recommissioned March 6, 1905. James R. Garfield, of Ohio, January 15, 1907, to take effect March 4, 1907. SECRETARY OF AGRICULTURE—James Wilson, of Iowa, continued from preceding administration. James Wilson, of Iowa, recommissioned March 6, 1905. SECRETARY OF COMMERCE AND LABOR—Victor H. Metcalf, of California, continued from preceding administration. Victor H. Metcalf, of California, recommissioned March 6, 1905. Oscar S. Straus, of New York, December 12, 1906; entered upon duties December 17, 1906.

**59th Congress**

1st Session: Dec. 4, 1905–June 30, 1906; 2d Session: Dec. 3, 1906–Mar. 3, 1907; Special Session of the Senate: Mar. 4, 1905—Mar. 18, 1905.

President pro tempore of the Senate: William P. Frye, of Maine (continued from preceding Congress). Speaker of the House: Joseph G. Cannon, of Illinois (reelected Dec. 4, 1905).

Senate: 57 Republican; 33 Democratic
House: 250 Republican; 136 Democratic

**60th Congress**

1st Session: Dec. 2, 1907–May 30, 1908; 2d Session: Dec. 7, 1908–Mar. 3, 1909.

President pro tempore of the Senate: Willliam P. Frye, of Maine (reelected Dec. 5, 1907). Speaker of the House: Joseph G. Cannon, of Illinois (reelected Dec. 2, 1907).

Senate: 61 Republican; 31 Democratic
House: 222 Republican; 164 Democratic

### Administration of WILLIAM H. TAFT

### March 4, 1909, TO MARCH 3, 1913

PRESIDENT—William H. Taft, of Ohio (Republican). VICE-PRESIDENT—James S. Sherman, of New York (died October 30, 1912). SECRETARY OF STATE—Robert Bacon, of New York, continued from preceding administration. Philander C. Knox, of Pennsylvania, March 5, 1909. SECRETARY OF THE TREASURY—George B. Cortelyou, of New York, continued from preceding administration. Franklin MacVeagh, of Illinois, March 5, 1909; entered upon duties March 8, 1909. SECRETARY OF WAR—Luke E. Wright, of Tennessee, continued from preceding administration. Jacob M. Dickinson, of Tennessee, March 5, 1909; entered upon duties March 12, 1909. Henry L. Stimson, of New York, May 16, 1911; entered upon duties May 22, 1911. ATTORNEY GENERAL—Charles J. Bonaparte, of Maryland, continued from preceding administration. George W. Wickersham, of New York, March 5, 1909. POSTMASTER GENERAL—George von L. Meyer, of Massachusetts, continued from preceding administration. Frank H. Hitchcock, of Massachusetts, March 5, 1909. SECRETARY OF THE NAVY—Truman H. Newberry, of Michigan, continued from preceding administration. George von L. Meyer, of Massachusetts, March 5, 1909. SECRETARY OF THE INTERIOR—James R. Garfield, of Ohio, continued from preceding administration. Richard A. Ballinger, of Washington, March 5, 1909. Walter Lowrie Fisher, of Illinois, March 7, 1911. SECRETARY OF AGRICULTURE—James Wilson, of Iowa, continued from preceding administration. James Wilson, of Iowa, recommissioned March 5, 1909. SECRETARY OF COMMERCE AND LABOR—Oscar S. Straus, of New York, continued from preceding administration. Charles Nagel, of Missouri, March 5, 1909.

**61st Congress**

1st Session: Mar. 15, 1909–Aug. 5, 1909; 2d Session: Dec. 6, 1909–June 25, 1910; 3d Session: Dec. 5, 1910–Mar. 3, 1911; Special Session of the Senate: Mar. 4, 1909–Mar. 6, 1909.

President pro tempore of the Senate: William P. Frye, of Maine (continued from preceding Congress). Speaker of the House: Joseph G. Cannon, of Illinois (reelected Mar. 15, 1909).

Senate: 61 Republican; 32 Democratic
House: 219 Republican; 172 Democratic

**62d Congress**

1st Session; Apr. 4, 1911–Aug. 22, 1911; 2d Session: Dec. 4, 1911–Aug. 26, 1912; 3d Session: Dec. 2, 1912–Mar. 3, 1913.

President pro tempore of the Senate: William P. Frye, of Maine (continued from preceding Congress). Charles Curtis, of Kansas (elected to serve Dec. 4–12, 1911). Augustus O. Bacon, of Georgia (elected to serve Jan. 15–17, 1912; Mar. 11–12, 1912; Apr. 8, 1912; May 10, 1912; May 30–June 3, 1912; June 13–July 5, 1912; Aug. 1–10, 1912; Aug. 27–Dec. 15, 1912; Jan. 5–18, 1913; Feb. 2–15, 1913). Jacob H. Gallinger, of New

Hampshire (elected to serve Feb. 12–14, 1912; April 26–27, 1912; May 7, 1912; July 6–31, 1912; Aug. 12–26, 1912; Dec. 16, 1912–Jan. 4, 1913; Jan. 19–Feb. 1, 1913; Feb. 16–Mar. 3, 1913). Henry C. Lodge, of Massachusetts (elected to serve Mar. 25–26, 1912). Frank B. Brandegee, of Connecticut (elected to serve May 25, 1912). Speaker of the House: James B. Clark, of Missouri (elected Apr. 4, 1911).

Senate: 51 Republican; 41 Democratic
House: 228 Democratic; 161 Republican; 1 other

### First Administration of WOODROW WILSON

### MARCH 4, 1913, TO MARCH 3, 1917

PRESIDENT—Woodrow Wilson, of New Jersey (Democratic). VICE-PRESIDENT—Thomas R. Marshall, of Indiana. SECRETARY OF STATE—Philander C. Knox, of Pennsylvania, continued from preceding administration. William Jennings Bryan, of Nebraska, March 5, 1913. Robert Lansing, of New York (counselor), ad interim, June 9, 1915. Robert Lansing, of New York, June 23, 1915. SECRETARY OF THE TREASURY—Franklin MacVeagh, of Illinois, continued from preceding administration. William Gibbs McAdoo, of New York, March 5, 1913; entered upon duties March 6, 1913. SECRETARY OF WAR—Henry L. Stimson, of New York, continued from preceding administration. Lindley M. Garrison, of New Jersey, March 5, 1913. Hugh L. Scott (United States Army), ad interim, February 12, 1916; served from February 11 to March 8, 1916. Newton D. Baker, of Ohio, March 7, 1916; entered upon duties March 9, 1916. ATTORNEY GENERAL—George W. Wickersham, of New York, continued from preceding administration. James Clark McReynolds, of Tennessee, March 5, 1913; entered upon duties March 6, 1913. Thomas Watt Gregory, of Texas, August 29, 1914; entered upon duties September 3, 1914. POSTMASTER GENERAL—Frank H. Hitchcock, of Massachusetts, continued from preceding administration. Albert Sidney Burleson, of Texas, March 5, 1913. SECRETARY OF THE NAVY—George von L. Meyer, of Massachusetts, continued from preceding administration. Josephus Daniels, of North Carolina, March 5, 1913. SECRETARY OF THE INTERIOR—Walter Lowrie Fisher, of Illinois, continued from preceding administration. Franklin Knight Lane, of California, March 5, 1913. SECRETARY OF AGRICULTURE—James Wilson, of Iowa, continued from preceding administration. David Franklin Houston, of Missouri, March 5, 1913; entered upon duties March 6, 1913. SECRETARY OF COMMERCE—Charles Nagel, of Missouri (Secretary of Commerce and Labor), continued from preceding administration. William C. Redfield, of New York, March 5, 1913. SECRETARY OF LABOR—Charles Nagel, of Missouri (Secretary of Commerce and Labor), continued from preceding administration. William Bauchop Wilson, of Pennsylvania, March 5, 1913.

**63d Congress**

1st Session: Apr. 7, 1913–Dec. 1, 1913; 2d Session: Dec. 1, 1913–Oct. 24, 1914; 3d Session: Dec. 7, 1914–Mar. 3, 1915; Special Session of the Senate: Mar. 4, 1913–Mar. 17, 1913.

President pro tempore of the Senate: James P. Clarke, of Arkansas (elected Mar. 13, 1913). Speaker of the House: James B. Clark, of Missouri (reelected Apr. 7, 1913).

Senate: 51 Democratic; 44 Republican; 1 other
House: 291 Democratic; 127 Republican; 17 other

**64th Congress**

1st Session: Dec. 6, 1915–Sept. 8, 1916; 2d Session: Dec. 4, 1916–Mar. 3, 1917.

President pro tempore of the Senate: James P. Clarke, of Arkansas (reelected Dec. 6, 1915); Willard Saulsbury, of Delaware (elected Dec. 14, 1916). Speaker of the House: James B. Clark, of Missouri (reelected Dec. 6, 1915).

Senate: 56 Democratic; 40 Republican
House: 230 Democratic; 196 Republican; 9 other

### Second Administration of WOODROW WILSON

### MARCH 4, 1917, TO MARCH 3, 1921

PRESIDENT—Woodrow Wilson, of New Jersey (Democratic). (Oath administered March 5, 1917.) VICE-PRESIDENT—Thomas R. Marshall, of Indiana. SECRETARY OF STATE—Robert Lansing, of New York, continued from preceding administration. Frank L. Polk, of New York (Under Secretary), ad interim, February 14, 1920, to March 13, 1920. Bainbridge Colby, of New York, March 22, 1920; entered upon duties March 23, 1920. SECRETARY OF THE TREASURY—William Gibbs McAdoo, of New York, continued from preceding administration. Carter Glass, of Virginia, December 6, 1918; entered upon duties December 16, 1918. David F. Houston, of Missouri, January 31, 1920; entered upon duties February 2, 1920. SECRETARY OF WAR—Newton D. Baker, of Ohio, continued from preceding administration. ATTORNEY GENERAL—Thomas Watt Gregory, of Texas, continued from preceding administration. A. Mitchell Palmer, of Pennsylvania, March 5, 1919. POSTMASTER GENERAL—Albert Sidney Burleson, of Texas, continued from preceding administration. Albert Sidney Burleson, of Texas, recommissioned January 24, 1918. SECRETARY OF THE NAVY—Josephus Daniels, of North Carolina, continued from preceding administration. SECRETARY OF THE INTERIOR—Franklin Knight Lane, of California, continued from preceding administration. John Barton Payne, of Illinois, February 28, 1920; entered upon duties March 13, 1920. SECRETARY OF AGRICULTURE—David Franklin Houston, of Missouri, continued from preceding administration. Edwin T. Meredith, of Iowa, January 31, 1920; entered upon duties February 2, 1920. SECRETARY OF COMMERCE—William C. Redfield, of New York, continued from preceding administration. Joshua Willis Alexander, of Missouri, December 11, 1919; entered upon duties December 16, 1919. SECRETARY OF LABOR—William Bauchop Wilson, of Pennsylvania, continued from preceding administration.

**65th Congress**

1st Session: Apr. 2, 1917–Oct. 6, 1917; 2d Session: Dec. 3, 1917–Nov. 21, 1918; 3d Session: Dec. 2, 1918–Mar. 3, 1919; Special Session of the Senate: Mar. 5, 1917–Mar. 16, 1917.

President pro tempore of the Senate: Willard Saulsbury, of Delaware (continued from preceding Congress). Speaker of the House: James B. Clark, of Missouri (reelected Apr. 2, 1917).

Senate: 53 Democratic; 42 Republican
House: 216 Democratic; 210 Republican; 6 other

**66th Congress**

1st Session: May 19, 1919–Nov. 19, 1919; 2d Session: Dec. 1, 1919–June 5, 1920; 3d Session: Dec. 6, 1920–Mar. 3, 1921.

President pro tempore of the Senate: Albert B. Cummins, of Iowa (elected May 19, 1919). Speaker of the House: Frederick H. Gillett, of Massachusetts (elected May 19, 1919).

Senate: 49 Republican; 47 Democratic
House: 240 Republican; 190 Democratic; 3 other

### Administration of WARREN G. HARDING

### MARCH 4, 1921, TO AUGUST 2, 1923

PRESIDENT—Warren G. Harding, of Ohio (Republican) (died August 2, 1923). VICE-PRESIDENT—Calvin Coolidge, of Massachusetts. SECRETARY OF STATE—Bainbridge Colby, of New York, continued from preceding administration. Charles Evans Hughes, of New York, March 4, 1921; entered upon duties March 5, 1921. SECRETARY OF THE TREASURY—David F. Houston, of Missouri, continued from preceding administration. Andrew W. Mellon, of Pennsylvania, March 4, 1921; entered upon duties March 5, 1921. SECRETARY OF WAR—Newton D. Baker, of Ohio, continued from preceding administration. John W. Weeks, of Massachusetts, March 5, 1921. ATTORNEY GENERAL—A. Mitchell Palmer, of Pennsylvania, continued from preceding administration. Harry M. Daugherty, of Ohio, March 5, 1921. POSTMASTER GENERAL—Albert Sidney Burleson, of Texas, continued from preceding administration. Will H. Hays, of Indiana, March 5, 1921. Hubert Work, of Colorado, March 4, 1922. Harry S. New, of Indiana, February 27, 1923; entered upon duties March 5, 1923. SECRETARY OF THE NAVY—Josephus Daniels, of North Carolina, continued from preceding administration. Edwin Denby, of Michigan, March 5, 1921. SECRETARY OF THE INTERIOR—John Barton Payne, of Illinois, continued from preceding administration. Albert B. Fall, of New Mexico, March 5, 1921. Hubert Work, of Colorado, February 27, 1923; entered upon duties March 5, 1923. SECRETARY OF AGRICULTURE—Edwin T. Meredith, of Iowa, continued from preceding administration. Henry C. Wallace, of Iowa, March 5, 1921. SECRETARY OF COMMERCE—Joshua Willis Alexander, of Missouri, continued from preceding administration. Herbert C. Hoover, of California, March 5, 1921. SECRETARY OF LABOR—William Bauchop Wilson, of Pennsylvania, continued from preceding administration. James J. Davis, of Pennsylvania, March 5, 1921.

### First Administration of CALVIN COOLIDGE

### AUGUST 3, 1923, TO MARCH 3, 1925

PRESIDENT—Calvin Coolidge, of Massachusetts (Republican). SECRETARY OF STATE—Charles Evans Hughes, of New York, continued from preceding administration. SECRETARY OF THE TREASURY—Andrew W. Mellon, of Pennsylvania, continued from preceding administration. SECRETARY OF WAR—John W. Weeks, of Massachusetts, continued from preceding administration. ATTORNEY GENERAL—Harry M. Daugherty, of Ohio, continued from preceding administration. Harlan F. Stone, of New York, April 7, 1924; entered upon duties April 9, 1924. POSTMASTER GENERAL—Harry S. New, of Indiana, continued from preceding administration. SECRETARY OF THE NAVY—Edwin Denby, of Michigan, continued from preceding administration. Curtis D. Wilbur, of California, March 18, 1924. SECRETARY OF THE INTERIOR—Hubert Work, of Colorado, continued from preceding administration. SECRETARY OF AGRICULTURE—Henry C. Wallace, of Iowa, continued from preceding administration (died October 25, 1924). Howard M. Gore, of West Virginia (Assistant Secretary), ad interim, October 26, 1924, to November 22, 1924. Howard M. Gore, of West Virginia, November 21, 1924; entered upon duties November 22, 1924. SECRETARY OF COMMERCE—

Herbert C. Hoover, of California, continued from preceding administration. SECRETARY OF LABOR—James J. Davis, of Pennsylvania, continued from preceding administration.

**67th Congress**

1st Session: Apr. 11, 1921–Nov. 23, 1921; 2d Session: Dec. 5, 1921–Sept. 22, 1922; 3d Session: Nov. 20, 1922–Dec. 4, 1922; 4th Session: Dec. 4, 1922–March 3, 1923; Special Session of the Senate: Mar. 4, 1921–Mar. 15, 1921.

President pro tempore of the Senate: Albert B. Cummins, of Iowa (reelected Mar. 7, 1921). Speaker of the House: Frederick H. Gillett, of Massachusetts (reelected Apr. 11, 1921).

Senate: 59 Republican; 37 Democratic
House: 303 Republican; 131 Democratic; 1 other

**68th Congress**

1st Session: Dec. 3, 1923–June 7, 1924; 2d Session: Dec. 1, 1924–Mar. 3, 1925.

President pro tempore of the Senate: Albert B. Cummins, of Iowa (continued from preceding Congress). Speaker of the House: Frederick H. Gillett, of Massachusetts (reelected Dec. 3, 1923).

Senate: 51 Republican; 43 Democratic; 2 other
House: 225 Republican; 205 Democratic; 5 other

## Second Administration of CALVIN COOLIDGE

### MARCH 4, 1925, TO MARCH 3, 1929

PRESIDENT—Calvin Coolidge, of Massachusetts (Republican). VICE-PRESIDENT—Charles G. Dawes, of Illinois. SECRETARY OF STATE—Charles Evans Hughes, of New York, continued from preceding administration. Frank B. Kellogg, of Minnesota, February 16, 1925; entered upon duties March 5, 1925. SECRETARY OF THE TREASURY—Andrew W. Mellon, of Pennsylvania, continued from preceding administration. SECRETARY OF WAR—John W. Weeks, of Massachusetts, continued from preceding administration. Dwight F. Davis, of Missouri, October 13, 1925; entered upon duties October 14, 1925. ATTORNEY GENERAL—James M. Beck, of Pennsylvania (Solicitor General), ad interim, March 4, 1925, to March 16, 1925. John G. Sargent, of Vermont, March 17, 1925; entered upon duties March 18, 1925. POSTMASTER GENERAL—Harry S. New, of Indiana, continued from preceding administration. Harry S. New, of Indiana, recommissioned March 5, 1925. SECRETARY OF THE NAVY—Curtis D. Wilbur, of California, continued from preceding administration. SECRETARY OF THE INTERIOR—Hubert Work, of Colorado, continued from preceding administration. Roy O. West, of Illinois, ad interim, July 25, 1928, to January 21, 1929. Roy O. West, January 21, 1929. SECRETARY OF AGRICULTURE—Howard M. Gore, of West Virginia, continued from preceding administration. William M. Jardine, of Kansas, February 18, 1925; entered upon duties March 5, 1925. SECRETARY OF COMMERCE—Herbert C. Hoover, of California, continued from preceding administration. William F. Whiting, of Massachusetts, ad interim, August 21, 1928, to December 11, 1928. William F. Whiting, December 11, 1928. SECRETARY OF LABOR—James J. Davis, of Pennsylvania, continued from preceding administration.

**69th Congress**

1st Session: Dec. 7, 1925–July 3, 1926; Nov. 10, 1926; 2d Session: Dec. 6, 1926–Mar. 3, 1927; Special Session of the Senate: Mar. 4, 1925–Mar. 18, 1925.

President pro tempore of the Senate: Albert B. Cummins, of Iowa (continued from preceding Congress); George H. Moses, of New Hampshire (elected Mar. 6, 1925). Speaker of the House: Nicholas Longworth, of Ohio (elected Dec. 7, 1925).

Senate: 56 Republican; 39 Democratic; 1 other
House: 247 Republican; 183 Democratic; 4 other

**70th Congress**

1st Session: Dec. 5, 1927–May 29, 1928; 2d Session: Dec. 3, 1928–Mar. 3, 1929.

President pro tempore of the Senate: George H. Moses, of New Hampshire (reelected Dec. 15, 1927). Speaker of the House: Nicholas Longworth, of Ohio (reelected Dec. 15, 1927).

Senate: 49 Republican; 46 Democratic; 1 other
House: 237 Republican; 195 Democratic; 3 other

## Administration of HERBERT C. HOOVER

### MARCH 4, 1929, TO MARCH 3, 1933

PRESIDENT—Herbert C. Hoover, of California (Republican). VICE-PRESIDENT—Charles Curtis, of Kansas. SECRETARY OF STATE—Frank B. Kellogg, of Minnesota, continued from preceding administration. Henry L. Stimson, of New York, March 4, 1929; entered upon duties March 29, 1929. SECRETARY OF THE TREASURY—Andrew W. Mellon, of Pennsylvania, continued from preceding administration. Ogden L. Mills, of New York, February 10, 1932; entered upon duties February 13, 1932. SECRETARY OF WAR—Dwight F. Davis, of Missouri, continued from preceding administration. James W. Good, of Illinois, March 5, 1929; entered upon duties March 6, 1929. Patrick J. Hurley, of Oklahoma, December 9, 1929. ATTORNEY GENERAL—John G. Sargent, of Vermont, continued from preceding administration. James DeWitt Mitchell, of Minnesota, March 5, 1929; entered upon duties March 6, 1929. POSTMASTER GENERAL—Harry S. New, of Indiana, continued from preceding administration. Walter F. Brown, of Ohio, March 5, 1929; entered upon duties March 6, 1929. SECRETARY OF THE NAVY—Curtis D. Wilbur, of California, continued from preceding administration. Charles F. Adams, of Massachusetts, March 5, 1929. SECRETARY OF THE INTERIOR—Roy O. West, of Illinois, continued from preceding administration. Ray L. Wilbur, of California, March 5, 1929. SECRETARY OF AGRICULTURE—William M. Jardine, of Kansas, continued from preceding administration. Arthur M. Hyde, of Missouri, March 5, 1929; entered upon duties March 6, 1929. SECRETARY OF COMMERCE—William F. Whiting, of Massachusetts, continued from preceding administration. Robert P. Lamont, of Illinois, March 5, 1929. Roy D. Chapin, of Michigan, ad interim, August 8, 1932, to December 14, 1932. Roy D. Chapin, of Michigan, December 14, 1932. SECRETARY OF LABOR—James J. Davis, of Pennsylvania, continued from preceding administration. William N. Doak, of Virginia, December 8, 1930; entered upon duties December 9, 1930.

**71st Congress**

1st Session: Apr. 15, 1929–Nov. 22, 1929; 2d Session: Dec. 2, 1929–July 3, 1930; 3d Session: Dec. 1, 1930–Mar. 3, 1931; Special Sessions of the Senate: Mar. 4, 1929–Mar. 5, 1929; July 7, 1930–July 21, 1930.

President pro tempore of the Senate: George H. Moses, of New Hampshire (continued from preceding Congress). Speaker of the House: Nicholas Longworth, of Ohio (reelected Apr. 15, 1929).

Senate: 56 Republican; 39 Democratic; 1 other
House: 267 Republican; 167 Democratic; 1 other

**72d Congress**

1st Session: Dec. 7, 1931–July 16, 1932; 2d Session: Dec. 15, 1932–Mar. 3, 1933.

President pro tempore of the Senate: George H. Moses, of New Hampshire (continued from preceding Congress). Speaker of the House: John N. Garner, of Texas (elected Dec. 7, 1931).

Senate: 48 Republican; 47 Democratic; 1 other
House: 220 Democratic; 214 Republican; 1 other

## First Administration of FRANKLIN DELANO ROOSEVELT

### MARCH 4, 1933, TO JANUARY 20, 1937

PRESIDENT—Franklin Delano Roosevelt, of New York (Democratic). VICE-PRESIDENT—John N. Garner, of Texas. SECRETARY OF STATE—Cordell Hull, of Tennessee, March 4, 1933. SECRETARY OF THE TREASURY—William H. Woodin, of New York, March 4, 1933. Henry Morgenthau, Jr., of New York (Under Secretary), ad interim, January 1, 1934, to January 8, 1934. Henry Morgenthau, Jr., of New York, January 8, 1934. SECRETARY OF WAR—George H. Dern, of Utah, March 4, 1933. ATTORNEY GENERAL—Homer S. Cummings, of Connecticut, March 4, 1933. POSTMASTER GENERAL—James A. Farley, of New York, March 4, 1933. SECRETARY OF THE NAVY—Claude A. Swanson, of Virginia, March 4, 1933. SECRETARY OF THE INTERIOR—Harold L. Ickes, of Illinois, March 4, 1933. SECRETARY OF AGRICULTURE—Henry A. Wallace, of Iowa, March 4, 1933. SECRETARY OF COMMERCE—Daniel C. Roper, of South Carolina, March 4, 1933. SECRETARY OF LABOR—Frances Perkins, of New York, March 4, 1933.

**73d Congress**

1st Session: March 9, 1933–June 15, 1933; 2d Session: Jan. 3, 1934–June 18, 1934; Special Session of the Senate: Mar. 4, 1933–Mar. 6, 1933.

President pro tempore of the Senate: Key Pittman, of Nevada (elected Mar. 9, 1933). Speaker of the House: Henry T. Rainey, of Illinois (elected Mar. 9, 1933).

Senate: 60 Democratic; 35 Republican; 1 other
House: 310 Democratic; 117 Republican; 5 other

**74th Congress**

1st Session: Jan. 3, 1935–Aug. 26, 1935; 2d Session: Jan. 3, 1936–June 20, 1936.

President pro tempore of the Senate: Key Pittman, of Nevada (reelected Jan. 7, 1935). Speaker of the House: Joseph W. Byrnes, of Tennessee (elected Jan. 3, 1935); William Bankhead, of Alabama (elected June 4, 1936).

Senate: 69 Democratic; 25 Republican; 2 other
House: 319 Democratic; 103 Republican; 10 other

## Second Administration of FRANKLIN DELANO ROOSEVELT

### JANUARY 20, 1937, TO JANUARY 20, 1941

PRESIDENT—Franklin Delano Roosevelt, of New York (Democratic). VICE-PRESIDENT—John N. Garner, of Texas. SECRETARY OF STATE—Cordell Hull, of Tennessee, continued from preceding administration. SECRETARY OF THE TREASURY—Henry Morgenthau, Jr., of New York, continued from preceding administration. SECRETARY OF WAR—George H. Dern, of Utah, continued from preceding administration (died August 27, 1936). Harry H. Woodring, of Kansas (Assistant Secretary), ad interim, September 25, 1936, to May 6, 1937. Harry H. Woodring, of Kansas, May 6, 1937. Henry L. Stimson, of New York, July 10, 1940. ATTORNEY GENERAL—Homer S. Cummings, of Connecticut, continued from preceding administration. Frank Murphy, of Michigan, ad interim, January 2, 1939, to January 17, 1939. Frank Murphy, of Michigan, January 17, 1939. Robert H. Jackson, of New York, January 18, 1940. POSTMASTER GENERAL—James A. Farley, of New York, continued from preceding administration. James A. Farley, of New York, recommissioned January 22, 1937. Frank C. Walker, of Pennsylvania, September 10, 1940. SECRETARY OF THE NAVY—Claude A. Swanson, of Virginia, continued from preceding administration (died July 7, 1939). Charles Edison, of New Jersey, Acting Secretary from August 5, 1939, to December 30, 1939. Charles Edison, of New Jersey (Assistant Secretary), ad interim, December 30, 1939, to January 11, 1940. Charles Edison, of New Jersey, January 11, 1940. Frank Knox, of Illinois, July 10, 1940. SECRETARY OF THE INTERIOR—Harold L. Ickes, of Illinois, continued from preceding administration. SECRETARY OF AGRICULTURE—Henry A. Wallace, of Iowa, continued from preceding administration. Claude R. Wickard, of Indiana, August 27, 1940; entered upon duties September 5, 1940. SECRETARY OF COMMERCE—Daniel C. Roper, of South Carolina, continued from preceding administration. Harry L. Hopkins, of New York, ad interim, December 24, 1938, to January 23, 1939. Harry L. Hopkins, of New York, January 23, 1939. Jesse H. Jones, of Texas, September 16, 1940; entered upon duties September 19, 1940. SECRETARY OF LABOR—Frances Perkins, of New York, continued from preceding administration.

**75th Congress**

1st Session: Jan. 5, 1937–Aug. 21, 1937; 2d Session: Nov. 15, 1937–Dec. 21, 1937; 3d Session: Jan. 3, 1938–June 16, 1938.

President pro tempore of the Senate: Key Pittman, of Nevada (continued from preceding Congress). Speaker of the House: William B. Bankhead, of Alabama (reelected Jan. 5, 1937).

Senate: 76 Democratic; 16 Republican; 4 other
House: 331 Democratic; 89 Republican; 13 other

**76th Congress**

Jan. 3, 1939–Aug. 5, 1939; 2d Session: Sept. 21, 1939–Nov. 3, 1939; 3d Session: Jan. 3, 1940–Jan. 3, 1941.

President pro tempore of the Senate: Key Pittman, of Nevada (continued from preceding Congress); William H. King, of Utah (elected Nov. 19, 1940). Speaker of the House: William B. Bankhead, of Alabama (reelected Jan. 3, 1940); Sam Rayburn, of Texas (elected Sept. 16, 1940).

Senate: 69 Democratic; 23 Republican; 4 other
House: 261 Democratic; 164 Republican; 4 other

---

## Third Administration of FRANKLIN DELANO ROOSEVELT

## JANUARY 20, 1941, TO JANUARY 20, 1945

PRESIDENT—Franklin Delano Roosevelt, of New York (Democratic). VICE-PRESIDENT—Henry A. Wallace, of Iowa. SECRETARY OF STATE—Cordell Hull, of Tennessee, continued from preceding administration. Edward R. Stettinius, of Virginia, November 30, 1944; entered upon duties December 1, 1944. SECRETARY OF THE TREASURY—Henry Morgenthau, Jr., of New York, continued from preceding administration. SECRETARY OF WAR—Henry L. Stimson, of New York, continued from preceding administration. ATTORNEY GENERAL—Robert H. Jackson, of New York, continued from preceding administration. Francis Biddle, of Pennsylvania, September 5, 1941. POSTMASTER GENERAL—Frank C. Walker, of Pennsylvania, continued from preceding administration. Frank C. Walker, of Pennsylvania, recommissioned January 27, 1941. SECRETARY OF THE NAVY—Frank Knox, of Illinois, continued from preceding administration (died April 28, 1944). James V. Forrestal, of New York, May 18, 1944. SECRETARY OF THE INTERIOR—Harold L. Ickes, of Illinois, continued from preceding administration. SECRETARY OF AGRICULTURE—Claude R. Wickard, of Indiana, continued from preceding administration. SECRETARY OF COMMERCE—Jesse H. Jones, of Texas, continued from preceding administration. SECRETARY OF LABOR—Frances Perkins, of New York, continued from preceding administration.

**77th Congress**

1st Session: Jan. 3, 1941–Jan. 2, 1942; 2d Session: Jan. 5, 1942–Dec. 16, 1942.

President pro tempore of the Senate: Pat Harrison, of Mississippi (elected Jan. 6, 1941); Carter Glass, of Virginia (elected July 10, 1941). Speaker of the House: Sam Rayburn, of Texas (reelected Jan. 3, 1941).

Senate: 66 Democratic; 28 Republican; 2 other
House: 268 Democratic; 162 Republican; 5 other

**78th Congress**

1st Session: Jan. 6, 1943–Dec. 21, 1943; 2d Session: Jan. 10, 1944–Dec. 19, 1944.

President pro tempore of the Senate: Carter Glass, of Virginia (continued from preceding Congress). Speaker of the House: Sam Rayburn, of Texas (reelected Jan. 6, 1943).

Senate: 57 Democratic; 38 Republican; 1 other
House: 222 Democratic; 208 Republican; 5 other

---

## Fourth Administration of FRANKLIN DELANO ROOSEVELT

## JANUARY 20, 1945, TO APRIL 12, 1945

PRESIDENT—Franklin Delano Roosevelt, of New York (Democratic) (died April 12, 1945). VICE-PRESIDENT—Harry S. Truman, of Missouri. SECRETARY OF STATE—Edward R. Stettinius, of Virginia, continued from preceding administration. SECRETARY OF THE TREASURY—Henry Morgenthau, Jr., of New York, continued from preceding administration. SECRETARY OF WAR—Henry L. Stimson, of New York, continued from preceding administration. ATTORNEY GENERAL—Francis Biddle, of Pennsylvania, continued from preceding administration. POSTMASTER GENERAL—Frank C. Walker, of Pennsylvania, continued from preceding administration. Frank C. Walker, of Pennsylvania, recommissioned February 6, 1945. SECRETARY OF THE NAVY—James V. Forrestal, of New York, continued from preceding administration. SECRETARY OF THE INTERIOR—Harold L. Ickes, of Illinois, continued from preceding administration. SECRETARY OF AGRICULTURE—Claude R. Wickard, of Indiana, continued from preceding administration. SECRETARY OF COMMERCE—Jesse H. Jones, of Texas, continued from preceding administration. Henry A. Wallace, of Iowa, March 1, 1945; entered upon duties March 2, 1945. SECRETARY OF LABOR—Frances Perkins, of New York, continued from preceding administration.

---

## First Administration of HARRY S TRUMAN

## APRIL 12, 1945, TO JANUARY 20, 1949

PRESIDENT—Harry S Truman, of Missouri (Democratic). SECRETARY OF STATE—Edward R. Stettinius, of Virginia, continued from preceding administration. James F. Byrnes, of South Carolina, July 2, 1945; entered upon duties July 3, 1945. George C. Marshall, of Pennsylvania, January 8, 1947; entered upon duties January 21, 1947. SECRETARY OF THE TREASURY—Henry Morgenthau, Jr., of New York, continued from preceding administration. Fred M. Vinson, of Kentucky, July 18, 1945; entered upon duties July 23, 1945. John W. Snyder, of Missouri, June 12, 1946; entered upon duties June 25, 1946. SECRETARY OF DEFENSE—James Forrestal, of New York, July 26, 1947; entered upon duties September 17, 1947. SECRETARY OF WAR—Henry L. Stimson, of New York, continued from preceding administration. Robert Porter Patterson, of New York, September 26, 1945; entered upon duties September 27, 1945. Kenneth C. Royall, of North Carolina, July 21, 1947; entered upon duties July 25, 1947, and served until September 17, 1947. ATTORNEY GENERAL—Francis Biddle, of Pennsylvania, continued from preceding administration. Tom C. Clark, of Texas, June 15, 1945; entered upon duties September 27, 1945. POSTMASTER GENERAL—Frank Walker, of Pennsylvania, from preceding administration. Robert E. Hannegan, of Missouri, May 8, 1945; entered upon duties July 1, 1945. Jesse M. Donaldson, of Missouri, December 16, 1947. SECRETARY OF THE NAVY—James V. Forrestal, of New York, continued from preceding administration; served until September 17, 1947. SECRETARY OF THE INTERIOR—Harold L. Ickes, of Illinois, continued from preceding administration. Julius A. Krug, of Wisconsin, March 6, 1946; entered upon duties March 18, 1946. SECRETARY OF AGRICULTURE—Claude R. Wickard, of Indiana, continued from preceding administration. Clinton P. Anderson, of New Mexico, June 2, 1945; entered upon duties June 30, 1945. Charles F. Brannan, of Colorado, May 29, 1948; entered upon duties June 2, 1948. SECRETARY OF COMMERCE—Henry A. Wallace, of Iowa, continued from preceding administration. William Averell Harriman, of New York, ad interim, September 28, 1946, to January 28, 1947. William Averell Harriman, of New York, January 28, 1947. Charles Sawyer, of Ohio, May 6, 1948. SECRETARY OF LABOR—Frances Perkins, of New York, continued from preceding administration. Lewis B. Schwellenbach, of Washington, June 1, 1945; entered upon duties July 1, 1945 (died June 10, 1948). Maurice J. Tobin, of Massachusetts, ad interim, August 13, 1948.

**79th Congress**

1st Session: Jan. 3, 1945–Dec. 21, 1945; 2d Session: Jan. 14, 1946–Aug. 2, 1946.

President pro tempore of the Senate: Kenneth McKellar, of Tennessee (elected Jan. 6, 1945). Speaker of the House: Sam Rayburn, of Texas (reelected Jan. 3, 1945).

Senate: 56 Democratic; 38 Republican; 1 other
House: 242 Democratic; 190 Republican; 2 other

**80th Congress**

1st Session: Jan. 3, 1947–Dec. 19, 1947; 2d Session: Jan. 6, 1948–Dec. 31, 1948.

President pro tempore of the Senate: Arthur H. Vandenberg, of Michigan (elected Jan. 4, 1947). Speaker of the House: Joseph W. Martin, Jr., of Massachusetts (elected Jan. 3, 1947).
Senate: 51 Republican; 45 Democratic
House: 245 Republican; 188 Democratic; 1 other

---

**Second Administration of HARRY S TRUMAN**

**JANUARY 20, 1949, TO JANUARY 20, 1953**

PRESIDENT—Harry S Truman, of Missouri (Democratic). VICE-PRESIDENT—Alben W. Barkley, of Kentucky. SECRETARY OF STATE—Dean G. Acheson, of Connecticut, January 19, 1949; entered upon duties January 21, 1949. SECRETARY OF THE TREASURY—John W. Snyder, of Missouri, continued from preceding administration. SECRETARY OF DEFENSE—James V. Forrestal, of New York, continued from preceding administration. Louis A. Johnson, of West Virginia, March 23, 1949; entered upon duties March 28, 1949. George C. Marshall, of Pennsylvania, September 20, 1950; entered upon duties September 21, 1950. Robert A. Lovett, of New York, September 14, 1951; entered upon duties September 17, 1951. ATTORNEY GENERAL—Tom C. Clark, of Texas, continued from preceding administration. J. Howard McGrath, of Rhode Island, August 19, 1949; entered upon duties August 24, 1949. James P. McGranery, of Pennsylvania, May 21, 1952; entered upon duties May 27, 1952. POSTMASTER GENERAL—Jesse M. Donaldson, of Missouri, continued from preceding administration. Jesse M. Donaldson, of Missouri, recommissioned February 8, 1949. SECRETARY OF THE INTERIOR—Julius A. Krug, of Wisconsin, continued from preceding administration. Oscar L. Chapman, of Colorado (Under Secretary), ad interim, December 1, 1949, to January 19, 1950. Oscar L. Chapman, of Colorado, January 19, 1950. SECRETARY OF AGRICULTURE—Charles F. Brannan, of Colorado, continued from preceding administration. SECRETARY OF COMMERCE—Charles Sawyer, of Ohio, continued from preceding administration. SECRETARY OF LABOR—Maurice J. Tobin, of Massachusetts, ad interim, continued from preceding administration. Maurice J. Tobin, of Massachusetts, recommissioned February 1, 1949.

**81st Congress**
1st Session: Jan. 3, 1949–Oct. 19, 1949; 2d Session: Jan. 3, 1950–Jan. 2, 1951.
President pro tempore of the Senate: Kenneth D. McKellar, of Tennessee (elected Jan. 3, 1949). Speaker of the House: Sam Rayburn, of Texas (elected Jan. 3, 1949).
Senate: 54 Democratic; 42 Republican
House: 263 Democratic; 171 Republican; 1 other

**82d Congress**
1st Session: Jan. 3, 1951–Oct. 20, 1951; 2d Session: Jan. 8, 1952—July 7, 1952.
President pro tempore of the Senate: Kenneth D. McKellar, of Tennessee (continued from preceding Congress). Speaker of the House: Sam Rayburn, of Texas (reelected Jan. 3, 1951).
Senate: 49 Democratic; 47 Republican
House: 234 Democratic; 199 Republican; 1 other

---

**First Administration of DWIGHT D. EISENHOWER**

**JANUARY 20, 1953, TO JANUARY 20, 1957**

PRESIDENT—Dwight D. Eisenhower, of New York (Republican). VICE-PRESIDENT—Richard M. Nixon, of California. SECRETARY OF STATE—John Foster Dulles, of New York, January 21, 1953. SECRETARY OF THE TREASURY—George M. Humphrey, of Ohio, January 21, 1953. SECRETARY OF DEFENSE—Charles E. Wilson, of Michigan, January 26, 1953; entered upon duties January 28, 1953. ATTORNEY GENERAL—Herbert Brownell, Jr., of New York, January 21, 1953. POSTMASTER GENERAL—Arthur E. Summerfield, of Michigan, January 21, 1953. SECRETARY OF THE INTERIOR—Douglas McKay, of Oregon, January 21, 1953. Frederick A. Seaton, of Nebraska, June 6, 1956; entered upon duties June 8, 1956. SECRETARY OF AGRICULTURE—Ezra Taft Benson, of Utah, January 21, 1953. SECRETARY OF COMMERCE—Sinclair Weeks, of Massachusetts, January 21, 1953. SECRETARY OF LABOR—Martin P. Durkin, of Maryland, January 21, 1953. James P. Mitchell, of New Jersey, ad interim, October 9, 1953, to January 19, 1954. James P. Mitchell, of New Jersey, January 19, 1954. SECRETARY OF HEALTH, EDUCATION, AND WELFARE—Oveta Culp Hobby, of Texas, April 10, 1953; entered upon duties April 11, 1953. Marion B. Folsom, of New York, July 20, 1955; entered upon duties August 1, 1955.

**83d Congress**
1st Session: Jan. 3, 1953—Aug. 3, 1953; 2d Session: Jan. 6, 1954–Dec. 2, 1954.
President pro tempore of the Senate: Styles Bridges, of New Hampshire (elected Jan. 3, 1953). Speaker of the House: Joseph W. Martin, Jr., of Massachusetts (elected Jan. 3, 1953).
Senate: 48 Republican; 47 Democratic; 1 other
House: 221 Republican; 211 Democratic; 1 other

**84th Congress**
1st Session: Jan. 5, 1955–Aug. 2, 1955; 2d Session: Jan. 3, 1956–July 27, 1956.
President pro tempore of the Senate: Walter F. George, of Georgia (elected Jan. 5, 1955). Speaker of the House: Sam Rayburn, of Texas (elected Jan. 5, 1955).
Senate: 48 Democratic; 47 Republican; 1 other
House: 232 Democratic; 203 Republican

---

**Second Administration of DWIGHT D. EISENHOWER**

**JANUARY 20, 1957, TO JANUARY 20, 1961**

PRESIDENT—Dwight D. Eisenhower, of Pennsylvania (Republican). VICE-PRESIDENT—Richard M. Nixon, of California. SECRETARY OF STATE—John Foster Dulles, of New York, continued from preceding administration. Christian A. Herter, of Massachusetts, April 21, 1959; entered upon duties April 22, 1959. SECRETARY OF THE TREASURY—George M. Humphrey, of Ohio, continued from preceding administration. Robert Bernerd Anderson, of Connecticut, July 2, 1957; entered upon duties July 29, 1957. SECRETARY OF DEFENSE—Charles E. Wilson, of Michigan, continued from preceding administration. Neil H. McElroy, of Ohio, August 19, 1957; entered upon duties October 9, 1957. Thomas S. Gates, Jr., of Pennsylvania, ad interim, December 1, 1959, to January 26, 1960. Thomas S. Gates, Jr., of Pennsylvania, January 26, 1960. ATTORNEY GENERAL—Herbert Brownell, Jr., of New York, continued from preceding administration. William P. Rogers, of Maryland, ad interim, November 8, 1957, to January 27, 1958. William P. Rogers, of Maryland, January 27, 1958. POSTMASTER GENERAL—Arthur E. Summerfield, of Michigan, continued from preceding administration. Arthur E. Summerfield, of Michigan, recommissioned February 4, 1957. SECRETARY OF THE INTERIOR—Frederick A. Seaton, of Nebraska, continued from preceding administration. SECRETARY OF AGRICULTURE—Ezra Taft Benson, of Utah, continued from preceding administration. SECRETARY OF COMMERCE—Sinclair Weeks, of Massachusetts, continued from preceding administration. Lewis L. Strauss, of New York, ad interim, November 13, 1958, to June 27, 1959. Frederick H. Mueller, of Michigan (Under Secretary), ad interim, July 21, 1959, to August 6, 1959. Frederick H. Mueller, of Michigan, August 6, 1959. SECRETARY OF LABOR—James P. Mitchell, of New Jersey, continued from preceding administration. SECRETARY OF HEALTH, EDUCATION, AND WELFARE—Marion B. Folsom, of New York, continued from preceding administration. Arthur S. Flemming, of Ohio, July 9, 1958; entered upon duties August 1, 1958.

**85th Congress**
1st Session: Jan. 3, 1957–Aug. 30, 1957; 2d Session: Jan. 7, 1958–Aug. 24, 1958.
President pro tempore of the Senate: Carl Hayden, of Arizona (elected Jan. 3, 1957). Speaker of the House: Sam Rayburn, of Texas (reelected Jan. 3, 1957).
Senate: 49 Democratic; 47 Republican
House: 233 Democratic; 200 Republican

**86th Congress**
1st Session: Jan. 7, 1959–Sept. 15, 1959; 2d Session: Jan. 6, 1960–Sept. 1, 1960.
President pro tempore of the Senate: Carl Hayden, of Arizona (continued from preceding Congress). Speaker of the House: Sam Rayburn, of Texas (reelected Jan. 7, 1959).
Senate: 64 Democratic; 34 Republican
House: 283 Democratic; 153 Republican

---

**Administration of JOHN F. KENNEDY**

**JANUARY 20, 1961, TO NOVEMBER 22, 1963**

PRESIDENT—John F. Kennedy, of Massachusetts (Democratic) (died November 22, 1963). VICE-PRESIDENT—Lyndon B. Johnson, of Texas. SECRETARY OF STATE—Dean Rusk, of New York, January 20, 1961. SECRETARY OF THE TREASURY—C. Douglas Dillon, of Washington, D.C., January 20, 1961. SECRETARY OF DEFENSE—Robert S. McNamara, of Michigan, January 20, 1961. ATTORNEY GENERAL—Robert F. Kennedy, of Massachusetts, January 20, 1961. POSTMASTER GENERAL—J. Edward Day, of California, January 20, 1961, to August 9, 1963. John A. Gronouski of Wisconsin, September 10, 1963. SECRETARY OF THE INTERIOR—Stewart L. Udall, of Arizona, January 20, 1961. SECRETARY OF AGRICULTURE—Orville L. Freeman, of Minnesota, January 20, 1961. SECRETARY OF COMMERCE—Luther H. Hodges, of North Carolina, January 20, 1961. SECRETARY OF LABOR—Arthur J. Goldberg, of Washington, D.C., January 20, 1961. W. Willard Wirtz, of Illinois, September 25, 1962. SECRETARY OF HEALTH, EDUCATION, AND WELFARE—Abraham A. Ribicoff, of Connecticut, January 21, 1961, to July 13, 1962. Anthony J. Celebrezze, of Ohio, July 31, 1962.

### First Administration of LYNDON B. JOHNSON
### NOVEMBER 22, 1963, TO JANUARY 20, 1965

PRESIDENT—Lyndon B. Johnson, of Texas (Democratic). SECRETARY OF STATE—Dean Rusk, of New York, continued from preceding administration. SECRETARY OF THE TREASURY—C. Douglas Dillon, of Washington, D.C., continued from preceding administration. SECRETARY OF DEFENSE—Robert S. McNamara, of Michigan, continued from preceding administration. ATTORNEY GENERAL—Robert F. Kennedy, of Massachusetts, continued from preceding administration. Nicholas Katzenbach, of Illinois, ad interim, Sept. 4, 1964. POSTMASTER GENERAL—John S. Gronouski, of Wisconsin, continued from preceding administration. SECRETARY OF THE INTERIOR—Stewart L. Udall, of Arizona, continued from preceding administration. SECRETARY OF AGRICULTURE—Orville L. Freeman of Minnesota, continued from preceding administration. SECRETARY OF COMMERCE—Luther H. Hodges, of North Carolina, continued from preceding administration to January 15, 1965. John T. O'Connor, of New Jersey, January 15, 1965. SECRETARY OF LABOR—W. Willard Wirtz, of Illinois, continued from preceding administration. SECRETARY OF HEALTH, EDUCATION, AND WELFARE—Anthony J. Celebrezze, of Ohio, continued from preceding administration.

**87th Congress**

1st Session: Jan. 3, 1961–Sept. 27, 1961; 2d Session: Jan. 10, 1962–Oct. 13, 1962.

President pro tempore of the Senate: Carl Hayden, of Arizona (continued from preceding Congress). Speaker of the House: Sam Rayburn, of Texas (reelected Jan. 3, 1961); John W. McCormack, of Massachusetts (elected Jan. 10, 1962).

Senate: 65 Democratic; 35 Republican
House: 263 Democratic; 174 Republican

**88th Congress**

1st Session: Jan. 9, 1963–Dec. 30, 1963; 2d Session: Jan. 7, 1964–Oct. 3, 1964.

President pro tempore of the Senate: Carl Hayden, of Arizona (continued from preceding Congress). Speaker of the House: John W. McCormack (reelected Jan. 9, 1963).

Senate: 67 Democratic; 33 Republican
House: 258 Democratic; 177 Republican

---

### Second Administration of LYNDON B. JOHNSON
### JANUARY 20, 1965 TO JANUARY 20, 1969

PRESIDENT—Lyndon B. Johnson, of Texas (Democratic). VICE-PRESIDENT—Hubert H. Humphrey, of Minnesota. SECRETARY OF STATE—Dean Rusk, of New York, continued from preceding administration. SECRETARY OF THE TREASURY—C. Douglas Dillon, of Washington, D.C., continued from preceding administration to March 31, 1965. Henry H. Fowler, of Virginia, April 1, 1965 to December 20, 1968. Joseph W. Barr, of Indiana, December 23, 1968. SECRETARY OF DEFENSE—Robert S. McNamara, continued from preceding administration. Clark Clifford, of Maryland, January 19, 1968. ATTORNEY GENERAL—Nicholas Katzenbach, of Illinois, ad interim, continued from preceding administration, confirmed on Feb. 10, 1965. Ramsey Clark, of Texas, March 2, 1967. POSTMASTER GENERAL—John A. Gronouski, of Wisconsin, continued from preceding administration. Lawrence O'Brien, of Massachusetts, August 29, 1965, to April 10, 1968. Marvin Watson, of Texas, April 10, 1968. SECRETARY OF THE INTERIOR—Stewart L. Udall, of Arizona, continued from preceding administration. SECRETARY OF AGRICULTURE—Orville L. Freeman, of Minnesota, continued from preceding administration. SECRETARY OF COMMERCE—John T. O'Connor, of New Jersey, continued from preceding administration to January 18, 1967. Alexander B. Trowbridge, of New York, May 23, 1967, to February 16, 1968. C. R. Smith, of New York, March 1, 1968. SECRETARY OF LABOR—W. Willard Wirtz, of Illinois, continued from preceding administration. SECRETARY OF HEALTH, EDUCATION, AND WELFARE—Anthony J. Celebrezze, of Ohio, continued from preceding administration. John W. Gardner, of New York, July 27, 1965. Wilbur J. Cohen, of Michigan, May 16, 1968. SECRETARY OF HOUSING AND URBAN DEVELOPMENT—Robert C. Weaver, of Washington, D.C., January 18, 1966 to January 1, 1969. Robert C. Wood, of Massachusetts, January 2, 1969. SECRETARY OF TRANSPORTATION—Alan S. Boyd, of Florida, January 16, 1967.

**89th Congress**

1st Session: Jan. 4, 1965–Oct. 23, 1965; 2d Session: Jan. 10, 1966–Oct. 22, 1966.

President pro tempore of the Senate: Carl Hayden, of Arizona (continued from preceding Congress). Speaker of the House: John W. McCormack, of Massachusetts (reelected Jan. 4, 1965).

Senate: 68 Democratic; 32 Republican
House: 295 Democratic; 140 Republican

**90th Congress**

1st Session: Jan. 10, 1967–Dec. 15, 1967; 2d Session: Jan. 15, 1968–Oct. 14, 1968.

President pro tempore of the Senate: Carl Hayden, of Arizona (continued from preceding Congress). Speaker of the House: John W. McCormack, of Massachusetts (reelected Jan. 10, 1967).

Senate: 64 Democratic; 36 Republican
House: 248 Democratic; 187 Republican

---

### First Administration of RICHARD M. NIXON
### JANUARY 20, 1969, TO JANUARY 20, 1973

PRESIDENT—Richard M. Nixon, of California (Republican). VICE-PRESIDENT—Spiro T. Agnew, of Maryland. SECRETARY OF STATE—William P. Rogers, of New York, January 22, 1969. SECRETARY OF THE TREASURY—David M. Kennedy, of Illinois, January 22, 1969 to February 10, 1971. John B. Connally, of Texas, February 11, 1971. George P. Shultz of Illinois, June 12, 1972. SECRETARY OF DEFENSE—Melvin R. Laird, of Wisconsin, January 22, 1969. ATTORNEY GENERAL—John N. Mitchell, of New York, January 22, 1969. Richard G. Kleindienst, of Arizona, ad interim, Feb. 15, 1972; took office June 12, 1972. POSTMASTER GENERAL—Winton M. Blount, of Alabama, January 22, 1969 to July 1, 1971. This office was then abolished as a cabinet post. SECRETARY OF THE INTERIOR—Walter J. Hickel, of Alaska, January 23, 1969. Fred J. Russell, of California, ad interim, Nov. 26, 1970. Rogers C. B. Morton, of Maryland, Jan. 29, 1971. SECRETARY OF AGRICULTURE—Clifford M. Hardin, of Nebraska, Jan. 22, 1969. Earl L. Butz, of Indiana, Dec. 2, 1971. SECRETARY OF COMMERCE—Maurice H. Stans, of New York, Jan. 22, 1969. Peter G. Peterson, of Illinois, Feb. 21, 1972. SECRETARY OF LABOR—George P. Shultz, of New York, Jan. 22, 1969. James D. Hodgson, of California, July 2, 1970. SECRETARY OF HEALTH, EDUCATION, AND WELFARE—Robert H. Finch, of California, Jan. 22, 1969. Elliot L. Richardson, of Massachusetts, June 15, 1970. SECRETARY OF HOUSING AND URBAN DEVELOPMENT—George W. Romney, of Michigan, Jan. 22, 1969. SECRETARY OF TRANSPORTATION—John A. Volpe, of Massachusetts, Jan. 22, 1969. Claude S. Brinegar, of California, Jan. 18, 1973.

**91st Congress**

1st Session: Jan. 3, 1969–Dec. 23, 1969; 2d Session: Jan. 19, 1970–Jan. 2, 1971.

President pro tempore of the Senate: Richard B. Russell, of Georgia (elected Jan. 3, 1969). Speaker of the House: John W. McCormack, of Massachusetts (reelected Jan. 3, 1969).

Senate: 57 Democratic; 43 Republican
House: 244 Democratic; 191 Republican

**92d Congress**

1st Session: Jan. 21, 1971–Dec. 17, 1971; 2d Session: Jan. 18, 1972–Oct. 18, 1972

President pro tempore of the Senate: James O. Eastland of Mississippi (elected July 28, 1972). (Richard B. Russell, continued from preceding Congress, died in office. Allen J. Ellender of Louisiana, who was elected Jan. 22, 1971, died in office.) Speaker of the House: Carl Albert, of Oklahoma (elected Jan. 21, 1971).

Senate: 54 Democratic; 44 Republican; 1 Independent-Democratic; 1 Conservative-Republican.
House: 255 Democratic; 180 Republican

---

### Second Administration of RICHARD M. NIXON
### JANUARY 20, 1973, TO AUGUST 9, 1974

PRESIDENT—Richard M. Nixon, of California (Republican). Resigned August 9, 1974. VICE PRESIDENT—Spiro T. Agnew, of Maryland. Resigned October 10, 1973. Gerald R. Ford, Jr., of Michigan, December 6, 1973. SECRETARY OF STATE—William P. Rogers, of Maryland, continued from preceding administration. Kenneth Rush, of New York (Deputy Secretary of State), ad interim, September 4, 1973. Henry A. Kissinger, of the District of Columbia, September 21, 1973. SECRETARY OF THE TREASURY—George P. Shultz, of Illinois, continued from preceding administration. William E. Simon, of New Jersey, April 30, 1974. SECRETARY OF DEFENSE—Melvin R. Laird, of Wisconsin, continued from preceding administration. Elliot L. Richardson, of Massachusetts, January 29, 1973. William P. Clements, Jr., of Texas, ad interim, May 26, 1973. James R. Schlesinger, of Virginia, June 28, 1973. ATTORNEY GENERAL—Richard G. Kleindienst, of Arizona, continued from preceding administration. Elliot L. Richardson, of Massachusetts, May 23, 1973. Robert H. Bork, of Pennsylvania (Solicitor General), ad interim, October 20, 1973. William B. Saxbe, of Ohio, Feb. 4, 1974. SECRETARY OF THE INTERIOR—Rogers C.B. Morton, of Maryland, continued from preceding administration. SECRETARY OF AGRICULTURE—Earl L. Butz, of Indiana, continued from preceding administration. SECRETARY OF COMMERCE—Frederick B. Dent, of South Carolina, ad interim, Jan. 18, 1973; took office Feb. 2, 1973. SECRETARY OF LABOR—James D. Hodgson, of California, continued from preceding administration. Peter J. Brennan, of New York, January 31, 1973. SECRETARY OF HEALTH, EDUCATION, AND WELFARE—Elliot L. Richardson, of Massachusetts, continued from preceding administration. Caspar W. Weinberger, of California, February 8, 1973. SECRETARY OF HOUSING AND URBAN DEVELOPMENT—George Romney, of Michigan, continued from preceding administration. James T. Lynn, of Ohio, January 31,

1973. SECRETARY OF TRANSPORTATION—Claude S. Brinegar, of California, continued from preceding administration.

### 93rd Congress

1st Session: Jan. 3, 1973-Dec. 22, 1973; 2nd Session: Jan. 21, 1974-Dec. 20, 1974.

President pro tempore of the Senate: James O. Eastland of Mississippi (continued from preceding Congress). Speaker of the House: Carl Albert, of Oklahoma (continued from preceding Congress).

Senate: 56 Democratic; 42 Republican; 1 Conservative-Republican; 1 Independent

House: 244 Democratic; 191 Republican; 1 Independent

---

## Administration of GERALD R. FORD, JR.

## AUGUST 9, 1974 TO JANUARY 20, 1977

PRESIDENT—Gerald R. Ford, Jr., of Michigan. VICE PRESIDENT—Nelson A. Rockefeller, of New York, December 19, 1974. SECRETARY OF STATE—Henry A. Kissinger, of the District of Columbia, continued from preceding administration. SECRETARY OF THE TREASURY—William E. Simon, of New Jersey, continued from preceding administration. SECRETARY OF DEFENSE—James R. Schlesinger, of Virginia, continued from preceding administration. Donald H. Rumsfeld, of Illinois, November 18, 1975. ATTORNEY GENERAL—William B. Saxbe, of Ohio, continued from preceding administration. Edward H. Levi, of Illinois, February 5, 1975. SECRETARY OF THE INTERIOR—Rogers C.B. Morton, of Maryland, continued from preceding administration. D. Kent Frizzell, of Kansas (Solicitor), ad interim, May 1, 1975. Stanley K. Hathaway of Wyoming, June 11, 1975. D. Kent Frizzell, of Kansas (Solicitor), ad interim, July 25, 1975. Thomas S. Kleppe, of North Dakota, October 9, 1975. SECRETARY OF AGRICULTURE—Earl L. Butz, of Indiana, continued from preceding administration. John A. Knebel, of Oklahoma, ad interim, October 4, 1976. John A. Knebel, November 5, 1976. SECRETARY OF COMMERCE—Frederick B. Dent, of South Carolina, continued from preceding administration. John K. Tabor, of Pennsylvania (Under Secretary), ad interim, March 12, 1975. Rogers C.B. Morton, of Maryland, April 25, 1975. Elliot L. Richardson, of Massachusetts, December 11, 1975. SECRETARY OF LABOR—Peter J. Brennan, of New York, continued from preceding administration. John T. Dunlop, of Massachusetts, March 6, 1975. Willie J. Usery, Jr., of Georgia, February 4, 1976. SECRETARY OF HEALTH, EDUCATION, AND WELFARE—Caspar W. Weinberger, of California, continued from preceding administration. Forrest David Mathews, of Alabama, June 26, 1975. SECRETARY OF HOUSING AND URBAN DEVELOPMENT—James T. Lynn, of Ohio, continued from preceding administration. Carla A. Hills, of California, March 5, 1975. SECRETARY OF TRANSPORTATION—Claude S. Brinegar, of California, continued from preceding administration. William T. Coleman, Jr., of Pennsylvania, March 3, 1975.

### 94th Congress

1st Session: Jan. 14, 1975-Dec. 19, 1975; 2nd Session: Jan. 19, 1976-Oct. 1, 1976.
President pro tempore of the Senate: James O. Eastland, of Mississippi (continued from preceding Congress). Speaker of the House: Carl Albert, of Oklahoma (continued from preceding Congress).
Senate: 61 Democratic; 37 Republican; 1 Conservative-Republican; 1 Independent

House: 291 Democratic; 144 Republican

---

## Administration of JIMMY CARTER

## JANUARY 20, 1977 TO JANUARY 20, 1981

PRESIDENT—Jimmy (James E.) Carter, of Georgia, VICE PRESIDENT—Walter F. Mondale, of Minnesota. SECRETARY OF STATE—Cyrus R. Vance, of New York, January 23, 1977. Edmund S. Muskie, of Maine, May 8, 1980. SECRETARY OF THE TREASURY—W. Michael Blumenthal, of Michigan, January 23, 1977. G. William Miller, of Oklahoma, August 6, 1979. SECRETARY OF DEFENSE—Harold Brown, of California, January 21, 1977. ATTORNEY GENERAL—Griffin B. Bell, of Georgia, January 26, 1977. Benjamin R. Civiletti, of Maryland, August 16, 1979. SECRETARY OF THE INTERIOR—Cecil R. Andrus, of Idaho, January 23, 1977. SECRETARY OF AGRICULTURE—Robert S. Bergland, of Minnesota, January 23, 1977. SECRETARY OF COMMERCE—Juanita M. Kreps, of North Carolina, January 23, 1977. Philip M. Klutznick, of Illinois, January 2, 1980. SECRETARY OF LABOR—F. Ray Marshall, of Texas, January 27, 1977. SECRETARY OF HEALTH AND HUMAN SERVICES—Joseph A. Califano, Jr., of the District of Columbia, January 25, 1977. Patricia R. Harris, of the District of Columbia, August 3, 1979. (On Sept. 27, 1979 Congress gave final approval to a bill establishing a cabinet-level Department of Education; the Department of Health, Education and Welfare is to be renamed the Department of Health and Human Resources) SECRETARY OF HOUSING AND URBAN DEVELOPMENT—Patricia R. Harris, of the District of Columbia, January 23, 1977. Moon Landrieu, of Louisiana, September 24, 1979. SECRETARY OF TRANSPORTATION—Brockman Adams, of Washington, January 23, 1977. Neil E. Goldschmidt, of Oregon, August 15, 1979. SECRETARY OF ENERGY—James R. Schlesinger, of Virginia, August 5, 1977. Charles W. Duncan, of Texas, August 24, 1979. SECRETARY OF EDUCATION—Shirley M. Hufstedler, of California, December 6, 1979.

### 95th Congress

1st Session: Jan. 4, 1977-Dec. 15, 1977; 2nd Session: Jan. 19, 1978-Oct. 15, 1978
President pro tempore of the Senate: James O. Eastland, of Mississippi (continued from preceding Congress). Deputy President pro tempore of the Senate: Hubert H. Humphrey,[1] of Minnesota. Speaker of the House: Thomas P. O'Neill, Jr., of Massachusetts.
Senate: 61 Democratic; 38 Republican; 1 Independent
House: 290 Democratic; 145 Republican

### 96th Congress

1st Session: Jan. 3, 1979-Jan. 3, 1980[2];
2nd Session: Jan. 3, 1980-Dec. 16, 1980

President pro tempore of the Senate: Warren G. Magnuson, of Washington. Speaker of the House: Thomas P. O'Neill, Jr., of Massachusetts. (continued from preceding Congress) Senate: 58 Democratic; 41 Republican; 1 Independent. House: 276 Democratic; 159 Republican.

---

[1]Office of Deputy President pro tempore was established January 5, 1977, pursuant to Senate Resolution 17, Ninety-fifth Congress. This office no longer exists since the death of Hubert H. Humphrey, Jan. 13, 1978. [2]The Senate adjourned sine die Dec. 20, 1979.

---

## Administration of RONALD W. REAGAN

## FROM JANUARY 20, 1981

PRESIDENT—Ronald W. Reagan, of California, VICE PRESIDENT—George H. W. Bush, of Texas, SECRETARY OF STATE—George P. Shultz, of California, July 16, 1982, SECRETARY OF THE TREASURY—Donald T. Regan, of New York, January 22, 1981, SECRETARY OF DEFENSE—Caspar W. Weinberger, of California, January 21, 1981, ATTORNEY GENERAL—William F. Smith, of California, January 23, 1981, SECRETARY OF THE INTERIOR—James G. Watt, of Colorado, January 23, 1981, SECRETARY OF AGRICULTURE—John R. Block, of Illinois, January 23, 1981, SECRETARY OF COMMERCE—Malcolm Baldrige, of Connecticut, January 23, 1981, SECRETARY OF LABOR—Raymond J. Donovan, of New Jersey, February 4, 1981, SECRETARY OF HEALTH AND HUMAN SERVICES—Richard S. Schweiker, of Pennsylvania, January 22, 1981, SECRETARY OF HOUSING AND URBAN DEVELOPMENT—Samuel R. Pierce, Jr., of New York, January 23, 1981, SECRETARY OF TRANSPORTATION—Andrew L. Lewis, Jr., of Pennsylvania, January 23, 1981, SECRETARY OF ENERGY—James B. Edwards, of South Carolina, January 23, 1981, SECRETARY OF EDUCATION—Terrell H. Bell, of Utah, January 23, 1981.

### 97th Congress

1st Session: Jan. 5, 1981—Dec. 16, 1981
2nd Session: Jan. 25, 1982—
President pro tempore of the Senate: Strom Thurmond of South Carolina Speaker of the House: Thomas P. O'Neill, Jr., of Massachusetts (continued from preceding Congress) Senate: 53 Republican; 46 Democratic; 1 Independent-Democrat. House: 244 Democratic; 191 Republican.

# THE PRESIDENTIAL BIOGRAPHIES

## George Washington

George Washington, 1st President (1789–1797), son of Augustine and Mary (Ball) Washington, was born on February 22, 1732, in Westmoreland County, Virginia. Of a family that migrated from England in 1658, George's father was a moderately well-to-do planter. He died when George was 11, and young Washington was brought up by his half-brother, Lawrence, whom he idolized and who took over the estate and functioned as a surrogate father.

George received a simple education at the parish church and at 16 entered the employ of Lord Thomas Fairfax as a land surveyor. Adept at mathematics and athletics, Washington in surveying Fairfax's vast holdings in mountainous western Virginia, learned to live in the wilderness, govern his helpers, and maintain accurate survey records on which land titles were based. In 1752, Lawrence Washington died. George inherited a share of Lawrence's lands, and he was commissioned (1753) a major and put in charge of training militia in southern Virginia. He immediately began to study histories of wars and books on military tactics.

Soon after, Washington emerged into public view when he volunteered for a hazardous and vital mission. Governor Robert Dinwiddie of Virginia was eager to warn the French that they must withdraw their troops from the Ohio River Valley, which the British hoped to settle. Bearing Dinwiddie's message, Washington, prudent and an excellent horseman, led a small party through the snow-covered wilderness to the successful completion of the mission.

At 22, Washington was promoted to lieutenant colonel as the French and Indian Wars commenced and was assigned as aide to British General Edward Braddock, a respected professional soldier, who led a disastrous expedition against the French at Fort Duquesne. Washington's personal skill in the battle was widely praised, and he was appointed (1755) colonel and entrusted with the defense of Virginia's 350-mile western frontier. At his urging, a new attack was made upon Fort Duquesne, and he again distinguished himself by capturing the French stronghold. With the French retreating into Canada, the fighting ceased, and Washington, now the most famous American-born soldier, retired to private life.

At Mount Vernon, which initially he leased from Lawrence's widow, he became at the age of 26, a country gentleman and successful businessman. He also commenced his political career by serving from 1759 to 1774 as a member of Virginia's House of Burgesses. This legislative background stood him well. A leader in opposition to British policy, Washington was a delegate to the First Continental Congress (1774-75) and, with the outbreak of the Revolutionary War, he was named commander-in-chief of the Continental forces.

Beset with obstacles seldom faced by military commanders, Washington described his troops as "raw militia, badly officered, and with no government." Since his troops preferred short-term enlistments and summer fighting to winter, he seldom commanded 10,000 men at one time. Weak in power, Congress supported Washington poorly, sometimes leaving him without adequate funds to pay his troops. Many subordinate officers were preoccupied with jealousies and intrigues.

Yet by ingenious retreats and thrusts, Washington kept his army afield, survived defeat at Germantown, a cruel winter at Valley Forge, and built up an able force that entrapped Cornwallis's army at Yorktown and forced its surrender. Washington emerged from the Revolution as the unrivaled hero and symbol of the new nation.

In 1783, he again retired to Mount Vernon, where life was pleasantly calm. However, by 1786, he like other leaders was distressed by the weaknesses of American government under the Articles of Confederation. When the Constitutional Convention gathered at Philadelphia in 1787, Washington received a hero's welcome as head of the Virginia delegation, and he was promptly elected president of the convention. In fashioning a strong Presidency, the convention, Pierce Butler wrote, "cast their eyes toward General Washington . . ."

After the Constitution was ratified, the first Electoral College met on February 4, 1789, and unanimously elected Washington President. On April 30, he was inaugurated at Federal Hall, in New York City, the capital. "I walk on untrodden ground," Washington said soon after beginning his new responsibilities. "There is scarcely any part of my conduct that may not hereafter be drawn into precedent."

Facing times that overflowed with crises, Washington left the republic far stronger and more confident than when he took office. An output of measures, highly impressive by today's standards, flowed from his administration. The Revolutionary debts of the states were assumed by the national government, a national currency was issued, and a Bank of the United States established to provide credit. Manufacture and trade were promoted by tariffs and bounties; inventions were protected by patent and copyright laws. A postal system was established; national security was improved by the reorganization of the army and the navy, the founding of West Point, and the construction of fortifications on the eastern seaboard and in the West. In the development of many of these measures, Washington was aided by his brilliant Secretary of the Treasury, Alexander Hamilton.

Hamilton's advocacy of a Bank of the United States touched off a dispute with Secretary of State Thomas Jefferson and Attorney General Edmund Randolph, who considered the bank unconstitutional because express authorization was not provided in the fundamental law. Washington sided with Hamilton, who argued that the national government could use all powers, except those denied by the Constitution. Time and again, where the Constitution was unclear, Washington exercised executive authority.

The President truly dominated the executive branch. With few exceptions, he prescribed the duties of his department heads and kept abreast of daily detail. So confident was he of his mastery that he brought together two of the most gifted and assertive department heads the nation has ever known—Jefferson and Hamilton. Washington succeeded outstandingly, where many of his successors have failed, in relations with Congress. He converted his popularity into major laws without tarnishing his prestige in political struggles. He prized the intrinsic dignity of the Presidency and gave the office a regal quality.

In 1793, Washington was reelected again by a unanimous electoral vote; his second term was to be more difficult than the first. War now raged between England and France, growing out of the French Revolution. Hamilton and Jefferson, in conflict over domestic questions, were also bitterly divided over the war. Each led a party reflecting his views: Hamilton—the Federalists, Jefferson—the Anti-Federalists (Democratic-Republicans). Hamilton's party sympathized with Britain and Jefferson's with France. As usual, Washington tried to be a moderating influence between his two strong secretaries. In weighing policy toward the war, he found convenience in meeting with all his secretaries simultaneously: and the institution known as the Cabinet was born.

On April 22, 1793, Washington issued a neutrality proclamation calling for "conduct friendly and impartial" to the warring nations. American vessels were barred from carrying war supplies to the belligerents. When the French minister to the United States, Citizen Genêt, attempted to outfit warships in American ports and to send them against the British, Washington requested that France recall its representative, because of his threat to American neutrality.

American relations with Britain also were badly deteriorating. British warships intercepted United States' vessels bearing food supplies to France, seizing their cargoes and impressing their seamen into the British navy. The British also refused to give up western frontier forts as they were obligated to under the treaty ending the Revolutionary War; instead, they stirred up the Indians in the surrounding area. To resolve these prickly questions, Washington dispatched Chief Justice John Jay to Britain. The resulting Jay Treaty dealt with trade and the frontier forts, but not with Britain's halting of American ships and seizure of seamen. Senate consideration of the treaty occasioned a bitter fight between the Federalists who supported it and the Anti-Federalists. Hostile newspapers called for Washington's impeachment. And some denounced him as an aristocrat and an enemy of true democracy. The Senate eventually approved the treaty.

In 1794, Washington demonstrated that he could enforce federal laws in the states when he put down the Whisky Rebellion by dispatching troops against farmers in western Pennsylvania who refused to pay federal taxes on whisky.

Declining to serve a third term, Washington issued his Farewell Address in 1796, announcing his retirement and warning against "permanent alliances" with foreign powers. Washington had gotten the U.S. Presidency off to a strong start, perhaps most fundamentally because of the bold, enterprising view he took of his office and his inspiring personal qualities. Washington retired to Mount Vernon, where he died on December 14, 1799.

## John Adams

John Adams, 2d President (1797–1801), was born October 30, 1735, in Braintree (now Quincy), Massachusetts. The son of a Puritan farmer, Adams was graduated (1755) from Harvard College. After teaching briefly, he read law, was admitted (1758) to the bar.

An opponent of the Stamp Act, he was elected (1771) to the Massachusetts colonial legislature. There he steadily resisted British colonial policies and in 1774, just prior to the American Revolution, he was chosen a delegate to the First Continental Congress. At the Second Continental Congress (1775), he pressed for American independence and persuaded Congress to organize the Continental Army and to appoint George Washington as commander-in-chief. Adams helped draft and defend the Declaration of Independence amid turbulent Congressional debates.

In 1778 Adams was dispatched to Paris to build ties between France and the struggling new nation, but his impatience, ready candor, and pride served him ill in diplomacy, and he returned home. A year later, he was elected to the convention that prepared the important Massachusetts state constitution. He returned (1780) to diplomacy as minister to the Netherlands, where he won recognition for the United States and, more important, negotiated a loan. With John Jay and Benjamin Franklin, Adams negotiated (1782) the Treaty of Paris with Great Britain that ended the American Revolution. Three years later, Congress named him the first United States minister to Britain. He was rebuffed by the British, and in 1788 he asked to be recalled.

Soon after his return to America, he was elected Vice-President under George Washington. Despite his characterization of his new post as "the most insignificant office that ever the invention of man contrived or his imagination conceived," Adams was a constructive influence in filling his duties in the Senate.

When Washington declined (1796) to serve a third Presidential term, the Federalists, led by Alexander Hamilton, supported Adams for the Presidency, while the Democratic-Republicans turned to Thomas Jefferson. Adams won by three votes.

At the outset, Adams stressed that his Presidency would be an extension of Washington's. He retained his predecessor's entire cabinet and, in his inaugural address, promised to continue the Washington policies. Despite these reassurances, Federalists became distrustful when Adams, deeming it necessary to improve relations with France, offered the ministry to that country to Jefferson.

When Jefferson declined, Adams was on the point of conferring the post upon another Democratic-Republican leader, James Madison. However, a cabinet upheaval loomed over the step, and Adams reconsidered. Although President, Adams was not leader of his party. Alexander Hamilton, who held no government post was the Federalist leader, and the loyalties of some cabinet members ran to him rather than to Adams.

The central problems and policies of the Adams administration derived from the French Revolution and the ensuing war between France and Britain. Both countries claimed the right to seize American vessels, and the French Directory went so far as to declare that all Americans serving on British vessels were pirates. Adams sought to steer a middle course between Hamilton and his strong partiality toward Britain and Jefferson's similar disposition toward France.

The President called Congress into special session to consider ways of keeping peace. To his cabinet he distributed a series of questions on the Franco-British situation, seeking advice before framing his message to Congress. The questions were leaked to Hamilton, who prepared replies that were submitted through the cabinet to Adams, who accepted their substance, proposing that defenses be strengthened.

Simultaneously, the President dispatched ministers to France to arrange a treaty. The French representatives demanded a bribe and a loan, touching off the sensational episode that became known as the XYZ Affair. Adams again asked his cabinet for advice, and again Hamilton surreptitiously supplied it, proposing a more vigorous policy toward France and closer ties with Britain. Adams accepted the former, but not the latter. Congress responded with actions just short of war, by declaring all treaties with France null and void, creating a Navy Department, and increasing the army and authorizing new ships.

Eager to keep peace, Adams moved to restore diplomatic relations with France. (Adams first nominated W. Vans Murray to become minister to France. The President acted without consulting the cabinet, which enraged the Hamiltonians in it. Federalists in the Senate raised various objections as a prelude to rejecting it. In a bold move, Adams replaced the Murray nomination with the proposal of a three-member peace commission. The step brought press and public opinion so strongly to the President's side that the commission was approved.) Fearful of an Anglo-American alliance, the French this time were cooperative and war was averted. Adams achieved his supreme goal of maintaining peace, but at the high price of alienating his ardently pro-British Federalist party.

In 1798, smarting under criticism of their opposition to France, the Federalists passed the repressive Alien and Sedition laws that were designed to limit and punish criticism of the government and its officers. Adams neither supported the laws' passage nor applied them. Nevertheless, anti-Federalist journalists were arrested and sentiment turned against the administration.

His successful avoidance of war with France alienated Federalist leaders who deemed Adams a traitor to his party. Jefferson, leader of the Democratic-Republicans, observed that the followers of Hamilton were only "a little less hostile" to Adams than to himself. After long, calculated delay, Adams dealt with his cabinet secretaries who, in effect, were Hamilton's spies. One, James McHenry, resigned after a stormy confrontation with Adams, and another, Timothy Pickering, was dismissed.

Without a party behind him, Adams made a poor showing in seeking reelection in 1800. Both Jefferson and Aaron Burr exceeded him in electoral votes (73 each), while Adams received 65. The election was ultimately decided by the House of Representatives.

So aggrieved was Adams by his defeat that he refused to remain in Washington for Jefferson's inauguration and returned home to Quincy. Subsequently the two Presidents—Jefferson and Adams—renewed their friendship. Adams lived longer than any other President, dying on July 4, 1826, a few months before his 91st birthday.

## Thomas Jefferson

Thomas Jefferson, 3d President (1801–1809), was born at Shadwell in Goochland County, Virginia, on April 13, 1743. His father was a planter, scholar, militia colonel, and a member of the House of Burgesses; his mother was a Virginia Randolph. Something of Jefferson's democratic impulse doubtless derived from the frontier influences of the Blue Ridge region in which he was reared. Educated by tutors and in local schools, Jefferson studied at William and Mary College, from which he was graduated (1762).

After leaving college, Jefferson studied law under George Wythe and was admitted (1767) to the bar. His practice was soon very successful, and in 1769, his political career began with his election to the House of Burgesses, in which he served until 1774. Not a brilliant speaker (later, as President, he abandoned the practice of delivering Congressional messages in person), Jefferson was brilliant at drafting laws and resolutions. As relations with the British deteriorated, Jefferson on the eve of the Revolution was a busy draftsman of protest documents. A triumph of revolutionary logic was his pamphlet "A Summary View of the Rights of British America," printed in 1774.

A year later, Jefferson was sent as a delegate to the Continental Congress. Always standing with those who were resolved to resist Great Britain, he was deputed to draft the Declaration of Independence, which with few changes Congress adopted on July 4, 1776.

Two months later, Jefferson resigned from Congress and returned to the Virginia House of Delegates, in which he served until 1779 when he was elected governor of Virginia, succeeding Patrick Henry. Disinclined toward the military life, he did not fight in the Revolutionary War. As a Virginia lawmaker, Jefferson was a powerful democratizing influence who moved his state away from virtual control by a few wealthy slaveholders. By amendment of the Virginia land laws, he effected a more equitable land distribution, which was the key to voting rights and educational opportunity. Even more important were his bills to assure religious freedom. Although he failed in his attempt to pass laws that would have gradually abolished slavery in Virginia, he remained opposed to that institution.

Jefferson resigned (1781) as governor, believing that the British army's threat to his state necessitated a military man to serve as chief executive. During a brief interval of private life, Jefferson began writing his *Notes on Virginia*, an extended statement of his beliefs.

He served (1784–89) in several diplomatic assignments and replaced Benjamin Franklin as minister to France. Jefferson sympathized openly with the French Revolution, believing it similar in essence to the American rebellion. His wide travel in Europe broadened his interests, particularly in architecture and agriculture.

Jefferson was abroad and did not participate in the Constitutional Convention of 1787, but his influence was felt in the quick preparation of the Bill of Rights; its omission from the original Constitution he had considered intolerable. He served as Secretary of State in Washington's first administration.

Jefferson was soon sharply at odds with the Secretary of the Treasury, Alexander Hamilton. After supporting several of Hamilton's early financial measures for the sake of unity, Jefferson, preferring an agricultural society, opposed Hamilton's plans to encourage manufacturing and trade and to found a national bank. In resisting Hamilton's broad interpretation of the Constitution to justify these measures, Jefferson advocated states' rights and "strict construction" of the Constitution, limiting the federal government's powers to those that the document specifically granted. Jefferson and Hamilton fought bitterly over foreign policy. Jefferson and the "Democratic-Republicans" who gathered as a party around him (and who were precursors of today's Democratic party) favored France, while Hamilton and the Federalists favored England. Late in 1793 their differences became so acute that Jefferson resigned.

He was elected (1796) Vice-President, with the Federalist John Adams as President. After four years of bitter party strife, Jefferson was elected (1800) President. His Vice-Presidential running mate, Aaron Burr, received the same number of electoral votes, and the election was referred to the House of Representatives. Thanks to the intervention of Hamilton, who advised Federalists to support Jefferson, the sage of Monticello won.

The first President to be inaugurated in Washington, Jefferson quickly set an example of simplicity. His inaugural address was an appeal for bipartisan cooperation—"We are all Republicans —we are all Federalists"—and his conception of government was largely negative, in the sense that he believed the federal government should deal chiefly with foreign affairs, leaving local matters to the states. Jefferson's view was that government should restrain men from harming one another, but otherwise leave them to their own concerns. Federal expenditures should be curtailed and excise taxes repealed.

Although Jefferson appointed followers such as James Madison as Secretary of State and Albert Gallatin as Secretary of the Treasury, he found the lesser offices, the infant bureaucracy, filled with Federalists. Noting that vacancies "by death are few; by resignations none," Jefferson foreshadowed the spoils system by replacing some Federalists in lesser offices with Democratic-Republicans. He refused to honor the Federalist appointment of "midnight judges" in the outgoing Adams' administration. Near the close of his Presidential tenure, Republicans held a majority of executive-branch appointments.

Through his party, Jefferson exerted strong control over Congress and accomplished the repeal of major Federalist statutes, including the Judiciary Act of 1801. His action was rebuked in *Marbury* v. *Madison*, the principle of which was that the Supreme Court may invalidate an act of Congress; Jefferson never accepted this principle. In pardoning those convicted of violating the Alien and Sedition laws, he asserted Presidential power over Congressional law. Heartily approving the use of the impeachment power against partisan Federalist judges, he was regretful of its failure when it was directed against Justice Samuel Chase, who had been impeached (1804) for discrimination against Jeffersonians.

The extraordinary diplomatic achievement of Jefferson's Presidency was the Louisiana Purchase (1803), which was negotiated by Robert Livingston and James Monroe. The temptation of acquiring a vast territory under favorable terms and of protecting the Mississippi's freedom of navigation overwhelmed Jefferson's devotion to strict Constitutional construction. Observing later that he "stretched the Constitution till it cracked," Jefferson submitted the purchase treaty to the Senate which readily approved it.

Jefferson was unsuccessful in seeking to acquire West Florida, chiefly because his lack of candor offended Congress. His reliance on diplomacy collapsed against the depredations of the Barbary pirates off North Africa. Ultimately, he dispatched a naval force and blockaded ports, and later he ordered frigates into action against the sultan of Morocco.

Aided by economic prosperity as well as political achievement, Jefferson was reelected in 1804 by an overwhelming majority. A major event in the second term was the trial of former Vice-President Aaron Burr, who was suspected by Jefferson of having politicked for the Presidency and now was accused of treasonable plottings. Burr's trial became a contest of wits between Jefferson and Chief Justice John Marshall. The latter's definition of treason made Burr's conviction impossible, to Jefferson's disgust.

Jefferson's diplomatic skill at peace-keeping was severely tested by the pressures of European war upon American neutrality. The Napoleonic decrees, British impressment of American seamen, and the audacity of a British frigate in firing on the United States' *Chesapeake*, combined to drive Jefferson to issue a proclamation denying British armed vessels the hospitality of United States waters.

In December 1807, Jefferson forced the Embargo Act through Congress; it prohibited exporting any produce from an American port or sailing any American ship to a foreign port. Enforcement of the act cast the administration in the role of exercising arbitrary power against key rights of the individual. Ironically, the exigencies of the Presidency brought Jefferson to violate the very values with which he was so long and so thoroughly identified—the sanctity of individual rights against governmental encroachment.

The embargo fell more heavily and injuriously upon the United States than upon France and England. Idle ships, unsold goods, and commercial unemployment fired opposition in New England, embittered the sections most loyal to Jefferson, and brought Congress to rebel against the President. Ultimately, Jefferson retreated by approving the Non-Intercourse Act of 1809 under which the embargo was partially raised.

Despite the rocky conclusion of his tenure, Jefferson handpicked his successor, Madison. He retired to Monticello, pursued scientific farming, counseled Presidents Madison and Monroe, and kept in touch with public affairs through a large correspondence. He died on July 4, 1826, on the same day as John Adams and on the 50th anniversary of the adoption of the Declaration of Independence.

## James Madison

James Madison, 4th President (1809–1817), was born on March 16, 1751, in Port Conway, Virginia, the son of a planter and justice of the peace, whose forebears had settled in Virginia in the 1600s. A frail and sickly child, Madison was educated by private tutors and graduated (1771) from the College of New Jersey (now Princeton). A year of postgraduate study there was devoted to Hebrew, history, and law.

Torn between the ministry and politics, he chose the latter and was elected (1774) to the Committee of Safety in Orange County, Virginia, an important organ of local government in the twilight of the colonial period. In 1776, Madison was a delegate to the Williamsburg convention that declared for independence and established a state government. Serving in Virginia's first legislative assembly, Madison met Thomas Jefferson and began a lifelong friendship. In 1778, Madison was a member of the executive council, and in 1779 the state legislature elected him to the Continental Congress.

Until 1788, Madison served either in the Virginia legislature or in Congress, where he quickly became convinced that the Continental Congress needed more power, particularly in financial affairs. Although only 36 years old, Madison represented (1787) Virginia at the Constitutional Convention in Philadelphia and took a leading part in the deliberations. Champion of a strong central government, he drafted the "Virginia Plan" on which the Constitution was based. Known as the "Father of the Constitution," Madison kept a journal of the convention—the most complete record available of the proceedings—and his knowledge of past governments and the inherent problems of federalism was invaluable. Madison was a member of the Virginia ratifying convention and, with John Jay and Alexander Hamilton, wrote *The Federalist*, a series of newspaper essays that are regarded as the best explanation of the American constitutional system.

In 1789, Madison defeated James Monroe for election to the new U.S. House of Representatives. One of its most able members, Madison drafted key legislation and played a leading part in preparing the first 10 amendments to the Constitution, known as the Bill of Rights. Soon convinced that Hamilton's policies were hurtful to farmers in the South and West, Madison joined Jefferson in founding the Democratic-Republican party. In 1797, Madison retired, briefly, from politics; however, outraged by the repressive Alien and Sedition Acts (1798), he drafted the Virginia Resolutions, condemning the acts and holding that the states could declare them unconstitutional.

Upon becoming President in 1801, Jefferson appointed Madison Secretary of State. He passed a busy apprenticeship in an administration that, like his own would be, was preoccupied with foreign affairs and the problems of European war. In 1808, after two Presidential terms, Jefferson, following the tradition of George Washington, declined a third term. He chose Madison to be his successor. Madison received 122 electoral votes to 47 for Federalist C. C. Pinckney.

Small and unimpressive in person, Madison at his inaugural, wrote Washington Irving, looked like "a withered little apple-John."

In its early months, Madison's administration was largely an inherited Presidency. He made no changes in Jefferson's cabinet, except to move Robert Smith from the Navy to the State Department. The cabinet, however, had an additional heritage, an old feud between Smith and Treasury Secretary Albert Gallatin. Eventually, Madison dismissed Smith and made Monroe his Secretary of State.

The war between Britain and France was continuing as were their depredations upon American shipping, despite Jefferson's policy of neutrality. In 1810, an act of Congress called for the resumption of trade with both France and Britain, but warned of American withdrawal if either power resumed shipping violations. France soon began such violations, and Britain stirred up the Indians in the West. In the House of Representatives, "hawks" such as Henry Clay and John Calhoun clamored for a war which, they believed would result in the annexation of Canada and Spanish Florida. New England was opposed to war; the rest of the nation demanded it; ultimately Madison called for war against Great Britain, and Congress declared it on June 18, 1812.

Later that year Madison was reelected President by 128 electoral votes to 89 for Mayor De Witt Clinton of New York City.

Both by his contemporaries and by historians, Madison is not rated as a good war President. Calhoun wrote of him, "Our President though a man of amiable manners and great talents has not I fear those commanding talents, which are necessary to control those about him." Madison was handicapped by poor field commanders and by acute sectional and factional differences. Northern Republicans hobbled his efforts to seize the remainder of the Floridas, and Southern Republicans were unenthusiastic about conquering Canada. Each party faction feared that out of conquered territory might come new states favoring the other. Federalists generally opposed "Mr. Madison's War."

In its early stage the war went badly for the United States. For two years, every thrust into Canada was foiled. Britain clamped a tight blockade upon the eastern coast. On August 24, 1814, British forces occupied and burned Washington, and the Madisons fled the White House. But then American fortunes brightened. A British thrust down Lake Champlain was repulsed, and Andrew Jackson won a thrilling victory at New Orleans. In the Treaty of Ghent, however, signed December 24, 1814, not a single U.S. war aim was achieved. At Madison's direction, the demand upon Britain to renounce impressments was dropped. The only demand imposed was that Britain leave occupied American territory.

The war's close saw the decline of the Federalist party, a decline speeded by Madison's adopting its key principles. He approved a new bank of the United States, a tariff act of 1816 to protect "infant industries," and the establishment of substantial military and naval forces on a permanent basis. However, Madison did not accept the Federalist plank of internal domestic improvements to be undertaken by the national government. Such ventures, he thought, necessitated a constitutional amendment.

After leaving the Presidency, Madison lived in retirement on his estate at Montpelier, Virginia. He was a member of the Virginia Constitutional Convention of 1829 and occasionally offered counsel to his successor, James Monroe. Madison died at Montpelier on June 28, 1836, and is buried nearby.

## James Monroe

James Monroe, 5th President (1817–1825), was born April 28, 1758, in Westmoreland County, Virginia, the eldest of five children of a circuit judge and planter. A student at William and Mary College when the Revolution broke out, Monroe joined the army, fought in major battles, and was wounded at Harlem Heights in New York and at the Battle of Trenton.

After the Revolution, Monroe studied law under Thomas Jefferson, then the governor of Virginia, and an important friendship between the two began. Monroe's political career commenced with his election (1780) to the Virginia legislature. Three years later he was elected to the Continental Congress, in which he opposed a highly centralized government but supported tariff-making by Congress. In 1786, he returned from Congress to serve in the Virginia Assembly.

Monroe was a state delegate to the Virginia convention that was called to ratify the new U.S. Constitution. So strong was his admiration for Jefferson that he moved to Charlottesville, Virginia, where he built Ash Lawn, not far from Jefferson's estate, Monticello.

Monroe ran unsuccessfully against James Madison for the first U.S. House of Representatives; however, the Virginia legislature elected him (1790) to the U.S. Senate. Allied with Jefferson and Madison, Monroe opposed the centralizing policies of Alexander Hamilton and, aided by Albert Gallatin and Aaron Burr, shared in the founding of the Democratic-Republican party. In 1794, Washington appointed Monroe minister to France, a country he deeply admired. He criticized Jay's (Anglo-American) Treaty so severely, however, that Washington, with whom he had previously clashed, recalled him in 1796.

From 1799 to 1802, Monroe was governor of Virginia. During Jefferson's Presidency, he was dispatched (1802) to Paris to help Robert R. Livingston arrange the Louisiana Purchase; the next year in Spain he aided in the unsuccessful negotiations for the purchase of the Floridas. In 1803 Jefferson named Monroe minister to Britain. From 1811 to 1816, he was Madison's Secretary of State.

In 1816, Monroe was elected President, winning easily over his Federalist opponent, Senator Rufus King of New York. He was reelected in 1820, with only one electoral vote cast against him.

Monroe's Presidency coincided with "the era of good feeling." After the election of 1816, the Federalist party disappeared and the Democratic-Republicans flourished as the country's only party. Thanks to fast developing industry and western settlement, the country prospered. Not even the depression of 1818 dampened the good feeling.

Few disturbing domestic political issues troubled Monroe's first Presidential years. He opposed "the American System" of House Speaker Henry Clay, who demanded internal domestic improvements and a protective tariff. A strict constructionist, Monroe in his first annual message declared that Congress lacked the constitutional power to establish a system of internal improvements. Subsequently, however, he modified his position by granting an appropriation to repair the Cumberland Road and approving the first harbor act. He also approved the 1824 tariff act and moved to a middle-of-the-road position on tariffs and domestic improvements.

In 1819, Missouri applied for admission to the Union as a slave state. A bitter legislative struggle followed on the questions of limiting slavery in Missouri and in the remainder of the Louisiana Purchase. Although sympathetic to the South, Monroe, in keeping with his view of the Presidency, did not involve himself in the struggle until a bill reached him. It provided for the admission of Missouri as a slave state, while banning slavery from much of the rest of the Louisiana Purchase.

Monroe doubted that Congress could constitutionally impose such a ban. His cabinet also had doubts but, ultimately, he decided to leave the question unresolved, signing the act that became known as the Missouri Compromise of 1820.

Attentive to the public's attitude toward his administration, Monroe traveled through the Northeast—a venture that increased his popularity—and later toured the South and Southwest. Monroe demonstrated unusual personal growth in the Presidency by moving away from the evident sectionalism of his first years toward national perspectives. With breadth of vision and a talent for conciliation, Monroe led a cabinet of strong personalities drawn from the country's major regions: John Quincy Adams (Secretary of State), John Calhoun (War), William Wirt (Attorney General), and William H. Crawford (Treasury).

In foreign affairs, the Monroe administration arranged with Great Britain to limit armaments on the Great Lakes and resolved a long-standing dispute with Newfoundland and Labrador over fishing rights. Monroe acquired (1819) Florida from Spain by the Adams-Onís Treaty, even though midway in the negotiations Andrew Jackson had invaded Florida (1818). Monroe also approved of the American Colonization Society settling Liberia; Monrovia was named for him.

A triumph of skillful Presidential leadership, the Monroe Doctrine began its evolution with the clamors for recognition by Spain's former Latin American colonies. Monroe dispatched special agents to those emerging countries and sought to associate Congress with his eventual policy. He recognized the former colonies and, on learning that European powers contemplated a reconquest of them, he and his cabinet developed the message to Congress of December 2, 1823, that set forth the doctrine. In effect, it threatened war against European powers that attempted to "extend their system to any portion of this hemisphere." Although Secretary of State Adams played an important part in the formulation of the doctrine, Monroe conceived the idea of a legislative message to convey it and drafted its central paragraphs.

After leaving office, Monroe retired to his estate near Leesburg, Virginia. He served as regent of the University of Virginia and was presiding officer of the Virginia Constitutional Convention in 1829. Financial distress, stemming from long years of public service, forced Monroe to move (1830) to New York City to live with his married daughter. He died there on July 4, 1831. Subsequently his remains were moved to Richmond, Virginia.

## John Quincy Adams

John Quincy Adams, 6th President (1825–1829), was born July 11, 1767, in Braintree (now Quincy), Massachusetts, the eldest son of the 2d President of the United States. Because his father had served as American diplomatic representative to several European countries during the Revolution, Adams received his early schooling abroad. His advanced learning enabled him to enter Harvard College as a junior and graduate in 1787. After reading law for three years, he was admitted to the bar.

But having few clients, Adams took up political journalism. He wrote articles replying to Tom Paine's *The Rights of Man,* which he considered too radical, and attacked the French Minister Edmond Genêt, who during the Washington administration urged the United States to join France in her war with Great Britain. In 1794, George Washington appointed the 27-year-old Adams minister to the Netherlands and, two years later, to Portugal. He served as minister to Prussia after his father became (1797) President.

With the advent (1801) of the Jefferson administration, Adams abandoned diplomacy and turned to politics as a Federalist; he was elected (1802) to the Massachusetts Senate but the Federalist leader there soon considered Adams "too unmanageable." A year later he was elected to the U.S. Senate from Massachusetts. In the Senate, he often voted with the Democratic-Republicans, although a Federalist, and he supported Jefferson's embargo policy to which other New England Federalists were bitterly opposed. When the end of Adams' term approached, the Federalists, feeling betrayed, elected (1808) another man to his place, and Adams immediately resigned.

He returned (1809) to diplomacy under James Madison, who appointed him minister to Russia. Near the end of his service there (1814), he became one of the U.S. commissioners who negotiated the Treaty of Ghent ending the War of 1812. In 1815 Madison appointed Adams minister to Britain; in 1817 James Monroe named him Secretary of State. Adams was a leading influence in the formulation of the Monroe Doctrine.

Just as Madison and Monroe had risen to the Presidency from the post of Secretary of State, Adams considered himself qualified for a similar ascent in the election of 1824. Proud, high-minded, and an independent in politics (which made party men look askance at him), Adams made little effort to obtain votes. Moreover, he faced formidable opponents: John Calhoun, Henry Clay, Andrew Jackson, and William Crawford. Calhoun soon withdrew from the Presidential race and was elected Vice-President. For President, Jackson received 99 electoral votes; Adams, 84; Crawford, 41; and Clay, 37. Since none of the candidates had won a majority, the House of Representatives had to choose among the three leading candidates.

Before the House voted, however, Jackson's followers charged that Adams had promised Clay a cabinet post in exchange for his support. Following his election, Adams appointed Clay Secretary of State, prompting Jacksonians in Congress to cry that Adams and Clay had made "a corrupt bargain." These circumstances assured Adams of unrelenting Jacksonian hostility.

In his inaugural address, Adams advocated an ambitious program of domestic improvements and, in his first annual message, he called for federal promotion of the arts and sciences, establishment of a national university and astronomical observatories, and support for scientific enterprises. Strict Northern constructionists were distressed by Adams' liberal interpretations of the Constitution, while Southerners were fearful that the logic of these Constitutional views might lead to federal abolition of slavery.

Neither by personality nor by circumstance was Adams sufficiently endowed to excel in two critical Presidential roles: as party leader and as legislative leader. Although his party controlled the House, the opposition ruled the Senate. Adams himself had little faith in his ability to command success in Congress. A simple proposal, such as his request for authority to dispatch a mission to the Panama Congress of Latin American states, encountered rough trouble in the legislature. A master of diatribe, John Randolph, launched a pointed attack on the supposed Adams-Clay "deal." Worse than Randolph's attack was the failure of anyone in the President's own party to defend him.

Adams made no attempt to soften Congressional opposition by the adroit use of patronage. Seemingly self-obstructive, his principles took precedence over party claims. His administration made only 12 removals from office, a degree of restraint that alienated friends and encouraged enemies. In other ways, too, Adams demonstrated that he was very little of a politician. His cabinet contained no one who had openly supported him for President. He even countenanced the aid openly given by one cabinet secretary to the future Presidential candidacy of Jackson.

The midterm Congressional elections went against Adams' interests, and for the first time in the history of the Presidency a large majority of Congress opposed the administration.

Adams' chief legislative success was the enactment (1828) of the "tariff of abominations," the high rates of which favored New England manufacturers and hurt Southern farmers, who had to pay more for imports. Southern resentment endangered Adams' chances for reelection.

The 1828 Presidential campaign was one of unparalleled bitterness. Adams did not answer—although his supporters did—the attacks of Jackson and his followers. Adams believed it beneath the dignity of the President to engage in political debate. Adams had no party of his own to cope with the well-organized opposition, and Jackson won an overwhelming victory: 178 electoral votes to 83 for Adams. But Adams did not regret leaving the Presidency.

After his Presidential term, Adams briefly enjoyed political retirement, until his election to the House of Representatives. Taking his seat in 1831, he served there for 17 years. He was the first Congressman to argue that slaves could be freed in time of war, an argument that Lincoln was to utilize in the Emancipation Proclamation.

Adams died of a paralytic stroke in the Speaker's Room of the House of Representatives on February 23, 1848. He is buried in Quincy, Massachusetts.

## Andrew Jackson

Andrew Jackson, 7th President (1829–1837), was born on March 15, 1767, in Waxhaw, South Carolina, the son of a linen weaver who, upon migrating to the United States from Ireland, became a farmer. Jackson's mother, too, was born in Ireland. In the frontier wilderness of the Carolinas, Jackson grew up with little education or refinement, and with a combative nature. But he was also energetic, self-confident, honest, and straightforward. He was genuinely the first of the "log-cabin" Presidents.

In the American Revolution, Jackson at 13 joined the South Carolina militia and was captured (1781) by the British. After the war, he read law and was admitted (1787) to the bar at the age of 20. In 1788, he became solicitor of the western district of North Carolina (now Tennessee) and soon excelled at sending law violators and debtors to jail. His success in public office rapidly enlarged his private law practice. Through successful land speculation, Jackson also increased his fortune, and he acquired the Hermitage, a plantation near Nashville.

Later that year, he was elected to the U.S. House of Representatives. His rough frontier manners won him attention and popularity, and he was appointed (1797) to the U.S. Senate at the age of 30. But impatient of the slow pace of life in Philadelphia (then the capital) and eager to care for his private affairs, Jackson resigned from the Senate the following year. The Tennessee legislature made his political retirement short lived by making him justice of the state supreme court (July 1798), and he served in that capacity until 1804. The pressures of creditors forced him to resign and devote himself to private affairs. By selling off land and winning steadily on his horses, Jackson withstood his creditors.

His already substantial public service had not compensated for his scanty formal education. A critic said that "his letters, with their crudities in spelling and grammar, would make the better educated angels weep." Nor did his temper diminish; he was party to many duels.

His service in the War of 1812 established him as a national military hero and a popular idol of the West. His best-known victory, at New Orleans, was gained after the treaty of peace had been signed, but before he had learned of it. In 1817 Jackson led a military expedition to Florida to guard the border, but he engaged and defeated the Seminole Indians in battle, pursuing them into northwest Florida. He ordered two British subjects, accused of inciting the Seminoles, hanged, thus precipitating diplomatic crises with Britain and Spain.

As a war hero, Jackson was attractive to politicians, and they began to talk of electing him President. In 1822 the Tennessee legislature nominated him to run for President in 1824 and, as a step in that direction, the legislature elected him to the U.S. Senate in 1823. Jackson again favorably impressed the Washington political community.

In the bitterly fought Presidential election of 1824, Jackson was one of five major candidates. Although he received more electoral votes than any of his rivals, he lacked a majority and the choice went to the House of Representatives. Supporters of Henry Clay in the House gave their votes to John Quincy Adams, who was elected. When Adams appointed Clay as Secretary of State, Jackson was convinced that he had been cheated out of the Presidency by "a corrupt bargain" between his two rivals.

The Presidential election of 1828 was even more bitter. It was the first election in which each Presidential nomination was made by state legislatures and mass meetings, instead of the traditional Congressional caucuses. Seeking reelection, Adams was the "National Republican" or Whig candidate. Jackson won easily, with 178 electoral votes to 83 for Adams.

His inaugural address was a true harbinger of Jackson's future policies. "The Federal Constitution," he said, "must be obeyed, state rights preserved, our national debts must be paid, direct taxes and loans avoided, and the Federal Union preserved." Jackson, who expressed and believed in the phrase "Let the people rule," invited the inaugural crowd into the White House. The results were disastrous: people grabbed up food and punch, stood on chairs, tore draperies, and broke china. The crowd's pressure endangered Jackson, who gladly escaped through a window.

Consistent with his desire for popular rule, Jackson became the first President to use the spoils system on a substantial scale. To Jackson's friend, Senator William L. Marcy of New York, is credited the slogan, "to the victor belong the spoils." Under the Jacksonian conception of spoils, experts were unnecessary for the conduct of government. The people could do its tasks and, best of all, members of the victorious party.

Although Jackson extolled popular rule, he also maximized his own personal rule as President, sometimes to the point of arbitrary power. He developed what became known as the "kitchen cabinet," a small group of personal advisers who were not in the cabinet but, in some cases, occupied subcabinet positions. The kitchen cabinet advised on policies and helped implement them; it tended to supplant the regular cabinet with which Jackson was chronically dissatisfied.

Jackson's revulsion to anything smacking of class privilege led him to attack the Bank of the United States. Although privately owned and managed, the bank, as chartered by Congress, had control over the nation's currency system. Jackson considered the act of Congress that had created the bank unconstitutional. On economic grounds, also, he opposed the bank. Jackson criticized it for failing to establish a "uniform and sound" currency, since he favored a "hard money" policy—one in which paper money would be based on specie (gold and silver).

In 1832 when Congress passed a bill rechartering the bank, Jackson vetoed it. Hitherto Presidents had restricted their use of the veto to constitutional grounds, but Jackson broke new ground by elaborating on the policy considerations prompting his action.

The election of 1832 was a landmark in Presidential history. For the first time, Presidential nominees were chosen by national conventions. The Democratic-Republican party broke into two parties. Jackson's opponents, who called themselves "National Republicans," nominated Henry Clay, while Jackson's followers continued to style themselves as "Republicans" or "Democratic-Republicans." The election was fought on the issue "Jackson or the Bank," and Jackson again won easily, with 219 electoral votes to 49 for Clay.

Spurred by his victory, Jackson continued to move against the Bank of the United States. He directed that government funds deposited with it be removed and placed in state banks, which opponents called "pet banks." "The dying monster," as Jackson called the Bank of the United States, was defeated after a savage fight and transformed itself into a state bank of Pennsylvania.

Meanwhile, banks having the use of government funds issued paper money in enormous quantities, prompting wild speculation. In 1836, Jackson suddenly issued his "specie circular," declaring that the government would accept only gold or silver in payment for public lands. He also required these banks to give up the money deposited with them, so that he might lend it to the states. The result was a disastrous panic that reached full force in the administration of his successor, Martin Van Buren.

Jackson also enhanced Presidential influence by his firm handling of the nullification crisis. In November 1832, South Carolina declared the high tariff acts of 1828 and 1832 null and void and threatened to secede. By proclamation, Jackson warned South Carolina that the law would be enforced and ordered troops and warships concentrated near Charleston. Congress passed a force bill, authorizing the President to employ the armed forces to collect tariffs. Eventually a new compromise tariff law was passed, and South Carolina withdrew its nullification of the tariff laws.

Jackson took a different course when Georgia disregarded the authority of the United States, as expressed by the Supreme Court. The Court had held unconstitutional a Georgia law concerning lands which by treaties had been given to the Indians. When Georgian authorities imprisoned a violator of the state law, Jackson refused to use the executive power to uphold the decision of the Supreme Court, and merely remarked, "John Marshall has made the decision; now let him enforce it." Some explain Jackson's position as one motivated by his long-standing distaste for Indians and for Marshall.

The audacious, enterprising, politically skillful Jackson remade the Presidency. His unprecedented use of spoils and the national nominating convention made it a party office. As a popular President and effective party leader, he became the first President to appeal to the people over the heads of their legislative representatives.

After leaving the Presidency, Jackson retired to the Hermitage and supported the Presidencies of his protégés—Van Buren and Polk. He died on June 8, 1845, and is buried at the Hermitage.

## Martin Van Buren

Martin Van Buren, 8th President 1837–1841), was born on December 5, 1782, in Kinderhook, New York, the son of a truck-farmer who was also tavern keeper. As a child, Van Buren enjoyed listening to his father's patrons discuss politics. At the age of 14, he left school to serve an apprenticeship in law offices at Kinderhook and Albany and was admitted to the bar in 1803.

While practicing in Kinderhook, he gained (1808) his first public office, being appointed surrogate of Columbia County by Gov. Daniel D. Tompkins. Van Buren rose rapidly in his New York political career, serving as state senator, attorney general, U.S. Senator, and delegate to the New York constitutional convention of 1821. An admirer of the ideas of Thomas Jefferson, Van Buren was a Democratic-Republican. As U.S. Senator (1821–28), he led in the fight against imprisonment for debt and the extension of the slave trade.

In 1828, Van Buren was elected governor of New York and gave invaluable support to the Presidential race of Andrew Jackson. A grateful Jackson named him Secretary of State but, more important, Van Buren rose to primacy among Jackson's advisers. Completely in accord with Jackson's policies, Van Buren in 1832 ran successfully for Vice-President, Jackson being reelected. As Jackson's chosen successor, Van Buren received the Democratic Presidential nomination in 1836 and won the election virtually unopposed.

Van Buren entered office pledged to follow the footsteps of his predecessor. The new President inherited not only policies but a legacy of problems as well. The worst of these was the feverish speculation in public lands that had developed in the latter days of the Jackson administration. Rich and poor alike, banks and their branches had all indulged in speculation. To check it, Jackson had issued the Specie Circular of July 1, 1836, that stipulated the government need only accept gold and silver in payment for public lands. Despite this restraint and others, a financial crash occurred (May 10, 1837) on Van Buren's 36th day in office. Bank closings and failures spread like plague, the nation having begun its first great depression.

Van Buren perceived neither the power nor the duty of the Presidency to help the people in their economic plight. Despite loud clamors of opposition, Van Buren held to Jackson's Specie Circular. His financial policies alienated conservative (or "bank") Democrats, especially in the politically important states of Virginia and New York. The rival Whig party denounced Van Buren for indifference and "heartlessness," pointing to his failure to issue paper money and resort to other relief measures that might have benefited the people and the economy. Van Buren, whose talents lay more in political manipulation than in persuasive public leadership, followed the practice of ignoring his critics. At this time, as throughout his political career, he was confident that "the sober second thought" of the people would support him.

Another Jacksonian inheritance was America's fiercest and costliest Indian war, the Seminole War in Florida. The great treasure of lives and money required to prosecute the eight-year war further diminished Van Buren's popularity. Even more costly, politically, was his policy toward Canada, since Americans sympathized with the Canadian rebellion of 1837. When British authorities seized an insurgent vessel in American waters, Van Buren resisted vociferous opinion that the country go to war with Great Britain. The President and his administration were derided as "tools of Victoria." In 1839, a border dispute between Maine and New Brunswick erupted, threatening war again, but Van Buren prevailed for peace with patience and tact.

Foreign policy, however, damaged his standing with the Southern base of his party. Facing pressures to annex the now independent Texas, he resisted because he did not want war with Mexico. He also opposed the extension of slavery, which the acquisition of Texas augured.

Dignified, courtly, and given to dandified dress and expensive tastes, Van Buren was a cartoonist's delight. But he was a leader with principles and convictions that he held to at the price of unpopularity and failure of reelection. His party bravely renominated him in 1840. In the boisterous "hard-cider" campaign of 1840, the Whigs delighted to chant that "Little Van" was "a used-up man." In his overwhelming defeat, Van Buren even lost his own state of New York.

Although driven from the Presidency, Van Buren remained active in politics for the next two decades. He continued to oppose annexation of Texas and approved the Wilmot Proviso, which barred slavery in territory acquired from Mexico. In 1848, he was the Presidential nominee of the Free-Soil party. Although defeated, he took so many votes in New York from the Democratic nominee, Lewis Cass, that the Whigs' Zachary Taylor was elected. Van Buren supported Democratic Presidents Pierce and Buchanan, as well as the prosecution of the Civil War. He died at his country estate of Lindenwald, near his birthplace, July 24, 1862.

## William Henry Harrison

William Henry Harrison, 9th President (March 4–April 4, 1841), was born at Berkeley, Charles City County, Virginia, on February 9, 1773. His father, a plantation owner and member of the Virginia aristocracy, was a signer of the Declaration of Independence.

Harrison attended Hampden-Sydney College and studied medicine in Philadelphia. Unattracted by the medical profession, he accepted an appointment by President Washington to the army as ensign in 1791.

Harrison served with distinction in the Indian campaigns of the Northwest Territory, rose to a captaincy, and in 1798 resigned his commission to settle at North Bend, Ohio, near Cincinnati. President John Adams appointed him secretary of the Northwest Territory. In 1799, he became the first territorial delegate to Congress.

For 12 years Harrison was territorial governor of Indiana and superintendent of Indian affairs. By negotiating vast land cessions from the Indians, he opened Ohio and Indiana to American settlement. When Tecumseh, a chieftain of the Shawnee Indians, and his brother the Shawnee Prophet objected to the land cessions, Harrison in November 1811 defeated the Indians in a formidable battle at Tippecanoe on the Wabash River. The battle made Harrison a national hero, admiringly called "Old Tippecanoe."

In the War of 1812, Harrison was commissioned a major general in command of forces in the Northwest. He took Detroit in September 1813, and in early October he established American hegemony in the West, when he defeated the combined Indian and British forces at the Thames River in Ontario, where Tecumseh was finally killed.

Harrison resigned his commission and as a war hero was elected in 1816 to the U.S. House of Representatives. He subsequently served in the Ohio Senate and in the U.S. Senate. Appointed minister to Colombia by President John Quincy Adams, Harrison was recalled when Andrew Jackson came to power. He retired to his farm at North Bend, and, to supplement his income, served as county recorder and clerk of the county court.

In 1836, Harrison's political fortunes recovered dramatically when the Whigs nominated him for President. Although defeated by Martin Van Buren, the Democratic candidate, Harrison ran an impressive race, carrying seven states. In 1840, the Whigs, including Daniel Webster and Henry Clay, nominated Harrison for President and John Tyler for Vice-President.

The 1840 Presidential campaign, famous for its slogan "Tippecanoe and Tyler too," is a classic of political demagoguery. Harrison's standing as a war hero, the absence of a platform, and diversionary political propaganda, enabled the Whigs to avoid the emerging issue of slavery. Van Buren, the incumbent, was portrayed drinking champagne from a crystal goblet at a table laden with costly viands and dinnerware. Harrison was seen content with a log cabin and hard cider. Aided also by the suffering of the Panic of 1837, Harrison scored an overwhelming victory.

His inaugural stirred enormous enthusiasm. His address, partly the work of Webster, prolix and abounding in classical allusions, was an extended statement of the Whig doctrine of the Presidency. Deferential to Congress, it viewed the legislators as the center of decision.

Harrison appointed a cabinet of high quality, headed by Daniel Webster as Secretary of State. On March 17, the President called a special session of Congress to meet on May 31 to act on the country's continuing financial distress. A week later, he took ill, developed pneumonia, and died, a month after his inauguration. Harrison was the first of our Presidents to die in office.

## John Tyler

John Tyler, 10th President (1841–1845), was born on March 29, 1790, in Charles City County, Virginia, the son of Judge John Tyler, a distinguished lawyer and governor of Virginia. Young Tyler graduated from William and Mary College at 17, was admitted to the bar at 19, and at 21 his public career began with his election to the Virginia House of Delegates.

Tyler moved steadily through a political career of remarkable breadth, as U.S. Congressman, Senator, governor of Virginia, and delegate to the important Virginia constitutional conventions of 1829 and 1830. In 1836, he was an unsuccessful candidate for the Vice-Presidency, but in the "Tippecanoe and Tyler too" campaign of 1840, with William Henry Harrison heading the Whig ticket, he ran again, this time successfully. Harrison died a month after his inauguration, and on April 4, 1841, Tyler became the first Vice-President to succeed to the Presidency.

Some chose to interpret the succession provision of the Constitution to mean that Tyler was only "Acting President," but he insisted upon the office's full title and powers. The reluctance to grant Tyler recognition was partly rooted in the unusual circumstances of his nomination. Tyler was an ex-Democrat who, as a legislator, had been a stubborn advocate of states' rights and consequently opposed to nationalistic Whig policies. The Whigs had nonetheless nominated him for the Vice-Presidency to attract Southern votes. They reasoned that, as Vice-President, Tyler would command no influence in the Harrison administration.

After Tyler became President, his ambiguous situation was further complicated by the presence in the Senate of Henry Clay, the heavy-handed but powerful leader of the Whig party. Clay was soon scornfully speaking of Tyler as "a President without a party." Tyler was also an obstacle to Clay's driving ambition to become President; if Tyler could be discredited to the point of being denied renomination, Clay might himself seize the prize.

Tyler, in a conciliatory step, retained the entire Harrison cabinet, which presumably should have satisfied the Whigs and Clay, but they were irreconcilable. A rift quickly developed over the Whig measure to reestablish a national bank. Twice Tyler vetoed the national bank bill. As a strict constitutionalist, he argued that a national bank must not be permitted to establish branches in the states without their prior consent. After the second bank veto, Tyler's entire cabinet resigned, with the exception of Daniel Webster, the Secretary of State. Webster remained only long enough to complete a treaty with Canada setting the northeast boundary of the United States.

With Clay now openly saying of the President that "I'll drive him before me," Tyler's own measures encountered rough treatment in Congress and his nominations to office were usually blocked.

Despite the deadlock with his own party, Tyler brought off some substantial achievements. He was adept at seizing upon issues that by their merit or popularity transcended partisanship. He was not unskilled at political maneuver and when a favorite project to annex Texas by treaty was lost—with every Whig but one voting against it —Tyler outmaneuvered his opponents and arranged for annexation by joint resolution.

A cultivated Southern gentleman, master of the good story and easy conversation, Tyler was attractive to Congressmen and, as a veteran legislator, experienced in dealing with them. Under his evident influence Congress passed a number of constructive laws. The Navy was thoroughly reorganized. A bureau was established for nautical charts and instruments, which later developed into the Naval Observatory. An act opening the way to initiating a national telegraphic system was passed, a step leading to the development of the Weather Bureau.

As President, Tyler excelled as an administrator and in employing his powers in foreign affairs. He conducted the government with a minimum of waste, although Congress provided no system for controlling public funds. Tyler brought the Seminole War to an end, entered into a treaty with China opening the doors of the Orient for the first time, and applied the Monroe Doctrine to Texas and Hawaii.

Despite his achievements, Tyler could muster only minor factional support for renomination in 1844. Withdrawing from the Presidential race, he retired to his estate, Sherwood Forest, in Virginia on the James River. There he lived in virtual retirement for 14 years, except for service as chancellor of the College of William and Mary from 1859 to 1861. In 1861, he proposed and presided over the secret North-South Conference held at Washington in an eleventh-hour effort to prevent the Civil War. When this failed, he advocated immediate secession and was elected a member of the congress of the Confederacy, but he died on January 18, 1862, before he could take his seat in that body.

## James Knox Polk

James Knox Polk, 11th President (1845–1849) was born on November 2, 1795, near Pineville in Mecklenburg County, North Carolina. Polk was of Scots-Irish stock, and his father soldiered in the Revolution. In 1806, the large and growing Polk family moved to central Tennessee, and Polk's schooling in that frontier district was fragmentary. Nevertheless, he entered the University of North Carolina at the age of 20, compiled an impressive record, and graduated in 1818. He studied law under Felix Grundy, the politician and noted criminal lawyer, was admitted to the bar, and practiced in Columbia, Tennessee.

An able orator in demand at political meetings, Polk became known as "the Napoleon of the Stump." This talent, as well as his friendship with Andrew Jackson, propelled him into a political career. In 1823 he was elected to the Tennessee House of Representatives, and in 1825 to the U.S. Congress, where he served seven consecutive terms, the last two as Speaker.

In 1839, he was elected governor of Tennessee. Although an ardent Jacksonian Democrat, he was defeated for reelection in 1841 and again in 1843.

Polk then turned to national politics, and when the Democratic national convention gathered in Baltimore in 1844, he was considered a serious candidate for the Vice-Presidency, but was unthought of for the Presidency. Circumstances, however, brought him an unexpected Presidential nomination: the first successful "dark horse" candidate in the history of the office.

Just before the convention met, former President Martin Van Buren issued a statement opposing the annexation of Texas, which offended both Western and Southern interests. This position eliminated Van Buren, the leading contender for the Democratic nomination. Polk's stand on Texas and the disputed territory of Oregon—"Reannexation of Texas and Reoccupation of Oregon" —won him the nomination and the election. Since Polk lacked national prominence, the rival Whig party's campaign slogan was, "Who is James Polk?" The Democrats countered with "54–40 or Fight!", a reference to the entire Oregon territory, which the United States, it was felt, should possess even at the price of war with Great Britain. In the election Polk narrowly defeated Henry Clay, the Whig candidate, by winning New York State.

His inaugural address exalted the Union and deplored sectional discord. More specifically, he opposed a tariff "for protection merely" and asserted uncompromisingly that the United States' title to Oregon was "clear and unquestionable."

The independent treasury bill of 1846, which he adroitly shepherded through Congress, reestablished a financial system that endured, with only minor modification, until the Federal Reserve System was established during Woodrow Wilson's administration.

The Walker Tariff Act of 1846, true to Polk's purpose, put most tariff duties on a revenue basis and used ad valorem in place of specific duties. Polk prevailed against political foes who foresaw only ruination for manufacturing and the public treasury.

Oregon proved a more difficult issue. Aided by Secretary of State James Buchanan and after long negotiations with Great Britain, Polk won a settlement that was something less than his campaign slogan had demanded. Buchanan proposed that the Oregon Territory be divided by extending to the Pacific coast the boundary provided by the 49th parallel. When Britain rejected the compromise, Polk boldly reasserted his claim to the entire Oregon Territory. Britain then acquiesced to the 49th parallel line, except for Vancouver Island, and the treaty that was signed (1846) incorporated this division.

The acquisition of California was a severe test of Polk's political skills. Aiming to secure the territory by purchases, he reasserted some longstanding damage claims against Mexico. Certain that Mexico could not pay her debt, he expected her to cede the territory. Mexico rejected any kind of bargain, and American troops under Gen. Zachary Taylor provoked hostilities along the Rio Grande. Polk asked Congress on May 9, 1846, for a declaration of war because of the unpaid claims and because Mexico had invaded American soil. The treaty at the end of the Mexican War ceded California and New Mexico to the United States, for which Mexico was paid $15 million, and the old damage claims were assumed by the United States. Polk's opponents charged that he had forced the war upon Mexico to extend slavery.

To induce Mexico to accept the treaty, Polk had asked Congress for $2 million to be used for "diplomatic purposes." The sum was to be devoted to paying the Mexican army, a step that was indispensable to acceptance of the treaty. David Wilmot offered a proviso to the appropriation, directing that slavery be excluded from any territory acquired through use of the funds made available to the President. Polk angrily termed Wilmot's proviso "a mischievous and foolish amendment," aimed at diplomatic embarrassment. After Polk threatened to veto it, the proviso was defeated, but it brought the building conflict between North and South into the open.

In foreign affairs, Polk extended the reach of the Monroe Doctrine from a prohibition of forcible foreign interference to any kind of interference in American affairs. He effectively opposed an invitation by the people of Yucatán in Mexico for Britain or Spain to exert sovereignty over their territory.

Polk was an exacting administrator who closely supervised the affairs of his departments. He bore unglادly the less palatable aspects of politics. He was contemptuous of the spoils system and, in a rare act for a President, vetoed two river-and-harbor bills, Congress's traditional and politically sacred pork-barrel method of legislation.

Serious and diligent almost to a fault, Polk had little time for pleasure and small talk. Secretive, particularly in dealing with Congress, he offended many by his reticence and sly maneuvers. He was lacking in personal magnetism and had few intimate friends, although Bancroft deemed him "generous and benevolent."

Just before taking office, Polk declared he would not be a candidate for reelection. He died on June 15, 1849, shortly after leaving office.

## Zachary Taylor

Zachary Taylor, 12th President (March 4, 1849–July 9, 1850) was born November 24, 1784, at Montebello, Orange County, Virginia. His father was a farmer and a colonel in the Revolution. When he was less than a year old, Taylor and his family migrated to Kentucky. There on the frontier, schools were little known, and Taylor absorbed a sketchy education from tutoring.

In 1808, he obtained a commission as first lieutenant in the army. During 40 years of military service, which ended when he was nominated for President, Taylor fought in the War of 1812, against the Indians in the Northwest and in Florida, and in the Mexican War. In the Seminole Indian War in Florida, the muscular, stocky Taylor became known as "Old Rough and Ready" to troops who admired his valor and candor. His distinction at the battle of Okeechobee against the Seminoles won him the rank of brevet brigadier general.

Taylor commanded the army in Texas, and a Mexican attack upon his forces in 1846 was used by Congress as justification for declaring war. After Taylor's victory at Monterrey, Mexico, President James K. Polk, distrustful of Taylor's independent spirit and his potential as a political rival, turned over most of Taylor's troops to a new commander. Santa Anna, the Mexican commander, learning of Taylor's weakened forces, attacked him at Buena Vista with troops that were numerically far superior. A stunning victory in an all-day battle made Taylor a national hero and immediately inspired both leading parties, the Democrats and the Whigs, to consider him as a candidate for the Presidential election of 1848.

As a lifelong soldier, Taylor had never voted, and his political views, if any existed, were unknown. Mindful of their victory with another military hero, W. H. Harrison in 1840, the Whigs in 1848 chose Taylor as their nominee over such other formidable contenders as Henry Clay and Daniel Webster.

Stressing that his administration would be nonpartisan and free from party pledges, Taylor defeated his Democratic opponent, Lewis Cass, and the Free-Soil nominee, Martin Van Buren, in the first election to be held simultaneously in all the states.

As President, Taylor was a potential force to check the widening breach between the North and South over slavery. He was a slave owner, but numbered among his closest counselors the antislavery Whig, Senator William H. Seward of New York. In addition, his electoral victory was fashioned by substantial support from both sections; he carried seven Northern and eight Southern states. His inaugural address urged Congress to work for conciliation of sectional controversies and offered a program no one could criticize: friendly relations in foreign affairs, an efficient army and navy, and encouragement of agriculture, commerce, and manufacture.

For all of this political insulation, Taylor had to face the fiery issue of the admission of new states to the Union on a free or slave basis. Thanks largely to his overriding nationalistic sentiment, Taylor quickly took an antislavery position, for above all he wanted to annex the territories won in the Mexican War. He wrote to Jefferson Davis that nature had excluded slavery from the new Southwest, and, in a Pennsylvania address, he assured Northerners they "need have no apprehension of the further extension of slavery."

Taylor dispatched a special emissary, Thomas Butler King, to counsel Californians in forming a constitution and applying for statehood. Similar assistance was given New Mexico. In special messages to Congress in 1850, he urged unconditional admission for California and statehood for New Mexico.

In a counterthrust, Southern legislators filibustered against the admission of California and insisted that all measures concerning territories ceded by Mexico be taken up in a single bill. Southern Whigs withdrew their support of Taylor, and such Southern leaders as Alexander Stephens and Robert Tombs threatened the President with secession.

In Congress, Henry Clay framed a series of bills known collectively as the Compromise of 1850 in an effort to placate both the North and the South. Taylor would doubtless have opposed the compromise, but following ceremonies connected with building the Washington Monument, he was stricken with cholera and died after a Presidential tenure of only 16 months.

In foreign affairs, Taylor's Secretary of State, John M. Clayton, negotiated the Clayton-Bulwer Treaty with Great Britain which guaranteed the neutrality of an isthmian canal. (The previous Polk administration had secured rights to build a canal across Nicaragua.)

## Millard Fillmore

Millard Fillmore, 13th President (July 10, 1850–March 3, 1853), was born in Locke (now Summerhill) in Cayuga County, New York, on January 7, 1800. The son of a frontier farmer who had migrated from Vermont, young Fillmore had scant schooling and was apprenticed to a wool carder. Intent upon studying law, he migrated to Buffalo, where he worked in a lawyer's office for room and board. In 1823, he was admitted to the bar and began practice in East Aurora, New York.

Fillmore's political career began with his election in 1828 to the New York State Assembly on an Anti-Mason ticket. He secured the passage of a law that abolished imprisonment for debt and formed a friendship with the Albany publisher and political leader, Thurlow Weed. In 1830, Fillmore moved back to Buffalo and a year later was elected to the first of four terms in the U.S. Congress. He supported the emerging Whig party and the nationalistic policies of Henry Clay. As chairman of the powerful Ways and Means Committee, he oversaw the 1842 tariff act that raised duties on manufactured goods. On the burning issue of slavery, he was a moderate.

In 1844, Fillmore ran as the Whig candidate for governor of New York but was unsuccessful and returned to his law practice. In 1846, he became the first chancellor of the University of Buffalo. A year later, he was elected comptroller of New York.

Fillmore's acceptability to both Northern and Southern Whigs and his backing by Henry Clay resulted in his election as Vice-President with Zachary Taylor in 1848. As Vice-President, he presided over the bitter Senate debates on the slavery compromise measures of 1850 with notable fairness. Midway in this political turbulence President Taylor died, and Fillmore became the second "accidental President."

The Taylor Cabinet promptly resigned. Fillmore's nomination of Daniel Webster of New Hampshire as Secretary of State and John Crittenden of Kentucky as Attorney General was indicative of the new President's preference for a moderate Whig position and his readiness to compromise in the growing conflict between North and South. In his message to Congress of August 6, 1850, Fillmore made a compelling plea for settlement by compromise. An opponent, Salmon Chase, credited the Presidential message with winning over six New England votes in the Senate and moving Congress down the compromise road.

Clay's "omnibus" compromise bill, unable to be passed as a whole, was separated into its several parts. These sections were soon enacted, and the President approved them believing that only through them could the Union be saved. Fillmore and Clay led not a united party, but rather one that represented a bipartisan coalition of Northern Democrats and Southern Whigs. To Southerners, a key element of the compromise was the new Fugitive Slave Law; Fillmore's approval of it cost him the support of Northern Whigs. Since the Presidency was Whig and Congress Democratic, little important legislation was passed, other than the Compromise of 1850.

In seeking renomination as the Whig standard-bearer in 1852, Fillmore enjoyed support from Southern Whigs. His rival, Webster, was backed by New Englanders, and another rival, General Winfield Scott, by an extreme antislavery group. When the Fillmore-Webster factions failed to unite, the nomination passed to Scott. Like other Presidents from Jackson to Lincoln, Fillmore was limited to one Presidential term by the slavery dispute, which prevented the Chief Executive from satisfying both the Northern and Southern wings of his party.

As President, Fillmore presented an image of cool-headedness and caution. His paramount political value was preservation of the Union, a goal to which he subordinated any specific interest or issue in the slavery controversy. From his deathbed, Henry Clay urged Fillmore's renomination, while Webster hailed his administration as one of the ablest.

Fillmore's advent to politics coincided with the emergence of the Whig party, and his departure with its demise. The 1852 elections were the last national campaign in which the Whigs were active. In 1856, Fillmore was the Presidential nominee of the American, or Know-Nothing, party. Stressing the value of unity and the dangers of sectionalism, he ran last in a three-way race. Always preferring conciliation to coercion, Fillmore opposed Lincoln's policies in the Civil War and supported Andrew Johnson's stand against radical reconstruction.

For all his lack of early advantages, Fillmore, according to a contemporary, possessed "a grace and polish of manner which fitted him for the most refined circles of the metropolis." Fillmore's political activities ended with the Reconstruction. He died on March 8, 1874. In 1969, a substantial body of Fillmore papers was discovered.

## Franklin Pierce

Franklin Pierce, 14th President (1853–1857), was born on November 23, 1804, in Hillsboro, New Hampshire. His father, Benjamin Pierce, served in the Revolution and later was a brigadier general in the state militia. He was also a two-term governor of New Hampshire and left a valuable heritage of political connections for his son, who, after study at nearby academies and at Phillips Exeter, entered Bowdoin College in Maine.

After graduating from Bowdoin in 1824, Pierce read law and was admitted to the bar in 1827. He began practice in Hillsboro and two years later commenced his political career by winning election as a Jacksonian Democrat to the New Hampshire House of Representatives. Reelected two years later, he also became Speaker. In 1833, he began a term in the U.S. House of Representatives and after a second term was elected to the U.S. Senate. He was the youngest member of that body, which then included such giants as Webster, Clay, and Calhoun. Because of his wife's poor health, Pierce resigned from the Senate in 1842 and resumed law practice in Concord, New Hampshire.

When the Mexican War broke out, Pierce, a staunch nationalist, inspired by his father's record in the Revolution, enlisted as a private. He advanced rapidly to brigadier general and served in key battles. In 1848, he resigned from the army, and two years later he became president of New Hampshire's Fifth State Constitutional Convention.

In 1852, Pierce became the Democratic Presidential nominee, a classic instance of a successful "dark horse" candidate. He received no votes until the 35th ballot and won on the 49th, as an acceptable compromise candidate in the deepening North-South split over slavery. An advocate of the Compromise of 1850, Pierce was regarded as a Northerner with Southern sympathies. Pierce was victorious over his Whig opponent, General Winfield Scott, by carrying every state but four, although with less than a 50,000 plurality.

By having avoided issues in his campaign, Pierce hoped to make his administration one of harmony. His cabinet was a perfect political balance of two conservative Southerners, two conservative Northerners, an antislavery Northerner, a states' rights Southerner, and a New England Whig. His inaugural address and early actions stressed objectives of general appeal. He promised a vigorous foreign policy and an economical and efficient administration. He called for a larger and better army and navy and reduction of the debt through use of the Treasury surplus. But Pierce's strategy of harmony was bedeviled by rising Northern sentiment against slavery and its expansion.

In foreign affairs, Pierce was an expansionist. His policies reflected his nationalism and, presumably, were designed to divert attention from domestic issues and gratify Southern hopes of introducing the slave economy into new territories. Accordingly, Pierce sought to convince Great Britain that under the Clayton-Bulwer Treaty she ought to withdraw from Nicaragua and Honduras. When negotiations failed, he tacitly supported a proslavery "filibustering" expedition against Nicaragua.

Pierce negotiated to acquire Hawaii, but the venture failed when the king of the islands died. Pierce's overtures to the Russians for the purchase of Alaska were unavailing. His administration's most brazen move was the Ostend Manifesto, a declaration by three proslavery American ministers calling for the annexation of Cuba. The public, the Senate, and the President's own party reacted indignantly to this move.

Pierce's foreign policies were not altogether blanketed with failure. A treaty was made with Japan in 1854, opening that country to American trading interests. James Gadsden, a special Presidential emissary, negotiated the purchase of land from Mexico that settled a boundary dispute and secured right-of-way for a southern railroad to the Pacific.

The President's preoccupation with foreign policy could not forestall a sudden, unexpected upsurge of the slavery issue. Leading Democratic Senators brought up a bill to organize Kansas and Nebraska as new territories out of the Indian lands, thus threatening the slender slavery truce.

When the Kansas-Nebraska Bill became law in 1854, both proslavery and antislavery settlers poured into the territory, and trouble quickly developed as both factions vied for control. Civil war erupted in Kansas when a free-soil group organized a government independent of the President's. Ultimately, Pierce ordered the free-soil government to cease and put federal troops at the disposal of the governor of Kansas. The Kansas experience served to reinforce the Democratic party's identification with slavery and to spur the rise of the new Republican party and the Know-Nothing party.

Pierce strove energetically to restore his crumbling popularity and win renomination. He launched an anti-British drive and demanded the recall of the British Minister Crampton for illegally recruiting troops in the United States for the Crimean War. But the Democratic national convention of 1856, apprehensive of rising Republican strength, looked for a "safer" man; it found him in James Buchanan, who, by having been abroad, had been untouched by the controversies of the Pierce era.

Although humiliated by his rejection for renomination, Pierce labored diligently to reduce and master problems before leaving office. He established a regular (proslavery) government in Kansas and, thanks to the continued presence of troops, he could proclaim that "peace now reigns in Kansas." A treaty was negotiated under which Britain agreed to abandon its interests in Central America except those in Honduras. The Senate, however, withheld its approval. Upon leaving office, Pierce at least had the satisfaction of seeing his party retain control of the Presidency and regain Congress.

After leaving the Presidency, Pierce traveled abroad to aid his wife's health. In the Civil War, having returned to Concord, he was an outspoken critic of Lincoln's, holding that war could have been averted by better leadership. The increasing unpopularity of his views relegated him to obscurity. His death on October 8, 1869, was almost unnoticed.

## James Buchanan

James Buchanan, 15th President (1857–1861), was born April 23, 1791, in Cove Gap, Pennsylvania, the second of 11 children and the son of a merchant-farmer. After graduation (1809) from Dickinson College in Carlisle, Pennsylvania, Buchanan studied law in Lancaster and began practice there in 1812. He volunteered for duty in the War of 1812 and helped defend the city of Baltimore.

Originally a Federalist, Buchanan was elected (1814) to the Pennsylvania House of Representatives. In 1816 he ran unsuccessfully for the U.S. Congress but, four years later, he won and began 10 years of service in that body. Joining the Democratic party, he supported the Presidential race of Andrew Jackson in 1824 and again in 1828, when Jackson won. Grateful for Buchanan's continued support, President Jackson appointed him (1831) minister to Russia. After negotiating America's first trade treaty with Russia, Buchanan returned to the United States, and in 1834 he was elected U.S. Senator.

Buchanan was a favorite-son candidate for the Democratic Presidential nomination of 1844, but he withdrew his name before the convention met. James K. Polk, who was elected, made Buchanan his Secretary of State in 1845. In this post,

Buchanan oversaw the negotiations that secured the southern half of the Oregon country and the vast territory in the Southwest from Mexico. His support of the annexation of Texas and the acquisition of Cuba led to the charge that he was a proslavery politician.

When the Whigs recaptured the Presidency in 1849, Buchanan retired to Wheatland, his estate near Lancaster. He was an unsuccessful aspirant for the Presidency in 1852. Franklin Pierce, who was nominated and elected, appointed Buchanan minister to Great Britain. By serving abroad, Buchanan avoided the fierce domestic political struggle over the Kansas-Nebraska Act and was, therefore, highly available in 1856 for the Democratic Presidential nomination. As the eventual nominee, Buchanan stressed the necessity of preserving the Union and avoided taking a stand on the slavery question. In a three-cornered race, Buchanan won only a popular plurality, although he secured a large majority of the electoral vote. He was a bachelor and the only Pennsylvanian to have become President.

Buchanan's plan for halting the worsening schism over slavery was revealed in his inaugural address and in the formation of his cabinet. In choosing his department heads, he preserved "the sacred balance," giving equal representation to slaveholding and nonslaveholding states. In his inaugural address, he declared that the question of slavery in the territories was a matter for the courts to determine, a view that he asserted confidently after learning how the pending Dred Scott case would be decided.

Buchanan hoped to deflect national attention from grievous domestic problems by fostering a dynamic foreign policy. He moved to acquire Cuba, but Congress failed to provide the necessary appropriations to begin negotiations. To avoid European intervention, he proposed to bolster the Benito Juarez government in Mexico, but Congress again would not lend financial support to the scheme.

Buchanan's image as a Northern man with Southern sympathies was affirmed by his accepting the Dred Scott decision as final and by his support of the proslavery Kansas constitution. Buchanan stressed that this constitution was republican in form and properly left the question of slavery up to popular determination once Kansas became a state. The President's stand divided the Democratic party into two great factions. It identified the administration with the Southern wing and ignited a revolt by the followers of Stephen A. Douglas.

The growing crisis of disunion was magnified when South Carolina moved toward secession. Buchanan rejected the advice of his military commanders to garrison Southern ports. (In his annual legislative message, however, he had emphatically denied the right of secession.) Simultaneously, he admitted an inability to deal with actual secession, since federal officers in South Carolina, through whom he enforced the law, had resigned. In a close construction of Presidential authority, Buchanan held that except for defending U.S. property in South Carolina and collecting customs, the Chief Executive lacked authority to act. Congress alone could decide whether existing laws were amendable for carrying out the Constitution.

Buchanan dispatched a personal agent, Caleb Cushing, to dissuade the South Carolinians from secession and again rejected military advice to reinforce the forts in Charleston harbor. A South Carolina convention, nevertheless, voted to secede and Major Robert Anderson moved his Federal troops from indefensible Fort Moultrie to Fort Sumter, a step that South Carolina spokesmen said violated a Presidential commitment to keep the status quo.

In the quickening tension, Buchanan's cabinet collapsed, with both Northern and Southern members resigning. The President filled the vacancies with Northern and border-state members, a harbinger of firmer policies. Buchanan sent reinforcements to Fort Sumter and announced his intent to hold it and keep peace until "the question shall have been settled by competent authority." Buchanan proposed new legislation to deal with the crisis, but Congress was unresponsive.

Buchanan retired into obscurity at Wheatland and died on June 1, 1868.

## Abraham Lincoln

Abraham Lincoln, 16th President (March 4, 1861–April 14, 1865), was born in a dirt-floor log cabin in Hardin (now Larue) County, Kentucky, on February 12, 1809. His father, Thomas, was a migratory frontier farmer and carpenter, who was nearly always poor and moved from Kentucky to Indiana and, eventually, to Illinois. Of Lincoln's mother, Nancy Hanks of Rockingham County, Virginia, little is known. She died when young Lincoln was nine, and his home seemed empty and lonely after her death, until his father married Sarah (Bush) Johnston, a widow, who brought affection to the family. Lincoln may have spoken of her when he said: "God bless my mother; all that I am or ever hope to be I owe to her."

Lincoln absorbed a scanty frontier education (his formal education probably totaled less than one year). Books were scarce, but Lincoln taught himself to read and was a close student of the family Bible. His boyhood readings in it provided the store of Biblical quotations and references that later abounded, with great effect, in his addresses and writings.

As a strong, large-boned youth of 6 feet, 4 inches, Lincoln was admirably suited for hard work, which he experienced in the full. He split logs for fence rails, plowed fields, cut corn, threshed wheat, and took a flat boat loaded with farm produce to New Orleans. As a boy, he showed talent as a speaker; his knack for telling stories and imitating local personalities made people gather to hear him, often at a store in which he was a clerk. His homely face and black coarse hair added fascination to what he said.

From 1831 to 1837, Lincoln was settled in New Salem, Illinois, a log-cabin community near Springfield. For a time he clerked in a store (which soon failed). As unemployment threatened, the Black Hawk War commenced, and Lincoln volunteered for service. His company elected him captain, but he saw no fighting except, he said, "with the mosquitoes."

Returning (1832) from the war, Lincoln groped for a way to make a livelihood. With a partner, he bought a grocery store in New Salem on credit. When the store failed and the partner died, Lincoln paid off the debts, an accomplishment that won him the nickname "Honest Abe." In 1833, Lincoln was appointed postmaster of New Salem, and eked out a living as a deputy to the county surveyor and from other odd-job fees.

Trying for the state legislature in 1834, Lincoln won as a Whig and served four successive two-year terms. His ready stories and sharp wit enabled him to excel in debate, and his leadership gifts were recognized in his selection as the Whig's floor leader. Simultaneous with his young political career, Lincoln read law and won (1836) his license to practice. In Springfield, he experienced a succession of partnerships, including one with William H. Herndon, who later became his biographer.

Lincoln "traveled the circuit," accompanying judges and fellow lawyers through the counties to try cases. The cases were heard in inns, which permitted Lincoln to indulge his talent for strong, effective argument when he thought his client was right.

Lincoln emerged in national politics when he was elected as a Whig to the U.S. House of Representatives and on December 6, 1847, took his seat in Congress where, to the displeasure of his constituents, he opposed President Polk and his conduct of the Mexican War. When his term ended on March 4, 1849, Lincoln did not dare run again because of the general unpopularity of his war views among his constituency. Convinced that his political career was ended, he returned to Springfield where, through hard work and a fast-growing practice, he became one of the best-known lawyers in Illinois in the 1850s.

In 1855, agitated by the national political issue of slavery, Lincoln again turned to politics. Opposed to slavery, although he was never an abolitionist, Lincoln spoke against the principal author of the Kansas-Nebraska Act, Illinois Senator Stephen A. Douglas, and supported the candidacies of legislators opposed to the act. In that same year, Lincoln ran unsuccessfully for the U.S. Senate. Believing that slavery was the negation of the nation's commitment to freedom and equality, he left the Whigs and joined the antislavery Republican party.

In 1858, Lincoln was nominated to run against Douglas for the U.S. Senate. In his speech at the Illinois Republican convention, Lincoln said that "I believe this government cannot endure permanently half slave and half free." The Senatorial contest included a series of debates between Lincoln and Douglas centered on the extension of slavery into free territory. Holding that he was not an abolitionist, Lincoln condemned slavery "as a moral, social, and political evil." Douglas won the election, but the debates gained Lincoln national attention.

In May 1860, the Republican national convention nominated Lincoln for President on the third ballot, after William H. Seward of New York had led on the first two ballots. Considered a moderate on the slavery question, Lincoln received 180 electoral votes to 72 for Breckinridge, 39 for Bell, and 12 for Douglas. Lincoln, elected President, was pledged not to abolish slavery, but to preserve the Union and to prevent the spread of slavery.

However, Southern secession began as soon as Lincoln's election was assured. On December 20, 1860, South Carolina passed a secession ordinance. By the time Lincoln was inaugurated (March 4, 1861), seven states had seceded and formed the Confederate government. Denying in his inaugural address that the federal government would interfere with slavery in states in which the Constitution protected it, he warned that he would use the full power of the nation to "hold, occupy, and possess" the "property and places belonging to the Federal government."

With the coming of war, Lincoln acted boldly and energetically. He called out the militia to suppress the "insurrection," expanded the regular army and navy, raised a volunteer army, closed the post office to "treasonable correspondence," imposed a blockade on Southern ports, and suspended the writ of habeas corpus in areas where Southern sympathizers were active. He also ordered the spending of unappropriated funds for purposes unauthorized by Congress.

For Lincoln's wartime Presidency, the Civil War was a severe test of the human spirit. A succession of battlefield defeats afflicted the North, and a substantial body of Northern opinion demanded peace. Many were willing to fight to preserve the Union, but not to destroy slavery. Others urged the destruction of slavery as the war's supreme goal. Lincoln had to keep the antislavery extremists in check to prevent the secession of the border states. Jealousies and frictions unsettled his cabinet. He appointed and removed a succession of field commanders in the vain hope of securing a major military victory.

In mid-1862, Lincoln decided to drop his reserve on the slavery question and issue a proclamation of emancipation. On the advice of Secretary of State Seward, he awaited a Northern victory. Seizing upon the dubious success of Union forces at Antietam (September 1862), Lincoln issued the proclamation on September 22. He declared that slaves in states in rebellion on January 1, 1863, would be free. Lincoln's action gave a clear-cut moral purpose to the war, setting the stage for the 13th Amendment to the Constitution (adopted in December 1865) that ended slavery throughout the United States.

The tide of the war ran strongly in the Union's favor in 1863 and 1864. Lincoln was renominated (1864), and easily defeated his Democratic opponent, General George B. McClellan, by an electoral vote of 212 to 21 and a popular majority that exceeded 400,000 votes. When Lincoln again took the oath of office (March 4, 1865), the end of the war was in sight, and his inaugural address outlined a postwar policy. He urged that, instead of vengeance, there be "malice toward none" and "charity for all." Pressed to decide if seceded states were in or out of the Union, Lincoln, in his last public address (April 11, 1865), said that the question was unimportant: the Southern states "finding themselves safely at home, it would be utterly immaterial whether they had ever been abroad."

On April 14, five days after Lee's surrender, Lincoln was mortally shot by John Wilkes Booth—an actor and fanatical supporter of the Confederacy—at Ford's Theater in Washington and died the next morning.

Lincoln as President withstood the trials of war with a granitic self-confidence. Yet he was a man of the purest humility, extraordinary wisdom, and shrewd judgment—a master politician in understanding and shaping public opinion. His lean, beautiful, moving prose brought to his Presidency an eloquence that no other incumbent has matched.

## Andrew Johnson

Andrew Johnson, 17th President (April 15, 1865–March 3, 1869), was born on December 29, 1808, at Raleigh, North Carolina. His father, who was a sexton, porter, and constable, died when Johnson was four, and at 10 he was apprenticed to a tailor. Thanks to the tailor's practice of employing someone to read aloud as his workmen stitched, and to the local newspaper and a few books, Johnson became familiar with American history and politics.

In 1826, Johnson moved to Greeneville, Tennessee, where he set up his own tailor shop. His efforts in organizing a workingman's party led to his election as alderman in opposition to the local slave-holding aristocracy's candidate. In 1830, he became mayor of Greeneville, and five years later he was elected to the Tennessee legislature and served continuously until 1843. Although formally unschooled, Johnson continued his political rise when elected (1843) to the U.S. House of Representatives in which he served for 10 years.

In Congress Johnson staunchly represented the interests of the "common people" and, in 1845, he introduced the first homestead bill for providing farms for landless citizens from public lands. Johnson's political beliefs were influenced by his fellow Tennessean, Andrew Jackson. Johnson's powerful voice and quick mind enhanced his popularity while provoking concern among Southern aristocrats who opposed his homestead policy. Johnson was elected (1853) Tennessee governor and U.S. Senator (1857), thus becoming one of the few major Southern officeholders of the time who had supported himself by manual labor. Although a slaveholder and a Democrat, Johnson defended the Union. In fact, he was the only Southern Senator not to resign and secede with his state. When Union armies won back (1862) control of western Tennessee, Lincoln appointed Johnson military governor of the state and, by 1864, he had organized a loyal government. This achievement won Johnson the Vice-Presidential nomination on Lincoln's Republican ticket in 1864.

Upon Lincoln's assassination, Johnson assumed the office of President in an atmosphere of grief and rage. Quickly moving to restore conditions of peace after the Civil War, Johnson disbanded most of the Federal army, revoked the blockade of the South, and restored trade. For the difficult problem of reestablishing local government in the seven states of the former Confederacy, Johnson faced rival Presidential and Congressional plans that had been formulated under Lincoln.

Although claiming to assert Lincoln's plan, Johnson actually altered it in some particulars. Unlike Lincoln, who had offered a general amnesty, Johnson required that 14 classes of persons—particularly the well-to-do—apply for pardon. But in judging the loyalty of a state government, Johnson required neither that there be a stipulated proportion of loyal voters nor that state legislatures or conventions take specific steps.

Under Johnson's stimulation, new state governments were organized, secession ordinances were repealed, and slavery abolished. The 13th Amendment was ratified (1865) by all Southern states, except Mississippi. The new governments, however, failed to extend suffrage to qualified blacks, as Johnson suggested. The President did not curb Southern police regulations that were aimed, presumably, at keeping order among blacks but quickened Northern suspicions of an attempt to restore slavery.

Congress, which had not been in session, met in December 1865. The Radical Republicans, who favored harsh reconstruction terms for the South, realized that they would be outnumbered if Southern legislators were seated. As a result, the Radicals refused to seat the Southerners, arguing that they had been illegally elected. Led by Congressman Thaddeus Stevens of Pennsylvania, the Radicals further contended that the Southern states had to come in as new states or continue to be regarded as conquered territory. However, in his message to Congress, Johnson viewed the states and the Constitution as intertwined: since the act of secession was null and void under the Constitution to begin with, Southern state functions had been in his view simply suspended, not destroyed.

In the conflict that developed, Congress' lawmaking powers were pitted against the President's veto power. Congress passed an act extending the Freedman's Bureau, but Johnson vetoed it. His veto of the Civil Rights Act, however, failed. The act aimed to guarantee the rights of freedmen against violation by state law. Congress also passed (1868) the 14th Amendment, which was designed to incorporate the substance of the act into the Constitution.

With the Congressional elections of 1866 in prospect, Johnson decided to present his case to the people and made his "swing around the circle," as it was known, through the East and Midwest in August and September. Although the venture began well, Johnson was provoked into making some ill-tempered remarks when goaded by Radical hecklers, and a hostile press ran biased accounts of his conduct. The election results imperiled Johnson: Congressional foes increased and, consequently, his veto power deteriorated.

Emboldened by its ability to overwhelm the President's veto power, Congress now began to encroach seriously on his domain. It circumvented the Presidential pardoning power, which Johnson had used on behalf of prominent Confederates, by excluding Confederates from office until Congress granted amnesty. The Tenure of Office Act (1867), which was passed despite Presidential veto, prohibited the Chief Executive from removing, without Senate consent, any officer appointed with the Senate's consent. The Supreme Court declined to review the act.

On August 12, 1867, Johnson suspended Secretary of War Edwin M. Stanton, a Radical informer, and appointed General Ulysses S. Grant as temporary secretary. But Grant was also a Radical sympathizer and, in January 1868, he returned his office to Stanton. On February 21, Johnson, formally removing Stanton, made General Lorenzo Thomas Secretary ad interim. Stanton, however, locked himself in his office to prevent Thomas from taking over, and the Senate refused to confirm Thomas' nomination.

A few days later, the House of Representatives voted 128 to 47 to impeach Johnson on 11 counts. A garish extravaganza of 11½ weeks' duration, the trial was presided over by Chief Justice Salmon P. Chase who, although wanting to be President with an intensity that Lincoln had once likened to insanity, proved to be a model of fairness. If the President was convicted, the new President was to be one of the Senate's own, Ben Wade of Ohio, its president pro tempore, who stood first in the line of succession under a law that dated back to 1792.

As the proceedings moved on, the case against Johnson proved thin and revealed that some Senators were more intent upon punishing him than seeing justice done. Fierce pressure was brought to bear on undecided Senators to build up the two-thirds vote required for conviction.

On May 16, the Senate voted on the eleventh charge, the one that Johnson's opponents believed the most likely to pass. As the vote proceeded, it became clear that the outcome would depend on the vote of Senator Edmund G. Ross of Kansas, who said "not guilty" and saved Johnson by a single vote. Votes were taken on only two other articles with identical results, and the trial ended.

In foreign affairs, Johnson and Secretary of State Seward achieved (1867) the purchase of Alaska from Russia and in 1865, by threat of force, they induced Napoleon III to withdraw his troops from Mexico. Maximilian, who was installed (1864) by Napoleon III as Mexico's emperor while the United States was distracted by the Civil War, was overthrown by Juarez.

For all of his travail, Johnson nonetheless aspired to be the Democratic nominee for President in 1868, but the party chose Governor Horatio Seymour of New York.

After leaving the White House, Johnson ran unsuccessfully for Congress in 1869 and 1872. In 1874, however, he was elected to the U.S. Senate, the only former President to become a Senator. Johnson served only in a special short session in March 1875. After returning to Tennessee, he suffered a paralytic stroke and died on July 31, 1875.

## Ulysses Simpson Grant

Ulysses Simpson Grant, 18th President (1869–1877), was born on April 27, 1822, in Point Pleasant, Ohio, the eldest son of a farmer and tanner. An excellent horseman but disinclined toward farm work, Grant applied to West Point.

An average student at West Point, Grant impressed his classmates as academically lazy and careless in dress. Graduating in 1843, he served with distinction in the Mexican War and attained the rank of first lieutenant.

After the war, Grant served in western posts and drank excessively, until his commanding officer ordered him either to reform or to resign. In 1854 he did resign and took up farming near St. Louis. Handicapped by poor land, Grant sold the farm in 1859 and became employed in a real estate office, but performed his main duty—collecting rents—poorly. He next worked, briefly, in the U.S. Customhouse, and in 1860 joined his father's hardware store in Galena, Illinois. As a storekeeper, he was unsuccessful, too.

At the outbreak of the Civil War, Grant, now 40 years old and unsettled, drilled a company of volunteers in Galena and then went to Springfield to work for the Illinois adjutant general. His request to the War Department for a colonelcy was ignored; however, in May 1861 the governor of Illinois appointed him colonel of the 21st Illinois Volunteers. By August, he was a brigadier general of volunteers and was given command of southwestern Missouri. An aggressive field commander, he swept through victories in Missouri, Kentucky, and Tennessee. In 1862, he gave the Union its first major victory when he captured Forts Henry and Donelson. At the latter fort he specified, "No terms other than an unconditional and immediate surrender can be accepted." This earned him the nickname "Unconditional Surrender Grant."

Grant moved on to larger commands and greater victories at Shiloh, Vicksburg, and Chattanooga. In March 1864, Lincoln made him a lieutenant-general, placed him in command of all the Union armies, and said of Grant that "he makes things git." Grant took personal command of the Army of the Potomac to confront the Confederates under General Robert E. Lee. Relentlessly applying superior manpower and force, Grant wore down the enemy and brought Lee to surrender at Appomattox, April 9, 1865. Generous in victory, Grant permitted the vanquished Confederates to keep their horses "for the spring plowing." Lavishly hailed in the victorious Union, Grant was made a full general in 1866, the first such designation since George Washington.

In 1868, Grant the military hero won the Republican nomination for President and triumphed easily over his Democratic opponent, Governor Horatio Seymour of New York. A newcomer to politics, Grant accepted the nomination in a note the brevity of which was unheard of for Presidential candidates, but it did contain the apt sentiment, "Let us have peace." Always a man of opinions, Grant declined to ride in the inaugural with the outgoing President, Andrew Johnson, owing to an estrangement that stemmed from Johnson's imbroglio with the War Department.

Unfamiliar and uneasy with politics, Grant conducted business in the executive mansion in a military style. Military aides did much of the work of the administration and Grant, upon issuing orders, expected battle-command compliance. To his misfortune, he did not readily perceive the subtle resistances and manipulations of civilian administrators.

Cabinet appointments, often used by a President to build support within his party, were devoted by Grant to the indulgence of his personal preferences. As Secretary of State he named his close friend Elihu Washburne. His military aide, John A. Rawlins, became Secretary of War. Grant sought to implant in the Treasury his friend, the merchant Alexander T. Stewart, who proved legally ineligible. Grant also made appointments with little regard to actual job fitness and soon had to redesign his Cabinet to recognize both party considerations and competence.

Aided by a distinguished Secretary of State, Hamilton Fish (Washburne's successor), Grant cleared up the serious controversies with Great Britain over the *Alabama* claims (when the United States claimed damages for British-supported Confederate cruisers) and carefully preserved the neutrality of the United States in Spain's suppression of Cuban insurrection. Grant made a bold, but embarrassingly futile, attempt to annex Santo Domingo, and when Charles Sumner, a powerful Republican leader, denounced Grant, he was removed as chairman of the Foreign Relations Committee; this break with Sumner was perhaps Grant's worst disaster in foreign affairs.

The Civil War left a heritage of bonds and other securities that were easy prey to manipulation by speculators. To foil them, Grant approved legislation establishing the policy of ultimate redemption of legal tender notes in coin. But the speculators and gamblers—especially Jim Fisk and Jay Gould—struck back by cornering gold on the market and by "buying" cronies and administrative associates of the President with favors. Grant, to whom defeat and submission were alien, released a flood of gold from the Treasury to overwhelm the corner. The victory was costly, resulting in the "Black Friday" of 1869, when thousands were ruined.

Never vindictive toward the South, Grant declined to enforce the 14th amendment, which had granted Negro rights. His detachment coincided with the beginnings of intimidation in the old Confederacy of Negro voters.

In 1872, Grant was unanimously renominated and won reelection against Horace Greeley, nominee of the Democrats as well as the Liberal Republicans, who were seeking both a more radical Reconstruction policy and a more competent administration.

Grant's second term was dominated by scandals. His private secretary, Orville Babcock, was implicated in the notorious Whisky Ring and suspected of wrongdoing in the Santo Domingo negotiations. Secretary of War William Belknap was revealed to have accepted bribes from a trader at an Indian post. Through the loyalty of Grant, both escaped punishment. Grant himself was criticized for coarse tastes, excessive appetite for material enjoyment, and low associations. He was seen in public with the "robber baron" Jim Fisk and offered the post of Chief Justice to the notorious political boss Roscoe Conkling.

Although Grant is rated as one of the worst Presidents, he nevertheless piloted the country and the Presidency through the difficult aftermath of Andrew Johnson's confrontation with Congress. He also overcame a severe financial crisis and brought Anglo-American relations into a new era of harmony and mutual respect.

In 1880 Grant was the candidate of Roscoe Conkling and the powerful Stalwart faction for the Republican Presidential nomination, but he was defeated on a late ballot by Garfield.

After leaving office, Grant settled in New York City and lost (1884) his savings in a fraudulent banking firm. A merciful Congress appointed him general at full pay and subsequently added retirement pay. While suffering from throat cancer, Grant wrote his memoirs. Published (2 vols., 1885–86) by Mark Twain, they were a remarkable financial success and rank among the great military narratives of history. Grant soon died, on July 23, 1885, but his courage and indomitable spirit in the face of grave illness had restored his family's security.

## Rutherford Birchard Hayes

Rutherford Birchard Hayes, 19th President (1877–1881), was born on October 4, 1822, in Delaware, Ohio. His father, a storekeeper from Vermont, died the year he was born. Raised by an uncle, Hayes graduated from Kenyon College (Ohio) as valedictorian. After study at Harvard Law School, he began the practice of law at Lower Sandusky (now Fremont), Ohio, and in 1849 he moved to Cincinnati.

Upon the outbreak of the Civil War, Hayes volunteered and was commissioned a major. Wounded four times, he advanced to the rank of major general. While on the battlefield, he was nominated for the U.S. House of Representatives and elected. A staunch Republican, he supported the Radical postwar reconstruction program and was reelected. However, he resigned from Congress to become governor of Ohio. Reelected twice, he ran on a platform in 1875 calling for "sound money" in opposition to Democratic monetary policy.

Hayes's hard-money position helped win him the Republican Presidential nomination in 1876 over the better-known James G. Blaine. Hayes defeated the Democratic nominee, Samuel J. Tilden, in a fiercely disputed election that threatened the country with civil war. Although Hayes received only a minority of the popular votes, a partisan election commission awarded him the office.

Hayes became President under a cloud of resentment over the dubious legitimacy of his incumbency. So restive was the country's mood that he took the oath of office privately, and the inaugural parade and ball were omitted. His shadowed Presidency coincided with a critical juncture in the nation's affairs. Wise statesmanship was needed to bring the stormy Reconstruction Period to an end.

Despite his electoral handicap, Hayes bravely faced problems and justified the boast of a forebear that "the name of Hayes began by valor." Days after his inauguration, Hayes removed federal troops from the South, thereby ending the period of Reconstruction. Wade, Blaine, and other leading Republicans angrily protested the step which imperiled the Republican "carpetbag" governments. These had made Hayes's election possible and could not exist without military protection. The wisdom of Hayes's policy was demonstrated by the end of violence and by the emergence of normalcy in the South.

Like other Presidents of his era, Hayes grappled with the problem of civil service reform. He offended the Stalwarts, the spoils-minded faction of his party, by declaring that appointments to office must be made on the basis of ability and tenure must be protected. Beginning with Secretary of the Interior Carl Schurz, Hayes's department heads applied these principles widely.

Hayes won admiration from "sound money" advocates for his devotion to the resumption of specie payments. The farmers of the Midwest and city workingmen, beset by the severe economic depression of 1876–77, widely favored soft money—"an irredeemable paper currency," and the "free coinage of silver." The House of Representatives passed bills for both in 1877. In a vigorous message of opposition to Congress, Hayes insisted upon resumption and payment of the public debt in gold. Hayes's action forestalled the Senate from passing a bill to postpone resumption. His veto, however, could not defeat the Bland-Allison bill calling upon the government to coin each month from $2 million to $4 million in silver dollars to be full legal tender.

Despite the business depression and political opposition, Hayes continued to accumulate a gold reserve, and on January 1, 1879, for the first time since the Civil War, the government declared that it would pay out gold, or "specie," in exchange for paper money.

Just as he showed little sympathy for the economically embattled farmer, Hayes was insensitive to the plight of labor in the economic depression. In 1877, with a railroad strike raging in 10 states, Hayes furnished state authorities with arms from national arsenals and, as commander-in-chief, transferred Federal troops from remote posts to the scenes of trouble.

Assertive toward Congress, Hayes vetoed a Chinese exclusion bill because it violated a treaty with China. He fought Congress successfully on "riders" to two appropriation bills. In an uncommon achievement for a President, he brought Congress to remove the riders.

Convinced that a President performed better if he served for only one term, Hayes in accepting the nomination in 1876 expressed his resolve to be a single-term President. Party leaders, dismayed by his bursts of independence, encouraged him to keep that resolve.

Hayes left office with the satisfaction of seeing the resentment over his flawed Presidential victory evaporate. His hard work, efficiency, and tough moral fiber impressed the public. After leaving office, he devoted his final years to education and philanthropy. He died in Fremont, Ohio, on January 17, 1893.

## James Abram Garfield

James Abram Garfield, 20th President (March 4, 1881–September 19, 1881), was born on November 19, 1831, in Orange, Ohio, the son of a frontier farmer. Fatherless at two, Garfield became "a self-made man," who supported his widowed mother by working on farms and as a carpenter.

At 18, Garfield began study at Hiram (Ohio) College and later transferred to Williams College, Williamstown, Massachusetts. Graduating in 1856, Garfield returned to Ohio and rose to a professorship of ancient languages and literature at Hiram College and served as president from 1857 to 1861.

With the outbreak of the Civil War, Garfield was commissioned a lieutenant colonel of an Ohio volunteer regiment. Serving at Chickamauga and as chief of staff to General Rosecrans, he rose to the rank of major general. In 1863 when he was elected to the U.S. House of Representatives, Garfield resigned from the army.

Serving for 17 years in the House, Garfield was a regular Republican of antislavery convictions and a firm advocate of Radical reconstruction. He was an influential member of key House committees on finance and military affairs and in 1876 was minority leader. Garfield was also a member of the Electoral Commission created by Congress to decide state contests in the disputed election of 1876.

In the Republican National Convention of 1880, Garfield, a compromise candidate, was nominated for President on the 36th ballot. A "dark horse," he had defeated ex-President Grant, whom the Stalwarts, a party faction, were promoting for a third term. Because Garfield was a member of a rival Republican faction, Chester A. Arthur, a Stalwart, was nominated for Vice-President.

The Stalwarts, headed by Senator Roscoe Conkling of New York, remained unappeased. Upon becoming President, Garfield became embroiled with Conkling in a war over patronage. Garfield sent to the Senate the nominations of men of his own choice for minor posts in the New York Custom House. Conkling felt the step violated pledges given in return for his acceptance of Garfield as Presidential nominee and invoked Senatorial courtesy to defeat the nominations.

Garfield's conflict with leading Republican personalities spread to the Post Office, where the "star route" frauds were uncovered. The Post Office scandalously overpaid certain persons operating these mail routes, including the chairman of the Republican National Committee. Despite intimidation, Garfield had prosecutions launched against offenders. He also withdrew all nominations for New York appointments, except for the Custom House, to stress Presidential independence and integrity in the appointive process.

Since Republican control of the Senate was insecure, the Republican caucus chose not to break with the President and supported his New York Custom House appointments. An outraged Conkling resigned from the Senate and invited the New York legislature to vindicate him.

Garfield approved the proposal of his Secretary of State James G. Blaine to call a conference of Latin-American nations to review the Clayton-Bulwer Treaty with Great Britain, entered into in 1850. Garfield and Blaine were eager to advance a proposed isthmian canal and to shake off the treaty's provision that called for Anglo-American control of the waterway.

Before the conference could take place, Garfield was shot on July 2, 1881, by Charles Guiteau, a Stalwart and an office-seeker disappointed by the deadlock over patronage. Garfield lingered on until September 19, 1881, when he died.

## Chester Alan Arthur

Chester Alan Arthur, 21st President (1881–1885), was born on October 5, 1830, at Fairfield, Vermont, the son of a Baptist clergyman. Arthur graduated from Union College, Schenectady, in 1848, where he was elected to Phi Beta Kappa. After teaching school in Vermont and serving as school principal in Cohoes, New York, Arthur moved to New York City to study law, and in 1854 was admitted to the bar.

A brilliant lawyer, Arthur won fame in two civil liberties lawsuits. One, a pre-Civil War case, held that a slave brought into New York became free. The other established that Negroes enjoyed the same rights on New York streetcars as whites.

Arthur, a staunch Republican, was rewarded in 1861 with the post of engineer-in-chief of New York State, and in the Civil War, he held further political positions as inspector general of New York troops and quartermaster of New York State. As such he helped organize the New York militia. After the war, in 1871, President Grant appointed him to the well-paid office of collector of the Port of New York, one of the choicest of political plums.

Competent and honest as the collector, Arthur, in the fashion of the day, ran the Custom House as an adjunct of Roscoe Conkling's New York Republican machine. Patronage was openly distributed, clerks freely attended party caucuses and conventions, got out the vote, and slacked on the job. Eventually, Arthur was removed by his fellow Republican, reform-minded President Rutherford Hayes.

At the Republican national convention of 1880, James Garfield was nominated for the Presidency, after the Conkling clique of New York Republicans, the Stalwarts, failed to nominate Grant for a third term. To sweeten the defeat, the convention chose Arthur, a leading Stalwart, for the Vice-Presidency.

Garfield's assassination soon after his inauguration made Arthur President.

Arthur is a classic instance of a man who became a better President than was generally expected. Forebodings of the day saw Arthur running the Presidency as a machine politician and spoilsman, and opening the hospitality of the White House to the Custom House loafers. Many ridiculed Arthur as a "dude" and "Gentleman Boss," owing to his courtly manners and dandified dress. But Arthur proved otherwise. His bearing as President was dignified, honorable, and constructive. His devotion to principle in the manner of his younger days as a civil liberties attorney quickly transformed his image into that of a man well capable of being President.

In addressing himself to the emerging problems of the day, especially the shabby morality of post-Civil War politics, Arthur suffered imposing handicaps; his cabinet was inherited from the rival Garfield faction, and he lacked a working majority in Congress. Matters worsened after the 1882 elections, when the Democrats won control of the House of Representatives.

Nevertheless, Arthur built a commendable record of effort and achievement. When he recommended the Civil Service Reform Act of 1883—the basis of the present-day personnel system—his former friends and colleagues felt betrayed because it drastically limited patronage.

He demonstrated courage and conscience in vetoing a Chinese exclusion bill that violated a treaty with China. Congress, however, overrode his veto. He also vetoed a river and harbor appropriation bill of 1882, contending that it wastefully committed public funds for improper local purposes. Congress again defeated his veto. His several defeats weakened his standing with professional politicians.

Arthur extracted from Congress laws to build a modern navy to replace the obsolete fleet dating back to the Civil War. He worked for tariff reform, and secured a new protective tariff act, with little reform. The Alaska Territory was organized. A treaty of friendship, commerce, and navigation was signed with Korea; a treaty for the construction of a canal with Nicaragua; and an agreement for a coaling and repair station at Pearl Harbor with Hawaii. Although lacking in drama, Arthur's administration was marked by growing prosperity in the country.

Arthur aspired to renomination for the Presidency in 1884, but his candidacy withered at an early stage. Professional politicians, bitter over his support of the civil service law, widely opposed him and reformers failed to support him.

At the end of his Presidential term, he returned to New York City where he resumed his law practice. He died on November 18, 1886, a little more than a year after leaving office, and was buried in Albany, New York.

## Grover Cleveland

Grover Cleveland, 22d (1885–1889) and 24th President (1893–1897), was born in Caldwell, New Jersey, on March 18, 1837. He was the fifth of nine children of a Presbyterian country minister and a relative of Moses Cleaveland, founder of Cleveland, Ohio. While a child, his family moved to Fayetteville and then to Clinton, in upstate New York. His father's death barred Cleveland from a college education. Heading west to seek his fortune, he proceeded no farther than Buffalo, where an uncle secured him a clerkship in a law office. In 1859, at the age of 22, he was admitted to the bar. When the Civil War erupted, Cleveland could not enlist because of the necessity of supporting his mother and sisters, and he borrowed money to hire a conscription substitute.

The industrious Cleveland entered politics as a ward worker for the Democratic party in Buffalo. In 1862, he was elected ward supervisor, and a year later he was appointed assistant district attorney of Erie County. His political career remained uneventful until 1871, when he was elected sheriff of Erie County, and in 1882, he was elected mayor of Buffalo. His efficiency and rigorous honesty ("Public office is public trust," he once said) won him rapid fame. After one year as mayor, he was chosen governor of New York.

In their national convention of 1884, the Democrats nominated Cleveland for President. His Republican opponent was the glamorous James G. Blaine and, in the ensuing campaign, the character of the candidates was viciously assailed. The Democratic party was described by the opposition as the party of "Rum, Romanism, and Rebellion." Offended Catholic voters supported Cleveland, and the "mugwumps," a reform wing of the Republican party, backed him, impressed by his reform record. Winning in a close race, Cleveland became the first Democratic President since the Civil War.

An awaiting question for his Presidency was whether Cleveland could transfer to the larger, more complex arena of national politics the atmosphere of probity and reform he so successfully cultivated in state and local officeholding. He was quickly tested by the new Civil Service Reform Law passed in the twilight of the previous administration. His "mugwump" supporters pressed for civil service reform, but from Cleveland's own party came a long line of Democratic office seekers, hungry for reward after 24 years of exclusion from Presidential patronage.

Pledged to "practical reform," Cleveland gave slow and reserved recognition to partisan demands. Simultaneously, he lent steady support to the new Civil Service Commission and induced Congress to repeal the Tenure of Office Act, a shadow upon the Presidency since 1867. He skillfully preserved Presidential independence in appointments, but his sturdy middle course served to offend both the politicians and the reformers.

Cleveland also championed the cause of tariff reform. Embarrassed by the substantial surplus in the Treasury, and convinced that it was fostered by excessive tariff rates, Cleveland called for tariff revision to diminish what he regarded as improper favoritism to protected industries.

Cleveland was renominated in 1888, and although he won a larger popular vote than his Republican opponent, Benjamin Harrison, the latter mustered a majority of the electoral vote to win the election.

In 1892, Cleveland regained the Presidency, a popular figure in the face of wide disgruntlement over the McKinley Tariff Act of 1890 and its high-rate structure. But the pleasure of victory was quickly displaced by the storms of economic crisis. From the Harrison administration, Cleveland inherited the forces that produced the Panic of 1893; bank failures, bankruptcies, and massive unemployment seized the economy. Cleveland resisted demands for inflation by Western and Southern Democrats and Populists and, instead, chose to combat the crisis through sound money policies and orthodox economic measures. Cleveland won a long, bitter fight only by receiving substantial Republican support, since the Democratic party was characterized by a cleavage between sound money and inflationary factions.

The animosities raised by the fight crippled Cleveland's chances for tariff reform. The Wilson-Gorman bill that finally passed so reflected the views of protectionist Democrats that Cleveland termed the legislation "party perfidy and party dishonor." Unwilling to sign the Wilson bill, Cleveland permitted it to become law without his signature.

Cleveland's sound money policy was beset by sharp declines in Treasury holdings of gold, and he was forced to replenish the reserves through large bond issues arranged with a syndicate of Eastern financiers. His vocal Democratic opponents charged the President with being in alliance with Wall Street.

In the wake of the Panic of 1893, strikes were widespread, and in 1894 striking employees of the Pullman Company and Eugene V. Debs' American Railway Union halted trains across the country. Violence erupted in Chicago, the center of the strike. In a historic intervention, the President declared that the strikers had interfered with the free flow of the mails, and regular army troops were dispatched to Chicago to enforce the laws. Governor J. P. Altgeld of Illinois, who did not want the troops, demanded their recall in vain.

In foreign affairs, Cleveland rejected the imperialist tendencies of recent American policy. He refused to deal with a new government in Hawaii, established by a revolution managed by American residents. Cleveland rejected domestic pressures to intervene in behalf of Cuban insurrectionists and make war with Spain; he ignored a Congressional resolution recognizing Cuba.

Cleveland was assertive in foreign affairs when what he regarded as legitimate American interests were at stake. In Venezuela's boundary dispute with Britain, he gave new precision to the Monroe Doctrine by articulating the hegemony of the United States in the Americas and our specific interest in the boundary dispute.

By the end of Cleveland's term, the "silver" or inflationary Democrats dominated his party and, at the national convention of 1896, they nominated—to Cleveland's great distress—William Jennings Bryan, the silver orator. Cleveland preferred the Republican nominee, William McKinley, and his sound-money policies, but he took no part in the campaign.

After leaving the Presidency, Cleveland lived in Princeton, New Jersey. He lectured at the University, served as a trustee, and in 1904 published *Presidential Problems,* one of the most penetrating books by a former President about the office. He died June 24, 1908, and fittingly, his last words were: "I have tried so hard to do right."

## Benjamin Harrison

Benjamin Harrison, 23d President (1889–1893), was born on August 20, 1833, at North Bend, Ohio. Of distinguished ancestry, he was the great-grandson of a signer of the Declaration of Independence, a grandson of President William Henry Harrison, and the son of a congressman. He studied at Miami University (Ohio), graduating in 1852, and was admitted to the bar the following year. In 1854 he moved to Indianapolis, where he practiced law and politics.

During the Civil War Harrison served with distinction on the battlefield and was brevetted brigadier general. A prosperous corporation lawyer in Indianapolis after the war, he was active in Republican politics and held various local and party offices. In 1876 he ran unsuccessfully for governor, but five years later he won a seat in the United States Senate.

His distinguished background, war record, and the importance of Indiana to Republican electoral strategy gained him the Presidential nomination in 1888. He received a majority of the electoral vote, although Grover Cleveland, running for re-election, won a plurality of the popular vote.

In the White House, Harrison and his Secretary of State, James G. Blaine, conducted an assertive foreign policy as the United States moved toward a posture of imperialism. A Pan-American Congress was highly successful. The United States established its claims in Samoa and checked German expansion there. Harrison was less successful, however, in a controversy with Great Britain over the killing of fur seals in the Bering Sea. Aggressive efforts to establish American rights to Mole St. Nicholas in Haiti failed. The Harrison administration also engaged in bitter negotiations with Chile following an attack on American sailors in Valparaiso; the United States demanded an apology and ultimately received it.

One of Harrison's fondest projects was the annexation of Hawaii. In his administration's closing days, he sent a treaty for that purpose to the Senate. His successor, Grover Cleveland, however, withdrew the treaty before the Senate voted.

In domestic affairs, Harrison was torn between the demands of the Civil Service Reform Act of 1883 and the more traditional spoils system. He followed a moderate course that displeased both the reformers and the organization politicians. On balance, his civil service record was statesmanlike. He appointed and retained Theodore Roosevelt as civil service commissioner, and angered the spoilsmen by adding 11,000 civil service positions to the classified list.

In legislation, Harrison was disinclined to oppose policies his party advocated in Congress. Since the party was in the hands of leaders he could not control, his impact upon the laws of the day was minor. Congress passed the McKinley Tariff Act, imposing the highest duties up to that time. Harrison, however, secured the insertion of a reciprocity provision, the act's only popular feature.

Harrison approved the Sherman Silver Purchase Act to help the silver industry. He signed a rivers and harbors act, a giant pork-barrel measure, and an act markedly increasing pension expenditures. He supported a federal elections bill, embodying several reforms, but it failed. Harrison also aided the Sherman Anti-Trust Act, passed to counteract popular feeling that the Republicans were the party of big business. However, this was insufficient to forestall the Democrats from winning control of the House in 1890, which further diminished Harrison's influence on legislation.

Opposed by party leaders and bosses, such as Quay, Platt, and "Czar" Reed, Harrison secured renomination in 1892 only with difficulty. They and other politicians were offended by his limited patronage policy and cold personality. His reserve, a frigid look darting from steel-gray eyes, and his brevity of response wore badly with politicians. Despite his manner, Harrison was a remarkably effective public speaker, bringing one observer to note: "Harrison can make a speech to 10,000 men, and every man of them will go away his friend. Let him meet the same 10,000 men in private, and every one will go away his enemy."

Party apathy, labor hostility to an administration heavily partial to business, and other factors caused Harrison's defeat in his race for reelection in 1892 against Cleveland.

After leaving the Presidency, Harrison continued to gain distinction as a lawyer, and in 1898 he represented Venezuela in her boundary dispute with Great Britain. He died in Indianapolis on March 13, 1901.

## William McKinley

William McKinley, 25th President (March 4, 1897–September 14, 1901), was born on January 29, 1843, at Niles, Ohio, the son of an iron-founder. After attending Poland Seminary (Ohio) and Allegheny College (Pennsylvania), McKinley taught school.

Following service in the Union Army in the Civil War, where he rose to the rank of major, McKinley studied at Albany (New York) Law School and was admitted to the bar in 1867; he soon moved to Canton, Ohio, where he began practice.

McKinley began his political career in 1869 by election as prosecuting attorney for Stark County, Ohio. In 1876, he was elected as a Republican to the U.S. House of Representatives, where he remained, except for one term, until 1891. As Congressman, McKinley sponsored the McKinley Tariff Act, which set record-high protective duties, and voted for the Bland-Allison (silver purchase) act.

Defeated for reelection in 1890, McKinley attracted the friendship and support of Mark Hanna, a powerful, wealthy Ohio Republican. Their lasting political partnership helped McKinley win election as governor in 1891 and reelection in 1893.

In 1896, McKinley's popularity and Hanna's shrewd management brought the Republican Presidential nomination to the governor. Pitted against him as the Democratic nominee was the colorful William Jennings Bryan whose free silver doctrines and Populist ties alarmed the business community and alienated many Democratic conservatives. Bryan, a superb orator, made a record number of speaking appearances. McKinley and Hanna, in contrast, perfected the "front porch" campaign; instead of the candidate going to the people, the people came to the candidate. Cooperating railroads gave excursion rates so low that one newspaper said that visiting McKinley was "cheaper than staying home."

McKinley's election was interpreted as a mandate for a high protective tariff and for a gold monetary standard, as opposed to a silver standard. Promptly after his inauguration, McKinley called a special session of Congress to act on the tariff; the Dingley Tariff Act resulted, the high duties of which delighted business. Not until 1900 was a monetary law enacted. It established the gold dollar as the United States standard and strictly limited the coinage of silver.

The monetary law was delayed by the Spanish-American War. When McKinley was inaugurated, Cuba was in revolt against Spain. The United States battleship *Maine* was blown up in Havana harbor, and McKinley was pressed to intervene. He did not want to go to war, nor fight legislators who were demanding war. Ultimately, he referred the problem to Congress, knowing that it favored war; Congress directed the President to intervene in Cuba to establish Cuban independence.

As a war President, McKinley was handicapped by an inadequate war department and army. Disease was more deadly and inefficiency more harassing than the Spanish enemy. Although the navy performed creditably, McKinley was fortunate in facing a weak enemy.

McKinley did not want to annex territory, but as in the coming of the war, his political style prevailed over his political ends. As a politician, he eschewed conflict. His natural kindliness and his background as a tariff negotiator adept at conciliating everyone ruled his approach to foreign affairs. As a public leader, famous for "keeping his ear close to the ground," he was seldom more than a half-step ahead of his constituents. Convinced from a tour of the Midwest that the people favored annexation, he instructed his peace negotiators accordingly. The Philippines, Guam, and Puerto Rico were ceded to the United States. Cuba was placed under American control until it could establish a government of its own. During the war, the Hawaiian Islands were annexed by joint resolution of Congress.

McKinley guided the country through its initial experiences as an imperial nation. A law to govern the new insular possessions was passed. The war department was reorganized. Rebellious Filipinos, seeking independence, were fought, and a commission headed by William Howard Taft was dispatched to the islands to set up the government of the United States there. In 1899 Secretary of State John Hay negotiated the Open Door policy with European nations with interests in China. But the Boxer Rebellion in China soon prompted intervention by many powers, including the United States.

In 1900, McKinley was reelected, upon defeating Bryan, this time to the cry of "a full dinner-pail for four years more." The war had turned the McKinley era into one of booming prosperity, and the election returns showed that the benign McKinley had the support of the people. The electorate also approved the new imperialism.

McKinley was at the crest of popularity and political vindication when he was shot by an anarchist, Leon Czolgosz, on September 6, 1901, at Buffalo, New York. He died on September 14.

McKinley's term, divided between the 19th century and the 20th, aptly symbolizes his contribution as a bridge between the old and the modern Presidency. With him ended the line of Presidents who had fought in the Civil War, and his popularity throughout the country signified that the breach between the North and South had been healed and was no longer a preoccupation of the Chief Executive. Likewise, he presided over the advent of a new era, in which the United States, through war with Spain, first took rank as a world power.

## Theodore Roosevelt

Theodore Roosevelt, 26th President (September 14, 1901–March 3, 1909), was born on October 27, 1858, in New York City, the son of a wealthy merchant of Dutch ancestry and of a mother of distinguished Georgian family whose brother served in the Confederate navy. Endowed with great energy, curiosity, and grit, Roosevelt was handicapped by frail health; however, by careful exercise, he built up unusual strength. He traveled widely and was educated by tutors until he entered Harvard (1876). After graduating (1880), he enrolled in Columbia Law School but, legal studies not proving of interest, turned to politics.

In 1881, at the age of 23, Roosevelt, as a Republican, was elected to the New York State Assembly. At first his fellow legislators looked askance at his expensive dress and pronounced sideburns, but his vitality and intelligence won their respect to the point that they elected (1882) him Republican minority leader. His disinclination to follow orders, however, prompted the party bosses to remove him. Roosevelt, nevertheless, remained highly influential in the assembly, working closely with Democratic Governor Grover Cleveland for the advancement of civil service reform.

In 1884, Roosevelt abandoned his political career in remorse over the deaths of his wife and mother, passing the next two years on his ranches in the Dakota Territory. There he developed his skills at riding and hunting and acquired Western flairs. In 1886, he remarried and returned to his home at Sagamore Hill (Oyster Bay) on Long Island. That year he also returned to politics, running unsuccessfully for mayor of New York City against overwhelming Democratic strength.

Roosevelt's speech-making for the Presidential candidacy of Benjamin Harrison was rewarded by Harrison's appointing him (1889) a member of the U.S. Civil Service Commission. Shrewd in cultivating publicity, Roosevelt brought the commission out of the shadows, interested the public in its work, and accomplished remarkable gains against the spoils system. As police commissioner of New York City (1895–97), he again used the power of publicity to restore discipline and stamp out police dishonesty.

In 1897 President William McKinley, for whom Roosevelt had campaigned the year before, appointed him Assistant Secretary of the Navy. Roosevelt worked to strengthen the navy but, when the United States and Spain went to war in 1898, Roosevelt resigned at once and organized the spectacular volunteer cavalry regiment that won fame as the "Rough Riders."

Roosevelt returned from Cuba a military hero and, with the Republican party in New York State besmirched by scandal, his nomination for governor was supported even by Boss Tom Platt, who was personally averse to the reform-minded Roosevelt. Elected, Roosevelt promoted reform legislation and forced through a law taxing the franchises of public service corporations. Large business interests were angered, and "Boss" Platt and other Republican leaders resolved to rid New York of Roosevelt by moving him into the 1900 national election as McKinley's running mate for the Vice-Presidency, presuming that in that office Roosevelt would be harmless and forgotten. Against his own inclinations, the governor accepted.

Ten months after the Republican victory that ensued, McKinley was assassinated, and Roosevelt became President at the early age of 42. Although he kept all members of McKinley's cabinet and said reassuringly that he would continue the late President's policies "absolutely unbroken," Roosevelt's zest and political skill soon broke the confines of this heritage, and business leaders, recalling his state reform policies, quavered.

In his first message to Congress (December 1901), Roosevelt addressed himself to the growing problem of business trusts, proposing not their prohibition, but regulation. His policy was illustrated by the government's suit (1902) against the Northern Securities Company, which J. P. Morgan interests had formed to control major railroads in the West. The company was charged with reducing competition, and the Supreme Court, upholding the government, ordered its dissolution. In all, the administration filed suits against 43 other corporations and achieved triumphs against the tobacco and oil trusts.

Roosevelt was the first President conspicuously friendly to labor. In 1902, facing a widespread anthracite coal strike and lacking express legal authority, Roosevelt nonetheless intervened, urging the disputants to arbitrate. When the miners agreed, but the mine-owners balked, Roosevelt threatened to have the army seize and operate the pits. Eventually a settlement was reached favorable to the miners, to whom public opinion was sympathetic. At Roosevelt's recommendation, Congress established (1903) a Department of Commerce and Labor.

In the foreign policy of his first term, Roosevelt used "the big stick"—the threat of force to advance his purposes. In 1902, he had applied the Monroe Doctrine when German and British naval forces threatened Venezuelan ports, trying to force payments of debts. Roosevelt warned Germany that the United States might use force if any Venezuelan territory was occupied. As a result, Germany withdrew her vessels, and a settlement was negotiated. In 1904, when Santo Domingo was staggering under European debts, the "Roosevelt Corollary" of the Monroe Doctrine was born. Under it, the United States announced that it was prepared to exercise "an international police power" in instances "of wrongdoing or impotence."

While negotiating (1903) to secure a strip of land across Panama—a prelude to the eventual construction of the canal—Roosevelt supported and recognized a revolutionary Panamanian government that signed the necessary treaty, and American troops protected this new government from Colombian forces.

Roosevelt was reelected (1904) by a record popular majority over the Democratic nominee, Judge Alton B. Parker. At the President's initiative, his often reluctant Congress passed a pure food law, a meat inspection law, and the Hepburn law that conferred on the Interstate Commerce Commission the power of railroad rate-making. Roosevelt promoted an aggressive conservation policy, which added enormous acreage to the national forests, and also promoted the reclamation and irrigation of arid lands.

Foreign affairs continued to be demanding during Roosevelt's second term. His mediation and strong personal influence brought the Russo-Japanese War to an end in 1905, an achievement that brought him the Nobel Peace Prize. Roosevelt, however, retained faith in the efficacy and value of a show of force. When relations with Japan deteriorated and possible attack on the Philippines was feared, he dispatched (1908) the fleet to the Far East and around the world. This step prompted several diplomatic agreements with Japan.

Roosevelt was the first President whose administration was continuously involved in major foreign policy, and his Square Deal program of social justice—he called his office "a bully pulpit"—was also the first of its kind. He was extraordinarily skillful at rallying public opinion; however, a contemporary cartoon that depicted him with large clenched teeth, a thick spiked club, and a belt full of pistols also tells much of his style. Audacious and innovative in legislative relations, he began the practice of supplementing his messages with actual drafts of bills, and he was the first of modern Presidents to appeal to public opinion to advance his measures in Congress.

After his election in 1904, Roosevelt declared that "under no circumstances" would he run again for President. He chose his Secretary of War, William Howard Taft, as his successor, and Taft was both nominated and elected.

After leaving office, Roosevelt went big-game hunting in Africa and, when he returned (1910) to the United States, he was approached by disgruntled progressive Republicans who felt that Taft had betrayed them. Failing to bring Taft around to his own progressive ways, Roosevelt broke with his protégé and, in 1912, he ran for a Presidential third term. After winning in Republican primaries, he was denied the nomination in the Taft-controlled convention. Roosevelt and his supporters bolted and formed the Bull Moose party. In the tumultuous campaign, Roosevelt survived an attempted assassination to run second in the three-way race that was easily won by the Democratic candidate: Woodrow Wilson.

In 1913 and 1914, Roosevelt made pioneering explorations in the Brazilian jungle. After the outbreak of World War I, he was an early advocate of preparedness against Germany and critical of Wilson's caution. When America entered the war, Roosevelt wanted to raise and lead an army division, but Wilson refused. Roosevelt opposed American entry into the League of Nations, which he considered an excessive limitation on national sovereignty. He would probably have been a leading contender for the Republican Presidential nomination in 1920 but for his unexpected death on January 6, 1919. He is buried at Sagamore Hill.

## William Howard Taft

William Howard Taft, 27th President (1909–1913), was born on September 15, 1857, in Cincinnati. His father, Alphonso Taft, had served as a judge in Ohio, as a cabinet officer under President Grant, and as U.S. minister to Austria and Russia. A huge, studious youth, William graduated (1878) with honors from Yale and (1880) from the Cincinnati Law School.

Admitted to the bar, he promptly moved into public service. He served (1881–82) as assistant prosecuting attorney for Hamilton County, Ohio. In 1882, President Chester Arthur appointed Taft, a Republican, collector of internal revenue for the first district, with headquarters in Cincinnati. Within a year he resigned, because he could not in good conscience discharge competent employees to open up jobs for Republicans.

After a brief return to private law practice, Taft resumed (1885) his public career as assistant solicitor for Hamilton County. He filled out a vacancy on the Superior Court in 1887, and the following year was elected for a five-year term. Except for the Presidency, this was the only office to which he was ever elected. He moved on to national prominence in 1890 when President Benjamin Harrison appointed him U.S. Solicitor General. Two years later, he became a United States Circuit Court judge, and his rulings occasionally displeased labor unions.

In 1900, Taft was thrust into a totally new endeavor—both for himself and for the nation—when President McKinley appointed him chairman of a commission to govern the Philippine Islands, which had been acquired in the Spanish-American War. Designated governor the following year, Taft was a model administrator, building roads and harbors, establishing civil courts, and installing organs of self-government. In 1904, President Theodore Roosevelt appointed Taft Secretary of War. In addition to presiding with marked competence over a complex department, he also became a kind of trouble-shooter, assisting in Roosevelt's Panamanian policies and in negotiations for concluding the Russo-Japanese War.

When Roosevelt declined (1908) to run, he recommended that Taft become his successor. Preferring appointment to the Supreme Court, Taft acquiesced after some hesitation. He easily defeated the Democratic Presidential nominee, William Jennings Bryan. The ponderous, good-humored Taft, cautious in action and conservative in temperament, illustrates the type of public figure who diminishes his exceptional record as administrator and judge in the Presidency.

At a disadvantage by being the heir to the scintillating Roosevelt, Taft suffered in the inevitable comparison. Almost immediately, he was confronted with a profound struggle in the House of Representatives, in which progressive Republicans, led by George Norris of Nebraska, overthrew "Cannonism"—the almost unlimited power wielded by House Speaker "Uncle Joe" Cannon. Taft declined to support the Norris forces, and they, after their victory, declined to cooperate with the President.

Taft had been elected on a platform pledged to revise the tariff. A believer in protection, he felt that somewhat reduced duties would help control the trusts. Summoning Congress into special session to deal with the tariff, he seemed highly restrained in promoting his views on Capitol Hill. Although the House enacted a bill with big tariff reductions, the Senate, led by the devoted protectionist Nelson W. Aldrich of Rhode Island worked to keep duties high. Although the eventual Payne-Aldrich Tariff Act lowered some rates slightly, the general rate level was undisturbed. Taft disapproved of the bill, but he signed it, deeming it the best that could be then secured.

Taft further damaged his standing with progressive Republicans in the dispute between Chief Forester Gifford Pinchot and Secretary of the Interior Richard Ballinger. Pinchot charged that Roosevelt's conservation policies were being desecrated by the Interior Department, which he accused of selling land concessions too cheaply to water and power companies, as well as of illegal transactions in the sale of Alaskan coal lands. Taft backed Ballinger, whose conduct was investigated and upheld by a Congressional committee. Taft then dismissed Pinchot, and angered progressive Republicans moved back toward Theodore Roosevelt.

Despite its political troubles, the Taft administration made solid accomplishments. The 16th Amendment (income tax) and the 17th (direct election of Senators) were added to the Constitution—the first new amendments since the aftermath of the Civil War. At Taft's initiative, Congress enlarged the powers of the Interstate Commerce Commission and created a commerce court, a children's bureau, the Postal Savings system, and a parcel post. The Department of Labor was also established, and Alaska achieved full territorial government. Taft took the first steps toward establishing a federal budget, by requesting his department heads to submit detailed reports of their financial needs.

Although the Theodore Roosevelt administration tends to be identified with an aggressive antitrust policy, Taft well outdid his predecessor. In four years, the Taft administration launched almost twice as many "trust-busting" prosecutions for violations of the Sherman Anti-Trust Act than Roosevelt had in almost eight years.

In foreign affairs, Secretary of State Philander Knox played a large part in promoting "dollar diplomacy," by which trade, finance, and commerce were used to increase America's diplomatic influence. The U.S. government negotiated loans with China, Honduras, Nicaragua, and other countries, as a step toward encouraging private bankers to make additional loans to these nations.

In 1910, Roosevelt returned from a hunting trip to Africa and hustled into the political arena. His speeches advocating a "new nationalism" attracted Republican progressives, while Republican conservatives moved behind Taft to win him renomination. The conservatives, or "Stand-Patters," proved too strong for the progressives, or insurgents, and the President defeated Roosevelt in 1912 by being renominated on the first ballot. Roosevelt and his followers then left the convention and organized the new Progressive, or "Bull Moose," party, with Roosevelt as its Presidential nominee. With the Republican vote so divided, the Democratic nominee, Woodrow Wilson, was elected. Taft received only 8 electoral votes, Roosevelt 88, and Wilson 435.

Upon leaving the Presidency, Taft became a Yale law professor in 1913, and that year he was also elected president of the American Bar Association. In World War I, he was joint chairman of the National War Labor Board. President Harding appointed him (1921) Chief Justice of the United States, which he deemed his greatest public honor. Taft served with distinction until 1930, when declining health forced his retirement. He died on March 8, 1930, and is buried in Arlington National Cemetery.

## Woodrow Wilson

Woodrow Wilson, 28th President (1913–1921), was born on December 28, 1856, at Staunton, Virginia. The son of a Presbyterian minister, Thomas Woodrow Wilson (his full name) was reared in an atmosphere of religious piety and respect for scholarship. Wilson entered Davidson College in North Carolina at the age of 17, transferring after a year to Princeton University, from which he was graduated (1879). He studied law at the University of Virginia, but withdrew (1881) from the school because of poor health.

In 1882, Wilson began to practice law in Atlanta; however, after a year of few clients and a discovered distaste for the commercial world, he returned to academic life and studied political science at Johns Hopkins University, where his thesis, *Congressional Government,* earned wide acclaim. After taking his Ph.D., he taught at Bryn Mawr College and Wesleyan University. In 1890, he became professor of jurisprudence and political economy at Princeton University. His reputation as a teacher and scholar having grown steadily, Wilson was named (1902) president of Princeton. Highly innovative as an administrator and tenacious in purpose against the most formidable odds, Wilson reorganized the curriculum, but suffered defeats in attempting to reform the eating clubs and revamp the graduate school.

Wilson's Princeton controversies resulted in his resignation as president, but the attendant publicity cast him as a fighter for democracy against the snobbery of privilege. New Jersey Democratic boss James Smith, Jr., and Colonel George Harvey, a party leader and publisher of *Harper's Weekly,* were both impressed with Wilson's political potential and secured (1910) his nomination for governor of New Jersey.

Once elected, Wilson fought Smith and his conservative organization and pushed through a primary election law, a corrupt practices act, an employer's liability law, an improved education law, and other legislation that suddenly placed New Jersey in the vanguard of progressivism.

Wilson's gubernatorial achievements also won national attention and established him in the confidence of William Jennings Bryan, who, despite three defeats for the Presidency, was still a dominant force in the Democratic party. At the 1912 national convention in Baltimore, Wilson won the Presidential nomination on the 46th ballot. Bryan's support was invaluable, and Wilson proved acceptable to the party's large progressive wing. With Republicans divided between Taft and Theodore Roosevelt, Wilson won the election easily.

His inaugural address (March 4, 1913) sounded progressive themes: "Here muster not the forces of party, but the forces of humanity." He immediately set a swift pace of initiative and activity, calling Congress into special session and addressing the two houses in person, thus breaking a century-long precedent. Wilson moved through Congress an extraordinary body of legislation that comprised his "New Freedom" program. A new tariff law lowered duties and removed them altogether on such commodities as wool, sugar, and iron ore. The Clayton Anti-Trust Act was passed (1914), and the Federal Trade Commission was established (also 1914) to regulate trusts and interstate trade. The Federal Reserve System was created (1913)—in effect, a central banking system empowered to provide a new currency and to facilitate the flow of capital through 12 reserve banks.

Wilson promoted this extraordinary legislative output with a generous investment of his own energies and skills. He worked closely with Democratic legislative leaders and the powerful committee chairmen. Adroit in using patronage, he was indefatigable in employing his own impressive powers of personal persuasion. He encouraged the revival of the long-dormant Congressional caucus as a forum in which his program might be presented to legislators for the purpose of organizing support. His exceptional gifts of articulation rallied attention to his program.

Wilson's early Presidential years were also preoccupied with foreign policy. He made amends for the recently assertive, if not highhanded, policies of the United States toward its Latin-American neighbors, assuring them (Mobile, Alabama, in 1913) that "the United States would never again seek one additional foot of territory by conquest." When the reform government of Francisco Madero in Mexico was overthrown, Wilson declined to recognize the new master, Victoriano Huerta, who had caused Madero's murder. Against raging turmoil within Mexico and intense pressure at home to intervene because of endangered American interests, Wilson nonetheless held to a policy of "watchful waiting" to permit the Mexican people to choose a government for themselves.

In August 1914, foreign policy compounded its demands on Wilson when World War I exploded. The President echoed the dominant sentiment of the nation when he proclaimed its neutrality. He was continuously buffeted in seeking to hold to this policy by the ravages of German submarines, by Britain's close administration of her blockade that often proved detrimental to American shipping interests, and by the solidifying of different segments of domestic opinion toward the belligerents. In 1915, neutrality was severely tested by the heavy loss of American life suffered when a German submarine sank the British passenger vessel *Lusitania*. Secretary of State William Jennings Bryan resigned, deeming Wilson's protest notes to Germany too strong; other Americans considered Wilson too detached and neutral by stating that there was such a thing as being "too proud to fight."

With Democrats promoting the slogan: "He kept us out of war," Wilson won reelection in 1916. However, he had declined to use neutrality as a campaign promise, and the defeat of Wilson's Republican opponent, Charles Evans Hughes, was a close race. Weeks before Wilson's second inauguration, Germany resumed unrestricted submarine warfare against all shipping, including American vessels. On April 2, 1917, Wilson went before Congress to request a declaration of war, averring that "the world must be made safe for democracy."

Wilson was an impressive war leader. Both for the United States and the world, he more than anyone articulated the purposes and the issues of the war. He infused the conflict with moral aspiration and harmonized its goals with his previous progressive domestic program. In a speech (January 8, 1918), he set forth the Fourteen Points that were his framework for a peace settlement. Among other things, he called for "a general association of nations," "open covenants of peace openly arrived at," freedom of the seas, arms reduction, and independence for various territories and countries. Wilson's guidelines afforded Germany a basis on which to appeal for peace.

Wilson personally headed the American delegation to the peace conference at Paris. Eager to make his Fourteen Points the center of the settlement, he believed that the United States should be represented by its head of government as the other major allies were. In the hard bargaining at the conference table, Wilson, to win acceptance of his plan for the League of Nations, and other of the Fourteen Points, had to make concessions and compromises.

He encountered more difficulty on his return to the United States, where he faced the task of securing Senate approval of the peace treaty and the League of Nations, for not only had Wilson been under criticism for excluding senators in the United States' delegation to the peace conference, but his general political position in the nation had weakened. He had asked for the election of Democrats to Congress in 1918 as a demonstration of popular confidence, but the voters responded by increasing Republican strength.

In the Senate, the peace treaty met fierce resistance from isolationists, such as Senators Hiram W. Johnson, James A. Reed, and William E. Borah as well as from many others, led by Henry Cabot Lodge, who were ready to approve the treaty but with important changes.

Deciding to take his fight for the league to the people, Wilson began (September 4, 1919) an ambitious speaking tour of the Midwest and Far West. Always frail in health, he had been weakened by the recent demands of office, and his doctors had advised against the trip. On September 25, following a speech at Pueblo, Colorado, Wilson collapsed from fatigue and tension aboard his train. The remainder of his tour was abandoned, and he returned to Washington. On October 3, he suffered a paralytic stroke.

The Presidency now sustained its longest and most difficult experience with an invalided Chief Executive. Seldom leaving his bed, Wilson did not call a cabinet meeting for more than six months, until April 13, 1920. The President's second wife, Mrs. Edith Bolling Wilson, not only guided his hand as he signed documents, but selected and digested the matters that were submitted for his personal attention.

From his sickbed, the President waged a losing fight for the peace treaty. The Senate Foreign Relations Committee, led by its chairman Senator Lodge, added 14 reservations, including one that declared the United States undertook no obligation to support the League of Nations. Wilson requested his Senate supporters to vote against the decimated treaty, but his term of office closed without its approval.

Repudiated at home, Wilson nevertheless was honored abroad as the recipient of the Nobel Peace Prize in 1920. He died in Washington on February 3, 1924, and is buried in the National Cathedral.

## Warren Gamaliel Harding

Warren Gamaliel Harding, 29th President (1921–1923), was born on November 2, 1865, in Blooming Grove, Ohio; he was the son of a homeopathic doctor and descended from an English family that had landed at Plymouth and migrated (1820) to Ohio. After study at local schools, Harding entered Ohio Central College, when he was only 14 years old and graduated three years later.

Harding moved (1882) with his parents to Marion, Ohio, where he taught briefly in a one-room schoolhouse; he also read law, sold insurance, and eventually turned to journalism. He soon became editor and part owner of the Marion *Star*. As editor, he was drawn into local political life and gained prominence as an orator. He was elected to the Ohio senate in 1900 and to the lieutenant governorship in 1904. He was the unsuccessful Republican candidate for governor in 1910, but five years later he was elected to the U.S. Senate. In Ohio politics, Harding became the close friend of Harry M. Daugherty, an astute political manager who desired to make Harding President, just as Mark Hanna in an earlier day had charted the course to the White House of his fellow Ohioan, William McKinley.

As Senator, Harding was a member of the Foreign Relations Committee and supported approval of the peace treaty of World War I, with reservations "sufficient to safeguard" American interests. Genial and good-looking, Harding enjoyed the fellowship of the Senate, but introduced no important legislation.

His emergence as a dark-horse, compromise nominee for the Presidency in 1920 was the outcome of deliberations by leading Republican Senators and party bosses in what Harry Daugherty called a "smoke-filled room" in Chicago's Blackstone Hotel. Conducting a "front-porch" campaign, Harding took no clear-cut stand on the leading issue: the League of Nations. He attacked it, but at the same time promised support for an "association of nations." He sidestepped domestic issues by promising a restoration of "normalcy." Harding easily defeated the Democratic nominee, James M. Cox.

Few Presidents have come into office facing more difficult tasks than Harding. The Versailles peace treaty was suspended uncertainly in the political air, having failed to win the Senate's approval under President Wilson. Powerful Republican Senators wanted to scrap the league; other legislators, who were eager to avoid future war, sought to salvage it. Substantial unemployment attended the changeover from a wartime to a peacetime economy. Harding approached these problems with a Presidential theory that looked to Congress and the cabinet for leadership; he rejected Wilson's performance as representing an encroachment on the powers of Congress.

Aided by a strong Secretary of State, Charles Evans Hughes, Harding was assertive in foreign affairs. The President moved quickly and energetically to break the impasse on the League of Nations. He made peace treaties with Germany and other enemy powers that omitted the league covenant. Harding's most conspicuous achievement in foreign policy was the Washington Disarmament Conference (1921), which resulted in treaties among the United States, Britain, France, Japan, and Italy that limited naval armament, restricted submarine use, and banned the use of poison gas in warfare.

The Harding era was marked by a surge of isolation; legislation was passed that for the first time placed quotas on immigration, and the Fordney-McCumber tariff act (1922) raised duties to record highs. Remaining aloof from European politics, the administration declined to take part in conferences at Geneva and The Hague. Unofficial American representatives on the Reparations Commission were withdrawn, and American troops stationed on the Rhine were gradually reduced. Harding himself, however, was a nonisolationist, and he repeatedly urged the promotion of peace through international friendship, as well as advocating American participation in the Permanent Court of International Justice at The Hague.

In domestic affairs, Harding largely acquiesced to what cabinet officers, Congress, and assertive group interests put forward for public policy. The excess profits tax was repealed, to the delight of business. The "farm bloc"—legislators of both parties devoted to agricultural interests—put through measures responsive to their needs.

Harding's cabinet included such strong and highly regarded public personalities as Secretary of State Hughes and Secretary of Commerce Herbert Hoover, as well as appointees who brought the administration into deep discredit. In addition, Harding had about him what became known as "the Ohio gang," whom he enjoyed as social companions and favored with responsible appointments.

Corruption set in and spread widely. Harding suffered a drastic shrinkage of political popularity not only because of betrayal by friends, but also due to deepening agricultural depression that brought heavy losses to Republicans in the 1922 Congressional elections, in which the Republican House majority fell from 165 to 15 and the Senate from 24 to 10.

In June 1923, Harding moved to restore his administration to public approval by embarking on a speaking tour through the West and Alaska. En route he received distressing news concerning the Senate investigation of oil leases, or what soon fanned out as the Teapot Dome scandal. Secretary of the Interior Albert B. Fall was subsequently convicted of accepting a bribe for leasing naval oil reserves to private oil interests. Harding's political manager, Attorney General Harry M. Daugherty, was implicated (but not convicted) in malfeasance in the Alien Property Custodian's Office. A friend and aide of Daugherty, Jesse W. Smith, committed suicide following revelations of settlements that Smith had arranged between the justice department and law violators.

In Seattle, Harding developed an illness that was attributed to food poisoning. His tour was suspended in San Francisco, where doctors said he was suffering from pneumonia. After a brief gain, Harding died there on August 2, 1923. There was no autopsy, and the precise cause of his death remains unknown. He was spared the humiliation of experiencing the trials of his two cabinet officials, Fall and Daugherty.

Historians generally rank Harding as one of the weakest of Presidents. But the qualities that made him weak also made him appealing to the bosses in the "smoke-filled room" and to a nation weary of Wilsonian zeal.

## Calvin Coolidge

Calvin Coolidge, 30th President (1923–1929), was born John Calvin Coolidge on July 4, 1872, in Plymouth Notch, Vermont. He was the son of John Calvin Coolidge, a farmer and shrewd, experienced politician who served in the Vermont legislature and held local offices. The son was graduated (1895) from Amherst College. He read law with a firm in Northampton, Massachusetts, was admitted (1897) to the bar, and soon opened his own office in Northampton.

In the tradition of the young smalltown lawyer, Coolidge entered politics as a Republican campaign worker in 1896. Three years later, he was elected a member of the Northampton City Council and, over the next five years, served as city solicitor and clerk of county courts. He was elected (1906) to the Massachusetts House of Representatives and reelected (1907).

Remarkable for his taciturnity—the very opposite of the stereotype extrovert politician—Coolidge moved up a career line of city and state politics with electoral invincibility. He was elected (1909) mayor of Northampton and reelected (1910). From 1912 to 1915, he served in the Massachusetts Senate, of which he was president for two terms. He was elected (1915) lieutenant governor and twice reelected. In 1918, he was elected governor.

In that office, Coolidge became a national figure by his resolute handling of the 1919 Boston police strike, declaring with cryptic force, "There is no right to strike against the public safety by anybody, anywhere, any time." By his firm action of calling in the militia, Coolidge suppressed the strike and won reelection overwhelmingly. The strike also helped boost him into the 1920 Vice-Presidential nomination. The Harding-Coolidge ticket won easily.

Upon Harding's death in 1923, Coolidge became President and the following year was elected to a full term. He commenced his tenure under extraordinarily difficult political circumstances. Scarcely had he declared his intention to carry out policies begun by Harding, when the Teapot Dome and other scandals of the previous administration were exposed. In this test, too, Coolidge was resolute, acting with fearless probity. He eluded the political temptation to shield the Harding administration against scandalous disclosure by bringing about the resignations of Harding's Attorney General, Harry Daugherty, and other important officials. Only three members of the Harding cabinet continued in office throughout the Coolidge administration.

Coolidge continued Harding's policy of responsiveness to the needs and interests of business. Declaring that "the business of America is business," Coolidge promoted a program of what he called "constructive economy." His principal policies were high tariffs, reduced income taxes, lowering the national debt, and strict governmental economy. So devoted was Coolidge to public thrift that he committed the rare political act of vetoing a (World War I) veterans' bonus bill, although Congress overrode him.

Paradoxically, Coolidge's bent for economy in government was enormously popular at a time when society, thanks to a soaring economy, was spendthrift. It was the era of rampant stock market speculation, freely countenanced Prohibition violations, "flaming youth," and the "jazz age." Champion of a rejected code of thrift and propriety, the President was a beloved figure—a reminder of old values that, although discarded, were still respected. In public addresses, Coolidge's pithy, apt expression of the old philosophy was widely appreciated. For example: "Let men in public office substitute the light that comes from the midnight oil for the limelight."

Distrustful of progressivism and opposed to legislation favoring any interest but business, Coolidge employed the veto in important instances where Congress transgressed his principles. For example, he vetoed legislation authorizing government operation of Muscle Shoals (Tennessee River rapids) for the production of electric power. Agriculture did not share in the booming prosperity, but suffered from falling prices and declining exports. Coolidge nonetheless twice vetoed legislation affording relief for farmers through government purchase of surplus products and sale abroad.

In foreign affairs, Coolidge, aided by Secretary of State Frank B. Kellogg, moved the country away from its isolationist tendencies. The secretary negotiated the Kellogg-Briand Pact, to which many nations subscribed, that sought to outlaw war. Although Coolidge opposed United States membership in the League of Nations, he favored joining the World Court. But when the Senate imposed unacceptable conditions, Coolidge dropped the project. A plan worked out by Vice-President Dawes and an international committee provided a new basis on which Germany might pay her World War I reparations.

Under Coolidge, relations with Mexico improved when Ambassador Dwight Morrow negotiated the settlement of old issues and obtained important concessions for American oil interests. With Japan, however, relations declined following Congress's passage of an immigration law that completely excluded Japanese; the President signed it under protest.

As the expected Republican Presidential nominee in 1928, Coolidge astounded the nation on August 2, 1927, by handing the press a slip of paper on which was written: "I do not choose to run for President in 1928." In his autobiography, he stated his conviction that "the chances of having wise and faithful public service are increased by a change in the Presidential office after a moderate length of time."

After leaving the Presidency, Coolidge returned to Northampton, where he wrote an autobiography and a series of daily newspaper articles that dealt mainly with political and economic topics. He was distressed by the coming of the depression in 1929, and it was reported that he felt he should have used the Presidency more assertively to have prevented it. He died on January 5, 1933.

## Herbert Clark Hoover

Herbert Clark Hoover, 31st President (1929–1933) and the first President from west of the Mississippi River, was born in West Branch, Iowa, on August 10, 1874. His father was a farmer and village blacksmith, and the family was strong in the Quaker faith. Orphaned at eight years of age, Hoover was raised by relatives in the West.

After graduation (1895) from Stanford University, Hoover became a successful mining engineer and businessman, with offices in New York, San Francisco, and London. His work took him all over the world and won him a fortune, as well as an international engineering and administrative reputation. In World War I, driven by his Quaker principles, he put aside his business affairs and administered to human suffering as chairman of the American Relief Commission with exceptional success that made him an international public figure.

In 1919, both the Republican and Democratic parties pressed Hoover to become their candidate for President the following year. Hoover clarified the question of his party affiliation by announcing that he was a Republican and that he would not be a candidate. In 1921, President Harding appointed him Secretary of Commerce, a post that Hoover continued in under President Coolidge.

As secretary, Hoover again functioned as a dynamic administrator with wide-ranging concerns. Under his hand, the Department of Commerce dramatically expanded its activities, and he oversaw conferences on foreign trade, industrial production, labor affairs, child welfare, and housing. The new industries of radio communication and aviation also came under his regulation.

When President Coolidge declined to run for reelection in 1928, Hoover easily won the Republican Presidential nomination. In a hard-fought campaign against his Democratic opponent, Governor Alfred E. Smith of New York, Hoover envisaged the day when poverty would be eliminated, and Americans would have "two chickens in every pot and a car in every garage." Impressed with Republican prosperity, voters expected even more of it from Hoover because of his genius for economic success. Elected overwhelmingly, he won 40 of the 48 states, with 444 electoral votes to Smith's 87.

Hoover's inaugural address sounded the notes of optimism. "In no nation," he said, "are the fruits of accomplishment more secure." He moved to help depression-ridden farmers by calling Congress into special session (April 1929) and bringing it to create a Federal Farm Board to encourage the growth of farm cooperatives and to absorb agricultural surpluses. Hoover also proposed an increase of tariff duties on farm imports to protect domestic markets. The resulting Hawley-Smoot Tariff Act not only incorporated Hoover's recommendations, but raised duties on many nonagricultural items. As a result, American foreign trade dropped, a contributing factor to the oncoming depression.

Seven months after Hoover's inaugural, the stock market crashed, and the upheaval of the Great Depression, which had long been building in the Harding-Coolidge era, exploded with devastating fury. Stocks collapsed in value, thousands became unemployed, fortunes evaporated overnight. The depression's root cause, in Hoover's view, was not material or political, but psychological: an erosion of confidence. Consequently, Hoover organized conferences with businessmen and labor leaders to spread reassurance and to secure their help in keeping wages and prices stable and avoiding strikes. The President aimed to improve confidence both by paring back federal expenditure and balancing the budget.

But the depression not only persisted but deepened. Unemployment reached a peak of one-fourth of the labor force. Bank failures rocketed, and mortgage foreclosures became commonplace. Reflecting his political philosophy, Hoover stressed the initiation of public works by states and localities to aid the unemployed. The Federal government, he believed, could help indirectly and, in 1932 at Hoover's request, Congress established the Reconstruction Finance Corporation (RFC), which made loans to banks to save them from bankruptcy and supported state relief programs.

Hoover also promoted conservation and federally administered public works programs to reduce unemployment. Federal flood control and navigation improvement projects were undertaken, and construction of Boulder (now Hoover) Dam on the Colorado River was begun. The Hoover administration substantially increased the acreage of national parks and forests, and it also launched major programs of public buildings and major highway construction.

In June 1932, some 15,000 veterans marched on Washington to pressure Congress into passing a bonus law. Opposing the bonus as financially unsound, Hoover eventually employed troops to drive the veterans out of the capital.

Under Hoover, American foreign policy tended toward forbearance and cooperation. He brought Congress to agree to a moratorium on war debt and reparation payments and also stressed goodwill in relations with Latin America. Following his election, he toured Latin America and as President removed the marines from an extended presence in Nicaragua. Hoover also concluded an agreement with Haiti that looked to the withdrawal of American troops in 1934.

Eager to promote disarmament, Hoover proposed that the principles of the London Naval Treaty of 1930 be extended to reduce land weapons; however, the proposal was declined by other nations. In 1931, when the Japanese invaded Manchuria and the League of Nations condemned Japan as an aggressor, Hoover announced that the United States would not recognize territorial aggrandizement that violated the Kellogg-Briand Pact.

A man whose motto was "Work is life," Hoover put in long hours at his desk and drove his staff hard. "He has the greatest capacity for assimilating and organizing information of any man I ever knew," said his Secretary of State, Henry L. Stimson. Yet a solution to the depression eluded this brilliant administrator. Hoover's critics contended that he overrelied on state, local, and private action, and was handicapped by a philosophical indisposition to exploit federal opportunities and resources.

With the nation still deep in depression, the Republicans dutifully renominated Hoover in 1932; however, his Democratic opponent, Franklin D. Roosevelt, promising a "new deal," defeated him by carrying 42 of the 48 states and by collecting 472 electoral votes to Hoover's 59.

After leaving the Presidency, Hoover was a vigorous critic of Roosevelt's New Deal, and later President Truman named Hoover chairman of the Famine Emergency Commission to report on the needs of many nations suffering from the ravages of World War II. Hoover made a similar study of Germany and Austria. In 1947, Truman appointed Hoover chairman of the Commission on Organization of the Executive Branch of the Government. Better known as "the Hoover Commission," the group proposed important changes in governmental organization and management. A second Hoover Commission was created in 1953. Hoover died on October 20, 1964, at age 90.

## Franklin Delano Roosevelt

Franklin Delano Roosevelt, 32d President (March 4, 1933–April 12, 1945), was born on January 30, 1882, at Hyde Park, New York, into a wealthy family which in the 1640s had migrated from Holland to New Amsterdam (later New York City). He was a fifth cousin of Theodore Roosevelt.

After studying at Groton and graduating from Harvard, Franklin extended his studies for another year and entered (1904) Columbia Law School. Admitted to the bar in 1907, Roosevelt evidenced little interest in the practice of law, but he soon discovered a keen taste for politics and won election (1910) as a Democrat to the New York Senate against great odds. As state senator, he demonstrated extraordinary adroitness as a political leader by thwarting party bosses who were bent on boosting a Tammany nominee into the U.S. Senate.

Following his vigorous campaign for Presidential aspirant Woodrow Wilson in 1912, Roosevelt was appointed Assistant Secretary of the Navy. Tammany secured its revenge two years later by helping defeat his quest in a primary for nomination to the U.S. Senate. Roosevelt's full emergence into national prominence was betokened by his nomination for the Vice-Presidency in 1920, with James M. Cox heading the ticket in an unsuccessful race.

Roosevelt returned to private life as vice-president of the Fidelity and Deposit Company of Maryland. A year later, he succumbed to poliomyelitis, which paralyzed him from the waist down. By great courage and effort, Roosevelt in time managed to walk a little by wearing braces on his legs and using crutches. In 1924, he surged back into national politics by nominating Alfred E. Smith for the Presidency, as a thrilled convention watched him master his crippling illness by walking slowly to the podium.

At Smith's insistence, Roosevelt ran (1928) for governor of New York and was barely elected. Reelected in 1930, Roosevelt won acclaim for his broad attack on the Great Depression with measures that were to find their counterparts in his subsequent program as President.

He received the Democratic Presidential nomination in 1932 and became the first nominee to make an acceptance speech at a national convention. Promising a "new deal" to bring the nation out of the depression, he easily defeated his Republican opponent, President Herbert Hoover.

At the moment of Roosevelt's inaugural, the depression was at its worst: breadlines of unemployed, mounting mortgage foreclosures, closed banks, and the widespread, gray despair that the country's complex paralyzing economic forces might never be fathomed and overcome.

Roosevelt created an immediate impression of action and initiative. He declared a "bank holiday," closing down the banks for federal inspection; those in good financial condition were permitted to reopen. The confidence of depositors, which had been shaken by rampant bank failures, was restored. He summoned Congress into special session, and between March 9 and June 16, 1933, the famous "100 Days," more legislation of major impact was passed than ever before.

The New Deal, as these accumulated economic and social measures became known, included relief for the unemployed, aid for farm mortgages, a civilian conservation corps, a Tennessee Valley Authority, a National Industrial Recovery Act, and an Agricultural Adjustment Act under which a price subsidy was provided to farmers who agreed to limit their output. Roosevelt's measures were directed to the unemployed, the farmer, labor, the young, the aged, and the Negro, all of whom suffered most acutely from the depression.

In advancing his program, Roosevelt gave a bravura performance as Presidential leader and politician. In "fireside chats," as his national radio addresses were called, he explained his purposes, actions, and plans. His press conferences were remarkably newsworthy and conducted with a skill and charm that left many reporters warmly disposed toward his administration. As legislative leader, Roosevelt was adept at attracting bipartisan support, at timing his measures well, and at exploiting his political opportunities. To the country, he appeared a confident leader whose easy humor and ready laughter were marks of self-possession in the face of national crisis.

In 1936, Roosevelt was overwhelmingly reelected, defeating the Republican nominee, Governor Alfred M. Landon of Kansas. Roosevelt's political fortunes now went into something of a tailspin, to the delight of his many foes and detractors, who considered him a "traitor to his class." The Supreme Court held such key measures as the National Industrial Recovery Act, the Agricultural Adjustment Act, and other laws unconstitutional. Roosevelt moved in 1937 to "pack the court." Although rebuffed, he did slow the pace of hostile court decisions.

Foreign policy was largely preoccupied with the war clouds gathering over Europe and the Pacific, culminating in Germany's invasion of Poland on September 1, 1939. Although restricted by neutrality legislation, Roosevelt sought to give "all aid short of war" to nations fighting the Axis. The neutrality laws were modified in the directions that Roosevelt urged. Isolationists, who believed the United States should remain uninvolved, attacked Roosevelt as bent upon bringing the United States into the struggle. When he shattered precedent by running for the Presidency for a third time, he was severely attacked and was driven to promise to try to keep the nation out of war. He prevailed over his Republican opponent, Wendell Willkie, but with reduced majorities.

Following France's surrender to Germany in June 1940, Roosevelt undertook bold initiatives to aid embattled Britain. He exchanged old American destroyers for American assumption of leases on several British bases in the Western Hemisphere. He promoted the Lend-Lease Act that authorized the provision of war supplies to any nation fighting the Axis. In a meeting with Winston Churchill in August 1941 on the high seas, the two leaders adopted the Atlantic Charter that attested to the ideals of freedom of the seas, the territorial integrity of nations, peaceful trade, freedom of choice of governmental form. Earlier in a speech on January 6, 1941, Roosevelt had declared that all men are entitled to at least four freedoms: freedom from want, freedom of worship, freedom of speech, and freedom from fear. The two documents provided a foundation of ideals and aims for the war.

With America's deepening commitment to the Allies, relations with Germany, Italy, and Japan deteriorated rapidly. On December 7, 1941, Japan attacked the United States fleet at Pearl Harbor and the nation found itself quickly at war with the Axis. Decisions of the utmost magnitude faced the President. After conferring with Churchill in Washington, for example, Roosevelt chose to concentrate on the defeat of Germany first, after which the full force of war was to be directed against Japan.

As commander-in-chief, Roosevelt was the chief architect of the North African invasion, which commenced on November 7, 1942. This was followed by invasions of Sicily and Italy, and finally the cross-channel, D-Day invasion of Normandy. In the latter enterprise, Roosevelt was under pressure from Joseph Stalin to create a second front quickly to relieve German pressure on the Russians. Stalin wanted the Normandy venture to begin before the President was convinced the Allies were prepared for it. Churchill preferred a thrust up through the Balkans to check the western surge of the Russians. Roosevelt remained the master of the decision.

The President furthered war diplomacy in a 1943 meeting with Churchill at Casablanca, where they agreed to accept only unconditional surrender by the Axis.

With the war at its peak, Roosevelt reluctantly ran (1944) for a fourth Presidential term, and he easily defeated his Republican opponent, Thomas E. Dewey. Roosevelt began his new term in obviously failing health, yet journeyed to Yalta in the Crimea to confer with Churchill and Stalin. The Crimea Declaration, which emerged from the conference, affirmed the principles of the Atlantic Charter and the objectives of the Casablanca conference. Plans for the defeat and occupation of Germany were drawn, and a future meeting at San Francisco was agreed on at which the United Nations would be organized as an enduring international structure. In return for Far East concessions, Russia agreed to enter the war against Japan.

In the weeks following the Yalta meeting, Roosevelt, whose wartime policies had assumed the continued goodwill and cooperation of the Soviet Union, grew restive with doubts over Soviet attitudes.

On April 12, 1945, about a month before Germany surrendered, Roosevelt suddenly died at Warm Springs, Georgia. He was buried at Hyde Park.

As President, Roosevelt employed the resources of his office with boldness and initiative. He delighted to break precedents and embark on new ways. His cabinet appointees were lively and resourceful, and he was given to employing both "Brain Trusters," who were usually academicians fertile in ideas, and wide-ranging White House assistants. Adroit in political controversy, he impressed fellow politicians with his canny sense of timing. Although given to deviousness, he unfailingly projected an air of rectitude. In the age of radio, he excelled at stirring public opinion, and as party leader he solidified the loyalties of such groups as labor and blacks to the Democratic party. These groups, joined with the South, city party organizations, and farmers constituted "the Roosevelt coalition," which endured for decades after its creator's death.

## Harry S Truman

Harry S Truman, 33d President (April 12, 1945–January 20, 1953), was born on May 8, 1884, in Lamar, Missouri. The oldest of three children of a farmer and livestock dealer, Truman was raised on a farm near Independence. A voracious reader of military history, he hoped to attend West Point, but was rejected because of unsatisfactory vision. After finishing high school, he worked as a timekeeper for a railroad construction gang, as a mail clerk for a Kansas City newspaper, and as a bookkeeper in Kansas City banks. In World War I, Truman helped recruit a field artillery regiment. He saw action in France, was discharged (1919) as a major, and later rose to a colonelcy in the reserves.

After the war, Truman invested in a men's clothing store, in Kansas City, but it failed in the farm depression of 1921. At this bleak moment, Truman turned to politics and secured an introduction to "Big Tom" Pendergast, Democratic boss of Kansas City. Impressed with Truman's political promise, Pendergast supported (1922) Truman's successful campaign for administrator of Jackson County; however, after a two-year term, Truman was defeated for reelection because of factional strife within his party. In his free time, Truman studied law at Kansas City Law School, and in 1926, he was elected presiding judge, serving in that capacity until 1934. Overseeing large projects of public works construction, he earned a reputation for probity and efficiency.

With Pendergast's backing, Truman was elected (1934) to the U.S. Senate. During a decade in the Senate, Truman strongly supported the New Deal, and during World War II he achieved national renown as chairman of the Senate's Special Committee to investigate the National Defense Program. The Truman Committee, as it was known, excelled at uncovering waste and inefficiency in war production.

In 1944, Truman won the Democratic Vice-Presidential nomination as a compromise choice in a spirited contest between several contenders. When President Roosevelt suddenly died, Truman became President at a critical moment in the nation's history. Within his first weeks as President, Germany surrendered and the United Nations was launched at the San Francisco conference as a postwar international organization. He met with the British and Soviet leaders at Potsdam, and made the grave decision to employ the atomic bomb against Japan to bring World War II to a quick conclusion.

Truman now had to lead the nation's reconversion from its wartime mobilization to a peacetime footing. In a message to Congress (September 6, 1945), he proposed a sweeping program (the "Fair Deal,") that was an extension of the New Deal. His proposals included an expanded social security system, a higher minimum wage, a permanent fair employment practices commission to protect minority rights, comprehensive housing legislation, government aid for scientific research, and public power projects on the Missouri, Columbia, and Arkansas rivers.

Few of Truman's proposals were enacted. In 1946, the Republicans gained control of both houses of Congress, and the President's program was blocked by a coalition of conservative Republicans and Democrats. His chief success was legislation for public housing that was passed with substantial help from the Senate Republican leader, Robert A. Taft. In 1947, Congress approved Truman's plan to unify the armed forces by creating the U.S. Department of Defense. In that same year, Congress passed the Taft-Hartley Labor Act, a far-ranging measure for regulating labor unions and labor-management relations. In a bitterly worded message, Truman vetoed the act but was overridden by Congress.

In foreign affairs, United States relations with the Soviet Union swiftly deteriorated as the Communists gained control in the nations of Eastern Europe. To check the Communist tide, Truman advanced a doctrine of American aid to nations that resisted either direct or indirect Communist aggression. The Truman Doctrine, as it became known, was prompted by Britain's inability to continue her aid to Greece and Turkey in their struggle against Communist actions, and American aid checked a Communist-supported civil war in Greece and bolstered Turkey's military strength.

In 1947, the Marshall Plan (European Recovery Program) extended the Truman Doctrine to speed the recovery of Western European economies from the devastation resulting from World War II. The Marshall Plan was a combination of European self-help supported by massive American outlays. The Soviet Union was invited to join the plan, but declined.

The continuing decline in American-USSR relations became known as "The Cold War," and the Truman administration's policy of applying counterforce—political, economic, or military—corresponding to the shifts and maneuvers of the Soviet Union was spoken of as the policy of "containment." Congress generously supported the President through appropriations and statutory authority.

While coping with the Cold War, Truman faced sharp political strife at home in the 1948 election. A segment of liberal Democrats formed the Progressive party and nominated Henry A. Wallace for President. Other liberal Democrats sought unsuccessfully to deny Truman the Democratic nomination. Conservative Southern Democrats formed the Dixiecrat party and nominated J. Strom Thurmond. Against mountainous odds and almost miraculously, Truman defeated the Republican nominee, Governor Thomas E. Dewey. Truman relied upon a "whistle-stop" campaign and rousing oratory that was directed at the Republican 80th Congress, which he characterized as "do-nothing" and "the worst in memory."

Foreign affairs dominated Truman's new term. A 1948 Communist coup in Czechoslovakia prompted Western European nations to draw together in their defenses and led to the creation of the North Atlantic Treaty Organization (NATO) under which the United States and other pact nations agreed that an attack on one member would be regarded as an attack on all member nations. An Anglo-American airlift thwarted the Communist blockade of Berlin in 1948.

In his inaugural address, Truman proposed "a bold new program" by which American technical and production skills could help "underdeveloped" areas. Implementation of the proposal began (1950) when Congress established the Point Four Program. In 1951, Truman initiated a foreign-aid program for Southeast Asian countries threatened by Communism. A Mutual Security program was also instituted to improve military defenses in many countries worldwide.

The Cold War became hot (June 25, 1950), when Communist North Korea invaded South Korea. Truman quickly responded by committing United States forces to South Korea's defense under UN auspices. Commanded by General Douglas MacArthur, UN forces overran most of North Korea, only to have Communist China enter the war. MacArthur proposed to bomb Communist bases in Manchuria, but Truman, who did not wish to extend the war, rejected the plan. When MacArthur publicly criticized the administration, Truman removed him from his command, igniting a furor of debate and criticism.

In domestic affairs, Truman fared little better with the new Democratic Congress than he had with the former Republican one. The Truman administration faced charges of Communist infiltration into the U.S. Department of State that were lodged by Senator Joseph McCarthy of Wisconsin. A House investigating committee made similar accusations about other agencies. As a result, Truman set up a federal loyalty board to deal with the problem, and the justice department launched prosecutions of American Communist leaders. The administration was hobbled by exposures of corruption among subordinates, who were generously defended by the President for reasons of friendship or party necessity.

On March 29, 1952, Truman announced that he would not seek reelection. Nevertheless, he campaigned strenuously for the unsuccessful Democratic nominee, Adlai E. Stevenson. After leaving office, Truman wrote his memoirs, which were published in two volumes, commented occasionally on national issues, and remained interested in the Democratic party. He died on December 26, 1972, and is buried at Independence, Missouri.

Winston Churchill credited President Truman with making "great and valiant decisions." Other admirers of his administration cited his courage and his gift of seeing issues divested of complication and of stating them in plain, blunt terms. His critics felt that his candor and affinity for strong language were undignified. Others considered him a man of the people, and Truman acknowledged these differences of opinion by once saying that he expected to be "cussed and discussed" for years to come.

## Dwight David Eisenhower

Dwight David Eisenhower, 34th President (1953–1961), was born in Denison, Texas, on October 14, 1890 as David Dwight Eisenhower. Of Swiss and German ancestry, Eisenhower's parents belonged to the River Brethren religious sect, which was opposed to war and violence. While young, Eisenhower moved to Abilene, Kansas; after graduating from high school, he worked in the local creamery where his father was engineer.

To the disappointment of his parents, Eisenhower entered West Point at the age of 21 and graduated in the 1915 class that included Omar Bradley and James Van Fleet. In World War I, he was commander of a tank training center near Gettysburg, Pennsylvania. His postwar career included service in the Canal Zone; study at the General Staff School at Fort Leavenworth, Kansas, and at the U.S. Army War College. Eisenhower became (1933) an aide of General Douglas MacArthur in the Philippines. Brilliance in field maneuvers won him assignment to the war plans division of the war department, and he became (1942) head of the operations division. At midyear, Eisenhower was named U.S. commander of the European Theater of Operations.

Eisenhower oversaw the North African invasion (November 1942) and directed the invasions of Sicily and Italy. He was named (1943) supreme commander of the Allied Expeditionary Force (AEF) that was organized for the Normandy invasion. He excelled at bringing proud, independent generals of various nations into working harmony and directing the military operations of an unprecedented scale that achieved (1945) the unconditional surrender of Germany. Made a five-star general (1944) and chief of staff of the U.S. Army (1945), Eisenhower played a leading part in the "unification" of the armed services under the newly established U.S. Department of Defense. He retired (1948) from active duty to become president of Columbia University.

After soundings made by both Democratic and Republican sources, Eisenhower announced (1948) his unavailability as a Presidential candidate. After 30 months he left his Columbia post to serve as NATO commander and to organize the forces of that alliance.

The approaching 1952 elections brought new pressures on Eisenhower to run for the Presidency, and he responded. He retired from the army to campaign successfully for the Republican nomination against Senator Robert A. Taft. Promising to "clean up the mess in Washington" and that "I shall go to Korea" to help end the war, the enormously popular "Ike" Eisenhower easily defeated his Democratic opponent, Adlai E. Stevenson. Eisenhower also helped his party win control of both houses of Congress. Soon after the election, he journeyed to Korea to observe the war firsthand.

From long observation of the Presidency during his military career, Eisenhower considered that the office was administered with excessive informality. As a result, he installed a staff system comparable to the military's and designated Sherman Adams, former governor of New Hampshire, as his chief White House aide. For the first time, the cabinet worked regularly according to a prearranged agenda, records of cabinet proceedings were kept, and each cabinet officer was responsible for monitoring problems and taking initiatives in his area of affairs.

Eisenhower was an apostle of what he termed Modern Republicanism, which, in its most ambitious projection, looked for major policy changes in his party. It called for the strengthening of federal social programs, and the President secured an expanded coverage of the social security system—its largest extension since its beginning under FDR. The minimum wage was also increased. Eisenhower was watchful that new measures did not encroach on state jurisdictions.

The President's domestic program included a 13-year highway building program that was urgently needed, because of a construction backlog that had accumulated during World War II. Eisenhower also succeeded in bringing Congress to modify the traditional rigid price supports of certain staple farm products.

In national security, the Eisenhower administration introduced "the new look" that shifted the emphasis of military expenditure from conventional forces and weapons to atomic weapons, which were regarded as more economical. In foreign affairs, an agreement was reached between the United States and Canada for joint development of the St. Lawrence Seaway.

More than most Presidents, Eisenhower faced substantial encroachment (or its threat) on his office and the functioning of the executive branch. Senator John Bricker of Ohio sponsored an amendment to curb the President's power to make treaties and executive agreements. After a strenuous fight, the President and his Secretary of State, John Foster Dulles, defeated the amendment.

Another Republican Senator, Joseph R. McCarthy of Wisconsin, steadily confronted the administration with accusations of subversion and Communist infiltration of the executive branch. Eisenhower, who declined to deal "in terms of personality," refrained from directly attacking McCarthy, a stand that prompted criticism. But when McCarthy charged that the United States Information Agency had Communist books in its European libraries, Eisenhower counseled students in an address at Dartmouth College: "Don't join the bookburners. . . . Don't be afraid to go to the library and read every book."

In foreign affairs, Eisenhower made important gains for peace and guided the Korean war to a close. He advanced (1953) the "Atoms for Peace" program, under which the world nations were to pool atomic energy information and output for peaceful purposes. The proposal led to the creation (1957) of the International Atomic Agency. The President proposed (1955) that the United States and the Soviet Union permit air inspection of each other's military installations, but the USSR declined.

On September 24, 1955, Eisenhower suffered a heart attack, the first of several illnesses with which he was afflicted during his years in office. His good recovery enabled him to run for a second term in 1956, when he again easily defeated Adlai Stevenson.

In his second term, Eisenhower sent (1957) Federal troops to Little Rock, Arkansas, to enforce school desegregation that was being resisted by Governor Orval Faubus. The nation suffered an economic recession in 1957 and 1958, but business improved markedly during the latter half of 1958. Eisenhower lost his chief assistant, Sherman Adams, in 1958, when Congressional investigations revealed that he had accepted gifts from a businessman who was under scrutiny by government agencies. Adams denied any wrongdoing, but resigned his White House post.

Eisenhower's hopes to develop a more peaceful international climate were defeated by repeated difficulties with the Communist world. The Soviet's launching (1957) of Sputnik I—the first manmade satellite—emboldened the Russians. Crisis in the Middle East evoked the "Eisenhower Doctrine," pledging American military aid to any Middle East nation that requested it to repel Communist aggression, and Eisenhower applied (1958) the doctrine to Lebanon. When Chinese Communists shelled Nationalist-held Quemoy island in 1958, the President committed American naval aid to protect Chinese Nationalist convoys.

Eisenhower met (1959) with Soviet Premier Nikita Khrushchev in a summit conference in the United States; however, a further summit conference at Paris (1960) was broken up by Khrushchev, because of an American U-2 reconnaissance aircraft that had been shot down over Russian territory. Following many provocations by Fidel Castro, Eisenhower broke off diplomatic relations with Cuba in 1961.

Eisenhower was the first President to be limited to two terms by the 22d Constitutional Amendment. Retiring to his farm in Gettysburg, Pennsylvania, Eisenhower wrote memoirs of his Presidential years and other books, supported Richard Nixon's Presidential campaigns, and discussed various political questions. He died on March 28, 1969, and is buried at Abilene, Kansas.

## John Fitzgerald Kennedy

John Fitzgerald Kennedy, 35th President (January 20, 1961–November 22, 1963) was born into a political family on May 29, 1917, in Brookline, Massachusetts. His paternal grandfather was a state senator and Boston ward boss, and his maternal grandfather was John F. ("Honey Fitz") Fitzgerald—Boston mayor, state senator, and U.S. Representative. Kennedy's father, Joseph P. Kennedy, was a self-made millionaire and ambassador to Great Britain during World War II.

After studies at the London School of Economics and Princeton, Kennedy graduated (1940) from Harvard, where he majored in political science and international relations. His senior thesis, *Why England Slept*, became a best-selling book.

At the outbreak of World War II, Kennedy enlisted in the Navy and served as commander of a PT boat in the South Pacific. In action off the Solomon Islands, a Japanese destroyer sank his boat. Kennedy heroically saved an injured member of his crew. After release from the Navy, Kennedy worked briefly as a reporter for the Hearst newspapers.

The World War II death of his older brother Joe, who had been expected to become the family politician, devolved that function on John Kennedy. He was elected (1946) to the U.S. House of Representatives, defeating eight opponents in the Democratic primary of the Massachusetts 11th district and easily overcoming his Republican opponent. As Congressman, Kennedy voted regularly for Truman's Fair Deal program. Reelected twice, Kennedy became (1952) Senator in an upset defeat of the popular Henry Cabot Lodge. Kennedy underwent (1954–55) operations to correct a spinal injury that he had sustained in the war; while recovering, he wrote *Profiles in Courage*, for which he won the Pulitzer Prize.

In 1956, Kennedy was a strong contender for the Vice-Presidential nomination, losing to Estes Kefauver in a close race. Kennedy was easily reelected (1958) to the Senate. From 1956 onward, however, he was busily preparing to make a Presidential race and eventually won the 1960 Democratic nomination, after scoring several crucial primary victories. In a hard-fought contest with his Republican opponent, Richard M. Nixon, Kennedy—a youthful, handsome, and wealthy figure with an attractive wife and a highly persuasive television style—won the election in the closest race of the century. Vital to his success were his televised debates with Nixon. At the age of 43, Kennedy became the youngest man ever elected President, and he was also the first Roman Catholic to occupy the office.

Kennedy's Presidential campaign had been geared largely to the industrial and urban states. On attaining office, he promoted legislative measures that he had promised to support if elected. Included in his recommendations to Congress were major educational legislation, medical aid for the aged, the creation of a Department of Urban Affairs, and an increase in the minimum wage.

He suffered severe resistance in the House of Representatives, where a conservative coalition of Republicans and Democrats thwarted much of his program. Because of this opposition, he long held back the promotion of major civil rights legislation. He sustained defeats on his farm bill, the urban department, health care for the aged, and education. His chief legislative triumph was the passage (1962) of the Trade Expansion Act, which gave the President broad powers to reduce tariffs to enable the United States to trade freely with the European Common Market.

In a rare step, President Kennedy sought to break the legislative logjam by seeking, with Speaker Sam Rayburn's help, to enlarge the House Rules Committee, at which point much legislation was stopped. The administration's position in the committee became somewhat improved following the fight, but not sufficiently to push key measures through.

Although blocked on Capitol Hill on civil rights legislation, Kennedy was diligent and ingenious in advancing civil rights policies through executive initiatives and actions. The Kennedy administration, with Robert Kennedy as Attorney General, was aggressive in prosecuting violations of the Supreme Court's school desegregation decisions; it directed U.S. marshals, the regular army, and the federalized National Guard to quell (1961) rioting against black and white "freedom riders" in Montgomery, Alabama; it employed the government contract to improve the civil rights standards of private employers; and it demanded that the civil service improve black recruitment and promotion. In televised appeals, the President promoted understanding of civil rights problems.

More than most modern Presidents, Kennedy was preoccupied with crisis, both foreign and domestic. In 1962, certain steel companies raised their prices, after Kennedy had induced labor to scale down its demands to check inflation. Outraged by management's action, the President moved forcefully against the companies involved and denounced them publicly. The companies withdrew the price rises, but the stock market soon underwent its sharpest drop since 1929. Within weeks, Kennedy faced a civil rights crisis in Mississippi, when the governor refused to obey a federal court order requiring that James Meredith, a black, be enrolled at the University. The President dispatched Federal troops and marshals, and Meredith was enrolled.

In foreign affairs, the President seemed never without crisis. Prepared and outfitted under American auspices, Cuban rebels invaded their homeland to overthrow the Communist-backed leader (1961), Fidel Castro. The assault was savagely repulsed, and Kennedy publicly took responsibility for the disaster. Berlin was a constant concern of the President. Aiming to end the Allied participation in control of the city, the Soviet Union and East Germany engaged in a series of maneuvers that culminated in the erection of the Berlin Wall, which sealed off escape from East to West Berlin. The President called up army reserves and dispatched military units to the border until the tense situation eased.

Kennedy faced (1961–62) spreading Communist penetration in Southeast Asia and made substantial commitments of American troops and matériel to the defense of South Vietnam and Thailand. Military advisers were sent to Laos.

Late in 1962, Kennedy became the first President to engage in a confrontation with another nuclear power. The Soviet Union built missile sites in Cuba from which it would have been possible to launch attacks on American cities. Kennedy imposed a blockade or "quarantine," barring the introduction of any offensive missiles to Cuba. The President also made clear that the United States would respond to any nuclear attack from Cuba on a Western Hemisphere nation by retaliating against the Soviet Union. After 14 days of intense deliberations by the President and his counselors and exchanges of messages with Russia, the crisis was resolved by Premier Khrushchev's ordering that the Cuban bases be dismantled and the missiles returned to Russia. In world eyes, Kennedy emerged from this crisis as a well-poised, rational, and resolute leader who had thoroughly excelled his Soviet opponent.

The Kennedy years were an era when young men were in charge of Presidential institutions. In his inaugural address, the President noted that a new generation was coming into power. Himself the first President born in the 20th century, Kennedy filled his chief posts with men in their 30s and early 40s. His administration he described as the "New Frontier." In foreign affairs, its chief innovations were establishment of the Peace Corps and the Latin-American Alliance for Progress and the nuclear test-ban treaty. In domestic affairs, he demonstrated new "vigor" in attacking urban problems. The Kennedy administration was also marked by new attention to American culture. Not since the days of Theodore Roosevelt did so many musicians, artists, writers, and scientists visit the White House.

For all of the power and majesty of his office, Kennedy displayed a remarkable gift for self-depreciation. A master of irony, both keen and gentle, he directed it at himself as well as at others. A capacity for self-criticism helped Kennedy maintain exceptional composure in crisis, to keep his assessments of problems and people in balance, and to question the well-settled responses of the past.

On November 22, 1963, the Kennedy era was suddenly ended in Dallas, Texas, where Lee Harvey Oswald murdered the President. An appalled nation and world mourned his death. He is buried at a simple site in Arlington National Cemetery.

## Lyndon Baines Johnson

Lyndon Baines Johnson, 36th President (November 22, 1963–January 20, 1969), was born on a farm near Stonewall, Texas, on August 27, 1908, the son of a state legislator and school teacher. The family moved (1913) to Johnson City, Texas, where young Johnson was educated in the local public schools. He taught (1928) grade school in Cotulla, Texas, and graduated (1930) from Southwest Texas State Teachers College. For the next two years, he taught public school in Houston.

Johnson began his political career in 1932 as secretary to a Texas Congressman and attended Georgetown University Law School in Washington. An enthusiastic supporter of the New Deal, Johnson became (1935) state director of the National Youth Administration in Texas. His first attempt at elective office was successful, when voters chose him to fill a vacancy in 1937 in the U.S. House of Representatives, and he was continuously reelected until 1948.

Immediately after the Japanese attack on Pearl Harbor, Johnson became the first member of Congress to go into uniform, entering active service in the U.S. Navy. He rose to lieutenant commander before being called back to Congress.

Johnson was elected (1948) to the U.S. Senate after winning the Democratic primary election by a hairline margin of 87 votes. Proving himself well-endowed with the gifts for legislative leadership and steeped in knowledge of Congressional procedures, Johnson rose rapidly in the Senate. He became (1951) Democratic whip, and he was elected (1953) Democratic leader, serving until 1960. He was reelected (1954) to the Senate and suffered a serious heart attack a year later. As Senate leader, Johnson was moderate in policy, extraordinarily persuasive, and skillful in effecting compromise. He was a top contender for the Democratic Presidential nomination in 1960, but it was won by John F. Kennedy, who chose him to be his Vice-President.

Kennedy's assassination on November 22, 1963, suddenly brought Johnson into the Presidency. Under these tragic circumstances, he quickly administered the office with a skill and self-possession that reassured the nation and the world. He guided through Congress the Civil Rights Act of 1964, a major education bill, a new tax law, and an economic opportunity act that declared "war on poverty."

In the 1964 Presidential elections, Johnson won an overwhelming victory over his Republican opponent, Barry M. Goldwater. Johnson received the largest percentage of popular votes ever accorded a President and perhaps, more important, he won lop-sided Democratic majorities in Congress.

Against this extraordinarily favorable legislative background, Johnson, with shrewd strategy and relentless drive, pushed legislation through Congress in 1965 and 1966 that instituted more innovations in domestic affairs than any other President in any other single session of Congress in this century. The "Great Society" program, as his platform became known, included medical care for the aged under social security, the first comprehensive aid-to-education law, a voting rights bill, a broad housing program, immigration reform, programs for highway beautification and for combating heart disease and cancer, and water and air pollution measures. After the 1966 Congressional elections that resulted in a loss of Democratic strength, the legislative output fell significantly.

The Presidential Succession Constitutional Amendment (25th) was adopted (1967) with Johnson's strong backing, and Congress passed (1968) a strong civil rights bill that included guarantees of open housing.

Crisis flared (1965) in the Dominican Republic, when the President dispatched U.S. marines to thwart a take-over by what he termed "a band of Communist conspirators."

The dominant preoccupation, however, of the Johnson administration was the Vietnamese war, which was already large in scale by the time that Johnson took office. When U.S. warships were alleged to have been attacked (1964) in the Gulf of Tonkin, Johnson ordered a bombing of North Vietnamese PT-boat bases, and Congress expressed approval in a broadly stated resolution. The President increased (1965) the numbers of American fighting men in Vietnam, although he encouraged the North Vietnamese to begin "unconditional negotiations."

In late 1967, additional U.S. troops were committed to the conflict. In the face of heavy Vietcong offensives in 1968 against South Vietnam cities, the President was criticized by "hawks" for restricting bombing in North Vietnam and by "doves" for not ending the bombing altogether. On March 31, the President announced a partial end to the bombing of North Vietnam and simultaneously appointed representatives to negotiate with the North Vietnamese in Paris. On October 31, Johnson ordered a complete halt to the bombing and shelling of North Vietnam.

Johnson pursued policies aiming toward improved relations with Eastern Europe and the Soviet Union, proposed treaties barring military activity in outer space and the proliferation of nations producing nuclear weapons, conducted a summit conference with Soviet Premier Kosygin at Glassboro, New Jersey, in 1967, and sought to prevent and terminate the Arab-Israeli war of 1967. In 1968, North Korea seized the U.S.S. *Pueblo*, precipitating a potentially major crisis that Johnson contained with diplomacy.

In a televised address (March 31, 1968), announcing a partial halt to the bombing of North Vietnam, Johnson also disclosed that he would "not accept the nomination of my party as your President."

Johnson's forte in the Presidency was clearly in the area of legislative relations, toward which his previous career was so strongly directed. "I am a compromiser and a manipulator," he once described himself. His perceptions of the nature of power moved him more to the backstage than to the frontstage of politics. "In every town," he once said, "there's some guy on top of the hill in a big white house who can get things done. I want to get that man on my side." As a public leader, he was handicapped by the unfriendliness toward him of many academics, the press, and American youth. Johnson did not have the great strength in the national party organization that Franklin D. Roosevelt enjoyed, nor did he have the personal organization for party affairs of John F. Kennedy. These deficiencies undoubtedly added to the troubles involved in his possible renomination in 1968. With roots in Populism and the Southwest, Johnson had difficulty winning national acceptance, particularly in the East. He died Jan. 22, 1973 and is buried near Johnson City, Texas.

## Richard Milhous Nixon

Richard Milhous Nixon, 37th President (January 20, 1969–August 9, 1974), was born of Quaker parentage in Yorba Linda, California, on January 9, 1913. When he was nine years old, the Nixon family moved to Whittier, California, where his father ran a combination grocery store and gas station. After graduating from Whittier College (1934) and Duke University Law School (1937), he practiced law in Whittier and worked briefly as an attorney for the Office of Price Administration in Washington, D. C. Following United States entry into World War II, he served (1942–46) as a naval officer.

Nixon's political career began in 1946, when a group of California Republicans urged him to run for Congress. He won a hard-fought contest (during which he accused his opponent, a New Deal Democrat, of being soft on Communism) and was reelected in 1948. In the House of Representatives, he contributed importantly to the development of the Marshall Plan and the Taft-Hartley act. He gained national prominence in 1948–49 by pressing an investigation by the House Un-American Activities Committee into charges that Alger Hiss, a former State Department official, had passed government information to Russian agents in the 1930s. In 1950, a federal district court convicted Hiss of perjury.

On the crest of the prominence attained by the Hiss case, Nixon was elected (1950) to the Senate from California. Two years later, Republicans nominated Nixon as the Vice-Presidential running mate of Dwight D. Eisenhower.

In 1960 Nixon was defeated by John F. Kennedy in a close race for the Presidency. The campaign witnessed the first televised debate between Presidential candidates. Turning to authorship, Nixon published (1962) *Six Crises*, a personal account of major interludes in his career. That year he also ran unsuccessfully against incumbent Edmund (Pat) Brown for governor of California.

He entered a crowded field of contestants for the 1968 Republican Presidential nomination, excelled in the primaries, and by forestalling defection of Southern delegates to his rival, Governor Ronald Reagan of California, won a first-ballot nomination. His selection of Governor Spiro T. Agnew of Maryland as a running mate and the firm adherence of Southern delegates, led by Strom Thurmond of South Carolina, to his nomination, prompted discussion that Nixon was pursuing a "Southern strategy."

Projecting a "New Nixon" image, he appealed to the nation's discontent with the Vietnam War and its concern for preserving law and order. In a close race, he defeated Hubert H. Humphrey, who led a divided Democratic party, and George C. Wallace, nominee of the American Independent party.

Nixon was engrossed, during his first term, in the Indo-China war. He sought a negotiated settlement, but despite both private and public talks in Paris, the war continued to drag on. In August, 1972, the American ground combat role ended in Vietnam as the last combat infantry unit was returned to the U.S. To replace the departing forces, the President depended on a policy of "Vietnamization," and American warplanes based throughout Southeast Asia.

To offset criticism that the United States was absorbed in Vietnam to the neglect of other parts of the world, the President visited several West European capitals in 1969, and he became the first President in nearly 25 years to visit a

Communist nation (Romania). His 1972 visits to Russia and China were hailed as historic moments in American diplomacy.

In domestic affairs Nixon was less successful in combating inflation. In August 1971, he instituted price and wage controls. It was the first time such constraints had been applied to the U.S. economy during peacetime, but by the time he left office in 1974, the economy was in a recession.

The President was reelected in 1972 by one of the greatest margins in U.S. history. He was helped by a disorganized Democratic party that was deeply split when old-line party leaders were routed in their effort to block the nomination of Sen. George McGovern of South Dakota.

Allegations of major scandals broke before the election, but apparently had little effect on the outcome. Not until the following year, when the bugging of Democratic headquarters in the Watergate Hotel was fully understood, did public opinion turn sharply downward.

In 1973 peace negotiations in Paris finally bore fruit, at least for the United States. Peace accords were signed in January which called for the end of all fighting and the withdrawal of American and other foreign troops from Vietnam and the rest of Indochina. What the President called "peace with honor" did not bring a halt in the fighting between North and South Vietnam or between Communist insurgents and government forces in Cambodia. U.S. bombing was halted with the peace treaty in Vietnam but continued in Cambodia until August when Nixon halted the bombing under heavy congressional pressure.

For the first time in years, Vietnam and other foreign crises were completely eclipsed by events in Washington. Although the White House initially wrote off the Watergate incident as of no major significance, the combined forces of the press, a Senate investigating committee, and a special prosecutor, eventually forced Nixon to resign in disgrace and left many of his former top assistants accused of obstruction of justice.

## Gerald R. Ford

Gerald Rudolph Ford, 38th President (August 9, 1974-January 20, 1977), is unique in American history. He was neither elected president nor vice president, but rather, was first appointed vice president under a new Constitutional amendment, when Vice President Agnew resigned in disgrace, and then became President when Nixon resigned.

Prior to becoming vice president, Ford had spent his entire political career in the U.S. House of Representatives, where he was the respected Republican House Minority Leader. After assuming the Presidency, Ford's popularity was initially very high, but continuing inflation, the pardon of former President Nixon, and the granting of limited amnesty to Vietnam-era draft evaders and deserters, quickly brought this "honeymoon" to an end.

President Ford was born in Omaha, Neb., on July 14, 1913. His mother and father were divorced shortly after his birth, and when his mother remarried, her second husband adopted the future president, renaming Leslie Lynch King, Jr., Gerald R. Ford, Jr.

Ford was raised in Grand Rapids, Mich.; was graduated from the University of Michigan, where he was captain of the football team; and received his law degree from Yale University.

In 1942 he entered the U.S. Navy, serving 47 months and participating for two years in 3d and 5th Fleet Carrier operations with the U.S.S. *Monterey*. After discharge, in 1946, Ford resumed his law practice briefly in Grand Rapids before being elected, in 1948, to the U.S. House of Representatives, a seat he retained for 25 years, through the election of 1972. In 1963, Ford was appointed by President Lyndon Johnson as a member of the Warren Commission to investigate the assassination of President Kennedy.

From the time of his entry into Congress, Gerald Ford's views tended toward the conservative. He voted against most social welfare legislation, in favor of weakened minimum wage bills, and he opposed forced school busing. He supported, however, key civil rights bills at the time of their final passage.

By 1959, Ford was gaining increasing party support for leadership of the House Republicans. In 1960, he was endorsed by Michigan Republicans as the state's favorite son for the G.O.P. vice-presidential nomination. By 1964, he had gained sufficient support to challenge successfully Rep. Charles R. Halleck for the post of House Minority Leader. Generally content with Ford's noncombative, middle-of-the-road approach to issues in his years as Minority Leader, his contituency continued to return him to Congress with majorities of over 60 per cent.

When, on October 12, 1973, Ford was nominated to succeed Spiro T. Agnew as Vice President, he willingly offered to make public any personal information or documentation asked for, including a full statement of net worth, as a way of removing any stigma attached to the office by the departed Vice President.

Richard M. Nixon resigned as President of the United States on August 9, 1974, and Gerald R. Ford was sworn in as his successor on the same day. Ford immediately moved to assure a stable transition of power, retaining Henry Kissinger as Secretary of State, meeting with foreign envoys to reaffirm the Nixon Administration's foreign policies, and conferring with members of the Cabinet, the National Security Council, and the government's economic advisors.

In 1975 President Ford twice escaped death at the hands of would-be assassins. In May when a U.S. merchant ship, the "Mayaguez", was fired on, boarded and seized by Cambodians, Ford reminded the world of his enormous power by ordering a swift attack by Marines which resulted in the rescue of the ship and its crew.

The nomination of an incumbent president by his own party is traditionally assured, but Ford had to meet a strong challenge from former Governor of California, Ronald Reagan. In August 1976, Ford was nominated on the first ballot as the Republican presidential candidate at the Republican National Convention in Kansas City, Missouri. In the November election, he was defeated by his Democratic opponent, Jimmy Carter.

## Jimmy Carter

Jimmy Carter, 39th President (January 20, 1977-January 20, 1981) was born in the small farming town of Plains, Georgia, on October 1, 1924. His father, James Earl Carter, had managed a dry goods store and brokered in peanuts; his mother Lillian, was a registered nurse. The Carter family roots in Georgia go back 150 years for eight generations.

The first member of his family to be graduated from high school, Jimmy Carter attended Georgia Southwestern College and Georgia Institute of Technology prior to his entrance into the U.S. Naval Academy at Annapolis. He graduated 59th in a class of 820 and for six years had a series of assignments which took him from battleships to submarines. In 1952 he was selected by Adm. Hyman G. Rickover to be a part of the Navy's nuclear submarine program. When his father died in 1953, Carter left the Navy and returned to Plains, where he took over the family's peanut warehousing business and built it into a thriving operation.

A deacon in the Plains Baptist Church and member of the local school board, Carter entered politics in 1962. He won a seat in the Georgia Senate that year, but it took a court suit to reverse irregularities that at first gave the primary to his opponent. He easily won a second term in 1964. In his bid for the governorship in 1966, he was third in a six-man primary contest. Encouraged by his showing, he campaigned again in 1970, winning the primary nomination and the election by a comfortable margin.

As governor, Carter reorganized that state's government, consolidating agencies and introducing a system of zero-based budgeting. He extended state hospital services and was a strong advocate of environmental protection. His stand on equal rights for "the poor, rural, black or not influential" brought Carter his first nationwide attention.

Barred by state law from a second term as governor, he announced in December 1974, one month before the end of his term, that he would run for President. For over a year, almost unnoticed by the press, Jimmy Carter was on the road. A good showing in the Iowa caucus in mid-January brought media attention; and his win in the New Hampshire primary launched a series of victories which eliminated the opposition and earned him the nomination on the first ballot at the Democratic convention, Carter won the close election against President Gerald Ford by holding together enough of the basic old Democratic coalition, namely labor, blacks and liberals.

One of Carter's first acts as President was to grant a pardon to almost all Vietnam draft evaders. A reorganization of the complex structure of departments and agencies was begun, and a new, Cabinet-level Department of Energy was created. A separate Department of Education was spun off from the Department of Health, Education and Welfare which has been renamed the Department of Health and Human Services.

Carter's program on energy was designed largely to reduce America's dependency on foreign oil. The President asked for a limit on imported oil, gradual price decontrol of domestically produced oil, and development of alternative sources of energy. He requested a tax on "gas guzzlers" and incentives for the purchase of small cars. Increases in coal production, greater use of solar energy and effective insulation were other key elements in the package. After long delays, significant portions of Carter's energy program were passed by Congress. Missing from the bills passed were penalties on heavy energy consumption.

In the area of foreign affairs, the effect of President Carter's policies and methods was immediate. Carter set his own course, giving a moral content to American foreign policy that had been missing in earlier years. He won respect in some quarters for concluding treaties that would turn the Panama Canal over to Panama by the year 2000 and for the restraint shown in coping with troubles in Iran, Afghanistan and Nicaragua. Carter strengthened ties between the United States and the Communist government of China, and after a lapse of almost 30 years, full diplomatic relations between the two nations were resumed in 1979.

The President's forthright championing of human rights and his outspoken defense of Soviet dissidents caused an immediate negative reaction in Moscow. Relations became increasingly strained by Western suspicions concerning a Soviet arms buildup and moves by Moscow in Africa. In spite of these differences, Carter and Soviet President Brezhnev negotiated to limit the nuclear arms race. Long, arduous sessions of the Strategic Arms Limitations Talks (SALT II) produced an agreement signed on June 15, 1979. The treaty got a mixed reaction in the U.S. Senate and it eventually was placed in limbo when the Soviets invaded Afghanistan.

In defense matters, Carter served notice on the Pentagon that he was in charge. He scrapped the B-1 bomber program, used his veto to block construction of a new nuclear aircraft carrier, and deferred production of the neutron bomb, although he reserved the option to produce it later. The President approved the development of the MX mobile ICBM in June 1979.

In the Middle East, the Carter Administration gained much in bringing Israel and Egypt to the 1978 Camp David peace negotiations. Some of the bloom came off Carter's Middle East success with the seizure of the American hostages in Tehran in November 1979 and the Soviet takeover of Afghanistan two months later. Carter called for a boycott of the Moscow Olympics and a cutback of exports to the USSR, thus cooling off U.S.-Soviet relations, but neither diplomatic pressure nor an aborted military rescue mission could free the U.S. hostages.

The events of late 1979 were working against Carter's chances of securing a second term. Part of the erosion of Carter's popularity came from the nation's sagging economy. Inflation was running in double-digit figures, interest rates were at an all-time high and the predictions were for a long-term recession. However, the President was able to defeat his Democratic challenger, Senator Edward Kennedy, in the primaries and win renomination.

In the three-man contest in November, Carter was overwhelmingly defeated by his Republican opponent, former Governor Ronald Reagan. The entry of John Anderson as an independent did not affect the outcome.

## Ronald Wilson Reagan

Ronald Wilson Reagan, 40th President (January 20, 1981- ), was born in the small, northwestern Illinois town of Tampico on February 6, 1911, and spent the period from his ninth to his 21st years in nearby Dixon. The area was a white Protestant, Republican stronghold in which his father, John Edward Reagan, eked out a living as a shoe salesman. Nellie Reagan, the President's mother, is remembered as a strong woman who held the family unit intact despite hard times and five moves in 14 years.

After graduation from high school, where extracurricular activities included football, acting and a stint as a lifeguard, Reagan attended nearby Eureka College, graduating in 1932 with a bachelor's degree in economics and sociology. Settling on show business as a career, he worked as a sportscaster for radio stations in Davenport and Des Moines, Iowa, until 1937, when on a vacation trip to Hollywood he made a successful screen test for Warner Brothers. His ensuing film career encompassed 50 movies in a quarter-century span that was interrupted during World War II by three years' service in the Army Air Force in California, where he worked on training films. His commercial feature film credits include *King's Row*, *Dark Victory* and *Knute Rockne–All American.*

After the War, Reagan, then a Democrat, was active in liberal causes and served six one-year terms as chairman of the Motion Picture Industry Council. In 1952 he married actress Nancy Davis, his first marriage to actress Jane Wyman having ended in divorce four years earlier.

In the 1950s, Reagan's political philosophy became increasingly conservative; in his autobiography, *Where's the Rest of Me?*, he credits actor George Murphy as being at this time key influence on his political thinking. Reagan began a television career in 1954 as host and an occasional performer on *General Electric Theater*, also becoming a spokesman for the company and, increasingly, for a variety of conservative viewpoints. From 1962 to 1965 he served as host for the TV series, *Death Valley Days;* the series' theme of rugged but decent individualists victoriously pursuing manifest destiny along the western frontier was perfectly attuned to the philosophy and image he was then developing.

During the 1960s, Reagan became ever more active in politics, joining the Republican party in 1962 and two years later delivering a notable speech in support of GOP presidential candidate Barry Goldwater, which won the admiration of conservatives throughout the nation. The speech also impressed California Republicans and helped pave the way to Reagan's gubernatorial nomination in 1966. In his first campaign for political office, Reagan defeated the incumbent Edmund B. ("Pat") Brown by a margin of nearly one million votes.

Reagan served eight years as governor of California. He left office in 1975, choosing not to run for a third term. In an era of unusual political ferment and polarization, and faced with an unfriendly Democratic legislature, Reagan as governor achieved some success in implementing his conservative ideas on tax and spending cuts, welfare reform and higher education. The California budget increased from $4.6 billion to $10.2 billion, but by the time Reagan left office there was a large surplus. Reagan did achieve reductions of welfare case loads, but payments to welfare recipients had been raised.

In 1968 Reagan made an unsuccessful, eleventh-hour attempt for the GOP presidential nomination. He tried again in 1976, but lost on the first ballot by a squeaky-thin, 1,181-1,070 margin to incumbent President Gerald R. Ford. Four years later, widespread impatience with persistent inflation and with President Jimmy Carter's handling of the Iranian hostage situation helped set the stage for Reagan's resounding victories at the GOP presidential nominating convention and later at the polls.

Reagan's presidency had hardly begun when an unsuccessful assassination attempt occurred on March 30, 1981; Reagan suffered a bullet wound in the chest from which he made a quick recovery.

Right from the beginning, the Reagan Administration took a tough stance in its relations with the Soviet Union and toward potential Communist expansion in the Americas. The less-than-smooth-running Reagan team had to learn quickly to deal with the realities of Latin American political upheaval and Middle East tangles. In November 1981 the President won Senate approval for the sale of AWACS surveillance aircraft to Saudi Arabia, a victory not without overtones for future Israeli-U.S. relations.

When Argentina seized the British Falkland Islands, Reagan sought neutral ground. When diplomacy failed to head off a military confrontation, the U.S. sided with the British. At the June 1982 Paris Summit, Reagan found Western leaders cool to his views. Some opposed additional nuclear arms and tended to blame their own economic problems on high U.S. interest rates and trade policies. They also rejected pleas for a ban on the sale of equipment to Russia for the Siberian natural gas pipeline. Reagan's decision later to allow U.S. grain sales to Russia did little to soothe feelings, Critical to any assessment of President Reagan's handling of foreign affairs was the outcome of U.S. pressure to end the carnage in Lebanon.

On the domestic side Reagan was quick to show impressive political skills. In his first test involving labor, he won out against striking air traffic controllers. For his "supply-side" economic policies, the President pushed through Congress a $35-billion cutback in Federal spending and broad reductions in personal and business income taxes. Six months later, these victories were forgotten as the nation's economy began to sag. Interest rates remained high, investment slumped and anticipated new revenues failed to appear.

By July 1982 the unemployment rate reached 9.8 percent—over 10 million persons were out of work. Its economic theories tarnished, the Administration reversed itself and attacked the Federal budget gap and asked for a three-year tax increase of $98 billion. With help from the Democratic leadership the Administration's new financial package was passed by Congress. Despite a record stock market rally in late August and a loosening of interest rates, the hoped-for lift to the nation's economy was slow in coming.

## MINORITY PRESIDENTS

SOURCE: U.S. Library of Congress and other sources

Under the Electoral College System, 15 Presidents have been elected who did not receive a majority of the popular votes cast. Three of them—John Quincy Adams, Rutherford B. Hayes, and Benjamin Harrison—actually trailed their opponents in the popular vote. The table shows the percentage of the popular vote received by the candidates.

| Year | Elected | Opponents | | |
|---|---|---|---|---|
| 1824 | Adams 30.54 | Jackson 43.13 | Clay 13.24 | Crawford 13.09 |
| 1844 | Polk 49.56 | Clay 48.13 | Birney 2.30 | ——— |
| 1848 | Taylor 47.35 | Cass 42.52 | Van Buren 10.13 | ——— |
| 1856 | Buchanan 45.63 | Frémont 33.27 | Fillmore 21.08 | Smith .01 |
| 1860 | Lincoln 39.79 | Douglas 29.40 | Breckinridge 18.20 | Bell 12.60 |
| 1876 | Hayes 48.04 | Tilden 50.99 | Cooper .97 | ——— |
| 1880 | Garfield 48.32 | Hancock 48.21 | Weaver 3.35 | Others .12 |
| 1884 | Cleveland 48.53 | Blaine 48.24 | Butler 1.74 | St. John 1.49 |
| 1888 | Harrison 47.86 | Cleveland 48.66 | Fisk 2.19 | Streeter 1.29 |
| 1892 | Cleveland 46.04 | Harrison 43.01 | Weaver 8.53 | Others 2.42 |
| 1912 | Wilson 41.85 | Roosevelt 27.42 | Taft 23.15 | Others 7.58 |
| 1916 | Wilson 49.26 | Hughes 46.12 | Benson 3.16 | Others 1.46 |
| 1948 | Truman 49.51 | Dewey 45.13 | Thurmond 2.40 | H. Wallace 2.38 |
| 1960 | Kennedy 49.71 | Nixon 49.55 | Unpledged .92 | Others .27 |
| 1968 | Nixon 43.16 | Humphrey 42.73 | G. Wallace 13.63 | Others .48 |

## UNCOMPLETED TERMS OF PRESIDENTS AND VICE-PRESIDENTS

| President | Term | Succeeded by |
|---|---|---|
| William H. Harrison | Mar. 4, 1841—Apr. 4, 1841 | John Tyler |
| Zachary Taylor | Mar. 5, 1849—July 9, 1850 | Millard Fillmore |
| Abraham Lincoln | Mar. 4, 1865—Apr. 15, 1865 (2d term) | Andrew Johnson |
| James A. Garfield | Mar. 4, 1881—Sept. 19, 1881 | Chester A. Arthur |
| William McKinley | Mar. 4, 1901—Sept. 14, 1901 (2d term) | Theodore Roosevelt |
| Warren G. Harding | Mar. 4, 1921—Aug. 2, 1923 | Calvin Coolidge |
| Franklin D. Roosevelt | Jan. 20, 1945—Apr. 12, 1945 (4th term) | Harry S Truman |
| John F. Kennedy | Jan. 20, 1961—Nov. 22, 1963 | Lyndon B. Johnson |
| Richard M. Nixon | Jan. 20, 1973—Aug. 9, 1974 (2d term) | Gerald R. Ford |

| Vice-President | Term |
|---|---|
| George Clinton | Mar. 4, 1809—Apr. 20, 1812 (2d term) |
| Elbridge Gerry | Mar. 4, 1813—Nov. 23, 1814 |
| John C. Calhoun[1] | Mar. 4, 1829—Dec. 28, 1832 |
| William R. King | Mar. 4, 1853—Apr. 18, 1853 |
| Henry Wilson | Mar. 4, 1873—Nov. 22, 1875 |
| Thomas A. Hendricks | Mar. 4, 1885—Nov. 25, 1885 |
| Garret A. Hobart | Mar. 4, 1897—Nov. 21, 1899 |
| James S. Sherman | Mar. 4, 1909—Oct. 30, 1912 |
| Spiro T. Agnew[2] | Jan. 20, 1973—Oct. 10, 1973 |

[1] Calhoun resigned to become a U.S. Senator. [2] Agnew resigned after pleading "no contest" to a charge of income tax evasion. He was succeeded by Gerald R. Ford, the first man to succeed to the office.

## LINCOLN'S GETTYSBURG ADDRESS

Four score and seven years ago our fathers brought forth on this continent, a new nation, conceived in Liberty, and dedicated to the proposition that all men are created equal.

Now we are engaged in a great civil war, testing whether that nation, or any nation so conceived and so dedicated, can long endure. We are met on a great battle-field of that war. We have come to dedicate a portion of that field, as a final resting place for those who here gave their lives that that nation might live. It is altogether fitting and proper that we should do this.

But, in a larger sense, we can not dedicate—we can not consecrate—we can not hallow—this ground. The brave men, living and dead, who struggled here, have consecrated it, far above our poor power to add or detract. The world will little note, nor long remember what we say here, but it can never forget what they did here. It is for us the living, rather, to be dedicated here to the unfinished work which they who fought here have thus far so nobly advanced. It is rather for us to be here dedicated to the great task remaining before us—that from these honored dead we take increased devotion to that cause for which they gave the last full measure of devotion—that we here highly resolve that these dead shall not have died in vain—that this nation, under God, shall have a new birth of freedom—and that government of the people, by the people, for the people, shall not perish from the earth.

## U.S. PRESIDENTIAL INDEX

**(F) = Federal Party; (D-R) = Democratic-Republican Party; (W) = Whig Party; (D) = Democratic Party; (R) = Republican Party.**

| President and Political Party | Place and Date of Birth | Parents | Ancestry | Religious Affiliation |
|---|---|---|---|---|
| 1. George Washington (favored F) | Westmoreland Co., Va.; Feb. 22, 1732 | Augustine and Mary (Ball) Washington | English | Episcopalian |
| 2. John Adams (F) | Braintree, Mass.; Oct. 30, 1735 | John and Susanna (Boylston) Adams | English | Unitarian |
| 3. Thomas Jefferson (D-R) | Goochland Co., Va.; Apr. 13, 1743 | Peter and Jane (Randolph) Jefferson | Welsh | No formal affiliation |
| 4. James Madison (D-R) | Port Conway, Va.; Mar. 16, 1751 | James and Eleanor (Conway) Madison | English | Episcopalian |
| 5. James Monroe (D-R) | Westmoreland Co., Va.; Apr. 28, 1758 | Spence and Elizabeth (Jones) Monroe | Scottish, Welsh | Episcopalian |
| 6. John Quincy Adams (D-R) | Braintree, Mass.; July 11, 1767 | John and Abigail (Smith) Adams | English | Unitarian |
| 7. Andrew Jackson (D) | Waxhaw, S.C.; Mar. 15, 1767 | Andrew and Elizabeth (Hutchinson) Jackson | Scots-Irish | Presbyterian |
| 8. Martin Van Buren (D) | Kinderhook, N.Y.; Dec. 5, 1782 | Abraham and Maria (Hoes) Van Buren | Dutch | Dutch Reformed |
| 9. William H. Harrison (W) | Charles City Co., Va.; Feb. 9, 1773 | Benjamin and Elizabeth (Bassett) Harrison | English | Episcopalian |
| 10. John Tyler (W) | Charles City Co., Va.; Mar 29, 1790 | John and Mary (Armistead) Tyler | English | Episcopalian |
| 11. James Knox Polk (D) | Mecklenburg Co., N.C.; Nov. 2, 1795 | Samuel and Jane (Knox) Polk | Scots-Irish | Presbyterian |
| 12. Zachary Taylor (W) | Orange Co., Va.; Nov. 24, 1784 | Richard and Sarah (Strother) Taylor | English | Episcopalian |
| 13. Millard Fillmore (W) | Locke, N.Y.; Jan. 7, 1800 | Nathaniel and Phoebe (Millard) Fillmore | English | Unitarian |
| 14. Franklin Pierce (D) | Hillsboro, N.H.; Nov. 23, 1804 | Benjamin and Anna (Kendrick) Pierce | English | Episcopalian |
| 15. James Buchanan (D) | Cove Gap, Pa.; Apr. 23, 1791 | James and Elizabeth (Speer) Buchanan | Scots-Irish | Presbyterian |
| 16. Abraham Lincoln (R) | Hardin Co., Ky.; Feb. 12, 1809 | Thomas and Nancy (Hanks) Lincoln | English | No formal affiliation |
| 17. Andrew Johnson (D) | Raleigh, N.C.; Dec. 29, 1808 | Jacob and Mary (McDonough) Johnson | Scottish, Irish, English | No formal affiliation |
| 18. Ulysses Simpson Grant (R) | Point Pleasant, Ohio; Apr. 27, 1822 | Jesse and Hannah (Simpson) Grant | Scottish, English | Methodist |
| 19. Rutherford B. Hayes (R) | Delaware, Ohio; Oct. 4, 1822 | Rutherford and Sophia (Birchard) Hayes | English, Scottish | No formal affiliation |
| 20. James Abram Garfield (R) | Orange, Ohio; Nov. 19, 1831 | Abram and Eliza (Ballou) Garfield | English, French Huguenot | Disciples of Christ |
| 21. Chester Alan Arthur (R) | Fairfield, Vt.; Oct. 5, 1830 | William and Malvina (Stone) Arthur | Scots-Irish, English | Episcopalian |
| 22., 24. Grover Cleveland (D) | Caldwell, N.J.; Mar. 18, 1837 | Richard and Ann (Neal) Cleveland | English, Scots-Irish | Presbyterian |
| 23. Benjamin Harrison (R) | North Bend, Ohio; Aug. 20, 1833 | John and Elizabeth (Irwin) Harrison | English | Presbyterian |
| 25. William McKinley (R) | Niles, Ohio; Jan. 29, 1843 | William and Nancy (Allison) McKinley | Scots-Irish, English | Methodist |
| 26. Theodore Roosevelt (R) | New York, N.Y.; Oct. 27, 1858 | Theodore and Martha (Bulloch) Roosevelt | Dutch, Scottish, English, Huguenot | Dutch Reformed |
| 27. William Howard Taft (R) | Cincinnati, Ohio; Sept. 15, 1857 | Alphonso and Louise (Torrey) Taft | English, Scots-Irish | Unitarian |
| 28. Woodrow Wilson (D) | Staunton, Va.; Dec. 28, 1856 | Joseph and Jessie (Woodrow) Wilson | Scots-Irish, Scottish | Presbyterian |
| 29. Warren G. Harding (R) | Blooming Grove, Ohio; Nov. 2, 1865 | George and Phoebe (Dickerson) Harding | English, Scots-Irish | Baptist |
| 30. Calvin Coolidge (R) | Plymouth Notch, Vt.; July 4, 1872 | John and Victoria (Moor) Coolidge | English | Congregationalist |
| 31. Herbert Clark Hoover (R) | West Branch, Iowa; Aug. 10, 1874 | Jesse and Huldah (Minthorn) Hoover | Swiss-German, English | Quaker |
| 32. Franklin D. Roosevelt (D) | Hyde Park, N.Y.; Jan. 30, 1882 | James and Sara (Delano) Roosevelt | Dutch, Huguenot, English | Episcopalian |
| 33. Harry S Truman (D) | Lamar, Mo.; May 8, 1884 | John and Martha (Young) Truman | English, Scots-Irish | Baptist |
| 34. Dwight D. Eisenhower (R) | Denison, Tex.; Oct. 14, 1890 | David and Ida (Stover) Eisenhower | Swiss-German | Presbyterian |
| 35. John F. Kennedy (D) | Brookline, Mass.; May 29, 1917 | Joseph and Rose (Fitzgerald) Kennedy | Irish | Roman Catholic |
| 36. Lyndon Baines Johnson (D) | Near Stonewall, Tex.; Aug. 27, 1908 | Samuel and Rebekah (Baines) Johnson | English | Disciples of Christ |
| 37. Richard Milhous Nixon (R) | Yorba Linda, Calif.; Jan. 9, 1913 | Frank and Hannah (Milhous) Nixon | English, Scots-Irish | Quaker |
| 38. Gerald R. Ford (R) | Omaha, Neb.; July 14, 1913 | Gerald R. and Dorothy (Gardner) Ford | English | Episcopalian |
| 39. Jimmy Carter (D) | Plains, Ga.; Oct. 1, 1924 | James Earl and Lillian (Gordy) Carter | English | Baptist |
| 40. Ronald W. Reagan (R) | Tampico, Ill.; Feb. 6, 1911 | John and Nelle (Wilson) Reagan | Irish, Scottish, English | Disciples of Christ |

| Occupation Prior to Politics | Elected From | Age at Inauguration | Date of Death and Place of Burial | Presidential Terms | Vice-President |
|---|---|---|---|---|---|
| Surveyor, Soldier, Planter | Virginia | 57 | Dec. 14, 1799; "Mount Vernon," Va. | Apr. 30, 1789–Mar. 3, 1793 | John Adams |
| | | | | Mar. 4, 1793–Mar. 3, 1797 | John Adams |
| Teacher, Lawyer | Massachusetts | 61 | July 4, 1826; Quincy, Mass. | Mar. 4, 1797–Mar. 3, 1801 | Thomas Jefferson |
| Planter, Lawyer | Virginia | 57 | July 4, 1826; "Monticello," Va. | Mar. 4, 1801–Mar. 3, 1805 | Aaron Burr |
| | | | | Mar. 4, 1805–Mar. 3, 1809 | George Clinton |
| Planter | Virginia | 57 | June 28, 1836; "Montpelier," Va. | Mar. 4, 1809–Mar. 3, 1813 | George Clinton |
| | | | | Mar. 4, 1813–Mar. 3, 1817 | Elbridge Gerry |
| Lawyer | Virginia | 58 | July 4, 1831; Richmond, Va. | Mar. 4, 1817–Mar. 3, 1821 | Daniel Tompkins |
| | | | | Mar. 4, 1821–Mar. 3, 1825 | Daniel Tompkins |
| Lawyer | Massachusetts | 57 | Feb. 23, 1848; Quincy, Mass. | Mar. 4, 1825–Mar. 3, 1829 | John Calhoun |
| Planter, Lawyer, Soldier | Tennessee | 61 | June 8, 1845; "Hermitage," Tenn. | Mar. 4, 1829–Mar. 3, 1833 | John Calhoun |
| | | | | Mar. 4, 1833–Mar. 3, 1837 | Martin Van Buren |
| Lawyer | New York | 54 | July 24, 1862; Kinderhook, N.Y. | Mar. 4, 1837–Mar. 3, 1841 | Richard Johnson |
| Soldier, Planter | Ohio | 68 | Apr. 4, 1841; North Bend, Ohio | Mar. 4, 1841–Apr. 4, 1841 | John Tyler |
| Lawyer | Virginia | 51 | Jan. 18, 1862; Richmond, Va. | Apr. 6, 1841–Mar. 3, 1845 | — |
| Lawyer | Tennessee | 49 | June 15, 1849; Nashville, Tenn. | Mar. 4, 1845–Mar. 3, 1849 | George Dallas |
| Soldier, Planter | Louisiana | 64 | July 9, 1850; near Louisville, Ky. | Mar. 4, 1849–July 9, 1850 | Millard Fillmore |
| Lawyer | New York | 50 | Mar. 8, 1874; Buffalo, N.Y. | July 10, 1850–Mar. 3, 1853 | — |
| Lawyer | New Hampshire | 48 | Oct. 8, 1869; Concord, N.H. | Mar. 4, 1853–Mar. 3, 1857 | William King |
| Lawyer | Pennsylvania | 65 | June 1, 1868; Lancaster, Pa. | Mar. 4, 1857–Mar. 3, 1861 | John Breckinridge |
| Lawyer | Illinois | 52 | Apr. 15, 1865; Springfield, Ill. | Mar. 4, 1861–Mar. 3, 1865 | Hannibal Hamlin |
| | | | | Mar. 4, 1865–Apr. 15, 1865 | Andrew Johnson |
| Tailor | Tennessee | 56 | July 31, 1875; Greeneville, Tenn. | Apr. 15, 1865–Mar. 3, 1869 | — |
| Soldier, Farmer, Clerk | Illinois | 46 | July 23, 1885; New York, N.Y. | Mar. 4, 1869–Mar. 3, 1873 | Schuyler Colfax |
| | | | | Mar. 4, 1873–Mar. 3, 1877 | Henry Wilson |
| Lawyer | Ohio | 54 | Jan. 17, 1893; Fremont, Ohio | Mar. 4, 1877–Mar. 3, 1881 | William Wheeler |
| Laborer, Professor | Ohio | 49 | Sept. 19, 1881; Cleveland, Ohio | Mar. 4, 1881–Sept. 19, 1881 | Chester Arthur |
| School Teacher, Lawyer | New York | 50 | Nov. 18, 1886; Albany, N.Y. | Sept. 19, 1881–Mar. 3, 1885 | — |
| Lawyer | New York | 47, 55 | June 24, 1908; Princeton, N.J. | Mar. 4, 1885–Mar. 3, 1889 | Thomas Hendricks |
| | | | | Mar. 4, 1893–Mar. 3, 1897 | Adlai Stevenson |
| Lawyer | Indiana | 55 | Mar. 13, 1901; Indianapolis, Ind. | Mar. 4, 1889–Mar. 3, 1893 | Levi Morton |
| School Teacher, Clerk, Lawyer | Ohio | 54 | Sept. 14, 1901; Canton, Ohio | Mar. 4, 1897–Mar. 3, 1901 | Garret Hobart |
| | | | | Mar. 4, 1901–Sept. 14, 1901 | Theodore Roosevelt |
| Historian, Rancher | New York | 42 | Jan. 6, 1919; Oyster Bay, N.Y. | Sept. 14, 1901–Mar. 3, 1905 | — |
| | | | | Mar. 4, 1905–Mar. 3, 1909 | Charles Fairbanks |
| Lawyer | Ohio | 51 | Mar. 8, 1930; Arlington, Va. | Mar. 4, 1909–Mar. 3, 1913 | James Sherman |
| Lawyer, University President | New Jersey | 56 | Feb. 3, 1924; Washington, D.C. | Mar. 4, 1913–Mar. 3, 1917 | Thomas Marshall |
| | | | | Mar. 4, 1917–Mar. 3, 1921 | Thomas Marshall |
| Newspaper Editor and Publisher | Ohio | 55 | Aug. 2, 1923; Marion, Ohio | Mar. 4, 1921–Aug. 2, 1923 | Calvin Coolidge |
| Lawyer | Massachusetts | 51 | Jan. 5, 1933; Plymouth, Vt. | Aug. 3, 1923–Mar. 3, 1925 | — |
| | | | | Mar. 4, 1925–Mar. 3, 1929 | Charles Dawes |
| Engineer, Relief Administrator | California | 54 | Oct. 20, 1964; West Branch, Iowa | Mar. 4, 1929–Mar. 3, 1933 | Charles Curtis |
| Lawyer | New York | 51 | April 12, 1945; Hyde Park, N.Y. | Mar. 4, 1933–Jan. 20, 1937 | John Garner |
| | | | | Jan. 20, 1937–Jan. 20, 1941 | John Garner |
| | | | | Jan. 20, 1941–Jan. 20, 1945 | Henry Wallace |
| | | | | Jan. 20, 1945–Apr. 12, 1945 | Harry Truman |
| Clerk, Haberdasher, Farmer | Missouri | 60 | Dec. 26, 1972; Independence, Mo. | Apr. 12, 1945–Jan. 20, 1949 | — |
| | | | | Jan. 20, 1949–Jan. 20, 1953 | Alben Barkley |
| Soldier | New York | 62 | Mar. 28, 1969; Abilene, Kan. | Jan. 20, 1953–Jan. 20, 1957 | Richard Nixon |
| | | | | Jan. 20, 1957–Jan. 20, 1961 | Richard Nixon |
| Author, Reporter | Massachusetts | 43 | Nov. 22, 1963; Arlington, Va. | Jan. 20, 1961–Nov. 22, 1963 | Lyndon Johnson |
| School Teacher | Texas | 55 | Jan. 22, 1973; near Johnson City, Texas | Nov. 22, 1963–Jan. 20, 1965 | — |
| | | | | Jan. 20, 1965–Jan. 20, 1969 | Hubert Humphrey |
| Lawyer | New York | 55 | — | Jan. 20, 1969–Jan. 20, 1973 | Spiro Agnew |
| | | | | Jan. 20, 1973–Aug. 9, 1974 | Gerald R. Ford |
| Lawyer | — | 61 | — | Aug. 9, 1974–Jan. 20, 1977 | Nelson Rockefeller |
| Businessman, Farmer | Georgia | 52 | — | Jan. 20, 1977–Jan. 20, 1981 | Walter Mondale |
| Actor, Broadcaster, Lecturer | California | 69 | — | Jan. 20, 1981 | George H. W. Bush |

## THE VICE-PRESIDENTS

For those Vice-Presidents who became Presidents—John Adams, Thomas Jefferson, Martin Van Buren, John Tyler, Millard Fillmore, Andrew Johnson, Chester A. Arthur, Theodore Roosevelt, Calvin Coolidge, Harry S. Truman, Lyndon B. Johnson, Richard M. Nixon, and Gerald R. Ford—see the Presidential biographies.

### Aaron Burr

Vice-President (1801–1805) to Thomas Jefferson ***Political Party:*** Democratic-Republican ***Born:*** Newark, New Jersey, February 6, 1756 ***Ancestry:*** English ***Religious Affiliation:*** Presbyterian ***Education:*** College of New Jersey (now Princeton University), 1772; thereafter briefly studied theology ***Wives:*** Married Mrs. Theodosia Prevost in 1782; she died in 1794. Married Mrs. Stephen Jumel in 1833; she petitioned for divorce a year later ***Children:*** Two by first wife ***Home:*** New York ***Occupations before Vice-Presidency:*** Revolutionary soldier, lawyer, politician, U.S. Senator (1791–1797) ***Age at Inauguration:*** 44 ***Outstanding Facts:*** In the Presidential election of 1800, an electoral vote tie between Aaron Burr and Thomas Jefferson threw the election into the House of Representatives, where, mainly through the efforts of Alexander Hamilton, the Presidency was finally won by Jefferson, with the Vice-Presidency going to Burr. In 1804, after Burr had been nominated for the governorship of New York, Hamilton again contributed to his defeat. Burr challenged Hamilton to a duel and killed him. This, as well as President Jefferson's suspicions that Burr had intrigued for the Presidency, effectively ended his political career. As Vice-President, Burr presided over the Senate with impartiality ***Occupation after Vice-Presidency:*** He became involved in a political conspiracy, the aims of which still remain unclear, and was tried for treason but acquitted. He left the country and schemed abroad but, frustrated in his plans, returned to the United States, where he again took up the practice of law ***Died:*** Sept. 14, 1836 ***Place of Burial:*** Princeton, N.J.

### George Clinton

Vice-President (1805–1812) to Thomas Jefferson and James Madison ***Political Party:*** Democratic-Republican ***Born:*** Little Britain (now Ulster County), New York, July 26, 1739 ***Ancestry:*** English, Scots-Irish ***Religious Affiliation:*** Presbyterian ***Education:*** Private tutoring ***Wife:*** Married Cornelia Tappen in 1770 ***Children:*** Six ***Home:*** New York ***Occupations before Vice-Presidency:*** Lawyer, Revolutionary soldier, politician, governor of New York (1777–1795, 1801–1804) ***Age at Inauguration:*** 65 ***Outstanding Facts:*** An advocate of state sovereignty, Clinton was one of the chief opponents of the Constitution. He hoped to be President but lost out to James Madison, to whom he was openly hostile. He spent much time in New York and was a poor presiding officer of the Senate. Clinton was the first Vice-President to die in office ***Died:*** April 20, 1812 ***Place of Burial:*** Washington, D.C.; reinterred (1908) in Kingston, Ulster County, N.Y.

### Elbridge Gerry

Vice-President (1813–1814) to James Madison ***Political Party:*** Democratic-Republican ***Born:*** Marblehead, Massachusetts, July 17, 1744 ***Ancestry:*** English ***Religious Affiliation:*** Episcopalian ***Education:*** Harvard College, 1762 ***Wife:*** Married Ann Thompson in 1786 ***Children:*** Nine ***Home:*** Massachusetts ***Occupations before Vice-Presidency:*** Merchant, politician, signer of the Declaration of Independence, governor of Massachusetts (1810–1812) ***Age at Inauguration:*** 63 ***Outstanding Facts:*** He socialized a great deal during his brief tenure and is now chiefly remembered for *gerrymander,* the term given to his attempt while governor of Massachusetts to redistrict the state in his party's favor ***Died:*** November 23, 1814 ***Place of Burial:*** Washington, D.C.

### Daniel D. Tompkins

Vice-President (1817–1825) to James Monroe ***Political Party:*** Democratic-Republican ***Born:*** Fox Meadow (now Scarsdale), New York, June 21, 1774 ***Ancestry:*** Scottish, English ***Religious Affiliation:*** Presbyterian ***Education:*** Columbia College, 1795 ***Wife:*** Married Hannah Minthorne in 1798 ***Children:*** Eight ***Home:*** New York ***Occupations before Vice-Presidency:*** Lawyer, politician, governor of New York (1807–1817) ***Age at Inauguration:*** 42 ***Outstanding Facts:*** He spent much time contesting court cases arising out of actions he took over expenditures made while he was governor of New York during the War of 1812 ***Occupation after Vice-Presidency:*** He continued contesting various court actions ***Died:*** June 11, 1825 ***Place of Burial:*** New York City

### John Caldwell Calhoun

Vice-President (1825–1832) to John Quincy Adams and Andrew Jackson ***Political Party:*** Democratic ***Born:*** Abbeville, South Carolina, March 18, 1782 ***Ancestry:*** Scots-Irish ***Religious Affiliation:*** Presbyterian ***Education:*** Yale College, 1804, studied (1805–1806) at Litchfield (Conn.) Law School ***Wife:*** Married Floride Calhoun in 1811 ***Children:*** Nine ***Home:*** South Carolina ***Occupations before Vice-Presidency:*** Lawyer, planter, U.S. Congressman (1811–1817), Secretary of War (1817–1825) ***Age at Inauguration:*** 42 ***Outstanding Facts:*** A strong supporter of Jackson, he opposed Adams throughout the latter's administration. In 1828 in his *South Carolina Exposition,* he set forth the principles of states' rights and nullification. Originally thought of as Jackson's successor, he broke with the President over a variety of issues, including the very nature of the federal union. Calhoun resigned as Vice-President upon being elected to the Senate in 1832. In the Senate he eloquently defended his states' rights principles and proslavery viewpoint in dramatic debates with Daniel Webster ***Occupations after Vice-Presidency:*** Senator (1832–1844, 1845–1850), Cabinet officer (Secretary of State, 1844–1845) ***Died:*** March 31, 1850 ***Place of Burial:*** Charleston, South Carolina

### Richard Mentor Johnson

Vice-President (1837–1841) to Martin Van Buren ***Political Party:*** Democratic ***Born:*** Beargrass Creek (a frontier settlement on the present location of Louisville), Kentucky, autumn of 1780 ***Ancestry:*** English ***Religious Affiliation:*** Baptist ***Education:*** Preparatory school and private instruction ***Wife:*** Johnson was a bachelor ***Home:*** Kentucky ***Occupations before Vice-Presidency:*** Lawyer, soldier, educator, politician, U.S. Congressman (1814–1819, 1829–1837), Senator (1819–1829) ***Age at Inauguration:*** 56 ***Outstanding Facts:*** A hero of the War of 1812, Johnson was said to be the slayer of Chief Tecumseh at the Battle of the Thames. Johnson has been the only Vice-President ever elected by the Senate; he failed to get enough electoral votes. *Occupations after Vice-Presidency:* Businessman, state legislator (1841-1842, 1850) *Died:* Nov. 19, 1850 *Place of Burial:* Frankfort, Ky.

**George Mifflin Dallas**

Vice-President (1845–1849) to James K. Polk *Political Party:* Democratic *Born:* Philadelphia, July 10, 1792 *Ancestry:* Scottish, English *Religious Affiliation:* Presbyterian *Education:* Princeton College, 1810 *Wife:* Married Sophia Chew in 1816 *Children:* Eight *Home:* Pennsylvania *Occupations before Vice-Presidency:* Lawyer, politician, diplomat *Age at Inauguration:* 52 *Outstanding Facts:* Although nominated as a protectionist, he cast (1846) the deciding vote for a lower tariff *Occupations after Vice-Presidency:* Lawyer, diplomat, writer *Died:* December 31, 1864 *Place of Burial:* Philadelphia

**William Rufus Devane King**

Vice-President (1853) to Franklin Pierce *Political Party:* Democratic *Born:* Sampson County, North Carolina, April 7, 1786 *Ancestry:* Scots-Irish, Huguenot *Religious Affiliation:* Presbyterian *Education:* University of North Carolina, 1803 *Wife:* King was a bachelor *Home:* Alabama *Occupations before Vice-Presidency:* Lawyer, politician, U.S. Congressman (1811–1816), Senator (1819–1844; 1848–1852), diplomat *Age at Inauguration:* 66 *Outstanding Facts:* Elected while recovering from tuberculosis in Cuba, he died shortly after his return. *Died:* April 18, 1853 *Place of Burial:* "Kings Bend," Ala.; reinterred in Selma, Ala.

**John Cabell Breckinridge**

Vice-President (1857–1861) to James Buchanan *Political Party:* Democratic *Born:* "Cabell's Dale" (near Lexington), Kentucky, January 21, 1821 *Ancestry:* English, Scots-Irish *Religious Affiliation:* Presbyterian *Education:* Centre College (Ky.), 1838; thereafter he studied law at Transylvania University *Wife:* Married Mary Cyrene Burch in 1843 *Children:* Five *Home:* Kentucky *Occupations before Vice-Presidency:* Lawyer, soldier, politician, U.S. Congressman (1851–1855) *Age at Inauguration:* 36 *Outstanding Facts:* The youngest man ever to become Vice-President, he was dignified beyond his years and ably presided over the Senate. Breckinridge tried to achieve some kind of compromise during the years prior to the Civil War. *Occupations after Vice-Presidency:* U.S. Senator (1861), Confederate soldier, Confederate Secretary of War (1865), lawyer, businessman *Died:* May 17, 1875 *Place of Burial:* Lexington, Kentucky

**Hannibal Hamlin**

Vice-President (1861–1865) to Abraham Lincoln *Political Party:* Republican *Born:* Paris, Maine, August 27, 1809 *Ancestry:* English *Religious Affiliation:* Unitarian *Education:* Preparatory studies *Wives:* Married Sarah Jane Emery in 1833; she died in 1855. Married her half-sister Ellen Vesta Emery in 1856 *Children:* Five by first wife, two by second wife *Home:* Maine *Occupations before Vice-Presidency:* Farmer, printer, lawyer, politician, U.S. Senator (1857–1861) *Age at Inauguration:* 51 *Outstanding Facts:* Hamlin was a staunch advocate of emancipation *Occupations after Vice Presidency:* Political appointee, lawyer, businessman, U.S. Senator (1869–1881), diplomat *Died:* July 4, 1891 *Place of Burial:* Bangor, Maine

**Schuyler Colfax**

Vice-President (1869–1873) to Ulysses S. Grant *Political Party:* Republican *Born:* New York City, March 23, 1823 *Ancestry:* English, Huguenot *Religious Affiliation:* Dutch Reformed *Education:* Grade school *Wives:* Married Evelyn Clark in 1844; she died in 1862. Married Ellen Wade in 1868 *Children:* One by second wife *Home:* Indiana *Occupations before Vice-Presidency:* Political appointee, journalist, U.S. Congressman (1855–1869), speaker of the House (1863–1869) *Age at Inauguration:* 45 *Outstanding Facts:* In 1870, midway through his term, he announced his retirement from political life, hoping that the public would demand that he remain. No such clamor developed, and Colfax rescinded his decision. Colfax failed of renomination. Later it was revealed that Colfax had been involved in the Credit Mobilier railroad scandal, which effectively ended his public career *Occupation after Vice-Presidency:* Lecturer *Died:* January 13, 1885 *Place of Burial:* South Bend, Indiana

**Henry Wilson**

Vice-President (1873–1875) to Ulysses S. Grant *Political Party:* Republican *Born:* Farmington, New Hampshire, February 16, 1812 *Ancestry:* Scots-Irish *Religious Affiliation:* Congregationalist *Education:* Little formal schooling *Wife:* Married Harriet Malvina Howe in 1840 *Children:* One *Home:* Massachusetts *Occupations before Vice-Presidency:* Indentured worker, school teacher, cobbler, businessman, newspaperman, politician, U.S. Senator (1855–1873) *Age at Inauguration:* 61 *Outstanding Facts:* As Vice-President ill health made his attendance in presiding over the Senate irregular, and he died in office *Died:* November 22, 1875 *Place of Burial:* Natick, Massachusetts

**William Almon Wheeler**

Vice-President (1877–1881) to Rutherford B. Hayes *Political Party:* Republican *Born:* Malone, New York, June 30, 1819 *Ancestry:* English *Religious Affiliation:* Presbyterian *Education:* Attended (1838–1840) the University of Vermont *Wife:* Married Mary King in 1845 *Children:* None *Home:* New York *Occupations before Vice-Presidency:* Lawyer, banker, businessman, politician, U.S. Congressman (1861–1863, 1869–1877) *Age at Inauguration:* 57 *Outstanding Facts:* Little known nationally when nominated for the office, he performed its major function, presiding over the Senate, with faithfulness *Occupation after Vice-Presidency:* Poor health resulted in general inactivity; unsuccessfully nominated for U.S. Senator in 1881 *Died:* June 4, 1887 *Place of Burial:* Malone, N.Y.

**Thomas Andrews Hendricks**

Vice-President (1885) to Grover Cleveland *Political Party:* Democratic *Born:* Zanesville, Ohio, September 7, 1819 *Ancestry:* Scottish, English, Huguenot *Religious Affiliation:* Episcopalian *Education:* Hanover College (Indiana), 1841 *Wife:* Married Eliza Morgan in 1845 *Children:* One *Home:* Indiana *Occupations before Vice-Presidency:* Lawyer, politician, defeated candidate for Vice-President in 1876 *Age at Inauguration:* 65 *Outstanding Fact:* He died 8 months after taking office. *Died:* Nov. 25, 1885 *Place of Burial:* Indianapolis, Ind.

**Levi Parsons Morton**

Vice-President (1889–1893) to Benjamin Harrison *Political Party:* Republican *Born:* Shoreham, Vermont, May 16, 1824 *Ancestry:* English *Religious Affiliation:* Episcopalian *Education:* Preparatory schools *Wives:* Married Lucy Young Kimball in 1856; she died in 1871 Married Anna Livingston Read Street in 1873 *Children:* One by first wife; six by second wife *Home:* New York *Occupations before Vice-Presidency:* Clerk, school teacher, businessman, U.S. Congressman (1879–1881), diplomat *Age at Inauguration:* 64 *Outstanding Fact:* He was passed over for renomination as Vice-President *Occupations after Vice-Presidency:* Real estate investor, banker, Governor of New York (1895–1897) *Died:* May 16, 1920 *Place of Burial:* Rhinebeck, N.Y.

### Adlai Ewing Stevenson

Vice-President (1893–1897) to Grover Cleveland *Political Party:* Democratic *Born:* Christian County, Kentucky, October 23, 1835 *Ancestry:* Scots-Irish *Religious Affiliation:* Presbyterian *Education:* Attended Centre College (Kentucky) two years *Wife:* Married Letitia Green in 1866 *Children:* Four *Home:* Illinois *Occupations before Vice-Presidency:* Lawyer, politician, U.S. Congressman (1875–1877, 1879–1881) *Age at Inauguration:* 57 *Outstanding Facts:* He presided with fairness over a Senate that had recently turned him down for a District of Columbia judicial post. A "soft money" advocate, he was unsympathetic to President Cleveland's monetary views but never embarrassed the administration with open disagreement *Occupations after Vice-Presidency:* Lawyer and politician *Died:* June 14, 1914 *Place of Burial:* Bloomington, Illinois

### Garret Augustus Hobart

Vice-President (1897–1899) to William McKinley *Political Party:* Republican *Born:* Long Branch, New Jersey, June 3, 1844 *Ancestry:* English, Dutch, Huguenot *Religious Affiliation:* Presbyterian *Education:* Rutgers College, 1863 *Wife:* Married Jennie Tuttle in 1869 *Children:* Two *Home:* New Jersey *Occupations before Vice-Presidency:* Lawyer, businessman, banker, politician *Age at Inauguration:* 52 *Outstanding Facts:* He presided over the Senate with ability. Hobart cast the deciding vote against granting the Philippine Is. independence *Died:* In office, Nov. 21, 1899 *Place of Burial:* Paterson, N.J.

### Charles Warren Fairbanks

Vice-President (1905–1909) to Theodore Roosevelt *Political Party:* Republican *Born:* Near Unionville Center, Ohio, May 11, 1852 *Ancestry:* English *Religious Affiliation:* Methodist *Education:* Ohio Wesleyan, 1872 *Wife:* Married Cornelia Cole in 1874 *Children:* Five *Home:* Indiana *Occupations before Vice-Presidency:* Newspaperman, railroad lawyer, politician, U.S. Senator (1897–1905) *Age at Inauguration:* 52 *Outstanding Facts:* Although Fairbanks and President Roosevelt represented opposite wings of the Republican Party, they maintained cordial relations *Occupations after Vice-Presidency:* Lawyer, unsuccessful candidate for Vice-Pres. in 1916 *Died:* June 4, 1918 *Place of Burial:* Indianapolis, Ind.

### James Schoolcraft Sherman

Vice-President (1909–1912) to William Howard Taft *Political Party:* Republican *Born:* Utica, New York, October 24, 1855 *Ancestry:* English *Religious Affiliation:* Dutch Reformed *Education:* Hamilton College, 1878 *Wife:* Married Carrie Babcock in 1881 *Children:* Three *Home:* New York *Occupations before Vice-Presidency:* Lawyer, banker, politician, U.S. Congressman (1887–1891, 1893–1909) *Age at Inauguration:* 53 *Outstanding Facts:* An affable man known as "Sunny Jim," he presided well over the Senate. Renominated but died before the election *Died:* October 30, 1912 *Place of Burial:* Utica, N.Y.

### Thomas Riley Marshall

Vice-President (1913–1921) to Woodrow Wilson *Political Party:* Democratic *Born:* North Manchester, Indiana, March 14, 1854 *Ancestry:* English *Religious Affiliation:* Presbyterian *Education:* Wabash College, 1873 *Wife:* Married Lois Irene Kimsey in 1895 *Children:* None *Home:* Indiana *Occupations before Vice-Presidency:* Lawyer, politician, governor of Indiana (1909–1913) *Age at Inauguration:* 58 *Outstanding Facts:* Marshall was the first Vice-President in nearly a century to succeed himself. While President Wilson was ill, Marshall acted as ceremonial head of state, but he refused to accept any of the President's powers. He was well known for his quip, "What this country needs is a good five-cent cigar" *Occupations after Vice-Presidency:* Lawyer, lecturer, political appointee *Died:* June 1, 1925 *Place of Burial:* Indianapolis, Ind.

### Charles Gates Dawes

Vice-President (1925–1929) to Calvin Coolidge *Political Party:* Republican *Born:* Marietta, Ohio, August 27, 1865 *Ancestry:* English *Religious Affiliation:* Congregationalist *Education:* Marietta College, 1884; Cincinnati Law School, 1886 *Wife:* Married Caro D. Blymer in 1889 *Children:* Four (two adopted) *Home:* Illinois *Occupations before Vice-Presidency:* Lawyer, banker, businessman, soldier, politician *Age at Inauguration:* 59 *Outstanding Facts:* Dawes shared the Nobel Peace Prize in 1925 for his work in attempting to settle through the Dawes Plan the problem of German reparations. A short-tempered man, he infuriated the Senate by telling that body it was time to change its antiquated rules *Occupations after Vice-Presidency:* Diplomat, public servant, banker, businessman *Died:* April 23, 1951 *Place of Burial:* Chicago

### Charles Curtis

Vice-President (1929–1933) to Herbert Hoover *Political Party:* Republican *Born:* Topeka, Kansas, January 25, 1860 *Ancestry:* American Indian, English, French *Religious Affiliation:* Episcopalian *Education:* High school *Wife:* Married Annie E. Baird in 1884 *Children:* Three *Home:* Kansas *Occupations before Vice-Presidency:* Lawyer, politician, U.S. Congressman (1893–1907), Senator (1907–1913, 1915–1929) *Age at Inauguration:* 69 *Outstanding Facts:* Lacking a close relationship with President Hoover, Curtis had little to say or do *Occupations after Vice-Presidency:* Lawyer, businessman *Died:* February 8, 1936 *Place of Burial:* Topeka, Kansas

### John Nance Garner

Vice-President (1933–1941) to Franklin D. Roosevelt *Political Party:* Democratic *Born:* Blossom Prairie, Texas, November 22, 1868 *Ancestry:* English, Welsh, Scottish *Religious Affiliation:* Methodist *Education:* High school *Wife:* Married Elizabeth Rheiner in 1895 *Children:* One *Home:* Texas *Occupations before Vice-Presidency:* Lawyer, businessman, banker, politician,

U.S. Congressman (1903–1933), Speaker of the House of Representatives (1931–1933) ***Age at Inauguration:*** 63 ***Outstanding Facts:*** Garner retained much of his influence with Congress while Vice-President and during his first term helped to obtain passage of much New Deal legislation. During his second term, he increasingly found himself out of sympathy with President Roosevelt's programs, and he was not renominated ***Occupations after Vice-Presidency:*** Businessman, banker, cattle rancher ***Died:*** November 7, 1967 ***Place of Burial:*** Uvalde, Texas

### Henry Agard Wallace

Vice-President (1941–1945) to Franklin D. Roosevelt ***Political Party:*** Democratic ***Born:*** Near Orient, Iowa, October 7, 1888 ***Ancestry:*** Scots-Irish ***Religious Affiliation:*** Episcopalian ***Education:*** Iowa State College, 1910 ***Wife:*** Married Ilo Browne in 1914 ***Children:*** Three ***Home:*** Iowa ***Occupations before Vice-Presidency:*** Editor, farmer, Secretary of Agriculture (1933–1940) ***Age at Inauguration:*** 52 ***Outstanding Facts:*** President Roosevelt cast the Vice-Presidency under Wallace into its most active role up to that time. Wallace served as good-will ambassador to Latin America, the Soviet Union, and the Far East. He also undertook various defense duties. However, his political and social views caused him to be viewed suspiciously by the Democratic Party and he failed of renomination ***Occupations after Vice-Presidency:*** Secretary of Commerce (1945–1946), author, farmer, defeated candidate for President in 1948 ***Died:*** November 18, 1965 ***Place of Burial:*** Des Moines, Iowa

### Alben William Barkley

Vice-President (1949–1953) to Harry S Truman ***Political Party:*** Democratic ***Born:*** Near Lowes, Kentucky, November 24, 1877 ***Ancestry:*** Scots-Irish ***Religious Affiliation:*** Methodist ***Education:*** Marvin College (Kentucky), 1897; attended University of Virginia Law School ***Wives:*** Married Dorothy Brower in 1903; she died in 1947. Married Mrs. Carleton S. Hadley in 1949 ***Children:*** Three by first wife ***Home:*** Kentucky ***Occupations before Vice-Presidency:*** Lawyer, politician, U.S. Senator (1927–1949) ***Age at Inauguration:*** 71 ***Outstanding Facts:*** Very popular, he was nicknamed "Veep" during his tenure. He was the only Vice-President to marry while in office. After President Truman announced he would not run again, Barkley attempted to win the Presidential nomination but failed ***Occupations after Vice-Presidency:*** Lawyer, U.S. Senator (1955–1956) ***Died:*** April 30, 1956 ***Place of Burial:*** Paducah, Kentucky

### Hubert Horatio Humphrey

Vice-President (1965–1969) to Lyndon B. Johnson ***Political Party:*** Democratic ***Born:*** Wallace, South Dakota, May 27, 1911 ***Ancestry:*** Welsh, Norwegian ***Religious Affiliation:*** Congregationalist ***Education:*** University of Minnesota, 1939; M.A., Louisiana State, 1940; began work for a Ph.D. ***Wife:*** Married Muriel Fay Buck in 1936 ***Children:*** Four ***Home:*** Minnesota ***Occupations before Vice-Presidency:*** Pharmacist, teacher, politician, U.S. Senator (1949–1965) ***Age at Inauguration:*** 53 ***Outstanding Facts:*** Humphrey was an energetic Vice-President and traveled widely as a spokesman of the United States. He was a vigorous defender of the Johnson administration. Humphrey ran unsuccessfully for the Presidency in 1968. ***Occupations after Vice-Presidency:*** College teaching, U.S. Senator (1971-1978) ***Died:*** January 13, 1978 ***Place of Burial:*** Minneapolis, Minnesota

### Spiro Theodore Agnew

Vice-President (1969–1973) to Richard M. Nixon ***Political Party:*** Republican ***Born:*** Baltimore, Maryland, November 9, 1918 ***Ancestry:*** Greek, English ***Religious Affiliation:*** Episcopalian ***Education:*** University of Baltimore Law School, 1947 ***Wife:*** Married Eleanor Isabel Judefind in 1942 ***Children:*** Four ***Home:*** Maryland ***Occupations before Vice-Presidency:*** Lawyer, politician, governor of Maryland (1967–1969) ***Age at Inauguration:*** 50 ***Outstanding Facts:*** Agnew resigned his office and pleaded "no contest" to one charge of income tax evasion after being implicated in a kickback scheme. He was the first Vice-President in history to resign under duress.

### Nelson Aldrich Rockefeller

Vice-President (1974-1977) to Gerald R. Ford ***Political Party:*** Republican ***Born:*** Bar Harbor, Maine, July 8, 1908 ***Ancestry:*** English, Scottish, German ***Religious Affilation:*** Baptist ***Education:*** Dartmouth College, 1930 ***Wives:*** Mary Todhunter Clark, June 23, 1930 (div. 1962), Margaretta Fitler Murphy, May 1963 ***Home:*** New York and Bar Harbor, Maine ***Occupation before Vice-Presidency:*** various government posts, four-term governor of New York ***Age at Inauguration:*** 66 ***Outstanding Facts:*** Nominated under the 25th Amendment by President Ford following resignation of Richard M. Nixon as President and Ford's assumption of the presidency ***Occupations after Vice Presidency:*** Art interests ***Died:*** January 26, 1979 ***Place of Burial:*** Pocantico Hills, New York

### Walter Frederick Mondale

Vice-President (1977-1981) to Jimmy Carter ***Political Party:*** Democratic ***Born:*** Ceylon, Minnesota, January 5, 1928 ***Ancestry:*** Norwegian ***Religious Affiliation:*** Methodist ***Education:*** University of Minnesota Law School, 1956 ***Wife:*** Married Joan Adams in 1955 ***Children:*** Three ***Home:*** Minnesota ***Occupation before Vice-Presidency:*** Lawyer, state attorney general, U.S. Senator (1965-1977) ***Age at Inauguration:*** 49 ***Outstanding Facts:*** His untraditional role as the President's personal international emissary added new responsibility and power to the previously passive, ceremonial role of the Vice-President ***Occupation after Vice-Presidency:*** Lawyer.

### George Herbert Walker Bush

Vice-President (1981- ) to Ronald W. Reagan ***Political Party:*** Republican ***Born:*** Milton, Massachusetts, June 12, 1924 ***Ancestry:*** English ***Religious Affiliation:*** Episcopal ***Education:*** Yale University, 1948 ***Wife:*** Married Barbara Pierce in 1945 ***Children:*** Five ***Home:*** Houston, Texas ***Occupation before Vice-Presidency:*** Oil industry businessman; member of US House of Representatives 1967-1971; U.S. Ambassador to the United Nations, 1971-1973; Chairman of the Republican National Committee 1973-1974; Head of U.S. Liaison Office in Beijing, China, 1974-1975; Director of the Central Intelligence Agency, 1975-1977; Chairman of bank in Houston, 1977-1980 ***Age at Inauguration:*** 56 ***Outstanding Facts:*** 1980 Republican presidential candidate from 1979 until 1980, when he withdrew from the race.

## THE FIRST LADIES

**Mrs. George Washington**—Born Martha Dandridge, daughter of a planter, in New Kent County, Virginia, on June 21, 1731. At 18, she married Daniel Parke Custis, heir to a large estate, and she bore him four children, two of whom died in infancy. After Custis died on July 8, 1757, leaving her reputedly the richest widow in Virginia, she married Colonel George Washington on January 6, 1759; at 27, she was eight months older than her second husband.

Besides adding substantially to his property (she provided 17,000 acres and 300 slaves, compared with his own estate of 5,000 acres and 49 slaves), she also gave him a happy domestic life. Small, plump, and cheerful, she was amply blessed with common sense, if not brilliance. When Washington became President, many contemporaries thought she humanized her austere husband—"Mrs. Washington is one of those unassuming characters which create love and esteem," Mrs. John Adams wrote to a sister.

In New York, then Philadelphia, where "Lady" Washington held sway in makeshift mansions while the new capital of Washington was being planned, she made an amiable hostess at the formal receptions and dinners her husband instituted as the social side of his official duties.

There were no children of her second marriage, but she was a doting mother to the offspring of her first husband, who were treated as his own by Washington. Although her daughter, Martha (Patsy) Parke Custis, died at 17, her son, John Parke Custis, married and had three daughters and a son. Mrs. Washington survived her husband two years, dying on May 22, 1802, at Mount Vernon, where she was buried.

**Mrs. John Adams**—Born Abigail Smith on November 11, 1744, in Weymouth, Massachusetts, the daughter of a Congregational minister. Although she had no formal schooling, she read much more widely than most girls, and first attracted the notice of her future husband by the breadth of her intellectual interests. But before they married on October 25, 1764, they were deeply in love, and theirs was a devoted union.

Shrewd, witty, and warm-hearted, Mrs. Adams was of inestimable help in furthering the careers of both her husband and her son, John Quincy Adams, the nation's sixth President: she is the only woman in American history to have been the wife of one President and the mother of another. She also won celebrity in her own right as a gifted letter-writer with a keen political instinct.

Mrs. Adams was the first First Lady to live in the Executive Mansion in Washington, moving there in November 1800 when most of the rooms were still unfinished; she gained lasting fame in American folklore by having her laundry set out to dry before the fire in the East Room, one of the few chambers where some warmth could be obtained. During the brief period before her husband's term expired on March 3, 1801, she had the distinction, too, of holding the first formal gathering in the Mansion—a reception on New Year's Day of 1801, when 135 callers were greeted in the crimson-hung Oval Room. Besides John Quincy, she had two other sons and a daughter; another daughter died in infancy. Mrs. Adams died at the Adams home in Quincy, Massachusetts, on October 28, 1818, and was buried there.

**Mrs. Thomas Jefferson**—Born Martha Wayles on October 30, 1748, in Charles City County, Virginia, the daughter of a wealthy lawyer and planter. At 18, she married a young Virginian, Bathurst Skelton, who died on September 30, 1768, leaving her with an infant son. No portrait or reliable facts about her have survived, but she was said to be musically inclined and well-off when she married Thomas Jefferson on January 1, 1772. Her firstborn child, and four of the six children she bore her second husband, died in early childhood. After just 10 years as Mrs. Jefferson, she died on September 6, 1782, and was buried at Monticello; so Jefferson had been a widower for 18 years when he became President.

Being opposed to elaborate state entertaining, he held such functions to a minimum, but when he did receive guests, often his hostess was Mrs. James (Dolley) Madison, the wife of his Secretary of State, or one of his two surviving daughters—Mrs. John Wayles Eppes and Mrs. Thomas Mann Randolph, whose eighth child, James Madison Randolph, was the first baby born in the Executive Mansion (on January 17, 1806).

**Mrs. James Madison**—Born Dolley Paine on May 20, 1768, the daughter of Virginia Quakers temporarily settled in North Carolina. When she was 15, her family moved to Philadelphia, and on January 7, 1790, she married John Todd, a Quaker lawyer who died three years later, leaving her with one son; another had already died. Strikingly handsome despite her plain garb, the young widow quickly attracted new suitors, among them "the great little Madison," as she described him in a letter. They were married on September 15, 1794, when he was 43 and she 26.

She soon blossomed forth in elegant dress, but with a warmth and simplicity of manner that made her one of the best loved figures of her day. As White House hostess during the Jefferson administration, then as First Lady, she reigned socially supreme in Washington from 1801 to 1817. The first Inaugural Ball, on March 4, 1809, marked her husband's assumption of the Presidency, and she appeared there in queenly yellow velvet, set off by a plumed satin headdress.

Dolley Madison put much effort into furnishing the Executive Mansion suitably, but her fine draperies were destroyed when the British burned the building on August 24, 1814. Mrs. Madison is supposed to have saved the famous Gilbert Stuart portrait of Washington from the flames and also her husband's invaluable notes describing the Constitutional Convention of 1787.

While the White House was being rebuilt, the Madisons lived in Octagon House, a private mansion. They had no children, and her one son grew up a ne'er-do-well. Upon leaving Washington, Mrs. Madison continued entertaining on a grand scale at Montpelier, her husband's Virginia plantation. She returned to Washington following his death, and took up residence in 1837 in a small house across Lafayette Square from the White House. Here she received homage till she died on July 12, 1849, and was buried at Montpelier.

**Mrs. James Monroe**—Born Elizabeth Kortright in New York City on June 30, 1768, the daughter of a former British Army captain. At 17, on February 16, 1786, she married James Monroe, 10 years her senior. Succeeding the popular Dolley Madison as First Lady, Mrs. Monroe precipitated a social storm.

Reserved and regal in manner, she refused to follow Mrs. Madison's custom of paying calls on capital hostesses, and she added to the outrage felt by much of Washington society by declining to make the White House's first wedding into an elaborate official ceremony; only relatives and close friends were invited to the marriage of the younger of the Monroes' two daughters, Maria, to Samuel L. Gouverneur on March 9, 1820. But during her husband's second term, Mrs. Monroe's policy of restricting the social obligations of the Presidential family to the receiving of guests, without any ritual paying of calls, won general approval, and it has been followed ever since. Mrs. Monroe died on September 23, 1830, at Oak Hill, her husband's Virginia plantation, and she was buried in Richmond.

**Mrs. John Quincy Adams**—Born Louisa Catherine Johnson in London on February 12, 1775, the daughter of a Marylander serving as a financial agent in England. In London, on July 27, 1797, she became the wife of John Quincy Adams, then serving his first diplomatic tour of duty abroad. The mother of three sons—the youngest, Charles Francis Adams, was the highly regarded American Minister to Great Britain during the Civil War—Mrs. Adams was plagued by ill health but made a gracious First Lady.

Much less stiff in manner than her husband, she was noted for her ornate headdresses and fashionable gowns when she received at the fortnightly levees held in the White House during her regime there. Besides her own sons and one daughter, her family during her years in the Executive Mansion also included the three orphaned children of one of her sisters, and many nieces and nephews paid frequent visits. Mrs. Adams died in the family's private residence in Washington on May 15, 1852, and was buried in Quincy, Massachusetts.

**Mrs. Andrew Jackson**—Born Rachel Donelson in 1767, the daughter of Colonel John Donelson of Virginia. When she was 13, her family moved to Kentucky, where she married Captain Lewis Robards in 1785. He proved a suspicious husband, and five years later he sought permission from the legislature to divorce her.

Mistakenly believing a divorce had been granted, she and Andrew Jackson were married near Natchez in 1791; then on discovering two years afterward that Robards had just obtained the divorce, they were remarried on January 17, 1794. As Jackson's fame spread, gossip about this unfortunate episode hurt his wife increasingly. He fought at least one duel to defend her honor (killing Charles Dickinson in Kentucky in 1806), but when the slander was revived in the scurrilous Presidential campaign of 1828, he could not protect her. Her death of a heart attack on December 22, 1828, just as he was preparing to leave for Washington, was widely blamed on scandalmongers. She was buried at The Hermitage, Jackson's home near Nashville.

A kindly woman fond of smoking a corncob pipe, though by no means illiterate as often charged, Mrs. Jackson had no children, but she and her husband adopted a nephew. During Jackson's administration, Mrs. Andrew Jackson Donelson, wife of his nephew, often served as his hostess.

**Mrs. Martin Van Buren**—Born Hannah Hoes on March 8, 1783, in Kinderhook, New York, where she knew her future husband from early childhood. Distant relatives on his mother's side, they were married February 21, 1807, and had four sons before she died in Albany on February 5, 1819; she was buried at Kinderhook. A widower for 18 years when he entered the Executive Mansion, Van Buren had as his official hostess Mrs. Abraham Van Buren, the South Carolina-born wife of his oldest son.

**Mrs. William Henry Harrison**—Born Anna Tuthill Symmes on July 25, 1775, near Morristown, New Jersey, the daughter of Colonel John Cleves Symmes, who later became a judge and large landholder in the Northwest Territory. When Lieutenant William Henry Harrison asked Colonel Symmes for his daughter's hand, the application was rejected on the ground that an Army officer could not support a wife. As a result, the couple ran off to be married by a justice of the peace on November 25, 1795.

While her husband advanced militarily and politically, Mrs. Harrison brought up 10 children. Because she had only recently recovered from an illness, she did not attend her husband's inauguration on March 4, 1841. She remained at the Harrison home in North Bend, Ohio, to complete her convalescence, expecting to be well enough by May to assume her duties as First Lady in Washington. But her husband took cold and died exactly one month after assuming office, and Mrs. Harrison never did move into the Executive Mansion. Surviving until February 25, 1864, when she died and was buried at North Bend, she outlived all but one of her children—John Scott Harrison, whose son Benjamin became President in 1889.

**Mrs. John Tyler**—The first Mrs. Tyler was born Letitia Christian in New Kent County, Virginia, on November 12, 1790. Married on March 29, 1813, she had eight children, one of whom died in infancy. Partially paralyzed by a stroke in 1839, she was unable to assume any social duties when her husband became President two years later. Her only appearance downstairs at the Executive Mansion came at the wedding of her daughter, Elizabeth, to William Nevison Waller on January 31, 1842. Mrs. Tyler died on September 10, 1842, in the White House and was buried at Cedar Grove, Virginia.

The role of official hostess during most of Tyler's administration was taken by his daughter-in-law, Mrs. Robert Tyler, a former actress born Priscilla Cooper in Bristol, Pennsylvania. But on June 26, 1844, the 54-year-old President married the 24-year-old Julia Gardiner, who in the nine months remaining to his term established herself as one of the nation's most flamboyant First Ladies. Born May 4, 1820, on Gardiner's Island, New York, she belonged to a wealthy society family, and she surrounded herself with a "court" of elegant young ladies when she began entertaining lavishly in Washington. The mother of seven children, she survived her husband 27 years; she died on July 10, 1889, in Richmond and was buried there beside him.

**Mrs. James Knox Polk**—Born Sarah Childress on September 4, 1803, in Murfreesboro, Tennessee, the daughter of a wealthy merchant. After attending the Female Academy in Salem, North Carolina, considered then to be the South's outstanding school for girls, she married James Polk on January 1, 1824.

A shrewd and ambitious woman, she had no children and devoted herself to advancing her husband's political career. As First Lady, she opened the Executive Mansion to the public two evenings a week, besides holding formal receptions and dinners frequently. Under her direction, the building received its first complete redecorating since Monroe's administration. Though a strict Presbyterian who frowned on dancing and Sunday visiting, she allowed wine to be served and was fond of showy clothes. Mrs. Polk survived her husband 42 years, dying on August 14, 1891, in Nashville, where she was buried.

**Mrs. Zachary Taylor**—Born Margaret Mackall Smith on September 21, 1788, in Calvert County, Maryland, the daughter of a planter. On June 21, 1810, she married Lieutenant Zachary Taylor and spent most of the next 35 years at frontier Army posts. She had six children, two of whom died in infancy. By the time her husband was elected President, ill health prevented her taking an active role as First Lady, and her youngest daughter, Mrs. William Wallace Bliss, acted as her father's official hostess. Mrs. Taylor died on August 18, 1852, near Pascagoula, Louisiana, and was buried beside her husband in Springfield, Kentucky.

**Mrs. Millard Fillmore**—The first Mrs. Fillmore was born Abigail Powers on March 13, 1798, in Stillwater, New York. The daughter of a Baptist minister, she met her future husband at a nearby academy when he appeared as a fellow pupil. Two years older than he, and much more cultivated, she helped him with his studies. They were married on February 5, 1826, and had two children.

In poor health when she became First Lady, she assigned her official duties to her daughter, Mary Abigail, her own contribution being her successful effort to secure funds from Congress for setting up a small library in the White House. At the inauguration ceremonies for her husband's successor, she caught a cold which developed into pneumonia, and she died in Washington on March 30, 1853. She was buried in Buffalo.

Five years later, on February 10, 1858, former President Fillmore married Mrs. Caroline C. McIntosh, the 44-year-old widow of a Troy, New York, merchant. The second Mrs. Fillmore, who had no children, survived her husband seven years, dying in Buffalo on August 11, 1881.

**Mrs. Franklin Pierce**—Born Jane Means Appleton on March 12, 1806, in Hampton, New Hampshire, the daughter of Jesse Appleton, who later became president of Bowdoin College. After the death of her father, she married Franklin Pierce on November 10, 1834. Frail and shy but with strict ideas of propriety, she had a tragic life. Two of her three sons died of infant ailments, and eight weeks before her husband's inauguration as President, their only remaining child—an 11-year-old boy whom she idolized—was killed in a train accident. She never recovered from this blow and spent her years in the White House secluded in her own room, pitifully writing pencil notes to her lost son.

For the limited official entertaining carried on during her husband's administration, her girlhood friend, Mrs. Abby L. Means, who had come to Washington as her companion, served as hostess. Mrs. Pierce died on December 2, 1863, in Andover, Massachusetts, and was buried in Concord, New Hampshire.

**Buchanan Administration**—James Buchanan, the nation's only bachelor President, had as his official hostess his orphaned niece, Miss Harriet Lane. A charming young woman with a taste for splendor, she entertained elaborately during her uncle's administration. Five years after leaving the White House, in 1866, she married Henry E. Johnson, a Baltimore banker.

**Mrs. Abraham Lincoln**—Born Mary Ann Todd on December 13, 1818, in Lexington, Kentucky, the daughter of a prosperous merchant. At 22, while visiting a married sister, Mrs. Ninian Edwards, in Springfield, Illinois, she became engaged to one of her brother-in-law's fellow legislators, the backwoods lawyer Abraham Lincoln. Under controversial circumstances—some say Lincoln failed to appear the first time the wedding was scheduled—the engagement was broken; but the marriage finally took place on November 4, 1842.

Lively and intelligent, Mrs. Lincoln was also quick-tempered to the point of emotional instability. In the White House, she aroused widespread criticism for her grasping attitude toward money and her poor judgment in choosing friends. She was so shocked by her husband's assassination that her behavior became increasingly erratic.

After leaving Washington, she brought about a new wave of newspaper abuse by attempting to sell her old clothes and jewelry. On May 19, 1875, a Chicago court adjudged her insane, and she was confined in a private sanitorium at Batavia, Illinois, for four months. Thereafter, she lived quietly abroad or with relatives until she died on July 16, 1882, in Springfield, where she was buried beside her husband. Of their four sons, only the oldest, Robert Todd Lincoln, survived her.

**Mrs. Andrew Johnson**—Born Eliza McCardle on October 4, 1810, in Leesburg, Tennessee, the daughter of a shoemaker. She was a 16-year-old schoolgirl living with her widowed mother in the Tennessee town of Greeneville when Andrew Johnson arrived to take up tailoring there; a few months later, on May 5, 1827, they were married. Finding he could hardly read and not write at all, she taught him these skills during the next several years. Mrs. Johnson had five children, one of whom died in infancy.

When her husband unexpectedly became President, she was a frail grandmother who told a White House visitor: "We are plain people from Tennessee temporarily in a high place, and you must not expect too much of us in a social way." During her husband's administration, the role of official hostess was shared by their two daughters, Mrs. David Patterson and Mrs. Daniel Stover. Mrs. Johnson died on January 15, 1876, in Greene County, Tennessee and was buried beside her husband in Greeneville.

**Mrs. Ulysses S. Grant**—Born Julia Boggs Dent on January 26, 1826, in St. Louis, Missouri, the daughter of Colonel Frederick Dent. She met her future husband while he was stationed at the nearby Jefferson Barracks, and they were married on August 22, 1848. The mother of three sons and a daughter, she took the hardships of being an Army wife cheerfully, even living in a tent at times when she joined her husband in the field during the Civil War, but she also enjoyed the glitter of capital society and entertained elaborately as First Lady. Her daughter, Nellie, became Mrs. Algernon Sartoris in a splendid White House wedding on May 21, 1874. Mrs. Grant died on December 14, 1902, in Washington and was buried beside her husband in Grant's Tomb in New York City.

**Mrs. Rutherford Birchard Hayes**—Born Lucy Ware Webb on August 28, 1831, in Chillicothe, Ohio, the daughter of a physician. A sweet-tempered and devout Methodist, she met her future husband while attending Wesleyan Female College in Cincinnati. He was a lawyer, eight years her senior, who called on her at the urging of his mother, who had already chosen Lucy Webb as the ideal candidate for her son's wife. Rutherford Hayes agreed, the marriage took place on December 30, 1852, and he gained a devoted companion who bore him one daughter and seven sons (three died in infancy). He also gave his country its first First Lady with a college diploma.

But for all her gentle submissiveness, Mrs. Hayes had strong temperance convictions. To please her, President Hayes banished wine from the White House during his administration, thereby inadvertently subjecting her to widespread ridicule as "Lemonade Lucy." Yet Mrs. Hayes was no hard-eyed reformer. She was a warm, friendly woman whose most lasting contribution in the White House was her initiation of annual Easter egg-rolling contests in 1878. She died of a stroke on June 25, 1889, at the Hayes home in Fremont, Ohio, and she was buried there.

**Mrs. James Abram Garfield**—Born Lucretia Rudolph on April 19, 1832, the daughter of the leading merchant in Hiram, Ohio. She met her future husband while attending a local academy her father had helped to found; after teaching a few years, she married James Garfield on November 11, 1858. They had seven children, two of whom died in infancy. Her tenure as First Lady was brief, but made memorable by tragedy. "The wife of the President is the bravest woman in the Universe," the New York *Herald* said of her. For she had only just recovered from a near-fatal attack of malaria and was convalescing at a seaside cottage in Elberon, New Jersey, when she received word on July 2, 1881, that her husband had been shot.

She immediately returned to Washington and displayed remarkable composure during the 80 days that he lingered on the brink of death. She traveled back to Elberon with him when he was moved there on September 6, and she was at his bedside when he died on September 19, 1881. Mrs. Garfield survived her husband 36 years. She died on March 14, 1918, in Pasadena, California, and was buried beside her husband in Cleveland.

**Mrs. Chester Alan Arthur**—Born Ellen Lewis Herndon on August 30, 1837, in Fredericksburg, Virginia, the daughter of Captain William Lewis Herndon of the U.S. Navy and explorer of the Amazon. Brought up in gracious Southern style, she was taken on a European tour at 16 and, while visiting New York City a few years later, met Chester Arthur; they were married on October 25, 1859. She had three children, one dying in infancy.

Beautiful and cultivated, she helped her Vermont-born husband develop a taste for elegance but did not live to reign as First Lady. She died of pneumonia in New York on January 12, 1880, ten months before her husband's nomination to the Vice-Presidency, and she was buried in Albany. Arthur's widowed sister, Mrs. John McElroy, served as his hostess while he was in the White House.

**Mrs. Grover Cleveland**—Born Frances Folsom on July 21, 1864, in Buffalo, New York, the daughter of Oscar Folsom, a lawyer who was killed in a buggy accident in 1875. Her father's partner, Grover Cleveland, then assumed responsibility for her. A tall, attractive young woman, she was attending Wells College when he became President in 1885. He was 48 years old and a bachelor. On June 2, 1886, they were married in the Blue Room of the White House, and this first Presidential wedding in the Executive Mansion was celebrated by the pealing of every church bell in Washington. (John Tyler, the only other President to marry while in office, had been wed at the Church of the Ascension in New York City.)

The 22-year-old Mrs. Cleveland won immediate popularity and was considered the most charming First Lady since Dolley Madison. Her friendliness drew large crowds to her public receptions. She had five children, the second—Esther, who later became Mrs. William Bosanquet—being the only Presidential child to be born in the White House (on September 9, 1893). Mrs. Cleveland survived her husband 39 years and, five years after his death, on February 10, 1913, she became the first Presidential widow to remarry. Her second husband was Thomas J. Preston, a Princeton professor of archaeology. She died on October 29, 1947, in Baltimore and was buried in Princeton.

**Mrs. Benjamin Harrison**—The first Mrs. Harrison was born Caroline (Carrie) Scott, on October 1, 1832, in Oxford, Ohio. She was the daughter of a Presbyterian minister who also conducted a school for girls. After teaching briefly, she married Benjamin Harrison on October 20, 1853; they had two children. As First Lady, she became the first President General of the National Society of the Daughters of the American Revolution. Prevented by ill health from taking an active social role, she died in the White House on October 25, 1892, and was buried in Indianapolis. The duties of official hostess during much of the Harrison administration were assumed by Mrs. Mary Scott Dimmick, a widowed niece of Mrs. Harrison's.

After leaving office, former President Harrison married Mrs. Dimmick in New York City on April 6, 1896; she was 37, and he was then 62. They had one child. The second Mrs. Harrison, a native of Honesdale, Pennsylvania, survived her husband 46 years, dying in New York on January 5, 1948.

**Mrs. William McKinley**—Born Ida Saxton on June 8, 1847, the daughter of a leading banker in Canton, Ohio. Charming but high-strung, she was, unconventionally, working as a cashier in her father's bank when she met a handsome newcomer to town, Major William McKinley; they were married on January 25, 1871. A year later, she gave birth to a daughter, then became pregnant again soon afterward. Before the birth of her second baby, her mother died, and Mrs. McKinley became severely depressed. The subsequent death of both her infant daughters left her a nervous invalid subject to frequent epileptic fits. Nevertheless, as her husband rose politically, she insisted on appearing with him at all social functions, and he became adept at shielding her when she suffered a seizure.

The nature of her illness was not generally known when she became First Lady, and her delicate health required many innovations in official entertaining. Despite protocol, she was seated beside the President at state dinners, and Mrs. Garret Hobart, wife of McKinley's Vice-

President during his first term, assisted her in many ceremonial duties. Mrs. McKinley survived her slain husband five years, dying on May 26, 1907, in Canton, where she was buried beside him.

**Mrs. Theodore Roosevelt**—The first Mrs. Roosevelt was born Alice Hathaway Lee on July 29, 1861, in Chestnut Hill, Massachusetts. As a charming girl of 17, she met her future husband while he was attending Harvard. They were married on October 27, 1880, soon after his graduation, when he was 22 and she 19. But two days after the birth of their first child—a daughter, also named Alice—she died (on February 14, 1884) of a previously unsuspected case of Bright's disease. Roosevelt lost his beloved young wife on the same day his mother died of typhoid fever.

He gradually recovered from the shock of this double tragedy after renewing his childhood friendship with Edith Kermit Carow. They were married in London, where she was temporarily living, on December 2, 1886. The daughter of a New York merchant, she had been born in Connecticut on August 6, 1861. The second Mrs. Roosevelt, who gave her husband four sons and another daughter, made an unusually poised and capable First Lady.

Besides coping with the antics of her high-spirited youngsters, she supervised an extensive remodeling of the White House which changed the mansion, her husband said, from "a shabby likeness of the ground floor of the Astor House into a simple and dignified dwelling for the head of a republic." In addition, she arranged an elegant East Room wedding when "Princess Alice" married Congressman Nicholas Longworth of Ohio on February 17, 1906. Mrs. Roosevelt died on September 30, 1948, at the family's summer home in Oyster Bay, New York, and she was buried there.

**Mrs. William Howard Taft**—Born Helen Herron on June 2, 1861, in Cincinnati, but always called Nellie. The daughter of Judge John Williamson Herron, she visited the White House at 17 as the guest of her father's former law partner, President Rutherford B. Hayes, and decided then that she would like to be First Lady. Studious as well as ambitious, she taught a few years before marrying William Howard Taft on June 19, 1886.

Two months after she did move into the White House, she suffered a stroke which prevented her from taking part in social activities for more than a year; then after her recovery, she and her husband celebrated their 25th wedding anniversary with an evening garden party for which the grounds of the Executive Mansion were spectacularly illuminated. Mrs. Taft left a lasting physical impression on Washington by sponsoring the planting of the capital's famous Japanese cherry trees, which she admired from the time of a diplomatic trip to Japan with her husband. The eldest of her three children, Robert A. Taft, became the distinguished Senator from Ohio. Mrs. Taft died on May 22, 1943, in Washington and was buried beside her husband in Arlington National Cemetery.

**Mrs. Woodrow Wilson**—The first Mrs. Wilson was born Ellen Louise Axson in Rome, Georgia, on May 15, 1860. Daughter of a Presbyterian minister, she married Wilson on June 24, 1885. An art student with a fondness for music and literature, she had a great influence on her husband; from their marriage to her death, they were never separated a day. They had three daughters, two of whom were married in the White House—Jessie, who became Mrs. Francis Bowes Sayre in an elaborate East Room ceremony on November 25, 1913, and Eleanor, who became Mrs. William Gibbs McAdoo at a smaller wedding in the Blue Room on May 7, 1914. The latter occasion was marred by the increasing weakness of Mrs. Wilson, who died in the White House on August 6, 1914.

Her death left the President so depressed by grief and loneliness that his physician, Dr. Cary T. Grayson, became alarmed until he, perhaps inadvertently, provided a cure. Dr. Grayson introduced Mrs. Edith Bolling Galt, an attractive 42-year-old widow, to Wilson's cousin, Miss Helen Woodrow Bones, who was temporarily serving as White House hostess. Miss Bones invited Mrs. Galt to tea in March of 1915. Just two months later, the President proposed marriage to Mrs. Galt, and they were married at her Washington home on December 18, 1915.

Born in Wytheville, Virginia, on October 15, 1872, the second Mrs. Wilson had been married to Norman Galt, a Washington jeweler, in 1896, then widowed twelve years later. As First Lady during World War I, she kept official entertaining to a minimum. After her husband was partly paralyzed by a stroke on October 2, 1919, she shielded him from visitors to the extent that she was called "the nation's first Lady President." She survived him 36 years, dying in Washington on December 28, 1961.

**Mrs. Warren Gamaliel Harding**—Born Florence Kling on August 15, 1860, the daughter of a banker who was the richest man in the small Ohio city of Marion. At 19, she eloped with Henry DeWolfe, the black sheep in an old local family. A year later, he abandoned her and an infant son, and she was forced to return to her stern father whose rule she had sought to escape.

After being divorced, she married Warren Harding on July 8, 1891; she was five years his senior. Then she took over the business side of the Marion *Star,* which Harding had recently acquired. Mrs. Harding was sometimes credited with inspiring her husband's political career, and in Ohio political circles she was known as "The Duchess." In the White House, failing health limited her social activities, but she survived her husband by a year, dying on November 21, 1924, in Marion, where she was buried.

**Mrs. Calvin Coolidge**—Born Grace Goodhue in Burlington, Vermont, on January 3, 1879, the daughter of a mechanical engineer. After graduating from the University of Vermont in 1902, she became a teacher at the Clarke Institute for the Deaf in Northampton, Massachusetts. An exceptionally warm person, she married the silent Calvin Coolidge on October 4, 1905, and was sometimes described as his most important asset.

In the White House, despite her husband's frugal management of menu planning, her charm won her wide popularity. She had two sons, but the younger, Calvin Jr., died at 16 of blood poisoning on July 7, 1924, less than a year after his father succeeded to the Presidency. Mrs. Coolidge died on July 8, 1957, in Northampton, and she was buried in Plymouth, Vermont.

**Mrs. Herbert Clark Hoover**—Born Lou Henry in Waterloo, Iowa, on March 29, 1874, the daughter of a banker who subsequently moved his family to Monterey, California. She entered Stanford University in 1894, planning to become a geology teacher, but she married Hoover, a fellow student, on February 10, 1899, and went to China with him. After living in many foreign lands, while her husband pursued his career, and raising two sons, Mrs. Hoover enjoyed settling in Washington in 1921, when her husband entered President Harding's Cabinet.

By the time she moved into the White House on March 4, 1929, she had a large circle of friends in the capital, and she entertained extensively as First Lady. But on January 1, 1930, she held what proved to be the last of the annual New Year's Day receptions in the Executive Mansion. When Mrs. John Adams had started the custom in 1801, 135 guests appeared to be greeted by the President and his wife; in 1930, more than 9,000 people sought admission, causing Mr. and Mrs. Hoover to make a point of being out of Washington over New Year's during the rest of his term. (His successor, President Franklin Roosevelt, formally discontinued these gatherings which had grown so unwieldy.) Mrs. Hoover died in New York City on January 7, 1944. The gravesite is located at West Branch, Iowa.

**Mrs. Franklin Delano Roosevelt**—Born Anna Eleanor Roosevelt on October 11, 1884, in New York City, the daughter of Theodore Roosevelt's younger brother, Elliott. Owing to the early death of both her parents, she was brought up by her maternal grandmother, Mrs. V. G. Hall. A shy and solitary child, she was educated in Europe; then on March 17, 1905, she married her fifth cousin, Franklin Roosevelt. They had six children, one son dying in infancy. After her husband's crippling attack of infantile paralysis in 1921, she took an increasingly active part in politics, serving as his eyes and ears at meetings he could not attend.

In the White House, she continued this role on a much broader scale, traveling thousands of miles to inspect coal mines and prisons and American military installations everywhere. A controversial figure as First Lady because of her outspoken support for humanitarian and civil rights causes, Mrs. Roosevelt broke with tradition by holding regular press conferences, lecturing widely, and writing a syndicated newspaper column, "My Day."

She won worldwide esteem as one of the century's outstanding women. President Truman, after her husband's death, appointed her to the United States delegation to the United Nations. She also served the world organization as chairman of its Commission for Human Rights. She died on November 7, 1962, in New York City, and was buried beside her husband at Hyde Park, New York.

**Mrs. Harry S Truman**—Born Elizabeth Virginia Wallace in Independence, Missouri, on February 13, 1885, but always called Bess. As a little girl with blond curls, she captivated her future husband at Sunday school in the First Prebyterian Church. Married on June 28, 1919, she had one daughter.

Unassuming and not fond of ceremony, Mrs. Truman tried to avoid personal publicity as First Lady. She was helped in her effort to live quietly by the fact that serious structural weaknesses were discovered in the White House during her residence there; and from November 1948 until March 1952, the Trumans lived across Pennsylvania Avenue in Blair House. After her husband left office, Mrs. Truman was happy to retire with him to the family home in Independence. She died on October 18, 1982 in Kansas City, Missouri, and was buried beside her husband at Independence.

**Mrs. Dwight David Eisenhower**—Born Mamie Geneva Doud on November 14, 1896, the daughter of a prosperous meat packer in Boone, Iowa. When she was 10, her family moved to Denver, but usually spent the colder months visiting San Antonio. Early in the winter of 1915, while at San Antonio, a young second lieutenant stationed at nearby Fort Sam Houston was introduced to the pretty and popular Miss Doud; on Valentine's Day, they became engaged, and they were married on July 1, 1916. For the next several decades, she lived at Army posts all over the world. She had two sons, but the older died at three.

A warm and friendly woman, Mrs. Eisenhower became accustomed to official entertaining during her Army years. But she described herself as "nonpolitical." After leaving the White House, she enjoyed retirement at the Gettysburg farm that was their first home.

After a massive stroke in late September 1979, she was hospitalized at Walter Reed Army Medical Center in Washington, D.C., where she died in her sleep on November 11, 1979. She was buried beside her husband in Abilene, Kansas.

**Mrs. John Fitzgerald Kennedy**—Born Jacqueline Lee Bouvier on July 28, 1929, in Southampton, New York, the daughter of John Vernon Bouvier 3d, a wealthy stockbroker. With generations of social prominence on both sides of her family, she attended private schools, had her own pony, and made a glittering début at Newport in 1947. (After the divorce of her parents in 1940, her mother married Hugh D. Auchincloss of Washington and Newport.) Then she went on to further study at Vassar, the Sorbonne, and George Washington University, from which she graduated in 1951. As the "Inquiring Camera Girl" for the Washington *Times-Herald*, she interviewed a young senator whom she had recently met at a dinner party; they were married on September 12, 1953, in St. Mary's Roman Catholic Church at Newport.

The nation's third youngest First Lady, she was 31 on moving into the White House. She won admiration everywhere for her tasteful redecoration of the White House and the glamorous receptions she arranged; this "Kennedy style" to which she contributed so much was a major ingredient in her husband's popularity.

With her two children, she lived in New York City after leaving the White House until her marriage on October 20, 1968, to Aristotle Socrates Onassis, the Greek shipping multimillionaire who died on March 15, 1975.

**Mrs. Lyndon Baines Johnson**—Born Claudia Alta Taylor on December 22, 1912, in Karnack, Texas, the daughter of Thomas Jefferson Taylor, a prosperous landowner and merchant. When she was two, a nursemaid called her Lady Bird—because she was "as purty as a lady bird"—and the nickname stuck. Brought up by an aunt after her mother died when she was five, she grew into a shy and nature-loving girl with an interest in studying.

Shortly after receiving a journalism degree from the University of Texas, she met the tall secretary to a Texas Congressman; and Lyndon Johnson proposed to her the next day. They were married two months later, on November 17, 1934. Mrs.

Johnson helped her husband along every step of his career. She provided the money for his first Congressional campaign (by borrowing against the $67,000 she was due to inherit from her mother), and she ran his Washington office while he took military leave during World War II.

In the White House, Mrs. Johnson's personal warmth was often credited with smoothing over difficulties caused by her husband's more abrasive personality. She showed a broader concern about public questions than any First Lady with the exception of Mrs. Franklin Roosevelt. Mrs. Johnson was particularly interested in promoting efforts to beautify the nation's cities and towns.

**Mrs. Richard Milhous Nixon**—Born Thelma Ryan on March 16, 1912, in Ely, Nevada, the daughter of a miner who took up farming a year later, and moved his family to Artesia, California. Her father always called her Pat, and the nickname stayed with her.

After graduating with honors from the University of Southern California in 1937, she taught commercial subjects at Whittier High School in Whittier, California, where she met her future husband in a local amateur theater group; they were married on June 21, 1940. Throughout his career, she has tirelessly supported him at every step. She gained valuable experience toward meeting her responsibilities while her husband was Vice-President under President Eisenhower.

Poised and imperturbable, she has brought up two daughters, the younger of whom, Julie, married David Eisenhower, grandson of the former President, in December 1968. Although she fulfilled her role of official hostess with grace, she generally shunned the limelight while in the White House. In 1976 she suffered a partial stroke.

**Mrs. Gerald R. Ford**—Born Elizabeth Anne Bloomer on April 8, 1918, in Chicago, Illinois, but moved to Grand Rapids, Michigan at the age of three. Mrs. Ford attended the Bennington School of Dance in Vermont and studied modern dance with Martha Graham. She spent two years in New York as a dancer in the Martha Graham Concert Group. In 1942, she returned to Grand Rapids and married William Warren. They were divorced in 1947. While in Grand Rapids she organized her own dance group and, in addition, became a model and fashion coordinator for a Grand Rapids department store. On October 15, 1948, she married Gerald R. Ford. The Fords have four children.

In Washington, Betty Ford was active in the Republican Wives Club, on the Board of Directors of the League of Republican Women in the District of Columbia, and as President of the Senate Red Cross Club. Mrs. Ford is noted for her candor in expressing her opinions and beliefs and is concerned with promoting equal opportunities for women.

**Mrs. Jimmy Carter** — Born Eleanor Rosalynn Smith on August 18, 1927, on her maternal grandfather's farm in Plains, Georgia, the daughter of town garage mechanic, Edgar Smith. While attending Georgia Southwestern College, Rosalynn studied interior decorating. She lived at home and helped her family from age 15 when she first went to work in a local beauty parlor. When 18-year-old Rosalynn married Jimmy Carter on July 7, 1946, she had known the U.S. Naval Academy midshipman for five years as her best friend's brother. The Carters have four children. Rosalynn enjoyed travelling from base to base until the death of Carter's father caused the couple's return to Plains in 1953 and catalyzed their first team effort in the family peanut business. Rosalynn deftly managed bookkeeping, office work, tax returns and helped to create a thriving business. Rosalynn profoundly influenced Carter's key presidential campaign strategy: to run in all possible primaries.

In the White House, Rosalynn demonstrated extraordinary determination and drive. She went along on presidential junkets both at home and abroad. On her own, she toured the U.S. in support of her favorite causes, campaigning and acting as observer for her husband; abroad she represented him at a presidential inauguration and a papal funeral. But more importantly, Rosalynn maintained her position as advisor to the President, a position which grew in both importance and visibility during the second half of the one-term Carter presidency.

**Mrs. Ronald Wilson Reagan** — Born Anne Frances Robbins on July 6, 1921, in New York City, the daughter of a New Jersey car salesman who left home soon after her birth. At the age of two, she was sent to live with relatives in Maryland to enable her mother, actress Edith Luckett, to pursue her career. Five years later, her mother married Dr. Loyal Davis, a prominent neurosurgeon in Chicago, who legally adopted Nancy when she was 14. Nancy has always been her nickname.

A leader in student government and dramatics at Girls' Latin School in Chicago, Nancy Davis also played forward on the field hockey team, while gaining a reputation for propriety. Upon graduation from Smith College, where she majored in drama, she pursued a career as a film actress in Hollywood. She became acquainted with Ronald Reagan after consulting with him on a Screen Actors Guild-related problem, and on March 1, 1952, they were married. They have two grown children, Patricia Ann and Ronald Prescott; President Reagan has two other children, a daughter, Maureen, and an adopted son, Michael, from a previous marriage.

Upon moving to Washington, Nancy Reagan arranged for a refurbishing of the Executive Mansion's public rooms and a complete redecorating of the family quarters. She and her husband are credited with bringing back to White House receptions a grand style of entertaining, with limousines, white tie and tails, and couturier gowns. Some of that glamorous world came close to being shattered in the ordeal of the attempted assassination of the President two months after the inauguration.

# U.S. PRESIDENTIAL ELECTIONS: 1789—1972

The first four Presidential elections (1789, 1792, 1796, and 1800) were held under Article II, Section 1, of the Constitution, which provided for the College of Electors to vote for two candidates —the one with the majority of votes was elected President, and the next highest became Vice-President. A tie in the Electoral College in 1800 led to the passage of the Twelfth Amendment, which provides for separate ballots for President and Vice-President.

Prior to the election of 1824, records of popular vote are scanty and inaccurate.

## ELECTION OF 1789

**The Political Scene:** The struggle over the ratification of the Constitution had led to the emergence of two political factions, the Federalists, who supported the new Constitution, and the Anti-Federalists, who opposed it.

**Nominations and Campaign:** George Washington, although identified with the Federalists, was unopposed for the Presidential nomination and received a unanimous vote from the 69 electors.

**Results of 1789 Election:**

| Presidential Candidate | Party | Electoral Votes |
|---|---|---|
| George Washington | None | 69 |
| John Adams | None | 34 |
| Other candidates | None | 35 |
| Votes not cast | — | 4 |

**Comments:** Rhode Island and North Carolina had not yet ratified the Constitution when the electors cast their ballots, and a deadlock between the Federalist Senate and the Anti-Federalist Assembly in New York prevented the choosing of any electors.

## ELECTION OF 1792

**The Political Scene:** Thomas Jefferson and James Madison in Virginia and George Clinton and Aaron Burr in New York provided the leadership of the Democratic-Republican party, which emerged in opposition to Alexander Hamilton's financial policy, to the Federalist emphasis on a strong central government, and to a loose or flexible interpretation of the Constitution.

**Nominations:** Both parties urged that Washington accept another term, but the Jeffersonians opposed Adams' re-election with Clinton's candidacy.

**The Campaign:** Adams was accused of being antidemocratic and a secret monarchist, but the real target of the Democratic-Republicans was Hamilton.

**Results of 1792 Election:**

| Presidential Candidate | Party | Electoral Votes |
|---|---|---|
| George Washington | Federalist | 132 |
| John Adams | Federalist | 77 |
| George Clinton | Democratic-Republican | 50 |
| Other candidates | — | 5 |
| Votes not cast | — | 3 |

## ELECTION OF 1796

**The Political Scene:** Washington, who deplored partisan politics, refused to consider another term, thus insuring the first real contest for the Presidency.

**Nominations:** Jefferson was the logical candidate for the Democratic-Republicans, but Hamilton was less than happy about the candidacy of John Adams of Massachusetts for the Federalists and hoped that Thomas Pinckney, the ostensible Federalist Vice-Presidential candidate, might win if Federalist electors in the South withheld their votes from Adams.

**The Campaign:** Adams electors in New England countered Hamilton's scheme by omitting Pinckney from their ballots. The unexpected result of the Federalist bickering was the election of Jefferson to the Vice-Presidency.

**Results of 1796 Election**

| Presidential Candidate | Party | Electoral Votes |
|---|---|---|
| John Adams | Federalist | 71 |
| Thomas Jefferson | Democratic-Republican | 68 |
| Thomas Pinckney | Federalist | 59 |
| Aaron Burr | Democratic-Republican | 30 |
| Other candidates | — | 48 |

## ELECTION OF 1800

**The Political Scene:** The wars of the French Revolution had created another area of disagreement between the Federalists, who favored Great Britain, and the Democratic-Republicans, who tended to support France. The apparent desire of some Federalist leaders for a war with France alarmed the nation.

**Nominations:** Congressional caucuses of each party chose the candidates: Adams and Pinckney for the Federalists and Jefferson and Burr for the Democratic-Republicans.

**The Campaign:** The Federalists gave their opponents a powerful campaign issue in the repressive Alien and Sedition Acts that Jefferson and Madison eloquently denounced in the Virginia and Kentucky Resolutions.

**Results of 1800 Election:**

| Presidential Candidate | Party | Electoral Votes |
|---|---|---|
| Thomas Jefferson | Democratic-Republican | 73 |
| Aaron Burr | Democratic-Republican | 73 |
| John Adams | Federalist | 65 |
| Charles C. Pinckney | Federalist | 64 |
| John Jay | Federalist | 1 |

**Comments:** Because the candidates for President and Vice-President were not separately nominated, Jefferson and Burr ended in a tie. The House of Representatives elected Jefferson on the 36th ballot after seven days of balloting. To prevent the situation from arising again, the Twelfth Amendment, ratified in 1804, provided for separate balloting for President and Vice-President. Jefferson's triumph ended the Federalist era and ushered in a quarter century of Democratic-Republican control of the Presidency.

## ELECTION OF 1804

**The Political Scene:** Jefferson's efficient administration and the acquisition of the vast Louisiana Territory gained his party almost universal support and led the more extreme Federalist leaders into the Essex Junto, an abortive scheme to separate the northeastern states from the Union.

**Nominations:** The Congressional caucuses of each party chose the candidates. A falling-out between Jefferson and Burr led to the latter's replacement as Vice-Presidential candidate by George Clinton of New York. Charles C. Pinckney of South Carolina and Rufus King of New York comprised the Federalist ticket.

**The Campaign:** The machinations of the Essex Junto all but destroyed the Federalist party; the only question remaining was the size of Jefferson's victory.

**Results of 1804 Election:**

| Presidential Candidate | Party | Electoral Votes | Vice-Presidential Candidate | Party | Electoral Votes |
|---|---|---|---|---|---|
| Thomas Jefferson | Democratic-Republican | 162 | George Clinton | Democratic-Republican | 162 |
| Charles C. Pinckney | Federalist | 14 | Rufus King | Federalist | 14 |

**Comments:** Jefferson won every electoral vote but those of Connecticut and Delaware and two in Maryland.

## ELECTION OF 1808

**The Political Scene:** The disastrous effects of the Embargo of 1808 on American commerce revived the Federalist party in New England and caused dissension among the Jeffersonians.
**Nominations:** It took considerable pressure by Jefferson to get the rebellious factions within his party to accept his choice of James Madison of Virginia to succeed him. Clinton of New York was again the Vice-Presidential candidate. Federalist leaders engineered the renomination of the 1804 ticket of Pinckney and King.
**The Campaign:** Running primarily on the Embargo issue, the Federalists considerably improved their showing over the previous election, but could not overcome the solid Democratic-Republican majority that had been created.

**Results of 1808 Election:**

| Presidential Candidate | Party | Electoral Votes | Vice-Presidential Candidate | Party | Electoral Votes |
|---|---|---|---|---|---|
| James Madison | Democratic-Republican | 122 | George Clinton | Democratic-Republican | 113 |
| Charles C. Pinckney | Federalist | 47 | Rufus King | Federalist | 47 |
| George Clinton | Democratic-Republican | 6 | Other candidates | — | 15 |
| Votes not cast | — | 1 | Votes not cast | — | 1 |

## ELECTION OF 1812

**The Political Scene:** Conflict with Great Britain over maritime rights and alleged incitement of Indian rebellion caused Madison to request a declaration of war in June 1812.
**Nominations:** The Republican congressional caucus, dominated by young "War Hawk" representatives from the frontier states, renominated Madison, a month before the war message. Elbridge Gerry of Massachusetts received the Vice-Presidential nomination. Insurgent Republicans in New York put up DeWitt Clinton, who thereupon received Federalist support but not an official endorsement. Jared Ingersoll of Pennsylvania ran with him.
**The Campaign:** Although Clinton tried to avoid running as a Peace-Federalist candidate, his strength clearly lay in the Northeast, the section most unenthusiastic about the war.

**Results of 1812 Election:**

| Presidential Candidate | Party | Electoral Votes | Vice-Presidential Candidate | Party | Electoral Votes |
|---|---|---|---|---|---|
| James Madison | Democratic-Republican | 128 | Elbridge Gerry | Democratic-Republican | 131 |
| DeWitt Clinton | Federalist | 89 | Jared Ingersoll | Federalist | 86 |
| Votes not cast | — | 1 | Votes not cast | — | 1 |

**Comments:** The vote of Pennsylvania together with the solid backing of the South and West elected Madison.

## ELECTION OF 1816

**The Political Scene:** The end of the War of 1812 and an economic boom assured the continued ascendancy of the Democratic-Republicans.
**Nominations:** The congressional caucus chose James Monroe of Virginia over William H. Crawford of Georgia in a close contest. The choice of Daniel D. Tompkins for the Vice-Presidency renewed the Virginia-New York alliance. Rufus King of New York, although not selected by any formal process, was considered the Federalist nominee.
**The Campaign:** King, the last Federalist candidate, received only the votes of Massachusetts, Connecticut, and Delaware in a campaign he hardly contested at all.

**Results of 1816 Election:**

| Presidential Candidate | Party | Electoral Votes | Vice-Presidential Candidate | Party | Electoral Votes |
|---|---|---|---|---|---|
| James Monroe | Democratic-Republican | 183 | Daniel D. Tompkins | Democratic-Republican | 183 |
| Rufus King | Federalist | 34 | John E. Howard | Federalist | 22 |
| Votes not cast | — | 4 | Other candidates | — | 12 |
| | | | Votes not cast | — | 4 |

**Comments:** Following Washington, Jefferson, and Madison, Monroe was the last of the Virginia dynasty and the last of the men of the revolutionary era to hold the Presidency.

## ELECTION OF 1820

**The Political Scene:** No great national issue disturbed the country enough for anyone to oppose Monroe's reelection.
**Nomination and Campaign:** Monroe received every electoral vote except that of William Plumer of New Hampshire.

**Results of 1820 Election:**

| Presidential Candidate | Party | Electoral Votes | Vice-Presidential Candidate | Party | Electoral Votes |
|---|---|---|---|---|---|
| James Monroe | Democratic-Republican | 231 | Daniel D. Tompkins | Democratic-Republican | 218 |
| John Quincy Adams | Independent | 1 | Other candidates | — | 14 |
| Votes not cast | — | 3 | Votes not cast | — | 3 |

**Comments:** The tradition that Plumer voted for John Quincy Adams in order to preserve for Washington alone the honor of a unanimous selection is of dubious validity; Plumer simply disliked Monroe and his policies.

## ELECTION OF 1824

**The Political Scene:** The "Era of Good Feelings" ended as the Democratic-Republican organization dissolved into sectional groupings.
**Nominations:** A poorly attended congressional caucus selected William H. Crawford of Georgia, while various state legislatures nominated Henry Clay of Kentucky, Andrew Jackson of Tennessee, John Quincy Adams of Massachusetts, and John C. Calhoun of South Carolina. Calhoun subsequently withdrew to run for the Vice-Presidency on Jackson's ticket.
**The Campaign:** Clay put forward his celebrated plan calling for a strong protective tariff, domestic improvements, and a national bank—policies that Adams also endorsed. Jackson relied on his popular appeal as a military hero.

**Results of 1824 Election:**

| Presidential Candidate | Party | Electoral Votes | Popular Vote Total | Popular Vote Percentage | Vice-Presidential Candidate and Electoral Votes | | Party |
|---|---|---|---|---|---|---|---|
| John Quincy Adams | None | 84 | 115,696 | 31.9 | John C. Calhoun | 182 | None |
| Andrew Jackson | None | 99 | 152,933 | 42.2 | Nathan Sanford | 30 | None |
| William H. Crawford | None | 41 | 46,979 | 12.9 | Nathaniel Macon | 24 | None |
| Henry Clay | None | 37 | 47,136 | 13.0 | Other candidates | 25 | — |

**Comments:** Since no candidate had gained a majority of the electoral vote, the House of Representatives, voting by states and with each state having one vote, chose Adams on the first ballot.

## ELECTION OF 1828

**The Political Scene:** More than two-thirds of the electorate had voted against Adams in 1824. This circumstance negated his hopes for a successful administration, and the Jacksonians commenced their plans to unseat him.

**Nominations:** The Tennessee legislature renominated Jackson in 1825, and the incumbent Vice-President Calhoun once again agreed to be his running mate. This is considered the first ticket of the modern Democratic party. Adams ran for reelection as a National Republican.

**The Campaign:** Although important differences on national questions divided Adams and Jackson, these issues disappeared in a welter of vituperative personal attacks against each standard-bearer.

**Results of 1828 Election:**

| Presidential Candidate | Party | Electoral Votes | Popular Vote Total | Popular Vote Percentage | Vice-Presidential Candidate and Electoral Votes | | Party |
|---|---|---|---|---|---|---|---|
| Andrew Jackson | Democratic | 178 | 647,292 | 56.0 | John C. Calhoun | 171 | Democratic |
| John Quincy Adams | National Republican | 83 | 507,730 | 44.0 | Richard Rush | 83 | National Republican |
| | | | | | William Smith | 7 | Democratic |

**Comments:** The election of Jackson, the frontier hero, represented a triumph for the West and the South. It also symbolized the arrival of the common people to political power.

## ELECTION OF 1832

**The Political Scene:** Internal disputes within Jackson's cabinet and the President's strong stand against nullification caused a break between Jackson and Calhoun. Jackson's veto of a bill rechartering the Bank of the United States, however, created the major issue in the campaign.

**Conventions and Nominees:** For the first time the national nominating convention was employed by the three parties in the field. All met at Baltimore, with the Anti-Masonic party holding the first convention (September 26, 1831) and choosing William Wirt of Maryland. The National Republicans nominated the legislative champion of the Bank of the United States—Henry Clay of Kentucky, while the Democrats unanimously endorsed Jackson and replaced Calhoun for the Vice-Presidency with Martin Van Buren of New York. The Democratic convention adopted a rule requiring a two-thirds vote of the whole convention for nomination. This remained in effect until 1936.

**The Campaign:** Clay attacked Jackson's veto of the bank bill and his opposition to internal improvements. He misjudged the popular temper; to the average voter, Jackson's bank policy was a blow against monopoly and privilege.

**Results of 1832 Election:**

| Presidential Candidate | Party | Electoral Votes | Popular Vote Total | Popular Vote Percentage | Vice-Presidential Candidate and Electoral Votes | | Party |
|---|---|---|---|---|---|---|---|
| Andrew Jackson | Democratic | 219 | 688,242 | 54.5 | Martin Van Buren | 189 | Democratic |
| Henry Clay | National Republican | 49 | 473,462 | 37.5 | John Sergeant | 49 | National Republican |
| John Floyd | Independent | 11 | — | — | Henry Lee | 11 | Independent |
| William Wirt | Anti-Masonic | 7 | 101,051 | 8.0 | Amos Ellmaker | 7 | Anti-Masonic |
| Votes not cast | — | 2 | — | — | William Wilkins | 30 | Independent |
| | | | | | Votes not cast | 2 | — |

**Comments:** The Anti-Masonic party, opposed to the Masons and other secret societies, was the first third party in American history. On December 28, 1832, following the election, Vice-President Calhoun resigned his office.

## ELECTION OF 1836

**The Political Scene:** Opponents of "King Andrew" Jackson formed the Whig party, taking the name of the antimonarchial English political party to emphasize Jackson's alleged autocratic tendencies.

**Conventions and Nominees:** Jackson desired his Vice-President Martin Van Buren of New York to succeed him, and the Democratic convention at Baltimore (May 20–22, 1835) unanimously ratified his choice. Richard M. Johnson of Kentucky was the Vice-Presidential candidate. The Whigs, lacking a leader with national appeal, nominated three sectional candidates (Daniel Webster of Massachusetts, Hugh L. White of Tennessee, and William Henry Harrison of Ohio) in an effort to throw the election into the House of Representatives.

**The Campaign:** Jackson's personality and the record of his administration provided the issues for the campaign. The influence of "Old Hickory" was probably decisive, since Van Buren received a bare majority of the popular vote. The Senate, for the only time in history, elected the Vice-President with 33 votes for Johnson, 16 for Granger.

**Results of 1836 Election:**

| Presidential Candidate | Party | Electoral Votes | Popular Vote Total | Popular Vote Percentage | Vice-Presidential Candidate and Electoral Votes | | Party |
|---|---|---|---|---|---|---|---|
| Martin Van Buren | Democratic | 170 | 764,198 | 50.9 | Richard M. Johnson | 147 | Democratic |
| William H. Harrison | Whig | 73 | 549,508 | 36.6 | Francis Granger | 77 | Whig |
| Hugh L. White | Whig | 26 | 145,352 | 9.7 | John Tyler | 47 | Democratic |
| Daniel Webster | Whig | 14 | 41,287 | 2.7 | William Smith | 23 | Independent |
| W. P. Mangum | Independent | 11 | — | — | | | |

## ELECTION OF 1840

**The Political Scene:** The Panic of 1837, which had been caused mainly by Jackson's erratic financial policies, fell with full force during Van Buren's administration, hurting his prospects for reelection.

**Conventions and Nominees:** The Whigs in Pennsylvania met at Harrisburg (May 4–5, 1840) to name William Henry Harrison of Ohio and John Tyler of Virginia as their ticket, while the Democrats convening at Baltimore (May 5–7) unanimously renominated Van Buren. The antislavery Liberty party in a convention at Albany, New York, nominated James G. Birney of New York and Thomas Earle of Pennsylvania.

**The Campaign:** The Whigs avoided any divisive issues and conducted a campaign of parades and ballyhoo, complete with the first memorable political slogan, "Tippecanoe and Tyler too."

**Results of 1840 Election:**

| Presidential Candidate | Party | Electoral Votes | Popular Vote Total | Popular Vote Percentage | Vice-Presidential Candidate and Electoral Votes | | Party |
|---|---|---|---|---|---|---|---|
| William H. Harrison | Whig | 234 | 1,275,612 | 52.9 | John Tyler | 234 | Whig |
| Martin Van Buren | Democratic | 60 | 1,130,033 | 46.8 | Richard Johnson | 48 | Democratic |
| James G. Birney | Liberty | — | 7,053 | .3 | Thomas Earle | — | Liberty |
| | | | | | L. W. Tazewell | 11 | Independent |
| | | | | | James K. Polk | 1 | Democratic |

**Comments:** Barely a month after his inauguration, Harrison became the first President to die in office and was succeeded by Tyler on April 6, 1841.

## ELECTION OF 1844

**The Political Scene:** In his one term Tyler managed to disrupt the Whig party and to secure the annexation of Texas, but he failed to settle the Oregon question.
**Conventions and Nominees:** The Whigs convened at Baltimore (May 1) to nominate Henry Clay for President and Senator Theodore Frelinghuysen of New Jersey for Vice-President. Later in the month at the same city, the Democrats chose the first "dark horse" nominee for the Presidency. Ex-President Van Buren had a clear majority on the early ballots but could not reach the required two-thirds vote. On the ninth ballot, the convention chose James K. Polk of Tennessee with George M. Dallas of Pennsylvania as the Vice-Presidential candidate. The Liberty party meeting at Buffalo, New York (August 1843), again named James G. Birney with Thomas Morris of Ohio as his running mate.
**The Campaign:** Polk, an ardent expansionist, favored the Texas annexation and the acquisition of Oregon with the slogan "Fifty-four forty or fight." Clay was hurt in the South by his wavering on Texas, and in the North by the defection of antislavery Whigs to the Liberty party.

**Results of 1844 Election:**

| Presidential Candidate | Party | Electoral Votes | Popular Vote Total | Popular Vote Percentage | Vice-Presidential Candidate |
|---|---|---|---|---|---|
| James K. Polk | Democratic | 170 | 1,339,368 | 49.6 | George M. Dallas |
| Henry Clay | Whig | 105 | 1,300,687 | 48.1 | Theodore Frelinghuysen |
| James G. Birney | Liberty | — | 62,197 | 2.3 | Thomas Morris |

**Comments:** Although far from conclusive, Polk's victory was regarded as a popular endorsement of a vigorous policy of expansion.

## ELECTION OF 1848

**The Political Scene:** Polk settled the Oregon dispute with Great Britain, led the nation through a successful war with Mexico, and secured a vast accretion of territory. Yet he left office immensely unpopular and with the question of the extension of slavery into the new territories threatening to divide the country.
**Conventions and Nominees:** Polk had renounced a second term and the Democratic convention meeting at Baltimore (May 1848) picked a ticket of Lewis Cass of Michigan and William O. Butler of Kentucky. Although most Whigs had opposed the Mexican War, it provided them with their party's two leading Presidential candidates, Generals Zachary Taylor and Winfield Scott. The convention at Philadelphia named Taylor of Louisiana with Millard Fillmore of New York. Antislavery dissidents from both parties formed the Free Soil party and, meeting at Buffalo (August 1848), nominated ex-President Martin Van Buren with Charles Francis Adams of Massachusetts as his running mate.
**The Campaign:** On the paramount issue, the Free Soilers opposed extension of slavery into the newly acquired territories, while Cass endorsed the concept of popular sovereignty, or letting the settlers decide. Taylor refused to take any stand at all, correctly counting on his war popularity to carry him to victory.

**Results of 1848 Election:**

| Presidential Candidate | Party | Electoral Votes | Popular Vote Total | Popular Vote Percentage | Vice-Presidential Candidate |
|---|---|---|---|---|---|
| Zachary Taylor | Whig | 163 | 1,362,101 | 47.3 | Millard Fillmore |
| Lewis Cass | Democratic | 127 | 1,222,674 | 42.4 | William O. Butler |
| Martin Van Buren | Free Soil | — | 291,616 | 10.1 | Charles Francis Adams |

**Comments:** Taylor died on July 9, 1850. The succession of Fillmore to the Presidency made possible the Compromise of 1850.

## ELECTION OF 1852

**The Political Scene:** Moderates in both parties had been alarmed by threats of disunion and vainly hoped the Compromise of 1850 would stifle the slavery agitation.
**Conventions and Nominees:** President Fillmore desired another term, but the Whigs again turned to a military hero, selecting General Winfield Scott of Virginia on the 53d ballot. The convention then named William A. Graham of North Carolina for the Vice-Presidency. The Democrats, who like the Whigs met at Baltimore in June, had a number of potential nominees, but none of the leaders could gain the necessary two-thirds majority. On the 49th ballot, "dark horse" Franklin Pierce of New Hampshire was named with William R. King of Alabama as the party's Vice-Presidential candidate. The remnants of the Free Soil party met in Pittsburgh in August to choose a ticket of John P. Hale of New Hampshire and George W. Julian of Indiana.
**The Campaign:** Both sides avoided the slavery question, and personalities dominated a rather listless campaign.

**Results of 1852 Election:**

| Presidential Candidate | Party | Electoral Votes | Popular Vote Total | Popular Vote Percentage | Vice-Presidential Candidate |
|---|---|---|---|---|---|
| Franklin Pierce | Democratic | 254 | 1,609,038 | 50.8 | William R. King |
| Winfield Scott | Whig | 42 | 1,386,629 | 43.8 | William A. Graham |
| John P. Hale | Free Soil | — | 156,297 | 4.9 | George Julian |

**Comments:** Scott was the last Presidential candidate of the Whig party.

## ELECTION OF 1856

**The Political Scene:** Despite their overwhelming victory in 1852, the Democrats found it more and more difficult to reconcile their Northern and Southern wings, while the Whigs disintegrated entirely. The passage of the Kansas-Nebraska Act led to the founding of the Republican party.
**Conventions and Nominees:** In their first national convention at Philadelphia in June, the Republicans nominated John C. Frémont of California and William L. Dayton of New Jersey. Although widely considered to be the ablest leader in the party, Stephen A. Douglas' sponsorship of the Kansas-Nebraska Act prevented his nomination by the Democratic convention at Cincinnati in June. On the 17th ballot a Northerner acceptable to the South, James Buchanan of Pennsylvania, was named with John C. Breckinridge of Kentucky as his running mate. The anti-immigrant, anti-Catholic, American (or Know-Nothing) party had nominated ex-President Fillmore and Andrew J. Donelson at its convention in Philadelphia in February.
**The Campaign:** The Republicans endorsed a protective tariff and condemned the extension of slavery into the territories. The Democratic platform supported the Kansas-Nebraska Act and the principle of popular sovereignty for the territories.

**Results of 1856 Election:**

| Presidential Candidate | Party | Electoral Votes | Popular Vote Total | Popular Vote Percentage | Vice-Presidential Candidate |
|---|---|---|---|---|---|
| James Buchanan | Democratic | 174 | 1,839,237 | 45.6 | John C. Breckinridge |
| John C. Frémont | Republican | 114 | 1,341,028 | 33.3 | William L. Dayton |
| Millard Fillmore | American | 8 | 849,872 | 21.1 | Andrew J. Donelson |

**Comments:** Frémont's 114 electoral votes—all from free states—demonstrated the sectional nature of the new Republican party.

## ELECTION OF 1860

**The Political Scene:** The Dred Scott decision, bloody fighting between sectional partisans in Kansas, and John Brown's raid on Harpers Ferry had widened the gulf between the free and slave states. Politicians in the states of the Deep South openly threatened secession if a Republican President was elected.
**Conventions and Nominations:** The Democrats meeting at Charleston (April 23–May 3, 1860) failed to nominate a candidate after 57 ballots, because the delegations of eight southern states withdrew in protest against the platform statement on slavery in the territories. Reassembling in Baltimore (June 18–23), the party nominated Stephen A. Douglas of Illinois and Benjamin Fitzpatrick of Alabama after further Southern defections. When Fitzpatrick declined to run, the national committee chose Herschel V. Johnson of Georgia. The Southern seceders, calling themselves the National Democratic party, convened in Baltimore on June 28 and nominated John Breckinridge of Kentucky and Joseph Lane of Oregon on a platform that endorsed slavery in the territories. The Constitutional Union party, which was composed mainly of former Whigs and was strongest in the border states, had met in Baltimore (May 9) to choose John Bell of Tennessee and Edward Everett of Massachusetts. Abraham Lincoln of Illinois required only three ballots to defeat preconvention favorite William H. Seward at the Republican convention in Chicago (May 18–20).
**The Campaign:** The Republicans promised congressional action to preserve freedom in the territories. Slavery and the sectional issues dominated the scene.

**Results of 1860 Election:**

| Presidential Candidate | Party | Electoral Votes | Popular Vote Total | Popular Vote Percentage | Vice-Presidential Candidate |
|---|---|---|---|---|---|
| Abraham Lincoln | Republican | 180 | 1,867,198 | 39.8 | Hannibal Hamlin |
| Stephen A. Douglas | Democratic | 12 | 1,379,434 | 29.4 | Herschel V. Johnson |
| John C. Breckinridge | National Democratic | 72 | 854,248 | 18.2 | Joseph Lane |
| John Bell | Constitutional Union | 39 | 591,658 | 12.6 | Edward Everett |

**Comments:** The division among his opponents seemed to insure Lincoln's election. Curiously, however, if all the popular votes cast for his opponents had been given to one man, Lincoln still would have won the electoral vote, because of the heavy distribution of his vote among the more populous states. A little more than a month after the election, South Carolina seceded from the Union.

## ELECTION OF 1864

**The Political Scene:** The apparent inability of the Union armies to end Confederate resistance increased the sentiment for peace, causing many leading Republicans to oppose Lincoln's renomination.
**Conventions and Nominees:** The Republicans (styling themselves the National Union party) met at Baltimore in June and renominated Lincoln. War-Democrat Andrew Johnson of Tennessee became the Vice-Presidential candidate. The Democrats meeting at Chicago in August nominated a ticket of General George B. McClellan of New Jersey and George H. Pendleton of Ohio.
**The Campaign:** The Democratic platform pronounced the war a failure and demanded a cessation of hostilities and the restoration of peace on the basis of the Federal Union of States. But spectacular Union victories at Mobile Bay, Atlanta, and in the Shenandoah Valley destroyed this peace platform, and insured Lincoln's victory.

**Results of 1864 Election:**

| Presidential Candidate | Party | Electoral Votes | Popular Vote Total | Popular Vote Percentage | Vice-Presidential Candidate |
|---|---|---|---|---|---|
| Abraham Lincoln | Republican | 212 | 2,219,362 | 55.1 | Andrew Johnson |
| George McClellan | Democratic | 21 | 1,805,063 | 44.9 | George Pendleton |
| Votes not cast | — | 1 | — | — | Votes not cast |

**Comments:** John Wilkes Booth assassinated Lincoln, who was succeeded on April 15, 1865, by Andrew Johnson.

## ELECTION OF 1868

**The Political Scene:** President Johnson and the Republican leadership fell out over Reconstruction policies. The Senate failed by one vote of removing the President by impeachment in May 1868.
**Conventions and Nominees:** The Republicans met (as the Union Republican party) at Chicago in May and selected General Ulysses S. Grant of Illinois with Schuyler Colfax of Indiana as his running mate. The Democrats meeting in Tammany Hall, New York City, in July drafted Horatio Seymour of New York after 21 ballots and complex maneuverings had failed to produce a candidate. The Vice-Presidential nod went to Francis P. Blair of Missouri.
**The Campaign:** In 1868 and for a generation thereafter, the Republicans used the "bloody shirt" tactic, attempting to label the Democrats as the party of secession and treason.

**Results of 1868 Election:**

| Presidential Candidate | Party | Electoral Votes | Popular Vote Total | Popular Vote Percentage | Vice-Presidential Candidate |
|---|---|---|---|---|---|
| Ulysses S. Grant | Republican | 214 | 3,013,313 | 52.7 | Schuyler Colfax |
| Horatio Seymour | Democratic | 80 | 2,703,933 | 47.3 | Francis P. Blair, Jr. |

**Comments:** Texas, Virginia, and Mississippi were not readmitted to the Union until 1870, therefore they cast no votes in this election. Grant greatly benefited from black votes in the South.

## ELECTION OF 1872

**The Political Scene:** Evidence of corruption within his administration and disagreement with his Southern policy led many Republicans to oppose Grant's renomination.
**Conventions and Nominees:** When it became apparent, however, that Grant would be renominated, a group of dissenters calling themselves the Liberal Republican party met at Cincinnati in May and nominated a ticket of Horace Greeley of New York and B. Gratz Brown of Missouri. Greeley's nomination provided a dilemma for the Democrats. Greeley had consistently criticized their party, but to nominate someone else would serve only to reelect Grant. Accordingly, the Democrats in convention at Baltimore in July accepted Greeley and Brown. The Republicans at Philadelphia in June had unanimously renominated Grant.
**The Campaign:** Although tariff and currency questions were debated to some extent, the Republicans relied on Grant's war record to overcome the scandals. Most Democratic voters reacted unenthusiastically to Greeley.

**Results of 1872 Election:**

| Presidential Candidate | Party | Electoral Votes | Popular Vote Total | Popular Vote Percentage | Vice-Presidential Candidate | Electoral Votes |
|---|---|---|---|---|---|---|
| Ulysses S. Grant | Republican | 286 | 3,597,375 | 55.6 | Henry Wilson | 286 |
| Horace Greeley | Democratic, Liberal Republican | — | 2,833,711 | 43.8 | B. Gratz Brown | 47 |
| Thomas A. Hendricks | Democratic | 42 | — | — | Other candidates | 19 |
| B. Gratz Brown | Democratic, Liberal Republican | 18 | — | — | Votes not cast | 14 |
| Other candidates | — | 3 | — | — | | — |
| Votes not cast | — | 17 | — | — | | — |

**Comments:** Greeley died after the election and his electoral votes went to other candidates.

## ELECTION OF 1876

**The Political Scene:** Growing national indignation at the scandals of Grant's second administration caused both parties to seek Presidential candidates associated with reform government.
**Conventions and Nominees:** The Republicans met at Cincinnati in June to select Rutherford B. Hayes of Ohio on the seventh ballot after the reform element had blocked the nomination of James G. Blaine. William A. Wheeler of New York was the Vice-Presidential candidate. Samuel J. Tilden of New York, who was acclaimed for his part in breaking up the notorious Tweed Ring, received a first-ballot nomination from the Democrats at St. Louis in June Thomas A. Hendricks of Indiana was named for the Vice-Presidency. The inflationary Greenback party named Peter Cooper of New York and Samuel F. Carey of Ohio.
**The Campaign:** Hayes's good record as governor of Ohio somewhat blunted Democratic efforts to capitalize on the corruption of the Grant regime. Tilden waged a very cautious campaign and probably did not pay enough attention to the "solid South."

**Results of 1876 Election:**

| Presidential Candidate | Party | Electoral Votes | Popular Vote Total | Popular Vote Percentage | Vice-Presidential Candidate |
|---|---|---|---|---|---|
| Rutherford B. Hayes | Republican | 185 | 4,035,924 | 47.9 | William A. Wheeler |
| Samuel J. Tilden | Democratic | 184 | 4,287,670 | 50.9 | Thomas A. Hendricks |
| Peter Cooper | Greenback | — | 82,797 | 1.0 | Samuel F. Carey |

**Comments:** When the returns came in, the 19 electoral votes of South Carolina, Florida, and Louisiana were in dispute. After months of controversy over rival sets of returns, Congress established an electoral commission composed of five senators, five representatives, and five members of the Supreme Court to determine the valid returns. The commissioners—eight Republicans and seven Democrats—voted along strict party lines to award the 19 votes and the Presidency to Hayes.

## ELECTION OF 1880

**The Political Scene:** Throughout the entire period of the "Gilded Age," few significant issues divided the two parties. This was particularly true in 1880 when, appealing to the veteran vote, both Republicans and Democrats nominated former generals.
**Conventions and Nominees:** The Republicans met in Chicago in June to choose "dark horse" James A. Garfield of Ohio on the 36th ballot, after reform or "Mugwump" delegates had blocked a proposed third term for Grant and a drive for James G. Blaine had collapsed. Chester A. Arthur of New York was named for the Vice-Presidency. Winfield S. Hancock of Pennsylvania and William H. English of Indiana comprised the ticket selected by the Democrats at Cincinnati in June. The Greenback party nominated a third general, James B. Weaver of Iowa, with B. J. Chambers of Texas named for the Vice-Presidency.
**The Campaign:** Personal attacks on the candidates characterized the campaign. The Democrats emphasized Garfield's involvement in the Crédit Mobilier Scandal, while the Republicans harped on Hancock's inexperience and naiveté.

**Results of 1880 Election:**

| Presidential Candidate | Party | Electoral Votes | Popular Vote Total | Popular Vote Percentage | Vice-Presidential Candidate |
|---|---|---|---|---|---|
| James A. Garfield | Republican | 214 | 4,454,433 | 48.3 | Chester A. Arthur |
| Winfield S. Hancock | Democratic | 155 | 4,444,976 | 48.2 | William English |
| James B. Weaver | Greenback | — | 308,649 | 3.3 | B. J. Chambers |

**Comments:** In July 1881 Charles J. Guiteau, a deranged and disappointed office-seeker, shot Garfield, who died on September 19, 1881. Arthur succeeded to the Presidency the following day.

## ELECTION OF 1884

**The Political Scene:** Although President by accident, Arthur made a respectable record in the office. He failed, however, to build up enough support for a nomination in his own right.
**Conventions and Nominees:** Despite a challenge from Arthur, James G. Blaine of Maine succeeded in this his third try for the Republican nomination. The Chicago convention meeting in June then picked John A. Logan of Illinois as his running mate. The Democrats convening in Chicago on July 8 nominated Grover Cleveland of New York and Thomas A. Hendricks of Indiana.
**The Campaign:** In what has been remembered as the dirtiest campaign in American history, Cleveland was charged with fathering an illegitimate child, and Blaine was abused for alleged shady practices while Speaker of the House. Many prominent "Mugwump" Republicans refused to support Blaine and endorsed Cleveland.

**Results of 1884 Election:**

| Presidential Candidate | Party | Electoral Votes | Popular Vote Total | Popular Vote Percentage | Vice-Presidential Candidate |
|---|---|---|---|---|---|
| Grover Cleveland | Democratic | 219 | 4,875,971 | 48.5 | Thomas A. Hendricks |
| James G. Blaine | Republican | 182 | 4,852,234 | 48.3 | John A. Logan |
| Benjamin F. Butler | Greenback | — | 175,066 | 1.7 | A. M. West |
| John P. St. John | Prohibition | — | 150,957 | 1.5 | William Daniel |

**Comments:** Just prior to election day, one of Blaine's supporters referred to the Democrats as the party of "Rum, Romanism and Rebellion," a slur on Irish Catholic voters that probably caused Blaine to lose New York State and, hence, the election.

## ELECTION OF 1888

**The Political Scene:** Cleveland's firm, honest, and conservative administration gained him a great deal of respect, but at the same time offended powerful pressure groups such as the Grand Army of the Republic and the tariff protectionists.
**Conventions and Nominees:** The Democrats renominated Cleveland by acclamation in St. Louis in June. Allen G. Thurman of Ohio joined him on the ticket. In a convention marked with much intrigues and bargaining, the Republicans named Benjamin Harrison of Indiana and Levi P. Morton of New York at Chicago in June.
**The Campaign:** The Democrats condemned the inequities of the high protective tariff. The Republicans replied that the system of protection served the interests of America over those of Europe.

**Results of 1888 Election:**

| Presidential Candidate | Party | Electoral Votes | Popular Vote Total | Popular Vote Percentage | Vice-Presidential Candidate |
|---|---|---|---|---|---|
| Benjamin Harrison | Republican | 233 | 5,445,269 | 47.8 | Levi P. Morton |
| Grover Cleveland | Democratic | 168 | 5,540,365 | 48.6 | Allen G. Thurman |
| Clinton B. Fisk | Prohibition | — | 250,122 | 2.2 | John A. Brooks |
| Aaron J. Streeter | Union Labor | — | 147,606 | 1.3 | C. E. Cunningham |

**Comments:** The Republicans managed to turn part of the Irish vote against Cleveland, when, on a pretext, a foolish letter favoring Cleveland over Harrison was obtained from the British Minister in Washington.

## ELECTION OF 1892

**The Political Scene:** Popular anger with veteran and tariff legislation combined with a growing militancy among farmers to hand the Republicans a stunning defeat in the midterm elections of 1890 and brighten Democratic prospects for regaining the Presidency.
**Conventions and Nominees:** Both parties met in June, the Democrats at Chicago and the Republicans at Minneapolis, to renominate their standard-bearers of 1888—Cleveland and Harrison. For the Vice-Presidency, the Democrats chose Adlai E. Stevenson of Illinois; the Republicans, Whitelaw Reid of New York. The Populist or People's party held its first national nominating convention at Omaha in July, endorsing James B. Weaver of Iowa and James G. Field of Virginia.
**Campaign Issues:** Debate centered on controversial measures of the Harrison administration together with the demand for the free and unlimited coinage of silver and the general agrarian unrest.

**Results of 1892 Election:**

| Presidential Candidate | Party | Electoral Votes | Popular Vote Total | Popular Vote Percentage | Vice-Presidential Candidate |
|---|---|---|---|---|---|
| Grover Cleveland | Democratic | 277 | 5,556,982 | 46.0 | Adlai E. Stevenson |
| Benjamin Harrison | Republican | 145 | 5,191,466 | 43.0 | Whitelaw Reid |
| James B. Weaver | Populist | 22 | 1,029,960 | 8.5 | James G. Field |
| John Bidwell | Prohibition | — | 271,111 | 2.2 | James B. Cranfill |

**Comments:** The Populists became the first third party since 1860 to win any electoral votes.

## ELECTION OF 1896

**The Political Scene:** The Panic of 1893 struck with full force after Cleveland's inauguration, and the subsequent "hard times" were blamed on the Democrats. It appeared possible that the Populists could replace the Democrats as the second major party.
**Conventions and Nominees:** The Republican convention at St. Louis in June nominated William McKinley of Ohio on the first ballot and Garrett Hobart of New Jersey as his running mate. The Democrats meeting at Chicago in July named William Jennings Bryan of Nebraska on the fifth ballot. Arthur Sewall of Maine was selected for the Vice-Presidential nomination. The Populists at their St. Louis convention in July accepted Bryan, but named Thomas E. Watson of Georgia for the Vice-Presidency.
**The Campaign:** Bryan's stand for the "free and unlimited coinage of silver" brought down on him the fury of the country's conservative interests. McKinley conducted a "front porch" campaign, but a strenuous and expensive effort was carried on in his behalf under the direction of Mark Hanna.

**Results of 1896 Election:**

| Presidential Candidate | Party | Electoral Votes | Popular Vote Total | Popular Vote Percentage | Vice-Presidential Candidate |
|---|---|---|---|---|---|
| William McKinley | Republican | 271 | 7,113,734 | 51.0 | Garret Hobart |
| William J. Bryan | Democratic-Populist | 176 | 6,516,722 | 46.7 | Arthur Sewall / Thomas E. Watson |
| John M. Palmer | National Democratic | — | 135,456 | .97 | Simon Buckner |
| Joshua Levering | Prohibition | — | 131,285 | .94 | Hale Johnson |

**Comments:** Bryan, whose "Cross of Gold" speech is perhaps the most famous ever made at a convention, failed to win any of the nation's industrial states, indicating the limited appeal of the free-silver issue.

## ELECTION OF 1900

**The Political Scene:** The successful conclusion of the Spanish-American War and returning prosperity buoyed Republican hopes for another Presidential victory.
**Conventions and Nominees:** At the Republicans' Philadelphia convention in June, McKinley was unanimously renominated and war hero Theodore Roosevelt of New York was selected for the Vice-Presidency. The Democrats met at Kansas City, Missouri, in July to choose Bryan again. Adlai E. Stevenson of Illinois was named for Vice-President. This year Eugene V. Debs of Indiana received the first of his five Presidential nominations by the Socialist party.
**The Campaign:** Theodore Roosevelt did most of the campaigning for the Republican ticket, stressing the "full dinner pail" of McKinley prosperity and the national pride in territories acquired from Spain. Bryan once more endorsed free silver, but called imperialism the paramount issue. He also criticized the growth of the giant trusts.

**Results of 1900 Election:**

| Presidential Candidate | Party | Electoral Votes | Popular Vote Total | Popular Vote Percentage | Vice-Presidential Candidate |
|---|---|---|---|---|---|
| William McKinley | Republican | 292 | 7,219,828 | 51.7 | Theodore Roosevelt |
| William J. Bryan | Democratic | 155 | 6,358,160 | 45.5 | Adlai E. Stevenson |
| John C. Wolley | Prohibition | — | 210,200 | 1.5 | Henry B. Metcalf |
| Eugene V. Debs | Socialist | — | 95,744 | .7 | Job Harriman |

**Comments:** McKinley, who was shot by anarchist Leon Czolgosz at the Pan-American Exposition in Buffalo, died on September 14, 1901. At the age of 42, Roosevelt became the youngest President in history.

## ELECTION OF 1904

**The Political Scene:** Roosevelt's moderately progressive policies, his energetic regimen, and his obvious relish of the Presidency made him the most popular President since Lincoln.
**Conventions and Nominees:** Mark Hanna's death early in 1904 removed the only man capable of challenging Roosevelt for the Presidential nomination. The Republican convention meeting at Chicago in June gave "T.R." its unanimous vote and chose Charles W. Fairbanks of Indiana to run with him. Having lost twice with the progressive Bryan, the Democrats turned to a more conservative candidate, Judge Alton B. Parker of New York. The convention, which met at St. Louis in July, then named Henry G. Davis of West Virginia for Vice-President.
**The Campaign:** Parker, who endorsed the gold standard, was portrayed by the Democrats as a safe, conservative candidate. A colorless figure, he could not hope to match Roosevelt's popular appeal.

**Results of 1904 Election:**

| Presidential Candidate | Party | Electoral Votes | Popular Vote Total | Popular Vote Percentage | Vice-Presidential Candidate |
|---|---|---|---|---|---|
| Theodore Roosevelt | Republican | 336 | 7,628,831 | 56.4 | Charles W. Fairbanks |
| Alton B. Parker | Democratic | 140 | 5,084,533 | 37.6 | Henry G. Davis |
| Eugene V. Debs | Socialist | — | 402,714 | 3.0 | Benjamin Hanford |
| Silas C. Swallow | Prohibition | — | 259,163 | 1.9 | George W. Carroll |

**Comments:** After his great victory, Roosevelt announced that he would not be a candidate for a third term, a pledge that was to haunt him in 1912.

## ELECTION OF 1908

**The Political Scene:** Roosevelt, the unchallenged leader of his party, determined to pick his successor. Following Parker's decisive defeat, the Democrats were ready to return to Bryan.

**Conventions and Nominees:** The Republican conclave at Chicago in June ratified Roosevelt's choice of his Secretary of War William Howard Taft of Ohio and named James S. Sherman of New York to run with him. The Democrats meeting at Denver in July picked a ticket of Bryan and John W. Kern of Indiana.

**The Campaign:** In a dull campaign, Bryan promised to revise the tariff downward; Taft replied that he also intended to work for a downward revision.

**Results of 1908 Election:**

| Presidential Candidate | Party | Electoral Votes | Popular Vote Total | Popular Vote Percentage | Vice-Presidential Candidate |
|---|---|---|---|---|---|
| William H. Taft | Republican | 321 | 7,679,114 | 51.6 | James S. Sherman |
| William J. Bryan | Democratic | 162 | 6,410,665 | 43.0 | John W. Kern |
| Eugene V. Debs | Socialist | — | 420,858 | 2.8 | Benjamin Hanford |
| Eugene W. Chafin | Prohibition | — | 252,704 | 1.7 | Aaron S. Watkins |

**Comments:** Bryan was the only major party candidate in American history to run three unsuccessful races for the Presidency.

## ELECTION OF 1912

**The Political Scene:** The opposition of progressive Republicans to Taft's policies led to an open rupture of the party, with Theodore Roosevelt leading the insurgents.

**Conventions and Nominees:** When the Republican convention meeting at Chicago in June decided a contest for disputed delegate seats in favor of Taft, Roosevelt ordered his delegates to abstain from voting. Taft and Sherman were renominated on the first ballot, but Roosevelt's delegates became the nucleus of the Progressive or "Bull Moose" party, which met in Chicago in August to nominate Roosevelt and Hiram Johnson of California. The Democrats convening in Baltimore (June 25–July 2) produced a drawn-out but exciting contest. Champ Clark of Missouri obtained a majority on the 10th ballot but could not reach the necessary two thirds. On the 46th ballot, the delegates chose Woodrow Wilson of New Jersey. Thomas R. Marshall of Indiana was selected for the Vice-Presidency.

**The Campaign:** With Wilson, Roosevelt, and Socialist nominee Eugene V. Debs all campaigning as reform candidates, the voters were asked to decide which man could best implement progressive policies. Wilson's New Freedom program emphasized dissolution of the great trusts and the return to free competition. Roosevelt's New Nationalism stressed regulation of big business by the federal government.

**Results of 1912 Election:**

| Presidential Candidate | Party | Electoral Votes | Popular Vote Total | Popular Vote Percentage | Vice-Presidential Candidate |
|---|---|---|---|---|---|
| Woodrow Wilson | Democratic | 435 | 6,301,254 | 41.8 | Thomas R. Marshall |
| Theodore Roosevelt | Progressive | 88 | 4,127,788 | 27.4 | Hiram Johnson |
| William H. Taft | Republican | 8 | 3,485,831 | 23.1 | { James S. Sherman<br>Nicholas M. Butler |
| Eugene V. Debs | Socialist | — | 901,255 | 6.0 | Emil Seidel |
| Eugene Chafin | Prohibition | — | 209,644 | 1.4 | Aaron S. Watkins |

**Comments:** Three-quarters of the popular vote went to the reform candidates, indicating the strength of the progressive movement in the country. The Republican split insured Wilson's election.

## ELECTION OF 1916

**The Political Scene:** The question of possible American involvement in World War I overshadowed the domestic controversies of the Wilson administration.

**Conventions and Nominees:** The Republicans nominated Charles Evans Hughes of New York and Charles W. Fairbanks of Indiana at their convention at Chicago in June. The Progressive party disintegrated when Theodore Roosevelt refused to be its candidate again. The Democrats at St. Louis in June renominated Wilson and Marshall.

**The Campaign:** The Democrats went before the electorate as the party of peace, using the slogan "Wilson and Peace with Honor, or Hughes with Roosevelt and War." Hughes had the difficult task of reconciling the belligerent Theodore Roosevelt with his antiwar supporters among German-Americans and other groups.

**Results of 1916 Election:**

| Presidential Candidate | Party | Electoral Votes | Popular Vote Total | Popular Vote Percentage | Vice-Presidential Candidate |
|---|---|---|---|---|---|
| Woodrow Wilson | Democratic | 277 | 9,131,511 | 49.3 | Thomas R. Marshall |
| Charles E. Hughes | Republican | 254 | 8,548,935 | 46.1 | Charles W. Fairbanks |
| Allan L. Benson | Socialist | — | 585,974 | 3.2 | George R. Kirkpatrick |
| J. Frank Hanly | Prohibition | — | 220,505 | 1.2 | Ira Landrith |

**Comments:** Wilson's carrying of California's electoral vote proved decisive.

## ELECTION OF 1920

**The Political Scene:** An immense reaction against the idealism of the Wilson years and the sacrifices entailed by World War I characterized the mood of the American people, who were anxious to return to normalcy.

**Conventions and Nominees:** The Republican choice fell upon "dark horse" Warren G. Harding, an Ohio editor, whose selection on the 10th ballot at Chicago on June 12, came after a meeting of party leaders in the famous "smoke-filled room" of the Blackstone Hotel. Calvin Coolidge of Massachusetts, who had won popular acclaim for his opposition to the Boston police strike, received the Vice-Presidential nod.

For the Democrats, Wilson probably desired a third nomination, but his physical incapacity and political unpopularity made this impossible. The San Francisco convention chose a relative unknown in James M. Cox of Ohio on the 44th ballot on July 6th and Franklin D. Roosevelt of New York, the possessor of a magnetic name, as his running mate.

**The Campaign:** The League of Nations was the most debated campaign topic, with Cox supporting American entry into the world body and Harding straddling the issue.

**Results of 1920 Election:**

| Presidential Candidate | Party | Electoral Votes | Popular Vote Total | Popular Vote Percentage | Vice-Presidential Candidate |
|---|---|---|---|---|---|
| Warren G. Harding | Republican | 404 | 16,153,115 | 60.3 | Calvin Coolidge |
| James M. Cox | Democratic | 127 | 9,133,092 | 34.1 | Franklin D. Roosevelt |
| Eugene V. Debs | Socialist | — | 915,490 | 3.4 | Seymour Stedman |
| Parley P. Christensen | Farmer-Labor | — | 265,229 | 1.0 | Max S. Hayes |

**Comments:** The massive Republican victory represented more of a rejection of Wilson and the Democrats than a personal mandate for Harding, who died in office after a scandal-marred administration and was succeeded by Calvin Coolidge on August 3, 1923.

## ELECTION OF 1924

**The Political Scene:** The cautious conservatism and New England frugality of Calvin Coolidge reduced the political capital the Democrats hoped to make out of the Harding administration's scandals.
**Conventions and Nominees:** The Republican convention at Cleveland in June chose Coolidge with Charles G. Dawes of Illinois. The Democratic convention in New York City lasted from June 24 through July 9, and the resulting contest between Alfred E. Smith and William Gibbs McAdoo led to the most ballots ever taken in a Presidential nominating convention. Finally after Smith and McAdoo had withdrawn, the delegates nominated John W. Davis of West Virginia on the 103d ballot. Charles W. Bryan of Nebraska was the Vice-Presidential selection. Dissident farm and labor elements in both parties formed the Progressive party, which named a ticket of Robert M. LaFollette of Wisconsin and Burton K. Wheeler of Montana at a convention held in Cleveland in July.
**The Campaign:** The bitter Democratic convention destroyed what little chance the party had of unseating Coolidge. Both major candidates concentrated their fire on LaFollette rather than each other.

**Results of 1924 Election:**

| Presidential Candidate | Party | Electoral Votes | Popular Vote Total | Popular Vote Percentage | Vice-Presidential Candidate |
|---|---|---|---|---|---|
| Calvin Coolidge | Republican | 382 | 15,719,921 | 54.0 | Charles G. Dawes |
| John W. Davis | Democratic | 136 | 8,386,704 | 28.8 | Charles W. Bryan |
| Robert M. LaFollette | Progressive | 13 | 4,832,532 | 16.6 | Burton K. Wheeler |

**Comments:** LaFollette won the electoral vote of Wisconsin.

## ELECTION OF 1928

**The Political Scene:** In the summer of 1927, Coolidge announced "I do not choose to run for President . . ." Despite the efforts of a "draft Coolidge" movement, most Republicans were willing to turn to another candidate.
**Conventions and Nominees:** The Republicans met at Kansas City, Missouri, in June and nominated a ticket of Herbert Hoover of California and Charles Curtis of Kansas. The Democrats meeting at Houston in June needed only one ballot to name Alfred E. Smith of New York for the Presidency and Joseph T. Robinson of Arkansas for the Vice-Presidency.
**The Campaign:** Smith, who differed with Hoover on the issues of prohibition, public power, and agriculture, found it difficult to make a dent in the public satisfaction with Republican prosperity.

**Results of 1928 Election:**

| Presidential Candidate | Party | Electoral Votes | Popular Vote Total | Popular Vote Percentage | Vice-Presidential Candidate |
|---|---|---|---|---|---|
| Herbert C. Hoover | Republican | 444 | 21,437,277 | 58.22 | Charles Curtis |
| Alfred E. Smith | Democratic | 87 | 15,007,698 | 40.8 | Joseph T. Robinson |
| Norman M. Thomas | Socialist | — | 265,583 | .7 | James Maurer |

**Comments:** Smith, the first Roman Catholic candidate nominated by a major party, lost many votes particularly in the South because of his religion, but gained many others for the same reason in the Northeast and Midwest.

## ELECTION OF 1932

**The Political Scene:** The Wall Street crash of 1929 and the subsequent economic depression made a Democratic victory almost certain and quickened the race for the party's nomination.
**Conventions and Nominees:** The Republicans meeting at Chicago in June renominated Hoover and Curtis. The Democrats held their convention during the same month in the same city. Franklin D. Roosevelt of New York, who had outdistanced a large field of contenders in the preconvention maneuvering, was nominated on the fourth ballot with John N. Garner of Texas as his running mate.
**The Campaign:** Roosevelt promised the country a New Deal and a willingness to experiment with different approaches in an effort to end the economic crisis. Hoover warned of even greater difficulties if the Democrats won.

**Results of 1932 Election:**

| Presidential Candidate | Party | Electoral Votes | Popular Vote Total | Popular Vote Percentage | Vice-Presidential Candidate |
|---|---|---|---|---|---|
| Franklin D. Roosevelt | Democratic | 472 | 22,829,501 | 57.4 | John Nance Garner |
| Herbert C. Hoover | Republican | 59 | 15,760,684 | 39.6 | Charles Curtis |
| Norman M. Thomas | Socialist | — | 884,649 | 2.2 | James Maurer |

**Comments:** Roosevelt's landslide victory carried into office many Democratic Congressmen who were to help implement his program.

## ELECTION OF 1936

**The Political Scene:** New Deal policies enraged political conservatives, but gained the Democrats many new supporters.
**Conventions and Nominees:** Delegates convening in Cleveland in June named a Republican ticket of Alfred M. Landon of Kansas and Frank Knox of Illinois. The Democrats met later in the month at Philadelphia to renominate Roosevelt and Garner by acclamation. The convention also abolished the two-thirds rule for choosing candidates, making a simple majority sufficient. Father Charles E. Coughlin, Dr. Francis Townsend, and Gerald L. K. Smith, all radical critics of the New Deal, formed the Union party at Cleveland in August and nominated William Lemke of North Dakota and Thomas C. O'Brien of Massachusetts.
**The Campaign:** The Republicans attacked Roosevelt and the New Deal for allegedly building a giant and wasteful bureaucracy. Roosevelt was content to run on his record.

**Results of 1936 Election:**

| Presidential Candidate | Party | Electoral Votes | Popular Vote Total | Popular Vote Percentage | Vice-Presidential Candidate |
|---|---|---|---|---|---|
| Franklin D. Roosevelt | Democratic | 523 | 27,757,333 | 60.8 | John Nance Garner |
| Alfred M. Landon | Republican | 8 | 16,684,231 | 36.5 | Frank Knox |
| William Lemke | Union | — | 892,267 | 2.0 | Thomas C. O'Brien |

**Comments:** Roosevelt won the most sweeping electoral victory in modern history, carrying every state but Maine and Vermont.

## ELECTION OF 1940

**The Political Scene:** With the outbreak of World War II in 1939, American neutrality once again became the dominant political issue in an election year.
**Conventions and Nominees:** The Republicans convened in Philadelphia in June. A tremendous groundswell of public opinion for Wendell L. Willkie of New York enabled him to overcome the early lead of Thomas E. Dewey and Robert A. Taft and win the nomination on the sixth ballot. His running mate was Charles L. McNary of Oregon. Roosevelt won his third nomination from the Democratic convention held in Chicago in July. At his insistence, Henry Wallace of Iowa replaced Garner for the Vice-Presidency.
**The Campaign:** The Democratic platform and Roosevelt were pledged against participation in foreign wars, except in

case of attack. Willkie endorsed most New Deal measures and did not differ substantially from Roosevelt on foreign policy, but he stressed that Roosevelt's attempt to win a third term threatened democratic government.

**Results of 1940 Election:**

| Presidential Candidate | Party | Electoral Votes | Popular Vote Total | Popular Vote Percentage | Vice-Presidential Candidate |
|---|---|---|---|---|---|
| Franklin D. Roosevelt | Democratic | 449 | 27,313,041 | 54.7 | Henry A. Wallace |
| Wendell L. Willkie | Republican | 82 | 22,348,480 | 44.8 | Charles L. McNary |

**Comments:** Roosevelt, destined to win a fourth term as well, was the only man to win more than two elections or to serve more than eight years as President.

## ELECTION OF 1944

**The Political Scene:** In the nation's third wartime election, Roosevelt benefited from the general reluctance "to change horses in midstream."

**Conventions and Nominees:** The Republicans held their convention at Chicago in June. Thomas E. Dewey of New York received all but one vote on the first ballot, and John W. Bricker of Ohio was the unanimous choice as his running mate. The Democrats convening at Chicago in July once again chose Roosevelt, but Wallace had earned the enmity of many party leaders, and the delegates turned to Harry S. Truman of Missouri for the Vice-Presidency.

**The Campaign:** The Republicans called for new political leadership for the work of peace and reconstruction, but agreed with the Democrats in the necessity of American participation in a postwar international organization.

**Results of 1944 Election:**

| Presidential Candidate | Party | Electoral Votes | Popular Vote Total | Popular Vote Percentage | Vice-Presidential Candidate |
|---|---|---|---|---|---|
| Franklin D. Roosevelt | Democratic | 432 | 25,612,610 | 53.3 | Harry S Truman |
| Thomas E. Dewey | Republican | 99 | 22,017,617 | 45.9 | John W. Bricker |

**Comments:** On April 12, 1945, Roosevelt died and was succeeded on the same day by Truman.

## ELECTION OF 1948

**The Political Scene:** Deep splits within the Democratic party and an apparent public desire for a change portended a Republican victory.

**Conventions and Nominees:** The Republicans meeting at Philadelphia in June again nominated Thomas E. Dewey. Earl Warren of California was the Vice-Presidential choice. The Democrats met in the same city the following month and unenthusiastically nominated a ticket of Truman and Alben W. Barkley of Kentucky. Several Southern delegations that were opposed to the party's civil rights platform bolted the convention and named a States' Rights or "Dixiecrat" ticket of Strom Thurmond of South Carolina for President and Fielding L. Wright of Mississippi for Vice-President. A fourth party, the Progressive, which was composed largely of liberal and left-wing Democrats critical of Truman's foreign policy, ran Henry A. Wallace of Iowa and Glenn Taylor of Idaho.

**The Campaign:** A distinct underdog because of the Dixiecrat and Progressive tickets, Truman undertook a vigorous campaign in which he castigated the Republican-controlled 80th Congress as a "do nothing" one. Dewey, who was indicated the certain winner in the public opinion polls, conducted a very cool and careful campaign.

**Results of 1948 Election:**

| Presidential Candidate | Party | Electoral Votes | Popular Vote Total | Popular Vote Percentage | Vice-Presidential Candidate |
|---|---|---|---|---|---|
| Harry S Truman | Democratic | 303 | 24,179,345 | 49.6 | Alben W. Barkley |
| Thomas E. Dewey | Republican | 189 | 21,991,291 | 45.1 | Earl Warren |
| J. Strom Thurmond | States' Rights | 39 | 1,176,125 | 2.4 | Fielding L. Wright |
| Henry A. Wallace | Progressive | — | 1,157,326 | 2.4 | Glenn Taylor |

**Comments:** Truman's upset victory reflected his ability to hold almost the entire labor and Negro vote and to carry the key Midwestern farm states of Ohio, Iowa, and Wisconsin.

## ELECTION OF 1952

**The Political Scene:** Truman announced early in the year that he would not be a candidate for a third term. In any case, the Korean War had dimmed his prospects of reelection.

**Conventions and Nominees:** General Dwight D. Eisenhower beat off the strong challenge of Robert A. Taft to win the nomination of the Republican convention that was held in Chicago in July. Richard M. Nixon of California received the Vice-Presidential designation. The Democrats convened in Chicago later in the same month and named a ticket of Adlai E. Stevenson of Illinois and John J. Sparkman of Alabama.

**The Campaign:** The Republicans used the slogan "Communism, Korea, and corruption," and Eisenhower promised a personal visit to Korea. Stevenson, a first-rate campaigner, was nonetheless forced on the defensive.

**Results of 1952 Election:**

| Presidential Candidate | Party | Electoral Votes | Popular Vote Total | Popular Vote Percentage | Vice-Presidential Candidate |
|---|---|---|---|---|---|
| Dwight D. Eisenhower | Republican | 442 | 33,936,234 | 55.1 | Richard M. Nixon |
| Adlai E. Stevenson | Democratic | 89 | 27,314,992 | 44.4 | John J. Sparkman |

**Comments:** Eisenhower carried the Republicans to victory in both houses of Congress, marking the only time since 1931 or after that the party has controlled the executive and legislative branches of government at the same time.

## ELECTION OF 1956

**The Political Scene:** Suffering a serious heart attack in September 1955, Eisenhower waited until the end of February 1956 before announcing that he would run for a second term.

**Conventions and Nominees:** Senator Estes Kefauver of Tennessee conducted an extensive primary campaign; however, he withdrew in favor of Stevenson a week before the Democrats met in Chicago in August. Kefauver then won a spirited contest with John F. Kennedy for the Vice-Presidency. The Republicans meeting in San Francisco in August renominated Eisenhower and Nixon.

**The Campaign:** Stevenson proposed the possibility of ending the draft system and an agreement with the Soviet Union on Cold War issues. In addition, the Democrats referred to Eisenhower's health and the possibility of Nixon's succession to the Presidency. The Republicans emphasized the "peace and prosperity" of the Eisenhower years.

**Results of 1956 Election:**

| Presidential Candidate | Party | Electoral Votes | Popular Vote Total | Popular Vote Percentage | Vice-Presidential Candidate |
|---|---|---|---|---|---|
| Dwight D. Eisenhower | Republican | 457 | 35,590,472 | 57.4 | Richard M. Nixon |
| Adlai E. Stevenson | Democratic | 73 | 26,022,752 | 42.0 | Estes Kefauver |
| Walter B. Jones | No party | 1 | — | — | — |

**Comments:** Eisenhower became the first winning Presidential candidate since Zachary Taylor in 1848 to fail to carry his party to victory in either the House of Representatives or the Senate.

## ELECTION OF 1960

**The Political Scene:** The mood of the country was somewhat restive, primarily because of economic recessions in 1953, 1957, and 1960, but also because of increasing disquiet over issues relating to civil rights and race relations.

**Conventions and Nominations:** John F. Kennedy of Massachusetts entered several Presidential primaries to disprove alleged liabilities of his youth and his Roman Catholic religion; victories in key contests in Wisconsin and West Virginia assured his first ballot victory at the Democratic Convention in Los Angeles (July 11–15), where he chose Lyndon B. Johnson of Texas as his running mate. Vice-President Richard Nixon of California easily overcame a challenge from Nelson Rockefeller of New York to win a first ballot endorsement from the Republican National Convention at Chicago (July 25–28).

**The Campaign:** Nixon emphasized the unity, strength, and stability that he claimed the Republicans had given the country during the previous eight years. Kennedy complained of stagnation and apathy in Washington and decline of American prestige abroad, promising to get the country moving again and, particularly, to revitalize the economy.

**Results of 1960 Election:**

| Presidential Candidate | Party | Electoral Votes | Popular Vote Total | Popular Vote Percentage | Vice-Presidential Candidate |
|---|---|---|---|---|---|
| John F. Kennedy .................... | Democratic | 303 | 34,226,731 | 49.7 | Lyndon B. Johnson |
| Richard M. Nixon .................... | Republican | 219 | 34,108,157 | 49.5 | Henry Cabot Lodge |
| Harry F. Byrd .................... | No party | 15 | 440,298 | .6 | — |

**Comments:** Kennedy built his victory on the large industrial states of the Northeast and key states in the South, where Johnson's candidacy helped. Kennedy was assassinated on November 22, 1963, in Dallas by Lee Harvey Oswald.

## ELECTION OF 1964

**The Political Scene:** In less than a year in office, Lyndon Johnson had compiled a record of legislative achievements that put him in excellent position for the campaign.

**Conventions and Nominees:** The Republican convention meeting at San Francisco in July witnessed the first victory for the conservative wing of the party in over a generation with the nomination of Barry M. Goldwater of Arizona. William Miller of New York was selected as his running mate. The Democrats convened at Atlantic City in August to nominate Johnson and Hubert H. Humphrey of Minnesota, both of whom were named by acclamation.

**The Campaign:** The Democrats were happy to run on the record of the Kennedy-Johnson administration, while depicting Goldwater as a dangerous reactionary, Goldwater assailed the Johnson administration for permitting a decline in government morality and efficiency and a deterioration of national prestige abroad.

**Results of 1964 Election:**

| Presidential Candidate | Party | Electoral Votes | Popular Vote Total | Popular Vote Percentage | Vice-Presidential Candidate |
|---|---|---|---|---|---|
| Lyndon B. Johnson .................... | Democratic | 486 | 43,129,484 | 61.1 | Hubert H. Humphrey |
| Barry M. Goldwater .................... | Republican | 52 | 27,178,188 | 38.5 | W. E. Miller |

**Comments:** Johnson gained a larger percentage of the popular vote than any candidate in modern times. Only Franklin Roosevelt in 1936 received more electoral votes.

## ELECTION OF 1968

**The Political Scene:** On March 31, Johnson announced he would not seek reelection following repeated attacks on his Vietnam war policy. Sen. Robert F. Kennedy was assassinated in June following his victory in the California primary. Ronald Reagan and Nelson Rockefeller challenged Richard Nixon for the Republican nomination.

**Conventions and Nominees:** The Republicans met in Miami in August and nominated Richard Nixon on the first ballot. Spiro T. Agnew was chosen for the Vice-Presidency. At a Chicago convention marred by much turbulence, the Democrats chose Hubert H. Humphrey of Minnesota; Edmund S. Muskie of Maine was the Vice-Presidential nominee. George C. Wallace of Alabama ran as Presidential candidate of the American Independent Party among other designations.

**The Campaign:** Nixon promised an honorable conclusion of the Vietnam war and the restoration of law and order throughout the country. Humphrey pledged to seek a political solution to the struggle in Vietnam and promised to work toward ending divisiveness in American life. Wallace, an extreme conservative, appeared to hope to force the election into the House of Representatives, where his electors might hold the balance of power.

**Results of 1968 Election:**

| Presidential Candidate | Party | Electoral Votes | Popular Vote Total | Popular Vote Percentage | Vice-Presidential Candidate |
|---|---|---|---|---|---|
| Richard M. Nixon .................... | Republican | 301 | 31,785,480 | 43.4 | Spiro T. Agnew |
| Hubert H. Humphrey .................. | Democratic | 191 | 31,275,165 | 42.7 | Edmund S. Muskie |
| George C. Wallace .................. | American Independent | 46 | 9,906,473 | 13.5 | Curtis E. LeMay |

**Comments:** Nixon received the lowest percentage of the popular vote for a successful candidate since 1912.

## ELECTION OF 1972

**The Political Scene:** The first Nixon administration reveled in its diplomatic gains abroad, while attempting to diminish the domestic problems of unemployment and inflation. The Democrats attacked Nixon's record on domestic affairs, along with hurling charges against the Committee to Reelect the President, accused of masterminding a break-in at the Democratic headquarters in the Watergate complex.

**Conventions and Nominees:** The Democrats met in Miami, Florida, in July and nominated Sen. George McGovern on the first ballot. His choice for Vice-President, Sen. Thomas F. Eagleton of Missouri, was endorsed by the convention's acclamation. Eagleton resigned from the ticket in late August, however, and was replaced by R. Sargent Shriver of Maryland. The Republicans met in Miami in August, and the incumbents were nominated without opposition.

**The Campaign:** Nixon did little active campaigning, using his spectacular trips to Moscow and Peking to give him exposure. McGovern had come from behind to win the Democratic nomination, but his campaign never regained its momentum when his first running mate, Sen. Thomas Eagleton, withdrew following disclosures that he had undergone shock treatment for depression. The Democrats were defeated in a near-record landslide.

**Results of 1972 Election:**

| Presidential Candidates | Party | Electoral Votes | Popular Vote Total | Popular Vote Percentage | Vice-Presidential Candidate |
|---|---|---|---|---|---|
| Richard M. Nixon ...................... | Republican | 520 | 47,167,319 | 60.7 | Spiro T. Agnew |
| George S. McGovern .................... | Democratic | 17 | 29,169,504 | 37.5 | R. Sargent Shriver |
| John G. Schmitz ...................... | American | — | 1,102,963 | 1.4 | Thomas J. Anderson |
| John Hospers ......................... | Libertarian | 1 | 2,691 | — | Theodora Nathan |

**Comments:** Division among the Democrats, with many party conservatives turning to Nixon, contributed to the Republican victory, along with apparent voter apathy regarding the Watergate issue.

## 1976 PRESIDENTIAL ELECTION RESULTS

| State | Electoral Vote | Popular Vote | | | | Percentages | | | |
|---|---|---|---|---|---|---|---|---|---|
| | | Carter | Ford | McCarthy | Other | Carter | Ford | McCarthy | Other |
| Alabama | 9 | 659,170 | 504,070 | — | 19,610 | 56 | 43 | — | 1 |
| Alaska | 3 | 44,058 | 71,555 | — | 7,961 | 36 | 58 | — | 6 |
| Arizona | 6 | 295,602 | 418,642 | 19,229 | 9,246 | 40 | 56 | 3 | 1 |
| Arkansas | 6 | 498,604 | 267,903 | 639 | 389 | 65 | 35 | — | — |
| California | 45 | 3,742,284 | 3,882,244 | 26,047 | 10,314 | 48 | 50 | — | 2 |
| Colorado | 7 | 460,801 | 584,278 | — | 179,242 | 43 | 54 | 2 | 1 |
| Connecticut | 8 | 647,895 | 719,261 | — | 19,199 | 47 | 52 | — | 1 |
| Delaware | 3 | 122,461 | 109,780 | 2,432 | 969 | 52 | 47 | 1 | — |
| Dist. Columbia | 3 | 137,818 | 27,873 | — | 3,139 | 82 | 17 | — | 1 |
| Florida | 17 | 1,636,000 | 1,469,531 | 23,643 | 21,457 | 52 | 47 | 1 | — |
| Georgia | 12 | 979,409 | 483,743 | — | — | 67 | 33 | — | — |
| Hawaii | 4 | 147,375 | 140,003 | — | 3,923 | 51 | 48 | — | 1 |
| Idaho | 4 | 126,549 | 204,151 | — | 10,232 | 37 | 60 | — | 3 |
| Illinois | 26 | 2,271,295 | 2,364,269 | 55,939 | 29,779 | 48 | 50 | 1 | 1 |
| Indiana | 13 | 1,014,714 | 1,185,958 | — | 21,690 | 46 | 53 | — | 1 |
| Iowa | 8 | 619,931 | 632,863 | 20,051 | 6,461 | 48 | 49 | 2 | 1 |
| Kansas | 7 | 430,421 | 502,752 | 13,185 | 11,487 | 45 | 53 | 1 | 1 |
| Kentucky | 9 | 615,717 | 531,852 | 6,837 | 12,736 | 53 | 46 | — | 1 |
| Louisiana | 10 | 661,365 | 587,446 | 6,490 | 22,082 | 52 | 46 | — | 2 |
| Maine | 4 | 232,279 | 236,320 | 10,874 | 3,495 | 48 | 49 | 2 | 1 |
| Maryland | 10 | 759,612 | 672,661 | — | — | 53 | 47 | — | — |
| Massachusetts | 14 | 1,429,475 | 1,030,276 | 65,637 | 22,170 | 56 | 40 | 3 | 1 |
| Michigan | 21 | 1,696,714 | 1,893,742 | 47,905 | 13,229 | 47 | 52 | 1 | — |
| Minnesota | 10 | 1,070,440 | 819,395 | 35,490 | 24,606 | 55 | 42 | 2 | 1 |
| Mississippi | 7 | 381,329 | 366,846 | 4,074 | 16,141 | 50 | 48 | — | 2 |
| Missouri | 12 | 998,387 | 927,443 | 24,029 | 3,741 | 51 | 48 | 1 | — |
| Montana | 4 | 149,259 | 173,703 | — | 5,772 | 45 | 53 | — | 2 |
| Nebraska | 5 | 233,293 | 359,219 | 9,383 | 4,854 | 38 | 59 | 2 | 1 |
| Nevada | 3 | 92,479 | 101,273 | — | 8,124 | 46 | 50 | — | 4 |
| New Hampshire | 4 | 147,645 | 185,935 | 4,095 | 1,952 | 43 | 55 | 1 | 1 |
| New Jersey | 17 | 1,444,653 | 1,509,688 | 32,717 | 27,414 | 48 | 50 | 1 | 1 |
| New Mexico | 4 | 201,148 | 211,419 | — | 4,023 | 48 | 51 | — | 1 |
| New York | 41 | 3,389,558 | 3,100,791 | — | 177,913 | 51 | 46 | — | 3 |
| North Carolina | 13 | 927,365 | 741,960 | — | 8,581 | 55 | 44 | — | 1 |
| North Dakota | 3 | 136,078 | 153,684 | 2,952 | 4,594 | 46 | 52 | — | 2 |
| Ohio | 25 | 2,009,959 | 2,000,626 | 58,267 | 41,604 | 49 | 49 | 1 | 1 |
| Oklahoma | 8 | 532,442 | 545,708 | 14,101 | — | 49 | 50 | 1 | — |
| Oregon | 6 | 490,407 | 492,120 | 40,207 | 7,142 | 48 | 48 | 4 | — |
| Pennsylvania | 27 | 2,328,677 | 2,205,604 | 50,584 | 35,922 | 50 | 48 | 1 | 1 |
| Rhode Island | 4 | 227,636 | 181,249 | — | 1,699 | 55 | 44 | — | 1 |
| South Carolina | 8 | 450,807 | 346,149 | — | 5,627 | 56 | 43 | — | 1 |
| South Dakota | 4 | 147,068 | 151,505 | — | 2,105 | 49 | 50 | — | 1 |
| Tennessee | 10 | 825,879 | 633,969 | 5,004 | 11,494 | 56 | 43 | — | 1 |
| Texas | 26 | 2,082,319 | 1,953,300 | 20,118 | 16,147 | 51 | 48 | 1 | — |
| Utah | 4 | 182,110 | 337,908 | 3,907 | 17,293 | 34 | 62 | 1 | 3 |
| Vermont | 3 | 77,798 | 100,387 | 4,001 | 1,716 | 42 | 55 | 2 | 1 |
| Virginia | 12 | 813,896 | 836,554 | — | 46,644 | 48 | 49 | — | 3 |
| Washington | 9 | 717,323 | 777,732 | 36,986 | 23,493 | 46 | 50 | 2 | 2 |
| West Virginia | 6 | 435,864 | 314,726 | — | — | 58 | 42 | — | — |
| Wisconsin | 11 | 1,040,232 | 1,004,987 | 34,943 | 21,174 | 49 | 48 | 2 | 1 |
| Wyoming | 3 | 62,239 | 92,717 | 624 | 763 | 40 | 59 | — | 1 |
| **Total Popular Votes** | | **40,825,839** | **39,147,770** | **680,390** | **949,348** | | | | |
| **Total Popular Votes, all candidates** | | | **81,603,346** | | | | | | |

**Minor candidates:** Roger McBride (Libertarian Party), 171,627; Lester G. Maddox (American Independent Party), 168,264; Thomas Anderson (American Party), 152,513; Peter Camejo (Socialist Workers Party), 90,287; Gus Hall (Communist Party), 58,692; Margaret Wright (People's Party), 49,014; Lyndon H. LaRouche (U.S. Labor Party), 40,043; Benjamin C. Bubar (Prohibition Party), 15,902; Jules Levin (Socialist Labor Party), 9,322; Frank P. Zeidler (Socialist Party), 5,991; Others, 187,693.

## ELECTION OF 1976

**The Political Scene:** Following the turmoil of the second Nixon administration, with the resignation of Spiro T. Agnew and then Nixon himself, Gerald R. Ford hoped to retain the Presidency, a position to which he had never been elected. The Democrats saw an opportunity to regain the White House by stressing the need for a return to "moral" government, while Eugene J. McCarthy of Minnesota, an independent, campaigned on a platform which called for the abolition of the two-party system, one which he felt made the government less responsive to the will of the people.

**Conventions and Nominees:** In July the Democrats met in New York City, with Jimmy Carter of Georgia virtually assured a first-ballot nomination after a string of primary victories. Walter F. Mondale of Minnesota was chosen the Vice-Presidential nominee. Incumbent Gerald R. Ford of Michigan successfully fought off a conservative challenge by Ronald W. Reagan of California in the Republicans' August convention in Kansas City, Missouri. Robert J. Dole of Kansas was selected by Ford to be his running mate. McCarthy picked Willam Clay Ford of Michigan to share his independent ticket.

**The Campaign:** Ford, as an appointed incumbent, hampered by the aftermath of the Watergate scandals and the 1974 economic recession, was unable to generate enthusiasm and loyalty within the Republican Party, even though he campaigned hard. Carter, an outsider from the Washington political scene, charged Ford with dealing ineffectively with high unemployment, and pledged to create more jobs, consider pardons for Vietnam draft evaders, reorganize the federal government, and develop a national energy policy. His televised debates with Ford helped convince many voters he was of presidential stature.

**RESULTS OF 1976 ELECTION**

| Presidential Candidate | Party | Electoral Votes | Popular Vote Total | Popular Vote Percentage | Vice-Presidential Candidates |
|---|---|---|---|---|---|
| Jimmy Carter | Democratic | 297 | 40,825,839 | 50.0+ | Walter F. Mondale |
| Gerald R. Ford | Republican | 240 | 39,147,770 | 47.9 | Robert J. Dole |
| Ronald Reagan | No Party | 1 | — | — | — |

**Comments:** Carter was the first President elected from a southern state since Zachary Taylor in 1848.

## FINAL 1980 PRESIDENTIAL ELECTION RESULTS

| | | Popular Vote | | | | Percentages | | | |
|---|---|---|---|---|---|---|---|---|---|
| State | Electoral Vote | Reagan | Carter | Anderson | Other | Reagan | Carter | Anderson | Other |
| Alabama | 9 | 654,192 | 636,730 | 16,481 | 34,526 | 49 | 47 | 1 | 3 |
| Alaska | 3 | 86,112 | 41,842 | 11,155 | 19,336 | 55 | 26 | 7 | 12 |
| Arizona | 6 | 529,688 | 246,843 | 76,952 | 20,462 | 61 | 28 | 9 | 2 |
| Arkansas | 6 | 403,164 | 398,041 | 22,468 | 13,909 | 48 | 47 | 3 | 2 |
| California | 45 | 4,522,994 | 3,082,943 | 739,618 | 237,383 | 52 | 36 | 9 | 3 |
| Colorado | 7 | 652,264 | 368,009 | 130,633 | 33,544 | 55 | 31 | 11 | 3 |
| Connecticut | 8 | 677,210 | 541,732 | 171,807 | 15,536 | 48 | 39 | 12 | 1 |
| Delaware | 3 | 111,252 | 105,754 | 16,288 | 2,374 | 47 | 45 | 7 | 1 |
| District of Columbia | 3 | 23,313 | 130,231 | 16,131 | 4,214 | 14 | 75 | 9 | 2 |
| Florida | 17 | 2,046,951 | 1,419,475 | 189,692 | 30,809 | 56 | 38 | 5 | 1 |
| Georgia | 12 | 654,168 | 890,955 | 36,055 | 15,627 | 41 | 56 | 2 | 1 |
| Hawaii | 4 | 130,112 | 135,879 | 32,021 | 5,275 | 43 | 45 | 10 | 2 |
| Idaho | 4 | 290,699 | 110,192 | 27,058 | 9,482 | 67 | 25 | 6 | 2 |
| Illinois | 26 | 2,358,049 | 1,981,413 | 346,754 | 63,505 | 50 | 42 | 7 | 1 |
| Indiana | 13 | 1,255,656 | 844,197 | 111,639 | 30,541 | 56 | 38 | 5 | 1 |
| Iowa | 8 | 676,026 | 508,672 | 115,633 | 17,330 | 51 | 39 | 9 | 1 |
| Kansas | 7 | 566,812 | 326,150 | 68,231 | 18,602 | 58 | 33 | 7 | 2 |
| Kentucky | 9 | 635,274 | 617,417 | 31,127 | 11,809 | 49 | 48 | 2 | 1 |
| Louisiana | 10 | 792,853 | 708,453 | 26,345 | 20,940 | 51 | 46 | 2 | 1 |
| Maine | 4 | 238,522 | 220,974 | 53,327 | 10,188 | 46 | 42 | 10 | 2 |
| Maryland | 10 | 680,606 | 726,161 | 119,537 | 14,192 | 44 | 47 | 8 | 1 |
| Massachusetts | 14 | 1,057,631 | 1,053,802 | 382,539 | 30,118 | 42 | 42 | 15 | 1 |
| Michigan | 21 | 1,915,225 | 1,661,532 | 275,223 | 57,745 | 49 | 43 | 7 | 1 |
| Minnesota | 10 | 873,268 | 954,173 | 174,997 | 49,478 | 43 | 47 | 8 | 2 |
| Mississippi | 7 | 441,089 | 429,281 | 12,036 | 9,344 | 50 | 48 | 1 | 1 |
| Missouri | 12 | 1,074,181 | 931,182 | 77,920 | 16,541 | 51 | 44 | 4 | 1 |
| Montana | 4 | 206,814 | 118,032 | 29,281 | 9,825 | 57 | 32 | 8 | 3 |
| Nebraska | 5 | 419,214 | 166,424 | 44,854 | 9,041 | 66 | 26 | 7 | 1 |
| Nevada | 3 | 155,017 | 66,666 | 17,651 | 4,358 | 64 | 27 | 7 | 2 |
| New Hampshire | 4 | 221,705 | 108,864 | 49,693 | 3,728 | 58 | 28 | 13 | 1 |
| New Jersey | 17 | 1,546,557 | 1,147,364 | 234,632 | 47,131 | 52 | 39 | 8 | 1 |
| New Mexico | 4 | 250,779 | 167,826 | 29,459 | 8,173 | 55 | 37 | 6 | 2 |
| New York | 41 | 2,888,831 | 2,728,372 | 467,801 | 116,955 | 46 | 44 | 8 | 2 |
| North Carolina | 13 | 915,018 | 875,635 | 52,800 | 12,380 | 49 | 47 | 3 | 1 |
| North Dakota | 3 | 193,695 | 79,189 | 23,640 | 4,592 | 64 | 26 | 8 | 2 |
| Ohio | 25 | 2,206,545 | 1,752,414 | 254,472 | 70,172 | 52 | 41 | 6 | 1 |
| Oklahoma | 8 | 695,570 | 402,026 | 38,284 | 13,828 | 61 | 35 | 3 | 1 |
| Oregon | 6 | 571,044 | 456,890 | 112,389 | 41,193 | 48 | 39 | 10 | 3 |
| Pennsylvania | 27 | 2,261,872 | 1,937,540 | 292,921 | 69,168 | 50 | 42 | 6 | 2 |
| Rhode Island | 4 | 154,793 | 198,342 | 59,819 | 3,013 | 37 | 48 | 14 | 1 |
| South Carolina | 8 | 439,277 | 428,220 | 13,868 | 6,893 | 49 | 48 | 2 | 1 |
| South Dakota | 4 | 198,343 | 103,855 | 21,431 | 4,074 | 61 | 32 | 6 | 1 |
| Tennessee | 10 | 787,761 | 783,051 | 35,991 | 10,813 | 49 | 48 | 2 | 1 |
| Texas | 26 | 2,510,705 | 1,881,147 | 111,613 | 38,171 | 55 | 42 | 2 | 1 |
| Utah | 4 | 439,687 | 124,266 | 30,284 | 9,915 | 73 | 20 | 5 | 2 |
| Vermont | 3 | 94,628 | 81,952 | 31,761 | 4,958 | 44 | 39 | 15 | 2 |
| Virginia | 12 | 989,609 | 752,174 | 95,418 | 28,831 | 53 | 40 | 5 | 2 |
| Washington | 9 | 865,244 | 650,193 | 185,073 | 41,884 | 50 | 37 | 11 | 2 |
| West Virginia | 6 | 334,206 | 367,462 | 31,691 | 4,356 | 45 | 50 | 4 | 1 |
| Wisconsin | 11 | 1,088,845 | 981,584 | 160,657 | 42,135 | 48 | 43 | 7 | 2 |
| Wyoming | 3 | 110,700 | 49,427 | 12,072 | 4,514 | 63 | 28 | 7 | 2 |
| **Total Popular Votes** | | **43,893,770** | **35,480,948** | **5,719,222** | **1,402,911** | | | | |
| **Total Popular Votes, all candidates** | | | **86,496,851** | | | | | | |

**Minor candidates:** John B. Anderson (Independent Party), 5,719,222; Ed Clark (Libertarian), 920,049; Barry Commoner (Citizens Party, 232,533; Andrew Pulley (Socialist Workers), 48,650; Guss Hall (Communist Party), 43,896; John R. Rarick (American Independent Party), 41,157; Percy L. Greaves, Jr. (American Party), 14,230; Deirdre Griswold (Workers World Party), 13,213; Benjamin C. Bubar (National Statesman Party), 7,127; David McReynolds (Socialist Party), 6,720; Maureen Smith (Peace and Freedom Party), 18,106; Ellen McCormack (Right to Life Party but known as Respect for Life Party in Kentucky), 32,319; Kurt Lynen (Middle Class Candidate Party), 3,694; Bill Gahres (Down with Lawyers Party), 1,718; Martin Wendelken (Independent [Wendelken] Party), 923; Harley J. McLain (Natural Peoples' League Party), 296.

## ELECTION OF 1980

**The Political Scene:** The Carter Administration was beset with the domestic problems of rampant inflation, high interest rates, and increasing unemployment, and on the foreign scene by the American hostages in Iran and the troublesome Middle East unrest despite the Camp David accords. Republicans and some elements in the Democratic Party criticized Carter for his ineptitude and lack of leadership, and in July 1980 he received a very low rating in a public opinion poll as a president.

**Conventions and Nominees:** The Republicans nominated Ronald Reagan on the first ballot at their convention in Detroit in July. In a surprise move Reagan picked George Bush, who as a presidential contender released his delegates shortly before the convention, as his vice presidential candidate, although momentum had built up behind former President Gerald Ford for the nomination. In August, incumbent Jimmy Carter easily won the nomination at the Democratic convention in New York City (after Edward M. Kennedy ended his candidacy only hours into the convention). Walter F. Mondale was again chosen as Carter's running mate.

**The Campaign:** The Reagan-Bush team campaigned feverishly throughout the states, while Carter, beleaguered by the Iranian hostage problem, campaigned little, leaving it mostly to Mondale, cabinet members and aides. The Reagan-Carter TV debates appeared to enhance Reagan's election chances. John B. Anderson, having lost his bid for the Republican presidential nomination, chose Democrat Patrick J. Lucey to share his Independent ticket.

**RESULTS OF 1980 ELECTION**

| Presidential Candidate | Party | Electoral Votes | Popular Vote Total | Popular Vote Percentage | Vice-Presidential Candidates |
|---|---|---|---|---|---|
| Ronald W. Reagan | Republican | 489 | 43,893,770 | 50.7+ | George H.W. Bush |
| Jimmy Carter | Democrat | 49 | 35,480,948 | 41.0+ | Walter F. Mondale |
| John B. Anderson | Independent* | 0 | 5,719,222 | 6.6 | Patrick J. Lucey |

* In New York, Anderson was the presidential candidate of the Liberal Party.

**Comments:** Carter became the third president (after Hoover and Ford) in modern times to be voted out of office after a single term.

## THE WHITE HOUSE OFFICE—1982 The White House, 1600 Pennsylvania Avenue, N.W., Washington, D.C. 20500

Counsellor to the President .......... Edwin Meese III
Chief of Staff and Assistant to the President ......... James A. Baker III
Deputy Chief of Staff and Assistant to the President ......... Michael K. Deaver
Assistant to the President and Press Secretary ................. James S. Brady
Assistant to the President for National Security Affairs .......... William P. Clark
Assistant to the President and Deputy to the Chief of Staff .... Richard G. Darman
Assistant to the President for Public Liaison .................. Elizabeth H. Dole
Assistant to the President for Legislative Affairs ............... Kenneth M. Duberstein
Counsel to the President ............ Fred F. Fielding
Assistant to the President for Cabinet Affairs ............... Craig L. Fuller
Assistant to the President for Communications ................ David R. Gergen
Assistant to the President for Policy Development .............. Edwin L. Harper
Assistant to the President and Director of Special Support Services Edward V. Hickey, Jr.
Deputy Counsellor to the President .... James E. Jenkins
Assistant to the President for Political Affairs ................ Edward J. Rollins
Assistant to the President for Presidential Personnel ............ Helene A. von Damm
Assistant to the President for Intergovernmental Affairs ......... Richard S. Williamson
Deputy Assistant to the President for Political Affairs ............... Lee Atwater
Deputy Assistant to the President and Director of Speechwriting ......... Aram Bakshian, Jr.
Deputy Assistant to the President and Director of Public Affairs ...... Michael Baroody
Deputy Assistant to the President for Public Liaison ............... Red Cavaney
Assistant Counsellor to the President .. T. Kenneth Cribb, Jr.
Deputy Counsel to the President ...... Richard A. Hauser
Deputy Assistant to the President for Intergovernmental Affairs ...... Alan F. Holmer
Deputy Assistant to the President for National Security Affairs ....... Robert C. McFarlane
Deputy Assistant to the President and Deputy to the Deputy Chief of Staff ...................... Michael A. McManus
Deputy Assistant to the President for Legislative Affairs (House) ...... M. B. Oglesby
Deputy Assistant to the President for Policy Development and Director of the Office of Policy Development ................... Roger B. Porter
Deputy Assistant to the President for Management and Director of the Office of Administration ..... John F. W. Rogers
Deputy Assistant to the President ..... James S. Rosebush
Deputy Assistant to the President and Deputy Press Secretary to the President ...................... Larry M. Speakes
Deputy Assistant to the President and Director of Media Relations and Planning ................... Karna Small Stringer
Deputy Assistant to the President for Legislative Affairs (Senate) ..... Pamela J. Turner
Deputy Assistant to the President for National Security Affairs ....... Charles P. Tyson
Deputy Press Secretary to the President ...................... Lyndon K. Allin
Special Assistant to the President and Director of Planning and Evaluation . Richard S. Beal
Special Assistant to the President for Communications ................ Joanna E. Bistany
Special Assistant to the President for Public Liaison ............... Morton C. Blackwell
Special Assistant to the President for Policy Development ........... Danny J. Boggs
Special Assistant to the President for Public Liaison .............. Robert F. Bonitati
Special Assistant to the President for Policy Development ........... Melvin B. Bradley
Special Assistant to the President for Public Liaison and Deputy Director of the Office of Public Liaison ....................... John F. Burgess
Special Assistant to the President for Policy Development ........... Robert B. Carleson
Special Assistant to the President and Special Assistant to the Chief of Staff ......................... James W. Cicconi
Associate Counsel to the President .... Sherrie M. Cooksey
Special Assistant to the President and Chief Speechwriter ........... Anthony Dolan
Special Assistant to the President for Legislative Affairs ............ John H. Dressendorfer
Special Assistant to the President for Public Liaison and Director of the 50 States Project .......... Thelma Duggin
Special Assistant to the President and Director, Office of Cabinet Affairs ... Becky Norton Dunlop
Personal Photographer to the President ...................... Michael A. W. Evans
Special Assistant to the President ..... David C. Fischer
Associate Counsel to the President .... Harold P. Goldfield
Special Assistant to the President for Policy Development ........... Wendell W. Gunn
Special Assistant to the President and Director of Presidential Advance William Henkel
Special Assistant to the President and Director of Correspondence .... Anne Higgins
Special Assistant to the President for Policy Development ........... Kevin R. Hopkins
Special Assistant to the President for Public Liaison ............... Dee Ann Jepsen
Special Assistant to the President for Legislative Affairs ............ Robert J. Kabel
Special Assistant to the President for Public Liaison ............... Virginia H. Knauer
Curator ......................... Clement E. Conger
Physician to the President ........... Daniel Ruge, M.D.
Chief Usher ...................... Rex W. Scouten

## U.S. GOVERNMENT OFFICIALS: ANNUAL SALARIES Source: Office of Personnel Management

| Executive Branch | | Legislative Branch | | Judicial Branch | |
|---|---|---|---|---|---|
| President | $200,000 | Speaker of the House | $79,125 | Chief Justice | $96,800 |
| Vice-President | 84,700 | President Pro Tem (Senate) | 68,575 | Associate Justices | 93,000 |
| Top Executive Positions[1] | | Majority and Minority Leaders | 68,575 | Judges of the U.S. Court of Appeals | 74,300 |
| I | 69,630 | Members of Congress | 60,662.50 | Judges of the U.S. District Court | 70,300 |
| II | 60,662.50 | Comptroller General | 60,662.50 | Director of the Administrative Office of the United States Courts | 70,300 |
| III | 59,500 | Heads of Other Legislative Agencies | 58,500 | | |
| IV | 58,500 | | | | |
| V | 57,500.50 | | | | |

[1] Top Executive positions are in levels I-V, ranging from Secretaries of Executive departments at level I to heads of major bureaus at level V; for a listing, see Sections 5312-5316 of Title 5, United States Code.

## THE U.S. CABINET: 1982

**Secretary of State:** George P. Shultz; b. Dec. 13, 1920, New York, N.Y.; ed. Princeton (B.A., 1942), MIT (Ph.D., 1949). After teaching for several years (1948-57) at MIT, he became Professor of Industrial Relations (1957-68) and later Dean (1962-68) of the Graduate School of Business, Univ. of Chicago. He initially served President Nixon as Secretary of Labor (1969-70), then resigned to become Director, Office of Budget and Manpower (1970-72), then from May 1972 to 1974, he assumed the position of Secretary of the Treasury. From early 1974 to 1982, he was affiliated with a large engineering firm. He assumed his cabinet post as Secretary of State on July 16, 1982.

**Secretary of the Treasury:** Donald T. Regan; b. Dec. 21, 1918, Cambridge, Mass.; ed. Harvard University (B.A., 1940). U.S. Marine Corps (1940-45); investment firm in 1946 as a trainee and then became its chief executive in 1971. Member of the policy committee of the Business Roundtable, the Council on Foreign Affairs, and the Committee for Economic Development. He assumed his cabinet post on Jan. 22, 1981.

**Secretary of Defense:** Caspar W. Weinberger; b. Aug. 18, 1917, San Francisco, Calif.; ed. Harvard College (A.B., 1938), Harvard Law School (LL.B., 1941). U.S. Army (1941-45); law clerk in the U.S. Court of Appeals (1945-47); attorney (1947-59 and 1959-1969); elected delegate to the Assembly of the California State Legislature (1952-58); California's director of finance (1968-1970); chairman of the Federal Trade Commission (Jan.-July 1970); deputy director then director of the Office of Management and Budget (1970-73); U.S. Secretary of Health, Education and Welfare (1973-75); corporate officer in an engineering firm (1975-1980). He assumed his cabinet post on Jan. 21, 1981.

**Attorney General:** William F. Smith; b. Aug. 26, 1917, Wilton, N.H.; ed. University of California (A.B., 1939), Harvard Law School (LL.B., 1942). U.S. Naval Reserve (1942-46); attorney (1946-1980). Member, board of trustees of a number of colleges, universities, educational institutes, and a member of several law organizations. Chairman and vice chairman of the California delegation to the Republican National Convention, in 1968, 1972, 1976 and 1980. He assumed his cabinet post on Jan. 23, 1981.

**Secretary of the Interior:** James G. Watt; b. Jan. 31, 1938, Lusk, Wyo.; ed. College of Commerce and Industry, University of Wyoming (1960). University of Wyoming Law School (J.D., 1962). Personal assistant, legislative assistant and counsel to the former U.S. Senator Simpson of Wyoming; secretary of the National Resources Committee and the Environmental Pollution Advisory Counsel; U.S. Chamber of Commerce (1966-69); special assistant, deputy assistant secretary, and then director of the Bureau of Outdoor Recreation, U.S. Department of the Interior (1969-1975); commissioner of the Federal Power Commission (1975-77), vice chairman of the Federal Power Commission (1977); president and chief legal officer of a legal foundation (1977). He assumed his cabinet post on Jan. 23, 1981.

**Secretary of Agriculture:** John R. Block; b. Feb. 15, 1935, Gilson, Ill.; ed. U.S. Military Academy (1957). U.S. Army (1957-1960); operated the family owned farms ever since. Illinois state director of agriculture (1977-1980), during which time he conducted a number of surveys on agriculture in Eastern Europe and the Far East; held offices in a variety of agriculture-related groups and advisory councils. He assumed his cabinet post on Jan. 23, 1981.

**Secretary of Commerce:** Malcolm Baldridge; b. Oct. 4, 1922, Omaha, Neb.; ed. Yale University (B.A., 1944). U.S. Army during World War II. Ranch hand and rodeo circuit rider; foundry foreman in a manufacturing company in 1947 and moved up the ranks before becoming the president in 1960. Corporate officer of another manufacturing company (1962-1980); member of boards of directors of several large corporations; member of the Business Council, the Council on Foreign Relations and the International Chamber of Commerce. He assumed his cabinet post on Jan. 23, 1981.

**Secretary of Labor:** Raymond J. Donovan; b. Aug. 31, 1930, Bayonne, N.J.; ed. Notre Dame Seminary (B.A., 1952). Associated with an insurance company (1953-58); joined construction company beginning in 1959 with primary responsibility for labor relations; member of several labor unions; advisor to several charitable organizations. He assumed his cabinet post on Feb. 4, 1981.

**Secretary of Health and Human Services:** Richard S. Schweiker; b. June 1, 1926, Norristown, Pa.; ed. Pennsylvania State University (B.A., 1950). U.S. Navy (1944-46). Businessman, then president of a construction materials company, beginning in 1950. Elected to the U.S. House of Representatives (1960-69); U.S. Senate (1969-1981). In Congress he was a member of many committees dealing with health matters; delegate or an alternate delegate to the Republican National Conventions in 1962, 1966, 1972, and Republican vice presidential nominee in 1976. He assumed his cabinet post on Jan. 22, 1981.

**Secretary of Housing and Urban Development:** Samuel R. Pierce, Jr.; b. Sept. 8, 1922, Glen Cove, Long Island, N.Y.; ed. Cornell University (1947), Cornell University (LL.B., 1949), New York University School of Law (M.A., 1952). U.S. Army during World War II. Assistant district attorney for New York County (1949); assistant U.S. attorney for the Southern District of New York (1953-55); assistant to the under secretary of the Department of Labor (1955-56); associate counsel and counsel with the Subcommittee on Antitrust of the Committee on the Judiciary of the U.S. House of Representatives (1956-57); judge of the New York Court of General Sessions (1959-60); private law practice (1960-1970) and (1973-1981); general counsel in the U.S. Department of Treasury (1970-73). He assumed his cabinet post on Jan. 23, 1981.

**Secretary of Transportation:** Andrew L. Lewis, Jr; b. Nov. 3, 1931, Philadelphia, Pa.; ed. Haverford College (B.S., 1953), Harvard Graduate School of Business (M.B.A., 1955). Production manager in 1955, then on the board of directors of a manufacturing company; until 1974, he held positions as a corporate officer in several construction materials manufacturing companies, and personnel placement company; trustee of a railroad company (1971-1980). Delegate to the Republican Nat'l Conventions in 1968, 1972, 1976, and 1980; deputy chairman of the Republican Nat'l Comm. (1980). He assumed his cabinet post on Jan. 23, 1981.

**Secretary of Energy:** James B. Edwards*; b. June 24, 1927, Hawthorne, Fla.; ed. College of Charleston (B.S., 1950), University of Louisville School of Dentistry (D.M.D., 1955). U.S. Maritime Service during World War II, U.S. Navy (1955-57), U.S. Naval Reserve (1957-1967). Practiced oral and maxillofacial surgery; elected for one term as a member of the South Carolina Senate in 1972; governor of South Carolina (1975-79); chairman of the National Governors' Association Subcommittee on Nuclear Energy (1978); chairman of the Southern Governors' Conference (1978). Member of several national dental organizations. He assumed his cabinet post on Jan. 23, 1981.

**Secretary of Education:** Terrell H. Bell; b. Nov. 11, 1921, Lava Hot Springs, Idaho; ed. Southern Idaho College of Education (B.A., 1946), University of Idaho (M.S., 1954), University of Utah (Ph.D.-educational administration, 1961). U.S. Marine Corps (1942-46). Athletic coach and teacher in a public high school (1946-47); superintendent of public schools at various times between 1947 and 1976; interim positions as professor and chairman of the Department of Educational Administration and superintendent of public instruction (1962-1970); deputy commissioner for school systems, U.S. Office of Education (1970-71); commissioner of higher education and chief executive officer for the State of Utah (1976-1980). He assumed his cabinet post on Jan. 23, 1981.

* Plans to resign in late 1982 to enter academe.

## FEDERAL EMPLOYMENT† SOURCE: Office of Personnel Management

| | Employees |
|---|---|
| **Total, All Agencies** | **2,846,323** |
| LEGISLATIVE BRANCH | 39,058 |
| Congress | 19,683 |
| Architect of the Capitol | 2,011 |
| General Accounting Office | 5,269 |
| Government Printing Office | 6,248 |
| Library of Congress | 5,172 |
| JUDICIAL BRANCH | 15,522 |
| EXECUTIVE BRANCH | 2,791,743 |
| Executive Office of the President | 1,634 |
| White House Office | 360 |
| Office of the Vice-President | 19 |
| Office of Management and Budget | 662 |
| Council of Economic Advisors | 37 |
| Executive Departments: | |
| State | 23,591 |
| Treasury | 122,846 |
| Defense: | |
| Military, Total | 895,785 |
| Department of the Army | 328,073 |
| Department of the Navy | 327,918 |
| Department of the Air Force | 239,794 |
| Civilian, Total | 112,654 |
| Justice | 54,448 |
| Interior | 74,033 |
| Agriculture | 114,336 |
| Commerce | 35,349 |
| Labor | 19,680 |
| Health and Human Services | 148,298 |
| Housing and Urban Development | 15,139 |
| Transportation | 51,255 |
| Energy | 18,825 |
| Education | 5,962 |
| ACTION | 1,613 |
| Environmental Protection Agency | 12,457 |
| Equal Employment Opportunity Commission | 3,287 |
| Federal Communications Commission | 2,042 |
| Federal Deposit Insurance Corporation | 3,290 |
| Federal Trade Commission | 1,559 |
| General Services Administration | 32,600 |
| International Communication Agency | 7,791 |
| Interstate Commerce Commission | 1,628 |
| National Aeronautics and Space Administration | 22,708 |
| National Labor Relations Board | 2,792 |
| Nuclear Regulatory Commission | 3,554 |
| Office of Personnel Management | 7,385 |
| Securities and Exchange Commission | 1,844 |
| Small Business Administration | 5,093 |
| Smithsonian Institution | 4,219 |
| Tennessee Valley Authority | 45,879 |
| U.S. Postal Service | 663,429 |
| Veterans Administration | 232,347 |

† List includes selected federal agencies with 1,500 or more employees. The total, however, represents all paid civilian employees of the U.S. government. Employees of the CIA, National Security Agency, and Special Youth Programs are not included. Data as of January 1982.

## HEADS OF FEDERAL DEPARTMENTS AND AGENCIES [1] (as of October 12, 1982)

| Departments and Agencies | Head |
|---|---|
| **ACTION** | Thomas W. Pauken |
| 806 Connecticut Avenue N.W. | Director |
| 20525 | |
| **Central Intelligence Agency** | William J. Casey |
| Washington, D.C. 20505 | Director |
| **Civil Aeronautics Board** | Dan McKinnon |
| 1825 Connecticut Ave. N.W. | Chairman |
| 20428 | |
| **Commission on Civil Rights** | Clarence M. Pendleton, Jr. |
| 1121 Vermont Ave. N.W. 20425 | Chairman |
| **Consumer Product Safety Commission** | Nancy H. Steorts |
| 1111 18th St. N.W. 20207 | Chairwoman |
| **Council of Economic Advisors** | Martin S. Feldstein |
| Executive Office Bldg. 20506 | Chairman |
| **Council on Environmental Quality** | A. Alan Hill |
| 722 Jackson Pl. N.W. 20006 | Chairman |
| **Department of Agriculture** | John R. Block |
| 14th St. and Independence Ave. S.W. 20250 | Secretary of Agriculture |
| Deputy Secretary | Richard E. Lyng |
| **Department of Commerce** | Malcolm Baldridge |
| 14th St. between Constitution Ave. and E St. N.W. 20230 | Secretary of Commerce |
| Deputy Secretary | Guy W. Fiske |
| Patent & Trademark Office | Gerald J. Mossinghoff |
| Crystal Plaza, Arlington, Va. | Commissioner |
| Bureau of Economic Analysis | George Jaszi |
| 1401 K St. N.W. 20230 | Director |
| Bureau of the Census | Bruce K. Chapman |
| Suitland, Md. 20233 | Director |
| National Bureau of Standards | Ernest Ambler |
| I-270 & Quince Orchard Rd., Gaithersburg, Md. 20234 | Director |
| National Oceanic and Atmospheric Administration | John V. Byrne |
| 6001 Executive Blvd., Rockville, Md. 20852 | Administrator |
| **Department of Defense** | Caspar W. Weinberger |
| The Pentagon 20301 | Secretary of Defense |
| Deputy Secretary of Defense | Frank C. Carlucci |
| Joint Chiefs of Staff | Gen. John W. Vessey, Jr. |
| | USA Chairman |
| Department of the Air Force | Verne Orr |
| The Pentagon 20330 | Secretary of the Air Force |
| Department of the Army | John O. Marsh, Jr. |
| The Pentagon 20310 | Secretary of the Army |
| Department of the Navy | John F. Lehman, Jr. |
| The Pentagon 20350 | Secretary of the Navy |
| Commandant of the Marine Corps | Gen. Robert H. Barrow |
| **Department of Education** | Dr. Terrel H. Bell |
| 400 Maryland Ave. S.W. 20202 | Secretary of Education |
| Under Secretary | Gary L. Jones** |
| **Department of Energy** | James B. Edwards[2] |
| 1110 Independence Ave. S.W. 20314 | Secretary of Energy |
| Deputy Secretary | W. Kenneth Davis |
| Federal Energy Regulatory Commission | Charles M. Butler, III |
| | Chairman |
| **Department of Health and Human Services** | Richard S. Schweiker |
| 200 Independence Ave. S.W. 20201 | Secretary of Health and Human Services |
| Under Secretary | David B. Swoap |
| Office of Human Development Services | Dorcas R. Hardy |
| | Ass't Sec. for Human Development Services |
| Food and Drug Administrations | Dr. Arthur H. Hayes, Jr. |
| 5600 Fishers Lane, Rockville, Md. 20857 | Commissioner |

| Departments and Agencies | Head |
|---|---|
| National Institutes of Health | Dr. James B. Wyngaarden |
| 9000 Rockville Pike, Bethesda, Md. 20205 | Director |
| Public Health Service | Dr. C. Everett Koop |
| 5600 Fishers Lane, Rockville, Md. 20857 | Surgeon General |
| Social Security Administration | John A. Svahn |
| 6401 Security Blvd., Baltimore, Md. 21235 | Commissioner |
| **Department of Housing and Urban Development** | Samuel R. Pierce, Jr. |
| 451 7th St. S.W. 20410 | Secretary of Housing and Urban Development |
| Under Secretary | Donald I. Hovde |
| **Department of the Interior** | James G. Watt |
| C St. between 18th and 19th Sts. N.W. 20240 | Secretary of the Interior |
| Under Secretary | Donald P. Hodel |
| Bureau of Indian Affairs | Kenneth L. Smith |
| | Ass't Sec.-Indian Affairs |
| Bureau of Mines | Robert C. Horton |
| | Director |
| Geological Survey | Dallas L. Peck |
| | Director |
| National Park Service | Russell E. Dickenson |
| | Director |
| **Department of Justice** | William F. Smith |
| Constitution Ave. and 10th St. N.W. 20530 | Attorney General |
| Deputy Attorney General | Edward C. Schmults |
| Solicitor General | Rex E. Lee |
| F.B.I. | William H. Webster |
| | Director |
| Immigration and Naturalization Service | Alan C. Nelson |
| | Commissioner |
| Drug Enforcement Administration | Francis M. Mullen, Jr.* |
| 1405 I St. N.W. 20537 | Administrator |
| **Department of Labor** | Raymond J. Donovan |
| 200 Constitution Ave. N.W. 20210 | Secretary of Labor |
| Under Secretary | Malcolm R. Lovell, Jr. |
| **Department of State** | George P. Shultz |
| 2201 C St. N.W. 20520 | Secretary of State |
| Deputy Secretary of State | Kenneth W. Dam |
| Chief of Protocol | Selwa Roosevelt |
| **Department of Transportation** | Andrew L. Lewis, Jr. |
| 400 7th St. S.W. 20590 | Secretary of Transportation |
| Deputy Secretary | Darrell M. Trent |
| U.S. Coast Guard | Vice Adm. James S. Gracey, USCG |
| | Commandant |
| Federal Aviation Administration | J. Lynn Helms |
| | Administrator |
| Federal Highway Administration | Ray A. Barnhart |
| | Administrator |
| Federal Railroad Administration | Robert W. Blanchette |
| | Administrator |
| **Department of the Treasury** | Donald T. Regan |
| 15th St. and Pennsylvania Ave. N.W. 20220 | Secretary of the Treasury |
| Deputy Secretary | Richard T. McNamar |
| Commissioner of Customs | William Von Raab |
| Bureau of Engraving and Printing | Harry R. Clements |
| | Director |
| Bureau of the Mint | Donna Pope |
| | Director |
| Internal Revenue Service | Roscoe L. Egger, Jr. |
| | Commissioner |
| Comptroller of the Currency | C. Todd Conover |
| Treasurer of the U.S. | Angela M. Buchanan |
| U.S. Secret Service | John R. Simpson |
| | Director |
| Bureau of Alcohol, Tobacco & Firearms | Stephen Higgens* |
| | Director |

[1]All addresses are Washington, D.C., unless otherwise noted. [2]Plans to resign in late 1982. * Acting ** Named or nominated but without Senate confirmation.

**District of Columbia** ............... Marion Barry
District Building, 14th & E Sts. N.W. 20004 — Mayor of the District of Columbia

**Environmental Protection Agency** ........... Anne McG. Gorsuch
401 M St. S.W. 20460 — Administrator

**Equal Employment Opportunity Commission** ................ Clarence Thomas
2401 E St. N.W. 20506 — Chairman

**Export-Import Bank of the United States** .......... William H. Draper III
811 Vermont Ave. N.W. 20571 — President & Chairman

**Farm Credit Administration** ......... Donald E. Wilkinson
490 L'Enfant Plaza East S.W. 20578 — Governor

**Federal Communications Commission** ........... Mark S. Fowler
1919 M St. N.W. 20554 — Chairman

**Federal Deposit Insurance Corporation** .................. William M. Isaac
550 17th St. N.W. 20429 — Chairman

**Federal Election Commission** ....... Frank P. Reiche
1325 K St. N.W. 20463 — Chairman

**Federal Maritime Commission** ....... Alan Green, Jr.
1100 L St. N.W. 20573 — Chairman

**Federal Mediation and Conciliation Service** ............. Kay McMurray
2100 K St. N.W. 20427 — Director

**Federal Reserve System, Board of Governors of the** ........... Paul A. Volcker
Constitution Ave. and 20th St. N.W. 20551 — Chairman

**Federal Trade Commission** ......... James C. Miller III
Pennsylvania Ave. and 6th St. N.W. 20580 — Chairman

**Foreign Claims Settlement Commission of the U.S.** ......... J. Raymond Bell
1111 20th St. N.W. 20579 — Chairman

**General Accounting Office** .......... Charles A. Bowsher
441 G St. N.W. 20548 — Comptroller General

**General Services Administration** ..... Gerald P. Carmen
18th and F Sts. N.W. 20405 — Administrator
Archivist of the U.S. .............. Robert M. Warner

**Government Printing Office** ......... Danford L. Sawyer
North Capitol and H Sts. N.W. 20401 — Public Printer

**Interstate Commerce Commission** .... Reese H. Taylor, Jr.
12th St. and Constitution Ave. N.W. 20423 — Chairman

**Library of Congress** ............... Daniel J. Boorstin
10 First St. S.E. 20540 — Librarian of Congress

Copyright Office.................. David L. Ladd
Crystal Mall Annex, Arlington, Va. 20559 — Register of Copyrights

**National Aeronautics and Space Administration** ........... James M. Beggs
400 Maryland Ave. S.W. 20546 — Administrator

**National Credit Union Administration** .............. Edgar F. Callahan
1776 G St. N.W. 20456 — Administrator

**National Foundation on the Arts and the Humanities**
National Endowment for the Arts ............. Francis S. M. Hodsell
2401 E St. N.W. 20520 — Chairman

National Endowment for the Humanities ............. William J. Bennett
806 15th St. N.W. 20506 — Chairman

**National Labor Relations Board** ...... John Van de Water
1717 Pennsylvania Ave. N.W. 20570 — Chairman

**National Mediation Board** .......... Robert D. Harris
1425 K St. N.W. 20572 — Chairman

**National Science Foundation** ........ John B. Slaughter
1800 G St. N.W. 20550 — Director

**National Security Council** ........... William P. Clark
Executive Off. Bldg. 20506 — Ass't to the President

**National Transportation Safety Board** ...... James E. Burnett
800 Independence Ave. S.W. 20594 — Chairman

**Nuclear Regulatory Commission** ..... Nunzio J. Palladino
1717 H St. N.W. 20555 — Chairman

**Occupational Safety and Health Review Commission** ...... Robert A. Rowland
1825 K St. N.W. 20006 — Chairman

**Office of Management and Budget** .......... David A. Stockman
Executive Office Building 20503 — Director

**Office of Personnel Management** .... Donald J. Devine
1900 E. St. N.W. 20415 — Director

**Office of Policy Development** ........ Edwin L. Harper
1600 Pennsylvania Ave. N.W. 20500 — Ass't to the Pres. for Development Policy

**Office of Technology Assessment** .... John H. Gibbons
600 Pennsylvania Ave. S.E. 20510 — Director

**Office of the United States Trade Representative** .......... William E. Brock
1800 G St. N.W. 20506 — United States Trade Representative

**Panama Canal Commission** ......... Michael Rhode, Jr.
425 13th St. N.W. 20004 — Secretary

**Postal Rate Commission** ........... Janet D. Steiger
2000 L St. N.W. 20268 — Chairman

**Securities and Exchange Commission** ........... John S. R. Shad
500 N. Capitol St. N.W. 20549 — Chairman

**Selective Service System** ........... Thomas K. Turnage
600 E St. N.W. 20435 — Director

**Small Business Administration** ...... James C. Sanders
1441 L St. N.W. 20416 — Administrator

**Smithsonian Institution** ............. S. Dillon Ripley
1000 Jefferson Drive S.W. 20560 — Secretary

**Synthetic Fuels Corporation U.S.** ..... Edward E. Noble
2121 K St. N.W. 20586 — Chairman

**Tennessee Valley Authority** ......... Charles H. Dean, Jr.
412 1st St. S.E. Knoxville, Tenn. 37902 — Chairman

**United States Arms Control and Disarmament Agency** ......... Eugene V. Rostow
320 21st St. N.W. 20451 — Director

**United States Information Agency** .... Charles Z. Wick
1750 Pennsylvania Ave. N.W. 20547 — Director

**United States International Development Cooperation Agency** .. M. Peter McPherson*
320 21st St. N.W. 20523 — Director

**United States International Trade Commission** .... Alfred E. Eckes, Jr.
701 E St. N.W. 20436 — Chairman

**United States Postal Service** ........ William F. Bolger
475 L'Enfant Plaza West S.W. 20260 — Postmaster General

**Veterans Administration** ............ Robert P. Nimmo[3]
810 Vermont Ave. N.W. 20420 — Administrator

* Acting [3] Resigned but not replaced.

## U.S. CONGRESSIONAL REPRESENTATIVES UNDER EACH APPORTIONMENT: 1790-1980

| State | 1790 | 1800 | 1810 | 1820 | 1830 | 1840 | 1850 | 1860 | 1870 | 1880 | 1890 | 1900 | 1910[1] | 1930 | 1940 | 1950 | 1960 | 1970 | 1980 |
|---|---|---|---|---|---|---|---|---|---|---|---|---|---|---|---|---|---|---|---|
| Alabama | .. | .. | .. | [2]1 | 3 | 5 | 7 | 7 | 6 | 8 | 8 | 9 | 9 | 10 | 9 | 9 | 9 | 8 | 7 | 7 |
| Alaska | .. | .. | .. | .. | .. | .. | .. | .. | .. | .. | .. | .. | .. | .. | .. | [2]1 | 1 | 1 | 1 |
| Arizona | .. | .. | .. | .. | .. | .. | .. | .. | .. | .. | .. | .. | [2]1 | 1 | 2 | 2 | 3 | 4 | 5 |
| Arkansas | .. | .. | .. | .. | [2]1 | 1 | 2 | 3 | 4 | 5 | 6 | 7 | 7 | 7 | 7 | 6 | 4 | 4 | 4 |
| California | .. | .. | .. | .. | .. | [2]2 | 2 | 3 | 4 | 6 | 7 | 8 | 11 | 20 | 23 | 30 | 38 | 43 | 45 |
| Colorado | .. | .. | .. | .. | .. | .. | .. | .. | [2]1 | 1 | 2 | 3 | 4 | 4 | 4 | 4 | 4 | 5 | 6 |
| Connecticut | 5 | 7 | 7 | 7 | 6 | 6 | 4 | 4 | 4 | 4 | 4 | 5 | 5 | 6 | 6 | 6 | 6 | 6 | 6 |
| Delaware | 1 | 1 | 1 | 2 | 1 | 1 | 1 | 1 | 1 | 1 | 1 | 1 | 1 | 1 | 1 | 1 | 1 | 1 | 1 |
| Florida | .. | .. | .. | .. | .. | [2]1 | 1 | 1 | 2 | 2 | 2 | 3 | 4 | 5 | 6 | 8 | 12 | 15 | 19 |
| Georgia | 3 | 2 | 4 | 6 | 7 | 9 | 8 | 8 | 7 | 9 | 10 | 11 | 11 | 12 | 10 | 10 | 10 | 10 | 10 | 10 |
| Hawaii | .. | .. | .. | .. | .. | .. | .. | .. | .. | .. | .. | .. | .. | .. | .. | [2]1 | 2 | 2 | 2 |
| Idaho | .. | .. | .. | .. | .. | .. | .. | .. | .. | [2]1 | 1 | 1 | 2 | 2 | 2 | 2 | 2 | 2 | 2 |
| Illinois | .. | .. | .. | [2]1 | 1 | 3 | 7 | 9 | 14 | 19 | 20 | 22 | 25 | 27 | 27 | 26 | 25 | 24 | 24 | 22 |
| Indiana | .. | .. | .. | [2]1 | 3 | 7 | 10 | 11 | 11 | 13 | 13 | 13 | 13 | 13 | 12 | 11 | 11 | 11 | 11 | 10 |
| Iowa | .. | .. | .. | .. | .. | [2]2 | 2 | 6 | 9 | 11 | 11 | 11 | 11 | 9 | 8 | 8 | 7 | 6 | 6 |
| Kansas | .. | .. | .. | .. | .. | .. | .. | 1 | 3 | 7 | 8 | 8 | 8 | 7 | 6 | 6 | 5 | 5 | 5 |
| Kentucky | .. | 2 | 6 | 10 | 12 | 13 | 10 | 10 | 9 | 10 | 11 | 11 | 11 | 11 | 9 | 9 | 8 | 7 | 7 | 7 |
| Louisiana | .. | .. | .. | [2]1 | 3 | 3 | 4 | 4 | 5 | 6 | 6 | 6 | 7 | 8 | 8 | 8 | 8 | 8 | 8 | 8 |
| Maine | .. | .. | .. | [3]7 | 7 | 8 | 7 | 6 | 5 | 5 | 4 | 4 | 4 | 4 | 3 | 3 | 3 | 2 | 2 | 2 |
| Maryland | 6 | 8 | 9 | 9 | 9 | 8 | 6 | 6 | 5 | 6 | 6 | 6 | 6 | 6 | 6 | 6 | 7 | 8 | 8 | 8 |
| Massachusetts | 8 | 14 | 17 | [3]13 | 13 | 12 | 10 | 11 | 10 | 11 | 12 | 13 | 14 | 16 | 15 | 14 | 14 | 12 | 12 | 11 |
| Michigan | .. | .. | .. | .. | [2]1 | 3 | 4 | 6 | 9 | 11 | 12 | 12 | 13 | 17 | 17 | 18 | 19 | 19 | 18 |
| Minnesota | .. | .. | .. | .. | .. | .. | [2]2 | 2 | 3 | 5 | 7 | 9 | 10 | 9 | 9 | 9 | 8 | 8 | 8 |
| Mississippi | .. | .. | .. | [2]1 | 1 | 2 | 4 | 5 | 5 | 6 | 7 | 7 | 8 | 8 | 7 | 7 | 6 | 5 | 5 | 5 |
| Missouri | .. | .. | .. | .. | 1 | 2 | 5 | 7 | 9 | 13 | 14 | 15 | 16 | 16 | 13 | 13 | 11 | 10 | 10 | 9 |
| Montana | .. | .. | .. | .. | .. | .. | .. | .. | .. | [2]1 | 1 | 1 | 2 | 2 | 2 | 2 | 2 | 2 | 2 |
| Nebraska | .. | .. | .. | .. | .. | .. | .. | [2]1 | 1 | 3 | 6 | 6 | 6 | 5 | 4 | 4 | 3 | 3 | 3 |
| Nevada | .. | .. | .. | .. | .. | .. | .. | [2]1 | 1 | 1 | 1 | 1 | 1 | 1 | 1 | 1 | 1 | 1 | 2 |
| New Hampshire | 3 | 4 | 5 | 6 | 6 | 5 | 4 | 3 | 3 | 3 | 2 | 2 | 2 | 2 | 2 | 2 | 2 | 2 | 2 | 2 |
| New Jersey | 4 | 5 | 6 | 6 | 6 | 6 | 5 | 5 | 5 | 7 | 7 | 8 | 10 | 12 | 14 | 14 | 14 | 15 | 15 | 14 |
| New Mexico | .. | .. | .. | .. | .. | .. | .. | .. | .. | .. | .. | .. | [2]1 | 1 | 2 | 2 | 2 | 2 | 3 |
| New York | 6 | 10 | 17 | 27 | 34 | 40 | 34 | 33 | 31 | 33 | 34 | 34 | 37 | 43 | 45 | 45 | 43 | 41 | 39 | 34 |
| North Carolina | 5 | 10 | 12 | 13 | 13 | 13 | 9 | 8 | 7 | 8 | 9 | 9 | 10 | 10 | 11 | 12 | 12 | 11 | 11 | 11 |
| North Dakota | .. | .. | .. | .. | .. | .. | .. | .. | .. | [2]1 | 1 | 2 | 3 | 2 | 2 | 2 | 2 | 1 | 1 |
| Ohio | .. | .. | [2]1 | 6 | 14 | 19 | 21 | 21 | 19 | 20 | 21 | 21 | 21 | 22 | 24 | 23 | 23 | 24 | 23 | 21 |
| Oklahoma | .. | .. | .. | .. | .. | .. | .. | .. | .. | .. | .. | [2]5 | 8 | 9 | 8 | 6 | 6 | 6 | 6 |
| Oregon | .. | .. | .. | .. | .. | .. | [2]1 | 1 | 1 | 1 | 2 | 2 | 3 | 3 | 4 | 4 | 4 | 4 | 5 |
| Pennsylvania | 8 | 13 | 18 | 23 | 26 | 28 | 24 | 25 | 24 | 27 | 28 | 30 | 32 | 36 | 34 | 33 | 30 | 27 | 25 | 23 |
| Rhode Island | 1 | 2 | 2 | 2 | 2 | 2 | 2 | 2 | 2 | 2 | 2 | 2 | 2 | 3 | 2 | 2 | 2 | 2 | 2 | 2 |
| South Carolina | 5 | 6 | 8 | 9 | 9 | 9 | 7 | 6 | 4 | 5 | 7 | 7 | 7 | 7 | 6 | 6 | 6 | 6 | 6 | 6 |
| South Dakota | .. | .. | .. | .. | .. | .. | .. | .. | .. | [2]2 | 2 | 2 | 3 | 2 | 2 | 2 | 2 | 2 | 1 |
| Tennessee | .. | [2]1 | 3 | 6 | 9 | 13 | 11 | 10 | 8 | 10 | 10 | 10 | 10 | 10 | 9 | 10 | 9 | 9 | 8 | 9 |
| Texas | .. | .. | .. | .. | .. | [2]2 | 2 | 4 | 6 | 11 | 13 | 16 | 18 | 21 | 21 | 22 | 23 | 24 | 27 |
| Utah | .. | .. | .. | .. | .. | .. | .. | .. | .. | .. | [2]1 | 1 | 2 | 2 | 2 | 2 | 2 | 2 | 3 |
| Vermont | .. | 2 | 4 | 6 | 5 | 5 | 4 | 3 | 3 | 3 | 2 | 2 | 2 | 2 | 1 | 1 | 1 | 1 | 1 | 1 |
| Virginia | 10 | 19 | 22 | 23 | 22 | 21 | 15 | 13 | 11 | 9 | 10 | 10 | 10 | 10 | 9 | 9 | 10 | 10 | 10 | 10 |
| Washington | .. | .. | .. | .. | .. | .. | .. | .. | .. | [2]1 | 2 | 3 | 5 | 6 | 6 | 7 | 7 | 7 | 8 |
| West Virginia | .. | .. | .. | .. | .. | .. | .. | .. | 3 | 4 | 4 | 5 | 6 | 6 | 6 | 6 | 5 | 4 | 4 |
| Wisconsin | .. | .. | .. | .. | .. | [2]2 | 3 | 6 | 8 | 9 | 10 | 11 | 11 | 10 | 10 | 10 | 10 | 9 | 9 |
| Wyoming | .. | .. | .. | .. | .. | .. | .. | .. | .. | [2]1 | 1 | 1 | 1 | 1 | 1 | 1 | 1 | 1 | 1 |
| Total | 65 | 106 | 142 | 186 | 213 | 242 | 232 | 237 | 243 | 293 | 332 | 357 | 391 | 435 | 435 | 435 | 437 | 435 | 435 | 435 |

[1] No apportionment was made in 1920. [2] The following representation was added after the several census apportionments indicated when new States were admitted and is included in the above table: First. Tennessee, 1. Second. Ohio, 1. Third. Alabama, 1; Illinois, 1; Indiana, 1; Louisiana, 1; Mississippi, 1. Fifth. Arkansas, 1; Michigan, 1. Sixth. California, 2; Florida, 1; Iowa, 2; Texas, 2; Wisconsin, 2. Seventh. Minnesota, 2; Oregon, 1. Eighth. Nebraska, 1; Nevada, 1. Ninth. Colorado, 1. Tenth. Idaho, 1; Montana, 1; North Dakota, 1; South Dakota, 2; Washington, 1; Wyoming, 1. Eleventh. Utah, 1. Twelfth. Oklahoma, 5. Thirteenth. Arizona, 1; New Mexico, 1. Seventeenth. Alaska, 1; Hawaii, 1. [3] Twenty Members were assigned to Massachusetts, but 7 of these were credited to Maine when that area became a State.

## 97th CONGRESS: January 5, 1981—

Democratic members are in roman, Republicans in *italics*.

### THE HOUSE OF REPRESENTATIVES

Democrats 241; *Republicans* 192; Vacant 2

**Speaker:** Thomas P. O'Neill, Jr., Mass.
**Majority Leader:** James C. Wright, Jr., Texas
**Majority Whip:** Thomas S. Foley, Wash.
**Minority Leader:** *Robert H. Michel*, Ill.
**Minority Whip:** *Trent Lott*, Miss.
**Clerk:** Edmund L. Henshaw, Jr.
**Sergeant at Arms:** Benjamin J. Guthrie
**Parliamentarian:** William Holmes Brown
**Doorkeeper:** James T. Molloy
**Postmaster:** Robert V. Rota
**Press Gallery Superintendent:** Benjamin C. West
**Chaplain:** Rev. James David Ford, D.D.

### THE SENATE

Democrats 45; *Republicans* 54; Independent-Democrat 1

**President:** *George H. W. Bush*
**President Pro Tempore:** *Strom Thurmond*, S.C.
**Majority Leader:** *Howard H. Baker, Jr.*, Tenn.
**Assistant Majority Leader:** *Theodore F. Stevens*, Alaska
**Minority Leader:** Robert C. Byrd, W. Va.
**Minority Whip:** Alan Cranston, Calif.
**Secretary:** William F. Hildenbrand
**Assistant Secretary:** William A. Ridgely
**Sergeant at Arms:** Howard S. Liebengood
**Secretary for the Majority:** Howard O. Greene, Jr.
**Secretary for the Minority:** Terrence E. Sauvain
**Chaplain:** Rev. Richard C. Halverson, LL.D.

## UNITED STATES HOUSE OF REPRESENTATIVES — 1982 ELECTION RESULTS

(as of November 3, 1982)

SOURCE: The Associated Press

### COMPOSITION BY PARTY

| | Pre-election | Post-election |
|---|---|---|
| Democrats | 241 | 266 |
| Republicans | 192 | 164 |
| Vacant | 2 | |
| Undecided as of Nov. 4, 1982 | | 5 |

* = Incumbent D = Democrat L = Liberal C = Conservative Unc = Uncontested
\+ = Winner R = Republican I = Independent RTL = Right to Life
U = Undecided
** = Incumbent from another district.
++ = Served as a Democrat in 97th Congress.

ALABAMA (D 5, R 2)

1st District
Gudac (D) .......... 51,844
Edwards (R)* ....... 85,254+

2nd District
Camp (D) ........... 80,389
Dickinson (R)* ..... 83,203+

3rd District
Nichols (D)* ....... Unc

4th District
Bevill (D)* ........ Unc

5th District
Flippo (D)* ....... 107,701+
Yambrek (R) ........ 23,950

6th District
Erdreich (D) ....... 87,540+
Smith (R)* ......... 73,682

7th District
Shelby (D)* ........ Unc

ALASKA (R 1)

At Large
Carlson (D) ........ 42,670
Young (R)* ......... 105,145+

ARIZONA (D 2, R 3)

1st District
Hegarty (D) ........ 41,174
McCain (R) ......... 88,879+

2nd District
Udall (D)* ......... 74,161+
Laos (R) ........... 28,713

3rd District
Bosch (D) .......... 58,267
Stump (R)* ++ ...... 100,959+

4th District
Earley (D) ......... 44,072
Rudd (R)* .......... 95,401+

5th District
McNulty (D) ........ 83,820+
Kolbe (R) .......... 82,317

ARKANSAS (D 2, R 2)

1st District
Alexander (D)* ..... 123,673+
Banks (R) .......... 67,232

2nd District
George (D) ......... 82,853
Bethune (R)* ....... 96,775+

3rd District
McDougal (D) ....... 69,236
Hammerschmidt (R)* . 133,998+

4th District
Anthony (D)* ....... 121,077+
Leslie (R) ......... 63,639

CALIFORNIA (D 29, R 16)

1st District
Bosco (D) .......... 106,379+
Clausen (R)** ...... 100,500

2nd District
Newmeyer (D) ....... 80,343
Chappie (R)** ...... 114,672+

3rd District
Matsui (D)* ......... Unc

4th District
Fazio (D)* .......... 117,131+
Canfield (R) ........ 66,016

5th District
Burton, P. (D)** .... 101,747+
Marks (R) ........... 70,593

6th District
Boxer (D) ........... 95,592+
McQuaid (R) ......... 87,118

7th District
Miller (D)* ......... 126,376+
Vallely (R) ......... 56,565

8th District
Dellums (D)* ........ 119,436+
Hutchinson (R) ...... 93,704

9th District
Stark (D)* .......... 103,073+
Kennedy (R) ......... 66,357

10th District
Edwards (D)* ........ 75,922+
Herriott (R) ........ 40,687

11th District
Lantos (D)* ......... 109,035+
Royer (R) ........... 75,847

12th District
Lynch (D) ........... 60,318
Zschau (R) .......... 112,395+

13th District
Mineta (D)* ......... 109,785+
Kelly (R) ........... 52,119

14th District
Reed (D) ............ 76,705
Shumway (R)* ........ 132,748+

15th District
Coelho (D)* ......... 84,630+
Bates (R) ........... 45,018

16th District
Panetta (D)* ........ 140,602+
Arnold (R) .......... 24,068

17th District
Tackett (D) ......... 67,576
Pashayan (R)* ....... 79,094+

18th District
Lehman (D) .......... 90,943+
Fondse (R) .......... 58,546

19th District
Frost (D) ........... 65,074
Lagomarsino (R)* .... 110,241+

20th District
Bethea (D) .......... 56,674
Thomas (R)** ........ 120,185+

21st District
Margolis (D) ........ 45,705
Fiedler (R)* ........ 135,808+

22nd District
Goldhammer (D) ...... 45,649
Moorhead (R)* ....... 142,504+

23rd District
Beilenson (D)* ...... 118,533+
Armor (R) ........... 80,299

24th District
Waxman (D)* ......... 86,912+
Zerg (R) ............ 41,151

25th District
Roybal (D)* ......... Unc

26th District
Berman (D) .......... 95,853+
Phillips (R) ........ 64,756

27th District
Levine (D) .......... 106,200+
Christensen (R) ..... 65,895

28th District
Dixon (D)* .......... 101,574+
Goerz (R) ........... 23,955

29th District
Hawkins (D)* ........ 96,017+
MacKaig (R) ......... 24,212

30th District
Martinez (D)* ....... 60,033+
Rousselot (R)** ..... 51,058

31st District
Dymally (D)* ........ 85,307+
Minturn (R) ......... 32,384

32nd District
Anderson (D)* ....... 83,755+
Lungren, B. (R) ..... 56,958

33rd District
Servelle (D) ........ 54,764
Dreier (R)** ........ 110,344+

34th District
Torres (D) .......... 67,569+
Jackson (R) ......... 50,180

35th District
Erwin (D) ........... 51,774
Lewis (R)** ......... 111,293+

36th District
Brown (D)* .......... 76,096+
Stark (R) ........... 64,005

37th District
Cross (D) ........... 67,551
McCandless (R) ...... 103,392+

38th District
Patterson (D)* ...... 72,853+
Dohr (R) ............ 60,349

39th District
Verges (D) .......... 46,129
Dannemeyer (R)* ..... 127,376+

40th District
Haseman (D) ......... 51,900
Badham (R)* ......... 141,112+

41st District
Brandenburg (D) ..... 57,793
Lowery (R)* ......... 137,212+

42nd District
Spellman (D) ....... 57,893
Lungren, D. (R)** .. 139,890+

43rd District
Archer (D) ......... 56,754+
Crean (R) .......... 54,838

44th District
Bates (D) .......... 77,339+
Gissendanner (R) ... 37,637

45th District
Hill (D) ........... 49,343
Hunter (R)** ....... 115,186+

COLORADO (D 3, R 3)

1st District
Schroeder (D)* ..... 91,952+
Decker (R) ......... 56,409

2nd District
Wirth (D)* ......... 98,735+
Buechner (R) ....... 57,840

3rd District
Kogovsek (D)* ...... 89,670+
Wiens (R) .......... 75,615

4th District
Bishop (D) ........ 44,623
Brown (R)* ......... 103,246+

5th District
Cronin (D) ......... 55,338
Kramer (R)* ........ 80,486+

6th District
Hogan (D) .......... 55,192
Swigert (R) ........ 95,513+

CONNECTICUT (D 4, R 2)

1st District
Kennelly (D)* ...... 126,601+
Klein (R) .......... 58,332

2nd District
Gejdenson (D)* ..... 96,202+
Guglielmo (R) ...... 73,283

3rd District
Morrison (D) ....... 89,848+
DeNardis (R)* ...... 88,384

4th District
Phillips (D) ....... 66,321
McKinney (R)* ...... 87,205+

5th District
Ratchford (D)* ..... 99,029+
Hanlon (R) ......... 70,054

6th District
Curry (D) .......... 92,063
Johnson (R) ........ 99,263+

DELAWARE (D 1)

At Large
Carper (D) ......... 98,672+
Evans (R)* ......... 87,063

FLORIDA (D 13, R 6)

1st District
Hutto (D)* ......... 80,707+
Bechtol (R) ........ 28,117

2nd District
Fuqua (D)* ......... 77,905+
McNeil (R) ......... 48,228

3rd District
Bennett (D)* ....... 71,551+
Grimsley (R) ....... 13,359

4th District
Chappell (D)* ...... 81,183+
Gaudet (R) ......... 40,143

5th District
Batchelor (D) ...... 65,296
McCollum (R)* ...... 98,766+

6th District
MacKay (D) ......... 85,783+
Havill (R) ......... 54,019

7th District
Gibbons (D) ........ 83,290+
Ayers (R) .......... 28,711

8th District
Young (R)** ......... Unc

9th District
Sheldon (D) ......... 89,974
Bilirakis (R) ....... 94,288+

10th District
Ireland (D)** ....... Unc

11th District
Nelson (D)** ........ 98,471+
Robinson (R) ........ 40,155

12th District
Culverhouse (D) ..... 73,493
Lewis (R) ........... 81,423+

13th District
Stevens (D) ......... 69,744
Mack (R) ............116,491+

14th District
Mica (D)** ..........128,567+
Mitchell (R) ........ 47,534

15th District
Stack (D) ........... 67,058
Shaw (R)** .......... 89,128+

16th District
Smith, L. (D) ....... 91,601+
Berkowitz (R) ....... 43,261

17th District
Lehman (D)** ........ Unc

18th District
Pepper (D)** ........ 69,853+
Nunez (R) ........... 28,460

19th District
Fascell (D)** ....... 72,174+
Rinker (R) .......... 49,946

GEORGIA (D 7, R 1, U 2)

1st District
Thomas (D) .......... 67,159+
Jones (R) ........... 36,406

2nd District
Hatcher (D) ......... Unc

3rd District
Ray (D) ............. 74,440+
Elliott (R) ......... 30,539

4th District
Levitas (D)* ........ U
Winder (R) .......... U

5th District
Hester (R) .......... U
Steele (R) .......... U

6th District
Wood (D) ............ 50,539
Gingrich (R)* ....... 62,454+

7th District
McDonald (D)* ....... 71,441+
Sellers (R) ......... 45,405

8th District
Rowland (D) ......... Unc

9th District
Jenkins (D)* ........ 85,092+
Sherwood (R) ........ 25,702

10th District
Barnard (D)* ........ Unc

HAWAII (D 2)

1st District
Heftel (D)* ......... Unc

2nd District
Akaka (D)* .......... Unc

IDAHO (R 2)

1st District
LaRocco (D) ......... 74,423
Craig (R)* .......... 86,165+

2nd District
Stallings (D) ....... 76,601
Hansen (R)* ......... 83,910+

ILLINOIS (D 12, R 10)

1st District
Washington (D)* ..... 154,042+
Taliasetto (R) ...... 5,327

2nd District
Savage (D)* ......... 119,763+
Sparks (R) .......... 17,206

3rd District
Russo (D)* .......... 104,693+
Murphy (R) .......... 24,550

4th District
Murer (D) ........... 50,077
O'Brien (R)** ....... 59,936+

5th District
Lipinski (D) ........ 94,134+
Partyka (R) ......... 26,272

6th District
Kennel (D) .......... 40,939
Hyde (R)* ........... 88,493+

7th District
Collins (D)* ........ 102,845+
Cheeks (R) .......... 15,350

8th District
Rostenkowski (D)* ... 113,536+
Hickey (R) .......... 21,717

9th District
Yates (D)* .......... 98,883+
Bertini (R) ......... 46,447

10th District
Chapman (D) ......... 60,633
Porter (R)* ......... 85,968+

11th District
Annunzio (D)* ....... 121,808+
Moynihan (R) ........ 44,733

12th District
De Fosse (D) ........ 37,027
Crane, P.M. (R)* .... 80,478+

13th District
Bily (D) ............ 46,749
Erlenborn (R)** ..... 108,614+

14th District
McGrath (D) ......... 53,862
Corcoran (R)** ...... 98,267+

15th District
Hall (D) ............ 53,331
Madigan (R)** ....... 105,030+

16th District
Schwerdtfeger (D) ... 66,777
Martin (R)* ......... 89,405+

17th District
Evans (D) ........... 93,807+
McMillan (R) ........ 83,793

18th District
Stephens (D) ........ 91,278
Michel (R)* ......... 97,405+

19th District
Gwinn (D) ........... 86,971
Crane, D.B. (R)** ... 94,547+

20th District
Durbin (D) .......... 100,758+
Findley (R)* ........ 99,345

21st District
Price (D)** ......... 88,660+
Gaffner (R) ......... 46,224

22nd District
Simon (D)** ......... 123,474+
Prineas (R) ......... 63,262

INDIANA (D 5, R 5)

1st District
Hall (D) ............ 89,369+
Krieger (R) ......... 66,921

2nd District
Sharp (D)** ........ 106,762+
Van Natta (R) ...... 82,813

3rd District
Bodine (D) ......... 81,671
Hiler (R)* ......... 85,774+

4th District
Miller (D) ......... 58,692
Coats (R)* ......... 107,336+

5th District
Maxwell (D) ........ 66,774
Hillis (R)* ........ 105,959+

6th District
Grabianowski (D) ... 70,421
Burton (R) ......... 129,363+

7th District
Bonney (D) ......... 69,957
Myers (R)* ......... 115,419+

8th District
McCloskey (D) ...... 99,975+
Deckard (R)* ....... 93,654

9th District
Hamilton (D)* ...... 120,591+
Coates (R) ......... 58,541

10th District
Jacobs (D)** ....... 110,443+
Carroll (R) ........ 55,421

IOWA (D 3, R 3)

1st District
Gluba (D) .......... 61,681
Leach (R)* ......... 89,499+

2nd District
Appel (D) .......... 68,536
Tauke (R)* ......... 98,420+

3rd District
Cutler (D) ......... 83,517
Evans (R)* ......... 103,973+

4th District
Smith (D)* ......... 118,354+
Readinger (R) ...... 60,583

5th District
Harkin (D)* ........ 92,982+
Danker (R) ......... 65,181

6th District
Bedell (D)* ........ 101,407+
Bremer (R) ......... 56,553

KANSAS (D 2, R 3)

1st District
Roth (D) ........... 50,978
Roberts (R)* ....... 115,621+

2nd District
Slattery (D) ....... 86,175+
Kay (R) ............ 64,164

3rd District
Kostar (D) ......... 53,218
Winn (R)* .......... 82,007+

4th District
Glickman (D)* ...... 106,157+
Caywood (R) ........ 35,311

5th District
Rowe (D) ........... 47,350
Whittaker (R)* ..... 102,219+

KENTUCKY (D 4, R 3)

1st District
Hubbard (D)* ....... Unc

2nd District
Natcher (D)* ....... 49,571+
Watson (R) ......... 17,561

3rd District
Mazzoli (D)* ....... 91,379+
Brown (R) .......... 45,169

4th District
Mann (D) ........... 61,576
Snyder (R)* ........ 73,572+

5th District
Davenport (D) ...... 28,265
Rogers (R)* ......... 52,951+

6th District
Mills (D) ........... 49,846
Hopkins (R)* ........ 68,895+

7th District
Perkins (D)* ........ 82,194+
Hamby (R) ........... 21,408

LOUISIANA (D 6, R 2)

1st District
Livingston (R)* ..... Unc

2nd District
Boggs (D)* .......... Unc

3rd District
Tauzin (D)* ......... Unc

4th District
Roemer (D)* ......... Unc

5th District
Huckaby (D)* ........ Unc

6th District
Moore (R)* .......... Unc

7th District
Breaux (D)* ......... Unc

8th District
Long (D)* ........... Unc

MAINE (R 2)

1st District
Kerry (D) ........... 119,019
McKernan (R) ........ 125,215+

2nd District
Dunleavy (D) ........ 67,967
Snowe (R)* .......... 134,473+

MARYLAND (D 6, R 2)

1st District
Dyson (D)* .......... 87,292+
Hopkins (R) ......... 38,414

2nd District
Long (D)* ........... 82,184+
Bentley (R) ......... 73,923

3rd District
Mikulski (D)* ....... 107,970+
Scherr (R) .......... 37,626

4th District
Aiken (D) ........... 47,200
Holt (R)* ........... 73,431+

5th District
Hoyer (D)* .......... 82,466+
Guthrie (R) ......... 21,044

6th District
Byron (D)* .......... 99,780+
Bartlett (R) ........ 34,685

7th District
Mitchell (D)* ....... 102,508+
Jones (R) ........... 13,881

8th District
Barnes (D)* ......... 117,722+
Spencer (R) ......... 47,386

MASSACHUSETTS (D 10, R 1)

1st District
Conte (R)* .......... Unc

2nd District
Boland (D)* ......... 118,320+
Swank (R) ........... 44,536

3rd District
Early (D)* .......... Unc

4th District
Frank (D)* .......... 121,632+
Heckler (R)** ....... 82,862

5th District
Shannon (D)* ........ Unc

6th District
Mavroules (D)* ...... 117,565+
Trimarco (R) ........ 85,755

7th District
Markey (D)* ......... 150,414+
Basile (R) .......... 43,043

8th District
O'Neill (D)* ........ 123,121+
McNamara (R) ........ 41,239

9th District
Moakley (D)* ........ 102,452+
Cochran (R) ......... 55,378

10th District
Studds (D)** ........ 137,379+
Conway (R) .......... 62,985

11th District
Donnelly (D) ........ Unc

MICHIGAN (D 12, R 6)

1st District
Conyers (D)* ........ Unc

2nd District
Sallade (D) ......... 52,427
Pursell (R)* ........ 106,379+

3rd District
Wolpe (D)* .......... 96,871+
Milliman (R) ........ 73,224

4th District
Masiokas (D) ........ 56,954
Siljander (R)* ...... 87,499+

5th District
Monsma (D) .......... 87,091
Sawyer (R)* ......... 98,287+

6th District
Carr (D) ............ 84,526+
Dunn (R)* ........... 78,132

7th District
Kildee (D)* ......... 118,538+
Darrah (R) .......... 36,303

8th District
Traxler (D)* ........ Unc

9th District
Warner (D) .......... 61,728
Vander Jagt (R)* .... 112,419+

10th District
Albosta (D)* ........ 101,818+
Reed (R) ............ 65,807

11th District
Bourland (D) ........ 69,193
Davis (R)* .......... 106,085+

12th District
Bonior (D)* ......... 104,166+
Contesti (R) ........ 52,301

13th District
Crockett (D)* ....... 108,396+
Gupta (R) ........... 13,848

14th District
Hertel (D) .......... Unc

15th District
Ford (D)* ........... 94,795+
Moran (R) ........... 33,815

16th District
Dingell (D)* ........ 113,896+
Haskins (R) ......... 39,277

17th District
Levin (D) ........... 115,881+
Rosen (R) ........... 55,462

18th District
Sipher (D) .......... 46,603
Broomfield (R)** .... 133,223+

MINNESOTA (D 5, R 2, U 1)

1st District
Penny (D) ........... 108,953+
Hagedorn (R)** ...... 101,957

2nd District
Nichols (D) ......... 103,635
Weber (R)** ......... 122,815+

3rd District
Saliterman (D) ...... 61,003
Frenzel (R)* ........ 166,771+

4th District
Vento (D)* ......... 153,615+
James (R) .......... 56,062

5th District
Sabo (D)* .......... 136,612+
Johnson (R) ........ 61,146

6th District
Sikorski (D) ....... 109,247+
Erdahl (R)** ....... 105,734

7th District
Wenstrom (D) ....... 106,894 U
Stangeland (R)* .... 107,880 U

8th District
Oberstar (D)* ...... 176,225+
Luce (R) ........... 53,464

MISSISSIPPI (D 3, R 2)

1st District
Whitten (D)* ....... 79,759+
Fawcett (R) ........ 32,418

2nd District
Clark (D) .......... 71,610
Franklin (R) ....... 73,764+

3rd District
Montgomery (D)* .... Unc

4th District
Dowdy (D)* ......... 80,633+
Williams (R) ....... 69,479

5th District
Coate (D) .......... 23,091
Lott (R)* .......... 82,897+

MISSOURI (D 6, R 3)

1st District
Clay (D)* .......... 102,605+
White (R) .......... 52,545

2nd District
Young (D)* ......... 100,773+
Dielmann (R) ....... 77,436

3rd District
Gephardt (D)* ...... 131,528+
Foristel (R) ....... 37,450

4th District
Skelton (D)* ....... 96,375+
Bailey (R)** ....... 79,639

5th District
Wheat (D) .......... 96,059+
Sharp (R) .......... 66,664

6th District
Russell (D) ........ 78,580
Coleman (R)* ....... 97,869+

7th District
Geisler (D) ........ 87,913
Taylor (R)* ........ 89,236+

8th District
Ford (D) ........... 80,989
Emerson (R)** ...... 86,443+

9th District
Volkmer (D)* ....... 99,248+
Mead (R) ........... 63,949

MONTANA (D 1, R 1)

1st District
Williams (D)* ...... 94,707+
Davies (R) ......... 60,222

2nd District
Lyman (D) .......... 62,217
Marlenee (R)* ...... 76,524+

NEBRASKA (R 3)

1st District
Donaldson (D) ...... 45,641
Bereuter (R)* ...... 136,298+

2nd District
Fellman (D) ........ 69,914
Daub (R)* .......... 91,900+

3rd District
Smith (R)* ......... Unc

NEVADA (D 1, R 1)

1st District
Reid (D) ........... 61,931+
Cavnar (R) ......... 45,693

2nd District
Gojack (D) ......... 52,188
Vucanovich (R) ..... 70,273+

NEW HAMPSHIRE (D 1, R 1)

1st District
D'Amours (D)* ...... 76,881+
Smith (R) .......... 61,876

2nd District
Dupay (D) .......... 37,726
Gregg (R)* ......... 92,218+

NEW JERSEY (D 9, R 5)

1st District
Florio (D)* ........ 109,747+
Dramesi (R) ........ 39,225

2nd District
Hughes (D)* ........ 105,014+
Mahoney (R) ........ 48,395

3rd District
Howard (D)* ........ 103,722+
Muhler (R) ......... 60,491

4th District
Merlino (D) ........ 76,532
Smith (R)* ......... 85,496+

5th District
Cammerzell (D) ..... 53,641
Roukema (R)** ...... 104,411+

6th District
Dwyer (D)** ........ 100,645+
Buckler (R) ........ 46,127

7th District
Levin (D) .......... 71,093
Rinaldo (R)** ...... 91,771+

8th District
Roe (D)* ........... 88,279+
Robertson (R) ...... 35,952

9th District
Torricelli (D) ..... 96,828+
Hollenbeck (R)* .... 83,869

10th District
Rodino (D)* ........ 78,444+
Lee (R) ............ 14,889

11th District
Minish (D)* ........ 105,658+
Redington (R) ...... 57,371

12th District
Connor (D) ......... 57,045
Courter (R)** ...... 117,870+

13th District
Callas (D) ......... 66,426
Forsythe (R)** ..... 100,033+

14th District
Guarini (D)* ....... 90,442+
Catrillo (R) ....... 27,379

NEW MEXICO (D 1, R 2)

1st District
Hartke (D) ......... 67,120
Lujan (R)* ......... 74,593+

2nd District
Chandler (D) ....... 50,651
Skeen (R)* ......... 71,324+

3rd District
Richardson (D) ..... 84,438+
Chambers (R) ....... 46,612

NEW YORK (D 20, R 14)

1st District
Eldon (D) .......... 47,226
Carney (R,C,RTL)* .. 80,223+

2nd District
Downey (D)* ........ 85,301+
Costello (R,C) ..... 48,978
VanDenEssen (RTL) .. 3,098

3rd District
Mrazek (D) ......... 90,815+
LeBoutillier (R,C)** 83,053
Bohner (RTL) ....... 4,150

4th District
Zimmerman (D,L) .... 63,161
Lent (R,C)* ........ 104,846+
Dunkle (RTL) ....... 5,753

5th District
Miller (D,L) ....... 66,764
McGrath (R,C)* ..... 100,115+
Boyle (RTL) ........ 4,973

6th District
Addabbo (D,L)** .... 94,327+
Scott (C) .......... 4,735

7th District
Rosenthal (D,L)** .. 81,122+
Lemishow (R,C,RTL) . 23,992

8th District
Scheuer (D,L)** .... 88,507+
Blume (R,C) ........ 10,900

9th District
Ferraro (D)* ....... 73,840+
Weigandt (R) ....... 19,917
Groves (C,RTL) ..... 6,347
Salargo (L) ........ 1,161

10th District
Schumer (D,L)** .... 86,977+
Marks (R,C) ........ 21,165
Bertolotti (RTL) ... 1,931

11th District
Towns (D) .......... 38,314+
Smith (R) .......... 5,248
Giagnacova (L) ..... 1,444
Caesar (C,RTL) ..... 1,321

12th District
Owens (D,L) ........ 43,045+
Katan (R) .......... 3,102
Rosenstroch (C) .... 940
Francis (RTL) ...... 475

13th District
Solarz (D,L)* ...... 66,610+
Nadrowski (R,RTL) .. 14,067
Gay (C) ............ 2,367

14th District
Zeferetti (D)** .... 50,601
Molinari (R,C)** ... 66,781+
Grillo (L) ......... 1,447

15th District
Lall (D,L) ......... 55,061
Green (R)** ........ 64,714+
Van Rossem (C) ..... 1,792

16th District
Rangel (D,L)** ..... 72,999+
Berns (C) .......... 1,225

17th District
Weiss (D,L)** ...... 109,090+
Antonelli (R,C,RTL) . 19,527

18th District
Garcia (D,L)** ..... 54,852+
Pichler (C) ........ 772

19th District
Biaggi (D,L,RTL)** .. Unc

20th District
Ottinger (D)** ..... 84,541+
Fossel (R,C) ....... 63,938
O'Grady (RTL) ...... 3,508

21st District
Strong (D) ......... 36,462
Fish (R,C,RTL) ..... 111,946+

22nd District
Peyser (D)** ....... 69,351
Gilman (R)** ....... 90,407+
Beck (C) ........... 5,188

23rd District
Stratton (D)** ..... 167,440+
Wicks (R) .......... 40,795
Dow (L) ............ 7,878

24th District
Esiason (D,L) ...... 47,988
Solomon (R,C,RTL)** 136,676+

25th District
Maxwell (D) ........ 66,496
Boehlert (R) ....... 87,509+
Thomas (RTL) ....... 2,712

26th District
Landy (D) .......... 46,381
Martin (R,C)** ..... 104,365+

27th District
Lytel (D,L) ........ 77,272
Wortley (R)** ...... 91,942+
Hunter (C) ......... 2,697
Hyrcza (RTL) ....... 1,941

28th District
McHugh (D,L)** ..... 97,886+
Crowley (R,C) ...... 73,580
Masterson (RTL) .... 1,926

29th District
Larsen (D) ......... 45,677
Horton (R)** ....... 115,370+
Lundberg (C) ....... 5,167

30th District
Benet (D) .......... 48,090
Conable (R)** ...... 117,603+
Baxter (C) ......... 3,849
Valone (RTL) ....... 2,860

31st District
Martin (D,L) ....... 43,318
Kemp (R,C)** ....... 131,710+

32nd District
LaFalce (D,L)** .... 114,827+
Walker (R,C) ....... 8,391
Hubbard (RTL) ...... 2,309

33rd District
Nowak (D,L)** ...... 124,632+
Pillich (R,C) ...... 19,673
Gallagher (RTL) .... 3,978

34th District
Lundine (D)** ...... 97,908+
Snyder (R,C) ....... 63,366
Ronan (RTL) ........ 2,428

NORTH CAROLINA (D 9, R 2)

1st District
Jones (D)* ......... 80,049+
McIntyre (R) ....... 17,464

2nd District
Valentine (D) ...... 59,745+
Marin (R) .......... 34,282

3rd District
Whitley (D)* ....... 68,579+
McDaniel (R) ....... 38,911

4th District
Andrews (D)* ....... 70,344+
Cobey (R) .......... 65,050

5th District
Neal (D)* .......... 88,154+
Bagnal (R) ......... 57,037

6th District
Britt (D) .......... 68,689+
Johnston (R)* ...... 58,234

7th District
Rose (D)* .......... 68,523+
Johnson (R) ........ 27,135

8th District
Hefner (D)* ........ 70,900+
Blake (R) .......... 50,869

9th District
Cornelius (D) ....... 47,337
Martin (R)* ......... 64,427+

10th District
Broyhill (R)* ...... Unc

11th District
Clarke (D) .......... 85,378+
Hendon (R)* ......... 84,062

NORTH DAKOTA (D 1)

At Large
Dorgan (D)* ......... 181,854+
Jones (R) ........... 71,466

OHIO (D 10, R 11)

1st District
Luken (D)** ......... 98,977+
Held (R) ............ 52,571

2nd District
Luttmer (D) ......... 67,858
Gradison (R)** ...... 120,807+

3rd District
Hall (D)* ........... Unc

4th District
Moon (D) ............ 57,529
Oxley (R)* .......... 104,995+

5th District
Sherck (D) .......... 70,118
Latta (R)* .......... 86,408+

6th District
Grimshaw (D) ........ 63,506
McEwen (R)* ......... 91,971+

7th District
Tackett (D) ......... 65,602
DeWine (R) .......... 87,763+

8th District
Griffin (D) ......... 49,623
Kindness (R)* ....... 97,620+

9th District
Kaptur (D) .......... 94,929+
Weber (R)* .......... 64,503

10th District
Buchanan (D) ........ 57,796
Miller (R)* ......... 99,639+

11th District
Eckart (D)** ........ 93,092+
Warner (R) .......... 56,578

12th District
Shamansky (D)* ...... 82,326
Kasich (R) .......... 88,600+

13th District
Pease (D)* .......... 92,266+
Martin (R) .......... 53,256

14th District
Seiberling (D)* ..... 113,300+
Mangels (R) ......... 50,376

15th District
Kostelac (D) ........ 46,611
Wylie (R)* .......... 104,416+

16th District
Orenstein (D) ....... 56,761
Regula (R)* ......... 109,408+

17th District
Tablack (D) ......... 80,212
Williams (R)** ...... 98,450+

18th District
Applegate (D)* ...... Unc

19th District
Feighan (D) ......... 111,459+
Anter (R) ........... 72,503

20th District
Oakar (D)* .......... 133,380+
LeJeune (R) ......... 17,715

21st District
Stokes (D)* ......... 132,431+
Shatteen (R) ........ 21,374

OKLAHOMA (D 5, R 1)

1st District
Jones (D)* .......... 76,379+
Freeman (R) ......... 61,704

2nd District
Synar (D)* .......... 111,815+
Striegel (R) ........ 42,297

3rd District
Watkins (D)* ........ 121,667+
Miller (R) .......... 26,343

4th District
McCurdy (D)* ........ 84,202+
Rutledge (R) ........ 44,351

5th District
Lane (D) ............ 42,453
Edwards (R)* ........ 98,976+

6th District
English (D)* ........ 102,851+
Moore (R) ........... 33,520

OREGON (D 3, R 2)

1st District
AuCoin (D)* ......... 114,842+
Moshofsky (R) ....... 98,015

2nd District
Willis (D) .......... 83,865
Smith, B. (R) ....... 104,284+

3rd District
Wyden (D)* .......... 153,248+
Phelan (R) .......... 42,119

4th District
Weaver (D)* ......... 114,983+
Anthony (R) ......... 79,660

5th District
McFarland (D) ....... 98,263
Smith, D. (R)**...... 103,213+

PENNSYLVANIA (D 13, R 9, U 1)

1st District
Foglietta (D)* ...... 100,426+
Marino (R) .......... 37,137

2nd District
Gray (D)* ........... 117,765+
Street (R) .......... 34,299

3rd District
Borski (D) .......... 90,889+
Dougherty (R)** ..... 88,617

4th District
Kolter (D) .......... 100,398+
Atkinson (R)** ...... 64,463

5th District
Burger (D) .......... 44,131
Schulze (R)* ........ 90,585+

6th District
Yatron (D)* ......... 107,976+
Martin (R) .......... 42,129

7th District
Edgar (D)* .......... 105,711+
Joachim (R) ......... 84,902

8th District
Kostmayer (D) ....... 83,145+
Coyne, J.K. (R)* .... 80,942

9th District
Duncan (D) .......... 49,525
Shuster (R)* ........ 92,521+

10th District
Rafalko (D) ......... 49,819
McDade (R)* ......... 103,095+

11th District
Harrison (D) ........ 90,502+
Nelligan (R)* ....... 78,505

12th District
Murtha (D)* ......... 95,479+
Toscano (R) ......... 53,607

13th District
Cunningham (D) ...... 59,632
Coughlin (R)* ....... 108,898+

14th District
Coyne, W.J. (D)*..... 119,127+
Clark (R) ........... 32,582

15th District
Orloski (D) ......... 58,286
Ritter (R)* ......... 79,770+

16th District
Mowery (D) ......... 37,519
Walker (R)* ........ 92,897+

17th District
Hochendoner (D) .... 61,952
Gekas (R) .......... 84,512+

18th District
Walgren (D)* ....... 101,363+
Jacob (R) .......... 84,406

19th District
Becker (D) ......... 41,779
Goodling (R)* ...... 100,935+

20th District
Gaydos (D)* ........ 125,720+
Ray (R) ............ 37,875

21st District
Andrezeski (D) ..... 79,340 U
Ridge (R) .......... 79,822 U

22nd District
Murphy (D)* ........ 122,640+
Paterra (R) ........ 32,034

23rd District
Calla (D) .......... 49,143
Clinger (R)* ....... 92,407+

RHODE ISLAND (D 1, R 1)

1st District
St. Germain (D)* ... 94,497+
Stallwood (R) ...... 59,537

2nd District
Aukerman (D) ....... 72,230
Schneider (R)* ..... 91,413+

SOUTH CAROLINA (D 3, R 3)

1st District
McLeod (D) ......... 51,525
Hartnett (R)* ...... 62,677+

2nd District
Mosely (D) ......... 50,652
Spence (R)* ........ 71,441+

3rd District
Derrick (D)* ....... Unc

4th District
Tyus (D) ........... 40,489
Campbell (R)* ...... 70,090+

5th District
Spratt (D) ......... 69,226+
Wilkerson (R) ...... 33,110

6th District
Tallon (D) ......... 61,183+
Napier (R)* ........ 55,744

SOUTH DAKOTA (D 1)

At Large
Daschle (D)** ...... 144,013+
Roberts (R)** ...... 133,986

TENNESSEE (D 6, R 3)

1st District
Cable (D) .......... 27,655
Quillen (R)* ....... 88,852+

2nd District
Duncan (R)* ........ Unc

3rd District
Bouquard (D)* ...... 85,049+
Byers (R) .......... 49,973

4th District
Cooper (D) ......... 93,506+
Baker (R) .......... 48,610

5th District
Boner (D)* ......... 109,270+
Steinhice (R) ...... 27,109

6th District
Gore (D)** ......... Unc

7th District
Clement (D) ........ 72,230
Sundquist (R) ...... 73,702+

8th District
Jones (D)** ........ 93,818+
Benson (R) ......... 31,525

9th District
Ford (D)** .......... 112,245+
Crawford (R) ....... 40,813

TEXAS (D 21, R 5, U 1)

1st District
Hall, S.D. (D)* ..... Unc

2nd District
Wilson (D)* ......... Unc

3rd District
McNees (D) .......... 28,015
Bartlett (R) ........ 98,704+

4th District
Hall, R.M. (D)* ..... 93,733+
Collumb (R) ......... 33,843

5th District
Bryant (D) .......... 52,049+
Devany (R) .......... 27,102

6th District
Gramm (D)* .......... Unc

7th District
Scroggins (D) ....... 17,839
Archer (R)* ......... 108,635+

8th District
Allee (D) ........... 37,983
Fields (R)* ......... 50,583+

9th District
Brooks (D)* ......... 78,960+
Lewis (R) ........... 35,409

10th District
Pickle (D)* ......... Unc

11th District
Leath (D)* .......... Unc

12th District
Wright (D)* ......... 74,945+
Ryan (R) ............ 34,558

13th District
Hightower (D)* ...... 85,708+
Slover (R) .......... 47,838

14th District
Patman (D)* ......... 76,091+
Wyatt (R) ........... 48,576

15th District
de la Garza (D)* .... Unc

16th District
Coleman (D) ......... 44,024+
Haggerty (R) ........ 36,064

17th District
Stenholm (D)* ....... Unc

18th District
Leland (D)* ......... 67,932+
Pickett (R) ......... 12,087

19th District
Hance (D)* .......... 89,552+
Hicks (R) ........... 19,976

20th District
Gonzalez (D)* ....... Unc

21st District
Stough (D) .......... 34,845
Loeffler (R)* ....... 106,218+

22nd District
Paul (R)* ........... Unc

23rd District
Kazen (D)* .......... 51,273+
Wentworth (R) ....... 41,340

24th District
Frost (D)* .......... 63,206+
Patterson (R) ....... 22,632

25th District
Andrews (D) ......... 63,903+
Faubion (R) ......... 40,063

26th District
Vandergriff (D) ..... 69,797 U
Bradshaw (R) ........ 69,363 U

27th District
Ortiz (D) ........... 66,548+
Luby (R) ............ 35,198

UTAH (R 3)

1st District
Dirks (D) ........... 66,029
Hansen (R)* ......... 111,792+

2nd District
Farley (D) .......... 78,633
Marriott (R)* ....... 91,599+

3rd District
Huish (I) ........... 32,601
Nielson (R) ......... 108,273+

VERMONT (R 1)

At Large
Kaplan (D) .......... 37,922
Jeffords (R)* ....... 112,756+

VIRGINIA (D 4, R 6)

1st District
McGlennon (D) ....... 62,380
Bateman (R) ......... 76,928+

2nd District
Whitehurst (R)* ..... Unc

3rd District
Waldrop (D) ......... 63,467
Bliley (R)* ......... 92,867+

4th District
Sisisky (D) ......... 80,679+
Daniel, R.W. (R)* ... 67,562

5th District
Daniel, Dan (D)* .... Unc

6th District
Olin (D) ............ 68,098+
Miller (R) .......... 66,526

7th District
Dorrier (D) ......... 46,500
Robinson (R)* ....... 76,744+

8th District
Harris (D) .......... 68,057
Parris (R)* ......... 69,616+

9th District
Boucher (D) ......... 76,112+
Wampler (R)* ........ 74,974

10th District
Lechner (D) ......... 75,444
Wolf (R)* ........... 86,389+

WASHINGTON (D 5, R 3)

1st District
Long (D) ............ 56,257
Pritchard (R)* ...... 116,656+

2nd District
Swift (D)* .......... 93,639+
Houchen (R) ......... 63,603

3rd District
Bonker (D)* ......... 91,721+
Quigg (R) ........... 56,267

4th District
Kilbury (D) ......... 40,563
Morrison (R)* ....... 100,771+

5th District
Foley (D)* .......... 103,392+
Sonneland (R) ....... 57,597

6th District
Dicks (D)* .......... 76,913+
Haley (R) ........... 39,911

7th District
Lowry (D)* .......... 118,385+
Dorse (R) ........... 47,949

8th District
Bland (D) ........... 54,818
Chandler (R) ........ 72,554+

WEST VIRGINIA (D 4)

1st District
Mollohan (D) ........ 79,289+
McCuskey (R) ........ 69,933

**continued on bottom of next page**

## UNITED STATES SENATE — 1982 ELECTION RESULTS (as of November 3, 1982)

SOURCE: The Associated Press

| | Pre-election | Offices Contested | Offices Won | Gain or Loss | 98th Congress |
|---|---|---|---|---|---|
| Democrats | 45 | 19 | 19 | 0 | 45 |
| Republicans | 54 | 13 | 13 | 0 | 54 |
| Independents | 1 | 1 | 0 | | |
| Undecided as of Nov. 4, 1982 | | | | | 1 |

* = Incumbent D = Democrat ID = Independent Democrat
\+ = Winner R = Republican L = Liberal
U = Undecided C = Conservative RTL = Right to Life

ARIZONA
DeConcini (D)* ..... 413,951+
Dunn (R) ........... 292,638

CALIFORNIA
Brown (D) .......... 3,441,142
Wilson (R) ......... 3,912,306+

CONNECTICUT
Moffett (D) ........ 493,237
Weicker (R)* ....... 538,678+

DELAWARE
Levinson (D) ....... 83,722
Roth (R)* .......... 105,472+

FLORIDA
Chiles (D)* ........ 1,612,567+
Poole (R) .......... 997,453

HAWAII
Matsunaga (D)* ..... 245,386+
Brown (R) .......... 52,071

INDIANA
Fithion (D) ........ 842,005
Lugar (R)* ......... 991,724+

MAINE
Mitchell (D)* ...... 278,568+
Emery (R) .......... 179,886

MARYLAND
Sarbanes (D)* ...... 691,358+
Hogan (R) .......... 412,610

MASSACHUSETTS
Kennedy (D)* ....... 1,249,014+
Shamie (R) ......... 784,062

MICHIGAN
Riegle (D)* ........ 1,713,220+
Ruppe (R) .......... 1,221,761

MINNESOTA
Dayton (D) ......... 834,967
Durenberger (R)* ... 941,505+

MISSISSIPPI
Stennis (D)* ....... 400,866+
Barbour (R) ........ 227,267

MISSOURI
Woods (D) .......... 755,800
Danforth (R)* ...... 782,485+

MONTANA
Melcher (D)* ....... 166,852+
Williams (R) ....... 128,654

NEBRASKA
Zorinsky (D)* ...... 360,197+
Keck (R) ........... 153,195

NEVADA
Cannon (D)* ........ 114,736
Hecht (R) .......... 120,354+

NEW JERSEY
Lautenberg (D) ..... 1,114,734+
Fenwick (R) ........ 1,050,977

NEW MEXICO
Bingaman (D) ....... 217,507+
Schmitt (R)* ....... 186,175

NEW YORK
Moynihan (D,L) ..... 3,135,096+
Sullivan (R,C,RTL) . 1,669,404

NORTH DAKOTA
Burdick (D)* ....... 160,713+
Knorr (R) .......... 87,804

OHIO
Metzenbaum (D)* .... 1,917,695+
Pfeifer (R) ........ 1,393,472

PENNSYLVANIA
Wecht (D) ......... 1,393,928
Heinz (R)* ........ 2,125,889+

RHODE ISLAND
Michaelson (D) .... 160,639 U
Chafee (R)* ....... 169,362 U

TENNESSEE
Sasser (D)*........ 779,058+
Beard (R) ......... 479,679

TEXAS
Bentsen (D)* ...... 1,802,806+
Collins (R) ....... 1,247,778

UTAH
Wilson (D) ........ 218,895
Hatch (R)* ........ 309,547+

VERMONT
Guest (D) ......... 78,447
Stafford (R)* ..... 83,259+

VIRGINIA
Davis (D) ......... 689,502
Trible (R) ........ 723,875+

WASHINGTON
Jackson (D)* ...... 870,307+
Jewett (R) ........ 306,522

WEST VIRGINIA
Byrd (D)* ......... 382,028+
Benedict (R) ...... 171,432

WISCONSIN
Proxmire (D)* ..... 987,371+
McCallum (R) ...... 526,887

WYOMING
McDaniel (D) ...... 72,453
Wallop (R)* ....... 94,690+

continued from page 176

2nd District
Staggers (D) ....... 87,506+
Hinkle (R) ......... 48,848

3rd District
Wise (D) ........... 81,669+
Staton (R)* ........ 58,914

4th District
Rahall (D)* ........ 90,679+
Harris (R) ......... 21,956

WISCONSIN (D 5, R 4)

1st District
Aspin (D)* ......... 94,445+
Jannson (R) ........ 59,450

2nd District
Kastenmeier (D)* .... 113,204+
Johnson (R) ......... 72,290

3rd District
Offner (D) .......... 75,021
Gunderson (R)* ...... 99,078+

4th District
Zablocki (D)* ....... Unc

5th District
Moody (D) ........... 98,958+
Johnston (R) ........ 54,523

6th District
Loehr (D) ........... 59,741
Petri (R)* .......... 110,375+

7th District
Obey (D)* ........... 121,998+
Zimmerman (R) ....... 57,483

8th District
Clusen (D) .......... 73,935
Roth (R)* ........... 101,023+

9th District
Sensenbrenner (R)* .. Unc

WYOMING (R 1)

At Large
Hommel (D) .......... 49,274
Cheney (R)* ......... 113,213+

## U.S. SENATORS WHOSE TERMS END IN 1985 or 1987

R = Republican D = Democrat

| | | |
|---|---|---|
| ALABAMA | Heflin (D) | 1985 |
| | Denton (R) | 1987 |
| ALASKA | Stevens (R) | 1985 |
| | Murkowski (R) | 1987 |
| ARIZONA | Goldwater (R) | 1987 |
| ARKANSAS | Pryor (D) | 1985 |
| | Bumpers (D) | 1987 |
| CALIFORNIA | Cranston (D) | 1987 |
| COLORADO | Armstrong (R) | 1985 |
| | Hart (D) | 1987 |
| CONNECTICUT | Dodd (D) | 1987 |
| DELAWARE | Bidden (D) | 1985 |
| FLORIDA | Hawkins (R) | 1987 |
| GEORGIA | Nunn (D) | 1985 |
| | Mattingly (R) | 1987 |
| HAWAII | Inouye (D) | 1987 |
| IDAHO | McClure (R) | 1985 |
| | Symms (R) | 1987 |
| ILLINOIS | Percy (R) | 1985 |
| | Dixon (D) | 1987 |
| INDIANA | Quayle (R) | 1987 |
| IOWA | Jepsen (R) | 1985 |
| | Grassley (R) | 1987 |
| KANSAS | Kassenbaum (R) | 1985 |
| | Dole (R) | 1987 |
| KENTUCKY | Huddleston (D) | 1985 |
| | Ford (D) | 1987 |
| LOUISIANA | Johnston (D) | 1985 |
| | Long (D) | 1987 |
| MAINE | Cohen (R) | 1985 |
| MARYLAND | Mathias (R) | 1987 |
| MASSACHUSETTS | Tsongas (D) | 1985 |
| MICHIGAN | Levin (D) | 1985 |
| MINNESOTA | Boschwitz (R) | 1985 |
| MISSISSIPPI | Cochran (R) | 1985 |
| MISSOURI | Eagleton (D) | 1987 |
| MONTANA | Baucus (D) | 1985 |
| NEBRASKA | Exon (D) | 1985 |
| NEVADA | Laxalt (R) | 1987 |
| NEW HAMPSHIRE | Humphrey (R) | 1985 |
| | Rudman (R) | 1987 |
| NEW JERSEY | Bradley (D) | 1985 |
| NEW MEXICO | Domenici (R) | 1985 |
| NEW YORK | D'Amato (R) | 1987 |
| NORTH CAROLINA | Helms (R) | 1985 |
| | East (R) | 1987 |
| NORTH DAKOTA | Andrews (R) | 1987 |
| OHIO | Glenn (D) | 1987 |
| OKLAHOMA | Boren (D) | 1985 |
| | Nickles (R) | 1987 |
| OREGON | Hatfield (R) | 1985 |
| | Packwood (R) | 1987 |
| PENNSYLVANIA | Specter (R) | 1987 |
| RHODE ISLAND | Pell (D) | 1985 |
| SOUTH CAROLINA | Thurmond (R) | 1985 |
| | Hollings (D) | 1987 |
| SOUTH DAKOTA | Pressler (R) | 1985 |
| | Abdnor (R) | 1987 |
| TENNESSEE | Baker (R) | 1985 |
| TEXAS | Tower (R) | 1985 |
| UTAH | Garn (R) | 1987 |
| VERMONT | Leahy (D) | 1987 |
| VIRGINIA | Warner (R) | 1985 |
| WASHINGTON | Gorton (R) | 1987 |
| WEST VIRGINIA | Randolph (D) | 1985 |
| WISCONSIN | Kasten (R) | 1987 |
| WYOMING | Simpson (R) | 1985 |

## GOVERNORS — 1982 ELECTION RESULTS (as of November 3, 1982)

SOURCE: The Associated Press

| | Pre-election | Offices Contested | Offices Won | Gain or Loss | Post-election |
|---|---|---|---|---|---|
| Democrats | 27 | 20 | 27 | + 7 | 34 |
| Republicans | 23 | 16 | 8 | - 8 | 15 |
| Undecided as of Nov. 4, 1982 | | | | | 1 |

* = Incumbent D = Democrat C = Conservative L = Liberal
\+ = Winner R = Republican ID = Independent Democrat
U = Undecided

| State | Candidate | Votes |
|---|---|---|
| ALABAMA | Wallace (D) | 640,796+ |
| | Folmar (R) | 433,492 |
| ALASKA | Sheffield (D) | 73,405+ |
| | Fink (R) | 61,050 |
| ARIZONA | Babbitt (D)* | 455,760+ |
| | Corbet (R) | 236,857 |
| ARKANSAS | Clinton (D) | 436,578+ |
| | White (R) | 358,291 |
| CALIFORNIA | Bradley (D) | 3,722,601 |
| | Deukmejian (R) | 3,775,576+ |
| COLORADO | Lamm (D)* | 626,041+ |
| | Fuhr (R) | 301,845 |
| CONNECTICUT | O'Neill (D)* | 570,476+ |
| | Rome (R) | 497,561 |
| FLORIDA | Graham (D)* | 1,715,164+ |
| | Befalis (R) | 933,181 |
| GEORGIA | Harris (D) | 732,686+ |
| | Bell (R) | 434,204 |
| HAWAII | Ariyoshi (D)* | 141,043+ |
| | Anderson (R) | 81,507 |
| | Fasi (ID) | 89,303 |
| IDAHO | Evans (D)* | 164,851+ |
| | Batt (R) | 161,274 |
| ILLINOIS | Stevenson (D) | 1,762,823 U |
| | Thompson (R)* | 1,771,409 U |
| IOWA | Conlin (D) | 482,858 |
| | Branstad (R) | 546,324+ |
| KANSAS | Carlin (D)* | 405,285+ |
| | Hardage (R) | 339,397 |
| MAINE | Brennan (D)* | 280,664+ |
| | Cragin (R) | 172,696 |
| MARYLAND | Hughes (D)* | 692,832+ |
| | Pascal (R) | 424,247 |
| MASSACHUSETTS | Dukakis (D) | 1,221,589+ |
| | Sears (R) | 749,306 |
| MICHIGAN | Blanchard (D) | 1,558,417+ |
| | Headlee (R) | 1,358,231 |
| MINNESOTA | Perpich (D) | 1,046,657+ |
| | Whitney (R) | 715,398 |
| NEBRASKA | Kerrey (D) | 274,517+ |
| | Thone (R)* | 267,026 |
| NEVADA | Bryan (D) | 128,133+ |
| | List (R)* | 100,138 |
| NEW HAMPSHIRE | Gallen (D)* | 132,503 |
| | Sununu (R) | 145,650+ |
| NEW MEXICO | Anaya (D) | 215,650+ |
| | Irick (R) | 190,521 |
| NEW YORK | Cuomo (D,L) | 2,617,352+ |
| | Lehrman (R,C) | 2,452,881 |
| OHIO | Celeste (D) | 1,979,388+ |
| | Brown (R) | 1,303,414 |
| OKLAHOMA | Nigh (D)* | 548,089+ |
| | Daxon (R) | 332,137 |
| OREGON | Kulongoski (D) | 366,767 |
| | Atiyeh (R)* | 624,343+ |
| PENNSYLVANIA | Ertel (D) | 1,754,567 |
| | Thornburgh (R)* | 1,868,219+ |
| RHODE ISLAND | Garrahy (D)* | 237,807+ |
| | Marzullo (R) | 76,076 |
| SOUTH CAROLINA | Riley (D)* | 466,347+ |
| | Workman (R) | 201,002 |
| SOUTH DAKOTA | O'Connor (D) | 81,487 |
| | Janklow (R)* | 195,653+ |
| TENNESSEE | Tyree (D) | 502,098 |
| | Alexander (R)* | 736,461+ |
| TEXAS | White (D) | 1,683,608+ |
| | Clements (R)* | 1,455,020 |
| VERMONT | Kunin (D) | 73,852 |
| | Snelling (R)* | 91,383+ |
| WISCONSIN | Earl (D) | 896,343+ |
| | Kohler (R) | 663,065 |
| WYOMING | Herschler (D)* | 106,424+ |
| | Morton (R) | 62,119 |

## STANDING CONGRESSIONAL COMMITTEES

### HOUSE OF REPRESENTATIVES

**Agriculture:** Agriculture and forestry in general, price stabilization, farm credit and security, crop insurance, meat and livestock inspections, soil conservation, and rural electrification.

**Appropriations:** Appropriation of money for the support of the government.

**Armed Services:** Matters relating to the national military establishment; Selective Service.

**Banking, Finance and Urban Affairs:** Financial matters other than taxes and appropriations, including price, commodity, rent, or services controls; deposit insurance, the Federal Reserve System.

**Budget:** To set ceilings for overall government spending.

**District of Columbia:** Municipal affairs (except appropriations) of the District.

**Education and Labor:** Measures relating to education and labor, including child labor and convict labor; wages and hours; arbitration of labor disputes; the school-lunch program.

**Foreign Affairs:** U.S. relations with other governments; the UN and international monetary organizations; the diplomatic service, foreign loans; interventions and declarations of war.

**Government Operations:** Budget and accounting measures other than appropriations; relationships of federal government with states and municipalities; reports of Comptroller General.

**House Administration:** General administration of the House and the Library of Congress.

**Interior and Insular Affairs:** Public lands in general; forest reserves and national parks; the Geological Survey; public mineral resources; irrigation; insular possessions; and American Indian affairs.

**Interstate and Foreign Commerce:** Commerce, communications, and transportation (except water transportation); interstate power transmission; railroad commerce and labor; civil aeronautics; inland waterways; petroleum and natural gas; securities and exchanges; public health; and the Weather Bureau.

**Judiciary:** Judicial proceedings in general; federal courts and judges; Constitutional amendments; civil rights; interstate compacts; immigration and naturalization; apportionment of representatives; Presidential succession; the Patent Office; bankruptcy, mutiny; protection of trade and commerce.

**Merchant Marine and Fisheries:** The merchant marine in general; navigation and pilotage laws; regulation of common carriers by water; the Coast Guard; the National Ocean Survey; oversees the activities of the Panama Canal Commission; fisheries and wildlife.

**Post Office and Civil Service:** Postal service and federal civil service; the census and collection of statistics; and the National Archives.

**Public Works and Transportation:** Public buildings and roads; flood control; improvement of rivers and harbors; public works for navigation, including bridges and dams; water power; and pollution of navigable waters.

**Rules:** Rules and order of business of the House; recesses and final adjournments of Congress; creation of committees.

**Science and Technology:** Scientific and astronautical research and development in general; the National Aeronautics and Space Administration and Council; the National Science Foundation; the Bureau of Standards.

**Small Business:** Assistance to and protection of small businesses.

**Standards of Official Conduct:** Regulations and standards for members, officers, and employees of the House.

**Veterans' Affairs:** Veterans' measures in general; pensions, armed forces life insurance, rehabilitation and education; and veterans' hospitals.

**Ways and Means:** Revenue and tax measures in general; customs; federal Social Security; reciprocal trade agreements.

### SENATE

**Agriculture, Nutrition, and Forestry:** Agriculture in general, including meat and livestock inspection, farm credit and security, soil conservation, crop insurances, and rural electrification; forestry and forest reserves.

**Appropriations:** Appropriation of money for the support of the government.

**Armed Services:** Matters relating to the national military establishment; the Panama Canal Commission.

**Banking, Housing, and Urban Affairs:** Financial matters other than appropriations and taxes; deposit insurance; Federal Reserve System.

**Budget:** To set ceilings for overall government spending.

**Commerce, Science, and Transportation:** Interstate and foreign commerce; merchant marine and navigation; Coast Guard; oceans, weather; fish and wildlife conservation; consumer product regulation; Bureau of Standards; science, engineering, and technology research and development.

**Energy and Natural Resources:** Energy policy, regulation, conservation, research and development; nuclear and solar energy.

**Environment and Public Works:** Environmental policy; water resources; flood control; public works; pollution control; highway construction and maintenance.

**Finance:** Revenue and tax matters in general; customs; reciprocal trade agreements; tariffs; import quotas; Social Security.

**Foreign Relations:** Relations with foreign nations, as well as treaties; interventions and declarations of war; diplomatic service; the U.N. and international monetary organizations.

**Governmental Affairs:** Budget and accounting measures other than appropriations; executive branch reorganizations; Comptroller General reports; postal service; census.

**Judiciary:** Judicial proceedings; federal courts and judges; Constitutional amendments; the Patent Office; immigration and naturalization; bankruptcy; apportionment of representatives.

**Labor and Human Resources:** Education, health, and public welfare; labor; aging; arts and humanities.

**Rules and Administration:** General administration of the Senate; federal elections; management of Library of Congress.

**Small Business:** Assistance to and protection of small businesses.

**Veterans' Affairs:** Veterans' hospitals, education, compensation, and welfare.

## CONGRESSIONAL JOINT COMMITTEES, COMMISSIONS AND BOARDS

Joint Committees on: Library, Printing, Taxation
Joint Economic Committee
Commission on Art and Antiquities of U.S. Senate
Commission on National Development in Postsecondary Education
Commission on Security and Cooperation in Europe
Commission on Wartime Relocation and Internment of Civilians
Consumer Product Safety Commission
Distric of Columbia Law Revision Commission
House Commission on Congressional Mailing Standards
House Office Building Commission
Japan United States Friendship Commission
Migratory Bird Conservation Commission
National Commission on Alcoholism and Other Alcohol-Related Problems
National Commission for Employment Policy
National Commission on Air Quality
National Commission of Social Security Reform
President's Commission on Mental Retardation
Senate Office Building Commission
Environmental Study Conference
North Atlantic Assembly
The Interparliamentary Union
Board for International Broadcasting
Board of Visitors to the Air Force Academy
Board of Visitors to the Coast Guard Academy
Board of Visitors to the Merchant Marine Academy
Board of Visitors to the Military Academy
Board of Visitors to the Naval Academy

## MEMBERS OF THE U.S. SUPREME COURT

SOURCE: Supreme Court of the United States and other sources

| | Place of Birth | Year of Birth | Education | Appointed by President | Date Oath Taken | Age at Oath | Date Service Ended | Service Ended By | Years of Service | Age at End of Term | Date of Death |
|---|---|---|---|---|---|---|---|---|---|---|---|
| **CHIEF JUSTICES** | | | | | | | | | | | |
| Jay, John | New York | 1745 | King's College (now Columbia University), grad. 1764 | Washington | Oct. 1789 | 44 | June 1795 | resigned | 5 | 49 | May 1829 |
| Rutledge, John* † | South Carolina | 1739 | Studied law at Middle Temple, London | Washington | | | | rejected | 0 | 56 | June 1800 |
| Ellsworth, Oliver | Connecticut | 1745 | Attended Yale College; College of New Jersey (now Princeton University), grad. 1766 | Washington | Mar. 1796 | 50 | Dec. 1800 | resigned | 4 | 55 | Nov. 1807 |
| Marshall, John | Virginia | 1755 | Attended College of William and Mary | Adams | Feb. 1801 | 45 | July 1835 | death | 34 | 79 | July 1835 |
| Taney, Roger Brooke | Maryland | 1777 | Dickinson College, Penn., grad. 1795 | Jackson | Mar. 1836 | 59 | Oct. 1864 | death | 28 | 87 | Oct. 1864 |
| Chase, Salmon Portland | New Hampshire | 1808 | Attended Cincinnati College; Dartmouth College, grad. 1826 | Lincoln | Dec. 1864 | 56 | May 1873 | death | 8 | 65 | May 1873 |
| Waite, Morrison Remick | Connecticut | 1816 | Yale College, grad. 1837 | Grant | Mar. 1874 | 57 | Mar. 1888 | death | 14 | 71 | Mar. 1888 |
| Fuller, Melville Weston | Maine | 1833 | Bowdoin College, grad. 1853; attended Harvard Law School | Cleveland | Oct. 1888 | 55 | July 1910 | death | 21 | 77 | July 1910 |
| White, Edward Douglass* | Louisiana | 1845 | Attended Mount St. Mary's College, Md.; Jesuit College in New Orleans, La.; and Georgetown College, Washington, D.C. | Taft | Dec. 1910 | 65 | May 1921 | death | 10 | 75 | May 1921 |
| Taft, William Howard | Ohio | 1857 | Yale College, grad. 1878; Cincinnati Law School, LL.B. 1880 | Harding | July 1921 | 63 | Feb. 1930 | retired | 8 | 72 | Mar. 1930 |
| Hughes, Charles Evans* | New York | 1862 | Attended Colgate University; Brown University, Rhode Island, grad. 1881; M.A. 1884; Columbia Law School, LL.B. 1884 | Hoover | Feb. 1930 | 67 | June 1941 | retired | 11 | 79 | Aug. 1948 |
| Stone, Harlan Fiske* | New Hampshire | 1872 | Amherst College, Mass., grad. 1894; M.A. 1897; Columbia Law School, LL.B. 1898 | Roosevelt, F. | July 1941 | 68 | Apr. 1946 | death | 4 | 73 | Apr. 1946 |
| Vinson, Frederick Moore | Kentucky | 1890 | Kentucky Normal College, grad.; Centre College, Ky., grad. 1909; LL.B. 1911 | Truman | June 1946 | 56 | Sept. 1953 | death | 7 | 63 | Sept. 1953 |
| Warren, Earl | California | 1891 | University of California, LL.B. 1912; J.D. 1914 | Eisenhower | Oct. 1953 | 62 | June 1969 | retired | 16 | 78 | July 1974 |
| Burger, Warren Earl | Minnesota | 1907 | Attended University of Minnesota; St. Paul College of Law, LL.B. 1931 | Nixon | June 1969 | 61 | — | — | — | — | — |
| **ASSOCIATE JUSTICES** | | | | | | | | | | | |
| Cushing, William | Massachusetts | 1732 | Harvard College, grad. 1751 | Washington | Sept. 1789 | 57 | Sept. 1810 | death | 20 | 77 | Sept. 1810 |
| Wilson, James | Scotland | 1742 | Attended University of St. Andrews (Scotland) | Washington | Sept. 1789 | 47 | Aug. 1798 | death | 8 | 56 | Aug. 1798 |
| Blair, John Jr. | Virginia | 1732 | College of William and Mary, grad. 1754; studied law at Middle Temple, London | Washington | Sept. 1789 | 57 | Jan. 1796 | resigned | 6 | 63 | Aug. 1800 |
| Iredell, James | England | 1751 | Private tutoring | Washington | Feb. 1790 | 39 | Oct. 1799 | death | 8 | 48 | Oct. 1799 |
| Johnson, Thomas | Maryland | 1732 | No formal education | Washington | Nov. 1791 | 59 | Sept. 1793 | resigned | 1 | 61 | Oct. 1819 |
| Paterson, William | Ireland | 1745 | College of New Jersey (now Princeton University), grad. 1763; M.A. 1766 | Washington | Feb. 1793 | 47 | Sept. 1806 | death | 13 | 61 | Sept. 1806 |
| Chase, Samuel | Maryland | 1741 | Private tutoring | Washington | Jan. 1796 | 55 | June 1811 | death | 15 | 70 | June 1811 |
| Washington, Bushrod | Virginia | 1762 | College of William and Mary, grad. 1778 | Adams, J. | Dec. 1798 | 36 | Nov. 1829 | death | 31 | 67 | Nov. 1829 |
| Moore, Alfred | North Carolina | 1755 | Attended private schools | Adams, J. | Oct. 1799 | 44 | Feb. 1804 | resigned | 4 | 48 | Oct. 1810 |
| Johnson, William | South Carolina | 1771 | College of New Jersey (now Princeton University), grad. 1778 | Jefferson | Apr. 1804 | 32 | Aug. 1834 | death | 30 | 63 | Aug. 1834 |
| Livingston, Brockholst | New York | 1757 | College of New Jersey (now Princeton University), grad. 1774 | Jefferson | Sept. 1806 | 49 | Mar. 1823 | death | 16 | 65 | Mar. 1823 |
| Todd, Thomas | Virginia | 1765 | Private tutoring | Jefferson | Mar. 1807 | 42 | Feb. 1826 | death | 18 | 60 | Feb. 1826 |
| Duvall, Gabriel | Maryland | 1752 | Dartmouth College, graduation date unknown | Madison | Feb. 1812 | | ? 1835 | resigned | 22 | 81 | Mar. 1844 |
| Story, Joseph | Massachusetts | 1779 | Harvard College, grad. 1798 | Madison | Nov. 1811 | 32 | Sept. 1845 | death | 33 | 65 | Sept. 1845 |
| Thompson, Smith | New York | 1768 | College of New Jersey (now Princeton University), grad. 1798 | Monroe | Dec. 1823 | 55 | Dec. 1843 | death | 20 | 75 | Dec. 1843 |
| Trimble, Robert | Virginia | 1776 | Attended Kentucky Academy (now Transylvania College | Adams, J. Q. | Apr. 1826 | 49 | Aug. 1828 | death | 2 | 51 | Aug. 1828 |
| McLean, John | New Jersey | 1784 | Private tutoring | Jackson | ? 1829 | 44 | Apr. 1861 | death | 32 | 76 | Apr. 1861 |

* Also served as associate justice: Rutledge (1789–91); White (1894–1910); Hughes (1910–16); Stone (1925–41). † Presided at Aug. 1795 term, but Senate refused to confirm him in December.

| Associate Justices | Place of Birth | Year of Birth | Education | Appointed by President | Date Oath Taken | Age at Oath | Date Service Ended | Service Ended By | Years of Service | Age at End of Term | Date of Death |
|---|---|---|---|---|---|---|---|---|---|---|---|
| Baldwin, Henry | Connecticut | 1780 | Yale College, grad. 1797 | Jackson | ? 1830 | 50 | Apr. 1844 | death | 14 | 64 | Apr. 1844 |
| Wayne, James M. | Georgia | 1790 | College of New Jersey (now Princeton University), grad. 1808 | Jackson | Jan. 1835 | 45 | July 1867 | death | 32 | 77 | July 1867 |
| Barbour, Philip P. | Virginia | 1783 | No record of formal education | Jackson | Mar. 1836 | 53 | Feb. 1841 | death | 5 | 58 | Feb. 1841 |
| Catron, John | Pennsylvania | 1786 | No record of formal education | Jackson | Mar. 1837 | 51 | May 1865 | death | 28 | 79 | May 1865 |
| McKinley, John | Virginia | 1780 | No record of formal education | Van Buren | ? 1837 | 57 | July 1852 | death | 15 | 72 | July 1852 |
| Daniel, Peter V. | Virginia | 1784 | Attended College of New Jersey (now Princeton Univ.) | Van Buren | Feb. 1841 | 57 | May 1860 | death | 19 | 76 | May 1860 |
| Nelson, Samuel | New York | 1792 | Middlebury College, grad. 1813 | Tyler | Mar. 1845 | 53 | Nov. 1872 | resigned | 27 | 80 | Dec. 1873 |
| Woodbury, Levi | New Hampshire | 1789 | Dartmouth College, grad. 1809 | Polk | May 1845 | 56 | Sept. 1851 | death | 5 | 61 | Sept. 1851 |
| Grier, Robert C. | Pennsylvania | 1794 | Dickinson College, grad. 1812 | Polk | Aug. 1846 | 52 | Feb. 1870 | resigned | 23 | 75 | Aug. 1870 |
| Curtis, Benjamin | Massachusetts | 1809 | Harvard College, grad. 1829 | Fillmore | Dec. 1851 | 42 | Sept. 1857 | resigned | 6 | 48 | Sept. 1874 |
| Campbell, John A. | Georgia | 1811 | University of Georgia, grad. 1826; Attended West Point, 1826–28 | Pierce | Mar. 1853 | 42 | Apr. 1861 | resigned | 8 | 50 | Mar. 1889 |
| Clifford, Nathan | New Hampshire | 1803 | Attended private schools | Buchanan | Jan. 1858 | 55 | July 1881 | death | 23 | 78 | July 1881 |
| Swayne, Noah Haynes | Virginia | 1804 | No record of formal education | Lincoln | Jan. 1862 | 57 | Jan. 1881 | retired | 18 | 76 | June 1884 |
| Miller, Samuel Freeman | Kentucky | 1816 | Transylvania University, Ky., grad. 1838 | Lincoln | July 1862 | 46 | Oct. 1890 | death | 28 | 74 | Oct. 1890 |
| Davis, David | Maryland | 1815 | Kenyon College, Ohio, grad. 1832; Yale Law School, LL.B. 1835 | Lincoln | Dec. 1862 | 47 | Mar. 1877 | resigned | 14 | 61 | June 1886 |
| Field, Stephen Johnson | Connecticut | 1816 | Williams College, Mass., grad. 1837 | Lincoln | May 1863 | 46 | Dec. 1897 | retired | 34 | 81 | Apr. 1899 |
| Strong, William | Connecticut | 1808 | Yale College, grad. 1828; M.A. 1831; attended Yale Law School | Grant | Mar. 1870 | 61 | Dec. 1880 | retired | 10 | 72 | Aug. 1895 |
| Bradley, Joseph P. | New York | 1813 | Rutgers College, grad. 1836 | Grant | Mar. 1870 | 57 | Jan. 1892 | death | 21 | 78 | Jan. 1892 |
| Hunt, Ward | New York | 1810 | Union College, N.Y., grad. 1828 | Grant | Jan. 1873 | 62 | Jan. 1882 | disabled | 9 | 71 | Mar. 1886 |
| Harlan, John Marshall | Kentucky | 1833 | Centre College, Ky., grad. 1850; studied law at Translyvania College, Ky. | Hayes | Dec. 1877 | 44 | Oct. 1911 | death | 33 | 78 | Oct. 1911 |
| Woods, William Burnham | Ohio | 1824 | Yale College, grad. 1845 | Hayes | Jan. 1881 | 56 | May 1887 | death | 6 | 62 | May 1887 |
| Matthews, Stanley | Ohio | 1824 | Kenyon College, Ohio, grad. 1840 | Garfield | May 1881 | 56 | Mar. 1889 | death | 7 | 64 | Mar. 1889 |
| Gray, Horace | Massachusetts | 1828 | Harvard College, grad. 1845; Harvard Law School, LL.B. 1849 | Arthur | Jan. 1882 | 53 | Sept. 1902 | death | 20 | 74 | Sept. 1902 |
| Blatchford, Samuel | New York | 1820 | Columbia College, grad. 1837 | Arthur | Apr. 1882 | 62 | July 1893 | death | 11 | 73 | July 1893 |
| Lamar, Lucius Quintus C. | Georgia | 1825 | Emory College, Ga., grad. 1845 | Cleveland | Jan. 1888 | 62 | Jan. 1893 | death | 5 | 67 | Jan. 1893 |
| Brewer, David Josiah | Asia Minor | 1837 | Yale College, grad. 1856; M.A. 1859; Albany (N.Y.) Law School, LL.B. 1858 | Harrison | Jan. 1890 | 52 | Mar. 1910 | death | 20 | 72 | Mar. 1910 |
| Brown, Henry Billings | Massachusetts | 1836 | Yale College, grad. 1856 | Harrison | Jan. 1891 | 54 | May 1906 | retired | 15 | 70 | Sept. 1913 |
| Shiras, George, Jr. | Pennsylvania | 1832 | Yale College, grad. 1853; Yale Law School, LL.B. 1854 | Harrison | Oct. 1892 | 60 | Feb. 1903 | retired | 10 | 71 | Aug. 1924 |
| Jackson, Howell Edmunds | Tennessee | 1832 | West Tennessee College, grad. 1849; attended University of Virginia; Cumberland University, Tenn., LL.B. 1856 | Harrison | Mar. 1893 | 60 | Aug. 1895 | death | 2 | 63 | Aug. 1895 |
| Peckham, Rufus Wheeler | New York | 1838 | Attended Albany (N.Y.) Academy | Cleveland | Jan. 1896 | 57 | Oct. 1909 | death | 13 | 70 | Oct. 1909 |
| McKenna, Joseph | Pennsylvania | 1843 | Benicia Collegiate Institute, Calif., grad. 1865 | McKinley | Jan. 1898 | 54 | Jan. 1925 | retired | 26 | 81 | Nov. 1926 |
| Holmes, Oliver Wendell | Massachusetts | 1841 | Harvard College, grad. 1861; LL.B. 1866 | Roosevelt, T. | Dec. 1902 | 61 | Jan. 1932 | retired | 29 | 90 | Mar. 1935 |
| Day, William Rufus | Ohio | 1849 | University of Michigan, grad. 1870 | Roosevelt, T. | Mar. 1903 | 53 | Nov. 1922 | retired | 19 | 73 | July 1923 |
| Moody, William Henry | Massachusetts | 1853 | Harvard College, grad. 1876; att. Harvard Law School | Roosevelt, T. | Dec. 1906 | 52 | Nov. 1910 | disabled | 3 | 56 | July 1917 |
| Lurton, Horace Harmon | Kentucky | 1844 | Attended Douglas University, Chicago (now University of Chicago); Cumberland University, Tenn., LL.B. 1867 | Taft | Jan. 1910 | 65 | July 1914 | death | 4 | 70 | July 1914 |
| Van Devanter, Willis | Indiana | 1859 | Attended Indiana Asbury (now De Pauw) University; Cincinnati Law School, LL.B. 1881 | Taft | Jan. 1911 | 51 | June 1937 | retired | 26 | 78 | Feb. 1941 |
| Lamar, Joseph Rucker | Georgia | 1857 | Bethany College, W. Va., grad. 1877; studied law, Washington and Lee University, Va. | Taft | Jan. 1911 | 53 | Jan. 1916 | death | 5 | 58 | Jan. 1916 |
| Pitney, Mahlon | New Jersey | 1858 | College of New Jersey (now Princeton University), grad. 1879 | Taft | Mar. 1912 | 54 | Dec. 1922 | resigned | 10 | 64 | Dec. 1924 |

| Associate Justices (cont.) | Place of Birth | Year of Birth | Education | Appointed by President | Date Oath Taken | Age at Oath | Date Service Ended | Service Ended By | Years of Service | Age at End of Term | Date of Death |
|---|---|---|---|---|---|---|---|---|---|---|---|
| McReynolds, James Clark | Kentucky | 1862 | Vanderbilt University, Tenn., grad. 1882; University of Virginia Law School, LL.B. 1884 | Wilson | Oct. 1914 | 52 | Jan. 1941 | retired | 26 | 78 | Aug. 1946 |
| Brandeis, Louis Dembitz | Kentucky | 1856 | Harvard Law School, LL.B. 1877 | Wilson | June 1916 | 59 | Feb. 1939 | retired | 22 | 82 | Oct. 1941 |
| Clarke, John Hessin | Ohio | 1857 | Western Reserve University, Ohio, grad. 1877 | Wilson | Oct. 1916 | 59 | Sept. 1922 | resigned | 5 | 65 | Mar. 1945 |
| Sutherland, George | England | 1862 | Studied law at the University of Michigan | Harding | Oct. 1922 | 60 | Jan. 1938 | retired | 15 | 75 | July 1942 |
| Butler, Pierce | Minnesota | 1866 | Carleton College, Minn., grad. 1887 | Harding | Jan. 1923 | 56 | Nov. 1939 | death | 16 | 73 | Nov. 1939 |
| Sanford, Edward Terry | Tennessee | 1865 | University of Tennessee, grad. 1883; Harvard University, M.A. 1889; Harvard Law School, LL.B. 1889 | Harding | Feb. 1923 | 57 | Mar. 1930 | death | 7 | 64 | Mar. 1930 |
| Roberts, Owen Josephus | Pennsylvania | 1875 | University of Pennsylvania, grad. 1895; LL.B. 1898 | Hoover | June 1930 | 55 | July 1945 | resigned | 15 | 70 | May 1955 |
| Cardozo, Benjamin Nathan | New York | 1870 | Columbia University, grad. 1889; M.A. 1890; attended Columbia Law School | Hoover | Mar. 1932 | 61 | July 1938 | death | 6 | 68 | July 1938 |
| Black, Hugo Lafayette | Alabama | 1886 | University of Alabama, Law School, LL.B. 1906 | Roosevelt, F. | Aug. 1937 | 51 | Sept. 1971 | retired | 34 | 85 | Sept. 1971 |
| Reed, Stanley Forman | Kentucky | 1884 | Kentucky Wesleyan College, grad. 1902; also Yale University, grad. 1906; studied law at Columbia University | Roosevelt, F. | Jan. 1938 | 53 | Feb. 1957 | retired | 19 | 72 | Apr. 1980 |
| Frankfurter, Felix | Austria | 1882 | City College of New York, grad. 1902; Harvard Law School, LL.B. 1906 | Roosevelt, F. | Jan. 1939 | 56 | Aug. 1962 | retired | 23 | 79 | Feb. 1965 |
| Douglas, William Orville | Minnesota | 1898 | Whitman College, Wash., grad. 1920; Columbia Law School, LL.B. 1925 | Roosevelt, F. | Apr. 1939 | 40 | Nov. 1975 | retired | 36 | 77 | Jan. 1980 |
| Murphy, Frank | Michigan | 1890 | University of Michigan, LL.B. 1914; studied law at Lincoln's Inn, London, and Trinity College, Dublin | Roosevelt, F. | Feb. 1940 | 49 | July 1949 | death | 9 | 59 | July 1949 |
| Byrnes, James Francis | South Carolina | 1879 | No record of formal education | Roosevelt, F. | July 1941 | 62 | Oct. 1942 | resigned | 1 | 63 | Apr. 1972 |
| Jackson, Robert Houghwout | New York | 1892 | Attended Albany (N.Y.) Law School | Roosevelt, F. | July 1941 | 49 | Oct. 1954 | death | 13 | 62 | Oct. 1954 |
| Rutledge, Wiley Blount | Kentucky | 1894 | University of Wisconsin, grad. 1914; University of Colorado, LL.B. 1922 | Roosevelt, F. | Feb. 1943 | 48 | Sept. 1949 | death | 6 | 55 | Sept. 1949 |
| Burton, Harold Hitz | Massachusetts | 1888 | Bowdoin College, Me., grad. 1909; Harvard Law School, LL.B. 1912 | Truman | Oct. 1945 | 57 | Oct. 1958 | retired | 13 | 70 | Oct. 1964 |
| Clark, Thomas Campbell | Texas | 1899 | University of Texas, grad. 1921; LL.B. 1922 | Truman | Aug. 1949 | 49 | June 1967 | retired | 18 | 67 | June 1977 |
| Minton, Sherman | Indiana | 1890 | Indiana University, LL.B. 1915 | Truman | Oct. 1949 | 58 | Oct. 1956 | retired | 7 | 65 | Apr. 1965 |
| Harlan, John Marshall | Illinois | 1899 | Princeton University, grad. 1920; Rhodes Scholar to Oxford University, 1921–23; New York Law School, LL.B. 1924 | Eisenhower | Mar. 1955 | 55 | Sept. 1971 | retired | 16 | 72 | Dec. 1971 |
| Brennan, William Joseph, Jr. | New Jersey | 1906 | University of Pennsylvania, grad. 1928; Harvard Law School, LL.B. 1931 | Eisenhower | Oct. 1956 | 50 | — | — | — | — | — |
| Whittaker, Charles Evans | Kansas | 1901 | University of Kansas City, LL.B. 1924 | Eisenhower | Mar. 1957 | 56 | Apr. 1962 | retired | 5 | 61 | Nov. 1973 |
| Stewart, Potter | Michigan | 1915 | Yale University, grad. 1937; attended Cambridge University, England; Yale Law School, LL.B. 1941 | Eisenhower | Oct. 1958 | 43 | July 1981 | retired | 23 | 66 | — |
| White, Byron Raymond | Colorado | 1917 | University of Colorado, grad. 1938; Rhodes Scholar, Oxford, England, 1939; Yale Law School, LL.B. 1946 | Kennedy | Apr. 1962 | 44 | — | — | — | — | — |
| Goldberg, Arthur Joseph | Illinois | 1908 | Northwestern University, grad. 1929; J.D. 1930 | Kennedy | Oct. 1962 | 54 | July 1965 | resigned | 3 | 56 | — |
| Fortas, Abe | Tennessee | 1910 | Southwestern College, grad. 1930; Yale Law School, LL.B. 1933 | Johnson | Oct. 1965 | 55 | May 1969 | resigned | 4 | 58 | Apr. 1982 |
| Marshall, Thurgood | Maryland | 1908 | Lincoln University, grad. 1929; Howard University, LL.B. 1933 | Johnson | Oct. 1967 | 59 | — | — | — | — | — |
| Blackmun, Harry Andrew | Minnesota | 1908 | Harvard College, grad. 1929; Harvard Law School, LL.B. 1932 | Nixon | June 1970 | 61 | — | — | — | — | — |
| Powell, Lewis Franklin, Jr. | Virginia | 1907 | Washington and Lee University, grad. 1929, LL.B., 1931; Harvard University, LL.M., 1932 | Nixon | Jan. 1972 | 64 | — | — | — | — | — |
| Rehnquist, William Hubbs | Wisconsin | 1924 | Stanford University, grad. 1948; M.A. Harvard University 1950; LL.B., Stanford 1952 | Nixon | Jan. 1972 | 47 | — | — | — | — | — |
| Stevens, John Paul | Illinois | 1920 | Univ. of Chicago, grad. 1941; Northwestern Univ. School of Law, J.D. 1947 | Ford | Dec. 1975 | 55 | — | — | — | — | — |
| O'Connor, Sandra Day | Texas | 1930 | Stanford University, grad. 1950; Stanford Univ. Law School, LL. B. 1952 | Reagan | Sept. 1981 | 51 | — | — | — | — | — |

## THE U.S. COURTS

Source: Administrative Office of the U.S.Courts

### SUPREME COURT OF THE UNITED STATES

Washington, D.C.

**Chief Justice** (Salary: $96,800): Warren E. Burger of Virginia.

**Associate Justices** (Salaries: $93,000): William J. Brennan, Jr., of New Jersey; Byron R. White of Colorado; Thurgood Marshall of New York; Harry A. Blackmun of Minnesota; Lewis F. Powell, Jr., of Virginia; William H. Rehnquist of Arizona; John P. Stevens of Illinois; Sandra Day O'Connor of Arizona.

### U.S. COURT OF APPEALS

(Salaries: $74,300)

**District of Columbia Circuit:** Spottswood W. Robinson III, Chief Judge; J. Skelly Wright, Edward Allen Tamm, George E. MacKinnon, Malcolm Richard Wilkey, Patricia M. Wald, Abner J. Mikva, Harry T. Edwards, Ruth B. Ginsburg, Robert H. Bork, Antonin Scalia.

**First Circuit** (Maine, Massachusetts, New Hampshire, Rhode Island, Puerto Rico): Frank M. Coffin, Chief Judge, Portland, Maine; Levin H. Campbell, Boston, Mass.; Hugh H. Bownes, Concord, N.H.; Stephen G. Breyer, Boston, Mass.

**Second Circuit** (Connecticut, New York, Vermont): Wilfred Feinberg, Chief Judge, New York, N.Y.; Irving R. Kaufman, George C. Pratt, both of New York, N.Y.; James L. Oakes, Brattleboro, Vt.; Ralph K. Winter, New Haven, Ct.; Thomas J. Meskill, New Britain, Ct.; Lawrence W. Pierce, Amalya L. Kearse, both of New York, N.Y.; Ellsworth Van Graafeiland, Rochester, N.Y.; Jon O. Newman, Hartford, Ct.; Richard J. Cardamone, Utica, N.Y.

**Third Circuit** (Delaware, New Jersey, Pennsylvania, Virgin Islands): Collins J. Seitz, Chief Judge, Wilmington, Del.; James Hunter III, Camden, N.J.; A. Leon Higginbotham, Arlin M. Adams, Dolores Korman Sloviter, Edward R. Becker, all of Philadelphia, Pa.; Ruggero J. Aldisert, Joseph F. Weis, Jr., both of Pittsburgh, Pa.; John J. Gibbons, Leonard I. Garth, both of Newark, N.J.

**Fourth Circuit** (Maryland, North Carolina, South Carolina, Virginia, West Virgina): Harrison L. Winter, Chief Judge, Baltimore, Md.; John D. Butzner, Jr., Richmond, Va.; Donald Stuart Russell, Spartanburg, S.C.; H. Emory Widener, Jr., Abingdon, Va.; Kenneth K. Hall, James M. Sprouse, both of Charleston, W. Va.; James Dickson Phillips, Jr., Durham, N.C.; Francis D. Murnaghan, Jr., Baltimore, Md.; Samuel J. Ervin III, Asheville, N.C.; Robert F. Chapman of Columbia, S.C.

**Fifth Circuit**[1] (Louisiana, Mississippi, Texas): Charles Clark, Chief Judge, Jackson, Miss.; Alvin B. Rubin, Baton Rouge, La.; Albert Tate, Jr., New Orleans, La.; Thomas G. Gee, Thomas M. Reavley, Samuel D. Johnson, Jr., Jerre S. Williams, William L. Garwood, all of Austin, Tex.; Henry A. Politz, Shreveport, La.; John R. Brown, Carolyn D. Randall, both of Houston, Tex.; Patrick E. Higgenbotham, Dallas, Tex.; E. Grady Jolly, Jackson, Miss.

**Sixth Circuit** (Kentucky, Michigan, Ohio, Tennessee): George Clifton Edwards, Jr., Chief Judge, Cincinnati, Ohio; Pierce Lively, Danville, Ky.; Albert J. Engel, Grand Rapids, Mich.; Gilbert S. Merritt, Nashville, Tenn.; Damon J. Keith, Cornelia Kennedy, both of Detroit, Mich.; Harry W. Wellford, Memphis, Tenn.; Boyce F. Martin, Jr., Louisville, Ky.; Leroy J. Contie, Jr., Akron, Ohio; Nathaniel R. Jones, Robert B. Krapansky, both of Cleveland, Ohio.

**Seventh Circuit** (Illinois, Indiana, Wisconsin): Walter J. Cummings, Chief Judge, Chicago, Ill.; Richard A. Posner, Richard D. Cudahy, Wilbur F. Pell, Jr., William J. Bauer, Harlington Wood, Jr., all of Chicago, Ill.; Jesse E. Eschbach, Fort Wayne, Ind.; John L. Coffey, Milwaukee, Wis.

**Eighth Circuit** (Arkansas, Iowa, Minnesota, Missouri, Nebraska, North Dakota, South Dakota): Donald Lay, Chief Judge, Omaha, Nebr.; Myron H. Bright, Fargo, N. Dak.; Donald R. Ross, Omaha, Nebr.; J. Smith Henley, Harrison, Ark.; Richard S. Arnold, Little Rock, Ark.; Theodore McMillian, St. Louis, Mo.; John R. Gibson, Kansas City, Mo.

**Ninth Circuit** (Arizona, California, Idaho, Montana, Nevada, Oregon, Washington, Alaska, Hawaii, Guam): James R. Browning, Chief Judge, San Francisco, Calif.; Eugene A. Wright, Betty B. Fletcher, Jerome J. Farris, all of Seattle, Wash.; Thomas Tang, Mary M. Schroeder, William C. Canby, Jr., all of Phoenix, Ariz.; Herbert Y.C. Choy, Honolulu, Hawaii; Alfred T. Goodwin, Otto R. Skopil, Jr., both of Portland, Oregon; J. Clifford Wallace, San Diego, Calif.; Joseph T. Sneed, Cecil F. Poole, both of San Francisco, Calif.; Anthony M. Kennedy, Sacramento, Calif.; J. Blaine Anderson, Boise, Idaho; Procter Hug, Jr., Reno, Nevada; Harry Pregerson, Arthur L. Alarcon, Warren J. Ferguson, Dorothy W. Nelson, William A. Norris, Stephen R. Reinhardt, all of Los Angeles, Calif.; Robert Boochever, Juneau, Alaska.

**Tenth Circuit** (Colorado, Kansas, New Mexico, Oklahoma, Utah, Wyoming): Oliver Seth, Chief Judge, Santa Fe, N. Mex.; William J. Holloway, Jr., Oklahoma City, Okla.; James E. Barrett, Cheyenne, Wyo.; William E. Doyle and Robert H. McWilliams, both of Denver, Colo.; Monroe McKay, Salt Lake City, Utah; James K. Logan, Olathe, Kansas; Stephanie K. Seymour, Tulsa, Okla.

**Eleventh Circuit** (Alabama, Florida, and Georgia): John C. Godbold, Chief Judge, Montgomery, Ala.; Frank M. Johnson, Jr., Montgomery, Ala.; Gerald B. Tjoflat, Jacksonville, Fla.; Phyllis A. Kravitch, Albert J. Henderson, James C. Hill, all of Atlanta, Ga.; Paul H. Roney, St. Petersburg, Fla.; Peter T. Fay, Miami, Fla.; Robert S. Vance, Birmingham, Ala.; Joseph W. Hatchett, Tallahassee, Fla.; R. Lanier Anderson III, Macon, Ga.; Thomas A. Clark, Tampa, Fla.

### U.S. DISTRICT COURTS

Judges of U.S. District Courts and the Chief Judge of the District of Columbia receive annual salaries of $70,300.

### U.S. TERRITORIAL JUDGES

The District Judges earn annual salaries of $70,300.

### U.S. COURT OF APPEALS FOR THE FEDERAL CIRCUIT*

717 Madison Place, N.W., Washington, D.C.
(Salaries: $74,300)

**Chief Judge:** Howard T. Markey, **Associate Judges:** Daniel M. Friedman, Giles S. Rich, Oscar H. Davis, Philip Nicholas, Jr., Shiro Kashiwa, Marion T. Bennett, Edward S. Smith, Jack R. Miller, Philip B. Baldwin, and Helen W. Nies.

### U.S. CLAIMS COURT†

717 Madison Place, N.W., Washington, D.C.
(Salaries: $57,500)

### U.S. COURT OF INTERNATIONAL TRADE

1 Federal Plaza, New York, N.Y.
(Salaries: $70,300)

**Chief Judge:** Edward D. Re, **Judges:** Paul P. Rao, Morgan Ford, Frederick Landis, James L. Watson, Herbert N. Maletz, Bernard Newman, Nils A. Boe.

---

[1] In accordance with the Panama Canal Treaty between the United States and Panama, which became effective October 1, 1979, 40% of the former Panama Canal Zone remains in the control of the U.S. Panama Canal Commission until December 31, 1999. The present Fifth Circuit continues its jurisdiction for this area.
*Former U.S. Court of Claims and U.S. Court of Customs and Patent Appeals were combined effective Oct. 1, 1982.
†Established Oct. 1, 1982.

## STATE AND LOCAL GOVERNMENT EXPENDITURES: PER CAPITA

Source: U.S. Bureau of the Census

| Year | Total general | Education | Highways | Public welfare | Health and hospitals | Police and fire |
|---|---|---|---|---|---|---|
| 1902 | $ 12.80 | $ 3.22 | $ 2.21 | $ .47 | $ .75 | $ 1.14 |
| 1913 | 21.23 | 5.93 | 4.31 | .53 | 1.11 | 1.70 |
| 1922 | 47.41 | 15.49 | 11.76 | 1.08 | 2.35 | 3.17 |
| 1932 | 62.15 | 18.50 | 13.93 | 3.55 | 3.65 | 4.23 |
| 1936 | 59.63 | 16.98 | 11.12 | 6.45 | 3.64 | 4.05 |
| 1940 | 69.85 | 19.97 | 11.91 | 8.75 | 4.61 | 4.54 |
| 1944 | 64.04 | 20.18 | 8.67 | 8.19 | 4.74 | 4.80 |
| 1946 | 78.00 | 23.74 | 11.83 | 9.97 | 5.79 | 5.47 |
| 1948 | 120.60 | 36.68 | 20.71 | 14.31 | 8.38 | 7.16 |
| 1950 | 150.22 | 47.31 | 25.07 | 19.38 | 11.52 | 8.34 |
| 1952 | 166.29 | 53.00 | 29.63 | 17.76 | 13.92 | 9.71 |
| 1954 | 189.06 | 65.01 | 34.04 | 18.84 | 14.83 | 10.98 |
| 1956 | 219.42 | 79.02 | 41.56 | 18.76 | 16.57 | 12.35 |
| 1958 | 258.76 | 91.84 | 49.43 | 22.03 | 19.97 | 14.33 |
| 1960 | 288.21 | 104.00 | 52.38 | 24.47 | 21.08 | 15.85 |
| 1962 | 324.00 | 119.56 | 55.74 | 27.36 | 23.37 | 17.51 |
| 1963 | 339.19 | 125.81 | 59.11 | 28.74 | 24.59 | 17.99 |
| 1964 | 362.20 | 137.38 | 60.96 | 30.13 | 25.66 | 18.74 |
| 1965 | 385.30 | 147.37 | 63.05 | 32.58 | 27.66 | 19.89 |
| 1966 | 422.97 | 169.95 | 65.20 | 34.50 | 30.17 | 21.19 |
| 1967 | 471.79 | 191.64 | 70.41 | 41.53 | 33.56 | 22.99 |
| 1968 | 512.41 | 205.93 | 72.46 | 49.32 | 37.76 | 25.18 |
| 1969 | 578.14 | 233.94 | 76.35 | 59.97 | 42.19 | 28.19 |
| 1970 | 646.20 | 259.39 | 80.83 | 72.23 | 47.57 | 32.07 |
| 1971 | 730.52 | 288.05 | 87.73 | 88.36 | 54.32 | 36.50 |
| 1972 | 801.38 | 311.60 | 91.29 | 101.18 | 61.79 | 41.07 |
| 1973 | 863.60 | 332.21 | 88.70 | 112.37 | 65.97 | 45.18 |
| 1974 | 941.19 | 358.74 | 94.36 | 118.67 | 75.43 | 48.85 |
| 1975 | 1082.58 | 412.24 | 105.71 | 132.11 | 88.43 | 56.54 |
| 1976 | 1195.99 | 452.89 | 111.37 | 151.89 | 96.37 | 62.56 |
| 1977 | 1268.37 | 475.22 | 106.80 | 166.14 | 104.20 | 67.82 |
| 1978 | 1361.90 | 507.91 | 112.85 | 179.49 | 114.41 | 73.87 |
| 1979 | 1488.05 | 542.70 | 129.22 | 190.36 | 128.20 | 78.84 |
| 1980 | 1629.48 | 588.11 | 147.07 | 208.77 | 142.05 | 84.82 |

## U.S. — BUDGET: 1789-1983

Source: U.S. Office of Management and Budget (in millions of dollars)

| Fiscal Year | Receipts | Outlays | Surplus or Deficit (—) |
|---|---|---|---|
| 1789–1849 | 1,160 | 1,090 | +70 |
| 1850–1900 | 14,462 | 15,453 | —991 |
| 1901 | 588 | 525 | +63 |
| 1902 | 562 | 485 | +77 |
| 1903 | 562 | 517 | +45 |
| 1904 | 541 | 584 | —43 |
| 1905 | 544 | 567 | —23 |
| 1906 | 595 | 570 | +25 |
| 1907 | 666 | 579 | +87 |
| 1908 | 602 | 659 | —57 |
| 1909 | 604 | 694 | —89 |
| 1910 | 676 | 694 | —18 |
| 1911 | 702 | 691 | +11 |
| 1912 | 693 | 690 | +3 |
| 1913 | 714 | 715 | —* |
| 1914 | 725 | 726 | —* |
| 1915 | 683 | 746 | —63 |
| 1916 | 761 | 713 | +48 |
| 1917 | 1,101 | 1,954 | —853 |
| 1918 | 3,645 | 12,677 | —9,032 |
| 1919 | 5,130 | 18,493 | —13,363 |
| 1920 | 6,649 | 6,358 | +291 |
| 1921 | 5,571 | 5,062 | +509 |
| 1922 | 4,026 | 3,289 | +736 |
| 1923 | 3,853 | 3,140 | +713 |
| 1924 | 3,871 | 2,908 | +963 |
| 1925 | 3,641 | 2,924 | +717 |
| 1926 | 3,795 | 2,930 | +865 |
| 1927 | 4,013 | 2,857 | +1,155 |
| 1928 | 3,900 | 2,961 | +939 |
| 1929 | 3,862 | 3,127 | +734 |
| 1930 | 4,058 | 3,320 | +738 |
| 1931 | 3,116 | 3,577 | —462 |
| 1932 | 1,924 | 4,659 | —2,735 |
| 1933 | 1,997 | 4,598 | —2,602 |
| 1934 | 3,015 | 6,645 | —3,630 |
| 1935 | 3,706 | 6,497 | —2,791 |
| 1936 | 3,997 | 8,422 | —4,425 |
| 1937 | 4,956 | 7,733 | —2,777 |
| 1938 | 5,588 | 6,765 | —1,177 |
| 1939 | 4,979 | 8,841 | —3,862 |
| 1940 | 6,361 | 9,456 | —3,095 |
| 1941 | 8,621 | 13,634 | —5,013 |
| 1942 | 14,350 | 35,114 | —20,764 |
| 1943 | 23,649 | 78,533 | —54,884 |
| 1944 | 44,276 | 91,280 | —47,004 |
| 1945 | 45,216 | 92,690 | —47,474 |
| 1946 | 39,327 | 55,183 | —15,856 |
| 1947 | 38,394 | 34,532 | +3,862 |
| 1948 | 41,774 | 29,773 | +12,001 |
| 1949 | 39,437 | 38,834 | +603 |
| 1950 | 39,485 | 42,597 | —3,112 |
| 1951 | 51,646 | 45,546 | +6,100 |
| 1952 | 66,204 | 67,721 | —1,517 |
| 1953 | 69,574 | 76,107 | —6,533 |
| 1954 | 69,719 | 70,890 | —1,170 |
| 1955 | 65,469 | 68,509 | —3,041 |
| 1956 | 74,547 | 70,460 | +4,087 |
| 1957 | 79,990 | 76,741 | +3,249 |
| 1958 | 79,636 | 82,575 | —2,939 |
| 1959 | 79,249 | 92,104 | —12,855 |
| 1960 | 92,492 | 92,223 | +269 |
| 1961 | 94,389 | 97,795 | —3,406 |
| 1962 | 99,676 | 106,813 | —7,137 |
| 1963 | 106,560 | 111,311 | —4,751 |
| 1964 | 112,662 | 118,584 | —5,922 |
| 1965 | 116,833 | 118,430 | —1,596 |
| 1966 | 130,856 | 134,652 | —3,796 |
| 1967 | 149,552 | 158,254 | —8,702 |
| 1968 | 153,671 | 178,833 | —25,161 |
| 1969 | 187,784 | 184,548 | +3,236 |
| 1970 | 193,743 | 196,588 | —2,845 |
| 1971 | 188,392 | 211,425 | —23,033 |
| 1972 | 208,649 | 232,021 | —23,373 |
| 1973 | 232,225 | 247,074 | —14,849 |
| 1974 | 264,932 | 269,620 | —4,688 |
| 1975 | 280,997 | 326,185 | —45,188 |
| 1976 | 300,005 | 366,439 | —66,434 |
| TQ | 81,773 | 94,729 | —12,956 |
| 1977 | 357,762 | 402,725 | —44,963 |
| 1978 | 401,997 | 450,836 | —48,839 |
| 1979 | 465,940 | 493,673 | —27,733 |
| 1980 | 520,050 | 579,613 | —59,613 |
| 1981 | 599,272 | 657,202 | —57,932 |
| 1982 est.[1] | 622,100 | 731,000 | —108,900 |
| 1983[1] | 646,500 | 761,500 | —115,000 |

* Less than $500,000. [1] Based on the 1983 budget from the Mid-Session Review in July 1982: Fiscal years through 1976 began on July 1 and ended the following June 30. Beginning with fiscal year 1977, each fiscal year begins on October 1 and ends on the following September 30. The Transition Quarter (TQ) refers to the 3-month period from the end of fiscal year 1976 on June 30, 1976, to the beginning of fiscal year 1977 on October 1, 1976.

Note: Data for 1789–1939 are for the administrative budget; 1940 and thereafter are for the unified budget.

## THE BUDGET DOLLAR

SOURCE: Office of Management and Budget
Fiscal Year 1983

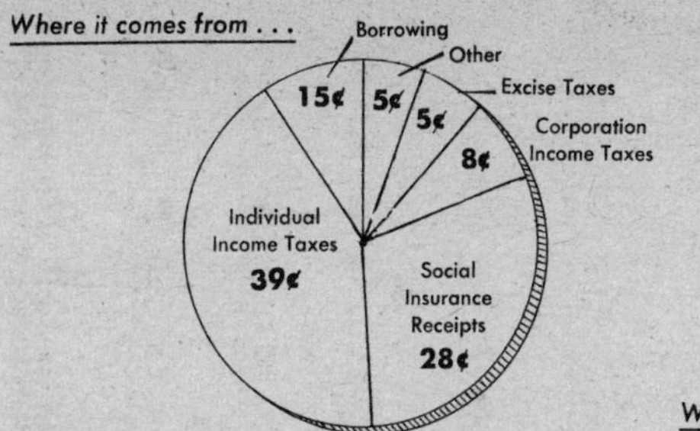


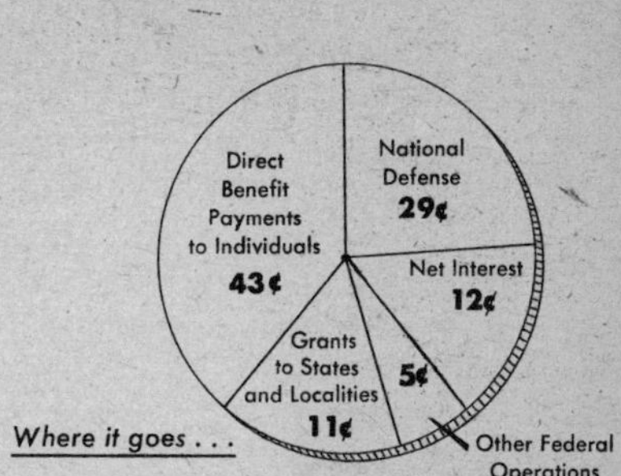


## FEDERAL GRANTS TO STATES[1]

SOURCE: Tax Foundation, Inc.

These comparisons of Federal tax burdens for aid payments per $1.00 of assistance do not actually indicate the entire costs which state and local governments incur for obtaining Federal grants. The comparisons, with few exceptions, do not take into account the costs to these governments of administering the programs for which the aid is granted, nor the amounts of matching funds which the state and local governments must make available out of their own revenue in order to qualify as recipients of these grants. In the last few years, it is estimated that state and local governments provided approximately $1.00 of matching funds for each $2.50 of Federal aid.

"PAYING STATES"[1]

Twenty-two states paid more in U.S. taxes to support grant programs than they received in aid in fiscal year 1982.

| State | Grants (millions) | Estimated tax burden for grants (millions) | Tax Burden for $1 of Aid: All Grants | Tax Burden for $1 of Aid: Rev. Sharing |
|---|---|---|---|---|
| Texas | $4,144.2 | $6,070.7 | $1.46 | $1.43 |
| Conn. | 1,180.0 | 1,665.7 | 1.41 | 1.51 |
| Fla. | 2,865.9 | 3,821.9 | 1.33 | 1.38 |
| Kansas | 772.5 | 990.2 | 1.28 | 1.17 |
| N.J. | 2,891.0 | 3,673.9 | 1.27 | 1.19 |
| Colo. | 994.2 | 1,249.3 | 1.26 | 1.20 |
| Ind. | 1,728.7 | 2,109.9 | 1.22 | 1.18 |
| N.H. | 306.1 | 370.2 | 1.21 | 1.22 |
| Ohio | 3,725.2 | 4,432.7 | 1.19 | 1.19 |
| Ill. | 4,610.0 | 5,441.4 | 1.18 | 1.21 |
| Iowa | 960.8 | 1,138.2 | 1.18 | .96 |
| Ariz. | 857.3 | 1,008.7 | 1.18 | .88 |
| Nev. | 340.9 | 397.9 | 1.17 | 1.69 |
| Wyo. | 199.9 | 231.4 | 1.16 | 1.19 |
| Nebr. | 516.9 | 601.5 | 1.16 | .91 |
| Va. | 1,884.1 | 2,128.4 | 1.13 | 1.10 |
| Mo. | 1,658.4 | 1,860.1 | 1.12 | 1.12 |
| Wash. | 1,738.5 | 1,924.8 | 1.11 | 1.43 |
| Calif. | 9,945.6 | 11,077.1 | 1.11 | 1.07 |
| Okla. | 1,040.4 | 1,129.0 | 1.09 | 1.07 |
| Oregon | 976.0 | 1,055.0 | 1.08 | .94 |
| Md. | 1,917.0 | 1,971.1 | 1.03 | 1.09 |

"RECEIVING STATES"

Twenty-eight states and the District of Columbia paid less in taxes to support grant programs than they received in aid.

| State | Grants (millions) | Estimated tax burden for grants (millions) | Tax Burden for $1 of Aid: All Grants | Tax Burden for $1 of Aid: Rev. Sharing |
|---|---|---|---|---|
| Penn. | $4,885.9 | $4,765.8 | $.98 | $1.00 |
| N.C. | 1,907.8 | 1,878.6 | .98 | .77 |
| Mich. | 4,106.6 | 3,923.7 | .96 | .98 |
| Hawaii | 443.0 | 416.4 | .94 | .92 |
| Minn. | 1,772.4 | 1,665.7 | .94 | .86 |
| S.C. | 1,007.5 | 925.4 | .92 | .67 |
| La. | 1,726.6 | 1,536.2 | .89 | .82 |
| Del. | 313.6 | 268.4 | .86 | .97 |
| Mass. | 2,888.9 | 2,480.1 | .86 | .85 |
| Idaho | 347.5 | 296.1 | .85 | .75 |
| Tenn. | 1,821.8 | 1,499.2 | .82 | .82 |
| Ga. | 2,167.1 | 1,767.5 | .82 | .81 |
| R.I. | 482.0 | 388.7 | .81 | .93 |
| Utah | 573.8 | 462.7 | .81 | .69 |
| Ala. | 1,463.4 | 1,166.0 | .80 | .74 |
| Wis. | 2,298.3 | 1,823.1 | .79 | .83 |
| Ky. | 1,423.7 | 1,129.0 | .79 | .70 |
| N.Y. | 10,374.3 | 7,643.9 | .74 | .78 |
| N.D. | 306.1 | 222.1 | .73 | .81 |
| Ark. | 882.0 | 638.5 | .72 | .66 |
| N. Mex. | 604.6 | 416.4 | .69 | .70 |
| Mont. | 428.3 | 286.9 | .67 | .74 |
| W. Va. | 940.8 | 629.3 | .67 | .72 |
| Maine | 536.0 | 351.7 | .66 | .63 |
| S.D. | 353.6 | 212.8 | .60 | .60 |
| Miss. | 1,083.1 | 647.8 | .60 | .48 |
| Alaska | 438.8 | 249.9 | .57 | .89 |
| Vt. | 279.2 | 157.3 | .56 | .56 |
| D.C. | 1,430.4 | 342.4 | .24 | .91 |

[1]Excludes shared revenues; includes general revenue sharing and trust fund aids.

## EXPENDITURE OF FEDERAL TAX DOLLARS (FISCAL YEAR 1982)*

SOURCE: Tax Foundation, Inc.

| Item | Worker's Share: Amount | Worker's Share: % of Total |
|---|---|---|
| **Total** | **$6,916** | **100.00** |
| Income security | 2,291 | 33.12 |
| National defense | 1,712 | 24.75 |
| Interest | 905 | 13.08 |
| Health | 670 | 9.69 |
| Education, training, employment and social services | 254 | 3.67 |
| Transportation | 194 | 2.80 |
| Veterans' benefits | 220 | 3.19 |
| Natural resources and environment | $115 | 1.67 |
| International affairs | 101 | 1.46 |
| Agriculture | 79 | 1.14 |
| Community and regional development | 76 | 1.10 |
| General science, space, & technology | 63 | .92 |
| Energy | 59 | .85 |
| General purpose fiscal assistance | 59 | .85 |
| General government | 47 | .68 |
| Administration of justice | 41 | .60 |
| Commerce and housing credit | 30 | .43 |

*Based on worker earning $25,000 a year as sole source of support for wife and two dependent children.

## THE U.S. BUDGET: RECEIPTS AND OUTLAYS (in billions of dollars)

SOURCE: U.S. Office of Management and Budget

| Description | 1978 Actual | 1979 Actual | 1980 Actual | 1981 Actual | 1982[1] Est | 1983[1] Est |
|---|---|---|---|---|---|---|
| **Receipts by source:** | | | | | | |
| Individual income taxes | 181.0 | 217.8 | 244.1 | 285.9 | 298.5 | 293.8 |
| Corporation income taxes | 60.0 | 65.7 | 64.6 | 61.1 | 49.9 | 58.3 |
| Social insurance taxes and contributions | 123.4 | 141.6 | 160.7 | 182.7 | 202.6 | 215.7 |
| Excise taxes | 18.4 | 18.7 | 24.3 | 40.8 | 37.8 | 40.1 |
| Estate and gift taxes | 5.3 | 5.4 | 6.4 | 6.8 | 8.1 | 6.0 |
| Customs duties | 6.6 | 7.4 | 7.2 | 8.1 | 9.2 | 9.5 |
| Miscellaneous receipts | 7.4 | 9.2 | 12.7 | 13.8 | 16.1 | 15.0 |
| Adjustment for Senate Finance Committee Bill | — | — | — | — | — | 8.1 |
| **Total receipts:** | **402.0** | **465.9** | **520.0** | **599.3** | **622.1** | **646.5** |
| **Outlays by function:** | | | | | | |
| National defense[2] | 105.2 | 117.7 | 145.8 | 159.8 | 187.7 | 221.5 |
| International affairs | 5.9 | 6.1 | 15.5 | 11.1 | 11.2 | 12.1 |
| General science, space, and technology | 4.7 | 5.0 | 6.1 | 6.4 | 7.0 | 7.6 |
| Energy | 5.9 | 6.9 | 36.4 | 10.3 | 6.0 | 4.2 |
| Natural resources and environment | 10.9 | 12.1 | 13.1 | 13.5 | 13.2 | 10.4 |
| Agriculture | 7.7 | 6.2 | 4.9 | 5.6 | 14.1 | 10.4 |
| Commerce and housing credit | 3.3 | 2.6 | 10.5 | 3.9 | 3.6 | 0.4 |
| Transportation | 15.4 | 17.5 | 20.2 | 23.4 | 21.2 | 19.9 |
| Community and regional development | 11.0 | 9.5 | 10.1 | 9.4 | 7.8 | 7.3 |
| Education, training, employment, and social services | 26.5 | 29.7 | 30.6 | 31.4 | 28.1 | 23.8 |
| Health | 43.7 | 49.6 | 59.8 | 66.0 | 73.8 | 78.5 |
| Income security | 146.2 | 160.2 | 224.2 | 225.1 | 249.1 | 259.3 |
| Veterans benefits and services | 19.0 | 19.9 | 21.2 | 23.0 | 24.2 | 24.2 |
| Administration of justice | 3.8 | 4.2 | 4.4 | 4.7 | 4.7 | 4.6 |
| General government | 3.7 | 4.2 | 4.6 | 4.6 | 5.3 | 5.0 |
| General purpose fiscal assistance | 9.6 | 8.4 | 8.7 | 6.9 | 6.5 | 6.5 |
| Interest | 44.0 | 52.6 | 64.5 | 82.5 | 99.9 | 111.1 |
| Allowances[3] | — | — | — | — | - 1.0 | - 4.7 |
| Undistributed offsetting receipts | -15.8 | -18.5 | - 21.9 | -30.3 | - 31.3 | - 40.8 |
| **Total outlays:** | **450.8** | **493.7** | **658.8** | **657.2** | **731.0** | **761.5** |
| **Budget deficit:** | **-48.8** | **-27.8** | **-138.8** | **-59.6** | **-108.9** | **-115.0** |

[1]Based on estimates of the 1983 Budget of the Mid-Session Review in July 1982. [2]Includes civilian and military pay raises for Department of Defense. [3]Includes allowances for civilian agency pay raises.

## FEDERAL, STATE & LOCAL GOVERNMENT FINANCES: 1929—1981

SOURCE: U.S. Department of Commerce, Bureau of Economic Analysis

(Billions of Dollars)

| | 1929 | 1939 | 1949 | 1959 | 1979 | 1980 | 1981* |
|---|---|---|---|---|---|---|---|
| **Total Government**** | | | | | | | |
| Receipts | 11.3 | 15.4 | 55.9 | 129.4 | 765.1 | 838.0 | 957.3 |
| Expenditures | 10.3 | 17.6 | 59.3 | 131.0 | 750.8 | 871.2 | 985.5 |
| Federal Government | | | | | | | |
| Receipts | 3.8 | 6.7 | 38.7 | 89.8 | 493.6 | 540.7 | 628.2 |
| Expenditures | 2.6 | 8.9 | 41.3 | 91.0 | 509.7 | 602.1 | 688.2 |
| State and Local Government | | | | | | | |
| Receipts | 7.6 | 9.6 | 19.5 | 46.4 | 352.0 | 385.9 | 416.8 |
| Expenditures | 7.8 | 9.6 | 20.2 | 46.9 | 321.5 | 357.8 | 385.0 |

*Preliminary. ** Total government is after subtraction of Federal grants-in-aid to state and local governments.

## STATE PER CAPITA INCOME: 1980 and 1981

SOURCE: U.S. Department of Commerce, Bureau of Economic Analysis

| Rank | State | 1980 Income | 1981 Income | Percent of National Average 1981 |
|---|---|---|---|---|
| | United States | $ 9,511 | $10,517 | 100 |
| | **States** | | | |
| 1. | Alaska | 12,759 | 14,190 | 135 |
| — | District of Columbia | 12,050 | 13,487 | 128 |
| 2. | Connecticut | 11,692 | 12,995 | 124 |
| 3. | New Jersey | 10,935 | 12,115 | 115 |
| 4. | California | 10,929 | 12,057 | 115 |
| 5. | Wyoming | 10,875 | 11,780 | 112 |
| 6. | Nevada | 10,723 | 11,633 | 111 |
| 7. | Maryland | 10,477 | 11,534 | 110 |
| 8. | Illinois | 10,479 | 11,479 | 109 |
| 9. | New York | 10,252 | 11,440 | 109 |
| 10. | Delaware | 10,291 | 11,279 | 107 |
| 11. | Washington | 10,355 | 11,266 | 107 |
| 12. | Massachusetts | 10,118 | 11,158 | 106 |
| 13. | Colorado | 10,033 | 11,142 | 106 |
| 14. | Hawaii | 10,091 | 11,096 | 106 |
| 15. | Michigan | 9,967 | 11,009 | 105 |
| 16. | Kansas | 9,864 | 10,870 | 103 |
| 17. | Minnesota | 9,765 | 10,747 | 102 |
| 18. | Texas | 9,528 | 10,743 | 102 |
| 19. | North Dakota | 8,626 | 10,525 | 100 |
| 20. | Rhode Island | 9,429 | 10,466 | 100 |
| 21. | Virginia | 9,406 | 10,445 | 99 |
| 22. | Pennsylvania | 9,427 | 10,373 | 99 |
| 23. | Ohio | 9,460 | 10,371 | 99 |
| 24. | Nebraska | 9,086 | 10,296 | 98 |
| 25. | Oklahoma | 9,066 | 10,210 | 97 |
| 26. | Iowa | 9,310 | 10,149 | 97 |
| 27. | New Hampshire | 9,119 | 10,073 | 96 |
| 28. | Wisconsin | 9,413 | 10,056 | 96 |
| 29. | Florida | 8,993 | 10,050 | 96 |
| 30. | Oregon | 9,296 | 9,991 | 95 |
| 31. | Missouri | 8,865 | 9,876 | 94 |
| 32. | Arizona | 8,814 | 9,693 | 92 |
| 33. | Montana | 8,652 | 9,676 | 92 |
| 34. | Indiana | 8,924 | 9,656 | 92 |
| 35. | Louisiana | 8,456 | 9,486 | 90 |
| 36. | Georgia | 8,041 | 8,960 | 85 |
| 37. | Idaho | 8,176 | 8,906 | 85 |
| 38. | South Dakota | 7,818 | 8,793 | 84 |
| 39. | North Carolina | 7,832 | 8,679 | 83 |
| 40. | Maine | 7,868 | 8,655 | 82 |
| 41. | New Mexico | 7,878 | 8,654 | 82 |
| 42. | Vermont | 7,810 | 8,654 | 82 |
| 43. | Tennessee | 7,702 | 8,604 | 82 |
| 44. | Kentucky | 7,662 | 8,455 | 80 |
| 45. | West Virginia | 7,814 | 8,334 | 79 |
| 46. | Utah | 7,681 | 8,308 | 79 |
| 47. | Alabama | 7,434 | 8,200 | 78 |
| 48. | South Carolina | 7,265 | 8,050 | 77 |
| 49. | Arkansas | 7,185 | 8,042 | 76 |
| 50. | Mississippi | 6,557 | 7,256 | 69 |

## INTERNAL REVENUE TAXES

**Source:** U.S. Internal Revenue Service

| Year | Collections | Cost of Collecting $100 | Tax per Capita |
|---|---|---|---|
| 1866 | $310,120,448 | $2.47 | $8.49 |
| 1868 | 190,374,926 | 4.90 | 4.98 |
| 1870 | 184,302,828 | 4.47 | 4.62 |
| 1873 | 113,504,013 | 5.83 | 2.64 |
| 1875 | 110,071,515 | 4.83 | 2.44 |
| 1876 | 116,768,096 | 4.09 | 2.53 |
| 1878 | 110,654,163 | 3.67 | 2.30 |
| 1880 | 123,981,916 | 3.63 | 2.47 |
| 1881 | 135,229,912 | 3.74 | 2.62 |
| 1883 | 144,553,345 | 3.53 | 2.67 |
| 1885 | 112,421,121 | 3.96 | 1.98 |
| 1886 | 116,902,896 | 3.68 | 2.02 |
| 1888 | 124,326,475 | 3.20 | 2.05 |
| 1890 | 142,594,697 | 2.87 | 2.26 |
| 1891 | 146,035,416 | 2.88 | 2.27 |
| 1893 | 161,004,990 | 2.62 | 2.40 |
| 1895 | 143,246,078 | 2.88 | 2.06 |
| 1896 | 146,830,616 | 2.78 | 2.07 |
| 1898 | 170,866,819 | 2.29 | 2.32 |
| 1900 | 295,316,108 | 1.58 | 3.88 |
| 1901 | 306,871,669 | 1.55 | 3.95 |
| 1903 | 230,740,925 | 2.07 | 2.86 |
| 1905 | 234,187,976 | 2.01 | 2.79 |
| 1906 | 249,102,738 | 1.90 | 2.92 |
| 1908 | 251,665,950 | 1.92 | 2.84 |
| 1910 | 289,957,220 | 1.74 | 3.14 |
| 1911 | 322,526,300 | 1.68 | 3.44 |
| 1913 | 344,424,454 | 1.59 | 3.54 |
| 1915 | 415,681,024 | 1.64 | 4.13 |
| 1916 | 512,723,288 | 1.40 | 5.03 |
| 1917 | 809,393,640 | 0.95 | 7.83 |
| 1918 | 3,698,955,821 | 0.33 | 35.38 |
| 1919 | 3,850,150,079 | 0.53 | 36.65 |
| 1921 | 4,595,357,062 | 0.72 | 42.34 |
| 1925 | 2,584,140,268 | 1.44 | 22.31 |
| 1926 | 2,835,999,892 | 1.23 | 24.16 |
| 1928 | 2,790,535,538 | 1.17 | 23.16 |
| 1929 | 2,939,054,375 | 1.17 | 24.14 |
| 1930 | 3,040,145,733 | 1.13 | 24.68 |
| 1932 | $1,557,729,043 | $2.17 | $12.47 |
| 1934 | 2,672,239,195 | 1.08 | 21.13 |
| 1935 | 3,299,435,572 | 1.29 | 25.91 |
| 1937 | 4,653,195,315 | 1.12 | 36.08 |
| 1939 | 5,181,573,953 | 1.13 | 39.55 |
| 1941 | 7,370,108,378 | 0.89 | 55.04 |
| 1943 | 22,371,385,497 | 0.44 | 163.00 |
| 1944 | 40,121,760,233 | 0.32 | 288.82 |
| 1945 | 43,800,387,576 | 0.33 | 311.82 |
| 1946 | 40,672,096,998 | 0.43 | 286.55 |
| 1948 | 41,864,542,295 | 0.44 | 284.39 |
| 1950 | 38,957,131,768 | 0.59 | 255.84 |
| 1951 | 50,445,686,315 | 0.49 | 325.71 |
| 1952 | 65,009,585,560 | 0.42 | 412.62 |
| 1954 | 69,919,990,791 | 0.38 | 428.89 |
| 1955 | 66,288,692,000 | 0.42 | 399.50 |
| 1957 | 80,171,917,000 | 0.38 | 466.16 |
| 1958 | 79,978,476,484 | 0.42 | 457.33 |
| 1959 | 79,797,972,806 | 0.44 | 448.73 |
| 1960 | 91,774,802,823 | 0.40 | 507.96 |
| 1961 | 94,401,086,398 | 0.44 | 513.91 |
| 1962 | 99,440,839,245 | 0.45 | 533.09 |
| 1963 | 105,925,395,281 | 0.47 | 559.74 |
| 1964 | 112,260,257,115 | 0.49 | 585.03 |
| 1965 | 114,434,633,721 | 0.52 | 588.95 |
| 1966 | 128,879,961,342 | 0.48 | 655.68 |
| 1967 | 148,374,814,552 | 0.45 | 746.68 |
| 1968 | 153,636,837,665 | 0.46 | 765.48 |
| 1969 | 187,919,559,668 | 0.40 | 927.19 |
| 1970 | 195,722,096,497 | 0.45 | 955.31 |
| 1971 | 191,647,198,138 | 0.51 | 925.63 |
| 1972 | 209,855,736,878 | 0.54 | 1,004.83 |
| 1973 | 237,787,204,058 | 0.49 | 1,130.11 |
| 1974 | 268,952,253,663 | 0.49 | 1,269.24 |
| 1975 | 293,822,725,772 | 0.54 | 1,375.84 |
| 1976 | 302,519,791,922 | 0.56 | 1,406.14 |
| 1977 | 358,139,416,730 | 0.50 | 1,647.91 |
| 1978 | 399,776,389,362 | 0.49 | 1,826.61 |
| 1979 | 460,412,185,013 | 0.46 | 2,083.32 |
| 1980 | 519,375,273,361 | 0.44 | 2,325.04 |
| 1981 | 606,799,120,630 | 0.41 | 2,686.55 |

## ADDRESSES OF U.S. INTERNAL REVENUE OFFICES

| If you are located in: | Send your return to: |
|---|---|
| Alabama, Florida, Georgia, Mississippi, South Carolina | Internal Revenue Service Center Atlanta, Georgia 31101 |
| Delaware, District of Columbia, Maryland, Pennsylvania | Internal Revenue Service Center Philadelphia, Pennsylvania 19255 |
| Michigan, Ohio | Internal Revenue Service Center Cincinnati, Ohio 45999 |
| Arkansas, Kansas, Louisiana, New Mexico, Oklahoma, Texas | Internal Revenue Service Center Austin, Texas 73301 |
| Illinois, Iowa, Missouri, Wisconsin | Internal Revenue Service Center Kansas City, Missouri 64999 |
| Connecticut, Maine, Massachusetts, New Hampshire, New York (except N.Y.C., and Nassau, Rockland, Suffolk, and Westchester counties), Rhode Island, Vermont | Internal Revenue Service Center Andover, Massachusetts 05501 |
| Indiana, Kentucky, North Carolina, Tennessee, Virginia, West Virginia | Internal Revenue Service Center Memphis, Tennessee 37501 |
| Alaska, Arizona, Colorado, Idaho, Minnesota, Montana, Nebraska, Nevada, North Dakota, Oregon, South Dakota, Utah, Washington, Wyoming | Internal Revenue Service Center Ogden, Utah 84201 |
| California, Hawaii | Internal Revenue Service Center Fresno, California 93888 |
| New York City and N.Y. counties of Nassau, Rockland, Suffolk, and Westchester; New Jersey | Internal Revenue Service Center Holtsville, New York 00501 |
| American Samoa | Internal Revenue Service Center Philadelphia, Pennsylvania 19255 |
| Guam | Commissioner of Revenue and Taxation Agana, Guam 96910 |
| Puerto Rico (or if excluding income under section 933), Virgin Islands: Non permanent residents | Internal Revenue Service Center Philadelphia, Pennsylvania 19255 |
| Virgin Islands: Permanent residents | Department of Finance, Tax Division Charlotte Amalie, St. Thomas Virgin Islands 00801 |

U.S. citizens with foreign addresses (except A.P.O. and F.P.O.) and those excluding income under sec. 911 or 931: file with Internal Revenue Service, Philadelphia, Pa. 19255

| U.S. citizens with A.P.O. or F.P.O. address of: | |
|---|---|
| Miami | Internal Revenue Service Center Atlanta, Georgia 31101 |
| New York | Internal Revenue Service Center Holtsville, New York 00501 |
| San Francisco | Internal Revenue Service Center Fresno, California 93888 |
| Seattle | Internal Revenue Service Center Ogden, Utah 84201 |

# TAX TIPS

Prepared by **H&R BLOCK** THE INCOME TAX PEOPLE

The tax tips discussed here are based on current tax law as of August 15, 1982. New tax legislation could result in changes.

The federal tax code requires that all deductions be substantiated. Good record-keeping is an important part of minimizing tax liability.

## INVESTMENTS, CAPITAL GAINS

For 1982, up to $100 ($200 on a joint return) of qualifying dividends may be excluded from income. Up to a total of $1,000 ($2,000 on a joint return) of interest earned on All Savers certificates is tax exempt if the certificates are held to maturity. Beginning in 1985, an exclusion of 15% of net interest up to $3,000 ($6,000 on a joint return) will be allowed.

U.S. series EE bonds may be a worthwhile investment. Interest earned is not taxable until the bonds mature (plus extensions) or are cashed. Or, you may elect to report the interest each year as it accrues. If the latter choice is made, all such interest in all future years is taxable as it accrues. This election may be wise when it is expected that gross income will be greater in the year(s) the bonds will be cashed than in the intervening years (such as bonds purchased for a child which will be used for his or her future). The first year the election is made, a return must be filed with a statement on the option chosen. Thereafter a return is filed or not, based on the usual filing requirements.

You may open a savings account or purchase stock to save for your child's college education or future without paying tax on the earnings. The security or savings must be in the child's name and neither the principal nor earnings can be used for the child's support or in any way used by you. You may be custodian of the investment. The child is not required to file a return for any year in which his or her investment income is less than $1,000 or gross income is less than $3,300. If the child is required to file, his or her tax on this income would most likely be less than the adult would have paid.

Sales of capital assets should be planned to gain the greatest possible tax advantage without sacrificing economic results. Try to avoid sales at a loss in the same year in which you will have a long-term gain. Only 40% of a net long-term capital gain is taxable, but gains and losses must be combined to determine the net gain or loss. To realize 100% of a long-term loss, sell short-term assets at a gain. (Only 50% of a net long-term loss is deductible against ordinary income.) Generally, property owned over one year is long term. Commodity futures are long term if held over 6 months.

## SELLING YOUR PRINCIPAL RESIDENCE

If you sell your home, all or part of any gain will not be taxed immediately if, within 24 months, you buy and occupy another home. The deferred gain reduces the basis of the new home. A taxpayer of age 55 or over on the date of sale may exclude up to $125,000 gain from sale of his or her principal residence. To qualify, you must have owned and lived in the home three of the five years ending on the date of sale. This election may be made only once in a lifetime.

If you sell your home on contract and cannot defer all or part of the gain, you may use the installment method. Gain is reported in the years that payments are received instead of all in the year of sale.

## PAYMENTS TO BENEFICIARIES

Life insurance proceeds paid because of the death of the insured, whether received in a lump sum or installments, generally are not taxable. If a surviving spouse elects to receive the proceeds in installments, up to $1,000 per year of the interest may be excluded from income. If you elect to receive interest only, it is fully taxable.

The first $5,000 of payments to beneficiaries of deceased employees made by or for an employer because of an employee's death is excludable from the income of the beneficiaries. The excludable amount may not exceed $5,000, regardless of the number of employers or the number of beneficiaries.

## END-OF-YEAR TAX PLANNING

It will generally be advantageous to defer receipt of income to later years, if possible.

Before the end of the year, you should estimate whether the total of your itemized deductions will exceed your zero bracket amount. If it will, it may be beneficial to pay any outstanding obligations that are deductible before the end of the year. If the total itemized deductions will not exceed the zero bracket amount, it will be better to postpone (if possible) payment of deductible obligations until the beginning of the new tax year.

Payment of various items, such as charitable contributions, medical expenses, and the fourth installment of estimated state and local income tax, can be timed to derive the greatest tax benefit. Interest generally may be deducted only in the year for which it is due. If medical expenses for 1982 are close to or exceed 3% of your income and deductions are itemized, you may reduce your tax liability by paying outstanding medical bills and having necessary optical and dental work done and paid for before the end of the year.

The amount of estimated unpaid tax at which estimated tax payments are required is $200 for 1982, $300 for 1983, $400 for 1984, and $500 for 1985 and later years. The interest rate on underpayments is 100% of the prime bank rate and will be adjusted semiannually.

## MARRIAGE PENALTY DEDUCTION

If both spouses are employed, a "marriage penalty" deduction may be claimed by a married couple on their joint tax return. This deduction is allowed regardless of whether you itemize. In 1982, 5% of up to $30,000 of the qualified earned income of the spouse having the lower earned income may be deducted.

## ADOPTION EXPENSES

Up to $1,500 of unreimbursed expenses incurred to adopt a child with special needs may be deducted on Schedule A. A qualified child is one for whom adoption assistance payments are made under section 473 of the Social Security Act.

## CHARITABLE CONTRIBUTIONS

You may deduct actual transportation expenses incurred in performing volunteer work for a charitable organization. In lieu of actual costs, you may deduct nine cents a mile plus parking fees and tolls. Also deductible are the cost and upkeep of uniforms required to be worn and equipment or supplies purchased to perform volunteer work. All items must be used solely for the charitable work.

You may deduct up to 50 percent of adjusted gross income for cash contributions made to churches, educational organizations, certain medical organizations, public organizations such as libraries and symphony orchestras, and other charities that receive most of their support from the general public or the government.

For 1982, if you do not itemize, you may deduct 25% of the first $100 ($50 MFS) of your charitable contributions. If you itemize, total contributions should be claimed on Schedule A as usual.

**CASUALTY LOSS**

Loss or damage to your property resulting from a sudden or unusual event such as severe weather, fire, accident or theft may be deductible. If you sustained such a loss in an area determined by the President to warrant federal disaster assistance, the loss may be claimed on your tax return for the year of the loss or the preceding year, whichever is more advantageous.

**AGE 65 BRINGS TAX BENEFITS**

You are allowed an additional personal exemption if you are 65 or older on the last day of the year. For tax purposes, you are considered 65 on the day before your 65th birthday.

You may be eligible for a tax credit if you are age 65 or older or are under age 65 and receive a pension or annuity from a public retirement system. The maximum credit is $375 for single individuals, $562.50 for married individuals filing a joint return, and $281.25 for married individuals filing a separate return. Married individuals must file a joint return to claim the credit unless they lived apart for the entire year.

**CLAIMING DEPENDENTS**

It is not always necessary to provide more than half of the support for a relative to claim him or her as a dependent. If you and one or more persons could claim the relative as a dependent, except for the support test and together contribute more than 50 percent of the support, you can agree to let any one who individually furnishes more than 10 percent of the support claim the dependent. The other contributors must sign Multiple Support Declarations (Form 2120) which are to be attached to the return of the individual who claims the exemption.

Parents who provide over half the total support of their working child (who is under 19 or is a student) may claim a dependent exemption regardless of the amount the child earns.

**DIVORCED TAXPAYERS**

Generally, the parent who has custody of the child for the greater part of the year is entitled to claim the exemption. There are two exceptions to this rule. The noncustody parent is entitled to the exemption if he or she:

1) contributed at least $600 toward each child's support during the year and the divorce decree or other agreement specifies that this parent is entitled to the exemption. Any agreement must be in writing. OR

2) provided $1,200 (or more) support for each child during the year and the parent having custody cannot prove that he or she provided more support.

Child support payments are neither deductible by the payer nor taxable to the recipient. If the decree does not specify an amount as child support, the entire payment is alimony. Alimony payments, generally, are deductible by the payer and taxable to the recipient. Deductible alimony is claimed as an adjustment, deductible regardless of whether deductions are itemized.

**EARNED-INCOME CREDIT**

Some individuals will qualify for the earned-income credit. If both your adjusted gross income and your earned income are less than $10,000 and you maintain your home for a qualifying child you may be eligible for this credit. Maximum credit is $500.

**OTHER CREDITS**

An investment credit is available when qualified business property is purchased. Employees may be able to claim this credit if required to use their own vehicles, tools, etc. in their work.

Residential energy credit is available for insulation, storm or thermal windows and certain energy saving devices installed in your home. Also for solar, wind or geothermal equipment. Energy investment credit is available to businesses for energy-conserving expenditures.

You may be able to claim a credit if you pay for the care of your child or disabled dependent that enables you to be gainfully employed.

**INDIVIDUAL RETIREMENT ACCOUNTS**

All taxpayers who have earned income, including those covered by an employer's qualified plan, may establish an Individual Retirement Account (IRA). If eligible, you may contribute and deduct up to the lesser of 100% of your compensation or $2,000 each year. In addition, the interest earned on your contributions is not taxable until it is withdrawn. Generally, any amount withdrawn before you reach age 59½ will be subject to a 10% penalty as well as being includable in income. If you become disabled or die, the penalty won't apply.

If your spouse received no earned income during the year, you may contribute to spousal IRAs. The maximum deduction and contribution for spousal IRAs is the lesser of 100% of compensation or $2,250. Your contribution may be divided between the accounts in any manner you choose, except the contribution to one spouse's account cannot exceed $2,000 per year. There is no longer a requirement that equal amounts be contributed to each spouse's account. You have until the due date of your tax return to establish and contribute to an IRA for that year.

**DEPRECIABLE ASSETS**

In years after 1980, recovery of the cost of property used for business or employment purposes will generally be more rapid and the computation more simple. In general, a larger investment credit will be earned in fewer years.

Beginning in 1982, an election will be available to deduct up to $5,000 of the cost of tangible personal property used for business or employment purposes. The allowable deduction increases to $10,000 by 1986. It is allowed in place of the recovery deduction (depreciation) and investment credit.

**INCOME EARNED ABROAD**

Income earned abroad by U.S. citizens and residents may be excluded up to $75,000 in 1982, increasing to $95,000 by 1986. In addition, excessive housing costs may be deductible.

**ESTATE AND GIFT TAXES**

Beginning in 1982, you can give up to $10,000 per year per recipient without incurring gift tax, unlimited amounts may be transferred between spouses without incurring gift or estate taxes, and by 1987 only estates valued in excess of $600,000 will be taxed.

## FEDERAL TAX COLLECTIONS

SOURCE: Tax Foundation, Inc. Based on official U.S. Government figures.

| | SELECTED FISCAL YEARS 1959-1982 (Figures in millions) | | | | | |
|---|---|---|---|---|---|---|
| SOURCE | 1959 | 1969 | 1979 | 1980 | 1981 | 1982* |
| **Total** | $77,520 | $182,575 | $450,817 | $500,950 | $581,596 | $606,449 |
| Income and profits taxes | 54,028 | 123,927 | 283,518 | 308,666 | 347,054 | 345,330 |
| Individual income | 36,719 | 87,249 | 217,841 | 244,069 | 285,917 | 298,578 |
| Corporate income and profits | 17,309 | 36,678 | 65,677 | 64,600 | 61,137 | 46,752 |
| Excise taxes | 10,760 | 15,543 | 18,479 | 24,619 | 40,420 | 42,993 |
| Alcoholic beverages | 3,002 | 4,556 | 5,531 | 5,705 | 5,688 | — |
| Tobacco products | 1,807 | 2,138 | 2,492 | 2,446 | 2,584 | — |
| Manufacturers' excises | 3,959 | 6,501 | 5,901 | 6,487 | 6,089 | — |
| Gasoline | 1,700 | 3,186 | 4,383 | 4,218 | 4,008 | — |
| Passenger automobiles[1] | 1,039 | 1,864 | — | 0.3 | 1.0 | — |
| Tires and tubes | 279 | 632 | 852 | 683 | 669 | — |
| Automobile and truck parts and accessories | 166 | 81 | 221 | 235 | 227 | — |
| Trucks and buses | 215 | 589 | 927 | 854 | 687 | — |
| Lubricating oils | 74 | 97 | 107 | 108 | 101 | — |
| Other manufacturers' excises | 464 | 0.9 | 117 | 8 | — | — |
| Retailers' excises | 408 | 225 | 552 | 560 | 587 | — |
| Miscellaneous excises | 383 | 1,923 | 3,563 | 6,359 | 19,774 | — |
| Telephone and telegraph | 690 | 1,316 | 1,340 | 1,118 | 999 | — |
| Transportation of persons | 227 | 224 | 1,282 | 1,566 | 1,281 | — |
| Other miscellaneous excises[2] | 179 | 1 | 941 | 0.3 | — | — |
| Estate and gift taxes | 1,333 | 3,491 | 5,411 | 6,389 | 6,787 | 7,162 |
| Employment taxes | 8,526 | 34,236 | 120,074 | 138,765 | 162,973 | 185,527 |
| Unemployment taxes[3] | 2,024 | 3,328 | 15,387 | 15,336 | 15,763 | 16,461 |
| Customs | 925 | 2,319 | 7,439 | 7,174 | 8,083 | 8,870 |
| Miscellaneous | 9 | 52 | 243 | 288 | 97 | 106 |

* Data for 1982 are estimated. [1] Repealed as of July 15, 1971. [2] Repealed as of June 22, 1965. Includes taxes on jewelry, furs, toilet preparations, luggage, handbags, and fuels used on inland waterways. [3] Includes state unemployment taxes deposited with the Treasury.

## PER CAPITA PROPERTY TAX COLLECTIONS

SOURCE: Bureau of the Census and the Tax Foundation

| State | Amount 1970 | Amount 1980 | Percent Increase | State | Amount 1970 | Amount 1980 | Percent Increase | State | Amount 1970 | Amount 1980 | Percent Increase |
|---|---|---|---|---|---|---|---|---|---|---|---|
| U.S. Avg. | $168 | $302 | 80 | Ky. | $ 69 | $135 | 97 | Ohio | $162 | $281 | 73 |
| Ala. | 39 | 79 | 100 | La. | 65 | 111 | 70 | Okla. | 93 | 151 | 63 |
| Alaska | 102 | 900 | 785 | Maine | 174 | 319 | 84 | Oreg. | 189 | 382 | 102 |
| Ariz. | 166 | 352 | 112 | Md. | 156 | 288 | 84 | Pa. | 119 | 249 | 110 |
| Ark. | 65 | 134 | 106 | Mass. | 250 | 555 | 122 | R.I. | 165 | 413 | 150 |
| Calif. | 262 | 274 | 4 | Mich. | 184 | 414 | 125 | S.C. | 61 | 160 | 160 |
| Colo. | 179 | 329 | 84 | Minn. | 171 | 324 | 90 | S.D. | 219 | 351 | 60 |
| Conn. | 238 | 473 | 98 | Miss. | 71 | 141 | 97 | Tenn. | 77 | 158 | 105 |
| Del. | 84 | 167 | 100 | Mo. | 137 | 215 | 57 | Texas | 128 | 280 | 118 |
| Fla. | 118 | 224 | 90 | Mont. | 216 | 455 | 111 | Utah | 135 | 235 | 74 |
| Ga. | 95 | 199 | 109 | Nebr. | 209 | 401 | 92 | Vt. | 164 | 377 | 130 |
| Hawaii | 98 | 193 | 96 | Nev. | 178 | 256 | 44 | Va. | 96 | 236 | 145 |
| Idaho | 127 | 227 | 79 | N.H. | 207 | 451 | 117 | Wash. | 155 | 290 | 87 |
| Ill. | 201 | 367 | 83 | N.J. | 242 | 499 | 106 | W.Va. | 70 | 137 | 95 |
| Ind. | 168 | 246 | 46 | N.M. | 81 | 142 | 75 | Wisc. | 220 | 361 | 64 |
| Iowa | 213 | 360 | 69 | N.Y. | 237 | 501 | 111 | Wy. | 206 | 552 | 168 |
| Kansas | 202 | 366 | 81 | N.C. | 79 | 171 | 117 | D.C. | 169 | 344 | 104 |
| | | | | N.D. | 175 | 269 | 54 | | | | |

## TAX BURDEN: SELECTED COUNTRIES

SOURCE: Tax Foundation, Inc. Based on OECD data

| Country | TAXES* AS % OF GROSS DOMESTIC PRODUCT 1970 | 1975 | 1980 | Country | TAXES* AS % OF GROSS DOMESTIC PRODUCT 1970 | 1975 | 1980 |
|---|---|---|---|---|---|---|---|
| Australia | 25.49 | 29.14 | 25.82[1] | Japan | 19.72 | 21.10 | 25.85 |
| Austria | 35.66 | 38.54 | 41.54 | Luxembourg | 31.94 | 43.57 | 47.56 |
| Belgium | 35.96 | 41.07 | 42.49 | Netherlands | 39.89 | 45.80 | 46.19 |
| Canada | 32.00 | 32.93 | 32.81 | New Zealand | 26.39 | 30.04 | 31.18[1] |
| Denmark | 40.23 | 41.05 | 45.14 | Norway | 39.19 | 44.82 | 47.36 |
| Finland | 32.18 | 36.15 | 34.46 | Portugal | 23.21 | 24.82 | 29.78 |
| France | 35.58 | 37.44 | 42.51 | Spain | 17.22 | 19.60 | 23.16 |
| Germany, West | 32.80 | 35.68 | 37.23 | Sweden | 40.99 | 44.24 | 49.87 |
| Greece | 24.30 | 24.64 | 27.69[1] | Switzerland | 23.81 | 29.61 | 30.74 |
| Ireland | 31.23 | 32.49 | 37.54 | Turkey | 17.63 | 20.67 | 20.84[1] |
| Italy | 27.91 | 28.98 | 30.09[1] | United Kingdom | 37.51 | 36.08 | 35.91 |
| | | | | United States | 30.10 | 30.18 | 30.69 |

[1] Data are for 1979.

## STATE INCOME TAX RATES AND EXEMPTIONS

SOURCE: Reprinted with permission from the *State Tax Guide*, published by Commerce Clearing House, Inc.

Five states have neither personal nor corporate income tax; they are Nevada, South Dakota, Texas, Washington, and Wyoming.

Under personal exemptions, additional exemptions for aged and/or blind are not included. All figures are as of July 1, 1982.

| State | Personal Exemptions | Individual Rates | Corporation Rates |
|---|---|---|---|
| ALABAMA | Single ....... $1,500<br>Married ...... 3,000<br>Dependent .... 300 | 1st $1,000........ 1.5% Next $2,000......... 4.5%<br>Next 2,000........ 3 Over 5,000......... 5 | 5%. Financial institutions 6% |
| ALASKA | | The Alaska personal income tax was repealed in September 1980, effective retroactive to January 1, 1979. Refunds are due persons who paid taxes in year 1979 and during 1980. Due to surplus state funds, all residents, adults and children, are eligible for special payments from oil earnings of Alaska Permanent Fund. Payment for 1982 was $1,000, estimate for 1983 is $356; applications for each year are due in October of each year. | Increments of 1% for each $10,000 up to $90,000; 9.4% for over $90,000. |
| ARIZONA | Single ....... $1,589<br>Married ...... 3,178<br>Dependent .... 954 | 1st $1,000........ 2% Next $1,000......... 6%<br>Next 1,000........ 3 Next 1,000......... 7<br>Next 1,000........ 4 Over 6,000......... 8<br>Next 1,000........ 5<br>Joint returns may split their income. | 1st $1,000 2.5%<br>2nd 1,000 4<br>3rd 1,000 5<br>4th 1,000 6.5<br>5th 1,000 8<br>6th 1,000 9<br>Over 6,000 10.5 |
| ARKANSAS | From tax:<br>Single ....... $17.50<br>Married ...... 35.00<br>Dependent .... 6.00 | 1st $2,999........ 1% Next $ 6,000......... 4.5%<br>Next 3,000........ 2.5 Next 10,000......... 6<br>Next 3,000........ 3.5 $25,000 and over.......... 7 | 1st $ 3,000 1%<br>2nd 3,000 2<br>Next 5,000 3<br>Next 14,000 5<br>Over 25,000 6 |
| CALIFOR-NIA | From tax:<br>Single ....... $35.00<br>Married ...... 70.00<br>Dependent .... 11.00 | 0-$ 2,850........ 1% $13,580-$15,710......... 7%<br>2,850- 4,990........ 2 15,710- 17,860......... 8<br>4,990- 7,130........ 3 17,860- 20,000......... 9<br>7,130- 9,290........ 4 20,000- 22,140........ 10<br>9,290- 11,430........ 5 22,140 and over........ 11<br>11,430- 13,580........ 6<br>Tax rates for heads of households range from 1% of taxable income not over $4,000 to 11% of taxable income over $23,750. | 9.6%.<br>Financial institutions, other than banks, are allowed limited offset for personal property taxes and license fees. |
| COLORADO | Single ....... $ 850<br>Married ...... 1,700<br>Dependent .... 850 | 0- $1,335........ 2.5% $ 8,011-$ 9,346......... 5.5%<br>1,335- 2,670........ 3 9,346- 10,681......... 6<br>2,670- 4,006........ 3.5 10,681- 12,017......... 6.5<br>4,006- 5,341........ 4 12,017- 13,352......... 7.5<br>5,341- 6,676........ 4.5 13,352 and over......... 8<br>6,676- 8,011........ 5<br>Surtax on intangible income over $5,000 ...................... 2%<br>Tax reduction credit applies to reduce the effective rate of tax ½ of 1% in each bracket up to $9,000. | 5%. |
| CONNECTI-CUT | Single ....... $100<br>Married, filing jointly...... 200<br>Married, filing separately .. 100 | Rates ranging from 1% on the net capital gains and dividends of at least $20,000, up to 9% on $100,000 and over. | 10% plus .31 of 1 mill per dollar of capital stock and surplus. Min. tax $250, max. tax $100,000. |
| DELAWARE | Single ....... $ 600<br>Married ...... 1,200<br>Dependent .... 600 | 1st $1,000........ 1.4% Next $ 5,000......... 8.2%<br>Next 1,000........ 2 Next 5,000......... 8.4<br>Next 1,000........ 3 Next 5,000......... 8.8<br>Next 1,000........ 4.2 Next 5,000......... 9.4<br>Next 1,000........ 5.2 Next 10,000........ 11<br>Next 1,000........ 6.2 Next 10,000........ 12.2<br>Next 2,000........ 7.2 Over 50,000........ 13.5<br>Next 2,000........ 8 | 8.7%. |
| D. OF COLUMBIA | Single ....... $1,000<br>Married ...... 2,000<br>Dependent .... 1,000 | 1st $1,000........ 2% Next $ 5,000......... 7%<br>Next 1,000........ 3 Next 3,000......... 8<br>Next 1,000........ 4 Next 4,000......... 9<br>Next 1,000........ 5 Next 8,000........ 10<br>Next 1,000........ 6 Over 25,000........ 11 | 9% plus 10% surtax. Minimum $25. |
| FLORIDA | No personal income tax. | | 5%. |
| GEORGIA | Single ....... $1,500<br>Married ...... 3,000<br>Dependent .... 700 | 1st $1,000........ 1% Next $ 2,000......... 4%<br>Next 2,000........ 2 Next 3,000......... 5<br>Next 2,000........ 3 Over 10,000......... 6<br>Rates are for married persons filing jointly. | 6%. |
| HAWAII | Single ....... $1,000<br>Married ...... 2,000<br>Dependent .... 1,000 | 1st $1,000...... No tax Next $ 4,000......... 7.5%<br>Next 1,000........ 2.25% Next 10,000......... 8.5<br>Next 1,000........ 3.25 Next 8,000......... 9.5<br>Next 1,000........ 4.5 Next 12,000........ 10.0<br>Next 1,000........ 5.0 Next 20,000........ 10.5<br>Next 2,000........ 6.5 Over 61,000........ 11.0 | 1st $25,000 5.85%<br>Over 25,000 6.435 |
| IDAHO | Single ....... $1,000<br>Married ...... 2,000<br>Dependent .... 1,000 | 1st $1,000........ 2% Next $1,000......... 5.5%<br>Next 1,000........ 4 Next 1,000......... 6.5<br>Next 1,000........ 4.5 Over 5,000......... 7.5<br>Additional $10 due from each person (joint returns deemed one person) filing return. Joint returns may split their income. | 6.5%. Additional tax $10. |
| ILLINOIS | Single ....... $1,000<br>Married ...... 2,000<br>Dependent .... 1,000 | 2.5% of taxable net income. | 4%. |
| INDIANA | Single ....... $1,000<br>Married ...... 2,000<br>Dependent .... 500 | 1.9% of federal adjusted gross income. | 3% + 4% supplemental income tax. |

| State | Personal Exemptions | Individual Rates | Corporation Rates |
|---|---|---|---|
| IOWA | From tax:<br>Single ....... $15.00<br>Married ...... 30.00<br>Dependent .... 10.00 | 0- $1,023...... 0.5%<br>1,023- 2,046........ 1.25<br>2,046- 3,069........ 2.75<br>3,069- 4,092........ 3.5<br>20,460- 25,575........ 9%<br>25,575- 30,690....... 10<br>30,690- 40,920....... 11<br>$ 4,092-$ 7,161......... 5%<br>7,161- 9,207......... 6<br>9,207- 15,345......... 7<br>15,345- 20,460......... 8<br>40,920- 76,725........ 12<br>76,725 and over........ 13<br>Tax brackets adjusted annually for inflation. | 1st $ 25,000 6%<br>Next 75,000 8<br>Next 150,000 10<br>Over 250,000 12<br>Financial institutions: 5% of taxable income. |
| KANSAS | Single ....... $1,000<br>Married ...... 2,000<br>Dependent .... 1,000 | 1st $2,000........ 2%<br>Next 1,000........ 3.5<br>Next 2,000........ 4<br>Next 2,000........ 5<br>Next $ 3,000......... 6.5%<br>Next 10,000......... 7.5<br>Next 5,000......... 8.5<br>Over 25,000......... 9.0 | 4.5% + 2¼% surtax over $25,000. |
| KEN-TUCKY | From tax:<br>Single ....... $20.00<br>Married ...... 40.00<br>Dependent .... 20.00 | 1st $3,000........ 2%<br>Next 1,000........ 3<br>Next 1,000........ 4<br>Next $3,000......... 5%<br>Over 8,000......... 6 | 1st $25,000 3%<br>Next 25,000 4<br>Next 50,000 5<br>Over 100,000 6 |
| LOUISI-ANA | Single ....... $ 6,000<br>Married ...... 12,000<br>Dependent .... 1,000 | 1st $10,000........ 2%<br>Next 40,000........ 4<br>Over 50,000........ 6<br>Joint returns may split their income. | Up to $ 25,000 4%<br>Next 25,000 4%<br>Next 50,000 6<br>Next 100,000 7<br>Over 200,000 8 |
| MAINE | Single ....... $1,000<br>Married ...... 2,000<br>Dependent .... 1,000 | 1% on the first $2,000 to 10% of taxable income over $25,000. | 1st $25,000 4.95%<br>Over 25,000 6.93 |
| MARYLAND | Single ....... $ 800<br>Married ...... 1,600<br>Dependent .... 800 | 1st $1,000........ 2%<br>Next 1,000........ 3<br>Next $1,000.......... 4%<br>Over 3,000.......... 5 | 7%. |
| MASSA-CHUSETTS | From earned income:<br>Single ....... $2,000<br>Married (joint return) ..... 2,000 plus up to $2,000 for spouse with lower income plus $800 if that spouse's income was under $2,000.<br>Dependent .... 700 | Interest, dividends, net capital gains.................... ... 10%<br>Earned income, annuities .................................. 5<br>(Plus 7.5% surtax) | 8.33% of net income plus $2.60 per $1,000 of tangible property, or $200 (whichever is greater), plus 14% surtax. |
| MICHIGAN | Single ....... $1,500<br>Married ...... 3,000<br>Dependent .... 1,500 | 4.6% of adjusted gross income. 1% surcharge imposed from April 1, 1982 to Sept. 30, 1982. | 2.35%. |
| MINNE-SOTA | From tax:<br>Single ....... $ 66<br>Married ...... 132<br>Dependent .... 66 | 0- $ 654........ 1.6%<br>654- 1,308........ 2.2<br>1,308- 2,614........ 3.5<br>2,614- 3,920........ 5.8<br>3,920- 5,226........ 7.3<br>5,226- 6,532........ 8.8<br>$ 6,532-$ 9,144........ 10.2%<br>9,144- 11,756........ 11.5<br>11,756- 16,327........ 12.8<br>16,327- 26,121........ 14.0<br>26,121- 35,915........ 15.0<br>Over 35,915........ 16.0<br>Plus surtax 7% for 1982; 3.5 % surtax for 1983. | 1st $25,000 9%<br>Over 25,000 12<br>6% rate after Jan. 1, 1983. |
| MISSIS-SIPPI | Single ....... $6,000<br>Married ...... 9,500<br>Dependent .... 1,500 | 1st $5,000........ 3%<br>Over 5,000........ 4 | 1st $5,000 3%<br>Over 5,000 4 |
| MISSOURI | Single ....... $1,200<br>Married ...... 2,400<br>Dependent .... 400 | 1st $1,000........ 1.5%<br>2nd 1,000........ 2<br>3rd 1,000........ 2.5<br>4th 1,000........ 3<br>5th 1,000........ 3.5<br>6th $1,000......... 4%<br>7th 1,000......... 4.5<br>8th 1,000......... 5.0<br>9th 1,000......... 5.5<br>Over 9,000......... 6.0 | 5%. |
| MONTANA | Single ....... $ 880<br>Married ...... 1,600<br>Dependent .... 880 | 1st $1,000........ 2%<br>Next 1,000........ 3<br>Next 2,000........ 4<br>Next 2,000........ 5<br>Next 2,000........ 6<br>Next 2,000........ 7<br>Next $ 4,000......... 8%<br>Next 6,000......... 9<br>Next 15,000......... 10<br>Over 35,000......... 11<br>(Plus 10% surtax.)<br>Tax brackets adjusted annually for inflation. | 6.75%. Minimum tax for corporations, $50, except $10 for small business corporations. |
| NEBRASKA | Federal personal exemptions already computed in the tax. | 17% of adjusted federal income tax liability. | 1st $50,000 4.25%<br>Over 50,000 5.95 |
| NEW HAMP-SHIRE | $1,200 | (Interest and dividend tax). 5% on income from interest and dividends. | 8%, plus surcharge 13.5%. Min. tax $250. |
| NEW JERSEY | Single ....... $1,000<br>Married ...... 2,000<br>Dependent .... 1,000 | 1st $20,000........ 2%<br>Over $20,000......... 2.5%<br>New York and Pennsylvania residents working in New Jersey are taxed at the same respective rate of their state of residence. | 9% on allocated net income of interstate corporations, plus additional tax on net worth. |

| State | Personal Exemptions | | Individual Rates | | Corporation Rates |
|---|---|---|---|---|---|
| NEW MEXICO | Single ....... | $1,000 | Rates range from 0.5% of net income for 1st $2,000 to 6.0% of net income over $100,000. | | 1st $1 million 4% |
| | Married ...... | 2,000 | | | 2nd $1 million 5% |
| | Dependent .... | 1,000 | | | Over $2 million 6% |
| NEW YORK | Single ....... | $ 800 | 1st $1,000.......... 2% | Next $ 2,000.......... 9% | 10% of net income, min. $250 or a tax on three alternative bases, whichever produces the greatest tax. |
| | Married ...... | 1,600 | Next 2,000.......... 3 | Next 2,000.......... 10 | |
| | Dependent .... | 800 | Next 2,000.......... 4 | Next 2,000.......... 11 | |
| | | | Next 2,000.......... 5 | Next 2,000.......... 12 | |
| | | | Next 2,000.......... 6 | Next 2,000.......... 13 | |
| | | | Next 2,000.......... 7 | Over 23,000.......... 14 | |
| | | | Next 2,000.......... 8 | | |
| NORTH CAROLINA | Single ....... | $1,100 | 1st $2,000.......... 3% | Next $ 4,000.......... 6% | 6%. |
| | Married ...... | 2,200 | Next 2,000.......... 4 | Over 10,000.......... 7 | |
| | Dependent .... | 800 | Next 2,000.......... 5 | | |
| NORTH DAKOTA | Single ....... | $1,000 | 1st $3,000.......... 1% | Next $ 4,000.......... 4% | 1st $ 3,000 2% |
| | Married ...... | 2,000 | Next 2,000.......... 2 | Next 18,000.......... 5 | Next 5,000 3 |
| | Dependent .... | 1,000 | Next 3,000.......... 3 | Over 30,000.......... 7.5 | Next 12,000 4 |
| | | | | | Next 10,000 5 |
| | | | | | Next 20,000 6 |
| | | | | | Over 50,000 7 |
| OHIO | Single ....... | $ 650 | 1st $5,000.......... 0.5% | Next $ 5,000.......... 2.5% | 4.71% of first $25,000 of net value; 8.92% of value over $25,000; or 5.5 mills per dollar of value, whichever is greater. Min., $150. |
| | Married ...... | 1,300 | Next 5,000.......... 1 | Next 20,000.......... 3 | |
| | Dependent .... | 650 | Next 5,000.......... 2 | Over 40,000.......... 3.5 | |
| | | | Plus surcharge 25% effective July 1, 1982. (1983 surcharge 12.5%.) | | |
| OKLAHOMA | Single ....... | $ 750 | 1st $2,000.......... 0.5% | Next $2,500.......... 4% | 4%. |
| | Married ...... | 1,500 | Next 3,000.......... 1 | Next 2,500.......... 5 | |
| | Dependent .... | 750 | Next 2,500.......... 2 | Remainder 2,500.......... 6 | |
| | | | Next 2,500.......... 3 | | |
| OREGON | Single ....... | $1,000 | 1st $ 500.......... 4.2% | Next $1,000.......... 8.6% | 7½%; minimum $10. |
| | Married ...... | 2,000 | Next 500.......... 5.3 | Next 1,000.......... 9.8 | |
| | Dependent .... | 1 000 | Next 1,000.......... 6.5 | Over 5,000.......... 10.8 | |
| | | | Next 1,000.......... 7.6 | | |
| PENNSYLVANIA | None | | No personal income tax. 2.2% of specified classes of income. | | 10.5%. (10% after Jan. 1, 1983.) |
| RHODE ISLAND | Single ....... | $1,000 | 19.24% of modified federal income tax liability. | | 8% of net income or 40¢ per $100 of corporate net worth, whichever is the greater. |
| | Married ...... | 2,000 | | | |
| | Dependent .... | 1 000 | | | |
| SOUTH CAROLINA | Single ....... | $ 800 | 1st $2,000.......... 2% | Next $ 2,000.......... 5% | 6%; banks 4.5%. |
| | Married ...... | 1,600 | Next 2,000.......... 3 | Next 2,000.......... 6 | |
| | Dependent .... | 800 | Next 2,000.......... 4 | Over 10,000.......... 7 | |
| TENNESSEE | None | | 6% on dividends and interest. | | 6%. |
| UTAH | Single ....... | $1,000 | 1st $1,500.......... 2.25% | Next 1,500... $169 + 5.75% | 4%. Minimum $25. |
| | Married ...... | 2,000 | Next 1,500.... $41 + 3.75 | Next 1,500.... 255 + 6.75 | |
| | Dependent .... | 1,000 | Next 1,500..... 98 + 4.75 | Over 7,500.... 356 + 7.75 | |
| | | | Rates are for married taxpayers filing jointly. | | |
| VERMONT | Single ....... | $1,000 | 24% of federal income tax liability. | | 1st $ 10,000 5% |
| | Married ...... | 2,000 | | | Next 15,000 6 |
| | Dependent .... | 1,000 | | | Next 225,000 7 |
| | | | | | Next 250,000 7.5 |
| | | | | | Min. $50. |
| VIRGINIA | Single ....... | $ 600 | 1st $3,000.......... 2% | Over $12,000.......... 5¾% | 6%. |
| | Married ...... | 1,200 | Next 2,000.......... 3 | | |
| | Dependent .... | 600 | Next 7,000.......... 5 | | |
| WEST VIRGINIA | Single ....... | $ 600 | 1st $2,000.......... 2.1% | Next $ 6,000.. $1,126 + 6.5% | 6%. |
| | Married ...... | 1,200 | 2nd 2,000..... 42 + 2.3 | Next 6,000... 1,516 + 6.8 | |
| | Dependent .... | 600 | 3rd 2,000..... 88 + 2.8 | Next 6,000... 1,924 + 7.2 | |
| | | | 4th 2,000.... 144 + 3.2 | Next 6,000... 2,356 + 7.5 | |
| | | | 5th 2,000.... 208 + 3.5 | Next 10,000... 2,806 + 7.9 | |
| | | | 6th 2,000.... 278 + 4.0 | Next 10,000... 3,596 + 8.2 | |
| | | | 7th 2,000.... 358 + 4.6 | Next 10,000... 4,416 + 8.6 | |
| | | | 8th 2,000.... 450 + 4.9 | Next 10,000... 5,276 + 8.8 | |
| | | | 9th 2,000.... 548 + 5.3 | Next 10,000... 6,156 + 9.1 | |
| | | | 10th 2,000.... 654 + 5.4 | Next 50,000... 7,066 + 9.3 | |
| | | | 11th 2,000.... 762 + 6.0 | Next 50,000.. 11,716 + 9.5 | |
| | | | Next 4,000.... 882 + 6.1 | Over 200,000.. 16,466 + 9.6 | |
| WISCONSIN | From tax: | | 1st $3,600.......... 3.4% | Next $ 3,600.......... 8.7% | 7.9% plus 10% surcharge for years 1982 and 1983. |
| | Single ....... | $20 | Next 3,600.......... 5.2 | Next 6,000.......... 9.1 | |
| | Married ...... | 40 | Next 3,700.......... 7.0 | Next 24,100.......... 9.5 | |
| | Dependent .... | 20 | Next 3,600.......... 8.2 | Over 48,200.......... 10.0 | |

## STATE SALES AND USE TAX RATES

SOURCE: *State Tax Guide,* Commerce Clearing House, Inc.

| State | Sales | Use* |
|---|---|---|
| Alabama[1] | 4% | 4% |
| Arizona[1] | 4% | 4% |
| Arkansas[1] | 3% | 3% |
| California[1] | 4¾% | 4¾% |
| Colorado[1] | 3% | 3% |
| Connecticut | 7½% | 7½% |
| D.C. | 6% | 6% |
| Florida[1] | 5% | 5% |
| Georgia[1] | 3% | 3% |
| Hawaii | 4% | 4% |
| Idaho | 3% | 3% |
| Illinois[1] | 4% | 4% |
| Indiana | 4% | 4% |
| Iowa | 3% | 3% |
| Kansas[1] | 3% | 3% |
| Kentucky[1] | 5% | 5% |
| Louisiana[1] | 3% | 3% |
| Maine | 5% | 5% |
| Maryland | 5% | 5% |
| Massachusetts | 5% | 5% |
| Michigan | 4% | 4% |
| Minnesota[1] | 4% | 4% |
| Mississippi | 5% | 5% |
| Missouri[1] | 3⅛% | 3⅛% |
| Nebraska[1] | 3½%[2] | 3½%[2] |
| Nevada[1] | 5¾% | 5¾% |
| New Jersey | 5% | 5% |
| New Mexico[1] | 3½% | 3½% |
| New York[1] | 4% | 4% |
| North Carolina[1] | 3% | 3% |
| North Dakota | 3% | 3% |
| Ohio[1] | 5% | 5% |
| Oklahoma[1] | 2% | 2% |
| Pennsylvania[1] | 6% | 6% |
| Rhode Island | 6% | 6% |
| South Carolina | 4% | 4% |
| South Dakota[1] | 4% | 4% |
| Tennessee[1] | 4½% | 4½% |
| Texas[1] | 4% | 4% |
| Utah[1] | 4% | 4% |
| Vermont | 4%[3] | 4%[3] |
| Virginia[1] | 3% | 3% |
| Washington [1] | 4½% | 4½% |
| West Virginia[1] | 5% | 5% |
| Wisconsin[1] | 5% | 5% |
| Wyoming[1] | 3% | 3% |

*As of June 1982. The list of states imposing sales and use taxes does not include Alaska and Delaware. Alaska imposes a business license (gross receipts) tax, and Delaware imposes a merchants' and manufacturers' license tax and a use tax on leases. Other states impose occupation, admission, license, or gross receipts taxes in addition to sales and use taxes. [1] Local tax rates are additional. [2]Sales and use tax rates increased to 3½% effective May 1, 1982 to Dec. 31, 1982. [3]Sales and use tax rates incresed to 4% effective July 1, 1982.

## CITY SALES TAX RATES

SOURCE: *All-State Sales Tax Reports,* published by Commerce Clearing House, Inc.

For these selected U.S. cities, the first rate given is the state sales tax applicable in the city. The second is the city or county rate. The third is the additional sales and use tax. The rates added together give total city sales tax rate.

| City | Sales Tax Rate |
|---|---|
| Atlanta | 3% + 1% |
| Birmingham | 4% + 1% |
| Buffalo | 4% + 3% |
| Chicago | 4% + 1% |
| Cincinnati | 5% + ½% |
| Cleveland | 5% + ½% |
| Dallas | 4% + 1% |
| Denver | 3% + 3% |
| Greensboro, N.C. | 3% + 1% |
| Houston | 4% + 1% |
| Kansas City, Mo. | 3⅛% + ½% |
| Los Angeles | 4¾% + 1¼% + 1% |
| Memphis | 4½% + 1½% |
| New Orleans | 3% + 2½% + 1½% |
| New York City | 4% + 4½% |
| Norfolk | 3% + 1% |
| Oklahoma City | 2% + 2% |
| Omaha | 3% + 1½% |
| Phoenix | 4% + 1% |
| Richmond | 3% + 1% |
| St. Louis | 3⅛% + 1% |
| Salt Lake City | 4% + ¾% + ¼% |
| San Antonio | 4% + 1% |
| San Diego | 4¾% + 1¼% + 1% |
| San Francisco | 4¾% + 1¼% + 1% |
| Seattle | 4½% + ½% |

## CITY INCOME TAXES

SOURCE: Commerce Clearing House, Inc.

FOR CITIES OVER 100,000 POPULATION

| | Present rate | Date of Introduction |
|---|---|---|
| **Alabama** | | |
| Birmingham | 1.0% | 1970 |
| **Kentucky** | | |
| Louisville | 2.2 | 1948 |
| **Maryland** | | |
| Baltimore | 50% of state income tax[1] | 1966 |
| **Michigan** | | |
| Detroit | 3.0[2] | 1962 |
| Flint | 1.0 | 1965 |
| Grand Rapids | 1.0 | 1967 |
| Lansing | 1.0 | 1968 |
| **Missouri** | | |
| Kansas City | 1.0 | 1964 |
| St. Louis | 1.0 | 1948 |
| **New York** | | |
| New York | 0.9% to 4.3%[3] | 1966 |
| **Ohio** | | |
| Akron | 2.0 | 1962 |
| Cincinnati | 2.0 | 1954 |
| Cleveland | 2.0 | 1947 |
| Columbus | 1.5 | 1947 |
| Dayton | 1.75 | 1949 |
| Toledo | 1.5 | 1955 |
| Youngstown | 2.0 | 1948 |
| **Pennsylvania** | | |
| Erie | 1.0 | 1948 |
| Philadelphia | 4 5/16 | 1939 |
| Pittsburgh | 2⅛ | 1976 |

[1]Individual income tax only. [2]1.5% for non-residents working in Detroit. [3]Plus surcharge of 2.5% to 5% effective June 15, 1982.

# FINANCE/INDUSTRY/LABOR

## FACTS ABOUT U.S. MONEY

**SOURCE: U.S. Treasury Department**

In the early days of our nation, before United States money was issued, there were in circulation English shillings, French louis d'ors, and Spanish doubloons, along with other units of those nations' money. This caused confusion and slowed up trade. The dollar was adopted (1785) by the Congress existing under the Articles of Confederation as the unit of our money, and the decimal system as the method of reckoning. In 1792 the United States monetary system was established, and the U.S. Mint began coining money at Philadelphia in 1793.

Many changes in the laws governing coinage and the denominations themselves have been made since the original 1792 act. Coins no longer in use include the half-cent, two-cent, three-cent, and 20-cent pieces, as well as the silver half dime. The five-cent nickel coin was introduced in 1866. Gold coins were struck from 1795 through 1933, in denominations ranging from $1 to $20. The minting and isssuance of gold coins were terminated by Section 5 of the Gold Reserve Act of 1934.

President Johnson signed (July 23, 1965) an historic bill providing for the first major change in U.S. coinage in more than a century. Silver was eliminated altogether from the dime and quarter and substanially reduced in the half dollar.

On Dec. 31, 1970, President Nixon signed the Bank Holding Company Act calling for the removal of all silver from silver dollars and half dollars. This legislation also authorized a silver dollar with a design emblematic of the symbolic eagle of the Apollo 11 landing on the Moon. Once adopted, a coin design may not be changed more often than once in 25 years without specific legislation.

The selection of coin designs is usually made by the Director of the Mint, with the approval of the Secretary of the Treasury. However, Congress has, in a few instances, prescribed them. For example, as a part of the bicentennial celebration of Washington's birth in 1932, Congress declared that the likeness of our first President should appear on the quarter dollar.

The Lincoln penny was the first portrait coin of a regular series minted by the United States. The 100th anniversary of Lincoln's birth aroused sentiment sufficiently strong to overcome a long-prevailing popular prejudice against the use of portraits on coins. A new reverse design was adopted in 1959, when the sesquicentennial of Lincoln's birth was observed. The familiar likeness on the obverse remains unchanged. Others which followed are the 25-cent coin, with Washington's profile, first minted in 1932; the five-cent piece honoring Jefferson, adopted in 1938; the FDR dime, introduced in 1946, and in 1971 the Eisenhower silver dollar, manufacture of which was discontinued in December 1978.

In July 1979, a new, smaller dollar coin was introduced whose size is between the half dollar and the quarter; its smaller size will save in the cost of dollar bill production and help the circulation of the little-used dollar coin. This coin bears the likeness of women's suffrage leader Susan B. Anthony.

Portraits of living persons on American coins are extremely rare and confined to a few commemorative issues of limited minting.

The year 1976 marked the 200th anniversary of American Independence. One of the most far-reaching Government observances was the issuance of specially designed dollars, half dollars, and quarters. Circulation commenced on July 4, 1975, and production ended on December 31, 1976.

The design selection used for American paper currency, including the selection of portraits, is a responsibility of the Secretary of the Treasury, who acts with the advice of the Director of the Bureau of Engraving and Printing, the Treasurer of the United States, and others. By tradition, portraits used on present paper money are those of deceased statesmen of assured historical significance.

The first regular issue of United States currency, the Demand notes that were issued in 1861, carried the portraits of Alexander Hamilton (first Secretary of the Treasury) on the $5 denomination and of Abraham Lincoln on the $10 denomination.

Those design features of U.S. paper currency that have historical or idealistic significance, as distinct from purely ornamental or security implications, include the following:

(1) The New Treasury Seal: Approved on January 29, 1968, the seal of the Department of the Treasury is found on the face of each note. Balance scales, a key, and a chevron with 13 stars appear on the seal, along with the date "1789," the year the Department was created.

(2) The obverse and reverse of the Great Seal of the United States are reproduced on the backs of $1 bills.

(3) Portraits of great Americans used on the face of currency.

(4) Pictures of famous buildings, monuments or events used on the back of currency.

All notes of the same denomination bear the same portrait. Designs on U.S. currency (Federal Reserve Notes) now in circulation are as follows:

| Denomination and Class | Portrait | Back |
|---|---|---|
| $1 Fed. Reserve Note ....... | Washington | Obverse and reverse of Great Seal of U.S. |
| $2 Fed. Reserve Note ....... | Jefferson | John Trumbull's "Declaration of Independence" |
| $5 Fed. Reserve Note ....... | Lincoln | Lincoln Memorial |
| $10 Fed. Reserve Note ....... | Hamilton | U.S. Treasury Building |
| $20 Fed. Reserve Note ....... | Jackson | White House |
| $50 Fed. Reserve Note ....... | Grant | U.S. Capitol |
| $100 Fed. Reserve Note ....... | Franklin | Independence Hall |

Notes of the higher denominations ($500, $1,000, $5,000, and $10,000) have not been printed for many years. As they are returned to Federal Reserve banks, they are removed from circulation and destroyed. The portraits selected for these small-sized notes were McKinley for the $500, Cleveland for the $1,000, Madison for the $5,000, and Chase for the $10,000.

The motto "In God We Trust" owes its presence on U.S. coins largely to the increased religious sentiment existing during the Civil War. Salmon P. Chase, then Secretary of the Treasury, received a number of appeals from devout persons throughout the country urging that the Deity be suitably recognized on our coins as it was on the coins of other nations.

The approved motto first made its appearance on the two-cent coin, authorized by Act of Congress (April 22, 1864), but its use has not been uninterrupted. In 1866 the motto was introduced on the double eagle, eagle, and half eagle gold coins and on the silver dollar, half dollar, and the quarter dollar pieces. It was included in the nickel five-cent design from 1866 to 1883, when it was dropped and not restored until the introduction of the Jefferson nickel in 1938. The motto has been in continuous use on the penny since 1909 and on the dime since 1916.

A law passed by the 84th Congress and approved by the President on July 11, 1955, provides that "In God We Trust" shall appear on all United States paper currency and coins.

By a joint resolution of the 84th Congress, approved by the President on July 30, 1956, "In God We Trust" was declared to be the official motto of the United States.

## COMPOUND INTEREST TABLE

**What a $1 deposit, compounded monthly, grows to over a thirty-year period.**

| | Interest Rates | | | | | | | | | | | | |
|---|---|---|---|---|---|---|---|---|---|---|---|---|---|
| Years | 5% | 5¼% | 5½% | 5¾% | 6% | 6¼% | 6½% | 6¾% | 7% | 7¼% | 7½% | 7¾% | 8% |
| 1 | 1.0512 | 1.0538 | 1.0564 | 1.0590 | 1.0617 | 1.0643 | 1.0670 | 1.0696 | 1.0723 | 1.0750 | 1.0776 | 1.0803 | 1.0830 |
| 1½ | 1.0778 | 1.0812 | 1.0858 | 1.0899 | 1.0939 | 1.0980 | 1.1021 | 1.1062 | 1.1104 | 1.1145 | 1.1187 | 1.1229 | 1.1270 |
| 2 | 1.1049 | 1.1105 | 1.1160 | 1.1216 | 1.1272 | 1.1328 | 1.1384 | 1.1441 | 1.1498 | 1.1555 | 1.1613 | 1.1671 | 1.1729 |
| 2½ | 1.1329 | 1.1399 | 1.1470 | 1.1542 | 1.1614 | 1.1686 | 1.1759 | 1.1833 | 1.1906 | 1.1981 | 1.2055 | 1.2130 | 1.2206 |
| 3 | 1.1615 | 1.1702 | 1.1789 | 1.1878 | 1.1967 | 1.2056 | 1.2147 | 1.2238 | 1.2329 | 1.2422 | 1.2514 | 1.2608 | 1.2702 |
| 3½ | 1.1908 | 1.2012 | 1.2117 | 1.2223 | 1.2330 | 1.2438 | 1.2547 | 1.2657 | 1.2767 | 1.2879 | 1.2991 | 1.3105 | 1.3219 |
| 4 | 1.2209 | 1.2331 | 1.2455 | 1.2579 | 1.2705 | 1.2832 | 1.2960 | 1.3090 | 1.3221 | 1.3353 | 1.3486 | 1.3621 | 1.3757 |
| 4½ | 1.2517 | 1.2658 | 1.2801 | 1.2945 | 1.3091 | 1.3238 | 1.3387 | 1.3538 | 1.3690 | 1.3844 | 1.4000 | 1.4157 | 1.4316 |
| 5 | 1.2834 | 1.2994 | 1.3157 | 1.3322 | 1.3489 | 1.3657 | 1.3828 | 1.4001 | 1.4176 | 1.4354 | 1.4533 | 1.4715 | 1.4898 |
| 5½ | 1.3158 | 1.3339 | 1.3523 | 1.3709 | 1.3898 | 1.4090 | 1.4284 | 1.4480 | 1.4680 | 1.4882 | 1.5087 | 1.5214 | 1.5504 |
| 6 | 1.3490 | 1.3693 | 1.3899 | 1.4108 | 1.4320 | 1.4536 | 1.4754 | 1.4976 | 1.5201 | 1.5429 | 1.5661 | 1.5896 | 1.6135 |
| 6½ | 1.3831 | 1.4057 | 1.4286 | 1.4519 | 1.4755 | 1.4996 | 1.5240 | 1.5489 | 1.5741 | 1.5997 | 1.6258 | 1.6522 | 1.6791 |
| 7 | 1.4180 | 1.4430 | 1.4683 | 1.4941 | 1.5204 | 1.5471 | 1.5742 | 1.6019 | 1.6300 | 1.6586 | 1.6877 | 1.7173 | 1.7474 |
| 7½ | 1.4539 | 1.4813 | 1.5092 | 1.5376 | 1.5666 | 1.5961 | 1.6261 | 1.6567 | 1.6879 | 1.7196 | 1.7520 | 1.7849 | 1.8185 |
| 8 | 1.4906 | 1.5206 | 1.5511 | 1.5823 | 1.6141 | 1.6466 | 1.6797 | 1.7134 | 1.7478 | 1.7829 | 1.8187 | 1.8552 | 1.8925 |
| 8½ | 1.5282 | 1.5609 | 1.5943 | 1.6284 | 1.6631 | 1.6987 | 1.7350 | 1.7721 | 1.8099 | 1.8485 | 1.8880 | 1.9283 | 1.9694 |
| 9 | 1.5668 | 1.6023 | 1.6386 | 1.6758 | 1.7137 | 1.7525 | 1.7922 | 1.8327 | 1.8742 | 1.9166 | 1.9599 | 2.0042 | 2.0495 |
| 9½ | 1.6064 | 1.6449 | 1.6842 | 1.7245 | 1.7658 | 1.8080 | 1.8512 | 1.8954 | 1.9407 | 1.9871 | 2.0346 | 2.0832 | 2.1329 |
| 10 | 1.6470 | 1.6885 | 1.7311 | 1.7747 | 1.8194 | 1.8652 | 1.9122 | 1.9603 | 2.0097 | 2.0602 | 2.1121 | 2.1652 | 2.2196 |
| 10½ | 1.6886 | 1.7333 | 1.7792 | 1.8263 | 1.8747 | 1.9243 | 1.9752 | 2.0274 | 2.0810 | 2.1361 | 2.1925 | 2.2505 | 2.3099 |
| 11 | 1.7313 | 1.7793 | 1.8287 | 1.8795 | 1.9316 | 1.9852 | 2.0402 | 2.0968 | 2.1549 | 2.2147 | 2.2760 | 2.3391 | 2.4039 |
| 11½ | 1.7750 | 1.8266 | 1.8796 | 1.9342 | 1.9903 | 2.0480 | 2.1075 | 2.1686 | 2.2315 | 2.2962 | 2.3627 | 2.4312 | 2.5016 |
| 12 | 1.8198 | 1.8750 | 1.9319 | 1.9904 | 2.0508 | 2.1129 | 2.1769 | 2.2428 | 2.3107 | 2.3807 | 2.4527 | 2.5269 | 2.6034 |
| 12½ | 1.8658 | 1.9248 | 1.9856 | 2.0483 | 2.1130 | 2.1798 | 2.2486 | 2.3196 | 2.3928 | 2.4683 | 2.5462 | 2.6265 | 2.7093 |
| 13 | 1.9130 | 1.9759 | 2.0408 | 2.1079 | 2.1772 | 2.2488 | 2.3227 | 2.3990 | 2.4778 | 2.5591 | 2.6431 | 2.7299 | 2.8195 |
| 13½ | 1.9613 | 2.0283 | 2.0976 | 2.1693 | 2.2434 | 2.3200 | 2.3992 | 2.4811 | 2.5658 | 2.6533 | 2.7438 | 2.8374 | 2.9341 |
| 14 | 2.0108 | 2.0821 | 2.1560 | 2.2324 | 2.3115 | 2.3934 | 2.4782 | 2.5660 | 2.6569 | 2.7509 | 2.8483 | 2.9491 | 3.0535 |
| 14½ | 2.0616 | 2.1374 | 2.2159 | 2.2974 | 2.3817 | 2.4692 | 2.5599 | 2.6538 | 2.7512 | 2.8522 | 2.9568 | 3.0653 | 3.1777 |
| 15 | 2.1137 | 2.1941 | 2.2776 | 2.3642 | 2.4541 | 2.5474 | 2.6442 | 2.7447 | 2.8489 | 2.9572 | 3.0695 | 3.1860 | 3.3069 |
| 15½ | 2.1671 | 2.2524 | 2.3409 | 2.4330 | 2.5286 | 2.6280 | 2.7313 | 2.8386 | 2.9501 | 3.0660 | 3.1864 | 3.3115 | 3.4414 |
| 16 | 2.2218 | 2.3121 | 2.4061 | 2.5038 | 2.6055 | 2.7112 | 2.8213 | 2.9358 | 3.0549 | 3.1788 | 3.3077 | 3.4419 | 3.5814 |
| 16½ | 2.2780 | 2.3735 | 2.4730 | 2.5766 | 2.6846 | 2.7971 | 2.9142 | 3.0363 | 3.1634 | 3.2958 | 3.4337 | 3.5774 | 3.7271 |
| 17 | 2.3355 | 2.4365 | 2.5418 | 2.6516 | 2.7662 | 2.8856 | 3.0102 | 3.1402 | 3.2757 | 3.4171 | 3.5645 | 3.7183 | 3.8786 |
| 17½ | 2.3945 | 2.5011 | 2.6125 | 2.7288 | 2.8502 | 2.9770 | 3.1094 | 3.2477 | 3.3921 | 3.5429 | 3.7003 | 3.8647 | 4.0364 |
| 18 | 2.4550 | 2.5675 | 2.6852 | 2.8082 | 2.9368 | 3.0712 | 3.2118 | 3.3588 | 3.5125 | 3.6732 | 3.8413 | 4.0169 | 4.2006 |
| 18½ | 2.5170 | 2.6357 | 2.7598 | 2.8899 | 3.0260 | 3.1685 | 3.3176 | 3.4738 | 3.6373 | 3.8084 | 3.9876 | 4.1751 | 4.3714 |
| 19 | 2.5806 | 2.7056 | 2.8366 | 2.9739 | 3.1179 | 3.2688 | 3.4269 | 3.5927 | 3.7665 | 3.9486 | 4.1395 | 4.3395 | 4.5492 |
| 19½ | 2.6458 | 2.7774 | 2.9155 | 3.0605 | 3.2126 | 3.3723 | 3.5398 | 3.7157 | 3.9002 | 4.0939 | 4.2971 | 4.5104 | 4.7342 |
| 20 | 2.7126 | 2.8511 | 2.9966 | 3.1495 | 3.3102 | 3.4790 | 3.6564 | 3.8429 | 4.0387 | 4.2446 | 4.4608 | 4.6880 | 4.9268 |
| 20½ | 2.7812 | 2.9268 | 3.0800 | 3.2412 | 3.4108 | 3.5892 | 3.7769 | 3.9744 | 4.1822 | 4.4008 | 4.6037 | 4.8727 | 5.1272 |
| 21 | 2.8514 | 3.0045 | 3.1657 | 3.3355 | 3.5144 | 3.7028 | 3.9013 | 4.1104 | 4.3307 | 4.5627 | 4.8071 | 5.0646 | 5.3357 |
| 21½ | 2.9235 | 3.0842 | 3.2537 | 3.4325 | 3.6211 | 3.8200 | 4.0298 | 4.2511 | 4.4845 | 4.7306 | 4.9902 | 5.2640 | 5.5527 |
| 22 | 2.9973 | 3.1660 | 3.3442 | 3.5324 | 3.7311 | 3.9410 | 4.1626 | 4.3966 | 4.6438 | 4.9047 | 5.1803 | 5.4173 | 5.7786 |
| 22½ | 3.0730 | 3.2501 | 3.4373 | 3.6352 | 3.8445 | 4.0658 | 4.2997 | 4.5471 | 4.8087 | 5.0852 | 5.3776 | 5.6868 | 6.0136 |
| 23 | 3.1507 | 3.3663 | 3.5329 | 3.7410 | 3.9613 | 4.1945 | 4.4134 | 4.7028 | 4.9795 | 5.2724 | 5.5825 | 5.9017 | 6.2582 |
| 23½ | 3.2302 | 3.4249 | 3.6311 | 3.8498 | 4.0816 | 4.3273 | 4.5877 | 4.8637 | 5.1563 | 5.4664 | 5.7951 | 6.1435 | 6.5127 |
| 24 | 3.3118 | 3.5157 | 3.7321 | 3.9618 | 4.2056 | 4.4643 | 4.7388 | 5.0302 | 5.3394 | 5.6676 | 6.0159 | 6.3854 | 6.7776 |
| 24½ | 3.3955 | 3.6090 | 3.8360 | 4.0771 | 4.3333 | 4.6056 | 4.8949 | 5.2024 | 5.5291 | 5.8762 | 6.2450 | 6.6369 | 7.0533 |
| 25 | 3.4813 | 3.7048 | 3.9427 | 4.1957 | 4.4650 | 4.7514 | 5.0562 | 5.3804 | 5.7254 | 6.0924 | 6.4829 | 6.8983 | 7.3402 |
| 25½ | 3.5692 | 3.8031 | 4.0523 | 4.3178 | 4.6006 | 4.9019 | 5.2228 | 5.5646 | 5.9288 | 6.3166 | 6.7928 | 7.1699 | 7.6387 |
| 26 | 3.6594 | 3.9041 | 4.1651 | 4.4434 | 4.7404 | 5.0570 | 5.3948 | 5.7551 | 6.1393 | 6.5491 | 6.9862 | 7.4523 | 7.9494 |
| 26½ | 3.7518 | 4.0077 | 4.2809 | 4.5727 | 4.8844 | 5.2172 | 5.5725 | 5.9521 | 6.3573 | 6.7901 | 7.2523 | 7.7458 | 8.2727 |
| 27 | 3.8466 | 4.1141 | 4.4000 | 4.7058 | 5.0327 | 5.3823 | 5.7561 | 6.1558 | 6.5831 | 7.0400 | 7.5285 | 8.0508 | 8.6092 |
| 27½ | 3.9438 | 4.2232 | 4.5224 | 4.8427 | 5.1856 | 5.5527 | 5.9457 | 6.3665 | 6.8169 | 7.2991 | 7.8153 | 8.3679 | 8.9594 |
| 28 | 4.0434 | 4.3353 | 4.6482 | 4.9836 | 5.3431 | 5.7285 | 6.1416 | 6.5844 | 7.0590 | 7.5677 | 8.1130 | 8.6974 | 9.3238 |
| 28½ | 4.1456 | 4.4504 | 4.7775 | 5.1286 | 5.5055 | 5.9099 | 6.3439 | 6.8098 | 7.3097 | 7.8462 | 8.4220 | 9.0399 | 9.7030 |
| 29 | 4.2503 | 4.5685 | 4.9104 | 5.2778 | 5.6727 | 6.0970 | 6.5529 | 7.0429 | 7.5693 | 8.1350 | 8.7428 | 9.3959 | 10.0976 |
| 29½ | 4.3577 | 4.6897 | 5.0467 | 5.4314 | 5.8450 | 6.2900 | 6.7688 | 7.2839 | 7.8381 | 8.4344 | 9.0758 | 9.7659 | 10.5083 |
| 30 | 4.4677 | 4.8192 | 5.1874 | 5.5894 | 6.0226 | 6.4872 | 6.9918 | 7.5332 | 8.1165 | 8.7448 | 9.4215 | 10.1505 | 10.9357 |

## GOLD PRODUCTION

SOURCE: U.S. Bureau of Mines (figures in 100,000 troy ounce units)

| | 1960 | 1965 | 1970 | 1975 | 1976 | 1977 | 1978 | 1979 | 1980 | 1981[1] |
|---|---|---|---|---|---|---|---|---|---|---|
| **South Africa** | **213.8** | **305.5** | **321.6** | **229.4** | **229.4** | **225.0** | **226.5** | **226.2** | **216.7** | **211.2** |
| **Canada** | **46.3** | **36.1** | **24.1** | **16.5** | **16.9** | **17.3** | **17.4** | **16.4** | **16.3** | **15.1** |
| **United States** | **16.8** | **17.1** | **17.4** | **10.5** | **10.5** | **11.0** | **10.0** | **10.0** | **10.0** | **13.0** |
| **USSR** | **41.0** | **50.3** | **65.0** | **75.0** | **77.0** | **78.5** | **80.0** | **81.6** | **83.0** | **84.2** |
| **Other Africa** | **19.7** | **16.0** | **14.6** | **13.1** | **10.7** | **10.3** | **9.2** | **8.5** | **8.0** | **7.7** |
| Ghana | 8.9 | 7.6 | 7.1 | 5.2 | 5.3 | 4.8 | 4.0 | 3.6 | 3.5 | 3.0 |
| Zimbabwe | 5.6 | 5.4 | 5.0 | 6.0 | 3.9 | 4.0 | 4.0 | 3.9 | 3.7 | 3.6 |
| Zaire | 3.1 | 0.9 | 1.8 | 1.0 | 0.9 | 0.8 | 0.8 | 0.7 | 0.4 | 0.7 |
| **Other Europe** | **6.0** | **3.3** | **3.0** | **5.1** | **5.3** | **4.5** | **4.3** | **4.6** | **4.9** | **3.8** |
| **Latin America** | **14.0** | **12.0** | **9.2** | **12.4** | **15.5** | **14.7** | **14.6** | **15.4** | **29.2** | **30.5** |
| Colombia | 4.3 | 3.2 | 2.0 | 3.1 | 3.0 | 2.6 | 2.5 | 2.7 | 5.1 | 5.4 |
| Mexico | 3.0 | 2.2 | 2.0 | 1.4 | 1.6 | 2.1 | 2.0 | 1.9 | 2.0 | 1.8 |
| Nicaragua | 2.1 | 2.0 | 1.2 | 0.7 | 0.8 | 0.7 | 0.7 | 0.6 | 0.6 | 0.5 |
| Peru | 1.4 | 1.0 | 1.1 | 0.8 | 1.2 | 1.0 | 1.0 | 1.4 | 1.5 | 2.2 |
| **Asia** | **11.6** | **11.7** | **12.6** | **10.6** | **18.6** | **19.9** | **21.9** | **23.1** | **25.5** | **28.6** |
| Philippines | 4.1 | 4.4 | 6.0 | 5.0 | 5.0 | 5.6 | 5.9 | 5.4 | 5.9 | 6.7 |
| Japan | 2.6 | 2.6 | 2.6 | 1.4 | 1.4 | 1.5 | 1.5 | 1.3 | 1.0 | 1.0 |
| India | 1.6 | 1.3 | 1.0 | 0.9 | 1.0 | 1.0 | 0.9 | 0.8 | 0.8 | 0.8 |
| **Oceania** | **12.4** | **10.3** | **7.6** | **12.1** | **12.7** | **14.2** | **14.3** | **12.6** | **10.3** | **11.0** |
| Australia | 10.9 | 8.8 | 6.2 | 5.3 | 5.0 | 6.2 | 6.5 | 6.0 | 5.4 | 5.3 |
| **World Total[2]** | **382** | **462** | **475** | **385** | **396** | **396** | **398** | **398** | **404** | **405** |

[1] Estimated. [2] Data may not add to total shown because of independent rounding.

## COMPANIES WITH THE LARGEST NUMBER OF COMMON STOCKHOLDERS

SOURCE: New York Stock Exchange (Figures rounded to nearest thousand)

EARLY 1982

| Company | Stockholders | Company | Stockholders |
|---|---|---|---|
| American Tel. & Tel. | 3,055,000 | Chrysler Corporation | 213,000 |
| General Motors | 1,122,000 | Niagara Mohawk Power | 210,000 |
| Exxon Corporation | 776,000 | Atlantic Richfield | 206,000 |
| International Business Machines | 742,000 | Northeast Utilities | 199,000 |
| General Electric | 502,000 | Standard Oil (Indiana) | 192,000 |
| General Tel. & Electronics | 476,000 | Virginia Electric & Power | 191,000 |
| Texaco Incorporated | 384,000 | Middle South Utilities | 188,000 |
| Sears, Roebuck | 354,000 | Ohio Edison | 183,000 |
| Southern Company | 351,000 | Occidental Petroleum | 176,000 |
| Ford Motor Co. | 342,000 | Long Island Lighting | 175,000 |
| American Electric Power | 340,000 | Union Electric | 175,000 |
| Gulf Oil | 302,000 | Consumers Power | 169,000 |
| Mobil Corporation | 292,000 | Westinghouse Electric | 168,000 |
| Commonwealth Edison | 275,000 | Pennsylvania Power & Light | 165,000 |
| Philadelphia Electric | 267,000 | BankAmerica | 165,000 |
| Pacific Gas & Electric | 255,000 | International Tel. & Tel. | 153,000 |
| Standard Oil of California | 247,000 | Southern California Edison | 152,000 |
| duPont de Nemours | 243,000 | Union Carbide Corp. | 150,000 |
| Tenneco Inc. | 238,000 | Dow Chemical | 144,000 |
| U.S. Steel | 236,000 | Columbia Gas System | 139,000 |
| Detroit Edison Co. | 235,000 | Duquesne Light | 138,000 |
| Public Service Electric & Gas | 233,000 | Pan American World Airways | 136,000 |
| Eastman Kodak | 221,000 | General Public Utilities | 136,000 |
| Consolidated Edison | 219,000 | Transamerica Corp. | 130,000 |
| RCA | 214,000 | Bethlehem Steel | 128,000 |

## U.S. CORPORATE PROFITS (In billions of dollars)

SOURCE: U.S. Department of Commerce, Bureau of Economic Analysis

| | Total pre-tax profits | Tax liability | After-tax profits | Dividends | Undistributed profits |
|---|---|---|---|---|---|
| 1929 | 10.0 | 1.4 | 8.6 | 5.8 | 2.8 |
| 1930 | 3.7 | .8 | 2.9 | 5.5 | −2.6 |
| 1931 | − .4 | .5 | − .9 | 4.1 | −4.9 |
| 1932 | −2.3 | .4 | −2.7 | 2.5 | −5.2 |
| 1933 | 1.0 | .5 | .4 | 2.0 | −1.6 |
| 1935 | 3.6 | 1.0 | 2.6 | 2.8 | − .2 |
| 1940 | 10.0 | 2.8 | 7.2 | 4.0 | 3.2 |
| 1945 | 19.8 | 10.7 | 9.1 | 4.6 | 4.5 |
| 1950 | 42.9 | 18.0 | 25.0 | 8.8 | 16.2 |
| 1955 | 49.2 | 22.0 | 27.2 | 10.3 | 16.9 |
| 1960 | 49.8 | 22.7 | 27.1 | 12.8 | 14.3 |
| 1965 | 77.2 | 30.9 | 46.3 | 19.1 | 27.2 |
| 1970 | 75.4 | 34.2 | 41.3 | 22.5 | 18.8 |
| 1971 | 86.6 | 37.5 | 49.0 | 22.9 | 26.1 |
| 1972 | 100.6 | 41.6 | 58.9 | 24.4 | 34.5 |
| 1973 | 125.6 | 49.0 | 76.6 | 27.0 | 49.6 |
| 1974 | 136.7 | 51.6 | 85.1 | 29.9 | 55.2 |
| 1975 | 132.1 | 50.6 | 81.5 | 30.8 | 50.7 |
| 1976 | 166.3 | 63.8 | 102.5 | 37.4 | 65.1 |
| 1977 | 192.6 | 72.6 | 120.0 | 39.9 | 80.1 |
| 1978 | 223.3 | 83.0 | 140.3 | 44.6 | 95.7 |
| 1979 | 255.4 | 87.6 | 167.8 | 50.2 | 117.6 |
| 1980 | 245.5 | 82.3 | 163.2 | 56.0 | 107.2 |
| 1981 | 230.2 | 76.4 | 153.9 | 63.1 | 90.7 |

## FOREIGN EXCHANGE RATES: 1949-1982 Source: Federal Reserve Bulletin (in U.S. cents)

| Year | United Kingdom (pound) | Canada (dollar) | Netherlands (guilder) | West Germany* (deutsche mark) | Switzerland (franc) | France† (franc) | Belgium (franc) | Japan‡ (yen) | Italy (lira) |
|---|---|---|---|---|---|---|---|---|---|
| 1949 | 368.72 | 92.88 | 34.53 | NA | 23.31 | .3017 | 2.20 | NA | .1699 |
| 1950 | 280.07 | 91.47 | 26.25 | 23.84 | 23.14 | .2858 | 1.99 | NA | .1601 |
| 1951 | 279.96 | 94.94 | 26.26 | 23.84 | 23.06 | .2856 | 1.99 | NA | .1600 |
| 1953 | 281.27 | 101.65 | 26.34 | 23.84 | 23.32 | .2856 | 2.00 | NA | .1600 |
| 1956 | 279.57 | 101.60 | 26.11 | 23.79 | 23.33 | .2855 | 2.00 | .2779 | .1600 |
| 1958 | 280.98 | 103.03 | 26.42 | 23.85 | 23.33 | .2858 | 2.00 | .2779 | .1601 |
| 1960 | 280.76 | 103.12 | 26.51 | 23.98 | 23.15 | 20.39 | 2.00 | .2778 | .1610 |
| 1962 | 280.78 | 93.56 | 27.76 | 25.01 | 23.12 | 20.41 | 2.01 | .2771 | .1611 |
| 1964 | 279.21 | 92.69 | 27.72 | 25.16 | 23.15 | 20.40 | 2.01 | .2763 | .1601 |
| 1966 | 279.30 | 92.81 | 27.63 | 25.01 | 23.11 | 20.35 | 2.01 | .2760 | .1601 |
| 1968 | 239.35 | 92.80 | 27.63 | 25.05 | 23.17 | 20.19 | 2.00 | .2774 | .1604 |
| 1970 | 239.59 | 95.80 | 27.65 | 27.42 | 23.20 | 18.09 | 2.01 | .2792 | .1595 |
| 1972 | 250.08 | 100.94 | 31.15 | 31.36 | 26.19 | 19.83 | 2.27 | .3300 | .1713 |
| 1974 | 234.03 | 102.26 | 37.27 | 38.72 | 33.69 | 20.81 | 2.57 | .3430 | .1537 |
| 1976 | 180.48 | 101.41 | 37.85 | 39.74 | 40.01 | 20.94 | 2.59 | .3374 | .1204 |
| 1977 | 174.49 | 94.11 | 40.75 | 43.08 | 41.71 | 20.34 | 2.79 | .3734 | .1133 |
| 1978 | 191.84 | 87.73 | 46.28 | 49.87 | 56.28 | 22.22 | 3.18 | .4798 | .1178 |
| 1979 | 212.24 | 86.18 | 49.82 | 54.52 | 60.09 | 23.49 | 3.41 | .4566 | .1203 |
| 1980 | 227.74 | 85.52 | 50.31 | 55.02 | 59.62 | 23.67 | 3.42 | .4412 | .1168 |
| 1981 | 202.43 | 83.40 | 40.00 | 44.19 | 50.83 | 18.38 | 2.69 | .4532 | .0878 |
| 1982 (April) | 177.20 | 81.62 | 37.60 | 41.72 | 50.96 | 16.01 | 2.21 | .4097 | .0757 |

*Beginning with June 1950. † Beginning with 1960, 100 old francs = 1 new franc. ‡ Beginning with November 1956. NA = Not Available.

## MONEY DEPRECIATION: ANNUAL RATES Source: International Monetary Fund

The value of money is here measured by reciprocals of official cost-of-living or consumer price indexes. (1970 = 100)

| | Indexes: Value of Money 1980 | Indexes: Value of Money 1981 | Rate of Depreciation 1970-81 |
|---|---|---|---|
| Switzerland | 62 | 58 | 5.1 |
| Germany, West | 61 | 57 | 5.2 |
| Malaysia | 56 | 51 | 6.2 |
| Tunisia | 55 | 51 | 6.3 |
| Austria | 54 | 51 | 6.4 |
| Egypt | 51 | 47 | 7.2 |
| Netherlands | 49 | 46 | 7.3 |
| Belgium | 49 | 46 | 7.4 |
| United States | 47 | 43 | 8.0 |
| India | 47 | 42 | 8.0 |
| Canada | 46 | 41 | 8.4 |
| Japan | 42 | 40 | 8.5 |
| Morocco | 45 | 40 | 8.7 |
| Venezuela | 44 | 38 | 9.1 |
| Sri Lanka | 43 | 37 | 9.5 |
| Sweden | 41 | 37 | 9.5 |
| Guatemala | 40 | 36 | 9.7 |
| Senegal | 38 | 36 | 9.7 |

| | Indexes: Value of Money 1980 | Indexes: Value of Money 1981 | Rate of Depreciation 1970-81 |
|---|---|---|---|
| France | 40 | 35 | 10.0 |
| Denmark | 39 | 35 | 10.0 |
| Australia | 37 | 34 | 10.4 |
| South Africa | 37 | 32 | 11.0 |
| Syria | 36 | 30 | 11.2 |
| Finland | 34 | 31 | 11.3 |
| Saudi Arabia | 32 | 31 | 11.3 |
| Kenya | 32 | 29 | 12.0 |
| New Zealand | 31 | 27 | 12.7 |
| Ecuador | 30 | 26 | 13.0 |
| Trinidad & Tobago | 29 | 26 | 13.2 |
| Philippines | 28 | 25 | 13.3 |
| United Kingdom | 28 | 25 | 13.5 |
| Iran | 30 | 24 | 13.7 |
| Italy | 27 | 23 | 14.2 |
| Ireland | 28 | 23 | 14.3 |
| Spain | 25 | 22 | 14.9 |
| Tanzania | 27 | 22 | 15.0 |

| | Indexes: Value of Money 1980 | Indexes: Value of Money 1981 | Rate of Depreciation 1970-81 |
|---|---|---|---|
| Greece | 26 | 21 | 15.2 |
| Nigeria | 24 | 20 | 15.7 |
| Korea, South | 22 | 18 | 17.3 |
| Indonesia | 19 | 17 | 17.3 |
| Jamaica | 19 | 17 | 17.4 |
| Mexico | 21 | 17 | 17.6 |
| Portugal | 19 | 16 | 18.3 |
| Yugoslavia | 18 | 13 | 20.4 |
| Colombia | 15 | 12 | 21.1 |
| Turkey | 7 | 5 | 31.5 |
| Peru | 7 | 4 | 33.7 |
| Brazil | 5 | 2 | 40.5 |
| Zaire | 3 | 2 | 40.6 |
| Ghana | 3 | 1 | 46.8 |
| Israel | 3 | 1 | 47.2 |
| Uruguay | * | * | 64.0 |
| Argentina | * | * | 128.8 |
| Chile | * | * | 130.4 |

*Less than 1.

## CENTRAL BANK DISCOUNT RATES

Source: International Monetary Fund (end of period quotations in percent per annum)

| | 1965 | 1967 | 1969 | 1971 | 1973 | 1975 | 1977 | 1978 | 1979 | 1980 | 1981 | 1982[1] |
|---|---|---|---|---|---|---|---|---|---|---|---|---|
| United States | 4.50 | 4.50 | 6.00 | 4.50 | 7.50 | 6.00 | 6.00 | 9.50 | 12.00 | 13.00 | 12.00 | 12.00 |
| United Kingdom | 6.00 | 8.00 | 8.00 | 5.00 | 13.00 | 11.25 | 7.00 | 12.50 | 17.00 | 14.00 | — | — |
| Industrial Europe | | | | | | | | | | | | |
| Austria | 4.50 | 3.75 | 4.75 | 5.00 | 7.75 | 6.00 | 5.50 | 4.50 | 3.75 | 6.75 | 6.75 | 6.75 |
| Belgium | 4.75 | 4.00 | 7.50 | 5.50 | 9.00 | 6.00 | 9.00 | 6.00 | 10.50 | 12.00 | 15.00 | 14.00 |
| France | 3.50 | 3.50 | 8.00 | 6.50 | 11.00 | 8.00 | 9.50 | 9.50 | 9.50 | 9.50 | 9.50 | 9.50 |
| Germany | 4.00 | 3.00 | 6.00 | 4.00 | 7.00 | 3.50 | 3.00 | 3.00 | 6.00 | 7.50 | 7.50 | 7.50 |
| Italy | 3.50 | 3.50 | 3.50 | 3.50 | 6.50 | 6.00 | 11.50 | 10.50 | 15.00 | 16.50 | 19.00 | 19.00 |
| Netherlands | 4.50 | 4.50 | 6.00 | 5.00 | 8.00 | 4.50 | 4.50 | 6.50 | 9.50 | 8.00 | 9.00 | 8.50 |
| Norway | 3.50 | 3.50 | 4.50 | 4.50 | 4.50 | 5.00 | 6.00 | 7.00 | 9.00 | 9.00 | 9.00 | 9.00 |
| Sweden | 5.50 | 6.00 | 7.00 | 5.00 | 5.00 | 6.00 | 8.00 | 6.50 | 9.00 | 10.00 | 11.00 | 11.00 |
| Switzerland | 2.50 | 3.00 | 3.75 | 3.75 | 4.50 | 3.00 | 1.50 | 1.00 | 2.00 | 3.00 | 6.00 | 6.00 |
| Canada | 4.75 | 6.00 | 8.00 | 4.75 | 7.25 | 9.00 | 7.50 | 10.75 | 14.00 | 17.26 | 14.66 | 14.59 |
| Japan | 5.48 | 5.84 | 6.25 | 4.75 | 9.00 | 6.50 | 4.25 | 3.50 | 6.25 | 7.25 | 5.50 | 5.50 |

[1]January.

## MONETARY TERMS

**Balance of Payment**—A nation's transactions with other nations, for trade, investment, tourism, foreign aid, and the like. A deficit occurs when more is paid out than a nation earns.

**Balance of Trade**—That part of the balance of payments covering exports and imports of goods.

**Devalue or Devaluation**—The act of changing a currency's par value downward.

**Exchange Control**—Government controls on purchase of foreign currencies for various purposes, aimed at protecting a nation's reserves.

**Foreign Exchange**—The term applied to foreign currencies.

**Foreign Exchange Market**—The market in which foreign currencies are bought and sold and the daily trading price in terms of dollars is set. It is not a specific place but rather a series of trading "desks," mainly at banks.

**Par Value**—The international value of a currency, expressed as so many ounces of gold or so many U.S. dollars and cents.

**Reserves**—A nation's holdings of gold plus certain foreign currencies.

**Reserve Currency**—A currency in which other nations hold part of their reserves.

**"Run" or "Attack"**—A mass wave of selling of a particular currency on the foreign exchange markets.

**Support**—Official intervention in the foreign exchange market by a nation's central bank to hold up the price of the nation's currency.

## U.S. GROSS NATIONAL PRODUCT†

SOURCE: U.S. Department of Commerce, Bureau of Economic Analysis

| | 1929 | 1933 | 1945 | 1955 | 1965 | 1975 | 1980 | 1981p |
|---|---|---|---|---|---|---|---|---|
| **Gross National Product** | **103.4** | **55.8** | **212.3** | **399.3** | **688.1** | **1528.8** | **2626.1** | **2922.2** |
| **GNP in Constant (1972) Dollars** | **314.7** | **222.1** | **559.0** | **654.8** | **925.9** | **1202.1** | **1480.7** | **1509.6** |
| **Personal Consumption Expenditures** | **77.3** | **45.8** | **119.5** | **253.7** | **430.2** | **980.4** | **1672.8** | **1858.1** |
| Durable goods | 9.2 | 3.5 | 8.0 | 38.6 | 62.8 | 132.9 | 211.9 | 232.0 |
| Nondurable goods | 37.7 | 22.3 | 71.9 | 122.9 | 188.6 | 409.3 | 675.7 | 743.4 |
| Services | 30.3 | 20.1 | 39.6 | 92.1 | 178.7 | 438.2 | 785.2 | 882.7 |
| **Gross Private Domestic Investment** | **16.2** | **1.4** | **10.6** | **68.4** | **112.0** | **189.1** | **395.3** | **450.6** |
| Fixed Investment | 14.5 | 3.0 | 11.7 | 62.4 | 102.5 | 200.6 | 401.2 | 432.4 |
| Nonresidential | 10.5 | 2.4 | 10.1 | 38.3 | 71.3 | 49.1 | 296.0 | 327.1 |
| Structures | 5.0 | 0.9 | 2.8 | 14.4 | 26.1 | 52.9 | 108.8 | 125.0 |
| Producers' durable equipment | 5.5 | 1.4 | 7.3 | 23.9 | 45.1 | 96.3 | 187.1 | 202.0 |
| Residential | 4.0 | 0.6 | 1.6 | 24.1 | 31.2 | 51.5 | 105.3 | 105.3 |
| Nonfarm structures | 3.8 | 0.5 | 1.4 | 23.0 | 29.9 | 49.5 | 100.3 | 99.8 |
| Farm structures | 0.2 | * | 0.1 | 0.6 | 0.6 | 0.9 | 2.0 | 2.3 |
| Producers' durable equipment | * | * | * | 0.4 | 0.7 | 1.1 | 3.0 | 3.2 |
| Change in business inventories | 1.7 | −1.6 | −1.0 | 6.0 | 9.5 | −11.5 | −5.9 | 18.2 |
| **Net exports of goods and services** | **1.1** | **0.4** | **−0.6** | **2.2** | **7.6** | **20.4** | **23.3** | **23.8** |
| **Government purchases** | **8.8** | **8.2** | **82.8** | **75.0** | **138.4** | **338.9** | **534.7** | **589.6** |
| Federal | 1.4 | 2.1 | 74.6 | 44.5 | 67.3 | 123.3 | 198.9 | 228.6 |
| National defense | — | — | 73.5 | 38.4 | 49.4 | 83.9 | 131.7 | 153.3 |
| Non-defense | — | — | 1.1 | 6.0 | 17.8 | 39.4 | 67.2 | 75.2 |
| State and local | 7.4 | 6.1 | 8.2 | 30.6 | 71.1 | 215.6 | 335.8 | 361.1 |

†In billions of dollars. * Less than $0.1 billion. p Provisional.

## GROSS DOMESTIC OR NATIONAL PRODUCT: SELECTED NATIONS 1980

SOURCE: Dr. Herbert Block, *The Planetary Product*

| | GNP Total ($ Millions) | GNP Per Capita (Dollars) | Population Mid-1980 (Millions) |
|---|---|---|---|
| **North America** | | | |
| **†Canada** | **235,333** | **9,864** | **23.86** |
| **UNITED STATES** | **2,626,500** | **11,596** | **226.51** |
| **Western Europe** | | | |
| †Austria | 53,358 | 7,127 | 7.49 |
| †Belgium | 85,064 | 8,619 | 9.87 |
| †Denmark | 50,745 | 9,878 | 5.14 |
| †Finland | 33,423 | 7,004 | 4.77 |
| †France | 508,085 | 9,479 | 53.60 |
| †Germany, West | 642,422 | 10,509 | 61.13 |
| †Greece | 29,311 | 3,089 | 9.49 |
| †Iceland | 1,600 | 7,018 | 0.23 |
| †Ireland | 12,423 | 3,770 | 3.30 |
| †Italy | 302,982 | 5,300 | 57.17 |
| †Luxembourg | 3,221 | 8,972 | 0.36 |
| †Netherlands | 99,421 | 7,048 | 14.11 |
| †Norway | 40,437 | 9,887 | 4.09 |
| †Portugal | 19,960 | 2,009 | 9.93 |
| †Spain | 114,825 | 3,022 | 38.00 |
| †Sweden | 92,335 | 11,111 | 8.31 |
| †Switzerland | 64,613 | 10,245 | 6.31 |
| †United Kingdom | 297,978 | 5,340 | 55.80 |
| **Africa** (Excluding Egypt) | | | |
| Algeria | 27,914 | 1,483 | 18.83 |
| Ethiopia | 3,846 | 118 | 32.59 |
| Gabon | 2,470 | 4,186 | 0.59 |
| Ghana | 6,084 | 501 | 12.13 |
| Ivory Coast | 7,483 | 932 | 8.03 |
| Kenya | 4,597 | 288 | 15.94 |
| Libya | 22,020 | 7,357 | 2.99 |
| Morocco | 12,691 | 605 | 20.97 |
| Nigeria | 54,271 | 704 | 77.09 |
| South Africa | 47,982 | 1,690 | 28.39 |
| Sudan | 6,458 | 346 | 18.67 |
| Tanzania | 3,532 | 197 | 17.91 |
| Tunisia | 7,811 | 1,207 | 6.47 |
| Uganda | 3,505 | 256 | 13.69 |
| Zaire | 4,140 | 142 | 28.92 |
| Zambia | 2,654 | 455 | 5.83 |
| Zimbabwe | 3,784 | 509 | 7.44 |
| **South Asia** | | | |
| Afghanistan | 3,115 | 207 | 15.03 |
| Bangladesh | 11,116 | 123 | 90.49 |
| Burma | 6,416 | 186 | 34.41 |
| India | 137,363 | 202 | 680.06 |
| Pakistan | 20,688 | 239 | 86.47 |
| Sri Lanka | 4,803 | 324 | 14.85 |
| **Near East** | | | |
| Egypt | 24,102 | 573 | 42.04 |
| Iran | 43,661 | 1,128 | 38.72 |
| Iraq | 35,615 | 2,666 | 13.36 |
| Israel | 18,995 | 5,052 | 3.76 |
| Jordan | 2,592 | 1,112 | 2.33 |
| Kuwait | 17,532 | 12,920 | 1.36 |
| Qatar | 5,508 | 31,838 | 0.17 |
| Saudi Arabia | 83,891 | 12,521 | 7.00 |
| Syria | 8,570 | 988 | 8.68 |
| †Turkey | 39,530 | 865 | 45.70 |
| United Arab Emirates | 9,556 | 10,600 | 0.90 |
| **East Asia** | | | |
| China, Rep. of (Taiwan) | 32,510 | 1,826 | 17.81 |
| Hong Kong | 19,194 | 3,952 | 4.86 |
| Indonesia | 63,111 | 417 | 151.20 |
| †Japan | 986,053 | 8,426 | 117.03 |
| Korea, South | 42,439 | 1,067 | 39.77 |
| Malaysia | 18,977 | 1,355 | 14.01 |
| Philippines | 28,809 | 589 | 48.88 |
| Singapore | 10,932 | 4,580 | 2.39 |
| Thailand | 28,504 | 601 | 47.42 |
| **Oceania** | | | |
| †Australia | 132,676 | 9,115 | 14.56 |
| †New Zealand | 19,496 | 6,227 | 3.13 |
| **Latin America** | | | |
| Argentina | 56,778 | 2,089 | 27.18 |
| Bolivia | 3,704 | 692 | 5.36 |
| Brazil | 251,500 | 2,067 | 121.65 |
| Chile | 20,710 | 1,880 | 11.01 |
| Colombia | 26,297 | 983 | 26.75 |
| Dominican Republic | 6,067 | 1,066 | 5.69 |
| Ecuador | 8,437 | 1,052 | 8.02 |
| Guatemala | 7,529 | 1,067 | 7.06 |
| Jamaica | 3,631 | 1,602 | 2.27 |
| Mexico | 138,006 | 2,045 | 67.50 |
| Panama | 3,212 | 1,680 | 1.91 |
| Peru | 21,082 | 1,200 | 17.61 |
| Uruguay | 4,990 | 1,704 | 2.93 |
| Venezuela | 51,044 | 3,398 | 15.02 |
| **Communist Countries** | | | |
| Albania | 2,160 | 805 | 2.68 |
| Bulgaria | 29,889 | 3,370 | 8.87 |
| China, People's Rep. | 592,000 | 576 | 1,027.00 |
| Cuba | 13,985 | 1,407 | 9.94 |
| Czechoslovakia | 85,000 | 5,542 | 15.34 |
| Germany, East | 99,619 | 5,945 | 16.76 |
| Hungary | 39,373 | 3,665 | 10.74 |
| Korea, North | 15,914 | 824 | 19.32 |
| Mongolia | 1,324 | 782 | 1.69 |
| Poland | 124,905 | 3,513 | 35.56 |
| Romania | 89,328 | 4,017 | 22.24 |
| USSR | 1,280,616 | 4,820 | 265.71 |
| Vietnam | 6,000 | 113 | 53.00 |
| Yugoslavia | 72,302 | 3,232 | 22.37 |
| **WORLD** | **10,490,220** | **2,338** | **4,486.92** |

†Gross Domestic Product

## OIL IMPORTS: 1980-1981 SOURCE: Social and Economic Statistics Administration, U.S. Dept. of Commerce

(Quantity in barrels, value in dollars.)

| Country of Origin | General Imports Calendar Year 1980 Net Quantity | F.a.s. Value |
|---|---|---|
| Canada | 75,691,312 | $ 2,207,042,980 |
| Guatemala | 640,229 | 19,633,968 |
| Mexico | 194,172,141 | 5,926,624,931 |
| Trinidad | 43,668,377 | 1,495,584,999 |
| Argentina | 355,423 | 9,162,400 |
| Brazil | 342,807 | 10,101,492 |
| Ecuador | 7,985,722 | 276,422,612 |
| Peru | 14,885,543 | 541,971,949 |
| Venezuela | 70,984,862 | 1,694,829,171 |
| Norway | 61,628,643 | 2,075,375,629 |
| United Kingdom | 56,779,053 | 1,922,460,779 |
| Iran | 8,475,152 | 285,188,277 |
| Iraq | 11,508,933 | 347,482,145 |
| Kuwait | 12,509,186 | 445,467,150 |
| Oman | 9,745,283 | 330,478,599 |
| Qatar | 7,091,334 | 236,265,427 |
| Saudi Arabia | 452,951,677 | 12,231,167,618 |
| Syria | 603,797 | 20,761,556 |
| United Arab Emirates | 66,101,253 | 1,971,678,898 |
| Brunei | 5,293,232 | 185,200,284 |
| China (PRC) | 763,970 | 18,808,941 |
| Indonesia | 120,916,467 | 3,698,759,377 |
| Malaysia | 19,972,628 | 705,158,245 |
| Algeria | 162,754,345 | 5,680,525,847 |
| Angola | 13,996,799 | 440,837,230 |
| Cameroon | 15,352,284 | 537,086,927 |
| Congo (Brazzaville) | 2,565,713 | 83,098,648 |
| Egypt | 12,406,854 | 400,159,288 |
| Gabon | 7,768,262 | 264,094,171 |
| Ghana | 299,010 | 10,273,046 |
| Libya | 197,487,324 | 7,010,060,598 |
| Nigeria | 311,659,797 | 10,625,616,660 |
| Tunisia | 1,774,505 | 51,894,424 |
| Zaire | 4,642,173 | 157,498,349 |
| Other Countries | 21 | 779 |
| **Total** | **1,974,774,111** | **$61,916,773,394** |

| Country of Origin | General Imports Calendar Year 1981 Net Quantity | F.a.s. Value |
|---|---|---|
| Canada | 57,187,701 | $ 1,932,182,000 |
| Mexico | 177,509,774 | 5,893,058,000 |
| Guatemala | 802,948 | 24,523,000 |
| Trinidad | 40,649,961 | 1,548,464,000 |
| Colombia | 142,722 | 3,634,000 |
| Venezuela | 70,556,836 | 2,008,013,000 |
| Ecuador | 14,380,901 | 487,457,000 |
| Peru | 10,913,942 | 399,435,000 |
| Brazil | 4,177,840 | 146,486,000 |
| Norway | 48,384,011 | 1,782,847,000 |
| United Kingdom | 134,266,730 | 4,932,989,000 |
| Turkey | 377,835 | 16,052,000 |
| Iraq | 4,088,178 | 161,449,000 |
| Syria | 2,141,567 | 74,316,000 |
| Kuwait | 2,222,571 | 74,253,000 |
| Saudi Arabia | 434,141,596 | 14,027,466,000 |
| Qatar | 3,057,287 | 106,196,000 |
| United Arab Emirates | 52,710,403 | 1,855,463,000 |
| Oman | 9,316,784 | 346,250,000 |
| Malaysia | 10,652,881 | 419,326,000 |
| Indonesia | 131,714,489 | 4,667,547,000 |
| Brunei | 8,335,681 | 321,329,000 |
| Algeria | 96,513,694 | 3,739,640,000 |
| Libya | 134,414,551 | 5,213,779,000 |
| Egypt | 9,243,055 | 332,932,000 |
| Cameroon | 15,375,580 | 564,847,000 |
| Ghana | 519,642 | 18,264,000 |
| Nigeria | 238,321,741 | 9,056,808,000 |
| Gabon | 12,054,085 | 417,031,000 |
| Angola | 23,883,515 | 841,304,000 |
| Congo | 8,390,936 | 283,502,000 |
| Zaire | 6,620,386 | 243,395,000 |
| Other Countries | 1,736 | 28,000 |
| **Total** | **1,763,071,559** | **$61,940,265,000** |

## LARGEST U.S. COMMERCIAL BANKS SOURCE: *Fortune* Magazine

| Bank | Assets[1] ($000) | Rank '81 | Rank '80 | Deposits ($000) | Deposits Rank | Loans[2] ($000) | Loans Rank |
|---|---|---|---|---|---|---|---|
| BankAmerica Corp. (San Francisco) | 121,158,350 | 1 | 2 | 94,369,453 | 1 | 71,236,237 | 2 |
| Citicorp (New York) | 119,232,000 | 2 | 1 | 72,125,000 | 2 | 77,139,000 | 1 |
| Chase Manhattan Corp. (New York) | 77,839,338 | 3 | 3 | 55,299,670 | 3 | 50,459,433 | 3 |
| Manufacturers Hanover Corp. (New York) | 59,108,519 | 4 | 4 | 42,462,035 | 4 | 37,448,484 | 4 |
| J.P. Morgan & Co. (New York) | 53,522,000 | 5 | 5 | 36,024,000 | 5 | 28,220,000 | 6 |
| Continental Illinois Corp. (Chicago) | 46,971,755 | 6 | 6 | 29,594,005 | 6 | 31,463,328 | 5 |
| Chemical New York Corp. | 44,916,933 | 7 | 7 | 29,429,577 | 7 | 27,789,275 | 7 |
| First Interstate Bancorp. (Los Angeles) | 36,982,091 | 8 | 9 | 27,407,174 | 8 | 20,795,103 | 9 |
| Bankers Trust New York Corp. | 34,213,010 | 9 | 8 | 23,345,022 | 11 | 18,504,025 | 11 |
| First Chicago Corp. | 33,562,442 | 10 | 10 | 25,554,923 | 9 | 20,020,357 | 10 |
| Security Pacific Corp. (Los Angeles) | 32,999,142 | 11 | 11 | 23,446,393 | 10 | 21,521,100 | 8 |
| Wells Fargo & Co. (San Francisco) | 23,219,189 | 12 | 12 | 16,853,927 | 12 | 16,936,490 | 12 |
| Crocker National Corp. (San Francisco) | 22,494,462 | 13 | 13 | 16,494,955 | 13 | 14,003,786 | 13 |
| Marine Midland Banks (Buffalo) | 18,682,474 | 14 | 15 | 14,095,704 | 14 | 10,799,319 | 14 |
| Mellon National Corp. (Pittsburgh) | 18,447,860 | 15 | 16 | 11,837,780 | 17 | 9,793,649 | 17 |

[1] As of December 31, 1981. [2] Net of unearned discount and loan loss reserve. Figure does not include direct lease financing.

## LARGEST DIVERSIFIED FINANCIAL COMPANIES SOURCE: *Fortune* Magazine

| Company | Assets[1] ($000) | Rank '81 | Rank '80 | Revenues ($000) | Revenues Rank | Net Income ($000) | Net Income Rank |
|---|---|---|---|---|---|---|---|
| Federal National Mortgage Assn. (Washington, D.C.) | 62,095,903 | 1 | 1 | 5,861,559 | 4 | (190,370) | 50 |
| Aetna Life & Casualty (Hartford) | 39,630,600 | 2 | 2 | 13,531,900 | 1 | 462,200 | 3 |
| American Express (New York) | 25,103,000 | 3 | 4 | 7,211,000 | 3 | 518,000 | 1 |
| Travelers (Hartford) | 23,982,300 | 4 | 3 | 9,800,800 | 2 | 360,100 | 5 |
| Merrill Lynch & Co. (New York) | 17,682,251 | 5 | 5 | 4,038,182 | 8 | 202,874 | 9 |
| H.F. Ahmanson (Los Angeles) | 15,048,826 | 6 | 6 | 1,564,248 | 20 | (51,307) | 48 |
| INA (Philadelphia) | 11,028,906 | 7 | 7 | 5,162,258 | 5 | 475,205 | 2 |
| Great Western Financial (Beverly Hills) | 10,646,435 | 8 | 8 | 1,173,973 | 28 | (15,420) | 38 |
| First Boston (New York) | 10,314,389 | 9 | 18 | 291,536 | 41 | 46,286 | 27 |
| Loews (New York) | 9,914,071 | 10 | 10 | 4,776,219 | 6 | 253,213 | 6 |
| First Charter Financial (Beverly Hills) | 9,750,034 | 11 | 9 | 1,003,800 | 30 | (55,654) | 49 |
| Lincoln National (Fort Wayne, Ind.) | 9,047,291 | 12 | 12 | 3,002,684 | 11 | 128,104 | 16 |
| Transamerica (San Francisco) | 9,042,342 | 13 | 11 | 4,155,887 | 7 | 223,336 | 7 |
| Imperial Corp. of America (San Diego) | 8,500,000 | 14 | 14 | 877,247 | 34 | (37,754) | 46 |
| American General (Houston) | 8,075,700 | 15 | 15 | 2,387,700 | 14 | 163,900 | 13 |
| Continental (New York) | 8,071,934 | 16 | 13 | 3,466,227 | 9 | 217,532 | 8 |

[1] As of December 31, 1981.

## LARGEST INDUSTRIAL CORPORATIONS

SOURCE: *Fortune* Magazine

| Company | Sales ($000) | Rank '81 | Rank '80 | Assets ($000) | Rank | Net Income ($000) | Rank |
|---|---|---|---|---|---|---|---|
| Exxon (New York) | 108,107,688 | 1 | 1 | 62,931,055 | 1 | 5,567,481 | 1 |
| Mobil (New York) | 64,488,000 | 2 | 2 | 34,776,000 | 3 | 2,433,000 | 3 |
| General Motors (Detroit) | 62,698,500 | 3 | 3 | 38,991,200 | 2 | 333,400 | 57 |
| Texaco (Harrison, N.Y.) | 57,628,000 | 4 | 4 | 27,489,000 | 5 | 2,310,000 | 5 |
| Standard Oil of California (San Francisco) | 44,224,000 | 5 | 5 | 23,680,000 | 7 | 2,380,000 | 4 |
| Ford Motor (Dearborn, Mich.) | 38,247,100 | 6 | 6 | 23,021,400 | 8 | (1,060,100) | 490 |
| Standard Oil (Indiana) (Chicago) | 29,947,000 | 7 | 9 | 22,916,000 | 9 | 1,922,000 | 7 |
| International Business Machines (Armonk, N.Y.) | 29,070,000 | 8 | 8 | 29,586,000 | 4 | 3,308,000 | 2 |
| Gulf Oil (Pittsburgh) | 28,252,000* | 9 | 7 | 20,429,000 | 11 | 1,231,000 | 14 |
| Atlantic Richfield (Los Angeles) | 27,797,436 | 10 | 11 | 19,732,539 | 13 | 1,671,290 | 9 |
| General Electric (Fairfield, Conn.) | 27,240,000 | 11 | 10 | 20,942,000 | 10 | 1,652,000 | 10 |
| E.I. du Pont de Nemours (Wilmington, Del.) | 22,810,000 | 12 | 15 | 23,829,000 | 6 | 1,401,000 | 12 |
| Shell Oil (Houston) | 21,629,000 | 13 | 12 | 20,118,000 | 12 | 1,701,000 | 8 |
| International Telephone & Telegraph (New York) | 17,306,189 | 14 | 13 | 15,052,377 | 16 | 676,804 | 24 |
| Phillips Petroleum (Bartlesville, Okla.) | 15,966,000 | 15 | 16 | 11,264,000 | 20 | 879,000 | 17 |

*Does not include excise taxes.

## LARGEST UTILITIES

SOURCE: *Fortune* Magazine

| Company | Assets[1] ($000) | Rank '81 | Rank '80 | Operating Revenues[2] ($000) | Rank | Net Income ($000) | Rank |
|---|---|---|---|---|---|---|---|
| American Telephone & Telegraph (New York) | 137,749,500 | 1 | 1 | 58,213,800 | 1 | 6,888,100 | 1 |
| General Telephone & Electronics (Stamford, Conn.) | 21,113,299 | 2 | 2 | 11,026,296 | 2 | 722,004 | 2 |
| Southern Company (Atlanta) | 12,415,034 | 3 | 3 | 4,256,237 | 7 | 325,979 | 10 |
| Pacific Gas & Electric (San Francisco) | 12,366,659 | 4 | 4 | 6,194,575 | 3 | 564,606 | 3 |
| American Electric Power (Columbus) | 11,567,039 | 5 | 5 | 4,192,645 | 8 | 368,279 | 7 |
| Commonwealth Edison (Chicago) | 11,196,823 | 6 | 6 | 3,737,311 | 11 | 449,894 | 5 |
| Southern California Edison (Rosemead, Calif.) | 8,728,543 | 7 | 7 | 4,054,356 | 9 | 489,912 | 4 |
| Middle South Utilities (New Orleans) | 8,318,556 | 8 | 9 | 2,771,788 | 21 | 281,483 | 11 |
| Consolidated Edison (New York) | 7,732,822 | 9 | 8 | 4,865,934 | 4 | 448,026 | 6 |
| Texas Utilities (Dallas) | 7,306,658 | 10 | 11 | 2,738,377 | 22 | 359,398 | 8 |
| Public Service Electric & Gas (Newark) | 7,277,089 | 11 | 10 | 3,471,652 | 15 | 264,137 | 13 |
| Virginia Electric & Power (Richmond) | 7,057,831 | 12 | 12 | 2,161,853 | 28 | 237,780 | 20 |
| Consumers Power (Jackson, Mich.) | 6,872,187 | 13 | 14 | 2,733,973 | 24 | 247,789 | 16 |
| Detroit Edison | 6,607,788 | 14 | 15 | 2,054,057 | 32 | 234,353 | 21 |
| Duke Power (Charlotte) | 6,531,044 | 15 | 13 | 1,908,454 | 33 | 336,251 | 9 |

[1]As of December 31, 1981. [2]Gross receipts from operations during fiscal 1981, including any non-utility revenues.

## LARGEST RETAILING COMPANIES

SOURCE: *Fortune* Magazine

| Company | Sales[1] ($000) | Rank '81 | Rank '80 | Assets ($000) | Rank | Net Income ($000) | Rank |
|---|---|---|---|---|---|---|---|
| Sears, Roebuck (Chicago)[2] | 27,357,400 | 1 | 1 | 34,509,400 | 1 | 650,100 | 1 |
| Safeway Stores (Oakland)[2] | 16,580,318 | 2 | 2 | 3,690,404 | 6 | 114,556 | 13 |
| K-Mart (Troy, Mich.) | 16,527,012 | 3 | 3 | 6,673,004 | 2 | 220,251 | 5 |
| J.C. Penney (New York) | 11,860,169 | 4 | 4 | 6,216,000 | 3 | 386,809 | 2 |
| Kroger (Cincinnati)[2] | 11,266,520 | 5 | 5 | 2,405,290 | 10 | 128,045 | 10 |
| F.W. Woolworth (New York)[2] | 7,223,241 | 6 | 6 | 3,141,965 | 7 | 81,870 | 21 |
| Lucky Stores (Dublin, Calif.) | 7,201,404 | 7 | 8 | 1,524,444 | 17 | 95,452 | 15 |
| American Stores Co. (Salt Lake City) | 7,096,590 | 8 | 9 | 1,356,328 | 21 | 64,552 | 24 |
| Federated Department Stores (Cincinnati) | 7,067,673 | 9 | 10 | 4,096,877 | 5 | 58,508 | 4 |
| Great Atlantic & Pacific Tea (Montvale, N.J.)[3] | 6,989,529 | 10 | 7 | 1,308,983 | 23 | (43,049) | 49 |
| Winn-Dixie Stores (Jacksonville)[4] | 6,200,167 | 11 | 12 | 924,776 | 28 | 95,395 | 16 |
| Montgomery Ward (Chicago)[2] | 5,742,491 | 12 | 11 | 4,116,593 | 4 | (124,120) | 50 |
| Southland (Dallas)[2] | 5,693,636 | 13 | 13 | 1,677,791 | 14 | 94,191 | 17 |
| Jewel Companies (Chicago) | 5,107,614 | 14 | 15 | 1,379,871 | 20 | 101,670 | 14 |
| Household Merchandising (Des Plaines, Ill.)[2]* | 5,079,932 | 15 | 14 | 1,354,299 | 22 | 53,262 | 27 |

[1]All figures are for the fiscal year ending January 31, 1982, unless otherwise noted. [2]Figures are for fiscal year ending December 31,1981. [3]Figures are for fiscal year ending February 28, 1981. [4]Figures are for fiscal year ending June 30, 1981. *Name changed from City Products on September 30, 1981.

## LARGEST LIFE INSURANCE COMPANIES

SOURCE: *Fortune* Magazine

| Company | Assets[1] ($000) | Rank '81 | Rank '80 | Premium & Annuity Income[2] ($000) | Rank | Life Insurance In Force[1] ($000) | Rank |
|---|---|---|---|---|---|---|---|
| Prudential (Newark)* | 62,498,540 | 1 | 1 | 9,935,180 | 1 | 456,174,632 | 1 |
| Metropolitan (New York)* | 51,757,845 | 2 | 2 | 5,131,318 | 2 | 393,590,726 | 2 |
| Equitable Life Assurance (New York)* | 36,758,160 | 3 | 3 | 2,400,771 | 8 | 223,874,676 | 3 |
| Aetna Life (Hartford) | 25,158,904 | 4 | 4 | 4,440,322 | 3 | 163,873,853 | 4 |
| New York Life* | 21,041,380 | 5 | 5 | 2,637,020 | 6 | 137,456,394 | 6 |
| John Hancock Mutual (Boston)* | 19,936,798 | 6 | 6 | 2,425,567 | 7 | 145,609,204 | 5 |
| Connecticut General Life (Bloomfield) | 15,103,332 | 7 | 7 | 2,810,410 | 5 | 90,809,773 | 9 |
| Travelers (Hartford) | 14,803,168 | 8 | 8 | 4,399,880 | 4 | 116,498,216 | 8 |
| Northwestern Mutual (Milwaukee)* | 12,154,318 | 9 | 9 | 1,244,436 | 12 | 70,133,741 | 11 |
| Teachers Insurance & Annuity (New York) | 11,439,344 | 10 | 10 | 1,791,958 | 9 | 9,072,398 | 45 |
| Massachusetts Mutual (Springfield)* | 10,022,231 | 11 | 11 | 1,224,967 | 14 | 55,978,807 | 13 |
| Bankers Life (Des Moines)* | 8,765,096 | 12 | 13 | 1,533,098 | 10 | 42,680,898 | 17 |
| Mutual of New York | 8,388,961 | 13 | 12 | 785,245 | 20 | 42,827,888 | 16 |
| New England Mutual (Boston) | 7,273,819 | 14 | 14 | 1,101,205 | 17 | 34,991,635 | 19 |
| Mutual Benefit (Newark)* | 6,619,044 | 15 | 15 | 1,158,830 | 16 | 46,732,485 | 14 |

[1]As of December 31, 1981. [2]Includes premium income from life, accident, and health policies, from annuities, and from contributions to deposit administration funds. *Mutual company.

## LEADING U.S. FARM CROPS

SOURCE: U.S. Department of Agriculture, Crop Reporting Board, SRS

| Crop | Unit | Production (in 1,000 units) 1980 | Production (in 1,000 units) 1981 | Yield per acre[2] 1980 | Yield per acre[2] 1981 |
|---|---|---|---|---|---|
| Corn for grain | Bushels | 6,644,841 | 8,200,951 | 91.0 | 109.9 |
| Sorghum for grain | Bushels | 579,197 | 880,266 | 46.3 | 64.1 |
| Oats | Bushels | 458,263 | 508,083 | 53.0 | 54.0 |
| Barley | Bushels | 360,956 | 478,301 | 49.6 | 52.3 |
| Wheat, total | Bushels | 2,374,306 | 2,793,436 | 33.4 | 34.5 |
| Winter | Bushels | 1,895,383 | 2,098,719 | 36.8 | 35.8 |
| Durum | Bushels | 108,395 | 185,940 | 22.4 | 32.3 |
| Other spring | Bushels | 370,528 | 508,777 | 25.3 | 30.6 |
| Rice | Cwt. | 146,150 | 185,370 | 4,413.0[1] | 4,873.0[1] |
| Rye | Bushels | 16,483 | 18,621 | 24.4 | 26.7 |
| Soybeans for beans | Bushels | 1,792,062 | 2,030,452 | 26.4 | 30.4 |
| Flaxseed | Bushels | 7,928 | 7,799 | 111.6 | 12.6 |
| Peanuts for nuts | Pounds | 2,307,847 | 3,948,985 | 1,650.0 | 2,654.0 |
| Sunflower seeds | Pounds | 3,741,640 | 4,487,410 | 1,016.0 | 1,177.0 |
| Popcorn | Pounds | 552,310 | 776,620 | 2,477.0 | 3,142.0 |
| Cotton, total | Bales | 11,122.1 | 15,733.2 | 404.0[1] | 546.0[1] |
| Hay | Tons | 131,027 | 143,105 | 2.2[1] | 2.38 |
| Beans, dry edible | Cwt. | 26,395 | 31,814 | 1,449.0[1] | 1,445.0[1] |
| Peas, dry edible | Cwt. | 3,285 | 2,290 | 2,433.0[1] | 2,120.0[1] |
| Potatoes | Cwt. | 302,857 | 333,682 | 262.0 | 271.0 |
| Sweetpotatoes | Cwt. | 10,953 | 12,622 | 107.0 | 115.0 |
| Tobacco | Pounds | 1,786,192 | 2,048,211 | 1,940.0 | 2,120.0 |
| Sugarbeets | Tons | 23,502 | 27,271 | 19.8 | 22.0 |
| Sugarcane | Tons | 26,963 | 29,846 | 36.8 | 39.6 |
| Coffee | Pounds | 1,440 | 2,240 | 850.0 | 1,320.0 |
| Hops | Pounds | 75,560 | 79,144 | 2,037.0 | 1,836.0 |
| Cranberries | Barrels | 2,697.5 | 2,664.0 | 116.3 | 115.1 |
| Apples, Com'l | Pounds | 8,828,400 | 7,645,300 | | |
| Peaches | Pounds | 3,079,600 | 2,788,600 | | |
| Pears | Tons | 897.3 | 893.4 | | |
| Grapes | Tons | 5,595.1 | 4,428.6 | | |
| Oranges | Boxes | 273,630 | 245,580 | | |
| Grapefruit | Boxes | 73,200 | 67,860 | | |
| Lemons | Boxes | 20,750 | 31,800 | | |
| Limes | Boxes | 1,100 | 1,200 | | |

[1]Yield in pounds. [2]Yield per acre figures not available for fruit.

## INCLUSIVE STATE—FARM PAYMENT TOTALS: 1981

SOURCE: U.S. Department of Agriculture, Agricultural Stabilization Conservation Service

| State | Amount | State | Amount | State | Amount |
|---|---|---|---|---|---|
| Alabama | $ 21,362,482 | Maine | $ 2,343,380 | Oregon | $ 19,335,685 |
| Alaska | 351,374 | Maryland | 2,960,800 | Pennsylvania | 11,877,714 |
| Arizona | 5,859,979 | Massachusetts | 836,993 | Rhode Island | 155,400 |
| Arkansas | 40,125,092 | Michigan | 17,263,136 | South Carolina | 15,929,453 |
| California | 23,367,705 | Minnesota | 79,120,737 | South Dakota | 89,039,859 |
| Colorado | 45,835,146 | Mississippi | 19,521,735 | Tennessee | 20,674,248 |
| Connecticut | 394,277 | Missouri | 105,401,471 | Texas | 317,618,384 |
| Delaware | 1,750,642 | Montana | 83,684,996 | Utah | 7,817,640 |
| Florida | 10,991,531 | Nebraska | 99,404,216 | Vermont | 1,561,798 |
| Georgia | 38,054,019 | Nevada | 3,742,660 | Virginia | 10,818,314 |
| Hawaii | 716,466 | New Hampshire | 714,065 | Washington | 37,297,087 |
| Idaho | 29,495,240 | New Jersey | 1,464,749 | West Virginia | 2,988,083 |
| Illinois | 49,234,860 | New Mexico | 24,975,151 | Wisconsin | 16,876,775 |
| Indiana | 27,890,286 | New York | 6,910,276 | Wyoming | 9,801,176 |
| Iowa | 58,170,133 | North Carolina | 15,547,429 | Puerto Rico | 642,063 |
| Kansas | 230,566,695 | North Dakota | 129,720,190 | Virgin Islands | 14,522 |
| Kentucky | 14,346,517 | Ohio | 24,089,349 | Undistributed | 2,767,744 |
| Louisiana | 15,436,123 | Oklahoma | 123,293,167 | Total | $1,920,159,012 |

## LIVESTOCK POPULATION ON U.S. FARMS AND RANCHES (as of January 1)

SOURCE: U.S. Department of Agriculture, Crop Reporting Board, SRS

| Year | CATTLE AND CALVES | SHEEP AND LAMBS | HOGS AND PIGS | CHICKENS[2] |
|---|---|---|---|---|
| 1959 | 92,322,000 | 32,606,000 | 58,045,000 | 387,002,000 |
| 1961[3] | 97,700,000 | 32,725,000 | 55,560,000 | 366,082,000 |
| 1963 | 104,488,000 | 29,176,000 | 62,726,000[1] | 375,575,000 |
| 1965 | 109,000,000 | 25,127,000 | 56,106,000 | 394,118,000 |
| 1967 | 108,783,000 | 23,953,000 | 57,125,000 | 425,571,000 |
| 1969 | 110,015,000 | 21,350,000 | 60,829,000 | 413,287,000 |
| 1971 | 114,578,000 | 19,731,000 | 67,285,000 | 433,280,000[1] |
| 1973 | 121,539,000 | 17,641,000 | 59,017,000 | 404,191,000 |
| 1975 | 132,028,000 | 14,515,000 | 54,693,000 | 384,101,000 |
| 1977 | 122,810,000 | 12,722,000 | 54,934,000 | 378,361,000 |
| 1979 | 110,864,000 | 12,365,000 | 60,356,000 | 396,933,000 |
| 1980 | 111,192,000 | 12,687,000 | 67,353,000 | 400,585,000 |
| 1981 | 114,321,000 | 12,936,000 | 64,512,000 | 392,110,000 |
| 1982 | 115,691,000 | 13,116,000 | 58,691,000 | 383,220,000 |

[1]Begins inventory as of December 1 preceding year. [2]Excludes commercial broilers. [3]Includes Alaska and Hawaii beginning 1961.

## U.S. PASSENGER CAR PRODUCTION: 1981

SOURCE: Motor Vehicle Manufacturers Association of the United States, Inc.

| Company | Automobile Production |
|---|---|
| AMERICAN MOTORS CORP. | 109,319 |
| Spirit | 35,143 |
| Concord | 49,480 |
| Eagle | 24,696 |
| CHRYSLER CORP. | 748,774 |
| Horizon | 139,014 |
| Reliant | 216,901 |
| Gran Fury | 7,448 |
| Caravelle | 2,139 |
| Total Plymouth | 365,502 |
| LeBaron | 52,478 |
| Chrysler | 4,862 |
| Total Chrysler-Plymouth | 422,842 |
| Omni | 125,650 |
| Aries | 170,139 |
| Dodge 400 | 13,817 |
| Diplomat | 12,644 |
| St. Regis | 3,682 |
| Total Dodge | 325,932 |
| FORD MOTOR CO. | 1,320,197 |
| LTD | 40,886 |
| Thunderbird | 64,328 |
| Granada | 103,702 |
| Fairmont | 176,246 |
| Escort | 353,162 |
| Mustang | 153,719 |
| Total Ford | 892,043 |
| Marquis | 65,720 |
| Cougar XR7 | 28,223 |
| Cougar/Monarch | 49,831 |
| Zephyr | 51,868 |
| Lynx | 117,991 |
| Capri | 50,336 |
| Lincoln | 26,651 |
| Mark | 25,640 |
| Continental | 11,894 |
| Total Lincoln-Mercury | 428,154 |
| GENERAL MOTORS CORP. | 3,904,083 |
| Chevrolet | 147,337 |
| Corvette | 27,990 |
| Monte Carlo | 139,899 |
| Celebrity/Malibu | 213,628 |
| Camaro | 99,059 |
| Citation | 300,652 |
| Cavalier/Monza | 139,837 |
| Chevette | 376,951 |
| Total Chevrolet | 1,445,353 |
| Pontiac | 10,064 |
| Grand Prix | 97,051 |
| Bonneville/LeMans & A6000 | 88,293 |
| Firebird | 48,961 |
| Phoenix | 96,597 |
| J-2000/Sunbird | 91,465 |
| T-1000 | 88,871 |
| Total Pontiac | 521,302 |
| Oldsmobile | 276,452 |
| Toronado | 43,929 |
| Supreme/Cierra | 385,674 |
| Omega | 132,268 |
| Firenza | 10 |
| Total Oldsmobile | 838,333 |
| Buick | 171,834 |
| Riviera | 58,275 |
| Century/Regal | 370,676 |
| Skylark | 239,175 |
| Total Buick | 839,960 |
| Cadillac | 155,622 |
| Eldorado | 57,861 |
| Seville | 23,344 |
| Cimarron | 22,308 |
| Total Cadillac | 259,135 |
| CHECKER MOTORS CORP. | 3,010 |
| VOLKSWAGEN OF AMERICA | 167,755 |
| TOTAL PASSENGER CARS | 6,253,138 |

## WORLD MOTOR VEHICLE PRODUCTION: 1981

SOURCE: U.N. *Monthly Bulletin of Statistics*, © United Nations, July 1982

| Country | Passenger Cars | Commercial Vehicles | Total |
|---|---|---|---|
| Japan | 6,978,000 | 4,206,000 | 11,184,000 |
| United States[1] | 6,256,000 | 1,690,000 | 7,946,000 |
| Germany, West | 3,590,500 | 311,700 | 3,902,200 |
| France | 2,953,500 | 473,300 | 3,426,800 |
| USSR | 1,323,600 | 873,600[2] | 2,197,200 |
| Italy | 1,250,800 | 164,900 | 1,415,700 |
| Canada | 820,900 | 528,700 | 1,349,600 |
| United Kingdom | 954,500 | 229,700 | 1,184,200 |
| Spain | 861,500 | 127,100 | 988,600 |
| Brazil | 661,800 | 97,700 | 759,500 |
| Mexico[3] | 357,300 | 171,500 | 428,800 |
| Australia[3] | 358,600 | 40,000 | 398,600 |
| Poland | 240,300 | 48,100 | 288,400 |
| Czechoslovakia | 180,700 | 85,600 | 266,300 |
| Yugoslavia | 175,400 | 73,000 | 248,400 |
| Sweden | 229,200 | — | 229,200 |
| Germany, East | 180,300 | 41,400 | 221,700 |
| Argentina[3] | 143,600 | 28,600 | 172,200 |
| India | 60,900 | 85,000 | 145,900 |
| Romania[4] | 67,200 | 33,600 | 100,800 |
| Netherlands | 77,900 | 12,100 | 90,000 |
| Austria | 7,000 | 6,300 | 13,300 |
| Hungary | — | 11,800 | 11,800 |

[1]Factory sales. [2]Excluding wheeled tractors. [3]Including assembly. [4]1980 figures.

## NEW ASSEMBLED PASSENGER CARS, TRUCKS AND BUSES IMPORTED INTO THE UNITED STATES: 1980

SOURCE: Motor Vehicle Manufacturers Association of the United States, Inc.

| | |
|---|---|
| Japan | 2,094,331 |
| Canada | 834,688 |
| Germany, West | 470,671 |
| Sweden | 61,889 |
| France | 47,396 |
| Italy | 46,899 |
| United Kingdom | 32,558 |
| Belgium | 40 |
| OTHERS | 3,146 |
| TOTAL | 3,591,618 |

## LARGEST PASSENGER CAR PRODUCER FOR EACH COUNTRY: 1980†

SOURCE: Motor Vehicle Manufacturers Association of the United States, Inc.

| Country | Producer | 1980 Production |
|---|---|---|
| Argentina | Ford Motor Argentina S.A. | 71,555 |
| Australia | General Motors-Holden's Ltd. | 110,822 |
| Belgium | General Motors Continental S.A. | 304,535 |
| Brazil | General Motors Brazil | 187,906 |
| Canada | General Motors | 512,330 |
| France | Regie Renault | 1,492,339 |
| West Germany | Volkswagenwerk A.G. | 1,232,164 |
| India | Hindustan Motors | 21,752 |
| Italy | Fiat Auto S.p.A. | 1,185,177 |
| Japan | Toyota Motor | 2,303,284 |
| Mexico | Volkswagen de Mexico | 113,033 |
| Netherlands | DAF-Volvo | 80,779 |
| Peru | Volkswagen | 4,337 |
| Poland | Fabryka Samochodow | 250,037 |
| Spain | Fasa-Renault | 343,678 |
| Sweden | A.B. Volvo | 169,566 |
| Turkey | Oyak (Renault) | 17,600 |
| United Kingdom | British Leyland | 395,820 |
| Venezuela | General Motors de Venezuela | 41,137 |
| Yugoslavia | Zavodi Crvena Zastava | 193,738 |

†Excluding United States.

## THE U.S. LABOR FORCE

SOURCE: U.S. Department of Labor, Bureau of Labor Statistics

| Year | TOTAL LABOR FORCE* Number | % of population | Total Civilian Employed |
|---|---|---|---|
| 1948 | 62,080,000 | 59.4 | 58,340,000 |
| 1950 | 63,858,000 | 59.9 | 58,918,000 |
| 1952 | 65,730,000 | 60.4 | 60,250,000 |
| 1954 | 66,993,000 | 60.0 | 60,109,000 |
| 1956 | 69,409,000 | 61.0 | 63,799,000 |
| 1958 | 70,275,000 | 60.4 | 63,036,000 |
| 1960 | 72,142,000 | 60.2 | 65,778,000 |
| 1961 | 73,031,000 | 60.2 | 65,746,000 |
| 1962 | 73,442,000 | 59.7 | 66,702,000 |
| 1963 | 74,571,000 | 59.6 | 67,762,000 |
| 1964 | 75,830,000 | 59.6 | 69,305,000 |
| 1965 | 77,178,000 | 59.7 | 71,088,000 |
| 1966 | 78,893,000 | 60.1 | 72,895,000 |
| 1967 | 80,793,000 | 60.6 | 74,372,000 |
| 1968 | 82,272,000 | 60.7 | 75,920,000 |
| 1969 | 84,240,000 | 61.1 | 77,902,000 |
| 1970 | 85,959,000 | 61.3 | 78,678,000 |
| 1971 | 87,198,000 | 61.0 | 79,367,000 |
| 1972 | 89,484,000 | 61.1 | 82,153,000 |
| 1973 | 91,756,000 | 61.4 | 85,064,000 |
| 1974 | 94,179,000 | 61.3 | 86,794,000 |
| 1975 | 95,955,000 | 61.8 | 85,846,000 |
| 1976 | 98,302,000 | 62.1 | 88,752,000 |
| 1977 | 101,142,000 | 62.8 | 92,017,000 |
| 1978 | 104,368,000 | 63.6 | 96,048,000 |
| 1979 | 107,050,000 | 64.1 | 98,824,000 |
| 1980 | 109,042,000 | 64.2 | 99,303,000 |
| 1981 | 110,812,000 | 64.3 | 100,397,000 |

*Persons 16 years of age and over; includes members of the armed forces.

## UNEMPLOYMENT RATES: BY SEX AND RACE

SOURCE: U.S. Department of Labor, Bureau of Labor Statistics

| Year | Unemployment Rate Total | Male | Female | White Total | Male | Female | Black and other Total | Male | Female |
|---|---|---|---|---|---|---|---|---|---|
| 1948 | 3.8 | 3.6 | 4.1 | 3.5 | 3.4 | 3.8 | 5.9 | 5.8 | 6.1 |
| 1950 | 5.3 | 5.1 | 5.7 | 4.9 | 4.7 | 5.3 | 9.0 | 9.4 | 8.4 |
| 1952 | 3.0 | 2.8 | 3.6 | 2.8 | 2.5 | 3.3 | 5.4 | 5.2 | 5.7 |
| 1954 | 5.5 | 5.3 | 6.0 | 5.0 | 4.8 | 5.6 | 9.9 | 10.3 | 9.3 |
| 1956 | 4.1 | 3.8 | 4.8 | 3.6 | 3.4 | 4.2 | 8.3 | 7.9 | 8.9 |
| 1958 | 6.8 | 6.8 | 6.8 | 6.1 | 6.1 | 6.2 | 12.6 | 13.8 | 10.8 |
| 1960 | 5.5 | 5.4 | 5.9 | 4.9 | 4.8 | 5.3 | 10.2 | 10.7 | 9.4 |
| 1961 | 6.7 | 6.4 | 7.2 | 6.0 | 5.7 | 6.5 | 12.4 | 12.8 | 11.8 |
| 1962 | 5.5 | 5.2 | 6.2 | 4.9 | 4.6 | 5.5 | 10.9 | 10.9 | 11.0 |
| 1963 | 5.7 | 5.2 | 6.5 | 5.0 | 4.7 | 5.8 | 10.8 | 10.5 | 11.2 |
| 1964 | 5.2 | 4.6 | 6.2 | 4.6 | 4.1 | 5.5 | 9.6 | 8.9 | 10.6 |
| 1965 | 4.5 | 4.0 | 5.5 | 4.1 | 3.6 | 5.0 | 8.1 | 7.4 | 9.2 |
| 1966 | 3.8 | 3.2 | 4.8 | 3.3 | 2.8 | 4.3 | 7.3 | 6.3 | 8.6 |
| 1967 | 3.8 | 3.1 | 5.2 | 3.4 | 2.7 | 4.6 | 7.4 | 6.0 | 9.1 |
| 1968 | 3.6 | 2.9 | 4.8 | 3.2 | 2.6 | 4.3 | 6.7 | 5.6 | 8.3 |
| 1969 | 3.5 | 2.8 | 4.7 | 3.1 | 2.5 | 4.2 | 6.4 | 5.3 | 7.8 |
| 1970 | 4.9 | 4.4 | 5.9 | 4.5 | 4.0 | 5.4 | 8.2 | 7.3 | 9.3 |
| 1971 | 5.9 | 5.3 | 6.9 | 5.4 | 4.9 | 6.3 | 9.9 | 9.1 | 10.9 |
| 1972 | 5.6 | 5.0 | 6.6 | 5.1 | 4.5 | 5.9 | 10.0 | 8.9 | 11.4 |
| 1973 | 4.9 | 4.2 | 6.0 | 4.3 | 3.8 | 5.3 | 9.0 | 7.7 | 10.6 |
| 1974 | 5.6 | 4.9 | 6.7 | 5.0 | 4.4 | 6.1 | 9.9 | 9.2 | 10.8 |
| 1975 | 8.5 | 7.9 | 9.3 | 7.8 | 7.2 | 8.6 | 13.8 | 13.6 | 13.9 |
| 1976 | 7.7 | 7.1 | 8.6 | 7.0 | 6.4 | 7.9 | 13.1 | 12.7 | 13.6 |
| 1977 | 7.1 | 6.3 | 8.2 | 6.2 | 5.5 | 7.3 | 13.1 | 12.3 | 13.9 |
| 1978 | 6.1 | 5.3 | 7.2 | 5.2 | 4.6 | 6.2 | 11.9 | 11.0 | 13.0 |
| 1979 | 5.8 | 5.1 | 6.8 | 5.1 | 4.5 | 5.9 | 11.3 | 10.4 | 12.3 |
| 1980 | 7.1 | 6.9 | 7.4 | 6.3 | 6.1 | 6.5 | 13.1 | 13.2 | 13.1 |
| 1981 | 7.6 | 7.4 | 7.9 | 6.7 | 6.5 | 6.9 | 14.2 | 14.1 | 14.3 |

## MINORITY GROUP PARTICIPATION IN THE U.S. LABOR MARKET: 1980 Preliminary

SOURCE: Equal Employment Opportunity Commission

% OF MINORITY WORKERS IN PARTICULAR CATEGORY[1]

| | Total | WHITE COLLAR Total | Professional | Technical | Clerical | Blue Collar | Service Workers |
|---|---|---|---|---|---|---|---|
| Black, Total[1] | 11.6% | 7.4% | 4.3% | 8.7% | 11.2% | 14.4% | 22.4% |
| Male | 6.1 | 2.5 | 1.9 | 3.7 | 2.0 | 9.8 | 10.1 |
| Female | 5.4 | 4.9 | 2.4 | 5.0 | 9.2 | 4.6 | 12.4 |
| Hispanic, Total | 5.4 | 3.3 | 1.9 | 3.5 | 4.6 | 7.5 | 7.9 |
| Male | 3.3 | 1.4 | 1.2 | 2.2 | 1.0 | 5.3 | 4.7 |
| Female | 2.1 | 1.9 | 0.7 | 1.3 | 3.6 | 2.2 | 3.2 |
| Asian or Pacific Islander, Total | 1.5 | 1.8 | 3.5 | 2.4 | 1.7 | 1.0 | 1.8 |
| Male | 0.8 | 0.9 | 2.2 | 1.5 | 0.4 | 0.6 | 0.9 |
| Female | 0.7 | 0.9 | 1.4 | 1.0 | 1.3 | 0.5 | 0.9 |
| American Indian or Alaskan Native, Total | 0.4 | 0.4 | 0.3 | 0.4 | 0.4 | 0.5 | 0.5 |
| Male | 0.3 | 0.2 | 0.2 | 0.2 | 0.2 | 0.4 | 0.2 |
| Female | 0.1 | 0.1 | 0.1 | 0.1 | 0.3 | 0.1 | 0.2 |
| All Minorities, Total | 18.9 | 12.8 | 10.0 | 15.1 | 17.9 | 23.5 | 32.6 |
| Male | 10.5 | 5.0 | 5.4 | 7.6 | 3.6 | 16.1 | 15.9 |
| Female | 8.5 | 7.8 | 4.6 | 7.5 | 14.3 | 7.4 | 16.8 |

[1]Percent of total employment in given occupational category.

## MINORITY GROUP EMPLOYEES IN U.S. LABOR MARKET: 1980 Preliminary

SOURCE: Equal Employment Opportunity Commission

Figures are in thousands

| | Total | WHITE COLLAR Total | Professional | Technical | Clerical | Blue Collar | Service Workers |
|---|---|---|---|---|---|---|---|
| Total U.S. Employees | 34,076 | 17,258 | 3,242 | 1,845 | 5,386 | 13,766 | 3,052 |
| Male | 20,115 | 8,557 | 2,037 | 1,104 | 929 | 10,187 | 1,372 |
| Female | 13,961 | 8,701 | 1,205 | 741 | 4,458 | 3,579 | 1,681 |
| Total Black Employees | 3,943 | 1,270 | 140 | 161 | 603 | 1,989 | 685 |
| Male | 2,086 | 426 | 62 | 69 | 109 | 1,353 | 307 |
| Female | 1,857 | 844 | 78 | 92 | 494 | 636 | 378 |
| Total Hispanics | 1,845 | 569 | 62 | 65 | 245 | 1,034 | 241 |
| Male | 1,121 | 247 | 39 | 40 | 52 | 732 | 142 |
| Female | 724 | 323 | 23 | 25 | 193 | 303 | 99 |
| Total Asian or Pacific Islander | 516 | 317 | 114 | 45 | 91 | 144 | 56 |
| Male | 267 | 160 | 70 | 27 | 22 | 79 | 28 |
| Female | 249 | 157 | 45 | 18 | 70 | 65 | 28 |
| Total American Indian or Alaskan Native | 143 | 61 | 9 | 7 | 24 | 68 | 14 |
| Male | 93 | 36 | 6 | 5 | 10 | 50 | 7 |
| Female | 50 | 25 | 3 | 2 | 14 | 18 | 7 |
| Total Minority Employees | 6,447 | 2,217 | 325 | 278 | 964 | 3,234 | 996 |
| Male | 3,567 | 869 | 177 | 140 | 193 | 2,213 | 484 |
| Female | 2,880 | 1,348 | 148 | 138 | 771 | 1,021 | 511 |

## PRINCIPAL U.S. LABOR UNIONS AND EMPLOYEE ASSOCIATIONS, 1981

SOURCE: U.S. Department of Labor, Bureau of Labor Statistics

The following is a list of selected labor unions with a 1980 membership of more than 100,000.

**International Brotherhood of Teamsters, Chauffeurs, Warehousemen, and Helpers of America,*** 25 Louisiana Avenue, N.W., Washington, D.C. 20001; **Membership:** 1,891,000

**National Education Association,*** 1201 16th St., N.W., Washington, D.C. 20036; **Membership:** 1,684,000

**International Union, United Automobile, Aerospace and Agricultural Implement Workers of America,** 8000 East Jefferson Ave., Detroit, Mich. 48214; **Membership:** 1,357,000

**United Food and Commercial Workers Union,** 1775 K St., N.W., Washington, D.C. 20006; **Membership:** 1,300,000

**United Steelworkers of America,** Five Gateway Center, Pittsburgh, Pa. 15222; **Membership:** 1,238,000

**American Federation of State, County and Municipal Employees,** 1625 L Street, N.W., Washington, D.C. 20036; **Membership:** 1,098,000

**International Brotherhood of Electrical Workers,** 1125 15th St., N.W., Washington, D.C. 20005; **Membership:** 1,041,000

**United Brotherhood of Carpenters and Joiners of America,** 101 Constitution Ave., N.W., Washington, D.C. 20001; **Membership:** 784,000

**International Association of Machinists and Aerospace Workers,** 1300 Connecticut Ave., N.W., Washington, D.C. 20036; **Membership:** 754,000

**Service Employees' International Union,** 2020 K St., N.W., Washington, D.C. 20006; **Membership:** 650,000

**Laborers' International Union of North America,** 905 16th St., N.W., Washington, D.C. 20006; **Membership:** 608,000

**American Federation of Teachers,** 11 Dupont Circle, Washington, D.C. 20036; **Membership:** 551,000

**Communications Workers of America,** 1925 K St., N.W., Washington, D.C. 20006; **Membership:** 551,000

**Amalgamated Clothing and Textile Workers of America,** 15 Union Square, New York, N.Y. 10003; **Membership:** 455,000

**International Union of Operating Engineers,** 1125 17th St., N.W., Washington, D.C. 20036; **Membership:** 423,000

**Hotel and Restaurant Employees and Bartenders International Union,** 120 E. Fourth St., Cincinnati, Oh. 45202; **Membership:** 400,000

**United Association of Journeymen and Apprentices of the Plumbing and Pipefitting Industry of the United States and Canada,** 901 Massachusetts Ave., N.W., Washington, D.C. 20001; **Membership:** 352,000

**International Ladies' Garment Workers Union,** 1710 Broadway, New York, N.Y. 10019; **Membership:** 323,000

**American Federation of Musicians,** 1500 Broadway, New York, N.Y. 10036; **Membership:** 299,000

**United Paperworkers International Union,** 702 Church St., Nashville, Tenn. 37202; **Membership:** 275,000

**American Federation of Government Employees,** 1325 Massachusetts Avenue, N.W., Washington, D.C. 20005; **Membership:** 255,000

**American Postal Workers Union,** 817 Fourteenth Street, N.W., Washington, D.C. 20005; **Membership:** 251,000

**United Mine Workers of America,*** 900 15th Street, N.W., Washington, D.C. 20005; **Membership:** 245,000

**International Union of Electrical, Radio, and Machine Workers,** 1126 16th St., N.W., Washington, D.C. 20036; **Membership:** 233,000

**National Association of Letter Carriers,** 100 Indiana Ave., N.W., Washington, D.C. 20001; **Membership:** 230,000

**Retail, Wholesale, and Department Store Union,** 30 East 29th St., New York, N.Y. 10016; **Membership:** 215,000

**National Association of Government Employees,*** 285 Dorchester Ave., Boston, Mass. 02127; **Membership:** 200,000

**United Transportation Union,** 14600 Detroit Avenue, Cleveland, Ohio, 44107; **Membership:** 190,000

**International Association of Bridge and Structural Iron Workers,** 1750 New York Ave., N.W., Suite 400, Washington, D.C. 20006; **Membership:** 184,000

**American Nurses Association,*** 2420 Pershing Rd., Kansas City, Mo. 64108; **Membership:** 180,000

**Brotherhood of Railway, Airline, and Steamship Clerks, Freight Handlers, Express and Station Employees,** 3 Research Place, Rockville, Md. 20850; **Membership:** 180,000

**International Association of Firefighters,** 1750 New York Avenue, N.W., Washington, D.C. 20006; **Membership:** 178,000

**International Brotherhood of Painters and Allied Trades of the United States and Canada,** 1750 New York Avenue, N.W., Washington, D.C. 20006; **Membership:** 164,000

**Amalgamated Transit Union,** 5025 Wisconsin Ave., N.W., Washington, D.C. 20016; **Membership:** 162,000

**United Electrical, Radio, and Machine Workers of America,*** 11 East 51st St., New York, N.Y. 10022; **Membership:** 162,000

**Sheet Metal Workers' International Association,** 1750 New York Ave., N.W., Washington, D.C. 20006; **Membership:** 161,000

**Bakery, Confectionary, and Tobacco Workers' International Union of America,** 10401 Connecticut Ave., Kensington, Md. 20795; **Membership:** 160,000

**Oil, Chemical, and Atomic Workers International Union,** P.O. Box 2812, 1636 Champa St., Denver, Colo. 80201; **Membership:** 154,000

**United Rubber, Cork, Linoleum, and Plastic Workers of America,** 87 South High St., Akron, Ohio 44308; **Membership:** 151,000

**Fraternal Order of Police,*** G—3136 Pasadena Ave., Flint, Mich. 48504; **Membership:** 150,000

**International Brotherhood of Boilermakers, Iron Ship Builders, Blacksmiths, Forgers, and Helpers,** 8th St. at State Ave., Kansas City, Kansas 66101; **Membership:** 145,000

**International Union of Bricklayers and Allied Craftsmen,** 815 15th St., N.W., Washington, D.C. 20005; **Membership:** 135,000

**Transport Workers Union of America,** 1980 Broadway, New York, New York 10023; **Membership:** 130,000

**National Alliance of Postal and Federal Employees,*** 1644 11th St., N.W., Washington, D.C. 20001; **Membership:** 125,000

**International Printing and Graphic Communications Union,** 1730 Rhode Island Avenue, N.W., Washington, D.C. 20036; **Membership:** 122,000

**International Woodworkers of America,** 1622 North Lombard St., Portland, Oregon 97217; **Membership:** 112,000

**Office and Professional Employees International Union,** 265 West 14th St., New York, N.Y. 10011; **Membership:** 107,000

**California State Employees Association,*** 1108 0 Street, Sacramento, Calif. 95814; **Membership:** 105,000

**Brotherhood of Maintenance of Way Employees,** 12050 Woodward Ave., Detroit, Mich. 48203; **Membership:** 102,000

* Independent—not members of AFL-CIO

## AVERAGE UNION HOURLY SCALE

SOURCE: U.S. Department of Labor, Bureau of Labor Statistics

| | Building | | Printing | | Local trucking | | |
|---|---|---|---|---|---|---|---|
| Year | Journeymen | Helpers and laborers | Book and job | Newspapers | Drivers | Helpers | Local transit workers |
| 1960 | $3.86 | $2.88 | $3.08 | $3.48 | $2.68 | $2.38 | $2.37 |
| 1965 | 4.64 | 3.54 | 3.58 | 3.94 | 3.26 | 2.90 | 2.88 |
| 1970 | 6.54 | 4.86 | 4.65 | 5.13 | 4.41 | 3.91 | 4.03 |
| 1972 | 7.69 | 5.68 | 5.49 | 6.09 | 5.49 | 4.90 | 4.68 |
| 1974 | 8.55 | 6.53 | 6.34 | 7.01 | 6.39 | 5.84 | 5.62 |
| 1976 | $ 9.92 | $7.54 | $7.41 | $8.17 | $7.42 | $6.67 | $6.63 |
| 1977 | 10.44 | 8.03 | 7.91 | 8.74 | 8.09 | 7.28 | 7.12 |
| 1978 | 11.05 | 8.54 | 8.51 | 9.23 | — | — | 7.53 |
| 1979 | 11.81 | 9.15 | — | — | 9.61 | 8.60 | 8.17 |
| 1980 | 12.72 | 9.80 | 10.29 | 10.97 | — | — | 9.01 |

## UNION CONTRACTS OF 1981

SOURCE: U.S. Department of Labor, Bureau of Labor Statistics

Major collective bargaining settlements in the private sector reached during 1981 provided average first-year wage adjustments of 9.8 percent, higher than the 9.5 percent average negotiated throughout 1980. Annual wage adjustments over the life of the contracts in this sector averaged 8.3 percent in 1981 and 7.1 percent in 1980. About 61 percent of the workers under 1980 settlements were covered by contracts with cost-of-living adjustment (COLA) clauses, slightly higher than the 58 percent for all major contracts negotiated in 1979.

First-year negotiated wage adjustments in contracts with COLA provisions averaged 9.8 percent, compared with 10.6 percent for contracts without such provisions. (Corresponding averages were 8.0 and 11.8 percent in 1980.) When negotiated wage adjustments are averaged over the life of the contracts, the annual rates in 1981 were 5.5 percent for contracts with COLA clauses and 8.8 percent for those without (compared with 5.0 and 10.4 percent in 1980).

In manufacturing, negotiated wage adjustments averaged 7.2 percent in the first contract year and 6.1 percent annually over the life of the agreements. In nonmanufacturing, the averages were higher, 11.2 and 8.8 percent, respectively. In the construction industry, first-year wage adjustments averaged 13.5 and 8.6 percent in all other industries combined. When negotiated wage changes for these contracts are averaged over the life of the agreements, the annual rate for construction was 11.5 percent, higher than the 6.7 percent for all other industries combined.

## UNEMPLOYMENT INSURANCE BENEFITS (1981 Calendar year)

SOURCE: U.S. Department of Labor

State unemployment insurance benefits for the totally unemployed are listed below. Where two figures are given for legal minimum and maximum benefits, the larger figures include dependents' allowances.

| | WEEKLY BENEFIT AMOUNTS | | | DURATION OF BENEFITS, WEEKS | |
|---|---|---|---|---|---|
| State | Average Unemployment Benefit | Legal Minimum | Legal Maximum | Actual Average | Legal Range |
| U.S. Avg. | $106.48 | — | — | 14.5† | — |
| Ala. | 77.46 | $15 | $ 90 | 11.1 | 11-26 |
| Alaska | 129.12 | 34-58 | 150-222 | 15.5 | 16-26 |
| Ariz. | 86.43 | 25 | 95 | 13.1 | 12-26 |
| Ark. | 92.47 | 31 | 136 | 12.2 | 10-26 |
| Calif. | 91.91 | 30 | 136 | 16.2 | 12-26* |
| Colo. | 122.07 | 25 | 176 | 11.7 | 7-26* |
| Conn. | 111.17 | 15-22 | 146-196 | 11.8 | 26-26* |
| Del. | 105.91 | 20 | 150 | 14.3 | 18-26 |
| D.C. | 130.85 | 13-14 | 206* | 20.5 | 17-34 |
| Fla. | 80.85 | 10 | 125 | 11.8 | 10-26 |
| Ga. | 83.47 | 27 | 115 | 9.2 | 4-26 |
| Hawaii | 117.72 | 5 | 169 | 14.0 | 26-26* |
| Idaho | 105.43 | 36 | 145 | 12.6 | 10-26 |
| Ill. | 132.95 | 45 | 148-198 | 18.4 | 26-26 |
| Ind. | 90.85 | 40 | 84-141 | 11.5 | 9-26 |
| Iowa | 122.09 | 17-18 | 146-176 | 13.2 | 15-26 |
| Kans. | 102.45 | 37 | 149 | 13.7 | 10-26 |
| Ky. | 105.50 | 22 | 140 | 14.2 | 15-26 |
| La. | 120.54 | 10 | 183 | 16.0 | 12-28 |
| Maine | 93.55 | 20-25 | 115-173 | 12.7 | 7-26* |
| Md. | 101.79 | 25-28 | 140 | 14.0 | 26-26 |
| Mass. | 104.79 | 12-18 | 156-234 | 14.8 | 9-30* |
| Mich. | 128.08 | 41-44* | 182 | 13.8 | 11-26 |
| Minn. | 125.99 | 30 | 177 | 14.8 | 11-26 |
| Miss. | 73.24 | 10 | 90 | 12.4 | 12-26 |
| Mo. | 91.45 | 15 | 105 | 13.1 | 10-26* |
| Mont. | $110.57 | $36 | $145 | 13.2 | 8-26 |
| Nebr. | 95.14 | 12 | 106 | 12.0 | 17-26 |
| Nev. | 106.66 | 16 | 136 | 13.8 | 11-26 |
| N.H. | 86.30 | 26 | 132 | 8.7 | 26-26 |
| N.J. | 106.23 | 20 | 145 | 14.9 | 15-26 |
| N.M. | 89.71 | 26 | 130 | 15.5 | 18-26* |
| N.Y. | 94.09 | 25 | 125 | 19.0 | 26-26 |
| N.C. | 91.60 | 15 | 152 | 9.6 | 13-26 |
| N.D. | 114.39 | 42 | 156 | 14.6 | 12-26 |
| Ohio | 127.87 | 10 | 147-233 | 14.7 | 20-26 |
| Okla. | 113.81 | 16 | 176 | 10.8 | 20-26* |
| Oreg. | 106.93 | 41 | 158 | 14.2 | 8-26 |
| Pa. | 126.27 | 35-40 | 190-198 | 16.6 | 26-30 |
| P.R. | 57.50 | 7 | 84 | 19.9 | 20-20* |
| R.I. | 98.75 | 35-40 | 143-163 | 14.2 | 12-26 |
| S.C. | 84.94 | 10 | 118 | 12.2 | 10-26 |
| S.D. | 103.94 | 28 | 129 | 12.2 | 18-26* |
| Tenn. | 81.96 | 20 | 110 | 12.9 | 12-26 |
| Texas | 100.22 | 21 | 147 | 13.0 | 9-26 |
| Utah | 114.57 | 10 | 166 | 14.5 | 10-36* |
| Vt. | 96.68 | 18 | 135 | 13.7 | 26-26 |
| Va. | 98.09 | 44 | 138 | 11.0† | 12-26 |
| Wash. | 119.22 | 45 | 163 | 15.8 | 16-30* |
| W. Va. | 109.98 | 18 | 194 | 15.7 | 28-28 |
| Wis. | 123.20 | 34 | 179 | 14.2 | 1-34* |
| Wyo. | 121.41 | 24 | 165 | 12.3 | 12-26* |

†Preliminary. *Provisional.

## EMPLOYMENT OUTLOOK IN 1990

| Occupation Title | Percent Change 1980-1990 Low | High |
|---|---|---|
| Accountants & auditors | 26.5 | 35.9 |
| Airplane pilots | 15.3 | 23.0 |
| Air traffic controllers | 16.1 | 18.5 |
| Architects | 32.7 | 41.0 |
| Bank tellers | 25.1 | 28.9 |
| Barbers | 7.3 | 22.4 |
| Bartenders | 18.5 | 25.5 |
| Bookkeepers, hand | 17.2 | 26.3 |
| Brick masons | 40.2 | 51.2 |
| Bus drivers | 13.9 | 15.1 |
| Buyers, retail & wholesale trade | 17.6 | 26.8 |
| Carpenters | 17.8 | 27.0 |
| Cashiers | 28.4 | 35.9 |
| Chemists | 20.6 | 27.6 |
| Clerks, file | 19.9 | 27.8 |
| general office | 15.8 | 24.1 |
| shipping | 15.0 | 24.6 |
| Commercial artists | 1.5 | 11.2 |
| Compositors & typesetters | − 9.6 | − 2.4 |
| Computer, peripheral equipment operators | 65.8 | 76.6 |
| Computer programmers | 48.9 | 60.8 |
| Computer systems analysts | 67.8 | 79.8 |
| Construction inspectors, public administration | 26.0 | 28.2 |
| Construction laborers (excl. carpenter helpers) | 20.2 | 30.9 |
| Cooks, institutional | 18.6 | 23.8 |
| restaurant | 25.0 | 32.4 |
| short order & specialty fast foods | 21.0 | 27.3 |
| Cosmetologists | 13.5 | 28.9 |
| Delivery & route workers | 11.1 | 20.1 |
| Dental hygienists | 39.2 | 42.3 |
| Dentists | 22.0 | 30.4 |
| Dieticians | 37.6 | 45.8 |
| Drafters | 27.9 | 38.5 |
| Drill press & boring machine operators | 18.6 | 34.2 |
| Economists | 42.0 | 50.1 |
| Electricians | 19.5 | 28.0 |
| Electroplaters | 17.7 | 27.3 |
| Employment interviewers | 47.9 | 63.7 |
| Engineers, chemical | 23.3 | 31.7 |
| civil | 25.8 | 31.3 |
| industrial | 25.8 | 37.5 |
| locomotive | − 0.3 | 9.3 |
| mechanical | 28.7 | 49.9 |
| stationary | 20.3 | 31.5 |
| Farmers & farm managers | − 17.1 | − 8.7 |
| Farm supervisors & laborers | − 20.1 | − 11.1 |
| Firefighters | 16.7 | 18.8 |
| Furniture upholsterers | 3.4 | 15.0 |
| Garbage collectors | 16.4 | 25.8 |
| Geologists | 30.1 | 38.2 |
| Guards & doorkeepers | 23.6 | 33.8 |
| Highway maintenance workers | 13.5 | 15.5 |
| Housekeepers, hotel & motel | 33.0 | 48.0 |
| Industrial truck operators | 14.9 | 23.2 |
| Insurance sales agents & representatives | 34.9 | 47.5 |
| Janitors & sextons | 18.2 | 27.2 |
| Jewelers & silversmiths | 15.9 | 27.2 |
| Lathe machine operators, metal | 19.0 | 34.2 |
| Lawyers | 25.8 | 39.4 |
| Librarians | 3.1 | 5.1 |
| Machine tool operators, combination | 17.1 | 32.5 |
| Machinists | 15.8 | 28.5 |
| Maids & servants, private household | − 6.1 | − 5.0 |
| Mail carriers | 7.7 | 11.7 |
| Mechanics, air conditioning, refrigeration & heating | 19.7 | 23.9 |
| aircraft | 15.2 | 22.3 |
| automobile | 24.4 | 32.9 |
| data processing machine | 93.2 | 112.4 |
| diesel | 23.5 | 31.1 |
| engineering equipment | 13.1 | 22.1 |
| maintenance | 18.1 | 26.3 |
| Medical laboratory technologists | 34.0 | 42.2 |
| Milling & planing machine operators | 14.8 | 31.9 |
| Musicians, instrumental | 15.5 | 19.7 |
| Nurses, licensed practical | 35.0 | 43.6 |
| professional (registered) | 39.6 | 46.5 |
| Office machine & cash register servicers | 59.8 | 73.5 |
| Opticians | 26.1 | 37.0 |
| Optometrists | 21.0 | 31.3 |
| Painters, construction & maintenance | 14.0 | 24.6 |
| Paralegal personnel | 108.8 | 138.8 |
| Parking attendants | 24.2 | 43.3 |
| Personnel & labor relations specialists | 15.1 | 21.9 |
| Pharmacists | 11.5 | 35.3 |
| Photoengravers & lithographers | 24.4 | 34.6 |
| Photographers | 14.9 | 24.5 |
| Physical therapists | 50.8 | 59.2 |
| Physicians, medical & osteopathic | 27.5 | 35.3 |
| Pipelayers | 18.4 | 30.5 |
| Plasterers | 29.6 | 39.9 |
| Plumbers & pipefitters | 15.2 | 23.8 |
| Police officers | 16.0 | 18.8 |
| Postal clerks | − 2.2 | 1.5 |
| Press & plate printers | 9.0 | 16.9 |
| Psychologists | 29.2 | 34.8 |
| Public relations specialists | 17.5 | 25.7 |
| Purchasing agents & buyers | 15.8 | 24.1 |
| Radio & television announcers | 28.4 | 33.5 |
| Real estate agents & representatives | 24.0 | 35.8 |
| Receptionists | 24.3 | 32.7 |
| Repairers, auto body | 23.1 | 30.8 |
| gas & electric appliance | 12.4 | 25.3 |
| instrument | 10.5 | 19.6 |
| maintenance, general utility | 20.5 | 29.8 |
| radio and TV service | 31.3 | 42.8 |
| Reporters & correspondents | 22.2 | 31.7 |
| Restaurant, cafe & bar managers | 15.3 | 22.1 |
| Roofers | 15.2 | 23.8 |
| Sailors & deckhands | 2.2 | 5.5 |
| Sales managers, retail trade | 18.4 | 28.6 |
| Secretaries | 28.3 | 37.4 |
| Sheet metal workers & tinsmiths | 15.7 | 24.3 |
| Social workers | 20.0 | 24.0 |
| Statisticians | 16.7 | 25.2 |
| Stenographers | − 8.3 | − 2.3 |
| Structural steel workers | 17.2 | 23.8 |
| Surveyors | 18.9 | 27.2 |
| Switchboard operators/ receptionists | 18.1 | 27.7 |
| Taxi drivers | − 3.0 | 10.0 |
| Teachers, college and university | − 11.4 | − 11.1 |
| elementary | 19.5 | 19.8 |
| preschool & kindergarten | 20.2 | 21.3 |
| secondary | 14.2 | 13.8 |
| vocational education | 22.8 | 26.5 |
| Technicians, medical | 35.0 | 43.6 |
| surgical | 39.3 | 45.4 |
| X-ray | 36.8 | 43.6 |
| Telephone installers & repairers | 7.4 | 21.8 |
| Telephone operators | 4.0 | 14.5 |
| Tire changers & repairers | 16.8 | 26.4 |
| Truck drivers | 24.5 | 32.5 |
| Typists | 17.5 | 24.6 |
| Veterinarians | 31.1 | 42.9 |
| Waiters & waitresses | 21.1 | 27.8 |
| Wirers, electronic | 14.4 | 25.1 |
| Wood machinists | 28.7 | 33.0 |
| Writers & editors | 22.5 | 33.0 |

## U.S. LICENSED COMMERCIAL NUCLEAR POWER PLANTS AS OF APRIL 1, 1982

SOURCE: Nuclear Regulatory Commission

| State | Name of Facility | Operating Company | Authorized Power Level (MWe) | Type* |
|---|---|---|---|---|
| Alabama | Farley 1 | Alabama Power Company | 829 | PWR |
| Alabama | Farley 2 | Alabama Power Company | 829 | PWR |
| Alabama | Browns Ferry 1 | TVA | 1,065 | BWR |
| Alabama | Browns Ferry 2 | TVA | 1,065 | BWR |
| Alabama | Browns Ferry 3 | TVA | 1,065 | BWR |
| Arkansas | Arkansas 1 | Arkansas Power & Light Company | 850 | PWR |
| Arkansas | Arkansas 2 | Arkansas Power & Light Company | 912 | PWR |
| California | Rancho Seco | Sacramento Municipal Utility District | 918 | PWR |
| California | San Onofre 1 | Southern California Edison Company | 430 | PWR |
| California | Humboldt Bay† | Pacific Gas & Electric Co. | 63 | BWR |
| Colorado | Ft. St. Vrain | Public Service Company of Colorado | 330 | HTGR |
| Connecticut | Haddam Neck | Connecticut Yankee Atomic Power Company | 575 | PWR |
| Connecticut | Millstone 1 | Northeast Nuclear Energy Company | 660 | BWR |
| Connecticut | Millstone 2 | Northeast Nuclear Energy Company | 830 | PWR |
| Florida | Crystal River 3 | Florida Power Corporation | 825 | PWR |
| Florida | St. Lucie 1 | Florida Power & Light Company | 802 | PWR |
| Florida | Turkey Point 3 | Florida Power & Light Company | 693 | PWR |
| Florida | Turkey Point 4 | Florida Power & Light Company | 693 | PWR |
| Georgia | Edwin I. Hatch 1 | Georgia Power Company | 786 | BWR |
| Georgia | Edwin I. Hatch 2 | Georgia Power Company | 795 | BWR |
| Illinois | Dresden 1† | Commonwealth Edison Company | 200 | BWR |
| Illinois | Dresden 2 | Commonwealth Edison Company | 794 | BWR |
| Illinois | Dresden 3 | Commonwealth Edison Company | 794 | BWR |
| Illinois | Quad-Cities 1 | Commonwealth Edison Company | 789 | BWR |
| Illinois | Quad-Cities 2 | Commonwealth Edison Company | 789 | BWR |
| Illinois | Zion 1 | Commonwealth Edison Company | 1,040 | PWR |
| Illinois | Zion 2 | Commonwealth Edison Company | 1,040 | PWR |
| Iowa | Duane Arnold | Iowa Electric Light & Power Company | 538 | BWR |
| Maine | Maine Yankee | Maine Yankee Atomic Power Company | 790 | PWR |
| Maryland | Calvert Cliffs 1 | Baltimore Gas & Electric Company | 845 | PWR |
| Maryland | Calvert Cliffs 2 | Baltimore Gas & Electric Company | 845 | PWR |
| Massachusetts | Pilgrim 1 | Boston Edison Company | 655 | BWR |
| Massachusetts | Yankee-Rowe | Yankee Atomic Electric Company | 175 | PWR |
| Michigan | Big Rock Point | Consumers Power Company | 72 | BWR |
| Michigan | Palisades | Consumers Power Company | 805 | PWR |
| Michigan | D.C. Cook 1 | Indiana & Michigan Electric Company | 1,054 | PWR |
| Michigan | D.C. Cook 2 | Indiana & Michigan Electric Company | 1,060 | PWR |
| Minnesota | Monticello | Northern States Power Company | 545 | BWR |
| Minnesota | Prairie Island 1 | Northern States Power Company | 530 | PWR |
| Minnesota | Prairie Island 2 | Northern States Power Company | 530 | PWR |
| Nebraska | Cooper Station | Nebraska Public Power District | 778 | BWR |
| Nebraska | Ft. Calhoun 1 | Omaha Public Power District | 457 | PWR |
| New Jersey | Oyster Creek 1 | Jersey Central Power & Light Company | 650 | BWR |
| New Jersey | Salem 1 | Public Service Electric & Gas Company | 1,090 | PWR |
| New Jersey | Salem 2 | Public Service Electric & Gas Company | Lower Power | PWR |
| New York | Indian Point 2 | Consolidated Edison Company of New York | 873 | PWR |
| New York | Nine Mile Point 1 | Niagara Mohawk Power Corporation | 610 | BWR |
| New York | Indian Point 3 | Power Authority of the State of New York | 873 | PWR |
| New York | Fitzpatrick | Power Authority of the State of New York | 821 | BWR |
| New York | Ginna | Rochester Gas & Electric Corporation | 490 | PWR |
| North Carolina | Brunswick 1 | Carolina Power & Light Comnpany | 821 | BWR |
| North Carolina | Brunswick 2 | Carolina Power & Light Company | 821 | BWR |
| North Carolina | McGuire 1 | Duke Power Company | 1,180 | PWR |
| Ohio | Davis-Besse 1 | Toledo Edison Company | 906 | PWR |
| Oregon | Trojan | Portland General Electric Company | 1,130 | PWR |
| Pennsylvania | Beaver Valley 1 | Duquesne Light Company | 852 | PWR |
| Pennsylvania | Three Mile I. 1 | Metropolitan Edison Company | 819 | PWR |
| Pennsylvania | Three Mile I. 2† | Metropolitan Edison Company | 906 | PWR |
| Pennsylvania | Peach Bottom 2 | Philadelphia Electric Company | 1,065 | BWR |
| Pennsylvania | Peach Bottom 3 | Philadelphia Electric Company | 1,065 | BWR |
| South Carolina | H.B. Robinson 2 | Carolina Power & Light Company | 700 | PWR |
| South Carolina | Oconee 1 | Duke Power Company | 887 | PWR |
| South Carolina | Oconee 2 | Duke Power Company | 887 | PWR |
| South Carolina | Oconee 3 | Duke Power Company | 887 | PWR |
| Tennessee | Sequoyah 1 | TVA | 1,140 | PWR |
| Tennessee | Sequoyah 2 | TVA | 1,140 | PWR |
| Vermont | Vermont Yankee 1 | Vermont Yankee Nuclear Power Corporation | 514 | BWR |
| Virginia | North Anna 1 | Virginia Electric & Power Company | 850 | PWR |
| Virginia | North Anna 2 | Virginia Electric & Power Company | 898 | PWR |
| Virginia | Surry 1 | Virginia Electric & Power Company | 822 | PWR |
| Virginia | Surry 2 | Virginia Electric & Power Company | 822 | PWR |
| Wisconsin | Lacrosse | Dairyland Power Cooperative | 50 | BWR |
| Wisconsin | Point Beach 1 | Wisconsin Electric Power Company | 497 | PWR |
| Wisconsin | Point Beach 2 | Wisconsin Electric Power Company | 497 | PWR |
| Wisconsin | Kewaunee | Wisconsin Public Service Corporation | 535 | PWR |

*PWR—Pressurized Water Reactor; BWR—Boiling Water Reactor; HTGR—High Temperature Gas Cooled Reactor † Shut down indefinitely.

## U.S. PRODUCTION AND CONSUMPTION OF ENERGY BY TYPE

SOURCE: Energy Information Administration, Department of Energy

| Fuel | Unit | Production 1979 | Production 1980 | Production 1981[1] | Consumption 1979 | Consumption 1980 | Consumption 1981[1] |
|---|---|---|---|---|---|---|---|
| Coal[2] | million short tons | 781.1 | 829.7 | 807.7 | 680.5 | 702.7 | 727.7 |
| | quadrillion Btu | 17.65 | 19.21 | 18.70 | 15.11 | 15.46 | 16.01 |
| Natural gas[3] | trillion cubic feet | 19.66 | 19.60 | 19.59 | 20.24 | 19.88 | 19.42 |
| | quadrillion Btu | 20.08 | 20.11 | 20.10 | 20.67 | 20.39 | 19.93 |
| Petroleum | million barrels | 3,121[4] | 3,146[4] | 3,125[4] | 6,757[5] | 6,242[5] | 5,840[5] |
| | quadrillion Btu | 18.10[4] | 18.25[4] | 18.13[4] | 37.12[5] | 34.20[5] | 32.00[5] |
| Natural Gas Plant Liquids | million barrels | 578 | 576 | 580 | — | — | — |
| | quadrillion Btu | 2.29 | 2.25 | 2.27 | — | — | — |
| Hydropower | billion kilowatt hours | 283.1[6] | 279.2[6] | 264.0[6] | 303.4[7] | 300.1[7] | 287.0[7] |
| | quadrillion Btu | 2.93[6] | 2.89[6] | 2.73[6] | 3.14[7] | 3.11[7] | 2.97[7] |
| Nuclear Power | billion kilowatt hours | 255.2 | 251.1 | 272.3 | 255.2 | 251.1 | 272.3 |
| | quadrillion Btu | 2.71 | 2.67 | 2.90 | 2.71 | 2.67 | 2.90 |
| Geothermal[8] | billion kilowatt hours | 3.9 | 5.1 | 5.7 | 3.9 | 5.1 | 5.7 |
| | quadrillion Btu | 0.08 | 0.11 | 0.12 | 0.08 | 0.11 | 0.12 |
| Wood & Waste[9] | billion kilowatt hours | 0.5 | 0.4 | 0.4 | 0.5 | 0.4 | 0.4 |
| | quadrillion Btu | 0.01 | ([10]) | ([10]) | 0.01 | ([10]) | ([10]) |
| Net Imports of Coal Coke | thousand short tons | — | — | — | 2,534 | −1,412 | −643 |
| | quadrillion Btu | — | — | — | 0.07 | −0.04 | −0.02 |
| Total Energy Production and Consumption | quadrillion Btu | 63.85 | 65.50 | 64.95 | 78.91 | 75.91 | 73.91 |

[1]Preliminary. [2]Bituminous coal, lignite, and anthracite. [3]Net dry natural gas. [4]Crude oil and lease condensate. [5]Refined petroleum products supplied including natural gas plant liquids and crude oil burned as fuel. [6]Electric utility and industrial generation of hydropower. [7]Electric utility and industrial generation of hydropower and net electricity imports. [8]Consumed by electric utilities. [9]Wood, refuse, and other vegetal fuels consumed by electric utilities. [10] Less than 0.005 quadrillion Btu.

## NUCLEAR POWER

SOURCE: International Atomic Energy Agency

During the 25 years which have lapsed since the 1955 Geneva Conference, a tremendous development effort has taken place in the nuclear power field. Roughly speaking, the first decade from 1955-1965 was marked by the emergence of several promising nuclear power systems which bridged the gap between prototypes and industrial plants. The second period from 1965 to the present witnessed the rapid introduction of large nuclear stations in the electric systems of industrial countries and the commissioning of a few nuclear power plants in some developing countries.

In 1956 there were in the world two power reactors with a total capacity of 0.6 MWe in two countries. By 1965, these members had risen to 44 reactors operating in 9 countries and with a total capacity of 4.9 MWe. By 1981, we find 261 stations with a capacity of over 144,483 MWe operating in 21 countries, and by 1995, 601 plants with close to 464,049 MWe in 33 states.

## ESTIMATED WORLD NUCLEAR POWER GROWTH*

| Country | 1981 No. Reactors | 1981 Capacity (1000 MWe) | 1995 est. No. Reactors | 1995 est. Capacity (1000 MWe) |
|---|---|---|---|---|
| Argentina | 1 | 0.3 | 5 | 2.8 |
| Belgium | 3 | 1.7 | 7 | 5.5 |
| Brazil | — | — | 3 | 3.1 |
| Bulgaria | 3 | 1.2 | 8 | 5.6 |
| Canada | 11 | 5.5 | 25 | 15.2 |
| Cuba | — | — | 2 | 0.8 |
| Czechoslovakia | 2 | 0.8 | 20 | 12.2 |
| Egypt | — | — | 1 | 0.6 |
| Finland | 4 | 2.2 | 5 | 3.2 |
| France | 26 | 18.1 | 74 | 73.2 |
| Germany, East | 5 | 1.7 | 15 | 5.9 |
| Germany, West | 14 | 8.6 | 32 | 29.2 |
| Hungary | — | — | 4 | 1.6 |
| India | 4 | 0.8 | 8 | 1.7 |
| Israel | — | — | 1 | 0.6 |
| Italy | 4 | 1.4 | 9 | 5.3 |
| Japan | 24 | 15.0 | 38 | 27.2 |
| Korea, South | 1 | 0.6 | 9 | 7.4 |
| Mexico | — | — | 2 | 1.3 |
| Netherlands | 2 | 0.5 | 2 | 0.5 |
| Pakistan | 1 | 0.1 | 1 | 0.1 |
| Philippines | — | — | 1 | 0.6 |
| Poland | — | — | 4 | 1.6 |
| Romania | — | — | 2 | 1.3 |
| South Africa | — | — | 2 | 1.8 |
| Spain | 4 | 2.0 | 18 | 15.1 |
| Sweden | 9 | 6.4 | 12 | 9.4 |
| Switzerland | 4 | 1.9 | 5 | 2.9 |
| Turkey | — | — | 1 | 0.7 |
| USSR | 35 | 14.0 | 72 | 50.9 |
| U.K. | 31 | 7.0 | 42 | 14.3 |
| United States | 73 | 54.7 | 169 | 160.7 |
| Yugoslavia | — | — | 2 | 1.6 |
| Total* | 261 | 144.5 | 601 | 464.0 |

*Does not include People's Republic of China, for which no information is available.

## ENERGY CONSUMPTION PER CAPITA IN 1980 (Kg of coal equivalent per capita)

SOURCE: U.N. *Statistical Yearbook* 1979/80; © United Nations

| Country | 1980 |
|---|---|
| Algeria | 808 |
| Argentina | 1,818 |
| Australia | 6,032 |
| Austria | 4,160 |
| Belgium | 6,037 |
| Brazil | 761 |
| Bulgaria | 5,678 |
| Canada | 10,241 |
| China | 602 |
| Cuba | 1,328 |
| Czechoslovakia | 6,482 |
| Denmark | 5,224 |
| Egypt | 496 |
| Finland | 5,135 |
| France (incl. Monaco) | 4,351 |
| Germany, East | 7,408 |
| Germany, West | 5,727 |
| Greece | 2,137 |
| Hungary | 3,850 |
| Iceland | 4,743 |
| India | 191 |
| Iran | 1,246 |
| Ireland | 2,955 |
| Israel | 2,367 |
| Italy (incl. San Marino) | 3,318 |
| Japan | 3,494 |
| Korea, North | 2,710 |
| Korea, South | 1,422 |
| Libya | 2,180 |
| Mexico | 1,770 |
| Netherlands | 6,208 |
| New Zealand | 3,453 |
| Nigeria | 144 |
| Norway | 6,437 |
| Philippines | 316 |
| Poland | 5,586 |
| Portugal | 1,097 |
| Romania | 4,593 |
| Saudi Arabia | 1,479 |
| South Africa | 2,595 |
| Spain | 2,539 |
| Sweden | 5,269 |
| Switzerland (incl. Liechtenstein) | 3,708 |
| Thailand | 371 |
| Tunisia | 536 |
| Turkey | 737 |
| United Kingdom | 4,942 |
| UNITED STATES | 10,410 |
| USSR | 5,595 |
| Uruguay | 945 |
| Venezuela | 3,375 |
| Yugoslavia | 2,049 |
| Zimbabwe | 618 |

## LARGEST FOREIGN INDUSTRIAL COMPANIES: 1981

SOURCE: *Fortune* magazine, August 23, 1982

| Rank '81 | Rank '80 | Company | Country | Industry | Sales ($000) |
|---|---|---|---|---|---|
| 1 | 1 | Royal Dutch/Shell Group | Netherlands-Britain | Petroleum | 82,291,728 |
| 2 | 2 | British Petroleum | Britain | Petroleum | 52,199,976 |
| 3 | 3 | ENI | Italy | Petroleum | 29,444,315 |
| 4 | 6 | Unilever | Britain-Netherlands | Food products; soaps, cosmetics | 24,095,898 |
| 5 | 5 | Française des Pétroles | France | Petroleum | 22,784,032 |
| 6 | 96 | Kuwait Petroleum | Kuwait | Petroleum | 20,556,871 |
| 7 | 9 | Elf-Aquitaine | France | Petroleum | 19,666,141 |
| 8 | 8 | Petróleos de Venezuela | Venezuela | Petroleum | 19,659,115 |
| 9 | 4 | Fiat | Italy | Motor vehicles and parts | 19,608,480 |
| 10 | 19 | Petrobrás (Petróleo Brasileiro) | Brazil | Petroleum | 18,946,056 |
| 11 | 20 | Pemex (Petróleos Mexicanos) | Mexico | Petroleum | 18,804,190 |
| 12 | 10 | Philips' Gloeilampenfabrieken | Netherlands | Electronics, appliances | 17,069,155 |
| 13 | 11 | Volkswagenwerk | Germany | Motor vehicles and parts | 16,822,215 |
| 14 | 13 | Daimler-Benz | Germany | Motor vehicles and parts | 16,281,398 |
| 15 | 23 | Nissan Motor | Japan | Motor vehicles and parts | 16,245,315 |
| 16 | 7 | Renault | France | Motor vehicles and parts | 16,229,762 |
| 17 | 12 | Siemens | Germany | Electronics: computers | 16,029,835 |
| 18 | 27 | Matsushita Electric Industrial | Japan | Electronics, appliances | 15,738,106 |
| 19 | 22 | Toyota Motor | Japan | Motor Vehicles | 15,712,540 |
| 20 | 26 | Hitachi | Japan | Electronics, appliances | 15,519,416 |
| 21 | 15 | Hoechst | Germany | Chemicals | 15,292,750 |
| 22 | 25 | Nippon Steel | Japan | Metal manufacturing—steel | 15,196,945 |
| 23 | 16 | Bayer | Germany | Chemicals | 14,985,272 |
| 24 | 29 | BAT Industries | Britain | Tobacco | 14,301,022 |
| 25 | 21 | Nestlé | Switzerland | Food products; beverages | 14,172,074 |
| 26 | 17 | BASF | Germany | Chemicals | 13,707,434 |
| 27 | 14 | Peugeot | France | Motor vehicles and parts | 13,396,308 |
| 28 | 24 | Imperial Chemical Industries | Britain | Chemicals | 13,338,305 |
| 29 | 18 | Thyssen | Germany | Metal refining—steel; industrial equipment | 13,063,961 |
| 30 | 28 | Mitsubishi Heavy Industries | Japan | Motor vehicles; industrial equipment | 12,408,234 |

## WORLD CRUDE PETROLEUM PRODUCERS

SOURCE: U.N. *Monthly Bulletin of Statistics*, © United Nations, July 1982

The list below is a compilation of the latest available figures on the oil production of selected countries. The figures for Communist countries are generally estimates. All figures are given in thousands of metric tons per average calendar month.

| Region and Country | 1973 | 1980 | 1981 |
|---|---|---|---|
| **North America:** | | | |
| Canada[1] | 7,336 | 5,867 | 5,184[2] |
| Barbados | N.A. | 3 | 2 |
| Cuba | N.A. | 23 | 30 |
| Mexico | 1,938 | 8,080 | 8,829 |
| Trinidad and Tobago | 734 | 915 | 822[3] |
| United States | 37,849 | 35,332 | 35,109 |
| **South America:** | | | |
| Argentina | 1,790 | 2,100 | 2,123[4] |
| Bolivia | 183 | 95 | 87 |
| Brazil | 690* | 760* | 891* |
| Colombia | 791 | 539[2] | 577 |
| Ecuador | 885 | 879 | 890[2] |
| Peru | 290 | 804 | 800 |
| Venezuela | 14,648 | 9,533 | 9,308 |
| **Europe:** | | | |
| Austria | 215 | 123 | 112 |
| Czechoslovakia | 14 | 8 | 7 |
| Denmark | 6 | 25 | 63 |
| France | 105 | 118 | 140 |
| Germany, West | 553 | 386 | 372 |
| Greece | N.A. | N.A. | 16 |
| Hungary | 166 | 169 | 169 |
| Italy | 87 | 150 | 122 |
| Netherlands | 124 | 107 | 111 |
| Norway | 132 | 2,034 | 1,965 |
| Romania | 1,191 | 958[5] | N.A. |
| Spain | 64 | 102 | 115 |
| United Kingdom | 31* | 6,706* | 7,253* |
| USSR | 35,753* | 50,250* | 50,750* |
| Yugoslavia | 278 | 352 | 365 |

| Region and Country | 1973 | 1980 | 1981 |
|---|---|---|---|
| **Africa:** | | | |
| Algeria | 4,229 | 3,952 | 3,042 |
| Angola | 680 | 619 | 596 |
| Congo | 174 | 220 | 258 |
| Egypt | 707 | 2,454 | 2,650 |
| Gabon | 633 | 742 | 638 |
| Libya | 8,740 | 7,177 | 4,488 |
| Nigeria | 8,480 | 8,517 | 5,932 |
| Tunisia | 324 | 469 | 451 |
| Zaire | N.A. | 85 | 83 |
| **Asia:** | | | |
| Bahrain | 284 | 202 | 193[6] |
| China | N.A. | 8,829 | 8,417 |
| India | 600 | 783 | 1,243 |
| Indonesia | 5,579 | 6,482 | 6,571 |
| Iran | 24,403 | 6,148 | 5,499 |
| Iraq | 8,295 | 10,822 | 3,741 |
| Israel | N.A. | N.A. | 1 |
| Japan | 58 | 36 | 33 |
| Kuwait | 12,702 | 7,128 | 4,726 |
| Malaysia | 362 | 1,096 | 1,025[6] |
| Oman | 1,219 | 1,180 | 1,331 |
| Pakistan | 36 | 41 | 40 |
| Qatar | 2,292 | 1,908 | 1,634 |
| Saudi Arabia | 31,482 | 41,310 | 40,900 |
| Syria | 462 | 708 | 768[6] |
| Turkey | 293 | 194 | 199 |
| United Arab Emirates | 6,813 | 7,015 | 6,132 |
| **Oceania:** | | | |
| Australia | 1,595 | 1,539 | 1,552 |
| New Zealand | N.A. | 29 | 34 |

*Includes natural gas liquids. N.A.: Data insufficient or not available. [1]Data include petroleum from tar sands. [2]Average for 11 months of 1981. [3]Average for 7 months of 1981. [4]Average for 8 months of 1981. [5]1980 Average. [6]Average for 6 months of 1981.

## U.S. METALS PRODUCTION

SOURCE: American Iron & Steel Institute; U.S. Bureau of Mines; Zinc Institute Inc. (figures in short tons)

| Year | Pig Iron and Ferroalloys | Steel Ingots[1] | Rolled Iron and Steel Products | Aluminum[2] | Copper[3] | Zinc[4] | Lead[3] |
|---|---|---|---|---|---|---|---|
| 1961 | 66,565,063 | 98,014,492 | 73,411,563 | 1,903,200 | 1,165,155 | 896,900 | 261,921 |
| 1965 | 90,918,000 | 131,461,601 | 99,304,221 | 2,754,500 | 1,351,734 | 1,078,300 | 301,147 |
| 1970 | 93,851,000 | 131,514,000 | N.A. | 3,976,148 | 1,719,657 | 961,153 | 571,767 |
| 1973 | 103,089,000 | 150,799,000 | N.A. | 4,529,116 | 1,717,940 | 687,861 | 603,024 |
| 1974 | 98,332,000 | 145,720,000 | N.A. | 4,903,000 | 1,597,000 | 590,181 | 663,870 |
| 1975 | 81,850,000 | 116,642,000 | N.A. | 3,879,000 | 1,413,000 | 445,916 | 621,464 |
| 1976 | 88,874,000 | 128,000,000 | N.A. | 4,251,000 | 1,606,000 | 535,953 | 609,546 |
| 1977 | 82,968,000 | 125,330,000 | N.A. | 4,539,000 | 1,504,000 | 434,054 | 592,491 |
| 1978 | 87,679,000 | 137,031,000 | N.A. | 4,804,000 | 1,496,000 | 445,879 | 583,845 |
| 1979 | 87,003,000 | 136,341,000 | N.A. | 5,023,000 | 1,591,000 | 537,427 | 579,334 |
| 1980 | 68,721,000[2] | 111,835,000[2] | N.A. | 5,130,000 | 1,302,000 | 358,609 | 607,370 |
| 1981 | 73,570,000 | 120,828,000 | N.A. | 4,950,000[5] | 1,685,000 | 376,780 | 496,040 |

[1]Plus castings. [2]Primary. [3]Recoverable from domestic mines. [4]Primary slab smelter output. [5]Preliminary.

## WORLD MINERAL-PRODUCTION LEADERS: 1981

SOURCE: U.N. *Monthly Bulletin of Statistics*, July 1982, © United Nations (Monthly averages in thousands of metric tons.)

| ITEM | COUNTRY AND PRODUCTION | | | |
|---|---|---|---|---|
| **Bauxite** | Australia (2,156) | Guinea (1,017)[1] | Jamaica (1,004)[1] | Suriname (311) |
| **Coal** | USSR (58,675) | U.S. (57,195) | Poland (13,210) | U.K. (10,649) |
| **Coal, Lignite & Brown** | E. Germany (21,500)[1] | USSR (13,333)[1] | W. Germany (10,885) | Czechoslovakia (7,935) |
| **Copper Ore** | U.S. (127.4) | Chile (89.9) | Philippines (76.9) | Zambia (61.4)[1] |
| **Crude Oil** | USSR (50,750) | Saudi Arabia (49,900) | U.S. (35,109) | Venezuela (9,308) |
| **Iron Ore** | USSR (20,167) | Australia (7,821) | U.S. (6,288) | Brazil (5,409) |
| **Lead Ore** | U.S. (37.0) | Australia (30.4) | Canada (27.7) | Mexico (13.1) |
| **Natural Gas**[2] | U.S. (1,739,443) | USSR (1,351,213) | Netherlands (222,524) | Canada (232,012)[1] |
| **Tin Concentrates** | Malaysia (4,988) | Thailand (3,832)[1] | Indonesia (2,613) | Bolivia (2,273)[1] |
| **Zinc Ore** | Canada (91.3) | Australia (30.7) | U.S. (25.4) | Japan (20.2) |

[1]1980 figures. [2]In terajoules.

## U.S. EXPORTS AND IMPORTS: GEOGRAPHIC AREAS

SOURCE: U.S. Dept. of Commerce, International Trade Administration

| Area | Exports (millions of $) | | | Imports (millions of $) | | | Trade Balance |
|---|---|---|---|---|---|---|---|
| | 1979 | 1980 | 1981 | 1979 | 1980 | 1981 | 1981 |
| Total | $181,816 | $220,626 | $233,677 | $206,327 | $244,871 | $261,305 | $-27,628 |
| Developed Countries | 110,579 | 130,849 | 135,840 | 111,514 | 125,306 | 141,506 | - 5,666 |
| Developing Countries | 62,983 | 81,125 | 88,972 | 92,345 | 117,025 | 116,343 | -27,371 |
| Communist Areas in Europe | 5,684 | 3,860 | 4,338 | 1,865 | 2,496 | 3,452 | + 886 |
| Canada | 33,096 | 35,395 | 39,564 | 38,099 | 41,459 | 46,414 | - 6,850 |
| Latin American Republics | 26,259 | 36,030 | 38,950 | 24,782 | 29,952 | 32,023 | + 6,927 |
| Other Western Hemisphere | 2,200 | 2,688 | 3,152 | 5,701 | 7,277 | 6,999 | - 3,847 |
| Western Europe | 53,514 | 67,512 | 65,377 | 41,684 | 46,602 | 51,855 | +13,522 |
| Japan | 17,581 | 20,790 | 21,823 | 26,243 | 30,714 | 37,612 | -15,789 |
| Near East | 11,030 | 11,900 | 14,962 | 14,988 | 18,672 | 18,543 | - 3,581 |
| East and South Asia | 18,436 | 23,722 | 23,448 | 24,913 | 29,854 | 33,980 | -10,482 |
| Australia and Oceania | 4,319 | 4,876 | 6,436 | 3,072 | 3,392 | 3,353 | + 3,083 |
| Africa | 6,299 | 9,060 | 11,097 | 24,377 | 34,410 | 27,071 | -15,974 |

## U.S. EXPORTS AND IMPORTS: PRINCIPAL COMMODITIES

SOURCE: U.S. Dept. of Commerce, International Trade Administration

| | Exports (millions of $) | | | Imports (millions of $) | | | Trade Balance |
|---|---|---|---|---|---|---|---|
| | 1979 | 1980 | 1981 | 1979 | 1980 | 1981 | 1981 |
| **Total** | $178,436 | $216,429 | $228,896 | $207,086 | $241,175 | $260,969 | $-32,073 |
| Excluding military grant aid | 178,271 | 216,273 | 228,834 | — | — | — | — |
| Crude foods | 15,787 | 19,362 | 21,075 | 7,689 | 7,662 | 7,206 | +13,869 |
| Manufactured foods | 7,581 | 9,516 | 10,244 | 9,624 | 10,397 | 10,857 | - 613 |
| Crude materials | 20,088 | 23,765 | 23,225 | 56,003 | 73,543 | 73,195 | -49,970 |
| Agricultural | 11,893 | 12,779 | 12,712 | 2,339 | 2,294 | 2,382 | +10,330 |
| Semimanufactures | 30,983 | 37,638 | 34,594 | 34,298 | 37,769 | 40,383 | - 5,789 |
| Finished manufactures | 103,997 | 126,150 | 139,758 | 99,473 | 111,804 | 129,327 | +10,431 |
| Excluding military grant aid | 103,832 | 125,994 | 139,696 | — | — | — | — |

## U.S. EXPORTS AND IMPORTS: SELECTED MERCHANDISE

SOURCE: U.S. Dept. of Commerce, International Trade Administration

| Exports (millions of $) | 1979 | 1980 | 1981 |
|---|---|---|---|
| Food and live animals | $22,251 | $27,744 | $30,291 |
| Grains and preparations | 14,454 | 18,079 | 19,457 |
| Wheat | 5,265 | 6,374 | 7,844 |
| Corn | 7,025 | 8,570 | 8,014 |
| Beverages and Tobacco | 2,337 | 2,663 | 2,915 |
| Crude Inedible Materials (nonfuel) | 20,756 | 23,791 | 20,993 |
| Mineral Fuels | 5,621 | 7,982 | 10,279 |
| Animal and Vegetable Oils | 1,845 | 1,946 | 1,750 |
| Chemicals | 17,308 | 20,740 | 21,187 |
| Machinery and Transport Equipment | 70,495 | 84,629 | 95,736 |
| Electronic Computers | 3,604 | 4,791 | 5,157 |
| Electrical Apparatus | 8,635 | 10,485 | 11,494 |
| Transport Equipment | 25,750 | 28,839 | 32,791 |
| Road Motor Vehicles & Parts | 15,077 | 14,590 | 16,214 |
| Aircraft, Parts and Accessories | 9,719 | 12,816 | 14,738 |

| Imports (millions of $) | 1979 | 1980 | 1981 |
|---|---|---|---|
| Food and live animals | $15,171 | $15,793 | $15,238 |
| Meat | 2,539 | 2,346 | 1,996 |
| Fish | 2,639 | 2,612 | 2,962 |
| Coffee | 3,820 | 3,872 | 2,622 |
| Beverages and Tobacco | 2,566 | 2,785 | 3,138 |
| Crude Inedible Materials (nonfuel) | 10,651 | 10,516 | 11,193 |
| Mineral Fuels | 60,061 | 82,924 | 81,417 |
| Chemicals | 7,458 | 8,594 | 9,446 |
| Machinery and Transport Equipment | 53,678 | 60,558 | 69,626 |
| Electrical Apparatus | 12,763 | 14,781 | 18,090 |
| Automobiles and Parts | 22,075 | 24,134 | 26,217 |
| Other Manufactured Goods | 51,098 | 55,970 | 63,471 |
| Paper | 3,356 | 3,587 | 3,875 |
| Metals | 17,457 | 18,717 | 22,333 |
| Textiles & Clothing | 8,092 | 8,921 | 10,583 |
| Footwear | 2,859 | 2,808 | 3,019 |

## LEADING U.S. TRADING PARTNERS: 1981

SOURCE: U.S. Department of Commerce, International Trade Administration (figures in millions of dollars)

**Export Trade**

| COUNTRY | VALUE | COUNTRY | VALUE |
|---|---|---|---|
| Canada | $39,564 | Netherlands | $8,595 |
| Japan | 21,823 | France | 7,341 |
| Mexico | 17,789 | Saudi Arabia | 7,327 |
| United Kingdom | 12,439 | Belg. and Lux. | 5,765 |
| West Germany | 10,277 | Venezuela | 5,445 |

**Import Trade**

| COUNTRY | VALUE | COUNTRY | VALUE |
|---|---|---|---|
| Canada | $46,414 | West Germany | $11,379 |
| Japan | 37,612 | Nigeria | 9,249 |
| Saudi Arabia | 14,391 | Taiwan | 8,049 |
| Mexico | 13,765 | Indonesia | 6,022 |
| United Kingdom | 12,835 | Hong Kong | 5,428 |

## VALUE OF U.S. EXPORTS AND IMPORTS

SOURCE: U.S. Department of Commerce, International Trade Administration (figures in millions of dollars)

| Year | Total Exports* | Total Imports | Trade Balance | Year | Total Exports* | Total Imports | Trade Balance | Year | Total Exports* | Total Imports | Trade Balance |
|---|---|---|---|---|---|---|---|---|---|---|---|
| 1981 | 223,677 | 261,305 | −27,628 | 1972 | 49,227 | 55,940 | −6,714 | 1963 | 22,467 | 17,207 | 5,260 |
| 1980 | 220,626 | 244,871 | −24,244 | 1971 | 43,573 | 45,784 | −2,210 | 1962 | 20,986 | 16,464 | +4,522 |
| 1979 | 181,651 | 206,256 | −24,605 | 1970 | 42,664 | 40,114 | +2,550 | 1961 | 20,226 | 14,761 | 5,465 |
| 1978 | 143,577 | 171,978 | −28,535 | 1969 | 37,332 | 36,043 | 1,289 | 1960 | 19,659 | 15,073 | 4,586 |
| 1977 | 121,150 | 147,685 | −26,535 | 1968 | 34,063 | 33,226 | 837 | 1959 | 16,426 | 15,690 | 736 |
| 1976 | 115,150 | 121,009 | − 5,859 | 1967 | 31,030 | 26,889 | 4,141 | 1958 | 16,375 | 13,392 | 2,983 |
| 1975 | 107,589 | 96,570 | +11,019 | 1966 | 29,490 | 25,618 | 3,872 | 1957 | 19,516 | 13,418 | 6,098 |
| 1974 | 97,997 | 100,648 | − 2,650 | 1965 | 26,742 | 21,427 | 5,315 | 1956 | 17,343 | 12,905 | 4,438 |
| 1973 | 70,873 | 69,832 | + 1,041 | 1964 | 25,832 | 18,749 | 7,083 | 1955 | 14,298 | 11,566 | 2,732 |

*Excluding aid in the form of military grants.

## U.S. SHARE OF WORLD TRADE: 1938-1981

SOURCE: United Nations *Monthly Bulletin of Statistics*, May 1982, © United Nations (figures in millions of dollars)

| Year | Total World Exports* | U.S. Exports | Year | Total World Imports* | U.S. Imports |
|---|---|---|---|---|---|
| 1981 | $1,946,057 | $228,961 | 1981 | $1,998,228 | $271,320 |
| 1980 | 1,992,924 | 216,668 | 1980 | 2,055,929 | 255,657 |
| 1979 | 1,643,947 | 178,578 | 1979 | 1,686,742 | 217,664 |
| 1978 | 1,302,004 | 141,154 | 1978 | 1,348,919 | 182,786 |
| 1977 | 1,126,638 | 119,042 | 1977 | 1,163,391 | 156,758 |
| 1976 | 896,400 | 113,323 | 1976 | 910,500 | 128,872 |
| 1975 | 873,408 | 106,157 | 1975 | 903,292 | 102,984 |
| 1974 | 767,900 | 97,144 | 1974 | 773,300 | 107,112 |
| 1973 | 517,900 | 70,223 | 1973 | 528,600 | 68,656 |
| 1972 | 372,300 | 48,968 | 1972 | 383,600 | 55,282 |
| 1971 | 314,100 | 43,492 | 1971 | 328,300 | 45,516 |
| 1970 | 313,871 | 42,590 | 1970 | 328,544 | 39,756 |
| 1969 | 243,500 | 37,462 | 1969 | 256,400 | 35,863 |
| 1968 | 212,500 | 34,199 | 1968 | 224,700 | 33,066 |
| 1967 | 189,900 | 31,243 | 1967 | 201,500 | 26,813 |
| 1966 | 180,600 | 29,998 | 1966 | 192,000 | 25,439 |
| 1965 | 164,800 | 27,189 | 1965 | 174,800 | 21,348 |
| 1964 | 152,200 | 26,300 | 1964 | 161,000 | 18,666 |
| 1963 | 135,400 | 23,104 | 1963 | 143,500 | 17,072 |
| 1962 | 141,400 | 21,446 | 1962 | 149,800 | 16,317 |
| 1960 | 128,000 | 20,412 | 1960 | 135,500 | 15,071 |
| 1958 | 108,100 | 17,755 | 1958 | 114,100 | 13,298 |
| 1953 | 82,700 | 15,661 | 1953 | 84,200 | 10,915 |
| 1948 | 57,500 | 12,545 | 1948 | 63,600 | 7,183 |
| 1938 | 23,500 | 3,064 | 1938 | 25,400 | 2,180 |

*Excluding trade of the Centrally Planned Economies.

## WORLD ECONOMIC SUMMARY: 1976-1981

SOURCE: United Nations *Monthly Bulletin of Statistics*, May 1982, © United Nations

| Item | Unit* | 1976 | 1981 |
|---|---|---|---|
| **Agricultural production:** | | | |
| Barley | Mil. tons | 187 | 160 |
| Coffee | 1,000 tons | 3,553 | 5,887 |
| Corn | Mil. tons | 333 | 445 |
| Cotton (lint) | Mil. tons | 12.1 | 15.4 |
| Eggs | Mil. tons | 23.9 | 28.4 |
| Meat | Mil. tons | 127 | 142 |
| Milk | Mil. tons | 438 | 471 |
| Potatoes | Mil. tons | 263 | 256 |
| Rice | Mil. tons | 350 | 408 |
| Tea | 1,000 tons | 1,586 | 1,855 |
| Tobacco | 1,000 tons | 5,669 | 5,289 |
| Wheat | Mil. tons | 425 | 454 |
| Wool, greasy | 1,000 tons | 2,596 | 2,822 |
| Rubber (natural) | 1,000 tons | 3,565 | 3,820† |
| Fish catches | Mil. tons | 72.1 | 72.2† |
| **Industrial Production:** | | | |
| Coal | Mil. tons | 1,940 | 2,740† |
| Crude petroleum | Mil. tons | 2,786 | 2,979† |
| Wheat flour[2] | Mil. tons | 128.7 | 137.5‡ |

| Item | Unit* | 1976 | 1981 |
|---|---|---|---|
| Sugar | Mil. tons | 83.6 | 91.0 |
| Sawnwood[1] | 1,000 cu.m. | 431 | 447‡ |
| Woodpulp | Mil. tons | 87.2 | 124.7‡ |
| Newsprint | Mil. tons | 22.5 | 24.6 |
| Cement | Mil. tons | 711 | 734 |
| Pig iron and ferroalloys | Mil. tons | 495 | 541† |
| Crude steel | Mil. tons | 648 | 755 |
| Tin[2,3,5] | 1,000 tons | 182 | 210 |
| Merchant vessels, launched[2,3,4] | Mil. gr.tons | 33.92 | 13.57† |
| Motor vehicles (passenger) | Millions | 23.93 | 27.72 |
| Electric energy | Bil. kw.-hr. | 6,775 | 8,044† |
| **External trade:** | | | |
| Imports, c.i.f. | Bil. U.S. dol. | 910.4 | 2,045.8† |
| Exports, f.o.b. | Bil. U.S. dol. | 896.5 | 2,001.7† |
| **Transport:** | | | |
| Railway freight | Bil. tons-km | 6,143 | 6,618‡ |
| Merchant shipping, loaded | Mil. tons | 3,346 | 3,778‡ |
| Civil aviation, km flown[4,6] | Millions | 7,830 | 9,440† |

*Data are in metric units. †Latest available figures are from 1980. ‡Latest available figures are from 1979. [1]Excludes Eastern Europe. [2]Excludes China. [3]Excludes East Germany. [4]Excludes USSR. [5]Excludes North Korea. [6]Includes ICAO members.

## WALL STREET GLOSSARY

SOURCE: New York Stock Exchange

**Assets:** Everything a corporation owns or has outstanding: cash, investments, money due it, materials and inventories (current assets); buildings and machinery (fixed assets); and patents and good will (intangible assets).

**Averages:** Various ways of measuring the trend of securities prices, the most popular of which is the Dow-Jones average of 30 industrial stocks listed on the New York Stock Exchange. The numbers are not true numerical averages, but take into account such factors as past splits, etc.

**Balance Sheet:** A condensed statement showing the nature and amount of a company's assets, liabilities, and capital on a given date. In dollar amounts, the balance sheet shows what the company owned, what it owed, and the ownership interest in the company of its stockholders.

**Bear:** Someone who believes the market will decline.

**Blue Chip:** Common stock in a company known nationally for the quality and wide acceptance of its products or services and its ability to make money and pay dividends.

**Bond:** Basically an IOU or promissory note of a corporation, usually issued in multiples of $1,000 or $5,000. A bond is evidence of a debt on which the issuing company usually promises to pay the bondholders a specified amount of interest for a specified length of time, and to repay the loan on the expiration date. In every case a bond represents debt—its holder is a creditor of the corporation and not a part owner as is the shareholder.

**Book Value:** An accounting term. Book value of a stock is determined from the company's records, by adding all assets (generally excluding intangibles), then deducting all debts and other liabilities, plus the liquidation price of any preferred issues. The sum arrived at is divided by the number of common shares outstanding and the result is book value per common share. Book value may have little or no significant relationship to market value.

**Bull:** One who believes the market will rise.

**Capital Gain or Capital Loss:** Profit or loss from the sale of a capital asset. Under current federal income tax laws, a capital gain may be either short-term (12 months or less) or long-term (more than 12 months). A short-term capital gain is taxed at the reporting individual's full income tax rate. A long-term capital gain is subject to a lower tax.

**Capitalization:** Total amount of the various securities issued by a corporation. Capitalization may include bonds, debentures, preferred and common stock. Bonds and debentures are usually carried on the books of the issuing company in terms of their par or face value. Preferred and common shares may be carried in terms of par or stated value. Stated value may be either an arbitrary figure decided upon by the directors, or may represent the amount received by the company from the sale of the securities at the time of issuance.

**Cash Flow:** Reported net income of a corporation *plus* amounts charged off for depreciation, depletion, amortization, extraordinary charges to reserves, which are bookkeeping deductions and not paid out in actual dollars and cents.

**Common Stock:** Securities that represent an ownership interest in a corporation. If the company has also issued preferred stock, both common and preferred have ownership rights, but the preferred normally has prior claim on dividends and, in the event of liquidation, assets. Claims of both common and preferred stockholders are junior to claims of bondholders or other creditors of the company. Common-stock holders assume greater risk than preferred-stock holders, but generally exercise greater control and may gain greater reward.

**Conglomerate:** A corporation that has diversified its operations usually by acquiring enterprises in widely varied industries.

**Convertible:** A bond, debenture, or preferred share that may be exchanged by the owner for common stock or another security, usually of the same company, in accordance with the terms of the issue.

**Dealer:** An individual or firm in the securities business acting as a principal rather than as an agent. Typically, a dealer buys for his own account and sells to a customer from his own inventory. The dealer's profit or loss is the difference between the price he pays and the price he receives for the same security.

**Discretionary Account:** An account in which the customer gives the broker or someone else discretion, which may be complete or within specific limits, as to the purchase and sales of securities or commodities including selection, timing, amount and price to be paid or received.

**Dollar Cost Averaging:** A system of buying securities at regular intervals with a fixed dollar amount. Under this system the investor buys by the dollars' worth rather than by the number of shares. If each investment is of the same number of dollars, payments buy more when the price is low and fewer when it rises. Thus temporary downswings in price benefit the investor if he continues periodic purchases in both good times and bad and the price at which the shares are sold is more than their average cost.

**Dow Theory:** A theory of market analysis based upon the performance of the Dow-Jones industrial and transportation stock price averages. The Theory says that the market is in a basic upward trend if these averages advance above a previous important high. When the averages dip, there is said to be a downward trend.

**Fiscal Year:** A corporation's accounting year. Due to the nature of their particular business, some companies do not use the calendar year for their bookkeeping.

**Growth Stock:** Stock of a company with prospects for future growth—a company whose earnings are expected to increase at a relatively rapid rate.

**Investment Banker:** Also known as an underwriter. He is the middleman between the corporation issuing new securities and the public. One or more investment bankers buy outright from a corporation a new issue of stocks or bonds. The group forms a syndicate to sell the securities to individuals and institutions. Investment bankers also distribute very large blocks of stocks or bonds.

**Investment Company:** A company or trust which uses its capital to invest in other companies. There are two principal types: the closed-end and the open-end, or mutual fund. Closed-end shares are readily transferable in the open market and are bought and sold like other shares. Open-end funds sell their own new shares to investors, stand ready to buy back their old shares, and are not listed.

**Legal List:** A list of investments selected by various states in which certain institutions and fiduciaries, such as insurance companies and banks, may invest.

**Liquidity:** The ability of the market in a particular security to absorb a reasonable amount of buying or selling at reasonable price changes. Liquidity is one of the most important characteristics of a good market.

**Listed Stock:** The stock of a company that is traded on a securities exchange and for which a listing application and a registration statement, giving detailed information about the company and its operations, have been filed with the Securities & Exchange Commission (SEC), unless otherwise exempted, and the exchange itself. The various stock exchanges have different standards for listing.

**Load:** The portion of the offering price of shares of open-end investment companies in excess of the value of the underlying assets which cover sales commissions and all other costs of distribution. The load is incurred only on purchase, there being, in most cases, no charge when the shares are sold (redeemed).

**Margin:** The amount paid by the customer when he uses his broker's credit to buy a security. Under Federal Reserve regulations, the initial margin required in the past years has ranged from 50 percent of the purchase price all the way to 100 percent.

**NASD:** The National Association of Securities Dealers, Inc., an association of brokers and dealers in the over-the-counter securities business.

**NYSE Common Stock Index:** A composite index covering price movements of all common stocks listed on the "Big Board." It is based on the close of the market December 31, 1965, as 50.00 and is weighted according to the number of shares listed for each issue. The index is computed continuously by the Exchange's Market Data System and printed on the ticker tape each half hour. Point changes in the index are converted to dollars and cents so as to provide a meaningful measure of changes in the average price of listed stocks. The composite index is supplemented by separate indexes for four industry groups: industrials, transportation, utilities, and finances.

**Option:** A right to buy (call) or sell (put) a fixed amount of a given stock at a specified price within a limited period of time. The purchaser hopes that the stock's price will go up (if he bought a call) or down (if he bought a put) by an amount sufficient to provide a profit greater than the cost of the contract and the commission and other fees required to exercise the contract. If the stock price holds steady or moves in the opposite direction, the price paid for the option is lost entirely.

**Over-the-Counter:** A market for securities made up of securities dealers who may or may not be members of a securities exchange. Thousands of companies have insufficient shares outstanding, stockholders, or earnings to warrant application for listing on a stock exchange. Securities of these companies are traded in the over-the-counter market between dealers who act either as principals or as brokers for customers. The over-the-counter market is the principal market for U.S. Government bonds and municipals.

**Par:** In the case of a common share, a dollar amount assigned to the share by the company's charter. Par value may also be used to compute the dollar amount of the common shares on the balance sheet. Par value has little significance so far as market value of common stock is concerned. Many companies today issue no-par stock, but give a stated per share value on the balance sheet. In the case of preferred shares and bonds, however, par is important. It often signifies the dollar value upon which dividends on preferred stocks and interest on bonds are figured. The issuer of a 6% bond promises to pay that percentage of the bond's par value annually.

**Point:** In the case of shares of stock, a point means $1. In the case of bonds, a point means $10.

**Portfolio:** Holdings of securites by an individual or institution. A portfolio may contain bonds, preferred stocks and common stocks of various types of enterprises.

**Preferred Stock:** A class of stock with a claim on the company's earnings before payment may be made on the common stock, usually also entitled to priority over common stock if the company liquidates. It is usually entitled to dividends at a specified rate before payment of a dividend on the common stock.

**Price-Earnings Ratio:** The price of a share of stock divided by earnings per share for a twelve-month period.

**Principal:** The person for whom a broker executes an order, or a dealer buying or selling for his own account. The term "principal" may also refer to a person's capital or to the face amount of a bond.

**Puts and Calls:** see **Option**

**Quotation:** Often shortened to "quote." The highest bid to buy and the lowest offer to sell a security in a given market at a given time. A "quote" on a stock might be "45¼ to 45½." This means that $45.25 is the highest price any buyer would pay at the time the quote was given on the floor of the Exchange, and that $45.50 was the lowest price that any seller would take at the same time.

**REIT:** Real Estate Investment Trust, an organization similar to an investment company but concentrating its holdings in real estate. The yield is generally liberal since REIT's are required to distribute as much as 90% of their income.

**Registration:** Before a public offering may be made of new securities by a company, or of outstanding securities by controlling stockholders—through the mails or in interstate commerce—the securities must be registered under the Securities Act of 1933. Registration statement is filed with the SEC by the issuer. It must disclose pertinent information relating to the company's operations, securities, management, and purpose of the public offering. Securities of railroads under jurisdiction of the Interstate Commerce Commission (ICC), and certain other types of securities, are exempted.

**Round Lot:** A unit of trading or a multiple thereof. On the New York Stock Exchange, the unit of trading is generally 100 shares in stocks and $1,000 par value in the case of bonds. In some inactive stocks, the unit of trading is 10 shares.

**Short Sale:** A person who believes a stock will decline and and sells it though he does not own any has made a short sale. Your broker borrows the stock so he can deliver the 100 shares to the buyer. The money value of the shares borrowed is deposited by your broker with the lender. Sooner or later you must cover your short sale by buying the same amount of stock you borrowed for return to the lender. If you are able to buy at a lower price than you sold it for, your profit is the difference between the two prices—not counting commissions and taxes. Stock exchange and federal regulations govern and limit the conditions under which a short sale may be made on a national securities exchange.

**Specialist:** A member of the New York Stock Exchange who has two functions: First, to maintain an orderly market in the stocks in which he is registered as a specialist. The Exchange expects the specialist to buy or sell for his own account, to a reasonable degree, when there is a temporary disparity between supply and demand. Second, the specialist acts as a broker's broker. When a commission broker on the exchange floor receives a limit order, he cannot wait at the particular post where the stock is traded until the price reaches the specified level. He leaves the order with the specialist, who will try to execute it in the market if and when the stock declines to the specified price. The specialist must always put his customers' interests first.

**Split:** The division of the outstanding shares of a corporation into a larger number of shares. A 3-for-1 split by a company with 1 million shares outstanding would result in 3 million shares outstanding. After the 3-for-1 split, each holder of 100 shares would have 300 shares.

**Take-Over:** The acquiring of one corporation by another – usually in a friendly merger but sometimes marked by a "proxy fight."

**Yield:** Also known as return. The dividends or interest paid by a company expressed as a percentage of the current price. A stock with a current market value of $40 a share paying dividends at the rate of $2.00 is said to return 5% ($2.00 – $40.00).

## WALL STREET INDEXES

**Dow Jones Industrial Average:** The addition of closing prices for 30 stocks divided by the current divisor. The divisor is never the number of stocks listed, but by reflecting splits, mergers, and bankruptcies, it is constantly revised.

**NASDAQ Composite Index:** The measure of all domestic common issues traded over-the-counter included in the NASDAQ System, exclusive of those listed on an exchange and those with only one market maker. The index is market value-weighted, in that the importance of each stock is proportional to its price times the number of shares outstanding.

**New York Stock Exchange Common Stock Index:** The current aggregate market value (sum of all shares times the price per share) divided by the adjusted base market value and multiplied by 50. The adjusted value reflects additions or deletions of listings, but remains unaffected by stock splits and dividends.

**Standard and Poor's Index:** The aggregate market value (price of each share times the number of shares) for 425 industrial stocks, expressed as one-tenth the percentage of the average market value relative to the average market value during the years 1941-43.

## THE AMERICAN SHAREHOLDER

The latest NYSE shareownership survey, conducted during 1975, revealed that almost 1 out of 5 shareowners had left the stock market since early 1970. U.S. shareowners numbered 25.3 million and included 1 out of 6 adult Americans in mid-1975. In this five-and-one-half-year period, the median age of shareowners increased by 5 years, from 48 to 53. For the first time since the Exchange began conducting shareownership surveys in 1952, the number of shareowners in the U.S. did not increase.

These 25 million shareowners held shares in some 11,000 publicly owned corporations and investment companies, which had 40.7 billion shares of stock outstanding at a total market value of $800 billion. While the number of shares of stock outstanding increased 12.6% from 36.2 billion in 1970, depressed economic conditions reduced the total market value of stocks outstanding, which declined 21.3% from $1.1 trillion in 1970.

Although the total number of U.S. shareowners declined 18.1%, the number of shareowners of NYSE-listed stocks declined only 1.9% to 18.0 million. Adult female shareowners slightly outnumbered adult males.

The average shareowner's income rose from $13,500 in early 1970 to $19,000 in mid-1975, paralleling changes in purchasing power. The incidence of shareowners with household incomes below $10,000 declined from 28.8% of all U.S. shareowners in 1970 to 14.6% in mid-1975.

| Year | Number of Shareowners (millions) | Percent of U.S. Population |
|---|---|---|
| 1952 | 6.5 | 4% |
| 1959 | 12.5 | 7 |
| 1962 | 17.0 | 9 |
| 1965 | 20.1 | 10 |
| 1971 | 31.9 | 17 |
| 1972 | 32.5 | 17 |
| 1973 | 31.7 | 15 |
| 1974 | 30.9 | 14 |
| 1975 | 25.3 | 11.9 |
| 1980 | 29.8 | 13.5 |
| 1981 | 32.3 | 14.4 |

## INSTITUTIONAL FAVORITES—1981

SOURCE: Standard & Poor's Corporation

The Standard & Poor's Corporation issues most favored by institutional investors are ranked here by the number of companies owning them.

| Issue | Ind. Div. Rate $ | % Yld. on Div. | P-E Ratio |
|---|---|---|---|
| Int'l Bus. Mach. | 3.44 | 5.7 | 9 |
| American Tel. & Tel. | 5.40 | 10.7 | 5 |
| Exxon Corp. | 3.00 | 11.0 | 5 |
| General Electric | 3.40 | 5.5 | 8 |
| Eastman Kodak | 3.50 | 4.8 | 10 |
| Atlantic Richfield | 2.40 | 6.3 | 6 |
| General Motors | 2.40 | 5.2 | 15 |
| Standard Oil (Ind.) | 2.80 | 6.9 | 6 |
| Schlumberger, Ltd. | .96 | 2.5 | 7 |
| Mobil Corp. | 2.00 | 8.6 | 5 |
| Xerox Corp. | 3.00 | 9.7 | 5 |
| Merck & Co. | 2.80 | 4.1 | 11 |
| Standard Oil of Cal. | 2.40 | 8.2 | 6 |
| Texaco Inc. | 3.00 | 10.2 | 4 |
| Minnesota Mng./Mfg. | 3.20 | 6.1 | 9 |
| Amer. Home Prods. | 2.20 | 5.9 | 11 |
| Halliburton Co. | 1.60 | 5.7 | 5 |
| Philip Morris | 2.40 | 4.7 | 8 |
| Phillips Petroleum | 2.20 | 7.1 | 6 |
| Dow Chemical | 1.80 | 9.0 | 8 |
| duPont (E.I.) de Nem. | 2.75 | 8.3 | 6 |
| Johnson & Johnson | 1.00 | 2.6 | 13 |
| Digital Equipment | — | — | 9 |
| Sears, Roebuck & Co. | 1.36 | 7.1 | 8 |
| Caterpillar Tractor | 2.70 | 7.2 | 7 |

| Issue | Ind. Div. Rate $ | % Yld. on Div. | P-E Ratio |
|---|---|---|---|
| Gen'l Tel. & Elect. | 2.84 | 10.6 | 6 |
| Pfizer, Inc. | 1.84 | 3.4 | 12 |
| Union Oil of Calif. | 1.00 | 3.0 | 7 |
| Procter & Gamble | 4.20 | 5.1 | 9 |
| Reynolds (R.J.) Indus. | 2.80 | 6.3 | 6 |
| Citicorp | 1.72 | 6.9 | 4 |
| Gulf Oil | 2.80 | 10.1 | 5 |
| Union Carbide | 3.40 | 7.9 | 5 |
| Coca-Cola | 2.48 | 7.3 | 9 |
| Tenneco, Inc. | 2.60 | 10.7 | 4 |
| Union Pacific | 1.80 | 5.3 | 9 |
| Bristol-Myers | 2.10 | 3.7 | 11 |
| K-Mart | 1.00 | 5.5 | 8 |
| Raytheon Co. | 1.40 | 3.8 | 9 |
| American Express | 2.20 | 5.4 | 7 |
| Int'l Tel. & Tel. | 2.68 | 11.6 | 5 |
| SmithKline Beckman | 2.32 | 3.6 | 11 |
| Abbott Laboratories | .84 | 2.9 | 12 |
| Standard Oil (Ohio) | 2.60 | 7.8 | 5 |
| Texas Utilities | 2.04 | 9.4 | 6 |
| Pepsico Inc. | 1.62 | 4.2 | 9 |
| Eli Lilly & Co. | 2.60 | 4.4 | 10 |
| Hewlett-Packard | .24 | .6 | 14 |
| Avon Products | 3.00 | 12.9 | 7 |
| Dart & Kraft | 3.60 | 6.8 | 7 |

| Issue | Ind. Div. Rate $ | % Yld. on Div. | P-E Ratio |
|---|---|---|---|
| Cigna Corp. | 2.30 | 6.7 | 5 |
| Emerson Electric | 2.00 | 4.5 | 10 |
| Aetna Life & Casualty | 2.52 | 7.5 | 5 |
| J.C. Penney | 2.00 | 5.2 | 7 |
| Morgan (J.P.) | 3.40 | 6.7 | 5 |
| Dresser Indus. | .80 | 4.4 | 5 |
| United Technologies | 2.40 | 6.4 | 6 |
| McDonald's Corp. | 1.20 | 1.7 | 9 |
| Monsanto Co. | 4.00 | 6.9 | 6 |
| Weyerhaeuser Co. | 1.30 | 5.5 | 23 |
| Commonwealth Edison | 2.80 | 13.6 | 6 |
| Int'l Paper | 2.40 | 6.8 | 10 |
| Baxter Travenol Lab. | .46 | 1.3 | 14 |
| Georgia-Pacific | 1.20 | 8.9 | 8 |
| Superior Oil | .20 | .7 | 12 |
| Deere & Co. | 2.00 | 8.0 | 11 |
| BankAmerica Corp. | 1.52 | 9.2 | 5 |
| Warner-Lambert | 1.40 | 6.7 | 8 |
| Amer. Hospital Sup. | .83 | 2.9 | 12 |
| Warner Communications | 1.00 | 2.0 | 9 |
| Aluminum Co. of Amer. | 1.80 | 7.8 | 12 |
| Central & So. West | 1.68 | 10.9 | 6 |
| Alcan Aluminium Ltd. | 1.80 | 10.2 | 20 |
| Burroughs Corp. | 2.60 | 8.1 | 7 |
| Houston Indus. | 2.16 | 11.9 | 5 |

## THE 50 LEADING STOCKS IN MARKET VALUE (AS OF DEC. 31, 1981)

SOURCE: New York Stock Exchange

| Issue | Listed Shares (in millions) | Market Value (in millions) |
|---|---|---|
| American Tel. & Tel. | 815.1 | $ 47,989 |
| Int'l Business Machines | 589.9 | 33,549 |
| Exxon Corp. | 906.4 | 28,211 |
| Schlumberger, N.V. | 302.2 | 16,850 |
| Standard Oil Co. (Ind.) | 304.3 | 15,825 |
| Standard Oil of Calif. | 342.1 | 14,668 |
| Shell Oil | 309.0 | 13,595 |
| General Electric | 231.5 | 13,338 |
| General Motors | 303.2 | 11,710 |
| Eastman Kodak | 162.7 | 11,569 |
| Atlantic Richfield | 239.5 | 11,225 |
| Mobil Corp. | 425.4 | 10,317 |
| Texaco Inc. | 274.3 | 9,052 |
| duPont de Nemours | 234.1 | 8,779 |
| Gulf Oil | 211.9 | 7,496 |
| Johnson & Johnson | 187.3 | 6,953 |
| Procter & Gamble | 82.9 | 6,677 |
| Union Oil of Calif. | 173.6 | 6,531 |
| Merck & Co. | 75.9 | 6,433 |
| Minnesota Mining & Mfg. | 118.0 | 6,431 |
| Phillips Petroleum | 154.4 | 6,255 |
| Halliburton Co. | 118.1 | 6,156 |
| American Home Products | 168.6 | 6,132 |
| Philip Morris Inc. | 125.4 | 6,113 |
| Getty Oil | 88.5 | 5,721 |
| Sun Company | 123.8 | $ 5,635 |
| Gen. Tel. & Elec. | 168.6 | 5,396 |
| Dow Chemical | 203.5 | 5,342 |
| Sears, Roebuck & Co. | 325.4 | 5,247 |
| Marathon Oil | 61.6 | 5,124 |
| Standard Oil (Ohio) | 120.9 | 5,018 |
| Union Pacific | 96.4 | 5,010 |
| Reynolds (R.J.) Indus. | 104.6 | 4,928 |
| Caterpillar Tractor | 88.6 | 4,917 |
| Superior Oil | 132.8 | 4,896 |
| Hewlett-Packard | 122.8 | 4,865 |
| Digital Equipment | 54.5 | 4,726 |
| SmithKline Corp. | 66.7 | 4,512 |
| Teledyne, Inc. | 32.3 | 4,479 |
| Pacific Tel. & Tel. | 224.5 | 4,462 |
| Tenneco Inc. | 130.1 | 4,343 |
| Coca-Cola Co. | 124.0 | 4,310 |
| Eli Lilly & Co. | 76.0 | 4,258 |
| Pfizer Inc. | 75.2 | 4,004 |
| Cities Service | 85.0 | 3,910 |
| American Express | 88.3 | 3,895 |
| Int'l Tel. & Tel. | 130.4 | 3,879 |
| Weyerhaeuser Co. | 128.6 | 3,730 |
| Aetna Life & Casualty | 81.2 | 3,575 |
| Tandy Corp. | 105.6 | 3,566 |
| TOTAL | 9,895.7 | $431,602 |

# REGULAR DIVIDEND PAYERS

SOURCE: Standard & Poor's Corporation

The following companies have paid quarterly, semi-annual, or annual dividends for 60 years or more. Dividends are for 1981.

| Company | Dividends Began | Dividend |
|---|---|---|
| Allied Chemical | 1887 | 2.350 |
| Amerada Hess | 1922 | .825 |
| American Brands | 1905 | 3.212 |
| American District Teleg. | 1903 | 1.460 |
| American Electric Power | 1909 | 2.260 |
| American Express | 1870 | 2.000 |
| American Home Products | 1919 | 1.900 |
| American Natural Res. | 1904 | 3.440 |
| American Sterilizer | 1914 | .350 |
| American Tel. & Tel. | 1881 | 5.300 |
| Amfac, Incorporated | 1898 | 1.440 |
| Anchor Hocking | 1914 | 1.360 |
| Arizona Public Service | 1920 | 2.200 |
| Atlantic City Electric | 1919 | 2.040 |
| Avon Products | 1919 | 3.000 |
| Baltimore Gas & Electric | 1910 | 2.620 |
| Bancal Tri-State | 1875 | 1.180 |
| Bank of N.Y. Company | 1785 | 3.050 |
| Bankers Trust N.Y. | 1904 | 1.849 |
| Bay State Gas | 1853 | 2.320 |
| Bell & Howell | 1915 | .960 |
| Bell Telephone of Canada | 1881 | 1.800 |
| Bemis Co. | 1922 | 1.600 |
| Borden, Incorporated | 1899 | 2.012 |
| Boston Edison | 1890 | 2.800 |
| Bristol-Myers | 1900 | 1.780 |
| British Petroleum | 1917 | 1.979 |
| Burroughs Corporation | 1895 | 2.600 |
| Campbell Soup | 1902 | 2.100 |
| Carpenter Technology | 1907 | 2.050 |
| Carter-Wallace | 1883 | .300 |
| Caterpillar Tractor | 1914 | 2.400 |
| CBI Indus. | 1913 | 1.550 |
| Ceco Corporation | 1921 | .900 |
| Central Hudson G. & E. | 1903 | 2.330 |
| Central Illinois Light | 1921 | 1.820 |
| Champion Spark Plug | 1919 | .800 |
| Chase Manhattan | 1848 | 3.100 |
| Chemical New York | 1827 | 2.500 |
| Chesebrough Ponds | 1883 | 1.520 |
| Cigna Corp. | 1867 | 1.700 |
| Cincinnati Bell | 1879 | 2.570 |
| Cincinnati Gas & Elec. | 1853 | 2.070 |
| Citicorp | 1813 | 1.525 |
| Cleveland Elec. Ill. | 1901 | 2.080 |
| Coca-Cola | 1893 | 2.320 |
| Colgate-Palmolive | 1895 | 1.140 |
| Combustion Engineer | 1911 | 1.550 |
| Commonwealth Edison | 1890 | 2.650 |
| Cone Mills | 1914 | 2.200 |
| Connecticut Natural Gas | 1851 | 1.900 |
| Consolidated Edison | 1885 | 1.480 |
| Consumers Power | 1913 | 2.360 |
| Continental Corporation | 1854 | 2.400 |
| Conwood Corporation | 1903 | 1.100 |
| Corning Glass Works | 1881 | 1.740 |
| CPC International | 1920 | 1.865 |
| Dayton Power & Light | 1919 | 1.820 |
| Delmarva Power and Light | 1921 | 1.520 |
| De Luxe Check Print | 1921 | .890 |
| Dentsply International | 1900 | .880 |
| Detroit Edison | 1909 | 1.620 |
| Diamond International | 1882 | 2.200 |
| Dome Mines, Ltd. | 1920 | .230 |
| Donnelley (RR) & Sons | 1911 | 1.280 |
| Dow Chemical | 1911 | 1.800 |
| Dow Jones & Company | 1906 | .920 |
| du Pont (EI) de Nemours | 1904 | 2.750 |
| Duquesne Light | 1913 | 1.825 |
| Eastman Kodak | 1902 | 3.500 |
| Emhart Corporation | 1902 | 2.400 |
| Equifax Incorporated | 1913 | 2.400 |
| Exxon Corporation | 1882 | 3.000 |
| Fidelity Union Banc | 1893 | 2.800 |
| First Atlanta | 1866 | .726 |
| First National Boston | 1784 | 1.666 |
| First Nat'l St. Bancorp. | 1812 | 2.095 |
| Fleet Financial Gr. | 1791 | 1.760 |
| Fort Howard Paper | 1922 | .880 |
| Foxboro Company | 1916 | .933 |
| Gatx Corporation | 1919 | 2.400 |
| General Bancshares | 1913 | .860 |
| General Electric | 1899 | 3.100 |
| General Foods | 1922 | 2.200 |
| General Mills | 1898 | 1.560 |
| General Motors | 1915 | 2.400 |
| Gillette Company | 1906 | 2.000 |
| Great Lakes Internat'l | 1920 | .710 |
| Great Northern Nekoosa | 1910 | 1.850 |
| Hackensack Water | 1886 | 2.200 |
| Handy & Harman | 1905 | .525 |
| Harcourt, Brace/Jov. | 1922 | .950 |
| Harris Bank Corporation | 1908 | 2.100 |
| Hawaiian Electric | 1901 | 2.690 |
| Heinz (H.J.) | 1911 | 1.310 |
| Heller (W.E.) Int'l | 1921 | 1.300 |
| Hercules, Incorporated | 1913 | 1.260 |
| Houghton Mifflin | 1908 | 1.600 |
| Household Int'l | 1917 | 1.612 |
| Hydraulic Company | 1903 | 1.660 |
| Idaho Power | 1917 | 2.520 |
| Ideal Basic Industries | 1911 | 1.700 |
| Ingersoll-Rand | 1910 | 3.400 |
| Interco, Incorporated | 1913 | 2.820 |
| Interfirst Corp. | 1875 | 1.050 |
| IBM | 1916 | 3.440 |
| Iowa Resources | 1909 | 2.720 |
| Irving Bank Corporation | 1865 | 3.040 |
| Jefferson-Pilot | 1913 | 1.490 |
| Johnson Controls | 1901 | 1.325 |
| Johnson & Johnson | 1905 | .850 |
| JWT Group | 1917 | 1.440 |
| Kansas City Power & Light | 1921 | 2.825 |
| K-Mart | 1913 | .950 |
| Kroger Company | 1902 | 1.520 |
| Lilly (Eli) & Company | 1885 | 2.300 |
| Lincoln National | 1920 | 3.000 |
| Louisville Gas & Elec. | 1913 | 2.160 |
| Manhattan Life Corp. | 1851 | .320 |
| Manufacturers Hanover | 1852 | 2.720 |
| May Department Stores | 1911 | 1.660 |
| Mellon Nat'l | 1895 | 2.090 |
| Melville Corporation | 1916 | 1.800 |
| Minn. Mining/Mfg. | 1916 | 3.000 |
| Mirro Corporation | 1902 | .960 |
| Mobil Corporation | 1902 | 2.000 |
| Monarch Machine Tool, Co. | 1913 | .800 |
| Morgan (J.P.) & Company | 1892 | 3.100 |
| Murphy (G.C.) | 1913 | 1.280 |
| Nabisco Brands | 1899 | 1.760 |
| National Fuel Gas | 1903 | 2.800 |
| National-Standard | 1916 | 1.240 |
| National Steel | 1907 | 2.000 |
| NCNB Corporation | 1903 | .820 |
| New York St. Elec. & Gas | 1910 | 1.940 |
| NL Industries | 1906 | .825 |
| NLT Corporation | 1920 | 1.320 |
| Norstar Bancorp. | 1804 | 1.950 |
| Northern States Power | 1910 | 2.420 |
| Oklahoma Gas & Electric | 1908 | 1.680 |
| Orange/Rockland Util. | 1908 | 1.640 |
| Owens-Illinois | 1907 | 1.560 |
| Pacific Gas & Electric | 1919 | 2.690 |
| Pacific Lighting | 1909 | 2.600 |
| Peavey Company | 1915 | 1.140 |
| J.C. Penney | 1922 | 1.840 |
| Pennwalt Corporation | 1863 | 2.200 |
| Pfizer, Incorporated | 1901 | 1.600 |
| Philadelphia Electric | 1902 | 1.900 |
| Potomac Electric Power | 1904 | 1.580 |
| PPG Industries | 1899 | 2.310 |
| Procter & Gamble | 1891 | 3.900 |
| Pub. Service of Colorado | 1907 | 1.660 |
| Pub. Serv. Elec. & Gas | 1907 | 2.440 |
| Quaker Oats | 1906 | 1.650 |
| Raybestos-Manhattan | 1895 | 1.100 |
| Republic Financial Serv. | 1906 | 1.150 |
| Republic of Texas | 1920 | 1.166 |
| Rexnord, Incorporated | 1894 | 1.080 |
| Reynolds (RJ) Industries | 1900 | 2.500 |
| Richardson-Vicks | 1922 | 1.070 |
| San Diego Gas & Electric | 1909 | 1.620 |
| Scott Paper | 1915 | 1.000 |
| Scoville Incorporated | 1856 | 1.520 |
| Security Pacific | 1881 | 2.150 |
| Shell Transport/Trade | 1898 | 2.171 |
| Sierra Pacific Power | 1916 | 1.460 |
| Singer Company | 1863 | .100 |
| Southeast Banking | 1908 | 1.000 |
| Southern Calif. Edison | 1909 | 3.030 |
| Southern New Eng. Tel. | 1891 | 4.080 |
| Springs Industries | 1898 | 1.020 |
| Squibb Corporation | 1902 | 1.215 |
| Standard Oil of Calif. | 1912 | 2.200 |
| Standard Oil, Indiana | 1894 | 2.600 |
| Stanley Works | 1877 | .720 |
| Stauffer Chemical | 1915 | 1.290 |
| Sterling Drug | 1902 | .980 |
| Sun Company, Inc. | 1904 | 2.025 |
| Teco Energy | 1900 | 1.680 |
| Texaco Incorporated | 1903 | 2.800 |
| Texas Commerce Bankshare | 1920 | .920 |
| Texas Utilities | 1917 | 1.850 |
| Times Mirror | 1892 | 1.720 |
| Timken Company | 1921 | 3.400 |
| Tokheim Corporation | 1920 | .540 |
| Toledo Edison | 1922 | 2.260 |
| Towle Manufacturing | 1917 | .440 |
| Travelers Corporation | 1864 | 1.440 |
| Tucson Electric Power | 1918 | 1.720 |
| UGI Corporation | 1885 | 1.410 |
| Union Carbide | 1918 | 3.300 |
| Union Electric | 1906 | 1.520 |
| Union Oil of California | 1916 | .850 |
| Union Pacific | 1900 | 1.600 |
| United Illuminating | 1900 | 2.740 |
| U.S. Gypsum | 1919 | 2.400 |
| U.S. Tobacco | 1912 | 2.400 |
| UpJohn Company | 1909 | 2.000 |
| Walker (H) Cons Hm | 1848 | 1.220 |
| Washington Gas Light | 1852 | 2.610 |
| Washington Water Power | 1899 | 2.280 |
| West Pt.-Pepperell | 1888 | 1.700 |
| Westvaco Corporation | 1892 | 1.146 |
| Woolworth, (F.W.) | 1912 | 1.800 |
| Wrigley, (Wm.) Jr. | 1913 | 2.240 |

# ENERGY: THE NATION'S FUTURE

## U.S. ENERGY SUPPLY AND DEMAND PROJECTIONS: 1985-1990
## (Quadrillion Btu per Year)

SOURCE: U.S. Department of Energy, Energy Information Administration

| | History | Projections | | |
|---|---|---|---|---|
| | 1980 | 1985 | 1990 | 1995 |
| World Oil Price | | | | |
| (1980 dollars per barrel) | 33.89 | 33.00 | 49.00 | 67.00 |
| Domestic Energy Supply | | | | |
| Oil | 20.6 | 19.3 | 20.0 | 21.2 |
| Gas | 19.8 | 18.6 | 18.2 | 18.7 |
| Coal | 18.7 | 21.9 | 27.1 | 33.7 |
| Nuclear | 2.7 | 5.4 | 7.6 | 8.6 |
| Other (hydropower, solar, and geothermal)[a] | 3.0 | 3.3 | 3.5 | 3.6 |
| Subtotal | 64.8 | 68.5 | 76.4 | 85.8 |
| Net Imports | | | | |
| Oil[b] | 13.3 | 14.7 | 12.0 | 10.6 |
| Gas | 1.0 | 0.9 | 0.7 | 0.7 |
| Coal | −2.5 | −2.7 | −3.5 | −4.2 |
| Subtotal[c] | 12.1 | 12.8 | 9.2 | 7.1 |
| Total Energy Supply | 76.8 | 81.3 | 85.7 | 93.0 |
| Domestic Energy Demand | | | | |
| Residential | 9.4 | 9.0 | 8.9 | 9.2 |
| Commercial | 6.8 | 7.0 | 7.3 | 8.0 |
| Industrial[d] | 23.2 | 26.4 | 28.3 | 30.4 |
| Transportation[e] | 19.0 | 18.9 | 18.2 | 18.3 |
| Total End-Use Demand | 58.5 | 61.3 | 62.7 | 65.9 |
| Stock Changes, Accounting Errors, and Generating and Transmission Losses | 18.3 | 20.0 | 23.0 | 27.0 |
| Total Energy Demand[f] | 76.8 | 81.3 | 85.7 | 93.0 |

[a]Includes gains from electricity generation, synthetics production, and petroleum cracking. Historical data excludes solar.
[b]Figure for 1980 includes imports for additions to the Strategic Petroleum Reserve.
[c]Includes 0.2 quadrillion Btu electricity imported in 1980.
[d]Includes refinery consumption of refined petroleum products and natural gas.
[e]Includes gas transmission losses.
[f]Total supply and consumption estimates include the use of wood to generate electrical power. All other fuel use of wood is at approximately 2 quadrillion Btu.

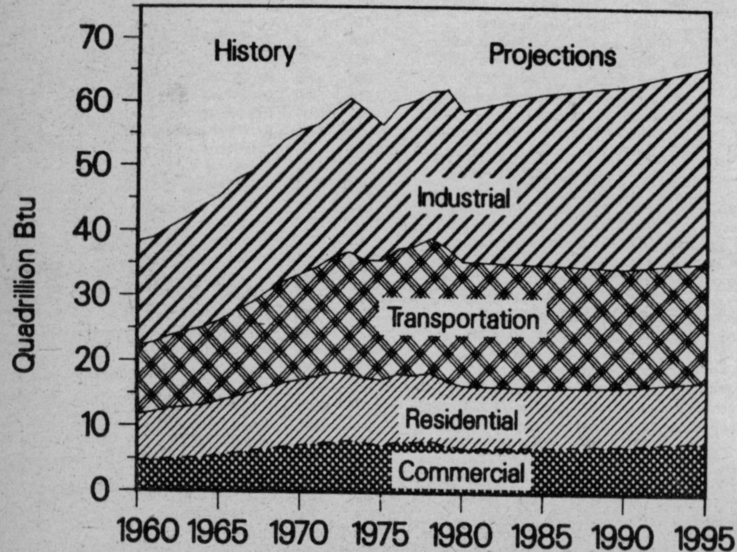

## MAJOR U.S. VEHICULAR TUNNELS

Source: Federal Highway Administration

### UNDERWATER TUNNELS

| State or City | Name and Location | Length Portal to Portal (Feet) |
|---|---|---|
| Alabama | Bankhead Tunnel at Mobile, Mobile River | 3,109 |
| Alabama | George C. Wallace Tunnel, Interstate 10, Mobile River | 3,000 |
| California | Posey Tube, Oakland Estuary | 3,500 |
| California | Webster St. Tube, Oakland Estuary | 3,350 |
| Louisiana | Harvey Tunnel Intracoastal Canal | 1,080 |
| Maryland | Baltimore Harbor Tunnel | 7,650 |
| Massachusetts | Sumner Tunnel, Boston Harbor | 5,650 |
| Massachusetts | Lt. Wm. F. Callahan, Jr. Tunnel, Boston Harbor | 5,047 |
| Michigan | Detroit-Windsor Tunnel | 5,160 |
| New York City | Holland Tunnel, Hudson River | 8,557 |
| New York City | Lincoln Tunnel, Hudson River | 8,215 |
| New York City | Lincoln Tunnel (3d Tube), Hudson River | 8,013 |
| New York City | Queens Midtown Tunnel, East River | 6,414 |
| New York City | Brooklyn-Battery Tunnel, Upper New York Bay | 9,117* |
| Texas | Baytown Tunnel, Houston Ship Channel | 3,009 |
| Texas | Washburn Tunnel, Houston Ship Channel | 2,936 |
| Virginia | Downtown Tunnel under Elizabeth River, Norfolk | 3,920 |
| Virginia | Midtown Tunnel under Elizabeth River, Norfolk | 4,194 |
| Virginia | Hampton Roads, near Norfolk, I-64 | 7,479 |
| Virginia | 2d Hampton Roads Tunnel near Norfolk, Interstate 64 | 7,500 |
| Virginia | Chesapeake Bay Crossing (Cape Charles to Cape Henry): | |
| Virginia | Baltimore Channel Tunnel | 5,450 |
| Virginia | Thimble Shoal Tunnel | 5,738 |

### LAND TUNNELS

| State or City | Name and Location | Length Portal to Portal (Feet) |
|---|---|---|
| Arizona | Mule Pass, Benson Douglas Highway | 1,400 |
| Arizona | Queen Creek Tunnel, Superior-Miami | 1,200 |
| California | Wawona, Yosemite Nat'l Park | 4,233 |
| California | Big Oak Flat, Yosemite Nat'l Park | 2,083 |
| California | Broadway, Low Level Twin Bore, Oakland | 2,944 |
| California | Caldecott (New) Tunnel No. 3, Oakland | 3,371 |
| California | Broadway, San Francisco | 1,616 |
| California | Park Presidio, San Francisco | 1,300 |
| California | Waldo Tunnel, Marin County | 1,000 |
| California | Elephant Butte, Plumas | 1,187 |
| California | International Airport Underpass, Los Angeles | 1,910 |
| Colorado | SN-WPH 81 G(1), near Idaho Springs—U.S. 6 | 1,036 |
| Colorado | 1-F Entrance Road, Mesa Verde Nat'l Park | 1,470 |
| Colorado | Eisenhower Memorial Tunnel, I-70 (2 bores) | 8,950† |
| Colorado | Interstate 70, near Glenwood Springs | 1,045 |
| Connecticut | West Rock Tunnel, near New Haven | 1,200 |
| D. C. | 9th Street Expressway | 1,600 |
| D. C. | Center Leg Mall Tunnel, I-395 | 3,400 |
| D. C. | Center Leg Air Rights Tunnel, I-395 (not open to traffic) | 1,200 |

### LAND TUNNELS (Cont.)

| State or City | Name and Location | Length Portal to Portal (Feet) |
|---|---|---|
| Hawaii | Kalihi Tunnel, Honolulu | 2,780 |
| Hawaii | Nuuanu-Pali Tunnel No. 1 | 1,000 |
| Massachusetts | John F. Fitzgerald Expressway, Boston | 2,335 |
| Massachusetts | Prudential Passageway, Boston | 1,980 |
| Minnesota | Lowry Hill Tunnel at Minneapolis—Interstate 94 | 1,500 |
| Nevada | Carlin Canyon Tunnel, near Elko on Interstate 80 | 1,400 |
| New York City | Battery Park | 2,300 |
| New York City | First Avenue | 1,377 |
| New York City | F.D.R. Drive (42–48 Sts.) | 1,600 |
| New York City | F.D.R. Drive (81–89 Sts.) | 2,400 |
| New York City | Park Avenue | 1,400 |
| New York City | 178–179 Sts., Cross-Town | 2,414 |
| North Carolina | Beaucatcher Tunnel, Asheville | 1,100 |
| North Carolina | Along Pigeon River, Haywood County | 1,035 |
| North Carolina | Along Pigeon River, Haywood County | 1,122 |
| North Carolina | Blue Ridge Parkway, near Waynesville | 820 |
| Ohio | Lytle Park Tunnel in Cincinnati—Interstate 71 | 850 |
| Oregon | Arch Cape, U.S. 101 | 1,228 |
| Oregon | Elk Creek Umpqua Highway, State Rt. 58 | 1,102 |
| Oregon | U.S. Route 26, Vista Ridge, Portland | 1,100 |
| Oregon | Sunset Tunnel | 779 |
| Oregon | Tooth Park, Route 30 | 837 |
| Pennsylvania | Squirrel Hill Tunnel, Pittsburgh | 4,225 |
| Pennsylvania | Armstrong Hill Tunnel, Pittsburgh | 1,325 |
| Pennsylvania | Liberty Tubes, Pittsburgh | 6,336 |
| Pennsylvania | Fort Pitt, Pittsburgh | 3,550 |
| Pa. Turnpike | Allegheny Tunnel | 6,070 |
| — | Tuscarora Tunnel | 5,326 |
| — | Kittatinny Tunnel | 4,727 |
| — | Blue Mountain | 4,339 |
| — | Evans Tunnel, NE Extensions | 4,379 |
| Rhode Island | Providence Reconverted Streetcar Tunnel | 1,793 |
| Tennessee | Bachman Tunnel, U.S. Route 41, Chattanooga | 1,027 |
| Tennessee | Wilcox Tunnel, Chattanooga | 1,312 |
| Utah | Copperfield Tunnel, Copperfield | 6,989 |
| Utah | Zion Nat'l Park Tunnel, Rt. 1, State Rt. 15 | 5,766 |
| Virginia | Colonial Parkway, Project 1D3 | 1,200 |
| Virginia | Route I-77, Big Walker Mountain | 4,200 |
| Washington | State Rt. 1-AW-3, Battery Street Tunnel, Seattle | 2,140 |
| Washington | State Rt. 2–639, U.S. 10—approach to Lake Washington, Seattle | 1,466 |
| Washington | Cayuse Pass Tunnel, Mt. Rainier | 510 |
| West Virginia | West Virginia Turnpike | 2,669 |
| West Virginia | I-70, Wheeling | 1,485 |
| West Virginia | East River Mountain Tunnel, near Bluefield—Interstate 77 | 5,700 |
| Wyoming | I-80, Green River | 1,137 |

### VEHICULAR TUNNELS UNDER CONSTRUCTION

| State or City | Name and Location | Length Portal to Portal (Feet) |
|---|---|---|
| Maryland | Fort McHenry Tunnel, Baltimore, I-95 under Patapsco River | 7,150 |
| Virginia | 2nd Downtown Tunnel, Norfolk, I-264, under Elizabeth River | 3,350 |

* Longest underwater U.S. vehicular tunnel. † Longest U.S. land vehicular tunnel.

## RAILROAD PASSENGER SERVICE

Source: Interstate Commerce Commission

| Year ended Dec. 31[1] | Average miles of road operated | Passengers carried (Thousands) | Total passenger-miles (Millions) | Revenues per passenger per mile* (Cents) | Revenues per passenger per mile† (Cents) | Passenger train-miles (Thousands) | Train-miles per train-hour | Percent passenger cars unserviceable |
|---|---|---|---|---|---|---|---|---|
| 1960 | 94,117 | 325,872 | 21,258 | 3.01 | 3.03 | 209,367 | 40.7 | 8.7 |
| 1965 | 76,993 | 298,877 | 17,389 | 3.18 | 3.14 | 172,344 | 41.3 | 7.9 |
| 1969 | 56,484 | 295,880 | 13,120 | 3.38 | 3.33 | 122,591 | 41.0 | 8.3 |
| 1970 | 49,533 | 283,970 | 12,169 | 3.60 | 3.63 | 107,106 | 41.0 | 7.8 |
| 1971[2] | 40,261 | 272,401 | 8,833 | 4.27 | 4.64 | 69,127 | 37.1 | 9.6 |
| 1972[2] | 29,398 | 261,099 | 8,560 | 4.76 | 5.31 | 60,993 | 38.3 | 15.3 |
| 1973[2] | 28,286 | 254,506 | 9,298 | 4.76 | 5.19 | 60,768 | 37.6 | 17.4 |
| 1974[2] | 31,344 | 274,298 | 10,337 | 5.22 | 5.85 | 64,368 | 38.2 | 17.1 |
| 1975[2] | 31,576 | 269,394 | 9,735 | 5.50 | 6.31 | 65,766 | 39.2 | 17.9 |
| 1976[2] | 34,474 | 271,581 | 10,307 | 5.72 | 6.30 | 66,487 | 31.2 | 16.9 |
| 1977[2] | 31,903 | 275,322 | 10,295 | 5.91 | 6.64 | 66,237 | 33.0 | 20.4 |
| 1978[2] | 30,369 | 281,069 | 10,223 | 5.95 | 6.62 | 64,190 | 32.3 | 19.6 |
| 1979[2] | 28,200 | 301,300 | 11,306 | 5.65 | 6.50 | 61,679 | 34.3 | N.A. |
| 1980[3] | 29,113 | 300,183 | 10,995 | 7.34 | 8.60 | 60,460 | 31.3 | N.A. |

[1] Effective Jan. 1, 1965, the revenue qualification of a Class I railroad was increased from average annual operating revenues of $3 million or more to $5 million or more; effective Jan. 1, 1976, this was again raised to $10 million or more. [2] Includes National Railroad Passenger Corp. (AMTRAK). [3] Preliminary. * Includes commutation. † Excludes commutation.

## INTERCITY BUS LINES

SOURCE: American Bus Association

| Summary of Operations | 1960 | 1964 | 1968 | 1972 | 1980 | 1981[5] |
|---|---|---|---|---|---|---|
| Operating companies | 1,150 | 1,100 | 1,050 | 1,000 | 1,330 | 1,470 |
| Buses | 20,974 | 20,500 | 21,000 | 21,400 | 21,400 | 21,200 |
| Miles of highway served[1] | 265,000 | 260,000 | 260,000 | 270,000 | 279,000 | 272,000 |
| Employees[2] | 45,000 | 46,800 | 47,300 | 49,100 | 49,100 | 49,400 |
| Total bus miles (millions) | 1,092 | 1,183 | 1,190 | 1,182 | 1,162 | 1,136 |
| Fare-paying passengers (millions) | 366 | 360 | 398 | 393 | 365 | 375 |
| Fare-paying passenger-miles (millions) | 19,300 | 23,300 | 24,500 | 25,600 | 27,400 | 26,900 |
| Operating revenue, all services ($ millions) | 556.2 | 686.7 | 797.6 | 974.4 | 1,943.0 | 2,074.6 |
| Operating expenses ($ millions) | 494.8 | 594.9 | 708.7 | 882.1 | 1,810.9 | 1,963.1 |
| Net operating revenue before income taxes ($ millions) | 61.4 | 91.8 | 88.9 | 92.3 | 132.1 | 111.5 |
| Operating ratio[3] | 89.0 | 86.6 | 88.9 | 90.5 | 93.2 | 94.6 |
| Taxes assigned to operations ($ millions)[4] | 53.2 | 63.5 | 67.9 | 84.1 | 111.3 | 123.7 |

[1]Includes duplication between carriers. [2]Operating companies only. [3]Operating expenses divided by operating revenues. [4]Excludes income taxes. [5]Preliminary.

## AMTRAK

The National Railroad Passenger Corporation (Amtrak) celebrated its 10th birthday in Fiscal 1981 with a record 16 percent revenue growth rate and a record 77 percent on-time performance that equaled the major airlines. With nearly 21 million passengers in 1981, Amtrak is the sixth-largest U.S. intercity carrier.

Amtrak's passenger car fleet serves 525 communities via a 23,000-mile national track system using right-of-way and operating agreements with existing freight railroads. Since 1976, Amtrak has owned and operated the 456-mile Northeast Corridor between Washington and Boston.

Amtrak earned $430.4 million in passenger revenue in Fiscal 1981 and $66.1 million in nonpassenger revenue including $16.6 million from real estate. The Corporation accepted the final delivery of 284 double-deck Superliner cars for service in Western states, and now operates new or completely rebuilt passenger cars on all its routes.

## CONRAIL

A private, for-profit corporation created by an Act of Congress, the Consolidated Rail Corporation (Conrail) began operations on April 1, 1976. It was conveyed most of the rail properties of the Central of New Jersey, Erie Lackawanna, Lehigh and Hudson River, Lehigh Valley, Penn Central, and Reading lines. In early 1982, Conrail operated over a 17,000 route-mile system in 16 Northeastern and Midwestern states, the District of Columbia, and two provinces of Canada.

Conrail is primarily a freight railroad, with rail linkages to carriers in other regions. In addition, Conrail operates certain rail commuter services under contract with local, regional or state authorities, and some intercity passenger trains under contract with Amtrak. However, as mandated in the 1981 Northeast Rail Service Act, Conrail will be relieved of its commuter service contractual obligations by Jan. 1, 1983.

Conrail's purpose is to create a viable, private-sector rail freight system in the Northeast and Midwest, providing efficient and essential rail service to customers.

## LONGEST RAILWAY TUNNELS

SOURCE: *Railway Directory and Yearbook*

There are considerable discrepancies in figures given by various authorities on precise tunnel lengths.

| Tunnel | Date of Opening | Length Miles | Length Yards | Operating Railway | Country |
|---|---|---|---|---|---|
| Seikan | U.C. | 33 | 810 | Japanese National | Japan |
| Dai-shimizu | March 18, 1982 | 13 | 1,403 | Japanese National | Japan |
| Simplon No. II | Oct. 16, 1922 | 12 | 559 | Swiss Federal & Italian State | Switzerland-Italy |
| Simplon No. I | June 1, 1906 | 12 | 537 | Swiss Federal & Italian State | Switzerland-Italy |
| New Kanmon | March 10, 1975 | 11 | 1,059 | Japanese National | Japan |
| Appenine | Apr. 22, 1934 | 11 | 892 | Italian State | Italy |
| Rokko | March 15, 1972 | 10 | 132 | Japanese National | Japan |
| Furka | U.C. | 9 | 1,003 | Swiss Federal | Switzerland |
| Gotthard | Jan. 1, 1882(a) | 9 | 562 | Swiss Federal | Switzerland |
| Lötschberg | July 15, 1913 | 9 | 140 | Bern-Lötschberg-Simplon | Switzerland |
| Hokuriku | June 10, 1962 | 8 | 1,055 | Japanese National | Japan |
| Mont Cenis (Fréjus) | Sept. 17, 1871 | 8 | 855 | Italian State | France-Italy |
| New Shimizu | Oct. 1, 1967 | 8 | 651 | Japanese National | Japan |
| Aki | March 10, 1975 | 8 | 141 | Japanese National | Japan |
| Cascade | Jan. 12, 1929 | 7 | 1,397 | Great Northern | United States |
| Kita-Kyushu | March 10, 1975 | 7 | 493 | Japanese National | Japan |
| Kubiki | Oct. 1, 1969 | 7 | 70 | Japanese National | Japan |
| Flathead | November 1970 | 6 | 5,275 | Great Northern | United States |
| Arlberg | Sept. 20, 1884 | 6 | 650 | Austrian Federal | Austria |
| Moffat | Feb. 27, 1928 | 6 | 373 | Denver & Rio Grande Western | United States |
| Shimizu | Sept. 1, 1981 | 6 | 35 | Japanese National | Japan |
| Kvineshei | Dec. 17, 1943(b) | 5 | 1,112 | Norwegian State | Norway |
| Bingo | March 10, 1975 | 5 | 915 | Japanese National | Japan |
| Rimutaka | Nov. 3, 1955 | 5 | 821 | New Zealand Government | New Zealand |
| Ricken | Oct. 1, 1910 | 5 | 608 | Swiss Federal | Switzerland |
| Grenchenberg | Oct. 1, 1915 | 5 | 581 | Swiss Federal(c) | Switzerland |
| Otira | Aug. 4, 1923 | 5 | 564 | New Zealand Government | New Zealand |
| Tauern | July 7, 1909 | 5 | 551 | Austrian Federal | Austria |
| Haegebostad | Dec. 17, 1943(b) | 5 | 467 | Norwegian State | Norway |
| Fukouka | March 10, 1975 | 5 | 458 | Japanese National | Japan |
| Ronco | Apr. 4, 1889 | 5 | 277 | Italian State | Italy |
| Hauenstein (Lower) | Jan. 8, 1916 | 5 | 95 | Swiss Federal | Switzerland |
| Connaught | Dec. 6, 1916 | 5 | 39 | Canadian Pacific | Canada |
| Karawanken | Oct. 1, 1906 | 4 | 1,683 | Austrian Federal | Austria-Yugoslavia |
| New Tanna | Oct. 1, 1964 | 4 | 1,663 | Japanese National | Japan |
| Somport | July 18, 1928 | 4 | 1,572 | French National | France-Spain |
| Tanna | Dec. 1, 1934 | 4 | 1,493 | Japanese National | Japan |
| Ulrikken | Aug. 1, 1964 | 4 | 1,338 | Norwegian State | Norway |
| Hoosac | Feb. 9, 1875 | 4 | 1,230 | Boston & Maine | United States |
| Monte Orso | Oct. 28, 1927 | 4 | 1,230 | Italian State | Italy |
| Lupacino | Sept. 24, 1958 | 4 | 1,178 | Italian State | Italy |
| Vivola | Oct. 28, 1927 | 4 | 1,004 | Italian State | Italy |
| Monte Adone | Apr. 22, 1934 | 4 | 760 | Italian State | Italy |
| Jungfrau | Aug. 1, 1912 | 4 | 750 | Jungfrau | Switzerland |
| Borgallo | Aug. 1, 1894 | 4 | 700 | Italian State | Italy |
| Severn | Sept. 1, 1886 | 4 | 628 | Western Region | Great Britain |
| Lusse (Vosges) | Aug. 9, 1937 | 4 | 474 | French National | France |
| Marianopoli | Aug. 1, 1885 | 4 | 42 | Italian State | Italy |

(a) For goods traffic; passengers: June 1, 1882. (b) These were wartime openings under German Occupation. Full traffic began March 1, 1944. (c) The Gronchenberg tunnel is owned but not worked by the Bern-Lötschberg-Simplon Railway.

## ESTIMATED AUTOMOBILE REGISTRATIONS: 1981 (in thousands)

SOURCE: U.S. Federal Highway Administration

| State | Registrations |
|---|---|
| Alabama | 2,140 |
| Alaska | 158 |
| Arizona | 1,458 |
| Arkansas | 1,072 |
| California | 14,019 |
| Colorado | 1,765 |
| Connecticut | 2,022 |
| Delaware | 324 |
| Dist. of Col. | 257 |
| Florida | 6,398 |
| Georgia | 2,938 |
| Hawaii | 525 |
| Idaho | 531 |
| Illinois | 6,390 |
| Indiana | 2,900 |
| Iowa | 1,670 |
| Kansas | 1,404 |
| Kentucky | 1,813 |
| Louisiana | 2,016 |
| Maine | 525 |
| Maryland | 2,393 |
| Massachusetts | 3,320 |
| Michigan | 5,326 |
| Minnesota | 2,345 |
| Mississippi | 1,269 |
| Missouri | 2,447 |
| Montana | 455 |
| Nebraska | 849 |
| Nevada | 492 |
| New Hampshire | 604 |
| New Jersey | 4,360 |
| New Mexico | 702 |
| New York | 6,978 |
| North Carolina | 3,421 |
| North Dakota | 370 |
| Ohio | 6,536 |
| Oklahoma | 1,844 |
| Oregon | 1,579 |
| Pennsylvania | 5,897 |
| Rhode Island | 557 |
| South Carolina | 1,541 |
| South Dakota | 371 |
| Tennessee | 2,597 |
| Texas | 7,606 |
| Utah | 682 |
| Vermont | 280 |
| Virginia | 3,137 |
| Washington | 2,344 |
| West Virginia | 978 |
| Wisconsin | 2,449 |
| Wyoming | 282 |
| **Total** | **124,336** |

## ESTIMATED LICENSED DRIVERS, BY SEX: 1981 (in thousands)

SOURCE: Federal Highway Administration

| State | Male Drivers | Female Drivers | Total Drivers |
|---|---|---|---|
| Alabama | 1,212 | 1,109 | 2,321 |
| Alaska | 126 | 97 | 223 |
| Arizona | 1,125 | 959 | 2,084 |
| Arkansas | 772 | 735 | 1,507 |
| California | 8,485 | 7,525 | 16,010 |
| Colorado | 1,076 | 997 | 2,073 |
| Connecticut | 1,083 | 1,122 | 2,205 |
| Delaware | 220 | 207 | 427 |
| Dist. of Col. | 187 | 156 | 343 |
| Florida | 3,816 | 3,536 | 7,352 |
| Georgia | 1,834 | 1,686 | 3,520 |
| Hawaii | 304 | 243 | 547 |
| Idaho | 345 | 310 | 655 |
| Illinois | 3,761 | 3,336 | 7,097 |
| Indiana | 1,897 | 1,787 | 3,684 |
| Iowa | 1,114 | 1,008 | 2,122 |
| Kansas | 871 | 826 | 1,697 |
| Kentucky | 1,112 | 974 | 2,086 |
| Louisiana | 1,197 | 1,088 | 2,285 |
| Maine | 392 | 360 | 752 |
| Maryland | 1,462 | 1,334 | 2,796 |
| Massachusetts | 1,826 | 1,811 | 3,637 |
| Michigan | 3,369 | 3,098 | 6,467 |
| Minnesota | 1,243 | 1,142 | 2,385 |
| Mississippi | 858 | 737 | 1,595 |
| Missouri | 1,708 | 1,583 | 3,291 |
| Montana | 336 | 271 | 607 |
| Nebraska | 578 | 533 | 1,111 |
| Nevada | 359 | 314 | 673 |
| New Hampshire | 353 | 324 | 677 |
| New Jersey | 2,604 | 2,413 | 5,017 |
| New Mexico | 437 | 455 | 892 |
| New York | 5,218 | 4,084 | 9,302 |
| North Carolina | 2,001 | 1,861 | 3,862 |
| North Dakota | 223 | 201 | 424 |
| Ohio | 4,244 | 2,783 | 7,027 |
| Oklahoma | 1,019 | 998 | 2,017 |
| Oregon | 1,080 | 950 | 2,030 |
| Pennsylvania | 3,830 | 3,315 | 7,145 |
| Rhode Island | 307 | 284 | 591 |
| South Carolina | 1,052 | 959 | 2,011 |
| South Dakota | 255 | 232 | 487 |
| Tennessee | 1,488 | 1,374 | 2,862 |
| Texas | 5,056 | 4,575 | 9,631 |
| Utah | 436 | 438 | 874 |
| Vermont | 186 | 166 | 352 |
| Virginia | 1,813 | 1,742 | 3,555 |
| Washington | 1,449 | 1,295 | 2,744 |
| West Virginia | 859 | 659 | 1,518 |
| Wisconsin | 1,581 | 1,454 | 3,035 |
| Wyoming | 197 | 166 | 363 |
| **Total** | **78,356** | **69,612** | **147,968** |

## WORLD MOTOR VEHICLE FATALITY RATES

(per 100,000 population)

SOURCE: *U.N. Demographic Yearbook* 1979, © United Nations

| Nation | Rate |
|---|---|
| Kuwait (1977) | 36.0 |
| Venezuela (1977) | 34.2 |
| Luxembourg (1978) | 29.5 |
| Austria (1978) | 28.9 |
| Australia (1977) | 27.2 |
| Belgium (1976) | 25.1 |
| Yugoslavia (1977) | 23.7 |
| Germany, West (1978) | 23.1 |
| Canada (1977) | 22.6 |
| France (1977) | 21.9 |
| UNITED STATES (1976) | 21.9 |
| New Zealand (1976) | 21.1 |
| Greece (1978) | 20.9 |
| Switzerland (1978) | 20.1 |
| Hungary (1978) | 19.9 |
| Czechoslovakia (1977) | 18.1 |
| Spain (1976) | 17.0 |
| Denmark (1978) | 16.9 |
| Netherlands (1978) | 16.7 |
| Panama (1977) | 16.6 |
| Mexico (1975) | 16.4 |
| Argentina (1977) | 16.1 |
| Jordan (1976) | 14.1 |
| Bulgaria (1978) | 14.1 |
| Israel (1978) | 13.9 |
| Sweden (1978) | 13.2 |
| Singapore (1978) | 12.8 |
| Iceland (1978) | 12.5 |
| England & Wales (1977) | 11.9 |
| Norway (1977) | 11.6 |
| Japan (1978) | 10.5 |

## AUTO CASUALTY RATES

SOURCE: International Road Federation

| | Vehicles per 1,000 pop. | Rates per 100 million vehicle-kilometers: Injuries | Deaths |
|---|---|---|---|
| Australia (1980) | 402 | 82[1] | 3.1[1] |
| Belgium (1980) | 320 | 162[1] | 6.3[1] |
| Canada (1979) | 423 | 109[3] | 2.9[3] |
| Denmark (1980) | 256 | 57 | 2.6 |
| Finland (1980) | 271 | 32[1] | 2.0[1] |
| France (1980) | 355 | 123 | 4.6 |
| Iceland (1979) | 357 | 61[2] | 2.3[2] |
| Italy (1980) | 308 | 86[2] | 3.3[2] |
| Japan (1980) | 202 | 153 | 2.2 |
| Netherlands (1979) | 288 | 95[2] | 3.5[2] |
| New Zealand (1980) | 415 | 87[2] | 3.8[2] |
| Norway (1979) | 292 | 71 | 2.6 |
| United Kingdom (1979) | 277 | 91[1] | 2.3[1] |
| United States (1979) | 541 | 113 | 2.1 |
| West Germany (1980) | 377 | 144 | 3.8 |

[1]1979. [2]1978. [3]1976.

## U.S. DEATHS AND DEATH RATES FROM MOTOR VEHICLE ACCIDENTS

SOURCE: National Center for Health Statistics

| Year | Number | Rate per 100,000 population |
|---|---|---|
| 1978 | 52,411 | 24.0 |
| 1977 | 49,510 | 22.9 |
| 1976 | 47,038 | 21.9 |
| 1975 | 45,853 | 21.5 |
| 1974 | 46,402 | 22.0 |
| 1972 | 56,278 | 27.0 |
| 1970 | 54,633 | 26.9 |

| | Atlanta | Baltimore | Birmingham | Boston | Buffalo | Chicago | Cincinnati | Cleveland | Dallas | Denver | Des Moines | Detroit | Houston | Indianapolis | Kansas City, Mo. |
|---|---|---|---|---|---|---|---|---|---|---|---|---|---|---|---|
| Akron | 672 | 331 | 702 | 653 | 207 | 366 | 230 | 33 | 1173 | 1385 | 707 | 190 | 1270 | 295 | 779 |
| Albuquerque | 1396 | 1889 | 1266 | 2194 | 1767 | 1289 | 1378 | 1581 | 639 | 422 | 994 | 1538 | 829 | 1272 | 790 |
| Atlanta | | 669 | 152 | 1068 | 877 | 695 | 461 | 686 | 805 | 1401 | 894 | 726 | 814 | 508 | 810 |
| Baltimore | 669 | | 787 | 399 | 345 | 687 | 494 | 351 | 1458 | 1701 | 1025 | 511 | 1449 | 580 | 1099 |
| Birmingham | 152 | 787 | | 1185 | 902 | 636 | 476 | 716 | 653 | 1282 | 808 | 741 | 662 | 480 | 706 |
| Boston | 1068 | 399 | 1185 | | 449 | 975 | 876 | 632 | 1819 | 1989 | 1311 | *699 | 1916 | 941 | 1456 |
| Buffalo | 877 | 345 | 902 | 449 | | 529 | 430 | 186 | 1373 | 1543 | 865 | *252 | 1470 | 495 | 1010 |
| Chicago | 695 | 687 | 656 | 975 | 529 | | 295 | 343 | 936 | 1016 | 338 | 275 | 1085 | 187 | 499 |
| Cincinnati | 461 | 494 | 476 | 876 | 430 | 295 | | 244 | 943 | 1169 | 571 | 265 | 1040 | 108 | 590 |
| Cleveland | 686 | 351 | 716 | 632 | 186 | 343 | 244 | | 1187 | 1357 | 679 | 167 | 1284 | 309 | 824 |
| Columbus | 549 | 408 | 579 | 769 | 323 | 359 | 107 | 137 | 1050 | 1233 | 695 | 189 | 1147 | 172 | 656 |
| Dallas | 805 | 1458 | 653 | 1819 | 1373 | 936 | 943 | 1187 | | 784 | 704 | 1188 | 242 | 882 | 499 |
| Denver | 1401 | 1701 | 1282 | 1989 | 1543 | 1016 | 1169 | 1357 | 784 | | 679 | 1284 | 1026 | 1061 | 604 |
| Des Moines | 894 | 1025 | 808 | 1311 | 865 | 338 | 571 | 679 | 604 | 679 | | 606 | 946 | 483 | 213 |
| Detroit | 726 | 511 | 741 | *699 | *252 | 275 | 265 | 167 | 1188 | 1284 | 606 | | 1337 | 277 | 751 |
| El Paso | 1427 | 2034 | 1275 | 2391 | 1945 | 1434 | 1524 | 1759 | 622 | 654 | 1139 | 1686 | 755 | 1423 | 935 |
| Hartford | 972 | 303 | 1090 | 102 | 380 | 903 | 752 | 562 | 1690 | 1883 | 1232 | 731 | 1752 | 822 | 1306 |
| Houston | 814 | 1449 | 662 | 1916 | 1470 | 1085 | 1040 | 1284 | 242 | 1026 | 946 | 1337 | | 997 | 741 |
| Indianapolis | 508 | 580 | 480 | 941 | 495 | 187 | 108 | 309 | 882 | 1061 | 483 | 277 | 997 | | 484 |
| Jacksonville | 314 | 793 | 426 | 1191 | 1067 | 1009 | 775 | 952 | 994 | 1708 | 1208 | 996 | 911 | 822 | 1123 |
| Kansas City, Mo. | 810 | 1099 | 706 | 1456 | 1010 | 499 | 590 | 824 | 499 | 604 | 213 | 751 | 741 | 484 | |
| Little Rock | 505 | 1086 | 386 | 1494 | 1048 | 644 | 618 | 862 | 325 | 957 | 573 | 896 | 441 | 562 | 405 |
| Los Angeles | 2197 | 2695 | 2056 | 3052 | 2606 | 2095 | 2186 | 2420 | 1403 | 1134 | 1801 | 2347 | 1553 | 2080 | 1596 |
| Louisville | 394 | 604 | 366 | 986 | 540 | 301 | 110 | 354 | 833 | 1120 | 569 | 375 | 930 | 114 | 516 |
| Memphis | 366 | 947 | 247 | 1355 | 909 | 544 | 479 | 723 | 464 | 1035 | 608 | 713 | 561 | 436 | 459 |
| Mexico City | 1800 | 2435 | 1648 | 2902 | 2456 | 2071 | 2026 | 2270 | 1149 | 1754 | 1852 | 2337 | 986 | 1983 | 1647 |
| Miami | 665 | 1144 | 765 | 1542 | 1418 | 1360 | 1126 | 1303 | 1309 | 2046 | 1559 | 1347 | 1216 | 1173 | 1470 |
| Milwaukee | 784 | 776 | 745 | 1064 | 618 | 91 | 384 | 432 | 1015 | 1040 | 361 | 364 | 1174 | 276 | 580 |
| Minneapolis/St. Paul | 1105 | 1097 | 1066 | 1385 | 939 | 412 | 705 | 753 | 956 | 841 | 252 | 685 | 1198 | 597 | 457 |
| Montgomery | 169 | 838 | 92 | 1236 | 979 | 748 | 568 | 793 | 650 | 1374 | 900 | 833 | 659 | 572 | 798 |
| Montreal | 1230 | 562 | 1289 | 324 | 393 | *848 | 820 | 576 | 1763 | *1862 | *1184 | *573 | 1860 | 885 | *1324 |
| Nashville | 256 | 725 | 205 | 1165 | 719 | 451 | 290 | 533 | 686 | 1158 | 638 | 555 | 783 | 294 | 554 |
| New Orleans | 493 | 1138 | 351 | 1536 | 1253 | 925 | 820 | 1063 | 498 | 1282 | 989 | 1085 | 359 | 805 | 821 |
| New York City | 855 | 187 | 974 | 216 | 445 | 843 | 659 | 507 | 1607 | 1851 | 1173 | 667 | 1636 | 729 | 1319 |
| Oklahoma City | 845 | 1321 | 726 | 1684 | 1308 | 797 | 844 | 1052 | 215 | 615 | 560 | 1049 | 457 | 743 | 347 |
| Omaha | 1012 | 1163 | 911 | 1449 | 1003 | 476 | 691 | 817 | 656 | 540 | 139 | 744 | 898 | 583 | 205 |
| Philadelphia | 766 | 97 | 884 | 304 | 365 | 762 | 578 | 426 | 1526 | 1770 | 1092 | 586 | 1546 | 648 | 1238 |
| Phoenix | 1810 | 2325 | 1658 | 2682 | 2236 | 1722 | 1816 | 2050 | 1005 | 818 | 1430 | 1977 | 1155 | 1710 | 1226 |
| Pittsburgh | 697 | 230 | 742 | 598 | 217 | 461 | 284 | 125 | 1232 | 1482 | 804 | 285 | 1319 | 354 | 937 |
| Portland, Ore. | 2654 | 2816 | 2552 | 3085 | 2639 | 2112 | 2405 | 2453 | 2043 | 1278 | 1819 | 2385 | 2233 | 2297 | 1846 |
| Providence | 1033 | 364 | 1151 | 45 | 444 | 967 | 813 | 626 | 1751 | 1944 | 1296 | 795 | 1813 | 883 | 1367 |
| Reno | 2408 | 2613 | 2288 | 2919 | 2482 | 1956 | 2173 | 2290 | 1677 | 1041 | 1623 | 2218 | 1867 | 2065 | 1639 |
| St. Louis | 558 | 817 | 476 | 1178 | 802 | 291 | 338 | 546 | 645 | 856 | 336 | 543 | 794 | 237 | 252 |
| Salt Lake City | 1900 | 2118 | 1781 | 2405 | 1958 | 1431 | 1644 | 1772 | 1241 | 512 | 1094 | 1700 | 1431 | 1536 | 1116 |
| San Francisco | 2523 | 2876 | 2393 | 3163 | 2716 | 2189 | 2402 | 2530 | 1806 | 1270 | 1852 | 2458 | 1955 | 2294 | 1874 |
| Seattle | 2756 | 2748 | 2575 | 3036 | 2590 | 2063 | 2356 | 2404 | 2112 | 1347 | 1773 | 2336 | 2302 | 2248 | 1872 |
| Toledo | 668 | 454 | 683 | 742 | 296 | 241 | 207 | 110 | 1154 | 1250 | 572 | 58 | 1247 | 221 | 717 |
| Topeka | 873 | 1162 | 764 | 1519 | 1073 | 562 | 653 | 887 | 505 | 541 | 276 | 814 | 745 | 547 | 63 |
| Tulsa | 783 | 1219 | 664 | 1650 | 1204 | 693 | 740 | 948 | 271 | 693 | 471 | 945 | 513 | 641 | 258 |
| Washington, D.C. | 630 | 39 | 748 | 437 | 359 | 687 | 492 | 351 | 1372 | 1696 | 1018 | 511 | 1410 | 564 | 1048 |

| | Los Angeles | Memphis | Milwaukee | Minneapolis | Montreal | Nashville | New Orleans | New York City | Philadelphia | Phoenix | Pittsburgh | St. Louis | Salt Lake City | San Francisco | Seattle | Washington, D.C. |
|---|---|---|---|---|---|---|---|---|---|---|---|---|---|---|---|---|
| Akron | 2368 | 709 | 455 | 776 | 597 | 519 | 1049 | 487 | 406 | 2003 | 105 | 532 | 1800 | 2541 | 2427 | 331 |
| Albuquerque | 806 | 1030 | 1370 | 1247 | *2111 | 1289 | 1137 | 2001 | 1918 | 454 | 1626 | 1040 | 611 | 1127 | 1482 | 1838 |
| Atlanta | 2197 | 366 | 784 | 1105 | 1230 | 256 | 493 | 855 | 766 | 1810 | 697 | 558 | 1900 | 2523 | 2756 | 630 |
| Baltimore | 2695 | 947 | 776 | 1097 | 562 | 725 | 1138 | 187 | 97 | 2325 | 230 | 817 | 2118 | 2876 | 2748 | 39 |
| Birmingham | 2056 | 247 | 745 | 1066 | 1289 | 205 | 351 | 974 | 884 | 1658 | 742 | 476 | 1781 | 2393 | 2575 | 748 |
| Boston | 3052 | 1355 | 1064 | 1385 | 324 | 1165 | 1536 | 216 | 304 | 2682 | 598 | 1178 | 2405 | 3163 | 3036 | 437 |
| Buffalo | 2606 | 909 | 618 | 939 | 393 | 719 | 1253 | 445 | 365 | 2236 | 217 | 802 | 1958 | 2716 | 2590 | 359 |
| Chicago | 2095 | 544 | 91 | 412 | *848 | 451 | 929 | 843 | 762 | 1722 | 461 | 291 | 1431 | 2189 | 2063 | 687 |
| Cincinnati | 2186 | 479 | 384 | 705 | 820 | 290 | 820 | 659 | 578 | 1816 | 284 | 338 | 1644 | 2402 | 2356 | 492 |
| Cleveland | 2420 | 723 | 432 | 753 | 576 | 533 | 1063 | 507 | 426 | 2050 | 125 | 546 | 1772 | 2530 | 2404 | 351 |
| Columbus | 2245 | 586 | 448 | 769 | 713 | 396 | 926 | 557 | 476 | 1882 | 182 | 409 | 1701 | 2459 | 2420 | 392 |
| Dallas | 1403 | 464 | 1015 | 956 | 1763 | 686 | 498 | 1607 | 1526 | 1005 | 1232 | 645 | 1241 | 1806 | 2112 | 1372 |
| Denver | 1134 | 1035 | 1040 | 841 | *1862 | 1158 | 1282 | 1851 | 1770 | 818 | 1482 | 856 | 512 | 1270 | 1347 | 1696 |
| Des Moines | 1801 | 608 | 361 | 252 | *1184 | 638 | 989 | 1173 | 1092 | 1430 | 804 | 336 | 1094 | 1852 | 1773 | 1018 |
| Detroit | 2347 | 713 | 364 | 685 | *573 | 555 | 1085 | 667 | 586 | 1977 | 285 | 543 | 1700 | 2458 | 2336 | 511 |
| El Paso | 798 | 1086 | 1513 | 1339 | *2280 | 1308 | 1114 | 2254 | 2173 | 400 | 1872 | 1180 | 869 | 1200 | 1740 | 1983 |
| Hartford | 2895 | 1226 | 992 | 1317 | 317 | 1027 | 1445 | 121 | 207 | 2530 | 477 | 1059 | 2326 | 3076 | 2955 | 342 |
| Houston | 1553 | 561 | 1174 | 1198 | 1860 | 783 | 359 | 1636 | 1546 | 1153 | 1319 | 794 | 1431 | 1955 | 2302 | 1410 |
| Indianapolis | 2080 | 436 | 276 | 597 | 885 | 294 | 805 | 729 | 648 | 1710 | 354 | 237 | 1536 | 2294 | 2245 | 564 |
| Jacksonville | 2397 | 673 | 1098 | 1419 | 1355 | 570 | 572 | 980 | 890 | 1999 | 865 | 872 | 2207 | 2799 | 3070 | 754 |
| Kansas City, Mo. | 1596 | 459 | 580 | 457 | *1324 | 554 | 821 | 1319 | 1238 | 1226 | 937 | 252 | 1116 | 1874 | 1872 | 1048 |
| Little Rock | 1701 | 139 | 723 | 825 | 1438 | 361 | 416 | 1282 | 1201 | 1330 | 897 | 353 | 1456 | 2027 | 2277 | 1047 |
| Los Angeles | | 1831 | 2176 | 1940 | *2920 | 2058 | 1901 | 2915 | 2721 | 398 | 2533 | 1848 | 734 | 403 | 1145 | 2644 |
| Louisville | 2107 | 369 | 390 | 711 | 930 | 180 | 710 | 769 | 688 | 1757 | 394 | 264 | 1632 | 2390 | 2362 | 596 |
| Memphis | 1831 | | 624 | 840 | 1299 | 222 | 401 | 1138 | 1057 | 1466 | 758 | 294 | 1534 | 2157 | 2331 | 908 |
| Mexico City | 2017 | 1547 | 2164 | 2104 | 2846 | 1769 | 1345 | 2622 | 2532 | 1625 | 2305 | 1794 | 2100 | 2419 | 2948 | 2396 |
| Miami | 2712 | 1011 | 1449 | 1770 | 1705 | 921 | 875 | 1330 | 1241 | 2314 | 1216 | 1223 | 2545 | 3075 | 3421 | 1105 |
| Milwaukee | 2176 | 624 | | 326 | *937 | 540 | 1013 | 932 | 851 | 1806 | 550 | 370 | 1455 | 2213 | 1977 | 776 |
| Minneapolis/St. Paul | 1940 | 840 | 326 | | *1258 | 861 | 1241 | 1253 | 1172 | 1630 | 871 | 546 | 1239 | 1997 | 1641 | 1097 |
| Montgomery | 2053 | 339 | 837 | 1158 | 1369 | 297 | 324 | 1024 | 935 | 1655 | 819 | 572 | 1873 | 2456 | 2667 | 799 |
| Montreal | *2920 | 1299 | *937 | *1258 | | 1109 | 1640 | 388 | 467 | *2550 | 611 | *1116 | *2273 | *3031 | *2697 | 600 |
| Nashville | 2058 | 222 | 540 | 861 | 1109 | | 530 | 949 | 868 | 1725 | 559 | 302 | 1670 | 2410 | 2512 | 686 |
| New Orleans | 1901 | 401 | 1013 | 1241 | 1640 | 530 | | 1325 | 1235 | 1503 | 1093 | 695 | 1739 | 2303 | 2610 | 1099 |
| New York City | 2915 | 1138 | 932 | 1253 | 388 | 949 | 1325 | | 92 | 2459 | 386 | 966 | 2267 | 3025 | 2904 | 225 |
| Oklahoma City | 1357 | 479 | 876 | 813 | 1671 | 738 | 678 | 1472 | 1391 | 987 | 1097 | 506 | 1108 | 1678 | 1962 | 1307 |
| Omaha | 1662 | 664 | 500 | 358 | *1317 | 756 | 1026 | 1312 | 1230 | 1335 | 942 | 454 | 955 | 1713 | 1667 | 1156 |
| Philadelphia | 2721 | 1057 | 851 | 1172 | 467 | 868 | 1235 | 92 | | 2464 | 305 | 885 | 2186 | 2944 | 2823 | 136 |
| Phoenix | 398 | 1466 | 1806 | 1630 | *2550 | 1725 | 1503 | 2459 | 2464 | | 2163 | 1478 | 653 | 800 | 1541 | 2274 |
| Pittsburgh | 2533 | 758 | 550 | 871 | 611 | 559 | 1093 | 386 | 305 | 2163 | | 591 | 1890 | 2648 | 2522 | 230 |
| Portland, Ore. | 970 | 2305 | 2026 | 1690 | *2746 | 2398 | 2541 | 2953 | 2872 | 1366 | 2571 | 2096 | 802 | 652 | 175 | 2797 |
| Providence | 2956 | 1287 | 1056 | 1381 | 342 | 1088 | 1506 | 182 | 268 | 2591 | 538 | 1120 | 2390 | 3140 | 3019 | 403 |
| Reno | 477 | 2041 | 1979 | 1773 | 2803 | 2192 | 2175 | 2765 | 2685 | 736 | 2394 | 1890 | 530 | 221 | 742 | 2618 |
| St. Louis | 1848 | 294 | 370 | 546 | *1116 | 302 | 695 | 966 | 885 | 1478 | 591 | | 1368 | 2126 | 2109 | 801 |
| Salt Lake City | 734 | 1534 | 1455 | 1239 | *2273 | 1670 | 1739 | 2267 | 2186 | 653 | 1890 | 1368 | | 759 | 871 | 2111 |
| San Francisco | 403 | 2157 | 2213 | 1997 | *3031 | 2410 | 2303 | 3025 | 2944 | 800 | 2648 | 2126 | 759 | | 827 | 2869 |
| Seattle | 1145 | 2331 | 1977 | 1641 | *2697 | 2512 | 2610 | 2904 | 2823 | 1541 | 2522 | 2109 | 871 | 827 | | 2748 |
| Toledo | 2313 | 686 | 330 | 651 | *631 | 497 | 1027 | 610 | 529 | 1943 | 228 | 509 | 1670 | 2428 | 2302 | 454 |
| Topeka | 1537 | 522 | 643 | 520 | *1387 | 617 | 884 | 1382 | 1301 | 1171 | 1000 | 315 | 1053 | 1811 | 1831 | 1111 |
| Tulsa | 1461 | 417 | 772 | 715 | *1518 | 634 | 689 | 1370 | 1289 | 1091 | 995 | 404 | 1191 | 1776 | 2038 | 1205 |
| Washington, D.C. | 2644 | 908 | 776 | 1097 | 600 | 686 | 1099 | 225 | 136 | 2274 | 230 | 801 | 2111 | 2869 | 2748 | |

* via Canadian routes.

# U.S. AIR DISTANCES

(See also, AIR DISTANCES BETWEEN MAJOR WORLD CITIES, pp. 234–235)

| | Atlanta | Birmingham | Boston | Buffalo | Charleston, S.C. | Chicago | Cincinnati | Cleveland | Dallas | Denver | Des Moines | Detroit | Houston | Indianapolis | Jacksonville | Kansas City, Mo. | Los Angeles | Louisville | Miami | Minneapolis | Nashville | New Orleans | New York City | Omaha | Philadelphia | Phoenix | Pittsburgh | Portland, Ore. | St. Louis | Salt Lake City | San Francisco | Seattle | Tulsa | Washington, D.C. |
|---|---|---|---|---|---|---|---|---|---|---|---|---|---|---|---|---|---|---|---|---|---|---|---|---|---|---|---|---|---|---|---|---|---|---|
| Albuquerque | 1272 | 1138 | 1972 | 1580 | 1539 | 1129 | 1251 | 1421 | 588 | 334 | 837 | 1364 | 754 | 1169 | 1488 | 720 | 664 | 1178 | 1698 | 983 | 1119 | 1029 | 1815 | 721 | 1753 | 330 | 1499 | 1107 | 942 | 484 | 896 | 1184 | 604 | 1653 |
| Amarillo | 999 | 866 | 1722 | 1338 | 1266 | 894 | 992 | 1173 | 334 | 358 | 626 | 1124 | 533 | 915 | 1219 | 481 | 937 | 915 | 1441 | 812 | 848 | 776 | 1560 | 526 | 1494 | 598 | 1244 | 1304 | 685 | 668 | 1157 | 1359 | 335 | 1391 |
| Atlanta | | 140 | 937 | 697 | 267 | 587 | 369 | 554 | 721 | 1212 | 739 | 596 | 701 | 426 | 285 | 676 | 1936 | 319 | 604 | 907 | 214 | 424 | 748 | 817 | 666 | 1592 | 521 | 2172 | 467 | 1583 | 2139 | 2182 | 678 | 543 |
| Billings | 1519 | 1425 | 1861 | 1473 | 1761 | 1073 | 1304 | 1369 | 1092 | 453 | 798 | 1283 | 1315 | 1204 | 1796 | 846 | 959 | 1275 | 2085 | 742 | 1309 | 1479 | 1760 | 703 | 1727 | 872 | 1479 | 686 | 1057 | 387 | 904 | 668 | 930 | 1669 |
| Birmingham | 140 | | 1052 | 776 | 402 | 578 | 406 | 618 | 581 | 1095 | 670 | 641 | 567 | 433 | 374 | 579 | 1802 | 331 | 665 | 862 | 182 | 312 | 864 | 732 | 783 | 1456 | 608 | 2066 | 400 | 1466 | 2013 | 2082 | 552 | 661 |
| Boston | 937 | 1052 | | 400 | 820 | 851 | 740 | 551 | 1551 | 1769 | 1159 | 613 | 1605 | 807 | 1017 | 1251 | 2596 | 826 | 1255 | 1123 | 943 | 1359 | 188 | 1282 | 271 | 2300 | 483 | 2540 | 1038 | 2099 | 2699 | 2493 | 1398 | 393 |
| Buffalo | 697 | 776 | 400 | | 699 | 454 | 393 | 173 | 1198 | 1370 | 760 | 216 | 1286 | 435 | 879 | 861 | 2198 | 483 | 1181 | 731 | 627 | 1086 | 292 | 883 | 279 | 1906 | 178 | 2156 | 662 | 1699 | 2300 | 2117 | 1023 | 292 |
| Burlington, Vt. | 951 | 1049 | 182 | 304 | 884 | 749 | 690 | 476 | 1501 | 1654 | 1049 | 516 | 1580 | 739 | 1079 | 1161 | 2485 | 780 | 1347 | 985 | 916 | 1361 | 260 | 1171 | 328 | 2202 | 445 | 2385 | 966 | 1969 | 2568 | 2333 | 1327 | 432 |
| Charleston, S.C. | 267 | 402 | 820 | 699 | | 757 | 506 | 609 | 981 | 1474 | 967 | 681 | 936 | 594 | 197 | 928 | 2203 | 500 | 482 | 1104 | 455 | 630 | 641 | 1058 | 562 | 1857 | 528 | 2425 | 704 | 1845 | 2405 | 2428 | 945 | 453 |
| Charlotte | 227 | 361 | 721 | 538 | 177 | 587 | 335 | 435 | 930 | 1358 | 819 | 504 | 927 | 428 | 341 | 803 | 2119 | 343 | 652 | 939 | 340 | 649 | 533 | 918 | 451 | 1783 | 362 | 2290 | 568 | 1727 | 2301 | 2285 | 853 | 330 |
| Cheyenne | 1229 | 1119 | 1735 | 1335 | 1486 | 891 | 1082 | 1199 | 726 | 96 | 583 | 1125 | 947 | 986 | 1493 | 560 | 882 | 1033 | 1763 | 642 | 1032 | 1131 | 1604 | 463 | 1556 | 663 | 1298 | 947 | 795 | 371 | 967 | 973 | 588 | 1477 |
| Chicago | 587 | 578 | 851 | 454 | 757 | | 252 | 308 | 803 | 920 | 309 | 238 | 940 | 165 | 863 | 414 | 1745 | 269 | 1188 | 355 | 397 | 833 | 713 | 432 | 666 | 1453 | 410 | 1758 | 262 | 1260 | 1858 | 1737 | 598 | 597 |
| Cincinnati | 369 | 406 | 740 | 393 | 506 | 252 | | 222 | 814 | 1094 | 510 | 235 | 892 | 100 | 626 | 541 | 1897 | 90 | 952 | 605 | 238 | 706 | 570 | 622 | 503 | 1581 | 257 | 1985 | 309 | 1453 | 2043 | 1972 | 661 | 404 |
| Cleveland | 554 | 618 | 551 | 173 | 609 | 308 | 222 | | 1025 | 1227 | 617 | 90 | 1114 | 263 | 770 | 700 | 2049 | 311 | 1087 | 630 | 459 | 924 | 405 | 739 | 360 | 1749 | 115 | 2055 | 492 | 1568 | 2166 | 2026 | 853 | 306 |
| Dallas | 721 | 581 | 1551 | 1198 | 981 | 803 | 814 | 1025 | | 663 | 632 | 999 | 225 | 763 | 908 | 451 | 1240 | 726 | 1111 | 862 | 617 | 443 | 1374 | 586 | 1299 | 887 | 1070 | 1633 | 547 | 999 | 1483 | 1681 | 236 | 1185 |
| Denver | 1212 | 1095 | 1769 | 1370 | 1474 | 920 | 1094 | 1227 | 663 | | 610 | 1156 | 879 | 1000 | 1467 | 558 | 831 | 1038 | 1726 | 700 | 1023 | 1082 | 1631 | 488 | 1579 | 586 | 1320 | 982 | 796 | 371 | 949 | 1021 | 550 | 1494 |
| Des Moines | 739 | 670 | 1159 | 760 | 967 | 309 | 510 | 617 | 632 | 610 | | 546 | 821 | 411 | 1023 | 180 | 1438 | 476 | 1333 | 235 | 525 | 827 | 1022 | 123 | 973 | 1155 | 715 | 1475 | 273 | 953 | 1550 | 1467 | 396 | 896 |
| Detroit | 596 | 641 | 613 | 216 | 681 | 238 | 235 | 90 | 999 | 1156 | 546 | | 1105 | 240 | 831 | 645 | 1983 | 316 | 1152 | 543 | 470 | 939 | 482 | 669 | 443 | 1690 | 205 | 1969 | 455 | 1492 | 2091 | 1938 | 813 | 396 |
| El Paso | 1291 | 1152 | 2072 | 1692 | 1552 | 1252 | 1335 | 1525 | 572 | 557 | 983 | 1479 | 676 | 1264 | 1473 | 839 | 701 | 1254 | 1643 | 1157 | 1169 | 983 | 1905 | 878 | 1836 | 346 | 1590 | 1286 | 1034 | 689 | 995 | 1376 | 674 | 1728 |
| Fargo | 1114 | 1060 | 1300 | 919 | 1317 | 569 | 820 | 835 | 972 | 642 | 397 | 745 | 1183 | 725 | 1399 | 549 | 1427 | 818 | 1716 | 214 | 902 | 1222 | 1210 | 390 | 1184 | 1225 | 949 | 1239 | 660 | 863 | 1446 | 1197 | 741 | 1140 |
| Houston | 701 | 567 | 1605 | 1286 | 936 | 940 | 892 | 1114 | 225 | 879 | 821 | 1105 | | 865 | 821 | 644 | 1374 | 803 | 968 | 1056 | 665 | 318 | 1420 | 794 | 1341 | 1017 | 1137 | 1836 | 679 | 1200 | 1645 | 1891 | 442 | 1220 |
| Indianapolis | 426 | 433 | 807 | 435 | 594 | 165 | 100 | 263 | 763 | 1000 | 411 | 240 | 865 | | 699 | 453 | 1809 | 107 | 1024 | 511 | 251 | 712 | 646 | 525 | 585 | 1499 | 330 | 1885 | 231 | 1356 | 1949 | 1872 | 591 | 494 |
| Jacksonville | 285 | 374 | 1017 | 879 | 197 | 863 | 626 | 770 | 908 | 1467 | 1023 | 831 | 821 | 699 | | 950 | 2147 | 594 | 326 | 1191 | 499 | 504 | 838 | 1098 | 758 | 1794 | 703 | 2439 | 751 | 1837 | 2374 | 2455 | 921 | 647 |
| Kansas City, Mo. | 676 | 579 | 1251 | 861 | 928 | 414 | 541 | 700 | 451 | 558 | 180 | 645 | 644 | 453 | 950 | | 1356 | 480 | 1241 | 413 | 473 | 680 | 1097 | 166 | 1038 | 1049 | 781 | 1497 | 238 | 925 | 1506 | 1506 | 216 | 945 |
| Knoxville | 155 | 235 | 818 | 548 | 316 | 454 | 219 | 400 | 767 | 1178 | 651 | 442 | 790 | 290 | 410 | 624 | 1941 | 188 | 736 | 792 | 161 | 547 | 632 | 745 | 552 | 1607 | 375 | 2115 | 392 | 1547 | 2121 | 2114 | 676 | 430 |
| Little Rock | 456 | 325 | 1259 | 913 | 723 | 552 | 524 | 740 | 293 | 780 | 478 | 723 | 388 | 483 | 690 | 325 | 1480 | 435 | 949 | 708 | 325 | 355 | 1081 | 492 | 1007 | 1137 | 779 | 1759 | 291 | 1148 | 1688 | 1785 | 231 | 892 |
| Los Angeles | 1936 | 1802 | 2596 | 2198 | 2203 | 1745 | 1897 | 2049 | 1240 | 831 | 1438 | 1983 | 1374 | 1809 | 2147 | 1356 | | 1829 | 2339 | 1524 | 1780 | 1673 | 2451 | 1315 | 2394 | 357 | 2136 | 825 | 1589 | 579 | 347 | 959 | 1266 | 2300 |
| Louisville | 319 | 331 | 826 | 483 | 500 | 269 | 90 | 311 | 726 | 1038 | 476 | 316 | 803 | 107 | 594 | 480 | 1829 | | 919 | 605 | 154 | 623 | 652 | 580 | 582 | 1508 | 344 | 1950 | 242 | 1402 | 1986 | 1943 | 582 | 476 |
| Memphis | 337 | 217 | 1137 | 803 | 604 | 482 | 410 | 630 | 420 | 879 | 485 | 623 | 484 | 384 | 590 | 369 | 1603 | 320 | 872 | 699 | 197 | 358 | 957 | 529 | 881 | 1263 | 660 | 1849 | 240 | 1250 | 1802 | 1867 | 341 | 765 |
| Miami | 604 | 665 | 1255 | 1181 | 482 | 1188 | 952 | 1087 | 1111 | 1726 | 1333 | 1152 | 968 | 1024 | 326 | 1241 | 2339 | 919 | | 1511 | 815 | 669 | 1092 | 1397 | 1019 | 1982 | 1010 | 2708 | 1061 | 2089 | 2594 | 2734 | 1176 | 923 |
| Minneapolis | 907 | 862 | 1123 | 731 | 1104 | 355 | 605 | 630 | 862 | 700 | 235 | 543 | 1056 | 511 | 1191 | 413 | 1524 | 605 | 1511 | | 697 | 1051 | 1018 | 290 | 985 | 1280 | 743 | 1427 | 466 | 987 | 1584 | 1395 | 626 | 934 |
| Nashville | 214 | 182 | 943 | 627 | 455 | 397 | 238 | 459 | 617 | 1023 | 525 | 470 | 665 | 251 | 499 | 473 | 1780 | 154 | 815 | 697 | | 469 | 761 | 607 | 685 | 1446 | 472 | 1969 | 254 | 1393 | 1963 | 1975 | 515 | 569 |
| New Orleans | 424 | 312 | 1359 | 1086 | 630 | 833 | 706 | 924 | 443 | 1082 | 827 | 939 | 318 | 712 | 504 | 680 | 1673 | 623 | 669 | 1051 | 469 | | 1171 | 847 | 1089 | 1316 | 919 | 2063 | 598 | 1434 | 1926 | 2101 | 548 | 966 |
| New York City | 748 | 864 | 188 | 292 | 641 | 713 | 570 | 405 | 1374 | 1631 | 1022 | 482 | 1420 | 646 | 838 | 1097 | 2451 | 652 | 1092 | 1018 | 761 | 1171 | | 1144 | 83 | 2145 | 317 | 2445 | 875 | 1972 | 2571 | 2408 | 1231 | 205 |
| Omaha | 817 | 732 | 1282 | 883 | 1058 | 432 | 622 | 739 | 586 | 488 | 123 | 669 | 794 | 525 | 1098 | 166 | 1315 | 580 | 1397 | 290 | 607 | 847 | 1144 | | 1094 | 1036 | 836 | 1371 | 354 | 833 | 1429 | 1369 | 352 | 1014 |
| Philadelphia | 666 | 783 | 271 | 279 | 562 | 666 | 503 | 360 | 1299 | 1579 | 973 | 443 | 1341 | 585 | 758 | 1038 | 2394 | 582 | 1019 | 985 | 685 | 1089 | 83 | 1094 | | 2083 | 259 | 2412 | 811 | 1925 | 2523 | 2380 | 1163 | 123 |
| Phoenix | 1592 | 1456 | 2300 | 1906 | 1857 | 1453 | 1581 | 1749 | 887 | 586 | 1155 | 1690 | 1017 | 1499 | 1794 | 1049 | 357 | 1508 | 1982 | 1280 | 1446 | 1316 | 2145 | 1036 | 2083 | | 1828 | 1005 | 1272 | 504 | 653 | 1114 | 932 | 1983 |
| Pittsburgh | 521 | 608 | 483 | 178 | 528 | 410 | 257 | 115 | 1070 | 1320 | 715 | 205 | 1137 | 330 | 703 | 781 | 2136 | 344 | 1010 | 743 | 472 | 919 | 317 | 836 | 259 | 1828 | | 2165 | 559 | 1668 | 2264 | 2138 | 917 | 192 |
| Portland, Ore. | 2172 | 2066 | 2540 | 2156 | 2425 | 1758 | 1985 | 2055 | 1633 | 982 | 1475 | 1969 | 1836 | 1885 | 2439 | 1497 | 825 | 1950 | 2708 | 1427 | 1969 | 2063 | 2445 | 1371 | 2412 | 1005 | 2165 | | 1723 | 636 | 534 | 145 | 1531 | 2354 |
| Raleigh | 356 | 491 | 609 | 490 | 220 | 642 | 396 | 428 | 1057 | 1463 | 902 | 510 | 1056 | 495 | 414 | 905 | 2237 | 429 | 695 | 996 | 457 | 776 | 426 | 1008 | 345 | 1903 | 330 | 2377 | 667 | 1829 | 2410 | 2367 | 972 | 233 |
| St. Louis | 467 | 400 | 1038 | 662 | 704 | 262 | 309 | 492 | 547 | 796 | 273 | 455 | 679 | 231 | 751 | 238 | 1589 | 242 | 1061 | 466 | 254 | 598 | 875 | 354 | 811 | 1272 | 559 | 1723 | | 1162 | 1744 | 1724 | 361 | 712 |
| Salt Lake City | 1583 | 1466 | 2099 | 1699 | 1845 | 1260 | 1453 | 1568 | 999 | 371 | 953 | 1492 | 1200 | 1356 | 1837 | 925 | 579 | 1402 | 2089 | 987 | 1393 | 1434 | 1972 | 833 | 1925 | 504 | 1668 | 636 | 1162 | | 600 | 701 | 917 | 1848 |
| San Antonio | 882 | 744 | 1766 | 1430 | 1122 | 1051 | 1039 | 1256 | 252 | 802 | 882 | 1238 | 189 | 999 | 1011 | 702 | 1204 | 949 | 1148 | 1110 | 823 | 507 | 1584 | 828 | 1507 | 849 | 1291 | 1720 | 792 | 1087 | 1490 | 1787 | 486 | 1388 |
| San Francisco | 2139 | 2013 | 2699 | 2300 | 2405 | 1858 | 2043 | 2166 | 1483 | 949 | 1550 | 2091 | 1645 | 1949 | 2374 | 1506 | 347 | 1986 | 2594 | 1584 | 1963 | 1926 | 2571 | 1429 | 2523 | 653 | 2264 | 534 | 1744 | 600 | | 678 | 1461 | 2442 |
| Seattle | 2182 | 2082 | 2493 | 2117 | 2428 | 1737 | 1972 | 2026 | 1681 | 1021 | 1467 | 1938 | 1891 | 1872 | 2455 | 1506 | 959 | 1943 | 2734 | 1395 | 1975 | 2101 | 2408 | 1369 | 2380 | 1114 | 2138 | 145 | 1724 | 701 | 678 | | 1560 | 2329 |
| Spokane | 1961 | 1865 | 2266 | 1888 | 2204 | 1508 | 1744 | 1796 | 1489 | 826 | 1240 | 1709 | 1704 | 1644 | 2237 | 1287 | 940 | 1717 | 2520 | 1166 | 1752 | 1898 | 2179 | 1146 | 2151 | 1019 | 1908 | 290 | 1500 | 550 | 727 | 229 | 1353 | 2100 |
| Syracuse | 781 | 875 | 264 | 138 | 738 | 592 | 514 | 303 | 1326 | 1508 | 898 | 354 | 1403 | 567 | 928 | 998 | 2336 | 603 | 1212 | 861 | 739 | 1187 | 194 | 1021 | 220 | 2044 | 268 | 2281 | 796 | 1835 | 2435 | 2238 | 1157 | 290 |
| Tulsa | 678 | 552 | 1398 | 1023 | 945 | 598 | 661 | 853 | 236 | 550 | 396 | 813 | 442 | 591 | 921 | 216 | 1266 | 582 | 1176 | 626 | 515 | 548 | 1231 | 352 | 1163 | 932 | 917 | 1531 | 361 | 917 | 1461 | 1560 | | 1058 |
| Washington, D.C. | 543 | 661 | 393 | 292 | 453 | 597 | 404 | 306 | 1185 | 1494 | 896 | 396 | 1220 | 494 | 647 | 945 | 2300 | 476 | 923 | 934 | 569 | 966 | 205 | 1014 | 123 | 1983 | 192 | 2354 | 712 | 1848 | 2442 | 2329 | 1058 | |
| Wichita | 776 | 658 | 1424 | 1036 | 1039 | 591 | 702 | 873 | 340 | 437 | 334 | 821 | 559 | 620 | 1031 | 177 | 1197 | 633 | 1297 | 546 | 594 | 677 | 1266 | 257 | 1204 | 879 | 950 | 1411 | 394 | 808 | 1369 | 1437 | 130 | 1106 |

## U.S. RAILROAD DISTANCES

| | Albuquerque | Atlanta | Baltimore | Birmingham | Boston | Buffalo | Chicago | Cincinnati | Cleveland | Dallas | Denver | Des Moines | Detroit | El Paso | Houston | Indianapolis | Jacksonville | Kansas City, Mo. | Los Angeles | Memphis | Miami | Mobile | New Orleans | New York City | Oklahoma City | Philadelphia | Pittsburgh | Portland, Ore. | St. Louis | St. Paul | Salt Lake City | San Francisco | Seattle | Washington, D.C. |
|---|---|---|---|---|---|---|---|---|---|---|---|---|---|---|---|---|---|---|---|---|---|---|---|---|---|---|---|---|---|---|---|---|---|---|
| Albuquerque | | 1554 | 2102 | 1388 | 2356 | 1862 | 1338 | 1528 | 1678 | 723 | 477 | 1108 | 1610 | 253 | 925 | 1430 | 1819 | 887 | 889 | 1135 | 2185 | 1369 | 1229 | 2216 | 648 | 2124 | 1776 | 1849 | 1190 | 1363 | 985 | 1209 | 2031 | 2047 |
| Amarillo | 374 | 1181 | 1728 | 1014 | 2028 | 1534 | 1010 | 1154 | 1339 | 370 | 465 | 780 | 1282 | 444 | 634 | 1056 | 1466 | 559 | 1216 | 761 | 1832 | 1016 | 876 | 1866 | 274 | 1775 | 1427 | 1837 | 816 | 1039 | 973 | 1537 | 2019 | 1690 |
| Altanta | 1554 | | 676 | 167 | 1091 | 934 | 734 | 490 | 750 | 825 | 1526 | 952 | 748 | 1471 | 856 | 585 | 350 | 890 | 2285 | 420 | 716 | 353 | 493 | 862 | 907 | 771 | 806 | 2798 | 612 | 1130 | 2051 | 2718 | 2824 | 638 |
| Baltimore | 2102 | 676 | | 799 | 416 | 395 | 796 | 582 | 459 | 1448 | 1822 | 1154 | 624 | 2095 | 1517 | 691 | 794 | 1198 | 2908 | 967 | 1160 | 1029 | 1154 | 187 | 1454 | 95 | 328 | 3030 | 920 | 1193 | 2310 | 3059 | 2937 | 38 |
| Billings | 1133 | 1921 | 2085 | 1788 | 2296 | 1802 | 1278 | 1559 | 1618 | 1491 | 656 | 1041 | 1550 | 1386 | 1755 | 1462 | 2226 | 1051 | 1452 | 1535 | 2592 | 1958 | 1924 | 2186 | 1394 | 2094 | 1747 | 961 | 1310 | 882 | 669 | 1418 | 903 | 2043 |
| Birmingham | 1388 | 167 | 799 | | 1215 | 925 | 651 | 481 | 741 | 658 | 1373 | 819 | 739 | 1304 | 718 | 503 | 438 | 737 | 2118 | 253 | 804 | 266 | 355 | 986 | 740 | 894 | 797 | 2665 | 479 | 1047 | 1906 | 2551 | 2691 | 761 |
| Boston | 2356 | 1091 | 416 | 1215 | | 494 | 1018 | 938 | 678 | 1864 | 2044 | 1376 | 746 | 2414 | 1933 | 962 | 1210 | 1469 | 3244 | 1382 | 1576 | 1444 | 1569 | 229 | 1743 | 321 | 668 | 3217 | 1202 | 1414 | 2532 | 3281 | 3159 | 454 |
| Buffalo | 1862 | 934 | 395 | 925 | 494 | | 524 | 444 | 184 | 1418 | 1550 | 882 | 252 | 1920 | 1554 | 468 | 1190 | 975 | 2750 | 938 | 1556 | 1191 | 1280 | 396 | 1249 | 415 | 260 | 2723 | 708 | 920 | 2038 | 2787 | 2665 | 434 |
| Butte | 1369 | 2157 | 2305 | 2024 | 2526 | 2032 | 1514 | 1795 | 1854 | 1727 | 892 | 1377 | 1780 | 1622 | 1991 | 1692 | 2462 | 1287 | 1216 | 1771 | 2828 | 2194 | 2160 | 2416 | 1631 | 2330 | 1983 | 725 | 1546 | 1112 | 433 | 1182 | 667 | 2273 |
| Cheyenne | 583 | 1532 | 1791 | 1399 | 2013 | 1519 | 995 | 1259 | 1335 | 941 | 106 | 652 | 1267 | 836 | 1205 | 1161 | 1877 | 702 | 1302 | 1186 | 2243 | 1569 | 1447 | 1903 | 845 | 1811 | 1463 | 1266 | 921 | 855 | 519 | 1268 | 1448 | 1759 |
| Chicago | 1338 | 734 | 796 | 651 | 1018 | 524 | | 281 | 340 | 968 | 1026 | 358 | 272 | 1396 | 1205 | 184 | 1083 | 451 | 2227 | 527 | 1449 | 917 | 921 | 908 | 794 | 816 | 468 | 2199 | 284 | 396 | 1514 | 2263 | 2141 | 764 |
| Cincinnati | 1528 | 490 | 582 | 481 | 938 | 444 | 281 | | 260 | 975 | 1252 | 639 | 258 | 1561 | 1110 | 109 | 840 | 616 | 2370 | 494 | 1206 | 747 | 836 | 755 | 880 | 664 | 316 | 2470 | 338 | 677 | 1778 | 2527 | 2422 | 544 |
| Cleveland | 1678 | 750 | 459 | 741 | 678 | 184 | 340 | 260 | | 1234 | 1366 | 698 | 164 | 1736 | 1370 | 283 | 1100 | 791 | 2555 | 754 | 1466 | 1007 | 1096 | 571 | 1065 | 479 | 131 | 2539 | 523 | 736 | 1854 | 2603 | 2481 | 427 |
| Columbia, S.C. | 1801 | 254 | 515 | 420 | 930 | 910 | 867 | 586 | 846 | 1078 | 1747 | 1173 | 844 | 1724 | 1110 | 681 | 280 | 1111 | 2538 | 673 | 646 | 607 | 747 | 701 | 1160 | 610 | 772 | 3019 | 833 | 1263 | 2272 | 2971 | 3045 | 476 |
| Dallas | 723 | 825 | 1448 | 658 | 1864 | 1418 | 968 | 975 | 1234 | | 835 | 738 | 1200 | 646 | 264 | 951 | 1096 | 517 | 1460 | 481 | 1462 | 646 | 506 | 1635 | 236 | 1543 | 1291 | 2227 | 711 | 997 | 1343 | 1930 | 2394 | 1410 |
| Denver | 477 | 1526 | 1822 | 1373 | 2044 | 1550 | 1026 | 1252 | 1366 | 835 | | 683 | 1298 | 730 | 1099 | 1154 | 1811 | 636 | 1353 | 1120 | 2177 | 1481 | 1341 | 1934 | 739 | 1842 | 1494 | 1372 | 914 | 886 | 570 | 1374 | 1554 | 1790 |
| Des Moines | 1108 | 952 | 1154 | 819 | 1376 | 882 | 358 | 639 | 698 | 738 | 683 | | 630 | 1166 | 1002 | 542 | 1301 | 221 | 1954 | 645 | 1667 | 988 | 1039 | 1266 | 565 | 1174 | 826 | 1918 | 340 | 259 | 1171 | 1920 | 1944 | 1122 |
| Detroit | 1610 | 748 | 624 | 739 | 746 | 252 | 272 | 258 | 164 | 1200 | 1298 | 630 | | 1668 | 1368 | 303 | 1098 | 723 | 2499 | 752 | 1464 | 1005 | 1094 | 648 | 1031 | 644 | 296 | 2505 | 489 | 668 | 1786 | 2535 | 2413 | 592 |
| Duluth | 1515 | 1202 | 1265 | 1119 | 1486 | 992 | 468 | 749 | 808 | 1149 | 1038 | 411 | 740 | 1577 | 1413 | 652 | 1551 | 632 | 2309 | 1031 | 1917 | 1374 | 1425 | 1376 | 976 | 1285 | 937 | 1820 | 726 | 152 | 1526 | 2275 | 1762 | 1233 |
| El Paso | 253 | 1471 | 2095 | 1304 | 2414 | 1920 | 1396 | 1561 | 1736 | 646 | 730 | 1166 | 1668 | | 827 | 1500 | 1764 | 945 | 814 | 1128 | 2130 | 1292 | 1152 | 2310 | 718 | 2190 | 1834 | 2002 | 1223 | 1425 | 1238 | 1284 | 2184 | 2056 |
| Fargo | 1605 | 1372 | 1435 | 1289 | 1656 | 1162 | 638 | 919 | 978 | 1239 | 1128 | 501 | 910 | 1667 | 1503 | 822 | 1721 | 722 | 2092 | 1121 | 2087 | 1464 | 1515 | 1546 | 1066 | 1454 | 1107 | 1601 | 816 | 242 | 1309 | 2058 | 1503 | 1403 |
| Houston | 925 | 856 | 1517 | 718 | 1933 | 1554 | 1205 | 1110 | 1370 | 264 | 1099 | 1002 | 1368 | 827 | | 1107 | 975 | 781 | 1641 | 616 | 1341 | 503 | 363 | 1703 | 500 | 1612 | 1426 | 2491 | 921 | 1261 | 1607 | 2111 | 2656 | 1478 |
| Indianapolis | 1430 | 585 | 691 | 503 | 962 | 468 | 184 | 109 | 283 | 951 | 1154 | 542 | 303 | 1500 | 1107 | | 935 | 518 | 2272 | 491 | 1301 | 769 | 858 | 811 | 782 | 719 | 371 | 2427 | 241 | 580 | 1680 | 2429 | 2325 | 653 |
| Jacksonville | 1819 | 350 | 794 | 438 | 1210 | 1190 | 1083 | 840 | 1100 | 1096 | 1811 | 1301 | 1098 | 1764 | 975 | 935 | | 1175 | 2578 | 691 | 366 | 472 | 612 | 981 | 1178 | 890 | 1052 | 3148 | 917 | 1479 | 2344 | 2989 | 3129 | 756 |
| Kansas City, Mo. | 887 | 890 | 1198 | 737 | 1469 | 975 | 451 | 616 | 791 | 517 | 636 | 221 | 723 | 945 | 781 | 518 | 1175 | | 1776 | 484 | 1541 | 926 | 873 | 1329 | 343 | 1237 | 889 | 1968 | 278 | 480 | 1206 | 1970 | 1954 | 1160 |
| Knoxville | 1556 | 197 | 545 | 254 | 961 | 737 | 574 | 296 | 553 | 903 | 1454 | 880 | 551 | 1549 | 972 | 388 | 547 | 818 | 2363 | 422 | 913 | 520 | 609 | 732 | 909 | 640 | 609 | 2726 | 540 | 970 | 2001 | 2720 | 2715 | 507 |
| Los Angeles | 889 | 2285 | 2908 | 2118 | 3244 | 2750 | 2227 | 2370 | 2555 | 1460 | 1353 | 1954 | 2499 | 814 | 1641 | 2272 | 2578 | 1776 | | 1942 | 2944 | 2106 | 1966 | 3082 | 1490 | 2991 | 2643 | 1188 | 2032 | 2157 | 783 | 470 | 1370 | 2906 |
| Louisville | 1463 | 474 | 696 | 392 | 1052 | 558 | 295 | 114 | 374 | 861 | 1188 | 614 | 372 | 1508 | 996 | 111 | 824 | 552 | 2306 | 380 | 1190 | 658 | 747 | 869 | 867 | 778 | 430 | 2460 | 274 | 691 | 1713 | 2462 | 2486 | 658 |
| Memphis | 1135 | 420 | 967 | 253 | 1382 | 938 | 527 | 494 | 754 | 481 | 1120 | 645 | 752 | 1128 | 616 | 491 | 691 | 484 | 1942 | | 1057 | 394 | 394 | 1153 | 487 | 1062 | 810 | 2496 | 305 | 879 | 1653 | 2298 | 2438 | 929 |
| Miami | 2185 | 716 | 1160 | 804 | 1576 | 1556 | 1449 | 1206 | 1466 | 1462 | 2177 | 1667 | 1464 | 2130 | 1341 | 1301 | 366 | 1541 | 2944 | 1057 | | 838 | 978 | 1347 | 1544 | 1256 | 1418 | 3514 | 1283 | 1845 | 2710 | 3355 | 3495 | 1122 |
| Mobile | 1369 | 353 | 1029 | 266 | 1444 | 1191 | 917 | 747 | 1007 | 646 | 1481 | 988 | 1005 | 1292 | 503 | 769 | 472 | 926 | 2106 | 394 | 838 | | 140 | 1215 | 871 | 1124 | 1063 | 2872 | 648 | 1222 | 1988 | 2553 | 2861 | 991 |
| Nashville | 1374 | 288 | 761 | 205 | 1177 | 745 | 446 | 301 | 561 | 720 | 1238 | 664 | 559 | 1367 | 855 | 298 | 637 | 602 | 2181 | 239 | 1003 | 471 | 560 | 948 | 726 | 856 | 617 | 2511 | 324 | 842 | 1892 | 2537 | 2537 | 723 |
| New Orleans | 1229 | 493 | 1154 | 355 | 1569 | 1280 | 921 | 836 | 1096 | 506 | 1341 | 1039 | 1094 | 1152 | 363 | 858 | 612 | 873 | 1966 | 394 | 978 | 140 | | 1355 | 742 | 1264 | 1152 | 2732 | 699 | 1273 | 1848 | 2436 | 2900 | 1115 |
| New York City | 2216 | 862 | 187 | 986 | 229 | 396 | 908 | 755 | 571 | 1635 | 1934 | 1266 | 648 | 2310 | 1703 | 811 | 981 | 1329 | 3082 | 1153 | 1347 | 1215 | 1355 | | 1592 | 91 | 439 | 3107 | 1051 | 1304 | 2422 | 3171 | 3049 | 225 |
| Oklahoma City | 648 | 907 | 1454 | 740 | 1743 | 1249 | 794 | 880 | 1065 | 236 | 739 | 565 | 1031 | 718 | 500 | 782 | 1178 | 343 | 1490 | 487 | 1544 | 871 | 742 | 1592 | | 1501 | 1153 | 2131 | 542 | 824 | 1247 | 1811 | 2293 | 1424 |
| Omaha | 1015 | 1025 | 1284 | 892 | 1506 | 1012 | 488 | 752 | 828 | 712 | 538 | 145 | 760 | 1140 | 976 | 654 | 1330 | 195 | 1809 | 679 | 1696 | 1062 | 1068 | 1396 | 538 | 1304 | 956 | 1773 | 414 | 348 | 1026 | 1775 | 1799 | 1252 |
| Philadelphia | 2124 | 771 | 95 | 894 | 321 | 415 | 816 | 664 | 479 | 1543 | 1842 | 1174 | 644 | 2190 | 1612 | 719 | 890 | 1237 | 2991 | 1062 | 1256 | 1124 | 1264 | 91 | 1501 | | 348 | 3015 | 959 | 1212 | 2330 | 3079 | 2957 | 133 |
| Pittsburgh | 1776 | 806 | 328 | 797 | 668 | 260 | 468 | 316 | 131 | 1291 | 1494 | 826 | 296 | 1834 | 1426 | 371 | 1052 | 889 | 2643 | 810 | 1418 | 1063 | 1152 | 439 | 1153 | 348 | | 2668 | 611 | 865 | 1982 | 2731 | 2610 | 296 |
| Portland, Ore. | 1849 | 2798 | 3030 | 2665 | 3217 | 2723 | 2199 | 2470 | 2539 | 2227 | 1372 | 1918 | 2505 | 2002 | 2491 | 2427 | 3148 | 1968 | 1188 | 2496 | 3514 | 2872 | 2732 | 3107 | 2131 | 3015 | 2668 | | 2187 | 1803 | 884 | 718 | 182 | 3025 |
| Richmond | 2038 | 579 | 155 | 735 | 570 | 550 | 862 | 581 | 544 | 1385 | 1833 | 1220 | 708 | 2031 | 1435 | 690 | 640 | 1197 | 2845 | 903 | 1006 | 932 | 1072 | 341 | 1390 | 250 | 413 | 3095 | 919 | 1258 | 2359 | 3108 | 3003 | 117 |
| St. Louis | 1190 | 612 | 920 | 479 | 1202 | 708 | 284 | 338 | 523 | 711 | 914 | 340 | 489 | 1223 | 921 | 240 | 917 | 278 | 2032 | 305 | 1283 | 648 | 699 | 1051 | 542 | 959 | 611 | 2187 | | 574 | 1440 | 2189 | 2213 | 882 |
| St. Paul | 1363 | 1130 | 1193 | 1047 | 1414 | 920 | 396 | 677 | 736 | 997 | 886 | 259 | 668 | 1425 | 1261 | 580 | 1479 | 480 | 2157 | 879 | 1845 | 1222 | 1273 | 1304 | 824 | 1212 | 865 | 1803 | 574 | | 1374 | 2123 | 1745 | 1161 |
| Salt Lake City | 985 | 2051 | 2310 | 1906 | 2532 | 2038 | 1514 | 1778 | 1854 | 1343 | 570 | 1171 | 1786 | 1238 | 1607 | 1680 | 2344 | 1206 | 783 | 1653 | 2710 | 1988 | 1848 | 2422 | 1247 | 2330 | 1982 | 884 | 1440 | 1374 | | 821 | 1066 | 2278 |
| San Antonio | 870 | 1066 | 1720 | 928 | 2125 | 1631 | 1208 | 1247 | 1447 | 271 | 1083 | 1009 | 1413 | 617 | 210 | 1164 | 1185 | 788 | 1431 | 753 | 1551 | 713 | 573 | 1906 | 507 | 1815 | 1535 | 2498 | 924 | 1268 | 1614 | 1901 | 2666 | 1681 |
| San Francisco | 1209 | 2718 | 3059 | 2551 | 3281 | 2787 | 2263 | 2527 | 2603 | 1930 | 1374 | 1920 | 2535 | 1284 | 2111 | 2429 | 2989 | 1970 | 470 | 2298 | 3355 | 2553 | 2436 | 3171 | 1811 | 3079 | 2731 | 718 | 2189 | 2123 | 821 | | 900 | 3028 |
| Seattle | 2031 | 2824 | 2937 | 2691 | 3159 | 2665 | 2141 | 2422 | 2481 | 2394 | 1554 | 1944 | 2413 | 2184 | 2656 | 2325 | 3129 | 1954 | 1370 | 2438 | 3495 | 2861 | 2900 | 3049 | 2293 | 2957 | 2610 | 182 | 2213 | 1745 | 1066 | 900 | | 2906 |
| Spokane | 1726 | 2514 | 2628 | 2381 | 2849 | 2355 | 1831 | 2112 | 2171 | 2084 | 1249 | 1634 | 2103 | 1979 | 2348 | 2015 | 2819 | 1644 | 1556 | 2128 | 3185 | 2551 | 2590 | 2739 | 1987 | 2647 | 2300 | 368 | 1903 | 1435 | 790 | 1086 | 310 | 2596 |
| Tucson | 565 | 1783 | 2407 | 1616 | 2726 | 2232 | 1708 | 1873 | 2048 | 958 | 1042 | 1478 | 1980 | 312 | 1139 | 1775 | 2076 | 1257 | 502 | 1440 | 2442 | 1604 | 1464 | 2586 | 1030 | 2494 | 2146 | 1690 | 1572 | 1737 | 1285 | 972 | 1872 | 2368 |
| Washington, D.C. | 2047 | 638 | 38 | 761 | 454 | 434 | 764 | 544 | 427 | 1410 | 1790 | 1122 | 592 | 2056 | 1478 | 653 | 756 | 1160 | 2906 | 929 | 1122 | 991 | 1115 | 225 | 1424 | 133 | 296 | 3025 | 882 | 1161 | 2278 | 3028 | 2906 | |
| Wichita | 721 | 986 | 1401 | 819 | 1681 | 1187 | 663 | 819 | 1003 | 408 | 580 | 433 | 935 | 791 | 672 | 721 | 1257 | 212 | 1563 | 566 | 1623 | 1053 | 913 | 1532 | 172 | 1440 | 1092 | 1971 | 481 | 692 | 1087 | 1884 | 2139 | 1363 |

## TOLL-FREE TELEPHONE NUMBERS

The following lists contain the toll-free telephone numbers for airlines, hotels, motels, and car rental companies. Airline companies often have local telephone numbers for reservations and information. If no local number is listed, dial 800 followed by the number given in the first column. In Atlanta and New York precede all 800 numbers with "1."

| AIRLINES | 800 Toll-Free Number | ATLANTA | CHICAGO | LOS ANGELES | NEW YORK | WASHINGTON, D.C. |
|---|---|---|---|---|---|---|
| Aer Lingus Irish | 223-6537 | | | | 212 557-1110 | |
| Aerocondor | | | | | | 800 327-0743 |
| Aeroflot | | | | | 212 661-4050 | 202 296-8060 |
| Aerolineas Argentinas | 327-0276 | | | | 212 974-3300 | 202 296-3863 |
| Aeromexico | 223-9780 | | | 213 380-6030 | 212 391-2900 | |
| Aero Perú | | | 312 726-2587 | 800 327-4363 | | |
| Air Canada | 327-4286 | | 312 527-3900 | 213 776-7000 | 212 869-1900 | 202 659-0198 |
| Air Florida | | 800 327-2971 | 800 327-2971 | | 800 327-2971 | 800 327-2971 |
| Air France | | 800 221-2110 | 312 782-6181 | 213 625-7171 | 212 247-0100 | 202 337-8711 |
| Air India | 223-7776 | | 312 782-6263 | | 212 751-6200 | |
| Air Jamaica | | 800 523-5585 | 312 527-3923 | 800 523-5618 | 212 421-9750 | |
| Air New Zealand | 421-5540 | | | 213 776-8790 | | |
| Air Panama Internacional | | | 312 564-5120 | 213 661-6286 | 800 329-2417 | |
| Alaska Airlines | 426-0333 | | | | | |
| Alitalia | 223-5730 | | 312 427-4720 | | 212 582-8900 | 202 393-2829 |
| American | 433-7300 | 404 521-2655 | 312 372-8000 | 213 935-6045 | 212 661-1500 | 202 393-2345 |
| Avianca | | | 312 346-8252 | 213 626-6656 | 212 399-0800 | 202 347-3626 |
| Aviateca International | | | 312 236-6941 | | | |
| Bahamasair | 327-8080 | | | | | |
| British Airways | | 800 327-9722 | 312 332-7744 | 213 272-8866 | 212 687-1600 | 202 393-5300 |
| B.W.I.A. International | | | | 800 327-7401 | 212 581-3200 | |
| CP Air | 426-7000 | | | 213 625-0131 | | |
| Capitol International | 223-6365 | | 312 347-0230 | 213 986-8445 | 212 883-0750 | |
| Cathay Pacific | | | | | 212 541-9750 | 202 833-9393 |
| China Airlines | | 0-WX-6935 | 312 427-2920 | 213 624-1161 | 212 581-6500 | 202 833-1760 |
| Commuter Airlines | | | | | 800 252-1490 | 800 847-1712 |
| Continental | 525-0280[1] | 800 525-0280 | 312 686-6500 | 213 772-6000 | 212 974-0028 | 202 628-6666 |
| Czechoslovak Air Lines | | | 312 372-1551 | | 212 682-5833 | |
| Delta Air Lines | | 404 765-5000 | 312 346-5300 | 213 386-5510 | 212 239-0700 | 202 920-5500 |
| Eastern Air Lines | | 404 435-1111 | 312 467-2900 | 213 380-2070 | (D) 212 986-5000<br>(I) 212 661-3500 | 202 393-4000 |
| Ecuatoriana Airlines | | | 312 332-0063 | 213 627-8844 | 212 247-8844 | |
| El Al Israel Airlines | 223-6280 | | | 800 223-6700 | 212 486-2600 | |
| Ethiopian Airlines | | 404 588-9476 | 312 663-4100 | 213 462-7291 | 212 867-0095 | 202 363-0207 |
| Finnair | | 800 223-5308 | 312 296-1144 | 800 223-5700 | 212 889-7070 | 800 223-5260 |
| Frontier Airlines | | 404 523-5487 | 312 686-6294 | 213 617-3606 | | |
| Gulf Air | | | 312 269-0076 | 213 879-3645 | 212 986-4500 | 202 296-2910 |
| Hawaiian Airlines | | 404 921-9339 | 312 236-5196 | 213 640-1040 | 212 355-4843 | 800 367-5320 |
| Iberia Air Lines of Spain | 221-9640 | | | 800 221-9741 | 212 793-3300 | |
| Icelandair | 223-5390 | | | 800 223-5500 | 212 757-8585 | 800 223-5190 |
| Japan Air Lines | 223-5405 | | 312 263-1384 | 213 620-9580 | 212 838-4400 | |
| KLM Royal Dutch Airlines | 223-5322 | | 312 346-3635 | 213 776-6300 | 212 759-3600 | |
| Korean Airlines | 223-1155 | 404 522-7461 | 312 558-9300 | 213 484-1900 | 212 371-4820 | |
| Kuwait Airlines | | | 312 263-3858 | 213 627-1485 | 212 581-9412 | 202 296-4644 |
| Lacsa | | | | 213 385-2272 | 212 245-6370 | |
| Lan-Chile Airlines | 327-3614 | | | | | |
| Lot Polish Airlines | | | 312 236-3388 | | 212 869-1074 | |
| Lufthansa German Airlines | 645-3880 | | | | 212 895-1277 | 800 645-3860 |
| Mexicana Airlines | 531-7921 | 404 237-8661 | 800 421-2150 | 213 646-9500 | | |
| Midway Airlines | | | 312 471-4710 | | 800 621-5700 | 800 621-5700 |
| National Airlines | see Pan Am | | | | | |
| New York Air | | | | | 212 565-1100 | 202 588-2300 |
| Northwest Orient | | (D) 404 577-3271<br>(I) 404 577-4843 | (D) 312 346-4900<br>(I) 312 346-6570 | (D) 213 380-1511<br>(I) 213 383-5480 | (D) 212 564-2300<br>(I) 212 563-7200 | (D) 202 337-0611<br>(I) 202 337-0666 |
| Olympic Airways | | 212 838-3600 | 212 838-3600 | 212 624-6441 | 212 838-3600 | 800 223-1226 |
| Ozark Air Lines | | 404 688-9565 | 312 726-4680 | | 212 586-3612 | 202 347-4744 |

[1]except Colo. (D) domestic. (I) international.

| AIRLINES | 800 Toll-Free Number | ATLANTA | CHICAGO | LOS ANGELES | NEW YORK | WASHINGTON, D.C. |
|---|---|---|---|---|---|---|
| Pakistan International | | | 312 263-3082 | | 212 949-0488 | 202 296-1755 |
| Pan Am | | 404 588-9619 | 312 332-4900 | 213 670-7301 | 212 973-4000 | 202 833-1000 |
| People Express | | | | | 212 772-0344 | 202 488-0981 |
| Philippine Airlines | 227-4600 | | | 800 652-1555 | | |
| Piedmont Airlines | | 404 681-3100 | 312 263-3656 | | 212 489-1460 | 202 347-1800 |
| Qantas Airways | 227-4500 | | | 800 622-0850 | | 202 223-3030 |
| Republic Airlines | | 404 762-5561 | 312 346-9860 | 213 772-5100 | 212 581-8851 | 202 347-0448 |
| Sabena Belgian World Airlines | 645-3790 | | | 800 645-1382 | 212 961-6200 | 800 645-3933 |
| SAS Scandinavian Airlines | 221-2350 | | | 213 655-8600 | 212 657-7700 | |
| Singapore Airlines | 421-3133 | | 312 332-6780 | 213 655-9270 | | |
| South African Airways | | 0-WX-6477 | 800 223-1160 | 800 622-0622 | 212 826-1245 | |
| Swissair | 221-4750 | | | | 212 995-8400 | |
| TAN-SAHSA Honduras Airlines | | | 312 236-3246 | 213 485-0261 | 212 730-0800 | 800 327-1225 |
| TAP The Airline of Portugal | 221-2061 | | | 800 221-7370 | 212 944-2100 | |
| Thai Airways International | 426-5204 | | | 800 426-5030 | | |
| Trans Australian Airlines | | | 312 329-1266 | 213 626-2352 | 800 227-4500 | |
| Trans World Airlines | | 404 522-5738 | (D) 312 558-7000<br>(I) 312 332-1118 | 213 484-2244 | 212 290-2121 | 202 737-7400 |
| Transamerica Airlines | 227-2888 | | | 800 772-2694 | | |
| UTA French Airlines | 221-2110 | 404 581-0520 | 312 782-6181 | 213 625-7171 | 212 247-0100 | |
| United Airlines | | 404 394-2234 | 312 569-3000 | 213 772-2121 | 212 867-3000 | 202 893-3400 |
| U.S. Air | | 800 245-1640 | 312 726-1201 | | 212 736-3200 | 202 783-4500 |
| Varig Brazilian Airlines | 223-5720 | | | 800 223-5720 | 212 682-3100 | |
| Viasa Venezuelan International Airways | | 800 327-5454 | 800 327-5454 | 800 327-5454 | 800 221-2150 | 800 221-2150 |
| Western Airlines | | | | 213 776-2311 | 212 966-1646 | 202 737-4825 |
| World Airways | 526-8340 | | 800 227-1057 | 800 772-2600 | 212 267-7111 | 202 298-7155 |
| Yugoslav (JAT) Airlines | | | 312 782-1322 | 213 388-0379 | 212 785-4050 | |

(D) domestic. (I) international.

| HOTELS and MOTELS | Telephone Number |
|---|---|
| Admiral Benbow Inns (except Tenn.) | 800 238-6877 |
| Americana Hotels (except N.Y.) | 800 228-3278 |
| Best Western Motels (except Ariz.) | 800 528-1234 |
| Days Inns (except Ga.) | 800 241-2340 |
| Econo Travel (except Va.) | 800 446-6900 |
| Four Seasons Hotels (except N.Y.) | 800 828-1188 |
| Friendship Inns of America Int'l | 800 453-4511 |
| Guest Quarters | 800 424-2900 |
| Hilton Hotels | |
| In Atlanta: | 404 659-1515 |
| In Boston: | 617 357-8320 |
| In Chicago: | 312 346-2772 |
| In Los Angeles: | 213 628-6231 |
| In New York City: | 212 594-4500 |
| Holiday Inns | 800 238-8000 |
| Howard Johnson Motor Lodges (except Okla.) | 800 654-2000 |
| Hyatt Hotels | 800 228-9000 |
| Imperial 400 Motels (except Texas) | 800 531-5300 |
| Marriott Hotels | 800 228-9290 |
| Master Hosts Inns (except Fla.) | 800 327-9073 |
| Omni International Hotels (except Ga.) | 800 241-5500 |
| Playboy Club-Hotels | 800 621-1116 |
| Princess Hotels | 800 223-1818 |
| Quality Inns (except Nebr.) | 800 228-5151 |
| Radisson Hotels (except Nebr.) | 800 228-9822 |
| Ramada Inns (except Nebr.) | 800 228-2828 |
| Red Carpet Inns of America (except Mich.) | 800 327-9073 |

| HOTELS and MOTELS | Telephone Number |
|---|---|
| Rockresorts | |
| In Atlanta: | 1 800 223-7637 |
| In Boston: | 1 800 223-7637 |
| In Chicago: | 312 266-0609 |
| In Los Angeles: | 213 846-9611 |
| In New York: | 212 586-4459 |
| Rodeway Inns of America | 800 228-2000 |
| Sheraton Hotels (except Mo.) | 800 325-3535 |
| Sonesta Hotels (except Mass.) | 800 343-7170 |
| Stouffer Hotels (except Ohio) | 800 321-6888 |
| Travelodge Motels (except Kans.) | 800 255-3050 |
| Treadway Inns (except N.J.) | 800 631-0182 |
| Trust Houses Forte Hotels (except N.Y.) | 800 223-5672 |
| Westin Hotels | 800 228-3000 |

**CAR RENTAL COMPANIES**

| | |
|---|---|
| Agency Rent-a-Car | 800 321-1972 |
| Ajax Rent-A-Car | 800 421-0896 |
| Avis Rent a Car | 800 331-1212 |
| Budget Rent A Car | 800 527-0700 |
| Dollar Rent-a-Car | 800 421-6868 |
| Econo-Car | 800 228-1000 |
| Greyhound Rent-a-Car | 800 327-2501 |
| Hertz Rent A Car | 800 654-3131 |
| National Car Rental | 800 328-4567 |
| Sears Rent a Car | 800 527-0770 |
| Thrifty Rent A Car | 800 331-4200 |

## THE NATIONAL PARK SYSTEM

SOURCE: National Park Service, U.S. Department of the Interior

| Park Service Areas | Number |
|---|---|
| National Parks | 48 |
| National Historical Parks | 26 |
| National Monuments | 78 |
| National Military Parks | 10 |
| National Battlefields | 10 |
| National Seashores | 10 |
| National Battlefield Parks | 3 |
| National Battlefield Sites | 1 |
| National Historic Sites | 62 |
| National Memorials | 23 |
| National Parkways | 4 |
| National Capital Parks | 1 |
| White House | 1 |
| National Recreation Areas | 17 |
| National Lakeshores | 4 |
| National Rivers (wild and scenic) | 11 |
| National Scenic Trail | 1 |
| National Preserves | 12 |
| "Other" Parks | 10 |
| National Mall | 1 |
| Total | 333 |

## OUR NATIONAL PARKS

**Acadia National Park, Maine;** (gross acreage, 39,055.75). Rugged coastal area on Mount Desert Island, highest elevation on eastern seaboard; picturesque Schoodic peninsula on mainland. Includes Isle au Haut. Sieur de Monts Nat'l Mon. est. 1916; est. as Lafayette Nat'l Park 1919; changed to Acadia Nat'l Park 1929. Visits (1981):3,402,973

**Arches National Park, Utah;** (gross acreage, 73,378.98). Extraordinary products of erosion in the form of giant arches, windows, pinnacles, and pedestals. Proclaimed as a nat'l mon. 1929; est. as a nat'l park 1971. Visits (1981): 326,508

**Badlands National Park, South Dakota;** (gross acreage, 243,302.33). Carved by erosion, this scenic landscape contains animal fossils of 40 million years ago, and supports bison, bighorn sheep, deer, and antelope. Authorized 1929; wilderness designated 1976; renamed nat'l park 1978. Visits (1981): 1,187,952

**Big Bend National Park, Texas;** (gross acreage, 741,118.40). Spectacular mountain and desert scenery; variety of unusual geological formations in the great bend of the Rio Grande. Authorized 1935; est. 1944. Visits (1981): 201,603

**Biscayne National Park, Florida;** (gross acreage, 180,127.65). Part of the only coral reefs in North America, this aquatic park contains a chain of islands, Biscayne Bay, and rare marine species. Authorized as a nat'l mon. 1968; est. as a nat'l park 1980. Visits (1981): 305,502

**Bryce Canyon National Park, Utah;** (gross acreage, 35,835.08). Along the edge of the Paunsaugunt Plateau of southern Utah stand innumerable highly colored and grotesque pinnacles, walls, and spires. Bryce Canyon Nat'l Mon. est. 1923; Utah Nat'l Park authorized 1924; changed to Bryce Canyon Nat'l Park 1928. Est. 1928. Visits (1981): 481,549

**Canyonlands National Park, Utah;** (gross acreage, 337,570.43). Geological wonderland of rock, spires, and mesas rising more than 7,800 feet. Extensive and sometimes large petroglyphs (stone carvings) chipped by prehistoric Indians about 1,000 years ago. Est. 1964. Visits (1981): 90,920

**Capitol Reef National Park, Utah;** (gross acreage, 241,904.26). Sixty-mile uplift of sandstone cliffs, with highly colored sedimentary formations dissected by narrow high-walled gorges. Dome-shaped white rock along the Fremont River accounts for the name. Proclaimed as a nat'l mon. 1937; est. as a nat'l park 1971. Visits (1981): 431,388

**Carlsbad Caverns National Park, New Mexico;** (gross acreage, 46,755.33). A series of connected caverns with countless magnificent and curious formations. Carlsbad Cave Nat'l Mon. est. 1923; Carlsbad Caverns Nat'l Park est. 1930. Visits (1981): 771,766

**Channel Islands National Park, California;** (gross acreage, 249,353.77). Est. as a nat'l mon. in 1938, and as a nat'l park in 1980, Channel Islands Nat'l Park is rich in marine life and aquatic recreation, and has the only northern fur seal breeding colony south of Alaska. Visits (1981): 109,417

**Crater Lake National Park, Oregon;** (gross acreage, 160,290.33). Lake of deepest blue in heart of once-active volcano, Mt. Mazama; encircled by multicolored lava walls 500 to 2,000 feet high. Est. 1902. Visits (1981): 536,719

**Denali National Park, Alaska;** (gross acreage, 4,698;583.00). Mount McKinley, highest mountain (20,320 feet) in North America; large glaciers of the Alaska Range; caribou, Dall sheep, moose, grizzly bears, wolves. Est. 1917. Visits (1981): 518,864

**Everglades National Park, Florida;** (gross acreage, 1,398,800.00). Largest remaining subtropical wilderness in conterminous United States; extensive fresh- and salt-water areas, open Everglades prairies, mangrove forests; abundant wildlife, including rare birds. Authorized 1934. Est. 1947. Visits (1981): 622,943

**Gates of the Arctic National Park, Alaska;** (gross acreage, 7,498,066.00). Contains broad valleys, meandering rivers, and the jagged peaks of the Central Brooks Range. Caribou, wolves, grizzly bears and Dall sheep share the habitat. Proclaimed a nat'l mon. 1978; est. as a nat'l park 1980.

**Glacier Bay National Park, Alaska** (gross acreage, 3,020,396) Noted for its glaciers, whales, brown bears, mountain goats, seals and eagles. Mount Fairweather is the highest peak in southeast Alaska. Proclaimed a nat'l mon. 1925; est. as a nat'l park 1980. Visits (1981): 119,372

**Glacier National Park, Montana;** (gross acreage, 1,013,594.67). Superb Rocky Mountain scenery, with numerous glaciers and lakes est peaks; forms part of Waterton-Glacier International Peace Park, est. 1932. Est. 1910. Visits (1981): 1,786,843

**Grand Canyon National Park, Arizona;** (gross acreage, 1,218,375.24). Most spectacular part of the Colorado River's greatest canyon; exposure of rocks representing vast geologic time. First Grand Canyon Nat'l Mon. est. 1908; nat'l park est. 1919. Marble Canyon and second Grand Canyon Nat'l Mons. and other lands absorbed 1975. Visits (1981): 2,693,194

**Grand Teton National Park, Wyoming;** (gross acreage, 310,516.23). Series of peaks comprising the most impressive part of the Teton range; once a noted landmark of Indians and "Mountain Men." Includes part of Jackson Hole; winter feeding ground of largest American elk herd. Est. 1929. Visits (1981); 3,598,454

**Great Smoky Mts. National Park, N.C.-Tenn.;** (gross acreage, 520,269.44). Loftiest range east of the Black Hills and one of the oldest uplands on earth. Diversified and luxuriant plant life, often of extraordinary size. Authorized 1926; est. for administration and protection only 1930; est. for full development 1934. Visits (1981): 12,006,847

**Guadalupe Mts. National Park, Texas;** (gross acreage, 76,293.06). Mountain mass rising from desert contains portions of the world's most extensive and significant Permian limestone fossil reef. Also features a tremendous earth fault, lofty peaks, unusual flora and fauna. Authorized 1966. Visits (1981): 142,641

**Haleakala National Park, Hawaii;** (gross acreage, 28,655.25). World-famous 10,023-foot Haleakala volcano (dormant), with one of the largest and most colorful craters known, in which grows a species of the rare silversword; native and migratory birdlife. Authorized 1960; est. 1961. Visits (1981): 644,661

**Hawaii Volcanoes National Park, Hawaii;** (gross acreage, 229,177.03). Scene of impressive active volcanism on the island of Hawaii; luxuriant vegetation at lower elevations; rare plants and animals. Est. as Hawaii Nat'l Park 1916; changed to Hawaii Volcanoes Nat'l Park 1961. Visits (1981): 2,368,907

**Hot Springs National Park, Arkansas;** (gross acreage, 5,825.79). Mineral hot springs (47), used in the treatment of certain ailments. Set aside as Hot Springs Reservation by federal government 1832; nat'l park est. 1921. Visits (1981): 5,301,994

**Isle Royale National Park, Michigan;** (gross acreage, 571,796.18). Forested island, distinguished for its wilderness character; moose and wolves; pre-Columbian copper mines. Authorized 1931; est. 1940. Visits (1981): 14,564

**Katmai National Park, Alaska;** (gross acreage, 3,678,929.00). Enlarged to provide more denning territory for the Alaska brown bear, this area was proclaimed a nat'l mon. in 1918 as a result of a 1912 volcanic eruption (Valley of Ten Thousand Smokes). Est. as a nat'l park 1980. Visits (1981): 13,140

**Kenai Fjords National Park, Alaska;** (gross acreage, 676,667.00). Rich in scenery and wildlife, this park has mountain goats, sea otters, Steller sea lions and seabirds, such as puffins. Proclaimed a nat'l mon. 1978; est. as a nat'l park 1980.

**Kings Canyon National Park, California;** (gross acreage, 460,136.20). Mountain wilderness dominated by two enormous canyons of the Kings River and by the summit peaks of the High Sierra. The former General Grant Nat'l Park, with its giant sequoias, is a detached section of the park. General Grant Nat'l Park est. 1890, abolished 1940, and its lands made part of Kings Canyon Nat'l Park; est. 1940. Visits (1981): 780,417

**Kobuk Valley National Park, Alaska;** (gross acreage, 1,749,037.00). The park, lying in northwest Alaska, includes the Salmon River, boreal forest, tundra and a 25 square-mile expanse of sand, the Great Kobuk Sand Dunes. Archeological sites reveal more than 10,000 years of human use. Proclaimed a nat'l mon. 1978, est. as a nat'l park 1980.

**Lake Clark National Park, Alaska;** (gross acreage, 2,633,933.00). The park contains the headwaters of the world's most important source of red salmon, two active volcanoes, lakes, glaciers and waterfalls; populated by a broad variety of wildlife. Proclaimed a nat'l mon. 1978; est. as a nat'l park 1980.

**Lassen Volcanic National Park, California;** (gross acreage, 106,372.36). Lassen Peak, which erupted between 1914 and 1921, exhibits volcanic phenomena. Lassen Peak and Cinder Cone Nat'l Mons. est. 1907; made part of Lassen Volcanic Nat'l Park 1916, when it was est. Visits (1981): 415,045

**Mammoth Cave National Park, Kentucky;** (gross acreage, 52,369.60). Series of underground passages, 146 miles explored; beautiful limestone, gypsum and cave onyx formations; deep pits and high domes; river 360 feet below surface. Authorized 1926; provided for minimum park area 1934; minimum area accepted for administration 1936; fully est. 1941. Visits (1981): 1,577,405

**Mesa Verde National Park, Colorado;** (gross acreage, 52,085.14). Best preserved prehistoric cliff dwellings in the United States. Est. 1906. Visits (1981): 590,127

**Mount Rainier National Park, Washington;** (gross acreage, 235,404.00). Greatest single-peak glacial system in the conterminous United States, radiating from the summit and slopes of an ancient volcano; dense forests, flowered meadows. Est. 1899. Visits (1981): 1,964,846

**North Cascades National Park, Washington;** (gross acreage, 504,780.94). Wild alpine region of jagged peaks, mountain lakes, and numerous glaciers. Est. 1968. Visits (1981): 865,849*

**Olympic National Park, Washington;** (gross acreage, 915,425.86). Mountain wilderness containing finest remnant of Pacific Northwest rain forest; active glaciers; rare Roosevelt elk. Mount Olympus Nat'l Mon. est. 1909; transferred from U.S. Dept. of Agriculture 1933; Olympic Nat'l Park est. 1938. Visits (1981): 2,754,514

**Petrified Forest National Park, Arizona;** (gross acreage, 93,492.57). Extensive natural exhibit of petrified wood; Indian ruins and petroglyphs; portion of colorful Painted Desert. Est. as a nat'l mon. 1906; changed to nat'l park 1962. Visits (1981): 751,432

**Redwood National Park, California;** (gross acreage, 109,255.54). Coastal redwood forests contain virgin groves of ancient trees. Park includes 40 miles of scenic Pacific coastline. Est. 1968. Visits (1981): 632,817

**Rocky Mountain National Park, Colorado;** (gross acreage, 266,942.71). One of the most diversified sections of the Front Range of the Rocky Mountains with 107 named peaks in excess of 11,000 feet. Est. 1915. Visits (1981): 2,917,080

**Sequoia National Park, California;** (gross acreage, 402,487.83). Great groves of giant sequoias, world's largest and among the oldest living things; magnificent High Sierra scenery, including Mount Whitney, highest mountain (14,494 feet) in conterminous United States. Est. 1890. Visits (1981): 1,083,377

**Shenandoah National Park, Virginia;** (gross acreage, 195,057.36). Outstanding portion of Blue Ridge with Skyline Drive traversing crest; magnificent vistas of historic Shenandoah Valley, Piedmont; hardwood forests; wealth of wildflowers. Authorized 1926; est. 1935. Visits (1981): 1,894,280

**Theodore Roosevelt National Park, North Dakota;** (gross acreage, 70,416.39). The park includes scenic badlands along the Little Missouri River, some original prairie grasslands, and part of Theodore Roosevelt's Elkhorn Ranch. Memorial park est. 1947; renamed 1978. Visits (1981): 710,349

**Virgin Islands National Park, V.I.;** (gross acreage, 14,694.73). St. John, an island of lush green hills and white sandy beaches; rich in tropical plant and animal life; pre-historic Carib Indian relics; remains of Danish colonial sugar plantations. Authorized 1956; est. 1956. Visits (1981): 841,258

**Voyageurs National Park, Minnesota;** (gross acreage, 219,128.00). Beautiful lakes and forests, interesting geology; historically used as passage between Great Lakes and Northwest Territory by French fur traders. Land area, 144,891.16 acres. Authorized 1971. Visits (1981): 261,722

**Wind Cave National Park, South Dakota;** (gross acreage, 28,292.08). Limestone caverns in scenic Black Hills, decorated by beautiful boxwork and calcite crystal formations; elk, deer, pronghorn, prairie dog towns and bison herd. Est. 1903. Visits (1981): 1,023,490

**Wrangell-St. Elias National Park, Alaska;** (gross acreage; 8,331,406.00). This park contains the largest collection of glaciers and peaks over 16,000 feet in North America. Wildlife includes caribou, Dall sheep, glacier bear, and trumpeter swans. Proclaimed a nat'l mon. 1978; est. a nat'l park 1980.

**Yellowstone National Park, Wyo.-Mont.-Idaho;** (gross acreage, 2,219,822.70). World's greatest geyser area; spectacular falls and canyons of the Yellowstone River; one of the world's greatest wildlife sanctuaries. First and largest nat'l park. Est. 1872. Visits (1981): 2,549,307

**Yosemite National Park, California;** (gross acreage, 760,917.18). Mountainous region of unusual beauty; Yosemite and other inspiring gorges with sheer granite cliffs; spectacular waterfalls; three groves of giant sequoias. Est. 1890. El Portal administrative site, 991.19 acres of federal land adjacent to the park, authorized 1958. Visits (1981): 2,616,260

**Zion National Park, Utah;** (gross acreage, 146,551.10). Outstanding colorful canyon and mesascenery; erosion and faulting patterns that create phenomenal shapes and landscapes; former volcanic activity. Zion Canyon, a vertical-walled chasm, readily accessible. Est. as Munkuntuweap Nat'l Mon. 1909; changed to Zion Nat'l Mon. 1918; est. as a nat'l park (including the Nat'l Mon. 1937) 1919. Visits (1981): 1,405,205

*** Acreage and visitor figures include those for Lake Chelan and Ross Lake National Recreation Areas.**

## THE U.S. PASSPORT

SOURCE: Department of State, Passport Services

A passport is your official identification as a citizen of the United States. Application for a passport should be made, in person, before a passport agent at one of the passport agencies located in Boston; Chicago; Honolulu; Houston; Los Angeles; Miami; New Orleans; New York; Philadelphia; San Francisco; Seattle; Stamford, Conn.; and Washington, D.C.; or a clerk of any federal court or state court of record or a judge or clerk of any probate court accepting applications; or a postal employee designated by the postmaster at a post office which has been selected to accept passport applications.

When you apply for a passport you must present the following items: proof of U.S. citizenship (a previously issued passport, birth certificate, or naturalization papers); two identical photographs taken within six months of the date of your application (have them taken by a professional photographer who knows the requirements concerning pose and size of prints); identification—a document such as a driver's license with your signature and your photograph or physical description on it. The fee for a passport is $10[1], plus a $5 execution fee. Allow about two to three weeks for processing of your application, longer if you apply during peak travel periods.

A passport is valid for five years[1] from the date of issue unless specifically limited to a shorter period by the Secretary of State. A new passport will be required for travel after expiration of the five-year period.

Application for a new passport must be made in person at the places listed above, or—under certain circumstances—a person who is the bearer of a passport issued within eight years prior to the date of his or her new application may apply for a subsequent passport by mail. The applicant must submit completed form DSP-82 (Application for Passport by Mail), which is available from travel agents and the places listed above, the previous passport, two new signed passport photographs, and a fee of $10. The applicant should carefully read the instructions on the application to determine his or her eligibility to use this form.

Loss or theft of a valid passport is a serious matter and should be reported in writing immediately to Passport Services, Department of State, Washington, D.C. 20524 or the nearest Passport Agency. If the passport holder is abroad when the loss occurs, he or she should notify the nearest U.S. consulate. Theft of a passport should also be reported to local police authorities.

Visas

A visa is official permission to visit a country granted by the government of that country. An American who plans to go abroad can check the general visa requirements for each country he or she plans to visit in a booklet entitled "Visa Requirements of Foreign Governments," which is available at any office accepting passport applications. Specific details should be obtained from the nearest embassy or consulate of the country in which you wish to do any traveling.

[1]Congressional approval has been requested to increase the passport fee and to extend the validity of the passport beyond five years.

## FOREIGN GOVERNMENT TOURIST OFFICES

**Australian Tourist Commission**
1270 Ave. of the Americas, Rm. 2908
New York, NY 10020

**Austrian National Tourist Office**
545 Fifth Avenue
New York, NY 10017

**Bahamas Tourist Office**
30 Rockefeller Plaza
New York, NY 10020

**Belgian National Tourist Office**
745 Fifth Avenue
New York, NY 10022

**Bermuda Government Official Travel Information Office**
630 Fifth Avenue
New York, NY 10020

**British Tourist Authority**
680 Fifth Avenue
New York, NY 10019

**Canadian Government Office of Tourism**
1251 Ave. of the Americas
New York, NY 10020

**Cedok Czechoslovak Travel Bureau**
10 East 40th Street
New York, NY 10016

**China International Travel Service**
Room 465, 60 East 42nd Street
New York, NY 10165

**Dominican Tourist Information Center, Inc.**
485 Madison Avenue
New York, NY 10022

**Egyptian Government Tourist Office**
630 Fifth Avenue
New York, NY 10020

**Finland National Tourist Office**
75 Rockefeller Plaza
New York, NY 10020

**French Government Tourist Office**
610 Fifth Avenue
New York, NY 10020

**German National Tourist Office**
630 Fifth Avenue
New York, NY 10022

**Greek National Tourist Organization**
645 Fifth Avenue
New York, NY 10022

**Haiti Government Tourist Bureau**
1270 Ave. of the Americas
New York, NY 10020

**India Government Tourist Office**
30 Rockefeller Plaza
New York, NY 10020

**Irish Tourist Board**
590 Fifth Avenue
New York, NY 10036

**Israel Government Tourism Administration**
350 Fifth Avenue
New York, NY 10016

**Italian Government Travel Office**
630 Fifth Avenue
New York, NY 10020

**Jamaica Tourist Board**
2 Hammarskjöld Plaza
New York, NY 10017

**Japan National Tourist Organization**
630 Fifth Avenue
New York, NY 10020

**Kenya Tourist Office**
60 East 56th Street
New York, NY 10022

**Korea National Tourism Corp.**
460 Park Avenue
New York, NY 10022

**Malaysian Tourist Center**
420 Lexington Avenue
New York, NY 10017

**Mexican National Tourist Council**
405 Park Avenue
New York, NY 10022

**Moroccan National Tourist Office**
521 Fifth Avenue
New York, NY 10017

**Panama Government Tourist Bureau**
630 Fifth Avenue
New York, NY 10020

**Polish National Tourist Office**
500 Fifth Avenue
New York, NY 10036

**Romanian National Tourist Office**
573 Third Avenue
New York, NY 10016

**(Russian) Intourist**
630 Fifth Avenue
New York, NY 10020

**Scandinavian National Tourist Office**
75 Rockefeller Plaza
New York, NY 10020

**South African Tourist Corporation**
610 Fifth Avenue
New York, NY 10020

**Spanish National Tourist Office**
665 Fifth Avenue
New York, NY 10022

**Sri Lanka (Ceylon) Tourist Board**
609 Fifth Avenue
New York, NY 10017

**Swiss National Tourist Office**
608 Fifth Avenue
New York, NY 10020

**Thailand Tourist Office**
5 World Trade Center
New York, NY 10048

**Turkish Government Tourism Office**
821 United Nations Plaza
New York, NY 10017

**Yugoslav State Tourist Office**
630 Fifth Avenue
New York, NY 10020

## FOREIGN CITY WEATHER

Two figures are given for each of the months, thus 88/73. The first figure is the average daily high temperature (°F) and the second is the average daily low temperature (°F) for the month. The **boldface** figures indicate the average number of days with rain for each month.

| | January | February | March | April | May | June | July | August | September | October | November | December |
|---|---|---|---|---|---|---|---|---|---|---|---|---|
| **ABIDJAN,** Ivory Coast | 88/73 **3** | 90/75 **4** | 90/75 **6** | 90/75 **9** | 88/75 **16** | 85/73 **18** | 83/73 **8** | 82/71 **7** | 83/73 **8** | 85/74 **13** | 87/74 **13** | 88/74 **6** |
| **ACAPULCO,** Mexico | 85/70 **0** | 87/70 **0** | 87/70 **0** | 87/71 **1** | 89/74 **4** | 89/76 **15** | 89/75 **11** | 89/75 **14** | 88/75 **18** | 88/74 **12** | 88/72 **4** | 87/70 **1** |
| **ACCRA,** Ghana | 87/73 **1** | 88/75 **2** | 88/76 **4** | 88/76 **6** | 87/75 **9** | 84/74 **10** | 81/73 **4** | 80/71 **3** | 81/73 **4** | 85/74 **6** | 87/75 **3** | 88/75 **2** |
| **ADDIS ABABA,** Ethiopia | 75/43 **2** | 76/47 **5** | 77/49 **8** | 77/50 **10** | 77/50 **10** | 74/49 **20** | 69/50 **28** | 69/50 **27** | 72/49 **21** | 75/45 **3** | 73/43 **2** | 73/41 **2** |
| **ALGIERS,** Algeria | 59/49 **11** | 61/49 **9** | 63/52 **9** | 68/55 **5** | 73/59 **5** | 78/65 **2** | 83/70 **1** | 85/71 **1** | 81/69 **4** | 74/63 **7** | 66/56 **11** | 60/51 **12** |
| **AMSTERDAM,** Netherlands | 40/34 **19** | 41/34 **15** | 46/37 **13** | 52/43 **14** | 60/50 **12** | 65/55 **12** | 69/59 **14** | 68/59 **14** | 64/56 **15** | 56/48 **18** | 47/41 **19** | 41/35 **19** |
| **ANKARA,** Turkey | 39/24 **8** | 42/26 **8** | 51/31 **7** | 63/40 **7** | 73/49 **7** | 78/53 **5** | 86/59 **2** | 87/59 **1** | 78/52 **3** | 69/44 **5** | 57/37 **6** | 43/29 **9** |
| **APIA,** Western Samoa | 86/75 **22** | 85/76 **19** | 86/74 **19** | 86/75 **14** | 85/74 **12** | 85/74 **7** | 85/74 **9** | 84/75 **9** | 84/74 **11** | 85/75 **14** | 86/74 **16** | 85/74 **19** |
| **ATHENS,** Greece | 54/42 **7** | 55/43 **6** | 60/46 **5** | 67/52 **3** | 77/60 **3** | 85/67 **2** | 90/72 **1** | 90/72 **1** | 83/66 **2** | 74/60 **4** | 64/52 **6** | 57/46 **7** |
| **BAGHDAD,** Iraq | 60/39 **4** | 64/42 **3** | 71/48 **4** | 85/57 **3** | 97/67 **1** | 105/73 **0** | 110/76 **0** | 110/76 **0** | 104/70 **0** | 92/61 **1** | 77/51 **3** | 64/42 **5** |
| **BALI,** Indonesia | 88/74 **19** | 88/74 **14** | 88/74 **13** | 88/74 **7** | 88/73 **5** | 87/71 **3** | 87/70 **1** | 87/70 **1** | 89/71 **1** | 90/73 **2** | 90/75 **6** | 88/74 **14** |
| **BANGKOK,** Thailand | 89/68 **1** | 91/72 **1** | 93/75 **3** | 95/77 **3** | 93/77 **9** | 91/76 **10** | 90/76 **13** | 90/76 **13** | 89/76 **15** | 88/75 **14** | 87/72 **5** | 87/68 **1** |
| **BARCELONA,** Spain | 56/42 **5** | 57/44 **7** | 61/47 **7** | 64/51 **8** | 71/57 **8** | 77/63 **5** | 81/69 **4** | 82/69 **5** | 78/65 **7** | 71/58 **8** | 62/50 **7** | 57/44 **6** |
| **BEIRUT,** Lebanon | 62/51 **15** | 63/51 **12** | 66/54 **9** | 72/58 **5** | 78/64 **2** | 84/74 **12** | 83/73 **11** | 84/74 **11** | 84/74 **9** | 85/74 **9** | 85/73 **12** | 85/73 **15** |
| **BELFAST,** Northern Ireland | 45/34 **22** | 47/34 **18** | 49/35 **20** | 53/39 **18** | 59/43 **17** | 64/49 **10** | 66/51 **18** | 65/51 **20** | 62/48 **17** | 55/42 **19** | 50/37 **21** | 46/35 **25** |
| **BELGRADE,** Yugoslavia | 37/27 **8** | 41/27 **6** | 53/35 **7** | 64/45 **9** | 74/53 **9** | 79/58 **9** | 84/61 **6** | 83/60 **7** | 76/55 **6** | 65/47 **8** | 52/39 **7** | 40/30 **9** |
| **BERLIN,** Germany | 35/26 **10** | 38/27 **8** | 46/32 **9** | 55/38 **9** | 65/46 **8** | 70/51 **9** | 74/55 **10** | 72/54 **10** | 66/48 **8** | 55/41 **8** | 43/33 **8** | 37/29 **11** |
| **BIARRITZ,** France | 54/40 **10** | 52/38 **11** | 63/43 **11** | 63/44 **11** | 69/53 **11** | 72/56 **10** | 80/66 **7** | 77/61 **7** | 77/58 **9** | 74/55 **11** | 58/44 **12** | 53/41 **14** |
| **BOGOTÁ,** Colombia | 67/48 **6** | 68/49 **7** | 67/50 **13** | 67/51 **20** | 66/51 **17** | 65/51 **16** | 64/50 **18** | 65/50 **16** | 66/49 **13** | 66/50 **20** | 66/50 **16** | 66/49 **15** |
| **BOMBAY,** India | 83/67 **1** | 83/67 **1** | 86/72 **1** | 89/76 **1** | 91/80 **1** | 89/79 **14** | 85/77 **21** | 85/76 **19** | 85/76 **13** | 89/76 **3** | 89/73 **1** | 87/69 **1** |
| **BONN,** West Germany | 39/30 **7** | 37/26 **6** | 50/35 **7** | 58/39 **14** | 67/46 **13** | 69/52 **19** | 73/56 **16** | 72/55 **17** | 67/50 **16** | 58/45 **16** | 47/37 **15** | 44/36 **15** |
| **BRASÍLIA,** Brazil | 80/65 **17** | 81/64 **20** | 82/64 **7** | 82/62 **10** | 79/56 **5** | 77/52 **0** | 78/51 **2** | 82/55 **0** | 87/60 **2** | 82/64 **16** | 82/66 **17** | 78/64 **16** |
| **BRINDISI,** Italy | 55/43 **10** | 57/43 **6** | 60/45 **5** | 65/50 **5** | 73/57 **5** | 80/64 **2** | 84/68 **1** | 84/69 **3** | 80/65 **4** | 70/58 **8** | 64/52 **10** | 58/46 **8** |
| **BUCHAREST,** Romania | 33/20 **6** | 38/24 **5** | 51/33 **6** | 63/41 **6** | 74/51 **8** | 81/58 **9** | 86/61 **7** | 86/60 **5** | 76/53 **5** | 65/44 **5** | 49/35 **6** | 37/26 **6** |
| **BUDAPEST,** Hungary | 35/26 **7** | 40/28 **6** | 51/36 **7** | 62/44 **8** | 72/52 **9** | 78/57 **8** | 82/61 **7** | 81/59 **6** | 74/53 **7** | 61/45 **8** | 47/37 **8** | 38/31 **9** |
| **BUENOS AIRES,** Argentina | 85/63 **7** | 83/63 **6** | 79/60 **7** | 72/53 **8** | 64/47 **7** | 57/41 **7** | 57/42 **8** | 60/43 **9** | 64/46 **8** | 69/50 **9** | 76/56 **9** | 82/61 **8** |
| **CAIRO,** Egypt | 65/47 **1** | 69/48 **1** | 75/52 **1** | 83/57 **1** | 91/63 **1** | 95/68 **0** | 96/70 **0** | 95/71 **0** | 90/68 **0** | 86/65 **1** | 78/58 **1** | 68/50 **1** |
| **CALCUTTA,** India | 80/55 **1** | 84/59 **2** | 93/69 **2** | 97/75 **3** | 96/77 **7** | 92/79 **13** | 89/79 **18** | 89/78 **18** | 90/78 **13** | 89/74 **6** | 84/64 **1** | 79/55 **1** |
| **CAPE TOWN,** South Africa | 78/60 **3** | 79/60 **2** | 77/58 **3** | 72/53 **6** | 67/49 **9** | 65/46 **9** | 63/45 **10** | 64/46 **9** | 65/49 **7** | 70/52 **5** | 73/55 **3** | 76/58 **3** |
| **CARACAS,** Venezuela | 75/56 **6** | 77/56 **2** | 79/58 **3** | 81/60 **4** | 80/62 **9** | 78/62 **14** | 78/61 **15** | 79/61 **15** | 80/61 **13** | 79/61 **12** | 77/60 **13** | 78/58 **10** |
| **CHARLOTTE AMALIE,** Virgin Islands | 82/73 **18** | 81/72 **13** | 82/73 **12** | 83/74 **13** | 85/76 **15** | 86/77 **15** | 87/78 **16** | 88/78 **19** | 87/78 **17** | 87/77 **18** | 85/76 **19** | 83/74 **18** |
| **COLOMBO,** Sri Lanka | 86/72 **7** | 87/72 **6** | 88/74 **8** | 88/76 **14** | 87/78 **19** | 85/77 **18** | 85/77 **12** | 85/77 **11** | 85/77 **13** | 85/75 **19** | 85/73 **16** | 85/72 **10** |
| **COPENHAGEN,** Denmark | 36/29 **9** | 36/28 **7** | 41/31 **8** | 50/37 **9** | 61/44 **8** | 67/51 **8** | 72/55 **9** | 69/54 **12** | 63/49 **8** | 53/42 **9** | 43/35 **10** | 38/32 **11** |
| **DARWIN,** Australia | 90/77 **20** | 90/77 **18** | 91/77 **17** | 92/76 **6** | 91/73 **1** | 88/69 **1** | 87/67 **0** | 89/70 **0** | 91/74 **2** | 93/77 **5** | 94/78 **10** | 92/78 **15** |
| **DJAKARTA,** Indonesia | 84/74 **18** | 84/74 **17** | 86/74 **15** | 87/75 **11** | 87/75 **9** | 87/74 **7** | 87/73 **5** | 87/73 **4** | 88/74 **5** | 87/74 **8** | 86/74 **12** | 85/74 **14** |
| **DUBLIN,** Ireland | 47/35 **13** | 47/35 **11** | 51/36 **10** | 54/38 **11** | 59/42 **11** | 65/48 **11** | 67/51 **13** | 67/51 **13** | 63/47 **12** | 57/43 **12** | 51/38 **12** | 47/36 **13** |
| **EDINBURGH,** Scotland | 43/35 **18** | 43/35 **15** | 47/36 **15** | 50/39 **16** | 55/43 **15** | 62/48 **15** | 65/52 **17** | 64/52 **17** | 60/48 **16** | 53/44 **18** | 47/39 **18** | 44/36 **17** |
| **FLORENCE,** Italy | 49/35 **9** | 53/36 **9** | 60/40 **7** | 68/46 **7** | 75/53 **9** | 84/58 **5** | 89/63 **4** | 88/62 **4** | 81/58 **6** | 69/51 **9** | 58/42 **10** | 50/37 **9** |
| **GENEVA,** Switzerland | 39/29 **10** | 43/30 **9** | 51/35 **10** | 58/41 **11** | 66/48 **12** | 73/55 **11** | 77/58 **9** | 76/57 **10** | 69/52 **10** | 58/44 **11** | 47/37 **11** | 40/31 **10** |
| **GUAYAQUIL,** Ecuador | 88/70 **20** | 87/71 **25** | 88/72 **24** | 89/71 **14** | 88/68 **9** | 87/68 **4** | 84/67 **2** | 86/65 **0** | 87/66 **2** | 86/68 **3** | 88/68 **4** | 88/70 **10** |
| **HAMBURG,** West Germany | 35/28 **12** | 37/30 **10** | 42/33 **10** | 51/39 **11** | 60/47 **9** | 67/53 **10** | 69/56 **12** | 67/55 **13** | 63/51 **10** | 53/44 **11** | 44/36 **11** | 38/31 **12** |
| **HAMILTON,** Bermuda | 68/58 **14** | 68/57 **13** | 68/57 **12** | 71/59 **9** | 76/64 **9** | 81/69 **9** | 85/73 **10** | 86/74 **13** | 84/72 **10** | 79/69 **12** | 74/63 **13** | 70/60 **15** |
| **HAVANA,** Cuba | 79/65 **6** | 79/65 **4** | 81/67 **4** | 84/69 **4** | 86/72 **7** | 88/74 **10** | 89/75 **9** | 89/75 **10** | 88/75 **11** | 85/73 **11** | 81/69 **7** | 79/67 **6** |
| **HELSINKI,** Finland | 27/17 **11** | 26/15 **8** | 32/22 **8** | 43/31 **8** | 55/41 **8** | 63/49 **9** | 71/57 **8** | 66/55 **12** | 57/46 **11** | 45/37 **12** | 37/30 **11** | 31/22 **11** |
| **HONG KONG** | 64/56 **4** | 63/55 **5** | 67/60 **7** | 75/67 **8** | 82/74 **13** | 85/78 **18** | 87/78 **17** | 87/78 **15** | 85/77 **12** | 81/73 **6** | 74/65 **2** | 68/59 **3** |
| **JERUSALEM,** Israel | 55/41 **9** | 56/42 **11** | 65/46 **3** | 73/50 **3** | 81/57 **1** | 85/60 **1** | 87/63 **0** | 87/64 **0** | 85/62 **1** | 81/59 **1** | 70/53 **4** | 59/45 **7** |
| **JOHANNESBURG,** South Africa | 78/58 **12** | 77/58 **9** | 75/55 **9** | 72/50 **4** | 66/43 **3** | 62/39 **1** | 63/39 **1** | 68/43 **1** | 73/48 **2** | 77/53 **7** | 77/55 **10** | 78/57 **11** |
| **KARACHI,** Pakistan | 77/55 **1** | 79/58 **1** | 85/67 **1** | 90/73 **1** | 93/79 **1** | 93/82 **1** | 91/81 **2** | 88/79 **2** | 88/77 **1** | 91/72 **1** | 87/64 **1** | 80/57 **1** |
| **KINGSTON,** Jamaica | 86/67 **3** | 86/67 **3** | 86/68 **2** | 87/70 **3** | 87/72 **4** | 89/74 **5** | 90/73 **4** | 90/73 **7** | 89/73 **6** | 88/73 **9** | 87/71 **5** | 87/69 **4** |
| **LAGOS,** Nigeria | 88/74 **2** | 89/77 **3** | 89/78 **7** | 89/77 **10** | 87/76 **16** | 85/74 **20** | 83/74 **16** | 82/73 **10** | 83/74 **14** | 85/74 **16** | 88/75 **7** | 88/75 **2** |
| **LA PAZ,** Bolivia | 63/43 **21** | 63/43 **18** | 64/42 **16** | 65/40 **9** | 64/37 **5** | 62/34 **2** | 62/33 **2** | 63/35 **4** | 64/38 **9** | 66/40 **9** | 67/42 **11** | 65/42 **18** |

| | January | February | March | April | May | June | July | August | September | October | November | December |
|---|---|---|---|---|---|---|---|---|---|---|---|---|
| **LAS PALMAS,** Canary Is. | 70/58 8 | 71/58 5 | 71/59 5 | 71/61 3 | 73/62 1 | 75/65 1 | 77/67 1 | 79/70 1 | 79/69 1 | 79/67 5 | 76/64 7 | 72/60 8 |
| **LENINGRAD,** USSR | 23/12 17 | 24/12 15 | 33/18 13 | 45/31 11 | 58/42 12 | 66/51 12 | 71/57 13 | 66/53 15 | 57/45 14 | 45/37 15 | 34/27 17 | 26/18 18 |
| **LIMA,** Peru | 82/66 1 | 83/67 1 | 83/66 1 | 80/63 1 | 74/60 1 | 68/58 1 | 67/57 1 | 66/56 2 | 68/57 1 | 71/58 1 | 74/60 1 | 78/62 1 |
| **LISBON,** Portugal | 56/46 9 | 58/47 8 | 61/49 10 | 64/52 7 | 69/56 6 | 75/60 2 | 79/63 1 | 80/64 1 | 76/62 4 | 69/57 7 | 62/52 10 | 57/47 10 |
| **LIVERPOOL,** England | 44/36 18 | 44/36 13 | 48/38 13 | 52/41 14 | 58/46 14 | 63/51 13 | 66/55 15 | 65/55 16 | 61/51 15 | 55/46 17 | 48/41 17 | 45/37 18 |
| **LONDON,** England | 44/35 17 | 45/35 13 | 51/47 11 | 56/40 14 | 63/45 13 | 69/51 11 | 73/55 13 | 72/54 13 | 67/51 13 | 58/44 14 | 49/39 16 | 45/36 16 |
| **MADRID,** Spain | 47/33 9 | 51/35 9 | 57/40 11 | 64/44 9 | 71/50 9 | 80/57 6 | 87/62 3 | 86/62 2 | 77/56 6 | 66/48 8 | 54/40 10 | 48/35 9 |
| **MANILA,** Philippines | 86/69 6 | 88/69 3 | 91/71 4 | 93/73 4 | 93/75 12 | 91/75 17 | 88/75 24 | 87/75 23 | 88/75 22 | 88/74 19 | 87/72 14 | 86/70 11 |
| **MARACAIBO,** Venezuela | 90/73 1 | 90/73 1 | 91/74 1 | 92/76 1 | 92/77 6 | 93/77 6 | 94/76 5 | 94/77 7 | 94/77 6 | 92/76 9 | 91/76 8 | 91/75 2 |
| **MARSEILLE,** France | 53/38 10 | 52/37 9 | 55/38 8 | 59/41 10 | 65/46 10 | 72/52 9 | 78/58 6 | 83/61 4 | 82/61 5 | 76/57 7 | 67/50 10 | 59/43 11 |
| **MELBOURNE,** Australia | 78/57 9 | 78/57 8 | 75/55 9 | 68/51 13 | 62/47 14 | 57/44 16 | 56/42 17 | 59/43 17 | 63/46 15 | 67/48 14 | 71/51 13 | 75/54 11 |
| **MEXICO CITY,** Mexico | 66/42 4 | 69/43 5 | 75/47 9 | 77/51 14 | 78/54 17 | 76/55 21 | 73/53 27 | 73/54 27 | 74/53 23 | 70/50 13 | 68/46 6 | 66/43 4 |
| **MILAN,** Italy | 40/29 7 | 47/33 6 | 56/38 6 | 66/46 6 | 72/54 9 | 80/61 6 | 84/64 6 | 82/63 6 | 76/58 6 | 64/49 7 | 51/39 7 | 42/33 7 |
| **MONTEVIDEO,** Uruguay | 83/62 6 | 82/61 5 | 78/59 5 | 71/53 6 | 64/48 6 | 59/43 5 | 58/43 6 | 59/43 7 | 63/46 6 | 68/49 6 | 74/54 6 | 79/59 7 |
| **MOSCOW,** USSR | 21/ 9 11 | 23/10 9 | 32/17 8 | 47/31 9 | 65/44 9 | 73/51 10 | 76/55 12 | 72/52 12 | 61/43 9 | 46/34 11 | 31/23 10 | 23/13 9 |
| **MUNICH,** West Germany | 33/23 10 | 37/25 9 | 45/31 10 | 54/37 13 | 63/45 13 | 69/51 14 | 72/54 14 | 71/53 13 | 64/48 11 | 53/40 10 | 42/31 9 | 36/26 11 |
| **NAIROBI,** Kenya | 77/54 5 | 79/55 6 | 77/57 11 | 75/58 16 | 72/56 17 | 70/53 9 | 69/51 6 | 70/52 7 | 75/52 6 | 76/55 8 | 74/56 15 | 74/55 11 |
| **NAPLES,** Italy | 54/42 11 | 55/43 11 | 60/46 6 | 67/50 6 | 73/56 6 | 81/62 3 | 86/67 1 | 86/67 3 | 81/63 6 | 72/56 9 | 63/49 11 | 57/45 11 |
| **NASSAU,** Bahamas | 77/65 6 | 77/64 5 | 79/66 5 | 81/69 6 | 84/71 9 | 87/74 12 | 88/75 14 | 89/76 14 | 88/75 15 | 85/73 13 | 81/70 9 | 79/67 6 |
| **NEW DELHI,** India | 70/44 2 | 75/49 2 | 87/58 1 | 97/68 1 | 105/79 2 | 102/83 4 | 96/81 8 | 93/79 8 | 93/75 4 | 93/65 1 | 84/52 1 | 73/46 1 |
| **NICE,** France | 56/40 8 | 56/41 8 | 59/45 8 | 64/49 7 | 69/56 8 | 76/62 5 | 81/66 2 | 81/66 5 | 77/62 6 | 70/55 9 | 62/48 7 | 58/43 8 |
| **NOUMEA,** New Caledonia | 86/72 10 | 85/73 12 | 85/72 16 | 83/70 13 | 79/66 15 | 77/64 13 | 76/62 13 | 76/61 12 | 78/63 8 | 80/65 7 | 83/68 7 | 86/70 6 |
| **ODESSA,** USSR | 28/22 7 | 31/26 4 | 39/32 5 | 52/41 6 | 67/55 6 | 74/62 7 | 79/65 6 | 78/65 5 | 68/56 4 | 57/47 5 | 43/35 5 | 33/27 6 |
| **OSLO,** Norway | 30/20 8 | 32/20 7 | 40/25 7 | 50/34 7 | 62/43 7 | 69/51 8 | 73/56 10 | 69/53 11 | 60/45 8 | 49/37 10 | 37/29 9 | 31/24 10 |
| **PALERMO,** Sicily, Italy | 58/47 14 | 60/47 10 | 62/49 7 | 67/53 5 | 83/59 5 | 82/66 1 | 86/71 1 | 87/72 1 | 83/69 4 | 75/62 10 | 67/55 9 | 61/50 11 |
| **PALMA,** Majorca, Spain | 57/42 8 | 59/43 8 | 62/45 8 | 66/49 5 | 73/55 5 | 80/61 3 | 84/66 1 | 86/67 2 | 81/64 6 | 74/57 8 | 65/50 9 | 59/44 10 |
| **PAPEETE,** Tahiti | 89/72 16 | 89/72 16 | 89/72 17 | 89/72 10 | 87/70 10 | 86/69 8 | 86/68 5 | 86/68 6 | 86/69 6 | 87/70 9 | 88/71 13 | 88/72 14 |
| **PARIS,** France | 42/32 15 | 45/33 13 | 52/36 15 | 60/41 14 | 67/47 13 | 73/52 11 | 76/55 12 | 75/55 12 | 69/50 11 | 59/44 14 | 49/38 15 | 43/33 17 |
| **PEKING,** China | 35/15 3 | 41/20 3 | 53/30 3 | 68/44 4 | 80/56 6 | 88/65 9 | 89/71 13 | 87/69 11 | 80/58 7 | 69/44 4 | 50/30 2 | 37/19 2 |
| **PHNOM PENH,** Cambodia | 87/70 1 | 90/72 1 | 93/74 3 | 94/76 6 | 92/76 14 | 91/76 15 | 89/75 16 | 89/76 17 | 88/76 19 | 87/76 17 | 86/74 9 | 86/71 4 |
| **PORT-AU-PRINCE,** Haiti | 87/68 3 | 88/68 5 | 89/69 7 | 89/71 11 | 90/72 13 | 92/73 8 | 94/74 7 | 93/73 11 | 91/73 12 | 90/72 12 | 88/71 7 | 87/69 3 |
| **PORT OF SPAIN,** Trinidad | 85/67 14 | 86/67 8 | 87/67 8 | 88/69 7 | 89/70 10 | 87/71 17 | 87/70 20 | 87/71 21 | 88/71 18 | 88/71 16 | 87/70 17 | 86/69 16 |
| **PRAGUE,** Czechoslovakia | 34/25 12 | 38/28 11 | 45/33 13 | 55/40 12 | 65/49 13 | 72/55 14 | 74/58 14 | 73/57 12 | 65/52 11 | 54/44 11 | 41/35 12 | 34/29 13 |
| **RANGOON,** Burma | 89/65 1 | 92/67 1 | 96/71 1 | 97/76 2 | 92/77 14 | 86/76 23 | 85/76 26 | 85/76 25 | 86/76 20 | 88/76 10 | 88/73 3 | 88/67 1 |
| **RIO DE JANEIRO,** Brazil | 84/73 13 | 85/73 11 | 83/72 12 | 80/69 10 | 77/66 10 | 76/64 7 | 75/63 7 | 76/64 7 | 75/65 11 | 77/66 13 | 79/68 13 | 82/71 14 |
| **ROME,** Italy | 54/39 8 | 56/39 11 | 62/42 5 | 68/46 6 | 74/55 6 | 82/60 3 | 88/64 2 | 88/64 3 | 83/61 6 | 73/53 9 | 63/46 8 | 56/41 9 |
| **SAIGON (HO CHI MINH CITY),** Vietnam | 89/70 2 | 91/71 1 | 93/74 2 | 95/76 4 | 92/76 16 | 89/75 21 | 88/75 23 | 88/75 21 | 88/74 21 | 88/74 20 | 87/73 11 | 87/71 7 |
| **SAN JUAN,** Puerto Rico | 80/70 20 | 80/70 15 | 81/70 15 | 82/72 14 | 84/74 16 | 85/75 17 | 85/75 19 | 85/76 20 | 86/75 18 | 85/75 18 | 84/73 19 | 81/72 21 |
| **SANTIAGO,** Chile | 85/53 0 | 84/52 0 | 80/49 1 | 74/45 1 | 65/41 5 | 58/37 6 | 59/37 6 | 62/39 5 | 66/42 3 | 72/45 3 | 78/48 1 | 83/51 0 |
| **SÃO PAULO,** Brazil | 81/63 19 | 82/64 17 | 81/62 15 | 78/58 10 | 73/54 10 | 71/51 8 | 71/49 6 | 73/51 8 | 74/54 11 | 76/57 13 | 79/59 14 | 80/61 13 |
| **SEOUL,** South Korea | 32/15 8 | 37/20 6 | 47/29 7 | 62/41 8 | 72/51 10 | 80/61 10 | 84/70 16 | 87/71 13 | 78/59 9 | 67/45 7 | 51/32 9 | 37/20 9 |
| **SEVILLE,** Spain | 59/41 8 | 62/44 9 | 67/48 9 | 73/51 8 | 80/57 5 | 89/63 2 | 96/67 1 | 97/68 1 | 89/64 3 | 78/57 5 | 67/49 9 | 60/44 8 |
| **SHANGHAI,** China | 46/33 6 | 47/34 9 | 55/40 9 | 66/50 9 | 77/59 9 | 82/67 11 | 90/74 9 | 90/74 9 | 82/66 11 | 74/57 4 | 63/45 6 | 53/36 6 |
| **SINGAPORE,** Singapore | 86/73 17 | 88/73 11 | 88/75 14 | 88/75 15 | 89/75 15 | 88/75 13 | 88/75 13 | 87/75 14 | 87/75 14 | 87/74 16 | 87/74 18 | 87/74 19 |
| **SOFIA,** Bulgaria | 34/22 6 | 39/25 6 | 51/32 8 | 62/41 8 | 70/49 11 | 76/54 9 | 82/57 7 | 82/56 6 | 74/50 6 | 63/42 7 | 50/35 7 | 37/26 7 |
| **STOCKHOLM,** Sweden | 31/23 8 | 31/22 7 | 37/26 7 | 45/32 6 | 57/41 8 | 65/49 7 | 70/55 9 | 66/53 10 | 58/46 8 | 48/39 9 | 38/31 9 | 33/26 9 |
| **SYDNEY,** Australia | 78/65 14 | 78/65 13 | 76/63 14 | 71/58 14 | 66/52 13 | 61/48 12 | 60/46 12 | 63/48 11 | 67/51 12 | 71/56 12 | 74/60 12 | 77/63 13 |
| **TAIPEI,** Taiwan, China | 66/54 9 | 65/53 13 | 70/57 12 | 77/63 14 | 83/69 12 | 89/73 13 | 92/76 10 | 91/75 12 | 88/73 10 | 81/67 9 | 75/62 7 | 69/57 8 |
| **TEHRAN,** Iran | 45/27 4 | 50/32 4 | 59/39 5 | 71/49 3 | 82/58 2 | 93/66 1 | 99/72 1 | 97/71 1 | 90/64 1 | 76/53 1 | 63/43 3 | 51/33 4 |
| **TEL AVIV,** Israel | 63/48 10 | 65/48 8 | 67/50 9 | 74/54 2 | 81/60 1 | 84/65 0 | 87/69 0 | 87/70 0 | 86/68 1 | 84/64 2 | 77/59 7 | 66/52 11 |
| **TOKYO,** Japan | 47/29 5 | 48/31 6 | 54/36 10 | 63/46 10 | 71/54 10 | 76/63 12 | 83/70 10 | 86/72 9 | 79/66 12 | 69/55 11 | 60/43 7 | 52/33 5 |
| **VALPARAISO,** Chile | 72/56 1 | 72/56 1 | 70/54 1 | 67/52 1 | 63/50 5 | 60/48 7 | 60/47 7 | 61/47 5 | 62/48 2 | 65/50 2 | 69/52 1 | 71/54 1 |
| **VENICE,** Italy | 43/33 6 | 46/35 5 | 54/41 6 | 63/49 5 | 71/57 8 | 78/64 8 | 82/67 8 | 82/67 5 | 78/62 5 | 65/52 7 | 54/43 7 | 46/37 7 |
| **VIENNA,** Austria | 34/26 8 | 38/28 7 | 47/34 7 | 57/41 9 | 66/50 9 | 71/56 9 | 75/59 9 | 73/58 10 | 66/52 7 | 55/44 8 | 44/36 8 | 37/30 9 |
| **WELLINGTON,** New Zealand | 69/56 10 | 69/56 9 | 67/54 11 | 63/51 13 | 58/47 16 | 55/44 17 | 53/42 18 | 54/43 17 | 57/46 15 | 60/48 14 | 63/50 13 | 67/54 12 |
| **ZURICH,** Switzerland | 48/14 11 | 52/15 11 | 62/22 14 | 70/32 14 | 77/39 14 | 83/47 15 | 86/51 15 | 84/49 14 | 78/42 11 | 68/32 14 | 57/25 12 | 49/16 13 |

## CUSTOMS HINTS

SOURCE: U.S. Customs Service

**Customs exemptions:** These apply only to articles brought back at the time of your return to the United States. You have a $300 exemption (subject to limitations on cigars, cigarettes, and liquor), if you are returning from a stay abroad of at least 48 hours (no minimum time limit for Mexico and American Virgin Islands), and you have not used the $300 exemption or any part of it within the preceding 30 days. Articles in excess of the $300 exemption up to $600 in value, based on the fair retail price of each item in the country of purchase, may be entered at a flat rate of 10%, if accompanying you at the time of your return, if acquired as an incident to your trip, if for personal or household use, and if properly declared to customs.

*Cigars and Cigarettes*—Not more than 100 cigars and 200 cigarettes (one carton) may be included in your exemption. Your cigarettes, however, may be subject to a tax imposed by state and local authorities. Products of Cuban tobacco may be brought in only if acquired in Cuba (FAC).

*Liquor*—One liter of alcoholic beverages may be included in the exemption if you are 21 years old or older. Importation varies with individual states.

**Articles imported in excess of your customs exemption:** Will be subject to duty unless the items are entitled to free entry or prohibited. After deducting your exemption and the value of any articles duty free, a flat rate of duty will be applied to the next $600 worth (fair retail value) of merchandise. Any dollar amount of an article over $600 will be dutiable at various rates of duty based on fair retail value. The flat rate of duty is 10% of fair retail value in the country of acquisition; 5% for articles purchased in certain U.S. Territories.

**Traveling back and forth across border:** If you cross the border at one point and then swing back into the United States to enter the foreign country at another point, you might lose your exemption unless certain requirements are met. Ask a customs officer about these.

**American Virgin Islands, American Samoa, Guam:** If you return either directly or indirectly from these places, you have a $600 customs exemption provided that not more than $300 of it is applied to merchandise obtained elsewhere than these insular possessions. Articles purchased elsewhere than in these islands cannot be mailed as duty-free articles under the exemption. These purchases must accompany the traveler in order to qualify as duty free up to $300.00. (The American Virgin Islands are exempt from the 48-hour minimum time requirement.) Articles whose value exceeds $600 and were acquired in the insular possessions will be assessed at a rate of 5%, and they may accompany you or be shipped home. These articles must be for your own use or for gifts. Four liters of alcoholic beverages may be included in this exemption provided that not more than one liter is acquired elsewhere than in these islands. Liquor cannot be mailed.

**Customs declarations:** All articles acquired abroad and in your possession at the time of your return must be declared to U.S. customs, either orally or in writing. Declaration forms 6059 B are distributed on planes and ships and should be prepared well in advance. Your declaration must include items that you are bringing back for another person at his request, any article that you intend to use or sell in your business, alterations or repairs of articles taken abroad, and gifts given to you while abroad. Wearing or using an article acquired abroad does not exempt it from duty, and it must be declared at the price you paid for it. The customs officer may make a reduction in value for wear and use.

**Necessary written declarations:** All articles acquired abroad must be declared in writing when their total value (including alterations and repairs) exceeds $300, when more than one liter of alcoholic beverages or more than 100 cigars and 200 cigarettes are included, when some of the items are intended for other than personal or household use, or when a customs duty or internal revenue tax is collectible on any article in your possession, or unaccompanied tourist purchases are being sent from U.S. insular possessions.

**Family declarations:** A family head may make a joint declaration for all members residing in the same household and returning with him as a group. A family may bring in articles free of duty valued up to $300 for each member (e.g., a family of seven: $2,100), even if the articles acquired by some members exceed their $300 exemptions. Returning infants and children are entitled to the same exemptions as adults (except for alcoholic beverages). Children born abroad who have never resided in the United States are not eligible for the exemption, but may claim Customs exemption as a nonresident.

**Value of articles:** You must declare the price actually paid for each article. If you do not know the price, say so. If an article was not purchased, state its fair value in the country where it was acquired. If you understate the value of an article or misrepresent an article, you may have to pay a penalty in addition to payment of duty.

**Preparation for customs:** It is helpful to make a list of items obtained abroad before reaching the port of entry. Retain sales slips and have these readily available for examination. Pack articles acquired abroad separately.

**Foreign-made articles taken abroad:** These are dutiable each time they are brought into our country unless you have acceptable proof of prior possession. Documents which fully describe the article, such as a bill of sale or an insurance policy may be considered. Items which may be readily identified by serial number or permanently affixed markings may be taken to the Customs office nearest you and registered before your departure to expedite free entry of these items when you return.

**Gifts:** These are connsidered to be for your personal use and may be included in your exemption. This proviso includes both gifts given to you while abroad and those you intend to give to others after your return. Gifts intended for business or promotional purposes may not be included. While abroad you may send gifts totaling $25 ($40 from U.S. insular possessions) retail value to people in the United States without duty or tax, provided that the addressee does not receive in a single day (at the customs processing station) gift parcels exceeding the $25 limitation. Write "unsolicited gift–Value under $25" in large letters on the outside of package as well as the retail value of the contents. Alcoholic beverages and tobacco products may not be sent, nor alcoholic perfumes valued at more than $5.

**Personal belongings sent home:** Personal belongings of U.S. origin taken abroad may be sent back by mail duty free if, on the outside wrapper or enclosed in the package, it is stated that the articles were taken out of the U.S. as personal effects and are being returned without having been repaired or altered while abroad. Mark packages: "American Goods Returned."

**Automobiles, boats, airplanes:** Vehicles taken abroad for noncommercial use may be returned duty free by proving they were taken out of this country. Proof may be the state registration for an automobile, the Federal Aviation Agency certificate of registration for an airplane, a yacht license or motorboat identification, or a customs registration certificate for any vehicle. Dutiable repairs or accessories acquired abroad must be declared. A leaflet entitled "Importing a Car" is available from any customs office for those considering purchase abroad of a foreign car.

**Household effects:** If you plan to reside overseas for more than one year, household effects may be sometimes duty free. Check with a customs office or U.S. consulate.

**$25 exemption:** If you are not entitled to the $300 exemption because of the 30-day or 48-hour limitations, you may bring in free of duty or tax articles that were acquired abroad for your personal or household use, if their total retail value does not exceed $25. This is an individual exemption that cannot be grouped on a family declaration. You may include any of the following in this exemption: 50 cigarettes, 10 cigars, four ounces of alcoholic beverages, or four ounces of alcoholic perfume. If the value of any article (or articles) exceeds $25, no article may be exempted from duty or tax.

**GSP:** Generalized System of Preferences (GSP) is designed to help improve the economy of 107 developing nations and 32 dependent territories by exempting certain items from import duty when brought into the U.S. from these areas. The brochure "GSP & The Traveler" or a customs office can provide further information.

### PROHIBITED AND RESTRICTED ARTICLES

Articles considered injurious to the general welfare are prohibited entry. Among these items are obscene publications, lottery tickets, wild birds, their eggs and feathers, endangered wildlife and items made from them, protected marine mammals, liquor-filled candies, switchblade knives.

**Narcotics** are also prohibited. If your medical condition requires drugs containing narcotics, you should carry a prescription or written statement from your doctor.

**Trademarked articles:** Foreign-made TM articles may be limited as to the quantity which may be brought into the U.S. if the registered TM has been recorded by an American trademark owner with U.S. Customs. Persons arriving in the U.S. with a TM article are allowed an exemption, usually one article, unless the TM owner allows a quantity over this amount.

**Fruits, plants, vegetables:** These, with cuttings, seeds, and unprocessed plant products, are either prohibited from entry or require an import license. Address applications to: Quarantines, U.S.D.A., Federal Center Bldg., Hyattsville, Md. 20782.

**Meats, livestock, poultry:** These items and their by-products (such as sausage, paté), are prohibited or restricted from entering the U.S., depending on the animal disease condition in the country of origin. Fresh meat is generally prohibited; canned meat is permitted if the inspector can determine that it is commercially canned, hermetically sealed, and can be kept without refrigeration. Other canned, cured, and dried meat is severely restricted from most countries. Cheese, except cottage cheese, may be brought into the country.

**Money or all types of negotiable instruments:** Any amount may be brought into or taken out of the United States. Persons importing or exporting an amount of more than $5,000 are required to file a report of the transaction with U.S. Customs. Ask a customs officer for the CF 4790 form at the time you arrive or depart with such amounts.

**Pets:** There are controls, restrictions and prohibitions on the entry of animals, birds, turtles, wildlife and all endangered species. Cats and dogs must be free of evidence of diseases communicable to man. Vaccination against rabies is not required for cats or dogs arriving from rabies-free countries. Personally owned pet birds may be entered (limit of two if of the Psittacine family), but APHIS and Public Health Service requirements must be met. This includes quarantine at any APHIS facility at specified locations, at the owner's expense. Advance reservations are required. For more information write: Veterinary Services, APHIS, U.S.D.A., Hyattsville, Md. 20782.

*Monkeys*—Live monkeys and other non-human primates may not be imported into the United States except by a registered importer for scientific, educational, or exhibition purposes.

**Biological materials:** Disease organisms and vectors for research and educational purposes require a permit. Write the Foreign Quarantine Program, Center for Disease Control, Atlanta, Ga. 30333.

**Prohibited merchandise:** Under a general license issued by Foreign Assets Control, tourists may import items for their personal use up to a value of $100 from the following countries: Cuba, North Korea, Vietnam, and Cambodia. This allowance may only be used once every six months, and the articles must accompany the visitor upon his return.

**Firearms and ammunition:** Up to three nonautomatic firearms may be taken out of the country and returned if they are registered with customs or field office of the Bureau of Alcohol, Tobacco and Firearms. Firearms and ammunition are subject to import restrictions. Contact the Bureau of Alcohol, Tobacco and Firearms, Department of the Treasury, Washington, D.C. 20226.

## HEALTH HINTS FOR TRAVELERS

SOURCE: U.S. Public Health Service

Under the International Health Regulations adopted by the World Health Organization a country, under certain conditions, may require International Certificates of Vaccination against Smallpox, Cholera, or Yellow Fever. For *direct* travel from the U.S. to many countries, no vaccinations are required—certain vaccinations are required by some countries in Africa and Asia. Some countries require vaccination against yellow fever or cholera if you arrive from an area infected with these diseases. No vaccinations are required to return to the U.S. from any country.

Required immunizations must be recorded in the International Certificates of Vaccination, form PHS-731. You can obtain this form with your passport application, from your local health department, or from the Superintendent of Documents, Government Printing Office, Washington, D.C. 20402, for 50 cents.

The Certificates must be signed by you and your physician or by a person under his supervision and be validated with an approved stamp. Validation of Cholera Certificates can be obtained at most health departments or from vaccinating physicians who possess a validation stamp. Yellow Fever vaccinations must be given at an officially designated Yellow Fever Vaccination Center and the Certificate validated by the Center that administers the vaccine. Information on the location of Yellow Fever Vaccination Centers is available from state and local health departments.

Smallpox has been eradicated. Smallpox vaccination should *not* be given for international travel. If you plan to travel to a country that requires vaccination as a condition for entry, you should consult your physician and obtain a signed, dated statement on the physician's letterhead stationery that smallpox vaccination is contraindicated for health reasons.

The Cholera Certificate is valid for 6 months beginning 6 days after 1 injection of vaccine or on the date of revaccination if within 6 months of the first injection.

The Yellow Fever Certificate is valid for 10 years beginning 10 days after primary vaccination or on the date of revaccination if within 10 years of the first injection.

Military personnel and their dependents, as well as other persons traveling under the auspices of the Department of Defense, are required to receive the immunizations as set forth by current service regulations.

### RECOMMENDED VACCINATIONS

Recommendations on the use of certain vaccines and prophylactic measures depend upon your immunization status, itinerary, the areas of the world to be visited, and the nature and duration of travel. Most international travelers probably do not need any additional vaccination or prophylaxis if their routine immunization status is up to date. In most developed countries such as Canada, Australia, New Zealand, and Europe, the risk to the health of the traveler will be no greater than that incurred while traveling throughout the United States. In the countries of Africa, Asia, South America, and in the countries of southern North America, the South Pacific, Middle East and Far East, living conditions and standards of sanitation and hygiene vary greatly. For travel to primarily tourist areas on itineraries which do not include travel in rural areas and consequently less risk of exposure to food or water of questionable quality, the risk of disease remains quite small. Travelers to smaller cities off the usual tourist routes and those who visit small villages or rural areas for extended periods are at greater risk of acquiring infectious diseases because of exposure to water and food of uncertain quality and closer contact with local residents who may harbor the organisms that cause such diseases. Typhoid is prevalent in many countries of Africa, Asia, and Central and South America. Vaccination is recommended for travel to areas off the usual tourist itinerary. The risk of contacting hepatitis-A varies with living conditions, the prevalence of hepatitis in the areas visited, and particularly the length of stay. Vaccination against plague is not indicated for most travelers to countries reporting cases, particularly if their travel is limited to urban areas with modern lodgings.

Measles is endemic in many countries. Persons traveling abroad for extended periods should be protected against measles either by prior disease or vaccination after the first birthday. Most persons born before 1957 are likely to have been infected naturally and generally need not be considered susceptible.

There is a risk of acquiring malaria when traveling to parts of the Caribbean, Central and South America, Africa, the Middle East, the Indian subcontinent, and the Far East. You are strongly advised to seek information from your health department or private physician concerning the need for protection against malaria and for instructions on how the prophylactic drugs should be taken.

You are advised to contact your local health department, physician or private or public agency that advises international travelers two weeks prior to departure to obtain current information on vaccinations required by and recommended for the countries to be visited.

**Unvaccinated Travelers:** A traveler who does not have the required vaccinations upon entering a country may be subject to vaccination, medical follow-up, and/or isolation.

**Exemption from Vaccination:** If a physician thinks that a particular vaccination should not be performed for medical reasons, the traveler should be given a signed, dated statement of the reasons on the physician's letterhead stationery.

### HEALTH PROTECTION HINTS

If you wear glasses, take along your lens prescription.

If you need medications regularly, take an adequate supply with you. Because of possible serious consequences to your health, do not buy medications "over the counter" unless you are familiar with the product.

If you have diabetes, are allergic to penicillin, or have any physical condition that may require emergency care, have some identification–a tag or bracelet or card–on your person at all times indicating this. Diabetics should take along an extra supply of medication. Drugs or medicines which must be taken should be accompanied by a letter from the traveler's physician.

Water can be considered safe only if it is obtained from adequately chlorinated sources, if boiled for ten minutes, or if treated with liquid chlorine laundry bleach or tincture of iodine.

Swimming in contaminated water may result in eye, ear, and certain intestinal infections. Generally only chlorinated pools can be considered safe places to swim.

Take it easy in unaccustomed conditions of heat and high altitudes.

It is wise to check with the local American Embassy or consulate for a list of acceptable doctors and dentists, and hospitals, if needed.

## WORLD CITIES: COST-OF-LIVING INDEX: 1981

SOURCE: *U.N. Monthly Bulletin of Statistics* (Special Table P), March 1982, © United Nations

Note: This table shows the relative cost-of-living comparison, based on prices for goods, services and housing for international UN officials stationed in various cities of the world. In the following table, the cost-of-living is based on New York City=100.

| City | Index | City | Index | City | Index |
|---|---|---|---|---|---|
| Afghanistan, Kabul | 77 | Germany, West, Bonn | 114 | Nicaragua, Managua | 110 |
| Argentina, Buenos Aires | 110 | Greece, Athens | 106 | Pakistan, Islamabad | 88 |
| Australia, Sydney | 102 | Guatemala, Guatemala | 99 | Panama, Panama City | 98 |
| Austria, Vienna | 115 | Guinea, Conakry | 141 | Paraguay, Asunción | 90 |
| Bangladesh, Dacca | 81 | Guyana, Georgetown | 84 | Peru, Lima | 104 |
| Barbados, Bridgetown | 97 | Haiti, Port-au-Prince | 94 | Philippines, Manila | 92 |
| Belgium, Brussels | 116 | Hungary, Budapest | 69 | Poland, Warsaw | 71 |
| Benin, Cotonou | 93 | India, New Delhi | 81 | Romania, Bucharest | 107 |
| Bolivia, La Paz | 104 | Indonesia, Jakarta | 109 | Senegal, Dakar | 97 |
| Brazil, Rio de Janeiro | 81 | Iraq, Baghdad | 99 | Singapore, Singapore | 99 |
| Bulgaria, Sofia | 100 | Italy, Rome | 88 | Spain, Madrid | 102 |
| Burma, Rangoon | 76 | Jamaica, Kingston | 72 | Sri Lanka, Colombo | 76 |
| Canada, Montréal | 82 | Japan, Tokyo | 156 | Sudan, Khartoum | 95 |
| Chile, Santiago | 132 | Kenya, Nairobi | 116 | Swaziland, Mbabane | 67 |
| Colombia, Bogotá | 107 | Korea, South, Seoul | 137 | Switzerland, Geneva | 138 |
| Cuba, Havana | 73 | Kuwait, Kuwait | 108 | Syria, Damascus | 135 |
| Cyprus, Nicosia | 77 | Liberia, Monrovia | 114 | Thailand, Bangkok | 84 |
| Czechoslovakia, Bratislava | 63 | Libya, Tripoli | 134 | Togo, Lomé | 84 |
| Denmark, Copenhagen | 117 | Madagascar, Antananarivo | 96 | Tunisia, Tunis | 110 |
| Dominican Rep., Santo Domingo | 89 | Malaysia, Kuala Lumpur | 84 | Turkey, Ankara | 72 |
| Ecuador, Quito | 80 | Malta, Valletta | 68 | United Kingdom, London | 123 |
| Egypt, Cairo | 97 | Mauritius, Port Louis | 75 | United States, Washington, DC | 95 |
| El Salvador, San Salvador | 98 | Mexico, Mexico City | 100 | Uruguay, Montevideo | 123 |
| Ethiopia, Addis Ababa | 99 | Morocco, Rabat | 101 | Venezuela, Caracas | 142 |
| Fiji, Suva | 91 | Nepal, Kathmandu | 84 | Yemen, San'a | 122 |
| France, Paris | 117 | Netherlands, The Hague | 117 | Yugoslavia, Belgrade | 92 |

## RATES OF CUSTOMS DUTY: 1982

SOURCE: U.S. Customs Service

This abbreviated list of popular items imported by tourists is intended to be used as an advisory guide only. The customs officer examining baggage at the point of entry determines the rates of duty on dutiable articles. Rates are often higher for items imported from certain Communist-controlled countries. These rates apply to those articles brought in after the $600 maximum has been reached and the 10% flat rate (5% for insular possessions) no longer applies.

**Item** — **Rate**

**Antiques:** produced prior to 100 years before the date of entry ..... Free
**Automobiles**, passenger .......... 2.8%
**Beads:**
imitation precious, and semi-precious stones ..... 4.7 to 11.4%
ivory .......... 8.5%
**Binoculars**, prism .......... Free
**Books** .......... Free
**Cameras:**
motion picture, over $50 each .......... 5.4%
still, over $10 each .......... 5.8%
cases, leather .......... 9.5%
lenses .......... 10.3%
**China:**
bone .......... 13.9%
nonbone, other than tableware .......... 14.3 to 26%
**China tableware**, nonbone, available in 77-piece sets:
valued not over $56 per set .......... 33.9%
valued over $56 per set .......... 15.8%
**Cigarette lighters, precious metal:**
pocket, valued at over 42 cents each .......... 12.1%
table .......... 9.3%
**Clocks**, valued over $5 but not over $10 ........ 58¢ + 12.4% + 4.8¢ for each jewel
valued over $10 each .......... 86¢ + 12.4% + 4.8¢ for each jewel
**Drawings** (done all by hand) ....... Free
**Earthenware tableware, household** available in 77-piece sets:
valued not over $38 per set .......... 19.7%
valued over $38 per set .......... 8.8%

**Item** — **Rate**

**Figurines, china** .......... 3.7 to 17.4%
**Fur:** wearing apparel .......... 7.3 to 14.3%
other manufactures of .......... 3.4 to 9.5%
**Furniture:**
wood, chairs .......... 6.6 to 7.3%
wood, other than chairs ...... 4.1%
**Gloves:**
wool, over $4 per dozen .......... 33¢ lb. + 16.6%
horsehide or cowhide .......... 15%
**Handkerchiefs**, cotton, plain ........ 23.2% to 4¢ lb. + 32.4%
**Ivory**, manufactures of .......... 5.3%
**Jade**, cut but not set .......... 2.4%
other articles of jade .......... 21%
**Jewelry**, precious metal or stone:
silver chief value, valued not over $18 per doz .......... 27.5%
other .......... 9.9%
**Leather:**
pocketbooks, bags ..... 7.3 to 9.9%
wallets .......... 6.1 to 10%
other manufactures of .. 5.3 to 8.4%
**Motorcycles** .......... 4.5%
**Musical instruments:**
music boxes .......... 6.2%
woodwind, except bagpipes ... 6.5%
**Paintings** (done all by hand) ....... Free
**Pearls**, loose or temporarily strung and without clasp:
genuine .......... Free
cultured .......... 2.4%
imitation .......... 15.5%
permanently or temporarily strung (with clasp attached or separate) ......... 9.9 to 21.3%
**Perfume** .......... 5¢ lb. + 6.6%
**Postage stamps** .......... Free
**Radios:**
transistors .......... 9.3 to 9.8%
other .......... 6%

**Item** — **Rate**

**Rattan:**
furniture .......... 14.9%
other manufactures of ...... 10.3%
**Records**, phonograph .......... 4.5%
**Shaver**, electric .......... 5.7%
**Shell**, manufactures of .......... 3.4%
**Shoes**, leather .......... 2.5 to 20%
**Sterling flatware and tableware:**
knives and forks 2.5¢ each + 7.4%
spoons and tableware ....... 10.3%
**Stereo equipment** .......... 5.1 to 6.5%
**Stones, cut but not set:**
diamonds not over one-half carat .......... Free
diamonds over one-half carat .......... Free
other .......... Free to 3.1%
**Sweaters**, of wool, over $5 per pound 31¢ lb. + 14.2 to 19.5%
**Tape recorders** .......... 4.9%
**Toys** .......... 13.6%
**Watches**, on $100 watch, duty varies from $3 to $13
**Wearing apparel:**
embroidered or ornamented ........ 18 to 41.3%
not embroidered, not ornamented
cotton, knit ........ 18.8 to 21%
cotton, not knit ...... 7.5 to 21%
linen, not knit .......... 6.8%
manmade fiber, knit ........ 21¢ lb. + 30.3% to 23¢ lb. + 32.5%
manmade fiber, not knit ..... 21¢ lb. + 25.4% to 23¢ lb. + 27.5%
silk, knit .......... 9.3%
silk, other .......... 14.6%
wool, knit ..... 31¢ lb. + 19.5% to 31¢ lb. + 28.8%
**Wood**, carvings and articles of .... 6.9%

### ALCOHOLIC BEVERAGES IMPORT RESTRICTIONS

**State laws:** Liquor may not be imported in violation of state law.

**Mail importations:** United States postal laws prohibit the shipment of alcoholic beverages by mail.

**Gift packages:** Alcoholic beverages may not be included in gift parcels sent to persons in the U.S.A. and are not entitled to free entry under the $25 gift exemption.

**Customs Exemption:** A returning resident 21 years or older may include in his $300 customs exemption one liter of alcoholic beverages free of duty and internal revenue tax. The importation must be for his own use or for a gift and not in violation of the laws of the state of arrival.

## MAJOR COMMERCIAL PASSENGER PLANES

| Country / Company and Type | Maximum Number of Passengers | Maximum Speed (MPH) | Wingspan (Feet) | Length (Feet) | Height (Feet) |
|---|---|---|---|---|---|
| **International Europe** | | | | | |
| Airbus Industrie A300 | 345 | 576 | 147.1 | 175.1 | 54.2 |
| Airbus Industrie A310 | 252 | 576 | 144.0 | 153.1 | 51.8 |
| **France** | | | | | |
| Aerospatiale A-300-B2 | 345 | 620 | 147.1 | 175.9 | 54.2 |
| Aerospatiale A-300-B4 | 345 | 620 | 147.1 | 175.9 | 54.2 |
| Aerospatiale A-310-200 | 255 | 620 | 144.0 | 153.1 | 51.9 |
| Aerospatiale Concorde | 140 | 1300 | 84.0 | 203.9 | 37.1 |
| **United Kingdom** | | | | | |
| BAe 146-100 | 90 | 480 | 86.4 | 85.8 | 28.2 |
| BAe 146-200 | 109 | 475 | 86.4 | 93.7 | 28.2 |
| BAC 1-11 200 | 89 | 576 | 88.5 | 93.5 | 24.5 |
| BAC 1-11 400 | 89 | 576 | 88.5 | 93.5 | 24.5 |
| BAC 1-11 475 | 89 | 541 | 93.5 | 93.5 | 24.5 |
| BAC 1-11 500 | 119 | 541 | 93.5 | 107.0 | 24.5 |
| HS Trident 1E | 115 | 605 | 94.8 | 114.8 | 27.8 |
| HS Trident 2E | 132 | 610 | 98.0 | 114.8 | 27.0 |
| HS Trident 3 | 160 | 605 | 98.0 | 131.1 | 28.2 |
| HS 748 | 60 | 281 | 98.5 | 67.0 | 24.8 |
| HS 748-2B | 60 | 281 | 102.5 | 67.0 | 24.8 |
| Viscount 700 | 64 | 268 | 93.7 | 81.1 | 26.8 |
| Viscount 800 | 76 | 271 | 93.7 | 85.7 | 26.8 |
| Viscount 810 | 73 | 301 | 93.7 | 85.7 | 26.8 |
| Concorde | 108 | 1350 | 83.8 | 203.8 | 37.1 |
| **Japan** | | | | | |
| Nihon YS-11 | 60 | 297 | 105.0 | 86.3 | 29.5 |
| **Netherlands** | | | | | |
| Fokker F27 MK500 | 60 | 298 | 95.2 | 82.2 | 28.6 |
| Fokker F27 MK600 | 48 | 298 | 95.2 | 77.3 | 27.9 |
| Fokker F28 MK3000 | 65 | 524 | 82.25 | 89.9 | 27.8 |
| Fokker F28 MK4000 | 85 | 524 | 82.25 | 97.1 | 27.8 |
| Fokker F28 MK6000 | 85 | 524 | 82.25 | 97.1 | 27.8 |
| **USSR** | | | | | |
| Ilyushin IL-18V | 110 | 425 | 122.7 | 117.8 | — |
| Ilyushin IL-62 | 186 | 560 | 142.0 | 174.2 | 40.5 |
| Tupolev TU-134 | 72 | 621 | 95.2 | 114.5 | 29.7 |
| Tupolev TU-144 | 130 | M.2.3 | 81.0 | 180.0 | — |
| Tupolev TU-154 | 164 | 559 | 123.3 | 157.2 | 37.5 |
| **United States** | | | | | |
| Boeing 707-320 B/C | 219 | 600 plus | 145.7 | 152.9 | 42.5 |
| Boeing 727-200 | 189 | 600 plus | 108.0 | 153.2 | 34.0 |
| Boeing 737-200 | 130 | 573 | 93.0 | 100.0 | 37.0 |
| Boeing 737-300 | 300 | 148 | 94.8 | 109.6 | 36.5 |
| Boeing 747 | 550 | 640 | 195.6 | 231.3 | 63.4 |
| Boeing 757 | 233 | 600 | 124.5 | 155.25 | 44.5 |
| Boeing 767 | 289 | 600 | 156.1 | 159.1 | 52.0 |
| General Dynamics Convair 880 | 107 | 600 | 120.0 | 129.0 | 42.0 |
| General Dynamics Convair 990 | 130 | 500 | 131.0 | 141.0 | 42.0 |
| Lockheed TriStar L-1011 | 400 | 620 | 155.4 | 177.7 | 55.4 |
| Lockheed TriStar L-1011-100 | 400 | 620 | 155.4 | 177.7 | 55.4 |
| Lockheed TriStar L-1011-200 | 400 | 620 | 155.4 | 177.7 | 55.4 |
| Lockheed TriStar L-1011-500 | 330 | 620 | 164.3 | 164.2 | 55.4 |
| McDonnell Douglas DC-9 Series 10 | 90 | 586 | 89.3 | 104.3 | 27.5 |
| McDonnell Douglas DC-9 Series 20 | 90 | 586 | 93.3 | 104.3 | 27.5 |
| McDonnell Douglas DC-9 Series 30 | 139 | 586 | 93.3 | 119.25 | 27.5 |
| McDonnell Douglas DC-9 Series 40 | 139 | 576 | 93.3 | 125.5 | 28.0 |
| McDonnell Douglas DC-9 Series 50 | 139 | 576 | 93.3 | 133.5 | 28.0 |
| McDonnell Douglas DC-9 Super 80 | 172 | 576 | 107.8 | 147.9 | 29.3 |
| McDonnell Douglas DC-10 Series 10 | 380 | 600 plus | 155.3 | 182.25 | 58.1 |
| McDonnell Douglas DC-10 Series 30 | 380 | 600 plus | 165.3 | 181.6 | 58.1 |
| McDonnell Douglas DC-10 Series 40 | 380 | 600 plus | 165.3 | 182.25 | 58.1 |

## OPERATIONS AT 30 TOP-RANKING U.S. AIRPORTS: FISCAL YEAR 1981

SOURCE: Federal Aviation Administration

| Tower | Rank | 1981 Operations† |
|---|---|---|
| Chicago O'Hare Int'l, Ill. | 1 | 677,553 |
| Atlanta International, Ga. | 2 | 614,641 |
| Long Beach, Calif. | 3 | 593,119 |
| Van Nuys, Calif. | 4 | 551,249 |
| Los Angeles Int'l, Calif. | 5 | 510,874 |
| Santa Ana, Calif. | 6 | 482,407 |
| Denver Stapleton Int'l, Colo. | 7 | 479,060 |
| Dallas-Ft. Worth Regional, Tex. | 8 | 466,917 |
| Oakland International, Calif. | 9 | 459,654 |
| Seattle Boeing, Wash. | 10 | 419,484 |
| Tamiami, Fla. | 11 | 407,276 |
| Fort Worth Meacham, Tex. | 12 | 396,381 |
| Denver Arapahoe County, Colo. | 13 | 393,362 |
| San Jose Municipal, Calif. | 14 | 375,615 |
| Opa Locka, Fla. | 15 | 369,737 |
| Houston Hobby, Tex. | 16 | 356,407 |
| Miami International, Fla. | 17 | 353,705 |
| Phoenix Sky Harbor Int'l, Ariz. | 18 | 352,546 |
| Honolulu, Hawaii | 19 | 351,892 |
| Washington National, D.C. | 20 | 349,590 |
| Pittsburgh Greater Int'l, Pa. | 21 | 347,845 |
| Torrance Municipal, Calif. | 22 | 336,843 |
| Philadelphia Int'l, Pa. | 23 | 335,875 |
| Las Vegas McCarran Int'l, Nev. | 24 | 333,355 |
| La Guardia, N.Y. | 25 | 332,456 |
| San Francisco, Calif. | 26 | 329,112 |
| Dallas Love Field, Tex. | 27 | 323,588 |
| Concord, Calif. | 28 | 320,809 |
| St. Louis Int'l, Mo. | 29 | 320,473 |
| Anchorage Merrill, Alaska | 30 | 312,251 |

†Takeoffs and landings.

## AIR DISTANCES BETWEEN MAJOR WORLD CITIES (See also, U.S. AIR DISTANCES, p. 221)

SOURCE: USAF Aeronautical Chart and Information Center (in statute miles)

| | Bangkok | Berlin | Cairo | Cape Town | Caracas | Chicago | Hong Kong | Honolulu | Istanbul | Lima | London | Madrid | Melbourne |
|---|---|---|---|---|---|---|---|---|---|---|---|---|---|
| Accra | 6,850 | 3,330 | 2,672 | 2,974 | 4,576 | 5,837 | 7,615 | 10,052 | 3,039 | 5,421 | 3,169 | 2,412 | 9,325 |
| Amsterdam | 5,707 | 360 | 2,015 | 5,997 | 4,883 | 4,118 | 5,772 | 7,254 | 1,372 | 6,538 | 222 | 921 | 10,286 |
| Anchorage | 6,022 | 4,545 | 6,116 | 10,478 | 5,353 | 2,858 | 5,073 | 2,778 | 5,388 | 6,385 | 4,491 | 5,181 | 7,729 |
| Athens | 4,930 | 1,121 | 671 | 4,957 | 5,815 | 5,447 | 5,316 | 8,353 | 352 | 7,312 | 1,488 | 1,474 | 9,297 |
| Auckland | 4,645 | 9,995 | 8,825 | 6,574 | 9,620 | 9,507 | 4,625 | 5,346 | 9,203 | 7,989 | 10,570 | 10,884 | 1,610 |
| Baghdad | 3,756 | 2,029 | 798 | 4,924 | 7,020 | 6,430 | 4,260 | 8,399 | 1,006 | 8,487 | 2,547 | 2,675 | 8,105 |
| Bangkok | — | 5,351 | 4,521 | 6,301 | 10,558 | 8,569 | 1,076 | 6,610 | 4,648 | 12,241 | 5,929 | 6,334 | 4,579 |
| Beirut | 4,272 | 1,689 | 341 | 4,794 | 6,520 | 6,097 | 4,756 | 8,536 | 614 | 7,972 | 2,151 | 2,190 | 8,579 |
| Belgrade | 5,073 | 623 | 1,147 | 5,419 | 5,587 | 5,000 | 5,327 | 7,882 | 500 | 7,169 | 1,053 | 1,263 | 9,578 |
| Berlin | 5,351 | — | 1,768 | 5,958 | 5,242 | 4,415 | 5,443 | 7,323 | 1,075 | 6,893 | 580 | 1,162 | 9,929 |
| Bombay | 1,870 | 3,915 | 2,717 | 5,103 | 9,034 | 8,066 | 2,679 | 8,036 | 3,000 | 10,389 | 4,478 | 4,689 | 6,101 |
| Buenos Aires | 10,490 | 7,395 | 7,360 | 4,285 | 3,155 | 5,582 | 11,478 | 7,554 | 7,608 | 1,945 | 6,907 | 6,236 | 7,219 |
| Cairo | 4,521 | 1,768 | — | 4,510 | 6,337 | 6,116 | 5,057 | 8,818 | 741 | 7,725 | 2,158 | 2,069 | 8,700 |
| Cape Town | 6,301 | 5,958 | 4,510 | — | 6,361 | 8,489 | 7,377 | 11,534 | 5,204 | 6,074 | 5,988 | 5,306 | 6,428 |
| Caracas | 10,558 | 5,242 | 6,337 | 6,361 | — | 2,500 | 10,171 | 6,024 | 6,050 | 1,699 | 4,662 | 4,351 | 9,703 |
| Chicago | 8,569 | 4,415 | 6,116 | 8,489 | 2,500 | — | 7,797 | 4,256 | 5,485 | 3,772 | 3,960 | 4,192 | 9,667 |
| Copenhagen | 5,361 | 222 | 1,964 | 6,179 | 5,215 | 4,263 | 5,392 | 7,101 | 1,252 | 6,886 | 595 | 1,289 | 9,936 |
| Denver | 8,409 | 5,092 | 6,846 | 9,331 | 3,078 | 920 | 7,476 | 3,346 | 6,164 | 3,986 | 4,701 | 5,028 | 8,755 |
| Frankfurt (W. Germany) | 5,581 | 270 | 1,817 | 5,815 | 5,022 | 4,344 | 5,709 | 7,450 | 1,160 | 6,660 | 408 | 885 | 10,133 |
| Helsinki | 4,903 | 689 | 2,069 | 6,490 | 5,658 | 4,442 | 4,867 | 6,818 | 1,330 | 7,349 | 1,135 | 1,835 | 9,448 |
| Hong Kong | 1,076 | 5,443 | 5,057 | 7,377 | 10,171 | 7,797 | — | 5,557 | 4,989 | 11,415 | 5,986 | 6,556 | 4,605 |
| Honolulu | 6,610 | 7,323 | 8,818 | 11,534 | 6,024 | 4,256 | 5,557 | — | 8,118 | 5,944 | 7,241 | 7,874 | 5,501 |
| Houston | 9,261 | 5,337 | 7,005 | 8,608 | 2,262 | 942 | 8,349 | 3,902 | 6,400 | 3,123 | 4,860 | 5,014 | 8,979 |
| Istanbul | 4,648 | 1,075 | 741 | 5,204 | 6,050 | 5,485 | 4,989 | 8,118 | — | 7,593 | 1,551 | 1,701 | 9,100 |
| Karachi | 2,305 | 3,365 | 2,222 | 5,153 | 8,502 | 7,564 | 2,977 | 8,059 | 2,457 | 9,943 | 3,928 | 4,152 | 6,646 |
| Keflavik | 6,300 | 1,505 | 3,267 | 7,107 | 4,269 | 2,942 | 6,044 | 6,085 | 2,578 | 5,965 | 1,188 | 1,802 | 10,552 |
| Kinshasa | 5,974 | 3,916 | 2,618 | 2,047 | 5,752 | 7,085 | 6,904 | 11,178 | 3,241 | 6,322 | 3,951 | 3,305 | 8,112 |
| Leningrad | 4,718 | 826 | 2,034 | 6,500 | 5,843 | 4,589 | 4,687 | 6,816 | 1,306 | 7,534 | 1,307 | 1,985 | 9,263 |
| Lima | 12,241 | 6,893 | 7,725 | 6,074 | 1,699 | 3,772 | 11,415 | 5,944 | 7,593 | — | 6,316 | 5,907 | 8,052 |
| Lisbon | 6,651 | 1,442 | 2,352 | 5,301 | 4,040 | 4,001 | 6,862 | 7,835 | 2,015 | 5,591 | 989 | 317 | 11,049 |
| London | 5,929 | 580 | 2,158 | 5,988 | 4,662 | 3,960 | 5,986 | 7,241 | 1,551 | 6,316 | — | 786 | 10,508 |
| Madrid | 6,334 | 1,162 | 2,069 | 5,306 | 4,351 | 4,192 | 6,556 | 7,874 | 1,701 | 5,907 | 786 | — | 10,766 |
| Melbourne | 4,579 | 9,929 | 8,700 | 6,428 | 9,703 | 9,667 | 4,605 | 5,501 | 9,100 | 8,052 | 10,508 | 10,766 | — |
| Mexico City | 9,793 | 6,054 | 7,677 | 8,516 | 2,234 | 1,688 | 8,789 | 3,791 | 7,106 | 2,635 | 5,558 | 5,642 | 8,420 |
| Montreal | 8,337 | 3,740 | 5,403 | 7,920 | 2,443 | 746 | 7,736 | 4,919 | 4,798 | 3,967 | 3,256 | 3,449 | 10,390 |
| Moscow | 4,394 | 1,001 | 1,770 | 6,277 | 6,176 | 4,984 | 4,443 | 7,049 | 1,087 | 7,855 | 1,556 | 2,140 | 8,965 |
| Nairobi | 4,481 | 3,947 | 2,217 | 2,543 | 7,179 | 8,012 | 5,447 | 10,740 | 2,957 | 7,821 | 4,229 | 3,840 | 7,159 |
| New Delhi | 1,812 | 3,598 | 2,752 | 5,769 | 8,837 | 7,486 | 2,339 | 7,413 | 2,837 | 10,430 | 4,178 | 4,528 | 6,340 |
| New York City | 8,669 | 3,980 | 5,598 | 7,801 | 2,124 | 714 | 8.061 | 4,969 | 5,022 | 3,635 | 3,473 | 3,596 | 10,352 |
| Oslo | 5,395 | 523 | 2,243 | 6,477 | 5,167 | 4,050 | 5,342 | 6,801 | 1,518 | 6,857 | 718 | 1,485 | 9,934 |
| Panama City | 10,871 | 5,856 | 7,118 | 7,021 | 867 | 2,321 | 10,089 | 5,254 | 6,756 | 1,454 | 5,285 | 5,081 | 9,027 |
| Paris | 5,877 | 549 | 1,973 | 5,782 | 4,735 | 4,145 | 5,992 | 7,452 | 1,400 | 6,367 | 215 | 652 | 10,442 |
| Peking | 2,027 | 4,600 | 4,687 | 8,034 | 8,978 | 6,625 | 1,195 | 5,084 | 4,407 | 10,365 | 5,089 | 5,759 | 5,632 |
| Rabat | 6,652 | 1,623 | 2,230 | 4,954 | 4,111 | 4,282 | 6,954 | 8,177 | 2,008 | 5,590 | 1,254 | 474 | 10,856 |
| Rio de Janeiro | 9,987 | 6,207 | 6,153 | 3,773 | 2,805 | 5,288 | 11,002 | 8,295 | 6,378 | 2,351 | 5,751 | 5,045 | 8,218 |
| Rome | 5,493 | 735 | 1,305 | 5,231 | 5,198 | 4,823 | 5,773 | 8,040 | 853 | 6,748 | 892 | 849 | 9,940 |
| Saigon (Ho Chi Minh City) | 467 | 5,771 | 4,987 | 6,534 | 10,905 | 8,695 | 938 | 6,302 | 5,102 | 12,180 | 6,345 | 6,779 | 4,168 |
| San Francisco | 7,930 | 5,673 | 7,436 | 10,248 | 3,908 | 1,860 | 6,904 | 2,397 | 6,711 | 4,516 | 5,369 | 5,806 | 7,850 |
| Santiago | 10,967 | 7,772 | 7,967 | 4,947 | 3,033 | 5,295 | 11,615 | 6,861 | 8,135 | 1,528 | 7,241 | 6,639 | 7,017 |
| Seattle | 7,455 | 5,060 | 6,809 | 10,205 | 4,096 | 1,737 | 6,481 | 2,681 | 6,077 | 4,961 | 4,799 | 5,303 | 8,176 |
| Shanghai | 1,797 | 5,231 | 5,188 | 8,062 | 9,508 | 7,071 | 760 | 4,947 | 4,975 | 10,665 | 5,728 | 6,386 | 4,991 |
| Shannon | 6,256 | 940 | 2,534 | 6,188 | 4,320 | 3,583 | 6,246 | 7,006 | 1,938 | 5,992 | 387 | 884 | 10,826 |
| Singapore | 887 | 6,167 | 5,143 | 6,007 | 11,408 | 9,376 | 1,608 | 6,728 | 5,379 | 11,689 | 6,747 | 7,079 | 3,767 |
| St. Louis | 8,763 | 4,676 | 6,370 | 8,549 | 2,414 | 265 | 7,949 | 4,134 | 5,744 | 3,589 | 4,215 | 4,426 | 9,476 |
| Stockholm | 5,141 | 505 | 2,084 | 6,422 | 5,422 | 4,288 | 5,115 | 6,873 | 1,347 | 7,109 | 892 | 1,613 | 9,693 |
| Tehran | 3,392 | 2,184 | 1,220 | 5,240 | 7,322 | 6,502 | 3,844 | 8,072 | 1,274 | 8,850 | 2,739 | 2,974 | 7,838 |
| Tokyo | 2,865 | 5,557 | 5,937 | 9,155 | 8,813 | 6,313 | 1,792 | 3,860 | 5,574 | 9,628 | 5,956 | 6,704 | 5,070 |
| Vienna | 5,252 | 323 | 1,455 | 5,656 | 5,374 | 4,696 | 5,432 | 7,632 | 791 | 6,990 | 767 | 1,124 | 9,802 |
| Warsaw | 5,032 | 322 | 1,588 | 5,934 | 5,563 | 4,679 | 5,147 | 7,368 | 858 | 7,212 | 901 | 1,425 | 9,609 |
| Washington D.C. | 8,807 | 4,182 | 5,800 | 7,892 | 2,051 | 2,598 | 8,157 | 4,839 | 5,225 | 3,504 | 3,676 | 3,794 | 10,174 |

| Mexico City | Montreal | Moscow | Nairobi | New Delhi | New York | Paris | Peking | Rio de Janeiro | Rome | San Francisco | Singapore | Stockholm | Tehran | Tokyo | Vienna | Warsaw |
|---|---|---|---|---|---|---|---|---|---|---|---|---|---|---|---|---|
| 6,677 | 5,146 | 4,038 | 2,603 | 5,279 | 5,126 | 2,988 | 7,359 | 3,501 | 2,624 | 7,688 | 7,183 | 3,835 | 3,874 | 8,594 | 3,100 | 3,440 |
| 5,735 | 3,426 | 1,337 | 4,136 | 3,958 | 3,654 | 271 | 4,890 | 5,938 | 807 | 5,465 | 6,526 | 701 | 2,533 | 5,788 | 581 | 681 |
| 3,776 | 3,133 | 4,364 | 8,287 | 5,709 | 3,373 | 4,697 | 3,997 | 8,145 | 5,263 | 2,005 | 6,678 | 4,102 | 5,654 | 3,463 | 4,856 | 4,601 |
| 7,021 | 4,737 | 1,387 | 2,827 | 3,120 | 4,938 | 1,305 | 4,757 | 6,030 | 654 | 6,792 | 5,629 | 1,498 | 1,539 | 5,924 | 801 | 996 |
| 8,274 | 10,231 | 9,018 | 7,315 | 6,420 | 10,194 | 10,519 | 5,626 | 8,259 | 10,048 | 7,692 | 3,848 | 9,732 | 7,935 | 5,017 | 9,886 | 9,676 |
| 8,082 | 5,768 | 1,583 | 2,431 | 1,966 | 6,007 | 2,405 | 3,925 | 6,938 | 1,836 | 7,466 | 4,427 | 2,164 | 431 | 5,199 | 1,781 | 1,752 |
| 9,793 | 8,337 | 4,394 | 4,481 | 1,812 | 8,669 | 5,877 | 2,027 | 9,987 | 5,493 | 7,930 | 887 | 5,141 | 3,392 | 2,865 | 5,252 | 5,032 |
| 7,707 | 5,405 | 1,514 | 2,420 | 2,479 | 5,622 | 1,987 | 4,352 | 6,478 | 1,368 | 7,302 | 4,935 | 1,931 | 913 | 5,598 | 1,401 | 1,459 |
| 6,610 | 4,305 | 1,066 | 3,328 | 3,270 | 4,526 | 902 | 4,634 | 6,145 | 449 | 6,296 | 5,833 | 1,010 | 1,741 | 5,720 | 309 | 516 |
| 6,054 | 3,740 | 1,001 | 3,947 | 3,598 | 3,980 | 549 | 4,600 | 6,207 | 735 | 5,673 | 6,167 | 505 | 2,184 | 5,557 | 323 | 322 |
| 9,739 | 7,524 | 3,132 | 2,811 | 722 | 7,811 | 4,367 | 2,953 | 8,334 | 3,846 | 8,406 | 2,427 | 3,880 | 1,743 | 4,196 | 3,725 | 3,601 |
| 4,580 | 5,597 | 8,369 | 6,479 | 9,823 | 5,279 | 6,857 | 11,994 | 1,231 | 6,925 | 6,455 | 9,870 | 7,799 | 8,565 | 11,411 | 7,334 | 7,656 |
| 7,677 | 5,403 | 1,770 | 2,217 | 2,752 | 5,598 | 1,973 | 4,687 | 6,153 | 1,305 | 7,436 | 5,143 | 2,084 | 1,220 | 5,937 | 1,455 | 1,588 |
| 8,516 | 7,920 | 6,277 | 2,543 | 5,769 | 7,801 | 5,782 | 8,034 | 3,773 | 5,231 | 10,248 | 6,007 | 6,422 | 5,240 | 9,155 | 5,656 | 5,934 |
| 2,234 | 2,443 | 6,176 | 7,179 | 8,837 | 2,124 | 4,735 | 8,978 | 2,805 | 5,198 | 3,908 | 11,408 | 5,422 | 7,322 | 8,813 | 5,374 | 5,563 |
| 1,688 | 746 | 4,984 | 8,012 | 7,486 | 714 | 4,145 | 6,625 | 5,288 | 4,823 | 1,860 | 9,376 | 4,288 | 6,502 | 6,313 | 4,696 | 4,679 |
| 5,918 | 3,605 | 971 | 4,156 | 3,640 | 3,857 | 642 | 4,503 | 6,321 | 953 | 5,473 | 6,195 | 325 | 2,287 | 5,415 | 540 | 417 |
| 1,438 | 1,639 | 5,501 | 8,867 | 7,730 | 1,631 | 4,900 | 6,385 | 5,866 | 5,887 | 953 | 9,079 | 4,879 | 7,033 | 5,815 | 5,395 | 5,322 |
| 5,945 | 3,650 | 1,261 | 3,865 | 3,811 | 3,857 | 295 | 4,853 | 5,932 | 595 | 5,700 | 6,386 | 745 | 2,346 | 5,831 | 388 | 559 |
| 6,101 | 3,845 | 554 | 4,282 | 3,247 | 4,126 | 1,192 | 3,956 | 6,872 | 1,370 | 5,435 | 5,759 | 248 | 2,062 | 4,872 | 895 | 569 |
| 8,789 | 7,736 | 4,443 | 5,447 | 2,339 | 8,061 | 5,992 | 1,195 | 11,002 | 5,773 | 6,904 | 1,608 | 5,115 | 3,844 | 1,792 | 5,432 | 5,147 |
| 3,791 | 4,919 | 7,049 | 10,740 | 7,413 | 4,969 | 7,452 | 5,084 | 8,295 | 8,040 | 2,397 | 6,728 | 6,873 | 8,072 | 3,860 | 7,632 | 7,368 |
| 749 | 1,605 | 5,925 | 8,746 | 8,388 | 1,419 | 5,035 | 7,244 | 5,015 | 5,702 | 1,648 | 9,954 | 5,227 | 7,442 | 6,685 | 5,609 | 5,609 |
| 7,106 | 4,798 | 1,087 | 2,957 | 2,837 | 5,022 | 1,400 | 4,407 | 6,378 | 853 | 6,711 | 5,379 | 1,347 | 1,274 | 5,574 | 791 | 858 |
| 9,249 | 6,997 | 2,600 | 2,708 | 678 | 7,277 | 3,817 | 3,020 | 8,082 | 3,306 | 8,078 | 2,942 | 3,340 | 1,194 | 4,313 | 3,175 | 3,052 |
| 4,614 | 2,317 | 2,083 | 5,404 | 4,749 | 2,597 | 1,402 | 4,951 | 6,090 | 2,068 | 4,196 | 7,181 | 1,352 | 3,568 | 5,497 | 1,813 | 1,745 |
| 7,915 | 6,378 | 4,328 | 4,234 | 4,692 | 6,378 | 3,742 | 7,002 | 4,105 | 3,186 | 8,920 | 6,132 | 4,388 | 3,612 | 8,307 | 3,619 | 3,910 |
| 6,276 | 4,005 | 396 | 4,230 | 3,069 | 4,291 | 1,350 | 3,789 | 7,028 | 1,460 | 5,523 | 5,575 | 431 | 1,926 | 4,733 | 986 | 642 |
| 2,635 | 3,967 | 7,855 | 7,821 | 10,430 | 3,635 | 6,367 | 10,365 | 2,351 | 6,748 | 4,516 | 11,689 | 7,109 | 8,850 | 9,628 | 6,990 | 7,212 |
| 5,396 | 3,255 | 2,433 | 4,013 | 4,844 | 3,377 | 904 | 6,040 | 4,777 | 1,163 | 5,679 | 7,393 | 1,862 | 3,288 | 6,943 | 1,432 | 1,720 |
| 5,558 | 3,256 | 1,556 | 4,229 | 4,178 | 3,473 | 215 | 5,089 | 5,751 | 892 | 5,369 | 6,747 | 892 | 2,739 | 5,956 | 767 | 901 |
| 5,642 | 3,449 | 2,140 | 3,840 | 4,528 | 3,596 | 652 | 5,759 | 5,045 | 849 | 5,806 | 7,079 | 1,613 | 2,974 | 6,704 | 1,124 | 1,425 |
| 8,420 | 10,390 | 8,965 | 7,159 | 6,340 | 10,352 | 10,442 | 5,632 | 8,218 | 9,940 | 7,850 | 3,767 | 9,693 | 7,838 | 5,070 | 9,802 | 9,609 |
| — | 2,315 | 6,671 | 9,218 | 9,119 | 2,086 | 5,723 | 7,772 | 4,769 | 6,374 | 1,889 | 10,331 | 5,965 | 8,182 | 7,036 | 6,316 | 6,335 |
| 2,315 | — | 4,397 | 7,267 | 7,012 | 333 | 3,432 | 6,541 | 5,082 | 4,102 | 2,544 | 9,207 | 3,667 | 5,879 | 6,470 | 4,007 | 4,021 |
| 6,671 | 4,397 | — | 3,928 | 2,703 | 4,680 | 1,550 | 3,627 | 7,162 | 1,477 | 5,884 | 5,236 | 764 | 1,534 | 4,663 | 1,039 | 716 |
| 9,218 | 7,267 | 3,928 | — | 3,371 | 7,365 | 4,020 | 5,720 | 5,556 | 3,340 | 9,598 | 4,636 | 4,299 | 2,709 | 6,996 | 3,625 | 3,800 |
| 9,119 | 7,012 | 2,703 | 3,317 | — | 7,319 | 4,103 | 2,350 | 8,747 | 3,684 | 7,691 | 2,574 | 3,466 | 1,584 | 3,638 | 3,467 | 3,277 |
| 2,086 | 333 | 4,680 | 7,365 | 7,319 | — | 3,638 | 6,867 | 4,805 | 4,293 | 2,574 | 9,539 | 3,939 | 6,141 | 6,757 | 4,233 | 4,271 |
| 5,722 | 3,418 | 1,024 | 4,446 | 3,726 | 3,686 | 838 | 4,395 | 6,462 | 1,248 | 5,196 | 6,249 | 260 | 2,462 | 5,238 | 839 | 661 |
| 1,496 | 2,542 | 6,720 | 8,043 | 9,422 | 2,213 | 5,388 | 8,939 | 3,296 | 5,916 | 3,326 | 11,692 | 5,956 | 8,011 | 8,441 | 6,031 | 6,175 |
| 5,723 | 3,432 | 1,550 | 4,020 | 4,103 | 3,638 | — | 5,138 | 5,681 | 688 | 5,579 | 6,676 | 964 | 2,624 | 6,054 | 643 | 853 |
| 7,772 | 6,541 | 3,627 | 5,720 | 2,350 | 6,867 | 5,138 | — | 10,778 | 5,076 | 5,934 | 2,754 | 4,197 | 3,496 | 1,305 | 4,664 | 4,340 |
| 5,612 | 3,537 | 2,579 | 3,733 | 4,841 | 3,636 | 1,125 | 6,206 | 4,589 | 1,184 | 5,995 | 7,348 | 2,084 | 3,263 | 7,174 | 1,546 | 1,866 |
| 4,769 | 5,082 | 7,162 | 5,556 | 8,747 | 4,805 | 5,681 | 10,778 | — | 5,704 | 6,621 | 9,776 | 6,638 | 7,368 | 11,535 | 6,124 | 6,453 |
| 6,374 | 4,102 | 1,477 | 3,340 | 3,684 | 4,293 | 688 | 5,076 | 5,704 | — | 6,259 | 6,231 | 1,229 | 2,126 | 6,140 | 476 | 819 |
| 9,718 | 8,558 | 4,798 | 4,874 | 2,268 | 8,889 | 6,303 | 2,072 | 10,290 | 5,943 | 7,829 | 682 | 5,534 | 3,851 | 2,689 | 5,687 | 5,454 |
| 1,889 | 2,544 | 5,884 | 9,598 | 7,691 | 2,574 | 5,579 | 5,934 | 6,621 | 6,259 | — | 8,449 | 5,372 | 7,362 | 5,148 | 5,992 | 5,854 |
| 4,094 | 5,436 | 8,770 | 7,180 | 10,518 | 5,106 | 7,224 | 11,859 | 1,820 | 7,391 | 5,926 | 10,190 | 8,120 | 9,185 | 10,711 | 7,760 | 8,059 |
| 2,340 | 2,289 | 5,217 | 9,006 | 7,046 | 2,409 | 5,012 | 5,432 | 6,890 | 5,680 | 679 | 8,074 | 4,731 | 6,686 | 4,793 | 5,381 | 5,222 |
| 8,033 | 7,067 | 4,248 | 5,951 | 2,646 | 7,384 | 5,772 | 645 | 11,339 | 5,679 | 6,150 | 2,363 | 4,837 | 3,974 | 1,097 | 5,281 | 4,963 |
| 5,172 | 2,873 | 1,863 | 4,563 | 4,529 | 3,086 | 563 | 5,288 | 5,597 | 1,247 | 5,040 | 7,089 | 1,135 | 3,117 | 6,064 | 1,153 | 1,258 |
| 10,331 | 9,207 | 5,236 | 4,636 | 2,574 | 9,539 | 6,676 | 2,754 | 9,776 | 6,231 | 8,449 | — | 5,993 | 4,106 | 3,304 | 6,039 | 5,846 |
| 1,425 | 978 | 5,248 | 8,231 | 7,736 | 878 | 4,398 | 6,792 | 5,218 | 5,073 | 1,744 | 9,544 | 4,552 | 6,766 | 6,407 | 4,955 | 4,942 |
| 5,965 | 3,667 | 764 | 4,299 | 3,466 | 3,939 | 964 | 4,197 | 6,638 | 1,229 | 5,372 | 5,993 | — | 2,217 | 5,091 | 771 | 504 |
| 8,182 | 5,879 | 1,534 | 2,709 | 1,584 | 6,141 | 2,624 | 3,496 | 7,386 | 2,126 | 7,362 | 4,106 | 2,217 | — | 4,775 | 1,983 | 1,878 |
| 7,036 | 6,479 | 4,663 | 6,996 | 3,638 | 6,757 | 6,054 | 1,305 | 11,535 | 6,140 | 5,148 | 3,304 | 5,091 | 4,775 | — | 5,689 | 5,346 |
| 6,316 | 4,007 | 1,039 | 3,625 | 3,467 | 4,233 | 643 | 4,664 | 6,124 | 476 | 5,992 | 6,039 | 771 | 1,983 | 5,689 | — | 347 |
| 6,335 | 4,021 | 716 | 3,800 | 3,277 | 4,271 | 853 | 4,340 | 6,453 | 819 | 5,854 | 5,846 | 504 | 1,878 | 5,346 | 347 | — |
| 1,883 | 490 | 4,873 | 7,550 | 7,500 | 203 | 3,841 | 6,965 | 4,783 | 4,496 | 2,444 | 9,667 | 4,135 | 6,340 | 6,792 | 4,436 | 4,471 |

## WORLD AVIATION RECORDS

SOURCE: National Aeronautic Association

### JET AND ROCKET AIRPLANES

**Date Record**

**1/10-11/62 Distance in a Straight Line**
U.S.: 12,532.28 miles
Major Clyde P. Evely, USAF
Boeing B52-H
Kadena, Okinawa, to Madrid, Spain

**6/6-7/62 Distance in a Closed Circuit**
U.S.: 11,336.92 miles
Captain William Stevenson, USAF
Boeing B52-H
Seymour-Johnson, North Carolina; Kindley, Bermuda; Sondrestrom, Greenland; Anchorage, Alaska; March AFB, California; Key West, Florida; Seymour-Johnson, N.C.

**8/31/77 Altitude**
USSR: 123,523.58 feet
Alexander Fedotov
E-226M Airplane
Podmoskovnoye, USSR

**7/17/62 Altitude (Rocket Powered)**
U.S.: 314,750 feet
Major Robert M. White, USAF
North American X-15-1 (NASA Aircraft)
Edwards Air Force Base, California

**7/28/76 Altitude in Horizontal Flight**
U.S.: 85,068.997 feet
Capt. Robert C. Helt, USAF
Lockheed SR-71

**7/28/76 Speed over a 15/25-Km. Course**
U.S.: 2,193.16 miles per hour
Capt. Eldon W. Joersz, USAF
Lockheed SR-71
Beale Air Force Base, California

**7/27/76 Speed over a Closed Circuit**
U.S.: 2,092.294 miles per hour
Major Adolphus H. Bledsoe, Jr., USAF
Lockheed SR-71
Beale Air Force Base, California

### PROPELLER-DRIVEN AIRPLANES

**Date Record**

**9/29/46 Distance in a Straight Line**
U.S.: 11,235.6 miles
Commander T. D. Davies, USN
Lockheed P2V-1 Monoplane
Perth, Australia to Columbus, Ohio

**12/5-8/81 Distance in a Closed Circuit**
U.S.: 10,007.1 S. Miles
Jerry D. Mullens
BD-2 Airplane
Oklahoma City/Jacksonville/Oklahoma City

**10/22/38 Altitude**
ITALY: 56,046 feet
Mario Pezzi
Caproni 161 Biplane
Montecelio, Italy

**8/14/79 Speed over a 3-Km. Course**
U.S.: 499.04 miles per hour
Steve Hinton
P-51D
Tonopah, Nevada

**4/9/51 Speed over a 15/25-Km. Course**
U.S.: 464.374 miles per hour
Jacqueline Cochran
North American P-51
Indio, California

**7/20-25/75 Speed around the World**
AUSTRALIA: 203.64 miles per hour
Pilot: D. N. Dalton; Copilot: T. Gwynne-Jones
Beechcraft Duke
Brisbane, Tarawa, Honolulu, San Jose, Toronto, Gander, Gatwick, Damascus, Dubai, Madras, Singapore, Darwin, Brisbane
Elapsed Time: 5 days, 2 hours, 19 minutes, 57 seconds

**Date Record**

### TURBOPROP AIRPLANES

**Date Record**

**2/20/72 Distance in a Straight Line**
U.S.: 8,732.09 miles
Lt. Col. Edgar L. Allison, Jr., USAF
Lockheed HC-130 Hercules
Ching-Chuan Kang, Taiwan to Scott AFB, Ill.

**11/4/72 Distance in a Closed Circuit**
U.S.: 6,278.05 miles
Cdr. Philip R. Hite, U.S. Navy
Lockheed RP-3D
NAS Patuxent River, Md.

**1/27/71 Speed over a 15/25-Km Course**
U.S.: 501.44 miles per hour
Commander D. H. Lilienthal, USN
Lockheed P3C Orion
NAS Patuxent River, Md.

**3/27/72 Altitude**
U.S.: 51,014 feet
Donald R. Wilson
LTV-L450F Airplane
Greenville, Texas

### WORLD COMMERCIAL AIRCRAFT SPEEDS

**Date Record**

**11/2/77 Barbados/London**
ENGLAND: 1,134.85 miles per hour
Captain Norman Todd
Concorde
Elapsed time: 3 h, 42 m, 5 s

**9/6/62 Chicago/Mexico City**
U.S.: 534.15 miles per hour
Captain D. W. Ledbetter
Boeing 720B
Elapsed time: 3 h, 10 m, 6.3 s

**4/30/60 London/Athens**
GREECE: 506.29 miles per hour
Captain P. Ioanides (Olympic Airways)
Comet DH-106-4B (SXDAK)
Elapsed time: 3 h, 13 m, 42 s

**6/5/62 London/Miami**
ENGLAND: 321.02 miles per hour
Captain G. N. Henderson (Cunard Eagle Airways); Captain P. Wilson
Boeing 707-465
Elapsed time: 13 h, 46 m, 38 s

**12/1/66 Los Angeles/Mexico City**
MEXICO: 597.88 miles per hour
Captain Rafael T. Zapata (Mexicana de Aviacion)
Boeing 727-64
Elapsed time 2 h, 36 m

**12/8/61 Los Angeles/New York**
U.S.: 636.8 miles per hour
Captain William Miller (American Airlines, Inc.)
Boeing 707B-123
Elapsed time: 3 h, 52 m, 43 s

**9/6/62 Mexico City/Chicago**
U.S.: 558.28 miles per hour
Captain E. Schlanser (American Airlines, Inc.)
Boeing 720B
Elapsed time: 3 h, 1 m, 53.2 s

**5/6/62 Miami/London**
ENGLAND: 419.94 miles per hour
Captain P. Wilson (Cunard Eagle Airways)
Captain M. Gudmundsson
Boeing 707-465
Elapsed time: 10 h, 31 m, 55 s

**5/28/60 Montreal/London**
CANADA: 565.29 miles per hour
Captain R. M. Smith (Trans-Canada Air Lines)
Douglas DC 8-40
Elapsed time: 5 h, 44 m, 42 s

**6/2/63 New York/Bergen**
NORWAY: 533.13 miles per hour
Captain B. Bjornstad (Scandinavian Airlines Systems)
Douglas DC-8
Elapsed time: 6 h, 32 m, 20 s

**Date Record**

**11/26/54 New York/Madrid**
SPAIN: 379.624 miles per hour
Captain C. I. Batida (Iberian Airlines)
Lockheed Super Constellation L-1049E
Elapsed time: 9 h, 29 m

**2/19/74 New York/Rio de Janeiro**
U.S.: 594.28 miles per hour
Capt. Theodore C. Patecell (Pan American World Airways)
Boeing 707-300 B/A
Elapsed time: 8 h, 5 m, 30 s

**6/3/60 New York/San Francisco**
AUSTRALIA: 510.092 miles per hour
Captain A. Yates (Quantas Empire Airways)
Boeing 707-138 VH-EBE
Elapsed time: 5 h, 3 m, 48.35 s

**8/18/78 Paris/Washington, D.C.**
FRANCE: 1,071.86 miles per hour
Captain Pierre Chanoine (Air France)
Concorde
Elapsed time: 3 h, 35 m, 15 s

**12/8/61 San Francisco/New York**
U.S.: 658 miles per hour
Captain T. F. Jonson (American Airlines, Inc.)
Boeing 707B-123
Elapsed time: 3 h, 55 m, 50 s

### NATIONAL COMMERCIAL AIRCRAFT SPEEDS

**Date Record**

**4/10/63 West to East Transcontinental:** 680.90 miles per hour
Captain Wylie H. Drummond (American Airlines, Inc.)
Boeing 707-123
Los Angeles International Airport/Idlewild Airport
Distance: 2,474 statute miles
Elapsed time: 3 h, 38 m

**8/15/62 East to West Transcontinental:** 575.52 miles per hour
Captain Gene Kruse (American Airlines, Inc.)
Boeing 707-720B
Idlewild Airport/Los Angeles International Airport
Distance: 2,474 statute miles
Elapsed time: 4 h, 19 m, 15 s

**8/5/47 Atlanta/Chicago:** 290.501 miles per hour
Captain H. T. Merrill (Eastern Air Lines)
Lockheed Constellation
Atlanta Municipal Airport/Chicago Municipal Airport
Distance: 590 miles; 2 hours, 1 minute, 55 seconds

**7/19/63 Atlanta/Los Angeles:** 566.82 miles per hour
Captain L. L. Caruthers (Delta Air Lines)
Douglas DC-8
Atlanta Municipal Airport/Los Angeles International Airport
Distance: 1,946 miles; 3 hours, 25 minutes, 59 seconds

**1/21/63 Atlanta/New York:** 589.64 miles per hour
Captain Michael Winicki (Delta Air Lines)
Douglas DC-8-51
Atlanta Municipal Airport/Idlewild Int'l Airport
Distance: 760 miles; 1 hour, 17 minutes, 20 seconds

**10/30/62 Baltimore/Los Angeles:** 563.46 miles per hour
Captain Howard U. Morton (American Airlines)
Boeing 707
Friendship Int'l Airport/Los Angeles Int'l Airport

Date Record

**4/29/65 Boston/Los Angeles:** 562.57 miles per hour
Captain George C. Dent (American Airlines)
Boeing 707
Logan Int'l Airport/Los Angeles Int'l Airport
Distance: 2,610 miles; 4 hours, 38 minutes, 21 seconds

**7/20/63 Boston/New York:** 414.61 miles per hour
Captain Peter C. Bals (American Airlines)
Convair 990
Logan Int'l Airport/Idlewild Int'l Airport
Distance: 186 miles; 00 hours, 26 minutes, 55 seconds

**8/5/47 Chicago/Atlanta:** 326.925 miles per hour
Captain H. T. Merrill (Eastern Air Lines)
Lockheed Constellation
Chicago Municipal Airport/Atlanta Municipal Airport
Distance: 590 miles; 1 hour, 48 minutes, 20 seconds

**2/16/65 Chicago/Boston:** 692.28 miles per hour
Captain Alden Young (American Airlines)
Convair 990
Chicago O'Hare Airport/Logan Int'l Airport
Distance: 865 miles; 1 hour, 14 minutes, 58 seconds

**4/20/65 Chicago/Fort Worth:** 548.85 miles per hour
Captain Glen L. Stockwell (American Airlines)
Boeing 727
O'Hare Int'l Airport/Greater Southwest Int'l Airport
Distance: 809 miles; 1 hour, 28 minutes, 26 seconds

**4/9/65 Chicago/Indianapolis:** 494.93 miles per hour
Captain P. G. Cook (American Airlines)
Boeing 707
O'Hare Int'l Airport/WEIR Cook Int'l Airport
Distance: 179 miles; 00 hours, 21 minutes, 42 seconds

**1/2–3/62 Chicago/Miami:** 588 miles per hour
Captain Dean Clifton (Delta Air Lines)
Convair 880
Chicago O'Hare Airport/Miami Int'l Airport
Distance: 1,184 miles; 2 hours, 1 minute

**10/28/65 Chicago/New York:** 644.36 miles per hour
Captain W. J. Callahan (American Airlines)
Boeing 727
O'Hare Int'l Airport/LaGuardia Airport
Distance: 733 miles; 1 hour, 8 minutes, 15 seconds

**2/3/65 Chicago/Washington, D.C.** 510.58 miles per hour
Captain A. B. Perriello (American Airlines)
Lockheed Electra L-188
O'Hare Int'l Airport/Washington National Airport
Distance: 612 miles; 1 hour, 11 minutes, 5 seconds

**3/12/65 Dallas/New York:** 686.73 miles per hour
Captain William F. Bonnell (American Airlines)
Boeing 707/720
Love Field/John F. Kennedy Int'l Airport
Distance: 1,384 miles; 2 hours, 6 minutes

Date Record

**2/18/65 Dallas/San Francisco:** 580.46 miles per hour
Captain W. R. Swain (American Airlines)
Boeing 707/720
Love Field/San Francisco Int'l Airport
Distance: 1,477 miles; 2 hours, 32 minutes, 40 seconds

**3/12/65 Dallas/Washington, D.C.:** 643.06 miles per hour
Captain W. T. Fleming (American Airlines)
Boeing 707/720
Love Field/Dulles Int'l Airport
Distance: 1,162 miles; 1 hour, 48 minutes, 25 seconds

**12/7/61 Los Angeles/Baltimore:** 657.68 miles per hour
Captain Stan Smith (American Airlines)
Boeing 707/123B
Los Angeles Int'l Airport/Friendship Airport
Distance: 2,329 miles; 3 hours, 32 minutes, 28 seconds

**11/26/65 Los Angeles/Boston:** 666.61 miles per hour
Captain Simon P. Bittner (American Airlines)
Boeing 707
Los Angeles Int'l Airport/Logan Int'l Airport
Distance: 2,610 miles; 3 hours, 54 minutes, 55 seconds

**4/9/63 Los Angeles/Chicago:** 672.80 miles per hour
Captain George R. Russon (American Airlines)
Boeing 707/123
Los Angeles Int'l Airport/O'Hare Int'l Airport
Distance: 1,746 miles; 2 hours, 35 minutes, 42 seconds

**3/9/65 Los Angeles/Dallas:** 689.00 miles per hour
Captain W. R. Hunt (American Airlines)
Boeing 707/123
Los Angeles Int'l Airport/Love Field
Distance: 1,245 miles; 1 hour, 48 minutes, 25 seconds

**7/16/47 Miami/Chicago:** 300.390 miles per hour
Captain H. T. Merrill (Eastern Air Lines)
Lockheed Constellation
36th Street Airport/Chicago Municipal Airport
Distance: 1,183 miles; 3 hours, 56 minutes, 22 seconds

**MAN-POWERED AIRCRAFT**

Date Record

**6/12/79 Duration, Distance**
U.S.: 2 hours, 49 minutes; 22.26 miles
Bryan Allen
Gossamer Albatross
Folkestone, England to Cap Gris-Nez, France

**BALLOONS (LARGE)**

Date Record

**8/12-17/78 Duration**
U.S.: 137 hrs., 5 min., 50 secs.; 3,107.61 miles
Ben L. Abruzzo, Maxie L. Anderson, Larry M. Newman; Double Eagle II
Presque Isle, Maine to Miserey, France

**11/9-12/81 Distance**
U.S.: 5,208.67 miles
Ben L. Abruzzo, Larry Newman, Rocky Aoki, Ron Clark
Raven Experimental
Nagashima, Japan to Covello, Calif.

Date Recod

**5/4/61 Altitude**
U.S.: 113,739.9 feet
Commander Malcolm D. Ross, USNR
"Lee Lewis Memorial"
Gulf of Mexico

**GLIDERS**

Date Record

**4/25/72 Distance in a Straight Line**
W. GERMANY: 907.7 miles
Hans Werner Grosse
ASK 12 Sailplane
Luebeck, W. Ger. to Biarritz, France.

**1/14/78 Distance to a Goal 779.36 miles**
NEW ZEALAND: Group Flight; David Wapier Speight, S. H. Georgeson, Bruce Lindsay Drake
Tower Peak Station to TeAraroa

**5/9/77 Distance to a Goal and Return**
U.S.: 1,015.81 miles
Karl Striedieck
ASW 17 Sailplane
Lock Haven, Pennsylvania

**2/25/61 Altitude above Sea Level**
U.S.: 46,267 feet
Paul F. Bikle
Schweizer SCG 123 E. Sailplane
Mojave, Lancaster, California

**2/25/61 Altitude Gained**
U.S.: 42,303 feet
Paul F. Bikle
Schweizer SGA 123 E. Sailplane
Mojave, Lancaster, California

**HELICOPTERS**

Date Record

**4/6–7/66 Distance in a Straight Line**
U.S.: 2,213.04 miles
Robert G. Ferry
Hughes YOH 6A helicopter
Culver City, California to Daytona Beach, Florida

**3/26/66 Distance in a Closed Circuit**
U.S.: 1,739.96 miles
Jack Schweibold
Hughes YOH-6A helicopter
Edwards AFB, California

**6/21/72 Altitude**
FRANCE: 40,820 feet
Jean Boulet
Alouette SA 315-001 "Lama" Helicopter
Istres, France

**11/4/71 Altitude in Horizontal Flight**
U.S.: 36,122 feet
CWO James K. Church, USA
Sikorsky CH-54B Helicopter
Stratford, Connecticut

**12/14/70 Speed over a 3 Km Course**
U.S.: 216.839 miles per hour
Byron Graham
Sikorsky S-67 Helicopter
Windsor Locks, Connecticut

**9/21/78 Speed over a 15/25 Km Course**
USSR: 228.91 Miles per hour
Gourguen Karapetyan
Helicopter A-10
Podmoskovnoye Aerodrome

**HANG GLIDING**

Date Record

**5/20/81 Distance in a Straight Line**
West Germany: 118.68 miles
Helmut Denz
Comet 165
Hippach-Rottenmann, Austria

**7/22/78 Gain in Altitude**
U.S.: 11,700 feet
George D. Worthington
Seagull 10 Meter
Cerro Gordo Peak, California

**7/21/77 Straight Distance to Goal**
U.S.: 95.44 miles
George D. Worthington
ASG-21 Albatross Sails
Cerro Gordo Peak, Calif. to Benton Station, Calif.

## BUSIEST WORLD AIRPORTS

SOURCE: International Civil Aviation Organization

Airports are ranked here according to their total passenger traffic (embarked plus disembarked) for 1980. USSR airports opened to domestic traffic exclusively are not included.

| Airport | Passengers (in millions) | Airport | Passengers (in millions) | Airport | Passengers (in millions) | Airport | Passengers (in millions) |
|---|---|---|---|---|---|---|---|
| Chicago (O'Hare) | 43.1 | New York (La Guardia) | 17.5 | Pittsburgh | 11.5 | New York (Newark) | 9.2 |
| Atlanta | 41.7 | Frankfurt (Main) | 16.8 | Rome (Fiumicino) | 10.8 | Seattle | 9.2 |
| Los Angeles | 33.1 | Osaka | 16.6 | Houston | 10.7 | Minneapolis | 9.0 |
| London (Heathrow) | 27.5 | Paris (Orly) | 15.7 | Madrid | 10.1 | Copenhagen | 8.6 |
| New York (Kennedy) | 26.8 | Toronto | 14.9 | Paris (De Gaulle) | 10.1 | Sydney | 8.4 |
| Dallas/Fort Worth | 21.5 | Boston (Logan) | 14.7 | Las Vegas | 9.9 | Saint Louis | 8.3 |
| San Francisco | 21.5 | Washington (Nat'l) | 14.5 | Detroit | 9.9 | Tokyo (New Tokyo Int'l) | 8.2* |
| Denver | 20.8 | Honolulu | 14.0 | London (Gatwick) | 9.7 | Tampa | 7.7 |
| Tokyo (Tokyo Int'l) | 20.7 | Mexico City | 11.9 | Philadelphia | 9.6 | Zürich | 7.6 |
| Miami | 20.5 | | | Amsterdam | 9.4 | Jeddah | 7.5 |

*Estimate

## MAJOR INTERNATIONAL AIRPORTS

SOURCE: International Civil Aviation Organization

Airports on the list are ranked according to the total international passenger traffic for 1980. *Estimated data.

| | | PASSENGERS (000) | | | COMMERCIAL OPERATIONS (000) | | |
|---|---|---|---|---|---|---|---|
| Airport | City | International | Domestic | Total | International | Domestic | Total |
| Heathrow | London | 23,381 | 4,090 | 27,471 | 208.7 | 64.3 | 273.0 |
| J.F. Kennedy | New York | 13,028 | 13,767 | 26,795 | 84.2 | 152.1 | 236.4 |
| Frankfurt-Main | Frankfurt | 11,773 | 5,012 | 16,785 | 139.8 | 68.7 | 208.5 |
| Schiphol | Amsterdam | 9,289 | 113 | 9,402 | 138.0 | 5.8 | 143.8 |
| De Gaulle | Paris | 8,841 | 1,270 | 10,110 | 90.0 | 12.6 | 102.6 |
| Gatwick | London | 8,665 | 1,039 | 9,704 | 90.3 | 33.0 | 123.4 |
| Orly | Paris | 8,594 | 7,076 | 15,670 | 93.5 | 81.7 | 175.2 |
| Miami Int'l | Miami | 8,438 | 12,067 | 20,505 | ... | ... | 297.5 |
| New Tokyo Int'l | Tokyo | 7,500* | 700* | 8,200* | ... | ... | .... |
| Zürich | Zürich | 7,235 | 392 | 7,627 | 109.8 | 8.7 | 118.5 |
| Hong Kong Int'l | Hong Kong | 6,813 | 0 | 6,813 | 54.6 | 0.2 | 54.8 |
| Toronto Int'l | Toronto | 6,716 | 8,152 | 14,869 | 65.4 | 111.2 | 176.6 |
| Kastrup | Copenhagen | 6,663 | 1,912 | 8,575 | 110.8 | 34.5 | 145.2 |
| Fiumicino | Rome | 6,600* | 4,165* | 10,765 | 80.7* | 65.7* | 146.4 |
| Singapore Int'l | Singapore | 6,292 | 0 | 6,292 | 68.2 | 0 | 68.2 |
| Los Angeles Int'l | Los Angeles | 5,676 | 27,386 | 33,062 | 46.4 | 364.3 | 410.7 |
| Palma de Mallorca | Palma de Mallorca | 5,478 | 1,818 | 7,296 | 47.3 | 23.6 | 70.9 |
| Düsseldorf | Düsseldorf | 5,116 | 1,926 | 7,042 | 51.6 | 34.1 | 85.7 |
| Bruxelles Nat'l | Brussels | 5,087 | 6 | 5,093 | 85.7 | 0.2 | 85.9 |
| Cairo Int'l | Cairo | 4,317 | 725 | 5,042 | 44.5 | 4.5 | 49.0 |
| Bangkok | Bangkok | 4,138 | 452 | 4,590 | 47.2 | 6.7 | 54.0 |
| Barajas | Madrid | 4,105 | 6,042 | 10,146 | 50.5 | 73.2 | 123.7 |
| Benito Juarez | Mexico City | 3,988* | 7,912* | 11,900 | ... | ... | 136.2 |
| Jeddah Int'l | Jeddah | 3,499 | 4,006 | 7,505 | ... | ... | .... |
| Cointrin | Geneva | 3,273 | 679 | 3,953 | 54.0 | 15.5 | 69.5 |
| Manchester Int'l | Manchester | 3,231 | 1,085 | 4,316 | 38.1 | 20.4 | 58.5 |
| München | Münich | 3,203 | 2,514 | 5,717 | 43.7 | 39.6 | 83.3 |
| Arlanda | Stockholm | 3,148 | 1,119 | 4,266 | 47.7 | 22.1 | 69.8 |
| Linate | Milan | 3,133* | 2,136* | 5,269 | 55.0* | 27.6* | 82.6 |
| O'Hare Int'l | Chicago | 2,883 | 40,256 | 43,138 | 28.4 | 617.2 | 645.6 |
| Ben Gurion | Tel Aviv | 2,800 | ..... | 2,800* | 20.7 | 8.1 | 28.8 |
| Schwechat | Vienna | 2,665 | 69 | 2,734 | 50.0 | 4.3 | 54.2 |
| Sheremetyevo | Moscow | 2,657 | 1,190 | 3,847 | 45.0 | 17.8 | 62.8 |

*Estimate

## AIRLINE TRAFFIC VOLUME

SOURCE: International Civil Aviation Organization

According to estimates released in March 1982 by the International Civil Aviation Organization for its 145 member states*, in 1981 the airlines carried 634 million passengers for a total of 943,000 million kilometers (586,000 million passenger miles on scheduled services), representing increases of 4.3 percent over 1980.

| Year | Miles Flown | Hours Flown | Passengers Carried | Passenger-Miles | Average Number of: Passengers per Aircraft | Miles Flown per Passenger | Miles Flown per hr. |
|---|---|---|---|---|---|---|---|
| | (In Millions) | | | | | | |
| 1981† | 5,720 | 14.6 | 634 | 586,000 | 103 | 924 | 391 |
| 1980 | 5,870 | 15.0 | 645 | 577,000 | 98 | 895 | 390 |
| 1979 | 5,690 | 14.9 | 652 | 565,000 | 99 | 867 | 382 |
| 1978 | 5,280 | 14.0 | 581 | 495,000 | 94 | 852 | 378 |
| 1977 | 5,030 | 13.3 | 517 | 430,000 | 85 | 830 | 377 |
| 1976 | 4,870 | 13.0 | 476 | 393,000 | 81 | 827 | 374 |
| 1975 | 4,670 | 12.6 | 436 | 357,000 | 77 | 820 | 371 |
| 1974 | 4,580 | 12.5 | 424 | 340,000 | 74 | 803 | 367 |
| 1973 | 4,670 | 12.7 | 404 | 323,000 | 69 | 799 | 367 |
| 1972 | 4,480 | 12.2 | 368 | 289,000 | 64 | 785 | 367 |
| 1971 | 4,390 | 12.0 | 333 | 252,000 | 58 | 757 | 365 |
| 1970 | 4,355 | 12.1 | 311 | 237,000 | 55 | 764 | 362 |
| 1969 | 4,170 | 11.8 | 293 | 222,000 | 52 | 745 | 356 |
| 1968 | 3,730 | 11.0 | 262 | 196,000 | 52 | 741 | 341 |
| 1967 | 3,290 | 10.2 | 233 | 169,500 | 52 | 727 | 320 |
| 1966 | 2,790 | 9.3 | 200 | 142,000 | 51 | 711 | 301 |
| 1965 | 2,550 | 8.7 | 177 | 123,000 | 48 | 696 | 292 |
| 1964 | 2,300 | 8.2 | 155 | 106,000 | 46 | 687 | 280 |
| 1963 | 2,130 | 7.9 | 135 | 91,500 | 43 | 674 | 270 |
| 1962 | 2,015 | 7.8 | 121 | 80,500 | 40 | 668 | 261 |
| 1961 | 1,940 | 8.0 | 111 | 72,500 | 38 | 656 | 242 |
| 1960 | 1,930 | 8.6 | 106 | 67,500 | 35 | 640 | 224 |
| 1959 | 1,920 | 9.0 | 99 | 61,000 | 32 | 615 | 214 |
| 1957 | 1,765 | 8.7 | 86 | 51,000 | 29 | 590 | 202 |
| 1955 | 1,425 | 7.3 | 68 | 38,000 | 27 | 562 | 196 |

*Except USSR †Preliminary

## SAFETY RECORD: U.S. SCHEDULED AIR CARRIERS—1972-1981

SOURCE: National Transportation Safety Board

| | | | | | Accident Rates | | | |
|---|---|---|---|---|---|---|---|---|
| | | | | | Per Million Aircraft-Miles | | Per 100,000 Aircraft-Hours | |
| Year | Total | Accidents Fatal | Fatalities | Aircraft Miles Flown (000) | Total Accidents | Fatal Accidents | Total Accidents | Fatal Accidents |
| 1972 | 46 | 7 | 186 | 2,347,864 | 0.020 | 0.003 | 0.813 | 0.124 |
| 1973 | 36 | 8 | 221 | 2,448,114 | 0.015 | 0.003 | 0.610 | 0.136 |
| 1974 | 43 | 7 | 460 | 2,258,136 | 0.019 | 0.003 | 0.767 | 0.110 |
| 1975 | 31 | 2 | 122 | 2,240,505 | 0.014 | 0.001 | 0.571 | 0.037 |
| 1976 | 22 | 2 | 38 | 2,319,967 | 0.009 | 0.001 | 0.394 | 0.036 |
| 1977 | 21[1] | 3 | 78 | 2,418,652 | 0.009 | 0.001 | 0.362 | 0.052 |
| 1978 | 21[1] | 5[1] | 160 | 2,520,165 | 0.008 | 0.002 | 0.348 | 0.083 |
| 1979 | 24[1,2] | 4 | 351 | 2,736,129 | 0.009 | 0.002 | 0.358 | 0.060 |
| 1980 | 15 | 0 | 0 | 2,890,000 | 0.005 | 0.000 | 0.215 | 0.000 |
| 1981[3] | 24[4] | 4 | 4 | 2,695,000 | 0.009 | 0.002 | 0.366 | 0.061 |

[1] Contains one accident involving a scheduled commercial operator. [2] Contains one accident involving a deregulated all-cargo air carrier. [3] Preliminary. [4] Contains two accidents involving deregulated all-cargo air carriers.

## SAFETY RECORD: WORLD SCHEDULED AIRLINES[1]

SOURCE: International Civil Aviation Organization

| Year | Number of Accidents: Passenger-carrying Aircraft | Number of Passengers Killed | Fatality Rate (per 100 million Pass.-mi.) | Fatal Accidents (per 100 million Mi. Flown) | Fatal Accidents† |
|---|---|---|---|---|---|
| 1950 | 27 | 581 | 3.15 | 3.02 | 0.54 |
| 1952 | 21 | 386 | 1.54 | 1.90 | 0.34 |
| 1954 | 28 | 443 | 1.36 | 2.19 | 0.42 |
| 1956 | 27 | 552 | 1.25 | 1.71 | 0.34 |
| 1958 | 30 | 609 | 1.15 | 1.65 | 0.34 |
| 1960 | 34 | 873 | 1.29 | 1.71 | 0.38 |
| 1962 | 29 | 778 | 1.97 | 1.44 | 0.37 |
| 1964 | 25 | 616 | 0.58 | 1.09 | 0.30 |
| 1966 | 31 | 1,001 | 0.70 | 1.12 | 0.33 |
| 1968 | 35 | 912 | 0.47 | 0.94 | 0.32 |
| 1970 | 28 | 687 | 0.29 | 0.64 | 0.23 |
| 1972 | 42 | 1,210 | 0.42 | 0.94 | 0.34 |
| 1973 | 36 | 862 | 0.27 | 0.77 | 0.28 |
| 1974 | 29 | 1,299 | 0.38 | 0.62 | 0.23 |
| 1975 | 20 | 443 | 0.13 | 0.43 | 0.16 |
| 1976 | 20 | 734 | 0.19 | 0.41 | 0.15 |
| 1977 | 24 | 516 | 0.11 | 0.48 | 0.18 |
| 1978 | 25 | 755 | 0.15 | 0.47 | 0.18 |
| 1979 | 31 | 879 | 0.16 | 0.55 | 0.21 |
| 1980 | 21 | 812 | 0.14 | 0.36 | 0.14 |
| 1981* | 17 | 365 | 0.06 | 0.30 | 0.12 |

†Per 100,000 aircraft hours. [1]Excluding USSR. *Preliminary figures.

## WORLD'S FASTEST TRAINS[1]

SOURCE: Donald M. Steffee

| Railroad | Train | From | To | Miles | Time (min.) | Speed (mph) |
|---|---|---|---|---|---|---|
| **Passenger** | | | | | | |
| French National | TGV (2 runs) | Lyon (Brotteaux) | Le Creusot | 76.6 | 40 | 114.9 |
| Japanese National | Hikari Train | Nagoya | Yokohama | 196.5 | 105 | 112.3 |
| British Rail | High Speed Train | London | Chippenham | 93.9 | 54 | 104.3 |
| German Federal | Three Trains | Hamm | Bielefeld | 41.7 | 24 | 104.2 |
| Amtrak | Six trains | Wilmington[2] | Baltimore | 68.4 | 45 | 91.2 |
| Italian State | Rapido | Chiusi | Rome | 91.9 | 65 | 84.8 |
| VIA (Canada) | Turbotrain (2 runs) | Kingston | Dorval | 165.8 | 120 | 82.9 |
| VIA (Canada) | Simco | Dorval | Kingston | 165.8 | 122 | 81.5 |
| Swedish State | No. 142 | Skvode | Laxa | 52.2 | 41 | 77.4 |
| **Freight** | | | | | | |
| British Rail | Freightliner | Carlisle | Wigan | 105.1 | 95½ | 66.2 |
| Union Pacific | BASV | North Platte | Cheyenne | 225.4 | 105 | 66.0 |
| French National | Freight Express | Orange | St. Rambert de Albon | 87.6 | 81 | 64.9 |

[1]Fastest run in each country. [2]Runs listed in both directions.

## FASTEST AMERICAN PASSENGER TRAINS

SOURCE: Donald M. Steffee

| Railroad | Train | From | To | Miles | Time (min.) | Speed (mph) |
|---|---|---|---|---|---|---|
| Amtrak | Five Trains | Wilmington | Baltimore | 68.4 | 45 | 91.2 |
| Amtrak | Metroliner 101 | Wilmington | Baltimore | 68.4 | 46 | 89.2 |
| Amtrak | Four Trains | Rensselaer | Hudson | 18.0 | 19 | 88.4 |
| Amtrak | Three trains | Baltimore[1] | Wilmington | 68.4 | 47 | 87.3 |
| Amtrak | Six trains | Baltimore[1] | Wilmington | 68.4 | 48 | 85.5 |
| Amtrak | Palmetto | BWI Station | Beltway Station | 19.7 | 14 | 84.4 |
| Amtrak | Three Trains | Wilmington | Baltimore | 68.4 | 49 | 83.8 |
| Amtrak | Valley Forge | Trenton | Newark (N.J.) | 48.1 | 35 | 82.5 |
| Amtrak | Cardinal | Baltimore | Wilmington | 68.4 | 50 | 82.1 |
| Amtrak | Southwest Limited | Garden City | Lamar | 99.9 | 73 | 82.1 |
| Amtrak | Four trains | Baltimore[1] | Wilmington | 68.4 | 51 | 80.5 |
| Amtrak | Three trains | Newark (N.J.) | Philadelphia | 80.5 | 60 | 80.5 |
| Amtrak | Three trains | Trenton | Newark (N.J.) | 48.1 | 36 | 80.2 |
| Amtrak | Cardinal | Wilmington | Aberdeen | 38.7 | 29 | 80.1 |
| Amtrak | No. 237 | Trenton | North Philadelphia | 27.9 | 21 | 79.7 |
| Conrail | Jersey Arrow | Princeton Jct. | Newark (N.J.) | 38.4 | 29 | 79.4 |
| Amtrak | Four trains | Wilmington | Baltimore | 68.4 | 52 | 78.9 |
| Amtrak | Two Trains | Metropark | Trenton | 33.9 | 26 | 78.2 |

[1]Runs listed in both directions.

## SELECTED MERCHANT FLEETS OF THE WORLD

SOURCE: U.S. Maritime Administration

| Country of Registry | Total† Number | Total† Gross Tons | Total† Dead-weight Tons |
|---|---|---|---|
| TOTAL—ALL COUNTRIES | 24,867 | 385,711 | 654,909 |
| **United States** | 864 | 16,020 | 24,090 |
| Privately-Owned | 578 | 13,467 | 21,103 |
| Government-Owned | 286 | 2,554 | 2,987 |
| Reserve Fleet | 253 | 2,211 | 2,620 |
| Other | 33 | 343 | 367 |
| **Algeria** | 68 | 1,236 | 1,842 |
| **Argentina** | 203 | 2,206 | 3,336 |
| **Australia** | 74 | 1,460 | 2,276 |
| **Austria** | 14 | 96 | 147 |
| **Bangladesh** | 33 | 298 | 422 |
| **Belgium** | 74 | 1,677 | 2,639 |
| **Brazil** | 313 | 4,611 | 7,720 |
| **British Colonies** | 202 | 2,767 | 4,310 |
| **Bulgaria*** | 108 | 1,095 | 1,620 |
| **Canada** | 102 | 646 | 980 |
| **Chile** | 47 | 570 | 938 |
| **China (People's Rep.)*** | 695 | 6,706 | 10,129 |
| **China (Republic of)** | 170 | 2,003 | 3,032 |
| **Colombia** | 41 | 272 | 356 |
| **Cuba*** | 90 | 687 | 935 |
| **Cyprus** | 395 | 1,719 | 2,507 |
| **Czechoslovakia*** | 16 | 154 | 229 |
| **Denmark** | 275 | 4,782 | 8,009 |
| **Ecuador** | 32 | 260 | 351 |
| **Egypt** | 87 | 413 | 552 |
| **Finland** | 175 | 2,178 | 3,553 |
| **France** | 345 | 10,981 | 19,539 |
| **Germany, East*** | 158 | 1,282 | 1,776 |
| **Germany, West** | 473 | 7,381 | 11,863 |
| **Ghana** | 29 | 199 | 262 |
| **Greece** | 2,928 | 40,502 | 69,559 |
| **Honduras** | 45 | 175 | 230 |
| **Hungary*** | 21 | 72 | 101 |
| **Iceland** | 36 | 71 | 109 |
| **India** | 370 | 5,704 | 9,221 |
| **Indonesia** | 254 | 1,053 | 1,490 |
| **Iran** | 55 | 1,062 | 1,757 |
| **Iraq** | 45 | 1,350 | 2,447 |
| **Ireland** | 25 | 138 | 207 |
| **Israel** | 39 | 471 | 634 |
| **Italy** | 622 | 10,256 | 17,269 |
| **Ivory Coast** | 19 | 180 | 236 |
| **Japan** | 1,762 | 36,730 | 62,001 |
| **Korea, North*** | 29 | 218 | 352 |
| **Korea, South** | 385 | 3,789 | 6,285 |
| **Kuwait** | 86 | 2,309 | 3,767 |
| **Lebanon** | 76 | 201 | 275 |
| **Liberia** | 2,271 | 78,743 | 153,342 |
| **Libya** | 27 | 836 | 1,530 |
| **Malaysia** | 73 | 651 | 949 |
| **Maldives** | 37 | 171 | 239 |
| **Mexico** | 61 | 836 | 1,278 |
| **Morocco** | 44 | 324 | 538 |
| **Netherlands** | 444 | 5,066 | 8,300 |
| **New Zealand** | 23 | 196 | 236 |
| **Nigeria** | 30 | 425 | 624 |
| **Norway** | 616 | 21,566 | 38,575 |
| **Pakistan** | 51 | 480 | 650 |
| **Panama** | 2,437 | 23,183 | 38,011 |
| **Peru** | 52 | 578 | 936 |
| **Philippines** | 235 | 1,731 | 2,757 |
| **Poland** | 318 | 3,175 | 4,686 |
| **Portugal** | 76 | 1,158 | 1,963 |
| **Romania*** | 191 | 1,625 | 2,408 |
| **Saudi Arabia** | 92 | 1,652 | 2,891 |
| **Singapore** | 622 | 7,148 | 11,754 |
| **Somalia** | 7 | 36 | 47 |
| **South Africa** | 29 | 606 | 767 |
| **Spain** | 509 | 6,907 | 12,235 |
| **Sweden** | 232 | 3,751 | 6,225 |
| **Switzerland** | 30 | 287 | 437 |
| **Thailand** | 68 | 323 | 489 |
| **Tunisia** | 19 | 115 | 164 |
| **Turkey** | 178 | 1,346 | 2,093 |
| **USSR**[1]* | 2,530 | 16,550 | 21,757 |
| **United Arab Emirates** | 12 | 105 | 193 |
| **United Kingdom** | 1,056 | 25,424 | 42,302 |
| **Venezuela** | 64 | 613 | 918 |
| **Vietnam** | 41 | 227 | 344 |
| **Yugoslavia** | 258 | 2,417 | 3,698 |
| **Zaire** | 8 | 77 | 116 |

† Oceangoing ships (1,000 gross tons and more) as of January 1, 1981. Tonnage in thousands. * Source material limited. [1] Includes 2 U.S. Government-owned ships transferred to USSR under lend-lease agreements.

## FOREIGN COMMERCE AT SELECTED U.S. PORTS: 1980

SOURCE: U.S. Corps of Engineers (figures in thousands of short tons of cargo)

| Port | Imports | Exports |
|---|---|---|
| **ATLANTIC COAST PORTS** | | |
| New Haven Harbor, Conn. | 729 | 263 |
| New Castle and vicinity, Del. | 5,344 | — |
| Wilmington Harbor, Del. | 1,175 | 906 |
| Canaveral Harbor, Fla. | 916 | 95 |
| Jacksonville Harbor, Fla. | 3,040 | 3,137 |
| Miami Harbor, Fla. | 854 | 1,605 |
| Port Everglades Harbor, Fla. | 1,808 | 241 |
| Savannah Harbor, Ga. | 4,203 | 4,864 |
| Portland Harbor, Maine | 9,110 | 41 |
| Baltimore Harbor and Channels, Md. | 14,452 | 21,665 |
| Fall River Harbor, Mass. | 728 | — |
| Port of Boston, Mass. | 5,192 | 836 |
| Salem Harbor, Mass. | 683 | — |
| Portsmouth Harbor, N.H. | 1,169 | 182 |
| Camden-Gloucester, N.J. | 1,265 | 732 |
| Paulsboro and vicinity, N.J. | 11,392 | 73 |
| Port of Albany, N.Y. | 1,950 | 540 |
| Port of New York, N.Y. and N.J. | 42,715 | 7,477 |
| Port of Wilmington, N.C. | 2,822 | 612 |
| Marcus Hook and vicinity, Pa. | 11,314 | 144 |
| Penn Manor and vicinity, Pa. | 2,788 | 91 |
| Philadelphia Harbor, Pa. | 21,726 | 7,632 |
| Providence River and Harbor, R.I. | 718 | 598 |
| Charleston Harbor, S.C. | 2,464 | 2,479 |
| Norfolk Harbor, Va. | 5,398 | 37,163 |
| Port of Newport News, Va. | 730 | 18,138 |
| San Juan Harbor, P.R. | 3,225 | 471 |
| **GULF COAST PORTS** | | |
| Mobile Harbor, Ala. | 8,471 | 9,316 |
| Tampa Harbor, Fla. | 4,229 | 18,468 |
| Baton Rouge, La. | 13,435 | 15,878 |
| Lake Charles (Calcasieu R. & Pass), La. | 3,939 | 3,301 |
| New Orleans, La. | 21,646 | 52,131 |
| Pascagoula Harbor, Miss. | 9,644 | 4,226 |
| Beaumont, Texas | 25,619 | 3,196 |
| Brownsville, Texas | 616 | 495 |
| Corpus Christi, Texas | 16,050 | 4,605 |
| Freeport Harbor, Texas | 13,022 | 1,299 |
| Galveston Channel, Texas | 1,915 | 5,538 |
| Harbor Island, Texas | 4,808 | 8 |
| Houston Ship Channel, Texas | 31,100 | 22,403 |
| Matagorda Ship Channel, Texas | 3,057 | 175 |
| Port Arthur, Texas | 13,688 | 2,896 |
| Texas City Channel, Texas | 11,745 | 827 |
| **PACIFIC COAST PORTS** | | |
| Skagway Harbor, Alaska | 718 | 358 |
| Long Beach Harbor, Calif. | 9,330 | 9,268 |
| Los Angeles Harbor, Calif. | 8,018 | 5,790 |
| Oakland Harbor, Calif. | 1,998 | 3,350 |
| Richmond Harbor, Calif. | 2,411 | 642 |
| San Francisco Harbor, Calif. | 722 | 797 |
| Stockton, Calif. | 358 | 1,372 |
| Barbers Point Harbor, Hawaii | 2,700 | 78 |
| Honolulu Harbor, Hawaii | 1,175 | 112 |
| Coos Bay, Oreg. | 2 | 4,951 |
| Port of Astoria, Oreg. | 205 | 1,046 |
| Port of Portland, Oreg. | 2,087 | 11,674 |
| Anacortes Harbor, Wash. | 5,155 | 117 |
| Everett Harbor & Snowhomish R., Wash. | 539 | 1,458 |
| Grays Harbor & Chehalis R., Wash. | 5 | 2,754 |
| Port Angeles Harbor, Wash. | 787 | 1,433 |
| Port of Longview, Wash. | 761 | 5,967 |
| Port of Vancouver, Wash. | 841 | 478 |
| Seattle Harbor, Wash. | 4,521 | 5,081 |
| Tacoma Harbor, Wash. | 2,454 | 9,433 |

## MAJOR WORLD SHIP CANALS

| Name | Location | Year Opened | Length (Miles) | Minimum Depth (Feet) | Minimum Width (Feet) |
|---|---|---|---|---|---|
| Baltic-White Sea | USSR: Povenets on Lake Onega to Belmorsk on White Sea | 1933 | 140 | 16 | NA |
| Cape Cod | U.S.: Buzzards Bay to Cape Cod Bay, Mass. | 1914 | 17.4 | 32 | 450 |
| Chesapeake and Delaware | U.S.: Delaware River to Chesapeake Bay | 1927 | 19 | 35 | 450 |
| Chicago Sanitary and Ship | U.S.: Lake Michigan to Des Plaines River, Ill. | 1900 | 33.8 | 20 | 160 |
| Corinth | Greece: Gulf of Athens to Gulf of Corinth | 1893 | 3.5 | 26.25 | 69 |
| Houston Ship | U.S.: Houston, Texas, to Gulf of Mexico | 1914 | 50 | 36 | 300 |
| Kiel (Nord-Ostsee) | Germany: North Sea to Baltic Sea | 1895 | 53.2 | 38 | 144 |
| Manchester Ship | England: Manchester to Mersey River | 1894 | 35.5 | 28 | 90 |
| Moscow | USSR: Moscow to Volga River | 1937 | 80 | 18 | 280 |
| North Sea | Netherlands: Amsterdam to IJmuiden | 1876 | 17.5 | 45 | 443 |
| Panama | Panama: Cristóbal on Atlantic Ocean to Balboa on Pacific Ocean | 1914 | 50.72 | 41.6 | 300 |
| St. Lawrence Seaway | U.S.-Canada: Atlantic Ocean to Great Lakes system | 1959 | 2,347* | 27 | 450 |
| Sault Sainte Marie (Canadian) | U.S.-Canada: Lake Huron to Lake Superior | 1895 | 1.38 | 27 | 150 |
| Sault Sainte Marie (American) | U.S.-Canada: Lake Huron to Lake Superior | 1855 | 1.8 | 27 | 80 |
| Suez | Egypt: Port Said on Mediterranean Sea to Suez on Gulf of Suez | 1869 | 100.76 | 42 | 196 |
| Terneuzen-Ghent | Belgium-Netherlands: Ghent to Scheldt Estuary at Terneuzen | 1827 | 11 | 29 | 164 |
| Volga-Baltic | USSR: Caspian Sea to Leningrad on Baltic Sea | 1964 | 225 | NA | NA |
| Volga-Don | USSR: Volga River to Don River, as linking waterway for Baltic-Black Sea route | 1952 | 62 | NA | NA |
| Welland | Canada: Lake Erie to Lake Ontario | 1932 | 27.6 | 27 | 80 |

* Distance from Strait of Belle Isle to Duluth, Minnesota. NA = Not Available.

## PANAMA CANAL USERS: 1980

SOURCE: *Statistical Abstract of the U.S.*, 1981

Commercial Ocean Traffic

| Nationality of vessel | Transits | Net tons (1,000) | Cargo (1,000 long tons) |
|---|---|---|---|
| UNITED STATES | 1,906 | 34,400 | 30,700 |
| United Kingdom | 870 | 11,600 | 10,200 |
| Greece | 1,552 | 18,800 | 24,300 |
| Japan | 1,133 | 16,600 | 10,500 |
| Liberia | 1,814 | 31,000 | 33,700 |
| Norway | 449 | 7,800 | 6,800 |
| Panama | 1,228 | 12,600 | 10,700 |
| U.S.S.R. | 544 | 3,400 | 2,000 |
| All Others | 4,011 | 45,900 | 38,300 |

## PANAMA CANAL TRAFFIC, 1950-1980

SOURCE: *Statistical Abstract of the U.S.*, 1981

| | Total Transits | Commercial Ocean Traffic: Transits | Commercial Ocean Traffic: Cargo (long tons) |
|---|---|---|---|
| 1950 | 5,900 | 5,400 | 28,900,000 |
| 1955 | 8,300 | 8,000 | 40,600,000 |
| 1960 | 12,100 | 10,800 | 59,300,000 |
| 1965 | 12,900 | 11,800 | 76,600,000 |
| 1970 | 15,500 | 13,700 | 114,300,000 |
| 1974 | 15,300 | 14,000 | 147,900,000 |
| 1975 | 14,700 | 13,600 | 140,100,000 |
| 1976 | 13,200 | 12,200 | 117,200,000 |
| 1977 | 13,100 | 11,900 | 123,000,000 |
| 1978 | 13,800 | 12,700 | 142,500,000 |
| 1979 | 14,400 | 12,900 | 154,100,000 |
| 1980 | 14,700 | 13,500 | 167,200,000 |

## WORLD CITIES: STANDARD TIME DIFFERENCES

When it is 12 noon in New York (Eastern Standard Time), the standard time in other cities is as follows:

| City | Time |
|---|---|
| Alexandria | 7:00 p.m. |
| Amsterdam | 6:00 p.m. |
| Anchorage | 7:00 a.m. |
| Athens | 7:00 p.m. |
| Auckland | 5:00 a.m.* |
| Baghdad | 8:00 p.m. |
| Bangkok | 12:00 Midnight |
| Barcelona | 6:00 p.m. |
| Basra | 8:00 p.m. |
| Beirut | 7:00 p.m. |
| Berlin | 6:00 p.m. |
| Bogotá | 12:00 Noon |
| Bombay | 10:30 p.m. |
| Boston | 12:00 Noon |
| Brussels | 6:00 p.m. |
| Bucharest | 7:00 p.m. |
| Budapest | 6:00 p.m. |
| Buenos Aires | 2:00 p.m. |
| Cairo | 7:00 p.m. |
| Calcutta | 10:30 p.m. |
| Cape Town | 7:00 p.m. |
| Caracas | 1:00 p.m. |
| Chicago | 11:00 a.m. |
| Copenhagen | 6:00 p.m. |
| Dakar | 5:00 p.m. |
| Damascus | 7:00 p.m. |
| Delhi | 10:30 p.m. |
| Denver | 10:00 a.m. |
| Jakarta | 12:00 Midnight |
| Dublin | 5:00 p.m. |
| Fairbanks | 7:00 a.m. |
| Frankfurt | 6:00 p.m. |
| Frobisher Bay | 1:00 p.m. |
| Gander | 1:30 p.m. |
| Geneva | 6:00 p.m. |
| Glasgow | 5:00 p.m. |
| Halifax | 1:00 p.m. |
| Hamilton (Bermuda) | 1:00 p.m. |
| Havana | 12:00 Noon |
| Helsinki | 7:00 p.m. |
| Ho Chi Minh City (Saigon) | 12:00 Midnight |
| Hong Kong | 1:00 a.m.* |
| Honolulu | 7:00 a.m. |
| Houston | 11:00 a.m. |
| Istanbul | 8:00 p.m. |
| Jerusalem | 7:00 p.m. |
| Johannesburg | 7:00 p.m. |
| Juneau | 9:00 a.m. |
| Karachi | 10:00 p.m. |
| Ketchikan | 9:00 a.m. |
| Kinshasa | 6:00 p.m. |
| Lima | 12:00 Noon |
| Lisbon | 5:00 p.m. |
| London (Greenwich) | 5:00 p.m. |
| Los Angeles | 9:00 a.m. |
| Madrid | 6:00 p.m. |
| Manila | 1:00 a.m.* |
| Melbourne | 3:00 a.m.* |
| Miami | 12:00 Noon |
| Monrovia | 5:00 p.m. |
| Montevideo | 2:00 p.m. |
| Moscow | 8:00 p.m. |
| New Orleans | 11:00 a.m. |
| Nome | 6:00 a.m. |
| Nouméa | 4:00 a.m.* |
| Oslo | 6:00 p.m. |
| Papeete | 7:00 a.m. |
| Paris | 6:00 p.m. |
| Peking | 1:00 a.m.* |
| Phoenix | 10:00 a.m. |
| Portland | 9:00 a.m. |
| Rangoon | 11:30 p.m. |
| Recife | 2:00 p.m. |
| Reykjavík | 5:00 p.m. |
| Rio de Janeiro | 2:00 p.m. |
| Rome | 6:00 p.m. |
| Salt Lake City | 10:00 a.m. |
| San Francisco | 9:00 a.m. |
| San Juan | 1:00 p.m. |
| Santiago | 1:00 p.m. |
| Seattle | 9:00 a.m. |
| Seoul | 2:00 a.m.* |
| Shanghai | 1:00 a.m.* |
| Singapore | 1:00 a.m.* |
| Stockholm | 6:00 p.m. |
| Suva | 5:00 a.m.* |
| Sydney | 3:00 a.m.* |
| Tehran | 8:30 p.m. |
| Tel Aviv | 7:00 p.m. |
| Tokyo | 2:00 a.m.* |
| Tucson | 10:00 a.m. |
| Valparaíso | 1:00 p.m. |
| Vancouver | 9:00 a.m. |
| Vienna | 6:00 p.m. |
| Vladivostok | 3:00 a.m.* |
| Warsaw | 6:00 p.m. |
| Washington, D.C. | 12:00 Noon |
| Whitehorse | 9:00 a.m. |
| Yokohama | 2:00 a.m.* |
| Zürich | 6:00 p.m. |

* = following day.

## LARGE PASSENGER LINERS

SOURCE: Cruise Lines International Association

| Ship Name | Line | Flag | Length, ft. | Tonnage | Max. No. Passengers |
|---|---|---|---|---|---|
| Norway | Norwegian Caribbean Lines | Norwegian | 1,035 | 69,500 | 2,000 |
| Queen Elizabeth 2 | Cunard Line, Ltd. | British | 963 | 67,140 | 1,909 |
| Canberra | P & O Cruises, Ltd. | British | 818 | 45,000 | 1,800 |
| Oriana | P & O Cruises, Ltd. | British | 804 | 42,000 | 1,800 |
| Oceanic | Home Lines Cruises | Panamanian | 774 | 39,241 | 1,034 |
| Festivale | Carnival Cruise Lines | Panamanian | 760 | 38,175 | 1,400 |
| Rotterdam | Holland America Cruises | Netherlands | 748 | 38,000 | 1,111 |
| Eugenio C. | Costa Cruises | Italian | 713 | 30,000 | 1,100 |
| Song of America | Royal Caribbean Cruise Line | Norwegian | 702 | 32,000 | 1,414 |
| Guglielmo Marconi | Chandris, Inc. | Italian | 700 | 27,900 | 1,000 |
| Galileo Galilei | Chandris, Inc. | Italian | 700 | 27,887 | 1,000 |
| Constitution | American Hawaii Cruises | U.S.A. | 682 | 30,090 | 800 |
| Oceanic Independence | American Hawaii Cruises | U.S.A. | 682 | 30,090 | 1,000 |
| Royal Viking Star | Royal Viking Line | Norwegian | 674 | 28,000 | 725 |
| Atlantic | Home Lines Cruises | Panamanian | 671 | 30,000 | 1,155 |
| Tropicale | Carnival Cruise Lines | Liberian | 660 | 30,000 | 1,022 |
| Sea Princess | P & O Cruises, Ltd. | British | 660 | 27,670 | 844 |
| Mardi Gras | Carnival Cruise Lines | Panamanian | 650 | 27,250 | 1,240 |
| Britanis | Chandris, Inc. | Greek | 642 | 25,245 | 1,545 |
| Rhapsody | Paquet Cruises | Bahamian | 642 | 24,500 | 893 |
| Carnivale | Carnival Cruise Lines | Panamanian | 640 | 27,250 | 1,350 |
| Maxim Gorki | Black Sea Shipping Co. | USSR | 639 | 25,000 | 728 |
| Song of Norway | Royal Caribbean Cruise Line | Norwegian | 635 | 23,005 | 1,170 |
| Nordic Prince | Royal Caribbean Cruise Line | Norwegian | 635 | 23,000 | 1,168 |
| Vistafjord | Norwegian American Cruises | Norwegian | 628 | 25,000 | 660 |
| Royal Odyssey | Royal Cruise Line | Greek | 627 | 25,500 | 806 |
| Emerald Seas | Eastern Steamship Lines | Panamanian | 622 | 24,458 | 920 |
| Sagafjord | Norwegian American Cruises | Norwegian | 620 | 24,000 | 500 |
| Veendam | Holland America Cruises | Panamanian | 617 | 23,500 | 713 |
| Volendam | Holland America Cruises | Panamanian | 617 | 23,500 | 717 |

## WORLD'S LEADING BRIDGES

SOURCE: American Society of Civil Engineers

Bridges listed here are grouped by type of construction and ranked by the length of their spans.

### SUSPENSION BRIDGES

| Bridge | Main Span Meters | Main Span Feet | Completion Date | Location |
|---|---|---|---|---|
| Humber | 1,410 | 4,626 | 1981 | Hull, England |
| Verrazano-Narrows | 1,298 | 4,260 | 1964 | New York City |
| Golden Gate | 1,280 | 4,200 | 1937 | San Francisco |
| Mackinac Straits | 1,158 | 3,800 | 1957 | Mackinaw City, Michigan |
| Bosporus | 1,074 | 3,524 | 1973 | Istanbul, Turkey |
| George Washington | 1,067 | 3,500 | 1931 | New York City |
| Tagus | 1,013 | 3,323 | 1966 | Lisbon, Portugal |
| Forth Road | 1,006 | 3,300 | 1964 | Scotland |
| Severn | 988 | 3,240 | 1966 | England/Wales |
| Tacoma Narrows | 853 | 2,800 | 1950 | Washington |
| Angostura | 712 | 2,336 | 1967 | Ciudad Bolívar, Venezuela |
| Kanmon Strait | 712 | 2,336 | 1973 | Honshu, Japan |
| San Francisco-Oakland | 704 | 2,310 | 1936 | San Francisco |
| Bronx-Whitestone | 701 | 2,300 | 1939 | New York City |
| Quebec | 668 | 2,190 | 1970 | Quebec, Canada |
| Delaware Memorial | | | 1951 | Wilmington, |
| I & II | 655 | 2,150 | 1968 | Delaware |
| Seaway Skyway | 655 | 2,150 | 1960 | New York-Ontario |
| Melville Gas Pipe | 610 | 2,000 | 1951 | Louisiana |
| Walt Whitman | 610 | 2,000 | 1957 | Philadelphia |
| Tancarville | 608 | 1,995 | 1959 | Le Havre, France |
| Lillebaelt | 600 | 1,968 | 1970 | Lillebaelt Strait, Denmark |
| Ambassador | 564 | 1,850 | 1929 | Detroit, Michigan |
| Throgs Neck | 549 | 1,800 | 1961 | New York City |
| Benjamin Franklin | 533 | 1,750 | 1926 | Philadelphia |
| Skojmen | 525 | 1,722 | 1972 | Narvik, Norway |
| Kvalsund | 525 | 1,722 | 1976 | Kvalsund, Norway |
| Kleve-Emmerich | 500 | 1,640 | 1965 | Emmerich, West Germany |
| Bear Mountain | 497 | 1,632 | 1924 | New York |
| Newport | 487 | 1,600 | 1969 | Rhode Island |
| Chesapeake | 487 | 1,600 | 1952 | Maryland |
| Williamsburg | 487 | 1,600 | 1903 | New York City |
| Brooklyn | 486 | 1,595 | 1883 | New York City |
| Lion's Gate | 472 | 1,550 | 1938 | British Columbia, Canada |
| Hirado | 465 | 1,526 | 1977 | Nagasaki, Japan |
| Mid-Hudson | 457 | 1,500 | 1930 | New York |
| Manhattan | 448 | 1,470 | 1909 | New York City |
| Triborough | 420 | 1,380 | 1937 | New York City |

*Under construction.

### CABLE-STAYED BRIDGES

| Bridge | Main Span Meters | Main Span Feet | Completion Date | Location |
|---|---|---|---|---|
| **Orthotropic Steel Deck** | | | | |
| Hooghly River | 457 | 1,500 | * | Calcutta, India |
| Saint Nazaire | 404 | 1,325 | 1975 | Brittany, France |
| Stretto di Rande | 400 | 1,312 | 1978 | Vigo, Spain |
| Luling | 376 | 1,235 | * | Louisiana |
| Dusseldorf | 367 | 1,204 | 1978 | Fleke, West Germany |
| Almoen | 366 | 1,201 | 1981 | Sweden |
| Yamatogawa | 355 | 1,165 | * | Osaka, Japan |
| Duisburg-Neuenkamp | 350 | 1,148 | 1970 | West Germany |
| West Gate | 336 | 1,102 | 1974 | Melbourne, Australia |
| Brazo Largo | 330 | 1,083 | 1977 | Guazu, Argentina |
| Zarate | 330 | 1,083 | 1977 | Palmas, Argentina |
| Kohlbrand | 325 | 1,066 | 1974 | Hamburg, West Germany |
| Knee | 320 | 1,050 | 1969 | Dusseldorf, West Germany |
| **Prestressed Concrete Deck** | | | | |
| Pasadas | 330 | 1,082 | * | Argentina-Paraguay |
| Brotonne | 320 | 1,050 | 1976 | Caudebec, France |
| Pasco, Kennewick | 299 | 981 | 1979 | Washington |
| Wadi-Kuf | 282 | 925 | 1972 | Beida, Libya |
| Tiel | 267 | 876 | 1975 | Waal, Netherlands |
| Manuel Belgrano | 245 | 804 | 1973 | Corrientes, Argentina |
| Rafael Urdaneta | 235 | 771 | 1962 | Maracaibo, Venezuela |
| Poleevera | 208 | 682 | 1967 | Genoa, Italy |

### STEEL TRUSS BRIDGES

| Bridge | Main Span Meters | Main Span Feet | Completion Date | Location |
|---|---|---|---|---|
| **Cantilever** | | | | |
| Quebec | 549 | 1,800 | 1918 | St. Lawrence River, Canada |
| Forth | 521 | 1,710 | 1889 | Scotland |
| Minato | 510 | 1,673 | 1974 | Osaka, Japan |
| Commodore J.J. Barry | 501 | 1,644 | 1974 | Pennsylvania |
| Greater New Orleans | 480 | 1,575 | 1958 | Louisiana |
| Howrah | 457 | 1,500 | 1943 | Calcutta, India |
| East Bay | 427 | 1,400 | 1936 | Oakland, Calif. |
| Baton Rouge | 376 | 1,235 | 1968 | Louisiana |
| Astoria | 376 | 1,235 | 1966 | Oregon |
| Tappan Zee | 369 | 1,212 | 1956 | New York |
| Longview | 366 | 1,200 | 1930 | Washington |
| Baltimore | 366 | 1,200 | 1976 | Maryland |
| Queensboro | 360 | 1,182 | 1908 | New York City |
| **Continuous** | | | | |
| Astoria | 376 | 1,235 | 1966 | Oregon |
| Oshima | 325 | 1,066 | 1976 | Japan |
| Tenmon | 300 | 984 | 1966 | Japan |
| Kuronoseto | 300 | 984 | 1974 | Japan |
| Dubuque | 258 | 945 | 1943 | Iowa |
| Braga Memorial | 256 | 840 | 1966 | Massachusetts |
| Earle | 252 | 825 | 1956 | Kentucky |
| Lincoln Trail | 252 | 825 | 1966 | Indiana |
| Cairo | 250 | 820 | 1975 | Illinois |
| **Simple Span** | | | | |
| Metropolis | 219 | 720 | 1917 | Illinois |
| Municipal | 204 | 668 | 1910 | St. Louis, Missouri |
| Elizabethtown | 179 | 586 | 1906 | Ohio |

*Under construction.

### LONGEST ARCHES

| Bridge | Main Span Meters | Main Span Feet | Completion Date | Location |
|---|---|---|---|---|
| **Steel** | | | | |
| New River Gorge | 518 | 1,700 | 1977 | West Virginia |
| Bayonne | 510 | 1,675 | 1931 | New Jersey |
| Sydney Harbor | 509 | 1,670 | 1932 | Sydney, Australia |
| Fremont | 383 | 1,255 | 1971 | Oregon |
| Zdakov | 380 | 1,244 | 1967 | Orlik, Czechoslovakia |
| Port Mann | 366 | 1,200 | 1964 | B.C., Canada |
| Runcorn | 330 | 1,082 | 1961 | Mersey, England |
| Birchenough | 329 | 1,080 | 1935 | Sabi, Zimbabwe |
| Glen Canyon | 313 | 1,028 | 1959 | Arizona |
| Lewiston-Queenston | 305 | 1,000 | 1962 | Niagara River, U.S.A.-Canada |
| Hellgate | 298 | 978 | 1916 | New York City |
| **Concrete** | | | | |
| KRK | 390 | 1,280 | 1974 | Zagreb, Yugoslavia |
| Gladesville | 305 | 1,000 | 1964 | Sydney, Australia |
| Amizade | 290 | 951 | 1964 | Foz do Ignacu, Brazil |
| Bloukrans | 272 | 892 | * | Southern Coast, S. Africa |
| Arrabida | 270 | 885 | 1963 | Oporto, Portugal |
| Sando | 264 | 866 | 1943 | Kramfors, Sweden |

## LONGEST BRIDGES IN THE WORLD

SOURCE: American Society of Civil Engineers

Measurements that determine the longest bridges in the world include the bridge span or spans, as well as its approach roads.

| Name of Bridge | Length in Feet | Completed | Location |
|---|---|---|---|
| Lake Pontchartrain Causeway II | 126,055 | 1969 | New Orleans-Lewisburg, La. |
| Lake Pontchartrain Causeway I | 125,827 | 1956 | New Orleans-Lewisburg, La. |
| Chesapeake Bay Bridge-Tunnel | 93,203 | 1964 | Cape Henry-Cape Charles, Va. |
| Presidente Costa e Silva Bridge | 45,866 | 1974 | Rio de Janeiro—Niteroi, Brazil |
| Marathon Key-Bahia Honda Key Bridge | 38,915 | 1910 | Florida Keys |
| San Mateo-Hayward Bridge I | 37,183 | 1929 | San Francisco Bay |
| San Mateo-Hayward Bridge II | 35,708 | 1967 | San Francisco Bay |
| Lake Maracaibo Bridge | 28,473 | 1962 | Punta Piedras-Punta Iguana, Venezuela |
| Transbay Bridge | 27,286 | 1936 | San Francisco-Oakland |
| Lake Pontchartrain Trestle | 24,927 | 1927 | Blind Bayou-Slidell, La. |
| Mackinac Straits Bridge | 23,390 | 1957 | Mackinaw City-St. Ignace, Mich. |
| James River Bridge | 23,177 | 1928 | Chuckatuck Creek-Newport News, Va. |
| Huey P. Long Bridge | 22,996 | 1935 | New Orleans |
| Sunshine Skyway (Structure C) | 22,373 | 1954 | St. Petersburg-Palmetto, Fla. |
| Richmond-San Rafael Bridge | 21,965 | 1957 | San Pablo Bay, Calif. |
| Astoria Bridge | 21,697 | 1966 | Pt. Ellice, Wash.-Astoria, Ore. |
| Chesapeake Bay Bridge | 21,286 | 1952 | Sandy Point-Kent Island, Md. |
| Öland Island Bridge | 19,882 | 1972 | Svinö-Möllstorp, Sweden |
| Oosterschelde Bridge | 16,475 | 1965 | Middelburg-Zierikzee, Netherlands |
| Tappan Zee Bridge | 16,013 | 1955 | South Nyack—Tarrytown, N.Y. |

## U.S. POPULATION AND AREA: 1790–1980

SOURCE: Bureau of the Census (Series P-25)

| Year | POPULATION Number (1,000) | Percent Increase | Per Square Mile[1] | AREA (1,000 sq. mi.) Land | Water |
|---|---|---|---|---|---|
| 1790 | 3,929 | (X) | 4.5 | 865 | 24 |
| 1800 | 5,308 | 35.1 | 6.1 | 865 | 24 |
| 1810 | 7,240 | 36.4 | 4.3 | 1,682 | 34 |
| 1820 | 9,638 | 33.1 | 5.6 | 1,749 | 39 |
| 1830 | 12,866 | 33.5 | 7.4 | 1,749 | 39 |
| 1840 | 17,069 | 32.7 | 9.8 | 1,749 | 39 |
| 1850 | 23,192 | 35.9 | 7.9 | 2,940 | 53 |
| 1860 | 31,443 | 35.6 | 10.6 | 2,970 | 53 |
| 1870 | 39,818 | 26.6 | 13.4 | 2,970 | 53 |
| 1880 | 50,156 | 26.0 | 16.9 | 2,970 | 53 |
| 1890 | 62,948 | 25.5 | 21.2 | 2,970 | 53 |
| 1900 | 75,995 | 20.7 | 25.6 | 2,970 | 53 |
| 1910 | 91,972 | 21.0 | 31.0 | 2,970 | 53 |
| 1920 | 105,711 | 14.9 | 35.6 | 2,969 | 53 |
| 1930 | 122,775 | 16.1 | 41.2 | 2,977 | 45 |
| 1940 | 131,669 | 7.2 | 44.2 | 2,977 | 45 |
| 1950 | 150,697 | 14.5 | 50.7 | 2,975 | 48 |
| 1960 | 179,323 | 18.5 | 50.5 | 3,541 | 74 |
| 1970 | 203,235 | 13.3 | 57.5 | 3,537 | 78 |
| 1980 | 226,547 | 11.4 | 63.9 | 3,544 | 79 |
| 1981* | 229,304 | 1.2 | 64.7 | 3,544 | 79 |

(X) Not applicable. [1] Land area only.
* As of July 1.

## CENTER OF POPULATION OF THE UNITED STATES: 1790–1980

SOURCE: Bureau of the Census

| Census Year | Approximate location |
|---|---|
| **Conterminous United States*** | |
| 1790 | 23 miles east of Baltimore, Md. |
| 1800 | 18 miles west of Baltimore, Md. |
| 1810 | 40 miles northwest by west of Washington, D.C. (in Virginia) |
| 1820 | 16 miles east of Moorefield, W. Va. |
| 1830 | 19 miles west-southwest of Moorefield, W. Va. |
| 1840 | 16 miles south of Clarksburg, W. Va. |
| 1850 | 23 miles southeast of Parkersburg, W. Va. |
| 1860 | 20 miles south by east of Chillicothe, Ohio |
| 1870 | 48 miles east by north of Cincinnati, Ohio |
| 1880 | 8 miles west by south of Cincinnati, Ohio (in Kentucky) |
| 1890 | 20 miles east of Columbus, Ind. |
| 1900 | 6 miles southeast of Columbus, Ind. |
| 1910 | In the city of Bloomington, Ind. |
| 1920 | 8 miles south-southeast of Spencer, Owen County, Ind. |
| 1930 | 3 miles northeast of Linton, Greene County, Ind. |
| 1940 | 2 miles southeast by east of Carlisle, Haddon township, Sullivan County, Ind. |
| 1950 | 8 miles north-northwest of Olney, Richland County, Ill. |
| **United States** | |
| 1950 | 3 miles northeast of Louisville, Clay County, Ill. |
| 1960 | In Clinton County, Ill. 6½ miles northwest of Centralia |
| 1970 | In St. Clair County, Ill. 5 miles east-southeast of Mascoutah |
| 1980 | In Jefferson County, Mo., a quarter mile west of De Soto. |

* Conterminous United States excludes Alaska and Hawaii.

## RESIDENT U.S. POPULATION BY STATE AND RANK, APRIL 1980 CENSUS

SOURCE: U.S. Bureau of the Census (Population in thousands)

| Rank | State | Population | Rank | State | Population | Rank | State | Population |
|---|---|---|---|---|---|---|---|---|
| 1 | California | 23,668 | 18 | Maryland | 4,217 | 35 | Nebraska | 1,570 |
| 2 | New York | 17,558 | 19 | Louisiana | 4,206 | 36 | Utah | 1,461 |
| 3 | Texas | 14,229 | 20 | Washington | 4,132 | 37 | New Mexico | 1,303 |
| 4 | Pennsylvania | 11,864 | 21 | Minnesota | 4,076 | 38 | Maine | 1,125 |
| 5 | Illinois | 11,427 | 22 | Alabama | 3,894 | 39 | Hawaii | 965 |
| 6 | Ohio | 10,798 | 23 | Kentucky | 3,661 | 40 | Rhode Island | 947 |
| 7 | Florida | 9,746 | 24 | South Carolina | 3,122 | 41 | Idaho | 944 |
| 8 | Michigan | 9,262 | 25 | Connecticut | 3,108 | 42 | New Hampshire | 921 |
| 9 | New Jersey | 7,635 | 26 | Oklahoma | 3,025 | 43 | Nevada | 800 |
| 10 | North Carolina | 5,882 | 27 | Iowa | 2,914 | 44 | Montana | 787 |
| 11 | Massachusetts | 5,737 | 28 | Colorado | 2,890 | 45 | South Dakota | 691 |
| 12 | Indiana | 5,490 | 29 | Arizona | 2,718 | 46 | North Dakota | 653 |
| 13 | Georgia | 5,463 | 30 | Oregon | 2,633 | 47 | District of Columbia | 638 |
| 14 | Virginia | 5,347 | 31 | Mississippi | 2,521 | 48 | Delaware | 594 |
| 15 | Missouri | 4,917 | 32 | Kansas | 2,364 | 49 | Vermont | 511 |
| 16 | Wisconsin | 4,706 | 33 | Arkansas | 2,286 | 50 | Wyoming | 470 |
| 17 | Tennessee | 4,591 | 34 | West Virginia | 1,950 | 51 | Alaska | 402 |

## STANDARD CONSOLIDATED STATISTICAL AREAS (SCSA's)

SOURCE: U.S. Bureau of the Census

| Rank 1980 | Standard Consolidated Statistical Area | 1980 Population | 1970 Population |
|---|---|---|---|
| 1. | New York-Newark-Jersey City, N.Y.-N.J.-Conn. | 16,121,297 | 17,035,270 |
| 2. | Los Angeles-Long Beach-Anaheim, Calif. | 11,497,568 | 9,980,859 |
| 3. | Chicago-Gary-Kenosha, Ill.-Ind.-Wis. | 7,869,542 | 7,726,039 |
| 4. | Philadelphia-Wilmington-Trenton, Pa.-Del.-N.J. | 5,547,902 | 5,627,719 |
| 5. | San Francisco-Oakland-San Jose, Calif. | 5,179,784 | 4,630,576 |
| 6. | Detroit-Ann Arbor, Mich. | 4,618,161 | 4,669,154 |
| 7. | Boston-Lawrence-Lowell, Mass.-N.H. | 3,448,122 | 3,526,349 |
| 8. | Houston-Galveston, Tex. | 3,101,293 | 2,169,128 |
| 9. | Cleveland-Akron-Lorain, Ohio | 2,834,062 | 2,999,811 |
| 10. | Miami-Fort Lauderdale, Fla. | 2,643,981 | 1,887,892 |
| 11. | Seattle-Tacoma, Wash. | 2,093,112 | 1,836,949 |
| 12. | Cincinnati-Hamilton, Ohio-Ky.-Ind. | 1,660,278 | 1,613,414 |
| 13. | Milwaukee-Racine, Wis. | 1,570,275 | 1,574,722 |
| 14. | Indianapolis-Anderson, Ind. | 1,305,911 | 1,249,874 |
| 15. | San Juan-Caguas, Puerto Rico | 1,260,337 | 1,078,398 |
| 16. | Providence-Fall River, R.I.-Mass. | 1,096,047 | 1,078,436 |
| 17. | Dayton-Springfield, Ohio | 1,013,955 | 1,040,137 |

## LARGEST U.S. METROPOLITAN AREAS (Rank by 1980 Census)

SOURCE: U.S. Bureau of the Census

| Rank 1980 | Standard Metropolitan Statistical Area | 1980 Population | 1970 Population |
|---|---|---|---|
| 1 | New York, N.Y.-N.J. | 9,119,737 | 9,973,716 |
| 2 | Los Angeles-Long Beach, Calif. | 7,477,657 | 7,041,980 |
| 3 | Chicago, Ill. | 7,102,328 | 6,974,755 |
| 4 | Philadelphia, Pa.-N.J. | 4,716,818 | 4,824,110 |
| 5 | Detroit, Mich. | 4,352,762 | 4,435,051 |
| 6 | San Francisco-Oakland, Calif. | 3,252,721 | 3,109,249 |
| 7 | Washington, D.C.-Md.-Va. | 3,060,240 | 2,910,111 |
| 8 | Dallas-Fort Worth, Tex. | 2,974,878 | 2,377,623 |
| 9 | Houston, Tex. | 2,905,350 | 1,999,316 |
| 10 | Boston, Mass. | 2,763,357 | 2,899,101 |
| 11 | Nassau-Suffolk, N.Y. | 2,605,813 | 2,555,868 |
| 12 | St. Louis, Mo.-Ill. | 2,355,276 | 2,410,884 |
| 13 | Pittsburgh, Pa. | 2,263,894 | 2,401,362 |
| 14 | Baltimore, Md. | 2,174,023 | 2,071,016 |
| 15 | Minneapolis-St. Paul, Minn.-Wis. | 2,114,256 | 1,965,391 |
| 16 | Atlanta, Ga. | 2,029,618 | 1,595,517 |
| 17 | Newark, N.J. | 1,965,304 | 2,057,468 |
| 18 | Anaheim-Sta. Ana-Garden Grove, Calif. | 1,931,570 | 1,421,233 |
| 19 | Cleveland, Ohio | 1,898,720 | 2,063,729 |
| 20 | San Diego, Calif. | 1,861,846 | 1,357,854 |
| 21 | Miami, Fla. | 1,625,979 | 1,267,792 |
| 22 | Denver-Boulder, Colo. | 1,619,921 | 1,239,545 |
| 23 | Seattle-Everett, Wash. | 1,606,765 | 1,424,605 |
| 24 | Tampa-St. Petersburg, Fla. | 1,569,492 | 1,088,549 |
| 25 | Riverside-San Bernardino-Ontario, Calif. | 1,557,080 | 1,139,149 |
| 26 | Phoenix, Ariz. | 1,508,030 | 971,228 |
| 27 | Cincinnati, Ohio-Ky.-Ind. | 1,401,403 | 1,387,207 |
| 28 | Milwaukee, Wis. | 1,397,143 | 1,403,884 |
| 29 | Kansas City, Mo.-Kans. | 1,327,020 | 1,273,926 |
| 30 | San Jose, Calif. | 1,295,071 | 1,065,313 |
| 31 | Buffalo, N.Y. | 1,242,573 | 1,349,211 |
| 32 | Portland, Ore.-Wash. | 1,242,187 | 1,007,130 |
| 33 | New Orleans, La. | 1,186,725 | 1,046,470 |
| 34 | Indianapolis, Ind. | 1,166,929 | 1,111,352 |
| 35 | Columbus, Ohio | 1,093,293 | 1,017,847 |
| 36 | San Antonio, Tex. | 1,071,954 | 888,179 |
| 37 | Fort Lauderdale-Hollywood, Fla. | 1,014,043 | 620,100 |
| 38 | Sacramento, Calif. | 1,014,002 | 803,793 |
| 39 | Rochester, N.Y. | 971,879 | 961,516 |
| 40 | Salt Lake City-Ogden, Utah | 936,255 | 705,458 |
| 41 | Providence-Warwick-Pawtucket, R.I.-Mass | 919,216 | 908,887 |
| 42 | Memphis, Tenn.-Ark.-Miss. | 912,887 | 834,103 |
| 43 | Louisville, Ky.-Ind. | 906,240 | 867,330 |
| 44 | Nashville-Davidson, Tenn. | 850,505 | 699,271 |
| 45 | Birmingham, Ala. | 847,360 | 767,230 |
| 46 | Oklahoma City, Okla. | 834,088 | 699,092 |
| 47 | Dayton, Ohio | 830,070 | 852,531 |
| 48 | Greensboro-Winston-Salem-High Point, N.C. | 827,385 | 724,129 |
| 49 | Norfolk-Virginia Beach-Portsmouth, Va.-N.C. | 806,691 | 732,600 |
| 50 | Albany-Schenectady-Troy, N.Y. | 795,019 | 777,977 |
| 51 | Toledo, Ohio-Mich. | 791,599 | 762,658 |
| 52 | Honolulu, Hawaii | 762,874 | 630,528 |
| 53 | Jacksonville, Fla. | 737,519 | 621,827 |
| 54 | Hartford, Conn. | 726,114 | 720,581 |
| 55 | Orlando, Fla. | 700,699 | 453,270 |
| 56 | Tulsa, Okla. | 689,628 | 549,154 |
| 57 | Akron, Ohio | 660,328 | 679,239 |
| 58 | Gary-Hammond-E. Chicago, Ind. | 642,781 | 633,367 |
| 59 | Syracuse, N.Y. | 642,375 | 636,596 |
| 60 | Northeast Pennsylvania | 640,396 | 621,882 |
| 61 | Charlotte-Gastonia, N.C. | 637,218 | 557,785 |
| 62 | Allentown-Bethlehem-Easton, Pa.-N.J. | 636,714 | 594,382 |
| 63 | Richmond, Va. | 632,015 | 547,542 |
| 64 | Grand Rapids, Mich. | 601,680 | 539,225 |
| 65 | New Brunswick-Perth Amboy-Sayreville, N.J. | 595,893 | 583,813 |
| 66 | West Palm Beach-Boca Raton, Fla. | 573,125 | 348,993 |
| 67 | Omaha, Nebr.-Iowa | 570,399 | 542,646 |
| 68 | Greenville-Spartanburg, S.C. | 568,758 | 473,454 |
| 69 | Jersey City, N.J. | 556,972 | 607,839 |
| 70 | Austin, Tex. | 536,450 | 360,463 |
| 71 | Youngstown-Warren, Ohio | 531,350 | 537,124 |
| 72 | Tucson, Ariz. | 531,263 | 351,667 |
| 73 | Raleigh-Durham, N.C. | 530,673 | 419,254 |
| 74 | Springfield-Chicopee-Holyoke, Mass.-Conn. | 530,668 | 541,752 |
| 75 | Oxnard-Simi Valley-Ventura, Calif. | 529,899 | 378,497 |
| 76 | Wilmington, Del.-N.J.-Md. | 524,108 | 499,493 |
| 77 | Flint, Mich. | 521,589 | 508,664 |
| 78 | Fresno, Calif. | 515,013 | 413,329 |
| 79 | Long Branch-Asbury Park, N.J. | 503,173 | 461,849 |
| 80 | Baton Rouge, La. | 493,973 | 375,628 |
| 81 | Tacoma, Wash. | 485,643 | 412,344 |
| 82 | El Paso, Tex. | 479,899 | 359,291 |
| 83 | Knoxville, Tenn. | 476,517 | 409,409 |
| 84 | Lansing-East Lansing, Mich. | 468,482 | 424,271 |
| 85 | Las Vegas, Nev. | 461,816 | 273,288 |
| 86 | Albuquerque, N. Mex. | 454,499 | 333,266 |
| 87 | Paterson-Clifton-Passaic, N.J. | 447,585 | 460,782 |
| 88 | Harrisburg, Pa. | 446,072 | 410,505 |
| 89 | Mobile, Ala. | 442,819 | 376,690 |
| 90 | Johnson City-Kingsport-Bristol, Tenn.-Va. | 433,638 | 373,591 |
| 91 | Charleston-North Charleston, S.C. | 430,301 | 336,036 |
| 92 | Chattanooga, Tenn.-Ga. | 426,540 | 370,857 |
| 93 | New Haven-West Haven, Conn. | 417,592 | 411,287 |
| 94 | Wichita, Kans. | 411,313 | 389,352 |
| 95 | Columbia, S.C. | 408,176 | 322,880 |
| 96 | Canton, Ohio | 404,421 | 393,789 |
| 97 | Bakersfield, Calif. | 403,089 | 330,234 |
| 98 | Bridgeport, Conn. | 395,455 | 401,752 |
| 99 | Little Rock-N. Little Rock, Ark. | 393,494 | 323,296 |
| 100 | Davenport-Rock Island-Moline, Iowa-Ill. | 383,958 | 362,638 |
| 101 | Fort Wayne, Ind. | 382,961 | 361,984 |
| 102 | York, Pa. | 381,255 | 329,540 |
| 103 | Shreveport, La. | 376,646 | 336,000 |
| 104 | Beaumont-Port Arthur, Tex. | 375,497 | 347,568 |
| 105 | Worcester, Mass. | 372,940 | 372,144 |
| 106 | Peoria, Ill. | 365,864 | 341,979 |
| 107 | Newport News-Hampton, Va. | 364,449 | 333,140 |
| 108 | Lancaster, Pa. | 362,346 | 320,079 |
| 109 | Stockton, Calif. | 347,342 | 291,073 |
| 110 | Spokane, Wash. | 341,835 | 287,487 |
| 111 | Des Moines, Iowa | 338,048 | 313,562 |
| 112 | Vallejo-Fairfield-Napa, Calif. | 334,402 | 251,129 |
| 113 | Augusta, Ga.-S.C. | 327,372 | 275,787 |
| 114 | Corpus Christi, Tex. | 326,228 | 284,832 |
| 115 | Madison, Wis. | 323,545 | 290,272 |
| 116 | Lakeland-Winter Haven, Fla. | 321,652 | 228,515 |
| 117 | Jackson, Miss. | 320,425 | 258,906 |
| 118 | Utica-Rome, N.Y. | 320,180 | 340,477 |
| 119 | Lexington-Fayette, Ky. | 318,136 | 266,701 |
| 120 | Colorado Springs, Colo. | 317,458 | 239,288 |
| 121 | Reading, Pa. | 312,509 | 296,382 |
| 122 | Huntington-Ashland, W. Va.-Ky.-Ohio | 311,350 | 286,935 |
| 123 | Evansville, Ind.-Ky. | 309,408 | 284,959 |
| 124 | Huntsville, Ala. | 308,593 | 282,450 |
| 125 | Trenton, N.J. | 307,863 | 304,116 |
| 126 | Binghamton, N.Y.-Pa. | 301,336 | 302,672 |
| 127 | Santa Rosa, Calif. | 299,827 | 204,885 |
| 128 | Santa Barbara-Santa Maria-Lompoc, Calif. | 298,660 | 264,324 |
| 129 | Appleton-Oshkosh, Wis. | 291,325 | 276,948 |
| 130 | Salinas-Seaside-Monterey, Calif. | 290,444 | 247,450 |
| 131 | Pensacola, Fla. | 289,782 | 243,075 |
| 132 | McAllen-Pharr-Edinburg, Tex. | 283,229 | 181,535 |
| 133 | Lawrence-Haverhill, Mass.-N.H. | 281,981 | 258,564 |
| 134 | South Bend, Ind. | 280,772 | 279,813 |
| 135 | Erie, Pa. | 279,780 | 263,654 |
| 136 | Rockford, Ill. | 279,514 | 272,063 |
| 137 | Kalamazoo-Portage, Mich. | 279,192 | 257,723 |
| 138 | Eugene-Springfield, Ore. | 275,226 | 215,401 |
| 139 | Lorain-Elyria, Ohio | 274,909 | 256,843 |
| 140 | Melbourne-Titusville-Cocoa, Fla. | 272,959 | 230,006 |
| 141 | Montgomery, Ala. | 272,687 | 225,911 |
| 142 | Charleston, W. Va. | 269,595 | 257,140 |
| 143 | Duluth-Superior, Minn.-Wis. | 266,650 | 265,350 |
| 144 | Modesto, Calif. | 265,902 | 194,506 |
| 145 | Ann Arbor, Mich. | 264,748 | 234,103 |
| 146 | Johnstown, Pa. | 264,506 | 262,822 |
| 147 | Hamilton-Middletown, Ohio | 258,787 | 226,207 |
| 148 | Daytona Beach, Fla. | 258,762 | 169,487 |
| 149 | Macon, Ga. | 254,623 | 226,782 |
| 150 | Salem, Ore. | 249,895 | 186,658 |

## VOTER PARTICIPATION: PRESIDENTIAL ELECTIONS PERCENTAGE OF VOTING AGE POPULATION; AND PERCENTAGE IN THE 25 LARGEST STATES

SOURCE: U.S. Bureau of the Census

| Sex: | 1980 election | 1976 election | 1972 election |
|---|---|---|---|
| Male | 59.1 | 59.6 | 64.1 |
| Female | 59.4 | 58.8 | 62.0 |
| **Race:** | | | |
| White | 60.9 | 60.9 | 64.5 |
| Black | 50.5 | 48.7 | 52.1 |
| Spanish origin* | 29.9 | 31.8 | 37.5 |

| Age: | 1980 election | 1976 election | 1972 election |
|---|---|---|---|
| 18–20 | 35.7 | 38.0 | 48.3 |
| 21–24 | 43.0 | 45.6 | 50.7 |
| 25–34 | 54.6 | 55.4 | 59.7 |
| 35–44 | 64.4 | 63.3 | 66.3 |
| 45–54 | 67.5 | 67.9 | 70.9 |
| 55–64 | 71.3 | 69.7 | 70.7 |
| 65–74 | 69.3 | 54.8 | 68.1 |
| 75 and over | 57.7 | 54.8 | 55.6 |

### Voter Participation in 25 Largest States in Population

| Voter Participation: | 1980 election | 1976 election | 1972 election |
|---|---|---|---|
| Alabama | 56.4 | 54.6 | N.A. |
| California | 53.8 | 54.8 | 66.0 |
| Connecticut | 67.6 | 64.4 | N.A. |
| Florida | 55.5 | 54.7 | 59.0 |
| Georgia | 53.5 | 54.1 | 49.2 |
| Illinois | 66.4 | 65.6 | 71.1 |
| Indiana | 61.6 | 64.8 | 68.9 |
| Iowa | 67.7 | 67.6 | N.A. |
| Kentucky | 56.9 | 55.6 | N.A. |
| Louisiana | 63.9 | 59.9 | N.A. |
| Maryland | 58.6 | 58.7 | N.A. |
| Massachusetts | 65.6 | 68.9 | 68.7 |
| Michigan | 64.1 | 64.0 | 65.1 |
| Minnesota | 73.3 | 75.4 | N.A. |
| Missouri | 67.3 | 63.1 | 65.4 |
| New Jersey | 59.6 | 59.1 | 66.7 |
| New York | 54.8 | 56.4 | 63.5 |
| North Carolina | 52.2 | 48.7 | 49.0 |
| Ohio | 60.7 | 59.5 | 65.6 |
| Pennsylvania | 54.9 | 57.3 | 61.0 |
| Tennessee | 56.7 | 55.2 | N.A. |
| Texas | 51.1 | 53.2 | 55.0 |
| Virginia | 55.2 | 55.2 | 49.3 |
| Washington | 61.2 | 64.4 | N.A. |
| Wisconsin | 74.5 | 72.4 | N.A. |

* Persons of Spanish origin can be of any race. NA = Not available.

## IMMIGRATION TO THE UNITED STATES

SOURCE: U.S. Immigration and Naturalization Service

| Years | Number |
|---|---|
| **1820** | 8,385 |
| **1821–1830** | 143,439 |
| **1831–1840** | 599,125 |
| **1841–1850** | 1,713,251 |
| **1851–1860** | 2,598,214 |
| **1861–1870** | 2,314,824 |
| **1871–1880** | 2,812,191 |
| **1881–1890** | 5,246,613 |
| **1891–1900** | 3,687,564 |
| **1901–1910** | 8,795,386 |
| **1911–1920** | 5,735,811 |
| **1921–1930** | 4,107,209 |
| **1931–1940** | 528,431 |
| **1941–1950** | 1,035,039 |
| **1951–1960** | 2,515,479 |
| **1961–1965** | 1,450,312 |
| **1966** | 323,040 |
| **1967** | 361,972 |
| **1968** | 454,448 |
| **1969** | 358,579 |
| **1970** | 373,326 |
| **1971** | 370,478 |
| **1972** | 384,685 |
| **1973** | 400,063 |
| **1974** | 394,861 |
| **1975** | 386,194 |
| **1976** | 398,613 |
| **1977** | 462,315 |
| **1978** | 601,442 |
| **1979** | 460,348 |

## IMMIGRATION BY COUNTRIES: 1820–1979

SOURCE: U.S. Immigration and Naturalization Service

| Countries | 1979 | Total (1820 to 1979) |
|---|---|---|
| **All countries** | 460,348 | 49,125,313 |
| **Europe** | 64,173 | 36,267,136 |
| Albania | 25 | 2,581 |
| Austria[1] | 507 | 4,316,149 |
| Hungary[1] | 528 | |
| Belgium | 646 | 203,064 |
| Bulgaria[4] | 127 | 67,954 |
| Czechoslovakia | 494 | 137,523 |
| Denmark | 378 | 364,538 |
| Estonia | 9 | 1,137 |
| Finland | 284 | 33,725 |
| France | 2,905 | 753,329 |
| Germany[1] | 7,166 | 6,984,909 |
| Great Britain | | |
| England | 14,336 | 3,192,894 |
| Scotland | 803 | 820,866 |
| Wales | 128 | 95,255 |
| Not specified | 270 | 805,092 |
| Greece | 5,942 | 660,828 |
| Ireland | 808 | 4,724,352 |
| Italy | 5,969 | 5,300,387 |
| Latvia | 13 | 2,568 |
| Lithuania | 23 | 3,875 |
| Luxembourg | 42 | 2,909 |
| Netherlands | 1,184 | 360,825 |
| Norway[2] | 438 | 856,912 |
| Poland[3] | 3,863 | 518,359 |
| Portugal | 7,068 | 452,422 |
| Romania | 1,180 | 172,071 |
| Spain | 3,285 | 262,836 |
| Sweden[2] | 764 | 1,272,689 |
| Switzerland | 774 | 349,877 |
| USSR | 1,919 | 3,375,233 |
| Yugoslavia[4] | 1,861 | 115,410 |
| Other Europe | 434 | 56,039 |
| **Asia** | 182,970 | 3,036,730 |
| China | 2,944 | 518,494 |
| India | 18,625 | 182,323 |
| Japan | 4,496 | 410,934 |
| Turkey | 1,306 | 386,861 |
| Other Asia | 155,599 | 1,538,118 |
| **America** | 197,123 | 9,247,834 |
| Canada & Newfoundland | 20,181 | 4,125,038 |
| Mexico | 52,479 | 2,176,206 |
| West Indies | 71,029 | 1,757,830 |
| Central America | 17,709 | 330,572 |
| South America | 35,715 | 748,739 |
| Other America | 10 | 109,449 |
| **Africa** | 11,212 | 143,271 |
| **Australia & New Zealand** | 2,476 | 120,984 |
| **Pacific Islands** | 135 | 24,706 |
| **Not specified** | 2,259 | 284,652 |

[1] Data for Austria-Hungary were not reported until 1861; Austria and Hungary have been recorded separately since 1905. From 1938 to 1945 inclusive, Austria was included with Germany. [2] From 1820 to 1868, the figures for Norway and Sweden were combined. [3] Poland was recorded as a separate country from 1820 to 1898 and again since 1920. [4] Bulgaria, Serbia, and Montenegro were first reported in 1899. Bulgaria has been reported separately since 1920, while the Serb, Croat, and Slovene Kingdom has been recorded as Yugoslavia since 1922. Data collected from country of last residence.

## WORLD POPULATION FACTS

SOURCE: *U.N. Demographic Yearbook 1979, Population and Vital Statistics Report April 1, 1982,* © United Nations

| Regions | Midyear Estimates (in Millions) 1950 | 1970 | 1975 | 1980 | 1981 | Annual % Increase (1970-81) |
|---|---|---|---|---|---|---|
| WORLD | 2,513 | 3,678 | 4,033 | 4,415 | 4,508 | 1.8 |
| Africa | 219 | 354 | 406 | 469 | 484 | 2.9 |
| Americas | 330 | 509 | 559 | 615 | 622 | 1.8 |
| Asia* | 1,380 | 2,091 | 2,319 | 2,558 | 2,625 | 2.1 |
| Europe* | 392 | 460 | 474 | 484 | 485 | 0.5 |
| Oceania | 13 | 19 | 21 | 23 | 23 | 1.8 |
| USSR | 180 | 244 | 254 | 267 | 268 | 0.9 |

* Excluding USSR.

## MOST POPULOUS URBAN AREAS

SOURCE: Various statistical reports

| City | Population | Year |
|---|---|---|
| New York, U.S. | 16,121,297 | 1980 |
| Mexico City, Mexico | 13,993,866 | 1978 (E) |
| São Paulo, Brazil | 12,588,439 | 1980 |
| Los Angeles, U.S. | 11,497,568 | 1980 |
| Shanghai, China | 11,320,000 | 1979 (E) |
| Buenos Aires, Argentina | 9,927,404 | 1980 |
| Paris, France | 9,878,524 | 1975 |
| Calcutta, India | 9,165,650 | 1981 |
| Rio de Janeiro, Brazil | 9,018,637 | 1980 |
| Peking (Beijing), China | 8,706,000 | 1979 (E) |
| Seoul, South Korea | 8,366,756 | 1980 |
| Tokyo, Japan | 8,349,209 | 1980 |
| Bombay, India | 8,227,332 | 1981 |
| Moscow, U.S.S.R. | 8,011,000 | 1979 |
| Chicago, U.S. | 7,869,542 | 1980 |
| Tianjin, China | 7,489,000 | 1979 (E) |
| London, U.K. | 6,696,008 | 1981 |
| Jakarta, Indonesia | 6,503,449 | 1980 |
| Delhi, India | 5,713,581 | 1981 |
| Philadelphia, U.S. | 5,547,902 | 1980 |
| Canton, China | 5,350,000 | 1979 (E) |
| San Francisco, U.S. | 5,179,784 | 1980 |
| Karachi, Pakistan | 5,103,000 | 1981 |
| Cairo, Egypt | 5,084,463 | 1976 |
| Detroit, U.S. | 4,618,161 | 1980 |
| Leningrad, U.S.S.R. | 4,588,000 | 1979 |
| Tehran, Iran | 4,496,159 | 1976 |
| Madras, India | 4,276,635 | 1981 |
| Bangkok, Thailand | 4,178,000 | 1975 (E) |
| Lima, Peru | 4,000,000 | 1972 |
| Chengdu, China | 3,850,000 | 1979 (E) |
| Wuhan, China | 3,832,487 | 1979 (E) |
| Santiago, Chile | 3,691,548 | 1978 (E) |
| Nanjing, China | 3,551,000 | 1979 (E) |
| Madrid, Spain | 3,520,320 | 1975 (E) |
| Dacca, Bangladesh | 3,458,602 | 1981 |
| Boston, U.S. | 3,448,122 | 1980 |
| Ho Chi Minh City (Saigon), Vietnam | 3,419,978 | 1979 |
| Jinan, China | 3,202,000 | 1979 (E) |
| Pusan, South Korea | 3,160,276 | 1980 |
| Houston, U.S. | 3,101,293 | 1980 |
| Washington, U.S. | 3,060,922 | 1980 |
| Sydney, Australia | 3,021,300 | 1976 |
| Athens, Greece | 3,016,457 | 1981 |
| Toronto, Canada | 2,998,947 | 1981 |
| Dallas-Ft. Worth, U.S. | 2,974,805 | 1980 |
| Lahore, Pakistan | 2,922,000 | 1981 |
| Bangalore, India | 2,913,537 | 1981 |
| Rome, Italy | 2,897,505 | 1977 (E) |
| Bogotá, Colombia | 2,855,065 | 1973 |
| Istanbul, Turkey | 2,853,539 | 1980 |
| Cleveland, U.S. | 2,834,062 | 1980 |
| Montréal, Canada | 2,828,349 | 1981 |
| Manila-Quezon City, Philippines | 2,792,239 | 1980 |
| Yokohama, Japan | 2,773,822 | 1980 |
| Xi'an, China | 2,760,000 | 1979 (E) |

(E) Estimated data.

## MOST POPULOUS COUNTRIES

SOURCE: *Population and Vital Statistics Report April 1, 1982,* © United Nations

| Country | Midyear 1980 Estimate (in Millions) | Density per Sq. Mi. | Area in Sq. Mi. |
|---|---|---|---|
| China | 994.91 | 269.6 | 3,691,000 |
| India | 663.60 | 522.8 | 1,269,339 |
| USSR | 265.54 | 30.7 | 8,649,490 |
| UNITED STATES | 227.66 | 62.8 | 3,623,420 |
| Indonesia | 148.03 | 187.8 | 788,430 |
| Brazil | 118.61 | 36.1 | 3,286,470 |
| Japan | 116.78 | 801.3 | 145,730 |
| Bangladesh | 88.66 | 1,608.3 | 55,126 |
| Nigeria | 84.50 | 222.6 | 379,628 |
| Pakistan | 81.45 | 237.6 | 342,750 |
| Mexico | 71.91 | 94.4 | 761,600 |
| Germany, West | 61.56 | 643.2 | 95,704 |
| Italy | 57.07 | 490.7 | 116,303 |
| United Kingdom | 55.94 | 592.6 | 94,399 |
| Vietnam | 53.74 | 418.5 | 128,405 |
| France | 53.71 | 255.7 | 210,038 |
| Philippines | 48.40 | 418.3 | 115,707 |
| Thailand | 47.17 | 237.7 | 198,455 |
| Turkey | 44.92 | 149.3 | 300,946 |
| Egypt | 42.20 | 109.1 | 386,659 |
| Korea, South | 38.12 | 998.6 | 38,175 |
| Iran | 37.45 | 58.9 | 636,293 |
| Spain | 37.43 | 191.0 | 195,988 |
| Poland | 35.58 | 294.7 | 120,725 |
| Burma | 33.64 | 128.5 | 261,789 |
| Ethiopia | 31.07 | 65.9 | 471,776 |
| South Africa | 29.29 | 62.0 | 472,359 |
| Colombia | 27.09 | 61.6 | 439,735 |
| Argentina | 27.06 | 25.3 | 1,068,296 |
| Zaire | 26.38 | 28.7 | 918,962 |
| Canada | 23.96 | 6.3 | 3,831,012 |
| Yugoslavia | 22.34 | 226.2 | 98,766 |
| Romania | 22.20 | 242.1 | 91,699 |
| Morocco | 20.05 | 116.3 | 172,413 |

## LARGEST COUNTRIES, BY GEOGRAPHICAL AREA

SOURCE: Various official reports

| Rank | Country | Area in Sq. Mi. |
|---|---|---|
| 1 | USSR | 8,649,490 |
| 2 | Canada | 3,831,012 |
| 3 | China (People's Rep.) | 3,691,000 |
| 4 | UNITED STATES | 3,623,420 |
| 5 | Brazil | 3,286,470 |
| 6 | Australia | 2,967,909 |
| 7 | India | 1,269,339 |
| 8 | Argentina | 1,068,296 |
| 9 | Sudan | 967,494 |
| 10 | Algeria | 919,591 |
| 11 | Zaire | 918,962 |
| 12 | Saudi Arabia | 829,995 |
| 13 | Indonesia | 788,430 |
| 14 | Mexico | 761,600 |
| 15 | Libya | 679,358 |
| 16 | Iran | 636,293 |
| 17 | Mongolia | 606,163 |
| 18 | Peru | 496,222 |
| 19 | Chad | 495,752 |
| 20 | Niger | 489,189 |
| 21 | Angola | 481,351 |
| 22 | South Africa | 472,359 |
| 23 | Ethiopia | 471,776 |
| 24 | Mali | 464,873 |
| 25 | Colombia | 439,735 |
| 26 | Bolivia | 424,163 |
| 27 | Mauritania | 397,954 |
| 28 | Egypt | 386,659 |

## MEDIAN INCOME DATA FOR STANDARD METROPOLITAN STATISTICAL AREAS OF 1,000,000 OR MORE POPULATION IN 1979*

SOURCE: U.S. Department of Commerce, Bureau of the Census

| | Median Income | | | Percent of Families below Poverty Level |
|---|---|---|---|---|
| SMSA's | Households | Families | Unrelated individuals 15 years and over | |
| Anaheim-Santa Ana-Garden Grove, Calif. | $22,180 | $25,482 | $ 9,672 | 4.9 |
| Atlanta, Ga. | 18,374 | 21,409 | 8,382 | 9.7 |
| Baltimore, Md. | 18,708 | 21,647 | 7,474 | 9.0 |
| Boston, Mass. | 18,265 | 22,580 | 6,673 | 8.0 |
| Buffalo, N.Y. | 17,663 | 20,889 | 6,616 | 7.6 |
| Chicago, Ill. | 19,388 | 22,898 | 8,227 | 9.5 |
| Cincinnati, Ohio-Ky.-Ind. | 18,236 | 21,492 | 7,391 | 8.1 |
| Cleveland, Ohio | 18,865 | 22,764 | 7,881 | 8.2 |
| Columbus, Ohio | 17,363 | 20,836 | 7,296 | 8.2 |
| Dallas-Fort Worth, Texas | 18,839 | 21,869 | 8,540 | 7.4 |
| Denver-Boulder, Colo. | 20,221 | 24,235 | 9,374 | 6.2 |
| Detroit, Mich. | 20,499 | 24,118 | 7,854 | 8.8 |
| Fort Lauderdale-Hollywood, Fla. | 16,534 | 19,646 | 8,432 | 6.1 |
| Houston, Texas | 20,587 | 23,959 | 10,112 | 8.3 |
| Indianapolis, Ind. | 18,726 | 21,842 | 7,676 | 7.6 |
| Kansas City, Mo.-Kansas | 19,179 | 22,715 | 8,693 | 6.0 |
| Los Angeles-Long Beach, Calif. | 17,826 | 21,334 | 8,364 | 10.1 |
| Miami, Fla. | 15,691 | 18,756 | 7,195 | 11.3 |
| Milwaukee, Wis. | 20,078 | 23,736 | 9,125 | 7.4 |
| Minneapolis-St. Paul, Minn.-Wis. | 20,890 | 24,793 | 8,909 | 4.4 |
| Nassau-Suffolk, N.Y. | 23,547 | 26,135 | 8,527 | 4.0 |
| New Orleans, La. | 16,048 | 19,028 | 7,491 | 14.6 |
| New York, N.Y.-N.J. | 15,613 | 19,794 | 7,773 | 14.7 |
| Newark, N.J. | 19,934 | 23,412 | 8,594 | 10.5 |
| Philadelphia, Pa.-N.J. | 17,856 | 21,489 | 6,825 | 9.3 |
| Phoenix, Ariz. | 17,925 | 20,920 | 8,255 | 6.2 |
| Pittsburgh, Pa. | 18,800 | 21,950 | 6,810 | 5.7 |
| Portland, Oreg.-Wash. | 18,540 | 22,102 | 7,990 | 6.1 |
| Riverside-San Bernardino-Ontario, Calif. | 17,141 | 19,707 | 6,754 | 8.8 |
| Sacramento, Calif. | 17,377 | 20,887 | 6,863 | 8.9 |
| St. Louis, Mo.-Ill. | 18,384 | 21,578 | 7,240 | 7.5 |
| San Antonio, Texas | 15,168 | 17,473 | 5,747 | 14.5 |
| San Diego, Calif. | 17,178 | 20,259 | 6,834 | 8.2 |
| San Francisco-Oakland, Calif. | 19,714 | 25,055 | 8,926 | 6.7 |
| San Jose, Calif. | 23,777 | 26,924 | 11,012 | 5.9 |
| Seattle-Everett, Wash. | 20,798 | 25,005 | 9,153 | 4.8 |
| Tampa-St. Petersburg, Fla. | 13,815 | 16,515 | 6,629 | 8.8 |
| Washington, D.C.-Md.-Va. | 23,344 | 27,515 | 11,138 | 6.1 |

*Figures are for calendar year 1979, as gathered in the 1980 census.

## U.S. METROPOLITAN AREA PER CAPITA INCOME: 1980

SOURCE: U.S. Department of Commerce, Bureau of Economic Analysis

**SMSA'S WITH HIGHEST INCOMES**

| Standard Metropolitan Statistical Area | Income |
|---|---|
| Anchorage, Alaska | $14,266 |
| Bridgeport-Stamford-Norwalk-Danbury, Connecticut | 14,197 |
| Casper, Wyoming | 14,072 |
| Midland, Texas | 13,761 |
| San Francisco-Oakland, California | 12,998 |
| Washington, D.C.-Maryland-Virginia | 12,871 |
| Reno, Nevada | 12,371 |
| San Jose, California | 12,297 |
| Nassau-Suffolk, New York | 12,258 |
| Seattle-Everett, Washington | 11,882 |
| Houston, Texas | 11,861 |
| Anaheim-Santa Ana-Garden Grove, California | 11,857 |
| Newark, New Jersey | 11,689 |
| West Palm Beach-Boca Raton, Florida | 11,554 |
| Hartford-New Britain-Bristol, Connecticut | 11,395 |
| Chicago, Illinois | 11,394 |
| Los Angeles-Long Beach, California | 11,350 |
| Minneapolis-St. Paul, Minnesota-Wisconsin | 11,329 |
| Denver-Boulder, Colorado | 11,301 |
| Sarasota, Florida | 11,287 |
| Cleveland, Ohio | 11,236 |
| Detroit, Michigan | 11,208 |
| New Brunswick-Perth Amboy-Sayreville, New Jersey | 11,174 |
| New York, New York-New Jersey | 11,087 |
| Dallas-Fort Worth, Texas | 11,041 |

**SMSA'S WITH LOWEST INCOMES**

| Standard Metropolitan Statistical Area | Income |
|---|---|
| State College, Pennsylvania | $7,153 |
| Johnson City-Kingsport-Bristol, Tennessee-Virginia | 7,147 |
| Anniston, Alabama | 7,090 |
| Danville, Virginia | 7,074 |
| Fort Smith, Arkansas-Oklahoma | 7,058 |
| Gainesville, Florida | 7,055 |
| Tuscaloosa, Alabama | 7,052 |
| Ocala, Florida | 6,966 |
| Athens, Georgia | 6,963 |
| Lawton, Oklahoma | 6,962 |
| Pascagoula-Moss Point, Mississippi | 6,911 |
| Biloxi-Gulfport, Mississippi | 6,903 |
| Clarksville-Hopkinsville, Tennessee-Kentucky | 6,903 |
| Florence, South Carolina | 6,811 |
| Bryan-College Station, Texas | 6,703 |
| Fayetteville, North Carolina | 6,697 |
| El Paso, Texas | 6,677 |
| Bloomington, Indiana | 6,647 |
| Alexandria, Louisiana | 6,643 |
| Las Cruces, New Mexico | 6,328 |
| Provo-Orem, Utah | 5,886 |
| Jacksonville, North Carolina | 5,876 |
| Brownsville-Harlingen-San Benito, Texas | 5,444 |
| Laredo, Texas | 5,439 |
| McAllen-Pharr-Edinburg, Texas | 4,808 |

## URBAN INTERMEDIATE BUDGET FOR A 4-PERSON FAMILY IN SELECTED METROPOLITAN AREAS: 1981 (in dollars)

SOURCE: U.S. Bureau of Labor Statistics, Autumn 1981 Urban Family Budgets and Comparative Indexes for Selected Urban Areas (USDL: 82-139)

| Metropolitan Areas | All Items | Food |
|---|---|---|
| Anchorage, Alaska | $31,390 | $6,586 |
| Atlanta, Ga. | 23,273 | 5,614 |
| Baltimore, Md. | 25,114 | 5,526 |
| Boston, Mass. | 29,213 | 5,918 |
| Buffalo, N.Y. | 26,473 | 5,890 |
| Chicago, Ill.-N.W. Ind. | 25,358 | 5,779 |
| Cincinnati, Ohio-Ky.-Ind. | 25,475 | 5,939 |
| Cleveland, Ohio | 25,598 | 5,859 |
| Dallas, Texas | 22,678 | 5,568 |
| Denver, Colo. | 24,820 | 5,480 |
| Detroit, Mich. | 25,208 | 5,886 |
| Honolulu, Hawaii | 31,893 | 7,626 |
| Houston, Texas | 23,601 | 5,816 |
| Kansas City, Mo.-Kans. | 24,528 | 5,727 |
| Los Angeles-Long Beach, Calif. | 25,025 | 5,700 |
| Milwaukee, Wis. | 26,875 | 5,660 |
| Minneapolis-St. Paul, Minn. | 25,799 | 5,607 |
| New York, N.Y.-N.E. N.J. | 29,540 | 6,578 |
| Philadelphia, Pa.-N.J. | 26,567 | 6,516 |
| Pittsburgh, Pa. | 24,717 | 6,040 |
| St. Louis, Mo.-Ill. | $24,498 | $6,081 |
| San Diego, Calif. | 24,776 | 5,569 |
| San Francisco-Oakland, Calif. | 27,082 | 5,905 |
| Seattle-Everett, Wash. | 25,881 | 5,880 |
| Washington, D.C.-Md.-Va. | 27,352 | 5,969 |
| Metropolitan Area Average | 25,893 | 5,915 |
| **Nonmetropolitan Areas** | | |
| Northeast | 25,839 | 5,772 |
| North Central | 23,191 | 5,434 |
| South | 21,829 | 5,450 |
| West | 24,402 | 5,518 |
| Nonmetropolitan Area Average | 23,238 | 5,521 |
| **URBAN U.S. AVERAGE** | 25,407 | 5,843 |

## WORLDWIDE COST OF LIVING—1981 (1970 = 100)

SOURCE: U.N. *Monthly Bulletin of Statistics*, June 1982

| Country | All Items | Food |
|---|---|---|
| Argentina (Buenos Aires) | 529,776.0 | 123,800.0 |
| Australia | 295.3 | 296.4 |
| Austria | 196.4 | 180.2 |
| Bahamas (Nassau)[1] | 203.7 | 232.2 |
| Bangladesh (Dacca)[1] | 469.0[2] | 459.6[2] |
| Barbados | 433.0 | 467.6 |
| Belgium | 219.0 | 189.5 |
| Brazil[1] | 3,071.6[5] | 3,436.5[5] |
| Canada | 243.7 | 293.6 |
| Chile (Santiago) | 502,215.0 | 572,281.0 |
| Costa Rica (San Jose) | 382.9 | 415.5 |
| Cyprus[3] | 147.8 | 144.0 |
| Czechoslovakia | 112.7 | 105.8 |
| Denmark[4] | 285.5 | 182.0 |
| El Salvador[4] | 134.7 | 140.8 |
| Fiji | 290.0 | 306.2 |
| Finland | 327.6 | 339.4 |
| France | 285.0 | 289.5 |
| Gambia (Banjul-Kambo St. Mary) | 283.4 | 305.4 |
| Germany, West | 174.0 | 160.8 |
| Ghana (Accra)[5] | 7,458.8 | 8,769.5 |
| Gibraltar[6] | 105.1 | 104.4 |
| Greece | 472.4 | 553.3 |
| Guadeloupe (Basse-Terre) | 302.2 | 322.7 |
| Guatemala[7] | 185.1 | 173.7 |
| Haiti (Port-au-Prince) | 335.7[2] | 381.1[2] |
| Honduras (Tegucigalpa) | 235.6 | 250.2 |
| Hong Kong[7] | 170.0 | 173.9 |
| Hungary | 162.5 | 170.7 |
| Ireland | 433.6 | 424.3 |
| Israel | 7,015.1 | 7,785.7 |
| Italy | 441.1 | 420.0 |
| Ivory Coast (Abidjan) | 351.8[5] | 400.1[5] |
| Japan | 248.1 | 246.7 |
| Jordan[7] | 208.0[5] | 175.5[5] |
| Korea, South | 555.8 | 663.7 |
| Liberia | 278.9[8] | 260.7[8] |
| Luxembourg | 205.5 | 195.9 |
| Madagascar (Antananarivo) | 316.8 | 345.3 |
| Malawi (Blantyre) | 268.5[5] | 294.0[5] |
| Malaysia (Peninsular) | 194.4 | 209.5 |
| Mexico[1] | 535.3 | 533.4 |
| Morocco[9] | 192.8 | 193.1 |
| Netherlands[7] | 142.8 | 131.1 |
| New Caledonia (Noumea) | 258.3 | 266.7 |
| New Zealand | 374.7 | 397.8 |
| Norway | 254.0 | 252.8 |
| Pakistan[10] | 347.1 | 353.7 |
| Panama (Panama City) | 211.2 | 231.8 |
| Papua New Guinea[10] | 238.5 | 248.7 |
| Philippines[1] | 331.1 | 308.2 |
| Portugal[3] | 269.9 | 274.3 |
| Spain | 474.8 | 423.6 |
| Sri Lanka (Colombo) | 282.9[5] | 309.1[5] |
| Sweden | 270.8 | 286.2 |
| Switzerland | 173.1 | 179.8 |
| Thailand (Bangkok, Metropolis) | 282.2 | 299.6 |
| Trinidad and Tobago | 388.5 | 417.5 |
| Tunisia (Tunis)[3] | 136.1 | 143.7 |
| United Kingdom | 403.6 | 429.2 |
| UNITED STATES[11] | 234.1 | 233.5 |
| Venezuela (Caracas) | 260.1 | 371.2 |
| Yugoslavia | 789.4 | 853.3 |
| Zimbabwe | 233.5 | 221.4 |

[1] 1972 = 100. [2] Aug. 1981. [3] 1977 = 100. [4] 1979 = 100. [5] Oct. 1981. [6] 1980 = 100. [7] 1975 = 100. [8] June 1981. [9] 1974 = 100. [10] 1971 = 100. [11] Beginning 1978, the series has been linked to the new urban wage earners-clerical workers, unadjusted. (CPI-W)

## THE AMERICAN CONSUMER: PERSONAL EXPENDITURES (1981)

SOURCE: U.S. Department of Commerce, Bureau of Economic Analysis

| | Personal Consumption Expenditures by Type of Product (Billions of Dollars) |
|---|---|
| **Total personal consumption expenditures** | **1,858.1** |
| **Durable goods** | **232.0** |
| Motor vehicles and parts | 98.2 |
| Furniture and household equipment | 92.7 |
| Other | 41.2 |
| **Nondurable goods** | **743.4** |
| Food | 382.1 |
| Clothing and shoes | 115.9 |
| Gasoline and oil | 94.5 |
| Other nondurable goods | 150.9 |
| Fuel oil and coal | 21.0 |
| Other | 129.9 |
| **Services** | **882.7** |
| Housing | 306.7 |
| Household operation | 126.3 |
| Electricity and gas | 62.8 |
| Other | 63.5 |
| Transportation | 68.8 |
| Other | 380.9 |

## CONSUMER PRICE INDEX* AND PURCHASING POWER OF THE CONSUMER DOLLAR (1967=100)

SOURCE: Bureau of Labor Statistics

| Year | All Items | Food & Beverages | Housing | Rent | Apparel & Upkeep | Trans-portation | Medical Care | Enter-tain-ment | Other Goods and Services | Purchasing power of the consumer dollar |
|---|---|---|---|---|---|---|---|---|---|---|
| 1968 | **104.2** | 103.6 | 104.0 | 102.4 | 105.4 | 103.2 | 106.1 | 105.7 | 105.2 | **.960** |
| 1970 | **116.3** | 114.7 | 118.2 | 110.1 | 116.1 | 112.7 | 120.6 | 116.7 | 116.8 | **.860** |
| 1972 | **125.3** | 123.2 | 128.1 | 119.2 | 122.3 | 119.9 | 132.5 | 126.5 | 127.5 | **.799** |
| 1973 | **133.1** | 139.5 | 133.7 | 124.3 | 126.8 | 123.8 | 137.7 | 130.0 | 132.5 | **.752** |
| 1974 | **147.7** | 158.7 | 148.8 | 130.6 | 136.2 | 137.7 | 150.5 | 139.8 | 142.0 | **.678** |
| 1975 | **161.2** | 172.1 | 164.5 | 137.3 | 142.3 | 150.6 | 168.6 | 152.2 | 153.9 | **.621** |
| 1976 | **170.5** | 177.4 | 174.6 | 144.7 | 147.6 | 165.5 | 184.7 | 159.8 | 162.7 | **.587** |
| 1977 | **181.5** | 188.0 | 186.5 | 153.5 | 154.2 | 177.2 | 202.4 | 167.7 | 172.2 | **.551** |
| 1978 | **195.4** | 206.3 | 202.8 | 164.0 | 159.6 | 185.5 | 219.4 | 176.6 | 183.3 | **.512** |
| 1979 | **217.4** | 228.5 | 227.6 | 176.0 | 166.6 | 212.0 | 239.7 | 188.5 | 196.7 | **.461** |
| 1980 | **246.8** | 248.0 | 263.3 | 191.6 | 178.4 | 249.7 | 265.9 | 205.3 | 214.5 | **.406** |
| 1981 | **272.4** | 267.3 | 293.5 | 208.2 | 186.9 | 280.0 | 294.5 | 221.4 | 235.7 | **.367** |

* Consumer Price Index for All Urban Consumers (CPI-U)

## AVERAGE U.S. RETAIL FOOD PRICES

SOURCE: Bureau of Labor Statistics (in cents)

| Year | Flour, wheat | Rice | White bread | Round steak | Rib roast | Chuck roast | Pork chops | Bacon sliced | Milk[1] | Butter | Cheese | Pota-toes | Sugar | Eggs | Coffee |
|---|---|---|---|---|---|---|---|---|---|---|---|---|---|---|---|
| | 10 lbs. | lb. | lb. | lb. | lb. | lb. | lb. | lb. | qt. | lb. | lb. | 15 lbs. | lb. | doz. | lb. |
| 1913 | 33 | 8.7 | 5.6 | 22.3 | 19.8 | 16.0 | 21.0 | 27.0 | 8.9 | 38.3 | 22.1 | 25.5 | 5.5 | 34.5 | 29.8 |
| 1918 | 67 | 12.9 | 9.8 | 36.9 | 30.7 | 26.6 | 39.0 | 52.9 | 13.9 | 57.7 | 35.9 | 48.0 | 9.7 | 56.9 | 30.5 |
| 1919 | 72 | 15.1 | 10.0 | 38.9 | 32.5 | 27.0 | 42.3 | 55.4 | 15.5 | 67.8 | 42.6 | 57.0 | 11.3 | 62.8 | 43.3 |
| 1920 | 81 | 17.4 | 11.5 | 39.5 | 33.2 | 26.2 | 42.3 | 52.3 | 16.7 | 70.1 | 41.6 | 94.5 | 19.4 | 68.1 | 47.0 |
| 1927 | 55 | 10.7 | 9.2 | 38.7 | 34.1 | 25.2 | 37.2 | 47.8 | 14.1 | 56.3 | 38.6 | 57.0 | 7.2 | 48.7 | 47.4 |
| 1930 | 46 | 9.5 | 8.6 | 42.6 | 36.4 | 28.6 | 36.2 | 42.5 | 14.1 | 46.4 | 36.6 | 54.0 | 6.1 | 44.5 | 39.5 |
| 1932 | 32 | 6.6 | 7.0 | 29.7 | 25.6 | 18.5 | 21.5 | 24.2 | 10.7 | 27.8 | 24.4 | 25.5 | 5.0 | 30.2 | 29.4 |
| 1934 | 49 | 8.0 | 8.3 | 28.1 | 23.6 | 17.5 | 25.5 | 29.1 | 11.2 | 31.5 | 25.0 | 34.5 | 5.5 | 32.5 | 26.9 |
| 1937 | 47.9 | 8.4 | 8.6 | 39.1 | 32.8 | 25.7 | 36.7 | 41.3 | 12.5 | 40.7 | 29.4 | 41.9 | 5.6 | 36.2 | 25.5 |
| 1939 | 37.9 | 7.7 | 7.9 | 36.0 | 29.5 | 23.4 | 30.4 | 31.9 | 12.2 | 32.5 | 25.3 | 37.1 | 5.4 | 32.1 | 22.4 |
| 1941 | 45.2 | 8.7 | 8.1 | 39.1 | 31.1 | 25.5 | 34.3 | 34.3 | 13.6 | 41.1 | 30.0 | 35.2 | 5.7 | 39.7 | 23.6 |
| 1942 | 52.8 | 12.1 | 8.7 | 43.5 | 34.0 | 29.3 | 41.4 | 39.4 | 15.0 | 47.3 | 34.8 | 51.3 | 6.8 | 48.4 | 28.3 |
| 1944 | 64.7 | 12.8 | 8.8 | 41.4 | 33.4 | 28.8 | 37.3 | 41.1 | 15.6 | 50.0 | 36.0 | 69.8 | 6.7 | 54.5 | 30.1 |
| 1946 | 70.8 | 14.0 | 10.4 | 52.1 | 43.1 | 36.6 | 48.5 | 53.3 | 17.6 | 71.0 | 50.1 | 70.2 | 7.7 | 58.6 | 34.4 |
| 1948 | 98.0 | 20.8 | 13.9 | 90.5 | 73.7 | 64.4 | 77.2 | 76.9 | 21.8 | 86.7 | 65.6 | 83.8 | 9.4 | 72.3 | 51.4 |
| 1950 | 98.2 | 16.8 | 14.3 | 93.6 | 74.3 | 61.6 | 75.4 | 63.7 | 20.6 | 72.9 | 51.8 | 69.2 | 9.7 | 60.4 | 79.4 |
| 1954 | 107.2 | 19.6 | 17.2 | 90.7 | 70.3 | 51.4 | 86.3 | 81.7 | 23.0 | 72.4 | 57.6 | 78.9 | 10.5 | 58.5 | 110.8 |
| 1956 | 106.6 | 17.2 | 17.9 | 88.2 | 70.1 | 48.4 | 78.2 | 57.3 | 24.2 | 72.1 | 57.2 | 101.6 | 10.6 | 60.2 | 103.4 |
| 1958 | 110.4 | 18.4 | 19.3 | 104.2 | 81.6 | 63.3 | 91.8 | 79.3 | 25.3 | 74.2 | 58.0 | 93.9 | 11.3 | 60.4 | 90.7 |
| 1960 | 110.8 | 18.6 | 20.3 | 105.5 | 81.7 | 61.6 | 85.8 | 65.5 | 26.0 | 74.9 | 68.6 | 107.7 | 11.6 | 57.3 | 75.3 |
| 1962 | 114.0 | 19.1 | 21.2 | 107.8 | 84.1 | 62.3 | 89.8 | 70.3 | 26.1 | 75.2 | 72.4 | 94.8 | 11.7 | 54.0 | 70.8 |
| 1964 | 113.4 | 18.8 | 20.7 | 103.9 | 82.8 | 56.8 | 88.0 | 66.7 | 26.4 | 74.4 | 73.4 | 113.6 | 12.8 | 53.9 | 81.6 |
| 1965 | 116.2 | 19.0 | 20.9 | 108.4 | 89.7 | 59.5 | 97.3 | 81.3 | 26.3 | 75.4 | 75.4 | 140.6 | 11.8 | 52.7 | 83.3 |
| 1966 | 118.8 | 19.0 | 22.2 | 110.7 | 93.2 | 62.2 | 106.3 | 95.4 | 27.8 | 82.2 | 84.4 | 112.4 | 12.0 | 59.9 | 82.3 |
| 1967 | 119.2 | 18.6 | 22.2 | 110.3 | 94.0 | 60.7 | 100.4 | 83.7 | 28.7 | 83.0 | 87.2 | 112.1 | 12.1 | 49.1 | 76.9 |
| 1968 | 116.8 | 18.8 | 22.4 | 114.3 | 98.8 | 63.5 | 102.9 | 81.4 | 30.3 | 83.6 | 88.8 | 114.5 | 12.2 | 52.9 | 76.4 |
| 1969 | 116.2 | 18.8 | 23.0 | 126.7 | 109.3 | 70.4 | 112.2 | 87.8 | 31.5 | 84.6 | 94.0 | 122.4 | 12.4 | 62.1 | 76.5 |
| 1970 | 117.9 | 19.1 | 24.3 | 130.2 | 111.7 | 72.5 | 116.2 | 94.9 | 33.0 | 86.6 | 100.7 | 134.5 | 13.0 | 61.4 | 91.1 |
| 1971 | 119.9 | 19.6 | 25.0 | 136.1 | 118.0 | 75.0 | 108.1 | 80.0 | 33.9 | 87.6 | 105.5 | 129.2 | 13.6 | 52.9 | 93.4 |
| 1972 | 119.2 | 19.6 | 24.7 | 147.7 | 129.5 | 82.1 | 124.6 | 96.2 | 34.5 | 87.1 | 108.6 | 138.9 | 13.9 | 52.4 | 92.7 |
| 1973 | 151.2 | 26.0 | 27.6 | 174.6 | 152.2 | 102.8 | 155.9 | 132.5 | 37.6 | 91.6 | 120.8 | 205.4 | 15.1 | 78.1 | 104.0 |
| 1974 | 205.0 | 44.0 | 34.5 | 179.8 | 158.5 | 102.1 | 156.5 | 132.0 | 39.2 | 94.6 | 145.8 | 249.6 | 32.3 | 78.3 | 122.9 |
| 1975 | 198.8 | 41.1 | 36.0 | 188.5 | 179.6 | 102.8 | 185.6 | 175.6 | 39.3 | 102.5 | 153.6 | 201.6 | 37.2 | 77.0 | 133.4 |
| 1976 | 185.2 | 37.5 | 35.3 | 178.3 | 177.4 | 96.9 | 184.8 | 171.1 | 41.4 | 126.1 | 173.0 | 219.0 | 24.0 | 84.1 | 187.3 |
| 1977 | 169.2 | 35.3 | 35.5 | 176.1 | 182.1 | 92.0 | 181.2 | 156.2 | 42.0 | 133.1 | 172.0 | 224.6 | 21.6 | 82.3 | 347.2 |
| 1978[2] | 169.0 | 40.2 | 35.8 | 189.5 | 200.2 | 103.3 | 193.2 | 173.2 | 42.8 | 139.6 | 92.3[3] | 198.0 | 23.9 | 81.5 | 339.5 |
| 1979 | Prices not available | | | | | | | | | | | | | | |
| 1980 | 209.1 | 51.2[4] | 50.9 | 276.9 | 294.5 | 181.9 | 195.3 | 146.5 | 52.5 | 187.8 | N.A. | 286.6 | 41.7[5] | 84.4[6] | 310.6[7] |
| 1981[8] | 218.0 | 54.5[4] | 52.0 | 291.0 | 309.0 | 178.0 | 213.0 | 175.0 | 53.0[9] | 99.5 | N.A. | 285.0 | 31.5[5] | 97.0[6] | 250.0[8] |

1) Milk — 1933 through 1973 = delivered milk; after 1973 milk purchased in grocery stores. 2) Data for 1978 are averages only for January through April. 3) American Process cheese. 4) White, long grain, uncooked rice. 5) White sugar, 33-80 oz. package. 6) Grade A large eggs. 7) Coffee, 100%, ground roast, 13.1-20 oz. can. 8) 1981 figures for December 1981 only. 9) Average for whole, skim and lowfat milk.

## THE CHANGING AMERICAN FOOD BASKET: 1914–1981

SOURCE: U.S. Department of Agriculture

The table indicates the amount of food that could be purchased through the years with one hour of labor.

| Item | Unit | 1914 | 1919 | 1929 | 1939 | 1949 | 1959 | 1969 | 1977 | 1981 |
|---|---|---|---|---|---|---|---|---|---|---|
| Bread, white | Lb. | 3.5 | 4.7 | 6.4 | 7.9 | 9.8 | 11.1 | 13.9 | 15.9 | 15.1 |
| Round steak | Lb. | 0.9 | 1.2 | 1.2 | 1.7 | 1.6 | 2.0 | 2.5 | 3.2 | 2.8 |
| Pork chops | Lb. | 1.0 | 1.1 | 1.5 | 2.1 | 1.9 | 2.6 | 2.8 | 3.1 | 3.8 |
| Sliced bacon | Lb. | 0.8 | 0.9 | 1.3 | 2.0 | 2.1 | 3.3 | 3.6 | 3.6 | 4.8 |
| Butter | Lb. | 0.6 | 0.7 | 1.0 | 1.9 | 1.9 | 2.9 | 3.8 | 4.2 | 4.0 |
| Cheese | Lb. | 1.0 | 1.1 | 1.4 | 2.5 | 2.4 | 3.8 | 3.4 | 3.3 | N.A. |
| Milk, fresh | Qt.[2] | — | — | — | 5.6 | 7.0 | 9.1 | 11.6 | 13.5 | 7.1 |
| Eggs, fresh | Doz. | 0.6 | 0.8 | 1.1 | 2.0 | 2.0 | 4.1 | 5.1 | 6.8 | 8.9 |
| Oranges | Doz.[3] | — | 0.9 | 1.3 | 2.2 | 2.7 | 3.3 | 3.8 | 4.4 | 21.0 |
| Potatoes | Lb. | 12.3 | 12.4 | 17.0 | 25.1 | 25.1 | 34.8 | 38.9 | 37.6 | 32.0 |
| Tomatoes[1] (canned) | — | — | 2.9 | 4.4 | 7.3 | 9.1 | 14.1 | 16.2 | 15.0 | 15.7 |
| Margarine | Lb. | — | 1.1 | 2.1 | 3.8 | 4.5 | 7.8 | 11.5 | 9.8 | 10.8 |

1) #2 can from 1914 to Sept. 1954; #303 can beginning Oct. 1954; 1 pound beginning in 1980.
2) ½ gallon beginning in 1980. 3) 1 pound beginning in 1980.

## AMERICAN FAMILY CHARACTERISTICS: 1981

Source: U.S. Bureau of Census

| Characteristic | Families | Per-cent |
|---|---|---|
| **All families** | **60,309,000** | **100.0** |
| White | 52,710,000 | 87.4 |
| Black and Other | 7,599,000 | 12.6 |
| Family Size: | | |
| 2 persons | 23,768,000 | 39.4 |
| 3 persons | 14,039,000 | 23.3 |
| 4 persons | 12,436,000 | 20.6 |
| 5 persons | 6,020,000 | 10.0 |
| 6 persons | 2,471,000 | 4.1 |
| 7 persons or more | 1,575,000 | 2.6 |
| Own Children under 18 Years Old: | | |
| No children | 29,082,000 | 48.2 |
| 1 child | 12,745,000 | 21.1 |
| 2 children | 11,592,000 | 19.2 |
| 3 children | 4,616,000 | 7.7 |
| 4 children or more | 2,274,000 | 3.8 |
| Residence: | | |
| Metropolitan | 40,203,000 | 66.7 |

| Characteristic | Families | Per-cent |
|---|---|---|
| Nonmetropolitan | 20,105,000 | 33.3 |
| Headed by Women | 9,082,000 | 15.1 |
| Age of Family Head: | | |
| Under 25 years | 3,770,000 | 6.3 |
| 25–34 years | 14,484,000 | 24.0 |
| 35–44 years | 12,475,000 | 20.7 |
| 45–54 years | 10,840,000 | 18.0 |
| 55–64 years | 9,554,000 | 15.8 |
| 65 years or older | 9,185,000 | 15.2 |
| Marital Status of Household Heads: | | |
| All Households | 82,368,000 | 100.0 |
| Married | 53,324,000 | 64.7 |
| Separated | 3,205,000 | 3.9 |
| Widowed | 10,785,000 | 13.1 |
| Divorced | 8,239,000 | 10.0 |
| Single | 10,021,000 | 12.2 |

## SEX RATIO OF U.S. POPULATION

Source: U.S. Bureau of the Census (males per 100 females). Figures relate to July 1, and include Armed Forces overseas

| Year | All ages | Under 15 years | 15 to 24 years | 25 to 44 years | 45 to 64 years | 65 or older |
|---|---|---|---|---|---|---|
| 1980 | **94.8** | 104.6 | 102.7 | 98.1 | 90.7 | 67.6 |
| 1979 | **94.9** | 104.5 | 102.7 | 98.1 | 90.7 | 67.8 |
| 1978 | **95.0** | 104.4 | 102.6 | 98.0 | 90.8 | 68.0 |
| 1976 | **95.2** | 104.3 | 102.5 | 97.8 | 90.9 | 68.6 |
| 1974 | **95.4** | 104.2 | 102.4 | 97.6 | 91.0 | 69.7 |
| 1972 | **95.6** | 104.0 | 102.2 | 97.3 | 91.2 | 70.6 |
| 1970 | **95.9** | 103.9 | 102.3 | 96.9 | 91.7 | 72.0 |
| 1968 | **96.2** | 103.7 | 102.2 | 96.9 | 92.4 | 73.8 |
| 1966 | **96.7** | 103.7 | 102.1 | 96.9 | 93.2 | 75.7 |
| 1964 | **97.1** | 103.6 | 101.8 | 97.0 | 94.1 | 77.9 |
| 1962 | **97.5** | 103.4 | 101.5 | 97.0 | 94.9 | 80.2 |
| 1960 | **97.8** | 103.4 | 101.4 | 96.9 | 95.7 | 82.6 |
| 1956 | **98.4** | 103.7 | 100.6 | 97.2 | 97.0 | 85.8 |
| 1950 | **99.3** | 103.8 | 100.0 | 97.2 | 100.1 | 89.5 |

## MARITAL STATUS OF ADULTS (Persons 14 years old and over)

Source: U.S. Bureau of Census

| Marital Status and Sex | 1955* | 1960 | 1970 | 1981 |
|---|---|---|---|---|
| **Total (millions)** | **107** | **114** | **147** | **174** |
| Single (millions) | 16 | 17 | 37 | 45 |
| Married (millions) | 79 | 84 | 94 | 105 |
| Widowed (millions) | 10 | 11 | 11 | 13 |
| Divorced (millions) | 2 | 3 | 5 | 11 |
| **Male, total (millions)** | **51** | **55** | **70** | **83** |
| Percent distribution | 100.0 | 100.0 | 100.0 | 100.0 |
| Single | 17.4 | 17.8 | 28.2 | 29.4 |
| Married | 76.1 | 76.0 | 66.6 | 63.0 |
| Wife separated | 1.5 | 1.7 | 1.3 | 1.9 |

| Martial Status and Sex | 1955* | 1960 | 1970 | 1981 |
|---|---|---|---|---|
| **Male, total** (cont.) | | | | |
| Widowed | 4.6 | 4.1 | 3.0 | 2.3 |
| Divorced | 1.9 | 2.1 | 2.2 | 5.3 |
| **Female, total (millions)** | **56** | **59** | **77** | **91** |
| Percent distribution | 100.0 | 100.0 | 100.0 | 100.0 |
| Single | 12.0 | 11.8 | 22.1 | 22.5 |
| Married | 71.9 | 71.3 | 62.0 | 58.5 |
| Husband separated | 2.5 | 2.2 | 2.2 | 2.9 |
| Widowed | 13.6 | 14.0 | 12.5 | 11.9 |
| Divorced | 2.4 | 2.9 | 3.5 | 7.1 |

* Excludes Alaska and Hawaii.

## U.S. MARRIAGE AND DIVORCE RATES

Source: National Center for Health Statistics

| Year | Marriages (thousands) | Divorces (thousands) | Marriage rate (per thousand) | Divorce rate (per thousand) |
|---|---|---|---|---|
| 1910 | 948 | 83 | 10.3 | 0.9 |
| 1915 | 1,008 | 104 | 10.0 | 1.0 |
| 1920 | 1,274 | 171 | 12.0 | 1.6 |
| 1925 | 1,188 | 175 | 10.3 | 1.5 |
| 1930 | 1,127 | 196 | 9.2 | 1.6 |
| 1935 | 1,327 | 218 | 10.4 | 1.7 |
| 1940 | 1,596 | 264 | 12.1 | 2.0 |
| 1945 | 1,613 | 485 | 12.2 | 3.5 |
| 1950 | 1,667 | 385 | 11.1 | 2.6 |
| 1955 | 1,531 | 377 | 9.3 | 2.3 |
| 1960 | 1,523 | 393 | 8.5 | 2.2 |
| 1963 | 1,654 | 428 | 8.8 | 2.3 |
| 1964 | 1,725 | 450 | 9.0 | 2.4 |
| 1965 | 1,800 | 479 | 9.3 | 2.5 |
| 1966 | 1,857 | 499 | 9.5 | 2.5 |
| 1967 | 1,927 | 523 | 9.7 | 2.6 |
| 1968 | 2,069 | 584 | 10.4 | 2.9 |
| 1969 | 2,145 | 639 | 10.6 | 3.2 |
| 1970 | 2,159 | 708 | 10.6 | 3.5 |
| 1971 | 2,190 | 773 | 10.6 | 3.7 |
| 1972 | 2,282 | 845 | 11.0 | 4.1 |
| 1973 | 2,284 | 915 | 10.9 | 4.4 |
| 1974 | 2,230 | 977 | 10.5 | 4.6 |
| 1975 | 2,153 | 1,036 | 10.1 | 4.9 |
| 1976 | 2,155 | 1,083 | 10.0 | 5.0 |
| 1977 | 2,178 | 1,091 | 10.0 | 5.0 |
| 1978 | 2,282* | 1,130 | 10.5 | 5.2 |
| 1979 | 2,331* | 1,181 | 10.6 | 5.4 |

*Beginning 1978, data include nonlicensed marriages registered in Calif.

## ILLEGITIMATE BIRTHS IN AMERICA

Source: National Center for Health Statistics (Figures in thousands)

| Categories | 1940 | 1950 | 1960 | 1965 | 1970 | 1975 | 1977 | 1978 | 1979 |
|---|---|---|---|---|---|---|---|---|---|
| Total Illegitimate Live Births | 89.5 | 141.6 | 224.3 | 291.2 | 398.7 | 447.9 | 515.7 | 543.9 | 597.8 |
| **By age of mother:** | | | | | | | | | |
| Under 15 years | 2.1 | 3.2 | 4.6 | 6.1 | 9.5 | 11.0 | 10.1 | 9.4 | 9.5 |
| 15 to 19 years | 40.5 | 56.0 | 87.1 | 123.1 | 190.4 | 222.5 | 239.7 | 239.7 | 253.2 |
| 20 to 24 years | 27.2 | 43.1 | 68.0 | 90.7 | 126.7 | 134.0 | 168.6 | 186.5 | 210.1 |
| 25 to 29 years | 10.5 | 20.9 | 32.1 | 36.8 | 40.6 | 50.2 | 62.4 | 70.0 | 80.6 |
| 30 to 34 years | 5.2 | 10.8 | 18.9 | 19.6 | 19.1 | 19.8 | 23.7 | 26.5 | 31.3 |
| 35 to 39 years | 3.0 | 6.0 | 10.6 | 11.4 | 9.4 | 8.1 | 8.8 | 9.4 | 10.6 |
| 40 and over | 1.0 | 1.7 | 3.0 | 3.7 | 3.0 | 2.3 | 2.3 | 2.3 | 2.5 |
| **By color of mother:** | | | | | | | | | |
| White | 40.3 | 53.5 | 82.5 | 123.7 | 175.1 | 186.4 | 220.1 | 233.6 | 263.0 |
| Nonwhite | 49.2 | 88.1 | 141.8 | 167.5 | 215.1 | 261.6 | 295.5 | 310.2 | 334.8 |

## DIVORCE LAWS 1981

SOURCE: Women's Bureau, U.S. Department of Labor and *The Book of the States* (1982-83) by the Council of State Governments

| | | "No fault" divorce (a) | | | "Traditional" Grounds for Absolute Divorce (b) | | | | | | | | | | | | Period before parties may remarry after final decree (f) | |
|---|---|---|---|---|---|---|---|---|---|---|---|---|---|---|---|---|---|---|
| State or other Jurisdiction | Residence required before filing suit for divorce(c) | Marriage break-down (d) | Separa-tion | Prior decree of limited divorce | Adul-tery | Mental and/or physical cruelty | Deser-tion | Alco-holism and/or drug addiction | Impo-tency | Non-support by husband | In-sanity | Preg-nancy at mar-riage | Big-amy | Un-explained ab-sence | Felony convic-tion or imprison-ment | Other | Plaintiff | Defendant |
| Alabama | 6 mos.(g) | * | 2 yrs.(h) | 2 yrs. | * | — | 1 yr. | * | * | * | 5 yrs. | * | — | — | * | (i) | 60 days(j) | 60 days(j) |
| Alaska | — | * | — | — | * | * | 1 yr. | * | * | * | 18 mos. | — | — | — | * | — | — | — |
| Arizona | 90 days | * | — | — | — | — | — | — | — | — | — | — | — | — | — | — | — | — |
| Arkansas | 60 days(k) | — | 3 yrs. | — | * | * | 1 yr. | * | * | *(l) | 3 yrs. | — | * | — | * | — | — | — |
| California | (m) | * | — | — | — | — | — | — | — | — | (n) | — | — | — | — | — | — | — |
| Colorado | 90 days | * | — | — | — | — | — | — | — | — | — | — | — | — | — | — | — | — |
| Connecticut | 1 yr.(o) | * | 18 mos. | — | * | * | 1 yr. | * | — | — | 5 yrs. | — | — | 7 yrs. | * | (p) | — | — |
| Delaware | 6 mos. | *(q) | — | — | (q) | (q) | (q) | (q) | — | — | (q) | — | (q) | — | (q) | (q) | — | — |
| Florida | 6 mos. | * | — | — | — | — | — | — | — | — | 3 yrs.(r) | — | — | — | — | — | — | — |
| Georgia | 6 mos. | * | — | — | * | * | 1 yr. | * | * | — | 2 yrs. | * | — | — | * | (p,s,t) | (u) | (u) |
| Hawaii | 3 mos. | * | 2 yrs.(h) | *(v) | — | — | — | — | — | — | — | — | — | — | — | — | — | — |
| Idaho | 6 wks. | * | 5 yrs. | — | * | * | * | * | — | * | 3 yrs. | — | — | — | * | — | — | — |
| Illinois | 90 days | — | — | — | * | * | 1 yr. | 2 yrs. | * | — | — | — | * | — | * | (w,x) | — | — |
| Indiana | 6 mos. | * | — | — | — | — | — | — | * | — | 2 yrs. | — | — | — | * | — | — | — |
| Iowa | 1 yr. | * | — | — | — | — | — | — | — | — | — | — | — | — | — | — | 1 yr.(j) | 1 yr.(j) |
| Kansas | 60 days | * | — | — | * | * | 1 yr. | * | — | * | 3 yrs. | — | — | — | * | — | 30 days | 30 days |
| Kentucky | 180 days(y) | * | — | — | — | — | — | — | — | — | — | — | — | — | — | — | — | — |
| Louisiana | (z) | — | 2 yrs. | *(aa) | * | — | — | — | — | — | — | — | — | — | * | — | — | — |
| Maine | 6 mos.(o) | * | — | — | * | * | 3 yrs. | * | * | * | — | — | — | — | — | — | — | — |
| Maryland | (ab) | — | (ac) | — | * | — | 1 yr. | — | * | — | 3 yrs. | — | — | — | * | (ad) | — | — |
| Massachusetts | (ae) | * | — | — | * | * | 1 yr. | * | * | * | — | — | — | — | * | — | — | — |
| Michigan | 180 days(o) | * | — | — | — | — | — | — | — | — | — | — | — | — | — | — | — | — |
| Minnesota | 180 days(o) | * | — | — | — | — | — | — | — | — | — | — | — | — | — | — | 6 mos.(j) | 6 mos.(j) |
| Mississippi | 1 yr. | * | — | — | * | * | 1 yr. | * | * | — | 3 yrs. | * | * | — | * | (s,af) | — | (ag) |
| Missouri | 90 days | * | — | — | — | — | — | — | — | — | — | — | — | — | — | — | — | — |
| Montana | 90 days | * | 180 days | — | — | — | — | — | — | — | — | — | — | — | — | — | — | — |
| Nebraska | 1 yr. | * | — | — | — | — | — | — | — | — | — | — | — | — | — | — | — | — |
| Nevada | 6 wks.(o) | * | 1 yr.(u) | — | — | — | — | — | — | — | 2 yrs. | — | — | — | — | — | — | — |
| New Hampshire | 1 yr.(o) | * | — | — | * | * | 2 yrs. | * | * | * | — | — | — | 2 yrs. | * | (ah,ai) | — | — |
| New Jersey | 1 yr. | — | 18 mos. | — | * | * | 1 yr. | * | — | — | 2 yrs. | — | — | — | * | (aj) | — | — |
| New Mexico | 6 mos. | * | — | — | * | * | * | — | — | — | — | — | — | — | — | — | — | — |
| New York | 1 yr.(o) | — | 1 yr.(h) | — | * | * | 1 yr. | — | (ak) | (al) | 5 yrs.(ak) | — | — | — | * | — | — | — |
| North Carolina | 6 mos. | — | 1 yr. | — | * | — | — | — | * | — | 3 yrs. | * | — | — | — | (i) | — | — |
| North Dakota | 1 yr. | * | — | 1 yr. | * | * | 1 yr. | * | * | *(l) | 5 yrs. | — | — | — | * | — | (u) | (u) |
| Ohio | 6 mos. | *(am) | 2 yrs. | — | * | * | 1 yr. | * | * | *(l) | 4 yrs. | — | * | — | * | (p,an) | — | — |
| Oklahoma | 6 mos.(ao) | * | — | — | * | * | 1 yr. | * | * | *(l) | 5 yrs. | * | — | — | * | (p,an) | 6 mos. | 6 mos. |
| Oregon | 6 mos. | * | — | — | — | — | — | — | — | — | — | — | — | — | — | — | 60 days | 60 days |
| Pennsylvania | 1 yr. | — | — | — | * | * | 2 yrs. | — | * | — | 3 yrs. | — | * | — | * | (j,s,ap) | — | (aq) |
| Rhode Island | 2 yrs. | — | 3 yrs. | — | * | * | 5 yrs.(at) | * | * | 1 yr. | — | — | — | * | — | (as,at) | 6 mos. | 6 mos. |
| South Carolina | 3 mos.(au) | — | 3 yrs. | — | * | * | 1 yr. | * | — | — | — | — | — | 7 yrs. | — | — | — | — |
| South Dakota | — | — | — | — | * | * | 1 yr. | 1 yr. | — | 1 yr. | 5 yrs. | — | — | — | * | — | — | — |
| Tennessee | 6 mos. | — | — | 2 yrs.(u) | * | * | 1 yr. | * | * | * | — | — | * | — | * | (x,av) | — | — |
| Texas | 6 mos. | * | 3 yrs. | — | * | * | 1 yr. | — | — | — | 3 yrs. | — | — | — | * | — | 30 days(j) | 30 days(j) |
| Utah | 3 mos. | — | 3 yrs.(h) | — | * | * | 1 yr. | * | * | *(j) | (aw) | — | — | — | * | — | — | — |
| Vermont | 6 mos.(ax) | — | 6 mos. | — | * | * | * | — | — | *(j) | 5 yrs. | — | — | — | — | — | — | — |

| State or other Jurisdiction | Residence required before filing suit for divorce(c) | "No fault" divorce (a): Marriage breakdown (d) | Separation | Prior decree of limited divorce | "Traditional" Grounds for Absolute Divorce (b): Adultery | Mental and/or physical cruelty | Desertion | Alcoholism and/or drug addiction | Impotency | Nonsupport by husband | Insanity | Pregnancy at marriage(e) | Bigamy | Unexplained absence | Felony conviction or imprisonment | Other | Period before parties may remarry after final decree (f): Plaintiff | Defendant |
|---|---|---|---|---|---|---|---|---|---|---|---|---|---|---|---|---|---|---|
| Virginia | 6 mos. | — | 1 yr. | (ay) | * | * | 1 yr. | — | — | — | — | — | — | — | * | — | — | — |
| Washington | — | * | — | — | — | — | — | — | — | — | — | — | — | — | — | — | — | — |
| West Virginia | 1 yr.(o) | — | 2 yrs. | — | * | * | 1 yr. | * | — | — | 3 yrs. | — | — | — | * | — | — | — |
| Wisconsin | 6 mos. | — | 1 yr. | 1 yr. | * | * | 1 yr. | 1 yr. | — | * | 1 yr. | — | — | — | * | — | 6 mos. | 6 mos. |
| Wyoming | 60 days(o) | — | 2 yrs.(az) | — | * | * | 1 yr. | * | * | * | 2 yrs. | * | — | — | * | (ba,bb) | — | — |
| District of Columbia | 6 mos. | — | 6 mos.(bc) | *(bd) | — | — | — | — | — | — | — | — | — | — | — | — | — | — |
| Puerto Rico | 1 yr.(o) | *(bc) | 2 yrs. | — | * | * | 1 yr. | * | * | — | 7 yrs. | — | — | 10 yrs. | * | (bf) | — | (bg) |

(a) "No fault" includes all proceedings where it is not necessary to prove one of the "traditional" grounds for divorce. In some states divorce can be obtained by the agreement of both parties; in others, unilaterally. (b) "Traditional" grounds enacted into English and American law during mid-1800s. (c) Local residence may also be required. (d) Expressed in statutes as irremediable or irretrievable breakdown of marriage relationship, irreconcilable differences, incompatibility, marriage insupportable because of discord, etc. (e) By another man; unknown to husband. (f) In contested divorce cases, many lawyers advise no remarriage until time for appeal has passed. (g) Two years for wife filing on grounds of nonsupport. (h) Under decree of separate maintenance and/or written separation agreement. (i) Crime against nature. (j) Except to each other. In Iowa, court can waive ban. (k) Three-month residency required before final judgment. (l) Grounds available to husband also. (m) No final decree until party is resident for 6 months. (n) Incurable. (o) In some cases, a lesser period of time may be allowed. (p) Fraud, force, or duress. (q) Grounds indicated, along with homosexuality, willful refusal to perform marriage obligations, and contracting venereal disease constitute basis for finding of marriage breakdown. (r) Mental incompetence. (s) Parties related by marriage or blood contrary to statute. (t) Mental incapacity at time of marriage. (u) In the discretion of the court. (v) After expiration of term of separation decree. (w) Loathsome disease. (x) Attempt on life of spouse by poison or other means showing malice. (y) No decree until parties have lived apart for 60 days. (z) Must be permanent residents (domiciliaries) of state and grounds must have occurred in state. (aa) Spouse who obtained separation may obtain absolute divorce 1 year after decree becomes final. Other party may obtain divorce 1 year and 60 days from date of separation decree. (ab) One year if cause occurred out of state; 2 years for insanity. (ac) Voluntary living apart for 1 year and no reasonable expectation of reconciliation, or living separate and apart without cohabitation or interruption for 3 years. (ad) Any cause which renders marriage null and void from the outset. (ae) One year if grounds occurred outside of Commonwealth. (af) Insanity or idiocy at time of marriage not known to other party. (ag) When divorce is granted on grounds of adultery, court may prohibit remarriage. Disability may be removed after 1 year upon satisfactory evidence of reformation. (ah) Membership in religious sect not believing in marriage. (ai) Wife out of state 10 years without husband's consent. (aj) Deviant sexual contact without consent of spouse. (ak) Grounds for annulment. (al) Grounds for separation. (am) On petition of both spouses, accompanied by separation agreement executed and confirmed by both spouses in court appearance not less than 90 days after filing of petition. (an) Defendant obtained divorce from plaintiff in another state. (ao) Five years for insanity and spouse in out-of-state facility. (ap) Remarriage after 2 years upon false but well-founded rumor of death of spouse. (If first spouse reappears, he or she may seek divorce for bigamy within 6 months.) (aq) If divorce is granted for adultery, the guilty party cannot marry the accomplice in adultery during lifetime of former spouse. (ar) Shorter period in court's discretion. (as) Void or voidable marriage; in case party is deemed civilly dead from crime or other circumstances, party may be presumed dead. (at) Gross misbehavior or wickedness. (au) If both parties residents; 1 year if one is a nonresident. (av) Refusal by wife to move to state with husband. (aw) Adjudication of permanent and incurable insanity. (ax) Two years if grounds are insanity. (ay) Limited divorce granted on the grounds of cruelty, reasonable apprehension of bodily hurt, willful desertion, or abandonment may be merged into an absolute divorce after 1 year. (az) Two years' separation without material fault by plaintiff. (ba) Husband guilty of conduct constituting vagrancy. (bb) Conviction of felony before marriage. (bc) Voluntary separation, involuntary separation, 1 year. (bd) Granted for 6 months' voluntary separation, 1 year involuntary separation, adultery, or cruelty. (be) By mutual consent. (bf) Attempt by either parent to corrupt son or prostitute daughter, or proposal by husband to prostitute wife. (bg) If remarriage before 301 days, she must present certificate showing pregnancy or nonpregnancy if she has given birth. If pregnant, former spouse presumed to be father.

## MEDIAN DURATION OF U.S. MARRIAGES PRIOR TO DIVORCE OR ANNULMENT (in years)

SOURCE: National Center for Health Statistics

| State* | 1950 | 1960 | 1970 | 1979 |
|---|---|---|---|---|
| Reporting States Average | 5.3 | 7.1 | 6.7 | 6.8 |
| Alabama | (NA) | 7.3 | 5.3 | 5.3 |
| Alaska | 5.0 | 6.2 | 5.4 | 5.2 |
| California | (NA) | (NA) | 6.8 | (NA) |
| Connecticut | (NA) | (NA) | 8.6 | 8.5 |
| Georgia | (NA) | 6.3 | 5.4 | 5.7 |
| Hawaii | (NA) | 6.3 | 7.2 | 6.0 |
| Idaho | 4.2 | 4.8 | 4.6 | 5.0 |
| Illinois | (NA) | (NA) | 6.6 | 6.5 |
| Iowa | 4.5 | 5.7 | 5.6 | 6.0 |
| Kansas | (NA) | 5.8 | 5.1 | 4.9 |
| Kentucky | (NA) | (NA) | 5.7 | 5.7 |
| Maryland | (NA) | 9.0 | 8.8 | 8.4 |
| Massachusetts | (NA) | (NA) | (NA) | 8.9 |
| Michigan | 6.6 | (NA) | 7.0 | 7.1 |
| Missouri | 5.2 | (NA) | 5.4 | 5.8 |
| Montana | (NA) | 5.1 | 5.1 | 5.3 |
| Nebraska | 5.7 | 6.3 | 6.0 | 6.3 |
| New Hampshire | (NA) | (NA) | (NA) | 7.1 |
| New York | (NA) | (NA) | 9.3 | 8.3 |
| Ohio | (NA) | (NA) | 6.3 | 6.2 |
| Oregon | 4.7 | 5.9 | 5.9 | 6.2 |
| Pennsylvania | (NA) | 9.2 | 8.1 | 7.9 |
| Rhode Island | (NA) | (NA) | 9.2 | 8.5 |
| South Carolina | (NA) | (NA) | (NA) | 7.3 |
| South Dakota | 4.8 | 6.3 | 5.9 | 5.9 |
| Tennessee | 4.6 | 6.3 | 5.6 | 5.8 |
| Utah | (NA) | 4.7 | 5.3 | 4.8 |
| Vermont | (NA) | (NA) | 8.3 | 7.9 |
| Virginia | 8.2 | 8.3 | 7.7 | 8.2 |
| Wisconsin | (NA) | 8.2 | 7.9 | 7.0 |
| Wyoming | 4.2 | 5.4 | 4.6 | 4.8 |

(NA) Not Available. *By reporting states only.

## MARRIAGE LAWS: 1981

SOURCE: Women's Bureau, U.S. Department of Labor and *The Book of States,* (1982-83), by the Council of State Governments

| State | Age at Which Marriage Can be Contracted without Parental Consent | | Age at Which Marriage Can be Contracted With Parental Consent | | Blood Test and Other Medical Requirements | | Waiting Period | |
|---|---|---|---|---|---|---|---|---|
| | Male | Female | Male | Female | Period between Examination and Issuance of License (days) | Scope of Medical Examination | Before Issuance of License | After Issuance of License |
| Alabama | 18 | 18 | 17(a) | 14(a) | 30 | (b) | — | — |
| Alaska | 18 | 18 | 16(c) | 16(c) | 30 | (b) | 3 da. | — |
| Arizona | 18 | 18 | 16(c) | 16(c) | 30 | (b) | (d) | — |
| Arkansas | 18 | 18 | 17(c) | 16(c) | 30 | (b) | 3 da. | — |
| California | 18 | 18 | 18(a,c) | 16(a,c) | 30 | (b,f,g,h) | — | — |
| Colorado | 18 | 18 | 16(c) | 16(c) | 30 | (b,g,i) | — | — |
| Connecticut | 18 | 18 | 16(c) | 16(c) | 35 | (b) | 4 da. | — |
| Delaware | 18 | 18 | 18(c) | 16(c) | 30 | (b) | — | (k) |
| Florida | 18 | 18 | 16(a,c) | 16(a,c) | 30 | (b) | 3 da. | — |
| Georgia | 18(l) | 18(l) | 16(c,l) | 16(c,l) | 30 | (b,f) | 3 da.(m) | — |
| Hawaii | 18 | 18 | 16 | 16(c) | 30 | (b) | — | — |
| Idaho | 18 | 18 | 16(c) | 16(c) | — | (g) | (o) | — |
| Illinois | 18 | 18 | 16(c) | 16(c) | 15 | (b,f) | 3 da. | — |
| Indiana | 18 | 18 | 17(c) | 17(c) | 30 | (b,f) | 3 da. | — |
| Iowa | 18 | 18 | 16 | 16 | 20 | (b) | 3 da. | — |
| Kansas | 18 | 18 | 18(c) | 18(c) | 30 | (b) | 3 da. | — |
| Kentucky | 18 | 18 | (a,q) | (a,q) | 15 | (b,f) | 3 da. | — |
| Louisiana | 18 | 18 | 18(c) | 16(c) | 10 | (b) | — | 72 hrs. |
| Maine | 18 | 18 | 16(c) | 16(c) | 60 | (b) | 5 da. | — |
| Maryland | 18 | 18 | 16(c) | 16(c) | — | — | 48 hrs. | — |
| Massachusetts | 18 | 18 | 18(c) | 18(c) | 30 | (b,g) | 3 da. | — |
| Michigan | 18 | 18 | (r) | 16 | 30 | (b) | 3 da. | — |
| Minnesota | 18 | 18 | 18 | 16(s) | — | — | 5 da. | — |
| Mississippi | 21 | 21 | 17(c) | 15(c) | 30 | (b) | 3 da. | — |
| Missouri | 18 | 18 | 15(c) | 15(c) | 15 | (b) | 3 da. | — |
| Montana | 18 | 18 | 18(c) | 18(c) | 20 | (b) | 5 da. | 3 da. |
| Nebraska | 19 | 19 | 17 | 17 | 30 | (b,g) | 2 da. | — |
| Nevada | 18 | 18 | 16(a,c) | 16(a,c) | — | — | — | — |
| New Hampshire | 18 | 18 | 14(s) | 13(s) | 30(t) | (b) | 3 da. | — |
| New Jersey | 18 | 18 | 16(c) | 16(c) | 30 | (b) | 72 hrs. | — |
| New Mexico | 18 | 18 | 16(c) | 16(c) | 30 | (b) | 72 hrs. | — |
| New York | 18 | 18 | 16 | 14(u) | 30 | (b,f) | — | 24 da.(v) |
| North Carolina | 18 | 18 | 16 | 16(c) | 30 | (b,g,w,x) | — | — |
| North Dakota | 18 | 18 | 16 | 16 | 30 | (b,y) | — | — |
| Ohio | 18 | 18 | 18(c) | 16(c) | 30 | (b) | 5 da. | — |
| Oklahoma | 18 | 18 | 16(c) | 16(c) | 30 | (b) | (o) | — |
| Oregon | 18 | 18 | 17 | 17 | 30 | (b) | — | (z) |
| Pennsylvania | 18 | 18 | 16(c) | 16(c) | 30 | (b,aa) | 3 da. | — |
| Rhode Island | 18 | 18 | 18(c) | 16(c) | 40 | (b,g,x) | — | — |
| South Carolina | 18 | 18 | 16(c) | 14(c) | — | — | 24 hrs. | — |
| South Dakota | 18 | 18 | 16(c) | 16(c) | 20 | (b) | — | — |
| Tennessee | 18 | 18 | 16(c) | 16(c) | 30 | (b) | 3 da.(ab) | — |
| Texas | 18 | 18 | 14(c) | 14(c) | 21 | (b) | — | — |
| Utah | 18 | 18 | 16(a) | 14(a) | 30 | (b) | — | — |
| Vermont | 18 | 18 | 16(c) | 16(c) | 30 | (b) | — | 5 da. |
| Virginia | 18 | 18 | 16(a,c) | 16(a,c) | 30 | (b) | — | — |
| Washington | 18 | 18 | 17(c) | 17(c) | — | (b,x,ac) | 3 da. | — |
| West Virginia | 18 | 18 | (q) | (q) | 30 | (b) | 3 da. | — |
| Wisconsin | 18 | 18 | 16 | 16 | 20 | (b) | 5 da. | — |
| Wyoming | 19 | 19 | 17(c) | 16(c) | 30 | (b) | — | — |
| District of Columbia | 18 | 18 | 16(a) | 16(a) | 30 | (b) | 3 da. | — |
| Puerto Rico | 21 | 21 | 18(c) | 16(c) | 10(ad) | (b,ac) | — | — |

**Note:** Common law marriage is recognized in Alabama, Colorado, Georgia, Idaho, Iowa, Kansas, Montana, Ohio, Oklahoma, Pennsylvania, Rhode Island, South Carolina, Texas, and the District of Columbia. (a) Parental consent not required if previously married. (b) Venereal diseases. (c) Legal procedure for younger persons to obtain license. (d) Blood test must be on record at least 48 hours before issuance of license. (f) Sickle cell anemia. (g) Rubella immunity. (h) Tay-Sachs disease. (i) Rh factor (k) Residents, 24 hours; nonresidents, 96 hours. (l) Parental consent is not needed regardless of age in cases of pregnancy or when couple has a living child born out of wedlock. (m) Unless parties are 18 years of age or over, or woman is pregnant, or applicants are the parents of a living child born out of wedlock. (o) Three days if parties are under 18 years of age. (q) Non minimum age. (r) No provision in the law for parental consent for males. (s) Permission of judge also required. (t) Maximum period between blood test and date of intended marriage. (u) If under 16 years of age, consent of family court judge also required. (v) However, marriage may not be solemnized within 3 days of date on which specimen for blood test was taken. (w) Mental competency. (x) Tuberculosis. (y) Some marriages prohibited if a party is severely retarded. (z) License valid 3 days after application signed and valid for 30 days thereafter. (aa) Court order needed if party is weakminded, insane, or of unsound mind. (ab) May be waived if certain conditions are met. (ac) Affidavit of mental competence required. Also, no epilepsy in Puerto Rico. (ad) Maximum time from blood test to expiration of license.

## SOCIAL SECURITY AND MEDICARE

SOURCE: U.S. Social Security Administration

The basic idea of Social Security is simple: During working years, employees, their employers, and self-employed people pay Social Security taxes. This money is used only to pay benefits to the 36 million people getting benefits and to pay administrative costs of the program.

Then, when today's workers' earnings stop or are reduced because of retirement, death, or disability, benefits will be paid to them from taxes paid by people in covered work and self-employment at that time.

Part of the contributions made go into a separate hospital insurance trust fund so that when workers and their dependents reach 65 they will have help in paying their hospital bills. Medicare is available also to people under 65 who have been entitled to Social Security disability benefits for 2 years or more and to insured people of any age and their dependents who need a kidney transplant or dialysis treatment because of permanent kidney failure. Medical insurance, also available, helps pay doctors' bills and other medical expenses. This program is financed out of premiums partially paid for by those who are enrolled with the majority of the cost paid for by the Federal Government. Under present law, the Federal share can never be less than one-half the cost of the program. Starting July 1, 1982, enrollees pay $12.20 a month for this protection.

Nine out of 10 working people in the United States are now building protection for themselves and their families under Social Security.

### FINANCING THE PROGRAMS

Federal retirement, survivors, and disability benefits and hospital insurance benefits are paid for by contributions based on earnings covered under Social Security.

If you are employed, you and your employer share the contributions. If you are self-employed, you pay contributions for retirement, survivors, and disability insurance at about 1½ times the rate for an employee. However, the hospital insurance contribution rate is the same for the employer, the employee, and the self-employed person.

As long as you have earnings that are covered by the law, you pay contributions regardless of your age and even if you are receiving Social Security benefits.

#### How Contributions Are Paid

If you are employed, your contribution is deducted from your wages each payday. Your employer sends it, with an equal amount as his own share of the contribution, to the Internal Revenue Service.

If you are self-employed and your net earnings are $400 or more in a year, you must report your earnings and pay your self-employment contribution each year when you file your individual income tax return. This is true even if you owe no income tax.

Your wages and self-employment income are entered on your individual record by the Social Security Administration. This record of your earnings will be used to determine your eligibility for benefits and the amount of cash benefits you will receive.

The maximum amount of earnings that can count for Social Security and on which you pay Social Security contributions is shown in the following table:

| Year | Amount | Year | Amount |
|---|---|---|---|
| 1937-50 | $3,000 | 1974 | 13,200 |
| 1951-54 | 3,600 | 1975 | 14,100 |
| 1955-58 | 4,200 | 1976 | 15,300 |
| 1959-65 | 4,800 | 1977 | 16,500 |
| 1966-67 | 6,600 | 1978 | 17,700 |
| 1968-71 | 7,800 | 1979 | 22,900 |
| 1972 | 9,000 | 1980 | 25,900 |
| 1973 | 10,800 | 1981 | 29,700 |
| | | 1982 | 32,400 |

Earnings over the maximums may have been reported to your Social Security record, but cannot be used to figure your benefit rate.

When you work for more than one employer in a year and pay Social Security contributions on wages over the Social Security maximum, you may claim a refund of the excess contributions on your income tax return for that year.

If you work for only one employer and he deducts too much in contributions, you should apply to the employer for a refund. A refund is made only when more than the required amount of contributions has been paid. Questions about contributions or refunds should be directed to the Internal Revenue Service. These tables show the schedule of contributions rates now in the law:

**SOCIAL SECURITY TAX RATES (In percent)**

| Year | OASI*[1] | DI*[2] | HI[3] | Total |
|---|---|---|---|---|
| | Employers & employees, each | | | |
| 1982-84 | 4.575 | .825 | 1.30 | 6.70 |
| 1985 | 4.750 | .950 | 1.35 | 7.05 |
| 1986-89 | 4.750 | .950 | 1.45 | 7.15 |
| 1990 & later | 5.100 | 1.100 | 1.45 | 7.65 |
| | Self-employed | | | |
| 1982-84 | 6.8125 | 1.2375 | 1.30 | 9.35 |
| 1985 | 7.1250 | 1.4250 | 1.35 | 9.90 |
| 1986-89 | 7.1250 | 1.4250 | 1.45 | 10.00 |
| 1990 & later | 7.6500 | 1.6500 | 1.45 | 10.75 |

*By allocation in law. [1]Old Age, Survivors Insurance. [2]Disability Insurance. [3]Hospital Insurance.

#### Social Security Cash Benefits

To get monthly cash payments for yourself and your family, or for your survivors to get payments in case of your death, you must first have credit for a certain amount of work under Social Security. This is measured in quarters of coverage. Credit may have been earned at any time after 1936.

In 1982, all employees and self-employed people earn one quarter of coverage for each $340 of their covered annual earnings. This quarter of coverage measure is increased each year to reflect increases in average wages. *No more than 4 quarters can be earned for any year, regardless of total earnings.*

For years before 1978, employees earned one quarter of coverage for a 3-month calendar quarter in which they were paid covered wages of $50 or more. Four quarters were counted for any year in which a person had $400 or more in self-employment income or in cash wages from farm work, or for any year a person had the maximum earnings that counted for Social Security.

You can be either fully or currently insured or both, depending on the total amount of credit you have for work under Social Security and the amount you have in the last 3 years.

If you stop working under Social Security before you have earned enough credit to be insured, no cash benefits will be payable to you. The earnings already credited to you will remain on your Social Security record; if you later return to work, regardless of your age, all your covered earnings will be considered.

#### Fully Insured

Just how much credit you must have to be fully insured depends upon the year you reach 62 or upon the date of your death or disabilty.

The amount of credit you will need is measured in quarters of coverage; but for convenience, the table on this page is given in years. The people in your Social Security office will be glad to give you further details if you have questions.

You are fully insured if you have credit for at least as many years as shown on the appropriate line of the following chart.

| When you reach 62 or become disabled | You will be fully insured if you have credit for this much work |
|---|---|
| 1979 | 7 |
| 1981 | 7½ |
| 1983 | 8 |
| 1987 | 9 |
| 1991 or later | 10 |

If you become disabled or die before reaching 62 you are fully insured if you have credit for ¼ year of work for each year after 1950 and up to the year of your disability or death. In counting the number of years after 1950, omit years before you were 22.

No one is fully insured with credit for less than 1½ years of work and no one needs more than 10 years of work to be fully insured.

### Currently Insured

You will be currently insured if you have Social Security credit for at least 1½ years of work within the 3 years before you die. If you leave a widow or widower and young children, they are eligible for monthly benefits if you were currently insured.

## AMOUNTS OF MONTHLY PAYMENTS

The amount of monthly Social Security benefits due you or your dependents or survivors is based on your covered earnings under Social Security over a period of years.

The exact amount of your benefit cannot be figured until there is an application for benefits, and all of your earnings up to the time of the application are considered.

A worker who doesn't get any benefits before 65 and who delays his retirement past age 65 will get a special credit that can mean a larger benefit. The credit adds 3 percent for each year (¼ of 1 percent for each month) from age 65 to age 70 (3 percent for people reaching 65 before 1982).

The law provides a special minimum benefit at retirement for some people who worked under Social Security more than 20 years. This provision helps people who had low incomes, but above a specified amount, in their working years. The amount of the special minimum depends on the number of years of coverage. For a worker retiring at 65 with 30 or more years of coverage, the minimum would be $289.00.

## DISABILITY PAYMENTS

If you become disabled before 65, you and certain members of your family may be eligible for benefits.

Do not wait too long after you are disabled to apply for benefits; if you wait more than a year, you may lose benefits. Payments may begin with the 6th full month of disability.

If you are found eligible for disability insurance benefits, you will remain eligible as long as you are disabled. When you reach 65, your benefit will be changed to retirement payments at the same rate.

### Who Is Considered Disabled?

A person is considered disabled only if he has a severe physical or mental condition which—

*prevents him from working, and*
*is expected to last (or has lasted) for at least 12 months or is expected to result in death.*

A person with a severe medical condition could be eligible even if he manages to do a little work.

### How Much Work Credit Is Required for a Disabled Worker?

If you become disabled before you are 24, you need credit for 1½ years of work in the 3 years before you become disabled.

If you become disabled between 24 and 31, you need Social Security credits for half the time after you are 21 and before you become disabled.

To get disability benefits if you become disabled at 31 or later, you must be fully insured and have credit for 5 years of work out of the 10 years ending when you become disabled.

People who become disabled because of blindness can get benefits without having to meet the requirement of substantial recent work.

## FAMILY PAYMENTS

Monthly payments can be made to certain dependents:
*When the worker gets retirement or disability benefits;*
*When the worker dies.*

These dependents are:

*Unmarried children under 18, or between 18 and 19 if they are full-time students at elementary or secondary schools;*

*Unmarried children 18 or over who were severely disabled before they reached 22 and who continue to be disabled;*

*A wife, husband, widow, or widower regardless of age, if caring for a child under 16 or disabled and the child gets payments based on the worker's record;*

*A wife 62 or widow 60 or older, even if there are no children entitled to payments;*

*A widow 50 or older (or widower 50 or older) who becomes disabled not later than 7 years after the death of the worker or not later than 7 years after the end of entitlement to benefits as a widow or widower with a child;*

*A husband 62 or over or widower 60 or over;*

*Dependent parents 62 or over after a worker dies.*

In addition to monthly benefits, a lump-sum payment of $255 may be made to an eligible spouse or child after the worker's death.

Payments may also be made to a divorced wife or husband at 62 or a surviving divorced wife or husband at 60 (or a disabled surviving divorced wife or husband 50 or older) if the marriage lasted at least 10 years.

Benefits also can be paid a dependent surviving divorced wife or husband at any age if she is caring for her deceased former husband's child under 18 or disabled who is entitled to benefits.

For more information about this provision, get in touch with your Social Security office.

Generally, a marriage must have lasted at least 1 year before dependents of a retired or disabled worker can get monthly benefits; survivors can get benefits in most cases if the marriage lasted at least 9 months.

**For Estimating Social Security Benefits on the Basis of Approximate Yearly Earnings for Those 62 Before 1979**

| Benefits can be paid to a: | $1,000 or less | $3,000 | $4,000 | $5,000 | $6,000 | $8,000 | $10,000 |
|---|---|---|---|---|---|---|---|
| Retired worker at 65 | 183.40 | 351.90 | 413.90 | 480.00 | 542.50 | 674.30 | 747.10 |
| Spouse at 65 or child | 91.70 | 176.00 | 189.80 | 240.00 | 271.30 | 337.20 | 373.60 |
| Spouse under 65 and one child each | 45.90 | 93.00 | 146.70 | 202.80 | 226.20 | 252.80 | 280.10 |
| Maximum family payment | 275.20 | 537.90 | 707.30 | 885.50 | 994.80 | 1179.90 | 1307.20 |

**Amount of Your Family's Benefits**

Cash benefits to your dependents, and to your survivors in case of your death, are figured from the amount of your retirement or disability benefit.

Permanently reduced benefits are received by:

*Workers and their wives who choose to start receiving retirement benefits while they are between 62 and 65; Widows and widowers who choose to start receiving benefits between 60 and 65 and*
*Disabled widows and disabled widowers 50 or older who receive benefits before they reach 65.*

The amount of the reduction depends on the number of months they receive benefits before they reach 65. On the average, people who choose to get benefits early will collect about the same value in total benefits over the years, but in smaller installments to take account of the longer period during which they will be paid.

If a person is entitled to monthly benefits based on the Social Security records of two or more workers, he will receive no more than the largest of the benefits.

The lump-sum payment at a worker's death is $255.

**Benefits Not Taxable**

Social Security benefits you receive are not subject to Federal income tax.

## AN APPLICATION IS NECESSARY

Before payments can start, an application must be filed.

When you are nearing 65 or if you become disabled, get in touch with your Social Security office.

It is important for you to inquire at your Social Security office 2 or 3 months before you reach 65, not only for the possibility of retirement benefits, but also for Medicare benefits, which are available whether or not you retire. If you wait until the month you reach 65 to apply for the medical insurance part of Medicare, you will lose at least one month of protection.

If you plan to retire *before* you reach 65, it is important to apply for benefits no later than the last day of the month you want benefits to begin. Generally, benefits payable for months before age 65 can start no earlier than the month you apply.

When a person who has worked under the Social Security law dies, some member of his family should get in touch with the Social Security office.

If you cannot come to the Social Security office write or telephone. A representative can arrange to visit you.

Long delay in filing an application can cause loss of some benefits, since back payments for monthly cash retirement or survivor benefits can be made for no more than 6 months.

An application for a lump-sum death payment must usually be made within 2 years of the worker's death.

## HEALTH INSURANCE (MEDICARE)

Nearly all people 65 and over are eligible for health insurance protection under Medicare, including some people who do not have enough credit for work covered by Social Security to qualify for monthly cash benefits.

Medicare also covers people who have been getting disability checks for 2 years or more and insured people and their dependents who need a kidney transplant or dialysis treatment because of permanent kidney failure.

There are two parts to Medicare: hospital insurance and, for those who choose, medical insurance.

**Eligibility for Hospital Insurance**

If you are 65 or over and are entitled to Social Security or railroad retirement benefits or if you are disabled and have been getting disability for 2 (consecutive) years or more, you are automatically eligible for hospital insurance; if you are not entitled to either of these benefits, you should ask about hospital insurance and medical insurance at your Social Security office.

People 65 or older who are not automatically entitled to hospital insurance can buy this protection for a monthly premium of $113 for the 12-month period starting July 1, 1982, although you will also have to purchase medical insurance.

After you establish your eligibility, you receive a health insurance card, which shows that you have hospital insurance, medical insurance, or both.

## YOUR HOSPITAL INSURANCE

Hospital insurance will help pay the cost of covered services for the following hospital and follow-up care:

*Up to 90 days of hospital care in a participating hospital during a "benefit period."[1] For the first 60 days of care in 1981, your hospital insurance will pay all but the first $260 of expenses. For the 61 through the 90th day of care, your hospital insurance will pay all but $65 daily for covered services. (There is a lifetime limit of payment for 190 days of care in mental hospitals.)*

*You also have 60 reserve days which can be used after you have exhausted your 90 days of hospital care in a "benefit period." Reserve days are not replaced after you use them. Hospital insurance pays all but $130 a day of your covered expenses during the reserve days.*

Hospital insurance in many cases also pays for up to 100 days of care in a participating skilled nursing facility after a hospital stay. Hospital insurance pays for all covered services for the first 20 days of care and all but $32.50 per day for up to 80 more days.

Unlimited home health "visits" from a participating home health agency when prescribed by your physician may also be covered.

## WHAT YOUR MEDICAL INSURANCE PAYS

Anyone who is 65 or older *or* entitled to hospital insurance is eligible for medical insurance. People who get monthly Social Security or railroad retirement benefits are automatically enrolled in medical insurance—unless they say they don't want it—at the same time they become entitled to hospital insurance. Other eligible people must apply for medical insurance at a Social Security office.

You will have protection at the earliest possible time if you enroll during the 3-month period just before the month you first become eligible for medical insurance. You may also enroll the month you become eligible and during the 3 following months, but your protection will not start until 1 to 3 months after that.

Anyone who declines enrollment in Medicare medical insurance during the initial enrollment period can enroll during a general enrollment period—the first 3 months of a year. The premium will be 10 percent higher for each full year a person could have had medical insurance but didn't choose to.

Medical insurance is financed with monthly premiums paid by those who are enrolled and by the Federal Government. The basic medical insurance premium is currently $12.20 a month for the 12-month period starting July 1, 1982.

If you wish to drop your medical insurance, you may give notice to do so at any time. You can re-enroll at any time.

## YOUR MEDICAL INSURANCE

Generally, your medical insurance will pay 80 percent of the approved charges for the following services after the first $75 in a calendar year.

*Physicians' and surgeons' services, no matter where you receive the services—in the doctor's office, in a clinic, in a hospital, or at home. (You do not have to meet the $75 deductible before your medical insurance will pay for X-ray or laboratory services of physicians when you are a bed patient in a hospital. The full reasonable charge will be paid, instead of 80 percent only if the physician accepts assignment.) Home health services even if you have not been in a hospital, the number of visits is unlimited. (Medical insurance pays the reasonable cost after you meet the $75 deductible.)*

*A number of other medical and health services, such as diagnostic tests, surgical dressings and splints, and rental or purchase of medical equipment.*

*Outpatient physical therapy services—whether or not you are homebound—furnished under supervision of a participating hospital, skilled nursing facility, home health agency, approved clinic, rehabilitation agency, or public health agency. All outpatient services of a participating hospital, including diagnostic tests or treatment.*

*Certain services by podiatrists (but not routine foot care or treatment of flat feet or partial dislocation). Limited services by chiropractors.*

[1]A "benefit period" begins the first time you enter a hospital after your hospital insurance starts. It ends after you have not been an inpatient for 60 days in a row in any hospital or in any facility that mainly provides skilled nursing or rehabilitation services.

## For More Medicare Information

For more information on the health insurance programs, get in touch with your Social Security office and ask for a copy of the leaflet, "A brief explanation of Medicare."

### MEDICAID

Both Medicare and Medicaid are part of the Social Security Act. They differ, however, in that the former is an insurance program intended to help those 65 (and some disabled people under 65), while Medicaid is designed for certain kinds of needy and low-income people: the aged (65 or older), the blind, the disabled, members of families with dependent children, and other cases involving children.

Medicaid programs, paid for by money from federal, state, and local taxes, were available in all states except Arizona as of April 1974. Under these programs, payment is made for at least the following services: inpatient hospital care; outpatient hospital services; other laboratory and X-ray services; skilled nursing home services; physicians' services; the screening, diagnosis, and treatment of children; and home health care services.

Medicaid can pay what Medicare does not pay for people who are eligible for both programs. For example, Medicaid can pay the $260 deductible amount for the first 60 days of hospital care under hospital insurance, and the $65 a day for the next 30 days of care. Medicaid also can pay the $75 deductible and the monthly premium for medical insurance.

## OLD-AGE, SURVIVORS, AND DISABILITY INSURANCE PROGRAM (Amounts in billions)

The estimated operations and status of the Old-Age Survivor Insurance (OASI) and Disability Insurance (DI) trust funds, combined, during calendar years 1981-85 under the five alternatives, are shown in this table together with figures on actual experience in 1980. The OASI Trust Fund is projected to be depleted in the near future under all five alternative sets of assumptions. Since under present law, none of the income to one trust fund can be allocated to the other trust fund, the projections of the combined OASI and DI Trust Fund operations for 1982-85 under each alternative are theoretical.

| Calendar Year | Income | Disbursements | Net increase in funds | Funds at end of year | Funds at beginning of year as a percentage of disbursements during year |
|---|---|---|---|---|---|
| Alternative I: | | | | | |
| 1980* | $119.7 | $123.5 | $− 3.8 | $26.5 | 25% |
| 1981 | 140.8 | 145.1 | − 4.3 | 22.2 | 18 |
| 1982† | 158.3 | 163.8 | − 5.5 | 16.7 | 14 |
| 1983† | 176.3 | 181.2 | − 4.9 | 11.8 | 9 |
| 1984† | 194.1 | 197.9 | − 3.7 | 8.1 | 6 |
| 1985† | 223.5 | 213.2 | 10.2 | 18.3 | 4 |
| Alternative II-A: | | | | | |
| 1980* | 119.7 | 123.5 | − 3.8 | 26.5 | 25 |
| 1981 | 140.2 | 145.1 | − 4.8 | 21.6 | 18 |
| 1982† | 156.6 | 164.1 | − 7.5 | 14.1 | 13 |
| 1983† | 173.1 | 181.5 | − 8.4 | 5.7 | 8 |
| 1984† | 190.1 | 198.2 | − 8.1 | − 2.4 | 3 |
| 1985† | 218.7 | 214.6 | 4.2 | 1.7 | − 1 |
| Alternative II-B: | | | | | |
| 1980* | 119.7 | 123.5 | − 3.8 | 26.5 | 25 |
| 1981 | 140.2 | 145.1 | − 4.8 | 21.6 | 18 |
| 1982† | 156.6 | 164.4 | − 7.8 | 13.8 | 13 |
| 1983† | 173.8 | 184.4 | −10.6 | 3.2 | 7 |
| 1984† | 191.1 | 206.0 | −15.0 | −11.7 | 2 |
| 1985† | 220.6 | 228.4 | − 7.9 | −19.6 | − 5 |
| Alternative III: | | | | | |
| 1980* | 119.7 | 123.5 | − 3.8 | 26.5 | 25 |
| 1981 | 141.1 | 145.1 | − 3.9 | 22.5 | 18 |
| 1982† | 158.5 | 167.3 | − 8.8 | 13.7 | 13 |
| 1983† | 174.2 | 192.6 | −18.4 | − 4.8 | 7 |
| 1984† | 196.0 | 220.1 | −24.1 | −28.9 | − 2 |
| 1985† | 229.9 | 249.7 | −19.7 | −48.6 | −12 |
| "Worst-case:" | | | | | |
| 1980* | 119.7 | 123.5 | − 3.8 | 26.5 | 25 |
| 1981 | 139.8 | 145.1 | − 5.3 | 21.1 | 18 |
| 1982† | 156.6 | 168.0 | −11.4 | 9.7 | 13 |
| 1983† | 170.0 | 194.3 | −24.3 | −14.6 | 5 |
| 1984† | 190.7 | 222.4 | −31.6 | −46.2 | − 7 |
| 1985† | 225.4 | 252.0 | −26.6 | −72.8 | −18 |

*1980 figures represent actual experience. †Figures are theoretical.

## OLD-AGE SURVIVORS (OASI), DISABILITY (DI), AND HEALTH INSURANCE (HI) PROGRAMS—1981-2000

Estimated Cost Rate as percent of taxable payroll*

| Calendar Year | OASI | DI | HI | Total | Total Tax Rate |
|---|---|---|---|---|---|
| Alternative II-A: | | | | | |
| 1981 | 9.89 | 1.41 | 2.27 | 13.57 | 13.30 |
| 1982 | 10.07 | 1.36 | 2.35 | 13.78 | 13.40 |
| 1983 | 10.04 | 1.29 | 2.43 | 13.76 | 13.40 |
| 1984 | 9.97 | 1.24 | 2.55 | 13.76 | 13.40 |
| 1985 | 9.90 | 1.20 | 2.67 | 13.77 | 14.10 |
| 1990 | 9.55 | 1.14 | 3.39 | 14.08 | 15.30 |
| 1995 | 9.43 | 1.16 | 4.27 | 14.85 | 15.30 |
| 2000 | 8.99 | 1.28 | 5.04 | 15.31 | 15.30 |
| Alternative II-B: | | | | | |
| 1981 | 9.89 | 1.41 | 2.27 | 13.57 | 13.30 |
| 1982 | 10.06 | 1.36 | 2.36 | 13.81 | 13.40 |
| 1983 | 10.15 | 1.31 | 2.46 | 13.91 | 13.40 |
| 1984 | 10.29 | 1.26 | 2.58 | 14.15 | 13.40 |
| 1985 | 10.38 | 1.25 | 2.73 | 14.36 | 14.10 |
| 1990 | 10.64 | 1.23 | 3.55 | 15.41 | 15.30 |
| 1995 | 10.47 | 1.23 | 4.55 | 16.25 | 15.30 |
| 2000 | 9.85 | 1.34 | 5.44 | 16.63 | 15.30 |

* Effective taxable payroll is slightly different for OASDI compared to HI, due to the different tax treatment of self-employment earnings.

## DISADVANTAGED: A DEFINITION

The level of family income used to determine whether or not a person is poor has been raised $850 (for an urban family of four) by the U.S. Department of Health and Human Services to reflect increases in consumer prices over the year.

The revised poverty-level guidelines for metropolitan and farm families became effective in April 1982.

Income levels for families of one through six persons are:

| Family Size | Income: Nonfarm* | Income: Farm* |
|---|---|---|
| 1 | $ 4,680 | $ 4,010 |
| 2 | 6,220 | 5,310 |
| 3 | 7,760 | 6,610 |
| 4 | 9,300 | 7,910 |
| 5 | 10,840 | 9,210 |
| 6 | 12,380 | 10,510 |

*For Continental U.S.

Income limits for families of more than six persons may be determined by adding for the nonfarm and farm levels these amounts for each additional person: $1,540 and $1,300 for the Continental U.S.

The federal poverty levels, in conjunction with the Lower Living Standard Income Levels for local areas set by the Bureau of Labor Statistics and based on family income data, are used by CETA† administrators to determine eligibility for CETA programs. The higher figure is the one used. The revised Lower Living Standard Income Levels will be issued for localities later.

The eligibility requirements for most CETA programs include the definition of "economically disadvantaged" containing provisions incorporating the federal poverty levels and the Lower Living Standard Income Levels.

The Labor Department's Employment and Training Administration (ETA) partially defines an economically disadvantaged person as one who is a member of a family whose income during the previous six months on an annualized basis does not exceed the poverty level or 70 percent of the Lower Living Standard Income Level—whichever is higher.

†The CETA program expired at the end of September 1982. In its place, Congress is considering legislation to establish a job training program.

## POVERTY IN THE UNITED STATES:

SOURCE: Bureau of the Census (numbers in millions)

| | Number below Poverty Level | | | | Percent below Poverty Level | | | |
|---|---|---|---|---|---|---|---|---|
| Year | Total | White | Black and Other Races | Black Only | Total | White | Black and Other Races | Black Only |
| **1980** | 29.3 | 19.7 | 9.6 | 8.6 | 13.0 | 10.2 | 29.8 | 32.5 |
| **1979*** | 26.1 | 17.2 | 8.9 | 8.1 | 11.7 | 9.0 | 28.4 | 31.0 |
| **1979** | 25.3 | 16.8 | 8.5 | 7.8 | 11.6 | 8.9 | 28.6 | 30.9 |
| **1978** | 24.5 | 16.3 | 8.2 | 7.6 | 11.4 | 8.7 | 22.8 | 30.6 |
| **1977** | 24.7 | 16.4 | 8.3 | 7.7 | 11.6 | 8.9 | 29.0 | 31.3 |
| **1976** | 25.0 | 16.7 | 8.3 | 7.6 | 11.8 | 9.1 | 29.4 | 31.1 |
| **1975** | 25.9 | 17.8 | 8.1 | 7.5 | 12.3 | 9.7 | 29.3 | 31.3 |
| **1974** | 23.4 | 15.7 | 7.6 | 7.2 | 11.2 | 8.6 | 28.3 | 30.3 |
| **1973** | 23.0 | 15.1 | 7.8 | 7.4 | 11.1 | 8.4 | 29.6 | 31.4 |
| **1972** | 24.5 | 16.2 | 8.3 | 7.7 | 11.9 | 9.0 | 31.9 | 33.3 |
| **1971** | 25.6 | 17.8 | 7.8 | 7.4 | 12.5 | 9.9 | 30.9 | 32.5 |
| **1970** | 25.4 | 17.5 | 7.9 | 7.5 | 12.6 | 9.9 | 32.0 | 33.5 |
| **1965** | 33.2 | 22.5 | 10.7 | NA | 17.3 | 13.3 | 47.1 | NA |

*Based on 1980 population controls. NA-Not available.

## FACTS ABOUT THE POOR

SOURCE: Community Services Administration

Based on 1981 population and 1980 income, there were 29,272,000 poor persons. Despite the fact that two out of every three poor persons are white, the incidence of poverty among non-whites was 29.8% as compared to 10.2% for whites. Children under 18 years of age make up 38.8% of the poor.

Between 1979 and 1980 the number of poor persons increased by 3.2 million. At the same time the number of poor persons aged 65 years and over increased by 190,000. (These are included in the 3.2 million.)

For the 6,217,000 poor families, the average income deficit in 1980 was $3,108. For the 6,227,000 poor unrelated individuals, the deficit averaged $1,669. Income deficit is the difference between a poor family's income and the poverty level, which in 1980 was $8,414 for a non-farm family of four and $7,170 for a farm family of four. The total amount of money required to bring all the poor to the poverty income level would be $29.7 billion.

## POVERTY IN AMERICA BY STATES

SOURCE: Bureau of Census

| State | Thousands of Poor Persons 1975 | 1979* | State | Thousands of Poor Persons 1975 | 1979* | State | Thousands of Poor Persons 1975 | 1979* |
|---|---|---|---|---|---|---|---|---|
| **Total** | 23,991 | 27,526 | Kentucky | 596 | 657 | North Dakota | 66 | 80 |
| Alabama | 587 | 684 | Louisiana | 720 | 777 | Ohio | 997 | 1,108 |
| Alaska | 23 | 39 | Maine | 126 | 140 | Oklahoma | 370 | 391 |
| Arizona | 314 | 331 | Maryland | 313 | 409 | Oregon | 204 | 291 |
| Arkansas | 392 | 417 | Massachusetts | 408 | 547 | Pennsylvania | 1,133 | 1,213 |
| California | 2,192 | 2,611 | Michigan | 821 | 1,004 | Rhode Island | 80 | 94 |
| Colorado | 230 | 289 | Minnesota | 324 | 370 | South Carolina | 478 | 479 |
| Connecticut | 204 | 262 | Mississippi | 607 | 600 | South Dakota | 88 | 107 |
| Delaware | 47 | 69 | Missouri | 565 | 592 | Tennessee | 660 | 760 |
| District of Columbia | 86 | 115 | Montana | 86 | 95 | Texas | 1,870 | 2,055 |
| Florida | 1,225 | 1,245 | Nebraska | 147 | 159 | Utah | 103 | 154 |
| Georgia | 883 | 869 | Nevada | 53 | 67 | Vermont | 63 | 56 |
| Hawaii | 67 | 92 | New Hampshire | 126 | 78 | Virginia | 513 | 594 |
| Idaho | 85 | 118 | New Jersey | 586 | 699 | Washington | 299 | 410 |
| Illinois | 1,150 | 1,284 | New Mexico | 223 | 222 | West Virginia | 270 | 276 |
| Indiana | 424 | 523 | New York | 1,671 | 2,344 | Wisconsin | 352 | 388 |
| Iowa | 225 | 266 | North Carolina | 788 | 827 | Wyoming | 33 | 37 |
| Kansas | 178 | 232 | | | | | | |

## AID TO FAMILIES WITH DEPENDENT CHILDREN

SOURCE: U.S. Department of Health, Education and Welfare (Data for December 1980)

| State | NUMBER OF RECIPIENTS | | | PAYMENTS TO RECIPIENTS | | | Percentage change from Dec. 1979 | |
|---|---|---|---|---|---|---|---|---|
| | | | | | Average per– | | | |
| | Families | Total | Children | Total | Family | Recipient | Recipients | Amount |
| **Total**[1] | 3,841,208 | 11,101,556 | 7,600,455 | $1,106,656,020 | $288.10 | $ 99.68 | 7.0 | 14.8 |
| Ala. | 63,246 | 178,322 | 127,684 | 6,967,928 | 110.17 | 39.07 | – .4 | .9 |
| Alaska | 6,606 | 15,931 | 10,882 | 2,590,514 | 392.15 | 162.61 | 5.5 | 31.3 |
| Ariz. | 21,573 | 59,809 | 43,589 | 3,809,666 | 176.59 | 63.70 | 19.7 | 26.8 |
| Ark. | 29,822 | 85,008 | 61,667 | 4,360,856 | 146.23 | 51.30 | .4 | 3.1 |
| Calif. | 511,486 | 1,498,216 | 996,054 | 220,451,580 | 431.00 | 147.14 | 10.1 | 27.8 |
| Colo. | 29,467 | 81,031 | 55,415 | 7,591,646 | 257.63 | 93.69 | 8.9 | 17.8 |
| Conn. | 49,407 | 139,685 | 96,240 | 18,308,524 | 370.57 | 131.07 | 2.9 | 14.7 |
| Del. | 12,404 | 34,243 | 23,555 | 2,817,520 | 227.15 | 82.28 | 5.1 | 5.9 |
| D.C. | 30,278 | 81,985 | 56,556 | 7,661,257 | 253.03 | 93.45 | –5.1 | –4.4 |
| Fla. | 103,315 | 279,392 | 199,015 | 18,229,236 | 176.44 | 65.25 | 12.8 | 16.0 |
| Ga. | 89,912 | 233,730 | 168,813 | 12,591,009 | 140.04 | 53.87 | 8.5 | 23.4 |
| Guam | 1,492 | 5,311 | 3,877 | 316,333 | 212.02 | 59.56 | 12.4 | 15.6 |
| Hawaii | 20,046 | 61,342 | 40,802 | 7,731,955 | 385.71 | 126.05 | 2.2 | 3.7 |
| Idaho | 7,503 | 20,326 | 13,845 | 2,064,949 | 275.22 | 101.59 | – .9 | 3.0 |
| Ill. | 222,937 | 691,434 | 482,773 | 62,903,873 | 282.16 | 90.98 | 4.6 | 8.4 |
| Ind. | 60,229 | 170,239 | 119,431 | 12,351,154 | 205.07 | 72.55 | 11.8 | 23.5 |
| Iowa | 40,476 | 111,287 | 73,907 | 12,553,542 | 310.15 | 112.80 | 13.6 | 15.3 |
| Kans. | 27,720 | 71,956 | 50,828 | 7,817,479 | 282.02 | 108.64 | 11.3 | 19.3 |
| Ky. | 67,159 | 175,071 | 122,437 | 12,478,662 | 185.81 | 71.28 | 6.7 | 22.5 |
| La. | 72,163 | 218,966 | 160,212 | 11,254,465 | 155.96 | 51.40 | 4.1 | 19.1 |
| Maine | 21,466 | 57,700 | 39,504 | 4,954,190 | 230.79 | 85.86 | –5.1 | – .9 |
| Md. | 80,823 | 220,316 | 148,989 | 19,304,624 | 238.85 | 87.62 | 5.0 | 17.5 |
| Mass. | 125,232 | 347,830 | 226,570 | 43,793,572 | 349.70 | 125.91 | –1.2 | 7.2 |
| Mich. | 246,648 | 752,578 | 494,459 | 96,243,119 | 390.20 | 127.88 | 16.4 | 21.3 |
| Minn. | 53,856 | 145,634 | 96,383 | 18,582,462 | 345.04 | 127.60 | 11.9 | 20.0 |
| Miss. | 59,814 | 176,253 | 129,704 | 5,257,257 | 87.89 | 29.83 | 2.8 | 5.8 |
| Mo. | 73,506 | 215,682 | 144,865 | 16,795,310 | 228.49 | 77.87 | 12.9 | 24.1 |
| Mont. | 7,136 | 19,883 | 13,621 | 1,646,790 | 230.77 | 82.82 | 8.7 | 12.0 |
| Nebr. | 13,573 | 37,541 | 25,900 | 3,890,757 | 286.65 | 103.64 | 10.6 | 24.8 |
| Nev. | 5,114 | 13,827 | 9,524 | 1,096,034 | 214.32 | 79.27 | 23.9 | 35.7 |
| N.H. | 8,647 | 23,648 | 15,636 | 2,377,068 | 274.90 | 100.52 | 9.7 | 17.2 |
| N.J.[1] | 152,383 | 469,010 | 322,034 | 49,908,100 | 327.52 | 106.41 | 2.8 | 13.1 |
| N.M. | 19,550 | 56,157 | 38,657 | 3,705,145 | 189.52 | 65.98 | 7.8 | 21.9 |
| N.Y. | 367,628 | 1,109,601 | 762,672 | 136,745,976 | 371.97 | 123.24 | 1.3 | 1.9 |
| N.C. | 80,074 | 201,828 | 142,638 | 13,014,235 | 162.53 | 64.48 | 4.3 | 5.5 |
| N.D. | 4,859 | 13,111 | 9,045 | 1,413,489 | 290.90 | 107.81 | 3.2 | 9.9 |
| Ohio | 200,243 | 572,347 | 380,365 | 50,348,940 | 251.44 | 87.97 | 16.9 | 16.9 |
| Okla. | 31,543 | 91,984 | 66,752 | 7,880,651 | 249.84 | 85.67 | 5.5 | 6.4 |
| Oreg. | 35,440 | 93,993 | 60,731 | 9,315,930 | 262.86 | 99.11 | –4.3 | –23.5 |
| Pa.[1] | 218,713 | 637,387 | 435,408 | 64,712,837 | 295.88 | 101.53 | 2.6 | 9.1 |
| P.R. | 46,245 | 169,697 | 118,368 | 2,812,545 | 60.82 | 16.57 | –2.9 | 14.9 |
| R.I. | 18,772 | 53,950 | 36,563 | 7,613,825 | 405.59 | 141.13 | 7.3 | 8.7 |
| S.C. | 57,643 | 156,080 | 110,573 | 6,685,505 | 115.98 | 42.83 | 4.5 | 21.8 |
| S.D. | 6,946 | 18,753 | 13,120 | 1,555,186 | 223.90 | 82.93 | –7.1 | –1.8 |
| Tenn. | 65,958 | 173,854 | 122,637 | 7,448,916 | 112.93 | 42.85 | 10.2 | 10.7 |
| Texas | 106,104 | 320,002 | 232,384 | 11,490,205 | 108.29 | 35.91 | 4.5 | 4.6 |
| Utah | 13,954 | 43,710 | 27,335 | 4,504,653 | 322.82 | 103.06 | 25.9 | 33.8 |
| Vt. | 8,129 | 24,251 | 15,379 | 2,839,074 | 349.25 | 117.07 | 14.7 | 21.2 |
| V.I. | 1,165 | 3,441 | 2,721 | 228,534 | 196.17 | 66.41 | 13.3 | 57.6 |
| Va. | 65,272 | 175,927 | 121,821 | 14,487,213 | 221.95 | 82.35 | 7.8 | 19.1 |
| Wash. | 61,639 | 173,339 | 108,234 | 23,434,682 | 380.19 | 135.20 | 20.9 | 27.2 |
| W. Va. | 28,026 | 79,971 | 60,820 | 4,970,373 | 177.35 | 62.15 | 3.8 | 5.6 |
| Wis. | 85,129 | 231,979 | 154,465 | 32,026,663 | 376.21 | 138.06 | 15.2 | 26.7 |
| Wyo. | 2,737 | 7,008 | 4,996 | 720,012 | 263.07 | 102.74 | 6.5 | 8.3 |

[1] Estimated data.

## DRUG LAW ENFORCEMENT

SOURCE: Drug Enforcement Administration (DEA)

| Item | STATE AND LOCAL ARRESTS | | | | DEA FEDERAL ARRESTS | | | |
|---|---|---|---|---|---|---|---|---|
| | 1977 | 1978 | 1979 | 1980 | 1977 | 1978 | 1979 | 1980 |
| Number of Arrests | 569,293 | 596,940 | 519,377 | 533,010 | 9,369 | 7,433 | 7,943 | 9,714 |
| Arrest Rate per 100,000 | 298.4 | 283.3 | 253.8 | 256.0 | | | | |
| Estimated % by Drug | | | | | | | | |
| Narcotics (heroin, cocaine) | 13.2% | 13.2% | 12.2% | 11.7% | 64.8% | 61.2% | 55.3% | 51.8% |
| Cannabis | 71.2% | 70.9% | 70.0% | 69.8% | 18.2% | 20.9% | 21.3% | 21.2% |
| Dangerous Drug | 15.6% | 15.9% | 17.8% | 18.4% | 16.5% | 17.2% | 21.2% | 24.4% |
| Other | – | – | – | – | .5% | .7% | 2.2% | 2.4% |
| Estimated % by Race | | | | | | | | |
| White | 77.0% | 76.5% | 76.7% | 75.6% | 80.6% | 80.1% | 81.2% | 83.4% |
| Nonwhite | 22.9% | 23.5% | 23.3% | 24.4% | 19.4% | 19.9% | 18.8% | 16.5% |
| Estimated % by Age | | | | | | | | |
| Under 21 | 50.7% | 50.4% | 48.3% | 43.5% | 8.2% | 5.6% | 6.2% | 5.3% |
| 21-24 | 23.2% | 23.0% | 23.6% | 24.4% | 26.5% | 16.7% | 18.2% | 16.3% |
| 25-29 | 14.5% | 14.3% | 15.0% | 16.5% | 28.4% | 27.6% | 26.7% | 23.3% |
| 30-39 | 8.4% | 6.3% | 9.6% | 11.4% | 25.2% | 34.1% | 32.9% | 32.9% |
| 40 or Older | 3.2% | 6.0% | 3.5% | 3.9% | 12.1% | 16.0% | 16.0% | 21.8% |
| Estimated % by Sex | | | | | | | | |
| Male | 86.1% | 86.3% | 85.5% | 86.6% | 85.8% | 87.2% | 87.7% | 85.8% |
| Female | 13.9% | 13.7% | 13.5% | 13.4% | 14.2% | 12.8% | 14.3% | 14.1% |

## DRUGS: USES AND ABUSES

SOURCE: Smith Kline & French

| Drugs | Pharmacologic Classification | Federal Controls | Medical Use | Potential for Physical Dependence | How Taken When Abused | Comments |
|---|---|---|---|---|---|---|
| Morphine (an opium derivative) | Central Nervous System Depressant | Narcotic: Schedule II Controlled Substances Act of 1970 | To relieve pain | Yes | Orally or by injection | Morphine is the standard against which other narcotic analgesics are compared. Legally available on prescription only. |
| Heroin (a morphine derivative) | Depressant | Narcotic: Schedule I C. S. A. of 1970 | To relieve pain | Yes | Sniffed or by injection | Not legally available in the United States. Used medically in some countries for relief of pain. |
| Codeine (an opium derivative) | Depressant | Narcotic C. S. A. of 1970 | To relieve pain and coughing | Yes | Orally (usually as cough syrup) | Preparations containing specified minimal amounts of codeine are classified as "exempt" narcotics (Schedule V) and can be obtained without prescription in some states. |
| Paregoric (preparation containing opium) | Depressant | Narcotic: Schedule II C. S. A. of 1970 | For sedation and to counteract diarrhea | Yes | Orally or by injection | Paregoric is often boiled to concentrate narcotic content prior to injection. Prescription only. |
| Meperidine (synthetic morphine-like drug) | Depressant | Narcotic: Schedule II C. S. A. of 1970 | To relieve pain | Yes | Orally or by injection | Shorter acting than morphine. Frequent dosing required. Withdrawal symptoms appear quickly. Prescription only. |
| Methadone (synthetic morphine-like drug) | Depressant | Narcotic: Schedule II C. S. A. of 1970 | To relieve pain | Yes | Orally or by injection | Longer acting than morphine. Withdrawal symptoms develop more slowly and are less intense and more prolonged. Prescription only. |
| Cocaine | Central Nervous System Stimulant | Schedule II C. S. A. of 1970 | Local anesthetic | No | Sniffed or by injection | |
| Marijuana | Hallucinogen | Schedule I | No | **No** | Smoked or orally | Available legally only for research. |
| Barbiturates (e.g., amobarbital, pentobarbital, secobarbital) | Depressant | Schedule II and III C. S. A. of 1970 | For sedation, sleep-producing, epilepsy, high blood pressure | Yes | Orally or by injection | Written prescription only. No refills for Schedule II barbiturates. For Schedule III barbiturates original prescription expires after 6 months. Only 5 refills permitted within this period. Dependence generally occurs only with the use of high doses for a protracted period of time. |
| Amphetamine drugs (e.g., amphetamine, dextroamphetamine, methamphetamine—also known as desoxyephedrine) | Stimulant | Schedule II C. S. A. of 1970 | For antiappetite, narcolepsy, hyperkinetic behavior disorders | No | Orally or by injection | Written prescription only. No refills permitted. |
| LSD (also mescaline, peyote, psilocybin, DMT, STP, THC) | Hallucinogen | Schedule I C. S. A. of 1970 | Medical research only | No | Orally or by injection | |

## U.S. INDEX OF CRIME Source: Federal Bureau of Investigation

**TRENDS BY GEOGRAPHIC REGION** (Percent change, 1981 over 1980)

| | Total | Violent | Property | Murder | Forcible Rape | Robbery | Aggravated Assault | Burglary | Larceny-Theft | Motor Vehicle Theft |
|---|---|---|---|---|---|---|---|---|---|---|
| Northeastern States | 0 | + 5 | − 1 | − 2 | + 2 | + 9 | 0 | − 3 | 0 | − 2 |
| North Central States | − 1 | − 3 | − 1 | − 5 | − 5 | 0 | − 6 | 0 | − 1 | − 4 |
| Southern States | + 1 | + 2 | + 1 | 0 | 0 | + 4 | + 1 | 0 | + 2 | − 2 |
| Western States | 0 | − 1 | 0 | − 7 | − 2 | + 3 | − 4 | 0 | + 1 | − 9 |
| TOTAL | 0 | + 1 | 0 | − 3 | − 1 | + 5 | − 2 | − 1 | 0 | − 4 |
| **TRENDS BY YEARS (Percent change 1968-1980, each year over previous year)** | | | | | | | | | | |
| 1970/1969 | + 9 | +12 | + 9 | + 8 | + 2 | +17 | + 8 | +11 | + 9 | + 6 |
| 1971/1970 | + 6 | +11 | + 6 | +11 | +11 | +11 | +10 | + 9 | + 5 | + 2 |
| 1972/1971 | − 4 | + 2 | − 5 | + 5 | +11 | − 3 | + 7 | − 1 | − 6 | − 6 |
| 1973/1972 | + 6 | + 5 | + 6 | + 5 | +10 | + 2 | + 7 | + 8 | + 5 | + 5 |
| 1974/1973 | +18 | +11 | +18 | + 5 | + 8 | +15 | + 8 | +18 | +21 | + 5 |
| 1975/1974 | +10 | + 5 | +10 | − 1 | + 1 | + 5 | + 6 | + 7 | +14 | + 2 |
| 1976/1975 | 0 | − 4 | + 1 | − 8 | + 1 | −10 | + 1 | − 5 | + 5 | − 4 |
| 1977/1976 | − 3 | + 2 | − 4 | + 2 | +11 | − 4 | + 6 | − 1 | − 6 | + 1 |
| 1978/1977 | + 2 | + 5 | + 2 | + 2 | + 7 | + 3 | + 7 | + 2 | + 1 | + 2 |
| 1979/1978 | + 9 | +11 | + 9 | +10 | +13 | +12 | +10 | + 6 | +10 | +11 |
| 1980/1979 | + 9 | +11 | + 9 | + 7 | + 8 | +18 | + 7 | +14 | + 8 | + 2 |
| 1981/1980 | 0 | + 1 | 0 | − 3 | − 1 | + 5 | − 2 | − 1 | 0 | − 4 |

## CRIME: U.S. CITIES (Offenses Known to the Police, 1980 and 1981)

Source: Federal Bureau of Investigation

Preliminary figures for cities over 100,000 population reporting more than 11,000 incidents.

| City | Crime Index 1980 | Crime Index 1981 |
|---|---|---|
| Akron, Ohio | 18,448 | 18,524 |
| Albuquerque, N. Mex. | 29,326 | 30,614 |
| Anaheim, Calif. | 17,131 | 17,202 |
| Anchorage, Alaska | 11,724 | 13,731 |
| Arlington, Texas | 11,341 | 11,541 |
| Atlanta, Ga. | 55,949 | 60,569 |
| Aurora, Colo. | 12,089 | 11,903 |
| Austin, Texas | 30,067 | 30,867 |
| Baltimore, Md. | 76,704 | 77,563 |
| Baton Rouge, La. | 26,226 | 25,917 |
| Beaumont, Texas | 11,346 | 13,242 |
| Berkeley, Calif. | 13,000 | 14,563 |
| Birmingham, Ala. | 35,403 | 34,249 |
| Boston, Mass. | 75,755 | 79,643 |
| Bridgeport, Conn. | 15,627 | 17,360 |
| Charlotte, N.C. | 26,196 | 29,646 |
| Chattanooga, Tenn. | 16,098 | 13,555 |
| Chicago, Ill. | 196,605 | 173,316 |
| Cincinnati, Ohio | 32,987 | 36,814 |
| Cleveland, Ohio | 57,002 | 60,721 |
| Colorado Springs, Colo. | 16,910 | 18,836 |
| Columbus, Ohio | 55,362 | 55,293 |
| Corpus Christi, Texas | 19,385 | 21,216 |
| Dallas, Texas | 106,010 | 111,585 |
| Dayton, Ohio | 26,593 | 27,053 |
| Denver, Colo. | 58,745 | 60,417 |
| Des Moines, Iowa | 19,369 | 19,974 |
| Detroit, Mich. | 127,423 | 143,107 |
| El Paso, Texas | 27,065 | 29,275 |
| Flint, Mich. | 21,201 | 23,649 |
| Fort Lauderdale, Fla. | 20,955 | 22,022 |
| Fort Wayne, Ind. | 15,101 | 13,112 |
| Fort Worth, Texas | 48,492 | 47,153 |
| Fresno, Calif. | 24,806 | 24,581 |
| Gary, Ind. | 12,446 | 12,268 |
| Grand Rapids, Mich. | 16,185 | 17,049 |
| Greensboro, N.C. | 12,462 | 12,018 |
| Hartford, Conn. | 23,648 | 24,732 |
| Hollywood, Fla. | 12,810 | 13,451 |
| Honolulu, Hawaii | 57,718 | 49,548 |
| Huntsville, Ala. | 13,144 | 12,078 |
| Indianapolis, Ind. | 37,220 | 33,898 |
| Jackson, Miss. | 16,209 | 18,585 |
| Jacksonville, Fla. | 42,890 | 45,070 |
| Jersey City, N.J. | 19,245 | 19,926 |
| Kansas City, Kansas | 17,495 | 18,123 |
| Kansas City, Mo. | 49,274 | 51,005 |
| Knoxville, Tenn. | 12,423 | 12,527 |
| Las Vegas, Nev. | 41,405 | 43,376 |
| Lexington, Ky. | 15,566 | 16,836 |
| Little Rock, Ark. | 17,851 | 18,781 |
| Long Beach, Calif. | 32,314 | 32,280 |
| Los Angeles, Calif. | 293,837 | 304,101 |
| Louisville, Ky. | 20,072 | 21,124 |
| Lubbock, Texas | 13,492 | 15,418 |
| Madison, Wis. | 14,796 | 14,898 |
| Memphis, Tenn. | 50,921 | 53,325 |
| Mesa, Ariz. | 12,098 | 11,170 |
| Miami, Fla. | 52,540 | 52,911 |
| Milwaukee, Wis. | 41,446 | 44,775 |
| Minneapolis, Minn. | 35,820 | 40,111 |
| Mobile, Ala. | 21,088 | 21,998 |
| Montgomery, Ala. | 12,852 | 11,512 |
| Nashville, Tenn. | 34,886 | 33,604 |
| New Haven, Conn. | 17,834 | 16,175 |
| New Orleans, La. | 53,575 | 52,158 |
| New York, N.Y. | 710,151 | 725,846 |
| Norfolk, Va. | 20,183 | 20,769 |
| Oakland, Calif. | 44,152 | 44,679 |
| Oklahoma City, Okla. | 36,191 | 35,128 |
| Omaha, Nebr. | 24,430 | 24,351 |
| Orlando, Fla. | 17,532 | 17,469 |
| Pasadena, Calif. | 11,675 | 11,305 |
| Paterson, N.J. | 14,260 | 14,713 |
| Peoria, Ill. | 12,098 | 11,822 |
| Philadelphia, Pa. | 101,144 | 100,592 |
| Phoenix, Ariz. | 88,523 | 81,371 |
| Pittsburgh, Pa. | 30,399 | 31,384 |
| Portland, Ore. | 40,833 | 50,432 |
| Providence, R.I. | 14,317 | 15,548 |
| Richmond, Va. | 21,493 | 24,765 |
| Riverside, Calif. | 15,626 | 15,361 |
| Rochester, N.Y. | 28,989 | 27,291 |
| Rockford, Ill. | 12,741 | 12,859 |
| Sacramento, Calif. | 34,699 | 36,681 |
| St. Louis, Mo. | 64,631 | 62,654 |
| St. Paul, Minn. | 22,134 | 22,799 |
| St. Petersburg, Fla. | 21,067 | 20,894 |
| Salt Lake City, Utah | 19,086 | 20,850 |
| San Antonio, Texas | 57,873 | 62,035 |
| San Bernardino, Calif. | 16,392 | 17,327 |
| San Diego, Calif. | 70,505 | 66,122 |
| San Francisco, Calif. | 70,424 | 71,812 |
| San Jose, Calif. | 51,831 | 54,514 |
| Santa Ana, Calif. | 19,033 | 20,712 |
| Savannah, Ga. | 14,656 | 15,369 |
| Seattle, Wash. | 53,294 | 55,764 |
| Shreveport, La. | 18,784 | 16,030 |
| South Bend, Ind. | 11,433 | 11,736 |
| Spokane, Wash. | 16,437 | 15,698 |
| Springfield, Mass. | 14,410 | 14,442 |
| Springfield, Mo. | 13,472 | 13,414 |
| Stockton, Calif. | 16,502 | 17,271 |
| Syracuse, N.Y. | 13,828 | 14,445 |
| Tacoma, Wash. | 16,516 | 16,193 |
| Tampa, Fla. | 38,903 | 40,856 |
| Toledo, Ohio | 34,047 | 34,091 |
| Tucson, Ariz. | 35,947 | 37,241 |
| Tulsa, Okla. | 32,017 | 30,260 |
| Virginia Beach, Va. | 15,069 | 15,337 |
| Washington, D.C. | 63,668 | 67,910 |
| Wichita, Kans. | 24,562 | 25,863 |
| Winston-Salem, N.C. | 12,973 | 12,611 |
| Yonkers, N.Y. | 11,522 | 11,212 |

## CAPITAL PUNISHMENT

### ABOLITION COUNTRIES[1]

| | |
|---|---|
| Australia | |
| Federal[2] | 1945 |
| New South Wales[2] | 1955 |
| Queensland[2] | 1922 |
| Tasmania[2] | 1968 |
| Austria | 1968 |
| Belgium[4] | 1867 |
| Bolivia | 1962 |
| Brazil | 1979 |
| Canada | 1976 |
| Colombia | 1910 |
| Costa Rica | 1870 |
| Denmark | 1978 |
| Dominican Republic | 1924 |
| Ecuador | 1897 |
| Finland[3] | 1949 |
| West Germany | 1949 |
| Honduras | 1957 |
| Iceland | 1940 |
| India (Travencore) | 1944 |
| Israel[2] | 1954 |
| Italy[3] | 1944 |
| Liechtenstein | (1798) |
| Luxembourg | 1979 |
| Mexico[5] | 1970 |
| Monaco | 1962 |
| Nepal | 1950 |
| Netherlands | 1886 |
| New Zealand | 1961 |
| Nicaragua | 1979 |
| Norway | 1905 |
| Panama | 1915 |
| Portugal | 1867 |
| San Marino | 1848 |
| Spain | 1978 |
| Sweden[3] | 1921 |
| Switzerland | 1942 |
| United Kingdom | 1969 |
| Uruguay | 1907 |
| Vatican City State | 1969 |
| Venezuela | 1864 |

[1]Capital punishment abolished de jure as of year indicated; if abolished only de facto, date in parentheses indicates year of last execution. [2]Death penalty retained for certain exceptional crimes other than murder, rape, burglary, robbery, arson, and kidnapping. [3]Death penalty retained for use in wartime or under military law. [4]One murderer executed during World War I in 1918. [5]Death penalty retained in 3 of 32 states.

| Death Penalty States | Year of Last Execution | Death Penalty States | Year of Last Execution |
|---|---|---|---|
| Ala. | 1965 | Mont. | 1943 |
| Ariz. | 1963 | Nebr. | 1959 |
| Ark. | 1964 | Nev. | 1979 |
| Calif. | 1967 | N.H. | 1939 |
| Colo. | 1967 | N.J.† | 1963 |
| Conn. | 1960 | N.M. | 1960 |
| Del. | 1946 | N.Y. | 1963 |
| Fla. | 1979 | N.C. | 1961 |
| Ga. | 1964 | Ohio | 1963 |
| Idaho | 1957 | Oklahoma | 1966 |
| Ill. | 1962 | Penn. | 1962 |
| Ind. | 1981 | S.C. | 1962 |
| Ky. | 1962 | S.D. | NA |
| La. | 1961 | Tenn. | 1960 |
| Md. | 1961 | Texas | 1964 |
| Miss. | 1964 | Utah | 1977 |
| Mo. | 1965 | Vt. | 1950 |
| | | Va. | 1962 |
| | | Wash. | 1963 |
| | | Wyo. | 1965 |

†Death penalty restored Aug. 1982.

### UNITED STATES*

In the United States, 13 states and the District of Columbia have no laws authorizing the use of the death penalty: Alaska, Hawaii, Iowa, Kansas, Maine, Massachusetts, Michigan, Minnesota, North Dakota, Oregon, Rhode Island, West Virginia and Wisconsin.

*Primary source: *Death-row Prisoners, 1981*, BJS bulletin NCJ-83191

Except for a few special cases, all states have abolished the *mandatory* death penalty for murder, rape, and other crimes. This is the result of landmark rulings of the U.S. Supreme Court in 1972 and 1976. In the 1972 "Furman vs. Georgia" case, the Court ruled that capital punishment could not be applied in an arbitrary manner. Since then, 35 states and the Federal government have revised their laws, and currently a total of 37 states have capital punishment laws on the books.

In 1976, the U.S. Supreme Court struck down two death penalty laws (Louisiana and North Carolina) because they contained mandatory death sentences. However, it upheld three laws (Georgia, Florida, and Texas) which allowed for discretion of the judge and jury in determining the sentence. Most death penalty states have modeled their laws in compliance with these decisions, referred to collectively as the "Gregg" rule.

According to the Bureau of Justice Statistics, the death-row population rose to 838 as of Dec. 31, 1981—the highest year-end total ever recorded. In contrast, only 77 persons were relieved of the death sentence during the year, and one person, Steven T. Judy of Indiana, was executed on March 9. Florida, Texas, and Georgia combined had nearly half of all prisoners on death row.

There were several new developments in 1981. On May 4, the U.S. Supreme Court ruled that protection against "double jeopardy" applies to capital punishment. Thus, a convict once sentenced to imprisonment could not be later sentenced to death for the same crime. Also in May, the Court ruled in "Estelle vs. Smith" that any pretrial psychiatric testimony in which a defendant had not been warned of his rights could not be used by the prosecution during sentencing. The Bureau of Justice Statistics projects that this ruling could affect nearly half of the death-row population in Texas. In addition, 1981 was the first year in which the states reported whether their death penalty laws provide for automatic appeal. All of them do, with the exception of Arkansas, New York, and the Federal government. Also in 1981 Oregon struck down its death penalty law on January 20, while Ohio restored its law on July 1.

Several major events also took place in August 1982. In New Jersey, Governor Kean signed a death penalty law on August 6, nearly a decade since the previous law had been voided by the "Furman" decision. On August 10, Frank J. Coppola was executed in Virginia, making him the fifth death-row inmate to be executed since 1977. On August 11 the *New York Times* reported death-row figures currently topping 1,000.

**Prisoners on Death Row as of December 31, 1981**

| State | Total | Law | State | Total | Law |
|---|---|---|---|---|---|
| Ala. | 16 | post-Furman[1] | Nebr. | 12 | post-Furman |
| Ariz. | 38 | post-Furman | Nev. | 12 | post-Gregg |
| Ark. | 23 | post-Furman | N.H. | — | post-Gregg |
| Calif. | 83 | post-Gregg | N.M. | 3 | post-Gregg |
| Colo. | 1 | post-Furman | N.C. | 17 | post-Gregg |
| Conn. | — | post-Furman | N.Y. | — | pre-Furman[1,2] |
| Del. | 4 | post-Gregg | Ohio | — | post-Gregg |
| Fla. | 161 | post-Furman | Okla. | 36 | post-Gregg |
| Ga. | 91 | post-Furman | Pa. | 11 | post-Furman |
| Idaho | 2 | post-Gregg | S.C. | 21 | post-Gregg |
| Ill. | 41 | post-Gregg | S.D. | — | post-Gregg |
| Ind. | 10 | post-Gregg | Tenn. | 21 | post-Gregg |
| Ky. | 9 | post-Gregg | Tex. | 144 | post-Furman |
| La. | 10 | post-Gregg | Utah | 3 | post-Gregg |
| Md. | 8 | post-Gregg | Vt. | — | pre-Furman[2] |
| Miss. | 27 | post-Gregg | Va. | 17 | post-Gregg |
| Mo. | 14 | post-Gregg | Wash. | — | post-Gregg |
| Mont. | 3 | post-Gregg | Wyo. | — | post-Gregg |

[1]Pre-Furman law for homicide by a person serving a life sentence. [2]Unchallenged because unused since "Furman" rule.

## EXECUTIONS IN THE UNITED STATES**

SOURCE: U.S. Dept. of Justice, Bureau of Justice Statistics

| Year | Prisoners Executed: Total | White | Black | Other |
|---|---|---|---|---|
| Total (1930-81) | 3,863 | 1,755 | 2,066 | 42 |
| Percent | 100.0 | 45.4 | 53.5 | 1.1 |
| 1981 | 1 | 1 | — | — |
| 1980 | — | — | — | — |
| 1979 | 2 | 2 | — | — |
| 1978 | — | — | — | — |
| 1977 | 1 | 1 | — | — |
| 1967 | 2 | 1 | 1 | — |
| 1966 | 1 | 1 | — | — |
| 1965 | 7 | 6 | 1 | — |
| 1964 | 15 | 8 | 7 | — |
| 1963 | 21 | 13 | 8 | — |
| 1962 | 47 | 28 | 19 | — |
| 1961 | 42 | 20 | 22 | — |
| 1960 | 56 | 21 | 35 | — |
| 1959 | 49 | 16 | 33 | — |
| 1958 | 49 | 20 | 28 | 1 |
| 1957 | 65 | 34 | 31 | — |
| 1956 | 65 | 21 | 43 | 1 |
| 1955 | 76 | 44 | 32 | — |
| 1954 | 81 | 38 | 42 | 1 |
| 1953 | 62 | 30 | 31 | 1 |
| 1952 | 83 | 36 | 47 | — |
| 1951 | 105 | 57 | 47 | 1 |
| 1950 | 82 | 40 | 42 | — |
| 1949 | 119 | 50 | 67 | 2 |
| 1948 | 119 | 35 | 82 | 2 |
| 1947 | 153 | 42 | 111 | — |
| 1946 | 131 | 46 | 84 | 1 |
| 1945 | 117 | 41 | 75 | 1 |
| 1944 | 120 | 47 | 70 | 3 |
| 1943 | 131 | 54 | 74 | 3 |
| 1942 | 147 | 67 | 80 | — |
| 1941 | 123 | 59 | 63 | 1 |
| 1940 | 124 | 49 | 75 | — |
| 1939 | 160 | 80 | 77 | 3 |
| 1938 | 190 | 96 | 92 | 2 |
| 1937 | 147 | 69 | 74 | 4 |
| 1936 | 195 | 92 | 101 | 2 |
| 1935 | 199 | 119 | 77 | 3 |
| 1934 | 168 | 65 | 102 | 1 |
| 1932 | 140 | 6[illegible] | 75 | 3 |
| 1930 | 155 | 90 | 65 | — |

**No executions took place 1968-1976.

# CIVIL RIGHTS/RACE

## CIVIL RIGHTS LEGISLATION

SOURCE: Congressional Quarterly Inc.

Six major civil rights bills have been passed by Congress since 1957. Highlights of these bills are:

**1957**—The Civil Rights Act of 1957 (HR 6127-PL 85-315) was the first civil rights legislation passed by Congress since the Reconstruction period. It prohibited action to prevent persons from voting in federal elections, authorizing the Attorney General to bring suit when a person was deprived of his voting rights. It also created a Civil Rights Commission and set up a Civil Rights Division in the Department of Justice.

**1960**—The Civil Rights Act of 1960 (HR 8601-PL 86-449) strengthened provisions of the 1957 Act for court enforcement of voting rights and required that voting records be preserved. It also contained limited criminal penalty provisions relating to bombing and to obstruction of federal court orders.

**1964**—The Civil Rights Act of 1964 (HR 7152-PL 88-352) prohibited discrimination on the basis of race, sex, or national origin in public accommodations and in federally assisted programs. It also prohibited discrimination by employers and unions.

**1965**—The Voting Rights Act of 1965 (S 1564-PL 89-110) authorized the Attorney General to appoint federal examiners to register voters in certain areas.

**1968**—A civil rights bill (HR 2516-PL 90-284) prohibited discrimination in the sale or rental of about 80 percent of all housing. It also protected persons exercising specified rights, such as attending school.

**1970**—A bill (HR 4249-PL 91-285) amended and extended the Voting Rights Act of 1965. It extended its application to Northern cities or counties where literacy tests are required.

**1975**—The Voting Rights Act was extended for seven years.

**1982**—The Voting Rights Act was extended for 25 years.

## U.S. POPULATION BY RACE AND SPANISH ORIGIN: 1980

SOURCE: Bureau of the Census: (1980 Census of Population—PC80-S1-3)

| | | | American Indian, Eskimo, and Aleut | | | | | |
|---|---|---|---|---|---|---|---|---|
| REGIONS AND STATES | White | Black | American Indian | Eskimo | Aleut | Chinese | Filipino | Japanese |
| United States, total | 188,340,790 | 26,488,218 | 1,361,869 | 42,149 | 14,177 | 806,027 | 774,640 | 700,747 |
| Northeast Region | 42,328,154 | 4,848,786 | 76,574 | 890 | 718 | 217,730 | 75,104 | 46,930 |
| Maine | 1,109,850 | 3,128 | 4,057 | 17 | 13 | 484 | 666 | 336 |
| N.H. | 910,099 | 3,990 | 1,297 | 41 | 14 | 790 | 314 | 448 |
| Vt. | 506,736 | 1,135 | 968 | 8 | 8 | 271 | 101 | 227 |
| Mass. | 5,362,836 | 221,279 | 7,483 | 129 | 131 | 25,015 | 3,073 | 4,483 |
| R.I. | 896,692 | 27,584 | 2,872 | 14 | 12 | 1,718 | 1,218 | 474 |
| Conn. | 2,799,420 | 217,433 | 4,431 | 68 | 34 | 4,691 | 3,132 | 1,864 |
| N.Y. | 13,961,106 | 2,401,842 | 38,117 | 330 | 285 | 148,104 | 33,956 | 24,524 |
| N.J. | 6,127,090 | 924,786 | 8,176 | 130 | 88 | 23,366 | 24,377 | 9,905 |
| Pa. | 10,654,325 | 1,047,609 | 9,173 | 153 | 133 | 13,291 | 8,267 | 4,669 |
| North Central Region | 52,183,794 | 5,336,542 | 246,456 | 1,286 | 763 | 72,905 | 79,945 | 44,426 |
| Ohio | 9,597,266 | 1,076,734 | 11,986 | 167 | 87 | 9,911 | 7,435 | 5,479 |
| Ind. | 5,004,567 | 414,732 | 7,681 | 107 | 47 | 3,974 | 3,625 | 2,356 |
| Ill. | 9,225,575 | 1,675,229 | 15,833 | 242 | 196 | 28,590 | 43,839 | 18,550 |
| Mich. | 7,868,956 | 1,198,710 | 39,702 | 208 | 128 | 10,993 | 11,162 | 5,859 |
| Wis. | 4,442,598 | 182,593 | 29,318 | 110 | 69 | 4,097 | 2,698 | 2,237 |
| Minn. | 3,936,948 | 53,342 | 34,841 | 118 | 67 | 4,835 | 2,675 | 2,790 |
| Iowa | 2,838,805 | 41,700 | 5,367 | 59 | 27 | 2,110 | 1,225 | 1,049 |
| Mo. | 4,346,267 | 514,274 | 12,127 | 119 | 73 | 4,290 | 4,029 | 2,651 |
| N.D. | 625,536 | 2,568 | 20,119 | 32 | 6 | 305 | 446 | 230 |
| S.D. | 638,955 | 2,144 | 45,081 | 17 | 3 | 269 | 282 | 262 |
| Nebr. | 1,490,569 | 48,389 | 9,147 | 26 | 24 | 1,106 | 867 | 1,378 |
| Kans. | 2,167,752 | 126,127 | 15,254 | 81 | 36 | 2,425 | 1,662 | 1,585 |
| South Region | 58,944,057 | 14,041,374 | 369,497 | 1,580 | 1,046 | 90,616 | 82,596 | 44,636 |
| Del. | 488,543 | 95,971 | 1,309 | 13 | 8 | 1,004 | 813 | 426 |
| Md. | 3,158,412 | 958,050 | 7,823 | 113 | 85 | 14,485 | 10,965 | 4,805 |
| D.C. | 171,796 | 448,229 | 996 | 19 | 16 | 2,475 | 1,297 | 752 |
| Va. | 4,229,734 | 1,008,311 | 9,093 | 156 | 87 | 9,360 | 18,901 | 5,207 |
| W. Va. | 1,874,751 | 65,051 | 1,555 | 37 | 18 | 881 | 1,313 | 404 |
| N.C. | 4,453,010 | 1,316,050 | 64,519 | 57 | 59 | 3,170 | 2,542 | 3,186 |
| S.C. | 2,145,122 | 948,146 | 5,666 | 70 | 22 | 1,388 | 3,697 | 1,414 |
| Ga. | 3,948,007 | 1,465,457 | 7,444 | 108 | 67 | 4,324 | 2,792 | 3,370 |
| Fla. | 8,178,387 | 1,342,478 | 18,981 | 199 | 136 | 13,471 | 14,212 | 5,565 |
| Ky. | 3,379,648 | 259,490 | 3,518 | 59 | 33 | 1,318 | 1,443 | 1,056 |
| Tenn. | 3,835,078 | 725,949 | 5,012 | 62 | 29 | 2,909 | 1,901 | 1,657 |
| Ala. | 2,869,688 | 995,623 | 7,483 | 50 | 28 | 1,503 | 960 | 1,394 |
| Miss. | 1,615,190 | 887,206 | 6,131 | 28 | 21 | 1,835 | 1,442 | 687 |
| Ark. | 1,890,002 | 373,192 | 9,346 | 48 | 17 | 1,275 | 921 | 754 |
| La. | 2,911,243 | 1,237,263 | 11,950 | 59 | 55 | 3,298 | 2,614 | 1,482 |
| Okla. | 2,597,783 | 204,658 | 169,297 | 107 | 60 | 2,461 | 1,687 | 1,975 |
| Texas | 11,197,663 | 1,710,250 | 39,374 | 395 | 305 | 25,459 | 15,096 | 10,502 |
| West Region | 34,884,785 | 2,261,516 | 669,342 | 38,393 | 11,650 | 424,776 | 536,995 | 564,755 |
| Mont. | 740,148 | 1,786 | 37,153 | 79 | 38 | 346 | 458 | 754 |
| Idaho | 901,641 | 2,716 | 10,418 | 76 | 27 | 905 | 680 | 2,585 |
| Wyo. | 447,716 | 3,364 | 7,088 | 27 | 10 | 392 | 253 | 600 |
| Colo. | 2,570,615 | 101,702 | 17,726 | 235 | 98 | 3,897 | 2,901 | 9,858 |
| N. Mex. | 976,465 | 24,042 | 104,634 | 88 | 55 | 1,441 | 1,182 | 1,280 |
| Ariz. | 2,240,033 | 75,034 | 152,610 | 138 | 109 | 6,820 | 3,363 | 4,074 |
| Utah | 1,382,550 | 9,225 | 19,158 | 81 | 17 | 2,730 | 928 | 5,474 |
| Nev. | 699,377 | 50,791 | 13,201 | 74 | 29 | 2,978 | 4,037 | 2,308 |
| Wash. | 3,777,296 | 105,544 | 58,159 | 1,251 | 1,361 | 18,113 | 24,363 | 26,369 |
| Oreg. | 2,490,192 | 37,059 | 26,587 | 407 | 315 | 8,033 | 4,257 | 8,429 |
| Calif. | 18,031,689 | 1,819,282 | 198,095 | 1,734 | 1,482 | 322,340 | 357,514 | 261,817 |
| Alaska | 308,455 | 13,619 | 21,849 | 34,135 | 8,063 | 521 | 3,095 | 1,589 |
| Hawaii | 318,608 | 17,352 | 2,664 | 68 | 46 | 56,260 | 133,964 | 239,618 |

## EMPLOYMENT IN URBAN POVERTY AREAS

SOURCE: Bureau of Labor Statistics

| U.S. Employment Status | TOTAL 1980* | TOTAL 1981 | WHITE 1980* | WHITE 1981 | BLACK AND OTHER 1980* | BLACK AND OTHER 1981 |
|---|---|---|---|---|---|---|
| **Total United States** | | | | | | |
| Civilian labor force | 106,940,000 | 108,670,000 | 93,600,000 | 95,052,000 | 13,340,000 | 13,618,000 |
| Unemployed | 7,637,000 | 8,273,000 | 5,884,000 | 6,343,000 | 1,752,000 | 1,930,000 |
| Unemployment rate (percent) | 7.1 | 7.6 | 6.3 | 6.7 | 13.1 | 14.2 |
| **Poverty Areas** | | | | | | |
| Civilian labor force | 16,973,000 | 17,100,000 | 12,293,000 | 12,371,000 | 4,680,000 | 4,729,000 |
| Unemployed | 1,692,000 | 1,831,000 | 927,000 | 988,000 | 766,000 | 844,000 |
| Unemployment rate (percent) | 10.0 | 10.7 | 7.5 | 8.0 | 16.4 | 17.8 |

*Data for 1980 have been revised to reflect 1980 census population controls.

| Asian and Pacific Islander | | | | | | | |
|---|---|---|---|---|---|---|---|
| Indian | Korean | Vietnamese | Hawaiian | Samoan | Guamanian | Spanish Origin | REGIONS AND STATES |
| 361,544 | 354,529 | 261,714 | 167,253 | 42,050 | 32,132 | 14,605,883 | United States, total |
| 120,761 | 68,152 | 24,855 | 3,786 | 804 | 1,637 | 2,604,261 | Northeast Region |
| 392 | 481 | 465 | 58 | 16 | 49 | 5,005 | Maine |
| 563 | 515 | 209 | 64 | 13 | 13 | 5,587 | N.H. |
| 343 | 288 | 85 | 18 | 8 | 14 | 3,304 | Vt. |
| 8,387 | 4,655 | 3,172 | 374 | 145 | 197 | 141,043 | Mass. |
| 851 | 592 | 314 | 71 | 14 | 51 | 19,707 | R.I. |
| 4,995 | 2,116 | 1,825 | 177 | 69 | 101 | 124,499 | Conn. |
| 60,511 | 34,157 | 6,644 | 1,566 | 296 | 773 | 1,659,245 | N.Y. |
| 29,507 | 12,845 | 2,884 | 632 | 92 | 234 | 491,867 | N.J. |
| 15,212 | 12,503 | 9,257 | 826 | 151 | 205 | 154,004 | Pa. |
| 85,119 | 62,149 | 36,633 | 5,174 | 1,242 | 2,154 | 1,276,405 | North Central Region |
| 13,105 | 7,257 | 3,509 | 768 | 117 | 232 | 119,880 | Ohio |
| 4,290 | 3,253 | 2,338 | 475 | 54 | 123 | 87,020 | Ind. |
| 35,711 | 23,980 | 7,025 | 1,063 | 187 | 606 | 635,525 | Ill. |
| 14,680 | 8,700 | 4,208 | 798 | 105 | 226 | 162,388 | Mich. |
| 3,657 | 2,643 | 2,249 | 383 | 48 | 153 | 62,981 | Wis. |
| 3,669 | 6,318 | 5,866 | 243 | 40 | 97 | 32,124 | Minn. |
| 2,147 | 2,259 | 2,476 | 182 | 59 | 70 | 25,536 | Iowa |
| 4,099 | 3,519 | 3,179 | 633 | 478 | 230 | 51,667 | Mo. |
| 294 | 342 | 283 | 46 | 13 | 20 | 3,903 | N.D. |
| 182 | 258 | 378 | 45 | 24 | 28 | 4,028 | S.D. |
| 928 | 993 | 1,432 | 160 | 27 | 105 | 28,020 | Nebr. |
| 2,357 | 2,627 | 3,690 | 378 | 90 | 264 | 63,333 | Kans. |
| 83,586 | 70,375 | 80,240 | 10,500 | 2,154 | 5,059 | 4,473,172 | South Region |
| 1,075 | 495 | 205 | 65 | 6 | 43 | 9,671 | Del. |
| 13,705 | 15,087 | 4,131 | 616 | 82 | 400 | 64,740 | Md. |
| 950 | 338 | 505 | 237 | 15 | 66 | 17,652 | D.C. |
| 8,483 | 12,550 | 10,000 | 903 | 270 | 535 | 79,873 | Va. |
| 1,641 | 587 | 253 | 74 | 14 | 27 | 12,707 | W. Va. |
| 4,718 | 3,581 | 2,391 | 839 | 241 | 500 | 56,607 | N.C. |
| 2,143 | 1,390 | 1,072 | 438 | 77 | 188 | 33,414 | S.C. |
| 4,347 | 5,970 | 2,294 | 778 | 177 | 409 | 61,261 | Ga. |
| 9,138 | 4,673 | 7,592 | 1,377 | 252 | 476 | 857,898 | Fla. |
| 2,226 | 2,102 | 1,090 | 342 | 129 | 265 | 27,403 | Ky. |
| 3,195 | 2,237 | 1,391 | 432 | 83 | 158 | 34,081 | Tenn. |
| 1,992 | 1,782 | 1,333 | 516 | 69 | 146 | 33,100 | Ala. |
| 1,163 | 576 | 1,281 | 330 | 22 | 76 | 24,731 | Miss. |
| 832 | 583 | 2,042 | 257 | 6 | 62 | 17,873 | Ark. |
| 2,873 | 1,729 | 10,877 | 563 | 121 | 214 | 99,105 | La. |
| 2,879 | 2,698 | 4,671 | 515 | 87 | 301 | 57,413 | Okla. |
| 22,226 | 13,997 | 29,112 | 2,218 | 503 | 1,193 | 2,985,643 | Texas |
| 72,078 | 153,853 | 119,986 | 147,793 | 37,850 | 23,282 | 6,252,045 | West Region |
| 162 | 301 | 275 | 135 | 24 | 48 | 9,974 | Mont. |
| 310 | 610 | 429 | 318 | 59 | 52 | 36,615 | Idaho |
| 176 | 235 | 167 | 102 | 15 | 29 | 24,499 | Wyo. |
| 2,298 | 5,316 | 4,026 | 861 | 173 | 567 | 339,300 | Colo. |
| 805 | 705 | 1,043 | 217 | 61 | 82 | 476,089 | N. Mex. |
| 2,101 | 2,446 | 1,989 | 804 | 147 | 354 | 440,915 | Ariz. |
| 830 | 1,319 | 2,108 | 844 | 763 | 80 | 60,302 | Utah |
| 622 | 2,044 | 1,123 | 609 | 135 | 253 | 53,786 | Nev. |
| 4,002 | 13,077 | 9,833 | 2,974 | 1,830 | 1,942 | 119,986 | Wash. |
| 1,938 | 4,427 | 5,564 | 1,488 | 244 | 387 | 65,833 | Oreg. |
| 57,989 | 103,891 | 89,587 | 23,091 | 20,096 | 17,662 | 4,543,770 | Calif. |
| 241 | 1,534 | 383 | 388 | 135 | 149 | 9,497 | Alaska |
| 604 | 17,948 | 3,459 | 115,962 | 14,168 | 1,677 | 71,479 | Hawaii |

## WOMEN'S RIGHTS: SOCIAL HISTORY OF AMERICAN WOMEN

**1821** Emma Willard founds the Troy Female Seminary, the first endowed school for girls in America.

**1848** Seneca Falls Convention held; Elizabeth Cady Stanton, Lucretia Mott and others draft the "Declaration of Sentiments," the first public protest against the inequality of the economic, political, and social positions of women in America.

**1849** Elizabeth Blackwell completes her training at Geneva Medical College and becomes the first woman ever to receive an M.D. degree.

**1868** New York women form the Working Women's Association to fight for better working conditions.

**1868** Susan B. Anthony and Elizabeth Cady Stanton found *The Revolution*, a newspaper with the motto; "Men, their rights and nothing more; women, their rights and nothing less!"

**1869** National Woman Suffrage Association founded; American Woman Suffrage Association founded; two organizations merge in 1890 to work for a voting rights amendment to the Constitution.

**1873** State of Illinois passes the first women's equal employment legislation.

**1890** Wyoming, the first territory to grant political equality to women, joins the Union.

**1917** Miss Jeannette Rankin of Montana becomes the first woman to serve in Congress.

**1920** Nineteenth Amendment to the Constitution adopted, giving women the right to vote.

**1963** Congress passes the Equal Pay Act which stipulates that equal pay must be given for equal work.

**1964** Under Title VII of the Civil Rights Act passed by Congress, discrimination based on sex by employers of 15 or more employees is prohibited.

**1972** Ms. magazine, written and edited by women, begins publication.

**1973** The Supreme Court issues two decisions rendering all state abortion laws unconstitutional.

**1973** The Senate July 23 passes a bill to protect consumers against unfair billing practices and to prohibit lenders from discriminating on the basis of sex or marital status in all credit transactions.

**1974** Little League Baseball allows girls to play.

**1976** The military academies of the Army, Air Force and Navy admit women to their freshman classes.

**1977** The National Women's Conference meets in Houston, Texas, in observance of International Women's Year.

**1978** Congress passes the Pregnancy Disability Bill, making pregnancy an insurable disability.

**1978** Congress passes a bill extending the time by three years three months for ratification of the Equal Rights Amendment.

**1982** Only 35 of the required 38 states ratify the Equal Rights Amendment before the extended deadline of June 30, 1982, thus the amendment dies.

## BLACK POPULATION OF LARGE U.S. CITIES

Source: Bureau of the Census

| Cities by Rank | Black Population 1970 | Black Population 1980 | % of Total Population |
|---|---|---|---|
| New York City, N.Y. | 1,668,115 | 1,784,124 | 25.2 |
| Chicago, Ill. | 1,102,620 | 1,197,000 | 39.8 |
| Detroit, Mich. | 660,428 | 758,939 | 63.1 |
| Philadelphia, Pa. | 653,791 | 638,878 | 37.8 |
| Los Angeles, Calif. | 503,606 | 505,208 | 17.0 |
| Washington, D.C. | 537,712 | 448,229 | 70.3 |
| Houston, Texas | 316,551 | 440,257 | 27.6 |
| Baltimore, Md. | 420,210 | 431,151 | 54.8 |
| New Orleans, La. | 267,308 | 308,136 | 55.3 |
| Memphis, Tenn. | 242,513 | 307,702 | 47.6 |
| Dallas, Texas | 210,238 | 265,594 | 29.4 |
| Cleveland, Ohio | 287,841 | 251,347 | 43.8 |
| St. Louis, Mo. | 254,191 | 206,386 | 45.6 |
| Newark, N.J. | 207,458 | 191,743 | 58.2 |
| Oakland, Calif. | 124,710 | 159,234 | 46.9 |
| Birmingham, Ala. | 126,388 | 158,223 | 55.6 |
| Indianapolis, Ind. | 134,320 | 152,626 | 21.8 |
| Milwaukee, Wis. | 105,088 | 146,940 | 23.1 |
| Jacksonville, Fla. | 118,158 | 137,324 | 25.4 |
| Cincinnati, Ohio | 125,070 | 130,467 | 33.8 |
| Boston, Mass. | 104,707 | 126,229 | 22.4 |
| Columbus, Ohio | 99,627 | 124,880 | 22.1 |
| Kansas City, Mo. | 112,005 | 122,699 | 27.4 |
| Richmond, Va. | 104,766 | 112,357 | 51.3 |
| Gary, Ind. | 92,695 | 107,644 | 70.8 |
| Nashville-Davidson, Tenn. | 87,851 | 105,942 | 23.3 |
| Pittsburgh, Pa. | 104,904 | 101,813 | 24.0 |
| Charlotte, N.C. | 72,972 | 97,627 | 31.0 |
| Jackson, Miss. | 61,063 | 95,357 | 47.0 |
| Buffalo, N.Y. | 94,329 | 95,116 | 26.6 |
| Norfolk, Va. | 87,261 | 93,987 | 35.2 |
| Fort Worth, Texas | 78,324 | 87,723 | 22.8 |
| Miami, Fla. | 76,156 | 87,110 | 25.1 |
| San Francisco, Calif. | 96,078 | 86,414 | 12.7 |
| Shreveport, La. | 62,152 | 84,627 | 41.1 |
| Louisville, Ky. | 86,040 | 84,080 | 28.2 |
| Baton Rouge, La. | 81,781 | 80,119 | 36.5 |
| San Diego, Calif. | 52,961 | 77,700 | 8.9 |
| Dayton, Ohio | 74,284 | 75,031 | 36.9 |
| Mobile, Ala. | 67,356 | 72,568 | 36.2 |
| Montgomery, Ala. | 44,523 | 69,765 | 39.2 |
| Flint, Mich. | 54,237 | 66,124 | 41.4 |
| East Orange, N.J. | 40,099 | 64,354 | 83.5 |
| Tampa, Fla. | 54,720 | 63,835 | 23.5 |
| Rochester, N.Y. | 49,647 | 62,332 | 25.8 |
| Jersey City, N.J. | 54,595 | 61,954 | 27.7 |
| Toledo, Ohio | 52,915 | 61,750 | 17.4 |
| Compton, Calif. | 55,781 | 60,812 | 74.8 |
| Denver, Colo. | 47,011 | 59,252 | 12.1 |
| Oklahoma City, Okla. | 50,103 | 58,702 | 14.6 |
| San Antonio, Texas | 50,041 | 57,654 | 7.3 |
| Inglewood, Calif. | 10,066 | 54,010 | 57.3 |
| Chattanooga, Tenn. | 42,610 | 53,716 | 31.7 |
| Winston-Salem, N.C. | 45,533 | 52,968 | 40.2 |
| East St. Louis, Ill. | 48,368 | 52,751 | 95.6 |
| Akron, Ohio | 48,205 | 52,719 | 22.2 |
| Greensboro, N.C. | 40,633 | 51,373 | 33.0 |
| Little Rock, Ark. | 33,396 | 51,091 | 32.2 |

## BLACK-AMERICAN HISTORY

**Year** **Event**

**1619** The first Negroes to be brought to the American colonies arrived in Virginia as indentured servants.

**1661** Virginia passed the first law making Negroes slaves.

**1663** Slavery was legally recognized in Maryland.

**1688** Quakers in Germantown, Pa., issued the first formal antislavery protest in the Western Hemisphere.

**1770** Crispus Attucks, a runaway slave, was killed in the Boston Massacre.

**1775** The Pennsylvania Abolition Society, the first antislavery society in America, was founded.

**1776** The Declaration of Independence was signed, the final version omitting an attack on slavery by Thomas Jefferson contained in the draft version.

The Continental Congress approved a proposal by General George Washington to permit the enlistment of free Negroes in the Continental Army. About 5,000 Negroes served in the War of Independence.

**1787** Congress barred the extension of slavery into the Northwest Territory.

**1791** Eli Whitney invented the cotton gin, spurring the expansion of cotton and the demand for slaves.

**1800** Gabriel Prosser, a Virginia slave, led an unsuccessful insurrection and was hanged with 24 conspirators.

**1807** British Parliament abolished the slave trade.
Congress barred the importation of new slaves into U.S. territory.

**1816** The American Colonization Society was formed to resettle free American Negroes in Africa.

**1820** Congress adopted the Missouri Compromise providing for the admission of Missouri into the Union as a slave state, and Maine's entry as a free state. All territory north of 36°30′ was declared free; all territory south of that line was left open to slavery.

**1827** The first Negro newspaper, *Freedom's Journal*, began publication in New York City.
Slavery was abolished in New York State.

**1830** The U.S. Census Bureau reported that 3,777 Negro heads of families owned slaves.

**1831** Federal and state troops crushed a slave rebellion in Southampton County, Va., led by Nat Turner. The rebellion, in which more than 50 whites and more than 100 slaves were killed, ended in the execution of Turner and led to the adoption of more rigid slave codes.

**1837** Institute for Colored Youth (later Cheyney State College) founded by Quakers in Philadelphia.

**1847** Frederick Douglass, a former slave and a lecturer with the Massachusetts Anti-Slavery Society, began publishing *North Star*, an abolitionist newspaper.

**1849** Harriet Tubman escaped from slavery in Maryland. She became one of the most venturesome conductors on the Underground Railroad, leading over 300 slaves to freedom.
Benjamin Roberts filed the first school integration suit on behalf of his daughter. The Massachusetts Supreme Court rejected the suit and established a "separate but equal" precedent.

**1850** The Compromise of 1850 admitted California to the Union as a free state but strengthened the Fugitive Slave Law, giving greater inducement for the apprehension of runaway slaves.

**1852** Harriet Beecher Stowe's novel *Uncle Tom's Cabin,* a vastly popular antislavery work, was published.

**1853** *Clotelle: or the President's Daughter* by historian William Wells Brown was published—the first novel by an American Negro.

**1854** James A. Healy was ordained a priest in Notre Dame cathedral, Paris. He later became America's first Negro Roman Catholic bishop.
Lincoln University was founded as Ashmun Institute in Oxford, Pa.

**1855** The first Negro to win elective office in the United States, John Mercer Langston, was elected clerk of Brownhelm Township, Lorain Co., O.

**1863** The Draft Riots took place in New York City. Blacks and abolitionists were attacked and killed.

**1865** By the end of the Civil War, some 186,000 Negroes had served with the Union forces.
The Thirteenth Amendment, freeing all slaves, was passed by Congress.
The Freedman's Bureau was organized to aid and protect newly freed blacks in the South.
Dr. John S. Rock, a Boston physician and lawyer, was the first Negro admitted to the bar of the United States Supreme Court.
Southern states passed the "Black Codes" in an attempt to restrict the freedom of emancipated slaves.

**1866** Charles L. Mitchell and Edward G. Walker were elected to the Massachusetts House of Representatives, becoming the first Negroes to serve in a U.S. legislature.

**1867** Morehouse College, Atlanta, Ga., and Howard University, Washington, D.C., were founded.

**1868** Oscar J. Dunn attained the highest elective office held by an American Negro up to that time, becoming lieutenant governor of Louisiana.

**1869** Ebenezer Don Carlos Basset was appointed minister to Haiti, the first Negro diplomat to represent the United States.

**1870** Hiram Revels was elected to fill the unexpired U.S. Senate term of Jefferson Davis of Mississippi, becoming the first Negro Senator. He served a year.
Joseph H. Rainey of South Carolina became the first Negro in the House of Representatives. He was subsequently reelected four times.

**1875** Congress passed a civil rights act prohibiting discrimination in such public accommodations as hotels and theaters.

**1877** Henry O. Flipper became the first Negro to graduate from West Point.

**1881** Tennessee passed a "Jim Crow" law instituting segregated railroad travel that set a trend among other states in the South.
Booker T. Washington opened Tuskegee Institute in Alabama.

**1883** The Supreme Court declared the 1875 Civil Rights Act unconstitutional.

**1890** Mississippi instituted restrictions on voting, including a poll tax and literacy tests, which were designed to disenfranchise Negroes. During the decade, other Southern states followed. Louisiana added (1898) the exclusionary device of the "grandfather clause," which set educational and property qualifications for voting but exempted those whose ancestors had been eligible to vote as of Jan. 1, 1867.

**1891** The Provident Hospital in Chicago—the first such interracial institution in America—was founded by Negro surgeon Daniel Hale Williams.

**1895** Frederick Douglass, the Negro abolitionist whom Lincoln had called "the most meritorious man of the 19th century," died.

**1896** The National Association of Colored Women was organized in Washington, D.C.; Mary Church Terrell served as its first president.

**1898** Four Negro regiments in the regular army compiled an excellent combat record during the Spanish-American War. Dismounted elements of the black Ninth and Tenth Cavalry rescued the Rough Riders from near annihilation.

**1905** Twenty-nine Negro intellectuals from 14 states, headed by Dr. W. E. B. DuBois, organized the Niagara Movement, which demanded the abolition of all racial distinctions. The meeting took place at Fort Erie, N.Y.

**1909** Matthew Henson, a Negro member of Admiral Peary's expedition, placed the American flag at the North Pole.

**1910** The National Association for the Advancement of Colored People (NAACP) was founded in New York.
The "Great Migration" of more than 2 million Southern blacks began.

**1911** The National Urban League was founded. It was originally made up of two groups: The Committee for Improving the Industrial Conditions of Negroes and The League for the Protection of Colored Women.

**1915** The Association for the Study of Negro Life and History was established by the "father of Negro history," Dr. Carter G. Woodson.

**1917** Ten thousand Negroes marched down Fifth Avenue in New York to protest the many lynchings in the South. The parade was led by W. E. B. DuBois. Race riots broke out in East St. Louis, Illinois.

**1920** The pioneer black nationalist Marcus Garvey inaugurated the International Convention of the Universal Negro Improvement Association (UNIA) in Harlem. UNIA reached its greatest influence during the following two years.

**1928** Oscar De Priest of Illinois was the first black Congressman from a northern state.

**1935** Mary McLeod Bethune organized the National Council of Negro Women.

1936 Negro track star Jesse Owen won four gold medals in the Olympics at Berlin.

1937 William H. Hastie became the first Negro to serve as a U.S. Federal judge.

Joe Louis became heavyweight boxing champion of the world, defeating Jim Braddock for the title.

1939 Contralto Marian Anderson, denied the use of Constitution Hall in Washington by the Daughters of the American Revolution, sang on Easter Sunday before 75,000 people at the Lincoln Memorial.

1940 Benjamin O. Davis, Sr., was appointed the first black general in the U.S. armed forces.

Dr. Charles R. Drew did notable research into blood preservation and discovered blood plasma.

1941 A Negro threat to stage a massive protest march on Washington resulted in the issuance of Executive Order 8802 prohibiting racial discrimination in defense industries or the government (but not the armed forces).

1942 The Congress of Racial Equality (CORE), an action-oriented civil rights group, was founded by James Farmer in Chicago.

1947 Statistics amassed by Tuskegee Institute indicated that in the period 1882–1947 3,426 Negroes were lynched in the United States. Of these, 1,217 were lynched in the 1890–1900 decade.

1948 President Truman issued Executive Order 9981 calling for "equality of treatment and opportunity" in the armed forces.

1949 William L. Dawson became the first Negro to head a Congressional committee.

1951 Ralph J. Bunche, who won a Nobel Peace Prize in 1950, was appointed Under-Secretary of the United Nations, the highest ranking American employed by the international body.

Private First Class William Thompson was awarded the Congressional Medal of Honor for bravery in the Korean War, the first Negro to win it since the Spanish-American War.

1952 A Tuskegee Institute report indicated that for the first time in 71 years of compilation, no lynchings were reported in the United States.

1954 In "Brown v. Board of Education of Topeka" the U.S. Supreme Court held that segregation in public education denied equal protection of the laws.

1955 A bus boycott in Montgomery, Ala., was led by Dr. Martin Luther King, Jr., after Rosa Parks was arrested for refusing to give up her seat to a white man.

1957 Central High School in Little Rock, Ark., was integrated by nine Negro children, but not until President Eisenhower had called in troops to keep order.

1960 Four Negro North Carolina A & T College freshmen occupied places at a Woolworth lunch counter, launching a wave of nonviolent sit-ins.

1961 CORE began "Freedom Rides" that rolled through the South, protesting segregation.

1962 The Albany (Ga.) Movement—a citywide attempt, supported by the Southern Christian Leadership Conference, Student Nonviolent Coordinating Committee, NAACP, and CORE, to abolish discrimination in all public facilities—was formed.

James Meredith desegregated the University of Mississippi, after President Kennedy dispatched troops and riots killed two persons.

1963 NAACP leader Medgar Evers was murdered in the doorway of his home in Jackson, Miss.

Birmingham, Ala.: The plight of Negroes in the South and throughout the nation was dramatized here as fire hoses, police dogs, and rough handling by the police, followed by bomb blasts in the black ghetto, became the order of the day. September 15: A bomb blast at the Sixteenth Street Baptist Church killed four girls.

June 11: President Kennedy declared that the black struggle for civil rights is a "moral issue."

August 28: The March on Washington in which more than 200,000 Americans from all walks of life converged on the nation's capital constituted one of the largest single protests in American history. The marchers gathered on the steps of the Lincoln Memorial to dramatize discontent with the Negro's plight.

1964 Three young civil-rights workers—Michael Schwerner, Andrew Goodman, and James E. Chaney—were murdered in Mississippi.

Riots exploded in Harlem and elsewhere.

1965 Malcolm X., former Black Muslim and advocate of black nationalism, was assassinated in New York City.

Thurgood Marshall was named as the first Negro Solicitor General of the United States.

President Johnson signed the Voting Rights Act, under which federal examiners are authorized to register black voters who have been refused by state officials.

Riots erupted in the Watts section of Los Angeles; 35 people were killed, 883 others were injured, and 3,598 were arrested. Damage totaled more than $220 million.

1966 Robert Weaver was appointed head of the Department of Housing and Urban Development (HUD), the first Negro ever to serve at cabinet level.

Constance Baker Motley, former borough president of Manhattan, became the first Negro woman to become a federal judge in American history.

The U.S. Supreme Court outlawed all poll taxes.

The concept of "Black Power" was adopted by CORE.

1967 Solicitor General Thurgood Marshall became the first Negro Supreme Court Justice.

At a four-day Black Power conference—the largest of its kind in American history—more than 400 people representing 45 civil rights groups from 36 cities convened in Newark, N.J., expressing viewpoints that ranged from moderate to militant.

1968 April 4: While standing on the balcony of a Memphis motel, Dr. Martin Luther King, Jr., was shot and killed by a sniper.

The Kerner Commission reported that "our nation is moving toward two societies, one black, one white—separate and unequal."

1969 Educational institutions acceded to demands by black students for more black studies.

James Earl Ray pleaded guilty to the assassination of Martin Luther King; sentenced to 99 years in prison.

1970 The killing in December 1969 of a Black Panther leader, Fred Hampton, led to a federal investigation and the subsequent conclusion that the Chicago police had exercised undue force.

1971 Samuel L. Gravely, Jr., was made the first black admiral in the U.S. Navy.

Thirteen Black Panthers, including two who fled to Algeria during the trial, were acquitted in New York City on charges of conspiring to bomb department stores and police stations and to murder policemen.

The six-month trial in New Haven of Bobby G. Seale, chairman of the Black Panther party, and Mrs. Ericka Huggins, a New Haven Panther, for crimes arising from the death of Alex Rackley, ended in a mistrial as the jury was unable to reach a verdict. Rackley, a Panther, died in May 1969.

1972 Over 8,000 delegates and observers met in Gary, Indiana as the first National Black Political Convention voted to set up a permanent representative body to set the direction for black political and social actions.

Angela Davis, accused of conspiracy to kidnap and murder, was acquitted.

The busing of children, both black and white, from one neighborhood school district to another became an important political issue. The Nixon administration supported and signed into law a bill which prohibited busing solely to achieve racial integration.

1975 Black Muslims agreed to accept white members.

1976 U.S. Supreme Court outlawed discrimination in commercially operated nonsectarian private schools.

1977 The TV dramatization of Alex Haley's book *Roots* was seen by the largest audience ever. The story chronicled the black author's family history from mid-eighteenth century African beginnings.

1978 U.S. Supreme Court ruled that the University of California Medical School at Davis must admit Allan P. Bakke, a 38-year-old white engineer, as the school's minority-admissions plan was inflexible and racially biased. The justices ruled, however, that race could be considered as a university admission factor. Black leaders expressed concern regarding the decision.

# PUBLIC HEALTH/MEDICINE

## FIRST AID

### CHOKING

CALL FOR MEDICAL HELP. If choking victim turns blue and cannot breathe or speak: Have him bend over with arms, upper torso and head hanging down.

Circle his waist just under ribcage, grasping your right wrist with your left hand.

Exert sudden pressure on his abdomen. The foreign object should be ejected.

### ARTIFICIAL RESPIRATION

CALL FOR MEDICAL HELP. Place patient on back, lift neck and tilt head back. Clear mouth of obstructions. Pinch nose and blow vigorously through mouth to make chest expand 12 times per minute without interruption. **Children to age 4**—proceed as above except: cover mouth and nose tightly with mouth. Puff to make chest expand 20 times per minute.

### POISONING

CALL FOR MEDICAL HELP. Dilute poison by giving milk or water. Get patient to vomit by tickling back of throat or giving syrup of ipecac or other emetic.

DO NOT MAKE PATIENT VOMIT IF:

Unconscious or in convulsion

Swallowed poison was: paint, lye, acid or other corrosive substance, kerosene or other petroleum product, furniture polish or household cleaner.

Give antidote as directed on poison container or by medical facility. If vomiting is desired but does not occur within 20 minutes, rush patient and poison container to nearest medical facility.

### BURNS

**Large or severe** — remove clothing from burned area unless stuck. Apply clean, dry cloth, no ointment or other medication. OBTAIN MEDICAL HELP IMMEDIATELY.

Patient may be given solution of 1 qt. water with 1 tsp. salt, ½ tsp. baking soda if conscious and not burned over more than half of body.

**Slight** — apply cold compresses until pain disappears. If skin is blistered, apply nonadhesive sterile dressing. **Chemical** — wash thoroughly with water. Follow first aid direction on container. CALL FOR MEDICAL HELP.

## EYES

KEEP PATIENT FROM RUBBING EYE.

**Chemicals** — flush with water and obtain medical help.

**Foreign body** — close eye for short time, then open and examine to see if tears have flushed it out. To examine, pull out lower lid, roll upper lid on matchstick. If still there, a moist cotton swab may be used to lift it out. If particle remains embedded, bandage eye shut and obtain medical help.

## CONVULSIONS

CALL FOR MEDICAL HELP.

Lay patient on side in bed or quiet place.

Place head lower than body.

Loosen clothing.

Do not give anything by mouth.

## FRACTURES

**Do Not** move patient with possible broken bones, especially if broken back or neck is suspected. Nerve and tissue damage, paralysis and death may result. OBTAIN MEDICAL HELP AT ONCE. If absolutely unavoidable, move patient completely flat and without bending neck or back out of position in which found. Bind padded splints to either side of arm or leg before moving. Use sling to support arm or pin sleeve to front of garment.

## BITES and STINGS

**Animal** — rinse with water, then wash with soap and water. Apply sterile dressing. CALL FOR MEDICAL HELP. **Poisonous snake** — keep patient quiet. CALL FOR MEDICAL HELP IMMEDIATELY. Apply band between bite and heart. **Insect** — remove stinger and use cold compresses. CALL FOR MEDICAL HELP in case of rash, vomiting, weakness, nose, throat or chest symptoms.

## FAINTING

Loosen clothing; massage arms and legs toward body.

Provide fresh air and keep warm.

Call for medical help if consciousness is not regained promptly. See doctor if fainting has been frequent.

Have patient rest for 10 minutes after regaining consciousness, longer if necessary.

## HEAD INJURIES

Keep patient quiet.

NOTIFY DOCTOR IN CASE OF:

Loss of consciousness at time of injury or later

Difficulty in rousing

Different-sized eye pupils

Severe and lasting headache

Convulsion

Persistent vomiting

Blood or other fluid coming from nose or ears

Paralysis of arms or legs

## SPRAINS

Rest and elevate injured limb. Use cold compresses to prevent swelling and pain.

Bandage joint to immobilize and allow healing.

A sling may be used to support an injured arm.

Check with doctor to be sure there is no fracture.

## CUTS and BRUISES

**Severe bleeding** — apply pressure using sterile pad or other clean cloth, adding more as necessary to contain bleeding. CALL FOR MEDICAL HELP IMMEDIATELY.

**Scrapes and small cuts** — clean with soap and water and apply disinfectant and sterile dressing.

**Bruises** — apply cold dressings to prevent swelling. If skin is broken, tetanus shots may be advisable.

## LONGEVITY IN THE UNITED STATES

SOURCE: 1979, 1980, and 1981 data from Statistical Bureau, Metropolitan Life Insurance Company; earlier years from the National Center for Health Statistics

The expectation of life at birth for the resident population of the United States increased to an all-time high in 1981. Preliminary life tables indicate that the average length of life for the total population decreased from 74.0 years in 1979 to 73.8 years in 1980 and rose to 74.1 years in 1981—a gain of 3.4 years since 1969-71 and of 14.9 years since 1929-31, when the average was only about 59 years.

The expected lifetime was 70.3 years for the male newborn and 77.9 years for the female. The infant mortality rate in 1981 declined to a new low of 11.7 per 1,000 live births.

### EXPECTATION OF LIFE IN THE U.S.: 1949-51 to 1981

| Age | 1949-51 | 1959-61 | 1969-71 | 1976 | 1979* | 1980* | 1981* |
|---|---|---|---|---|---|---|---|
| 0-1 | 68.1 | 69.9 | 70.7 | 72.8 | 74.0 | 73.8 | 74.1 |
| 1 | 69.2 | 70.7 | 71.2 | 72.9 | 74.0 | 73.7 | 74.0 |
| 15 | 55.9 | 57.3 | 57.7 | 59.3 | 60.4 | 60.1 | 60.3 |
| 25 | 46.6 | 47.9 | 48.4 | 50.0 | 51.1 | 50.7 | 50.9 |
| 35 | 37.3 | 38.5 | 39.1 | 40.6 | 41.7 | 41.3 | 41.6 |
| 45 | 28.5 | 29.5 | 30.1 | 31.5 | 32.5 | 32.2 | 32.4 |
| 55 | 20.6 | 21.4 | 22.0 | 23.2 | 24.2 | 23.8 | 24.0 |
| 65 | 13.8 | 14.4 | 15.0 | 16.0 | 16.9 | 16.5 | 16.7 |

*Preliminary (based on results of the 1980 census).

### EXPECTATION OF LIFE—UNITED STATES: 1978

SOURCE: National Center for Health Statistics

| AGE | Total (years) | White | | All Other | | Age | Total (years) | White | | All other | |
|---|---|---|---|---|---|---|---|---|---|---|---|
| | | Male | Female | Male | Female | | | Male | Female | Male | Female |
| Birth | 73.3 | 70.2 | 77.8 | 65.0 | 73.6 | 43 | 33.7 | 30.8 | 37.1 | 28.1 | 34.4 |
| 1 | 73.3 | 70.1 | 77.6 | 65.5 | 74.0 | 44 | 32.8 | 29.9 | 36.1 | 27.3 | 33.5 |
| 2 | 72.4 | 69.2 | 76.7 | 64.6 | 73.1 | 45 | 31.9 | 29.1 | 35.2 | 26.5 | 32.7 |
| 3 | 71.5 | 68.3 | 75.7 | 63.7 | 72.1 | 46 | 31.0 | 28.2 | 34.3 | 25.8 | 31.8 |
| 4 | 70.5 | 67.3 | 74.8 | 62.8 | 71.2 | 47 | 30.1 | 27.3 | 33.4 | 25.0 | 31.0 |
| 5 | 69.5 | 66.3 | 73.8 | 61.8 | 70.2 | 48 | 29.3 | 26.5 | 32.5 | 24.3 | 30.2 |
| 6 | 68.6 | 65.4 | 72.8 | 60.8 | 69.3 | 49 | 28.4 | 25.6 | 31.6 | 23.5 | 29.3 |
| 7 | 67.6 | 64.4 | 71.8 | 59.9 | 68.3 | 50 | 27.6 | 24.8 | 30.7 | 22.8 | 28.5 |
| 8 | 66.6 | 63.4 | 70.8 | 58.9 | 67.3 | 51 | 26.7 | 24.0 | 29.8 | 22.1 | 27.8 |
| 9 | 65.6 | 62.4 | 69.9 | 57.9 | 66.3 | 52 | 25.9 | 23.2 | 29.0 | 21.4 | 27.0 |
| 10 | 64.6 | 61.5 | 68.9 | 57.0 | 65.4 | 53 | 25.1 | 22.4 | 28.1 | 20.8 | 26.2 |
| 11 | 63.7 | 60.5 | 67.9 | 56.0 | 64.4 | 54 | 24.3 | 21.6 | 27.3 | 20.1 | 25.5 |
| 12 | 62.7 | 59.5 | 66.9 | 55.0 | 63.4 | 55 | 23.5 | 20.8 | 26.4 | 19.5 | 24.7 |
| 13 | 61.7 | 58.5 | 65.9 | 54.0 | 62.4 | 56 | 22.7 | 20.1 | 25.6 | 18.9 | 24.0 |
| 14 | 60.7 | 57.5 | 64.9 | 53.1 | 61.4 | 57 | 22.0 | 19.3 | 24.7 | 18.3 | 23.3 |
| 15 | 59.7 | 56.6 | 64.0 | 52.1 | 60.4 | 58 | 21.2 | 18.6 | 23.9 | 17.7 | 22.5 |
| 16 | 58.8 | 55.6 | 63.0 | 51.1 | 59.5 | 59 | 20.5 | 17.9 | 23.1 | 17.1 | 21.8 |
| 17 | 57.8 | 54.7 | 62.0 | 50.2 | 58.5 | 60 | 19.7 | 17.2 | 22.3 | 16.5 | 21.2 |
| 18 | 56.9 | 53.8 | 61.1 | 49.3 | 57.5 | 61 | 19.0 | 16.5 | 21.5 | 16.0 | 20.5 |
| 19 | 56.0 | 52.9 | 60.1 | 48.3 | 56.6 | 62 | 18.3 | 15.8 | 20.7 | 15.5 | 19.9 |
| 20 | 55.0 | 52.0 | 59.1 | 47.4 | 55.6 | 63 | 17.6 | 15.2 | 19.9 | 15.1 | 19.3 |
| 21 | 54.1 | 51.1 | 58.2 | 46.5 | 54.7 | 64 | 17.0 | 14.6 | 19.2 | 14.6 | 18.6 |
| 22 | 53.2 | 50.2 | 57.2 | 45.7 | 53.7 | 65 | 16.3 | 14.0 | 18.4 | 14.1 | 18.0 |
| 23 | 52.2 | 49.3 | 56.2 | 44.8 | 52.8 | 66 | 15.7 | 13.4 | 17.7 | 13.6 | 17.3 |
| 24 | 51.3 | 48.4 | 55.3 | 43.9 | 51.8 | 67 | 15.0 | 12.8 | 16.9 | 13.1 | 16.7 |
| 25 | 50.4 | 47.5 | 54.3 | 43.1 | 50.9 | 68 | 14.4 | 12.2 | 16.2 | 12.5 | 16.0 |
| 26 | 49.5 | 46.5 | 53.3 | 42.2 | 49.9 | 69 | 13.7 | 11.6 | 15.5 | 12.0 | 15.4 |
| 27 | 48.5 | 45.6 | 52.4 | 41.4 | 49.0 | 70 | 13.1 | 11.1 | 14.8 | 11.6 | 14.8 |
| 28 | 47.6 | 44.7 | 51.4 | 40.5 | 48.1 | 71 | 12.5 | 10.6 | 14.1 | 11.1 | 14.2 |
| 29 | 46.6 | 43.8 | 50.4 | 39.7 | 47.1 | 72 | 12.0 | 10.1 | 13.4 | 10.7 | 13.7 |
| 30 | 45.7 | 42.8 | 49.5 | 38.8 | 46.2 | 73 | 11.4 | 9.6 | 12.7 | 10.4 | 13.2 |
| 31 | 44.8 | 41.9 | 48.5 | 37.9 | 45.2 | 74 | 10.9 | 9.1 | 12.1 | 10.0 | 12.8 |
| 32 | 43.8 | 41.0 | 47.5 | 37.1 | 44.3 | 75 | 10.4 | 8.6 | 11.5 | 9.8 | 12.5 |
| 33 | 42.9 | 40.0 | 46.6 | 36.2 | 43.4 | 76 | 9.8 | 8.2 | 10.9 | 9.5 | 12.2 |
| 34 | 41.9 | 39.1 | 45.6 | 35.4 | 42.5 | 77 | 9.4 | 7.8 | 10.3 | 9.3 | 11.9 |
| 35 | 41.0 | 38.2 | 44.6 | 34.5 | 41.5 | 78 | 9.0 | 7.4 | 9.8 | 9.1 | 11.7 |
| 36 | 40.1 | 37.2 | 43.7 | 33.7 | 40.6 | 79 | 8.5 | 7.1 | 9.3 | 8.9 | 11.6 |
| 37 | 39.1 | 36.3 | 42.7 | 32.9 | 39.7 | 80 | 8.1 | 6.7 | 8.8 | 8.8 | 11.5 |
| 38 | 38.2 | 35.4 | 41.8 | 32.0 | 38.8 | 81 | 7.8 | 6.4 | 8.3 | 8.7 | 11.3 |
| 39 | 37.3 | 34.5 | 40.8 | 31.2 | 37.9 | 82 | 7.4 | 6.1 | 7.9 | 8.6 | 11.1 |
| 40 | 36.4 | 33.6 | 39.9 | 30.4 | 37.0 | 83 | 7.1 | 5.8 | 7.5 | 8.5 | 10.9 |
| 41 | 35.5 | 32.6 | 38.9 | 29.6 | 36.1 | 84 | 6.7 | 5.5 | 7.1 | 8.2 | 10.5 |
| 42 | 34.6 | 31.7 | 38.0 | 28.9 | 35.3 | 85 over | 6.4 | 5.3 | 6.7 | 7.8 | 9.9 |

### INFANT AND NEONATAL DEATH RATES IN THE UNITED STATES: 1978

SOURCE: National Center for Health Statistics (Deaths per 1,000 live births)

| State | Infant Deaths[1] | Neonatal Deaths[2] | State | Infant Deaths[1] | Neonatal Deaths[2] | State | Infant Deaths[1] | Neonatal Deaths[2] | State | Infant Deaths[1] | Neonatal Deaths[2] |
|---|---|---|---|---|---|---|---|---|---|---|---|
| Ala. | 16.1 | 11.0 | Ill. | 15.7 | 10.9 | Mont. | 11.6 | 7.3 | R.I. | 13.6 | 10.6 |
| Alaska | 14.4 | 9.4 | Ind. | 13.1 | 8.6 | Nebr. | 13.0 | 9.1 | S.C. | 18.6 | 12.4 |
| Ariz. | 13.1 | 9.0 | Iowa | 12.6 | 8.9 | Nev. | 12.5 | 8.6 | S.D. | 13.5 | 9.4 |
| Ark. | 16.4 | 10.5 | Kans. | 12.5 | 8.7 | N.H. | 10.4 | 8.0 | Tenn. | 14.8 | 10.5 |
| Calif. | 11.8 | 7.7 | Ky. | 12.7 | 8.6 | N.J. | 13.0 | 9.3 | Texas | 14.3 | 9.8 |
| Colo. | 11.2 | 6.9 | La. | 17.3 | 12.0 | N.M. | 14.1 | 9.0 | Utah | 11.4 | 7.8 |
| Conn. | 11.6 | 9.3 | Maine | 10.4 | 6.1 | N.Y. | 14.0 | 10.1 | Vt. | 10.4 | 8.0 |
| Del. | 13.2 | 9.6 | Md. | 14.7 | 11.1 | N.C. | 16.6 | 11.4 | Va. | 13.8 | 9.7 |
| D.C. | 27.3 | 20.2 | Mass. | 11.1 | 8.1 | N.D. | 13.5 | 9.6 | Wash. | 12.5 | 7.9 |
| Fla. | 14.1 | 9.3 | Mich. | 13.8 | 9.2 | Ohio | 13.3 | 9.2 | W.Va. | 15.1 | 10.3 |
| Ga. | 15.4 | 10.3 | Minn. | 12.0 | 8.3 | Okla. | 14.3 | 9.0 | Wis. | 11.2 | 7.6 |
| Hawaii | 11.1 | 7.6 | Miss. | 18.7 | 12.3 | Oreg. | 12.9 | 7.7 | Wyo. | 13.0 | 8.1 |
| Idaho | 11.7 | 7.3 | Mo. | 14.8 | 10.8 | Pa. | 13.7 | 10.5 | U.S. avg. | 13.8 | 9.5 |

[1] Under 1 yr. [2] Under 28 days.

## LEADING CAUSES OF DEATH IN THE UNITED STATES: 1978

SOURCE: National Center for Health Statistics

| Rank | Cause of Death | Number of Deaths | Death Rate per 100,000 Population |
|---|---|---|---|
| | ALL CAUSES | 1,927,788 | 883.4 |
| 1. | Heart Diseases | 729,510 | 334.3 |
| 2. | Cancer | 396,992 | 181.9 |
| 3. | Cerebrovascular diseases | 175,629 | 80.5 |
| 4. | Accidents | 105,561 | 48.4 |
| | Motor Vehicular | 52,411 | 24.0 |
| | All Other | 53,150 | 24.4 |
| 5. | Influenza & Pneumonia | 58,319 | 26.7 |
| 6. | Diabetes Mellitus | 33,841 | 15.5 |
| 7. | Cirrhosis of Liver | 30,066 | 13.8 |
| 8. | Arteriosclerosis | 28,940 | 13.3 |
| 9. | Suicide | 27,294 | 12.5 |
| 10. | Diseases of Early Infancy | 22,033 | 10.1 |
| | All Other Causes | 319,603 | 146.5 |

## DEATH RATES FOR SPECIFIED CAUSES, BY COLOR AND SEX: UNITED STATES, 1978

SOURCE: National Center for Health Statistics

(Rate per 100,000 population in specified group)

| | Total | | | White | | | All Other | | |
|---|---|---|---|---|---|---|---|---|---|
| | Both sexes | Male | Female | Both sexes | Male | Female | Both sexes | Male | Female |
| All causes | 883.4 | 994.4 | 778.3 | 895.7 | 999.8 | 796.5 | 805.1 | 959.7 | 664.5 |
| Major cardiovascular diseases | 442.7 | 472.8 | 414.2 | 459.5 | 489.2 | 431.2 | 335.5 | 365.6 | 308.1 |
| Diseases of heart | 334.3 | 375.3 | 295.5 | 348.6 | 390.8 | 308.4 | 242.8 | 273.8 | 214.7 |
| Hypertension | 2.5 | 2.4 | 2.6 | 2.3 | 2.2 | 2.4 | 3.7 | 3.8 | 3.6 |
| Cerebrovascular diseases | 10.4 | 9.6 | 20.3 | 18.4 | 15.3 | 21.4 | 13.5 | 13.2 | 13.7 |
| Arteriosclerosis | 13.3 | 10.9 | 9.7 | 12.8 | 15.7 | 10.1 | 8.0 | 8.7 | 7.3 |
| Cancer | 181.9 | 203.5 | 161.4 | 186.6 | 206.4 | 167.7 | 152.0 | 184.9 | 122.1 |
| Accidents | 48.4 | 69.6 | 28.3 | 47.9 | 68.3 | 28.5 | 51.3 | 78.2 | 26.8 |
| Motor vehicle addidents | 24.0 | 35.9 | 12.7 | 24.4 | 36.2 | 13.1 | 21.8 | 34.1 | 10.6 |
| All other accidents | 24.4 | 33.7 | 15.5 | 23.5 | 32.1 | 15.4 | 29.5 | 44.1 | 16.3 |
| Influenza and pneumonia | 1.9 | 1.6 | 2.1 | 2.0 | 1.7 | 2.3 | 0.9 | 0.9 | 0.9 |
| Cirrhosis of liver | 13.8 | 18.6 | 9.3 | 13.2 | 17.8 | 8.8 | 17.5 | 23.3 | 12.3 |
| Diabetes mellitus | 15.5 | 13.1 | 17.8 | 15.0 | 12.9 | 17.0 | 18.7 | 14.7 | 22.5 |
| Suicide | 12.5 | 19.0 | 6.3 | 13.4 | 20.2 | 6.9 | 6.9 | 11.1 | 3.1 |
| Homicide | 9.4 | 14.9 | 4.1 | 5.9 | 9.2 | 2.9 | 31.2 | 52.6 | 11.8 |
| Bronchitis, emphysema, and asthma | 10.0 | 14.4 | 5.9 | 10.8 | 15.5 | 6.4 | 5.0 | 7.3 | 2.9 |
| Tuberculosis, all forms | 1.3 | 1.8 | 0.9 | 1.1 | 1.4 | 0.7 | 3.0 | 4.3 | 1.7 |

## DEATH RATES IN AMERICA 1978 (per 100,000)

SOURCE: National Center for Health Statistics

| | Total | | | White | | | All Other | | |
|---|---|---|---|---|---|---|---|---|---|
| Age Group | Both sexes | Male | Female | Both sexes | Male | Female | Both sexes | Male | Female |
| All ages[1] | 883.4 | 994.4 | 778.3 | 895.7 | 999.8 | 796.5 | 805.1 | 959.7 | 664.5 |
| Under 1 year | 1,434.4 | 1,591.7 | 1,269.6 | 1,218.3 | 1,359.6 | 1,069.7 | 2,456.7 | 2,708.5 | 2,206.5 |
| 1-4 | 69.2 | 78.2 | 59.9 | 62.7 | 71.7 | 53.3 | 99.0 | 108.1 | 89.7 |
| 5-9 | 33.4 | 38.9 | 27.8 | 31.4 | 36.3 | 26.3 | 43.0 | 51.5 | 34.4 |
| 10-14 | 34.3 | 43.7 | 24.6 | 33.0 | 41.8 | 23.7 | 40.9 | 53.1 | 28.6 |
| 15-19 | 100.9 | 145.3 | 55.3 | 101.8 | 146.9 | 55.2 | 96.0 | 136.1 | 55.9 |
| 20-24 | 134.7 | 203.1 | 66.5 | 126.3 | 190.8 | 61.0 | 184.0 | 278.4 | 97.2 |
| 25-29 | 131.8 | 192.2 | 72.5 | 115.7 | 168.3 | 63.0 | 233.7 | 356.7 | 128.5 |
| 30-34 | 139.7 | 192.9 | 87.8 | 120.6 | 165.0 | 76.4 | 270.5 | 402.3 | 159.7 |
| 35-39 | 189.4 | 254.0 | 127.9 | 161.7 | 215.3 | 109.6 | 381.6 | 548.8 | 244.8 |
| 40-44 | 296.1 | 382.8 | 213.8 | 257.2 | 329.1 | 187.5 | 562.6 | 784.7 | 380.9 |
| 45-49 | 471.6 | 608.5 | 341.4 | 428.5 | 553.8 | 307.8 | 779.7 | 1,021.3 | 570.1 |
| 50-54 | 742.4 | 980.9 | 520.5 | 683.7 | 906.6 | 474.5 | 1,216.8 | 1,610.3 | 877.4 |
| 55-59 | 1,115.9 | 1,490.1 | 774.3 | 1,046.0 | 1,404.8 | 716.5 | 1,734.2 | 2,266.7 | 1,271.5 |
| 60-64 | 1,774.2 | 2,411.5 | 1,212.8 | 1,695.2 | 2,318.2 | 1,143.4 | 2,537.7 | 3,339.1 | 1,867.3 |
| 65-69 | 2,463.0 | 3,439.3 | 1,685.2 | 2,412.7 | 3,394.5 | 1,628.2 | 2,878.3 | 3,814.8 | 2,150.3 |
| 70-74 | 3,787.4 | 5,241.5 | 2,724.9 | 3,684.9 | 5,166.9 | 2,612.5 | 4,877.9 | 5,984.5 | 3,980.1 |
| 75-79 | 6,024.2 | 8,065.8 | 4,713.2 | 5,393.8 | 7,996.2 | 4,564.3 | 7,547.7 | 8,724.1 | 6,620.7 |
| 80-84 | 8,954.0 | 11,597.1 | 7,509.4 | 9,080.7 | 11,821.8 | 7,606.7 | 7,573.2 | 9,419.8 | 6,372.9 |
| 85 and over | 14,700.7 | 17,258.9 | 13,541.2 | 15,316.0 | 18,100.3 | 14,079.0 | 9,228.7 | 10,678.2 | 8,449.0 |

[1]Figures for age not stated included in "All ages" but not distributed among age groups.

## U.S. DEATHS FROM ACCIDENTS

SOURCE: National Center for Health Statistics

| Type of Accident | Deaths per 100,000 Population 1970 | 1973 | 1978 |
|---|---|---|---|
| **All Accidents** | **56.4** | **55.2** | **48.4** |
| Railway Accidents | 0.4 | 0.4 | 0.3 |
| Motor vehicle accidents | 26.9 | 26.5 | 24.0 |
| Motor vehicle traffic | 26.3 | 25.9 | 23.5 |
| Vehicle pedestrian | 4.4 | 4.3 | 3.7 |
| Other road vehicle accidents | 0.1 | 0.1 | 0.1 |
| Water transport accidents | 0.8 | 0.8 | 0.7 |
| Air and space transport accidents | 0.8 | 0.8 | 0.9 |
| Accidental poisoning | | | |
| By solid and liquid substances | 1.8 | 1.8 | 1.4 |
| By gases and vapors | 0.8 | 0.8 | 0.8 |
| Accidental falls | 8.3 | 7.9 | 6.3 |
| Fall from one level to another | 2.4 | 2.0 | 1.8 |
| Fall on the same level | 0.4 | 0.3 | 0.2 |
| Unspecified falls | 5.6 | 5.5 | 4.3 |
| Accidents caused | | | |
| By fire and flames | 3.3 | 3.1 | 2.8 |
| By firearms | 1.2 | 1.2 | 0.8 |
| Accidents mainly of industrial type | | | |
| Cutting or piercing instruments | 0.1 | 0.1 | 0.1 |
| Explosive material | 0.3 | 0.2 | 0.2 |
| Hot substances, etc. | 0.1 | 0.1 | 0.1 |
| Electric current | 0.6 | 0.5 | 0.5 |
| Other | 1.9 | 1.8 | 1.6 |
| Inhalation and ingestion of objects | 1.4 | 1.4 | 1.4 |
| Accidental drowning | 3.1 | 3.4 | 2.7 |
| Complications due to medical procedures | 1.8 | 1.7 | 1.4 |
| All other accidents | 2.8 | 2.5 | 2.5 |

## U.S. HOMICIDES AND SUICIDES

SOURCE: National Center For Health Statistics

| Item | 1960 Male | 1960 Female | 1965 Male | 1965 Female | 1970 Male | 1970 Female | 1978 Male | 1978 Female |
|---|---|---|---|---|---|---|---|---|
| **Homicide** | **6,269** | **2,195** | **8,148** | **2,564** | **13,278** | **3,570** | **15,838** | **4,594** |
| Assault by: | | | | | | | | |
| Firearms and explosives | 3,460 | 1,167 | 4,807 | 1,351 | 9,209 | 2,004 | 10,997 | 2,389 |
| Cutting and piercing instruments | 1,442 | 394 | 1,847 | 445 | 2,229 | 551 | 2,729 | 783 |
| Other means | 1,069 | 631 | 1,216 | 768 | 1,512 | 1,010 | 1,854 | 1,414 |
| Intervention of police | 242 | 3 | 271 | — | 328 | 5 | 257 | 8 |
| Execution | 56 | — | 7 | — | — | — | 1 | — |
| **Suicide** | **14,539** | **4,502** | **15,490** | **6,017** | **16,629** | **6,851** | **20,188** | **7,106** |
| Poisoning | 2,631 | 1,699 | 3,179 | 2,816 | 3,299 | 3,285 | 3,105 | 2,912 |
| Hanging and strangulation | 2,576 | 79 | 2,453 | 744 | 2,422 | 831 | 2,759 | 753 |
| Firearms and explosives | 7,879 | 1,138 | 8,457 | 1,441 | 9,704 | 2,068 | 12,830 | 2,557 |
| Other | 1,453 | 875 | 1,401 | 1,016 | 1,204 | 667 | 1,494 | 884 |

—Represents zero.

## ACCIDENTAL DEATH RATES: BY NATIONS

SOURCE: U.N. *Demographic Yearbook*, 1979 (Table 21), © United Nations

| Nation | Latest Year Available | Accidental Deaths per 100,000 Population* |
|---|---|---|
| France | 1977 | 70.6 |
| Austria | 1978 | 68.9 |
| Hungary | 1978 | 68.9 |
| Luxembourg | 1978 | 61.2 |
| Belgium | 1976 | 60.5 |
| Czechoslovakia | 1977 | 59.4 |
| Kuwait | 1977 | 59.1 |
| Germany, East | 1978 | 58.9 |
| Venezuela | 1977 | 57.9 |
| Poland | 1978 | 54.7 |
| Ecuador | 1976 | 54.4 |
| Iceland | 1978 | 53.7 |
| New Zealand | 1976 | 51.2 |
| Northern Ireland | 1977 | 49.1 |
| Germany, West | 1978 | 49.0 |
| Canada | 1977 | 48.1 |
| Australia | 1977 | 48.0 |
| Sweden | 1978 | 47.0 |
| UNITED STATES | 1976 | 46.9 |
| Switzerland | 1978 | 46.6 |
| Greece | 1978 | 46.2 |
| Norway | 1977 | 46.0 |
| Yugoslavia | 1977 | 44.4 |
| Scotland | 1977 | 44.2 |
| Costa Rica | 1978 | 44.1 |
| Uruguay | 1978 | 44.0 |
| Trinidad & Tobago | 1977 | 43.1 |
| Bulgaria | 1978 | 41.8 |
| Ireland | 1976 | 40.0 |
| Denmark | 1978 | 38.9 |
| Guatemala | 1977 | 38.7 |
| Mauritius | 1978 | 38.7 |
| Spain | 1976 | 37.3 |
| Panama | 1977 | 34.4 |
| Jordan | 1976 | 31.4 |
| Israel | 1978 | 29.7 |
| England & Wales | 1977 | 29.3 |
| Malta | 1978 | 27.9 |
| Netherlands | 1978 | 27.9 |
| Japan | 1978 | 26.2 |
| Chile | 1976 | 24.8 |
| Egypt | 1976 | 23.9 |
| Singapore | 1978 | 23.8 |
| Paraguay | 1977 | 20.1 |
| Argentina | 1977 | 19.5 |
| Hong Kong | 1978 | 15.5 |

*Based on population estimates for the designated year.

## INTERNATIONAL SUICIDE RATES (per 100,000 population)

SOURCE: United Nations *Demographic Yearbook*, 1979 (Table 21), © United Nations

| Nation | Year | Rate |
|---|---|---|
| Romania | 1978 | 66.5 |
| Hungary | 1978 | 43.1 |
| Austria | 1978 | 24.8 |
| Switzerland | 1978 | 23.9 |
| Denmark | 1978 | 23.3 |
| Germany, West | 1978 | 22.2 |
| Czechoslovakia | 1977 | 21.3 |
| Sweden | 1978 | 19.0 |
| Luxembourg | 1978 | 18.5 |
| Japan | 1978 | 17.7 |
| Belgium | 1976 | 16.6 |
| France | 1977 | 16.5 |
| Yugoslavia | 1977 | 14.5 |
| Canada | 1977 | 14.2 |
| Bulgaria | 1978 | 13.6 |
| Poland | 1978 | 13.3 |
| UNITED STATES | 1976 | 12.5 |
| Iceland | 1978 | 11.6 |
| Singapore | 1978 | 11.4 |
| Norway | 1977 | 11.4 |
| Australia | 1977 | 11.1 |
| Uruguay | 1978 | 10.5 |
| Trinidad & Tobago | 1977 | 8.7 |
| Hong Kong | 1978 | 8.3 |
| Scotland | 1977 | 8.1 |
| England & Wales | 1977 | 8.0 |
| Argentina | 1977 | 7.8 |
| Mauritius | 1978 | 7.7 |
| Chile | 1976 | 5.7 |
| Ireland | 1976 | 5.7 |
| Israel | 1978 | 5.6 |
| Northern Ireland | 1977 | 4.6 |
| Venezuela | 1977 | 4.6 |
| Costa Rica | 1978 | 4.1 |
| Spain | 1976 | 4.1 |
| Greece | 1978 | 2.9 |
| Ecuador | 1976 | 2.7 |
| Malta | 1978 | 2.1 |
| Netherlands | 1978 | 2.1 |
| Guatemala | 1977 | 1.9 |
| Panama | 1977 | 1.9 |
| Paraguay | 1977 | 1.8 |
| Mexico | 1975 | 1.7 |
| Barbados | 1977 | 1.6 |
| Kuwait | 1977 | 0.4 |
| Guyana | 1976 | 0.3 |
| Jordan | 1976 | 0.2 |
| Egypt | 1976 | 0.1 |

## VENEREAL DISEASE

SOURCE: American Social Health Association

Venereal disease, or more accurately, sexually transmissible disease, encompasses 20 conditions of which gonorrhea, nongonococcal urethritis/cervicitis, genital herpes, syphilis, cytomegalovirus and group B streptococcal disease are the most dangerous. It is estimted that over ten million persons were affected with some form of VD this year. Complications from prolonged and untreated infection with some forms of VD can lead to serious medical conditions, some of which can be permanently debilitating and even fatal.

Most venereal diseases can be completely cured although at least two are viral and cannot. Genital herpes is spreading at an alarming rate, and is associated with cervical cancer in women and brain damage in newborn babies. With vaccines for any of the venereal diseases still some way off, major attention is given to educating the public. The American Social Health Association produces and distributes, films, literature and other material suited for home, classroom or clinic. Additionally, the VD National Hotline, an information and referral service in the continental U.S. is 800-227-8922 (Calif., 800-982-5883), provides service 8 AM-8 PM, M-F, 10 AM-6 PM, S/Sun.

## REFERENCE CHART: LEADING CANCER SITES, 1982 (ESTIMATED)

SOURCE: American Cancer Society. All figures rounded to nearest 1,000.

| Site | Estimated New Cases 1982 | Estimated Deaths 1982 | Warning Signal: If you have one, see your doctor | Safeguards | Comment |
|---|---|---|---|---|---|
| BREAST | 113,000 | 37,000 | Lump or thickening in the breast or unusual discharge from nipple. | Regular checkup. Monthly breast self-examination. | The leading cause of cancer death in women. |
| COLON AND RECTUM | 123,000 | 57,000 | Change in bowel habits; bleeding. | Regular checkup, including digital, occult blood and proctoscopic exams, especially after age 40. | Because of accuracy of available tests, is potentially a highly curable disease. |
| LUNG | 129,000 | 111,000 | Persistent cough, or lingering respiratory ailment | 80% of lung cancer would be prevented if no one smoked cigarettes. | The leading cause of cancer death among men and rising mortality among women. |
| ORAL (INCLUDING PHARYNX) | 27,000 | 9,000 | Sore that does not heal. Difficulty in swallowing. | Regular checkup. | Many more lives should be saved because the mouth is easily accessible to visual examination by physicians and dentists. |
| SKIN | 15,000[1] | 7,000 | Sore that does not heal, or change in wart or mole. | Regular checkup, avoidance of over-exposure to sun. | Skin cancer is readily detected by observation, and diagnosed by simple biopsy. |
| UTERUS | 55,000[2] | 10,000 | Unusual bleeding or discharge. | Regular checkup, including pelvic examination with Pap test. | Uterine cancer mortality has declined 70% during the last 40 years with wider application of the Pap test. Postmenopausal women with abnormal bleeding should be checked. |
| KIDNEY AND BLADDER | 55,000 | 19,000 | Urinary difficulty bleeding, in which case consult doctor at once | Regular checkup with urinalysis. | Protective measures for workers in high-risk industries are helping to eliminate one of the important causes of these cancers. |
| LARYNX | 11,000 | 4,000 | Hoarseness—difficulty in swallowing. | Regular checkup, including larygoscopy. | Readily curable if caught early. |
| PROSTATE | 73,000 | 23,000 | Urinary difficulty | Regular checkup, including palpation. | Occurs mainly in men over 60, the disease can be detected by palpation at regular checkup. |
| STOMACH | 24,000 | 14,000 | Indigestion | Regular checkup. | An 80% decline in mortality in 50 years, for reasons yet unknown. |
| LEUKEMIA | 24,000 | 16,000 | Leukemia is cancer of blood-forming tissues and is characterized by the abnormal production of immature white blood cells. Acute lymphocytic leukemia strikes mainly children and is treated by drugs which have extended life from a few months to as much as ten years. Chronic leukemia strikes usually after age 25 and progresses less rapidly. | | |
| LYMPHOMAS | 40,000 | 21,000 | These cancers arise in the lymph system and include Hodgkin's Disease and lymphosarcoma. Some patients with lymphatic cancers can lead normal lives for many years. Five-year survival rate for Hodgkin's Disease increased from 25% to 54% in 20 years. | | |

[1]Only melanoma. Estimate new cases of non-melanoma skin cancer over 400,000. [2]If carcinoma in situ is included, cases total over 100,000.

### PROGRESS AGAINST CANCER

| Category | 1937 | 1981 |
|---|---|---|
| Saved (alive five years after treatment) | Fewer than one in five | One in three |
| Uterine cancer | Chief cause of cancer death in women | Death rate cut more than 70% since 1930. Could be reduced more |
| Lung cancer | Mounting: no prospect of control | Still mounting: but upward of 80% could be prevented |
| Research support | Less than $1,000,000 | Over $1,000,000,000 |
| Cancer clinics and registries approved by American College of Surgeons | 240 in United States and Canada | Over 800, plus expansion of teaching, research, treatment centers |
| State control measures | Seven states | All 50 states |
| Chemotherapy | Almost no research | Major research attack has produced more than 40 useful drugs |

One in two patients could be saved today by early diagnosis and prompt treatment.

## CANCER DEATH RATES AROUND THE WORLD

SOURCE: American Cancer Society

Death Rates per 100,000 Population—1976-77.

| Male Cancer Death Rates | | Male Cancer Death Rates | | Female Cancer Death Rates | | Female Cancer Death Rates | |
|---|---|---|---|---|---|---|---|
| Uruguay* | 294.6 | Hong Kong | 229.1 | Uruguay* | 180.3 | Israel | 141.3 |
| Scotland | 269.8 | Ireland* | 225.2 | Denmark | 170.9 | Sweden | 140.9 |
| Belgium* | 266.7 | New Zealand | 221.0 | Scotland | 165.8 | Costa Rica* | 139.5 |
| Netherlands | 261.6 | UNITED STATES | 213.6 | Hungary | 163.6 | Iceland | 138.7 |
| Hungary | 256.9 | Poland | 213.4 | Ireland* | 161.0 | Argentina** | 137.2 |
| France* | 255.7 | Argentina** | 212.5 | England & Wales | 156.0 | UNITED STATES | 136.3 |
| England & Wales | 251.5 | Germany, East* | 211.8 | Austria | 155.3 | Canada | 135.3 |
| Austria | 248.7 | Canada | 211.2 | Germany, West | 154.8 | Switzerland | 134.2 |
| Germany, West | 244.8 | Australia | 210.7 | Chile | 153.8 | Germany, East* | 133.8 |
| Singapore | 242.1 | Chile | 197.7 | New Zealand | 150.7 | Norway | 131.2 |
| Switzerland | 236.8 | Sweden | 197.5 | Northern Ireland | 150.4 | Venezuela | 130.3 |
| Denmark | 232.1 | Spain* | 192.5 | Belgium* | 147.7 | Australia | 129.2 |
| Northern Ireland | 229.6 | Norway | 188.0 | Netherlands | 142.6 | Singapore | 127.7 |

*1976 only. **1977 only.

## ADJUSTED HOSPITAL EXPENSE PER INPATIENT DAY: COMMUNITY HOSPITALS, 1968-1980

Source: American Hospital Association

Expenses per day related to inpatient care adjusted to exclude those expenses incurred for outpatient care.

| Hospital Size All Community | 1968 | 1970 | 1972 | 1974 | 1976 | 1978 | 1979 | 1980 |
|---|---|---|---|---|---|---|---|---|
| **Hospitals** | **$55.80** | **$73.73** | **$94.87** | **$113.55** | **$151.79** | **$194.34** | **$217.34** | **$245.12** |
| 6-24 Beds | 41.98 | 59.68 | 75.76 | 83.44 | 117.46 | 152.34 | 176.19 | 203.49 |
| 25-49 Beds | 41.10 | 54.15 | 68.68 | 82.73 | 113.42 | 151.68 | 172.05 | 197.14 |
| 50-99 Beds | 45.24 | 58.85 | 72.98 | 86.58 | 117.95 | 149.68 | 170.12 | 190.98 |
| 100-199 Beds | 51.11 | 65.87 | 84.31 | 101.06 | 135.04 | 172.50 | 193.55 | 215.16 |
| 200-299 Beds | 56.22 | 74.32 | 92.43 | 111.35 | 148.37 | 186.94 | 206.90 | 239.17 |
| 300-399 Beds | 59.24 | 77.96 | 99.34 | 116.80 | 155.99 | 200.70 | 223.27 | 247.86 |
| 400-499 Beds | 60.67 | 79.68 | 100.23 | 122.11 | 160.35 | 208.78 | 234.15 | 263.01 |
| 500 or more Beds | 66.27 | 87.37 | 115.34 | 136.73 | 179.80 | 228.53 | 254.17 | 288.03 |

## HOSPITAL COSTS IN COMMUNITY HOSPITALS

Source: American Hospital Association

| Year | Adjusted Expenses per Inpatient Day | Average Length of Stay (Days) | Average Adjusted Expense per Patient Stay |
|---|---|---|---|
| 1963 | $ 35.11 | 7.7 | $270.35 |
| 1965 | 40.56 | 7.8 | 316.37 |
| 1967 | 49.46 | 8.3 | 410.52 |
| 1969 | 64.26 | 8.3 | 533.36 |
| 1971 | 83.43 | 8.0 | 667.44 |
| 1972 | 94.87 | 7.9 | 749.47 |
| 1973 | 102.44 | 7.8 | 799.03 |
| 1974 | $113.55 | 7.8 | $ 885.69 |
| 1975 | 133.81 | 7.7 | 1030.34 |
| 1976 | 151.79 | 7.7 | 1168.78 |
| 1977 | 173.98 | 7.6 | 1322.25 |
| 1978 | 194.34 | 7.6 | 1474.41 |
| 1979 | 217.34 | 7.6 | 1641.48 |
| 1980 | 245.12 | 7.6 | 1851.04 |

## ABORTION AND THE LAW

On January 22, 1973, the U.S. Supreme Court issued two landmark rulings in *Roe v. Wade* and *Doe v. Bolton* which declared the abortion laws of Texas and Georgia, respectively, unconstitutional. As a result of these decisions, state abortion laws are subject to the Court's three-fold guidelines (each of which determines the states' power to regulate abortion based on the trimester of pregnancy in question).

Since that time, state legislatures and the Congress have set up parental and spousal consent requirements or funding regulations pursuant to their legitimate interests "in the health of the mother and the potential life of the fetus." In a 1976 decision, the Court ruled that the State cannot, in all cases, require parental consent to abortions for minors. The Court did decide, however, that statutory provisions requiring written consent of the aborting mother, and requiring recordkeeping and reporting which "are reasonably directed to the preservation of maternal health and that properly respect a patient's confidentiality and privacy," are constitutional. During 1981, the High Court decided that a statute which requires a physician to notify an immature, unemancipated minor's parents of her intent to abort was not unconstitutional. The Court also affirmed an Indiana federal court decision upholding the constitutionality of an Indiana law requiring that all second trimester abortions be performed in hospitals.

In two 1977 decisions, *Maher v. Roe* and *Beal v. Doe*, the Court ruled that states have no Constitutional or statutorial obligation to provide Medicaid funding for elective non-therapeutic abortion. The Court maintained that "the State unquestionably has a 'strong and legitimate interest in encouraging normal childbirth...' an interest honored over the centuries." Such "sensitive" issues, declared the Court, are properly decided by the legislature in a democratic society. In June 1980, the Supreme Court, in *Harris v. McRae* and *Williams v. Zbarag*, extended its ruling by determining that neither Congress nor the States need provide funding for medically necessary abortions. Resolving a much contested element in the abortion controversy, the Court further declared that such funding restrictions are not violative of the First Amendment's Establishment Clause just because it "may coincide with the religious tenets of the Roman Catholic Church."

## ABORTION DEBATE: 1982

Since 1973, opponents of abortion have sought to reverse the Court's decisions through legislation. The primary goal of the Right-to-Life Movement has been to pass a Constitutional Amendment which would permit the outlawing of abortion. Since *Roe v. Wade*, various types of amendments have been introduced in Congress. One type sought to make it clear that an unborn child was a person whose rights are to be protected to the same extent as those of any already-born United States citizen. Another approach was to return to the States the power to enact or not enact abortion-prohibiting or limiting legislation. The focus in 1982, however, was on a "federalism amendment" which would specifically reject the holdings in *Roe v. Wade* by declaring "[t]he right to abortion is not secured by this Constitution." This amendment would then permit both the Federal government and the States to restrict abortion, with the understanding that a State law can be "more restrictive than a" Federal statute. For the first time since 1973, the full Senate Judiciary Committee voted favorably on a Right-to-Life Amendment when it voted 10-7 in behalf of this federalist amendment.

A second avenue of abortion regulation, significant during 1982, was Senator Jesse Helms' Human Life Bill which contains a legislative finding that human life begins at conception, and which includes various other provisions, which if passed, would virtually remove all Federal government encouragement, whether through the use of funds, insurance benefits or educational subsidies, of abortion. This bill reached the Senate floor for debate, but it was tabled after a several-day filibuster.

Various other abortion-related legislation has emanated at the Federal, state and even local levels. Many of such enactments have met with court challenges. These include:

**Funding Restrictions:** In 1976, Congress enacted the "Hyde Amendment" to the Labor-HEW Appropriations bill to cut off, in most cases, federal funds for abortion provided through the Medicaid program. Various versions, more or less restrictive than the 1976 bill, had been enacted by each successive Congress. A number of states had also continued to prohibit the use of public funds for abortion. Court challenges were brought against the Hyde Amendment and some of the state laws which restricted government funding of abortions. In two 1977 decisions, the U.S. Supreme Court held that funding of non-medically necessary abortions is not mandated by either the Constitution or the Medicaid provisions of the Social Security Act. Subsequently, two federal judges, one each from Illinois and New York, declared the Hyde Amendment unconstitutional. The Illinois judge also ruled unconstitutional an Illinois statute prohibiting state funding of medically necessary abortions. In June 1980, the Court, extending the reasoning of the 1977 cases, decided that neither Congress nor the States was constitutionally compelled, nor were the States required by the Medicaid statute, to provide funding for medically necessary abortions. Its opinion also affirmed that "abortion is inherently different from other medical procedures because no other medical procedure involves the purposeful termination of a potential life." In order to circumvent the effect of permitting states to prohibit abortion funding, abortion advocates have sued to have abortion funding restrictions declared violative of *state* constitutions. The New Jersey Supreme Court, joining the prior declarations of the Massachusetts and California high courts, decided that its respective state constitution, as compared with the United States Constitution, affords a greater degree of protection to a woman's decision to have an abortion.

**Miscellaneous Requirements:** The Supreme Court has ruled that parental and spousal vetoes of a woman's choice to abort are unconstitutional. However, in 1981 in *H.L. v. Matheson* the highest tribunal declared that a law which mandates "possible" notification of parents of a minor who is seeking an abortion, and is a dependent, unemancipated child making "no claim or showing as to her maturity or as to her relation with her parents" is constitutional. The Court voted that such a statute serves to preserve "family integrity and [protect] adolescents."

The Supreme Court has agreed to hear in the 1982-83 term arguments in two cases on the validity of a number of abortion-related regulations. These include a mandated detailing of fetal development and a required 24-hour waiting period before a woman undergoes an abortion.

# AIR POLLUTION IN U.S. AIR QUALITY CONTROL AREAS: 1980

SOURCE: Environmental Protection Agency

## OZONE/OXIDANT

Note: The new ozone standard is 0.12 ppm, daily maximum hour.

| Metropolitan Area | Number of Stations: Total Valid | Number of Stations: Exceeding Daily Standard | Range of Max. (ppm)* Daily Values |
|---|---|---|---|
| New York | 9 | 8 | 0.15–0.18 |
| Los Angeles | 14 | 13 | 0.11–0.38 |
| Chicago | 13 | 8 | 0.10–0.15 |
| Philadelphia | 4 | 4 | 0.14–0.18 |
| Detroit | 6 | 2 | 0.11–0.13 |
| San Francisco | 13 | 4 | 0.05–0.18 |
| Boston | 2 | 1 | 0.11–0.15 |
| Washington, D.C. | 6 | 3 | 0.12–0.19 |
| Cleveland | 4 | 0 | 0.09–0.12 |
| St. Louis | 14 | 12 | 0.07–0.18 |

* ppm = parts per million.

## CARBON MONOXIDE

Note: The 8-hour standard is 10 milligrams per cubic meter, arithmetic mean.

| Metropolitan Area | Number of Stations: Total Valid | Number of Stations: Exceeding Annual Standard | Range of Max. 8-Hour Values (Mg/m³)* |
|---|---|---|---|
| New York | 10 | 3 | 4.5–15.0 |
| Los Angeles | 17 | 11 | 5.6–24.9 |
| Chicago | 5 | 1 | 5.2–13.6 |
| Philadelphia | 4 | 0 | 2.5– 8.2 |
| Detroit | 6 | 0 | 4.6– 8.3 |
| San Francisco | 10 | 1 | 4.3–10.3 |
| Boston | 3 | 1 | 4.6– 9.7 |
| Washington, D.C. | 6 | 1 | 5.3–11.0 |
| Cleveland | 2 | 1 | 8.3–11.0 |
| St. Louis | 12 | 2 | 5.0–13.7 |

* $Mg/m^3$ = milligrams per cubic meter.

## SULFUR DIOXIDE

Note: The primary annual standard is 80 $\mu g/m^3$, arithmetic mean.

| Metropolitan Area | Number of Stations: Total Valid | Number of Stations: Exceeding Annual Standard | Range of Annual Mean (μg/m³)* |
|---|---|---|---|
| New York | 31 | 0 | 9–59 |
| Los Angeles | 10 | 0 | 20–28 |
| Chicago | 7 | 0 | 29–43 |
| Philadelphia | 6 | 0 | 22–48 |
| San Francisco | 3 | 0 | 7– 9 |
| Detroit | 17 | 0 | 10–46 |
| Boston | 4 | 0 | 17–56 |
| Washington, D.C. | 7 | 0 | 24–36 |
| Cleveland | 8 | 0 | 23–47 |
| St. Louis | 14 | 0 | 21–59 |

* $\mu g/m^3$ = micrograms per cubic meter.

## TOTAL SUSPENDED PARTICULATES

Note: The primary annual standard is 75 $\mu g/m^3$, geometric mean.

| Metropolitan Area | Number of Stations: Total Valid | Number of Stations: Exceeding Annual Standard | Range of Annual Mean (μg/m³)* |
|---|---|---|---|
| New York | 30 | 0 | 37– 67 |
| Los Angeles | 7 | 7 | 86–127 |
| Chicago | 5 | 21 | 43–250 |
| Philadelphia | 20 | 1 | 40–132 |
| Detroit | 38 | 4 | 43–138 |
| San Francisco | 11 | 0 | 41– 64 |
| Boston | 13 | 0 | 34– 74 |
| Washington, D.C. | 23 | 0 | 40– 67 |
| Cleveland | 47 | 15 | 48–143 |
| St. Louis | 31 | 18 | 50–167 |

* $\mu g/m^3$ = micrograms per cubic meter.

# WORLDWIDE TANKER* CASUALTIES, 1973 TO 1981

SOURCE: Tanker Advisory Center, New York, N.Y.

| Year | Accidental Oil Spills: Number | Accidental Oil Spills: Tons | Total Losses: Number | Total Losses: DWTs (millions) | Total Losses: No. of Fatalities | Tankers: Number | Tankers: DWTs (millions) |
|---|---|---|---|---|---|---|---|
| 1973 | 36 | 84,458 | 12 | 0.682 | 70 | 3,750 | 218.9 |
| 1974 | 48 | 67,115 | 14 | 0.536 | 94 | 3,928 | 253.6 |
| 1975 | 45 | 188,042 | 22 | 0.815 | 90 | 4,140 | 296.2 |
| 1976 | 29 | 204,235 | 20 | 1.172 | 226 | 4,237 | 336.7 |
| 1977 | 49 | 213,080 | 20 | 1.000 | 113 | 4,229 | 369.0 |
| 1978 | 35 | 260,488 | 17 | 0.913 | 148 | 4,137 | 380.4 |
| 1979 | 65 | 723,533 | 26 | 2.501 | 306 | 3,945 | 376.0 |
| 1980 | 32 | 135,635 | 15 | 1.703 | 132 | 3,898 | 375.7 |
| 1981 | 33 | 45,285 | 20 | 1.086 | 73 | 3,937 | 372.5 |

* Includes tankers, oil/ore and bulk/oil ships of 6,000 deadweight tons.

# MEDICAL CARE INDEXES

SOURCE: U.S. Bureau of Labor Statistics

| Year | All medical care items* | Physicians' services | Dental services | Optometric examination and eyeglasses | Hospital daily service charges | Prescriptions and drugs |
|---|---|---|---|---|---|---|
| 1935 | **36.1** | 39.2 | 40.8 | 56.7 | 11.9 | 70.7 |
| 1945 | **42.1** | 46.0 | 49.6 | 63.9 | 16.2 | 74.8 |
| 1955 | **64.8** | 65.4 | 73.0 | 77.0 | 41.5 | 94.7 |
| 1960 | **79.1** | 77.0 | 82.1 | 85.1 | 56.3 | 104.5 |
| 1962 | **83.5** | 81.3 | 84.7 | 89.2 | 64.9 | 101.7 |
| 1964 | **87.3** | 85.2 | 89.4 | 90.9 | 72.4 | 100.5 |
| 1965 | **89.5** | 88.3 | 92.2 | 92.8 | 76.6 | 100.2 |
| 1966 | **93.4** | 93.4 | 95.2 | 95.3 | 84.0 | 100.5 |
| 1967 | **100.0** | 100.0 | 100.0 | 100.0 | 100.0 | 100.0 |
| 1968 | **106.1** | 105.6 | 105.5 | 103.2 | 113.2 | 100.2 |
| 1969 | **113.4** | 112.9 | 112.9 | 107.6 | 127.9 | 101.3 |
| 1970 | **120.6** | 121.4 | 119.4 | 113.5 | 143.9 | 103.6 |
| 1971 | **128.4** | 129.8 | 127.0 | 120.3 | 160.8 | 105.4 |
| 1972 | **132.5** | 133.8 | 132.3 | 124.9 | 102.0† | 105.6 |
| 1973 | **137.7** | 138.2 | 136.4 | 129.5 | 105.6† | 105.9 |
| 1974 | **150.5** | 150.9 | 146.8 | 138.6 | 115.1† | 109.6 |
| 1975 | **168.6** | 169.4 | 161.9 | 149.6 | 132.3† | 118.8 |
| 1976 | **184.7** | 188.5 | 172.2 | 158.9 | 148.7† | 126.0 |
| 1977 | **202.4** | 206.0 | 185.1 | 168.2 | 164.1† | 134.1 |
| 1978 | **219.4** | 223.1 | 198.1 | — | — | 143.5 |
| 1979 | **239.7** | 243.6 | 214.8 | — | — | 153.8 |
| 1980 | **265.9** | 269.3 | 240.2 | — | — | 168.1 |
| 1981 | **294.5** | 299.0 | 263.3 | — | — | — |

* 1967 = 100 †Hospital Service Charges (January 1972 = 100)

## MILESTONES OF MEDICINE

| Date | Milestone | Discoverer | Nationality |
|---|---|---|---|
| 6th cent. B.C. | First recorded dietary and sanitary laws | Book of Leviticus | Hebrew |
| 5th–4th cent. B.C. | Medicine moves from realm of superstition to that of observation; emergence of the idea of nature as healer | Hippocrates | Greek |
| 4th cent. B.C. | Beginning of a systematic study of anatomy | Herophilus | Greek |
| 2d cent. A.D. | Correlation of extant medical knowledge into a single great system that influenced medical thought until the 16th century | Clarissimus Galen | Greco-Roman |
| 9th or 10th cent. | First-known description of smallpox and differentiation between that disease and measles; the approach was used until the 18th century | Rhazes or Rasis | Persian |
| 16th cent. | Reaffirmation of nature as prime healer; also, beginning of chemotherapy | Paracelsus | Swiss |
| 1543 | Publication of **De humani corporis fabrica**, first anatomy textbook based entirely on observation, rather than on Galen's writings | Andreas Vesalius | Flemish |
| c. 1590 | Invention of the microscope | Zacharias Janssen | Dutch |
| 1628 | Discovery of blood circulation | William Harvey | English |
| c. 1648 | Founding of biochemistry | Jan Baptista van Helmont | Flemish |
| 1661 | Discovery that capillaries are vein-artery junctions, thus completing the explanation of blood circulation | Marcello Malpighi | Italian |
| 1736 | First successful appendectomy | Claudius Amyand | French |
| 1757–66 | Established physiology as a branch of science | Albrecht von Haller | Swiss |
| 1796 | First successful antitoxin vaccination (for smallpox) | Edward Jenner | English |
| 1800 | Founding of histology—the study of tissues | Marie F. X. Bichat | French |
| 1816 | Invention of the stethoscope | René Laënnec | French |
| 1822 | Description of the process of digestion | William Beaumont | American |
| 1838–39 | Establishment of cell theory founding of cytology | Matthias Schleiden, Theodor Schwann | German |
| 1842 | Use of ether as an anesthetic during surgery | Crawford W. Long | American |
| 1844 | Use of nitrous oxide as anesthetic during surgery | Horace Wells | American |
| 1857 | Development of the pasteurization process began | Louis Pasteur | French |
| 1860 | Experiments that finally destroyed the idea of spontaneous generation | Louis Pasteur | French |
| 1865 | Introduction of surgical antisepsis | Joseph Lister | English |
| 1866 | Invention of the clinical thermometer | Thomas C. Allbut | English |
| 1870–1909 | Founding of neuroanatomy | Camillo Golgi | Italian |
| c. 1872 | Founding of bacteriology | Ferdinand Cohn | German |
| 1877 | Publication of postulates for determining the etiology of diseases | Robert Koch | German |
| 1883–84 | Discovery of the bacillus that causes diphtheria | Edwin Klebs, Friedrich Löffler | German |
| 1890–95 | Founding of serology and immunology | Paul Ehrlich, Emil von Behring | German |
| 1894 | Discovery of bubonic plague's causative bacillus | Alexandre Yersin<br>S. Kitasato | French<br>Japanese |
| 1892, 1895 | Founding of virology | Dmitri Ivanovski<br>(Independently, M. Beijerinck) | Russian<br>Dutch |
| 1895 | Publication of **Studies in Hysteria**; founding of psychoanalysis | Sigmund Freud | Austrian |
| 1895 | Discovery of X rays | Wilhelm Roentgen | German |
| 1897 | Development of method for making a differential blood count | Paul Ehrlich | German |
| 1901 | Establishment of etiology of yellow fever | Walter Reed and others | American |
| 1906 | Development of specific test for syphilis | August Wassermann and others<br>(Independently, Lazlo Detre) | German<br>Hungarian |
| 1906 | Passage of U.S. Pure Food Law—the first legislation of its kind | Harvey W. Wiley | American |
| 1912 | Discovery of vitamins | Casimir Funk | American, b. Poland |
| 1915 | Discovery of pellagra cure | Joseph Goldberger | American, b. Austria-Hungary |
| 1921 | Isolation of insulin for use in diabetic therapy | Frederick Banting, Charles Best | Canadian |
| 1926 | Discovery of liver extract (vitamin $B_1$) | George Minot, William Murphy | American |
| 1928 | Invention of artificial respirator ("iron lung") | Philip Drinker, Louis Shaw | American |
| 1928 | Discovery of penicillin | Alexander Fleming | Scottish |
| c. 1932 | First use of sulfa drugs in therapy | Gerhard Domagk | German |
| 1940 | Discovery of the Rh factor | Karl Landsteiner | American, b. Austria |
| 1943 | Discovery of streptomycin and its use in treating tuberculosis | Selman Waksman | American |
| 1944 | Introduction of corrective heart surgery to enable survival of "blue babies" | Alfred Blalock, Helen Taussig | American |
| 1949 | Cortisone introduced into medical therapy | Philip Hench and others | American |
| 1953 | Establishment of cryosurgery in which body temperature is lowered to slow circulation, allowing dry-heart surgery | Henry Swan | American |
| 1954 | Introduction of open-heart surgery | C. Walton Lillehei | American |
| 1954 | Development of hypodermic poliomyelitis vaccine | Jonas Salk | American |
| 1955 | Development of oral poliomyelitis vaccine | Albert Sabin | American |
| 1963 | First use of artificial heart for circulating blood during heart surgery | Michael De Bakey | American |
| 1967 | First surgical transplant of a human heart | Christiaan Barnard | South African |
| 1969 | Deciphering of structure of gamma globulin—one of the body's chief defenders against diseases | Gerald Edelman and others | American |
| 1972 | Research into the structure of antibodies | Gerald Edelman<br>Rodney R. Porter | American<br>English |
| 1978 | First "test-tube" baby born | Patrick Steptoe,<br>Robert Edwards | English |
| 1979 | First synthesis of a biologically active human protein, **Interferon** | Kari Cantell<br>Charles Weissmann<br>Walter Gilbert | Finnish<br>Swiss<br>American |

# MEDICAL GLOSSARY

**Abscess:** Collection of pus in a tissue cavity resulting from a localized infection associated with cellular disintegration.

**Anemia:** Decrease in the number of circulating red blood cells or in their hemoglobin (oxygen-carrying pigment) content. Can result from excessive bleeding or blood destruction (either inherited or disease caused) or from decreased blood formation (either nutritional deficiency or disease). In one form, sickle-cell anemia, it is inherited, occurring almost wholly among blacks. Pernicious anemia is caused by inability to absorb vitamin $B_{12}$.

**Angina:** Choking pain. Angina pectoris: chest pain resulting from insufficient blood circulation through the vessels supplying blood to the heart, precipitated by exertion or emotion and usually relieved by a vasodilator drug.

**Arteriosclerosis:** Generalized thickening, loss of elasticity, and hardening of the body's small and medium-size arteries.

**Atherosclerosis:** Arteriosclerosis in which fatty plaques build up in the lining of the arteries, narrowing the passageway and making the arterial walls thick and stiff.

**Asthma:** Disease characterized by repeated attacks of shortness of breath, with wheezing, cough, and choking feeling due to a spasmodic narrowing of the small bronchi.

**Biopsy:** Removal of a small piece of tissue from the living body for microscopic or chemical examination to assist in disease diagnosis.

**Bronchitis:** Acute or chronic inflammation of the bronchi (tubular passages leading to the lung cavities).

**Cancer:** Malignant disease in which abnormal tissue develops. The tumor may grow, invade nearby tissues and organs, and spread through the body via the lymph and blood vessels.

**Cataract:** Opacity of the normally transparent eye lens; this condition leads to impaired vision and stems from hereditary, nutritional, inflammatory, toxic, traumatic, or degenerative causes.

**Catheterization:** Introduction of a tubular instrument called a catheter into a body cavity for purposes of injecting fluids (as in intravenous therapy), of withdrawing fluids (as in bladder catheterization), or for observing body functions (as in cardiac catheterization).

**Cerebrospinal Fluid Examination:** Chemical, miscroscopic, and bacteriological examination of a sample of the usually clear and colorless liquid bathing the brain and spinal cord. The sample is usually removed by needle puncture of the lumbar spine.

**Cirrhosis:** Chronic liver ailment that results in a progressive destruction of liver cells and impairment of the organ's functions.

**Computerized Axial Tomography (CAT Scan):** The use of serial X-ray beams, recorders, and a computer to construct a visual, 3-dimensional description of any portion of the body for identification of abnormal structures or processes.

**Conjunctivitis:** Acute or chronic inflammation of the conjunctiva (the delicate transparent membrane lining the eyelids and covering the exposed surface of the eyeball). It results from exposure of the tissue to bacteria, viruses, or allergens or to other physical or chemical irritants.

**Cyst:** Any normal or abnormal sac in the body, especially one containing a liquid or semiliquid material.

**Cystic Fibrosis:** An inherited disease of the mucous-secreting glands that appears in infancy. Respiratory, excretory, and digestive functions are impaired by the copious production of thick secretions. There is no cure, but modern antibiotics and respiratory therapy enable children to live into adulthood.

**Cystitis:** Acute or chronic inflammation of the urinary bladder, caused by infection or irritation. The symptoms are frequent voiding accompanied by burning sensation and, sometimes, blood in the urine.

**Diabetes (Mellitus):** Hereditary or acquired disease of the insulin-secreting cells of the pancreas. Symptoms are thirst, weight loss, and frequent urination. Diabetes is diagnosed by use of urine and blood sugar tests. It is treated by regulating the sugar in the blood with diet, oral drugs, or, when necessary, with regular injections of insulin. Severe diabetes, if untreated, results in kidney failure, blindness, and death.

**Eczema:** Inflammatory skin disease that produces a great variety of lesions, such as vesicles, thickening of skin, watery discharge, and scales and crusts, with itching and burning sensations. Eczema is caused by allergy, infections, and nutritional, physical, and sometimes unknown factors.

**Edema:** Excessive accumulation of water and salt in the tissue spaces, caused by kidney or heart disease (generalized edema) or by local circulatory impairment stemming from inflammation, trauma, or neoplasm (localized edema).

**Electrocardiogram (ECG or EKG):** Graphic tracing of the electric current that is produced by the rhythmic contraction of the heart muscle. Visually, a periodic wave pattern is produced. Changes in the wave pattern may appear in the course of various heart diseases; the tracing is obtained by applying electrodes to specific spots on the skin of the chest and limbs.

**Electroencephalogram (EEG):** Graphic recording of the electric current created by the activity of the brain. The electrodes are placed on the scalp.

**Embolism:** Blocking of a blood vessel by a dislodged blood clot (after surgery), a fat globule (after a fracture), gas bubbles (after sudden decompression), clumps of bacteria (in certain infections), or by other matter.

**Emphysema (Pulmonary):** Lung disease characterized by over distention of the air sacs of the lungs (alveoli), their loss of elasticity, and destruction of the walls separating them. It results in a reduction of the respiratory surface, chronic shortness of breath, wheezing, and cough.

**Epilepsy:** Disease characterized by sudden and brief (in some forms momentary) convulsions, which are associated with impairment or loss of consciousness, psychic or sensory disturbances, and autonomic nervous system disturbances.

**Gangrene:** A form of necrosis (tissue death) due to an inadequate blood supply. Infection may also occur.

**Gastritis:** Acute or chronic inflammation of the lining of the stomach. It may be caused by the ingestion of alcohol, spices, medicines, chemicals, foods, as well as by infections or allergy.

**Gastroscopy:** Direct visualization of the inside of the stomach interior by means of an optical instrument called a gastroscope.

**Gastrointestinal Series (G.I. Series):** Serial X-ray examination of the stomach and intestines.

**Glaucoma:** Eye disease characterized by an increase in the internal pressure in the eye, caused by alteration of the intraocular fluid flow and resulting in visual impairment. If untreated, it may lead to blindness.

**Goiter:** Enlargement of the thyroid gland that shows as a swelling at the base of the neck. Goiter is often associated with iodine deficiency (endemic goiter), or with excessive secretion of thyroid hormones (exophthalmic goiter).

**Gout:** A disturbance of body chemistry, manifested by elevated uric acid blood levels and excessive deposits in tissues, particularly joints and cartilages. It is characterized by repeated attacks of acute and very painful inflammation of joints, especially those of the big toe but also of ankles, knees, wrists, and elbows.

**Hematoma:** Swelling produced by a collection of blood escaping from a ruptured blood vessel, resulting from trauma or injury. It is generally located under the skin and subcutaneous tissue, or under the bones of the skull.

**Hemorrhage (Bleeding):** Copious blood loss from the body. If sufficiently severe or unchecked, it will lead to faintness, shock, and death.

**Hemorrhoids (Piles):** Abnormal dilatation of the veins of the rectum and anus, causing local swelling, pain, itching, and bleeding.

**Hepatitis:** Liver inflammation, caused by infection or toxic substances. It is characterized by clay-colored stools, dark urine, fever, and jaundice (yellow coloration of the skin and white of the eye).

**Hernia:** Protrusion of a portion of an organ or tissue through an abnormal body opening. Inguinal hernia is one of the most common and consists of an intestinal loop protruding at the groin.

**Hypertension:** Disease characterized by elevated blood pressure, resulting from the functional or pathological narrowing of the peripheral small arteries. Except in limited instances, its cause is generally unknown.

**Immunotherapy:** A method of treating certain diseases by stimulating the body's natural immune response, resulting in partial or total immunization.

**Intestinal Obstruction:** Blockage of the normal flow of the intestinal contents, caused by a twist of a loop of the bowel or by a tumor, cancer, or foreign body.

**Kidney Failure (Renal Failure):** Severe impairment of the excretory function of the kidney. The acute form occurs most frequently after a crushing injury, transfusion of mismatched blood, severe burns, shock, generalized infections, obstetric accidents, and some kinds of poisoning.

**Laboratory Procedures:** Laboratory tests performed to assist in the diagnosis and treatment of disease. Usually these tests are carried out on samples of blood, urine, or other body fluids. The most common are:

**Blood Count:** Determination of the number and percentage of red and white blood cells from a blood sample that is obtained by puncturing a vein or the skin. It consists of a red blood cell (RBC) count, white blood cell (WBC) count, and platelet count.

**Blood Grouping:** Classification of red blood cells by the demonstration of specific antigens in the blood. Always done prior to transfusion.

**Blood Chemistry:** Determination of the content of various blood chemicals; the most usual are: sugar, for diabetes; urea nitrogen (BUN), for kidney or liver disease; uric acid, for gout; and cholesterol, for vascular and liver disease.

**Blood Culture:** Investigation to detect the presence of pathogenic germs by special culturing in artificial media.

**Urinalysis (Urine Analysis):** Examination of urine constituents, both normal (urea, uric acid, total nitrogen, ammonia, chlorides, phosphate, and others) and abnormal (albumin, glucose, acetone, bile, blood, cells, and bacteria).

**Meningitis:** Inflammation of the enveloping membranes of the brain or spinal cord, caused by virus, bacteria, yeasts, fungi, or protozoa. It may occur as a serious complication of another infection.

**Metabolism:** The total of the physical and chemical processes occurring in the living organism by which its substance is produced, maintained, and exchanged with transformation of energy; this energy itself provides fuel for all body functions and heat production.

**Metastasis:** Transfer of a disease (usually cancer) or the causative agent of a disease (e.g. bacteria or cancer cells) from one organ or part of the body to another, through the blood or lymph vessels.

**Multiple Sclerosis:** A chronic and slowly progressive disease of unknown cause that is characterized by patches of fibrous tissue degeneration in brain and spinal cord, causing various nervous system symptoms. The disease's course is marked by occasional periods of worsening or improvement.

**Muscular Dystrophy:** An inherited disease that involves the progressive weakness and degeneration of voluntary skeletal muscle fibers without nerve involvement.

**Myocarditis:** Inflammation of the heart muscle that may be caused by a number of infectious diseases, toxic chemicals, drugs, and traumatic agents.

**Necrosis:** Localized death of tissue, following interruption of the blood supply to the area.

**Nephritis:** Acute or chronic inflammatory disease of the kidneys, which usually follows some form of infection or toxic chemical poisoning. It impairs renal function, causing malaise, headache, edema, high blood pressure, and excretion of albumin in the urine.

**Neuralgia:** Brief attack of severe shooting pain along the course of one or more peripheral nerves, usually without clear physical cause.

**Neuritis:** Inflammation or degeneration of one or more peripheral nerves, causing pain, tenderness, tingling sensations, numbness, paralysis, muscle weakness, and wasting and disappearance of reflexes in the area involved. The cause may be infectious, toxic, nutritional (vitamin $B_1$ deficiency), or unknown.

**Pancreatitis:** Inflammation of the pancreas, either mild or acute and fulminating. The chronic form is characterized by recurrent attacks of diverse severity. Symptoms are sudden abdominal pain, tenderness and distention, vomiting and, in severe cases, shock and circulatory collapse.

**Pap Smear (Papanicolau Smear):** Method of staining a specimen of various body secretions—especially cervical but also respiratory, digestive, or genitourinary—to detect cancer by examining the cells in the smear. The procedure is named for its developer.

**Parkinsonism (Paralysis Agitans):** A usually chronic condition, marked by muscular rigidity, immobile face, excessive salivation, and tremor. These symptoms characterize Parkinson's disease; however, they are also observed in the course of treatment with certain psychotropic drugs or following encephalitis, or trauma.

**Pericarditis:** Acute or chronic inflammation of the pericardium (fibrous sac surrounding the heart), caused by infection, trauma, myocardial infarction, cancer, or complication from other diseases.

**Peritonitis:** Acute or chronic inflammation of the serous membrane lining and covering the visceral organs. Its symptoms are abdominal pain and tenderness, nausea, vomiting, moderate fever, and constipation. It is usually caused by infectious agents or foreign matter entering the abdominal cavity from the intestinal tract (perforation), female genital tract, bloodstream, or an external source (wound).

**Phlebitis:** Condition caused by inflammation of a vein wall, usually resulting in the formation of a blood clot inside the vessel. Phlebitis produces pain, swelling, and stiffness of the affected part, generally a limb.

**Pleurisy:** Acute or chronic inflammation of the pleura (serous membranes lining the thoracic cavity and covering the lungs). It often accompanies inflammatory lung diseases and may be caused by infection or cancer.

**Pneumonia:** An acute inflammation of the lungs, usually caused by bacterial or viral infection. Chills, sharp chest pain, shortness of breath, cough, rusty sputum, fever, and headache are primary symptoms.

**Pneumothorax:** Accumulation of air or gas in the space between the lungs and the chest wall, resulting in collapse of the lung.

**Polycythemia:** An abnormal increase in the number of circulating red blood cells.

**Polyp:** A protruding excrescence or growth from a mucous membrane, usually of the nasal passages but also of the uterine cervix, alimentary tract, or vocal cords.

**Psoriasis:** Chronic, occasionally acute, recurrent skin disease of unknown cause, characterized by thickened red skin patches that are covered with whitish shiny scales (plaques). Psoriasis usually affects the scalp, elbows, knees, back, and buttocks.

**Pulmonary Edema:** An acute condition in which fluid collects in the alveoli and tissues of the lungs. If severe, respiration is impaired and death may rapidly ensue. Pulmonary edema often accompanies congestive heart disease.

**Rheumatic Fever:** Disease characterized by initial sore throat, chills, high fever, and painful inflammation of large joints. Frequently cardiac complications follow, leading to permanent organic heart disease.

**Rickets:** A nutritional disease of children and infants caused by a deficiency of vitamin D. It is marked by irritability, decalcification of the bones, and skeletal deformity. Bowed legs, knock knees, and pigeon breast may occur.

**Sciatica:** A severe pain along the sciatic nerve, which extends from the buttock along the back of the thigh and leg to the ankle.

**Spinal Curvature:** A marked displacement of any portion of the spine, which may be caused by disease or mechanical deviation of the bones or muscles of the spine, hips, or legs.

**Septicemia:** Presence of bacteria or bacterial toxins in the circulating blood caused by the breakdown of local defenses, permitting a circumscribed infection to spread.

**Silicosis:** Occupational disease, usually chronic, causing fibrosis of the lungs. It results from inhalation of the dust of stone, flint, or sand that contains silica (quartz).

**Slipped Disk:** An acute or chronic condition, caused by the traumatic or degenerative displacement and protrusion of the softened central core of an intervertebral disk (cartilagenous disk between the spine bones), especially of the lower back. Symptoms are low back pain, which frequently extends to the thigh; muscle spasm; and tenderness.

**Spastic Paralysis (Cerebral Palsy):** A condition most commonly stemming from birth injury. Associated with nonprogressive brain damage, cerebral palsy is characterized by spastic, jerky voluntary movements, or constant involuntary and irregular writhing.

**Stroke (Cerebral Apoplexy):** A sudden attack of paralysis, with disturbance of speech and thought. It is caused by the destruction of brain substance, as the result of brain hemorrhage, vascular damage, intravascular clotting, or local circulatory insufficiency.

**Tardive Dyskinesia (TD):** A condition in which there are repeated involuntary movements of the extremities, face, jaw, and tongue. TD afflicts many people who have taken antipsychotic medications for prolonged periods of time. It is disfiguring and usually not reversible.

**Thermography:** A diagnostic technique for locating the presence of underlying tumors by recording infrared radiations that emanate from the body surface: tumors radiate more heat than the surrounding tissues.

**Thrombophlebitis:** Condition caused by the inflammation of a vein complicated by the formation of an intravascular blood clot (thrombus). Circulation is diminished in the affected area, usually an arm or a leg.

**Thrombosis:** Formation, development, or presence of a blood clot inside an artery or vein. This condition can be serious, if it affects the blood vessels of vital organs, such as the brain, heart, or lungs.

**Toxic Shock Syndrome:** A severe, life-threatening systemic infection caused by staphylococcal organisms. The infection may be associated with the use of "high-absorbency" tampons.

**Tumor:** A swelling or growth of new tissue; it develops independently of surrounding structures and serves no specific function of its own.

**Uremia:** Toxic clinical condition in which renal insufficiency allows the retention of urinary waste products in the circulating blood.

**Varicose Veins:** Abnormally distended and lengthened superficial veins caused by slowing and obstruction of the normal blood backflow. Varicose veins are most commonly observed in the legs, anus and rectum (hemorrhoids), and scrotum (varicocele).

## MODERN DRUG ADVANCES

**Acyclovir**—Antiviral drug effective in preliminary studies for treatment of herpes infections.

**Adrenocorticosteroids**—More than 20 synthetic adrenal hormones and their chemical derivatives. They are used primarily in the treatment of "collagen diseases" (e.g., rheumatoid arthritis) and in the suppression of certain inflammatory diseases or immunological processes.

**Allopurinol**—An oral drug used in suppressing the symptoms of gout.

**Ampicillin**—A "broad-spectrum" semisynthetic penicillin effective in the treatment of many infections.

**Antithyroid Agents**—A group of unrelated compounds, ranging from propylthiouracil to radio-iodide; used for treating hyperthyroidism.

**BCG (Bacille Calmette-Guérin)**—A nonvirulent strain of tubercle bacillus used in vaccines for immunization against tuberculosis and experimentally in controlling some forms of cancer.

**Chloramphenicol**—An important broad-spectrum antibiotic that is used to treat typhoid fever, certain types of food poisoning, and other infections caused by micro-organisms that are resistant to other antibiotics.

**Chloroquin Compounds**—Antimalarial and antiamebic.

**Chlorpromazine and Other Tranquilizers**—Over 30 compounds with mild depressant action on the brain, used in certain mental illnesses and anxiety states, and for antinauseant and sedative effects.

**Clomiphene Citrate**—A drug that improves fertility, sometimes causing multiple births.

**Diphenhydramine and 30 Other Antihistaminics**—Employed mainly in treating certain allergic conditions and also for antiemetic and sedative effects.

**Estrogen-Progestogen Contraceptives**—Oral contraceptive agents.

**Ganglionic Blocking Agents, Mostly Quaternary Ammonium Compounds**—Used in the treatment of certain types of hypertension.

**Griseofulvin**—A drug taken orally that is effective against many fungal infections of the skin and fingernails and toenails.

**Heptavax B**—A viral vaccine for people at risk of developing hepatitis B (formerly called serum hepatitis).

**Hydantoin**—A drug used to prevent or reduce seizures in epilepsy and other conditions.

**Immune Globulin**—A protein derived from human blood that, when injected into persons exposed to certain infectious diseases, confers temporary immunity.

**Interferon**—A protein, produced by the white blood cells, that activates immune systems, prevents an invading virus from reproducing itself within the host cell, and changes membranes of the invaded cell to interfere with the virus's ability to infect other cells. It was recently synthesized and is being used experimentally in the treatment of certain cancers and viruses.

**Isoniazid**—The most important drug in the treatment and prophylaxis of tuberculosis.

**Isoproterenol**—Used in the treatment of bronchial asthma, particularly to relieve the bronchial-tube spasm.

**Lidocaine and Other Local Anesthetics**—Injected locally to anesthetize tissues prior to minor surgical operations.

**Lithium**—A drug found effective in the treatment of manic-depressive psychoses.

**Meperidine**—A powerful pain-relieving drug.

**Methantheline and Other Anticholinergics**—Parasympatholytic agents used in cases of peptic ulcer and to decrease hypermotility (or spasm) of the gastrointestinal tract.

**Methicillin**—The first penicillin effective against staph (staphylococcus) infections that are resistant to ordinary penicillin.

**Oral Antidiabetes Agents**—Drugs that stimulate the pancreas to produce more insulin, given to treat mild diabetes.

**Propranolol**—A drug for heart-rhythm disorders, angina, and hypertension. It also reduces incidence of fatal heart attacks.

**Rauwolfia and Veratrum Alkaloids**—Principles of plant origin used in treating hypertension or as a tranquilizer.

**Streptomycin**—An important antibiotic, and one of the primary drugs for treating tuberculosis.

**Sulfonamide**—A drug used in the treatment of infections of the respiratory and urinary tracts and in certain types of meningitis.

**Synthetic Anticoagulants**—Used to prevent formation or extension of blood clots within arteries and veins.

**Ten Basic Penicillins, Plus Salts and Esters**—Antibacterial drugs that are used primarily to treat infections of the skin, respiratory tract, and of the genitourinary tract.

**Tetracycline Derivatives, Plus Salts and Esters**—Used in the treatment of a wide variety of infections caused by many different types of micro-organisms.

**Thiazide Diuretics**—Drugs used to remove excess fluid from the body in certain types of heart and kidney diseases and in the treatment of hypertension (high blood pressure).

**Timolol**—A drug similar to propanolol used to prevent the recurrence of a heart attack.

**Trihexyphenidyl, Amantadine Hydrochloride, L-Dopa, and Other Anti-Parkinsonism Agents**—Used to relieve the muscle symptoms in patients with Parkinson's disease.

## PSYCHIATRIC TERMS

SOURCE: American Psychiatric Association

**Alienation:** The estrangement felt in cultural settings one views as foreign, unpredictable, or unacceptable.

**Anal Character:** In psychoanalysis a pattern of behavior in an adult that originates in the anal eroticism of infancy and is characterized by such traits as excessive orderliness, miserliness, and obstinacy.

**Anorexia Nervosa:** A disorder marked by severe and prolonged refusal to eat, resulting in significant weight loss, amenorrhea or impotence, disturbance of body image, and an intense fear of becoming obese. Most frequently encountered in girls and young women.

**Anxiety:** Apprehension, the source of which is largely unknown or unrecognized. It is different from fear, which is the emotional response to a consciously recognized and usually external danger.

**Autistic Child:** In child psychiatry, a child who responds chiefly to inner thoughts, who does not relate to his environment, and whose overall functioning is immature and often appears retarded.

**Blocking:** Difficulty in recollection, or interruption of a train of thought or speech, caused by unconscious emotional factors.

**Catatonic State (catatonia):** Immobility with muscular rigidity and inflexibility. The catatonic state is almost always a symptom of schizophrenia.

**Community Mental Health Center (CMHC):** A mental health delivery system providing community-based services. Regulations require that the following services be provided: inpatient, outpatient, partial hospitalization, services for children and the elderly, half-way houses, alcohol and drug abuse programs, emergency services, follow-up care, assistance to the courts and other public agencies, and consultation and education.

**Compensation:** (1) An unconscious defense mechanism by which a person attempts to make up for real or imagined deficiencies. (2) A conscious process in which a person attempts to compensate for real or imagined deficiencies, including skills or physical or psychological attributes.

**Complex:** A cluster of ideas that share a common emotional tone. These ideas are largely unconscious but greatly affect attitudes and associations. Examples include:

*Inferiority complex:* Feelings of inferiority stemming from real or imagined physical or social inadequacies that may cause anxiety or other adverse reactions. The individual may overcompensate by excessive ambition or by the development of special skills, often in the very field in which he was originally handicapped.

*Oedipus complex:* Attachment of the child for the parent of the opposite sex, accompanied by envious and aggressive feelings toward the parent of the same sex. These feelings are largely repressed (i.e., made unconscious) because of the fear of displeasing the parent of the same sex. In its original use, the term applied only to the male child.

**Compulsion:** An insistent, repetitive, and unwanted urge to perform an act that is contrary to the person's ordinary conscious wishes or standards. Failure to perform the compulsive act results in anxiety.

**Defense Mechanism:** A specific process, operating unconsciously, that is employed to seek relief from emotional conflict and freedom from anxiety.

**Depression:** Psychiatrically, a morbid sadness, dejection, or melancholy; to be differentiated from grief, which is realistic and proportionate to what has been lost. A depression may be a symptom of any psychiatric disorder or may constitute its principal manifestation.

**Ego:** In psychoanalytic theory, one of the three major divisions of human personality, the others being the *id* and *superego*. The *ego*, commonly identified with consciousness of self, is the mental agent mediating among three contending forces: the external demands of social pressure or reality; the primitive instinctual demands arising from the *id* imbedded as it is in the deepest level of the unconscious; and the claims of the *superego*, born of parental and social prohibitions and functioning as an internal censor or "conscience."

**Empathy:** An objective awareness of the feelings, emotions, and behavior of another person. To be distinguished from sympathy, which is usually nonobjective and noncritical.

**Epilepsy:** A disorder characterized by periodic seizures, and sometimes accompanied by a loss of consciousness. May be caused by organic or emotional disturbances.

*Major epilepsy (grand mal):* Characterized by gross convulsive seizures, with loss of consciousness.

*Minor epilepsy (petit mal):* Characterized by brief seizures with limited lapses of consciousness.

**Euphoria:** An exaggerated feeling of physical and emotional well-being inconsonant with reality.

**Extroversion:** A state in which attention and energies are largely directed outward from the self, as opposed to interest primarily directed toward the self, as in introversion.

**Family Therapy:** Psychiatric treatment of a family, usually begun when one member develops a mental disorder.

**Free Association:** In psychoanalytic therapy, spontaneous, uncensored verbalization by the patient of whatever comes to mind.

**Fugue:** A major state of personality dissociation characterized by amnesia and physical flight from the immediate environment.

**Homosexuality:** Sexual attraction or relations between members of the same sex.

*Latent homosexuality:* A condition characterized by unconscious homosexual desires.

*Overt homosexuality:* Homosexuality that is consciously recognized or practiced.

**Hypnosis:** A state of increased receptivity to suggestion and direction, initially induced by the influence of another person. The degree may vary from mild suggestibility to a trance state so profound as to be used for anesthesia in surgical operations.

**Hypochondriasis:** Overconcern with the state of physical or emotional health, accompanied by various bodily complaints without demonstrable organic pathology.

**Hysterical Personality:** A personality type characterized by shifting emotional feelings, susceptibility to suggestion, impulsive behavior, attention seeking, and immaturity.

**Id:** *See* **Ego.**

**Inhibition:** Interference with or restriction of activities; the result of an unconscious defense against forbidden instinctual drives.

**Insight:** A person's understanding of the origin, nature, and mechanisms of his attitudes and behavior. Insight is the self-knowledge that is the goal of mental health care.

**Mania:** A suffix denoting a pathological preoccupation with some desire, idea, or activity; a morbid compulsion. Some frequently encountered manias are *dipsomania*, compulsion to drink alcoholic beverages; *egomania*, pathological preoccupation with self; *kleptomania*, compulsion to steal; *pyromania*, morbid compulsion to set fires.

**Manic-Depressive Reaction (bi-polar disorder):** One of a group of psychiatric disorders marked by conspicuous mood swings from elation to depression. The condition is classified as a psychosis but exists in mild forms.

*Depressed phase:* Characterized by depression of mood with retardation and inhibition of thought processes and physical activity.

*Manic phase:* Characterized by heightened excitability, acceleration of thought, speech, and bodily motion, and by elation or grandiosity of mood, and irritability.

**Masochism:** Pleasure derived from undergoing physical or psychological pain inflicted by oneself or by others. It may be consciously sought or unconsciously arranged or invited. Present to some degree in most human relations and to greater degrees in most psychiatric disorders. It is the converse of sadism, in which pain is inflicted on another; the two tend to coexist in the same individual.

**Narcissism (narcism):** Self-love, as opposed to object-love (love of another person). Some degree of narcissim is considered healthy and normal, but an excess interferes with relations with others.

**Obsession:** Persistent, unwanted idea or impulse that cannot be eliminated by logic or reasoning.

**Overcompensation:** A conscious or unconscious process in which a real or imagined physical or psychological deficit is overcome by exaggerated correction.

**Paranoid State:** Characterized by delusions of persecution. A paranoid state may be of short duration or chronic.

**Phobia:** An obsessive, unrealistic fear of an external object or situation. Some of the common phobias are *acrophobia*, fear of heights; *agoraphobia*, fear of open places; *claustrophobia*, fear of closed spaces; *mysophobia*, fear of dirt and germs; *xenophobia*, fear of strangers.

**Projective Test:** A psychological test, used as a diagnostic tool. One of the most common projective tests is the Rorschach (inkblot) test.

**Psychoanalysis:** A theory of human development and behavior, a method of research, and a system of psychotherapy, originally described by Sigmund Freud (1856–1939). Through analysis of free associations and interpretation of dreams, emotions and behavior are traced to the influence of repressed instinctual drives in the unconscious. Psychoanalytic treatment seeks to eliminate or diminish the undesirable effects of unconscious conflicts by making the patient aware of their existence, origin, and inappropriate expression.

**Psychoneurosis:** One of the two major categories of emotional illness, the other being psychosis. It is usually less severe than a psychosis, with minimal loss of contact with reality.

**Psychosis:** A major mental disorder of organic and/or emotional origin in which there is a departure from normal patterns of thinking, feeling, and acting. Commonly characterized by loss of contact with reality, distortion of perception, regressive behavior and attitudes, diminished control of elementary impulses and desires, and delusions and hallucinations. Chronic and generalized personality deterioration may occur.

**Psychosomatic:** Adjective to denote the constant and inseparable interdependence of the psyche (mind) and the soma (body). Most commonly used to refer to illnesses in which the manifestations are primarily physical with at least a partial emotional cause.

**Psychotherapy:** A form of mental treatment that is based primarily upon communication with the patient, rather than on the use of drugs, surgery, or physical measures such as electric or insulin shock.

**Regression:** A partial or symbolic return to more infantile patterns of behavior or reaction.

**Repression:** A defense mechanism, operating unconsciously, that banishes unacceptable ideas, emotions, or impulses from consciousness or that keeps out of consciousness what has never been conscious.

**Sadism:** *See* **Masochism.**

**Schizophrenia:** A severe emotional disorder of psychotic depth marked by a retreat from reality with delusions, hallucinations, emotional disharmony, and regressive behavior. Formerly called dementia praecox. Its prognosis has improved in recent years.

**Shock Treatment:** A form of psychiatric treatment in which electric current, insulin, or carbon dioxide is administered to the patient, causing a brief convulsive reaction. It may improve the outcome of mental illness.

**Sublimation:** A defense mechanism, operating unconsciously, by which instinctual but consciously unacceptable drives are diverted into personally and socially acceptable channels.

**Superego:** *See* **Ego.**

**Unconscious:** That part of the mind the content of which is only rarely subject to awareness. It is the repository for knowledge that has never been conscious or that may have been conscious briefly and was then repressed.

## PATIENT CARE EPISODES IN MENTAL HEALTH FACILITIES

SOURCE: National Institute for Mental Health

Patient care episodes are defined as the number of residents in inpatient facilities at the beginning of the year (or the number of persons on the rolls of noninpatient facilities) plus the total additions to these facilities during the year. Total additions during the year include new admissions, readmissions, and returns from long-term leave. The index, patient care episodes, therefore, is not equal to a true annual prevalence rate nor the annual prevalence of treated mental disorder, since episodes of care are counted rather than cases. This index does present useful measures of the volume of services utilized by persons with mental disorders and as such are useful in describing the distribution of episodes by age, sex, modality and type of facility.

While trend data on day care episodes by type of facility are not available for more than a few years, such data are available for inpatient and outpatient episodes as illustrated below. The number of inpatient and outpatient care episodes in mental health facilities in 1979 – 6.4 million – was almost four times greater than the approximately 1.7 million episodes in 1955.

**Number and percent distribution of inpatient and outpatient care episodes[1], in selected mental health facilities, by type of facility: United States, 1955, 1965, 1975, 1977, and 1979**

| | | Inpatient Services of: | | | | | Outpatient Psychiatric Services of: | |
|---|---|---|---|---|---|---|---|---|
| Year | Total All[1] Facilities | State & County Mental Hospitals | Private Mental[2] Hospitals | Gen. Hosp. Psychiatric Service (non-VA) | VA Psychiatric Inpatient Services | Federally Assisted Comm. Men. Health Cen. | Federally Assisted Comm. Men. Health Cen. | Other |
| | | | | **Number of Patient Care Episodes** | | | | |
| 1979 | 6,403,915 | 528,695 | 184,919 | 571,725[3] | 217,507[3] | 298,897[4] | 1,949,602 | 2,652,570 |
| 1977 | 6,392,979 | 574,226 | 184,189 | 571,725 | 217,507 | 268,966 | 1,741,729 | 2,834,637 |
| 1975 | 6,409,357 | 598,993 | 165,237 | 565,696 | 214,264 | 246,891 | 1,584,968 | 3,033,308 |
| 1965 | 2,636,525 | 804,926 | 125,428 | 519,328 | 115,843 | 130,088 | 622,906 | 1,693,848 |
| 1955 | 1,675,352 | 818,832 | 123,231 | 265,934 | 88,355 | — | — | 379,000 |
| | | | | **Percent Distribution** | | | | |
| 1979 | 100.0 | 8.3 | 2.9 | 8.9 | 3.4 | 4.7 | 30.4 | 41.4 |
| 1977 | 100.0 | 8.6 | 2.8 | 8.6 | 3.3 | 4.1 | 26.2 | 46.4 |
| 1975 | 100.0 | 9.3 | 2.6 | 8.8 | 3.3 | 3.9 | 24.7 | 47.4 |
| 1965 | 100.0 | 30.5 | 4.8 | 19.7 | 4.4 | — | — | 40.6 |
| 1955 | 100.0 | 48.9 | 7.3 | 15.9 | 5.3 | — | — | 22.6 |

[1] In order to present trends on the same set of facilities over this interval, it has been necessary to exclude from this table the following: private psychiatric office practice; psychiatric service modes of all types in hospitals or outpatient clinics of Federal agencies other than the VA (e.g., Public Health Service, Indian Health Service, Department of Defense Bureau of Prisons, etc.); inpatient service modes of multiservice facilities not shown in this table; all partial care episodes, and outpatient episodes of VA hospitals. [2] Includes estimates of episodes of care in residential treatment centers for emotionally disturbed children. [3] 1977 figures. [4] 1978 figures.

Source (All years except 1979): The National Institute of Mental Health, Statistical Note 154—Provisional data on patient care—episodes in mental health facilities, 1955-1977, September 1980

Source (1979): Unpublished provisional data from the National Institute of Mental Health.

## RECOMMENDED DAILY DIETARY ALLOWANCES FOR AMERICANS

The schedule is designed for the maintenance of good nutrition of normally active Americans in a temperate climate. The following abbreviations are used: Gm. for gram; Mg. for milligram; I.U. for International Unit.

| Family Members | Weight (Pounds) | Height Feet Inches | Calories | Protein (Gms.) | Calcium (Gms.) | Iron (Mg.) | Vitamin A (I.U.) | Thiamine (Mg.) | Riboflavin (Mg.) | Niacin (Mg. Equiv.) | Ascorbic Acid (Mg.) | Vitamin D (I.U.) |
|---|---|---|---|---|---|---|---|---|---|---|---|---|
| **MEN** | | | | | | | | | | | | |
| 18–35 years | 154 | 5–9 | 2,900 | 70 | 0.8 | 10 | 5,000 | 1.2 | 1.7 | 19 | 70 | — |
| 35–55 years | 154 | 5–9 | 2,600 | 70 | 0.8 | 10 | 5,000 | 1.0 | 1.6 | 17 | 70 | — |
| 55–75 years | 154 | 5–9 | 2,200 | 70 | 0.8 | 10 | 5,000 | 0.9 | 1.3 | 15 | 70 | — |
| **WOMEN** | | | | | | | | | | | | |
| 18–35 years | 128 | 5–4 | 2,100 | 58 | 0.8 | 15 | 5,000 | 0.8 | 1.3 | 14 | 70 | — |
| 35–55 years | 128 | 5–4 | 1,900 | 58 | 0.8 | 15 | 5,000 | 0.8 | 1.2 | 13 | 70 | — |
| 55–75 years | 128 | 5–4 | 1,600 | 58 | 0.8 | 10 | 5,000 | 0.8 | 1.2 | 13 | 70 | — |
| **CHILDREN** | | | | | | | | | | | | |
| 1–3 years | 29 | 2–10 | 1,300 | 32 | 0.8 | 8 | 2,000 | 0.5 | 0.8 | 9 | 40 | 400 |
| 3–6 years | 40 | 3–6 | 1,600 | 40 | 0.8 | 10 | 2,500 | 0.6 | 1.0 | 11 | 50 | 400 |
| 6–9 years | 53 | 4–1 | 2,100 | 52 | 0.8 | 12 | 3,500 | 0.8 | 1.3 | 14 | 60 | 400 |
| **BOYS** | | | | | | | | | | | | |
| 9–12 years | 72 | 4–7 | 2,400 | 60 | 1.1 | 15 | 4,500 | 1.0 | 1.4 | 16 | 70 | 400 |
| 12–15 years | 98 | 5–1 | 3,000 | 75 | 1.4 | 15 | 5,000 | 1.2 | 1.8 | 20 | 80 | 400 |
| 15–18 years | 134 | 5–8 | 3,400 | 85 | 1.4 | 15 | 5,000 | 1.4 | 2.0 | 22 | 80 | 400 |
| **GIRLS** | | | | | | | | | | | | |
| 9–12 years | 72 | 4–7 | 2,200 | 55 | 1.1 | 15 | 4,500 | 0.9 | 1.3 | 15 | 80 | 400 |
| 12–15 years | 103 | 5–2 | 2,500 | 62 | 1.3 | 15 | 5,000 | 1.0 | 1.5 | 17 | 80 | 400 |
| 15–18 years | 117 | 5–4 | 2,300 | 58 | 1.3 | 15 | 5,000 | 0.9 | 1.3 | 15 | 70 | 400 |

## DESIRABLE WEIGHTS FOR ADULT MEN AND WOMEN

| Height (in shoes, 1-in. heels) FT. IN. | MEN WEIGHT (LB.) IN INDOOR CLOTHING* Small Frame | Medium Frame | Large Frame |
|---|---|---|---|
| 5 2 | 112–120 | 118–129 | 126–141 |
| 5 3 | 115–123 | 121–133 | 129–144 |
| 5 4 | 118–126 | 124–136 | 132–148 |
| 5 5 | 121–129 | 127–139 | 135–152 |
| 5 6 | 124–133 | 130–143 | 138–156 |
| 5 7 | 128–137 | 134–147 | 142–161 |
| 5 8 | 132–141 | 138–152 | 147–166 |
| 5 9 | 136–145 | 142–156 | 151–170 |
| 5 10 | 140–150 | 146–160 | 155–174 |
| 5 11 | 144–154 | 150–165 | 159–179 |
| 6 0 | 148–158 | 154–170 | 164–184 |
| 6 1 | 152–162 | 158–175 | 168–189 |
| 6 2 | 156–167 | 162–180 | 173–194 |
| 6 3 | 160–171 | 167–185 | 178–199 |
| 6 4 | 164–175 | 172–190 | 182–204 |

* For nude weight, deduct 5–7 lbs. (male) or 2–4 lbs. (female).

| Height (in shoes, 2-in. heels) FT. IN. | WOMEN WEIGHT (LB.) IN INDOOR CLOTHING* Small Frame | Medium Frame | Large Frame |
|---|---|---|---|
| 4 10 | 92–98 | 96–107 | 104–119 |
| 4 11 | 94–101 | 98–110 | 106–122 |
| 5 0 | 96–104 | 101–113 | 109–125 |
| 5 1 | 99–107 | 104–116 | 112–128 |
| 5 2 | 102–110 | 107–119 | 115–131 |
| 5 3 | 105–113 | 110–122 | 118–134 |
| 5 4 | 108–116 | 113–126 | 121–138 |
| 5 5 | 111–119 | 116–130 | 125–142 |
| 5 6 | 114–123 | 120–135 | 129–146 |
| 5 7 | 118–127 | 124–139 | 133–150 |
| 5 8 | 122–131 | 128–143 | 137–154 |
| 5 9 | 126–135 | 132–147 | 141–158 |
| 5 10 | 130–140 | 136–151 | 145–163 |
| 5 11 | 134–144 | 140–155 | 149–168 |
| 6 0 | 138–148 | 144–159 | 153–173 |

## RECOMMENDED FOOD QUANTITIES IN TERMS OF SERVINGS

SOURCE: U.S. Department of Agriculture

Here follows a table of food groups and approximate amounts of foods as served per person per day, according to low-cost and moderate-cost plans. Servings allow for some plate waste. In addition to the food groups mentioned, some fats and oils (available in butter and margarine) and sugar (in its own form or in sweets and preserves) should be included in most diets.

| | | | NUMBER OF SERVINGS PER PERSON PER DAY | | | | | | | |
|---|---|---|---|---|---|---|---|---|---|---|
| | | | | | | | Woman | | Man | |
| Food Group | Unit | Plan | Child 1–6 years[1] | Child 6–12 years[1] | Girl 12–20 years | Boy 12–20 years | 20–55 years | 55 years and over | 20–55 years | 55 years and over |
| Meat, poultry, fish or alternates | 1 oz. cooked lean meat, 1 egg, ½ cup cooked dry beans, or 2 tbsp. peanut butter | Low Cost | 3–3½ | 4–4½ | 4½–5 | 4½–6 | 5½–6 | 3½–4½ | 5½–6 | 4½–5½ |
| | | Moderate | 3½–4½ | 5–7 | 7 | 7–8 | 7½ | 5½–6½ | 7½–8 | 7 |
| Milk, cheese, ice cream, ice milk | 1 8-oz. cup of milk as beverage or in cooking or cheese or ice cream | Low Cost | 2¼ | 2¼–3 | 4 | 4 | 2 | 2 | 2 | 2 |
| | | Moderate | 3 | 3 | 4 | 4 | 2 | 2 | 2 | 2 |
| Vegetables and fruits | ½ cup or equivalent vegetable or fruit as served | Low Cost | 2–3½ | 4½–5½ | 5–6 | 5½–6½ | 4½–5½ | 3½–4½ | 5–6 | 4–5 |
| | | Moderate | 2½–4 | 4½–6 | 5½–6½ | 6–7½ | 5–6 | 4–4½ | 5½–7 | 5–6 |
| Cereal and bakery products | 1 slice of bread or other bakery products with equal flour; 1 oz. ready-to-eat cereal; or ¾ cup cooked cereal or cereal product | Low Cost | 5–7 | 8–9 | 8–9 | 14–16 | 7–8 | 5–7 | 12–14 | 8–9 |
| | | Moderate | 4–6 | 8–9 | 7–8 | 13–15 | 7–8 | 4–5 | 11–13 | 7–8 |

[1] Smaller amount is for younger children.

# EARTH: FACTS/FIGURES

## EARTH: THIRD PLANET FROM THE SUN

The Earth, our planet, is located at an average distance of 93 million miles from the Sun, which it orbits 365.2564 days, the "sidereal year," when measured in one way or in 365.2422 days, the "tropical year," by another way. (The calendar year of 365.2425 days was chosen to agree closely with the latter.) The Earth completes one rotation on its axis in 23 hours, 56 minutes, and 4 seconds, and its equator is inclined 23 degrees and 27 minutes to the plane of the ecliptic. The equatorial diameter of the Earth is 7,926 miles; its polar diameter is 7,900 miles. The Earth's average density is 5.52 grams/cm$^3$.

The circumference of the Earth around the equator has been estimated at 24,900 miles, while its circumference around the poles is thought to be about 24,820 miles. From these dimensions, it is obvious that the Earth is not a true sphere, but rather a *geoid*—a triaxial ellipsoid that is nearly spherical but flattened at the poles. Small bulges produce four "corners"—at Ireland, off Peru, south of Africa, and near New Guinea. Space-satellite measurements have further indicated two "dimples" in the Northern Hemisphere, giving the Earth a slightly pearlike appearance.

The Earth has an average density of 5.52 grams/cm$^3$ and an estimated mass of 5.883 x $10^{21}$ tons and an estimated volume of 2.6 x $10^{11}$ cubic miles. Its total surface area is approximately 197,272,000 square miles, of which the land area makes up only about 57,200,000 square miles. The average land elevation is 2,700 feet; the average ocean depth is 12,500 feet.

It is generally believed that the Earth and the other planets are 4.6 billion years old, although the oldest rocks found on the Earth are only 3.7 billion years old. Scientists have given names to the various geological time periods of Earth's history.

The largest segments of geologic time are called eras and are named according to the type of life that then existed. Eras are divided into periods, which are further divided into epochs. The period names usually refer to locations where rocks of the specific period were first studied (e.g., Devonian signifies Devonshire, England; Cretaceous, the chalk deposits that are found on both sides of the English Channel). Other names, such as Ordovician and Silurian, are actually the names of Celtic tribes that inhabited parts of Wales where rocks from this time interval were first studied.

| Era | Period, Epoch | Age (Millions of Years Ago) | Evolution of Life |
|---|---|---|---|
| Cenozoic | Quaternary, Recent & Pleistocene | 0 to 2.5 | Man |
| | Tertiary, Pliocene | 2.5 to 12 | Higher Mammals |
| | Tertiary, Miocene | 12 to 25 | |
| | Tertiary, Oligocene | 25 to 36 | |
| | Tertiary, Eocene | 36 to 58 | |
| | Tertiary, Paleocene | 58 to 63 | |
| Mesozoic | Cretaceous | 63 to 135 | Modern Vegetation |
| | Jurassic | 135 to 200 | Birds |
| | Triassic | 200 to 230 | Mammals |
| Paleozoic | Permian | 230 to 280 | |
| | Carboniferous | 280 to 345 | Reptiles |
| | Devonian | 345 to 405 | Amphibians |
| | Silurian | 405 to 425 | Land Plants |
| | Ordovician | 425 to 500 | Agnathans, Fishes |
| | Cambrian | 500 to 570 | Invertebrate Animals |
| Pre-Cambrian | Late Pre-Cambrian | 570 to 700 | Higher Algae |
| | Upper Pre-Cambrian | 700 to 1600 | |
| | Middle Pre-Cambrian | 1600 to 2700 | Unicellular Organisms |
| | Lower Pre-Cambrian | 2700 to 3500 | Blue-green Algae |
| | Archaean | 3500+ | Bacteria |

### THE EARTH'S INTERIOR

The core at the Earth's center is the least-known part of the interior; our knowledge of it stems mostly from study of seismic (earthquake) waves and their propagation. However, it is known that the solid inner core of iron is surrounded by a liquid outer core of iron. The inner core, which has a radius of about 850 miles, is believed to have a very high pressure and high temperature (about 10,000° F) and a density of about 13.5 grams/cm$^3$ (13.5 times the density of water). The outer core has a thickness of about 1,200 miles. Surrounding the outer core is the mantle, which is 1,800 miles thick. The boundary between the mantle and the core is called the Gutenberg-Wiechert Discontinuity.

The mantle has an average density of 5 grams/cm$^3$ and consists of three layers: the plastic inner mantle that surrounds the liquid core, a transition region, and the outer solid mantle. The uppermost region of the Earth's interior is called the crust and is separated from the outer mantle by the Mohorovicic Discontinuity (or M-Discontinuity). The crust consists of continental crust and oceanic crust. The continental crust is composed of relatively light silicon rocks, such as granite, andesite, and various grades of metamorphic rocks known under the general name of *sial* (aluminum silicate, with silicon oxide comprising 60%) which has an average density of 2.7 grams/cm$^3$. The continental crust has an average thickness of 23 miles, reaching 40 to 45 miles under high mountain chains. The oceanic crust is composed of heavier basaltic rocks that contain greater proportions of metallic oxides, such as magnesium and iron, under the general name of *sima* (magnesium silicate, with silicon oxide comprising only 46%) which has an average density of 3.0 grams/cm$^3$. The oceanic crust has an average thickness of 4 miles. As well as being lighter and much thicker, the continental crust is considerably older than the ocean crust.

### EARTH'S WATER-COVERED SURFACE

The oceans (hydrosphere) cover some 140 million square miles—70 percent of the Earth's total surface area—to an average depth of 12,500 feet. There are 340 million cubic miles of liquid water on the Earth's surface—making our planet a truly water-covered one. The greatest ocean depth is found in the Marianas Trench in the Western Pacific, being more than 37,500 feet deep.

Chemically, the ocean consists of water (96.5%) and numerous dissolved salts (3.5%), of which common salt (2.8%) is easily the most abundant. The principal elements in seawater are chlorine, sodium, magnesium, sulfur, oxygen, calcium, potassium, bromine, strontium, boron, and smaller amounts of carbon, fluorine, and iodine.

The features of the ocean floor, which result from deformations of the Earth's crust, are either elevations—ridges, rises, seamounts, and sills—or depressions—troughs, trenches, basins, and deeps. For example, the Atlantic Ocean is divided into two troughs by a north-south ridge, the Mid-Atlantic Ridge, which extends into both hemispheres. On either side of the ridge, depths exceeding 16,000 feet exist.

### THE EARTH'S ATMOSPHERE

For its first 60 miles, the Earth's atmosphere has a nearly homogeneous composition consisting of the following gases:

| Constituent | Percent by Volume |
|---|---|
| Nitrogen ($N_2$) | 78.084 |
| Oxygen ($O_2$) | 20.946 |
| Argon (Ar) | 0.934 |
| Carbon dioxide ($CO_2$) | 0.033 |
| Neon (Ne) | 0.000018 |
| Helium (He) | 0.000005 |
| Methane ($CH_4$) & Krypton (Kr) | 0.000001 |

Water vapor ($H_2O$) varies within the lower atmosphere (the lowest 7 miles) from 0 to 4 percent, but it generally is present in concentrations of 0.1 to 1 percent. Water vapor is rarely found above the lower atmosphere.

Above 60 miles, the atmosphere is no longer homogeneous, but rather successive layers consisting of atomic oxygen (O), helium (He), and hydrogen (H).

Incoming solar radiation reaching our planet heats up the Earth's surface to about −18° F. At this temperature, the Earth emits infrared radiation into space in all directions; however, the carbon dioxide and water vapor molecules in the Earth's lower atmosphere absorb and then reemit this infrared radiation. Part of the reemitted infrared radiation is directed downward and strikes the Earth's surface, increasing the surface temperature to a value of about 60° F, which is the Earth's actual mean temperature, averaged over the entire year. The absorption and reemission of infrared radiation by $CO_2$ and $H_2O$ is known as the "Greenhouse Effect" or greenhouse temperature enhancement.

The Earth's neutral atmosphere can be divided into five distinct regions, depending on the region's temperature gradient, which is the variation of temperature with height within a particular atmospheric region. That is, a positive temperature gradient means that temperature increases with height; a negative temperature gradient means that temperature decreases with height; an undefined temperature gradient means that the density of molecules is too low to give a meaningful value to the temperature.

| Atmospheric Region | Height | Temperature Gradient |
|---|---|---|
| Troposphere | 0 to 7 miles | Negative |
| Stratosphere | 7 to 30 miles | Positive |
| Mesosphere | 30 to 50 miles | Negative |
| Thermosphere | 50 to 300 miles | Positive |
| Exosphere | Above 300 miles | Undefined |

The troposphere contains about two-thirds of the total mass of the atmosphere. Within this layer, the temperature decreases with increasing height at a "lapse rate" of about 3.5° F per 1,000 feet. The decrease of temperature with height results from the atmosphere's being heated by solar radiation mainly from below. Whenever there is warmer below cooler air, vertical motions in the atmosphere result, since warm air is lighter than cool air. Such a condition causes vertical wind motions or convective currents within the troposphere. All of our weather, such as clouds and precipitation, occurs in the troposphere.

At the top of the troposphere, the temperature (about −75° F) stops decreasing with height, and the stratosphere begins. Within the stratosphere, the temperature increases with height from heating that is caused by the absorption of solar ultraviolet radiation by the stratospheric ozone layer. Since ozone absorbs most of the incoming solar ultraviolet radiation, this lethal radiation does not reach the surface, where it would adversely affect life.

At the top of the stratosphere, the temperature reaches its maximum of about 35° F, and the mesosphere begins. Within the mesosphere, the temperature decreases approximately 1.5° F per 1,000 feet. The temperature minimum of the entire atmosphere, about −130° F, is found at the top of the mesosphere.

Above this mesopause, the thermosphere begins. This is a region in which the temperature increases with height because of the absorption and subsequent heating of solar X rays and short wavelength ultraviolet radiation. The temperature of the higher layers of the thermosphere can reach about 2000° F. However, at the extremely low density prevailing in this region temperature is a somewhat meaningless concept. Above the thermosphere is the exosphere, which is the top of the Earth's neutral atmosphere.

In addition to the neutral atmosphere of Earth, there are several regions consisting of large amounts of positive atomic nuclei or ions and negative electrons. The absorption of solar X rays and ultraviolet radiation results in the ionization of the air, which, in turn, results in several ionized layers known as the ionosphere. Another region of charged particles—protons and electrons—comprises the Van Allen Radiation belts, which surround the Earth at distances from about 1250 to 3000 miles and 8000 to 12,000 miles. The protons and electrons are held within the radiation belts by the Earth's magnetic field. Most of the electrons and protons in the belt's outer portion come from the Sun in the form of the solar wind.

There is evidence to suggest that the Earth originally had an atmospheric composition similar to that of Jupiter: mostly hydrogen and helium, some methane and ammonia, and no oxygen. It is possible that life began in this atmosphere. However, at some point in the past, the entire original atmosphere was lost and the present one developed. It is believed that nitrogen came from the Earth's interior via volcanic outgassing, as did the carbon dioxide and water vapor in the present atmosphere. Most of the oxygen in our atmosphere was probably produced by plant photosynthesis. Atmospheric argon was produced by the decay of radioactive potassium in rocks and minerals in the Earth's interior.

## ORIGIN OF LIFE ON EARTH

The Earth and the other planets are thought to be about 4.6 billion years old. The earliest known fossil records of living organisms on our planet are about 3 billion years old. It is estimated that life existed on our planet some 3.5 to 4 billion years ago, suggesting that up to 1 billion years elapsed before life evolved on Earth from the material then available. Fundamental to an understanding of the origin of life is knowledge of the chemical makeup of living cells.

Two types of molecules—proteins and nucleic acids—play basic functional roles in living cells. Proteins are large complex molecules consisting of a number of amino acids that are joined together to form a long chain. An amino acid is a carbon compound containing an acid group (—COOH) and a basic amino group ($-NH_2$). Some 21 different amino acids have been found in proteins. Enzymes are the biochemical catalysts that control many metabolic processes. Enzymes are proteins in which the amino-acid chain has been folded into a very specific shape.

Nucleic acids are formed in the cell nucleus, but some are produced in other cell parts. Like proteins, nucleic acids are complex molecules composed of chains of simpler units. The fundamental unit of nucleic acids is a complex molecule called a nucleotide, which consists of three separate parts: residues of a nitrogenous base, a sugar with five carbon atoms, and phosphoric acid.

In a given nucleic acid, all of the sugar residues are the same. They are either all ribose or all deoxyribose. When the sugar residues are all ribose, the nucleic acids are called ribonucleic acids (RNA) and, when they all are deoxyribose, the nucleic acids are called deoxyribonucleic acids (DNA). Both DNA and RNA are produced in the nuclei of nearly all living cells but, whereas RNA leaves the nucleus and enters the surrounding cytoplasm, essentially all the DNA remains within the nucleus.

Nucleic acids are the key materials for all terrestrial life forms, their presence being fundamental to life processes. DNA is the principal component of genes and chromosomes, passed from parents to offspring. The sequence of nucleotides in DNA comprises the genetic code, which determines the type and amount of protein synthesized in a particular living cell. Hence, it appears that the formation of nucleic acids is related to the origin of life. It has been suggested that viruses, which are larger than a single molecule but smaller than a cell nucleus, represent an intermediate stage between nonliving and living systems. However, the modern virus, which needs to inhabit a cell in order to live, is presumed to be a development of a more primitive precursor.

The probable inorganic elements and conditions on Earth during its first billion years, which together combined to form life, were first discussed by the Russian biochemist A. I. Oparin in his 1924 publication *The Origin of Life*. Oparin described the gradual step-by-step evolution of life from the simple inorganic elements of hydrogen, carbon, nitrogen, and oxygen. A somewhat similar view was expressed (1928) independently by the English biochemist J. B. S. Haldane. The first attempts to simulate early conditions on Earth and produce biological compounds in the laboratory were largely failures. Although oxygen is now the second most abundant gas in the Earth's atmosphere, accounting for some 21% by volume, it was probably not always so abundant.

If oxygen were as abundant in the past as it is today, then carbon would be present mainly as carbon dioxide. Oparin suggested that atmospheric carbon probably existed originally in the reduced form—methane ($CH_4$)—and not in oxidized form—carbon dioxide ($CO_2$). Similarly, nitrogen, now present in free state and accounting for some 78% by volume of the atmosphere, would have been in the reduced form of ammonia ($NH_3$). Like Oparin, but for entirely different reasons, Haldane also concluded that the Earth's primitive atmosphere probably contained little if any free oxygen but consisted mainly of carbon dioxide, ammonia, and water vapor.

In 1952, the American chemist H. C. Urey showed that the Earth's primitive atmosphere should have consisted of methane, ammonia, water vapor, and free hydrogen gas. Urey and S. Miller began a series of lab experiments attempting to synthesize the gases of his theoretical atmosphere into complex organic molecules. After exposing gases to ultraviolet radiation, to simulate the sun's radiation, Urey and Miller reported (1953) that they had successfully produced several amino acids, as well as other organic compounds of biological interest.

From similar laboratory experiments made by P. H. Abelson (1956) and by Pavlovskaya and A. G. Pasinsky (1957) in the USSR, it has been established that amino acids can be produced by passing an electrical discharge (simulating lightning discharges in the Earth's primitive atmosphere) through various gas mixtures other than those used by Urey and Miller. Provided the gaseous system has overall reducing characteristics, amino acids are always formed. Other experiments have shown that amino acids can even be formed in aqueous solutions.

As life evolved on Earth, it appears certain that later stages took place in a liquid water environment. This is evidenced by the presence of large amounts of water in all living organisms and the fact that the calcium/potassium ratio in seawater and blood is roughly similar. Furthermore the earliest organisms would have required the protection of the oceans from the damaging solar ultraviolet radiation. It seems likely that the primitive organisms in the oceans started to obtain hydrogen necessary for the synthesis of amino acids and other organic molecules by dissociating water using light energy. This is an important stage in the evoluton of life since free oxygen was released into the atmosphere. Once oxygen and then ozone built up in the atmosphere, the land was effectively shielded from solar ultraviolet. At this stage organisms appear to have emerged from the sea and colonized land.

Laboratory experiments have shown that amino acids and nucleic acids could have been synthesized in a reducing atmosphere of hydrogen, methane, ammonia, and water vapor. It is now believed that the Earth originally had such an atmosphere when life originated.

## ANCIENT SUPERCONTINENTS

American scientists of the Environmental Science Services Administration reported in 1969 that they had established that Australia and Antarctica, which are now separated by about 2,000 miles of water, were once part of an ancient supercontinent.

The scientists, Walter Sproll and Dr. Robert S. Dietz, having processed oceanographic data obtained in 1967 by U.S. and Australian scientists during a global cruise of the Coast and Geodetic Survey Ship *Oceanographer*, relate that there was a fit between the two continents.

Sproll and Dietz are supporters of the continental-drift theory: that the continents constantly drift about 1–6 in. each year in the earth's mantle—the part of the earth's interior that rests between the molten central core and the crust. Among the scientists who espouse this theory, some believe that there was once a single supercontinent they call Pangaea; others, including Sproll and Dietz, contend that there were two supercontinents, which they refer to as Gondwana and Laurasia.

Supporters of the two-continent theory believe that Gondwana was composed of Australia, Antarctica, Africa, India, South America, Madagascar, and various submerged fragments, while Laurasia is thought to have consisted of North America and Eurasia.

It was generally believed of the two continents that southern Australia was once linked with another land mass, but opinions differed as to which one. Antarctica was the popular choice, but some thought it was Madagascar; others contended that it was the east coast of Africa, while still others believed it to have been the southwestern coast of South America.

Sproll and Dietz reported that their study shows that the south coast of Australia once joined Antarctica and identifies the exact position of fit: the SE end of Australia—including Tasmania—fitted into Antarctica's Ross Sea, while the SW end reached to just off Antarctica's Knox Coast; the concave Great Bight of Australia fitted against the convex outline of Wilkes Land.

"Recent geophysical findings on the ocean floor have demonstrated to the satisfaction of most earth scientists that the continents were once together," the ESSA scientists said. "About 200 to 250 million years ago, they commenced to separate and slowly drifted to their present scattered locations around the globe. One of the last units to be sundered—the Australia-Antarctica split—may have occurred as late as 40 million years ago.

The fit of continents is not the only evidence of continental drift. There is a very significant fit of rock formations and other geological structures in landmasses now separated by oceans. Studies of the past positions of the magnetic poles also indicate relative movement between continents. Again the scattered distribution of certain animals and plants in the distant past as well as that of ancient climatic zones can only be satisfactorily explained by continental drift: the discovery in Antarctica of a fossilized bone of an extinct amphibian points to a much milder Antarctic climate in the past.

Continental drift is now explained in terms of plate tectonics. The earth's outer shell is divided into at least 15 rigid rock segments, known as plates, that extend downward through the earth's crust and float on a semi-molten layer of the upper mantle. Seven of the plates are of major size and in most cases carry a continental landmass with surrounding ocean floor and island arcs. The plates are slowly moving relative to each other, driven by powerful forces within the earth's mantle. The movements of the plates have produced the present continent locations. At their boundaries plates are either slowly separating with new material added from the mantle, are converging with one plate being ground down and consumed under another, or are gliding past each other. Almost all earthquake, volcanic, and mountain-building activity closely follows these boundaries and is related to movements between them.

## THE CONTINENTS

| Name | Area (in square miles) | Percent of World's Land | Highest Point (in feet) | Lowest Point (in feet) |
|---|---|---|---|---|
| Asia | 17,129,000 | 29.7 | Mount Everest (29,028), Nepal-China | Dead Sea (1,296 below sea level), Israel-Jordan |
| Africa | 11,707,000 | 20.0 | Kibo (19,340), a peak of Mount Kilimanjaro, Tanzania | Lake Assal, Djibouti (510 below sea level) |
| North America | 9,363,000 | 16.3 | Mount McKinley (20,320), Alaska | Death Valley (282 below sea level), California |
| South America | 6,886,000 | 12.0 | Aconcagua (22,831), Argentina | Salinas Grandes (131 below sea level), Valdés Pen., Argentina |
| Europe | 4,057,000 | 7.0 | El'brus (18,510), USSR | Caspian Sea (92 below sea level), USSR |
| Australia | 2,942,000 | 5.1 | Mount Kosciusko (7,316), New South Wales | Lake Eyre (52 below sea level), South Australia |
| Antarctica | 5,500,000 | 9.6 | Vinson Massif (16,864) | Sea level |

## PREHISTORIC CREATURES

**Allosaurus:** This predator of 125 million years ago was the giant of its day: 34-feet long, more than eight feet high, and with a reach of about 15 feet above the ground. It had a massive skull that was nearly a yard long and a lower jaw hinged far back, enabling it to swallow food in unchewed lumps. Allosaurus remains have been found in Utah, Wyoming, and other Rocky Mountain states.

**Anatosaurus** *(Trachodon):* This 30-foot, duck-billed dinosaur lived in North America about 100 million years ago. It had a long narrow skull, a ducklike bill, and at the back of the jaws up to 2,000 grinding teeth, which were continuously replaced as they wore out. The anatosaurus could swim and wade, as evidenced by its webbed feet and deep oarlike tail.

**Apatosaurus** *(Brontosaurus):* This quadruped dinosaur probably grew to more than 70 feet in length and 30 tons in weight. Because of its size, the apatosaurus (as well as the brachiosaurus) had a huge pelvis and long, heavy shoulder blades. It had a short but deep body, a long neck, a massive tail, and a relatively tiny brain weighing about one pound. The apatosaurus was herbivorous and semiaquatic; as its nostrils were situated high on its head it could stand almost fully submerged. It lived about 125 million years ago in Colorado, Wyoming, Texas, and other Western states.

**Archaeopteryx:** Appearing about 150 million years ago, the archaeopteryx was the earliest known bird and was about the size of our crow. Although it had feathers, its bony tail, toothed jaws, and the claws on its forelimbs were reptilian. But its hindlimbs were birdlike, thus it could walk and run like a chicken. The archaeopteryx was probably warm-blooded, had weak flying muscles, and a gliding flight.

**Baluchitherium:** The largest land mammal ever to have lived. Found in Oligocene (circa 28–30 million years ago) deposits of Western and Central Asia, it was over 16 feet tall and weighed several tons; its head alone was over 4 feet long. Baluchitherium was related to the modern rhinoceros, but unlike the rhino it had no horns, long limbs, and a long neck, which would have suited it for swift running and browsing on leaves on the higher branches of trees.

**Brachiosaurus:** Ranging from 60 to 80 feet in length and weighing up to 80 tons, the brachiosaurus was one of the largest land animals that ever lived. The dinosaur's front legs were massive; consequently, its shoulders were high and sloped giraffe-fashion to the hips. Since its nostrils were located on a raised area of the head, the creature could breathe while standing in deep water. The brachiosaurus, which fed on vegetation, lived in Colorado, adjacent areas, and eastern Africa more than 125 million years ago.

**Camptosaurus:** Appearing in North America about 125 million years ago, the camptosaurus ranged between four and 15 feet in length. It had strong hind limbs; small, stout forelimbs; and a broad hand with full fingers. Its femur was curved, suggesting that this dinosaur sometimes walked on all fours. The camptosaurus was a non-predatory planteater, with a flat, beak-like mouth.

**Coelacanth:** This subgroup of lobe-finned fishes ranged in weight from 125 to 150 pounds and were strong, armed with sharp teeth, and active. Early coelacanths were freshwater fish, but later forms were marine. They first appeared about 350 million years ago and were thought to have become extinct about 65 million years ago. However, in 1938 a fisherman caught a 4½-foot coelacanth off the coast of South Africa, and since then several other specimens have been caught.

**Compsognathus:** This dinosaur was no larger than a big fowl, and two-thirds of its body was neck and tail. Its toes were long and clawed, and its small jaws were lined with sharp teeth. This slender bipedal creature preyed on small reptiles, on the Baltic coast of what is now Germany, about 125 million years ago.

**Eohippus** *(Hyracotherium):* As its name implies, the "dawn *(eo)* horse *(hippus)*" was the earliest-known horse, appearing about 60 million years ago on the Great Plains of North America. The species varied from 10 to 20 inches high; all of these horses had four toes on each front foot and three on each hind foot. The eohippus was lightly built; its hindquarters were high and its simple teeth were suited for browsing on leaves. Some species of the eohippus migrated to Europe about 50 million years ago, becoming ancestors of the Old World horse. By the time that the Indians reached North America, the New World horse had become extinct.

**Hesperornis:** This flightless water bird ranged from Europe to North America about 100 million years ago. The hesperornis had an elongated body, about 6 feet long, with feet that enabled it to swim. It had a long bill, possibly toothed, and preyed on fish. Although its ancestors probably had wings, those of the hesperornis were useless evolutionary remnants.

**Iguanodon:** This genus of herbivorous dinosaurs varied in length from 15 to 30 feet and reached a height of 15 feet. All specimens had narrow bodies. They walked on hind feet, which had three large toes and one small one, and used their long heavy tails for balancing. Their small "forefeet" were five-fingered and had a thumb that was shaped into a bony spike. Iguanodon remains have been found in Europe and North Africa; the genus flourished between 100 and 140 million years ago.

**Kronosaurus:** Similar to the sperm whale of today, the kronosaurus paddled through Australian seas about 70 million years ago. Its neck was comparatively short, and its elongated skull measured 12 feet. The kronosaurus had large eyes and temporal openings, nostrils in front of the eyes, an almost solid palate, and long sharp teeth.

**Lystrosaurus:** A member of the dicynodont group of mammal-like reptiles, this animal is dated from the early Triassic Age (circa 220 million years ago) of both South Africa and Asia. It is believed that the dicynodonts may in general have preferred to live in marshy country, but Lystrosaurus is the only one which may have been aquatic to any extent. All dicynodonts were herbivorous and were the most common land animals of their time.

**Megatherium:** The largest of the extinct giant ground sloths, it flourished in both North and South America during the Pleistocene (circa 1.5 million to 10,000 years ago). This early mammal was slightly larger than the modern elephant and possessed extremely massive limbs. Its teeth grew continually throughout life and were adapted for a leaf-eating diet. It had a short, massive neck and tail, but a relatively long trunk. Its hands possessed powerful claws, which probably served to draw branches down towards its extensible tongue; the animal appears to have walked on the outside of its knuckles.

**Pteranodon:** This flying reptile lived between 85 and 100 million years ago, ranging from present-day Kansas to Europe and possibly around the world. Its body was small, bulking to about that of a small turkey. Its jaws formed a long toothless beak, and the back of the skull extended into a bony crest that was between about four and six feet long. The pteranodon's large wingspread, about 25 feet, and pelicanlike gular pouch gave it a most unreptilian appearance.

**Stegosaurus:** This "plated dinosaur" was a quadruped, about 20 feet long and weighing about 2 tons. It had short forelegs, two rows of bony plates down its back, and long pointed spikes on its tail. The brain of the stegosaurus, about the size of a walnut, weighed only about 2½ ounces. The bony plates, together with its tail spikes, may have been used for defense against predators; alternatively they may have functioned as heat exchangers. This herbivorous dinosaur roamed the American West about 125 million years ago.

**Triceratops:** This dinosaur was also herbivorous and also lived in the American West, about 100 million years ago. The head of the triceratops was about eight feet long and sheltered a two-pound brain. Its body, which was about 20 feet long, was bulky and shaped like a barrel. The dinosaur's four legs were of equal size. The name *triceratops* is derived from the creature's three horns: one on the nose and one over each eye.

**Tyrannosaurus:** The "tyrant" dinosaur was a flesh-eater and well equipped for predation with six-inch teeth that were housed in a four-foot-long skull. Existing for a short time, about 85 million years ago, this dinosaur was 40 feet long and 19 feet tall. It weighed up to eight tons. Its forelimbs were reduced to such a degree that it is believed that they were not utilitarian; therefore, the creature's predation was probably restricted to its use of its jaws and powerful clawed hind legs.

**Uintatherium:** The uintatheres were primitive rhinoceros-like ungulates of late Paleocene and Eocene times (circa 50 to 60 million years ago), and are distantly related to the elephants. Their long, low skulls were characterized by a number of large, horn-like bony swellings; they possessed large, saber-like upper canine teeth which were presumably very effective as defensive weapons.

## FOSSIL MAN

Remains of what have been claimed to be man's earliest ancestors were found on two continents in 1934 and 1961. Fossil bones found at sites in India, Pakistan and Kenya were classified as **Ramapithecus** and **Kenyapithecus.** However on present evidence **Ramapithecus** from Asia now seems to be more closely related to the orang-utan than to humans.

The oldest bones to be placed with certainty in the category "Hominidae," or the family of Man, are about 4 million years old. Hominid remains have been found in several locations. Many anthropologists have given their finds a different name (e.g., Zinjanthropus, Paranthropus, Plesianthropus), but today some scientists believe that all of these individuals who lived between 3 million and 4 million B.C. have the same general characteristics and can be called by the general genus name, Australopithecus, or "southern ape." Others disagree and classify them differently.

The different genus and species names are given in the chart below to indicate that they probably represent different branches of the same group.

The brain of Australopithecus was about the same size as that of a modern large ape—less than half that of modern man. In spite of his apelike traits, Australopithecus walked erect.

Some of the specimens found by L. S. B. Leakey in 1960 have been given the classification name Homo, the genus to which modern man belongs. Homo habilis was only 3½ to 4½ feet tall but had a larger brain and more manlike features.

Homo erectus, sometimes called Pithecanthropus or "ape man" (e.g., Java Man, Peking Man), was probably the direct ancestor of modern man, Homo sapiens. He appeared at least 1½ million years ago and was structurally similar to us although he lacked a forehead and possessed a bony shelf over his eyes and a small chin. He made tools and knew how to use fire.

The next major evolutionary advance came approximately 100,000 years ago with the appearance of Neanderthal Man in Europe and Western Asia. He, too, was short in stature and had low brows, but his brain was equal in size to that of modern man, and he possessed a language. He was not a settler, but instead hunted widely.

At about 35,000 B.C., as the Neanderthals were disappearing, modern man, Homo sapiens (e.g., Cromagnon), appeared in Europe, but may have existed earlier in Western Asia and Africa. He was taller and more delicate, and he fashioned intricate tools and clothing and drew paintings of his environment. However, it was not until 10,000 years ago that Homo sapiens became a domesticator of animals, a farmer, and a settler.

### MAJOR FOSSIL MAN DISCOVERIES

| Year | Scientific Name | Period and Estimated Date (B.C.) | Location | Remains | Discoverer |
|---|---|---|---|---|---|
| 1848 | Homo Neanderthalensis (Gibraltar Man) | Upper Pleistocene 50,000–120,000 | Forbes Quarry, Gibraltar | skull | Lieutenant Flint |
| 1856 | Homo neanderthalensis (Neanderthal Man) | Upper Pleistocene 50,000 | Neander Valley, nr. Dusseldorf, Germany | skull, bones | Johann C. Fuhlrott |
| 1868 | Homo sapiens (Cromagnon) | Upper Pleistocene 28,000 | Cromagnon, France | 4 skeletons, 1 fetus | Louis Lartet |
| 1891 | Pithecanthropus erectus (Java Man) | Lower Pleistocene 700,000 | Trinil, Java | skull, femur | Eugene Dubois |
| 1907 | Homo heidelbergensis (Heidelberg Man) | Middle Pleistocene 450,000 | Mauer, nr. Heidelberg, Germany | lower jaw | Otto Schoetensack |
| 1921 | Homo rhodensiensis (early H. sapiens) | Middle/Upper Pleistocene 120,000 | Broken Hill (Kabwe) Zambia | skull parts of skeletons | T. Zwigelaar |
| 1921–37 | Sinanthropus pekinensis (Peking Man) | Middle Pleistocene 450,000 | Choukoutien, nr. Peking, China | skulls, teeth, bones | Davidson Black |
| 1924 | Australopithecus africanus (Southern Ape) | Pleistocene 2,750,000 | Taung, South Africa | skull | M. de Bruyn |
| 1929–34 | Mt. Carmel Man | Upper Pleistocene 50,000 | Tabun and Skhul, Israel | parts of 16 skeletons | Dorothy Garrod |
| 1935–55 | Early Homo sapiens (Swanscombe Skull) | Middle Pleistocene 250,000 | Swanscombe, Kent, England | parts of skull | A. T. Marston |
| 1938 | Paranthropus robustus | Lower Pleistocene c. 2,000,000 | Kromdraai, Transvaal | skull part, bones | G. Terblanche |
| 1953–60 | Neanderthal Man | Upper Pleistocene 50,000 | Shanidar, Iraq | skeletons | Ralph Solecki |
| 1959 | Zinjanthropus boisei (Nutcracker Man) | Lower Pleistocene c. 1,750,000 | Olduvai, Tanzania | skull | Mary D. Leakey |
| 1960 | Homo habilis | Lower Pleistocene c. 1,750,000 | Olduvai, Tanzania | skull fragments | Louis S. B. Leakey |
| 1960 | Homo erectus or early Homo sapiens | Middle Pleistocene 350,000 | Petralona, Greece | skull | 6 local people |
| 1967–72 | Australopithecus boisei, Australopithecus africanus, Homo sapiens | Upper Pliocene 4,000,000-2,000,000 | Omo Valley, Ethiopa | various remains | Y. Coppens, F. C. Howell, and teams |
| 1968–80 | Australopithecus boisei, Homo habilis, Homo erectus | Pleistocene 2,200,000–1,300,000 | Koobi Fora (formerly East Rudolf), Kenya | 150 specimens | Richard Leakey and team |
| 1971 | Early Homo erectus or Homo sapiens? (Arago Man) | Middle Pleistocene 300,000 | Arago, France | skull, jaws, pelvis | H. de Lumley |
| 1973–80 | Australopithecus afarensis | Upper Pliocene 3,800,000-3,000,000 | Afar, Ethiopia | various remains, including partial skeleton "Lucy" | Y. Coppens, M. Taieb, D. Johanson, and teams |
| 1975–80 | Australopithecus afarensis | Upper Pliocene 3,800,000-3,500,000 | Laetoli, Tanzania | footprints, jaws, teeth, 8 adults, 3 children | Mary Leakey and team |
| 1976 | early Homo sapiens | Middle/Upper Pleistocene 120,000 | Laetoli, Tanzania | skull | M. Leakey and team |
| 1978 | early Homo sapiens | Middle Pleistocene 150,000 | Dali, China | skull | not reported |

## MAXIMUM LIFE-SPANS OF ANIMALS

**The list below reflects the maximum life-span of various animals while in captivity.**

| Years | Animal | Years | Animal | Years | Animal | Years | Animal |
|---|---|---|---|---|---|---|---|
| 190 | Giant Tortoise | 37 | Chimpanzee | 25 | Tiger | 17 | Goat |
| 138 | Eastern Box Turtle | 36 | Toad | 25 | Zebra | 16 | Bullfrog |
| 84 | Elephant | 33 | Gorilla | 23 | Leopard | 16 | Cheetah |
| 80 | Freshwater Oyster | 31 | Gibbon | 23 | Domestic Cat | 16 | Kangaroo |
| 68 | Owl | 31 | Grizzly Bear | 22 | Domestic Dog | 15 | Pronghorn |
| 55 | Eagle | 30 | Dolphin | 20 | Cougar | 15 | Reindeer |
| 51 | Pelican | 30 | Lion | 20 | Cow | 15 | Timber Wolf |
| 50 | Domestic Horse | 28 | Giraffe | 20 | Moose | 14 | Chicken |
| 46 | Jackass | 28 | Sea Lion | 20 | Rattlesnake | 14 | Coyote |
| 45 | Baboon | 25 | Black Bear | 20 | Sheep | 13 | Rabbit |
| 41 | Polar Bear | 25 | Camel | 19 | Beaver | 10 | Pig |

## THE ANIMAL KINGDOM

This classification system of living animals is one of many types available. Subphyla are included only for phylum Chordata, subclasses only for class Mammalia, and orders only for Eutheria in class Mammalia.

SUBKINGDOM PROTOZOA—one-celled animals
- **Phylum Protozoa**—acellular animals (protozoans)
  - Class Mastigophora (Flagellata)–flagellates
  - Class Sarcodina (Rhizopoda)–sarcodines (Amoeba)
  - Class Sporozoa–spore-forming parasites
  - Class Ciliophora (Ciliata)–ciliates (Paramecium)

SUBKINGDOM MESOZOA—certain wormlike parasites
- **Phylum Mesozoa**—mesozoans

SUBKINGDOM PARAZOA—pore-perforated bodies
- **Phylum Porifera**—sponges
  - Class Calcarea–chalky sponges
  - Class Hexactinellida–glass sponges
  - Class Demospongiae–horny sponges

SUBKINGDOM METAZOA—multi-cellular animals
- **Phylum Coelenterata** (Cnidaria)—coelenterates
  - Class Hydrozoa–hydroids (Portuguese man-of-war)
  - Class Scyphozoa–jellyfish
  - Class Anthozoa–sea anemones and corals
- **Phylum Ctenophora**—ctenophores
  - Class Tentaculata–with tentacles
  - Class Nuda–without tentacles
- **Phylum Platyhelminthes**—flatworms
  - Class Turbellaria–free-living flatworms
  - Class Trematoda–flukes
  - Class Cestoda–tapeworms
  - Class Gnathostomulida–gnathostomulids
- **Phylum Nemertea**—nemertines (ribbon worms)
  - Class Anopla–unarmed proboscis
  - Class Enopla–armed proboscis
- **Phylum Acanthocephala**—thorny-headed worms
- **Phylum Aschelminthes**—aschelminths
  - Class Rotifera (Rotatoria)–rotifers
  - Class Gastrotricha–gastrotrichs
  - Class Kinorhyncha (Echinodera)–kinorhynchs
  - Class Nematoda–nematodes (roundworms)
  - Class Nematomorpha–horsehair worms
  - Class Priapulida–priapulids
- **Phylum Sipunculida**—sipunculids
- **Phylum Bryozoa** (Ectoprocta)—bryozoans
  - Class Phylactolaemata–fresh-water
  - Class Gymnolaemata–salt-water
- **Phylum Entoprocta**—entoprocts
- **Phylum Phoronida**—phoronids
- **Phylum Brachiopoda**—brachiopods
  - Class Inarticulata–without teeth
  - Class Articulata–with teeth
- **Phylum Mollusca**—mollusks
  - Class Amphineura–chitons
  - Class Monoplacophora–monoplacophs
  - Class Gastropoda–gastropods (snails, slugs)
  - Class Scaphopoda–tooth shells
  - Class Bivalvia (Lamellibranchia)–bivalve mollusks
  - Class Cephalopoda–cephalopods (squids, octopi)
- **Phylum Echiurida**—echiuroid marine worms
- **Phylum Annelida**—segmented worms
  - Class Polychaeta–sand-and bristleworms
  - Class Mysostomaria–mysostomarians
  - Class Oligochaeta–earthworms
  - Class Hirudinea–leeches
  - Class Archiannelida–no external segments
- **Phylum Onychophora**—velvet worms
- **Phylum Tardigrada**—tardigrades (water bears)
- **Phylum Pentastomida**—tongue worms
- **Phylum Arthropoda**—arthropods
  - Class Merostomata–horseshoe & king crabs
  - Class Arachnida–spiders, ticks, mites, scorpions
  - Class Pycnogonida (Pantopoda)–sea spiders
  - Class Crustacea–crustaceans
  - Class Chilopoda–centipedes
  - Class Diplopoda–millipedes
  - Class Pauropoda–pauropods
  - Class Symphyla–symphylids (garden centipede)
  - Class Insecta–insects
- **Phylum Chaetognatha**—arrowworms
- **Phylum Pogonophora**—beard worms
- **Phylum Hemichordata**—hemichordates
  - Class Enteropneusta–acorn worms
  - Class Pterobranchia–pterobranchs
  - Class Planctosphaeroidea–planctosphaera
- **Phylum Echinodermata**—echinoderms
  - Class Echinoidea–sea urchins, sand dollars
  - Class Holothuroidea–sea cucumbers
  - Class Crinoidea–crinoids (sea lilies, feather stars)
  - Class Asteroidea–starfish
  - Class Ophiuroidea–brittle & basket stars
- **Phylum Chordata**—chordates
  - **Subphylum Urochordata (Tunicata)**—tunicates
    - Class Ascidiacea–sea squirts
    - Class Thaliacea–salps
    - Class Larvacea–larvaceans
  - **Subphylum Cephalochordata**—lancelets
  - **Subphylum Vertebrata (Craniata)**—vertebrates
    - Class Agnatha–jawless vertebrates
    - Class Chondrichthyes (Elasmobranchii)–cartilaginous fish (sharks, rays)
    - Class Osteichthyes–bony fish
    - Class Amphibia–amphibians
    - Class Reptilia–reptiles
    - Class Aves–birds
    - Class Mammalia–mammals
      - Subclass Prototheria–egg laying mammals (monotremes)
      - Subclass Theria–viviparous (live-bearing) mammals
        - Infraclass Metatheria–pouched mammals (marsupials)
        - Infraclass Eutheria–placental mammals
          - Order Insectivora–moles, shrews, hedgehogs
          - Order Dermoptera–flying lemurs (colugos)
          - Order Chiroptera–bats
          - Order Primates–lemurs, monkeys, apes, man
          - Order Edentata–sloths, anteaters, armadillos
          - Order Pholidota–pangolins
          - Order Lagomorpha–rabbits, hares, pikas
          - Order Rodentia–rodents
          - Order Cetacea–whales, dolphins, porpoises
          - Order Carnivora–carnivores (dogs, cats)
          - Order Pinnipedia–seals, sea lions, walruses
          - Order Tubulidentata–aardvark
          - Order Proboscidea–elephants
          - Order Hyracoidea–hyraxes (coneys)
          - Order Sirenia–sea cows (manatee, dugong)
          - Order Perissodactyla–odd-toe ungulates (horses, zebras, tapirs, rhinoceroses)
          - Order Artiodactyla–even-toed ungulates (cattle, deer, sheep, goats, pigs, camels)

## ANIMAL GESTATION PERIODS AND LITTERS

SOURCE: Grace Davall, Assistant Curator, Mammals and Birds, New York Zoological Society

| Animal | Gestation Period | Litter Size |
|---|---|---|
| AMERICAN BUFFALO (BISON) | 270–285 days | 1 |
| BABOON | 6 months | 1–2 |
| BLACK BEAR | 7 months | 1–4 |
| CAMEL | 12–13 months | 1 |
| CAT | 63 days | 1–6 |
| CHIMPANZEE | 226 days | 1–2 |
| CHINCHILLA | 105–111 days | 1–4 |
| COW | 280 days | 1–2 |
| DEER (WHITE-TAIL) | 7 months | 2 |
| DOG | 61 days | 1–12 |
| DOLPHIN | 9 months | 1 |
| ELEPHANT | 21 months | 1 |
| FOX | 49–55 days | 1–8 |
| GERBIL | 14 days | 1–7 |
| GIRAFFE | 14–15 months | 1 |
| GORILLA | 8½ months | 1 |
| HAMSTER | 16–19 days | 2–12 |
| HORSE | 11 months | 1 |
| KANGAROO | 38–39 days | 1–2 |
| LION | 108 days | 1–4 |
| MACAQUE | 160–170 days | 1–2 |
| MINK | 48–51 days | 4–8 |
| MOUSE | 19–21 days | 1–9 |
| OPOSSUM | 12–13 days | 4–13 |
| OTTER | 9½–12½ months | 1–4 |
| PIG | 112–115 days | 4–6 |
| RABBIT | 1 month | 1–13 |
| RACCOON | 63 days | 1–6 |
| SHEEP | 150 days | 1–3 |
| SKUNK | 52 days | 4–7 |
| SQUIRREL | 44 days | 2–5 |
| TIGER | 100–108 days | 2–4 |
| WOLF | 60–63 days | 1–13 |
| YAK | just over 9 months | 1 |
| ZEBRA | 11–12 months | 1 |

## ENDANGERED WILDLIFE

**Source:** Office of Endangered Species, U.S. Dept. of the Interior

Anyone wishing to know the status of any animal should contact the Office of Endangered Species, Dept. of the Interior, Washington, D.C. 20240. Below is a selection from official List of Endangered Fauna, including the 109 native to the United States.

**BONY FISHES** (Class *Osteichthyes/Phylum Chordata*)

**Sturgeons & Paddlefishes** (Order: *Acipenseriformes*): 1. Sturgeon, Shortnose.

**Trout, Salmon & Relatives** (Order: *Salmoniformes*): 1. Ala Balik; 2. Cisco, Longjaw; 3. Trout, Arizona (Apache); 4. Trout, Gila; 5. Trout, Greenback cutthroat; 6. Trout, Lahontan cutthroat; 7. Trout, Paiute cutthroat.

**Carps, Minnows & Relatives** (Order: *Cypriniformes*): 1. Ayumodoki; 2. Bonytail, Pahranagat; 3. Chub, Humpback; 4. Chub, Mohave; 5. Cicek; 6. Cui-ui; 7. Dace, Kendall Warm Springs; 8. Dace, Moapa; 9. Squawfish, Colorado River; 10. Tanago, Miyako; 11. Woundfin.

**Sticklebacks** (Order: *Solenichthyiformes*): 1. Stickleback, Unarmored threespine.

**Silversides, Topminnows & Relatives** (Order: *Atheriniformes*): 1. Gambusia, Big Bend; 2. Gambusia, Clear Creek; 3. Gambusia, Pecos; 4. Killifish, Pahrump; 5. Pupfish, Comanche Springs; 6. Pupfish, Devil's Hole; 7. Pupfish, Owens River; 8. Pupfish, Tecopa; 9. Pupfish, Warm Springs; 10. Topminnow, Gila.

**Perches & Relatives** (Order: *Perciformes*): 1. Darter, Fountain; 2. Darter, Maryland; 3. Darter, Okaloosa; 4. Darter, Watercress; 5. Pike, Blue.

**AMPHIBIANS** (Class *Amphibia/Phylum Chordata*)

**Salamanders** (Order: *Urodela*): 1. Salamander, Desert slender; 2. Salamander, Santa Cruz long-toed; 3. Salamander, Texas blind. **Frogs** (Order: *Anura*): 1. Frog, Stephen Island; 2. Frog, Israel painted; 3. Toad, Houston.

**REPTILES** (Class *Reptilia/Phylum Chordata*)

**Turtles** (Order: *Testudinata*): 1. Terrapin, River (Tuntong); 2. Tortoise, Galapagos; 3. Tortoise, Madgascar radiated; 4. Tortoise, Short-necked (swamp); 5. Turtle, Aquatic box; 6. Turtle, Atlantic Ridley; 7. Turtle, Hawksbill; 8. Turtle, Leatherback.

**Crocodiles** (Order: *Crocodilia*): 1. Alligator, American; 2. Crocodile, Cuban; 3. Crocodile, Morelet's.

**Lizards & Snakes** (Order: *Squamata*): 1. Lizard, Day gecko; 2. Lizard, Round Island day gecko; 3. Lizard, Anegada ground iguana; 4. Lizard, Barrington land iguana; 5. Lizard, Blunt-nosed leopard; 6. Snake, Jamaica boa; 7. Snake, Puerto Rican boa; 8. Snake, San Francisco garter.

**BIRDS** (Class *Aves/Phylum Chordata*)

**Albatrosses, Petrels & Relatives** (Order: *Procellariiformes*): 1. Albatross, Short-tailed; 2. Cahow (Bermuda petrel); 3. Petrel, Hawaiian dark-rumped.

**Pelicans** (Order: *Pelecaniformes*): 1. Pelican, Brown.

**Ducks, Geese, Swans & Relatives** (Order: *Anseriformes*): 1. Duck, Hawaiian (koloa); 2. Duck, Laysan; 3. Duck, Mexican; 4. Duck, White-winged wood; 5. Goose, Aleutian Canada; 6. Goose, Hawaiian (nene).

**Eagles, Falcons, Vultures & Relatives** (Order: *Falconiformes*): 1. Condor, Andean; 2. Condor, California; 3. Eagle, Monkey-eating; 4. Eagle, Southern bald; 5. Eagle, Spanish imperial; 6. Falcon, American peregrine; 7. Falcon, Arctic peregrine; 8. Goshawk, Christmas Island; 9. Hawk, Anjouan Island sparrow; 10. Hawk, Galapagos; 11. Hawk, Hawaiian (io); 12. Kite, Florida Everglade.

**Pheasants, Grouse, Curassows & Relatives** (Order: *Galliformes*): 1. Curassow, Red-billed; 2. Curassow, Trinidad white-headed; 3. Guan, Horned; 4. Megapode, Maleo; 5. Megapode, LaPerouse's; 6. Pheasant, Bar-tailed; 7. Pheasant, Blyth's tragopan; 8. Pheasant, Brown-eared; 9. Pheasant, Cabot's tragopan; 10. Pheasant, Chinese monal; 11. Pheasant, Edward's; 12. Pheasant, Imperial; 13. Pheasant, Mikado; 14. Pheasant, Palawan peacock; 15. Pheasant, Sclater's monal; 16. Pheasant, Swinhoe's; 17. Pheasant, Western tragopan; 18. Pheasant, White-eared; 19. Prairie Chicken, Attwater's greater; 20. Quail, Masked bobwhite.

**Cranes, Rails, Bustards & Relatives** (Order: *Gruiformes*): 1. Bustard, Great Indian; 2. Coot, Hawaiian; 3. Crane, Hooded; 4. Crane, Japanese; 5. Crane, Mississippi sandhill; 6. Crane, Siberian white; 7. Crane, Whooping; 8. Gallinule, Hawaiian; 9. Kagu (rail); 10. Rail, Auckland Island; 11. Rail, California clapper; 12. Rail, Light-footed clapper; 13. Rail, Yuma clapper; 14. Wanderer, Plains; 15. Takahe.

**Plovers, Snipes, Gulls & Relatives** (Order: *Charadriiformes*): 1. Curlew, Eskimo; 2. Gull, Audouin's; 3. Stilt, Hawaiian; 4. Tern, California least.

**Pigeons, Doves, Sandgrouse & Relatives** (Order: *Columbiformes*): 1. Dove, Cloven-feathered; 2. Dove, Grenada; 3. Dove, Palau ground; 4. Pigeon, Azores wood; 5. Pigeon, Chatham Island; 6. Pigeon, Puerto Rican plain.

**Parrots** (Order: *Psittaciformes*): 1. Parrot, Puerto Rican; 2. Parakeet, Splendid.

**Owls** (Order: *Strigiformes*): 1. Owl, Anjouan scops; 2. Owl, Palau; 3. Owl, New Zealand laughing.

**Goatsuckers & Relatives** (Order: *Caprimulgiformes*): 1. Whip-poor-will, Puerto Rican.

**Woodpeckers, Puffbirds, Barbets & Relatives** (Order: *Piciformes*): 1. Woodpecker, Imperial; 2. Woodpecker, Ivory-billed; 3. Woodpecker, Red-cockaded.

**Perching Birds—Sparrows, Larks, Thrushes & Relatives** (Order: *Passeriformes*): 1. Bulbul, Mauritius olivaceous; 2. Crow, Hawaiian (alala); 3. Cuckoo-Shrike, Mauritius; 4. Cuckoo-Shrike, Reunion; 5. Finch, Sao Miguel bullfinch; 6. Flycatcher, Chatham Island robin; 7. Flycatcher, Eyrean grass-wren; 8. Flycatcher, Grey-necked rock-fowl; 9. Flycatcher, Palau fantail; 10. Flycatcher, Seychelles black; 11. Flycatcher, Tahiti; 12. Flycatcher, Western bristlebird; 13. Flycatcher, White-necked rock-fowl; 14. Flycatcher (Tyrant), Euler's; 15. Flycatcher (Tyrant), Scarlet-breasted robin; 16. Flycatcher (Tyrant), Tinian monarch; 17. Grackle, Slender-billed; 18. Honeycreeper, Akiapolaau; 19. Honeycreeper, Crested (akohekohe); 20. Honeycreeper, Hawaii akepa (akepa); 21. Honeycreeper, Kauai akialoa; 22. Honeycreeper, Maui parrotbill; 23. Honeycreeper, Maui akepa (akepuie); 24. Honeycreeper, Molokai creeper (kakawahie); 25. Honeycreeper, Oahu creeper (alauwahio); 26. Honeycreeper, Ou; 27. Honeycreeper, Palila; 28. Honeycreepers, Laysan & Nihoa finches; 29. Honeycreepers, Kauai & Maui nukupuus; 30. Honey-eater, Helmeted; 31. Honey-eater, Kauai Oo (oo aa); 32. Scrub-bird, Noisy; 33. Sparrow, Cape Sable; 34. Sparrow, Dusky seaside; 35. Sparrow, Santa Barbara song; 36. Starling, Ponape Mountain; 37. Starling, Rothschild's (myna); 38. Thrasher, White-breasted; 39. Thrush, Large Kauai; 40. Thrush, Molokai (olomau); 41. Thrush, Seychelles magpie-robin; 42. Thrush, Small Kauai (puaiohi); 43. Thrush, Western whipbird; 44. Warbler, Nihoa millerbird; 45. Warbler, Bachman's; 46. Warbler, Kirtland's.

**MAMMALS** (Class *Mammalia/Phylum Chordata*)

**Bats** (Order: *Chiroptera*): 1. Bat, Indiana; 2. Bat, Hawaiian hoary.

**Primates** (Order: *Primates*): 1. Avahis; 2. Aye-aye; 3. Colobus, Red; 4. Colobus, Zanzibar red; 5. Gibbon, Kloss; 6. Gibbon, Pileated; 7. Gorilla; 8. Indris; 9. Langur, Douc; 10. Langur, Pagi Island; 11. Lemurs; 12. Lemurs, Gentle; 13. Lemurs, Sportive & Weasel; 14. Lemurs, Dwarf; 15. Lemurs, Mouse; 16. Lemurs, Fork-marked; 17. Macaque, Lion-tailed; 18. Mangabey, Tana River; 19. Marmoset, Goeldi's; 20. Monkey, Spider; 21. Monkey, Spider; 22. Orangutan; 23. Sifakas; 24. Tamarins, Golden-rumped; (Golden Marmosets); 25. Uakari.

**Rodents** (Order: *Rodentia*): 1. Rat, Morro Bay kangaroo; 2. Mouse, Salt marsh harvest; 3. Prairie dog, Utah; 4. Squirrel, Delmarva fox.

**Whales, Dolphins & Porpoises** (Order: *Cetacea*): 1. Whale, Blue; 2. Whale, Bowhead; 3. Whale, Finback; 4. Whale, Gray; 5. Whale, Humpback; 6. Whale, Right; 7. Whale, Sei; 8. Whale, Sperm.

**Carnivores** (Order: *Carnivora*): 1. Bear, Mexican grizzly; 2. Cat, Tiger; 3. Cheetah; 4. Cougar, Eastern; 5. Dog, Asiatic wild; 6. Ferret, Black-footed; 7. Fox, Northern kit; 8. Fox, San Joaquin kit; 9. Hyaena, Barbary; 10. Hyaena, Brown; 11. Jaguar; 12. Leopard; 13. Leopard, Formosan clouded; 14. Leopard, Snow; 15. Lion, Asiatic; 16. Lynx, Spanish; 17. Margay; 18. Marten, Formosan yellow-throated; 19. Ocelot; 20. Otter, Cameroon clawless; 21. Otter, Giant; 22. Otter, La Plata; 23. Panther, Florida; 24. Serval, Barbary; 25. Tiger; 26. Wolf, Eastern timber; 27. Wolf, Northern Rocky Mountain; 28. Wolf, Red; 29. Wolf, Maned.

**Sirenians** (Order: *Sirenia*): 1. Manatee, Florida.

**Even-Toed Ungulates** (Order: *Artiodactyla*): 1. Anoa; 2. Banteng; 3. Bison, Wood; 4. Deer, Columbian white-tailed; 5. Deer, Key; 6. Deer, Marsh; 7. Deer, McNeill's; 8. Deer, Swamp; 9. Gazelle, Cuviers; 10. Pronghorn, Sonoran; 11. Hartebeest, Swayne's; 12. Ibex, Pyrenean; 13. Impala, Black-faced.

## LONG FOREIGN RIVERS

| River | Empties Into | Length (in miles) |
|---|---|---|
| Amazon | Atlantic Ocean | 3,915 |
| Amu-Dar'ya | Aral Sea | 1,616 |
| Amur-Shilka-Onon | Tatar Strait | 2,744 |
| Angara | Yenisey River | 1,135 |
| Araguaia | Tocantins River | 1,367 |
| Athabasca | Lake Athabasca | 765 |
| Belaya | Kama River | 889 |
| Brahmaputra | Bay of Bengal | 1,700 |
| Chang Jiang (Yangtze) | East China Sea | 3,900 |
| Churchill | Hudson Bay | 1,000 |
| Congo (Zaire) | Atlantic Ocean | 2,718 |
| Cubango-Okovango | Okovango Swamps | 994 |
| Danube | Black Sea | 1,775 |
| Darling | Murray River | 1,160 |
| Dnieper | Black Sea | 1,368 |
| Dniester | Black Sea | 876 |
| Don | Sea of Azov | 1,222 |
| Dvina, Northern | White Sea | 809 |
| Ebro | Mediterranean Sea | 565 |
| Elbe | North Sea | 724 |
| Euphrates | Persian Gulf | 1,700 |
| Fraser | Strait of Georgia | 850 |
| Ganges | Bay of Bengal | 1,550 |
| Huang He (Yellow) | Yellow Sea | 2,877 |
| Indigirka | East Siberian Sea | 1,228 |
| Indus | Arabian Sea | 1,800 |
| Irrawaddy | Bay of Bengal | 1,325 |
| Japurá | Amazon River | 1,500 |
| Kama | Volga River | 1,262 |
| Kasai | Congo River | 1,338 |
| Kolyma | East Siberian Sea | 1,562 |
| Lena | Laptev Sea | 2,734 |
| Limpopo | Indian Ocean | 995 |
| Loire | Bay of Biscay | 628 |
| Mackenzie-Peace-Finlay | Beaufort Sea | 2,635 |
| Madeira | Amazon River | 2,013 |
| Magdalena | Caribbean Sea | 1,000 |
| Mekong | South China Sea | 2,610 |
| Meuse | North Sea | 590 |
| Murray-Darling | Indian Ocean | 2,310 |
| Negro | Amazon River | 1,400 |
| Nelson-Saskatchewan | Hudson Bay | 1,600 |
| Niger | Gulf of Guinea | 2,548 |
| Nile-Kagera | Mediterranean Sea | 4,145 |
| Ob'-Irtysh-Black Irtysh | Gulf of Ob' (Kara Sea) | 3,362 |
| Oder | Baltic Sea | 538 |
| Oka | Volga River | 918 |
| Olenek | Laptev Sea | 1,411 |
| Orange | Atlantic Ocean | 1,350 |
| Orinoco | Atlantic Ocean | 1,600 |
| Ottawa | St. Lawrence River | 790 |
| Paraguay | Paraná River | 1,584 |
| Paraná-La Plata | Atlantic Ocean | 2,450 |
| Peace-Finlay | Slave River | 1,195 |
| Pechora | Pechora Sea | 1,124 |
| Pilcomayo | Paraguay River | 1,000 |
| Po | Adriatic Sea | 420 |
| Purus | Amazon River | 1,995 |
| Rhine | North Sea | 820 |
| Rhone | Gulf of Lions | 505 |
| Rio Grande | Gulf of Mexico | 1,885 |
| St. Lawrence | Gulf of St. Lawrence | 1,900 |
| Salween | Gulf of Martaban | 1,770 |
| São Francisco | Atlantic Ocean | 1,811 |
| Saskatchewan | Lake Winnipeg | 1,205 |
| Seine | English Channel | 482 |
| Selenga | Lake Baykal | 920 |
| Si | South China Sea | 1,650 |
| Sungari | Amur River | 1,130 |
| Syr-Dar'ya–Naryn | Aral Sea | 1,359 |
| Tagus (Tajo, Tejo) | Atlantic Ocean | 565 |
| Tigris | Euphrates River | 1,181 |
| Tisza | Danube River | 800 |
| Tocantins | Pará River | 1,677 |
| Ural | Caspian Sea | 1,509 |
| Uruguay | Río de La Plata | 994 |
| Vistula | Gulf of Gdańsk | 664 |
| Volga | Caspian Sea | 2,194 |
| Volta | Atlantic Ocean | 710 |
| Yangtze (Chang Jiang) | East China Sea | 3,900 |
| Yellow (Huang He) | Yellow Sea | 2,877 |
| Yenisey | Kara Sea | 2,543 |
| Yenisey-Angara | Kara Sea | 3,100 |
| Yukon | Bering Sea | 1,979 |
| Zambezi | Indian Ocean | 1,600 |

## OCEANS AND SEAS

| Ocean | Area (in square miles) | Percent of World's Water | Greatest Depth (in feet) |
|---|---|---|---|
| Pacific | 64,186,000 | 46 | Mariana Trench, off the Mariana Islands, 36,198 |
| Atlantic | 31,862,000 | 22.9 | Puerto Rico Trench, (Milwaukee Deep), off Puerto Rico, 28,374 |
| Indian | 28,350,000 | 20.3 | Java Trench, off Java, 25,344 |
| Arctic | 5,427,000 | 3.9 | Eurasia Basin, north of Svalbard, 17,880 |

| Sea | Area (in square miles) | Greatest Depth (in feet) |
|---|---|---|
| Caribbean | 970,000 | 24,720 |
| Mediterranean Sea | 969,000 | 16,896 |
| South China Sea | 895,000 | 15,000 |
| Bering Sea | 875,000 | 15,800 |
| Gulf of Mexico | 600,000 | 12,300 |
| Sea of Okhotsk | 590,000 | 11,070 |
| East China Sea | 482,000 | 9,500 |
| Sea of Japan | 389,000 | 12,280 |
| Hudson Bay | 317,500 | 846 |
| North Sea | 222,000 | 2,200 |
| Black Sea | 185,000 | 7,365 |
| Red Sea | 169,000 | 7,200 |
| Baltic Sea | 163,000 | 1,506 |

## ELEMENTS IN SEAWATER

SOURCE: U.S. Office of Saline Water

| Element | Milligrams per Kilogram* |
|---|---|
| Chlorine | 18,980 |
| Sodium | 10,561 |
| Magnesium | 1,272 |
| Sulfur | 884 |
| Calcium | 400 |
| Potassium | 380 |
| Bromine | 65 |
| Carbon | 28 |
| Strontium | 13 |
| Boron | 4.6 |
| Silicon | 0.02–4.0 |
| Fluorine | 1.4 |
| Nitrogen (compound) | 0.01–0.7 |
| Aluminum | 0.5 |
| Rubidium | 0.2 |
| Lithium | 0.1 |
| Phosphorus | 0.001–0.10 |
| Barium | 0.05 |
| Iodine | 0.05 |
| Arsenic | 0.01 –0.02 |
| Iron | 0.002–0.02 |
| Manganese | 0.001–0.01 |
| Copper | 0.001–0.01 |
| Zinc | 0.005 |
| Lead | 0.004 |
| Selenium | 0.004 |
| Cesium | 0.002 |
| Uranium | 0.0015 |
| Molybdenum | 0.0005 |
| Thorium | 0.0005 |
| Cerium | 0.0004 |
| Silver | 0.0003 |
| Vanadium | 0.0003 |
| Lanthanum | 0.0003 |
| Yttrium | 0.0003 |
| Nickel | 0.0001 |
| Scandium | 0.00004 |
| Mercury | 0.00003 |
| Gold | 0.000006 |

* Parts per million.

## MAJOR GLACIERS OF THE WORLD

Based on statistics from "Fluctuation of Glaciers 1965-70," © IAHS/UNESCO, 1973, and other sources.

| Name | Locality | *Area (sq. mi.) | *Length (mi.) |
|---|---|---|---|
| Aletsch | Swiss Alps | 45 | 15 |
| Amundsen | Antarctica | — | 60 |
| Baltoro | Asia (Karakoram) | 290 | 35 |
| Beardmore | Antarctica | 130 | 100 |
| Bering | Alaska | — | 125 |
| Bivachnyy | Asia (Pamir) | 75 | 15 |
| Chisana | Alaska | 135 | 30 |
| Columbia | Alaska | 110 | 40 |
| Denman | Antarctica | — | 70 |
| Fedchenko | Asia (Pamir) | 350 | 45 |
| Gangotri | Asia (Himalaya) | 115 | 20 |
| Garmo | Asia (Pamir) | 60 | 15 |
| Geographical Society | Asia (Pamir) | 50 | 15 |
| Grum-Grzhimaylo | Asia (Pamir) | 60 | 25 |
| Hispar | Asia (Karakoram) | 240 | 35 |
| Hofsjökull† | Iceland | 260 | — |
| Hubbard | Alaska-Yukon | — | 75 |
| Humboldt | Greenland | — | 70 |
| Inyl'chek, Yuzh. | Asia (Tien Shan) | 110 | 40 |
| Jostedalsbreen† | Norway | 485 | 60 |
| Kahiltna | Alaska | — | 45 |
| Lambert | Antarctica | — | 270 |
| Langjökull† | Iceland | 265 | 40 |
| Logan | Alaska-Yukon | — | 70 |
| Malaspina | Alaska-Yukon | 1,350 | 75 |
| Muir | Alaska | 400 | 15 |
| Muldrow | Alaska | 735 | 45 |
| Mýrdalsjökull† | Iceland | 180 | 30 |
| Nabesna | Alaska | 775 | 50 |
| Petermann | Greenland | — | 90 |
| Rennick | Antarctica | 185 | 160 |
| Rider | Greenland | 125 | — |
| Rimo | Asia (Karakoram) | 200 | 30 |
| Robert Scott | Antarctica | — | 90 |
| Shackleton | Antarctica | — | 90 |
| Shamrock | Alaska | 40 | 15 |
| Siachen | Asia (Karakoram) | 450 | 50 |
| Svartisen | Norway | 200 | 20 |
| Tasman | New Zealand | 50 | 20 |
| Temir-su | Asia (Tien Shan) | 45 | 25 |
| Totten | Antarctica | — | 45 |
| Triumvirate | Alaska | 170 | 30 |
| Vatnajökull† | Iceland | 2,200 | 90 |
| Zemu | Asia (Himalaya) | 50 | 20 |
| Zeravshan | Asia (Turkestan) | 45 | 15 |

* Approximate, subject to continuous revision. † Icefield.

## LARGE LAKES OF THE WORLD

| Lake | Continent | Area (in sq. miles) | Length (in miles) | Max. Depth (in ft.) |
|---|---|---|---|---|
| Caspian Sea | Asia-Europe | 143,243 | 746 | 3,264 |
| Superior | N. America | 31,700 | 383 | 1,301 |
| Victoria | Africa | 26,724 | 250 | 270 |
| Aral Sea | Asia | 25,676 | 266 | 256 |
| Huron | N. America | 23,010 | 247 | 748 |
| Michigan | N. America | 22,300 | 321 | 923 |
| Tanganyika | Africa | 12,650 | 420 | 4,700 |
| Baykal | Asia | 12,162 | 395 | 5,316 |
| Great Bear | N. America | 12,096 | 190 | 1,356 |
| Nyasa (Malawi) | Africa | 11,555 | 360 | 2,320 |
| Great Slave | N. America | 11,269 | 300 | 2,015 |
| Chad | Africa | 10,000–4,000* | 175–125 | 25–15 |
| Erie | N. America | 9,910 | 241 | 209 |
| Winnipeg | N. America | 9,417 | 265 | 60 |
| Ontario | N. America | 7,340 | 193 | 775 |
| Ladoga | Europe | 7,104 | 124 | 738 |
| Balkhash | Asia | 7,027 | 376 | 87 |
| Maracaibo | S. America | 5,120 | 110 | 100 |
| Bangweulu | Africa | 4,500–1,900* | 50 | — |
| Dongting | Asia | 4,500–1,500* | 80 | — |
| Onega | Europe | 3,710 | 154 | 377 |
| Eyre | Australia | 3,500–0* | 110 | — |
| Titicaca | S. America | 3,200 | 120 | 1,000 |
| Nicaragua | N. America | 3,100 | 100 | 230 |
| Athabasca | N. America | 3,064 | 200 | 400 |
| Reindeer | N. America | 2,568 | 143 | — |
| Tonle Sap | Asia | 2,500–1,000* | 85 | 40–5 |
| Turkana (Rudolf) | Africa | 2,463 | 160 | 240 |
| Issyk-Kul' | Asia | 2,425 | 114 | 2,303 |
| Urmia | Asia | 2,300–1,500* | 90 | 50 |
| Torrens | Australia | 2,230* | 120 | — |
| Vänern | Europe | 2,156 | 85 | 328 |
| Winnipegosis | N. America | 2,075 | 125 | 38 |
| Albert | Africa | 2,075 | 100 | 160 |
| Kariba | Africa | 2,050 | 175 | 295 |
| Nettilling | N. America | 1,956 | 65 | — |
| Chany | Asia | 1,931–965* | 56 | 39–23 |
| Nipigon | N. America | 1,872 | 70 | 540 |
| Gairdner | Australia | 1,825–0* | 100 | — |
| Mweru | Africa | 1,800 | 75 | 60 |
| Manitoba | N. America | 1,794 | 140 | 12 |
| Taymyr | Asia | 1,737 | 125 | 85 |
| Kyoga | Africa | 1,700 | 75 | 25 |
| Khanka | Asia | 1,700 | 59 | 33 |
| Lake of the Woods | N. America | 1,679 | 70 | 70 |
| Peipus | Europe | 1,400 | 87 | 50 |
| Qinghai | Asia | 1,625 | 70 | 125 |
| Nasser-Nubia | Africa | 1,550 | 350 | — |
| Dubawnt | N. America | 1,480 | 70 | — |
| Van | Asia | 1,470 | 80 | — |
| Wollaston | N. America | 1,035 | 70 | — |
| Great Salt | N. America | 940 | 75 | 27 |

* Max. and min. of fluctuating water area.

## GREAT WORLD DESERTS

| Desert | Location | Size |
|---|---|---|
| Arabian (Eastern) | North Africa-Red Sea coast | c. 70,000 sq. mi. |
| Atacama | Northern Chile | c. 140,000 sq. mi.; c. 600 mi. long |
| Colorado | Southern California | c. 2,500 sq. mi. |
| Dasht-i-Kavir | Iran | c. 450 mi. long; c. 175 mi. wide |
| Dasht-i-Lut | Iran | c. 300 mi. long; c. 175 mi. wide |
| Death Valley | California | c. 140 mi. long; c. 10 mi. wide |
| Gibson | Western Australia | c. 250,000 sq. mi. |
| Gobi | China and Mongolia | c. 500,000 sq. mi.; c. 1,000 mi. long |
| Great Salt Lake | Utah | c.125 mi. long; c. 80 mi. wide |
| Great Sandy | Western Australia | c. 150,000 sq. mi. |
| Great Victoria | Western and South Australia | c. 250,000 sq. mi. |
| Kalahari | Southern Africa | c. 225,000 sq.mi. |
| Kara-Kum | Turkmen SSR, USSR | c. 115,000 sq. mi.; c. 650 mi. long |
| Kyzyl-Kum | Uzbek & Kazakh SSR, USSR | c. 100,000 sq. mi. |
| Mojave | Southern California | c. 15,000 sq.mi. |
| Namib | South-West African coast | c. 800 mi. long; c. 60 mi. wide |
| Nefud (An Nafud) | Northern Arabia | c. 180 mi. long; c. 140 mi. wide |
| Negev | Southern Israel | c. 5,000 sq. mi. |
| Nubian | Northern Sudan | c.150,000 sq. mi. |
| Rub al Khali | Southern Arabia | c. 235,000 sq.mi. |
| Sahara | Northern Africa | c. 3,500,000 sq. mi; c. 3,100 mi. long; c. 1,100 mi. wide |
| Sechura | Peruvian coast | c. 10,000 sq. mi. |
| Simpson | Central Australia | c. 45,000 sq.mi. |
| Syrian (El Hamad) | Northern Arabia, Iraq, Jordan & Syria | c. 450 mi. long; c. 350 mi. wide |
| Taklamakan | Xinjiang Uygur Aut. Reg., China | c. 180,000 sq. mi.; c. 500 mi. long; c. 300 mi. wide |
| Thar (Great Indian) | India and Pakistan | c. 500 mi. long; c. 275 mi.wide |
| Vizcaíno | Baja California Sur, Mexico | c. 6,000 sq. mi. |

## HIGH MOUNTAIN PEAKS

(See page 301 for U. S. peaks over 14,000 feet)

| Name | Location | Feet |
|---|---|---|
| **ASIA** | | |
| Everest (Chomolungma) | Nepal-China (Tibet) | 29,028 |
| K2 (Godwin-Austen) | Pakistan-China | 28,250 |
| Kanchenjunga I | Nepal-India | 28,208 |
| Lhotse | Nepal-China (Tibet) | 27,923 |
| Makalu | Nepal-China (Tibet) | 27,824 |
| Kanchenjunga II | Nepal-India | 27,803 |
| Lhotse Shar | Nepal-China (Tibet) | 27,504 |
| Dhaulagiri I | Nepal | 26,810 |
| Manaslu I (Kutang) | Nepal | 26,760 |
| Cho Oyu I | Nepal-China (Tibet) | 26,750 |
| Nanga Parbat I | Pakistan | 26,660 |
| Annapurna I | Nepal | 26,504 |
| Gasherbrum I | Pakistan | 26,470 |
| Broad Peak | Pakistan | 26,400 |
| Gasherbrum II | Pakistan | 26,362 |
| Gosainthan (Shisha Pangma) | China (Tibet) | 26,291 |
| Gasherbrum IV | Pakistan | 26,181 |
| Gasherbrum III | Pakistan | 26,090 |
| Annapurna II | Nepal | 26,041 |
| Gyachung Kang | Nepal-China (Tibet) | 25,990 |
| Nanga Parbat II | Pakistan | 25,953 |
| Himalchuli | Nepal | 25,895 |
| Disteghil Sar | Pakistan | 25,868 |
| Nuptse | Nepal | 25,850 |
| Khinyang Chhish | Pakistan | 25,760 |
| Masherbrum | Pakistan | 25,660 |
| Nanda Devi | India | 25,645 |
| Cho Oyu II | Nepal-China (Tibet) | 25,611 |
| Chomo Lönzo | China (Tibet) | 25,558 |
| Rakaposhi | Pakistan | 25,550 |
| Batura Muztagh I | India (Kashmir) | 25,540 |
| Kanjut Sar | India (Kashmir) | 25,460 |
| Kamet | India-China (Tibet) | 25,447 |
| Namzha Parwa | China (Tibet) | 25,445 |
| Dhaulagiri II | Nepal | 25,429 |
| Saltoro Kangri | Pakistan | 25,400 |
| Batura Muztagh II | Pakistan | 25,361 |
| Gurla Mandhada | China (Tibet) | 25,355 |
| Ulu Muztag | China (Sinkiang-Tibet) | 25,340 |
| Trivor | Pakistan | 25,330 |
| Kungur | China (Sinkiang) | 25,325 |
| Jannu | Nepal | 25,294 |
| Dhaulagiri III | Nepal | 25,271 |
| Tirich Mir | Pakistan | 25,230 |
| Saser Kangri I | India (Kashmir) | 25,170 |
| Chogolisa | Pakistan | 25,148 |
| Dhaulagiri IV | Nepal | 25,135 |
| Kangchungtse (Makalu II) | Nepal-China (Tibet) | 25,128 |
| Dhaulagiri V | Nepal | 24,992 |
| Rathong | Nepal-India | 24,912 |
| Gongga Shan | China | 24,790 |
| Annapurna III | Nepal | 24,787 |
| Kula Kangri | Bhutan-China (Tibet) | 24,784 |
| Changtse | China (Tibet) | 24,780 |
| Muztagata | China (Sinkiang) | 24,757 |
| Annapurna IV | Nepal | 24,688 |
| Communism Peak | USSR | 24,590 |
| Noshaq | Pakistan-Afghanistan | 24,581 |
| Jongsong Peak | India-China (Tibet) | 24,472 |
| Malubiting | Pakistan | 24,470 |
| Pobeda Peak | USSR | 24,406 |
| Chomo Lhari | Bhutan-China (Tibet) | 23,997 |
| Muztag | China (Sinkiang) | 23,891 |
| Anyêmaqên | China | 23,490 |
| Demavend | Iran | 18,376 |
| Ararat | Turkey | 16,946 |
| Djaja (Carstensz) | Indonesia (New Guinea) | 16,503 |
| Klyuchevskaya Sopka | USSR | 15,584 |
| Kinabalu | Malaysia (Sabah) | 13,455 |
| Kerintji | Indonesia (Sumatra) | 12,484 |
| Fuji | Japan | 12,389 |
| Semeru | Indonesia (Java) | 12,060 |
| **AFRICA** | | |
| Kilimanjaro (Kibo) | Tanzania | 19,340 |
| Kenya (Batian) | Kenya | 17,058 |
| Kilimanjaro (Mawenzi) | Tanzania | 16,896 |
| Margherita (Ruwenzori) | Uganda-Zaire | 16,795 |
| Ras Dashan | Ethiopia | 15,157 |
| Meru | Tanzania | 14,979 |
| Karisimbi | Rwanda-Zaire | 14,787 |
| Elgon (Wagagai) | Kenya-Uganda | 14,178 |
| Toubkal | Morocco | 13,665 |
| Cameroon (Fako Peak) | Cameroon | 13,350 |
| Teide | Canary Is. | 12,198 |
| **AUSTRALIA and OCEANIA** | | |
| Wilhelm | Papua New Guinea | 14,793 |
| Mauna Kea | US (Hawaii) | 13,796 |
| Mauna Loa | US (Hawaii) | 13,680 |
| Cook (Aorangi) | New Zealand | 12,349 |
| Kosciusko | Australia | 7,316 |

**ANTARCTICA**

| Name | Feet | Name | Feet |
|---|---|---|---|
| Vinson Massif | 16,864 | Markham | 14,285 |
| Tyree | 16,289 | Bell | 14,117 |
| Gardner | 15,374 | Mackellar | 14,098 |
| Kirkpatrick | 14,856 | Anderson | 13,990 |
| Elizabeth | 14,698 | Bentley | 13,934 |

| Name | Location | Feet |
|---|---|---|
| **EUROPE (including Caucasus)** | | |
| El'brus | USSR | 18,510 |
| Shkhara | USSR | 17,064 |
| Dykh-Tau | USSR | 17,054 |
| Koshtan-Tau | USSR | 16,877 |
| Dzhangi-Tau | USSR | 16,565 |
| Kazbek | USSR | 16,558 |
| Mont-Blanc | France | 15,771 |
| Dufourspitze (Mte. Rosa) | Switz.-Italy | 15,203 |
| Dom (Mischabel) | Switz. | 14,911 |
| Lyskamm | Switz.-Italy | 14,852 |
| Weisshorn | Switz. | 14,780 |
| Täschhorn | Switz. | 14,733 |
| Matterhorn | Switz. | 14,692 |
| Mont-Maudit | France-Italy | 14,649 |
| Dent-Blanche | Switz. | 14,293 |
| Nadelhorn | Switz. | 14,196 |
| Grand-Combin | Switz. | 14,154 |
| Lenzspitze | Switz. | 14,098 |
| Finsteraarhorn | Switz. | 14,022 |
| Rimpfischhorn | Switz. | 13,776 |
| Aletschhorn | Switz | 13,763 |
| Jungfrau | Switz. | 13,642 |
| Gran Paradiso | Italy | 13,323 |
| Piz Bernina | Switz.-Italy | 13,284 |
| Grossglockner | Austria | 12,457 |
| Mulhacén | Spain | 11,411 |
| Etna | Italy | 11,053 |
| Zugspitze | Germany-Austria | 9,721 |
| Olympus (Mytikas) | Greece | 9,570 |
| Glittertind | Norway | 8,110 |
| Ben Nevis | UK (Scotland) | 4,406 |
| Vesuvius | Italy | 4,190 |
| **NORTH AMERICA** | | |
| Logan | Canada | 19,524 |
| Citlaltépetl (Orizaba) | Mexico | 18,855 |
| St. Elias | Canada-US | 18,008 |
| Popocatépetl | Mexico | 17,887 |
| Iztaccíhuatl | Mexico | 17,343 |
| Lucania | Canada | 17,147 |
| King Peak | Canada | 16,971 |
| Steele | Canada | 16,644 |
| Wood | Canada | 15,885 |
| Vancouver | Canada-US | 15,700 |
| Fairweather | Canada-US | 15,300 |
| Toluca (Zinantécatl) | Mexico | 15,015 |
| Walsh | Canada | 14,780 |
| La Malinche | Mexico | 14,635 |
| Nevada de Colima | Mexico | 14,205 |
| Cofre de Perote | Mexico | 14,050 |
| Tajumulco | Guatemala | 13,845 |
| Robson | Canada | 12,972 |
| Chirripó Grande | Costa Rica | 12,530 |
| Parícutin | Mexico | 10,400 |
| **SOUTH AMERICA** | | |
| Aconcagua | Argentina | 22,831 |
| Ojos del Salado | Argentina | 22,546 |
| Bonete | Argentina-Chile | 22,572 |
| Tupungato | Argentina-Chile | 22,310 |
| Pissis | Argentina | 22,245 |
| Mercedario | Argentina | 22,211 |
| Huascarán | Peru | 22,205 |
| Llullaillaco | Argentina-Chile | 22,057 |
| Cumbre del Libertador Gen. San Martín | Argentina | 22,047 |
| Ancohuma | Bolivia | 21,489 |
| Sajama | Bolivia | 21,391 |
| Nacimiento | Argentina | 21,302 |
| Illampu | Bolivia | 21,276 |
| Illimani | Bolivia | 21,184 |
| Coropuna | Peru | 21,079 |
| Nevados de Huandoy | Peru | 20,981 |
| Toro | Argentina-Chile | 20,932 |
| Chimborazo | Ecuador | 20,561 |
| Cotopaxi | Ecuador | 19,347 |
| El Misti | Peru | 19,199 |

# DAMS, MAN-MADE LAKES, HYDROELECTRIC PLANTS

SOURCE: Water and Power Resources Service, Dept. of the Interior

## HIGHEST DAMS

TE = Earth; ER = Rockfill; PG = Gravity; VA = Arch; MV = Multiarch; UC = Under Construction

| Name of Dam | | Height Meters | Height Feet | Year Completed |
|---|---|---|---|---|
| 1. Rogun, USSR | ER | 325 | 1,066 | UC |
| 2. Nurek, USSR | TE | 300 | 984 | UC |
| 3. Grande Dixence, Switzerland | PG | 285 | 935 | 1962 |
| 4. Inguri, USSR | VA | 272 | 892 | UC |
| 5. Chicoasén, Mexico | ER | 265 | 869 | 1981 |
| 6. Vaiont, Italy | VA | 265 | 869 | 1961 |
| 7. Tehri, India | ER | 261 | 856 | UC |
| 8. Kinshaw, India | TE-ER | 253 | 830 | UC |
| 9. Mica, Canada | TE-ER | 242 | 794 | 1972 |
| 10. Sayano-Shushensk, USSR | VA-PG | 242 | 794 | 1980 |
| 11. Mihoesti, Romania | TE-ER | 242 | 794 | UC |
| 12. Chivor, Colombia | ER- | 237 | 778 | 1975 |
| 13. Mauvoisin, Switzerland | VA | 237 | 777 | 1957 |
| 14. Oroville, U.S.A. | TE | 235 | 770 | 1968 |
| 15. Chirkey, USSR | VA | 233 | 764 | 1977 |
| 16. Bhakra, India | PG | 226 | 741 | 1963 |
| 17. El Cajón, Honduras | VA | 226 | 741 | UC |
| 18. Hoover, U.S.A. | VA-PG | 221 | 726 | 1936 |
| 19. Contra, Switzerland | VA | 220 | 722 | 1965 |
| 20. Dabaklamm, Austria | VA | 220 | 722 | UC |
| 21. Piva (Mratinje), Yugoslavia | VA | 220 | 722 | 1975 |
| 22. Dworshak, U.S.A. | PG | 219 | 717 | 1974 |
| 23. Glen Canyon, U.S.A. | VA | 216 | 710 | 1964 |
| 24. Toktogul, USSR | PG | 215 | 705 | 1978 |
| 25. Daniel Johnson, Canada | MV | 214 | 703 | 1968 |
| 26. San Roque, Philippines | TE | 210 | 689 | UC |
| 27. Luzzone, Switzerland | VA | 208 | 682 | 1963 |
| 28. Keban, Turkey | TE-ER-PG | 207 | 679 | 1974 |

## LARGEST DAMS

Based on total volume of dam structure.

| Name of Dam | Volume (Thousands) Cubic Meters | Volume (Thousands) Cubic Yards | Year Completed |
|---|---|---|---|
| 1. New Cornelia Tailings, U.S.A. | 209,500 | 274,026 | 1973 |
| 2. Pati (Chapetón), Argentina | 200,000 | 261,590 | UC |
| 3. Tarbella, Pakistan | 121,720 | 159,203 | 1976 |
| 4. Fort Peck, U.S.A. | 96,049 | 125,628 | 1940 |
| 5. Yacyretá-Apipe, Paraguay-Argentina | 81,000 | 105,944 | UC |
| 6. Guri (Raul Leoni), Venezuela | 78,000 | 102,014 | UC |
| 7. Rogun, USSR | 75,500 | 98,750 | UC |
| 8. Atatürk, Turkey | 75,000 | 98,096 | UC |
| 9. Oahe, U.S.A. | 70,339 | 92,000 | 1963 |
| 10. Mangla, Pakistan | 65,651 | 85,872 | 1967 |
| 11. Gardiner, Canada | 65,440 | 85,592 | 1968 |
| 12. Afsluitdijk, Netherlands | 63,400 | 82,927 | 1932 |
| 13. Oroville, U.S.A. | 59,639 | 78,008 | 1968 |
| 14. San Luis, U.S.A. | 59,383 | 77,670 | 1967 |
| 15. Nurek, USSR | 58,000 | 75,861 | UC |
| 16. Garrison, U.S.A. | 50,843 | 66,500 | 1956 |
| 17. Cochita, U.S.A. | 50,230 | 65,698 | 1975 |
| 18. Tabka (Thawra), Syria | 46,000 | 60,168 | 1976 |
| 19. Bennett W.A.C., Canada | 43,733 | 57,201 | 1967 |
| 20. Tucuruí, Brazil | 43,000 | 56,242 | UC |
| 21. Boruca, Costa Rica | 43,000 | 56,242 | UC |
| 22. High Aswan (Sadd-el-Aali), Egypt | 43,000 | 56,242 | 1970 |
| 23. San Roque, Philippines | 43,000 | 56,242 | UC |
| 24. Kiev, USSR | 42,841 | 56,034 | 1964 |
| 25. Dantiwada Left Embankment, India | 41,040 | 53,680 | 1965 |
| 26. Saratov, USSR | 40,400 | 52,843 | 1967 |
| 27. Mission Tailings 2, U.S.A. | 40,088 | 52,435 | 1973 |

## GREATEST MAN-MADE LAKES

| Name of Dam | Capacity Millions of Cubic Meters | Capacity Thousands of Acre-Feet | Year Completed |
|---|---|---|---|
| 1. Owen Falls, Uganda | 204,800 | 166,000 | 1954 |
| 2. Kariba, Zimbabwe | 181,592 | 147,218 | 1959 |
| 3. Bratsk, USSR | 169,270 | 137,220 | 1964 |
| 4. High Aswan (Sadd-el-Aali), Egypt | 168,000 | 136,200 | 1970 |
| 5. Akosombo, Ghana | 148,000 | 120,000 | 1965 |
| 6. Daniel Johnson, Canada | 141,851 | 115,000 | 1968 |
| 7. Guri (Raul Leoni), Venezuela | 136,000 | 110,256 | UC |
| 8. Krasnoyarsk, USSR | 73,300 | 59,425 | 1967 |
| 9. Bennett W.A.C., Canada | 70,309 | 57,006 | 1967 |
| 10. Zeya, USSR | 68,400 | 55,452 | UC |
| 11. Cabora Bassa, Mozambique | 63,000 | 51,075 | 1974 |
| 12. LaGrande 2, Canada | 61,720 | 50,037 | UC |
| 13. LaGrande 3, Canada | 60,020 | 48,659 | UC |
| 14. Ust'-Ilimsk, USSR | 59,300 | 48,075 | 1980 |
| 15. Volga-V.I. Lenin, USSR | 58,000 | 47,020 | 1955 |
| 16. Caniapiscau, Canada | 53,790 | 43,608 | UC |
| 17. Pati (Chapetón), Argentina | 53,700 | 43,535 | UC |
| 18. Upper Wainganga, India | 50,700 | 41,103 | UC |
| 19. São Felix, Brazil | 50,600 | 41,022 | UC |
| 20. Bukhtarma, USSR | 49,740 | 40,325 | 1960 |
| 21. Atatürk (Karababa), Turkey | 48,000 | 38,914 | UC |
| 22. Cerros Colorados, Argentina | 48,000 | 38,914 | 1973 |
| 23. Irkutsk, USSR | 46,000 | 37,290 | 1956 |
| 24. Tucuruí, Brazil | 36,375 | 29,489 | UC |
| 25. Vilyuy, USSR | 35,900 | 29,104 | 1967 |
| 26. Sanmenxia, China | 35,400 | 28,700 | 1960 |
| 27. Hoover, U.S.A. | 35,200 | 28,537 | 1936 |

## LARGEST HYDROELECTRIC PLANTS

**MW = Megawatts**

| Name of Dam | Rated Capacity MW Present | Rated Capacity MW Ultimate | Year of Initial Operation |
|---|---|---|---|
| 1. Itaipu, Brazil-Paraguay | — | 12,600 | UC |
| 2. Grand Coulee, U.S.A. | 6,430 | 10,080 | 1942 |
| 3. Guri (Raul Leoni), Venezuela | 2,800 | 10,060 | 1968 |
| 4. Tucuruí, Brazil | — | 6,480 | UC |
| 5. Sayano-Shushensk, USSR | — | 6,400 | 1980 |
| 6. Krasnoyarsk, USSR | 6,096 | 6,096 | 1968 |
| 7. Corpus-Christi, Argentina-Paraguay | — | 6,000 | UC |
| 8. LaGrande 2, Canada | — | 5,328 | UC |
| 9. Churchill Falls, Canada | 5,225 | 5,225 | 1971 |
| 10. Bratsk, USSR | 4,100 | 4,600 | 1964 |
| 11. Ust'-Ilimsk, USSR | 3,675 | 4,500 | 1974 |
| 12. Cabora Bassa, Mozambique | 2,075 | 4,150 | 1974 |
| 13. Yacyretá-Apipe, Argentina-Paraguay | — | 4,050 | UC |
| 14. Rogun, USSR | — | 3,600 | UC |
| 15. Randolph-Hunting, U.S.A. | — | 3,575 | UC |
| 16. Paulo Afonso, Brazil | 1,524 | 3,409 | 1955 |
| 17. Pati (Chapetón), Argentina | — | 3,300 | UC |
| 18. Brumley Gap, U.S.A. | 3,200 | 3,200 | 1973 |
| 19. Inga I, Zaire | 360 | 2,820 | 1974 |
| 20. Gezhouba, China | — | 2,715 | UC |
| 21. John Day, U.S.A. | 2,160 | 2,700 | 1969 |
| 22. Nurek, USSR | 900 | 2,700 | 1976 |
| 23. Revelstroke, Canada | — | 2,700 | UC |
| 24. São Simao, Brazil | 2,680 | 2,680 | 1979 |
| 25. Ilha Solteira, Brazil | 2,650 | 2,650 | 1973 |
| 26. LaGrande 4, Canada | — | 2,637 | UC |
| 27. Mica, Canada | 1,736 | 2,610 | 1976 |
| 28. Volgograd-22nd Congress, USSR | 2,560 | 2,560 | 1958 |
| 29. Itaparica, Brazil | — | 2,500 | UC |
| 30. Bennett W.A.C., Canada | 2,116 | 2,416 | 1969 |
| 31. Chicoasén, Mexico | — | 2,400 | 1980 |
| 32. Atatürk, Turkey | — | 2,400 | UC |
| 33. LaGrande 3, Canada | — | 2,304 | UC |
| 34. Volga-V.I. Lenin, USSR | 2,300 | 2,300 | 1955 |
| 35. Iron Gates I, Romania-Yugoslavia | 2,300 | 2,300 | 1970 |
| 36. Fos do Areia, Brazil | 2,250 | 2,250 | UC |
| 37. Itumbiara, Brazil | — | 2,124 | UC |
| 38. Bath County, U.S.A. | — | 2,100 | UC |
| 39. High Aswan (Saad-el-Aali), Egypt | 2,100 | 2,100 | 1967 |
| 40. Tarbella, Pakistan | 1,400 | 2,100 | 1977 |
| 41. Piedra de Aquila, Argentina | — | 2,100 | UC |
| 42. Chief Joseph, U.S.A. | 2,069 | 2,069 | 1956 |
| 43. Salto Santiago, Brazil | — | 2,031 | 1980 |
| 44. McNary, U.S.A. | 980 | 2,030 | 1954 |
| 45. Green River, U.S.A. | — | 2,000 | 1980 |

## VOLCANOES

Key to letters: (E) Last eruption, with year in parentheses; (R) Rumbling; (St) Steaming; (D) Dormant.

| Name | Location | Height (in feet) |
|---|---|---|
| **AFRICA** | | |
| Kibo (Kilimanjaro) (D) | Tanzania | 19,340 |
| Cameroon Mt. (E-1959) | Cameroon | 13,350 |
| El Teide (St) | Canary Is. | 12,172 |
| Nyiragongo (E-1977) | Zaire | 11,385 |
| Nyamulagira (E-1976) | Zaire | 10,028 |
| Fogo (E-1951) | Cape Verde Is. | 9,281 |
| Piton de la Fournaise (E-1981) | Réunion | 8,632 |
| Tristan da Cunha (E-1961) | South Atlantic | 6,760 |
| Teneguia (D) | Canary Is. | 2,006 |
| **ANTARCTICA** | | |
| Deception Island (E-1970) | | — |
| Erebus (E-1981) | | 12,450 |
| Melbourne (St) | | 8,500 |
| **ASIA and AUSTRALASIA** | | |
| Klyuchevskaya (E-1962) | USSR | 15,584 |
| Kerintji (St) | Indonesia | 12,484 |
| Fuji (D) | Japan | 12,389 |
| Rindjani (E-1964) | Indonesia | 12,224 |
| Tolbachik (E-1941) | USSR | 12,080 |
| Semeru (E-1981) | Indonesia | 12,060 |
| Ichinskaya (St) | USSR | 11,880 |
| Kronotskaya (D) | USSR | 11,575 |
| Koryakskaya (E-1957) | USSR | 11,339 |
| Slamet (E-1953) | Indonesia | 11,247 |
| Raung (St) | Indonesia | 10,932 |
| Shiveluch (E-1964) | USSR | 10,771 |
| Dempo (St) | Indonesia | 10,364 |
| Agung (E-1964) | Indonesia | 10,308 |
| Sundoro (D) | Indonesia | 10,285 |
| Tjareme (E-1938) | Indonesia | 10,098 |
| Gede (E-1949) | Indonesia | 9,705 |
| Apo (D) | Philippines | 9,369 |
| Merapi (E-1969) | Indonesia | 9,551 |
| Bezymyannaya (E-1961) | USSR | 9,514 |
| Marapi (D) | Indonesia | 9,485 |
| Tambora (D) | Indonesia | 9,353 |
| Mayon (E-1978) | Philippines | 7,940 |
| Alaid (E-1981) | USSR | 7,674 |
| Ulawun (E-1980) | Papua New Guinea | 7,546 |
| Galunggung (E-1982) | Indonesia | 7,155 |
| Sinila (E-1979) | Indonesia | c. 7,000 |
| Gamalama (E-1980) | Indonesia | 5,625 |
| Bulosan (E-1978) | Philippines | 5,140 |
| Usu (E-1978) | Japan | 2,390 |
| Taal (E-1977) | Philippines | 990 |
| **MID-PACIFIC** | | |
| Mauna Kea (D) | Hawaii | 13,796 |
| Mauna Loa (E-1975) | Hawaii | 13,680 |
| Kilauea (E-1977) | Hawaii | 4,077 |
| **EUROPE** | | |
| Etna (E-1981) | Sicily, Italy | 11,053 |
| Askja (E-1961) | Iceland | 4,954 |
| Hekla (E-1981) | Iceland | 4,892 |
| Vesuvius (St) | Italy | 4,190 |
| Stromboli (E-1971) | Lipari Is., Italy | 3,038 |
| Surtsey (E-1967) | Iceland | 570 |
| Eldfell (E-1973) | Iceland | 327 |
| **NORTH AMERICA** | | |
| Popocatépetl (St) | Mexico | 17,887 |
| Colima (St) | Mexico | 14,205 |
| Wrangell (St) | Alaska | 14,163 |
| Torbert (E-1953) | Alaska | 11,413 |
| Spurr (E-1953) | Alaska | 11,069 |
| Lassen (D) | California | 10,457 |
| Paricutín (D) | Mexico | 10,400 |
| Redoubt (E-1966) | Alaska | 10,197 |
| Iliamna (St) | Alaska | 10,016 |
| Shishaldin (St) | Aleutians | 9,387 |
| St. Helens (E-1980-82) | Washington | 8,364 |
| Pavlof (E-1981) | Alaska | 8,261 |
| Veniaminof (D) | Alaska | 8,225 |
| Griggs (St) | Alaska | 7,600 |
| El Chichón (E-1982) | Mexico | 7,300 |
| Mageik (St) | Alaska | 7,250 |
| Douglas (St) | Alaska | 7,064 |
| Katmai (E-1962) | Alaska | 6,715 |
| Kukak (St) | Alaska | 6,700 |
| Makushin (D) | Aleutians | 6,680 |
| Pogromni (E-1964) | Aleutians | 6,568 |
| Martin (E-1960) | Alaska | 6,050 |
| Trident (E-1963) | Alaska | 6,010 |
| Augustine (E-1976) | Alaska | 3,999 |
| **CENTRAL AMERICA and CARIBBEAN** | | |
| Tajumulco (R) | Guatemala | 13,845 |
| Tacaná (R) | Guatemala | 13,428 |
| Acatenango (R) | Guatemala | 12,992 |
| Fuego (E-1978) | Guatemala | 12,582 |
| Santa Maria (R) | Guatemala | 12,362 |
| Atitlan (R) | Guatemala | 11,565 |
| Irazú (E-1964) | Costa Rica | 11,260 |
| San Pedro (R) | Guatemala | 9,921 |
| Poás (St) | Costa Rica | 8,930 |
| Pacaya (E-1970) | Guatemala | 8,346 |
| Izalco (E-1967) | El Salvador | 6,184 |
| Soufrière (E-1979) | St. Vincent | 4,048 |
| **SOUTH AMERICA** | | |
| Guallatiri (E-1959) | Chile | 19,882 |
| Lascar (E-1951) | Chile | 19,652 |
| Cotopaxi (St) | Ecuador | 19,347 |
| Misti (D) | Peru | 19,199 |
| Cayambe (D) | Ecuador | 18,996 |
| Tupungatito (E-1959) | Chile | 18,504 |
| Sangay (E-1946) | Ecuador | 17,159 |
| Tungurahua (R) | Ecuador | 16,512 |
| Cotacachi (E-1955) | Ecuador | 16,204 |
| Pichincha (D) | Ecuador | 15,696 |
| Purace (E-1950) | Colombia | 15,604 |
| Lautaro (St) | Chile | 11,090 |
| Llaima (E-1955) | Chile | 10,239 |
| Villarrica (E-1964) | Chile | 9,318 |
| Osorno (R) | Chile | 8,730 |
| Shoshuenco (E-1960) | Chile | 7,743 |

## WORLD WATERFALLS

| Location and Name | | Height[1] (in feet) |
|---|---|---|
| **AFRICA** | | |
| Aughrabies[3] | S. Africa | 482 |
| Baratieri | Ethiopia | 460 |
| Chirombo[2] | Zambia | 880 |
| Dianzundu (Duque de Braganca) | Angola | 344 |
| Finca | Ethiopia | 508 |
| Howick | S. Africa | 358 |
| Kalambo[2 3] | Tanz.-Zambia | 726 |
| Karkloof[2] | S. Africa | 350 |
| Livingstone[2] | Zaire | 875 |
| Lofoi | Zaire | 1,115 |
| Magwa | S. Africa | 450 |
| Maletsunyane | Lesotho | 630 |
| Murchison[2] | Uganda | 400 |
| Ruacana | Angola | 406 |
| Stanley[2] | Zaire | 200 |
| Tisisat[3] | Ethiopia | 140 |
| Tsitza | S. Africa | 375 |
| Tugela[2] | S. Africa | 3,110 |
| Verme | Ethiopia | 229 |
| Victoria[2 3] | Zimbabwe-Zambia | 355 |
| **ASIA** | | |
| Diyaluma | Sri Lanka | 600 |
| Jog (Gersoppa)[2 3] | India | 830 |
| Kegon | Japan | 330 |
| Kirindi Ela | Sri Lanka | 347 |
| Kurundu Oya | Sri Lanka | 620 |
| Laksapana | Sri Lanka | 377 |
| Nachi | Japan | 430 |
| Ramboda | Sri Lanka | 329 |
| Ratna Ella | Sri Lanka | 305 |
| Sivasamudram (Kaveri)[2] | India | 320 |
| Yudaki | Japan | 335 |
| **OCEANIA** | | |
| Akaka | Hawaii (US) | 420 |
| Barron | Australia | 770 |
| Bowen[2] | New Zealand | 540 |
| Helena | New Zealand | 860 |
| Leura[2] | Australia | 308 |
| Stirling | New Zealand | 505 |
| Sutherland[2] | New Zealand | 1,904 |
| Tully[2] | Australia | 972 |
| Wentworth[2] | Australia | 518 |
| Wollomombi[2] | Australia | 1,580 |
| **EUROPE** | | |
| Aurstapet[2] | Norway | 794 |
| Gastein[2] | Austria | 486 |
| Gavarnie | France | 1,385 |
| Giessbach[2] | Switz. | 1,312 |
| Glomach | UK (Scotland) | 370 |
| Golling[2] | Austria | 203 |
| Iffigen | Switz. | 394 |
| Kile[2] | Norway | 1,840 |
| Krimml[2] | Austria | 1,246 |
| Låtefoss[2] | Norway | 541 |
| Mardalsfoss (E.)[2] | Norway | 1,696 |
| Mardalsfoss (W.) | Norway | 1,535 |
| Marmore[2] | Italy | 525 |
| Mongefossen[2] | Norway | 2,539 |
| Reichenbach[2] | Switz. | 656 |
| Rjoandefoss[2] | Norway | 1,847 |
| Rjukenfoss | Norway | 983 |

[1] Height means total drop whether in one or more leaps. [2] Falls consisting of more than one leap.
[3] Falls that diminish greatly seasonally.

| Location and Name | | Height[1] (in feet) |
|---|---|---|
| Simme[2] | Switz. | 459 |
| Skjeggedalsfoss | Norway | 525 |
| Skykkjedalsfoss | Norway | 820 |
| Søtefoss | Norway | 896 |
| Stalheimsfoss | Norway | 413 |
| Staubbach | Switz. | 984 |
| Stäuber | Switz. | 590 |
| Stigfoss | Norway | 590 |
| Toce[2] | Italy | 470 |
| Trümmelbach[2] | Switz. | 1,312 |
| Tyssefoss[2] | Norway | 1,749 |
| Tyssestrengene[2] | Norway | 2,795 |
| Vermafoss | Norway | 1,248 |
| Vettisfoss[2] | Norway | 1,214 |
| Vøringfoss | Norway | 597 |
| **NORTH AMERICA** | | |
| Basaseachic | Mexico | 1,000 |
| Bridalveil | US (Calif.) | 620 |
| Chequaga | US (N.Y.) | 156 |
| Churchill | Canada (Newf.) | 245 |
| Comet | US (Wash.) | 320 |
| Cumberland | US (Ky.) | 68 |
| Della | Canada (B.C.) | 1,443 |
| Fairy | US (Wash.) | 700 |
| Fall Creek | US (Tenn.) | 256 |
| Feather | US (Calif.) | 640 |
| Grand | Canada (N. Br.) | 75 |
| Grand | Canada (Ont.) | 150 |
| Granite | US (Wash.) | 350 |
| Illilouette | US (Calif.) | 370 |
| Juanacatlán, Salto de[3] | Mexico | 70 |
| Jumatán | Mexico | 394 |
| Manitou | US (Wis.) | 165 |
| Minnehaha[3] | US (Minn.) | 52 |
| Missouri (Great Falls)[2] | US (Mont.) | 90 |
| Montmorency | Canada (Que.) | 274 |
| Multnomah[2] | US (Oreg.) | 620 |
| Narada | US (Wash.) | 168 |
| Necaxa | Mexico | 540 |
| Nevada | US (Calif.) | 594 |
| Niagara[2]: | | |
| American | US (N.Y.) | 167 |
| Canadian (Horseshoe) | U.S.-Canada | 158 |
| Palouse | US (Wash.) | 198 |
| Panther | Canada (Alta.) | 600 |
| Passaic (Great Falls)[3] | US (N.J.) | 70 |
| Potomac (Great Falls)[2] | US (Md.-Va.) | 90 |
| Ribbon[3] | US Calif.) | 1,612 |
| Saint Anthony | US (Minn.) | 60 |
| Seven | US (Colo.) | 266 |
| Shawinigan | Canada (Que.) | 150 |
| Shoshone[2,3] | US (Idaho) | 210 |
| Silver Strand | US (Calif.) | 1,170 |
| Sluiskin | US (Wash.) | 300 |
| Snoqualmie | US (Wash.) | 270 |
| Tahquamenon[2] | US (Mich.) | 88 |
| Takakkaw[2] | Canada (B.C.) | 1,650 |
| Taughannock | US (N.Y.) | 215 |
| Tower | US (Wyo.) | 132 |
| Twin[2,3] | US (Idaho) | 125 |
| Vernal | US (Calif.) | 317 |
| Virginia | Canada (N.W.T.) | 315 |
| Xico | Mexico | 256 |
| Yellowstone[2] | | |
| Upper | US (Wyo.) | 109 |
| Lower | | 308 |
| Yosemite[2] | US (Calif.) | 2,425 |
| Upper | | 1,430 |
| **SOUTH AMERICA** | | |
| Angel[2] | Venezuela | 3,212 |
| Upper | | 2,648 |
| Anta, Cascada da | Brazil | 665 |
| Candelas, Cataratas de | Colombia | 984 |
| Glass | Brazil | 1,325 |
| Grande | Arg.-Uruguay | 75 |
| Grande | Brazil | 140 |
| Great | Guyana | 500 |
| Iguazú (Iguaçu)[2] | Brazil | 237 |
| Itiquira | Brazil | 395 |
| Kaieteur[2] | Guyana | 822 |
| highest | | 741 |
| King Edward VIII | Guyana | 850 |
| King George VI | Guyana | 1,600 |
| Kukenaam[2] | Venezuela | 2,000 |
| Marina[2] | Guyana | 500 |
| Papagaio | Brazil | 350 |
| Patos-Maribondo | Brazil | 115 |
| Paulo Afonso[2] | Brazil | 275 |
| Roraima[3] | Guyana | 1,500 |
| Sete Quedas (Guairá) | Brazil-Parag. | 360 |
| Tequendama | Colombia | 482 |
| Urubupungá | Brazil | 33 |

[1] Height means total drop whether in one or more leaps. [2] Falls consisting of more than one leap. [3] Falls that diminish greatly seasonally.

## OUTSTANDING WORLDWIDE WEATHER EXTREMES

SOURCE: National Oceanic & Atmospheric Administration

### TEMPERATURE EXTREMES

Temperature extremes for any place on Earth are determined by a number of factors, including altitude, latitude, and physical characteristics. For an extreme to be recorded, an observation must be made at the precise time and place of occurrence; consequantity, more extreme temperatures undoubtedly have occurred.

THE HOTTEST

| Area | Max. (°F.) | Place | Elevation (Ft.) | Date |
|---|---|---|---|---|
| Africa | 136 | Al'Aziziyah, Libya | 380 | Sept. 13, 1922 |
| North America | 134 | Death Valley, California | -178 | July 10, 1913 |
| Asia | 129 | Tirat Tsvi, Israel | -722 | June 21, 1942 |
| Australia | 128 | Cloncurry, Queensland | 622 | Jan. 16, 1889 |
| Europe | 122 | Seville, Spain | 26 | Aug. 4, 1881 |
| South America | 120 | Rivadavia, Argentina | 676 | Dec. 11, 1905 |
| Oceania | 108 | Tuguegarao, Philippines | 72 | Apr. 29, 1912 |
| Antarctica | 58 | Esperanza, Palmer Peninsula | 26 | Oct. 20, 1956 |

THE COLDEST

| Area | Min. (°F.) | Place | Elevation (Ft.) | Date |
|---|---|---|---|---|
| Antarctica | —127 | Vostok Station | 11,220 | Aug. 24, 1960 |
| Asia | — 90 | Oymyakon, USSR | 2,625 | Feb. 6, 1933 |
| Greenland | — 87 | Northice Station | 7,690 | Jan. 9, 1954 |
| North America | — 81 | Snag, Yukon, Canada | 1,925 | Feb. 3, 1947 |
| Europe | — 67 | Ust'-Shchugor, USSR | 279 | date unknown |
| South America | — 27 | Sarmiento, Argentina | 879 | June 1, 1907 |
| Africa | — 11 | Ifrane, Morocco | 5,364 | Feb. 11, 1935 |
| Australia | — 8 | Charlotte Pass, New South Wales | NA | July 22, 1947 |

### RAINFALL EXTREMES

The total annual precipitation recorded at a place may vary greatly from year to year. The rainiest places show the greatest variations from year to year in actual amounts. The drier places show the greatest variation taken as a percentage of the mean value. At Cherrapunji, India, for example, the greatest amount of precipitation in a calendar year was 905.1 inches. The least was 282.6 inches, a difference of over 600 inches. At Arica, Chile, half of the total rainfall recorded from 1931 through 1960 fell in the single year of 1959. No rain at all fell in 19 of the 30 years. Because of such fluctuations, the average annual precipitation may be greatly influenced by the available years of record; the longer the record, the more reliable is the average.

THE WETTEST

| Area | Average Annual Rainfall (Inches) | Place | Elevation (Ft.) | Years of Record |
|---|---|---|---|---|
| Oceania | 460.0 | Mt. Waialeale, Hawaii | 5,075 | 33 |
| Asia | 450.0 | Cherrapunji, India | 4,309 | 75 |
| Africa | 404.6 | Debundscha, Cameroon | 30 | 33 |
| South America | 354.0 | Quibdó, Colombia | 240 | 11–17 |
| North America | 262.1 | Henderson Lake, Br. Col. | 12 | 15 |
| Europe | 182.8 | Crkvice, Yugoslavia | 3,337 | 23 |
| Australia | 179.0 | Tully, Queensland | 220 | 32 |

THE DRIEST

| Area | Average Annual Rainfall (Inches) | Place | Elevation (Ft.) | Years of Record |
|---|---|---|---|---|
| South America | 0.03 | Arica, Chile | 95 | 60 |
| Africa | 0.1 | Wadi Halfa, Sudan | 410 | 40 |
| Antarctica | 0.8 | South Pole Station | 9,186 | 11 |
| North America | 1.2 | Bataques, Mexico | 16 | 15 |
| Asia | 1.8 | Aden, P.D.R. Yemen | 22 | 51 |
| Australia | 4.05 | Mulka, South Australia | NA | 35 |
| Europe | 6.4 | Astrakhan, USSR | 45 | 26 |
| Oceania | 8.93 | Puako, Hawaii | 5 | 14 |

## WORLD'S TALLEST BUILDINGS

*Under construction. SOURCE: Council on Tall Buildings and Urban Habitat

| Building | Location | Height (in feet) | Stories |
|---|---|---|---|
| Sears Tower | Chicago | 1,454 | 110 |
| World Trade Center (Twin Towers) | New York City | 1,350 | 110 |
| Empire State | New York City | 1,250 | 102 |
| Standard Oil (Indiana) | Chicago | 1,136 | 80 |
| John Hancock | Chicago | 1,127 | 100 |
| Texas Commerce Plaza | Houston | 1,049 | 75 |
| Chrysler | New York City | 1,046 | 77 |
| American International | New York City | 950 | 66 |
| First Bank Tower | Toronto | 935 | 72 |
| 40 Wall Tower | New York City | 927 | 71 |
| Citicorp Center | New York City | 914 | 59 |
| Water Tower Place | Chicago | 859 | 74 |
| United California Bank | Los Angeles | 858 | 62 |
| RCA Rockefeller Center | New York City | 850 | 70 |
| First National Bank | Chicago | 844 | 60 |
| Transamerica | San Francisco | 843 | 48 |
| U. S. Steel | Pittsburgh | 841 | 64 |
| One Chase Manhattan Plaza | New York City | 813 | 60 |
| Pan American | New York City | 808 | 59 |
| Woolworth | New York City | 792 | 57 |
| Palace of Science and Culture | Warsaw | 790 | 42 |
| John Hancock Tower | Boston | 790 | 60 |
| M.L.C. Centre | Sydney, Australia | 786 | 70 |
| Commerce Court West | Toronto | 784 | 57 |
| Bank of America | San Francisco | 778 | 32 |
| 3 First National Plaza | Chicago | 775 | 58 |
| IDS Center | Minneapolis | 772 | 57 |
| One Penn Plaza | New York City | 766 | 57 |
| Maine Montparnasse | Paris | 751 | 64 |
| Prudential Center | Boston | 750 | 52 |
| Federal Reserve | Boston | 750 | 32 |
| Exxon | New York City | 750 | 54 |
| First International Plaza | Houston | 748 | 55 |
| 1 Liberty Plaza (U.S. Steel) | New York City | 743 | 54 |
| Ikebukuro Office Tower | Tokyo | 742 | 60 |
| 20 Exchange Place (Citibank) | New York City | 741 | 55 |
| Renaissance 1 | Detroit | 739 | 73 |
| Security Pacific National Bank | Los Angeles | 738 | 57 |
| Toronto Dominion Bank Tower | Toronto | 736 | 56 |
| One Astor Plaza | New York City | 730 | 54 |
| 9 West 57th Street | New York City | 725 | 50 |
| Peachtree Center Plaza | Atlanta | 723 | 71 |
| Carlton Centre | Johannesburg | 722 | 50 |
| Detroit Plaza Hotel | Detroit | 720 | 73 |
| One Shell Plaza | Houston | 714 | 52 |
| First International | Dallas | 710 | 56 |
| Shinjuku Center | Tokyo | 709 | 55 |
| Terminal Tower | Cleveland | 708 | 52 |
| Union Carbide | New York City | 707 | 52 |
| General Motors | New York City | 705 | 50 |
| Metropolitan Life | New York City | 700 | 50 |
| Atlantic Richfield Plaza A & B | Los Angeles | 699 | 52 |
| One Shell Square | New Orleans | 697 | 51 |
| 500 Fifth Avenue | New York City | 697 | 58 |
| Shinjuku Mitsui | Tokyo | 696 | 55 |
| IBM | Chicago | 695 | 52 |
| Neiman-Marcus | Chicago | 690 | 65 |
| 55 Water Street | New York City | 687 | 53 |
| Chemical Bank Trust | New York City | 687 | 50 |
| Three Allen Center* | Houston | 685 | 50 |
| One Houston Center | Houston | 681 | 46 |
| Chanin | New York City | 680 | 55 |
| Gulf+Western | New York City | 679 | 44 |
| Marine Midland Bank | New York City | 677 | 52 |
| Southern Bell | Atlanta | 677 | 46 |
| Metropolitan Tower | New York City | 675 | 50 |
| Lincoln Building | New York City | 673 | 55 |
| Georgia Pacific Tower* | Atlanta | 673 | 52 |
| McGraw-Hill | New York City | 670 | 51 |
| 1633 Broadway | New York City | 670 | 48 |
| Bank of Oklahoma Tower | Tulsa | 667 | 50 |
| Shinjuku Nomura | Tokyo | 666 | 53 |
| Civic Center | Chicago | 662 | 38 |
| First City Tower | Houston | 662 | 49 |
| Overseas-Chinese Banking Corp. | Singapore | 660 | 52 |
| Shinjuku Sumitomo | Tokyo | 656 | 52 |
| Parque Central Torre Oficinas | Caracas | 656 | 56 |
| 1100 Milam | Houston | 651 | 47 |
| One Miracle Mile | Chicago | 650 | 60 |
| Ukraine Hotel | Moscow | 650 | 34 |
| American Brands | New York City | 648 | 47 |
| Lake Point Towers | Chicago | 645 | 70 |
| A.T.&T. | New York City | 645 | 37 |
| 1000 Lakeshore Plaza | Chicago | 640 | 60 |
| Irving Trust | New York City | 640 | 53 |
| Belmont Centre* | Kuala Lumpur | 632 | 50 |

## SELECTED WORLD STRUCTURES

SOURCE: Amer. Society of Civil Engineers

| Structure | Location | Height in Feet |
|---|---|---|
| **Polish National TV Service Tower** | Plock, Poland | 2,120 |
| **KTHI-TV** | Fargo, N.D. | 2,063 |
| **CN Communication Tower** | Toronto | 1,815 |
| **Ostankino TV tower** | Near Moscow, USSR | 1,762 |
| **Moscow TV tower** | USSR | 1,732 |
| **B.R.E.N. Tower** | Nevada | 1,527 |
| **Loran Mast** | Snaefellsnes, Iceland | 1,378 |
| **Danish Government Navigational Mast** | Thule, Greenland | 1,345 |
| **Peking Radio Antenna** | China | 1,312 |
| **Tower Zero** | N.W. Cape, Western Australia | 1,271 |
| **TV antenna** | Emley Moor, England | 1,265 |
| **TV antenna** | Belmont, England | 1,265 |
| **Zender Lopik TV Antenna** | Near Lopik, Netherlands | 1,253 |
| **American Electric Power smokestack** | Cresap, W. Va. | 1,206 |
| **Utah Copper Div. of Kennecott Copper Corp. Magna Smelter Chimney** | Great Salt Lake, Utah | 1,200 |
| **East Berlin Antenna** | East Germany | 1,185 |
| **Television Center** | Moscow | 1,179 |
| **TV tower** | Vinnitsa, Ukraine, USSR | 1,150 |
| **Loran Tower** | Tomil, Yap Island | 1,100 |
| **CHCHTV Antenna** | Hamilton, Canada | 1,093 |
| **TV tower** | Tokyo | 1,092 |
| **Leningrad antenna** | USSR | 1,065 |
| **TV Antenna** | Kojál, Czechoslovakia | 1,033 |
| **Weather tower** | Obninsk, USSR | 1,027 |
| **Lakihegg Antenna** | Lakihegg, Hungary | 1,006 |
| **ITA Antenna** | Brynychain, Wales | 1,000 |
| **Conemaugh Station Chimney (pair)** | Johnstown, Pa. | 1,000 |
| **TV antenna** | Black Hill, Scotland | 1,000 |
| **TV antenna** | Durris, Scotland | 1,000 |
| **TV antenna** | Anglia-Mendlesham, England | 1,000 |
| **ITA Antenna** | Strabane, Northern Ireland | 1,000 |
| **Factory chimney** | Cracow, Poland | 985 |
| **Eiffel Tower (with TV antenna, 1052)** | Paris | 984 |
| **TV Tower** | Munich | 951 |
| **Exxon Co. Oil Platform** | Santa Barbara, Calif. | 945 |
| **TV Tower** | Hamburg, Germany | 856 |
| **Ohio Edison Company Chimney** | Stratton, Ohio | 853 |
| **General Post Office Antennae (pair)** | Rugby, England | 820 |
| **TV antenna** | Stuttgart, Germany | 767 |
| **Radio tower** | Transvaal, Rep. of So. Africa | 760 |
| **BBC Antenna, Crystal Palace** | London | 710 |
| **TV antenna** | West Berlin | 696 |
| **National Cathedral Tower** | Washington, D.C. | 660 |
| **Gateway Arch** | St. Louis | 630 |
| **Tour du Maine** | Paris | 607 |
| **Space Needle** | Seattle | 606 |
| **Donauturm** | Vienna | 597 |
| **Radio Luxembourg Antenna** | Junglinster | 591 |
| **Post Office Tower** | London | 580 |
| **San Jacinto Column** | Houston | 570 |
| **Tower of the First Methodist Church** | Chicago | 568 |
| **Washington Monument** | Washington, D.C. | 555 |
| **American Smelting and Refining smokestack** | Tacoma, Wash. | 535 |
| **Ulm Cathedral** | West Germany | 530 |
| **Vertical Assembly Building** | Cape Canaveral, Fla. | 525 |
| **Cathedral of Learning** | Pittsburgh | 523 |
| **Blackpool Tower** | England | 519 |
| **Cologne Cathedral** | West Germany | 515 |
| **Mole Antonelliana** | Turin, Italy | 510 |
| **Kaknastornet Tower** | Stockholm | 502 |

## EARTH'S EXTREMES Source: National Geographic Society

| | |
|---|---|
| Wettest spot | Mt. Waialeale, Hawaii; greatest annual average, 460 inches (12-month record, Cherrapunji, India: 1,042 inches between Aug. 1860 and July 1861) |
| Driest spot | Atacama Desert, Chile; rainfall barely measurable |
| Coldest spot | Vostok, Antarctica; -127°F. recorded in 1960; Plateau Station, Antarctica; annual average; —70°F. |
| Hottest spot | Al'Aziziyah, Libya; 136°F. recorded in 1922. Dalol, Danakil Depression, Ethiopia; annual average temperature; 94°F. |
| Northernmost town | Ny Alesund, Spitsbergen, Norway |
| Southernmost town | Puerto Williams, Chile |
| Highest town | Wenquan, China; 16,732 feet |
| Lowest town | Villages along the Dead Sea; 1,299 feet below sea level |
| Largest gorge | Grand Canyon, Colorado River, Arizona; 277 miles long, 600 feet to 18 miles wide, 1 mile deep |
| Deepest gorge | Hells Canyon, Snake River, Idaho; 7,900 feet deep |
| Strongest surface wind | 231 mph; recorded in 1934 at Mount Washington, New Hampshire |
| Greatest tides | Bay of Fundy, Nova Scotia; 53 feet |

## PRINCIPAL WORLD ISLANDS

| Island | Area (in sq. miles) |
|---|---|
| Greenland | 840,000 |
| New Guinea | 305,000 |
| Borneo | 290,000 |
| Madagascar | 226,400 |
| Baffin (Canada) | 195,928 |
| Sumatra (Indonesia) | 164,000 |
| Japan | 145,730 |
| Philippines | 115,707 |
| New Zealand | 103,736 |
| Great Britain (U.K.) | 88,764 |
| Honshu (Japan) | 88,000 |
| Victoria (Canada) | 83,896 |
| Ellesmere (Canada) | 75,767 |
| Celebes (Indonesia) | 72,986 |
| South (N.Z.) | 58,393 |
| Java (Indonesia) | 48,842 |
| North (N.Z.) | 44,187 |
| Newfoundland (Canada) | 42,031 |
| Cuba | 40,533 |
| Luzon (Philippines) | 40,420 |
| Iceland | 39,768 |
| Mindanao (Philippines) | 36,537 |
| Moluccas (Indonesia) | 32,307 |
| Novaya Zemlya (USSR) | 31,900 |
| Ireland | 31,743 |
| Sakhalin (USSR) | 29,500 |
| Hispaniola (Haiti and Dominican Rep.) | 29,399 |
| Hokkaido (Japan) | 28,983 |
| Banks (Canada) | 27,038 |
| Tasmania (Australia) | 26,383 |
| Ceylon (Sri Lanka) | 25,332 |
| Svalbard (Norway) | 23,957 |
| Devon (Canada) | 21,331 |
| Bismarck Arch. (PNG) | 18,976 |
| Marajó (Brazil) | 17,991 |
| Tierra del Fuego (Chile and Argentina) | 17,900 |
| Axel Heiberg (Canada) | 16,671 |
| Melville (Canada) | 16,274 |
| Southampton (Canada) | 15,913 |
| Solomons | 15,600 |
| New Siberian Is. (USSR) | 14,672 |
| Severnaya Zemlya (USSR) | 14,285 |
| New Britain (PNG) | 14,100 |
| Taiwan (Formosa) (China) | 13,836 |
| Kyushu (Japan) | 13,770 |
| Hainan (China) | 13,127 |
| Prince of Wales (Canada) | 12,872 |
| Spitsbergen (Norway) | 12,355 |
| Vancouver (Canada) | 12,079 |
| Timor | 11,527 |
| Sicily (Italy) | 9,926 |
| Somerset (Canada) | 9,570 |
| Sardinia (Italy) | 9,301 |
| Fiji | 7,055 |
| Shikoku (Japan) | 6,860 |
| New Caledonia (France) | 6,530 |
| Hawaiian (U.S.) | 6,450 |
| Nordaustlandet (Norway) | 6,409 |
| Franz Josef Land (USSR) | 6,216 |
| Kuriles (USSR) | 6,025 |
| Bahamas | 5,382 |
| Samar (Philippines) | 5,050 |
| New Hebrides (Vanuatu) | 5,700 |
| Negros (Philippines) | 4,906 |
| Falklands (U.K.) | 4,618 |
| Palawan (Philippines) | 4,550 |
| Panay (Philippines) | 4,446 |
| Jamaica | 4,232 |
| Aleutians (Alaska, U.S.) | 4,201 |
| Hawaii (U.S.) | 4,038 |
| Viti Levu (Fiji) | 4,010 |
| Cape Breton (Canada) | 3,981 |
| Mindoro (Philippines) | 3,759 |
| Kodiak (Alaska, U.S.) | 3,670 |
| Cyprus | 3,572 |
| Puerto Rico (U.S.) | 3,435 |
| Corsica (France) | 3,352 |
| New Ireland (PNG) | 3,340 |
| Crete (Greece) | 3,218 |
| Galápagos (Ecuador) | 3,075 |
| Anticosti (Canada) | 3,066 |
| Wrangel (USSR) | 2,819 |
| Hebrides (U.K.) | 2,812 |
| Canaries (Spain) | 2,808 |
| Leyte (Philippines) | 2,786 |
| Kerguélen (France) | 2,700 |
| Andamans (India) | 2,448 |
| Guadalcanal (Solomon Islands) | 2,180 |
| Bali (Indonesia) | 2,171 |
| Prince Edward (Canada) | 2,170 |
| Balearics (Spain) | 1,936 |
| Trinidad (Trinidad & Tobago) | 1,864 |
| Ryukyus (Japan) | 1,767 |
| Madura (Indonesia) | 1,752 |
| Cape Verde | 1,557 |
| South Georgia (U.K.) | 1,450 |
| Euboea (Greece) | 1,411 |
| Long (N.Y., U.S.) | 1,401 |
| Socotra (PDR Yemen) | 1,400 |
| Samoa | 1,209 |
| Gotland (Sweden) | 1,153 |
| Western Samoa | 1,133 |
| Manitoulin (Canada) | 1,068 |
| Réunion (France) | 969 |
| Azores (Portugal) | 902 |
| Juventud (I. of Pines) (Cuba) | 849 |
| Bioko (Fernando Po) (Equat. Guinea) | 779 |
| Tenerife (Spain) | 745 |
| Maui (Hawaii, U.S.) | 729 |
| Mauritius | 720 |
| Skye (U.K.) | 670 |
| Savaii (W. Samoa) | 662 |
| Zanzibar (Tanzania) | 641 |
| Oahu (Hawaii, U.S.) | 608 |
| Guadeloupe (France) | 584 |
| Alands (Finland) | 581 |
| Kauai (Hawaii, U.S.) | 553 |
| Shetlands (U.K.) | 552 |
| Rhodes (Greece) | 542 |
| Faeroes (Denmark) | 540 |
| Marquesas (France) | 492 |
| Carolines (Pacific Is.) | 463 |
| Okinawa (Japan) | 454 |
| Upolu (W. Samoa) | 433 |
| Martinique (France) | 425 |
| Tahiti (France) | 402 |
| Pemba (Tanzania) | 380 |
| Orkneys (U.K.) | 372 |
| Madeiras (Portugal) | 307 |
| Dominica | 290 |
| Tonga | 270 |
| Molokai (Hawaii, U.S.) | 261 |
| Bahrain | 240 |
| St. Lucia | 238 |
| Corfu (Greece) | 229 |
| Isle of Man (U.K.) | 227 |
| Bornholm (Denmark) | 227 |
| Singapore | 226 |
| Guam (U.S.) | 212 |
| Isle Royale (Mich., U.S.) | 196 |
| Virgins (U.S.-U.K.) | 192 |
| Marianas (excluding Guam) (Pacific Is.) | 184 |
| Curacao (Neth. Antilles) | 182 |
| Barbados | 166 |
| Isle of Wight (U.K.) | 145 |
| Lanai (Hawaii, U.S.) | 140 |
| St. Vincent | 131 |
| Maltese | 122 |
| Grenada | 120 |
| Tobago (Trinidad & Tobago) | 116 |
| Antigua | 108 |
| Martha's Vineyard (Mass., U.S.) | 93 |
| Elba (Italy) | 87 |
| Seychelles | 85 |
| Channel (U.K.) | 74 |
| Marshalls (Pacific Is.) | 70 |
| Easter (Chile) | 63 |
| Staten (N.Y., U.S.) | 58 |
| Tutuila (Amer. Samoa) | 53 |
| St. Helena (U.K.) | 47 |
| Nantucket (Mass., U.S.) | 46 |
| Hong Kong | 30 |
| Manhattan (N.Y., U.S.) | 22 |
| Bermudas | 21 |
| Iwo Jima (Japan) | 7.8 |
| Nauru | 7.7 |
| Governors (N.Y., U.S.) | 180 acres |

## GEOGRAPHIC CENTERS OF THE UNITED STATES

SOURCE: U.S. Geological Survey

Because there is neither a generally accepted definition of a geographic center nor a completely satisfactory method for determining it, there may be as many geographic centers of a state or country as there are definitions of the term.

No marked or monumented point has been established by any government agency as the geographic center of either the 50 states, the conterminous United States, or the North American Continent. However, a monument was erected in Lebanon, Kansas, by a group of citizens who had hired engineers to determine the "geographic center" of the United States.

Sometimes confused with the geographic center of the United States is the reference point for all property lines and city, county, State, and international boundaries on the North American Continent that are tied to the National Triangulation networks of the United States, Canada, Mexico, and Central America. This point is Meades Ranch Triangulation station located at latitude 39°13′26.686″, longitude 98°32′30.506″, about 12 miles north of Lucas, Kansas. It is the base point or origin of geodetic positions and directions in the triangulation net of the United States because it is at the junction of the main east-west transcontinental triangulation arc stretching from the Atlantic to the Pacific Coasts and the main north-south arc, which follows approximately the 98th meridian from the Canadian border to the Rio Grande.

In determining the centers of the states, islands adjacent to their coastlines and large bodies of water on their boundaries were excluded.

The geographic centers and positions listed below should be considered as estimates. The center of the United States (without Alaska and Hawaii) is approximately Lebanon, Kansas.

| Center | Latitude (N) | Longitude (W) |
|---|---|---|
| **Conterminous United States** (48 States) Near Lebanon, Smith County, Kansas | 39°50′ | 98°35′ |
| **Continental United States** (49 States) Near Castle Rock, Butte County, South Dakota | 44°59′ | 103°38′ |
| **The United States** (50 States) West of Castle Rock, Butte County, South Dakota | 44°58′ | 103°46′ |
| **North American Continent** 6 miles west of Balta, Pierce County, North Dakota | 48°10′ | 100°10′ |

| State | Geographic Center |
|---|---|
| Alabama | 12 miles southwest of Clanton |
| Alaska | 63°50′N., 152°00′W., 60 miles northwest of Mt. McKinley |
| Arizona | 55 miles east-southeast of Prescott |
| Arkansas | 12 miles northwest of Little Rock |
| California | 35 miles east of Madera |
| Colorado | 30 miles northwest of Pikes Peak |
| Connecticut | at East Berlin |
| Delaware | 11 miles south of Dover |
| District of Columbia | near Fourth and L Streets NW |
| Florida | 12 miles north-northwest of Brooksville |
| Georgia | 18 miles southeast of Macon |
| Hawaii | 20°15′N., 156°20′W., off Maui Island |
| Idaho | at Custer, southwest of Challis |
| Illinois | 28 miles northeast of Springfield |
| Indiana | 14 miles north-northwest of Indianapolis |
| Iowa | 5 miles northeast of Ames |
| Kansas | 15 miles northeast of Great Bend |
| Kentucky | 3 miles north-northwest of Lebanon |
| Louisiana | 3 miles southeast of Marksville |
| Maine | 18 miles north of Dover-Foxcroft |
| Maryland | 4½ miles northwest of Davidsonville |
| Massachusetts | north part of city of Worcester |
| Michigan | 5 miles north-northwest of Cadillac |
| Minnesota | 10 miles southwest of Brainerd |
| Mississippi | 9 miles west-northwest of Carthage |
| Missouri | 20 miles southwest of Jefferson City |
| Montana | 12 miles west of Lewistown |
| Nebraska | 10 miles northwest of Broken Bow |
| Nevada | 26 miles southeast of Austin |
| New Hampshire | 3 miles east of Ashland |
| New Jersey | 5 miles southeast of Trenton |
| New Mexico | 12 miles south-southwest of Willard |
| New York | 12+ miles south of Oneida and 26+ miles southwest of Utica |
| North Carolina | 10 miles northwest of Sanford |
| North Dakota | 5 miles southwest of McClusky |
| Ohio | 25 miles north-northeast of Columbus |
| Oklahoma | 8 miles north of Oklahoma City |
| Oregon | 25 miles south-southeast of Prineville |
| Pennsylvania | 2½ miles southwest of Bellefonte |
| Rhode Island | 1 mile south-southwest of Crompton |
| South Carolina | 13 miles southeast of Columbia |
| South Dakota | 8 miles northeast of Pierre |
| Tennessee | 5 miles northeast of Murfreesboro |
| Texas | 15 miles northeast of Brady |
| Utah | 3 miles north of Manti |
| Vermont | 3 miles east of Roxbury |
| Virginia | 5 miles southwest of Buckingham |
| Washington | 10 miles west-southwest of Wenatchee |
| West Virginia | 4 miles east of Sutton |
| Wisconsin | 9 miles southeast of Marshfield |
| Wyoming | 58 miles east-northeast of Lander |

## EXTREME POINTS OF THE UNITED STATES

SOURCE: U.S. Geological Survey

The geographic center of an area may be defined as the center of gravity of the surface, or that point on which the surface of the area would balance if it were a cardboardlike plane of uniform thickness. Extreme points are measured from the various centers of the U.S. Because many factors, such as curvature of the earth, large bodies of water, and irregular surfaces, affect the determination of centers of gravity, the following positions should be considered as approximations only.

| Location | Direction from Geographic Center | Coordinates | | Distance from Geographic Center (in miles) |
|---|---|---|---|---|
| | | Latitude (N) | Longitude (W) | |
| From geographic center of United States near Lebanon, Smith County, Kansas, 39°50′, 98°35′ to— | | | | |
| Lake of the Woods, Minnesota | Northeast | 49°23′ | 95°09′ | 680 |
| Key West, Florida | Southeast | 24°33′ | 81°48′ | 1,436 |
| West Quoddy Head, Maine | East | 44°49′ | 66°57′ | 1,640 |
| Cape Alava, Washington | West | 48°10′ | 124°44′ | 1,412 |
| From geographic center of United States (including Alaska) near Castle Rock, Butte County, S.D., 44°59′, 103°38′ to— | | | | |
| Point Barrow, Alaska | Northwest | 71°23′ | 156°29′ | 2,504 |
| Key West, Florida | Southeast | 24°33′ | 81°48′ | 1,865 |
| West Quoddy Head, Maine | East | 44°49′ | 66°57′ | 1,779 |
| Cape Wrangell, Attu Island, Alaska | Northwest | 52°55′ | 172°27′(E) | 3,623 |
| From geographic center of United States (including Alaska and Hawaii) west of Castle Rock, S.D., 44°58′, 103°46′ to— | | | | |
| Point Barrow, Alaska | Northwest | 71°23′ | 156°29′ | 2,502 |
| Ka Lae (South Cape), Hawaii Island, Hawaii | Southwest | 18°56′ | 155°41′ | 3,456 |
| West Quoddy Head, Maine | East | 44°49′ | 66°57′ | 1,785 |
| Cape Wrangell, Attu Island, Alaska | Northwest | 52°55′ | 172°27′(E) | 3,620 |

## U.S. COASTLINE & SHORELINE

Source: National Ocean Survey, National Oceanic and Atmospheric Administration

General coastline figures represent lengths of the seacoast outline. The coastlines of sounds and of bays are included to a point where they narrow to the width of 30 minutes of latitude, and the distance across at such point is included. Tidal shorelines include the outer coast, offshore islands, sounds, bays, and rivers to the head of tidewater or to a point where tidal waters narrow to a width of 100 feet.

| | Coastline | Shoreline |
|---|---|---|
| **UNITED STATES** | **12,383** | **88,633** |
| (without Alaska and Hawaii) | 4,993 | 53,677 |
| **Atlantic** | **2,069** | **28,673** |
| Maine | 228 | 3,478 |
| New Hampshire | 13 | 131 |
| Massachusetts | 192 | 1,519 |
| Rhode Island | 40 | 384 |
| Connecticut | — | 618 |
| New York | 127 | 1,850 |
| New Jersey | 130 | 1,792 |
| Pennsylvania | — | 89 |
| Delaware | 28 | 381 |
| Maryland | 31 | 3,190 |
| Virginia | 112 | 3,315 |
| North Carolina | 301 | 3,375 |
| South Carolina | 187 | 2,876 |
| Georgia | 100 | 2,344 |
| Florida (Atlantic only) | 580 | 3,331 |
| **Gulf of Mexico** | **1,631** | **17,141** |
| Florida (Gulf only) | 770 | 5,095 |
| Alabama | 53 | 607 |
| Mississippi | 44 | 359 |
| Louisiana | 397 | 7,721 |
| Texas | 367 | 3,359 |

| | Coastline | Shoreline |
|---|---|---|
| **Pacific** | **7,623** | **40,298** |
| California | 840 | 3,427 |
| Oregon | 296 | 1,410 |
| Washington | 157 | 3,026 |
| Hawaii | 750 | 1,052 |
| Alaska (Pacific only) | 5,580 | 31,383 |
| Alaska (Arctic only) | 1,060 | 2,521 |
| EXTRATERRITORIAL | | |
| **Atlantic** | | |
| Navassa | 5 | 5 |
| Puerto Rico | 311 | 700 |
| Virgin Islands | 117 | 175 |
| **Pacific** | | |
| Baker Island | 3 | 3 |
| Guam Islands | 78 | 110 |
| Howland Island | 4 | 4 |
| Jarvis Island | 5 | 5 |
| Johnston Island | 5 | 5 |
| Midway Island | 20 | 33 |
| Palmyra Island | 9 | 16 |
| Samoa Islands | 76 | 126 |
| Wake Island | 12 | 20 |

## AVERAGE AND EXTREME U.S. ELEVATIONS

Source: U.S. Geological Survey

| State or Territory | Mean Elevation (feet) | HIGH Point | Mean Elevation (feet) | LOW Point | Mean Elevation (feet) |
|---|---|---|---|---|---|
| Alabama | 500 | Cheaha Mountain | 2,407 | Gulf of Mexico | (1) |
| Alaska | 1,900 | Mount McKinley | 20,320 | Pacific Ocean | (1) |
| American Samoa | 1,300 | Lata Mountain (Tau I.) | 3,160 | Pacific Ocean | (1) |
| Arizona | 4,100 | Humphreys Peak | 12,633 | Colorado River | 70 |
| Arkansas | 650 | Magazine Mountain | 2,753 | Ouachita River | 55 |
| California | 2,900 | Mount Whitney | 14,494 | Death Valley | —282 |
| Colorado | 6,800 | Mount Elbert | 14,433 | Arkansas River | 3,350 |
| Connecticut | 500 | Mount Frissell (So. Slope) | 2,380 | Long Island Sound | (1) |
| Delaware | 60 | On Ebright Road (New Castle County) | 442 | Atlantic Ocean | (1) |
| District of Columbia | 150 | Tenleytown (NW part) | 410 | Potomac River | 1 |
| Florida | 100 | Sec. 30, T. 6N., R. 20W. | 345 | Atlantic Ocean | (1) |
| Georgia | 600 | Brasstown Bald | 4,784 | Atlantic Ocean | (1) |
| Guam | 330 | Mount Lamlam | 1,329 | Pacific Ocean | (1) |
| Hawaii | 3,030 | Mauna Kea | 13,796 | Pacific Ocean | (1) |
| Idaho | 5,000 | Borah Peak | 12,662 | Snake River | 710 |
| Illinois | 600 | Charles Mound | 1,235 | Mississippi River | 279 |
| Indiana | 700 | Franklin Township (Wayne County) | 1,257 | Ohio River | 320 |
| Iowa | 1,100 | Sec. 29, T. 100 N., R. 41 W. | 1,670 | Mississippi River | 480 |
| Kansas | 2,000 | Mount Sunflower | 4,039 | Verdigris River | 680 |
| Kentucky | 750 | Black Mountain | 4,145 | Mississippi River | 257 |
| Louisiana | 100 | Driskill Mountain | 535 | New Orleans | —5 |
| Maine | 600 | Mount Katahdin | 5,268 | Atlantic Ocean | (1) |
| Maryland | 350 | Backbone Mountain | 3,360 | Atlantic Ocean | (1) |
| Massachusetts | 500 | Mount Greylock | 3,491 | Atlantic Ocean | (1) |
| Michigan | 900 | Mount Curwood | 1,980 | Lake Erie | 572 |
| Minnesota | 1,200 | Eagle Mountain | 2,301 | Lake Superior | 602 |
| Mississippi | 300 | Woodall Mountain | 806 | Gulf of Mexico | (1) |
| Missouri | 800 | Taum Sauk Mountain | 1,772 | St. Francis River | 230 |
| Montana | 3,400 | Granite Peak | 12,799 | Kootenai River | 1,800 |
| Nebraska | 2,600 | Johnson Township (Kimball County) | 5,426 | SE corner of state | 840 |
| Nevada | 5,500 | Boundary Peak | 13,143 | Colorado River | 470 |
| New Hampshire | 1,000 | Mount Washington | 6,288 | Atlantic Ocean | (1) |
| New Jersey | 250 | High Point | 1,803 | Atlantic Ocean | (1) |
| New Mexico | 5,700 | Wheeler Peak | 13,161 | Red Bluff Reservoir | 2,817 |
| New York | 1,000 | Mount Marcy | 5,344 | Atlantic Ocean | (1) |
| North Carolina | 700 | Mount Mitchell | 6,684 | Atlantic Ocean | (1) |
| North Dakota | 1,900 | White Butte | 3,506 | Red River | 750 |
| Ohio | 850 | Campbell Hill | 1,550 | Ohio River | 433 |
| Oklahoma | 1,300 | Black Mesa | 4,973 | Little River | 287 |
| Oregon | 3,300 | Mount Hood | 11,239 | Pacific Ocean | (1) |
| Pennsylvania | 1,100 | Mount Davis | 3,213 | Delaware River | (1) |
| Puerto Rico | 1,800 | Cerro de Punta | 4,389 | Atlantic Ocean | (1) |
| Rhode Island | 200 | Jerimoth Hill | 812 | Atlantic Ocean | (1) |
| South Carolina | 350 | Sassafras Mountain | 3,560 | Atlantic Ocean | (1) |
| South Dakota | 2,200 | Harney Peak | 7,242 | Big Stone Lake | 962 |
| Tennessee | 900 | Clingmans Dome | 6,643 | Mississippi River | 182 |
| Texas | 1,700 | Guadalupe Peak | 8,749 | Gulf of Mexico | (1) |
| Utah | 6,100 | Kings Peak | 13,528 | Beaverdam Creek | 2,000 |
| Vermont | 1,000 | Mount Mansfield | 4,393 | Lake Champlain | 95 |
| Virginia | 950 | Mount Rogers | 5,729 | Atlantic Ocean | (1) |
| Virgin Islands | 750 | Crown Mountain (St. Thomas) | 1,556 | Atlantic Ocean | (1) |
| Washington | 1,700 | Mount Rainier | 14,410 | Pacific Ocean | (1) |
| West Virginia | 1,500 | Spruce Knob | 4,863 | Potomac River | 240 |
| Wisconsin | 1,050 | Timms Hill | 1,951 | Lake Michigan | 581 |
| Wyoming | 6,700 | Gannett Peak | 13,804 | Belle Fourche River | 3,100 |

(1) = Sea level.

## PRINCIPAL U.S. RIVERS

SOURCE: U.S. Geological Survey

| River | Empties Into: | Length (in miles) |
|---|---|---|
| Mississippi-Missouri-Red Rock | Gulf of Mexico | 3,741 |
| Missouri-Red Rock | Mississippi River | 2,564 |
| Mississippi | Gulf of Mexico | 2,348 |
| Missouri | Mississippi River | 2,315 |
| Yukon (U.S.-Canada) | Bering Sea | 1,979 |
| St. Lawrence (U.S.-Canada) | Atlantic Ocean | 1,900 |
| Rio Grande (U.S.-Mexico) | Gulf of Mexico | 1,885 |
| Arkansas | Mississippi River | 1,450 |
| Colorado (U.S.-Mexico) | Gulf of California | 1,450 |
| Brazos | Gulf of Mexico | 1,309 |
| Ohio-Allegheny | Mississippi River | 1,306 |
| Columbia (U.S.-Canada) | Pacific Ocean | 1,243 |
| Red (Okla.-Tex.-Ark.-La.) | Mississippi River | 1,222 |
| Mississippi, Upper | to mouth of Missouri River | 1,171 |
| Snake | Columbia River | 1,000 |
| Ohio | Mississippi River | 981 |
| Pecos | Rio Grande | 926 |
| Canadian | Arkansas River | 906 |
| Tennessee-N. Fk. Holston | Ohio River | 900 |
| Colorado (Texas) | Gulf of Mexico | 894 |
| Columbia, Upper (U.S.-Canada) | to mouth of Snake River | 890 |
| Kuskokwim | Bering Sea | 800 |
| Tanana | Yukon River | 800 |
| North Canadian | Canadian River | 784 |
| Kansas-Republican-Arikaree | Missouri River | 743 |
| Green (Wyo.-Colo.-Utah) | Colorado River | 730 |
| Milk (U.S.-Canada) | Missouri River | 729 |
| Trinity | Gulf of Mexico | 715 |
| James (N. Dak.-S. Dak.) | Missouri River | 710 |
| Cimarron | Arkansas River | 698 |
| Cumberland | Ohio River | 687 |
| White (Mo.-Ark.) | Mississippi River | 685 |
| North Platte | Platte River | 680 |
| Yellowstone | Missouri River | 671 |
| Tennessee | Ohio River | 652 |
| Mobile-Alabama-Coosa | Gulf of Mexico | 639 |
| Gila | Colorado River | 630 |
| Washita | Red River | 626 |
| Ouachita | Red River | 605 |
| Little Missouri | Missouri River | 560 |
| Smoky Hill | Kansas River | 560 |
| Porcupine (U.S.-Canada) | Yukon River | 555 |
| Koyukuk | Yukon River | 554 |
| Red River of the North (U.S.-Canada) | Lake Winnipeg | 545 |
| Tombigbee | Mobile River | 525 |
| Apalachicola-Chattahoochee | Gulf of Mexico | 524 |
| White (S. Dak.-Nebr.) | Missouri River | 507 |
| Osage-Marais des Cygnes | Missouri River | 496 |
| Pend Oreille-Clark Fork | Columbia River | 490 |
| Pearl | Gulf of Mexico | 490 |
| Powder | Yellowstone River | 486 |
| Kootenai (U.S.-Canada) | Columbia River | 485 |
| Wabash | Ohio River | 475 |
| Innoko | Yukon River | 463 |
| Susquehanna | Chesapeake Bay | 458 |
| Neosho | Arkansas River | 450 |
| South Platte | Platte River | 442 |
| Santee-Wateree-Catawba | Atlantic Ocean | 438 |
| Pee Dee-Yadkin | Atlantic Ocean | 435 |
| Niobrara | Missouri River | 431 |
| Wisconsin | Mississippi River | 430 |

## LARGE U.S. LAKES

SOURCE: U.S. Geological Survey and Statistics Canada

Natural U.S. lakes with areas of 100 sq. mi. or more are listed

| Lake | State | Area (sq. mi.) |
|---|---|---|
| **Superior** | Canada, Minnesota, Wisconsin, and Michigan | 31,700 |
| **Huron** | Canada and Michigan | 23,010 |
| **Michigan** | Wisconsin, Illinois, Indiana, and Michigan | 22,400 |
| **Erie** | Canada, Michigan, Ohio, Pennsylvania, and New York | 9,910 |
| **Ontario** | Canada and New York | 7,340 |
| **Lake of the Woods** | Minnesota and Canada | 1,679 |
| **Great Salt**[a] | Utah | 1,361[b] |
| **Iliamna** | Alaska | 1,000 |
| **Okeechobee** | Florida | 700 |
| **Pontchartrain**[a] | Louisiana | 625 |
| **Becharof** | Alaska | 458 |
| **Red Lake** (Upper and Lower) | Minnesota | 451 |
| **Champlain** | New York, Vermont, and Canada | 435 |
| **St. Clair** | Michigan and Canada | 432 |
| **Salton Sea**[a] | California | 374[b] |
| **Rainy** | Minnesota and Canada | 360 |
| **Teshekpuk** | Alaska | 315 |
| **Naknek** | Alaska | 242 |
| **Winnebago** | Wisconsin | 215 |
| **Mille Lacs** | Minnesota | 207 |
| **Flathead** | Montana | 197 |
| **Tahoe** | California and Nevada | 193 |
| **Leech** | Minnesota | 176 |
| **Pyramid**[a] | Nevada | 168[b] |
| **Pend Oreille** | Idaho | 148 |
| **Ugashik** (Upper and Lower) | Alaska | 147 |
| **Upper Klamath** | Oregon | 142 |
| **Utah** | Utah | 140 |
| **Bear** (including Mud Lake) | Idaho and Utah | 136 |
| **Yellowstone** | Wyoming | 134 |
| **Moosehead** | Maine | 117 |
| **Tustumena** | Alaska | 117 |
| **Clark** | Alaska | 110 |
| **Winnibigoshish** | Minnesota | 109 |
| **Dall** | Alaska | 100 |

[a] Salty. [b] Variable.

## HIGHEST U.S. MOUNTAIN PEAKS

SOURCE: U.S. Geological Survey

| Peak | State | Elevation |
|---|---|---|
| Mt. McKinley | Alaska | 20,320 |
| Mt. St. Elias | Alaska | 18,008 |
| Mt. Foraker | Alaska | 17,400 |
| Mt. Bona | Alaska | 16,421 |
| Mt. Blackburn | Alaska | 16,390 |
| Mt. Sanford | Alaska | 16,237 |
| South Buttress | Alaska | 15,885 |
| Mt. Vancouver | Alaska | 15,700 |
| Mt. Churchill | Alaska | 15,638 |
| Mt. Fairweather | Alaska | 15,300 |
| Mt. Hubbard | Alaska | 15,015 |
| Mt. Bear | Alaska | 14,831 |
| East Buttress | Alaska | 14,730 |
| Mt. Hunter | Alaska | 14,573 |
| Mt. Alverstone | Alaska | 14,565 |
| Browne Tower | Alaska | 14,530 |
| Mt. Whitney | California | 14,494 |
| Mt. Elbert | Colorado | 14,433 |
| Mt. Massive | Colorado | 14,421 |
| Mt. Harvard | Colorado | 14,420 |
| Mt. Rainier | Washington | 14,410 |
| Mt. Williamson | California | 14,375 |
| Blanca Peak | Colorado | 14,345 |
| La Plata Peak | Colorado | 14,336 |
| Uncompahgre Peak | Colorado | 14,309 |
| Crestone Peak | Colorado | 14,294 |
| Mt. Lincoln | Colorado | 14,286 |
| Grays Peak | Colorado | 14,270 |
| Mt. Antero | Colorado | 14,269 |
| Torreys Peak | Colorado | 14,267 |
| Castle Peak | Colorado | 14,265 |
| Quandary Peak | Colorado | 14,265 |
| Mt. Evans | Colorado | 14,264 |
| Longs Peak | Colorado | 14,255 |
| Mt. Wilson | Colorado | 14,246 |
| White Mtn. | California | 14,246 |
| North Palisade | California | 14,242 |
| Shavano Peak | Colorado | 14,229 |
| Mt. Belford | Colorado | 14,197 |
| Mt. Princeton | Colorado | 14,197 |
| Crestone Needle | Colorado | 14,197 |
| Mt. Yale | Colorado | 14,196 |
| Mt. Bross | Colorado | 14,172 |
| Kit Carson Mtn. | Colorado | 14,165 |
| Mt. Wrangell | Alaska | 14,163 |
| Mt. Shasta | California | 14,162 |
| Mt. Sill | California | 14,162 |
| El Diente Peak | Colorado | 14,159 |
| Maroon Peak | Colorado | 14,156 |
| Tabeguache Mtn. | Colorado | 14,155 |
| Mt. Oxford | Colorado | 14,153 |
| Mt. Sneffels | Colorado | 14,150 |
| Mt. Democrat | Colorado | 14,148 |
| Capitol Peak | Colorado | 14,130 |
| Pikes Peak | Colorado | 14,110 |
| Snowmass Mtn. | Colorado | 14,092 |
| Windom Peak | Colorado | 14,087 |
| Mt. Russell | California | 14,086 |
| Mt. Eolus | Colorado | 14,084 |
| Mt. Columbia | Colorado | 14,073 |
| Mt. Augusta | Alaska | 14,070 |
| Missouri Mtn. | Colorado | 14,067 |
| Humboldt Peak | Colorado | 14,064 |
| Mt. Bierstadt | Colorado | 14,060 |
| Sunlight Peak | Colorado | 14,059 |
| Handies Peak | California | 14,058 |
| Split Mt. | Colorado | 14,048 |
| Culebra Peak | Colorado | 14,047 |

## U.S. TEMPERATURE EXTREMES

SOURCE: National Oceanic and Atmospheric Administration

### HIGHEST TEMPERATURES

Greenland Ranch, Calif., with 134° on July 10, 1913, holds the record for the highest temperature ever officially recorded in the United States. This station is located in Death Valley, which is about 140 miles long, four to 16 miles wide, and runs north and south in southeastern California and southwestern Nevada. Death Valley is below sea level and flanked by towering mountain ranges with Mt. Whitney, rising to 14,495 feet, less than 100 miles to the west. It has the hottest summers in the Western Hemisphere and is the only known place in the United States where nighttime temperatures sometimes remain above 100°.

In the United States the station normally having the highest annual average is Key West, Fla., 78.2°; the highest summer average, Death Valley, Calif., 98.2°; and the highest winter normal temperature is 72.8° for Honolulu, Hawaii.

Amazing temperature rises of 40° to 50° in a few minutes occasionally may be brought about by Chinook winds. Some outstanding extreme temperature rises in short periods are:

12 hours: 83°, Granville, N. Dak., Feb. 21, 1918, from —33° to 50° from early morning to late afternoon.

15 minutes: 42°, Fort Assiniboine, Mont., Jan. 19, 1892, from —5° to 37°.

7 minutes: 34°, Kipp, Mont., Dec. 1, 1896; observer also reported that a total rise of 80° occurred in a few hours and that 30 inches of snow disappeared in one-half day.

2 minutes: 49°, Spearfish, S. Dak., Jan. 22, 1943, from —4° at 7:30 a.m., to 45° at 7:32 a.m.

### HIGHEST TEMPERATURES IN CONTERMINOUS UNITED STATES BY MONTHS

| Month | Temp. (°F.) | Year | Day | State | Place | Elevation Feet |
|---|---|---|---|---|---|---|
| Jan. | 98 | 1936 | 17 | Texas | Laredo | 421 |
| Feb.* | 105 | 1963 | 3 | Ariz. | Montezuma | 735 |
| Mar.* | 108 | 1954 | 31 | Texas | Rio Grande City | 168 |
| Apr. | 118 | 1898 | 25 | Calif. | Volcano Springs | —220 |
| May* | 124 | 1896 | 27 | Calif. | Salton | —263 |
| June*† | 127 | 1896 | 15 | Ariz. | Ft. Mohave | 555 |
| July | 134 | 1913 | 10 | Calif. | Greenland Ranch | —178 |
| Aug.† | 127 | 1933 | 12 | Calif. | Greenland Ranch | —178 |
| Sept. | 126 | 1950 | 2 | Calif. | Mecca | —175 |
| Oct.* | 116 | 1917 | 5 | Ariz. | Sentinel | 685 |
| Nov.* | 105 | 1906 | 12 | Calif. | Craftonville | 1,759 |
| Dec. | 100 | 1938 | 8 | Calif. | La Mesa | 539 |

* Two or more occurrences, most recent given. † Slightly higher temperatures in old records are not used owing to lack of information.

### RECORD HIGHEST TEMPERATURES BY STATES

| State | Temp. (°F.) | Date | Station | Elevation Feet |
|---|---|---|---|---|
| Ala. | 112 | Sept. 5, 1925 | Centerville | 345 |
| Alaska | 100 | June 27, 1915 | Fort Yukon | 420 |
| Ariz. | 127 | July 7, 1905* | Parker | 345 |
| Ark. | 120 | Aug. 10, 1936 | Ozark | 396 |
| Calif. | 134 | July 10, 1913 | Greenland Ranch | —178 |
| Colo. | 118 | July 11, 1888 | Bennett | 5,484 |
| Conn. | 105 | July 22, 1926 | Waterbury | 400 |
| Del. | 110 | July 21, 1930 | Millsboro | 20 |
| D.C. | 106 | July 20, 1930* | Washington | 112 |
| Fla. | 109 | June 29, 1931 | Monticello | 207 |
| Ga. | 113 | May 27, 1978 | Greenville | 860 |
| Hawaii | 100 | Apr. 27, 1931 | Pahala | 850 |
| Idaho | 118 | July 28, 1934 | Orofino | 1,027 |
| Ill. | 117 | July 14, 1954 | E. St. Louis | 410 |
| Ind. | 116 | July 14, 1936 | Collegeville | 672 |
| Iowa | 118 | July 20, 1934 | Keokuk | 614 |
| Kans. | 121 | July 24, 1936* | Alton (near) | 1,651 |
| Ky. | 114 | July 28, 1930 | Greensburg | 581 |
| La. | 114 | Aug. 10, 1936 | Plain Dealing | 268 |
| Maine | 105 | July 10, 1911* | North Bridgton | 450 |
| Md. | 109 | July 10, 1936* | Cumberland & Frederick | 623; 325 |
| Mass. | 107 | Aug. 2, 1975 | New Bedford & Chester | 120; 640 |
| Mich. | 112 | July 13, 1936 | Mio | 963 |
| Minn. | 114 | July 6, 1936* | Moorhead | 904 |
| Miss. | 115 | July 29, 1930 | Holly Springs | 600 |
| Mo. | 118 | July 14, 1954* | Warsaw & Union | 687; 560 |
| Mont. | 117 | July 5, 1937 | Medicine Lake | 1,950 |
| Nebr. | 118 | July 24, 1936* | Minden | 2,169 |
| Nev. | 122 | June 23, 1954* | Overton | 1,240 |
| N.H. | 106 | July 4, 1911 | Nashua | 125 |
| N.J. | 110 | July 10, 1936 | Runyon | 18 |
| N. Mex. | 116 | July 14, 1934* | Orogrande | 4,171 |
| N.Y. | 108 | July 22, 1926 | Troy | 35 |
| N.C. | 109 | Sept. 7, 1954* | Weldon | 81 |
| N. Dak. | 121 | July 6, 1936 | Steele | 1,857 |
| Ohio | 113 | July 21, 1934* | Gallipolis (near) | 673 |
| Okla. | 120 | July 26, 1943* | Tishomingo | 670 |
| Oreg. | 119 | Aug. 10, 1898 | Pendleton | 1,074 |
| Pa. | 111 | July 10, 1936* | Phoenixville | 100 |
| R.I. | 104 | Aug. 2, 1975 | Providence | 51 |
| S.C. | 111 | June 28, 1954* | Camden | 170 |
| S. Dak. | 120 | July 5, 1936 | Gannvalley | 1,750 |
| Tenn. | 113 | Aug. 9, 1930* | Perryville | 377 |
| Tex. | 120 | Aug. 12, 1936 | Seymour | 1,291 |
| Utah | 116 | June 28, 1892 | Saint George | 2,880 |
| Vt. | 105 | July 4, 1911 | Vernon | 310 |
| Va. | 110 | July 15, 1954 | Balcony Falls | 725 |
| Wash. | 118 | Aug. 5, 1961* | Ice Harbor Dam | 475 |
| W. Va. | 112 | July 10, 1936* | Martinsburg | 435 |
| Wis. | 114 | July 13, 1936 | Wisconsin Dells | 900 |
| Wyo. | 114 | July 12, 1900 | Basin | 3,500 |

* Also on earlier dates at the same or other places.

### LOWEST TEMPERATURES

In the United States, the lowest temperature on record, —79.8°, was recorded at Prospect Creek Camp, which is located in the Endicott Mountains of northern Alaska. The lowest temperature in the 48 states, —69.7°, occurred at Rogers Pass (Lewis and Clark County, Montana), which is mountainous and heavily forested terrain, about a half mile east of and 140 feet below the summit of the Continental Divide.

The lowest average annual temperature recorded in the United States is 9.3° at Barrow, Alaska, on the Arctic coast. Barrow also has the coolest summers (June, July, August) with an average of 36.4°. The lowest average winter (December, January, February) temperature is —15.7° at Barter Island on the Arctic coast of northeast Alaska. In Hawaii, average annual temperatures range from 44.0° at Mauna Loa Slope Observatory (elevation 11,146 feet) on the island of Hawaii to 76.6° at Honolulu on the island of Oahu.

In the 48 states, Mt. Washington, N.H. (elevation 6,262 feet) has the lowest mean annual temperature, 26.9° F, and the lowest mean summer (June, July, August) temperature, 46.8°. A few stations in the Northeast and upper Rockies have mean annuals in the high 30's, and at the same stations in the latter area summers may average in the high 40's. Winter (December, January, February) mean temperatures are lowest in northeastern North Dakota where the average is 5.9° at the Langdon Experiment Farm and northwestern Minnesota where the average is 6.1° at Hallock.

In continental areas of the Temperate Zone, 40° to 50° temperature falls in a few hours caused by advection (horizontal shifting) of cold air masses are not uncommon. Following these large drops, radiation sometimes may cause a further temperature fall resulting in remarkable changes. Some outstanding extreme temperature falls are:

24 hours: 100°, Browning, Mont., Jan. 23–24, 1916, from 44° to –56°.

12 hours: 84°, Fairfield, Mont., Dec. 24, 1924, from 63° at noon to –21° at midnight.

2 hours: 62°, Rapid City, S. Dak., Jan. 12, 1911, from 49° at 6 a.m., to –13° at 8 a.m.

27 minutes: 58°, Spearfish, S. Dak., Jan. 22, 1943, from 54° at 9 a.m., to –4° at 9:27 a.m.

15 minutes: 47°, Rapid City, S. Dak., Jan. 10, 1911, from 55° at 7 a.m. to 8° at 7:15 a.m.

### LOWEST TEMPERATURES IN CONTERMINOUS UNITED STATES BY MONTHS

| Month | Temp. (°F.) | Year | Day | State | Place | Elevation Feet | Month | Temp. (°F.) | Year | Day | State | Place | Elevation Feet |
|---|---|---|---|---|---|---|---|---|---|---|---|---|---|
| Jan. | -70 | 1954 | 20 | Mont. | Rogers Pass | 5,470 | July* | 10 | 1911 | 21 | Wyo. | Painter | 6,800 |
| Feb. | -66 | 1933 | 9 | Mont. | Riverside | 6,700 | Aug.* | 5 | 1910 | 25 | Mont. | Bowen | 6,080 |
| Mar. | -50 | 1906 | 17 | Wyo. | Snake River | 6,862 | Sept.* | -9 | 1926 | 24 | Mont. | Riverside | 6,700 |
| Apr. | -36 | 1945 | 5 | N. Mex. | Eagle Nest | 8,250 | Oct. | -33 | 1917 | 29 | Wyo. | Soda Butte | 6,600 |
| May | -15 | 1964 | 7 | Calif. | White Mtn. 2 | 12,470 | Nov. | -53 | 1959 | 16 | Mont. | Lincoln 14 NE | 5,130 |
| June | 2 | 1907 | 13 | Calif. | Tamarack | 8,000 | Dec.* | -59 | 1924 | 19 | Mont. | Riverside | 6,700 |

* Two or more occurrences, most recent given.

### RECORD LOWEST TEMPERATURES BY STATES

| State | Temp. (°F.) | Date | Station | Elevation Feet | State | Temp. (°F.) | Date | Station | Elevation Feet |
|---|---|---|---|---|---|---|---|---|---|
| Ala. | —27 | Jan. 30, 1966 | New Market | 760 | Nebr. | —47 | Feb. 12, 1899 | Camp Clarke | 3,700 |
| Alaska | —80 | Jan. 23, 1971 | Prospect Creek Camp | 1,100 | Nev. | —50 | Jan. 8, 1937 | San Jacinto | 5,200 |
| Ariz. | —40 | Jan. 7, 1971 | Hawley Lake | 8,180 | N.H. | —46 | Jan. 28, 1925 | Pittsburg | 1,575 |
| Ark. | —29 | Feb. 13, 1905 | Pond | 1,250 | N.J. | —34 | Jan. 5, 1904 | River Vale | 70 |
| Cal. | —45 | Jan. 20, 1937 | Boca | 5,532 | N. Mex. | —50 | Feb. 1, 1951 | Gavilan | 7,350 |
| Colo. | —60 | Jan. 1, 1979* | Maybell | 5,920 | N.Y. | —52 | Feb. 18, 1979* | Old Forge | 1,720 |
| Conn. | —32 | Feb. 16, 1943 | Falls Village | 585 | N.C. | —29 | Jan. 30, 1966 | Mt. Mitchell | 6,525 |
| Del. | —17 | Jan. 17, 1893 | Millsboro | 20 | N. Dak. | —60 | Feb. 15, 1936 | Parshall | 1,929 |
| D.C. | —15 | Feb. 11, 1899 | Washington | 112 | Ohio | —39 | Feb. 10, 1899 | Milligan | 800 |
| Fla. | — 2 | Feb. 13, 1899 | Tallahassee | 193 | Okla. | —27 | Jan. 18, 1930 | Watts | 958 |
| Ga. | —17 | Jan. 27, 1940 | CCC Camp F-16 | 1,000 | Oreg. | —54 | Feb. 10, 1933* | Seneca | 4,700 |
| Hawaii | 14 | Jan. 2, 1961 | Haleakala, Maui Island | 9,750 | Pa. | —42 | Jan. 5, 1904 | Smethport | 1,500 |
| Idaho | —60 | Jan. 18, 1943 | Island Park Dam | 6,285 | R.I. | —23 | Jan. 11, 1942 | Kingston | 100 |
| Ill. | —35 | Jan. 22, 1930 | Mount Carroll | 817 | S.C. | —20 | Jan. 18, 1977 | Caesars Head | 3,100 |
| Ind. | —35 | Feb. 2, 1951 | Greensburg | 954 | S. Dak. | —58 | Feb. 17, 1936 | McIntosh | 2,277 |
| Iowa | —47 | Jan. 12, 1912 | Washta | 1,157 | Tenn. | —32 | Dec. 30, 1917 | Mountain City | 2,471 |
| Kans. | —40 | Feb. 13, 1905 | Lebanon | 1,812 | Tex. | —23 | Feb. 8, 1933* | Seminole | 3,275 |
| Ky. | —34 | Jan. 28, 1963 | Cynthiana | 684 | Utah | —50 | Jan. 5, 1913* | Strawberry Tunnel | |
| La. | —16 | Feb. 13, 1899 | Minden | 194 | | | | east portal | 7,650 |
| Maine | —48 | Jan. 19, 1925 | Van Buren | 510 | Vt. | —50 | Dec. 30, 1933 | Bloomfield | 915 |
| Md. | —40 | Jan. 13, 1912 | Oakland | 2,461 | Va. | —29 | Feb. 10, 1899 | Monterey | — |
| Mass. | —34 | Jan. 18, 1957 | Birch Hill Dam | 840 | Wash. | —48 | Dec. 30, 1968 | Mazama | 2,120 |
| Mich. | —51 | Feb. 9, 1934 | Vanderbilt | 785 | | | | Winthrop | 1,765 |
| Minn. | —59 | Feb. 16, 1903* | Pokegama Dam | 1,280 | W. Va. | —37 | Dec. 30, 1917 | Lewisburg | 2,200 |
| Miss. | —19 | Jan. 30, 1966 | Corinth | 420 | Wis. | —54 | Jan. 24, 1922 | Danbury | 908 |
| Mo. | —40 | Feb. 13, 1905 | Warsaw | 700 | Wyo. | —63 | Feb. 9, 1933 | Moran | 6,770 |
| Mont. | —70 | Jan. 20, 1954 | Rogers Pass | 5,470 | | | | | |

* Also on earlier dates at the same or other places.

## WIND CHILL

Source: National Oceanic and Atmosphereic Administration

A very strong wind combined with a temperature slightly below freezing can have the same chilling effect as a temperature nearly 50°F lower in a calm atmosphere. Arctic explorers and military experts have developed what is called the "wind-chill factor," which shows the combined effects of wind and temperature as equivalent calm-air temperatures. In effect, the index describes the cooling power of the air on exposed flesh. The wind-chill table here shows this cooling power for various combinations of wind and temperature, and will help you gauge how much protection you really need.

**Directions:** 1) Find actual (calm) air temperature across top of table. 2) Determine wind speed and follow across to correct calm-air temperature. Number given is **equivalent temperature.**

For example, a 10° temperature with a 20 mph wind equals the equivalent of —24 degrees.

### WIND CHILL

Equivalent Temperatures (°F)

| Windspeed (Miles per hour) | | | | | | | | | | | | | | | | | |
|---|---|---|---|---|---|---|---|---|---|---|---|---|---|---|---|---|---|
| Calm | 35 | 30 | 25 | 20 | 15 | 10 | 5 | 0 | —5 | —10 | —15 | —20 | —25 | —30 | —35 | —40 | —45 |
| 5 | 33 | 27 | 21 | 16 | 12 | 7 | 1 | —6 | —11 | —15 | —20 | —26 | —31 | —35 | —41 | —47 | —54 |
| 10 | 21 | 16 | 9 | 2 | —2 | —9 | —15 | —22 | —27 | —31 | —38 | —45 | —52 | —58 | —64 | —70 | —77 |
| 15 | 16 | 11 | 1 | —6 | —11 | —18 | —25 | —33 | —40 | —45 | —51 | —60 | —65 | —70 | —78 | —85 | —90 |
| 20 | 12 | 3 | —4 | —9 | —17 | —24 | —32 | —40 | —46 | —52 | —60 | —68 | —76 | —81 | —88 | —96 | —103 |
| 25 | 7 | 0 | —7 | —15 | —22 | —29 | —37 | —45 | —52 | —58 | —67 | —75 | —83 | —89 | —96 | —104 | —112 |
| 30 | 5 | —2 | —11 | —18 | —26 | —33 | —41 | —49 | —56 | —63 | —70 | —78 | —87 | —94 | —101 | —109 | —117 |
| 35 | 3 | —4 | —13 | —20 | —27 | —35 | —43 | —52 | —60 | —67 | —72 | —83 | —90 | —98 | —105 | —113 | —123 |
| 40 | 1 | —4 | —15 | —22 | —29 | —36 | —45 | —54 | —62 | —69 | —76 | —87 | —94 | —101 | —107 | —116 | —128 |
| 45 | 1 | —6 | —17 | —24 | —31 | —38 | —46 | —54 | —63 | —70 | —78 | —87 | —94 | —101 | —108 | —118 | —128 |
| 50 | 0 | —7 | —17 | —24 | —31 | —38 | —47 | —56 | —63 | —70 | —79 | —88 | —96 | —103 | —110 | —120 | —128 |

VERY COLD

BITTER COLD

EXTREME COLD

## U.S. CITY WEATHER | Source: National Climatic Center

| City | Record Temperature High (F°) | Record Temperature Low (F°) | Annual Average: Precip. (Water equiv.) (in.) | Annual Average: Snow and Sleet (in.) | Annual Average: Wind Speed (mph) | First Freeze Date 32 F° or less: Average | First Freeze Date 32 F° or less: Earliest on record | Last Freeze Date 32 F° or less: Average | Last Freeze Date 32 F° or less: Latest on record | Elevation of Station (feet) |
|---|---|---|---|---|---|---|---|---|---|---|
| Albany | 104 | —28 | 36.46 | 65.7 | 8.8 | Oct. 13 | Sept. 23 | Apr. 27 | May 20 | 292 |
| Albuquerque | 105 | —17 | 8.33 | 10.7 | 9.0 | Oct. 29 | Oct. 11 | Apr. 16 | May 18 | 5,314 |
| Atlanta | 103 | — 9 | 48.66 | 1.5 | 9.1 | Nov. 12 | Oct. 24 | Mar. 24 | Apr. 15 | 1,034 |
| Baltimore | 107 | — 7 | 41.62 | 21.9 | 9.5 | Oct. 26 | Oct. 8 | Apr. 15 | May 11 | 155 |
| Birmingham | 107 | —10 | 53.46 | 1.2 | 7.4 | Nov. 10 | Oct. 17 | Mar. 17 | Apr. 21 | 630 |
| Bismarck | 114 | —45 | 16.15 | 38.4 | 10.6 | Sept. 22 | Sept. 6 | May 11 | May 30 | 1,660 |
| Boise | 111 | —23 | 11.97 | 21.7 | 9.0 | Oct. 12 | Sept. 9 | May 6 | May 31 | 2,868 |
| Boston | 104 | —18 | 41.55 | 41.9 | 12.6 | Nov. 7 | Oct. 5 | Apr. 8 | May 3 | 29 |
| Buffalo | 99 | —21 | 35.19 | 88.6 | 12.3 | Oct. 25 | Sept. 23 | Apr. 30 | May 24 | 706 |
| Burlington, Vt. | 101 | —30 | 32.54 | 78.4 | 8.8 | Oct. 3 | Sept. 13 | May 10 | May 24 | 340 |
| Charleston, W. Va. | 108 | —24 | 43.66 | 28.8 | 6.5 | Oct. 28 | Sept. 29 | Apr. 18 | May 11 | 951 |
| Charlotte | 104 | — 5 | 45.00 | 5.6 | 7.6 | Nov. 4 | Oct. 15 | Apr. 2 | Apr. 16 | 769 |
| Cheyenne | 100 | —38 | 14.48 | 52.0 | 13.3 | Sept. 27 | Aug. 25 | May 18 | June 18 | 6,141 |
| Chicago | 105 | —23 | 33.47 | 40.7 | 10.3 | Oct. 26 | Sept. 25 | Apr. 20 | May 14 | 623 |
| Cincinnati | 102 | —19 | 40.40 | 23.2 | 9.1 | Oct. 25 | Sept. 28 | Apr. 15 | May 25 | 877 |
| Cleveland | 103 | —19 | 34.15 | 51.5 | 10.8 | Nov. 2 | Sept. 29 | Apr. 21 | May 14 | 805 |
| Columbia, S.C. | 107 | — 2 | 45.23 | 1.8 | 6.9 | Nov. 3 | Oct. 4 | Mar. 30 | Apr. 21 | 225 |
| Columbus, Ohio | 106 | —20 | 36.98 | 27.7 | 8.7 | Oct. 31 | Oct. 7 | Apr. 16 | May 9 | 833 |
| Concord, N.H. | 102 | —37 | 38.13 | 64.1 | 6.7 | Sept. 24 | Sept. 13 | May 17 | June 6 | 346 |
| Dallas-Ft. Worth, Tex. | 112 | — 8 | 32.11 | 2.7 | 11.1 | Nov. 21 | Oct. 27 | Mar. 16 | Apr. 13 | 596 |
| Denver | 105 | —30 | 14.60 | 60.1 | 9.0 | Oct. 14 | Sept. 16 | May 2 | May 28 | 5,332 |
| Des Moines | 110 | —30 | 31.49 | 33.2 | 11.1 | Oct. 10 | Sept. 28 | Apr. 20 | May 11 | 963 |
| Detroit | 105 | —24 | 31.49 | 31.7 | 10.2 | Oct. 21 | Sept. 23 | Apr. 23 | May 12 | 626 |
| El Paso | 109 | — 8 | 8.47 | 4.4 | 9.6 | Nov. 11 | Oct. 31 | Mar. 13 | Apr. 11 | 3,916 |
| Great Falls | 107 | —49 | 14.83 | 57.7 | 13.1 | Sept. 26 | Sept. 7 | May 14 | June 8 | 3,657 |
| Hartford | 102 | —26 | 43.00 | 53.1 | 9.0 | Oct. 15 | Sept. 27 | Apr. 22 | May 10 | 179 |
| Houston | 108 | 5 | 47.07 | 0.4 | 7.6 | Dec. 11 | Oct. 25 | Feb. 5 | Mar. 27 | 108 |
| Indianapolis | 107 | —25 | 39.98 | 21.3 | 9.7 | Oct. 22 | Sept. 27 | Apr. 23 | May 27 | 808 |
| Jackson | 107 | — 5 | 50.96 | 0.8 | 7.7 | Nov. 8 | Oct. 9 | Mar. 18 | Apr. 25 | 331 |
| Jacksonville | 105 | 10 | 51.75 | Trace | 8.6 | Dec. 16 | Nov. 3 | Feb. 6 | Mar. 31 | 31 |
| Juneau | 90 | —22 | 53.95 | 109.1 | 8.5 | Oct. 21 | Sept. 9 | Apr. 22 | June 8 | 24 |
| Kansas City, Mo. | 113 | —22 | 36.66 | 19.7 | 10.2 | Oct. 26 | Sept. 30 | Apr. 7 | May 6 | 1,025 |
| Little Rock | 110 | —13 | 48.17 | 5.3 | 8.2 | Nov. 15 | Oct. 23 | Mar. 16 | Apr. 13 | 265 |
| Los Angeles | 110 | 23 | 11.94 | Trace | 7.4 | — | Dec. 9 | — | Jan. 21 | 104 |
| Louisville | 107 | —20 | 42.94 | 17.3 | 8.4 | Oct. 25 | Oct. 15 | Apr. 10 | Apr. 19 | 488 |
| Memphis | 106 | —13 | 48.74 | 5.7 | 9.2 | Nov. 5 | Oct. 17 | Mar. 20 | Apr. 15 | 284 |
| Miami | 100 | 26 | 59.21 | — | 9.1 | — | — | — | Feb. 6 | 12 |
| Milwaukee | 105 | —25 | 30.18 | 45.2 | 11.8 | Oct. 23 | Sept. 20 | Apr. 25 | May 27 | 693 |
| Minneapolis-St. Paul | 108 | —34 | 26.62 | 45.8 | 10.6 | Oct. 13 | Sept. 3 | Apr. 29 | May 24 | 838 |
| Mobile | 104 | — 1 | 63.26 | 0.4 | 9.3 | Dec. 12 | Nov. 15 | Feb. 17 | Mar. 20 | 221 |
| Nashville | 107 | —15 | 46.61 | 10.9 | 7.9 | Oct. 31 | Oct. 7 | Apr. 3 | Apr. 24 | 605 |
| New Orleans | 102 | 7 | 58.93 | 0.2 | 8.4 | Dec. 3 | Nov. 11 | Feb. 15 | Apr. 8 | 30 |
| New York City | 106 | —15 | 43.56 | 29.1 | 9.4 | Nov. 12 | Oct. 19 | Apr. 7 | Apr. 24 | 87 |
| Norfolk | 105 | 2 | 45.22 | 7.2 | 10.6 | Nov. 21 | Nov. 7 | Mar. 22 | Apr. 14 | 30 |
| Oklahoma City | 113 | —17 | 31.71 | 9.2 | 12.9 | Nov. 7 | Oct. 7 | Apr. 1 | May 3 | 1,304 |
| Omaha | 114 | —32 | 28.48 | 32.5 | 10.9 | Oct. 20 | Sept. 24 | Apr. 14 | May 11 | 982 |
| Philadelphia | 106 | —11 | 41.18 | 20.3 | 9.6 | Nov. 17 | Oct. 19 | Mar. 30 | Apr. 20 | 28 |
| Phoenix | 118 | 16 | 7.41 | Trace | 6.1 | Dec. 11 | Nov. 4 | Jan. 27 | Mar. 3 | 1,107 |
| Pittsburgh | 103 | —20 | 36.21 | 45.5 | 9.4 | Oct. 20 | Oct. 10 | Apr. 21 | May 4 | 1,225 |
| Portland, Me. | 103 | —39 | 42.15 | 74.3 | 8.8 | Sept. 27 | Sept. 17 | May 12 | May 31 | 63 |
| Portland, Ore. | 107 | — 3 | 37.98 | 7.5 | 7.8 | Dec. 1 | Oct. 26 | Feb. 25 | May 4 | 39 |
| Providence | 104 | —17 | 40.90 | 37.8 | 10.8 | Oct. 26 | Oct. 3 | Apr. 14 | Apr. 24 | 62 |
| Reno | 106 | —19 | 7.65 | 26.8 | 6.4 | Oct. 2 | Aug. 30 | May 14 | June 25 | 4,400 |
| Richmond | 107 | —12 | 43.77 | 14.3 | 7.6 | Nov. 8 | Oct. 5 | Apr. 2 | May 11 | 177 |
| Sacramento | 115 | 17 | 17.33 | Trace | 8.3 | Dec. 11 | Nov. 4 | Jan. 24 | Mar. 14 | 25 |
| St. Louis | 115 | —23 | 36.70 | 17.8 | 9.5 | Oct. 20 | Sept. 28 | Apr. 15 | May 10 | 564 |
| Salt Lake City | 107 | —30 | 15.63 | 58.1 | 8.7 | Nov. 1 | Sept. 25 | Apr. 12 | Apr. 30 | 4,227 |
| San Francisco | 106 | 20 | 18.88 | Trace | 10.5 | — | Dec. 11 | — | Jan. 21 | 18 |
| Seattle | 100 | 0 | 40.30 | 15.2 | 9.3 | Dec. 1 | Oct. 19 | Feb. 23 | Apr. 3 | 450 |
| Spokane | 108 | —30 | 16.19 | 54.0 | 8.7 | Oct. 12 | Sept. 13 | Apr. 20 | May 16 | 2,365 |
| Washington, D.C. | 106 | —15 | 40.00 | 16.8 | 9.2 | Nov. 10 | Oct. 2 | Mar. 29 | May 12 | 65 |
| Wichita | 114 | —22 | 30.06 | 16.3 | 12.6 | Nov. 1 | Sept. 27 | Apr. 5 | Apr. 21 | 1,340 |
| Wilmington, Del. | 107 | —15 | 43.63 | 20.1 | 9.1 | Oct. 26 | Sept. 27 | Apr. 18 | May 9 | 80 |

## U.S. CITY WEATHER II

SOURCE: National Climatic Center (data based on normals for 1936-1975)

| City | AVERAGE MONTHLY TEMPERATURES (in °F) | | | | | | | | | | | | |
|---|---|---|---|---|---|---|---|---|---|---|---|---|---|
| | Jan. | Feb. | Mar. | April | May | June | July | Aug. | Sept. | Oct. | Nov. | Dec. | ANNUAL |
| Albany | 23.0° | 23.7° | 33.5° | 46.5° | 58.4° | 67.7° | 72.5° | 70.2° | 62.7° | 51.4° | 39.7° | 27.7° | 48.1° |
| Albuquerque | 34.5 | 39.5 | 46.3 | 54.8 | 63.8 | 73.3 | 77.1 | 75.1 | 68.4 | 56.8 | 43.9 | 35.1 | 55.7 |
| Atlanta | 43.5 | 45.6 | 52.6 | 61.3 | 69.6 | 76.4 | 78.5 | 77.8 | 73.1 | 62.9 | 52.0 | 44.7 | 61.5 |
| Baltimore | 33.2 | 35.0 | 42.6 | 53.6 | 63.1 | 72.1 | 76.8 | 75.3 | 68.5 | 57.3 | 46.0 | 36.4 | 55.0 |
| Birmingham | 45.6 | 47.1 | 55.0 | 62.9 | 70.7 | 77.8 | 79.9 | 79.6 | 75.2 | 64.6 | 53.4 | 46.3 | 63.2 |
| Bismarck | 8.1 | 12.2 | 25.3 | 42.9 | 54.6 | 64.1 | 70.6 | 68.5 | 57.9 | 45.7 | 28.6 | 15.4 | 41.1 |
| Boise | 29.9 | 35.5 | 42.3 | 49.6 | 57.8 | 65.4 | 74.5 | 72.5 | 62.7 | 52.3 | 40.6 | 32.1 | 51.3 |
| Boston | 28.9 | 29.1 | 36.9 | 46.9 | 57.7 | 67.0 | 72.6 | 70.7 | 64.0 | 54.2 | 43.5 | 32.6 | 50.3 |
| Buffalo | 25.1 | 24.5 | 32.3 | 43.3 | 54.6 | 64.7 | 70.3 | 68.9 | 62.6 | 51.8 | 40.0 | 29.5 | 47.3 |
| Burlington, Vt. | 18.0 | 18.4 | 29.3 | 42.6 | 55.2 | 64.8 | 69.7 | 67.3 | 59.6 | 48.8 | 36.6 | 23.3 | 44.5 |
| Charleston, W. Va. | 36.6 | 38.0 | 46.0 | 56.0 | 64.8 | 72.3 | 76.0 | 74.8 | 69.3 | 58.0 | 46.7 | 38.2 | 56.4 |
| Charlotte | 42.0 | 43.9 | 51.0 | 60.0 | 68.9 | 76.0 | 78.7 | 77.4 | 72.2 | 61.6 | 50.9 | 43.1 | 60.5 |
| Cheyenne | 26.1 | 27.7 | 32.4 | 41.4 | 51.0 | 61.0 | 67.7 | 66.4 | 57.3 | 46.4 | 35.2 | 28.6 | 45.1 |
| Chicago | 24.7 | 27.1 | 36.4 | 47.8 | 58.2 | 68.4 | 73.8 | 72.5 | 65.6 | 54.5 | 40.4 | 29.4 | 49.9 |
| Cincinnati | 30.8 | 33.6 | 41.7 | 53.5 | 63.3 | 71.9 | 75.5 | 74.2 | 67.3 | 56.3 | 43.6 | 34.4 | 53.9 |
| Cleveland | 27.5 | 27.8 | 35.9 | 47.0 | 58.3 | 67.9 | 72.2 | 70.6 | 64.6 | 53.8 | 41.6 | 31.3 | 49.9 |
| Columbia, S.C. | 46.6 | 48.1 | 55.1 | 63.5 | 71.9 | 78.5 | 80.8 | 79.9 | 75.1 | 64.5 | 54.4 | 47.2 | 63.8 |
| Columbus, Ohio | 29.4 | 30.8 | 40.0 | 51.1 | 61.9 | 70.9 | 74.8 | 72.9 | 66.6 | 55.0 | 42.3 | 32.4 | 52.3 |
| Concord, N.H. | 21.3 | 22.8 | 31.9 | 44.4 | 56.2 | 64.9 | 70.0 | 67.3 | 59.7 | 49.2 | 37.5 | 25.6 | 45.9 |
| Dallas-Ft. Worth, Tex. | 45.6 | 48.8 | 56.9 | 65.2 | 72.7 | 80.9 | 84.5 | 84.6 | 77.8 | 67.8 | 56.1 | 47.7 | 65.7 |
| Denver | 30.1 | 32.8 | 38.7 | 47.4 | 56.7 | 66.6 | 72.6 | 71.3 | 62.6 | 51.6 | 39.6 | 32.3 | 50.2 |
| Des Moines | 20.8 | 24.7 | 36.3 | 50.4 | 61.5 | 71.1 | 76.1 | 73.7 | 65.3 | 54.2 | 38.5 | 26.1 | 49.9 |
| Detroit | 25.3 | 25.8 | 34.5 | 46.7 | 58.1 | 68.2 | 73.0 | 71.1 | 64.2 | 53.1 | 40.1 | 29.5 | 49.2 |
| El Paso | 44.7 | 49.3 | 55.6 | 63.8 | 72.2 | 80.8 | 81.9 | 80.2 | 74.8 | 64.7 | 52.5 | 45.2 | 63.8 |
| Great Falls | 21.2 | 26.1 | 31.4 | 43.3 | 53.3 | 60.9 | 69.7 | 67.9 | 57.6 | 48.3 | 34.8 | 27.1 | 45.1 |
| Hartford | 27.1 | 27.7 | 36.9 | 47.9 | 59.0 | 67.9 | 73.1 | 70.9 | 63.7 | 53.3 | 42.1 | 30.4 | 50.0 |
| Houston | 53.2 | 54.6 | 62.0 | 67.9 | 74.3 | 79.8 | 82.4 | 81.3 | 77.5 | 70.2 | 59.6 | 55.5 | 68.2 |
| Indianapolis | 28.5 | 30.8 | 40.1 | 52.0 | 62.5 | 71.8 | 75.7 | 73.7 | 66.9 | 55.5 | 42.0 | 31.9 | 52.6 |
| Jackson | 48.4 | 50.9 | 57.3 | 65.3 | 72.6 | 79.6 | 81.8 | 81.5 | 76.9 | 66.5 | 55.7 | 49.5 | 65.5 |
| Jacksonville | 55.0 | 56.6 | 61.8 | 67.5 | 73.7 | 78.5 | 80.4 | 80.1 | 77.1 | 68.9 | 60.6 | 54.9 | 67.9 |
| Juneau | 22.2 | 27.3 | 31.2 | 38.4 | 46.4 | 52.8 | 55.5 | 54.1 | 49.0 | 41.5 | 32.0 | 26.9 | 39.8 |
| Kansas City, Mo. | 29.7 | 33.1 | 43.2 | 55.5 | 65.3 | 74.7 | 79.5 | 78.0 | 70.0 | 59.1 | 44.7 | 33.6 | 55.6 |
| Little Rock | 41.7 | 44.8 | 52.9 | 62.5 | 70.1 | 78.2 | 81.3 | 80.5 | 74.1 | 63.8 | 51.9 | 43.8 | 62.1 |
| Los Angeles | 54.6 | 55.9 | 56.9 | 59.3 | 62.1 | 64.9 | 68.3 | 69.5 | 68.5 | 65.2 | 60.4 | 56.4 | 61.8 |
| Louisville | 34.7 | 36.8 | 45.6 | 56.3 | 66.0 | 74.6 | 78.3 | 76.8 | 70.4 | 58.9 | 46.4 | 37.2 | 56.9 |
| Memphis | 41.3 | 44.1 | 52.2 | 62.1 | 70.5 | 78.2 | 81.2 | 80.0 | 74.1 | 63.5 | 51.6 | 43.6 | 61.9 |
| Miami | 67.5 | 68.0 | 71.3 | 74.9 | 78.0 | 80.9 | 82.2 | 82.7 | 81.6 | 77.8 | 72.3 | 68.5 | 75.5 |
| Milwaukee | 20.9 | 23.2 | 32.6 | 44.3 | 54.3 | 64.5 | 70.7 | 69.7 | 62.5 | 51.5 | 37.7 | 26.1 | 46.5 |
| Minneapolis-St. Paul | 13.2 | 16.7 | 29.6 | 45.7 | 57.9 | 67.8 | 73.1 | 70.7 | 61.5 | 50.0 | 33.0 | 19.5 | 44.9 |
| Mobile | 51.9 | 54.4 | 60.1 | 67.1 | 74.3 | 80.3 | 81.8 | 81.5 | 78.1 | 68.9 | 58.9 | 53.1 | 67.6 |
| Nashville | 39.1 | 41.0 | 49.5 | 59.5 | 68.2 | 76.3 | 79.4 | 78.3 | 72.2 | 61.1 | 48.9 | 41.1 | 59.6 |
| New Orleans | 54.3 | 56.5 | 61.7 | 68.9 | 75.4 | 80.8 | 82.2 | 82.0 | 78.8 | 70.7 | 60.7 | 55.6 | 69.0 |
| New York City | 32.3 | 32.7 | 40.6 | 51.1 | 61.9 | 70.9 | 76.1 | 74.6 | 68.0 | 58.0 | 46.7 | 35.7 | 54.1 |
| Norfolk | 41.6 | 42.3 | 48.8 | 57.4 | 66.7 | 74.7 | 78.6 | 77.5 | 72.4 | 62.2 | 52.1 | 43.6 | 59.8 |
| Oklahoma City | 37.2 | 40.8 | 49.8 | 60.2 | 68.2 | 77.0 | 81.4 | 81.1 | 73.7 | 62.7 | 49.4 | 39.9 | 60.1 |
| Omaha | 22.0 | 26.5 | 37.5 | 51.7 | 62.7 | 72.3 | 77.4 | 75.1 | 66.3 | 55.0 | 39.3 | 27.5 | 51.1 |
| Philadelphia | 33.1 | 33.8 | 41.6 | 52.2 | 63.0 | 71.8 | 76.6 | 74.7 | 68.4 | 57.5 | 46.2 | 36.2 | 54.6 |
| Phoenix | 51.6 | 55.4 | 60.5 | 67.7 | 76.0 | 85.2 | 90.8 | 89.0 | 83.6 | 71.7 | 59.8 | 52.4 | 70.3 |
| Pittsburgh | 30.7 | 31.3 | 39.9 | 51.1 | 62.0 | 70.6 | 74.6 | 72.8 | 66.6 | 55.2 | 43.2 | 33.6 | 52.7 |
| Portland, Me. | 22.4 | 23.4 | 32.3 | 42.8 | 53.2 | 62.4 | 68.2 | 66.6 | 59.6 | 49.6 | 38.6 | 26.9 | 45.5 |
| Portland, Ore. | 38.5 | 43.0 | 45.9 | 50.6 | 57.0 | 60.2 | 65.8 | 65.3 | 62.7 | 54.0 | 45.7 | 41.1 | 52.5 |
| Providence | 29.4 | 29.3 | 37.6 | 47.5 | 57.8 | 66.9 | 72.7 | 71.0 | 63.9 | 54.0 | 43.4 | 32.6 | 50.5 |
| Reno | 31.8 | 36.6 | 41.2 | 47.4 | 54.9 | 62.5 | 70.2 | 68.5 | 60.7 | 50.9 | 41.0 | 33.4 | 49.9 |
| Richmond | 38.0 | 39.4 | 46.9 | 56.9 | 66.1 | 74.0 | 77.6 | 76.1 | 69.9 | 58.9 | 48.7 | 39.7 | 57.7 |
| Sacramento | 44.9 | 49.8 | 53.1 | 58.1 | 64.5 | 70.8 | 75.4 | 74.3 | 71.6 | 63.4 | 52.9 | 45.7 | 60.4 |
| St. Louis | 31.7 | 34.8 | 44.3 | 56.1 | 65.9 | 75.1 | 79.3 | 77.5 | 70.1 | 59.0 | 45.3 | 35.3 | 56.2 |
| Salt Lake City | 28.0 | 33.2 | 40.7 | 49.0 | 58.3 | 68.1 | 77.2 | 75.4 | 65.1 | 53.1 | 40.5 | 31.4 | 51.7 |
| San Francisco | 48.0 | 50.9 | 52.9 | 54.6 | 57.3 | 60.3 | 61.5 | 62.0 | 62.9 | 60.0 | 54.3 | 49.3 | 56.2 |
| Seattle | 38.2 | 42.2 | 43.9 | 48.1 | 55.0 | 59.9 | 64.4 | 63.8 | 59.6 | 51.8 | 44.6 | 40.5 | 51.0 |
| Spokane | 26.8 | 31.7 | 39.4 | 47.6 | 55.8 | 62.5 | 70.2 | 68.7 | 59.5 | 48.7 | 37.0 | 30.4 | 48.2 |
| Washington, D.C. | 36.1 | 37.7 | 45.7 | 56.1 | 65.8 | 74.3 | 78.4 | 76.9 | 70.3 | 59.6 | 48.4 | 38.4 | 57.3 |
| Wichita | 31.6 | 35.2 | 44.7 | 56.3 | 65.4 | 75.3 | 80.3 | 79.3 | 70.9 | 59.6 | 45.2 | 35.0 | 56.5 |
| Wilmington, Del. | 32.6 | 33.1 | 41.9 | 52.2 | 62.7 | 71.4 | 76.0 | 74.1 | 67.9 | 56.8 | 45.7 | 35.2 | 54.2 |

## THE NATIONAL WEATHER SERVICE

Although people are critical of the weather forecaster's failures, they seldom generously acknowledge his successes. Employing a vast network of radar stations, professional and amateur weather observers, orbiting satellites, and other sources of data on a regular basis, the National Weather Service, a major program element of the National Oceanic and Atmospheric Administration (in the Department of Commerce) has the impressive record of 87% accurate rain predictions for the same day and 83% for the next. The national average of success in forecasting shows that today's and tonight's temperatures are correct within about 3½ degrees and tomorrow's to within about 4.2 degrees.

The National Weather Service employs about 5000 full-time people at 400 facilities within the 50 states and at 14 overseas stations. Its physical facilities are valued at approximately $75 million.

The National Meteorological Center receives the following observational reports daily: 20,000 synoptic and 29,000 hourly from surface observation; 3,000 synoptic from ships; 4,100 atmospheric soundings; 3,200 aircraft reports; and all available cloud and temperature data from weather satellites.

## HURRICANE NAMES: 1983

**Atlantic Ocean, Caribbean Sea, Gulf of Mexico**

Alicia, Barry, Chantal, Dean, Erin, Felix, Gabrielle, Hugo, Iris, Jerry, Karen, Luis, Marilyn, Noel, Opal, Pablo, Roxanne, Sebastien, Tanya, Van, Wendy.

**Eastern North Pacific**

Andres, Blanca, Carlos, Delores, Enrique, Fefa, Guillermo, Hilda, Ignacio, Jimena, Kevin, Linda, Marty, Nora, Olaf, Pauline, Rick, Sandra, Terry, Vivian, Waldo.

## METEOROLOGICAL GLOSSARY

**Anticyclone**—An area of high pressure from which air spirals in all directions, usually accompanied by good weather. Anticyclones circulate in a clockwise direction in the northern hemisphere and in a counterclockwise direction in the southern (as seen from above).

**Blizzard**—A fall of fine, powdery snow accompanied by low temperatures and strong winds, often with low visibility and large accumulations.

**Blizzard warning**—Considerable amounts of snow will fall, with winds of at least 35 mph and temperatures not higher than 20°F.

**Blowing snow**—Snow lifted from the ground by the wind enough to restrict visibility.

**Cold wave warning**—A rapid and dramatic drop in temperature during the following 24 hrs requiring substantially increased protection for agricultural, industrial, commercial and social activities.

**Convection**—Motion of air produced by thermal or mechanical instability in the atmosphere.

**Coriolis force**—The force, apparently resulting from the earth's rotation, that causes high-pressure weather systems to circulate in a clockwise direction in the northern hemisphere and in a counterclockwise direction in the southern.

**Cyclone**—A rotary, usually columnar or funnel-shaped atmospheric system having its lowest pressure at the center of a circulating mass of air and water vapor. Cyclones circulate in a counterclockwise direction in the northern hemisphere and in a clockwise direction in the southern (as seen from above).

**Drifting snow**—Snow blown into significant drifts by strong winds either during or after a snowfall.

**Eddy**—(Within a fluid mass) a circulation pattern independent of the surrounding fluid.

**Freezing drizzle**—A light freezing rain.

**Freezing rain**—Another name for an ice storm.

**Gale warning**—Winds of 38–55 mph may be expected, with attendant strong wave action at sea.

**Hail**—Precipitation in the form of ice (hailstones) formed by the accumulation of sub-freezing water on a growing ice particle either by repeated circulation aloft or by long descent through layers of super-cooled water in clouds.

**Hazardous driving (travelers') warning**—Falling, blowing, or drifting snow, freezing rain or drizzle, sleet or strong winds will make driving dangerous.

**Heavy snow warning**—A fall of four inches or more in a 12-hr period or of six inches or more in a 24-hr period.

**Hurricane**—A well-defined weather system with winds of more than 74 mph and pronounced rotary circulation at the surface.

**Hurricane warning**—Winds of 74 mph or more may be expected within 24 hrs or high water or high waves may endanger life and property.

**Hurricane watch**—A hurricane that is nearby may affect the area: prepare for action if a hurricane warning is issued.

**Ice storm**—A winter storm in which falling rain rapidly freezes on all surfaces, causing hazardous driving conditions.

**Inversion**—A meteorological system in which temperature increases with an increase in altitude, the reverse of a normal system at lower altitudes.

**Lightning**—A discharge of electricity between clouds or between clouds and the earth resulting from an equalization between positively and negatively charged masses.

**Livestock (stockmen's) warnings**—Livestock will require protection from snow or ice accumulations, from a rapid drop in temperature, or from strong winds.

**Neutercane**—A storm, similar to and formerly identified as a cyclone or tropical storm, observed by weather satellites in areas of the oceans where hurricanes do not usually occur.

**Ridge**—An elongated high-pressure atmospheric system.

**Seeding**—The sprinkling of crystals, usually of silver iodide, into clouds and tropical storm formations in order to induce sudden freezing of super-cooled water vapor with a resultant release of latent heat of fusion, raising of cloud temperatures, and attendant reduction in maximum wind speeds. In some experiments, the intention of seeding is to increase the height and volume of storm clouds, thus dissipating the storm's energy over a wider area.

**Severe blizzard warning**—Considerable amounts of snow will fall, with winds of at least 45 mph and temperature not higher than 10°F.

**Sleet storm**—A winter storm in which falling rain freezes before striking the surface, usually bouncing on the ground.

**Small-craft warning**—Wind and water action may threaten the safety of small boats, which are best advised to remain in or return to port.

**Snow flurries**—Intermittent light snow for short periods with minimal accumulations.

**Snow squalls**—Brief, heavy snowfalls accompanied by gusty winds.

**Storm warning**—Winds of 55–74 mph may be expected, with attendant dangerous wave action at sea.

**Thunder**—A sound produced when lightning suddenly heats the surrounding air and causes it to expand with explosive force.

**Thunderstorm**—An atmospheric disturbance of varying severity, often accompanied by rain and characteristically by lightning. Thunderstorms are caused by unstable thermal convection currents of air that carry water vapor aloft creating a chimney-like effect. Exchanges of heated and cooled air and water increase and accelerate the effect, with attendant formation of ice and snow at upper altitudes and precipitation as water on the ground.

**Tornado**—A violently rotating column of air, moving counterclockwise at an estimated 300 mph, descending from a thunderstorm cloud system in a characteristically funnel-shaped form.

**Tornado warning**—A tornado has been sighted and all are advised to seek shelter.

**Tornado watch**—Tornadoes are expected to develop.

**Tropical depression**—A weather system with winds of not more than 39 mph and some circulation at the surface.

**Tropical disturbance**—Ill-defined weather phenomenon without strong wind and little or no circulation, sometimes better developed at higher altitudes.

**Tropical storm**—A well-defined weather system with winds of 39–73 mph and strong circulation at the surface.

**Trough**—An elongated low-pressure atmospheric system.

**Waterspout**—A tornado over water, in which water vapor is sucked skyward in a funnel-shaped vortex.

**Wind-chill factor**—The combined effect of temperature and wind velocity as compared with equivalent temperature in calm air.

## NATIONAL OCEANIC AND ATMOSPHERIC ADMINISTRATION

The National Oceanic and Atmospheric Administration (NOAA) was formed on October 3, 1970, to explore, map and chart the ocean and its resources; to manage, use, and conserve those resources; and to describe, monitor, and predict conditions in all environments. It also is to issue warnings against impending destructive natural events while developing beneficial methods and assessing the consequences of environmental modification.

Among its principal functions and activities, NOAA reports the weather of the U.S. and provides weather forecasts to the general public, issues warning bulletins against destructive natural events, and provides services for such weather-sensitive activities as aviation, marine activities, and agriculture.

NOAA prepares and issues nautical and aeronautical charts and geodetic surveys. It conducts a broad range of research programs on the environment, including the use of satellites. The agency promotes wise and balanced management of the Nation's coastal zone, including the awarding of grants to states for their own development of their coastal zones. The agency also administers the Marine Mammal Protection Act of 1972.

The National Sea Grant program, which provides grants to institutions for marine research, education, and advisory services, is administered by the NOAA. It is also developing a system of data buoys for obtaining and disseminating marine environment data. Additionally, it tests and evaluates oceanographic instruments and maintains a national reference center for their specifications and characteristics.

## DAYLIGHT SAVING TIME

In enacting the Uniform Time Act of 1966 (amended in 1972), the Congress made the observance of advanced (daylight) time automatic throughout the country for the six-month period extending from the last Sunday of April to the last Sunday of October.

That law, however, allows a state which falls in one time zone to exempt itself as a whole, and a state which falls in more than one time zone to exempt itself as a whole, or only that part in the most easterly zone, from the observance of advanced time. In 1981, in addition to the territories, only Arizona, Hawaii and the eastern time zone of Indiana did not observe daylight saving time from April 26 to October 25.

Faced with the energy crisis in 1974, the U.S. government required the use of daylight saving time throughout the year and, as amended later in 1974, it was temporarily observed from January 6 to October 27, 1974, and from February 23 to October 26, 1975.

Time-zone boundaries in the United States have been defined—and from time to time relocated—since 1918 by the Interstate Commerce Commission and by the Department of Transportation beginning in 1967. Prior to 1966, however, a number of communities in the vicinity of the defined boundaries chose not to recognize them. When the Uniform Time Act became effective in 1967 those communities were confronted with a problem. With its automatic advanced (daylight) feature, the 1966 act required a far greater degree of nationwide recognition of the boundaries defined by DOT. The result has been active urging by state, local, and municipal governments, as well as hundreds of requests from private citizens, for the relocation of time zones boundaries.

## STANDARD TIME ZONES

**Time zone boundaries for the United States are defined by the Secretary of Transportation under the Standard Time Act (1918) as amended by the Uniform Time Act (1966). In the map below, reading from east to west, when it is 5:00 P.M. Atlantic Time (a zone that runs along the Maine-New Brunswick border, and includes Puerto Rico and the Virgin Islands in the Caribbean), it is 4:00 P.M. Eastern Time; 3:00 P.M. Central Time; 2:00 P.M. Mountain Time; 1:00 P.M. Pacific Time; 12 noon Yukon Time; 11:00 A.M. Alaska-Hawaii Time; and 10:00 A.M. Bering Time (which includes Nome and Western Alaska). Thus, there is a seven-hour time difference between Nome, Alaska, and San Juan, Puerto Rico.**

## LATITUDE AND LONGITUDE OF U.S. CITIES

Source: National Ocean Survey

| City and State | Lat. ° ′ | Long. ° ′ |
|---|---|---|
| Akron, Ohio | 41 05 | 81 31 |
| Albany, N.Y. | 42 39 | 73 45 |
| Albuquerque, N.M. | 35 05 | 106 39 |
| Allentown, Pa. | 40 36 | 75 28 |
| Amarillo, Tex. | 35 12 | 101 50 |
| Anchorage, Alaska | 61 12 | 149 48 |
| Ann Arbor, Mich. | 42 17 | 83 45 |
| Asheville, N.C. | 35 35 | 82 33 |
| Atlanta, Ga. | 33 45 | 84 24 |
| Augusta, Ga. | 33 28 | 81 58 |
| Austin, Tex. | 30 16 | 97 45 |
| Baltimore, Md. | 39 17 | 76 37 |
| Bangor, Me. | 44 48 | 68 46 |
| Baton Rouge, La. | 30 27 | 91 11 |
| Biloxi, Miss. | 30 23 | 88 53 |
| Birmingham, Ala. | 33 31 | 86 49 |
| Bismarck, N.D. | 46 48 | 100 47 |
| Boise, Idaho | 43 37 | 116 12 |
| Boston, Mass. | 42 21 | 71 03 |
| Brattleboro, Vt. | 42 51 | 72 33 |
| Bridgeport, Conn. | 41 11 | 73 11 |
| Buffalo, N.Y. | 42 52 | 78 52 |
| Butte, Mont. | 46 01 | 112 32 |
| Casper, Wyo. | 42 51 | 106 19 |
| Charleston, S.C. | 32 47 | 79 56 |
| Charlotte, N.C. | 35 14 | 80 51 |
| Chattanooga, Tenn. | 35 03 | 85 19 |
| Cheyenne, Wyo. | 41 08 | 104 49 |
| Chicago, Ill. | 41 52 | 87 38 |
| Cincinnati, Ohio | 39 06 | 84 31 |
| Cleveland, Ohio | 41 30 | 81 42 |
| Columbus, Ohio | 39 58 | 83 00 |
| Concord, N.H. | 43 12 | 71 32 |
| Dallas, Tex. | 32 47 | 96 48 |
| Dayton, Ohio | 39 45 | 84 11 |
| Daytona Beach, Fla. | 29 12 | 81 01 |
| Denver, Colo. | 39 45 | 104 59 |
| Des Moines, Iowa | 41 35 | 93 37 |
| Detroit, Mich. | 42 20 | 83 03 |
| Dubuque, Iowa | 42 30 | 90 40 |
| Duluth, Minn. | 46 47 | 92 06 |
| Durham, N.C. | 36 00 | 78 54 |
| El Paso, Tex. | 31 46 | 106 29 |
| Eugene, Ore. | 44 03 | 123 05 |
| Fairbanks, Alaska | 64 48 | 147 51 |
| Fargo, N.D. | 46 53 | 96 47 |
| Flagstaff, Ariz. | 35 11 | 111 39 |
| Fort Wayne, Ind. | 41 04 | 85 08 |
| Fort Worth, Tex. | 32 45 | 97 20 |
| Gainesville, Fla. | 29 39 | 82 19 |
| Galveston, Tex. | 29 18 | 94 48 |
| Gary, Ind. | 41 36 | 87 20 |
| Grand Rapids, Mich. | 42 58 | 85 40 |
| Green Bay, Wisc. | 44 30 | 88 00 |
| Greenville, S.C. | 34 50 | 82 24 |
| Harrisburg, Pa. | 40 15 | 76 52 |
| Hartford, Conn. | 41 46 | 72 40 |
| Honolulu, Hawaii | 21 20 | 158 00 |
| Houston, Tex. | 29 45 | 95 22 |
| Indianapolis, Ind. | 39 46 | 86 10 |
| Iowa City, Iowa | 41 39 | 91 31 |
| Jacksonville, Fla. | 30 19 | 81 39 |
| Joplin, Mo. | 37 05 | 94 30 |
| Juneau, Alaska | 58 18 | 134 24 |
| Kalamazoo, Mich. | 42 17 | 85 35 |
| Kansas City, Mo. | 39 05 | 94 35 |
| Knoxville, Tenn. | 35 58 | 83 55 |
| Lancaster, Pa. | 40 02 | 76 18 |
| Las Vegas, Nev. | 36 10 | 115 09 |
| Lincoln, Nebr. | 40 49 | 96 42 |
| Little Rock, Ark. | 34 45 | 92 17 |
| Los Angeles, Calif. | 34 03 | 118 14 |
| Louisville, Ky. | 38 14 | 85 45 |
| Macon, Ga. | 32 50 | 83 37 |
| Madison, Wisc. | 43 04 | 89 23 |
| Memphis, Tenn. | 35 09 | 90 03 |
| Miami, Fla. | 25 47 | 80 12 |
| Milwaukee, Wisc. | 43 02 | 87 54 |
| Minneapolis, Minn. | 44 59 | 93 16 |
| Mobile, Ala. | 30 42 | 88 03 |
| Montgomery, Ala. | 32 23 | 86 19 |
| Montpelier, Vt. | 44 16 | 72 35 |
| Nashville, Tenn. | 36 10 | 86 47 |
| Newark, N.J. | 40 44 | 74 10 |
| New Haven, Conn. | 41 18 | 72 55 |
| New Orleans, La. | 29 57 | 90 04 |
| New York, N.Y. | 40 45 | 74 00 |
| Niagara Falls, N.Y. | 43 05 | 79 03 |
| Nome, Alaska | 64 30 | 165 25 |
| Norfolk, Va. | 36 51 | 76 17 |
| Oakland, Calif. | 37 48 | 122 16 |
| Oklahoma City, Okla. | 35 28 | 97 31 |
| Omaha, Nebr. | 41 16 | 95 56 |
| Peoria, Ill. | 40 41 | 89 35 |
| Philadelphia, Pa. | 39 57 | 75 09 |
| Phoenix, Ariz. | 33 27 | 112 04 |
| Pittsburgh, Pa. | 40 26 | 80 00 |
| Pocatello, Idaho | 42 52 | 112 27 |
| Portland, Me. | 43 39 | 70 15 |
| Portland, Ore. | 45 31 | 122 41 |
| Providence, R.I. | 41 50 | 71 25 |
| Provo, Utah | 40 14 | 111 39 |
| Reno, Nev. | 39 31 | 119 48 |
| Richmond, Va. | 37 32 | 77 26 |
| Rochester, N.Y. | 43 09 | 77 36 |
| St. Louis, Mo. | 38 38 | 90 12 |
| Salt Lake City, Utah | 40 45 | 111 53 |
| San Francisco, Calif. | 37 47 | 122 25 |
| Santa Fe, N.M. | 35 41 | 105 56 |
| Savannah, Ga. | 32 04 | 81 05 |
| Seattle, Wash. | 47 37 | 122 20 |
| Shreveport, La. | 32 30 | 93 44 |
| Sioux Falls, S.D. | 43 32 | 96 43 |
| Syracuse, N.Y. | 43 03 | 76 09 |
| Tallahassee, Fla. | 30 26 | 84 16 |
| Texarkana, Tex. | 33 25 | 94 02 |
| Topeka, Kans. | 39 03 | 95 40 |
| Tulsa, Okla. | 36 09 | 96 00 |
| Tucson, Ariz. | 32 13 | 110 58 |
| Utica, N.Y. | 43 07 | 75 13 |
| Washington, D.C. | 38 54 | 77 01 |
| Wichita, Kans. | 37 41 | 97 20 |
| Wilmington, Del. | 39 45 | 75 33 |

## SUNRISE AND SUNSET: 1983

Source: U.S. Naval Observatory

Note: To determine Daylight Saving Time, add one hour to all times; e.g., sunrise at 20° latitude on January 2 is 7:35 D.S.T.

To determine sunrise or sunset for any location, follow these directions:

(1) From the table directly above, determine the latitude and longitude of the city closest to you;

(2) From the tables below, read the sunrise or sunset time for the desired date at the correct latitude (given in degrees at the top of the table);

(3) Determine your time zone:

(a) Eastern Time Zone: If longitude is less than 75°, subtract four minutes from the time on the table for each degree. If it is greater than 75°, add four minutes for each degree.

(b) Central Time Zone: If longitude is less than 90°, subtract four minutes from the time on the table for each degree. If it is greater, add four minutes for each degree.

(c) Rocky Mountain Time: If longitude is less than 105°, subtract four minutes from the time on the table for each degree. If it is greater, add four minutes for each degree.

(d) Pacific Time: If longitude is less than 120°, subtract four minutes from the time on the table for each degree. If it is greater, add four minutes for each degree.

**SUNRISE (UPPER LIMB)**

| Date | | +20° h m | +30° h m | +35° h m | +40° h m | +46° h m | +50° h m |
|---|---|---|---|---|---|---|---|
| Jan. | −2 | 6 34 | 6 55 | 7 07 | 7 21 | 7 42 | 7 59 |
| | 2 | 6 35 | 6 56 | 7 08 | 7 22 | 7 42 | 7 59 |
| | 6 | 6 36 | 6 57 | 7 09 | 7 22 | 7 42 | 7 58 |
| | 10 | 6 37 | 6 57 | 7 09 | 7 22 | 7 41 | 7 56 |
| | 14 | 6 38 | 6 57 | 7 08 | 7 21 | 7 39 | 7 54 |
| | 18 | 6 38 | 6 56 | 7 07 | 7 19 | 7 37 | 7 51 |
| | 22 | 6 38 | 6 55 | 7 05 | 7 17 | 7 33 | 7 47 |
| | 26 | 6 37 | 6 54 | 7 03 | 7 14 | 7 30 | 7 42 |
| | 30 | 6 36 | 6 52 | 7 01 | 7 11 | 7 26 | 7 37 |
| Feb. | 3 | 6 35 | 6 50 | 6 58 | 7 07 | 7 21 | 7 32 |
| | 7 | 6 34 | 6 47 | 6 55 | 7 03 | 7 16 | 7 25 |
| | 11 | 6 32 | 6 44 | 6 51 | 6 59 | 7 10 | 7 19 |
| | 15 | 6 30 | 6 41 | 6 47 | 6 54 | 7 04 | 7 12 |
| | 19 | 6 27 | 6 37 | 6 42 | 6 49 | 6 57 | 7 04 |
| | 23 | 6 25 | 6 33 | 6 38 | 6 43 | 6 51 | 6 57 |
| | 27 | 6 22 | 6 29 | 6 33 | 6 37 | 6 44 | 6 49 |
| Mar. | 3 | 6 19 | 6 25 | 6 28 | 6 31 | 6 37 | 6 41 |
| | 7 | 6 16 | 6 20 | 6 23 | 6 25 | 6 29 | 6 32 |
| | 11 | 6 12 | 6 15 | 6 17 | 6 19 | 6 22 | 6 24 |
| | 15 | 6 09 | 6 11 | 6 12 | 6 13 | 6 14 | 6 15 |
| | 19 | 6 06 | 6 06 | 6 06 | 6 06 | 6 06 | 6 06 |
| | 23 | 6 02 | 6 01 | 6 00 | 6 00 | 5 59 | 5 58 |
| | 27 | 5 59 | 5 56 | 5 55 | 5 53 | 5 51 | 5 49 |
| | 31 | 5 55 | 5 51 | 5 49 | 5 47 | 5 43 | 5 40 |
| Apr. | 4 | 5 52 | 5 47 | 5 44 | 5 40 | 5 36 | 5 32 |
| | 8 | 5 48 | 5 42 | 5 38 | 5 34 | 5 28 | 5 23 |
| | 12 | 5 45 | 5 37 | 5 33 | 5 28 | 5 21 | 5 15 |
| | 16 | 5 42 | 5 33 | 5 28 | 5 22 | 5 13 | 5 06 |
| | 20 | 5 39 | 5 29 | 5 23 | 5 16 | 5 06 | 4 58 |
| | 24 | 5 36 | 5 24 | 5 18 | 5 10 | 4 59 | 4 51 |
| | 28 | 5 33 | 5 21 | 5 13 | 5 05 | 4 53 | 4 43 |
| May | 2 | 5 31 | 5 17 | 5 09 | 5 00 | 4 46 | 4 36 |
| | 6 | 5 28 | 5 13 | 5 05 | 4 55 | 4 41 | 4 29 |
| | 10 | 5 26 | 5 10 | 5 01 | 4 50 | 4 35 | 4 22 |
| | 14 | 5 25 | 5 08 | 4 58 | 4 46 | 4 30 | 4 16 |
| | 18 | 5 23 | 5 05 | 4 55 | 4 43 | 4 25 | 4 11 |
| | 22 | 5 22 | 5 03 | 4 52 | 4 39 | 4 21 | 4 06 |
| | 26 | 5 21 | 5 01 | 4 50 | 4 37 | 4 17 | 4 02 |
| | 30 | 5 20 | 5 00 | 4 48 | 4 34 | 4 14 | 3 58 |
| June | 3 | 5 20 | 4 59 | 4 47 | 4 33 | 4 12 | 3 55 |
| | 7 | 5 20 | 4 58 | 4 46 | 4 31 | 4 10 | 3 53 |

SUNRISE (UPPER LIMB)

| Date | | +20° | +30° | +35° | +40° | +46° | +50° |
|---|---|---|---|---|---|---|---|
| | | h m | h m | h m | h m | h m | h m |
| June | 11 | 5 20 | 4 58 | 4 45 | 4 31 | 4 09 | 3 51 |
| | 15 | 5 20 | 4 58 | 4 45 | 4 30 | 4 09 | 3 50 |
| | 19 | 5 21 | 4 59 | 4 46 | 4 31 | 4 09 | 3 50 |
| | 23 | 5 22 | 5 00 | 4 47 | 4 32 | 4 09 | 3 51 |
| | 27 | 5 23 | 5 01 | 4 48 | 4 33 | 4 11 | 3 52 |
| July | 1 | 5 24 | 5 02 | 4 49 | 4 34 | 4 13 | 3 54 |
| | 5 | 5 25 | 5 04 | 4 51 | 4 37 | 4 15 | 3 57 |
| | 9 | 5 27 | 5 06 | 4 53 | 4 39 | 4 18 | 4 01 |
| | 13 | 5 28 | 5 08 | 4 56 | 4 42 | 4 21 | 4 05 |
| | 17 | 5 30 | 5 10 | 4 58 | 4 45 | 4 25 | 4 09 |
| | 21 | 5 31 | 5 12 | 5 01 | 4 48 | 4 29 | 4 14 |
| | 25 | 5 33 | 5 14 | 5 04 | 4 51 | 4 33 | 4 19 |
| | 29 | 5 34 | 5 17 | 5 07 | 4 55 | 4 38 | 4 24 |
| Aug. | 2 | 5 35 | 5 19 | 5 10 | 4 59 | 4 43 | 4 30 |
| | 6 | 5 37 | 5 22 | 5 13 | 5 02 | 4 47 | 4 35 |
| | 10 | 5 38 | 5 24 | 5 16 | 5 06 | 4 52 | 4 41 |
| | 14 | 5 39 | 5 26 | 5 19 | 5 10 | 4 57 | 4 47 |
| | 18 | 5 41 | 5 29 | 5 22 | 5 14 | 5 02 | 4 53 |
| | 22 | 5 42 | 5 31 | 5 25 | 5 18 | 5 07 | 4 59 |
| | 26 | 5 43 | 5 33 | 5 28 | 5 21 | 5 12 | 5 05 |
| | 30 | 5 44 | 5 35 | 5 31 | 5 25 | 5 17 | 5 11 |
| Sept. | 3 | 5 45 | 5 38 | 5 34 | 5 29 | 5 22 | 5 17 |
| | 7 | 5 45 | 5 40 | 5 36 | 5 33 | 5 27 | 5 23 |
| | 11 | 5 46 | 5 42 | 5 39 | 5 36 | 5 32 | 5 29 |
| | 15 | 5 47 | 5 44 | 5 42 | 5 40 | 5 37 | 5 35 |
| | 19 | 5 48 | 5 46 | 5 45 | 5 44 | 5 42 | 5 41 |
| | 23 | 5 49 | 5 48 | 5 48 | 5 48 | 5 47 | 5 47 |

| Date | | +20° | +30° | +35° | +40° | +46° | +50° |
|---|---|---|---|---|---|---|---|
| | | h m | h m | h m | h m | h m | h m |
| Sept. | 27 | 5 50 | 5 51 | 5 51 | 5 52 | 5 52 | 5 53 |
| Oct. | 1 | 5 51 | 5 53 | 5 54 | 5 56 | 5 57 | 5 59 |
| | 5 | 5 52 | 5 55 | 5 57 | 5 59 | 6 03 | 6 05 |
| | 9 | 5 53 | 5 58 | 6 00 | 6 04 | 6 08 | 6 11 |
| | 13 | 5 54 | 6 00 | 6 04 | 6 08 | 6 13 | 6 18 |
| | 17 | 5 55 | 6 03 | 6 07 | 6 12 | 6 19 | 6 24 |
| | 21 | 5 57 | 6 05 | 6 10 | 6 16 | 6 24 | 6 30 |
| | 25 | 5 58 | 6 08 | 6 14 | 6 20 | 6 30 | 6 37 |
| | 29 | 6 00 | 6 11 | 6 18 | 6 25 | 6 35 | 6 44 |
| Nov. | 2 | 6 02 | 6 14 | 6 21 | 6 29 | 6 41 | 6 50 |
| | 6 | 6 04 | 6 17 | 6 25 | 6 34 | 6 47 | 6 57 |
| | 10 | 6 06 | 6 20 | 6 29 | 6 39 | 6 52 | 7 04 |
| | 14 | 6 08 | 6 24 | 6 33 | 6 43 | 6 58 | 7 10 |
| | 18 | 6 10 | 6 27 | 6 37 | 6 48 | 7 04 | 7 17 |
| | 22 | 6 13 | 6 30 | 6 41 | 6 52 | 7 09 | 7 23 |
| | 26 | 6 15 | 6 34 | 6 44 | 6 57 | 7 14 | 7 29 |
| | 30 | 6 18 | 6 37 | 6 48 | 7 01 | 7 19 | 7 35 |
| Dec. | 4 | 6 20 | 6 40 | 6 52 | 7 05 | 7 24 | 7 40 |
| | 8 | 6 23 | 6 43 | 6 55 | 7 09 | 7 28 | 7 45 |
| | 12 | 6 25 | 6 46 | 6 58 | 7 12 | 7 32 | 7 49 |
| | 16 | 6 27 | 6 49 | 7 01 | 7 15 | 7 35 | 7 52 |
| | 20 | 6 30 | 6 51 | 7 03 | 7 17 | 7 38 | 7 55 |
| | 24 | 6 32 | 6 53 | 7 05 | 7 19 | 7 40 | 7 57 |
| | 28 | 6 33 | 6 55 | 7 07 | 7 21 | 7 41 | 7 58 |
| | 32 | 6 35 | 6 56 | 7 08 | 7 22 | 7 42 | 7 59 |
| | 36 | 6 36 | 6 57 | 7 09 | 7 22 | 7 42 | 7 58 |

SUNSET (UPPER LIMB)

| Date | | +20° | +30° | +35° | +40° | +46° | +50° |
|---|---|---|---|---|---|---|---|
| | | h m | h m | h m | h m | h m | h m |
| Jan. | −2 | 17 30 | 17 09 | 16 57 | 16 43 | 16 22 | 16 06 |
| | 2 | 17 32 | 17 12 | 17 00 | 16 46 | 16 26 | 16 09 |
| | 6 | 17 35 | 17 15 | 17 03 | 16 49 | 16 30 | 16 14 |
| | 10 | 17 38 | 17 18 | 17 06 | 16 53 | 16 34 | 16 19 |
| | 14 | 17 40 | 17 21 | 17 10 | 16 57 | 16 39 | 16 24 |
| | 18 | 17 43 | 17 25 | 17 14 | 17 02 | 16 45 | 16 30 |
| | 22 | 17 45 | 17 28 | 17 18 | 17 07 | 16 50 | 16 37 |
| | 26 | 17 48 | 17 32 | 17 22 | 17 11 | 16 56 | 16 43 |
| | 30 | 17 50 | 17 35 | 17 26 | 17 16 | 17 02 | 16 50 |
| Feb. | 3 | 17 53 | 17 38 | 17 30 | 17 21 | 17 07 | 16 57 |
| | 7 | 17 55 | 17 42 | 17 34 | 17 26 | 17 13 | 17 04 |
| | 11 | 17 57 | 17 45 | 17 38 | 17 30 | 17 19 | 17 10 |
| | 15 | 17 59 | 17 48 | 17 42 | 17 35 | 17 25 | 17 17 |
| | 19 | 18 01 | 17 51 | 17 46 | 17 40 | 17 31 | 17 24 |
| | 23 | 18 03 | 17 54 | 17 50 | 17 44 | 17 37 | 17 31 |
| | 27 | 18 04 | 17 57 | 17 53 | 17 49 | 17 43 | 17 38 |
| Mar. | 3 | 18 06 | 18 00 | 17 57 | 17 53 | 17 48 | 17 44 |
| | 7 | 18 07 | 18 03 | 18 00 | 17 58 | 17 54 | 17 51 |
| | 11 | 18 08 | 18 05 | 18 04 | 18 02 | 17 59 | 17 58 |
| | 15 | 18 09 | 18 08 | 18 07 | 18 06 | 18 05 | 18 04 |
| | 19 | 18 11 | 18 10 | 18 10 | 18 10 | 18 10 | 18 10 |
| | 23 | 18 12 | 18 13 | 18 14 | 18 14 | 18 16 | 18 17 |
| | 27 | 18 13 | 18 15 | 18 17 | 18 19 | 18 21 | 18 23 |
| | 31 | 18 14 | 18 18 | 18 20 | 18 23 | 18 26 | 18 29 |
| Apr. | 4 | 18 15 | 18 20 | 18 23 | 18 27 | 18 32 | 18 36 |
| | 8 | 18 16 | 18 23 | 18 26 | 18 31 | 18 37 | 18 42 |
| | 12 | 18 17 | 18 25 | 18 30 | 18 35 | 18 42 | 18 48 |
| | 16 | 18 18 | 18 27 | 18 33 | 18 39 | 18 47 | 18 54 |
| | 20 | 18 20 | 18 30 | 18 36 | 18 43 | 18 53 | 19 01 |
| | 24 | 18 21 | 18 32 | 18 39 | 18 47 | 18 58 | 19 07 |
| | 28 | 18 22 | 18 35 | 18 42 | 18 51 | 19 03 | 19 13 |
| May | 2 | 18 24 | 18 38 | 18 46 | 18 55 | 19 08 | 19 19 |
| | 6 | 18 25 | 18 40 | 18 49 | 18 59 | 19 14 | 19 25 |
| | 10 | 18 27 | 18 43 | 18 52 | 19 03 | 19 19 | 19 31 |
| | 14 | 18 28 | 18 45 | 18 55 | 19 07 | 19 23 | 19 37 |
| | 18 | 18 30 | 18 48 | 18 58 | 19 11 | 19 28 | 19 43 |
| | 22 | 18 32 | 18 50 | 19 01 | 19 14 | 19 33 | 19 48 |
| | 26 | 18 33 | 18 53 | 19 04 | 19 18 | 19 37 | 19 53 |
| | 30 | 18 35 | 18 55 | 19 07 | 19 21 | 19 41 | 19 58 |
| June | 3 | 18 36 | 18 57 | 19 09 | 19 24 | 19 44 | 20 02 |
| | 7 | 18 38 | 18 59 | 19 12 | 19 26 | 19 48 | 20 05 |
| | 11 | 18 39 | 19 01 | 19 14 | 19 28 | 19 50 | 20 08 |
| | 15 | 18 40 | 19 02 | 19 15 | 19 30 | 19 52 | 20 11 |
| | 19 | 18 41 | 19 04 | 19 17 | 19 32 | 19 54 | 20 12 |
| | 23 | 18 42 | 19 04 | 19 17 | 19 33 | 19 55 | 20 13 |
| | 27 | 18 43 | 19 05 | 19 18 | 19 33 | 19 55 | 20 13 |
| July | 1 | 18 43 | 19 05 | 19 18 | 19 33 | 19 54 | 20 13 |

| Date | | +20° | +30° | +35° | +40° | +46° | +50° |
|---|---|---|---|---|---|---|---|
| | | h m | h m | h m | h m | h m | h m |
| July | 5 | 18 44 | 19 05 | 19 18 | 19 32 | 19 53 | 20 11 |
| | 9 | 18 43 | 19 04 | 19 17 | 19 31 | 19 52 | 20 09 |
| | 13 | 18 43 | 19 03 | 19 15 | 19 29 | 19 49 | 20 06 |
| | 17 | 18 42 | 19 02 | 19 14 | 19 27 | 19 46 | 20 02 |
| | 21 | 18 41 | 19 00 | 19 11 | 19 24 | 19 43 | 19 58 |
| | 25 | 18 40 | 18 58 | 19 09 | 19 21 | 19 39 | 19 53 |
| | 29 | 18 39 | 18 56 | 19 06 | 19 17 | 19 34 | 19 48 |
| Aug. | 2 | 18 37 | 18 53 | 19 02 | 19 13 | 19 29 | 19 42 |
| | 6 | 18 35 | 18 50 | 18 59 | 19 09 | 19 24 | 19 35 |
| | 10 | 18 32 | 18 46 | 18 55 | 19 04 | 19 18 | 19 29 |
| | 14 | 18 30 | 18 43 | 18 50 | 18 59 | 19 11 | 19 21 |
| | 18 | 18 27 | 18 39 | 18 46 | 18 53 | 19 05 | 19 14 |
| | 22 | 18 24 | 18 35 | 18 41 | 18 48 | 18 58 | 19 06 |
| | 26 | 18 21 | 18 30 | 18 36 | 18 42 | 18 51 | 18 58 |
| | 30 | 18 18 | 18 26 | 18 30 | 18 36 | 18 43 | 18 50 |
| Sept. | 3 | 18 14 | 18 21 | 18 25 | 18 29 | 18 36 | 18 41 |
| | 7 | 18 11 | 18 16 | 18 19 | 18 23 | 18 28 | 18 32 |
| | 11 | 18 07 | 18 11 | 18 14 | 18 16 | 18 21 | 18 24 |
| | 15 | 18 03 | 18 06 | 18 08 | 18 10 | 18 13 | 18 15 |
| | 19 | 18 00 | 18 01 | 18 02 | 18 03 | 18 05 | 18 06 |
| | 23 | 17 56 | 17 56 | 17 56 | 17 57 | 17 57 | 17 57 |
| | 27 | 17 52 | 17 51 | 17 51 | 17 50 | 17 49 | 17 49 |
| Oct. | 1 | 17 49 | 17 46 | 17 45 | 17 43 | 17 41 | 17 40 |
| | 5 | 17 45 | 17 41 | 17 39 | 17 37 | 17 34 | 17 31 |
| | 9 | 17 42 | 17 37 | 17 34 | 17 31 | 17 26 | 17 23 |
| | 13 | 17 39 | 17 32 | 17 29 | 17 25 | 17 19 | 17 14 |
| | 17 | 17 35 | 17 28 | 17 23 | 17 19 | 17 12 | 17 06 |
| | 21 | 17 33 | 17 24 | 17 19 | 17 13 | 17 05 | 16 58 |
| | 25 | 17 30 | 17 20 | 17 14 | 17 07 | 16 58 | 16 51 |
| | 29 | 17 27 | 17 16 | 17 09 | 17 02 | 16 52 | 16 43 |
| Nov. | 2 | 17 25 | 17 12 | 17 05 | 16 57 | 16 46 | 16 35 |
| | 6 | 17 23 | 17 10 | 17 02 | 16 53 | 16 40 | 16 30 |
| | 10 | 17 22 | 17 07 | 16 58 | 16 49 | 16 35 | 16 24 |
| | 14 | 17 21 | 17 05 | 16 56 | 16 45 | 16 30 | 16 18 |
| | 18 | 17 20 | 17 03 | 16 53 | 16 42 | 16 26 | 16 13 |
| | 22 | 17 19 | 17 01 | 16 51 | 16 39 | 16 22 | 16 09 |
| | 26 | 17 19 | 17 00 | 16 50 | 16 37 | 16 20 | 16 05 |
| | 30 | 17 19 | 17 00 | 16 49 | 16 36 | 16 17 | 16 02 |
| Dec. | 4 | 17 20 | 17 00 | 16 48 | 16 35 | 16 16 | 16 00 |
| | 8 | 17 21 | 17 00 | 16 48 | 16 35 | 16 15 | 15 59 |
| | 12 | 17 22 | 17 01 | 16 49 | 16 35 | 16 15 | 15 58 |
| | 16 | 17 23 | 17 02 | 16 50 | 16 36 | 16 15 | 15 58 |
| | 20 | 17 25 | 17 04 | 16 51 | 16 37 | 16 17 | 16 00 |
| | 24 | 17 27 | 17 06 | 16 53 | 16 39 | 16 19 | 16 02 |
| | 28 | 17 29 | 17 08 | 16 56 | 16 42 | 16 21 | 16 04 |
| | 32 | 17 32 | 17 11 | 16 59 | 16 45 | 16 25 | 16 08 |
| | 36 | 17 34 | 17 14 | 17 02 | 16 48 | 16 29 | 16 12 |

**CALENDARS: 1801-2030** Select the desired year from the table below. The number shown with each year tells you the calendar to use for that year.

| | | | | |
|---|---|---|---|---|
| 1801...5 | 1847...6 | 1893...1 | 1939...1 | 1985...3 |
| 1802...6 | 1848..14 | 1894...2 | 1940...9 | 1986...4 |
| 1803...7 | 1849...2 | 1895...3 | 1941...4 | 1987...5 |
| 1804...8 | 1850...3 | 1896..11 | 1942...5 | 1988..13 |
| 1805...3 | 1851...4 | 1897...6 | 1943...6 | 1989...1 |
| 1806...4 | 1852..12 | 1898...7 | 1944..14 | 1990...2 |
| 1807...5 | 1853...7 | 1899...1 | 1945...2 | 1991...3 |
| 1808..13 | 1854...1 | 1900...2 | 1946...3 | 1992..11 |
| 1809...1 | 1855...2 | 1901...3 | 1947...4 | 1993...6 |
| 1810...2 | 1856..10 | 1902...4 | 1948..12 | 1994...7 |
| 1811...3 | 1857...5 | 1903...5 | 1949...7 | 1995...1 |
| 1812..11 | 1858...6 | 1904..13 | 1950...1 | 1996...9 |
| 1813...6 | 1859...7 | 1905...1 | 1951...2 | 1997...4 |
| 1814...7 | 1860...8 | 1906...2 | 1952..10 | 1998...5 |
| 1815...1 | 1861...3 | 1907...3 | 1953...5 | 1999...6 |
| 1816...9 | 1862...4 | 1908..11 | 1954...6 | 2000..14 |
| 1817...4 | 1863...5 | 1909...6 | 1955...7 | 2001...2 |
| 1818...5 | 1864..13 | 1910...7 | 1956...8 | 2002...3 |
| 1819...6 | 1865...1 | 1911...1 | 1957...3 | 2003...4 |
| 1820..14 | 1866...2 | 1912...9 | 1958...4 | 2004..12 |
| 1821...2 | 1867...3 | 1913...4 | 1959...5 | 2005...7 |
| 1822...3 | 1868..11 | 1914...5 | 1960..13 | 2006...1 |
| 1823...4 | 1869...6 | 1915...6 | 1961...1 | 2007...2 |
| 1824..12 | 1870...7 | 1916..14 | 1962...2 | 2008..10 |
| 1825...7 | 1871...1 | 1917...2 | 1963...3 | 2009...5 |
| 1826...1 | 1872...9 | 1918...3 | 1964..11 | 2010...6 |
| 1827...2 | 1873...4 | 1919...4 | 1965...6 | 2011...7 |
| 1828..10 | 1874...5 | 1920..12 | 1966...7 | 2012...8 |
| 1829...5 | 1875...6 | 1921...7 | 1967...1 | 2013...3 |
| 1830...6 | 1876..14 | 1922...1 | 1968...9 | 2014...4 |
| 1831...7 | 1877...2 | 1923...2 | 1969...4 | 2015...5 |
| 1832...8 | 1878...3 | 1924..10 | 1970...5 | 2016..13 |
| 1833...3 | 1879...4 | 1925...5 | 1971...6 | 2017...1 |
| 1834...4 | 1880..12 | 1926...6 | 1972..14 | 2018...2 |
| 1835...5 | 1881...7 | 1927...7 | 1973...2 | 2019...3 |
| 1836..13 | 1882...1 | 1928...8 | 1974...3 | 2020..11 |
| 1837...1 | 1883...2 | 1929...3 | 1975...4 | 2021...6 |
| 1838...2 | 1884..10 | 1930...4 | 1976..12 | 2022...7 |
| 1839...3 | 1885...5 | 1931...5 | 1977...7 | 2023...1 |
| 1840..11 | 1886...6 | 1932..13 | 1978...1 | 2024...9 |
| 1841...6 | 1887...7 | 1933...1 | 1979...2 | 2025...4 |
| 1842...7 | 1888...8 | 1934...2 | 1980..10 | 2026...5 |
| 1843...1 | 1889...3 | 1935...3 | 1981...5 | 2027...6 |
| 1844...9 | 1890...4 | 1936..11 | 1982...6 | 2028..14 |
| 1845...4 | 1891...5 | 1937...6 | 1983...7 | 2029...2 |
| 1846...5 | 1892..13 | 1938...7 | 1984...8 | 2030...3 |

## 1

**JANUARY**
S M T W T F S
1 2 3 4 5 6 7
8 9 10 11 12 13 14
15 16 17 18 19 20 21
22 23 24 25 26 27 28
29 30 31

**FEBRUARY**
S M T W T F S
1 2 3 4
5 6 7 8 9 10 11
12 13 14 15 16 17 18
19 20 21 22 23 24 25
26 27 28

**MARCH**
S M T W T F S
1 2 3 4
5 6 7 8 9 10 11
12 13 14 15 16 17 18
19 20 21 22 23 24 25
26 27 28 29 30 31

**APRIL**
S M T W T F S
1
2 3 4 5 6 7 8
9 10 11 12 13 14 15
16 17 18 19 20 21 22
23 24 25 26 27 28 29
30

**MAY**
S M T W T F S
1 2 3 4 5 6
7 8 9 10 11 12 13
14 15 16 17 18 19 20
21 22 23 24 25 26 27
28 29 30 31

**JUNE**
S M T W T F S
1 2 3
4 5 6 7 8 9 10
11 12 13 14 15 16 17
18 19 20 21 22 23 24
25 26 27 28 29 30

**JULY**
S M T W T F S
1
2 3 4 5 6 7 8
9 10 11 12 13 14 15
16 17 18 19 20 21 22
23 24 25 26 27 28 29
30 31

**AUGUST**
S M T W T F S
1 2 3 4 5
6 7 8 9 10 11 12
13 14 15 16 17 18 19
20 21 22 23 24 25 26
27 28 29 30 31

**SEPTEMBER**
S M T W T F S
1 2
3 4 5 6 7 8 9
10 11 12 13 14 15 16
17 18 19 20 21 22 23
24 25 26 27 28 29 30

**OCTOBER**
S M T W T F S
1 2 3 4 5 6 7
8 9 10 11 12 13 14
15 16 17 18 19 20 21
22 23 24 25 26 27 28
29 30 31

**NOVEMBER**
S M T W T F S
1 2 3 4
5 6 7 8 9 10 11
12 13 14 15 16 17 18
19 20 21 22 23 24 25
26 27 28 29 30

**DECEMBER**
S M T W T F S
1 2
3 4 5 6 7 8 9
10 11 12 13 14 15 16
17 18 19 20 21 22 23
24 25 26 27 28 29 30
31

## 2

**JANUARY**
S M T W T F S
1 2 3 4 5 6
7 8 9 10 11 12 13
14 15 16 17 18 19 20
21 22 23 24 25 26 27
28 29 30 31

**FEBRUARY**
S M T W T F S
1 2 3
4 5 6 7 8 9 10
11 12 13 14 15 16 17
18 19 20 21 22 23 24
25 26 27 28

**MARCH**
S M T W T F S
1 2 3
4 5 6 7 8 9 10
11 12 13 14 15 16 17
18 19 20 21 22 23 24
25 26 27 28 29 30 31

**APRIL**
S M T W T F S
1 2 3 4 5 6 7
8 9 10 11 12 13 14
15 16 17 18 19 20 21
22 23 24 25 26 27 28
29 30

**MAY**
S M T W T F S
1 2 3 4 5
6 7 8 9 10 11 12
13 14 15 16 17 18 19
20 21 22 23 24 25 26
27 28 29 30 31

**JUNE**
S M T W T F S
1 2
3 4 5 6 7 8 9
10 11 12 13 14 15 16
17 18 19 20 21 22 23
24 25 26 27 28 29 30

**JULY**
S M T W T F S
1 2 3 4 5 6 7
8 9 10 11 12 13 14
15 16 17 18 19 20 21
22 23 24 25 26 27 28
29 30 31

**AUGUST**
S M T W T F S
1 2 3 4
5 6 7 8 9 10 11
12 13 14 15 16 17 18
19 20 21 22 23 24 25
26 27 28 29 30 31

**SEPTEMBER**
S M T W T F S
1
2 3 4 5 6 7 8
9 10 11 12 13 14 15
16 17 18 19 20 21 22
23 24 25 26 27 28 29
30

**OCTOBER**
S M T W T F S
1 2 3 4 5 6
7 8 9 10 11 12 13
14 15 16 17 18 19 20
21 22 23 24 25 26 27
28 29 30 31

**NOVEMBER**
S M T W T F S
1 2 3
4 5 6 7 8 9 10
11 12 13 14 15 16 17
18 19 20 21 22 23 24
25 26 27 28 29 30

**DECEMBER**
S M T W T F S
1
2 3 4 5 6 7 8
9 10 11 12 13 14 15
16 17 18 19 20 21 22
23 24 25 26 27 28 29
30 31

## 3

**JANUARY**
S M T W T F S
1 2 3 4 5
6 7 8 9 10 11 12
13 14 15 16 17 18 19
20 21 22 23 24 25 26
27 28 29 30 31

**FEBRUARY**
S M T W T F S
1 2
3 4 5 6 7 8 9
10 11 12 13 14 15 16
17 18 19 20 21 22 23
24 25 26 27 28

**MARCH**
S M T W T F S
1 2
3 4 5 6 7 8 9
10 11 12 13 14 15 16
17 18 19 20 21 22 23
24 25 26 27 28 29 30
31

**APRIL**
S M T W T F S
1 2 3 4 5 6
7 8 9 10 11 12 13
14 15 16 17 18 19 20
21 22 23 24 25 26 27
28 29 30

**MAY**
S M T W T F S
1 2 3 4
5 6 7 8 9 10 11
12 13 14 15 16 17 18
19 20 21 22 23 24 25
26 27 28 29 30 31

**JUNE**
S M T W T F S
1
2 3 4 5 6 7 8
9 10 11 12 13 14 15
16 17 18 19 20 21 22
23 24 25 26 27 28 29
30

**JULY**
S M T W T F S
1 2 3 4 5 6
7 8 9 10 11 12 13
14 15 16 17 18 19 20
21 22 23 24 25 26 27
28 29 30 31

**AUGUST**
S M T W T F S
1 2 3
4 5 6 7 8 9 10
11 12 13 14 15 16 17
18 19 20 21 22 23 24
25 26 27 28 29 30 31

**SEPTEMBER**
S M T W T F S
1 2 3 4 5 6 7
8 9 10 11 12 13 14
15 16 17 18 19 20 21
22 23 24 25 26 27 28
29 30

**OCTOBER**
S M T W T F S
1 2 3 4 5
6 7 8 9 10 11 12
13 14 15 16 17 18 19
20 21 22 23 24 25 26
27 28 29 30 31

**NOVEMBER**
S M T W T F S
1 2
3 4 5 6 7 8 9
10 11 12 13 14 15 16
17 18 19 20 21 22 23
24 25 26 27 28 29 30

**DECEMBER**
S M T W T F S
1 2 3 4 5 6 7
8 9 10 11 12 13 14
15 16 17 18 19 20 21
22 23 24 25 26 27 28
29 30 31

## 4

**JANUARY**
S M T W T F S
1 2 3 4
5 6 7 8 9 10 11
12 13 14 15 16 17 18
19 20 21 22 23 24 25
26 27 28 29 30 31

**FEBRUARY**
S M T W T F S
1
2 3 4 5 6 7 8
9 10 11 12 13 14 15
16 17 18 19 20 21 22
23 24 25 26 27 28

**MARCH**
S M T W T F S
1
2 3 4 5 6 7 8
9 10 11 12 13 14 15
16 17 18 19 20 21 22
23 24 25 26 27 28 29
30 31

**APRIL**
S M T W T F S
1 2 3 4 5
6 7 8 9 10 11 12
13 14 15 16 17 18 19
20 21 22 23 24 25 26
27 28 29 30

**MAY**
S M T W T F S
1 2 3
4 5 6 7 8 9 10
11 12 13 14 15 16 17
18 19 20 21 22 23 24
25 26 27 28 29 30 31

**JUNE**
S M T W T F S
1 2 3 4 5 6 7
8 9 10 11 12 13 14
15 16 17 18 19 20 21
22 23 24 25 26 27 28
29 30

**JULY**
S M T W T F S
1 2 3 4 5
6 7 8 9 10 11 12
13 14 15 16 17 18 19
20 21 22 23 24 25 26
27 28 29 30 31

**AUGUST**
S M T W T F S
1 2
3 4 5 6 7 8 9
10 11 12 13 14 15 16
17 18 19 20 21 22 23
24 25 26 27 28 29 30
31

**SEPTEMBER**
S M T W T F S
1 2 3 4 5 6
7 8 9 10 11 12 13
14 15 16 17 18 19 20
21 22 23 24 25 26 27
28 29 30

**OCTOBER**
S M T W T F S
1 2 3 4
5 6 7 8 9 10 11
12 13 14 15 16 17 18
19 20 21 22 23 24 25
26 27 28 29 30 31

**NOVEMBER**
S M T W T F S
1
2 3 4 5 6 7 8
9 10 11 12 13 14 15
16 17 18 19 20 21 22
23 24 25 26 27 28 29
30

**DECEMBER**
S M T W T F S
1 2 3 4 5 6
7 8 9 10 11 12 13
14 15 16 17 18 19 20
21 22 23 24 25 26 27
28 29 30 31

## 5

**JANUARY**
S M T W T F S
1 2 3
4 5 6 7 8 9 10
11 12 13 14 15 16 17
18 19 20 21 22 23 24
25 26 27 28 29 30 31

**FEBRUARY**
S M T W T F S
1 2 3 4 5 6 7
8 9 10 11 12 13 14
15 16 17 18 19 20 21
22 23 24 25 26 27 28

**MARCH**
S M T W T F S
1 2 3 4 5 6 7
8 9 10 11 12 13 14
15 16 17 18 19 20 21
22 23 24 25 26 27 28
29 30 31

**APRIL**
S M T W T F S
1 2 3 4
5 6 7 8 9 10 11
12 13 14 15 16 17 18
19 20 21 22 23 24 25
26 27 28 29 30

**MAY**
S M T W T F S
1 2
3 4 5 6 7 8 9
10 11 12 13 14 15 16
17 18 19 20 21 22 23
24 25 26 27 28 29 30
31

**JUNE**
S M T W T F S
1 2 3 4 5 6
7 8 9 10 11 12 13
14 15 16 17 18 19 20
21 22 23 24 25 26 27
28 29 30

**JULY**
S M T W T F S
1 2 3 4
5 6 7 8 9 10 11
12 13 14 15 16 17 18
19 20 21 22 23 24 25
26 27 28 29 30 31

**AUGUST**
S M T W T F S
1
2 3 4 5 6 7 8
9 10 11 12 13 14 15
16 17 18 19 20 21 22
23 24 25 26 27 28 29
30 31

**SEPTEMBER**
S M T W T F S
1 2 3 4 5
6 7 8 9 10 11 12
13 14 15 16 17 18 19
20 21 22 23 24 25 26
27 28 29 30

**OCTOBER**
S M T W T F S
1 2 3
4 5 6 7 8 9 10
11 12 13 14 15 16 17
18 19 20 21 22 23 24
25 26 27 28 29 30 31

**NOVEMBER**
S M T W T F S
1 2 3 4 5 6 7
8 9 10 11 12 13 14
15 16 17 18 19 20 21
22 23 24 25 26 27 28
29 30

**DECEMBER**
S M T W T F S
1 2 3 4 5
6 7 8 9 10 11 12
13 14 15 16 17 18 19
20 21 22 23 24 25 26
27 28 29 30 31

## 6

**JANUARY**
S M T W T F S
1 2
3 4 5 6 7 8 9
10 11 12 13 14 15 16
17 18 19 20 21 22 23
24 25 26 27 28 29 30
31

**FEBRUARY**
S M T W T F S
1 2 3 4 5 6
7 8 9 10 11 12 13
14 15 16 17 18 19 20
21 22 23 24 25 26 27
28

**MARCH**
S M T W T F S
1 2 3 4 5 6
7 8 9 10 11 12 13
14 15 16 17 18 19 20
21 22 23 24 25 26 27
28 29 30 31

**APRIL**
S M T W T F S
1 2 3
4 5 6 7 8 9 10
11 12 13 14 15 16 17
18 19 20 21 22 23 24
25 26 27 28 29 30

**MAY**
S M T W T F S
1
2 3 4 5 6 7 8
9 10 11 12 13 14 15
16 17 18 19 20 21 22
23 24 25 26 27 28 29
30 31

**JUNE**
S M T W T F S
1 2 3 4 5
6 7 8 9 10 11 12
13 14 15 16 17 18 19
20 21 22 23 24 25 26
27 28 29 30

**JULY**
S M T W T F S
1 2 3
4 5 6 7 8 9 10
11 12 13 14 15 16 17
18 19 20 21 22 23 24
25 26 27 28 29 30 31

**AUGUST**
S M T W T F S
1 2 3 4 5 6 7
8 9 10 11 12 13 14
15 16 17 18 19 20 21
22 23 24 25 26 27 28
29 30 31

**SEPTEMBER**
S M T W T F S
1 2 3 4
5 6 7 8 9 10 11
12 13 14 15 16 17 18
19 20 21 22 23 24 25
26 27 28 29 30

**OCTOBER**
S M T W T F S
1 2
3 4 5 6 7 8 9
10 11 12 13 14 15 16
17 18 19 20 21 22 23
24 25 26 27 28 29 30
31

**NOVEMBER**
S M T W T F S
1 2 3 4 5 6
7 8 9 10 11 12 13
14 15 16 17 18 19 20
21 22 23 24 25 26 27
28 29 30

**DECEMBER**
S M T W T F S
1 2 3 4
5 6 7 8 9 10 11
12 13 14 15 16 17 18
19 20 21 22 23 24 25
26 27 28 29 30 31

## 7

**JANUARY**

| S | M | T | W | T | F | S |
|---|---|---|---|---|---|---|
|  |  |  |  |  |  | 1 |
| 2 | 3 | 4 | 5 | 6 | 7 | 8 |
| 9 | 10 | 11 | 12 | 13 | 14 | 15 |
| 16 | 17 | 18 | 19 | 20 | 21 | 22 |
| 23 | 24 | 25 | 26 | 27 | 28 | 29 |
| 30 | 31 |  |  |  |  |  |

**FEBRUARY**

| S | M | T | W | T | F | S |
|---|---|---|---|---|---|---|
|  |  | 1 | 2 | 3 | 4 | 5 |
| 6 | 7 | 8 | 9 | 10 | 11 | 12 |
| 13 | 14 | 15 | 16 | 17 | 18 | 19 |
| 20 | 21 | 22 | 23 | 24 | 25 | 26 |
| 27 | 28 |  |  |  |  |  |

**MARCH**

| S | M | T | W | T | F | S |
|---|---|---|---|---|---|---|
|  |  | 1 | 2 | 3 | 4 | 5 |
| 6 | 7 | 8 | 9 | 10 | 11 | 12 |
| 13 | 14 | 15 | 16 | 17 | 18 | 19 |
| 20 | 21 | 22 | 23 | 24 | 25 | 26 |
| 27 | 28 | 29 | 30 | 31 |  |  |

**APRIL**

| S | M | T | W | T | F | S |
|---|---|---|---|---|---|---|
|  |  |  |  |  | 1 | 2 |
| 3 | 4 | 5 | 6 | 7 | 8 | 9 |
| 10 | 11 | 12 | 13 | 14 | 15 | 16 |
| 17 | 18 | 19 | 20 | 21 | 22 | 23 |
| 24 | 25 | 26 | 27 | 28 | 29 | 30 |

**MAY**

| S | M | T | W | T | F | S |
|---|---|---|---|---|---|---|
| 1 | 2 | 3 | 4 | 5 | 6 | 7 |
| 8 | 9 | 10 | 11 | 12 | 13 | 14 |
| 15 | 16 | 17 | 18 | 19 | 20 | 21 |
| 22 | 23 | 24 | 25 | 26 | 27 | 28 |
| 29 | 30 | 31 |  |  |  |  |

**JUNE**

| S | M | T | W | T | F | S |
|---|---|---|---|---|---|---|
|  |  |  | 1 | 2 | 3 | 4 |
| 5 | 6 | 7 | 8 | 9 | 10 | 11 |
| 12 | 13 | 14 | 15 | 16 | 17 | 18 |
| 19 | 20 | 21 | 22 | 23 | 24 | 25 |
| 26 | 27 | 28 | 29 | 30 |  |  |

**JULY**

| S | M | T | W | T | F | S |
|---|---|---|---|---|---|---|
|  |  |  |  |  | 1 | 2 |
| 3 | 4 | 5 | 6 | 7 | 8 | 9 |
| 10 | 11 | 12 | 13 | 14 | 15 | 16 |
| 17 | 18 | 19 | 20 | 21 | 22 | 23 |
| 24 | 25 | 26 | 27 | 28 | 29 | 30 |
| 31 |  |  |  |  |  |  |

**AUGUST**

| S | M | T | W | T | F | S |
|---|---|---|---|---|---|---|
|  | 1 | 2 | 3 | 4 | 5 | 6 |
| 7 | 8 | 9 | 10 | 11 | 12 | 13 |
| 14 | 15 | 16 | 17 | 18 | 19 | 20 |
| 21 | 22 | 23 | 24 | 25 | 26 | 27 |
| 28 | 29 | 30 | 31 |  |  |  |

**SEPTEMBER**

| S | M | T | W | T | F | S |
|---|---|---|---|---|---|---|
|  |  |  |  | 1 | 2 | 3 |
| 4 | 5 | 6 | 7 | 8 | 9 | 10 |
| 11 | 12 | 13 | 14 | 15 | 16 | 17 |
| 18 | 19 | 20 | 21 | 22 | 23 | 24 |
| 25 | 26 | 27 | 28 | 29 | 30 |  |

**OCTOBER**

| S | M | T | W | T | F | S |
|---|---|---|---|---|---|---|
|  |  |  |  |  |  | 1 |
| 2 | 3 | 4 | 5 | 6 | 7 | 8 |
| 9 | 10 | 11 | 12 | 13 | 14 | 15 |
| 16 | 17 | 18 | 19 | 20 | 21 | 22 |
| 23 | 24 | 25 | 26 | 27 | 28 | 29 |
| 30 | 31 |  |  |  |  |  |

**NOVEMBER**

| S | M | T | W | T | F | S |
|---|---|---|---|---|---|---|
|  |  | 1 | 2 | 3 | 4 | 5 |
| 6 | 7 | 8 | 9 | 10 | 11 | 12 |
| 13 | 14 | 15 | 16 | 17 | 18 | 19 |
| 20 | 21 | 22 | 23 | 24 | 25 | 26 |
| 27 | 28 | 29 | 30 |  |  |  |

**DECEMBER**

| S | M | T | W | T | F | S |
|---|---|---|---|---|---|---|
|  |  |  |  | 1 | 2 | 3 |
| 4 | 5 | 6 | 7 | 8 | 9 | 10 |
| 11 | 12 | 13 | 14 | 15 | 16 | 17 |
| 18 | 19 | 20 | 21 | 22 | 23 | 24 |
| 25 | 26 | 27 | 28 | 29 | 30 | 31 |

## 8

**JANUARY**

| S | M | T | W | T | F | S |
|---|---|---|---|---|---|---|
| 1 | 2 | 3 | 4 | 5 | 6 | 7 |
| 8 | 9 | 10 | 11 | 12 | 13 | 14 |
| 15 | 16 | 17 | 18 | 19 | 20 | 21 |
| 22 | 23 | 24 | 25 | 26 | 27 | 28 |
| 29 | 30 | 31 |  |  |  |  |

**FEBRUARY**

| S | M | T | W | T | F | S |
|---|---|---|---|---|---|---|
|  |  |  | 1 | 2 | 3 | 4 |
| 5 | 6 | 7 | 8 | 9 | 10 | 11 |
| 12 | 13 | 14 | 15 | 16 | 17 | 18 |
| 19 | 20 | 21 | 22 | 23 | 24 | 25 |
| 26 | 27 | 28 | 29 |  |  |  |

**MARCH**

| S | M | T | W | T | F | S |
|---|---|---|---|---|---|---|
|  |  |  |  | 1 | 2 | 3 |
| 4 | 5 | 6 | 7 | 8 | 9 | 10 |
| 11 | 12 | 13 | 14 | 15 | 16 | 17 |
| 18 | 19 | 20 | 21 | 22 | 23 | 24 |
| 25 | 26 | 27 | 28 | 29 | 30 | 31 |

**APRIL**

| S | M | T | W | T | F | S |
|---|---|---|---|---|---|---|
| 1 | 2 | 3 | 4 | 5 | 6 | 7 |
| 8 | 9 | 10 | 11 | 12 | 13 | 14 |
| 15 | 16 | 17 | 18 | 19 | 20 | 21 |
| 22 | 23 | 24 | 25 | 26 | 27 | 28 |
| 29 | 30 |  |  |  |  |  |

**MAY**

| S | M | T | W | T | F | S |
|---|---|---|---|---|---|---|
|  |  | 1 | 2 | 3 | 4 | 5 |
| 6 | 7 | 8 | 9 | 10 | 11 | 12 |
| 13 | 14 | 15 | 16 | 17 | 18 | 19 |
| 20 | 21 | 22 | 23 | 24 | 25 | 26 |
| 27 | 28 | 29 | 30 | 31 |  |  |

**JUNE**

| S | M | T | W | T | F | S |
|---|---|---|---|---|---|---|
|  |  |  |  |  | 1 | 2 |
| 3 | 4 | 5 | 6 | 7 | 8 | 9 |
| 10 | 11 | 12 | 13 | 14 | 15 | 16 |
| 17 | 18 | 19 | 20 | 21 | 22 | 23 |
| 24 | 25 | 26 | 27 | 28 | 29 | 30 |

**JULY**

| S | M | T | W | T | F | S |
|---|---|---|---|---|---|---|
| 1 | 2 | 3 | 4 | 5 | 6 | 7 |
| 8 | 9 | 10 | 11 | 12 | 13 | 14 |
| 15 | 16 | 17 | 18 | 19 | 20 | 21 |
| 22 | 23 | 24 | 25 | 26 | 27 | 28 |
| 29 | 30 | 31 |  |  |  |  |

**AUGUST**

| S | M | T | W | T | F | S |
|---|---|---|---|---|---|---|
|  |  |  | 1 | 2 | 3 | 4 |
| 5 | 6 | 7 | 8 | 9 | 10 | 11 |
| 12 | 13 | 14 | 15 | 16 | 17 | 18 |
| 19 | 20 | 21 | 22 | 23 | 24 | 25 |
| 26 | 27 | 28 | 29 | 30 | 31 |  |

**SEPTEMBER**

| S | M | T | W | T | F | S |
|---|---|---|---|---|---|---|
|  |  |  |  |  |  | 1 |
| 2 | 3 | 4 | 5 | 6 | 7 | 8 |
| 9 | 10 | 11 | 12 | 13 | 14 | 15 |
| 16 | 17 | 18 | 19 | 20 | 21 | 22 |
| 23 | 24 | 25 | 26 | 27 | 28 | 29 |
| 30 |  |  |  |  |  |  |

**OCTOBER**

| S | M | T | W | T | F | S |
|---|---|---|---|---|---|---|
|  | 1 | 2 | 3 | 4 | 5 | 6 |
| 7 | 8 | 9 | 10 | 11 | 12 | 13 |
| 14 | 15 | 16 | 17 | 18 | 19 | 20 |
| 21 | 22 | 23 | 24 | 25 | 26 | 27 |
| 28 | 29 | 30 | 31 |  |  |  |

**NOVEMBER**

| S | M | T | W | T | F | S |
|---|---|---|---|---|---|---|
|  |  |  |  | 1 | 2 | 3 |
| 4 | 5 | 6 | 7 | 8 | 9 | 10 |
| 11 | 12 | 13 | 14 | 15 | 16 | 17 |
| 18 | 19 | 20 | 21 | 22 | 23 | 24 |
| 25 | 26 | 27 | 28 | 29 | 30 |  |

**DECEMBER**

| S | M | T | W | T | F | S |
|---|---|---|---|---|---|---|
|  |  |  |  |  |  | 1 |
| 2 | 3 | 4 | 5 | 6 | 7 | 8 |
| 9 | 10 | 11 | 12 | 13 | 14 | 15 |
| 16 | 17 | 18 | 19 | 20 | 21 | 22 |
| 23 | 24 | 25 | 26 | 27 | 28 | 29 |
| 30 | 31 |  |  |  |  |  |

## 9

**JANUARY**

| S | M | T | W | T | F | S |
|---|---|---|---|---|---|---|
|  | 1 | 2 | 3 | 4 | 5 | 6 |
| 7 | 8 | 9 | 10 | 11 | 12 | 13 |
| 14 | 15 | 16 | 17 | 18 | 19 | 20 |
| 21 | 22 | 23 | 24 | 25 | 26 | 27 |
| 28 | 29 | 30 | 31 |  |  |  |

**FEBRUARY**

| S | M | T | W | T | F | S |
|---|---|---|---|---|---|---|
|  |  |  |  | 1 | 2 | 3 |
| 4 | 5 | 6 | 7 | 8 | 9 | 10 |
| 11 | 12 | 13 | 14 | 15 | 16 | 17 |
| 18 | 19 | 20 | 21 | 22 | 23 | 24 |
| 25 | 26 | 27 | 28 | 29 |  |  |

**MARCH**

| S | M | T | W | T | F | S |
|---|---|---|---|---|---|---|
|  |  |  |  |  | 1 | 2 |
| 3 | 4 | 5 | 6 | 7 | 8 | 9 |
| 10 | 11 | 12 | 13 | 14 | 15 | 16 |
| 17 | 18 | 19 | 20 | 21 | 22 | 23 |
| 24 | 25 | 26 | 27 | 28 | 29 | 30 |
| 31 |  |  |  |  |  |  |

**APRIL**

| S | M | T | W | T | F | S |
|---|---|---|---|---|---|---|
|  | 1 | 2 | 3 | 4 | 5 | 6 |
| 7 | 8 | 9 | 10 | 11 | 12 | 13 |
| 14 | 15 | 16 | 17 | 18 | 19 | 20 |
| 21 | 22 | 23 | 24 | 25 | 26 | 27 |
| 28 | 29 | 30 |  |  |  |  |

**MAY**

| S | M | T | W | T | F | S |
|---|---|---|---|---|---|---|
|  |  |  | 1 | 2 | 3 | 4 |
| 5 | 6 | 7 | 8 | 9 | 10 | 11 |
| 12 | 13 | 14 | 15 | 16 | 17 | 18 |
| 19 | 20 | 21 | 22 | 23 | 24 | 25 |
| 26 | 27 | 28 | 29 | 30 | 31 |  |

**JUNE**

| S | M | T | W | T | F | S |
|---|---|---|---|---|---|---|
|  |  |  |  |  |  | 1 |
| 2 | 3 | 4 | 5 | 6 | 7 | 8 |
| 9 | 10 | 11 | 12 | 13 | 14 | 15 |
| 16 | 17 | 18 | 19 | 20 | 21 | 22 |
| 23 | 24 | 25 | 26 | 27 | 28 | 29 |
| 30 |  |  |  |  |  |  |

**JULY**

| S | M | T | W | T | F | S |
|---|---|---|---|---|---|---|
|  | 1 | 2 | 3 | 4 | 5 | 6 |
| 7 | 8 | 9 | 10 | 11 | 12 | 13 |
| 14 | 15 | 16 | 17 | 18 | 19 | 20 |
| 21 | 22 | 23 | 24 | 25 | 26 | 27 |
| 28 | 29 | 30 | 31 |  |  |  |

**AUGUST**

| S | M | T | W | T | F | S |
|---|---|---|---|---|---|---|
|  |  |  |  | 1 | 2 | 3 |
| 4 | 5 | 6 | 7 | 8 | 9 | 10 |
| 11 | 12 | 13 | 14 | 15 | 16 | 17 |
| 18 | 19 | 20 | 21 | 22 | 23 | 24 |
| 25 | 26 | 27 | 28 | 29 | 30 | 31 |

**SEPTEMBER**

| S | M | T | W | T | F | S |
|---|---|---|---|---|---|---|
| 1 | 2 | 3 | 4 | 5 | 6 | 7 |
| 8 | 9 | 10 | 11 | 12 | 13 | 14 |
| 15 | 16 | 17 | 18 | 19 | 20 | 21 |
| 22 | 23 | 24 | 25 | 26 | 27 | 28 |
| 29 | 30 |  |  |  |  |  |

**OCTOBER**

| S | M | T | W | T | F | S |
|---|---|---|---|---|---|---|
|  |  | 1 | 2 | 3 | 4 | 5 |
| 6 | 7 | 8 | 9 | 10 | 11 | 12 |
| 13 | 14 | 15 | 16 | 17 | 18 | 19 |
| 20 | 21 | 22 | 23 | 24 | 25 | 26 |
| 27 | 28 | 29 | 30 | 31 |  |  |

**NOVEMBER**

| S | M | T | W | T | F | S |
|---|---|---|---|---|---|---|
|  |  |  |  |  | 1 | 2 |
| 3 | 4 | 5 | 6 | 7 | 8 | 9 |
| 10 | 11 | 12 | 13 | 14 | 15 | 16 |
| 17 | 18 | 19 | 20 | 21 | 22 | 23 |
| 24 | 25 | 26 | 27 | 28 | 29 | 30 |

**DECEMBER**

| S | M | T | W | T | F | S |
|---|---|---|---|---|---|---|
| 1 | 2 | 3 | 4 | 5 | 6 | 7 |
| 8 | 9 | 10 | 11 | 12 | 13 | 14 |
| 15 | 16 | 17 | 18 | 19 | 20 | 21 |
| 22 | 23 | 24 | 25 | 26 | 27 | 28 |
| 29 | 30 | 31 |  |  |  |  |

## 10

**JANUARY**

| S | M | T | W | T | F | S |
|---|---|---|---|---|---|---|
|  |  | 1 | 2 | 3 | 4 | 5 |
| 6 | 7 | 8 | 9 | 10 | 11 | 12 |
| 13 | 14 | 15 | 16 | 17 | 18 | 19 |
| 20 | 21 | 22 | 23 | 24 | 25 | 26 |
| 27 | 28 | 29 | 30 | 31 |  |  |

**FEBRUARY**

| S | M | T | W | T | F | S |
|---|---|---|---|---|---|---|
|  |  |  |  |  | 1 | 2 |
| 3 | 4 | 5 | 6 | 7 | 8 | 9 |
| 10 | 11 | 12 | 13 | 14 | 15 | 16 |
| 17 | 18 | 19 | 20 | 21 | 22 | 23 |
| 24 | 25 | 26 | 27 | 28 | 29 |  |

**MARCH**

| S | M | T | W | T | F | S |
|---|---|---|---|---|---|---|
|  |  |  |  |  |  | 1 |
| 2 | 3 | 4 | 5 | 6 | 7 | 8 |
| 9 | 10 | 11 | 12 | 13 | 14 | 15 |
| 16 | 17 | 18 | 19 | 20 | 21 | 22 |
| 23 | 24 | 25 | 26 | 27 | 28 | 29 |
| 30 | 31 |  |  |  |  |  |

**APRIL**

| S | M | T | W | T | F | S |
|---|---|---|---|---|---|---|
|  |  | 1 | 2 | 3 | 4 | 5 |
| 6 | 7 | 8 | 9 | 10 | 11 | 12 |
| 13 | 14 | 15 | 16 | 17 | 18 | 19 |
| 20 | 21 | 22 | 23 | 24 | 25 | 26 |
| 27 | 28 | 29 | 30 |  |  |  |

**MAY**

| S | M | T | W | T | F | S |
|---|---|---|---|---|---|---|
|  |  |  |  | 1 | 2 | 3 |
| 4 | 5 | 6 | 7 | 8 | 9 | 10 |
| 11 | 12 | 13 | 14 | 15 | 16 | 17 |
| 18 | 19 | 20 | 21 | 22 | 23 | 24 |
| 25 | 26 | 27 | 28 | 29 | 30 | 31 |

**JUNE**

| S | M | T | W | T | F | S |
|---|---|---|---|---|---|---|
| 1 | 2 | 3 | 4 | 5 | 6 | 7 |
| 8 | 9 | 10 | 11 | 12 | 13 | 14 |
| 15 | 16 | 17 | 18 | 19 | 20 | 21 |
| 22 | 23 | 24 | 25 | 26 | 27 | 28 |
| 29 | 30 |  |  |  |  |  |

**JULY**

| S | M | T | W | T | F | S |
|---|---|---|---|---|---|---|
|  |  | 1 | 2 | 3 | 4 | 5 |
| 6 | 7 | 8 | 9 | 10 | 11 | 12 |
| 13 | 14 | 15 | 16 | 17 | 18 | 19 |
| 20 | 21 | 22 | 23 | 24 | 25 | 26 |
| 27 | 28 | 29 | 30 | 31 |  |  |

**AUGUST**

| S | M | T | W | T | F | S |
|---|---|---|---|---|---|---|
|  |  |  |  |  | 1 | 2 |
| 3 | 4 | 5 | 6 | 7 | 8 | 9 |
| 10 | 11 | 12 | 13 | 14 | 15 | 16 |
| 17 | 18 | 19 | 20 | 21 | 22 | 23 |
| 24 | 25 | 26 | 27 | 28 | 29 | 30 |
| 31 |  |  |  |  |  |  |

**SEPTEMBER**

| S | M | T | W | T | F | S |
|---|---|---|---|---|---|---|
|  | 1 | 2 | 3 | 4 | 5 | 6 |
| 7 | 8 | 9 | 10 | 11 | 12 | 13 |
| 14 | 15 | 16 | 17 | 18 | 19 | 20 |
| 21 | 22 | 23 | 24 | 25 | 26 | 27 |
| 28 | 29 | 30 |  |  |  |  |

**OCTOBER**

| S | M | T | W | T | F | S |
|---|---|---|---|---|---|---|
|  |  |  | 1 | 2 | 3 | 4 |
| 5 | 6 | 7 | 8 | 9 | 10 | 11 |
| 12 | 13 | 14 | 15 | 16 | 17 | 18 |
| 19 | 20 | 21 | 22 | 23 | 24 | 25 |
| 26 | 27 | 28 | 29 | 30 | 31 |  |

**NOVEMBER**

| S | M | T | W | T | F | S |
|---|---|---|---|---|---|---|
|  |  |  |  |  |  | 1 |
| 2 | 3 | 4 | 5 | 6 | 7 | 8 |
| 9 | 10 | 11 | 12 | 13 | 14 | 15 |
| 16 | 17 | 18 | 19 | 20 | 21 | 22 |
| 23 | 24 | 25 | 26 | 27 | 28 | 29 |
| 30 |  |  |  |  |  |  |

**DECEMBER**

| S | M | T | W | T | F | S |
|---|---|---|---|---|---|---|
|  | 1 | 2 | 3 | 4 | 5 | 6 |
| 7 | 8 | 9 | 10 | 11 | 12 | 13 |
| 14 | 15 | 16 | 17 | 18 | 19 | 20 |
| 21 | 22 | 23 | 24 | 25 | 26 | 27 |
| 28 | 29 | 30 | 31 |  |  |  |

## 11

**JANUARY**

| S | M | T | W | T | F | S |
|---|---|---|---|---|---|---|
|  |  |  | 1 | 2 | 3 | 4 |
| 5 | 6 | 7 | 8 | 9 | 10 | 11 |
| 12 | 13 | 14 | 15 | 16 | 17 | 18 |
| 19 | 20 | 21 | 22 | 23 | 24 | 25 |
| 26 | 27 | 28 | 29 | 30 | 31 |  |

**FEBRUARY**

| S | M | T | W | T | F | S |
|---|---|---|---|---|---|---|
|  |  |  |  |  |  | 1 |
| 2 | 3 | 4 | 5 | 6 | 7 | 8 |
| 9 | 10 | 11 | 12 | 13 | 14 | 15 |
| 16 | 17 | 18 | 19 | 20 | 21 | 22 |
| 23 | 24 | 25 | 26 | 27 | 28 | 29 |

**MARCH**

| S | M | T | W | T | F | S |
|---|---|---|---|---|---|---|
| 1 | 2 | 3 | 4 | 5 | 6 | 7 |
| 8 | 9 | 10 | 11 | 12 | 13 | 14 |
| 15 | 16 | 17 | 18 | 19 | 20 | 21 |
| 22 | 23 | 24 | 25 | 26 | 27 | 28 |
| 29 | 30 | 31 |  |  |  |  |

**APRIL**

| S | M | T | W | T | F | S |
|---|---|---|---|---|---|---|
|  |  |  | 1 | 2 | 3 | 4 |
| 5 | 6 | 7 | 8 | 9 | 10 | 11 |
| 12 | 13 | 14 | 15 | 16 | 17 | 18 |
| 19 | 20 | 21 | 22 | 23 | 24 | 25 |
| 26 | 27 | 28 | 29 | 30 |  |  |

**MAY**

| S | M | T | W | T | F | S |
|---|---|---|---|---|---|---|
|  |  |  |  |  | 1 | 2 |
| 3 | 4 | 5 | 6 | 7 | 8 | 9 |
| 10 | 11 | 12 | 13 | 14 | 15 | 16 |
| 17 | 18 | 19 | 20 | 21 | 22 | 23 |
| 24 | 25 | 26 | 27 | 28 | 29 | 30 |
| 31 |  |  |  |  |  |  |

**JUNE**

| S | M | T | W | T | F | S |
|---|---|---|---|---|---|---|
|  | 1 | 2 | 3 | 4 | 5 | 6 |
| 7 | 8 | 9 | 10 | 11 | 12 | 13 |
| 14 | 15 | 16 | 17 | 18 | 19 | 20 |
| 21 | 22 | 23 | 24 | 25 | 26 | 27 |
| 28 | 29 | 30 |  |  |  |  |

**JULY**

| S | M | T | W | T | F | S |
|---|---|---|---|---|---|---|
|  |  |  | 1 | 2 | 3 | 4 |
| 5 | 6 | 7 | 8 | 9 | 10 | 11 |
| 12 | 13 | 14 | 15 | 16 | 17 | 18 |
| 19 | 20 | 21 | 22 | 23 | 24 | 25 |
| 26 | 27 | 28 | 29 | 30 | 31 |  |

**AUGUST**

| S | M | T | W | T | F | S |
|---|---|---|---|---|---|---|
|  |  |  |  |  |  | 1 |
| 2 | 3 | 4 | 5 | 6 | 7 | 8 |
| 9 | 10 | 11 | 12 | 13 | 14 | 15 |
| 16 | 17 | 18 | 19 | 20 | 21 | 22 |
| 23 | 24 | 25 | 26 | 27 | 28 | 29 |
| 30 | 31 |  |  |  |  |  |

**SEPTEMBER**

| S | M | T | W | T | F | S |
|---|---|---|---|---|---|---|
|  |  | 1 | 2 | 3 | 4 | 5 |
| 6 | 7 | 8 | 9 | 10 | 11 | 12 |
| 13 | 14 | 15 | 16 | 17 | 18 | 19 |
| 20 | 21 | 22 | 23 | 24 | 25 | 26 |
| 27 | 28 | 29 | 30 |  |  |  |

**OCTOBER**

| S | M | T | W | T | F | S |
|---|---|---|---|---|---|---|
|  |  |  |  | 1 | 2 | 3 |
| 4 | 5 | 6 | 7 | 8 | 9 | 10 |
| 11 | 12 | 13 | 14 | 15 | 16 | 17 |
| 18 | 19 | 20 | 21 | 22 | 23 | 24 |
| 25 | 26 | 27 | 28 | 29 | 30 | 31 |

**NOVEMBER**

| S | M | T | W | T | F | S |
|---|---|---|---|---|---|---|
| 1 | 2 | 3 | 4 | 5 | 6 | 7 |
| 8 | 9 | 10 | 11 | 12 | 13 | 14 |
| 15 | 16 | 17 | 18 | 19 | 20 | 21 |
| 22 | 23 | 24 | 25 | 26 | 27 | 28 |
| 29 | 30 |  |  |  |  |  |

**DECEMBER**

| S | M | T | W | T | F | S |
|---|---|---|---|---|---|---|
|  |  | 1 | 2 | 3 | 4 | 5 |
| 6 | 7 | 8 | 9 | 10 | 11 | 12 |
| 13 | 14 | 15 | 16 | 17 | 18 | 19 |
| 20 | 21 | 22 | 23 | 24 | 25 | 26 |
| 27 | 28 | 29 | 30 | 31 |  |  |

## 12

**JANUARY**

| S | M | T | W | T | F | S |
|---|---|---|---|---|---|---|
|  |  |  |  | 1 | 2 | 3 |
| 4 | 5 | 6 | 7 | 8 | 9 | 10 |
| 11 | 12 | 13 | 14 | 15 | 16 | 17 |
| 18 | 19 | 20 | 21 | 22 | 23 | 24 |
| 25 | 26 | 27 | 28 | 29 | 30 | 31 |

**FEBRUARY**

| S | M | T | W | T | F | S |
|---|---|---|---|---|---|---|
| 1 | 2 | 3 | 4 | 5 | 6 | 7 |
| 8 | 9 | 10 | 11 | 12 | 13 | 14 |
| 15 | 16 | 17 | 18 | 19 | 20 | 21 |
| 22 | 23 | 24 | 25 | 26 | 27 | 28 |
| 29 |  |  |  |  |  |  |

**MARCH**

| S | M | T | W | T | F | S |
|---|---|---|---|---|---|---|
|  | 1 | 2 | 3 | 4 | 5 | 6 |
| 7 | 8 | 9 | 10 | 11 | 12 | 13 |
| 14 | 15 | 16 | 17 | 18 | 19 | 20 |
| 21 | 22 | 23 | 24 | 25 | 26 | 27 |
| 28 | 29 | 30 | 31 |  |  |  |

**APRIL**

| S | M | T | W | T | F | S |
|---|---|---|---|---|---|---|
|  |  |  |  | 1 | 2 | 3 |
| 4 | 5 | 6 | 7 | 8 | 9 | 10 |
| 11 | 12 | 13 | 14 | 15 | 16 | 17 |
| 18 | 19 | 20 | 21 | 22 | 23 | 24 |
| 25 | 26 | 27 | 28 | 29 | 30 |  |

**MAY**

| S | M | T | W | T | F | S |
|---|---|---|---|---|---|---|
|  |  |  |  |  |  | 1 |
| 2 | 3 | 4 | 5 | 6 | 7 | 8 |
| 9 | 10 | 11 | 12 | 13 | 14 | 15 |
| 16 | 17 | 18 | 19 | 20 | 21 | 22 |
| 23 | 24 | 25 | 26 | 27 | 28 | 29 |
| 30 | 31 |  |  |  |  |  |

**JUNE**

| S | M | T | W | T | F | S |
|---|---|---|---|---|---|---|
|  |  | 1 | 2 | 3 | 4 | 5 |
| 6 | 7 | 8 | 9 | 10 | 11 | 12 |
| 13 | 14 | 15 | 16 | 17 | 18 | 19 |
| 20 | 21 | 22 | 23 | 24 | 25 | 26 |
| 27 | 28 | 29 | 30 |  |  |  |

**JULY**

| S | M | T | W | T | F | S |
|---|---|---|---|---|---|---|
|  |  |  |  | 1 | 2 | 3 |
| 4 | 5 | 6 | 7 | 8 | 9 | 10 |
| 11 | 12 | 13 | 14 | 15 | 16 | 17 |
| 18 | 19 | 20 | 21 | 22 | 23 | 24 |
| 25 | 26 | 27 | 28 | 29 | 30 | 31 |

**AUGUST**

| S | M | T | W | T | F | S |
|---|---|---|---|---|---|---|
| 1 | 2 | 3 | 4 | 5 | 6 | 7 |
| 8 | 9 | 10 | 11 | 12 | 13 | 14 |
| 15 | 16 | 17 | 18 | 19 | 20 | 21 |
| 22 | 23 | 24 | 25 | 26 | 27 | 28 |
| 29 | 30 | 31 |  |  |  |  |

**SEPTEMBER**

| S | M | T | W | T | F | S |
|---|---|---|---|---|---|---|
|  |  |  | 1 | 2 | 3 | 4 |
| 5 | 6 | 7 | 8 | 9 | 10 | 11 |
| 12 | 13 | 14 | 15 | 16 | 17 | 18 |
| 19 | 20 | 21 | 22 | 23 | 24 | 25 |
| 26 | 27 | 28 | 29 | 30 |  |  |

**OCTOBER**

| S | M | T | W | T | F | S |
|---|---|---|---|---|---|---|
|  |  |  |  |  | 1 | 2 |
| 3 | 4 | 5 | 6 | 7 | 8 | 9 |
| 10 | 11 | 12 | 13 | 14 | 15 | 16 |
| 17 | 18 | 19 | 20 | 21 | 22 | 23 |
| 24 | 25 | 26 | 27 | 28 | 29 | 30 |
| 31 |  |  |  |  |  |  |

**NOVEMBER**

| S | M | T | W | T | F | S |
|---|---|---|---|---|---|---|
|  | 1 | 2 | 3 | 4 | 5 | 6 |
| 7 | 8 | 9 | 10 | 11 | 12 | 13 |
| 14 | 15 | 16 | 17 | 18 | 19 | 20 |
| 21 | 22 | 23 | 24 | 25 | 26 | 27 |
| 28 | 29 | 30 |  |  |  |  |

**DECEMBER**

| S | M | T | W | T | F | S |
|---|---|---|---|---|---|---|
|  |  |  | 1 | 2 | 3 | 4 |
| 5 | 6 | 7 | 8 | 9 | 10 | 11 |
| 12 | 13 | 14 | 15 | 16 | 17 | 18 |
| 19 | 20 | 21 | 22 | 23 | 24 | 25 |
| 26 | 27 | 28 | 29 | 30 | 31 |  |

## 13

**JANUARY**

| S | M | T | W | T | F | S |
|---|---|---|---|---|---|---|
|  |  |  |  |  | 1 | 2 |
| 3 | 4 | 5 | 6 | 7 | 8 | 9 |
| 10 | 11 | 12 | 13 | 14 | 15 | 16 |
| 17 | 18 | 19 | 20 | 21 | 22 | 23 |
| 24 | 25 | 26 | 27 | 28 | 29 | 30 |
| 31 |  |  |  |  |  |  |

**FEBRUARY**

| S | M | T | W | T | F | S |
|---|---|---|---|---|---|---|
|  | 1 | 2 | 3 | 4 | 5 | 6 |
| 7 | 8 | 9 | 10 | 11 | 12 | 13 |
| 14 | 15 | 16 | 17 | 18 | 19 | 20 |
| 21 | 22 | 23 | 24 | 25 | 26 | 27 |
| 28 | 29 |  |  |  |  |  |

**MARCH**

| S | M | T | W | T | F | S |
|---|---|---|---|---|---|---|
|  |  | 1 | 2 | 3 | 4 | 5 |
| 6 | 7 | 8 | 9 | 10 | 11 | 12 |
| 13 | 14 | 15 | 16 | 17 | 18 | 19 |
| 20 | 21 | 22 | 23 | 24 | 25 | 26 |
| 27 | 28 | 29 | 30 | 31 |  |  |

**APRIL**

| S | M | T | W | T | F | S |
|---|---|---|---|---|---|---|
|  |  |  |  |  | 1 | 2 |
| 3 | 4 | 5 | 6 | 7 | 8 | 9 |
| 10 | 11 | 12 | 13 | 14 | 15 | 16 |
| 17 | 18 | 19 | 20 | 21 | 22 | 23 |
| 24 | 25 | 26 | 27 | 28 | 29 | 30 |

**MAY**

| S | M | T | W | T | F | S |
|---|---|---|---|---|---|---|
| 1 | 2 | 3 | 4 | 5 | 6 | 7 |
| 8 | 9 | 10 | 11 | 12 | 13 | 14 |
| 15 | 16 | 17 | 18 | 19 | 20 | 21 |
| 22 | 23 | 24 | 25 | 26 | 27 | 28 |
| 29 | 30 | 31 |  |  |  |  |

**JUNE**

| S | M | T | W | T | F | S |
|---|---|---|---|---|---|---|
|  |  |  | 1 | 2 | 3 | 4 |
| 5 | 6 | 7 | 8 | 9 | 10 | 11 |
| 12 | 13 | 14 | 15 | 16 | 17 | 18 |
| 19 | 20 | 21 | 22 | 23 | 24 | 25 |
| 26 | 27 | 28 | 29 | 30 |  |  |

**JULY**

| S | M | T | W | T | F | S |
|---|---|---|---|---|---|---|
|  |  |  |  |  | 1 | 2 |
| 3 | 4 | 5 | 6 | 7 | 8 | 9 |
| 10 | 11 | 12 | 13 | 14 | 15 | 16 |
| 17 | 18 | 19 | 20 | 21 | 22 | 23 |
| 24 | 25 | 26 | 27 | 28 | 29 | 30 |
| 31 |  |  |  |  |  |  |

**AUGUST**

| S | M | T | W | T | F | S |
|---|---|---|---|---|---|---|
|  | 1 | 2 | 3 | 4 | 5 | 6 |
| 7 | 8 | 9 | 10 | 11 | 12 | 13 |
| 14 | 15 | 16 | 17 | 18 | 19 | 20 |
| 21 | 22 | 23 | 24 | 25 | 26 | 27 |
| 28 | 29 | 30 | 31 |  |  |  |

**SEPTEMBER**

| S | M | T | W | T | F | S |
|---|---|---|---|---|---|---|
|  |  |  |  | 1 | 2 | 3 |
| 4 | 5 | 6 | 7 | 8 | 9 | 10 |
| 11 | 12 | 13 | 14 | 15 | 16 | 17 |
| 18 | 19 | 20 | 21 | 22 | 23 | 24 |
| 25 | 26 | 27 | 28 | 29 | 30 |  |

**OCTOBER**

| S | M | T | W | T | F | S |
|---|---|---|---|---|---|---|
|  |  |  |  |  |  | 1 |
| 2 | 3 | 4 | 5 | 6 | 7 | 8 |
| 9 | 10 | 11 | 12 | 13 | 14 | 15 |
| 16 | 17 | 18 | 19 | 20 | 21 | 22 |
| 23 | 24 | 25 | 26 | 27 | 28 | 29 |
| 30 | 31 |  |  |  |  |  |

**NOVEMBER**

| S | M | T | W | T | F | S |
|---|---|---|---|---|---|---|
|  |  | 1 | 2 | 3 | 4 | 5 |
| 6 | 7 | 8 | 9 | 10 | 11 | 12 |
| 13 | 14 | 15 | 16 | 17 | 18 | 19 |
| 20 | 21 | 22 | 23 | 24 | 25 | 26 |
| 27 | 28 | 29 | 30 |  |  |  |

**DECEMBER**

| S | M | T | W | T | F | S |
|---|---|---|---|---|---|---|
|  |  |  |  | 1 | 2 | 3 |
| 4 | 5 | 6 | 7 | 8 | 9 | 10 |
| 11 | 12 | 13 | 14 | 15 | 16 | 17 |
| 18 | 19 | 20 | 21 | 22 | 23 | 24 |
| 25 | 26 | 27 | 28 | 29 | 30 | 31 |

## 14

**JANUARY**

| S | M | T | W | T | F | S |
|---|---|---|---|---|---|---|
|  |  |  |  |  |  | 1 |
| 2 | 3 | 4 | 5 | 6 | 7 | 8 |
| 9 | 10 | 11 | 12 | 13 | 14 | 15 |
| 16 | 17 | 18 | 19 | 20 | 21 | 22 |
| 23 | 24 | 25 | 26 | 27 | 28 | 29 |
| 30 | 31 |  |  |  |  |  |

**FEBRUARY**

| S | M | T | W | T | F | S |
|---|---|---|---|---|---|---|
|  |  | 1 | 2 | 3 | 4 | 5 |
| 6 | 7 | 8 | 9 | 10 | 11 | 12 |
| 13 | 14 | 15 | 16 | 17 | 18 | 19 |
| 20 | 21 | 22 | 23 | 24 | 25 | 26 |
| 27 | 28 | 29 |  |  |  |  |

**MARCH**

| S | M | T | W | T | F | S |
|---|---|---|---|---|---|---|
|  |  |  | 1 | 2 | 3 | 4 |
| 5 | 6 | 7 | 8 | 9 | 10 | 11 |
| 12 | 13 | 14 | 15 | 16 | 17 | 18 |
| 19 | 20 | 21 | 22 | 23 | 24 | 25 |
| 26 | 27 | 28 | 29 | 30 | 31 |  |

**APRIL**

| S | M | T | W | T | F | S |
|---|---|---|---|---|---|---|
|  |  |  |  |  |  | 1 |
| 2 | 3 | 4 | 5 | 6 | 7 | 8 |
| 9 | 10 | 11 | 12 | 13 | 14 | 15 |
| 16 | 17 | 18 | 19 | 20 | 21 | 22 |
| 23 | 24 | 25 | 26 | 27 | 28 | 29 |
| 30 |  |  |  |  |  |  |

**MAY**

| S | M | T | W | T | F | S |
|---|---|---|---|---|---|---|
|  | 1 | 2 | 3 | 4 | 5 | 6 |
| 7 | 8 | 9 | 10 | 11 | 12 | 13 |
| 14 | 15 | 16 | 17 | 18 | 19 | 20 |
| 21 | 22 | 23 | 24 | 25 | 26 | 27 |
| 28 | 29 | 30 | 31 |  |  |  |

**JUNE**

| S | M | T | W | T | F | S |
|---|---|---|---|---|---|---|
|  |  |  |  | 1 | 2 | 3 |
| 4 | 5 | 6 | 7 | 8 | 9 | 10 |
| 11 | 12 | 13 | 14 | 15 | 16 | 17 |
| 18 | 19 | 20 | 21 | 22 | 23 | 24 |
| 25 | 26 | 27 | 28 | 29 | 30 |  |

**JULY**

| S | M | T | W | T | F | S |
|---|---|---|---|---|---|---|
|  |  |  |  |  |  | 1 |
| 2 | 3 | 4 | 5 | 6 | 7 | 8 |
| 9 | 10 | 11 | 12 | 13 | 14 | 15 |
| 16 | 17 | 18 | 19 | 20 | 21 | 22 |
| 23 | 24 | 25 | 26 | 27 | 28 | 29 |
| 30 | 31 |  |  |  |  |  |

**AUGUST**

| S | M | T | W | T | F | S |
|---|---|---|---|---|---|---|
|  |  | 1 | 2 | 3 | 4 | 5 |
| 6 | 7 | 8 | 9 | 10 | 11 | 12 |
| 13 | 14 | 15 | 16 | 17 | 18 | 19 |
| 20 | 21 | 22 | 23 | 24 | 25 | 26 |
| 27 | 28 | 29 | 30 | 31 |  |  |

**SEPTEMBER**

| S | M | T | W | T | F | S |
|---|---|---|---|---|---|---|
|  |  |  |  |  | 1 | 2 |
| 3 | 4 | 5 | 6 | 7 | 8 | 9 |
| 10 | 11 | 12 | 13 | 14 | 15 | 16 |
| 17 | 18 | 19 | 20 | 21 | 22 | 23 |
| 24 | 25 | 26 | 27 | 28 | 29 | 30 |

**OCTOBER**

| S | M | T | W | T | F | S |
|---|---|---|---|---|---|---|
| 1 | 2 | 3 | 4 | 5 | 6 | 7 |
| 8 | 9 | 10 | 11 | 12 | 13 | 14 |
| 15 | 16 | 17 | 18 | 19 | 20 | 21 |
| 22 | 23 | 24 | 25 | 26 | 27 | 28 |
| 29 | 30 | 31 |  |  |  |  |

**NOVEMBER**

| S | M | T | W | T | F | S |
|---|---|---|---|---|---|---|
|  |  |  | 1 | 2 | 3 | 4 |
| 5 | 6 | 7 | 8 | 9 | 10 | 11 |
| 12 | 13 | 14 | 15 | 16 | 17 | 18 |
| 19 | 20 | 21 | 22 | 23 | 24 | 25 |
| 26 | 27 | 28 | 29 | 30 |  |  |

**DECEMBER**

| S | M | T | W | T | F | S |
|---|---|---|---|---|---|---|
|  |  |  |  |  | 1 | 2 |
| 3 | 4 | 5 | 6 | 7 | 8 | 9 |
| 10 | 11 | 12 | 13 | 14 | 15 | 16 |
| 17 | 18 | 19 | 20 | 21 | 22 | 23 |
| 24 | 25 | 26 | 27 | 28 | 29 | 30 |
| 31 |  |  |  |  |  |  |

## HOLIDAYS AND COMMEMORATED DAYS FOR 1983

Days in parentheses are not legal holidays. *—Holiday observed on following Monday; **—Holiday observed on preceding Friday. Note: applies to all states immediately following symbol. †Legal holiday in Pa.

### January

1/ New Year's Day (All states & Canada); (*—ID); (**—AL, AK, AZ, AR, CT, DE, DC, GA, HI, IL, IN, IA, KS, KY, ME, MD, MI, MN, NE, NV, NH, NJ, NM, ND, PA, SC, SD, VT, VA, WV)
1/ Martin Luther King Day (**—VA)
8/ (Battle of New Orleans Day) (LA)
15/ Martin Luther King Day (FL, MA); (**—CT, DC, IL, MD, NJ, PA, SC)
17/ Martin Luther King's Birthday (MI, OH)
17/ Robert E. Lee's Birthday (AL, MS)
17/ Lee-Jackson Day (VA)
19/ Robert E. Lee's Birthday (AR, FL, GA, NC, SC)
Confederate Heroes Day (TX)

### February

2/ (Groundhog Day)
7/ Abraham Lincoln's Birthday (DE, OR)
12/ Abraham Lincoln's Birthday (CA, CO, FL, MO, MT, NY, UT, WA); (**—AK, CT, IL, IN, KS, MD, NJ, NM, VT, WV)
14/ Abraham Lincoln's Birthday (AZ)
14/ (St. Valentine's Day)
15/ Susan B. Anthony's Birthday (FL)
15/ Mardi Gras Day (AL, LA)
21/ George Washington's Birthday (All states except HI, ID, LA, MN, NE, OH, PA, SD, WI, WY)
Combined celebration of birthdays of George Washington & Abraham Lincoln (OH, SD, WI, WY); called Presidents' Day (HI, ID, MN, NE, PA)

### March

1/ Town Meeting Day (VT)
2/ Texas Independence Day (TX)
17/ (St. Patrick's Day)
25/ Maryland Day (MD)
26/ Prince Jonah Kuhio Kalanianaole Day (**—HI)
28/ Seward's Day (AK)

### April

1/ Good Friday (CT, DE, FL, HI, IN, LA, MD, NJ, ND, TN); (Canada)
Good Friday Afternoon (KY, WI)
2/ Pascua Florida Day (FL)
4/ Easter Monday (NC); (Canada)
12/ Anniversary of signing of Halifax Resolves (NC)
13/ Thomas Jefferson's Birthday (AL)
18/ Patriot's Day (ME, MA)
21/ San Jacinto Day (TX)
22/ Arbor Day (NE)
25/ Confederate Memorial Day (AL, MS)
25/ Fast Day (NH)
26/ Confederate Memorial Day (FL, GA)

### May

1/ (May Day)
3/ Primary Election Day (IN)
4/ Rhode Island Independence Day (RI)
8/ Harry S Truman's Birthday (*—MO)
8/ (Mother's Day)
10/ Confederate Memorial Day (NC, SC)
17/ Primary Election Day (PA)
20/ Anniversary of Mecklenburg Declaration of Independence (NC)
21/ (Armed Forces Day)
23/ Victoria Day (Canada)
30/ Memorial Day (All states except AL, LA, MS, SC, VA)
30/ Confederate Memorial Day (VA)

### June

3/ Jefferson Davis' Birthday (FL, GA, SC)
6/ Jefferson Davis' Birthday (AL, MS)
11/ King Kamehameha I Day (**—HI)
14/ (Flag Day)†
19/ Emancipation Day (TX)
19/ (Father's Day)
20/ West Virginia Day (WV)

### July

1/ Dominion Day (Canada)
4/ Independence Day (All states)
4/ (Indian Rights Day) (WI)
24/ Pioneer Day (UT)

### August

1/ Colorado Day (CO)
7/ American Family Day (AZ)
8/ Victory Day (RI)
16/ Bennington Battle Day (VT)
19/ Admission Day (HI)
27/ Lyndon B. Johnson's Birthday (TX)
30/ Huey P. Long Day (LA)

### September

5/ Labor Day (All states & Canada)
8/ (Rosh Hashanah)
9/ Admission Day (CA)
11/ (Grandparents' Day)
12/ Defenders' Day (MD)
13/ Primary Election Day (WI)
17/ Yom Kippur (NC)
24/ (Indian Day) (OK)

### October

9/ (Leif Erikson Day)
10/ Columbus Day (All states except AK, AR, HI, IA, KS, KY, LA, MN, MS, NV, ND, OR, SC, SD, WA)
10/ Discoverers' Day (HI)
10/ Farmers' Day (FL)
10/ Pioneer's Day (SD)
10/ Thanksgiving Day (Canada)
12/ Columbus Day (MD)
18/ Alaska Day (AK)
24/ (United Nations Day)
31/ Nevada Day (NV)
31/ (Halloween)

### November

1/ (All Saints' Day) (LA)
8/ (Election Day)
11/ Veterans Day (All states except KY); called Armistice Day (MS, RI, WI)
Remembrance Day (Canada)
24/ Thanksgiving Day (All states)
25/ Thanksgiving Friday (IL, IN, IA, KS, KY, ME, MN, NE, NH, OK, TX, WA)

### December

24/ Christmas Eve (TX); (**—AR, KY)
25/ Christmas Day (All states & Canada); (*—AL, AK, AZ, AR, CA, CO, CT, DE, DC, GA, HI, ID, IL, IN, IA, LA, MD, ME, MI, MN, MT, NE, NV, NJ, NM, OK, PA, SC, SD, TX, VT, VA)
26/ Boxing Day (Canada)

## NEW WORLD EXPLORERS

### NORTH AMERICA

**c. 1000** . . . Leif Ericsson (Norway) possibly sailed to Labrador and Newfoundland, from Greenland; others theorize that he reached Virginia, Nova Scotia, or New England

**c. 1010** . . . Thorfinn Karlsefni (Iceland) sailed from Greenland to North America, probably Labrador or New England

**1497–98** . . . John Cabot (England) sailed to North America, probably Cape Breton Island or Newfoundland

**1513** . . . Juan Ponce de León (Spain) sailed to near St. Augustine, Florida, and south to Miami Bay

**1519** . . . Alonso de Pineda (Spain) explored the Gulf of Mexico from Florida to the mouth of the Rio Grande

**1524** . . . Giovanni da Verrazano (France) explored North American coast, probably from North Carolina to Maine, entering New York Bay

**1528** . . . Pánfilo de Narváez (Spain) explored Florida from Tampa Bay as far as Tallahassee

**1534–36** . . . Jacques Cartier (France) sailed to Strait of Belle Isle, Newfoundland, and discovered Prince Edward Island; he also discovered St. Lawrence River as far as Quebec and Montreal (1535–36)

**1536** . . . Alvar Nuñez Cabeza de Vaca (Spain), shipwrecked on Texas coast, traveled as far as New Mexico, Arizona, and possibly California

**1538–39** . . . Francisco de Ulloa (Spain) explored Gulf of California to its head, proving that present-day Baja California is a peninsula

**1538–41** . . . Hernando de Soto (Spain) began (1539) exploring southern coast of United States, as far inland as Mississippi River, Arkansas, and Oklahoma

**1539** . . . Marcos de Niza (Spain) explored southeastern Arizona and perhaps New Mexico

**1540–42** . . . Francisco Vásquez de Coronado (Spain) explored New Mexico, Texas Panhandle, Oklahoma, and Kansas

**1542** . . . Juan Rodríguez Cabrillo (Spain) discovered California mainland, landing at San Diego Bay

**1565** . . . Pedro Menéndez de Avilés (Spain) founded St. Augustine, Florida, and explored Gulf Coast

**1576–78** . . . Sir Martin Frobisher (England) explored Frobisher Bay, South Baffin Island, and Hudson Strait in northeastern Canada

**1577–79** . . . Sir Francis Drake (England) sailed from Chile to Washington, stopping at San Francisco Bay

**1585–87** . . . John Davis (England) discovered Cumberland Sound off Baffin Island in northeastern Canada

**1598–1605** . . . Juan de Oñate (Spain) explored New Mexico (1598), Oklahoma, and the plains around Wichita, Kansas (1601), and went down the Colorado River to the Gulf of California (1605)

**1602** . . . Bartholomew Gosnold (England) explored eastern coast from Maine to Narragansett Bay, naming Cape Cod

**1603–9** . . . Samuel de Champlain (France) explored St. Lawrence River as far as Lachine (1603), New England south to Martha's Vineyard (1603–6); founded Quebec (1608); and discovered Lake Champlain (1609)

**1607–9** . . . John Smith (England) helped to found (1607) Jamestown, Virginia, and explored adjacent areas

**1609–10** . . . Henry Hudson (Netherlands) sailed up Chesapeake, Delaware, and New York Bays; under English flag, he sailed through Greenland, Labrador, Hudson Strait and Bay (1610)

**1634** . . . Jean Nicolet (France) explored Lake Michigan, Green Bay, and Fox River, Wisconsin

**1673** . . . Louis Jolliet, Father Jacques Marquette (France) navigated Mississippi, Arkansas, and Illinois Rivers to Chicago; first to establish the existence of a waterway from St. Lawrence River to the Gulf of Mexico

**1678–79** . . . Frère Louis Hennepin (France) explored Great Plains and the upper Mississippi River region

**1678–80** . . . Daniel Greysolon Duluth (Du Lhut) (France) claimed Lake Superior and upper Mississippi region for France; his treatment of the Indians gained their lasting friendship

**1679–82** . . . Robert Cavalier de La Salle (France) crossed Great Lakes and navigated Mississippi River to its mouth

**1691–92** . . . Henry Kelsey (England) explored the area around Reindeer Lake in western Canada

**1692** . . . Arnout Viele (France) explored the area from the Great Lakes to the Ohio River

**1701** . . . Antoine de la Mothe Cadillac (France) explored upper Michigan; founded Detroit

**1710–18** . . . Jean Baptiste le Moyne, sieur de Bienville (France), founded Mobile (1710) and New Orleans (1718)

**1731–43** . . . Pierre Gautier de Varennes, sieur de la Vérendrye (Canada), explored central Canada, Red River country, and the Missouri River (1731–34); discovered Lake Manitoba (1739) in central Canada; and traveled probably as far as the Black Hills in north central United States (1742–43)

**1769–79** . . . Daniel Boone (United States) explored Kentucky territory (1769–71) and blazed the Wilderness Road (1775)

**1770–72** . . . Samuel Hearne (England) opened areas of north central Canada, around Great Slave Lake and Coppermine River

**1775–76** . . . Silvestre Vélez de Escalante (Spain) explored Arizona and Colorado; first white man known to travel in Utah

**1792** . . . Robert Gray (United States) discovered Columbia River in northwestern United States

**1789–93** . . . Sir Alexander Mackenzie (Canada) followed Mackenzie River in Canada to Arctic Ocean (1789); explored elsewhere in Canada, making first overland crossing of North America to the Pacific, north of Mexico (1793)

**1797–1810** . . . David Thompson (Canada) explored Rocky Mountains and all of the Columbia River system

**1803–6** . . . Meriwether Lewis, William Clark (United States) navigated Missouri River to Bismarck, North Dakota, traveled west through the mountains to the Clearwater, Snake, and Columbia Rivers as far as the Pacific Ocean

**1805–7** . . . Zebulon Pike (United States) explored Minnesota (1805) and southwestern United States, sighted Pikes Peak (1806)

**c. 1807** . . . John Colter (United States) crossed Teton Range in the Rocky Mountains, and discovered Yellowstone area

**1819–27** . . . Sir John Franklin (England) explored northern Canada to the Arctic

**1825** . . . James Bridger (United States) discovered Great Salt Lake in Utah

**1825–27** . . . Jedediah Smith (United States) traveled from Great Salt Lake to Colorado River and San Diego, California; on return trip, he crossed Sierra Nevada and Great Salt Desert

**1832–35** . . . Benjamin Bonneville (United States) helped open Rocky Mountain territory

**1842–45** . . . John Frémont, Kit Carson (United States) explored Oregon, Nevada, and California

### SOUTH AND CENTRAL AMERICA

**1492–1502** . . . Christopher Columbus (Spain) discovered America: Bahamas, Cuba, and Hispaniola in the Caribbean (1492); Venezuela (1498); and Honduras (1502)

**1499** . . . Alonso de Ojeda (Spain) explored northeastern coast of South America

**1499–1509** . . . Vicente Pinzón (Spain) explored coast of Brazil and discovered mouth of the Amazon River in Brazil (1499–1500); skirted along Yucatán, Honduras, and Venezuela (1508–9)

**1500** . . . Pedro Alvarez Cabral (Portugal) reached coast of Brazil, possibly before Pinzón

**1501–2** . . . Amerigo Vespucci (Portugal) discovered Río de la Plata, explored about 6,000 miles of South American coast; he was the first to suggest that America was not part of Asia

**1513** . . . Vasco Núñez de Balboa (Spain) discovered the Pacific Ocean by crossing Isthmus of Panama

**1516** . . . Juan Díaz de Solís (Spain) sailed up Río de la Plata and explored Uruguay

**1517** . . . Francisco Fernández de Córdoba (Spain) discovered Yucatán in Mexico

**1519** . . . Gil González Dávila and Andrés Niño (Spain) explored Pacific coast of Central America from Panama to Nicaragua

**1519–21** . . . Hernán Cortés (Spain) discovered Aztec capital Tenochtitlán (now Mexico City) and conquered Mexico

**1520** . . . Ferdinand Magellan (Spain) explored Río de la Plata and Patagonia in Argentina, and discovered the strait at the tip of South America that bears his name

**1524–33** . . . Francisco Pizarro (Spain) explored the San Juan River between Colombia and Ecuador; conqueror of Peru (1532–33)

**1526–30** . . . Sebastian Cabot (Spain) explored Río de la Plata country along Paraguay, Plata, and Paraná Rivers

**1530–35** . . . Nikolaus Federmann (Germany) explored northwestern Venezuela and interior of Colombia through the Andes

**1533** . . . Sebastián de Belalcázar (Spain) explored and conquered Ecuador and southeastern Colombia

**1535–37** . . . Diego de Almagro (Spain) explored from Peru south through the Andes as far as Coquimbo and the Atacama Desert in Chile

**1535–37** . . . Pedro de Mendoza (Spain) explored Río de la Plata and founded Buenos Aires (1536)

**1536** . . . Gonzalo Jiménez de Quesada (Spain) founded Bogotá, Colombia, and explored the Magdalena River, Colombia

**1541** . . . Francisco de Orellana (Spain) floated down the Amazon's entire length

**1549–52** . . . Pedro de Valdivia (Spain) explored Chile, founding Concepción and Valdivia (1552)

**1595** . . . Sir Walter Raleigh (England) explored Orinoco River, penetrating 300 miles into Guiana's interior

**1616** . . . Willem C. Schouten (Netherlands) rounded and named Cape Horn at the tip of South America, avoiding the Strait of Magellan

**1799–1804** . . . Alexander von Humboldt (Germany) explored source of Orinoco and Amazon Rivers, establishing the connecting systems of the two

# STARS/PLANETS/SPACE

## ORIGIN AND EVOLUTION OF THE UNIVERSE

One of the major and perhaps most fundamental problems in astronomy is to develop a theory of the origin and evolution of the universe, based on actual observations of stars and galaxies and on known physical laws, in the attempt to determine how the universe changes with time. Cosmology deals with the physical structure of the universe, and with the origin of the universe and of its subsystems—that is, galaxies and systems of galaxies. Several different theories of the origin and evolution of the universe have been suggested.

The Einstein-Friedmann relativistic theories of cosmology, which were first formulated (1922) by Alexander Friedmann, a Russian physicist, are based on Einstein's theory of general relativity. The relativistic theorists postulate a universe that is in constant motion and originated from one infinitesimal point and subsequently expanded. The expansion of the universe refers to the mutual recession of galaxies from each other, with a recessional velocity proportional to their distance from one another. The observational evidence for the recession of galaxies from one another was first discovered by the American astronomer Edwin Hubble in the late 1920s.

Most astronomers believe that the whole universe originated in a cataclysmic explosion. This is the basis of the "big-bang" theory. From the moment of the big bang the universe has expanded and as the galaxies formed they shared in this expansion. At the very beginning, the temperature in the universe was extremely high. As it decreased, particles of radiation (photons) and of matter were created. Within only a few minutes electrons and the nuclei of hydrogen, deuterium, and helium had been produced. Matter and radiation continued to cool and after many thousands of years the immense clouds of matter that had formed were able to condense into galaxies and stars.

According to the relativistic concept, the geometry of space determines the kind of expansion of the universe. If the curvature of space is positive, which means that space is finite, the relativistic equations predict that the expansion of the universe will come to a halt at some finite time. Thereafter, the universe will begin to contract with increasing velocity until it reaches its initial primordial state of very high density and very high temperature. This concept is sometimes referred to as a "closed" universe. If the curvature of space is negative, the expansion could be permanent; the universe could expand forever. In this "open" universe idea, even after the last star has stopped shining and the entire universe is in total darkness, the universe will still be expanding.

According to the "steady-state" or "continuous creation" theory of cosmology, galaxies recede from one another, but their spatial density remains constant. According to this theory, there is a continuous creation of new matter (hydrogen atoms) throughout space. The newly created matter subsequently condenses to form new stars and galaxies between the older galaxies, and a steady state or constant spatial density with time is maintained. In the steady-state concept, the universe had no beginning and has no end.

However, we can determine an upper limit for the age of the universe, since its rate of expansion has been continually slowing up. This is considered evidence of the primordial explosion postulated as first putting the universe in motion. Based on the present rate of the expansion, it appears that the age of the universe is between about 10 and 20 billion years.

The big-bang theory predicts that the radiation originally created in the big bang should by now have cooled to a very low temperature. It should in fact be observed as black-body radiation characteristic of a temperature of about 3 kelvin (−270°C), i.e., as very high frequency radio waves (microwaves) of very low intensity. In 1965, A. A. Penzias and R. W. Wilson of the Bell Telephone Laboratories in New Jersey, made an accidental discovery of major cosmological importance. They detected a background microwave emission of uniform intensity coming from all parts of the sky that corresponded to a temperature of about 3 kelvin. This is believed to be the relic radiation from the original big bang of the universe. Molecules found in interstellar space can be used as a cosmic thermometer: spectral measurements of CN absorption confirm the existence of the 3-kelvin universal background radiation.

Further evidence for the big bang comes from studies on the abundance of helium in the universe. Most of the helium in the universe is thought to have formed within minutes of the big bang. The amount predicted by theory is very close to what has been observed: helium forms about 25% (by mass) of the matter in the universe, hydrogen about 73%, with oxygen, carbon and other elements making up the balance.

According to the big-bang theory, the number of galaxies per volume of space should have been much greater in the early stages of the universe's evolution than it is today. The steady-state model holds that the number of galaxies per volume of space should be statistically the same everywhere at all times. Martin Ryle, the British Astronomer Royal, has presented very substantial radio astronomical evidence against the steady-state theory, based on counts of the numbers of radio galaxies that are very distant in space (looking farther out into space is really like looking back into time).

At present it appears that the balance of the observational evidence is against the steady-state concept and in favor of the big-bang theory.

## STARS AND GALAXIES

Stars are the basic elements in the universe. More than 90 percent of the mass of our own galaxy—the Milky Way—is in the form of stars; the rest of the matter is interstellar hydrogen gas and dust that form stars. The mass of the Sun—the star of our solar system—is $2 \times 10^{30}$ kg. The range of masses observed for most stars varies from 0.05 of the Sun's mass to 60 times the Sun's mass. The range of luminosity or absolute magnitude (brightness) varies from a tiny fraction of the Sun's luminosity for white dwarf stars to over a million times the Sun's luminosity for the most luminous stars. The range of stellar radii varies from 1/70,000 of the Sun's radius for neutron stars to over 1,000 times the Sun's radius for supergiants. The Sun's density is about 1.4 grams/cm$^3$ (a little heavier than water). White dwarfs may be over 1 million times as dense as the Sun and neutron stars even more dense; supergiants can be only one-millionth as dense as the Sun.

Multiple star systems consist of more than two stars linked by gravitational forces. Galactic or open clusters are loosely bound stellar systems with up to a few hundred stars. Globular or closed clusters are tightly bound spherical star clusters with maybe over a million stars. Galaxies are the largest stellar systems and are regarded as the basic mass elements of the universe. Galaxies, which occur in clusters, contain from a billion to a thousand billion stars each. It has been estimated that there are at least 10 billion galaxies in the universe. From observations, it appears that there are three distinct types. In spiral galaxies, spiral arms of gas and dust are distinctly visible. In elliptical galaxies, there are no visible spiral arms or gas, and the exterior shape is either elliptical or spherical. Irregular galaxies have no definite shape.

In 1944 Walter Baade reported that stars in the nucleus of spiral galaxies are different from the stars in the arms of the galaxy. Stars within the spiral arms are called Population I stars and are young and bluish in color. Population II stars are found in the galactic nucleus and galactic halo and are old and reddish in color.

Red giants are cool red stars that have undergone expansion; their luminosity may be well over 1,000 times the Sun's luminosity, and their radius several hundred times the Sun's radius. The red giant has already converted about 50 percent of its hydrogen into helium by thermonuclear processes. As this energy source becomes exhausted, expansion halts and contraction to a white dwarf may occur. White dwarfs have low luminosity, relatively high surface temperature and extremely high density. They are dying stars and are gradually cooling to become "black dwarfs" or nonluminous chunks of mass. The Sun will become a white dwarf in billions of years time.

The process by which a star dies depends on its mass. When its energy is exhausted, a star with a mass below 1.4 times the Sun's mass will become a white dwarf. One with a mass between 1.4 and about 3 times the Sun's mass will contract through the white-dwarf stage and become a tiny immensely dense neutron star. Supernovae are stars that suddenly increase their luminosity by more than 10 million times. The supernova luminosity increase reflects the fact that the star is exploding—literally blowing itself up. It is believed that the remnant of at least one supernova (the Crab Nebula) is a neutron star, which forms the pulsating radio source or "pulsar" observed in that region of the sky.

## QUASARS

Quasars ("quasi-stellar radio sources") were first discovered in 1961 as starlike objects emitting extremely intense radio radiation. In 1963 optical astronomers identified these objects with faint sources of light. Since then hundreds of quasars have been found, all well beyond our galaxy. Over 99% are undetectable radio sources and are sometimes referred to as QSOs ("quasi-stellar objects"). It is still a most challenging problem to understand the physical process that leads to the tremendous radio emission in some quasars and the lack of it in others. The discovery that most quasars emit intense infrared radiation and X-rays must also now be explained.

In 1963, Maarten Schmidt, of the California Institute of Technology, discovered one of the main characteristics of quasars: a large red shift in the location of the emission lines in their spectra. It is generally accepted that these large red shifts are caused by the cosmological expansion of the universe. The red shift is used to determine the distance of receding extragalactic objects. The measured red shift of quasars would place them at a few billion light years—in fact, the most distant objects in the universe.

This interpretation also implies that to be detectable on Earth quasars must emit a thousand times more energy than an entire galaxy, containing about 100 billion stars. The radiative emission from quasars in the visible and in the short radio-wavelength region varies with time. The time scale and amplitude of these brightness variations place a limit on the geometrical size of the emitting object. Thus, the center of activity in a quasar is in the order of a few light months or less in diameter, compared to 100,000 light years for a galaxy. Detailed studies have been made of the complex emission lines and absorption lines that occur in the spectra of quasars. These studies indicate that the compact active region lies at the center of a group of dense, rapidly moving clouds of gas, which are enveloped in low density gas. Evidence is indeed accumulating that quasars lie at the centers of galaxies.

Despite the theories advanced, the actual origin of the tremendous energy output of quasars remains unknown. One theory is that the energy is generated in a compact cluster of stars by supernova explosions, numerous collisions between the closely packed stars, and by pulsars. In another theory the active center contains a supermassive black hole of a billion solar masses; the energy is released when gas and stars are drawn into the black hole.

Of late, there has been a growing awareness that quasars show similarities to Seyfert galaxies, which are a galaxy class characterized by the small size and high luminosity of their nuclei. Their outer parts, however, are inconspicuous. Since quasars appear photographically similar and have similar emission spectra to Seyfert galaxies, it appears that these two celestial phenomena may somehow be related.

## PULSARS

In 1967 a new class of astronomical object was discovered by a Cambridge University group: a rapidly pulsating radio source, or "pulsar." The radio signals from this object, located in the constellation Vulpecula, were periodic in nature, consisting of brief radio pulses that were separated by about 1.3 seconds. Since then, more than 300 pulsars have been discovered.

The most interesting property of pulsars is the extreme regularity of their radio-emission period, which ranges from 0.033 to over 4 seconds. It was believed that this time period between radio pulses was remarkably constant, varying by not more than a few parts per million annually; however, recently it has been found that the periods of most pulsars are lengthening very slightly due to the transfer of internal rotational energy to the surroundings. Two of these pulsars have been identified with the remnants of exploding stars, the Crab Nebula and one in the constellation of Vela. These two pulsars have the shortest periods of any known—0.033 and 0.089 second, respectively—but their periods are increasing more rapidly than those of any other pulsars. A pulsar's radio pulses are of very short duration compared to the time periods between those pulses, which typically are some thousandths of a second.

Optical astronomers have gone to considerable lengths to determine if pulsars emit optical pulses as well as radio pulses. At the present time, only the Crab Nebula pulsar and the very faint Vela pulsar have been observed to emit periodic pulses of light. The former also emits X-rays, ultraviolet, and infrared radiation.

A pulsar is assumed to be a rapidly rotating neutron star, which is a very dense star with an intense magnetic field. The gravitational collapse of a massive dying star causes it to implode as a supernova and vast quantities of energy are given off. Any remaining core could be a pulsar, with a mass between 1.4 and about 3 times the Sun's mass but a diameter of only about 10 miles (the Sun's diameter is 865,000 miles). This kind of star rotates so rapidly that it can complete one rotation on its axis in less than a thousandth of a second.

## STELLAR AND GALACTIC TERMS

**Absolute Magnitude**—Apparent magnitude that a star would have at a distance of 10 parsecs.

**Albedo**—Reflecting power of a nonluminous body.

**Apparent Magnitude**—A measure of the observed light flux received from a star or other object at Earth.

**Astronomical Unit (AU)**—The average distance between the Sun and the Earth. It is equal to 92,957,000 miles and is often used as a unit of measurement.

**Bands (in spectra)**—Emission or absorption lines, usually in the spectra of chemical compounds or radicals, coalesced into broad emission or absorption bands.

**Binary Star**—System of two stars revolving about a common center of gravity.

**Black Body**—A hypothetical perfect radiator that absorbs and reemits all radiation incident upon it.

**Clouds of Magellan**—Two neighboring galaxies visible to the naked eye from southern latitudes.

**Cosmic Rays**—Atomic nuclei (mostly protons) that are observed to strike the Earth's atmosphere with exceedingly high energies, probably from supernovae.

**Cosmological Red Shift**—Red shift of spectral lines in celestial objects arising from the expansion of the universe which, when interpreted with a cosmological model, indicates the distance of those objects.

**Cosmology**—The study of the organization and evolution of the universe.

**Dark Nebula**—A cloud of interstellar dust that obscures the light of more distant stars and appears as an opaque curtain.

**Diffuse Nebula**—A reflection or emission nebula produced by interstellar matter (not a planetary nebula).

**Emission Nebula**—A gaseous nebula that derives its visible light from the fluorescence of ultraviolet light from a star in or near the nebula.

**Extragalactic**—Beyond the galaxy.

**Gamma Rays**—Photons (of electromagnetic radiation) of energy higher than that of X rays—the most energetic form of electromagnetic radiation.

**Gravitational Force**—Force of attraction between two bodies, directly proportional to product of their masses, inversely proportional to square of distance between them.

**"Heavy" Elements**—In astronomy, usually those elements of greater atomic number than helium.

**Hertzsprung-Russell Diagram**—A basic classification of the properties of stars in which luminosity is related to effective surface temperature or star color.

**Infrared Radiation**—Electromagnetic radiation of wavelength longer than the longest visible (red) wavelengths but shorter than radio wavelengths.

**Interstellar Dust**—Microscopic solid grains, believed to be mostly dielectric compounds of hydrogen and other common elements, in interstellar space.

**Interstellar Gas**—Sparse gas in interstellar space.

**Kelvin Temperature Scale**—An absolute temperature scale, the zero point of which is $-273.15°$ C; temperature in kelvin = temperature in °C − 273.15.

**Law of the Red Shifts**—The relation between the radial velocity and distance of a remote galaxy: the radial velocity is proportional to the galaxy distance.

**Light-year**—The distance light travels in a vacuum in one year; 1 LY = $9.46 \times 10^{12}$ km, or about $6 \times 10^{12}$ mi.

**Luminosity**—The rate of radiation of electromagnetic energy into space by a star or other object.

**Magnitude**—A measure of the amount of light flux received from a star or other luminous object.

**Nebula**—Cloud of interstellar gas or dust.

**Neutron Stars**—A near-final stage in stellar evolution at which nuclear energy sources are exhausted, central densities are nuclear densities, and the stars are supported by degenerate neutron pressure. Rotating neutron stars are of current interest as pulsar models.

**Nova**—Suddenly exploding or erupting star gradually fading to original brightness.

**Nuclear Transformation**—Transformation of one atomic nucleus into another.

**Occultation**—An eclipse of a star or planet by the moon or some other celestial body, as seen from Earth.

**Parsec**—The distance of an object that would have a stellar parallax of one second of arc; 1 parsec = 3.26 light-years.

**Planetary Nebula**—A shell of gas ejected from, and enlarging about, a certain kind of extremely hot star.

**Population I and II**—Two classes of stars (and star systems) classified according to their spectral characteristics, chemical compositions, radial velocities, ages, and galaxy locations.

**Proton-Proton Reaction**—A chain of thermonuclear reactions by which hydrogen nuclei are built up into nuclei of helium, so producing huge amounts of energy.

**Radio Waves**—The lowest-energy electromagnetic radiation, lying beyond the infrared region of the spectrum. Narrow bands that can pass through the Earth's atmosphere are used in radio astronomy.

**Recurrent Nova**—A nova that has been known to erupt more than once.

**Red Shift, Redshift**—A shift to longer wavelengths of the light from a celestial body; produced by Doppler shift due to body's recession from Earth.

**Seyfert Galaxies**—Galaxies having very bright nuclei and inconspicuous spiral arms. Their spectra show strong emission lines.

**Solar Wind**—Flow of high-energy particles (mainly protons and electrons) from the Sun.

**Spectral Class (or Type)**—A classification of a star according to the characteristics of its spectrum.

**Spectrograph**—An instrument for photographing a spectrum; usually attached to a telescope to photograph the spectrum of a star.

**Spectroscope**—An instrument for directly viewing the spectrum of a light source.

**Spectrum**—The array of colors or wavelengths obtained when light from a source is dispersed, as in passing it through a prism or grating.

**Stellar Evolution**—The changes that take place in the sizes, luminosities, structures, and the like of stars as they age.

**Supergiants**—Very bright stars that have undergone considerable expansion.

**Ultraviolet Radiation**—Electromagnetic radiation of wavelengths shorter than the shortest visible (violet) wavelengths and in the approximate range 10 to 300 nanometers.

**X rays**—Electromagnetic radiation lying between gamma rays and ultraviolet radiation in energy: totally absorbed by Earth's atmosphere.

## THE TWENTY BRIGHTEST STARS*

**The 20 brightest stars—stars with smallest apparent magnitude—contain one triple-star system and nine binary systems. The table gives the stars, their distance in parsecs, and the apparent and absolute magnitude of the stars and their components.**

| | | APPARENT VISUAL MAGNITUDES OF COMPONENTS | | | ABSOLUTE VISUAL MAGNITUDES OF COMPONENTS | | |
|---|---|---|---|---|---|---|---|
| **Star** | **Distance (Parsecs)** | **1st** | **2d** | **3d** | **1st** | **2d** | **3d** |
| Sirius | 2.7 | −1.47 | + 8.5 | — | +1.4 | +11.4 | — |
| Canopus | 34 | −0.73 | — | — | −3.3 | — | — |
| Arcturus | 11 | −0.06 | — | — | −0.3 | — | — |
| α Centauri | 1.3 | −0.00 | + 1.4 | +10.7 | +4.4 | + 5.8 | +15 |
| Vega | 8.0 | +0.04 | — | — | +0.6 | — | — |
| Rigel | 261 | +0.08 | + 6.6 | — | −7.0 | − 0.4 | — |
| Capella | 14 | +0.09 | + 0.5 | — | +0.1 | + 0.4 | — |
| Procyon | 3.4 | +0.34 | +10.8 | — | +2.6 | +13.0 | — |
| Betelgeuse | 199 | +0.41v | — | — | −5.5 | — | — |
| Achernar | 23 | +0.47 | — | — | −1.6 | — | — |
| β Centauri | 101 | +0.59 | + 4 | — | −4.4 | − 0.8 | — |
| Altair | 4.9 | +0.77 | — | — | +1.9 | — | — |
| α Crucis | 86 | +0.79 | + 1.9 | — | −3.9 | − 3.5 | — |
| Aldebaran | 20 | +0.86 | +13 | — | −0.3 | +12 | — |
| Spica | 80 | +0.96 | — | — | −3.5 | — | — |
| Antares | 132 | +1.08 | + 5.1 | — | −4.5 | − 0.3 | — |
| Pollux | 11 | +1.15 | — | — | +0.2 | — | — |
| Fomalhaut | 7.0 | +1.16 | + 6.5 | — | +1.7 | + 7.3 | — |
| β Crucis | 175 | +1.24v | — | — | −5.0 | — | — |
| Deneb | 460 | +1.26 | — | — | −7.0 | — | — |

* For information about the Sun, see page 321. v=variable magnitude.

## THE NEAREST STARS*

The following list gives the star, its distance in parsecs (a parsec is equal to 3.26 light-years), and the apparent and absolute magnitudes of the star and its components. The apparent magnitude is the brightness of the star as observed from Earth, while the absolute magnitude is the brightness that the star would have at a distance of 10 parsecs. The larger the magnitude, the fainter the star. A first-magnitude star appears roughly 2.5 times as bright as a second-magnitude star. A zero magnitude star is 2.5 times as bright as a first-magnitude star, and a —1 star is 2.5 times as bright as a zero-magnitude star.

| Star | Distance (Parsecs) | APPARENT VISUAL MAGNITUDES OF COMPONENTS | | | ABSOLUTE VISUAL MAGNITUDES OF COMPONENTS | | |
|---|---|---|---|---|---|---|---|
| | | 1st | 2d | 3d | 1st | 2d | 3d |
| Proxima | 1.31 | 10.7 | — | — | 15.1 | — | — |
| α Centauri | 1.31 | 0.00 | + 1.4 | +10.7 | + 4.4 | + 5.8 | +15 |
| Barnard's Star | 1.80 | + 9.54 | — | — | +13.2 | — | — |
| Wolf 359 | 2.33 | +13.5 | — | — | +16.7 | — | — |
| Lalande 21185 | 2.48 | + 7.48 | — | — | +10.5 | — | — |
| Sirius | 2.67 | — 1.47 | + 8.5 | — | + 1.4 | +11.4 | — |
| Luyten 726–8 | 2.73 | +12.5 | +12.9 | — | +15.4 | +15.8 | — |
| Ross 154 | 2.91 | +10.6 | — | — | +13.3 | — | — |
| Ross 248 | 3.16 | +12.24 | — | — | +14.7 | — | — |
| ε Eridani | 3.28 | + 3.68 | — | — | + 6.1 | — | — |
| Ross 128 | 3.31 | +11.13 | — | — | +13.5 | — | — |
| Luyten 789–6 | 3.31 | +12.28 | — | — | +14.6 | — | — |
| Procyon | 3.37 | + 0.34 | +10.7 | — | + 2.6 | +13.0 | — |
| 61 Cygni | 3.43 | + 5.19 | + 6.02 | — | + 7.5 | + 8.4 | — |
| ε Indi | 3.43 | + 4.71 | — | — | + 7.0 | — | — |
| Σ 2398 | 3.53 | + 8.90 | + 9.69 | — | +11.1 | +11.9 | — |
| BD+43°44 | 3.56 | + 8.07 | +11.04 | — | +10.3 | +13.2 | — |
| Lac 9352 | 3.59 | + 7.43 | — | — | + 9.6 | — | — |
| τ Ceti | 3.65 | + 3.49 | — | — | + 5.7 | — | — |
| BD+5°1668 | 3.77 | +10.9 | — | — | +13.0 | — | — |
| Lac 8760 | 3.83 | + 6.76 | — | — | + 8.8 | — | — |
| Kapteyn's Star | 3.90 | + 8.81 | — | — | +10.8 | — | — |
| Kruger 60 | 3.93 | + 9.85 | +11.3 | — | +11.9 | +13.3 | — |
| Ross 614 | 4.03 | +11.13 | +14.8 | — | +13.1 | +16.8 | — |
| BD—12°4523 | 4.10 | +10.13 | — | — | +12.0 | — | — |
| v. Maanen's Star | 4.24 | +12.36 | — | — | +14.3 | — | — |

* For information about the Sun, see page 321.

## THE CONSTELLATIONS

Constellations are areas of the sky with configurations of stars supposedly resembling a particular object, person, or animal. The bright stars within a given constellation are named with a Greek letter plus the genitive of the constellation, with the brightest star getting the first Greek letter, alpha; the second brightest getting the second Greek letter, beta; and the like. The following table gives the constellation, its genitive, its English name or description, and the abbreviation for it.

| Constellation | Genitive | English name or description | Abbreviation |
|---|---|---|---|
| Andromeda | Andromedae | Chained Maiden | And |
| Antlia | Antliae | Air pump | Ant |
| Apus | Apodis | Bird of Paradise | Aps |
| Aquarius | Aquarii | Water bearer | Aqr |
| Aquila | Aquilae | Eagle | Aql |
| Ara | Arae | Altar | Ara |
| Aries | Arietis | Ram | Ari |
| Auriga | Aurigae | Charioteer | Aur |
| Boötes | Boötis | Herdsman | Boo |
| Caelum | Caeli | Chisel | Cae |
| Camelopardalis | Camelopardalis | Giraffe | Cam |
| Cancer | Cancri | Crab | Cnc |
| Canes Venatici | Canum Venaticorum | Hunting dogs | CVn |
| Canis Major | Canis Majoris | Great dog | CMa |
| Canis Minor | Canis Minoris | Little dog | CMi |
| Capricornus | Capricorni | Sea goat | Cap |
| •Carina | Carinae | Keel of Argonauts' ship | Car |
| Cassiopeia | Cassiopeiae | Queen of Ethiopia | Cas |
| Centaurus | Centauri | Centaur | Cen |
| Cepheus | Cephei | King of Ethiopia | Cep |
| Cetus | Ceti | Whale | Cet |
| Chamaeleon | Chamaeleontis | Chameleon | Cha |
| Circinus | Circini | Compasses | Cir |
| Columba | Columbae | Dove | Col |
| Coma Berenices | Comae Berenices | Berenice's hair | Com |
| Corona Australis | Coronae Australis | Southern crown | CrA |
| Corona Borealis | Coronae Borealis | Northern crown | CrB |
| Corvus | Corvi | Crow | Crv |
| Crater | Crateris | Cup | Crt |
| Crux | Crucis | Cross (southern) | Cru |
| Cygnus | Cygni | Swan | Cyg |
| Delphinus | Delphini | Dolphin | Del |
| Dorado | Doradûs | Swordfish | Dor |
| Draco | Draconis | Dragon | Dra |
| Equuleus | Equulei | Little horse | Equ |
| Eridanus | Eridani | River | Eri |
| Fornax | Fornacis | Furnace | For |
| Gemini | Geminorum | Twins | Gem |
| Grus | Gruis | Crane | Gru |
| Hercules | Herculis | Hercules | Her |
| Horologium | Horologii | Clock | Hor |
| Hydra | Hydrae | Sea serpent | Hya |
| Hydrus | Hydri | Water snake | Hyi |
| Indus | Indi | Indian | Ind |
| Lacerta | Lacertae | Lizard | Lac |
| Leo | Leonis | Lion | Leo |
| Leo Minor | Leonis Minoris | Little lion | LMi |
| Lepus | Leporis | Hare | Lep |
| Libra | Librae | Balance | Lib |
| Lupus | Lupi | Wolf | Lup |
| Lynx | Lyncis | Lynx | Lyn |
| Lyra | Lyrae | Lyre | Lyr |
| Mensa | Mensae | Table Mountain | Men |
| Microscopium | Microscopii | Microscope | Mic |
| Monoceros | Monocerotis | Unicorn | Mon |
| Musca | Muscae | Fly | Mus |
| Norma | Normae | Rule | Nor |
| Octans | Octantis | Octant | Oct |
| Ophiuchus | Ophiuchi | Serpent bearer | Oph |
| Orion | Orionis | Orion, the hunter | Ori |
| Pavo | Pavonis | Peacock | Pav |
| Pegasus | Pegasi | Pegasus, the winged horse | Peg |
| Perseus | Persei | Perseus, hero who saved Andromeda | Per |
| Phoenix | Phoenicis | Phoenix | Phe |
| Pictor | Pictoris | Easel | Pic |

| Constellation | Genitive | English name or description | Abbreviation |
|---|---|---|---|
| Pisces | Piscium | Fishes | Psc |
| Piscis Austrinus | Piscis Austrini | Southern fish | PsA |
| *Puppis | Puppis | Stern of the Argonauts' ship | Pup |
| *Pyxis | Pyxidis | Compass on the Argonauts' ship | Pyx |
| Reticulum | Reticuli | Net | Ret |
| Sagitta | Sagittae | Arrow | Sge |
| Sagittarius | Sagittarii | Archer | Sgr |
| Scorpius | Scorpii | Scorpion | Sco |
| Sculptor | Sculptoris | Sculptor's tools | Scl |
| Scutum | Scuti | Shield | Sct |
| Serpens | Serpentis | Serpent | Ser |
| Sextans | Sextantis | Sextant | Sex |
| Taurus | Tauri | Bull | Tau |
| Telescopium | Telescopii | Telescope | Tel |
| Triangulum | Trianguli | Triangle | Tri |
| Triangulum Australe | Trianguli Australis | Southern triangle | TrA |
| Tucana | Tucanae | Toucan | Tuc |
| Ursa Major | Ursae Majoris | Great bear | UMa |
| Ursa Minor | Ursae Minoris | Little bear | UMi |
| *Vela | Velorum | Sails of the Argonauts' ship | Vel |
| Virgo | Virginis | Virgin | Vir |
| Volans | Volantis | Flying fish | Vol |
| Vulpecula | Vulpeculae | Fox | Vul |

* The four constellations Carina, Puppis, Pyxis, and Vela originally formed the single constellation Argo Navis.

## SUPERNOVAE, BLACK HOLES AND THE GUM NEBULA

Astronomers have recently added two new objects to the growing list of strange and puzzling objects speculated about or found in the universe. A "black hole" is the hypothetical result of a runaway or uncontrolled gravitational collapse of a star or collection of stars. Eventually, if its contraction is not halted, a collapsing object will reach a limiting size, called the Schwarzschild radius, which depends upon the mass of the object. For the Sun the Schwarzschild radius would be under two miles. As the object continues to contract to less than its Schwarzschild radius it becomes a black hole. The gravitational forces exerted by this object are so strong that no matter or radiation can escape from it. The light emanating from this object is trapped and effectively removed from the "observable universe."

A supernova occurs when a star has evolved to such an unstable state that it blows itself up. The energy released in the holocaust is almost beyond comprehension. The material ejected with immense force from the exploding star forms a huge shell of gas which sweeps up interstellar gas as it expands. This is known as a supernova remnant. What remains of the star is possibly its dense central core. Astrophysicists have speculated that the core of a supernova can become either a neutron star or a black hole. The final mass of the remnant star determines whether gravitational collapse will stop at the stable neutron star stage, instead of running away and becoming a black hole. It is believed that if the star's mass is greater than about 3.0 times the Sun's mass a black hole should readily form. (Neutron stars should form for stars whose mass is above 1.4 times the Sun's mass.) A black hole almost certainly exists in the binary star Cygnus X-1 and maybe in other X-ray binaries. There is also possible evidence of massive black holes at the centers of certain galaxies, notably M87, that would tear apart and swallow stars in the immediate surroundings.

Nebulae are extended bright luminosities in the sky. Some nebulae are the glowing remnants of supernovae. Other nebulae are clouds of ionized hydrogen surrounding hot stars, which cause them to glow continuously. Such objects surrounding hot stars are called Stromgren spheres. The Gum Nebula (discovered by the Australian astronomer, Colin S. Gum, in 1952) combines certain characteristics of the other two types of nebulae. It is about 2,600 light-years across in its longest dimension and appears to be somewhat elliptical in shape. A group of astronomers from NASA and Kitt Peak National Observatory proposes that the Gum Nebula is a fossil Stromgren sphere produced by a supernova that exploded 11,000 years ago, giving off a tremendous blast of ultraviolet radiation, which ionized interstellar hydrogen clouds for hundreds of light years around. What is now glowing is not the material that was originally ejected from the supernova, but the interstellar hydrogen gas that was there before the supernova explosion. Unlike Stromgren spheres that are continuously being ionized by hot stars, the fossil Gum Nebula is gradually decaying, as the ionized hydrogen gas recombines in the absence of a new ionizing source.

## INTERSTELLAR MOLECULES

Within the last 25 years astronomers have found that there is a continuous exchange of material between stars and the interstellar medium. Stars are continually being formed from interstellar hydrogen and other gas, mixed with dust: diffuse interstellar material somehow collects into cool dense clouds which may eventually contract under gravitational forces forming stars and, possibly, planetary systems. As stars evolve, material is ejected from them, e.g., in supernovae, to again become part of the interstellar medium.

The first interstellar molecules ever found—CH, $CH^+$, and CN (cyanogen)—were diatomic (consisting of only two atoms) and were found more than 40 years ago by optical astronomers.

In March 1951 radio astronomers detected interstellar atomic hydrogen (H) and in 1963 they discovered the hydroxyl radical (OH) in the interstellar medium. Up to this time no one had ever detected a polyatomic molecule (consisting of three or more atoms). The formation of molecules more complex than diatomic molecules in interstellar space was believed to be rare, since interstellar densities and temperatures are so low that molecule formation is very difficult.

This idea was upset in 1968 when radio astronomers detected interstellar ammonia ($NH_3$). In early 1969 radio astronomers detected interstellar water vapor ($H_2O$). In March 1969 interstellar formaldehyde ($H_2CO$)—the first polyatomic organic molecule—was discovered by radio astronomers. On March 13, 1970, a Naval Research Laboratory Aerobee rocket detected molecular hydrogen ($H_2$) in interstellar space.

Interstellar atomic hydrogen (H) has been observed by radio astronomers since 1951, but molecular hydrogen had previously eluded detection. In 1970 radio astronomers also found interstellar carbon monoxide (CO), hydrogen cyanide (HCN), cyanoacetylene ($HC_3N$), formic acid (HCOOH), and methanol or wood alcohol ($CH_3OH$). Another molecule, originally called "X-ogen" has since been identified as HCO . At present over 50 interstellar molecules have been detected, including deuterium (heavy hydrogen), hydrogen sulfide ($H_2S$), acetaldehyde ($CH_3CHO$), and silicon monoxide (SiO). Large numbers are found in massive dense interstellar clouds, known as "giant molecular complexes", associated with dense clumps of dust.

Additional evidence for the existence of extraterrestrial organic molecules was given in December 1970, when it was announced that a meteorite that fell near Murchison, Victoria, Australia, on September 28, 1969, is believed to contain five of the 20 most common amino acids—glycine, alanine, glutamic acid, valine, and proline. This finding demonstrates that complex amino acids, the basic building blocks of proteins, can be and have been formed outside the Earth by natural chemical processes.

Hence, in recent years, astronomers have found that the interstellar medium is interspersed with molecules, a proportionately high fraction of which are organic compounds. As star and planet formation take place, these organic compounds may play an important role in the chemical evolution and origin of life.

## OUR LOCAL GROUP OF GALAXIES

Our local group of galaxies contains over 30 members that cover a region about 3 million light-years in diameter. The largest members are both spiral galaxies—our Milky Way galaxy and the Andromeda galaxy (M31). All together, there are three spirals, four irregulars, 11 ellipticals, and many dwarf irregulars and dwarf ellipticals. Some of our local galaxies are listed below, with apparent magnitude, distance in thousand parsecs (kiloparsecs), galactic diameter in kiloparsecs, and absolute magnitude.

| Galaxy | Visual magnitude | Distance (kilopcs) | Diameter (kilopcs) | Absolute magnitude |
|---|---|---|---|---|
| The Milky Way | — | — | 30 | (—21) |
| Large Magellanic Cloud | 0.9 | 48 | 10 | —17.7 |
| Small Magellanic Cloud | 2.5 | 56 | 8 | —16.5 |
| Ursa Minor system | — | 70 | 1 | (—9) |
| Sculptor system | 8.0 | 83 | 2.2 | —11.8 |
| Draco system | — | 100 | 1.4 | (—10) |
| Fornax system | 8.3 | 190 | 6.6 | —13.3 |
| Leo II system | 12.04 | 230 | 1.6 | —10.0 |
| Leo I system | 12.0 | 280 | 1.5 | —10.4 |
| NGC 6822 | 8.9 | 460 | 2.7 | —14.8 |
| NGC 147 | 9.73 | 570 | 3 | —14.5 |
| NGC 185 | 9.43 | 570 | 2.3 | —14.8 |
| NGC 205 | 8.17 | 680 | 5 | —16.5 |
| NGC 221 (M32) | 8.16 | 680 | 2.4 | —16.5 |
| IC 1613 | 9.61 | 680 | 5 | —14.7 |
| Andromeda galaxy | 3.47 | 680 | 40 | —21.2 |
| NGC 598 (M33) | 5.79 | 720 | 17 | —18.9 |
| Maffei 1 | 11.0 | 1000 | — | —19.0 |

## ASTRONOMICAL INSTRUMENTATION

The most important property of a telescope is its ability to gather light so that objects that are too remote or too faint to be seen with the naked eye are detectable. The light-gathering power of a telescope varies according to the total surface area of either the objective lens or the mirror in the telescope.

There are two main classes of telescopes that gather visible light: reflectors and refractors. In a reflector, a large curved mirror gathers the light; in a refractor, a large objective lens accomplishes this feat. The largest reflecting telescope now in operation has a 236" mirror; the largest refracting telescope has a 40" objective lens. The Schmidt camera is an optical system that utilizes both a mirror and a lens; it produces excellent star images over a large area of the sky and is in widespread use around the world.

In 1931, K. G. Jansky encountered interference in the form of radio radiation coming from an unknown source, which subsequent investigation showed was the Milky Way. In 1936, Grote Reber built the first antenna that was specifically designed to receive these cosmic radio waves. In 1942, radio radiation was first received from the Sun. After World War II, the technique of making radio astronomical observations was rapidly developed, especially in Australia, England, the Netherlands, and more recently in the United States. The 328-foot radio telescope at Bonn, West Germany is the world's largest fully steerable radio telescope.

In a radio telescope, the radiowave gathering is done by a parabolic metallic reflector, called a "dish," which focuses waves onto an antenna, or by a dipole antenna. Sensitivity is increased by using an array of such antennas.

Radio signals have been observed to come from the Sun, the Moon, certain planets, from the center of our galaxy, and from other galaxies. In addition, strong radio signals are given off by quasars while rapidly pulsating radio signals are received from pulsars. Radio signals can be used to determine both the surface and lower-atmosphere temperatures of the planets.

Other types of radio emission offer insight into the physical processes within the upper atmosphere of the planets and the Sun, as well as certain physical processes within galaxies. Signals at certain discrete radio wavelengths are caused by the presence of certain interstellar molecules. The amount and distribution of these molecules in space are determinable by using radio telescopes.

Radar astronomy systems consist of a powerful radio transmitter, capable of transmitting high-power radio signals out into space over long distances, and a sensitive antenna, with which the return radar echo is detectable. This returning radar echo can provide information about lunar and planetary surfaces, planetary atmospheres and rotation periods, and the precise values of the distances of different solar system objects. X-ray astronomy gains data from satellites and from rocket and balloon flights, X-rays being absorbed by the atmosphere. Since 1962 over 3,000 X-ray sources have been detected inside and outside our Galaxy and include supernova remnants, quasars, binary systems, and possible black holes.

Only a few bands of infrared wavelengths from space can penetrate the atmosphere. Special detectors of this radiation, on the ground and in rockets, have shown that huge quantities of infrared rays are emitted from dying stars and from stars being born.

## MAJOR ASTRONOMICAL FACILITIES

This list includes the world's major astronomical observing facilities: reflecting and refracting optical telescopes, radio telescopes, and radar astronomy systems. UC = Under construction.

### REFLECTING OPTICAL AND INFRARED (IR) TELESCOPES AND SCHMIDT CAMERAS

| Mirror Diameter (Inches) | Observatory | In Operation Since |
|---|---|---|
| 236 | Special Astrophysical Observatory, Mount Pastukhov, USSR | 1976 |
| 200 | Palomar Observatory, Mount Palomar, California | 1948 |
| 176* | Smithsonian Astrophysical Observatory, Mount Hopkins, Arizona | 1979 |
| 165 | Roque de los Muchachos Observatory, La Palma, Canaries | UC |
| 158 | Kitt Peak National Observatory, Tucson, Arizona | 1974 |
| 158 | Cerro Tololo Observatory, La Serena, Chile | 1976 |
| 153 | Siding Spring Observatory, Siding Spring, NSW, Australia | 1975 |
| 153 | (IR) Unit of Royal Obs., Edinburgh, Mauna Kea, Hawaii | 1979 |
| 142 | Canada-France-Hawaii Telescope, Mauna Kea, Hawaii | 1979 |
| 142 | European Southern Observatory, La Silla, Chile | 1976 |
| 138 | National Astronomical Observatory, Calar Alto, Spain | UC |
| 126 | (IR) Mauna Kea Observatory, Mauna Kea, Hawaii | 1979 |
| 120 | Lick Observatory, Mount Hamilton, California | 1959 |
| 107 | McDonald Observatory, Fort Davis, Texas | 1968 |
| 102 | Crimean Astrophysical Observatory, Nauchnyy, Ukrainian SSR | 1960 |
| 100 | Las Campanas Observatory, La Serena, Chile | 1977 |
| 100 | Hale Observatory, Mount Wilson, California | 1917 |
| 98 | Roque de los Muchachos Observatory, Canaries; originally at Royal Greenwich Observatory, England | 1967 |
| 95 | Space Telescope for Earth orbit, NASA/ESA | UC |
| 90 | Steward Observatory, University of Arizona, Tucson, Arizona | 1969 |
| 88 | Mauna Kea Observatory, University of Hawaii, Mauna Kea, Hawaii | 1970 |
| 84 | Kitt Peak National Observatory, Tucson, Arizona | 1961 |

* Light-gathering power of the six 72" mirrors in the Multiple Mirror Telescope.

| Mirror Diameter (Inches) | Observatory | In Operation Since |
|---|---|---|
| 83 | McDonald Observatory, Fort Davis, Texas | 1938 |
| 83 | National Astronomical Observatory, Nat. Univ. of Mexico, Baja California | 1977 |
| 79 | (53″ Schmidt) Karl Schwarzschild Obs., Tautenburg, East Germany | 1960 |
| 77 | Observatoire de Haute-Provence, Saint Michel, France | 1958 |
| 74 | David Dunlap Observatory, Richmond Hill, Ontario, Canada | 1935 |
| 74 | South African Astronomical Observatory, Sutherland, South Africa | 1948 |
| 74 | Mount Stromlo Observatory, Canberra, Australia | 1955 |
| 74 | Kottamia Observatory, c/o Helwan Observatory, Helwan, Egypt | 1960 |
| 74 | Okayama Astrophysical Observatory, Kamogata-Cho, Japan | 1960 |
| 72 | Dominion Astrophysical Observatory, Victoria, British Columbia | 1918 |
| 72 | Astrophysical Observatory, University of Padua, Asiago, Italy | 1973 |
| 72 | (48″ Schmidt) Palomar Observatory, Mount Palomar, California | 1948 |
| 72 | (48″ Schmidt) Unit of Royal Obs., Edinburgh, Siding Spring Obs., New South Wales | 1973 |
| 72 | Lowell Observatory, Flagstaff, Arizona | 1965 |
| 64 | (39″ Schmidt) European Southern Obs., La Silla, Chile | 1972 |
| 61 | Agassiz Station, Harvard College Observatory, Cambridge, Massachusetts | 1934 |
| 61 | Cordoba Astronomical Observatory, Bosque Alegre Station, Argentina | 1942 |
| 61 | U.S. Naval Observatory, Flagstaff, Arizona | 1963 |
| 61 | Lunar and Planetary Laboratory, Tucson, Arizona | 1965 |
| 60 | Hale Observatory, Mount Wilson, California | 1908 |
| 60 | Boyden Observatory, Bloemfontein, South Africa | 1930 |
| 60 | Steward Observatory, Tucson, Arizona | 1964 |
| 60 | Lunar and Planetary Laboratory, Tucson, Arizona | 1967 |
| 60 | Palomar Observatory, Mount Palomar, California | 1970 |
| 60 | Cerro Tololo Observatory, La Serena, Chile | 1967 |
| 60 | (39″ Schmidt) Uppsala University Obs., Kvistaberg, Sweden | 1963 |
| 59 | (41″ Schmidt) Tokyo Astronomical Obs., Kiso, Japan | 1976 |

## REFRACTING TELESCOPES

| Lens Diameter (Inches) | Observatory | In Operation Since |
|---|---|---|
| 40 | Yerkes Observatory, Williams Bay, Wisconsin | 1897 |
| 36 | Lick Observatory, Mount Hamilton, California | 1888 |
| 33 | Observatory of Physical Astronomy, Meudon, France | 1893 |
| 32 | Astrophysical Observatory, Potsdam, Germany | 1899 |
| 30 | Nice Observatory, Nice, France | 1880 |
| 30 | Allegheny Observatory, Pittsburgh, Pennsylvania | 1914 |
| 28 | Old Royal Greenwich Observatory, Greenwich, England | 1894 |
| 26.5 | University Observatory, Vienna, Austria | 1878 |
| 26 | U.S. Naval Observatory, Washington, D.C. | 1873 |
| 26 | Leander-McCormick Observatory, Charlottesville, Virginia | 1883 |
| 26 | Royal Greenwich Observatory, Herstmonceux, England | 1897 |

## RADIO TELESCOPES

| Antenna Diameter (Feet) | Observatory | In Operation Since |
|---|---|---|
| 1000 | Arecibo Observatory, Arecibo, Puerto Rico | 1963 |
| 400 | University of California, Hat Creek, California | 1960 |
| 360 × 70 | Ohio State-Ohio Wesleyan Radio Observatory, Delaware, Ohio | 1962 |
| 328 × 131(2) | Lebedev Physics Institute, Serpukhov, USSR | 1963 |
| 328 | Max Planck Institute, Bonn, West Germany | 1971 |
| 300 | National Radio Astronomy Observatory, Green Bank, West Virginia | 1962 |
| 250 | Nuffield Radio Ast. Lab., Jodrell Bank, England | 1957 |
| 210 | Australian Nat. Radio Astron. Observatory (CSIRO), Parkes New South Wales | 1961 |
| 210 | Jet Propulsion Laboratory, Goldstone, California | 1968 |
| 150 | Naval Research Laboratory, Sugar Grove, West Virginia | |
| 150 | Algonquin Radio Observatory, Lake Traverse, Ontario | 1967 |
| 140 | National Radio Astronomy Observatory, Green Bank, West Virginia | 1964 |
| 130 | California Institute of Technology, Owens Valley, California | 1968 |
| 125 × 85 | Nuffield Radio Astronomy Lab., Jodrell Bank, England | 1964 |
| 120 | Haystack Observatory, NE Radio Observatory Corp., Westford, Massachusetts | 1963 |
| 120 | University of Illinois, Danville, Illinois | 1971 |
| 118 | Heinrich Hertz Institute, Berlin-Adlershof, Germany | 1958 |
| 90(2) | California Institute of Technology, Owens Valley, California | 1958 |
| 88 | Stanford Research Institute Chatanika, Alaska | |
| 85 | University of Michigan, Dexter, Michigan | 1959 |
| 85(3) | Jet Propulsion Laboratory, Goldstone, California | 1960 |
| 85 | Harvard Radio Astronomy Station, Fort Davis, Texas | 1961 |
| 85 | University of California, Hat Creek, California | 1962 |
| 85(2) | National Radio Astronomy Observatory, Green Bank, West Virginia | 1964 |
| 17 mile array | National Radio Astronomy Obs., Socorro, New Mexico | 1980 |
| 3.1 mile array | Mullard Radio Astronomy Obs., Cambridge, England | 1972 |
| 1.9 mile radio-heliograph | Culgoora Solar Radio Obs., (CSIRO), Narrabri, New South Wales | 1968 |
| 1 mile array | Westerbork Radio Observatory, Westerbork, Netherlands | 1970 |
| 1 mile array | Mullard Radio Astron. Observatory, Cambridge, England | 1964 |
| 1 mile array | Molonglo Radio Observatory, Sydney University, Hoskinstown, New South Wales | 1960 |

## RADAR ASTRONOMY SYSTEMS

| Antenna Diameter (Feet) | Observatory | Peak Power (Kilowatts) |
|---|---|---|
| 1000 | Arecibo Observatory, Arecibo, Puerto Rico | 2,500 |
| 250 | Nuffield Radio Ast. Lab., Jodrell Bank, Macclesfield, England | 60 |
| 120 | Haystack Observatory, NE Radio Observatory Corp, Westford, Massachusetts | 400 |
| 85 | Jet Propulsion Laboratory, Goldstone, California | 100 |
| 84 | Millstone Lincoln Laboratory, Massachusetts Institute of Technology, Westford, Massachusetts | 5,000 |

## THE SUN, OUR NEAREST STAR

The Sun is of great importance because of its dominant influence on the Earth and the other planets and its role in the beginning and maintenance of life on our planet. But it is also important because the Sun is the only star near enough to be observed in any detail. Astronomers have inferred that physical processes on other stars are similar to those processes observed on the Sun.

This star is directly responsible for many phenomena on our planet, including the origin and survival of life, clouds, atmospheric motion and weather, and the thermal structure and composition of the Earth's atmosphere and the atmospheres of the other planets. Several billion years ago solar ultraviolet radiation supplied the energy needed to synthesize inorganic elements into the first organic molecules that formed the basis for life on Earth.

The average surface temperature of our planet, which must be within certain limits if life is to flourish and evolve, is determined by the amount of visible solar radiation the Earth's surface receives. Visible solar radiation causes water to evaporate from our oceans, and this atmospheric water vapor eventually condenses to form clouds and precipitation. Solar heating is responsible for the large-scale motions of the atmosphere and ocean, as well as small-scale phenomena, such as cumulus cloud formation. Solar X rays and ultraviolet radiation determine the temperature of the upper atmospheres of the planets, as well as the structure of planetary ionospheres.

Solar electrons and protons reaching the vicinity of the Earth, via solar wind or solar flares, are trapped by the Earth's magnetic field, forming the Van Allen radiation belts. Solar-emitted particles that collide with the atoms in our upper atmosphere cause auroral displays.

Solar particles are also responsible for radio and shortwave communication fadeouts, since clouds of these solar particles embedded in the Earth's upper atmosphere interfere with the radio reflection characteristics of the ionosphere. Sudden increases in the emission of solar X rays and energetic particles, during periods of high solar activity, may prove dangerous to astronauts orbiting above the protective blanket of atmosphere that shields life at the Earth's surface from the lethal solar radiation and particle flux.

It is believed that the formation of the Sun, the planets, and other stars began with the condensation of an interstellar gas cloud; this cloud consisted almost completely of pure hydrogen with a very small percentage of heavier elements that were produced during the explosion and ejections of exploding stars (supernovae). In fact, the interstellar medium is constantly being supplied with material rich in heavy elements that have been ejected from supernovae.

As a star contracts out of the interstellar cloud under gravitational forces, the temperature and pressure at the star's center (core) increase until the temperature reaches about 10 million degrees. At this temperature, four hydrogen nuclei in the star's core fuse together to form a single helium nucleus. However, four hydrogen nuclei weigh a little more than one helium nucleus. This small amount of mass has been converted to energy. Every second the Sun converts some 616 million tons of hydrogen into 612 million tons of helium. This thermonuclear reaction provides the tremendous amount of energy that the Sun radiates out in all directions into space in the form of electromagnetic radiation: X rays; ultraviolet, visible, and infrared rays; and radio waves. Every square meter of the Sun's surface emits 64 million watts into space.

Its high temperature causes the Sun to be a gaseous body or, more precisely, a plasma—the fourth state of matter that is attained when electrically neutral atoms break up into positively charged nuclei and negatively charged electrons. The diameter of the Sun is about 864,900 miles—more than 109 times that of the Earth. The Sun's mass is $2 \times 10^{30}$ kg—or approximately 333,000 times the mass of the Earth. The mean density of the Sun is 1.4 grams/$cm^3$—only about one-quarter of the Earth's density—suggesting that the Sun primarily consists of very light elements. The period of the Sun's rotation on its axis depends on the solar latitude, being least (25 days) at the equator; its average rotation period is 27 days.

It is difficult to obtain any evidence that is based on direct observation about the core of the Sun. All of our knowledge of the solar core reflects theoretical considerations: it is a region of very high pressure and temperature, and thermonuclear reactions occur there. The solar energy is transported from the core by radiative processes, in which atoms absorb, reemit, and scatter the radiation. Close to the surface the energy is carried by large looping convection currents in the unstable region known as the convective zone. Shock waves from this zone carry energy into the solar atmosphere.

The solar surface (photosphere or "sphere of light") is what we see when looking up at the Sun. By using high-resolution telescopes, the convection currents' tops can actually be observed on the photosphere. The solar surface is not as smooth as had been thought; it is actually covered with a fine cellular structure (granulation), which is caused by the top of the convection cells breaking across the photosphere. Spectacular gaseous eruptions (prominences) from the surface can extend up to an altitude of 500,000 miles in great arching filaments.

Other photospheric features include sunspots and solar flares, which are discussed below. The convective motions are very important, because they appear to be the source of the mechanical energy that is responsible for heating and the observed temperature increase within the solar atmosphere. The immense temperature—2,000,000°C—of the outer layer of the atmosphere (the corona) has no dependence on the heat flowing from the photosphere.

The solar atmosphere consists of two regions: the chromosphere and the corona. The chromosphere is 6,000 to 9,000 miles thick, and its lower part is simply an extension of the photosphere at about 6,000° C, the density decreasing very considerably. The upper chromosphere has a temperature that approaches 100,000° C.

The corona, which surrounds the chromosphere, is the region that is observed during a total solar eclipse, when the Moon, which has the same angular size in the sky as the Sun, passes directly in front of it, blocking out the photospheric radiation and permitting the fainter light of the corona to be observed.

The solar atmosphere permeates through the interplanetary medium via a constant stream of solar protons and electrons ("solar wind"). The protons and electrons have enough energy by virtue of the high temperature of the solar atmosphere to escape from the Sun's gravitational field. The solar wind streams radially outward from the Sun, and is a regular feature of the Sun. Study of the X-ray emissions from the corona have revealed large low-density regions, known as coronal holes, usually extending as winding structures from the polar regions. They appear to be the source of the high-speed particles of the solar wind.

Complicated magnetic fields occur in the region extending from the convective zone to the corona and beyond. There is much evidence that magnetic fields are of considerable importance on the Sun. Their most spectacular manifestations are related to photospheric solar activity, particularly prominences, sunspots and solar flares. Sunspots are complicated hydromagnetic phenomena displaying very strong magnetic fields; they appear dark against the bright photosphere because their temperatures are several thousand degrees lower.

Associated with sunspots are solar flares, energetic phenomena that produce both electromagnetic radiation and solar particle emission. These flares occur because their material has gained enough energy—via solar magnetic fields—to be ejected from the Sun and shot into space. One of the remarkable features of both sunspots and solar flares is that they increase then decrease in number in an 11-year cycle of solar activity. Also associated with this cycle are increased emissions of solar X rays and centimeter radio waves.

In recent years, it has been shown from studies of the frictional atmospheric drag on orbiting satellites and from direct *in situ* measurements with instruments on board rockets and satellites that the temperature, composition, and density of the Earth's upper atmosphere is strongly responsive to changes in solar geometry and the level of solar activity. Some of these responses follow diurnal, 27-day (solar rotation period), and 11-year (sunspot cycle) variations.

## THE PLANETS

It is thought that about 4.6 billion years ago, the Earth was formed from the same interstellar gas cloud that gave birth to the other planets of the solar system and the Sun. The gas cloud was mostly hydrogen, with heavier elements making up only a small fraction of its composition. As the gas cloud contracted under gravitational forces, the temperature and pressure of the central core increased tremendously until thermonuclear reactions—the conversion of hydrogen into helium with the accompanying release of huge amounts of light and heat energy—began, and a star, the Sun, formed. Dust grains in the now disk-shaped cloud constantly collided and coalesced into ever larger bodies, which in turn consolidated into planets surrounded by gaseous atmospheres.

During the following 4.6 billion years, the planets and their atmospheres have changed and evolved significantly. The following is a brief survey of the planets in our solar system, with the exception of the Earth, which is discussed in the section *Earth: Facts/Figures.*

**MERCURY** is the second smallest planet in the solar system and the closest to the Sun. This combination provides for a hot and gravitationally "weak" planet that cannot retain a gaseous atmosphere. Mercury rotates within a period of 58.65 days, or exactly two thirds of its period of revolution around the Sun: 88 days.

The U.S. Mariner 10 space probe has relayed to Earth invaluable information and photographs as it flew within 500 miles of Mercury. The surface resembles that of the Moon in being heavily cratered, little eroded, and with smooth areas similar but smaller than the lunar *maria.* The surface material has a low density. Thus the average density, measured accurately by Mariner 10, of 5.5 grams/cc implies a large core of heavy material, possibly iron. The planet could therefore be similar in composition to the Earth. An iron core would mean that Mercury has a magnetic field and in fact a very weak magnetic field was detected by the probe.

No gaseous atmosphere greater than 100-billionths that of the Earth was revealed. Traces of helium were detected but this gas would be rapidly boiled off. Measurements of surface temperature gave a daytime maximum of 350°C (660°F) and a night-time minimum of −170°C (−270°F). Mercury therefore has a greater surface temperature range than any other planet, although its maximum is less than that of Venus.

**VENUS,** "Earth's twin" in size and mass, is otherwise unlike it. Its surface is hot (about 890°F on dark and light side and from pole to pole), waterless, corrosive and lifeless, with a pressure averaging 90 terrestrial atmospheres (equivalent to an ocean depth of 1/2 mile) and gentle surface winds of 1 to 2 mph. It has no moon, no magnetic field, no aurorae and no radiation belts. Only about 2% of incident solar radiation reaches its surface, while 75% is reflected; the rest is absorbed in atmosphere and clouds. A "greenhouse effect" makes the surface abnormally hot. Atmospherically absorbed heat drives convective currents and strong winds aloft, creating wind speeds in excess of 400 mph in the middle of the cloud zone and about 200 mph atop the clouds.

Although no liquid or solid particles exist below about 21 miles, surface visibility is probably less than 1/2 mile (molecular light scattering) and a bright Venusian midday would compare to one heavily overcast on Earth. From 21 to about 31 miles there is smog and haze. The cloud layer lies at 31-41 miles and consists of tiny liquid droplets of sulfuric acid, tinged yellow with tiny grains of sulfur.

US and Soviet Space missions to Venus by Mariner, Pioneer Venus, and Venera craft have greatly increased our knowledge, especially of surface and atmospheric features. Venera probes first descended through the opaque clouds to transmit data from the surface of Venus in 1970. Pictures of a rocky landscape were returned in 1975. A soil analysis by the 1982 Venera mission revealed that the brownish surface rock is composed mainly of highly alkaline potassium basalts.

Radar images of an extensive area of the surface have been obtained by Earth-bound radio telescopes but now almost the entire surface has been mapped using a radar altimeter aboard the orbiting Pioneer Venus 1. This has revealed that the surface of Venus is remarkably flat: 60% of its surface lies within 500 m (1640 ft.) above or below the average surface level; the comparable figure for Earth is 25%.

Most of the surface consists of rolling upland plains in which shallow circular features, up to 500 miles across, appear. These are assumed to be impact craters produced in the very distant past. Rising well above the upland plains are two large "continents" and some smaller "islands," with jagged mountain ranges and extensive high plateaus. The highest feature on Venus, Maxwell Montes, lies on the northern continent and towers 36,000 ft above the mean surface level. It is probably a shield volcano. There is other evidence of past volcanism on Venus, although no current activity has been observed. The remainder of the surface is smooth lowland plains, equivalent to Earth's ocean-basin floors but much shallower and less extensive. Several tectonically disturbed regions have been found, including a giant 1400-mile-long rift valley near the equator.

Venus condensed too close to the Sun ever to have possessed much water. The ambient surface temperature of 890°F is too hot for water-bearing minerals such as micas and amphiboles to be stable. Probably there have never been oceans, or sedimentary rocks such as limestone. It is also doubtful that there has ever been life. Water and life have greatly altered Earth's primitive atmosphere, locking up most of its $CO_2$ in the hydrosphere and carbonate rocks. Were this $CO_2$ released on Earth our atmosphere would be much like that of Venus in bulk, pressure and composition.

The atmosphere of Venus is about 97% $CO_2$, 3% $N_2$, with traces of $H_2O$, $O_2$, noble gases, CO, $SO_2$, and others. In its lesser gases it is inhomogeneous in its upper reaches where photochemical reactions occur, but is homogeneous below about 21 miles, where no liquid or solid particles condense. Both Earth and Venus lost their original hydrogen and helium in the "protoplanet" stage. Were all of the atmospheric water of Venus to condense onto a level, cool surface, its depth would be about 1.5 feet.

Like Earth, Venus has an ionosphere. Unlike Earth's it persists at night, and there is an ionopause—i.e., a sharp *upper* boundary where the ionosphere reacts with the solar wind, in the absence of a magnetosphere. The atmosphere of Venus is very dynamic in its upper reaches, driven by the solar energy absorbed. At both poles there is a huge zone of down-flowing air.

The cause of the anomalous 243-day *retrograde* rotation of Venus is unknown. The once suspected spin-orbit resonance control by Earth has been discounted. Venus' spin vector is apparently aligned with the angular momentum vector of the solar system.

The slow rotation means that, unlike Earth, Venus is quite round with no equatorial bulge and no flattening at the poles. The planet probably has a molten iron core but its slow rotation precludes the existence of a magnetic field.

**MARS,** in direct contrast to Venus, with its hot, heavy, and opaque atmosphere, has one that is cold, thin, and transparent and readily permits observation of the planet's surface features. As observed from Earth, Mars's main surface features include white polar caps and bright and dark regions all of which show seasonal variations.

The bright areas, which constitute almost three-quarters of the total Martian surface area, give the planet its familiar ruddy color. The bright areas are believed to be siliceous, as was found from data sent back in 1971 from the Soviet probe Mars III. The dark areas cover roughly one third of the planet's surface.

Infrared observations have shown that the average temperature of the whole planet is −45° F, with a maximum equatorial noon temperature of 80° F. The daily temperature variation from noon to midnight at the equator is about 180° F, suggesting that the Martian atmosphere is very thin and thus does not retain heat. With an atmosphere much thinner than ours, the atmospheric surface pressure is only 7.7 mbar (Viking readings). Because the Martian atmosphere is so thin, it changes temperature rapidly, thus bringing about the large temperature contrasts that play a major role in driving the high Martian winds.

In 1971 three orbiting Mars probes were launched: two Russian (Mars II and III) and one American (Mariner 9). Mars III deposited a transmitter on the surface of the planet, but this failed almost immediately after arrival. Mariner 9 remained in orbit for almost a year and sent back photographs and scientific information that drastically altered man's ideas about the planet. Only half of the surface, mainly in the southern hemisphere, is substantially cratered. In the northern hemisphere, observed by Mariner 9, four immense volcanic mountains were found as well as a vast system of canyons, tributary gullies, and narrow channels. These features are far greater in scale than anything seen on earth. The largest volcanic mountain, Olympus Mons, the biggest known in the solar system, is more than 300 miles in diameter at the base and about 16 miles high. The sparsely cratered northern regions, strewn with wind-blown debris, are plains of lava that flooded the surface at different times after its earliest history. The heavily cratered southern terrain was also modified by volcanic activity.

Apparently, contrary to earlier ideas, there has been internal activity in the planet, maybe quite recently. This is also suggested by the series of huge canyons, 50 to 75 miles wide and 3 to 4 miles deep stretching along the equator to the east of the volcanic regions.

At the eastern extreme of the canyons lies a large area of chaotic terrain, first observed by Mariner 6 and 7. It is an irregular jumble of topographic forms, possibly the result of some kind of collapse related to that of the canyons. Channels, hundreds of miles long, extend from this terrain in a northwesterly direction. They also appear in other areas on the planet's surface. The channels may have been cut by large amounts of flowing water. The Viking spacecraft have since shown that in Mars' earliest history flowing water was significant in shaping its features. Since then, although surface dust and other debris have been extensively and continuously redistributed by high-speed winds, wind erosion of the surface has been negligible, leaving features sharply defined.

The bright circular region, Hellas, roughly 1000 miles across, is an example of basinlike depressions seen in several regions of the Martian surface. Mariner 7 showed it to be almost devoid of topographical features. It is exceptionally low—over a mile below the mean Martian elevation. Mariner 9 indicated that Hellas probably serves as a collection center for dust and may also be a source of dust.

The lower atmosphere can become filled with dust when the Martian winds become really strong. The dust storms are phenomena whose explanation may be similar to that of the initial stages of a hurricane. When Mariner 9 and the Soviet Mars probes reached Mars, the greatest dust storm in more than a century was raging. The mapping of the Martian surface was consequently delayed for almost three months.

The polar caps appear as a white cover over the north and south poles. This cover grows and recedes with seasonal regularity, alternating from one hemisphere to the other once every Martian year (687 Earth days). The Mariner 7 photographs showed snow-filled craters of the southern polar cap in sharp relief with snow-covered crater rims. The Viking orbiters have indicated that the residual (summer) northern and probably the southern caps are predominantly water ice not frozen carbon dioxide as hitherto suspected. The amount of water vapor in the atmosphere, although very small, was found to increase with latitude, reaching a peak at the edge of the polar caps. In addition infrared measurements showed that the surface temperature (about −70° C) is not cold enough for solid carbon dioxide to form.

The landings of Viking 1 and 2 on Mars on July 20 and September 3, 1976, respectively, have greatly increased our store of Martian information. The mission's purpose was to probe the planet's interior, surface properties, weather, atmosphere and biology. Photographs from the two Viking orbiters and the two landers have shown Mars as a planet that, like Earth, has been shaped by great forces, and have revealed Mars' characteristics to a greater degree than any other unmanned exploration of Mars has been able to accomplish.

Landing site locales were finalized only after the two spacecraft went into orbit around Mars. Viking 1 landed near a region heavily scoured by what are believed to have been ancient floods, while Viking 2 is on a vast flat plain pocked by fewer craters. The color pictures transmitted to earth showed a bright faintly pink sky and a salmon-pink surface. The dry pink dust covering most of the rock-strewn desert-like surface is composed of a mixture of iron-rich clay minerals and carbonate minerals, iron oxide probably giving Mars its red appearance.

The inorganic analysis of Martian soil showed the presence of silicon, iron, calcium, aluminum, titanium, and sulfur (in order of abundance). Analysis of the atmosphere found it to contain 95% carbon dioxide, 2.7% nitrogen, 1.6% argon, and traces of oxygen and water vapor. The presence of argon showed that there was probably a much denser atmosphere and hence a very different climate from today's. The discovery of nitrogen increases the possibility of some form of life having evolved.

Viking landers are the first spacecraft ever sent to another planet with equipment specifically designed to search for alien life forms. Information from biology experiments on Mars are inconclusive but could suggest "the possibility of biological activity in the samples being incubated." Life on Mars has of yet been neither confirmed nor ruled out, but if it does exist, it has made a different adaptation than life forms on Earth.

**JUPITER** has a dense, cloudy atmosphere of hydrogen and helium, with about 90% hydrogen and 2% $CH_4$ and $NH_3$ and traces of ethane and acetylene. It rotates rapidly (in approximately 9 hours 50 minutes), is flattened 1/15, has a low mean density, great mass, a large fraction of the solar system's angular momentum and 16 satellites. Its interior has a small rock-metal core, a liquid monatomic hydrogen "metallic" mantle 28,000 miles thick, and a liquid diatomic hydrogen mantle overlying that. Parallel clouds characterize its visible surface, divided into white-yellowish zones and reddish-brown belts. They probably consist of $H_2O$, ammonia, and $NH_4SH$ crystals. Cloud-top temperatures average about −220°F.

Jupiter's central temperature theoretically is about 54,000°F and the planet radiates about two times as much energy as it receives, due possibly to continuing contraction.

The Great Red Spot – 24,000 × 9,000 miles – is an immense hurricane-like atmospheric disturbance, poorly understood. Other smaller, ephemeral spots are known. Since 1954 radio astronomers have detected radio signals, arising in strong magnetic fields and in Jupiter's magnetosphere. This magnetosphere is huge, complex and interacts with the solar wind, Jupiter's atmosphere, and the surface of Io (one of the planet's satellites). A "plasma torus" near Io's orbit surrounds Jupiter, containing ionized sulfur, with a temperature of 180,000°F. A "flux tube" connects Jupiter's magnetic poles and Io, and a powerful electric current flows (possibly as great as 5 million amperes). A system of rings lies in the equatorial plane.

The elongated satellite, Amalthea, is dark like an asteroid (166 × 88 miles). Io is fantastic! Seven currently active volcanoes were found spewing umbrella-shaped plumes up to 180 miles. Its surface is orange-red with no impact craters, but over 100 huge caldera-like depressions and lava flows—a "young" surface, renewed about every 10 million years.

Io and Europa are composed of rock; Ganymede and Callisto are composed of mixtures of "water-ice" and rock. Europa has few craters, Ganymede more, and craters are "shoulder-to-shoulder" on Callisto. Europa has a cracked, ice-encrusted surface. Ganymede, larger than Mercury, is also ice-encrusted, with a contorted, involuted and faulted pattern of lines and ridges. Icy Callisto has a huge bull's-eye formation (1,600 miles across), with concentric mountain ridges around a 200-mile central basin.

**SATURN,** the second largest planet in the solar system, has an internal and atmospheric structure similar to that of Jupiter. But it may have a greater amount of hydrogen and methane, as well as a smaller amount of ammonia in its atmosphere. The density of Saturn is very low.

First discovered by Galileo, the superb rings of Saturn have the appearance of a large, extremely thin, and flat circular sheet, lying centered on the planet in the equatorial plane. There are three prominent rings; the outer ring A is separated from the brightest ring, B, by a narrow gap called Cassini's Division. Interior to ring B is a faint, semitransparent one known as the "Crepe," or ring C. The rings are only about five miles thick and are probably composed of innumerable particles of ice.

Our knowledge of Saturn, its satellites, and ring system increased dramatically with the Pioneer 11 (1979) and Voyager 1 and 2 encounters (1980, 1981). Voyager 1 found considerable internal structure in the rings. Ring B in particular has numerous individual ringlets of particles and also some bizarre dark "spokes" that rotate with the rings around the planet. Several fainter rings exist. The narrow 300-mile-wide F ring, discovered by Pioneer 11, lies just outside the A ring. Voyager 1 pictures of this ring showed strands of material, not concentric but kinked and apparently intertwined. A highly tenuous belt, the G ring, is thought to lie beyond the F ring while evidence was found for the D and E rings, previously reported as lying inside (D) and outside the bright trio. The rings of Saturn are very large in extent. Ring A has an outer radius of 85,000 miles; that of ring G could be 95,000 miles.

Saturn has at least 17 satellites, five of the smallest and most recently discovered lying within the ring system. The largest satellite, Titan, is about the size of Mercury; it is the only satellite in the solar system observed to date that has an appreciable atmosphere, mainly of nitrogen and some methane, with a surface pressure which may be similar to that of Earth.

**URANUS** and **NEPTUNE** are the third- and fourth-largest planets, respectively, in the solar system. Because of their great distance from the Sun, little is known about either of them. Their mass can be calculated from the orbital period of their satellites. Their diameters have recently been recalculated by balloon measurement (Uranus: 32,-200 miles) and by a stellar occultation (Neptune: 30,800 miles).

Uranus was the first planet to be discovered with the aid of a telescope. It was discovered in 1781 by William Herschel. Neptune was telescopically discovered in 1846 by J. G. Galle; this discovery was based on orbital changes of Uranus brought about by the gravitational pull of Neptune. These gravitational perturbations were calculated by J. C. Adams and U. J. Leverrier.

Spectroscopic observations of their atmospheres have established the presence of molecular hydrogen and helium, as in the atmospheres of Jupiter and Saturn, and an increased proportion of methane.

Uranus has a system of five known moons, Neptune has two. Neptune's larger moon, Triton, Jupiter's Ganymede and Callisto, and Saturn's Titan comprise the four largest moons of the solar system.

Observations in 1977 and 1978 indicate that Uranus is surrounded by at least eight rings lying in its equatorial plane, similar to but much narrower than Saturn's rings.

**PLUTO**, the most distant and smallest planet in the solar system, was discovered in 1930 by C. W. Tombaugh. Although little is yet known about Pluto, it appears to be a small low-density body, too cold and small to retain an appreciable atmosphere and probably covered in a layer of methane ice.

Pluto has the most eccentric orbit in the solar system, bringing it at times closer to the Sun than Neptune. Because of its orbit, some theorists have suggested that Pluto may in fact be a runaway moon of Neptune.

In 1978 a moon was discovered in orbit around Pluto. The orbital distance and period of this moon has led to the first reasonably accurate measurement of Pluto's mass (0.2% of Earth's mass). Additional measurements now indicate a diameter of 1,500–2,000 miles.

## THE SPECTRAL SEQUENCE

**The spectral class or spectral type of a star is a classification that depends on the star's color or surface temperature. The spectral class and corresponding star color, approximate surface temperature, and principal features of the star's spectrum are:**

| Spectral Class | Color | Approximate Surface Temperature (K) | Principal Features of Spectrum |
|---|---|---|---|
| O | blue | >30,000 | Relatively few absorption lines in observable spectrum. Lines of ionized helium, nitrogen, silicon, and other atoms. Weak hydrogen lines. |
| B | blue-white | 11,000–30,000 | Lines of neutral helium, ionized silicon, oxygen, and magnesium. Hydrogen lines more pronounced. |
| A | white | 7,500–11,000 | Strong lines of hydrogen. Weak lines of ionized magnesium, silicon, iron, titanium, calcium, and others. Weak lines of some neutral metals. |
| F | white to yellowish | 6,000–7,500 | Hydrogen lines still conspicuous. Lines of ionized calcium, iron, and chromium, and of neutral iron and chromium. Lines of other neutral metals. |
| G | yellow | 5,000–6,000 | Very strong lines of ionized calcium. Many lines of ionized and neutral metals. Hydrogen lines weaker. |
| K | orange to red | 3,500–5,000 | Lines of neutral metals predominate. Hydrogen lines are quite weak. Bands of molecular titanium oxide. |
| M | red | <3,500 | Strong lines of neutral metals and strong bands of titanium oxide dominate. |

## IMPORTANT PLANETARY PROBES

| Name of probe | Launching Local date | Launching Rocket | Weight, lbs. | Period, min. | Inclination, degrees | Perigee, miles | Apogee, miles | Results of mission—Remarks |
|---|---|---|---|---|---|---|---|---|
| | | | | SOVIET UNION | | | | |
| Venera I | 12 Feb. 1961 | — | 1,417 | 300 days | 0.58 | 0.7183 A.U. | 1.0190 A.U. | In solar orbit; Venus probe; radio contact lost at 4.6 million miles. |
| Mars I | 1 Nov. 1962 | — | 1,965 | 519 days | 2.683 | 0.9237 A.U. | 1.604 A.U. | In solar orbit; Mars probe; radio contact lost at 66 million miles. |
| Zond I | 2 Apr. 1964 | — | 1,700 | | | solar orbit | | In solar orbit; probe aimed at Venus; failed to send back information on its target. |
| Zond II | 30 Nov. 1964 | — | | | | solar orbit | | In orbit; probe aimed at Mars; failed to send back information on its target. |
| Venera II | 12 Nov. 1965 | — | 2,123 | | | solar orbit | | In solar orbit; failed to send back data. |
| Venera III | 16 Nov. 1965 | — | 2,116 | | duration of flight: 105 days | | | First space probe to impact on a planet; entry capsule sent back no data after landing. |
| Venera IV | 12 June 1967 | — | 2,433 | | duration of flight: 128 days | | | Instrumented capsule deployed parachute 18.10.67. |

| | | | | | | | | |
|---|---|---|---|---|---|---|---|---|
| **Venera V** | 5 Jan. 1969 | — | 2,500 | | | — | | Instrumented capsule deployed parachute 16.5.69. |
| **Venera VI** | 10 Jan. 1969 | — | 2,500 | | | — | | Instrumented capsule deployed parachute 17.5.69. |
| **Venera VII** | 16 Aug. 1970 | — | 2,500 | | | — | | Instrumented capsule transmitted data for 23 minutes 15.12.70. |
| **Mars II** | 19 May 1971 | — | — | | duration of flight: 18 hrs. | | | Orbited Mars 27.11.72; sent back close-range photos. |
| **Mars III** | 28 May 1971 | — | — | | duration of flight: 11 days | | | Instrumented capsule televised signals from surface. |
| **Venera VIII** | 26 Mar. 1972 | — | — | | | — | | Ceased transmitting on entering atmosphere. |
| **Mars IV** | 21 July 1973 | — | 10,250 | | | — | | Failed to go into Martian orbit. |
| **Mars V** | 25 July 1973 | — | 10,250 | | | — | | Went into orbit March 1974. |
| **Mars VI** | 5 Aug. 1973 | — | 10,250 | | | — | | Released descent module: ceased functioning. |
| **Mars VII** | 9 Aug. 1973 | — | 10,250 | | | — | | Failed to go into orbit. |
| **Venera IX** | 6 June 1975 | — | — | | duration of flight: 139 days | | | Descent modules landed on Venus at sites of different terrain, relaying data and clear photos of surface. |
| **Venera X** | 14 June 1975 | — | — | | duration of flight: 134 days | | | |
| **Venera XIII** | 30 Oct. 1981 | — | — | | duration of flight: 121 days | | | Descent modules relayed detailed data and photographs and analyzed soil samples. |
| **Venera XIV** | 4 Nov. 1981 | — | — | | duration of flight: 121 days | | | |
| | | | | **UNITED STATES** | | | | |
| **Pioneer 5** | 11 Mar. 1960 | Thor-Able | 95 | 312 days | 3.55 | 0.8161 A.U. | 0.995 A.U. | In solar orbit; launched toward Venus; studied interplanetary space. |
| **Mariner 2** | 26 Aug. 1962 | Atlas-Agena B | 446 | 348 days | 1.66 | 0.7046 A.U. | 1.299 A.U. | In solar orbit; passed within 22,000 miles of Venus. |
| **Mariner 3** | 5 Nov. 1964 | Atlas-Agena D | 575 | 448.7 days | 0.524 | 0.6150 A.U. | 0.8155 A.U. | In solar orbit; final speed too low. |
| **Mariner 4** | 28 Nov. 1964 | Atlas-Agena D | 575 | 567.2 days | 2.540 | 1.1089 A.U. | 1.5730 A.U. | In solar orbit; highly successful; 22 photographs of Mars sent back in mid-July 1965. |
| **Pioneer 6** | 16 Dec. 1965 | TAID | 139 | 311.3 days | 0.1695 | 0.814 A.U. | 0.985 A.U. | In solar orbit; studied Sun and interplanetary space. |
| **Pioneer 7** | 17 Aug. 1966 | TAID | 139 | 402.9 days | 0.097 | 1.010 A.U. | 1.125 A.U. | In solar orbit; studied Sun and interplanetary space. |
| **Mariner 5** | 14 June 1967 | Atlas-Agena D | 540 | | duration of flight: 127 days | | | In solar orbit; Venus probe; fly-by on 19.10.67. |
| **Pioneer 8** | 13 Dec. 1967 | TAID | 145 | — | — | 1.0 A.U. | 1.1 A.U. | In solar orbit; studied Sun and interplanetary space. |
| **Mariner 6** | 24 Feb. 1969 | Atlas-Agena D | — | | duration of flight: 156 days | | | Passed within 2,000 miles of Mars on 31.7.69; relayed data and photos. |
| **Mariner 7** | 27 Mar. 1969 | Atlas-Agena D | — | | duration of flight: 130 days | | | Passed within 2,000 miles of Mars on 5.8.69; sent photographs back to Earth. |
| **Mariner 9** | 30 May 1971 | Atlas Centaur | 2,200 | 12 hrs. | 65 | 800 | 11,000 | Entered Mars orbit 14.11.71; sent photographs and instrument readings to Earth. |
| **Pioneer 10** | 2 Mar. 1972 | Atlas Centaur | 570 | — | — | — | — | Flew past Jupiter 4.12.73 relaying data and photos of planets and satellites. |
| **Pioneer 11** | 6 Apr. 1973 | Atlas Centaur | 570 | — | — | — | — | Investigated asteroid belt; passed Jupiter 3.12.74; passed Saturn 1.9.79. |
| **Mariner 10** | 3 Nov. 1973 | Atlas Centaur | — | — | — | — | — | Relayed data and photos of Venus, photos of Mercury. |
| **Viking 1** | 20 Aug. 1975 | Titan 3E/Centaur | 7,550 | | entered Mars orbit 6/19/76; landed July 20, 1976 | | | Orbiters studied atmosphere, photographed surface; landers studied surface geology and chemistry, testing soil for signs of life. |
| **Viking 2** | 9 Sept. 1975 | Titan 3E/Centaur | 7,550 | | entered Mars orbit 8/7/76; landed Sept. 3, 1976 | | | |
| **Voyager 1** | 5 Sept. 1977 | Titan 3 E/Centaur | 1,820 | — | flew by Jupiter March 1979, Saturn Nov. 1980 | | | Studied and photographed atmospheres, ring systems and surfaces of main satellites in great detail. |
| **Voyager 2** | 20 Aug. 1977 | Titan 3 E/Centaur | 1,820 | — | flew by Jupiter July 1979, Saturn Aug. 1981 | | | |
| **Pioneer Venus 1** | 20 May 1978 | Atlas Centaur | | — | entered Venus orbit 4/12/78 | | | Orbiter plus multiprobe atmospheric entry craft studied Venusian atmosphere and surface. |
| **Pioneer Venus 2** | 8 Aug. 1978 | Atlas Centaur | | — | entered atmosphere 9/12/78; following payload of probes | | | |

## THE MOON

The Moon is the closest celestial body to the Earth, at a mean distance of 238,857 miles. Because of its elliptical orbit, the Moon reaches a minimum distance—or perigee—of 221,463 miles and a maximum distance—apogee—of 252,710 miles. The Moon revolves around the Earth in 27 days 7 hours 43 minutes. The Moon's rotation about its axis is equal to its period of revolution, hence the Moon always shows the Earth the same face. However, since its revolution around the Earth is not uniform, speeding up at perigee and slowing down at apogee, and because its equator is inclined 6 degrees to the plane of its orbit, about 59 percent of the Moon's surface is visible at different times from the Earth. The Moon's mass is 1/81 of the Earth's mass, and its radius of 1,080 miles makes it about one-fourth of the Earth's radius. The mean density of the Moon is 3.34 grams/$cm^3$.

The Moon is visible, as are the Earth and the other planets, by virtue of its reflection of solar radiation. However, the Moon is a relatively poor reflector, with an albedo, or reflectivity, of only 7 percent. At full moon, the Earth is between the Sun and the Moon (although usually not in the same plane), and the whole lunar disk facing the Earth is completely illuminated. At new moon, the Moon is between the Sun and the Earth (usually not in the same plane), and the Sun's rays illuminate only the hemisphere facing it, leaving the side facing the Earth in complete darkness, making it invisible from Earth. After new moon, the waxing thin crescent turns into first quarter. Following full moon, the waning gibbous turns into last quarter, then into new moon again.

The origin of the Moon is still a major area of debate. Three different mechanisms have been suggested for its origin: independent formation in Earth orbit, formation via fission of the Earth, and capture by Earth's gravitational field after formation elsewhere.

In the independent-formation theory, the Moon is supposed to have been formed by accretion of small masses from the original interstellar gas cloud that gave birth to the Sun, the Earth, and other planets. The major difficulty with this hypothesis is the disparity in mean density between the Earth and the Moon. This density difference, which is generally believed to represent a difference in the composition—specifically in the proportion of metallic iron and silicates—makes it difficult to explain why objects accumulating in the same part of the gas cloud should have such different compositions.

In 1898, G. H. Darwin, the astronomer son of Sir Charles Darwin, concluded that the Earth and the Moon might have once formed one body that rotated at high speed (about five hours). This rapid rotation might have led to fission into one large and one or more smaller bodies, the latter eventually forming the Moon. However, mathematical objections to this theory have led modern astronomers to abandon it.

According to some hypotheses, the first large solid bodies to form in the solar system were approximately the size of the Moon. These bodies collided, forming the planets. The Moon is considered to be one of these bodies, which escaped destruction by accretion and was later gravitationally captured by the Earth.

The lunar surface is divided into bright highland areas (comprising about two thirds of the total surface) and dark lowland areas, called *maria*, because they were originally thought to be seas. Craters are the most conspicuous and most plentiful of all lunar surface features. The near side of the Moon has more *maria* than the far side, which is almost entirely covered by highland regions. The major mechanisms believed to be responsible for crater formation are meteoritic impact and lunar volcanism. Impact craters appear to be of two types. Primary craters stem from the actual impact of meteoritic material; secondary craters result in part from the rain of heavy debris ejected from the primary ones. Craters may also be formed by collapse triggered by seismic quakes, which result from the impact of a large meteorite. The frequency with which craters are found on the bright highland areas is more than 15 times that of their incidence on the dark lowland *maria*. It is known that the Moon, and also possibly Mars, Mercury, and Earth, suffered very intense bombardment by massive bodies (planetesimals) about 4 billion years ago. Shortly after this, volcanic lava flooded gigantic basins on the Moon's surface, covering many craters and creating the *maria*. Seismic waves indicate activity (moonquakes) still occurring in the Moon's core but its present thick rigid outer layers prevent any surface fracturing.

Lunar rilles, or deep canyons, some of them more than 100 miles long, were thought to be remnants of long-dried-out rivers on the Moon but are probably collapse features. One of them, the Hadley Rille, was studied at close range by the astronauts of Apollo 15 in 1971.

Mascons—dense lunar mass concentrations—were accidentally discovered in 1968 during analysis of small changes in the motion of Langley Research Center's Lunar Orbiter 5 during 80 consecutive orbits around the Moon. Five conspicuous mascons, ranging from 25 to 100 miles in extent and perhaps 25 miles below the lunar surface, were detected under all five large circular *maria* on the side of the Moon facing the Earth—Mare Imbrium, Mare Serenitatis, Mare Crisium, Mare Nectaris, and Mare Humorum. A sixth mascon is located in the central part of the lunar disk, between Sinus Aestuum and Sinus Medii. There is also some evidence that a large mascon exists under Mare Orientale. Mascons are absent from the bright lunar highlands and from the irregularly shaped *maria*. Both the presence of these features under every ringed *mare*, except Sinus Iridum, and their relative absence elsewhere, suggest a physical relationship.

In 1969, six more mascons were discovered—in Mare Smythii, Mare Humboldtianum, Mare Orientale, the ringed plain Grimaldi, and in two unnamed *maria*. As with the other mascons, the new mascons were discovered as lunar-orbiting spacecraft speeded up in passing over certain areas, which were revealed as places where the lunar gravitational attraction was stronger than average.

Due to the Moon's smaller mass, its gravitational attraction is only one sixth of the Earth's. Since the Moon is a weak gravitational body, it is believed that it could not retain any atmosphere it may have originally had for any length of time, since the atoms and molecules of the lunar atmosphere could easily drift off the planet. Observations first made with Apollo instruments have, however, revealed the presence of helium, neon, argon, and radon in very minute quantities.

The large day-to-night temperature variation observed on the Moon also suggests that it does not have an appreciable atmosphere. A planetary atmosphere acts as a heat insulator that keeps the planet's surface from experiencing wide temperature extremes from day to night. The day-to-night temperature variations on the Moon range from 300° F in the lunar equatorial region at noon to —220° F before sunrise—a daily change of over 500° F.

The samples of lunar material brought back by the Apollo astronauts consist of basaltic igneous rocks; breccias, which are composed of soil and rock fragments compacted into coherent rock; and lunar soil. The soil is a mixture of crystalline and glassy fragments with a variety of interesting shapes; it also contains fragments of iron meteorites. Most of the breccia rock fragments are similar to the larger igneous rocks and apparently were derived from them; the rocks in turn were probably once part of the underlying lunar bedrock.

The igneous rocks from the Moon contain the minerals pyroxene, plagioclase, ilmenite, olivine, and cristobalite. Three new minerals were found in these igneous rocks: pyroxmanganite, ferropseudobrookite, and a chromium-titanium compound. All of the lunar rocks were found to have unusually high concentrations of chromium, titanium, scandium, zirconium, hafnium, and yttrium, and very low concentrations of sodium. Many elements such as potassium, rubidium, cesium, chlorine, and thallium, which exist in great abundance in Earth rocks, were found to be very deficient in the lunar rocks.

Radioactive isotopic dating of the igneous rocks brought back by the astronauts shows that they were formed 3.3 to 3.7 billion years ago. In May 1970, G. Wasserburg reported that an Apollo 12 rock was found to be 4.6 billion years old, making it the oldest rock yet found on the Moon or Earth. For the soil and breccia such dating gives an age of 4.4 to 4.6 billion years. The existence of complex biological molecules in the lunar samples would be of tremendous significance, but some of the most sophisticated and sensitive analytical techniques ever devised failed to detect any. Lacking an atmosphere and an appreciable magnetic field, the moon is exposed to ultraviolet radiation as well as high-energy cosmic rays and the solar wind.

## MODERN PLANETARY DATA

| | Distance from Sun in Astronomical Units[1] | Period of Revolution Around Sun | Diameter[2] | Mass[3] | Density[6] (grams/cm³) |
|---|---|---|---|---|---|
| MERCURY | 0.387 | 87.97 Days | 0.38 | 0.055 | 5.5 |
| VENUS | 0.723 | 224.70 Days | 0.95 | 0.815 | 5.25 |
| EARTH | 1.000 | 365.25 Days | 1.00 | 1.00 | 5.517 |
| MARS | 1.524 | 1.88 Years | 0.53 | 0.107 | 3.94 |
| JUPITER | 5.203 | 11.86 Years | 11.20 | 317.9 | 1.330 |
| SATURN | 9.539 | 29.45 Years | 9.36 | 95.2 | 0.706 |
| URANUS | 19.18 | 84.01 Years | 4.06 | 14.6 | 1.21 |
| NEPTUNE | 30.06 | 164.79 Years | 3.88 | 17.2 | 1.67 |
| PLUTO | 39.44 | 247.7 Years | 0.23(?) | 0.002 | 0.8(?) |

| | Period of Rotation ($^H$ = hours; $^M$ = minutes) | Amount of Incident Solar Radiation[4] | Albedo[5] | Observed Surface Temp. | Number of Satellites |
|---|---|---|---|---|---|
| MERCURY | 58.65 Days | 6.7 | 0.06 | 660°F (Dayside) | 0 |
| VENUS | 243 Days (retrograde) | 1.9 | 0.76 | 890°F | 0 |
| EARTH | $23^H 56^M 4^S$ | 1.0 | 0.36 | 70°F | 1 |
| MARS | $24^H 37^M 23^S$ | 0.43 | 0.16 | — 45°F | 2 |
| JUPITER | $9^H 50^M$* | 0.04 | 0.73 | —220°F (Cloud-top) | 16 |
| SATURN | $10^H 14^M$** | 0.01 | 0.76 | —290°F (Cloud-top) | 17 |
| URANUS | $10^H 49^M$ (retrograde) | 0.003 | 0.93 | —350°F (Cloud-top) | 5 |
| NEPTUNE | $15^H 48^M$ | 0.001 | 0.84 | —360°F (Cloud-top) | 2 |
| PLUTO | 6.39 Days | 0.0006 | 0.8(?) | —380°F | 1 |

[1] The astronomical unit, defined as the mean distance from the Earth to the Sun, is approximately 93 million miles. [2] Diameter in terms of the Earth's diameter: 7,926 miles. [3] Mass in terms of the Earth's mass: $1.3 \times 10^{25}$ pounds. [4] Amount of solar radiation falling on the planet in terms of the solar radiation the Earth receives: about 1.4 kilowatts falling on every square meter of the upper atmosphere per second. [5] The albedo is the percentage of the incoming solar radiation that is reflected back to space by the planet and its atmosphere. [6] Density of water is 1.0 gram/cm³. * For the latitudes greater than 12°, the rotation period is $9^H 55^M$. ** For temperate latitudes, the rotation period is $10^H 38^M$.

## SATELLITES OF THE SOLAR SYSTEM

| Planet | | Satellites | Distance from the Planet (Miles) | Period of Revolution* (Days) | Radius (Miles) | Mass (Pounds) |
|---|---|---|---|---|---|---|
| Earth | 1 | Moon | 238,850 | 27.32 | 1,080 | $162 \times 10^{21}$ |
| ‡Mars | 1 | Phobos | 5,810 | 0.32 | 8.4×6.5×6 | — |
| | 2 | Deimos | 14,595 | 1.26 | 4.7×3.7×3.4 | — |
| †Jupiter | 1 | Io | 262,075 | 1.77 | 1,130 | $160 \times 10^{21}$ |
| | 2 | Europa | 416,980 | 3.55 | 980 | $104 \times 10^{21}$ |
| | 3 | Ganymede | 665,130 | 7.15 | 1,650 | $339 \times 10^{21}$ |
| | 4 | Callisto | 1,169,820 | 16.69 | 1,500 | $209 \times 10^{21}$ |
| | 5 | Amalthea | 112,470 | 0.50 | 60 | — |
| | 6 | Hestia | 7,131,940 | 250.57 | 30 | — |
| | 7 | Hera | 7,292,940 | 259.7 | 9 | — |
| | 8 | Poseidon | 14,594,300 | 739 | 6 | — |
| | 9 | Hades | 14,687,200 | 758 | 6 | — |
| | 10 | Demeter | 7,282,700 | 259 | 6 | — |
| | 11 | Pan | 14,036,000 | 692 | 6 | — |
| | 12 | Adrastea | 13,199,000 | 631 | 6 | — |
| | 13 | Leda | 6,906,700 | 240 | — | — |
| ††Saturn | 1 | Mimas | 115,320 | 0.94 | 150 | $0.09 \times 10^{21}$ |
| | 2 | Enceladus | 147,950 | 1.37 | 180 | $0.15 \times 10^{21}$ |
| | 3 | Tethys | 183,150 | 1.89 | 310 | $0.14 \times 10^{21}$ |
| | 4 | Dione | 234,580 | 2.74 | 340 | $2.20 \times 10^{21}$ |
| | 5 | Rhea | 327,590 | 4.52 | 470 | $5.06 \times 10^{21}$ |
| | 6 | Titan | 759,090 | 15.95 | 1,600 | $301 \times 10^{21}$ |
| | 7 | Hyperion | 921,340 | 21.28 | 150 | $0.68 \times 10^{21}$ |
| | 8 | Iapetus | 2,212,200 | 79.33 | 450 | $2.20 \times 10^{21}$ |
| | 9 | Phoebe | 8,047,700 | 550.34 | 60 | — |
| Uranus | 1 | Ariel | 119,200 | 2.52 | 250 | $2.64 \times 10^{21}$ |
| | 2 | Umbriel | 166,020 | 4.14 | 190 | $1.10 \times 10^{21}$ |
| | 3 | Titania | 272,390 | 8.70 | 340 | $8.80 \times 10^{21}$ |
| | 4 | Oberon | 364,270 | 13.46 | 310 | $5.72 \times 10^{21}$ |
| | 5 | Miranda | 81,000 | 1.41 | 90 | $.02 \times 10^{21}$ |
| Neptune | 1 | Triton | 220,700 | 5.88 | 1,150 | $308 \times 10^{21}$ |
| | 2 | Nereid | 3,456,000 | 360 | 90 | $0.07 \times 10^{21}$ |
| Pluto | 1 | 1978-P-1 (Charon) | 12,000 | 6.39 | c.400 | — |

* Around planets. ‡ Satellites are roughly ellipsoidal: principal radii are given.
† A 14th satellite of Jupiter was discovered in 1979 and a 15th and 16th in 1980.
†† An additional 8 satellites of Saturn were discovered 1979, 1980; one is identified with Janus, reported 1966.

## THE ASTEROIDS OR MINOR PLANETS

Between the orbits of Mars and Jupiter are found several thousand small rocky bodies, density 2–2.5 grams/cm³, orbiting the Sun. Ceres was the first to be discovered in 1801, and is also the largest (620 miles in diameter). Some 2,000 asteroids—minor planets—have now been catalogued and their orbits determined. However, there may be as many as 50,000 asteroids in the asteroid belt, most of which probably have diameters of less than a mile.

Because of their large number and planetary positions, it was originally thought that asteroids were the remnants of an exploded planet; however, since the total mass of the asteroids is less than 1/1000 of the Earth's mass, it is unlikely. Evidence shows that most asteroids have a surface consisting of very primitive material (carbonaceous chondrites) so that they may be the solid primordial remnants of the original dust from which the Sun and Earth and other planets condensed.

Many asteroids are not confined to the zone between Mars and Jupiter but have highly eccentric orbits. Hermes and Icarus pass close to Earth's orbit, Hidalgo close to Saturn's. Chiron, discovered 1977 by C. Kowall, orbits between Saturn and Uranus and has been recognized as an asteroid rather than a comet.

## COMETS

Comets are bodies that move around the Sun, most of them in highly elliptical orbits. As a comet approaches the Sun, a somewhat transparent envelope of gas and dust called the *coma* appears around the small compact icy nucleus. The nucleus and coma comprise the comet's head. If the comet comes within two astronomical units of the Sun, it may develop a luminous tail—a long straight gaseous one that always points away from the Sun and a shorter broad dust tail that also curves away from the Sun.

Spectroscopic analysis of the comet's head shows the existence of the following neutral molecules and atoms: $H_2O$, OH, C, O, CO, CH, CN, NH, $NH_2$, Fe, and Ni. The following ionized molecules are found in the comet's tail: $CH^+$, $CO^+$, $CO_2^+$, and $N_2^+$. In addition, large amounts of dust are found in both the head and tail.

The comet's head may be as large as 500,000 miles across, and some comet tails are more than 10 million miles long. Comets circle the Sun in one of three types of orbits: elliptical, parabolic, or hyperbolic. Comets with elliptical orbits are periodic comets: they will continually orbit the Sun, as do the planets. Parabolic or hyperbolic orbits are probably caused by strong planetary perturbation.

The exact origin of comets is unknown. There may be hundreds of millions of comet nuclei in a huge region (Oort cloud) centered on the Sun but way beyond the orbit of Pluto. Occasionally, one may become perturbed and enter into close orbit around the Sun. Comet nuclei, which are only a few miles in diameter, are believed to consist of rocky fragments and frozen gases. As it approaches the Sun, solar radiation and heat cause the frozen gases in the nucleus to vaporize, forming the coma and later, as it comes still closer to the Sun, the tail.

The coma and head shine as sunlight is scattered by the dust and is also reradiated by fluorescent gas molecules. The gas is ionized by the solar wind streaming out radially from the Sun, carrying the gas ions with it and forming the long gaseous tail.

An enormous cloud of hydrogen, 10 times as large as the Sun, was discovered around comet Bennett in April 1970 by the National Aeronautics and Space Administration's Orbiting Geophysical Observatory (OGO) 5 satellite during a special maneuver to view the comet with a hydrogen-sensing device. Comet Bennett had become visible over portions of the United States and Britain late in March. Its huge hydrogen gas envelope—not visible from Earth—is about 8 million miles across and is probably the largest entity ever observed orbiting the Sun.

The existence of large amounts of hydrogen around comets was first discovered in January 1970 by Orbiting Astronomical Observatory (OAO) 2 when it observed a cloud around the comet Tago-Sato-Kosaka. Hydrogen is the most abundant element in the universe, and the vast amounts of it measured by the OAO and OGO satellites clearly show it to be a major constituent of comets. So it now appears that the newly discovered hydrogen clouds are a fourth feature to be added to the classical three components of a comet: the center, or nucleus; the coma; and the tail, which streams out thousands, sometimes millions of miles, always in a direction away from the Sun.

Hailey's Comet, which was last seen from Earth in 1910, should reappear again in 1986.

## SOME PERIODIC COMETS

| Comet | Period (Years) | Perihelion Distance* | Average Distance from Sun* |
|---|---|---|---|
| Encke | 3.3 | 0.339 | 2.21 |
| Grigg-Skjellerup | 5.12 | 0.855 | 2.89 |
| Tempel-2 | 5.27 | 1.37 | 3.0 |
| Giacobini-Zinner | 6.3 | 0.94 | 3.4 |
| Faye | 7.42 | 1.644 | 3.8 |
| Whipple | 7.44 | 2.47 | 3.8 |
| Comas Solá | 8.94 | 1.87 | 4.3 |
| Väisälä | 11.28 | 1.745 | 4.79 |
| Neujmin-1 | 17.9 | 1.54 | 6.8 |
| Crommelin | 27.9 | 0.744 | 9.2 |
| Olbers | 69.6 | 1.18 | 16.9 |
| Pons-Brooks | 70.9 | 0.775 | 17.2 |
| Hailey | 76.0 | 0.587 | 17.9 |

* In astronomical units.

## METEORS

Meteors are small, usually highly fragile particles that enter the Earth's atmosphere at great speeds. A meteor will burn up or vaporize from frictional heating as it enters the atmosphere. A burning meteor is popularly referred to as a "shooting star" or "falling star." A meteor is called a *meteoroid* before it enters the Earth's atmosphere; meteors the size of dust particles are called *micrometeorites*. A *fireball* is a bright glowing meteor that is brilliant enough to cast shadows on the ground. A *bolide* is a fireball that explodes in the atmosphere.

In general, an observer at any one location may observe between five and 10 meteors an hour; however, worldwide, there are some 200,000 visible meteors a day that collectively represent a mass influx of about 10 tons. In addition micrometeorites may account for some 100 tons of extraterrestrial matter that falls to Earth each day.

Meteors usually become visible at about 70 miles above the Earth's surface. Larger bodies may not completely burn up in the Earth's atmosphere and survive the trip through the atmosphere to Earth. These survivors are called *meteorites*, and may weigh as much as 60 tons; they are fundamentally different from meteors both in their origin and in their composition, which is stony, or iron-nickel, or a mixture of these.

Meteor showers occur each year as the Earth runs into patches of particle swarms that are scattered about in the Earth's orbit. When the Earth runs into one of these swarms, meteors appear to burst out in all directions from a particular radiant point. The Leonid meteor showers of November 12, 1799, and November 13, 1833, produced some 300,000 meteors per hour. The Leonid shower on the morning of November 17, 1966, may have produced as many as 2,500 meteors per minute.

Analysis of orbits and periods indicates that meteor showers may be associated with the disintegration of comets. Meteorites are probably closely related to asteroids. Meteor showers, which are named after the constellations in which their radiant point appears to lie, usually are visible for several days before and after their date of maximum occurrence. Meteors associated with meteor showers are usually completely disintegrated within the Earth's upper atmosphere.

## PRINCIPAL METEOR SHOWERS

| Meteor Stream | Date of Maximum Occurrence | Maximum Hourly Rate | Associated Comet |
|---|---|---|---|
| Quadrantids | Jan. 3 | 110 | |
| Lyrids | Apr. 22 | 12 | 1861 I |
| η Aquarids | May 5 | 21 | Halley? |
| Arietids | June 8* | 40 | |
| ζ Perseids | June 9* | 30 | |
| β Taurids | June 30* | 20 | Encke |
| δ Aquarids | July 28 | 35 | |
| Perseids | Aug. 12 | 68 | 1862 III |
| Draconids | Oct. 10 | — | 1933 III, Giacobini-Zinner |
| Orionids | Oct. 21 | 30 | Halley? |
| Taurids | Nov. 8 | 12 | Encke |
| Andromedids | Nov. 10 | — | Biela |
| Leonids | Nov. 17 | 10 | 1866 I |
| Geminids | Dec. 14 | 58 | |
| Ursids | Dec. 22 | 5 | Tuttle |

* Daytime showers.

## ASTRONOMICAL PHENOMENA: 1983

Source: U.S. Naval Observatory

The times in the following tables, dealing with the Moon, with eclipses, and with the seasons, are all given in Greenwich (England) Mean Time (GMT); the new day "begins" at 00 hours 00 minutes (midnight) at the Greenwich meridian and lasts 23 hours and 59 minutes, until one minute before the next day begins. In the United States, there are eight standard time zones, which differ from the Greenwich Mean Time by a fixed number of hours.

To convert any GMT value to that of a particular time zone, subtract from the GMT the number of hours in the table below. If the number of hours to be subtracted is greater than the GMT value, then add 24 hours to the GMT before subtracting. This will then give the time for the preceding day. If the difference is between 00 and 11 hours, the time is A.M.; if the difference is between 12 and 23 hours the time is P.M.

| Local Time Zone | To Convert from GMT |
|---|---|
| Eastern Daylight | Subtract 4 hours |
| Eastern Standard/Central Daylight | Subtract 5 hours |
| Central Standard/Mountain Daylight | Subtract 6 hours |
| Mountain Standard/Pacific Daylight | Subtract 7 hours |
| Pacific Standard/Yukon Daylight | Subtract 8 hours |
| Yukon Standard/Alaska and Hawaii Daylight | Subtract 9 hours |
| Alaska and Hawaii Standard | Subtract 10 hours |
| Bering Standard | Subtract 11 hours |

**PHASES OF THE MOON: 1983** d = day; h = hour; m = minute (Universal Time or GMT)

| New Moon | | | | First Quarter | | | | Full Moon | | | | Last Quarter | | | |
|---|---|---|---|---|---|---|---|---|---|---|---|---|---|---|---|
| | d | h | m | | d | h | m | | d | h | m | | d | h | m |
| Jan. | 14 | 05 | 08 | Jan. | 22 | 05 | 33 | Jan. | 28 | 22 | 26 | Jan. | 6 | 04 | 00 |
| Feb. | 13 | 00 | 32 | Feb. | 20 | 17 | 32 | Feb. | 27 | 08 | 58 | Feb. | 4 | 19 | 17 |
| Mar. | 14 | 17 | 43 | Mar. | 22 | 02 | 25 | Mar. | 28 | 19 | 27 | Mar. | 6 | 13 | 16 |
| Apr. | 13 | 07 | 58 | Apr. | 20 | 08 | 58 | Apr. | 27 | 06 | 31 | Apr. | 5 | 08 | 38 |
| May | 12 | 19 | 25 | May | 19 | 14 | 17 | May | 26 | 18 | 48 | May | 5 | 03 | 43 |
| June | 11 | 04 | 37 | June | 17 | 19 | 46 | June | 25 | 08 | 32 | June | 3 | 21 | 07 |
| July | 10 | 12 | 18 | July | 17 | 02 | 50 | July | 24 | 23 | 27 | July | 3 | 12 | 12 |
| Aug. | 8 | 19 | 18 | Aug. | 15 | 12 | 47 | Aug. | 23 | 14 | 59 | Aug. | 2 | 00 | 52 |
| Sept. | 7 | 02 | 35 | Sept. | 14 | 02 | 24 | Sept. | 22 | 06 | 36 | Aug. | 31 | 11 | 22 |
| Oct. | 6 | 11 | 16 | Oct. | 13 | 19 | 42 | Oct. | 21 | 21 | 53 | Sept. | 29 | 20 | 05 |
| Nov. | 4 | 22 | 21 | Nov. | 12 | 15 | 49 | Nov. | 20 | 12 | 29 | Oct. | 29 | 03 | 37 |
| Dec. | 4 | 12 | 26 | Dec. | 12 | 13 | 09 | Dec. | 20 | 02 | 00 | Nov. | 27 | 10 | 50 |
| | | | | | | | | | | | | Dec. | 26 | 18 | 52 |

PERIGEE (Moon closest to Earth)

| | d | h | | d | h | | d | h |
|---|---|---|---|---|---|---|---|---|
| Jan. | 28 | 11 | May | 16 | 16 | Sept. | 6 | 05 |
| Feb. | 25 | 22 | June | 13 | 06 | Oct. | 4 | 11 |
| Mar. | 25 | 22 | July | 11 | 10 | Nov. | 1 | 03 |
| Apr. | 21 | 08 | Aug. | 8 | 19 | Nov. | 26 | 02 |
| | | | | | | Dec. | 22 | 18 |

APOGEE (Moon farthest from Earth)

| | d | h | | d | h | | d | h |
|---|---|---|---|---|---|---|---|---|
| Jan. | 14 | 05 | May | 4 | 13 | Aug. | 22 | 09 |
| Feb. | 10 | 08 | June | 1 | 08 | Sept. | 18 | 17 |
| Mar. | 9 | 23 | June | 28 | 23 | Oct. | 16 | 08 |
| Apr. | 6 | 18 | July | 26 | 07 | Nov. | 13 | 03 |
| | | | | | | Dec. | 11 | 01 |

**SEASONS 1983**

Spring begins — Mar. 21: 04 h: 39 m
Summer begins — June 21: 23 h: 09 m
Autumn begins — Sept. 23: 14 h: 42 m
Winter begins — Dec. 22: 10 h: 30 m

**SUN DISTANCES 1983**

Perihelion (Earth closet to sun) — Jan. 2
Aphelion (Earth farthest from sun) — July 6

**ECLIPSES: 1983** h = hour; m = minute

**JUNE 11 — TOTAL ECLIPSE OF THE SUN**

Visible in Madagascar, extreme S.E. Asia, Indonesia, Australia, West of New Zealand.

| | |
|---|---|
| Eclipse begins | June 11: 02 h: 09.5 m |
| Central eclipse at local apparent noon | June 11: 04 h: 33.4 m |
| Eclipse ends | June 11: 07 h: 15.8 m |

**JUNE 25 — PARTIAL ECLIPSE OF THE MOON**

Visible in the Americas, Australia.

| | |
|---|---|
| Moon enters penumbra | June 25: 05 h: 43.0 m |
| Middle of the eclipse | June 25: 08 h: 22.3 m |
| Moon leaves penumbra | June 25: 11 h: 01.6 m |

**DECEMBER 4 — ANNULAR ECLIPSE OF THE SUN**

Visible in extreme N.E. of North America; N.E. of South America, British Isles, Iceland; Southern Europe, Africa, S.W. Asia.

| | |
|---|---|
| Eclipse begins | Dec. 4: 09 h: 41.0 m |
| Central eclipse at local apparent noon | Dec. 4: 12 h: 19.6 m |
| Eclipse ends | Dec. 4: 15 h: 19.9 m |

**DECEMBER 19-20 — PENUMBRAL ECLIPSE OF THE MOON**

Visible in South America, North America, Greenland, Africa, Europe, Asia.

| | |
|---|---|
| Moon enters penumbra | Dec. 19: 23 h: 45.9 m |
| Middle of the eclipse | Dec. 20: 01 h: 49.0 m |
| Moon leaves penumbra | Dec. 20: 03 h: 52.3 m |

**CONFIGURATIONS OF THE BRIGHT PLANETS: 1983**

To locate the bright planets, their location in degrees north or south of the Moon is given. All times are GMT.

| | d | h | | | d | h | | | d | h | |
|---|---|---|---|---|---|---|---|---|---|---|---|
| Jan. | 7 | 12 | Saturn 2° S | | 29 | 19 | Jupiter 0.6° S | | 7 | 20 | Mercury 10° S |
| | 9 | 22 | Jupiter 2° S | May | 16 | 01 | Venus 1.5° N | | 10 | 07 | Saturn 1.7° S |
| | 15 | 19 | Venus 1.8° N | | 23 | 23 | Saturn 1.8° S | | 12 | 18 | Jupiter 0.9° S |
| | 17 | 04 | Mars 3° N | | 26 | 21 | Jupiter 0.8° S | Oct. | 3 | 07 | Venus 9° S |
| Feb. | 3 | 21 | Saturn 2° S | June | 9 | 10 | Mercury 0.8° S | | 3 | 16 | Mars 4° S |
| | 6 | 13 | Jupiter 1.5° S | | 14 | 11 | Venus 1.5° S | | 5 | 03 | Mercury 4° S |
| | 10 | 15 | Mercury 2° N | | 20 | 03 | Saturn 2° S | | 7 | 23 | Saturn 1.4° S |
| | 15 | 02 | Venus 4° N | | 22 | 21 | Jupiter 1.2° S | | 10 | 11 | Jupiter 0.4° S |
| | 15 | 06 | Mars 5° N | July | 13 | 08 | Venus 6° S | Nov. | 1 | 04 | Mars 4° S |
| Mar. | 3 | 06 | Saturn 1.7° S | | 17 | 09 | Saturn 2° S | | 1 | 06 | Venus 5° S |
| | 6 | 03 | Jupiter 1.0° S | | 19 | 23 | Jupiter 1.4° S | | 7 | 07 | Jupiter 0.2° N |
| | 16 | 06 | Mars 5° N | Aug. | 7 | 12 | Mars 1.8° S | | 29 | 15 | Mars 4° S |
| | 17 | 06 | Venus 5° N | | 10 | 01 | Venus 12° S | | 30 | 21 | Venus 2° S |
| | 30 | 14 | Saturn 1.5° S | | 10 | 11 | Mercury 6° S | Dec. | 2 | 04 | Saturn 0.9° S |
| Apr. | 2 | 13 | Jupiter 0.6° S | | 13 | 18 | Saturn 1.9° S | | 6 | 03 | Mercury 0.9° S |
| | 14 | 15 | Mercury 6° N | | 16 | 06 | Jupiter 1.3° S | | 28 | 00 | Mars 3° S |
| | 16 | 07 | Venus 4° N | Sept. | 5 | 02 | Mars 3° S | | 29 | 16 | Saturn 0.6° S |
| | 26 | 19 | Saturn 1.6° S | | 5 | 14 | Venus 13° S | | 30 | 19 | Venus 0.7° N |

## U.S. SPACE PROGRAM

Source: National Aeronautics and Space Administration

### SCIENTIFIC AND APPLICATIONS SATELLITES

**Applications Technology Satellites**—The Applications Technology Satellites (ATS) are designed to test in space promising techniques and equipment for use in future meteorological, navigation, and communications satellite systems. The satellites also carry scientific experiments such as instruments to measure radiation in space. The approximately 1,600-pound spacecraft was designed to include from 100 to 300 pounds of experimental equipment. A larger model, ATS-6, launched in 1974, weighs 3,000 pounds. Its transmitter was turned off in 1979. Orbits are at synchronous (approximately 22,235-mile) altitude.

**Biosatellites**—The biosatellites carried into space a wide variety of plants and animals ranging from microorganisms to primates. The experiments were aimed primarily at studying the biological effects of zero gravity—or weightlessness and removal of living things from the influence of the Earth's rotation. They have contributed to knowledge in genetics, evolution, and physiology, and have provided new information about the effects of prolonged flight in space.

**Discoverer**—Discoverer is a U.S. military satellite program that, since its inception (February 28, 1959), has provided valuable data in such areas as radiation, meteoroids, and air density in space near Earth, as well as in aerospace medicine. A major contribution of the program was the development of the technology for midair recovery or sea recovery of packages sent from an orbiting satellite to Earth.

**Dynamics Explorer**—The dual spacecraft, Dynamics Explorer A and B, were launched Aug. 3, 1981. Dynamics Explorer was designed to study the Earth's near-space environment. The mission of the two spacecraft, which are at different orbital altitudes, is the study of the space around Earth from the limits of the upper atmosphere to distances far out in the Earth's magnetic field. Their function is to lay the preliminary foundation for a future mission that will provide a comprehensive assessment of the energy balance in near-Earth space.

**Early Bird**—Early Bird (launched April 6, 1965) was the world's first operational commercial communications satellite. Early Bird was guided by Earth stations into a nearby stationary position (relative to Earth's surface) over the Atlantic. From that point, it was able to furnish communications service (including telecasts) between Europe and North America.

**Earth Resources Technology Satellites (LANDSAT)**—LANDSAT is a technology development program designed to provide comprehensive observation of the Earth's surface. The spacecraft carry television cameras and radiometric scanners which collect global data on the earth's environment: the condition of the atmosphere and oceans, major ecological changes, and variations in weather systems. The 2,100-pound satellite circles the Earth four times a day and has a lifetime of more than a year to cover all four seasons and to account for seasonally-induced variations in the Earth's surface. The satellite's cameras view a 115-mile swath running north to south as the satellite orbits the Earth. The first spacecraft was launched in 1972, the second in 1975, the third in 1978, and the fourth in 1982. The third is still transmitting and the fourth will be able to transmit geological data due to improved resolution.

**Echo**—Echo 1 (orbited August 12, 1960) proved that it is possible to communicate between distant areas on Earth by reflecting radio microwaves from a manmade satellite. Echo 1 was fabricated of aluminum-vapor-coated polyester film 0.0005 inch thick. It was 100 feet in diameter and weighed 123½ pounds. Echo 2 (launched January 25, 1964) was 135 feet in diameter and weighed 565 pounds. Made up of a laminate of aluminum foil and polymer plastic about 0.00075 inch thick, it was 20 times as rigid as Echo 1.

**Explorers**—Explorers comprise the largest group of satellites in the United States space program. Explorer 1 (launched February 1, 1958) was the nation's first satellite. It made one of the most significant contributions of the Space Age, confirming existence of the previously theorized Van Allen radiation belts—a zone of intense radiation surrounding the Earth.

Generally, Explorers are small satellites carrying a limited number of experiments. Their orbits vary to serve the particular purposes of the experiments. Their designs also differ.

Explorers have been put into orbit to measure the thin wisps of air in the upper atmosphere; determine air density by latitude and altitude; provide data on the composition of Earth's ionosphere, including the presence of electrons, which enable the ionosphere to bounce back certain radio waves, thus making possible long-range radio communications on Earth; study the composition, density, pressure, and other properties of the upper atmosphere; provide information on micrometeoroids (small particles of matter in space), and measure the small variations in Earth's gravity field and fix more precisely the locations of points on Earth.

**High Energy Astronomy Observatory (HEAO)**—The HEAO program studies some of the most intriguing mysteries of the universe – pulsars, black holes, neutron stars, quasars and supernovae. HEAO 1, launched Aug. 12, 1977, and HEAO 3, launched September 20, 1979, were designed to perform celestial surveys, mapping the sky for sources and background of X-rays. HEAO 2, launched Nov. 13, 1978, a celestial pointing mission, was to spend one year studying individual X-ray objects in detail by using an advanced X-ray telescope.

**Interplanetary Explorers**—Interplanetary Explorers are a special class of Explorers to provide data on radiation and magnetic fields between the Earth and Moon. The information has been of value to science and contributed to planning for the Apollo program that landed American explorers on the Moon.

**Nimbus**—Advanced equipment intended for use in future operational weather satellites is tested in Nimbus, a research and development project. Nimbus 1 (launched August 28, 1964) was equipped with advanced television cameras and with a high-resolution infrared observation system. The cameras provided daylight pictures; the infrared equipment, night pictures. Nimbus 1 ceased operation about a month after operation.

The thousands of day and night pictures taken by Nimbus 1 have contributed significantly not only to study and tracking of hurricanes and other weather phenomena but also to geology, geography, oceanography, and other earth sciences.

Nimbus 2 (launched May 15, 1966) contained equipment not only for providing day and night pictures of the Earth and its clouds but also for measuring the Earth's heat balance. Heat balance refers to how much of the Sun's radiation the Earth absorbs and how much it reflects back into the atmosphere. The Nimbus 2 experiment represents the first time such information was obtained on a global basis. Study of heat balance data may increase understanding of how storms are born, develop, and die.

Nimbus 3 (launched April 14, 1969), and Nimbus 4 (launched April, 1970), were both powered by a nuclear system, contained equipment to determine the variation of temperature with height within the atmosphere. Nimbus 5 (launched December 1972) carries instruments to measure temperature in clouds as an indicator of their height. Nimbus 6 was launched on June 12, 1975, and Nimbus 7, an advanced pollution-monitoring satellite, was lofted on October 24, 1978.

**Orbiting Astronomical Observatory (OAO)**—Man's study of the universe has been narrowly circumscribed because the atmosphere blocks or distorts much electromagnetic radiation (X-rays, infrared rays, ultraviolet rays) from space. These emissions can tell much about the structure, evolution, and composition of celestial bodies. OAO has made it possible to observe the universe in ultraviolet wavelengths for extended periods from a vantage point above the haze of the atmosphere that contains 99 percent of Earth's air.

**Orbiting Geophysical Observatory (OGO)**—Orbiting Geophysical Observatories are designed to broaden significantly knowledge about the Earth and space and how the Sun influences and affects both. The approximately 1,000-pound OGO furnishes many times the data provided by smaller satellites such as the Explorers.

The principal advantage of OGO is that it makes possible the observation of numerous phenomena simultaneously for prolonged periods of time. This permits study in depth of the relationships between the phenomena. For example, while some OGO experiments report on the erratic behavior of the Sun, others may describe concurrent fluctuations in Earth and interplanetary magnetic fields, space radiation, and properties of the Earth's atmosphere.

**Orbiting Solar Observatory (OSO)**—OSO is a series of satellites intended for intensive study of the Sun and solar phenomena from a point above the disruptive effects of the atmosphere. The observatory is designed to carry such instruments as X-ray and Lyman Alpha spectrometers, neutron flux sensors, and gamma-ray monitors. Data from OSO have provided deeper insight into the functioning of the Sun, and suggest that techniques could be developed for forecasting the major solar flares that flood space with intensities of radiation lethal to man and detrimental to instruments.

**Pegasus**—Named for the winged horse of Greek mythology, Pegasus satellites are among the heaviest and largest of U.S. spacecraft. Deployed in space, the great wings of the Pegasus satellites span 96 feet while the center section, resembling the fuselage of an airplane, is 71 feet long. The wings are designed to report punctures by micrometeoroids, tiny particles of matter speeding through space. Data from Pegasus satellites not only have advanced man's understanding of space but are aiding him in design of large craft intended for prolonged missions in space.

**Relay**—Project Relay demonstrated the feasibility of intercontinental and transoceanic transmission of telephone, television, teleprint, and facsimile radio signals via a medium-altitude (several thousand to 12,000 miles) active-repeater (radio-equipped) satellite.

**Solar Maximum Mission**—This 5,000-pound spacecraft was launched on a Delta rocket on February 14, 1980, to study solar phenomena during the period of maximum solar flares and related phenomena.

**Solar Mesosphere Explorer**—The Solar Mesosphere Explorer was launched from Vandenberg Air Force Base, Calif., Oct. 6, 1981. The SME is an atmospheric research satellite designed to study reactions between sunlight, ozone and other chemicals in the atmosphere and how concentrations of ozone are transported in the atmosphere in the region from 30 kilometers (19 miles) to 90 km (55 mi.) altitude. One year orbital operation is planned.

**Syncom**—NASA's Project Syncom (for *syn*chronous *com*munication) demonstrated the feasibility of employing synchronous-orbit active-repeater satellites for global communication. Syncom satellites have been used in many experiments and public demonstrations.

**Telstar**—Telstar—like Relay—was an experiment using active-repeater satellites in medium-altitude orbits. Because the two satellites differed in important structural and other features, they permitted comparison of different designs. This contributed to the acquisition of information needed to develop equipment for an operational communications satellite system.

**TIROS**—Originally a research and development project, TIROS has evolved into an operational weather observation system. TIROS stands for *T*elevision and *I*nfra-*R*ed *O*bservation *S*atellite. The first TIROS satellite was launched on April 1, 1960. Since then, TIROS 1 and subsequent satellites have proved themselves the most effective storm detection system known. They have provided meteorologists with more than half a million usable cloud-cover pictures, enabling them to track, forecast, and analyze storms. Through TIROS observations, the U.S. Weather Service has issued thousands of storm bulletins to countries throughout the world.

Continued progress has been made in improving the observations made by TIROS and in making these observations available to weather services of other nations. TIROS satellites now provide almost global coverage as compared to the coverage of about 25 percent of the Earth's surface at the program's inception. They can provide high-quality pictures of Earth's cloud cover. Some are equipped with an automatic picture transmission (APT) system that permits receipt of TIROS cloud-cover photographs on the ground with relatively inexpensive ground equipment.

In addition to contributing significantly to the discovery and tracking of hurricanes and other weather phenomena, TIROS satellites are providing valuable data for meteorological research. Such research may lead to long-range weather forecasts and perhaps greater understanding of how hurricanes and other destructive storms breed and how their development can be curbed. TIROS pictures of the Earth are proving useful in geography and geology, in showing the magnitude of river and sea ice, and in furnishing information on snowcover and thus spring flooding.

**TOS and NOAA**—NASA's research and development work with meteorological satellites has led to the world's first operational weather satellite system, called TOS (for *T*IROS *O*perational *S*atellite). The TOS system is furnishing weathermen daily with pictures of the weather over nearly the whole Earth. TOS and an improved version called ITOS are financed, managed, and operated by the Weather Service, a part of the National Oceanic and Atmospheric Administration (NOAA) of the United States Department of Commerce. A new advanced TIROS-N satellite was launched on October 13, 1978. After the first spacecraft, the remainder of this series received NOAA designations: NOAA-6 was launched in 1979 and NOAA-7 in 1980.

**Transit and the Navy Navigation Satellite System**—Transit was a Department of Defense experimental navigation satellite program designed to lead to a worldwide operational navigation-satellite system for American military ships. The operational system, consisting of four satellites that are properly positioned relative to each other, is intended to provide accurate data for navigational fixes on an average of once every 1¾ hours. The system is designed to allow users to determine their precise position on Earth regardless of weather and time of day.

**Vanguard**—The first Vanguard satellite went into orbit in 1958. Among the valuable data acquired from this satellite was information regarding the relatively slight but significant distortion referred to as the "pear shape" of the Earth. Two other Vanguards were successfully launched in 1959 in this now completed program. The Vanguards provided valuable information on Earth and its space environment, including such phenomena as Earth's magnetic field, the Van Allen radiation belts, and micrometeoroids.

## UNMANNED INTERPLANETARY MISSIONS

**Lunar Orbiter**—Lunar Orbiter 1 (launched August 10, 1966) was the first of a series of spacecraft designed to orbit the Moon and return closeup pictures and other information about Earth's only natural satellite. The photographs and other information returned to Earth by Lunar Orbiter spacecraft contributed to manned landings on the Moon and added significantly to knowledge. Analysis of Lunar Orbiter 5's motions around the Moon led to the surprise discovery of lunar mascons.

**Mariner**—Mariner 9 orbited Mars in 1971–72, sending back via television 7,000 photographs of the Martian surface. Mariner 10, launched in November 1973, flew by Venus and Mercury in February and March 1974, returning the first close-up pictures of those planets. After orbiting around the Sun, Mariner 10 again flew by Mercury on September 21, 1974, and for a third time on March 16, 1975.

**Pioneer**—Pioneer was the designation of NASA's first series of long-distance spacecraft. Of these, the most notable was Pioneer 5 (launched March 11, 1960), with which radio communication was maintained until June 26, 1960, when the craft was about 22.5 million miles from Earth—a record for the period.

NASA opened a new series of Pioneer experiments with the launch of Pioneer 6 (December 16, 1965). The series is designed to monitor on a continuing basis phenomena of interplanetary space such as radiation, magnetic fields, and the solar wind.

Some Pioneers are investigating space between Earth and Venus; others, between Earth and Mars. The knowledge gained is expected to advance scientific understanding and contribute to planning for manned interplanetary space flights.

Pioneer 10 (launched March 2, 1972) observed Jupiter close up in December, 1973 after passing beyond the orbit of Mars and through the Asteroid belt. Ultimately it should escape the solar system. Pioneer 11, launched March 6, 1973, followed a similar flight path, with a Jupiter encounter Dec. 4, 1974. Pioneer 11 flew past Saturn's rings in Sept. 1979.

Pioneer Venus 1 (launched May 20, 1978) and Pioneer Venus 2 (launched Aug. 8, 1978) began the most extensive study ever made of Venus upon arrival at the planet in December 1978. Swinging into orbit on Dec. 4, Pioneer Venus 1 was to sample upper atmospheric composition, make radar measurements of the surface elevations and roughness, and take daily ultraviolet and infrared pictures of the atmosphere for one Venusian year (225 Earth days) or more. On December 9, the four probes and transporter bus that comprised Pioneer Venus 2 plunged into the Venusian clouds at widely separated points for detailed measurements of the atmosphere from top to bottom.

**Ranger**—NASA's Project Ranger made possible the greatest single advance in lunar knowledge since Galileo first studied the Moon through a telescope more than three centuries ago. In the program, Ranger spacecraft telecast to Earth 17,255 closeups of the Moon. Features as small as 10 inches across on the lunar surface were made visible to man for the first time.

Ranger 7 through Ranger 9, the last of the Ranger series, began telecasting pictures when they were about 20 minutes away from the Moon and continued to telecast until crashing onto the surface. The Rangers with the television packages were about 5 feet in diameter at their hexagonal base and approximately 8¼ feet long. Cruising in space with appendages extended, Ranger spanned 15 feet across its winglike solar panels and measured 10¼ feet to the far edge of its dish-shaped antenna.

**Surveyor**—Surveyor was designed to decelerate from the lunar approach velocity of 6,000 mph (or 9,000 feet per second) to a touchdown speed of about 3½ mph.

The first Surveyors were designed as engineering test spacecraft intended primarily to test soft-landing techniques. Their legs were instrumented to return data on the Moon's surface hardness, and each carried a single scanning television camera which have transmitted over 90,000 photos of the lunar surface.

**Viking**—A decade of planning and work came to fruition with the landing of robot spacecraft on Mars to conduct detailed scientific investigation of the planet, including the search for life. After an 11-month journey, Viking 1 touched down on the boulder-strewn Martian plain called Chryse on July 20, 1976. On Sept. 3, its sister ship, Viking 2, landed at Utopia, about 1,600 km (1,000 mi.) nearer to Mars' polar cap.

Specially designed cameras on the craft took closeup pictures of the planet; miniature weather stations monitored the thin Martian air; other instruments noted magnetism, radiation; and Martian soil was analyzed in miniaturized biology laboratories aboard the spacecraft. The "life" experiments data both satisfied and puzzled scientists. The presence of compounds which were conceivably of biological origin was indicated by the data but the organic analysis data did not support that conclusion.

The end of the normal missions of the two spacecraft occurred in mid-November when solar conjunction produced a blackout of Viking-to-Earth communications. By mid-December, there was a return to post-conjunction operations, and the beginning of the "extended missions" which ended in 1978. The landers continued to operate during a "continued mission" phase through February 1979 and mission planners have advocated a plan to keep Viking Lander 1 operating on a reduced schedule through 1989.

**Voyager**—Two Voyager spacecraft, carrying instruments to conduct 11 science experiments, were launched on Aug. 20 and Sept. 5, 1977, toward Jupiter, Saturn and the outer reaches of the solar system. Voyager 1, launched on the later date, reached Jupiter on March 5, 1979, and almost immediately made two major discoveries – a ring around Jupiter and active volcanoes on Io, the planet's closest satellite. Boosted toward Saturn, Voyager 1 also examined three other satellites – Europa, Ganymede and Callisto; Voyager 2 made its closest approach to Jupiter on July 9, 1979, also surveyed Callisto, Ganymede, Europa and Amalthea. Both spacecraft continued to observe Jupiter as they headed for Saturn.

Voyager 1 explored Saturn and its ring and moon system in November 1980. Voyager 2 followed in turn in August 1981. Voyager 2 is now heading for Uranus and should reach the distant planet in January 1986.

## MANNED SPACE-FLIGHT PROGRAMS

**Project Mercury**—Project Mercury placed the first Americans into space. The pioneering project was organized (October 5, 1958) to orbit a manned spacecraft, investigate man's reaction to, and abilities in, space flight, and recover both man and spacecraft.

Project Mercury experiments demonstrated that the high-gravity forces of launch and of atmosphere entry as well as weightlessness in orbit for as much as 34 hours do not impair man's ability to control a spacecraft. It proved that man not only augments the reliability of spacecraft controls but also can conduct scientific observations and experiments that expand and clarify information from instruments.

**Project Gemini**—Project Gemini markedly extended the technology and experience gained through Project Mercury and vastly increased knowledge about space, Earth, and man. The last of the Gemini missions was Gemini 12 (completed November 15, 1966). In achieving all of its major objectives, the Gemini project demonstrated that man can maneuver his craft in space; leave his craft and do useful work in space if he is properly clothed and equipped; rendezvous (find and come near) and dock (link up) his craft with another vehicle in space; function effectively during prolonged space flight of a least two weeks and return to Earth in good physical condition; and control his spacecraft during its descent from orbit and land it within a selected area on Earth.

**Project Apollo**—Its goals: land American explorers on the Moon and bring them safely back to Earth (which was successfully accomplished by Apollo 11 in July 1969), and establish the technology to meet other national interests in space. The Apollo spacecraft is made up of three sections or modules:

1. COMMMAND MODULE—The command module is designed to accommodate three astronauts in a "shirt-sleeve" environment; i.e., the astronauts are able to work, eat, and sleep in the module without pressure suits. The command module, like the crew compartment of an airliner, has windows, and contains controls and instruments (including a computer) of various kinds to enable the astronauts to pilot their craft. The command module weighs about 5 tons. It stands 11 feet tall and has a base diameter of about 13 feet.

2. SERVICE MODULE—The service module is equipped with rocket engines and fuel supplies to enable the astronauts to propel their craft into and out of lunar orbit and to change their course in space. The service module weighs 24 tons. It is 23 feet long and 13 feet in diameter.

3. LUNAR MODULE—The lunar module (LM) is the space ferry that takes two Apollo astronauts down to the Moon and carries them from the Moon's surface into lunar orbit and rendezvous with the Apollo command and service modules in lunar orbit. At launch from Earth, the LM weighs about 14½ tons. It is some 20 feet high and has a base diameter of 13 feet. After the two-man crew of the LM returns to the command module, the LM is jettisoned in lunar orbit.

**Skylab**—Skylab was America's first orbiting space laboratory, launched by NASA on May 14, 1973. Eleven days later, the first of three scheduled manned missions made a rendezvous with the space station, activating its extensive facilities to conduct solar astronomy experiments, to relay informaton on Earth's ecological systems and to study the effects of weightlessness on industrial processes. Most important, however, was the medical and life sciences information obtained from observation of the three-man crews as they lived in space for prolonged periods of time. The Skylab II (actually the first *manned* Skylab) mission lasted 28 days; its success prompted NASA to extend Skylab III's mission (launched July 28, 1973 to 59 days. A fourth (third manned) and final Skylab mission was launched on November 16, 1973, and the crew spent 84 days in space. Skylab descended from orbit and broke up over Australia on July 11, 1979.

**Apollo Soyuz Test Project**—The first international manned space flight was made by United States and U.S.S.R. spacecraft July 15-24, 1975. Its objective was to accomplish spacecraft rendezvous, docking, undocking, crew transfer, interaction of control centers, and interaction of spacecraft crews. The planned joint activities were carried out successfully and the many ceremonial activities were televised as were many of the other activities.

**Space Shuttle**—The key element in the United States' future Space Transportation System made its first appearance as the first Space Shuttle orbiter, the Enterprise, was rolled out at the NASA/Rockwell International facility at Palmdale, Calif., in September 1976. The spacecraft successfully completed a series of unmanned flight tests in 1977. The first U.S. manned space shuttle flight began when Columbia was launched from Kennedy Space Center, Florida, on April 12, 1981. Two days and 38 earth orbits later, it landed its two-man crew safely at Edwards Air Force Base in California. Three additional manned test flights were made prior to the first "operational" shuttle flight presently scheduled for November 1982.

The agency has 78 active astronauts, of which 19 are in candidate status. Of the 78, 42 are mission specialists and the remainder are pilots.

## MANNED SPACE FLIGHTS

| Spacecraft | Launching Date | Astronauts | Revolutions | Flight Time | Flight Highlights |
|---|---|---|---|---|---|
| USSR Vostok I | Apr. 12, 1961 | Yuri A. Gagarin | 1 | 1 hr. 48 mins. | First manned flight. |
| U.S. Mercury-Redstone 3 | May 5, 1961 | Alan B. Shepard, Jr. | Suborbital | 0 hrs. 15 mins. | First American in space. |
| U.S. Mercury-Redstone 4 | July 21, 1961 | Virgil I. Grissom | Suborbital | 0 hrs. 16 mins. | Evaluated spacecraft functions. |
| USSR Vostok II | Aug. 6, 1961 | Gherman S. Titov | 16 | 25 hrs. 18 mins. | More than 24 hours in space. |
| U.S. Mercury-Atlas 6 | Feb. 20, 1962 | John H. Glenn | 3 | 4 hrs. 55 mins. | First American in orbit. |
| U.S. Mercury-Atlas 7 | May 24, 1962 | M. Scott Carpenter | 3 | 4 hrs. 56 mins. | Landed 250 miles from target. |
| USSR Vostok III | Aug. 11, 1962 | Andrian G. Nikolayev | 60 | 94 hrs. 22 mins. | First group flight (Vostok III and IV). |
| USSR Vostok IV | Aug. 12, 1962 | Pavel R. Popovich | 45 | 70 hrs. 57 mins. | Came within 3.1 miles of Vostok III on first orbit. |
| U.S. Mercury-Atlas 8 | Oct. 3, 1962 | Walter M. Schirra, Jr. | 6 | 9 hrs. 13 mins. | Landed 5 miles from target. |
| U.S. Mercury-Atlas 9 | May 15, 1963 | L. Gordon Cooper, Jr. | 22 | 34 hrs. 20 mins. | First long flight by an American. |
| USSR Vostok V | June 14, 1963 | Valery F. Bykovsky | 76 | 119 hrs. 6 mins. | Second group flight (Vostok V and VI). |
| USSR Vostok VI | June 16, 1963 | Valentina V. Tereshkova | 45 | 70 hrs. 50 mins. | Passed within 3 miles of Vostok V; first woman in space. |
| USSR Voskhod I | Oct. 12, 1964 | Komarov; Feoktistov; Yegorov | 15 | 24 hrs. 17 mins. | First 3-man craft. |
| USSR Voskhod II | Mar. 18, 1965 | Leonov; Belyayev | 16 | 26 hrs. 2 mins. | First man outside spacecraft in 10-minute "walk" (Leonov). |
| U.S. Gemini 3 | Mar. 23, 1965 | V. I. Grissom; J. W. Young | 3 | 4 hrs. 53 mins. | First manned orbital maneuvers. |
| U.S. Gemini 4 | June 3, 1965 | J. A. McDivitt; E. H. White, II | 62 | 97 hrs. 48 mins. | 21-minute "space walk" (White). |
| U.S. Gemini 5 | Aug. 21, 1965 | L. G. Cooper, Jr.; C. Conrad, Jr. | 120 | 190 hrs. 56 mins. | First extended manned flight. |
| U.S. Gemini 7 | Dec. 4, 1965 | F. Borman; J. A. Lovell, Jr. | 206 | 330 hrs. 35 mins. | Longest space flight at the time. |
| U.S. Gemini 6-A | Dec. 15, 1965 | W. M. Schirra, Jr.; T. P. Stafford | 16 | 25 hrs. 52 mins. | World's first successful space rendezvous. |
| U.S. Gemini 8 | Mar. 16, 1966 | N. A. Armstrong; D. R. Scott | 6.5 | 10 hrs. 42 mins. | World's first docking (to Agena target); mission cut short. |
| U.S. Gemini 9-A | June 3, 1966 | T. P. Stafford; E. A. Cernan | 44 | 72 hrs. 21 mins. | Rendezvous, extravehicular activity, precision landing. |
| U.S. Gemini 10 | July 18, 1966 | J. W. Young; M. Collins | 43 | 70 hrs. 47 mins. | Rendezvous with 2 targets; Agena package retrieved. |
| U.S. Gemini 11 | Sept. 12, 1966 | C. Conrad, Jr.; R. F. Gordon, Jr. | 44 | 71 hrs. 17 mins. | Rendezvous and docking. |
| U.S. Gemini 12 | Nov. 11, 1966 | J. A. Lovell, Jr., E. E. Aldrin, Jr. | 59 | 94 hrs. 35 mins. | 3 successful extravehicular trips. |
| USSR Soyuz 1 | Apr. 23, 1967 | Vladimir M. Komarov | 17 | 26 hrs. 40 mins. | Heaviest manned craft; crashed, killing Komarov. |
| U.S. Apollo 7 | Oct. 11, 1968 | W. M. Schirra, Jr.; D. F. Eisele; R. Walter Cunningham | 163 | 260 hrs. 9 mins. | First manned flight of Apollo spacecraft. |
| USSR Soyuz 3 | Oct. 26, 1968 | Georgi T. Beregovoi | 60 | 94 hrs. 51 mins. | Rendezous with unmanned Soyuz 2. |
| U.S. Apollo 8 | Dec. 21, 1968 | F. Borman; Wm. A. Anders; James A. Lovell, Jr. | Moon orbital (10 revolutions) | 147 hrs. | First manned voyage around Moon. |
| USSR Soyuz 4 | Jan. 14, 1969 | Vladimir A. Shatalov | 45 | 71 hrs. 14 mins. | Rendezvous with Soyuz 5. |

**MANNED SPACE FLIGHTS (Cont.)**

| Spacecraft | Launching Date | Astronauts | Revolutions | Flight Time | Flight Highlights |
|---|---|---|---|---|---|
| USSR Soyuz 5 | Jan. 15, 1969 | Volynov; Khrunov; Yeliseyev | 46 | 72 hrs. 46 mins. | Cosmonauts transfer to Soyuz 4. |
| U.S. Apollo 9 | Mar. 3, 1969 | J. A. McDivitt; D. R. Scott; Russell L. Schweickart | 151 | 241 hrs. 1 min. | First docking with Lunar Module within Earth's atmosphere. |
| U.S. Apollo 10 | May 18, 1969 | Stafford; Cernan; Young | 31 (Moon) | 192 hrs. 3 mins. | Descent to within 9 miles of Moon. |
| U.S. Apollo 11 | July 16, 1969 | Neil A. Armstrong<br>Edwin E. Aldrin, Jr.<br>Michael Collins | Moon orbital for Command Module (31 revolutions) | 195 hrs. 18 mins. | Armstrong and Aldrin, in Lunar Module, land in Sea of Tranquility. Collins remained in lunar orbit in Command Module. Remained on Moon for 21 hours, 36 minutes. |
| USSR Soyuz 6 | Oct. 11, 1969 | G. S. Shonin; V. N. Kubasov | 79 | 118 hrs. 42 mins. | Welding of metals in space. |
| USSR Soyuz 7 | Oct. 12, 1969 | Filipchenko; Volkov; Gorbatko | 79 | 118 hrs. 41 mins. | Tests for building an orbiting space laboratory. |
| USSR Soyuz 8 | Oct. 13, 1969 | V. A. Shatalov; A. S. Yeliseyev | 79 | 118 hrs. 50 mins. | Test for building an orbiting space laboratory. |
| U.S. Apollo 12 | Nov. 14, 1969 | Charles Conrad, Jr.; A. L. Bean; R. F. Gordon, Jr. | Moon orbital for Command Module (45 revolutions) | 244 hrs. 36 mins. | Conrad and Bean, in Lunar Module, land in Sea of Storms. Gordon remained in lunar orbit in Command Module. |
| U.S. Apollo 13 | Apr. 11, 1970 | J. A. Lovell, Jr.; F. W. Haise, Jr.; John L. Swigert, Jr. | Swung around Moon; returned to Earth | 142 hrs. 52 mins. | Power failure en route to Moon led to the termination of the scheduled lunar landing of Lovell and Haise. |
| USSR Soyuz 9 | June 1, 1970 | Nikolayev; Sevastyanov | 286 | 424 hrs. 59 mins. | Studied physical reactions to extended space travel. |
| U.S. Apollo 14 | Jan. 31, 1971 | Alan B. Shepard, Jr.; Stuart A. Roosa; Edgar D. Mitchell | Moon orbital for Command Module (34 revolutions) | 216 hrs. 0.2 mins. | Shepard and Mitchell, in Lunar Module, land in Fra Mauro area. Roosa remained in lunar orbit in Command Module. |
| USSR Soyuz 10 | Apr. 22, 1971 | Shatalov; Yeliseyev; Rukavishnikov | 32 | 47 hrs. 46 mins. | Aborted after linking up with unmanned satellite Salyut 1. |
| USSR Soyuz 11 | June 6, 1971 | Dobrovolsky; Volkov; Patsayev | 360 | 570 hrs. 22 mins. | Docked with Salyut 1; dead on return. |
| U.S. Apollo 15 | July 26, 1971 | David R. Scott<br>Alfred M. Worden<br>James B. Irwin | Moon orbital for Command Module (64 revolutions) | 295 hrs. 12 mins. | Scott and Irwin, in Lunar Module, landed in Hadley Rille and explored in Lunar Rover. Worden, from Command Module, performed experiments and first deep space walk. |
| U.S. Apollo 16 | Apr. 16, 1972 | Charles M. Duke, Jr.<br>Thomas K. Mattingly<br>John W. Young | Moon orbital for Command Module (74 revolutions) | 265 hrs. 51 mins. | Young and Duke spent 71 hours, two minutes on the Moon's surface. They returned with 214 pounds of lunar rock and soil. |
| U.S. Apollo 17 | Dec. 7, 1972 | Eugene A. Cernan<br>Ronald E. Evans<br>Harrison H. Schmitt | Moon orbital for Command Module (75 revolutions) | 301 hrs. 51 mins. | Cernan and Schmitt spent a record 74 hours and 59 mins. on Moon and returned with 250 pounds of lunar material. |
| U.S. Skylab 2 | May 25, 1973 | Charles "Pete" Conrad, Jr. J. P. Kerwin; P. J. Weitz | 393 | 672 hrs. 49 mins. | First manned flight to Skylab space station. |
| U.S. Skylab 3 | July 28, 1973 | Alan L. Bean, Owen K. Garriott, Jack R. Lousma | 852 | 1427 hrs. 9 mins. | Second manned flight to space station demonstrating man's ability to function for long periods in space. |
| USSR Soyuz 12 | Sept. 27, 1973 | V. G. Lazarev; O. G. Makarov | 29 | 47 hrs. 16 mins. | Testing of modifications in spacecraft. |
| USSR Soyuz 13 | Dec. 18, 1973 | P. I. Klimuk; V. V. Lebedev | 119 | 188 hrs. 55 mins. | Cosmonauts grew nutritive protein samples. |
| U.S. Skylab 4 | Nov. 16, 1973 | G. P. Carr; Wm. R. Pogue; Edward G. Gibson | 1,214 | 2017 hrs. 17 mins. | Weightless for 84 days, the astronauts each "grew" an inch. |
| USSR Soyuz 14 | July 3, 1974 | Popovich; Artyukhin | N.A. | 377 hrs. 30 mins. | Occupied Salyut 3. |
| USSR Soyuz 15 | Aug. 26, 1974 | Sarafanov; Demin | N.A. | 48 hrs. 12 mins. | Failed to achieve a link-up with Salyut 3. |
| USSR Soyuz 16 | Dec. 2, 1974 | Filipchenko; Rukavishnikov | 96 | 142 hrs. 24 mins. | ASTP precursor flight to check out new Soyuz designs. |

| | | | | | |
|---|---|---|---|---|---|
| USSR Soyuz 17 | Jan. 11, 1975 | Grechko; Gubarev | N.A. | 709 hrs. 20 mins. | Occupied Salyut 4 and set Soviet duration record. |
| USSR Soyuz 18 | May 24, 1975 | Klimuk; Sevastyanov | N.A. | 1512 hrs. (est.) | Conducted experiments with Salyut 4. |
| USSR Soyuz 19<br>U.S. Apollo 18 | July 15, 1975<br>July 15, 1975 | Leonov; Kubasov<br>Stafford; Slayton; Brand | 96 Earth orbits<br>136 Earth orbits | 143 hrs. 31 mins.<br>217 hrs. 30 mins. | ASTP joint flight, U.S. and USSR link up in space and hold a joint news conference. |
| USSR Soyuz 21 | July 6, 1976 | Volynov; Zholobov | N.A. | 50 days | Conducted experiments with Salyut 5. |
| USSR Soyuz 22 | Sept. 15, 1976 | Bykovsky; Aksenov | N.A. | 8 days | Photographed Earth's surface. |
| USSR Soyuz 23 | Oct. 14, 1976 | Zudov; Rozhdestvensky | N.A. | 2 days | Failed to achieve link-up with Salyut 5. |
| USSR Soyuz 24 | Feb. 7, 1977 | Gorbatko; Glazkov | N.A. | 425 hrs. 23 mins. | Conducted experiments with Salyut 5. |
| USSR Soyuz 25 | Oct. 9, 1977 | Kovalenak; Ryumin | N.A. | 48 hrs. 46 mins. | Failed to dock with Salyut 6. |
| USSR Soyuz 26 | Dec. 10, 1977 | Romanenko; Grechko | 1600 (approx.) | 96 days, 10 hrs. | Docked with Salyut 6. Returned to Earth March 16, 1978. |
| USSR Soyuz 27 | Jan. 10, 1978 | Dzhanibekov; Makarov | N.A. | 6 days | Docked with Salyut 6. Returned to Earth Jan. 16. |
| USSR Soyuz 28 | March 2, 1978 | Gubarev; Remek (Czech) | N.A. | 7 days | Docked with Salyut 6. Returned to Earth, March 10. |
| USSR Soyuz 29 | June 15, 1978 | Kovalenak; Ivanchenkov | N.A. | 139 days, 15 hrs. | Docked with Salyut 6. Returned to Earth Nov. 2. |
| USSR Soyuz 30 | June 27, 1978 | Klimuk; Hermaszewski (Pole) | N.A. | 8 days | Docked with Salyut 6. Returned to Earth, July 5. |
| USSR Soyuz 31 | Aug. 26, 1978 | Bykovsky; Jaehn (E. Ger.) | N.A. | 8 days | Docked with Salyut 6. Returned to Earth Sept. 3. |
| USSR Soyuz 32 | Feb. 25, 1979 | Lyakhov; Ryumin | N.A. | 175 days | Docked with Salyut 6 space station; resupplied three times. Returned to Earth on Aug. 19, in Soyuz 34. |
| USSR Soyuz 33 | Apr. 10, 1979 | Rukavishnikov; Ivanov (Bulgarian) | N.A. | 2 days | Aborted attempt to ferry two cosmonauts to the Salyut 6 space station. Returned to Earth, Apr. 12. |
| USSR Soyuz 35 | Apr. 9, 1980 | Ryumin; Popov | N.A. | 185 days | Docked with Salyut 6 space station. In orbit for record endurance space flight. Returned to Earth, Oct. 11. |
| USSR Soyuz 36 | May 25, 1980 | Kubasov; Farkas (Hungarian) | N.A. | 7 days | Link-up with Salyut 6. Returned to Earth, June 3. |
| USSR Soyuz T2 | June 5, 1980 | Malyshev; Aksenov | N.A. | 4 days | Link-up with Salyut 6. Returned to Earth, June 9. |
| USSR Soyuz 37 | July 23, 1980 | Gorbatko; Tuan (Vietnamese) | N.A. | 8 days | Link-up with Salyut 6. Returned to Earth, July 31. |
| USSR Soyuz 38 | Sept. 18, 1980 | Romanenko, Mendez (Cuban) | N.A. | 8 days | Link-up with Salyut 6. Returned to Earth, Sept. 26. |
| USSR Soyuz T-3 | Nov. 27, 1980 | Kizim; Makarov; Strekalov | N.A. | 13 days | Link-up with Salyut 6. Test of upgraded Soyuz. Returned to Earth, Dec. 10. |
| USSR Soyuz T-4 | Mar. 12, 1981 | Kovalyonok; Savinykh | N.A. | 75 days | Link-up with Salyut 6. Returned to Earth, May 26. |
| USSR Soyuz 39 | Mar. 22, 1981 | Dzhanibekov; Gurragcha (Mongolian) | N.A. | 8 days | Link-up with Salyut 6. Returned to Earth, Mar. 30. |
| U.S. Columbia (STS-1) | Apr. 12, 1981 | J.W. Young; R.L. Crippen | 36 | 54 hrs. 22 mins. | First space shuttle test flight. Returned to Earth, Apr. 14 |
| USSR Soyuz 40 | May 14, 1981 | Popov; Prunariu (Romanian) | N.A. | 8 days | Link-up with Salyut 6. Returned to Earth May 22. |
| U.S. Columbia (STS-2) | Nov. 12, 1981 | J. H. Engle; R. H. Truly | 36 | 54 hrs. 13 mins. | Space shuttle test flight. Returned to Earth Nov. 14. |
| U.S. Columbia (STS-3) | Mar. 22, 1982 | J. R. Lousma; C. G. Fullerton | 129 | 8 days, 4 mins. | Space Shuttle test flight. Returned to Earth Mar. 30. |
| USSR Soyuz T5 | May 13, 1982 | A. Berezovnoy; V. Lebedev | — | — | Link-up with Salyut 7. Still in orbit as of Aug. 1, 1982. |
| USSR Soyuz T6 | June 24, 1982 | V. Dzhanibekov; A. Ivanchenkov; J. Chretien (French) | N.A. | 8 days | Link-up with Salyut 7. Returned to Earth July 2, 1982. |
| U.S. Columbia (STS-4) | June 27, 1982 | T. Mattingly; H. Hartsfield | 112 | 7 days, 70 mins. | Space shuttle test flight. Returned to Earth July 4, 1982. |

# SCIENCE: PAST/PRESENT

## ENGINEERING ACHIEVEMENTS

The following is a list of engineering projects that have received the American Society of Civil Engineers' Outstanding Civil Engineering Achievement Award.

**St. Lawrence Seaway and Power Project.** A swath for ocean-going vessels from the Atlantic to the Great Lakes, serving America's and Canada's energy and navigational needs.

**John F. Kennedy International Airport, 1961**–Handles nearly all of New York's international air traffic.

**Intercontinental Ballistic Missile Program, 1962**–This program involved ICBM installations in 14 states.

**Ohio River Basin Clean Streams Program, 1963**–This complex of facilities for pollution control affected the economy of more than 1,500 municipalities in eight states adjacent to 1,000 miles of waterways in the Ohio River Basin.

**The Glen Canyon Unit of the Colorado River Project, 1964**–Rising 710 feet, the dam is only 16 feet less than Hoover Dam in height; its concrete volume is greater.

**Chesapeake Bay Bridge-Tunnel, 1965** – This engineering achievement crosses over and under the open sea and links the Eastern Shore of Virginia with the mainland. Its 12.5 miles of low-level trestle, four man-made islands, two mile-long tunnels, a high and medium-level bridge and several miles of approach roads make up the project.

**NASA Complex 39, 1966**–This huge complex, the Apollo-Saturn assembly and launch facility at Cape Kennedy (Merritt Island), Florida, is dominated by the world's second largest building: the Vehicle Assembly Building.

**St. Louis Gateway Arch, 1967**–This 630-foot stainless steel arch commemorates the "Gateway to the West."

**San Mateo Hayward Bridge, 1968**–Spans San Francisco Bay, is located 17 miles south of the city, accommodates 50,000 vehicles daily, and is 6.7 miles long.

**Oroville Dam and Powerplant, 1969**–This dam on California's Feather River is 770 ft. high, the world's third largest.

**Middletown, Ohio, Armco Steelworks, 1970**–This steelmaking complex was cited for construction innovations, techniques, materials, and pollution control.

**World Trade Center, 1971**–When built, these twin towers were the world's two tallest buildings (110 stories, 1,350 feet high).

**California State Water Project, 1972**–The project to deliver 4.23 million acre-feet of water throughout California. Its major aqueduct extends 444 miles.

**Ludington Pumped Storage Project, 1973**–Water from Lake Michigan is pumped up to a reservoir from which it rushes through the turbines of the power plant, with a generating capacity of over 1.8 million kw of electricity.

**Land Reclamation Program of Fulton County, Ill., 1974** – Sludge is barged down the Illinois River to Fulton County, and pumped 11 miles underground until converted into liquid fertilizer.

**The Keowee-Toxaway Project, 1975** – of the Duke Power Co., in the western part of North and South Carolina, a 700-million-dollar power generating complex that includes two hydroelectric projects and a major nuclear generating station, generating over 3.4 million kw of electricity.

**Lower Snake River Project, 1976** – a 140-mile development in southeastern Washington, is designed to facilitate navigation and generate power through the construction of four dams and the Lewiston levee and parkway system.

**Superior, Wis., Midwest Energy Terminal, 1977**–The nation's largest western coal transshipment terminal, this complex was designed to receive, store, and load coal from rail cars onto Great Lakes carriers for Detroit's fuel needs.

**Trans-Alaska Pipeline, 1978** — An 800-mile system of highway, 48-inch steel pipeline from Prudhoe Bay to Valdez, eight pump stations along the route, and storage and tanker facilities at Valdez harbor.

**Nation's Capital Metro Transit System, 1979**–Some 30 miles of subway connecting suburban Maryland and Virginia with various sections of Washington, D.C.

**Shell Oil's Cognac offshore drilling platform, 1980**—Located off the coast of Louisiana, this is the tallest oil rig–1,265 ft. tall–and is capable of a daily peak oil production of 50,000 barrels and 150 mil. cu. ft. of gas.

**Industry Hills Civic-Recreation-Conservation Area, 1981**–(City of Industry, Calif.)–A badly scarred 600-acre hill formation was transformed into an impressive multi-purpose area to meet vital needs of the community.

**Louisiana Offshore Oil Port (LOOP), 1982**–America's first oil superport, 18 miles off the coast of Louisiana, built in water depths of 105–115 feet, capable of handling supertankers and 1.4 million barrels of oil daily.

## PERIODIC TABLE OF ELEMENTS

The periodic table, first devised by the Russian chemist Dmitri I. Mendeleev (1834–1907) in 1869, is shown here in its present form. It is an orderly classification of the elements based on physical and chemical similarities. The atomic number of each element denotes the number of protons (positive charge) in the nucleus of its atoms as well as the number of electrons (negative charge) in its orbital shells when the atoms are neutral. In general, the higher the atomic number, the heavier the element. The table is arranged so that elements in the same vertical column possess similar properties (this similarity is related to the number of outer or valence electrons). Elements in the same horizontal row have the same number of electron shells. Numbers in brackets are atomic numbers of undiscovered elements.

| | Group IA | IIA | IIIB | IVB | VB | VIB | VIIB | VIII | VIII | VIII | IB | IIB | IIIA | IVA | VA | VIA | VIIA | Inert Gases |
|---|---|---|---|---|---|---|---|---|---|---|---|---|---|---|---|---|---|---|
| 1 | H 1 | | | | | | | | | | | | | | | | | He 2 |
| 2 | Li 3 | Be 4 | | | | | | | | | | | B 5 | C 6 | N 7 | O 8 | F 9 | Ne 10 |
| 3 | Na 11 | Mg 12 | | | | | | | | | | | Al 13 | Si 14 | P 15 | S 16 | Cl 17 | Ar 18 |
| 4 | K 19 | Ca 20 | Sc 21 | Ti 22 | V 23 | Cr 24 | Mn 25 | Fe 26 | Co 27 | Ni 28 | Cu 29 | Zn 30 | Ga 31 | Ge 32 | As 33 | Se 34 | Br 35 | Kr 36 |
| 5 | Rb 37 | Sr 38 | Y 39 | Zr 40 | Nb 41 | Mo 42 | Tc 43 | Ru 44 | Rh 45 | Pd 46 | Ag 47 | Cd 48 | In 49 | Sn 50 | Sb 51 | Te 52 | I 53 | Xe 54 |
| 6 | Cs 55 | Ba 56 | La 57 | Hf 72 | Ta 73 | W 74 | Re 75 | Os 76 | Ir 77 | Pt 78 | Au 79 | Hg 80 | Tl 81 | Pb 82 | Bi 83 | Po 84 | At 85 | Rn 86 |
| 7 | Fr 87 | Ra 88 | Ac 89 | 104 | 105 | 106 | 107 | (108) | (109) | (110) | (111) | (112) | (113) | (114) | (115) | (116) | (117) | (118) |

| | | | | | | | | | | | | | | |
|---|---|---|---|---|---|---|---|---|---|---|---|---|---|---|
| LANTHANIDE SERIES | Ce 58 | Pr 59 | Nd 60 | Pm 61 | Sm 62 | Eu 63 | Gd 64 | Tb 65 | Dy 66 | Ho 67 | Er 68 | Tm 69 | Yb 70 | Lu 71 |
| ACTINIDE SERIES | Th 90 | Pa 91 | U 92 | Np 93 | Pu 94 | Am 95 | Cm 96 | Bk 97 | Cf 98 | Es 99 | Fm 100 | Md 101 | No 102 | Lr 103 |

## ELEMENTS AND THEIR DISCOVERERS

| Element and Symbol | Atomic Number | Atomic Weight | Discoverer and Date |
|---|---|---|---|
| Actinium (Ac) | 89 | (227)* | A. Debierne (1899) |
| Aluminum (Al) | 13 | 27.0 | F. Wöhler (1827) |
| Americium (Am) | 95 | (243) | G. Seaborg et al. (1944) |
| Antimony (Sb) | 51 | 121.8 | B. Valentine (1604) |
| Argon (Ar) | 18 | 39.9 | W. Ramsay and J. Rayleigh (1894) |
| Arsenic (As) | 33 | 74.9 | A. Magnus (1250) (?) |
| Astatine (At) | 85 | (210) | E. Segrè et al. (1940) |
| Barium (Ba) | 56 | 137.3 | H. Davy (1808) |
| Berkelium (Bk) | 97 | (247) | S. Thompson et al. (1949) |
| Beryllium (Be) | 4 | 9.0 | N. Vauquelin (1798) |
| Bismuth (Bi) | 83 | 209.0 | C. Geoffroy the Younger (1753) |
| Boron (B) | 5 | 10.8 | H. Davy et al. (1808) |
| Bromine (Br) | 35 | 79.9 | A. Balard (1826) |
| Cadmium (Cd) | 48 | 112.4 | F. Stromeyer (1817) |
| Calcium (Ca) | 20 | 40.1 | H. Davy (1808) |
| Californium (Cf) | 98 | (251) | S. Thompson et al. (1950) |
| Carbon (C) | 6 | 12.0 | Prehistoric |
| Cerium (Ce) | 58 | 140.1 | J. Berzelius and W. d'Hisinger (1803) |
| Cesium (Cs) | 55 | 132.9 | R. Bunsen and G. Kirchhoff (1860) |
| Chlorine (Cl) | 17 | 35.5 | K. Scheele (1774) |
| Chromium (Cr) | 24 | 52.0 | N. Vauquelin (1797) |
| Cobalt (Co) | 27 | 58.9 | G. Brandt (c.1735) |
| Copper (Cu) | 29 | 63.5 | Prehistoric |
| Curium (Cm) | 96 | (247) | G. Seaborg et al. (1944) |
| Dysprosium (Dy) | 66 | 162.5 | L. de Boisbaudran (1886) |
| Einsteinium (Es) | 99 | (254) | A. Ghiorso et al. (1952) |
| Erbium (Er) | 68 | 167.3 | C. Mosander (1843) |
| Europium (Eu) | 63 | 152.0 | E. Demarçay (1896) |
| Fermium (Fm) | 100 | (257) | A. Ghiorso et al. (1952) |
| Fluorine (F) | 9 | 19.0 | H. Moissan (1886) |
| Francium (Fr) | 87 | (223) | M. Perey (1939) |
| Gadolinium (Gd) | 64 | 157.3 | J. C. de Marignac (1880) |
| Gallium (Ga) | 31 | 69.7 | L. de Boisbaudran (1875) |
| Germanium (Ge) | 32 | 72.6 | C. Winkler (1886) |
| Gold (Au) | 79 | 197.0 | Prehistoric |
| Hafnium (Hf) | 72 | 178.5 | D. Coster and G. von Hevesy (1923) |
| Helium (He) | 2 | 4.0 | J. C. P. Janssen and N. Lockyer (1868) |
| Holmium (Ho) | 67 | 164.9 | J. Soret and M. Delafontaine (1878) |
| Hydrogen (H) | 1 | 1.0 | H. Cavendish (1766) |
| Indium (In) | 49 | 114.8 | F. Reich and T. Richter (1863) |
| Iodine (I) | 53 | 126.9 | B. Courtois (1811) |
| Iridium (Ir) | 77 | 192.2 | S. Tennant (1803) |
| Iron (Fe) | 26 | 55.8 | Prehistoric |
| Krypton (Kr) | 36 | 83.8 | W. Ramsay and M. Travers (1898) |
| Lanthanum (La) | 57 | 138.9 | C. Mosander (1839) |
| Lawrencium (Lr) | 103 | (257) | A. Ghiorso et al. (1961) |
| Lead (Pb) | 82 | 207.2 | Prehistoric |
| Lithium (Li) | 3 | 6.9 | A. Arfvedson (1817) |
| Lutetium (Lu) | 71 | 175.0 | G. Urbain (1907) |
| Magnesium (Mg) | 12 | 24.3 | Recognized by J. Black (1755) |
| Manganese (Mn) | 25 | 54.9 | Recognized by K. Scheele et al. (1774) |
| Mendelevium (Md) | 101 | (258) | A. Ghiorso et al. (1955) |
| Mercury (Hg) | 80 | 200.6 | Prehistoric |
| Molybdenum (Mo) | 42 | 95.9 | K. Scheele (1778) |
| Neodymium (Nd) | 60 | 144.2 | C. von Welsbach (1885) |
| Neon (Ne) | 10 | 20.2 | W. Ramsay and M. Travers (1898) |
| Neptunium (Np) | 93 | (237) | E. McMillan and P. Abelson (1940) |
| Nickel (Ni) | 28 | 58.7 | A. Cronstedt (1751) |
| Niobium (Columbium) (Nb) | 41 | 92.9 | C. Hatchett (1801) |
| Nitrogen (N) | 7 | 14.0 | D. Rutherford (1772) |
| Nobelium (No) | 102 | (255) | A. Ghiorso et al. (1958) |
| Osmium (Os) | 76 | 190.2 | S. Tennant (1803) |
| Oxygen (O) | 8 | 16.0 | J. Priestley (1774) |
| Palladium (Pd) | 46 | 106.4 | W. Wollaston (1803) |
| Phosphorus (P) | 15 | 31.0 | H. Brand (1669) |
| Platinum (Pt) | 78 | 195.1 | D. de Ulloa (1735) |
| Plutonium (Pu) | 94 | (244) | G. Seaborg et al. (1940) |
| Polonium (Po) | 84 | (209) | P. and M. Curie (1898) |
| Potassium (K) | 19 | 39.1 | H. Davy (1807) |
| Praseodymium (Pr) | 59 | 140.9 | C. von Welsbach (1885) |
| Promethium (Pm) | 61 | (145) | J. Marinsky et al. (1947) |
| Protactinium (Pa) | 91 | 231.0 | K. Fajans and A. H. Göhring (1913) |
| Radium (Ra) | 88 | 226.1 | P. and M. Curie (1898) |
| Radon (Rn) | 86 | (222) | E. Rutherford (thoron) (1899)<br>E. Dorn (radon) (1900) |
| Rhenium (Re) | 75 | 186.2 | W. Noddack et al. (1925) |
| Rhodium (Rh) | 45 | 102.9 | W. Wollaston (1803) |
| Rubidium (Rb) | 37 | 85.5 | R. Bunsen and G. Kirchhoff (1861) |
| Ruthenium (Ru) | 44 | 101.1 | K. Claus (or Klaus) (1844) |
| Samarium (Sm) | 62 | 150.4 | L. de Boisbaudran (1879) |
| Scandium (Sc) | 21 | 45.0 | L. Nilson (1879) |
| Selenium (Se) | 34 | 79.0 | J. Berzelius (1817) |
| Silicon (Si) | 14 | 28.1 | J. Berzelius (1824) |
| Silver (Ag) | 47 | 107.9 | Prehistoric |
| Sodium (Na) | 11 | 23.0 | H. Davy (1807) |
| Strontium (Sr) | 38 | 87.6 | H. Davy (1808) |
| Sulfur (S) | 16 | 32.1 | Prehistoric |
| Tantalum (Ta) | 73 | 180.9 | A. Ekeberg (1802) |
| Technetium (Tc) | 43 | (97) | E. Segrè and C. Perrier (1937) |
| Tellurium (Te) | 52 | 127.6 | M. von Reichenstein (1782) |
| Terbium (Tb) | 65 | 158.9 | C. Mosander (1843) |
| Thallium (Tl) | 81 | 204.4 | W. Crookes (1861) |
| Thorium (Th) | 90 | 232.0 | J. Berzelius (1828) |
| Thulium (Tm) | 69 | 168.9 | P. Cleve (1879) |
| Tin (Sn) | 50 | 118.7 | Prehistoric |
| Titanium (Ti) | 22 | 47.9 | W. Gregor (1791) |
| Tungsten (Wolfram) (W) | 74 | 183.9 | J. and F. d'Elhuyar (1783) |
| Uranium (U) | 92 | 238.0 | E. M. Peligot (1841) |
| Vanadium (V) | 23 | 51.0 | A. del Rio (1801) |
| Xenon (Xe) | 54 | 131.3 | W. Ramsay and M. Travers (1898) |
| Ytterbium (Yb) | 70 | 173.0 | C. Marignac (1878) |
| Yttrium (Y) | 39 | 88.9 | J. Gadolin (1794) |
| Zinc (Zn) | 30 | 65.4 | Prehistoric |
| Zirconium (Zr) | 40 | 91.2 | M. Klaproth (1789) |
| Unnilquadium (Unq) | 104 | (257) | A. Ghiorso et al.<br>G. Flerov et al. |
| Unnilpentium (Unp) | 105 | (262) | |
| Unnilhexium (Unh) | 106 | (262) | |
| Unnilseptium (Uns) | 107 | (261) | G. Flerov et al. (1976) |

* A number in parentheses under "Atomic Weight" is the mass number of the longest-lived isotope.

The systematic naming of new elements of atomic number number greater than 103 was first introduced in 1978. Prior to this, there had been a dispute between teams of scientists in the U.S. and the U.S.S.R., both claiming to have discovered element 104 (now known as unnilquadium). Both teams supplied different names: **rutherfordium** from the U.S. and **kurchatovium** from the U.S.S.R.

## SELECTED NATIONAL ACADEMIES OF SCIENCE

| Institution | Founded |
|---|---|
| National Academy of Sciences (Rome) | 1603 |
| The Royal Society (London) | 1660 |
| Academy of Sciences (Paris) | 1666 |
| The Royal Danish Academy of Sciences and Letters (Copenhagen) | 1742 |
| Royal Academy of Sciences, Letters, and Fine Arts of Belgium (Brussels) | 1772 |
| Royal Society of Edinburgh | 1783 |
| Royal Irish Academy (Dublin) | 1786 |
| Hungarian Academy of Sciences (Budapest) | 1825 |
| Austrian Academy of Science (Vienna) | 1847 |
| The Norwegian Academy of Science and Letters in Oslo | 1857 |
| National Academy of Sciences (Washington, D. C.) | 1863 |
| Yugoslav Academy of Sciences and Arts (Zagreb) | 1867 |
| Japan Academy (Tokyo) | 1879 |
| Royal Society of Canada (Ottawa) | 1882 |
| National Academy of Science (Mexico City) | 1884 |
| Brazilian Academy of Sciences (Rio de Janeiro) | 1916 |
| Academy of Athens | 1926 |
| Academia Sinica (Taipei) | 1928 |
| National Academy of Sciences of Buenos Aires | 1937 |
| Academy of the Socialist Republic of Rumania (Bucharest) | 1948 |
| Academy of Finland (Helsinki) | 1947 |
| Chinese Academy of Sciences (Peking) | 1949 |
| Czechoslovak Academy of Sciences (Prague) | 1952 |
| Polish Academy of Sciences (Warsaw) | 1952 |
| Australian Academy of Science (Canberra) | 1954 |
| Israel Academy of Sciences and Humanities (Jerusalem) | 1961 |
| Academy of Sciences of Cuba (Havana) | 1962 |

## LANDMARKS OF SCIENCE

| Date | Landmark | Discoverer | Nationality |
|---|---|---|---|
| 5th cent. B.C. | The atomic structure of matter postulated | Democritus | Greek |
| 5th cent. B.C. | Postulation of causality in nature: the belief that every natural event has a natural cause | Leucippus | Greek |
| c. 300 B.C. | Compilation of **Elements:** the first formal statement of geometric principles | Euclid | Greek |
| 3d cent. B.C. | Discovery of the laws of floating bodies, establishing the discipline of hydrostatics | Archimedes | Greek |
| c. 230 B.C. | First measurement of the Earth's circumference (accomplished without astronomical instruments) | Eratosthenes | Greek |
| 3d cent. B.C. | Observations and calculations leading to the conclusions that the Earth is smaller than the Sun, rotates on an inclined axis, and revolves around the Sun; also, explanation of the seasons | Aristarchus of Samos | Greek |
| 2d cent. B.C. | Measurement of size and distance of the Sun and the Moon | Hipparchus | Greek |
| 2d cent. A.D. | Synthesis of current astronomical knowledge in the **Almagest,** which provided a system of celestial mechanics | Claudius Ptolemaeus (Ptolemy) | Greek |
| 9th cent. A.D. | Establishment of the theory of numbers | Al-Khowarizmi | Arabian |
| 1530 | Publication of **De re metallica,** establishing the science of mineralogy | Georg Bauer (Agricola) | German |
| 1543 | Publication of **De revolutionibus orbium coelestium;** the solar system described as heliocentric | Mikolaj Kopernik (Copernicus) | Polish |
| 1559 | First cylindrical-projection map (commonly known as Mercator's projection), establishing mapmaking | Gerhard Kremer (Mercator) | Flemish |
| 1589–92 | Discovery of the laws of motion concerning falling bodies, the pendulum, and the inclined plane | Galileo Galilei | Italian |
| 1600 | Publication of **De magnete:** the basis for future work on magnetism and electricity | William Gilbert or Gylberde | English |
| 1609/1619 | Discovery of the three fundamental laws of planetary motion | Johannes Kepler | German |
| 1614 | Invention of logarithms as a powerful method of arithmetical calculation | John Napier | Scottish |
| 1619 | Formulation of analytic geometry | René Descartes | French |
| 1620 | Publication of **Novum Organum,** elucidating first formal theory of inductive logic | Francis Bacon | English |
| 1643 | Proof that air has weight; invention of the barometer | Evangelista Torricelli | Italian |
| 1661 | Formulation of the modern concept of the distinction between chemical elements and compounds | Robert Boyle | Anglo-Irish |
| 1662 | Discovery of law (Boyle's law) governing relation between pressure and volume of a gas | Robert Boyle | Anglo-Irish |
| c. 1670 | Discovery of the calculus: the most powerful mathematical tool | Isaac Newton [Independently (1675–76) by Gottfried Leibniz, German] | English |
| 1676 | First measurement of the velocity of light | Olaus Römer | Danish |
| 1687 | Publication of **Philosophiae naturalis principia mathematica,** establishing the laws of gravitation and universal laws of motion | Isaac Newton | English |
| 1690 | Propounding of the wave theory of light | Christiaan Huygens | Dutch |
| 1733 | Distinction between two kinds of electricity (later called positive and negative); establishment of the fundamental law of electric charges | C. F. Du Fay | French |
| 1735 | Publication of **Systema naturae:** the foundation of taxonomy | Karl von Linné (Carolus Linnaeus) | Swedish |
| c. 1789 | Discovery of true nature of combustion | Antoine Lavoisier | French |
| 1795 | Publication of **Theory of the Earth,** which paved the way to modern geological science | James Hutton | Scottish |
| 1799 | Discovery of the law of definite proportions of elements by weight in chemical compounds | Joseph Proust | French |
| 1801 | **Disquisitiones Arithmeticae** advances number theory | Karl F. Gauss | German |
| 1802 | Discovery of the dark lines in the solar spectrum | William Wollaston [Independently (1814) by Joseph von Fraunhofer, German] | English |
| 1803 | Proposal of an atomic theory of matter to explain the laws of chemical combination | John Dalton | English |
| 1815 | Establishment of stratigraphic geology for dating geological formations | William Smith | English |
| 1820 | Discovery of electromagnetism | Hans Christian Oersted | Danish |
| 1825–26 | Formulation of non-Euclidean geometry | Nikolai I. Lobachevski [Independently (1825–26) by Janos Bolyai, Hungarian] | Russian |
| 1827 | Statement of the law (Ohm's law) of electric conduction | Georg S. Ohm | German |
| 1828 | First synthesis of an organic compound from inorganic material | Friedrich Wöhler | German |
| 1831 | Discovery of electromagnetic induction | Michael Faraday [Independently (c. 1830) by Joseph Henry, American] | English |
| 1840s | Formulation of the law of the conservation of energy (also known as the first law of thermodynamics) | Julius R. von Mayer<br>James P. Joule<br>Hermann L. F. von Helmholtz | German<br>English<br>German |
| 1850 | Formulation of the concept of entropy: the second law of thermodynamics | Rudolf J. E. Clausius | German |
| 1850s | Establishment of the science of spectroscopy | Gustav R. Kirchhoff<br>Robert W. Bunsen | German<br>German |
| 1852 | Formulation of the concept of chemical valence | Edward Frankland | English |
| 1855 | Founding of the science of oceanography | Matthew F. Maury | American |

**LANDMARKS OF SCIENCE (Continued)**

| Date | Landmark | Discoverer | Nationality |
|---|---|---|---|
| 1859 | Publication of **Origin of Species,** setting forth the idea of natural selection of living things | Charles Darwin [Independently (1858) by A. R. Wallace, English] | English |
| 1861 | Establishment of organic chemistry as the chemistry of carbon compounds | Friedrich A. Kekulé | German |
| 1864 | Formulation of the mathematical theory of electromagnetic radiation | James C. Maxwell | Scottish |
| 1865 | Formulation of the fundamental laws of genetics | Gregor J. Mendel | Austrian |
| 1869 | Formulation of the periodic table of elements | Dmitri I. Mendeleev | Russian |
| 1884 | Formulation of the concepts of transfinite mathematics and the development of set theory, the basis of modern mathematical analysis | Georg Cantor | German |
| 1884 | Establishment of the concept of ionic dissociation in solution (ionization) | Svante A. Arrhenius | Swedish |
| 1887 | Propagation of electromagnetic waves (radio waves): demonstration that these waves travel at the velocity of light | Heinrich R. Hertz | German |
| 1895 | Discovery of X-rays | Wilhelm K. Roentgen | German |
| 1896 | Discovery of radioactivity in uranium | Antoine H. Becquerel | French |
| 1897 | Discovery of the electron | Joseph J. Thomson | English |
| 1900 | Postulation of quantum theory | Max Planck | German |
| 1901 | Enunciation of the idea of evolution by mutation | Hugo Marie De Vries | Dutch |
| | Established nature of radioactive disintegration | Ernest Rutherford | English, b. New Zealand |
| 1905–15 | Postulation of the special and general theories of relativity | Albert Einstein | American, b. Germany |
| 1905–16 | Completion of first cloud chamber for observing nuclear particles | Charles T. R. Wilson | Scottish |
| 1911 | Discovery of superconductivity | Heike Kammerlingh-Onnes | Dutch |
| 1911 | Formulation of the concept of the planetary atom | Niels H. D. Bohr | Danish |
| 1913 | Establishment of the concept of atomic number and that it is equal to the charge on the nucleus | Henry G. J. Moseley | English |
| 1913 | Completion of **Principia Mathematica,** a major contribution to symbolic logic | Bertrand A. W. Russell<br>Alfred North Whitehead | English<br>English |
| 1916 | First relativistic theory of "black holes" formed by high-density matter | Karl Schwarzschild | German |
| 1924–26 | Formulation of wave mechanics | Louis V. de Broglie<br>Erwin Schroedinger | French<br>German |
| 1925 | Formulation of matrix mechanics | Werner Heisenberg | German |
| 1926 | Publication of **Conditioned Reflexes** | Ivan Petrovich Pavlov | Russian |
| 1931 | Postulation of existence of the neutrino | Wolfgang Pauli | German |
| 1932 | Discovery of the neutron | James Chadwick | English |
| 1932 | Discovery of the positron | Carl D. Anderson | American |
| 1934 | Neutron bombardment of uranium leading to the production of transuranium elements | Enrico Fermi | American, b. Italy |
| 1938 | First nuclear fission of uranium | Lise Meitner<br>Otto Hahn<br>Fritz Strassmann | Austrian-Swedish<br>German<br>German |
| 1942 | Controlled nuclear fission of uranium | Enrico Fermi and others | American, b. Italy |
| 1945 | Explosion of first atomic bomb | J. Robert Oppenheimer and others | American |
| 1947 | Development of carbon-14 dating | Willard F. Libby | American |
| 1948 | Construction of the transistor | John Bardeen, Walter H. Brattain, & William Shockley | American |
| 1951 | First power-producing, nuclear-fission reactor | Atomic Energy Commission | American |
| 1951 | Explosion of first nuclear-fusion (hydrogen) bomb | Atomic Energy Commission | American |
| 1953 | Deciphering the double-helix structure of deoxyribonucleic acid (DNA) in the chromosome | Francis Crick, Maurice Wilkins, &<br>James Watson | English<br>American |
| 1954 | Construction of first maser | Charles H. Townes | American |
| 1955 | Production and detection of the antiproton | Emilio G. Segré<br>Owen Chamberlain | American, b. Italy<br>American |
| 1958 | Discovery of belts of high-energy radiation surrounding the Earth | James A. Van Allen | American |
| 1960 | First demonstration of laser action | Theodore H. Maiman | American |
| 1961 | Classification of elementary particles using group theory; leading to quark hypothesis | Murray Gell-Mann<br>Yuval Ne'eman | American<br>Israeli |
| 1962 | Prediction of Josephson effect | Brian David Josephson | British |
| 1967 | Deciphering the structure of ribonuclease (RNA) | David Harker and others | American |
| 1968 | Synthesizing of ribonuclease molecule | R. Bruce Merrifield and others<br>Ralph F. Hirschman and others | American<br>American |
| 1969 | First men on the moon | Neil Armstrong<br>Edwin Aldrin | American<br>American |
| 1971 | Discovery of reverse transcriptase for synthesizing DNA from RNA | H. Temin | American |
| 1973 | Theory unifying electromagnetic and weak forces | Sheldon Lee Glashow<br>Steven Weinberg<br>Abdus Salam | American<br>American<br>Pakistani |
| 1974 | Detection of psi particle | Sam Ting and others<br>Burt Richter and others | American<br>American |
| 1976 | Completion of gene synthesis | Har Gobind Khorana | American, b. India |
| 1978 | Discovery that some animal genes are interrupted in structure with genetic material of unknown function | P. Chambon and others | French |
| 1981 | Successful launch of reusable space shuttle | NASA | American |

## THE BASIS OF MEASUREMENT

The International System of Units (Système International, SI) is the modernized version of the metric system, established by international agreement to provide a logical and interconnected framework for all measurements in science, industry, and commerce. The seven base units here given are the foundation for the entire system, and all other units are derived from them. (Use of metric weights and measures was legalized in the United States in 1866, and our customary units of weights and measures are defined in terms of the meter and kilogram.)

**Length**—*Meter.* The meter is defined as 1,650,763.73 wavelengths in vacuum of the orange-red line of the spectrum of krypton-86.

**Time**—*Second.* The second is defined as the duration of 9,192,631,770 cycles of the radiation associated with a specified transition of the cesium atom.

**Mass**—*Kilogram.* The standard for the kilogram is a cylinder of platinum-iridium alloy kept by the International Bureau of Weights and Measures at Paris. A duplicate at the National Bureau of Standards serves as the mass standard for the United States. The kilogram is the only base unit still defined by an artifact.

**Temperature**—*Kelvin.* The Kelvin scale has its base at absolute zero and has a fixed point at the triple point of water defined as 273.16 kelvins. This triple point, at which water forms an interface of solid, liquid, and vapor, is defined as 0. 01° C on the Celsius or centigrade scale, and 32.02° F on the Fahrenheit scale.

**Electric Current**—*Ampere.* The ampere is defined as the magnitude of the current that, when flowing through each of two long parallel wires separated by one meter in free space, results in a force between the two wires (due to their magnetic fields) of $2 \times 10^{-7}$ newton for each meter of length. (A newton is the unit of force of such size that a body of one kilogram mass would experience an acceleration of one meter per second per second.)

**Luminous Intensity**—*Candela.* The candela is defined as the luminous intensity of 1/600,000 of a square meter of a radiating cavity at the temperature of solidifying platinum (2,042 K).

**Amount of Substance**—*Mole.* The mole is defined as the amount of a substance containing as many elementary units (specified as atoms, molecules, ions, electrons, photons, and so forth) as there are carbon atoms in 0.012 kilogram of carbon-12.

## TABLES OF METRIC WEIGHTS AND MEASURES

### LINEAR MEASURE

| | |
|---|---|
| 10 millimeters (mm) | = 1 centimeter (cm) |
| 10 centimeters | = 1 decimeter (dm) = 100 millimeters |
| 10 decimeters | = 1 meter (m.) = 1,000 millimeters |
| 10 meters | = 1 dekameter (dam) |
| 10 dekameters | = 1 hectometer (hm) = 100 meters |
| 10 hectometers | = 1 kilometer (km) = 1,000 meters |

### AREA MEASURE

| | |
|---|---|
| 100 square millimeters | = 1 square centimeter |
| 10,000 square centimeters | = 1 square meter = 1,000,000 square millimeters |
| 100 square meters | = 1 are (a) |
| 100 ares | = 1 hectare (ha) = 10,000 |
| 100 hectares | = 1 square kilometer = 1,000,000 square meters |

### VOLUME MEASURE

| | |
|---|---|
| one liter | = 0.001 cubic meter |
| 10 milliliters (ml) | = 1 centiliter (cl) |
| 10 centiliters | = 1 deciliter (dl) = 100 milliliters |
| 10 deciliters | = 1 liter (l) = 1,000 milliliters |

### VOLUME MEASURE (Cont.)

| | |
|---|---|
| 10 liters | = 1 dekaliter (dal) |
| 10 dekaliters | = 1 hectoliter (hl) = 100 liters |
| 10 hectoliters | = 1 kiloliter (kl) = 1,000 liters |

### WEIGHT

| | |
|---|---|
| 10 milligrams (mg) | = 1 centigram (cg) |
| 10 centigrams | = 1 decigram (dg) = 100 milligrams |
| 10 decigrams | = 1 gram (g) = 1,000 milligrams |
| 10 grams | = 1 dekagram (dag) |
| 10 dekagrams | = 1 hectogram (hg) = 100 grams |
| 10 hectograms | = 1 kilogram (kg) = 1,000 grams |
| 1,000 kilograms | = 1 metric ton (t) |

### CUBIC MEASURE

| | |
|---|---|
| 1,000 cubic millimeters | = 1 cubic centimeter |
| 1,000 cubic centimeters | = 1 cubic decimeter = 1,000,000 cubic millimeters |
| 1,000 cubic decimeters | = 1 cubic meter = 1 stere = 1,000,000 cubic centimeters = 1,000,000,000 cubic millimeters |

## TABLES OF EQUIVALENTS

The name of a unit enclosed in brackets [1 chain] indicates (1) that the unit is not in current use in the United States, or (2) that the unit is believed to be based on "custom and usage" rather than on formal definition. Equivalents involving decimals are, in most instances, rounded off to the third decimal place except where exact equivalents are so designated.

| | |
|---|---|
| 1 angstrom[1] | 0.1 millimicron (exactly).<br>0.000 1 micron (exactly).<br>0.000 000 1 millimeter (exactly).<br>0.000 000 004 inch. |
| 1 cable's length | 120 fathoms.<br>720 feet.<br>219.456 meters (exactly). |
| 1 centimeter | 0.393 7 inch. |
| 1 chain (Gunter's or surveyor's) | 66 feet.<br>20.1168 meters (exactly). |
| [1 chain] (engineer's) | 100 feet.<br>30.48 meters (exactly). |
| 1 decimeter | 3.937 inches. |
| 1 dekameter | 32.808 feet. |
| 1 fathom | 6 feet.<br>1.8288 meters (exactly). |
| 1 foot | 0.3048 meter (exactly). |
| 1 furlong | 10 chains (surveyor's).<br>660 feet.<br>220 yards.<br>⅛ statute mile.<br>201.168 meters (exactly). |
| [1 hand] | 4 inches. |
| 1 inch | 2.54 centimeters (exactly). |
| 1 kilometer | 0.621 mile. |
| 1 league (land) | 3 statute miles.<br>4.828 kilometers. |
| 1 link (Gunter's or surveyor's) | 7.92 inches (exactly).<br>0.201 168 meter (exactly). |
| [1 link (engineer's)] | 1 foot.<br>0.3048 meter (exactly). |
| 1 meter | 39.37 inches.<br>1.094 yards. |
| 1 micron (μ [the Greek letter mu]) | 0.001 millimeter (exactly).<br>0.000 039 37 inch. |
| 1 mil | 0.001 inch (exactly).<br>0.025 4 millimeter (exactly). |
| 1 mile (statute or land) | 5,280 feet.<br>1.609 kilometers. |
| 1 mile (nautical, international) | 1.852 kilometers (exactly).<br>1.151 statute miles.<br>0.999 U.S. nautical miles. |
| 1 millimeter | 0.039 37 inch. |
| 1 millimicron (mμ [the English letter m in combination with the Greek letter mu]) | 0.001 micron (exactly).<br>0.000 000 039 37 inch. |
| 1 point (typography) | 0.013 837 inch (exactly).<br>1/72 inch (approximately).<br>0.351 millimeter. |
| 1 rod, pole, or perch | 16½ feet.<br>5½ yards.<br>5.0292 meters (exactly). |
| 1 yard | 0.9144 meter (exactly). |

### AREAS OR SURFACES

| | |
|---|---|
| 1 acre | 43,560 square feet.<br>4,840 square yards.<br>0.405 hectare. |
| 1 are | 119.599 square yards.<br>0.025 acre. |
| 1 hectare | 2.471 acres. |
| [1 square (building)] | 100 square feet. |
| 1 square centimeter | 0.155 square inch. |
| 1 square decimeter | 15.500 square inches. |
| 1 square foot | 929.030 square centimeters. |
| 1 square inch | 6.4516 square centimeters (exactly). |
| 1 square kilometer | 0.386 square mile.<br>247.105 acres. |
| 1 square meter | 1.196 square yards.<br>10.764 square feet. |
| 1 square mile | 258.999 hectares. |
| 1 square millimeter | 0.002 square inch. |
| 1 square rod, sq. pole, or sq. perch | 25.293 square meters. |
| 1 square yard | 0.836 square meter. |

## CAPACITIES OR VOLUMES

| | |
|---|---|
| 1 barrel, liquid | 31 to 42 gallons.[2] |
| 1 barrel, standard for fruits, vegetables, and other dry commodities except cranberries | 7,056 cubic inches.<br>105 dry quarts.<br>3.281 bushels. |
| 1 barrel, standard, cranberry | 5,286 cubic inches.<br>86 45/64 dry quarts.<br>2.709 bushels, struck measure. |
| 1 bushel (U.S.), struck measure | 2,150.42 cubic inches.<br>35.239 liters. |
| [1 bushel, heaped (U.S.)] | 2,747.715 cubic inches.<br>1.278 bushels, struck measure.[3] |
| [1 bushel (British Imperial) (struck measure)] | 1.032 U.S. bushels.<br>2,219.36 cubic inches. |
| 1 cord (firewood) | 128 cubic feet. |
| 1 cubic centimeter | 0.061 cubic inch. |
| 1 cubic decimeter | 61.024 cubic inches. |
| 1 cubic foot | 7.481 gallons.<br>28.316 cubic decimeters. |
| 1 cubic inch | 0.554 fluid ounce.<br>4.433 fluid drams.<br>16.387 cubic centimeters. |
| 1 cubic meter | 1.308 cubic yards. |
| 1 cubic yard | 0.765 cubic meter. |
| 1 cup, measuring | 8 fluid ounces.<br>½ liquid pint. |
| 1 dram, fluid or liquid (U.S.) | ⅛ fluid ounce.<br>0.226 cubic inch.<br>3.697 milliliters.<br>1.041 British fluid drachms. |
| 1 dekaliter | 2.642 gallons.<br>1.135 pecks. |
| 1 gallon (U.S.) | 231 cubic inches.<br>3.785 liters.<br>0.833 British gallon.<br>128 U.S. fluid ounces. |
| [1 gallon (British Imperial)] | 277.42 cubic inches.<br>1.201 U.S. gallons.<br>4.546 liters.<br>160 British fluid ounces. |
| 1 gill | 7.219 cubic inches.<br>4 fluid ounces.<br>0.118 liter. |
| 1 hectoliter | 26.418 gallons.<br>2.838 bushels. |
| 1 liter | 1.057 liquid quarts.<br>0.908 dry quart.<br>61.024 cubic inches. |
| 1 milliliter | 0.271 fluid dram.<br>16.231 minims.<br>0.061 cubic inch. |
| 1 ounce, fluid or liquid (U.S.) | 1.805 cubic inches.<br>29.574 milliliters.<br>1.041 British fluid ounces. |
| [1 ounce, fluid (British)] | 0.961 U.S. fluid ounce.<br>1.734 cubic inches.<br>28.412 milliliters. |
| 1 peck | 8.810 liters. |
| 1 pint, dry | 33.600 cubic inches.<br>0.551 liter. |
| 1 pint, liquid | 28.875 cubic inches (exactly).<br>0.473 liter. |
| 1 quart, dry (U.S.) | 67.201 cubic inches.<br>1.101 liters.<br>0.969 British quart. |
| 1 quart, liquid (U.S.) | 57.75 cubic inches (exactly).<br>0.946 liter.<br>0.833 British quart. |
| [1 quart (British)] | 69.354 cubic inches.<br>1.032 U.S. dry quarts.<br>1.201 U.S. liquid quarts. |
| 1 tablespoon | 3 teaspoons.<br>4 fluid drams.<br>½ fluid ounce. |
| 1 teaspoon | ⅓ tablespoon.<br>1⅓ fluid drams. |

## WEIGHTS OR MASSES

| | |
|---|---|
| 1 assay ton[4] | 29.167 grams. |
| 1 carat | 200 milligrams.<br>3.086 grains. |
| 1 dram, apothecaries | 60 grains.<br>3.888 grams. |
| 1 dram, avoirdupois | 27 11/32 (= 27.344) grains.<br>1.772 grams. |
| 1 grain | 64.798 91 milligrams (exactly). |
| 1 gram | 15.432 grains.<br>0.035 ounce, avoirdupois. |
| 1 hundredweight, gross or long[5] | 112 pounds.<br>50.802 kilograms. |
| 1 hundredweight, net or short | 100 pounds.<br>45.359 kilograms. |
| 1 kilogram | 2.205 pounds. |
| 1 microgram (μg [the Greek letter mu in combination with the letter g]) | 0.000 001 gram (exactly). |
| 1 milligram | 0.015 grain. |
| 1 ounce, avoirdupois | 437.5 grains (exactly).<br>0.911 troy or apothecaries ounce.<br>28.350 grams. |
| 1 ounce, troy or apothecaries | 480 grains.<br>1.097 avoirdupois ounces.<br>31.103 grams. |
| 1 pennyweight | 1.555 grams. |
| 1 point | 0.01 carat.<br>2 milligrams. |
| 1 pound, avoirdupois | 7 000 grains.<br>1.215 troy or apothecaries pounds.<br>453.592 37 grams (exactly). |
| 1 pound, troy or apothecaries | 5 760 grains.<br>0.823 avoirdupois pound.<br>373.242 grams. |
| 1 ton, gross or long[5] | 2,240 pounds.<br>1.12 net tons (exactly).<br>1.016 metric tons. |
| 1 ton, metric | 2,204.623 pounds.<br>0.984 gross ton.<br>1.102 net tons. |
| 1 ton, net or short | 2,000 pounds.<br>0.893 gross ton.<br>0.907 metric ton. |

[1] The angstrom is basically defined as $10^{-10}$ meter. [2] There are a variety of "barrels," established by law or usage. For example, federal taxes on fermented liquors are based on a barrel of 31 gallons; many state laws fix the "barrel for liquids" at 31½ gallons; one state fixes a 36-gallon barrel for cistern measurement; federal law recognizes a 40-gallon barrel for "proof spirits"; by custom, 42 gallons comprise a barrel of crude oil or petroleum products for statistical purposes, and this equivalent is recognized "for liquids" by four states. [3] Frequently recognized as 1¼ bushels, struck measure. [4] The assay ton bears the same relation to the milligram that a ton of 2,000 pounds avoirdupois bears to the ounce troy; hence the weight in milligrams of precious metal obtained from one assay ton of ore gives directly the number of troy ounces to the net ton. [5] The gross or long ton and hundredweight are used commercially in the United States to only a limited extent, usually in restricted industrial fields. These units are the same as the British "ton" and "hundredweight."

## ROMAN NUMERALS

These are letter symbols used to represent numbers. The seven basic letters and their number equivalents are: I=1, V=5, X=10, L=50, C=100, D=500, M=1,000. All other numbers (there is no zero) are formed using combinations of these letters (reading left to right, highest to lowest) which, when added together, produce the desired total: MCLX=1,160; LXXI=71; XVIII=18, etc.

In most cases a subtraction principle is used to show numbers containing 4's and 9's. Thus, instead of using four consecutive similar letters (IIII, XXXX or CCCC), only one letter is shown, followed by a larger value letter from which the smaller is to be subtracted. Examples of these cases are: IV=4, IX=9, XL=40, XC=90, CD=400, CM=900. 494 is written CDXCIV, 1979 becomes MCMLXXIX.

The addition of a bar line over the Roman numeral increases its value 1,000 times. $\overline{\text{V}}$ represents 5,000, $\overline{\text{XIX}}$ is 19,000, $\overline{\text{LVI}}$ is 56,000. A large number such as 145,262 converts to $\overline{\text{CXLV}}$CCLXII.

## BINARY NUMBERS

This number system utilizes only two symbols, 1 and 0. The location of these symbols in the binary number indicates the presence (1) or absence (0) of a certain number of units which, when added together, produce a total numerical value. The number of units to be added is determined by the length of the binary number and the location(s) of the 1 symbol. The extreme right-hand place stands for one unit; each successive place to the left represents double (2 times) the quantity of the place to its right.

| Number of Units | 32 | 16 | 8 | 4 | 2 | 1 | Add | Total Value |
|---|---|---|---|---|---|---|---|---|
| BINARY 1= | | | | | | 1 | 1 | 1 |
| NUMBERS 10= | | | | | 1 | 0 | 2+0 | 2 |
| 101= | | | | 1 | 0 | 1 | 4+0+1 | 5 |
| 1010= | | | 1 | 0 | 1 | 0 | 8+0+2+0 | 10 |
| 11001= | | 1 | 1 | 0 | 0 | 1 | 16+8+0+0+1 | 25 |
| 101110= | 1 | 0 | 1 | 1 | 1 | 0 | 32+0+8+4+2+0 | 46 |

## UNIT CONVERSIONS

| To Convert | Into | Multiply By |
|---|---|---|
| Acre | hectare | 0.4047 |
| Acres | square feet | 43,560.0 |
| Acres | square miles | $1.562 \times 10^{-3}$ |
| Ampere-hours | coulombs | 3,600.0 |
| Angstrom unit | inch | $3.937 \times 10^{-9}$ |
| Angstrom unit | micron | $1 \times 10^{-4}$ |
| Astronomical unit | kilometers | $1.495 \times 10^{8}$ |
| Atmospheres | cms of mercury | 76.0 |
| Bolt (U.S. cloth) | meters | 36.576 |
| BTU | horsepower-hrs | $3.931 \times 10^{-4}$ |
| BTU | kilowatt-hrs | $2.928 \times 10^{-4}$ |
| BTU/hr | watts | 0.2931 |
| Bushels | cubic inches | 2,150.4 |
| Calories, gram (mean) | BTU (mean) | $3.9685 \times 10^{-3}$ |
| Centares | square meters | 1.0 |
| Centimeters | kilometers | $1 \times 10^{-5}$ |
| Centimeters | meters | $1 \times 10^{-2}$ |
| Centimeters | millimeters | 10.0 |
| Centimeters | feet | $3.281 \times 10^{-2}$ |
| Centimeters | inches | 0.3937 |
| Chain | inches | 792.0 |
| Circumference | radians | 6.283 |
| Coulombs | faradays | $1.036 \times 10^{-5}$ |
| Cubic centimeters | cubic inches | 0.06102 |
| Cubic centimeters | pints (U.S. liq.) | $2.113 \times 10^{-3}$ |
| Cubic feet | cubic meters | 0.02832 |
| Cubic feet/min | pounds water/min. | 62.43 |
| Cubic feet/sec | gallons/min. | 448.831 |
| Cubits | inches | 18.0 |
| Days | seconds | 86,400.0 |
| Degrees (angle) | radians | $1.745 \times 10^{-2}$ |
| Degrees/sec. | revolutions/min. | 0.1667 |
| Dynes | grams | $1.020 \times 10^{-3}$ |
| Dynes | joules/meter (newtons) | $1 \times 10^{-5}$ |
| Ell | inches | 45.0 |
| Em, pica | inch | 0.167 |
| Ergs | BTU | $9.480 \times 10^{-11}$ |
| Ergs | foot-pounds | $7.3670 \times 10^{-8}$ |
| Ergs | kilowatt-hours | $2.778 \times 10^{-14}$ |
| Faradays/sec. | amperes (absolute) | 96,500 |
| Fathoms | feet | 6.0 |
| Feet | centimeters | 30.48 |
| Feet | meters | 0.3048 |
| Feet | miles (nautical) | $1.645 \times 10^{-4}$ |
| Feet | miles (statute) | $1.894 \times 10^{-4}$ |
| Feet/min. | centimeters/sec. | 0.5080 |
| Feet/sec. | knots | 0.5921 |
| Feet/sec. | miles/hour | 0.6818 |
| Foot-pounds | BTU | $1.286 \times 10^{-3}$ |
| Foot-pounds | kilowatt-hours | $3.766 \times 10^{-7}$ |
| Furlongs | miles (U.S.) | 0.125 |
| Furlongs | feet | 660.0 |
| Gallons | liters | 3.785 |
| Gallons of water | pounds of water | 8.3453 |
| Gallons/min. | cubic feet/hour | 8.0208 |
| Grams | ounces (avoirdupois) | $3.527 \times 10^{-2}$ |
| Grams | ounces (troy) | $3.215 \times 10^{-2}$ |
| Grams | pounds | $2.205 \times 10^{-3}$ |
| Hand | centimeters | 10.16 |
| Hectares | acres | 2.471 |
| Hectares | square feet | $1.076 \times 10^{5}$ |
| Horsepower | BTU/min. | 42.44 |
| Horsepower | kilowatts | 0.7457 |
| Horsepower | watts | 745.7 |
| Hours | days | $4.167 \times 10^{-2}$ |
| Hours | weeks | $5.952 \times 10^{-3}$ |
| Inches | centimeters | 2.540 |
| Inches | miles | $1.578 \times 10^{-5}$ |
| International ampere | ampere (absolute) | 0.9998 |
| International volt | volts (absolute) | 1.0003 |
| Joules | BTU | $9.480 \times 10^{-4}$ |
| Joules | ergs | $1 \times 10^{7}$ |
| Kilograms | pounds | 2.205 |
| Kilometers | feet | 3,281.0 |
| Kilometers | meters | 1,000.0 |
| Kilometers | miles | 0.6214 |
| Kilometers/hr. | knots | 0.5396 |
| Kilowatts | horsepower | 1.341 |
| Kilowatt-hours | BTU | 3,413.0 |
| Knots | feet/hour | 6,080.0 |
| Knots | nautical miles/hr. | 1.0 |
| Knots | statute miles/hr. | 1.151 |
| League | miles (approximately) | 3.0 |
| Light year | miles | $5.9 \times 10^{12}$ |
| Links (surveyor's) | inches | 7.92 |
| Liters | cubic centimeters | 1,000.0 |
| Liters | cubic inches | 61.02 |
| Liters | gallons (U.S. liq.) | 0.2642 |
| Liters | milliliters | 1,000.0 |
| Liters | pints (U.S. liq.) | 2.113 |
| Meters | centimeters | 100.0 |
| Meters | feet | 3.281 |
| Meters | kilometers | $1 \times 10^{-3}$ |
| Meters | miles (nautical) | $5.396 \times 10^{-4}$ |
| Meters | miles (statute) | $6.214 \times 10^{-4}$ |
| Meters | millimeters | 1,000.0 |
| Microns | meters | $1 \times 10^{-6}$ |
| Miles (nautical) | feet | 6,080.27 |
| Miles (statute) | feet | 5,280.0 |
| Miles (nautical) | kilometers | 1.853 |
| Miles (statute) | kilometers | 1.609 |
| Miles (nautical) | miles (statute) | 1.1516 |
| Miles (statute) | miles (nautical) | 0.8684 |
| Miles/hour | feet/min. | 88.0 |
| Milligrams/liter | parts/million | 1.0 |
| Milliliters | liters | $1 \times 10^{-3}$ |
| Millimeters | inches | $3.937 \times 10^{-2}$ |
| Newtons | dynes | $1 \times 10^{5}$ |
| Ohms (international) | ohms (absolute) | 1.0005 |
| Ounces | grams | 28.349527 |
| Ounces | pounds | $6.25 \times 10^{-2}$ |
| Ounces (troy) | ounces (avoirdupois) | 1.09714 |
| Parsec | miles | $19 \times 10^{12}$ |
| Parsec | kilometers | $3.084 \times 10^{13}$ |
| Pints (liq.) | cubic centimeters | 473.2 |
| Pints (liq.) | cubic inches | 28.87 |
| Pints (liq.) | gallons | 0.125 |
| Pints (liq.) | quarts (liq.) | 0.5 |
| Pounds | kilograms | 0.4536 |
| Pounds | ounces | 16.0 |
| Pounds | ounces (troy) | 14.5833 |
| Pounds | pounds (troy) | 1.21528 |
| Pounds/sq. inch | grams/sq. cm. | 70.31 |
| Quarts (dry) | cubic inches | 67.20 |
| Quarts (liq.) | cubic inches | 57.75 |
| Quarts (liq.) | gallons | 0.25 |
| Quarts (liq.) | liters | 0.9463 |
| Quires | sheets | 25.0 |
| Radians | degrees | 57.30 |
| Radians | minutes | 3,438.0 |
| Reams | sheets | 500.0 |
| Revolutions | degrees | 360.0 |
| Revolutions/min. | degrees/sec. | 6.0 |
| Rods | meters | 5.029 |
| Rods | feet | 16.5 |
| Rods (surveyor's measure) | yards | 5.5 |
| Seconds | minutes | $1.667 \times 10^{-2}$ |
| Slug | pounds | 32.17 |
| Tons (long) | kilograms | 1,016.0 |
| Tons (short) | kilograms | 907.1848 |
| Tons (long) | pounds | 2,240.0 |
| Tons (short) | pounds | 2,000.0 |
| Tons (long) | tons (short) | 1.120 |
| Tons (short) | tons (long) | 0.89287 |
| Volt (absolute) | statvolts | $3.336 \times 10^{-3}$ |
| Watts | BTU/hour | 3.4129 |
| Watts | horsepower | $1.341 \times 10^{-3}$ |
| Watts (international) | watts (absolute) | 1.0002 |
| Yards | meters | 0.9144 |
| Yards | miles (nautical) | $4.934 \times 10^{-4}$ |
| Yards | miles (statute) | $5.682 \times 10^{-4}$ |

## MULTIPLES AND SUBMULTIPLES

| Prefix | Symbol | Equivalent | Factor |
|---|---|---|---|
| atto- | a | quintillionth part | $\times 10^{-18}$ |
| femto- | f | quadrillionth part | $\times 10^{-15}$ |
| pico- | p | trillionth part | $\times 10^{-12}$ |
| nano- | n | billionth part | $\times 10^{-9}$ |
| micro- | $\mu$ | millionth part | $\times 10^{-6}$ |
| milli- | m | thousandth part | $\times 10^{-3}$ |
| centi- | c | hundredth part | $\times 10^{-2}$ |
| deci- | d | tenth part | $\times 10^{-1}$ |
| deca- | da | tenfold | $\times 10$ |
| hecto- | h | hundredfold | $\times 10^{2}$ |
| kilo- | k | thousandfold | $\times 10^{3}$ |
| mega- | M | millionfold | $\times 10^{6}$ |
| giga- | G | billionfold | $\times 10^{9}$ |
| tera- | T | trillionfold | $\times 10^{12}$ |

# TABLES OF UNITED STATES CUSTOMARY WEIGHTS AND MEASURES

## LINEAR MEASURE

12 inches (in.) = 1 foot (ft.)
3 feet = 1 yard (yd.)
5½ yards = 1 rod (rd.), pole, or perch (16½ ft.)
40 rods = 1 furlong (fur.) = 220 yards = 660 feet
8 furlongs = 1 statute mile (mi.) = 1,760 yards = 5,280 feet
3 land miles = 1 league
5,280 feet = 1 statute or land mile
6,076.11549 feet = 1 international nautical mile

## AREA MEASURE

Squares and cubes of units are sometimes abbreviated by using "superior" figures. For example, $ft^2$ means square foot, and $ft^3$ means cubic foot.

144 square inches = 1 square foot
9 square feet = 1 square yard = 1,296 square inches
30¼ square yards = 1 square rod = 272¼ square feet
160 square rods = 1 acre = 4,840 square yards = 43,560 square feet
640 acres = 1 square mile
1 mile square = 1 section (of land)
6 miles square = 1 township = 36 sections = 36 square miles

## CUBIC MEASURE

1,728 cubic inches = 1 cubic foot
27 cubic feet = 1 cubic yard

## LIQUID MEASURE

When necessary to distinguish the liquid pint or quart from the dry pint or quart, the word "liquid" or the abbreviation "liq." should be used in combination with the name or abbreviation of the liquid unit.

4 gills (gi.) = 1 pint (pt.) (= 28.875 cubic inches)
2 pints = 1 quart (qt.) (= 57.75 cubic inches)
4 quarts = 1 gallon (gal.) (= 231 cubic inches) = 8 pints = 32 gills

## APOTHECARIES FLUID MEASURE

60 minims (min.) = 1 fluid dram (fl. dr.) (= 0.2256 cubic inch)
8 fluid drams = 1 fluid ounce (fl. oz.) (= 1.8047 cubic inches)
16 fluid ounces = 1 pint (= 28.875 cubic inches) = 128 fluid drams
2 pints = 1 quart (= 57.75 cubic inches) = 32 fluid ounces = 256 fluid drams
4 quarts = 1 gallon (= 231 cubic inches) = 128 fluid ounces = 1,024 fluid drams

## DRY MEASURE

When necessary to distinguish the dry pint or quart from the liquid pint or quart, the word "dry" should be used in combination with the name or abbreviation of the dry unit.

2 pints = 1 quart (= 67.2006 cubic inches)
8 quarts = 1 peck (pk.) (= 537.605 cubic inches) = 16 pints
4 pecks = 1 bushel (bu.) (= 2,150.42 cubic inches) = 32 quarts

## AVOIRDUPOIS WEIGHT

When necessary to distinguish the avoirdupois dram from the apothecaries dram, or to distinguish the avoirdupois dram or ounce from the fluid dram or ounce, or to distinguish the avoirdupois ounce or pound from the troy or apothecaries ounce or pound, the word "avoirdupois" or the abbreviation "avdp." should be used in combination with the name or abbreviation of the avoirdupois unit.

(The "grain" is the same in avoirdupois, troy, and apothecaries weights.)

27 11/32 grains = 1 dram (dr.)
16 drams = 1 ounce (oz.) = 437½ grains
16 ounces = 1 pound (lb.) = 256 drams = 7,000 grains
100 pounds = 1 hundredweight (cwt.)*
20 hundredweights = 1 ton (tn.) = 2,000 pounds*

In "gross" or "long" measure, the following values are recognized:

112 pounds = 1 gross or long hundredweight*
20 gross or long hundredweights = 1 gross or long ton = 2,240 pounds*

## TROY WEIGHT

24 grains = 1 pennyweight (dwt.)
20 pennyweights = 1 ounce troy (oz. t.) = 480 grains
12 ounces troy = 1 pound troy (lb. t.) = 240 pennyweights = 5,760 grains

## APOTHECARIES WEIGHT

20 grains = 1 scruple (s. ap.)
3 scruples = 1 dram apothecaries (dr. ap.) = 60 grains
8 drams apothecaries = 1 ounce apothecaries (oz. ap.) = 24 scruples = 480 grains
12 ounces apothecaries = 1 pound apothecaries (lb. ap.) = 96 drams apothecaries = 288 scruples = 5,760 grains

## GUNTER'S OR SURVEYOR'S CHAIN MEASURE

7.92 inches = 1 link (li.)
100 links = 1 chain (ch.) = 4 rods = 66 ft.
80 chains = 1 statute mile = 320 rods = 5,280 ft.

* When the terms "hundredweight" and "ton" are used unmodified, they are commonly understood to mean the 100-pound hundredweight and the 2,000-pound ton, respectively; these units may be designated "net" or "short" when necessary to distinguish them from the corresponding units in gross or long measure.

# TEMPERATURE CONVERSIONS

The table offers temperature conversions that range from the freezing point of water (32° F., 0° C.) to its boiling point (212° F., 100° C.). For conversions below or beyond that range, apply these formulas: to convert Fahrenheit degrees into Celsius, subtract 32, multiply by 5, and divide by 9; to convert Celsius into Fahrenheit, multiply by 9, divide by 5, and add 32. A Fahrenheit degree is smaller than a Celsius degree, one Fahrenheit degree being 5/9 of a Celsius degree.

| °F | °C | °F | °C | °F | °C | °F | °C | °F | °C |
|---|---|---|---|---|---|---|---|---|---|
| 32 | 0 | 53 | 11·7 | 72 | 22·2 | 89·6 | 32 | 103 | 39·4 |
| 33·8 | 1 | 54 | 12·2 | 73 | 22·8 | 90 | 32·2 | 104 | 40 |
| 35·6 | 2 | 55 | 12·8 | 73·4 | 23 | 91 | 32·8 | 105 | 40·6 |
| 36·5 | 2·5 | 56 | 13·3 | 74 | 23·3 | 91·4 | 33 | 105·8 | 41 |
| 37·4 | 3 | 57 | 13·9 | 75 | 23·9 | 92 | 33·3 | 106 | 41·1 |
| 38 | 3·3 | 57·2 | 14 | 75·2 | 24 | 93 | 33·9 | 107 | 41·7 |
| 39 | 3·9 | 58 | 14·4 | 76 | 24·4 | 94 | 34·4 | 107·6 | 42 |
| 39·2 | 4 | 59 | 15 | 77 | 25 | 95 | 35 | 108 | 42·2 |
| 40 | 4·4 | 60 | 15·6 | 78 | 25·6 | 96 | 35·6 | 109 | 42·8 |
| 41 | 5 | 61 | 16·1 | 79 | 26·1 | 96·8 | 36 | 110 | 43·3 |
| 42 | 5·6 | 62 | 16·7 | 80 | 26·7 | 97 | 36·1 | 111 | 43·9 |
| 43 | 6·1 | 63 | 17·2 | 80·6 | 27 | 97·3 | 36·3 | 112 | 44·4 |
| 44 | 6·7 | 64 | 17·8 | 81 | 27·2 | 98 | 36·7 | 113 | 45 |
| 45 | 7·2 | 65 | 18·3 | 82 | 27·8 | 98·6 | 37 | 114 | 45·6 |
| 46 | 7·8 | 66 | 18·9 | 82·4 | 28 | 99 | 37·2 | 115 | 46·1 |
| 46·4 | 8 | 66·2 | 19 | 83 | 28·3 | 99·5 | 37·5 | 116 | 46·7 |
| 47 | 8·3 | 67 | 19·4 | 84 | 28·9 | 100 | 37·8 | 117 | 47·2 |
| 48 | 8·9 | 68 | 20 | 85 | 29·4 | 100·4 | 38 | 118 | 47·8 |
| 48·2 | 9 | 69 | 20·6 | 86 | 30 | 101 | 38·3 | 118·4 | 48 |
| 50 | 10 | 69·8 | 21 | 87 | 30·6 | 101·8 | 38.8 | 119 | 48·3 |
| 51 | 10·6 | 70 | 21·1 | 88 | 31·1 | 102 | 38·9 | 120 | 48·9 |
| 52 | 11·1 | 71 | 21·7 | 89 | 31·7 | 102·2 | 39 | 121 | 49·4 |

| °F | °C | °F | °C | °F | °C | °F | °C | °F | °C |
|---|---|---|---|---|---|---|---|---|---|
| 122 | 50 | 140 | 60 | 160 | 71·1 | 180 | 82·2 | 197 | 91·7 |
| 123 | 50·6 | 141 | 60·6 | 161 | 71·7 | 181 | 82·8 | 198 | 92·2 |
| 124 | 51·1 | 142 | 61·1 | 161·6 | 72 | 182 | 83·3 | 199 | 92·8 |
| 125 | 51·7 | 143 | 61·7 | 162 | 72·2 | 183 | 83·9 | 199·4 | 93 |
| 125·6 | 52 | 144 | 62·2 | 163 | 72·8 | 183·2 | 84 | 200 | 93·3 |
| 126 | 52·2 | 145 | 62·8 | 164 | 73·3 | 184 | 84·4 | 201 | 93·9 |
| 127 | 52·8 | 146 | 63·3 | 165 | 73·9 | 185 | 85 | 202 | 94·4 |
| 128 | 53·3 | 147 | 63·9 | 166 | 74·4 | 186 | 85·6 | 203 | 95 |
| 129 | 53·9 | 148 | 64·4 | 167 | 75 | 186·8 | 86 | 204 | 95·6 |
| 130 | 54·4 | 149 | 65 | 168 | 75·6 | 187 | 86·1 | 204·8 | 96 |
| 131 | 55 | 150 | 65·6 | 168·8 | 76 | 188 | 86·7 | 205 | 96·1 |
| 132 | 55·6 | 151 | 66·1 | 169 | 76·1 | 188·6 | 87 | 206 | 96·7 |
| 133 | 56·1 | 152 | 66·7 | 170 | 76·7 | 189 | 87·2 | 207 | 97·2 |
| 134 | 56·7 | 152·6 | 67 | 171 | 77·2 | 190 | 87·8 | 208 | 97·8 |
| 134·6 | 57 | 153 | 67·2 | 172 | 77·8 | 190·4 | 88 | 208·4 | 98 |
| 135 | 57·2 | 154 | 67·8 | 173 | 78·3 | 191 | 88·3 | 209 | 98·3 |
| 136 | 57·8 | 155 | 68·3 | 174 | 78·9 | 192 | 88·9 | 210 | 98·9 |
| 136·4 | 58 | 156 | 68·9 | 175 | 79·4 | 193 | 89·4 | 210·2 | 99 |
| 137 | 58·3 | 156·2 | 69 | 176 | 80 | 194 | 90 | 211 | 99·4 |
| 138 | 58·9 | 157 | 69·4 | 177 | 80·6 | 195 | 90·6 | 212 | 100 |
| 138·2 | 59 | 158 | 70 | 178 | 81·1 | 195·8 | 91 | | |
| 139 | 59·4 | 159 | 70·6 | 179 | 81·7 | 196 | 91·1 | | |

# SCIENCE GLOSSARY

## PHYSICS AND ATOMIC ENERGY

**Absolute temperature**—Temperature scale on which the zero point is absolute zero (−273.15° C).

**Acceleration**—Rate of change of velocity; increase or decrease in velocity per unit of time.

**Alpha particle**—Low-speed, low-penetration helium nucleus emitted during disintegration of radioactive elements.

**Anode**—The positive electrode in an electric cell or an electron tube.

**Angstrom**—A unit of length: 1/100,000,000 centimeter.

**Atom**—Smallest part of a chemical element that takes part in a chemical change.

**Atomic number**—Number of protons in an atomic nucleus.

**Atomic weight**—Ratio of the average mass per atom of an element to 1/12 of the mass of an atom of carbon 12.

**Beta particle**—High-speed, high-penetration electron emitted during radioactive disintegration.

**British thermal unit (BTU)**—The amount of heat required to raise the temperature of one pound of water through one Fahrenheit degree.

**Calorie**—The amount of heat required to raise the temperature of one gram of water through 1° C.

**Cathode**—The negative electrode in an electric cell or an electron tube.

**Celsius scale**—A temperature scale on which the range between the freezing point of water, 0°, and the boiling point, 100°, is divided into 100 equal degrees. Also called the *Centigrade* scale.

**Centrifugal force**—The apparent force experienced by a body moving in a curved path that seems to act outward from the center of the path.

**Doppler effect**—Apparent change in frequency of sound waves or light waves caused by relative motion of the source toward or away from an observer, and by motion of an observer toward or from a stationary source.

**Electron**—Negatively charged, stable elementary particle.

**Fission**—Specifically, the splitting of an atomic nucleus into two parts of approximately the same size, accompanied by the release of great amounts of energy.

**Fusion, nuclear**—Union of two light atomic nuclei to form a heavier, more complex one, accompanied by the release of great amounts of energy. Also called *thermonuclear fusion*.

**Gamma rays**—Shortwave, high-frequency electromagnetic radiation emitted during disintegration of radioactive elements.

**Gravity**—Attraction of the earth or a celestial body for other bodies at or near its surface.

**Half life**—The time required for half of a radioactive substance to decay.

**Hertz**—Unit of frequency equal to 1 cycle per second.

**Infrared**—Electromagnetic radiation with wavelengths longer than visible red.

**Ion**—Charged atom or molecule produced by loss or gain of electrons from the outer orbits.

**Ionization**—Any process resulting in the formation of ions from atoms or molecules.

**Joule**—Unit of energy equal to the work done when a force of one newton moves through one meter.

**Kinetic energy**—Energy due to motion.

**Liquid**—Fluid phase of matter in which the surface is free, the volume is definite, and the shape is determined by the container.

**Magnetic field**—Space permeated by magnetic lines of force.

**Magnetic pole**—One of the two points in a magnet or a celestial body where magnetism seems to concentrate.

**Mass Number**—Sum of the numbers of protons and neutrons in the nucleus of an atom.

**Matter**—Anything that has mass and occupies space.

**Meson**—Any of a group of elementary particles of small mass and very short life.

**Neutron**—Neutral particle found in the nuclei of atoms with a mass number greater than 1.

**Newton**—Unit of force equal to the force required to give a mass of 1 kilogram on acceleration of 1 meter per second per second.

**Nuclear reactor**—Device for starting and regulating nuclear fission for the purpose of producing heat.

**Nucleon**—Particle found in the structure of an atom's nucleus; a proton or neutron.

**Nucleus**—Central, positively charged part of an atom.

**Ohm**—Unit of electrical resistance.

**Photoelectric effect**—Emission of electrons by certain substances when struck by light or other electromagnetic radiation.

**Photon**—A quantum of radiation.

**Physical change**—An alteration that includes no change in the molecular composition of a substance.

**Physics**—The study of matter and energy and the interchange of energy among material things.

**Positron**—Positive electron.

**Proton**—Positively charged, stable particle found in the nuclei of all atoms.

**Quantum mechanics**—Modern mathematical form of the quantum theory.

**Quantum theory**—Theory that all energy is lost or gained in discrete amounts (quanta).

**Quark**—Type of particle with fractional electron charge, postulated to be components of other particles.

**Radar**—Electronic system for detecting distant objects by means of transmitted high-frequency radio waves and their reflection from the objects.

**Radiation**—Electromagnetic waves, or particles emitted from nuclei.

**Radioactivity**—Disintegration of the nuclei of the atoms of certain elements, during which electromagnetic waves and elementary particles are emitted.

**Relative density**—Ratio of density of a substance to the density of water. Formerly *specific gravity*.

**Relativity**—(1) Einstein's special theory: All motion is relative to observer, and velocity of light in space is constant regardless of motion of light source or observer. Mass may be changed into energy and vice versa according to the law $E = mc^2$ (2) Einstein's general theory: gravitation is a consequence of curved space.

**Resistance**—Opposition to passage of electric current offered by an electrical conductor.

**Spectroscope**—Optical instrument for the study of spectra.

**Spectrum**—Band of electromagnetic radiation in which the constituent parts are arranged according to their wavelengths or their frequencies.

**Transformer**—Device for changing the voltage of alternating current.

**Transistor**—Device made of semiconductor materials for the control of the flow of electric current.

**Ultrasonic**—Having a frequency above that audible to human beings: above about 20,000 hertz (cycles per second).

**Ultraviolet**—Electromagnetic radiation with wavelengths shorter than visible violet but longer than X-rays.

**Velocity**—Rate of motion in a given direction.

**Watt hour**—The energy of 1 watt acting for 1 hour.

**Wavelength**—Distance between two successive points of a wave in the same phase, such as crest to crest.

**X-rays**—Electromagnetic radiations of short wavelength and high penetration of matter.

## MATHEMATICS

**Additive inverse of a number**—A number with its sign changed to minus if originally plus, or vice versa.

**Algorism (Algorithm)**—In modern mathematics, any systematic method or procedure for computation.

**Analog computer**—A calculating device in which problems are solved by analogy rather than by digital counting.

**Analytic geometry**—The technique of dealing with geometry in terms of algebra.

**Antilogarithm**—The number corresponding to a given logarithm, e.g., 2 is the logarithm of 100, therefore, 100 is the antilogarithm of 2.

**Axiom**—In a system of mathematics or logic, a proposition or statement from which secondary propositions or statements are derived.

**Binary arithmetic**—A system of calculation in which the only numerals used are 0 and 1, and all real numbers are represented as powers of 2.

**Bit**—Condensation of *binary digit*. In computer and information theory, a single binary digit, either 0 or 1.

**Boolean algebra**—An algebra obeying special laws that make it suitable for such uses as the study of logic and planning switching circuits.

**Calculus**—Generally, any system of mathematical calculation, or any system of operations involving symbols, e.g., calculus of finite differences, calculus of probabilities, and the like. Specifically, a method of mathematical analysis (developed independently by Isaac Newton and Gottfried Leibniz) involving the rate of change of a variable function.

**Cardinal number**—Zero and the counting numbers 1, 2, 3, 4, . . . , as distinguished from the ordinal numbers.

**Cartesian coordinates**—Two or three lines intersecting at right angles and providing a reference system for locating points in two or three dimensional space; used in analytic geometry.

**Compound interest**—Interest paid periodically on the sum of a given principle and its accruing interest.

**Decimal number system**—The ordinary number system (sometimes called the Arabic system) that denotes real numbers according to the place values for multiples of 10 plus the digits 0 through 9.

**Derivative**—A measure of the rate at which one mathematical variable changes in response to changes in a related variable.

**Digital computer**—A calculating machine in which mathematical operations are performed by individually tallying every digit.

**Duodecimal system**—A system of numeration in which the base is 12. The numbers 10 and 11 of the decimal system are rendered in the duodecimal system by arbitrary symbols, two of which in use are *t* (called dek) and *e* (called el).

**Function**—In classical algebra, a variable $y$ so related to another variable $x$, that for each value given to $x$ there is a value that may be determined for $y$.

**Hardware**—The electronic equipment used in a computer system, in contrast to the software.

**Infinity**—A quantity that is greater than any assignable quantity.

**Integral**—Mathematical function used in calculus for finding the area under a curve.

**Intersection**—That portion of two or more sets common to all the sets considered.

**Iterative procedure**—A means of approximating the solution to an equation by repeating a given procedure several times to get successively closer answers, each based on the preceding approximation.

**Logarithm**—The exponent of the power to which a number is to be raised to produce a given number. Thus, using the base 10, the logarithm of 100 is 2, because the exponent of the power to which 10 must be raised in order to equal 100 is 2 ($10^2 = 100$).

**Machine language**—The characters and symbols and the rules for combining them that convey information and instruction to a computer for processing.

**Matrix**—Usually a rectangular array of numbers, including several columns and rows, that can be manipulated as though it were a single quantity.

**Modular arithmetic**—A form of arithmetic dealing with the remainders left over when all the numbers considered are divided by a single number, the modulus.

**Multiplicative inverse of a number**—The reciprocal of that number; for example, 1/5 is the reciprocal of 5.

**Non-Euclidean geometry**—Any of several geometries that substitute other postulates for Euclid's fifth postulate (in effect, through a point outside a given line, only one line may be drawn parallel to the given line).

**Open sentence**—An equation containing one or more unknown quantities.

**Ordinal number**—A number that indicates position or relation; thus, 2d, 3d, 8th.

**Postulate**—An unproved assumption accepted as basic to a mathematical system, and from which, in combination with other postulates, the propositions of the system are derived, or in terms of which the propositions are proved.

**Problem language**—The language used by a programmer to state the problem to be solved by a computer.

**Program**—A sequence of steps to be executed by a computer to solve a given problem.

**Reciprocal**—The number that results when 1 is divided by a given number. Thus, the reciprocal of 2 is ½; the reciprocal of 4 is ¼; and the reciprocal of a fraction is the fraction inverted, thus the reciprocal of ⅘ is 5/4.

**Repeating decimal**—A nonterminating decimal in which a pattern of numbers is established and is followed by a continuous repetition of the digit or pattern of digits, thus: .222222222222, .777777777777, .151515151515, .234523452345; a repeating decimal is also called a recurring decimal, periodic decimal, or circulating decimal.

**Scalar**—A quantity indicating magnitude but not direction, in contrast to a vector.

**Set**—A collection of objects, symbols, or ideas with some common property or attribute.

**Slide rule**—A computing device usually consisting of a frame and a horizontal slide, on both of which are printed scales graduated logarithmically. Also, usually, a transparent runner, or indicator, containing a hairline that is used to enable accurate reading of the results obtained by manipulation of the slide within the frame.

**Software**—Programs, procedures, and routines that support and augment a computer system.

**Symbolic logic**—Logic performed with the use of symbols subject to certain predetermined rules.

**Topology**—The study of those properties of geometric figures that remain unchanged despite radical distortions of considered figures.

**Transformation**—A rule for transforming one set of values into another; for example, $y = 2x$ transforms each x into a y twice as large.

**Truth set**—A set of solutions to an equation or group of equations.

**Union**—The total of all the members of all the sets of the union being considered.

**Vector**—A quantity having direction as well as magnitude. Thus, velocity is a vector because it is specified by its direction as well as its magnitude.

## CHEMISTRY

**Acid**—A substance that in aqueous solution turns blue litmus red, furnishes hydrogen ions, and contains hydrogen, which can be replaced by a metal.

**Alkali**—A water-soluble base that ionizes strongly to form hydroxide ions.

**Anion**—A negative ion.

**Base**—A substance that in aqueous solution turns red litmus blue, furnishes hydroxyl ions, and reacts with an acid to form a salt and water only.

**Buffer**—A solution containing either a weak acid and its salt or a weak base and its salt, thereby resisting changes in acidity or basicity.

**Carbohydrate**—A compound of carbon, hydrogen, and oxygen, usually having hydrogen and oxygen in the proportion of 2 to 1.

**Catalyst**—A substance that alters the rate at which a chemical reaction takes place, but which itself remains unchanged.

**Cation**—A positive ion.

**Chemical change**—Change in a substance involving a change in its identity due to an increase, decrease, or rearrangement of the atoms within its molecules; opposed to physical change, in which the substance keeps its identity.

**Colloid**—Dispersion in a medium of particles that are very small aggregates of molecules. Also called *colloidal suspension.*

**Combustion**—Any chemical change that produces heat and, usually, light. Most commonly, the combination of the oxygen of the air with a substance: *burning.*

**Compound**—A homogeneous substance composed of two or more chemical elements, the proportions of which by weight are fixed and invariable.

**Cracking**—A method of changing the constituents of petroleum, using pressure, heat, and catalysts, in which the hydrocarbons of high molecular weight are broken down into those of lower molecular weight.

**Crystal**—A solid in which the component molecules, atoms, or ions are oriented in a definite and repeated geometric pattern.

**Deliquescent substance**—A substance that absorbs moisture from the air and dissolves in the water so absorbed.

**Deuterium**—An isotope of hydrogen of mass number 2.

**Distillation**—Vaporization of a liquid, followed by condensation of the vapor.

**Electrolysis**—Chemical decomposition of a substance by an electric current passed through the substance in dissolved or molten state.

**Element**—A substance which cannot be decomposed by ordinary types of chemical change, or made by chemical union.

**Emulsion**—Dispersion of minute droplets of one liquid (that does not dissolve) in another.

**Ester**—Organic compounds corresponding to inorganic salts, derived by replacing hydrogen of an acid by an organic group.

**Fixation of nitrogen**—The combination of atmospheric nitrogen with other elements to form chemical compounds.

**Formula**—The combination of chemical symbols showing the composition of a chemical element or compound.

**Hard water**—Water that contains chemicals in solution that react with soap to form a precipitate and which therefore only lathers with difficulty.

**Hydrocarbon**—A compound containing only carbon and hydrogen.

**Hydrolysis**—Chemical reaction of a substance with water.

**Ion**—An atom or group of atoms possessing an electrical charge.

**Isomers**—Molecules that have the same number and kinds of atoms but different molecular configurations.

**Isotopes**—Atoms of the same atomic number which differ in the number of neutrons in the nucleus.

**Molecular weight**—Relative weight of a molecule compared to the weight of an atom of carbon taken as exactly 12.00; the sum of the atomic weights of the atoms in a molecule.

**Molecule**—The smallest unit of a substance that can exist free, and retain all the chemical properties of that substance.

**Osmosis**—Diffusion of a solvent through a semipermeable membrane into a more concentrated solution.

**Oxidation**—A process in which an atom or group of atoms loses electrons; combination with oxygen.

**pH**—A symbol for the logarithm of the reciprocal of the hydrogen ion concentration of a solution; thus, an indication of the acidity or basicity of a solution. A neutral solution has a pH of 7; an acid solution has a pH lower than seven, an alkaline, higher.

**Photosynthesis**—A chemical change that utilizes light energy; e.g., the production in plants of starch from carbon dioxide and water in sunlight.

**Polymorphism**—The ability of a substance to exist in two or more crystalline forms.

**Precipitate**—An insoluble solid deposited from a solution.

**Protein**—Complex organic compounds of very high molecular weight that compose a large part of all living matter; protein molecules invariably contain the elements of carbon, hydrogen, oxygen, and nitrogen.

**Radical**—A group of atoms that functions as a unit in chemical change.

**Reduction**—A process in which an atom or group of atoms gains electrons: loss of oxygen or combination with hydrogen.

**Salt**—A compound made up of the positive ion of a base and the negative ion of an acid.

**Solution**—A homogeneous mixture of two or more substances of dissimilar molecular structure. In a solution there is a dissolving medium—*solvent*—and a dissolved substance—*solute.*

**Standard conditions**—0° C and 1 atmosphere (760 mm, or 29.92 in. of mercury) pressure.

**Synthesis**—The formation of a compound from its elements or from simpler compounds.

**Tritium**—An isotope of hydrogen of mass number 3.

**Valence**—A number that represents the combining power of an atom or radical referred to hydrogen as a standard.

## MULTIPLICATION AND DIVISION TABLE

**A number in the top line (14) multiplied by a number in the extreme left hand column (13) produces the number where the top line and side line meet (182).**

**A number in the table (208) divided by the number at the top of the same column (13) results in the number (16) in the extreme left hand column. A number in the table (208) divided by the number at the extreme left (16) results in the number (13) at the top of the column.**

| 1 | 2 | 3 | 4 | 5 | 6 | 7 | 8 | 9 | 10 | 11 | 12 | 13 | 14 | 15 | 16 | 17 | 18 | 19 | 20 | 21 | 22 | 23 | 24 | 25 |
|---|---|---|---|---|---|---|---|---|---|---|---|---|---|---|---|---|---|---|---|---|---|---|---|---|
| 2 | 4 | 6 | 8 | 10 | 12 | 14 | 16 | 18 | 20 | 22 | 24 | 26 | 28 | 30 | 32 | 34 | 36 | 38 | 40 | 42 | 44 | 46 | 48 | 50 |
| 3 | 6 | 9 | 12 | 15 | 18 | 21 | 24 | 27 | 30 | 33 | 36 | 39 | 42 | 45 | 48 | 51 | 54 | 57 | 60 | 63 | 66 | 69 | 72 | 75 |
| 4 | 8 | 12 | 16 | 20 | 24 | 28 | 32 | 36 | 40 | 44 | 48 | 52 | 56 | 60 | 64 | 68 | 72 | 76 | 80 | 84 | 88 | 92 | 96 | 100 |
| 5 | 10 | 15 | 20 | 25 | 30 | 35 | 40 | 45 | 50 | 55 | 60 | 65 | 70 | 75 | 80 | 85 | 90 | 95 | 100 | 105 | 110 | 115 | 120 | 125 |
| 6 | 12 | 18 | 24 | 30 | 36 | 42 | 48 | 54 | 60 | 66 | 72 | 78 | 84 | 90 | 96 | 102 | 108 | 114 | 120 | 126 | 132 | 138 | 144 | 150 |
| 7 | 14 | 21 | 28 | 35 | 42 | 49 | 56 | 63 | 70 | 77 | 84 | 91 | 98 | 105 | 112 | 119 | 126 | 133 | 140 | 147 | 154 | 161 | 168 | 175 |
| 8 | 16 | 24 | 32 | 40 | 48 | 56 | 64 | 72 | 80 | 88 | 96 | 104 | 112 | 120 | 128 | 136 | 144 | 152 | 160 | 168 | 176 | 184 | 192 | 200 |
| 9 | 18 | 27 | 36 | 45 | 54 | 63 | 72 | 81 | 90 | 99 | 108 | 117 | 126 | 135 | 144 | 153 | 162 | 171 | 180 | 189 | 198 | 207 | 216 | 225 |
| 10 | 20 | 30 | 40 | 50 | 60 | 70 | 80 | 90 | 100 | 110 | 120 | 130 | 140 | 150 | 160 | 170 | 180 | 190 | 200 | 210 | 220 | 230 | 240 | 250 |
| 11 | 22 | 33 | 44 | 55 | 66 | 77 | 88 | 99 | 110 | 121 | 132 | 143 | 154 | 165 | 176 | 187 | 198 | 209 | 220 | 231 | 242 | 253 | 264 | 275 |
| 12 | 24 | 36 | 48 | 60 | 72 | 84 | 96 | 108 | 120 | 132 | 144 | 156 | 168 | 180 | 192 | 204 | 216 | 228 | 240 | 252 | 264 | 276 | 288 | 300 |
| 13 | 26 | 39 | 52 | 65 | 78 | 91 | 104 | 117 | 130 | 143 | 156 | 169 | 182 | 195 | 208 | 221 | 234 | 247 | 260 | 273 | 286 | 299 | 312 | 325 |
| 14 | 28 | 42 | 56 | 70 | 84 | 98 | 112 | 126 | 140 | 154 | 168 | 182 | 196 | 210 | 224 | 238 | 252 | 266 | 280 | 294 | 308 | 322 | 336 | 350 |
| 15 | 30 | 45 | 60 | 75 | 90 | 105 | 120 | 135 | 150 | 165 | 180 | 195 | 210 | 225 | 240 | 255 | 270 | 285 | 300 | 315 | 330 | 345 | 360 | 375 |
| 16 | 32 | 48 | 64 | 80 | 96 | 112 | 128 | 144 | 160 | 176 | 192 | 208 | 224 | 240 | 256 | 272 | 288 | 304 | 320 | 336 | 352 | 368 | 384 | 400 |
| 17 | 34 | 51 | 68 | 85 | 102 | 119 | 136 | 153 | 170 | 187 | 204 | 221 | 238 | 255 | 272 | 289 | 306 | 323 | 340 | 357 | 374 | 391 | 408 | 425 |
| 18 | 36 | 54 | 72 | 90 | 108 | 126 | 144 | 162 | 180 | 198 | 216 | 234 | 252 | 270 | 288 | 306 | 324 | 342 | 360 | 378 | 396 | 414 | 432 | 450 |
| 19 | 38 | 57 | 76 | 95 | 114 | 133 | 152 | 171 | 190 | 209 | 228 | 247 | 266 | 285 | 304 | 323 | 342 | 361 | 380 | 399 | 418 | 437 | 456 | 475 |
| 20 | 40 | 60 | 80 | 100 | 120 | 140 | 160 | 180 | 200 | 220 | 240 | 260 | 280 | 300 | 320 | 340 | 360 | 380 | 400 | 420 | 440 | 460 | 480 | 500 |
| 21 | 42 | 63 | 84 | 105 | 126 | 147 | 168 | 189 | 210 | 231 | 252 | 273 | 294 | 315 | 336 | 357 | 378 | 399 | 420 | 441 | 462 | 483 | 504 | 525 |
| 22 | 44 | 66 | 88 | 110 | 132 | 154 | 176 | 198 | 220 | 242 | 264 | 286 | 308 | 330 | 352 | 374 | 396 | 418 | 440 | 462 | 484 | 506 | 528 | 550 |
| 23 | 46 | 69 | 92 | 115 | 138 | 161 | 184 | 207 | 230 | 253 | 276 | 299 | 322 | 345 | 368 | 391 | 414 | 437 | 460 | 483 | 506 | 529 | 552 | 575 |
| 24 | 48 | 72 | 96 | 120 | 144 | 168 | 192 | 216 | 240 | 264 | 288 | 312 | 336 | 360 | 384 | 408 | 432 | 456 | 480 | 504 | 528 | 552 | 576 | 600 |
| 25 | 50 | 75 | 100 | 125 | 150 | 175 | 200 | 225 | 250 | 275 | 300 | 325 | 350 | 375 | 400 | 425 | 450 | 475 | 500 | 525 | 550 | 575 | 600 | 625 |

## FOREIGN WEIGHTS AND MEASURES

| Name of Unit | Country | U.S. Equivalent |
|---|---|---|
| **Ardeb** | Egypt | 43.55 gals. |
| **Arroba** | Costa Rica | 25.35 lbs. |
| **Bak (opium)** | Laos | 57.9 grains |
| **Barril** | Mexico | 16.72 gals. |
| **Batman** | Iran | 6.546 lbs. |
| **Beswa** | Afghanistan | 116.8 sq. yds. |
| **Bhara** | Malaysia | 400.0 lbs. |
| **Bocoy** | Cuba | 18.214 bu. |
| **Botella** | Honduras | 1.216 pts. |
| **Bu** | Japan | .011930 in. |
| **Caballería** | El Salvador | 111.11 acres |
| **Cable (nautical)** | United Kingdom | 200.0 yds. |
| **Cajuela** | Costa Rica | 3.74 gals. |
| **Cân** | South Vietnam | 1.333 lbs. |
| **Candy** | Burma | 18,000.0 lbs. |
| **Caneca** | Cuba | 4.784 gals. |
| **Cántaro (wine)** | Spain | 3.572 gals. |
| **Cape inch** | South Africa | 1.033 ins. |
| **Capicha** | Iran | 2.32 qts. |
| **Carga** | El Salvador | 200.0 lbs. |
| **Carga** | Mexico | 308.6 lbs. |
| **Case (bananas)** | Western Samoa | 72.0 lbs. |
| **Catty** | Indonesia | 1.3616 lbs. |
| **Centner** | Denmark | 110.231 lbs. |
| **Chang** | Mongolia | 3.50 yds. |
| **Cheung** | Hong Kong | 4.063 yds. |
| **Chi** | South Korea | 1.423 sq. ins. |
| **Cho** | Japan | 119.30 yds. |
| **Chum** | Malaysia | 1.475 ins. |
| **Chupak** | Malaysia | 1.0 qt. |
| **Cuadra** | Ecuador | 91.9 yds. |
| **Cuadra** | Peru | 2.47 acres |
| **Cuarta** | Costa Rica | 8.228 ins. |
| **Cuartilla** | Ecuador | 50.7 lbs. |
| **Cuartillo (oil)** | Mexico | .890 pt. |
| **Cubito** | Somalia | 22.0 ins. |
| **Cuerdo** | Puerto Rico | .971 acre |
| **Dariba** | Egypt | 43.55 bu. |
| **Dawulla** | Ethiopia | 220.46 lbs. |
| **Dékare** | Bulgaria | .247 acre |
| **Dhira** | Syria | 29.5 ins. |
| **Dira** | Saudi Arabia | 17.3 ins. |
| **Djuim** | Byelorussian SSR | 1.0 in. |
| **Dönüm** | Cyprus | 1,600.0 sq. yds. |
| **Dönüm, metric** | Israel | 1,196.0 sq. yds. |
| **Doppelzentner** | West Germany | 220.462 lbs. |
| **Dra (textiles)** | Jordan | 26.8 ins. |
| **Du** | Mongolia | 5.72 qts. |
| **El** | Surinam | 2.26 ft. |
| **Fan che** | Mainland China | 1.19599 sq. ft. |
| **Fanega** | Paraguay | 63.4 gals. |
| **Farsakh-song** | Iran | 3.88 mi. |
| **Fatar** | Muscat and Oman | Span from first finger to thumb |
| **Fen** | Mainland China | .1312 in. |
| **Frasila** | Tanzania | 36.0 lbs. |
| **Fuder** | West Germany | 220.0 gals. |
| **Fun** | Hong Kong | .14625 in. |
| **Fuss** | West Germany | 12.36 ins. |
| **Gallon** | Haiti | .8326 gal. |
| **Gang** | South Vietnam | .4306 sq. ft. |
| **Gantang** | Sabah | 1.0 gal. |
| **Gaz** | Iran | 1.14 yds. |
| **Gazi jerib** | Afghanistan | 29.0 ins. |
| **Gian sheng** | Mainland China | 27.4961 bu. |
| **Gong qing** | Mainland China | 2.471054 acres |
| **Grain, colonial** | Mauritius | .819 grain |
| **Gun** | Hong Kong | 1.333 lbs. |
| **Gurraf** | Libya | 2.03 qts. |
| **Habba (gold)** | Sudan | 1.543 grains |
| **Hand (height of horses)** | United Kingdom | 4.0 ins. |
| **Heml** | Egypt | 550.3 lbs. |
| **Hold (agriculture)** | Hungary | 1.422 acres |
| **Izenbi** | Morocco | 2,153.0 sq. yds. |
| **Jemba** | Malaysia | 144.0 sq. ft. |
| **Jin** | Mainland China | 1.1023 lbs. |
| **Jutro, katastarsko** | Yugoslavia | 1.422 acres |
| **Kala** | Morocco | 19.69 ins. |
| **Kantang** | Cambodia | 1.650 gals. |
| **Kantar** | Lebanon | 565.3 lbs. |
| **Kantar** | Egypt | 99.05 lbs. |
| **Ken** | Japan | 1.988 yds. |
| **Kettle** | Sierra Leone | 8.79 qts. |
| **Kilates (troy)** | Philippines | 3.09 grains |
| **Kin** | Japan | 1.32 lbs. |
| **Koku** | Japan | 39.68 gals. |
| **Kosh** | Nepal | 2.0 mi. |
| **Kung chang** | China (Taiwan) | 10.9361 yds. |
| **Kwien** | Thailand | 440.0 gals. |
| **Kwintal** | Poland | 220.46 lbs. |
| **Legua** | Cuba | 2.635 mi. |
| **Legua** | Uruguay | 3.2 mi. |
| **Leaguer** | South Africa | 127.0 gals. |
| **Lei (Chinese mi.)** | Hong Kong | 706–745.0 yds. |
| **Lelong** | Malaysia | 2,400.0 sq. ft. |
| **Li** | Mainland China | 546.8 yds. |
| **Li** | South Korea | 2.440 mi. |
| **Libra** | Spain | 1.014 lbs. |
| **Livre, colonial** | Seychelles | 1.079 lbs. |
| **Load (cocoa)** | Sierra Leone | 60.0 lbs. |
| **Ma (Chinese yd.)** | Hong Kong | 35.10 ins. |
| **Manzana** | Guatemala | 1.74 acres |
| **Marco** | Mexico | 1.015 oz. |
| **Marco real** | Spain | 1.591 acres |
| **Maund (Imperial)** | Aden | 82.28 lbs. |
| **Mecate** | Costa Rica | 21.942 yds. |
| **Medida** | Honduras | 2.527 qts. |
| **Meripeninkulma** | Finland | 1.15 mi. |
| **Mid (oil)** | Jordan | 15.8 qts. |
| **Mil** | Sweden | 6.214 mi. |
| **Mile (geographical)** | Indonesia | 4.60 mi. |
| **Milla legal** | Argentina | 1.0 mi. |
| **Misura** | Libya | 4.36 gals. |
| **Mu** | Mainland China | .16474 acre |
| **Mud** | Netherlands | 2.471 acres |
| **Mudu (rice)** | Nigeria | 2.5 lbs. |
| **Nim-man** | Iran | 3.272 lbs. |
| **Oke** | Saudi Arabia | 2.8 lbs. |
| **Onza** | Honduras | 1.014 oz. |
| **Ounce, Amsterdam** | Indonesia | 1.089 oz. |
| **Peninkulma (mil)** | Finland | 6.21 mi. |
| **Phăn** | South Vietnam | 2.583 sq. ft. |
| **Pié** | Argentina | 1.0 ft. |
| **Pied anglais** | Haiti | 1.0 ft. |
| **Pipa** | Dominican Republic | 15.75 bu. |
| **Pond** | Surinam | 1.102 lbs. |
| **Poud (grain)** | USSR | 36.11 lbs. |
| **Pulgada** | Philippines | 1.0 in. |
| **Quintal** | Angola | 220.5 lbs. |
| **Quintal** | El Salvador | 100.0 lbs. |
| **Raummeter** | Austria | 1.308 cu. yds. |
| **Ri** | Japan | 2.440 mi. |
| **Roupi (textiles)** | Cyprus | 3.00 ins. |
| **Rute** | West Germany | 4.12 yds. |
| **Sâa** | Libya | 26.13 gals. |
| **Saco (coffee)** | Colombia | 137.8 lbs. |
| **Saco (coffee)** | Peru | 152.1 lbs. |
| **Seer** | Nepal | 2.057 lbs. |
| **Shaku** | Japan | .635 fl. oz. |
| **Shō** | Japan | 1.587 qts. |
| **Sildarmál (herring)** | Iceland | 4.12 bu. |
| **Solar** | Ecuador | .43 acre |
| **Stone** | United Kingdom | 14.0 lbs. |
| **Stoop (beer)** | Netherlands | 1.32 gals. |
| **Sun** | Japan | 1.19303 ins. |
| **Tael** | Cambodia | 1.323 avoir. oz. |
| **Tanan** | Thailand | .880 qt. |
| **Tartous** | Syria | 1,099.0 sq. yds. |
| **Tercia** | El Salvador | 1.0 ft. |
| **Thail (opium)** | Indonesia | 1.241 avoir. oz. |
| **Thŏn** | South Vietnam | 2.870 sq. yds. |
| **To** | Japan | 3.968 gals. |
| **Tola (standard)** | Pakistan | 180.0 grains |
| **Tomme** | Denmark | 1.030 ins. |
| **Tondeland** | Denmark | 1.363 acres |
| **Tonne** | Schleswig-Holstein, W. Ger. | 1.35 acres |
| **Tonneau de mer** | Belgium | 100.0 cu. ft. |
| **Topo (usual)** | Peru | .86 acre |
| **Tuuma** | Finland | 1.0 in. |
| **Ud** | Sudan | 2.54 yds. |
| **Uyên (rice)** | South Vietnam | .880 qt. |
| **Vara** | Chile | 32.91 ins. |
| **Vara** | Paraguay | 2.84 ft. |
| **Vara** | Spain | 2.74 ft. |
| **Voet, Amsterdam** | Netherlands | .928 ft. |
| **War** | Aden | 1.0 yd. |
| **Wari** | Kenya | 1.0 yd. |
| **Wine gallon** | Barbados | .83267 gal. |
| **Wizna** | Malta | 8.750 lbs. |
| **Yang** | South Korea | 1.32 oz. |
| **Yarda** | Colombia | 35.43 ins. |
| **Yen** | South Vietnam | 13.33 lbs. |
| **Zentner** | Austria | 220.46 lbs. |
| **Zoll** | West Germany | 1.03 ins. |

## SQUARES, CUBES, SQUARE ROOTS, AND CUBE ROOTS

| No. | Squares | Cubes | Square roots | Cube roots | No. | Squares | Cubes | Square roots | Cube roots |
|---|---|---|---|---|---|---|---|---|---|
| **1** | 1 | 1 | 1.0000000 | 1.0000000 | **51** | 2601 | 132651 | 7.1414284 | 3.7084298 |
| **2** | 4 | 8 | 1.4142136 | 1.2599210 | **52** | 2704 | 140608 | 7.2111026 | 3.7325111 |
| **3** | 9 | 27 | 1.7320508 | 1.4422496 | **53** | 2809 | 148877 | 7.2801099 | 3.7562858 |
| **4** | 16 | 64 | 2.0000000 | 1.5874011 | **54** | 2916 | 157464 | 7.3484692 | 3.7797631 |
| **5** | 25 | 125 | 2.2360687 | 1.7099759 | **55** | 3025 | 166375 | 7.4161985 | 3.8029525 |
| **6** | 36 | 216 | 2.4494896 | 1.8171206 | **56** | 3136 | 175616 | 7.4833148 | 3.8258624 |
| **7** | 49 | 343 | 2.6457513 | 1.9129312 | **57** | 3249 | 185193 | 7.5498344 | 3.8485011 |
| **8** | 64 | 512 | 2.8284271 | 2.0000000 | **58** | 3364 | 195112 | 7.6157731 | 3.8708766 |
| **9** | 81 | 729 | 3.0000000 | 2.0800837 | **59** | 3481 | 205379 | 7.6811457 | 3.8929965 |
| **10** | 100 | 1000 | 3.1622777 | 2.1544347 | **60** | 3600 | 216000 | 7.7459667 | 3.9148676 |
| **11** | 121 | 1331 | 3.3166248 | 2.2239801 | **61** | 3721 | 226981 | 7.8102497 | 3.9364972 |
| **12** | 144 | 1728 | 3.4641016 | 2.2894286 | **62** | 3844 | 238328 | 7.8740079 | 3.9578915 |
| **13** | 169 | 2197 | 3.6055513 | 2.3513347 | **63** | 3969 | 250047 | 7.9372539 | 3.9790571 |
| **14** | 196 | 2744 | 3.7416574 | 2.4101422 | **64** | 4096 | 262144 | 8.0000000 | 4.0000000 |
| **15** | 225 | 3375 | 3.8729833 | 2.4662121 | **65** | 4225 | 274625 | 8.0622577 | 4.0207256 |
| **16** | 256 | 4096 | 4.0000000 | 2.5198421 | **66** | 4356 | 287496 | 8.1240384 | 4.0412401 |
| **17** | 289 | 4913 | 4.1231056 | 2.5712816 | **67** | 4489 | 300763 | 8.1853528 | 4.0615480 |
| **18** | 324 | 5832 | 4.2426407 | 2.6207414 | **68** | 4624 | 314432 | 8.2462113 | 4.0816551 |
| **19** | 361 | 6859 | 4.3588989 | 2.6684016 | **69** | 4761 | 328509 | 8.3066239 | 4.1015661 |
| **20** | 400 | 8000 | 4.4721360 | 2.7144177 | **70** | 4900 | 343000 | 8.3666003 | 4.1212853 |
| **21** | 441 | 9261 | 4.5825757 | 2.7589243 | **71** | 5041 | 357911 | 8.4261498 | 4.1408178 |
| **22** | 484 | 10648 | 4.6904158 | 2.8020393 | **72** | 5184 | 373248 | 8.4852814 | 4.1601676 |
| **23** | 529 | 12167 | 4.7958315 | 2.8438670 | **73** | 5329 | 389017 | 8.5440037 | 4.1793390 |
| **24** | 576 | 13824 | 4.8989795 | 2.8844991 | **74** | 5476 | 405224 | 8.6023253 | 4.1983364 |
| **25** | 625 | 15625 | 5.0000000 | 2.9240177 | **75** | 5625 | 421875 | 8.6602540 | 4.2171633 |
| **26** | 676 | 17576 | 5.0990195 | 2.9624960 | **76** | 5776 | 438976 | 8.7177979 | 4.2358236 |
| **27** | 729 | 19683 | 5.1961524 | 3.0000000 | **77** | 5929 | 456533 | 8.7749644 | 4.2543210 |
| **28** | 784 | 21952 | 5.2915026 | 3.0365889 | **78** | 6084 | 474552 | 8.8317609 | 4.2726586 |
| **29** | 841 | 24389 | 5.3851648 | 3.0723168 | **79** | 6241 | 493039 | 8.8881944 | 4.2908404 |
| **30** | 900 | 27000 | 5.4772256 | 3.1072325 | **80** | 6400 | 512000 | 8.9442719 | 4.3088695 |
| **31** | 961 | 29791 | 5.5677644 | 3.1413806 | **81** | 6561 | 531441 | 9.0000000 | 4.3267487 |
| **32** | 1024 | 32768 | 5.6568542 | 3.1748021 | **82** | 6724 | 551368 | 9.0553851 | 4.3444815 |
| **33** | 1089 | 35937 | 5.7445626 | 3.2075343 | **83** | 6889 | 571787 | 9.1104336 | 4.3620707 |
| **34** | 1156 | 39304 | 5.8309519 | 3.2396118 | **84** | 7056 | 592704 | 9.1651514 | 4.3795191 |
| **35** | 1225 | 42875 | 5.9160798 | 3.2710663 | **85** | 7225 | 614125 | 9.2195445 | 4.3968296 |
| **36** | 1296 | 46656 | 6.0000000 | 3.3019272 | **86** | 7396 | 636056 | 9.2736185 | 4.4140049 |
| **37** | 1369 | 50653 | 6.0827625 | 3.3322218 | **87** | 7569 | 658503 | 9.3273791 | 4.4310476 |
| **38** | 1444 | 54872 | 6.1644140 | 3.3619754 | **88** | 7744 | 681472 | 9.3808315 | 4.4479602 |
| **39** | 1521 | 59319 | 6.2449980 | 3.3912114 | **89** | 7921 | 704969 | 9.4339811 | 4.4647451 |
| **40** | 1600 | 64000 | 6.3245553 | 3.4199519 | **90** | 8100 | 729000 | 9.4868330 | 4.4814047 |
| **41** | 1681 | 68921 | 6.4031242 | 3.4482172 | **91** | 8281 | 753571 | 9.5393920 | 4.4979414 |
| **42** | 1764 | 74088 | 6.4807407 | 3.4760266 | **92** | 8464 | 778688 | 9.5916630 | 4.5143574 |
| **43** | 1849 | 79507 | 6.5574385 | 3.5033981 | **93** | 8649 | 804357 | 9.6436508 | 4.5306549 |
| **44** | 1936 | 85184 | 6.6332496 | 3.5303483 | **94** | 8836 | 830584 | 9.6953597 | 4.5468359 |
| **45** | 2025 | 91125 | 6.7082039 | 3.5568933 | **95** | 9025 | 857375 | 9.7467943 | 4.5629026 |
| **46** | 2116 | 97336 | 6.7823300 | 3.5830479 | **96** | 9216 | 884736 | 9.7979590 | 4.5788570 |
| **47** | 2209 | 103823 | 6.8556546 | 3.6088261 | **97** | 9409 | 912673 | 9.8488578 | 4.5947009 |
| **48** | 2304 | 110592 | 6.9282032 | 3.6342411 | **98** | 9604 | 941192 | 9.8994949 | 4.6104363 |
| **49** | 2401 | 117649 | 7.0000000 | 3.6593057 | **99** | 9801 | 970299 | 9.9498744 | 4.6260650 |
| **50** | 2500 | 125000 | 7.0710678 | 3.6840314 | **100** | 10000 | 1000000 | 10.0000000 | 4.6415888 |

## DECIMAL EQUIVALENTS OF COMMON FRACTIONS

| 8ths | 16ths | 32ds | 64ths | Equivalent | 8ths | 16ths | 32ds | 64ths | Equivalent | 8ths | 16ths | 32ds | 64ths | Equivalent |
|---|---|---|---|---|---|---|---|---|---|---|---|---|---|---|
| | | | 1 | .015625 | | | | 23 | .359375 | | | | 45 | .703125 |
| | | 1 | 2 | .031250 | 3 | 6 | 12 | 24 | .375000 | | | 23 | 46 | .718750 |
| | | | 3 | .046875 | | | | 25 | .390625 | | | | 47 | .734375 |
| | 1 | 2 | 4 | .062500 | | | 13 | 26 | .406250 | 6 | 12 | 24 | 48 | .750000 |
| | | | 5 | .078125 | | | | 27 | .421875 | | | | 49 | .765625 |
| | | 3 | 6 | .093750 | | 7 | 14 | 28 | .437500 | | | 25 | 50 | .781250 |
| | | | 7 | .109375 | | | | 29 | .453125 | | | | 51 | .796875 |
| 1 | 2 | 4 | 8 | .125000 | | | 15 | 30 | .468750 | | 13 | 26 | 52 | .812500 |
| | | | 9 | .140625 | | | | 31 | .484375 | | | | 53 | .828125 |
| | | 5 | 10 | .156250 | 4 | 8 | 16 | 32 | .500000 | | | 27 | 54 | .843750 |
| | | | 11 | .171875 | | | | 33 | .515625 | | | | 55 | .859375 |
| | 3 | 6 | 12 | .187500 | | | 17 | 34 | .531250 | 7 | 14 | 28 | 56 | .875000 |
| | | | 13 | .203125 | | | | 35 | .546875 | | | | 57 | .890625 |
| | | 7 | 14 | .218750 | | 9 | 18 | 36 | .562500 | | | 29 | 58 | .906250 |
| | | | 15 | .234375 | | | | 37 | .578125 | | | | 59 | .921875 |
| 2 | 4 | 8 | 16 | .250000 | | | 19 | 38 | .593750 | | 15 | 30 | 60 | .937500 |
| | | | 17 | .265625 | | | | 39 | .609375 | | | | 61 | .953125 |
| | | 9 | 18 | .281250 | 5 | 10 | 20 | 40 | .625000 | | | 31 | 62 | .968750 |
| | | | 19 | .296875 | | | | 41 | .640625 | | | | 63 | .984375 |
| | 5 | 10 | 20 | .312500 | | | 21 | 42 | .656250 | 8 | 16 | 32 | 64 | 1.000000 |
| | | | 21 | .328125 | | | | 43 | .671875 | | | | | |
| | | 11 | 22 | .343750 | | 11 | 22 | 44 | .687500 | | | | | |

## INVENTORS AND INVENTIONS

| Invention | Date | Inventor | Country |
|---|---|---|---|
| abacus | c. 500 B.C. | unknown | China (?) |
| achromatic lens | 1758 | John Dolland | England |
| adding machine | 1642 | Blaise Pascal | France |
| adding machine (commercial) | 1885 | William Burroughs | U.S. |
| addressing machine | 1893 | J. S. Duncan | U.S. |
| aerosol spray | 1941 | Lyle D. Goodhue | U.S. |
| air brake | 1869 | George Westinghouse | U.S. |
| air conditioning | 1911 | Willis H. Carrier | U.S. |
| air-cushion vehicle | 1877 | J. I. Thornycroft | England |
| airplane | 1903 | Orville and Wilbur Wright | U.S. |
| airplane (multimotored) | 1913 | Igor Sikorsky | Russia |
| airship (nonrigid) | 1852 | Henri Giffard | France |
| airship (rigid) | 1900 | Ferdinand von Zeppelin | Germany |
| automatic pilot | 1929 | William Green | U.S. |
| automobile (electric) | 1891 | William Morrison | U.S. |
| automobile (internal combustion) | 1887 | Gottlieb Daimler<br>Karl Benz (independently) | Germany<br>Germany |
| Babbitt metal | 1839 | Isaac Babbitt | U.S. |
| Bakelite | 1907 | Leo H. Baekeland | U.S. |
| balloon | 1783 | J. M. and J. E. Montgolfier | France |
| barbed wire | 1874 | Joseph F. Glidden | U.S. |
| barometer | 1643 | Evangelista Torricelli | Italy |
| battery (electric) | 1800 | Alessandro Volta | Italy |
| benday process | 1879 | Benjamin Day | U.S. |
| Bessemer converter | 1856<br>1857 | Henry Bessemer<br>William Kelly (independently) | England<br>U.S. |
| betatron | 1939 | Donald W. Kerst | U.S. |
| bicycle | 1816 | Karl D. von Sauerbronn | Germany |
| bifocal lens | 1780 | Benjamin Franklin | U.S. |
| blast furnace | 1828 | J. B. Neilson | Scotland |
| bottlemaking machine | 1903 | Michael Owens | U.S. |
| Braille | 1829 | Louis Braille | France |
| breech-loading rifle | 1810 | John Hall | U.S. |
| bubble chamber | 1952 | Donald A. Glaser | U.S. |
| bulldozer | 1923 | unknown | U.S. |
| bullet (rifle) | 1849 | Claude E. Minié | France |
| Bunsen burner | 1855 | Robert W. Bunsen | Germany |
| calculating machine (digital) | 1823 | Charles Babbage | England |
| camera (photographic) | 1822 | Joseph N. Niepce | France |
| carburetor | 1892 | Gottlieb Daimler | Germany |
| cash register | 1879 | James Ritty | U.S. |
| cathode-ray tube | 1878 | William Crookes | England |
| cellophane | c. 1900 | Jacques Brandenberger | Switzerland |
| celluloid | 1855 | Alexander Parkes | England |
| cement (portland) | 1824 | Joseph Aspdin | England |
| chronometer | 1735 | John Harrison | England |
| clock (pendulum) | 1656 | Christiaan Huygens | Holland |
| cloud chamber | 1911 | Charles T. R. Wilson | Scotland |
| color photography | 1881 | Frederic E. Ives | U.S. |
| combine (harvesting, threshing, cleaning) | 1911 | Benjamin Holt | U.S. |
| compressed-air rock drill | 1871 | Simon Ingersoll | U.S. |
| computer (differential analyzer) | 1928 | Vannevar Bush | U.S. |
| computer (electronic) | 1946 | J. Presper Eckert<br>John W. Mauchly | U.S. |
| condensed milk | 1853 | Gail Borden | U.S. |
| cotton gin | 1793 | Eli Whitney | U.S. |
| cylinder lock | 1865 | Linus Yale, Jr. | U.S. |
| cultivator | 1820 | Henry Burden | U.S. |
| daguerrotype | 1837 | Louis J. M. Daguerre | France |
| dictating machine | 1885 | Charles S. Taintor | U.S. |
| diesel engine | 1892 | Rudolf C. K. Diesel | Germany |
| disc brake | 1902 | Ferdinand W. Lanchester | England |
| dynamite | 1866 | Alfred B. Nobel | Sweden |
| electric flatiron | 1882 | Henry W. Seely | U.S. |
| electric generator | 1832 | Hippolyte Pixii | France |
| electric motor | 1822 | Michael Faraday | England |
| electric shaver | 1928 | Jacob Schick | U.S. |
| electric stove | 1896 | William S. Hadaway, Jr. | U.S. |
| electric vacuum cleaner | 1907 | James M. Spangler | U.S. |
| electromagnet | 1824 | William Sturgeon | England |
| electron microscope | 1939 | Vladimir K. Zworykin | U.S. |
| electroplating | 1805 | Luigi Brugnatelli | Italy |
| electrotype | 1839 | Moritz-Hermann Jacobi | Russia |
| elevator (passenger) | 1852 | Elisha G. Otis | U.S. |
| evaporated milk | 1880 | John B. Meyenberg | U.S. |
| firearm magazine | 1854 | Horace Smith and Daniel B. Wesson | U.S. |
| flanged railway rail | 1831 | Robert L. Stevens | U.S. |
| flying shuttle | 1733 | John Kay | England |
| frequency-modulation (FM) broadcasting | 1933 | Edwin H. Armstrong | U.S. |
| galvanometer | 1819 | Johann S. C. Schweigger | Germany |
| gas engine (four-cycle) | 1876 | Nikolaus August Otto | Germany |
| geiger counter | 1913 | Hans W. Geiger | England |
| glider | 1853 | George Cayley | England |
| gramophone (disc record) | 1887 | Emile Berliner | U.S. |
| gyrocompass | 1911 | Elmer A. Sperry | U.S. |
| halftone engraving process | 1886 | Frederic E. Ives | U.S. |
| helicopter (man-carrying) | 1907 | Paul Cornu | France |
| holography | 1949 | Denis Gabor | England |
| hydraulic press | 1795 | Joseph Brahmah | England |
| hydrometer | 1768 | Antoine Baumé | France |
| hydroplane | 1911 | Glenn H. Curtis | U.S. |
| internal combustion engine | 1859 | Jean J. E. Lenoir | France |
| internal combustion engine (high speed) | 1880 | Gottlieb Daimler | Germany |
| iron lung | 1928 | Philip Drinker and Louis A. Shaw | U.S. |
| jet engine | 1937 | Frank Whittle | England |
| kaleidoscope | 1816 | David Brewster | Scotland |
| knitting machine | c. 1589 | William Lee | England |
| lamp (incandescent) | 1879 | Thomas A. Edison | U.S. |
| lamp (mercury vapor) | 1901 | Peter C. Hewitt | U.S. |
| lamp (neon) | 1910 | Georges Claude | France |

| Invention | Date | Inventor | Country |
|---|---|---|---|
| laser | 1960 | Theodore H. Naiman | U.S. |
| lathe (engine-driven) | 1800 | Henry Maudslay | England |
| Leyden jar | 1746 | John Bevis<br>Pieter van Musschenbroek | England<br>Holland |
| life preserver | 1805 | John Edwards | England |
| lightning rod | 1752 | Benjamin Franklin | American colonies |
| linoleum | 1860 | Frederick Walton | England |
| linotype | 1884 | Ottmar Mergenthaler | U.S. |
| lithography | 1798 | Aloys Senefelder | Germany |
| long-playing (LP) record | 1948 | Peter C. Goldmark | U.S. |
| machine gun | 1862 | Richard J. Gatling | U.S. |
| match (friction) | 1827 | John Walker | England |
| match (safety) | 1855 | J. E. Lundstrom | Sweden |
| metronome | 1816 | Johann N. Mälzel | Austria |
| micrometer | 1636 | William Gascoigne | England |
| microphone | c. 1877 | Thomas A. Edison | U.S. |
| microscope | 1590 | Zacharias Janssen | Holland |
| miner's lamp | 1815 | Humphry Davy | England |
| monotype | 1887 | Tolbert Lanston | U.S. |
| motion pictures | 1872 | Eadweard Muybridge and John D. Isaacs | U.S. |
| motorcycle | 1885 | Edward Butler | England |
| mowing machine | 1810 | Peter Gaillard | U.S. |
| multiplying machine | 1671 | Gottfried W. von Leibniz | Germany |
| nitroglycerine | c. 1846 | Ascanio Sobrero | Italy |
| nylon | 1935 | Wallace H. Carothers | U.S. |
| oleomargarine | 1868 | Hippolyte Mége-Mouriz | France |
| parachute | 1783 | Louis S. Lenormand | France |
| parking meter | 1935 | Carlton C. Magee | U.S. |
| percussion cap | 1816 | Joshua Shaw | U.S. |
| phonograph (cylindrical record) | 1877 | Thomas A. Edison | U.S. |
| photocell | 1895 | Julius Elster and Hans Geitel | Germany |
| phototype-setting machine | 1945 | E. G. Klingberg<br>Fritz Stadelmann<br>H. R. Freund | U.S. |
| plow, iron | 1784 | James Small | England |
| plow (wooden) | c. 2500 B.C. | unknown | Egypt |
| polarizing glass (Polaroid) | 1932 | Edwin H. Land | U.S. |
| printing press (screw type) | c. 1450 | Johann Gutenberg | Germany |
| printing with movable type | 11th century | Pi-sheng | China |
| prism spec-troscope | 1859–60 | Gustave Kirchhoff and Robert Bunsen | Germany |
| pump (air) | 1650 | Otto von Guericke | Germany |
| radar | 1935 | Robert A. Watson-Watt | England |
| radio-telegraph | 1895 | Guglielmo Marconi | Italy |
| radio-telephone | 1902 | Reginald A. Fessenden | U.S. |
| railway (electric) | 1881 | Werner von Siemens | Germany |
| railway signal (block) | 1863 | Ashbel Welch and Robert Stewart | U.S. |
| railway sleep-ing car | 1859 | George M. Pullman | U.S. |
| reaper | 1826 | Patrick Bell | Scotland |
| refrigerator | 1858 | Ferdinand Carré | France |
| revolver | 1831 | Samuel Colt | U.S. |
| rifle | 1520 | August Kotter | Germany |
| roller bearings | c. 1496 | Leonardo da Vinci | Italy |
| rolling mill | c. 1496 | Leonardo da Vinci | Italy |
| safety pin | 1849 | Walter Hunt | U.S. |
| sail | c. 3000 B.C. | unknown | Egypt |
| saw (circular) | 1777 | Samuel Miller | England |
| screw propeller | 1804 | John C. Stevens | U.S. |
| self-starter (automo-bile) | 1911 | Charles F. Kettering | U.S. |
| sewing machine | 1790 | Thomas Saint | England |
| shrapnel shell | 1784 | Henry Shrapnel | England |
| silencer (firearm) | 1908 | Hiram P. Maxim | U.S. |
| slide rule | c. 1620 | William Oughtred | England |
| spinning machine | 1764 | James Hargreaves | England |
| sprinkler (fire) | 1723 | Ambrose Godfrey | England |
| steamboat | 1783 | Marquis de Jouffroy d'Abbans | France |
| steam engine | 1628 | Edward Somerset | England |
| steam engine (con-densing) | 1765 | James Watt | Scotland |
| steam hammer | 1839 | James Nasmyth | Scotland |
| stereoscope | 1838 | Charles Wheatstone | England |
| stereotyping | 1725 | William Ged | Scotland |
| stock ticker | 1870 | Thomas A. Edison | U.S. |
| storage battery | 1803 | Johann W. Ritter | Germany |
| street car | 1834 | Thomas Davenport | U.S. |
| submarine detector | 1917 | Max Mason | U.S. |
| switchboard | 1877 | Edgar T. Holmes | U.S. |
| tank, military | 1914 | Ernest D. Swinton | England |
| tape recorder (magnetic) | 1899 | Valdemar Poulsen | Denmark |
| telegraph (multiwire) | 1809 | Samuel T. von Soemmering | Germany |
| telegraph (single wire) | 1835 | Samuel F. B. Morse | U.S. |
| telegraph cable (sub-marine) | 1866 | Cyrus W. Field | U.S. |
| telephone | 1876 | Alexander G. Bell | U.S. |
| telescope | 1608 | Hans Lippershey | Holland |
| telescope (reflecting) | 1661 | James Gregory | Scotland |
| television | 1926 | James Logie Baird | Scotland |
| television iconoscope scanner | 1938 | Vladimir K. Zworykin | U.S. |
| thermometer (air and water) | c. 1592 | Cornelius Drebbel | Holland |
| thermometer (mercury) | 1714 | Gabriel D. Fahrenheit | Germany |
| threshing machine | 1732 | Michael Menzies | Scotland |
| tire (pneu-matic) | 1843 | Robert W. Thompson | England |
| toaster (auto-matic) | 1918 | Charles Strite | U.S. |
| tractor | 1825 | Robert Keeley | England |
| transformer (electric) | 1885 | William Stanley | U.S. |
| transistor | 1948 | J. Bardeen<br>W. H. Brattain<br>W. Shockley | U.S.<br>U.S.<br>U.S. |
| typecasting machine | 1836 | David Bruce | U.S. |
| typewriter | 1714 | Henry Mill | England |
| vacuum bottle | 1873 | James Dewar | England |
| vacuum tube (diode) | 1904 | John A. Flemming | England |
| vacuum tube (triode) | 1906 | Lee De Forest | U.S. |
| vulcanized rubber | 1839 | Charles Goodyear | U.S. |
| Wankel engine | 1957 | Felix Wankel | Germany |
| warship (steam) | c. 1860 | John Ericsson | U.S. |
| washing machine | 1858 | Hamilton E. Smith | U.S. |
| weaving machine | 1733 | John Kay | England |
| wirephoto | 1881 | Shelford Bidwell | England |
| xerography | 1948 | Chester Carlson | U.S. |
| X-ray tube (hot-filament) | 1913 | William D. Coolidge | U.S. |
| zipper | 1893 | Whitcomb L. Judson | U.S. |

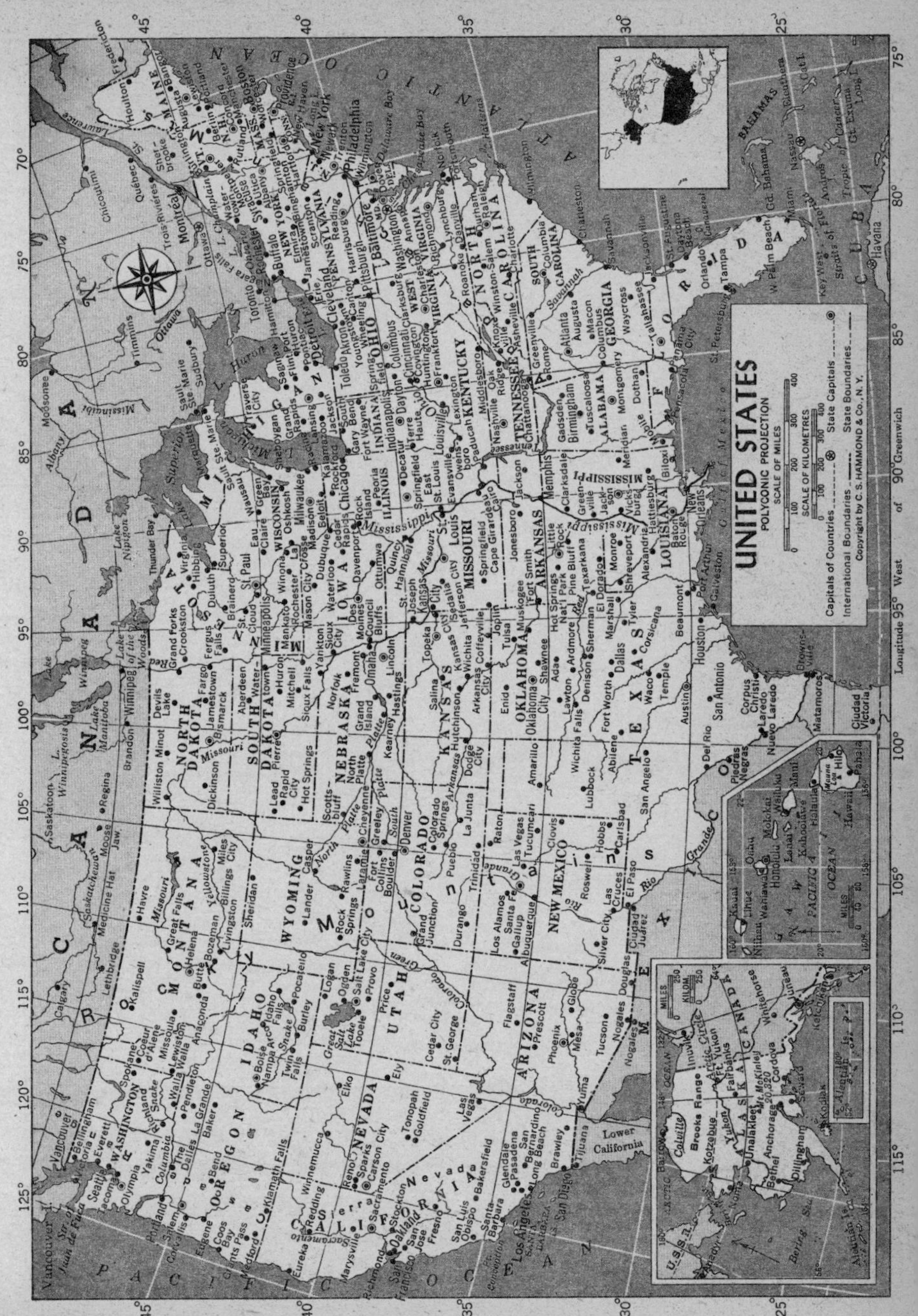
UNITED STATES
POLYCONIC PROJECTION
SCALE OF MILES
0 100 200 300 400
SCALE OF KILOMETRES
0 100 200 300 400
Capitals of Countries
State Capitals
International Boundaries
State Boundaries
Copyright by C. S. HAMMOND & Co., N. Y.
Longitude 95° West of 90° Greenwich
C A N A D A
A T L A N T I C O C E A N
P A C I F I C O C E A N
M E X I C O
Gulf of Mexico
WASHINGTON
OREGON
CALIFORNIA
NEVADA
IDAHO
MONTANA
WYOMING
UTAH
ARIZONA
COLORADO
NEW MEXICO
NORTH DAKOTA
SOUTH DAKOTA
NEBRASKA
KANSAS
OKLAHOMA
TEXAS
MINNESOTA
IOWA
MISSOURI
ARKANSAS
LOUISIANA
WISCONSIN
ILLINOIS
MICHIGAN
INDIANA
OHIO
KENTUCKY
TENNESSEE
MISSISSIPPI
ALABAMA
GEORGIA
FLORIDA
SOUTH CAROLINA
NORTH CAROLINA
VIRGINIA
WEST VIRGINIA
PENNSYLVANIA
NEW YORK
MAINE
BAHAMAS
CUBA
Lower California
ALASKA
PACIFIC OCEAN
Hawaii

ALABAMA
MILES
0 20 40 60
KILOMETERS
0 20 40 60
State Capitals
County Seats
Longitude West of Greenwich
© Copyright HAMMOND INCORPORATED, Maplewood, N.J.
88° 87° 86° 85°
35° 34° 33° 32° 31°
TENNESSEE
GEORGIA
FLORIDA
MISSISSIPPI
GULF OF MEXICO
PICKWICK LANDING DAM
CHICKAMAUGA AND CHATTANOOGA NAT'L MIL. PK.
KENNESAW MT. NAT'L BATTLEFIELD PK.
HORSESHOE BEND NAT'L MIL. PK.
REDSTONE ARSENAL
RUSSELL CAVE N.M.
WILSON DAM
WHEELER DAM
GUNTERSVILLE DAM
WALTER F. GEORGE DAM
ANNISTON ARMY DEPOT
FT. McCLELLAN
MAXWELL A.F.B.
GUNTER A.F.B.
CRAIG A.F.B.
FT. RUCKER
BROOKLEY A.F.B.
Cheaha Mtn. 2,407
LAUDERDALE
LIMESTONE
MADISON
JACKSON
COLBERT
FRANKLIN
LAWRENCE
MORGAN
MARSHALL
DE KALB
MARION
WINSTON
CULLMAN
ETOWAH
CHEROKEE
WALKER
BLOUNT
CALHOUN
FAYETTE
LAMAR
JEFFERSON
ST. CLAIR
CLEBURNE
TUSCALOOSA
PICKENS
SHELBY
TALLADEGA
CLAY
RANDOLPH
BIBB
CHAMBERS
GREENE
HALE
CHILTON
COOSA
TALLAPOOSA
PERRY
AUTAUGA
ELMORE
LEE
SUMTER
DALLAS
MACON
RUSSELL
MARENGO
LOWNDES
MONTGOMERY
BULLOCK
CHOCTAW
WILCOX
BARBOUR
BUTLER
CRENSHAW
PIKE
CLARKE
MONROE
COFFEE
DALE
HENRY
WASHINGTON
CONECUH
ESCAMBIA
COVINGTON
GENEVA
HOUSTON
MOBILE
BALDWIN
Montgomery
Birmingham
Huntsville
Mobile
Tuscaloosa
Florence
Sheffield
Tuscumbia
Decatur
Athens
Gadsden
Anniston
Selma
Dothan
Chattanooga
Atlanta
Columbus
Pensacola
Rome
Corinth
Phenix City
Opelika
Auburn
Prichard
Chickasaw
Bessemer
Fairfield
Hueytown
Homewood
Mtn. Brook
Tarrant
Leeds
Jasper
Cullman
Hartselle
Guntersville
Albertville
Scottsboro
Ft. Payne
Jacksonville
Talladega
Sylacauga
Alexander City
Prattville
Enterprise
Ozark
Troy
Eufaula
Andalusia
Opp
Greenville
Brewton
Atmore
Demopolis
Northport
Lanett
Wheeler Lake
Pickwick Lake
Guntersville L.
L. M. Smith L.
Bankhead L.
Logan Martin Lake
Weiss Res.
Martin L.
Demopolis Lake
West Point Res.
L. Harding
Lake Eufaula
Lake Seminole
Allatoona Lake
Mobile Bay
Perdido Bay
East Bay
Choctawhatchee Bay
Mississippi Sound
Grants Pass
Santa Rosa Island
Dauphin Island
Tennessee R.
Tombigbee R.
Black Warrior R.
Alabama R.
Coosa R.
Tallapoosa R.
Cahaba R.
Chattahoochee R.
Conecuh R.
Pea R.
Sepulga R.
Escambia R.
Perdido R.
Mobile R.
Tensaw R.
Sipsey R.
Elk R.
Etowah R.
Choctawhatchee R.
Sand Mtn.
Lookout Mtn.
CUMBERLAND PLAT.

# THE FIFTY STATES

## ALABAMA

Site of the first Confederate capital in the proverbial "Heart of Dixie," Alabama is a traditionally agricultural state in the Southern mold. A continuing concerted drive toward greater economic diversification in the state began in the 1930s, after costly boll weevil infestations and other problems demonstrated that the state was relying too heavily on cotton. Today, Birmingham has become the South's largest iron and steel producing center, while the Redstone Arsenal and George C. Marshall Space Flight Center in Huntsville have emerged as important research installations; in a single decade (1950-60), Huntsville's population more than quadruppled.

Hydroelectric power provided by the Tennessee Valley Authority has been a key factor in Alabama's growing industrialization. Tourist attractions include the Alabama Space and Rocket Center at Huntsville, Bellingrath Gardens near Mobile, the famed Mardi Gras celebration held in Mobile, the Mound State Monument (Moundsville) and the George Washington Carver Museum at Tuskegee Institute, a school founded by Booker T. Washington, a former slave.

The state's diverse topography ranges from the Appalachian highlands in the northeast to the broad coastal plain comprising about two-thirds of the total area; in the plain's central region is the fertile "Black Belt." Swamps, bayous, and sandy beaches also mark the varied terrain. The state's abbreviated coastline is dominated by Mobile Bay; Dauphin Island lies at the bay's entrance. About 65 percent of the state is forested.

Mound Builders, who lived in the Alabama region in prehistoric times, were followed by a number of Indian tribes, including the Chickasaws, Cherokees, and Creeks. Spaniards Cabeza de Vaca and Hernando De Soto were among the region's early European explorers. The first permanent European settlement was made (1702) by Frenchmen at Fort Louis near present-day Mobile; it served as the capital of the Louisiana Territory until 1722. Other French settlements followed, but in 1763 France lost the region to the British.

After the American Revolution, England ceded to the United States all of the Alabama region except the southernmost British West Florida area that included Mobile; this region, together with East Florida, went to Spain.

In 1817, after a short period as part of the Territory of Mississippi, the region was organized as the Alabama Territory. Settlers spurred by the virtual ending of Indian troubles in the area helped the new territory's growth; statehood came in 1819. Slave-supported plantation farming, aided by the recent invention of the cotton gin, soon emerged as the main factor in the state's economy.

Alabama seceded from the Union and joined the Confederacy in 1861; Montgomery was briefly the Confederate capital. The state suffered a great deal from both the Civil War and the harsh, chaotic Reconstruction.

In the middle of the twentieth century, there were spectacular and sometimes bloody confrontations between supporters and opponents of racial segregation. Martin Luther King, Jr., led opponents of segregation in a boycott of Montgomery buses in 1955-56, in the 1963 demonstrations in Birmingham, and in a march from Selma to Montgomery in 1965. In 1978, a suspect in the 1963 bombing of a black church in Birmingham was convicted. Democratic Governor George Wallace temporarily retired from politics in 1979 and was succeeded by Forrest James, a Democrat with no segregationist identity.

The U.S. Supreme Court in a nationally important 1980 decision ruled that the city of Mobile could select its officials through *at-large* elections.

**Full name:** State of Alabama. **Origin of name:** From the Indian, Alba Amo meaning "I' Clear the Thicket." **Inhabitant:** Alabamian. **Capital:** Montgomery. **State motto:** Andemus Jura Nostra Defendere (We Dare Defend Our Rights). **Flag:** Red cross of St. Andrew on white field. **Seal:** A circled map of Alabama with boundaries & rivers. **Flower:** Camellia. **Bird:** Yellowhammer. **Tree:** Southern pine. **Song:** "Alabama." **Nickname:** Yellowhammer State and The Heart of Dixie.

**Governor:** Forrest James, Jr. **Annual salary:** $50,000. **Term:** 4 years. **Current term expires:** Jan. 1983. **Voting requirements:** 18 yrs. old & U.S. citizen; resident of state 10 days. **U.S. Congressmen:** 7 **Entered Union:** 1819 (22nd state).

**Location & boundaries:** Southeastern state: bounded on the north by Tennessee; on the east by the Chattahoochee River & Georgia; on the south by Florida & the Gulf of Mexico; & on the west by Mississippi. **Total area:** 51,705 sq. mi. (ranks 29th). **Extreme length:** 330 mi. **Extreme breadth:** 200 mi. **Coastline:** 53 mi. **Chief rivers:** Mobile, Alabama, Tombigbee, Coosa. **Major lakes:** Wheeler, Guntersville, Wilson, Martin, Mitchell. **No. of counties:** 67.

**Population (1980 census):** 3,893,888 (ranks 22nd). **Pop. increase (1970-80):** 13.1%. **Largest cities:** Birmingham, Mobile, Montgomery, Huntsville. **Pop. density:** 75.3 per sq. mi. (ranks 26th). **Pop. distribution: White**—2,869,688; **Black**—995,623; **Am. Indian, Eskimo and Aleut**—7,561; **Asian and Pacific Islander**—9,695; **Other**—7,494; **Spanish origin**—33,100. **Marriage rate (1979):** 12.9 per 1,000 people. **Divorce rate:** 7.0 per 1,000 people.

**State finances (1980). Revenue:** $4,154,000,000. **Expenditures:** $4,002,000,000. **State taxes:** $477.32 per capita. **State personal income tax:** Yes. **Public debt (1980):** $265.38 per capita. **Federal aid (1980):** $399.65 per capita. **Personal income (1981):** $8,200.

**Sectors of the economy (% of labor force employed in 1970):** Manufacturing (29%), Wholesale & retail trade (19%), Government (17%), Services (9%), Educational Services (7%), Construction (7%). **Leading products:** primary & fabricated metals, transportation equipment, machinery, food, textiles, apparel, paper, chemicals. **Minerals:** coal, cement, stone, petroleum. **Agricultural products:** broilers, cattle, eggs, corn, soybeans, peanuts. **Fishing:** shrimp, red snappers, blue crabs. **Avg. farm (1981):** 217 acres. **Avg. value of farm per acre:** $935.

**Highway expenditures per capita (1980):** $104.96. **Persons per motor vehicle (1981):** 1.29. **Minimum age for driver's license:** 16. **Gasoline tax:** 11¢ per gallon. **Diesel tax:** 12¢ per gallon. **Motor vehicle deaths (1980):** 24.2 per 100,000 people.

**Birthrate (1979):** 16.6 per 1,000 people. **Infant mortality rate per 1,000 births (1978):** 16.1. **Physicians per 100,000 pop. (1979):** 124. **Dentists per 100,000 pop. (1979):** 35. **Acceptable hospital beds (1979):** 6.5 per 1,000 people. **State expenditures per capita for health and hospitals (1980):** $87.50.

**Education expenditures (1977-78):** $445.55 per capita annually. **No. of pupils in public schools (1980):** 753,000. **No. of institutions of higher learning (1978-79):** 58. **Public school expenditure per pupil in attendance (1978-79):** $1,563. **Avg. salary of public school teachers (1979-80):** $13,830. **No. full-time teachers (1980):** 35,250. **Educational attainment of adult population (1976):** 12.2 median yrs. of school completed: 6.8% with less than 5 years of education; 10.3% with 4 yrs. of college.

**Telephones (1979):** 50 per 100 people. **State Chamber of Commerce:** Alabama Chamber of Commerce, 468 South Perry Street, P.O. Box 76, Montgomery, Alabama 36195.

## ALASKA

Alaska is a land of great extremes: first among the states in area, last in population. One of the nation's biggest bargains (Alaska's purchase price

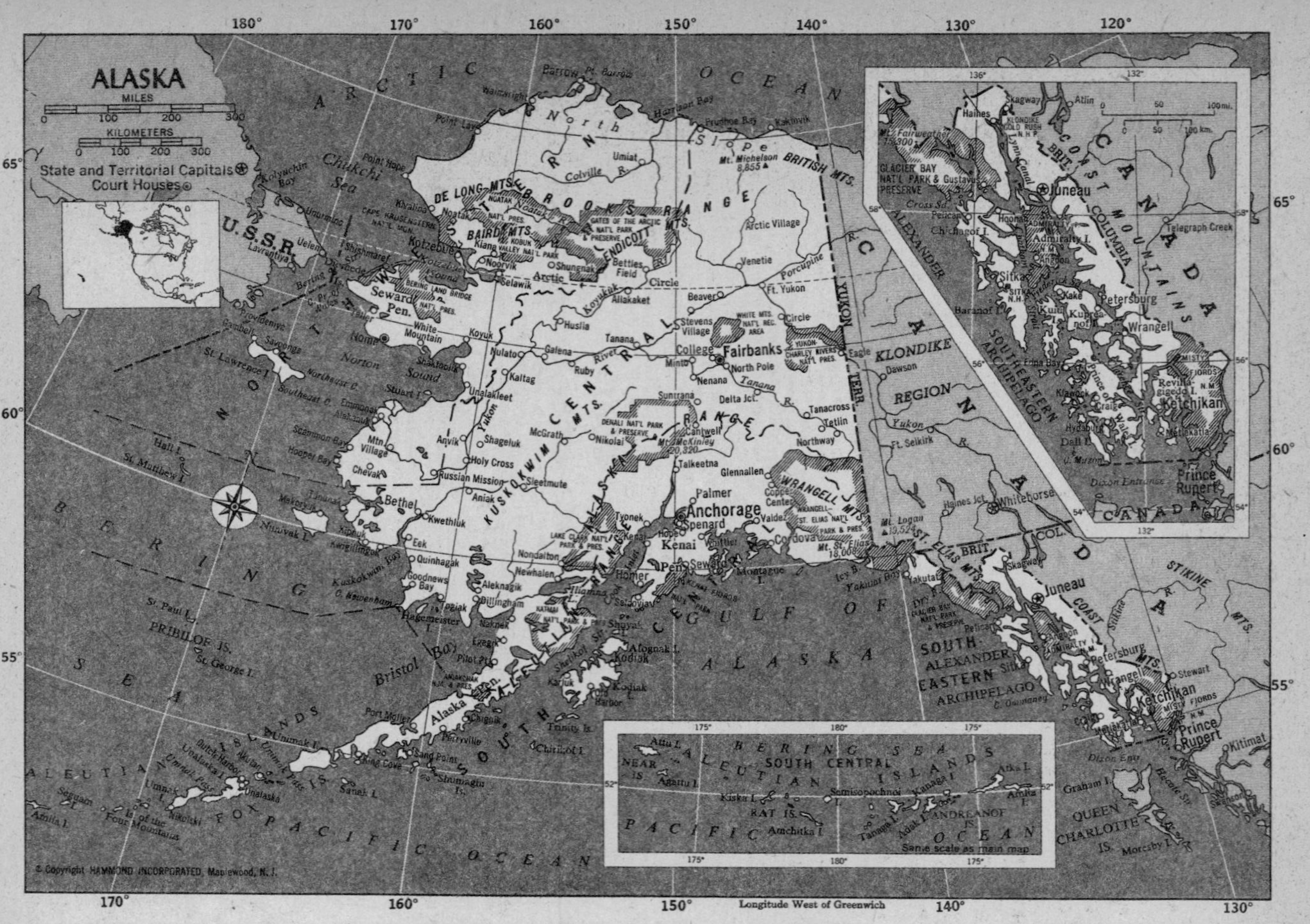
ALASKA
MILES
0 100 200 300
KILOMETERS
0 100 200 300
State and Territorial Capitals
Court Houses
ARCTIC OCEAN
BERING SEA
PACIFIC OCEAN
GULF OF ALASKA
CANADA
U.S.S.R.
BROOKS RANGE
ALASKA RANGE
YUKON TERR.
BRIT. COLUMBIA
KLONDIKE REGION
SOUTHEASTERN ARCHIPELAGO
ALEUTIAN ISLANDS
Juneau
Anchorage
Fairbanks
Nome
Ketchikan
Sitka
Kodiak
Mt. McKinley 20,320
Mt. Logan 19,524
Mt. St. Elias 18,008
Same scale as main map
Longitude West of Greenwich
© Copyright HAMMOND INCORPORATED, Maplewood, N.J.

was less than 2¢ an acre), it is potentially one of the richest states—particularly in view of the spectacular oil strikes in Prudhoe Bay off the state's frigid Arctic (or North) Slope. Many believe that these strikes will fulfill the century-long promise of "The Last Frontier"; the find has already been called "one of the largest petroleum accumulations known to the world today." In 1969 about $900 million was bid for oil-land leases.

During the next decade, oil revenues so glutted state coffers that in April 1980 the state enacted a plan to share the wealth directly with Alaska's 400,000 residents. The state income tax was virtually abolished and each Alaskan was to receive annually at least $50 for every year he lived in the state since 1959. In early September 1980, the Alaska Supreme Court struck down the tax-exemption portion of the these plans to fruition. Governor Hammond countered the decision by an April law. Later that month the State Legislature voted overwhelmingly to repeal the state personal income tax. In October 1980, the Alaskan Supreme Court upheld the royalty sharing plan, but the U.S. Supreme Court voided it on June 14, 1982, because of the length of the residency restrictions. The legislature then passed a new law without residency length bias.

Alaska's awesome terrain has long challenged explorers and settlers. The state, which entered the Union in 1959, is cut into isolated areas by its craggy coast and high mountains, principally the Brooks Range in the north (an extension of the Rocky Mountains) and the Alaska Range in the south, which includes Mount McKinley, the highest peak in North America. Alaskans have attempted unsuccessfully to have the famed mountain renamed Mount Denali.

Sticking out into the sea in the northwest is the Seward Peninsula. Off the peninsula, in the Bering Strait, is U.S.-owned Little Diomede Island, separated from the USSR's Big Diomede by about two miles. Alaska is separated from the nearest state, Washington, by about 500 miles.

The Alaskan climate is widely variable. The southeast coast, protected by mountains from the north winds and influenced by the warm Japan Current, is generally temperate and rainy, while interior summers are short and very hot (with exceptionally long days), and the winters very cold.

Major tourist attractions include Denali National Park, site of Mount McKinley, Glacier Bay National Park, with its awesome ice sheet and the magnificent Inland Passage in the southeast Panhandle region.

Captain Vitus Bering, a Dane who explored for Russia, is thought to have been the first white man to visit Alaska (1741), after passing close to it on an earlier voyage. At this time there were about 75,000 Indians, Eskimos, and Aleuts in Alaska; some prehistoric campsites date back to the Ice Age.

Though several nations tried to get a foothold in the region, mainly for the trade in sea otter pelts it might support, Russia prevailed, establishing Alaska's first white settlement on Kodiak Island in 1784. By the 1850s, Russia, facing increased competition from Americans, British, and Canadians, plus a dwindling supply of fur-bearing animals, wanted to sell. In 1867, U.S. Secretary of State William H. Seward agreed to buy—for $7.2 million—thereby becoming a target of ridicule. Many Americans dubbed Alaska "Seward's Folly" or "Seward's Icebox," considering it a frozen wasteland that was relatively valueless.

But gold was discovered (1896) at Klondike in neighboring Yukon Territory, and in Alaska itself at Nome (1899) and at Fairbanks (1902). Settlement was spurred as prospectors poured in and the economy was strengthened—but the lasting gains were few.

During World War II, the region's importance as a military outpost was dramatized when the Japanese briefly occupied some of the Aleutians—the war's only North American enemy occupation. Today, Alaska contains the Distant Early Warning system (DEW line) and other defense installations, including military bases. Roughly half the state's personal income is from government sources, and 97 percent of the land is Federally owned.

With a long coastline punctuated by many bays and fjords, Alaska is a leading state in commercial fishing. Forest products account for a considerable share of the state's revenue, while the value of agricultural products remains far more potential than actual. Only a small fraction of the state's potential cropland of 2 to 3 million acres has so far been developed. Tourism is a major industry.

On Good Friday, March 27, 1964, an exceptionally powerful earthquake struck the south-central part of the state, killing 114 and causing property damage estimated at $750 million.

In 1971 Congress passed the Alaska Native Land Claims Settlement Act to extinguish the nearly 100-year old claims of Alaska's 64,000 Eskimos, Indians and Aleuts by providing 40 million acres of land and approximately $925 million in compensation. An enrollment of eligible natives began in 1972.

Construction on the $4.5-billion Trans-Alaska pipeline project, first proposed in 1969 and delayed by legal suits brought by environmentalists finally began in 1974. In June 1977 oil began to flow from Prudhoe Bay on the Arctic Ocean through the 799-mile, 48-inch hot-oil pipeline to the Gulf of Alaska port of Valdez. To get that oil to the American consumer, President Carter in January 1980 announced plans for a pipeline to extend from a Washington state port, where it was to receive oil from Alaska by sea, to Minnesota. In April 1982, Washington's governor rejected an application to build the pipeline in his state.

A proposed trans-Canadian pipeline to deliver natural gas from the Alaskan North Slope to the lower forty-eight states has been approved by the United States and Canada. In January 1980 the Alberta Gas Trunk Line Co., Ltd. announced plans to begin construction of a segment of the pipeline from Calgary to the U.S. border, while the Pacific Gas and Electric Co. was expected to extend the line to Oregon. Financing problems have delayed the enormous project, however.

On December 2, 1980, President Carter signed into law a bill designating over 104 million acres of Alaskan land as national parks, monuments and preserves. Among the new national parks created are Gates of the Arctic, Kenai Fjords, Kobuk Valley, Lake Clark and Wrangell-St. Elias. In certain areas oil, gas and mineral exploration and exploitation would be permitted.

Plans begun in 1974 to move the capital of Alaska from Juneau to Willow, a site chosen in 1977, have been delayed by the Alaska Legislature. State Senator Bill Ray and his supporters have blocked the move, citing the high cost to the Alaskans.

**Full name:** State of Alaska. **Origin of name:** From Aleutian word meaning "Great Land." **Inhabitant:** Alaskan. **Capital:** Juneau. **State motto:** North to the Future. **Flag:** Blue field with seven gold stars, representing the Big Dipper; eighth star represents the North Star. **Seal:** Rising sun shines on lake, fishing boat, merchant ship, forests, mining & agricultural activities, symbols of Alaskan resources & occupations. **Flower:** Forget-me-not. **Bird:** Willow ptar-

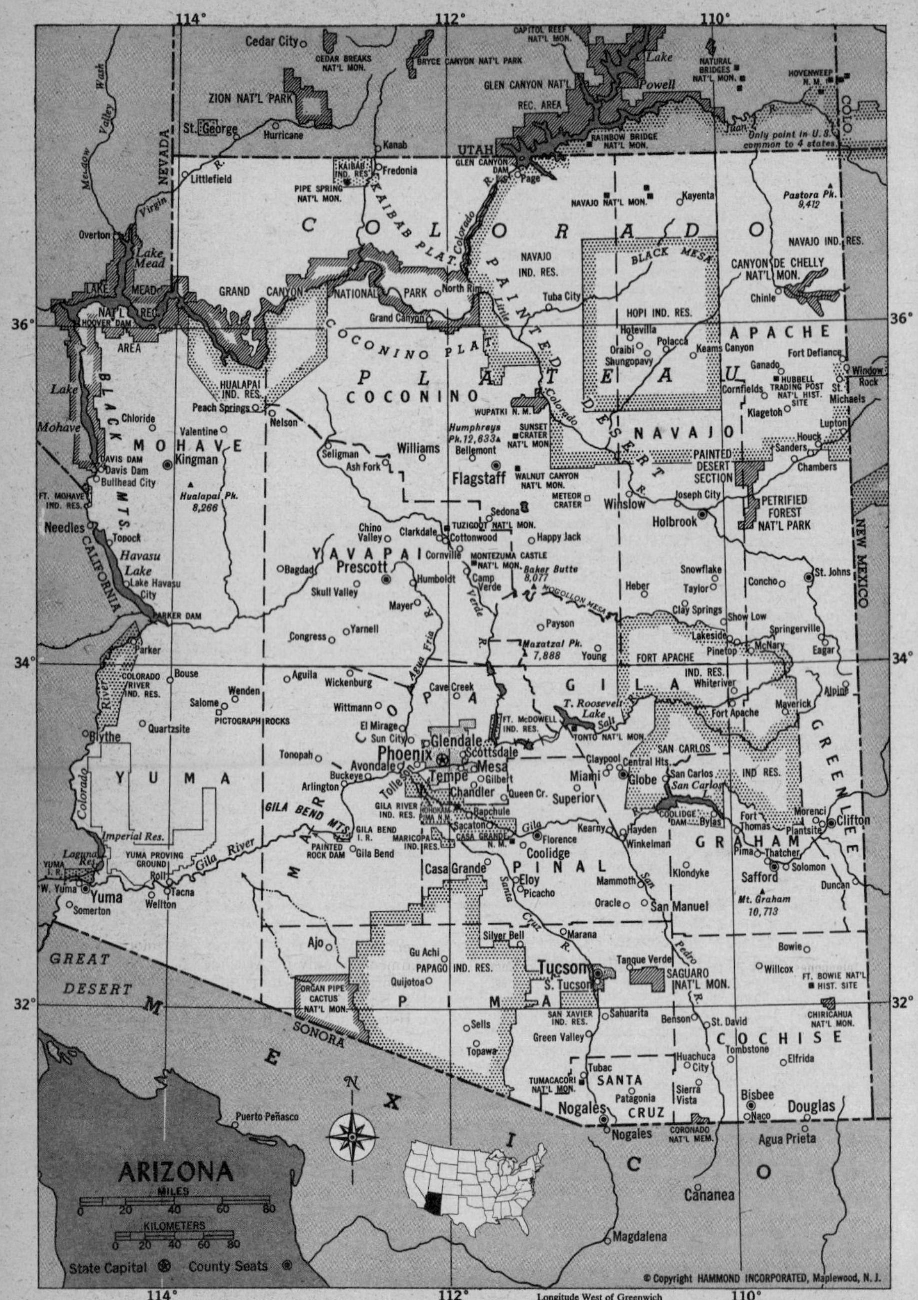
114°
112°
110°
36°
34°
32°
Cedar City
CEDAR BREAKS NAT'L MON.
BRYCE CANYON NAT'L PARK
CAPITOL REEF NAT'L MON.
Lake Powell
NATURAL BRIDGES NAT'L MON.
HOVENWEEP N.M.
ZION NAT'L PARK
GLEN CANYON NAT'L REC. AREA
St. George
Hurricane
RAINBOW BRIDGE NAT'L MON.
Only point in U.S. common to 4 states
COLO.
Kanab
UTAH
GLEN CANYON DAM
NEVADA
Littlefield
KAIBAB IND. RES.
Fredonia
Page
PIPE SPRING NAT'L MON.
Meadow Valley Wash
Virgin R.
KAIBAB PLAT.
NAVAJO NAT'L MON.
Kayenta
Pastora Pk. 9,412
Overton
C O L O R A D O
Lake Mead
BLACK MESA
NAVAJO IND. RES.
CANYON DE CHELLY NAT'L MON.
LAKE MEAD NAT'L REC. AREA
HOOVER DAM
GRAND CANYON NATIONAL PARK
North Rim
Tuba City
Chinle
Grand Canyon
HOPI IND. RES.
Hotevilla
Oraibi
Shungopavy
Polacca
Keams Canyon
A P A C H E
Fort Defiance
COCONINO PLAT.
Ganado
Window Rock
P L A T E A U
HUBBELL TRADING POST NAT'L HIST. SITE
St. Michaels
Cornfields
Lake Mohave
HUALAPAI IND. RES.
COCONINO
WUPATKI N.M.
Klagetoh
Peach Springs
Nelson
Chloride
Valentine
Humphreys Pk. 12,633
SUNSET CRATER NAT'L MON.
PAINTED DESERT
N A V A J O
Lupton
Houck
Sanders
BLACK MTS.
M O H A V E
Kingman
Seligman
Ash Fork
Williams
Bellemont
Flagstaff
PAINTED DESERT SECTION
Chambers
DAVIS DAM
Davis Dam
Bullhead City
WALNUT CANYON NAT'L MON.
METEOR CRATER
Winslow
Joseph City
PETRIFIED FOREST NAT'L PARK
FT. MOHAVE IND. RES.
Hualapai Pk. 8,266
Sedona
Holbrook
NEW MEXICO
Needles
Topock
TUZIGOOT NAT'L MON.
Chino Valley
Clarkdale
Cottonwood
Happy Jack
CALIFORNIA
Havasu Lake
Y A V A P A I
Cornville
MONTEZUMA CASTLE NAT'L MON.
Bagdad
Prescott
Humboldt
Camp Verde
Baker Butte 8,077
Snowflake
St. Johns
Lake Havasu City
Skull Valley
MOGOLLON MESA
Heber
Taylor
Concho
Mayer
Verde R.
Clay Springs
Show Low
PARKER DAM
Yarnell
Payson
Springerville
Congress
Lakeside
Pinetop
McNary
Parker
Mazatzal Pk. 7,888
Young
FORT APACHE IND. RES.
Eagar
COLORADO RIVER IND. RES.
Bouse
Aguila
Wickenburg
Agua Fria R.
Cave Creek
G I L A
Whiteriver
Alpine
Wenden
Salome
PICTOGRAPH ROCKS
Wittmann
T. Roosevelt Lake
Salt
Fort Apache
Maverick
Quartzsite
El Mirage
FT. McDOWELL IND. RES.
TONTO NAT'L MON.
GREENLEE
Blythe
Sun City
Glendale
Scottsdale
SAN CARLOS IND. RES.
Tonopah
Phoenix
Avondale
Mesa
Claypool
Central Hts.
Y U M A
Buckeye
Tolleson
Tempe
Gilbert
Miami
Globe
San Carlos
San Carlos L.
Arlington
Chandler
Queen Cr.
Superior
Colorado
GILA BEND MTS.
GILA RIVER IND. RES.
Bapchule
COOLIDGE DAM
Bylas
Morenci
Clifton
Sacaton
Gila
Kearny
Hayden
Fort Thomas
Plantsite
Imperial Res.
GILA BEND I. R.
MARICOPA IND. RES.
CASA GRANDE N.M.
Florence
Winkelman
G R A H A M
PAINTED ROCK DAM
Gila Bend
Coolidge
Pima
Thatcher
Laguna Res.
YUMA PROVING GROUND
Gila River
Casa Grande
P I N A L
Klondyke
Safford
Solomon
YUMA I. R.
Roll
Eloy
Mammoth
W. Yuma
Yuma
Tacna
Picacho
Duncan
Wellton
Oracle
San Manuel
Mt. Graham 10,713
Somerton
Santa Cruz R.
Marana
Silver Bell
Pedro
Bowie
GREAT DESERT
Ajo
Gu Achi
Tanque Verde
PAPAGO IND. RES.
Tucson
SAGUARO NAT'L MON.
Willcox
FT. BOWIE NAT'L HIST. SITE
Quijotoa
ORGAN PIPE CACTUS NAT'L MON.
S. Tucson
P I M A
SAN XAVIER IND. RES.
Sahuarita
Benson
St. David
CHIRICAHUA NAT'L MON.
SONORA
Sells
Green Valley
C O C H I S E
Topawa
Huachuca City
Tombstone
Elfrida
M E X I C O
Tubac
TUMACACORI NAT'L MON.
SANTA CRUZ
Patagonia
Sierra Vista
Bisbee
Naco
Douglas
Puerto Peñasco
Nogales
CORONADO NAT'L MEM.
Agua Prieta
Cananea
Magdalena
ARIZONA
MILES
0 20 40 60 80
KILOMETERS
0 20 40 60 80
State Capital
County Seats
© Copyright HAMMOND INCORPORATED, Maplewood, N. J.
Longitude West of Greenwich

migan. **Tree:** Sitka spruce. **Song:** "Alaska's Flag." **Nickname:** The Great Land.

**Governor:** Jay S. Hammond. **Annual salary:** $74,196. **Term:** 4 years. **Current term expires:** Dec. 1982. **Voting requirements:** 18 yrs. old & U.S. citizen; resident of state 30 days. **U.S. Congressmen:** 1. **Entered Union:** 1959 (49th state).

**Location & boundaries:** Pacific state: bounded on the north by the Arctic Ocean; on the east by Canada; on the south by the Pacific Ocean; & on the west by the Bering Sea & Arctic Ocean. **Total area:** 591,004 sq. mi. (ranks 1st). **Extreme length:** 2,200 mi. **Extreme breadth:** 1,200 mi. **Coastline:** 6,640 mi. **Chief rivers:** Yukon, Tanana, Kuskokwim. **Major lakes:** Iliamna, Becharof, Tustumena. **No. of boroughs:** 10.

**Population (1980 census):** 401,851 (ranks 50th). **Pop. increase (1970-80):** 32.8%. **Largest cities:** Anchorage, Fairbanks, Juneau, Sitka. **Pop. density:** 0.7 per sq. mi. (ranks 50th). **Pop. distribution: White**—308,455; **Black**—13,619; **Am. Indian, Eskimo and Aleut**—64,047; **Asian and Pacific Islander**—8,035; **Other**—6,325; **Spanish origin**—9,497. **Marriage rate (1979):** 12.3 per 1,000 people. **Divorce rate:** 8.6 per 1,000 people.

**State finances (1980). Revenue:** $3,230,000,000. **Expenditures:** $2,033,000,000. **State taxes:** $3,594.02 per capita. **State personal income tax:** No. (In 1980, Alaska eliminated all personal income taxes.) **Public debt (1980):** $3,861.38 per capita. **Federal aid (1980):** $1,099.66 per capita. **Personal income (1981):** $14,190.

**Sectors of the economy (% of labor force employed in 1970):** Government (37%), Wholesale & retail trade (19%), Educational Services (11%), Construction (9%), Services (8%), Manufacturing (7%). **Leading products:** seafood, timber, pulp, oil, gas, petrochemicals. **Minerals:** petroleum & natural gas, coal, sand & gravel. **Agricultural products:** dairy items, eggs, cattle, hay, vegetables, wool. **Fishing:** salmon, halibut, crab, shrimp, scallops. **Avg. farm (1981):** 4,000 acres. **Avg. value of farm per acre:** N.A.

**Highway expenditures per capita (1980):** $433.81. **Persons per motor vehicle (1981):** 1.55. **Minimum age for driver's license:** 16. **Gasoline tax:** 8¢ per gallon. **Diesel tax:** 8¢ per gallon. **Motor vehicle deaths (1980):** 22.0 per 100,000 people.

**Birthrate (1979):** 22.4 per 1,000 people. **Infant mortality rate per 1,000 births (1978):** 14.4. **Physicians per 100,000 pop. (1979):** 118. **Dentists per 100,000 pop. (1979):** 56. **Acceptable hospital beds (1979):** 4.2 per 1,000 people. **State expenditures per capita for health and hospitals (1980):** $121.66.

**Education expenditures (1977-78):** $1,120.47 per capita annually. **No. of pupils in public schools (1980):** 88,000. **No. of institutions of higher learning (1978-79):** 16. **Public school expenditure per pupil in attendance (1978-79):** $4,112. **Avg. salary of public school teachers (1979-80):** $27,930. **No. full-time teachers (1980):** 5,600. **Educational attainment of adult population (1976):** 12.7 median yrs. of school completed: 2.8% with less than 5 years of education; 17.6% with 4 yrs. of college.

**Telephones (1979):** 36 per 100 people. **State Chamber of Commerce:** Alaska State Chamber of Commerce, 310 Second Street, Juneau, Alaska 99801.

## ARIZONA

Arizona, the last mainland state to join the Union (1912), lies west of the Continental Divide and consists of three general areas: the desert in the southwest, the central highlands, and the Colorado Plateau in the northwest. Almost all of the state is within the Colorado drainage basin. Its principal tourist attraction, the awesome Grand Canyon, is one of the world's natural wonders: a multicolored fissure 217 miles long, four to eight miles wide at the brim, and about a mile deep.

The warm, dry, and reputedly health-restoring climate of the state's southern region—which includes Arizona's two largest cities, Phoenix and Tucson—has made it a popular winter resort area (as well as the site of many senior citizen retirement communities). Tourism is one of the leading industries in Arizona. In 1979 it contributed over $2 billion to the state's economy and provided over 68,000 jobs.

In addition to the Grand Canyon, state attractions include Hoover Dam, Lake Mead, 15 national monuments, various Indian villages and reservations (the state has the nation's largest Indian population: about 152,800), Oak Creek Canyon, legendary Tombstone, the Petrified Forest, and the Painted Desert. A new addition to the list is legendary London Bridge, which a private group has re-erected at Lake Havasu City.

Bolstered by defense contracts, manufacturing has lately become the state's leading industry, followed by mining and agriculture. The electronics industry is important in the Tucson and Phoenix areas. Cotton is the major farm crop. Arizona produces a number of metals, including more than half of the country's supply of copper. The state is a major producer of molybdenum. The Black Mesa open pit coal mine on the Navajo Reservation provides fuel for a power plant which sends electricity to southern California.

Mummies and ancient human relics—such as baskets and cloth—have been found in a strikingly well-preserved condition in Arizona. Several Indian cultures lived there from about 25,000 to 10,000 B.C., and the ancestors of the modern Navajos (or Navahos) and Apaches lived in northern Arizona. One of the oldest continuously inhabited settlements in the country, the community of Oraibi was built sometime in the 1100s by Hopi Indians, over 5,000 of whom presently live on a reservation in northeast Arizona. The first white men were 16th-century Spanish explorers. Missions were established as early as 1692. The United States obtained (1848) most of the land from Mexico following the Mexican War; the rest was included in the Gadsden Purchase (1853).

Arizona was organized as a territory in 1863, with the capital at Prescott (1865-67), then Tucson (1867-77), Prescott again (1877-89), and finally at Phoenix. Over many years, various bloody conflicts raged in Arizona—between the whites and the Apaches, whose leaders included the fabled fighters Cochise and Geronimo, between Confederate and Union troops during the Civil War, between labor and management during violent strikes in the mining communities, and between cattlemen and sheepmen in the range wars that continued until the turn of the century. Yet another subject of contention through the years has been the water rights along the Colorado River claimed not only by Arizona but by Nevada and California as well; distribution now follows a 1963 U.S. Supreme Court ruling.

Hopi and Navajo Indians of northeastern Arizona have been feuding for years over ownership of 1.8 million acres of desert plateau which acts as a buffer between the much smaller Hopi reservation and the Navajo nation which surrounds it. The U.S. Supreme Court ruled in the early 1960s that the two tribes should share the land equally. However, following congressional action, the tract was divided between the Hopi and the Navajo in April 1981.

**Full name:** State of Arizona. **Origin of name:** From the Indian, Alekzon, meaning "Small Spring." **Inhabitant:** Arizonan. **Capital:** Phoenix. **State motto:** Ditat Deus (God Enriches). **Flag:** A copper-colored star centered on radiating red & yellow stripes & a horizontal blue bar. **Seal:** Miner standing in mountains symbolizes state's mineral industry; irrigated fields & cow represent agriculture. **Flower:** Saguaro cactus. **Bird:** Cactus wren. **Tree:** Paloverde. **Song:** "Arizona." **Nickname:** Grand Canyon State.

**Governor:** Bruce E. Babbitt. **Annual salary:** $50,000. **Term:** 4 years. **Current term expires:** Jan. 1983. **Voting requirements:** 18 yrs. old &

ARKANSAS
MILES
0 10 20 30 40 50 60
KILOMETERS
0 10 20 30 40 50 60
State Capital
County Seats
MISSOURI
OKLAHOMA
TEXAS
LOUISIANA
MISSISSIPPI
TENN.
KY.
BENTON
CARROLL
BOONE
MARION
BAXTER
FULTON
IZARD
SHARP
RANDOLPH
CLAY
GREENE
LAWRENCE
CRAIGHEAD
MISSISSIPPI
POINSETT
WASHINGTON
MADISON
NEWTON
SEARCY
STONE
INDEPENDENCE
JACKSON
CRAWFORD
FRANKLIN
JOHNSON
POPE
VAN BUREN
CLEBURNE
WHITE
WOODRUFF
CROSS
CRITTENDEN
SEBASTIAN
LOGAN
YELL
CONWAY
FAULKNER
PERRY
LONOKE
PRAIRIE
MONROE
ST. FRANCIS
LEE
PHILLIPS
SCOTT
POLK
MONTGOMERY
GARLAND
SALINE
PULASKI
JEFFERSON
ARKANSAS
HOT SPRING
GRANT
DALLAS
CLEVELAND
LINCOLN
DESHA
DREW
HOWARD
PIKE
CLARK
SEVIER
LITTLE RIVER
HEMPSTEAD
NEVADA
OUACHITA
CALHOUN
BRADLEY
ASHLEY
CHICOT
MILLER
LAFAYETTE
COLUMBIA
UNION
Little Rock
Fayetteville
Ft. Smith
Hot Springs
Pine Bluff
Texarkana
El Dorado
Jonesboro
Memphis
Longitude West of Greenwich
© Copyright HAMMOND INCORPORATED, Maplewood, N.J.

U.S. citizen; resident of state 50 days; registered. **U.S. Congressmen:** 5. **Entered Union:** 1912 (48th state).

**Location & boundaries:** Southwestern state: bounded on the north by Utah; on the east by New Mexico; & on the south by Mexico; & on the west by Baja California (Mexico), the Colorado River, California & Nevada. **Total area:** 114,000 sq. mi. (ranks 6th). **Extreme length:** 395 mi. **Extreme breadth:** 340 mi. **Chief rivers:** Colorado, Little Colorado, Gila. **Major lakes:** Mohave, Theodore Roosevelt, Lake Mead. **No. of counties:** 14.

**Population (1980 census):** 2,718,425 (ranks 29th). **Pop. increase (1970-80):** 53.1%. **Largest cities:** Phoenix, Tucson, Mesa, Tempe. **Pop. density:** 23.8 per sq. mi. (ranks 40th). **Pop. distribution: White**—2,240,033; **Black**—75,034; **Am. Indian, Eskimo and Aleut**—152,857; **Asian and Pacific Islander**—22,098; **Other**—227,844; **Spanish origin**—440,915. **Marriage rate (1979):** 12.1 per 1,000 people. **Divorce rate:** 8.2 per 1,000 people.

**State finances (1980). Revenue:** $3,187,000,000. **Expenditures:** $2,637,000,000. **State Taxes:** $619.72 per capita. **State personal income tax:** Yes. **Public debt (1980):** $34.59 per capita. **Federal aid (1980):** $302.75 per capita. **Personal income (1981):** $9,693.

**Sectors of the economy (% of labor force employed in 1974):** Wholesale & retail trade (21%), Government (19%), Services (15%), Manufacturing (14%), Educational Services (8%), Construction (7%). **Leading products:** electrical & other machinery; transportation equipment; food; primary metals; printing & publishing; stone, clay & glass products. **Minerals:** copper, sand & gravel, molybdenum, silver, cement. **Agricultural products:** cattle, dairy products, cotton lint, hay, lettuce. **Avg. farm (1981):** 5,465 acres. **Avg. value of farm per acre:** $282.

**Highway expenditures per capita (1980):** $124.03. **Persons per motor vehicle (1981):** 1.33. **Minimum age for driver's license:** 16. **Gasoline tax:** 10¢ per gallon. **Diesel tax:** 10¢ per gallon. **Motor vehicle deaths (1980):** 34.8 per 100,000 people.

**Birthrate (1979):** 19.1 per 1,000 people. **Infant mortality rate per 1,000 births (1978):** 13.1. **Physicians per 100,000 pop. (1979):** 187. **Dentists per 100,000 pop. (1979):** 49. **Acceptable hospital beds (1979):** 4.3 per 1,000 people. **State expenditures per capita for health and hospitals (1980):** $57.41.

**Education expenditures (1977-78):** $581.28 per capita annually. **No. of pupils in public schools (1980):** 510,000. **No. of institutions of higher learning (1978-79):** 23. **Public school expenditure per pupil in attendance (1978-79):** $1,720. **Avg. salary of public school teachers (1979-80):** $18,200. **No. full-time teachers (1980):** 29,000. **Educational attainment of adult population (1976):** 12.6 median yrs. of school completed: 3.3% with less than 5 years of education; 15.7% with 4 yrs. of college.

**Telephones (1979):** 53 per 100 people. **State Chamber of Commerce:** Arizona Chamber of Commerce, 3216 N. Third Street, Suite 103, Phoenix, Arizona 85012.

## ARKANSAS

Gracing the Arkansas terrain are rugged hills, scenic valleys and streams, and impressive hardwood and pine forests. In the south and east are the generally flat West Gulf Coastal and Mississippi Alluvial Plains, while highlands make up the northwestern region. Magazine Mountain (2,853 feet) is the state's highest point. About three-fifths of the land is wooded, forming the basis for a sizable timber industry. Resources include two large national forests, the Ozark and Ouachita.

Arkansas ranks among the national leaders in cotton, rice, soybean and livestock production; it also contains one of the world's most famous spas (Hot Springs), as well as North America's first diamond mine, near Murfreesboro. No longer commercially operative, the mine is today a state park, popular among tourists; anyone finding a diamond there (up to five carats) is allowed to keep it. Another tourist attraction is the old health resort town of Eureka Springs in the Ozark region of northwestern Arkansas. Excellent hunting and fishing also contribute to the state's increasingly significant tourism business as do such attractions as the Old Arsenal in Little Rock's MacArthur Park, which marks the birthplace of one of the most famous of Arkansans, General Douglas MacArthur.

The production of oil, the state's major mineral, is another important element in the economy. Arkansas is the nation's chief producer of bauxite ore, from which aluminum is extracted. A further vital asset is an abundant water supply, convertible to hydroelectric power. A modern navigational system on the Arkansas River connects the Gulf of Mexico and Little Rock, now a foreign trade zone, the 14th such zone established in the United States, and the only one on an inland waterway.

The so-called Bluff Dwellers of about A.D. 500 are considered to have been the first inhabitants of the Arkansas region, followed by the culturally superior Mound Builders and, later, by Quapaw, Osage, and Caddo Indians.

The first Europeans to visit (1541) the area were Spanish explorers led by Hernando De Soto. Frenchmen arrived more than a century later: Marquette and Jolliet exploring (1673) the land around the mouth of the Arkansas River, and La Salle claiming (1682) for France the Arkansas region and the rest of the Mississippi Valley. In 1686, Henri de Tonti established Arkansas Post, the first permanent settlement. The United States obtained all of what is now Arkansas as part of the Louisiana Purchase (1803).

Much of the region's early history is shared with Louisiana, of which it was a part until 1812, when it was attached to the Territory of Missouri. Settlement was spurred by the cotton boom of 1818, and a year later Arkansas Territory, incorporating part of present-day Oklahoma, was created. The 1830s saw the emergence of the slavery-supported plantation system as the state's primary economic force. The virtual absence of Indian troubles encouraged immigration, and between 1830 and 1840 population tripled.

Statehood came (1836) at a time when the slavery issue was more and more seriously dividing the nation. In March 1861, the Arkansas convention voted to remain in the Union, but when President Lincoln asked for troops, the state refused and two months later decided to secede. Many relatively small battles were fought in the state, and from 1864-65 there existed two separate state governments: one at Little Rock controlled by the Union and a Confederate one at Washington, Arkansas. Recovery in the postwar period was slow in coming, and not helped by the violence-engendering struggle (1872-74) for the governorship between Republicans Elisha Baxter and Joseph Brooks, a struggle won by Baxter only after Presidential intervention.

On the cultural scene, the Arkansas Arts Center in Little Rock offers exhibits, plays, and classes in painting, sculpture, dance, photography, music and drama. The Arkansas Symphony Orchestra was established in 1966.

In addition to a fine public school system, there is the Arkansas School for the Deaf, established about 1866 as the Arkansas Deaf-Mute Institute, and the Arkansas School for the Blind. Arkansas Enterprises for the Blind opened in 1947 a rehabilitation center providing personal adjustment, pre-vocational and vocational training for the blind and visually impaired. It has served persons from the fifty states and over twenty-four foreign countries.

In 1966 the state made political history by electing a transplanted New Yorker, Winthrop Rockefeller (now deceased), governor on the Republican ticket, climaxing a six-year effort on his part to

CALIFORNIA
MILES
0 40 80 120
KILOMETERS
0 40 80 120
State Capitals County Seats
Longitude West of Greenwich
124° 122° 120° 118° 116°
42° 40° 38° 36° 34° 32°
Counties indicated by numbers:
1 ALAMEDA
2 AMADOR
3 CALAVERAS
4 CONTRA COSTA
5 LAKE
6 MARIN
7 MERCED
8 NAPA
9 ORANGE
10 SACRAMENTO
11 SAN FRANCISCO
12 SAN JOAQUIN
13 SOLANO
14 STANISLAUS
15 SUTTER
16 YUBA
SAN FRANCISCO AND VICINITY
0 10 20 mi.
0 10 20 km.
MARIN
SOLANO
CONTRA COSTA
ALAMEDA
SAN MATEO
SANTA CLARA
PT. REYES NAT'L SEASHORE
MUIR WOODS N.M.
GOLDEN GATE NAT'L REC. AREA
San Pablo Bay
Vallejo
Collinsville
Pittsburg
Antioch
Oakley
Martinez
Rodeo
Novato
San Anselmo
San Rafael
Mill Valley
Richmond
El Cerrito
Albany
Berkeley
Piedmont
Oakland
Alameda
San Pablo
Cogcord
Pleasant Hill
Walnut Creek
Brentwood
San Leandro
Castro Valley
Livermore
Pleasanton
Hayward
Fremont
Newark
Menlo Park
Palo Alto
Mountain View
Sunnyvale
San Jose
Alum Rock
Sta. Clara
Los Altos
Redwood City
San Carlos
San Mateo
Burlingame
San Bruno
Millbrae
Pacifica
S. San Francisco
Daly City
SAN FRANCISCO
Pillar Pt.
Half Moon Bay
PACIFIC OCEAN
LOS ANGELES AND VICINITY
0 10 20 mi.
0 10 20 km.
LOS ANGELES
ORANGE
RIVERSIDE
Santa Susana
San Fernando
Thousand Oaks
Van Nuys
Burbank
Glendale
Mt. Wilson
Pasadena
Arcadia
Monrovia
Hollywood
Beverly Hills
Alhambra
W. Covina
Upland
Ontario
Pomona
Santa Monica
Sta. Monica B.
Inglewood
S. Gate
Pico Rivera
Whittier
Downey
Norwalk
Hawthorne
Compton
Manhattan Beach
Redondo Beach
Torrance
Gardena
Carson
Lakewood
Long Beach
San Pedro Bay
Huntington Beach
Fullerton
Anaheim
Buena Park
Corona
Orange
Santa Ana
Garden Grove
Costa Mesa
El Toro
Irvine
Newport Beach
Laguna Beach
© Copyright HAMMOND INCORPORATED
CRATER LAKE NAT'L PK.
OREGON
OREGON CAVES N.M.
Medford
Rogue R.
DEL NORTE
Happy Camp
Crescent City
REDWOOD NAT'L PK.
Klamath
Orick
Orleans
HOOPA VALLEY I.R.
Hoopa
HUMBOLDT
Arcata
Eureka
Fortuna
Rohnerville
Rio Dell
Ferndale
C. Mendocino
Garberville
SISKIYOU
Yreka
Montague
Dorris
Tulelake
LAVA BEDS N.M.
Clear Lake Res.
Goose L.
Alturas
Cedarville
Weed
Mt. Shasta 14,162
Mt. Shasta
McCloud
Dunsmuir
Canby
MODOC
Pondosa
Adin
SHASTA
Clair Engle L.
Shasta L.
SHASTA DAM
Salyer
Weaverville
TRINITY
Central Valley
Project City
Hayfork
Redding
Anderson
Burney
LASSEN
LASSEN VOLCANIC NAT'L PK.
Lassen Pk. 10,457
Eagle L.
Susanville
Chester
Westwood
Honey L.
Red Bluff
TEHAMA
Greenville
Herlong
ROUND VALLEY IND. RES.
Corning
Black Butte Res.
Keddie
Quincy
PLUMAS
Portola
Pyramid L.
PYRAMID LAKE IND. RES.
MENDOCINO
Fort Bragg
Willits
GLENN
Orland
Chico
Mulberry
Paradise
BUTTE
Oroville
Downieville
SIERRA
Mendocino
Willows
Potter Valley
Ukiah
Colusa
Williams
COLUSA
Marysville
S. Oroville
NEVADA
Truckee
Reno
Nevada City
Grass Valley
Carson City
Pt. Arena
Hopland
Clear L.
Lakeport
Yuba City
Linda
PLACER
Tahoe City
L. Tahoe
SONOMA
Cloverdale
Healdsburg
Calistoga
YOLO
Woodland
Auburn
Roseville
EL DORADO
Placerville
S. Lake Tahoe
Guerneville
Santa Rosa
St. Helena
Winters
Folsom
Sacramento
Markleeville
ALPINE
Bodega B.
PT. REYES NAT'L SEASHORE
Petaluma
Napa
Vacaville
Fairfield
Jackson
Novato
Sonoma
Vallejo
Galt
Lodi
San Andreas
Bridgeport
Pt. Reyes
San Rafael
Golden Gate
Martinez
Berkeley
Oakland
TUOLUMNE
Stockton
Manteca
Sonora
Mono L.
NEVADA
YOSEMITE NAT'L PARK
Lee Vining
MONO
SAN FRANCISCO
San Mateo
Redwood City
SAN MATEO
Tracy
Oakdale
Modesto
Hughson
MARIPOSA
DEVILS POSTPILE N.M.
Santa Clara
San Jose
Los Gatos
SANTA CRUZ
SANTA CLARA
Turlock
Atwater
Merced
Mariposa
PAIUTE IND. RES.
Bishop
Santa Cruz
Watsonville
Los Banos
Dos Palos
Chowchilla
MADERA
North Fork
Big Pine
Monterey B.
Hollister
SAN BENITO
Madera
Firebaugh
KINGS CANYON NAT'L PARK
Seaside
Salinas
Mendota
Clovis
Fresno
Independence
Pacific Grove
Carmel
Monterey
Soledad
PINNACLES NAT'L MON.
Kerman
Sanger
Selma
SEQUOIA NAT'L PARK
Mt. Whitney 14,494
Lone Pine
Owens L.
MONTEREY
King City
Hanford
Dinuba
Visalia
INYO MTS.
DEATH VALLEY
PANAMINT RA.
DEATH VALLEY NAT'L MON.
DEATH VALLEY N.M. (Devil's Hole)
Lowest Pt. in N. A. 282 Ft. Below Sea Level
Las Vegas
Lake Mead
HOOVER DAM
Boulder City
Coalinga
Tulare
Lindsay
Corcoran
Porterville
Tulare L.
TULE R. I. R.
INYO
Avenal
KINGS
Delano
TULARE
Trona
Shoshone
Tecopa
LAKE MEAD NAT'L RECREATION AREA
Lake Mohave
Paso Robles
SAN LUIS OBISPO
Morro Bay
Estero B.
Pt. Buchon
Atascadero
San Luis Obispo
Arroyo Grande
Grover City
Guadalupe
KERN
McFarland
Wasco
Shafter
Oildale
Bakersfield
Lamont
Arvin
Buena Vista L.
Ford City
Taft
China Lake
Ridgecrest
SAN BERNARDINO
FORT IRWIN
Baker
Cima
DAVIS DAM
Kelso
Tehachapi
Mojave
Los Angeles Aqueduct
EDWARDS A.F.B.
MOJAVE DESERT
Mojave R.
Barstow
FT. MOHAVE IND. RES.
Needles
Santa Maria
Orcutt
VANDENBERG A.F.B.
SANTA BARBARA
Lompoc
VENTURA
Lancaster
Quartz Hill
Pt. Arguello
Pt. Conception
Isla Vista
Santa Barbara
Sta. Barbara Chan.
Montecito
Fillmore
Sta. Paula
Ventura
Oxnard
Pt. Hueneme
Palmdale
LOS ANGELES
Newhall
Adelanto
GEORGE A.F.B.
Victorville
TWENTYNINE PALMS MARINE BASE
Amboy
Essex
ARIZONA
Havasu L.
CHEMEHUEVI VALLEY IND. RES.
Parker Dam
San Miguel I.
Santa Rosa I.
Sta. Cruz I.
CHAN. IS. NAT'L PARK
SANTA BARBARA IS.
LOS ANGELES
Glendale
Pasadena
Santa Monica
Torrance
Long Beach
Pomona
San Bernardino
Highland
Redlands
Yucaipa
Twentynine Palms
JOSHUA TREE NAT'L MON.
Desert Hot Springs
Anaheim
Riverside
Corona
Santa Ana
Banning
Palm Sprs.
Indio
Coachella
Hemet
RIVERSIDE
Laguna Beach
San Pedro Chan.
Santa Catalina I.
San Clemente
CAMP PENDLETON
Mt. Palomar 6,140
Salton Sea
Colorado R.
COLORADO RIVER IND. RES.
Blythe
San Nicolas I.
Gulf of Sta. Catalina
Oceanside
Vista
Leucadia
Escondido
SAN DIEGO
IMPERIAL
IMPERIAL VALLEY
Calipatria
Westmorland
Brawley
Imperial Res.
San Clemente I.
La Jolla
Pacific Beach
SAN DIEGO
Coronado
Imperial Beach
La Mesa
El Cajon
National City
Chula Vista
CAMPO I. R.
El Centro
IMPERIAL DAM
YUMA I. R.
Yuma
Calexico
Mexicali
Tijuana
BAJA CALIFORNIA
Laguna Salada
MEXICO
PACIFIC OCEAN

build a two-party system in this traditionally Democratic state. Rockefeller served two terms, but lost to a political unknown, Dale Bumpers, in a third term bid in 1970.

In November 1978, Pine Bluff was chosen for the location of a proposed nerve gas plant. According to the plan, production of nerve gas shells and bombs probably would not begin before 1982.

In May and June 1980 thousands of Cuban refugees were housed at Fort Chaffee near Barling. On two occasions rioting broke out and scores of Cubans escaped temporarily into the surrounding area. The refugees were resettled throughout the nation during 1981.

**Full name:** State of Arkansas. **Origin of name:** From Algonquian name of the Quapaw Indians. **Inhabitant:** Arkansan. **Capital:** Little Rock. **State motto:** Regnat Populus (The People Rule). **Flag:** Star-studded blue & white diamond on a red field; diamond shape represents Arkansas, the only diamond-producing state. **Seal:** Shield design has steamboat, plow, beehive & sheaf of wheat, symbolizing industry & agriculture; angel of mercy & sword of justice guard American eagle; goddess of liberty stands above. **Flower:** Apple blossom. **Bird:** Mockingbird. **Tree:** Pine. **Song:** "Arkansas." **Nickname:** Land of Opportunity.

**Governor:** Frank D. White. **Annual salary:** $35,000. **Term:** 2 years. **Current term expires:** Jan. 1983. **Voting requirements:** 18 yrs. old & U.S. citizen; registered in county of residence. **U.S. Congressmen:** 4. **Entered Union:** 1836 (25th state).

**Location & boundaries:** South Central state: bounded on the north by Missouri; on the east by the Mississippi River & the states of Missouri, Tennessee & Mississippi; on the south by Louisiana; & on the west by Texas & Oklahoma. **Total area:** 53,187 sq. mi. (ranks 27th). **Extreme length:** 275 mi. **Extreme breadth:** 240 mi. **Chief rivers:** Mississippi, Arkansas, Ouachita, White. **Major lakes:** Bull Shoals, Ouachita, Beaver, Norfork. **No. of counties:** 75.

**Population (1980 census):** 2,286,435 (ranks 33rd). **Pop. increase (1970-80):** 18.9%. **Largest cities:** Little Rock, Fort Smith, N. Little Rock, Pine Bluff. **Pop. density:** 43.0 per sq. mi. (ranks 35th). **Pop. distribution: White**—1,890,002; **Black**—373,192; **Am. Indian, Eskimo and Aleut**—9,411; **Asian and Pacific Islander**—6,732; **Other**—6,176; **Spanish origin**—17,873. **Marriage rate (1979):** 11.9 per 1,000 people. **Divorce rate:** 9.3 per 1,000 people.

**State finances (1980). Revenue:** $2,295,000,000. **Expenditures:** $2,148,000,000. **State taxes:** $507.99 per capita. **State personal income tax:** Yes. **Public debt (1980):** $158.68 per capita. **Federal aid (1980):** $408.80 per capita. **Personal income (1981):** $8,042.

**Sectors of the economy (% of labor force employed in 1970):** Manufacturing (26%), Wholesale and retail trade (19%), Government (15%), Services (8%), Educational Services (8%), Construction (7%). **Leading products:** food, lumber & wood, paper products, electrical machinery, chemicals, furniture & fixtures, apparel. **Minerals:** petroleum, natural gas, bauxite, stone, bromine, sand & gravel. **Agricultural products:** broilers, cattle, eggs, soybeans, rice, cotton lint. **Avg. farm (1981):** 280 acres. **Avg. value of farm per acre:** $1,061.

**Highway expenditures per capita (1980):** $164.75. **Persons per motor vehicle (1981):** 1.40. **Minimum age for driver's license:** 16. **Gasoline tax:** 9.5¢ per gallon. **Diesel tax:** 10.5¢ per gallon. **Motor vehicle deaths (1980):** 25.7 per 100,000 people.

**Birthrate (1979):** 16.7 per 1,000 people. **Infant mortality rate per 1,000 births (1978):** 10.5. **Physicians per 100,000 pop. (1979):** 119. **Dentists per 100,000 pop. (1979):** 33. **Acceptable hospital beds (1979):** 5.6 per 1,000 people. **State expenditures per capita for health and hospitals (1980):** $61.28.

**Education expenditures (1977-78):** $374.28 per capita annually. **No. of pupils in public schools (1980):** 450,000. **No. of institutions of higher learning (1978-79):** 34. **Public school expenditure per pupil in attendance (1978-79):** $1,348. **Avg. salary of public school teachers (1979-80):** $12,783. **No. full-time teachers (1980):** 25,500. **Educational attainment of adult population (1976):** 12.2 median yrs. of school completed: 6.0% with less than 5 years of education; 9.1% with 4 yrs. of college.

**Telephones (1979):** 47 per 100 people. **State Chamber of Commerce:** Arkansas State Chamber of Commerce, 911 Wallace Building, Little Rock, Arkansas 72201.

## CALIFORNIA

California, the most populous of the states, is the national leader in agriculture, commercial fishing, and motor vehicle ownership. It ranks first in manufacturing and third in land area and oil production.

The heart of the state is the fertile Central Valley, fenced in by two long north-south mountain ranges: the Sierra Nevada (on the east) and the Coast Range. Several small forested ranges of the Klamath Mountains cover the northwestern corner of the state, while below the Coast Range are the Los Angeles Ranges, and below these, the San Diego Ranges. More than 40 percent of the land is forested. Other important land areas are the Cascade Mountains extending northward from the Central Valley and the Basin and Range Region of the southeast and extreme northeast; within the southeastern part of this region are the Mojave and Colorado deserts.

Both the highest mountain peak in the conterminous United States, Mt. Whitney (14,494 feet) and the lowest point in the hemisphere (282 feet below sea level) can be seen from Dante's View, 5,475 feet high and about 3 miles east of that lowest point. Two island groups lie off the coast: the Santa Barbara (or Channel) Islands, consisting of eight major islands 20 to 60 miles from the southern mainland, and the six small rugged Farallon Islands, about 30 miles west of San Francisco. California's main harbors are San Francisco and San Diego Bays and the man-made Los Angeles harbor, San Pedro Bay. Great extremes mark the climate, with many areas enjoying generally mild and sunny weather, partially befouled in urban areas by palls of smog.

There were about 130,000 Indians living in the California region when Juan Rodriguez Cabrillo, a Portuguese in Spanish employ, discovered it in 1542. English interest in the area began with Sir Francis Drake, who claimed (1579) it for Queen Elizabeth I, but the first permanent European settlement was made by Spaaniards, who established 21 missions northward along the coast from San Diego (1769) to Sonoma (1823). In 1812, Russian fur-traders from Alaska came down and established Fort Ross on the state's northern coast, but they did not prevail. In 1822, after Mexico won its independence from Spain, California became a Mexican province, and its social, economic, and political life was centered around large cattle ranches. The first organized group of American settlers came to the region by land in 1841; the United States offered to buy the province, but Mexico refused to sell. U.S. forces occupied the area early in the Mexican War, with Mexico formally ceding its claims in 1848.

Less than two weeks before the treaty was signed, an event of massive importance occurred at John A. Sutter's sawmill near Coloma: the discovery of gold, which set off the famous Gold Rush of '49. In the following seven years, the region produced $450 million worth of gold, while the population jumped from about 15,000 to almost 300,000. This influx virtually secured American possession of the territory. San Francisco, for example, grew from an outpost to a great city, in a turbulent, often lawless, atmosphere. Vigilante groups filled the "law-and-order" gap until more stable government was established, beginning with admission of California into the Union as a free state, under terms of the Compromise of 1850. Meanwhile, California's mountain-walled isolation was rapidly ending: the telegraph reached the area in 1861, and

COLORADO
MILES
KILOMETERS
State Capitals
County Seats
Longitude West of Greenwich
© Copyright HAMMOND INCORPORATED, Maplewood, N.J.

eight years later direct rail connection was made with the rest of the country.

The late 19th and early 20th centuries were marked by continued population growth, soaring land values, and economic-rooted social tensions between American-born Californians, Mexican-Americans and Oriental immigrants. Manufacturing, especially the canning and packing of food, increased greatly; and Hollywood became the world motion picture capital.

More recently, defense-contract industries, electronics and senior citizen retirement communities have played particularly large roles in the state's economy. Tourist attractions include Disneyland (in Anaheim), San Francisco's Golden Gate Bridge, scenic Lake Tahoe on the Nevada border, the Napa Valley wine-producing district, the Monterey-Carmel area with its renowned Seventeen Mile Drive, William Randolph Hearst's estate at San Simeon, the coastal highway between Big Sur and Morro Bay, 17 national forests, six national parks, and many scenic beaches.

With 20 million residents in 1970, California overtook New York as the most populous state. The 1980 census reported a population of 23,667,565, representing an increase of eighteen and a half percent for the decade. As a result, California has gained two additional seats in the U.S. House of Representatives.

During the 1960s, California's migrant farm workers, mostly Mexican-Americans, were organized by the United Farm Workers Organizing Committee (the union is now the United Farm Workers of America). The long, and sometimes bitterly resisted struggle was led by Cesar Chavez. In the mid-1970s, the United Farm Workers competed for worker loyalty with the Teamsters Union. The two groups settled their dispute in 1977 with a five-year agreement.

In the spring of 1978 a taxpayers' revolt against heavy government spending and high tax rates culminated in the adoption, by 65% of the vote, of Proposal 13, a state constitutional amendment andating a 57% reduction in property taxes, and limiting the authority of state and local governments to raise taxes. No drastic reduction in government services followed initially—largely because the state was able to divide a huge surplus with local governments. In 1980, however, California voters rejected by a 3-2 margin another initiative (Proposition 9) which sought to reduce state income tax rates by half. Howard Jarvis, author of both propositions, has suggested he would continue his efforts in this matter by mounting an assault on state pension funds. In 1982 voters limited income tax increases to the inflation rate.

In the early summer of 1981 an infestation of the Mediterranean fruit fly appeared in Santa Clara County. During August the "Medfly," which is extremely destructive to fruit crops, spread to the Central Valley despite aerial spraying with insecticides and the destruction of infected fruit.

**Full name:** State of California. **Origin of name:** From an imaginary island in a 16th-century Spanish romance. **Inhabitant:** Californian. **Capital:** Sacramento. **State motto:** Eureka (I Have Found It). **Flag:** a bear & a red star on white field with red horizontal bar at the bottom. **Seal:** Grizzly bear stands near seated figure of Minerva; a miner, ships & peaks of Sierra Nevada in background; state motto. **Flower:** Golden poppy. **Bird:** California Valley quail. **Tree:** California redwood. **Song:** "I Love You, California." **Nickname:** Golden State.

**Governor:** Edmund G. Brown, Jr. **Annual salary:** $49,100. **Term:** 4 years. **Current term expires:** Jan. 1983. **Voting requirements:** 18 yrs. old & U.S. citizen; state resident 29 days. **U.S. Congressmen:** 45. **Entered Union:** 1850 (31st state).

**Location & boundaries:** Pacific state: bounded on the north by Oregon; on the east by Nevada & Arizona; on the southeast by the Colorado River; on the south by Mexico; & on the west by the Pacific Ocean. **Total area:** 158,706 sq. mi. (ranks 3rd). **Extreme length:** 1775 mi. **Extreme breadth:** 1360 mi. **Coastline:** 1,264 mi. **Chief rivers:** Sacramento, San Joaquin, Klamath. **Major lakes:** Salton Sea, Tahoe, Goose. **No. of counties:** 58.

**Population (1980 census):** 23,667,565 (ranks 1st). **Pop. increase (1970-80):** 18.5%. **Largest cities:** Los Angeles, San Diego, San Francisco, San Jose. **Pop. density:** 149.1 per sq. mi. (ranks 14th). **Pop. distribution: White**—18,031,689; **Black**—1,819,282; **Am. Indian, Eskimo and Aleut**—201,311; **Asian and Pacific Islander**—1,253,987; **Other**—2,362,293; **Spanish origin**—4,543,770. **Marriage rate (1979):** 8.8 per 1,000 people. **Divorce rate:** 6.1 per 1,000 people.

**State finances (1980). Revenue:** $36,087,000,000. **Expenditures:** $32,812,000,000. **State taxes:** $818.23 per capita. **State personal income tax:** Yes. **Public debt (1980):** $353.28 per capita. **Federal aid (1980):** $368.56 per capita. **Personal income (1981):** $12,057.

**Sectors of the economy (% of labor force employed in 1970):** Manufacturing (22%), Wholesale and retail trade (21%), Government (18%), Services (9%), Educational Services (8%), Construction (5%). **Leading products:** transportation equipment, food, machinery, ordnance & accessories, fabricated metals, printing & publishing. **Minerals:** petroleum, natural gas, cement, sand & gravel. **Agricultural products:** cattle, dairy items, hay, tomatoes, cotton lint. **Fishing:** tuna, salmon, crabs. **Avg. farm (1981):** 423 acres. **Avg. value of farm per acre:** $1,735.

**Highway expenditures per capita (1980):** $65.52. **Persons per motor vehicle (1981):** 1.33. **Minimum age for driver's license:** 16. **Gasoline tax:** 7¢ per gallon. **Diesel tax:** 7¢ per gallon. **Motor vehicle deaths (1980):** 23.2 per 100,000 people.

**Birthrate (1979):** 16.7 per 1,000 people. **Infant mortality rate per 1,000 births (1978):** 11.8. **Physicians per 100,000 pop. (1979):** 226. **Dentists per 100,000 pop. (1979):** 63. **Acceptable hospital beds (1979):** 4.8 per 1,000 people. **State expenditures per capita for health and hospitals (1980):** $72.07.

**Education expenditures (1977-78):** $614.51 per capita annually. **No. of pupils in public schools (1980):** 3,951,000. **No. of institutions of higher learning (1978-79):** 262. **Public school expenditure per pupil in attendance (1978-79):** $2,052. **Avg. salary of public school teachers (1979-80):** $19,770. **No. full-time teachers (1980):** 212,900. **Educational attainment of adult population (1976):** 12.7 median yrs. of school completed: 3.3% with less than 5 years of education; 16.8% with 4 yrs. of college.

**Telephones (1979):** 61 per 100 people. **State Chamber of Commerce:** California Chamber of Commerce, 1027 10th Street, P.O. Box 1736, Sacramento, California 95808.

## COLORADO

Colorado, the Centennial State, is the state with the highest overall elevation; it has more than 1,000 peaks that soar at least 10,000 feet, including legendary Pikes Peak. In the east are the high plains, while the Rockies' peaks and ranges make up the central region; and in the west is the Colorado Plateau. The Continental Divide runs generally north and south through the west-central part of the state. As is typical of mountainous areas, there are great extremes of climate, yet a surprisingly diverse agriculture.

This state is part of the *real* Old West, not the West of romanticized Westerns. Ruthlessly competitive gold mining (starting in 1858) and silver mining (1875) and the decades-long wresting of crops from the arid land shaped Colorado and defined its character.

Many metals are mined in the mountains. Molybdenum, which hardens steel and is used in rocketry, is the state's most valuable: Colorado holds over half of the world's supply. Oil shale is the state's most important undeveloped resource.

Food and machinery are the state's two main industries. Only California has more irrigated

CONNECTICUT
MASSACHUSETTS
RHODE ISLAND
NEW YORK
LITCHFIELD
HARTFORD
TOLLAND
WINDHAM
NEW LONDON
MIDDLESEX
NEW HAVEN
FAIRFIELD
LONG ISLAND SOUND
LONG ISLAND
ATLANTIC OCEAN
TACONIC MTS.
Hartford
New Haven
Bridgeport
Waterbury
Stamford
Norwalk
New London
Norwich
Middletown
Meriden
New Britain
Bristol
Danbury
Torrington
Manchester
Willimantic
Greenwich
Stratford
Milford
Mt. Frissell 2,380
Mohawk Mtn. 1,682
Bear Hill 1,281
Connecticut R.
Housatonic River
Thames R.
Naugatuck River
Fishers I.
Gardiners I.
Plum I.
The Race
MILES
KILOMETERS
State Capital
Longitude West of Greenwich
© Copyright HAMMOND INCORPORATED, Maplewood, N.J.

acreage; however, two-thirds of Colorado's farm output consists of livestock and livestock products. It leads in the refining of beet sugar.

Cliff-dwelling Indians are believed to have built (c. A.D. 100) Colorado's first civilization in the Mesa Verde plateau, which lies in the southwest corner of the state; they carved irrigation ditches and built many-storied pueblos.

In the 1500s, Spanish explorers became the first Europeans to visit the region but, not finding gold, they did not stay. The United States got the eastern and central areas of Colorado as part of the Louisiana Purchase and the western part as a result of the Mexican War.

The gold rush of the late 1850s was followed by the Civil War. With fewer Federal troops in the area, the intense fighting between whites and the Arapaho and Cheyenne Indians posed the very real threat of general lawlessness.

The establishment (1861) of the Colorado Territory was a step toward unity and stability, and the advent of the railroads in the 1870s was another. Statehood came in 1876. This was the era in which the New York journalist Horace Greeley sponsored a Colorado farming colony and advised, "Go West, young man!"

The 1880s brought fiscal health and early growth as a state, but trouble and renewed bloodshed characterized the next decade.

Silver prices dropped badly after the repeal of the Sherman Silver Purchase Act (1893), and many great mines closed, leaving behind ghost towns with colorful names such as Cripple Creek and Eureka. Range warfare was rife, and bitter hassles took place over railway franchises. Long-simmering labor-management conflict came to a head in 1914 in a battle near Trinidad between striking coal miners and the militia in which innocent women and children were killed. Subsequent reforms included regular government inspection of mines.

The state's economy advanced sharply after both World Wars. In between were more years of struggle: the great Wall Street fiasco of 1929 was accompanied, in Colorado, by drought and high winds which created a disastrous dust bowl.

Today, Colorado is prosperous. Denver is an important business center, missile-plant site, and headquarters for Federal agencies. In addition, U.S. coins are minted there, while the National Bureau of Standards laboratory at Boulder has expanded greatly in recent years. Scientists at an observation station near Climax are studying the earth's atmosphere and conducting space research.

Because of the state's magnificent scenery, tourism has developed into a major industry. Tourist attractions include Rocky Mountain and Mesa Verde National Parks, a dozen national forests, hunting and fishing, Balanced Rock in the Garden of the Gods, Royal Gorge on the Arkansas River, the ski center of Vail, Buffalo Bill's Grave on Lookout Mountain, and cultural festivals at Aspen and Central City.

The U..S. Air Force Academy, founded in 1958, is located at Colorado Springs. In 1976 the academy admitted the first female cadets.

Exxon's giant shale oil project near Parachute was discontinued in May 1982. Work on the smaller Union Oil Company shale oil project continues as the only remaining active synfuels development in the state.

**Full name:** State of Colorado. **Origin of name:** From Spanish for "Colored Red." **Inhabitant:** Coloradan. **Capital:** Denver. **State motto:** Nil Sine Numine (Nothing Without Providence). **Flag:** A red letter C encloses gold ball & rests against blue, white & blue bars. **Seal:** A triangular figure, representing "all seeing" eye of God, bound rods, three mountains & pick & hammer. **Flower:** Rocky Mountain columbine. **Bird:** Lark bunting. **Tree:** Blue spruce. **Song:** "Where the Columbines Grow." **Nickname:** Centennial State.

**Governor:** Richard D. Lamm. **Annual salary:** $50,000. **Term:** 4 years. **Current term expires:** Jan. 1983. **Voting requirements:** 18 yrs. old & U.S. citizen; resident of state and precinct, 32 days. **U.S. Congressmen:** 6. **Entered Union:** 1876 (38th state).

**Location & boundaries:** Rocky Mountain state: bounded on the north by Wyoming & Nebraska; on the east by Nebraska & Kansas; on the south by Oklahoma & New Mexico; & on the west by Utah. **Total area:** 104,091 sq. mi. (ranks 8th). **Extreme length:** 387 mi. **Extreme breadth:** 276 mi. **Chief rivers:** Colorado, Arkansas, South Platte, Rio Grande. **Major lakes:** Blue Mesa, Dillon, John Martin, Granby. **No. of counties:** 63.

**Population (1980 census):** 2,889,735 (ranks 28th). **Pop. increase (1970-80):** 30.8%. **Largest cities:** Denver, Colorado Springs, Aurora, Lakewood. **Pop. density:** 27.8 per sq. mi. (ranks 38th). **Pop. distribution: White**—2,570,615; **Black**—101,702; **Am. Indian, Eskimo and Aleut**—18,059; **Asian and Pacific Islander**—29,897; **Other**—168,561; **Spanish origin**—339,300. **Marriage rate (1979):** 11.8 per 1,000 people. **Divorce rate:** 6.0 per 1,000 people.

**State finances (1980). Revenue:** $3,366,000,000. **Expenditures:** $2,805,000,000. **State taxes:** $516.06 per capita. **State personal income tax:** Yes. **Public debt (1980):** $159.40 per capita. **Federal aid (1980):** $334.04 per capita. **Personal income (1981):** $11,142.

**Sectors of the economy (% of labor force employed in 1970):** Wholesale and retail trade (22%), Government (20%), Manufacturing (15%), Educational Services (10%), Services (8%), Construction (7%). **Leading products:** food; machinery; transportation equipment; electrical equipment; printing & publishing; stone, clay & glass items; fabricated metals; chemicals; lumber. **Minerals:** molybdenum, petroleum, coal, sand & gravel. **Agricultural products:** cattle, hay, dairy items, wheat, sugar beets, sheep. **Avg. farm (1981):** 1,377 acres. **Avg. value of farm per acre:** $412.

**Highway expenditures per capita (1980):** $116.16. **Persons per motor vehicle (1981):** 1.22. **Minimum age for driver's license:** 21. **Gasoline tax:** 9¢ per gallon. **Diesel tax:** 9¢ per gallon. **Motor vehicle deaths (1980):** 24.5 per 100,000 people.

**Birthrate (1979):** 17.0 per 1,000 people. **Infant mortality rate per 1,000 births (1978):** 11.2. **Physicians per 100,000 pop. (1979):** 199. **Dentists per 100,000 pop. (1979):** 61. **Acceptable hospital beds (1979):** 5.2 per 1,000 people. **State expenditures per capita for health and hospitals (1980):** $121.15.

**Education expenditures (1977-78):** $596.97 per capita annually. **No. of pupils in public schools (1980):** 543,000. **No. of institutions of higher learning (1978-79):** 41. **Public school expenditure per pupil in attendance (1978-79):** $2,205. **Avg. salary of public school teachers (1979-80):** $16,400. **No. full-time teachers (1980):** 32,300. **Educational attainment of adult population (1976):** 12.8 median yrs. of school completed: 1.3% with less than 5 years of education; 19.4% with 4 yrs. of college.

**Telephones (1979):** 57 per 100 people. **State Chamber of Commerce:** Colorado Association of Commerce and Industry, 1390 Logan Street, Suite 308, Denver, Colorado 80203.

## CONNECTICUT

Connecticut, one of the smallest states in area, is one of the most varied and most prosperous. Generally rectangular in shape, the state is divided by the Connecticut River and its fertile valley into two almost equal regions. Gently rolling hills rise from the southern coastal plain to an average elevation of about 1,000 feet at the northern boundary.

Highly industrialized cities contrast with the scenic, typically New England countryside, 60 percent of which is forested. The southern shore has a number of excellent harbors, and several small islands lie off the coast. The southern section, particularly Fairfield County, is home for many who work in New York City.

Among Connecticut's attractions are Yale University at New Haven, the American Dance Festival at Connecticut College in New London, and this hemisphere's first school for the deaf, at Hartford.

About 7,000 members of the Algonquian Indian family were living in Connecticut before the Europeans came; of these, the Pequot were most powerful. Uncas, chief of the Mohican branch of the Pequots, was immortalized by James Fenimore Cooper in *The Last of the Mohicans*. Relations between the Indians and early settlers were mostly friendly, except for the brief Pequot War (1637) and the more serious King Philip's War (1675-76).

Dutch navigator Adriaen Block was the first European of record to visit the state (1614), sailing up the Connecticut River. In 1633, colonists from Holland set up a trading post (near present-day Hartford), but the Dutch lost control of the area to the English; Puritans from the Massachusetts Bay Colony established the first permanent settlement at the site of modern Windsor that same year, and another at Wethersfield in 1634. English settlements at Hartford and Saybrook began in 1635, and representatives of the three "River Towns" of Windsor, Wethersfield, and Hartford united to form the Connecticut Colony and adopt (1639) the "Fundamental Orders" that gave citizens the right to elect government officials and omitted the religious test for citizenship; the document thus anticipated the U.S. Constitution and is considered the world's first written constitution.

Meanwhile, a wholly new colony came into being with the establishment of New Haven (1638) and other communities in the southern part of Connecticut; called the New Haven Colony, it was more rigidly Puritan than the older colony. In 1662, the Connecticut Colony procured an unusually democratic royal charter resembling the "Fundamental Orders" and providing for the incorporation (1665) of the New Haven Colony, which strongly opposed absorption but reluctantly acquiesced under threat of an alternative take-over by New York. Sir Edmund Andros, who had been named British governor of New England by James II, demanded surrender of the colony's charter; he arrived in Hartford in 1687 to seize the document, but the townspeople are said to have hidden it in the legendary Charter Oak tree.

Connecticut patriots, including Nathan Hale and Governor Jonathan Trumbull, took on a leading role in the Revolutionary War, and the colony served as the Continental Army's major supply area. After the war Connecticut gave up its claims to all western land except the so-called "Western Reserve." Statehood dates from 1788, but boundary disputes with New York, Massachusetts, and Rhode Island persisted until the present borders were established in 1799. Jefferson's Embargo Act of 1807 was highly unpopular in Connecticut, as it was elsewhere in New England. The state's contribution to the Union cause in the Civil War was exceptional; five times the quota of men volunteered.

Most early Connecticut colonists wrested their living from the land and made their own clothes and tools. Enterprising "Yankee peddlers" with horse and rig toured the nation, hawking well-turned wares. During and after the Civil War, better transportation and sharply increased immigration served to shift the economic focus from agriculture to industry. The state, sometimes called "The Arsenal of the Nation," became one of the most industrialized in the country. Its business pioneers included revolver inventor Samuel Colt, rubber magnate Charles Goodyear, and Eli Whitney, who innovated mass production of firearms and manufactured (1793) the cotton gin that proved a boon to the textile industry.

Often called the Insurance Capital of the World, Hartford is the headquarters city for nearly 40 firms in that field.

Connecticut is a leader in the production of such vital items as ball and roller bearings, electronic goods, chemicals and plastics, jet engines, helicopters, and nuclear submarines. United Technologies Corp., the state's largest employer with ten divisions and subsidiaries, and the Electric Boat Division of General Dynamics in Groton are important contributors to the nation's aerospace and submarine production. Electric Boat launched the world's first nuclear submarine in 1954. Shifting emphasis to commercial production has helped the state's numerous defense contractors withstand military cutbacks in the 1970s.

In the southwest section the industrial base is shifting from traditional skilled industry and manufacturing. A number of major companies have established headquarters facilities in the state, including Xerox, IBM, General Electric, Pepsico and Union Carbide. Connecticut ranks very high among the states in per capita income, and in the proportionate number of white-collar and professional workers in the work force.

**Full name:** State of Connecticut. **Origin of name:** From the Indian, Quinnehtukqut, meaning "Beside the Long Tidal River." **Inhabitant:** Nutmegger. **Capital:** Hartford. **State motto:** Qui Transtulit Sustinet (He Who Transplanted Still Sustains). **Flag:** State seal on blue field. **Seal:** Three grapevines symbolize transplanting of culture & traditions of Europe to the colony. **Flower:** Mountain laurel. **Bird:** Robin. **Tree:** White oak. **Song:** "Yankee Doodle." **Nickname:** Constitution State.

**Governor:** William A. O'Neill **Annual salary:** $42,000. **Term:** 4 years. **Current term expires:** Jan. 1983. **Voting requirements:** 18 yrs. old & U.S. citizen; resident of state. **U.S. Congressmen:** 6. **Entered Union:** 1788 (5th state).

**Location & boundaries:** New England state: bounded on the north by Massachusetts; on the east by Rhode Island; on the south by Long Island Sound; & on the west by New York. **Total area:** 5,018 sq. mi. (ranks 48th). **Extreme length:** 100 mi. **Extreme breadth:** 50 mi. **Coastline:** 253 mi. **Chief rivers:** Connecticut, Housatonic, Thames. **Major lake:** Candlewood. **No. of counties:** 8.

**Population (1980 census):** 3,107,576 (ranks 25th). **Pop. increase (1970-80):** 2.5%. **Largest cities:** Bridgeport, Hartford, New Haven, Waterbury. **Pop. density:** 619.3 per sq. mi. (ranks 4th). **Pop. distribution: White**—2,799,420; **Black**—217,433; **Am. Indian, Eskimo and Aleut**—4,533; **Asian and Pacific Islander**—18,970; **Other**—67,220; **Spanish origin**—124,499. **Marriage rate (1979):** 8.2 per 1,000 people. **Divorce rate:** 4.5 per 1,000 people.

**State finances (1980). Revenue:** $3,472,000,000. **Expenditures:** $3,341,000,000. **State taxes:** $591.92 per capita. **State personal income tax:** No, except on capital gains and dividends. **Public debt (1980):** $1,248.13 per capita. **Federal aid (1980):** $372.25 per capita. **Personal income (1981):** $12,995.

**Sectors of the economy (% of labor force employed in 1973):** Manufacturing (34%), Wholesale & retail trade (22%), Services (14%), Government (14%), Educational Services (8%), Construction (5%). **Leading products:** transportation equipment, electrical and other machinery, primary and fabricated metals, chemicals, instruments. **Agricultural products:** dairy items, eggs, tobacco. forest and nursery truck crops. **Avg. farm (1981):** 120 acres. **Avg. value of farm per acre:** $2,533.

**Highway expenditures per capita (1980):** $79.34. **Persons per motor vehicle (1981):** 1.42. **Minimum age for driver's license:** 16. **Gasoline tax:** 11¢ per gallon. **Diesel tax:** 11¢ per gallon. **Motor vehicle deaths (1980):** 18.5 per 100,000 people.

**Birthrate (1979):** 12.4 per 1,000 people. **Infant mortality rate per 1,000 births (1978):** 9.3. **Physicians per 100,000 pop. (1979):** 242. **Dentists per 100,000 pop. (1979):** 73. **Acceptable hospital beds (1979):** 5.9 per 1,000 people. **State expenditures per capita for health and hospitals (1980):** $89.12.

**Education expenditures (1977-78):** $467.39 per capita annually. **No. of pupils in public schools (1980):** 545,000. **No. of institutions of higher learning (1978-79):** 47. **Public school expenditure per**

**pupil in attendance (1978-79):** $2,136. **Avg. salary of public school teachers (1979-80):** $16,939. **No. full-time teachers (1980):** 40,350. **Educational attainment of adult population (1976):** 12.6 median yrs. of school completed: 2.1% with less than 5 years of education; 18.3% with 4 yrs. of college.

**Telephones (1979):** 64 per 100 people. **State Chamber of Commerce:** Connecticut Business & Industry Association, Inc., 370 Asylum Street, Hartford, Connecticut 06103.

## DELAWARE

Although only Rhode Island is smaller in size and few states are less populous, Delaware has a disproportionate worth because of its natural assets and strategic proximity to New York, Philadelphia, Baltimore, and Washington. This location and the state's convenient incorporation laws have made Delaware the home of about 70,000 chartered firms, including some of the country's largest.

The state is part of the Delmarva Peninsula separating Delaware and Chesapeake Bays, the peninsula being shared with Maryland and Virginia. Almost all of the state consists of a part of the Atlantic Coastal Plain extending from Florida to New Jersey; the exception is that part of the Piedmont Plateau crossing the state's northern tip and having a maximum width of about 10 miles. Rolling hills in the north slope to a nearly sea-level plain. The state has the nation's lowest mean elevation, and along the southern border is a 30,000-acre swamp. The climate is moderate though humid, with few prolonged periods of extreme temperature.

Before the Europeans arrived, the region was inhabited by the Lenni-Lenape (later called Delaware) Indians, of Algonquian linguistic stock. Although others from Europe may have preceded him, explorer Henry Hudson is credited with Delaware's discovery (1609). A year later, Captain Samuel Argall of Virginia named Delaware Bay for his colony's governor, Thomas West, Baron De La Warr. Several countries vied for control of the state; Swedes made the first permanent settlement (1638) at Fort Christina (now Wilmington); but New Sweden, as the colony as a whole was called, gave way (1655) to Dutch forces led by New Netherland Governor Peter Stuyvesant. The English seized the colony in 1664, administering it under the Duke of York until 1682. It was then annexed to Pennsylvania as The Three Lower Counties. In 1704 it became semiautonomous, and fought in the American Revolution as a separate state. It later became (1787) the first state to ratify the U.S. Constitution.

Meanwhile, the Wilmington area developed into the hub of the flour-milling business and, in 1802, Eleuthère Irénée du Pont established a gunpowder mill on nearby Brandywine Creek that was the foundation of the state's enormous chemical industry. British ships shelled Lewes during the War of 1812, but there was little damage. Great tensions were created in Delaware by the advent of the Civil War, for it was a border state, condoning slavery but remaining loyal to the Union. Antiadministration and neutralist views were common; true secessionists were rare throughout the conflict.

Aided by fertile soil and an abundant water supply, agriculture has long been an important part of Delaware's economy, although far superseded over the years by manufacturing, chiefly of chemicals, transportaion equipment, and food and food products. In the 1950s, there was a new surge of industrial expansion, while the population increased by about 40 percent. Among historical attractions are Fort Christina Monument, Hagley Museum, and Winterthur Museum, in and near Wilmington; central New Castle, a unique survival of a colonial capital, almost unchanged; Dover, with notable public and private buildings; and Lewes, site of the first attempted settlement. Recreation areas include Cape Henlopen, Delaware Seashore, and Trap Pond State Parks. Rehoboth Beach and Bethany Beach are popular seashore resort areas.

Because the Delaware Bay contains a deep natural channel, a sheltered area, and a convenient route to major east coast oil refineries, the state has frequently been mentioned as a prime site for construction of a deepwater terminal. In 1971, under former Republican Gov. Russell W. Peterson, who later was named chairman of the President's Council on Environmental Quality, the state enacted a broad zoning law which flatly prohibited off-shore ports in state waters and refineries and other heavy industry in its coastal zone.

Supporters argue that the law spells out a policy of moderate growth and is needed to protect Delaware's environment and tourist industry. Environmentalists have introduced amendments to clarify the language of the 1971 acts which remain intact despite continuing opposition from petroleum companies and industrially related groups.

In November 1978, Dover Air Force Base was the scene of the return of the 913 bodies from Jonestown, Guyana, after the mass murder-suicides there. The base's mortuary staff, plus military pathologists and graves registration experts from the Washington area, undertook the difficult task of identifying and embalming the corpses. Base personnel took on a more pleasant mission in early 1980, as they hosted the six U.S. diplomats spirited out of Iran by Canadian embassy officials in Tehran. The diplomats spent two days in seclusion at Dover before returning to their homes.

**Full name:** State of Delaware. **Origin of name:** From Lord De La Warr, English governor of Virginia. **Inhabitant:** Delawarean. **Capital:** Dover. **State motto:** Liberty & Independence. **Flag:** State seal in a buff diamond on a blue field with date Delaware ratified Constitution. **Seal:** A sheaf of wheat, an ear of corn, an ox, a soldier & a farmer under the crest of a ship. **Flower:** Peach blossom. **Bird:** Blue Hen Chicken. **Tree:** American holly. **Song:** "Our Delaware." **Nicknames:** Blue Hen State; Diamond State; First State.

**Governor:** Pierre S. du Pont IV. **Annual salary:** $35,000. **Term:** 4 years. **Current term expires:** Jan. 1985. **Voting requirements:** 18 yrs. old & U.S. citizen; state resident, 1 year; county, 3 mos.; district, 30 days. **U.S. Congressmen:** 1. **Entered Union:** 1787 (1st state).

**Location & boundaries:** Middle Atlantic state: bounded on the north by Pennsylvania; on the east by New Jersey, Delaware Bay & the Atlantic Ocean; & on the south & west by Maryland. **Total area:** 2,044 sq. mi. (ranks 49th). **Extreme length:** 96 mi. **Extreme breadth:** 35 mi. **Coastline:** 28 mi. **Chief rivers:** Delaware, Nanticoke, Christina. **Major lakes:** None; but many small lakes and ponds. **No. of counties:** 3.

**Population (1980 census):** 594,317 (ranks 47th). **Pop. increase (1970-80):** 8.4%. **Largest cities:** Wilmington, Newark, Dover, Elsmere. **Pop. density:** 290.8 per sq. mi. (ranks 7th). **Pop. distribution: White**—488,543; **Black**—95,971; **Am. Indian, Eskimo and Aleut**—1,330; **Asian and Pacific Islander**—4,132; **Other**—52,49; **Spanish origin**—9,671. **Marriage rate (1979):** 7.5 per 1,000 people. **Divorce rate:** 5.3 per 1,000 people.

**State finances (1980). Revenue:** $970,000,000. **Expenditures:** $886,000,000. **State taxes:** $866.75 per capita. **State personal income tax:** Yes. **Public debt (1980):** $1,755.46 per capita. **Federal aid (1980):** $463.22 per capita. **Personal income (1981):** $11,279.

**Sectors of the economy (% of labor force employed in 1970):** Manufacturing (30%), Wholesale and retail trade (19%), Government (15%), Services (8%), Educational Services (8%), Construction (8%). **Leading products:** chemicals & related items, food, apparel, primary & fabricated metals, textile mill items, auto-

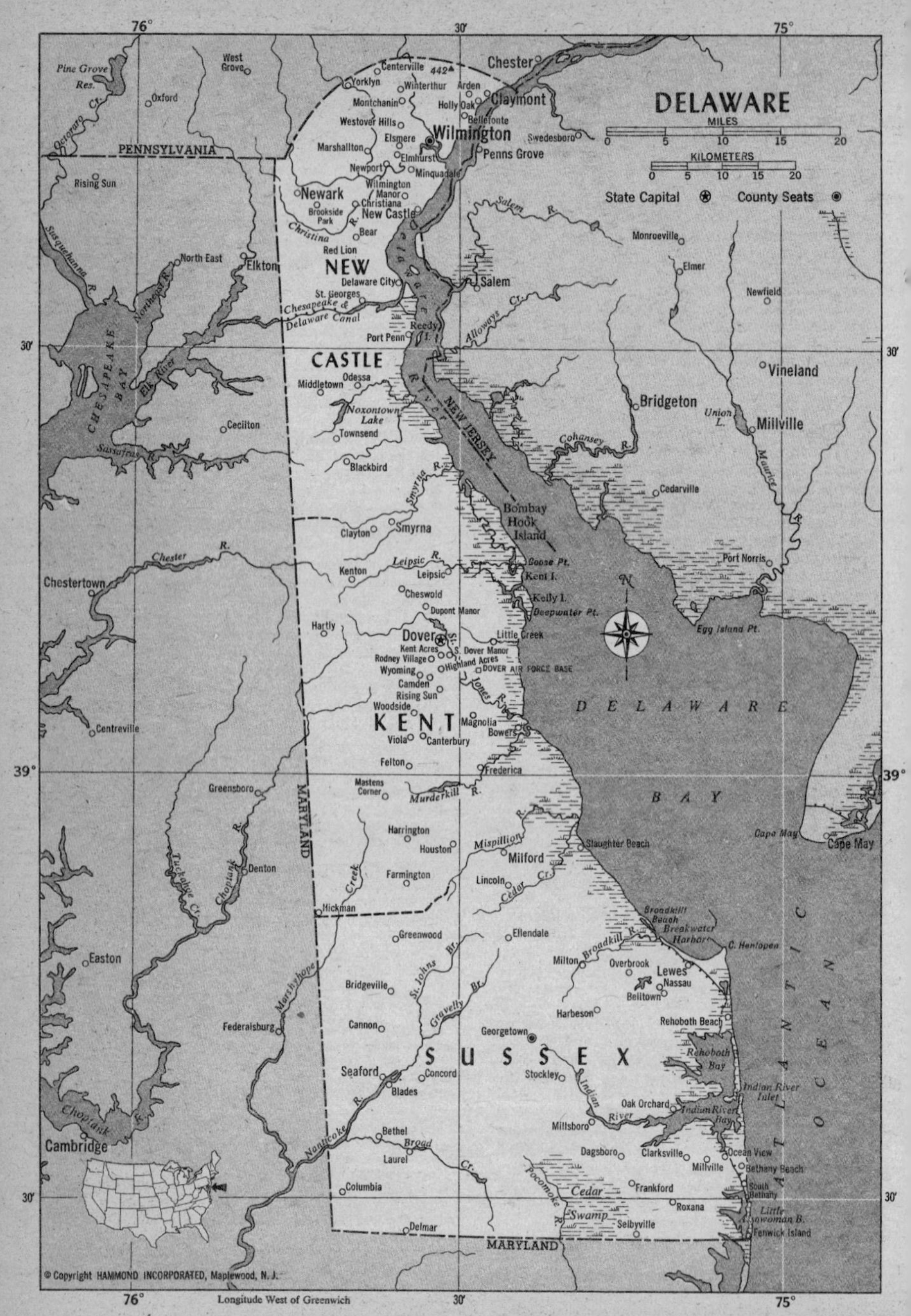
DELAWARE
MILES
KILOMETERS
State Capital
County Seats
NEW CASTLE
KENT
SUSSEX
PENNSYLVANIA
MARYLAND
NEW JERSEY
DELAWARE BAY
ATLANTIC OCEAN
CHESAPEAKE BAY
Wilmington
Dover
Georgetown
Newark
New Castle
Smyrna
Milford
Lewes
Seaford
Rehoboth Beach
Cape May
© Copyright HAMMOND INCORPORATED, Maplewood, N. J.
Longitude West of Greenwich

mobiles, paper. **Agricultural products:** broilers, dairy items, corn, soybeans, potatoes. **Fishing:** clams, crabs. **Avg. farm (1981):** 186 acres. **Avg. value of farm per acre:** $1,931.

**Highway expenditures per capita (1980):** $147.12. **Persons per motor vehicle (1981):** 1.48. **Minimum age for driver's license:** 16. **Gasoline tax:** 11¢ per gallon. **Diesel tax:** 11¢ per gallon. **Motor vehicle deaths (1980):** 25.1 per 100,000 people.

**Birthrate (1979):** 15.3 per 1,000 people. **Infant mortality rate per 1,000 births (1978):** 13.2. **Physicians per 100,000 pop. (1979):** 160. **Dentists per 100,000 pop. (1979):** 46. **Acceptable hospital beds (1979):** 7.1 per 1,000 people. **State expenditures per capita for health and hospitals (1980):** $81.88.

**Education expenditures (1977-78):** $613.57 per capita annually. **No. of pupils in public schools (1980):** 99,000. **No. of institutions of higher learning (1978-79):** 10. **Public school expenditure per pupil in attendance (1978-79):** $2,368. **Avg. salary of public school teachers (1979-80):** $16,789. **No. full-time teachers (1980):** 7,100. **Educational attainment of adult population (1976):** 12.5 median yrs. of school completed: 1.8% with less than 5 years of education; 15.5% with 4 yrs. of college.

**Telephones (1979):** 64 per 100 people. **State Chamber of Commerce:** Delaware State Chamber of Commerce, Inc., 1102 West Street, Wilmington, Delaware 19801.

## FLORIDA

Florida, southernmost of the continental states, is a low-lying peninsula with a coastline second in length only to Alaska's, measuring 1,350 miles—580 on the Atlantic coast and 770 on the Gulf. The state has an average elevation of 100 feet. Curving southwestward for about 200 miles off the southern coast are the Florida Keys, including Elliott Key and Key Largo at the north and Key West at the south.

Indians are thought to have inhabited this region about 10,000 years ago. In 1513 Juan Ponce de León, a Spanish explorer said to be searching for the legendary Fountain of Youth, landed on the east coast and mistakenly thought his find was an island. He named it and claimed it for Spain. Except for an interlude of British rule (1763-1783), Spain kept a tenuous hold until 1819, when the United States bought the Spanish claim. Florida became a state in 1845, seceded from the Union in 1861, and was readmitted in 1868.

Florida's early development was severely hampered by two bloody and costly wars with the Seminole Indians, who were not defeated until 1842. Many never surrendered, but fled instead to the Everglades wilderness, became the core of a new tribe, and, eventually, were settled on reservations. In May 1970, the Seminoles were awarded $12,347,500 for land taken from them by U.S. military forces. The Indians estimate there are now 1,500 Seminoles in Florida and 3,500 in Oklahoma.

Among the fastest-growing states in the nation, Florida has risen in population from 2.8 million in 1950 to over 9.7 million in 1980. Land values and industry have grown proportionately, but rapid expansion has created such problems for the state as attempting to keep pace with the spiraling demand for new facilities.

Tourism, with 36 million visitors in 1981, is the state's leading industry, thanks to one of the mildest and most comfortable climates east of the Mississippi and an abundance of swimming, fishing, and other recreational resources. In 1979 tourism was responsible for over $10 billion in business receipts, and generated 316,000 jobs. Resort centers along the "Gold Coast" include Miami Beach (a suburb of Miami), Palm Beach, Daytona Beach, and Fort Lauderdale. West coast resorts along the Gulf of Mexico include Clearwater, St. Petersburg, Sarasota, the Fort Myers area and Naples. Formerly a winter industry, tourism is now significant all year round. Walt Disney World, built on a 43-square-mile site near Orlando, is the state's newest attraction; eight times as large as California's Disneyland, it is the world's largest non-governmental construction project. Retirees have flocked to the state and those over 65 years of age constitute 17 percent of the population.

Everglades National Park, at Florida's southern tip, draws many visitors. The 2,185-square-mile preserve contains the country's largest remaining tropical wilderness and a multitude of plant and animal types. Other attractions include Cypress Gardens near Winter Haven, Monkey Jungle near Goulds (a Miami suburb), and the Ringling Museum of Art in Sarasota.

Commercial fishing is a major industry in the state, although much of the water is given over to sport fishermen. There are more kinds of fish in the waters in or off Florida than anywhere else in the country. The state is also important agriculturally; its leading crop—oranges—is worth over $600 million a year. Mining of phosphate is also significant.

An important connection point for North, Central, and South American air traffic, Florida has about 485 airports; Miami International is one of the busiest in the world in passenger traffic.

Natural dangers the state faces include crop damage by droughts and early frosts, and seasonal (July-October) hurricanes. Destructive hurricanes struck Florida in 1926, 1928, 1935, 1941, and 1964. Today, many Federal programs have been implemented to help arm the state against these tropical storms.

Cape Canaveral (called Cape Kennedy from 1963 to 1973) was the launching site of most U.S. space vehicles, including the first manned vehicle to land on the moon (1969), the first orbiting laboratory (Skylab 1973), the first joint venture with the Soviet Union (1975), and first orbiting of the reusable space shuttle, the Columbia (1981).

All Florida courts were open in 1977 to news coverage by television and still picture cameras, thus making the state's judicial system the most open to media coverage in the nation.

In 1980, Florida voters adopted a constitutional amendment to increase from $5,000 to $25,000 the homestead exemption from property taxes. The state compensated local governments for lost revenue out of a large surplus.

Tens of thousands of Cuban refugees journeyed in small boats from Mariel, Cuba, to Key West in May 1980. Many were then transferred to Eglin Air Force Base, near Fort Walton Beach in Florida's Panhandle region, before being sent to permanent settlement sites throughout the nation. Starting in 1980, large numbers of Haitian refugees have entered the state illegally.

**Full name:** State of Florida. **Origin of name:** From Spanish, Pascua Florida, meaning "Feast of Flowers." **Inhabitant:** Floridian. **Capital:** Tallahassee. **State motto:** In God We Trust. **Flag:** State seal lies on white field crossed by diagonal red bars. **Seal:** Sun, steamboat & Indian girl strewing flowers. **Flower:** Orange blossom. **Bird:** Mockingbird. **Tree:** Sabal palm. **Song:** "Old Folks at Home." **Nickname:** Sunshine State.

**Governor:** Robert Graham. **Annual salary:** $65,000. **Term:** 4 years. **Current term expires:** Jan. 1983. **Voting requirements:** 18 yrs. old & U.S. citizen; resident of state and county. **U.S. Congressmen:** 19. **Entered Union:** 1845 (27th state).

**Location & boundaries:** South Atlantic state: bounded on the north by Alabama, the Chattahoochee River, Georgia & St. Mary's River; on the east by the Atlantic Ocean; on the south by the Straits of Florida; & on the west by the Gulf of Mexico, the Perdido River &

FLORIDA
MILES
KILOMETERS
State Capital
County Seats
Counties indicated by numbers:
1 ESCAMBIA
2 GADSDEN
3 GILCHRIST
4 HILLSBOROUGH
5 JEFFERSON
6 PINELLAS
7 SEMINOLE
8 SUMTER
GEORGIA
ALA
Moultrie
Waycross
Brunswick
Bainbridge
Donalsonville
Folkston
Okefenokee Swamp
Tallahassee
Jacksonville
Jacksonville Beach
St. Augustine
Gainesville
Palatka
Ocala
Daytona Beach
De Land
Orlando
Sanford
Winter Park
Cocoa
Melbourne
Lakeland
Clearwater
Tampa
St. Petersburg
Bradenton
Sarasota
Ft. Myers
Ft. Pierce
W. Palm Beach
Ft. Lauderdale
Hollywood
Miami
Miami Beach
Hialeah
Coral Gables
Key West
L. Okeechobee
Big Cypress Swamp
EVERGLADES NATIONAL PARK
Florida Bay
FLORIDA KEYS
Straits of Florida
ATLANTIC OCEAN
GULF OF MEXICO
Longitude West of Greenwich
WESTERN PART OF FLORIDA
Same scale as main map
ALABAMA
Pensacola
Panama City
Ft. Lauderdale
Plant City
Bartow
Kissimmee
Titusville
Vero Beach
Naples
Punta Gorda
Marianna
Chipley
Crestview
DeFuniak Springs
Apalachicola
Port St. Joe
30°
28°
26°
84°
82°
80°

Alabama. **Total area:** 58,664 sq. mi. (ranks 22nd). **Extreme length:** 447 mi. **Extreme breadth:** 361 mi. **Coastline:** 399 mi. on Atlantic; 798 mi. on Gulf Coast. **Chief rivers:** St. Johns, Apalachicola, Suwannee. **Major lakes:** Okeechobee, George, Kissimmee. **No. of counties:** 67.

**Population (1980 census):** 9,746,342 (ranks 7th). **Pop. increase (1970-80):** 43.5%. **Largest cities:** Jacksonville, Miami, Tampa, St. Petersburg. **Pop. density:** 166.1 per sq. mi. (ranks 11th). **Pop. distribution: White**—8,178,387; **Black**—1,342,478; **Am. Indian, Eskimo and Aleut**—19,316; **Asian and Pacific Islander**—56,756; **Other**—143,055; **Spanish origin**—857,898. **Marriage rate (1979):** 11.7 per 1,000 people. **Divorce rate:** 7.9 per 1,000 people.

**State finances (1980). Revenue:** $8,223,000,000. **Expenditures:** $7,387,000,000. **State taxes:** $493.25 per capita. **State personal income tax:** No. **Public debt (1980):** $269.70 per capita. **Federal aid (1980):** $292.53 per capita. **Personal income (1981):** $10,050.

**Sectors of the economy (% of labor force employed in 1970):** Wholesale and retail trade (24%), Government (16%), Manufacturing (14%), Services (12%), Construction (9%), Educational Services (7%). **Leading products:** apparel products; transportation equipment; fabricated metal products; chemicals; paper items; food; printing & publishing; electrical machinery; limestone, clay & glass items; fabricated metals. **Minerals:** phosphate rock, stone, clay. **Agricultural products:** dairy items, cattle, citrus, tomatoes, sugarcane for sugar & seed, winter vegetables. **Fishing:** oysters and scallops, crabs, lobsters, shrimp. **Avg. farm (1981):** 341 acres. **Avg. value of farm per acre:** $1,507.

**Highway expenditures per capita (1980):** $97.26. **Persons per motor vehicle (1981):** 1.24. **Minimum age for driver's license:** 16. **Gasoline tax:** 8¢ per gallon. **Diesel tax:** 8¢ per gallon. **Motor vehicle deaths (1980):** 29.0 per 100,000 people.

**Birthrate (1979):** 13.7 per 1,000 people. **Infant mortality rate per 1,000 births (1978):** 14.1. **Physicians per 100,000 pop. (1979):** 188. **Dentists per 100,000 pop. (1979):** 50. **Acceptable hospital beds (1979):** 5.8 per 1,000 people. **State expenditures per capita for health and hospitals (1980):** $65.16.

**Education expenditures (1977-78):** $438.04 per capita annually. **No. of pupils in public schools (1980):** 1,495,000. **No. of institutions of higher learning (1978-79):** 77. **Public school expenditure per pupil in attendance (1978-79):** $1,657. **Avg. salary of public school teachers (1979-80):** $15,200. **No. full-time teachers (1980):** 82,400. **Educational attainment of adult population (1976):** 12.4 median yrs. of school completed: 3.7% with less than 5 years of education; 13.7% with 4 yrs. of college.

**Telephones (1979):** 59 per 100 people. **State Chamber of Commerce:** Florida Chamber of Commerce, 311 S. Calhoun Street, P.O. Box 5497, Tallahassee, Florida 32301.

## GEORGIA

The largest state east of the Mississippi, and the last of the 13 Colonies to be founded, Georgia consists of three main land regions: in the north is a small section of the Appalachian Mountains; the Piedmont Plateau constitutes the middle; and in the south, coastal flatlands make up about three-fifths of the state's total area. Landmarks include the Okefenokee Swamp, one of the country's largest.

Mound Builders were the first known inhabitants of the Georgia region, followed in modern times by Creek and Cherokee Indians. Spanish explorer De Soto is thought to have been the first European to visit (1540) the area, but British claims soon conflicted with those of Spain; in 1733, English philanthropist James Oglethorpe led a group of his countrymen in launching the first permanent settlement at Savannah as an asylum for debtors. England ended the Spanish threat in 1742, as forces under Oglethorpe defeated their rivals in the battle of Bloody Marsh.

The sale of rum and the introduction of Negro slaves into the region were at first outlawed, but by about 1750 new legislation ended these restrictions. Many foreigners were among the early immigrants, soon followed by settlers mainly from Virginia and the Carolinas.

After the American Revolution, Georgia became a stronghold of slavery and cotton culture—fostered by the invention of the cotton gin, in 1793, by Eli Whitney, who was living near Savannah. Georgia seceded in 1861, and suffered great damage in the Civil War. The war ended slavery, but black Georgians suffered many disabilities until the civil rights movement of the 1950s and 1960s.

Changes in social patterns are evident. Public accommodations throughout the state are generally desegregated, in accordance with law, as are most school systems, although residential housing patterns in many areas limit the amount of actual school integration. In 1980 violence occurred between blacks and whites in rural Wrightsville.

As in many other parts of the country, Georgians expressed concern over busing pupils to achieve racial balance in schools. In February, 1972, classroom boycotts to protest busing cut into school attendance at Augusta. There were efforts to promote a statewide boycott, but they failed.

Georgia, the first state (1943) to grant 18-year-olds the right to vote, in 1973 lowered from 21 to 18 the legal age for adults.

Georgia is today involved in the same agriculture-to-industry transformation which the South as a whole is undergoing. Its extensive resources include a wealth of largely untapped hydroelectric power and some of the most valuable marble and gravel deposits in the country. Favorable climate, natural resources and an abundant labor supply have caused many industries to establish plants in the state. Industrialization has brought efforts at unionization, and resistance to these efforts. In 1980, the mayor and police chief of Milledgevile settled out of court with a union which had sued them for alleged illegal surveillance of union organizers. Georgia is the nation's largest supplier of peanuts and poultry, and also ranks high in textiles, egg production, lumber, cotton, peaches, and tobacco production, while Atlanta has become one of the South's most important transportation and distributing centers.

Tourism is another significant revenue source, and is aided by such attractions as the Chattahoochee and Oconee National Forests, picturesque Savannah, the Sea Island beach resorts, FDR's "Little White House" at Warm Springs, and Andersonville Prison Park and National Cemetery on the site of the infamous Confederate prison. A major attraction is the enormous Confederate Memorial carving, the world's largest single piece of sculpture, cut into the sheer north face of historic Stone Mountain, near Atlanta; the work, centerpiece of a 3,200-acre park, depicts General Robert E. Lee, Confederate President Jefferson Davis, and General Stonewall Jackson.

Former Gov. Jimmy Carter, often hailed as one of the South's "new breed" of young progressive chief executives, was inaugurated as President of the United States in 1977, the first Southern president since the Civil War. At the end of his term in January 1981, he returned to his hometown of Plains.

**Full name:** State of Georgia. **Origin of name:** In honor of King George II of England. **Inhabitant:** Georgian. **Capital:** Atlanta. **State motto:** Wisdom, Justice & Moderation. **Flag:** State seal on a vertical blue bar; Confederate flag to the right. **Seal:** Arch representing state constitution; three columns with Georgia's motto; date 1776 is year Georgia signed Declaration of Independence. **Flower:** Cherokee rose. **Bird:** Brown thrasher. **Tree:** Live oak. **Song:** "Georgia." **Nickname:** Peach State and The Empire State of the South.

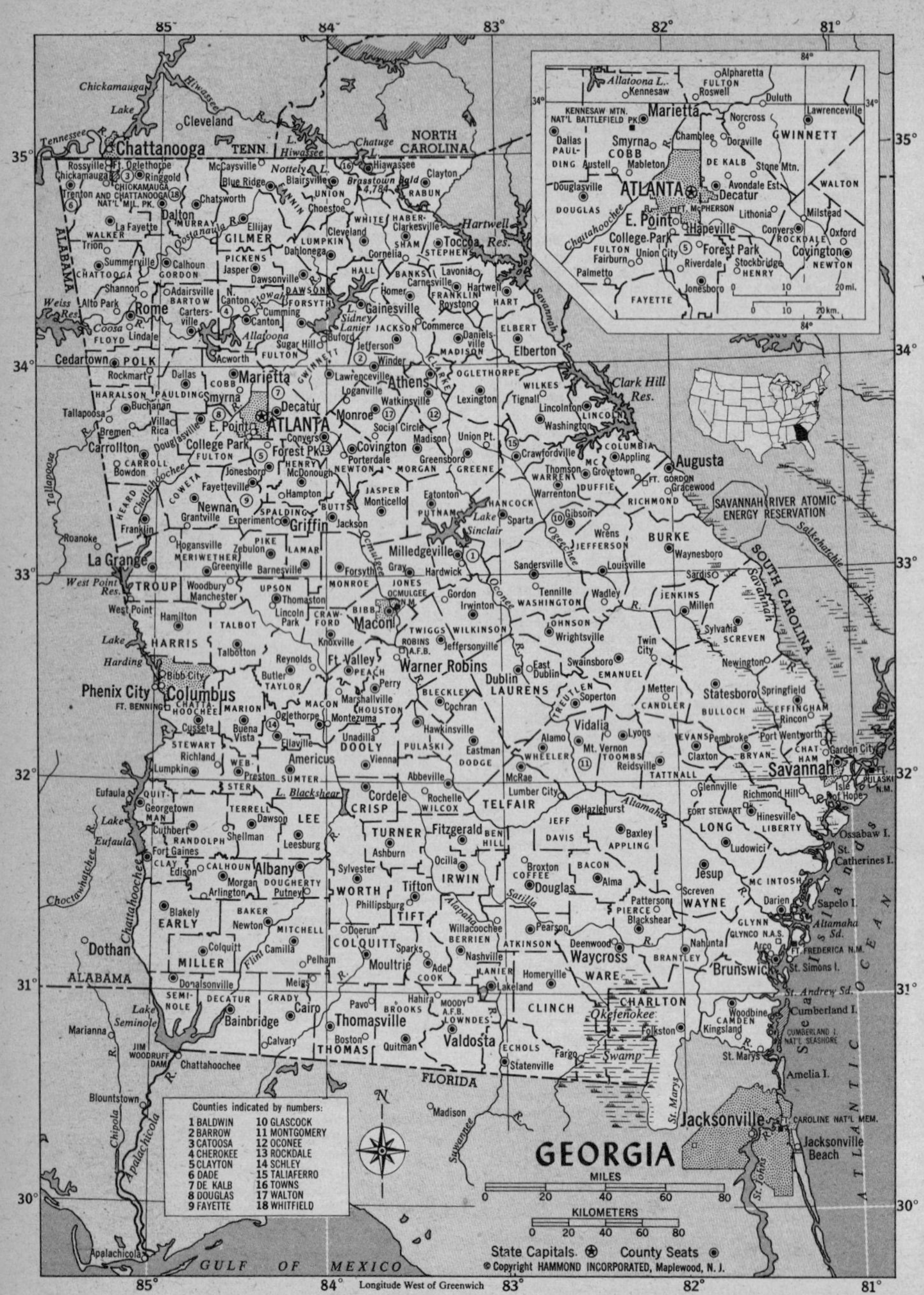
GEORGIA
Counties indicated by numbers:
1 BALDWIN
2 BARROW
3 CATOOSA
4 CHEROKEE
5 CLAYTON
6 DADE
7 DE KALB
8 DOUGLAS
9 FAYETTE
10 GLASCOCK
11 MONTGOMERY
12 OCONEE
13 ROCKDALE
14 SCHLEY
15 TALIAFERRO
16 TOWNS
17 WALTON
18 WHITFIELD
MILES
0 20 40 60 80
KILOMETERS
0 20 40 60 80
State Capitals.
County Seats
© Copyright HAMMOND INCORPORATED, Maplewood, N. J.
Longitude West of Greenwich
85° 84° 83° 82° 81°
35° 34° 33° 32° 31° 30°
ALABAMA
TENN.
NORTH CAROLINA
SOUTH CAROLINA
FLORIDA
GULF OF MEXICO
ATLANTIC OCEAN
SAVANNAH RIVER ATOMIC ENERGY RESERVATION
Chattanooga
Cleveland
Dalton
Rome
Marietta
ATLANTA
Decatur
E. Point
College Park
Forest Pk.
Athens
Gainesville
Augusta
Macon
Milledgeville
Columbus
Phenix City
Warner Robins
Albany
Americus
Valdosta
Waycross
Brunswick
Savannah
Jacksonville
Thomasville
Dothan
La Grange
Griffin
Newnan
Carrollton
Cedartown
Statesboro
Vidalia
Dublin
Tifton
Moultrie
Bainbridge
Cairo
Cordele
Fitzgerald
Douglas
Jesup
Hinesville
Elberton
Toccoa
Okefenokee Swamp
Clark Hill Res.
Hartwell Res.
Lake Sinclair
L. Sidney Lanier
L. Blackshear
Lake Seminole
JIM WOODRUFF DAM
Savannah R.
Altamaha R.
Chattahoochee R.
Flint R.
Ocmulgee R.
Oconee R.
Ogeechee R.
Satilla R.
St. Marys R.
Cumberland I.
St. Simons I.
Sapelo I.
St. Catherines I.
Ossabaw I.
Amelia I.
Jacksonville Beach
Allatoona L.
Kennesaw
KENNESAW MTN. NAT'L BATTLEFIELD PK.
Smyrna
COBB
Austell
Mableton
Douglasville
DOUGLAS
FULTON
Fairburn
Union City
Hapeville
Forest Park
Riverdale
Jonesboro
FAYETTE
Palmetto
Roswell
Alpharetta
Duluth
Norcross
Doraville
Chamblee
GWINNETT
Lawrenceville
DE KALB
Stone Mtn.
Avondale Ests.
Lithonia
Conyers
ROCKDALE
Covington
NEWTON
Oxford
Milstead
WALTON
HENRY
Stockbridge
FT. McPHERSON
0 10 20 mi.
0 10 20 km.

**Governor:** George D. Busbee. **Annual salary:** $65,934. **Term:** 4 years. **Current term expires:** Jan. 1983. **Voting requirements:** 18 yrs. old & U.S. citizen. **U.S. Congressmen:** 10. **Entered Union:** 1788 (4th state).

**Location & boundaries:** South Atlantic state: bounded on the north by Tennessee & North Carolina; on the east by South Carolina, the Atlantic Ocean & the Savannah, Tugaloo & Chattooga Rivers; on the south by St. Mary's River & Florida; & on the west by Florida, Alabama & the Chattahoochee River. **Total area:** 58,910 sq. mi. (ranks 21st). **Extreme length:** 315 mi. **Extreme breadth:** 250 mi. **Coastline:** 100 mi. **Chief Rivers:** Altamaha, Chattahoochee, Savannah. **Major lakes:** Lanier, Allatoona, Seminole. **No. of counties:** 159.

**Population (1980 census):** 5,463,105 (ranks 13th). **Pop. increase (1970-80):** 19.1%. **Largest cities:** Atlanta, Columbus, Savannah, Macon. **Pop. density:** 92.7 per sq. mi. (ranks 21st). **Pop. distribution: White**—3,948,007; **Black**—1,465,457; **Am. Indian, Eskimo and Aleut**—7,619; **Asian and Pacific Islander**—24,461; **Other**—18,721; **Spanish origin**—61,261. **Marriage rate (1979):** 13.4 per 1,000 people. **Divorce rate:** 6.5 per 1,000 people.

**State finances (1980). Revenue:** $5,194,000,000. **Expenditures:** $4,901,000,000. **State taxes:** $499.44 per capita. **State personal income tax:** Yes. **Public debt (1980):** $257.07 per capita. **Federal aid (1980):** $433.87 per capita. **Personal income (1981):** $8,960.

**Sectors of the economy (% of labor force employed in 1970):** Manufacturing (27%), Wholesale and retail trade (20%), Government (16%C, Services (9%), Educational Services (7%), Construction (7%). **Leading products:** textile mill items, apparel, food, transportation equipment, lumber, pulp & paper products, chemicals. **Minerals:** clays, stone, cement, sand & gravel. **Agricultural products:** broilers, eggs, cattle, peanuts, tobacco, corn. **Fishing:** shrimp. **Avg. farm (1981):** 263 acres. **Avg. value of farm per acre:** $915.

**Highway expenditures per capita (1980):** $128.45. **Persons per motor vehicle (1981):** 1.43. **Minimum age for driver's license:** 16. **Gasoline tax:** 7.5¢ per gallon. **Diesel tax:** 7.5¢ per gallon. **Motor vehicle deaths (1980):** 27.6 per 100,000 people.

**Birthrate (1979):** 17.2 per 1,000 people. **Infant mortality rate per 1,000 births (1978):** 15.4. **Physicians per 100,000 pop. (1979):** 144. **Dentists per 100,000 pop. (1979):** 42. **Acceptable hospital beds (1979):** 5.7 per 1,000 people. **State expenditures per capita for health and hospitals (1980):** $73.14.

**Education expenditures (1977-78):** $388.40 per capita annually. **No. of pupils in public schools (1980):** 1,068,000. **No. of institutions of higher learning (1978-79):** 72. **Public school expenditure per pupil in attendance (1978-79):** $1,485. **Avg. salary of public school teachers (1979-80):** $14,732. **No. full-time teachers (1980):** 59,000. **Educational attainment of adult population (1976):** 12.3 median yrs. of school completed: 8.0% with less than 5 years of education; 12.3% with 4 yrs. of college.

**Telephones (1979):** 55 per 100 people. **State Chamber of Commerce:** Georgia Chamber of Commerce, 1200 Commerce Building, Atlanta, Georgia 30335.

## HAWAII

Hawaii, 50th state to join (1959) the Union, is a chain of 132 islands near the center of the North Pacific Ocean, about 2,400 miles from San Francisco. The islands were formed by volcanoes erupting from the ocean floor; there are some still-active volcanoes at the easterly end of the island chain, which extends 1,523 miles, and may be divided into three groups: the sand and coral islands of the northwest, rock islets in the center, and the eight major islands at the southeast end.

The eight major islands make up all except three square miles of the entire area: Hawaii, Oahu, Maui, Kahoolawe, Lanai, Molokai, Kauai, and Niihau. Hawaii is the largest of these islands (4,038 sq. mi.), while Oahu has the highest population (over 79 percent of the state's total). On Oahu are Honolulu and Pearl Harbor. Of these eight islands, only Kahoolawe is uninhabited; it is used as a target island for bombing and artillery training. The coastline of the islands is approximately 750 miles long. Cooling trade winds make for a pleasantly mild climate all year round. Rainfall varies from hundreds of inches in the mountains to less than 10 inches in the lowlands.

A melting pot of nationalities and racial groups, Hawaii was first settled by seagoing Polynesians, most likely from the Marquesas Islands, during the eighth century. The early Hawaiians, who practiced a religion that included human sacrifice and idolatry, developed a feudal form of government. Europe learned of the islands after British explorer Captain James Cook came upon them (1778); he named them the "Sandwich Islands" in honor of the Earl of Sandwich.

Local chieftain King Kamehameha I took control (1795) of the main islands—except Kauai and Niihau—after thirteen years of warfare with other aspirants. The other two islands accepted his rule in 1810.

Missionaries were active on the islands in the 1800s. In 1840, the Kingdom of Hawaii adopted its first constitution. The growth of the vital sugar and pineapple industries increased U.S. business and political involvement, leading to the establishment (1900) of Hawaii as a United States Territory following annexation (1898). The present population includes significant numbers of Polynesians, Chinese, Filipinos, and Japanese, as well as Caucasians.

The "date which will live in infamy"—Dec. 7, 1941—saw the Japanese attack on Pearl Harbor, which drew the nation into World War II.

Hawaii has since consolidated its importance as a strategic U.S. military outpost: Army, Navy, and Air Force units of the Pacific are under a single command located there. The salaries of military personnel and civilians employed at this command constitute one of Hawaii's principal sources of income. Tourism is the major revenue source. Sugar and pineapple are still exported but are diminishing in the face of foreign competition.

The building boom which critics say created a "concrete jungle" in Waikiki to provide for the tourists is now shifting toward housing for local residents, giving rise to cries of "urban sprawl." There is considerable focus on environmental quality control, with frequent calls for preserving the land. In addition, there is growing concern over the traditional land development pattern. Most of the undeveloped land has been in the hands of a few owners who in the past leased but would not sell to private individuals, who then built homes on their leaseholds. With pressure on landowners to sell rather than lease, and with escalating land values, the future of the real estate market is uncertain.

In addition to such pleasures as swimming, boating and surfing, the islands have much to offer the scientist, historian and general sightseer, including the Bishop Museum in Honolulu—an important center for Polynesian studies; Iolani Palace in Honolulu, the only royal palace in the United States; the world's most active volcano, Kilauea, on Hawaii Island; the extinct Haleakala Crater on Maui Island; and the Waimea Canyon on Kauai Island, often called the "Grand Canyon of the Pacific." The cliff Nuuanu Pali (1,188 feet high) offers a fine view of Oahu's northeast coast.

In 1981-82 the growing Hawaiian economy experienced problems for the first time. Tourists from the mainland declined in numbers because of the recession and increased air fares. Increased travel from Japan partially offset the mainland falloff. Sugarcane production has been cut back with the fall in sugar prices. However, military spending has held up.

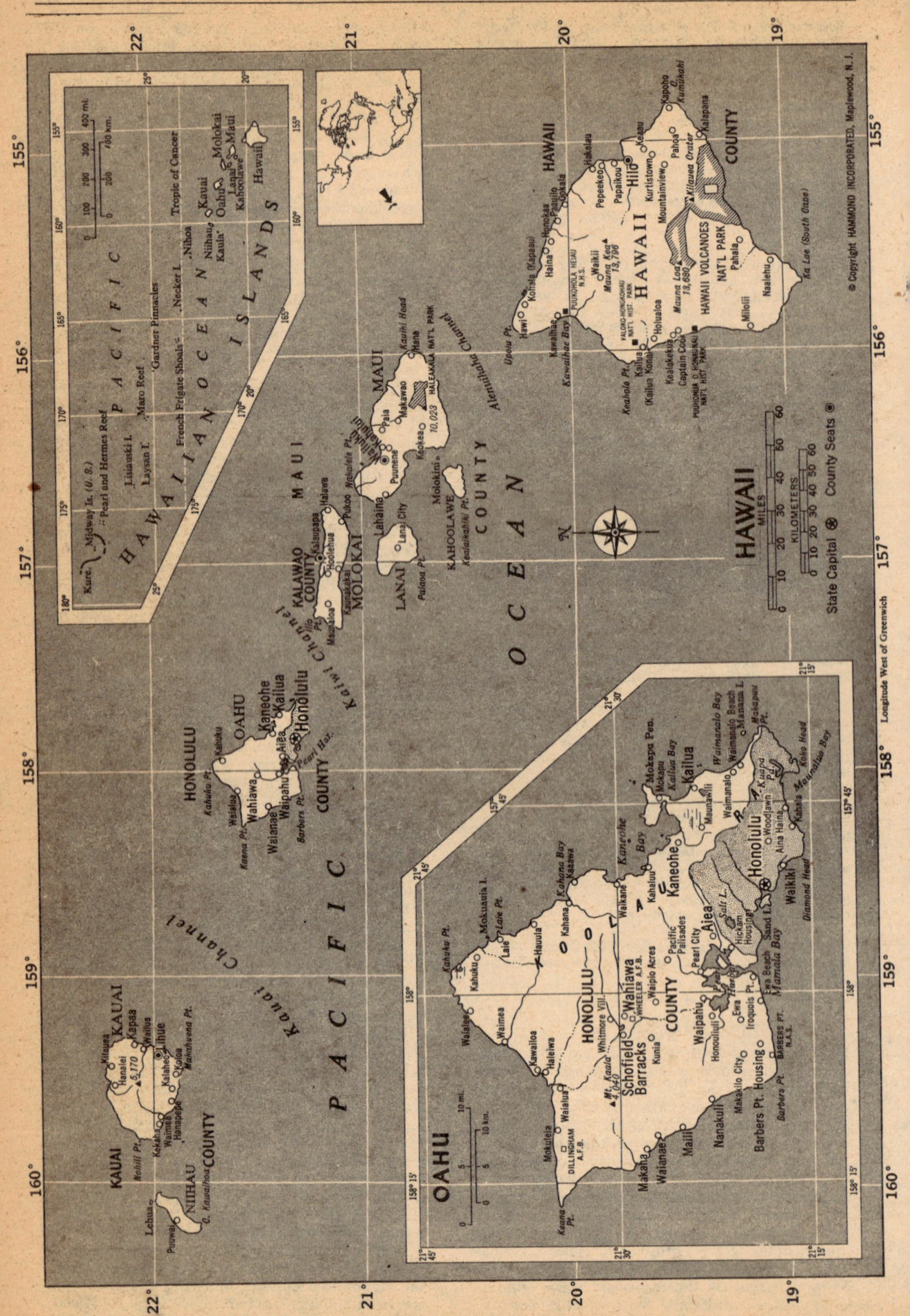
HAWAII
PACIFIC OCEAN
HAWAIIAN ISLANDS
KAUAI
NIIHAU
OAHU
MOLOKAI
LANAI
MAUI
KAHOOLAWE
HAWAII
KAUAI COUNTY
HONOLULU COUNTY
KALAWAO COUNTY
MAUI COUNTY
HAWAII COUNTY
Honolulu
Hilo
Kauai Channel
Kaiwi Channel
Alenuihaha Channel
Tropic of Cancer
State Capital
County Seats
MILES
KILOMETERS
Longitude West of Greenwich
© Copyright HAMMOND INCORPORATED, Maplewood, N.J.

**Full name:** State of Hawaii. **Origin of name:** Perhaps from native name of the Polynesians' original home. **Inhabitant:** Hawaiian. **Capital:** Honolulu. **State motto:** Ua Mau Ke Ea O Ka Aina I Ka Pono (The Life of the Land Is Perpetuated in Righteousness). **Flag:** Eight alternating white, red & blue bars, representing main islands of state; Union Jack in upper left. **Seal:** Coat of arms of Hawaiian monarchy with King Kamehameha I on right & goddess of liberty on left. **Flower:** Hibiscus. **Bird:** Hawaiian goose. **Tree:** Candlenut (kukui). **Song:** "Hawaii Ponoi." **Nickname:** Aloha State.

**Governor:** George R. Ariyoshi. **Annual salary:** $59,400. **Term:** 4 years. **Current term expires:** Dec. 1982. **Voting requirements:** 18 yrs. old & U.S. citizen. **U.S. Congressmen:** 2. **Entered Union:** 1959 (50th state).

**Location & boundaries:** Pacific state composed of a chain of 132 islands, located about 2,397 miles SW of San Francisco; major islands from east to west are Hawaii, Maui, Kahoolawe, Lanai, Molokai, Oahu, Kauai & Niihau. **Total area:** 6,471 sq. mi. (ranks 47th). **Coastline:** 750 mi. **No. of counties:** 5 (inc. Kalawao County—a leprosy settlement).

**Population (1980 census):** 964,691 (ranks 39th). **Pop. increase (1970-80):** 25.3%. **Largest cities:** Honolulu, Pearl City, Kailua, Hilo. **Pop. density:** 149.1 per sq. mi. (ranks 15th). **Pop. distribution: White**—318,608; **Black**—17,352; **Am. Indian, Eskimo and Aleut**—2,778; **Asian and Pacific Islander**—583,660; **Other**—42,602; **Spanish origin**—71,479. **Marriage rate (1979):** 12.8 per 1,000 people. **Divorce rate:** 5.5 per 1,000 people.

**State finances (1980). Revenue:** $1,895,000,000. **Expenditures:** $1,660,000,000. **State taxes:** $1,034.59 per capita. **State personal income tax:** Yes. **Public debt (1980):** $1,931.83 per capita. **Federal aid (1980):** $480.15 per capita. **Personal income (1981):** $11,096.

**Sectors of the economy (% of labor force employed in 1975):** Wholesale and retail trade (24%), Government (23%), Services (21%), Construction (8%), Manufacturing (7%). **Leading products:** food, printing & publishing, stone, clay, glass items, fabricated metals, lumber & wood. **Agricultural products:** dairy items, cattle, hogs, sugarcane, pineapples, vegetables. **Fishing:** Aku, Ahi, Akule, tuna, big-eyed scad, marlin. **Avg. farm (1981):** 457 acres. **Avg. value of farm per acre:** N.A.

**Highway expenditures per capita (1980):** $105.28. **Persons per motor vehicle (1981):** 1.62. **Minimum age for driver's license:** 15. **Gasoline tax:** 13.5¢ per gallon in Hawaii Cty., 15¢ in Honolulu Cty., 12.5¢ in Kauai Cty., 14.5¢ in Maui Cty. **Diesel tax:** 13.5¢ per gallon in Hawaii Cty., 15¢ in Honolulu Cty., 12.5¢ in Kauai Cty., 14.5¢ in Maui Cty. **Motor vehicle deaths (1980):** 19.3 per 100,000 people.

**Birthrate (1979):** 19.2 per 1,000 people. **Infant mortality rate per 1,000 births (1978):** 11.1. **Physicians per 100,000 pop. (1979):** 203. **Dentists per 100,000 pop. (1979):** 68. **Acceptable hospital beds (1979):** 4.0 per 1,000 people. **State expenditures per capita for health and hospitals (1980):** $136.60.

**Education expenditures (1977-78):** $541.03 per capita annually. **No. of pupils in public schools (1980):** 167,000. **No. of institutions of higher learning (1978-79):** 12. **Public school expenditure per pupil in attendance (1978-79):** $2,133. **Avg. salary of public school teachers (1979-80):** $18,875. **No. full-time teachers (1980):** 8,750. **Educational attainment of adult population (1976):** 12.7 median yrs. of school completed: 5.5% with less than 5 years of education; 16.8% with 4 yrs. of college.

**Telephones (1979):** 47 per 100 people. **State Chamber of Commerce:** The Chamber of Commerce of Hawaii, Dillingham Building, 735 Bishop Street, Honolulu, Hawaii 96813.

## IDAHO

Idaho is a rugged, mountainous state that does not yield its resources easily. It has the nation's deepest canyon (Hells Canyon, on the Oregon border), as well as 50 mountain peaks more than 10,000 feet high. There are three main regions: the southern, dominated by the Snake River plains and desolate volcanic terrain; the central, a primitive area of craggy mountains and canyons, dominated by the Salmon River Mountains; and the northern region, featuring the Cabinet Mountains and the Selkirk Mountains lying on the Canadian border. Forests of fir, pine, spruce, and other varieties cover about 40 percent of the state. Many peaceful, relatively unspoiled lakes set off the rough beauty of these areas and of the snow-capped mountains.

Indians are thought to have been living in the area 10,000 years ago. The region was acquired by the United States in the Louisiana Purchase (1803) and explored two years later by Lewis and Clark, who crossed the Bitterroot Range and camped near the present site of Lewiston (founded 1861). Throughout the 1860s, Idaho experienced a gold rush that drew scores of prospectors but left a legacy of ghost towns. Mining, however, is still important; Idaho ranks first nationally in the production of silver, antimony, garnets, and cobalt.

In the 1870s, the growing white occupation of Indian lands—particularly for cattle ranging—led to a series of battles between U.S. forces and the Nez Percé, Bannock, and Sheepeater tribes. Idaho gained statehood in 1890.

During the 1890s, disputes between miners and mineowners often resulted in violence and bloodshed. In 1892, in the Coeur d'Alene area, unionized miners used dynamite and guns to fight nonunion men and mineowners. There was violence again in 1899. Governor Frank Steunenberg declared martial law then and called in Federal troops to restore order. Six years later, Steunenberg, no longer in office, was murdered by a member of the Western Federation of Miners; the confessed killer, defended by Clarence Darrow in a famous trial, was sentenced to life imprisonment.

Despite ravages by forest fires (including a 78,000-acre blaze in 1967) and troublesome mountain pine beetle infestations, agriculture is still the state's leading industry; crops include potatoes, wheat, apples, corn, barley, and hops. In 1979, the state's small poultry industry was devastated by the discovery of PCBs in chicken feed.

Irrigation, which has been crucially important, was begun on a large scale under the Federal government's Carey Act (1894) and Reclamation Act (1902). By 1950, Idaho had more than 5,000 diversion dams, 360 reservoirs (with 5 million acre-feet of water capacity), and more than 15,000 miles of irrigation canals and ditches. In 1968, the Idaho Power Company completed Hells Canyon Dam in the Snake River Valley, which also includes Oxbow and Brownlee dams. In recent years thousands of acres of new land have been brought into cultivation on high desert plateaus in the Boise area, largely possible through increased water pumping efficiency. With the completion of the Snake River navigation project in 1975, Idaho now has water access to the Pacific Ocean.

Manufacturing has been steadily increasing, particularly the dehydrating and freezing of potatoes of which Idaho produces about one-fourth of the nation's yield. Nearly 75 percent of this crop is now processed before it goes to the consumer.

Tourism, now the third-ranked industry, is also on the rise, with an estimated 6 million yearly visitors.

Soda Springs, Champagne Springs, Steamboat Spring, and Hooper Spring boast ice-cold, as well as hellishly hot, water discharges. Lava Hot Springs, the site of a state park, has yielded mineral-rich waters since Indian times.

Other attractions of Idaho include the Craters of the Moon National Monument; scenic Coeur d'Alene, Pend Oreille and Priest Lakes in the Panhandle country of northern Utah; Sun Valley that offers skating, swimming, skiing and other attractions; and the Sawtooth Mountains in central Idaho, wherre a new national recreation area was created in 1972. In 1978 Federal legislation established the large new Gospel-Hump Wilderness Area in north-central Idaho.

In June 1976 the Teton dam burst in the eastern

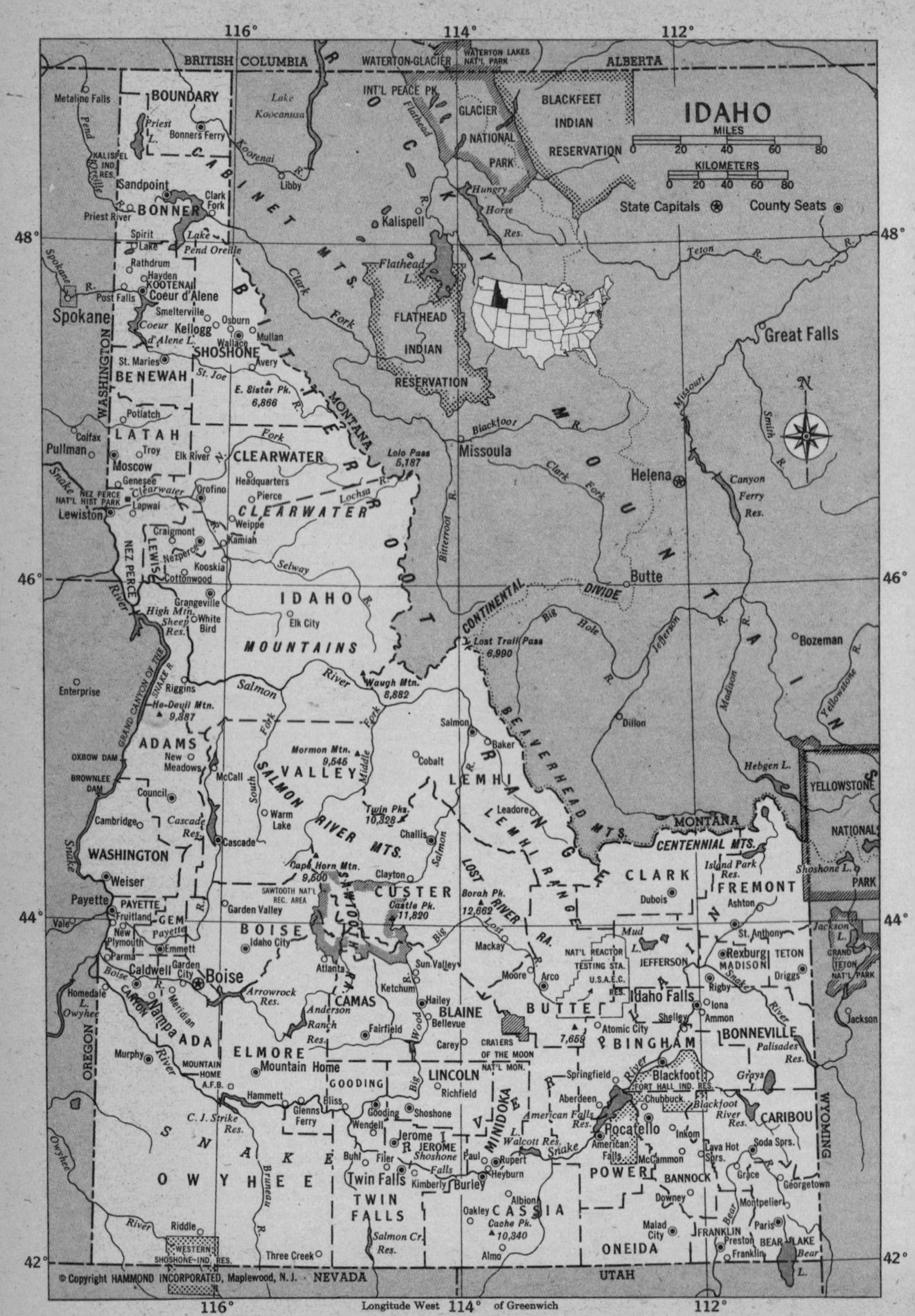
IDAHO
MILES
KILOMETERS
State Capitals
County Seats
BRITISH COLUMBIA
ALBERTA
WATERTON-GLACIER INT'L PEACE PK.
WATERTON LAKES NAT'L PARK
GLACIER NATIONAL PARK
BLACKFEET INDIAN RESERVATION
FLATHEAD INDIAN RESERVATION
WASHINGTON
OREGON
MONTANA
WYOMING
NEVADA
UTAH
YELLOWSTONE NATIONAL PARK
BOUNDARY
BONNER
KOOTENAI
SHOSHONE
BENEWAH
LATAH
CLEARWATER
NEZ PERCE
LEWIS
IDAHO
ADAMS
VALLEY
LEMHI
WASHINGTON
PAYETTE
GEM
BOISE
CUSTER
CLARK
FREMONT
JEFFERSON
MADISON
TETON
BUTTE
BINGHAM
BONNEVILLE
CAMAS
BLAINE
ELMORE
ADA
CANYON
GOODING
LINCOLN
MINIDOKA
JEROME
TWIN FALLS
CASSIA
POWER
BANNOCK
CARIBOU
OWYHEE
ONEIDA
FRANKLIN
BEAR LAKE
Spokane
Boise
Helena
Missoula
Butte
Great Falls
Bozeman
Dillon
Kalispell
Libby
Lewiston
Moscow
Coeur d'Alene
Sandpoint
Pocatello
Idaho Falls
Twin Falls
Nampa
Caldwell
Mountain Home
Salmon
Burley
Rexburg
Blackfoot
BITTERROOT RANGE
BEAVERHEAD MTS.
LEMHI RANGE
LOST RIVER RA.
SALMON RIVER MTS.
SAWTOOTH RA.
CENTENNIAL MTS.
CABINET MTS.
CLEARWATER MTS.
IDAHO MOUNTAINS
CONTINENTAL DIVIDE
ROCKY MOUNTAINS
SNAKE RIVER PLAIN
Borah Pk. 12,662
Castle Pk. 11,820
Lolo Pass 5,187
Lost Trail Pass 6,990
He-Devil Mtn. 9,387
GRAND CANYON OF THE SNAKE R.
CRATERS OF THE MOON NAT'L MON.
NAT'L REACTOR TESTING STA. U.S.A.E.C. RES.
SAWTOOTH NAT'L REC. AREA
MOUNTAIN HOME A.F.B.
FORT HALL IND. RES.
WESTERN SHOSHONE IND. RES.
NEZ PERCE NAT'L HIST. PARK
© Copyright HAMMOND INCORPORATED, Maplewood, N.J.
116°
114°
112°
48°
46°
44°
42°
Longitude West 114° of Greenwich

part of the state, causing an estimated one billion dollars damage. Loss of human life was relatively light, but thousands of acres of farmland were destroyed and much of the Idaho cattle industry was temporarily wiped out by floodwaters. Reports indicate the collapse was in part due to poor design.

The eruption of Mount St. Helens in the neighboring state of Washington dumped volcanic ash on northern Idaho in May 1980.

In 1982, it was announced that the Kellogg silver mine, the nation's largest, would be closed because of low silver prices.

**Full name:** State of Idaho. **Origin of name:** Probably from the Indian word meaning "Gem of the Mountains." **Inhabitant:** Idahoan. **Capital:** Boise. **State motto:** Esto Perpetua (It Is Forever). **Flag:** State seal centered on blue field. **Seal:** Woman holding scales & a spear; miner; trees & river; elk's head; horns of plenty & sheaves of grain. **Flower:** Syringa. **Bird:** Mountain bluebird. **Tree:** Western pine. **Song:** "Here We Have Idaho." **Nickname:** Gem State.

**Governor:** John V. Evans. **Annual salary:** $40,000. **Term:** 4 years. **Current term expires:** Jan. 1983. **Voting requirements:** 18 yrs. old & U.S. citizen; state resident for 30 days; registered. **U.S. Congressmen:** 2. **Entered Union:** 1890 (43rd state).

**Location & boundaries:** Rocky Mountain state: bounded on the north by Canada; on the east by Montana & Wyoming; on the south by Utah & Nevada; & on the west by Oregon, the Snake River & Washington. **Total area:** 83,564 sq. mi. (ranks 13th). **Extreme length:** 483 mi. **Extreme breadth:** 310 mi. **Chief rivers:** Snake, Salmon, Clearwater. **Major lakes:** Pend Oreille, Coeur d'Alene, Priest. **No. of counties:** 44.

**Population (1980 census):** 944,038 (ranks 41st). **Pop. increase (1970-80):** 32.4%. **Largest cities:** Boise, Pocatello, Idaho Falls, Lewiston. **Pop. density:** 11.3 per sq. mi. (ranks 43rd). **Pop. distribution: White**—901,641; **Black**—2,716; **Am. Indian, Eskimo and Aleut**— 10,521; **Asian and Pacific Islander**—5,948; **Other**—23,109; **Spanish origin**—36,615. **Marriage rate (1979):** 14.8 per 1,000 people. **Divorce rate:** 7.1 per 1,000 people.

**State finances (1980). Revenue:** $1,108,000,000. **Expenditures:** $1,041,000,000. **State taxes:** $519.43 per capita. **State personal income tax:** Yes. **Public debt (1980):** $346.75 per capita. **Federal aid (1980):** $391.51 per capita. **Personal income (1981):** $8,906.

**Sectors of the economy (% of labor force employed in 1970):** Wholesale and retail trade (23%), Government (17%), Manufacturing (15%), Educational Services (9%), Services (8%), Construction (7%). **Leading products:** food; lumber & chemicals; electronics; printing & publishing; stone, clay & pumice. **Minerals:** silver, phosphate rock, lead, zinc. **Agricultural products:** potatoes, cattle, sheep, dairy items, wheat, hay, sugar beets. **Avg. farm (1981):** 636 acres. **Avg. value of farm per acre:** $717.

**Highway expenditures per capita (1980):** $153.87. **Persons per motor vehicle (1981):** 1.09. **Minimum age for driver's license:** 16. **Gasoline tax:** 12.5¢ per gallon. **Diesel tax:** 12.5¢ per gallon. **Motor vehicle deaths (1980):** 35.1 per 100,000 people.

**Birthrate (1979):** 22.1 per 1,000 people. **Infant mortality rate per 1,000 births (1978):** 7.3. **Physicians per 100,000 pop. (1979):** 108. **Dentists per 100,000 pop. (1979):** 55. **Acceptable hospital beds (1979):** 3.9 per 1,000 people. **State expenditures per capita for health and hospitals (1980):** $53.45.

**Education expenditures (1977-78):** $465.21 per capita annually. **No. of pupils in public schools (1980):** 204,000. **No. of institutions of higher learning (1978-79):** 9. **Public school expenditure per pupil in attendance (1978-79):** $1,517. **Avg. salary of public school teachers (1979-80):** $14,109. **No. full-time teachers (1980):** 10,050. **Educational attainment of adult population (1976):** 12.6 median yrs. of school completed: 1.5% with less than 5 years of education; 13.5% with 4 yrs. of college.

**Telephones (1979):** 54 per 100 people. **State Chamber of Commerce:** Idaho Association of Commerce & Industry, 805 Idaho St., Suite 414, P.O. Box 389, Boise, Idaho 83701.

---

## ILLINOIS

Illinois, the nation's fifth most populous state, consists almost entirely of gently rolling plains that slope gradually from north to south, although there is a range of relatively small hills, known as the Shawnee Hills (or the "Illinois Ozarks"), in the southern part of the state. In the north is Chicago, with 28.8 miles of shoreline along Lake Michigan; it is the state's largest city by far, and the country's second largest after New York. More than 60 percent of the state's population lives in or around Chicago.

Fertile soil, excellent drainage, and a long growing season have made Illinois one of the nation's major agricultural states, despite a climate that also includes spring and summer tornadoes and wide temperature extremes. The state is usually first or second (to Iowa) in corn and soybean production, and a leading producer of hogs.

Manufacturing and mining are other important revenue sources for the state, which ranks high in oil and coal production and has the nation's largest soft coal reserves. Since 1842, Illinois has been the country's leading producer of fluorspar, or fluorite, which is used in making steel.

Transportation has been a key factor in the state's growth, thanks to its strategic position between the two seaboards and its proximity to important waterways, including Lake Michigan (and the Saint Lawrence Seaway) and the Mississippi River. Canals and an extensive highway system have also helped. Chicago has been the nation's railroad hub for many years, and today is a leading air travel center.

Prehistoric Indians called Mound Builders lived in the Illinois region and left a legacy of more than 10,000 burial and temple mounds. Later inhabitants included a union of Indian tribes known as the "Illinois Confederacy." The Frenchmen Marquette and Jolliet were the first Europeans of record (1673) to visit the region and, two years later, Marquette founded a mission at the Indian town of Kaskaskia, near the present site of Utica. The first permanent European settlement, founded (1699) by French priests of the Seminary of Foreign Missions, was at Cahokia. The territory was ceded by France to Britain in 1763. In 1779, during the Revolutionary War, the Commonwealth of Virginia set up the "County of Illinois." The area passed to the Northwest Territory in 1787. The first county, St. Clair, was established in 1790. Illinois became a territory in 1809 and entered the Union as a state in 1818.

Early landmarks in the state's history included the growing migration of eastern settlers following the opening (1825) of the Erie Canal; the Black Hawk War (1832), which virtually ended Indian troubles in the area; and the "Lincoln" years (1831-60), during which Abraham Lincoln rose from New Salem laborer to Springfield lawyer and president-elect. Lincoln's seven 1858 debates on the slavery issue with prominent Democrat Stephen A. Douglas, which were held in seven different Illinois towns, did not win him the Senate seat both men were seeking, but instead won him the national attention that led to his becoming the nation's Civil War President.

Illinois made great economic advances after the Civil War, despite such setbacks as the Chicago fire (October 1871) and a number of serious labor disputes, particularly the Haymarket Square Riot (1886) and the Pullman strike (1894).

Industry boomed during World War II, which also served to put the state into the vanguard of the Atomic Age: in 1942, at the University of Chicago, Enrico Fermi and other scientists set off the world's first controlled atomic reaction.

The state's current problems are many but not unique. There have been racial tensions in the major cities, and critical unemployment in some cities. In recent years, Chicago has been plagued

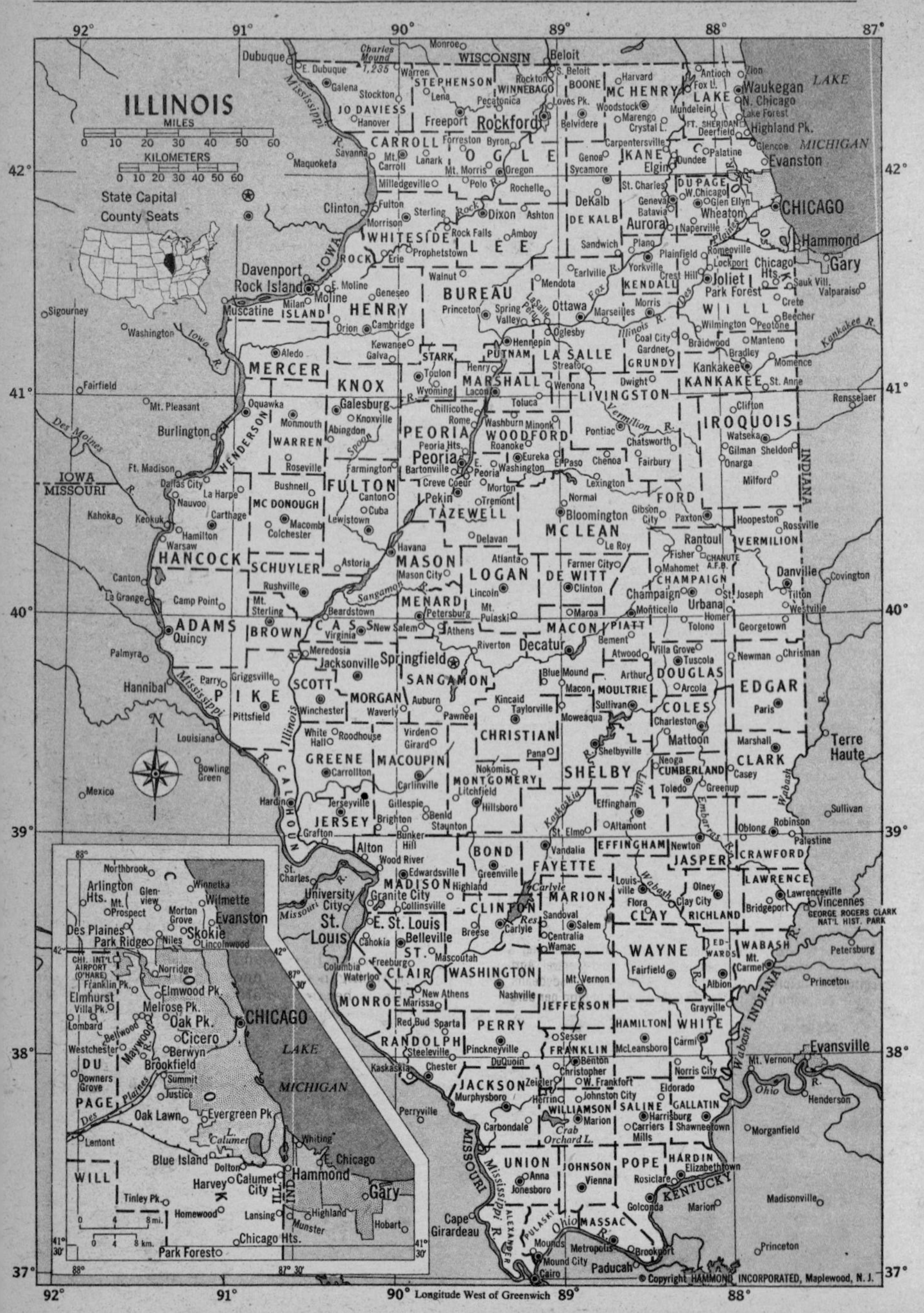
ILLINOIS
MILES
0 10 20 30 40 50 60
KILOMETERS
0 10 20 30 40 50 60
State Capital
County Seats
92°
91°
90°
89°
88°
87°
42°
41°
40°
39°
38°
37°
Longitude West of Greenwich
WISCONSIN
IOWA
MISSOURI
INDIANA
KENTUCKY
LAKE MICHIGAN
Charles Mound 1,235
Mississippi R.
Illinois R.
Rock R.
Fox R.
Des Plaines R.
Kankakee R.
Vermilion R.
Spoon R.
Sangamon R.
Kaskaskia R.
Embarras R.
Wabash R.
Ohio R.
Iowa R.
Des Moines R.
Missouri R.
Carlyle Res.
Crab Orchard L.
JO DAVIESS
STEPHENSON
WINNEBAGO
BOONE
MC HENRY
LAKE
CARROLL
OGLE
DE KALB
KANE
DU PAGE
COOK
WHITESIDE
LEE
ROCK ISLAND
HENRY
BUREAU
LA SALLE
KENDALL
WILL
GRUNDY
MERCER
KNOX
STARK
PUTNAM
MARSHALL
KANKAKEE
LIVINGSTON
HENDERSON
WARREN
PEORIA
WOODFORD
IROQUOIS
FULTON
TAZEWELL
MC LEAN
FORD
HANCOCK
MC DONOUGH
SCHUYLER
MASON
LOGAN
DE WITT
CHAMPAIGN
VERMILION
ADAMS
BROWN
CASS
MENARD
MACON
PIATT
PIKE
SCOTT
MORGAN
SANGAMON
MOULTRIE
DOUGLAS
EDGAR
COLES
CHRISTIAN
SHELBY
CLARK
CUMBERLAND
GREENE
MACOUPIN
MONTGOMERY
JERSEY
CALHOUN
BOND
FAYETTE
EFFINGHAM
JASPER
CRAWFORD
MADISON
CLINTON
MARION
CLAY
RICHLAND
LAWRENCE
ST. CLAIR
WASHINGTON
WAYNE
EDWARDS
WABASH
MONROE
JEFFERSON
HAMILTON
WHITE
RANDOLPH
PERRY
FRANKLIN
JACKSON
WILLIAMSON
SALINE
GALLATIN
UNION
JOHNSON
POPE
HARDIN
ALEXANDER
PULASKI
MASSAC
Dubuque
Galena
Freeport
Rockford
Beloit
Waukegan
Evanston
CHICAGO
Hammond
Gary
Joliet
Aurora
Elgin
Wheaton
DeKalb
Dixon
Sterling
Clinton
Davenport
Rock Island
Moline
Muscatine
Ottawa
Kankakee
Galesburg
Peoria
Pekin
Bloomington
Burlington
Keokuk
Macomb
Champaign
Urbana
Danville
Decatur
Springfield
Jacksonville
Quincy
Hannibal
Mattoon
Charleston
Terre Haute
Alton
Belleville
E. St. Louis
St. Louis
Granite City
Vincennes
Mt. Vernon
Carbondale
Marion
Evansville
Cape Girardeau
Paducah
Cairo
GEORGE ROGERS CLARK NAT'L. HIST. PARK
CHANUTE A.F.B.
Arlington Hts.
Des Plaines
Park Ridge
Skokie
Wilmette
Winnetka
Northbrook
CHI. INT'L AIRPORT (O'HARE)
Elmhurst
Oak Pk.
Cicero
Berwyn
Maywood
Oak Lawn
Evergreen Pk.
Blue Island
Harvey
Calumet City
Whiting
E. Chicago
Chicago Hts.
Park Forest
© Copyright HAMMOND INCORPORATED, Maplewood, N. J.

by civil unrest and corruption, and there have been violence, security problems and a number of escapes from Illinois prisons.

The state's tourist attractions include Old Town, the Art Institute, the Sears Tower, the world's tallest building, and the Museum of Science and Industry in Chicago; the reconstructed state park in New Salem, where Lincoln lived (1831-37); the Lincoln home and tomb in Springfield; the Dickson Indian Mounds near Havana; historic Galena, site of the Ulysses S. Grant home; the former Mormon settlement of Nauvoo; and Shawnee National Forest. Chain O'Lakes, a group of lakes in the northeastern part of the state, is a popular summer resort area.

**Full name:** State of Illinois. **Origin of name:** From Indian name meaning "The Men." **Inhabitant:** Illinoisan. **Capital:** Springfield. **State motto:** State Sovereignty—National Union. **Flag:** Adaptation of state seal centered on white field. **Seal:** An American eagle holds shield with stars & stripes, representing 13 original states; olive branch stands for peace; prairies & rising sun represent plains of Illinois. **Flower:** Native violet. **Bird:** Cardinal. **Tree:** Oak. **Song:** "Illinois." **Nickname:** Prairie State.

**Governor:** James R. Thompson. **Annual salary:** $58,000. **Term:** 4 years. **Current term expires:** Jan. 1983. **Voting requirements:** 18 yrs. old & U.S. citizen; resident of state, county, and district 30 days. **U.S. Congressmen:** 22. **Entered Union:** 1818 (21st state).

**Location & boundaries:** Midwestern state: bounded on the north by Wisconsin; on the east by Lake Michigan, Indiana & the Wabash River; on the southeast by Kentucky; on the southwest by Missouri; & on the west by the Mississippi River, Missouri & Iowa. **Total area:** 56,345 sq. mi. (ranks 24th). **Extreme length:** 381 mi. **Extreme breadth:** 211 mi. **Shoreline:** 63 mi. **Chief rivers:** Mississippi, Illinois, Kaskaskia. **Major lakes:** Michigan, Chain O'Lakes. **No. of counties:** 102.

**Population (1980 census):** 11,426,596 (ranks 5th). **Pop. increase (1970-80):** 2.8%. **Largest cities:** Chicago, Rockford, Peoria, Springfield. **Pop. density:** 203.0 per sq. mi. (ranks 10th). **Pop. distribution: White**—9,225,575; **Black**—1,675,229; **Am. Indian, Eskimo and Aleut**—16,271; **Asian and Pacific Islander**—159,551; **Other**—341,835; **Spanish origin**—635,525. **Marriage rate (1979):** 9.7 per 1,000 people. **Divorce rate:** 4.6 per 1,000 people.

**State finances (1980). Revenue:** $12,730,000,000. **Expenditures:** $12,429,000,000. **State taxes:** $619.47 per capita. **State personal income tax:** Yes. **Public debt (1980):** $549.76 per capita. **Federal aid (1980):** $391.73 per capita. **Personal income (1981):** $11,479.

**Sectors of the economy (% of labor force employed in 1970):** Manufacturing (30%), Wholesale and retail trade (20%), Government (13%), Services (7%), Educational Services (7%), Construction (5%). **Leading products:** machinery, food, electrical machinery, primary & fabricated metals, chemicals, printing & publishing. **Minerals:** coal; petroleum; stone, sand & gravel. **Agricultural products:** hogs, cattle, dairy items, corn, soybeans, wheat. **Avg. farm (1981):** 274 acres. **Avg. value of farm per acre:** $2,133.

**Highway expenditures per capita (1980):** $118.38. **Persons per motor vehicle (1981):** 1.49. **Minimum age for driver's license:** 16. **Gasoline tax:** 7.5¢ per gallon. **Diesel tax:** 7.5¢ per gallon. **Motor vehicle deaths (1980):** 17.3 per 100,000 people.

**Birthrate (1979):** 16.4 per 1,000 people. **Infant mortality rate per 1,000 births (1978):** 15.7. **Physicians per 100,000 pop. (1979):** 182. **Dentists per 100,000 pop. (1979):** 54. **Acceptable hospital beds (1979):** 6.4 per 1,000 people. **State expenditures per capita for health and hospitals (1980):** $56.66.

**Education expenditures (1977-78):** $504.27 per capita annually. **No. of pupils in public schools (1980):** 1,986,000. **No. of institutions of higher learning (1978-79):** 154. **Public school expenditure per pupil in attendance (1978-79):** $2,202. **Avg. salary of public school teachers (1979-80):** $17,931. **No. full-time teachers (1980):** 122,100. **Educational attainment of adult population (1976):** 12.5 median yrs. of school completed: 2.6% with less than 5 years of education; 13.7% with 4 yrs. of college.

**Telephones (1979):** 66 per 100 people. **State Chamber of Commerce:** Illinois State Chamber of Commerce, 20 North Wacker Drive, Chicago, Illinois 60606.

## INDIANA

Although it is the smallest state in the continental United States west of the Alleghenies, Indiana ranks among the national leaders in population, agriculture, and manufacturing. Huge steel mills and oil refineries make the state's 45-mile Lake Michigan waterfront one of the world's great industrial centers, while the fertile plains of the central region produce an abundance of food (especially grain crops) for market and livestock. Mining, especially of coal and oil, is also significant; and the state's vast southern quarries produce two-thirds of the nation's building limestone. The automotive industry maintains a large number of plants in the state.

There are three main land regions: the Great Lakes Plain in the north, the central Till Plains (the largest single area), and, in the south, the Interior Low Plateau, characterized by hills, ridges, knolls, caves, and waterfalls. (The two plains regions are subdivisions of the Central Lowlands.) The generally mild, humid climate is marked by occasional temperature extremes.

The first inhabitants of the Indiana region were the prehistoric Mound Builders, followed by a number of Indian tribes, chiefly the Miamis. Many of the Indians came into the area from the east after losing their land to the white settlers. The first European of record to visit the region was Robert Cavelier, Sieur de La Salle, who made two explorations (1679, 1681) and paved the way for French fur-trading posts (in the 1720s) and the first European permanent settlement at Vincennes (fortified 1732). The English sharply challenged French control, however, and by the 1763 Treaty of Paris they gained dominance in the area; in 1774 the British government attached the territory to the province of Quebec.

During the American Revolution, George Rogers Clark and a small army financed by Virginia Governor Patrick Henry captured (1778) Vincennes from the British, lost it, and then in the following year recaptured it. Virginia relinquished (1784) its claim to the Northwest Territory, of which Indiana was the south central part; three years later, the Northwest Ordinance provided for the territory's government, the permanent exclusion of slavery, and basic individual rights. Indiana Territory was created as an entity separate from Ohio in 1800 and initially included the present states of Indiana, Illinois, and Wisconsin, as well as parts of Michigan and Minnesota. After Michigan and Illinois became separate territories (1805, 1809), Indiana had almost the same boundaries as it has today. (The present boundaries were finally established when statehood was attained, in 1816.)

Indian troubles in the area were serious and persistent during the whole early period of white settlement. Anthony Wayne's victory at Fallen Timbers in Ohio (1794) brought peace but it was short-lived. Governor William Henry Harrison, who played a primary role in Indiana's early development, purchased (1809) for the Federal Government nearly 3 million acres of Indian lands in southern Indiana; this outraged the Shawnee chief Tecumseh, who led several tribes on the warpath. Troops led by Harrison won (1811) the Battle of Tippecanoe (near present-day Lafayette) and, during the War of 1812, defeated combined Indian and British forces in the Battle of the Thames, at Moraviantown, Ontario. Thus was British influence in the region ended, and the Indian threat virtually broken.

Indiana's famous "Hoosier" personality was forged in the first half of the 19th century, and its

INDIANA
MILES
0 10 20 30 40 50
KILOMETERS
0 10 20 30 40 50
State Capital
County Seats
© Copyright HAMMOND INCORPORATED, Maplewood, N. J.
Longitude West of Greenwich
88°
87°
86°
85°
41°
40°
39°
38°
CHICAGO
Lake Michigan
MICHIGAN
OHIO
ILLINOIS
KENTUCKY
CINCINNATI
Covington
Louisville
INDIANA DUNES NAT'L LAKESHORE
GEORGE ROGERS CLARK NAT'L HIST. PARK
LINCOLN BOYHOOD NAT'L MEM.
GRISSOM A.F.B.
BAKALAR A.F.B.
INDIANAPOLIS
South Bend
Gary
Hammond
Fort Wayne
Evansville
Terre Haute
Muncie
Anderson
Kokomo
Lafayette
Richmond
Bloomington
LAKE
PORTER
LAPORTE
ST. JOSEPH
ELKHART
LAGRANGE
STEUBEN
NOBLE
DEKALB
STARKE
MARSHALL
KOSCIUSKO
WHITLEY
ALLEN
NEWTON
JASPER
PULASKI
FULTON
MIAMI
WABASH
HUNTINGTON
WELLS
ADAMS
BENTON
WHITE
CASS
CARROLL
HOWARD
GRANT
BLACKFORD
JAY
WARREN
TIPPECANOE
CLINTON
TIPTON
MADISON
DELAWARE
RANDOLPH
FOUNTAIN
MONTGOMERY
BOONE
HAMILTON
HENDRICKS
MARION
HANCOCK
HENRY
WAYNE
VERMILLION
PARKE
PUTNAM
MORGAN
JOHNSON
SHELBY
RUSH
FAYETTE
UNION
FRANKLIN
VIGO
CLAY
OWEN
MONROE
BROWN
BARTHOLOMEW
DECATUR
RIPLEY
DEARBORN
SULLIVAN
GREENE
LAWRENCE
JACKSON
JENNINGS
OHIO
SWITZERLAND
KNOX
DAVIESS
MARTIN
ORANGE
WASHINGTON
SCOTT
JEFFERSON
CLARK
PIKE
DUBOIS
FLOYD
GIBSON
WARRICK
CRAWFORD
HARRISON
POSEY
VANDERBURGH
SPENCER
PERRY
Kankakee R.
Iroquois R.
Wabash R.
Tippecanoe
Eel R.
Mississinewa
White R.
Ohio River
Kentucky R.
Maumee
St. Joseph R.
Monroe Res.
L. Shafer
L. St. Marys
Cataract L.
Morse Res.

hallmarks were rustic simplicity, self-sufficient isolation, and an almost reflexive conservatism. Attempts were made, most notably at New Harmony (1814), to reorganize society fundamentally along idealistic lines; although the experiments failed, they were the basis for the eventual development in the state of enlightened social and legal institutions and practices. The Hoosier spirit has been immortalized by such authors as Edward Eggleston, James Whitcomb Riley, Booth Tarkington, and George Ade, as well as songwriter Paul Dresser ("On the Banks of the Wabash") and artist John T. McCutcheon, whose cartoon "Injun Summer" has become a classic of its kind. And although his themes were more universal, novelist Theodore Dreiser (*Sister Carrie, An American Tragedy*) was also a Hoosier, and the brother of Paul Dresser.

Internal strife, led by the proslavery Knights of the Golden Circle, marked the Civil War period in Indiana, which, however, largely supported the Union cause. Except for occasional raids, the state saw little action.

Indiana's first public port opened in 1970 on Lake Michigan near Portage after a prolonged battle between proponents of industrial expansion and environmentalists over destruction of the unique dunelands between Gary and Michigan City. A compromise produced the Dunes National Lakeshore.

While the port permits worldwide waterborne trade via the St. Lawrence Seaway, much greater tonnage moves on the Ohio River, where there is a port at Mount Vernon; another port is under construction near Jeffersonville.

Raillroads and trucks remain the most important transport in Indiana, where Indianapolis is favored by being the crossroads of five interstate highways. Virtually all livestock now moves by truck, and there have been forecasts that Indianapolis will become the largest collecting point in the nation for meat animals.

Hoosiers also brag of the Army Finance Center at Ft. Benjamin Harrison, largest U.S. military building aside from the Pentagon.

Indiana's major tourist attractions include the Dunes National Lakeshore near Gary; the Motor Speedway and Hall of Fame at Indianapolis; the Lincoln Boyhood National Memorial, the Lincoln State Park near Lincoln City; the well-preserved Indian earthworks at Mounds State Park near Anderson; the Rappite and Owenite communal settlements at New Harmony; and the George Rogers Clark National Historical Park at Vincennes. Claremont is the site of Raceway Park, home of drag racing.

In 1980, the United States Supreme Court ruled that the boundary between Indiana and Kentucky was the high-water mark of the Ohio River as it was in 1792—not, as Kentucky claimed, the contemporary high-water mark. The ruling made it impossible for Kentucky to sue to stop construction of a nuclear power plant at Marble Hill, Indiana, but Kentucky gained jurisdiction over some land on the Indiana side of the river.

**Full name:** State of Indiana. **Origin of name:** Denoted that state was domain of Indians. **Inhabitant:** Hoosier. **Capital:** Indianapolis. **State motto:** The Crossroads of America. **Flag:** Gold torch & 19 gold stars on blue field. **Seal:** Pioneer scene represents westward expansion. **Flower:** Peony. **Bird:** Cardinal. **Tree:** Tulip poplar. **Song:** "On the Banks of the Wabash Far Away." **Nickname:** Hoosier State.

**Governor:** Robert D. Orr. **Annual salary:** $48,000. **Term:** 4 years. **Current term expires:** Jan. 1985. **Voting requirements:** 18 yrs. old & U.S. citizen; resident of state 30 days; township 60 days; precinct 30 days. **U.S. Congressmen:** 10. **Entered Union:** 1816 (19th state).

**Location & boundaries:** Midwestern state: bounded on the north by Lake Michigan & Michigan; on the east by Ohio; on the southeast & south by the Ohio River & Kentucky; & on the west by the Wabash River & Illinois. **Total area:** 36,185 sq. mi. (ranks 38th). **Extreme length:** 280 mi. **Extreme breadth:** 160 mi. **Shoreline:** 45 mi. **Chief rivers:** Wabash, Ohio, White. **Major lakes (other than border-forming):** Monroe Reservoir, Mississinewa Reservoir, Wawasee. **No. of counties:** 92.

**Population (1980 census):** 5,490,260 (ranks 12th). **Pop. increase (1970-80):** 5.7%. **Largest cities:** Indianapolis, Fort Wayne, Gary, Evansville. **Pop. density:** 151.7 per sq. mi. (ranks 13th). **Pop. distribution: White**—5,004,567; **Black**—414,732; **Am. Indian, Eskimo and Aleut**—7,835; **Asian and Pacific Islander**—20,488; **Other**—42,557; **Spanish origin**—87,000. **Marriage rate (1979):** 11.0 per 1,000 people. **Divorce rate:** 7.7 per 1,000 people.

**State finances (1980). Revenue:** $4,794,000,000. **Expenditures:** $4,867,000,000. **State taxes:** $491.03 per capita. **State personal income tax:** Yes. **Public debt (1980):** $110.67 per capita. **Federal aid (1980):** $292.90 per capita. **Personal income (1981):** $9,656.

**Sectors of the economy (% of labor force employed in 1970):** Manufacturing (36%), Wholesale and retail trade (19%), Government (13%), Educational Services (8%), Services (6%), Construction (5%). **Leading products:** electrical & other machinery, transportation equipment, food, chemicals, primary & fabricated metals. **Minerals:** coal, cement, stone, petroleum. **Agricultural products:** hogs, cattle, dairy items, corn, soybeans, wheat. **Avg. farm (1981):** 193 acres. **Avg. value of farm per acre:** $1,972.

**Highway expenditures per capita (1980):** $117.53. **Persons per motor vehicle (1981):** 1.42. **Minimum age for driver's license:** 16. **Gasoline tax:** 11.1¢ per gallon. **Diesel tax:** 11.1¢ per gallon. **Motor vehicle deaths (1980):** 21.2 per 100,000 people.

**Birthrate (1979):** 16.2 per 1,000 people. **Infant mortality rate per 1,000 births (1978):** 13.1. **Physicians per 100,000 pop. (1979):** 126. **Dentists per 100,000 pop. (1979):** 43. **Acceptable hospital beds (1979):** 5.9 per 1,000 people. **State expenditures per capita for health and hospitals (1980):** $57.71.

**Education expenditures (1977-78):** $443.79 per capita annually. **No. of pupils in public schools (1980):** 1,057,000. **No. of institutions of higher learning (1978-79):** 66. **Public school expenditure per pupil in attendance (1978-79):** $1,690. **Avg. salary of public school teachers (1979-80):** $15,754. **No. full-time teachers (1980):** 58,400. **Educational attainment of adult population (1976):** 12.4 median yrs. of school completed: 1.9% with less thhan 5 years of education; 11.0% with 4 yrs. of college.

**Telephones (1979):** 57 per 100 people. **State Chamber of Commerce:** Indiana State Chamber of Commerce, Inc., Indiana Commerce Center, One North Capitol, Suite 200, Indianapolis, Indiana 46204.

## IOWA

With about two-thirds of its land mass between 800 and 1,400 feet above sea level, Iowa is a gently rolling plain quilted almost entirely by farms. The border-forming Mississippi and Missouri Rivers provide an abundant water supply and transportation routes.

The soil of Iowa is considered the finest in America and accounts for the fact that Iowa produces a tenth of the nation's food suppply. It alternately shares the lead with Illinois in corn and soybean production, and is a major producer of oats. The state's high crop yield supports the country's largest livestock industry; Iowa is the leading hog state and ranks high in cattle. It is also a leader in the production of butter and cheese.

Because of the soil's economic importance, floods and the quest of greater productivity have made Iowans conservation conscious. In fact, in 1960 it was recognized that only a quarter of the state's water supply was being effectively harnessed.

As impressive as Iowa's agriculture is, manufacturing income is greater. Farm machinery, electronic equipment, mobile homes and home appliances are important products of the state's

IOWA
MILES
KILOMETERS
State Capital
County Seats
MINNESOTA
WISCONSIN
ILLINOIS
MISSOURI
NEBRASKA
S. DAKOTA
MISSISSIPPI
LYON
OSCEOLA
DICKINSON
EMMET
KOSSUTH
WINNEBAGO
WORTH
MITCHELL
HOWARD
WINNESHIEK
ALLAMAKEE
SIOUX
O'BRIEN
CLAY
PALO ALTO
HANCOCK
CERRO GORDO
FLOYD
CHICKASAW
FAYETTE
CLAYTON
PLYMOUTH
CHEROKEE
BUENA VISTA
POCAHONTAS
HUMBOLDT
WRIGHT
FRANKLIN
BUTLER
BREMER
BLACK HAWK
BUCHANAN
DELAWARE
DUBUQUE
WOODBURY
IDA
SAC
CALHOUN
WEBSTER
HAMILTON
HARDIN
GRUNDY
TAMA
BENTON
LINN
JONES
JACKSON
CLINTON
MONONA
CRAWFORD
CARROLL
GREENE
BOONE
STORY
MARSHALL
IOWA
JOHNSON
CEDAR
SCOTT
MUSCATINE
HARRISON
SHELBY
AUDUBON
GUTHRIE
DALLAS
POLK
JASPER
POWESHIEK
POTTAWATTAMIE
CASS
ADAIR
MADISON
WARREN
MARION
MAHASKA
KEOKUK
WASHINGTON
LOUISA
MILLS
MONTGOMERY
ADAMS
UNION
CLARKE
LUCAS
MONROE
WAPELLO
JEFFERSON
HENRY
DES MOINES
FREMONT
PAGE
TAYLOR
RINGGOLD
DECATUR
WAYNE
APPANOOSE
DAVIS
VAN BUREN
LEE
Des Moines
Longitude West of Greenwich
© Copyright HAMMOND INCORPORATED, Maplewood, N. J.

industries. The chief industrial centers are Des Moines; Cedar Rapids, site of its first nuclear power plant (1974); Dubuque and Waterloo. Except for gypsum—Iowa is the nation's third-largest producer—mining is not significant.

The state's climate is of the continental, long-summer type, marked by great extremes; there is generally less precipitation in the western regions than in the eastern.

A civilization of Mound Builders—sedentary farmers who lived in permanent villages—predated the Indians in Iowa; the Effigy Mounds National Monument contains numerous examples of their building in bird, animal, and serpentine forms. The first Europeans to visit the region were Jacques Marquette and Louis Jolliet (1673); almost a century later (1788), the Indians allowed Julien Dubuque, a French-Canadian, to mine lead in the area of the city named for him. The United States obtained control of the state under the Louisiana Purchase (1803). Formation of Iowa Territory dates from 1838.

There was much fighting between white settlers and Indians of the area. A rich strip of land 50 miles wide along the Mississippi was won from the Sauk and Fox in 1832, after Black Hawk and his braves were defeated in battle. Other areas were taken from the Indians in 1836 and 1837. The Sioux ceded their claims in 1851, although an outlaw band of their numbers six years later killed 33 settlers in the Spirit Lake Massacre.

When Iowa became (1846) a state, its capital was at Iowa City; the more centrally located Des Moines became the capital in 1857. It was at this time, too, that the state's present boundaries were drawn up.

Iowa was strongly anti-slavery during the antebellum period and was a center for abolitionist activity. The state was staunchly pro-Union during the Civil War and provided a large number of troops for the Union cause.

From the beginning, the character of Iowa has been a paradoxical amalgam of free-thinking liberalism and close-to-the-vest conservatism. Education has long had a high priority in the state, resulting in the nation's lowest illiteracy rate. Iowa has 3 state-supported universities, over 30 private colleges and approximately 10 private junior colleges. In 1965 a system of 15 area community colleges and vocational-technical schools was established.

Iowa's tourist attractions include the Amana, 20 miles southwest of Cedar Rapids; the Effigy Mounds National Monument, famed for its Indian mounds in the shapes of birds and animals; and the Herbert Hoover National Historic Site east of Iowa City.

**Full name:** State of Iowa. **Origin of name:** From name of Sioux tribe—the Ioways or Aiouez—meaning "Sleepy Ones." **Inhabitant:** Iowan. **Capital:** Des Moines. **State motto:** Our Liberties We Prize & Our Rights We Will Maintain. **Flag:** Vertical blue, white & red bars; flying eagle carrying state motto. **Seal:** Prairie scene represents Iowa's pioneer days; an eagle flies over scene carrying streamer with state motto. **Flower:** Wild rose. **Bird:** Eastern goldfinch. **Tree:** Oak. **Song:** "The Song of Iowa." **Nickname:** Hawkeye State.

**Governor:** Robert D. Ray. **Annual salary:** $60,000. **Term:** 4 years. **Current term expires:** Jan. 1983. **Voting requirements:** 18 yrs. old & U.S. citizen; resident of state; registration 10 days before election. **U.S. Congressmen:** 6. **Entered Union:** 1846 (29th state).

**Location & boundaries:** Midwestern state: bounded on the north by Minnesota; on the east by the Mississippi River, Wisconsin & Illinois; on the south by the Des Moines River & Missouri; & on the west by the Missouri River, Nebraska, the Big Sioux River & South Dakota. **Total area:** 56,275 sq. mi. (ranks 25th). **Extreme length:** 324 mi. **Extreme breadth:** 210 mi. **Chief rivers:** Des Moines, Mississippi, Missouri, Big Sioux. **Major lakes:** Clear, Spirit, Storm Red Rock. **No. of counties:** 99.

**Population (1980 census):** 2,913,808 (ranks 27th). **Pop. increase (1970-80):** 3.1%. **Largest cities:** Des Moines, Cedar Rapids, Davenport, Sioux City. **Pop. density:** 51.8 per sq. mi. (ranks 32nd). **Pop. distribution: White**— 2,838,805; **Black**—41,700; **Am. Indian, Eskimo and Aleut**—5,453; **Asian and Pacific Islander**—11,577; **Other**—15,852; **Spanish origin**—25,536. **Marriage rate (1979):** 9.6 per 1,000 people. **Divorce rate:** 3.9 per 1,000 people.

**State finances (1980). Revenue:** $3,479,000,000. **Expenditures:** $3,412,000,000. **State taxes:** $599.67 per capita. **State personal income tax:** Yes. **Public debt (1980):** $130.79 per capita. **Federal aid (1980):** $341.27 per capita. **Personal income (1981):** $10,149.

**Sectors of the economy (% of labor force employed in 1970):** Wholesale and retail trade (22%), Manufacturing (20%), Government (14%), Educational Services (9%), Services (7%), Construction (5%). **Leading products:** food; electrical & other machinery; chemicals; printing & publishing; primary & fabricated metals; stone, clay & glass items. **Minerals:** cement; stone, sand & gravel; gypsum. **Agricultural products:** cattle, hogs, dairy items, corn, soybeans, hay. **Avg. farm (1981):** 286 acres. **Avg. value of farm per acre:** $1,941.

**Highway expenditures per capita (1980):** $168.70. **Persons per motor vehicle (1981):** 1.25. **Minimum age for driver's license:** 16. **Gasoline tax:** 13¢ per gallon. **Diesel tax:** 15.5¢ per gallon. **Motor vehicle deaths (1980):** 21.5 per 100,000 people.

**Birthrate (1979):** 16.1 per 1,000 people. **Infant mortality rate per 1,000 births (1978):** 12.6. **Physicians per 100,000 pop. (1979):** 122. **Dentists per 100,000 pop. (1979):** 50. **Acceptable hospital beds (1979):** 7.4 per 1,000 people. **State expenditures per capita for health and hospitals (1980):** $77.54.

**Education expenditures (1977-78):** $542.93 per capita annually. **No. of pupils in public schools (1980):** 529,000. **No. of institutions of higher learning (1978-79):** 62. **Public school expenditure per pupil in attendance (1978-79):** $2,107. **Avg. salary of public school teachers (1979-80):** $15,550. **No. full-time teachers (1980):** 35,600. **Educational attainment of adult population (1976):** 12.5 median yrs. of school completed: .9% with less than 5 years of education; 12.8% with 4 yrs. of college.

**Telephones (1979):** 59 per 100 people. **State Chamber of Commerce:** Iowa Manufacturers Association, 706 Employers Mutual Building, 717 Mulberry Street, Des Moines, Iowa 50309.

## KANSAS

The popular notion that Kansas consists wholly of flat prairie land is false; the land, in fact, rises from an elevation of about 700 feet in the southeast to more than 4,000 feet in the northwest, where the foothills of the Rockies begin. Three main land regions make up the state: the Great Plains, covering the western two-thirds; the Dissected Till Plains, covering a small area in the northeast corner; and the Southeastern Plains, often subdivided by geographers into the Osage Plains in the east and the Flint Hills in the west. Thousands of rolling hills between 100 and 400 feet high dot the state's terrain, which also features many valleys and picturesque chalk and sandstone formations. The relatively small natural water area is augmented by more than a hundred artificial lakes.

The eastern half of Kansas contains the overwhelmingly larger part of the population: the three largest cities—Wichita, Kansas City, and Topeka—are all in this section. Kansas City, on the eastern border, adjoins Kansas City, Missouri, but the two are separate municipalities.

A number of Indian tribes—including the Kansa, Wichita, Pawnee, and Comanche—were living in the Kansas region before the coming (1541) of the first European, Spanish explorer Francisco Vásquez de Coronado; he and his men were seeking the gold of a land called Quivira and, finding none, departed without establishing settlements. La Salle's far-reaching land claims (1682) on behalf of France included the Kansas region but, although French fur traders dealt with area Indians in the years immediately following,

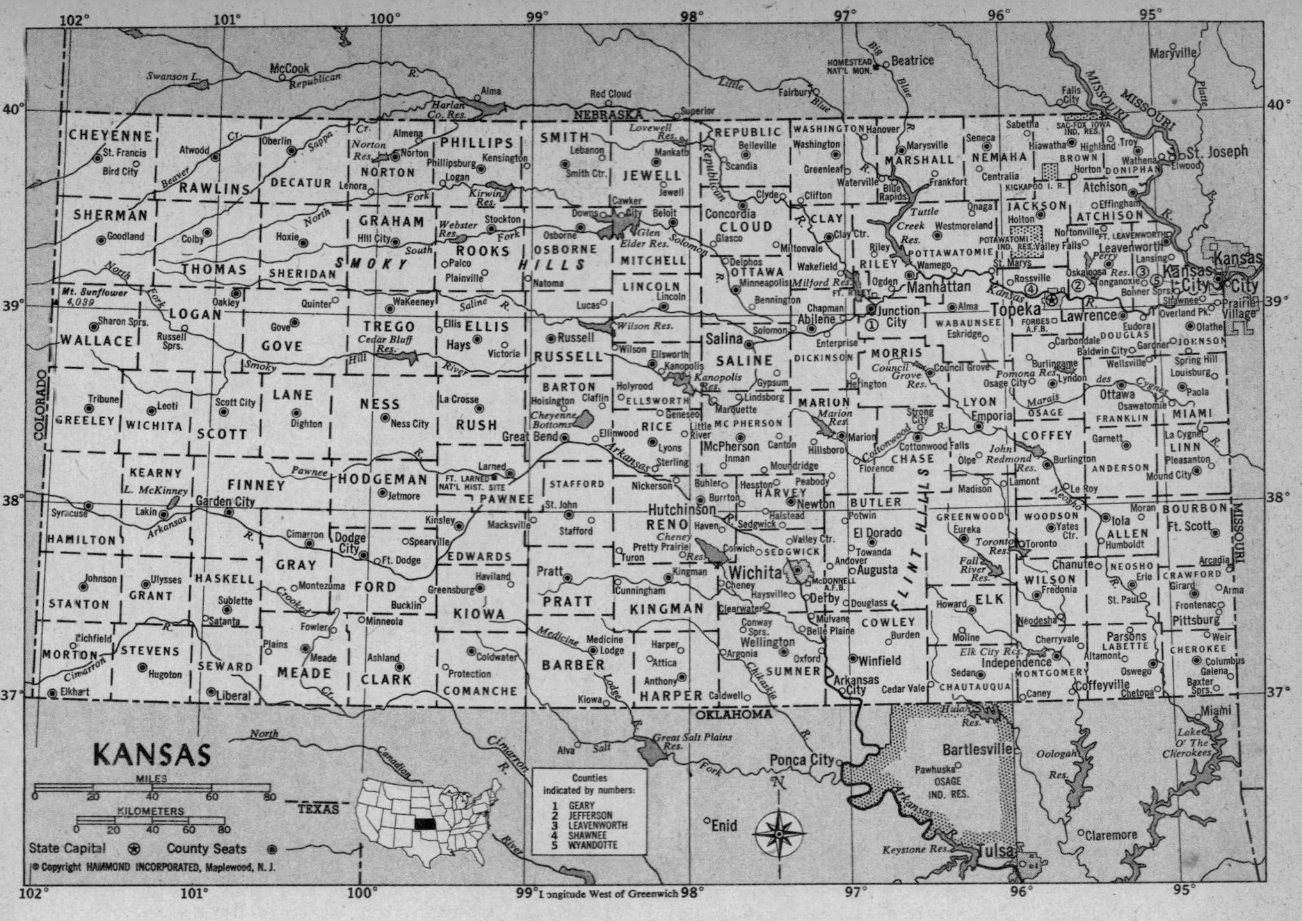
KANSAS
MILES
0 20 40 60 80
KILOMETERS
0 20 40 60 80
State Capital
County Seats
© Copyright HAMMOND INCORPORATED, Maplewood, N. J.
Counties indicated by numbers:
1 GEARY
2 JEFFERSON
3 LEAVENWORTH
4 SHAWNEE
5 WYANDOTTE
Longitude West of Greenwich
NEBRASKA
MISSOURI
COLORADO
OKLAHOMA
TEXAS
CHEYENNE
RAWLINS
DECATUR
NORTON
PHILLIPS
SMITH
JEWELL
REPUBLIC
WASHINGTON
MARSHALL
NEMAHA
BROWN
DONIPHAN
SHERMAN
THOMAS
SHERIDAN
GRAHAM
ROOKS
OSBORNE
MITCHELL
CLOUD
CLAY
RILEY
POTTAWATOMIE
JACKSON
ATCHISON
WALLACE
LOGAN
GOVE
TREGO
ELLIS
RUSSELL
LINCOLN
OTTAWA
DICKINSON
WABAUNSEE
DOUGLAS
JOHNSON
GREELEY
WICHITA
SCOTT
LANE
NESS
RUSH
BARTON
ELLSWORTH
SALINE
MORRIS
LYON
OSAGE
FRANKLIN
MIAMI
HAMILTON
KEARNY
FINNEY
HODGEMAN
PAWNEE
STAFFORD
RICE
MC PHERSON
MARION
CHASE
COFFEY
ANDERSON
LINN
STANTON
GRANT
HASKELL
GRAY
FORD
EDWARDS
KIOWA
PRATT
RENO
HARVEY
BUTLER
GREENWOOD
WOODSON
ALLEN
BOURBON
MORTON
STEVENS
SEWARD
MEADE
CLARK
COMANCHE
BARBER
HARPER
KINGMAN
SEDGWICK
SUMNER
COWLEY
ELK
CHAUTAUQUA
WILSON
MONTGOMERY
NEOSHO
LABETTE
CRAWFORD
CHEROKEE
Topeka
Wichita
Kansas City
Salina
Hutchinson
Dodge City
Garden City
Manhattan
Lawrence
Emporia

the Indians retained actual possession of the land. France yielded its claim to West Louisiana (including Kansas) to Spain in 1763, and Spain retroceded it to France (1800), which three years later sold it in the Louisiana Purchase to the United States.

Lewis and Clark, Zebulon M. Pike, and Major Stephen H. Long made (1803-19) the first serious explorations of the area, but their reports were incomplete and such as to discourage immediate American settlement. Erroneously considered a part of the "Great American Desert," the Kansas region was primarily used (1825-42) as a resettlement area for uprooted Indian tribes.

With the establishment of the Santa Fe Trail (1821), which cut across the region diagonally from northeast to southwest, and the Oregon Trail (c. 1830), which traversed part of the northeastern region, the first permanent non-Indian settlements (Fort Leavenworth-1827, Fort Scott-1842, and Fort Riley-1853) were founded as outposts to protect travelers against Indian raids.

The passage of the Kansas-Nebraska Act (1854), repealing the slavery-prohibiting Missouri Compromise of 1821 in favor of "squatter sovereignty," thrust Kansas into a bloody tug-of-war between proslavery and antislavery forces who rushed into the territory and fought savagely for political control. This was the era of "Bleeding Kansas," which saw the free-state "Jayhawkers" (including famed abolitionist John Brown) pitted against the advocates of slavery; the Jayhawkers ultimately won out and, in 1861 Kansas entered the Union as a free state.

Often called the Nation's Breadbasket, Kansas is the leading wheat producer and flour miller as well as one of the most important mining states. Today, Kansas is moving toward economic diversification, and manufacturing has now surpassed agriculture as the primary revenue source. The massive wheat and cattle raising operations have spawned an impressive manufacturing segment producing farm and heavy equipment. Hesston Corporation is now a world leader in farm machinery and exemplifies Kansas' growth in this area.

The production of transportation equipment is the major industrial activity. Wichita produces more than half of the nation's aircraft, while Topeka is a center for the manufacture and repair of railroad cars, and is also a major tire production center. Kansas' strategic location in the center of America makes it attractive to industries with nationwide distribution.

Occasional periods of drought or flood have prompted a massive program of flood control, water conservation and utilization. More than 30 federal reservoirs have been constructed or authorized along with dozens of watershed districts.

The reservoirs and lesser impoundments assure cities and industries of a stable water supply and provide facilities for camping, fishing, swimming, boating and water skiing. There are state park facilities at many of the reservoirs and an outstanding system of roadside parks.

Among the top tourist attractions is the Dwight D. Eisenhower Center at Abilene, featuring the boyhood home, Museum, Presidential Library, and Chapel where the former President and World War II commander is buried. Reconstruction of Early Day Front Street at Dodge City and Old Ft. Larned are other tourist attractions.

As a result of the food shortage of recent years, thousands of acres of Kansas farmland were pressed back into production. Bumper crops of wheat, corn and sorghum were harvested in 1976 and 1977, both here and abroad, with the result that U.S. stockpiles were at their highest level in many years and prices dropped sharply in the face of a lessening demand for American grains abroad. Kansas farmers were among the leaders of the American Agriculture movement, which withheld grain and influenced the price support increases of 1978. Corn and wheat production in 1979 and 1980 again hit record highs.

In the fall of 1979, a controversial Federal court order requiring the Wichita public schools to reassign thousands of pupils in order to improve racial balance was implemented with no serious incidents. However, a violent racial confrontation between blacks and the Wichita police, unrelated to the school reassignment order, took place on April 22, 1980.

**Full name:** State of Kansas. **Origin of name:** From name of Sioux tribe, meaning "People of the South Wind." **Inhabitant:** Kansan. **Capital:** Topeka. **State motto:** Ad Astra per Aspera (To the Stars through Difficulties). **Flag:** Blue field with wreath & yellow sunflower over state seal. **Seal:** Rising sun represents east; buffalo, log cabin, riverboat, wagon & plowing farmer suggest early history of region. **Flower:** Sunflower. **Bird:** Western meadowlark. **Tree:** Cottonwood. **Song:** "Home on the Range." **Nickname:** Sunflower State.

**Governor:** John Carlin. **Annual salary:** $45,000. **Term:** 4 years. **Current term expires:** Jan. 1983. **Voting requirements:** 18 yrs. old & U.S. citizen; resident of state and voting area; registration 20 days before election. **U.S. Congressmen:** 5. **Entered Union:** 1861 (34th state).

**Location & boundaries:** Midwestern state: bounded on the north by Nebraska; on the east by the Missouri River & Missouri; on the south by Oklahoma; & on the west by Colorado. **Total area:** 82,277 sq. mi. (ranks 14th). **Extreme length:** 411 mi. **Extreme breadth:** 208 mi. **Chief rivers:** Arkansas, Missouri, Kansas. **Major lakes:** Tuttle Creek, Cedar Bluff, Cheney, Perry. **No. of counties:** 105.

**Population (1980 census):** 2,364,236 (ranks 32nd). **Pop. increase (1970-80):** 5.1%. **Largest cities:** Wichita, Kansas City, Topeka, Overland Park. **Pop. density:** 28.7 per sq. mi. (ranks 37th). **Pop. distribution: White**—2,167,752; **Black**—126,127; **Am. Indian, Eskimo and Aleut**—15,371; **Asian and Pacific Islander**—15,078; **Other**—38,880 **Spanish origin**—63,333. **Marriage rate (1979):** 10.5 per 1,000 people. **Divorce rate:** 5.4 per 1,000 people.

**State finances (1980). Revenue:** $2,419,000,000. **Expenditures:** $2,254,000,000. **State taxes:** $666.15 per capita. **State personal income tax:** Yes. **Public debt (1980):** $185.42 per capita. **Federal aid (1980):** $345.44 per capita. **Personal income (1981):** $10,870.

**Sectors of the economy (% of labor force employed in 1975):** Wholesale and retail trade (18.7%), Government (16.9%), Manufacturing (15.8%), Services (13.1%). **Leading products:** aerospace equipment, food, chemicals, crude oil & natural gas items, machinery, printing & publishing. **Minerals:** petroleum, helium, natural gas & gas liquids. **Agricultural products:** cattle, hogs, dairy items, wheat, sorghum grain, hay. **Avg. farm (1981):** 653 acres. **Avg. value of farm per acre:** $590.

**Highway expenditures per capita (1980):** $160.19. **Persons per motor vehicle (1981):** 1.16. **Minimum age for driver's license:** 16. **Gasoline tax:** 8¢ per gallon. **Diesel tax:** 10¢ per gallon. **Motor vehicle deaths (1980):** 25.2 per 100,000 people.

**Birthrate (1979):** 16.5 per 1,000 people. **Infant mortality rate per 1,000 births (1978):** 12.5. **Physicians per 100,000 pop. (1979):** 150. **Dentists per 100,000 pop. (1979):** 46. **Acceptable hospital beds (1979):** 7.8 per 1,000 people. **State expenditures per capita for health and hospitals (1980):** $64.25.

**Education expenditures (1977-78):** $516.97 per capita annually. **No. of pupils in public schools (1980):** 418,000. **No. of institutions of higher learning (1978-79):** 52. **Public school expenditure per pupil in attendance (1978-79):** $1,978. **Avg. salary of public school teachers (1979-80):** $14,513. **No. full-time teachers (1980):** 27,900. **Educational attainment of adult population (1976):** 12.6 median yrs. of school completed: 1.0% with less than 5 years of education; 14.6% with 4 yrs. of college.

**Telephones (1979):** 61 per 100 people. **State Chamber of Commerce:** Kansas Assn. of Commerce and Industry, 500 First National Tower, One Townsite Plaza, Topeka, Kansas 66603.

## KENTUCKY

Kentucky, renowned for the quality of its tobacco, whiskey, and racehorses, was the first state west of the Alleghenies to be settled by pioneers. A state of sometimes bizarre contrasts, Kentucky has the nation's gold reserves (at Fort Knox) and many fine farms and estates, yet much of its land has been devastated by reckless lumbering and strip-mining practices, and in some eastern areas chronic unemployment prevails. Two Kentuckians, Abraham Lincoln and Jefferson Davis, were the opposing presidents in the Civil War.

Roughly triangular in shape, the state consists of the Appalachian Plateau (known locally as the Cumberland Plateau and constituting the largest single area—more than a fourth of the total), the northcentral Bluegrass Region, the Pennyroyal Region (or Southwestern Mississippian Embayment), the Western Coal Field, and the East Gulf Coastal Plain (or Jackson Purchase Region), which makes up the state's western tip. A double hairpin turn in the Mississippi River separates a small bit of extreme southwestern Kentucky from the rest of the state. Most of the state's surface is a much-furrowed plain sloping gently to the west. The state's northern boundary, the Ohio River, has been shifting gradually north- and westward for centuries. Kentucky thus had stood to gain territory with the border's expansion, but the Supreme Court ruled in January 1980 that the boundary remains fixed at its original position regardless of the movement of the Ohio River.

About half the land is farmed, and agriculture (especially tobacco) is still important, although it has been surpassed in recent years by manufacturing. Commercial fishing is limited, while mining continues as a major activity; Kentucky ranks as the country's leading coal producer. Spurred by the building of new roads, tourism is also a significant revenue source; attractions include Mammoth Cave National Park, Abraham Lincoln Birthplace National Historical Site, Daniel Boone National Forest, Natural Bridge, Cumberland Gap National Historic Park, the Bluegrass Region around Lexington, historic Harrodsburg, and the annual Kentucky Derby at Louisville.

Indians are thought to have lived in the forests of what is now western Kentucky as long as 15,000 years ago. Although other Europeans visited the region during the latter part of the 17th century, the first serious exploration of record was conducted (1750) by Dr. Thomas Walker, who passed through, and named, Cumberland Gap. About this time, a number of Indian tribes—including the Cherokee, Iroquois, and Shawnee—who were using the region as hunting grounds strongly resisted the advance of the white man. Daniel Boone explored eastern Kentucky (1767) and later spent two years in the Bluegrass Region. In 1773 he led a group of settlers into Kentucky, but Indians forced him out. James Harrod established (1774) the first permanent non-Indian settlement at Harrodsburg; in the following year Daniel Boone, acting as an agent for the Transylvania Company, returned to hack out the Wilderness Road and establish Boonesboro.

Indian raids were a continuing menace until General Anthony Wayne's victory in the Battle of Fallen Timbers in Ohio (1794) virtually ended them. Kentucky was originally a county of Virginia known as Fincastle before gaining statehood in 1792. The 1795 Pinckney's Treaty with Spain and the 1803 Louisiana Purchase made travel on the Mississippi more secure and aided development.

Kentucky's growth has been marked by conflict and violence. Kentuckians fought hard against the Alien and Sedition Acts (1798), vigorously supported the War of 1812 and the Mexican War (1846-48), and, although neutral in the Civil War, supplied each side with thousands of troops. The slavery issue, a particularly contentious one for a slaveholding state containing many abolitionists, was officially resolved in 1865 with the adoption of the 13th Constitutional Amendment. Lesser conflicts included the Hatfield-McCoy wrangle (1882-96), troubles surrounding the assassination of Democratic gubernatorial candidate William Goebel (1900), the so-called Black Patch War (1904-09) between tobacco farmers and buyers, and frequent strife between mine owners and the United Mine Workers.

In response to the energy crisis forced in the early 1970s by the oil shortage and rising prices, coal mines were reopened, resulting in a drop in the state's unemployment. After two methane gas explosions which claimed 26 lives in 1976, a mine safety bill was passed.

**Full name:** Commonwealth of Kentucky. **Origin of name:** From Wyandot name, Ken-tah-teh, meaning "Land of Tomorrow." **Inhabitant:** Kentuckian. **Capital:** Frankfort. **State motto:** United We Stand, Divided We Fall. **Flag:** State seal on a blue field. **Seal:** Two men greeting each other; state motto. **Flower:** Goldenrod. **Bird:** Cardinal. **Tree:** Kentucky coffee tree. **Song:** "My Old Kentucky Home." **Nickname:** Bluegrass State.

**Governor:** John Y. Brown, Jr. **Annual salary:** $52,000. **Term:** 4 years. **Current term expires:** Dec. 1983. **Voting requirements:** 18 yrs. old & U.S. citizen; resident of state, one year. **U.S. Congressmen:** 7. **Entered Union:** 1792 (15th state).

**Location & boundaries:** Southeastern state: bounded on the north by the Ohio River, Illinois, Indiana & Ohio; on the east by the Big Sandy & Tug Fork Rivers, West Virginia & Virginia; on the south by Tennessee; & on the west by the Mississippi River & Missouri. **Total area:** 40,409 sq. mi. (ranks 37th). **Extreme length:** 350 mi. **Extreme breadth:** 175 mi. **Chief rivers:** Ohio, Kentucky, Tennessee. **Major lakes:** Kentucky, Barkley & Cumberland Reservoirs. **No. of counties:** 120.

**Population (1980 census):** 3,660,257 (ranks 23rd). **Pop. increase (1970-80):** 13.7%. **Largest cities:** Louisville, Lexington, Owensboro, Covington. **Pop. density:** 90.6 per sq. mi. (ranks 22nd). **Pop. distribution: White**—3,379,648; **Black**—259,490; **Am. Indian, Eskimo and Aleut**—3,610; **Asian and Pacific Islander**—9,971; **Other**—8,714; **Spanish Origin**—27,403. **Marriage rate (1979):** 9.6 per 1,000 people. **Divorce rate:** 4.5 per 1,000 people.

**State finances (1980). Revenue:** $4,168,000,000. **Expenditures:** $4,569,000,000. **State taxes:** $585.89 per capita. **State personal income tax:** Yes. **Public debt (1980):** $829.08 per capita. **Federal aid (1980):** $399.51 per capita. **Personal income (1981):** $8,455.

**Sectors of the economy (% of labor force employed in 1970):** Manufacturing (26%), Wholesale and retail trade (19%), Government (16%), Educational Services (8%), Services (7%), Construction (7%). **Leading products:** food, chemicals, tobacco items, machinery, primary & fabricated metals, transportation equipment. **Minerals:** coal, petroleum, stone, natural gas. **Agricultural products:** cattle, hogs, tobacco, dairy items, corn, hay. **Avg. farm (1981):** 144 acres. **Avg. value of farm per acre:** $991.

**Highway expenditures per capita (1980):** $246.96. **Persons per motor vehicle (1981):** 1.40. **Minimum age for driver's license:** 16. **Gasoline tax:** 9.5¢ per gallon. **Diesel tax:** 9.5¢ per gallon. **Motor vehicle deaths (1980):** 22.4 per 100,000 people.

**Birthrate (1979):** 16.7 per 1,000 people. **Infant mortality rate per 1,000 births (1978):** 12.7. **Physicians per 100,000 pop. (1979):** 134. **Dentists per 100,000 pop. (1979):** 42. **Acceptable hospital beds (1979):** 5.1 per 1,000 people. **State expenditures per capita for health and hospitals (1980):** $69.91.

**Education expenditures (1977-78):** $406.04 per capita annually. **No. of pupils in public schools (1980):** 671,000. **No. of institutions of higher learning (1978-79):** 42. **Public school expenditure per pupil in attendance (1978-79):** $1,502. **Avg. salary of public**

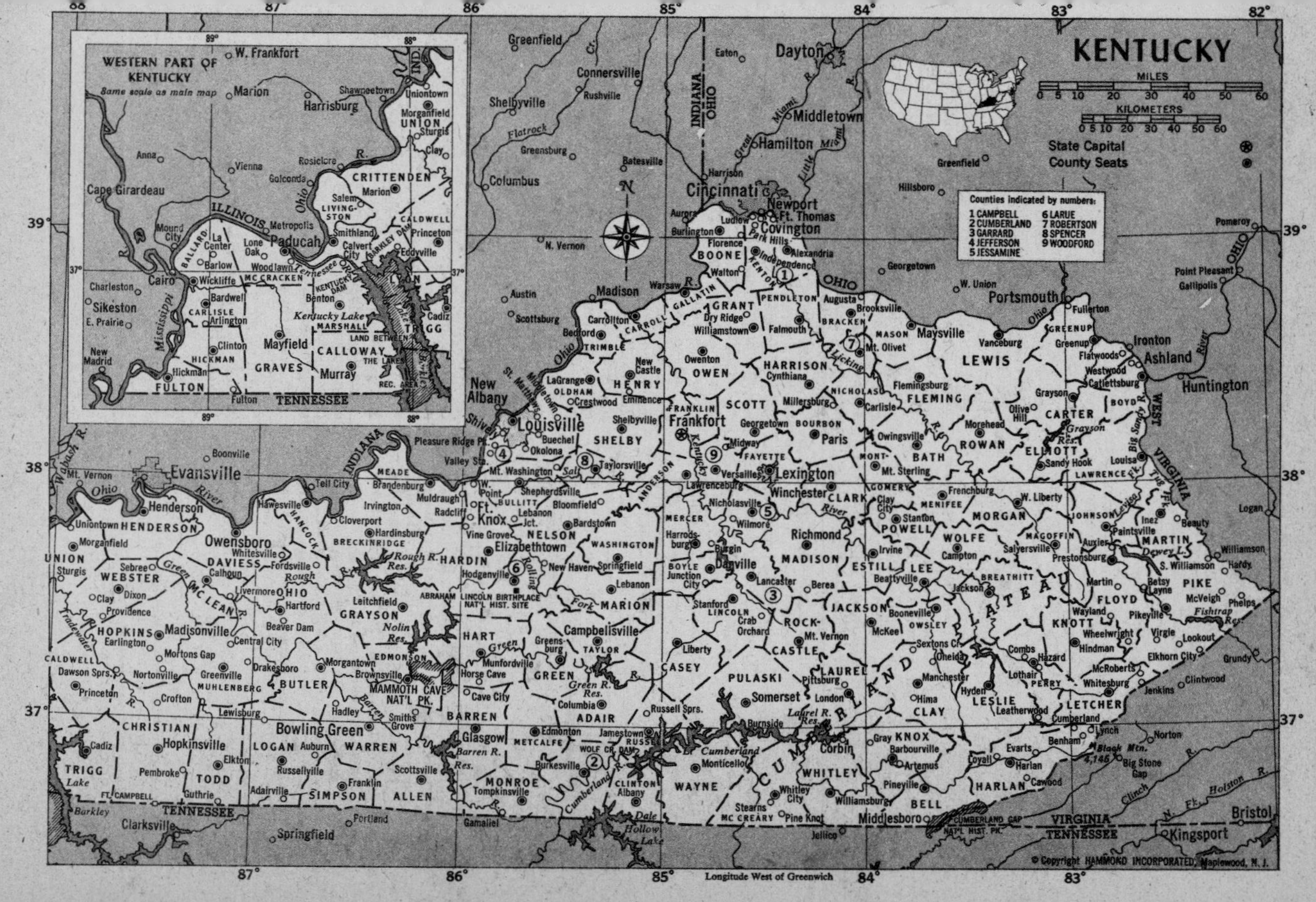
KENTUCKY
MILES
KILOMETERS
State Capital
County Seats
Counties indicated by numbers:
1 CAMPBELL
2 CUMBERLAND
3 GARRARD
4 JEFFERSON
5 JESSAMINE
6 LARUE
7 ROBERTSON
8 SPENCER
9 WOODFORD
WESTERN PART OF KENTUCKY
Same scale as main map
Longitude West of Greenwich
© Copyright HAMMOND INCORPORATED, Maplewood, N.J.

**school teachers (1979-80):** $15,260. **No. full-time teachers (1980):** 36,400. **Educational attainment of adult population (1976):** 12.1 median yrs. of school completed: 5.7% with less than 5 years of education; 10.0% with 4 yrs. of college.

**Telephones (1979):** 48 per 100 people. **State Chamber of Commerce:** Kentucky Chamber of Commerce, Versailles Rd., P.O. Box 817, Frankfort, Kentucky 40602.

## LOUISIANA

With its French and Spanish background, Louisiana is rich in history and among the nation's leaders in oil and natural gas, salt, sulphur, commercial fishing, fur trapping and rice, sugar cane and sweet potato production. The Michoud plant at New Orleans was a vital rocket-assembly installation during NASA's earth orbit and Apollo moon shots, contributing to the emergence of manufacturing as a major industry in the state.

New Orleans lies 100 miles up the Mississippi River from the Gulf of Mexico. It has been the nation's second-busiest seaport since 1840 but is perhaps better known as the site of the annual Mardi Gras. The world's longest bridge, the 24-mile Lake Pontchartrain Causeway, connects New Orleans to Mandeville. A sizeable timber industry is fed by extensive forest lands.

In the north are low rolling hills, and in the east many bluffs dot the river plain. Coastal marshes and sluggish streams (bayous) are features of the southern terrain. The Mississippi Delta, a fertile sedimentary deposit, comprises a third of the state's total area.

Indians are thought to have lived in the northern part of the Louisiana region over 3,000 years ago. Spanish explorer Cabeza de Vaca may have visited the area about 1530, and Hernando De Soto did so (1540-42). Approximately 12,000 Indians were then living in the region.

In 1682 Robert Cavelier, Sieur de La Salle, reached the mouth of the Mississippi and claimed all the land drained by it and its tributaries for King Louis XIV of France.

Permanent French settlement of the Louisiana region began (1699) with its founding as a royal colony and the establishment of a community near present-day Biloxi, Mississippi. In 1717 the area was granted to a company headed by John Law, who initially centered his development in the region that is now Arkansas, but then moved south. New Orleans was founded in 1718 and four years later became the capital. Law's venture spurred immigration, but eventually failed.

French control of the region gave way (1762) to Spanish; France regained possession in 1800. Three years later, Napoleon Bonaparte, seeking funds to support his European military activities, sold the land to the United States, as part of the vast Louisiana Purchase. In 1804 the territory was divided at the state's present northern border: the northern portion, now made up of other states, was at first called the District of Louisiana, then the Territory of Louisiana, and later Missouri Territory; the southern portion, originally the Territory of Orleans, became the present state of Louisiana. The period between 1760 and 1790 was marked by an influx of French-speaking Acadians, or Cajuns, from what is now Nova Scotia, who settled mainly in the southern region.

In the early 19th century, the natives of Louisiana were a heterogeneous mixture of French, Spanish, Isleños from the Canary Islands, and Germans. Although the Louisianians generally did not welcome the coming of the Americans, they did unite behind Andrew Jackson to defeat (1815) the British in the Battle of New Orleans at the end of the War of 1812. The state, which entered the Union in 1812, was enlarged by the settlement of the West Florida Controversy, which had stemmed from conflicting Spanish and American land claims involving portions of Florida, Alabama, Mississippi, and Louisiana; the Transcontinental Treaty of 1819 gave control of the disputed regions to the United States.

Early statehood was marked by the advent of the Mississippi steamboat trade and its attendant prosperity, and by the rise of plantation agriculture. The Civil War and the Reconstruction period brought considerable hardship and chaos. White rule was ultimately reestablished and farm tenancy and sharecropping replaced the plantation system. The discovery of oil (1901) and natural gas (1916) greatly aided the state's economic recovery.

The 1927 Mississippi flood, which forced 300,000 people from their homes, remains the worst on record. But the 1973 high water flooded nearly four million acres of Louisiana for months before the crisis ebbed away into the Gulf. Enormous damage was averted by the levee system.

Huey P. Long, elected governor in 1927 and assassinated in 1935, remains the state's most renowned political figure. His term as governor launched a political dynasty that continued even after he was killed. As governor and later (1930) as U.S. senator, Long was an advocate of a "Share the Wealth" program that challenged powerful Louisiana oil interests. He was responsible for much material progress but also was blamed for considerable political corruption. His brother Earl served three terms as governor, and his son Russell was a United States senator.

Louisiana today is becoming increasingly industrialized, often to the detriment of its tradition-ripe picturesqueness. One reason for the spurt is that the state grants 10-year tax exemptions to new industries. Tourism also has grown, and today accounts for over $2 billion annually. Over 70,000 jobs are dependent on the travel industry. Those seeking to preserve the traces of the past were heartened by the Federal government's refusal (July 1969) to grant funds for part of a highway system that would have "seriously impaired the historic quality of New Orleans' famed French Quarter." An alternate route was not acceptable because of its disruptive effects on the city, excessive costs, and construction hazards to the city's river levee. The ruling was believed to be the first denial of Federal funds for a highway on the basis of preserving a historic area.

The Louisiana Offshore Oil Port (Loop) has been constructed 18 miles off Grand Isle. Tankers too large to dock at any existing U.S. ports unload their cargo at the superport, and the oil is sent to the mainland by pipeline. The port was completed in mid-1981.

On March 10, 1980, David C. Treen was inaugurated as Louisiana's first Republican governor in 103 years. He had been elected by a slim margin in a run-off on Dec. 8, 1979, having promised to end the state's notorious political corruption.

**Full name:** State of Louisiana. **Origin of name:** In honor of King Louis XIV of France. **Inhabitant:** Louisianian. **Capital:** Baton Rouge. **State motto:** Union, Justice & Confidence. **Flag:** State seal & motto on a blue field. **Seal:** Mother pelican feeding brood. **Flower:** Magnolia. **Bird:** Brown pelican. **Tree:** Bald cypress. **Song:** "Give Me Louisiana." **Nickname:** Pelican State.

**Governor:** David C. Treen. **Annual salary:** $73,400. **Term:** 4 years. **Current term expires:** March 1984. **Voting requirements:** 18 yrs. old & U.S. citizen; resident of state 1 yr.; county, 6 mos.; district, 3 mos.; valid I.D. **U.S. Congressmen:** 8. **Entered Union:** 1812 (18th state).

**Location & boundaries:** Gulf state: bounded on the north by Arkansas; on the east by the Mississippi & Pearl Rivers & Mississippi; on

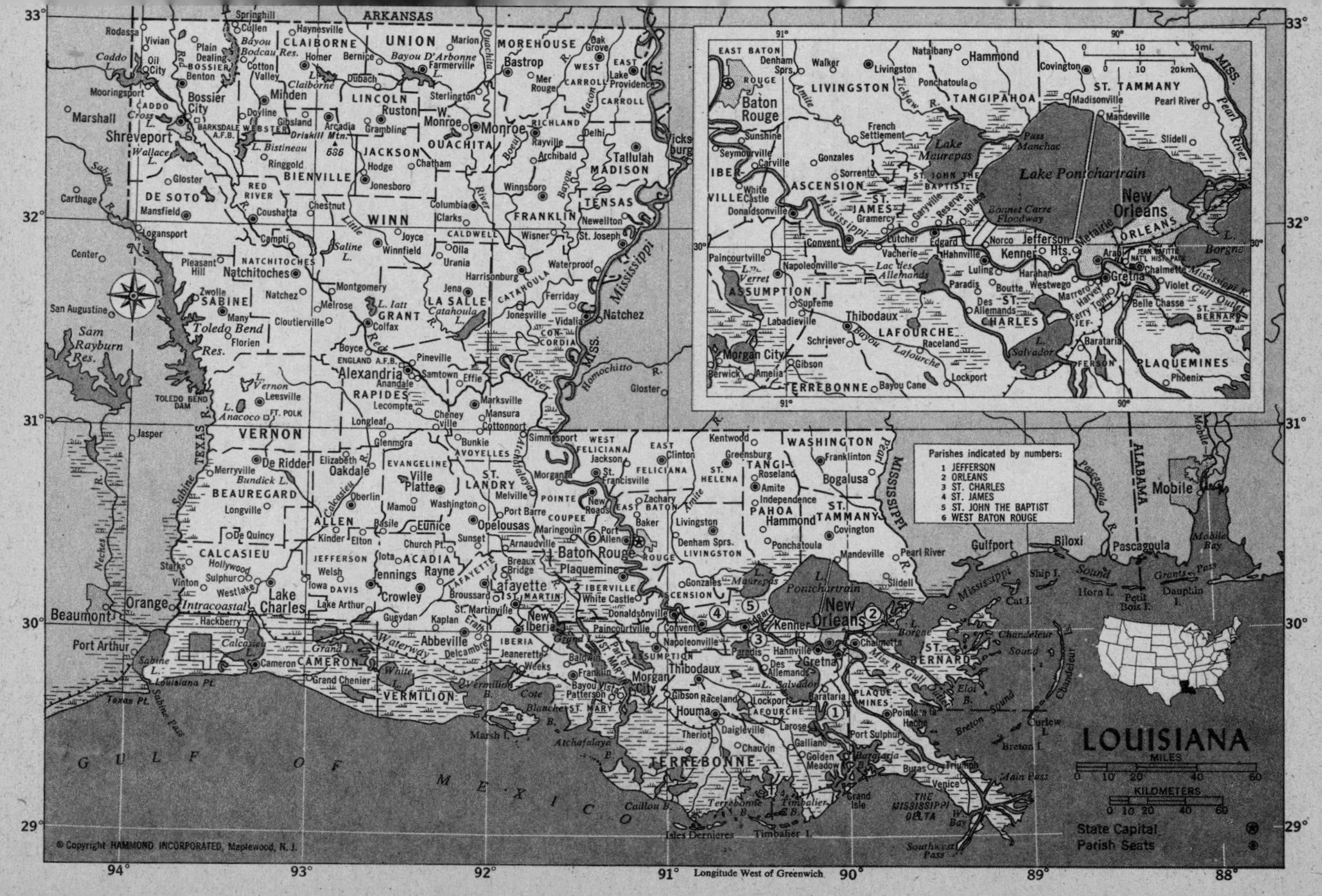
LOUISIANA
MILES
KILOMETERS
State Capital
Parish Seats
Parishes indicated by numbers:
1 JEFFERSON
2 ORLEANS
3 ST. CHARLES
4 ST. JAMES
5 ST. JOHN THE BAPTIST
6 WEST BATON ROUGE
ARKANSAS
MISSISSIPPI
ALABAMA
TEXAS
GULF OF MEXICO
Longitude West of Greenwich
© Copyright HAMMOND INCORPORATED, Maplewood, N.J.
Shreveport
Monroe
Alexandria
Baton Rouge
New Orleans
Lafayette
Lake Charles
Lake Pontchartrain
Mobile
Biloxi
Gulfport

the southeast & south by the Gulf of Mexico; & on the west by Texas & the Sabine River. **Total area:** 47,752 sq. mi. (ranks 31st). **Extreme length:** 237 mi. **Extreme breadth:** 236.5 mi. **Coastline:** 397 mi. **Chief rivers:** Mississippi, Atchafalaya, Red, Ouachita. **Major lakes:** Pontchartrain, Grand, White. **No. of parishes (counties):** 64.

**Population (1980 census):** 4,206,312 (ranks 19th). **Pop. increase (1970-80):** 15.4%. **Largest cities:** New Orleans, Baton Rouge, Shreveport, Lafayette. **Pop. density:** 88.1 per sq. mi. (ranks 23rd). **Pop. distribution: White**—2,911,243; **Black**—1,237,263; **Am. Indian, Eskimo and Aleut**—12,064; **Asian and Pacific Islander**—23,771; **Other**—19,631; **Spanish origin**—99,105. **Marriage rate (1979):** 10.3 per 1,000 people. **Divorce rate:** 3.8 per 1,000 people.

**State finances (1980). Revenue:** $5,412,000,000. **Expenditures:** $4,887,000,000. **State taxes:** $570.22 per capita. **State personal income tax:** Yes. **Public debt (1980):** $708.14 per capita. **Federal aid (1980):** $371.66 per capita. **Personal income (1981):** $9,486.

**Sectors of the economy (% of labor force employed in 1970):** Wholesale & retail trade (21%), Government (17%), Manufacturing (16%), Services (10%), Educational Services (9%), Construction (8%). **Leading products:** chemicals, food, petroleum and paper items, transportation equipment, lumber, primary metals. **Minerals:** petroleum, natural gas, sulfur. **Agricultural products:** cattle, dairy items, rice, sugar cane, soybeans. **Fishing:** shrimp, menhaden, oysters. **Avg. farm (1981):** 273 acres. **Avg. value of farm per acre:** $1,519.

**Highway expenditures per capita (1980):** $147.86. **Persons per motor vehicle (1981):** 1.47. **Minimum age for driver's license:** 15. **Gasoline tax:** 8¢ per gallon. **Diesel tax:** 8¢ per gallon. **Motor vehicle deaths (1980):** 29.0 per 100,000 people.

**Birthrate (1979):** 19.7 per 1,000 people. **Infant mortality rate per 1,000 births (1978):** 17.3. **Physicians per 100,000 pop. (1979):** 134. **Dentists per 100,000 pop. (1979):** 42. **Acceptable hospital beds (1979):** 5.9 per 1,000 people. **State expenditures per capita for health and hospitals (1980):** $105.86.

**Education expenditures (1977-78):** $442.47 per capita annually. **No. of pupils in public schools (1980):** 786,000. **No. of institutions of higher learning (1978-79):** 32. **Public school expenditure per pupil in attendance (1978-79):** $1,604. **Avg. salary of public school teachers (1979-80):** $14,020. **No. full-time teachers (1980):** 53,700. **Educational attainment of adult population (1976):** 12.3 median yrs. of school completed: 8.7% with less than 5 years of education; 1115% with 4 yrs. of college.

**Telephones (1979):** 52 per 100 people. **State Chamber of Commerce:** Louisiana Association of Business & Industry, P.O. Box 3988, Baton Rouge, Louisiana 70821.

---

## MAINE

Four-fifths of Maine is covered by softwood forests that feed an enormous wood-processing industry. There are three general land areas: the White Mountains region in the northwest, the New England Uplands extending through the heart of the state, and the coastal lowlands of the southeast. Many bays and harbors dot the craggy, convoluted coastline. Southwest of Portland, the rockbound coast is supplanted by sandy beaches. Sailors coasting downwind from Boston gave the shore its nickname, "Down East." Fishermen are attracted by the state's 2,500 lakes and ponds and 5,000 rivers and streams. The commercial lobster industry is famed throughout the nation. Waterpower availability is correspondingly excellent. Ten mountains rise more than 4,000 feet; undersea peaks form 400 offshore islands.

The climate is marked by generally severe winters, and summer evenings occasionally so cool that people heat their homes. Yet this very ruggedness of terrain and climate has proved an asset in drawing tourists. Tourism is responsible for $900 million in business revenues and 34,000 jobs. Skiing, camping, sailing, fishing, hunting, and other outdoor activities are especially popular, and many city-worn visitors seek out the unspoiled Allagash wilderness, the 92-mile-long Allagash Wilderness Waterway, and Mount Katahdin (5,268 ft.) in Baxter State Park, which is the first place in the nation to catch the rays of the rising sun. Other attractions include Bar Harbor on Mount Desert Island, most of which is part of Acadia National Park and the many historic and picturesque towns, such as Bath, Kennebunk, Rockland, Eastport and Searsport, which dot the coast.

Maine may have been sighted by Norse explorer Leif Ericsson as early as A.D. 1000, and English-employed Italian sea captain John Cabot is considered to have been the first European to reach the area, in 1498. Giovanni da Verrazano sailed along the coast in 1524. Thousands of Abnaki and Etchemin Indians were living there at the time. They peaceably coexisted with the earliest settlers but occasionally joined together to fight off raiding Iroquois. The legendary city of Norumbega, thought to have contained vast riches, drew adventurers up the Penobscot River, upon which the city was said to have been located. The Abnaki were greatly reduced in number by a smallpox epidemic which broke out at the time of the first English settlements. The French established a settlement on the St. Croix River in 1604, but the post was abandoned.

Maine lands were granted (1622) by the Council for New England (successor to the Plymouth Company) to two wealthy Englishmen, Sir Ferdinando Gorges and Captain John Mason. Gorgeana (now York) became (1641) the first chartered English city in the New World. After Gorges' death (1647), Maine was largely neglected. Its settlers came under the jurisdiction of Massachusetts, which later bought (1677) the proprietary rights of Gorges' heirs for about $6,000. French efforts to control the region ended with the Treaty of Paris (1763), terminating the French and Indian Wars that had begun in 1689. Many coastal towns suffered French and Indian attacks during the long conflict.

Revolt against England was in the air in the 1760s because of taxes and restrictions. In 1774, Maine men followed Boston's example of a year earlier and burned a supply of British tea (York Tea Party). The first naval encounter of the American Revolution took place (June 1775) off Machias, as patriots captured the British ship *Margaretta.* Maine was the scene of a disastrous attempt to capture the British garrison at Castine on the Penobscot River in 1779. The eastern part of the state passed under British control during the War of 1812.

Maine stayed a part of Massachusetts until 1820, when it was admitted to the Union as a free state under the terms of the Missouri Compromise, thus balancing Missouri's admission as a slave state. A long-simmering boundary dispute with New Brunswick was settled by the Webster-Ashburton Treaty (1842), which ended the bloodless Aroostook War.

Maine was the first state to outlaw (1851) alcohol, which remained illegal until 1934. From 1909 to 1955, to keep the state's hydroelectric power within its borders and thus attract new industries, the sale of such power outside the state was prohibited. The state's textile business has declined since the 1920s, while the food-processing industry has grown significantly. Lobsters, canned sardines, potatoes, and blueberries are among the state's most famous products, as well as shoes, beet sugar and wood pulp and paper. Papermill products dominate the state's economy. The Bath Iron Works facilities for shipbuilding and repair at Bath and Portland are world-renowned. Mining is limited, despite large deposits of granite, limestone, slate and abrasive garnets. The communications

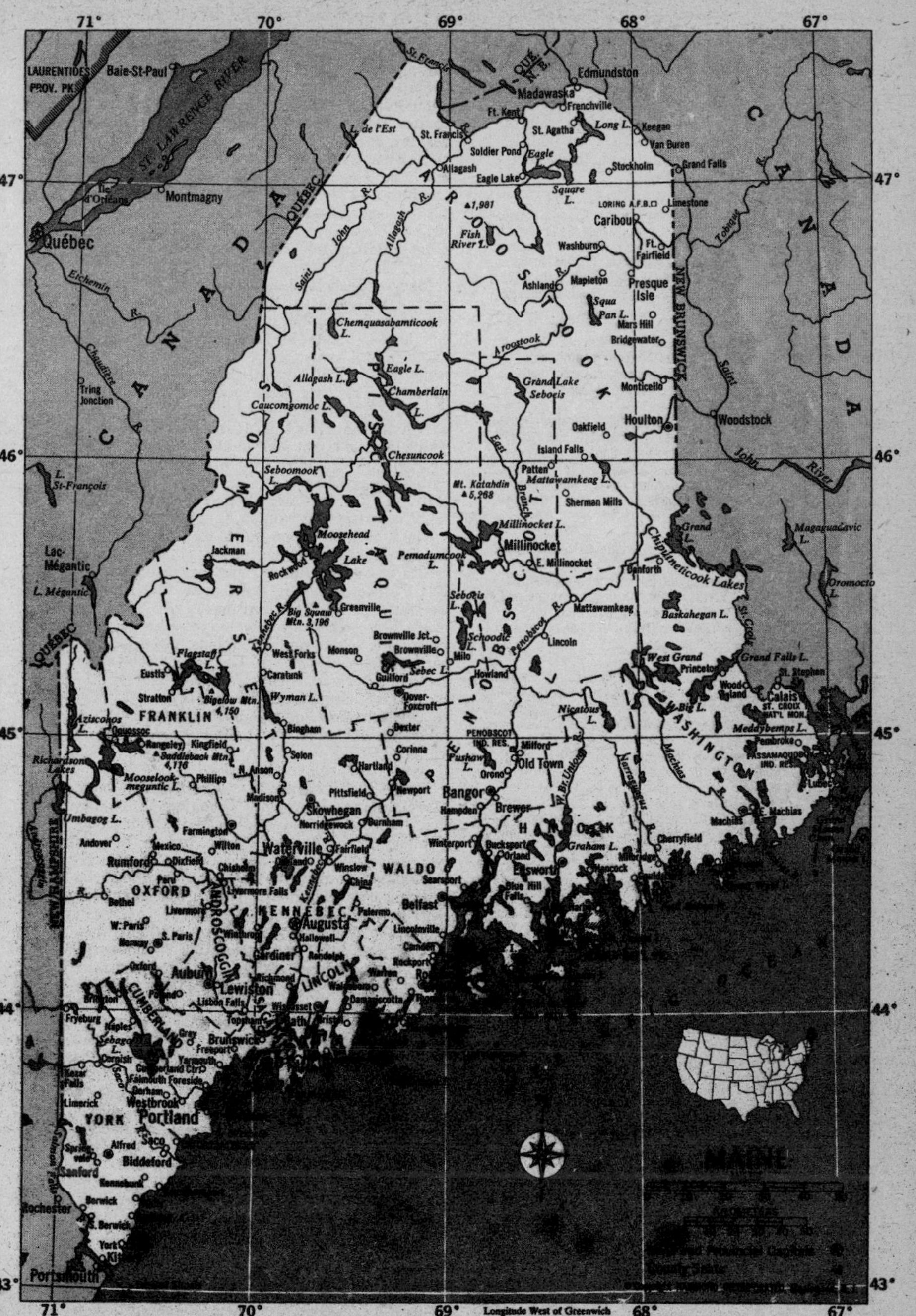
MAINE
Augusta
Portland
Bangor
Lewiston
Auburn
Waterville
Presque Isle
Caribou
Houlton
Millinocket
Moosehead Lake
Mt. Katahdin 5,268
Québec
NEW BRUNSWICK
CANADA
Longitude West of Greenwich

satellite station near Andover (completed 1962) is part of a worldwide satellite communications system.

In March 1980 members of the Penobscot Indian tribe approved an $81 million settlement proposal for their claims to half of Maine's territory.

In a referendum in March 1980, Maine voters strengthened a five-year-old ban on slot machines operated for profit to eliminate even those gambling devices operated for charity.

**Full name:** State of Maine. **Origin of name:** From name of ancient province in France. **Inhabitant:** Mainer. **Capital:** Augusta. **State motto:** Dirigo (I Guide). **Flag:** State seal on a blue field. **Seal:** Farmer & seaman represent two chief occupations; pine tree symbolizes forests; moose, wildlife; northern star stands for northern location. **Flower:** White pine cone & tassel. **Bird:** Chickadee. **Tree:** White pine. **Stone:** Tourmaline. **Song:** "State of Maine Song." **Nickname:** Pine Tree State.

**Governor:** Joseph E. Brennan. **Annual salary:** $35,000. **Term:** 4 years. **Current term expires:** Jan. 1983. **Voting requirements:** 18 yrs. old & U.S. citizen; resident of state and municipality of registration. **U.S. Congressmen:** 2. **Entered Union:** 1820 (23rd state).

**Location & boundaries:** New England state: bounded on the north & east by Canada; on the south by New Hampshire & the Atlantic Ocean; & on the west by New Hampshire & Canada. **Total area:** 33,265 sq. mi. (ranks 39th). **Extreme length:** 332 mi. **Extreme breadth:** 207 mi. **Coastline:** 228 mi. **Chief rivers:** Androscoggin, Kennebec, Penobscot, St. Croix. **Major lakes:** Moosehead, Chesuncook, Sebago, Rangeley. **No. of counties:** 16.

**Population (1980 census):** 1,125,027 (ranks 38th). **Pop. increase (1970-80):** 13.2%. **Largest cities:** Portland, Lewiston, Bangor, Auburn. **Pop. density:** 33.8 per sq. mi. (ranks 36th). **Pop. distribution: White**— 1,109,850; **Black**—3,128; **Am Indian, Eskimo and Aleut**—4,087; **Asian and Pacific Islander**—2,947; **Other**—4,648; **Spanish origin**—5,005. **Marriage rate (1979):** 10.9 per 1,000 people. **Divorce rate:** 5.6 per 1,000 people.

**State finances (1980). Revenue:** $1,369,000,000. **Expenditures:** $1,326,000,000. **State taxes:** $550.36 per capita. **State personal income tax:** Yes. **Public debt (1980):** $649.13 per capita. **Federal aid (1980):** $464.43 per capita. **Personal income (1981):** $8,655.

**Sectors of the economy (% of labor force employed in 1970):** Manufacturing (32%), Wholesale and retail trade (20%), Government (15%), Educational Services (8.2%) Services (7%), Construction (6%). **Leading products:** paper items, leather items, food, textile items, lumber & wood, transportation equipment, printing & publishing. **Minerals:** sand & gravel, cement, stone, peat. **Agricultural products:** broilers, dairy items, potatoes, hay, apples. **Fishing:** lobster, ocean perch, clams. **Avg. farm (1981):** 195 acres. **Avg. value of farm per acre:** $612.

**Highway expenditures per capita (1980):** $134.41. **Persons per motor vehicle (1981):** 1.51. **Minimum age for driver's license:** 15. **Gasoline tax:** 9¢ per gallon. **Diesel tax:** 9¢ per gallon. **Motor vehicle deaths (1980):** 23.6 per 100,000 people.

**Birthrate (1979):** 14.9 per 1,000 people. **Infant mortality rate per 1,000 births (1978):** 10.4. **Physicians per 100,000 pop. (1979):** 146. **Dentists per 100,000 pop. (1979):** 45. **Acceptable hospital beds (1979):** 6.3 per 1,000 people. **State expenditures per capita for health and hospitals (1980):** $54.28.

**Education expenditures (1977-78):** $434.99 per capita annually. **No. of pupils in public schools (1980):** 221,000. **No. of institutions of higher learning (1978-79):** 27. **Public school expenditure per pupil in attendance (1978-79):** $1,609. **Avg. salary of public school teachers (1979-80):** $17,340. **No. full-time teachers (1980):** 15,150. **Educational attainment of adult population (1976):** 12.5 median yrs. of school completed: 1.2% with less than 5 years of education; 13.6% with 4 yrs. of college.

**Telephones (1979):** 54 per 100 people. **State Chamber of Commerce:** Maine State Chamber of Commerce, One Canal Plaza, Box 65, Portland, Maine 04112.

## MARYLAND

Maryland has been called "America in Miniature" because, although small in area, it is uncommonly diverse and rich in history. Hills, valleys, rolling plains, swamps, and plateaus are all found there, and contrasting life-styles abound: from tobacco farmers in the southern part of the state to the missile makers of the highly industrialized Baltimore area, where more than half of the state's population lives. It was from Maryland that Washington, D.C. received (1791) part of its land (the rest was ceded by Virginia); when the capital was threatened by Confederate forces, Maryland became the scene of much fighting, including one of the bloodiest Civil War battles of all: Antietam (1862). Earlier, during the War of 1812, Marylander Francis Scott Key, watching the British bombardment of Baltimore's Fort McHenry, was inspired to write "The Star-Spangled Banner."

Maryland's coastline along the Atlantic Ocean is short, but Chesapeake Bay, which divides the state into an Eastern and Western Shore, provides many fine harbors, and a number of important islands dot the bay. A section of the Atlantic Coastal Plain, sometimes called "Tidewater Maryland," makes up all of the low-lying Eastern Shore. Fishing is a significant industry, and wild fowl abound.

Indians, mainly of the Algonquian family, were living in what is now Maryland before John Cabot, probably the region's first European explorer, sailed along the eastern coast in 1498. Virginian William Claiborne established the first settlement, a fur-trading post, on Kent Island.

The Maryland region was named for Henrietta Maria, queen consort of Charles I, who granted it (1632) to George Calvert, first Baron Baltimore. But Calvert died the same year, and his son Cecilius, second Baron Baltimore, was given the grant. He soon began developing the colony as both an income source and a religious haven for persecuted fellow Catholics. The Act of Toleration (1649) was passed in behalf of the Catholics, but when the Puritans gained control of the area they repealed this instrument (1654). A short civil war followed (1655), from which the Puritans emerged victors. In 1657 a compromise briefly restored the proprietorship to Lord Baltimore.

The English government eventually (1691) made Maryland a royal province. Commercial development proceeded rapidly in the next century, particularly in the Baltimore area. Indian troubles were infrequent and comparatively mild. Boundary quarrels with Pennsylvania were settled by the drawing of the Mason-Dixon Line (1767). Marylanders staged (1774) a Boston-style "tea party" in Annapolis, protesting British rule, and fought so well in the American Revolution that George Washington nicknamed Maryland "The Old Line State," in honor of its dependable "troops of the line." The state, which entered the Union in 1788, prospered early, thanks largely to the famous Baltimore clipper ships and the opening (1830) of the Baltimore and Ohio Railroad, first in the hemisphere to carry both passengers and freight.

During the Civil War, Maryland was a sharply divided slave state that remained loyal to the Union under great pressure; the state's inherited racial problems are compounded by such factors as inadequate urban housing and public apathy.

Maryland becomes increasingly less a part of the Old South and seems to grow smaller every year. Expressways now link all areas of the state; two of them serve the rapidly developing Baltimore-Washington corridor, while Interstate 70 reaches into Western Maryland and the dual-lane U.S. 50 and U.S. 13 funnel traffic through the Eastern Shore. The Francis Scott Key Bridge opened in 1977. It is Baltimore's second harbor crossing and teams with the Harbor Tunnel. A second span of the Chesapeake Bay Bridge opened in 1973.

Maryland's tourist attractions include a wide va-

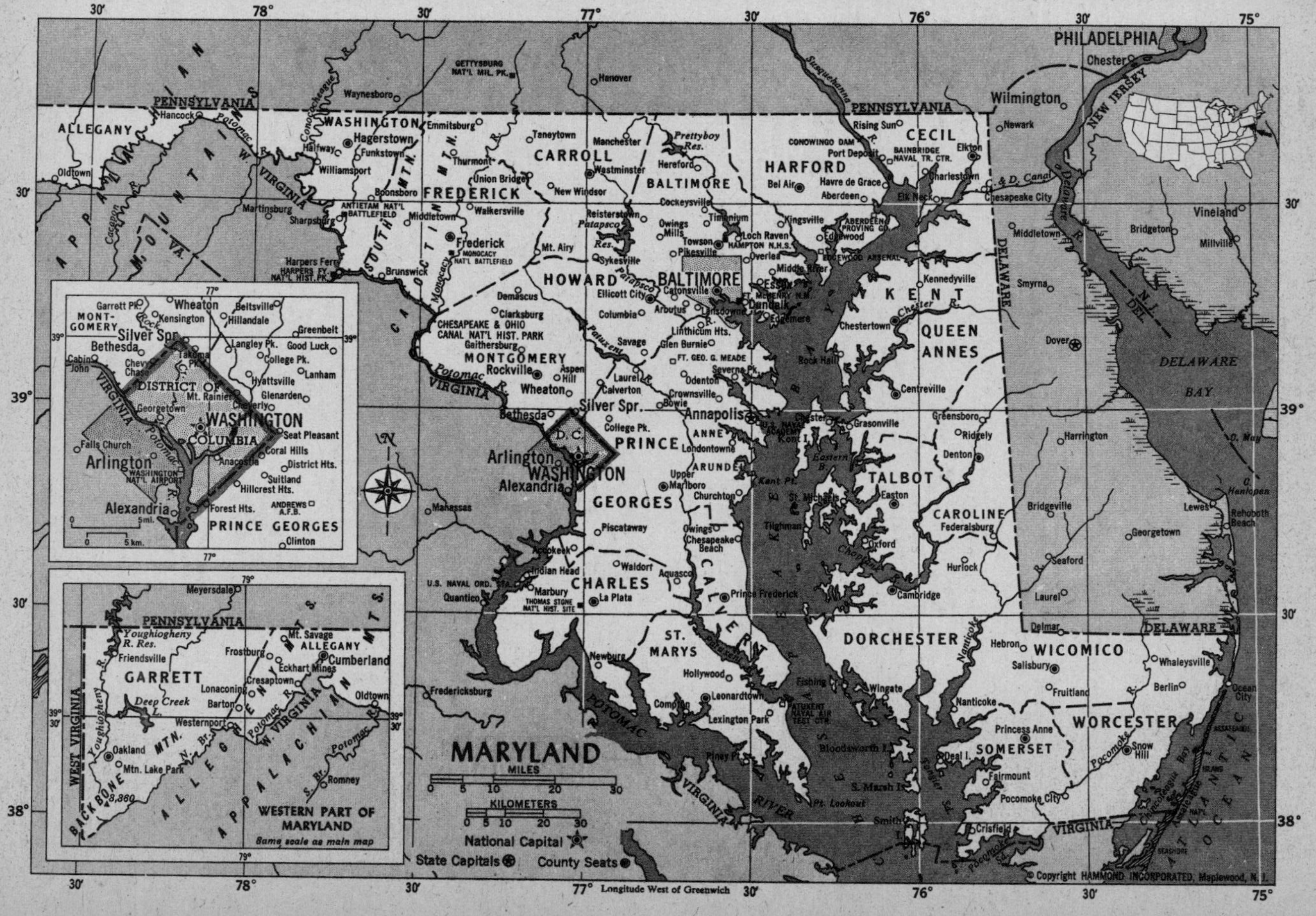
MARYLAND
MILES
KILOMETERS
National Capital
State Capitals
County Seats
Longitude West of Greenwich
WESTERN PART OF MARYLAND
Same scale as main map
© Copyright HAMMOND INCORPORATED, Maplewood, N.J.
PENNSYLVANIA
DELAWARE
NEW JERSEY
VIRGINIA
W. VIRGINIA
WEST VIRGINIA
PHILADELPHIA
DELAWARE BAY
ALLEGANY
WASHINGTON
FREDERICK
CARROLL
BALTIMORE
HARFORD
CECIL
HOWARD
MONTGOMERY
PRINCE GEORGES
ANNE ARUNDEL
CHARLES
CALVERT
ST. MARYS
KENT
QUEEN ANNES
TALBOT
CAROLINE
DORCHESTER
WICOMICO
SOMERSET
WORCESTER
GARRETT
DISTRICT OF COLUMBIA
WASHINGTON
Baltimore
Annapolis
Wilmington
Dover
Frederick
Hagerstown
Cumberland
Salisbury
Arlington
Alexandria

riety of parks and forests stretching from Appalachia to the Atlantic Ocean. Annapolis is the site of the U.S. Naval Academy, with the nation's oldest statehouse in use and more original colonial buildings than any other U.S. city. Ocean City is the state's seashore resort. Columbia, the planned city built by James Rouse halfway between Baltimore and Washington, is renowned among urbanologists throughout the world.

In 1975 Maryland's Governor Mandel and five associates were indicted by a Federal grand jury on charges of mail fraud and "racketeering" activity. The trial ended abruptly in 1976 with two separate cases of tampering. A second trial held in 1977 resulted in conviction, and Mandel was sentenced to four years in prison. The sentence was voided when the 4th U.S. Circuit Court of Appeals set aside his conviction on technical grounds on January 11, 1979, but, following a review, it was reinstated on July 20. Mandel entered prison on May 19, 1980. President Reagan commuted his sentence in 1981 and he was released on December 20. In a separate charge filed in January 1980, the state alleged that Governor and Mrs. Mandel, upon leaving the governor's mansion in 1977, had illegally removed such state property as furniture and liquor.

**Full name:** State of Maryland. **Origin of name:** From Queen Henrietta Maria of England, wife of Charles I. **Inhabitant:** Marylander. **Capital:** Annapolis. **State motto:** "Fatti maschi, parole femine" ("Manly deeds, womanly words"). **Flag:** Geometric black & gold pattern in opposite quarters; red & white crosses in the others. **Seal:** Shield with coats of arms of Calvert & Crossland families; farmer represents Maryland; fisherman, Lord Baltimore's Avalon colony in Newfoundland. **Flower:** Black-eyed Susan. **Bird:** Baltimore oriole. **Tree:** White oak. **Song:** "Maryland, My Maryland." **Nickname:** Old Line State.

**Governor:** Harry R. Hughes. **Annual salary:** $60,000. **Term:** 4 years. **Current term expires:** Jan. 1983. **Voting requirements:** 18 yrs. old & U.S. citizen; resident of state and county 30 days. **U.S. Congressmen:** 8. **Entered Union:** 1788 (7th state).

**Location & boundaries:** Middle Atlantic seaboard state: bounded on the north by Pennsylvania; on the east by Delaware & the Atlantic Ocean; on the south by the Potomac River, Virginia & West Virginia; & on the west by West Virginia. **Total area:** 10,460 sq. mi. (ranks 42nd). **Extreme length:** 198.6 mi. **Extreme breadth:** 125.5 mi. **Coastline:** 31 mi. (coastline including Chesapeake Bay, 3,190 mi.). **Chief rivers:** Potomac, Susquehanna, Patuxent. **Major lakes:** Deep Creek Lake (man-made). **No. of counties:** 23, plus 1 independent city.

**Population (1980 census):** 4,216,975 (ranks 18th). **Pop. increase (1970-80):** 7.5%. **Largest cities:** Baltimore, Rockville, Hagerstown, Bowie. **Pop. density:** 403.2 per sq. mi. (ranks 5th). **Pop. distribution: White**—3,158,412; **Black**—958,050; **Am. Indian, Eskimo and Aleut**—8,021; **Asian and Pacific Islander**—64,276; **Other**—27,687; **Spanish origin**—64,740. **Marriage rate (1979):** 11.1 per 1,000 people. **Divorce rate:** 4.1 per 1,000 people.

**State finances (1980). Revenue:** $5,564,000,000. **Expenditures:** $5,435,000,000. **State taxes:** $654.84 per capita. **State personal income tax:** Yes. **Public debt (1980):** $830.70 per capita. **Federal aid (1980):** $447.29 per capita. **Personal income (1981):** $11,534.

**Sectors of the economy (% of labor force employed in 1970):** Manufacturing (20%), Government (26%), Wholesale and retail trade (19%), Educational Services (8%), Services (7%), Construction (7%). **Leading products:** food and kindred products, primary metals, electrical equipment and supplies, transportation equipment, chemical and allied products, apparel, printing. **Agricultural products:** dairy items, broilers, cattle, corn, hay, tobacco. **Fishing:** oysters, crabs, clams. **Avg. farm (1981):** 160 acres. **Avg. value of farm per acre:** $2,556.

**Highway expenditures per capita (1980):** $171.41 **Persons per motor vehicle (1981):** 1.48. **Minimum age for driver's license:** 16. **Gasoline tax:** 11¢ per gallon. **Diesel tax:** 11¢ per gallon. **Motor vehicle deaths (1980):** 17.9 per 100,000 people.

**Birthrate (1979):** 14.0 per 1,000 people. **Infant mortality rate per 1,000 births (1978):** 14.7. **Physicians per 100,000 pop. (1979):** 257. **Dentists per 100,000 pop. (1979):** 59. **Acceptable hospital beds (1979):** 5.9 per 1,000 people. **State expenditures per capita for health and hospitals (1980):** $119.01.

**Education expenditures (1977-78):** $581.44 per capita annually. **No. of pupils in public schools (1980):** 750,000. **No. of institutions of higher learning (1978-79):** 54. **Public school expenditure per pupil in attendance (1978-79):** $2,349. **Avg. salary of public school teachers (1979-80):** $18,440. **No. full-time teachers (1980):** 47,400. **Educational attainment of adult population (1976):** 12.6 median yrs. of school completed: 2.1% with less than 5 years of education; 18.6% with 4 yrs. of college.

**Telephones (1979):** 62 per 100 people. **State Chamber of Commerce:** Maryland Chamber of Commerce, 60 West Street, Annapolis, Maryland 21401.

## MASSACHUSETTS

Today a key New England state, Massachusetts was also one of the most important of the 13 Colonies. It was at Plymouth in 1620 that the Pilgrims landed. And the Boston Massacre (1770) and Tea Party (1773) were major, irreversible steps on the road to the American War of Independence, which began at Lexington and Concord in 1775. Statehood dates from 1788.

The topography of the state is unusually varied. The eastern third is a low coastal plain that includes the Cape Cod peninsula and the islands due south: the Elizabeth Islands, Martha's Vineyard, and Nantucket. The New England Uplands, part of a high plateau stretching from Maine to New Jersey, extend westward for roughly 50 miles. Due west of this area is the Connecticut Valley, which extends from Massachusetts to southern Connecticut; the Connecticut River flows through it, providing fine soil for farming. Farther west lies the Berkshire Valley, surrounded by the Berkshire Hills and, near the northwestern border, the Taconic Mountains.

Besides its historic sites, the state's attractions include the Museum of Fine Arts and Symphony Hall in Boston, Sturbridge Village with its reconstructed early 19th-century community, the summer Tanglewood music festival in the Berkshires, and literary landmarks, such as the homes of Emerson, Hawthorne and Thoreau in Concord. Cape Cod is a leading Eastern summer resort area, with long, sandy beaches and picturesque towns. To the south, the islands of Martha's Vineyard and Nantucket are vacationers' favorites because of their beauty and charm. North of Boston, the art colony town of Rockport and the fishing port of Gloucester are visited by many tourists.

Norsemen including Leif Ericsson may have visited the region about A.D. 1000, but this remains more conjecture than fact. In 1602 English explorer Bartholomew Gosnold landed on Cuttyhunk Island in the Elizabeth chain and gave Cape Cod its name, and Captain John Smith explored the coast in 1614. Oddly enough, the arrival of the Pilgrims at Plymouth six years later, after a brief stop at what is now Provincetown, was purely accidental; the *Mayflower's* destination was a point south of the Hudson River, but a severe storm diverted the ship north. Because this area was beyond the bounds of the sponsoring company in London, a provisional instrument of government called the "Mayflower Compact" was drawn up. Designed to serve until more permanent institutions could be established, this covenant of the Massachusetts Bay Colony, as the settlement was called, formed the foundation of American democracy. But it was not originally a very democratic democracy, because while the Puritans insisted on religious freedom for themselves, they denied it to others, and some they banished from the colony. Roger Williams and the Reverend Thomas Hooker were

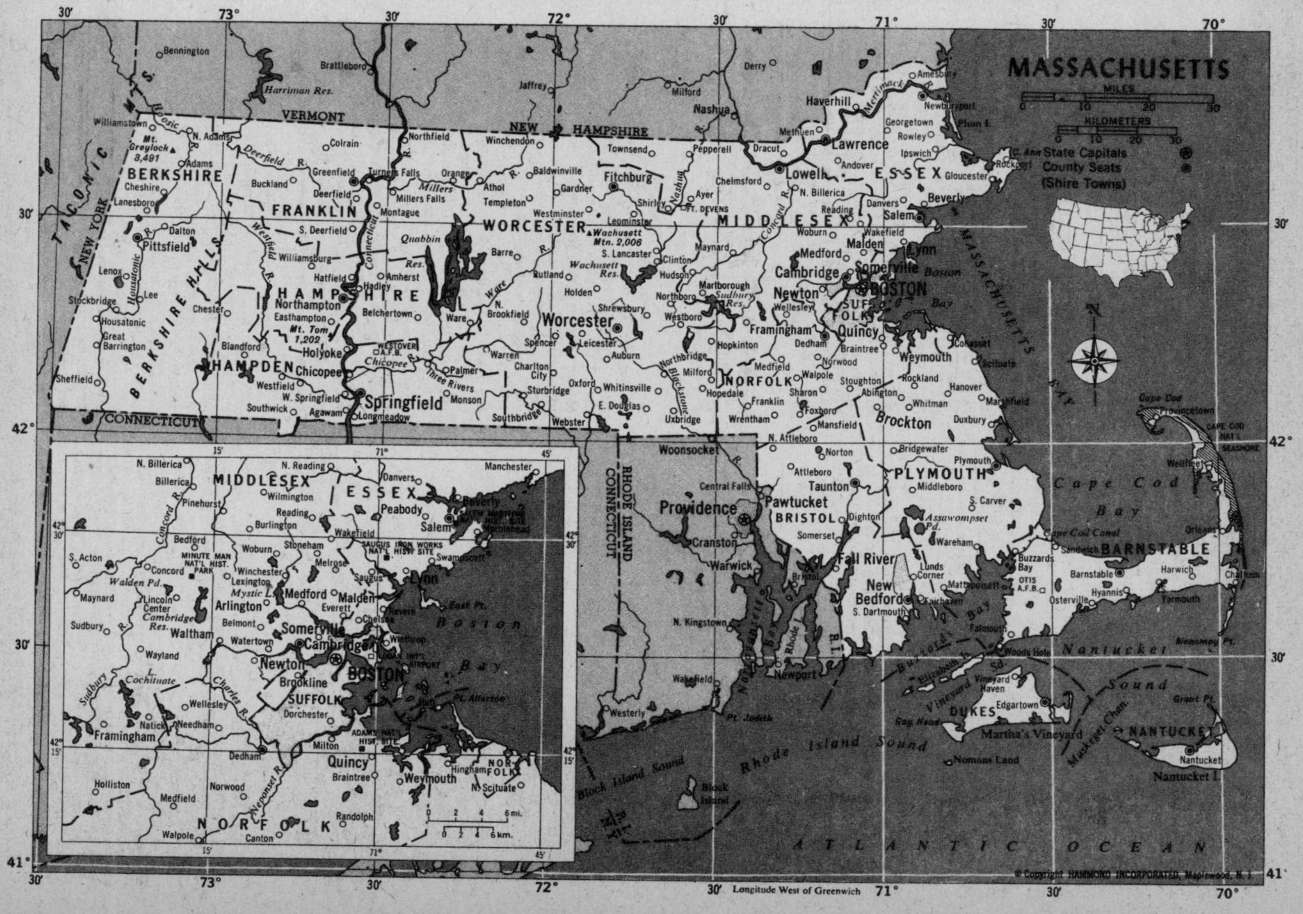
MASSACHUSETTS
MILES
KILOMETERS
State Capitals
County Seats
(Shire Towns)
© Copyright HAMMOND INCORPORATED, Maplewood, N. J.
Longitude West of Greenwich
ATLANTIC OCEAN
MASSACHUSETTS BAY
Cape Cod Bay
Rhode Island Sound
Nantucket Sound
NEW HAMPSHIRE
VERMONT
NEW YORK
CONNECTICUT
RHODE ISLAND
BERKSHIRE
FRANKLIN
HAMPSHIRE
HAMPDEN
WORCESTER
MIDDLESEX
ESSEX
SUFFOLK
NORFOLK
PLYMOUTH
BRISTOL
BARNSTABLE
DUKES
NANTUCKET
BOSTON
Springfield
Worcester
Providence
Brockton
Lowell
Lawrence
Fall River
New Bedford
Pittsfield
Boston Bay

exiled in 1636, and settled in Rhode Island and Connecticut respectively. Puritan oppression climaxed with the Salem witch trials at the end of the seventeenth century; about 20 persons accused of witchcraft were put to death.

Indian troubles began with an engagement with the Pequot Indians in 1637. In 1675-76, settlers and Wampanoag Indians, led by Metacom, who was known as King Philip, battled in "King Philip's War," which the colonists won at great expense. At various times from 1689 to 1763, the colonists fought against the French and their Indian allies, and ultimately prevailed. Soon after, they began resisting the royal tax laws, setting the stage for general revolt. In 1775 General George Washington arrived in Cambridge to assume command of the Continental Army. A year later, he routed the redcoats from Boston in the war's first major American victory. Then the scene of battle shifted to New York, New Jersey, and Pennsylvania.

The American Revolution was followed in Massachusetts by hard times. There came a business depression, and friction between the legislature and farmers, many of whom suffered foreclosures for debts and taxes; an insurrection (1786-87) led by former army captain Daniel Shays became known as Shays' Rebellion. But prosperity gradually returned, only to fade away again as Jefferson's 1807 Embargo Act, intended to keep the country from involvement in European wars, seriously hurt the state's sea-oriented economy. As it happened, the precaution was a failure: war came anyway in 1812, and Massachusetts turned to manufacturing for its principal livelihood.

Over the years, steady influxes of immigrants provided a plentiful source of labor, and workers were often exploited. Labor unions fought hard for recognition, and there were strikes, occasionally marked by violence as in the 1912 textile strike at Lawrence. Governor Calvin Coolidge gained national prominence when he broke a policemen's strike in Boston in 1919.

Today Massachusetts still ranks among the national leaders in manufacturing, as well as commercial fishing. The electronics industry, tourism, and its many private colleges and universities are important to the state's economy.

**Full name:** Commonwealth of Massachusetts. **Origin of name:** From Algonquian name, Massa-dchu-es-at, meaning "Great-Hill-Small-Place." **Inhabitant:** Bay Stater. **Capital:** Boston. **State motto:** Ense Petit Placidam Sub Libertate Quietem (By the Sword We Seek Peace, but Peace Only under Liberty). **Flag:** State seal on white field is on one side; other side has green pine tree on blue field. **Seal:** Coat of arms of Commonwealth of Massachusetts; Indian points arrow downward, symbolizing peace; star over his right shoulder represents Massachusetts as a state. **Flower:** Mayflower. **Bird:** Chickadee. **Tree:** American elm. **Song:** "Hail Massachusetts." **Nickname:** Bay State.

**Governor:** Edward J. King. **Annual salary:** $40,000. **Term:** 4 years. **Current term expires:** Jan. 1983. **Voting requirements:** 18 yrs. old & U.S. citizen; resident of state. **U.S. Congressmen:** 11. **Entered Union:** 1788 (6th state).

**Location & boundaries:** New England state: bounded on the north by Vermont & New Hampshire; on the east by the Atlantic Ocean; on the south by the Atlantic Ocean, Rhode Island & Connecticut; on the west by New York. **Total area:** 8,284 sq. mi. (ranks 45th). **Extreme length:** 190 mi. **Extreme breadth:** 110 mi. **Coastline:** 192 mi. **Chief rivers:** Connecticut, Merrimack, Charles, Housatonic. **Major lakes:** Assawompset Pond; Quabbin, Wachusett Reservoirs. **No. of counties:** 14.

**Population (1980 census):** 5,737,037 (ranks 11th). **Pop. increase (1970-80):** 0.8%. **Largest cities:** Boston, Worcester, Springfield, New Bedford. **Pop. density:** 692.5 per sq. mi. (ranks 3rd). **Pop. distribution: White**—5,362,836; **Black**—221,279; **Am. Indian, Eskimo and Aleut**—7,743; **Asian and Pacific Islander**—49,501; **Other**—95,678; **Spanish origin**—141,043. **Marriage rate (1979):** 7.8 per 1,000 people. **Divorce rate:** 3.0 per 1,000 people.

**State finances (1980). Revenue:** $7,457,000,000. **Expenditures:** $7,336,000,000. **State taxes:** $684.56 per capita. **State personal income tax:** Yes. **Public debt (1980):** $1,008.35 per capita. **Federal aid (1980):** $503.13 per capita. **Personal income (1981):** $11,158.

**Sectors of the economy (% of labor force employed in 1970):** Manufacturing (29%), Wholesale and retail trade (20%), Government (15%), Educational Services (9%), Services (6%), Construction (5%). **Leading products:** electrical machinery, apparel, leather items, fabricated metals, printing, food. **Agricultural products:** dairy items, poultry, greenhouse & nursery items, vegetables, tobacco. **Fishing:** haddock, flounder, scallops. **Avg. farm (1981):** 117 acres. **Avg. value of farm per acre:** $1,641.

**Highway expenditures per capita (1980):** $73.74. **Persons per motor vehicle (1981):** 1.51. **Minimum age for driver's license:** 17. **Gasoline tax:** 10.8¢ per gallon. **Diesel tax:** 10.8¢ per gallon. **Motor vehicle deaths (1980):** 15.4 per 100,000 people.

**Birthrate (1979):** 12.2 per 1,000 people. **Infant mortality rate per 1,000 births (1978):** 11.1. **Physicians per 100,000 pop. (1979):** 258. **Dentists per 100,000 pop. (1979):** 71. **Acceptable hospital beds (1979):** 7.8 per 1,000 people. **State expenditures per capita for health and hospitals (1980):** $106.88.

**Education expenditures (1977-78):** $475.86 per capita annually. **No. of pupils in public schools (1980):** 980,000. **No. of institutions of higher learning (1978-79):** 119. **Public school expenditure per pupil in attendance (1978-79):** $2,629. **Avg. salary of public school teachers (1979-80):** $22,500. **No. full-time teachers (1980):** 79,700. **Educational attainment of adult population (1976):** 12.6 median yrs. of school completed: 2.4% with less than 5 years of education; 16.8% with 4 yrs. of college.

**Telephones (1979):** 58 per 100 people. **State Chamber of Commerce:** Massachusetts Commonwealth Chamber of Commerce, c/o Worcester Chamber of Commerce, 350 Mechanics Tower, Worcester, Massachusetts 01608.

## MICHIGAN

Michigan, one of the world's largest producer of automobiles and among the most populous of the states, extends across two peninsulas and consists of two land regions: the Great Lakes Plain that makes up all of the mitten-shaped Lower Peninsula (where 90 percent of the people live) and the eastern portion of the irregularly shaped Upper Peninsula and the Superior Upland that comprise the rest. The state is touched by four of the five Great Lakes (all but Ontario) and has a longer shoreline than any other inland state.

Dividing the peninsulas and linking Lakes Michigan and Huron are the Straits of Mackinac, crossed by one of the world's longest suspension bridges. Largest among the state's approximately 500 islands is the 209-square-mile Isle Royale (a national park) in Lake Superior. Many mountains, forests, rivers, and waterfalls make the state a sportsman's paradise. The somewhat moist climate is marked by well-defined seasons.

Several Indian tribes were living in the Michigan region when the first European, Étienne Brulé of France, arrived (1618). Other Frenchmen, including Marquette, Jolliet, and La Salle, followed, and the first permanent settlement was established (1668) at Sault Sainte Marie. By 1700 there were French missions, fur-trading posts, and forts on both peninsulas; Fort Pontchartrain (founded 1701) was to become the city of Detroit. But the French were more interested in the lucrative pelt trade than in extensive development of the territory; while Mackinac Island became a busy trading center, most of the rest of the region remained sparsely settled and vulnerable to attack by the British, who gained possession in 1763. The Indians in the area, who had lived in peace with the French, detested the British and tried to drive them out, but eventually they joined with them to fight the Americans in the American Revolution and in the War of 1812.

MICHIGAN
MILES
0 10 20 40 60 80
KILOMETERS
0 20 40 60 80
State Capital
County Seats
ISLE ROYALE (NAT'L PARK)
KEWEENAW
Same scale as main map.
LAKE SUPERIOR
ONTONAGON
GOGEBIC
IRON
HOUGHTON
WISCONSIN
Same scale as main map.
OAKLAND
WAYNE
WASHTENAW
ONTARIO
Pontiac
Troy
Royal Oak
Warren
Birmingham
Southfield
Oak Park
Novi
Farmington
Ferndale
Northville
Livonia
Highland Pk.
Hamtramck
Plymouth
Dearborn Hts.
DETROIT
Garden City
Westland
Dearborn
Windsor
Ann Arbor
Ypsilanti
Inkster
Lincoln Pk.
River Rouge
Wyandotte
Trenton
Grosse Ile
Mt. Clemens
Sterling Hts.
Roseville
St. Clair Shores
Grosse Pte. Park
SELFRIDGE A.F.B.
MACOMB
KEWEENAW PEN.
LAKE SUPERIOR
BARAGA
MARQUETTE
Marquette
IRON
ALGER
SCHOOLCRAFT
LUCE
CHIPPEWA
Sault Ste. Marie
DELTA
MACKINAC
DICKINSON
MENOMINEE
WISCONSIN
GARDEN PEN.
DOOR PEN.
Green Bay
LAKE MICHIGAN
EMMET
CHEBOYGAN
PRESQUE ISLE
CHARLEVOIX
LEELANAU
ANTRIM
OTSEGO
MONTMORENCY
ALPENA
BENZIE
GRAND TRAVERSE
KALKASKA
CRAWFORD
OSCODA
ALCONA
MANISTEE
WEXFORD
MISSAUKEE
ROSCOMMON
OGEMAW
IOSCO
MASON
LAKE
OSCEOLA
CLARE
GLADWIN
ARENAC
HURON
OCEANA
NEWAYGO
MECOSTA
ISABELLA
MIDLAND
BAY
TUSCOLA
SANILAC
MUSKEGON
KENT
MONTCALM
GRATIOT
SAGINAW
LAPEER
ST. CLAIR
OTTAWA
IONIA
CLINTON
SHIAWASSEE
GENESEE
MACOMB
ALLEGAN
BARRY
EATON
INGHAM
LIVINGSTON
OAKLAND
VAN BUREN
KALAMAZOO
CALHOUN
JACKSON
WASHTENAW
WAYNE
BERRIEN
CASS
ST. JOSEPH
BRANCH
HILLSDALE
LENAWEE
MONROE
Lansing
Grand Rapids
Saginaw
Flint
Kalamazoo
Battle Creek
Jackson
Muskegon
Bay City
Midland
Pontiac
Royal Oak
DETROIT
Dearborn
Windsor
Ann Arbor
Port Huron
Monroe
Toledo
Milwaukee
CHICAGO
Gary
Hammond
South Bend
LAKE HURON
LAKE ERIE
CANADA
ONTARIO
INDIANA
OHIO
WISCONSIN ILLINOIS
© Copyright HAMMOND INCORPORATED, Maplewood, N.J.
Longitude West of Greenwich

Michigan, initially part of the Northwest Territory and then of Indiana Territory, was made a separate territory in 1805, with Detroit as its capital (succeeded by Lansing in 1847). Statehood was delayed by a boundary dispute with Ohio and Southern opposition to forming another free state. Compromises broke the impasse, as Michigan's admission (1837) was offset by that of slave state Arkansas, while Ohio was given the disputed land in return for awarding to Michigan the Upper Peninsula, which had been a part of the Territory of Wisconsin.

Michigan's development as a state was rapid, and a number of important roads, rail lines, and canals were soon built—including the vital Soo Ship Canal at Sault Sainte Marie (completed 1855), which allows ships to travel between Lakes Huron and Superior; these new routes spurred the state's mining industry. In the political sphere, the Republican party was founded in 1854 at Jackson, and abolitionist sentiment was strong throughout the state which contributed 100,000 troops to the Union cause during the Civil War.

Today Michigan is both a center of tourism and industry. Greenfield Village in Detroit's suburban Dearborn, to which Ford moved some of early America's famous landmarks, including the courthouse where Abraham Lincoln practiced, attracts over a million sightseers annually. Mackinac Island, near the meeting place of Lakes Michigan and Huron, has been a famous resort for 150 years. The spectacular, colorful turning of the Upper Peninsula's forests in fall attract thousands there, and the state has many annual events aimed at attracting others. Summer resorts abound along both the inland and Great Lakes. The National Park Service maintains three facilities: Isle Royale National Park, Pictured Rocks National Lakeshore and Sleeping Bear Dunes National Lakeshore.

The United Automobile, Aerospace and Agricultural Implement Workers of America (UAW), now the nation's third-largest union with over 1.3 million members, got its start in the famed "Sit-Down Strikes" of the 1930s with workers refusing to leave auto plants until their fledgling union was recognized as bargaining agent. UAW international headquarters are in Detroit.

Social reforms, including open housing, have occurred in a number of Michigan communities in recent years and the new constitution created an independent Civil Rights Commission with police powers. A state referendum in 1976 banned the use of throwaway containers for beer and soft drinks.

The recession of 1980-82 was particularly damaging to the state's auto industry, whose grip on the American market had already been shaken by foreign competitors. The state topped the nation in unemployment during August 1982 when Michigan's jobless rate reached 15.2 percent.

**Full name:** State of Michigan. **Origin of name:** From Michigama, meaning "Great Water." **Inhabitant:** Michiganian. **Capital:** Lansing. **State motto:** Si Quaeris Peninsulam Amoenam, Circumspice (If You Seek a Pleasant Peninsula, Look Around You). **Flag:** State seal on a blue field. **Seal:** Sun rising over water & man in field appear on shield supported by an elk & a moose. **Flower:** Apple blossom. **Bird:** Robin. **Tree:** White pine. **Song:** "Michigan, My Michigan." **Nickname:** Wolverine State.

**Governor:** William G. Milliken. **Annual salary:** $70,000. **Term:** 4 years. **Current term expires:** Jan. 1983. **Voting requirements:** 18 yrs. old & U.S. citizen; registered resident of state 30 days. **U.S. Congressmen:** 18. **Entered Union:** 1837 (26th state).

**Location & boundaries:** Midwestern state: bounded on the north by Lake Superior, the Straits of Mackinac & Lake Huron; on the east by Lakes Huron & St. Clair, Canada & Lake Erie; on the south by Ohio & Indiana; & on the west by Wisconsin & Lake Michigan. **Total area:** 58,527 sq. mi. (ranks 23rd). **Extreme length:** Upper peninsula 334 mi.; lower peninsula 286 mi. **Extreme breadth:** Upper peninsula 215 mi.; lower peninsula 200 mi. **Shoreline:** 2,232 mi. **Chief rivers:** Grand, Kalamazoo, Escanaba, Saginaw. **Major lakes (other than border-forming):** Houghton, Torch, Charlevoix, Burt. **No. of counties:** 83.

**Population (1980 census):** 9,262,078 (ranks 8th). **Pop. increase (1970-80):** 4.3%. **Largest cities:** Detroit, Grand Rapids, Warren, Flint. **Pop. density:** 158.3 per sq. mi. (ranks 12th). **Pop. distribution: White**—7,868,956; **Black**—1,198,710; **Am. Indian, Eskimo and Aleut**—40,038; **Asian and Pacific Islander**—56,731; **Other**—93,909; **Spanish origin**—162,388. **Marriage rate (1979):** 9.7 per 1,000 people. **Divorce rate:** 4.8 per 1,000 people.

**State finances (1980). Revenue:** $12,357,000,000. **Expenditures:** $12,634,000,000. **State taxes:** $642.43 per capita. **State personal income tax:** Yes. **Public debt (1980):** $314.98 per capita. **Federal aid (1980):** $423.89 per capita. **Personal income (1981):** $11,009.

**Sectors of the economy (% of labor force employed in 1970):** Manufacturing (36%), Wholesale and retail trade (19%), Government (14%), Educational Services (8%), Services (6%), Construction (5%). **Leading products:** primary & fabricated metals, food, electrical machinery, paper. **Minerals:** iron ore, cement, sand & gravel, copper. **Agricultural products:** cattle, poultry, dairy items, corn, hay, wheat. **Fishing:** whitefish, chubs, lake herring. **Avg. farm (1981):** 175 acres. **Avg. value of farm per acre:** $1,232.

**Highway expenditures per capita (1980):** $106.56. **Persons per motor vehicle (1981):** 1.41. **Minimum age for driver's license:** 16. **Gasoline tax:** 11¢ per gallon. **Diesel tax:** 9¢ per gallon. **Motor vehicle deaths (1980):** 18.9 per 100,000 people.

**Birthrate (1979):** 15.7 per 1,000 people. **Infant mortality rate per 1,000 births (1978):** 13.8. **Physicians per 100,000 pop. (1979):** 154. **Dentists per 100,000 pop. (1979):** 53. **Acceptable hospital beds (1979):** 5.4 per 1,000 people. **State expenditures per capita for health and hospitals (1980):** $96.53.

**Education expenditures (1977-78):** $587.44 per capita annually. **No. of pupils in public schools (1980):** 1,807,000. **No. of institutions of higher learning (1978-79):** 96. **Public school expenditure per pupil in attendance (1978-79):** $2,682. **Avg. salary of public school teachers (1979-80):** $18,830. **No. full-time teachers (1980):** 95,200. **Educational attainment of adult population (1976):** 12.5 median yrs. of school completed: 1.8% with less than 5 years of education; 12.6% with 4 yrs. of college.

**Telephones (1979):** 60 per 100 people. **State Chamber of Commerce:** Michigan State Chamber of Commerce, Business and Trade Center, Suite 400, 200 North Washington Square, Lansing, Michigan 48933.

## MINNESOTA

Site of the headwaters of the Mississippi, Minnesota is one of the most scenic states in the nation, rich in natural resources and boasting more than 15,000 lakes. Manufacturing, mainly of farm products, has in recent years become the leading industry, while improved techniques and new copper, nickel, and taconite finds signal a resurgence in mining. Tourism is today a major revenue producer for the state, which also ranks high agriculturally, with livestock and corn recently surpassing wheat in importance. Politically, Minnesota has gained a reputation for voter independence, experimentation in local government, and the institution of Scandinavian-type cooperatives.

Duluth has the nation's largest inland harbor and, since the completion of the St. Lawrence Seaway and Power Project (1959), the port has handled an increasingly significant amount of foreign trade. In Minneapolis are the central offices of the University of Minnesota, one of the largest universities in the country, while in Rochester is the famous Mayo Clinic, an international center of medical practice and research. About half of the state's population is centered in the "Twin Cities" of Minneapolis and St. Paul.

Minnesota's topography is marked by rolling prairies, fertile valleys, high bluffs, deep pine

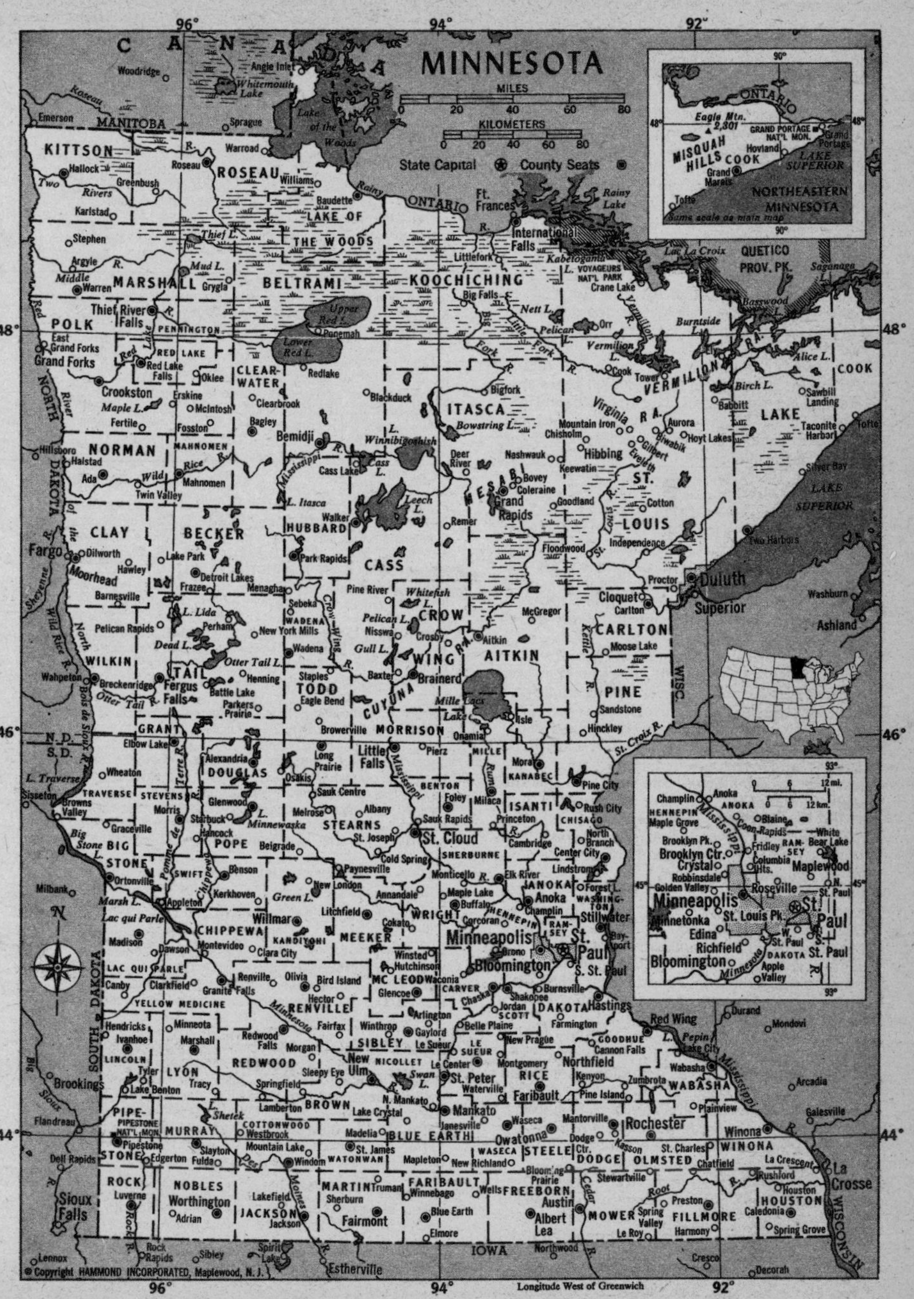
MINNESOTA
MILES
KILOMETERS
State Capital
County Seats
CANADA
MANITOBA
ONTARIO
Lake of the Woods
Rainy Lake
NORTHEASTERN MINNESOTA
Same scale as main map
MISQUAH HILLS
Eagle Mtn. 2,301
GRAND PORTAGE NAT'L MON.
Grand Portage
COOK
Grand Marais
Hovland
Tofte
LAKE SUPERIOR
QUETICO PROV. PK.
VOYAGEURS NAT'L PARK
KITTSON
ROSEAU
LAKE OF THE WOODS
MARSHALL
BELTRAMI
KOOCHICHING
POLK
PENNINGTON
RED LAKE
CLEARWATER
ITASCA
LAKE
NORMAN
MAHNOMEN
ST. LOUIS
CLAY
BECKER
HUBBARD
CASS
CROW WING
AITKIN
CARLTON
PINE
WILKIN
OTTER TAIL
TODD
MORRISON
MILLE LACS
KANABEC
GRANT
DOUGLAS
TRAVERSE
STEVENS
POPE
STEARNS
BENTON
SHERBURNE
ISANTI
CHISAGO
BIG STONE
SWIFT
ANOKA
WASHINGTON
CHIPPEWA
KANDIYOHI
MEEKER
WRIGHT
HENNEPIN
RAMSEY
LAC QUI PARLE
YELLOW MEDICINE
RENVILLE
MC LEOD
CARVER
SCOTT
DAKOTA
GOODHUE
WABASHA
LINCOLN
LYON
REDWOOD
SIBLEY
NICOLLET
LE SUEUR
RICE
PIPESTONE
MURRAY
COTTONWOOD
BROWN
BLUE EARTH
WASECA
STEELE
DODGE
OLMSTED
WINONA
ROCK
NOBLES
JACKSON
MARTIN
FARIBAULT
FREEBORN
MOWER
FILLMORE
HOUSTON
NORTH DAKOTA
SOUTH DAKOTA
IOWA
WISCONSIN
WISC.
N.D.
S.D.
Duluth
Superior
St. Paul
Minneapolis
St. Cloud
Rochester
Bloomington
Mankato
Moorhead
Fargo
Grand Forks
International Falls
Bemidji
Brainerd
Hibbing
Virginia
Winona
La Crosse
Sioux Falls
Red Wing
Willmar
Austin
Albert Lea
Faribault
Owatonna
Northfield
New Ulm
Fergus Falls
Crookston
Thief River Falls
Little Falls
Stillwater
Hastings
Worthington
Fairmont
Brookings
Longitude West of Greenwich
96°
94°
92°
90°
48°
46°
45°
44°
93°
© Copyright HAMMOND INCORPORATED, Maplewood, N.J.

woods, and wilderness areas. The two main land regions are the Superior Upland (or, locally, the "arrowhead country"), consisting of a roughly triangular northeastern land segment, and the Central Lowlands, comprising the rest except, in the south, a small projection of the Wisconsin Driftless Area and two small projections of the Dissected Till Plains. The state's continental climate has a relatively low mean temperature, and is subject to wide and often sudden fluctuation.

The timber industry, which flourished from about 1870 to the early 1900s, was vital to the state's early development, while incidentally fostering the well-known legend of Paul Bunyan.

The state's major tourist attractions are Voyageur's National Park and Grand Portage National Monument, both associated with the fur trade of the 1700s; Lumbertown USA at Brainerd; and the lake and winter sports centers of the North Country.

The first inhabitants of the Minnesota region are thought to date from about 20,000 years ago. Norsemen may have visited in the 14th century, but the first Europeans of record to do so were the French fur traders and missionaries, beginning with Radisson and Groseilliers (1659-61) and including La Salle, Marquette and Jolliet, and Daniel Greysolon—Sieur Du Lhut, or Duluth—who claimed (1679) the region for King Louis XIV.

Principal Indian tribes in the region at the time were the Sioux in the west and south and the Ojibwa in the heavily wooded northern section; the two groups, often at war with one another, were generally friendly to the French, who built up a vast pelt-marketing empire but ultimately lost it (1763) to the British.

Serious American development began after the War of 1812, with the powerful American Fur Company leading the way. Eastern Minnesota at this time was still part of the Northwest Territory, while the western region had been acquired (1803) as part of the Louisiana Purchase. A short-lived Spanish claim to the region (dating from 1762) was never effectively enforced. The year 1819 saw the building of Fort St. Anthony (later called Fort Snelling), and in 1832 Henry R. Schoolcraft discovered the source of the Mississippi at Lake Itasca. Six years later, Pierre Parrant settled on the site of present-day St. Paul.

In 1849 the Minnesota region—which in whole or part had been successively a portion of the French, English, and Spanish empires, the Northwest Territory, and seven U.S. territories—was made a territory in its own right. A comprehensive Indian treaty (1851) and statehood (1858) both spurred settlement, which was not deterred by a brief, ill-fated Sioux uprising in 1862.

In the 1890s, the mining of the high-grade iron ore of the Mesabi Ranges became a major industry. As the rich Mesabi mines dwindled after World War II, iron companies began to mine a low-grade ore called taconite, which abounds in Minnesota, and to extract high-grade iron pellets from it. Extraction leaves useless tailings, which contain asbestos and other dangerous substances.

Tailings caused a near-crisis in the city of Silver Bay. In 1975, the Reserve Mining Company, one of Silver Bay's largest employers, was ordered by a Federal court to stop dumping tailings into Lake Superior. At first, the company claimed that it would have to go out of business, thus ruining Silver Bay's economy. Eventually, a compromise allowed the company a "reasonable time" to change. In 1980, the company opened a land dump, linked to its plant by a slurry system, and ended dumping in the lake. The case concluded in April 1982 when the Federal court accepted an agreement by Reserve Mining to pay Silver Bay, Two Harbors, Beaver Bay and Duluth $1,840,000 for filtering lake water.

Declining production in the great steel-making centers, brought on by decreased demand and foreign competition, has resulted in serious cutbacks in Mesabi iron ore mining. Severe unemployment and out-migration has been the result in 1982.

**Full name:** State of Minnesota. **Origin of name:** From the Sioux meaning "Sky-Tinted Water." **Inhabitant:** Minnesotan. **Capital:** St. Paul. **State motto:** L'Etoile du Nord (The Star of the North). **Flag:** State seal & 19 gold stars on blue field. **Seal:** Indian riding into sunset, farmer plowing field, waterfall, forest. **Flower:** Pink & white lady's-slipper. **Bird:** Common loon. **Tree:** Norway (Red) pine. **Song:** "Hail! Minnesota." **Nickname:** North Star State.

**Governor:** Albert H. Quie. **Annual salary:** $66,500. **Term:** 4 yrs. **Current term expires:** Jan. 1983. **Voting requirements:** 18 yrs. old & U.S. citizen; registered state resident 20 days. **U.S. Congressmen:** 8. **Entered Union:** 1858 (32nd state).

**Location & boundaries:** Northern Midwestern state: bounded on the north by Canada; on the east by Lake Superior, Wisconsin & the Mississippi River; on the south by Iowa; & on the west by South Dakota, North Dakota & Red River of the North. **Total area:** 84,402 sq. mi. (ranks 12th). **Extreme length:** 406 mi. **Extreme breadth:** 358 mi. **Coastline:** 180 mi. **Chief rivers:** Mississippi, Red River of the North, Minnesota. **Major lakes:** Superior, Red, Lake of the Woods. **No. of counties:** 87.

**Population (1980 census):** 4,075,970 (ranks 21st). **Pop. increase (1970-80):** 7.1%. **Largest cities:** Minneapolis, St. Paul, Duluth, Bloomington. **Pop. density:** 48.3 per sq. mi. (ranks 33rd). **Pop. distribution: White**—3,936,948; **Black**—53,342; **Am. Indian, Eskimo and Aleut**—35,026; **Asian and Pacific Islander**—26,533; **Other**—25,299; **Spanish origin**—32,124. **Marriage rate (1979):** 9.1 per 1,000 people. **Divorce rate:** 3.7 per 1,000 people.

**State finances (1980). Revenue:** $5,700,000,000. **Expenditures:** $5,418,000,000. **State taxes:** $785.52 per capita. **State personal income tax:** Yes. **Public debt (1980):** $507.70 per capita. **Federal aid (1980):** $408.44 per capita. **Personal income (1981):** $10,747.

**Sectors of the economy (% of labor force employed in 1970):** Wholesale and retail trade (22%), Manufacturing (21%), Government (15%), Educational Services (9%), Services (7%), Construction (6%). **Leading products:** food; electrical & other machinery; printing & publishing; paper items; chemicals; stone, clay & glass items. **Minerals:** iron ore, taconite, sand & gravel, cement, stone. **Agricultural products:** cattle, hogs, dairy items, corn, soybeans. **Fishing:** yellow pike, lake herring, tullibee. **Avg. farm (1981):** 286 acres. **Avg. value of farm per acre:** $1,231.

**Highway expenditures per capita (1980):** $133.11. **Persons per motor vehicle (1981):** 1.30. **Minimum age for driver's license:** 16. **Gasoline tax:** 13¢ per gallon. **Diesel tax:** 13¢ per gallon. **Motor vehicle deaths (1980):** 20.8 per 100,000 people.

**Birthrate (1979):** 16.1 per 1,000 people. **Infant mortality rate per 1,000 births (1978):** 12.0. **Physicians per 100,000 pop. (1979):** 185. **Dentists per 100,000 pop. (1979):** 62. **Acceptable hospital beds (1979):** 7.5 per 1,000 people. **State expenditures per capita for health and hospitals (1980):** $80.55.

**Education expenditures (1977-78):** $577.79 per capita annually. **No. of pupils in public schools (1980):** 751,000. **No. of institutions of higher learning (1978-79):** 65. **Public school expenditure per pupil in attendance (1978-79):** $2,368. **Avg. salary of public school teachers (1979-80):** $17,310. **No. full-time teachers (1980):** 48,200. **Educational attainment of adult population (1976):** 12.5 median yrs. of school completed: 1.1% with less than 5 years of education; 13.3% with 4 yrs. of college.

**Telephones (1979):** 57 per 100 people. **State Chamber of Commerce:** Minnesota Association of Commerce and Industry, 200 Hanover Bldg., 480 Cedar Street, St. Paul, Minnesota 55101.

## MISSISSIPPI

Without renouncing the history that has been both its pride and its handicap, this Deep South state has begun to rework its economic and social structures after a period of transition that began during the Great Depression.

MISSISSIPPI
MILES
0 10 20 30 40 50 60
KILOMETERS
0 10 20 30 40 50 60
State Capitals
County Seats
92°
91°
90°
89°
88°
35°
34°
33°
32°
31°
TENNESSEE
ARKANSAS
LOUISIANA
ALABAMA
Memphis
W. Memphis
Forrest City
Collierville
Horn Lake
Olive Branch
DESOTO
Hernando
Byhalia
BENTON
Ashland
Corinth
ALCORN
Iuka
Woodall Mtn. 806
Pickwick L.
TIPPAH
Ripley
Blue Mountain
PRENTISS
Booneville
TISHOMINGO
Wheeler
Belmont
Baldwyn
Red Bay
Marianna
Tunica
TUNICA
Arkabutla L.
Coldwater
TATE
Senatobia
Holly Springs
MARSHALL
UNION
New Albany
BRICES CROSS ROADS NAT'L BATTLEFIELD SITE
Helena
Crenshaw
Como
Sardis
Sardis Lake
Oxford
LAFAYETTE
PONTOTOC
Pontotoc
TUPELO NAT'L BATTLEFIELD
LEE
Tupelo
ITAWAMBA
Fulton
Verona
Plantersville
Shannon
Hamilton
DeWitt
Friars Point
Jonestown
Clarksdale
COAHOMA
Marks
Lambert
QUITMAN
Batesville
PANOLA
Crowder
Water Valley
Enid Lake
Pine Bluff
Arkansas River
White R.
Mississippi
Tutwiler
Charleston
YALOBUSHA
CALHOUN
Houlka
Nettleton
MONROE
Amory
Star City
Shelby
Mound Bayou
Rosedale
Merigold
Cleveland
Dumas
SUNFLOWER
Sumner
Webb
TALLAHATCHIE
Coffeeville
Grenada Lake
Bruce
Pittsboro
CHICKASAW
Okolona
Houston
Vardaman
Calhoun City
Aberdeen
Sulligent
Drew
Ruleville
Grenada
GRENADA
Tie Plant
Warren
Monticello
Benoit
Boyle
Shaw
BOLIVAR
McGehee
FLOWER
LEFLORE
Duck Hill
WEBSTER
Walthall
Maben
CLAY
West Point
COLUMBUS A.F.B.
Columbus
Dermott
Sunflower
Itta Bena
Greenwood
MONTGOMERY
Winona
Eupora
Mathiston
Starkville
Indianola
Carrollton
CARROLL
Vaiden
Kilmichael
CHOCTAW
Ackerman
State College
OKTIBBEHA
LOWNDES
Reform
Greenville
Moorhead
Inverness
Leland
Lake Village
Arcola
WASHINGTON
Isola
Belzoni
HUMPHREYS
Tchula
Lexington
ATTALA
Weir
Brooksville
Crossett
Eudora
Hollandale
Midnight
HOLMES
Durant
Kosciusko
Ethel
Louisville
WINSTON
NOXUBEE
Macon
Aliceville
Anguilla
Rolling Fork
Goodman
Noxapater
Shuqualak
Bastrop
Lake Providence
Mayersville
SHARKEY
Yazoo City
YAZOO
Pickens
LEAKE
Carthage
Philadelphia
Scooba
DeKalb
KEMPER
Demopolis
Lake
Bentonia
MADISON
NESHOBA
ISSAQUENA
Canton
Lena
Union
Okatibbee Res.
Lauderdale
Livingston
Rayville
Delhi
Tallulah
Flora
Madison
Sebastopol
Ross Barnett Res.
SCOTT
Decatur
NEWTON
Marion
York
VICKSBURG NAT'L MIL. PARK
Ridgeland
Bolton
Tougaloo
Clinton
Jackson
Morton
Forest
Meridian
LAUDERDALE
Vicksburg
WARREN
Raymond
Brandon
Pelahatchie
Newton
Hickory
Winnsboro
HINDS
Whitfield
RANKIN
Enterprise
Utica
Terry
Piney Woods
SMITH
Raleigh
JASPER
Paulding
Stonewall
Quitman
Butler
Port Gibson
CLAIBORNE
Crystal Springs
COPIAH
Mendenhall
Magee
Bay Springs
CLARKE
Alcorn College
Hazlehurst
SIMPSON
Taylorsville
Heidelberg
Shubuta
JEFFERSON
Fayette
Wesson
Mount Olive
COVINGTON
Collins
Laurel
JONES
Ellisville
Sandersville
Waynesboro
Ferriday
Vidalia
Natchez
Brookhaven
LAWRENCE
Monticello
Prentiss
FRANKLIN
Meadville
Bude
LINCOLN
JEFFERSON DAVIS
Moselle
WAYNE
Buckatunna
ADAMS
Roxie
State Line
Homochitto R.
Summit
McComb
Morgantown
Sumrall
Petal
PERRY
Richton
Crosby
AMITE
Gloster
Foxworth
Columbia
Hattiesburg
GREENE
Beaumont
WILKINSON
Liberty
Fernwood
Magnolia
Tylertown
MARION
Purvis
New Augusta
Leakesville
Citronelle
Woodville
Centreville
PIKE
WALTHALL
Osyka
LAMAR
Lumberton
Brooklyn
McLain
FORREST
Kentwood
Lucedale
GEORGE
Clinton
Franklinton
PEARL RIVER
Poplarville
Wiggins
Perkinston
STONE
Jackson
Bogalusa
McNeill
McHenry
Amite
Carriere
HARRISON
JACKSON
Mobile
Baton Rouge
Hammond
Covington
Picayune
HANCOCK
Gulfport
D'Iberville
KEESLER A.F.B.
Ocean Sprs.
GULF ISLANDS NAT'L SEASHORE
Escatawpa
Moss Pt.
Bayou La Batre
Pass Christian
Long Beach
Biloxi
Pascagoula
Mississippi Sound
Bay St. Louis
Lakeshore
Waveland
Slidell
L. Maurepas
Lake Pontchartrain
New Orleans
Plaquemine
Cat I.
Ship I.
Horn I.
Petit Bois I.
Dauphin I.
GULF ISLANDS NAT'L SEASHORE
Mobile Bay
© Copyright HAMMOND INCORPORATED, Maplewood, N. J.
Longitude West of Greenwich

In 1936, wealthy lumberman Hugh White became governor and instituted a "Balance Agriculture with Industry" (BAWI) program which allowed cities to issue bonds and build plants for private industry. By 1965, industrial employment had inched ahead of agricultural employment.

Tourists from outside the state enrich Mississippi's economy by over $800 million yearly as they flock to the beaches of the Gulf Coast winter resort area and other attractions.

The petroleum industry has become a major factor since the discovery of oil in the Tinsley field in 1939. Mississippi is a leading producer of oil and natural gas in the U.S.

The state is made up of two main land regions: the flat and fertile Delta area along the Mississippi River in northwest Mississippi and the rolling hills which cover most other areas, though broken by occasional river valleys. The Bay of St. Louis and Biloxi or Back Bay break the coastline and a chain of small islands lie offshore.

Mississippi was inhabited by the Choctaw, Chickasaw, Natchez and Yazoo Indians before De Soto explored it for Spain in 1540. French explorers La Salle, Iberville and Bienville came later.

The French ceded Mississippi to the British under the treaty of Paris in 1763 but the Spanish claimed it along with West Florida in 1781. Spanish influence virtually ended in 1798 when Mississippi flew the United States flag as a territory of the new republic.

The early settlement of the state was handicapped by conflicting land claims, Indian troubles and the Yazoo Land Fraud in which Georgia, claiming the region, sold lots to speculators. Georgia finally ceded its claim to the Federal Government in 1802 and the Louisiana Purchase in 1803 insured free access to the Mississippi River. Mississippi became a state in 1817.

By the time the Civil War began, Mississippi was among the wealthiest states in the nation. Property assessments totaled $509 million in 1860. By 1880 property assessments had fallen to $110 million. Not until 1920 did assessments reach the pre-Civil War level.

Most black people were effectively disfranchised until the passage of the Federal Voting Rights Act of 1965.

Attacks on segregation brought turbulence. Two persons were killed in rioting at the University of Mississippi; NAACP leader Medgar Evers was shot to death in ambush at his Jackson home in 1963; and three civil rights workers were killed in 1964 near Philadelphia, Miss. However, the state joined the FBI in a massive crackdown on the Ku Klux Klan group behind much of the trouble, and tensions then eased.

Massive public school desegregation came later and Mississippi experienced less trouble than Northern and Eastern states under similar orders. Mississippi experienced some campus unrest as the 1960s closed and two persons were shot to death in a riot at Jackson State College in 1970.

In recent years blacks have made important gains, with an improvement in job opportunities and an increase in numbers elected to public office. The 1979 elections increased the number of blacks in the legislature from four to seventeen.

Mississippi's recent bid for trade with Middle Eastern and South American countries has paid off in massive sales of such products as farm machinery, food products, soybeans and cotton.

The Tennessee-Tombigbee Waterway project, one of a number of such measures cancelled by President Carter as an economy move, was reinstated after Congressional pressure was brought to bear. The project, estimated to cost $1.8 billion, is expected to be a shot in the arm for Mississippi's economy.

**Full name:** State of Mississippi. **Origin of name:** From the Indian, Maesi, meaning "Large," & Sipu, meaning "River." **Inhabitant:** Mississippian. **Capital:** Jackson. **State motto:** Virtute et Armis (By Valor & Arms). **Flag:** Horizontal red, white & blue bars with Confederate battle flag in upper left. **Seal:** American eagle holds olive branch, representing peace, & three arrows, symbolizing war. **Flower:** Magnolia. **Bird:** Mockingbird. **Tree:** Magnolia. **Song:** "Go, Mississippi." **Nickname:** Magnolia State.

**Governor:** William F. Winter. **Annual salary:** $53,000. **Term:** 4 years. **Current term expires:** Jan. 1984. **Voting requirements:** 18 yrs. old & U.S. citizen; resident of state and county for 1 year, resident 6 months in election district or municipality. **U.S. Congressmen:** 5. **Entered Union:** 1817 (20th state).

**Location & boundaries:** Southeastern state bounded on the north by Tennessee; on the east by Alabama; on the south by the Gulf of Mexico & Louisiana; & on the west by the Mississippi River, Louisiana & Arkansas. **Total area:** 47,689 sq. mi. (ranks 32nd). **Extreme length:** 352 mi. **Extreme breadth:** 188 mi. **Coastline:** 44 mi. **Chief rivers:** Mississippi, Yazoo, Pearl, Big Black. **Major lakes:** Grenada, Barnett, Sardis, Enid, Okatibbee Reservoirs. **No. of counties:** 82.

**Population (1980 census):** 2,520,638 (ranks 31st). **Pop. increase (1970-80):** 13.7%. **Largest cities:** Jackson, Biloxi, Meridian. **Pop. density:** 52.9 per sq. mi. (ranks 31st). **Pop. distribution: White**—1,615,190; **Black**—887,206; **Am. Indian, Eskimo and Aleut**—6,180; **Asian and Pacific Islander**—7,142; **Other**—4,650; **Spanish origin**—24,731. **Marriage rate (1979):** 11.2 per 1,000 people. **Divorce rate:** 5.6 per 1,000 people.

**State finances (1980). Revenue:** $2,885,000,000. **Expenditures:** $2,691,000,000. **State taxes:** $498.98 per capita. **State personal income tax:** Yes. **Public debt (1980):** $323.30 per capita. **Federal aid (1980):** $467.26 per capita. **Personal income (1981):** $7,256.

**Sectors of the economy (% of labor force employed in 1970):** Manufacturing (26%), Wholesale and retail trade (18%), Government (18%), Educational Services (9%), Construction (8%), Services (7%). **Leading products:** food, lumber & wood, apparel, chemicals, transportation equipment. **Minerals:** petroleum, natural gas, sand & gravel. **Agricultural products:** cattle, broilers, eggs, cotton lint, soybeans, cottonseed. **Fishing:** menhaden, shrimp, oysters. **Avg. farm (1981):** 265 acres. **Avg. value of farm per acre:** $1,047.

**Highway expenditures per capita (1980):** $147.11. **Persons per motor vehicle (1981):** 1.54. **Minimum age for driver's license:** 15. **Gasoline tax:** 9¢ per gallon. **Diesel tax:** 10¢ per gallon. **Motor vehicle deaths (1980):** 27.6 per 100,000 people.

**Birthrate (1979):** 18.9 per 1,000 people. **Infant mortality rate per 1,000 births (1978):** 18.7. **Physicians per 100,000 pop. (1979):** 106. **Dentists per 100,000 pop. (1979):** 32. **Acceptable hospital beds (1979):** 6.5 per 1,000 people. **State expenditures per capita for health and hospitals (1980):** $69.83.

**Education expenditures (1977-78):** $422.67 per capita annually. **No. of pupils in public schools (1980):** 472,000. **No. of institutions of higher learning (1978-79):** 46. **Public school expenditure per pupil in attendance (1978-79):** $1,610. **Avg. salary of public school teachers (1979-80):** $12,300. **No. full-time teachers (1980):** 29,100. **Educational attainment of adult population (1976):** 12.1 median yrs. of school completed: 7.9% with less than 5 years of education; 11.5% with 4 yrs. of college.

**Telephones (1979):** 47 per 100 people. **State Chamber of Commerce:** Mississippi Economic Council, 656 N. State Street, P.O. Box 1849, Jackson, Mississippi 39205.

## MISSOURI

Traditional "Gateway to the West," centrally located Missouri owes much of its industrial and agricultural importance to the nation's two largest rivers—the Mississippi and Missouri—which form part of the state's borders while facilitating transportation and enriching its soil. Lead mining, in which the state ranks first nationally, has been important in the region for 200 years, being conducted chiefly in the Viburnum and Bixby areas.

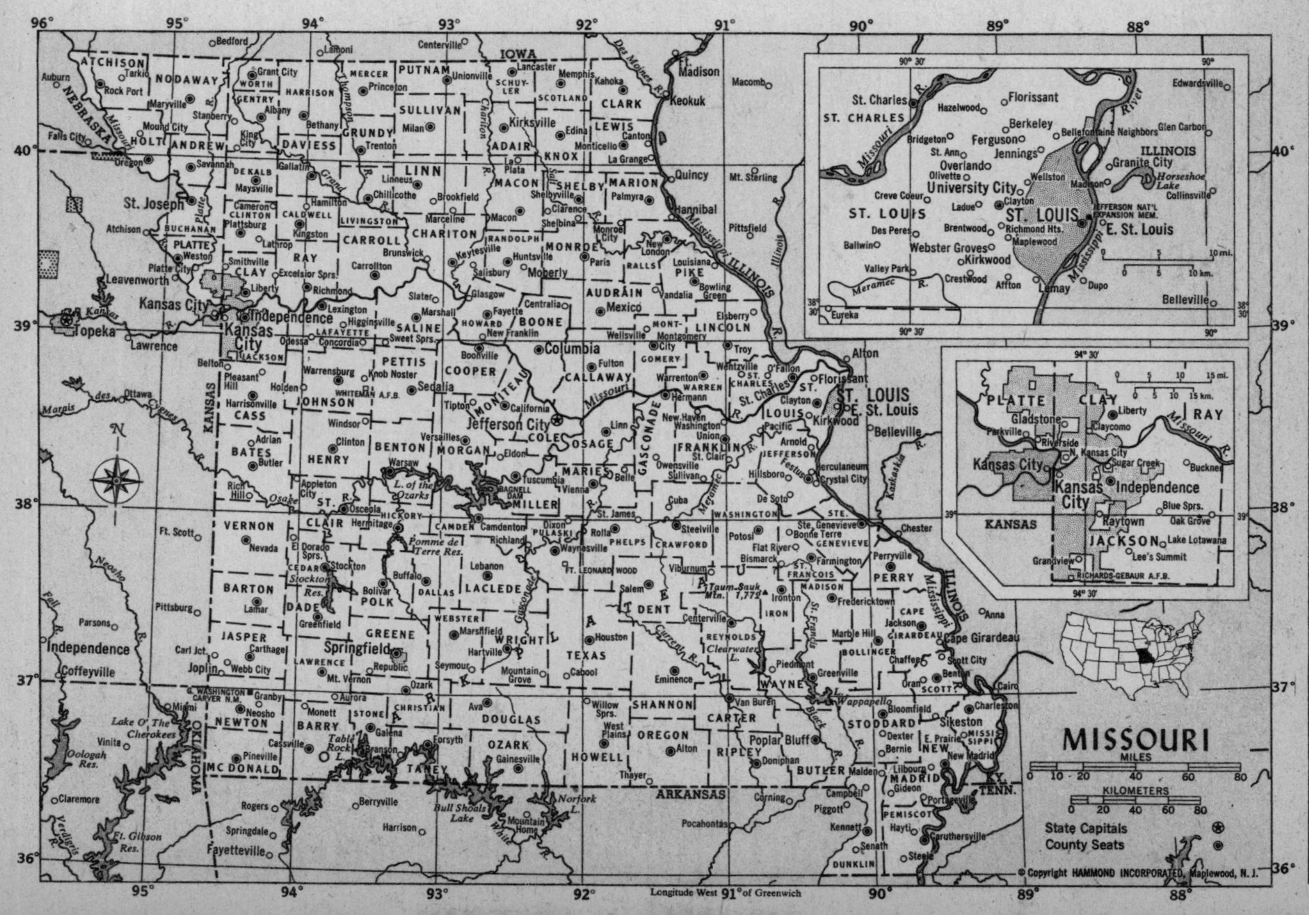
MISSOURI
MILES
0 10 20 40 60 80
KILOMETERS
0 20 40 60 80
State Capitals
County Seats
© Copyright HAMMOND INCORPORATED, Maplewood, N. J.
Longitude West 91° of Greenwich
IOWA
ILLINOIS
KANSAS
NEBRASKA
OKLAHOMA
ARKANSAS
KY.
TENN.
Jefferson City
Kansas City
Independence
St. Joseph
Springfield
Columbia
ST. LOUIS
E. St. Louis
St. Charles
Florissant
University City
Webster Groves
Kirkwood
Clayton
PLATTE
CLAY
RAY
JACKSON
Liberty
Gladstone
Raytown
Lee's Summit
Grandview

Most of the state's manufacturing activity is concentrated in and around St. Louis and Kansas City.

The state is made up of four principal land regions: the Dissected Till Plains, lying north of the Missouri; the Osage Plains in the west; the West Gulf Coastal Plain (known locally as the Mississippi Alluvial Plain), covering the southeastern corner; and the Ozark Plateau, making up most of the southern section and constituting the largest single region. The Dissected Till and Osage Plains are considered subdivisions of the Central Lowlands. Ten major artificial lakes formed by dams in the Ozark region have helped make that area a popular vacationland, contributing greatly to the state's $2 billion annual tourism business. Although two-thirds of the state was once covered by forests, today only half that amount remains, including Mark Twain and Clark National Forests.

The Mound Builders, the earliest known inhabitants of the Missouri region, predated the Osage and Missouri Indians, who were living there when the first European explorers—Frenchmen Marquette and Jolliet—visited (1673). France's claim to the entire Mississippi Valley, including what is now Missouri, was based on La Salle's travels in 1682. In the following years, French fur trading posts were established along the river, and the working of the lead mines was begun. Established about 1735, Ste. Genevieve was the first permanent white settlement.

Having met defeat in the French and Indian Wars, France secretly yielded (1762) to Spain all its territory west of the Mississippi; even so, Frenchmen Laclede and Chouteau founded St. Louis two years later. Napoleon regained (1800) possession of the region for France, then sold it three years later as part of the Louisiana Purchase. A year later, in 1804, President Thomas Jefferson sent Meriwether Lewis and William Clark westward up the Missouri River on the famous expedition that tied the United States together as a continental nation. The area was briefly a district of the Territory of Indiana, but was made a separate territory in 1805, comprising at that time all U.S. land west of the Mississippi and north of 33° north latitude and therefore including the future state of Missouri.

The question of admitting Missouri to the Union became bound up, in Congress, with the volatile slavery issue. Bitter controversy was arduously resolved by the Missouri Compromise (1820), which provided for the admission of Missouri (1821) as a slave state and Maine as a free one, while banning slavery in the rest of the Louisiana Purchase north of 36°30′N. Missouri was at this time the nation's western frontier, and fur trading was still its foremost economic pursuit. The state's six northwestern counties were added by the Platte Purchase (1837). An unusual boundary dispute between Missouri and Illinois was settled early in 1970, giving Illinois the site of Old Kaskaskia, the state's original capital, now an island as a result of shifts by the Mississippi River. Illinois received Kaskaskia and Beaver islands, and Missouri, Cottonwoods and Roth islands.

The years preceding the Civil War were marked by growing prosperity in an increasingly tense political climate. The town of Independence became the starting point of the much-traveled Santa Fe and Oregon Trails, while St. Louis prospered as a thriving inland port. St. Joseph was the eastern starting point of the briefly active (1860-61) Pony Express. But bitter Missouri-Kansas border wars over the slavery issue had begun, and although Missouri voted (February 1861) not to secede from the Union, Missourians were sharply divided in their allegiances, supplying both sides with troops.

Missouri today seeks to attract new industry by stressing its central location, good transportation facilities, availability of labor, and relatively low taxes. Tourism has emerged in recent years as one of Missouri's leading businesses.

Missouri's tourist and vacation attractions include the Gateway Arch which is part of the Jefferson National Expansion Memorial in St. Louis, Wilson's Creek National Battlefield near Springfield, the George Washington Carver National Monument near Carthage, the Ozark National Scenic Riverways, Hannibal on the Mississippi of Mark Twain fame, and the Lake of the Ozarks vacation country.

**Full name:** State of Missouri. **Origin of name:** From name of Sioux tribe. **Inhabitant:** Missourian. **Capital:** Jefferson City. **State motto:** Salus Populi Suprema Lex Esto (Let the Welfare of the People Be the Supreme Law). **Flag:** State seal centered on horizontal red, white & blue bars. **Seal:** Two grizzly bears hold shields of United States & Missouri; 24 stars represent Missouri's entrance into Union. **Flower:** Hawthorn. **Bird:** Bluebird. **Tree:** Flowering dogwood. **Song:** "Missouri Waltz." **Nickname:** Show-Me State.

**Governor:** Christopher S. Bond. **Annual salary:** $55,000. **Term:** 4 years. **Current term expires:** Jan. 1985. **Voting requirements:** 18 yrs. old & U.S. citizen; registered to vote fourth Wednesday prior to election. **U.S. Congressmen:** 9. **Entered Union:** 1821 (24th state).

**Location & boundaries:** Southern Midwestern state: bounded on the north by Iowa; on the east by Illinois, Kentucky, Tennessee & the Mississippi River; on the south by Arkansas; & on the west by Oklahoma, Kansas, Nebraska & the Missouri River. **Total area:** 69,697 sq. mi. (ranks 19th). **Extreme length:** 284 mi. **Extreme breadth:** 308 mi. **Chief rivers:** Missouri, Mississippi, Osage. **Major lakes:** Lake of the Ozarks; Stockton, Taneycomo, Clearwater, and Wappapello lakes; Table Rock & Pomme de Terre Reservoirs. **No. of counties:** 114 & the city of St. Louis.

**Population (1980 census):** 4,916,759 (ranks 15th). **Pop. increase (1970-80):** 5.1%. **Largest cities:** St. Louis, Kansas City, Springfield, Independence. **Pop. density:** 70.5 per sq. mi. (ranks 27th). **Pop. distribution: White**—4,346,267; **Black**—514,274; **Am. Indian, Eskimo and Aleut**—12,319; **Asian and Pacific Islander**—23,108; **Other**—21,476; **Spanish origin**—51,667. **Marriage rate (1979):** 10.9 per 1,000 people. **Divorce rate:** 5.7 per 1,000 people.

**State finances (1980). Revenue:** $4,258,000,000. **Expenditures:** $3,996,000,000. **State taxes:** $425.98 per capita. **State personal income tax:** Yes. **Public debt (1980):** $207.01 per capita. **Federal aid (1980):** $345.39 per capita. **Personal income (1981):** $9,876.

**Sectors of the economy (% of labor force employed in 1970):** Manufacturing (24%), Wholesale and retail trade (22%), Government (15%), Educational Services (8%), Services (7%), Construction (6%). **Leading products:** transportation equipment, food, chemicals, printing & publishing, machinery, fabricated metals. **Minerals:** stone, cement, lead, iron ore. **Agricultural products:** cattle, hogs, dairy items, corn, soybeans, hay. **Avg. farm (1981):** 265 acres. **Avg. value of farm per acre:** $941.

**Highway expenditures per capita (1980):** $107.85. **Persons per motor vehicle (1981):** 1.49. **Minimum age for driver's license:** 16. **Gasoline tax:** 7¢ per gallon. **Diesel tax:** 7¢ per gallon. **Motor vehicle deaths (1980):** 23.9 per 100,000 people.

**Birthrate (1979):** 15.7 per 1,000 people. **Infant mortality rate per 1,000 births (1978):** 14.8. **Physicians per 100,000 pop. (1979):** 158. **Dentists per 100,000 pop. (1979):** 48. **Acceptable hospital beds (1979):** 7.1 per 1,000 people. **State expenditures per capita for health and hospitals (1980):** $68.46.

**Education expenditures (1977-78):** $389.73 per capita annually. **No. of pupils in public schools (1980):** 847,000. **No. of institutions of higher learning (1978-79):** 84. **Public school expenditure per pupil in attendance (1978-79):** $1,856. **Avg. salary of public school teachers (1979-80):** $14,225. **No. full-time teachers (1980):** 55,200. **Educational attainment of adult population (1976):** 12.4 median yrs. of school completed: 2.5% with less than 5 years of education; 11.8% with 4 yrs. of college.

**Telephones (1979):** 58 per 100 people. **State Chamber of Commerce:** Missouri Chamber of Commerce, P.O. Box 149, Jefferson City, Missouri 65102.

## MONTANA

As its Spanish name suggests, Montana is a mountainous region: the Rocky Mountains cover the western two-fifths of the state and the high, gently rolling Great Plains make up the rest. The state is large, ranking fourth nationally in area, but it is sparsely populated. The Rockies' Bitterroot Range, marking the Montana-Idaho boundary, is one of the most rugged and remote areas in the country. Many of the state's mountains are thick with forests below the timber line; fir, pine, and spruce abound. The state is an important producer of Christmas trees for national markets.

Montana's climate is generally cool to cold, and dry. Tourists—mainly hunters, fishermen, and dude ranch patrons—have been coming to the state in growing numbers, attracted by plentiful fish and game and the varied scenery. As an industry, tourism has become increasingly vital in recent years. Attractions include Glacier National Park, 11 national forests, the Lewis and Clark Cavern (one of the country's largest), Big Hole National Battlefield, the Custer Battlefield National Monument, Bighorn Canyon National Recreation Area, the Flathead Lake vacation area, and a number of annual rodeos and Indian ceremonials. Yellowstone National Park, most of which is in Wyoming, has three entrances in Montana.

Arapaho, Blackfoot, Cheyenne, Crow, Atsina, Bannock, Kalispel, Kutenai, and Shoshoni Indians were living in the region before the arrival of the first Europeans, who were probably fur trappers of the Hudson Bay Company or the Northwest Company. In 1805, Lewis and Clark explored the area on their journeys to and from the Pacific Coast. The American Fur Company, in 1829 and 1846, built two of Montana's earliest non-Indian settlements: Forts Union and Benton.

The major Indian wars (1867-77) included the famous 1876 Battle of Little Bighorn, popularly known as "Custer's Last Stand," in which Cheyennes and Sioux killed General Custer and more than 200 of his men. But the Indians' moment of glory was something of a brief one, for in 1877, when Chief Joseph and his Nez Percé warriors surrendered to Federal troops near the Canadian border, Indian resistance in Montana virtually ended. Today, the state has some 37,000 Indians, almost all of whom live on seven reservations.

The United States obtained most of Montana as part of the Louisiana Purchase (1803). The remaining northwestern section passed into U.S. hands following the 1846 treaty with England. Montana was originally part of the Territory of Idaho, created in 1863; Montana Territory came into being in 1864. Statehood came in 1889.

Much of Montana's early history was bound up with mining, which is still a leading industry: oil, coal, copper, and sand and gravel are important products. The capital of Helena was originally a mining camp called Last Chance Gulch. The Anaconda Company branched out from Butte ("the riccest hill on earth") to become a giant conglomerate of its day, with interests in railroading, journalism, banking, and other fields.

Another of Montana's major occupations, ranching, came into its own in 1866 when a cattleman by the name of Nelson Story drove his herd of a thousand longhorn from Texas to Montana, setting an example that many others soon followed. The coming of the railroad in 1883 was another impetus. But the severe winter of 1886-87 spelled disaster; thousands of cattle perished in subzero blizzards. Although the industry eventually recovered, for a long time profit margins were narrow. Ranching is economically important: the state has over three times as many cattle (including calves) and almost as many sheep as it has people.

Montana today is attempting to attract new industry while preserving clean air and water. The aims have touched off a clash between environmentalists and the energy companies which are developing reserves of strippable coal.

In May 1980, volcanic ash from the eruption of Mount St. Helens in Washington fell thickly in six counties in western Montana. Streets became impassable, and schools and businesses were closed.

**Full name:** State of Montana. **Origin of name:** From Spanish word meaning "Mountainous." **Inhabitant:** Montanan. **Capital:** Helena. **State motto:** Oro y Plata (Gold & Silver). **Flag:** State seal on blue field. **Seal:** A plow, pick & shovel rest on soil, symbolizing Montana's agricultural & mineral industries; Great Falls of Missouri River & mountain scenery. **Flower:** Bitterroot. **Bird:** Western meadowlark. **Tree:** Ponderosa pine. **Song:** "Montana." **Nicknames:** Treasure State; the Big Sky Country; Land of the Shining Mountains.

**Governor:** Ted Schwinden. **Annual salary:** $47,023. **Term:** 4 years. **Current term expires:** Dec. 1985. **Voting requirements:** 18 yrs. old & U.S. citizen; registered resident of state & county 30 days. **U.S. Congressmen:** 2. **Entered Union:** 1889 (41st state).

**Location & boundaries:** Rocky Mountain state: bounded on the north by Canada; on the east by North Dakota & South Dakota; on the south by Wyoming & Idaho; & on the west by Idaho. **Total area:** 147,046 sq. mi. (ranks 4th). **Extreme length:** 570 mi. **Extreme breadth:** 315 mi. **Chief rivers:** Missouri, Yellowstone, Kootenai. **Major lakes:** Flathead; Fort Peck & Canyon Ferry Reservoirs. **No. of counties:** 56.

**Population (1980 census):** 786,690 (ranks 44th). **Pop. increase (1970-80):** 13.3%. **Largest cities:** Billings, Great Falls, Butte-Silver Bow, Missoula. **Pop. density:** 5.3 per sq. mi. (ranks 48th). **Pop. distribution: White**—740,148; **Black**—1,786; **Am. Indian, Eskimo and Aleut**—37,270; **Asian and Pacific Islander**—2,503; **Other**—4,983; **Spanish origin**—9,974. **Marriage rate (1979):** 10.4 per 1,000 people. **Divorce rate:** 6.5 per 1,000 people.

**State finances (1980). Revenue:** $1,153,000,000. **Expenditures:** $1,005,000,000. **State taxes:** $553.69 per capita. **State personal income tax:** Yes. **Public debt (1980):** $393.31 per capita. **Federal aid (1980):** $584.35 per capita. **Personal income (1981):** $9,676.

**Sectors of the economy (% of labor force employed in 1970):** Wholesale and retail trade (22%), Government (21%), Manufacturing (10%), Educational Services (10%), Services (7%), Construction (6%). **Leading products:** lumber & wood; primary metals; food; petroleum & coal items; printing & publishing; stone, clay & glasss items; chemiicals. **Minerals:** copper, petroleum, lead & zinc, sand & gravel, phosphate rock, silver, gold. **Agricultural products:** cattle, dairy items, sheep, wheat, hay, barley, flax seed, sugar beets. **Avg. farm (1981):** 2,598 acres. **Avg. value of farm per acre:** $239.

**Highway expenditures per capita (1980)):** $237.22. **Persons per motor vehicle (1981):** 1.09. **Minimum age for driver's license:** 15. **Gasoline tax:** 9¢ per gallon. **Diesel tax:** 11¢ per gallon. **Motor vehicle deaths (1980):** 41.3 per 100,000 people.

**Birthrate (1979):** 17.9 per 1,000 people. **Infant mortality rate per 1,000 births (1978):** 11.6. **Physicians per 100,000 pop. (1979):** 127. **Dentists per 100,000 pop. (1979):** 27. **Acceptable hospital beds (1979):** 6.7 per 1,000 people. **State expenditures per capita for health and hospitals (1980):** $63.87.

**Education expenditures (1977-78):** $641.48 per capita annually. **No. of pupils in public schools (1980):** 153,000. **No. of institutions of higher learning (1978-79):** 13. **Public school expenditure per pupil in attendance (1978-79):** $2,215. **Avg. salary of public school teachers (1979-80):** $15,080. **No. full-time teachers (1980):** 9,950. **Educational attainment of adult population (1976):** 12.6 median yrs. of school completed: 1.2% with less than 5 years of education; 14.2% with 4 yrs. of college.

**Telephones (1979):** 56 per 100 people. **State Chamber of Commerce:** Montana Chamber of Commerce, 110 Neill Avenue, P.O. Box 1730, Helena, Montana 59624.

## NEBRASKA

Nebraska is rich with grass (with more forage varieties than any other state) and grain; agriculture is its mainstay. The grassy Sand Hills make up the

MONTANA
CANADA
MILES
0 10 20 40 60 80 100
KILOMETERS
0 20 40 60 80 100
State Capital ⊛ County Seats ●
Longitude West of Greenwich
© Copyright HAMMOND INCORPORATED, Maplewood, N. J.

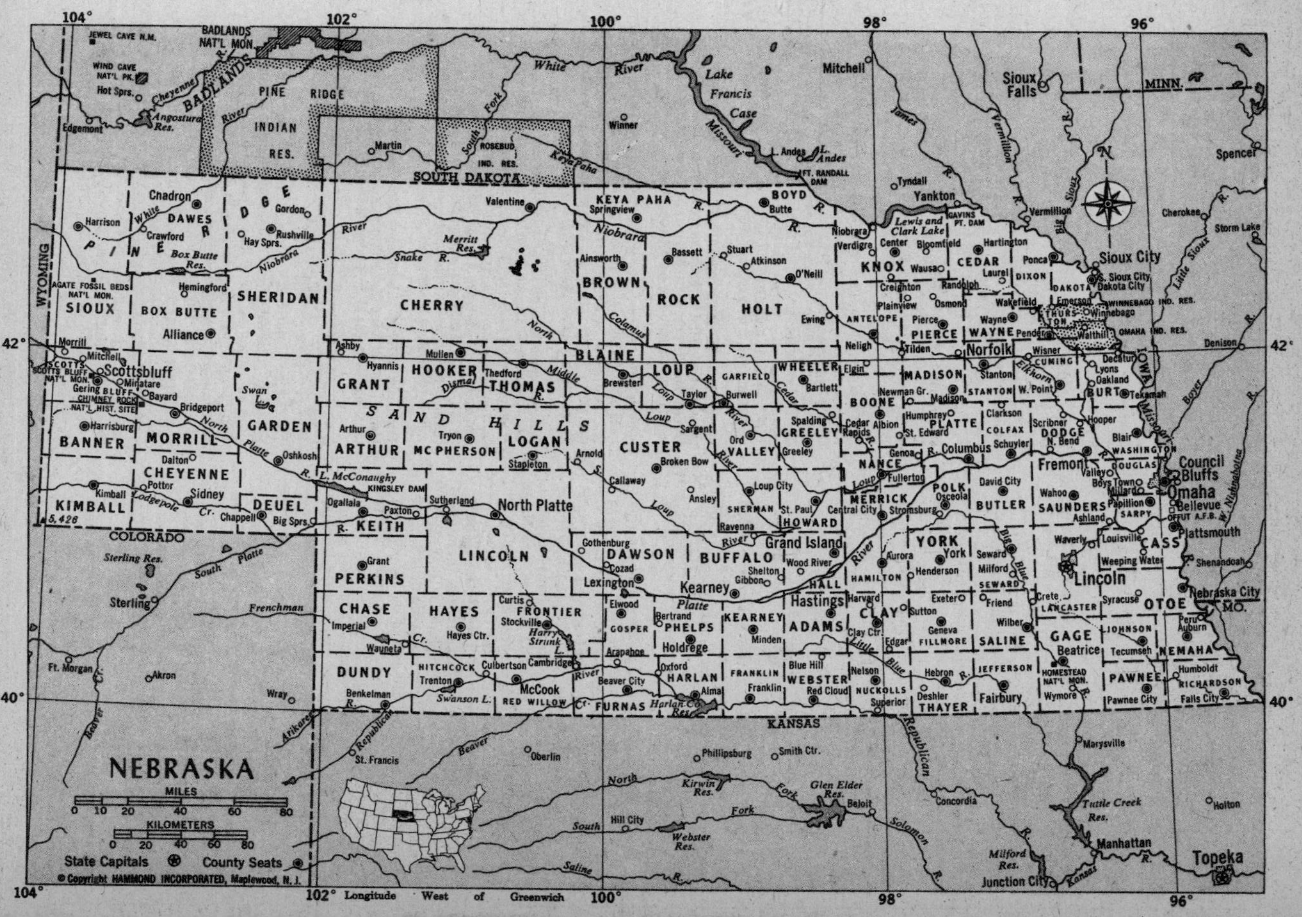
NEBRASKA
MILES
0 10 20 40 60 80
KILOMETERS
0 20 40 60 80
State Capitals
County Seats
© Copyright HAMMOND INCORPORATED, Maplewood, N. J.
Longitude West of Greenwich
SOUTH DAKOTA
IOWA
MO.
KANSAS
COLORADO
WYOMING
MINN.
Lincoln
Omaha
Council Bluffs
Sioux City
Sioux Falls
Topeka
Grand Island
North Platte
Scottsbluff
Kearney
Hastings
Norfolk
Columbus
Fremont
Beatrice

state's central region, and rolling farmland, found in the east, rises gradually from 840 feet above sea level to 5,300 feet in the western High Plains region. A portion of the South Dakota Badlands takes up about 1,000 square miles of the northwest corner of the state. The climate of Nebraska is one of extremes: severe winters and sweltering summers.

Nebraska annually harvests large crops of corn, sorghum, oats, wheat, rye, soybeans, alfalfa and dry edible beans. Omaha, with its surrounding area, forms the nation's largest meat-packing center, and it is the second-largest cattle market of both the United States and the world.

The state's numerous rivers and lakes are vitally important to its agricultural and allied processing industries. Many conservation practices, such as dam construction, systematic tree-planting, and irrigation, are widely employed to keep the land productive. Larger farms, more modern equipment, and improved farming techniques have resulted in vastly increased production even with a smaller farm population.

Judging by stone tool and weapon remnants that have been unearthed, the first inhabitants of Nebraska arrived between 10,000 and 25,000 years ago. In the early 1700s, Spanish and French explorers found, among others, the Omaha and Oto Indians living peacefully along the region's rivers. The buffalo-hunting Pawnee, however, battled other tribes—especially the Sioux—but were generally friendly to whites. The Sioux, Arapaho, and Cheyenne Indians constituted the white settlers' principal resistance, waging a losing battle to keep their hunting grounds.

The United States gained possession of the area with the Louisiana Purchase (1803). Pioneers going west along the Oregon Trail, which followed the Platte Valley, stimulated trading and settlement; many early Nebraskans earned a living supplying food, lodging, and fresh mounts. Scotts Bluff National Monument and Chimney Rock National Historic Site are landmarks along the Trail. Statehood came in 1867.

Early times were very hard for settlers. There was bitter, protracted conflict between them and the cattlemen, who wanted the land for their herds. (This struggle was not fully resolved until the 1904 Kinkaid Act gave over the last of the state's open range land to the homesteaders.) And there were harsh blows from nature: blizzards, locust infestations, and droughts. Homestead National Monument near Beatrice commemorates the pioneer spirit of the 19th-century farmers who settled the Great Plains region.

World War I brought prosperity, but hard times returned: depression and drought hit the state simultaneously. Overextended farmers faced foreclosure. Violence was averted by the enactment of a series of farm mortgage moratorium acts; New Deal legislation also helped. In 1937, the Nebraska legislature was reorganized into a "one house" (unicameral) system, under which state senators are elected on a nonpartisan basis.

Border disputes with Iowa have plagued Nebraska ever since the Missouri River was made the dividing line (1867). Through the years, the river's shifting has transferred parcels of land from one state to the other.

**Full name:** State of Nebraska. **Origin of name:** From Omaha Indian name for the Platte River. **Inhabitant:** Nebraskan. **Capital:** Lincoln. **State motto:** Equality Before the Law. **Flag:** State seal on blue field. **Seal:** Blacksmith represents mechanical arts; settler's cabin, growing corn & shocks of grain stand for agriculture; steamboat & train symbolize transportation. **Flower:** Goldenrod. **Bird:** Western meadowlark. **Tree:** Cottonwood. **Song:** "Beautiful Nebraska." **Nickname:** Cornhusker State.

**Governor:** Charles Thone. **Annual salary:** $40,000. **Term:** 4 years. **Current term expires:** Jan. 1983. **Voting requirements:** 18 yrs. old & U.S. citizen; state resident and registered voter. **U.S. Congressmen:** 3. **Entered Union:** 1867 (37th state).

**Location & boundaries:** Midwestern state: bounded on the north by South Dakota; on the east by Iowa, the Missouri River & Missouri; on the south by Kansas; on the southwest by Colorado; & on the west by Wyoming. **Total area:** 77,355 sq. mi. (ranks 15th). **Extreme length:** 415 mi. **Extreme breadth:** 205 mi. **Chief rivers:** Missouri, North Platte, South Platte. **Major lakes:** Lewis & Clark, McCoonaughy. **No. of counties:** 93.

**Population (1980 census):** 1,569,825 (ranks 35th). **Pop. increase (1970-80):** 5.7%. **Largest cities:** Omaha, Lincoln, Grand Island, North Platte. **Pop. density:** 20.3 per sq. mi. (ranks 41st). **Pop. distribution: White**—1,490,569; **Black**—48,389; **Am. Indian, Eskimo and Aleut**—9,197; **Asian and Pacific Islander**—6,996; **Other**—14,855; **Spanish origin**—28,020. **Marriage rate (1979):** 8.9 per 1,000 people. **Divorce rate:** 4.0 per 1,000 people.

**State finances (1980). Revenue:** $1,506,000,000. **Expenditures:** $1,392,000,000. **State taxes:** $520.23 per capita. **State personal income tax:** Yes. **Public debt (1980):** $126.97 per capita. **Federal aid (1980):** $347.68 per capita. **Personal income (1981):** $10,296.

**Sectors of the economy (% of labor force employed in 1970):** Wholesale and retail trade (22%), Government (16%), Manufacturing (14%), Educational Services (9%), Services (7%), Construction (6%). **Leading products:** food, electrical & other machinery, chemicals, fabricated metal items, printing & publishing, primary metals, transportation equipment. **Agricultural products:** cattle, hogs, dairy items, corn, hay, wheat, sorghums. **Avg. farm (1981):** 744 acres. **Avg. value of farm per acre:** $660.

**Highway expenditures per capita (1980):** $168.51. **Persons per motor vehicle (1981):** 1.23. **Minimum age for driver's license:** 16. **Gasoline tax:** 13.7¢ per gallon. **Diesel tax:** 13.7¢ per gallon. **Motor vehicle deaths (1980):** 25.2 per 100,000 people.

**Birthrate (1979):** 16.7 per 1,000 people. **Infant mortality rate per 1,000 births (1978):** 13.0. **Physicians per 100,000 pop. (1979):** 145. **Dentists per 100,000 pop. (1979):** 61. **Acceptable hospital beds (1979):** 7.6 per 1,000 people. **State expenditures per capita for health and hospitals (1980):** $75.11.

**Education expenditures (1977-78):** $503.56 per capita annually. **No. of pupils in public schools (1980):** 279,000. **No. of institutions of higher learning (1978-79):** 31. **Public school expenditure per pupil in attendance (1978-79):** $2,198. **Avg. salary of public school teachers (1979-80):** $14,236. **No. full-time teachers (1980):** 20,500. **Educational attainment of adult population (1976):** 12.6 median yrs. of school completed: 1.0% with less than 5 years of education; 14.3% with 4 yrs. of college.

**Telephones (1979):** 61 per 100 people. **State Chamber of Commerce:** Nebraska Association of Commerce & Industry, 1008 Terminal Bldg., P.O. Box 81556, Lincoln, Nebraska 68501.

## NEVADA

Except for its northeast and southeast corners, Nevada lies entirely within the Great Basin, a broad plateau averaging 5,500 feet in elevation and broken by mountain ranges. The Sierra Nevadas on the California border interrupt moisture-carrying clouds from the Pacific, making Nevada the driest state in the country; its average annual rainfall is only 3.73 inches. Much of the state is uninhabited, sagebrush-covered desert dotted by alkali sinks in which rivers have dried up. Only seven states have fewer inhabitants than Nevada, which in 1980 had but 7.2 persons per square mile. However, the 1980 census revealed that Nevada is the fastest-growing state in the nation.

Nevada's minimal agriculture depends largely on irrigation. Most crops go for livestock feed. Leading income sources have been, first, tourism, then mining—followed by a modest mineral and metals processing industry. In the Reno area, warehousing, aided by a free port law, is growing substantially. Thanks mainly to legalized gambling, spectacular entertainment and lenient di-

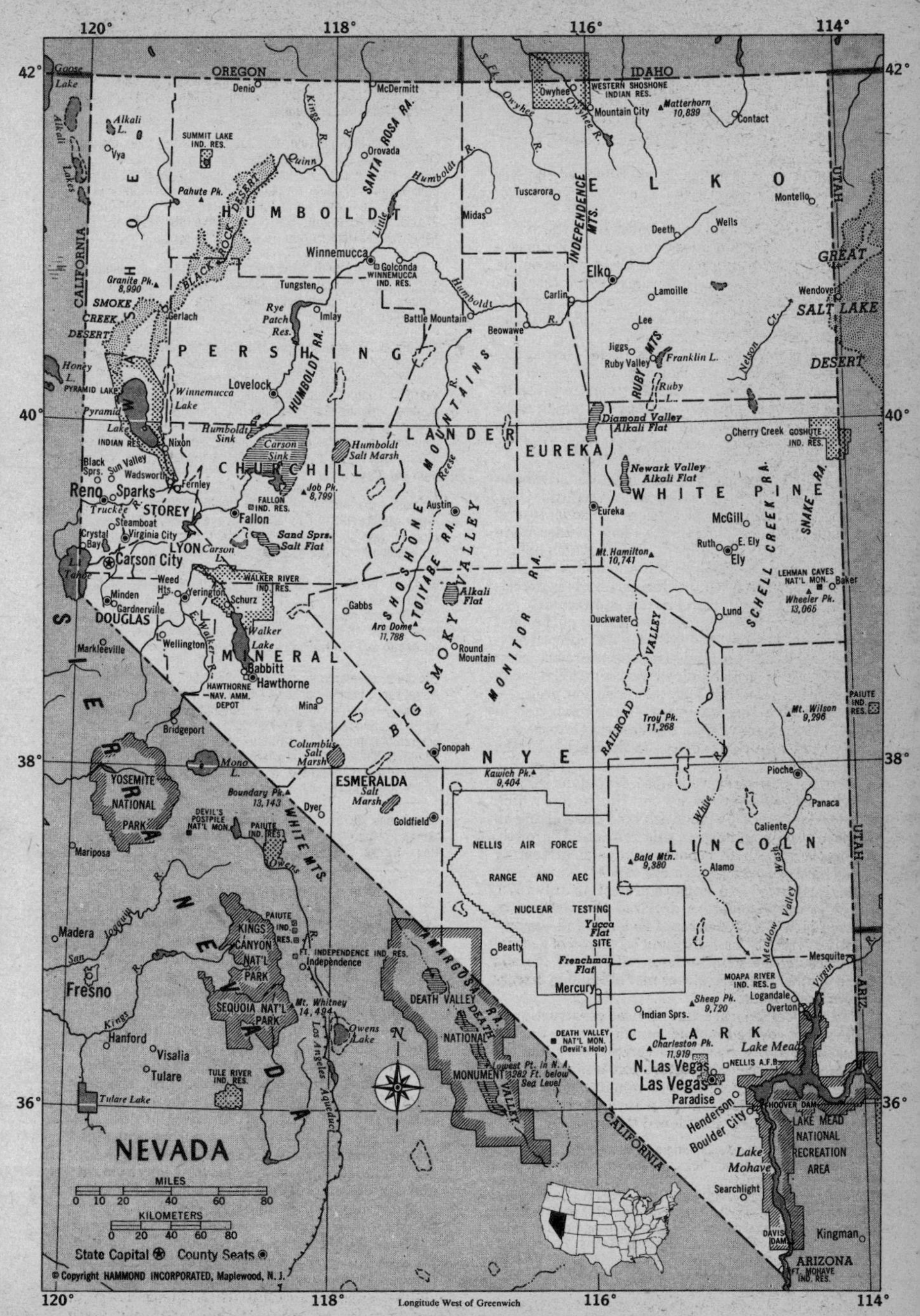
NEVADA
OREGON
IDAHO
UTAH
ARIZONA
CALIFORNIA
HUMBOLDT
ELKO
PERSHING
LANDER
EUREKA
CHURCHILL
WHITE PINE
STOREY
LYON
DOUGLAS
MINERAL
NYE
ESMERALDA
LINCOLN
CLARK
Reno
Sparks
Carson City
Winnemucca
Elko
Lovelock
Fallon
Tonopah
Goldfield
Las Vegas
N. Las Vegas
Ely
Pioche
Hawthorne
Austin
Eureka
Yerington
Minden
Henderson
Boulder City
Mesquite
NELLIS AIR FORCE RANGE AND AEC NUCLEAR TESTING SITE
LAKE MEAD NATIONAL RECREATION AREA
DEATH VALLEY NATIONAL MONUMENT
YOSEMITE NATIONAL PARK
KINGS CANYON NAT'L PARK
SEQUOIA NAT'L PARK
GREAT SALT LAKE DESERT
Lake Tahoe
Pyramid Lake
Walker Lake
Lake Mead
Lake Mohave
Boundary Pk. 13,143
Wheeler Pk. 13,066
Mt. Whitney 14,494
Lowest Pt. in N. A. 282 Ft. below Sea Level
MILES
0 10 20 40 60 80
KILOMETERS
0 20 40 60 80
State Capital
County Seats
© Copyright HAMMOND INCORPORATED, Maplewood, N. J.
Longitude West of Greenwich
120° 118° 116° 114°
42° 40° 38° 36°

vorce laws, tourism today accounts for billions of dollars in revenue. The Las Vegas and Reno metropolitan areas, where nearly four of every five Nevadans live, are the principal tourist attractions. Others include Lake Tahoe on the California-Nevada border, Pyramid Lake, Hoover Dam, Lake Mead National Recreation Area and Death Valley National Monument.

Indians are thought to have inhabited the Nevada region between 10,000 and 20,000 years ago. In more recent times, the Shoshoni, Washoe, Northern Paiute, and other tribes lived there.

In 1775 a Spanish missionary named Francisco Garcés passed through what is now Nevada on his way to the West Coast. In the early 1800s, trappers searched the area for new fur sources. John C. Frémont and Kit Carson explored (1843-45) the Great Basin and Sierra Nevada.

The United States obtained (1848) the region, following the Mexican War, and the first permanent settlement (1851) was a Mormon trading post called Mormon Station (now Genoa). Amid the conflicting pressures of the Civil War, Nevada was made a state (1864), although the territory did not meet the population requirement.

In 1859 the discovery of the Comstock (silver and gold) Lode, near what became Virginia City, brought an influx of both settlers and adventurers. During the next 20 years, the lode yielded more than $300 million of mineral wealth which helped the Union to win the Civil War and was the basis of many American fortunes. Today Nevada is the nation's leading producer of barite and mercury.

The Federal Government owns 87% of the land in Nevada. The first Federal irrigation project anywhere was the Newlands Irrigation Project, completed in 1907, which helped west central Nevada's agriculture. Another Federal irrigation project—the Southern Nevada Project—was completed in 1971. In the early 1950s, the Federal Government began to test nuclear devices on Federal land in the Nevada desert.

As the 1970s drew to a close, Nevadans became increasingly annoyed by the limitation which Federal ownership of so much land was putting on agriculture, commercial, and residential growth. Moreover, in 1979, reports that nuclear testing may have caused a high rate of cancer in areas near the test site led to a storm of protest. In July 1979, the Nevada legislature declared the state to be owner of 49,000,000 acres of Federal land—apparently in order to facilitate judicial review of Federal policies. Three months later, officials of Nevada and of other Western states met at Reno to discuss common problems.

In 1980, a Federal study advised construction in Nevada of covered mobile launching sites for MX missiles. Many Nevadans complained that the plan would encourage saturation bombing of Nevada in the event of war, and announced their outright opposition to the plan in 1981. In October President Reagan abandoned the proposal.

**Full name:** State of Nevada. **Origin of name:** From Spanish for "Snow-Clad." **Inhabitant:** Nevadan. **Capital:** Carson City. **State motto:** All for Our Country. **Flag:** Blue field with gold & green insignia in upper left; words "Battle Born" recall that Nevada gained statehood during Civil War. **Seal:** Plow & sheaf of wheat represent Nevada's agricultural resources; quartz mill, mine tunnel & carload of ore symbolize mineral wealth of state; 36 stars. **Flower:** Sagebrush. **Animal:** Nelson (Desert) bighorn sheep. **Bird:** Mountain bluebird. **Tree:** Single-leaf piñon. **Song:** "Home Means Nevada." **Nickname:** Silver State.

**Governor:** Robert F. List. **Annual salary:** $57,000. **Term:** 4 years. **Current term expires:** Dec. 1982. **Voting requirements:** 18 yrs. old & U.S. citizen; state resident 30 days. **U.S. Congressmen:** 2. **Entered Union:** 1864 (36th state).

**Location & boundaries:** Rocky Mountain state: bounded on the north by Oregon & Idaho; on the east by Utah & Arizona; & on the south & west by California. **Total area:** 110,561 sq. mi. (ranks 7th). **Extreme length:** 483 mi. **Extreme breadth:** 320 mi. **Chief rivers:** Humboldt, Colorado, Truckee. **Major lakes:** Pyramid, Walker, Tahoe, Mead. **No. of counties:** 17.

**Population (1980 census):** 800,493 (ranks 43rd). **Pop. increase (1970-80):** 63.8%. **Largest cities:** Las Vegas, Reno, North Las Vegas. **Pop. density:** 7.2 per sq. mi. (ranks 47th). **Pop. distribution: White**—699,377; **Black**—50,791; **Am. Indian, Eskimo and Aleut**—13,304; **Asian and Pacific Islander**—14,109; **Other**—21,603; **Spanish origin**—53,786. **Marriage rate (1979):** 147.4 per 1,000 people. **Divorce rate:** 16.8 per 1,000 people.

**State finances (1980). Revenue:** $1,221,000,000. **Expenditures:** $1,098,000,000. **State taxes:** $596.50 per capita. **State personal income tax:** No. **Public debt (1980):** $660.79 per capita. **Federal aid (1980):** $402.25 per capita. **Personal income (1981):** $11,633.

**Sectors of the economy (% of labor force employed in 1970):** Services (22%), Wholesale and retail trade (19%), Government (18%), Construction (8%), Educational Services (6%), Manufacturing (5%). **Leading products:** stone, clay & glass items; chemicals; printing & publishing; food items; lumber; electrical machinery; fabricated metals. **Minerals:** copper, gold, sand & gravel, diatomite. **Agricultural products:** sheep, cattle, hay, alfalfa seed, wheat, dairy items. **Avg. farm (1981):** 3,100 acres. **Avg. value of farm per acre:** $271.

**Highway expenditures per capita (1980):** $188.34. **Persons per motor vehicle (1981):** 1.16. **Minimum age for driver's license:** 16. **Gasoline tax:** 10.25¢ per gallon. **Diesel tax:** 12¢ per gallon. **Motor vehicle deaths (1980):** 43.3 per 100,000 people.

**Birthrate (1979):** 17.6 per 1,000 people. **Infant mortality rate per 1,000 births (1978):** 12.5. **Physicians per 100,000 pop. (1979):** 138. **Dentists per 100,000 pop. (1979):** 49. **Acceptable hospital beds (1979):** 4.1 per 1,000 people. **State expenditures per capita for health and hospitals (1980):** $52.70.

**Education expenditures (1977-78):** $487.53 per capita annually. **No. of pupils in public schools (1980):** 150,000. **No. of institutions of higher learning (1978-79):** 6. **Public school expenditure per pupil in attendance (1978-79):** $2,124. **Avg. salary of public school teachers (1979-80):** $16,980. **No. full-time teachers (1980):** 8,700. **Educational attainment of adult population (1976):** 12.6 median yrs. of school completed: 1.2% with less than 5 years of education; 13.1% with 4 yrs. of college.

**Telephones (1979):** 63 per 100 people. **State Chamber of Commerce:** Nevada Chamber of Commerce Association, P.O. Box 2806, Reno, Nevada 89505.

## NEW HAMPSHIRE

New Hampshire is a relatively small but well wooded and scenic state of mountains, lakes, and rapid rivers that provide a good water supply and large hydroelectric-power potential. There are three main land areas: the coastal lowlands covering the southeast corner; the New England Uplands, covering most of the southwest, west central, and south central area; and the White Mountains region in the north, which includes Mount Washington, the Northeast's highest peak (6,288 feet). Near the coast are the rough-hewn Isles of Shoals, three of which belong to New Hampshire. The state's largest harbor is at Portsmouth, near the mouth of the Piscataqua. The climate features cool summers with low humidity and winters marked by heavy snowfall. The ocean tempers the weather along the 17.8 mile Atlantic coastline, shortest of any state bordering an ocean.

About 5,000 Indians were living in the New Hampshire region before the Europeans came. The various tribes coexisted peacefully but often banded together to fight the Iroquois. The first explorers in the area are thought to have been Captain Martin Pring (1603), Samuel de Champlain (1605), and Captain John Smith (1614). Permanent settlement began in 1623, when David

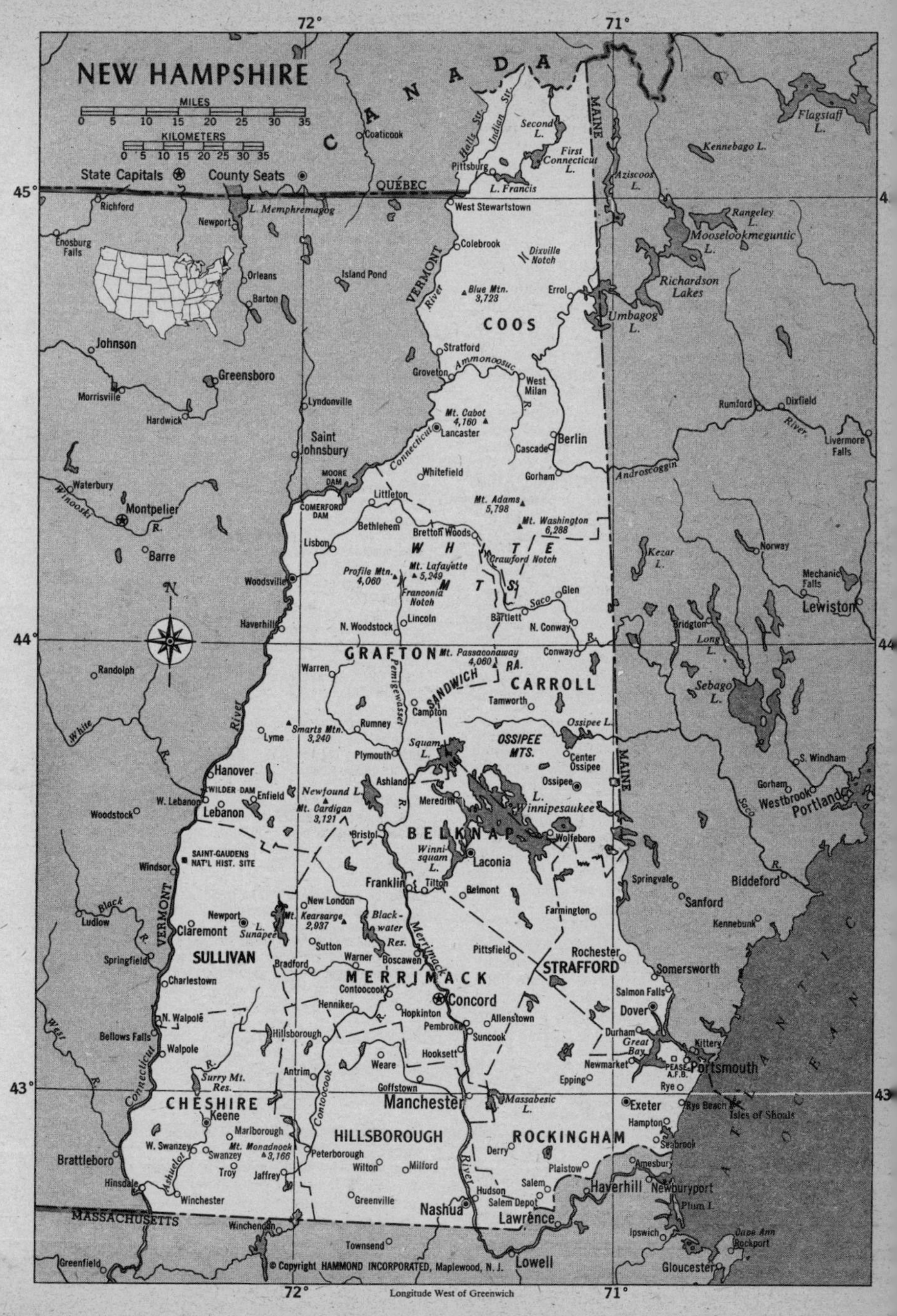
NEW HAMPSHIRE
MILES
KILOMETERS
State Capitals
County Seats
CANADA
QUÉBEC
VERMONT
MAINE
MASSACHUSETTS
COOS
GRAFTON
CARROLL
BELKNAP
SULLIVAN
MERRIMACK
STRAFFORD
CHESHIRE
HILLSBOROUGH
ROCKINGHAM
WHITE MTS.
SANDWICH RA.
OSSIPEE MTS.
Concord
Manchester
Nashua
Portsmouth
Keene
Laconia
Berlin
Lancaster
Dover
Exeter
Mt. Washington 6,288
Mt. Adams 5,798
Mt. Lafayette 5,249
Mt. Cabot 4,160
Blue Mtn. 3,723
Mt. Passaconaway 4,060
Mt. Kearsarge 2,937
Mt. Monadnock 3,166
Mt. Cardigan 3,121
Smarts Mtn. 3,240
Profile Mtn. 4,060
L. Winnipesaukee
ATLANTIC OCEAN
Isles of Shoals
© Copyright HAMMOND INCORPORATED, Maplewood, N. J.
Longitude West of Greenwich

Thomson established Little Harbour, now in the town of Rye. Captain John Mason, who had a hand in the founding (1630) of Portsmouth, gave New Hampshire its name. Though the state was once part of Massachusetts, it became a separate royal colony in 1679; the two states had the same governor from 1699 to 1741. New Hampshire established an independent government (1776), one designed to be only temporary but which in fact operated until 1784, when the present constitution was adopted. New Hampshire was the ninth state to ratify the U.S. Constitution (1788), and the one that made that document legal.

Complicated boundary disputes with all its neighbors have marked New Hampshire's history. Royal orders eventually defined the Massachusetts (1741) and New York (1764) boundaries, while the state's northern border was set by the Webster-Ashburton Treaty (1842), which established the international line between the United States and Canada. But not until a 1934 U.S. Supreme Court ruling was the Vermont boundary decided. A border dispute with Maine over 2,400 acres of coastal waters that began in 1974 was resolved in 1976, when the U.S. Supreme Court awarded the bulk of the disputed territory to Maine.

The state is one of the most industrialized in the nation, based on the percentage of its population working in manufacturing. The electronic, chemical, and machinery industries are major employers.

New Hampshire, with its beneficial tax climate, is experiencing an influx of new industrial development, especially in the southern sections along the Massachusetts border. In the absence of a general sales or income tax, state government is financed through the state-operated liquor monopoly, pari-mutuel betting on racing, state taxes on business profits and rooms and meals. Education is funded by the local property tax.

Tourism, meanwhile, has mushroomed into an annual $900-million business. One fifth of the land is in public parklands, including 724,000 acres of the White Mountain National Forest, which extends into Maine. Hiking, boating, and camping are popular, and the state has more than 60 ski lifts. Attractions include Strawbery Banke, a preservation project that has restored about 30 buildings and homes of the original settlement at Portsmouth, N.H., the Lakes Region around Lake Winnipesaukee, the Kancamagus Highway between Lincoln and Conway, Daniel Webster's birthplace near Franklin, the Mount Washington Cog Railway, the first (1869) in North America, and the famous "Old Man of the Mountain" granite head profile at Franconia, the state's official emblem.

New Hampshire today functions as an exceptionally democratic entity, with the state's 222 towns (nicknamed "little republics") using the traditional town meeting to provide a forum for all voters. The state, which for decades had a sometimes disputed reputation as a political bellwether, has been relieved of its position as the first to hold a presidential primary by Puerto Rico, which in 1980 held its first such election.

Nuclear power remains controversial in New Hampshire. In 1976 construction began on a nuclear power plant in the environmentally sensitive seacoast area at Seabrook. Anti-nuclear power forces from all over New England focused on the issue, and in May 1977, a mass occupation of the construction site resulted in the arrest of 1,414 demonstrators by authorities. In October 1979 and again in May 1980, protestors renewed attempts to occupy the site, but their repeated assaults were repelled by state troopers and National Guardsmen armed with nightsticks and high-pressure water hoses. Some injuries were reported.

**Full name:** State of New Hampshire. **Origin of name:** From the English county of Hampshire. **Inhabitant:** New Hampshirite. **Capital:** Concord. **State motto:** Live Free or Die. **Flag:** State seal on a blue field. **Seal:** A reproduction of Revolutionary War frigate "Raleigh" is surrounded by nine stars in a laurel wreath to symbolize victory. **Flower:** Purple lilac. **Bird:** Purple finch. **Tree:** White birch. **Songs:** "Old New Hampshire" & "New Hampshire, My New Hampshire." **Nickname:** Granite State.

**Governor:** Hugh J. Gallen. **Annual salary:** $51,830. **Term:** 2 years. **Current term expires:** Jan. 1983. **Voting requirements:** 18 yrs. old & U.S. citizen; registered voter and state resident. **U.S. Congressmen:** 2. **Entered Union:** 1788 (9th state).

**Location & boundaries:** New England state: bounded on the north by Canada; on the east by Maine & the Atlantic Ocean; on the south by Massachusetts; & on the west by Vermont, Canada & the Connecticut River. **Total area:** 9,279 sq. mi. (ranks 44th). **Extreme length:** 180 mi. **Extreme breadth:** 93 mi. **Coastline:** 17.8 mi. **Chief rivers:** Connecticut, Merrimack, Androscoggin. **Major lake:** Winnipesaukee. **No. of counties:** 10.

**Population (1980 census):** 920,610 (ranks 42nd). **Pop. increase (1970-80):** 24.8%. **Largest cities:** Manchester, Nashua, Concord, Portsmouth. **Pop. density:** 99.2 per sq. mi. (ranks 20th). **Pop. distribution: White**— 910,099; **Black**—3,990; **Am. Indian, Eskimo and Aleut**—1,352; **Asian and Pacific Islander**—2,929; **Other**—2,240; **Spanish origin**—5,587. **Marriage rate (1979):** 10.2 per 1,000 people. **Divorce rate:** 5.9 per 1,000 people.

**State finances (1980). Revenue:** $894,000,000. **Expenditures:** $889,000,000. **State taxes:** $290.44 per capita. **State personal income tax:** No, except on interest & dividends. **Public debt (1980):** $976.17 per capita. **Federal aid (1980):** $375.19 per capita. **Personal income (1981):** $10,073.

**Sectors of the economy (% of labor force employed in 1970):** Manufacturing (36%), Wholesale and retail trade (19%), Government (14%), Educational Services (8%), Construction (7%), Services (6%). **Leading products:** leather items, electrical & other machinery, textile mill items, paper items, food items, printing & publishing. **Agricultural products:** dairy items, eggs, cattle, hay, apples, potatoes. **Avg. farm (1981):** 151 acres. **Avg. value of farm per acre:** $1,046.

**Highway expenditures per capita (1980):** $140.22. **Persons per motor vehicle (1981):** 1.27. **Minimum age for driver's license:** 16. **Gasoline tax:** 14¢ per gallon. **Diesel tax:** 14¢ per gallon. **Motor vehicle deaths (1980):** 21.1 per 100,000 people.

**Birthrate (1979):** 14.5 per 1,000 people. **Infant mortality rate per 1,000 births (1978):** 10.4. **Physicians per 100,000 pop. (1979):** 159. **Dentists per 100,000 pop. (1979):** 53. **Acceptable hospital beds (1979):** 5.1 per 1,000 people. **State expenditures per capita for health and hospitals (1980):** $59.34.

**Education expenditures (1977-78):** $398.13 per capita annually. **No. of pupils in public schools (1980):** 169,000. **No. of institutions of higher learning (1978-79):** 24. **Public school expenditure per pupil in attendance (1978-79):** $1,860. **Avg. salary of public school teachers (1979-80):** $12,930. **No. full-time teachers (1980):** 9,600. **Educational attainment of adult population (1976):** 12.6 median yrs. of school completed: 1.1% with less than 5 years of education; 15.3% with 4 yrs. of college.

**Telephones (1979):** 58 per 100 people. **State Chamber of Commerce:** Business and Industry Association of New Hampshire, 23 School Street, Concord, New Hampshire 03301.

## NEW JERSEY

New Jersey's importance is disproportionate to its modest size. Strategically located, amid many rich markets, the state has extraordinary transportation facilities and a correspondingly large volume of interstate traffic: railway trackage, highways, tunnels, and bridges abound. The nation's most densely populated state, it is a manufacturing giant with limited but valuable farming and fishing industries.

Many sandy beaches, coupled with a generally mild climate marked by ocean breezes, have made New Jersey popular with vacationers, and tourism is today a major industry. Attractions include such resort areas as Atlantic City and Wildwood, as well

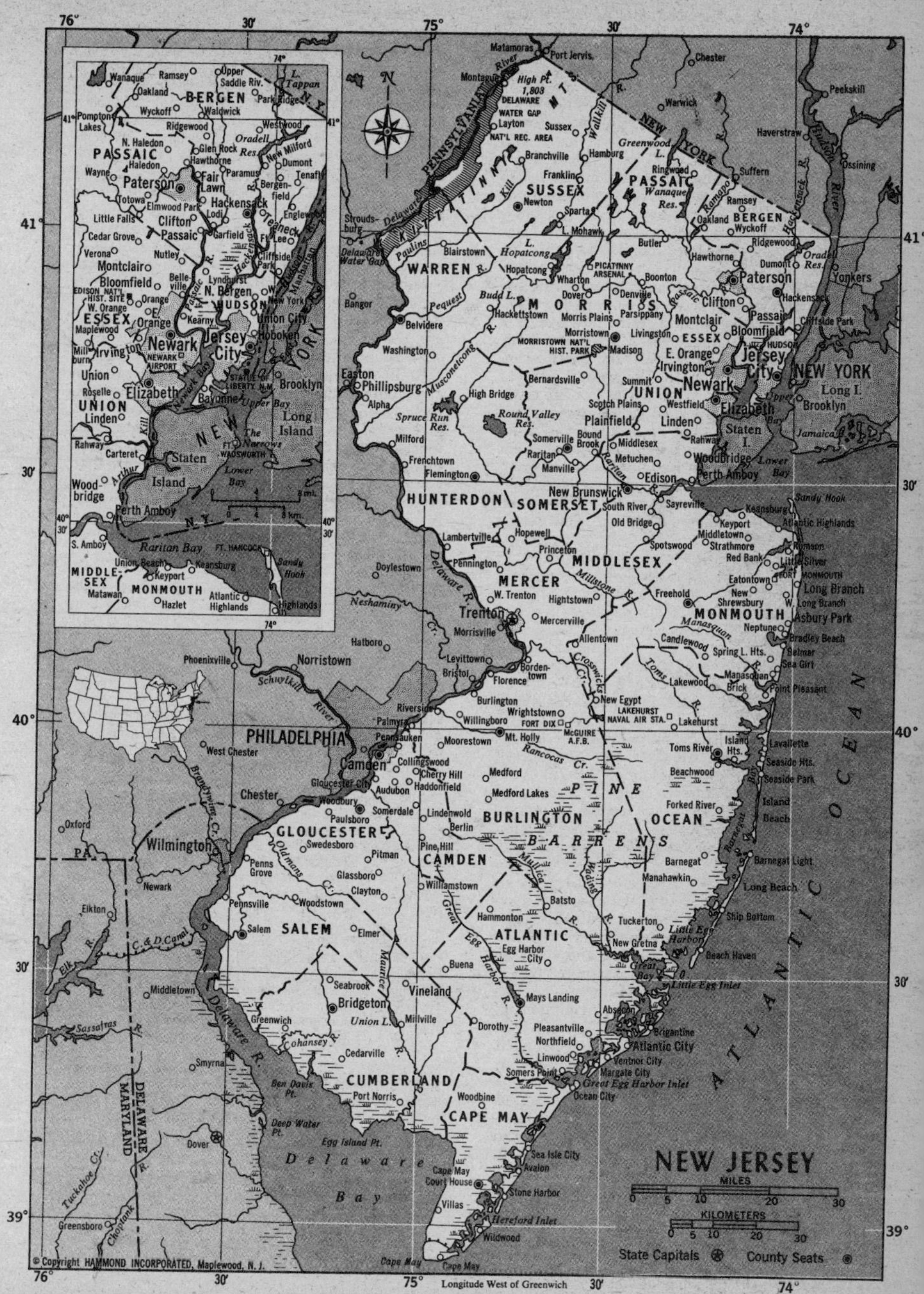
NEW JERSEY
MILES
0 5 10 20 30
KILOMETERS
0 5 10 20 30
State Capitals
County Seats
Longitude West of Greenwich
76° 30' 75° 30' 74°
41° 30' 40° 30' 39°
ATLANTIC OCEAN
PHILADELPHIA
NEW YORK
PENNSYLVANIA
DELAWARE
MARYLAND
SUSSEX
PASSAIC
BERGEN
WARREN
MORRIS
ESSEX
HUDSON
UNION
HUNTERDON
SOMERSET
MIDDLESEX
MERCER
MONMOUTH
BURLINGTON
OCEAN
GLOUCESTER
CAMDEN
SALEM
ATLANTIC
CUMBERLAND
CAPE MAY
PINE BARRENS
KITTATINNY MTS.
High Pt. 1,803
DELAWARE WATER GAP NAT'L REC. AREA
MORRISTOWN NAT'L HIST. PARK
PICATINNY ARSENAL
LAKEHURST NAVAL AIR STA.
FORT DIX
McGUIRE A.F.B.
FORT MONMOUTH
Trenton
Newark
Jersey City
Paterson
Elizabeth
Camden
Atlantic City
Wilmington
Delaware Bay
Delaware R.
Hudson River
Raritan Bay
Sandy Hook
Long I.
Staten I.
Brooklyn
Yonkers
Peekskill
Ossining
Haverstraw
Suffern
Port Jervis
Matamoras
Chester
Warwick
Newton
Sparta
Hopatcong
Dover
Boonton
Morristown
Belvidere
Phillipsburg
Easton
Flemington
Somerville
New Brunswick
Perth Amboy
Edison
Plainfield
Princeton
Freehold
Asbury Park
Long Branch
Toms River
Lakewood
Mt. Holly
Burlington
Woodbury
Salem
Bridgeton
Vineland
Millville
Mays Landing
Cape May Court House
Cape May
Wildwood
Ocean City
Tuckerton
Beach Haven
Barnegat Light
Hammonton
Norristown
Chester
Dover
© Copyright HAMMOND INCORPORATED, Maplewood, N. J.

as the Thomas A. Edison National Historic Site in West Orange, the Walt Whitman House in Camden, the Garden State Arts Center in Telegraph Hill Park, and several ski areas.

Before the coming of the Europeans, the region was inhabited by Lenni-Lenape (later called Delaware) Indians of the Algonquian group. The area's early colonial history is bound up with that of New York (then New Netherland), of which it was a part. With the passing of power from Dutch to English hands (1664), New Jersey began to emerge as a more distinct entity. Proprietorship of lands between the Hudson and Delaware Rivers was granted by James II to Lord John Berkeley and Sir George Carteret, who then offered territory to settlers in return for sworn allegiance to the king and payment of quitrent (fixed rent). Berkeley eventually sold (1676) his land share to a group of Quakers, who then agreed with Carteret to divide the region into East and West Jersey, the line running southeastward from the Delaware River near the Water Gap to the Atlantic Ocean near Little Egg Harbor. Carteret owned East Jersey—about three-eighths of the total area—until his death (1680), while West Jersey became the nation's first Quaker settlement. Control of both Jerseys eventually reverted to England which governed it jointly with New York from 1702 to 1738, when Lewis Morris was made governor of New Jersey alone.

The region remained turbulent for many years. A decade of virtual lawlessness began in 1745, ended only by the advent of the French and Indian War of the mid-1750s, which served to unify New Jerseyans against a common enemy. Because of its location between New York City and Philadelphia, New Jersey was the scene of many important battles of the American Revolution. In 1783 Princeton served briefly as the nation's capital. Statehood dates from 1787.

After the Revolution, many scientific breakthroughs took place in the state, and the country's first model factory town was founded in 1791 at the site of the present Paterson, under the auspices of Alexander Hamilton's Society for the Establishment of Useful Manufactures. (A few years later, Hamilton was killed in Weehawken in a notorious duel with Aaron Burr.)

The state was sharply divided by the Civil War. Most New Jerseyans accepted the ending of slavery, but many businessmen were against the war because of the profitable Southern market. When peace came, the state's population and economy continued their rapid growth, interrupted by the Panic of 1873. Powerful special-interest groups grasped undue political control, bringing a counterwave of reform under Governor Woodrow Wilson, who was elected in 1910. But after Wilson left in 1913 to become president, much of the impetus toward reform in the state withered away.

The institution (1966) of a general sales tax has helped lighten the state's severe financial problems, as has the March 1970 hike in that tax, from three to five percent. One side effect of these measures has been to detract somewhat from the state's traditionally favorable tax climate which, together with streamlined corporation laws, has been a vital weapon in the continuing battle with other states for new industry. New Jersey enacted an income tax in 1976 as a replacement for portions of local property tax burdens, and in December 1977 the tax was made permanent.

Large-scale urban-renewal projects that would eliminate blight while creating jobs are seen as a means of alleviating a major part of the problem. A vast $300-million Hackensack Meadowlands project built on land from ten different north Jersey towns opened in 1976, with the National Football League Giants and the Cosmos professional soccer team as the major long-term tenants and including a racetrack. In 1981 an indoor sports arena was opened, housing the New Jersey Nets basketball team (formerly the New York Nets). The New Jersey Devils hockey team (formerly the Colorado Rockies) followed in 1982. Port Jersey, a 707-acre, $160-million industrial center with a 17-berth terminal for containerships has been planned for the New Jersey side of Upper New York Bay, adjoining the U.S. Military Ocean Terminal in Bayonne.

In mid-1977 the courts lifted the ban on drilling East Coast offshore oil leases, and exploration commenced by the end of the year. After six months there had been no announcement of any profitable strikes in the Baltimore Canyon off the New Jersey Coast. Since that time, however, both Texaco Inc. and the U.S. Geological Survey have announced offshore gas finds.

In 1976 New Jersey passed a constitutional amendment authorizing the establishment of gambling casinos in Atlantic City as a means of rejuvenating the ailing resort and rebuilding the tourist industry in general. The first casino opened in May 1978 and has proved successful. Since then additional casinos have opened and others are being constructed. Though the casinos have attracted thousands of new visitors to the resort, there have been complaints that organized crime figures have penetrated the city.

**Full name:** State of New Jersey. **Origin of name:** From Channel Island of Jersey. **Inhabitant:** New Jerseyite. **Capital:** Trenton. **State motto:** Liberty & Prosperity. **Flag:** State seal on yellow field. **Seal:** Three plows & goddess Ceres holding a cornucopia represent agriculture; a horse's head lies above sovereign's helmet. **Flower:** Purple violet. **Bird:** Eastern goldfinch. **Tree:** Red oak. **Song:** (unofficial) "New Jersey Loyalty Song." **Nickname:** Garden State.

**Governor:** Thomas H. Kean. **Annual salary:** $85,000. **Term:** 4 years. **Current term expires:** Jan. 1986. **Voting requirements:** 18 yrs. old & U.S. citizen; resident of state & county 30 days. **U.S. Congressmen:** 14. **Entered Union:** 1787 (3rd state).

**Location & boundaries:** Middle Atlantic state: bounded on the north by New York; on the east by New York, the Hudson River & the Atlantic Ocean; on the south by Delaware Bay; on the southwest by Delaware & the Delaware River; & on the west by Pennsylvania & the Delaware River. **Total area:** 7,787 sq. mi. (ranks 46th). **Extreme length:** 166 mi. **Extreme breadth:** 57 mi. **Coastline:** 130 mi. **Chief rivers:** Raritan, Delaware, Hudson, Passaic. **Major lakes:** Hopatcong, Budd, Culvers. **No. of counties:** 21.

**Population (1980 census):** 7,364,823 (ranks 9th). **Pop. increase (1970-80):** 2.7%. **Largest cities:** Newark, Jersey City, Paterson, Elizabeth. **Pop. density:** 945.8 per sq. mi. (ranks 1st). **Pop. distribution: White**—6,127,090; **Black**—924,786; **Am. Indian, Eskimo and Aleut**—8,394; **Asian and Pacific Islander**—103,842; **Other**—200,046; **Spanish origin**—491,867. **Marriage rate (1979):** 7.5 per 1,000 people. **Divorce rate:** 3.2 per 1,000 people.

**State finances (1980). Revenue:** $8,882,000,000. **Expenditures:** $8,537,000,000. **State taxes:** $579.28 per capita. **State personal income tax:** Yes. **Public debt (1980):** $886.31 per capita. **Federal aid (1980):** $384.65 per capita. **Personal income (1981):** $12,115.

**Sectors of the economy (% of labor force employed in 1970):** Manufacturing (32%), Wholesale and retail trade (19%), Government (14%), Services (7%), Educational Services (7%), Construction (5%). **Leading products:** chemicals, machinery, food items, primary & fabricated metals, transportation equipment, apparel. **Agricultural products:** dairy items, cattle, tomatoes, potatoes, corn, hay, asparagus. **Fishing:** clams, flounder, oysters. **Avg. farm (1981):** 110 acres. **Avg. value of farm per acre:** $2,998.

**Highway expenditures per capita (1980):** $59.11. **Persons per motor vehicle (1981):** 1.51. **Minimum age for driver's license:** 17. **Gasoline tax:** 8¢ per gallon. **Diesel tax:** 8¢ per gallon. **Motor vehicle deaths (1980):** 15.2 per 100,000 people.

**Birthrate (1979):** 13.2 per 1,000 people. **Infant mortality rate per 1,000 births (1978):** 13.0. **Physicians per 100,000 pop. (1979):** 184.

**Dentists per 100,000 pop. (1979):** 66. **Acceptable hospital beds (1979):** 5.9 per 1,000 people. **State expenditures per capita for health and hospitals (1980):** $67.46.

**Education expenditures (1977-78):** $504.37 per capita annually. **No. of pupils in public schools (1980):** 1,246,000. **No. of institutions of higher learning (1978-79):** 63. **Public school expenditure per pupil in attendance (1978-79):** $2,818. **Avg. salary of public school teachers (1979-80):** $17,976. **No. full-time teachers (1980):** 87,300. **Educational attainment of adult population (1976):** 12.4 median yrs. of school completted: 2.7% with less than 5 years of education; 14.9% with 4 yrs. of college.

**Telephones (1979):** 66 per 100 people. **State Chamber of Commerce:** New Jersey State Chamber of Commerce, 5 Commerce Street, Newark, New Jersey 07102.

## NEW MEXICO

New Mexico is a land of great contrast. It is rich in history yet in the forefront of the Atomic Era—the world's first A-bomb, produced at Los Alamos, was exploded (1945) at Trinity Site near Alamogordo. Three major cultures intermingle—Spanish, Indian, and Anglo-American—and within each is a variety of types and subcultures.

Indians are thought to have lived in this region between 20,000 and 25,000 years ago. In 1980, a total of 104,000 Indians—mainly Navajo, Apache, and Pueblo—were to be found in New Mexico, living much as their ancestors had, despite a few modern trappings. Within the state is the country's largest Indian reservation (more than 16 million acres), which is inhabited by Navajos. At Gallup each August is held the colorful Inter-tribal Indian Ceremonial.

Sharp contrasts also mark the face of the land, a complex blending of deserts, rugged blue-rimmed mesas, and forested mountain regions, with an average mean elevation of 5,700 feet. The generally thin, dry air cools rapidly at night, making for wide daily temperature variations. Because of the great ranges in altitude and rainfall, the state supports six distinct life zones and a correspondingly large variety of plants and animals.

Water is generally scarce in New Mexico, and irrigation difficult. Much of the land, however, is devoted to grazing, sustaining a sizable ranching industry. Cotton lint is the main crop in the irrigated areas. In the dry-farming regions (about two-thirds of the state's farmland), hay and wheat are among the significant outputs. Dry-farmers are gradually shifting to irrigation, as more dams and wells are built. In the river valleys, especially along the Rio Grande, fruits and vegetables are grown.

Francisco Vásquez de Coronado, in search of the fabled "Seven Cities of Cibola," explored (1540-42) the region that became New Mexico, but found no treasure. In 1598 the first Spanish colony was established at the Pueblo of San Juan de Los Caballeros. Santa Fe was founded in 1610 and made provincial capital. Roman Catholic missionaries set up schools in the region. Subjected to harsh treatment and forbidden to worship their gods, the Pueblo Indians revolted in 1680; Spain regained control in 1692. Mexico governed from 1821 until the United States took possession via the 1848 Mexican treaty and the 1853 Gadsden Purchase. Vital to early-day commerce, the Santa Fe Trail between New Mexico and Missouri was opened in 1821; today, east of Santa Fe, the Trail is still in use as U.S. 85.

The surrender (1886) of Geronimo terminated the Apache Wars and marked the virtual end of area Indian troubles. During the 1880s, the mining and ranching industries boomed. New Mexico entered the Union in 1912.

New Mexico is one of the largest energy-producing states in the nation. The state is the leading producer of potash and uranium. It has almost half of the nation's uranium reserves and large deposits of low-sulphur coal and natural gas. Historically, it has been a massive exporter of energy, sending out of the state more than half the electricity it has produced, about three-quarters of the gas generated and almost all of the petroleum pumped in the state.

Since 1945, the state has been a leader in the field of energy research and development. It helps the nation solve its energy needs through research conducted by Los Alamos Scientific Laboratory and Sandia Laboratories in the nuclear, solar and geothermal fields.

The increased demand for domestic energy and the pattern of growth it shares with other states of the sunbelt have brought problems as well as prosperity. School systems are overcrowded and there is a housing shortage in some places. Urban sprawl is spreading around Grants, Albuquerque and Santa Fe, intensifying the contrast between the relatively low economic level of the rural areas and the prosperity of some cities and mining communities. As a result, political power, which has been in the hands of agricultural interests (ranching is still the state's chief industry), is shifting to represent newcomers from out of state and the growing Mexican-American population.

Tourist attractions in New Mexico include the Carlsbad Caverns National Park, Inscription Rock at El Morro National Monument, and the ruins of Fort Union, which in its day was one of the largest U.S. military outposts on the southwest frontier. Other National Park Service facilities are Bandelier National Monument, Capulin Mountain National Monument, Chaco Canyon National Monument, Gila Cliff Dwellings National Monument, Salinas National Monument, and White Sands National Monument. Santa Fe and Taos attract thousands of visitors every year. At Lincoln are mementos of Billy the Kid, the outlaw who was involved (1878) in the Lincoln County cattle war. And near Aztec are Indian ruins, including a 500-room, E-shaped pueblo dating from A.D. 800-1200.

In February 1980 a prison revolt at the New Mexico state penitentiary left more than 30 inmates dead and about 90 prisoners and guards injured. During the 36-hour siege, convicts turned on one another, torturing and killing suspected informers. The worst U.S. prison riot since that at Attica, New York, nine years before, it focused national attention on the explosive atmosphere in many of the nation's prisons.

In June 1981, the western part of Valencia County was detached to form the new county of Cibola with Grants as its county seat.

**Full name:** State of New Mexico. **Origin of name:** From the Aztec, Mexitli, meaning "War God." **Inhabitant:** New Mexican. **Capital:** Santa Fe. **State motto:** Crescit Eundo (It Grows As It Goes). **Flag:** Stylized red sun, symbol of Zia pueblo of Indians, on a yellow field. **Seal:** Two eagles represent annexation of New Mexico by the United States; scroll under eagles bears state's motto. **Flower:** Yucca. **Bird:** Roadrunner. **Tree:** Piñon or nut pine. **Gem:** Turquoise. **Vegetable:** Chile and Pinto Beans. **Song:** "O, Fair New Mexico." **Nickname:** Land of Enchantment.

**Governor:** Bruce King. **Annual salary:** $60,000. **Term:** 4 years. **Current term expires:** Dec. 1982. **Voting requirements:** 18 yrs. old & U.S. citizen; registered state resident 42 days (30 days for Pres. election). **U.S. Congressmen:** 3. **Entered Union:** 1912 (47th state).

**Location & boundaries:** Southwestern state: bounded on the north by Colorado; on the east by Oklahoma & Texas; on the south by Texas & Mexico; & on the west by Arizona. **Total area:** 121,5993 sq. mi. (ranks 5th). **Extreme length:** 391 mi. **Extreme breadth:** 352 mi. **Chief rivers:** Rio Grande, San Juan, Pecos, Canadian. **Major lakes:**

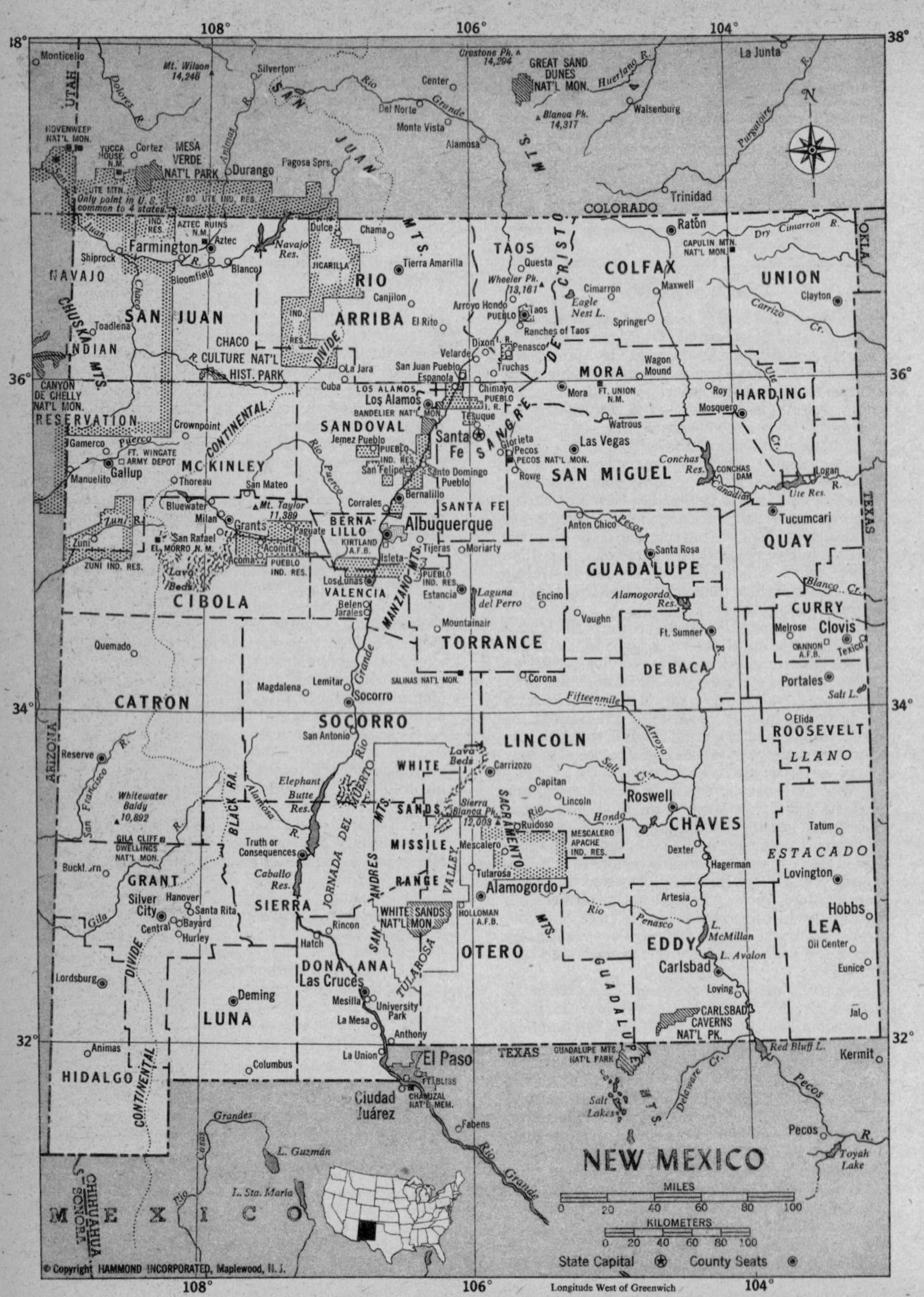
NEW MEXICO
COLORADO
UTAH
ARIZONA
TEXAS
OKLA.
MEXICO
CHIHUAHUA
SONORA
SAN JUAN
RIO ARRIBA
TAOS
COLFAX
UNION
MC KINLEY
SANDOVAL
MORA
HARDING
SAN MIGUEL
SANTA FE
BERNALILLO
CIBOLA
VALENCIA
TORRANCE
GUADALUPE
QUAY
CURRY
DE BACA
CATRON
SOCORRO
LINCOLN
ROOSEVELT
CHAVES
GRANT
SIERRA
OTERO
EDDY
LEA
LUNA
DONA ANA
HIDALGO
Santa Fe
Albuquerque
Farmington
Gallup
Los Alamos
Las Vegas
Roswell
Clovis
Alamogordo
Las Cruces
Carlsbad
Hobbs
El Paso
Ciudad Juárez
MILES
0 20 40 60 80 100
KILOMETERS
0 20 40 60 80 100
State Capital
County Seats
Longitude West of Greenwich
108°
106°
104°
38°
36°
34°
32°
© Copyright HAMMOND INCORPORATED, Maplewood, N. J.

Navajo, Conchas, Cochiti, Elephant Butte Reservoir. **No. of counties:** 33.

**Population (1980 census):** 1,302,981 (ranks 37th). **Pop. increase (1970-80):** 28.1%. **Largest cities:** Albuquerque, Santa Fe, Las Cruces. **Pop. density:** 10.7 per sq. mi. (ranks 44th). **Pop. distribution: White**—976,465; **Black**—24,042; **Am. Indian, Eskimo and Aleut**—104,777; **Asian and Pacific Islander**—6,816; **Other**—187,868; **Spanish origin**—476,089; **Marriage rate (1979):** 13.1 per 1,000 people. **Divorce rate:** 8.0 per 1,000 people.

**State finances (1980). Revenue:** $2,183,000,000. **Expenditures:** $1,744,000,000. **State taxes:** $712.34 per capita. **State personal income tax:** Yes. **Public debt (1980):** $544.45 per capita. **Federal aid (1980):** $432.55 per capita. **Personal income (1981):** $8,654.

**Sectors of the economy (% of labor force employed in 1970):** Government (27%), Wholesale and retail trade (21%), Educational Services (12%), Services (11%), Construction (7%), Manufacturing (7%). **Leading products:** food items, petroleum & coal items, electronics, apparel. **Minerals:** coal, lead, zinc, gold, petroleum, silver, natural gas, potassium salts, copper, uranium, molybdenum. **Agricultural products:** cattle, sheep, dairy items, cotton lint, hay, sorghum, grain, poultry. **Avg. farm (1981):** 3,434 acres. **Avg. value of farm per acre:** $203.

**Highway expenditures per capita (1980):** $158.20. **Persons per motor vehicle (1981):** 1.19. **Minimum age for driver's license:** 15. **Gasoline tax:** 9¢ per gallon. **Diesel tax:** 9¢ per gallon. **Motor vehicle deaths (1980):** 46.6 per 100,000 people.

**Birthrate (1979):** 20.6 per 1,000 people. **Infant mortality rate per 1,000 births (1978):** 14.1. **Physicians per 100,000 pop. (1979):** 147. **Dentists per 100,000 pop. (1979):** 41. **Acceptable hospital beds (1979):** 4.7 per 1,000 people. **State expenditures per capita for health and hospitals (1980):** $104.41.

**Education expenditures (1977-78):** $589.72 per capita annually. **No. of pupils in public schools (1980):** 271,000. **No. of institutions of higher learning (1978-79):** 19. **Public school expenditure per pupil in attendance (1978-79):** $1,942. **Avg. salary of public school teachers (1979-80):** $19,245. **No. full-time teachers (1980):** 15,600. **Educational attainment of adult population (1976):** 12.5 median yrs. of school completed: 5.7% with less than 5 years of education; 15.3% with 4 yrs. of college.

**Telephones (1979):** 46 per 100 people. **State Chamber of Commerce:** Association of Commerce and Industry of New Mexico, 117 Quincy, N.E., Albuquerque, New Mexico 87108.

## NEW YORK

New York is a state of superlatives, ideally located and richly endowed. In many respects, it is a nerve center of the nation, a major marketplace, and a national leader in manufacturing, finance, fashion, art, and communications. Second to California in population, New York is the region that George Washington foresaw as a "seat of empire"—hence its nickname, the Empire State. New York City, the nation's largest city, was the first U.S. capital (1789-90), and Washington was first inaugurated (1789) there.

Roughly triangular in shape, the state has a highly diversified terrain, with many lakes, wooded hills, and fertile valleys. Most of the area south of the Mohawk Valley falls within the province of the Appalachian Plateau, which covers more than half the state and slopes upward from northwest to southeast. New York's land features include the scenic Adirondack Mountains in the north and the Catskill range in the south, as well as imposing Niagara Falls. New York is the only state to border both the Atlantic Ocean and the Great Lakes.

Florentine explorer Giovanni da Verrazano is thought to have discovered New York by entering New York Bay in 1524. In 1609 Henry Hudson, an Englishman in the employ of the Dutch, sailed up the river bearing his name and the same year Samuel de Champlain discovered what is now Lake Champlain. The Dutch West India Company began (1624) settlement of the region, then called New Netherland, at Fort Orange (now Albany). Soon after, Governor Peter Minuit is said to have bought Manhattan Island from the Indians for trinkets worth about $24.

Indian troubles, misgovernment, and other woes hindered the colony's development. As a countermeasure, the Dutch began (1629) the "patroon" (landholder's) system that tended to concentrate economic and governmental power in the hands of a few. Squabbling broke out among the patroons, other settlers, and the home company, and Minuit was recalled (1631) for granting the patroons undue privileges. He then entered the service of Sweden; its colony (New Sweden), along the Delaware River south of Dutch interests, was viewed by the Dutch as a territorial threat. Minuit's successors—Wouter Van Twiller and Willem Kieft—were failures, but Peter Stuyvesant for a time did better. In 1655 he captured New Sweden for the Dutch and reorganized New Amsterdam (now New York City). Stuyvesant was a strict Calvinist whose tactics often provoked resentment.

Meanwhile, English penetration of Long Island and the southeastern part of what is now the mainland state was steadily progressing. In the north and west of the state, Canadian French allied themselves with the Huron Indians, but met with hostility from the Iroquois. Comprised of five tribes confederated about 1570, the Iroquois greatly influenced the struggle for control of the region between France and England that ensued after the Dutch surrender (1664) of the land to the British. New Netherland thus became the colonies New York and New Jersey, granted by King Charles II to his brother, the Duke of York (later James II). The Dutch recaptured New York in 1673, but had to yield it again a year later.

The period was marked by the development of English governmental institutions, amid a welter of conflicts and confrontations. A popular legislative assembly was formed in 1683, after years of struggle by townspeople wanting a meaningful voice in their government; but two years later the assembly was dissolved by James II. In 1686 the king sought to combine New York, New Jersey, and the New England colonies under the vice-regal authority of governor general Edmund Andros, but Andros was very unpopular, and when the king was dethroned in England in 1688, Andros was forced out of power by irate citizens. New York City merchant Jacob Leisler, hoping to foster more democratic government, then seized control, but was soon replaced by a royal governor and executed.

New York played a major role in the French and Indian Wars (1689-1763) in which France was helped by Algonquian Indians, while the Iroquois aided the English. The region also saw much action in the American Revolution and the War of 1812. (Statehood dates from 1788.) With the opening of the Erie Canal (1825), which linked the Hudson and the Great Lakes, the state entered an era of great prosperity, reinforced a few years later by the massive industrial demands of the Civil War. The state contributed more men (nearly 500,000), supplies, and money to the Union cause than any other.

The postwar period was marked by continued industrialization, large-scale immigration, and a corrupt political climate that often led to ineffective reform pressures: it was the notorious era of Boss Tweed and Tammany Hall. The most successful reform efforts were those made between World Wars I and II.

Recent important state developments include a $1 billion state office building complex called the Empire State Plaza in Albany; the Artpark near

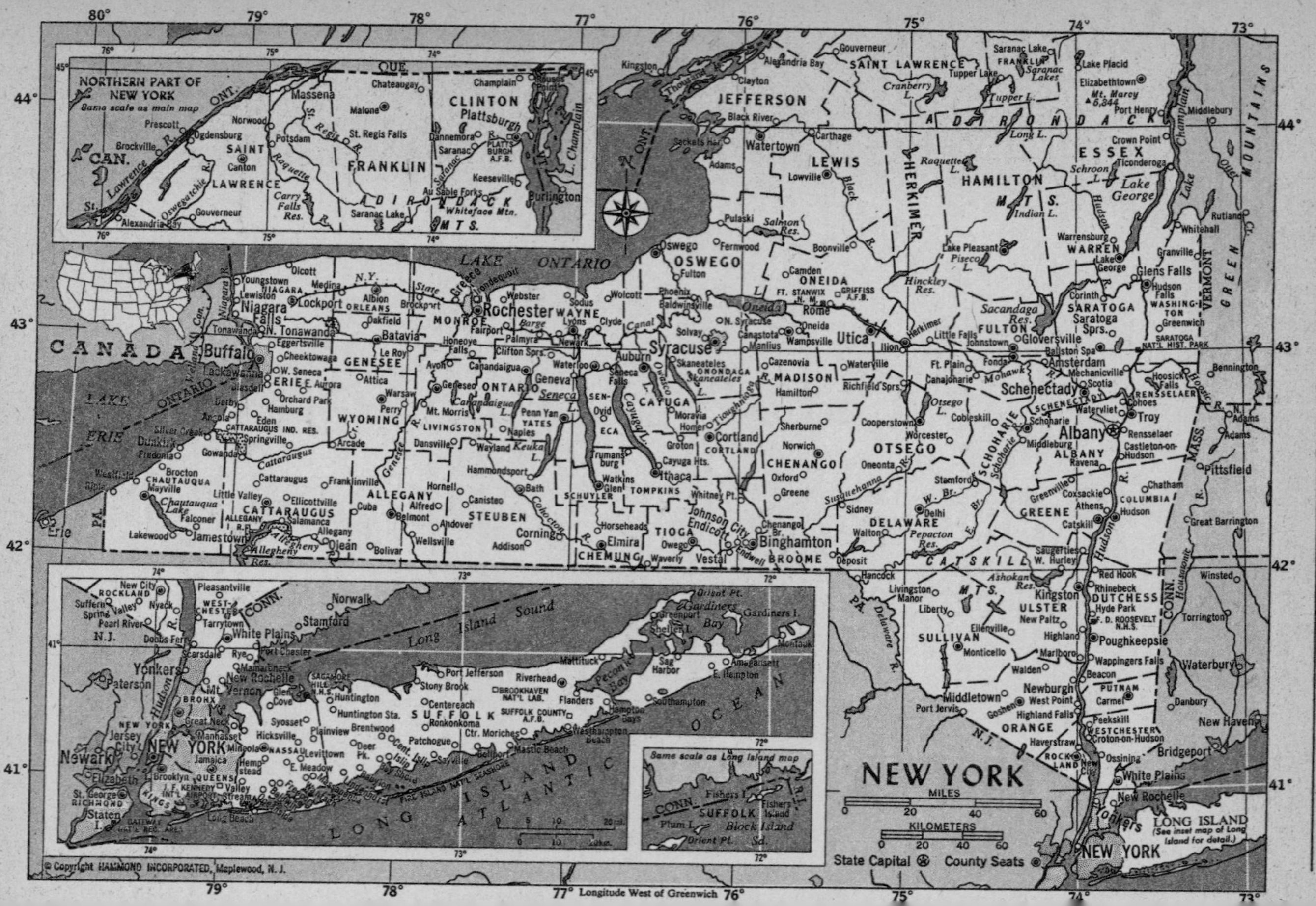
NEW YORK
MILES
KILOMETERS
State Capital
County Seats
NORTHERN PART OF NEW YORK
Same scale as main map
LONG ISLAND
(See inset map of Long Island for detail.)
Same scale as Long Island map
Longitude West of Greenwich
© Copyright HAMMOND INCORPORATED, Maplewood, N. J.

Niagara Falls, an area devoted to the visual and performing arts, with summer artists-in-residence; and the expansion of the higher education system. The State University of New York is the largest higher education system in the country, with 21 campuses throughout the state and an enrollment of over 225,000.

In 1978, residents of the Love Canal area in Niagara Falls learned they were living on top of a chemical time-bomb. Leakage from toxic wastes dumped 30 years before by the Hooker Chemical Corp., forced 239 families to evacuate the area. In May 1980, the Environmental Protection Agency revealed that 30 percent of Love Canal residents suffered from chromosome damage linked to higher incidences of miscarriages, birth defects and cancer. However, in 1981 New York State health officials reported that cancer rates were no higher among Love Canal residents than among other Niagara Falls residents. A federal report in 1982 stated that that area was again habitable following cleanup.

**Full name:** State of New York. **Origin of name:** In honor of the Duke of York. **Inhabitant:** New Yorker. **Capital:** Albany. **State motto:** Excelsior (Ever Upward). **Flag:** State coat of arms on blue field. **Seal:** Coat of arms surrounded with legend "The Great Seal of State of New York." Coat of arms has figures representing Liberty & Justice, a typical New York river scene & an eagle perched on globe. **Flower:** Rose. **Bird:** Bluebird. **Tree:** Sugar maple. **Gem:** Garnet. **Song:** "I Love New York." **Nickname:** Empire State.

**Governor:** Hugh L. Carey. **Annual salary:** $85,000. **Term:** 4 years. **Current term expires:** Dec. 1982. **Voting requirements:** 18 yrs. old & U.S. citizen; resident of state and county for 30 days; registered. **U.S. Congressmen:** 34. **Entered Union:** 1788 (11th state).

**Location & boundaries:** Middle Atlantic state; bounded on the north by the St. Lawrence River & Canada; on the east by Vermont, Massachusetts & Connecticut; on the south by the Atlantic Ocean, New Jersey, the Delaware River & Pennsylvania; & on the west by Pennsylvania, Lake Erie, Niagara River, Lake Ontario & Canada. **Total area:** 49,108 sq. mi. (ranks 30th). **Extreme length (exclusive of Long Island):** 20 mi. **Extreme breadth:** 310 mi. **Coastline:** 127 mi. on Atlantic; 371 mi. on Lakes Ontario & Erie. **Chief rivers:** St. Lawrence, Hudson, Mohawk. **Major lakes:** Finger Lakes, Champlain, Erie, Ontario. **No. of counties:** 62.

**Population (1980 census):** 17,558,072 (ranks 2nd). **Pop. increase (1970-80):** −3.7%. **Largest cities:** New York, Buffalo, Rochester, Yonkers. **Pop. density:** 357.5 per sq. mi. (ranks 6th). **Pop. distribution: White**—13,961,106; **Black**—2,401,842; **Am. Indian, Eskimo and Aleut**—38,732; **Asian and Pacific Islander**—310,531; **Other**—845,077; **Spanish origin**—1,659,245. **Marriage rate (1979):** 8.1 per 1,000 people. **Divorce rate:** 3.7 per 1,000 people.

**State finances (1980). Revenue:** $27,199,000,000. **Expenditures:** $24,978,000,000. **State taxes:** $724.31 per capita. **State personal income tax:** Yes. **Public debt (1980):** $1,346.48 per capita. **Federal aid (1980):** $545.01 per capita. **Personal income (1981):** $11,440.

**Sectors of the economy (% of labor force employed in 1970):** Manufacturing (24%), Wholesale and retail trade (20%), Government (17%), Services (8%), Educational Services (8%), Construction (5%). **Leading products:** printing & publishing, apparel, machinery, instruments, transportation equipment, food items. **Minerals:** cement, stone, sand & gravel, salt. **Agricultural products:** dairy items, poultry, fruit, vegetables. **Fishing:** clams, scallops, flounder. **Avg. farm (1981):** 192 acres. **Avg. value of farm per acre:** $749.

**Highway expenditures per capita (1980):** $63.51. **Persons per motor vehicle (1981):** 2.20. **Minimum age for driver's license:** 17. **Gasoline tax:** 8¢ per gallon. **Diesel tax:** 10¢ per gallon. **Motor vehicle deaths (1980):** 14.9 per 100,000 people.

**Birthrate (1979):** 13.4 per 1,000 people. **Infant mortality rate per 1,000 births (1978):** 14.0. **Physicians per 100,000 pop. (1979):** 261. **Dentists per 100,000 pop. (1979):** 74. **Acceptable hospital beds (1979):** 7.5 per 1,000 people. **State expenditures per capita for health and hospitals (1980):** $110.24.

**Education expenditures (1977-78):** $570.88 per capita annually. **No. of pupils in public schools (1980):** 2,864,000. **No. of institutions of higher learning (1978-79):** 286. **Public school expenditure per pupil in attendance (1978-79):** $3,180. **Avg. salary of public school teachers (1979-80):** $19,600. **No. full-time teachers (1980):** 183,100. **Educational attainment of adult population (1976):** 12.5 median yrs. of school completed: 3.0% with less than 5 years of education; 16.0% with 4 yrs. of college.

**Telephones (1979):** 54 per 100 people. **State Chamber of Commerce:** Business Council of New York State, Washington at Dove, Albany, New York 12207.

## NORTH CAROLINA

One of the 13 Colonies and the Southeast's foremost industrial state, North Carolina presents an unusual amalgam of tradition and progress. It is a leader in both small-farm agriculture and business-applied research, and the nation's major producer of tobacco and tobacco products. The state also ranks high as a producer of textiles, bricks, wood products, and seafood. The first sustained airplane flight, by Orville and Wilbur Wright, took place (1903) near Kitty Hawk. Today, the state boasts of its famous "Research Triangle" at the University of North Carolina, Duke University, and North Carolina State University; the schools use their pooled resources to assist industry.

The state is topographically similar to South Carolina, sharing the same three principal land regions: (from east to west) the Atlantic Coastal Plain, the Piedmont Plateau, and the Blue Ridge Mountains. Mount Mitchell is the highest peak east of the Mississippi. Beyond the state's coastline are the islands, reefs, sheltered sounds, dunes, and capes of the Outer Banks, including Capes Fear and Hatteras—the latter so treacherous to ships that it is often called the graveyard of the Atlantic. About 60 percent of the state is forested.

The headwaters of the scenic New River in North Carolina were saved from inundation by power company dams in legislation enacted in Congress in 1976 and backed by every major environmental group in the country. The river is considered one of the oldest in the Western Hemisphere.

Much of North Carolina's early history is shared with South Carolina, of which it was a part until 1712. Highlights of this period include Sir Walter Raleigh's unsuccessful attempts (1585, 1587) to establish a colony on Roanoke Island. Although it lasted only about a year, Raleigh's initial settlement was the first English colony in the New World; when all members of his second settlement (1587-?) disappeared, it came to be called the "Lost Colony"; among the missing was Virginia Dare, first child of English parentage born in America.

Among the region's problems were Culpeper's Rebellion (1677), involving colonists angered by the English Navigation Acts; and the Cary Rebellion (1708), brought about by Quakers and other dissenters who refused to support the established Anglican church. In 1705, French Huguenots from Virginia established North Carolina's first permanent settlement at Bath.

Growth in the Carolinas was slow. Swamps and dense forests made land communication difficult, and there were serious Indian troubles, especially during the Tuscarora War (1711-13). Pirates, too, were a hindrance, often menacing the colony's seabound trade; the slaying (1718) of the infamous "Blackbeard" (Edward Teach) in a battle near Ocracoke Island eased the problem. From 1712 to 1729, the proprietors appointed separate governors to administer North and South Carolina. A bitter North Carolina-Virginia boundary dispute was settled in 1728. Dissatisfied with the proprietary system, England eventually made (1729) the region a royal colony, a move that marked a period of

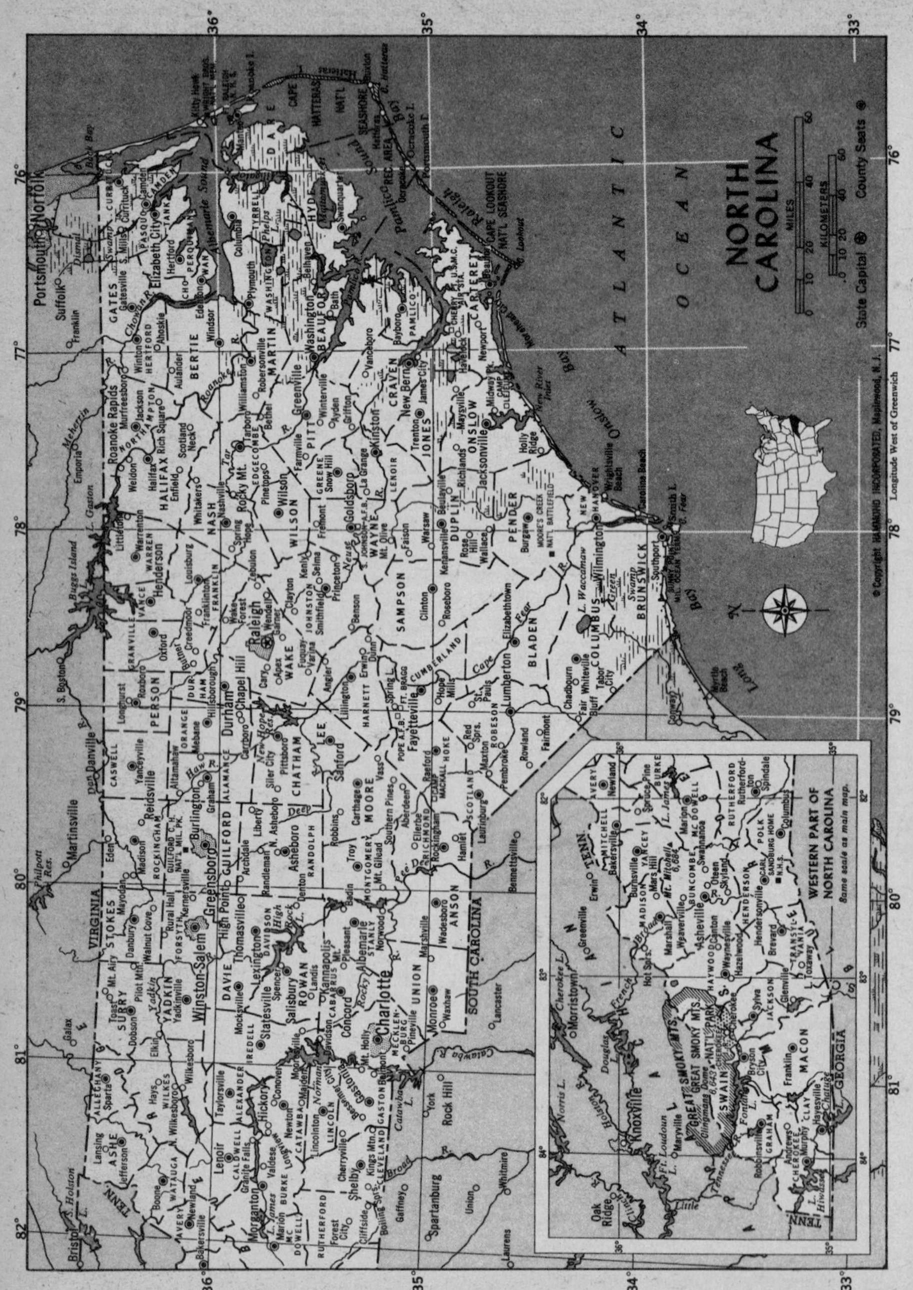
NORTH CAROLINA
ATLANTIC OCEAN
MILES
KILOMETERS
State Capital
County Seats
WESTERN PART OF NORTH CAROLINA
Same scale as main map.
© Copyright HAMMOND INCORPORATED, Maplewood, N.J.
Longitude West of Greenwich
VIRGINIA
SOUTH CAROLINA
GEORGIA
TENN.
Raleigh
Charlotte
Greensboro
Winston-Salem
Durham
Wilmington
Fayetteville
Asheville
Knoxville

progress in which farming and industry expanded as the population rose.

North Carolina contributed troops and materials to help England in its various colonial wars, while a persistent east-west sectionalism began to develop; this rift was caused by sharp differences in geography, politics, economics, and religion. Indian troubles were virtually ended in 1761 by a treaty with the Cherokees, but their final removal from the area did not begin until 1835. In 1768 irate back-country farmers, protesting taxes they considered excessive, organized the short-lived Regulator Movement for reform. The insurgents were eventually suppressed (1771) at Alamance by the provincial militia.

During the American Revolution, there was relatively little fighting on the state's soil, but many North Carolinians saw action elsewhere. In 1779 North Carolina annexed an area of present-day Tennessee settled by the Watauga Association, which lay immediately beyond North Carolina's present border. North Carolina administered the region until 1784, when it ceded its claim to the United States. The "Watauga" settlers then established the independent state of Franklin. Failing to gain official recognition, the new state's territory was again absorbed in 1789 by North Carolina, which later that same year ceded it once more to the Federal government; North Carolina's statehood dates from that year.

From 1815 to 1835, North Carolina languished in backwardness and apathy, and came to be called the "Rip Van Winkle State"; this period was followed until 1860 by one of progress, which saw a resurgence of political democracy and a lessening of unproductive sectionalism.

Despite the presence of considerable pro-Union and antislavery sentiment, North Carolina joined the Confederacy after the Civil War began. During the conflict, the port of Wilmington became a haven for Confederate blockade-runners. In the postwar period, Reconstruction was followed by the return of white supremacy and a suffrage amendment (1900) that again disenfranchised the Negro.

Among modern North Carolina's most pressing preoccupations is the continued strengthening and diversification of its economy, to curb reliance upon any single factor, such as tobacco. Another task is the peaceable achievement of racial integration. A majority of the rural and small-city school districts in the state are headed toward complete desegregation, but in the larger cities, such as Charlotte, Raleigh, Winston-Salem, and Durham, breaking down the dual systems has been difficult because there are more all-black schools and more rigid residential patterns.

The U.S. Supreme Court, in an historic ruling in the spring of 1971, upheld U.S. District Judge James B. McMillan's ruling that busing was a legitimate tool to use in ending racial segregation. The decision was applied to several school districts and by the fall, few racially identifiable schools remained in the state.

A conflict between extremist groups in Greensboro resulted in the deaths of five persons in November 1979. The slayings occurred at an anti-Ku Klux Klan rally sponsored by the Workers' Viewpoint Organization (WVO), a left-wing group also known as the Communist Workers party, U.S.A. As the protest rally began in a black area of Greensboro, Klansmen and American Nazi party members appeared and taunted the demonstrators. The two groups fought with each other and exchanged gunfire resulting in the deaths. Police arrested 15 Klansmen and American Nazis for allegedly killing five of the anti-Klan group; some were indicted for murder or felonious rioting in December. On November 17, 1980, a trial jury in Greensboro acquitted the six defendants of the charges.

**Full name:** State of North Carolina. **Origin of name:** In honor of Charles I of England. **Inhabitant:** North Carolinian. **Capital:** Raleigh. **State motto:** Esse Quam Videri (To Be Rather Than to Seem). **Flag:** Gold scrolls & NC (separated by white star) on blue bar; a red & white horizontal bar to right. **Seal:** Liberty holds scroll inscribed "Constitution"; seated figure of plenty; date "May 20, 1775." **Flower:** Dogwood. **Bird:** Cardinal. **Tree:** Pine. **Song:** "The Old North State." **Nickname:** Tar Heel State.

**Governor:** James B. Hunt, Jr. **Annual salary:** $57,864. **Term:** 4 years. **Current term expires:** Jan. 1985. **Voting requirements:** 18 yrs. old & U.S. citizen; resident of state and district, 30 days. **U.S. Congressmen:** 11. **Entered Union:** 1789 (12th state).

**Location & boundaries:** South Atlantic state: bounded on the north by Virginia; on the east by the Atlantic Ocean; on the south by South Carolina & Georgia; & on the west by Tennessee. **Total area:** 52,669 sq. mi. (ranks 28th). **Extreme length:** 503 mi. **Extreme breadth:** 187 mi. **Coastline:** 301 mi. **Chief rivers:** Yadkin, Cape Fear, Neuse, Roanoke. **Major lakes:** Fontana, Mattamuskeet, Norman. **No. of counties:** 100.

**Population (1980 census):** 5,881,813 (ranks 10th). **Pop. increase (1970-80):** 15.7%. **Largest cities:** Charlotte, Greensboro, Raleigh, Winston-Salem. **Pop. density:** 111.7 per sq. mi. (ranks 17th). **Pop. distribution: White**—4,453,010; **Black**—1,316,050; **Am. Indian, Eskimo and Aleut**—64,635; **Asian and Pacific Islander**—21,168; **Other**—19,566; **Spanish origin**—56,607. **Marriage rate (1979):** 8.0 per 1,000 people. **Divorce rate:** 4.9 per 1,000 people.

**State finances (1980). Revenue:** $6,202,000,000. **Expenditures:** $5,733,000,000. **State taxes:** $547.39 per capita. **State personal income tax:** Yes. **Public debt (1980):** $215.48 per capita. **Federal aid (1980):** $327.71 per capita. **Personal income (1981):** $8,679.

**Sectors of the economy (% of labor force employed in 1970):** Manufacturing (36%), Wholesale and retail trade (18%), Government (13%), Services (8%), Educational Services (7%), Construction (7%). **Leading products:** textile items, tobacco items, furniture & fixtures, food items, electrical machinery, chemicals, apparel. **Agricultural products:** broilers, dairy items, tobacco, corn, soybeans. **Fishing:** shrimp, menhaden, crabs. **Avg. farm (1981):** 126 acres. **Avg. value of farm per acre:** $1,331.

**Highway expenditures per capita (1980):** $107.36. **Persons per motor vehicle (1981):** 1.27. **Minimum age for driver's license:** 16. **Gasoline tax:** 12¢ per gallon. **Diesel tax:** 12¢ per gallon. **Motor vehicle deaths (1980):** 25.6 per 100,000 people.

**Birthrate (1979):** 15.0 per 1,000 people. **Infant mortality rate per 1,000 births (1978):** 16.6. **Physicians per 100,000 pop. (1979):** 150. **Dentists per 100,000 pop. (1979):** 38. **Acceptable hospital beds (1979):** 5.7 per 1,000 people. **State expenditures per capita for health and hospitals (1980):** $76.21.

**Education expenditures (1977-78):** $464.77 per capita annually. **No. of pupils in public schools (1980):** 1,139,000. **No. of institutions of higher learning (1978-79):** 126. **Public school expenditure per pupil in attendance (1978-79):** $1,712. **Avg. salary of public school teachers (1979-80):** $14,711. **No. full-time teachers (1980):** 60,700. **Educational attainment of adult population (1976):** 12.2 median yrs. of school completed: 6.4% with less than 5 years of education; 11.8% with 4 yrs. of college.

**Telephones (1979):** 53 per 100 people. **State Chamber of Commerce:** North Carolina Citizens Association, Wake County Office Building, P.O. Box 2508, Raleigh, North Carolina 27602.

## NORTH DAKOTA

North Dakota is the most rural of the states, with more than 90 percent of the land in farms. Agriculture and mining are two of its economic mainstays. Only Kansas and Oklahoma produce more wheat, and the state's coal and oil reserves are among the nation's largest. Manufacturing is limited but growing, with food processing leading the way. Tourism is aided by excellent hunting and fishing and such attractions as the Theodore Roosevelt National Park in the Badlands, the International Peace Gardens on the Canadian border, and numerous historic sites including Fort Abercrombie (established 1857), the first U.S. military post in the region. Giant Lake Sakakawea, extending 180 miles upstream from Garrison Dam on the Missouri River, provides sailing and other water sports. A number of rodeos and fairs take place in the state in the summer and early fall.

Three main regions make up the state: the Red River Valley, comprising a ten-to-forty-mile-wide strip along the eastern border; the Young Drift Plains, just west of this strip; and, covering the state's southwestern half, the Great Plains (also known locally as the Missouri Plateau). The state's continental climate is marked by wide temperature variation, light-to-moderate precipitation, and considerable windiness.

North Dakota's prestatehood history is shared with that of South Dakota. Various Sioux tribes inhabited the land. The first Europeans to explore the area were the Sieur de la Vérendrye and sons who visited in 1738, four years before their travels in South Dakota. First settlement attempts were made (1812) at Pembina by Scottish and Irish families. After statehood (1889) separated it from its sister state, North Dakota experienced a spurt in population, growing from about 191,000 in 1890 to more than 577,000 in only 20 years. Immigrants from Norway, Germany, Russia and other parts of Europe poured into the state by the thousands.

The Nonpartisan League was founded in 1915 by farmers who advocated state involvement in the storage and processing of grain to break the power of out-of-state interests, increased funds for rural schools, and tax incentives to improve farms. The legislature which took office in 1919 was controlled by persons elected with the League's support; they enacted the League's educational and tax programs, and established a state-owned bank, a state-owned flour mill, and a state-owned grain elevator.

Work was begun in 1968 on the first stage of an irrigation system to carry water through nearly 2,000 miles of canals to irrigate a million acres of North Dakota soil. The entire project is expected to cost over $500 million. The Lonetree Reservoir and Dam project has come under fire from the Federal Government, the State of Minnesota, and the Canadian government, so work has been halted on the partially completed construction. A bill to reauthorize the project failed to pass in the U.S. Congress in November 1981.

The $9-million Omega all-weather navigation system permitting any ship or aircraft with a proper receiver to determine its exact position was completed near Lamoure in 1973. Unique in North America, it is one of the few in the world.

The energy crisis has resulted in the exploitation, chiefly by strip mining, of the coal reserves in the western part of the state, over the objections of environmentalists.

President Reagan approved an important project for North Dakota on August 5, 1981. A $2-billion coal gasification plant is to be built at Beulah in Mercer County. The facility will convert lignite from the extensive deposits nearby into synthetic gas for transmission throughout the nation.

**Full name:** State of North Dakota. **Origin of name:** From the Sioux meaning "Alliance with Friends." **Inhabitant:** North Dakotan. **Capital:** Bismarck. **State motto:** Liberty & Union, Now & Forever, One & Inseparable. **Flag:** Eagle with American shield on breast, holding sheaf of arrows in left claw & olive branch in right & carrying in beak a banner inscribed "E Pluribus Unum"; above eagle is sunburst enclosing 13 stars, beneath is scroll inscribed "North Dakota"—all on blue field with yellow fringe. **Seal:** Elm tree & setting sun; plow, sheaves of wheat & anvil symbolize agriculture; bow & arrows & Indian hunting a buffalo represent North Dakota's history. **Flower:** Wild prairie rose. **Bird:** Western meadowlark. **Tree:** American elm. **Song:** "North Dakota Hymn." **Nickname:** Flickertail State and The Sioux State.

**Governor:** Allen I. Olson. **Annual salary:** $47,000. **Term:** 4 years. **Current term expires:** Jan. 1985. **Voting requirements:** 18 yrs. old & U.S. citizen; resident of state and precinct 30 days. **U.S. Congressmen:** 1. **Entered Union:** 1889 (39th state).

**Location & boundaries:** Northern Midwestern state: bounded on the north by Canada; on the east by Minnesota at the Red River of the North; on the south by South Dakota; & on the west by Montana. **Total area:** 70,702 sq. mi. (ranks 17th). **Extreme length:** 360 mi. **Extreme breadth:** 210 mi. **Chief rivers:** Red River of the North, Missouri, Sheyenne. **Major lakes:** Devils, Sakakawea Reservoir. **No. of counties:** 53.

**Population (1980 census):** 652,717 (ranks 46th). **Pop. increase (1970-80):** 5.7%. **Largest cities:** Fargo, Bismarck, Grand Forks, Minot. **Pop. density:** 9.2 per sq. mi. (ranks 45th). **Pop. distribution: White**—625,536; **Black**—2,568; **Am. Indian, Eskimo and Aleut**—20,157; **Asian and Pacific Islander**—1,979; **Other**—2,455; **Spanish origin**—3,903. **Marriage rate (1979):** 9.2 per 1,000 people. **Divorce rate:** 3.2 per 1,000 people.

**State finances (1980). Revenue:** $1,013,000,000. **Expenditures:** $910,000,000. **State taxes:** $569.47 per capita. **State personal income tax:** Yes. **Public debt (1980):** $335.80 per capita. **Federal aid (1980):** $524.88 per capita. **Personal income (1981):** $10,525.

**Sectors of the economy (% of labor force employed in 1970):** Wholesale and retail trade (23%), Government (19%), Educational Services (11%), Services (7%), Construction (6%), Manufacturing (5%). **Leading products:** food items, printing & publishing, machinery. **Minerals:** petroleum, sand & gravel, natural gas, lignite coal. **Agricultural products:** cattle, dairy items, poultry, potatoes, sugar beets, wheat, barley, hay. **Avg. farm (1981):** 1,043 acres. **Avg. value of farm per acre:** $423.

**Highway expenditures per capita (1980):** $211.82. **Persons per motor vehicle (1981):** 1.02. **Minimum age for driver's license:** 16. **Gasoline tax:** 8¢ per gallon. **Diesel tax:** 8¢ per gallon. **Motor vehicle deaths (1980):** 23.1 per 100,000 people.

**Birthrate (1979):** 17.9 per 1,000 people. **Infant mortality rate per 1,000 births (1978):** 13.5. **Physicians per 100,000 pop. (1979):** 126. **Dentists per 100,000 pop. (1979):** 47. **Acceptable hospital beds (1979):** 9.0 per 1,000 people. **State expenditures per capita for health and hospitals (1980):** $75.16.

**Education expenditures (1977-78):** $553.50 per capita annually. **No. of pupils in public schools (1980):** 114,000. **No. of institutions of higher learning (1978-79):** 16. **Public school expenditure per pupil in attendance (1978-79):** $1,977. **Avg. salary of public school teachers (1979-80):** $13,544. **No. full-time teachers (1980):** 8,150. **Educational attainment of adult population (1976):** 12.5 median yrs. of school completed: 1.7% with less than 5 years of education; 12.2% with 4 yrs. of college.

**Telephones (1979):** 63 per 100 people. **State Chamber of Commerce:** Greater North Dakota Association—State Chamber of Commerce, 808 Third Avenue, South, P.O. Box 2467, Fargo, North Dakota 58108.

## OHIO

A leading industrial state and the first to be carved out of the Northwest Territory, Ohio enjoys a variety of important natural resources and a strategic location near many rich markets. Predominantly a producer of iron and steel and their products, the state also ranks high in mining and agriculture (especially livestock). It is among the most populous of states, and only Virginia has produced more U.S. Presidents than Ohio, which claims eight.

Four land regions make up the state: the Appalachian Plateau, making up almost all of the eastern half; the fertile Till Plains, constituting the bulk of the western half; a five-to-50-mile-wide strip of the Great Lakes Plain bordering Lake Erie; and, in the south, an extension of Kentucky's Bluegrass Region forming a small wedge between the plateau and the lowlands. The climate is generally temperate but marked somewhat by extremes and

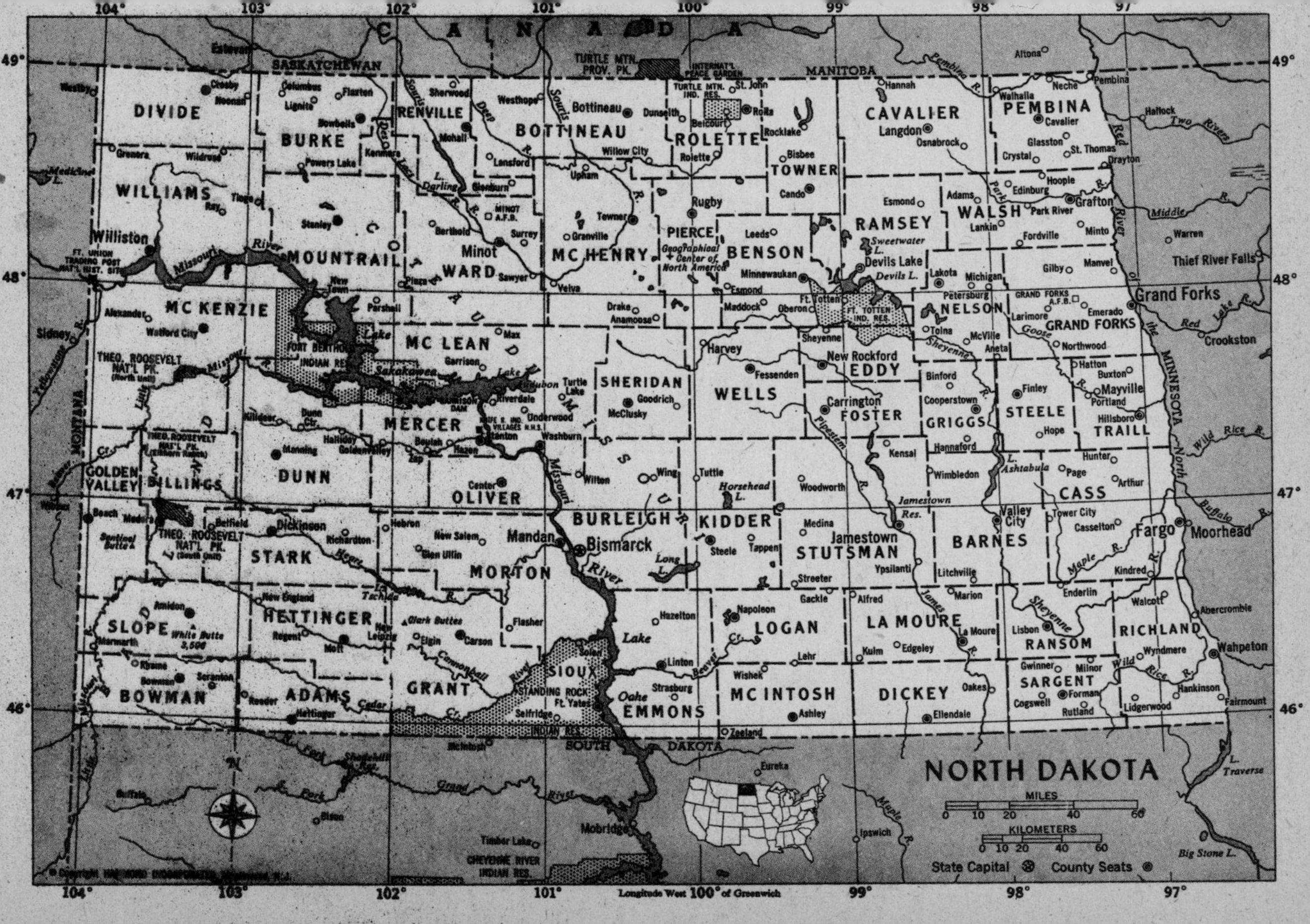
NORTH DAKOTA
MILES
0 10 20 40 60
KILOMETERS
0 10 20 40 60
State Capital
County Seats
CANADA
MANITOBA
SASKATCHEWAN
MINNESOTA
MONTANA
SOUTH DAKOTA
DIVIDE
BURKE
RENVILLE
BOTTINEAU
ROLETTE
TOWNER
CAVALIER
PEMBINA
WILLIAMS
MOUNTRAIL
WARD
MC HENRY
PIERCE
BENSON
RAMSEY
WALSH
NELSON
GRAND FORKS
MC KENZIE
MC LEAN
SHERIDAN
WELLS
EDDY
FOSTER
GRIGGS
STEELE
TRAILL
DUNN
MERCER
OLIVER
BURLEIGH
KIDDER
STUTSMAN
BARNES
CASS
GOLDEN VALLEY
BILLINGS
STARK
MORTON
SLOPE
HETTINGER
GRANT
SIOUX
EMMONS
LOGAN
LA MOURE
RANSOM
RICHLAND
BOWMAN
ADAMS
MC INTOSH
DICKEY
SARGENT
Bismarck
Fargo
Grand Forks
Minot
Williston
Jamestown
Mandan
Devils Lake
Valley City
Dickinson
Wahpeton
Moorhead
Missouri River
Lake Sakakawea
Longitude West 100° of Greenwich

sudden changes. Many dams and reservoirs have been built as a bulwark against disasters such as the floods of 1913 that killed about 500 persons and caused some $150 million in property loss.

Early Amerindian peoples are thought to have lived in the Ohio region between 5,000 and 7,000 years ago, followed by the Adena and Hopewell Mound Builders (c. 800 B.C.—A.D. 1300).

Algonquian and Iroquois Indians were living in the region when the first Europeans arrived. Robert Cavelier, Sieur de La Salle, passed through about 1670, providing a basis for French claims to the region that were sharply contested by the British, who claimed all the territory extending westward from their colonies. Victory in the French and Indian Wars (1689-1763) gave England the upper hand until the American Revolution. Massachusetts, Connecticut, and Virginia land claims in the area were resolved by the Northwest Ordinance (1787). A band of New Englanders led by General Rufus Putnam established (1788) the first permanent white settlement at Marietta. Early settlers were beset by serious Indian troubles that were largely ended after troops under General Anthony Wayne won (1794) the Battle of Fallen Timbers, near present-day Toledo. The Division Act of 1800 created the Indiana Territory out of the western part of the region, then still called the Northwest Territory. In 1803, Ohio entered the Union. A border dispute with the Territory of Michigan gave rise (1835) to the "Toledo War" but, before any actual fighting broke out, Congress awarded the area—about 520 square miles along Lake Erie—to Ohio. At present another land controversy between the two states—over a 200-square-mile area beneath Lake Erie that is rich in oil and natural gas—remains to be resolved. The state's southern boundary, the Ohio River, has been receding gradually north-and westward for centuries. Fortunately for Ohio, the U.S. Supreme Court ruled in January 1980 that the boundary is to remain fixed at its original position regardless of the river's shifting course.

Ohio was in the forefront of events leading to the Civil War. The abolition movement began at St. Clairsville, and many Ohioans helped slaves escape to Canada via the Underground Railroad. Although there was relatively little actual fighting on its soil, Ohio contributed heavily to the Union cause. In the postwar period the state rapidly emerged as an industrial power while retaining its agricultural status. In the years just prior to the turn of the century, big business became inordinately involved in Ohio politics, causing discontent among the less well-off. Labor troubles developed that culminated in Jacob S. Coxey's march on Washington, D.C. (1894) and a voting shift toward reform candidates. More recent troubles of this nature include major strikes during the mid-1930s, 1949, and 1959.

Tourism, aided by a surge in new highway construction, has developed into a valuable revenue-producer, now bringing in over $3 billion a year. Attractions include numerous state park and recreation areas, prehistoric Indian mounds, and historic sites such as Commodore Perry's Victory and International Peace Memorial at Put-in-Bay on Lake Erie, which commemorates his vital victory there during the War of 1812. Annual events include the All-American Soap Box Derby, held in Akron each summer.

In 1979 Honda Motor Company Ltd. of Japan opened a motorcycle assembly plant (its first in the U.S.) northwest of Columbus. At nearby Marysville, Honda plans to construct an auto assembly complex to employ about 2,000 persons. It is scheduled to open in 1982 or 1983.

The 1982 economic recession resulted in a 12.7 percent unemployment rate for the state in August 1982.

**Full name:** State of Ohio. **Origin of name:** From Iroquois name meaning "Great." **Inhabitant:** Ohioan. **Capital:** Columbus. **State motto:** With God, All Things Are Possible. **Flag:** Pennant-shaped flag; white-bordered red circle & white stars on a blue triangle, with red & white bars. **Seal:** Sheaf of wheat; bundle of arrows; sun rising behind mountains, indicating Ohio was first state west of Allegheny Mountains. **Flower:** Scarlet carnation. **Bird:** Cardinal. **Tree:** Buckeye. **Song:** "Beautiful Ohio." **Nickname:** Buckeye State.

**Governor:** James A. Rhodes. **Annual salary:** $60,000. **Term:** 4 years. **Current term expires:** Jan. 1983. **Voting requirements:** 18 yrs. as of election day & U.S. citizen; resident of state 30 days. **U.S. Congressmen:** 21. **Entered Union:** 1803 (17th state).

**Location & boundaries:** Midwestern state; bounded on the north by Michigan & Lake Erie; on the east by Pennsylvania & West Virginia; on the south by West Virginia, Kentucky & the Ohio River & on the west by Indiana. **Total area:** 41,330 sq. mi. (ranks 35th). **Extreme length:** 230 mi. **Extreme breadth:** 210 mi. **Shoreline:** 312 mi. **Chief rivers:** Ohio, Miami, Muskingum. **Major lakes:** Erie, Grand. **No. of counties:** 88.

**Population (1980 census):** 10,797,624 (ranks 6th). **Pop. increase (1970-80):** 1.3%. **Largest cities:** Cleveland, Columbus, Cincinnati, Toledo. **Pop. density:** 261.3 per sq. mi. (ranks 9th). **Pop. distribution: White**—9,597,266; **Black**—1,076,734; **Am. Indian, Eskimo and Aleut**—12,240; **Asian and Pacific Islander**—47,813; **Other**—63,366; **Spanish origin**—119,880. **Marriage rate (1979):** 9.3 per 1,000 people. **Divorce rate:** 5.5 per 1,000 people.

**State finances (1980). Revenue:** $12,180,000,000. **Expenditures:** $11,397,000,000. **State taxes:** $441.48 per capita. **State personal income tax:** Yes. **Public debt (1980):** $371.86 per capita. **Federal aid (1980):** $317.97 per capita. **Personal income (1981):** $10,371.

**Sectors of the economy (% of labor force employed in 1970):** Manufacturing (36%), Wholesale and retail trade (19%), Government (13%), Educational Services (7%), Services (6%), Construction (5%). **Leading products:** transportation equipment, primary & fabricated metals, machinery, rubber & plastic items. **Minerals:** bituminous coal, limestone, sand & gravel, salt, oil. **Agricultural products:** millk, hogs, cattle & calves, corn, soybeans. **Fishing:** yellow perch, catfish, white bass, yellow pike. **Avg. farm (1981):** 173 acres. **Avg. value of farm per acre:** $1,727.

**Highway expenditures per capita (1980):** $76.83. **Persons per motor vehicle (1981):** 1.35. **Minimum age for driver's license:** 16. **Gasoline tax:** 11.7¢ per gallon. **Diesel tax:** 11.7¢ per gallon. **Motor vehicle deaths (1980):** 18.8 per 100,000 people.

**Birthrate (1979):** 15.6 per 1,000 people. **Infant mortality rate per 1,000 births (1978):** 13.3. **Physicians per 100,000 pop. (1979):** 157. **Dentists per 100,000 pop. (1979):** 49. **Acceptable hospital beds (1979):** 5.9 per 1,000 people. **State expenditures per capita for health and hospitals (1980):** $89.96.

**Education expenditures (1977-78):** $455.08 per capita annually. **No. of pupils in public schools (1980):** 1,960,000. **No. of institutions of higher learning (1978-79):** 133. **Public school expenditure per pupil in attendance (1978-79):** $1,917. **Avg. salary of public school teachers (1979-80):** $15,800. **No. full-time teachers (1980):** 111,800. **Educational attainment of adult population (1976):** 12.4 median yrs. of school completed: 1.7% with less than 5 years of education; 11.5% with 4 yrs. of college.

**Telephones (1979):** 56 per 100 people. **State Chamber of Commerce:** Ohio Chamber of Commerce, 17 South High Street, 8th Floor, Columbus, Ohio 43215.

## OKLAHOMA

Oil-rich Oklahoma, the nation's Indian Territory in the early 19th century, has one of the largest Indian populations of any state, 169,000 in 1980. Generally considered an agricultural state, even though the value of its manufacturing and mining output exceeds cash farm revenue, the state earns more from livestock and livestock products (especially cattle) than it does from crops. Manufacturing, although becoming more diverse, is still based largely on the processing of the state's farm

OHIO
MILES
0 10 20 30 40 50
KILOMETERS
0 10 20 30 40 50
State Capital
County Seats
84°
83°
82°
81°
42°
41°
40°
39°
38°
DETROIT
CANADA
LAKE ERIE
ONTARIO
MICHIGAN
INDIANA
PA.
WEST VIRGINIA
KENTUCKY
Ohio River
Toledo
Cleveland
Columbus
Dayton
Cincinnati
Akron
Youngstown
Canton
Springfield
Lima
Mansfield
Sandusky
Lorain
Hamilton
Zanesville
Marietta
Portsmouth
Steubenville
Warren
WILLIAMS
FULTON
LUCAS
OTTAWA
DEFIANCE
HENRY
WOOD
SANDUSKY
ERIE
HURON
LORAIN
CUYAHOGA
GEAUGA
LAKE
ASHTABULA
TRUMBULL
PORTAGE
SUMMIT
MEDINA
MAHONING
COLUMBIANA
STARK
WAYNE
ASHLAND
RICHLAND
CRAWFORD
SENECA
HANCOCK
PUTNAM
PAULDING
VAN WERT
ALLEN
WYANDOT
MARION
HARDIN
AUGLAIZE
MERCER
SHELBY
LOGAN
UNION
DELAWARE
MORROW
KNOX
HOLMES
COSHOCTON
TUSCARAWAS
CARROLL
JEFFERSON
HARRISON
BELMONT
GUERNSEY
MUSKINGUM
LICKING
FRANKLIN
MADISON
CHAMPAIGN
CLARK
MIAMI
DARKE
PREBLE
MONTGOMERY
GREENE
FAYETTE
PICKAWAY
FAIRFIELD
PERRY
MORGAN
NOBLE
MONROE
WASHINGTON
ATHENS
HOCKING
VINTON
ROSS
CLINTON
WARREN
BUTLER
HAMILTON
CLERMONT
BROWN
HIGHLAND
ADAMS
PIKE
SCIOTO
JACKSON
GALLIA
LAWRENCE
MEIGS
Campbell Hill 1,550
HAMILTON
CLERMONT
KENTUCKY
Cincinnati
Covington
Newport
84°30'
LAKE ERIE
CLEVELAND
Parma
CUYAHOGA
SUMMIT
LAKE
81°30'
41°30'
N
Longitude West of Greenwich

and mineral products. Most industry is located in and around Oklahoma City and Tulsa, which also rank among the world's foremost gas and oil centers. The state ranks third in the nation in natural gas production.

Topographically, the state is largely a rolling plain sloping from northwest to southeast, with a mean altitude of 1,300 feet. About three-fourths of the state, especially the central area, consists of the Osage Plains section of the Central Lowlands. The Great Plains region, making up the northwestern panhandle, slopes from 4,973 feet at Black Mesa in the west (the state's highest point) to about 287 feet in the extreme Southeast. Vast wheat fields and broad grazing lands characterize much of the terrain, punctuated by such features as the Wichita, Arbuckle, Ouachita, and Ozark mountains in the southwest, southcenter, southeast and northeast, respectively. A segment of the West Gulf Coastal Plains covers the extreme southeastern corner of the state. A quarter of the land is forested, but only pine and hardwood in the southeast are commercially significant.

Various bands of buffalo-hunting Indians roamed the Oklahoma region before the coming of the first European, Spanish explorer Coronado, who crossed (1541) what is today the Oklahoma panhandle. All the area except it came under U.S. sovereignty via the Louisiana Purchase (1803), and a year later that part of the purchase north of present-day Louisiana was made the District of Louisiana, governed as part of Indiana Territory. The district became in turn the Territory of Louisiana (1805) and the Missouri Territory (1812).

In 1819, Arkansas Territory, including the present state of Oklahoma, was formed from a part of Missouri Territory. A few years later, the U.S. Government designated part of the region Indian Territory and used it for the forcible resettlement of the Five Civilized Tribes (Cherokee, Choctaw, Chickasaw, Creek, and Seminole), who had been living in relatively close contact witth white men of the southeastern states for more than 100 years. Some of these Indians pursued farming in the traditional Southern mold, even maintaining slaves. When the Civil War erupted, the Indians were caught up in it, fighting on both sides and suffering invasions from both Confederate and Union forces.

After the war, the five tribes were punished collectively for those Indians who had supported the Confederacy; the western part of the Indian Territory was taken from them, and much of it was assigned to other tribes in the country that the government wanted resettled. White encroachments, led by Kansas-bound Texas cattlemen, soon followed despite laws and Indian treaties; a number of cattle trails, including the famed Chisholm Trail, were forged across the state. The first railroad across the region (built 1870-72) brought still more white settlers. The influx was legalized when a large strip of land was opened for settlement on April 22, 1889. Some of the settlers who entered before the proper time were called "sooners," giving rise to Oklahoma's nickname, the Sooner State.

The western section of present-day Oklahoma was made Oklahoma Territory in 1890, and for a time Oklahoma and Indian (the "twin") Territories existed side by side. The Indians wanted separate admission to the Union, as the state of Sequoyah, but in 1907 the territories were merged and admitted as a single state.

Oklahoma's advances in the economic sphere include expanding aeroospace facilities in Tulsa, several tire manufacturing plants, one of the world's largest paper mills at Valliant in the southeastern section, and Western Electric, General Motors and Honeywell plants, the FAA center and Wilson & Co., all in Oklahoma City. The state's economy boomed during the seventies and its government finances are in excellent shape.

The Arkansas River navigation project, the largest single domestic project ever undertaken by the Army Corps of Engineers, has made Tulsa a port city via a new channel and system of locks dredged from Tulsa across Arkansas to the Mississippi River. In agriculture, conservation methods have been inaugurated since the Dust Bowl days of the 1930s and, in some areas, irrigation is used to offset frequent droughts. Wheat, hay, cotton, sorghum, soybeans, corn and peanuts are the principal crops.

Tourism in recent years has boomed with an increased advertising program, with much of the emphasis put on the state parks, lodges and recreation areas located on the system of large man-made lakes. Lake Texoma and Lake O' the Cherokees are favorites. Other tourist attractions include the Will Rogers Memorial (at Claremore, near his birthplace at Oologah), the Philbrook Art Center (Tulsa), Indian City U.S.A. (near Anadarko) with authentic copies of Indian villages of the early 1800s, Tsa-La-Gi Cherokee Indian village (Tahlequah) where "The Trail of Tears" pageant depicting the Cherokee removal to Oklahoma is performed during the summer, Chickasaw National Recreation Area near Sulphur, and the National Cowboy Hall of Fame and Western Heritage Center (Oklahoma City).

**Full name:** State of Oklahoma. **Origin of name:** From Choctaw meaning "Red People." **Inhabitant:** Oklahoman. **Capital:** Oklahoma City. **State motto:** Labor Omnia Vincit (Labor Conquers All Things). **Flag:** Symbols of war & peace on a blue field. **Seal:** Indian & white man shaking hands before justice, representing cooperation of all people of state; large star has symbols of the Five Civilized Tribes from the southeastern states, forced by the government to resettle in this region. **Flower:** Mistletoe. **Bird:** Scissor-tailed flycatcher. **Tree:** Redbud. **Song:** "Oklahoma!" **Nickname:** Sooner State.

**Governor:** George Nigh. **Annual salary:** $48,000. **Term:** 4 years. **Current term expires:** Jan. 1983. **Voting requirements:** 18 yrs. old & U.S. citizen; resident of state; registered with County Election Board. **U.S. Congressmen:** 6. **Entered Union:** 1907 (46th state).

**Location & boundaries:** South Central state: bounded on the north by Colorado & Kansas; on the east by Missouri & Arkansas; on the south by Texas & the Red River; & on the west by Texas & New Mexico. **Total area:** 69,956 sq. mi. (ranks 18th). **Extreme length:** 464 mi. **Extreme breadth:** 230 mi. **Chief rivers:** Red, Arkansas, Cimarron, Canadian. **Major lakes:** Texoma, Eufaula, Oologah Reservoir. **No. of counties:** 77.

**Population (1980 census):** 3,025,290 (ranks 26th). **Pop. increase (1970-80):** 18.2%. **Largest cities:** Oklahoma City, Tulsa, Lawton. **Pop. density:** 43.2 per sq. mi. (ranks 34th). **Pop. distribution: White**—2,597,783; **Black**—204,658; **Am. Indian, Eskimo and Aleut**—169,464; **Asian and Pacific Islander**—17,274; **Other**—36,087; **Spanish origin**—57,413. **Marriage rate (1979):** 15.4 per 1,000 people. **Divorce rate:** 7.9 per 1,000 people.

**State finances (1980). Revenue:** $3,433,000,000. **Expenditures:** $3,249,000,000. **State taxes:** $587.12 per capita. **State personal income tax:** Yes. **Public debt (1980):** $504.38 per capita. **Federal aid (1980):** $349.69 per capita. **Personal income (1981):** $10,210.

**Sectors of the economy (% of labor force employed in 1974):** Government (20%), Manufacturing (14.4%), Wholesale & retail trade (14.8%), Services (12.7%), Educational Services (9%), Construction (4.2%). **Leading products:** food items; machinery; petroleum and coal items; stone, clay & glass items; transportation equipment; fabricated metals; apparel. **Minerals:** petroleum and coal, natural gas & natural gas liquids, cement. **Agricultural products:** cattle, dairy items, hogs, wheat, hay, sorghum grain. **Avg. farm (1981):** 481 acres. **Avg. value of farm per acre:** $662.

**Highway expenditures per capita (1980):** $124.03. **Persons per motor vehicle (1981):** 1.11. **Minimum age for driver's license:** 16.

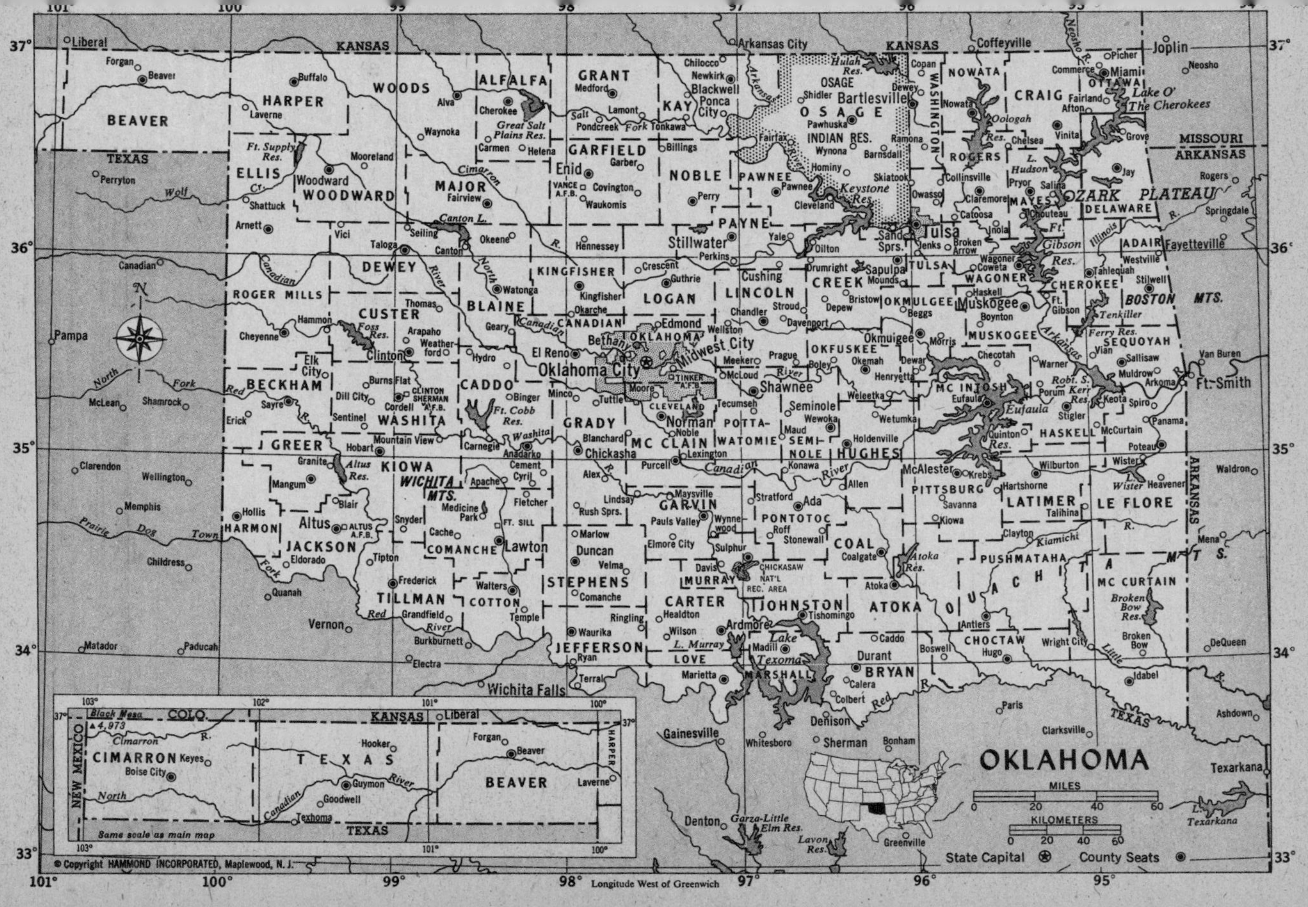
OKLAHOMA
MILES
KILOMETERS
State Capital
County Seats
Longitude West of Greenwich
Same scale as main map
© Copyright HAMMOND INCORPORATED, Maplewood, N. J.

**Gasoline tax:** 6.6¢ per gallon. **Diesel tax:** 6.5¢ per gallon. **Motor vehicle deaths (1980):** 31.7 per 100,000 people.

**Birthrate (1979):** 17.0 per 1,000 people. **Infant mortality rate per 1,000 births (1978):** 14.3. **Physicians per 100,000 pop. (1979):** 128. **Dentists per 100,000 pop. (1979):** 42. **Acceptable hospital beds (1979):** 5.8 per 1,000 people. **State expenditures per capita for health and hospitals (1980):** $67.11.

**Education expenditures (1977-78):** $434.15 per capita annually. **No. of pupils in public schools (1980):** 579,000. **No. of institutions of higher learning (1978-79):** 43. **Public school expenditure per pupil in attendance (1978-79):** $1,941. **Avg. salary of public school teachers (1979-80):** $13,550. **No. full-time teachers (1980):** 34,950. **Educational attainment of adult population (1976):** 12.4 median yrs. of school completed: 2.9% with less than 5 years of education; 11.7% with 4 yrs. of college.

**Telephones (1979):** 57 per 100 people. **State Chamber of Commerce:** Oklahoma State Chamber of Commerce, 4020 N. Lincoln Blvd., Oklahoma City, Oklahoma 73105.

## OREGON

With more than 30 million acres of trees (nearly half the state's total area), Oregon is the nation's leading lumber state. Its awesome scenery includes mountains, plains, lush valleys, and immense forests. The 400-mile Pacific coast is marked by the thickly forested Coast Range and the Klamath Mountains that parallel it.

There are four other general land areas: the Cascade Mountains, the Willamette Valley between the coastal elevations and the Cascades, the Columbia Plateau, and the Basin and Range Region.

The Cascade Range is a climatic dividing line: there is mild, moist weather in the west, and in the east dry weather that is warmer in summer and colder in winter than the west's.

Except for the section in the southeast known as the Basin and Range Region, the entire area east of the Cascades is called the Columbia Plateau; this plateau, comprising two-thirds of the state, was formed thousands of years ago when lava gushed forth from the Earth's crust, which has since been covered by rolling plains, and, along the desolate southern edge, the Harney Desert. It was across these plains that settlers from the East came, along the Oregon Trail.

Portland, 100 miles inland, is reached from the Pacific via the Columbia River, and is one of the West Coast's major ports; the Portland area contains about half of Oregon's total population.

Oregon produces about a fifth of the nation's lumber and a majority of our plywood. Centered in the Willamette Valley, wood processing is the state's leading manufacturing industry.

There is some mining in the state, principally of nickel, gemstones, and construction materials. Agriculture, shipping, fishing (mainly for Chinook and silver salmon), metal and food processing, and tourism are also economically significant. Attractions include Hells Canyon, Mount Hood, and Crater Lake, a brilliantly blue, clear body of water that is the principal feature of the national park bearing its name; the nation's deepest lake (1,932 feet), it is six miles wide and was formed 6,600 years ago when the peak of Mount Mazama, in which the lake is set, collapsed after violent volcanic activity. Another tourist attraction is Kah-Nee-Ta Vacation Resort in the Warm Springs Indian Reservation, which was developed by 2,000 Northwest tribesmen; it offers hot mineral baths, swimming, fishing, and riding.

Chinook, Tillamook, Clackama, and Multnomah Indians were among the Oregon Country's earliest known inhabitants. Spanish seamen, sailing from Mexico to the Philippines, are thought to have been the first Europeans to sight the Oregon coast, in the 1500s and 1600s. Captain Cook, seeking the Northwest Passage to the Atlantic, charted some of the coastline in 1778. The Columbia River was discovered in 1792, and the Lewis and Clark expedition passed through the region in 1805.

The nineteenth century was marked by the conflict of British and American claims to the area that were eventually resolved by treaty in 1846. Two years later, Oregon became a territory, which until 1853 also included present-day Washington. Statehood came in 1859. In 1860 the discovery of gold in what is now Idaho turned Portland into a vital trade center for the Pacific Northwest. Transcontinental rail service came to Oregon in 1883.

In the early part of the 20th century, a series of reform measures were enacted in what came to be known as the Oregon System; this system, designed to make government more responsive to those governed, featured a referendum amendment, a direct primary, and a recall provision. Oregon women were given the vote in 1912.

The state also has developed a broad program for improving the environment and has given its Department of Environmental Quality the power to enforce the regulations. In addition, Oregon has adopted a Scenic Waterways plan for state ownership of land along many rivers in the state as well as a law for public ownership of the ocean beaches. Oregon was a pioneer in outlawing throwaway beverage containers and fluorocarbon aerosol cans. One of the first states to abolish criminal penalties for the possession of small amounts of marijuana, Oregon in 1979 legalized the sale of marijuana for legitimate medical purposes.

The great eruption of Mount St. Helens volcano in neighboring Washington on May 18, 1980, had little effect on Oregon, but the lesser eruption of May 24 sprayed dust and ash over parts of northern Oregon, damaging crops and making roads impassable.

The nationwide 1981-82 slump in new housing starts produced widespread distress in Oregon's lumber industry.

**Full name:** State of Oregon. **Origin of name:** Probably from Spanish, Orejon, meaning "Big-eared men." **Inhabitant:** Oregonian. **Capital:** Salem. **State motto:** The Union. **Flag:** State seal & lettering in yellow on a blue field. **Seal:** Departing British man-of-war & arriving American merchant ship symbolize end of British influence & rise of American power; sheaf of grain, pickax & plow represent mining & agriculture. **Flower:** Oregon grape. **Bird:** Western meadowlark. **Fish:** Chinook salmon; **Rock:** Thunderegg. **Tree:** Douglas fir. **Song:** "Oregon, My Oregon." **Nickname:** Beaver State.

**Governor:** Victor G. Atiyeh. **Annual salary:** $55,423. **Term:** 4 years. **Current term expires:** Jan. 1983. **Voting requirements:** 18 yrs. old & U.S. citizen; must be registered and resident of state 20 days prior to election. **U.S. Congressmen:** 5. **Entered Union:** 1859 (33rd state).

**Location & boundaries:** Pacific state: bounded on the north by the Columbia River & Washington; on the east by Idaho & the Snake River; on the south by Nevada & California; & on the west by the Pacific Ocean. **Total area:** 97,073 sq. mi. (ranks 10th). **Extreme length:** 295 mi. **Extreme breadth:** 395 mi. **Coastline:** 360 mi. **Chief rivers:** Columbia, Snake, Willamette. **Major lakes:** Upper Klamath, Malheur, Crater. **No. of counties:** 36.

**Population (1980 census):** 2,633,149 (ranks 30th). **Pop. increase (1970-80):** 25.9%. **Largest cities:** Portland, Eugene, Salem. **Pop. density:** 27.1 per sq. mi. (ranks 39th). **Pop. distribution: White**—2,490,192; **Black**—37,059; **Am. Indian, Eskimo and Aleut**—27,309; **Asian and Pacific Islander**—34,767; **Other**—43,336; **Spanish origin**—65,833. **Marriage rate (1979):** 8.7 per 1,000 people. **Divorce rate:** 7.0 per 1,000 people.

**State finances (1980). Revenue:** $4,041,000,000. **Expenditures:** $3,456,000,000. **State taxes:** $552.74 per capita. **State personal**

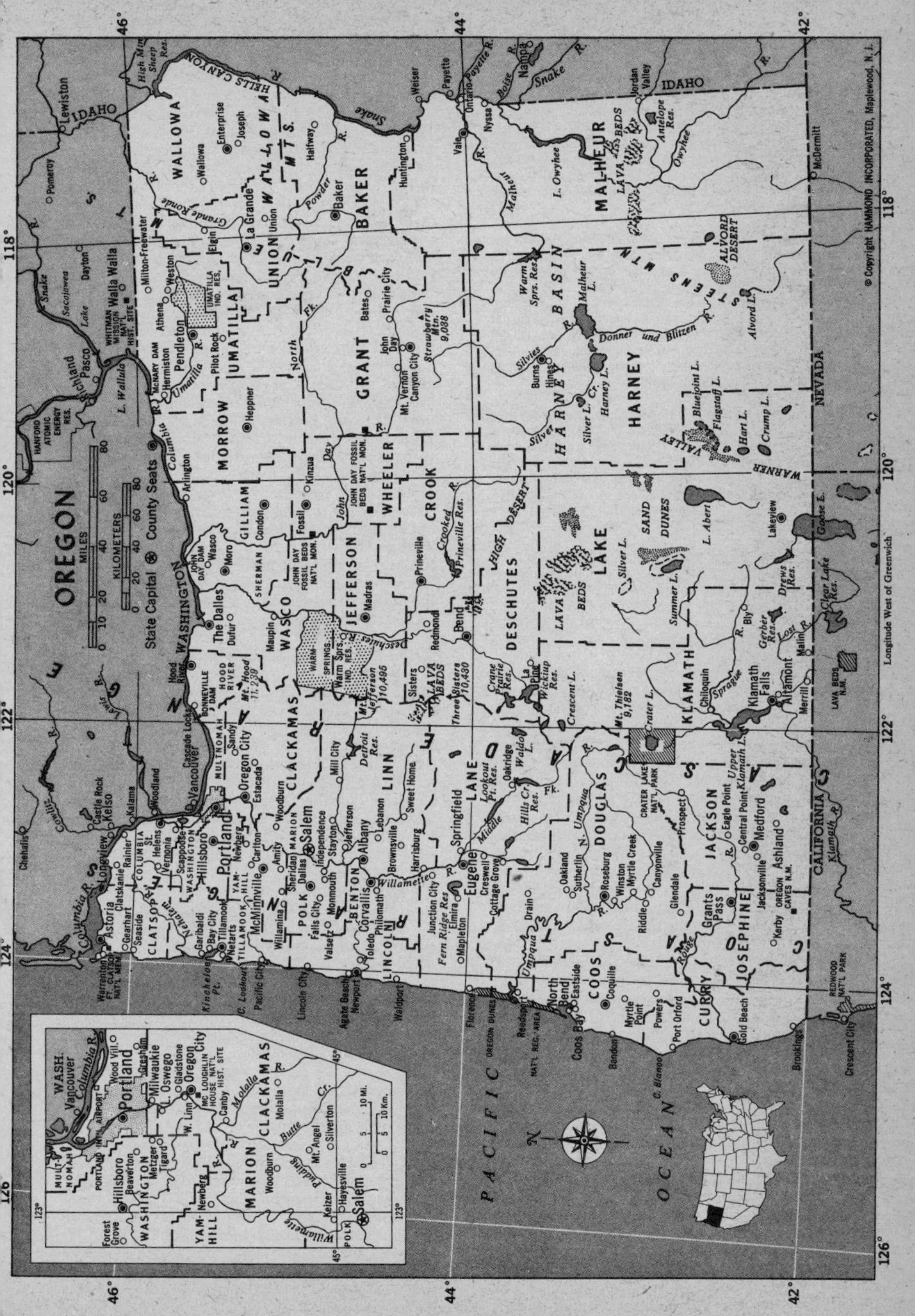
OREGON
MILES
KILOMETERS
State Capital ⊛ County Seats
WASHINGTON
IDAHO
NEVADA
CALIFORNIA
PACIFIC OCEAN
CLATSOP
COLUMBIA
TILLAMOOK
WASHINGTON
MULTNOMAH
HOOD RIVER
WASCO
SHERMAN
GILLIAM
MORROW
UMATILLA
UNION
WALLOWA
BAKER
GRANT
WHEELER
JEFFERSON
CROOK
DESCHUTES
HARNEY
MALHEUR
LAKE
KLAMATH
JACKSON
JOSEPHINE
CURRY
COOS
DOUGLAS
LANE
LINN
BENTON
LINCOLN
POLK
MARION
YAMHILL
CLACKAMAS
Portland
Salem
Eugene
Medford
Bend
Pendleton
Baker
Klamath Falls
Mt. Hood 11,239
Mt. Jefferson 10,495
Three Sisters 10,480
Mt. Thielsen 9,182
Strawberry Mtn. 9,038
CRATER LAKE NAT'L PARK
HELLS CANYON
WALLOWA MTS.
STEENS MTN
HIGH DESERT
ALVORD DESERT
Longitude West of Greenwich
© Copyright HAMMOND INCORPORATED, Maplewood, N.J.

**Income tax:** Yes. **Public debt (1980):** $1,855.79 per capita. **Federal aid (1980):** $385.51 per capita. **Personal income (1981):** $9,991.

**Sectors of the economy (% of labor force employed in 1970):** Wholesale and retail trade (22%), Manufacturing (21%), Government (17%), Educational Services (10%), Services (7%), Construction (6%). **Leading products:** lumber & wood items, food items, paper items, machinery, fabricated metals, printing & publishing. **Agricultural products:** wheat, livestock, barley, oats, hops, legumes, potatoes, berries, fruits, nuts, truck crops, dairy and poultry products, sugar beets, corn, green beans and peppermint. **Fishing:** salmon, tuna, bottom fish (sole, rockfish, halibut, cod, etc.) and shellfish. **Avg. farm (1981):** 517 acres. **Avg. value of farm per acre:** $605.

**Highway expenditures per capita (1980):** $163.89. **Persons per motor vehicle (1981):** 1.24. **Minimum age for driver's license:** 16. **Gasoline tax:** 8¢ per gallon. **Diesel tax:** 8¢ per gallon. **Motor vehicle deaths (1980):** 24.5 per 100,000 people.

**Birthrate (1979):** 16.5 per 1,000 people. **Infant mortality rate per 1,000 births (1978):** 12.9. **Physicians per 100,000 pop. (1979):** 177. **Dentists per 100,000 pop. (1979):** 69. **Acceptable hospital beds (1979):** 4.4 per 1,000 people. **State expenditures per capita for health and hospitals (1980):** $80.68.

**Education expenditures (1977-78):** $616.61 per capita annually. **No. of pupils in public schools (1980):** 463,000. **No. of institutions of higher learning (1978-79):** 43. **Public school expenditure per pupil in attendance (1978-79):** $2,487. **Avg. salary of public school teachers (1979-80):** $17,070. **No. full-time teachers (1980):** 26,250. **Educational attainment of adult population (1978):** 12.7 median yrs. of school completed: 1.1% with less than 5 years of education; 15.4% with 4 yrs. of college.

**Telephones (1979):** 55 per 100 people. **State Chamber of Commerce:** Associated Oregon Industries, Inc., 1149 Court Street, N.E., P.O. Box 12519, Salem, Oregon 97309.

## PENNSYLVANIA'

Called the "Keystone State" because of its central location among the 13 Colonies, Pennsylvania is today an important economic center and a rich repository of Americana. The state, which enjoys an abundant water supply, is the nation's fourth most populous, and manufacturing, mining, farming, and tourism are all important to its economy.

Pennsylvania produces nearly all the country's hard coal and a fourth of its steel. Oil is also important, although not so much so as in the 1890s; the first oil well in the world was drilled (1859) near Titusville. Dairy farming flourishes today in the northeast, as does cattle raising in the southwest; throughout the fertile, well-farmed southeast countryside can be seen the highly decorated barns of the Pennsylvania Dutch.

Pittsburgh was the home (1920) of the first radio broadcasting station, and the first electric computer was built (1945) in Philadelphia; these cities, along with Erie, provide the state with three fine ports. Philadelphia is the dominantly large city of the eastern region (as Pittsburgh is of the western).

Roughly rectangular, the state is crossed from west to east by the Erie Lowland, Appalachian Plateau (by far the largest single region), Great Appalachian Valley, Blue Ridge, Piedmont Plateau, New England Uplands, and Atlantic Coastal Plain. Among the many attractions are 495 state park and recreation areas, as well as Valley Forge and Gettysburg Battlefield national shrines, scenes of decisive events in the American Revolution and the Civil War.

The state's early history is shared in large part with neighboring Delaware, which it once contained. Swedes made the first permanent settlement (1643) in the Pennsylvania region at Tinicum Island in the Schuylkill River, but Swedish rule soon gave way (1655) to Dutch. The English supplanted the Dutch in 1664, as King Charles II put the region under the control of his brother James, Duke of York. In 1681, the king granted the region to Quaker William Penn, naming it after Penn's father, an admiral in the Royal Navy to whom the king was indebted. Penn's era, which except for a brief interruption (1692-94) lasted until his death in 1718, was an enlightened and fruitful one.

The so-called Charter of Privileges (1701) gave Pennsylvania the most liberal of colonial governments, and there shortly followed a cultural flowering as well. Benjamin Franklin of Philadelphia published *The Pennsylvania Gazette* (1729-1766) and the *Poor Richard's Almanack* (1732-1757), in addition to pursuing his interest in politics and science. The nation's first magazine, *The American Magazine, or A Monthly View of the Political State of the British Colonies*, was established (1741) in Philadelphia. Penn's notably fair-minded dealings with the Indians, including his famous treaty, kept the region free of the usual frontier bloodshed. But Penn's successors—especially his son Thomas, who took over in 1746—lacked his vision and conciliatory gifts, and troubles with the French and Indians lasted from 1754 until the suppression of Pontiac's Rebellion in 1763. Pennsylvania was involved at various times in boundary disputes with four other colonies: Maryland, Virginia, Connecticut, and New York. The bitterest wrangle was the one with Connecticut over the Wyoming Valley, which gave rise to the Pennamite Wars (1769-71 and 1784). The northwestern "Erie triangle" was bought first from the Indians, and later from the Federal Government, following a 1789 agreement with New York setting the northern border at the 42nd parallel; the parcel was purchased to secure an Erie port for the colony. The establishment of the Mason-Dixon line (1767) settled Pennsylvania's differences with Maryland and Virginia.

After the American Revolution, in which Pennsylvania played a central role, settlement increased in the western region and in the upper Susquehanna Valley. The country's first paved road, the Philadelphia-Lancaster Turnpike, was completed in 1794. In 1811, a Robert Fulton steamboat was launched at Pittsburgh and became the first to traverse the Ohio and Mississippi rivers. The Schuylkill Canal, one of the nations first long canals (completed 1825), connected Philadelphia and Reading.

The state strongly supported the Union in the Civil War; only New York contributed more troops.

The most widespread flood in the state's history struck in 1972, when Hurricane Agnes, diminished to a tropical storm, remained stationary over the central part of the state for 24 hours. Officials termed it the worst natural disaster in the state's history. In 1975 the Susquehanna again overflowed in the wake of Hurricane Eloise, with damage estimated at over $200 million.

On March 28, 1979, a reactor cooling system at the Three Mile Island nuclear power plant south of Harrisburg malfunctioned in the nation's worst nuclear accident in history. The possibility of a core meltdown or an explosion of the hydrogen gas bubble that had formed in the overheated reactor posed a real threat to nearby residents. Although neither catastrophe occurred, some 144,000 people were evacuated at a cost of $18 million. A 12-member commission appointed by President Carter to investigate the accident issued its report in October 1979: It blamed the plant operator Metropolitan Edison for, among other things, failing to train its personnel adequately to cope with malfunctions. However, the study also concluded that the accident had caused no significant health problems. The Nuclear Regulatory Commission fined Metropolitan Edison $155,000, and only a tie vote on the

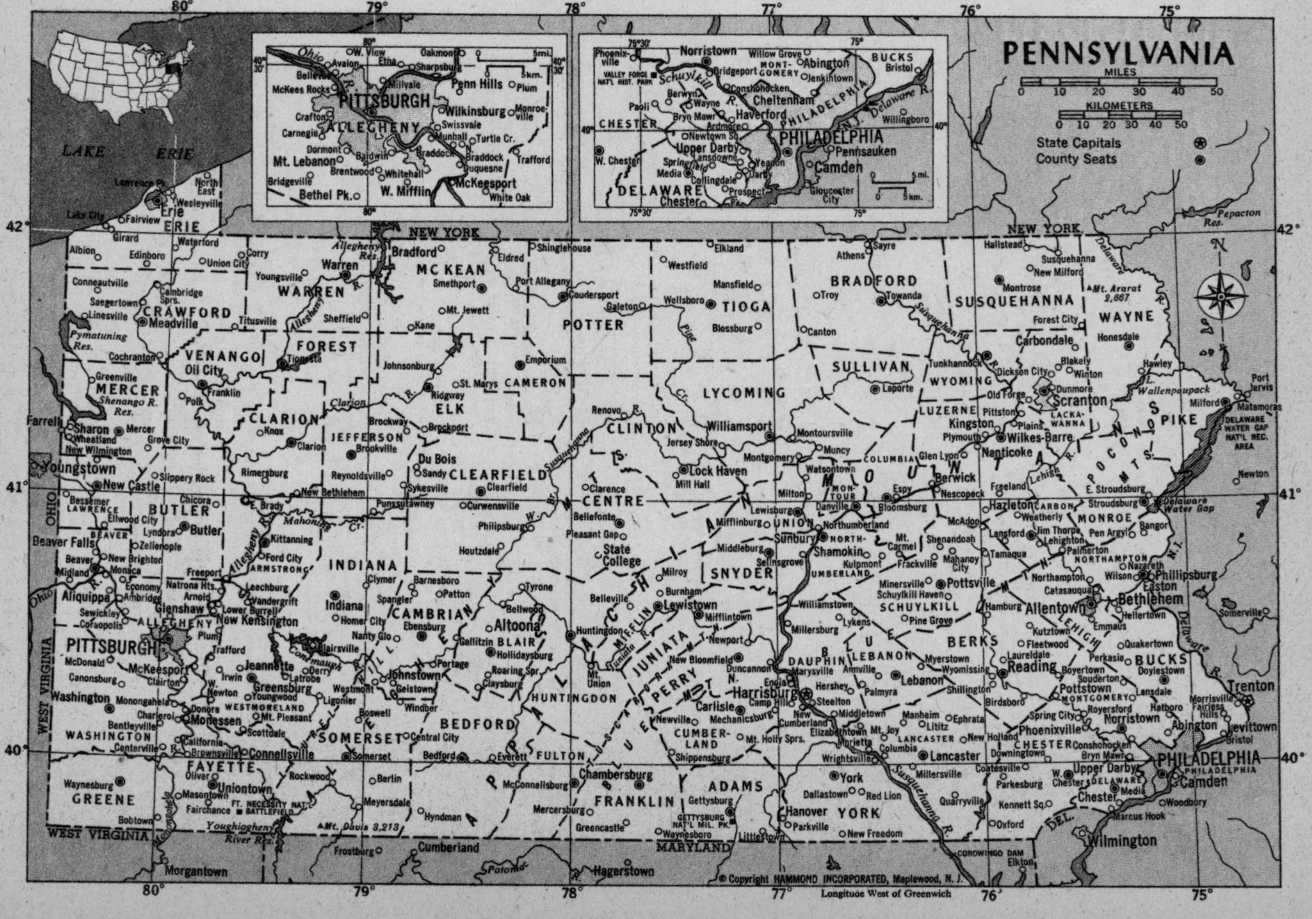
PENNSYLVANIA
MILES
0 10 20 30 40 50
KILOMETERS
0 10 20 30 40 50
State Capitals
County Seats
ERIE
CRAWFORD
WARREN
MC KEAN
POTTER
TIOGA
BRADFORD
SUSQUEHANNA
WAYNE
PIKE
MERCER
VENANGO
FOREST
ELK
CAMERON
CLINTON
LYCOMING
SULLIVAN
WYOMING
LUZERNE
MONROE
LAWRENCE
BUTLER
CLARION
JEFFERSON
CLEARFIELD
CENTRE
UNION
COLUMBIA
CARBON
NORTHAMPTON
LEHIGH
BEAVER
ARMSTRONG
INDIANA
CAMBRIA
BLAIR
HUNTINGDON
JUNIATA
SNYDER
SCHUYLKILL
BERKS
BUCKS
ALLEGHENY
WESTMORELAND
PERRY
DAUPHIN
LEBANON
WASHINGTON
SOMERSET
BEDFORD
FULTON
FRANKLIN
ADAMS
YORK
LANCASTER
CHESTER
DELAWARE
PHILADELPHIA
GREENE
FAYETTE
Harrisburg
Pittsburgh
Philadelphia
Erie
Scranton
Wilkes-Barre
Allentown
Bethlehem
Reading
Lancaster
Altoona
Johnstown
LAKE ERIE
NEW YORK
MARYLAND
WEST VIRGINIA
OHIO
© Copyright HAMMOND INCORPORATED, Maplewood, N. J.
Longitude West of Greenwich

panel saved the utility company from losing its license. The NRC also cited Babcock & Wilcox, designer of the damaged reactor, for failure to report safety information that may have avoided or lessened the malfunction.

A second accident at Three Mile Island took place in February 1980 when about 1,000 gallons of radioactive water leaked into an auxiliary building. Small amounts of radioactivity were released into the atmosphere and 11 workers were evacuated during the 90-minute crisis, but no health injury was reported.

In November 1981, it was reported that it would take six years and $1 billion to clean up the site.

**Full name:** Commonwealth of Pennsylvania. **Origin of name:** In honor of William Penn, father of the founder. **Inhabitant:** Pennsylvanian. **Capital:** Harrisburg. **State motto:** Virtue, Liberty & Independence. **Flag:** State seal & motto supported by two horses on gold-bordered blue field. **Seal:** Eagle, ship, plow & sheaves of wheat stand for strength, commerce & agricultural abundance; stalk of corn & olive branch represent peace & plenty. **Flower:** Mountain laurel. **Bird:** Ruffed grouse. **Tree:** Hemlock. **Song:** None. **Nickname:** Keystone State.

**Governor:** Richard L. Thornburgh. **Annual salary:** $66,000. **Term:** 4 years. **Current term expires:** Jan. 1983. **Voting requirements:** 18 yrs. old & U.S. citizen; resident of state (or district) for 30 days prior to election day. **U.S. Congressmen:** 23. **Entered Union:** 1787 (2nd state).

**Location & boundries:** Middle Atlantic state: bounded on the north by New York; on the east by the Delaware River, New York & New Jersey; on the southeast by Delaware & the Delaware River; on the south by Maryland & West Virginia; on the west by West Virginia & Ohio; & on the northwest by Lake Erie. **Total area:** 45,308 sq. mi. (ranks 33rd). **Extreme length:** 307 mi. **Extreme breadth:** 169 mi. **Shoreline:** 51 mi. **Chief rivers:** Delaware, Allegheny, Susquehanna. **Major lakes:** Erie, Wallenpaupack; Pymatuning & Bear Creek Reservoirs. **No. of counties:** 67.

**Population (1980 census):** 11,863,895 (ranks 4th). **Pop. increase (1970-80):** 0.5%. **Largest cities:** Philadelphia, Pittsburgh, Erie, Allentown. **Pop. density:** 261.8 per sq. mi. (ranks 8th). **Pop. distribution: White**—10,654,325; **Black**—1,047,609; **Am. Indian, Eskimo and Aleut**—9,459; **Asian and Pacific Islander**—64,381; **Other**—90,954; **Spanish origin**—154,004. **Marriage rate (1979):** 8.0 per 1,000 people. **Divorce rate:** 3.4 per 1,000 people.

**State finances (1980). Revenue:** $14,004,000,000. **Expenditures:** $12,644,000,000. **State taxes:** $610.16 per capita. **State personal income tax:** No. **Public debt (1980):** $534.92 per capita. **Federal aid (1980):** $380.52 per capita. **Personal income (1981):** $10,373.

**Sectors of the economy (% of labor force employed in 1970):** Manufacturing (34%), Wholesale and retail trade (19%), Government (13%), Educational Services (7%), Services (6%), Construction (5%). **Leading products:** primary and fabricated metals, food items, machinery, chemicals, apparel. **Minerals:** coal, cement, stone, sand & gravel. **Agricultural Products:** dairy items, cattle, hogs, hay, corn, oats, wheat. **Avg. farm (1981):** 145 acres. **Avg. value of farm per acre:** $1,447.

**Highway expenditures per capita (1980):** $73.14. **Persons per motor vehicle (1981):** 1.66 **Minimum age for driver's license:** 17. **Gasoline tax:** 11¢ per gallon. **Diesel tax:** 11¢ per gallon. **Motor vehicle deaths (1980):** 17.6 per 100,000 people.

**Birthrate (1979):** 13.5 per 1,000 people. **Infant mortality rate per 1,000 births (1978):** 13.7. **Physicians per 100,000 pop. (1979):** 183. **Dentists per 100,000 pop. (1979):** 55. **Acceptable hospital beds (1979):** 7.3 per 1,000 people. **State expenditures per capita for health and hospitals (1980):** $77.09.

**Education expenditures (1977-78):** $433.00 per capita annually. **No. of pupils in public schools (1980):** 1,900,000. **No. of institutions of higher learning (1978-79):** 178. **Public school expenditure per pupil in attendance (1978-79):** $2,524. **Avg. salary of public school teachers (1979-80):** $17,270. **No. full-time teachers (1980):** 130,500. **Educational attainment of adult population (1976):** 12.4 median yrs. of school completed: 2.3% with less than 5 years of education; 11.9% with 4 yrs. of college.

**Telephones (1979):** 62 per 100 people. **State Chamber of Commerce:** Pennsylvania Chamber of Commerce, 222 North Third Street, Harrisburg, Pennsylvania 17101.

## RHODE ISLAND

Rhode Island, the nation's smallest state, is not an island, although many small islands are contained within it, including one in Narragansett Bay, Aquidneck Island.

The Bay, which extends inland 28 miles from the Atlantic Ocean, is the predominant feature of the state's eastern section, which comprises about two-thirds of the total area and includes Providence, Pawtucket, and most of Rhode Island's other major cities. The remaining northeastern third of the state is rough, hilly terrain rising east to northwest from 200 to 800 feet above sea level—this section being a part of the New England Uplands, which extend from Maine to Connecticut. Offshore, ten miles south of the mainland, is Block Island, an important navigation landmark. Sixty-seven percent of the state's area is forested, but mostly with "restocked" trees not yet suitable for lumber. Damaging hurricanes occasionally plague the coast.

Once dominated economically by the textile industry, Rhode Island has added many new industries, in a continuing drive toward greater diversification. The Providence area is a major center for the manufacture of jewelry and silverware. Small commercial fishing fleets operate out of several ports.

Explorer Giovanni da Verrazano is thought to have been the first European to visit (1524) the region. Adriaen Block explored there in 1614. In 1636, Roger Williams, looking for a place where "persons distressed for conscience" could go, left Puritan-controlled Massachusetts and founded Providence, the state's first settlement. Two years later Williams organized the country's first Baptist congregation.

Despite harsh, costly combat with the Indians in King Philip's War (1675-76), the region prospered, thanks in large measure to the "triangular trade"—vessels carried rum from Newport to Africa, slaves from there to the West Indies, and molasses from there to Newport, where it was made into rum. Later, Rhode Island renounced slavery, prohibiting (1774) the importation of slaves; it also strongly backed the Union in the Civil War. The economic gap that the passing of the triangular trade left was soon filled by the rapid growth of manufacturing, spurred by Samuel Slater's pioneering in mechanized textile production and by a heavy influx of French Canadian, Italian, Portuguese and Polish immigrants who provided an ample labor pool.

From its beginnings, Rhode Island has been famous for its insistence on political and religious freedom, attracting oppressed and refuge-seeking settlers, and the state's rebellious, iconoclastic character streak soon became evident. In 1769, Newport rebels scuttled the British revenue ship *Liberty* and, three years later, in protest to British trade and navigation laws, a group of Providence men burned the English ship *Gaspee* to the water's edge in Narragansett Bay where it had run aground. The colony was the first of the original 13 to declare independence from England. Rhode Island was the last of the original 13 states to ratify (1790) the Constitution.

Rhode Island also balked at Jefferson's Embargo Act of 1807, and in the War of 1812 it refused to allow its militia to serve outside its borders. Thomas Wilson Dorr and other Rhode Islanders made an abortive revolution in 1842 ("Dorr's Rebellion"), which nonetheless effected a small measure of legislative reform.

In the late 1800s Newport became a fashionable summer home for the very rich, and many palatial

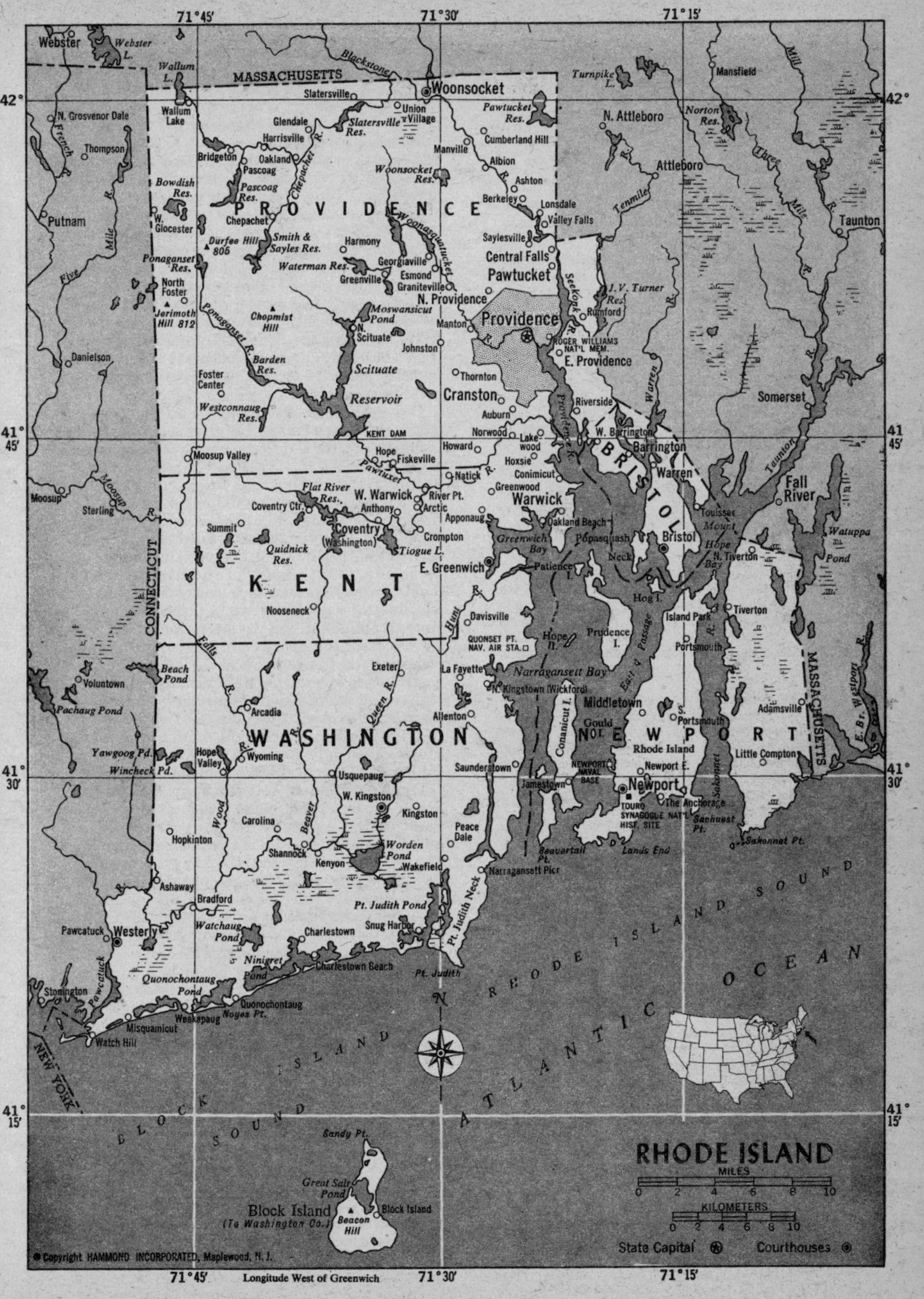
RHODE ISLAND
MILES
0 2 4 6 8 10
KILOMETERS
0 2 4 6 8 10
State Capital
Courthouses
© Copyright HAMMOND INCORPORATED, Maplewood, N. J.
Longitude West of Greenwich
71°45'
71°30'
71°15'
42°
41° 45'
41° 30'
41° 15'
MASSACHUSETTS
CONNECTICUT
NEW YORK
PROVIDENCE
KENT
WASHINGTON
BRISTOL
NEWPORT
RHODE ISLAND SOUND
BLOCK ISLAND SOUND
ATLANTIC OCEAN
Narragansett Bay
Webster
Webster L.
Wallum L.
Wallum Lake
Blackstone
Slatersville
Woonsocket
Union Village
Pawtucket Res.
Turnpike L.
Mansfield
N. Grosvenor Dale
Glendale
Slatersville Res.
Harrisville
Cumberland Hill
N. Attleboro
Norton Res.
Thompson
Bridgeton
Oakland
Pascoag
Chepachet R.
Manville
Albion
Attleboro
Woonsocket Res.
Ashton
Bowdish Res.
Pascoag Res.
Berkeley
Lonsdale
Valley Falls
Taunton
Putnam
W. Glocester
Chepachet
Durfee Hill 805
Smith & Sayles Res.
Harmony
Saylesville
Central Falls
Pawtucket
Ponaganset Res.
Waterman Res.
Georgiaville
Esmond
Greenville
Graniteville
N. Providence
Seekonk R.
J. V. Turner Res.
Rumford
North Foster
Jerimoth Hill 812
Chopmist Hill
Moswansicut Pond
Manton
Providence
N. Scituate
Johnston
ROGER WILLIAMS NAT'L MEM.
E. Providence
Danielson
Barden Res.
Scituate Reservoir
Thornton
Foster Center
Cranston
Westconnaug Res.
Auburn
Riverside
Somerset
KENT DAM
Norwood
Lakewood
W. Barrington
Barrington
Hope
Fiskeville
Howard
Hoxsie
Warren
Fall River
Moosup Valley
Natick
Conimicut
Moosup
Sterling
Flat River Res.
W. Warwick
River Pt.
Greenwood
Warwick
Coventry Ctr.
Anthony
Arctic
Apponaug
Touisset
Mount Hope
Summit
Coventry (Washington)
Crompton
Oakland Beach
Popasquash Neck
Bristol
Watuppa Pond
Quidnick Res.
Tiogue L.
Greenwich Bay
N. Tiverton
Hope Bay
E. Greenwich
Patience I.
Hog I.
Nooseneck
Tiverton
Davisville
Island Park
QUONSET PT. NAV. AIR STA.
Hope I.
Prudence I.
Portsmouth
Beach Pond
Exeter
La Fayette
Voluntown
N. Kingstown (Wickford)
East Passage
Pachaug Pond
Arcadia
Queen R.
Allenton
Middletown
S. Portsmouth
Adamsville
Conanicut I.
Gould I.
Rhode Island
Yawgoog Pd.
Wincheck Pd.
Hope Valley
Wyoming
Saunderstown
NEWPORT NAVAL BASE
Newport E.
Little Compton
Usquepaug
Jamestown
Newport
W. Kingston
TOURO SYNAGOGUE NAT'L HIST. SITE
The Anchorage
Sakonnet R.
Sachuest Pt.
Kingston
Carolina
Peace Dale
Hopkinton
Wood R.
Beaver R.
Worden Pond
Beavertail Pt.
Lands End
Sakonnet Pt.
Shannock
Kenyon
Wakefield
Narragansett Pier
Ashaway
Bradford
Pt. Judith Pond
Pt. Judith Neck
Pawcatuck
Westerly
Watchaug Pond
Charlestown
Snug Harbor
Ninigret Pond
Charlestown Beach
Pt. Judith
Stonington
Quonochontaug Pond
Quonochontaug
Noyes Pt.
Weekapaug
Misquamicut
Watch Hill
Sandy Pt.
Great Salt Pond
Block Island
(To Washington Co.)
Beacon Hill

mansions were built, some of which are now open for tourists to visit. Today Newport is the country's yachting capital, host to the America's Cup, Newport-Bermuda, and transatlantic races. In 1976, Newport was the first port of welcome for the spectacular fleet of Tall Ships, which sailed from throughout the world to commemorate the bicentennial of the United States. The flotilla assembled was one of the largest ever.

Rhode Island is presently trying to broaden its economic base by expanding its tourist industry. Music festivals and dramas highlight the summer's entertainment possibilities, along with fishing tournaments and regattas.

Newport, with its great mansions and the Touro Synagogue National Historic Site, and the offshore vacation resort of Block Island are major tourist attractions.

**Full name:** State of Rhode Island & Providence Plantations. **Origin of name:** In honor of the Isle of Rhodes: name chosen by General Court of Colony. **Inhabitant:** Rhode Islander. **Capital:** Providence. **State motto:** Hope. **Flag:** Golden anchor & 12 gold stars on white field. **Seal:** State motto printed above anchor, symbolizing hope; date 1636 was year Roger Williams founded Providence. **Flower:** Violet. **Bird:** Rhode Island red. **Tree:** Red maple. **Song:** "Rhode Island." **Nickname:** Little Rhody.

**Governor:** John Joseph Garrahy. **Annual salary:** $49,500. **Term:** 2 years. **Current term expires:** Jan. 1983. **Voting requirements:** 18 yrs. old & U.S. citizen; resident of city or town 30 days; positive identification. **U.S. Congressmen:** 2. **Entered Union:** 1790 (13th state).

**Location & boundaries:** New England state: bounded on the north & east by Massachusetts; on the west by Connecticut; & on the south by New York where Block Island Sound meets Long Island Sound in the Atlantic Ocean. **Total area:** 1,212 sq. mi. (ranks 50th). **Extreme length:** 48 mi. **Extreme breadth:** 37 mi. **Coastline:** 40 mi. **Chief rivers:** Sakonnet, Blackstone, Woonasquatuket, Pawtuxet. **Major lakes:** Worden Pond, Scituate Reservoir. **No. of counties:** 5.

**Population (1980 census):** 947,154 (ranks 40th). **Pop. increase (1970-80):** −0.3%. **Largest cities:** Providence, Warwick, Cranston, Pawtucket. **Pop. density:** 781.5 per sq. mi. (ranks 2nd). **Pop. distribution: White**—896.692; **Black**—27,584; **Am. Indian, Eskimo and Aleut**—2,898; **Asian and Pacific Islander**— 5,303; **Other**—14,677; **Spanish origin**— 19,707. **Marriage rate (1979):** 7.9 per 1,000 people. **Divorce rate:** 3.9 per 1,000 people.

**State finances (1980). Revenue:** $1,393,000,000. **Expenditures:** $1,361,000,000. **State taxes:** $581.61 per capita. **State personal income tax:** Yes. **Public debt (1980):** $1,544.98 per capita. **Federal aid (1980):** $504.04 per capita. **Personal income (1981):** $10,466.

**Sectors of the economy (% of labor force employed in 1970):** Manufacturing (35%), Wholesale and retail trade (19%), Government (16%), Educational Services (8%), Services (6%), Construction (5%). **Leading products:** jewelry & silverware, textile items, primary metals, machinery, fabricated metals, electrical equipment, rubber and plastic items. **Avg. farm (1981):** 87 acres. **Avg. value of farm per acre:** $2,693.

**Highway expenditures per capita (1980):** $55.30. **Persons per motor vehicle (1981):** 1.48. **Minimum age for driver's license:** 16. **Gasoline tax:** 12¢ per gallon. **Diesel tax:** 12¢ per gallon. **Motor vehicle deaths (1980):** 13.6 per 100,000 people.

**Birthrate (1979):** 12.8 per 1,000 people. **Infant mortality rate per 1,000 births (1978):** 13.6. **Physicians per 100,000 pop. (1979):** 206. **Dentists per 100,000 pop. (1979):** 56. **Acceptable hospital beds (1979):** 6.5 per 1,000 people. **State expenditures per capita for health and hospitals (1980):** $145.89.

**Education expenditures (1977-78):** $484.31 per capita annually. **No. of pupils in public schools (1980):** 149,000. **No. of institutions of higher learning (1978-79):** 13. **Public school expenditure per pupil in attendance (1978-79):** $2,450. **Average salary of public school teachers (1979-80):** $20,615. **No. full-time teachers (1980):** 10,800. **Educational attainment of adult population (1976):** 12.4 median yrs. of school completed: 3.4% with less than 5 years of education; 14.9% with 4 yrs. of college.

**Telephones (1979):** 57 per 100 people. **State Chamber of Commerce:** Rhode Island Chamber of Commerce Federation, 91 Park Street, Providence, Rhode Island 02908.

## SOUTH CAROLINA

South Carolina, where the Civil War began, was the first state to secede from the Union. One of the 13 Colonies, it is particularly rich in historic sites, which help draw a growing number of tourists annually. Vivid contrasts often confront the visitor: inlet-dotted swampland gives way to hill country, and estates graced by handsome Georgian homes are set off by poor areas in which shacks are not uncommon. Hilton Head Island and Myrtle Beach are prime vacation spots. Charleston is famous for its historic homes, churches and other buildings. A major U.S. Marine Corps training center is located at Parris Island, near Beaufort. Fort Jackson at Columbia is a major U.S. Army training base.

Vast projects such as the Atomic Energy Commission's $1.2-billion Savannah River Plant (near Aiken) underscore South Carolina's transition from a basically agrarian economy to one in which industry plays the leading part. Livestock raising and commercial fishing are also significant.

Two main land regions make up the roughly triangular-shaped state: the "low country," making up two-thirds of the total area and consisting of a part of the Atlantic Coastal Plain rising northwest from the ocean to a fall line running parallel to the coast and bisecting Columbia; and the "up country," consisting of a portion of the Piedmont Plateau and, in the extreme northwest, a small segment of the Blue Ridge Mountains of the Appalachian range. South of the Santee River's mouth are the Sea Islands, a long chain of offshore isles reaching down the rest of the state's length. Water is abundant, and the sharp drops in the land surface make the state rich in hydroelectric-power potential. About two-thirds of the land is forested, contributing to a sizable timber industry.

Giovanni da Verrazano is thought to have been the first to explore (1524) the coast of the region that later became North and South Carolina; an initial Spanish settlement (1526) at Winyah Bay suffered a malaria outbreak and did not endure.

The first English settlement in present-day South Carolina was made (1670) at Albemarle Point on the Ashley River, but poor conditions drove settlers to the site of Charleston (originally Charles Town). There grew the core of a prosperous though ultimately unstable economy based on the slave-supported cultivation of rice and indigo. Although North and South Carolina were officially a single province, they had separate governors until 1691; from that year until 1712, a sole governor was based at Charleston while his deputy governed North Carolina. After 1712, North and South Carolina were governed independently again, and in 1729 they officially became separate royal provinces; the boundary between them was not defined, however, until 1815.

South Carolina, in the years before the American Revolution, progressed economically despite wars with the Spanish and French, and with pirates and Indians; there was a revolt against proprietary rule in 1719, and a slave uprising in 1739. An influx of Germans, Swiss, and Scots-Irish—from abroad and from neighboring states—helped settle the uplands and the lower middle country. Social and economic differences between the small-scale farmers of the up country and the plantation lords of the low country gave rise to regional disputes, culminating in the Regulator Movement for up country reforms. Statehood dates from 1788.

The early part of the 19th century in South Carolina was marked by a decline in agriculture and an increasingly contentious dialogue between the state and the Federal government on the issue of states' rights. South Carolina's Nullification Act

SOUTH CAROLINA
MILES
0 20 40 60
KILOMETERS
0 20 40 60
State Capital
County Seats
ATLANTIC OCEAN
NORTH CAROLINA
GEORGIA
Longitude West of Greenwich
© Copyright HAMMOND INCORPORATED, Maplewood, N.J.
OCONEE
PICKENS
GREENVILLE
SPARTANBURG
CHEROKEE
YORK
CHESTER
LANCASTER
CHESTERFIELD
MARLBORO
DILLON
MARION
HORRY
ANDERSON
ABBEVILLE
LAURENS
UNION
FAIRFIELD
KERSHAW
DARLINGTON
FLORENCE
GREENWOOD
NEWBERRY
McCORMICK
SALUDA
LEXINGTON
RICHLAND
LEE
SUMTER
WILLIAMSBURG
GEORGETOWN
EDGEFIELD
AIKEN
CALHOUN
CLARENDON
BERKELEY
ORANGEBURG
BARNWELL
BAMBERG
DORCHESTER
CHARLESTON
ALLENDALE
HAMPTON
COLLETON
JASPER
BEAUFORT
Columbia
Charleston
Greenville
Spartanburg
Florence
Savannah
Augusta
Charlotte

(1832) declared a new, higher U.S. tariff act null and void; the immediate issue was resolved (1833) by compromise, but the larger question of the division of power between nation and state remained. A leading national figure of the period was South Carolina's Senator John C. Calhoun, who defended not only the values and rights of his own state, but of the South as a whole. After South Carolina led the way to secession (1860), Confederate artillery fire on Federal troops at Fort Sumter in Charleston Harbor started (April 12, 1861) the Civil War.

During the conflict, there was much fighting along the state's coast, and a Union blockade of Charleston Harbor crippled the economy. In 1865, troops led by General William T. Sherman marched across the state, destroying many plantations and burning Columbia. Reconstruction brought a measure of material recovery, but there was also much waste and political corruption. White supremacy and Negro disenfranchisement soon returned.

In 1979 the nation's only commercial nuclear waste disposal facility in operation was at Barnwell, S.C. To prevent the state from becoming a national nuclear dumping ground, Gov. Richard Riley in October ordered a severe reduction in the amount of out-of-state nuclear waste to be processed at Barnwell. In 1981 the Reagan Administration rejected a plan for federal acquisition of the Barnwell plant. In October 1981, President Reagan lifted a ban placed on commercial reprocessing of used nuclear fuel that had been imposed by President Carter in 1977. The Barnwell facility will provide this service.

**Full name:** State of South Carolina. **Origin of name:** In honor of Charles I of England. **Inhabitant:** South Carolinian. **Captial:** Columbia. **State mottoes:** Animis Opibusque Parati (Prepared in Mind & Resources); Dum Spiro, Spero (While I Breathe, I Hope). **Flag:** White palmetto & crescent on blue field. **Seal:** Palmetto tree, symbolizing successful defense (1776) of fort on Sullivan's Island against British; figure of hope carrying laurel branch across sword-covered beach. **Flower:** Carolina (Yellow) jessamine. **Bird:** Carolina wren. **Tree:** Palmetto. **Song:** "Carolina." **Nickname:** Palmetto State.

**Governor:** Richard W. Riley. **Annual salary:** $60,000. **Term:** 4 years. **Current term expires:** Jan. 1983. **Voting requirements:** 18 yrs. old & U.S. citizen; resident of state; registration 30 days before election. **U.S. Congressmen:** 6. **Entered Union:** 1788 (8th state).

**Location & boundaries:** South Atlantic state: bounded on the north & northeast by North Carolina; on the east by the Atlantic Ocean; & on the south & west by Georgia & the Savannah River. **Total area:** 31,113 sq. mi. (ranks 40th). **Extreme length:** 273 mi. **Extreme breadth:** 210 mi. **Coastline:** 281 mi. **Chief rivers:** Pee Dee, Santee, Edisto, Savannah. **Major lakes:** Marion, Moultrie, Murray. **No. of counties:** 46.

**Population (1980 census):** 3,121,833 (ranks 24th). **Pop. increase (1970-80):** 20.5%. **Largest cities:** Columbia, Charleston, North Charleston, Greenville. **Pop. density:** 100.3 per sq. mi. (ranks 19th). **Pop. distribution: White**—2,145,122; **Black**—948,146; **Am. Indian, Eskimo and Aleut**—5,758; **Asian and Pacific Islander**—11,807; **Other**—8,375; **Spanish origin**—33,414. **Marriage rate (1979):** 18.2 per 1,000 people. **Divorce rate:** 4.7 per 1,000 people.

**State finances (1980). Revenue:** $3,484,000,000. **Expenditures:** $3,325,000,000. **State taxes:** $538.01 per capita. **State personal income tax:** Yes. **Public debt (1980):** $621.11 per capita. **Federal aid (1980):** $341.27 per capita. **Personal income (1981):** $8,050.

**Sectors of the economy (% of labor force employed in 1970):** Manufacturing (36%), Wholesale and retail trade (17%), Government (15%), Services (9%), Educational Services (7%), Construction (7%). **Leading products:** textile items, chemicals, paper items, food items, machinery, lumber & wood items. **Agricultural products:** dairy items, cattle, tobacco, soybeans, cotton, peaches, corn. **Fishing:** shrimp, oysters, crabs. **Avg. farm (1981):** 188 acres. **Avg. value of farm per acre:** $930.

**Highway expenditures per capita (1980):** $86.55. **Persons per motor vehicle (1981):** 1.54. **Minimum age for driver's license:** 16. **Gasoline tax:** 13¢ per gallon. **Diesel tax:** 13¢ per gallon. **Motor vehicle deaths (1980):** 27.3 per 100,000 people.

**Birthrate (1979):** 17.3 per 1,000 people. **Infant mortality rate per 1,000 births (1978):** 18.6. **Physicians per 100,000 pop. (1979):** 134. **Dentists per 100,000 pop. (1979):** 36. **Acceptable hospital beds (1979):** 5.4 per 1,000 people. **State expenditures per capita for health and hospitals (1980):** $95.95.

**Education expenditures (1977-78):** $444.86 per capita annually. **No. of pupils in public schools (1980):** 623,000. **No. of institutions of higher learning (1978-79):** 61. **Public school expenditure per pupil in attendance (1978-79):** $1,692. **Avg. salary of public school teachers (1979-80):** $13,632. **No. full-time teachers (1980):** 32,600. **Educational attainment of adult population (1976):** 12.2 median yrs. of school completed: 6.9% with less than 5 years of education; 10.4% with 4 yrs. of college.

**Telephones (1979):** 50 per 100 people. **State Chamber of Commerce:** South Carolina Chamber of Commerce, Bankers Trust Tower, 1301 Gervais Street, Suite 520, P.O. Box 11278, Columbia, South Carolina 29211.

---

## SOUTH DAKOTA

South Dakota contains (near Castle Rock) the geographical center of the United States, as well as the largest gold mine in the world, Homestake, at the town of Lead. Rich in Old West lore, with such place names as Belle Fourche, Deadwood, and Wounded Knee, the state is home for 45,000 Indians (mostly Sioux), living on 8,400 square miles of reservations. Within the state's borders is one of the country's most famous landmarks and tourist attractions, Mount Rushmore, in the Black Hills; carved into its granite face, at an altitude of more than a mile, are 60-foot-high busts of Presidents Washington, Jefferson, Lincoln, and Theodore Roosevelt. Badlands National Park contains fantastic pinnacles and canyons in a desert setting.

The state, which has less than five percent forested land, is cut by the Missouri into broadly contrasting, irregularly shaped halves. In the west are the Badlands, the spectacular Black Hills, and the rolling grasslands of the Great Plains, while in the east are the rich farmlands that continue to make agriculture South Dakota's main industry. There is a heavy emphasis on livestock, including large numbers of cattle, hogs and sheep. Manufacturing consists mainly of meat processing. Sioux Falls is the headquarters of Earth Resource Observation Systems (EROS), the national air and space photography organization.

Early inhabitants were the Mound Builders, dating from about 1200. Living there after 1600 were the Arikara Indians, an advanced agricultural people, eventually forced out by the more warlike Sioux, or Dakota, Indians. South Dakota and southwestern North Dakota were part of the vast territory claimed (1682) for France by Robert Cavelier, Sieur de La Salle, but Frenchmen did not actually visit the region until 1742-43, when the brothers François and Louis Joseph Vérendyre made explorations and planted a lead plate at the site of what is now Pierre. The area was ceded to Spain in 1762, and toward the end of the century it became part of the St. Louis fur-trading empire. Napolean Bonaparte reclaimed (1800) the territory for France, but three years later sold it to the United States, as part of the Louisiana Purchase.

The Lewis and Clark Expedition explored the region which is now the Dakotas in 1804 and 1806. Fort Pierre, the first non-Indian settlement (1817), became a major fur-trading center, and in 1831 the first steamboat on the upper Missouri began operations.

Dakota Territory—comprising both Dakotas and parts of Montana and Wyoming—was created in

SOUTH DAKOTA
MILES
0 10 20 40 60 80
KILOMETERS
0 10 20 40 60 80
State Capital
County Seats
© Copyright HAMMOND INCORPORATED, Maplewood, N.J.
Longitude West 100° of Greenwich
NORTH DAKOTA
MINNESOTA
IOWA
NEBRASKA
MONTANA
WYOMING
HARDING
PERKINS
CORSON
CAMPBELL
MC PHERSON
BROWN
MARSHALL
ROBERTS
DAY
GRANT
CODINGTON
DEUEL
HAMLIN
CLARK
SPINK
EDMUNDS
WALWORTH
FAULK
POTTER
SULLY
HYDE
HAND
BEADLE
KINGSBURY
BROOKINGS
BUTTE
MEADE
ZIEBACH
DEWEY
STANLEY
HUGHES
HAAKON
JONES
LYMAN
BUFFALO
JERAULD
SANBORN
MINER
LAKE
MOODY
LAWRENCE
PENNINGTON
CUSTER
FALL RIVER
SHANNON
JACKSON
BENNETT
MELLETTE
TODD
TRIPP
GREGORY
BRULE
AURORA
DAVISON
HANSON
MC COOK
MINNEHAHA
CHARLES MIX
DOUGLAS
HUTCHINSON
TURNER
LINCOLN
YANKTON
BON HOMME
CLAY
UNION
Pierre
Rapid City
Sioux Falls
Aberdeen
Watertown
Mitchell
Huron
BLACK HILLS

1861. In 1868, the Sioux—their way of life disrupted by the decline of the buffalo herds—made a treaty with the U.S., accepting a food subsidy and a reservation which included the Black Hills. But the discovery of gold in the Black Hills caused non-Indian prospectors to pour in. Open war broke out between the Sioux and the prospectors. The Sioux agreed in 1876 to abandon the Black Hills, after the government threatened to cut off their food supply. Rough mining towns grew up, and population soared from about 98,000 (1880) to nearly 350,000 (1890). North and South Dakota were admitted to the Union on November 2, 1889.

The Pine Ridge Indian Reservation was the focus of recurring violence in the early 1970s. Wounded Knee, the site of a massacre of Indians in 1890, was the scene of a 71-day takeover by members of the militant American Indian Movement (AIM) in 1973. There were also numerous incidents on the reservation, including the shooting deaths of two FBI agents in 1975, for each of which a member of AIM was sentenced to life imprisonment in 1977. On June 13, 1979, the U.S. Court of Claims ruled that the removal of the Sioux from the Black Hills in 1876 had violated the tribe's constitutional rights as well as its treaty rights. The Federal Government was ordered to pay the Sioux $17,500,000 for the loss of the Black Hills—and to pay it with interest because of the constitutional violation. The total was estimated to be about $100,000,000—the largest award ever made to a U.S. Indian tribe. The government appealed to the Supreme Court but lost the review on June 30, 1980. Militant Sioux occupied Black Hills campsites on April 4, 1981, near Rapid City.

**Full name:** State of South Dakota. **Origin of name:** From the Sioux meaning "Alliance with Friends." **Inhabitant:** South Dakotan. **Capital:** Pierre. **State motto:** Under God The People Rule. **Flag:** State seal surrounded by gold circle, stylized sun & lettering in yellow on a blue field. **Seal:** Smelter chimney, represents mining; plowman stands for farming; riverboat symbolizes transportation. **Flower:** Pasqueflower. **Bird:** Ringnecked pheasant. **Tree:** Black Hills spruce. **Song:** "Hail, South Dakota." **Nickname:** Coyote State; Sunshine State.

**Governor:** William J. Janklow. **Annual salary:** $49,025. **Term:** 4 yrs. **Current term expires:** Jan. 1983. **Voting requirements:** 18 yrs. old & U.S. citizen; registered to vote 15 days before election; county resident. **U.S. Congressmen:** 1. **Entered Union:** 1889 (40th state).

**Location & boundaries:** Northern Midwestern state: bounded on the north by North Dakota; on the east by Minnesota, Iowa & Big Sioux & Red Rivers; on the south by Nebraska & the Missouri River; & on the west by Wyoming & Montana. **Total area:** 77,116 sq. mi. (ranks 16th). **Extreme length:** 380 mi. **Extreme breadth:** 245 mi. **Chief rivers:** Missouri, James, Cheyenne. **Major lakes:** Lewis & Clark, Big Stone. **No. of counties:** 66.

**Population (1980 census):** 690,768 (ranks 45th). **Pop. increase (1970-80):** 3.7%. **Largest cities:** Sioux Falls, Rapid City, Aberdeen. **Pop. density:** 9.0 per sq. mi. (ranks 46th). **Pop. distribution: White**—638,955; **Black**—2,144; **Am. Indian, Eskimo and Aleut**—45,101; **Asian and Pacific Islander**—1,728; **Other**—2,250; **Spanish origin**—4,028. **Marriage rate (1979):** 13.0 per 1,000 people. **Divorce rate:** 3.9 per 1,000 people.

**State finances (1980). Revenue:** $762,000,000. **Expenditures:** $740,000,000. **State Taxes:** $392.06 per capita. **State personal income tax:** No. **Public debt (1980):** $1,035.18 per capita. **Federal aid (1980):** $636.24 per capita. **Personal income (1981):** $8,793.

**Sectors of the economy (% of labor force employed in 1970):** Wholesale and retail trade (22%), Government (19%), Educational Services (10%), Services (7%), Construction (5%), Manufacturing (4%). **Leading products:** food items; printing & publishing; machinery; stone, clay & glass items; lumber; fabricated metals. **Agricultural products:** cattle, hogs, dairy items, wheat, corn, hay. **Avg. farm (1981):** 1,184 acres. **Avg. value of farm per acre:** $290.

**Highway expenditures per capita (1980):** $209.10. **Persons per motor vehicle (1981):** 1.14. **Minimum age for driver's license:** 16. **Gasoline tax:** 13¢ per gallon. **Diesel tax:** 13¢ per gallon. **Motor vehicle deaths (1980):** 33.0 per 100,000 people.

**Birthrate (1979):** 18.9 per 1,000 people. **Infant mortality rate per 1,000 births (1978):** 13.5. **Physicians per 100,000 pop. (1979):** 102. **Dentists per 100,000 pop. (1979):** 43. **Acceptable hospital beds (1979):** 8.1 per 1,000 people. **State expenditures per capita for health and hospitals (1980):** $58.01.

**Education expenditures (1977-78):** $473.92 per capita annually. **No. of pupils in public schools (1980):** 128,000. **No. of institutions of higher learning (1978-79):** 18. **Public school expenditure per pupil in attendance (1978-79):** $1,699. **Avg. salary of public school teachers (1979-80):** $12,870. **No. full-time teachers (1980 est.):** 8,900. **Educational attainment of adult population (1976):** 12.5 median yrs. of school completed: 1.1% with less than 5 years of education; 11.4% with 4 yrs. of college.

**Telephones (1979):** 56 per 100 people. **State Chamber of Commerce:** South Dakota Chamber of Commerce, P.O. Box 190, Pierre, South Dakota 57501.

## TENNESSEE

Traces of Tennessee's traditionally hardy frontier spirit remain today in its museums and restored buildings, as well as in the character and life-style of many Tennesseans themselves. The first state to be created out of national territory, Tennessee came to be called the Volunteer State because of its readiness to furnish troops in the War of 1812 and the Mexican War. Its history and culture have been deeply influenced by its three main land regions—East, Middle, and West Tennessee.

In East Tennessee, with the heaviest population outside of the major urban areas in the state, are the Great Smoky Mountains and the eastern slope of the Cumberland Mountains, both in the Appalachian range. Middle Tennessee consists of the fertile Nashville Basin and an elevated plain (the Highland Rim) and the western slope of the Cumberlands, which divide the two sections of the state, the features being part of the Interior Low Plateaus. Middle Tennesseans of this gently rolling bluegrass region tend to identify with the Old South. West Tennessee lies between the western bend of the Tennessee River and the Mississippi River and includes a portion of the East Gulf Coastal Plain and a thin strip of the Mississippi Alluvial Plain. Here farming predominates. About half of the state is forested.

Tennessee, once a basically rural region, has become a largely industrial state. Chemicals, textiles, and food and metal products are among the major manufactures. Nissan, a Japanese corporation, is building a major truck manufacturing facility at Smyrna, southeast of Nashville. Massive hydroelectric installations, developed (beginning 1933) by the Tennessee Valley Authority (TVA), provide power for Tennessee and six other states. Mining, lumbering, cotton, tobacco, and livestock are also vital elements of the state's economy.

Indians similar to the Mound Builders are thought to have been the early inhabitants of the Tennessee region. The Chickasaw, Cherokee, and Shawnee were among the tribes living there when the first Europeans, led by De Soto, arrived in 1540. De Soto was soon followed by countryman Juan Pardo, but the Spaniards were seeking gold and did not settle. A long period of French-British contention over the land was foreshadowed by the arrival in the same year (1673) of Marquette and Jolliet, and Englishmen James Needham and Gabriel Arthur. In 1682, La Salle and his party paused in their exploration of the Mississippi Valley and built Fort Prudhomme at the mouth of the Hatchie River.

Spurred by reports of scouts such as Daniel Boone, a steady stream of settlers from Virginia and the Carolinas soon began to enter the region. French influence waned, and by 1763 the British were in control, despite strong resistance from the

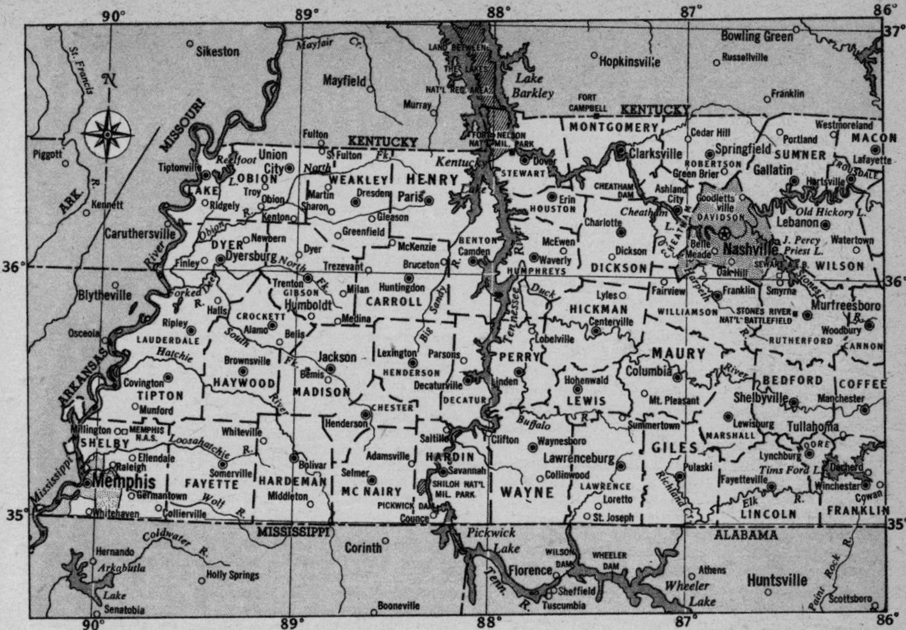

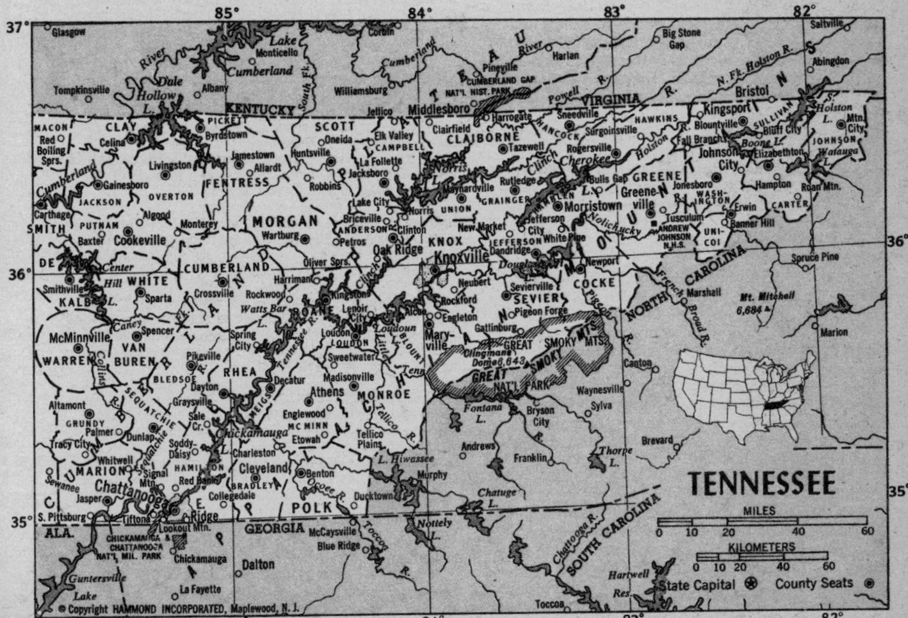

# TENNESSEE

MILES
0 10 20 40 60

KILOMETERS
0 10 20 40 60

State Capital ⊛ County Seats ⊙

Longitude West of Greenwich

Cherokees. Between 1772 and 1790 several abortive attempts were made by settlers to establish self-government and achieve statehood.

In 1790 Congress organized the region into the "Territory of the United States South of the River Ohio," commonly called the Southwest Territory. Tennessee entered the Union in 1796.

Tennessee began life as a state with what Jefferson called the nation's "least imperfect and most republican" constitution. By 1800, immigration had swelled the population to 100,000, and the coming of steam and rail transportation did much to develop the state's economy. When the Cherokees and the Chickasaws were forced to move west in the late 1830s, another, smaller wave of immigration ensued. Politically, the new state's dominant figure was Andrew Jackson, who served as a U.S. representative and senator from Tennessee before becoming (1829) president.

Although a slaveholding state, Tennessee was at first pro-Union in the years before the Civil War, but after Fort Sumter a referendum was held and two-thirds of the people backed secession (1861). Tennessee was the last Confederate state to secede, and the first to be readmitted.

The Reconstruction Era triggered a strong reaction that included the founding (1866) of the Ku Klux Klan in Pulaski and the adoption (1870) of a new constitution limiting Negro suffrage via a poll tax. On the farms, a tenancy system replaced the plantations, and the state's crippled economy turned toward increased industrialization for new life. In 1878, the worst yellow-fever epidemic in U.S. history hit Memphis, killing thousands.

Among the state's attractions is Great Smoky Mountains National Park, which it shares with North Carolina. Parts of five states can be seen from Lookout Mountain on the Tennessee River near Chattanooga. The Historic State Capital and a reproduction of the Parthenon are in Nashville, the home of the famed "Grand Ole Opry." The new Opry House and Opryland, U.S.A., a 300-acre theme park are popular tourist attractions. Libertyland, a theme park at Memphis, was opened during the nation's bicentennial. Memphis is also the site of Graceland, Elvis Presley's home.

In 1973, six years after the repeal of the ban on the teaching of the theory of evolution, a new version was enacted. It requires that equal emphasis be given to Genesis in the classroom as well as other theories of man's origin. The original law resulted in the 1925 trial of biology teacher John Scopes in the little town of Dayton, Tenn. The trial pitted Clarence Darrow for the defense against special prosecutor William Jennings Bryan.

The Clinch River nuclear energy project was opposed by President Carter as unnecessary, too expensive and, as a producer of plutonium as a byproduct, a substance likely to cause proliferation of atomic weapons technology. Nevertheless, after much controversy, a House committee approved going ahead with the reactor early in 1979. President Reagan's budget for 1982 pledged $222 million for the breeder reactor

Lamar Alexander replaced Governor Ray Blanton on January 17, 1979 (three days before the appointed inauguration day), to stop further convicted criminals from being granted executive clemency. Blanton's clemency grants were in question because of their possible link to a Federal probe of his administration's alleged clemency-for-sale scandal. On April 10, the Tennessee Court of Criminal Appeals upheld 52 grants of clemency allowed by Blanton the day before he left office. Six persons (Blanton not among them) were indicted in connection with the pardon sales. Following conviction by a federal jury on charges of selling state liquor licenses during his administration, Blanton was sentenced to three years in prison and fined $11,000 on August 14, 1981.

On May 1, 1982, President Reagan opened the Knoxville World's Fair, scheduled to run 184 days. The theme of the fair, whose exhibits stress energy-related topics, was "Energy Turns the World."

**Full name:** State of Tennessee. **Origin of name:** From Tennese, name of leading Cherokee town. **Inhabitant:** Tennessean. **Capital:** Nashville. **State motto:** Agriculture & Commerce. **Flag:** Three white stars in a white-bordered blue circle on a red field; narrow white & blue stripe at right. **Seal:** Plow, sheaf of wheat & cotton plant represent agriculture; riverboat symbolizes commerce; Roman numerals indicate Tennessee was 16th state to be admitted to Union. **Flower:** Iris. **Bird:** Mockingbird. **Tree:** Tulip poplar. **Song:** "The Tennessee Waltz," "When It's Iris Time in Tennessee," "Tennessee, My Homeland Tennessee," "My Tennessee," & "Oh! Tennessee." **Nickname:** Volunteer State.

**Governor:** Lamar Alexander. **Annual salary:** $68,226. **Term:** 4 years. **Current term expires:** Jan. 1983. **Voting requirements:** 18 yrs. old & U.S. citizen; resident of state for 20 days. **U.S. Congressmen:** 9. **Entered Union:** 1796 (16th state).

**Location & boundaries:** Southeastern state: bounded on the north by Kentucky & Virginia; on the east by North Carolina; on the south by Georgia, Alabama & Mississippi; & on the west by Arkansas, Missouri & the Mississippi River. **Total area:** 42,144 sq. mi. (ranks 34th). **Extreme length:** 432 mi. **Extreme breadth:** 110 mi. **Chief rivers:** Mississippi, Tennessee, Cumberland. **Major lakes:** Watts, Chickamauga, Douglas, Cherokee. **No. of counties:** 95.

**Population (1980 census):** 4,591,120 (ranks 17th). **Pop. increase (1970-80):** 16.9%. **Largest cities:** Memphis, Nashville, Knoxville, Chattanooga. **Pop. density:** 108.9 per sq. mi. (ranks 18th). **Pop. distribution: White**—3,835,078; **Black**—725,949; **Am. Indian, Eskimo and Aleut**—5,103; **Asian and Pacific Islander**—13,963; **Other**—10,657; **Spanish origin**—34,081. **Marriage rate (1979):** 13.5 per 1,000 people. **Divorce rate:** 6.8 per 1,000 people.

**State finances (1980). Revenue:** $4,028,000,000. **Expenditures:** $3,874,000,000. **State taxes:** $411.02 per capita. **State personal income tax:** No. **Public debt (1980):** $306.24 per capita. **Federal aid (1980):** $353.66 per capita. **Personal income (1981):** $8,604.

**Sectors of the economy (% of labor force employed in 1973):** Wholesale and retail trade (16.9%), Government (15.8%), Services (13.9%), Manufacturing (13.8%), Educational Services (7%), Construction (6.1%). **Leading products:** chemicals, food items, electrical equipment, apparel, textile items, primary metals. **Minerals:** stone, coal, zinc, cement, copper. **Agricultural products:** cattle, soybeans, dairy items, cotton, tobacco. **Avg. farm (1981):** 142 acres. **Avg. value of farm per acre:** $1,024.

**Highway expenditures per capita (1980):** $132.76. **Persons per motor vehicle (1981):** 1.38. **Minimum age for driver's license:** 16. **Gasoline tax:** 9¢ per gallon. **Diesel tax:** 12¢ per gallon. **Motor vehicle deaths (1980):** 25.1 per 100,000 people.

**Birthrate (1979):** 15.6 per 1,000 people. **Infant mortality rate per 1,000 births (1978):** 14.8. **Physicians per 100,000 pop. (1979):** 158. **Dentists per 100,000 pop. (1979):** 48. **Acceptable hospital beds (1979):** 6.8 per 1,000 people. **State expenditures per capita for health and hospitals (1980):** $62.96.

**Education expenditures (1977-78):** $404.28 per capita annually. **No. of pupils in public schools (1980):** 863,000. **No. of institutions of higher learning (1978-79):** 76. **Public school expenditure per pupil in attendance (1978-79):** $1,548. **Avg. salary of public school teachers (1979-80):** $13,905. **No. full-time teachers (1980):** 45,200. **Educational attainment of adult population (1976):** 12.2 median yrs. of school completed: 6.4% with less than 5 years of education; 10.5% with 4 yrs. of college.

**Telephones (1979):** 53 per 100 people. **State Chamber of Commerce:** State Chamber Division of the Tennessee Taxpayers Assoc., 706 Church Street, Suite 242, Nashville, Tennessee 37203.

## TEXAS

Second largest of the states and third most populous, Texas is a fiercely independent land of awesome expanses and great natural resources. It leads the nation in the production of oil, sulfur, cattle, sheep and cotton, and ranks high in natural gas, fishing and electric power. Texas is also a major agricultural state, as well as a major industrial region. It contains the facilities of 19 of the top 20 U.S. chemical companies, and is the home of the Lyndon B. Johnson Space Center (near Houston) and other space age projects. And while keeping pace technologically, it can also claim a richly varied heritage, having flown the flags of six nations: Spain, France, Mexico, the Republic of Texas, the Confederate States of America, and the United States.

Among the state's many tourist attractions are two national parks, Big Bend with outstanding desert scenery and Guadalupe Mountains with rugged mountain and canyon topography. Padre Island National Seashore stretches for 80 miles along the Gulf shore. Historic sites include the Alamo, San Antonio Missions National Historic Park, Fort Davis National Historic Site, and the Lyndon B. Johnson National Historic Site.

The state consists of four main land regions: the West Gulf Coastal Plain, the largest single area, making up more than two-fifths of the total area and consisting of a 150-to 350-mile-wide strip of land in the east and southeast extending from the Gulf of Mexico to the Balcones Escarpment; the Central Lowland, known locally as the Osage Plains and extending southward to a line running roughly from Fort Worth, through Abilene, to Big Springs and including the southern fringe of the Texas panhandle; the Great Plains, reaching mostly westward (but also north and southward) from the Central Lowland into New Mexico and including the bulk of the panhandle; and the Basin and Range (or Trans-Pecos) Region, making up the westernmost part of the state below New Mexico and including high, rugged, partly arid plains crossed by spurs of the Rocky Mountains; in this region are the Guadalupe Mountains and the state's highest point, Guadalupe Peak (8,749 feet).

Texas has more farmed area than any other state, and about half the land consists of forest, woodland, or brush land. The state's widely varied climate ranges from the warm, damp, subtropical Gulf Coast and lower Rio Grande Valley to the continental weather of the northern panhandle. Hot, dry weather is typical of the far south as are frequent droughts. Narrow sand bars, enclosing shallow lagoons, lie along the coast and afford some protection against ocean storms and tidal waves. The U.S.-Mexican border, where it follows the Rio Grande has been a continuing problem for the state, because the riverbed shifts occasionally, cutting off land from one or the other country. These shifts have given rise to nearly a century of minor but annoying border disputes. In August 1970, however, Presidents Nixon and Diaz met in Mexico and announced agreement on current disputes and ways to prevent future ones. New, major reservoirs, including giant Amistad Reservoir, built in cooperation with Mexico, will prevent any substantial change in the Rio Grande.

Indians inhabited what is now Texas about 20,000 years before the coming of the Europeans. Spaniards (including Cabeza de Vaca and Francisco Vásquez Coronado) visited the region in the 16th and 17th centuries, settling (1682) at Ysleta (near present-day El Paso). Spain increased its settlement efforts after French explorer Robert Cavelier, Sieur de La Salle, established (1685) a short-lived colony near Matagorda Bay. The first Spanish mission, San Francisco de los Tejas, was founded in 1690 and others soon followed, but generally Spain's efforts to exploit the region's wealth and convert the Indians were not very successful. After the Louisiana Purchase (1803) gave the United States a common border with Texas, Americans began challenging Spanish rule there.

Moses Austin secured (1821) a grant from local authorities permitting him, as an *empresario*, to bring in American settlers; when he died that same year, his son, Stephen F. Austin, established the first permanent Anglo-American settlement at San Felipe de Astin. Often called the "Father of Texas," Austin brought approximately 8,000 colonists to the region. Other *empresarios* brought hundreds more, and during the next 15 years the total approached 30,000. Preoccupied with its birth as an independent republic (1824), Mexico was not effective in curbing what it saw as a growing encroachment on its territory, despite an 1830 law restricting immigration, and the establishment of customs stations and a military force in Texas.

The Anglo-Americans were moved to action when Antonio López de Santa Anna set up (1835) a Mexican dictatorship in Texas; the Texans then proclaimed (1836) a provisional government at Washington-on-the-Brazos and turned command of the revolutionary army over to Sam Houston. Santa Anna and his men quickly gained the upper hand in the struggle, recapturing San Antonio, which had initially fallen to the Texans; the Mexican victory came despite the famous heroic defense of the Alamo by greatly outnumbered Texans (including Davy Crockett and Jim Bowie). After more than 300 Texas prisoners were shot at Goliad, Houston rallied his still relatively small army and, with a surprise attack, won (April 21, 1836) the Battle of San Jacinto, ending the war and bringing to birth the Independent Republic of Texas.

Under its famed Lone Star flag, Texas remained independent for nearly a decade, with Houston serving as president. The country was beset by many grave problems, including Indian and Mexican raids and a money shortage. The issue of annexation by the United States, which most Texans favored, arose early. Slavery, condoned in Texas, made the issue highly controversial: the Southern states favored annexation, while the Northern ones opposed it. Annexation, which came in 1845, precipitated the Mexican War (1846-48).

Settlers, drawn by inexpensive land, came to Texas in great numbers in the pre-Civil War period. Partly because of its slave-holding status but more importantly because of states' rights views, the state sided with the Confederacy, seceding in 1861. Texas saw little action during the war, but contributed 50,000 troops and much matériel to the Southern cause. The state suffered much during the excesses of Reconstruction.

The development of modern Texas was spurred by the growth of the cattle industry, the coming of the railroad, and the discovery, among others before it, of the spectacular Spindletop oil field (1901) near Beaumont. The state's vast petroleum resources spurred the growth of a huge chemical industry. After World War II, Texas became a leader in the aircraft and electronic industries. Texas today, while enjoying great growth, faces serious challenges, such as ways to irrigate with surface water its dry western areas where shrinking underground supplies now help to grow vast crops.

Texas shrimp fishermen, together with the Ku Klux Klan, were enjoined by a Federal District Court judge in May 1981 from intimidating Vietnamese refugee fishermen at Galveston Bay. The American fishermen had complained of unfair competition from the Vietnamese and feared that the bay would be overfished. Witnesses at the trial

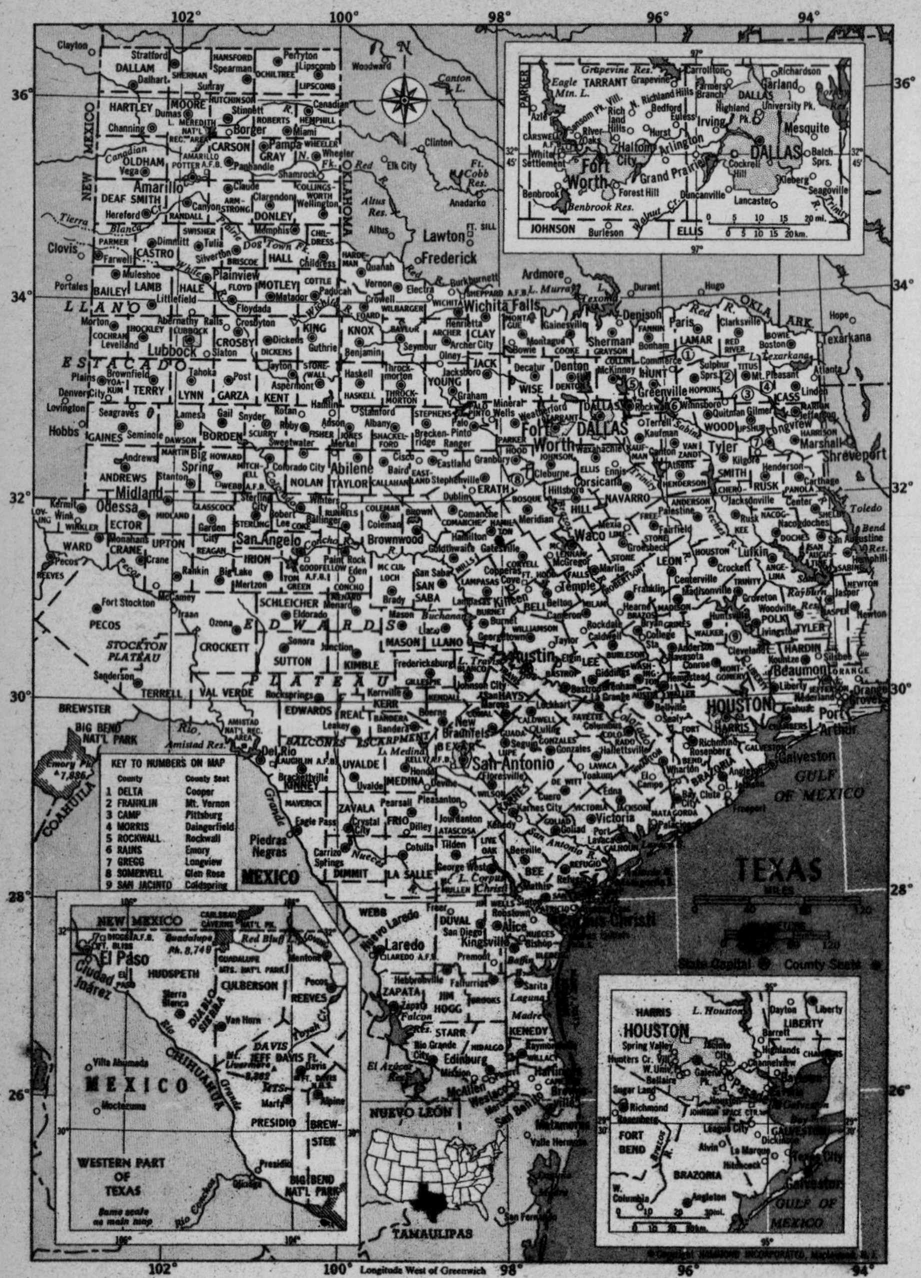
TEXAS
KEY TO NUMBERS ON MAP
County / County Seat
1 DELTA Cooper
2 FRANKLIN Mt. Vernon
3 CAMP Pittsburg
4 MORRIS Daingerfield
5 ROCKWALL Rockwall
6 RAINS Emory
7 GREGG Longview
8 SOMERVELL Glen Rose
9 SAN JACINTO Coldspring
WESTERN PART OF TEXAS
Same scale as main map
GULF OF MEXICO
MEXICO
NEW MEXICO
OKLAHOMA
LLANO ESTACADO
EDWARDS PLATEAU
STOCKTON PLATEAU
BALCONES ESCARPMENT
NUEVO LEON
TAMAULIPAS
COAHUILA
CHIHUAHUA
Amarillo
Lubbock
Midland
Odessa
Abilene
San Angelo
Wichita Falls
Fort Worth
DALLAS
Austin
Waco
San Antonio
HOUSTON
Beaumont
Port Arthur
Galveston
Corpus Christi
Laredo
El Paso
Brownsville
Tyler
Texarkana
Shreveport
Longitude West of Greenwich

testified that native shrimpers and the Klan had threatened Vietnamese fishermen and burned three of their boats.

The U.S. Supreme Court in June 1982, declared invalid a Texas law that allowed local districts to bar the children of illegal aliens from school or to charge them tuition. It is estimated that five percent of the state's population are illegal aliens, mostly Mexican.

The August 1982 decline in value of the Mexican peso brought on hardship to businesses operating along the Rio Grande international border. Mexicans no longer purchased goods in Texas stores because of the decreased value of their currency.

On September 9, 1982, the first successful test flight of a private corporation space rocket *Conestoga 1* took place at Matagorda Island on the Gulf Coast. A previous attempt in August 1981 had failed.

**Full name:** State of Texas. **Origin of name:** From the Indian meaning "Friends" or "Allies." **Inhabitant:** Texan. **Capital:** Austin. **State motto:** Friendship. **Flag:** Single star on vertical blue bar with a red & a white bar to the right. **Seal:** Single star with branch of oak, representing strength, on left; olive branch, symbolizing peace, to the right. **Flower:** Bluebonnet. **Bird:** Mockingbird. **Tree:** Pecan. **Song:** "Texas, Our Texas." **Nickname:** Lone Star State.

**Governor:** William P. Clements, Jr. **Annual salary:** $85,000. **Term:** 4 years. **Current term expires:** Jan. 1983. **Voting requirements:** 18 yrs. old & U.S. citizen; registered resident of state. **U.S. Congressmen:** 27. **Entered Union:** 1845 (28th state).

**Location & boundaries:** Southwestern state: bounded on the north by Oklahoma & the Red River; on the northeast by Arkansas; on the east by Louisiana & the Sabine River; on the south by the Gulf of Mexico, the Rio Grande River & Mexico, & on the west by New Mexico. **Total area:** 266,807 sq. mi. (ranks 2nd). **Extreme length:** 801 mi. **Extreme breadth:** 773 mi. **Coastline:** 367 mi. **Chief rivers:** Rio Grande, Red, Pecos, Brazos, Colorado. **Major lakes:** Texoma, Toledo Bend, Amistad, Falcon. **No. of counties:** 254.

**Population (1980 census):** 14,229,288 (ranks 3rd). **Pop. increase (1970-80):** 27.1%. **Largest cities:** Houston, Dallas, San Antonio, El Paso. **Pop. density:** 53.3 per sq. mi. (ranks 29th). **Pop. distribution: White**—11,197,663; **Black**—1,710,250; **Am. Indian, Eskimo and Aleut**—40,074; **Asian and Pacific Islander**—120,306; **Other**—1,160,090; **Spanish origin**—2,985,643. **Marriage rate (1979):** 12.9 per 1,000 people. **Divorce rate:** 6.9 per 1,000 people.

**State finances (1980). Revenue:** $12,924,000,000. **Expenditures:** $11,487,000,000. **State taxes:** $475.03 per capita. **State personal income tax:** No. **Public debt (1980):** $173.50 per capita. **Federal aid (1980):** $278.38 per capita. **Personal income (1981):** $10,743.

**Sectors of the economy (% of labor force employed in 1970):** Wholesale and retail trade (22%), Manufacturing (19%), Government (16%), Services (9%), Educational Services (8%), Construction (8%). **Leading products:** chemicals, petroleum & coal items, food items, transportation equipment, machinery, primary & fabricated metals. **Minerals:** petroleum, natural gas & natural gas liquids, cement. **Agricultural products:** cattle, sheep, swine, dairy items, mohair, sorghum grain, cotton lint, rice, wheat, oats, barley, pecans. **Fishing:** shrimp, oysters, menhaden. **Avg. farm (1981):** 746 acres. **Avg. value of farm per acre:** $492.

**Highway expenditures per capita (1980):** $118.61. **Persons per motor vehicle (1981):** 1.32. **Minimum age for driver's license:** 16. **Gasoline tax:** 5¢ per gallon. **Diesel tax:** 6.5¢ per gallon. **Motor vehicle deaths (1980):** 30.7 per 100,000 people.

**Birthrate (1979):** 19.0 per 1,000 people. **Infant mortality rate per 1,000 births (1978):** 14.3. **Physicians per 100,000 pop. (1979):** 152. **Dentists per 100,000 pop. (1979):** 42. **Acceptable hospital beds (1979):** 5.6 per 1,000 people. **State expenditures per capita for health and hospitals (1980):** $57.87.

**Education expenditures (1977-78):** $498.05 per capita annually. **No. of pupils in public schools (1980):** 2,882,000. **No. of institutions of higher learning (1978-79):** 147. **Public school expenditure per pupil in attendance (1978-79):** $2,073. **Avg. salary of public school teachers (1979-80):** $14,763. **No. full-time teachers (1980):** 164,000. **Educational attainment of adult population (1976):** 12.4 median yrs. of school completed: 6.0% with less than 5 years of education; 13.7% with 4 yrs. of college.

**Telephones (1979):** 55 per 100 people. **State Chamber of Commerce:** Texas State Chamber of Commerce, 815 Brazos, Suite 801, Austin, Texas 78701.

## UTAH

Utah is a rough-hewn, scenically spectacular state consisting of two relatively arid regions (eastern and western), divided by the rain-catching Wasatch Range of the Rocky Mountains. In the west is the Great Basin, which includes the Great Salt Lake (about 75 miles long and 30 miles wide) and the 4,000-square-mile Great Salt Lake Desert. East of the Wasatch Range are the Uinta Mountains (with 11 peaks that rise more than 13,000 feet) and the awesome, many-hued Colorado Plateau. Most of the towns and cities, situated at the base of the mountains, enjoy a pleasant climate with few temperature extremes.

A number of factors—mainly scarcity of water—have limited the state's agricultural growth. Nearly three-quarters of the annual farm revenue comes from livestock and livestock products. Hay, wheat, barley and cherries are the main crops. The struggle for better irrigation in Utah began with the early Mormon settlers and still goes on.

Stimulated by the demands of World War II, manufacturing has become increasingly vital. Leading manufactures include food products; fabricated steel; stone, clay and glass products; missiles; chemicals; and in recent years, electronics equipment. In rural communities, the fabric and apparel industries are active.

In the last ten years, distribution services have become an important part of the Utah economy. Since the state legislature eliminated all taxes on inventories, the state has become an important shipping and receiving point for the entire Western market.

Tourism is important, attracting visitors to the Great Salt Lake; Arches, Bryce Canyon, Canyonlands, Capitol Reef and Zion National Parks; Natural Bridges, Cedar Breaks, Dinosaur, Rainbow Bridge and Timpanogos National Monuments, Glen Canyon National Recreation Area, and Golden Spike National Historic Site.

Disfavored by the agrarian Mormons, mining got off to a slow start, but in 1863 huge deposits of copper, silver, and lead were unearthed in Bingham Canyon, which contains the largest open-pit copper mine in the country. The industry came into its own with the coming of the railroad in 1869. Utah leads the nation in gold production, and coal mining is important. Since 1948, significant quantities of oil, natural gas and uranium have been found. In 1980 an important gas field was opened in the Overthrust Belt near the Wyoming border east of Ogden. Recent discoveries of large oil-shale and tar-sands deposits have raised hopes of further energy development, but uncertainties in the economy and a lagging technology have slowed the exploitation of these resources.

Archaeological findings (1968) in the Great Basin at Hogup Cave, 75 miles northwest of Salt Lake City, show that there was continuous Indian habitation in the area from 6400 B.C. to A.D. 1600. An even older human habitation, Danger Cave near Wendover, was excavated a decade ago and dates to 9000 B.C. Some doubt exists as to whether or not Spanish explorers visited the region in 1540 when they explored the Grand Canyon, but it has been established that in 1776 two Spanish Franciscan friars—Silvestre Velez de Escalante and Francisco Atanasio Dominguez—did explore the area. They recommended colonization, but Spain was apparently not interested. Between 1811 and 1840 British and American fur trappers hunted their prey there.

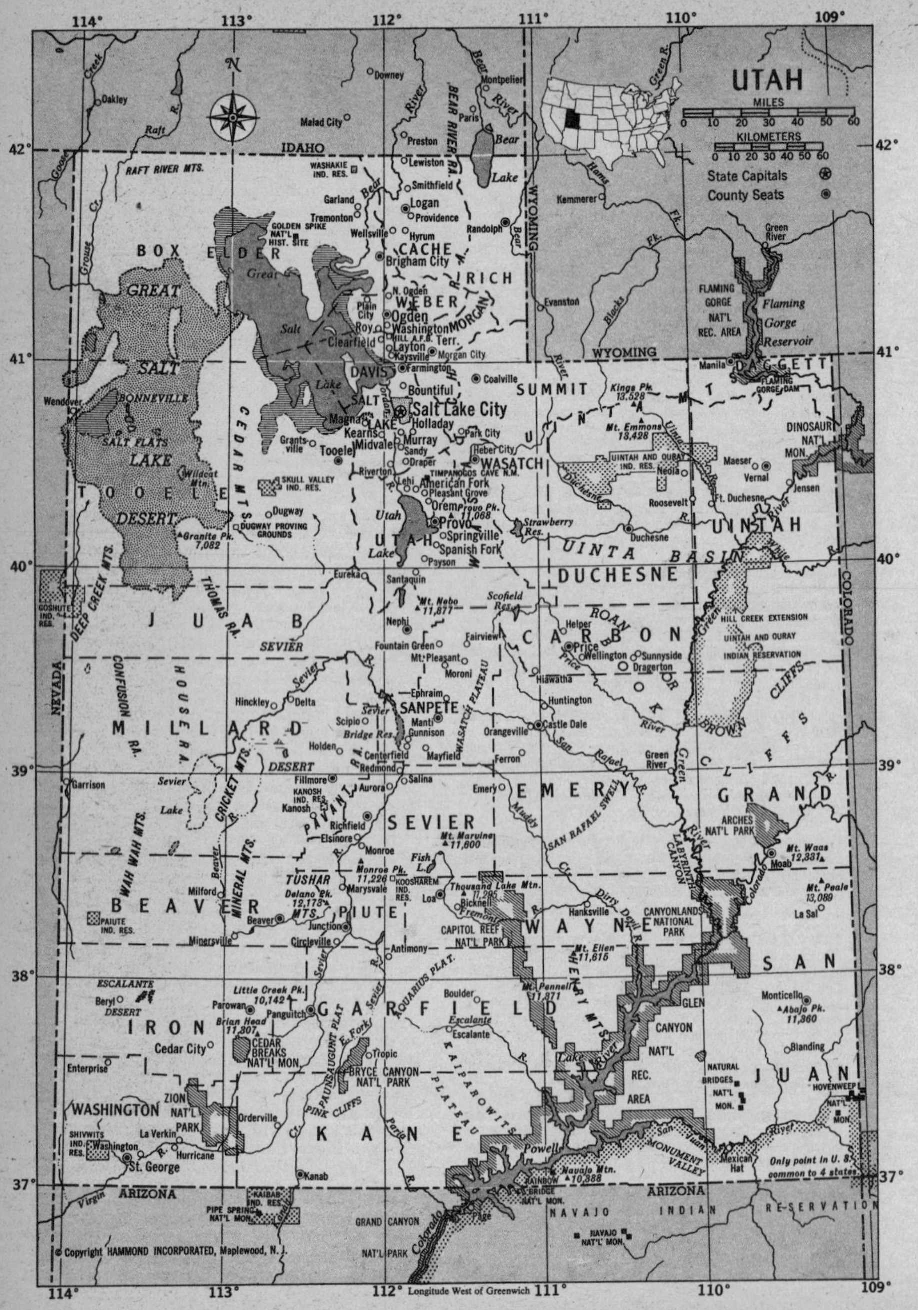
UTAH
MILES
KILOMETERS
State Capitals
County Seats
IDAHO
WYOMING
NEVADA
COLORADO
ARIZONA
Salt Lake City
BOX ELDER
CACHE
RICH
WEBER
MORGAN
DAVIS
SALT LAKE
SUMMIT
DAGGETT
TOOELE
WASATCH
UTAH
DUCHESNE
UINTAH
JUAB
CARBON
MILLARD
SANPETE
EMERY
GRAND
SEVIER
BEAVER
PIUTE
WAYNE
IRON
GARFIELD
SAN JUAN
WASHINGTON
KANE
GREAT SALT LAKE DESERT
BONNEVILLE SALT FLATS
UINTA BASIN
Only point in U. S. common to 4 states
© Copyright HAMMOND INCORPORATED, Maplewood, N. J.
Longitude West of Greenwich

Permanent occupation of the territory was begun in 1847 by the persecuted Mormons—members of the Church of Jesus Christ of Latter-day Saints—who had emigrated from New York via Missouri, Ohio, and Illinois to Utah in search of "a [secluded] gathering place for Zion." From the time of its founding (1847) Salt Lake City has been the world headquarters of the L.D.S. church.

The Utah region at that time belonged to Mexico, but after the Mexican War (1846-48), it became the property of the United States. At least 70 percent of the state's area is still federally owned and administered, and about ten percent of the people work for Federal agencies.

Two Indian wars were fought: the Walker War (1853-54) and the Black Hawk War (1865-68), involving a number of tribes but principally the Utes, who were eventually placed on a reservation in the Uinta basin.

As early as 1849 Utah asked to be admitted to the Union, but Congress refused—mainly because the Mormon practice of polygamy was frowned upon.

The dismissal of the Mormon leader, Brigham Young, as territorial governor led to the "Utah" or "Mormon" War (1857-58). Federal troops were dispatched to the area, but there was more bad feeling than actual fighting. When the Civil War broke out in 1861, the troops were recalled and peace reigned, although there remained a residue of bitterness between the Mormon stronghold and the "outside" world which time has gradually erased. Utah finally entered the Union in 1896.

Some residents of St. George have filed claims against the Energy Department charging that nuclear blasts which occurred some 25 years ago at the Nevada Testing Site caused cancer deaths among members of their families who lived in the area. In 1982, a U.S. District Court ordered a new trial for Utah sheep ranchers as plaintiffs in a suit that they had unsuccessfully brought against the Federal government in 1956 over the poisoning of their animals by atomic testing in 1953.

The Federal government's planned deployment of the MX missile system in the state brought vigorous objections from Utahns. Both the Mormon church and U.S. Senator Jake Garn protested the move in 1981. In October, President Reagan dropped the plan.

**Full name:** State of Utah. **Origin of name:** From the Indian tribe of Utes. **Inhabitant:** Utahn. **Capital:** Salt Lake City. **State motto:** Industry. **Flag:** State seal in a gold circle on blue field. **Seal:** Beehive on shield represents industry; sego lilies surrounding beehive symbolize time when Mormon pioneers ate lily bulbs to avoid starvation. **Flower:** Sego lily. **Bird:** Seagull. **Tree:** Blue spruce. **Song:** "Utah, We Love Thee." **Nickname:** Beehive State.

**Governor:** Scott M. Matheson. **Annual salary:** $48,000. **Term:** 4 years. **Current term expires:** Dec. 1984. **Voting requirements:** 18 yrs. old & U.S. citizen; state resident 30 days. **U.S. Congressmen:** 3. **Entered Union:** 1896 (45th state).

**Location & boundaries:** Rocky Mountain state: bounded on the north by Idaho; on the northeast by Wyoming; on the east by Colorado; on the south by Arizona; & on the west by Nevada. **Total area:** 84,899 sq. mi. (ranks 11th). **Extreme length:** 345 mi. **Extreme breadth:** 2755 mi. **Chief rivers:** Colorado, Green, Sevier. **Major lakes:** Great Salt Lake, Utah, Sevier, Bear Lake. **No. of counties:** 29.

**Population (1980 census):** 1,461,037 (ranks 36th). **Pop. increase (1970-80):** 37.9%. **Largest cities:** Salt Lake City, Provo, Ogden. **Pop. density:** 17.2 per sq. mi. (ranks 42nd). **Pop. distribution:** **White**—1,382,550; **Black**—9,225; **Am. Indian, Eskimo and Aleut**—19,256; **Asian and Pacific Islander**—15,076; **Other**—34,930; **Spanish origin**—60,302. **Marriage rate (1979):** 12.2 per 1,000 people. **Divorce rate:** 5.6 per 1,000 people.

**State finances (1980). Revenue:** $1,889,000,000. **Expenditures:** $1,755,000,000. **State taxes:** $537.82 per capita. **State personal income tax:** Yes. **Public debt (1980):** $367.61 per capita. **Federal aid (1980):** $374.73 per capita. **Personal income (1981):** $8,307.

**Sectors of the (% of labor force employed in 1970):** Government (25%), Wholesale and retail trade (22%), Manufacturing (15%), Educational Services (12%), Services (7%), Construction (6%). **Leading products:** food items; stone, clay, & glass items; machinery; printing & publishing; fabricated metals; petroleum & coal items. **Minerals:** copper, petroleum, coal, molybdenum. **Agricultural products:** cattle, dairy items, turkeys, hay, wheat, barley. **Avg. farm (1981):** 969 acres. **Avg. value of farm per acre:** $567.

**Highway expenditures per capita (1980):** $156.67. **Persons per motor vehicle (1981):** 1.46. **Minimum age for driver's license:** 16. **Gasoline tax:** 11¢ per gallon. **Diesel tax:** 11¢ per gallon. **Motor vehicle deaths (1980):** 22.9 per 100,000 people.

**Birthrate (1979):** 30.1 per 1,000 people. **Infant mortality rate per 1,000 births (1978):** 11.4. **Physicians per 100,000 pop. (1979):** 164. **Dentists per 100,000 pop. (1979):** 64. **Acceptable hospital beds (1979):** 3.5 per 1,000 people. **State expenditures per capita for health and hospitals (1980):** $79.62.

**Education expenditures (1977-78):** $621.42 per capita annually. **No. of pupils in public schools (1980):** 339,000. **No. of institutions of higher learning (1978-79):** 14. **Public school expennditure per pupil in attendance (1978-79):** $2,114. **Avg. salary of public school teachers (1979-80):** $15,690. **No. full-time teachers (1980):** 12,600. **Educational attainment of adult population (1976):** 12.8 median yrs. of school completed: 0.7% with less than 5 years of education; 17.5% with 4 yrs. of college.

**Telephones (1979):** 53 per 100 people. **State Chamber of Commerce:** None.

## VERMONT

Vermont, the only New England state lacking an ocean coastline, is noted for the independence of thought and action that stem, in part, from this relative insularity; there is much truth to the saying, "Vermonters will do nothing that you tell them to; most anything that you ask them to."

Four main land areas make up the state: the extensively forested Green Mountains, forming a north-south backbone through the center (and inspiring the state's French-rooted name); the White Mountains in the northeast, Lake Champlain and the Champlain Valley in the northwest, and the Taconic Hills in the southwest. Many lakes, ponds, streams, and rivers—including the eastern-border-forming Connecticut River—provide an abundant water supply. Forests cover about 60 percent of the area.

Called a "state in a very natural state" by poet Robert Frost (who lived the latter part of his life near Ripton), Vermont is famous for the rustic charm of its towns and villages, winding roads, covered bridges, and largely unspoiled scenery. In the early 1900s, manufacturing began to replace agriculture in importance through small-scale industralization: only a quarter of the state's land is now devoted to agriculture. Maple sugar and syrup and the finest marble in the United States are among Vermont's better-known products, while an important source of the nation's asbestos is located in the Hyde Park region. Machine tools, electronic equipment, computer components and armaments are the state's leading industrial products.

Four-season tourism has grown enormously in recent years, generating nearly $1 billion in income. Attractions include the Green Mountain National Forest, Shelburne and Bennington museums, a multitude of ski resorts, and many state parks.

French explorer Samuel de Champlain was most likely the first European to visit the region, discovering (1609) the lake now bearing his name. The British established (1724) the first permanent settlement at Fort Dummer (near present-day Brattleboro), and the English assumed control at

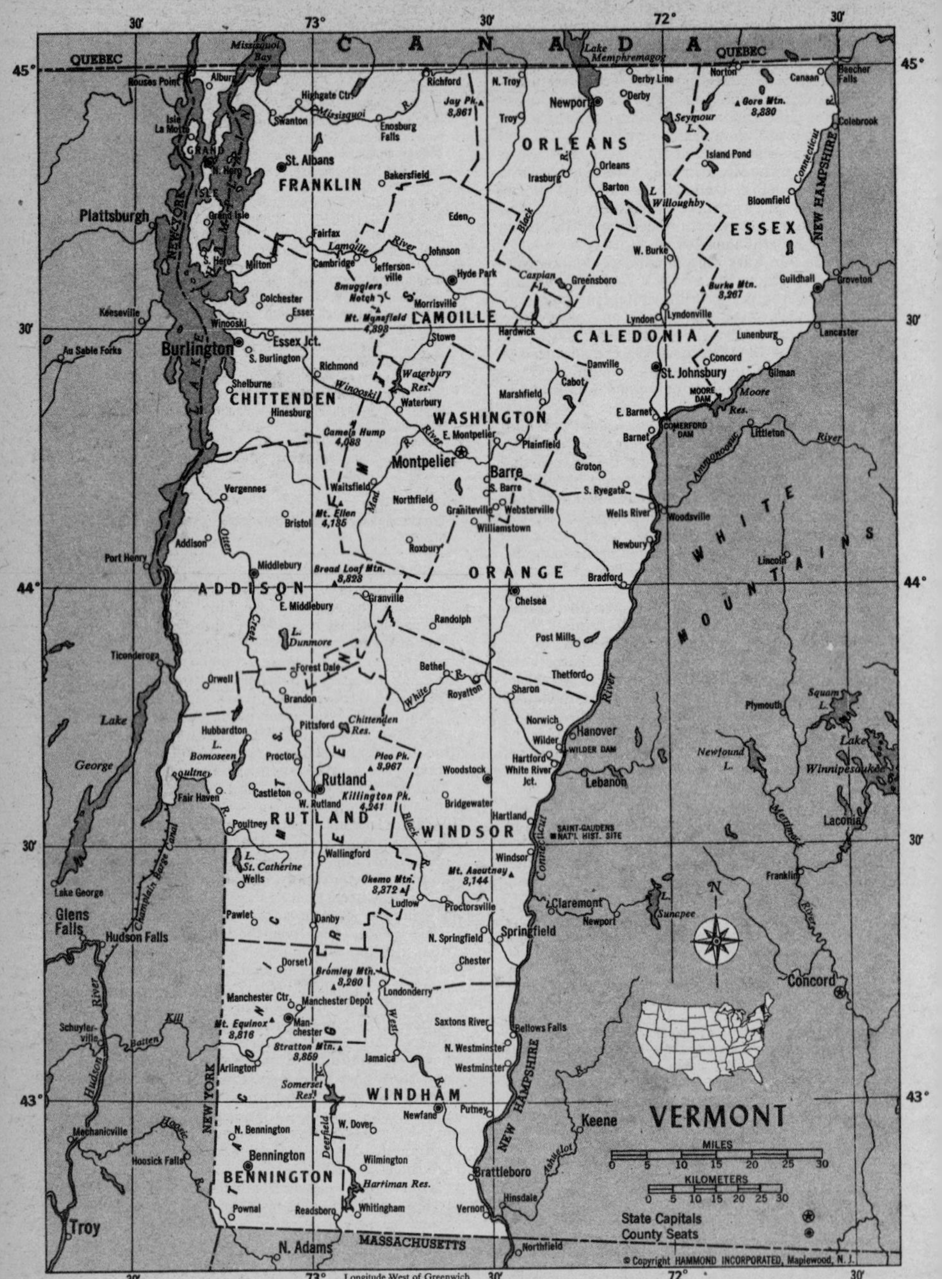

VERMONT
CANADA
QUEBEC
NEW YORK
NEW HAMPSHIRE
MASSACHUSETTS
FRANKLIN
ORLEANS
ESSEX
LAMOILLE
CALEDONIA
CHITTENDEN
WASHINGTON
ADDISON
ORANGE
RUTLAND
WINDSOR
WINDHAM
BENNINGTON
GREEN MTS.
WHITE MOUNTAINS
Montpelier
Burlington
St. Albans
Newport
St. Johnsbury
Barre
Rutland
Bennington
Brattleboro
Springfield
Middlebury
Jay Pk. 3,861
Gore Mtn. 3,330
Burke Mtn. 3,267
Mt. Mansfield 4,393
Camels Hump 4,083
Mt. Ellen 4,135
Bread Loaf Mtn. 3,823
Pico Pk. 3,967
Killington Pk. 4,241
Okemo Mtn. 3,372
Mt. Ascutney 3,144
Bromley Mtn. 3,260
Mt. Equinox 3,816
Stratton Mtn. 3,859
Lake Champlain
Lake Memphremagog
Lake George
Connecticut River
Lake Winnipesaukee
MILES
0 5 10 15 20 25 30
KILOMETERS
0 5 10 15 20 25 30
State Capitals
County Seats
Longitude West of Greenwich
© Copyright HAMMOND INCORPORATED, Maplewood, N. J.

the end of the French and Indian War (1763). Beginning in the mid-1700s New Hampshire and New York made conflicting claims on the region, and violence erupted when Ethan Allen and his "Green Mountain Boys" resisted New York officers who sought to take possession of the territory.

These differences were soon overshadowed by the American Revolution, in which the Vermonters played an important part, including the capture of Fort Ticonderoga and Crown Point. In 1777, Vermont proclaimed its independence, drawing up the first state constitution that outlawed slavery and established universal manhood suffrage without property qualifications. Land disputes continued, but were finally ended (1791) when Vermont paid New York a $30,000 claims settlement and was admitted to the Union, the first state to be added to the original 13.

The Embargo Act of 1807 and the War of 1812 were unpopular with Vermonters, who relied heavily on trade with Canada. But involvement in the war was unavoidable. Invasion by the British from Canada was averted when Americans, led by Captain Thomas Macdonough, gained a vital naval victory on Lake Champlain in 1814. Two years later, disastrous frosts ruined the state's crops, and thousands of farmers went west; immigration, which had been significant, fell sharply and never regained its former level.

Abolition was popular in the state, which strongly supported Abraham Lincoln in the 1860 presidential election. Vermont's casualties in the Civil War, as a proportion of the male population, were among the heaviest of any Northern state.

Historically a Republican state, Vermont has increasingly become a state in which the two parties are in close balance. The first Democratic governor was elected in 1962 and served until 1968. A second Democrat was elected for two terms beginning in 1972. The Republicans recaptured the governor's chair in 1976, 1978 and 1980, although in 1976 they lost control of the House of Representatives for the first time since the early 19th century. The House seat was regained by the GOP with the 1978 elections. The first Democratic U.S. Senator in the state's history was elected in 1974.

**Full name:** State of Vermont. **Origin of name:** From the French words meaning "Green Mountain." **Inhabitant:** Vermonter. **Capital:** Montpelier. **State motto:** Freedom & Unity. **Flag:** State seal on a blue field. **Seal:** Pine tree with 14 branches represents 13 original states & Vermont; cow & sheaves of wheat stand for dairying & agriculture; wavy lines at top & bottom symbolize sky & sea. **Flower:** Red clover. **Bird:** Hermit thrush. **Tree:** Sugar maple. **Song:** "Hail, Vermont." **Nickname:** Green Mountain State.

**Governor:** Richard A. Snelling. **Annual salary:** $45,000. **Term:** 2 years. **Current term expires:** Nov. 1982. **Voting requirements:** 18 yrs. old & U.S. citizen; registered state resident. **U.S. Congressmen:** 1. **Entered Union:** 1791 (14th state).

**Location & boundaries:** New England state: bounded on the north by Canada; on the east by New Hampshire & the Connecticut River; on the south by Massachusetts; & on the west by New York & Lake Champlain. **Total area:** 9,614 sq. mi. (ranks 43rd). **Extreme length:** 159 mi. **Extreme breadth:** 86 mi. **Chief rivers:** Connecticut, Winooski, Lamoille. **Major lake:** Champlain. **No. of counties:** 14.

**Population (1980 census):** 511,456 (ranks 48th). **Pop. increase (1970-80):** 15.0%. **Largest cities:** Burlington, Rutland, South Burlington. **Pop. density:** 53.2 per sq. mi.(ranks 30th). **Pop. distribution: White**—506,736; **Black**—1,135; **Am. Indian, Eskimo and Aleut**—984; **Asian and Pacific Islander**—1,355; **Other**—1,246; **Spanish origin**—3,304. **Marriage rate (1979):** 10.5 per 1,000 people. **Divorce rate:** 4.6 per 1,000 people.

**State finances (1980). Revenue:** $711,000,000. **Expenditures:** $676,000,000. **State taxes:** $521.17 per capita. **State personal income tax:** Yes. **Public debt (1980):** $1,280.15 per capita. **Federal aid (1980):** $694.87 per capita. **Personal income (1981):** $8,654.

**Sectors of the economy (% of labor force employed in 1970):** Manufacturing (24%), Wholesale and retail trade (18%), Government (15%), Educational Services (11%), Services (8%), Construction (8%). **Leading products:** machinery, food items, computer components, printing, stone items, lumber, wood & paper items, rubber & plastic items. **Agricultural products:** dairy items, cattle, apples, hay, maple items. **Avg. farm (1981):** 220 acres. **Avg. value of farm per acre:** $751.

**Highway expenditures per capita (1980):** $142.19. **Persons per motor vehicle (1981):** 1.42. **Minimum age for driver's license:** 18. **Gasoline tax:** 11¢ per gallon. **Diesel tax:** 14¢ per gallon. **Motor vehicle deaths (1980):** 26.8 per 100,000 people.

**Birthrate (1979):** 15.2 per 1,000 people. **Infant mortality rate per 1,000 births (1978):** 13.6. **Physicians per 100,000 pop. (1979):** 211. **Dentists per 100,000 pop. (1979):** 58. **Acceptable hospital beds (1979):** 5.7 per 1,000 people. **State expenditures per capita for health and hospitals (1980):** $84.70.

**Education expenditures (1977-78):** $532.54 per capita annually. **No. of pupils in public schools (1980):** 97,000. **No. of institutions of higher learning (1978-79):** 21. **Public school expenditure per pupil in attendance (1978-79):** $1,976. **Avg. salary of public school teachers (1979-80):** $13,070. **No. full-time teachers (1980):** 7,400. **Educational attainment of adult population (1976):** 12.5 median yrs. of school completed: 0.9% with less than 5 years of education; 15.7% with 4 yrs. of college.

**Telephones (1979):** 52 per 100 people. **State Chamber of Commerce:** Vermont State Chamber of Commerce, P.O. Box 37, Montpelier, Vermont 05602.

## VIRGINIA

Virginia, home of the first English settlement in North America (Jamestown, 1607), is a state particularly rich in American history. A Virginian, Richard Henry Lee, introduced (June 7, 1776) the motion for separation of the 13 Colonies from England; Virginian Thomas Jefferson was the main author of the Declaration of Independence; and Virginian George Washington led the way to victory in the American Revolution. Eight U.S. Presidents were Virginians, including four of the first five: Washington (1st), Jefferson (3rd), James Madison (4th), and James Monroe (5th); the latter three, in office 24 consecutive years, made up the so-called "Virginia Dynasty." Famed Chief Justice John Marshall was also a Virginian.

The state, which is named for Elizabeth I ("The Virgin Queen"), has acquired several nicknames including "The Mother of States," because all or part of eight other states were formed from western territory it once claimed: West Virginia, Kentucky, Illinois, Indiana, Michigan, Minnesota, Ohio, and Wisconsin. In the American Revolution, General Charles Cornwallis's surrender (1781) to Washington at Yorktown virtually ended hostilities. During the Civil War, Virginia was the central battleground. Among the major battles fought within it were First and Second Bull Run (Manassas), Fredericksburg, Chancellorsville, the Wilderness, Petersburg, and Richmond; Confederate General Robert E. Lee, another Virginian, surrendered at Appomattox (April 9, 1865).

Roughly triangular in shape, the state has four principal land regions (west to east): the Appalachian Plateau, the Great Appalachian Valley (known also locally as the Valley of Virginia, a series of ridges and valleys including the historic Shenandoah Valley), the Piedmont Plateau (the largest single area), and the Atlantic Coastal Plain, also called the Tidewater Region. Prominent local features of the Appalachian range include the Allegheny Mountains along the western border and the Blue Ridge range rising between the Valley and Piedmont sections. Across Chesapeake Bay, making up the lower part of the Delmarva

VIRGINIA
MILES
0 10 20 40 60
KILOMETERS
0 10 20 40 60
National Capital
State Capitals
County Seats
Independent Cities *Bristol
WESTERN PART OF VIRGINIA
Same scale as main map
WASHINGTON D.C.
Longitude West of Greenwich
© Copyright HAMMOND INCORPORATED, Maplewood, N.J.
ATLANTIC OCEAN
CHESAPEAKE BAY
NORTH CAROLINA
Richmond
Norfolk
Virginia Beach
Newport News
Hampton
Portsmouth
Chesapeake
Alexandria
Arlington
Fredericksburg
Charlottesville
Lynchburg
Roanoke
Danville
Petersburg
Harrisonburg
Staunton
Winchester
Bristol
Delmarva Peninsula
DELAWARE
MARYLAND
W. VA.
KENTUCKY
TENN.

Peninsula, is the state's Eastern Shore. About two-thirds of the land is forested.

Significant agriculture includes fruit, hay, corn, peanuts, and tobacco, the largest crop and a crucial factor in the state's development. Leading manufactures include chemical and tobacco products. Fishing and, to a lesser degree, mining (especially of coal) are considerable, as is tourism. Attractions include the reconstructed colonial town of Williamsburg, Washington's birthplace (Wakefield) and residence (Mount Vernon), Jefferson's Monticello, old Alexandria, Virginia Beach, Shenandoah National Park and the Skyline Drive, Arlington National Cemetery, Cumberland Gap National Historical Park, Assateague Island National Seashore at Chincoteague, and various Civil War battlegrounds.

Indians of three major language groups (Algonquian, Siouan, and Iroquoian) were living in the region when the first British arrived, about 25 years after an unsuccessful settlement by Spanish Jesuits. English settlement proceeded despite great hardship, mainly through the efforts of such men as Captain John Smith and Thomas West, Baron De La Warr, Virginia's first governor. The House of Burgesses, first legislative body in the New World, convened (1619) at Jamestown, and five years later Virginia became England's first royal colony. The importation of Negroes, first as indentured servants and later as slaves, was begun. The production and exportation of tobacco, which was first cultivated (1612) by John Rolfe, spurred the colony's growth, and the plantation became the earliest social unit. Rolfe's marriage (1614) to Pocahontas helped induce a brief period of peace with the Indians, but there were massacres in 1622 and 1644, and not until Lord Dunmore's War (1774) did Indian troubles decrease.

At the time of Sir William Berkeley's governorship (1641-52, 1660-77), the colony was thriving, with freeholders and merchants controlling the government. Hard times came (1660) with the Restoration's Navigation Acts, which stipulated the exclusive use of English ships and ports for the tobacco trade, causing initial transport bottlenecks, price drops, and widespread discontent. This unrest was aggravated by Berkeley's increasingly unpopular practices (including a slacking of vigilance against the Indians), and an abortive revolt (Bacon's Rebellion, 1676) was mounted; when Berkeley harshly overreacted, England recalled him.

Inflamed by such orators as Patrick Henry ("Give me liberty or give me death!"), Virginians in the 18th century traveled a path of inevitable revolt and, after Washington's final military victory had decided the issue, they provided the first Federal leadership. In 1788 Virginia ratified the Constitution and relinquished all its western land claims except Kentucky and West Virginia (Kentucky became an independent state in 1792, as did West Virginia in 1863; two counties were added to the latter state in 1866). Virginia seceded from the Union in 1861 and was readmitted in 1870.

A new constitution was drafted (1902) that imposed a poll tax, virtually disenfranchising Blacks, but state and Federal court decisions in the 1960s held the poll tax unconstitutional as a requisite for voting, and a new state constitution approved by voters in 1970 eliminated the tax.

Virginia undertook "massive resistance" to public school desegregation after the Supreme Court's 1954 desegregation ruling, and a few schools were temporarily closed to avoid integration. During the 1960s and 1970s racial tensions have sharply declined. Tension was renewed, however, when federal courts issued orders for massive busing of pupils, climaxed by the decision of a U.S. District Judge ordering the consolidation of the school systems of Richmond and two adjacent, mostly white counties. That order later was overturned.

**Full name:** Commonwealth of Virginia. **Origin of name:** In honor of Queen Elizabeth of England, the "Virgin Queen." **Inhabitant:** Virginian. **Capital:** Richmond. **State motto:** Sic Semper Tyrannis (Thus Always to Tyrants). **Flag:** State seal on blue field. **Seal:** State motto; standing figure representing virtue, dressed as woman warrior, standing triumphant over figure of tyranny. **Flower:** American Dogwood. **Bird:** Cardinal. **Tree:** American Dogwood. **Song:** "Carry Me Back to Old Virginia." **Nickname:** Old Dominion State.

**Governor:** Charles S. Robb. **Annual salary:** $75,000. **Term:** 4 years. **Current term expires:** Jan. 1986. **Voting requirements:** 18 yrs. old & U.S. citizen; registered in precinct of residence. **U.S. Congressmen:** 10. **Entered Union:** 1788 (10th state).

**Location & boundaries:** South Atlantic state: bounded on the north by Maryland; on the west by West Virginia & Kentucky; on the south by Tennessee & North Carolina; & on the east by the Atlantic Ocean. **Total area:** 40,767 sq. mi. (ranks 36th). **Extreme length:** 440 mi. **Extreme breadth:** 200 mi. **Coastline:** 342 mi.; 112 mi. along the Atlantic Ocean & 230 mi. along Chesapeake Bay. **Chief rivers:** James, Potomac, Rappahannock. **Major lakes:** Smith Mountain, John H. Kerr Reservoir. **No. of counties:** 95.

**Population (1980 census):** 5,346,818 (ranks 14th). **Pop. increase (1970-80):** 14.9%. **Largest cities:** Norfolk, Virginia Beach, Richmond, Newport News. **Pop. density:** 131.2 per sq. mi. (ranks 16th). **Pop. distribution: White**—4,229,734; **Black**—1,008,311; **Am. Indian, Eskimo and Aleut**—9,336; **Asian and Pacific Islander**—66,209; **Other**—32,689; **Spanish origin**—79,873. **Marriage rate (1979):** 11.3 per 1,000 people. **Divorce rate:** 4.5 per 1,000 people.

**State finances (1980). Revenue:** $5,656,000,000. **Expenditures:** $5,393,000,000. **State taxes:** $513.15 per capita. **State personal income tax:** Yes. **Public debt (1979):** $360.32 per capita. **Federal aid (1980):** $338.12 per capita. **Personal income (1981):** $10,445.

**Sectors of the economy (% of labor force employed in 1970):** Government (24%), Manufacturing (22%), Wholesale and retail trade (18%), Services (8%), Educational Services (8%), Construction (7%). **Leading products:** chemicals, textile items, apparel, food items, transportation equipment, furniture & fixtures, electrical equipment & supplies. **Minerals:** coal, stone, sand & gravel, lime. **Fishing:** crabs, oysters, menhaden. **Agricultural products:** livestock & livestock items, dairy items, poultry & poultry items, tobacco, corn, hay. **Avg. farm (1981):** 169 acres. **Avg. value of farm per acre:** $1,080.

**Highway expenditures per capita (1980):** $155.92. **Persons per motor vehicle (1981):** 1.44. **Minimum age for driver's license:** 16. **Gasoline tax:** 11¢ per gallon. **Diesel tax:** 11¢ per gallon. **Motor vehicle deaths (1980):** 19.5 per 100,000 people.

**Birthrate (1979):** 14.8 per 1,000 people. **Infant mortality rate per 1,000 births (1978):** 13.8. **Physicians per 100,000 pop. (1979):** 170. **Dentists per 100,000 pop. (1979):** 49. **Acceptable hospital beds (1979):** 6.0 per 1,000 people. **State expenditures per capita for health and hospitals (1980):** $105.01.

**Education expenditures (1977-78):** $461.75 per capita annually. **No. of pupils in public schools (1980):** 1,013,000. **No. of institutions of higher learning (1978-79):** 71. **Public school expenditure per pupil in attendance (1978-79):** $1,870. **Avg. salary of public school teachers (1979-80):** $14,600. **No. full-time teachers (1980):** 60,400. **Educational attainment of adult population (1976):** 12.4 median yrs. of school completed: 4.6% with less than 5 years of education; 16.4% with 4 yrs. of college.

**Telephones (1979):** 53 per 100 people. **State Chamber of Commerce:** Virginia State Chamber of Commerce, 611 East Franklin Street, Richmond, Virginia 23219.

## WASHINGTON

Washington, traditional gateway to Alaska and the Far East, is a leader in the vital areas of aircraft production, nuclear research, lumbering, and actual and potential waterpower production. It is also a land of rugged beauty that particularly appeals to lovers of the great outdoors.

The Cascade Mountains, running north and south, divide the state in two, the eastern part comprising about three-fifths of the total area. The

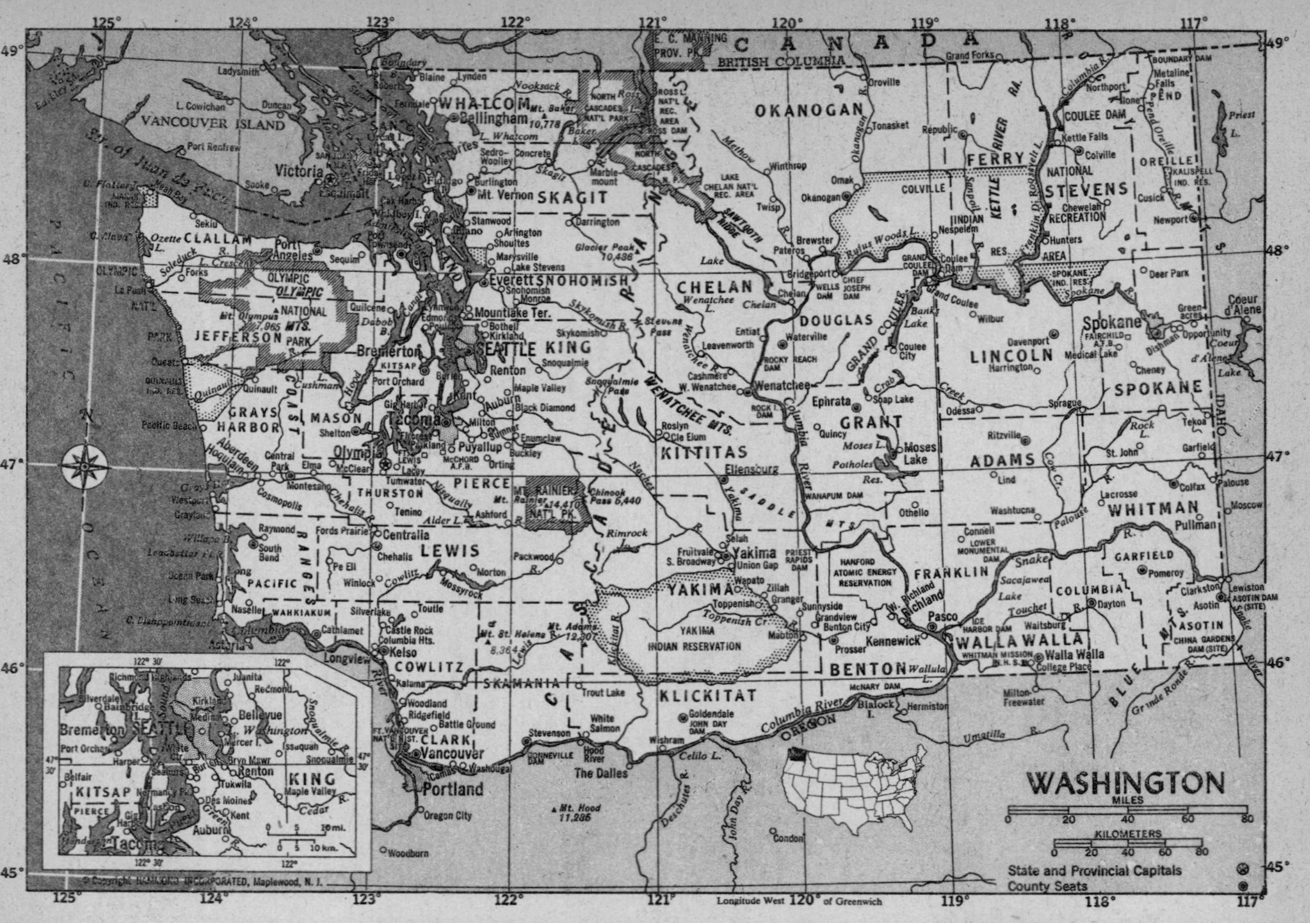
WASHINGTON
MILES
KILOMETERS
State and Provincial Capitals
County Seats
Longitude West 120° of Greenwich
CANADA
BRITISH COLUMBIA
IDAHO
OREGON
PACIFIC OCEAN
VANCOUVER ISLAND
Str. of Juan de Fuca
OKANOGAN
FERRY
STEVENS
PEND OREILLE
SPOKANE
LINCOLN
DOUGLAS
CHELAN
WHATCOM
SKAGIT
SNOHOMISH
KING
KITTITAS
GRANT
ADAMS
WHITMAN
GARFIELD
COLUMBIA
ASOTIN
WALLA WALLA
FRANKLIN
BENTON
YAKIMA
KLICKITAT
SKAMANIA
CLARK
COWLITZ
LEWIS
PIERCE
THURSTON
MASON
KITSAP
JEFFERSON
CLALLAM
GRAYS HARBOR
PACIFIC
WAHKIAKUM
Olympia
Seattle
Tacoma
Spokane
Yakima
Vancouver
Portland
Victoria
Bellingham
Everett
Bremerton
Wenatchee
Ellensburg
Kennewick
Pasco
Richland
Walla Walla
Pullman
Aberdeen
Hoquiam
Centralia
Longview
Kelso
The Dalles
Columbia River
Snake R.
HANFORD ATOMIC ENERGY RESERVATION
YAKIMA INDIAN RESERVATION
OLYMPIC NATIONAL PARK
MT. RAINIER NAT'L PK.
Mt. Rainier 14,410
Mt. Baker 10,778
Glacier Peak 10,436
Mt. Adams 12,307
Mt. St. Helens 8,364
Mt. Olympus 7,965
Mt. Hood 11,235
WENATCHEE MTS.
SADDLE MTS.
BLUE MTS.
COAST RANGES
CASCADE RANGE
GRAND COULEE
COULEE DAM
KING
Bellevue
Renton
Kirkland
© Copyright HAMMOND INCORPORATED, Maplewood, N. J.

Olympic Mountains make up the northwest corner of the state, while the Puget Sound Lowland lies between the Olympic Mountains on the west and the Cascades on the east. In the southwest corner is the Coast Range, which extends south into Oregon. East of the Cascades are the Rocky Mountains in the north and the Columbia Plateau in the south.

Most of the state's larger cities, including Seattle and Tacoma, are in the western region along Puget Sound, an unusual 200-mile-long arm of the Pacific Ocean; it varies in width up to 40 miles and harbors more than 300 islands. This area has a milder climate than any other in the country that is as far north. Generally, the weather is drier in the east than in the west, which receives moist Pacific winds and considerable rainfall. Principal irrigated regions are in the Columbia Basin and the valleys of the Walla Walla, Snake, and Yakima rivers. The Lower Granite Dam and Lock System extends navigation on the Columbia and Snake rivers as far inland as Lewiston, Idaho.

Washington is a leading producer of apples, wheat, and hops. Livestock and livestock products make up a third of the total farm revenue, while commercial fishing is significant. Mineral production, including coal and stone, accounted for $251 million in 1978. Aircraft, lumber and food industries dominate the manufacturing sector of the economy.

Today, the state is trying to diversify and stabilize its industry, with less dependency on federal defense contracts. One area of concentration is the brisk tourist trade, which has gained greatly in recent years as more facilities are built to augment the exceptional hunting, fishing, and skiing available. Mount Rainier and Olympic National Parks, and the Grand Coulee Dam National Recreation Area, are among the major attractions. Seattle Center, consisting of structures from the 1962 Century 21 Exposition, includes a monorail and 606-foot "Space Needle." Whitman Mission National Historic Site denotes the place Marcus Whitman founded an Indian mission in 1836; it is also the site of the 1847 Indian massacre in which Whitman and others were killed.

A part of the Oregon country claimed by both Britain and the United States in the 1830s, Washington became U.S. territory by a compromise treaty with Britain in 1846. It became a state in 1889.

The period after World War I was one of discontent and strife in the labor field. There were many disputes, especially between businessmen and the Industrial Workers of the World (IWW); violence erupted at Centralia. During World War II, the state's sizable Japanese-American population suffered discrimination and disruption; over 15,000 people were displaced eastward.

In 1979, Gov. Dixy Lee Ray closed a nuclear waste dump near Hanford, accusing users of carelessness in shipments. The dump was reopened after Gov. Ray made an agreement with the governors of the other two states with similar dumps—Richard Riley of South Carolina and Robert List of Nevada—to require dump users to certify that each shipment met all Federal and state standards.

In March 1980, Mount St. Helens, a volcano which had been dormant since 1857, began to rumble and to spew out smoke and ash. Tremors and thunderstorms followed, and Gov. Ray ordered the area five miles around the mountain evacuated. An eruption on May 18 blew 1,300 feet off the mountain, spewed volcanic ash throughout western Washington and into Idaho and Montana, sent streams of mud through low-lying areas, overturned 2,500 acres of timber, and killed 60 people. The ash disabled vehicles and closed hundreds of miles of highways. A stream of mud moved slowly down the Toutle River, and Spirit Lake filled up with mud and ash and was cut in half by a dam of debris. Steam and ash continued out of the mountain; the ground rumbled; an eruption on May 24 blew 200 feet off the mountain, spreading more ash and mud. On the night of June 12-13, a third major eruption sent pebbles of pumice the size of marbles into the air; pebble fallout forced the evacuation of the entire town of Cougar.

On July 22, after almost six weeks of silence, and following a series of increasingly frequent earthquakes, Mount St. Helens spewed forth ash three times within a two-hour period. This trio of eruptions resulted in the lava dome being completely blown apart and a new, glowing inner crater being revealed. The volcano continued intermittent activity throughout 1981 and into 1982.

In April 1982, Governor John Spellman rejected an application to allow the Northern Tier Pipeline Company to build an oil unloading terminal at Port Angeles and a pipeline under Puget Sound. The pipeline would have transported Alaskan oil to the Midwest.

**Full name:** State of Washington. **Origin of name:** In honor of George Washington. **Inhabitant:** Washingtonian. **Capital:** Olympia. **State motto:** Alki (By & By). **Flag:** State seal on green field. **Seal:** Portrait of George Washington & date 1889, the year state was admitted to Union. **Flower:** Western rhododendron. **Bird:** Willow goldfinch. **Tree:** Western hemlock. **Song:** "Washington, My Home." **Nickname:** Evergreen State.

**Governor:** John Spellman. **Annual salary:** $63,000. **Term:** 4 years. **Current term expires:** Jan. 1983. **Voting requirements:** 18 yrs. old & U.S. citizen; resident of state for 30 days. **U.S. Congressmen:** 8. **Entered Union:** 1889 (42nd state).

**Location & boundaries:** Pacific state: bounded on the north by Canada; on the east by Idaho; on the south by Oregon & the Columbia River; & on the west by the Pacific Ocean. **Total area:** 68,139 sq. mi. (ranks 20th). **Extreme length:** 358 mi. **Extreme breadth:** 240 mi. **Coastline:** 157 mi. **Chief rivers:** Columbia, Snake, Yakima. **Major lakes:** Chelan, Franklin D. Roosevelt. **No. of counties:** 39.

**Population (1980 census):** 4,132,180 (ranks 20th). **Pop. increase (1970-80):** 21.1%. **Largest cities:** Seattle, Spokane, Tacoma. **Pop. density:** 60.6 per sq. mi. (ranks 28th). **Pop. distribution: White—** 3,777,296; **Black—**105,544; **Am. Indian, Eskimo and Aleut—** 60,771; **Asian and Pacific Islander—**102,503; **Other—**84,049; **Spanish origin—**119,986. **Marriage rate (1979):** 12.0 per 1,000 people. **Divorce rate:** 6.9 per 1,000 people.

**State finances (1980). Revenue:** $6,324,000,000. **Expenditures:** $5,715,000,000. **State taxes:** $706.40 per capita. **State personal income tax:** No. **Public debt (1980):** $387.51 per capita. **Federal aid (1980):** $395.02 per capita. **Personal income (1981):** $11,266.

**Sectors of the economy (% of labor force employed in 1970):** Manufacturing (22%), Wholesale and retail trade (22%), Government (19%), Educational Services (9%), Services (7%), Construction (6%). **Leading products:** transportation equipment, machinery, food items, lumber & wood, paper items, chemicals, primary metals, printing & publishing. **Agricultural products:** dairy items, cattle, poultry, wheat, apples, hay. **Fishing:** salmon, oysters, crabs. **Avg. farm (1981):** 413 acres. **Avg. value of farm per acre:** $854.

**Highway expenditures per capita (1980):** $149.63. **Persons per motor vehicle (1981):** 1.25. **Minimum age for driver's license:** 16. **Gasoline tax:** 12¢ per gallon. **Diesel tax:** 12¢ per gallon. **Motor vehicle deaths (1980):** 23.5 per 100,000 people.

**Birthrate (1979):** 16.4 per 1,000 people. **Infant mortality rate per 1,000 births (1978):** 12.5. **Physicians per 100,000 pop. (1979):** 178. **Dentists per 100,000 pop. (1979):** 68. **Acceptable hospital beds (1979):** 3.9 per 1,000 people. **State expenditures per capita for health and hospitals (1980):** $62.20.

**Education expenditures (1977-78):** $622.25 per capita annually. **No. of pupils in public schools (1980):** 758,000. **No. of institutions of higher learning (1978-79):** 49. **Public school expenditure per pupil in attendance (1978-79):** $2,575. **Avg. salary of public school teachers (1979-80):** $19,488. **No. full-time teachers (1980):**

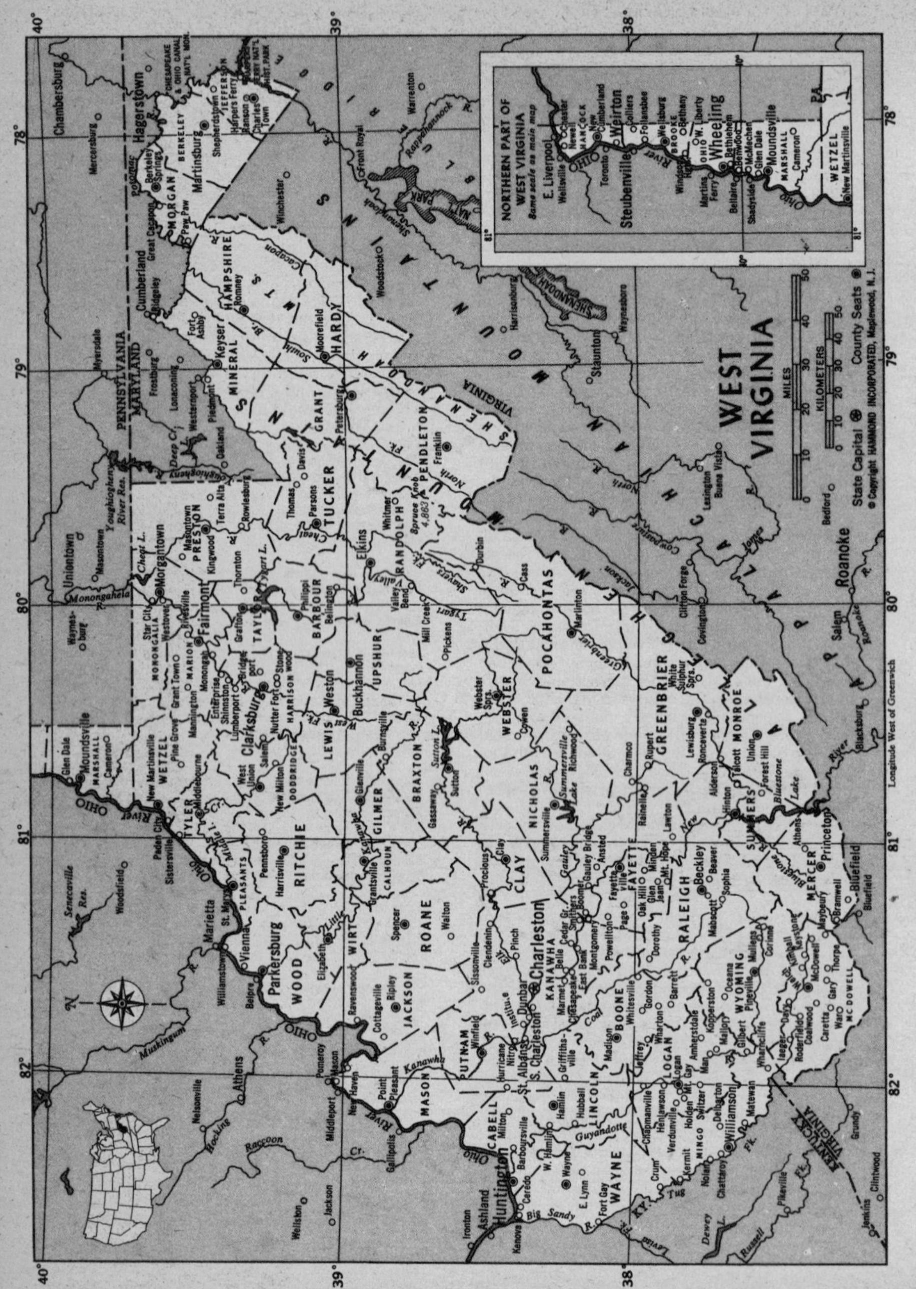
WEST VIRGINIA
NORTHERN PART OF WEST VIRGINIA
Same scale as main map
MILES
0 10 20 30 40 50
KILOMETERS
0 10 20 30 40 50
State Capital
County Seats
© Copyright HAMMOND INCORPORATED, Maplewood, N.J.
Longitude West of Greenwich

38,900. **Educational attainment of adult population (1976):** 12.7 median yrs. of school completed: 1.0% with less than 5 years of education; 16.1% with 4 yrs. of college.

**Telephones (1979):** 56 per 100 people. **State Chamber of Commerce:** Association of Washington Business, P.O. Box 658, Olympia, Washington 98507.

## WEST VIRGINIA

West Virginia, second leading coal producer in the U.S., has rugged, ravine-slashed terrain and highly irregular boundaries. There are two main land regions: the Appalachian Plateau constitutes more than 80 percent of its area, and the Great Appalachian Valley consists of a wide strip along the eastern border and includes an expanse of the Allegheny Mountains and a small section of the Blue Ridge. Most of the state's coal, oil, gas, and salt deposits are in the plateau region. Moderately cold winters, warm summers, and adequate rainfall are features of the climate, but the craggy land is not conducive to large-scale farming.

Manufacturing and commerce buttress the state's mineral-oriented economy. The state's numerous glass factories include the Fostoria works at Moundsville and the Fenton plant at Williamstown. The Ohio and Kanawha Valleys are vital chemical centers. Fine scenery, mineral springs, and 40 state parks make for a sizable tourism business. Attractions include the Harpers Ferry National Historical Park, the National Radio Astronomy Observatory at Green Bank, the famous White Sulphur Springs Spa, the Monongahela National Forest, and Wheeling's Oglebay Park.

West Virginia's early history is largely shared with Virginia, of which it was a part until Virginia joined the Confederacy in 1861; the western counties then adopted their own government and sided with the Union; statehood dates from 1863. Two counties were added to the state in 1866.

Indians known as Mound Builders were the region's earliest inhabitants, but they were gone long before the advent of the Europeans in the 1670s. Several Indian tribes continued, however, to use the area as hunting grounds. Welsh, Scots-Irish, and Germans may have lived in the region before him, but credit is often given to Morgan Morgan for having established (1731) the first known permanent settlement on Mill Creek in the eastern panhandle. In 1742 coal was discovered on the Coal River, an event that was a major determinant of West Virginia's destiny. The Indians' hold on the region virtually ended in 1774 but fighting erupted three years later and continued until 1794.

When the state broke away from Virginia, many West Virginians, including General Thomas J. (Stonewall) Jackson, remained loyal to the mother state. A famous long-running (1882-96) feud between the Hatfields of West Virginia and the McCoys of Kentucky resulted in many killings and involved the governors of those states in an acrimonious rift.

Industrial expansion marked the late 19th and early 20th centuries, despite serious labor disputes, especially in the coal mining industry. Not until the 1930s were the mines unionized and working conditions appreciably improved.

A public employee strike for union recognition in 1968 resulted in mass dismissals of state highway workers. The coal mines were shut down 45 days in late 1971 as the United Mine Workers negotiated a new contract. Wildcat strikes have erupted in the mines over such issues as safety and health benefits. Some 25,000 coal miners stayed off the job for three weeks in early 1974 in a protest over gas rationing measures at the height of the fuel crisis.

Recently the coal industry has come under attack by labor activists charging that priority is given to production and profits over the health of miners, and by environmentalists who charge the state's land is being destroyed for the benefit of out-of-state interests.

In 1975 there was a major resurgence in the state's coal industry. In 1976 progress was slowed by a wildcat strike which began in Logan, spreading to eight other states before it ended. With the announcement of President Carter's energy program in 1977, increased importance was placed on West Virginia's industry, but again production was hampered by a series of wildcat strikes. In a long strike, the United Mine Workers shut down the mines from December 1977 to March 1978. And 5,200 wildcat strikers stayed off the job for 11 days in February and March 1980. The UMW coal strike of 1981 lasted 72 days, with the miners returning to work on June 8.

**Full name:** State of West Virginia. **Origin of name:** In honor of the "Virgin Queen," Elizabeth I of England. **Inhabitant:** West Virginian. **Capital:** Charleston. **State motto:** Montani Semper Liberi (Mountaineers Are Always Free). **Flag:** State seal on blue-bordered white field. **Seal:** Rock (with date June 20, 1863, when state entered Union) stands between farmer & miner, symbolizing state's industries. **Flower:** Big rhododendron. **Bird:** Cardinal. **Tree:** Sugar maple. **Songs:** "The West Virginia Hills," "This Is My West Virginia," & "West Virginia, My Home Sweet Home." **Nickname:** Mountain State.

**Governor:** John D. Rockefeller IV. **Annual salary:** $60,000. **Term:** 4 years. **Current term expires:** Jan. 1984. **Voting requirements:** 18 yrs. old & U.S. citizen; resident of state, 30 days. **U.S. Congressmen:** 4. **Entered Union:** 1863 (35th state).

**Location & boundaries:** Southeastern state: bounded on the north by the Ohio River, Pennsylvania, Maryland & the Potomac River; on the east by Maryland & Virginia; on the south by Virginia; & on the west by Kentucky, Ohio & the Ohio River. **Total area:** 24,231 sq. mi. (ranks 41st). **Extreme length:** 265 mi. **Extreme breadth:** 237 mi. **Chief rivers:** Ohio, Potomac, Kanawa. **Major lake:** East Lynn Reservoir. **No. of counties:** 55.

**Population (1980 census):** 1,950,279 (ranks 34th). **Pop. increase (1970-80):** 11.8%. **Largest cities:** Charleston, Huntington, Wheeling. **Pop. density:** 80.5 per sq. mi. (ranks 25th). **Pop. distribution: White**—1,874,751; **Black**—65,051; **Am. Indian, Eskimo and Aleut**—1,610; **Asian and Pacific Islander**—5,194; **Other**—3,038; **Spanish origin**—12,707. **Marriage rate (1979):** 9.4 per 1,000 people. **Divorce rate:** 5.3 per 1,000 people.

**State finances (1980). Revenue:** $2,640,000,000. **Expenditures:** $2,679,000,000. **State taxes:** $625.38 per capita. **State personal income tax:** Yes. **Public debt (1980):** $931.53 per capita. **Federal aid (1980):** $486.85 per capita. **Personal income (1981):** $8,334.

**Sectors of the economy (% of labor force employed in 1970):** Manufacturing (23%), Wholesale and retail trade (19%), Government (17%), Educational Services (8%), Services (7%), Construction (7%). **Leading products:** chemicals; stone, clay & glass items; primary & fabricated metals; food items; machinery; printing & publishing. **Minerals:** coal, natural gas & natural gas liquids, stone. **Agricultural products:** cattle, dairy items, hay, apples, corn. **Avg. farm (1981):** 210 acres. **Avg. value of farm per acre:** $751.

**Highway expenditures per capita (1980):** $295.65. **Persons per motor vehicle (1981):** 1.41. **Minimum age for driver's license:** 16. **Gasoline tax:** 10.5¢ per gallon. **Diesel tax:** 10.5¢ per gallon. **Motor vehicle deaths (1980):** 26.8 per 100,000 people.

**Birthrate (1979):** 15.9 per 1,000 people. **Infant mortality rate per 1,000 births (1978):** 15.1. **Physicians per 100,000 pop. (1979):** 133. **Dentists per 100,000 pop. (1979):** 39. **Acceptable hospital beds (1979):** 7.2 per 1,000 people. **State expenditures per capita for health and hospitals (1980):** $63.83.

**Education expenditures (1977-78):** $456.62 per capita annually. **No. of pupils in public schools (1980):** 384,000. **No. of institutions of higher learning (1978-79):** 28. **Public school expenditure per pupil in attendance (1978-79):** $1,905. **Avg. salary of public school teachers (1979-80):** $14,282. **No. full-time teachers (1980):** 20,800. **Educational attainment of adult population (1976):** 12.1 median yrs. of school completed: 5.0% with less than 5 years of education; 9.2% with 4 yrs. of college.

WISCONSIN
MILES
0 10 20 40 60
KILOMETERS
0 20 40 60
State Capitals County Seats
© Copyright HAMMOND INCORPORATED, Maplewood, N. J.
Longitude West of Greenwich
93° 92° 91° 90° 89° 88° 87°
47° 46° 45° 44° 43° 42°
LAKE SUPERIOR
LAKE MICHIGAN
MINNESOTA
IOWA
ILLINOIS
MICHIGAN
MESABI RA.
APOSTLE ISLANDS NAT'L. LAKESHORE
APOSTLE ISLANDS
EFFIGY MOUNDS NAT'L MON.
Timms Hill 1,951
Rib Mtn. 1,941
DOUGLAS
BAYFIELD
IRON
ASHLAND
VILAS
BURNETT
WASHBURN
SAWYER
PRICE
ONEIDA
FLORENCE
FOREST
MARINETTE
POLK
BARRON
RUSK
LINCOLN
LANGLADE
TAYLOR
ST. CROIX
DUNN
CHIPPEWA
MARATHON
MENOMINEE
OCONTO
PIERCE
PEPIN
EAU CLAIRE
CLARK
SHAWANO
DOOR
BUFFALO
TREMPEALEAU
WOOD
PORTAGE
WAUPACA
OUTAGAMIE
BROWN
KEWAUNEE
JACKSON
MANITOWOC
LA CROSSE
MONROE
JUNEAU
ADAMS
WAUSHARA
WINNEBAGO
CALUMET
MARQUETTE
GREEN LAKE
FOND DU LAC
SHEBOYGAN
VERNON
RICHLAND
SAUK
COLUMBIA
DODGE
WASHINGTON
OZAUKEE
CRAWFORD
IOWA
DANE
JEFFERSON
WAUKESHA
MILWAUKEE
GRANT
LAFAYETTE
GREEN
ROCK
WALWORTH
RACINE
KENOSHA
Duluth
Superior
Ashland
Ironwood
Hayward
Rhinelander
Wausau
Eau Claire
Green Bay
Appleton
Oshkosh
Stevens Point
Wisconsin Rapids
La Crosse
Sheboygan
Manitowoc
Fond du Lac
Madison
Janesville
Beloit
Racine
Kenosha
MILWAUKEE
Waukesha
Wauwatosa
West Allis
Dubuque
Rockford
Freeport
Elgin
Evanston
CHICAGO
Winona
Rochester
Red Wing
Marinette
Menominee
Escanaba
Iron Mountain
Mississippi R.
Wisconsin R.
Chippewa R.
Wolf R.
Fox R.
Rock R.
L. Winnebago
Petenwell Flowage
Castle Rock Flowage
Chippewa Flowage
Flambeau Flowage
Holcombe Flowage
L. Mendota
L. Koshkonong
RACINE
Franksville
Sturtevant
Union Grove
Waterford
Muskego
Franklin
Oak Creek
S. Milwaukee
Cudahy
St. Francis
Greenfield
Greendale
Hales Cors.
New Berlin
Brookfield
Elm Grove
Menomonee Falls
Germantown
Thiensville
Mequon
Brown Deer
Glendale
Whitefish Bay
Shorewood
Fox Point
Bayside
Oconomowoc
Hartland
Pewaukee
Delafield
Sussex
Lannon
Butler
Dousman
Mukwonago
N. Prairie
Palmyra
E. Troy
Wind L.
Okauchee
Lebanon

**Telephones (1979):** 44 per 100 people. **State Chamber of Commerce:** West Virginia Chamber of Commmerce, 1101 Kanawha Valley Bldg., P.O. Box 2789, Charleston, West Virginia 25330.

## WISCONSIN

Although Wisconsin is best known as the leading U.S. dairy state, manufacturing today represents its major economic activity; top products include nonelectrical machinery and the many pulp and paper items that the state's forests make possible. Wisconsin is also the country's largest supplier of beer, with brewers concentrated most heavily in the Milwaukee area. Politically, the state has gained a reputation for progress and reform.

The land itself, rich and diverse, consists of two principal regions: the Superior Upland in the north and the Central Lowlands, covering the lower two-thirds of the state and consisting of the Wisconsin Driftless Area in the west and the Great Lakes Plain in the east. Rolling hills, ridges, and fertile valleys and plains, punctuated by many clear lakes, have made Wisconsin famous for its scenic beauty, and, despite past exploitation, forests still cover almost half the state. By far the largest part of the population lives in the southeastern region. The state's climate is marked by sharply defined seasons that are tempered somewhat by Lakes Superior and Michigan.

Tourist attractions include the Apostle Islands National Lakeshore, the scenic Door Peninsula, and the gorge at Wisconsin Dells.

Frenchman Jean Nicolet was the first European to explore the Wisconsin region, landing (1634) at Green Bay in search of a fur-trading fortune and the legendary "Northwest Passage" to the Orient. At the time, Ottawa, Huron, and other Indians from the east were forcing indigenous Indians (including the Winnebago) westward, and only the Menominees were settled there. The arrival of Nicolet and other Frenchmen soon after established France's claim to the region that was valid until 1763, when the British gained possession.

After the American Revolution, England ceded (1783) the region to the United States, but the British retained actual control until after the War of 1812. A part of the Northwest Territory until 1800, the Wisconsin region became, successively, a part of the territories of Indiana (1800-09), Illinois (1809-18), and Michigan (1818-36). When it was made a separate territory in 1836, Wisconsin included its present area in addition to parts of Iowa, Minnesota, and sections of North and South Dakota east of the Missouri and White Earth Rivers. In 1838, the territory west of the Mississippi was organized as the Territory of Iowa, Wisconsin retaining its present area and a northward extension to Lake of the Woods in what is now Minnesota. A decade later, Wisconsin entered the Union.

Wisconsin's Indian troubles reached a climax in the Black Hawk War (1832), which virtually ended the Indian threat in the area and caused a settlement boom. There followed a substantial influx of immigrants—especially Germans, Irish, English, and Welsh. Liberal leaders, like Carl Schurz, settled in Wisconsin and added to the intellectual development of the state. In 1871, Wisconsin was hit by the great Peshtigo forest fire, the worst natural disaster in its history, which killed more than 1,000 persons and destroyed more than $5 million worth of property. An extensive reforestation program is part of Wisconsin's current far-reaching conservation efforts.

Wisconsin is the home of the three major league sports teams. The Green Bay Packers have won the NFL championship eleven times and the Milwaukee Bucks became the NBA champions in 1971. Major league baseball returned to the state in 1970 when the Seattle club of the American League became the Milwaukee Brewers.

In 1976 Wisconsin became the first of the 1976 primary states to hold an open presidential primary election. The Democratic National Committee decided in 1978 to bar open primaries in this state as well as in Michigan and Montana.

**Full name:** State of Wisconsin. **Origin of name:** From an Indian name. **Inhabitant:** Wisconsinite. **Capital:** Madison. **State motto:** Forward. **Flag:** State seal on a blue field. **Seal:** A sailor & a miner hold shield with symbols representing Wisconsin's industries; badger is state's nickname; horn of plenty; pyramid of lead. **Flower:** Wood violet. **Bird:** Robin. **Tree:** Sugar maple. **Rock:** Granite. **Mineral:** Galena. **Domestic Animal:** Dairy Cow. **Song:** "On, Wisconsin!" **Nickname:** Badger State.

**Governor:** Lee Sherman Dreyfus. **Annual salary:** $65,801. **Term:** 4 years. **Current term expires:** Jan. 1983. **Voting requirements:** 18 yrs. old & U.S. citizen; registered 10 days. **U.S. Congressmen:** 9. **Entered Union:** 1848 (30th state).

**Location & boundaries:** Midwestern state: bounded on the north by Lake Superior & the state of Michigan; on the east by Lake Michigan; on the south by Illinois; & on the west by Iowa, Minnesota, the Mississippi River & the St. Croix River. **Total area:** 56,153 sq. mi. (ranks 26th). **Extreme length:** 315 mi. **Extreme breadth:** 289 mi. **Shoreline:** 785 mi. **Chief rivers:** Mississippi, Wisconsin, St. Croix, Black, Fox. **Major lakes:** Winnebago, Poygan, Mendota, Pentenwell, Castle Rock. **No. of counties:** 72.

**Population (1980 census):** 4,705,521 (ranks 16th). **Pop. increase (1970-80):** 6.5%. **Largest cities:** Milwaukee, Madison, Green Bay, Racine. **Pop. density:** 83.8 per sq. mi. (ranks 24th). **Pop. distribution: White**—4,442,598; **Black**—182,593; **Am. Indian, Eskimo and Aleut**—29,497; **Asian and Pacific Islander**—18,165; **Other**—32,482; **Spanish origin**—62,981. **Marriage rate (1979):** 8.4 per 1,000 people. **Divorce rate:** 3.6 per 1,000 people.

**State finances (1980). Revenue:** $6,588,000,000. **Expenditures:** $6,074,000,000. **State taxes:** $715.48 per capita. **State personal income tax:** Yes. **Public debt (1980):** $519.87 per capita. **Federal aid (1980):** $430.00 per capita. **Personal income (1981):** $10,056.

**Sectors of the economy (% of labor force employed in 1970):** Manufacturing (31%), Wholesale and retail trade (20%), Government (14%), Educational Services (8%), Services (6%), Construction (5%). **Leading products:** machinery, food items, transportation equipment, paper items, primary & fabricated metals. **Agricultural products:** dairy items, cattle, hogs, hay, corn, oats. **Fishing:** whitefish, lake herring, chubs, carp, buffalo. **Avg. farm (1981):** 200 acres. **Avg. value of farm per acre:** $1,105.

**Highway expenditures per capita (1980):** $108.35. **Persons per motor vehicle (1981):** 1.56. **Minimum age for driver's license:** 16. **Gasoline tax:** 13¢ per gallon. **Diesel tax:** 13¢ per gallon. **Motor vehicle deaths (1980):** 20.7 per 100,000 people.

**Birthrate (1979):** 15.5 per 1,000 people. **Infant mortality rate per 1,000 births (1978):** 11.2. **Physicians per 100,000 pop. (1979):** 151. **Dentists per 100,000 pop. (1979):** 58. **Acceptable hospital beds (1979):** 6.1 per 1,000 people. **State expenditures per capita for health and hospitals (1980):** $70.67.

**Education expenditures (1977-78):** $569.07 per capita annually. **No. of pupils in public schools (1980):** 831,000. **No. of institutions of higher learning (1978-79):** 62. **Public school expenditure per pupil in attendance (1978-79):** $2,400. **Avg. salary of public school teachers (1979-80):** $16,300. **No. full-time teachers (1980):** 56,000. **Educational attainment of adult population (1976):** 12.5 median yrs. of school completed: 1.4% with less than 5 years of education; 12.7% with 4 yrs. of college.

**Telephones (1979):** 55 per 100 people. **State Chamber of Commerce:** Wisconsin Association of Manufacturers & Commerce, 111 E. Wisconsin Ave., Suite 1600, Milwaukee, Wisconsin 53202.

## WYOMING

Wyoming, an awesome, sparsely settled state of alternating plains and mountains, is crossed by the Continental Divide—the junction of the Great Plains and the Rocky Mountains, which slash across the state's rectangle from the northwest corner to the center of the southern boundary.

The plains-mountains dividing line is less marked in the central and northern "intermon-

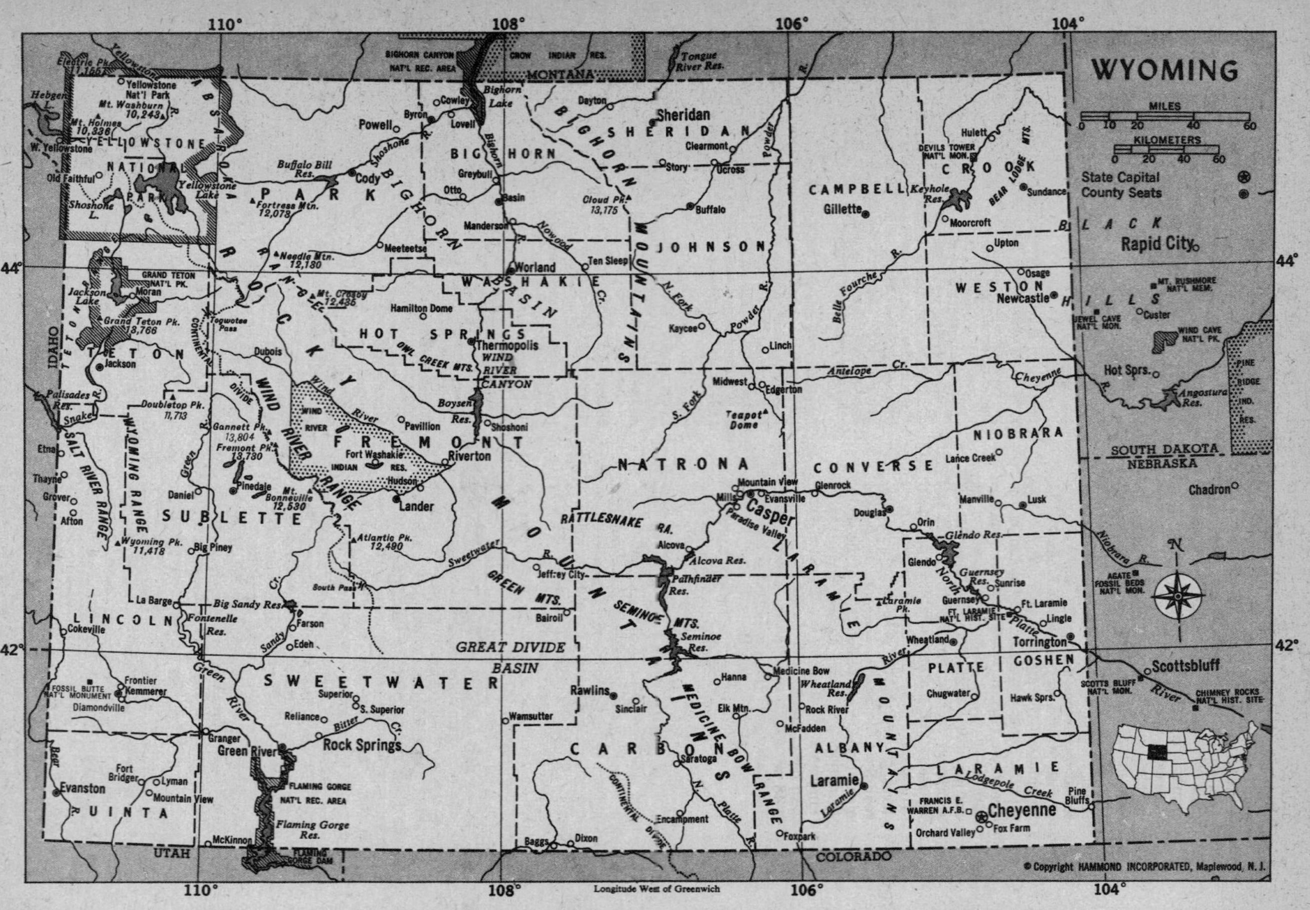
WYOMING
MILES
KILOMETERS
State Capital
County Seats
Rapid City
Scottsbluff
Chadron
Hot Sprs.
Custer
SOUTH DAKOTA
NEBRASKA
MONTANA
IDAHO
UTAH
COLORADO
CROOK
WESTON
CAMPBELL
NIOBRARA
CONVERSE
GOSHEN
PLATTE
LARAMIE
ALBANY
CARBON
NATRONA
JOHNSON
SHERIDAN
BIG HORN
WASHAKIE
HOT SPRINGS
PARK
FREMONT
SWEETWATER
SUBLETTE
TETON
LINCOLN
UINTA
YELLOWSTONE NATIONAL PARK
Cheyenne
Laramie
Casper
Sheridan
Gillette
Rock Springs
Green River
Rawlins
Evanston
Sundance
Newcastle
Lusk
Douglas
Torrington
Wheatland
Buffalo
Worland
Thermopolis
Basin
Cody
Powell
Lander
Riverton
Pinedale
Jackson
Kemmerer
Kaycee
Midwest
Edgerton
Medicine Bow
Saratoga
Encampment
Baggs
Dixon
BIGHORN MOUNTAINS
ROCKY MOUNTAINS
WIND RIVER RANGE
LARAMIE MOUNTAINS
MEDICINE BOW RANGE
WYOMING RANGE
SALT RIVER RANGE
GREEN MTS.
SEMINOE MTS.
RATTLESNAKE RA.
GREAT DIVIDE BASIN
CONTINENTAL DIVIDE
Gannett Pk. 13,804
Fremont Pk. 13,730
Grand Teton Pk. 13,766
Cloud Pk. 13,175
Atlantic Pk. 12,490
Wyoming Pk. 11,418
Teapot Dome
Flaming Gorge Res.
Yellowstone Lake
Boysen Res.
Pathfinder Res.
Seminoe Res.
Glendo Res.
Keyhole Res.
Buffalo Bill Res.
Bighorn Lake
Jackson Lake
DEVILS TOWER NAT'L MON.
FOSSIL BUTTE NAT'L MONUMENT
FRANCIS E. WARREN A.F.B.
Longitude West of Greenwich
© Copyright HAMMOND INCORPORATED, Maplewood, N.J.

tane" areas. The horizons are distant, and the land generally high—its average altitude of 6,700 feet is second only to Colorado's. The spectacular Devil's Tower—the country's first national monument—is a volcanic plug in the northeastern plains that stands 865 feet above its 415-foot base and can be seen for many miles.

The face of the land provides a clue to its economy. Short, tough grass covers much of the terrain, 80 percent of which is used for cattle and sheep grazing (Wyoming is second only to Texas in wool production). Recent consolidations have increased the size but decreased the number of farms and ranches within the state. About 20 percent of the farms produce commercial crops; the others are devoted to livestock production.

The growth of agriculture, however, is limited by the state's water supply. Although Wyoming has sufficient precipitation and underground springs to foster crop growth, as late as 1966 only ten percent of these resources were being utilized effectively. The perennial problem is distribution: in some places, where the soil is suitable for farming, the streamflow and precipitation are too light, while many large rivers like the Yellowstone and Tongue run through steep, rocky canyons.

More important to the state than agriculture is mining. In 1975, the assessed valuation on minerals was 48 percent of the entire state valuation. With the rise in oil prices, Wyoming has become one of the most intensively explored states in the Union. The Overthrust Belt near the Utah border shows great promise. Oil and oil products are among Wyoming's leading industries. Other minerals include bentonite, trona, coal, uranium, and iron ore. Wyoming is the second largest uranium producing state. Devastated by the conversion of railroad locomotives to diesel power, coal is making a comeback following formulation of emission standards which make Wyoming's low sulphur coal very much in demand. The state's coal reserves are estimated at 36 billion tons, of which two-thirds is recoverable through strip mining and underground mining methods.

John Colter, a fur-trapper and a member of the Lewis and Clark expedition (1804-06), is the first European known to have entered the state; in 1807 he explored the Yellowstone area and brought back news of its geysers and hot springs.

The Union Pacific Railroad was built (1867-68) across southern Wyoming, following the coal deposits and bringing in laborers to work the mines. The scant farmland caused many homesteaders to bypass Wyoming, leaving it open for cattlemen, who enjoyed bonanza days from 1865 to 1887.

Rustlers, declining market prices, and the severe winter of 1886-87 in which one-sixth of the herds starved all helped to curtail the cattle industry's dominance. About this time, sheep raising began to increase, leading to conflict between sheepmen and cattlemen over grazing rights.

Today tourism is increasingly vital to Wyoming's economy: over nine million persons—including many sportsmen—visit the state annually. Yellowstone and Grand Teton National Parks are prime attractions. Other National Park Service facilities are Devils Tower and Fossil Butte National Monuments; Bighorn Canyon and Flaming Gorge National Recreation Areas; and Fort Laramie National Historic Site. Wyoming has been decisively thrust into the missile age by Warren AFB (Cheyenne), one of the largest in the nation's ICBM complex.

**Full name:** State of Wyoming. **Origin of name:** Named after Wyoming Valley, Pennsylvania; Indian word means "Alternating Mountains & Valleys." **Inhabitant:** Wyomingite. **Capital:** Cheyenne. **State motto:** Equal Rights. **Flag:** State seal & buffalo on a red-&-white-bordered blue field. **Seal:** Woman & motto, "Equal Rights," symbolize equal treatment women have had in state; two men represent Wyoming's livestock & mining industries; dates Wyoming became territory & state. **Flower:** Indian paintbrush. **Bird:** Meadowlark. **Tree:** Cottonwood. **Song:** "Wyoming." **Nickname:** Equality State.

**Governor:** Ed Herschler. **Annual salary:** $55,000. **Term:** 4 years. **Current term expires:** Jan. 1983. **Voting requirements:** 18 yrs. old & U.S. citizen; resident of state & registered to vote before or at primary for general election. **U.S. Congressmen:** 1. **Entered Union:** 1890 (44th state).

**Location & boundaries:** Rocky Mountain state: bounded on the north by Montana; on the east by South Dakota & Nebraska; on the south by Colorado & Utah; & on the west by Utah, Idaho & Montana. **Total area:** 97,809 sq. mi. (ranks 9th). **Extreme length:** 365 mi. **Extreme breadth:** 265 mi. **Chief rivers:** North Platte, Bighorn, Green, Snake. **Major lakes:** Yellowstone, Jackson, Flaming Gorge Reservoir. **No. of counties:** 23.

**Population (1980 census):** 469,557 (ranks 49th). **Pop. increase (1970-80):** 41.3%. **Largest cities:** Casper, Cheyenne, Laramie. **Pop. density:** 4.8 per sq. mi. (ranks 49th). **Pop. distribution: White**—447,716; **Black**—3,364; **Am. Indian, Eskimo and Aleut**—7,125; **Asian and Pacific Islander**—1,969; **Other**—10,642; **Spanish origin**—24,499. **Marriage rate (1979):** 14.4 per 1,000 people. **Divorce rate:** 7.8 per 1,000 people.

**State finances (1980). Revenue:** $937,000,000. **Expenditures:** $797,000,000. **State taxes:** $824.04 per capita. **State personal income tax:** No. **Public debt (1980):** $770.48 per capita. **Federal aid (1980):** $406.34 per capita. **Personal income (1981):** $11,780.

**Sectors of the economy (% of labor force employed in 1970):** Government (22%), Wholesale and retail trade (20%), Educational Services (11%), Services (9%), Construction (7%), Manufacturing (6%). **Leading products:** petroleum & coal items; food items; stone, clay & glass items; lumber & wood; printing & publishing. **Minerals:** petroleum, natural gas, sodium salts, iron ore, uranium. **Agricultural products:** cattle, sheep, wool, hay, sugarbeets, wheat. **Avg. farm (1981):** 3,804 acres. **Avg. value of farm per acre:** $164.

**Highway expenditures per capita (1980):** $316.80. **Persons per motor vehicle (1981):** 0.98. **Minimum age for driver's license:** 16. **Gasoline tax:** 8¢ per gallon. **Diesel tax:** None. **Motor vehicle deaths (1980):** 52.0 per 100,000 people.

**Birthrate (1979):** 21.7 per 1,000 people. **Infant mortality rate per 1,000 births (1978):** 13.0. **Physicians per 100,000 pop. (1979):** 107. **Dentists per 100,000 pop. (1979):** 49. **Acceptable hospital beds (1979):** 5.3 per 1,000 people. **State expenditures per capita for health and hospitals (1980):** $69.83.

**Education expenditures (1977-78):** $720.43 per capita annually. **No. of pupils in public schools (1980):** 98,000. **No. of institutions of higher learning (1978-79):** 8. **Public school expenditure per pupil in attendance (1978-79):** $2,759. **Avg. salary of public school teachers (1979-80):** $16,830. **No. full-time teachers (1980):** 5,600. **Educational attainment of adult population (1976):** 12.6 median yrs. of school completed: 1.2% with less than 5 years of education; 14.5% with 4 yrs. of college.

**Telephones (1979):** 56 per 100 people. **State Chamber of Commerce:** None.

# REPRESENTATIVE AMERICAN CITIES

## ALBUQUERQUE

**Location:** North-central New Mexico, on upper Rio Grande **County:** Bernalillo **City Area:** 100 sq. miles (259 sq. kilometers) **Altitude:** 5,354 feet (1631.9 meters)
**Mayor:** Harry Kinney **Chief Administrative Officer:** Frank Kleinhenz
**City Population:** 331,767 (1980 census) **Metro Area Population:** 454,499 (1980 census)
**Daily Newspapers:** 2 **No. of Radio Stations:** 22 **No. of TV Stations:** 6
**City Chamber of Commerce:** Greater Albuquerque Chamber of Commerce, 401 2nd Street, NW, Albuquerque, New Mexico 87102

Albuquerque, seat of Bernalillo County, is the largest city in New Mexico; a fast-growing center of trade, clean industry, and Federal agencies; and a health resort. On a per capita basis, more solar-heated homes stand here than in any other large U.S. city.

The old town of Albuquerque was founded in 1706 and named for the Duke of Alburquerque. After the Mexican War (1846-48), New Mexico was organized as a U.S. territory. Albuquerque was occupied by Confederate forces briefly in 1862. The new Albuquerque was mapped out in 1880 in connection with railroad construction.

After World War II, the city grew rapidly, primarily because of Sandia Laboratory (a nuclear weapons laboratory and the city's largest employer) and Kirtland Air Force Base, a nuclear effects research laboratory and satellite tracking station. Lovelace Foundation for medical research is also located here. Albuquerque now has railroad shops, lumber mills, and food-processing plants. Manufactures include brick and tile, wood products, Indian jewelry, clothing, and business machines. Several national electronic firms have opened facilities recently. New office buildings and hotels are being constructed and a major redevelopment of the downtown area is underway.

Of historic interest is the Old Town Plaza, laid out by Spanish settlers in 1706. Some of the buildings are two centuries old and have recently been restored. The Church of San Felipe de Neri (1706), once used as a fortress against the Indians, is in the Old Town. Other attractions are the University of New Mexico, founded in 1889, with pueblo-style buildings; the Ernie Pyle Memorial Branch Library, former home of the war correspondent; the annual state fair; and the magnificent vistas from the Sandia Peak Aerial Tramway.

## ATLANTA

**Location:** Northwest Georgia, at foot of Blue Ridge Mountains, about 75 miles from northern border **County:** mostly in Fulton, part in DeKalb **City Area:** 136 sq. miles (352 sq. kilometers) **Altitude:** 1,050 feet (319.1 meters)
**Mayor:** Andrew Young
**City Population:** 425,022 (1980 census) **Metro Area Population:** 2,029,618 (1980 census)
**Daily Newspapers:** 3 **No. of Radio Stations:** 19 **No. of TV Stations:** 6
**City Chamber of Commerce:** Atlanta Chamber of Commerce, 1300 North Omni International, Atlanta, Georgia 30303

Atlanta, seat of Fulton County and capital and largest city of Georgia, is the leading commercial, industrial, and distribution center of the southeastern United States. It is also a port of entry and cultural center.

The first settler, Hardy Ivy, built a cabin on former Creek Indian land in 1833. The town, founded as Terminus in 1837, was later called Marthasville and in 1845 assumed the name Atlanta. It is said that the name was given it by railroad builder J. E. Thomson for its location at the end of the Western and Atlantic Railroad. It was incorporated as a city in 1847.

An important Confederate communications center during the Civil War, Atlanta fell to General W. T. Sherman on September 2, 1864, and on November 15 was put to the torch and almost completely destroyed. After the war, a new city was constructed and industrialization proceeded rapidly. In 1868 Atlanta became the state capital.

Today there are more than 1,500 manufacturing plants in the area. Products include automobiles, airplanes, chemicals, furniture, steel, paper, fertilizers, soft drinks, and processed foods. Atlanta is a major garment manufacturing center and is the home of the Apparel Mart, opened in 1979 as a showcase for southeastern clothing buyers. It is also a financial center and home of a Federal Reserve district bank. The National Center for Disease Control of the U.S. Public Health Service has its national headquarters here.

A billion-dollar building boom has included major privately financed projects plus several public facilities: a stadium and coliseum are in operation; the $70-million Georgia World Congress convention complex opened in September 1976 and is being expanded. The Atlanta Memorial Arts Center opened in 1968 and the High Museum of Art will occupy a new building in 1983. The Metropolitan Atlanta Rapid Transit Authority's $2.1-billion Federally financed subway system started services July 1, 1979. The 52-story Georgia-Pacific Tower will open in 1982.

In recent years Atlanta has developed its international trade, with 16 foreign banks, 31 consulates annd 18 trade, tourism and foreign chambers of commerce offices. Atlanta's new William B. Hartsfield International Airport is the global air hub of the southeast and the world's second busiest airport.

Of historic interest are the capitol and state library; the state archives building; the Cyclorama of the Battle of Atlanta; Oakland Cemetery of Civil War dead; Martin Luther King, Jr., National Historic Site; Fort Peachtree; Fort McPherson; and Wren's Nest, the home of Joel Chandler Harris, noted fabulist.

## BALTIMORE

**Location:** In Maryland, 40 miles northeast of Washington, D.C., on the Patapsco River **County:** Baltimore is an independent city **City Area:** 79 sq. miles (205 sq. kilometers) **Altitude:** 20 feet (6.1 meters)
**Mayor:** William Donald Schaefer
**City Population:** 786,775 (1980 census) **Metro Area Population:** 2,174,023 (1980 census)
**Daily Newspapers:** 2 **No. of Radio Stations:** 24 **No. of TV Stations:** 3
**City Chamber of Commerce:** Greater Baltimore Committee, Inc., Suite 900, Two Hopkins Plaza, Charles Center, Baltimore, Maryland 21201

Baltimore, largest city in Maryland, is an industrial and commercial center and major seaport. Named for Lord Baltimore, first proprietor of Maryland, it was settled in the early 1600s and officially founded in 1729.

The shipbuilding industry grew highly profitable during the Revolution and War of 1812. The famous Baltimore clippers were built in the early 1800s. During the First and Second World Wars, the city was a major shipbuilder and supply port.

Baltimore was the site of the Continental Congress after the British occupation of Philadelphia (1777-78). The city's location, near the eastern terminus of the National Road that eventually ran from Cumberland to St. Louis, helped it develop into a major center of commerce. The opening in 1825 of the Erie Canal, in New York State, diverting trade, led to the chartering of the Baltimore & Ohio Railroad to bolster Baltimore's position.

During the Civil War, Maryland remained in the Union, but many Baltimore residents were pro-Southern and in 1861 some of them attacked Union troops. The city suffered a disastrous fire in 1904 but emerged as a better-planned metropolis.

Of historic interest are the Maryland Historical Society; the Baltimore Cathedral, the 175-year-old U.S. Frigate Constellation; Edgar Allan Poe's grave in Westminster Churchyard, and Ft. McHenry.

Today Baltimore handles the fourth largest volume of foreign trade of any American port. It has attracted diverse industries, including sugar and food processing. Petroleum and chemicals, aircraft, guided missiles, and steel and gypsum products are important industries. Bethlehem Steel Company's Sparrows Point complex, the largest tidewater steel plant in the world, is located here.

Baltimore, which suffers from the deterioration and shrinking population common to all Eastern cities, has attacked these problems vigorously. Through careful planning, long-term renewal efforts have begun to reverse the trend without adding to the city's debt load. A 8.5 mile subway is under construction and a major program of urban redevelopment has reshaped the downtown area. Charles Center, begun twenty years ago, is virtually complete, as is the Civic Center. In the Inner Harbor area, an Academy of Science has been completed, the Convention Center opened in August 1979, the Harborplace Shopping Pavilions opened in July 1980, and the National Aquarium opened in 1981.

To ease traffic jams plaguing the city's harbor tunnel, a $100-million federal grant was approved in 1980 for construction of a second connection, to be named Fort McHenry Tunnel.

## BIRMINGHAM

**Location:** North-central Alabama, in the Jones Valley at the foot of Red Mt. **County:** Jefferson **City Area:** 98.4 sq. miles (254.9 sq. kilometers) **Altitude:** 600 feet (182.3 meters)
**Mayor:** Richard Arrington
**City Population:** 284,413 (1980 census) **Metro Area Population:** 847,360 (1980 census)
**Daily Newspapers:** 2 **No. of Radio Stations:** 17 **No. of TV Stations:** 5
**City Chamber of Commerce:** Birmingham Area Chamber of Commerce, P.O. Box 10127, Birminghhm, Alabama 35202

Birmingham, seat of Jefferson County, is Alabama's principal industrial city and the South's leading iron-and-steel center.

Named after Birmingham, England, the city was founded and incorporated in 1871. A decade earlier the iron ore, coal, and limestone deposits in the region were used by Confederate forces to produce cannonballs and rifles. As railroads expanded and the steel industry developed, Birmingham prospered. A financial panic briefly interrupted its growth in 1900.

Since World War II, the city's economy has undergone diversification. Birmingham, "the Pittsburgh of the South," is now a leader in transportation equipment, construction materials, chemicals, and food processing.

Birmingham experienced a building boom during the 1960s; a $37.5-million civic center includes a coliseum, music hall, theater, and exhibit hall. Development of the University of Alabama in Birmingham is entering its final phase of completion on a 236-acre site adjacent to downtown. The $100-million complex of 40 buildings is expected to outstrip U.S. Steel as the area's biggest employer. By 1990, an estimated 50,000 people will be either an employee, a student, or both.

Of interest is the Arlington Historical Shrine, one of Alabama's few remaining antebellum homes. Overlooking the city on nearby Red Mountain is a giant statue of Vulcan, the largest iron figure ever cast. The Birmingham Museum of Art has recently been enlarged. The city is also the home of the Southern Research Institute, which has a technical staff of 360.

## BOSTON

**Location:** In Massachusetts, on Massachusetts Bay, between Neponset River and the mouths of the Charles and Mystic rivers **County:** Suffolk **City Area:** 49.9 sq. miles (129.2 sq. kilometers) **Altitude:** 27 feet (8.2 meters)
**Mayor:** Kevin H. White
**City Population:** 562,994 (1980 census) **Metro Area Population:** 2,763,357 (1980 census)
**Daily Newspapers:** 3 **No. of Radio Stations:** 23 **No. of TV Stations:** 9
**City Chamber of Commerce:** Greater Boston Chamber of Commerce, 125 High Street, Boston, Massachusetts 02110

Boston, seat of Suffolk County and capital of Massachusetts, is New England's largest city. It was settled in 1630 by Puritan colonists. It became the center of American Puritanism and a fount of culture and intellect. The Boston Public Latin School, founded in 1635, and Harvard College, founded the following year in nearby Cambridge, were the first American schools.

An important commercial center because of its busy harbor, Boston became a leader in opposing British rule. Among pre-Revolutionary War actions were the Boston Massacre (1770) and the Boston Tea Party (1773). The Battle of Bunker Hill, one of the first of the Revolution, was fought close by in June 1775.

After the war, Boston prospered steadily and became a city in 1822. Prominent families such as the Cabots, Lowells, and Lodges ("the Boston Brahmins") made fortunes in shipping, textiles, and shoes. Because of the cultivated tastes of wealthy Bostonians, the city became known as "the Athens of America." Despite the conservative and wealthy atmosphere, however, it was a center of abolitionism before the Civil War.

A 19th-century flood of immigrants, largely Irish at first, converted Boston into a thriving industrial metropolis. Although it declined during the first half of the 20th century, primarily because industries moved to the South, Boston remained a cultural center and is still the financial and trading center of New England, a leading port, and an important market for fish, seafood, and wool. The electronics industry has helped revived Boston's economy.

Boston is also noted for its hospitals and its universities, among them Northeastern, Boston University and Boston College, as well as Harvard and MIT across the Charles River in Cambridge. In October 1979 the John F. Kennedy Library was dedicated.

History-steeped Boston has many points of interest from colonial and Revolutionary War times, including the Old North Church, Old South Meeting House, Old State House, Paul Revere House, King's Chapel, Boston Common and Faneuil Hall.

Downtown has undergone major redevelopment in recent years, with the building of commercial and residential high-rises, the Government Center and the renovation of Faneuil Hall Marketplace, including Quincy, South and North Markets, the Downtown Crossing Pedestrian shopping mall, and Boston Waterfront Park.

## BUFFALO

**Location:** Western New York, at mouth of Niagara River on Lake Erie **County:** Erie **City Area:** 42.6 sq. miles (110.3 sq. kilometers) **Altitude:** 585 feet (177.8 meters)
**Mayor:** James D. Griffin
**City Population:** 357,870 (1980 census) **Metro Area Population:** 1,242,573 (1980 census)
**Daily Newspapers:** 1 **No. of Radio Stations:** 19 **No. of TV Stations:** 5
**City Chamber of Commerce:** Buffalo Area Chamber of Commerce, 107 Delaware Ave., Buffalo, New York 14202

Buffalo, seat of Erie County and second largest city in New York State, was named after a local creek, which in turn derived its name from that of an Indian who once lived in the area.

A village was laid out on the site of the present city by Joseph Ellicott for the Holland Land Company in 1803. Almost completely destroyed by fire during the War of 1812, Buffalo grew slowly until the opening of the Erie Canal in 1825 after whiich it mushroomed. Buffalo was chartered as a city in 1832, became an important transportation center, a major Great Lakes port, and since the opening of the St. Lawrence Seaway, a world port.

The city has had a long association with the Presidency. Millard Fillmore, Buffalo resident, was elected Vice-President in 1848 and two years later became President after the death of Zachary Taylor. Grover Cleveland, mayor of Buffalo in 1881, was elected President in 1884 and 1892. During the 1901 Pan-American Exposition, President McKinley was assassinated in Buffalo.

Industry in the Buffalo area has flourished, largely because of hydroelectric power from Niagara Falls augmented by the Niagara Power Project, one of the largest hydroelectric power projects in the world. Buffalo is the largest grain-milling center in the world. Bethlehem Steel and General Motors are the two largest industrial employers in the area, while the State University at Buffalo is the largest service employer.

Downtown Buffalo has undergone a tremendous facelift in the past ten years. In Oct. 1978, the Buffalo Convention Center was completed, strengthening the Niagara Frontier as a prime localle for conventions. The 6.4-mile light rail rapid transit system is underway and will be completed by 1984.

Of interest in the area are nearby Niagara Falls; the Buffalo Museum of Science, Historical Museum, and Zoological Gardens; the Albright-Knox Art Gallery; Botanical Gardens; and Niagara Square.

Buffalo's professional sports teams include the Bills (NFL), Sabres (NHL), Bisons (Eastern-League baseball), and Stallions (indoor soccer).

### CHARLESTON

**Location:** In southeastern part of South Carolina, along coast, on peninsula between Ashley and Cooper Rivers **County:** Charleston **City Area:** 20.6 sq. miles (53.5 sq. kilometers) **Altitude:** sea level
**Mayor:** Joseph P. Riley, Jr.
**City Population:** 69,510 (1980 census) **Metro Area Population:** 430,301 (1980 census)
**Daily Newspapers:** 1 **No. of Radio Stations:** 11 **No. of TV Stations:** 3
**City Chamber of Commerce:** Charleston Trident Chamber of Commerce, P.O. Box 975, Charleston, South Carolina 29402

Charleston is a major Atlantic seaport and, as one of America's oldest cities, a leading tourist center. It was originally called Charles Towne in honor of Charles II by the English settlers who first landed in 1670 at Albemarle Point, about 7 miles from modern Charleston. Ten years later they moved to Oyster Point, where the city had been laid out according to the Grande Modell sent from England by the Lords Proprietor. It was incorporated in 1783 as Charleston and became the economic and social center of the region.

By the time of the Revolution, Charleston was the most important city south of Philadelphia. It was a wealthy cultural center to which French Huguenots and other non-English immigrants gave a cosmopolitan touch.

Charleston's role in the Civil War began when the South Carolina ordinance of secession was passed there in December 1860. The city's harbor was also the site of the first hostile act of the war: the firing on Fort Sumter on April 12, 1861. Although under continuous siege from 1863 to 1865, Charleston did not fall to Union forces until February 1865.

Despite the ravages of two wars, disastrous fires, a violent earthquake in 1886, and periodic hurricanes, Charleston has retained many historic buildings and colonial mansions. Of interest are: Fort Sumter, a national monument since 1948; Patriot's Point, a naval museum; the Dock Street Theater, opened in 1735; the original Catfish Row, made famous in Gershwin's *Porgy and Bess*; the Charleston Museum, founded in 1773; the Huguenot Church built in 1680 and rebuilt in 1844, and numerous antebellum homes in the peninsula city. Nearby are notable plantation homes and three world famous gardens: Cypress, Magnolia and Middleton. Charles Towne Landing (a park, pavilion, and natural zoo), was established at the time of the city's tricentennial anniversary in 1970.

The city's growing economy is linked to port and transportation expansion and commerce; diversified business, industrial, and education centers; and military installations and facilities maintained by the Army, Navy, Air Force, and the Coast Guard. New construction projects, such as the proposed Charleston Convention Center and a $13-million hotel, will bring in more tourists and more tax revenue, revitalizing the downtown area. However, controversy over the location of the convention center site, on land surrounded by areas under restoration, has held up construction.

Spoleto Festival USA, "the world's most comprehensive art festival," has become an annual event, featuring music, drama, ballet, films, opera, dance and visual arts.

### CHICAGO

**Location:** Northeastern corner of Illinois on shore of Lake Michigan **County:** Cook **City Area:** 228.1 sq. miles (590.8 sq. kilometers) **Altitude:** 578.5 feet (175.8 meters)
**Mayor:** Jane Byrne
**City Population:** 3,005,072 (1980 census) **Metro Area Population:** 7,102,328 (1980 census)
**Daily Newspapers:** 2 **No. of Radio Stations:** 26 **No. of TV Stations:** 9
**City Chamber of Commerce:** Chicago Association of Commerce and Industry, 130 S. Michigan Ave., Chicago, Illinois 60603

Chicago, seat of Cook County, Illinois, is the largest city between the Eastern seaboard and the Pacific Coast, the most important Great Lakes port, the center of the nation's largest industrial area, and the world's largest railroad terminal. Its O'Hare International Airport is considered the world's busiest.

Father Marquette and Louis Jolliet visited the site of Chicago in 1673, but more than a century elapsed before a trading post was established, by Jean Baptiste Point du Sable. He was succeeded in 1804 by the first permanant non-Indian settler, John Kinzie, who is usually regarded as the "father of Chicago."

The Erie Canal, which was opened in 1825, stimulated growth and helped convert Chicago into a prosperous commercial town. Incorporated as a city in 1837, it developed into a major rail hub and the nation's mid-continent shipping center soon after the arrival of the railroads in the 1840s. By the time of the Civil War, meatpacking had become a leading industry.

In 1871 the city was almost completely destroyed by a great fire. It was quickly rebuilt, and its booming industry attracted immigrants from all over the world. In the 1890s Chicago replaced Philadelphia as the nation's second-largest city. Labor problems led to violent eruptions, such as the Haymarket Riot of 1886 and Pullman strikes in 1894.

Chicago is a leading producer of steel, telephone equipment, appliances, electrical machinery, plastic products, and diesel engines. It boasts a Federal Reserve district bank, the Midwest Stock Exchange, the Chicago Mercantile Exchange, and the Chicago Board of Trade–the world's largest commodity futures market.

The skyscraper was Chicago's contribution to American architecture. The first skyscraper, designed by William Le Baron Jenney, was built here in 1883, and of the world's ten tallest buildings, four are in Chicago. Two of the nation's greatest architects, Louis H. Sullivan and Frank Lloyd Wright, worked in Chicago.

Landmarks of interest in the Chicago area include the Sears Tower, the world's tallest skyscraper; the Chicago Mercantile Exchange, a major international commodity and monetary market; the Merchandise Mart, the largest commercial building in the world; the Art Institute; the Museum of Science and Industry; the Shedd Aquarium; the Adler Planetarium; the Oriental Institute Museum of the University of Chicago; the Lincoln Park and Brookfield Zoos; and the Water Tower, one of the few structures to survive the 1871 fire. In 1974 the Chagall mosaic was unveiled at the First National Bank Plaza; it consists of a colorful wall of glass and stone from all over the world. Since then, monumental outdoor sculpture by such notables as Picasso, Calder, Bertoia, Noguchi, Oldenburg, Moore and Miró have been unveiled in Chicago.

Scheduled for completion in 1989 is the Illinois Center, the nation's largest planned urban development. The Center is situated northeast of the Loop and borders the lakeshore. The daytime working population will total 80,000, some of whom will reside in the Center's high-rise apartment buildings.

### CINCINNATI

**Location:** Southwestern Ohio, on Ohio River **County:** Hamilton **City Area:** 78 sq. miles (202 sq. kilometers) **Altitude:** 550 feet (167.1 meters)
**Mayor:** David Mann **City Manager:** Sylvester Murray
**City Population:** 385,457 (1980 census) **Metro Area Population:** 1,401,403 (1980 census)
**Daily Newspapers:** 2 **No. of Radio Stations:** 30 **No. of TV Stations:** 6
**City Chamber of Commerce:** Greater Cincinnati Chamber of Commerce, 120 West Fifth Street, Cincinnati, Ohio 45202

Cincinnati, seat of Ohio's Hamilton County, is an industrial, commercial, and cultural center. The first settlers arrived in 1788 and named it Losantiville. In 1790 General Arthur St. Clair, first governor of thee Northwest Territory, renamed it Cincinnati for the Society of the Cincinnati, which was formed by Continental Army officers at the end of the American Revolution. Cincinnati was the first seat of the legislature of the Northwest Territory; it was incorporated in 1802 and chartered as a city in 1819.

Completion of the Miami Canal (1827) and the Ohio and Erie Canal in the 1830s increased tthe growth of Cincinnati and its importance as a shipping center. The city was also a major station on the Underground Railroad.

Cincinnati suffered disastrous floods in 1884 and 1937. The Cincinnati riot (March 28-31, 1884) was the result of a crime wave and corrupt politics. Later the notorious political boss G. B. Cox took control, but a reform movement in the 1920s led to the establishment (1924) of the city-manager type of government.

Located on the Ohio River, Cincinnati is a major manufacturing center and a leading producer of machine tools, soap products, and playing cards. Cosmetics, radar equipment, automobiles, jet engines, and metal goods also are important to the economy. In 1976 the Environmental Protection Agency Laboratory opened here.

Recent additions to the refurbished downtown area are the new Westin Hotel, Atrium One and the First National Bank Center. The architecturally renowned Union Terminal has been given a new lease on life as an urban shopping mall.

Riverfront Stadium, built in 1970, houses the Cincinnati Bengals Football Team and the Cincinnati Reds Baseball Team. The Cincinnati Zoo and the Cincinnati Art Museum are prime attractions of the city.

## CLEVELAND

**Location:** Northeastern Ohio, on Lake Erie at mouth of the Cuyahoga River **County:** Cuyahoga **City Area:** 76 sq. miles (196.8 sq. kilometers) **Altitude:** 680 feet (206.6 meters)
**Mayor:** George V. Voinovich
**City Population:** 573,822 (1980 census) **Metro Area Population:** 1,898,720 (1980 census)
**Daily Newspapers:** 1 **No. of Radio Stations:** 27 **No. of TV Stations:** 6
**City Chamber of Commerce:** Greater Cleveland Growth Association, 690 Union Commerce Building, Cleveland, Ohio 44115

Cleveland, seat of Cuyahoga County and largest city in Ohio, is a port of entry on Lake Erie. It was laid out in 1796 by General Moses Cleaveland, an ancestor of President Grover Cleveland. Three years later a permanent settlement was established by Lorenzo Carter, and in 1836 Cleveland was chartered as a city.

After the completion of the Ohio and Erie Cannal in the 1830s and the arrival of the railroad in 1851, Cleveland became a significant link between the interior of Ohio and eastern markets. Coal from Pennsylvania and iron ore shipped from Minnesota by way of the Great Lakes made the city an important iron and steel producer. It also developed into the main refining area for Pennsylvania oil, and in 1870 John D. Rockefeller began his oil dynasty in Cleveland. Immigrants from all over the world settled in the city to work in the industries.

Mainstays of the economy today are the manufacture of machine tools and fabricated metal products with iron and steel a close third. Automobile parts, electrical equipment and chemicals are also important.

Cleveland has experienced a decline common to many large northern cities. However, cooperative efforts have produced an almost new downtown skyline, with new commercial and federal and local government buildings. Standard Oil of Ohio is erecting a 46-story headquarters building. The old flats area along the river has been restored, providing evening entertainment in the many restaurants and pubs. The Playhouse Square area is being restored.

The Cuyahoga River, Lake Erie, and the air itself have had a reputation for pollution, but extensive efforts to clean up the environment have met with great success.

Of special interest is the Emerald Necklace—a system of parks, trails, and bridle paths looping the city—along with the downtown Convention Center and Municipal Stadium. The East Side's University Circle area is a cultural center housing the Art Museum, Museum of Natural History, Western Reserve Historical Society Museum and Severance Hall, home of the world-renowned Cleveland Orchestra.

In December 1978, the city failed to pay $14 million worth of promissory notes that had fallen due and thus became the first major U.S.. city to default since the Great Depression. To generate additional revenue, voters approved a 50% increase in city income taxes in February 1979. The increase, plus a 20% lay-off of municipal employees, enabled the city to retire $3.5 million of debt and renegotiation of the notes saved Cleveland from bankruptcy. A three-year financial recovery plan began in April 1980.

## COLUMBUS

**Location:** Central Ohio, on Scioto River **County:** Franklin **City Area:** 183.9 sq. miles (476.3 sq. kilometers) **Altitude:** 780 feet (237.0 meters)
**Mayor:** Tom Moody
**City Population:** 565,032 (1980 census) **Metro Area Population:** 1,093,293 (1980 census)
**Daily Newspapers:** 2 **No. of Radio Stations:** 23 **No. of TV Stations:** 4
**City Chamber of Commerce:** Columbus Area Chamber of Commerce, 37 North High Street, P.O. Box 1527, Coluumbus, Ohio 43216

Columbus, capital of Ohio and seat of Franklin County, is the state's largest city in area. It was laid out to be the capital in 1812, a position it assumed four years later, and chartered as a city in 1834. A feeder canal (1831) to the Ohio and Erie Canal, along with the National Road (1833), spurred development. By the middle of the 19th century the railroad had arrived, making Columbus a commercial and transportation center.

During the Civil War Columbus was an assembly point for recruits and the site of a Union arsenal. A cemetery at Camp Chase, a Civil War prison, contains the graves of 2,260 Confederate soldiers. By the end of the century the city was a leader in the manufacture of buggies, producing about 20,000 a year. In 1913 the Scioto River flooded, causing the death of more than 100 people.

Today about 20 percent of the working population is employed by the federal, state, or municipal government. Because it is the capital of a populous state and the home of a major university (Ohio State), Columbus was the only large northern city to boast of a 1980 census population increase. Industry is also a large employer; among the city's products are coal-mining machinery, concrete mixers, auto parts, paints, shoes, glassware, and refrigerators. Columbus is the headquarters of the Battelle Memorial Institute, an organization engaged in scientific, technological, and economic research.

Several downtown construction projects have generated excitement and confidence about Columbus as a place to work, to shop, and to live. Completion of the Ohio Center (convention center) and the Capitol South recreation, hotel and retail center insure continued growth of the downtown area.

## DALLAS

**Location:** Northeastern Texas on Trinity River, about 75 miles south of Oklahoma border **County:** Dallas **City Area:** 350 sq. miles (906.5 sq. kilometers) **Altitude:** 481 feet (146.2 meters)
**Mayor:** Jack Evans **City Manager:** Charles Anderson
**City Population:** 904,078 (1980 census) **Metro Area Population:** 2,974,878 (1980 census)
**Daily Newspapers:** 2 **No. of Radio Stations:** 19 **No. of TV Stations:** 8
**City Chamber of Commerce:** Dallas Chamber of Commerce, 1507 Pacific Avenue, Dallas, Texas 75201

Dallas, seat of Dallas County and second largest city in Texas, is the financial and commercial center of the Southwest.

John Neely Bryan settled here in 1841 and later founded Dallas, probably naming it after George M. Dallas, then Vice President under James K. Polk. In 1858 followers of the French social philosopher Charles Fourier abandoned their nearby socialist community, La Réunion, and moved to Dallas. Two years later a fire destroyed most of the town, but residents quickly rebuilt it. During the Civil War the Confederate Army had quartermaster, commissary, and administrative headquarters here.

Oil was discovered in eastern Texas in the 1930s, increasing the growth of Dallas, which was the site of the Texas Centennial Exposition in 1936. During and after World War II, population boomed following introduction of first the aircraft and then the electronics industries. Today the city's economy is highly diversified, with a strong manufacturing base and many corporate headquarters of the electronics, oil, gas, finance and insurance industries.

Dallas is the home of the annual Texas state fair, the Cotton Bowl football stadium, the NFL Dallas Cowboys, the Mavericks basketball team, the Tornado soccer team, and shares with Fort Worth the American Baseball League's Texas Rangers. Dallas hosts annually final matches of the $100,000 World Championship of Tennis, the Byron Nelson Golf Classic, the U.S. Karate National Championships, and the Avon Futures Tennis Finals.

Another advantage which Dallas has created for itself is its role as a tourist/convention center. Its role as a merchandise distribution center helped make it a major buyers' market. Dallas/Fort Worth Airport is one of the world's largest airports.

Dallas is also the cultural center of Texas. Each year the city is host to the Metropolitan Opera and the USA Film Festival. Dallas has its own Opera and Symphony as well. There are other community enterprises in tthe cultural field including the Summer Musicals, the Ballet, the Civic Chorus, the Dallas Theatre Center, Theatre Three, and a new upsurge in professional theatre groups working in six theatres.

## DENVER

**Location:** North-central Colorado, on South Platte River **County:** Denver; city and county are coextensive **City Area:** 117 sq. miles (303 sq. kilometers) **Altitude:** 5,280 feet (1604.5 meters)
**Mayor:** William H. McNichols, Jr.
**City Population:** 492,365 (1980 census) **Metro Area Population:** 1,619,921 (1980 census)
**Daily Newspapers:** 2 **No. of Radio Stations:** 35 **No. of TV Stations:** 6
**City Chamber of Commerce:** Denver Chamber of Commerce, 1301 Welton, Denver, Colorado 80204

Denver, capital and largest city of Colorado, is a major commercial and financial center. It was settled in 1858 after the discovery of placer gold at the junction of the South Platte River and Cherry Creek, and named for James W. Denver, governor of the Kansas Territory, which then included eastern Colorado.

Denver was incorporated in 1861 and became the capital of the Colorado Territory six years later. During the 1870s and 1880s rich lodes of silver, gold, and copper were found in the Rockies, bringing fortune seekers to the area. The city boasted plush opera houses with singers imported from the East, makeshift boarding houses, and noisy saloons, such as the famous Silver Dollar.

By the end of the 19th century, Denver was beginning to develop into a large processing, shipping, and distributing point for an extensive agricultural area, making mining and metalworking less important. A federal mint has been in operation for more than a century. Today the aerospace industry makes a significant contribution to Denver's economy, and food processing is also a major occupation. In addition, the city is the regional center for many federal agencies. The Atomic Energy Commission's Rocky Flats plant is nearby, and the federal Solar Energy Research Instituute opened in 1978 in nearby Golden, Colo. Denver is fast becoming a national energy capital, rivalling Houston in importance. The city is the center for the development of the West's energy resources—oil, gas, coal, shale oil, uranium, synthetic fueels and solar energy. As a result, new office construction is booming in Denver.

Military establishments in the area include Lowry Air Force Base; the Air Force Accounting and Finance Center; the army's Rocky Mountain Arsenal; and Fitzsimmons General Hospital. The Air Force Academy is in Colorado Springs, less than 100 miles south of Denver.

Denver, which maintains the largest system of public parks and recreational facilities in the world, is a tourist mecca. Of interest are the Colorado State Historical Museum, the tomb of Buffalo Bill, the Cody Museum, and the $6.1-million Denver Art Museum, a block-square, fortresslike structure set against a distant backdrop of Rocky Mountains, and the Denver Botanic Gardens. Nearby is Red Rocks Park with its famous Easter sunrise service. Denver is the home of the Denver Broncos football team and the Denver Nuggets basketball team.

## DETROIT

**Location:** Southeastern Michigan, on Detroit River, between Lakes St. Clair and Erie, 18 miles north of Lake Erie **County:** Wayne **City Area:** 139.6 sq. miles (361.6 sq. kilometers) **Altitude:** 581 feet (176.6 meters)
**Mayor:** Coleman A. Young
**City Population:** 1,203,339 (1980 census) **Metro Area Population:** 4,352,762 (1980 census)
**Daily Newspapers:** 2 **No. of Radio Stations:** 37 **No. of TV Stations:** 9
**City Chamber of Commerce:** Greater Detroit Chamber of Commerce, 150 Michigan Ave., Detroit, Michigan 48226

Detroit, seat of Wayne County, is the largest city in Michigan and one of the largest in the United States. Antoine de la Mothe Cadillac established a French fort (Pontchartrain) and settlement on the site in 1701.

The settlement took the name Detroit from the French word for "strait," because it was on the water link between Lake Erie and Lake St. Clair. Detroit was ceded to the British in 1763, turned over to the United States in 1796, destroyed by fire in 1805, rebuilt, and occupied by the British for a year during the War of 1812. It became an important commercial center after the opening of the Erie Canal in 1825.

From 1837, when Michigan became a state, until 1847, Detroit was the capital. It was connected by rail to Chicago in 1852 and to New York two years later. The city was a key terminus of the Underground Railroad.

Detroit assumed great importance after the middle of the 19th century because of its shipping, shipbuilding, and manufacturing.

Today, Greater Detroit serves as international headquarters for General Motors, American Motors, Ford and Chrysler. But with the auto industry in a severe slump, the unemployment rate in the "Motor City" soared to nearly twice the national average during the recession of 1980-82. The Detroit-Pontiac-Flint corridor produces some 25 percent of all the cars and trucks built in the United States. Detroit is linked to Windsor, Ont., by a bridge over and a tunnel under the Detroit River.

The city also is international headquarters for the United Automobile, Aerospace and Agricultural Implement Workers of America (UAW), which has been embroiled in many labor disputes.

Detroit has had two major racial riots. One in 1943 and the other in 1967.

Renaissance Center, a $350-million complex along Detroit's downtown riverfront, the new Joe Louis Arena, and the Senator Philip A. Hart Plaza are three of the new construction projects completed in recent years. The Horace E. Dodge & Son Memorial Fountain, designed by Isamu Noguchi, has become the center of community activity and the permanent home of Detroit's famous international ethnic festivals. The city was host to the 1980 Republican convention.

The Detroit Symphony Orchestra, Detroit Institute of Arts, and the Detroit Zoo are rated among the nation's best. Henry Ford Museum and Greenfield Village, which contains Thomas A. Edison's original laboratories and many early American landmarks, attract more than 1.6 million visitors annually to suburban Dearborn. Belle Isle, a 1,000-acre park in the Detroit River, is a major recreation center, with gardens, a conservatory, children's zoo and aquarium among attractions.

## FORT WORTH

**Location:** Northern Texas, at the junction of the Clear and West forks of the Trinity River about 30 miles west of Dallas **Counties:** Tarrant, Hood, Wise, Parker and Johnson **City Area:** 250 sq. miles (647.5 sq. kilometers) **Altitude:** 670 feet (203.6 meters)
**Mayor:** Bob Bolen **City Manager:** Robert Herchert
**City Population:** 385,164 (1980 census) **Metro Area Population:** 2,974,878 (1980 census)
**Daily Newspapers:** 3 **No. of Radio Stations:** 22 **No. of TV Stations:** 9
**City Chamber of Commerce:** Fort Worth Chamber of Commerce, 700 Throckmorton, Fort Worth, Texas 76102

Fort Worth, often considered in conjunction with nearby Dallas, is the seat of Tarrant County and a prime cog in the massive North Texas industrial complex, serving as a transportation center, oil-pipeline hub and a major grain and livestock market. It is one of the nation's largest producers of aircraft, an outgrowth of World War II, when aircraft assembly first flourished there.

Settlement of the area began in 1843. Four years later

Camp Worth (later Fort Worth) was established by Major Ripley A. Arnold as a frontier outpost to protect settlers against Comanche Indian raids; it was named in honor of Major General William J. Worth, then commander of U.S. troops in Texas, and proved of great use to the Army during the Mexican War.

After the Army departed (1853), the town suffered a brief decline, but soon began to boom. Cowboys driving Longhorn cattle up the Chisholm Trail to the railheads of Kansas would bed their herds outside of Fort Worth and go into town for supplies and relaxation. This brought a heavy influx of merchants and contributed much to the city's growth, which was further spurred by the coming of the railroad in 1876, three years after the city's incorporation. Meat-packing and the milling and shipping of grain were the mainstays of the fledgling town's economy. With the 20th century, came widespread industrialization and a continuing trend toward greater diversification. Besides those mentioned, other of the city's chief industries include brewing, electronics, food processing, and the manufacture of automobiles, containers, furniture, leather goods and machinery.

Despite the bustle of its industry, Fort Worth today retains a distinctive, easy-going Western flavor. It is known all over the world as "Cowtown" or "Where the West Begins," and is committed to retainingg its Western heritage. Fort Worth has become increasingly involved in the arts, rivaling Dallas as the state's cultural leader. Its attractions include Casa Mañana, a theater-in-the-round that presents Broadway productions; a renowned museum complex including the Fort Worth Art Museum, the Kimbell Art Museum, the Amon Carter Museum of Western Art, and the Fort Worth Museum of Science and History; the Fort Woorth Opera and Symphony; and Trinity Park. In addition, the area boasts the Fort Worth Water Garden Park, the Will Rogers Memorial Complex, and the Tarrant County Convention Center. Fort Worth is host to the Van Cliburn Piano Competition and the Colonial Invitational Golf Tournament and is the home of Six Flags Over Texas. Popular annual events include the Southwestern Exposition, Fat Stock Show and Rodeo.

### HONOLULU

**Location:** In Hawaii, in Pacific Ocean, 2,397 miles southwest of San Francisco **County:** Honolulu **City Area:** 608 sq. miles (574.7 sq. kilometers) **Altitude:** 21 feet (6.4 meters)
**Mayor:** Eileen R. Anderson **Managing Director:** Andrew I.T. Chang
**City Population:** 365,048 (1980 census) **Metro Area Population:** 762,874 (1980 census)
**Daily Newspapers:** 2 **No. of Radio Stations:** 36 **No. of TV Stations:** 5
**City Chamber of Commerce:** The Chamber of Commerce of Hawaii, Dillingham Building, 735 Bishop Street, Honolulu, Hawaii 96813

Honolulu, capital and principal city of Hawaii, is on the island of Oahu at the crossroads of the Pacific. (The name "Honolulu" is Hawaiian for "sheltered harbor.") Although Honolulu city and county are usually thought of as consisting of Oahu only, Honolulu is technically the most far-reaching city in the nation, with boundaries extending officially 1,381 miles northwest to Kure Island.

Honolulu became the seat of the Kamehameha dynasty, which had succeeded in unifying the Hawaiian Islands in 1810, and in 1845 it was named the permanent capital of the Kingdom of Hawaii. During the 19th century, American and European whalers and sandalwood traders came to Honolulu, and it was occupied successively by Russian, British, and French forces. It developed into an important commercial city after U.S. annexation of Hawaii in 1898.

In the early 20th century, the U.S. Navy established its famous base at Pearl Harbor, now the headquarters of the U.S. Pacific Fleet. Honolulu was bombed during Japan's surprise attack on Pearl Harbor on Dec. 7, 1941, and during World War II became a major staging area for U.S. forces in the Pacific.

The postwar years saw a tourist boom coupled with a diversification of industry. The military continued as a mainstay of the economy, but tourism surpassed it as the leading industry. In 1979 alone, 3.9 million visitors came to the islands. However, high air fares and the economic recession on the mainland caused the number of tourists to decline in 1980-82.

Numerous new high-rise office buildings have changed the skyline and helped revitalize downtown Honolulu. Harbor facilities have been expanded and the Honolulu International Airport has been enlarged.

Structures of interest in the city are Iolani Palace, former home of Hawaii's monarchs and the only royal palace in the U.S.; the state capitol; the Bishop Museum (of Polynesian Ethnology and Natural History); Washington Place, former private home of Queen Lilioukalani; and the Neal Blaisdell Center, a 22-acre complex of public buildings.

### HOUSTON

**Location:** Southeastern Texas, on Houston Ship Channel, 50 miles from Gulf of Mexico **Counties:** Brazoria, Harris, Fort Bend, Liberty, Montgomery and Waller. **City Area:** 556.3 sq. miles (1440.8 sq. kilometers) **Altitude:** 49 feet (15 meters)
**Mayor:** Katherine J. Whitmire
**City Population:** 1,595,138 (1980 census) **Metro Area Population:** 2,905,350 (1980 census)
**Daily Newspapers:** 2 **No. of Radio Stations:** 33 **No. of TV Stations:** 6
**City Chamber of Commerce:** Houston Chamber of Commerce, 1100 Milam, 25th Floor, Houston, Texas 77002

Houston, seat of Harris County, is the leading industrial metropolis not only of Texas but also of the surrounding region. It is the largest city in the Southwest and South, the fifth largest in the nation and the country's third-largest seaport.

Founded in 1836 by J. K. and A. C. Allen, the city was named for General Sam Houston, hero of the Battle of San Jacinto (1836), by which Texas gained independence from Mexico. The city served as capital of the Republic of Texas from 1837 until 1840.

The discovery of oil in Southeast Texas at Spindletop in 1901 and the opening of the man-made Houston Ship Channel in 1914 stimulated the rapid development of the Houston area.

Strategically situated in an area rich in oil, gas, sulfur, salt, lime, timber, industrial soil, seawater and freshwater, the Houston metropolitan area ranks first in the nation in petroleum refining, petrochemical manufacturing, manufacturing and distribution of petroleum equipment and pipeline transmission of oil and gas.

Houston, which became the U.S. center of manned spacecraft activities in the early 1960s, has experienced increasing economic diversification over the past two decades. The city emerged as a corporate center in the 1960s, and since 1970 over 200 major companies have moved their headquarters, subsidiaries or divisions to Houston, capitalizing on the growing nucleus of energy, space and medical technology available in the area.

The Texas Medical Center is an $823-million complex of 28 institutions and organizations on 506 acres in central Houston. More than 80 research firms maintain research facilities in Houston. The number of life, earth, and physical scientists in metropolitan Houston has risen to 14,900, up 158 percent since 1970, while technical engineers have increased 146 percent in the same period, to stand at 44,200.

In addition, the city is growing in prominence in international business. More than 54 foreign banks maintain representative offices in Houston, and 50 nations maintain consular offices there. Houston Intercontinental Airport provides direct service to Europe, the Middle East, South and Central America, the Caribbean, Mexico and Canada.

Bordering the City of Houston on the southeast is the Lyndon B. Johnson Space Center, a $202-million complex for astronaut training, equipment testing, and flight control for the Skylab and Space Shuttle programs.

Houston's Nina Vance Alley Theatre is nationally known, performing repertory works as well as new plays. Elegant Jones Hall for the Performing Arts features the Houston Symphony Society, the Houston Ballet, and the Houston Grand Opera; all tour nationally. The Astrodome, a huge, enclosed and air-conditioned arena, has convertible seating arrangements which allow the presentation of widely varied sports events. The Summit, another sports and entertainment arena, is located in Houston's Greenway Plaza.

Houston is home of the Houston Astros of the National Baseball League, the Houston Oilers of the American Conference of the National Football League and the Houston Rockets of the National Basketball Association.

Prominent tourist attractions in the area include the Harris County Domed Stadium and Astrohall; Astroworld, a 65-acre family amusement park; the Museum of Fine Arts and several other museums; Johnson Space

Center; and San Jacinto Battleground, plus the battleship Texas, a veteran of two World Wars.

### INDIANAPOLIS

**Location:** In central Indiana, on White River **County:** Marion **City Area:** 379.4 sq. miles (982.6 sq. kilometers) **Altitude:** 710 feet (215.8 meters)
**Mayor:** William H. Hudnut, III
**City Population:** 700,807 (1980 census) **Metro Area Population:** 1,166,929 (1980 census)
**Daily Newspapers:** 2 **No. of Radio Stations:** 25 **No. of TV Stations:** 6
**City Chamber of Commerce:** Indianapolis Chamber of Commerce, 320 North Meridian Street, Indianapolis, Indiana 46204

Indianapolis, seat of Marion County and capital of Indiana, is the largest city in the state. Its name combines "Indiana" with "polis," the Greek term for "city." It was settled in 1820.

Indianapolis grew slowly until the arrival of the first railroad in 1847. Toward the end of the 19th century the discovery of nearby natural gas, plus the beginning of the automobile industry, helped the city's expansion. On Jan. 1, 1970, the City of Indiannapolis merged with surrounding Marion County in the nation's first major city-county consolidation to occur without a popular referendum since modern New York City was formed in 1898.

Leading products are processed foods, electronics equipment, automotive parts, heavy machinery, and pharmaceuticals. Indianapolis is also a major insurance center, with offices of more than 70 firms.

Indianapolis might be called the educational hub of Indiana. It includes the Indiana University Medical School and Center, Butler University, Indiana Central University, Indiana University/Purdue University at Indianapolis (IUPUI), and Marian College.

Urban renewal has made enormous changes in the city's skyline in the last ten years. Indianapolis has kept its famous Soldiers' and Sailors' Monument on Monument Circle, but the city is now dominated by such structures as the Indiana National Bank Tower, Indiana Bell Telephone Building, the Market Square Arena, a new Hyatt Hotel, the new Federal Building, and the Indiana Convention and Exposition Center. A new $70-million domed stadium is under construction.

Three of Indianapolis' newest points of interest are: the Museum of Art, the Indiana State Museum, and the Children's Museum, the largest of its kind in the nation. Indianapolis is national headquarters for the American Legion and the home of the Army Finance Center at Fort Harrison. Tourist attractions include the homes of President Benjamin Harrison, James Whitcomb Riley and Booth Tarkington. Eagle Creek Park is the country's largest municipal park.

The city is the amateur sports capital of the United States and is the home of the Indianapolis 500 motor speedway track. Indianapolis is also the home of the Amateur Athletic Union, Kiwanis, the American Legion and the U.S. Automobile Club.

### JACKSONVILLE

**Location:** Northeastern Florida, on St. Johns River and Atlantic Ocean **County:** Duval **City Area:** 841 sq. miles (2178 sq. kilometers) **Altitude:** 20 feet (6.1 meters)
**Mayor:** Jake N. Godbold
**City Population:** 540,920 (1980 census) **Metro Area Population:** 737,519 (1980 census)
**Daily Newspapers:** 2 **No. of Radio Stations:** 24 **No. of TV Stations:** 6
**City Chamber of Commerce:** Jacksonville Chamber of Commerce, P.O. Box 329, Jacksonville, Florida 32201

Jacksonville, Florida's most populous city, is the nation's largest in area (841 square miles). A vital seaport with over 80 miles of berthing space and a sizable U.S. Navy installation, the city is a major financial, industrial and transportation center of the Southeast.

Among Jacksonville's chief industries are the manufacturing and/or processing of food products, wood products, computer components, fertilizer, paper, furniture and cigars. It is generally the last port of call for steamships from the North that are bound for the Southern Hemisphere and Far East.

French and Spanish colonization of the Jacksonville region dates from the latter part of the 16th century. Except for a brief period of British rule (1763-1783), Spain managed to maintain tenuous dominion until 1819, when the U.S. bought its claim to the Florida peninsula. Originally known as Cowford (during the English period), the community was eventually renamed for Andrew Jackson, Florida's first territorial governor. It was incorporated in 1832.

Early development of the area was hampered by Florida's two costly wars with the Seminole Indians, and by the Civil War, which brought widespread destruction and periodic occupation by Union forces. Industry's recognition of the city's strategic location and moderate climate spurred recovery in the postwar period, though progress was stalled by a yellow-fever epidemic (1888) and a fire (1901) that destroyed 147 city blocks. Since 1940 the city has expanded greatly, and in 1968 it was consolidated with Duval County. During the 1950s Jacksonville gained the title of "insurance capital of the South."

Jacksonville's nearby beaches, with thousands of accommodations, are popular summer attractions, especially for inland Southerners. Other favorites with visitors are the Jacksonville Art Museum and Symphony Orchestra, the Jacksonville Museum of Arts and Sciences, the Cummer Gallery of Art, the Jacksonville Zoological Park, the Coliseum and the Gator Bowl. Among its historical sites are the Fort Caroline National Monument, site of the state's first French settlement in 1564, and the Delius House, home of the famed British composer.

### KANSAS CITY

**Location:** Western Missouri, on Kansas-Missouri border, on Kansas and Missouri rivers **Counties:** Jackson, Clay, Platte **City Area:** 316 sq. miles (818 sq. kilometers) Altitude: 750 feet (227.9 meters)
**Mayor:** Richard L. Berkley **City Manager:** Robert A. Kipp
**City Population:** 448,159 (1980 census) **Metro Area Population:** 1,327,020 (1980 census)
**Daily Newspapers:** 2 **No. of Commercial Radio Stations (AM):** 14 **No. of TV Stations:** 5
**City Chamber of Commerce:** Chamber of Commerce of Greater Kansas City, 600 CharterBank Center, 920 Main Street, Kansas City, Missouri 64105

Kansas City, Missouri's second largest metropolis, is an important industrial, transportation, commercial, and banking center. It is separated from Kansas City, Kansas, by the state line, but both are served by the same railroad terminals and transit and telephone systems.

The area was explored by the French early in the 18th century and toward the end of the century by Daniel Morgan Boone (son of the famous frontiersman), who was probably the first American to set foot in the vicinity. François Chouteau established a trading post in 1826, and a settlement later developed known as Westport Landing. The city was incorporated in 1850 as the Town of Kansas, it became the City of Kansas in 1853, and under a new charter (1889) was named Kansas City. Its name reflects its location on the Kansas (Kaw) River, which in turn honors an Indian tribe.

Kansas City grew into an important trade and transportation hub for pioneers migrating westward over the Oregon and Santa Fe Trails; it was an early center of the nation's cattle business. In 1865 the railroad arrived, and four years later Hannibal Bridge, the first structure to span the Missouri River, was opened.

Today Kansas City is a major market for winter wheat and cattle. Its stockyards are among the nation's busiest. It leads the nation in the manufacture of vending machines, is the country's second largest assembly center for cars and trucks, and is an important warehousing center.

Landmarks of interest include the Liberty Memorial, the Nelson Gallery and Atkins Museum of Fine Arts, Swope Park with its zoo, Country Club Plaza, Crown Center, and the Livestock Yards.

### LOS ANGELES

**Location:** Southwestern California, between Santa Monica and San Pedro bays, near the Pacific coast **County:** Los Angeles **City Area:** 464 sq. miles (1201.8 sq. kilometers) **Altitude:** 275 feet (83.6 meters)
**Mayor:** Thomas Bradley

**City Population:** 2,966,731 (1980 census) **Metro Area Population:** 7,477,657 (1980 census)
**Daily Newspapers:** 2 **No. of Commercial Radio Stations (AM):** 54 **No. of TV Stations:** 18
**City Chamber of Commerce:** Los Angeles Area Chamber of Commerce, 404 South Bixel Street, Los Angeles, California 90017

Los Angeles, seat of California's Los Angeles County, is the nation's third-largest city, but its metropolitan area ranks second only to New York in population.

Gaspar de Portolá led an expedition to the site in 1769, and in 1781 El Pueblo de Nuestra Señora la Reina de los Angeles de Porciuncula (The Town of Our Lady the Queen of the Angels of Porciuncula) was founded. The name was later shortened to Los Angeles.

In 1846 during the Mexican War, U.S. military forces took the town. Four years later, Los Angeles was incorporated as a city; that same year California entered the Union. It was soon linked with the Eastern seaboard as railroads arrived: the Southern Pacific in 1876 and the Santa Fe nine years later. Discovery of oil in the 1890s stimulated commercial growth, and the opening of the Panama Canal in 1914 brought further expansion. The motion-picture industry grew up in the early 20th century and more recent years have seen the establishment of television studios.

The Los Angeles area is rich in agricultural resources and well known for its citrus fruit. It ranks third nationally in manufacturing, finance, and trade, and leads the U.S. in production of aircraft and aircraft parts. In addition, Greater Los Angeles is the nation's sportswear center and the world's second largest garment manufacturer. Other important industries are food processing and the production of machinery, chemicals, and electronics equipment. As a port Los Angeles handles the largest cargo tonnage of deep-sea vessels on the Pacific Coast and is a major fishing complex. In 1979, it was reported that 16 industrial corporations with sales exceeding $1 billion were headquartered in the Los Angeles area.

Los Angeles County has the heaviest per-capita concentration of automobiles in the world, and the city is famous for its vast system of freeways radiating from the center of town to outlying areas. Dozens of independent municipalities are incorporated in the county, some completely surrounded by the city. Shore areas include Santa Monica, Manhattan Beach, Hermosa Beach, Redondo Beach, and Long Beach. The industrial section includes Lynwood, Downey, Norwalk, and Torrance.

Los Angeles is the home of a $33.5 million Music Center, the Los Angeles County Museum of Art and the recently constructed Los Angeles Convention Center.

Of interest to the thousands of tourists who flock to the Los Angeles area are Disneyland, at nearby Anaheim, considered the biggest attraction in the West; Mount Wilson Observatory; Mission San Gabriel Arcángel, dedicated in 1771; Santa Catalina Island; the Hollywood Bowl; Griffith Park with its zoo, golf course, and observatory; and Laguna Beach.

Los Angeles will host the 1984 Summer Olympics. The decision by the city to ratify a contract with the International Olympic Committee came after 15 months of conflict between the two over who would bear financial responsibility. Under a compromise incorporated into the agreement, Los Angeles would have no financial liability. The burden would be shared by the U.S. Olympic Committee and a private group.

The city celebrated a year-long bicentennial observance which culminated on September 4, 1981, the 200th anniversary of its founding. Art shows, ballet and plays were be presented under the slogan "L.A.'s the Place."

## LOUISVILLE

**Location:** Northwest Kentucky, at the falls of the Ohio River **County:** Jefferson **City Area:** 65.2 sq. miles (168.9 sq. kilometers) **Altitude:** 477 feet (144.9 meters)
**Mayor:** Harvey I. Sloane
**City Population:** 298,840 (1980 census) **Metro Area Population:** 906,240 (1980 census)
**Daily Newspapers:** 2 **No. of Radio Stations:** 17 **No. of TV Stations:** 6
**City Chamber of Commerce:** Louisville Area Chamber of Commerce, 300 West Liberty, Louisville, Kentucky 40202

Louisville, seat of Jefferson County, is the largest city in Kentucky and a major Southern industrial center. The city lies over a mammoth glacial deposit called an "aquifer," which is drawn upon for water.

Laid out in 1773 by General George Rogers Clark and settled six years later, it was named Louisville in 1780 by the Virginia legislature in honor of King Louis XVI of France. Two years later at Louisville, General Clark built Fort Nelson, which served as headquarters for his expeditions to the Northwest. It was then widely known as the "Settlement at the Falls."

Louisville was incorporated as a city in 1828 and grew into an important river port after the opening of the Louisville and Portland Canal in 1830. Arrival of the railroad in 1851 enhanced its position as a transportation center. During the Civil War it was a major Union base, despite the divided loyalties of its citizens.

Today the city has the world's largest electrical appliance and neoprene plants. Other important industries are the manufacture of bourbon whiskey, aluminum products, bathroom fixtures, tobacco processing, auto and truck manufacturing, and meat-packing. The American Printing House for the Blind, the world's largest publisher of Braille books and magazines and talking books, is located in Louisville. More than $300-million in private and public funds have been committed to the redevelopment of the downtown area. A $120-million Galleria office, shopping and apartment complex opened in 1982, and the $70-million Riverfront development is under construction.

Of historic interest are the grave of George Rogers Clark, in Cave Hill Cemetery, and the site of Fort Nelson. The state's tourist attractions include Churchill Downs, scene of the annual Kentucky Derby; the State Fair Grounds; the Louisville Zoological Garden featuring a children's zoo, and the Filson Club, which houses a Kentucky history museum.

## MEMPHIS

**Location:** Southwestern corner of Tennessee, on Mississippi River
**County:** Shelby **City Area:** 290 sq. miles (651.1 sq. kilometers)
**Altitude:** 275 feet (83.6 meters)
**Mayor:** Wyeth Chandler **Chief Administrative Officer:** Wallace Madewell
**City Population:** 646,174 (1980 census) **Metro Area Population:** 912,887 (1980 census)
**Daily Newspapers:** 2 **No. of Radio Stations:** 24 **No. of TV Stations:** 4
**City Chamber of Commerce:** Memphis Area Chamber of Commerce, 555 Beale Street, P.O. Box 224, Memphis, Tennessee 38101

Memphis, seat of Shelby County, is the largest city in Tennessee and a port of entry. It is the commercial center for much of Tennessee, Arkansas, and Mississippi, as well as parts of Missouri and Alabama. It was named after the ancient Egyptian city.

According to tradition, De Soto crossed the Mississippi River in 1540 at the site of this Tennessee city. In 1682 La Salle built Fort Prudhomme overlooking the river, and for almost a century the area was involved in the imperial rivalries of Great Britain, France, and Spain. The United States built Fort Adams in 1797, and in 1819 Memphis was laid out. Thirty years later it was incorporated as a city, having become an important port noted for its gambling casinos and glittering wealth.

The fall of Memphis to Union forces on June 6, 1862, ended the city's early prosperity. After the Civil War, yellow-fever epidemics caused about 25,000 people to flee.

Today it is a major hardwood-lumber center and manufacturer of furniture and flooring. It is also a major distribution center, a leading cotton and livestock market and home of the Memphis Cotton Exchange. The city's products include rubber goods, cottonseed oil, textiles, farm machinery, drugs, and livestock feeds. It is headquarters for Federal Express, Plough, Inc., Holiday Inns of America, Inc. and Cook Industries, grain exporters, and the site of a Sharp Electronics Corporation plant.

The Tennessee Chute Project has provided Memphis with a dam connecting the mainland to Presidents Island in the Mississippi and has given the city a stillwater harbor with two barge terminals. A 963-acre industrial park is now on the island; across the harbor is the 6,800-acre Frank C. Pidgeon Industrial Park.

Of interest in Memphis is Confederate Park, which contains ramparts used in defense against Union gunboats in 1862, and Beale Street, which was immortalized by jazz composer W.C. Handy. It is the site of Graceland, the mansion and gravesite of Elvis Presley. Mud Island, with its park, museum, scale model of the Mississippi River system and amphitheatre, opened in 1982. Memphis is the only four-time winner of the Ernest T. Trigg (Cleanest City in the Nation) Award.

### MIAMI

**Location:** Southeastern Florida, on Biscayne Bay **County:** Dade **City Area:** 34 sq. miles (88.1 sq. kilometers) **Altitude:** 25 feet (7.6 meters)
**Mayor:** Maurice A. Ferre **City Manager:** Howard Gary
**City Population:** 346,865 (1980 census) **Metro Area Population:** 1,625,979 (1980 census)
**Daily Newspapers:** 4 **No. of Radio Stations:** 23 **No. of TV Stations:** 8
**City Chamber of Commerce:** Greater Miami Chamber of Commerce, 391 N.E. 15 St., Miami, Florida 33132

Miami, seat of Florida's Dade County, is an international banking and trade center, and the focal point of a world-famous resort area. The city was founded in 1870 at the site of Fort Dallas, which the United States had built in the 1830s during the war against the Seminoles. "Miami" is an Indian word meaning "big water."

In 1896 the financier Henry M. Flagler extended the Florida East Coast Railroad to Miami, built the Royal Palm Hotel, and dredged the city's harbor. The city was incorporated the same year. By 1910 it was booming.

During the 1920s the Miami region was the scene of wild land speculation in which many fortunes were lost. However, the city continued to grow, despite disastrous hurricanes in 1926 and 1935.

Miami has the largest population of Cuban refugees in the United States—in excess of 500,000. The 1980 boat exodus of thousands of new Cuban refugees strained the resources of Miami's existing first-and second-generation Cuban community. An additional influx of sea-borne refugees from Haiti also taxed public services in the South Florida metropolis.

A major rail, air and shipping point, Miami is considered the principal gateway to Latin America; the Dodge Island passenger terminal is home base for the many cruise ships serving South America and the Caribbean. The Greater Miami Foreign-Trade Zone is the largest of its kind in the U.S.

Although tourism is the leading industry in the area, the city is the nation's third largest garment manufacturing center. Concrete, metal, electronics, meat products, and commercial fishing also make substantial contributions to the economy. Miami's booming trade with Latin America and the Caribbean has been spurred by the siting of more than 80 international and Edge Act banks in the city. The U.S. Environmental Science Services Administration's Oceanographic and Meteorological Laboratories have made Miami a world leader in undersea studies. Construction of the $900-million, 20.5-mile elevated rail system, linking downtown Miami with its suburbs, began in June 1979.

Greater Miami, which consists of over two dozen independent municipalities, is renowned for its luxurious resort hotels and fine beaches. Recently, many of the visitors have come from Latin America and Europe. Tourist attractions include Bicentennial-New World Center Park, the Museum of Science, the Miami Seaquarium, and Vizcaya, formerly the estate of James Deering and now the Dade County Art Museum. Everglades National Park, a preserve for tropical birds and flora, is nearby. The area has year-round horse racing at Hialeah, Gulfstream and Calder racetracks. Miami is home to the annual Orange Bowl Festival and January 1 football classic, and to the National Football League's Miami Dolphins.

### MILWAUKEE

**Location:** Southeastern Wisconsin, on Lake Michigan **County:** Milwaukee **City Area:** 96.5 sq. miles (249.9 sq. kilometers) **Altitude:** 581 feet (176.6 meters)
**Mayor:** Henry W. Maier
**City Population:** 636,236 (1980 census) **Metro Area Population:** 1,397,143 (1980 census)
**Daily Newspapers:** 2 **No. of Radio Stations:** 23 **No. of TV Stations:** 6
**City Chamber of Commerce:** Metropolitan Milwaukee Association of Commerce, 756 North Milwaukee Street, Milwaukee, Wisconsin 53202

Milwaukee, seat of Milwaukee County and largest city in Wisconsin, is a leading Great Lakes port and major industrial metropolis.

French missionaries and the French explorer La Salle visited the site in the late 17th century. French Canadian fur traders came to barter with the Indians, and in 1795 the North West Company established a trading post. The first permanent settler, Solomon Juneau, an agent of the American Fur Company, arrived in 1818. His settlement and several neighboring villages merged after 1835 to form Milwaukee, which was incorporated as a city in 1846. Its name is derived from an Indian term interpreted to mean either "gathering place by the waters" or "beautiful land."

The city's excellent harbor, accessible raw materials, and growing population made it a shipping and industrial center, and German immigrants, arriving after 1848, stimulated its political, economic, and social development.

Milwaukee produces more beer than any other city and is the home of three of the four largest breweries. However, machinery manufacturing is the area's largest industry. Milwaukee is also a significant grain market and meat packer.

Of interest in the city are the Greek Orthodox Annunciation Church, designed by Frank Lloyd Wright; the War Memorial Center, on the lakeshore, designed by Eero Saarinen and housing the Milwaukee Art Center; the Milwaukee County Zoo, one of the most modern in the nation; the Mitchell Park Botanical Conservatory, three domed buildings for display of plants under arid, moist and temperate conditions; and the world-famous breweries, which offer tours to the public. A $12-million Performing Arts Center with a large park and fountains is the home of the Milwaukee Symphony Orchestra and the Repertory Theatre. MECCA, the Milwaukee Exposition and Convention Center and Arena, one of Milwaukee's newest buildings, has won national attention because of its artistic design and colors.

Milwaukee has gained recognition from national organizations for cleanliness and beautification for many years and is one of the safest areas in the nation.

### MINNEAPOLIS

**Location:** East-central Minnesota, on both sides of Mississippi River at Falls of St. Anthony **County:** Hennepin **City Area:** 58.8 sq. miles (152.2 sq. kilometers) **Altitude:** 815 feet (247.7 meters)
**Mayor:** Donald Fraser **Chief Administrative Officer:** Lyle Schwartzkopf
**City Population:** 370,951 (1980 census) **Metro Area Population:** 2,114,256 (1980 census)
**Daily Newspapers:** 1 **No. of Radio Stations:** 35 **No. of TV Stations:** 5
**City Chamber of Commerce:** Greater Minneapolis Chamber of Commerce, 15 South Fifth Street, Minneapolis, Minnesota 55402

Minneapolis, seat of Hennepin County, is the largest city in Minnesota and an important industrial and railroad center. It is contiguous to St. Paul, its twin city and the state capital.

Father Louis Hennepin visited the site in 1680 and gave the Falls of Saint Anthony their name. In 1819 the U.S. government established Fort Snelling, and two years later a sawmill was built at the falls. The village of St. Anthony was soon settled on the east bank of the Mississippi River, while Minneapolis grew up (c. 1847) on the west bank. Minneapolis, from the local Indian "minnea," or water, combined with "polis," Greek for city, was incorporated as a town in 1856 and as a city the following year. In 1872 St. Anthony was annexed.

During the 1890s the lumber business thrived as logs were floated downstream to the sawmills of Minneapolis from the great forests of the north. Minneapolis was also known as the "Flour City of the World" until a change in freight rates after World War I shifted the center of the flour-milling industry to Buffalo.

Today the city is the home of the Minneapolis Grain Exchange, the world's largest cash grain market, and headquarters for a Federal Reserve district bank. Leading industries are electronics, computers, control instruments, food processing, printing and publishing.

Minneapolis and St. Paul constitute the financial and industrial center of a large area rich in natural resources, power, and transportation facilities. The two cities are connected by a massive freeway system that runs through the suburban areas, plus a $300-million Minneapolis Gateway Center in the Loop. A new $65-million domed stadium is in use in the downtown area. The Minneapolis area has 25 industrial parks and a 12-acre river terminal to handle shipping and storage of grain, fertilizer, petroleum products, sand gravel, salt and coal.

The major landmarks in Minneapolis are the 57-story IDS skyscraper and Nicollet Mall. Within the city are 153 parks with 22 lakes; Minnehaha Park with its Stevens House, dating from 1849; the Tyrone Guthrie Theater; the $5.5-million Walker Art Center; the Minneapolis Institute of Arts; and the Minnesota Orchestra's new concert hall.

### NASHVILLE

**Location:** Northcentral Tennessee, on Cumberland River **County:** Davidson **City Area:** 533 sq. miles (1380.5 sq. kilometers) **Altitude:** 500 feet (152.4 meters)
**Mayor:** Richard H. Fulton
**City Population:** 455,651 (1980 census) **Metro Area Population:** 850,505 (1980 census)
**Daily Newspapers:** 2 **No. of Radio Stations:** 30 **No. of TV Stations:** 5
**City Chamber of Commerce:** Nashville Area Chamber of Commerce, 161 Fourth Avenue, North, Nashville, Tennessee 37219

Nashville, capital of Tennessee and seat of Davidson County, is sometimes called "the Athens of the South" because of its numerous educational institutions and its many buildings of Classical Greek design. The city is an important regional center for finance, industry and transportation, as well as a significant music recording center and the home of the Grand Ole Opry. Principal manufactures include shoes, apparel, books, magazines, chemicals, glass aerostructures, tires and trucks. Nissan Motors of Japan is building a truck plant in Smyrna, southeast of Nashville.

The first settlement on the site of present-day Nashville was made in 1779, with the building of Fort Nashborough, a frontier outpost named for Revolutionary War hero General Francis Nash, who was killed in the Battle of Germantown. The small community grew quickly and in 1784 was incorporated under its present name; it was chartered as a city in 1806.

Nashville's role as a vital trade depot was enhanced in 1796 by the entry of Tennessee into the Union, and in the 1850s by the coming of the railroads. During the Civil War, the city served as a Confederate military headquarters, but fell to Union forces in 1862 and remained under their control despite efforts in 1864 by troops under Confederate General John B. Hood to recapture the city.

Nashville was slow to recover from the effects of war and the period of so-called "carpetbag rule" that followed. In the late 1870s, however, the pace of progress quickened as industry became an increasingly large factor in the city's economy. In the period 1870-1890 the population tripled, from 25,865 to 76,168. After 1900 industry developed more slowly, until the advent of World War II, which acted as a spur to growth.

The city's many attractions include a full-size replica of the Parthenon, in Centennial Park; Andrew Jackson's home, The Hermitage; Tennessee State Museum, containing relics of wars in which Tennesseeans have fought; the Belle Meade Mansion, a plantation home dating from 1853; the Country Music Hall of Fame and Museum; Ryman Auditorium amd Opryland, U.S.A., new home of the Grand Ole Opry and a 110-acre theme park with live entertainment, rides and exhibits.

### NEWARK

**Location:** Northeastern New Jersey, on Passaic River and Newark Bay **County:** Essex **City Area:** 24 sq. miles (62.2 sq. kilometers) **Altitude:** 55 feet (16.7 meters)
**Mayor:** Kenneth A. Gibson
**City Population:** 329,248 (1980 census) **Metro Area Population:** 1,965,304 (1980 census)
**Daily Newspapers:** 1 **No. of Radio Stations:** 2 **No. of TV Stations:** 2
**City Chamber of Commerce:** Greater Newark Chamber of Commerce, 50 Park Place, Newark, New Jersey 07102

Newark, seat of Essex County and largest city in New Jersey, is an important industrial and commercial center. It was settled in 1666 by Puritans from Connecticut led by Robert Treat and is said to have been named after the town of Newark, England, although some contend its name was New Ark and had a religious connotation.

During the Revolutionary War, the city was the scene of several skirmishes; General George Washington passed through in 1776 leading his troops south to the Delaware River.

Newark's industrial growth began in the early 19th century. The arrival of railroads and canals in the 1830s stimulated the expansion of shoemaking and tanning and the development of the jewelry, insurance, and shipbuilding industries. After 1880 swarms of immigrants arrived, living in hastily built tenements. In 1915 Port Newark opened; during World War I Newark was the nation's leading shipbuilding city.

Today Newark is the country's third leading insurance center. A significant factor in its economic life is the Port of New York Authority, which operates Port Newark and Newark International Airport. Among the city's products are leather goods, jewelry, malt liquors, plastics, electrical equipment, auto parts, and chemicals.

Of interest in the city are Trinity Cathedral, the Sacred Heart Cathedral (begun in 1898), the First Presbyterian Church (1791); and the old County courthouse (1906), designed by Cass Gilbert.

Newark began to deteriorate economically and politically in the 1930s, a process which continued for 30 years or more. The city suffered the same ills which plagued many of the country's major cities—an exodus of population and business from the central city, with the concommitant drop in revenues, and a high unemployment rate among the remaining population, which is now over 75 percent black and Hispanic. Newark is fighting hard to lure business back to the downtown area and to improve the lot of its underprivileged citizens. Local efforts aided by the receipt of large federal health-care funds have dramatically reduced the death rate over a ten-year period since the mid 60s.

The Prudential and Mutual Benefit life insurance companies have since built new headquarters here, Blue Cross-Blue Shield of New Jersey is also headquartered here, and Public Service Electric and Gas Company, a major utility, has replaced its downtown headquarters with a new $60-million, 27-story corporate complex on an adjacent site. Since then millions of dollars have been spent to rebuild the city. The New Jersey Institute of Technology expanded its facilities. In 1974 New Jersey College of Medicine and Dentistry, Essex County College, Seton Hall and Rutgers University began construction of university facilities. In 1976 construction was completed at Seton Hall Law School, the School of Dentistry, Rutgers University and Essex County College.

### NEW ORLEANS

**Location:** Southeastern Louisiana, on Mississippi River, near Lake Pontchartrain, about 100 miles from Gulf of Mexico **Parish:** Orleans **City Area:** 366 sq. miles (947.9 sq. kilometers) **Altitude:** 5 feet (1.5 meters)
**Mayor:** Ernest N. Morial **Chief Administrative Officer:** Reynaud Rochon
**City Population:** 557,927 (1980 census) **Metro Area Population:** 1,186,725 (1980 census)
**Daily Newspapers:** 1 **No. of Radio Stations:** 17 **No. of TV Stations:** 5
**City Chamber of Commerce:** Chamber of Commerce of New Orleans and the River Region, P.O. Box 30240, New Orleans, Louisiana 70190

New Orleans, coextensive with Louisiana's Orleans Parish (county), is one of the largest cities in the South, the nation's second largest port, and the third largest port in the world. It was founded in 1718 by the Sieur de Bienville and named for Philippe II, duke of Orleans. Four years later it became the capital of the French colony of Louisiana. In 1762 the city passed to Spain, but remained culturally French.

New Orleans was returned to France in 1800 and in 1803 came under U.S. jurisdiction with the Louisiana Purchase. It developed into a flourishing cotton and slave-trade center, and was an important stopover on the southern routes to the West. After Andrew Jackson's victory over the British at New Orleans (January 8, 1815), the city's prosperity reached great heights, and New Orleans became famous for gaiety and elegance. (Today its colorful Mardi Gras, which is held every February, is one of the country's best-known festivals.)

In 1862 the city fell to Admiral David G. Farragut and did not fully recover from occupation by Union troops under General Benjamin Butler and the subsequent Reconstruction era until the end of World War I. Discovery of oil and the renewed commercial importance of sugar and cotton helped the city regain prosperity.

Today New Orleans is a leading banking and business center of the New South. It has the world's largest sugar refinery and is surrounded, offshore and on, by some of the most productive sources of oil in the nation. Other important industries are aerospace and shipbuilding.

The city's Vieux Carré, the French quarter, which comprised the original settlement, is a popular tourist attraction. Among the points of interest are Royal Street (Rue Royale) and the French Market on Decatur Street. Dixieland jazz was born on Bourbon Street.

Other landmarks include the Hibernia Tower, 33-story International Trade Mart, and the 52-story One Shell Square. The $178-million air-conditioned Superdome, the largest in the world, was dedicated August 3, 1975. The downtown area is being developed with five large-scale multi-use projects, provided for by some $1 billion in investments by private and public sectors. These projects are the Poydras Plaza, the International Rivercenter, the Pan-American Life Insurance Company Headquarters, the Canal Place, and the Piazza D'Italia.

On April 24, 1981, the Bureau of International Expositions in Paris approved New Orleans as the site for the 1984 World's Fair. The exposition will be located along the riverfront and will cost $69 million to construct.

## NEW YORK CITY

**Location:** Southeastern New York, at mouth of Hudson River **Counties:** New York, Bronx, Kings, Queens, and Richmond **City Area:** 320 sq. miles (828.8 sq. kilometers) **Altitude:** 55 feet (16.7 meters)
**Mayor:** Edward I. Koch
**City Population:** 7,071,639 (1980 census) **Metro Area Population:** 9,119,737 (1980 census)
**Daily Newspapers:** 9 **No. of Radio Stations:** 58 **No. of TV Stations:** 9
**City Chamber of Commerce:** New York Chamber of Commerce and Industry, 200 Madison Avenue, New York, New York 10016

New York, the nation's largest city and richest port, is a national leader in business, finance, manufacturing, communications, service industries, fashion, and the arts. It is also one of the world's largest cities, one of the world's leading ports, and headquarters of the United Nations.

As the financial headquarters of the world, New York is the home of some of the world's largest corporations and the New York and American Stock Exchanges.

As a cultural capital and influential arbiter of taste, the city has its renowned theater district and the cultural complex of Lincoln Center for the Performing Arts. It also has innumerable museums, art galleries, and related attractions, as well as scientific collections, libraries, and educational institutions.

Giovanni da Verrazano, a Florentine, was probably the first European to visit (1524) the site of New York. Henry Hudson's explorations (1609) up the river named after him led to the first permanent European settlements. In 1625 the colony of New Netherland was established, with its capital, New Amsterdam, located at the southern tip of Manhattan Island. The following year Peter Minuit of the Dutch West India Company bought the entire island from the Indians for the equivalent of about $24 in trinkets and beads. In 1664 the English seized the city for the Duke of York, for whom it was renamed. Later the Dutch regained control for a brief period (1673-74).

New York was active in the colonial opposition to British rule, and during the first year of the Revolution several battles were fought in the area. In 1776 the British captured the city and controlled it for the rest of the war.

New York, the first capital (1789-90) of the United States under the Constitution, was the site of George Washington's first inauguration. Until 1797 the city was also the capital of New York State.

The opening of the Erie Canal (1825) accelerated the growth of the city, already the nation's largest, and established its dominance over Boston and Philadelphia. By 1840 New York was the country's leading port.

During the 19th century, the city expanded northward from the tip of Manhattan, until by 1874 it covered the entire island. That same year saw annexation of parts of Westchester County that later formed the Bronx. New York assumed its present boundaries in 1898, after annexing Brooklyn, Queens County and Staten Island.

New York's best known attractions include Central Park, the Bronx Zoo and Botanical Gardens, the Aquarium at Coney Island, Hayden Planetarium, the Fifth Avenue shops, the Broadway theatrical district, the United Nations Headquarters, Radio City Music Hall, the Statue of Liberty and the Staten Island ferry, Rockefeller and Lincoln Centers, Madison Square Garden, Yankee and Shea Stadiums, South Street Seaport, Greenwich Village, Chinatown and the Financial District, the Metropolitan Museum of Art, St. Patrick's Cathedral and the World Trade Center.

New York City was host to the 1980 Democratic Convention on August 11-14, which saw the renomination of Jimmy Carter and Walter Mondale to the presidency and vice-presidency.

During the 1980s work will begin on the massive Westway project, a combined interstate highway and parkland project along the lower Manhattan shoreline of the Hudson River. The project is expected to cost $2.3 billion by completion. The city is also constructing a large convention center on Manhattan's West Side.

## NORFOLK

**Location:** southeastern Virginia, at the mouth of Chesapeake Bay
**County:** independent city **City Area:** 54.2 sq. miles (140.4 sq. kilometers) **Altitude:** 10 feet (3 meters)
**Mayor:** Vincent J. Thomas **City Manager:** Julian F. Hirst
**City Population:** 266,979 (1980 census) **Metro Area Population:** 806,691 (1980 census)
**Daily Newspapers:** 2 **No. of Radio Stations:** 18 **No. of TV Stations:** 5
**City Chamber of Commerce:** Norfolk Chamber of Commerce, 480 Bank Street, Norfolk, Virginia 23510

Norfolk, Virginia's largest city and a world seaport, is adjoined by the city of Portsmouth on the opposite bank of the Elizabeth River and by nearby Newport News, the three communities making up the Port of Hampton Roads, one of the world's finest natural harbors.

Norfolk is the home of the nation's largest naval base, and the Norfolk Naval Shipyard (actually in Portsmouth) has the greatest number of dry docks of any U.S. shipyard. The city is also headquarters for the Fifth Naval District, the Atlantic Fleet, the Second Fleet, and for NATO's Supreme Allied Command, Atlantic (SACLANT). The city's major economic activities include shipping, shipbuilding and repair, meat-packing, fishing and automobile assembly. Among its chief manufactures are lumber and wood products, fertilizer, cement, chemicals, clothing and food products.

Norfolk was established in 1682 by the Virginia colonial government, on the site of an Indian village. It was made a borough in 1736, incorporated as a town in 1805 amd chartered as a city in 1845. It was completely demolished in the American Revolution—first bombarded by British warships anchored in the Elizabeth River, then razed by fleeing Virginians to prevent its use by the British. (Only St. Paul's Church, dating from 1739, survived the flames; it stands today, with a cannonball still embedded in one of its walls.) The city suffered a severe yellow-fever epidemic in 1855, and in 1861, during the Civil War, it was once again bombarded—this time by Union forces. In 1862 it was captured and occupied for the duration. the famous fight between the *Monitor* and the *Merrimack* took place that year in Hampton Roads.

The postwar period saw Norfolk become an increasingly vital international trading center, thanks largely to its development as a major rail terminus. Coal and grain exports have grown dramatically in recent years. Visitors are attracted to the city by the excellent bathing and fishing opportunities it affords, as well as its many historic buildings. Other attractions include the General Douglas MacArthur Memorial, the 114-acre Lafayette Zoological Park, the azalea gardens at Gardens-by-the-Sea, and the Chrysler Museum. The waterfront area is undergoing a major redevelopment, and will contain the headquarters of the Cousteau Society.

## OKLAHOMA CITY

**Location:** Central Oklahoma, on North Canadian River **Counties:** Oklahoma, Canadian, Cleveland and McClain **City Area:** 621 miles (1,608 sq. kilometers) **Altitude:** 1,207 feet (366.8 meters)

**Mayor:** Patience Latting **City Manager:** Scott Johnson
**City Population:** 403,136 (1980 census) **Metro Area Population:** 834,088 (1980 census)
**Daily Newspapers:** 3 **No. of Radio Stations:** 24 **No. of TV Stations:** 8
**City Chamber of Commerce:** Oklahoma City Chamber of Commerce, One Santa Fe Plaza, Oklahoma City, Oklahoma 73102

Oklahoma City, seat of Oklahoma County and state capital, is the largest municipality in Oklahoma. It is also the state's financial, commercial, and industrial center.

The city's origin is one of the most colorful in American history. When the first land run into Indian Territory took place on April 22, 1889, a small Santa Fe Railroad water and coaling station blossomed into a city of 10,000 people between noon and sundown. The name of the city and territory means "red people" and had been proposed by a Choctaw chief in 1866 to designate the area set off for Indians. Oklahoma City was incorporated in 1890 and became the state capital in 1910.

Oil was struck in 1928, and it soon became apparent that rich oil and gas lands lay beneath the city itself. An extensive system of oil wells in the metropolitan area, reaching almost to the governor's mansion, is a large factor in the city's economy.

Oklahoma City is a rapidly growing regional, national and international marketing center. The U.S. Customs Bureau opened an office in 1967 to expedite exports and imports. Industry includes meat packing, including the headquarters of Wilson & Co., electronics components and the production of transportation equipment and oil field supplies. General Motors opened a huge auto assembly plant in 1979. The city also is noted as a convention site.

Oklahoma City has grown into an aeronautical complex with such Federal Aviation Administration facilities as the Aeronautical Center and Civil Aeromedical Institute. Nearby is Tinker Air Force Base with equipment and inventory of over $2 billion.

Of interest are the National Cowboy Hall of Fame and Western Heritage Center, with western art and a recreation of a western scene; the State Historical Society Building and Museum; the zoo; Kirkpatrick Center, with its science, air and space museum; and the State Capitol. The Oklahoma National Stockyards, the nation's largest cattle feeder market, has been designated as a national historical landmark. The National Finals rodeo is held here every December.

## OMAHA

**Location:** East-central Nebraska, on Missouri River **County:** Douglas City **Area:** 87.8 sq. miles (226.5 sq. kilometers) **Altitude:** 1,063 feet (324 meters)
**Mayor:** Mike Boyle
**City Population:** 313,911 (1980 census) **Metro Area Population:** 570,399 (1980 census)
**Daily Newspapers:** 1 **No. of Radio Stations:** 19 **No. of TV Stations:** 7
**City Chamber of Commerce:** Greater Omaha Chamber of Commerce, 1606 Douglas, Omaha, Nebraska 68102

Omaha, seat of Douglas County, is the largest city in Nebraska. It is an important cattle market and meatpacking center. It took its name from the Omaha Indians living nearby, who were known as "those who go upstream or against the current."

Omaha's history is associated with the opening of the West beginning with Lewis and Clark's conference with the Indians in 1804. A trading post was set up by Jean Pierre Cabanne in 1825, and the first settlement came in 1846-47, when the Mormons spent the winter there on their way to Utah. The city was officially founded in 1854 after Indians ceded the present Douglas County to the United States. Three years later Omaha was incorporated as a city and was capital of the Nebraska Territory from 1855 to 1867.

As a supply point for westward migration, Omaha grew quickly. The Union Pacific Railroad arrived in 1865, augmenting river traffic and making Omaha, on the west bank of the Missouri, a major transportation and shipping center.

Despite floods, droughts, and a plague of grasshoppers later in the 19th century, the city continued to expand. Today it is an important market for livestock and farm produce and has large meat-packing and food-processing plants, grain elevators, and stockyards. It also has oil refineries, a large lead smelter, and factories manufacturing farm implements and appliances.

The headquarters of the Strategic Air Command are located here as are the regional headquarters of the Farm Credit Administration and the Reconstruction Finance Corporation. Boys Town, the youth community founded by Father Edward J. Flanagan in 1917, is 11 miles west of the city.

Of interest are Fort Omaha, built in 1868, and the Mormon Cemetery with the Winter Quarters Monument. Riverview Park contains a monument to Friedrich von Schiller and Levi Carter Park has a lake and picnic grounds. The Joslyn Art Museum contains paintings by many of the world's greatest artists.

## PHILADELPHIA

**Location:** Southeastern Pennsylvania, at the junction of the Delaware and Schuylkill rivers, 88 miles from Atlantic Ocean **County:** Philadelphia **City Area:** 129 sq. miles (334.1 sq. kilometers) **Altitude:** 100 feet (30.4 meters)
**Mayor:** William J. Green **Managing Director:** W. Wilson Goode
**City Population:** 1,688,210 (1980 census) **Metro Area Population:** 4,716,818 (1980 census)
**Daily Newspapers:** 3 **No. of Radio Stations:** 22 **No. of TV Stations:** 7
**City Chamber of Commerce:** The Greater Philadelphia Chamber of Commerce, 1346 Chestnut Street, Suite 800, Philadelphia, Pennsylvania 19107

Philadelphia, coextensive with Philadelphia County, is the largest city in Pennsylvania and the fourth largest in the nation. The site was originally settled by Swedes early in the 17th century. In 1682 William Penn founded a Quaker settlement, naming it Philadelphia from the Greek phrase for "brotherly love."

The city was the largest and wealthiest in the 13 Colonies and served, except during a brief British occupation, as the capital from 1777 to 1788—the period of the adoption of the Articles of Confederation (1778) and the drafting of the United States Constitution (1787). From 1790 to 1800 it was the capital of the United States. Philadelphia was the site of both Banks of the United States—the first from 1791 to 1811, and the second from 1816 to 1836. It was also an important center of the abolition movement and a major station on the Underground Railroad.

Philadelphia was host to the 1876 Centennial Exposition, commemorating the 100th anniversary of American independence, and the 1926 Sesquicentennial Exposition. In 1982 the city celebrated its 300th anniversary with a visit of the "Tall Ships."

Today its diversified economy includes such industries as printing and publishing, and the manufacture of machinery, chemicals, clothing, carpets, instruments and textiles. It is the largest petroleum refining center on the East Coast and the second largest in the nation. It has the largest freshwater port in the world, with 50 miles of waterfront, and is also a major financial center.

A major renovation of the waterfront, referred to as Penn's Landing, has been completed, and a University City Science Center has opened. Ground was broken in April 1972 for a $300-million complex called Market Street East, which has transformed Philadelphia's main shopping street from City Hall to Independence Mall into a mall and transportation center. In November 1975 the Chestnut Street Transitway opened to transform the 10 blocks between 8th and 18th streets into a buses-only transitway and a modern shrub-lined pedestrian promenade and shopping mall.

There are numerous historic monuments in the city. Independence Hall, where the Declaration of Independence was signed, is in Independence National Park. Nearby is Congress Hall, seat of Congress from 1790 to 1800; Carpenters' Hall, meeting place for the First Continental Congress; the First and Second U.S. Banks; the Jacob Graff House; old City Hall; and the Merchants' Exchange. Other points of interest are Elfreth's Alley, one of the nation's oldest streets; Christ Church; the Society Hill area; and the Betsy Ross House. Fairmount Park, one of the largest in the world, contains many historic monuments and a famous zoo. Among the city's many outstanding museums are the world-famous Museum of Art, the Franklin Institute Science Museum and the University Museum.

## PHOENIX

**Location:** South-central Arizona on Salt River **County:** Maricopa **City Area:** 325 sq. miles (842 sq. kilometers) **Altitude:** 1,117 feet (340.4 meters)
**Mayor:** Margaret Hance **City Manager:** Marvin Andrews
**City Population:** 789,704 (1980 census) **Metro Area Population:** 1,508,030 (1980 census)
**Daily Newspapers:** 2 **No. of Radio Stations:** 35 **No. of TV Stations:** 7
**City Chamber of Commerce:** Phoenix Metropolitan Chamber of Commerce, 34 W. Monroe Street, Phoenix, Arizona 85003

Phoenix, seat of Maricopa County and state capital, is the largest city in Arizona and one of the fastest growing in the nation. Because Phoenix grew up on a site that showed traces of an ancient Hohokam Indian settlement, it was named after the mythological bird that rose from its own ashes.

The area was probably visited by the Spanish explorers Cabeza de Vaca in 1536, Marcos de Niza in 1539, and Coronado in 1540. John Y. T. Smith established a hay camp on the Salt River in 1866, and the following year Phoenix was officially founded. It was incorporated as a city in 1881 and replaced Prescott as the territorial capital in 1889, two years after the first railroad arrived. In 1912 Arizona was admitted to the Union, and Phoenix became the state capital.

The completion in 1911 of Roosevelt Dam, part of the first successful large-scale irrigation project in the country, made it possible to grow citrus fruits, dates and other crops in the desert climate. The city has also prospered from rich mineral deposits in the region. Since 1945 electronics, computer, aircraft, furniture, steel, aluminum and chemical manufacturing have become important.

In 1972 the Phoenix Civic Plaza, a $19-million commercial and cultural complex, and the 40-story Valley National Bank Building, Arizona's tallest, were completed.

Abundant sunshine has made Phoenix a health resort and winter vacationland. Of interest in the area are the city's museums; nearby South Mountain Park; and Taliesin West, home of the late Frank Lloyd Wright and now an architectural school directed by Mrs. Wright. An annual rodeo simulates the atmosphere of the Old West each spring.

Phoenix has a mushrooming population—people are moving into this city at a rate of more than 400 a day. Newcomers are discovering that the reasons they moved away—air pollution, traffic congestion, inflation, overburdened utilities and suburban sprawl—are problems that already exist in Phoenix. Major long-range plans for the city are in the beginning stages, with redevelopment and "in-filling" of areas within the inner city being the new direction taken.

As Phoenix has mushroomed in population and development, so it has in athletic stature. Professional sports teams such as the National Basketball Association Phoenix Suns have found a home in the Valley of the Sun and are popular drawing cards.

## PITTSBURGH

**Location:** Southwestern Pennsylvania, at junction where the Allegheny and Monongahela rivers form the Ohio River **County:** Allegheny **City Area:** 55.5 sq. miles (143.8 sq. kilometers) **Altitude:** 745 feet (226.4 meters)
**Mayor:** Richard S. Caliguiri
**City Population:** 423,959 (1980 census) **Metro Area Population:** 2,263,894 (1980 census)
**Daily Newspapers:** 2 **No. of Radio Stations:** 28 **No. of TV Stations:** 6
**City Chamber of Commerce:** The Greater Pittsburgh Chamber of Commerce, 411 Seventh Avenue, Pittsburgh, Pennsylvania 15219

Pittsburgh, seat of Allegheny County, is the second largest city in Pennsylvania, an important inland port, and one of the world's great steel centers.

It was founded on the site of Shannopin, an Indian settlement that was a fur-trading post in the late 17th century. In the 18th century the French built Fort Duquesne on the site, and after it fell to the British it was renamed Fort Pitt in honor of William Pitt. The fort withstood attack in 1763 during Pontiac's Rebellion, and in the ensuing years a village grew up around it.

When the Northwest Territory opened up, the village became an important trading and shipping center. Anthony Wayne negotiated (1795) with Indian tribes in the area, allowing Pittsburgh to develop in peace. It was incorporated as a city in 1816. Completion of the Pennsylvania Canal in 1837 and rail lines in 1851 further stimulated industrial and commercial development. One of the world's first cable suspension bridges was constructed here in 1847.

In 1936 Pittsburgh suffered the most disastrous flood of its history when the Allegheny and the Monongahela rivers rose 46 feet, inundating much of the business and industrial district, paralyzing the city, and taking 45 lives. Damages amounted to $25 million.

The city is headquarters for some of the country's biggest corporations. Among them are U.S. Steel, Gulf Oil, Rockwell International, Heinz foods, Westinghouse, Alcoa, PPG Industries, and Koppers Co. The reactors for the Nautilus and Skate, the first nuclear submarines, were built here.

Pittsburgh's revolutionary urban-renewal program began when public-spirited citizens formed the Allegheny Conference on Community Development in 1943. Demolition work began in 1950 for the famous Gateway Center and $22-million Civic Auditorium with a retractable dome. The program has been eminently successful in rebuilding the Golden Triangle—the triangular-shaped business district bounded by the Allegheny, Monongahela, and Ohio rivers. It has also been so successful in controlling smoke emitted by the steelmaking and other industrial complexes that Pittsburgh is no longer "Smoky City," a nickname it bore for more than a century. The recent Renaissance II program has been responsible for a surge of massive construction projects. Among them are the $35-million David L. Lawrence Convention Center, opened in 1981; the $150-million PPG Headquarters Building; the Liberty Center office-hotel complex; the Dravo building; and the One Oxford Centre complex.

Pittsburgh has a fine park system. City landmarks include the Carnegie-Mellon University, established by Andrew Carnegie in 1895; the University of Pittsburgh and its Cathedral of Learning, noted for its medical and law schools; the Buhl Planetarium and Institute of Popular Science; and Highland Park, site of the Pittsburgh Zoo and a memorial to Stephen Foster, who was born there. Heinz Hall for the Performing Arts opened in September 1971. It is home for the Pittsburgh Symphony, Pittsburgh Opera, Civic Light Opera, Pittsburgh Ballet and Pittsburgh Youth Symphony.

The bold skyline of Pittsburgh is clearly visible from the top of Mount Washington reached from the south bank of the Monongahela by the "incline," one of two in the city, which acts as a near-verticle tramway up the steep slope.

## PORTLAND

**Location:** Northwestern Oregon, near the junction of the Willamette and Columbia rivers **Counties:** Multnomah and Washington **City Area:** 107 sq. miles (277 sq. kilometers) **Altitude:** 77 feet (23.4 meters)
**Mayor:** Francis Ivancie
**City Population:** 366,383 (1980 census) **Metro Area Population:** 1,242,287 (1980 census)
**Daily Newspapers:** 3 **No. of Radio Stations:** 27 **No. of TV Stations:** 6
**City Chamber of Commerce:** Portland Chamber of Commerce, 824 S.W. 5th Avenue, Portland, Oregon 97204

Portland, seat of Multnomah County and largest city in Oregon, is a trading, transportation, and manufacturing center, an important deepwater port with shipyards and the world's third-largest floating dry dock.

When it was founded in 1845, a coin was flipped to decide whether it should be named after Boston, Massachusetts or Portland, Maine. Incorporated in 1851, it expanded with the establishment of the salmon industry after the Civil War, the arrival of the railroad (1883), the Alaska gold rush (1897-1900), and the Lewis and Clark Centennial Exposition (1905). A disastrous fire in 1873 destroyed part of the city, but it was rapidly rebuilt. The city made history in 1889 with the first long-distance transmission of electricity; power from a plant on the Willamette Falls at Oregon City was sent over wires to light the streets of Portland. During World War II, Portland emerged as a major shipbuilding port.

Today the city is a major export point for wheat, wool, bauxite and lumber, and the leading manufacturer of specialized lumbering equipment. Also important to the city's economy are the numerous chemical industries. Portland has become a major electronics manufacturing center. It is the home of Tektronics, a major producer of display and signal equipment.

Portland instituted a popularly elected regional government that embraces parts of three counties. The reorganization is the first of its kind in the nation, and calls for a two-tiered government of municipal, county and other local jurisdictions and a regional government.

A $16-million transit mall was completed in the central business district in late 1977. The mall provides partial separation of buses, pedestrians and cars for improved transportation flow and lower pollutant levels in the downtown area. A new transit project is the $161-million light rail route which will extend 15 miles from downtown Portland to a suburb.

Of interest in Portland are the annual rose festival, the Pacific International Livestock Exposition, the Portland Zoo, the Portland Art Museum, and the fine views of various mountains, occasionally including distant Mount Rainier and Mount Jefferson. Mount Tabor, an extinct volcanic crater, is located in Portland.

## PROVIDENCE

**Location:** Northeastern Rhode Island, at the head of the Narragansett Bay, on Providence River **County:** Providence **City Area:** 20 sq. miles (51.8 sq. kilometers) **Altitude:** 80 feet (24.3 meters)
**Mayor:** Vincent A. Cianci, Jr.
**City Population:** 156,804 (1980 census) **Metro Area Population:** 919,216 (1980 census)
**Daily Newspapers:** 2 **No. of Radio Stations:** 7 **No. of TV Stations:** 4
**City Chamber of Commerce:** Greater Providence Chamber of Commerce, 10 Dorrance Street, Providence, Rhode Island 02903

Providence, seat of Providence County and state capital, is the largest city in Rhode Island and a port of entry. It was founded by Roger Williams in 1636 after he was exiled from Massachusetts. The Narragansett Indians granted him title to the site, which he named in gratitude for "God's merciful providence." Early settlers formed (1638) a "Proprietors Company" cooperative.

The settlement developed slowly during the 17th century and suffered much destruction during King Philip's War (1675-76) when Indians raided it and burned more than a third of its homes. Later, however, Providence developed into an important commercial center, and many families amassed fortunes as ships engaged in the West Indian trade.

Providence served the patriotic cause during the Revolutionary War and signed the Rhode Island Independence Act two months before the signing of the Declaration of Independence. After the War of 1812, Providence became a jewelry and textile manufacturing center. In 1832 the city charter became effective.

In 1842 Thomas Wilson Dorr, a Providence man, led a rebellion that collapsed; however, it was influential in the formation of a more democratic state constitution. In 1900 Providence became Rhode Island's sole capital, having been joint capital with other communities since colonial days.

Today Providence is still noted as a jewelry manufacturing center. Silverware, textiles, machinery, metal products, and rubber goods are also important products.

Among the city's historic structures are the old market building (1773), the Stephen Hopkins House (c. 1755), the John Brown House (1786), the Arcade (1828), and the First Baptist Meetinghouse (1775). Roger Williams Park contains a museum of natural history and a natural amphitheater where concerts are given.

Providence is the home of Brown University, Providence College, Rhode Island College, and Rhode Island School of Design, one of the country's leading art schools.

## ROCHESTER

**Location:** Western New York State, at the mouth of the Genesee River on Lake Ontario, 65 miles east of Buffalo **County:** Monroe **City Area:** 36 sq. miles (93.2 sq. kilometers) **Altitude:** 510 feet (154.9 meters)
**Mayor:** Thomas P. Ryan, Jr. **City Manager:** Peter Korn
**City Population:** 295,011 (1970 census), 262,766 (1976 est.) **Metro Area Population:** 961,516 (1970 census), 970,200 (1977 est.)
**Daily Newspapers:** 3 **No. of Radio Stations:** 16 **No. of TV Stations:** 5
**City Chamber of Commerce:** Rochester Area Chamber of Commerce, Inc., 55 St. Paul Street, Rochester, New York 14604

Rochester, seat of Monroe County, is situated on the falls of the Genesee River, the New York State Barge Canal and Lake Ontario. Known as the home of Eastman Kodak, Bausch & Lomb, R. T. French, and Xerox, the city enjoys an unusually diverse economy; major industries include machinery, optical goods, foundry products, nurseries, food packing and processing, leather goods, printing and publishing. It also has great natural beauty, its many parks and gardens earning for it the nickname, "The Flower City."

The Rochester region was originally the home of the Seneca Indians. In 1789 Ebenezer Allen built a mill at the falls of the Genesee, on land he had been granted on condition he serve the Senecas' needs. But the mill failed, and Allen's land was sold to Colonel Nathaniel Rochester and two friends. In 1811 Colonel Rochester laid out the village and a year later the first white settlement was made; its original name, Rochesterville, was shortened in 1812. The village was incorporated in 1817, the city in 1834.

Blessed with abundant waterpower, and the rich yields of the Genesee Valley, a significant milling industry developed and played a large part in Rochester's early growth. The industry's success was assured by the opening of the Erie Canal to the city in 1823.

Before the Civil War, the city was in the forefront of the anti-slavery movement and a station on the Underground Railroad; it was in Rochester that black abolitionist Frederick Douglass published a newspaper, *The North Star.* The period 1850-1900 saw the decline of milling as the city's chief economic pursuit, and the rise of the nursery trade and a number of technical industries to take its place. In 1916 the city was extended northward, in a strip along the banks of the Genesee, to Lake Ontario.

Among the city's attractions are the Eastman Kodak Company, whose plants are open to tours; the George Eastman House of Photography; the Rochester Museum of Arts and Sciences; the Strassenburgh Planetarium; Eastman Theatre, home of the Rochester Philharmonic and the Susan B. Anthony House, commemorating the women's rights pioneer and former Rochester resident.

## SACRAMENTO

**Location:** North-central California, at the confluence of the Sacramento and American rivers, 90 miles northeast of San Francisco **County:** Sacramento **City Area:** 93.8 sq. miles (242.9 sq. kilometers) **Altitude:** 17 feet (5.2 meters)
**Mayor:** Phillip Isenberg **City Manager:** Walter Slipe
**City Population:** 275,741 (1980 census) **Metro Area Population:** 1,014,002 (1980 census)
**Daily Newspapers:** 2 **No. of Radio Stations:** 16 **No. of TV Stations:** 6
**City Chamber of Commerce:** Sacramento Metropolitan Chamber of Commerce, P.O. Box 1017, Sacramento, California 95805

Sacramento, capital of California and seat of Sacramento County, is a rare amalgam of industrial strength and natural beauty, and the focal point of the profusely fertile Sacramento Valley. Fruits, vegetables, cattle and dairy products abound, supporting a large food packing and processing industry. Other important resources include oil, natural gas, timber, lead, pottery clay and a plentiful supply of waterpower for generating electricity. In 1963 the city opened deep-water port facilities, with direct access to the Pacific Ocean. The city is also an important missile development and electronics center.

The history of Sacramento is rich in drama and color, dating from its founding in 1839 by John Augustus Sutter, a German-born Swiss citizen who received permission from the Mexican governor to establish a colony for fellow Swiss immigrants. Originally called New Helvetia, it received its present name (from the river which ran beside it) in 1848, when it was laid out as a town.

The following year brought the new community immediate and widespread renown, when gold was discovered (by James W. Marshall) on Sutter's property, triggering the legend-engendering Gold Rush of 1849. Fortune followed fame in swift abundance, as Sacramento became the supply center for prospectors, in an often ruthless seller's market. (Ironically, the Gold Rush brought only impoverishment to Sutter himself, as hordes of prospectors pillaged his property and put him heavily in debt.)

Sacramento was incorporated as a town in 1850 and selected as the state capital four years later. City incorporation came in 1863.

From 1849 to 1862, Sacramento was plagued by a series of disasters, including a serious fire and three devastating floods; yet always the town came back to flourish anew. Over the years, the development of flood control techniques has greatly aided the city's growth. A hub of river transport since its inception, Sacramento also became (in 1856) the terminus of California's first railroad and (in 1860) the western terminus of the Pony Express. In 1863 the Central Pacific Railroad began laying track east from Sacramento to meet the westward-reaching Union Pacific, and six years later the link was made, giving the country its first transcontinental rail route.

In 1978, a comprehensive plan was issued to guide public and private efforts in developing and revitalizing the center city. A $30-million redevelopment project is under way in an effort by retailers to move back into the downtown area.

Among Sacramento's many attractions are old Fort Sutter, built by Sutter and now maintained as a museum; the 1860 State Capitol; the old Governor's Mansion; the Crocker Art Gallery; Old Sacramento, a re-creation of the original city, including restaurants, theaters, shops and such museums as the Pony Express Museum and the Railroad Museum.

## ST. LOUIS

**Location:** East-central Missouri, near junction of Mississippi and Missouri rivers **County:** St. Louis is an independent city **City Area:** 61 sq. miles (158 sq. kilometers) **Altitude:** 455 feet (138.3 meters)
**Mayor:** Vincent Schoemehl, Jr.
**City Population:** 453,085 (1980 census) **Metro Area Population:** 2,355,276 (1980 census)
**Daily Newspapers:** 2 **No. of Radio Stations:** 26 **No. of TV Stations:** 6
**City Chamber of Commerce:** St. Louis Regional Commerce and Growth Association, 10 Broadway, St. Louis, Missouri 63102

St. Louis, the largest city in Missouri and the Mississippi River Valley, is surrounded by, but independent of, St. Louis County.

In 1763 the French fur trader Pierre Laclede chose the site for a trading post and a year later dispatched René Auguste Chouteau to build it. It was named St. Louis after Louis IX, the patron saint of France.

The settlement, which became part of the United States in 1803 with the Louisiana Purchase, was an important point of embarkation for expeditions to the West, such as that of Lewis and Clark in 1804. Incorporated in 1808, it did not expand rapidly until after the War of 1812, when immigrants coming by flatboat began to settle the West. Great Americans associated with the city include Charles Lindbergh, Thomas Hart Benton and Joseph Pulitzer.

Today manufacturing is the most important aspect of the economy. The St. Louis industrial area is the only one in the nation producing six basic metals: iron, lead, zinc, copper, aluminum, and magnesium. The city is also a major center for chemical industries and research. St. Louis has been second only to Detroit in automobile assembly; it has one of the pioneer aerospace manufacturers; and it has the world's largest brewery, Anheuser-Busch, Inc.

In 1966 St. Louis completed its 50,000-seat Busch Memorial Stadium. The following year the Jefferson National Expansion Memorial, a project of the National Park Service, was dedicated. The city erected the 630-foot stainless steel Gateway Arch, tallest monument in the country, as part of the memorial. The Arch attracts between 2-and 4-million visitors a year.

St. Louis, like many other cities, is seeking to rejuvenate its downtown area. In the Laclede's Landing section on the riverfront, old warehouses are being restored, and new restaurants and nightspots have revived night life in the area. A $25-million Convention Center, completed in 1977, and new hotels are bringing more visitors to the city.

Points of interest in St. Louis include the Old Courthouse, scene of the Dred Scott case; Forest Park; the Missouri Botanical Garden; the Municipal Opera; the McDonnell Planetarium; and the Powell Symphony Hall.

## ST. PAUL

**Location:** Eastern Minnesota, adjacent to Minneapolis at the junction of the Minnesota River with the Mississippi **County:** Ramsey **City Area:** 55.45 sq. miles (143.6 sq. kilometers) **Altitude:** 687 feet (209.4 meters)
**Mayor:** George Latimer
**City Population:** 270,230 (1980 census) **Metro Area Population:** 2,114,256 (1980 census)
**Daily Newspapers:** 2 **No. of Radio Stations:** 36 **No. of TV Stations:** 5
**City Chamber of Commerce:** St. Paul Area Chamber of Commerce, Suite 701, North Central Tower, St. Paul, Minnesota 55101

St. Paul, capital of Minnesota and seat of Ramsey County, is contiguous with Minneapolis, with which it forms the Twin Cities metropolitan area, home for about half the state's population. A port of entry and a major transportation and industrial center, the city is situated on bluffs overlooking the Mississippi, close to the head of navigation. Its diverse economy includes meat packing, printing, publishing, steel fabrication, and the manufacture of automobiles, machinery, petroleum products, aerospace equipment, computers, food products, abrasives and cosmetics.

Permanent white settlement in the area began in 1819 with the establishment of an army post on the Minnesota River, on the site of Mendota, now a St. Paul suburb. The following year, the post was moved across the river, where Josiah Snelling built Fort St. Anthony, later named Fort Snelling. Thanks to its strategic location and a large supply of game, fur-trading flourished at Mendota, as did the trading of food and dry goods. After treaties with the Indians paved the way for settlement, many traders, lumbermen and others came from the East to make the area home.

In 1838 a community was begun on the site of present-day St. Paul, which was originally named Pig's Eye, after one of the settlers, a French-Canadian trader named Pierre "Pig's Eye" Parrant. But it soon came to be called St. Paul, in honor of the church built there in 1841 by Father Lucian Galtier. St. Paul was made the capital of Minnesota Territory in 1849, and was incorporated five years later. It was made the state capital in 1858, when Minnesota was admitted to the Union. With the advent of the railroad and the ready availability of immigrant labor (especially German and Irish), St. Paul's early prosperity was assured.

Among the city's attractions are the Capitol Building, which has the world's largest supported marble dome; the Cathedral of St. Paul; Town Square Park, a unique four level glass enclosed park; Landmark Center; William L. McKnight Omnitheatre; the St. Paul Arts and Science Center; Minnesota Museum of Art; St. Paul Civic Center; and, on the outskirts of the city, Fort Snelling State Park, Como Park Conservatory and Zoo, and Minnesota Zoological Gardens. The major annual events in Saint Paul include the Saint Paul Winter Carnival with ice sculpture contests, dog sled and snowmobile racing and parades and the St. Patrick's Day Parade, one of the largest in the country.

## SALT LAKE CITY

**Location:** North-central Utah, southeast of the Great Salt Lake, at the foot of the Wasatch range **County:** Salt Lake **City Area:** 56 sq. miles (145 sq. kilometers) **Altitude:** 4,260 feet (1294.5 meters)
**Mayor:** Ted Wilson
**City Population:** 163,697 (1980 census) **Metro Area Population:** 936,255 (1980 census)
**Daily Newspapers:** 2 **No. of Radio Stations:** 23 **No. of TV Stations:** 6
**City Chamber of Commerce:** Salt Lake Area Chamber of Commerce, 19 East Second South, Salt Lake City, Utah 84111

Salt Lake City, seat of Salt Lake County, is Utah's capital, its largest city, and headquarters of the 4 million members of the Mormon faith—the Church of Jesus Christ of Latter-day Saints. It was founded in 1847 by the Mormon leader Brigham Young. Mormon settlers soon transformed the arid region into irrigated farmland.

After 1849 Salt Lake City (called Great Salt Lake City until 1868) was a supply point for California-bound pioneers. A link to the transcontinental railroad in 1870 brought non-Mormons to the city and contributed to its growth. When Utah entered the Union in 1896, Salt Lake City became its capital.

Today the metropolis is an important distribution point for a rich agricultural and mining area, as well as an important air and rail hub. Its industries include printing and publishing, oil refining, copper refining, and the smelting of copper and iron. Electronics manufacturing is increasingly becoming an important industry. Major employers are Hill Air Force Base, 30 miles to the north, local defense industries, and the Kennecott Copper Corp.

The city lies at the foot of the beautiful Wasatch Mountains. The magnificent Utah State Capitol with its copper dome houses noted works of art and many interesting exhibits. The Salt Palace, a $17-million civic auditorium complex, was completed in 1969, since enlarged.

Centrally located Temple Square contains the most important buildings of the Mormon Church—the Mormon Temple, a mammoth granite structure designed under Brigham Young's direction and built between 1853 and 1893; and the Tabernacle, housing one of the world's largest organs.

Now completed is the tallest building in Salt Lake City, a 28-story office building for the Mormon church. A multimillion dollar arts project is the latest phase of the city's building boom. The Bicentennial Arts Center includes a concert hall for the Utah Symphony and a performing arts center. Recently completed is Crossroads Plaza, a downtown shopping mall-hotel complex.

## SAN ANTONIO

**Location:** South-central Texas, on the San Antonio River about 190 miles west of Houston **County:** Bexar **City Area:** 267 sq. miles (692 sq. kilometers) **Altitude:** 701 feet (231.3 meters)
**Mayor:** Henry Cisneros **City Manager:** Louis C. Fox
**City Population:** 786,023 (1980 census) **Metro Area Population:** 1,071,954 (1980 census)
**Daily Newspapers:** 3 **No. of Radio Stations:** 20 **No. of TV Stations:** 5
**City Chamber of Commerce:** Greater San Antonio Chamber of Commerce, 602 East Commerce Street, P.O. Box 1628, San Antonio, Texas 78296

San Antonio, port of entry and seat of Bexar County, has developed into the banking and commerce hub of south central Texas, while retaining its history-rich Spanish-Mexican character, redolent of the days when Indian, Spanish, Mexican, Texan and United States forces all sought dominion there. Only 154 miles from the U.S.-Mexico border at Laredo, it is a bilingual city whose old missions and historic landmarks offer charming contrast to its modern factories, refineries and military installations.

Although the federal government is San Antonio's largest employer, tourism, farming, stock-raising, food processing and diversified manufacture are also important to its economy. The city's mild climate and natural beauty have made it a popular winter resort.

The site of San Antonio had been known to the Spanish, and to the Coahuiltecan Indians, long before 1718, when a military expedition led by Martín de Alarcón, Spanish governor of Coahuila and Texas, founded a town and fort there, the Villa (and Presidio) de Béjar. At the same time, missionaries founded the Mission San Antonio de Valero nearby; in 1724 the mission was moved from its original site to where the Alamo stands today.

In 1731 Spanish colonists from the Canary Islands founded San Fernando de Béjar, just west of Alarcón's settlement. By 1791 the three settlements—Villa de Béjar, Mission San Antonio de Valero and San Fernando de Béjar—came to be known as one, San Antonio de Béjar (later, simply, San Antonio).

The settlement grew in prominence and was the principal objective of the Mexican and Texas Revolutions (1821, 1836). In the latter conflict, on March 6, 1836, the famous battle of the Alamo took place, in which all of the nearly 200 defenders (including Davy Crockett) were killed by Mexican forces numbering over 2,400. However, the following month, spurred by the battlecry "Remember the Alamo!," the Texans gained ultimate victory at San Jacinto, and the Texas republic was born; a year later, San Antonio was incorporated.

During the later part of the 19th century, the town became a major cattle center, where herds were assembled and started on overland drives up the Chisholm Trail to the Kansas railheads. San Antonio's prosperity was aided by the advent of the railroad and, later, by the increased military presence there.

Among the city's attractions are the Alamo; La Villita, a reconstructed old Spanish settlement; the historic Governor's Palace and San Fernando Cathedral, both restored; the Arneson River Theater; and the Tower of the Americas, built during HemisFair '68. San Antonio is the home of five major universities and has one of the largest medical centers in the country at the University of Texas (San Antonio campus).

## SAN DIEGO

**Location:** Southern California, on east side of San Diego Bay **County:** San Diego **City Area:** 319.5 sq. miles (810.7 sq. kilometers)
**Altitude:** sea level
**Mayor:** Pete Wilson **City Manager:** Ray Blair
**City Population:** 875,538 (1980 census) **Metro Area Population:** 1,861,846 (1980 census)
**Daily Newspapers:** 2 **No. of Commercial Radio Stations (AM):** 11
**No. of TV Stations:** 5
**City Chamber of Commerce:** San Diego Chamber of Commerce, 110 W. "C" Street, Suite 1600, San Diego, California 92101

San Diego, seat of San Diego County, is a port of entry and the oldest permanent European settlement in California. The city has risen rapidly in size, from fifteenth largest in the country in 1970, and now ranks as the eighth largest in the United States.

Since Juan Rodriguez Cabrillo sailed into its bay in 1542, the area has been under four flags—that of Spain, Mexico, California, and the United States. In 1769 San Diego de Alcalá Mission was established by Junípero Serra, a Franciscan missionary. A settlement grew up and was incorporated (1850) as a city after California became part of the Union.

San Diego's excellent natural harbor has made it an important commercial center and the site of several large navy installations. It is the distribution and processing hub for the surrounding farm and dairy region and has a wide variety of manufactures. It is the home of the Atlas missile, an aircraft producer, and it is an important oceanographic and health sciences center. San Diego has a large electronics industry. Recently 30 new companies have located in San Diego because of the availability of land and workers. Its magnificent climate and proximity to Mexico have made tourism significant.

San Diego's Balboa Park contains an art gallery, the Reuben H. Fleet Space Theater and Science Center, gardens, a zoo, and some buildings from the Panama-California International Exposition (1915-16) and the California Pacific International Exposition (1935-36). In the Old Town area is a state park containing adobes from the Spanish and Mexican era, and Heritage Park with its Victorian buildings. The Mission Bay park includes boat landings, water ski, fishing and swimming areas, hotels and Sea World, a huge marine animal amusement park.

A 16-mile trolley line, linking downtown San Diego with the Mexican border at Tijuana, opened in July 1981. The new light rail system is expected to carry 30,000 passengers daily.

## SAN FRANCISCO

**Location:** West-central California, on a peninsula between Pacific Ocean and San Francisco Bay **County:** San Francisco **City Area:** 46.3 sq. miles (119.9 sq. kilometers) **Altitude:** 65 feet (19.6 meters)
**Mayor:** Dianne Feinstein **Chief Administrative Officer:** Roger Boas
**City Population:** 678,974 (1980 census) **Metro Area Population:** 3,252,721 (1980 census)
**Daily Newspapers:** 2 **No. of Commercial Radio Stations (AM):** 16
**No. of TV Stations:** 9
**City Chamber of Commerce:** San Francisco Chamber of Commerce, 465 California Street, San Francisco, California 94104

San Francisco, coextensive with California's San Francisco County, is the financial center of the West and, together with the San Francisco Bay area, the largest port on the Pacific Coast.

In 1579 Sir Francis Drake stopped in the vicinity on his voyage around the world. In 1776 a mission, later known as Mission Dolores, and fort were founded at a site chosen by Juan Bautista de Anza. In 1846, during the Mexican

War, a U.S. naval force under John Montgomery took Yerba Buena, the settlement that had grown up. The following year the community assumed the name of its bay, which, according to tradition, had been named after St. Francis of Assisi by Spanish voyagers in 1595.

In 1848 the California gold rush began and a flood of fortune seekers, adventurers, and settlers brought a period of lawlessness, during which San Francisco's waterfront section became notorious as the Barbary Coast, and vigilantes were organized to restore order. Newcomers from all over the world, including China, gave the city a cosmopolitan air. It was incorporated in 1850 and linked with the East by railroads in 1869.

On April 18, 1906, a disastrous earthquake and fire almost completely destroyed the city; an estimated 700 persons perished.

The opening of the Panama Canal, which stimulated trade, was celebrated by the Panama-Pacific Exposition of 1915. By 1939, the year of the Golden Gate International Exposition, San Francisco had become the leading industrial and commercial center of the Pacific Coast. During the Second World War, the city was the major mainland supply point and port of embarkation for the struggle in the Pacific.

San Francisco is the home of the Pacific Coast Stock Exchange and a Federal Reserve district bank. More than 65 industrial parks lie within a 50-mile radius of the city. Major industries include food processing, shipbuilding, petroleum refining, and the manufacture of metal products and chemicals. The city is also a noted cultural center.

Situated among steep hills, San Francisco is a colorful city of lovely vistas, graceful bridges, ornate mansions, imposing public buildings, and unusual districts. The Golden Gate Bridge (1937) links the city with Marin County to the north. San Francisco's scenic hills now hold apartment complexes and shopping centers, but despite the changes the city maintains its warm personality.

On December 2, 1981, the city opened the $126-million George Moscone Convention Center in the rejuvenated "South of Market" area.

San Francisco is famous for its fine restaurants; its temporarily shutdown cable car system, preserved as a historic landmark; Chinatown—the country's largest—with its Oriental architecture, tearooms, and temples; Telegraph Hill, where in earlier times a signal tower sent word to the city of the arrival of ships and is now crowned with the Coit Memorial Tower; and Nob Hill, once the home of millionaires, is the site of the Cable Car Barn. Also of interest are Fisherman's Wharf, with its fishing fleet and seafood restaurants; the nearby National Maritime Museum and its historic ships; Ghirardelli Square and the Cannery, converted factories housing shops and restaurants; the Cow Hollow district, scene of art, book and specialty shops in an area of Victorian houses; and Golden Gate Park, with its planetarium, museum of natural history, aquarium, and flower gardens. The Cow Palace is the home of political conventions, sports events, and livestock exhibitions. In 1980 San Francisco celebrated the opening of the Louise M. Davies Symphony Hall, a fitting home for the great San Francisco Symphony.

## SAN JOSE

**Location:** Western California, about 40 miles southeast of San Francisco in the Santa Clara Valley **County:** Santa Clara **City Area:** 156.6 sq. miles (405.6 sq. kilometers) **Altitude:** 70 feet (21.3 meters)
**Mayor:** Tom McEnery **City Manager:** Francis Fox
**City Population:** 629,546 (1980 census) **Metro Area Population:** 1,295,071 (1980 census)
**Daily Newspapers:** 2 **No. of Radio Stations:** 15 **No. of TV Stations:** 3
**City Chamber of Commerce:** San Jose Chamber of Commerce, One Paseo De San Antonio, San Jose, California 95113

San Jose, seat of Santa Clara County, is virtually contiguous with the city of Santa Clara, the two communities together forming the focal point of the "Silicon Valley" area, the nation's leading producer of semi-conductors. Plants producing high technology devices, computers, aerospace equipment and advanced electronic apparatus line the streets and highways of this fast-growing region. The San Jose metropolitan area ranks second in California and eighth in the nation in manufacturing, as measured by value of shipments.

San Jose (originally the Pueblo de San José de Guadalupe) was founded in 1777 by José Joaquin Moraga, as a Spanish military supply base, and soon also became an ecclesiastical center. After the territory came under U.S. control, San Jose was made (in 1849) California's first capital, although statehood was not officially achieved until 1850, the year San Jose also became the state's first incorporated city. It remained the capital until 1851, when the seat of state government shifted to Benicia.

In its early years, San Jose served as a supply base for gold prospectors and as a bustling fruit trade depot. The coming of the railroad (in 1864), connecting the community to San Francisco, consolidated its importance as a distribution point for the increasingly bountiful produce of the Santa Clara Valley. This in turn gave rise to the growth of industries to equip the region's faams and service the needs of a growing populace.

Between 1940 and 1960, San Jose's population increased three-fold; from 1960 to 1970, it more than doubled, making San Jose-Santa Clara one of the nation's largest urban areas. The increase between 1970 and 1980 amounted to 36 percent for the city. This rapid growth was seen as a plus by developers, politicians and retailers. However, the growth has led to the decay of the downtown area, air pollution and traffic congestion. A rethinking of San Jose's growth future came with former Mayor Hayes' reelection. Initial efforts at "in-filling" and redevelopment of areas within the city, instead of continued urban sprawl, appears to be successful.

Places of interest in San Jose include the Municipal Rose Garden; Winchester Mystery House; Kelley Park with Happy Hollow Park/Zoo and the Japanese Friendship Garden; the San Jose Historical Museum; Rosicrucian Egyptian Museum; and nearby, the Lick Observatory (atop Mount Hamilton), and Mission Santa Clara de Asis, dating from 1777.

## SEATTLE

**Location:** West-central Washington, on Puget Sound and west shore of Lake Washington **County:** King **City Area:** 92 sq. miles (238 sq. kilometers) **Altitude:** 10 feet (3.0 meters)
**Mayor:** Charles Royer
**City Population:** 493,846 (1980 census) **Metro Area Population:** 1,606,765 (1980 census)
**Daily Newspapers:** 2 **No. of Radio Stations:** 34 **No. of TV Stations:** 5
**City Chamber of Commerce:** Seattle Chamber of Commerce, 215 Columbia Street, Seattle, Washington 98104

Seattle, seat of King County, is Washington's largest city and the largest in the Pacific Northwest. It is a manufacturing, trade, and transportation center, and a major port of entry. The city is situated on seven hills and is flanked by the majestically beautiful Cascade and Olympic Mountains. Within its limits are four lakes, 48 parks and more than 22 miniparks.

Seattle began as a small lumber settlement in 1851. It was platted two years later and named for a chief of the Duwamish and Suquamish Indians. Incorporated in 1869, it remained a small lumber town until the arrival of the railroad in 1884. Subsequent strikes, anti-Chinese riots, and a great fire in 1889 did not prevent the city from growing rapidly. With the 1897-98 Alaska gold rush, Seattle became a boom town and was the nation's chief link with Alaska. Further growth came with the Alaska-Yukon-Pacific Exposition (1909), the opening of the Panama Canal (1914), and the completion (1917) of a canal and locks making the city both a saltwater and freshwater port. In 1919 the Industrial Workers of the World (IWW) led a general strike in Seattle, long a center of the radical labor movement. A series of various municipal scandals led to the election in 1926 of a reform candidate, Bertha K. Landis, the first woman mayor of a large American city.

World War II made the city a center of aircraft manufacturing and shipbuilding. The Boeing Company is the largest employer in the area. Although the region underwent a severe recession in the early 1970s due to a slackening of the aerospace industry, the area's economy and the aircraft industry revived late in the decade. The construction of the trans-Alaska crude oil pipeline did much to bolster Seattle's economy. Other important industries today are electronics, printing, food processing, lumber, chemical products, metal goods and machinery.

The Seattle downtown area has taken on a new look.

Since 1970 almost half of the downtown has been rebuilt. Seattle has become an important cultural center on the West Coast. It boasts a first-rate Opera House, the Seattle Symphony Orchestra, several active theater companies, and a fine arts museum. Of interest in the city is the Seattle Center, site of the 1962 World's Fair. It is connected to the downtown area by a monorail line and contains the opera house, arena, coliseum, and International Fountain, the world-famous 606-foot Space Needle, and the Pacific Science Center. Also of interest are Pike Place Market, Underground Seattle and the old Pioneer Square district.

Seattle is the home of the Mariners Baseball Team, the Seahawks Football Team, the Supersonics Basketball Team, the Sounders Soccer Team, the Breakers hockey team, and the Smashers Volleyball Team.

### TAMPA

**Location:** On the west coast of Florida at the mouth of the Hillsboro River on Tampa Bay. **County:** Hillsborough **City Area:** 84.5 sq. miles (218.9 sq. kilometers) **Altitude:** 15 feet (4.6 meters)
**Mayor:** Bobb Martinez
**City Population:** 271,523 (1980 census) **Metro Area Population:** 1,569,492 (1980 census)
**Daily Newspapers:** 1 **No. of Radio Stations:** 9 **No. of TV Stations:** 4
**City Chamber of Commerce:** Greater Tampa Chamber of Commerce, P.O. Box 420, Tampa, Florida 33601

Tampa, the closest port to the Panama Canal, is located on Tampa Bay, an inlet of the Gulf of Mexico. Once known almost exclusively as a vacation spot and a source of fine cigars, Tampa, which is the seat of Hillsborough County, today has also emerged as one of Florida's most industrialized cities and the trade center of the state's west coast. Its economy ranges from food processing and phosphate shipping to the manufacture of a wide variety of goods, including beer, fertilizer, paint, cement, cigars, fabricated steel, and electronic equipment. Nearby is MacDill Air Force Base, headquarters for the U.S. Readiness Command. Tampa International Airport, which is served by 16 airlines, has been called "the best airport in the world" in the press. The Tampa City Center and Plaza on the Mall projects highlight the downtown redevelopment activities.

At least two Spanish explorers, and probably more, visited the site of Tampa in the 16th century: Panfilo de Narváez (1528) and Hernando de Soto (1539). Seminole Indians successfully resisted white men's efforts to settle in the area until 1823, when a contingent of U.S. troops established Fort Brooke there. By 1831 the settlement that had grown up around the fort had come to be known by its former Indian name of Tampa; it was incorporated in 1849. During the Civil War, Tampa was bombarded by gunboats.

Development of Tampa began in earnest in 1885 with the coming of Henry B. Plant's narrow-gauge South Florida Railroad—and his port improvements and tourism promotions. The economy got another boost when the manufacture of cigars was begun (in 1886) at Ybor City, which soon became a part of Tampa proper. Tourism was spurred in 1891 by the completion of the lavish, Moorish-style Tampa Bay Hotel, which today houses the University of Tampa. In 1898, during the Spanish-American War, Tampa served as the embarkation point for Colonel "Teddy" Roosevelt and his "Rough Riders." In the mid-1920s the man-made Davis Islands in Tampa Bay were completed, providing choice sites for hotels, residences and various resort facilities.

Among Tampa's attractions are Ybor city, the city's Latin quarter, famous for its Spanish restaurants and shops, Adventure Island theme park, and the Busch Gardens, Florida's second-largest tourist attraction. Tampa Museum, opened in July 1979, is the city's first major public effort at a permanent art museum. The Center for Science and Industry, which opened in October 1981, has already won the Owen Corning Energy Conservation Award for its energy conservation design and for its use of solar panels. The Gasparilla Festival, a one-day event in honor of the allleged pirate José Gaspar, is celebrated in February with a mock invasion of the city.

### WASHINGTON, D.C.

**Location:** Between Virginia and Maryland, on Potomac River **City Area:** 68.2 sq. miles (176.7 sq. kilometers) **Altitude:** 72 feet (21.9 meters)
**Mayor:** Marion S. Barry, Jr. **City Administrator:** Elijah B. Rogers
**City Population:** 638,432 (1980 census) **Metro Area Population:** 3,060,240 (1980 census)
**Daily Newspapers:** 2 **No. of Radio Stations:** 32 **No. of TV Stations:** 8
**City Chamber of Commerce:** District of Columbia Chamber of Commerce, 425 13th Street, N.W., Suite 829, Washington, D.C. 20004

Washington, D.C., is not only the capital of the United States but an important business and financial center, with over 1,800 professional and trade associations headquartered there. Since 1895, when Georgetown became part of Washington, it has been coextensive with the District of Columbia. Washington's large government work force insures a more recession-proof climate than in other major markets.

The District was established by Congress in 1790-91, and George Washington selected the exact site for the "Federal City," which was designed by Pierre L'Enfant and laid out by Andrew Ellicott. Maryland and Virginia ceded land for the District, and the capital moved there from Philadelphia in 1800. Thomas Jefferson was the first President to be inaugurated in Washington.

During the War of 1812, the city fell to the British, who burned the Capitol, White House, and other public buildings. During the Civil War, the city was threatened by Confederate forces.

1878 marked the end of home rule for the district, with city officials thereafter being appointed by the President. Since 1961, however, when residents were given the right to vote in Presidential elections, Washingtonians have sought to increase local self-governmment and national political representation. Residents were allowed to elect their own school board in 1968, and full home rule followed in 1975. Under the Nixon Administration, the District of Columbia was granted non-voting representation in Congress, with Walter E. Fauntroy sworn in on April 19, 1971, as Washington's first Representative in nearly 100 years. And in an historic move, Congress voted in 1978 to approve a constitutional amendment giving the District full elected representation in both the House and the Senate. The amendment gives Washington two Senators—expanding the Senate from 100 to 102—and either one or two Representatives, based on the District's 1980 census. The amendment must now be ratified by at least 38 state legislatures by the summer of 1985 for it to become law.

Washington, with its broad tree-shaded thoroughfares and open vistas, has many imposing buildings. The Capitol and White House are the most historic. Other leading tourist attractions are the Washington Monument and Lincoln and Jefferson Memorials. The many additional points of interest in or near the city include the Library of Congress; the National Archives, which houses the Declaration of Independence, the Constitution, and the Bill of Rights; the Supreme Court Building; Constitution Hall; the Smithsonian Institution; the National Gallery of Art; the numerous embassies; the John F. Kennedy Center for the Performing Arts; the Pentagon; the U.S. Naval Observatory; and Mount Vernon. The fashionable Georgetown area was designated a national monument in 1967.

The Arlington Memorial Bridge across the Potomac River connects Washington with Arlington National Cemetery. Among the city's beautiful parks are West Potomac Park, which includes the Tidal Basin with the famous Japanese cherry trees; East Potomac Park; Rock Creek Park and the adjoining National Zoological Park; and Anacostia Park.

Washington's Metro, the computerized subway which first opened in 1976, is one of the most advanced systems in the world. Lines have since been extended to National Airport and to the suburbs. Metro suffered its first fatal accident on January 13, 1982, when a derailment killed three passengers.

Public and private redevelopment has given downtown Washington a new face. Currently under way is the joint $500-million public-private Pennsylvania Avenue Development Plan for combined residential-commercial use. The $60-million expansion of the Sheraton Washington Hotel (formerly the Sheraaton Park) in northwest Washington was completed in 1980. In 1980, construction began on a $99-million convention center north of the Mall that officials hope will one day attract the city's first national political convention.

## U.S. OUTLYING AREAS

The areas under United States sovereignty or otherwise associated with some type of American jurisdiction extend through the Caribbean and almost across the Pacific. From east to west, the Virgin Islands of the United States, in the Caribbean, lie 160° from the Palau Islands in the American-administered Trust Territory of the Pacific Islands, nearly halfway around the world. The distance between Point Barrow in northern Alaska, 71.5° north of the equator, and American Samoa in the southwest Pacific, 14° south of the equator, is nearly half of that from pole to pole.

**American Samoa**—*Status:* Unorganized unincorporated territory. *Population:* 32,395 (1980 census). *Area:* 83 sq. mi. *Seat of government:* Pago Pago (3,058).

American Samoa consists of six small Pacific islands in that part of the Samoan islands lying east of 171°W., plus Swains Island, 250 miles north of Tutuila. It is roughly 2,200 miles southwest of Hawaii and 1,600 miles northeast of the northern tip of New Zealand.

In 1977 American Samoa held its first popular election for governor. The victor, Peter Tali Coleman, a native of the islands, was inaugurated on January 3, 1978. He was reelected on November 4, 1980. There is a legislature, the *Fono*, with limited authority, the House of Representatives being elected by universal suffrage, the Senate by the native chiefs. Samoan society is rigidly stratified, and the chiefs, of whom there are some 600 of varying ranks, have firm, paternalistic control over their followers.

The six islands in the Samoan group came under American hegemony in 1899, when Great Britain and Germany renounced their claims in favor of the United States, and Swains was added in 1925. American Samoa's native inhabitants are U.S. nationals; they are not American citizens but may migrate freely to the United States. In October 1978, President Carter signed into law an act of Congress giving the islands a nonvoting delegate to the U.S. House of Representatives. Fofo I. F. Sunia was elected as the island group's first delegate on November 18, 1980.

**Guam**—*Status:* Organized unincorporated territory. *Population:* 105,821 (1980 census). *Area:* 212 sq. mi. *Capital:* Agana (881).

This island in the western Pacific is the most southerly of the Marianas, 1,300 miles east of the Philippines and 1,475 miles south of Japan, at 13°27′N. and 144°47′E. Of volcanic origin, it is mountainous in the south, a plateau in the north. The climate is tropical, with moderately heavy rainfall. The indigenes—the Chamorros—make up about half the population. Most of the rest are military or other government transients. English is the official language. About 95 percent of the native Guamanians are Roman Catholics.

U.S. military installations and tourism are the most significant factors in the economy. Guam is the only American territory without excise duties (except for tobacco, liquid fuel, and liquor).

Guam's administration is under the U.S. Department of the Interior. Its people are U.S. citizens (however, they do not vote in national elections but do have a nonvoting delegate in the House of Representatives). The governor and lieutenant governor are elected by the people. There is an elected unicameral legislature. On August 4, 1979, Guam residents rejected a proposed constitution drafted in December 1977 which allowed the island more self-government. Most islanders felt that it did not provide residents with the same rights as other Americans.

**Howland, Baker, and Jarvis Islands**—*Status:* Unincorporated possession. *Population:* Uninhabited. *Area:* 2.77 sq. mi.

These three small islands are situated in the South Pacific: Howland at 48°N.,176°38′W., Baker at 0°15′N., 176°27′W. and Jarvis at 0°23′S.,160°02′W. Howland and Baker are coral atolls about 35 miles apart and some 2,000 miles southwest of Honolulu. Jarvis lies some 1,500 miles south of Honolulu. They had rich guano deposits that were worked by American interests in the 1850s; however, when that industry faded, the islands had no value until the trans-Pacific aviation era began in the 1930s. In 1934 the United States reasserted its claim to them, based on the fact that they had been mentioned in the Guano Act of 1856.

**Johnston Atoll**—*Status:* Unincorporated possession. *Population:* 327 (1980 census). *Area:*.91 sq. mi.

This Pacific atoll lies 715 miles southwest of Honolulu, at 16°45′N. and 169°30′W. It consists of a reef around four islets. Johnston was annexed in 1858 by both the United States and the Kingdom of Hawaii. A quantity of guano was removed during the next 50 years, and for a long time the area was also a bird reservation. It was taken over by the U.S. Navy in 1934.

In 1958 and 1962 it was the site of high-altitude nuclear tests. In 1971 the Defense Department started to move 13,000 tons of nerve and mustard gas stored on Okinawa to igloo-shaped structures on Johnston.

**Kingman Reef**—*Status:* Unincorporated possession. *Population:* Uninhabited. *Area:* .01 sq. mi.

This bare reef in the Pacific lies 35 miles northwest of Palmyra Island and 1,000 miles south of Honolulu at 6°24′S., 162°22′W. It was annexed by the United States in 1922 and placed under the U.S. Navy in 1934.

**Midway Islands**—*Status:* Unincorporated possession. *Population:* 468 (1980 census). *Area:* 1.9 sq. mi.

Midway is near the western end of the Hawaiian chain, 1,200 miles northwest of Honolulu, at 28°12′-17′N. and 177°19′-26′W. It consists of an atoll with two islets.

Made a possession in 1867 and placed under the U.S. Navy in 1903, Midway was the scene of one of the great air/sea battles of World War II. Today it is a naval installation; its chief executive is a naval officer. Midway is noted as a nesting site for seabirds.

**Navassa Island**—*Status:* Unincorporated possession. *Population:* Uninhabited. *Area:* 2 sq. mi.

Navassa lies in the Caribbean between Jamaica and Haiti, 30 miles west of the latter. It was certified in 1865 as appertaining to the United States under the Guano Act of 1856. A presidential proclamation of 1916 declared it to be under the sole jurisdiction of the United States and reserved it for lighthouse purposes. It is administered by the Coast Guard.

**Palmyra Island**—*Status:* Unincorporated possession. *Population:* Uninhabited. *Area:* 3.85 sq. mi.

An atoll of more than 50 islets, Palmyra is located in the Pacific 1,000 miles south of Honolulu, at 5°52′N. and 162°06′W. It is covered with dense foliage, coconut trees, and pisonis grandis, a 100-foot-tall balsalike tree.

Claimed by the Kingdom of Hawaii in 1862, the atoll was annexed by the United States with Hawaii in 1898. Excluded from Hawaii's boundaries when the latter became a state in 1959, it was placed under the administration of the U.S. Secretary of the Interior in 1961. In 1979 the U.S. government proposed purchasing the privately-owned island for use as a nuclear waste storage site.

**Puerto Rico**—*Status:* Commonwealth (Estado Libre Asociado). *Population:* 3,196,520 (1980 census). *Area:* 3,435 sq. mi. *Capital:* San Juan (424,600).

Puerto Rico, 885 miles southeast of the southern coast of Florida, is the easternmost island of the Greater Antilles in the Caribbean. It is separated from the Dominican Republic to the west by the 61 miles of Mona Passage. To the east, St. Thomas of the U.S. Virgin Islands is 34 miles away. Among the offshore islands are Vieques and Culebra to the east, Mona to the west.

The island is crossed by mountain ranges and ringed by a coastal plain that is 15 miles wide at its broadest. The climate is mildly tropical. Rainfall is moderate in the coastal areas, but heavier in the interior mountains.

Many of the people are of mixed African-Spanish descent. (The original Arawak Indians were destroyed in the 16th century.) English and Spanish are the official languages, but Spanish is commonly spoken. Roman Catholicism predominates.

Before World War II, the Puerto Rican economy was based on sugar and such related products as rum. Needlework, mostly piecework produced by women at home, was the second most important activity, and tobacco growing the third. Unemployment was high, poverty widespread; however, after the war a determined drive was begun to foster industrialization on the island.

Under then Governor Rexford Guy Tugwell and the Puerto Rican legislative leader Luis Muñoz Marin, the framework for economic expansion was established. In 1948, "Operation Bootstrap" commenced, giving tax exemptions to new or expanded industry. By 1971 the program had attracted $2 billion in industrial investments and 2,000 plants. However, while the successor program continued to expand incentives, the federal government froze $13 million in loans to Puerto Rican businesses in 1981.

Today, income from manufacturing is more than three times that from agriculture, although sugar, coffee, tobacco, and rum are still produced and exported. Among the industries attracted by the tax abatement and lower wage scales in Puerto Rico are textiles and apparel, leather and shoes, electronic components, pharmaceuticals, tuna canning, and—increasingly—such heavy industries as metal products and petrochemicals.

In addition, tourist facilities and tourism have greatly expanded. Despite the general economic advance, unemployment continues to be much higher than in the United States. Many Puerto Ricans have been dependent on federal food stamp programs and on CETA jobs; both were cut back in 1981.

Puerto Ricans are U.S. citizens and, if they migrate to this country, vote subject only to local electoral requirements. Puerto Rico does not send members to Congress (although it has a Resident Commissioner in the House of Representatives who may introduce legislation but does not have a vote) and Puerto Rico is not liable to federal taxation.

Beginning in 1948 (as the first elected governor), Luis Muñoz Marin—leader of the Popular Democratic party and the force behind "Operation Bootstrap"—served four terms, retiring in 1964. During this period the main minority faction was the Statehood Republican party, which advocated U.S. statehood for Puerto Rico as opposed to the commonwealth status championed by the Popular Democrats. In a plebiscite held in 1967, the vote was 60.5 percent for continuation of commonwealth status, and 38.9 percent for statehood.

In the 1968 gubernatorial election, however, Luis A. Ferré, long a prominent Statehood Republican, who ran as the candidate of the New Progressive party (which he had helped form during the plebiscite campaign), won with more than 44 percent of the vote. Although Ferré's platform advocated statehood for Puerto Rico, he had made it clear that such a step would depend on a plebiscite "separate from the general elections." In 1972 Ferré was defeated by Rafael Hernández-Colón of the Popular Democratic party, but in 1976 the New Progressives returned to power under Carlos Romero Barcelo. In 1980 Romero-Barcelo narrowly won reelection over Hernandez-Colon. The race was so close that Hernandez-Colon had been declared the apparent winner; a recount tipped the election to the incumbent by a vote of 47.4%-47.2%.

Although advocates of Puerto Rican independence have had little impact at the polls, there has long been such a movement on the island. Perhaps its leading figure was the Harvard-educated Pedro Albizu Campos, who died in 1965, aged 73. A leader of the Nationalist party in Puerto Rico, in 1950 he staged an abortive armed revolt, which included an attempt by some of his followers to assassinate President Truman.

Columbus claimed the island for Spain in 1493 on his second voyage to the New World. Spanish colonization began under Ponce de León in 1508. Occupied by American troops during the Spanish-American War, the island was ceded to the United States by Spain in 1898. Congress provided for its civil government by the Foraker Act of 1900 and granted Puerto Ricans U.S. citizenship in 1917 by an "Organic Act," known as the Jones Act. In 1947 Puerto Rico obtained the right to elect its governor. Commonwealth status in free association with the United States was achieved in 1952. Operating under a constitution much like that of the United States, Puerto Rico has an elected legislature consisting of a Senate and a House of Representatives. In 1977, the Puerto Rican legislature provided for the selection of delegates to the Democratic and Republican conventions by presidential primary. More than 600,000 voters participated in the 1980 election of delegates to the two parties' national conventions.

Migration from Puerto Rico to the mainland has varied with the economic conditions here and on the island. It was very heavy during much of the 1950s, and the 1970 censuss counted more than 1.8 million persons of Puerto Rican birth in the United States. Substantial numbers of Puerto Ricans have also returned to the island from the United States.

In September 1978, the United Nations Decolonization Committee passed a Cuban-sponsored resolution calling for self-determination for Puerto Rico, recommending that it be included on the UN's list of non-governing territories as a U.S. colony. In response, committees in both houses of Congress approved resolutions in 1979 reaffirming American support of self-determination for the island's people. In January 1982,

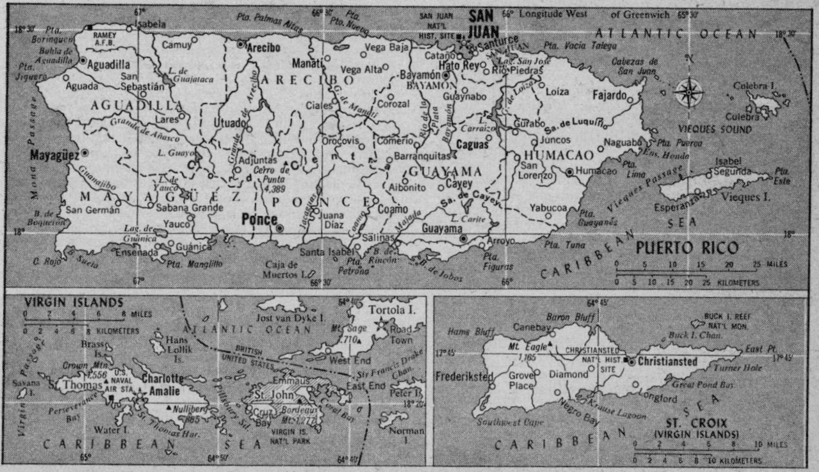

President Reagan, after meeting with Puerto Rican officials, reaffirmed his support for statehood if approved by a majority of islanders in referendum. He added that the language and rich culture of Puerto Rico would not be jeopardized by entry into the Union.

**Trust Territory of the Pacific Islands**—*Status:* UN Trust Territory. *Population:* 133,732 (1980 census) *Area:* 8,511 sq. mi. including lagoons (707 sq. mi. of land). *Administrative Center:* Saipan, Northern Mariana Islands.

These islands and atolls, generally known as Micronesia, are scattered over an area of more than three million sq. mi. There are more than 3,000 of them, about 100 inhabited. They stretch 2,300 miles from some 500 miles east of the Philippines almost as far east as the international date line, from about 1° to 22°N. and from 130° to 172°E. The islands fall into three major groups—the Carolines (including the Palau Islands), the Marshalls, and the Marianas (excluding Guam). A number of the islands were the scene of bitter fighting during World War II—Peleliu in the Carolines, Saipan in the Marianas, Kwajalein in the Marshalls. Bikini and Enewetak in the Marshalls have been used as nuclear-test sites.

Subsistence agriculture (coconuts, cassava, copra, bananas, yams) and fishing are the main economic activities; copra and fish are the chief exports. Tourism is being developed.

The area is under the jurisdiction of the U.S. Secretary of the Interior; administrative authorityy is vested in a high commissioner who is appointed by the president. Following the establishment of the new island governments beginning in 1976 (see below), the duties of the high commissioner were limited to carrying out UN Trust Territory policy.

Beginning in 1565 the islands gradually came under tenuous Spanish control. Strong German penetration into the Marshall Islands in the late nineteenth century resulted in the sale of the whole area to Germany by Spain in 1899. Following Germany's defeat in the First World War, they were placed under Japanese mandate. In 1947, following the end of World War II, they entered the UN Trusteeship system under American administration as a "strategic" trust: one in which military bases are permissible.

For many years after assuming its trusteeship, the United States neglected the area, permitting the Japanese-built road system and sanitary facilities to deteriorate. In 1966, the World Health Organization reported that health conditions were bad; the United States has pledged improvements in this field.

In 1969, Secretary of the Interior Hickel visited the islands and promised immediate steps would be taken to increase the territory's self-government and assure that equal wages would be paid to Micronesians and Americans for doing comparable work. At the same time, it was reported that a political status commission, appointed by the Trust Territory-wide Congress of Micronesia in 1967, had recommended that the territory be made a self-governing nation in free association with the United States or, failing that, seek complete independence. An offer by the United States of "Commonwealth status" like that of Puerto Rico was rejected by the Congress of Micronesia in 1970. The Trust Territory's Congress of Micronesia was dissolved in 1978. The United States government signed agreements with the emergent governments of the Marshall Islands, the Federated States of Micronesia and Belau (see below) in October-November 1980. These agreements provided "free association status" with the United States for the new nations, under which the United States would retain military responsibility for the region. The agreements require approval by the U.S. president, Senate and the citizens of the new nations. The new arrangement also requires the approval of the United Nations.

In 1975 the **Northern Mariana Islands** (1980 population: 16,758) voted in favor of future commonwealth status and in 1976 the U.S. Congress approved a plan making the islands a commonwealth associated with the United States. Following a March 1977 referendum approving a new constitution—providing for an elected bicameral legislature and an elected governor—Carlos S. Camacho became the islands' first democratically elected chief executive, and the first native islander to administer the Northern Marianas in over 400 years of foreign domination. He was succeeded by Pedro P. Tenorio in 1982. The bicameral Legislature consists of a 9-member Senate and a 14-member House of Representatives. The administrative center is on Saipan.

In a July 12, 1978, referendum, four of the six island districts of the Trust Territory—Ponape, Yap, Kosrae and Truk—voted to accept "free association" with the U.S. as the **Federated States of Micronesia (FSM)** (1980 population: 73,755). The new federation officially came into being on May 10, 1979. Such status entails continued American financial support for 15 years, with Washington to retain responsibility for defense; otherwise the islands will become fully self-governing when the United States terminates its UN Trusteeship. Tosiwo Nakayama was elected president on May 11, 1979. The federal Congress consists of a Senate and a House of Representatives. A fifth state, Faichuk, was created in 1981 from parts of Truk. The capital is Kolonia on Ponape.

The **Marshall Islands** (1980 population: 31,042) electorate rejected membership in the FSM in the July 1978 referendum. Under May 1, 1979 constitution, legislation is the function of the 33-member *Nitijela* which meets at the government center on Majuro atoll. The president is Amata Kabua. Bikini and Kwajalein, scene of postwar nuclear tests, are located in the Marshalls. Negotiations between the United States and the Marshall Islands over the future political status of the islands broke down in July 1982.

The Palau group, now the **Republic of Belau (Palau)** (1980 population: 12,177), also rejected inclusion in the FSM. Under the republican constitution of 1979, the government consists of a president and a bicameral legislature consisting of an 18-member Senate and a 16-member House of Delegates. In elections held on November 4, 1980, Haruo I. Remeliik was elected president and took office on January 1, 1981. The seat of government is on Koror.

**Virgin Islands**—*Status:* Organized unincorporated territory. *Population:* 95,591 (1980 census). *Area:* 133 sq. mi. *Capital:* Charlotte Amalie (11,756), on St. Thomas.

The Virgin Islands of the United States form the western end of the Lesser Antilles between the Caribbean and the Atlantic, about 34 miles east of Puerto Rico. They comprise nearly 100 islands and cays, but only three islands are significant—St. Thomas (27 sq. mi.), St. Croix (82 sq. mi.), and St. John (19 sq. mi.). The United States bought the Virgin Islands from Denmark for $25 million in 1917.

St. Thomas is mountainous, with many harbors, of which Charlottte Amalie is one of the finest in the Caribbean. The climate is subtropical, moderated by the trade winds. Rainfall is variable and sometimes so light as to cause drought. Seventy percent of the popuulation is black, many of whom are immigrants from other Antillean islands. Of the rest, considerably more than half are from the United States. English is the official language.

Since the phasing out of the peasant-based sugarcane agriculture, there has been little farming on the islands. Tourism is the major industry, and the area has the greatest number of cruise-ship calls in the world. Oil refining and bauxite processing are important; labor-intensive light industry has been introduced. More than half the island of St. John is occupied by the Virgin Islands National Park.

The U.S. Department of the Interior has jurisdiction over the islands. The governor has been elected since 1970. Juan Luis became governor in January 1978 on the death of Cyril E. King. Virgin Islanders are U.S. citizens, but cannot vote in national elections and have no Congressional representation, except for a non-voting delegate in the House since April 1972. In March 1979 voters rejected a proposed constitution. A new draft of the constitution failed to gain acceptance in a November 1981 referendum.

**Wake Island**—*Status:* Possession. *Population:* 302 (1980 census). *Area:* 2.5 sq. mi. *Administrative Center:* Wake Islet.

Wake lies in the Pacific some 2,000 miles west of Honolulu and 1,500 miles northeast of Guam, at 19°17'N. and 166°35'E. It is an atoll comprising three islets—Wake, Wilkes, and Peale. They are formed of coral built up on the rim of an underwater volcano; the land averages only 12 feet above sea level. Waves driven by 200-knot winds from Typhoon Sarah swept over the three islets in 1967.

The island has an aviation base with a 9,800-foot runway. Responsibility for its civil administration was vested in the U.S. Secretary of the Interior in 1962, but since 1974 has been under the Air Force Department.

Wake Island was annexed in 1899. It was attacked by the Japanese on December 7, 1941, and later that month fell after an heroic defense by the small Marine garrison.

## U.S. TERRITORIAL ACQUISITIONS, POSSESSIONS, AND LEASEHOLDS

| Year | Acquisition |
|---|---|
| — | **Gross Area (888,685 sq. mi.)** Original territory of the first 13 states and their claims, including part of drainage basin of Red River of the North, south of the 49th parallel, sometimes considered part of Louisiana Purchase; completely acquired by independence treaty (1783; ratified, 1784) with Great Britain. |
| 1803 | **Gross Area (827,192 sq. mi.)** Louisiana Purchase acquired from France for about $15 million (60 million francs); total payment, including interest: $23,213,567.73. |
| 1819 | **Gross Area (72,003 sq. mi.)** Florida and adjacent areas purchased from Spain for amount not exceeding $5 million; treaty ratified 1821. |
| 1845 | **Gross Area (390,144 sq. mi.)** Independent Republic of Texas annexed and admitted as a state. |
| 1846 | **Gross Area (285,580 sq. mi.)** Oregon Territory acquired by treaty with Great Britain, terminating joint occupation. |
| 1848 | **Gross Area (529,017 sq. mi.)** Mexican Cession acquired out of the Mexican War; the United States paid $15 million. |
| 1853 | **Gross Area (29,640 sq. mi.)** Gadsden Purchase negotiated with Mexico for $10 million; treaty ratified 1854. |
| 1858 | **Gross Area (.91 sq. mi.)** By terms of the Guano Island Act (1856), stipulating that the United States could take possession of any uninhabited guano island, Johnston and Sand Islands in the Pacific were claimed; they constitute a possession. |
| 1862 | **Gross Area (3.85 sq. mi.)** Palmyra Island, 1,000 miles south of Honolulu, annexed by Hawaii but not included in the state; it constitutes a possession. |
| 1863 | **Gross Area (1 sq. mi.)** Under the Guano Island Act (1856), the Swan Islands in the Caribbean were claimed by the United States. The U.S. recognized Honduran sovereignty over the islands on September 1, 1972. |
| 1865 | **Gross Area (2 sq. mi.)** Under the Guano Island Act (1856), Navassa in the Caribbean was claimed; it constitutes a possession. |
| 1867 | **Gross Area (586,412 sq. mi.)** Alaska purchased from Russia for $7.2 million. |
| | **Gross Area (1.9 sq. mi )** Midway Islands, 1,200 miles NW of Honolulu, annexed; they are a possession. |
| 1898 | **Gross Area (6,450 sq. mi.)** Independent Republic of Hawaii annexed. |
| | **Gross Area (212 sq. mi.)** Guam, in the Western Pacific area, conquered from Spain and formally annexed by peace treaty (ratified, 1899); it constitutes an organized unincorporated territory. |
| | **Gross Area (115,707 sq. mi.)** Philippines conquered from Spain; peace treaty (ratified, 1899) stipulated payment of $20 million for the islands; the Philippines became independent on July 4, 1946. |
| | **Gross Area (3,435 sq. mi.)** Puerto Rico conquered from Spain and formally annexed by peace treaty (ratified, 1899); granted commonwealth status by Act of Congress on July 25, 1952. |
| 1899 | **Gross Area (2.5 sq. mi.)** Wake Island in Central Pacific claimed; it constitutes a possession. |
| 1899 | **Gross Area (83 sq. mi.)** American Samoa acquired by partition treaty (ratified, 1900) with Great Britain and Germany; it constitutes an unorganized, unincorporated territory. |
| 1903 | **Gross Area (647 sq mi.)** Canal Zone leased from Panama (treaty ratified, 1904); United States paid $10 million supplemented by annual amounts of $250,000 (1913-33); $430,000 (1934-55); $1.93 million (1956-1971); $2.095 million (1972); and $2.33 million (1974 to date). Under the terms of the 1977 treaty, the Canal Zone reverted to Panama on October 1, 1979. |
| | **Gross Area (30 sq. mi.)** Guantanamo leased from Cuba for coaling and naval station. |
| 1914 | **Gross Area (4.6 sq. mi.)** Corn Islands leased for 99 years from Nicaragua for payment of $3 million; treaty (ratified, 1916) included perpetual right to construct and maintain a ship canal through Lake Nicaragua. The canal rights and the lease of the islands were terminated on April 25, 1971. |
| 1916 | **Gross Area (133 sq. mi.)** Virgin Islands purchased from Denmark for $25 million by treaty (ratified in 1917); they constitute an organized unincorporated territory. |
| 1919 | **Gross Area (each less than 0.5 sq. mi.)** By terms of the Guano Island Act (1856), Quita Sueño Bank, Roncador Cay, and Serrana Bank in the Caribbean were claimed; 1928 treaty provided Colombia with fishing rights in adjacent waters. On September 8, 1972, the United States renounced all claims. |
| 1922 | **Gross Area (.01 sq. mi.)** Kingman Reef in the South Pacific annexed by Act of Congress; it constitutes a possession. |
| 1925 | **Gross Area (1.33 sq. mi.)** Swains Island in the Pacific annexed by Resolution of Congress and incorporated in American Samoa. |
| 1934 | **Gross Area (2.77 sq. mi. combined)** U.S. control of Howland, Baker, and Jarvis islands in the South Pacific was reasserted under terms of the Guano Island Act (1856); they are possessions. |
| 1939 | **Gross Area (27 sq. mi.)** Canton and Enderbury Islands, 1,660 miles SW of Honolulu, controlled jointly by Britain and the United States. They are to be ceded to Kiribati, when the 1979 draft treaty comes into force. |
| 1947 | **Gross Land Area (707 sq. mi )** Trust Territory of the Pacific Islands, about 3,000 Micronesian islands and atolls including the Caroline, Marshall, and Mariana groups (except Guam) placed under U.S. jurisdiction by UN Trusteeship System. |
| 1952 | **Gross Area (848 sq. mi.)** Ryukyu Islands, including Okinawa, under U.S. jurisdiction by peace treaty with Japan; other islands included in treaty but returned to Japan by an agreement, June 26, 1968, are: Volcano Islands, including Iwo Jima (11 sq. mi.), Bonin Islands (40 sq. mi.), Marcus Island (1 sq. mi.), Rosario Island (less than 0.5 sq. mi.), and Parece Vela. All of the remaining territory was formally returned to Japan on May 15, 1972. |
| 1968 | **Gross Area (193 acres)** Mexico ceded to the United States the northern half of Cordova Island in the Rio Grande in return for the Chamizal (630 acres) on December 13, 1968, readjusting the border near El Paso, Texas. |

## ADMISSION DATES OF STATES TO THE UNION

|  |  |  |  |  |  |
|---|---|---|---|---|---|
| Delaware | Dec. 7, 1787 | Louisiana | April 30, 1812 | West Virginia | June 20, 1863 |
| Pennsylvania | Dec. 12, 1787 | Indiana | Dec. 11, 1816 | Nevada | Oct. 31, 1864 |
| New Jersey | Dec. 18, 1787 | Mississippi | Dec. 10, 1817 | Nebraska | March 1, 1867 |
| Georgia | Jan. 2, 1788 | Illinois | Dec. 3, 1818 | Colorado | Aug. 1, 1876 |
| Connecticut | Jan. 9, 1788 | Alabama | Dec. 14, 1819 | North Dakota | Nov. 2, 1889 |
| Massachusetts | Feb. 6, 1788 | Maine | March 15, 1820 | South Dakota | Nov. 2, 1889 |
| Maryland | April 28, 1788 | Missouri | Aug. 10, 1821 | Montana | Nov. 8, 1889 |
| South Carolina | May 23, 1788 | Arkansas | June 15, 1836 | Washington | Nov. 11, 1889 |
| New Hampshire | June 21, 1788 | Michigan | Jan. 26, 1837 | Idaho | July 3, 1890 |
| Virginia | June 26, 1788 | Florida | March 3, 1845 | Wyoming | July 10, 1890 |
| New York | July 26, 1788 | Texas | Dec. 29, 1845 | Utah | Jan. 4, 1896 |
| North Carolina | Nov. 21, 1789 | Iowa | Dec. 28, 1846 | Oklahoma | Nov. 16, 1907 |
| Rhode Island | May 29, 1790 | Wisconsin | May 29, 1848 | New Mexico | Jan. 6, 1912 |
| Vermont | March 4, 1791 | California | Sept. 9, 1850 | Arizona | Feb. 14, 1912 |
| Kentucky | June 1, 1792 | Minnesota | May 11, 1858 | Alaska | Jan. 3, 1959 |
| Tennessee | June 1, 1796 | Oregon | Feb. 14, 1859 | Hawaii | Aug. 21, 1959 |
| Ohio | March 1, 1803 | Kansas | Jan. 29, 1861 | | |

# CANADA

**Area:** 3,831,012 sq. mi. **Population:** 24,343,181 (1981 census)

**Official Name:** Canada **Capital:** Ottawa **Nationality:** Canadian **Language:** English and French are both official languages. About 13% of the population is bilingual; 67% speaks English only, 18% French only, and 2% other languages, such as Italian, German and Ukrainian **Religion:** Roman Catholic 46%, United Church 18% and Anglican 12%. The rest is made up of Presbyterian, Lutheran, Baptist, Jewish, etc. **Flag:** A single red maple leaf with eleven points, centered on a white square; flanked by vertical red bars one half the width of the square. **Anthem:** O Canada **Currency:** Canadian Dollar (1.24 per U.S. $1 as of August 30, 1982)

**Location:** North America, occupying all of the continent north of the United States except for Alaska and the French islands of St. Pierre and Miquelon, in the Gulf of St. Lawrence. The second largest country in the world, Canada is bordered on the north by the Arctic Ocean; on the east by Baffin Bay, Davis Strait and the Atlantic Ocean; on the south by the United States; and on the west by the Pacific Ocean and Alaska **Features:** The Shield, a rugged area of pre-Cambrian rock, covers most of eastern and central Canada, or roughly half the entire country. To the north is the Arctic Archipelago and to the west of the Shield is a vast prairie region stretching to the Canadian Rockies. Westernmost Canada, which comprises most of British Columbia, is laced with towering mountain ranges **Chief Rivers:** Mackenzie, Yukon, St. Lawrence, Nelson, Columbia, Churchill

**Head of State:** Queen Elizabeth II, represented by a governor-general, Edward R. Schreyer, born 1936, assumed office 1979 **Head of Government:** Prime Minister Pierre Elliott Trudeau, born 1921, elected Feb. 18, 1980 **Effective Date of Present Constitution:** The British North America Act of 1867 (renamed the Constitution Act—1867) is Canada's constitution. The Act was "patriated" by the United Kingdom, with a new charter of rights and other new provisions, and was proclaimed by Queen Elizabeth II in Ottawa on April 17, 1982 **Legislative Body:** Parliament (bicameral), consisting of a Senate and a House of Commons. The Senate is composed of a maximum of 104 members, appointed until age 75 by the governor-general on the advice of the prime minister. The House of Commons has 282 members, elected for 5 years **Local Government:** 10 provinces, governed by a premier and an elected legislature. There are also 2 large northern territories, Yukon and the Northwest Territories. Yukon is governed by a federal government commissioner and a council of 7 elected members. The Northwest Territories are governed by a commissioner and a council of 9, of whom 5 are appointed and 4 elected

**Ethnic Composition (1971):** 44.6% of the population is of British Isles descent; 28.7% of French origin; German 6.1%; Italian, 3.4%; Ukrainian 2.7%; Netherlands 2.0% and others 12.5% **Population Distribution:** 75.5% urban **Density:** 6.4 inhabitants per square mile

**Largest Cities (M.A. = Metropolitan Areas as of 1981 census):** Toronto, 599,217 (M.A. 2,998,947); Montreal, 980,354 (M.A. 2,828,349); Vancouver, 414,281 (M.A. 1,268,183); Ottawa, 295,163 (M.A. 717,978); Winnipeg, 564,473 (M.A. 584,842); Edmonton, 532,246 (M.A. 657,057); Quebec, 166,474 (M.A. 576,075); Hamilton, 306,434 (M.A. 542,095); Calgary, 592,743 (M.A. 592,743); Kitchener, 139,734 (M.A. 287,801); London, 254,280 (M.A. 283,668); Halifax, 114,594 (M.A. 277,727); Windsor, 192,083 (M.A. 246,110); Victoria, 64,379 (M.A. 233,481); Sudbury, 91,829 (M.A. 149,923); Regina, 162,613 (M.A. 164,313)

**Per Capita Income:** $11,519* (1981) **Gross National Product (GNP):** $331,338 million (1981) **Economic Statistics:** Manufacturing accounts for 21.6% of Gross National Product (chief industries: motor vehicles manufacturers, pulp and paper mills, meat slaughtering and processors, petroleum refining, iron and steel mills, motor vehicles parts and accessories manufacturers, dairy products industry, sawmills and planing mills, miscellaneous machinery and equipment manufacturers, and smelting and refining); about 27.8% is derived from public administration and services; 22.8% from trade and finance; 9.8% from primary industries (agriculture, forestry, fishing, trapping, and mining) **Minerals and Mining:** Crude petroleum, copper, nickel, iron ore, zinc, natural gas, natural gas by-products, sand and gravel, and coal, are exploited in large quantities. Value of mineral production: $32.4 billion (1980) **Labor Force:** 10,888,000 employed (June 1982) with 19.5% employed in manufacturing, 37% in services and public administration, 7.5% in primary industries and 22% in trade and finance. Unemployment 11.8% (July 1982) **Average industrial earnings:** $379.21 per week (Feb. 1982). The average monthly wage for agricultural workers is $700.00 with board (Feb. 1981) **Foreign Trade:** Exports, chiefly motor vehicles and parts, crude petroleum, fabricated metals, other machinery and equipment, other fabricated inedible materials, metal ores and concentrates, wheat, totaled $83.7 billion in 1981. Imports, chiefly machinery and equipment, motor vehicles and parts, crude petroleum, food, fabricated metals and other fabricated inedible materials, totaled $78.9 billion **Principal Trade Partners:** United States, Britain, Japan, West Germany, Venezuela, Italy, France, Australia, Netherlands, Saudi Arabia

**Vital Statistics:** Birthrate, 15.2 per 1,000 of population; death rate, 7.0 (1981) **Life Expectancy:** males 70.2, females 77.5 **Health Statistics:** 5.1 hospital beds per 1,000 inhabitants (1980-81) **Infant Mortality:** 10.9 per 1,000 births (1979) **Education Statistics:** 14,205 public primary and secondary schools, with combined enrollment of 4,671,701 (1980-81) **Enrollment in Higher Education:** 619,513 (1980) **GDP Expended on all forms of Education:** 8.2%

**Transportation:** Surfaced roads total 712 938 km; earth roads 171 336; total roads 884 273 **Passenger Cars:** 13,717,152 (1980) **Railway Mileage (in km):** 67 725.0 of first main track; total 94 051.3 **Principal Ports:** Vancouver, Sept Iles, Port Cartier, Montreal, Halifax, Quebec City, Saint John, Hamilton, Baie Comeau, Sarnia **Major Airlines:** Air Canada, the government line, and Canadian Pacific Airlines, a private carrier, operate domestic and international services

**Communications:** There are both government and privately owned radio and TV stations **No. of Radio Stations:** 737 AM; 470 FM; 10 short wave: 98.4% of homes have radios (excludes car radios) **No. of TV Stations:** 1,100: 97.8% (1981) of homes have TVs; 81.2% have color TVs **No. of Telephones:** 16,531,000 (1980): 97.6% (19811) of homes have telephones **No. of Newspapers:** 123 dailies (1980); daily circulation 5,424,500 (1980)

**Weights and Measures:** Old British standards with gradual implementation of the metric system **Travel Requirements:** for entry into Canada, proper identification or valid passport

*All monetary figures for Canada are in Canadian dollars

---

On April 17, 1982, Britain's Queen Elizabeth II proclaimed a new Canadian constitution, supplanting the British North America Act of 1867, in a grand ceremony in Ottawa. The new constitution ends the anachronistic requirement of submitting constitutional amendments to Britain's Parliament for approval and also for the first time guarantees equal rights for women, ethnic and religious minorities, and the disabled. Patriation—i.e., to bring the constitution solely under Canadian jurisdiction—was a singular victory for Prime Minister Pierre Elliott Trudeau, whose government painstakingly negotiated with provincial leaders to iron out differences over amendment procedures and the wording of the bill of rights. In November 1981, the nine English-speaking provinces finally approved the proposed document. The lone holdout was the French-speaking province of Quebec, whose premier René Lévesque condemned the constitution and led about 12,000 protestors in a demonstration through Montreal on the day the Queen signed the historic document.

During his successful campaign to oust the Progressive Conservative government of Prime Minister Joe Clark in 1980, Liberal party leader Pierre Elliott Trudeau pledged that he would be a 'caretaker' prime minister, and not serve out his full five-year term. He declared his goal was to lay the constitutional basis for a strong, united Canadian confederation that he and his party had always envisioned—a "just society" for all Canadians. His campaign broadened traditional Liberal support in Quebec to include the economically hard-pressed Maritime provinces, and the crucial Ontario vote to ensure his return to office.

But Trudeau faces an uphill battle in seeking to bind the nation together. Clark's concessions to the oil and mineral-rich Western provinces was a genuine recognition that the provinces have been eco-

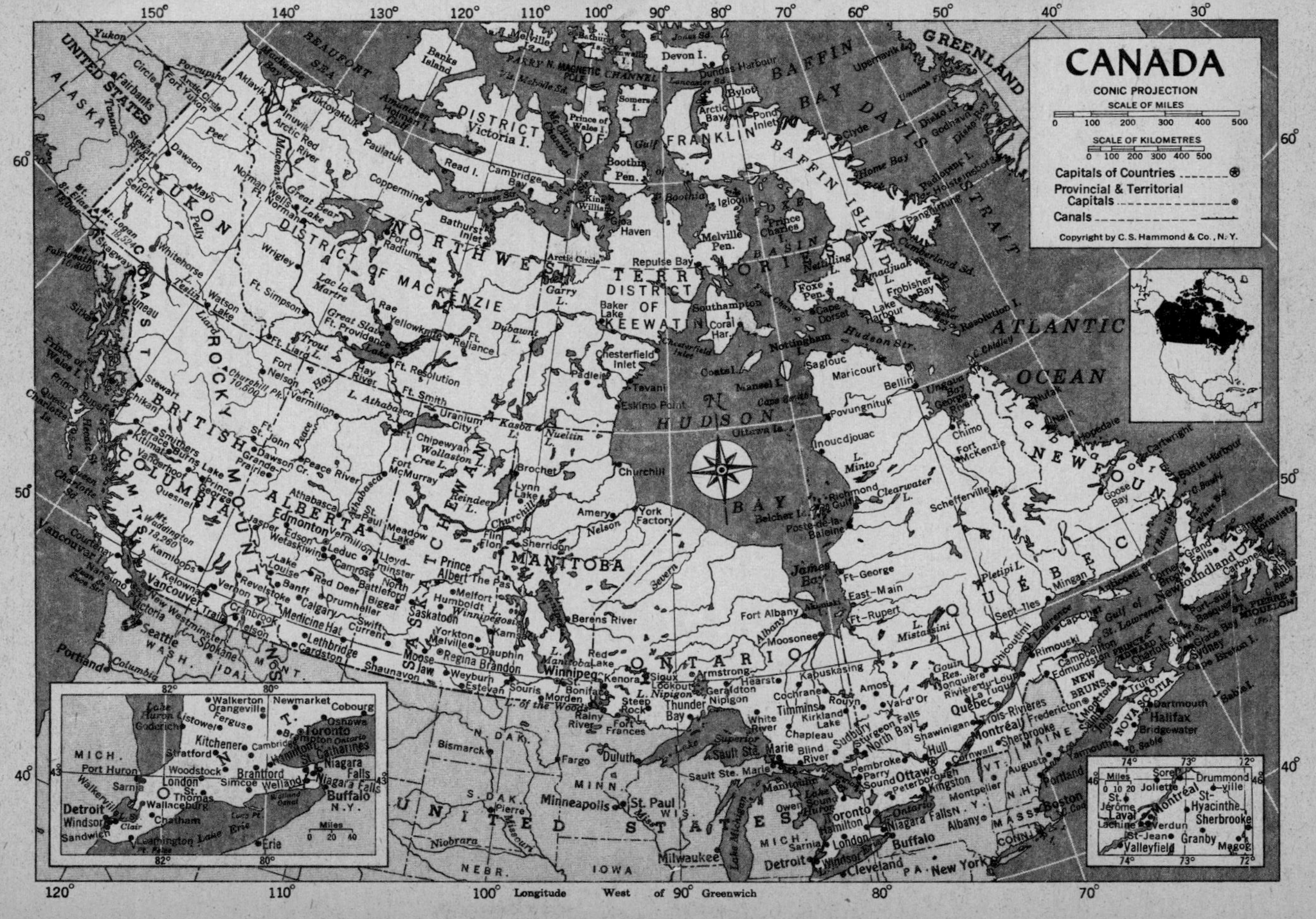
CANADA
CONIC PROJECTION
SCALE OF MILES
SCALE OF KILOMETRES
Capitals of Countries
Provincial & Territorial Capitals
Canals
Copyright by C. S. Hammond & Co., N.Y.
ATLANTIC OCEAN
HUDSON BAY
GREENLAND
UNITED STATES
BRITISH COLUMBIA
ALBERTA
MANITOBA
ONTARIO
QUEBEC
YUKON
NORTHWEST TERRITORIES
DISTRICT OF MACKENZIE
DISTRICT OF KEEWATIN
BAFFIN BAY
DAVIS STRAIT
BEAUFORT SEA
Longitude West of 90° Greenwich

nomically and politically dominated by the "Eastern" establishment. Clark had promised greater powers to the provinces, and despite his belief in a strong central government, Trudeau cannot ignore the clamor of the ten disparate local governments for more control over their own affairs.

Trudeau's biggest immediate problem remains Quebec. Since 1976, when the separatist *Parti Québécois* won a majority in the provincial assembly, Premier René Lévesque has pursued a policy calculated to make Quebec an independent state. In 1979, Lévesque called for accepting a "sovereign" Quebec within an economic association with Canada, moderating demands for total independence in order to gain acceptance of greater autonomy for the province by the rest of the nation. When Quebec's National Assembly called a referendum on association for 1980, Trudeau came out in support of Quebec Liberal leader Claude Ryan's proposals for more provincial autonomy within the federal system. He attacked the referendum as a ploy by Lévesque and the PQ to gain a yes vote by presenting independence as autonomy. On May 20, 1980, fully 58 percent of those Quebecers who turned out voted *non* to sovereignty-association, with only 42 percent casting *oui* ballots. These results had been preceeded by a Liberal resurgence in local by-elections, in recent opinion polls showing separatist sentiment waning, and by the December 21, 1979 ruling of Canada's Supreme Court striking down Quebec's Bill 101—making French the official and primary language of that province—as unconstitutional. Nevertheless, the PQ, at its convention in Montreal in February 1982, reaffirmed its goal of independence.

In October 1980 the Trudeau government launched a farreaching national energy program designed to make Canada energy self-sufficient by the end of the decade. The plan called for increased Canadianization of oil and natural gas companies operating in the country. By 1990 the government hopes to increase domestic ownership of the oil industry from the present 35% to 50%. To encourage the takeover the government boosted taxes on all oil companies while offering tax incentives for exploration only to companies substantially controlled by Canadian interests. The policy, while popular in Canada, drew charges of discrimination from U.S. and other foreign oil executives, a complaint voiced publicly by President Reagan. The energy plan also calls for development of synthetic fuels, construction of hydroelectric power plants and an Alaska Highway natural gas pipeline, and tapping the oil-rich Beaufort Sea. However, all these expensive projects have been threatened by the recent world oil glut, which has forced government planners to sharply reduce earnings and revenue projections on which the projects were based. One such project, the $13-billion Alsands synthetic crude oil facility in Alberta that had been in the planning stages for five years, was scrapped in April 1982.

**HISTORY:** Although the Vikings are believed to have visited Canada about A.D. 1000, the first recorded landing was made by John Cabot in 1497. Cabot, an Italian-born explorer in the service of Henry VII of England, landed near Newfoundland and claimed the area for the English king. In 1534, Jacques Cartier planted a cross on the Gaspé Peninsula and claimed the region for France. The intense rivalry that followed as each country tried to extend its claims was to dominate the history of Canada for more than two centuries

**1689-1763:** French and Indian Wars, a series of colonial wars in North America that reflect Anglo-French rivalry in Europe, culminate in the loss of French control of Canada and the establishment of British rule

**1774:** Quebec Act is passed, reversing favored treatment accorded British in Quebec and providing for preservation of French culture; the act is to prove instrumental in maintaining loyalty of Canada to Britain following outbreak of the American Revolution

**1791:** Constitutional Act divides Lower Canada, now southern Quebec, from Upper Canada, now southern Ontario, and establishes limited self-government

**1837-41:** Rebellions in the two Canadas and growing movement for responsible government cause British government to reunite the two Canadas

**1867:** British North America Act establishes Dominion of Canada, a confederation of Nova Scotia, New Brunswick, and Lower and Upper Canada, the latter two becoming the provinces of Quebec and Ontario, respectively. (The other components of present-day Canada are added in subsequent years, the last, Newfoundland, not until 1949.)

**1914-18:** Canada fights on Allied side in World War I; issue of conscription arouses strong opposition from French Canadians, deepening split between the French-and English-speaking

**1931:** Statute of Westminster establishes equality of Canadian Parliament with that of Britain

**1939-45:** Canada plays vital role in World War II and emerges as one of the major nations of the world

**1957:** Conservatives, led by John Diefenbaker, take office after 22 years of Liberal party rule

**1963:** Liberals, led by Lester Pearson, return to power

**1967:** French President Charles de Gaulle, on a visit to Canada, calls for a "free Quebec" during speech in Montreal; his speech prompts a sharp rebuke from the Canadian government, causing the French leader to cut short his Canadian visit

**1968:** Pearson retires and is succeeded by Pierre Elliott Trudeau, a French Canadian lawyer and former justice minister; new elections are held in which decisive Liberal victory gives Canada its first majority government in six years

**1969:** Canada opens negotiations with Communist China for the establishment of diplomatic relations between the two countries; Commons passes government-sponsored language bill requiring bilingual federal facilities wherever 10 percent of the people of any district speak French

**1970:** Government invokes wartime powers after separatist terrorists kidnap British diplomat and Quebec labor minister, who is subsequently slain

**1971:** Trudeau and Kosygin sign a protocol agreement in Moscow calling for regular, high-level consultations; Communist China and Canada exchange ambassadors

**1974:** Trudeau reelected with parliamentary majority

**1975:** Wage and price controls are imposed for three years

**1976:** The death penalty is abolished throughout Canada. *Parti Québécois* takes the Quebec provincial elections

**1977:** Bill establishing French as primary language in government and education introduced into Quebec's National Assembly. Berger Commission calls for 10-year halt to construction of natural gas pipeline in Northwest until native land claims settled. Citizenship Act becomes law

**1978:** Soviet nuclear-powered satellite crashes in northern Canada; radiation threat minimal. Trudeau introduces new federal constitution to supercede 1867 Dominion Act. Government halts all development in northern Yukon, considers measures to protect caribou migration. Four western provinces join Ontario in opposing any future economic association with an independent Quebec

**1979:** Progressive Conservatives come to power under Joe Clark, ending 11-year term of Prime Minister Trudeau. Task Force on Canadian Unity report calls for recognition of Quebec's right to self-determination and secession, proposes granting province powers to "protect and develop its distinctive character" within the Canadian federation. U.S. and Canada sign pact on disputed Atlantic and Pacific fishing grounds; but "fish war" continues with seizure of U.S. tuna boats and American ban on Canadian tuna imports as treaty is stalled in U.S. Senate. Supreme Court Dec. 13 voids Quebec's French-language Bill 101 as unconstitutional. U.S. and Canada agree to pollution controls along border to prevent "acid rain." Clark government is defeated Dec. 13. Yukon territorial council becomes legislative assembly and appoints a cabinet, in step towards provincial status

**1980:** Ottawa announces Jan. 29 that Canadian diplomats aided six Americans to escape Tehran after takeover of U.S. Embassy. Joe Clark's Progressive Conservatives are defeated in Feb. 18 general elections; Liberals win majority in parliament, as Pierre Trudeau gains new term as prime minister. Federal report issued March 6 rejects provincial status for Northwest Territories for the immediate future. Voters reject Quebec sovereignty in May 20 referendum. Trudeau and Alberta's Premier Peter Lougheed break off talks July 25 on federal energy policy and price increases for province's oil and natural gas. In September Canada and the U.S. sign a bilateral tax treaty, at the conclusion of eight years of negotiation, resolving such competing claims as the taxation of citizens of one country living and earning income in the other. Some 40,000 non-essential federal employees go on strike Sept. 29-Oct. 14 to win a 24.7% pay hike over two years but failing to

ALBERTA
MILES
KILOMETERS
Provincial Capital
Edmonton
Calgary
Red Deer
Lethbridge
Medicine Hat
Grande-Prairie
Peace River
Lloydminster
Ft. McMurray
Jasper
Banff
JASPER NATIONAL PARK
BANFF NAT'L PK.
WATERTON LAKES NAT'L PARK
WOOD BUFFALO NATIONAL PARK
ALBERTA NORTHERN PART
N.W. TERRITORIES
BR. COLUMBIA
SASKATCHEWAN
MONTANA
IDAHO
WASH.
Longitude West of Greenwich
© C.S. HAMMOND & Co., Maplewood, N.J.

achieve demands for a cost-of-living escalator clause and a shorter work week

**1981:** Joe Clark is renamed Progressive Conservative party leader Feb. 27, but by reduced margin. In March President Reagan visits Trudeau in his first trip outside the U.S. as president; Reagan draws hecklers upset over U.S. policy in El Salvador and failure to resolve acid rain problem; the two leaders sign an agreement renewing for five years the North American Air Defense Command (NORAD). In May Canada agrees to sell the Soviet Union minimum of 25 million metric tons of wheat and feed grains for an estimated $5 billion by 1986; the five-year pact is the longest ever entered into by the two countries. On Sept. 1, federal government and Alberta reach accord on oil prices. In October Parliament study panel issues report calling acid rain problem the greatest threat to the continent in history; blames the U.S. for much of it and calls for stricter anti-pollution standards. In November English-speaking provinces approve proposed constitution; Quebec protests

**1982:** In March Ontario Appeals Court Judge Bertha Wilson is appointed first woman justice of Canada Supreme Court. Progressive Conservatives protest a Liberal omnibus energy bill by boycotting the House of Commons March 2-17, an unprecedented parliamentary maneuver that suspended Commons business for two weeks; Trudeau denounces tactic as "fascistic." Britain's Queen Elizabeth II proclaims new Canadian constitution April 17; Quebecers protest. World oil glut, depressed economy forces cancellation of long-planned Alberta Alsands oil sands project in April. Unemployment in July rises to 11.8%, a postwar high. Government in May announces additional tax concessions to ailing oil industry

## ALBERTA

**Area:** 255,284 square miles **Population:** 2,237,724 (1981 census); population density: 8.8 per sq. mi.; urban, 75.0%; rural 25.0% as of 1976 census **Capital:** Edmonton **Major Cities (Metropolitan Areas as of 1981 census):** Edmonton, 657,057; Calgary, 592,743

**Ethnic Composition:** British Isles, 47%; German, 14%; Ukrainian, 8%; Scandinavian, 6%; French, 6%; Netherlands, 4%; and Native Indian, 3%; other, 12% **Religion:** United Church, 28%; Roman Catholic, 24%; Anglican, 10%; Lutheran, 8%; Presbyterian, 4%; other, 26%

**Vital Statistics (per 1,000 population):** birthrate, 17.8 (1981); death rate, 5.5 (1981); marriage rate, 10.0 (1980); divorce rate, 3.6 (1980); infant mortality per 1,000 live births, 11.4 (1978)

**Location and Geography:** Except for the northeast corner and the mountainous fringe on its western border, Alberta is underlain with arable soil, and irrigation has made the semi-arid far south and east productive for agricultural purposes. Most of the province is now very fertile agricultural land

**Government:** Alberta became a province in 1905 and is represented in the federal government by 21 members in the House of Commons and 6 Senators. The provincial government is unicameral with a Legislative Assembly of 78 members. At present, there are 73 Progressive Conservatives, 3 members of the Social Credit party, one New Democrat and one Independent in the legislature **Premier:** Honourable Peter Lougheed **Salary and Allowance:** $93,205.80

**Education (1980-81):** In Alberta, there are 1,482 public primary and secondary schools; 24,295 teachers; and 426,916 students. Total full-time winter session students enrolled at 5 universities, 29,988 (1980), and 16,950 (1980) full-time students enrolled at 18 Alberta community colleges

**Net value of production in goods-producing industries (1978 est.):** $17,705,185,000. Mining represented 51.5% of this total, construction 24.2%, agriculture 7.7% and manufacturing 14.4%. Value of oil and natural gas production is increasing annually and has made the province Canada's leading producer of mineral products with a value of $16,845,250,000 (1980). In 1980 Alberta produced 87.4% of the crude petroleum, 93.8% of the natural gas and 32% of the coal in the nation **Leading manufacturing industries (1978):** slaughtering and meat processors, petroleum refining, dairy products industries, chemical & chemical products industries, pulp and paper mills **Average industrial earnings (Feb. 1982):** $417.94 per week **Cash receipts from farming operations (1980):** $3,234,774,000; 39.5% derived from cattle and calves, 18.2% from wheat, 10.3% from rapeseed, 9.1% from barley, and 4.6% from dairy products **Families with incomes over $15,000 (1979):** 81.6% **Per capita personal income (1979):** $9,717 **Unemployment:** 7.0% (May 1982)

**Provincial Finances:** Gross general revenue (est., fiscal year 1980-81): $10,530,000,000, gross general expenditures (est., fiscal year 1980-81): $6,548,000,000

**Daily newspapers:** 9 with a circulation of 480,300 (1980) **Telephones in service (1980):** 1,727,000 **Radio stations (1980):** 110 **Homes with radios (1981):** 98.6% **Homes with TVs (1981):** 96.8%

**Hospital beds (1980-81):** 16,245 (5.6 beds per 1,000 population) **Residents per physician (Dec. 1980):** 3,406

**Motor vehicles (1980):** 1,659,079 **Residents per motor vehicle (1980):** 1.3 **Motor vehicle deaths (1979):** 698

The first European to explore Alberta was Pierre Boucher, Sieur de Boucherville, in 1751. Boucher was an agent of the English Hudson's Bay Company, but it was not until over forty years later, in 1795, that the Company and its rival, the French Northwest Company, established the first European settlements in the province. Both of the companies set up their trading posts near Edmonton, although trapping activities were concentrated further north.

In 1869 the government of the region was transferred from the Hudson's Bay Company to the newly formed Dominion of Canada, but widespread settlement was delayed until the Canadian Pacific Railroad reached the province in the mid-1880's. After the railroad made eastern markets accessible, settlers—mostly ranchers and farmers—began trickling into the region. They found that although it is far north in latitude, most of the land in Alberta is fertile.

With the development and introduction of early-ripening Marquis wheat in the early part of the 20th century, settlers poured into the west, coming in almost equal numbers from the U.S., the U.K., eastern Canada, and northern Europe. Alberta's population rose from 73,000 in 1901 to 374,000 in 1911. Since then its population has risen steadily, although less spectacularly.

Following World War II, the agricultural nature of the province began to change with the discovery of new oil fields near Leduc in 1947.

Alberta's long-term supplies of petroleum are assured by the vast reserves of oil recoverable from Alberta's oil sands. The largest oil sands deposit is found in northeastern Alberta and two plants, Suncor and Syncrude, are currently producing from these deposits. Plans for a third facility, the $13-billion Alsands project, were scrapped in April 1982 because of the worldwide oil glut and economic recession.

Abundant deposits of natural gas are found in Alberta and the province produces approximately 95% of Cananda's pentanes plus propane and butanes. Alberta also has reserves of more than 100 billion tons of high quality coking coal.

Revenues from the sale of petroleum and natural gas enabled the Alberta government to establish the Alberta Heritage Savings Trust Fund in 1976. The Fund was created to invest a portion of the province's non-renewable resource revenue to provide economic and social benefits to Albertans. To protest the federal government's oil price controls, Alberta, which provides Canada with 85% of its domestic oil, cut production sharply in 1981. The Trudeau government responded by raising taxes on petroleum to help pay for more imported oil. On September 1, the two governments reached a five-year accord on oil prices. However, in 1982, amid the oil glut, Premier Peter Lougheed and the Canadian Petroleum Association urged revision of the pact.

## BRITISH COLUMBIA

**Area:** 366,253 square miles **Population:** 2,744,467 (1981 census); population density (1981 census): 7.5 per sq. mi.; urban, 76.9%; rural 23.1% **Capital:** Victoria **Major Cities (Metropolitan Areas as of 1981 census):** Vancouver, 1,268,183; Victoria, 233,481

**Ethnic Composition:** British Isles, 58%; German, 9%; Scandinavian, 5%; French, 4%; Netherlands, 3%; Ukrainian, 3%; Italian,

BRITISH COLUMBIA
MILES
0 25 50 100 150
KILOMETERS
0 25 50 100 150
Provincial and State Capitals
BRITISH COLUMBIA NORTHERN PART
PACIFIC OCEAN
QUEEN CHARLOTTE SOUND
HECATE STRAIT
Longitude West of Greenwich
© C. S. HAMMOND & Co., Maplewood, N. J.

2%; and Native Indians, 2% **Religion:** United Church, 25%; Roman Catholic, 19%; Anglican, 18%; Lutheran, 6%; Presbyterian, 5%; Baptist, 3%; no religion, 13%

**Vital Statistics (per 1,000 population):** birthrate, 14.5 (1981); death rate, 7.2 (1981); marriage rate, 9.0 (1980); divorce rate, 3.6 (1980); infant mortality per 1,000 live births, 12.7 (1978)

**Location and Geography:** Parallel ranges of mountains and fertile valleys cover all but the northeast corner of the province. There is also a deeply indented Pacific shoreline. Because it is warmed by the Japanese Current, the climate of the coastal region is moderate

**Government:** British Columbia became a province in 1871 and is represented in the federal government by 28 members in the House of Commons and 6 Senators. The provincial government is unicameral with a Legislative Assembly of 57 members. In May 1979, 31 members of the Social Credit party and 26 members of the New Democratic party were elected to the legislature **Premier:** Honourable William R. Bennett **Salary and allowance:** $76,527

**Education (1980-81):** In British Columbia, there are 1,600 public primary and secondary schools; 28,272 teachers; and 491,796 students **Colleges:** Six degree-granting universities, 20 community colleges with a combined enrollment of 48,040 (1980); a total of 1,943 (1980) community college teachers and a total of 3,086 university teachers

**Value added in goods-producing industries (1978):** $11,176,110,000; manufacturing represents 49.7% and construction 22%. Slightly more than half of the manufacturing total comes from wood industries and paper and allied industries. Mining, which accounted for 20% of the province's industry in the 1940's, now accounts for only 10.6% **Leading manufacturing industries (1978):** Pulp and paper mills, sawmills and planing mills, and veneer and plywood mills **Average industrial earnings (March 1982):** $431.66 per week **Value of fishery products (1980):** $165,069,000 **Cash receipts from farming operations (1980):** $749,120,000, of which 23.1% is derived from dairy products, and 16.3% from poultry and eggs **Families with incomes of $16,000 and over (1979):** 74.9% **Per capita personal income (1979):** $9,821 **Unemployment (May 1982):** 10.9%

**Provincial Finances:** Gross general revenue (fiscal year 1980-81): $6,529,000,000; gross general expenditure, $6,385,000,000

**Daily Newspapers:** 22 **Combined circulation (1980):** 563,900 **Telephones (1980):** 1,910,000 **Homes with radios (1981):** 98.3% **Homes with TVs (1981):** 96.5%

**Hospital beds (1980-81):** 18,767 (5.8 beds per 1,000 population) **Physicians (Dec. 31, 1980):** 5,265 (510 residents per physician)

**Motor vehicles (1980):** 1,672,575 **Residents per motor vehicle (1980):** 1.6 **Motor vehicle deaths (1979):** 743

---

The first European to visit what is now the province of British Columbia was a Spaniard, Juan Perez, who came while on a voyage in search of the Northwest Passage. Two years later Capt. James Cook explored and established the general outline of the northwest coast. Cook stopped only briefly on the coast of Vancouver Island, but while there he obtained several sea-otter pelts from the Indians. When he arrived in Macao, on the south China coast, and traded the pelts, the potential profits of the sea-otter became clear. Soon after Cook published an account of his voyage, a legion of trading ships descended on the coast, setting the stage for a decades-long controversy between Spain and England over which was the rightful claimant to the area.

With the coming of trappers and traders after the 1790's, English control was established, and the merged Northwest and Hudson Bay Companies controlled the region until the middle of the nineteenth century. In 1849 and 1858 Vancouver Island and mainland British Columbia, respectively, were made English colonies. In 1866 the two were united and agreed to become part of the Dominion of Canada in 1871 on condition that a transcontinental railroad be built.

The completion of the railroad in 1885 spurred the development of agriculture, forestry and mining. The economy received a second boost in 1914 when the Panama Canal opened, giving Vancouver direct sea-borne access to European markets.

During the twentieth century the province has continued to grow. The demands of World War II sparked spectacular growth in the forest industries, hydroelectric power, and manufacturing. These additional jobs contributed to a trebling of the population since 1941.

In 1975, the New Democratic party was unseated by the Social Credit party headed by William Bennett. The "Socreds" pledged to repeal the Mineral Royalties Act of the previous administration.

In 1982, amid a severe recession, particularly in the province's forestry and energy industries, Premier Bennett curbed spending and taxes and spurred offshore oil and gas development.

## MANITOBA

**Area:** 250,999 square miles **Population:** 1,026,241 (1981 census); population density 4.1; urban, 69.9%; rural, 30.1% **Capital:** Winnipeg **Largest Cities:** Winnipeg, Metropolitan Area 584,842 (1981 census); Brandon, 36,242 (1981 census)

**Ethnic Composition:** British Isles, 42%; German, 12%; Ukrainian, 12%; French, 9%; Native Indian, 4%; Polish, 4% and Scandinavian, 4% **Religion:** United Church, 26%; Roman Catholic, 25%; Anglican, 12%; Lutheran, 7%; Mennonite, 6%; Ukrainian Catholic, 6%

**Vital Statistics (per 1,000 population):** birthrate, 16.5 (1981); death rate, 8.6 (1981); marriage rate, 7.6 (1980); divorce rate, 2.2 (1980); infant mortality per 1,000 live births, 13.7 (1978)

**Location and Geography:** Located between Ontario and Saskatchewan, Manitoba is a vast plain which rises gradually to the west and south. On the southern prairie the fertility of the land varies greatly, from the black gumbo of the Red River valley to sandy soil in the southwest and stonier soil between Lakes Winnipeg and Manitoba

**Government:** Manitoba became a province in 1870 **No. of representatives in Parliament:** 14 members in the House of Commons and 6 Senators **Type of legislature:** Unicameral with a Lieutenant-Governor, Executive Council and a Legislative Assembly of 57 members **Current government:** Standings in the legislature as of Nov. 17, 1981: 34 New Democrats, 23 Progressive Conservatives **Premier:** Honourable Howard Pawley **Salary and allowance:** $47,371.23

**Education (1980-81):** In Manitoba, there are 720 public primary and secondary schools; 11,771 teachers; and 196,215 students **Colleges:** Seven degree-granting universities and eight post-secondary non-university institutions with a combined enrollment of 18,710

**Value added in goods-producing industries (1978):** $3,262,587,000; manufacturing represented 41.0% of this total, construction 21.3%, agriculture 19.8%, and electric power 10.0% **Value of manufacturing shipment (1980):** $4,250,972,000 **Leading manufacturing industries:** slaughtering and meat processing, agricultural implements, dairy products, feed, publishing and printing, and metal stamping and pressing industry **Average industrial earnings (March 1982):** $334.21 per week **Cash receipts from farming operations (1980):** $1,404,568,000 with 24% from cattle and calves, 24.1% derived from wheat, 8.2% from hogs, 5.7% from barley, 6.7% from rapeseed, 5.3% from dairy products and 6.2% from flaxseed **Per capita personal income (1979):** $8,198 **Unemployment (May 1982):** 7.6%

**Provincial Finances:** Estimated gross general revenue (fiscal year 1980-81): $2,269,000,000; estimated gross general expenditure, $2,418,000,000

**Daily newspapers:** 8 **Total circulation (1980):** 283,500 **Number of telephones (1980):** 703,000 **Homes with radios (1981):** 98.6% **Homes with TVs (1981):** 96.8%

**Hospital beds (1980-81):** 6,233 (5.7 beds per 1,000 population) **Physicians (Dec. 31, 1980):** 1,878 (population per physician, 547)

**Motor Vehicles (1980):** 656,435 **Residents per motor vehicle (1980):** 1.6 **Motor vehicle deaths (1979):** 205

---

Despite the fact that it is known as a "prairie province," only a small southern portion of Manitoba's 250,999 square miles is actually treeless grassland. The remainder ranges from forest land, to lakes, subarctic tundra, and—most surprisingly of all for a "prairie" province—nearly 400 miles of salt-water coast on Hudson Bay. Its name and reputation derives from the fact that only the prairie area south of the infertile Pre-Cambrian shield is suitable for large-scale settlement.

Manitoba is bounded on the south by the U.S., on the west by Saskatchewan, on the north by the

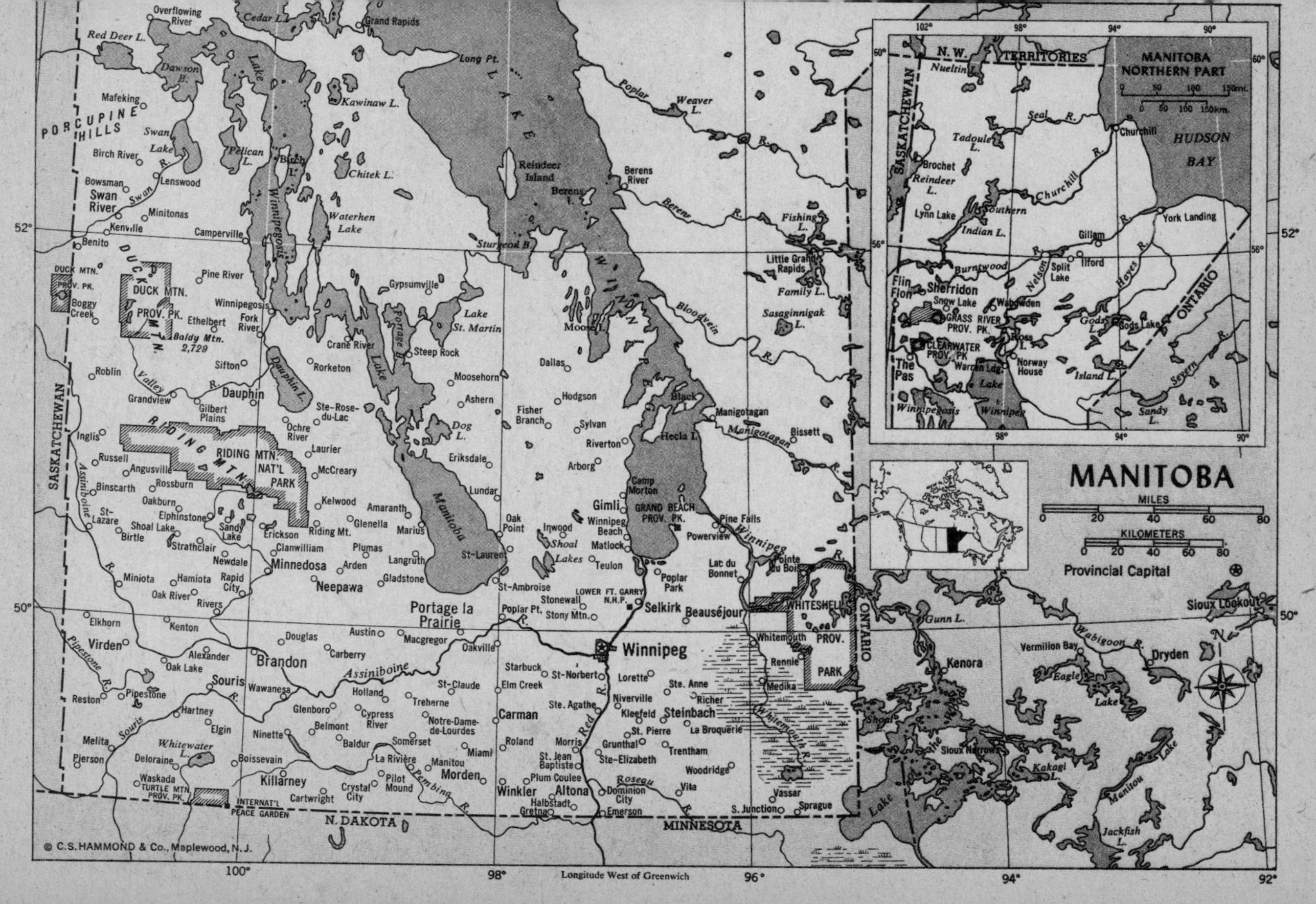
MANITOBA
MILES
KILOMETERS
Provincial Capital
MANITOBA NORTHERN PART
HUDSON BAY
N. W. TERRITORIES
SASKATCHEWAN
ONTARIO
MINNESOTA
N. DAKOTA
Churchill
York Landing
Gillam
Split Lake
Ilford
Norway House
Flin Flon
Sherridon
The Pas
Lynn Lake
Brochet
GRASS RIVER PROV. PK.
CLEARWATER PROV. PK.
LAKE WINNIPEG
Lake Winnipegosis
Lake Manitoba
Dauphin L.
Cedar L.
Grand Rapids
Berens River
Reindeer Island
Hecla I.
GRAND BEACH PROV. PK.
WHITESHELL PROV. PARK
RIDING MTN. NAT'L PARK
DUCK MTN. PROV. PK.
TURTLE MTN. PROV. PK.
INTERNAT'L PEACE GARDEN
PORCUPINE HILLS
Winnipeg
Selkirk
Beauséjour
Steinbach
Gimli
Portage la Prairie
Brandon
Dauphin
Swan River
Neepawa
Minnedosa
Virden
Souris
Killarney
Morden
Winkler
Carman
Altona
Emerson
Kenora
Dryden
Sioux Lookout
Red R.
Assiniboine
Winnipeg R.
Longitude West of Greenwich
© C.S.HAMMOND & Co., Maplewood, N.J.

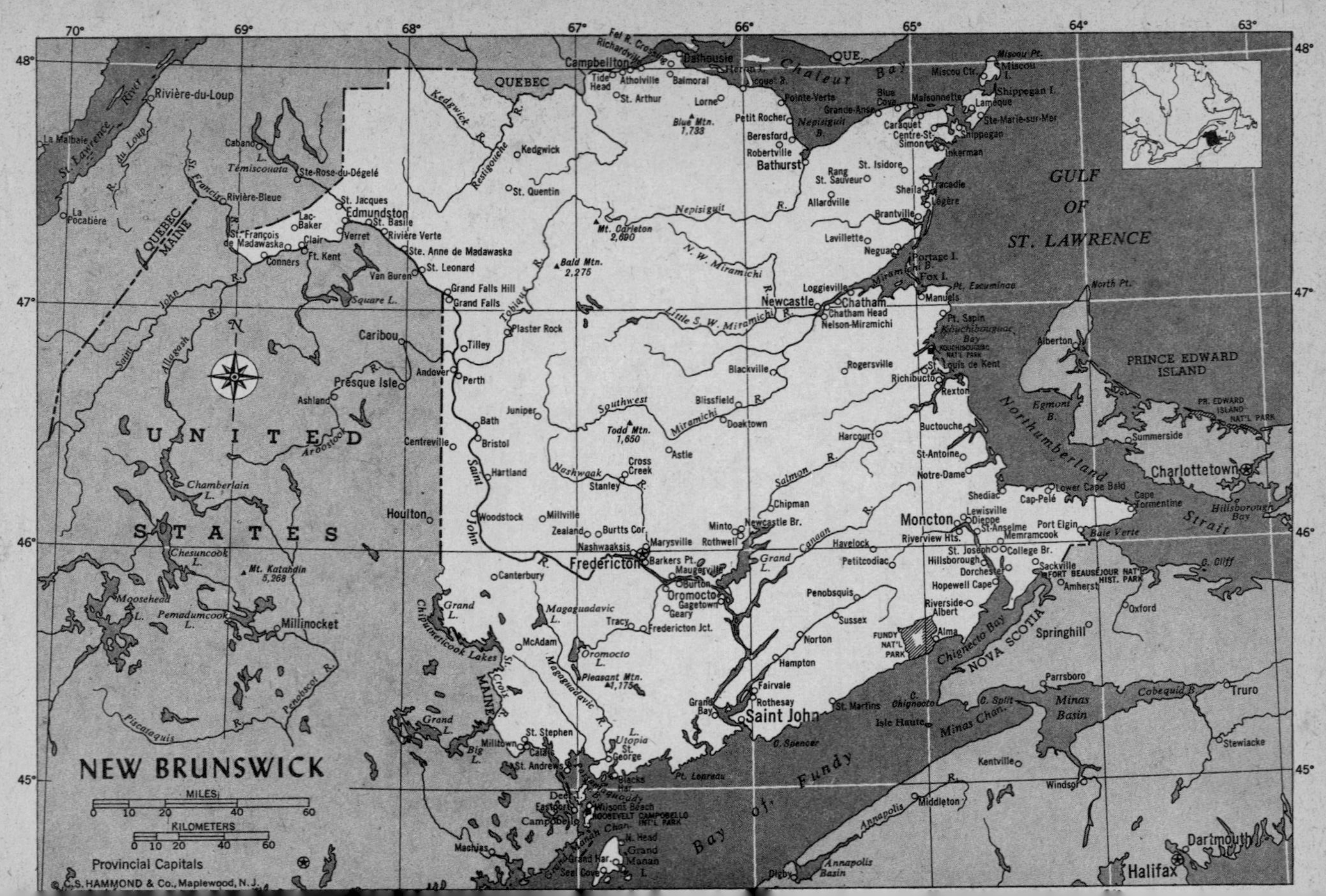
NEW BRUNSWICK
Provincial Capitals
MILES
KILOMETERS
C.S. HAMMOND & Co., Maplewood, N.J.
GULF OF ST. LAWRENCE
PRINCE EDWARD ISLAND
NOVA SCOTIA
QUEBEC
MAINE
UNITED STATES
Bay of Fundy
Northumberland Strait
Chaleur Bay
Fredericton
Saint John
Moncton
Bathurst
Newcastle
Chatham
Campbellton
Dalhousie
Edmundston
Woodstock
Charlottetown
Halifax
Dartmouth
Truro
Amherst
Springhill
Sackville
Sussex
St. Stephen
Grand Falls
Caribou
Presque Isle
Houlton
Millinocket
Rivière-du-Loup
Mt. Katahdin 5,268
Mt. Carleton 2,690
Minas Basin
Saint John R.

Keewatin District, and on the east by Ontario, but it was through its Hudson Bay sea coast that early European explorers, trappers, and settlers first came to the province. The first European to enter the territory was probably Sir Thomas Button in 1612. Nearly 60 years later, in 1670, the Hudson's Bay Company began building forts in the area, principally at the mouths of the Nelson and Churchill rivers. Throughout the 18th century the area was affected by the feud between the English Hudson's Bay Company and the French Northwest Company. The feud between the two fur-trading companies continued until 1821 when the rivals amalgamated.

Until the advent of the steamship and railroad in the mid-19th century, white men came to the provinces mostly as trappers and traders. An exception was the historic Red River Settlement (now Winnipeg), which was established in 1812, but it was not until the late 1860's that steam navigation from the north and railroads from the south and east made the area accessible to large numbers of settlers.

In 1870 the province of Manitoba was organized. It was linked by rail to the U.S. in 1878 and with eastern Canada in 1881, and the population, which was a mere 25,000 in 1871, grew to 250,000 in 1901 and 700,000 in 1931.

Like their prairie neighbors in both Canada and the U.S., Manitobans suffered during the 1920s and '30s, but since the hard years of the Great Depression, the growth of mineral, forest, and manufacturing industries, and the return of markets for its agricultural products have helped the province become one of Canada's richest. While it was once solely dependent on agriculture, its economy is now substantially diversified. Manufacturing accounts for over 40 percent of the province's net produced value; agriculture less than 20 percent.

In 1969 the New Democratic party won control after eleven years of Conservative rule. The NDP introduced public automobile insurance, medicare, and other wide-ranging social programs.

An upset victory in the October 1977 elections returned the Progressive Conservatives to office after eight years.

The NDP was returned to power in the November 1981 elections, winning 34 of 57 seats. The economic recession was said to have contributed to the fall of the Conservatives.

## NEW BRUNSWICK

**Area:** 28,354 square miles **Population:** 696,403 (1981 census); population density 24.6 per square mile; urban, 52%; rural, 48% Capital: Fredericton **Major cities (1981 census) populations:** Fredericton, 43,723; Moncton, 54,743; Saint John, Metropolitan Area: 114,048

**Ethnic Composition:** British Isles, 58%; French, 37% **Religion:** Roman Catholic, 52%; Baptist, 14%; United Church, 13%; Anglican, 11%

**Vital Statistics (per 1,000 population):** birthrate, 15.7 (1981); death rate, 7.6 (1981); marriage rate, 7.5 (1980); divorce rate, 1.9 (1980); infant mortality per 1,000 live births, 11.8 (1978)

**Location and Geography:** Nearly rectangular in shape, New Brunswick has an extensive sea coast: on the Bay of Chaleur on the north, the Gulf of St. Lawrence and Northumberland Strait on the east, and the Bay of Fundy on the south. Much of the soil is rocky and unfit for agriculture, but generous rainfall produces prolific forest growth. The Bay of Fundy, which separates New Brunswick and Nova Scotia, has the world's highest tides, and there are proposals to harness these to produce electric power

**Government:** New Brunswick became a province in 1867 and is represented in the federal government by 10 members in the House of Commons and 10 Senators. The provincial government is unicameral with a Legislative Assembly of 58 members. Present standings in the legislature are: 30 Progressive Conservatives and 27 Liberals **Premier:** Honourable Richard Hatfield **Salary and allowance:** $57,500

**Education (1980-81):** In New Brunswick, there are 465 public primary and secondary schools; 7,970 teachers; and 152,697 students **Colleges:** Four degree-granting universities with a total enrollment of 12,264 (1980). There are 9 campuses known as New Brunswick Community Colleges with a total enrollment of 1,390 (1980)

**Value added in goods-producing industries (1978 actual):** $1,744,700,000. Manufacturing represented 44.9% of this total, construction 28%, electric power 8%, mining 7.5%, forestry 5.0%, agriculture 3.6% **Leading manufacturing industries (1978):** pulp and paper mills, sawmills and planing mills, and fishery products **Average industrial earnings (March 1982):** $339.39 per week **Cash receipts from farming operations (1980):** $153,889,000 **Families with incomes over $10,000 (1979):** 74.8% **Per capita personal income (1979):** $6,472 **Unemployment (May 1982):** 15.3%

**Provincial Finances:** Estimated gross general revenue (fiscal year 1980-81): $1,609,000,000; estimated gross general expenditure, $1,691,000,000

**Daily newspapers (1980):** 6 **Circulation:** 156,400 **Telephones in service (1980):** 390,000 **Homes with radios (1981):** 98.6% **Homes with TVs (1981):** 98.6%

**Hospital beds (1980-81):** 4,237 (6.0 beds per 1,000 population) **Physicians (Dec. 31, 1980):** 786 (population per physician, 902)

**Motor vehicles (1980):** 364,236 **Residents per motor vehicle (1980):** 1.9 **Motor vehicle deaths (1979):** 258

There was little settlement of New Brunswick during the French period, and for 20 years following the beginning of British rule (1763), the sea coasts and river valleys were largely left to the fur traders. Then the *Loyalists*, escaping from the rebelling American Colonies southward, settled the area in 1783. At that time the County of Sunbury was split from Nova Scotia and made a separate province named New Brunswick, after the family name of the reigning monarch, George III.

Other immigrations brought Scottish farmers and laborers and immigrants from Great Britain after the Napoleonic wars of the next century. By 1842 the population had swelled to 74,000.

The 600 mile long New Brunswick coast and the softwood forests of the interior encouraged the development of lumbering, shipbuilding, and fisheries and, helped by preferential tariffs and trade agreements with England, the colony was initially prosperous. Its resources were a mixed blessing, however, for they hindered the development of a well balanced economy and political system.

By 1866 declining economic fortunes forced the colony into a not wholly welcome union with the nascent Dominion of Canada. A major railroad link with Montreal was established as a result of a pre-unification agreement, but its promise of economic salvation was dimmed as the coming of the steamship, and the depletion of its forest reserves brought economic ruin to many provincial industries.

Since World War II some success has occurred in developing a more balanced economy. Although still heavily oriented towards extractive industries and their exportation, the province has attempted to develop manufacturing industries for processing the raw materials. The service sector accounts for 70 percent of provincial employment.

On January 9, 1982, an earthquake, registering 5.9 on the Richter scale, the largest to hit the eastern part of the continent in more than 125 years, was epicentered at Woodstock.

## NEWFOUNDLAND

**Area:** 156,184 square miles **Population:** 567,681 (1981 census); population density 3.6; urban 58.9%; rural 41.1% **Capital:** St. John's **Major cities:** St. John's, Metropolitan Area (1981 census), 154,820; Corner Brook, 24,339

**Ethnic Composition:** British Isles, 94%; French, 3% **Religion:** Roman Catholic, 37%; Anglican, 28%; United Church, 19%

**Vital Statistics (per 1,000 population):** birthrate, 19.9 (1981); death rate, 5.4 (1981); marriage rate, 6.5 (1980); divorce rate, 1.0 (1980); infant mortality per 1,000 live births, 12.2

**Location and Geography:** Newfoundland includes the island of Newfoundland (43,359 square miles) and the coast of Labrador (112,828 square miles) on the mainland. They are separated by the Strait of Belle Isle which is nine and a half miles wide at its narrowest point. The island's surface is low, rolling, and rocky. Its highest point is Lewis Hill (2,672 feet) in the Northern peninsula. The west coast and river valleys are thickly forested

**Government:** Newfoundland became a province in 1949 and is represented in the federal government by 7 members in the House of Commons and 6 Senators. The provincial government is unicameral with a House of Assembly of 52 members. In April 1982, 44 Progressive Conservatives and 8 Liberals were elected to the house **Premier:** Honourable Brian Peckford **Salary and allowance:** $75,204

**Education (1980-81):** In Newfoundland, there are 665 public primary and secondary schools; 7,978 teachers; and 142,800 students **Colleges:** One degree-granting university and six non-university post-secondary institutions with enrollment of 7,855

**Value added in goods-producing industries (1978):** $1,413,543,000. Construction represented 22.4% of this total; mining 23.4%, manufacturing 27.9%, electric power 13.9% and fisheries 8.4%. (The development of the huge iron ore deposits in Labrador has boosted Newfoundland to 6th position in the nation's production of minerals. In 1980 production was valued at $1,083,319,000. Iron ore contributed 89% of the total and represented 53.3% of the total Canadian production.) **Value of manufacturing shipments (1980):** $1,044,029,000 **Leading manufacturing industry:** fishery products **Average industrial earnings (March 1982):** $362.57 per week **Families with incomes over $12,000 (1979):** 67.1% **Per capita personal income (1979):** $5,862 **Unemployment (May 1982):** 17.0%

**Provincial Finances:** Estimated gross general revenue (fiscal year 1980-81): $1,505,000,000; estimated gross general expenditure, $336,000,000

**Daily newspapers (1980):** 3 **Circulation:** 54,200 **Telephones in service (1980):** 259,000 **Homes with radios (1981):** 96.6% **Homes with TVs (1981):** 97.3%

**Hospital beds (1980-81):** 3,315 (5.0 beds per 1,000 population) **Physicians (Dec. 31, 1980):** 866 (population per physician, 674)

**Motor Vehicles (1980):** 212,198 **Residents per motor vehicle (1980):** 2.8 **Motor vehicle deaths (1979):** 106

---

Newfoundland, which consists of the island of Newfoundland itself and the coast of Labrador, is a land of great natural resources. Huge forests of spruce and pine cover much of the area; the inland wilderness has an abundance of wildlife; great mineral wealth lies hidden beneath the surface; hydroelectric power is abundant; and the Grand Banks, in which it is located, is a fishing ground of legendary richness.

Despite these resources, the history of Newfoundland is largely one of great promise only partially fulfilled. It was discovered by John Cabot in 1497, and Sir Humphrey Gilbert made a formal claim for Britain in 1583, but the island remained a distant outpost visited only by fishing boats until the end of the 18th century. By then a court system and land-based commerce had been established, but by 1850 the population had only increased to 30,000.

Fishing and forestry gave the island limited prosperity through the 1860s and '70s, and fueled by this the small province chose not to join the Canadian nation when it was granted dominion status in 1867. The question of union was taken up again in the 1890s, but by then the province's precarious economic condition made it impossible. It remained independent until February 16, 1934 when, after surveying the province's debts, Britain reestablished direct rule, which was then maintained until Newfoundland was united with Canada in 1949.

Many economists today believe that Newfoundland's continuing economic problems can be solved only by developing resource industries and increasing the volume of local processing and refining, as opposed to the continuing export of raw natural resources. A jurisdictional dispute between Ottawa and the province has thus far held up development of the offshore Hibernia oilfield, expected to be Canada's largest.

Provincial elections on April 6, 1982, saw Premier Brian Peckford's Progressive Conservatives increase their majority in the 52-member assembly to 44, with the Liberals winning the remaining 8 seats.

## NOVA SCOTIA

**Area:** 21,425 square miles **Population:** 847,442 (1981 census); population density 39.6; urban 55.8%; rural 44.2% **Capital:** Halifax **Major city populations (1981 census):** Halifax, Metropolitan Area 277,727; Dartmouth, 62,277

**Ethnic Composition:** British Isles, 77%; French, 10%; German, 5% **Religion:** Roman Catholic, 36%; United Church, 21%; Anglican, 17%; Baptist, 13%; Presbyterian, 5%

**Vital Statistics (per 1,000 population):** birthrate, 14.2 (1981); death rate, 7.6 (1981); marriage rate, 8.0 (1980); divorce rate, 2.7 (1980); infant mortality per 1,000 live births, 11.9 (1978)

**Location and Geography:** The province is a 359.6-mile long peninsula. The Atlantic coast is generally rocky; the slopes facing the Bay of Fundy and Gulf of St. Lawrence, sheltered from the Atlantic storms by a series of low ridges that run through the center of the province, consist of fertile plains and river valleys. Cape Breton Island, the northeast portion of the province, is mostly rugged upland and is divided almost in two by the saltwater Bras d'Or Lake, in reality a land-enclosed extension of the sea

**Government:** Nova Scotia became a province in 1867 and is represented in the federal government by 11 members in the House of Commons and 10 Senators. The provincial government is unicameral with a House of Assembly of 52 members. As of October 1981, there were 37 Progressive Conservatives, 13 Liberals, one New Democrat, and one Independent in the house **Premier:** Honourable John M. Buchanan, Q.C. **Salary and Allowance:** $55,600

**Education (1980-81):** In Nova Scotia there are 600 public primary and secondary schools; 10,896 teachers; and 185,568 students **Colleges:** 10 degree-granting universities and 14 colleges with a combined enrollment of 19,194 in 1980

**Value added in goods-producing industries (1978):** $2,052,910,000. Manufacturing represents 46.8% of this total; construction, 25.7%; fisheries, 9.5%; and mining, 5.8%. The province vies with British Columbia each year as the nation's leading producer of fish products. These in 1980 had a total value of $214,370,000 (prelim.) **Leading manufacturing industries (1978):** Petroleum refining, fish products industry, pulp and paper mills, dairy products **Average industrial earnings (March 1982):** $322.88 per week **Cash Receipts from farming operations (1980):** $202,458,000, with 27.6% derived from dairy products, 32.7% from livestock, 16.9% from crops, 18.8% from poultry and eggs **Families with incomes over $10,000 (1979):** 75.9% **Per capita personal income (1979):** $7,088 **Unemployment (May 1982):** 14.0%

**Provincial Finances:** Estimated general revenue (fiscal year 1980-81 est.): $1,874,000,000; estimated gross general expenditure, fiscal year 1980-81 est., $2,025,000,000

**Daily newspapers (1980):** 7 **Circulation:** 194,400 **Telephones in service (1980):** 499,000 **Homes with radios (1981):** 98.1% **Homes with TVs (1981):** 98.1%

**Hospital beds (1980-81):** 5,447 (5.9 beds per 1,000 populationn) **Physicians (Dec. 31, 1980):** 1,588 (population per physician approx. 539)

**Motor vehicles (1980):** 530,018 **Residents per motor vehicle (1980):** 1.6 **Motor vehicle deaths (1979):** 208

---

John Cabot is regarded, on the basis of his 1497 visit to Cape Breton Island, as the "discoverer" of Nova Scotia, despite the belief that Norsemen and European fishermen probably visited the island centuries before. Britain's claim to Nova Scotia began with Cabot's visit, but its sovereignty was contested by France until Halifax was firmly established as a naval and military base in 1749, and the Acadians were expelled in 1755. The fall of the French stronghold of Louisbourg on Cape Breton Island in 1758 secured British control. Following the American Revolution, nearly 30,000 "Loyalists" emigrated to Nova Scotia, becoming its first citizens. The province was a founding member of the Canadian confederation.

Population growth, increased trade, and wealth marked the first half of the 19th century. But today

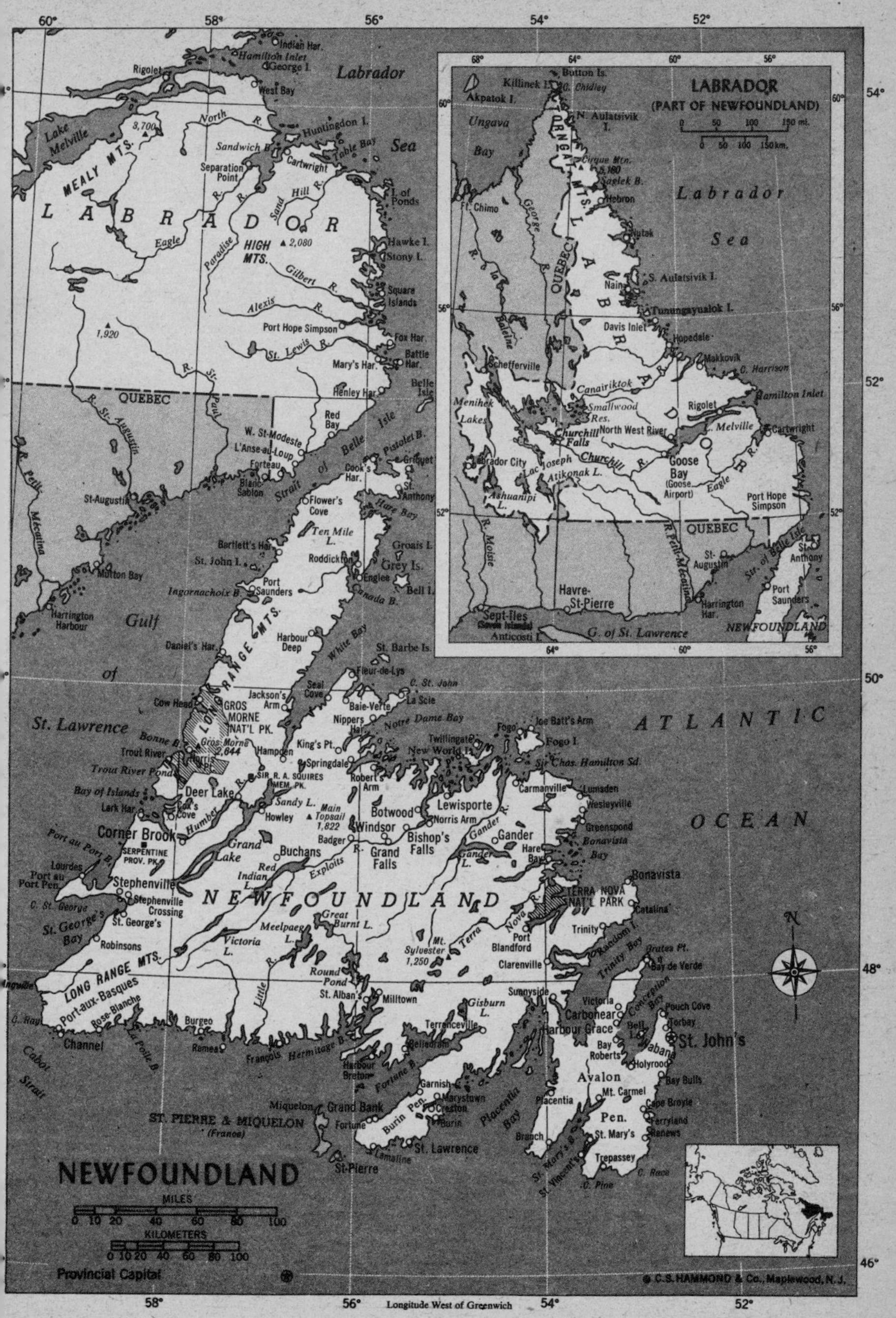
NEWFOUNDLAND
LABRADOR
(PART OF NEWFOUNDLAND)
Labrador Sea
Gulf of St. Lawrence
ATLANTIC OCEAN
Provincial Capital
Longitude West of Greenwich
© C.S. HAMMOND & Co., Maplewood, N.J.

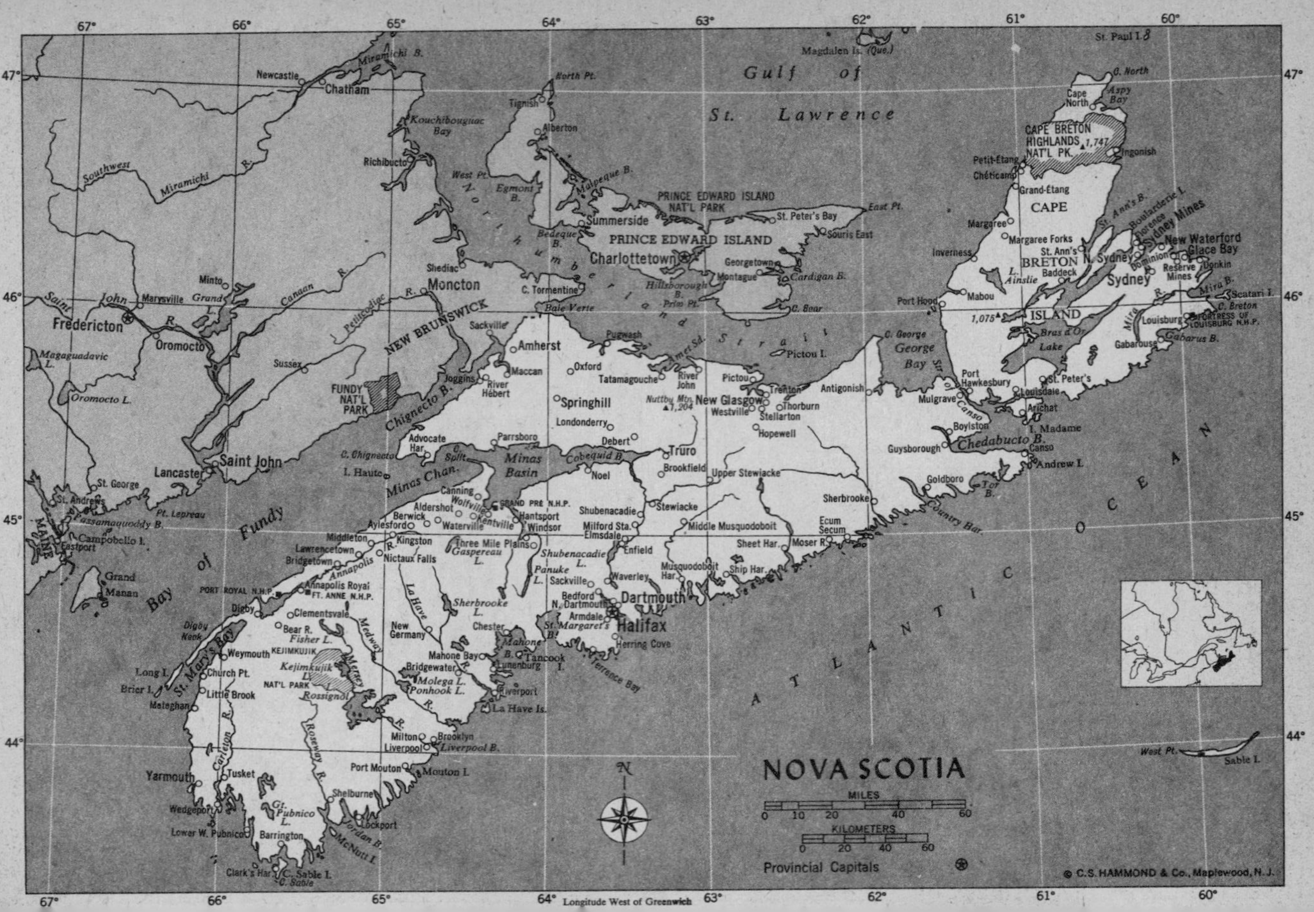
NOVA SCOTIA
MILES
KILOMETERS
Provincial Capitals
Longitude West of Greenwich
© C.S. HAMMOND & Co., Maplewood, N. J.
Gulf of St. Lawrence
Bay of Fundy
ATLANTIC OCEAN
PRINCE EDWARD ISLAND
NEW BRUNSWICK
CAPE BRETON ISLAND
MAINE
Halifax
Dartmouth
Charlottetown
Fredericton
Saint John
Moncton
Sydney
Truro
Yarmouth
Amherst
Springhill
New Glasgow
Sable I.

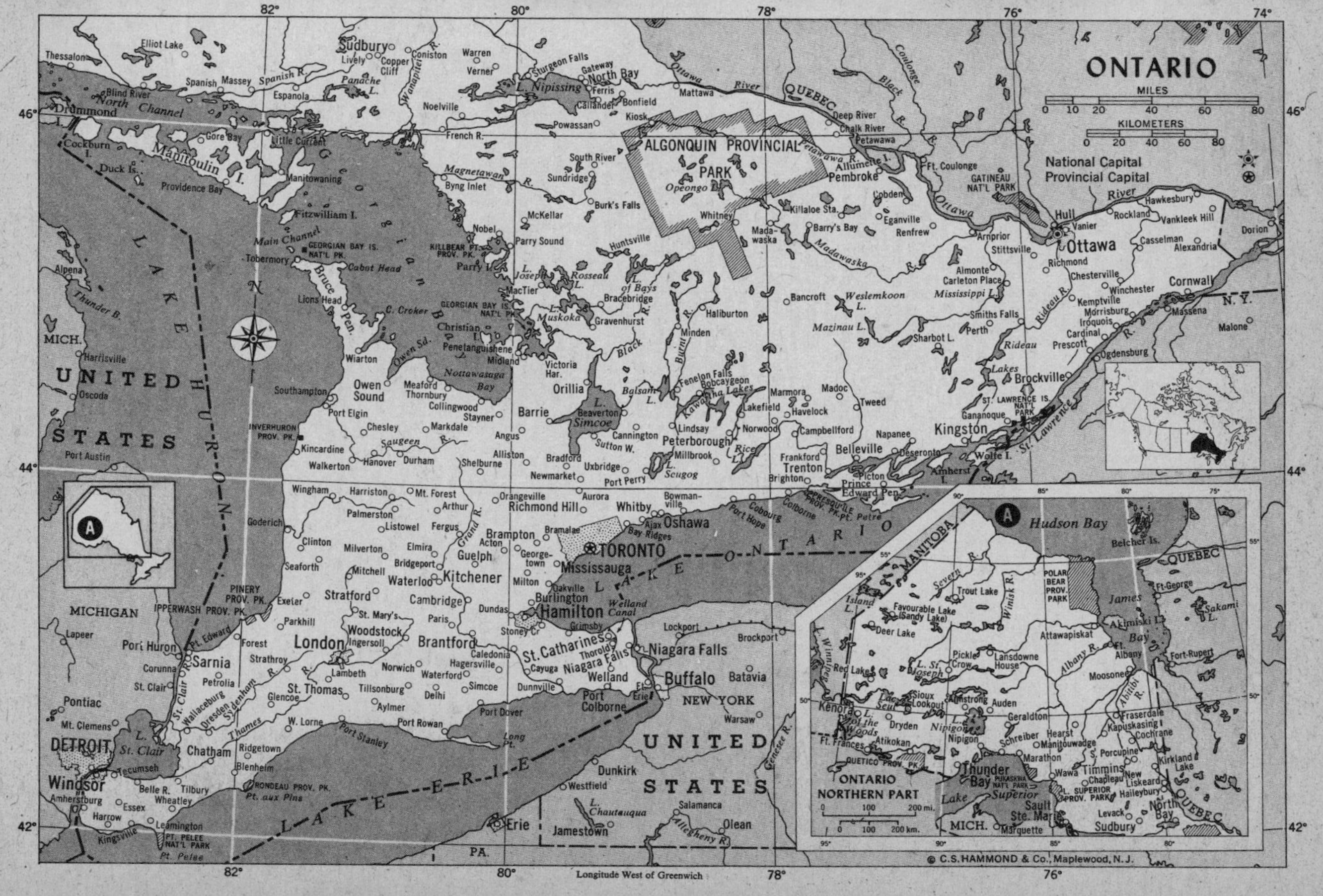
ONTARIO
MILES
KILOMETERS
National Capital
Provincial Capital
ALGONQUIN PROVINCIAL PARK
LAKE HURON
LAKE ONTARIO
LAKE ERIE
UNITED STATES
NEW YORK
MICHIGAN
QUEBEC
Georgian Bay
Ottawa
TORONTO
Hamilton
Kingston
London
Windsor
DETROIT
Sudbury
North Bay
Buffalo
Niagara Falls
Manitoulin I.
Bruce Pen.
ONTARIO NORTHERN PART
Hudson Bay
James Bay
MANITOBA
Longitude West of Greenwich
© C.S. HAMMOND & Co., Maplewood, N.J.

Nova Scotia shares many of the problems of its neighboring provinces. Its economy is largely dependent on low-technology industries such as fishing and mining, and though the federal government is attempting to diversify the economy, unemployment and economic disparity between the Maritime Provinces and the rest of Canada remains.

In April 1981 some 3.2 million acres off the coast of Nova Scotia were opened to offshore oil exploration.

A growing vacationland, Nova Scotia has two national parks and nine designated historic parks.

## ONTARIO

**Area:** 412,580 square miles **Population:** 8,625,107 (1981 census); population density, 20.9; urban, 81.2% rural, 18.8% **Capital:** Toronto **Major Cities (Metropolitan areas as of 1981 census):** Toronto, 2,998,947; Ottawa, 717,978; Hamilton, 542,095; St. Catharines-Niagara Falls, 304,353; London, 283,668; Kitchener, 287,801; Sudbury, 149,923; Thunder Bay, 121,379; Oshawa, 154,217

**Ethnic Composition:** British Isles, 59%; French, 10%; German, 6%; Italian, 6% **Religion:** Roman Catholic, 33%; United Church, 22%; Anglican, 16%; Presbyterian, 7%; Baptist, 4%; Lutheran, 3%

**Vital Statistics (per 1,000 population):** birthrate, 14.3 (1981); death rate, 7.3 (1981); marriage rate, 8.0 (1980); divorce rate, 2.6 (1980); infant mortality per 1,000 live births, 11.3 (1978)

**Location and Geography:** Located in the center of Canada, Ontario is a geographic and cultural transition between eastern Quebec and the midwestern prairie provinces. It has a freshwater shoreline of 1,700 miles on the Great Lakes and St. Lawrence River and 750 miles of salt-water shorelines on Hudson and James Bays. The northern part is within the Canadian Shield, but nearly 17.5 million acres are arable

**Government:** Ontario became a province in 1867 and is represented in the federal government by 95 members in the House of Commons and 24 Senators. The provincial government is unicameral with a Legislative Assembly of 125 members. At present, the standings in the House are: 70 Progressive Conservatives, 34 Liberals, and 21 New Democrats **Premier:** Honourable William G. Davis **Salary and allowance:** $81,600

**Education (1980-81):** In Ontario, there are 4,867 public primary and secondary schools; 99,273 teachers; and 1,751,273 students **Colleges:** 21 degree-granting universities and 30 non-university post-secondary institutions with enrollment of 226,728 (1980)

**Value added in goods-producing industries (1978):** $38,719,051,000, 37.4% of Canada's total; manufacturing contributed 71.8%; construction, 14.5%; mining, 3.7%; and agriculture, 4.3%. The province is the second-largest producer of mineral products with a total value of $4,660,572,000 in 1980 **Value of manufacturing shipments (1980):** $80,991,160,000, 48.9% of the national total Leading manufacturing industries: motor vehicles and their parts and accessories, iron and steel mills and petroleum refining **Average industrial earnings (March 1982):** $374.07 per week **Cash receipts from farming operations (1980):** $4,370,039,000, with 27.1% derived from cattle and calves, dairy products 15.9%, hogs 10.8%, tobacco 4.5%, poultry 5.7% and vegetables 4.4% **Families with incomes over $12,000 (1979):** 82.2% **Per capita personal income (1979):** $9,608 **Unemployment (May 1982):** 8.7%

**Provincial finances:** Estimated gross general revenue (fiscal year 1980-81): was $17,341,000,000; estimated gross general expenditure, $17,787,000,000

**Daily newspapers:** 46 English and 1 French **Combined circulation (1980):** 2,346,300 **Telephones in service (1980):** 6,180,000 **Homes with radios (1981):** 98.0% **Homes with TVs (1981):** 97.9%

**Hospital beds (1980-81):** 48,442 (4.8 beds per 1,000 population) **Physicians (Dec. 31, 1980):** 16,664 (population per physician, 516)

**Motor vehicles (1980):** 4,647,820 **Residents per motor vehicle (1980):** 1.9 **Motor vehicle deaths (1978):** 1,653

Ontario was the site of the first European settlement in the interior of North America. In 1639 a combined Jesuit mission, French fort, and Norman town, called Sainte-Marie Among the Hurons, was established on the River Wye, nearly 800 miles from Quebec. The colony lasted for ten years, when it was burned by its founders in the face of attacking Iroquois, who with the Huron Indians were the settlers' chief rivals in the fur trade. Archaeologists and historians have recently restored the outpost on its site 90 miles north of Toronto.

At the time of the founding of Sainte-Marie, Huronia was the most densely populated area of what is now Canada. It was the home of 30,000 Hurons, who controlled the best trade routes and acted as middlemen, trading for furs with more distant tribes and with white settlements on the St. Lawrence River.

In 1774, eleven years after cession to England, the Quebec Act made the area a western extension of Quebec. Loyalist refugees from the American Revolution settled the area around the St. Lawrence, and in 1791 a division was effected, Upper Canada being the future Ontario.

During the War of 1812 the Loyalists defended their lands against the U.S., the town of York (renamed Toronto in 1834) suffering invasion and burning by U.S. forces. After the war, emigration by U.S. and British citizens seeking land brought rapid population expansion. The fur trade was slowly replaced with lumbering and wheat production, and by the mid-19th century the economy began to boom as development of railroads and canal systems started a major transportation network. The establishment of the Dominion of Canada in 1867 and of the capital of Ottawa added to the importance of the province.

Today Ontario is the largest province in terms of wealth and population. Its industrial production accounts for nearly 40 percent of the national income and it is the major industrial center of Canada, producing 97 percent of the motor vehicle parts, and over 90 percent of all office and store machinery, motor vehicles and household radios and televisions manufactured domestically. Yet the province's farming, lumber and fishing are still vitally important to the Canadian economy. And its famous lake regions have made Ontario a favorite summer and winter vacationland for Canadians and Americans alike.

For all its wealth, Ontario still suffers from some unemployment. With proposals for independence in Quebec, however, Ontario's position as the center of commerce and industry for Canada has been enhanced by the exodus of businesses from its eastern neighbor.

The provincial elections of March 18, 1981, saw Premier William Davis' Progressive Conservative party increase its control of the government by 12 additional seats in the legislature.

## PRINCE EDWARD ISLAND

**Area:** 2,184 square miles **Population:** 122,506 (1981 census); population density, 56.1; urban, 37.1%; rural, 62.9% **Capital:** Charlottetown (1981 census), 15,282

**Ethnic Composition:** British Isles, 83%; French 14% **Religion:** Roman Catholic, 46%; United Church, 25%; Presbyterian, 12%; Anglican, 6%; Baptist, 6%

**Vital Statistics (per 1,000 population):** birthrate, 16.1 (1981); death rate, 7.9 (1981); marriage rate, 7.5 (1980); divorce rate, 1.3 (1980); infant mortality per 1,000 live births, 7.6

**Location and Geography:** Separated from the mainland by Northumberland Strait, nine to 25 miles wide, the island is about 120 miles in length and has an average width of 20 miles. The irregular coastline has many large bays and deep inlets and all inland waters are tidal except for one river and one lake. The rich soil is of a distinctive red color; more than half of the area is farmed. There is no mining and forestland is limited to small farm woodlots

**Government:** Prince Edward Island became a province in 1873 and is represented in the federal government by four members in the House of Commons and four Senators. The provincial government is unicameral with a Legislative Assembly of 32 members. Current standings in the legislature are: 21 Progressive Conservatives and 11 Liberals **Premier:** Honourable James M. Lee **Salary and allowance:** $57,700

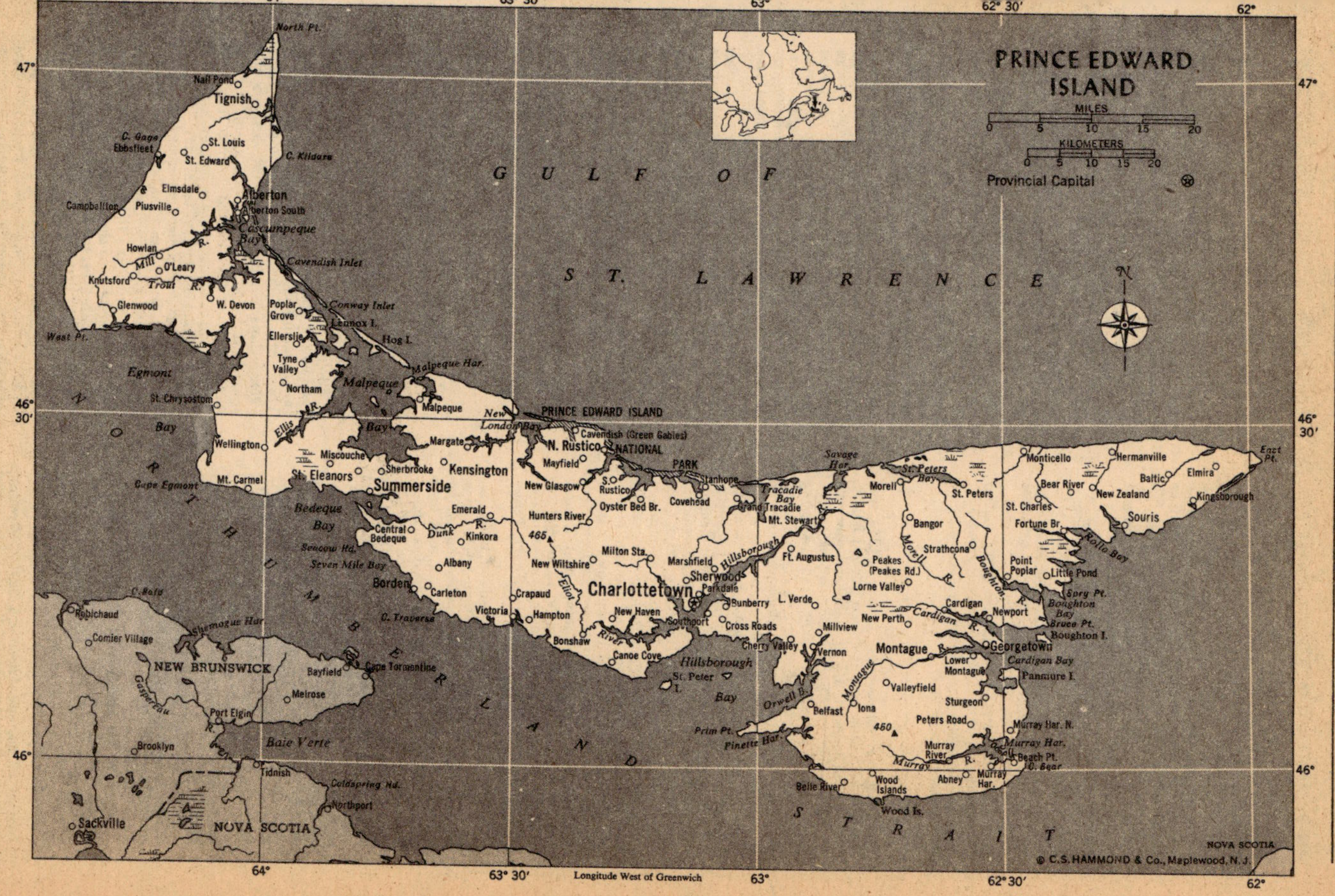
PRINCE EDWARD ISLAND
MILES
KILOMETERS
Provincial Capital
GULF OF ST. LAWRENCE
NORTHUMBERLAND STRAIT
NEW BRUNSWICK
NOVA SCOTIA
PRINCE EDWARD ISLAND NATIONAL PARK
Charlottetown
Summerside
Kensington
Montague
Georgetown
Souris
Tignish
Alberton
O'Leary
Borden
N. Rustico
Cavendish (Green Gables)
Sherwood
Parkdale
Southport
Hillsborough Bay
Bedeque Bay
Egmont Bay
Malpeque Bay
Cardigan Bay
Rollo Bay
North Pt.
East Pt.
West Pt.
Sackville
Baie Verte
Cape Tormentine
Longitude West of Greenwich
© C.S. HAMMOND & Co., Maplewood, N.J.

**Education (1980-81):** On Prince Edward Island, there are 70 public primary and secondary schools; 1,448 teachers; and 26,834 students. In 1980 full-time enrollment in one degree-granting university and two post-secondary non-university institutions was 1,988

**Value added in goods-producing industries (1978):** $229,980,000. Agriculture represented 22.9% of the total; construction, 33.8%; manufacturing, 27.6%; and fisheries, 10.2% **Leading manufacturing industries:** fish products, dairy products **Average industrial earnings (March 1982):** $276.65 per week **Cash receipts from farming operations (1980):** $141,507,000, with 31.8% derived from potatoes, 18.6% from cattle and calves, 14.1% from hogs, and 15.3% from dairy products **Per capita personal income (1979):** $6,057 **Unemployment (May 1982):** 15.1%

**Provincial Finances:** Estimated gross general revenue (fiscal year 1980-81): $342,000,000; estimated gross general expenditure, $336,000,000

**Daily Newspapers (1980):** 3 **Combined circulation:** 35,000 **Number of telephones in service (1980):** 67,000 **Homes with radios (1981):** 100% **Homes with TVs (1981):** 94.3%

**Hospital beds (1980-81):** 757 (5.3 beds per 1,000 population) **Physicians (Dec. 31, 1980):** 152 (population per physician, 816)

**Motor Vehicles (1980):** 68,750 **Residents per motor vehicle:** 1.8 **Motor vehicle deaths (1979):** 29

---

The great explorer Jacques Cartier, in 1534, was the first European to visit Prince Edward Island. The French called it Ile St. Jean and used the island as a fishery. When the British took over in 1758 most of the nearly 5,000 Acadians living there were deported. The British divided their newly won territory into lots which were granted to persons in Britain, largely Scots, who had a claim on the patronage of the Crown. Few of the new owners fulfilled their obligation to develop their holdings, however, and a century of struggle followed between tenant farmers and nonresident proprietors. It was resolved only after Confederation in 1873 when the Dominion government advanced $800,000 to the provincial government to buy out the landlords and resell the land to tenants. The development of Prince Edward Island was further delayed by its separation from Nova Scotia in 1769 by the British government. Despite the fact that an 1864 meeting in Charlottetown eventually led to the Canadian Confederation, ironically Prince Edward Island itself did not enter the Dominion until 1873.

The province has abundant good soil, and today agriculture remains a principal industry. However, farmers have become overly dependent on potatoes, a crop that generates 32% of total farm income. Silver fox farming originated on the island. From 1910 to 1940 the island was world-famous for the breed, which is now virtually extinct there. Although its isolation from the mainland has made the island increasingly attractive to tourists, it must import its energy needs and thus pays more for electricity and other power sources than any other province. A replica of the house from *Anne of Green Gables*, found in the Prince Edward Island National Park, is a favorite of travelers. Fort Amherst National Historic Park, at Rocky Point, contains earthworks of the fort built by the British after its capture from the French in 1758.

By the mid-1980s, the Ministry of Veterans Affairs is to be relocated to Charlottetown, thus becoming the first federal ministry to be transferred from Ottawa.

James M. Lee succeeded J. Angus MacLean as premier in 1981.

---

## QUEBEC

**Area:** 595,857 square miles **Population:** 6,438,403 (1981 census); population density, 10.8; urban, 79.1%; rural, 20.9% Capital: Québec **Major cities (Metropolitan areas as of 1981 census):** Montréal, 2,828,349; Québec, 576,075; Chicoutimi-Jonquière, 135,172, Laval, 268,335; Longueuil, 124,320; Montréal-Nord, 94,914; Sherbrooke, 115,983; Verdun, 61,287; La Salle, 76,299; Ste-Foy, 68,883; Hull, 56,225; St-Laurent, 65,900; Trois Rivières, 111,453; St-Léonard, 79,429

**Ethnic Composition:** French, 79%; British Isles, 11% **Religion:** Roman Catholic, 87%; United Church, 3%; Anglican, 3%

**Vital Statistics (per 1,000 population):** birthrate, 14.9 (1981); death rate, 6.7 (1981); marriage rate, 7.1 (1980); divorce rate, 2.2 (1980); infant mortality per 1,000 live births, 11.9

**Location and Geography:** The province's northern four-fifths lies in the Canadian Shield, a lake-dotted, partly wooded, rolling plateau. The St. Lawrence Lowlands have climate and soil well suited for general farming. The Appalachian region, south of the St. Lawrence River and including the Gaspé peninsula, is a succession of plateaus and plains, much of it arable and the remainder wooded

**Government:** Québec became a province in 1867 and is represented in the federal government by 75 members in the House of Commons and 24 Senators. The provincial government is unicameral with a National Assembly of 122 members. As of April 5, 1982, the standings in the legislature were: *Parti Québécois* 79, Liberals 43 **Prime Minister:** Honourable René Lévesque **Salary and allowance:** $88,221

**Education (1980-81):** In Quebec, there are 2,677 public primary and secondary schools; 73,000 teachers; and 1,083,580 students **Colleges:** Seven degree-granting universities and 83 post-secondary non-university institutions with a total enrollment of 221,526

**Value added in goods-producing industries (1978):** $22,272,497,000; manufacturing represented 65.7% of this total and construction, 18.5% **Value of manufactured shipments (1980):** $43,927,066,000, 26.5% of the national total **Leading manufacturing industries (1978):** pulp and paper, petroleum refining, dairy products, smelting and refining **Average industrial earnings (March 1982):** $377.83 per week **Mineral production (1980 prel. est.):** $2,501,085,000 **Cash Receipts from farming operations (1980):** $2,236,505,000; dairy products contributed 35.4%; hogs, 21.8%; cattle and calves, 11.4%; and poultry, 9.2% Families with incomes over $12,000: 78.8% **Per capita personal income (1979):** $8,341 **Unemployment (May 1982):** 13.8%

**Provincial Finances:** Estimated gross general revenue (fiscal year 1980-81): $17,534,000,000; estimated gross general expenditure, $19,044,000,000

**Daily newspapers:** 10 French language, three English **Combined Circulation (1980):** 1,144,100 **Telephones in service (1980):** 4,131,000 **Homes with radios (1981):** 99% **Homes with TVs (1981):** 98.8%

**Hospital beds (1980-81):** 49,035 (4.6 beds per 1,000 population) **Physicians (Dec. 31, 1980):** 12,160 (population per physician, 520)

**Motor vehicles (1980):** 3,787,433 **Residents per motor vehicle (1980):** 1.7 **Motor vehicle deaths (1979):** 1,718

---

It was at Quebec that Cartier landed in 1534, proclaiming French sovereignty. In 1608 Champlain established a settlement at the site of Quebec City, and by 1750 65,000 French-Canadian descendants of the original settlers inhabited the land around the St. Lawrence River. When New France, subject of the crown of France, was ceded to Britain in 1763, and the colony officially became the "province of Quebec," it was a land where French law, religion and custom were firmly entrenched. The confusion created by the co-existence of French-Canadian and British rule was somewhat resolved in 1774 by an act guaranteeing maintenance of French civil law and customs, freedom of worship and education, but the problem remains a source of great controversy to this day.

The French nationalist sentiment has become increasingly strident since the late 1950s. French-speaking Canadians have insisted on greater control of their province's industry and commerce, with demands of some that Quebec become a separate nation. In 1974, the legislature gave voice to the separatists' demands and established French as the province's official language.

In 1976 the separatist *Parti Québécois* (PQ) led by René Lévesque won a majority in the provincial assembly. Premier Lévesque promptly announced his government's intention to seek independence—a goal that thus far has proved elusive. In 1978

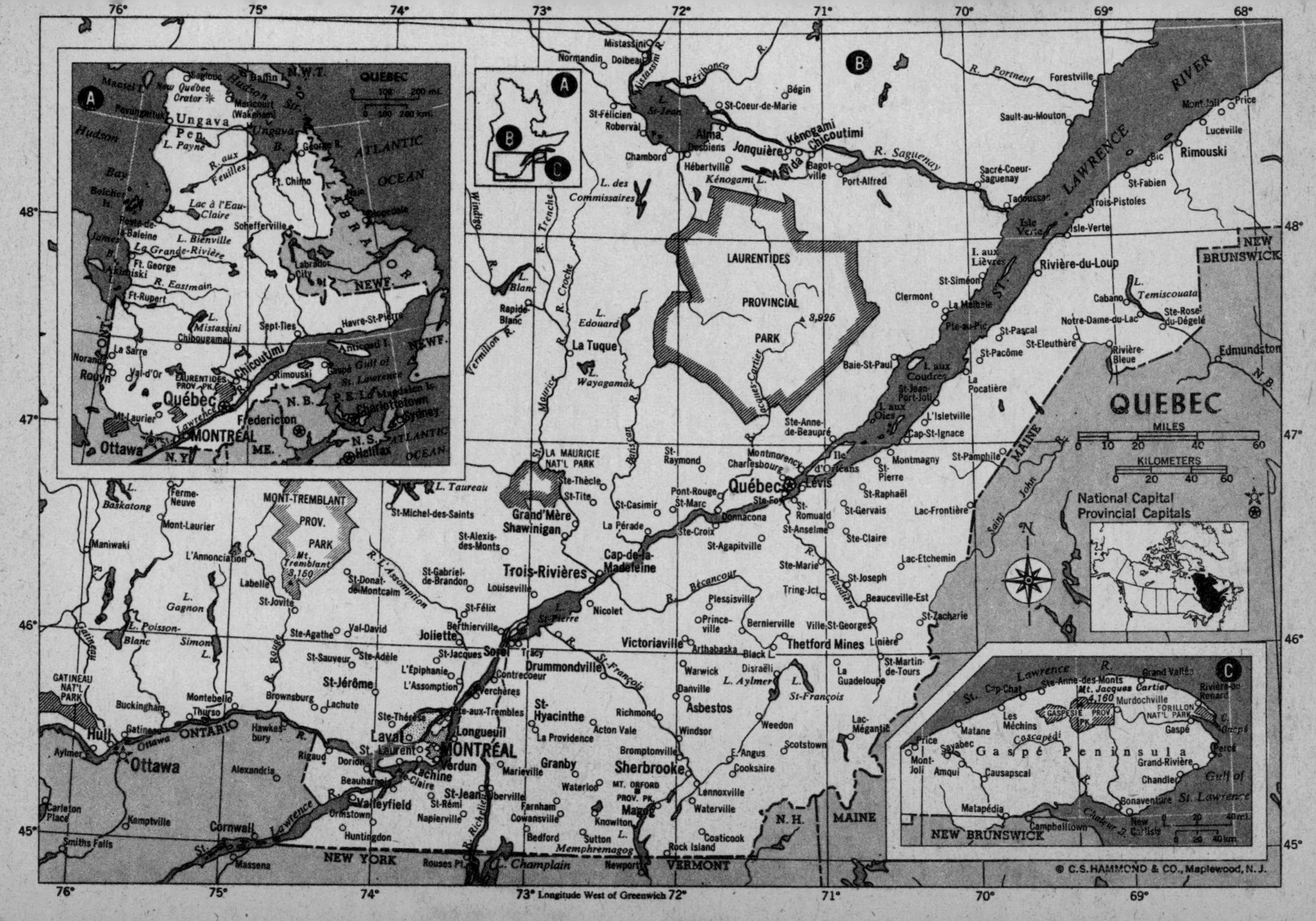
QUEBEC
MILES
KILOMETERS
National Capital
Provincial Capitals
ST. LAWRENCE RIVER
NEW BRUNSWICK
MAINE
N.H.
VERMONT
NEW YORK
ONTARIO
LAURENTIDES PROVINCIAL PARK
3,926
MONT-TREMBLANT PROV. PARK
Mt. Tremblant 3,150
LA MAURICIE NAT'L PARK
GATINEAU NAT'L PARK
MT. ORFORD PROV. PK.
Québec
Lévis
Montréal
Ottawa
Hull
Aylmer
Laval
Longueuil
St. Laurent
Verdun
Lachine
Valleyfield
St-Jean
Sherbrooke
Granby
St-Hyacinthe
Drummondville
Sorel
Joliette
St-Jérôme
Trois-Rivières
Cap-de-la-Madeleine
Shawinigan
Grand'Mère
La Tuque
Victoriaville
Thetford Mines
Asbestos
Chicoutimi
Kénogami
Jonquière
Alma
Roberval
Chambord
St-Félicien
Mistassini
Dolbeau
Normandin
Rivière-du-Loup
Rimouski
Mont-Joli
Price
Luceville
Bic
Trois-Pistoles
Isle-Verte
Tadoussac
Forestville
Sault-au-Mouton
Baie-St-Paul
La Malbaie
Montmagny
Edmundston
Lac-Mégantic
Magog
Coaticook
Cornwall
Hawkesbury
Buckingham
Maniwaki
Mont-Laurier
L. Témiscouata
L. St-Jean
R. Saguenay
L. Champlain
L. Memphremagog
Gaspé Peninsula
Gaspé
Percé
Gulf of St. Lawrence
Mt. Jacques Cartier 4,160
GASPÉSIE PROV. PK.
FORILLON NAT'L PARK
Hudson Bay
Ungava Pen.
LABRADOR
ATLANTIC OCEAN
73° Longitude West of Greenwich 72°
© C.S. HAMMOND & CO., Maplewood, N.J.

French was established as the primary language of government, education and legal record; however, the law subsequently was struck down by the federal Supreme Court. In May 1980 Quebecers, including a majority of the French-speakers, voted down by a 3-2 margin a PQ-sponsored referendum on a "sovereign-association" plan that would have given Quebec greater self-government while maintaining economic ties to the rest of the Canadian federation. With this setback, Lévesque called for a new Canadian constitution that would guarantee Quebec's right to self-determination. However, the new constitution agreed upon by the federal government and the English-speaking provinces in November 1981 proved unacceptable to Lévesque, who led 12,000 Quebecers in a demonstration through Montreal on April 17, 1982, the day Britain's Queen Elizabeth proclaimed the historic document in ceremonies at Ottawa.

In April 1981, the PQ won 80 of 122 seats in the provincial assembly and the right to govern for another five years; by-elections in April 1982 trimmed its majority to 79. Meanwhile Premier Lévesque urged his party to step up its separatist campaign. At a PQ special convention in February 1982, delegates reaffirmed the goal of eventual independence. The administration has also raised the possibility that an independent Quebec might join Canada, the U.S., and Mexico in a North American economic association.

## SASKATCHEWAN

**Area:** 251,699 square miles **Population:** 968,313 (1981 census); population density, 3.8; urban, 55.5%; rural, 44.5% **Capital:** Regina **Major cities (1981 census: Metropolitan areas):** Regina, 164,313; Saskatoon, 154,210

**Ethnic Composition:** British Isles, 42%; German, 19%; Ukrainian, 9%; Scandinavian, 6%; French, 6%; and Native Indian, 4% **Religion:** United Church, 30%; Roman Catholic, 28%; Lutheran, 10%; Anglican, 9%; Ukrainian Catholic, 4%; Mennonite, 3%

**Vital Statistics (per 1,000 population):** birthrate, 17.5 (1981); death rate, 7.4 (1981), marriage rate, 7.8 (1980); divorce rate, 1.9 (1980); infant mortality per 1,000 live births, 14.3 (1978)

**Location and Geography:** Situated between Manitoba and Alberta, the southern portion of the province consists of a rolling plain. The northern third begins the Canadian shield

**Government:** Saskatchewan became a province in 1905 and is represented in the federal government by 14 members in the House of Commons and six Senators. The provincial government is unicameral with a Legislative Assembly of 64 members. Present standings in the legislature: 55 Progressive Conservatives and 9 New Democrats **Premier:** Honourable Grant Devine **Salary and allowance:** $65,472

**Education (1980-81):** In Saskatchewan there are 964 public primary and secondary schools; 11,574 teachers; and 197,280 students **Colleges:** Three degree-granting universities and 3 community colleges, and technical and vocational institutes, with an enrollment of 16,270 (1980)

**Value added in goods-producing industries (1978 actual):** $4,537,325,000; agriculture represented 38.2% of this total, mining 26.8%, construction 18.6%, and manufacturing 12.5% **Value of Mineral Shipments (1980):** $2,290,347,000 **Leading manufacturing industries:** slaughtering and meat processing, agricultural implement industry, sawmills and planing mills, printing and publishing **Average industrial earnings (March 1982):** $359.93 per week **Cash receipts from farming operations (1980):** $3,149,267,000; with 55.3% derived from wheat, 18.3% from cattle and calves, and 4.4% from barley **Families with incomes over $10,000 (1979):** 78.2% **Per capita personal income (1979):** $8,335 **Unemployment (May 1982):** 5.5%

**Provincial Finances:** Estimated gross general revenue (fiscal year 1980-81): $2,670,000,000; estimated gross general expenditure, $2,438,000,000

**Daily newspapers (1980):** 5 **Combined circulation:** 161,500 **Telephones in service (1980):** 625,000 **Homes with radios (1981):** 99.1% **Homes with TVs (1981):** 97.5%

**Hospital beds (1980-81):** 7,747 (6.9 beds per 1,000 population) **Physicians (Dec. 31, 1980):** 1,442 (population per physician, 677)

**Motor Vehicles (1980):** 683,955 **Residents per motor vehicle (1980):** 1.4 **Motor vehicle deaths (1979):** 272

The first European to reach what is now Saskatchewan and to see the vast buffalo herds that roamed the central plains was Henry Kelsey, an agent of the Hudson's Bay Company. In 1690 he was sent into the Northwest to explore the vast territory and ensure the Company's fur supply by pacifying the Indians. For two centuries fur trading continued, and settlement only began in 1870 with the building of the railroad and the practice of homesteading.

Today the province has Canada's largest area of occupied agricultural land. Yet, after the disasters of the dust bowl of the 1930s, diversification has been a priority and now 65 percent of the province's gross product is from industry, only 35 percent from farming. Petroleum, mining and manufacturing are the major industries; farms are large and highly mechanized. Saskatchewan's potash deposits are the world's largest.

In April 1982, the Progressive Conservative party, led by Grant Devine, won 55 of 64 seats in the provincial assembly, ousting the socialist New Democratic party after 11 years of rule.

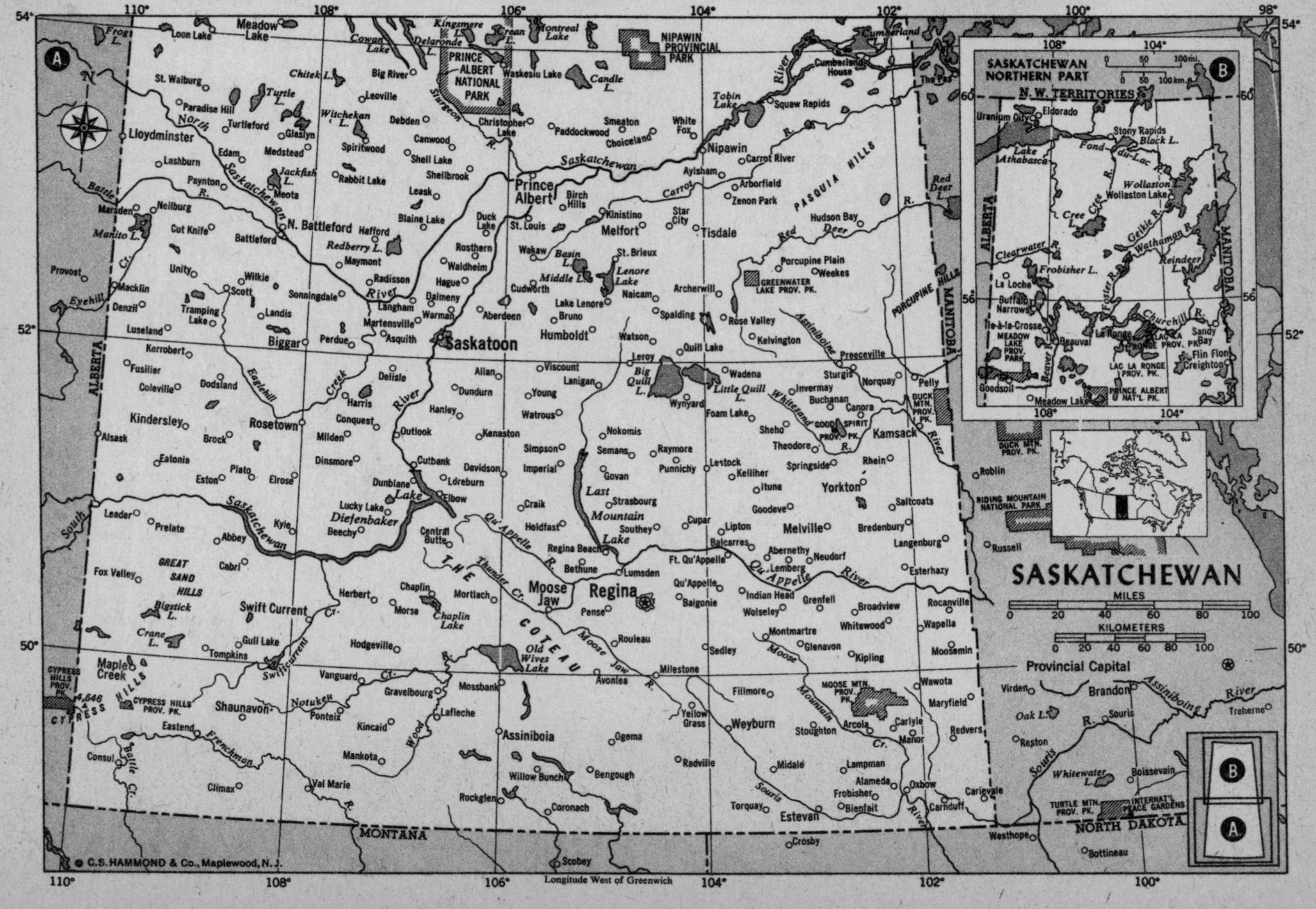
SASKATCHEWAN
MILES
KILOMETERS
Provincial Capital
SASKATCHEWAN NORTHERN PART
N. W. TERRITORIES
ALBERTA
MANITOBA
MONTANA
NORTH DAKOTA
Regina
Saskatoon
Prince Albert
Moose Jaw
Swift Current
Yorkton
Lloydminster
N. Battleford
PRINCE ALBERT NATIONAL PARK
NIPAWIN PROVINCIAL PARK
Longitude West of Greenwich
© C.S. HAMMOND & Co., Maplewood, N.J.

## PRINCIPAL CANADIAN AGRICULTURAL CROPS Source: Statistics Canada

| | Area in Acres | | Yield per Acre | | Total Production | |
|---|---|---|---|---|---|---|
| | 1980 | 1981 | 1980 | 1981 | 1980 | 1981 |
| | | | Bushels | | Bushels | |
| Winter wheat | 680,000 | 750,000 | 48.0 | 49.9 | 32,642,000 | 37,400,000 |
| Spring wheat | 23,642,200 | 25,622,000 | 25.4 | 29.7 | 599,907,000 | 759,955,000 |
| Durum wheat | 3,100,000 | 3,850,000 | 23.0 | 26.9 | 71,400,000 | 103,600,000 |
| All wheat | 27,422,200 | 30,222,000 | 25.7 | 29.8 | 703,949,000 | 900,955,000 |
| Oats for grain | 3,742,000 | 4,337,000 | 52.5 | 53.4 | 196,317,000 | 231,509,000 |
| Barley for grain | 11,453,000 | 13,320,000 | 45.2 | 46.1 | 517,104,000 | 614,708,000 |
| Fall rye | 719,000 | 1,045,000 | 23.2 | 34.6 | 16,654,000 | 36,153,000 |
| Spring rye | 47,000 | 67,000 | 21.1 | 26.4 | 990,000 | 1,770,000 |
| All rye | 766,000 | 1,112,400 | 23.0 | 34.1 | 17,644,000 | 37,923,000 |
| Mixed grains | 1,431,600 | 1,437,000 | 56.4 | 53.2 | 80,778,000 | 76,399,000 |
| Flaxseed | 1,420,000 | 1,150,000 | 12.9 | 16.3 | 18,300,000 | 18,800,000 |
| Rapeseed | 5,140,000 | 3,580,000 | 21.3 | 22.1 | 109,500,000 | 79,150,000 |
| Corn for grain | 2,367,500 | 2,614,000 | 90.4 | 93.6 | 213,920,000 | 244,648,000 |
| Buckwheat | 118,500 | 116,000 | 10.6 | 17.5 | 1,259,000 | 2,035,000 |
| Peas, dry | 122,000 | 125,000 | 22.9 | 28.4 | 2,790,000 | 3,550,000 |
| Soybeans | 700,000 | 710,000 | 37.4 | 32.7 | 26,204,000 | 23,200,000 |
| | | | Cwt | | | |
| Beans, dry, white | 95,000 | 100,000 | 16.3 | 12.3 | 1,550,000 | 1,230,000 |
| | | | Pounds | | | |
| Mustard seed | 229,000 | 186,000 | 873.0 | 978.0 | 200,000,000 | 182,000,000 |
| Sunflower seed | 338,000 | 299,000 | 1,083.0 | 1,286.0 | 366,000,000 | 384,400,000 |
| | | | Tons | | | |
| Tame hay | 13,534,000 | 13,405,000 | 1.93 | 2.18 | 26,179,000 | 29,204,000 |
| Fodder corn | 1,202,200 | 1,130,300 | 13.10 | 13.62 | 15,749,000 | 15,396,000 |
| Sugar beets | 65,430 | 72,610 | 14.84 | 18.38 | 971,100 | 1,334,000 |

## CANADA: PRINCIPAL TRADE PARTNERS Source: Statistics Canada

| | EXPORTS ($000,000 in Canadian dollars) | | | | IMPORTS ($000,000 in Canadian dollars) | | |
|---|---|---|---|---|---|---|---|
| Country | 1980 | 1979 | 1978 | Country | 1980 | 1979 | 1978 |
| United States | 46,825 | 43,439 | 36,455 | United States | 48,414 | 45,420 | 35,246 |
| Japan | 4,370 | 4,077 | 3,052 | Japan | 2,792 | 2,157 | 2,268 |
| United Kingdom | 3,192 | 2,589 | 1,985 | Saudi Arabia | 2,446 | 1,242 | 749 |
| Germany, West | 1,637 | 1,368 | 782 | Venezuela | 2,190 | 1,505 | 1,283 |
| USSR | 1,535 | 763 | 567 | United Kingdom | 1,971 | 1,929 | 1,600 |
| Netherlands | 1,428 | 1,082 | 563 | Germany, West | 1,449 | 1,556 | 1,244 |
| France | 997 | 620 | 460 | France | 770 | 778 | 684 |
| Belgium/Luxembourg | 987 | 668 | 475 | Italy | 610 | 636 | 525 |
| Italy | 981 | 729 | 481 | Hong Kong | 574 | 427 | 332 |
| Brazil | 893 | 422 | 417 | China, Rep. of | 557 | 522 | 397 |
| China, People's Rep. | 866 | 596 | 503 | Switzerland | 521 | 323 | 285 |
| Australia | 663 | 557 | 412 | Australia | 507 | 466 | 350 |
| Venezuela | 653 | 671 | 686 | Sweden | 415 | 383 | 325 |
| Korea, South | 504 | 364 | 216 | Korea, South | 414 | 463 | 363 |
| Mexico | 483 | 236 | 229 | South Africa | 350 | 240 | 149 |
| Cuba | 415 | 257 | 218 | Brazil | 348 | 313 | 248 |
| Algeria | 393 | 215 | — | Mexico | 345 | 208 | 185 |
| Switzerland | 373 | 184 | — | Netherlands | 262 | 252 | 227 |
| India | 348 | 226 | — | Iraq | 254 | 74 | — |
| Poland | 346 | 262 | 224 | Belgium/Luxembourg | 251 | 241 | 202 |

## SALARIES OF SENIOR MEMBERS OF HOUSE OF COMMONS

| Position | Sessional Allowance | Expense Allowance | Salary | Total |
|---|---|---|---|---|
| Prime Minister | $46,400 | $15,500 | $53,000 | $114,900 |
| Cabinet Ministers and Leaders of Opposition in the House of Commons | 46,400 | 15,500 | 35,600 | 97,500 |
| Members of Parliament | 46,400 | 15,500* | — | 61,900* |

*Certain members for larger northern constituencies have larger expense allowances.

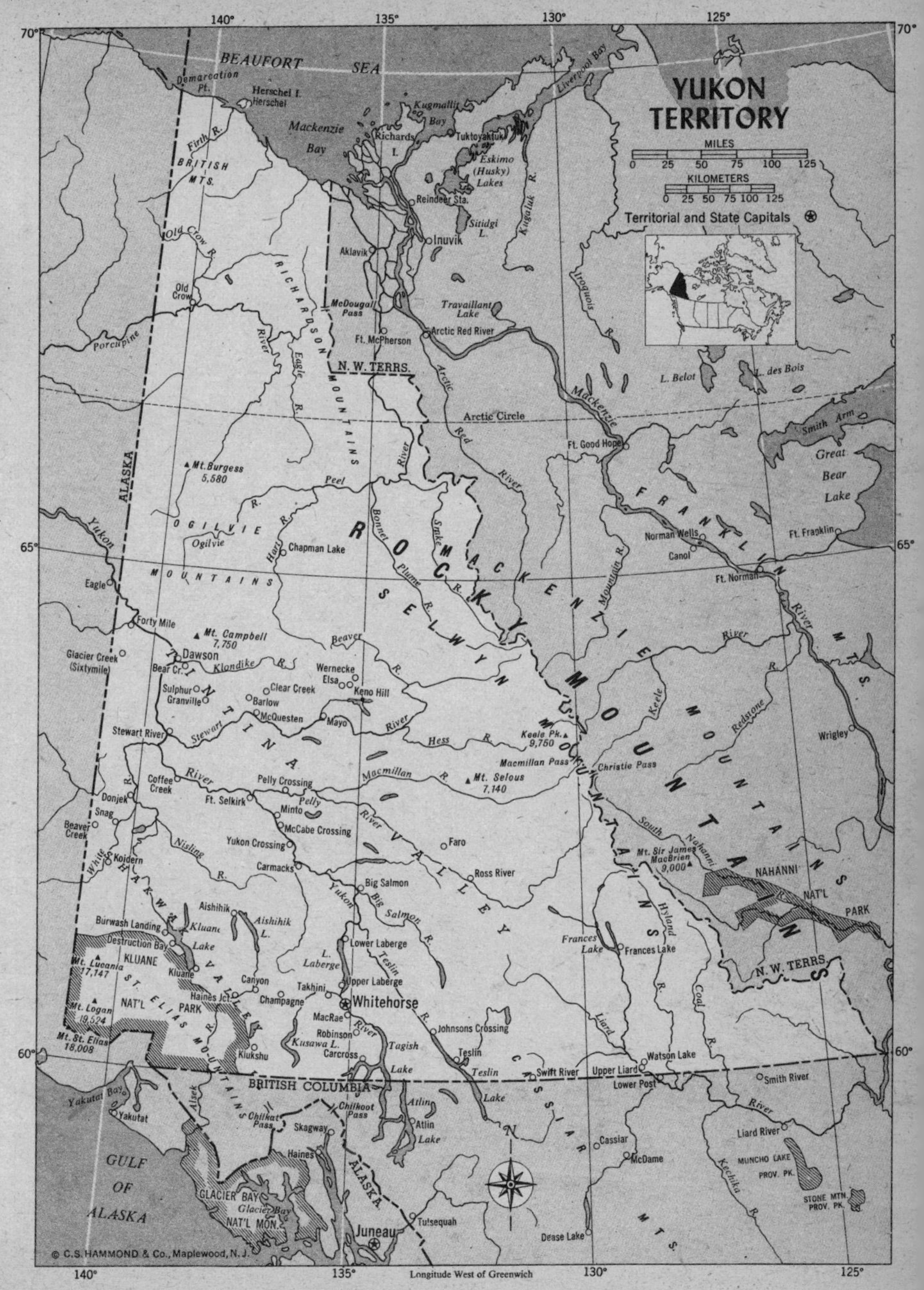
YUKON TERRITORY
MILES
0 25 50 75 100 125
KILOMETERS
0 25 50 75 100 125
Territorial and State Capitals
BEAUFORT SEA
Mackenzie Bay
Demarcation Pt.
Herschel I.
Herschel
Richards I.
Kugmallit Bay
Tuktoyaktuk
Liverpool Bay
Eskimo (Husky) Lakes
Reindeer Sta.
Sitidgi L.
Kugaluk R.
Inuvik
Aklavik
Firth R.
BRITISH MTS.
Old Crow R.
Old Crow
RICHARDSON MOUNTAINS
McDougall Pass
Travaillant Lake
Ft. McPherson
Arctic Red River
Porcupine
River
Eagle R.
N. W. TERRS.
Iroquois R.
L. Belot
L. des Bois
Mackenzie
Arctic Circle
Arctic Red River
Smith Arm
Great Bear Lake
Ft. Good Hope
ALASKA
Mt. Burgess 5,580
Peel R.
Bonnet Plume R.
Snake R.
OGILVIE MOUNTAINS
Ogilvie
Hart R.
Chapman Lake
ROCKY
MACKENZIE MOUNTAINS
FRANKLIN MTS.
Norman Wells
Canol
Ft. Franklin
Ft. Norman
Mountain R.
Yukon
Eagle
Forty Mile
Mt. Campbell 7,750
SELWYN
Glacier Creek (Sixtymile)
Dawson
Bear Cr.
Klondike R.
Beaver R.
Wernecke
Elsa
Keno Hill
Clear Creek
Sulphur
Granville
Barlow
McQuesten
Mayo
Stewart River
Stewart
River
Hess R.
Keele Pk. 9,750
Macmillan Pass
Christie Pass
Keele
Redstone
Wrigley
TINTINA
Coffee Creek
River
Pelly Crossing
Macmillan R.
Mt. Selous 7,140
Donjek
Snag
Beaver Creek
Ft. Selkirk
Pelly
Minto
River
McCabe Crossing
Yukon Crossing
Faro
Nisling
South Nahanni
Mt. Sir James MacBrien 9,000
NAHANNI NAT'L PARK
White
Koidern
Carmacks
R.
VALLEY
Ross River
Big Salmon
SHAKWAK
Aishihik
Aishihik L.
Yukon
Big Salmon R.
Hyland R.
Frances Lake
Frances Lake
Burwash Landing
Kluane Lake
Destruction Bay
Mt. Lucania 17,147
KLUANE NAT'L PARK
Kluane
L. Laberge
Lower Laberge
Teslin
N. W. TERRS.
Coal R.
Mt. Logan 19,524
ST. ELIAS MOUNTAINS
Canyon
Haines Jct.
Champagne
Takhini
Upper Laberge
Whitehorse
Johnsons Crossing
Liard
Mt. St. Elias 18,008
MacRae
Robinson
Kusawa L.
Carcross
Tagish Lake
River
Teslin
Klukshu
Teslin Lake
Swift River
CASSIAR MTS.
Upper Liard
Watson Lake
Lower Post
Smith River
BRITISH COLUMBIA
Yakutat Bay
Yakutat
Alsek
Chilkat Pass
Chilkoot Pass
Skagway
Atlin
Atlin Lake
Cassiar
River
Liard River
GULF OF ALASKA
Haines
ALASKA
McDame
MUNCHO LAKE PROV. PK.
Kechika R.
GLACIER BAY
Glacier Bay
NAT'L MON.
Tulsequah
STONE MTN. PROV. PK.
Juneau
Dease Lake
© C.S. HAMMOND & Co., Maplewood, N.J.
Longitude West of Greenwich
140° 135° 130° 125°
70° 65° 60°

NORTHWEST TERRITORIES
MILES
0 50 100 200 300 400
KILOMETERS
0 50 100 200 300 400
State and Territorial Capitals
All islands in Hudson and James Bays lie within the District of Keewatin.
Longitude West 100° of Greenwich
© C.S. HAMMOND & Co., Maplewood, N.J.
ARCTIC OCEAN
GREENLAND
(KALÂTDLIT-NUNÂT)
(Denmark)
QUEEN ELIZABETH ISLANDS
SVERDRUP IS.
PARRY ISLANDS
Beaufort Sea
Baffin Bay
Davis Strait
Hudson Strait
Hudson Bay
FRANKLIN
Baffin Island
DISTRICT OF KEEWATIN
DISTRICT OF MACKENZIE
DISTRICT Victoria Island
MACKENZIE MTS.
YUKON TERR.
ALASKA
UNITED STATES
BROOKS RA.
BRITISH COLUMBIA
ALBERTA
SASKATCHEWAN
MANITOBA
QUEBEC
Ungava Peninsula
Banks I.
Ellesmere Island
Devon I.
Great Bear Lake
Great Slave Lake
Yellowknife
Whitehorse
Juneau
Arctic Circle

## CANADIAN IMPORTS BY LEADING COMMODITIES

SOURCE: Statistics Canada

($000,000 in Canadian dollars)

| | 1981* | 1980 | 1979 |
|---|---|---|---|
| Motor vehicles and parts | 15,956.1 | 13,478.6 | 15,160.9 |
| Other equipment tools | 9,947.9 | 8,078.1 | 6,998.4 |
| Crude petroleum | 7,839.7 | 6,919.1 | 4,497.2 |
| Food, feed, beverages and tobacco | 4,982.2 | 4,689.7 | 4,161.0 |
| Special industry machinery | 4,573.6 | 4,330.2 | 3,440.6 |
| Chemicals | 3,813.8 | 3,354.2 | 3,240.3 |
| General purpose machinery | 2,721.0 | 2,420.6 | 2,250.0 |
| Agricultural machinery and tractors | 2,395.8 | 2,092.0 | 2,115.1 |
| Electronic computers | 2,328.1 | 1,652.8 | 1,103.5 |
| Iron and steel | 2,275.8 | 1,414.8 | 1,668.8 |
| Non-ferrous metals | 2,196.3 | 2,578.7 | 1,923.7 |
| Metal ores, concentrates and scrap | 1,877.8 | 2,125.0 | 1,130.2 |
| Fruits and vegetables | 1,802.1 | 1,497.6 | 1,462.0 |
| Textiles | 1,425.6 | 1,275.5 | 1,390.7 |
| Aircraft, with engines | 1,252.7 | 860.4 | 679.4 |
| Wood and paper | 1,173.6 | 918.3 | 974.8 |
| Special transactions, trade | 929.7 | 763.0 | 566.7 |
| Coal | 833.7 | 811.2 | 865.0 |
| Machine tools, metalworking | 719.3 | 539.5 | 338.5 |
| Meat and fish | 688.8 | 662.0 | 667.6 |
| Raw sugar | 469.4 | 499.5 | 236.2 |

*Ranked by value.

## CANADIAN EXPORTS BY LEADING COMMODITIES

SOURCE: Statistics Canada

($000,000 in Canadian dollars)

| | 1981* | 1980 | 1979 |
|---|---|---|---|
| Motor vehicles and parts | 13,071.5 | 10,818.5 | 11,899.7 |
| Wood and paper | 12,630.6 | 12,457.9 | 11,620.8 |
| Food, feed, beverages and tobacco | 9,207.0 | 7,960.8 | 6,068.6 |
| Non-ferrous metals | 5,417.4 | 6,070.0 | 3,652.4 |
| Cereals and preparations | 5,327.8 | 4,793.7 | 3,075.9 |
| Chemicals | 4,639.6 | 4,054.7 | 3,321.8 |
| Natural gas | 4,370.1 | 3,983.8 | 2,889.1 |
| Newsprint paper | 4,326.2 | 3,681.9 | 3,221.8 |
| Metal ores, concentrates and scrap | 4,082.5 | 4,209.1 | 3,894.6 |
| Wood pulp and similar pulp | 3,820.3 | 3,870.4 | 3,083.3 |
| Wheat | 3,723.4 | 3,795.7 | 2,180.3 |
| Lumber, softwood | 2,913.2 | 3,262.9 | 3,820.8 |
| Industrial machinery | 2,735.6 | 2,175.8 | 1,949.0 |
| Petroleum and coal products | 2,642.0 | 2,324.3 | 1,885.3 |
| Crude petroleum | 2,505.0 | 2,899.1 | 2,404.6 |
| Iron and steel | 2,316.8 | 2,039.1 | 1,598.6 |
| Other equipment and tools | 2,307.5 | 1,974.6 | 1,746.7 |
| Meat and fish | 2,111.6 | 1,765.8 | 1,719.9 |
| Fertilizers and fertilizer materials | 1,343.2 | 1,253.8 | 987.3 |
| Agricultural machinery and tractors | 884.6 | 876.0 | 847.7 |
| Nickel and alloys | 694.5 | 818.5 | 576.3 |
| Copper and alloys | 688.8 | 999.0 | 612.6 |
| Special transactions, trade | 670.7 | 228.1 | 166.2 |
| Textiles | 266.6 | 233.9 | 177.8 |

*Ranked by value.

## CANADA: POPULATION, 1851-1981

SOURCE: Statistics Canada

| | 1851 | 1871 | 1891 | 1931 | 1951 | 1971 | 1981 |
|---|---|---|---|---|---|---|---|
| Newfoundland | — | — | — | — | 361,416 | 522,104 | 567,681 |
| Prince Edward Island | 62,678[1] | 94,021 | 109,078 | 88,038 | 98,429 | 111,641 | 122,506 |
| Nova Scotia | 276,854 | 387,800 | 450,396 | 512,846 | 642,584 | 788,960 | 847,442 |
| New Brunswick | 193,800 | 285,594 | 321,263 | 408,219 | 515,697 | 634,557 | 696,403 |
| Quebec | 890,261 | 1,191,516 | 1,488,535 | 2,874,662 | 4,055,681 | 6,027,764 | 6,438,403 |
| Ontario | 952,004 | 1,620,851 | 2,114,321 | 3,431,683 | 4,597,542 | 7,703,106 | 8,625,107 |
| Manitoba | — | 25,228 | 152,560 | 700,139 | 776,541 | 988,247 | 1,026,241 |
| Saskatchewan | — | — | —[2] | 921,785 | 831,728 | 926,242 | 968,313 |
| Alberta | — | — | —[2] | 731,605 | 939,501 | 1,627,874 | 2,237,724 |
| British Columbia | 55,000 | 36,247 | 98,173 | 694,263 | 1,165,210 | 2,184,621 | 2,744,467 |
| Yukon | — | — | — | 4,230 | 9,096 | 18,388 | 23,153 |
| Northwest Territory | 5,700 | 48,000 | 98,967 | 9,316 | 16,004 | 34,807 | 45,741 |
| Total Canada | 2,436,297 | 3,689,257 | 4,833,239 | 10,376,786 | 14,009,429 | 21,568,311 | 24,343,181 |

[1]1848 figure. [2]Included with the Northwest Territories.

## LARGEST CANADIAN CITIES

SOURCE: Statistics Canada

| | 1851 | 1901 | 1951 | 1961 | 1971 | 1976 | 1981 |
|---|---|---|---|---|---|---|---|
| Calgary, Alberta | — | 4,091 | 129,060 | 249,641 | 403,343* | 471,397 | 592,743 |
| Edmonton, Alberta | — | — | 159,631 | 218,027 | 438,152 | 461,594 | 532,246 |
| Halifax, Nova Scotia | 20,740 | 40,832 | 85,589 | 92,511 | 122,035 | 117,882 | 114,594 |
| Hamilton, Ontario | 14,112 | 52,634 | 208,321 | 273,991 | 309,173 | 312,003 | 306,434 |
| London, Ontario | — | 37,981 | 95,343 | 169,569 | 223,222 | 240,412 | 254,280 |
| Montreal, Quebec | 57,715 | 267,730 | 1,021,520 | 1,191,062 | 1,214,352 | 1,080,546 | 980,354 |
| Ottawa, Ontario | — | 59,928 | 202,045 | 268,206 | 302,341 | 304,462 | 295,163 |
| Quebec, Quebec | 42,052 | 68,840 | 164,016 | 171,979 | 187,833* | 177,082 | 166,474 |
| Regina, Saskatchewan | — | — | 71,319 | 112,141 | 139,479* | 149,608 | 162,613 |
| Saint John, N.B. | 22,745 | 40,711 | 50,779 | 55,153 | 89,039 | 85,956 | 80,521 |
| St. John's, Newfoundland | — | — | 52,873 | 63,533 | 88,414* | 86,653 | 83,770 |
| Toronto, Ontario | 30,775 | 208,040 | 675,754 | 672,407 | 712,786 | 633,318 | 599,217 |
| Vancouver, British Columbia | — | 26,133 | 344,833 | 384,522 | 426,298* | 409,734 | 414,281 |
| Windsor, Ontario | — | 12,153 | 120,049 | 114,367 | 203,300 | 196,526 | 192,083 |
| Winnipeg, Manitoba | — | 42,340 | 235,710 | 265,429 | 504,150* | 560,874 | 564,473 |

*Revised, based on 1976 areas.

# WORLD NATIONS

## AFGHANISTAN

**Area:** 250,775 sq. mi. **Population:** 13,051,358 (1979 census—excl. approx. 2,500,000 nomads)

**Official Name:** Democratic Republic of Afghanistan **Capital:** Kabul **Nationality:** Afghan **Languages:** Pushtu, spoken by the Pathans, and Dari, a Persian dialect spoken by the Tajiks, are official languages **Religion:** About 99% of the population are Moslems, most of whom belong to the Sunni sect **Flag:** Three equal horizontal stripes of black, red and green with the national coat of arms set near the hoist at the intersection of the black and red stripes **Anthem:** National Anthem (no words) **Currency:** Afghani (50.6 per U.S. $1)

**Location:** Central Asia. Landlocked Afghanistan is bordered by the USSR on the north, China on the extreme northeast, Pakistan on the east and south, and Iran on the west **Features:** The towering Hindu Kush range and its parallel extensions run through the center of the country from northeast to southwest. Mountains and desert country are interspersed by small, fertile valleys irrigated by snow-fed mountain streams **Chief Rivers:** Helmand, Farah Rud, Hari Rud, Khulm, Amu Darya

**Head of State and Government:** President Babrak Karmal, born 1929, named head of state, prime minister, Chairman of the Revolutionary Council and General Secretary of the People's Democratic party, following the Soviet-backed coup of December 1979. On June 11, 1981, Karmal relinquished the post of Prime Minister and turned it over to Sultan Ali Kishtmand **Effective Date of Present Constitution:** April 1980 (provisional constitution) **Legislative Body:** Revolutionary Council of 57 members. The Loya Jirgah (Supreme Council) is to be elected under the terms of the provisional constitution of 1980 **Local Government:** 26 provinces, each headed by a governor

**Ethnic Composition:** The Pathans (Pushtus) make up about half the total population; the rest is made up largely of Tajiks, Uzbeks, Hazara, and Turkmen **Population Distribution:** 15% urban **Density:** 52 inhabitants per sq. mi.

**Largest Cities:** (1979 census) Kabul 913,164, Kandahar 178,409, Herat 140,323, Mazar-e-Sharif 103,372

**Per Capita Income:** $207 (1980) **Gross National Product (GNP):** $3.1 billion (1980) **Economic Statistics:** about 53% of GNP comes from agriculture (wheat, corn, fruit, nuts, barley, rice, cotton, sugar beets and cane) and animal husbandry (sheep, cattle, goats); 16% from trade and services; 11% from industry and handicrafts (textiles, cement, flour, sugar, fruit processing, hand-woven carpets); 20% from other activities **Minerals and Mining:** Fields of natural gas in northern Afghanistan are being developed with Soviet assistance. There are large coal deposits; known deposits of iron ore, chromite and beryl are unexploited; lapis lazuli of world-renowned quality is produced. Hydroelectricity is an important source of energy **Labor Force:** 5,000,000 (1980), with 68% in agriculture, and 10% in industry **Foreign Trade:** Exports, chiefly fruit, karakul skins, natural gas, wool and carpets, totaled $322 million in 1979. Imports, mainly textiles, used clothing, petroleum products, tea, tires, thread, sugar and medicine, totaled $420 million **Principal Trade Partners:** USSR, Japan, West Germany, Britain, India, Pakistan, Czechoslovakia

**Vital Statistics:** Birthrate, 45.2 per 1,000 of pop. (1978); death rate, 21.1 **Life Expectancy:** 40.3 years **Health Statistics:** 5,879 inhabitants per hospital bed (1976); 28,313 per physician (1974) **Illiteracy:** 88% **Infant Mortality:** 185 per 1,000 births **Primary and Secondary School Enrollment:** 1,168,095 (1980) **Enrollment in Higher Education:** 13,797 (1980) **GNP Expended on Education:** 1.3% (1974)

**Transportation:** Paved roads total 1,900 mi. (1975) **Motor Vehicles:** 60,436 (1980) **Passenger Cars:** 31,722 **Railway Mileage:** None **Ports:** None **Major Airlines:** Ariana Afghan Airlines operates international flights **Communications: Radio Transmitters:** 8 **Receivers:** 823,000 (1977) **Television Stations:** 1 **Telephones:** 31,000 (1978) **Newspapers:** 17 dailies, 4 per 1,000 inhabitants (1977)

**Weights and Measures:** Metric system and local units are used **Travel Requirements:** The U.S. Government advises against travel to Afghanistan (1980)

Divided by tribal loyalties and the country's mountainous terrain, many in Afghanistan live now as their forefathers did: as herdsmen, nomads, and farmers. The cities, especially the capital, Kabul, show tentative signs of modernity, but the gap between the way urban and rural Afghans live and think has long been a major problem in attempts to consolidate the national mosaic.

Afghanistan's modern history has seen tribal rebellions, bloody royal successions and military coups, but no foreign interference ever had resulted in virtually total conquest until the Soviet Union invaded in late December 1979, and quickly became an occupying force—beset, however, by guerrilla resistance in the countryside.

King Mohammed Zahir Shah, who succeeded his assassinated father in 1933 at the age of 19, was a near-prisoner of relatives for years. He did not assume full governmental powers until 1963. Zahir attempted to introduce reforms and presented his people with the first democratic constitution in 1964. Lasting political changes did not take place, however, and a two-year drought in 1971-72 brought an already poor economy to a crisis condition, sealing the fate of the monarchy.

In July 1973 a group of young military officers deposed the king and proclaimed a republic. The leader of the coup, Lt. Gen. Mohammad Daud Khan, a cousin of the king and a former prime minister (1953-1963), became both president and prime minister of the new republic. The constitution of 1964 was put aside and rule by decree instituted. In April 1978 President Daud, members of his family and some 100 police officers and other officials were among an undetermined number who were killed as leftist military elements overthrew the government in two days of fierce fighting in Kabul. The rebels set up a Revolutionary Council to run the country by decree and installed a civilian, Nur Mohammad Taraki, general secretary of the Marxist Khalq Party, as president and prime minister of what became "the Democratic Republic of Aghanistan." On Dec. 5, Taraki signed a 20-year Afghan-USSR friendship treaty in Moscow.

Protesting the Taraki government's atheistic policies, village tribesmen began sporadic attacks on government forces in 1978. Without forming a united front, fervent but poorly armed Moslem bands gained control of an estimated 22 of the country's 28 provinces in 1979. In Herat, Moslems and defecting troops rioted in March and killed hundreds of loyal troops; a government response with helicopter gunships caused an estimated 20,000 deaths in the city.

The Revolutionary Council named Hafizulla Amin as prime minister in March 1979; six months later, in a shootout that took 60 lives at Kabul's People's House, Taraki was apparently slain and Amin became president. But in a Dec. 27 coup backed by Soviet troops, Babrak Karmal, back from exile in Eastern Europe, was installed as head of state, and Amin was executed for "crimes against the people." A 3½-hour battle preceded the takeover of Radio Kabul by the Soviets.

By the start of 1980 the Soviet troops had fanned out to control towns, passes, and key roads throughout the country, but many thousands of Moslem "holy warriors," or *mujahidin*—organized into some 60 guerrilla groups—established effective resistance.

By 1981, the nation's gross national product had declined by more than two thirds. As the Soviets destroyed food stores, the rebels began to shift the focus of their operations from the countryside to the towns, for a time even holding Kandahar,

Afghanistan's second-largest city. In the spring of 1982, the resistance, though disunited, appeared as persistent as ever, mounting several major attacks with a few miles of Kabul. With defections having reduced the Afghan army to a third of its 1979 complement of 100,000, defense of the regime devolved more and more on Soviet troops.

**HISTORY:** Afghanistan has suffered invasions from east and west—by Persians, Greeks, Mongols, and Turks. Among the foreign conquerors was Alexander the Great, in the 4th century B.C. After him came the independent kingdom of Bactria, which lasted until the middle of the 2nd century B.C. Buddhism spread from the east but was superseded by Islam in the 7th century A.D., after which several Moslem kingdoms were set up

**11th cent.:** Mahmud of Ghazni, an Afghan Moslem, forms kingdom stretching from Caspian Sea to the Ganges River

**13th cent.:** Genghis Khan and his hordes overrun the country

**18th cent.:** Persians under Nadir Shah conquer Afghanistan; after Nadir's death in 1747, Ahmad Shah unifies the country for the first time and sets up the Durrani dynasty

**1838-42:** Attempts by Emir Dost Mohammed to exploit Anglo-Russian rivalry in central Asia and to seize control of British possessions in India lead to first Afghan War, which ends with British withdrawal from Afghanistan

**1878-80:** Dost Mohammed's son, Shere Ali, turns to Russia for aid, setting off second Afghan War with Britain; Shere Ali is ousted and replaced by Anglophile Abd ur-Rahman

**1907:** Anglo-Russian agreement guarantees independence of Afghanistan under British influence

**1926-29:** Afghanistan becomes kingdom, with Amanullah as first king; he attempts to modernize the country but ultra-conservative elements force him to abdicate

**1930-33:** His successor, Mohammed Nadir Shah, continues reforms until killed; Mohammed Zahir Shah becomes king

**1964-65:** A new, liberal constitution goes iito effect and parliamentary elections are held for the first time

**1973:** King Mohammed Zahir Shah is overthrown by brother-in-law, General Mohammad Daud Khan; Daud proclaims Afghanistan a republic, declares himself president and prime minister

**1974:** Daud and Brezhnev sign a joint statement of interest in a collective Asian security system

**1975:** Daud nationalizes all banks and land reform laws are announced. Increased foreign aid is received

**1978:** Daud killed as leftist military coup succeeds; Nur Mohammad Taraki becomes president and prime minister. Rural Moslem conservatives begin guerrilla warfare

**1979:** U.S. Ambassador Adolph Dubs, kidnapped by rebels, is killed in a rescue attempt by government security officers. Hafizullah Amin becomes prime minister in March and advances to president in a coup on Sept. 16, when Taraki reportedly is killed. In a Dec. 27 coup, Babrak Karmal becomes head of state, and Amin is executed. Soviet troops, airlifted into Kabul, win a battle for Radio Kabul, which announces the coup

**1980:** Soviet troops occupy the country, but a widespread guerrilla resistance arises. Economy declines precipitously

**1982:** Guerrillas remain active in and near Kabul and in remote regions. Soviet troop commitment estimated at 85,000

## ALBANIA

**Area:** 11,100 sq. mi. **Population:** 2,591,000 (1979 census)

**Official Name:** People's Socialist Republic of Albania **Capital:** Tirana **Nationality:** Albanian **Languages:** Albanians are divided into two main language groups: Gheg, north of the river Shkumbi, and Tosk in the south. The official language is based on Tosk. Greek is spoken by the Greek minority in the south **Religion:** 50% Moslem, 20% Orthodox, 10% Roman Catholic. In 1967, however, all religious institutions were closed by the government **Flag:** A red field, with a double-headed black eagle and a gold-edged, five-pointed star above it **Anthem:** Anthem of the Flag **Currency:** Lek (7 per U.S. $1)

**Location:** Southeast Europe, on the west coast of the Balkan peninsula. Albania is bordered on the north and east by Yugoslavia, on the south by Greece, and on the west by the Adriatic Sea **Features:** About 20% of the country consists of a flat-to-rolling coastal plain. Most of the country, however, consists of hills and mountains, frequently covered with scrub forest **Chief Rivers:** Drin, Mat, Shkumbi, Semun, Vijosë

**Political Leader:** First Secretary of the Albanian (Communist) Party of Labor: Enver Hoxha, born 1908; in power since 1945 as First Secretary of the Central Committee **Head of State:** Chairman of the Presidium of the People's Assembly: Haxhi Lleshi, born 1913, reelected by People's Assembly 1978 **Head of Government:** Chairman of the Council of Ministers (premier): Adil Carcani, appointed 1982 **Effective Date of Present Constitution:** 1977 **Legislative Body:** People's Assembly (unicameral), consisting of 250 members, elected for 4 years. The People's Assembly is nominally the supreme organ of government, but in practice meets only a few days each year. Real power is vested in the Politburo and Central Committee of the Communist party **Local Government:** 27 districts with locally elected people's councils

**Ethnic Composition:** The population is homogeneous, with a small Greek minority **Population Distribution:** 34% urban (1971) **Density:** 233 inhabitants per sq. mi.

**Largest Cities:** (1979 census) Tirana 189,100, Durrës 66,300, Shkodër 65,000, Elbasan 61,200, Vlorë 56,200

**Per Capita Income:** $805 (1980) **Gross National Product (GNP):** $2.2 billion (1980) **Economic Statistics:** GNP components are not available. In 1968, however, industrial production accounted for 61.5% of total production in the country; the principal industries are oil refining, chemicals, fertilizers, construction materials, textiles, pig iron, processed minerals, and agricultural products. Agricultural production is chiefly devoted to corn, sugar beets, wheat, cotton, tobacco, and livestock **Minerals and Mining:** Chrome ore, oil, coal, copper, iron, and nickel are exploited and are among Albania's chief exports. Hydroelectric and thermoelectric plants provide the country with full electrification **Labor Force:** In 1972, 343,228 workers were employed in the socialist sector of the economy, with about 30% in industry and 60% in agriculture **Foreign Trade:** Exports, chiefly chrome ores, crude petroleum, bitumen, olives, fruit and tobacco, amounted to $151 million in 1978. Imports, chiefly machinery and equipment, rolled steel and wheat, totaled about $173 million **Principal Trade Partners:** Yugoslavia, Greece, Italy

**Vital Statistics:** Birthrate, 33.3 per 1,000 of pop.; death rate, 8.1 (1971) **Life Expectancy:** 69 years **Health Statistics:** 156 inhabitants per hospital bed; 966 per physician (1977) **Infant Mortality:** 86.8 per 1,000 births (1965) **Illiteracy:** 25% **Education Statistics:** 1,429 schools with a combined enrollment of 750,000 pupils (1975) **Enrollment in Higher Education:** 28,668 (1971) **GNP Expended on Education:** N.A.

**Transportation:** There were 800 mi. of paved roads in 1975 **Motor Vehicles:** 10,100 (1967) **Passenger Cars:** 2,600 (1967) **Railway Mileage:** 188 **Ports:** Durrës, Vlorë **Major Airlines:** Albtransport operates international flights **Communications: Radio Transmitters:** 36 **Receivers:** 200,000 (1977) **Television Transmitters:** 1 **Receivers:** 4,500 (1976) **Telephones:** 10,150 (1963) **Newspapers:** 2 dailies, 45 copies per 1,000 inhabitants (1976)

**Weights and Measures:** Metric system **Travel Requirements:** (1971) Passport, visa obtainable in Paris or Rome

Albania's present, like its past, is influenced by its forbidding hills and poor soil. In a land unattractive to migrants, the Albanians have preserved their ancient culture. But the land cannot feed the people; Albania is a food-importing nation. Fearful of strangers, Albania must depend on strangers for its survival.

Since 1946, Albania has been dominated by the Albanian Party of Labor—a party fanatically devoted to Marxist-Leninist ideology. The Party's leaders have rejected calls for de-Stalinization and for détente with the West and have maintained a rigid police state. The government has fallen out, successively, with Yugoslavia, the Soviet Union and China, as these states have moved away from ideological rigidity.

At the beginning of the 20th century, Albania was part of the Ottoman Empire. Serbia took from that Empire much territory inhabited by ethnic Albanians before an alarmed Austria, in 1912, helped the rest of the country to win independence. After World War I, Albania was caught up in the rivalry between Yugoslavia and Italy; the latter annexed Albania in 1939.

Nominally independent under Communist rule in 1946, Albania was virtually a Yugoslav satellite. The two countries joined in aiding Communist guerrillas in Greece. But Albania broke with Yugoslavia in 1947 and ended the Greek adventure, after Yugoslavia broke with the Soviet Union. Territorial claims against Yugoslavia and loyalty to Joseph Stalin led Albania to remain in the Soviet camp, and the Soviet Union took over the task of supplying most of Albania's food.

In 1961, however, Albania's relations with the Soviet Union soured because of Soviet policies of de-Stalinization. Albania turned to Communist China for friendship and food. For practical reasons Albania resumed relations with Yugoslavia in 1970 and with Greece in 1971. Later, China's course became increasingly pragmatic, and Albania criticized the lack of devotion to the Communist cause. After Mao's death in 1976, Albania became hostile to his successors, and in 1978 China ended its aid to Albania. Albania's leaders sought to develop other foreign markets and scheduled an increase of 25% in foreign trade.

**HISTORY:** Around 300 B.C., the Illyrian kingdom covered much of what is now Albania. Greek colonies were established along the coast, but the hinterland remained independent. In the 6th century A.D., while nominally under Byzantine rule, Albania was invaded by the Slavs and in the 9th century was annexed to Bulgaria. The Turks conquered the country in the 15th century

**1912-20:** Albania proclaims its independence with the support of Austria-Hungary. During World War I, Albania is occupied by Allied troops but reasserts its independence

**1925-28:** Ahmed Zogu, chief of the Mat district, seizes power with Yugoslav support. He rules as president until 1928, when he establishes a monarchy and becomes King Zog I

**1939:** Italy occupies Albania and unites it with Italian crown

**1946:** Albania becomes a people's republic under the leadership of Enver Hoxha, head of the Communist resistance group during the Italian occupation

**1955-60:** Backed by the USSR, Albania joins the Warsaw Pact and the United Nations. Relations with the Soviet Union soon cool, however, as Moscow attempts to improve relations with Yugoslavia, behind whose frontiers live more than 750,000 ethnic Albanians; estrangement is sharpened by Albania's support for Peking in Sino-Soviet ideological split

**1961:** USSR breaks diplomatic relations with Albania

**1968:** Albania withdraws from Warsaw Pact

**1970:** Albania signs trade pact with Yugoslavia

**1971:** Greece and Albania resume full diplomatic relations

**1976:** A new constitution is approved by People's Assembly

**1978:** Chinese aid ended

**1981:** Albania's new five-year plan (1981-85) sets moderate increases of about 35% for agricultural and industrial output. Premier Mehmet Shehu dies, reportedly a suicide

## ALGERIA

**Area:** 919,591 sq. mi. **Population:** 19,130,000 (1979 est.)

**Official Name:** Democratic and Popular Republic of Algeria **Capital:** Algiers **Nationality:** Algerian **Languages:** Arabic is the official and principal language. French is also widely spoken and serves as a quasi-official language. Berber dialects are spoken by one-fourth the population **Religion:** 99% Moslem; Islam was declared the state religion in 1976 **Flag:** A red star in a red crescent in center of background of green (left hand of flag) and white (right hand) **Anthem:** We Pledge **Currency:** Algerian dinar (4.5 per U.S. $1)

**Location:** North Africa. Algeria is bordered on the north by the Mediterranean Sea, on the east by Tunisia and Libya, on the south by Niger and Mali, and on the west by Mauritania, Western Sahara, and Morocco **Features:** Two mountain chains, the Tell Atlas and the Saharan Atlas. The mountains of the Tell Atlas rise from a narrow coastal plain along the Mediterranean and are separated from the Saharan Atlas by a corridor of semiarid plateaus dotted with salt marshes and shallow salt lakes. To the south lies the Sahara itself, broken only by a few oases **Chief River:** Chéliff

**Head of State and of Government:** President: Chadli Bendjedid, born 1929, elected 1979. He is assisted by Premier Mohamed Ben Ahmed Abdelghani, appointed 1979 **Effective Date of Present Constitution:** 1976 **Legislative Body:** A new National Popular Assembly of 261 members was elected in February 1977 for 5-year terms **Local Government:** 31 departments (wilayas)

**Ethnic Composition:** The population is of Arabo-Berber stock **Population Distribution:** 52% urban **Density:** 20.8 inhabitants per sq. mi.

**Largest Cities:** (1978 census) Algiers 1,365,400, Oran 491,900, Constantine 335,100, Annaba 255,900, Blida 160,900

**Per Capita Income:** $1,483 (1980) **Gross National Product (GNP):** $28 billion (1980) **Economic Statistics:** In 1976, 7% of the GNP came from agriculture (wheat, vineyard, orchards), livestock raising (sheep, cattle, donkeys, mules, horses, pigs, goats) and fishing; 35% from trade and services; and 44% from mining and industry (food processing and beverages, textiles, leather, chemicals, building materials, steel, and engineering) **Minerals and Mining:** Vast deposits of oil and gas, iron ore, phosphates, and coal; small amounts of lead, zinc and copper **Labor Force:** 4 million (1978 est.), of which 50% is engaged in agriculture, 20% in industry, and the rest in services **Foreign Trade:** Exports, chiefly petroleum, natural gas, fruit and wine, totaled $8.2 billion in 1979. Imports, mainly textiles, cereals, chemicals, motor vehicles, iron and steel products, sugar, machinery, and electrical apparatus, totaled $8.2 billion **Principal Trade Partners:** United States, France, West Germany, Italy, Japan, Spain, Canada

**Vital Statistics:** Birthrate, 47.5 per 1,000 of pop. (1980); death rate, 13.5 **Life Expectancy:** 55 years (1977) **Health Statistics:** 356 inhabitants per hospital bed, 5,592 per physician (1977) **Infant Mortality:** 70.8 per 1,000 births **Illiteracy:** 74% **Primary and Secondary School Enrollment:** 3,400,531 (1976) **Enrollment in Higher Education:** 59,100 (1977) **GNP Expended on Education:** 9% (1977)

**Transportation:** Paved roads total 22,125 mi. (1977) **Motor Vehicles:** 440,800 (1975) **Passenger Cars:** 286,100 **Railway Mileage:** 2,423 **Ports:** Algiers, Oran, Annaba, Bejaia, Arzew **Major Airlines:** Air Algérie operates international and domestic flights **Communications: Radio Transmitters:** 30 **Receivers:** 3,000,000 (1976) **Television Transmitters:** 75 **Receivers:** 525,000 (1976) **Telephones:** 346,000 (1978) **Newspapers:** 4 dailies, 13 copies per 1,000 inhabitants (1977)

**Weights and Measures:** Metric system **Travel Requirements:** Passport, tourist visa, $5.25, valid for 3 months, 4 photos

Algeria won independence from France in a long struggle organized by a disciplined party—the National Liberation Front (NLF). Independence brought one-party rule, economic dislocation, and a period of military control. The NLF is a party of Islam, socialism, and concern for the aspirations of the Third World in general and of the Arab states in particular. It is strident in its support of those it considers oppressed, and has made Algeria a haven for many kinds of self-proclaimed revolutionaries—including airplane hijackers. Israel is a favorite target of Algerian rhetoric, although not of Algerian military action. Ironically, Algeria's only actual military adventure is that against Morocco—in support of the Polisario movement for Western Saharan independence.

Despite its ideology, Algeria must trade with the capitalist West. Its economy was ruined by the departure of its European inhabitants after independence, and recovery is incomplete. Fortunately, Algeria has oil and gas which the West needs.

France agreed to independence in 1962, after a plebiscite showed a majority to favor "independence in cooperation with France." Benyoussef Ben Khedda, who had headed the NLF's exile government, became Premier. But his power was broken by Ahmed Ben Bella, a firebrand NLF official who had spent most of the struggle in a French jail. Ben Bella established a one-party system that tended toward personal dictatorship. He was deposed in 1965 by Colonel Houari Boumédienne, who established military rule within the NLF framework.

Boumédienne created most of the salient features of the new Algeria. Finding that cooperation with France was working to France's advantage, he ended it in 1971. Then, he increased trade with the United States, although he had broken diplomatic relations with the U.S. in 1967 because of U.S. support for Israel. Discontent of NLF leaders with military rule led to the adoption of a new constitution in 1976 and to ratification by the voters of the NLF's choice of Boumédienne as President. The constitution did not bring democracy, but it broadened the limits within which divergent views were tolerated.

The system of semi-democratic one-party rule was tried and found workable in 1978, when Boumédienne died after weeks in a coma. As the constitution provided, Rabah Bitat became the interim president, and in 1979 Col. Chadli Bendjedid was elected to the office.

Algeria shored up its relations with France by concluding a new trade agreement in February 1982. By its terms Algeria agreed to increase sales of liquefied natural gas to 300 billion cubic feet annually and to buy $2 billion worth of automobile assembly plants and other industrial products from France.

**HISTORY:** In prehistoric times, Algeria was inhabited by a mixture of peoples from whom the Berbers of today are probably descended. About 1200 B.C. the Phoenicians made settlements in the area, and it eventually fell under the control of Carthage. After the destruction of Carthage in 146 B.C., the Romans gradually gained control of the entire North African coast. With the weakening of the Roman Empire, Algeria fell prey to Vandals from Europe and eventually to the Arabs

**7th cent.:** Algeria, along with the rest of North Africa, falls to Moslem conquerors from Arabia. Islam takes root

**11th cent.:** Saharan nomads sweep into the country and destroy farms and pastures, forcing the coastal Berbers into seafaring and piracy. The Berbers spread through North Africa and, in the Moorish Conquest, move to the Iberian peninsula to occupy much of Spain

**16th cent.:** Spain gains a foothold in Algeria and Algerians turn to Turkish corsairs for help in 1518. Turkish rule is established

**1830:** France sends an expedition to pacify turbulent tribes along the coast and in the interior. French naval forces seize Algiers, depose the bey, and establish French rule

**1942:** Allies invade North Africa during World War II

**1954-61:** Discontent with French rule erupts in a widespread rebellion. Rebel leaders form a "provisional government of Algeria" in Cairo, but the fighting continues until the opening of peace talks with the French

**1962-63:** Algeria becomes an independent republic. Benyoussef Ben Khedda, premier of the provisional government in exile, takes control but is ousted by Vice-Premier Ahmed Ben Bella who later becomes President under one-party constitution

**1965:** A military revolt led by Colonel Houari Boumédienne overthrows Ben Bella. A revolutionary council assumes power; Ben Bella placed in "comfortable" confinement

**1967-68:** Algeria declares war on Israel, but no Algerian troops take part in Middle East fighting. Boumédienne fosters closer economic and military ties with USSR

**1969:** Algeria accuses U.S. State Department and CIA of involvement in a conspiracy to overthrow the government

**1971:** French oil companies in Algeria partly nationalized; France ends "special relations" with Algeria

**1973:** The United States arranges to import 1 billion cubic feet of Algerian liquefied natural gas daily for 25 years

**1974:** Algeria resumes diplomatic relations with U.S. after severance in 1967

**1976:** Algerian troops clash with Moroccan and Mauritanian forces in Western Sahara. New constitution approved and elections held. Boumédienne elected President

**1978:** Boumédienne dies

**1979:** Chadli Bendjedid elected President

**1980:** Ben Bella is freed after 15 years' imprisonment

## ANDORRA

**Area:** 188 sq. mi. **Population:** 32,000 (1980 est.)

**Official Name:** Principality of Andorra **Capital:** Andorra la Vella **Nationality:** Andorran **Languages:** Catalan is the official language. French and Spanish are spoken **Religion:** Roman Catholic **Flag:** Vertical blue, yellow, and red stripes, with the national coat of arms in the center **Anthem:** The Great Charlemagne **Currency:** French franc (6.1 per U.S. $1) and Spanish peseta (104 per U.S. $1)

**Location:** Eastern Pyrenees, between France and Spain **Features:** Drained by the Valira River, Andorra consists of narrow valleys and gorges, bounded by high peaks **Chief Rivers:** Valira

**Head of State:** Andorra is a co-principality under the joint sovereignty of the president of France and the Spanish bishop of Urgel, each of whom is represented by a viguier, or agent **Head of Government:** Oscar Ribas Reig, elected by the General Coouncil to head the newly created Executive Council on Jan. 8, 1982 **Legislative Body:** Parliament (unicameral 28-member General Council) **Effective Date of Present Constitution:** 1866 Plan of Reform **Local Government:** 7 parishes, each with an elected council

**Ethnic Composition:** Native Andorrans, who constitute one-third of the population, are of Catalan stock. The rest of the population is primarily Spanish and French **Population Distribution:** 81% urban **Density:** 170 inhabitants per sq. mi. **Largest Towns:** (1977 est.) Andorra la Vella 19,764, Sant Juliá 3,510, Encamp 2,268

**Per Capita Income:** N.A. **Gross National Product (GNP):** N.A. **Economic Statistics:** Tourism is the chief source of income. Cereals, potatoes, livestock raising and tobacco are dominant, while tobacco processing is the chief industry. Timber production and building are also important activities. There is considerable smuggling of merchandise shipped between France and Spain **Minerals and Mining:** Small amounts of iron ore and lead are mined **Labor Force:** 9,500, with about 80% in local industries and 20% in agriculture **Foreign Trade:** Principal exports are timber, cattle and derivatives, and furniture; the chief imports are fuel, perfumes, clothing, radio and television sets. Imports in 1979 totaled $840 million **Principal Trade Partners:** France, Spain

**Vital Statistics:** Birthrate, 17.4 per 1,000 of pop. (1980); death rate, 4.6 **Life Expectancy:** 70 years **Health Statistics:** N.A. **Infant Mortality:** .16 per 1,000 births **Illiteracy:** negligible **Primary and Secondary School Enrollment:** 5,555 (1975) **Enrollment in Higher Education:** N.A. **GNP Expended on Education:** N.A.

**Transportation:** Surfaced roads total 77 mi. **Motor Vehicles:** 9,346 (1970) **Passenger Cars:** Over 25,000 **Railway Mileage:** None **Ports:** None **Major Airlines:** No air service **Communications: Radio Stations:** 4 **Licenses:** 7,000 (1977) **Television Stations:** None **Receivers:** 3,000 (1976) **Telephones:** 4,000 (1977) **Newspapers:** One daily established in 1974

**Weights and Measures:** Metric system **Travel Requirements:** See *France* **International Dialing Code:** 33

Modern tourism, bringing over three million visitors a year, has altered the formerly leisurely pace of life in Andorra. Tourist access to the tiny state in the fastness of the Pyrenees has been made possible with the opening of modern highways from France and Spain in the last thirty years.

Motoring tourists—and automobile traffic in general—are especially important to Andorra, which obtains more than a third of its revenue from gasoline taxes and automobile fines. Tourism as an industry supplements Andorran wool-combing, spinning, tobacco processing, and the manufacture of sandals. Smuggling of goods from France into Spain is also a substantial industry.

What draws tourists is the attraction of towering passes; peaks topped with snow as late as June; a countryside dotted with sheep, goats, and mules; and bargains. Despite the state's need of revenue, there is no income tax.

**HISTORY:** According to tradition, Charlemagne granted the people of Andorra a charter because of their help in battling the Moors. In 843 Charles the Bald made the Spanish count of Urgel overlord of Andorra. In 1278 the bishop of Urgel was made joint suzerain after contending that Andorra was part of the endowment of his cathedral. The rights of the count eventually passed by inheritance to Henry IV of France and eventually to the presidents of France

**1793:** French revolutionary government renounces its claims to Andorra

**1806:** Napoleon restores co-principality at Andorrans' request

**1933:** Suffrage is granted to all men over the age of 25

**1941:** Suffrage is restricted to heads of families

**1970:** Limited women's suffrage granted

**1971:** New bishop of Urgel installed as the 80th co-prince

**1982:** An Executive Council assumes administrative functions for the first time

## ANGOLA

**Area:** 481,351 sq. mi. **Population:** 7,000,000 (1978 est.)

**Official Name:** People's Republic of Angola **Capital:** Luanda **Nationality:** Angolan **Languages:** Portuguese is the official language. A number of African languages, chiefly of Bantu origin, are commonly spoken **Religion:** Animist 84%, Roman Catholic 12%, Protestant 4% **Flag:** Two equal horizontal stripes of red over black, with yellow five-pointed star, machete, and half a cogwheel in the center **Anthem:** National Anthem (no words) **Currency:** Kwanza (30.8 per U.S. $1)

**Location:** West-central Africa. Bounded by the Atlantic Ocean on the west, Namibia on the south, and Zaire and Zambia on the north and east. The exclave of Cabinda lies on the Atlantic coast north of the Congo River mouth **Features:** A narrow coastal strip rises sharply toward an interior plateau, which ranges from 3,000 to 5,000 feet in elevation. A highland area of 6,000 to 7,000 feet lies in the west-central region. Cabinda consists of a low-lying rain forest **Chief Rivers:** Cubango, Cuanza, Cunene, Cuango, Cassai, Cuando, Congo, Cuito

**Head of State and of Government:** President: José Eduardo dos Santos, born 1942, elected 1979 **Effective Date of Present Constitution:** 1975 **Legislative Body:** National People's Assembly with

206 members **Local Government:** 18 provinces, with appointed commissars and elected assemblies

**Ethnic Composition:** Predominantly indigenous Bantus, with the Ovimbundu constituting 38%, Kimbundu 23%, Bakongo 13%. Only 30,000 Portuguese remained at independence **Population Distribution:** N.A. **Density:** 14.5 inhabitants per sq. mi.

**Largest Cities:** (1972 est.) Luanda 540,000; (1970 census) Huambo 61,885; Lobito 59,528; Benguela 40,996; Lubango 31,674; Malanje 31,599; Cabinda 21,124

**Per Capita Income:** $558 (1980) **Gross National Product (GNP):** $3.7 billion (1980) **Economic Statistics:** The economy remains heavily dependent upon agriculture (subsistence and cash crops such as coffee, sisal, cotton, wheat, sugar, and tobacco, with fish and timber of importance). Industry (cement, oil refining, paper, agricultural processing, and metal products) has declined since independence **Minerals and Mining:** Iron ore and diamonds are exploited, and petroleum is being produced in the Cabinda exclave **Labor Force:** Total currently unknown, with an estimated 80% in agriculture, and 10% in industry **Foreign Trade:** Exports, chiefly petroleum, coffee, iron ore, diamonds, cotton, and fish meal, totaled $1.7 billion in 1980. Imports, mainly machinery, textiles, transportation and construction equipment, iron and steel products, rice, and electrical products, totaled $1.5 billion **Principal Trade Partners:** Western & Eastern Europe, United States

**Vital Statistics:** Birthrate, 47.6 per 1,000 of pop. (1980); death rate, 23.1 **Life Expectancy:** 38.5 years **Health Statistics:** 322 inhabitants per hospital bed; 15,404 per physician (1972) **Infant Mortality:** 24.1 per 1,000 births **Illiteracy:** 85% **Education Statistics:** N.A. **Higher Education:** N.A. **GNP Expended on Education:** N.A.

**Transportation:** Surfaced roads total 8,371 mi. (1974) **Motor Vehicles:** 163,000 (1973) **Passenger Cars:** 127,300 **Railway Mileage:** 1,895 **Ports:** Lobito, Luanda, Moçamades, Cabinda **Major Airlines:** TAAG (Angolan Airlines) **Communications: Radio Transmitters:** 43 (1976) **Receivers:** 118,000 (1977) **Television Transmitters:** 1 **Telephones:** 28,000 (1978) **Newspapers:** 5 dailies, 19 copies per 1,000 inhabitants (1976)

**Weights and Measures:** Metric system **Travel Requirements:** No U.S. representation in Angola. Contact Angola UN Mission in New York for travel information

---

Fifteen years of rebellion against colonial ruule culminated in the granting of Angolan independence by Portugal on November 11, 1975. However, independence did not bring peace to Angola, the largest and most important territory of the former Portuguese overseas empire. Three factions contended for power in this resource-rich country: the Marxist-oriented Popular Movement for the Liberation of Angola (MPLA), the pro-Western National Front for the Liberation of Angola (FNLA), and the pro-Western National Union for the Total Independence of Angola (UNITA). The MPLA, backed by the Soviet Union and Cuba, held the Angolan capital, Luanda, while the pro-Western forces occupied most of the country north and south of the capital.

Initially, following independence, the pro-Western forces scored military successes against the MPLA in the central area around Luanda. Particularly important was the contribution to the MPLA of trained manpower by Cuba and of arms by the USSR. South African armed forces crossed into Angola from Namibia to aid FNLA and UNITA.

Late in 1975 the military tide turned in favor of the MPLA as a result of the massive Soviet and Cuban assistance. The situation grew increasingly grim for the pro-Western factions when the U.S. Senate voted to cut off covert financial aid to the combatants. By 1976 the MPLA forces had overrun most of Angola. However, UNITA and FNLA continued to wage guerrilla warfare. South African troops withdrew into Namibia but have since continued to launch air and land attacks on SWAPO (South-West African People's Organization) units based in Angola.

The violent conditions of this period resulted in the flight of most of the Portuguese population. The departure of the educationally and technically advanced segment of Angolan society resulted in a drastic decline in the economic life of the country.

The leader of the MPLA, Agostinho Neto, a poet and doctor, became president of independent Angola in November 1975. Faced with massive economic problems, he sought better relations with Western governments, but because of the continued presence of Cuban troops in the country, the United States withheld diplomatic relations.

Although Angola has good agricultural land, food and clothing, as well as other goods, are in short supply. Many small farmers produce only enough for themselves; why raise crops to sell when they can't buy anything with the money? Moreover, drought has affected the maize-growing areas severely. On the other hand, production from oil wells off the coast of Cabinda has increased to such an extent that petroleum provides about 80% of the country's export income. Swelling revenues from this source have made possible increasing imports of food and of machinery and raw materials needed for industrial revival.

**HISTORY:** Prior to the coming of the Portuguese in 1483, present-day Angola was part of the African Kingdom of the Kongo. During the 16th century Portugal established trading posts along the coast and exploited Angola as a prime source of the lucrative slave trade. The Dutch captured and held the Angolan port cities for seven years until the Portuguese recaptured them in 1648

**1884-85:** At Berlin Conference the Portuguese receive "right of occupation" to Angola while losing all claims in central Africa

**1910-20:** Portugal begins serious colonizing effort in Angola

**1926:** Portuguese Republic overthrown. Subsequent authoritarian regime of Salazar tightens Portuguese rule over colony

**1961:** Rebellion against Portugal breaks out, beginning 15-year violent struggle for independence

**1975:** Portugal grants Angolan independence. Rival factions battle for supremacy

**1976:** Marxist MPLA group wins control of Angola

**1978:** Cuban troops lead government offensive against pro-Western guerrillas

**1979:** President Neto dies Sept. 10 and is succeeded by his Minister of Planning, José Eduardo dos Santos, a Soviet-educated petroleum engineer

**1980:** MPLA launches purge of all anti-Marxist elements. Benguela railway is reopened for first time since 1975, but is still subject to disruptive UNITA attacks

**1981:** Angola links departure of Cubans to independence for Namibia. Economic relations with Western nations expand

**1982:** Ten-year economic cooperation agreement with USSR calls for building a 450,000-kw. hydroelectric station. South African elite unit wipes out SWAPO supply base inside Angola

## ANTIGUA AND BARBUDA

**Area:** 171 sq. mi. **Population:** 76,213 (Barbuda—1,200) (1981 est.)

**Official Name:** Antigua and Barbuda **Capital:** St. John's **Nationality:** Antiguan, Barbudan **Languages:** English is the official language. A patois is commonly spoken **Religion:** Christian, chiefly Anglican **Flag:** A red field bearing an inverted triangle whose base corresponds to the top edge of the flag and whose apex is at the center of the bottom edge. The triangle is composed of three horizontal stripes of white (bottom), light blue, and black (top), the latter bearing a rising yellow sun **Anthem:** National Anthem **Currency:** East Caribbean Dollar (2.7 per U.S. $1)

**Location:** Eastern Caribbean. The three islands of Antigua, Barbuda and Redonda are situated in the Leeward Islands, 250 miles southeast of Puerto Rico **Features:** Antigua is low lying for the most part, but there are rolling hills in the south and west. The deeply indented coastline has several natural harbors. Barbuda is a flat coral island. The rocky islet of Redonda is uninhabited. The tropical climate is tempered by sea breezes, and Antigua has a drier climate than most of the West Indies

**Head of State:** Queen Elizabeth II, represented by a governor-general, Sir Wilfred Ebenezer Jacobs **Head of Government:** Prime Minister Vere C. Bird, Sr., appointed Nov. 1, 1981 **Effective Date of Present Constitution:** Nov. 1, 1981 **Legislative Body:** Parliament (bicameral) consists of a 17-member House of Representatives, elected for 5 years, and a Senate, appointed by the governor-general (11 on the advice of the prime minister, 4 on the advice of the opposition leader, one on the advice of the Barbuda Council, and one at his own discretion) **Local Government:** Barbuda, through its Council, possesses exclusive responsibility for certain island functions

**Ethnic Composition:** Mainly of African descent **Population Distribution:** 34% urban **Density:** 446 inhabitants per sq. mi.

**Largest City:** (1980 est.) St. John's 25,000

**Per Capita Income:** $1,000 (1978) **Gross Domestic Product (GDP):** $73 million (1978) **Economic Statistics:** Tourism accounts for 40% of GDP. Agriculture (sea-island cotton, livestock, fruits and vegetables) contributes 5%. Sugarcane planting is being revived. Manufacturing (clothing, rum, consumer products) provides 7%. An oil refinery is expected to be operational in 1982, and a sugar refinery should reopen in the near future **Minerals and Mining:** Offshore oil resources are to be explored **Labor Force:** Tourism provides 60% of employment **Foreign Trade:** Exports, chiefly clothing, rum, fruit, and lobsters, totaled $11 million in 1979. Imports, mainly fuel, food and machinery, totaled $60 million **Principal Trade Partners:** Britain, United States, Commonwealth Caribbean countries

**Vital Statistics:** Birthrate, 16.5 per 1,000 of pop. (1980); death rate, 5.6 **Life Expectancy:** 62 years **Health Statistics:** 140 inhabitants per hospital bed; 2,333 per physican (1976) **Infant Mortality:** 31.5 per 1,000 births (1980) **Illiteracy:** 11% (1960) **Primary and Secondary School Enrollment:** 20,000 (1977) **Enrollment in Higher Education:** N.A. **GDP Expended on Education:** N.A.

**Transportation:** Surfaced roads total 150 mi. **Motor Vehicles:** N.A. **Railway Mileage:** None **Ports:** St. John's **Major Airlines:** LIAT operates service internationally and between Antigua and Barbuda **Communications: Radio Transmitters:** 3 **Receivers:** 16,000 (1977) **Television Transmitters:** 2 **Receivers:** 15,000 (1977) **Telephones:** 3,000 (1977) **Newspapers:** 2 weeklies, 137 copies per 1,000 inhabitants (1976)

**Weights and Measures:** British system **Travel Requirements:** N.A. **Direct Dialing Code:** 809

---

The tourism industry dominates the life of the new Caribbean nation of Antigua and Barbuda. The islands' delightful climate and beautiful beaches attracted over 86,000 long-stay visitors in 1980, while another 107,000 people stopped at the country in cruise ships. The total number of hotel rooms is expected to reach 2,600 by 1983.

The path to independence was made difficult by separatist sentiment on the part of Barbuda's inhabitants. The smaller island, which is 25 miles north of Antigua, was granted a substantial degree of autonomy under terms of the revised draft constitution for the new nation in early 1981. Nevertheless, Barbudans threatened to secede throughout the pre-independence months of 1981. However, the dual-island state achieved nationhood on November 1, without suffering division.

The government of Antigua and Barbuda is led by Prime Minister Vere Bird, who has been active in island politics since 1945. His Antigua Labour party has controlled Antiguan government since 1960, except for the years 1971 to 1976.

**HISTORY:** Arawak Indians were the earliest known inhabitants, but were driven out by the Caribs from South America. Columbus landed on Antigua in 1493, but the Spanish were unsuccessful in attempting colonization in 1520. The island was settled by Englishmen from St. Kitts in 1632. Barbuda was colonized from Antigua in 1661. English Harbour, on Antigua's southern coast, served as the Royal Navy's main base and dockyard in the West Indies from 1725 to 1854

**1871:** Antigua, including Barbuda, is administered as part of the Federation of the Leeward Islands, until the abolition of the Federation in 1956

**1958:** Antigua participates in the Federation of the West Indies until its dissolution in 1962

**1967:** Antigua becomes an Associated State with complete control of its internal affairs, while Britain retains control of the islands' external relations and deefense

**1980:** Constitutional talks, leading to independence, are held in London

**1981:** Independence is proclaimed on Nov. 1, despite Barbudan objections to terms of the constitution. Longtime political leader, Vere Bird, becomes Antigua and Barbuda's first prime minister

---

## ARGENTINA

**Area:** 1,068,296 sq. mi. **Population:** 27,862,771 (1980 census)

**Official Name:** Argentine Republic **Capital:** Buenos Aires **Nationality:** Argentine **Languages:** Spanish is the official and principal language. Italian, French, and German are also frequently heard **Religion:** About 95% of the population belongs to the Roman Catholic Church, which is officially recognized in the Constitution. There are small minorities of Protestants and Jews **Flag:** Horizontal stripes of blue, white, and blue, with the sun on the white stripe **Anthem:** Argentine National Anthem, beginning "Hear, mortals, the sacred cry of Liberty" **Currency:** New Argentine peso (20,000 per U.S. $1)

**Location:** Southern South America. Argentina is bordered on the north by Bolivia and Paraguay, on the northeast by Brazil and Uruguay, on the east and south by the Atlantic Ocean, and on the west by Chile. Argentina claims the Falkand (Malvinas), South Georgia, South Orkney and South Sandwich Islands in the South Atlantic, as well as a large sector in Antarctica **Features:** The heartland of Argentina is the rich, temperate plains area known as the Pampas, which fans out from the east-central sectorr of the country. The north consists of subtropical lowlands, while the west is dominated by the Andean Mountains and the south by the Patagonian steppe and the rainy Tierra del Fuego **Chief Rivers:** Paraná, Negro, Salado, Colorado, Chubut

**Head of State and Government:** President: Maj. Gen. Reynaldo Benito Antonio Bignone, born 1928, took office on July 1, 1982. A separate 3-man military junta is the supreme ruling body of the state. The president is assisted by a mixed civilian-military cabinet **Effective Date of Present Constitution:** Although the constitution of 1853 is still in effect, its provisions have been made subject to the Statutes of the Revolution, issued after a military coup in 1966 and to other changes following the 1976 coup **Legislative Body:** The National Congress was dissolved in 1976 **Local Government:** 22 provinces, 1 national territory, and 1 federal district, each administered by an appointed governor

**Ethnic Composition:** 97% of the population is of European origin; persons of Arab descent, Indians and mestizos constitute about 3% **Population Distribution:** 81.1% urban (1975) **Density:** 26 inhabitants per sq. mi.

**Largest Cities:** (1980 census—Metropolitan Areas) Buenos Aires 9,927,404, Córdoba 982,018, Rosario 954,606, Mendoza 596,796, La Plata 560,341, San Miguel de Tucumán 496,914

**Per Capita Income:** $2,089 (1980) **Gross National Product (GNP):** $57 billion (1980) **Economic Statistics:** In 1975, 48% of the GNP came from trade and services; 36% from industry (iron and steel, automobiles, machinery, chemicals, cement); 11% from agriculture (meat, hides, grain, fruits); and 8% from mining and construction **Minerals and Mining:** Oil and natural gas supply domestic needs; copper, low-grade iron ore and small amounts of coal, lead, zinc, silver, bismuth, vanadium, beryllium, tantalite, and tungsten are mined **Labor Force:** 10,800,000 in 1978, of which 25% is employed in manufacturing and 19% in agriculture **Foreign Trade:** Exports, chiefly grains, meat, wool, hides, linseed oil and other agricultural products totaled $7.8 billion in 1979. Imports, mainly machinery and equipment, iron and steel products, chemicals, textiles and fuels, totaled $6.7 billion **Principal Trade Partners:** United States, Brazil, West Germany, Netherlands, Italy, Britain, Japan, USSR

**Vital Statistics:** Birthrate, 25.2 per 1,000 of pop. (1978); death rate, 8.9 **Life Expectancy:** 68 years **Health Statistics:** 176 inhabitants per hospital bed; 479 per physician (1972) **Infant Mortality:** 40.8 per 1,000 births (1970) **Illiteracy:** 7% **Primary and Secondary School Enrollment:** 4,945,515 (1977) **Enrollment in Higher Education:** 619,950 **GNP Expended on Education:** 1.6% (1976)

**Transportation:** Paved roads total 23,000 mi. (1975) **Motor Vehicles:** 3,500,000 (1976) **Passenger Cars:** 2,027,500 (1974) **Railway Mileage:** 25,794 **Ports:** Buenos Aires, Bahía Blanca, La Plata, Rosario **Major Airlines:** Aerolíneas Argentinas is the major international and domestic carrier **Communications: Radio Transmitters:** 567 (1976) **Receivers:** 10,000,000 (1977) **Television Transmitters:** 82 **Receivers:** 4,500,000 (1974) **Telephones:** 2,404,000 (1978) **Newspapers:** 142 dailies, 179 copies per 1,000 inhabitants (1976)

**Weights and Measures:** Metric system **Travel Requirements:** Passport and visa required. Check embassy or consulate for specific requirements. No fee **International Dialing Code:** 54

---

Extending 2,300 miles from north to south and with an Atlantic coastline 1,600 miles long, Argentina is the second-largest country on the South American continent, after Brazil. Its topography and climate are as varied as those of the United States, the terrain ranging from the subtropical lowlands of the north to the towering Andean Mountains in the west and the bleak Patagonian steppe and rainy Tierra del Fuego in the south. More than 60 percent of the country's area is suitable for agriculture, of which about 8 percent is under cultivation and the remainder is pastureland upon which a massive livestock population thrives (there are currently more than two animals for every Argentine man, woman and child). The heartland of Argentina is the rich, temperate plains area known as the Pampas, which fans out for almost 500 miles from Buenos Aires in the east-central sector; here is found some of the richest topsoil in the world.

Politically, the dominant factor of life in Argentina has been turmoil. In the early months of 1976, Argentina was a country on the edge of anarchy, racked by daily kidnappings and bombings. Its treasury, down to its last foreign reserves, was about to default on its overseas debt. Then, on March 24, in a bloodless coup led by the Commander in Chief of the army, Jorge Rafael Videla, the military deposed Isabel Perón, the first woman chief of state in the Americas, from the presidency, her inept government falling along with her.

Mrs. Perón had come into power on the death of her husband, Juan Perón, in July 1974. He had returned to Argentina in June 1973, after 18 years of exile, which had been preceded by an 11-year rule as Argentina's president. He was reelected to the presidency in September of that year, with his wife as vice-president.

After the ouster of Mrs. Perón, Videla was sworn in as president on March 29, 1976. Executive power was entrusted to a military junta that set two goals: crushing terrorism and reviving the economy. Despite the opposition of President Videla and other moderates there followed a wave of uncontrolled kidnappings and arrests by security forces of the army. In 1981 a report of the United Nations Human Rights Commission stated that Argentina accounted for more than half of 11,000 to 13,000 people reported missing around the world. Amnesty International has placed the number of missing in Argentina as high as 15,000 to 20,000. Adolfo Pérez Esquivel, an Argentine champion of human rights who had formerly been held in jail for over a year without being charged with any crime, was awarded the Nobel Peace Prize in 1980. He accepted it in the name of the missing persons.

A new "Professional Associations Law," aimed at curbing the political thrust of the trade unions, which were the backbone of Peronist power, took effect Nov. 16, 1979.

In October 1980 the military junta nominated Gen. Roberto Eduardo Viola to succeed President Videla. Viola, a moderate opposed by hard-line members of the military, was sworn in for a three-year term on March 29, 1981. Viola promised a return to civilian rule, and perhaps because of this and his failure to shore up the country's faltering economy, the junta seized the opportunity during Viola's illness late in 1981 to replace him with Gen. Leopoldo Galtieri.

By the early 1980s, Argentina's economy had reached a critical stage brought on by declining industrial production, unemployment, a growing balance-of-payments deficit, and continuing inflation. In 1981 the peso was devalued from 2,300 to 6,500 to the dollar. Some of the country's largest industrial and banking concerns have suffered financial collapse.

Against this background, on April 2, 1982, Argentine forces seized the British-held Falkland Islands about 250 miles away. The islands, called the Malvinas by the Argentines, have been claimed by them since 1833, when Britain captured them. Despite efforts in the United Nations and elsewhere to mediate in this crisis, Britain sent an armada into the South Atlantic to dislodge the Argentines, who refused to end the occupation of the islands. In the early round of clashes, torpedoes sank the Argentine cruiser *General Belgrano*, and soon afterward an air-launched Argentine missle destroyed the British destroyer *Sheffield*. British troops landed at Port San Carlos on East Falkland Island on May 22, and pushed east to the Falkland capital of Stanley. Argentine forces were encircled and forced to capitulate on June 14.

Following the Falkland surrender, Galtieri resigned from the junta and from the presidency. He was succeeded as president by General Reynaldo Benito Antonio Bignone.

**HISTORY:** The treeless plains of the Pampas were inhabited by fierce nomadic Indian tribes of unknown origin for centuries before 1516, when a band of eight conquistadors led by Juan Díaz de Solís landed on the shores of Río de la Plata. Magellan and Sebastian Cabot soon followed on other voyages of exploration and in 1580 Juan de Garay reached what is now Buenos Aires by way of Paraguay. By the 18th century Buenos Aires had become the capital of a vast Spanish viceroyalty that included Argentina

**1810:** Argentine revolutionists depose Spanish viceroy and form their own government

**1817-19:** General José de San Martín crosses the Andes with 5,000 men, defeats Spanish forces at Battle of Maipú (1818), and goes on to liberate Chile and Peru. New Argentine constitution sets off civil war between "federalists" and "unitarians," with the latter favoring a central government dominated by Buenos Aires

**1829:** Juan Manuel de Rosas, the federalist leader, establishes one-man rule

**1845-52:** Rosas interferes in neighboring countries; aided by Brazil, Uruguay, France and Britain, Justo José de Urquiza overthrows Rosas, who flees to England

**1880-81:** Long struggle between Buenos Aires and federalist forces ends, with the city becoming a federal district; settlers end Indians' resistance by virtually wiping them out

**1916-30:** Period of vast immigration and prosperity begins; Hipólito Irigoyen, leader of the Radicals, a bourgeois reform party, is elected president and enacts wide social-reform legislation. He is succeeded in 1922 by another Radical, but returns to power in 1928. Two years later he is overthrown by the military

**1943-45:** The latest in a string of military coups places Colonel Juan Domingo Perón in a relatively unimportant post as labor secretary. Perón, effecting sweeping social and economic reforms, wins popularity among masses; he is thrown in jail by frightened military men. Released after nine days, Perón asks for election

**1946:** Perón wins election. A widower, he takes as his second wife Eva Duarte, a radio star, who helps Perón establish trade unions along militant, Fascist lines

**1952-55:** Eva Perón dies (1952); Perón, unsettled, faces charges of immorality and corruption. After thwarting several coups, he is overthrown and makes his way to Spain

**1973:** Following a long succession of civilian and military presidents, Perón returns from exile on June 20 and, running on a coalition ticket, is elected president in September

**1974:** Perón dies and is succeeded by his wife, Isabel Perón

**1976:** Coup topples Mrs. Perón's government. Argentina is governed by a junta led by Gen. Jorge Rafael Videla

**1979:** Jacobo Timerman, publisher of *La Opinión* and outspoken critic of the government, is exiled

**1980:** Argentina defies U.S. call for grain embargo against USSR

**1981:** Gen. Roberto Eduardo Viola is sworn in as president on March 29, but is replaced on Dec. 11 by Gen. Leopoldo Galtieri. Isabel Perón is convicted on charges of misappropriating government funds, then is released and allowed to go into exile

**1982:** Following an unsuccessful round of talks with Britain on sovereignty over the Falkland Islands, Argentina seizes them on April 2. The two nations go to war and Britain retakes the islands on June 14. Galtieri resigns as president and is succeeded by Gen. Reynaldo Bignone. Peso is devalued

## AUSTRALIA

**Area:** 12,967,909 sq. mi. **Population:** 14,574,488 (1981 census)

**Official Name:** Commonwealth of Australia **Capital:** Canberra **Nationality:** Australian **Languages:** English **Religion:** 36% Anglican, 31% Roman Catholic, 10% Methodist, 9% Presbyterian, 2% Baptist, 12% others **Flag:** A blue field, with the Union Jack in the upper left corner, a large, 7-pointed white star directly beneath, and five smaller white stars in the right half **Anthem:** God Save the Queen **National Song:** Advance Australia Fair **Currency:** Australian dollar (0.94 per U.S. $1)

**Location:** An island continent between the Indian and Pacific oceans, lying southeast of Asia. It is bounded on the north by the Torres Strait and the Timor Sea, on the east by the Coral and Tasman seas, and on the south and west by the Indian Ocean. The continent and the island of Tasmania, off the eastern part of the south coast, make up the Commonwealth of Australia **Features:** The continent is roughly a low, irregular plateau, with a flat, arid center. The south-eastern quarter of the continent is a huge fertile plain covering some 500,000 sq. mi. Relatively low mountains lie close to the east coast **Chief Rivers:** Murray, Darling, Murrumbidgee, Burdekin, Fitzroy, Ord

**Head of State:** Queen Elizabeth II, represented by a governor-general, Sir Ninian Martin Stephens, appointed 1982 **Head of Government:** Prime Minister John Malcolm Fraser, born 1930, took office in 1975 **Effective Date of Present Constitution:** 1900 **Legislative Body:** Federal Parliament (bicameral), consisting of a Senate and House of Representatives. There are 64 Senators, elected for 6-year terms. The House consists of 125 members, elected every three years **Local Government:** 6 states, each headed by a governor appointed by the sovereign and with an elected legislature, premier, and a cabinet. There is also one internal territory, one capital territory, and six external territories

**Ethnic Composition:** The population is mainly of British origin; Aborigines (excluding mixed-bloods) number 40,000 **Population Distribution:** 86% urban **Density:** 4.9 inhabitants per sq. mi.

**Largest Cities (Metropolitan Areaa):** (1976 census) Sydney 3,021,300, Melbourne 2,603,000, Brisbane 957,000, Adelaide 900,000, Perth 805,000, Canberra 215,400, Hobart 162,000

**Per Capita Income:** $9,115 (1980) **Gross Domestic Product (GDP):** $133 billion (1980) **Economic Statistics:** About 30% of GDP comes from industry (steel, automobiles, ships, textiles, chemicals, petroleum refining, electrical equipment). Agriculture and mining, however, are the mainstays of the economy. Australia is the world''s foremost wool-growing country, producing almost one-third of the world's wool, and is a leading producer of meats and dairy products. Mining, which accounts for 3% of GDP, plays an important role in the country's export trade **Minerals and Mining:** Australia is a major world producer of coal, iron ore, bauxite, copper, gold, silver, tin, nickel, lead, zinc, manganese, antimony, cobalt, titanium, salt and uranium. A major diamond field is to be exploited. Australian wells provide 50% of the nation's crude oil requirements. About 90% of indigenous oil production is from offshore wells in the Bass Strait, discovered in 1964 and estimated to have reserves of 1,500 million barrels. There have been several natural gas finds; reserves are estimated at 20 trillion cu. ft. of gas **Labor Force:** 6.2 million (1978), of which 22% is employed in manufacturing, 6% in agriculture, and 51% in services **Foreign Trade:** Exports, chiefly wool, wheat, meat, dairy products, iron ore and other minerals, totaled $22.5 billion in 1980. Imports, mainly machinery and transportation equipment, manufactured goods, chemicals, mineral fuels, crude materials, food and beverages, totaled $20.7 billion **Principal Trade Partners:** Japan, United States, Britain, West Germany, New Zealand, Canada, Singapore, France, USSR

**Vital Statistics:** Birthrate, 15.3 per 1,000 of pop. (1980); death rate, 7.3 **Life Expectancy:** 74 years **Health Statistics:** 80 inhabitants per hospital bed; 650 per physician (1977) **Infant Mortality:** 10.7 per 1,000 births **Illiteracy:** Negligible **Primary and secondary school enrollment:** 2,725,463 (1976) **Enrollment in Higher Education:** 274,738 (1975) **GNP Expended on Education:** 6.3% (1975)

**Transportation:** Paved roads total 261,170 mi. (1973) **Motor Vehicles:** 8,526,700 (1978) **Passenger Cars:** 6,819,000 **Railway Mileage:** 25,166 **Ports:** Sydney, Melbourne, Newcastle, Port Kembla, Fremantle, Port Hedland, Port Adelaide, Dampier, Brisbane **Major Airlines:** Qantas Airways is the major international carrier; domestic flights are operated by Trans-Australia Airlines and the privately-owned Ansett Airlines of Australia **Communications: Radio Transmitters:** 240 **Receivers:** 14,600,000 (1977) **Television Transmitters:** 198 **Receivers:** 4,785,000 (1976) **Telephones:** 6,677,000 (1979) **Newspapers:** 60 dailies, 310 copies per 1,000 inhabitants (1977)

**Weights and Measures:** British standards are being replaced by the metric system **Travel Requirements:** Passport; visa valid for 48 months or life of passport; no fee **International Dialing Code:** 61

---

Political and economic pressures of the postwar era, enhanced by the communications revolution of the times, have propelled Australia out of easygoing isolation into an increasing involvement in world and regional affairs.

Australia is one of the foremost donors of foreign aid compared with the national income. Much of this aid goes to Papua New Guinea, which became independent on September 16, 1975. The emergence of new independent island states in the South Pacific has thrust demands for leadership on Australia as the most advanced and affluent power in its geopolitical sphere.

Ties between Australians and the "mother country," Britain, loosened significantly in World War II when it became clear that the hard-pressed British forces were unable to defend Australia against the Japanese onslaught. Americans filled the breach, and from that time on the Australians have looked toward the United States as the guarantor of national security. The new relationship was cemented after the war in the ANZUS (Australia, New Zealand, United States) Treaty of Mutual Security.

Japan has emerged as Australia's foremost customer overseas, taking more than one-fourth of the country's total exports. Japan's late Prime Minister Masayoshi Ohira, in a 1979 visit, expressed hopes for making further deals for long-term supply of raw materials and discussed formation of a Pacific Basin Community.

Assistance to the country's 40,000 full-blood aborigines and 150,000 part-aborigines has been stepped up, but advancement programs have foundered because of administrative problems. Aborigines have been demanding a greater say in their own affairs. In November 1978, the government agreed to grant Northern Territory aborigines a 4.25 percent royalty (estimated $11 million per year) on uranium oxide extracted from a ranger site.

The application of postwar technology to the exploitation of vast mineral resources revolutionized the Australian economy. By the 1970s, Australia had become the leading supplier of lead and zinc, the chief iron ore exporter and furnished 90 percent of the world's rutile and zircon.

At the outset of the 1980s, the country was literally riding a minerals boom as the world sought energy sources other than costly oil. Ranked second (behind the U.S.) in coal exports, Australia was expected to advance to No. 1 in a few years. Uranium, shale, and natural gas exports also were to rise sharply. It was announced in 1980 that a diamond field discovered two years earlier in Western Australia was one of the world's largest and richest, with "pipes" larger than any in South Africa. About 60% of the stones are of gem quality.

Development of underground wealth required massive importation of capital, principally from Japan, Britain and the United States. A major consequence has been a nationalist backlash against the extent of foreign ownership of business, particularly in the mining industry. The government therefore assumed the right to veto foreign takeover bids for Australian companies and to supervise mineral exportation negotiations.

Progress in manufacturing was less impressive as Australia entered the 1980's, the heavily protected auto industry being especially troubled. Prime Minister Malcolm Fraser's conservative-leaning coalition government, installed in 1975, was barely hanging on to control by early 1982, as double-digit inflation threatened the economy.

**HISTORY:** Long before it was first sighted by European explorers in the 17th century, Australia was inhabited by primitive native groups with various languages and customs. In 1770, Captain James Cook explored the east coast of the continent and claimed it for Britain. Within 50 years, the whole of Australia became a British dependency, serving as a penal colony and dumping ground for British criminals and undesirables

**1851-59:** Gold strikes in Victoria and New South Wales in 1851 attract thousands of new settlers; within two decades the rising population is settled in six self-governing colonies

**1901:** Constitution providing for federation of colonies is approved by British Parliament; Commonwealth of Australia comes into being

**1914-18:** Australia fights on Allied side during World War I

**1939-45:** Australia fights alongside Allies in World War II

**1946-48:** Immigrants, numbering 2 million by 1965, begin to pour into Australia

**1952-54:** Australia signs Pacific defense pact (ANZUS) with New Zealand and United States and joins SEATO

**1972:** The first Labor Party government in 23 years is elected, recognizes the People's Republic of China

**1975:** The Labor Party government is dismissed. Liberal-Country Party coalition government is elected by a large majority vote. Papua New Guinea is granted independence

**1977:** Liberal-Country Party government of Prime Minister Malcolm Fraser decisively reelected

**1978:** One of the world's richest diamond fields is found in west

**1979:** January cyclone devastates north Queensland
**1980:** Liberal-Country Party coalition loses Senate to Labor Party opposition, but retains bare majority in the House
**1981:** Ties to U.S. strengthened with agreement to allow American B-52s to refuel at Darwin
**1982:** Huge one-year increase (37%) in foreign investment in Australia, mainly in farmland, causes concern and protests

## AUSTRIA

**Area:** 32,375 sq. mi. **Population:** 7,555,338 (1981 census)

**Official Name:** Republic of Austria **Capital:** Vienna **Nationality:** Austrian **Languages:** German is the official and principal language. Slovenian, Croatian, and Hungarian are spoken by small minorities **Religion:** 90% Roman Catholic **Flag:** Red, white, and red horizontal stripes, with the national emblem centered on the white stripe **Anthem:** Land of Mountains, Land on the River **Currency:** Schilling (16.4 per U.S. $1)

**Location:** Central Europe. Landlocked Austria is bordered by West Germany and Czechoslovakia on the north, Hungary on the east, Yugoslavia and Italy on the south, and Switzerland and Liechtenstein on the west **Features:** The country is 70% mountainous, with the Alps and their outliers dominating the west and south. The east and Vienna are located in the Danube basin **Chief Rivers:** Danube, Inn, Mur, Drau, Enns

**Head of State:** President Rudolf Kirchschlaeger, born 1915, re-elected 1980 **Head of Government:** Chancellor Bruno Kreisky, born 1911, took office April 1970, reappointed May 1979 **Effective Date of Present Constitution:** 1920, reinstated 1945 **Legislative Body:** Federal Assembly (bicameral parliament), consisting of the Federal Council (upper house), or *Bundesrat*, with 58 members, and the National Council (lower house), or *Nationalrat*, with 183 members. Members of the Upper House are appointed by provincial diets for 4-to 6-year terms; members of the Lower House are elected for 4 years **Local Government:** 9 provinces, each administered by an elected governor and provincial legislature

**Ethnic Composition:** Austrians are generally of South Germanic stock, with Slavic admixtures. The only sizeable minority group consists of some 70,000 Slovenes in Carinthia **Population Distribution:** 52% urban **Density:** 233 inhabitants per sq. mi.

**Largest Cities:** (1981 census) Vienna 1,515,666, Graz 243,405, Linz 197,962, Salzburg 138,213, Innsbruck 116,100

**Per Capita Income:** $7,127 (1980) **Gross Domestic Product (GDP):** $53 billion (1980) **Economic Statistics:** About 61% of GDP comes from industry (machinery, iron and steel, food and beverages, electronics, chemicals, textiles, ceramics, stone and glass, and metal goods); 5% from agriculture and forestry **Minerals and Mining:** Iron ore, petroleum, magnesite, lignite, and natural gas **Labor Force:** 2,875,000 (1980), of which 49% is employed in industry and crafts, 18% in agriculture and forestry, and 18% in trade and communications **Foreign Trade:** Exports, mainly machinery, iron and steel, textiles, chemicals, wood and paper, totaled $15 billion in 1979. Imports, chiefly machinery, transportation equipment, textiles, mineral fuels and chemicals, totaled $20 billion **Principal Trade Partners:** West Germany, Switzerland, Italy, Britain, United States, Sweden, Netherlands, France, USSR, Poland, Yugoslavia

**Vital Statistics:** Birthrate, 12 per 1,000 of pop. (1980); death rate, 12.2 **Life Expectancy:** 73 years **Health Statistics:** 89 inhabitants per hospital bed; 429 per physician (1977) **Infant Mortality:** 13.9 per 1,000 births (1977) **Illiteracy:** Negligible **Primary and Secondary School Enrollment:** 1,263,298 (1976) **Enrollment in Higher Education:** 104,525 (1975) **GNP Expended on Education:** 5.7% (1976)

**Transportation:** Surfaced roads total 20,357 mi. **Motor Vehicles:** 2,526,700 (1978) **Passenger Cars:** 2,040,300 **Railway Mileage:** 4,081 **Ports:** None **Major Airlines:** Austrian Airlines operates international and domestic flights **Communications: Radio Transmitters:** 412 **Licenses:** 2,068,000 (1977) **Television Transmitters:** 461 **Licenses:** 1,772,000 (1976) **Telephones:** 2,443,000 (1977) **Newspapers:** 31 dailies, 336 copies per 1,000 inhabitants (1977)

**Weights and Measures:** Metric system **Travel Requirements:** Passport, no visa for 3 months **International Dialing Code:** 43

Once the core of the Hapsburg Empire that covered much of Central and Southern Europe, Austria has been reduced by wars to a relatively small state and, by its geographical position, to a land that is officially neutral between East and West. But its actual sympathies and economic ties lie with the West.

Because Austria was forced by Hitler's 1938 *Anschluss* to become part of the Nazi war machine, the victors of World War II granted it a special state treaty in 1955, which specified the country's official neutrality.

But most of Austria's trade is with Western Europe. After the European Economic Community (EC) was organized in 1958, Austria sought association with it, despite the objections of the Soviet Union, which argued that association was incompatible with neutrality. Austria joined the European Free Trade Association in 1960, and, over token Soviet opposition, negotiated a special agreement with the EC in 1973.

Internal politics have been influenced by an almost equal division of voting strength between the People's party—which professes Christian values and respect for property— and the Socialist party. From 1945 to 1966, the People's party had a plurality, but not a majority, in the *Nationalrat* and governed in coalition with the Socialists. The two parties madee this arrangement because neither trusted the small Freedom party, which held the rest of the seats, and because memories of the chaos of the 1930s caused a desire for stability. This "grand coalition" ended in 1966, when a special election gave the People's party a one-seat majority; the Socialists were offered a coalition, but imposed conditions which the winners thought unreasonable. In 1970 the Socialists won a plurality, but not a majority, and formed a minority government with Bruno Kreisky as chancellor after attempts to reorganize the grand coalition broke down. This government remained in office after winning majorities in the elections of 1971, 1975 and 1979. There is little real difference between the parties, and the economy has remained basically capitalist, but with much state intervention.

Aside from the basic industries, an important source of income in Austria is tourism, as visitors are attracted to Alpine ski slopes and lakes and to city attractions such as the summer festival in Mozart's native city, Salzburg, and the spring festival week in Vienna.

**HISTORY:** Austria was settled by various tribes in prehistoric times and was subject to numerous invasions long before the Roman conquest around 15 B.C. About A.D. 800 it became a province of Charlemagne's empire and was joined to the Holy Roman Empire two centuries later. German-speaking rulers sponsored migrations, and the German language became predominant. By the end of the 13th century most of Austria was firmly under the rule of the Hapsburgs, who were to build a huge empire in central and southern Europe. By 1815, Austria had also become the leading power in the German Confederation, only to lose that position half a century later
**1848:** Nationalistic minorities in the Austrian Empire revolt against the monarchy but are subdued by Austrian forces
**1866:** Austro-Prussian War ends in Austrian defeat and terminates Austrian influence in German Confederation
**1867:** Hungary gains equal rights with Austria under a dual monarchy
**1914-18:** On June 28, 1914, a Serbian nationalist assassinates Archduke Francis Ferdinand, triggering World War I; Austria is allied with Germany and other Central Powers and shares in their defeat; Hapsburg monarchy collapses and Austria is proclaimed a republic
**1932-34:** Engelbert Dollfuss becomes chancellor and opposes *Anschluss* (union) with Germany; the outlawed Nazi party carries out his assassination (1934)
**1938:** Hitler annexes Austria to Germany
**1945:** United States, USSR, Britain, and France divide Austria into occupation zones following World War II. People's party wins elections; forms coalition with Socialist party
**1955:** Occupation forces leave and Austria proclaims permanent neutrality
**1966:** The conservative People's Party gains absolute majority in parliamentary election, ending 20-year rule of Socialist-conservative coalition
**1969:** Parliament, by overwhelming majority, ratifies treaty to prevent spread of nuclear weapons. Austria and Italy agree to give major autonomy to the 230,000 German-speaking inhabitants of the Italian province of Alto Adige. Socialists win plurality in Parliment; their leader, Bruno Kreisky, becomes chancellor
**1976:** 12th Winter Olympics are held in Innsbruck

* For flags of ANGOLA, ANTIGUA & BARBUDA, CAPE VERDE, COMOROS, DJIBOUTI and DOMINICA see page 517

* For flags of GRENADA, GUINEA-BISSAU and KIRIBATI see page 517

* For flags of MOZAMBIQUE and PAPUA NEW GUINEA see page 517

* For flags of ST. LUCIA, ST. VINCENT, SÃO TOMÉ E PRÍNCIPE, SEYCHELLES, SOLOMON IS., SURINAME, TUVALU and VANUATU see next page.

YEMEN (PEOPLES REP.)
YEMEN ARAB REP.
YUGOSLAVIA
ZAIRE
INDEPENDENT NATIONS 1974-1982
ZAMBIA
GRENADA (1974)
GUINEA-BISSAU (1974)
MOZAMBIQUE (1975)
CAPE VERDE (1975)
COMOROS (1975)
SÃO TOMÉ E PRÍNCIPE (1975)
PAPUA NEW GUINEA (1975)
ANGOLA (1975)
SURINAME (1975)
SEYCHELLES (1976)
DJIBOUTI (1977)
SOLOMON ISLANDS (1978)
TUVALU (1978)
DOMINICA (1978)
ST. LUCIA (1979)
KIRIBATI (1979)
ST. VINCENT & GRENS. (1979)
ZIMBABWE (1980)
VANUATU (1980)
BELIZE (1981) flag appears on page 513
ANTIGUA & BARBUDA (1981)
10 PM 11 PM MID-NIGHT 1 AM 2 AM 3 AM 4 AM 5 AM 6 AM 7 AM 8 AM 9 AM 10 AM 11 AM NOON 1 PM 2 PM 3 PM 4 PM 5 PM 6
NOTE: Standard time zones in the U.S.S.R. are always advanced one hour.
INTERNATIONAL DATE LINE
MONDAY
SUNDAY
GREENWICH
MERIDIAN
STANDARD
TIME
ZONES
Areas using half hour deviations.
Areas not using zone system.
6 PM 7 PM 8 PM 9 PM 10 PM
90° E 120° E 150° E 180° 150° W 120° W 90° W 60° W 30° W 0° 30° E 60° E 90° E
60° N 40° N 20° N 0° 20° S 40° S
TIME ZONES OF THE WORLD

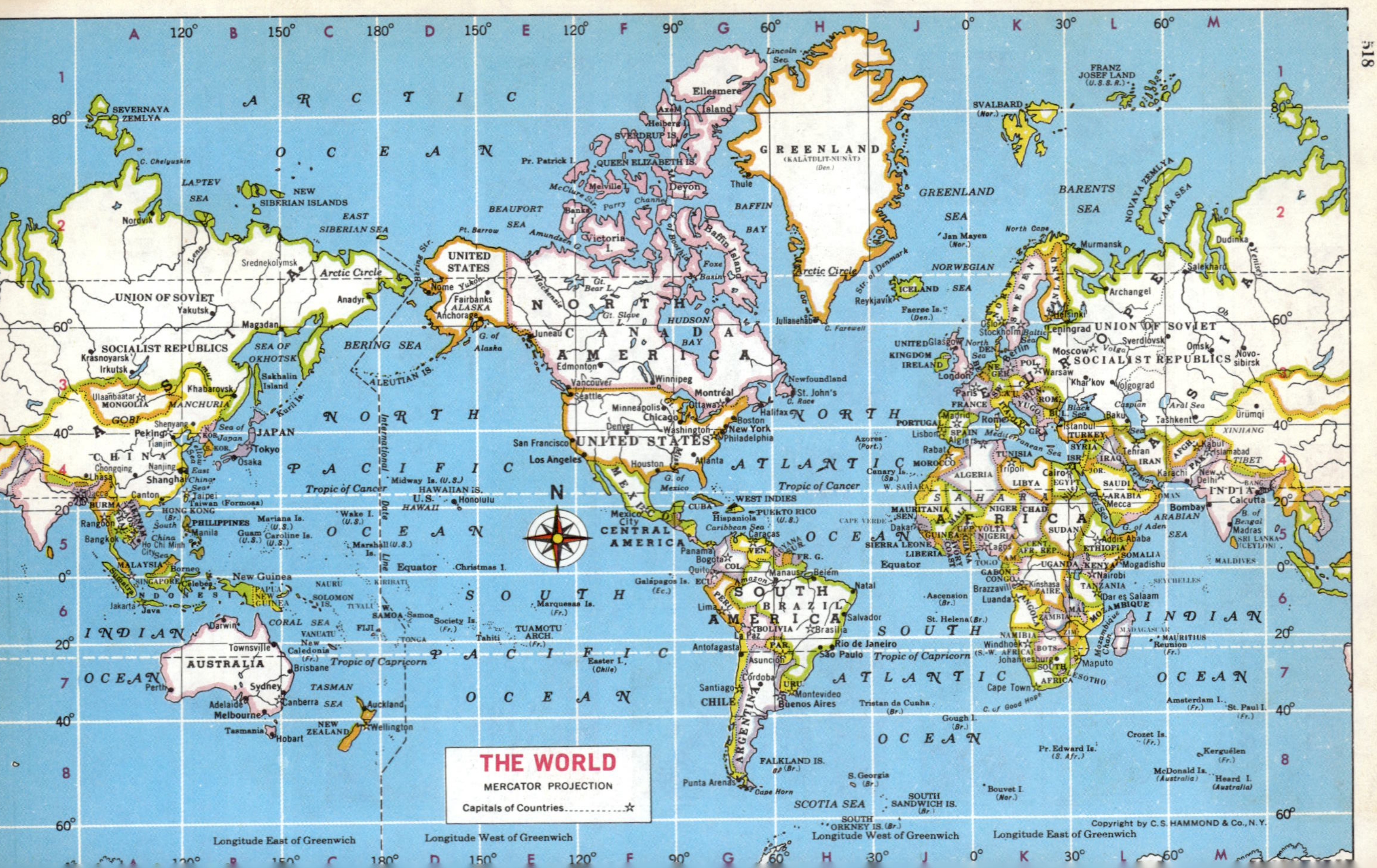
THE WORLD
MERCATOR PROJECTION
Capitals of Countries ............ ☆
ARCTIC OCEAN
NORTH PACIFIC
SOUTH PACIFIC OCEAN
NORTH ATLANTIC OCEAN
SOUTH ATLANTIC OCEAN
INDIAN OCEAN
NORTH AMERICA
SOUTH AMERICA
AFRICA
EUROPE
ASIA
AUSTRALIA
UNION OF SOVIET SOCIALIST REPUBLICS
UNITED STATES
CANADA
GREENLAND
CHINA
INDIA
BRAZIL
ARGENTINA
CENTRAL AMERICA
Tropic of Cancer
Equator
Tropic of Capricorn
Arctic Circle
International Date Line
Longitude East of Greenwich
Longitude West of Greenwich
Copyright by C.S. HAMMOND & Co., N.Y.

EUROPE
LAMBERT AZIMUTHAL EQUAL-AREA PROJECTION
SCALE OF MILES
0 100 200 300 400 500 600
SCALE OF KILOMETRES
0 100 200 300 400 500 600
Capitals of Countries
International Boundaries
Internal Boundaries
Copyright by C.S. HAMMOND & CO., N.Y.
Longitude West D of Greenwich 0° Longitude East E of Greenwich
ATLANTIC OCEAN
BRITISH ISLES
NORTH SEA
BALTIC SEA
BARENTS SEA
BLACK SEA
CASPIAN SEA
MEDITERRANEAN SEA
TYRRHENIAN SEA
IONIAN SEA
ADRIATIC SEA
AEGEAN SEA
SEA OF AZOV
Bay of Biscay
English Channel
Arctic Circle
ICELAND
NORWAY
SWEDEN
FINLAND
DENMARK
UNITED KINGDOM
SCOTLAND
ENGLAND
WALES
NO. IRELAND
IRELAND
NETH.
BELG.
LUX.
FRANCE
SPAIN
PORTUGAL
ANDORRA
MONACO
SWITZ.
LIECHT.
AUSTRIA
ITALY
SAN MARINO
VATICAN CITY
WEST GERMANY
EAST GERMANY
POLAND
CZECHOSLOVAKIA
HUNGARY
ROMANIA
YUGOSLAVIA
BULGARIA
ALBANIA
GREECE
TURKEY
AFRICA
GIBRALTAR (Br.)
MALTA
UNION OF SOVIET SOCIALIST REPUBLICS
RUSSIAN SOVIET FEDERATED SOCIALIST REPUBLIC
WHITE RUSSIAN S.S.R.
UKRAINIAN S.S.R.
LITHUANIAN S.S.R.
LATVIAN S.S.R.
EST. S.S.R.
MOLD. S.S.R.
GEORGIAN S.S.R.
ARMENIAN S.S.R.
AZERBAIDZHAN S.S.R.
Moscow
Leningrad
London
Paris
Berlin
Bonn
Warsaw
Prague
Vienna
Budapest
Bucharest
Sofia
Belgrade
Athens
Rome
Madrid
Lisbon
Oslo
Stockholm
Helsinki
Copenhagen
Dublin
Brussels
Amsterdam
Bern
Tirane
Reykjavik
Crete
Sicily
Sardinia
Corsica
Kola Pen.
Faeroe Is. (Den.)
Shetland Is.
Orkney Is.
Lofoten Is.

EUROPE
FRANCE
SPAIN
PORTUGAL
ITALY
YUGOSLAVIA
ALBANIA
ROMANIA
BULGARIA
TURKEY
U. S. S. R.
CASPIAN SEA
BLACK SEA
IRAN
IRAQ
SYRIA
LEBANON
ISRAEL
JORDAN
CYPRUS
KUWAIT
Persian Gulf
SAUDI ARABIA
Tropic of Cancer
RED SEA
YEMEN ARAB REP.
PEOP. DEM. REP. YEMEN
Gulf of Aden
MEDITERRANEAN SEA
Corsica
Sardinia
Sicily
Crete
MALTA
Balearic Is.
Madrid
Barcelona
Lisbon
Marseille
Rome
Naples
Athens
Istanbul
Ankara
Tehran
Baghdad
Damascus
Beirut
Riyadh
Mecca
Aden
GIBRALTAR
Str. of Gibraltar
Tangier (Tanger)
Rabat
Casablanca
Fez
Meknès
Marrakech
MOROCCO
Atlas Mountains
Algiers
Oran
Constantine
Tunis
TUNISIA
ALGERIA
LIBYA
Tripoli
Benghazi
G. of Sidra
Cyrenaica
Tripolitania
Fezzan
Libyan Desert
Kufra Oasis
EGYPT
CAIRO
Alexandria
Port Said
Suez
Aswan
Lake Nasser
Nubian Desert
SAHARA
Ahaggar
Tassili n'Ajjer
Tibesti
Tahat 9,852
Emi Koussi 11,204
Jebel 'Uweinat 6,345
WESTERN SAHARA
Canary Is. (Sp.)
Madeira (Port.)
MAURITANIA
Nouakchott
MALI
Timbuktu
Bamako
NIGER
Niamey
Niger
CHAD
L. Chad
N'Djamena
SUDAN
Khartoum
Omdurman
Port Sudan
Blue Nile
White Nile
ETHIOPIA
Addis Ababa
Ogaden
DJIBOUTI
SOMALIA
Mogadishu
KENYA
Nairobi
Kenya 17,058
UGANDA
Kampala
L. Victoria
L. Turkana
RWANDA
ZAIRE
Kisangani
CONGO
Ubangi
CENTRAL AFRICAN REPUBLIC
Bangui
CAMEROON
Yaoundé
Cameroon 13,350
NIGERIA
Lagos
Kano
Ibadan
Benue
BENIN
TOGO
GHANA
Accra
Kumasi
L. Volta
UPPER VOLTA
Ouagadougou
IVORY COAST
Abidjan
LIBERIA
Monrovia
SIERRA LEONE
Freetown
GUINEA
Conakry
GUINEA-BISSAU
Bissau
GAMBIA
Banjul
SENEGAL
Dakar
C. Verde
EQUATORIAL GUINEA
GABON
Libreville
SÃO TOMÉ E PRÍNCIPE
Gulf of Guinea
Equator

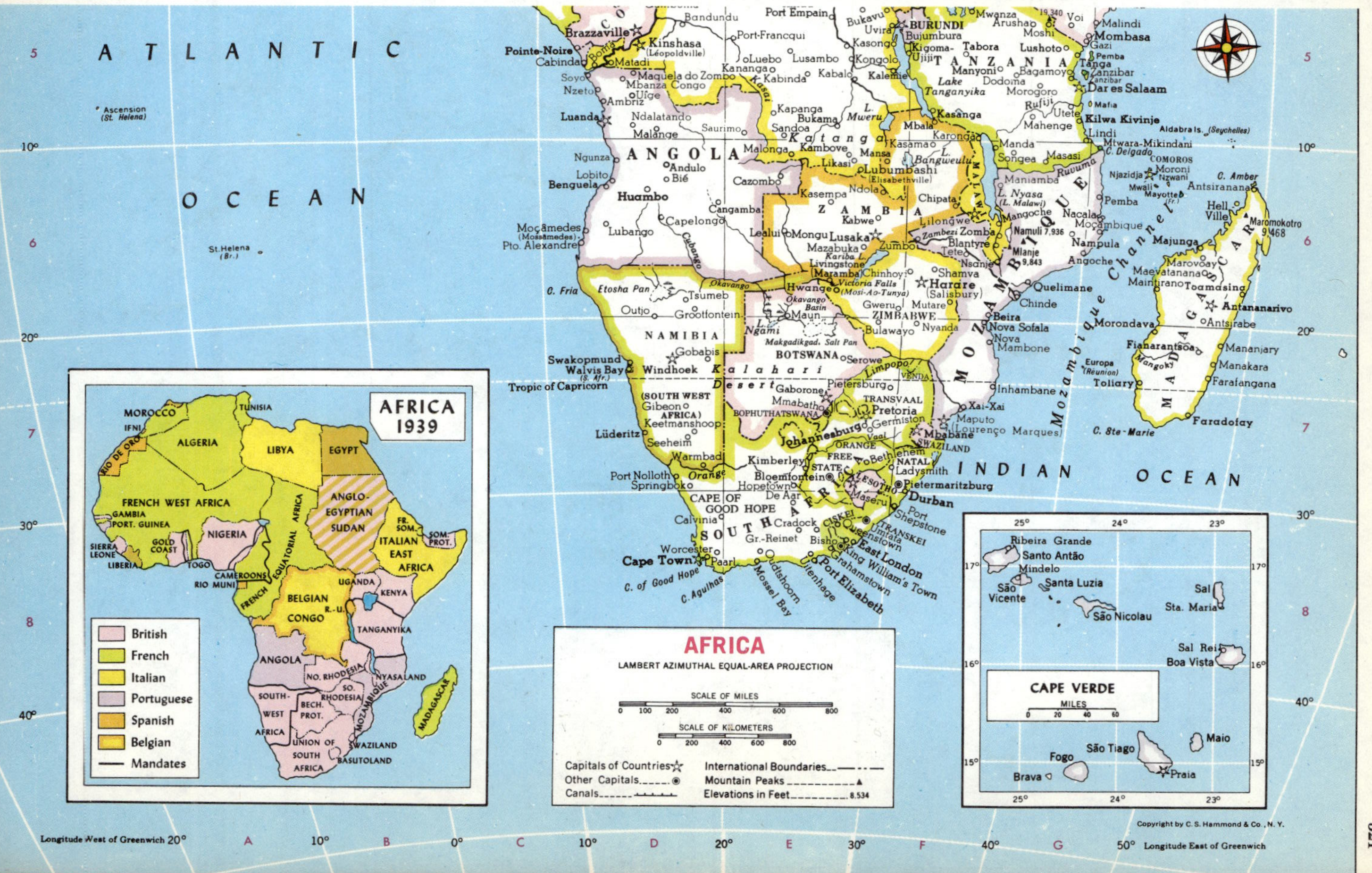
AFRICA
LAMBERT AZIMUTHAL EQUAL-AREA PROJECTION
SCALE OF MILES
0 100 200 400 600 800
SCALE OF KILOMETERS
0 200 400 600 800
Capitals of Countries
Other Capitals
Canals
International Boundaries
Mountain Peaks
Elevations in Feet 8,534
ATLANTIC OCEAN
INDIAN OCEAN
Mozambique Channel
Ascension (St. Helena)
St. Helena (Br.)
Tropic of Capricorn
ANGOLA
ZAMBIA
NAMIBIA (SOUTH WEST AFRICA)
BOTSWANA
ZIMBABWE
MOZAMBIQUE
MALAWI
TANZANIA
BURUNDI
MADAGASCAR
SOUTH AFRICA
LESOTHO
SWAZILAND
BOPHUTHATSWANA
TRANSVAAL
ORANGE FREE STATE
NATAL
CAPE OF GOOD HOPE
TRANSKEI
CISKEI
VENDA
Katanga
Kalahari Desert
Brazzaville
Kinshasa (Léopoldville)
Pointe-Noire
Cabinda
Matadi
Luanda
Benguela
Lobito
Huambo
Moçâmedes (Mossâmedes)
Lubumbashi (Elisabethville)
Lusaka
Harare (Salisbury)
Bulawayo
Windhoek
Walvis Bay (S. Afr.)
Swakopmund
Lüderitz
Gaborone
Pretoria
Johannesburg
Kimberley
Bloemfontein
Durban
Pietermaritzburg
East London
Port Elizabeth
Cape Town
C. of Good Hope
C. Agulhas
Maputo (Lourenço Marques)
Beira
Lilongwe
Blantyre
Zomba
Dar es Salaam
Zanzibar
Mombasa
Antananarivo
Toamasina
Mahajanga
Toliary
Moroni
COMOROS
Aldabra Is. (Seychelles)
Europa (Réunion)
C. Ste-Marie
C. Amber
Maromokotro 9,468
Mbabane
Maseru
AFRICA 1939
MOROCCO
IFNI
RIO DE ORO
ALGERIA
TUNISIA
LIBYA
EGYPT
FRENCH WEST AFRICA
GAMBIA
PORT. GUINEA
SIERRA LEONE
LIBERIA
GOLD COAST
TOGO
NIGERIA
CAMEROONS
RIO MUNI
FRENCH EQUATORIAL AFRICA
ANGLO-EGYPTIAN SUDAN
FR. SOM.
SOM. PROT.
ITALIAN EAST AFRICA
BELGIAN CONGO
R.-U.
UGANDA
KENYA
TANGANYIKA
NYASALAND
NO. RHODESIA
SO. RHODESIA
ANGOLA
MOZAMBIQUE
SOUTH-WEST AFRICA
BECH. PROT.
UNION OF SOUTH AFRICA
SWAZILAND
BASUTOLAND
MADAGASCAR
British
French
Italian
Portuguese
Spanish
Belgian
Mandates
CAPE VERDE
MILES
0 20 40 60
Ribeira Grande
Santo Antão
Mindelo
São Vicente
Santa Luzia
São Nicolau
Sal
Sta. Maria
Sal Rei
Boa Vista
Maio
São Tiago
Praia
Fogo
Brava
Copyright by C. S. Hammond & Co., N. Y.
Longitude West of Greenwich 20°
Longitude East of Greenwich

ATLANTIC OCEAN
PACIFIC OCEAN
ARCTIC OCEAN
BERING SEA
SEA OF OKHOTSK
SEA OF JAPAN
BARENTS SEA
KARA SEA
LAPTEV SEA
NORTH SEA
BALTIC SEA
BLACK SEA
CASPIAN SEA
MEDITERRANEAN SEA
ADRIATIC SEA
AEGEAN SEA
RED SEA
North Pole
Arctic Circle
Greenland
Iceland
Spitsbergen
Svalbard (Spitsbergen)
Franz Josef Ld.
Novaya Zemlya
Severnaya Zemlya
New Siberian Is.
Wrangel I.
Aleutian Is.
Kuril Is.
Sakhalin
Kamchatka Pen.
Honshu
UNITED STATES
ALASKA
Bering Str.
UNION OF SOVIET SOCIALIST REPUBLICS
RUSSIAN SOVIET FEDERATED SOCIALIST REPUBLIC
SIBERIA
KAZAKH S.S.R.
UZBEK S.S.R.
TURKMEN S.S.R.
MONGOLIA
INNER MONGOLIA
CHINA
TIBET
XINJIANG
AFGHANISTAN
PAKISTAN
IRAN (PERSIA)
IRAQ
SYRIA
TURKEY
SAUDI ARABIA
JAPAN
Kolyma Range
Sikhote-Alin
Tian Shan
Altun Shan
Kunlun Shan
Caucasus
Ural Mts.
Lena
Yenisey
Ob'
Irtysh
Amur
Volga
Don
Dnieper
Danube
L. Baykal
L. Balkhash
Aral Sea
MOSCOW
Leningrad
Kiev
Warsaw
Berlin
Prague
Vienna
Budapest
Bucharest
Sofia
Istanbul
Ankara
Athens
Rome
Paris
LONDON
Brussels
Amsterdam
Copenhagen
Stockholm
Oslo
Helsinki
Hamburg
Milan
Glasgow
Edinburgh
Dublin
Belfast
Tehran
Baghdad
Cairo
Alexandria
Beirut
PEKING
SHANGHAI
TOKYO
Yokohama
Osaka
Kyoto
Nagoya
Kobe
Seoul
Vladivostok
Tashkent
Alma-Ata
Novosibirsk
Omsk
Sverdlovsk
Chelyabinsk
Irkutsk
Krasnoyarsk
Volgograd (Stalingrad)
Astrakhan
Riga
Tallinn
Kabul
Lahore
Chongqing
Chengdu
Wuhan
Nanjing
Shenyang
Xi'an
Lanzhou
Taiyuan

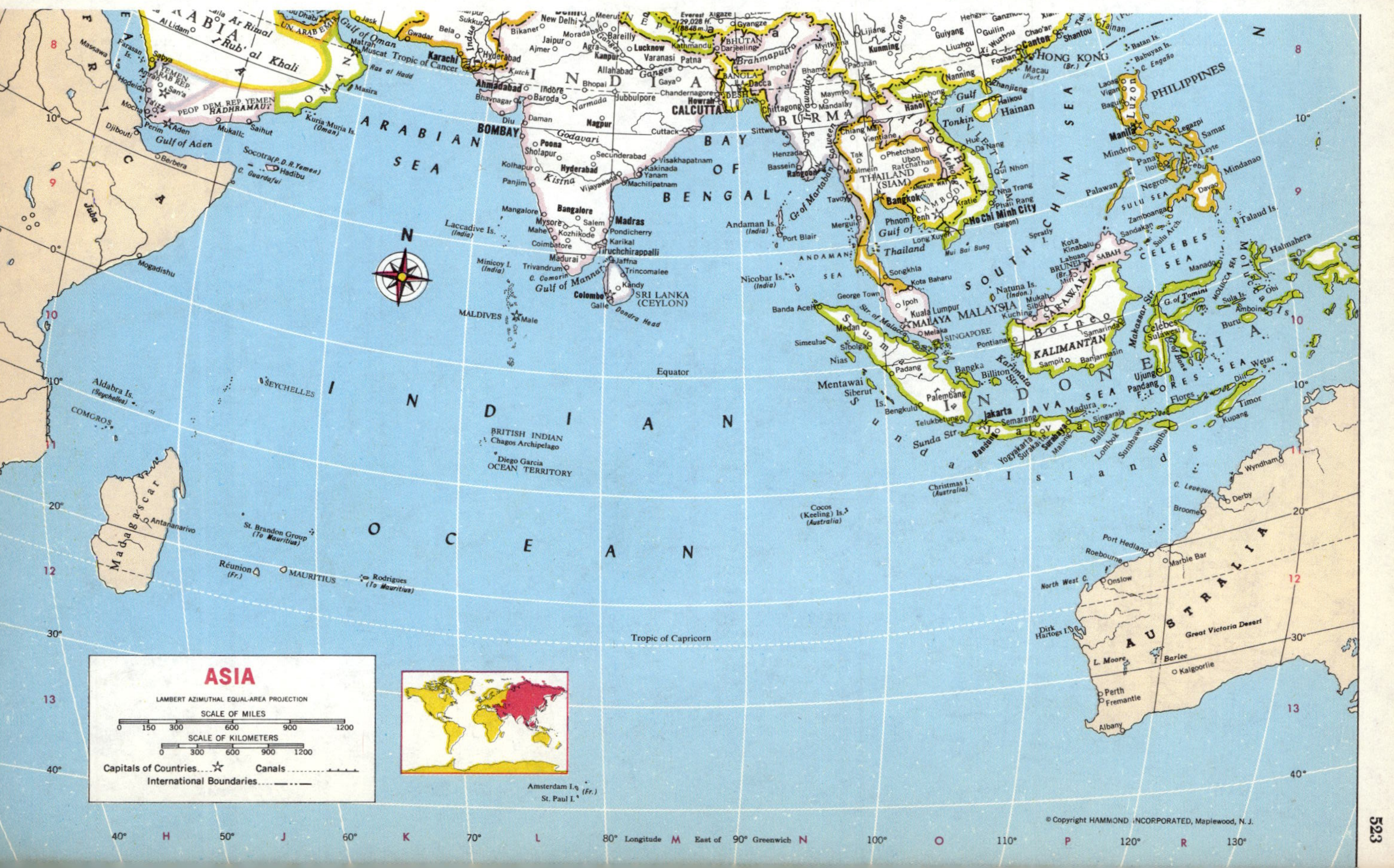
ASIA
LAMBERT AZIMUTHAL EQUAL-AREA PROJECTION
SCALE OF MILES
0 150 300 600 900 1200
SCALE OF KILOMETERS
0 300 600 900 1200
Capitals of Countries ☆
Canals
International Boundaries
INDIAN OCEAN
ARABIAN SEA
BAY OF BENGAL
SOUTH CHINA SEA
ANDAMAN SEA
JAVA SEA
CELEBES SEA
SULU SEA
INDIA
BURMA
THAILAND (SIAM)
MALAYSIA
PHILIPPINES
AUSTRALIA
AFRICA
ARABIA
SRI LANKA (CEYLON)
MALDIVES
SEYCHELLES
MAURITIUS
BRITISH INDIAN OCEAN TERRITORY
Madagascar
Great Victoria Desert
Tropic of Cancer
Tropic of Capricorn
Equator
Longitude East of Greenwich
© Copyright HAMMOND INCORPORATED, Maplewood, N.J.

THE NEAR and MIDDLE EAST
CONIC PROJECTION
SCALE OF MILES
0 100 200 300 400
KILOMETERS
0 100 200 300 400
Capitals of Countries
International Boundaries
Other Boundaries
55° Longitude East of 60° Greenwich
Copyright by C. S. HAMMOND & Co., N. Y.
BLACK SEA
CASPIAN SEA
MEDITERRANEAN SEA
ARABIAN SEA
PERSIAN GULF
GULF OF OMAN
RED SEA
G. of Aden
TURKEY
SYRIA
LEBANON
ISRAEL
JORDAN
IRAQ
IRAN
AFGHANISTAN
PAKISTAN
INDIA
SAUDI ARABIA
KUWAIT
BAHRAIN
QATAR
UN. ARAB EMIRATES
OMAN
YEMEN ARAB REP.
PEOPLES DEM. REP. OF YEMEN
EGYPT
SUDAN
ETHIOPIA
DJIBOUTI
CYPRUS
LIBYA
CHINA
SINKIANG
U. S. S. R.
Ankara
Tehran
Baghdad
Riyadh
Kabul
Cairo
Damascus
Beirut
Amman
Jerusalem
Al Kuwait
Manama
Doha
Abu Dhabi
Muscat
Aden
Sa'ada
Khartoum
Nicosia
Islamabad
Rub' al Khali
Nubian Desert
Arabian Desert
Libyan Desert
Great Indian Desert
Dasht-i-Kavir
Dasht-i-Lut
Kara-Kum Desert
Kyzyl-Kum Desert
Nefud
Tropic of Cancer

SOUTH AMERICA
LAMBERT AZIMUTHAL EQUAL-AREA PROJECTION
SCALE OF MILES
0 100 200 400 600
SCALE OF KILOMETERS
0 200 400 600
Capitals of Countries
International Boundaries
Copyright by C. S. HAMMOND & Co., N. Y.
CARIBBEAN SEA
NETHERLANDS ANTILLES
Willemstad
BARBADOS
Bridgetown
GRENADA
Port of Spain
TRINIDAD & TOBAGO
ATLANTIC OCEAN
PACIFIC OCEAN
Equator
Tropic of Capricorn
Longitude West of Greenwich
COLOMBIA
VENEZUELA
GUYANA
SURINAME
FR. GUIANA
ECUADOR
PERU
BRAZIL
BOLIVIA
PARAGUAY
CHILE
ARGENTINA
URUGUAY
FALKLAND ISLANDS (Br.)
Stanley
Pta. Gallinas
Sta. Marta
Barranquilla
Cartagena
Colón
Panamá
G. of Panamá
Montería
Maracaibo
Medellín
Cucuta
Bucaramanga
Manizales
Bogotá
Tunja
Buenaventura
I. Malpelo (Col.)
Cali
Neiva
Popayán
Pasto
Quito
Guayaquil
Riobamba
Cuenca
G. de Guayaquil
Sullana
Piura
Chiclayo
Pta. de Aguja
Cajamarca
Trujillo
Iquitos
Marañon
Huánuco
Cerro de Pasco
Huacho
Lima
Callao
Huancayo
Ayacucho
Pisco
Ica
Pta. Huacas
Puno
Arequipa
Mollendo
Tacna
Arica
Iquique
Tocopilla
Antofagasta
Taltal
Copiapó
La Serena
Ovalle
Valparaíso
Santiago
Rancagua
Talca
Concepción
Chillán
Angol
Temuco
Valdivia
Puerto Montt
Ancud
I. de Chiloé
ARCHIPIÉLAGO de los CHONOS
Aysén
I. Campana
I. Wellington
I. Madre de Dios
Santa Inés
I. Hoste
Cape Horn
Punta Arenas
Tierra del Fuego
Ushuaia
I. de los Estados
I. San Félix (Chile)
I. San Ambrosio (Chile)
I. Alejandro Selkirk
I. Robinson Crusoe
Is. Juan Fernández (Chile)
Coro
Pto. Cabello
Caracas
Valencia
Barquisimeto
Cumaná
Carúpano
Mérida
San Cristóbal
Pto. Carreño
Puerto Ayacucho
Ciudad Bolívar
Orinoco
Georgetown
Paramaribo
Nieuw Nickerie
Cayenne
Oyapock
I. de Maraca
Macapá
I. de Marajó
Belém
São Luiz
Parnaíba
Fortaleza
Mocajuba
Tocantins
Caxias
Teresina
Mocoró
Natal
João Pessoa
Juazeiro de Ceará
Campina Grande
Caruarú
Recife
Maceió
Aracajú
Alagoinhas
Salvador (Bahia)
Jequié
Ilhéus
Porto Nacional
Carinhanha
Brasília
Goiás
Anápolis
Goiânia
Ipamerí
Montes Claros
Araguarí
Uberaba
Belo Horizonte
Vitória
Campos
C. de São Tomé
Juiz de Fora
Ribeirão Preto
Tres Lagôas
Marília
Campinas
São Paulo
Niterói
Rio de Janeiro
Cabo Frio
Santos
Londrina
Curitiba
Paranaguá
Joinville
Florianópolis
Passo Fundo
Caxias do Sul
Pôrto Alegre
L. dos Patos
Pelotas
Santa Maria
Uruguaiana
Livramento
Bagé
Óbidos
Santarém
Parintins
Itacoatiara
Manaus
Amazon
Negro
Japurá
Putumayo
Pto. Cordoba
Benjamin Constant
Juruá
Purús
Madeira
Tapajós
Xingú
Conceição do Araguaia
Araguaia
Rio Branco
Pôrto Velho
Roosevelt
Boa Vista
Branco
Cobija
Guaporé
Beni
Mamoré
Trinidad
Lake Titicaca
La Paz
Cochabamba
Oruro
L. Poopó
Sucre
Potosí
Uyuni
Tarija
Santa Cruz
Pto. Suárez
Corumbá
Mato Grosso
Cuiabá
Paraguay
Aquidauana
Campo Grande
Maracajú
Mariscal Estigarribia
Pto. Casado
Concepción
Asunción
Rosario
Villarrica
Encarnación
Posadas
Pilcomayo
Ollague
Jujuy
Salta
Tucumán
Formosa
San Pedro
Resistencia
Corrientes
Santiago del Estero
Catamarca
La Rioja
Goya
Salado
Córdoba
San Juan
Santa Fe
Paraná
Concordia
Aconcagua
Villa María
Rosario
Mendoza
Río Cuarto
S. Rafael
Mercedes
Buenos Aires
Avellaneda
La Plata
Río de la Plata
C. San Antonio
Salto
Paysandú
Melo
Durazno
Minas
Montevideo
Santa Rosa
Azul
Tandil
Mar del Plata
Bahía Blanca
Colorado
Neuquén
Negro
Viedma
San Carlos de Bariloche
G. San Matías
Pto. Madryn
Chubut
Comodoro Rivadavia
G. San Jorge
C. Tres Puntas
Buenos Aires
San Julián
Bahía Grande
Gallegos

ARCTIC OCEAN
ATLANTIC OCEAN
PACIFIC
North Pole
GREENLAND SEA
GREENLAND
(KALÂTDLIT-NUNÂT)
(Den.)
KING CHRISTIAN IX LAND
KING FREDERIK VI COAST
KING CHRISTIAN X LAND
KING FREDERIK VIII LAND
KNUD RASMUSSEN LAND
Arctic Circle
C. Farewell
Denmark Str.
ICELAND
Reykjavík
Faeroe Is. (Den.)
Jan Mayen (Nor.)
UNITED KINGDOM
LINCOLN SEA
Baffin Bay
Davis Strait
LABRADOR SEA
Hudson Strait
Baffin Island
Ellesmere I.
QUEEN ELIZABETH ISLANDS
SVERDRUP IS.
Axel Heiberg I.
Devon I.
Melville I.
Banks I.
Victoria I.
BEAUFORT SEA
Amundsen Gulf
Gulf of Boothia
BOOTHIA PEN.
MELVILLE PEN.
Foxe Basin
Southampton I.
Hudson Bay
James Bay
Belcher Is.
NORTHWEST TERRITORIES
CANADA
YUKON TERR.
BRITISH COLUMBIA
ALBERTA
SASKATCHEWAN
MANITOBA
ONTARIO
QUEBEC
NEWFOUNDLAND
Labrador
NOVA SCOTIA
NEW BRUNSWICK
Great Bear Lake
Great Slave L.
L. Athabasca
L. Winnipeg
Mackenzie
Yukon
Coast Mountains
QUEEN CHARLOTTE IS.
Vancouver I.
ALEXANDER ARCH.
UNITED STATES
ALASKA
Brooks Range
Mt. McKinley 20,320
Fairbanks
Anchorage
Juneau
Kodiak I.
ALASKA PEN.
Bristol Bay
BERING SEA
Bering Strait
Norton Sd.
Nunivak I.
St. Matthew I.
St. Lawrence I.
Wrangel I.
ASIA
U.S.S.R.
Anadyr
G. of Anadyr
Winnipeg
Edmonton
Calgary
Regina
Vancouver
Montreal
Québec
Toronto
Ottawa
Halifax
St. John's
Seattle
Portland
Chicago
Detroit
New York
Boston
Philadelphia
Washington
MONT.
WYO.
IDAHO
WASH.
OREG.
N. DAK.
S. DAK.
NEBR.
MINN.
IOWA
WIS.
MICH.
ILL.
OHIO
PA.
N.Y.
MAINE
Lake Superior
Huron
Missouri
Hecate Str.
Dixon Entr.
C. Mendocino

NORTH AMERICA
LAMBERT AZIMUTHAL EQUAL-AREA PROJECTION
SCALE OF MILES
0 100 200 400 600 800
SCALE OF KILOMETERS
0 200 400 600 800
Capitals of Countries
International Boundaries
Other Boundaries
Canals
Copyright by C. S. HAMMOND & Co., N. Y.
UNITED STATES
MEXICO
Gulf of Mexico
CARIBBEAN SEA
WEST INDIES
BAHAMAS
CUBA
JAMAICA
Hispaniola
HAITI
GUATEMALA
HONDURAS
NICARAGUA
EL SALVADOR
COSTA RICA
PANAMA
COLOMBIA
VENEZUELA
SOUTH
ATLANTIC
PACIFIC OCEAN
Gulf of California
LOWER CALIFORNIA
Sierra Madre Occidental
Tropic of Cancer
Equator
GALÁPAGOS IS. (Ecuador)
REVILLAGIGEDO IS. (Mex.)
Clipperton (Fr.)
Cocos I. (C.R.)
Malpelo I. (Col.)
Bermuda (Br.)
TEXAS
Mexico City
Havana
New Orleans
Longitude 100° West of Greenwich

# PACIFIC OCEAN

LAMBERT AZIMUTHAL EQUAL-AREA PROJECTION

NAUTICAL MILES: 0 200 400 600 800 1000 1200

STATUTE MILES: 0 200 400 600 800 1000 1200

KILOMETERS: 0 400 800 1200

Capitals of Countries ☆

Other Capitals ◉

**1979:** Socialist Party wins majority in Parliament; Kreisky is sworn in to his 4th term as chancellor

## BAHAMAS

**Area:** 5,382 sq. mi. **Population:** 223,455 (1980 census)

**Official Name:** Commonwealth of the Bahamas **Capital:** Nassau **Nationality:** Bahamian **Language:** English **Religion:** There are Baptist, Methodist, Anglican, and Roman Catholic congregations **Flag:** Three horizontal stripes, the upper and lower aquamarine, the middle gold, with a black equilateral triangle on the hoist **Anthem:** March on, Bahamaland **Currency:** Bahamian dollar (1.00 per U.S. $1)

**Location:** An archipelago located in the northern portion of the West Indies in the Atlantic **Features:** The Bahamas include 700 islands and 2,000 rocks and cays, but less than 30 of the islands are inhabited. The islands are generally low and flat, with many splendid beaches. The climate is pleasantly warm throughout the year

**Head of State:** Queen Elizabeth II, represented by acting governor-general Gerald C. Cash, born 1917 **Head of Government:** Prime Minister Lynden O. Pindling, appointed 1973 **Effective Date of Present Constitution:** July 1973 **Legislative Body:** A General Assembly consists of a Senate with 16 members and a House of Assembly with 38 elected members **Local Government:** 18 districts, administered by appointed commissioners

**Ethnic Composition:** 85% Negro; the rest are of British, Canadian, and U.S. descent **Population Distribution:** 58% urban **Density:** 42 inhabitants per sq. mi.

**Largest Cities:** (1980 census) Nassau 135,437, Freeport 22,301

**Per Capita Income:** $4,534 (1980) **Gross National Product (GNP):** $1.1 billion (1980) **Economic Statistics:** Tourism is the main source of income **Minerals and Mining:** Salt is extracted from brine by solar radiation; cement and petroleum products are produced **Labor Force:** 101,000 (1979). In 1970, 20% were in industry, 7% in agriculture, and the rest in trade and services **Foreign Trade:** Exports, mainly petroleum products, cement, alcoholic beverages, pulpwood, pharmaceuticals, crawfish, and salt extracted from brine by solar radiation totaled about $2.4 billion in 1977. Imports of food, drink, tobacco, crude oil, manufactured articles, and animals totaled $2.1 billion **Principal Trade Partners:** United States, Saudi Arabia, Nigeria, Angola, Libya, Canada, Britain

**Vital Statistics:** Birthrate, 21.6 per 1,000 of pop. (1980); death rate, 4.7 per 1,000 **Life Expectancy:** 68.8 years **Infant Mortality:** 31.9 per 1,000 births **Illiteracy:** 7% **Health Statistics:** 253 inhabitants per hospital bed; 1,507 per physician (1977) **Primary and Secondary School Enrollment:** 31,928 (1976) **Enrollment in Higher Education:** 2,160 (1975) **GNP Expended on Education:** 5.4% (1973)

**Transportation:** Surfaced roads total about 1,000 mi. **Motor Vehicles:** 46,000 (1977) **Passenger Cars:** 42,800 **Railway Mileage:** None **Ports:** Nassau, Freeport **Major Airlines:** Nassau is served by numerous international carriers, and Bahamasair services the Family Islands **Communications: Radio Transmitters:** 5 **Receivers:** 97,000 (1977) **Television Transmitters:** 1 **Telephones:** 66,000 (1978) **Newspapers:** 3 dailies, 118 copies per 1,000 inhabitants (1976)

**Weights and Measures:** British and metric systems **Travel Requirements:** Passport and visa not required of tourist with onward/return ticket and citizenship identification **Direct Dialing Code:** 809

After three centuries as a British colony, the Bahamas became an independent nation on July 10, 1973. The new country at the same time became an independent member of the British Commonwealth—the 33rd British possession to gain its freedom since World War II. Bahamian Prime Minister Lynden O. Pindling and his ruling Progressive Liberal Party had received a mandate for independence in elections held in September 1972. The party was formed in 1953 by blacks discontented with the policies of the white-dominated government.

In opposition to Pindling's ruling party is the Free National Movement, made up of whites and black PLP dissidents.

Because of the warm climate and beautiful beaches, tourism is the major industry. The islands host over 1,900,000 visitors a year.

A real estate boom drove land prices up so high that in 1979 the government restricted land sales for foreigners. Some $250 million in construction was expected in a three-year span ending in 1982.

Citrus fruit, bananas, and vegetables are grown, but most food must still be imported. Pulpwood, cement, rum, and salt are exported. Nassau, the capital, is a major center for banking and insurance and for corporate operations. There is one bank for every 600 Bahamians.

The influx of refugees from Haiti had become a problem by 1980, when they constituted one tenth of the total population. Bahamian efforts to repatriate them were hampered by Haiti's slowness in granting re-entry permits. In 1981, when Bahamian authorities arrested 390 immigrants, Haiti banned all travel between the two countries, bringing repatriation to a standstill.

**HISTORY:** On Oct. 12, 1492, Christopher Columbus made his first landfall in the Western Hemisphere at San Salvador (now known as Watling Island) in the Bahamas. At the time the islands were inhabited by the Arawak Indians

**1647:** First permanent European settlement in the Bahamas
**1860:** Royal Victoria Hotel first attracts winter tourists
**1964:** Bahamas granted complete internal self-government
**1973:** Britain grants independence July 10
**1979:** Land sales to foreigners are restricted
**1982:** Labor unrest increases; walkout in March disrupts telephone, air transportation, and other services. Prime Minister Pindling's Progressive Liberal party retains power in election victory

## BAHRAIN

**Area:** 255 sq. mi. **Population:** 350,798 (1981 census)

**Official Name:** State of Bahrain **Capital:** Manama **Nationality:** Bahraini **Languages:** Predominantly Arabic; English used widely **Religion:** Moslem, the Sunni sect predominating in urban centers and the Shi'a sect in rural areas **Flag:** Red, with vertical serrated white band on the hoist **Anthem:** "National Anthem" **Currency:** Bahraini dinar (0.38 per U.S. $1)

**Location:** Southwest Asia. Eleven islands in the Persian Gulf. The main island, Bahrain, and those nearby lie 15 miles east of the coast of Saudi Arabia and the same distance west of the coast of Qatar

**Head of State:** Emir Isa ibn Salman al Khalifa, born 1933, became emir in 1961 **Head of Government:** Prime Minister: Sheikh Khalifa ibn Salman al Khalifa, born 1935, took office 1973 **Effective Date of Present Constitution:** 1973 **Legislative Body:** Rule is by the emir's decree **Local Government:** 6 municipalities—4 urban, each administered by a partly elected municipal council; and 2 rural

**Ethnic Composition:** 80% Arab, with about 12% Indians, Pakistanis, and Iranians and about 3,000 Europeans **Population Distribution:** 78% urban **Density:** 1,376 inhabitants per sq. mi.

**Largest Cities:** (1981 census) Manama 115,054, Muharraq 57,688

**Per Capita Income:** $2,397 (1980) **Gross Domestic Product (GDP):** $913 million (1980) **Economic Statistics:** Petroleum refining and the production of crude oil are the most important economic resources. Over 50% of the oil refined is piped from Saudi Arabia. There is in addition an aluminum smelter, a major dry dock and smaller industrial plants. The islands produce dates, fruit, and vegetables **Minerals and Mining:** Considerable deposits of natural gas exist, in addition to oil deposits **Labor Force:** 140,000 (1980 est.), with 5% in agriculture and 90% in industry (chiefly petroleum and aluminum refining) **Foreign Trade:** Exports, chiefly crude oil, totaled $2.4 billion in 1979. Imports, including machinery, foods, chemicals, industrial equipment, and vehicles, totaled $2.3 billion **Principal Trade Partners:** Britain, Saudi Arabia, United States, Japan, UAE

**Vital Statistics:** Birthrate, 46 per 1,000 of pop. (1974); death rate, 9 **Infant Mortality:** 23 per 1,000 births (1974) **Health Statistics:** 270 inhabitants per hospital bed; 218 per physician (1977) **Illiteracy:** 48% **Primary and Secondary School Enrollment:** 45,640 (1976) **Enrollment in Higher Education:** 703 (1975) **GNP Expended on Education:** 4.6% (1975)

**Transportation:** Paved roads total 61 mi. **Motor Vehicles:** 54,700 (1978) **Passenger Cars:** 41,200 **Ports:** Sitra, Mina Salman **Major Airlines:** Gulf Air and several international companies service the country **Communications: Radio Transmitters:** 4 **Receivers:** 100,000 (1977) **Television Transmitters:** 1 **Receivers:** 31,000 (1976) **Telephones:** 40,000 (1978) **Newspapers:** 1 daily, 11 weeklies, 29 copies per 1,000 inhabitants

**Weights and Measures:** Metric system, plus local measures **Travel Requirements:** Passport and visa required, $14 fee **International Dialing Code:** 973

Bahrain consists of a number of desert islands in the west central Persian Gulf, chief among these being Bahrain, Muharraq, Sitra, Umm Na'san, and the Hawar group. Bahrainis, who are Moslem Arabs, constitute about 63 percent of the population. There are also Arabs from elsewhere, Iranians, Indians, and Europeans.

The oil industry and transit trade are the mainstays of the economy. There is a large refinery on Sitra, and trade passes through Manama and Mina Salman, a duty-free transit center. "Offshore" service banking is a source of revenue.

Internally, the ruler, or emir, wields almost absolute power. In 1970 a Council of State was established, responsible to the ruler and serving at his pleasure. In 1971 Bahrain declared independence, ending its special relationship with Britain. Iran informally became Bahrain's protector, but in Dec. 1981 Bahrain turned away from Iran and signed a joint security pact with Saudi Arabia.

**HISTORY:** Bahrain may have been "Dilmun," a trade center mentioned in Sumerian records, but little is known of its history before it was occupied by Portugal (1501-1602). The present dynasty was founded in 1783 by an adventurer from Arabia

**1820:** British protectorate status begins

**1971:** Bahrain declares independence on August 15, and is admitted to the UN and the Arab League

**1973:** New constitution is in effect

**1975:** National Assembly is dissolved by Emir Khalifa

**1982:** Bahrain and five other Arab states sign regional defense plan

## BANGLADESH

**Area:** 55,126 sq. mi. **Population:** 87,052,024 (1981 census)

**Official Name:** People's Republic of Bangladesh **Capital:** Dacca **Nationality:** Bangladeshi **Languages:** Bengali (Bangla) is official; English is also widely used **Religion:** About 83% Moslem and 16% Hindu, with some Buddhists and Christians **Flag:** Rectangular, in bottle green, with a red circle, slightly left of center, on the green body **Anthem:** Amar Sonar Bangla (My Golden Bengal) by Rabindranath Tagore **Currency:** Taka (21.4 per U.S. $1)

**Location:** Bangladesh is bordered on the north, east, and west by India, on the southeast by Burma, and on the south by the Bay of Bengal **Features:** a subtropical alluvial plain, with many river valleys and deltas. Average annual temperature 49°F-80°F. Jute fields, rice paddies, tea plantations, tropical jungles, and swamps are prominent features of its landscape **Chief Rivers:** Ganges and Brahmaputra

**Head of State and Government:** Chief Martial Law Administrator: Lt. Gen. Hussain Mohammad Ershad, born 1930, took power following the military coup of March 24, 1982. There is a figurehead president, Abul Fazal Mohammad Assanuddin Chowdhury **Effective Date of Present Constitution:** The 1972 Constitution has been suspended **Legislative Body:** Gen. Ershad has assumed full legislative power **Local Government:** 19 districts grouped into 4 divisions

**Ethnic Composition:** The population is overwhelmingly Bengali, with a few tribal peoples in the hills near the Burma border **Population Distribution:** 10% urban (1974) **Density:** 1,579 inhabitants per sq. mi.

**Largest Cities:** (1981 census—Metropolitan Areas) Dacca 3,458,602, Chittagong 1,388,475, Khulna 623,184, Rajshahi 171,600

**Per Capita Income:** $123 (1980) **Gross National Product (GNP):** $11 billion (1980) **Economic Statistics:** In 1979 about 54% of GNP was from agriculture (jute, rice, tea, sugarcane, chillies, wheat, and tobacco) and 12% from industry **Minerals and Mining:** There are large reserves of natural gas and some deep-lying coal **Labor Force:** 31,500,000 (1980), with 74% engaged in agriculture; some 11% are employed in industry **Foreign Trade:** Exports are chiefly raw jute and jute products, hides and skins and tea, and totaled about $757 million in 1979. Imports, chiefly fuels, machinery, clothing, foodstuffs, and chemicals, totaled $1.9 billion **Principal Trade Partners:** United States, Britain, India, Japan, USSR, UAE

**Vital Statistics:** Birthrate, 49.5 per 1,000 of pop. (1975); death rate, 28.1 **Life Expectancy:** 47 years **Health Statistics:** 4,505 inhabitants per hospital bed; 12,709 per physician (1977) **Infant Mortality:** 139 per 1,000 births **Illiteracy:** 74% **Primary and Secondary School Enrollment:** 11,800,209 (1976) **Enrollment in Higher Education:** 121,155 **GNP Expended on Education:** 1.4% (1975)

**Transportation:** Paved roads total 2,511 miles **Motor Vehicles:** 83,700 (1978) **Passenger Cars:** 53,200 **Railway Mileage:** 1,806 **Ports:** Chittagong, Chalna **Major Airlines:** Biman (Air Bangladesh) operates both international and domestic services **Communications: Radio Transmitters:** 12 **Receivers:** 500,000 (1977) **Television Stations:** 7 **Telephones:** 101,000 (1978) **Newspapers:** 28 dailies (1976)

**Weights and Measures:** Metric system and British standards **Travel Requirements:** Passport and visa required

In December 1970 the Awami League, a Bengali nationalist party concentrated in East Pakistan and led by the enormously popular Sheik Mujibur Rahman, won a majority of the seats in the Pakistan National Assembly. This unexpectedly strong showing in the first national elections held in Pakistan since independence emphasized the fissure between the Bengalis in East Pakistan and their rulers in Islamabad.

The old state of Bengal, now Bangladesh, has been a perennial disaster zone. It has virtually no industry, and the market for jute—its main export crop—has declined steadily with the introduction of synthetic fibers. Its population density is among the highest in the world, and most of its people live at the subsistence level. Bengalis long resented the relative prosperity of West Pakistan, contending it was the result of exploitative economic policies.

Demands for Bengali autonomy came to a head in the campaign of the Awami League. Sheik Mujib's six-point program called for a loose federation amounting to internal self-government for the Bengalis.

On March 1, 1971, Pakistan's President Yahya Khan announced that the convening of the National Assembly would be postponed. Leaders of the Awami League claimed they were being cheated of the fruits of the election, which had made them the majority party of Pakistan.

Widespread rioting and strikes in the Bengali province ensued, and on March 25, President Yahya Khan ordered the national army into the province to crush the separatist movement by force and arrest Sheik Mujib as a traitor. The next day, before his arrest, Sheik Mujib in a radio broadcast declared the independence of Bangladesh. The East Bengal Regiment of the army promptly defected to form the Bangladesh armed forces. For a few days the national army was pinned down. On April 10 a constituent assembly of the Awami League candidates elected to the National Assembly convened and confirmed the declaration of Bengali independence, naming Sheik Mujib president of the republic. But a military campaign of great ferocity, resulting in a death toll in the hundreds of thousands, quickly subdued the Bangladesh forces and cowed the population. In addition, several million Bengalis fled to neighboring India, and an occupation army remained.

Reports of clashes between Indian and Pakistani forces began to be heard. On December 3, Pakistani planes attacked western Indian military airfields, and Indian troops launched an attack in Bangladesh. Three days later India recognized the Bangladesh provisional government. After a whirlwind Indian campaign, the Pakistani forces in Bangladesh surrendered on December 16.

Sheik Mujib, freed from jail in Pakistan, returned to Bangladesh early in 1972, and on January 12 was named prime minister. The Sheik rapidly lost his charismatic hold as Bangladesh suffered from a disintegrating economy, corruption and famine.

Following the assassination of Sheik Mujib during a military coup in August 1975, Bangladesh experienced the turmoil of two new leaders within a period of two and a half months. Khandakar Mushtaque Ahmed was sworn in as president, but was forced to resign in November. Mohammad Sayem, chief justice of the Supreme Court, succeeded to the presidency. On assuming office, Sayem dissolved parliament.

Public opinion in Bangladesh, and especially in the armed forces, on which the Sayem regime largely depended for support, was divided in the first part of 1976 among four main forces: the supporters of Gen. Ziaur Rahman, the army chief of staff; the supporters of the late Sheik Mujib and the Awami League; the Islamic right; and the left-wing National Socialist party.

Taking advantage of these divisive conditions, General Rahman assumed full power as chief martial law administrator on November 30, 1976, and arrested at least 11 prominent political leaders, including former Pres. Khandakar Mushtaque Ahmed. National elections that had been promised for early 1977 were postponed. On April 21, 1977, General Rahman was sworn in as president following the resignation of Sayem. On October 2, 1977, at Dacca Airport, dissident junior officers attempted unsuccessfully to overthrow the government. Reports put the death toll at over 200.

In a field of 10 candidates, General Rahman won a five-year presidential term on June 3, 1978, by garnering about 75 percent of the votes cast. In February 1979, his Bangladesh Nationalist party swept 207 of the 300 contested parliament seats in national elections. The Awami League was left far behind, winning only 40 seats. Martial law was lifted and parliament restored.

The country turned into the 1980s with its food production rising and food imports down by 50%. "Exporting" of workers helped the economy as 100,000 Bangladeshi men sent money home from jobs in Persian Gulf states. Overpopulation, maldistribution of wealth, and corruption in the government and the marketplace remained major problems.

In the early hours of May 30, 1981, President Rahman was killed by army officers led by Maj. Gen. Manzur in an attempt to seize power. The coup was crushed promptly and Vice President Abdus Sattar assumed office. Elected handily in presidential elections in November, he was deposed on March 24, 1982, by the military, led by army chief of staff, Gen. Hussain Mohammad Ershad. Declaring that he hoped democracy could be restored in two years, Ershad banned political activity and instituted harsh penalties for such transgressions as smuggling, tax evasion, and "profiteering."

**HISTORY:** In the 12th century, Moslem invaders brought Islam to Bengal, part of which is now Bangladesh. Moslem power and culture in the Indian subcontinent reached their zenith under the Mogul empire (1526-1857). Despite cultural interchange with the Hindus, the Moslem community continued to maintain its distinct identity under British rule

**1970:** In November a massive cyclone kills 200,000

**1971:** The Awami League, a Bengali nationalist party, leads a movement and civil war for Bengali independence

**1972:** Awami leader Sheik Mujibur Rahman is named prime minister. New constitution effected for independent Bangladesh

**1973:** First parliamentary elections held; Awami League controls the National Assembly

**1975:** Sheik Mujib is assassinated in a military coup and Khandakar Mushtaque Ahmed is named president. He is forced to resign during a power struggle within the army, and Mohammad Sayem assumes the presidency. Sayem dissolves parliament

**1977:** Gen. Ziaur "Zia" Rahman is sworn in as president. Coup attempt by dissident officers fails

**1978:** Gen. Ziaur Rahman is elected to presidency for five-year term

**1979:** President Rahman's Bangladesh Nationalist party wins parliamentary elections. Martial law lifted

**1981:** Ziaur Rahman killed in abortive coup (May); Vice President Abdus Sattar, a civilian, succeeds him, wins November presidential election by wide margin

**1982:** Economic problems weaken Sattar in confrontation with military, who depose him in March. Army chief H.M. Ershad suspends constitution, imposes strict anti-corruption laws

## BARBADOS

**Area:** 166 sq. mi. **Population:** 249,000 (1980 census)

**Official Name:** Barbados **Capital:** Bridgetown **Nationality:** Barbadian **Languages:** English is the official and universal language **Religion:** About 70% of the population belongs to the Anglican Church. The rest are mainly Methodists, Moravians, and Roman Catholics **Flag:** Vertical bands of blue, gold, and blue, with a black trident centered on the gold band **Anthem:** National Anthem of Barbados, beginning "In plenty and in time of need" **Currency:** Barbadian dollar (2.01 per U.S. $1)

**Location:** West Indies. The most easterly of the Caribbean islands, Barbados lies immediately east of the Windward Islands and about 270 miles northeast of the mainland of South America **Features:** The island, which is of coral origin, is relatively flat, rising gently from the west coast in a series of terraces to a ridge in the center **Chief Rivers:** None

**Head of State:** Queen Elizabeth II, represented by a governor-general, Sir Deighton Harcourt Lisle Ward **Head of Government:** Prime Minister John Michael Geoffrey ("Tom") Adams, born 1932, appointed 1976 **Effective Date of Present Constitution:** 1966 **Legislative Body:** Parliament (bicameral), consisting of a House of Assembly and a Senate. The House of Assembly is composed of 27 members, elected for 5 years. The Senate consists of 21 members, 12 of whom are appointed by the governor-general on the advice of the prime minister, 2 on the advice of the leader of the opposition, and 7 appointed by the governor-general to represent various social and economic groups **Local Government:** 11 parishes and the city of Bridgetown

**Ethnic Composition:** About 80% of the population is of African descent; 4% is white, mainly of British origin **Population Distribution:** 4% urban **Density:** 1,500 inhabitants per sq. mi.

**Largest City:** (1980 census) Bridgetown 7,552 (Metropolitan Area 99,953)

**Per Capita Income:** $2,294 (1980) **Gross Domestic Product (GDP):** $654 million (1980) **Economic Statistics:** In 1980 about 10% of GDP was derived from agriculture (sugarcane), fishing and animal husbandry, and 32% from industry (sugar, rum, molasses, electronic parts) **Minerals and Mining:** Limestone and coral are quarried for domestic needs; there are small quantities of natural gas **Labor Force:** 103,900 (1980), of which 10% is employed in agriculture and 25% in industry and commerce **Foreign Trade:** Exports, chiefly sugar, rum, molasses and clothing, totaled $147 million in 1979. Imports, mainly food, machinery, transportation equipment, chemicals and petroleum products, totaled $424 million **Principal Trade Partners:** Britain, United States, Canada, West Indies, Japan

**Vital Statistics:** Birthrate, 17 per 1,000 of pop. (1979); death rate, 8.5 **Life Expectancy:** 71 years **Health Statistics:** 119 inhabitants per hospital bed; 1,471 per physician (1976) **Infant Mortality:** 25.1 per 1,000 births **Illiteracy:** 1% **Primary and Secondary School Enrollment:** 62,666 (1976) **Enrollment in Higher Education:** 1,417 (1973) **GNP Expended on Education:** 7.5% (1976)

**Transportation:** Paved roads total 840 mi. **Motor Vehicles:** 29,100 (1977) **Passenger Cars:** 25,300 **Railway Mileage:** None **Ports:** Bridgetown **Major Airlines:** Barbados is served by numerous international airlines **Communications: Radio Transmitters:** 1 **Receivers:** 100,000 (1977) **Television Transmitters:** 1 **Receivers:** 48,000 (1976) **Telephones:** 53,000 (1978) **Newspapers:** 1 daily, 115 copies per 1,000 inhabitants (1976)

**Weights and Measures:** Metric system **Travel Requirements:** Passport or proof of citizenship **Direct Dialing Code:** 809

Four centuries ago, the Portuguese sailors who sighted the 21-mile-long strip of coral first noticed its trees, their long branches drooping to the ground, and gave their name, Barbados—the bearded fig tree—to the island. The name is the only sign that Barbados has not always been British, perhaps even more British than Britain.

Nevertheless, since it won independence in 1966, the West Indian country has moved to expand its regional and hemispheric ties. It was admitted to the United Nations immediately after gaining independence and has also joined the Organization of American States and the Inter-American Development Bank.

In recent years the Barbadian economy, once totally dependent on the sugar crop, has been diversified by the development of tourism and light manufacturing, both of which were vigorously promoted by the Barbados Labour party government of Prime Minister J. M. G. ("Tom") Adams, elected in 1976 and returned to power over Democratic Labour party opposition in 1981.

**HISTORY:** Although both Arawak and Carib Indians had at one time inhabited Barbados, the island was uninhabited when the first white settlers arrived from England in 1627. In less than a decade slaves were brought from Africa to work the sugar plantations, which continue to serve as the mainstay of the island's economy. Slavery was abolished in 1834, but the island's political life continued to be dominated by a small white upper class until well into the 20th century

**1954:** Sir Grantley Adams, a Negro Barbadian and founder of the Barbados Labour party, becomes the first prime minister

**1966:** Barbados achieves full independence

**1968-69:** Barbados joins Caribbean Free Trade Area and Inter-American Development Bank

**1973:** Prime ministers of Barbados, Trinidad and Tobago, Guyana, and Jamaica establish CARICOM, a Caribbean common market

**1976:** J.M.G. Adams is appointed prime minister following election victory of his Barbados Labour party

**1982:** U.S. President Ronald Reagan meets Caribbean leaders, describes $1-billion area aid plan on visit to Barbados (April)

## BELGIUM

**Area:** 11,781 sq. mi. **Population:** 9,863,374 (1981 est.)

**Official Name:** Kingdom of Belgium **Capital:** Brussels **Nationality:** Belgian **Languages:** French, Flemish (Dutch), and German are the official and principal spoken languages. Flemish is spoken by the Flemings (Dutch) in the north and west, and French by the Walloons in the south and east; Brussels is bilingual **Religion:** The population is predominantly Roman Catholic, but there are several Protestant denominations and a Jewish community **Flag:** Vertical stripes of black, yellow, and red **Anthem:** La Brabançonne ("Song of Brabant") **Currency:** Belgian franc (44 per U.S. $1)

**Location:** Northwest Europe. Belgium is bordered by the Netherlands and the North Sea on the north, by Germany and Luxembourg on the east, and by France on the southwest and west **Features:** Although generally flat, Belgium has increasingly hilly and forested terrain toward the Ardennes region in the southeast **Chief Rivers:** Scheldt, Meuse

**Head of State:** King Baudouin I, born 1930, ascended the throne 1951 **Head of Government:** Premier Wilfried Martens, born 1936, appointed 1981 **Effective Date of Present Constitution:** 1831, amended December 1970 **Legislative Body:** Parliament (bicameral), consisting of a Senate and Chamber of Representatives. The Senate, consisting of 181 members elected for 4 years, is partly elected directly and in part chosen by provincial councils and fellow senators. The Chamber, with 212 members, is elected by direct universal suffrage for 4 years **Local Government:** 9 provinces and 589 (1976) communes, with considerable autonomy in local matters. Four regions have been established: Flanders and Wallonia, each with a large degree of autonomy, and Brussels and a German-speaking region with lesser powers

**Ethnic Composition:** Flemings 58%, French (Walloons) 41%, Germans 1% **Population Distribution:** 95% urban **Density:** 837 inhabitants per sq. mi.

**Largest Cities:** (1979 est.) Brussels 1,015,710, Ghent 243,523, Charleroi 224,229, Liège 224,136, Antwerp 197,305

**Per Capita Income:** $8,619 (1980) **Gross Domestic Product (GDP):** $85 billion (1980) **Economic Statistics:** 32% of the GNP comes from industry (steel, metal manufacturing, nonferrous metal, textile, diamond cutting, chemical, glass), and 3% from agriculture (livestock, sugar beets, hay, potatoes, grain) **Minerals and Mining:** Coal is the only mineral resource of major importance. Iron, lead, zinc, copper, manganese, and phosphates are mined in small quantities **Labor Force:** 4 million (1978), with 47% in services, 30% in industry, 8% in construction, 3% in agriculture and 12% in civil service **Foreign Trade:** Exports, chiefly chemicals, textiles, diamonds, iron and steel products, machinery, automotive vehicles, glass, and nonferrous metals, totaled $53.1 billion in 1979. Imports, mainly grains, ores, petroleum, chemicals, textiles, diamonds, metals and products, machinery, electrical equipment and automotive vehicles, totaled $56.9 billion **Principal Trade Partners:** West Germany, Netherlands, France, Italy, United States, Britain, Switzerland

**Vital Statistics:** Birthrate, 12.7 per 1,000 of pop. (1980); death rate, 11.6 **Life Expectancy:** 72 years **Health Statistics:** 111 inhabitants per hospital bed; 474 per physician (1977) **Infant Mortality:** 11.2 per 1,000 births **Illiteracy:** 3% **Primary and Secondary School Enrollment:** 1,773,614 (1976) **Enrollment in Higher Education:** 159,660 (1975) **GNP Expended on Education:** 6.2% (1976)

**Transportation:** Paved roads total 32,800 mi. **Motor Vehicles:** 3,272,300 (1978) **Passenger Cars:** 2,973,400 **Railway Mileage:** 2,620 **Ports:** Antwerp, Zeebrugge, Ghent, Ostend **Major Airlines:** Sabena airline operates both domestic and international services **Communications: Radio Transmitters:** 55 **Licenses:** 4,077,000 (1977) **Television Transmitters:** 30 **Licenses:** 2,646,000 (1976) **Telephones:** 3,271,000 (1978) **Newspapers:** 27 dailies, 241 copies per 1,000 inhabitants (1977)

**Weights and Measures:** Metric system **Travel Requirements:** Passport, no visa for 3 months **International Dialing Code:** 32

The geography of Belgium has brought it misfortune and fortune: the misfortune of having a largely low-lying countryside that served as a route for foreign armies, and the fortune of a location in Western Europe that helps to make the country a key trading and manufacturing center.

In its military misadventures, Belgium was the scene of Caesar's conquest of the Gallic tribes; the site of Napoleon's ultimate defeat, at Waterloo; and the stage for invasion by German armies in both world wars. But conflict also brought Belgium independence; the Belgians revolted against Dutch domination in 1830.

The northern part of the country, in which Belgian basic industry is largely situated, is inhabited by Dutch-speaking Flemings. Most of the rest of Belgium is Walloon country, where French is spoken. Currently the Flemings are dominant, with a majority in both the Senate and Chamber. The bilingual nature of the land has led to much friction.

In 1970, in order to reduce linguistic tensions, the unitary constitution of 1831 was revised to recognize "three cultural communities: French, Dutch, and German." Four linguistic regions—the Flemish and Walloon areas, a small German area along the border of West Germany, and bilingual Brussels—were created. Each has a council with limited authority over education, culture, and the economy. But proposals to increase their authority have been the most divisive issue of the 1970s. In 1980 the coalition government granted more self-governing powers to the Flemish and Walloon areas, but postponed consideration of similar status for Brussels to a later time.

Dependent on trade, Belgium has been a leader in the movement for European integration. It merged its customs with those of Luxembourg in 1921. The Netherlands joined this union to form *Benelux* by an agreement which took full effect in 1950. The Benelux countries joined the European Economic Community in 1958, and their earlier experience has helped to guide the Community. European integration helped to make Belgium prosperous in the 1960s; the Walloon region gained new industries.

In addition to industry, Belgium has gained as the headquarters of major international organizations—NATO, which had run out of its welcome in France, and the European Community, which is headquartered in Brussels.

**HISTORY:** Belgium, named after ancient Celtic settlers, the Belgae, was conquered by Julius Caesar about 50 B.C. and later formed part of Charlemagne's empire. Ruled by Burgundy in the 15th century, it passed to the Hapsburgs of Austria and then of Spain. In the 16th century, the Low Countries (including modern Belgium, Luxembourg, and the Netherlands) revolted against Spanish rule. But while the northern and predominantly Protestant Netherlands provinces won their independence, Belgium remained under Spanish rule until the 18th century

**1713:** Belgium is ceded to Austria by the Treaty of Utrecht, which ends the War of the Spanish Succession

**1792-97:** French armies invade Belgium; country is ceded to France by Treaty of Campo Formio

**1815:** Belgium is united with the Netherlands by Treaty of Paris

**1830-39:** Belgians revolt against affiliation with Protestant Netherlands, a provisional government declares Belgium independent; Dutch invade Belgium but are forced by Britain and France to recognize the country's independence. Belgian Parliament chooses Prince Leopold of Saxe-Coburg-Gotha as ruler of the new kingdom

**1885-1908:** Leopold II becomes absolute monarch of Congo Free State. Belgium reluctantly annexed the area in 1908

**1914-18:** Germans invade and occupy neutral Belgium

**1940-44:** Germany again invades Belgium; King Leopold III surrenders unconditionally. Belgian cabinet sets up government-in-exile in London and declares surrender illegal; Belgian underground continues to fight German invaders

**1950-51:** Belgian electorate votes for return of king, but uprisings against Leopold by Socialists and Liberals force him to abdicate in favor of his son, Baudouin
**1960:** Belgium grants Congo independence
**1968:** Cultural-language conflict between Flemish and French-speaking population (Walloons) leads to fall of center-right coalition government; new coalition of Christian Socialists and Socialists is formed
**1969:** Cultural conflict continues to simmer as Senate studies constitutional reform proposals for regional autonomy
**1970:** Belgium amends constitution giving autonomous cultural and economic powers to each of the two communities, Flemings and Walloons
**1973:** Heretofore provisional double presidency (one Fleming, one Walloon) is made permanent part of Socialist party structure
**1974:** Iran's withdrawal from joint oil refining project adds to Belgium's economic woes and topples Leburton government. Leo Tindemans forms three-party coalition government
**1975:** Severe inflation and 6 percent unemployment force wage-price measures
**1977:** Tindemans' coalition government wins April election after cabinet crisis brought on by withdrawal of leftist Walloons
**1978:** Linguistic tensions trouble coalition, but crisis is resolved. Belgian Army enters Zaire to rescue victims of violence
**1979:** Wilfried Martens becomes premier in five-party coalition
**1980:** Greater authority is given to Flemish and Walloon regions
**1981:** Marc Eyskins replaces Martens as premier; Christian Democratic-Liberal coalition is formed after elections; Martens again becomes premier
**1982:** Socialist-led strike protesting government's austerity measures paralyzes Wallonia on Feb. 8, but has little effect in Flanders

## BELIZE

**Area:** 8,867 sq. mi. **Population:** 144,857 (1980 census)

**Official Name:** Belize **Capital:** Belmopan **Nationality:** Belizean **Languages:** English is the official language. Most inhabitants speak a Creole dialect of English. Spanish, Carib and Maya are the first languages of certain groups **Religion:** 60% are Roman Catholic; 40% are Protestant **Flag:** A blue field with a white circle in the center containing a coat of arms. Two red horizontal bars cross the full length of the flag at top and bottom **Anthem:** Lands of the Free **Currency:** Belize dollar (2 per U.S. $1)

**Location:** On the east coast of Central America, bounded on the east by the Bay of Honduras of the Caribbean Sea, on the south and west by Guatemala, and on the northwest by Mexico. It has a swampy coast that rises gradually toward the interior, which is dominated by tropical jungle growth

**Head of State:** Queen Elizabeth II, represented by a governor-general, Dr. Minita Gordon **Head of Government:** Prime Minister George C. Price, born 1919, appointed Sept. 21, 1981 **Effective Date of Present Constitution:** 1981 **Legislative Body:** National Assembly (bicameral), consisting of an 18-member House of Representatives elected for 5 years and a Senate composed of 8 appointed members **Local Government:** 6 districts, with district officers; municipalities are administered by elected bodies

**Ethnic Composition:** 51% "Creole" (African and mixed-African descent), 22% Mestizo (Spanish-Maya), 19% Amerindian. There are some people of East Indian, German and Spanish descent **Population Distribution:** N.A. **Density:** 16 inhabitants per sq. mi.

**Largest Cities:** (1980 census) Belize City 39,887, Orange Walk 8,441, Corozal 6,862, Dangriga 6,627, Belmopan 2,932

**Per Capita Income:** $1,048 (1980) **Gross Domestic Product (GDP):** $163 million (1980) **Economic Statistics:** In 1979 about 24% of GDP was from agriculture (sugar, citrus fruit, rice, tobacco, beef, honey and bananas), and 20% from industry (clothing, construction materials, beverages and cigarettes). The fishing industry is important. Some timber is still produced **Minerals and Mining:** Drilling for oil began in 1977 in offshore and onshore areas **Labor Force:** 34,500, with 39% in agriculture, 20% in services, 14% in manufacturing and 8% in commerce **Foreign Trade:** Exports, chiefly sugar, molasses, citrus fruit, fish, timber and clothing, totaled $102 million in 1979. Imports, mainly food, machinery and transport equipment, manufactured goods and fuels, totaled $133 million **Principal Trade Partners:** United States, Britain, Canada, Caribbean countries, Mexico

**Vital Statistics:** Birthrate, 38.7 per 1,000 of pop. (1973); death rate, 5.3 (1974) **Life Expectancy:** 60 years **Health Statistics:** 226 inhabitants per hospital bed; 3,261 per physician (1977) **Infant Mortality:** 33.7 per 1,000 births (1972) **Illiteracy:** 7% **Primary and Secondary School Enrollment:** 41,260 (1979) **Enrollment in Higher Education:** 121 (1974) **GNP Expended on Education:** 3.6% (1974)

**Transportation:** Paved roads total 185 mi. **Motor Vehicles:** 10,900 (1977) **Passenger Cars:** 7,500 **Railway Mileage:** None **Ports:** Belize City, Dangriga **Major Airlines:** Belize is served by Central American and U.S. airlines **Communications: Radio Transmitters:** 6 **Receivers:** 85,000 (1977) **Television Stations:** None **Telephones:** 6,000 (1978) **Newspapers:** 2 dailies, 45 copies per 1,000 inhabitants (1976)

**Weights and Measures:** Imperial system **Travel Requirements:** Passport and visa not required of tourist with onward/return ticket and citizenship identification **International Dialing Code:** 501

Belize, formerly British Honduras, existed for over a century as a little-known outpost of the globe-encircling British Empire. The colony's chief claim to fame was as an important source of mahogany, the strong cabinet wood prized by furniture makers. Though Belize is only slightly smaller than New Hampshire in area, its isolation and physical drawbacks prevented it from becoming a populous and economically valuable possession of the British crown. Empire builders of the nineteenth century, approaching the shore from the Caribbean Sea, were greeted by a flat and swampy coastal plain and, on landing, suffered from a hot and humid climate, prone to hurricanes. In addition, Britain never possessed clear and uncontested title to the lonesome piece of Central American real estate.

The dispute over ownership of Belize dates back to the seventeenth century, when British log cutters waged intermittent warfare with neighboring Spanish settlers, until the final British victory in 1798. In the nineteenth century, Guatemala pressed its claim to the area as an inheritor of the Spanish claim. When negotiations with Guatemala broke down in 1981, Britain decided to act anyway, and on Sept. 21 Belize became independent. Thus the last British toehold on the American mainland was relinquished.

Since World War II, the Belizean economy has diversified into new fields. Mahogany and chicle, once the mainstays of the area's livelihood, have declined in relative importance as a result of uncontrolled cutting and of hurricane damage. Sugarcane, citrus fruit, rice, bananas, livestock and fish are now the dominant products of Belize. Tourism holds promise for the future.

The history of Belize in the nineteenth century provided an interesting footnote to the American Civil War. In 1869, refugees from the defeated Confederacy established sugar plantations in the Stann Creek and Toledo districts. A latter-day migration from Anglo-America occurred after World War II, when Mennonite farmers from Canada settled in the interior of Belize.

**HISTORY:** The Mayan civilization spread into the area of Belize several centuries B.C. and flourished until about A.D. 1000. European contact began in 1502, when Columbus sailed along the coast. The first recorded European settlement was begun by shipwrecked English seamen in 1638. Over the next 150 years, more English settlements were established, although the settlers suffered sporadic attacks by pirates, Indians and neighboring Spanish settlers
**1798:** Settlers defeat Spaniards in Battle of St. George's Cay, establishing *defacto* British control
**1859:** Britain and Guatemala sign treaty establishing common border. Treaty later declared null and void by Guatemala
**1862:** The Crown Colony of British Honduras is established
**1964:** Internal self-government is attained
**1973:** British Honduras is renamed Belize
**1975:** Guatemala threatens invasion. UN General Assembly adopts resolution recognizing Belize's right to self-determination and calls for negotiations between Britain and Guatemala
**1977:** Britain rushes troops to Belize to counter Guatemalan invasion threats
**1981:** British-Guatemalan negotiations on independence for Belize break down, but the former colony becomes free anyway, on Sept. 21. Guatemala refuses to recognize the new nation

## BENIN

**Area:** 43,483 sq. mi. **Population:** 3,567,000 (1980 est.)

**Official Name:** People's Republic of Benin **Capital:** Porto Novo

**Nationality:** Beninese or Beninois **Languages:** French is the official language; the most common African dialects are Fon, Mina, Yoruba, and Dendi **Religion:** Animists 65%, Christians 15%, Moslems 13% **Flag:** A green flag with a red five-pointed star in the upper left **Anthem:** The New Dawn **Currency:** CFA Franc (305 per U.S. $1)

**Location:** West Africa. Benin is bordered on the north by Upper Volta and Niger, on the east by Nigeria, on the south by the Bight of Benin, and on the west by Togo **Features:** A 75-mile coastline of sandy beaches and lagoons is unbroken by natural harbors; north of it is a flat area that is the main oil palm region; further inland, a swampy depression is succeeded by hills, plateaus, and the Atakora Mountains, which stretch into Togo **Chief Rivers:** Ouémé, Mono, Couffo

**Head of State and of Government:** President: Col. Ahmed (Mathieu) Kérékou, born 1933, assumed power in 1972; he also is defense minister **Effective Date of Present Constitution:** August 1977 **Legislative Body:** A 336-member unicameral National Revolutionary Assembly **Local Government:** 6 provinces

**Ethnic Composition:** Of some 42 distinctive African groups the main ones are the Fon, Yoruba, Adja, Bariba, Peul, and Somba **Population Distribution:** 14% urban (1975) **Density:** 82 inhabitants per sq. mi.

**Largest Cities:** (1979 census) Cotonou 327,595, Porto-Novo 131,989, Parakou 60,797, Abomey 50,170

**Per Capita Income:** $340 (1980) **Gross National Product (GNP):** $1.1 billion (1980) **Economic Statistics:** In 1978, 33% of GDP came from agriculture (coffee, cotton, peanuts, cassava, fish, yams, corn, oil palm products); 16% from industry (palm oil products, textiles, kenaf, beverages, furniture, ceramics and cement) and mining **Minerals and Mining:** Some low-grade iron ore and limestone deposits are located in the north. Offshore oil deposits are being exploited **Labor Force:** 1.5 million with 85% in agriculture **Foreign Trade:** Exports, chiefly palm kernel oil, cotton, and cocoa beans, totaled $230 million in 1980. Imports, chiefly food products, textiles, machinery, vehicles, and iron and steel products, totaled $435 million **Principal Trade Partners:** France, United States, West Germany, Netherlands, Nigeria, Japan, Britain, Ivory Coast

**Vital Statistics:** Birthrate, 48.8 per 1,000 of pop. (1980); death rate, 19 **Life Expectancy:** 40 years **Health Statistics:** 750 inhabitants per hospital bed; 27,417 per physician (1977) **Infant Mortality:** 109.6 per 1,000 births **Illiteracy:** 80% **Primary and Secondary School Enrollment:** 348,723 (1977) **Enrollment in Higher Education:** 2,118 (1975) **GNP Expended on Education:** 7.4% (1976)

**Transportation:** Paved roads total 446 mi. **Motor Vehicles:** 26,500 (1976) **Passenger Cars:** 17,000 **Railway Mileage:** 360 **Ports:** Cotonou **Major Airlines:** Air Afrique provides intercontinental and regional services **Communications: Radio Transmitters:** 5 (1976) **Receivers:** 150,000 (1977) **Television Stations:** 1 **Receivers:** 10,000 **Telephones:** 10,000 (1975) **Newspapers:** 1 daily, 0.3 copies per 1,000 inhabitants (1976)

**Weights and Measures:** Metric system **Travel Requirements:** Passport and visa required. Transit visa $3.00 for 24 hours; 1-3 days, $3.00, 2 photos

In addition to being one of the smallest, poorest, and most densely populated countries in West Africa, Benin has the unenviable distinction of having had more changes of government than any other newly independent African nation.

Counting the government that was in office when the former French territory won independence in 1960 under the name Dahomey, there were 11 governments between 1960 and 1972. Six of these were installed by military coups. In many cases, governments resigned or were ousted simply because they could not meet a payroll.

In 1970 the government sought to bring a measure of stability to the country by creating a civilian presidential commission which consisted of three former leaders who had served as president or premier in the past. Starting with Hubert Maga, as first president, the chairmanship of the commission was to rotate every two years.

According to schedule Mr. Maga stepped down in May 1972 and was replaced by Justin Ahomadegbe. Five months later, however, the transfer of power by military coup was again the case. On October 26 junior and middle-grade army officers seized power, replacing Ahomadegbe's regime with an 11-man military government headed by then Maj. Mathieu Kérékou.

The Kérékou government represented a clear break from earlier regimes. Persons long in positions of power were swept aside and replaced by a younger generation. A guiding principle of "Marxist-Leninist Scientific Socialism" was proclaimed by President Kérékou and some changes in the political and economic system began to appear. Reports of corruption, incompetence in government and attempted coups followed by wholesale arrests continue to come from Benin, however.

In elections held Nov. 20, 1979, for a National Revolutionary Assembly, more than 80 percent of the electorate voted. The count was overwhelmingly in favor of the single list of candidates of the People's Revolutionary party of Benin (PRPB).

Much of Benin's political instability has been caused by the country's weak economy and dependence on French aid. Producing only a small quantity of palm products, cotton and cocoa beans for export, Benin has been unable to earn enough revenue to meet development requirements. Imports greatly exceed exports, and membership in the French franc pool is all that makes such a deficit viable. Some hope for improvement is seen in the development of petroleum resources.

**HISTORY:** In the 17th century, the powerful Kingdom of Abomey gained dominance over neighboring kingdoms; it maintained its pre-eminent position until the late 19th century, when it was occupied by the French. Abomey armies, which included an elite corps of women soldiers, warred constantly with Yorubas in the east and raided Ashanti territory to the west. Until well into the 19th century, much of the fighting was stimulated by the slave trade, since prisoners were readily sold to European slavers

**1851:** French make treaty with King Gezo of Cotonou, where they establish trading post

**1892-1904:** French crush Abomey rebellion, push inland, and make country part of French West Africa

**1958-59:** Territory of Dahomey becomes autonomous state within French community; constitution is adopted and in National Assembly elections Hubert Maga becomes premier

**1960:** Dahomey becomes fully independent, with Maga as president

**1963:** Maga government is forced to resign in coup led by Col. (later General) Christophe Soglo, army chief of staff, who forms provisional government

**1964:** Sourou Migan Apithy is elected president

**1965:** Dissension among government leaders prompts second coup by General Soglo; provisional civilian government is formed and elections are announced, but Soglo again intervenes, proclaims himself president and premier

**1967:** Soglo government is overthrown by military junta

**1968:** Military regime returns government to civilian administration headed by Emile-Derlin Zinsou

**1972:** Dahomey's first peaceful transition of power is aborted by the country's fifth coup since independence. Maj. Mathieu Kérékou assumes power

**1975:** Rebellion led by Minister of Labor quashed. Dahomey is renamed the People's Republic of Benin by President Kérékou

**1979:** In November first general elections for a National Revolutionary Assembly are held in accordance with the new constitution

**1980:** Kérékou signs agreement for cooperation with Libya

**1981:** Joint commission with Nigeria is reactivated to settle border disputes and control smuggling

**1982:** Fifty thousand people attend mass led by Pope John Paul II and hear Kérékou give an anti-imperialist lecture

## BHUTAN

**Area:** 18,147 sq. mi. **Population:** 1,301,000 (1980 est.)

**Official Name:** Kingdom of Bhutan **Capital:** Thimphu **Nationality:** Bhutanese **Languages:** Dzongka, a Tibetan dialect, is the official and principal language; Nepali and tribal dialects are also spoken **Religion:** About 75% are Mahayana Buddhists and many live in Buddhist monasteries; the Nepalese of southern Bhutan (25%) are predominantly Hindu **Flag:** Divided diagonally with saffron to the left and red to the right, with a white dragon outlined in black in the center **Anthem:** National Anthem, beginning "In the sandal-wood ornamented Kingdom of Dragonland" **Currencies:** Ngultrum (9.9 per U.S. $1) and Indian rupee (9.3 per U.S. $1)

**Location:** Eastern Himalayas of Central Asia. Bhutan is bordered by China (Tibet) on the north and northwest, and by India on the east, west and south **Features:** The undemarcated northern boundary with Tibet stretches along 300 miles of snow-capped peaks that are almost inaccessible. The inner Himalayan region in central Bhutan contains densely populated, fertile valleys; the Duar Plain of southern Bhutan contains dense forests **Chief Rivers:** Manas, Sankosh, Tongsa, Torsa, Raidak

**Head of State and of Government:** King Jigme Singye Wangchuk, born 1955, ascended the throne 1972. The king governs with the aid of a 5-man council of ministers **Effective Date of Present Constitution:** No formal written constitution **Legislative Body:** Tsongdu (unicameral national assembly), consisting of 150 members, 40 appointed by the king, 10 by the organizations of lamas, and the rest nominated by villages for 3-year terms **Local Government:** 4 regions under appointed governors

**Ethnic Composition:** Bhutanese, or Bhotias, who are ethnically related to the Tibetans, make up 60% of the population. Nepalese constitute about 25% and the rest consist of various tribal groups, including the Lepcha, an indigenous people, and the Santal, descendants of migrants from India **Population Distribution:** The population is chiefly rural **Density:** 72 inhabitants per sq. mi.

**Largest Cities:** (1970 est.) Thimphu 50,000, Paro Dzong 35,000, Taga Dzong 18,000, Punakha 12,000, Bumthang 10,000

**Per Capita Income:** $80 (1979) **Gross National Product (GNP):** $100 million (1979 est.) **Economic Statistics:** The economy is still at a primitive level and many transactions are on a barter basis. The country is self-sufficient in food; the main crops are rice, wheat, and barley, and together with butter from yaks provide a sufficient diet. Large forests provide the potential for lumber and paper-processing plants, and several turbulent rivers furnish a potential source of hydroelectric power. Bhutan's first 5-year development plan was begun in 1961 with the aid of India, the fourth plan covered the years 1976-1981 **Minerals and Mining:** Copper, dolomite, graphite, and coal deposits have been discovered **Labor Force:** Virtually the entire working population is engaged in agriculture and pastoral activities **Foreign Trade:** Almost all external trade is with India, chiefly exports ($1 million) of rice, dolomite and handicrafts, and imports ($1.4 million) of textiles and light equipment

**Vital Statistics:** Birthrate, 43 per 1,000 of pop. (1980); death rate, 20.6 **Life Expectancy:** 43.6 years **Health Statistics:** N.A. **Infant Mortality:** N.A. **Illiteracy:** 95% **Primary and Secondary School Enrollment:** 20,357 (1976) **Enrollment in Higher Education:** Bhutanese students are studying in India, New Zealand, Australia and the U.S. **GNP Expended on Education:** N.A.

**Transportation:** Paved roads total 250 mi. **Motor Vehicles:** N.A. **Passenger Cars:** N.A. **Railway Mileage:** None **Ports:** None **Major Airlines:** An Indian airline operates flights from Hashimara, West Bengal, to Paro Dzong **Communications:** Teleprinter and postal services link Bhutan with India and the rest of the world **Radio Transmitters:** 1 A.M. station **Licenses:** 110,000 (1976) **Television:** None **Telephones:** 1,000 **Newspapers:** A weekly government newspaper is published in 3 languages

**Weights and Measures:** Traditional and metric standards are used **Travel Requirements:** Tourists are admitted only in grooups by prearrangement with the Ministry of Tourism, Thimphu. Passport, visa, smallpox and cholera immunizations are required. India requires special passes to enter Bhutan.

---

Well into the 20th century, the Buddhist kingdom of Bhutan was still living in the 19th, content to be isolated politically from the rest of the world. In 1959 the Chinese takeover of Tibet, Bhutan's northern neighbor, jolted the country into closing its trade routes to Tibet and into building a road to the south.

It took six days then, on the back of a mule, to travel from Bhutan to India. The same trip now, by bus, takes five hours. With the help of foreign, mainly Indian, aid and advisers, similar advances have been made in other sectors in the agrarian kingdom. Where only 2,600 of Bhutan's people had gone even to primary school a decade ago, now 20,000 are studying in schools of all levels. About 500 have studied abroad at universities and returned to Bhutan.

Bhutan's king from 1952 to 1972 was Jigme Dorji Wangchuk, whose name means "fearless thunderbolt master of the cosmic powers." Despite his awesome appellation, the king was surprisingly informal and genuinely loved by his people. To give his rule a popular base, he persuaded the National Assembly to pass a bill (dropped by his successor) empowering it by a two-thirds vote to replace the king with the next in the royal line of succession if the monarch loses the assembly's confidence. After his death, he was succeeded by his son, Jigme Singye Wangchuk.

Bhutan is largely independent and insists that it is not an Indian protectorate, though by a treaty of 1949 it "agrees to be guided by the government of India in regard to external relations." Until 1978, Bhutan was under an agreement to sell its goods only to India. Bhutan has no plans to open its mountain border with China; it has diplomatic missions only at the United Nations, in India and in Bangladesh.

Bhutan's people are thinly spread over a beautiful, mountainous country. Most Bhutanese live as farmers on their own land, bartering for what they need. Since 1974, Bhutanese planners have permitted group tours of rich travelers—a maximum of 200 at a time—who stay in excellent new facilities. In 1979 some 1,500 tourists put $700,000 into Bhutan's economy.

**HISTORY:** Bhutan's early history is obscure. In the 16th century it was conquered by Tibet and nominally came under a dual spiritual and temporal rule. In the 19th century the southern part of the country was occupied by the British and annexed to India, and Britain began paying Bhutan an annual subsidy. In 1907 Sir Ugyen Wangchuk, a former local governor, established a hereditary monarchy, and in a 1910 treaty Bhutan agreed to British direction of its external affairs

**1949:** India signs treaty with Bhutan assuming Britain's role in subsidizing kingdom and directing its foreign relations; India returns areas annexed by Britain in 1865

**1959:** Communist China publishes maps showing parts of Bhutan as Chinese territory; Communist spokesmen claim Bhutan belongs to greater Tibet. Indian government warns that any attack on Bhutan will be regarded as an act of aggression against India

**1971:** Bhutan iis admitted to the United Nations

**1973:** Bhutan signs agreement with UN under which Bhutan will receive $2.5 million in aid to carry out projects under third five-year plan

**1974:** King Jigme Singye Wangchuk formally crowned

---

## BOLIVIA

**Area:** 424,163 sq. mi. **Population:** 5,916,000 (1981 est.)

**Official Name:** Republic of Bolivia **Capital:** La Paz is the administrative capital, Sucre the legal and judicial capital **Nationality:** Bolivian **Languages:** Spanish, the official language, is spoken by about 55% of the population (but only 36% as a mother tongue). The rest speak a variety of Indian dialects, chiefly Quechua and Aymara **Religion:** The population is about 95% Roman Catholic **Flag:** Red, yellow, and green horizontal stripes, with the national coat of arms on the yellow stripe **Anthem:** National Anthem, beginning "Bolivians, provident destiny" **Currency:** Bolivian peso (43.2 per U.S. $1)

**Location:** South America. Landlocked Bolivia is bordered on the north and east by Brazil, on the south by Paraguay and Argentina, and on the west by Chile and Peru **Features:** The country is divided into three distinct regions: the Altiplano, a bleak plateau lying between two ranges of the Andes Mountains and one of the world's highest inhabited regions; an intermediate region (yungas) containing the eastern mountain slopes and valleys, and the Amazon-Chaco lowlands (llanos) **Chief Rivers:** Beni, Guaporé-Iténez, Mamoré-Río Grande, Pilcomayo, Paraguay

**Head of State and of Government:** President: Gen. Guido Vildoso Calderón, sworn in July 21, 1982. **Effective Date of Present Constitution:** 1967 (suspended July 1980) **Legislative Body:** Bicameral National Congress (disbanded July 1980) with 27 Senators and 117 Deputies **Local Government:** 9 departments, each headed by an appointed prefect

**Ethnic Composition:** 65% Amerindian (mainly Quechua aand Aymará), 10% of European origin, 25% of mixed origin (Cholo) **Population Distribution:** 42% urban **Density:** 13.9 inhabitants per sq. mi.

**Largest Cities:** (1976 census) La Paz 635,283, Santa Cruz 254,682, Cochabamba 204,684, Oruro 124,213, Sucre 63,625

**Per Capita Income:** $692 (1980) **Gross National Product (GNP):** $3.7 billion (1980) **Economic Statistics:** In 1977 about 28% of GNP came from agriculture (sugar, corn, potatoes, wheat, and rice); 10% from manufacturing (food processing, textiles, leather goods, cement, and glass ceramics); 14% from mining; 13% from trade and services; 9% from transportation **Minerals and Mining:** Mining is the most important element of the nation's economy and accounts for the major share of the country's exports. Tin still dominates these exports, which also include lead, zinc, silver, copper, tungsteen, bismuth, antimony, gold, petroleum, natural gas, and sulphur **Labor Force:** 2.8 million (1977); 70% in agriculture, 10% in services and utilities, 7% in manufacturing, 3% in mining, 10% other **Foreign Trade:** Exports, chiefly tin, natural gas, petroleum, tungsten, silver, antimony, copper, lead, zinc, sugar, cotton and coffee, totaled $777 million in 1979. Imports, mainly machinery, vehicles, iron and steel, and food staples, totaled $1 billion **Principal Trade Partners:** United States, Argentina, West Germany, Britain, Brazil, Japan, Switzerland, Netherlands

**Vital Statistics:** Birthrate, 48 per 1,000 of pop. (1976); death rate, 18 **Life Expectancy:** 52 years **Health Statistics:** 526 inhabitants per hospital bed; 2,117 per physician (1975) **Infant Mortality:** 77.3 per 1,000 births **Illiteracy:** 37% **Primary and Secondary School Enrollment:** 1,050,931 (1976) **Enrollment in Higher Education:** 51,585 (1976) **GNP Expended on Education:** 3.2% (1976)

**Transportation:** Paved roads total 714 mmi. **Motor Vehicles:** 68,000 (1978) **Passenger Cars:** 38,600 **Railway Mileeage:** 2,400 **Ports:** None **Major Airlines:** Lloyd Aéreo Boliviano (LAB) operates domestic and international services **Communications: Radio Trans- mitters:** 136 **Receivers:** 440,000 (1977) **Television Transmitters:** 8 **Receivers:** 100,000 (1976) **Telephones:** 49,000 (1974) **Newspapers:** 13 dailies, 26 copies per 1,000 inhabitants (1976)

**Weights and Measures:** Metric system; old Spanish units are still used **Travel Requirements:** Passport and tourist visa, 90-day extendable, no fee **International Dialing Code:** 591

---

Often called the "Tibet of South America," landlocked Bolivia is made up of three distinct topographical regions: a mineral-rich high plateau region, an extensively farmed middle region of semitropical rain forests and somewhat drier valleys, and the sparsely populated Amazon-Chaco lowlands.

Bolivia is among the poorest countries in Latin America, with its Andean Indian peasants and its miners widely separated from the urban minorities of European origin.

Signs of economic and social advance, however, include skyscraper office buildings, modern jet airliner service between La Paz and the tropical lowlands, and the large growth in primary school enrollment.

Bolivia's economy is based on natural gas and petroleum, which make the country self-sufficient in energy, and nonferrous minerals, including tin, of which Bolivia is one of the world's leadinng producers. Mining accounts for more than 60% of the country's export earnings. Because of political instability and technical difficulties, production and exports of tin declined by nearly a third from 1977 to 1980, bringing on a severe recession. By 1982 Bolivia was beset by a host of economic troubles including a $3.8-billion foreign debt and a record balance-of-payments deficit.

From 1943, when the pro-miner National Revolutionary Movement (MNR) led a revolt against poor working conditions and suppression of strikes, power shifted back and forth between the MNR and rightist military juntas. In August 1971 the regime of Gen. Juan José Torres was overthrown by Col. Hugo Banzer Suárez with support of both the MNR and the rightist Bolivian Socialist Falange. By foiling a series of attempts to unseat him and by establishing (in 1974) an all-military government, Banzer attained a relatively long period of political stability. In 1978, in response to a popular cry for more democratic government, he opened the way for a presidential election. Gen. Juan Pereda Asbún, backed by Banzer, received more than half of the popular votes, but the electoral court declared the election void on the grounds of fraud. Pereda then seized power in a coup, but he was soon deposed and Gen. David Padilla Arancibia was named interim president.

Because no candidate received a majority in the election held in July 1979, the National Congresss chose Walter Guevara Arze as the first civilian president in 10 years. However, when he was toppled by a coup in November, Lidia Gueiler Tejada, president of the Chamber of Deputies, was selected to serve as interim president until a new election scheduled for June 29, 1980. A former president, Hernán Siles Zuazo, won a plurality in the 1980 election, but not a majority, of votes. Before the National Congress could meet on August 3 to choose a president, a three-man military junta seized power on July 17 and proclaimed Gen. Luis García Meza as president. This coup and reign of terror against political opponents that ensued were condemned by Bolivia's Andean Pact partners. García Meza was removed from office by a reconstituted junta which assumed power Aug. 4, 1981.

**HISTORY:** The Bolivian Altiplano was a center of Indian life long before the days of the Incas, who conquered the region in the 13th century. The Spanish conquest began in the 1530s, and the Indians were soon virtually enslaved to work the rich silver mines of Upper Peru, as Bolivia was then called. Following the occupation of Spain by Napoleon in 1809, Upper Peru became one of the first Spanish colonies to revolt against Spain

**1824-26:** Revolutionary army under Antonio José de Sucre, chief lieutenant of Simón Bolívar, defeats Spanish forces at Ayacucho. Bolivian independence is proclaimed in 1825

**1879-84:** Bolivia and Peru fight Chile in War of the Pacific. Chile is victorious and Bolivia is forced to cede province of Atacama, nation's only coastal territory

**1903:** After bitter conflict, Bolivia cedes large rubber-tree area on Acre River to Brazil

**1932-35:** Discovery of oil at the foot of the Bolivian Andes precipitates Chaco War with Paraguay, which lays claim to region. More than 100,000 lives are lost on both sides; a defeated Bolivia loses three-quarters of disputed Chaco Boreal area to Paraguay

**1943:** Economic unrest culminates in widespread strikes by miners; pro-miner Movement of the National Revolution (MNR) stages revolt and takes power

**1951-56:** Victor Paz Estenssoro, the MNR candidate, wins presidential elections but is prevented from taking office by military junta; he is finally swept into power by a party-led uprising

**1964-66:** Second administration headed by Paz is overthrown and a military junta installed. Air Force General René Barrientos Ortuño is elected president in 1966

**1967:** Cuban guerrilla leader Ernesto "Che" Guevara, who had been waging a "liberation" movement in Bolivia, is executed

**1969:** Barrientos is killed in helicopter crash and is succeeded by Vice-President Luis Adolfo Siles Salinas; Siles is ousted, however, in coup led by General Alfredo Ovando Candia

**1970-71:** Ovando regime is overthrown in leftist coup led by General Juan José Torres. Torres is overthrown in rebel uprising; Col. Hugo Banzer Suárez is appointed president

**1980:** June election results in plurality, but not majority, for Hernán Siles Zuazo. Before congress can pick a new president, a military junta seizes power and names Gen. García Meza as head of state. Bolivia's output of tin is the lowest since 1965

**1981:** Following revolts in July, García Meza is deposed by junta which assumes full power and names Gen. Celso Torrelio Villa as president. A counter coup in August fails. Senior government officers are linked to the cocaine trade

**1982:** Government announces austerity measures to relieve economic crisis, touching off protests by labor. President Torrelio shuffles cabinet to produce a civilian majority. Torrelio resigns and a 3-man military junta names Gen. Guido Vildoso Calderón as president

---

## BOTSWANA

**Area:** 224,764 sq. mi. **Population:** 936,600 (1981 census)

**Official Name:** Republic of Botswana **Capital:** Gaborone **Nationality:** Botswana **Languages:** English is the official language; Setswana is the main African language. Various dialects of the Khoisan "click" language are spoken by the Bushmen; Afrikaans is also used **Religion:** About 15% Christian; the rest practice tribal religions **Flag:** A blue field divided by a black horizontal band edged in white **Anthem:** Our Land **Currency:** Pula (0.93 per U.S. $1)

**Location:** Southern Africa. Landlocked Botswana is bordered by Namibia on the north and west, by Zambia and Zimbabwe on the east, and by South Africa on the southeast and south **Features:** Most of the country is a tableland, with a mean altitude of 3,300 feet. The Kalahari Desert covers much of the southwest; in the northwest the waters of the Okavango River form a great inland delta, known as the Okavango Swamps, which extend over 6,500 sq. mi. **Chief Rivers:** Okavango, Molopo, Shashi, Limpopo

**Head of State and of Government:** President: Dr. Quett K.J. Masire, born 1925, elected by the National Assembly in July 1980 **Effective**

**Date of Present Constitution:** September 30, 1966 **Legislative Body:** Parliament (unicameral), consisting of a 36-member National Assembly. Of the total membership, 32 are directly elected and 4 chosen by the elected members. The constitution also provides for a House of Chiefs, which plays an advisory role in government affairs **Local Government:** 9 districts and 4 independent towns, governed by local councils

**Ethnic Composition:** 94% are Bantu (Tswana), grouped into 8 main tribes, 5% Bushmen, and 1% Europeans **Population Distribution:** 16% urban **Density:** 4.1 inhabitants per sq. mi.

**Largest Cities:** (1981 census) Gaborone 59,700, Francistown 31,100, Selebi-Pikwe 30,200

**Per Capita Income:** $407 (1980) **Gross National Product (GNP):** $321 million (1980) **Economic Statistics:** In 1979, 29% of GNP came from animal husbandry (cattle, goats, sheep) and agriculture (corn, sorghum); and 10% from mining **Minerals and Mining:** Diamonds, manganese, copper and copper/nickel, and coal are mined **Labor Force:** About 385,000, with most in agriculture **Foreign Trade:** Exports, chiefly diamonds, livestock, hides and skins, copper, nickel, canned meats, beans and sorghum, totaled $383 million in 1979. Imports, chiefly cereals, petroleum products, textiles, sugar, and motor vehicles, totaled $381 million **Principal Trade Partners:** South Africa, Britain, Zambia, Zimbabwe

**Vital Statistics:** Birthrate, 50.9 per 1,000 of pop. (1980); death rate, 17.4 **Life Expectancy:** 55 years **Health Statistics:** 328 inhabitants per hospital bed; 10,476 per physician (1976) **Infant Mortality:** 24.1 **Illiteracy:** 65% **Primary and Secondary School Enrollment:** 141,863 (1976) **Enrollment in Higher Education:** 469 (1975) **GNP Expended on Education:** 9.22PC (1975)

**Transportation:** Paved roads total 500 mi. **Motor Vehicles:** 17,600 (1978) **Passenger Cars:** 5,000 **Railway Mileage:** 450 **Ports:** None **Major Airlines:** Air Botswana operates domestic flights and maintains services to South Africa and Zambia **Communications: Radio Transmitters:** 6 **Receivers:** 63,000 (1977) **Television:** None **Telephones:** 10,000 (1978) **Newspapers:** 2 dailies, 24 per 1,000 inhabitants (1977)

**Weights and Measures:** Metric system **Travel Requirements:** Passport, no visa

---

Since gaining independence in 1966, the former British protectorate of Bechuanaland has seen its previously bleak economic prospects brightened by the discovery of substantial mineral wealth—diamonds, copper, and nickel.

The mineral wealth found in the country's arid northeastern area includes a diamond "pipe" (the core of an ancient volcano) at Orapa, which is one of the largest ever discovered anywhere. However, diamond mining provides jobs for less than 10% of Botswana's working population. Therefore, nearly half of the job seekers are forced to seek employment as migrant workers in South Africa. Still, with new industry this impoverished nation hopes to gain economic independence that will significantly add to its political independence.

Nearly surrounded by white-ruled areas, Botswana previously had seemed destined to be no more than a cattle ranch for South Africa. As head of a newly independent black African state, Botswana's late president, Sir Seretse Khama, had asserted opposition to South Africa's racist policies, but acknowledged his country's economic dependence on its southern neighbor. Still, Botswana is devoted to strengthening its commercial and psychological ties with Zambia and other independent states of black Africa, while refusing to have diplomatic relations with Pretoria.

Relations between Botswana and white-ruled Zimbabwe Rhodesia became strained as a result of incidents arising out of the guerrilla war between Zimbabwe Rhodesian black nationalists and Zimbabwe Rhodesian security forces. The Botswana deeply resented the infiltration of Zimbabwe Rhodesian security forces into their country. Eventually independence for Zimbabwe in 1980 brought an end to the incursions and opened new opportunities for trade and communications for Botswana.

Sir Seretse, an Oxford-educated lawyer, caused a controversy in his homeland as well as in South Africa by his marriage to an Englishwoman in 1948. However, his popularity gained him victory in the preindependence elections of 1965. He maintained a policy of non-racial democracy for Botswana. Sir Seretse was reelected overwhelmingly for a third term as president Oct. 20, 1979. He died on July 13, 1980, and was succeeded by Dr. Quett K.J. Masire, Vice President and Finance Minister under Sir Seretse.

**HISTORY:** Little is known of the origins of Botswana's peoples. The early inhabitants, the Bushmen, who now are dying out, have no recorded history. The ancestors of most of the present-day population, the Botswana, probably arrived centuries ago in Bantu migrations from Central or East Africa. In the 19th century, the great chief Khama III loosely united the Botswana against incursions of the neighboring Matabele people and Boer trekkers from the Transvaal. Under British protection, the southern area was made part of the South African Cape Colony, while the northern part, known as Bechuanaland, remained under direct British administration until it became independent Botswana

**1909:** Constitution of Union (now Republic) of South Africa is drafted, with a provision that Bechuanaland and other British protectorates in southern Africa, Basutoland (now Lesotho) and Swaziland, will some day be included in the union

**1920-61:** Advisory councils, one representing Africans, the other, Europeans, are established by British Central Authority. Central Authority establishes a Joint Advisory Council with African and European membership, which resolves to form legislative council to assist in governing the territory. A constitution for this purpose is promulgated

**1965:** New constitution is made effective and general elections are held for new National Assembly; seat of government is moved from Mafeking in South Africa to Gaborone

**1966:** Bechuanaland becomes independent member of the British Commonwealth and adopts name of Botswana. Sir Seretse Khama, grandson of Chief Khama III and leader of the Botswana Democratic party, is elected president

**1977:** UN Security Council adopts a resolution demanding the cessation of all hostile acts against Botswana by Rhodesia

**1979:** Khama is reelected president for a third term by a big margin. Drought and hoof-and-mouth disease hurt cattle industry

**1980:** Sir Seretse dies and is succeeded by Dr. Quett K.J. Masire. Satellite tracking station begins operation at Khale

**1981:** Increased diamond production offsets declining output of copper and nickel

---

## BRAZIL

---

**Area:** 3,286,470 sq. mi. **Population:** 119,098,992 (1980 census)

**Official Name:** Federative Republic of Brazil **Capital:** Brasília **Nationality:** Brazilian **Languages:** Portuguese is the official and principal language. In central and southern Brazil, Italian, German, and Japanese immigrants still use their native languages **Religion:** About 93% of the population is Roman Catholic. There are about 8 million Protestants and 150,000 Jews **Flag:** Green, with a yellow diamond enclosing a blue globe containing 23 white stars and a white band inscribed with the words "Ordem e Progresso" (Order and Progress) **Anthem:** Brazilian National Hymn, beginning "From peaceful Ypiranga's banks" **Currency:** Cruzeiro (156 per U.S. $1)

**Location:** South America. The fifth-largest nation in the world, Brazil is bordered by every country in South America except Chile and Ecuador. It is bounded by French Guiana, Suriname, Guyana, Venezuela, and Colombia on the north, by Peru, Bolivia, and Paraguay on the west, and by Uruguay and Argentina on the south **Features:** The country is divided into four distinct major regions: the northern tropical basin of the Amazon, which flows more than 1,500 miles within the country, bordered on the north by the Guiana Highlands; the semiarid scrub land of the northeast; the agricultural and mineral heartland of the south-central plains, plateaus and highlands; and the narrow coastal belt, fringed by interior mountain ranges, extending from Natal to Porto Alegre **Chief Rivers:** Amazon, São Francisco, Paraná, Uruguay, Paraguay

**Head of State and of Government:** President João Baptista de Oliveira Figueiredo, born 1918, inaugurated on Mar. 15, 1979, following selection by Electoral College in 1978 **Effective Date of Present Constitution:** January 24, 1967, extensively revised in 1969 **Legislative Body:** National Congress (bicameral), composed of the Chamber of Deputies and the Senate **Local Government:** 22 states, each with an indirectly elected governor and legislature, 4 federal territories, and 1 federal district

**Ethnic Composition:** The primary elements are 60% European, 8% African and a complex mixture (30%) of both **Population Distribution:** 68% urban **Density:** 36.2 inhabitants per sq. mi.

**Largest Cities:** (1980 census—Metropolitan Areas) São Paulo 12,588,439, Rio de Janeiro 9,018,637, Belo Horizonte 2,541,788, Recife 2,348,362, Pôrto Alegre 2,232,370, Salvador 1,772,018

**Per Capita Income:** $2,067 (1980) **Gross National Product (GNP):** $251.5 billion (1980) **Economic Statistics:** 38% of GNP comes from industry (food processing, chemicals, textiles, metallurgical producits, vehicles annd accessories, electrical and communications equipment), mining and construction; 50% from services; 12% from agriculture (rice, corn, coffee, sugarcane, cocoa, soybeans, livestock, manioc, cotton) **Minerals and Mining:** Large deposits of iron, manganese, and bauxite; nickel, lead, tin, asbestos, chrome ore, gold, tungsten, and copper are also important. Coal and petroleum production is supplemented by imports **Labor Force:** Approximately 38,000,000 (1978); of which 38% is employed in agriculture, 24% in industry **Foreign Trade:** Exports, chiefly coffee, soybeans, cotton, iron ore, cane sugar, pine wood, corn, and cocoa beans, totaled $20.1 billion in 1980. Imports, mainly wheat, crude petroleum, machinery, chemicals, metals and heavy equipment, totaled $23 billion **Principal Trade Partners:** United States, West Germany, Argentina, Italy, Netherlands, United Kingdom, France, Japan, Saudi Arabia, Canada, Poland

**Vital Statistics:** Birthrate, 36 per 1,000 of pop. (1980); death rate, 7.8 **Life Expectancy:** 61 years **Health Statistics:** 245 inhabitants per hospital bed; 2,117 per physician (1975) **Infant Mortality:** about 83 per 1,000 births **Illiteracy:** 17% **Primary and Secondary School Enrollment:** 20,968,339 (1974) **Enrollment in Higher Education:** 1,316,640 (1976) **GNP Expended on Education:** 2.3% (1976)

**Transportation:** Paved roads total 47,000 mi. **Motor Vehicles:** 8,698,500 (1978) **Passenger Cars:** 7,123,900 **Railway Mileage:** 20,447 **Ports:** Santos, Rio de Janeiro, Vitória, Salvador, Rio Grande, Recife, Paranagua, Macapá **Major Airlines:** VARIG and Cruzeiro do Sul operate domestic and international services **Communications: Radio Transmitters:** 962 **Receivers:** 16,980,000 (1975) **Television Transmitters:** 120 **Receivers:** 10,680,000 (1975) **Telephones:** 5,525,000 (1978) **Newspapers:** 318 dailies, 45 copies per 1,000 inhabitants (1977)

**Weights and Measures:** Metric system **Travel Requirements:** Passport and visa required. Tourists need onward/return ticket or financial guarantee **International Dialing Code:** 55

---

Long considered the country of the future, Brazil has begun to grow visibly through industrialization within its vast geographical outline. Since 1930 the activist governments of the country, the largest in Latin America and the fifth largest in the world in area, have—despite wide ideological differences—followed roughly similar policies of industrial development and national integration of the huge hinterland and the urban coast. As a result, Brazil is the industrial leader of South America.

For all its economic progress, Brazil has had more than its share of political upheaval. It has been by turns a Portuguese colony, an independent empire, a republic, a dictatorship, and, up to 1964, a representative democracy. Since the ousting of a civilian president, João Goulart, in that year, Brazil has had a succession of military presidents.

Leaving the economy largely under civilian management, the first three military administrations reformed the tax structure, began the reorganization of the state's inefficient bureaucracy, shifted some resources to the country's backward regions, attracted large amounts of U.S. and other foreign investment capital, and whipped up the pace of industrial expansion. The result is often described as Brazil's "economic miracle."

Brazil's economy fared less well under the fourth military administration, in which Ernesto Geisel, a career artillery general, served a five-year term that ended in 1979. The nation's industrial and farm exports were still growing, but these advantages were offset by increased imports, strikes, and the rapidly rising cost of living.

Gen. João Baptista Figueiredo, who had been the chief of intelligence, was sworn in as president on March 15, 1979. He had been elected five months earlier in Brazil's first contested presidential election since the coup that ousted Goulart. The print media—but not television and radio—received full freedom during the campaign.

Figueiredo inherited the economic problems of his predecessor. Almost immediately he had to send troops to restore calm and bring about a settlement of a strike by 180,000 metalworkers in São Paulo. More strikes ensued in the following years. In February 1981 labor leader Luis Inacio da Silva was tried and convicted under national security laws by a military court for his role in fomenting a long metalworkers strike in 1980 which shut down Brazil's automobile industry.

At the root of the labor discontent has been the cost of living which has been rising at an annual rate of over 100%. The increasing cost of imported oil, strikes, financing of the huge national debt, urban unemployment, and loss of coffee crops due to drought and frost have brought about a precarious economy. In 1981-82, the once-booming automobile industry was in a deep recession.

To combat soaring energy costs, the government in 1979 instituted a six-year plan for development of vehicles that run on alcohol which can be produced from Brazil's bountiful sugarcane crop. In the area of nuclear energy, Brazil is buying eight power plants and a uranium reprocessing facility from West Germany.

In his inauguration speech, Figueiredo had announced his "unswerving purpose" of restoring democracy to Brazil in tthe future. In August 1979, he signed a law granting amnesty to political prisoners and exiles except those held for "acts of terrorism". A Party Reform Bill was passed dissolving the two existing parties but enabling establishment of the Social Democratic Party, which supports the government, and four new opposition parties that would be allowed as long as they were democratic and in accord with the constitution.

**HISTORY:** In 1500 Pedro Alvares Cabral landed on the Brazilian coast and claimed the land for Portugal. The first Portuguese governor-general of Brazil was appointed in 1549. In 1727 coffee was introduced in Brazil. In 1808 King John VI, fleeing the Napoleonic invasion of Portugal, arrived in Rio de Janeiro, and in 1815 all Portuguese dominions were designated the United Kingdom of Portugal, Brazil, and the Algarves. The king returned to Portugal in 1821, leaving behind Dom Pedro, his son, as regent

**1822:** Dom Pedro, later Pedro I, declares Brazil independent of Portugal and assumes title of emperor
**1840:** Dom Pedro II begins his 40-year rule as emperor
**1888:** Slavery is abolished and 700,000 slaves are emancipated
**1889:** The monarchy is toppled by a bloodless revolution and Brazil becomes a republic
**1930:** Getúlio Vargas comes to power through a revolution and establishes dictatorial rule
**1942:** Brazil enters WW II and declares war against Axis powers
**1945-54:** Military coup topples the Vargas dictatorship and restores democracy. In 1951 Vargas again becomes president. Faced with army opposition and impeachment, he commits suicide in 1954
**1956-61:** Presidency of Juscelino Kubitschek; capital moved from Rio de Janeiro to Brasília
**1964:** The elected government of João Goulart is ousted in a military coup led by General Humberto de Alencar Castelo Branco
**1974:** General Ernesto Geisel "elected" as the fourth successive president from the military
**1979:** General João Baptista de Oliveira Figueiredo sworn in as president after winning a two-party contest in late 1978
**1981:** President Figueiredo signs a $388-million trade and credit agreement with France. Inflation continues at an annual rate of over 100%
**1982:** Daniel K. Ludwig, ailing 84-year-old American financier, abandons billion-dollar Jari industrial project in Amazon basin; mounting financial problems and disputes with government officials are cited as reasons. Merger of Brazil's two largest opposition political parties is approved by Supreme Electoral Tribunal, opening door for first fully free elections in 16 years in November

---

## BULGARIA

**Area:** 42,823 sq. mi. **Population:** 8,862,000 (1980 est.)

**Official Name:** People's Republic of Bulgaria **Capital:** Sofia **Nationality:** Bulgarian **Languages:** Bulgarian is the official and principal language; Turkish, Greek, and Armenian are spoken by minority groups **Religion:** Bulgarian Orthodox 85%, Moslem 13%; other denominations are Roman Catholicism, Protestantism, and Judaism. The government is officially atheist **Flag:** Horizontal stripes of white, green, and red, with the state emblem, a lion framed by wheatstalks, located on the white stripe near the hoist **Anthem:** Mila Rodino (Dear Fatherland) national anthem (1964) **Currency:** Lev (0.85 per U.S. $1)

**Location:** Southeast Europe, on the eastern part of the Balkan peninsula. Bulgaria is bordered on the north by Romania, on the east by the Black Sea, on the south by Turkey and Greece, and on the west by Yugoslavia **Features:** The country is divided into several roughly parallel east/west zones: the Danubian tableland in the north; the Stara Planina (Balkan) Mountains through the central part; and the Thracian Plain and Rhodope Mountains in the south and southwest **Chief Rivers:** Danube, Maritsa, Iskur, Tundzha

**Political Leader and Head of State:** Todor Zhivkov, born 1911; General Secretary of the Central Committee of the Communist party since 1954, reelected 1981. In 1971 he was elected chairman of the State Council **Head of Government:** Georgi (Grisha) Filipov, appointed 1981, Chairman of the Council of Ministers (premier). The Chairman of the National Assembly is Stanko Todorov **Effective Date of Present Constitution:** May 1971 **Legislative Body:** Parliament (unicameral National Assembly), consisting of 400 members elected for 5 years. Although the National Assembly is nominally the supreme organ of state power, real power is, in fact, wielded by the Politburo and Secretariat of the Communist party **Local Government:** 27 provinces and one city commune, each governed by an elective people's council

**Ethnic Composition:** 85% of the population consists of ethnic Bulgarians; the only sizable minority is the Turks, who make up about 9%. Macedonians, Armenians, Gypsies, and Greeks constitute smaller ethnic groups **Population Distribution:** 61% urban **Density:** 207 inhabitants per sq. mi.

**Largest Cities:** (1975 census) Sofia 965,355, Plovdiv 305,091, Varna 269,980, Ruse 171,264, Burgas 148,236

**Per Capita Income:** $3,370 (1980) **Gross National Product (GNP):** $30 billion (1980) **Economic Statistics:** About 43% of GNP comes from industry (food processing, engineering and metallurgy, textiles, chemicals, rubber); 20% from agriculture (wheat, corn, barley, sugar beets); 7% from commerce; and the rest from other activities **Minerals and Mining:** Lead, iron ore, zinc, and copper are produced in substantial quantities. Large coal reserves exist but the coal is of low caloric value **Labor Force:** 4.7 million (1980), of which 26% is employed in industry, and 26% in agriculture **Foreign Trade:** Exports, mainly foodstuffs, machines and equipment and dairy products, fuels, raw materials and minerals, rose oil, totaled $9 billion in 1979. Imports, chiefly machines and equipment, fuels, minerals, raw materials, metals, animal and vegetable products, totaled $8.6 billion **Principal Trade Partners:** USSR, East Germany, Czechoslovakia, West Germany, Poland, Romania, Greece

**Vital Statistics:** Birthrate, 14.3 per 1,000 of pop. (1980); death rate 10.7 **Life Expectancy:** 71 years **Health Statistics:** 115 inhabitants per hospital bed; 443 per physician (1977) **Infant Mortality:** 19.9 per 1,000 births (1977) **Illiteracy:** 5% **Primary and Secondary School Enrollment:** 1,317,659 (1976) **Enrollment in Higher Education:** 128,593 (1975) **GNP Expended on Education:** 5.4% (1976)

**Transportation:** Surfaced roads total 7,884 mi. **Motor Vehicles:** 39,000 (1967) **Passenger Cars:** 11,400 (1967) **Railway Mileage:** 3,780 **Ports:** Burgas, Varna **Major Airlines:** Bulgarian Airlines-Balkan operates domestic and international services **Communications: Radio Transmitters:** 34 **Licenses:** 1,299,000 (1977) **Television Transmitters:** 154 **Licenses:** 1,546,000 (1976) **Telephones:** 1,032,000 (1978) **Newspapers:** 12 dailies, 237 copies per 1,000 inhabitants (1977)

**Weights and Measures:** Metric system **Travel Requirements:** Passport and visa required; transit visa, up to 30 hours, $9.00; tourist visa, 30 hours-2 months, $14.00

---

Long one of the more backward countries of Eastern Europe, Bulgaria has sought to modernize itself under Communist rule along several directions. The country has expanded its industry, often in close coordination with the Soviet Union. Bulgaria and Romania are the only East European countries in which Soviet troops were not stationed.

Bulgaria produces early fruits and vegetables for the Soviet bloc. The country's Black Sea coast has been developed as a summer resort area.

At the 10th congress of the Bulgarian Communist party, held in April 1971 and attended by Soviet leader Leonid Brezhnev, a new constitution and a new party program were adopted. The congress reaffirmed the dominance of Todor Zhivkov, the veteran Communist party boss, and hailed the country's solidarity with the Soviet Union. But in the 1970s the government had to deal with domestic unrest on the part of workers seeking higher pay and better living conditions. The 12th Communist party congress of April 1981 recognized the country's poor economic performance in recent years, but other than calling for improvements in production, did nothing to resolve the problems.

**HISTORY:** Bulgaria, part of ancient Thrace and Moesia, was settled by Slavic tribes in the 6th century. In the 7th century the Slavs were conquered by Turkic-speaking Bulgars, who in time fully merged with the Slavs and whose domain continued to expand until the early part of the 11th century, when the Bulgarian state was annexed by the Byzantine Empire. Bulgaria again became a major Balkan power in the 12th and 13th centuries. In the 14th century, however, it was overrun by the Ottoman Turks and remained under their rule for 5 centuries

**1876:** Bulgarians revolt against Turkish rule but rebellion is crushed by brutal Turkish reprisals

**1878:** A large Bulgaria is created under Treaty of San Stefano ending Russo-Turkish Wars. However, treaty is revised by Congress of Berlin, making northern Bulgaria a principality under Turkish suzerainty and leaving southern Bulgaria, known as Eastern Rumelia, under direct Turkish rule

**1885-1908:** Alexander of Battenberg, first prince of Bulgaria, annexes Eastern Rumelia. His successor, Prince Ferdinand of Saxe-Coburg-Gotha, profiting from revolution of Young Turks in 1908, proclaims Bulgaria's independence

**1912-13:** Bulgaria, allied with Serbia, Greece, and Montenegro, enters first Balkan War against Turkey, which is expelled from all of Europe except the Constantinople area. Bulgarian claims to Macedonia result in second Balkan War, with Bulgaria fighting the armies of Serbia, Romania, Greece, and Turkey; Bulgaria is defeated and loses territory to all its enemies

**1915-1918:** Bulgaria enters World War I on side of Germany and Austria-Hungary, is defeated and loses territory

**1941-44:** Bulgaria joins Axis powers in World War II, declaring war on Britain and United States but not on USSR; in 1944 USSR declares war on Bulgaria and occupies country; Communists seize power with Soviet help

**1946-48:** Monarchy is abolished and a people's republic established. Industry is nationalized and resistance to collectivization of agriculture is broken

**1955:** Bulgaria joins Warsaw Pact

**1969:** Zhivkov regime launches campaign against Western influences in arts and culture and warns against anti-Soviet "revisionist" nationalism

**1971:** New constitution and new Bulgarian Communist Party program adopted

**1976:** Bulgaria meets with other Balkan nations for first conference on Balkan cooperation since WW II

**1978:** Diplomatic problems arise over steel dumping and assassinations of Bulgarian exiles

**1981:** 12th party congress reelects Zhivkov as secretary-general

## BURMA

**Area:** 261,789 sq. mi. **Population:** 33,640,000 (1980 est.)

**Official Name:** Socialist Republic of the Union of Burma **Capital:** Rangoon **Nationality:** Burmese **Languages:** Burmese, the official language, is spoken by 80%; the rest speak a variety, including Tamil, Hindi, Chinese, Shan, Karen, Kachin, Chin and Kayah; English is used in business **Religion:** 85% of the people are Buddhists; minority religions are Hinduism, Islam, Christianity, and animism **Flag:** A red field with a blue rectangle in the upper left corner containing a cog wheel and ear of paddy surrounded by 14 white stars **Anthem:** Our Free Homeland **Currency:** Kyat (7.6 per U.S. $1)

**Location:** Southeast Asia. Burma is bordered on the north and northeast by China, on the east by Laos and Thailand, on the south by the Andaman Sea and the Bay of Bengal, and on the west by Bangladesh and India **Features:** The country is rimmed on the north, east, and west by mountain ranges forming a giant horseshoe. Enclosed within this mountain barrier is a central basin containing most of the country's agricultural land and population. The Salween River, cutting deep gorges through the Shan Plateau and Karenni hills in the east separates the narrow Tenasserim coast from the central basin. A similar narrow coastal strip lies in the west between the Bay of Bengal and the Arakan Yoma mountain range **Chief Rivers:** Irrawaddy, Salween, Sittang, Mekong

**Head of State and of Government:** President: U San Yu, born 1918, chairman of the Council of State, elected by the People's Assembly

Nov. 9, 1981. He is assisted by a Cabinet headed by Prime Minister U Maung Maung Kha, elected 1977 **Effective Date of Present Constitution:** January 1974 **Legislative Body:** Parliament (unicameral People's Assembly) with 464 members elected for 4-year terms **Local Government:** 7 states and 7 divisions. Since March 1974, Peoples Councils have been elected at various local levels

**Ethnic Composition:** Burmans, ethnically related to the Tibetans, make up about 72% of the population; the Karens (7%), the Shans (6%), the Kachins (2%), and the Chins (2%) are the next largest ethnic groups. Chinese (3%) and Hindus and Pakistanis (6%) constitute the other major ethnic groups **Population Distribution:** 19% urban **Density:** 129 inhabitants per sq. mi.

**Largest Cities:** (1973 census) Rangoon 2,015,230, Mandalay 417,938, Moullmein 171,970, Bassein 126,041, Pegu 123,586

**Per Capita Income:** $186 (1980) **Gross National Product (GNP):** $6.4 billion (1980) **Economic Statistics:** In 1980, 27% of GNP came from agriculture, fishing, and forestry, and 10% from industry **Minerals and Mining:** Burma is rich in minerals, but production is low; petroleum, copper and tin are exploited; small quantities of tungsten, lead, zinc, nickel, cobalt, and precious stones are produced **Labor Force:** 12.2 million, of which 67% is employed in agriculture, and 9% in industry **Foreign Trade:** Exports, chiefly rice, teak and various ores, totaled $414 million in 1979. Imports, mainly textiles, machinery, transport equipment, and foodstuffs, totaled $714 million **Principal Trade Partners:** Singapore, Japan, Indonesia, West Germany, China, Hong Kong, France, Britain, United States

**Vital Statistics:** Birthrate, 38.6 per 1,000 pop. (1980); death rate 14.3 **Life Expectancy:** 57 years **Health Statistics:** 1,125 inhabitants per hospital bed; 5,121 per physician (1977) **Infant Mortality:** 62.7 per 1,000 births **Illiteracy:** 22% **Education Statistics:** 18,670 primary and secondary schools with a total enrollment of 4,370,987 (1976) **Enrollment in Higher Education:** 56,083 (1975) **GNP Expended on Education:** 1.7% (1976)

**Transportation:** Surfaced roads total 13,000 mi. **Motor Vehicles:** 82,200 (1978) **Passenger Cars:** 39,900 **Railway Mileage:** 2,040 **Ports:** Rangoon, Sittwe, Bassein, Moulmein, Tavoy, Mergui **Major Airlines:** Burma Airways operates both domestic and international services **Communications: Radio Transmitters:** 6 **Licenses:** 693,000 (1977) **Television Transmitters:** 1 **Telephones:** 34,000 (1978) **Newspapers:** 7 dailies, 11 copies per 1,000 inhabitants (1976)

**Weights and Measures:** British weights and measures as well as local units are used **Travel Requirements:** Passport; visa; tourist visa, one week, $4.85, 3 photos

---

A neglected adjunct of imperial India until 1937, Burma started its modern nationhood doubly colonialized: by the British and by the Indians, who ran the lower levels of government and, with the Chinese, dominated commerce.

The Japanese occupation of Burma during World War II turned the lush, rich land into a battlefield on which Burmese nationalists first fought the British and then the Japanese, whom they found to be worse oppressors.

The inability of the government to mollify the rebellious hill peoples, the demise of the coalition which had ruled since 1948, and the prevalence of corruption led to the unopposed military take-over of General Ne Win in 1958. He gave Burma two years of comparatively able government and then returned authority to civilians. While U Nu's faction won a convincing victory, the country's troubles proved too powerful for his new government.

In 1962 Ne Win again took over, jailing many politicians and banning all parties but the army's. The 15-man Revolutionary Council began broad nationalization, driving out Indians and generally sealing off Burma. The replacement of Indians and Chinese with Burmese proved politically popular but economically disastrous.

Under a new constitution adopted in 1974, Ne Win was elected president, and in 1978 he was reelected for another four-year term. The 1978 national elections gave the appearance of unity, since all candidates were members of Burma's single party, the Socialist Program party. Burma was beset, however, by internal disunity, underscored by stepped-up guerrilla strife.

Despite an economic upturn in the early 1980s, a 1982 UN study reported that Burma was neither producing nor importing enough food to meet the basic caloric needs of its citizens. Leftist insurgents remained active, and government military forays were having little effect in suppressing a large-scale illicit opium operation in the west. Ne Win stepped down as president in late 1981, but retained power through his continued chairmanship of the Socialist Program party.

**HISTORY:** A Mongoloid race from Tibet, the Burmese moved southward before the 9th century and settled along the Irrawaddy. In the 11th century, King Anawratha established supremacy over the Irrawaddy delta and introduced Hinayana Buddhism. His kingdom fell to Kublai Khan in 1287, after which it passed to the Shans, who ruled until 1546 as tributaries of China. Following the rise of new Burmese dynasties, Burma was once again unified, only to be annexed piecemeal by Britain in the 19th century

**1937:** Burma obtains dominionlike status

**1942-45:** Japan invades Burma during World War II and expels the British from most of the country. U.S., British, and Chinese forces mount a counterattack and expel the Japanese

**1948:** The Union of Burma is set up as an independent republic. U Nu becomes the first premier

**1962:** General Ne Win takes over from U Nu

**1970:** Government troops clash with rebels in northern Burma

**1971:** Large Karen minority plans new drive against government; Chinese-backed Burmese Communists launch widespread attacks on troop positions in northeast Burma

**1974:** New constitution adopted by referendum. Ne Win installed as president

**1976:** Karen rebels and Communist Shan insurgents renew fighting. Military plot to overthrow Ne Win aborted

**1978:** Ne Win reelected for second four-year term. About 200,000 Moslems flee into Bangladesh

**1979:** Burma leaves the nonaligned nations movement, saying it was disillusioned by Cuban handling of a summit meeting

**1980:** Ne Win declares political amnesty, frees 5,000 prisoners. U Nu returns from exile

**1981:** Ne Win gives up presidency, retains chairmanship of ruling party; U San Yu elected president

## BURUNDI

**Area:** 10,747 sq. mi. **Population:** 4,021,910 (1979 census)

**Official Name:** Republic of Burundi **Capital:** Bujumbura **Nationality:** Burundi **Languages:** Kirundi (Rundi), a Bantu tongue, and French are the official languages; Swahili is the trade language **Religion:** 60% are Christians, chiefly Roman Catholic; 2% Moslems and the rest are animists **Flag:** A white saltire (diagonal cross) with green and red quarters, and a white circle in the center bearing 3 red six-pointed stars outlined in green **Anthem:** Dear Burundi, O Sweet Land **Currency:** Burundi franc (90 per U.S. $1)

**Location:** East-central Africa. Burundi is bordered by Rwanda on the north, Tanzania on the east and south, Lake Tanganyika on the southwest, and Zaire on the northwest **Features:** Most of the country consists of grassy uplands and high plateaus. The Ruzizi River Valley and Lake Tanganyika, both along the western boundary with the Congo, constitute part of the Great Rift Valley **Chief Rivers:** Kagera, Ruvubu, Malagarazi, Ruzizi

**Head of State and Government:** President: Col. Jean-Baptiste Bagaza, born 1946, seized power in 1976 and appointed president **Effective Date of Present Constitution:** 1981 **Legislative Body:** None **Local Government:** 8 provinces, each headed by a governor

**Ethnic Composition:** 85% are Bahutu (Hutu), farmers of Bantu origin; 14% are Tutsi (Watusi, Batutsi), a tall warrior people of Hamitic origin; and 1% Twa (Batwa), aboriginal pygmies **Population Distribution:** 2% urban **Density:** 374 inhabitants per sq. mi.

**Largest Cities:** (1979 census) Bujumbura 141,000, Gitega 19,500, Bururi 7,800

**Per Capita Income:** $143 (1980) **Gross National Product (GNP):** $633 million (1980) **Economic Statistics:** In 1979, 63% of GNP was derived from agriculture (coffee, cotton, tea, bananas, sweet potatoes, cassava, millet and sorghum); and 13% from industry (chiefly food processing and textiles) **Minerals and Mining:** Bastnaesite, used for the manufacture of color TV tubes, and small amounts of cassiterite, tungsten, and gold are mined. Important nickel deposits are to be exploited **Labor Force:** 2,000,000 (1976), with 95% in agriculture **Foreign Trade:** Exports, chiefly coffee, cotton, tea, hides, and minerals, totaled $133 million in 1980. Imports, mainly textiles and leather, vehicles, machinery, food products, petroleum, consumer goods, totaled $127 million **Principal Trade Partners:** United States, Belgium, Luxembourg, West Germany, France, Kenya, Tanzania, Britain, Italy

**Vital Statistics:** Estimated birthrate, 46.8 per 1,000 of pop. (1975);

death rate, 20.4 **Life Expectancy:** 45 years **Health Statistics:** 857 inhabitants per hospital bed; 45,432 per physician (1975) **Infant Mortality:** 140 per 1,000 births **Illiteracy:** 86% **Primary and Secondary School Enrollment:** 274,9311 (1976) **Enrollment in Higher Education:** 1,002 (I975) **GNP Expended on Education:** 2.2% (1976)

**Transportation:** Of some 4,800 miles of road only about 190 miles are paved **Motor Vehicles:** 7,300 (1976) **Passenger Cars:** 5,100 **Railway Mileage:** None **Ports:** None **Major Airlines:** Air Burundi provides service to neighboring countries **Communications: Radio Transmitters:** 7 **Receivers:** 107,000 (1977) **Television:** None **Telephones:** 5,000 (1977) **Newspapers:** 1 daily (1976)

**Weights and Measures:** Metric system **Travel Requirements:** Passport, visa, $11 fee, 3 pictures

---

One of Africa's least-known and poorest countries, Burundi was until independence in 1962 the southern half of the former Belgian trust territory of Ruanda-Urundi. The landlocked country—Bujumbura, the capital, is nearly 1,000 miles by lake-rail routes from the nearest seaport, Dar es Salaam, in Tanzania—remains a geophysical, ethnic and economic twin of neighboring Rwanda.

Like Rwanda, Burundi is small, densely populated, heavily eroded, and the home of diverse peoples—the tall Tutsi (better known as Watusi), the traditional ruling minority; the medium-height Hutu, the majority peasant folk; and the dwindling pygmy Twa. However, in contrast to Rwanda where the majority Hutu rule, in Burundi the minority Tutsi caste has control and is reluctant to better the lives of the Hutu masses. As a result, foreign assistance to Burundi is less than half that provided to Rwanda, since donors assume their aid would end up serving the Tutsi elite.

The overthrow of the monarchy and proclamation of a republic in 1966 by a young Tutsi prime minister, Capt. Michel Micombero, opened the way to relative stability and concentration on needed economic development. While there have been gains in fiscal stability, Burundi continues to depend primarily on a small and fluctuating production of coffee.

Discontent among the Hutu has been an obstacle to more rapid development. In 1970 an alleged Hutu plot to massacre the Tutsi and seize power led to executions. In 1972-73 hostilities between the ruling Tutsis and the more numerous Hutus escalated, as Hutu tribesmen entered the country from Tanzania and Rwanda.

Burundi is aligned with the leftist-leaning nations of Africa, including neighboring Tanzania. In 1981 the government seized all television sets (Burundi has no transmission facilities) to halt reception of Western- oriented programs from Zairre.

**HISTORY:** Burundi's earliest inhabitants, the pygmy Twa, were supplanted by the Hutu, a Bantu people, who, in turn, were subjugated in the 15th or 16th century by the Tutsi, a tall, warrior people, coming probably from Ethiopia. Although Burundi was visited briefly by European explorers, it was not until the late 19th century that serious efforts at colonization were attempted

**1899:** Burundi is made part of German East Africa

**1916:** Belgian forces from the Congo defeat Germans, occupy Burundi and Rwanda

**1923-61:** Burundi and Rwanda become Belgian mandated territory known as Ruanda-Urundi which in 1946 is made United Nations trusteeship

**1962:** Kingdom of Burundi attains full independence under Mwami Mwambutsa IV

**1965:** Premier Pierre Ngendandumwe assassinated; Dr. Pie Masumbuko becomes acting premier

**1966:** Premier Michel Micombero deposes King Ntare V, declares himself President of Republic

**1972-73:** Tutsi-Hutu war results in more than 100,000 deaths

**1976:** Armed forces seize control of government and name Col. Jean- Baptiste Bagaza as president

**1979:** Approximately 85 missionaries, mostly Catholic, are expelled in June on grounds of preaching against the government

**1981:** Government begins to resettle scattered peasants in villages

## CAMBODIA (KAMPUCHEA)

**Area:** 69,898 sq. mi. **Population:** 5,756,141 (1981 est.)

**Official Name:** Democratic Kampuchea (functions in countryside); People's Republic of Kampuchea (pro-Vietnamese, in Phnom Penh) **Capital;** Phnom Penh **Nationality:** Cambodian or Kampuchean **Languages:** Cambodian, or Khmer, is the official aand predominant language **Religion:** The vast majority practice Theravada Buddhism **Flag (Democratic Kampuchea):** Red, with a stylized yellow three-towered temple in the middle **Flag (People's Republic):** Red, with a stylized yellow five-towered temple in the middle **Currency:** Riel

**Location:** Southeast Asia. Cambodia is bounded by Thailand and Laos on the north, by Vietnam on the southeast, by the Gulf of Thailand on the southwest, and by Thailand on the west **Features:** The country largely consists of a saucer-shaped alluvial plain drained by the Mekong River and shut off by mountains **Chief Rivers:** Mekong, Stung Sen

**Head of State (Democratic Kampuchea):** Prince Norodom Sihanouk, born 1922, is president of the coalition government established on June 22, 1982. Khieu Samphan serves as vice-president, and Son Sann is prime minister **Head of State (People's Republic):** President Heng Samrin, born 1931, is Chairman of the Council of State and Secretary General of the People's Revolutionary party of Kampuchea. Chan Si, born 1932, is Chairman (Prime Minister) of the Council of Ministers **Effective Date of Constitution (People's Rep.):** June 1981 **Legislative Body (People's Rep.):** National Assembly of 117 members, elected for 5-year terms **Local Government:** 19 provinces

**Ethnic Composition:** Cambodians, or Khmer, make up about 87% of the population; Chinese 5%, and Chams (Moslems descended from the people of the ancient kingdom of Champa) make up the rest **Density:** 82 inhabitants per sq. mi.

**Largest Cities:** Phnom Penh 600,000 (1970 est.); reported to be c. 400,000 in 1981; (1972 est.) Battambang 80,000, Kompong Cham 50,000, Pursat 20,000

**Per Capita Income:** $125 (1980) **Gross National Product (GNP):** $719 million (1980) **Economic Statistics:** In normal times overwhelmingly agricultural (rice, rubber, beans, corn), with a little industry (textiles, cement, rubber products) **Minerals and Mining:** Phosphates, gemstones and gold were produced, and there are known quantities of unexploited iron ore, manganese, and phosphates **Foreign Trade:** Rubber and dried fish are known exports, and oil and machinery are imported **Principal Trade Partners:** Vietnam, Laos, Soviet Bloc

**Transportation:** Paved roads totaled 1,600 mi. in 1975 **Railway Mileage:** 400 (1975) **Port:** Kompong Som **Communications:** Government owned

**Weights and Measures:** Metric system **Travel Requirements:** No U.S. relations exist, and tourists are not accepted at present

---

During 22 years of existence as an independent nation, caught in the middle of the East-West political and military struggle in Southeast Asia, Cambodia managed to walk the tightrope of neutrality. Its success was credited to the diplomatic skill of Prince Norodom Sihanouk, who started as a youthful king under the French, abdicated to fill a more active political role as premier, and then became the country's first chief of state.

Sihanouk managed to maintain Cambodia's neutrality even as the Vietnam War intruded increasingly on—and over—the eastern border. Then, in March 1970, while he was out of the country, his government was overthrown in a coup led by Lt. Gen. Lon Nol.

Within a month, Cambodia's small and ill-equipped army was fighting the Vietnamese Communists and Prince Sihanouk was forming a government in exile based in Peking. The war went badly for the Cambodians, who appealed to the world for help against the enemy's sudden consolidation of its enclaves in the east. Late in April there was a response: South Vietnamese and American troops drove across the border to smash the sanctuaries. Many Vietnamese Communists moved west and assumed control of large sections of the country, including the temples at Angkor. Phnom Penh itself was often isolated from the only seaport.

In mid-1973, the United States was hoping to nudge Cambodia's exiled Prince Sihanouk and Khmer insurgent leaders into serious peace talks with members of General Lon Nol's regime. The diplomatic pressure was being brought to bear against a backdrop of urgency caused by the steady advance of Communist troops toward Phnom Penh and the imminent end of U.S. bombing raids in the country. It was at this time that the Pentagon admitted having secretly bombed Communist forces in Cambodia as early as 1969 and supplying false statistics to the U.S. Senate.

The war, with U.S. help, continued through 1974 and into 1975, with Khmer Rouge forces moving ever closer to the capital city of Phnom Penh. The end came swiftly in April 1975, with the departure of President Lon Nol and the evacuation of U.S. civilians and embassy personnel. According to Cambodian estimates, nearly 800,000 people had been killed in the war and 200,000 wounded.

In the following months, refugees who escaped to Thailand reported that hundreds of thousands of people had been forcibly moved from the cities to rural areas. Almost the entire population of Phnom Penh—a city swollen by 2 million refugees—was evacuated and put to work in the rice fields. Refugees spoke of long forced marches, starvation and wholesale killings by the Khmer Rouge.

In January 1976 a new constitution went into effect and the state took a new name: Democratic Kampuchea. Elections were held on March 20 and a People's Representative Assembly of 250 was selected. Prince Sihanouk, who had returned to Phnom Penh in late 1975, announced his resignation as Head of State on April 5 and Khieu Samphan became President of the State Presidium. In September 1977, Pol Pot ended his country's virtual isolation by making a trip to Peking, where he was identified as the Secretary of the Central Committee of the Cambodian Communist Party, Prime Minister and the prime force in making sweeping changes.

Under Pol Pot—he had been Saloth Sar, a schoolteacher, according to Prince Sihanouk—the country's economy and manpower were reshaped drastically. All lands and means of production belonged to the state. Private plots, permitted even in China and the USSR, were forbiddeen. Wages were paid as foood rations, but they were meager, and no money was circulated. The foremost economic activity was the rebuilding of irrigation canals and dikes that had been destroyed in the civil war.

The outside world was ignored, except for China, which sent technical advisers and delivered supplies through Kompong Som, Cambodia's only port. Reports carried to neighboring countries said that the harsh treatment had produced a high death toll—somewhere between 500,000 and 2 million. U.S. President Carter accused Cambodia of being the world's worst violator of human rights.

Enemies for centuries, Cambodia and Vietnam fought frequent border clashes in 1977 and 1978. In December 1978, Vietnamese troops moved steadily across Cambodia with, Hanoi said, the aid of Cambodian insurgents. On Jan. 9, 1979, Phnom Penh fell, and Pol Pot's government was replaced with the Hanoi-backed People's Revolutionary Council of Cambodia. A Cambodian, Heng Samrin took over as president, and he declared that "during the last three years, they [the Khmer Rouge under Pol Pot] killed millions." Entire villages and communes had been slaughtered, he said. On Feb. 18, he signed a treaty of friendship with Vietnam.

Despite the change in governments, the fighting continued. Khmer Rouge loyalists fled into the jungles or mixed with the population, and Pol Pot reportedly was with them. The Khmer Rouge then mounted a stubborn resistance, cutting the roads and thus denying supplies to Vietnam troops, but they pursued a policy of avoiding big-scale confrontations. Estimates were that Vietnam had 100,000 soldiers in Cambodia, while the Pol Pot forces had 40,000 to 50,000 men and were receiving some aid through Thailand.

Possibly as many as 3 million Cambodians died from 1975 through 1979. Fearing that another 2 million or more might starve because crops had not been planted or were destroyed in the fighting, UNICEF and the International Red Cross took charge of receiving food from 51 nations. Massive tie-ups in ports and warehouses occurred in early 1980, but distribution became more effective toward the end of the year, and, in 1981, a UN study reported that the threat of widespread starvation and malnutrition had receded.

The fighting continued, as several anti-Vietnamese groups other than the Pol Pot forces also became active in the resistance. Early in 1981, the exiled Sihanouk began efforts to unite the opposition, and by 1982, the move for a coalition of anti-Samrin factions was being supported by China, several Southeast Asian nations, and, with qualifications, by the United States. By June, the coalition government became a reality. Early that year, Vietnamese troop strength in Cambodia was estimated at 200,000 and that of all resistance forces at less than 50,000.

**HISTORY:** Modern Cambodia is what remains of the great Khmer Empire, which by the 1200s stretched across Southeast Asia from the South China Sea westward into Burma. By the 1800s the Khmer holdings had been steadily reduced to the present size of Cambodia bby the invasions of the Vietnamese and Siamese

**1863:** French protectorate is established over Cambodia

**1887:** Cambodia is incorporated in the Union of Indo-China

**1945:** Japanese invade Cambodia, driving out the Vichy French

**1946:** French return and grant Cambodia autonomy within the French Union

**1953-54:** Cambodia becomes independent, leaves French Union

**1970:** Prince Sihanouk is ousted by Lon Nol in pro-Western coup; U.S. and South Vietnamese troops enter Cambodia in drive against North Vietnamese forces. U.S. ground forces are later withdrawn. Cambodia is declared a republic

**1971:** United States expands bombing strikes and troop-ferrying missions; South Vietnamese driven from Cambodia

**1973:** Pentagon admits it conducted 14 months (1969/70) of secret bombings in Cambodia. Bombing halted Aug. 15

**1974:** Khmer Rouge insurgents intensify military operations. The U.S. airlifts supplies to government

**1975:** U.S. triples its airlift to overcome effect of insurgents' blockade of roads into Phnom Penh and of Mekong River. April 1: Lon Nol leaves country. Government resistance begins to crumble. April 16: Government surrenders and insurgents enter Phnom Penh. War ends. May 14: U.S. air, sea and ground forces battle Cambodians after seizure of the American merchant ship *Mayaguez* in the Gulf of Siam. The ship and crew of 39 are freed

**1976:** New constitution goes into effect. Prince Sihanouk resigns as head of state. Hundreds of thousands reported to have died during forced movement of population from cities into countryside, beginning in 1975

**1977:** Pol Pot identified as nation's leader

**1978:** Border clashes with Vietnam and Thailand intensify

**1979:** Phnom Penh falls, Pol Pot's government ("Democratic Kampuchea") retreats to remote areas, and the Vietnam-backed People's Revolutionary Council takes over, with Heng Samrin as president of the "People's Republic of Kampuchea"

**1980:** UNICEF and the Red Cross direct a famine-relief effort. Khieu Samphan emerges as leader of Pol Pot forces

**1981:** Threat of famine eases. Anti-Communist insurgents, led by former premier Son Sann, become active. Soviet-led attempt to give Pol Pot UN seat to Samrin regime fails

**1982:** Vietnam troops lead major spring offensive, score successes against rebels near Thai border, but fail to wipe them out. Sihanouk, Khieu Samphan and Son Sann form anti-Samrin, anti-Vietnam coalition government ("Democratic Kampuchea")

## CAMEROON

**Area:** 183,568 sq. mi. **Population:** 8,503,000 (1980 est.)

**Official Name:** United Republic of Cameroon **Capital:** Yaoundé **Nationality:** Cameroonian **Languages:** French (spoken by 75%) and English (25%) are both official languages; 24 African languages are spoken **Religion:** 33% Christian (mainly in the south); 15%

Moslem (mainly in the north); the rest are animists **Flag:** Vertical green, red, and yellow stripes, with a yellow star in the center of the red stripe **Anthem:** O, Cameroon, Cradle of Our Ancestors **Currency:** CFA Franc (305 per U.S. $1)

**Location:** West-central Africa. Cameroon is bordered by Lake Chad on the north, by Chad and the Central African Republic on the east, by the Congo, Gabon, and Equatorial Guinea on the south, by the Gulf of Guinea on the west, and by Nigeria on the west and northwest **Features:** Of the country's four distinct regions, the south consists of a low coastal plain with equatorial rain forests, the center forms a transitional plateau, the west is an area of mountainous forests, and the north is low rolling savanna **Chief Rivers:** Sanaga, Nyong

**Head of State and of Government:** President Ahmadou Ahidjo, born 1924, elected 1960, reelected to fifth 5-year term in April 1980, assisted by a cabinet headed by the premier, Paul Biya, appointed 1975 **Effective Date of Present Constitution:** May 1972 **Legislative Body:** National Asseembly (unicameral), consisting of 120 members elected by universal suffrage for 5 years **Local Goverment:** 7 provinces with appointed governors

**Ethnic Composition:** Estimates of the number of tribal groups run as high as 200. The main divisions are the Bantus and semi-Bantus, which include the Beti and Bamiléké; the Sudanese, mainly Kirdis; and the Arab Foulbé. Pygmies inhabit the equatorial forest **Population Distribution:** 28% urban **Density:** 46 inhabitants per sq. mi.

**Largest Cities:** (1976 census) Douala 458,426, Yaoundé 313,706, N'Kongsamba 71,298, Maroua 67,187

**Per Capita Income:** $600 (1980) **Gross Domestic Product (GDP):** $4.9 billion (1980) **Economic Statistics:** 33% of GDP came from agriculture (coffee, cocoa, bananas, cotton, peanuts, livestock, rubber, palm oil) and 24% from industry (aluminum, paper, chemicals) **Minerals and Mining:** Large deposits of bauxite ore, iron ore, and limestone; traces of mica and phosphates; small deposits of tin and gold. Petroleum and natural gas exploitation is important **Labor Force:** Over 3 million; 75% in agriculture **Foreign Trade:** Exports, chiefly coffee, cocoa beans, aluminum, petroleum, wood, cotton, and rubber, totaled $1.6 billion in 1980. Imports, mainly vehicles and transportation equipment, industrial machinery and other capital goods, consumer goods, food, beverages, and tobacco, totaled $1.8 billion **Principal Trade Partners:** EC countries (mainly France), United States, Japan, adjacent African nations

**Vital Statistics:** Birthrate, 42.3 per 1,000 of pop. (1980); death rate, 19.4 **Life Expectancy:** 44 years **Health Statistics:** 372 inhabitants per hospital bed; 15,820 per physician (1977) **Infant Mortality:** 137 per 1,000 births **Illiteracy:** 81% **Primary and Secondary School Enrollment:** 1,375,548 (1977) **Enrollment in Higher Education:** 7,191 (1975) **GNP Expended on Education:** 4.6% (1976)

**Transportation:** Paved roads total about 1,338 miles **Motor Vehicles:** 134,900 (1978) **Passenger cars:** 73,700 **Railway Mileage:** 727 **Ports:** Douala, Tiko, Victoria, Kribi **Major Airlines:** Cameroon Airlines operates international and domestic services **Communications: Radio Transmitters:** 10 **Receivers:** 240,000 (1977) **Television:** None **Telephones:** 22,000 (1973) **Newspapers:** 3 dailies, 5 copies per 1,000 inhabitants (1976)

**Weights and Measures:** Metric system **Travel Requirements:** Passport; tourist visa, valid 20-30 days, $14.42 fee, 2 photos

---

Cameroon has been one of the main racial crossroads of Africa as a result of Bantu migrations from the east and links to the Sahara caravan trade to the north. Extending nearly 800 miles in length from the Gulf of Guinea to Lake Chad, the country is a cross section of Africa from desert north through central plateau and grasslands to southern rain forest.

Formerly a German colony, Cameroon was divided between France and Britain after World War I, with the French getting about four-fifths of the area. The country was reunited as a federal republic in 1961, after a UN plebiscite had resulted in the addition of the northern part of former British Cameroons to Nigeria.

The two areas, West Cameroon (formerly British) and the larger East Cameroon (formerly French) were governed as constituent states, each with its own legislature. The new constitution which went into effect in May 1972 established a unitary state with a strong executive authority and an elected national assembly.

Cameroon is the only African country in which both French and English are official languages. The Federal University of Cameroon, established in Yaoundé in 1962, is the first in Africa to teach courses in French and English, as well as one of the first to establish a medical school.

Cameroon has been one of Africa's "quiet" countries, in which the single-party government of President Ahmadou Ahidjo has maintained a measure of political and economic stability.

Before Cameroon became an independent republic in 1960, the former French eastern area was torn by a terrorist revolt. Protracted rebel activities in the central part of the country were suppressed in 1970. Despite the diversity of its peoples, cultures, and religions, however, Cameroon has escaped the coups and civil wars that have plagued neighboring countries.

Cameroon's great diversity of tropical produce—timber, cocoa, coffee, rubber, palm oil, cotton, and a wide range of food crops—has been the basis for an economic growth that has been averaging nine percent a year. Although France remains the country's chief partner in trade and investment, British, American, West German, and Japanese interests have been attracted by the favorable economic and investment climate. Petroleum production began in 1978, but President Ahidjo has cautioned his people not to "give in to the mirage of oil." He emphasizes the need for continuing agricultural development.

Education and health services also are increasing and Cameroonians take pride in the fact that 70 percent of the country's children attend school, a high rate for developing Africa.

**HISTORY:** The country was given its name by 15th century Portuguese explorers. Impressed with the number of shrimp in one of the rivers, they called it Rio dos Camarões (River of Shrimp) and extended the name to the entire region. After being made a German colony in the late 19th century, the country was occupied during World War I by the French and British, who divided it under League of Nations mandates

**1946:** French and British mandates are converted into United Nations Trusteeships

**1959:** UN General Assembly votes end of French trusteeship

**1960:** On Jan. 1, French Cameroon becomes independent Cameroon Republic; draft constitution is approved by referendum; National Assembly names Premier Ahmadou Ahidjo president

**1961:** In UN-supervised plebiscites, southern part of British Cameroons votes for reunification with Cameroon Republic, northern part for union with Nigeria; federation of East and West Camerooon is established

**1966:** After unification of major political parties in East and West Cameroon, all opposition parties are dissolved or join in single new party, the Cameroon National Union

**1971:** Political trials and executions end 10-year guerrilla insurrection

**1980:** President Ahidjo is reelected to his fifth five-year term. Influx of refugees from Chad poses serious food-supply problem for Cameroon government

**1981:** Five Nigerian soldiers killed in border dispute with Cameroon

---

## CANADA

(See separate Canada section)

---

## CAPE VERDE

**Area:** 1,557 sq. mi. **Population:** 296,093 (1980 census)

**Official Name:** Republic of Cape Verde **Capital:** Praia **Nationality:** Cape Verdean **Languages:** Officially Portuguese, with most speaking a dialect, Crioulo **Religion:** 65% Roman Catholic, and 30% animist **Flag:** Two horizontal stripes, yellow over green, with a red vertical stripe at the hoist, the latter having an emblem of a black star over a yellow seashell, framed by two cornstalks **Anthem:** This Is Our Beloved Country **Currency:** Cape Verdean escudo (52 per U.S. $1)

**Location:** In the Atlantic Ocean, 390 miles west of Dakar, Senegal, off the coast of Africa, centering on 16°N. and 24°W. Ten islands and 5 islets comprise the nation **Features:** Summer climate is extremely hot and there is a lack of potable water. Three of the main islands are flat; the other seven are mountainous, volcanic in origin **Chief Rivers:** No large rivers

**Head of State:** President Aristides Pereira, named 1975, reelected 1981 **Head of Government:** Premier Pedro Pires, appointed 1975 **Effective Date of Constitution:** 1980 **Legislative Body:** National Assembly (unicameral), with 56 mmembers **Local Government:** 14 *concelhos*

**Ethnic Composition:** 71% are Creoles (mulattoes) of mixed African annd Portuguese descent, 28% are Africans, and 1% Europeans **Population Distribution:** 20% urban **Density:** 190 inhabitants per sq. mi.

**Largest Cities:** (1980 census) Praia 37,480, Mindelo 36,265

**Per Capita Income:** $233 (1979) **Gross Domestic Product (GDP):** $71 million (1979 est.) **Economic Statistics:** The main economic function of the country is ship and aircraft refueling. The soil is poor and dry, and although some food (corn, beans, coffee, sugar) is grown, much must be imported. Fishing is important **Minerals and Mining:** Salt, pozzolana (used in making cements) **Labor Force:** 84,869 in 1970, with 67% in agriculture, and 5% in industry **Foreign Trade:** Exports, chiefly fish products, bananas, salt, coffee, pozzolana, totaled $3 million in 1980. Imports, chiefly corn, wheat, cement, petroleum products, totaled $98 million **Principal Trade Partners:** Portugal, EC, Angola, United States

**Vital Statistics:** Birthrate, 27.6 per 1,000 of pop. (1975); death rate, 9.4 **Life Expectancy:** 45 years **Health Statistics:** 516 per hospital bed; 7,750 per physician (1977) **Infant Mortality:** 104.9 per 1,000 births **Illiteracy:** 63% **Primary and Secondary School Enrollment:** 71,790 (1972) **Enrollment in Higher Education:** N.A. **GNP Expended on Education:** 1.5% (1972)

**Transportation:** Paved roads total 380 mi. **Motor Vehicles:** 4,000 (1977) **Passenger Cars:** 3,100 **Railway Mileage:** None **Ports:** Mindelo, Praia **Major Airlines:** T.A.P. provides international service, and Cape Verde Air Transport domestic service **Communications: Radio Transmitters:** 6 **Receivers:** 40,000 (1977) **Television:** None **Telephones:** 2,000 (1977) **Newspapers:** Three, several times a week

**Weights and Measures:** Metric system **Travel Requireemeents:** Passport; tourist visa, valid 30 days, $13.50 fee, 1 photo

---

Cape Verde became independent on July 5, 1975, ending 515 years of Portuguese rule. In 1460 the Portuguese navigators Diego Gomes and Antonio da Noli discovered Maio and São Tiago Islands, and in 1462 the first settlers landed on São Tiago.

Aristedes Pereira and Pedro Pires, heroes of the guerrilla war waged against Portugal in Guinea-Bissau, were named president and premier, respectively, in 1975.

These overpopulated islands have been afflicted with disastrous drought and famine in recent years. Since the mid-1900s, an estimated 300,000 Cape Verdeans have emigrated because of the difficulty of earning a living. In 1981 a $4-million refrigerating plant was opened as a step in building up a modern fisheries industry.

**HISTORY:** The islands were discovered in 1460 by Portuguese navigators in the service of Prince Henry the Navigator. Settlement began two years later. The archipelago was a center for the slave trade with the West African coast

**1975:** On June 30, the Party for the Independence of Guinea-Bissau and Cape Verde (PAIGC) is the only political group to run candidates for the 56-member Assembly at the first general election

**1976:** Cape Verde and USSR sign pact granting reciprocal use of each other's ports

**1979:** UN Food and Agriculture Organization grants $908,000 in emergency food aid to the drought-stricken nation

**1980:** National Assembly approves a constitution to replace provisional laws. Coup in Guinea-Bissau chills close relations between Cape Verde and that country

**1981:** The name of PAIGC is changed to PAICV (African party for the Independence of Cape Verde)

---

## CENTRAL AFRICAN REPUBLIC

**Area:** 236,293 sq. mi. **Population:** 2,370,000 (1978 est.)

**Official Name:** Central African Repubiic **Capital:** Bangui **Nationality:** Central African **Languages:** French is the official language; Sangho is the national language **Religion:** 40% Protestant, 28% Roman Catholic, 24% animist, 8% Moslem **Flag:** Horizontal bars of blue, white, green, and yellow, bisected by a vertical red bar. A yellow star appears on the blue band at the upper left **Anthem:** La Renaissance **Currency:** CFA Franc (305 per U.S. $1)

**Location:** In the center of the African continent. The landlocked country is borderred by Chad on the north, Sudan on the east, Zaire and Congo on the south, and Cameroon on the west **Features:** The country is a huge, well-watered plateau drained by 2 major river systems **Chief Rivers:** Ouham, Ubangi, Kotto, Lobaye, Sangha

**Head of State and of Government:** President of the Military Committee: Gen. André-Dieudonne Kolingba, took power on Sept. 1, 1981 **Effective Date of Present Constitution:** Feb. 6, 1981; suspended Sept. 1 **Legislative Body:** suspended **Local Government:** 14 prefectures

**Ethnic Composition:** Of some 80 different ethnic groups, the main ones (66%) are the Banda in the east-central area; the Baya and the Mandjia in the west and in the west-central area; 7% are M'baka **Population Distribution:** 20% urban **Density:** 10 inhabitants per sq. mi.

**Largest Cities:** (1975 census) Bangui 279,792, Bambari 31,285, Bouar 29,5288, Berberati 27,285, Bossangoa 25,150

**Per Capita Income:** $182 (1980) **Grross National Product (GNP):** $451 million (1980) **Economic Statistics:** Agriculture (cotton, coffee, rice, tobacco, rubber, peanuts, palm oil) and livestock (cattle, sheep, goats, pigs, poultry) make up 34% of the GNP; diamond and uranium mining, and small-scale manufacturing (textiles, beer, shoes, bicycles and motor bikes, plastics) 16%; and trade and services 29% **Minerals and Mining:** Diamonds, uranium and gold are exploited. Deposits of iron ore, zinc, copper, and tin exist **Labor Force:** 87% of the population is engaged in farming **Foreign Trade:** Exports, chiefly diamonds, wood, cotton, and coffee, totaled $108 million in 1980. Imports, mainly machinery and equipment, textiles, and petroleum products, totaled $100 million **Principal Trade Partners:** France, other EC countries, United States, Japan, Cameroon, Congo

**Vital Statistics:** Birthrate, 41.5 per 1,000 of pop. (1980); death rate, 19 **Life Expectancy:** 41 years **Health Statistics:** 522 inhabitants per hospital bed; 20,833 peer physician (1975) **Infant Mortality:** 190 per 1,000 births **Illiteracy:** 82% **Primary and Secondary School Enrollment:** 245,307 (1975) **Enrollment in Higher Education:** 555 **GNP Expended on Education:** 3.9% (1973)

**Transportation:** Paved roads total 180 mi. **Motor Vehicles:** 16,400 (1977) **Passenger Cars:** 12,400 **Railway Mileage:** None 3Ports: None **Major Airlines:** Air Centrafrique operates domestic services **Communications: Radio Transmitters:** 4 (1976) **Receivers:** 80,000 (1977) **Television Transmitters:** 1 **Telephones:** 5,000 (1973) **Newspapers:** 1

**Weights and Measures:** Metric system **Travel Requirements:** Passport, visa

---

Isolation in the heart of Africa constitutes the main problem of the Central African Republic (the Central African Empire from 1976 until 1979), a problem that is compounded by a paucity of resources and a small population.

Most of the former French colony of Ubangi-Shari is a plateau of 2,000-foot ellevation, a condition that makes for a relatively temperate climate during the dry season. Stretches of grassy savanna and woodland, in which there is an abundance of wildlife, give the land a magnificent beauty.

With modern techniques, cotton production has increased more than three times to 60,000 metric tons a year and provides a major export. Diamond production and small quantities of coffee and peanuts have also added to exports and income.

While the diamonds may be shipped by air, the other products must be transported at considerable cost by road or river to the nearest ports. Aid from France, the World Bank, and other sources has helped improve roads and create small industry, but clearly a rail link is needed for further crop expansion and development of timber resources.

The recent exploitation of uranium at Bakouma, 540 miles east of Bangui, has brightened economic prospects and, with new exploration indicating deposits of iron ore, manganese, and copper, has heightened the need for a railroad.

On becoming fully independent Aug. 13, 1960, the Central African Republic adopted a parliamentary form of government. David Dacko became president. His cousin, Col. Jean-Bédel Bokassa, a former French army sergeant, led a military coup in 1966 which dissolved the national assembly and established Bokassa as head of the ruling revolutionary council. Ten years later, he proclaimed himself emperor and was crowned in a $22-million ceremony in December 1977. He ruled by imperial decree and sometimes with brutal discipline.

One government decree, that students wear state uniforms, prompted protest demonstrations in the capital in January 1979, resulting in 12 deaths. Amnesty International reportedd the killing of more than 100 schoolchildren following their arrest for further rioting in April.

Emperor Bokassa was overthrown with French assistance on Sept. 20, 1979, in a bloodless coup led by David Dacko who resumed the presidency he had held from 1960 to 1965. Dacko formed the single-party Central African Democratic Union and was elected to a six-year term as president on March 15, 1981. Demonstrators claimed that the election had been rigged, and Dacko had to declare a state of emergency to stop the rioting. On September 1, Dacko was toppled by a military group headed by Gen. André Kolingba.

**HISTORY:** For centuries, what is now the Central African Empire was a crossroads for numerous migrations by various groups, mainly of Bantu origin. In the 19th century, French expeditions penetrated the country, which was named Ubangi-Shari after its two main rivers. Early in the 20th century, the countrry was joined with Chad and became one of the territories of French Equatorial Africa

**1946:** French constitutional reform confers French citizenship on people of Ubangi-Shari

**1958:** In a referendum, Ubangi-Shari votes to become an autonomous republic within the French Community. The Central African Republic is proclaimed, with Barthélémy Boganda as president

**1959:** Boganda, founder of the republic and its mass political party, Social Evolution Movement of Black Africa, is killed in plane crash and succeeded by his cousin, David Dacko

**1960-65:** Republic becomes a fully independent nation under President Dacko, who dissolves all political parties. He is reelected in an election in which he is the only candidate

**1966:** Colonel Jean-Bedel Bokassa, chief of staff of the armed forces, overthrows Dacko government, ousts Communist Chinese mission, and establishes rule by revolutionary council

**1970:** C.A.R. resumes relations with Zaire and Chad

**1972:** Congress of the sole political party appoints Bokassa president for life

**1976:** Bokassa escapes assassination attempt in February. He dismisses Domitien and declares his country a parliamentary monarchy with himself as emperor

**1979:** David Dacko leads a bloodless coup to unseat Bokassa and drive him out of the country

**1981:** In Feb. 1 referendum 97% of population approves new constitution. Dacko is elected to a six-year term. Army overthrows Dacko on on Sept. 1 and names Gen. André Kolingba in his place

**1982:** Government reports a coup attempt; arrests and executes many followers of Ange Patasse, leader of the opposition who gains asylum in the French Embassy

## CHAD

**Area:** 495,752 sq. mi. **Population:** 4,309,000 (1978 est.)

**Official Name:** Republic of Chad **Capital:** N'Djamena **Nationality:** Chadian **Languages:** French is the official language. An Arabic dialect is spoken in northern and central Chad; in the south the main tribal languages are Sara, Massa, and Moudang **Religion:** More than 50% of the population is Moslem, 40% animist, and 5% Christian **Flag:** Vertical stripes of blue, yellow, aand red **Anthem:** La Tchadienne, beginning "Chadians, Stand up and Set to Work!" **Currency:** CFA Franc (305 per U.S. $1)

**Location:** North-Central Africa. Landlocked Chad is bordered by Libya on the north, Sudan on the east, the Centrral African Republliic on the south, and by Niger, Nigeria, and Cameroon on the west **Features:** The country is shaped like a shallow basin, rimmed by mountain ranges on the north and east. The northern part of the country is desert, the central part a savanna, and the south tropical, with wooded savanna. Lake Chad on the western border is believed to be the remnant of an inland sea **Chief Rivers:** Shari, Logone

**Head of State and of Government:** Hissen Habré took power when his military forces captured N'Djamena, the capital, on June 7, 1982 **Effective Date of Present Constitution:** 1962; suspended 1975 **Legislative Body:** None **Local Government:** 14 prefectures, under appointed governors

**Ethnic Composition:** The population is about evenly divided between the northern and eastern people, of predominantly Sudanic origin, and the Nilotic southerners **Population Distribution:** 18% urban **Density:** 9 inhabitants per sq. mi.

**Largest Cities:** (1972 est.) N'Djamena 179,000, Sarh 43,700, Moundou 39,600, Abécher 28,100

**Per Capita Income:** $97 (1980) **Gross National Product (GNP):** $451 million (1980) **Economic Statistics:** In 1973 about 50% of GNP came from agriculture (cotton, sorghum, rice, sugar, peanuts, gum arabic, livestock) and fishing, 8% from industry and mining, and 23% from trade and services **Minerals and Mining:** Natron, a low-grade salt, is the only exploited mineral. Traces of shale oil, uranium, kaolin, and tungsten have been found in the north. Petroleum has been discovered **Labor Force:** 1.3 million (1970), with about 88% in agriculture **Foreign Trade:** Exports, chiefly cotton and cattle, totaled $134 million in 1980. Imports, mainly mineral products (including petroleum products), foodstuffs and beverages, electrical machinery and parts, textiles, and transportation equipment, totaled $170 million **Principal Trade Partners:** Nigeria, France, Japan

**Vital Statistics:** Birthrate, 43.9 per 1,000 of pop. (1980); death rate, 20.8 **Life Expectancy:** 43 years **Health Statistics:** 1,140 inhabitants per hospital bed; 44,382 per physician (1974) **Infant Mortality:** 160 per 1,000 births **Illiteracy:** 94% **Primary and Secondary School Enrollment:** 230,462 (1976) **Enrollment in Higher Education:** 547 (1975) **GNP Expended on Education:** 2.4% (1976)

**Transportation:** Paved roads total 150 mi. **Motor Vehicles:** 12,100 (1973) **Passenger Cars:** 5,800 **Railway Mileage:** None **Ports:** None **Major Airlines:** 1 Air Chad is the domestic carrier **Communications: Radio Transmitters:** 3 **Receivers:** 80,000 (1977) **Television Transmitters:** 1 **Telephones:** 7,000 (1977) **Newspapers:** 4 dailies, 0.4 copies per 1,000 inhabitants (1975)

**Weights and Measures:** Metric system **Travel Requirements:** (1971) Passport, visa, $6.25; 3 photos, round-trip ticket

The remote outpost of former French Equatorial Africa, landlocked Chad suffers from isolation, internal strife, and a loss of arable land.

With its productive area more than 1,000 miles from any seaport, Chad is difficult to reach except by air. There is no railroad and a good part of the network of dirt roads and tracks is impassable during the rainy season.

Since 1968 Arab guerrillas in the northern and eastern part of the country have waged a rebellion against the Bantu-dominated government. Some 3,500 French troops were sent to help the Chadian government quell the revolt, an action that has raaised controversy both in France and in Africa. French forces actively fighting the rebels were withdrawn in 1971.

The chief cause of the nomadic northerners' enmity toward the Chadian government was the fact that it had been dominated by southerners—Negroid river peoples whom the Arabs traditionally scorned as slaves. In addition, the northerners, mainly the Toubous, resented the government's tax on their cattle.

The regime of François Tombalbaye, which had been in power since 1962, was toppled by a military coup in 1975. General Félix Malloum, the new Bantu ruler, became the object of a coup attempt himself in 19799 when the Moslem premier, Hissen Habré, led a move to oust him.

For months control passed from one provisional government to another. On Nov. 10 a transitional government of national unity was formed with Goukouni Oueddei as president and Habré as defense minister. The power struggle between these rival Moslem leaders was quieted for only a few months, however. On March 22, 1980, guerrilla forces loyal to the president and the minister fought each other in the streets of N'Djamena, using tanks, artillery and rockets. the number of persons killed, both military and civilian, ran into the hundreds. An estimated 70,000 refugees crossed the Shari River into Cameroon.

Efforts of the Organization of African Unity and France failed to bring about a settlement of the civil war. A short-lived cease-fire was arranged late in 1980. Libya's revolutionary leader, Col. Muammar el-Qaddafi, sent tanks into N'Djamena on

Dec. 16 to support Goukouni Oueddei and compel Habré's forces to abandon the city. Libya talked of a "merger" of Chad with Libya, but late in 1981, at Chad's request, Libyan forces withdrew, to be replaced by Nigerian, Senegalese and Zairian troops provided by the OAU.

Following the Libyan withdrawal, Habré launched a military offensive to retake power with Egyptian and Sudanese support. On June 7, 1982, his forces retook N'Djamena, driving Goukouni into exile. His newly gained power was limited to the capital and the northern desert areas of the country, however, as southern tribesmen declined allegiance to the new regime.

In addition to the ravages of political strife, the economy of Chad has been badly injured by prolonged drought. Thousands of persons have died, cattle have perished and former grazing lands have become sandy desert. Production of cotton, the chief export crop, has declined greatly.

**HISTORY:** Chad is believed to have been a center of ancient cultures before the southward encroachment of the Sahara. The varied ethnic make-up of present-day Chadians is evidence also of a succession of migrations and invasions in past centuries by Bantu southerners, Sudanese Moslems, and Nilotic peoples. Throughout the ages, Chad was the domain of conquerors and warrior slave traders, some of whom held sway until the late 19th century. Among the last of these was Rabah Amoney, a Sudanese ex-slave turned slave merchant and chieftain, whose conquest of the Bornu Kingdom was to lead to French intervention

**1897-1900:** Traditional rulers, threatened by Rabah's army, seek protection of French, whose forces march across the Sahara from Algeria, defeat Sudanese, and impose own rule

**1910:** Chad is made one of the four territories of French Equatorial Africa, along with Gabon, the present Congo (Brazzaville), and Ubangi-Shari (now the Central African Empire)

**1940:** Chad becomes first territory to rally to Free French

**1959-60:** Chad becomes autonomous member of French Community. On Aug. 11, 1960, complete independence and the Republic of Chad are proclaimed

**1962:** All opposition parties are banned under new constitution and single-party rule is set up by Chadian Progressive party, led by President François Tombalbaye

**1963:** State of emergency is declared after abortive coup d'état and arrest of Moslem leaders; constitutional amendments are adopted and new elections are held in an effort to heal the rift between Moslem north and Bantu south

**1969:** Moslem guerrillas step up attacks on government installations as Arab-Bantu split widens; President Tombalbaye calls in French troops to help quell growing revolt

**1973:** UN reports Chad is most severly affected of the sub-Saharan countries suffering from drought

**1975:** President Tombalbaye assassinated (April 13). Military junta headed by Gen. Félix Malloum takes control

**1979-1980:** Malloum is ousted in coup and rival factions battle for control of country; one provisional government follows another in rapid succession; hundreds of persons are killed in streetfighting in the capital in March 1980. Libyan tanks and troops invade Chad to support Goukouni Oueddei's bid for control

**1981:** Libya withdraws its troops from Chad. France pledges support for its former colony and urges formation of an African peacekeeping force

**1982:** Habré, with support of Egypt and Sudan, seizes power in N'Djamena after his shock troops rout Goukouni's army. Goukouni goes into exile. Southern tribes threaten to secede

## CHILE

**Area:** 292,256 sq. mi. **Population:** 11,406,000 (1982 est.)

**Official Name:** Republic of Chile **Capital:** Santiago **Nationality:** Chilean **Languages:** The official and virtually universal language is Spanish **Religion:** 90% Roman Catholic **Flag:** A white horizontal stripe over a longer red stripe, with a blue square in the upper left corner containing a 5-pointed white star **Anthem:** National Anthem; refrain "Sweet Country, receive the pledge" **Currency:** Chilean peso (39 per U.S. $1)

**Location:** Southwest coast of South America. Chile is bordered on the north by Peru, on the east by Argentina and Bolivia, on the south by Drake Passage, and on the west by the Pacific Ocean **Features:** The country stretches some 2,650 miles along the Pacific coast and is at no point wider than 250 miles. The north is desert, the central region agricultural, and the south is forest land. The towering Andes dominate most of the eastern frontier **Chief Rivers:** Loa, Maule, Bio-Bio, Valdivia

**Head of State and of Government:** President: Maj. Gen. Augusto Pinochet Ugarte, born 1915, assumed power September 1973 as head of a 4-man military junta, formally assumed title on March 11, 1981 for 8 years **Effective Date of Present Constitution:** March 1981 **Legislative Body:** Congress (dissolved) **Local Government:** 12 regions, subdivided into 40 provinces, and the metropolitan region of Santiago

**Ethnic Composition:** About 68% of the population is of Spanish-Indian descent, 30% of European (mainly Spanish) descent, and less than 1% Indian **Population Distribution:** 80% urban **Density:** 39 inhabitants per sq. mi.

**Largest Cities:** (1978 est.) Santiago 3,691,548, Valparaiso 620,180, Concepción 518,950, Viña del Mar 262,100, Talcahuano 204,100, Antofagasta 157,000, Temuco 156,900

**Per Capita Income:** $1,880 (1980) **Gross National Product (GNP):** $20.7 billion (1980) **Economic Statistics:** In 1979, 50% of GNP was derived from trade and services; 21% from industry (paper and paper products, iron and steel, petrochemicals, chemicals, and metal products); 11% from mining; and 9% from agriculture (wheat, wine grapes, potatoes, sugar beets, tobacco, fruit), forestry and fishing **Minerals and Mining:** Chile is one of the world's leading copper producers; iron ore is second in importance; natural nitrates, iodine, molybdenum and coal are also exploited **Labor Force:** 3,500,000 (1978), with 28% in agriculture **Foreign Trade:** Exports, mainly copper and copper manufactures, iron ore, pulp and paper, fishmeal, wine, seafood, wool, and fruit, totaled $3.8 billion in 1979. Imports, mainly machinery and equipment, agricultural products, and transport equipment, totaled $4.2 billion **Principal Trade Partners:** United States, Latin American Free Trade Association, EC, Japan

**Vital Statistics:** Birthrate, 21.5 per 1,000 of pop. (1979); death rate, 6.8 **Life Expectancy:** 67 years **Health Statistics:** 282 inhabitants per hospital bed; 1,636 per physician (1977) **Infant Mortality:** 39.7 per 1,000 births (1978) **Illiteracy:** 8% **Primary and Secondary School Enrollment:** 2,729,375 (1977) **Enrollment in Higher Education:** 149,647 (1975) **GNP Expended on Education:** 3.7% (1975)

**Transportation:** Paved roads total 5,750 mi. **Motor Vehicles:** 527,000 (1978) **Passenger Cars:** 335,800 **Railway Mileage:** 5,511 **Ports:** Valparaiso, Arica, Antofagasta, Coquimbo, Iquique, Talcahuano **Major Airlines:** LAN-Chile, the government-owned airline, operates domestic and international services **Communications: Radio Transmitters:** 167 **Receivers:** 2,000,000 (1977) **Television Transmitters:** 56 **Receivers:** 1,700,000 **Telephones:** 514,013 (1978) **Newspapers:** 42 dailies (1977); 94 copies per 1,000 inhabitants (1972)

**Weights and Measures:** Metric system **Travel Requirements:** Passport, no visa up to 3 months **International Dialing Code:** 56

Chile has long had an outstanding potential—immense natural resources and a relatively sophisticated population—but efforts to match living standards to promise have fallen short. Inflation, once chronic and at runaway rates—it rose 340 percent in 1975, for instance—has been brought down to a manageable 30-40 percent a year, but at the expense of large-scale unemployment and other social problems.

Nature is largely responsible for the economic and social status of Chile, a land dominated by the geological immaturity of the Andes, a mountain range that runs the entire length of the long and narrow country. Relatively "new" and earthquake-prone, the Andes yield the copper and other metals that account for more than half of Chile's foreign-exchange earnings.

Politically, Chile has also been a victim of abrupt change and contrasts. The pride of South American democracies from 1932 until the 1970s, the country since 1973 has seen its military employ coercion at the expense of human rights to remove all vestiges of the Marxist experiment of Salvador Allende Gossens. Allende in 1970 became the first Marxist to be elected president in South America, but on September 11, 1973, one week after the third anniversary of Allende's election, a military junta staged the first successful coup against a civilian government in Chile since 1927. President Allende was reported to have committed suicide. A year later it was learned that the United States had funneled more than $8 million through the CIA to anti-Allende groups.

The current military regime, headed by Chile's president, Gen. Augusto Pinochet Ugarte, is facing world criticism for political repression, torture and news censorship. The regime continues to hold political prisoners, but, under pressure from the U.S. and other democratic nations, the number has been reduced. The junta's aim has been to entrench political power by dictatorial rule, and Pinochet has succeeded in establishing an "authoritarian democracy."

After the UN General Assembly reported that Chile was violating human rights, President Pinochet ordered a national referendum on Jan. 4, 1978, that upheld his government. Despite this support, the government eased up by restoring some autonomy to civil judges and by limiting the president's punitive powers. Also, an amnesty program was set in motion, leading to pardons or voluntary exile for some prisoners.

In 1980, Chile set out to improve its international image, both within and outside Latin America. Diplomatic relations were restored with Great Britain, and a year later the new Reagan Administration in the United States lifted trade sanctions against Chile.

On Sept. 11, 1980, the seventh anniversary of the military coup that overthrew Allende, a national plebiscite was held on a new constitution which would give Pinochet greater powers and an additional eight-year term in office, with an option to serve another term after that. In spite of strong opposition by former President Frei and followers of Allende, Pinochet received two thirds of the votes cast. (Blank ballots were counted as "yes" votes.)

Despite the rising cost of imported fuel, the loss of foreign investment capital and a large foreign debt, Chile has made considerable economic progress since 1973. Gross national product has been increasing at an annual rate of more than 8 percent compared to a drop of 12 percent in 1974. The balance of payments is on the plus side, and inflation and unemployment have been declining. Foreign investors, including such large U.S. companies as Anaconda, Dow Chemical and Exxon, have been returning to Chile. Development of the wood-products industry is helping to alleviate dependence on a one-product (copper) economy.

**HISTORY:** Prior to the Spanish conquest of Chile in the 16th century, the northern portion of the country was under the rule of the Inca Empire and the south was mainly controlled by the Araucanian Indians, who were to prove fiercely hostile to the Spanish colonists until almost the end of the 19th century. During most of its colonial history, Chile was a captaincy general dependent on the viceroyalty of Peru

**1817-18:** Argentine revolutionist José de San Martín brings an army over the Andes from Argentina to Chile and, in 1818, defeats Spanish army at Battle of Maipú. Bernardo O'Higgins, who had been chosen supreme director, formally proclaims Chile's independence (Feb. 12)

**1879-83:** Chile defeats Peru and Bolivia in the War of the Pacific, acquiring the mineral-bearing northern desert region

**1891-1925:** Internal struggle between executive and legislative branches culminates in overthrow of President José Balmaceda (1891); congressional dictatorship lasts until 1925

**1932-38:** President Arturo Alessandri, elected for second term, institutes a kind of state capitalism in efforts to wipe out aftermath of 1929 depression; however, he turns to repressive measures and alienates working class

**1946-48:** Economic dislocations lead to riots and strikes encouraged by aggressive Communist activity

**1964-68:** Eduardo Frei Montalva is elected president and his Christian Democratic Party wins control of Chamber of Deputies after defeating coalition of Marxist parties. Frei launches reforms

**1969:** National discontent becomes manifest in congressional elections, when Frei's party retains majority in lower house but loses more than a third of its former seats; right-wing National party scores heavy gains

**1970:** Salvador Allende Gossens becomes the first Marxist to be elected president of a Latin American country

**1971:** Government nationalizes all U.S. copper investments

**1973:** On September 11, Allende government is overthrown by a military junta. Allende dies in coup. State of siege declared

**1974:** Military junta returns to private ownership 150 companies nationalized by left-wing Allende government. CIA bankrolling of anti-Allende groups is revealed

**1978:** Referendum shows wide support for Pinochet; opposition charges fraud. Government declares amnesty for political prisoners and exiles and lifts state of siege. Border disputes with neighbors continue; Bolivia breaks diplomatic relations, alleging Chile has hindered negotiations to grant it a corridor to Pacific

**1979:** Chile refuses to extradite three army officers to U.S. to stand trial on charges of complicity in the 1976 murder in Washington, D.C., of Orlando Letelier, prominent exiled leader of opposition to the Pinochet regime

**1980:** Voters approve new constitution

**1981:** Pinochet begins an 8-year term as president on March 11; continues ban on political party activities

**1982:** Despite reports by UN and other human-rights groups that Chile's record has not improved, Reagan Administration moves to resume U.S. military aid to Pinochet regime

## CHINA (PEOPLE'S REPUBLIC)

**Area:** 3,691,000 sq. mi. **Population:** 982,550,000 (1980 est.)

**Official Name:** People's Republic of China **Capital:** Peking (Beijing) **Nationality:** Chinese **Languages:** Chinese, spoken with many regional phonetical differences but written with a uniform script, is the principal language. Mandarin, based on the Peking dialect, forms the basis of the new national language being promoted by the government; Shanghai, Cantonese, Fukienese, and Hakka dialects are spoken in the south. Among the national minorities, the Tibetans have their own highly distinctive language and script, while the Uigurs of Xinjiang (Sinkiang) speak a Turkic language **Religion:** Freedom of religion is guaranteed under the constitution. The 3 long-established religions are Confucianism, Buddhism, and Taoism; the average Chinese has practiced a mixture of all 3 faiths. About 5% of the people are Moslems, and there is a very small minority of Christians **Flag:** A red field with a gold star and an arc of 4 smaller stars to the right in the upper left corner **Anthem:** Anthem beginning, "March on, brave people of our nation," set to the music of The March of the Volunteers **Currency:** Yuan (renminbi) (1.87 per U.S. $1)

**Location:** East Asia. China, the third-largest country in the world after the USSR and Canada, is bounded on the north by Mongolia and the USSR; on the east by the USSR, North Korea, the Yellow Sea, and the East China Sea; on the south by the South China Sea, Vietnam, Laos, Burma, India, Bhutan, and Nepal; and on the west by Afghanistan, Pakistan, and the USSR **Features:** Two-thirds of the country is mountainous or semidesert. The eastern part consists of fertile plains and deltas **Chief Rivers:** Chang Jiang (Yangtze), Huang (Yellow), Amur, Xi (Si)

**Head of State:** Executive responsibility is vested in a State Council, headed by the premier. Control is exercised by the Standing Committee of the Central Committee's Politburo, within the National People's Congress **Head of Government:** Premier Zhao Ziyang, born 1919, elected by the National People's Congress, Sept. 1980 **Head of Party:** Hu Yaobang, born 1915, Chairman of the Politburo of the Communist party **Effective Date of Present State Constitution:** Jan. 1, 1980 **Legislative Body:** National People's Congress (unicameral), consisting of 3,497 members elected for 5-year terms. The provinces elect 1 deputy for every 800,000 inhabitants; municipalities directly under central authority elect 1 deputy for every 100,000 inhabitants. Ethnic minorities are represented by 381 deputies, the armed forces by 505 deputies, and overseas Chinese by 35 deputies **Local Government:** 21 provinces, 5 autonomous regions, and 3 municipalities directly under central authority. Revolutionary committees and people's congresses are the principal local organs of power

**Ethnic Composition:** 94% Han Chinese; 6% Chuang, Uigur, Hui, Yi, Tibetan, Miao, Manchu, Mongol, Korean, and numerous lesser minorities **Population Distribution:** 20% urban **Density:** 266 inhabitants per sq. mi.

**Largest Cities:** (1979 est.) Shanghai 11,320,000, Peking (Beijing) 8,706,000, Tianjin 7,489,000, Canton 5,350,000, Chengdu 3,850,000, Wuhan 3,832,487, Nanjing 3,551,000, Jinan 3,202,000, Xian 2,760,000, Shenyang 2,690,000

**Per Capita Income:** $576 (1980) **Gross National Product (GNP):** $592 billion (1979) **Economic Statistics:** Agriculture is still the foundation of the economy. GNP components are not available but official figures disclosed in 1971 indicate that industrial capacity is still comparatively small. The State Statistical Bureau had estimated $409 billion for the gross value of industrial, transport and agricultural production in 1979. Grain output for 1980 was 318 million

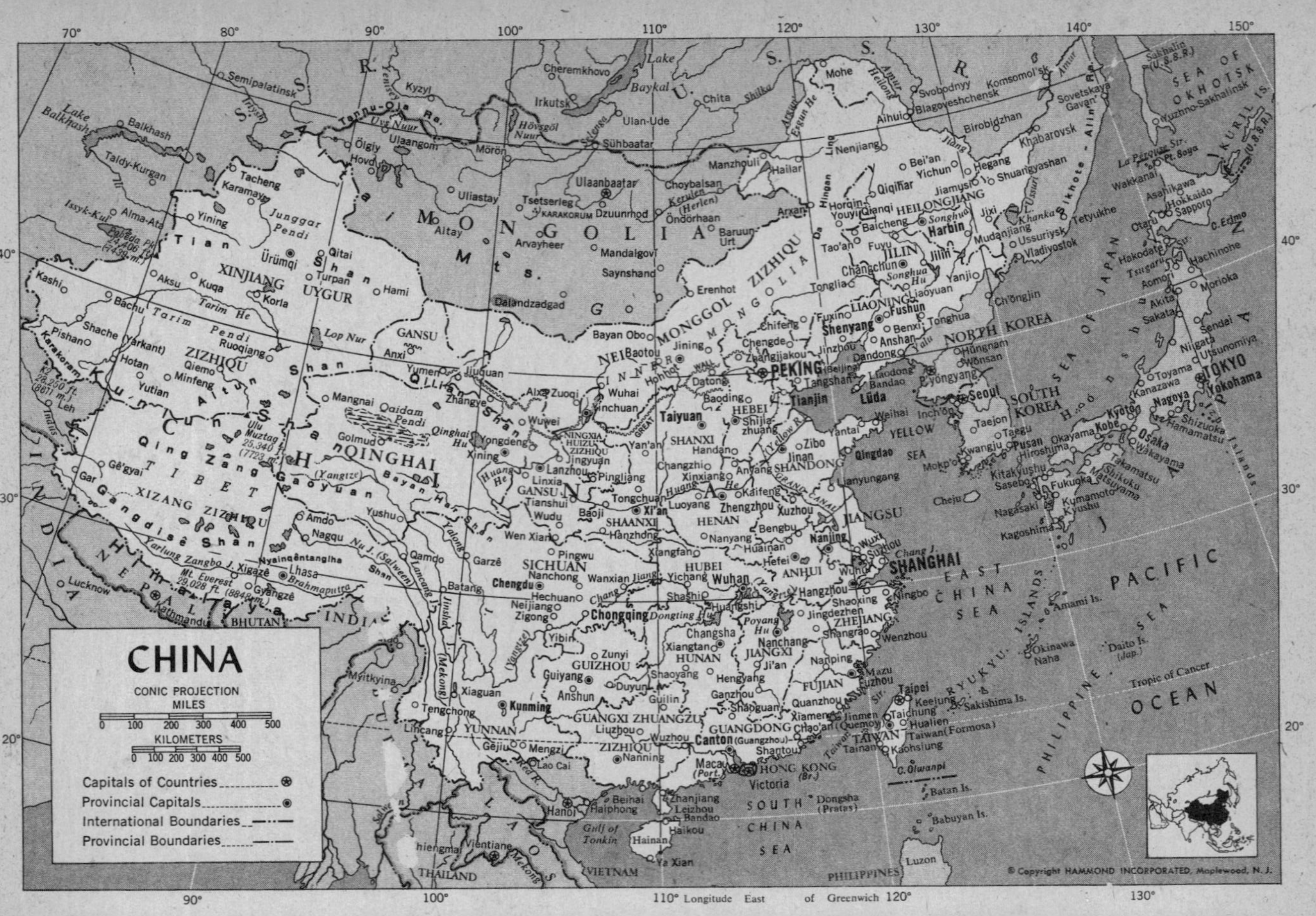
CHINA
CONIC PROJECTION
MILES
0 100 200 300 400 500
KILOMETERS
0 100 200 300 400 500
Capitals of Countries
Provincial Capitals
International Boundaries
Provincial Boundaries
© Copyright HAMMOND INCORPORATED, Maplewood, N.J.
110° Longitude East of Greenwich 120°

metric tons; chemical fertilizer, 12 million metric tons; cotton cloth, 13.5 billion meters; petroleum output, more than 106 million metric tons **Minerals and Mining:** Coal, petroleum, iron ore, tin, molybdenum, tungsten, mercury, manganese, antimony **Labor Force:** The working age population is about 476 million, with 75% in agriculture **Foreign Trade:** Exports are estimated at about $15.5 billion for 1980, with imports of about $16.6 billion. Exports are chiefly agricultural and food products, coal, oil products, minerals, and textiles. Imports are mainly wheat, chemical fertilizers, iron and steel, transport equipment, machinery, advanced technology equipment, insecticides, cotton, pulp, consumer goods and rubber **Principal Trade Partners:** Japan, Hong Kong, West Germany, Romania, Singapore, Britain, United States, Malaysia, Canada, France, Australia

**Vital Statistics:** Birthrate, 17.9 per 1,000 pop. (1979); death rate, 6.2 **Life Expectancy:** 68 years **Illiteracy:** 45%. **Health Statistics:** 503 inhabitants per hospital bed; 2,602 per physician (1978) **Infant Mortality:** N.A. **Primary and Secondary School Enrollment:** 203,274,000 (1980) **Enrollment in Higher Education:** 1,144,000 **GNP Expended on Education:** N.A.

**Transportation:** Surfaced roads total 551,800 mi. **Motor Vehicles:** N.A. **Passenger Cars:** N.A. **Railway Mileage:** 32,000 **Ports:** Shanghai, Tianjin, Lüda, Canton **Major Airlines:** The Civil Aviation Administration of China operates domestic flights and international flights abroad **Communications: Radio Transmitters:** 250 **Receivers:** 45,000,000 (1978) **Television Transmitters:** 120 **Receivers:** 1,250,000 (1978) **Telephones:** 5,000,000 (1978) **Newspapers:** 278 (1979)

**Weights and Measures:** Metric System and local standards **Travel Requirements:** Passport, visa; contact Chinese Embassy, Washington, D.C.

---

Developments of the early 1970s made the world aware that domestic conditions in the world's most populous country had stabilized and that its Communist leaders were trying to bring China out of the isolation that they had imposed on it after 1949, when they won the long Civil War and drove the Nationalists from the mainland to Taiwan.

The 1960s had seen China become a nuclear power, but it had also witnessed the ideological turmoil and economic disasters of the Cultural Revolution— the attempt by party Chairman Mao Zedong, begun in 1966, to impose a purer form of communism at all levels of Chinese society. After 1969, with Mao's consent, a reshuffled, more pragmatic leadership had been established, with the widely respected Zhou Enlai as premier, and the momentum of the Cultural Revolution slowed down.

The Peking regime initiated a fresh approach in foreign affairs in April 1971 by inviting an American table-tennis team, with accompanying journalists, to tour China. After April 1972 there came a small but steady flow of Americans and other Western nationals, and Peking climaxed their visits in July by arranging to receive President Nixon. The new Peking policy also led to formal diplomatic relations with Japan in 1972, culminating six years later in a 10-year treaty of peace and friendship.

Relations had been established with Canada, Italy, and a number of smaller countries; more Chinese delegations had been sent abroad; more foreign trade agreements had been signed; and Chinese diplomatic missions in foreign countries, which operated without ambassadors during the Cultural Revolution, had been restaffed.

Trade with the United States began in 1972 following the lifting of the American trade embargo, and by 1981 had reached about $5.5 billion. In May 1979, China concluded an agreement on establishing formal commercial relations with the United States, which provided for the lowering of United States tariff restrictions on Chinese imports and the granting of a most-favored nation trade status (approved February 1, 1980).

The death of Premier Zhou Enlai in January 1976, came at a time of domestic crisis and of mounting debate between moderates and radicals. After major rioting occurred in April, the Politburo gave the radicals a brief victory, dismissing the most influential moderate, Deng Xiaoping, a protégé of Zhou, from all of his posts. Hua Guofeng was elevated to the premiership, and became Mao Zedong's political heir when Mao died in September 1976.

Hua's first task, after Mao's death, was to resolve the conflict between radical and moderate factions in the party. Late in 1976, he moved decisively against the radicals, known as the "Gang of Four," led by Mao's widow, Jiang Jing, who along with her supporters plus the cohorts of the late Lin Biao were tried in 1980-81 and given sentences ranging from 16 years to suspended death sentences. From late 1976 to mid 1977, in an apparent effort to liberalize Maoist doctrine along pragmatic lines, Deng Xiaoping was brought back into the government as first deputy premier. Together with Chairman Hua and the honorary head of state, Ye Jianying, he became part of China's ruling triumvirate.

Deng's power grew not only with the elevation of his protégés to key party and government positions but also with his plan for the implementation of the "four modernizations"—rapid development of agriculture, industry, defense, and technology. The plan included granting more state aid to poorer areas, the centralization of state planning, the return of private plots to the farmers, a wage increase of 60 percent in the industrial sphere, the upgrading of military hardware and effectiveness, and the advancement of lagging science, technology and education. By 1980, the program was modified to make it more economically viable. Experiments in industrial profit incentives and local accountability proved successful enough for nationwide application. In place of fulfilling arbitrary state quotas, industries were rewarded for quantity, quality and talent, with excess profits after taxes (an innovation) to remain with the industry. Also, workers were given the right to elect and dismiss plant managers. Similar incentives were introduced in agriculture, by far the largest economic sector, with farmers allowed to sell to the state or trade on the free markets any produce beyond what they were contracted to grow.

On February 17, 1979, China invaded Vietnam, an ancient enemy which had become a satellite of the USSR. Four weeks of fighting resulted in no territorial gains, heavy casualties on both sides, and a drain on both economies.

China's chief defense goal, openly professed, has been to achieve parity with the Soviet Union and the United States. The Peking regime has called for the introduction of foreign technology and the purchase of foreign weapons as part of a modernization effort for its military.

Relations with the United States improved in 1978 with the announcement of the formal establishment of official diplomatic relations between the two countries, effective on March 1, 1979. At the same time, the announcement included the abrogation of the mutual defense treaty between the United States and the offshore Republic of China and the termination of formal diplomatic relations with Taiwan. By 1981, mutual airline and shipping agreements between the People's Republic and the United States were implemented, further bolstering China's growing trade and its developing tourist industry. An estimated 80,000 U.S. visitors arrived during 1981.

But the years 1980-82 proved also that innovations on the domestic front were to provide no instant panacea. Both inflation and unemployment were growing and there were serious failures on the heavy industry front, due in part to bottlenecks in transportation and raw materials production.

An austerity plan, announced in February 1981, included reductions in capital construction, in the budget for oil and coal production, and in the importation of foreign equipment. Expensive foreign contracts for large industrial facilities were either cancelled or modified, but many of these were reactivated in 1982, as China's planners appeared to be having second thoughts about the new policy. Early in 1982, several contracts were signed with Western oil concerns, which agreed to drill for oil in offshore Chinese waters under terms very beneficial to China.

In 1980, four members of the party's Politburo, elevated by Mao, were ousted and Zhao Ziyang replaced Hua Guofeng as premier. Early in 1981, Hua surrendered to Deng Xiaoping his position as head of the party's powerful Military Commission and, in June, was demoted from the chairmanship of the Politburo to a junior vice chairman's post, then ousted in September 1982. Deng's protégé, Hu Yaobang, became the new chairman. In September 1982, the title of chairman was abolished, and Hu became General Secretary. In 1982 a new constitution was promulgated (the fourth since 1949), in which many of the innovations of 1966-69 were abandoned.

These developments, together with the posthumous rehabilitation of the reputation of Liu Shaoqi, who was chief of state before Mao dismissed him in 1969, seemed to mark progressive stages in the "de-Mao-ification" of China. In 1981 and 1982, attacks on Mao himself were finally heard, although the criticism centered on "mistakes" in his concept of party and government administration after 1966 and did not yet demean him in his role as the "father" of China's revolution.

In China's relations with the superpowers, the stance of bitter hostility toward the USSR and of growing political accommodation with the United States that had marked the decade of the 1970s began to shift in the early 1980s. Friendly discussions were held with the Soviets and their satellite, Mongolia, following an overture from Soviet Premier Brezhnev early in 1982. Meanwhile, relations with the United States soured as President Reagan, fulfilling a campaign promise, initiated a new program of military aid to Nationalist China (Taiwan). Though the plan was scaled down in 1982 in answer to strong objections from Peking, signs of strain persisted. In mid-1982, China renewed its demand that U.S. troops withdraw from South Korea.

In pursuit of its long-term goal of reabsorbing Taiwan, Peking abandoned the stick in favor of the carrot, offering in late 1981 a nine-point reunification plan that promised Taiwan a considerable measure of autonomy. Though the proposal was quickly rejected, the People's Republic declared a broad amnesty for Nationalists imprisoned on the mainland and, in June 1982, announced that it had released more than 4,000 prisoners, some of whom had been held as "spies and traitors" for over 30 years.

**HISTORY:** The home of the oldest continuing civilization on earth, China has a recorded history dating back more than 2,000 years before the birth of Christ. By the advent of the Christian era, the Chinese had lived under a succession of dynasties that succeeded in unifying the country and protecting it from the outside world by building the Great Wall. In the end, however, the wall was to prove useless against invaders

**1644:** Manchu (Ching) dynasty is established, completing the gradual conquest of China by the Manchu peoples of the north

**1839-42:** Britain provokes Opium War and defeats Chinese; China opens ports and grants extraterritorial rights to British traders, cedes Hong Kong to Britain

**1894-95:** China and Japan war for control over their co-protectorate of Korea; a defeated China is forced to cede Formosa (Taiwan), Liaotung peninsula, and Pescadores to Japan

**1898-1900:** Resentment against foreign influence erupts in Boxer Rebellion; revolt is quelled after intervention by European, U.S., and Japanese forces. U.S. Open Door policy, calling for equal treatment for all nations in Chinese ports and respect for China's territorial integrity, wins lip service from European powers

**1911-12:** Manchu dynasty is overthrown in revolution led by Sun Yatsen; a republic is established with Sun as president

**1917-30:** Civil war breaks out between supporters of Sun's Kuomintang Party in the south and the national government and its warlords in the north; Kuomintang army, led by Chiang Kai-shek, sweeps north and defeats warlords. A new civil war breaks out, however, after Chiang breaks alliance formed by Sun with Chinese Communists

**1931-39:** Japan, taking advantage of turmoil in China, invades Manchuria and sets up puppet government. In 1934, some 100,000 Communist troops led by Mao Zedong, Lin Biao, and Zhou Enlai, begin 6,000-mile "long march" to the north to avoid encirclement by Kuomintang army. Kuomintang and Communists later agree to truce to repel Japanese, but agreement collapses and sporadic fighting resumes

**1945-49:** U.S. attempts to mediate civil war fail; Communists launch offensive and drive Chiang's forces from mainland to Taiwan; People's Republic of China is proclaimed Oct. 1, 1949

**1950:** China overruns Tibet; Chinese forces intervene on side of North Korea in Korean War

**1960-64:** Growing rift between USSR and "hard-line" Chinese leaders unfolds. China explodes its first nuclear bomb

**1966-67:** Mao Zedong launches "Cultural Revolution" in attempt to reverse trend toward "revisionist" Communism. New policy is marked by widespread purge of leading officials and wave of terrorism by Mao's youthful followers, known as Red Guards. China explodes its first hydrogen bomb

**1969:** Chinese and Soviet troops exchange fire along borders

**1971:** People's Republic of China replaces Nationalist China (Taiwan) in the UN. Lin Biao, Mao's designated successor, dies following an abortive coup

**1972:** Nixon visits China, meets Zhou Enlai and Mao Zedong

**1975:** China adopts a revised constitution. U.S. President Ford and Secretary of State Kissinger visit China

**1976:** Mao Zedong, Zhou Enlai and Zhu De die. Hua Guofeng confirmed premier and chairman of Communist party. Tangshan earthquake kills an estimated 700,000

**1977:** Deng Xiaoping returns to Politburo

**1979:** Deng Xiaoping visits the United States and signs scientific and cultural exchange agreement. China invades Vietnam in February. China and the U.S. establish formal diplomatic relations on March 1. Hua Guofeng visits Western Europe

**1980:** China admitted to International Monetary Fund and World Bank. Hua Guofeng meets President Carter in Tokyo. U.S. reopens consulates in Shanghai and Canton. National People's Congress convenes and elects Zhao Ziyang as premier to replace Hua Guofeng. Deng Xiaoping and several vice premiers resign from State Council, though Deng's protégés win new posts

**1981:** Sixteen members of the "Gang of Four" and cohorts of Lin Biao tried and sentenced. Central Committee of the party elects Hu Yaobang, a Deng colleague, as chairman of the seven-member Politburo; Hua Guofeng is demoted. Vice Premier Soong Ching-ling (Sun Yat Sen's widow) dies. Peking's nine-point reunification plan rejected by Taiwan

**1982:** New draft constitution abandons principles of Cultural Revolution. U.S. military aid to Taiwan strains relations with Washington. U.S. Vice President Bush visits Peking (May). Over a million homeless in second year of heavy floods in South China. Associates of Deng and Hu get more top posts as streamlining of government is announced. The 12th Congress of the Communist Party meets in early Sept. and adopts new party constitution. Politburo membership is increased and chairmanship titles are abolished. 157-member Central Advisory Commission is established, with Deng as chairman. Hua Guofeng is ousted from Politburo

## NATIONALIST CHINA (TAIWAN)

**Area:** 13,971 sq. mi. **Population:** 18,031,825 (1980 census)

**Official Name:** Republic of China **Capital:** Taipei **Nationality:** Chinese **Languages:** Mandarin Chinese is the official language; native Taiwanese speak a variant of the Amoy dialect, although the Hakka dialect is used in northwestern Taiwan; Japanese and English are also widely used by the inhabitants **Religion:** The predominant religion (93%) is a blend of Buddhism, Confucianism and Taoism. 4.5% are Christians **Flag:** A red field with a blue rectangle in the upper left corner containing a 12-pointed white sun **Anthem:** National Anthem of the Republic of China, beginning "Our aim shall be to found a free land" **Currency:** New Taiwan yuan (dollar) (38.5 per U.S. $1)

**Location:** The seat of the Republic of China is the island of Taiwan, 90 miles off the southeast coast of the Chinese mainland. In addition to the island proper, Taiwan comprises 14 islands in the Taiwan group and 63 in the Penghu group, known as the Pescadores. The islands of Quemoy and Matsu, just off Fukien province on the China mainland, are also under the control of the Republic of China. Taiwan, also known as Formosa, is bordered on the north by the East China Sea, on the east by the Pacific Ocean, on the south and southwest by the South China Sea, and on the west by the Taiwan (Formosa) Strait **Features:** About two-thirds of the island of Taiwan is composed of rugged foothills and mountain chains. The mountains, towering along the eastern coast, run from northeast to southwest. A flat coastal plain, running from north to south, occupies the western third and supports most of the population **Chief Rivers:** Cho-shui, Tan-shui, Hsia-tan-shui

**Head of State:** President Chiang Ching-kuo, born 1910, elected 1978 **Head of Government:** Premier Sun Yün-hsüan, born 1913, appointed 1978 **Effective Date of Present Constitution:** 1947 **Legislative Body:** The National Assembly (unicameral); its members (elected 1947) are serving indefinitely. Of the original 3,045 there are now 1,185. The 5 branches of government are the Legislative, Executive, Control, Examination, and Judicial yuans. The Legislative Yuan is the highest body and now has 410 members; both it and the National Assembly have some parliamentary function, and are dominated by the Nationalist party (the Kuomintang) under its chairman, the premier **Local Government:** The Provincial Government is under a governor appointed by the national government. There is an elective Provincial Assembly with limited powers

**Ethnic Composition:** With the exception of about 250,000 aborigines of Indonesian origin, the Taiwanese are descendants of Chinese who migrated from the provinces of Fukien and Kwangtung of mainland China during the past 3 centuries; post-World War II refugees from the mainland constitute about 14% of the population **Population Distribution:** 77% urban (1975) **Density:** 1,291 inhabitants per sq. mi.

**Largest Cities:** (1981 est.) Taipei 2,238,841; (1979 est.) Kaohsiung 1,002,000, Taichung 549,000, Tainan 525,000, Keelung 343,000

**Per Capita Income:** $1,826 (1980) **Gross National Product (GNP):** $32.5 billion (1980 est.) **Economic Statistics:** 30% of GNP comes from industry (textiles, electronics, plastics, furniture, other goods), and 12% from agriculture (rice, sweet potatoes, bananas, sugarcane, pineapple, peanuts, and soybeans are the major crops) **Minerals and Mining:** Taiwan is deficient in minerals with the exception of coal. There are reserves of volcanic sulphur and deposits of natural gas and petroleum **Labor Force:** 6.5 million (1980), 39% employed in manufacturing, mining and construction, 35% in commerce and services, 26% in agriculture **Foreign Trade:** Exports, chiefly textiles, chemicals, metals and machinery, plywood, sugar, bananas, and canned mushrooms, totaled $19.8 billion in 1980. Imports, chiefly machinery, chemicals, transportation equipment, soybeans, raw cotton, timber, crude oil, and wheat, totaled $19.7 billion **Principal Trade Partners:** United States, Japan, Hong Kong, West Germany, Australia, Britain, Singapore, Canada, Thailand, Saudi Arabia, South Korea, Kuwait

**Vital Statistics:** Birthrate, 23 per 1,000 of pop (1980); death rate, 5 **Life Expectancy:** 72 years **Health Statistics:** 580 inhabitants per hospital bed; 1,377 per physician **Infant Mortality:** 14 per 1,000 births **Illiteracy:** 10% **Education Statistics:** 3,269 primary and secondary schools, with combined enrollment of 3,932,000 (1975) **Enrollment in Higher Education:** 282,300 **GNP Expended on Education:** 4.8%

**Transportation:** Surfaced roads total 5,496 mi. (1974) **Motor Vehicles:** 2,600,000 (1976) **Passenger Cars:** 122,517 (1974) **Railway Mileage:** 2,795 (1978) **Ports:** Kaohsiung, Keelung, Hualien, Taichung, Suao **Major Airlines:** China Airlines operates domestic and international services **Communications: Radio Stations:** 111 **Receivers:** 3,000,000 **Television Stations:** 3 **Receivers:** 747,444 **Telephones:** 1,689,000 (1979) **Newspapers:** 31 dailies, 80 copies per 1,000 inhabitants

**Weights and Measures:** Metric system and local units are used **Travel Requirements:** Passport, visa **International Dialing Code:** 886

---

The government of the Republic of China, defeated on mainland China by the Communists in 1949, established itself on Taiwan, with the goal of regaining power over all of China. That goal, with time, has become more and more remote. In the meantime, with the help of massive American aid, the government has built Taiwan into a prosperous, industrialized island state.

In 1971 a steady stream of countries switched diplomatic recognition from Taiwan to Communist China. With the shift in U.S. policy on China and American support for the seating of Peking in the United Nations, the Nationalist diplomatic position underwent further erosion. Nationalist China was eventually expelled from the UN and replaced by the Communist-led People's Republic of China.

Because of its insistence that it was not only the government of Taiwan, 90 miles off the China mainland, but also the only legal government of all China, the Nationalist regime would not sanction elections that would change the central leadership. But it has held local elections.

The government has been dominated by the Kuomintang, or Nationalist party, and the party in turn was dominated by President Chiang Kai-shek until his death in April 1975. Criticism of government policies and officials is permitted in moderation under what has become a permanent, if limited, state of martial law.

Taiwan, which was devastated when China regained control from Japan after World War II, is flourishing, if overpopulated, with a rapidly growing industrial sector. Its people, the vast majority of whom are native-born Taiwanese, enjoy one of the higher standards of living in Asia. Economic development is due in no small measure to the fact that the island has enjoyed U.S. military protection and received U.S. military aid.

In a November 1977 election for local offices, independent candidates scored their largest, if still limited, victory since 1949. Moreover, the unusual fairness of the election was seen as reflecting a decision by the government to allow native Taiwanese a greater share in the political process than did Chiang Kai-shek.

When President Yen Chia-kan (C.K. Yen) retired in March 1978 the National Assembly named Premier Chiang Ching-kuo to succeed him. Sun Yün-hsüan was named premier in May.

Formal diplomatic relations between Taiwan and the United States were terminated on March 1, 1979, while cultural, commercial and quasi-official relations continued. Meanwhile, Taiwan's trade with the United States was increasing rapidly, totaling $11.8 billion in 1980, 45 percent above the 1978 level. Its worldwide trade was growing even faster, approaching $40 billion in 1980.

Though the U.S.-Taiwan mutual defense treaty was abrogated in 1979, President Reagan in 1981 fulfilled a campaign promise by offering increased arms aid, including modern military equipment. In January 1982, the package was somewhat scaled down in the wake of vigorous Peking objections.

In late 1981, Peking put forward a reunification plan which offered Taiwan an extraordinary degree of autonomy as a province of the People's Republic. Taiwan's prompt rejection was followed by a Peking proposal to establish air, sea, and mail links.

**HISTORY:** Chinese emigration to Taiwan began in the 7th century. In the 16th century the Portuguese arrived, naming the island Formosa, meaning "beautiful." The Dutch assumed control in 1641 but were driven out in 1662 by Ming dynasty forces fleeing the Manchu takeover in mainland China. In 1683 Taiwan, too, fell to the Manchus. At the end of the Sino-Japanese War of 1894-95 it was ceded to Japan, which held it until the conclusion of World War II, when it was restored to China

**1949:** The Nationalist government of Chiang Kai-shek and remnants of his army flee to Taiwan, as the Communist forces of Mao Zedong gain control of the Chinese mainland

**1950:** President Truman orders U.S. Seventh Fleet to patrol the Taiwan Strait, thwarting a planned invasion of Taiwan by Communist China

**1955:** Following shelling of Nationalist-held offshore islands, the United States pledges to defend Taiwan and the Pescadores

**1965:** Because of Taiwan's impressive economic growth, U.S. aid is terminated except for surplus-food shipments

**1966:** Chiang Kai-shek is reelected president for fourth term

**1969:** Chiang Ching-kuo, elder son of Chiang Kai-shek, is named deputy premier

**1971:** Nationalist China replaced in UN by Mainland China

**1972:** Chiang Kai-shek is reelected president for fifth term; Chiang Ching-kuo is named premier

**1973:** U.S. announces gradual withdrawal of its forces on Taiwan as relations with Communist China improve

**1974:** U.S. pledges to "safeguard the security of Taiwan"

**1975:** Generalissimo Chiang Kai-shek, 87, dies of a heart attack in Taipei, April 5, and Yen Chia-kan (C.K. Yen) succeeds him

**1978:** Yen Chia-kan retires; Chiang Ching-kuo succeeds him in presidency

**1979:** American and Taiwan embassies are closed on March 1, quasi-official offices are established in each country
**1980:** Taiwan loses membership in both the International Monetary Fund and the World Bank. Premier Sun Yün-hsüan visits Costa Rica, Panama and the Dominican Republic
**1981:** Peking offers considerable autonomy to Taiwan as part of reunification plan; Taiwan rejects proposal
**1982:** Protests by Peking result in modification of major new U.S. military aid package for Taiwan

## COLOMBIA

**Area:** 439,735 sq. mi. **Population:** 28,776,000 (1980 est.)

**Official Name:** Republic of Colombia **Capital:** Bogotá **Nationality:** Colombian **Languages:** Spanish is the official language and is spoken by all but a few Indian tribes **Religion:** Roman Catholicism is the state religion and that of 95% of the population **Flag:** The top half of the flag is yellow; the bottom half consists of a blue stripe and red stripe of equal widths **Anthem:** National Anthem, beginning "O unwithering glory, immortal joy" **Currency:** Colombian peso (62 per U.S. $1)

**Location:** Northwest South America. Colombia is bordered on the north by the Caribbean Sea, on the east by Venezuela and Brazil, on the south by Peru and Ecuador, and on the west by the Pacific Ocean and Panama **Features:** Colombia is divided by the Andes Mountains into flat coastal areas, a highland or plateau area, and an eastern plains area **Chief Rivers:** Magdalena, Cauca, Amazon

**Head of State and of Government:** President Belisario Betancur Cuartas, took office Aug. 7, 1982 **Effective Date of Present Constitution:** August 1886 **Legislative Body:** Congress (bicameral), consisting of a Senate and a Chamber of Representatives. The Senate has 112 members; the Chamber has 199 members **Local Government:** 22 departments, the Special District of Bogotá, 3 intendencies, and 5 commissaries, under appointed governors and administrators

**Ethnic Composition:** 58% mixed European and Indian descent, 20% European stock, 14% European and African descent, 4% African stock, and 1% Indian **Population Distribution:** 60% urban **Density:** 65 inhabitants per sq. mi.

**Largest Cities:** (1973 census) Bogotá 2,855,065, Medellín 1,070,924, Cali 898,253, Barranquilla 661,009, Cartagena 292,512, Bucaramanga 291,661, Manizales 199,904

**Per Capita Income:** $983 (1980) **Gross National Product (GNP):** $26.3 billion (1980) **Economic Statistics:** 26% of GNP comes from agriculture (coffee, rice, cotton, potatoes, bananas, sugar); and 19% from industry (food, beverages, tobacco, textiles, chemicals, metal products and machinery) **Minerals and Mining:** Petroleum, gold, coal, salt, limestone, sand and gravel, platinum and emeralds are exploited **Labor Force:** Wage earners totaled 9,000,000 (1981), with 27% in agriculture and 21% in industry **Foreign Trade:** Exports, chiefly coffee, crude petroleum, agricultural products, textiles, cattle, and emeralds, totaled $3.8 billion in 1980. Imports, chiefly machinery and electronic equipment, chemicals, transport vehicles, metals and metal products, totaled $5.4 billion **Principal Trade Partners:** United States, West Germany, Japan, Netherlands, Italy, Britain, Sweden, the Andean Group

**Vital Statistics:** Birthrate, 33.8 per 1,000 of pop. (1980); death rate, 7.9 **Life Expectancy:** 63 years **Health Statistics:** 620 inhabitants per hospital bed; 1,969 per physician (1977) **Infant Mortality:** 39.5 per 1,000 births **Illiteracy:** 19% **Primary and Secondary School Enrollment:** 5,776,638 (1977) **Enrollment in Higher Education:** 186,635 (1975) **GNP Expended on Education:** 1.9% (1976)

**Transportation:** Paved roads total 5,092 mi. **Motor Vehicles:** 558,100 (1977) **Passenger Cars:** 453,600 **Railway Mileage:** 2,134 **Ports:** Buenaventura, Sta. Marta, Barranquilla, Cartagena, Tumaco **Major Airlines:** Avianca operates domestic and international services **Communications: Radio Transmitters:** 340 **Receivers:** 2,930,000 (1977) **Television Transmitters:** 3 **Receivers:** 1,700,000 (1976) **Telephones:** 1,410,000 (1978) **Newspapers:** 42 dailies (1976), 69 copies per 1,000 inhabitants (1974)

**Weights and Measures:** Metric system **Travel Requirements:** Passport, tourist card valid for visits up to 90 days, 2 photos **International Dialing Code:** 57

Colombia, in effect, is a federation of city-states that are reflections of the isolation imposed by the Andes. Traditionally, the economy has been based on coffee on the rocks: Small farmers strive to raise quality coffee beans on the steep and rocky slopes of the Andes. Their crop accounts for the largest part of the nation's legal exports. In recent years, however, the illicit growing and exporting of marijuana and cocaine has risen fast as a major economic activity, estimated at from $1 billion to $2 billion a year even in the face of a government crackdown.

Colombia's social problems are staggering; its population is growing by 2.1 percent a year, despite efforts to expand family-planning programs, and its cities are swelling because of migration from rural areas. (Bogotá's population has doubled in the past 10 years.)

With illiteracy widespread, Colombia has a high unemployment rate and the income distribution of her population is highly skewed in favor of the upper fifth of the population. Access to health services and the quality of health care are even more unequally distributed.

Colombia's people are as varied as its geography. The top hundred or so families are basically European, and American-educated. The bulk of the people are of part-Indian stock, and some are descendants of African slaves. About 18 percent of the population is black or mulatto. There are small groups of nomads who wander the deserts of the northern fringe of the land as well as primitive Amazon Indians in the forests of the south. Indians make up 1 percent of the population.

Politically, Colombia is the largest working democracy in Latin America. Its 28 million people are still awed by *La Violencia*, the bloody period of anarchy from 1948 to 1958, which cost about 200,000 lives. Its cause is still debated. *La Violencia* gave the Spanish language a new word, *bogotazo*, referring to the sudden eruption of violence in the capital on April 9, 1948, an uprising not clearly linked to a specific cause.

In any event, the civil war led first to the military dictatorship (1953-57) of General Gustavo Rojas Pinilla, then to a return to democracy on the basis of cooperation between the two traditional parties, the Liberals and the Conservatives, who began to rotate the presidency. Colombia permits its notably ineffectual Communist party to operate openly and legally.

With the advent to power of President Misael Pastrana Borrero in August 1970, following an election bitterly contested by General Rojas, Colombia began to achieve substantial progress for the people as a whole. In 1973, however, there were renewed indications that the violence that had marked so much of her history was not yet dead. After a number of bloody guerrilla actions, the government adopted several emergency security measures, including the establishment of special groups within the armed forces to pursue guerrilla bands operating in rural areas.

The 1974 elections offered the first open polls after 16 years of alternate rule by Liberals and Conservatives. Alfonso López Michelsen, the Liberal party candidate, won a constitutional mandate for a four-year term in coalition with the Conservatives. His term was marred somewhat by strikes of workers and students and by attacks and kidnappings by left-wing guerrillas.

The Liberals were again big winners in the 1978 congressional elections, and their candidate, Julio César Turbay Ayala, won the presidency in a close race. He became involved very soon in the twin problems of increased terrorism and rising drug traffic. On January 1, 1979, guerrillas of the M-19 group seized 5,300 weapons from the main Bogotá military arsenal. M-19, the Movement of April 19, got its name from the date in 1970 on which General Rojas was defeated for the presidency. Its original members were radical followers of Rojas. M-19 advocates establishing a socialist state through force of arms. In the wake of the arsenal raid, soldiers arrested several hundred left-wing guerrillas and imprisoned them.

M-19 struck again on February 27, 1980, as a group of masked young men and women shot their way into the Dominican Republic's embassy in Bogotá where a diplomatic reception was being held. They demanded $50 million ransom and release of 311 political prisoners as part of the price for freeing more than 50 hostages, among whom were the Spanish-born U.S. ambassador, Diego C. Asencio, and top-level diplomats of 15 other countries. During two months of negotiations, many of the hostages, including all of the women, were released gradually. The Uruguayan ambassador escaped on March 17, breaking a leg in jumping from a second-story window. For its part, the Colombian government speeded up the trials of political prisoners and acquitted many. On April 27 the siege ended peacefully when the 16 guerrillas settled for an alleged ransom of $2.5 million from unknown sources and safe escort to Cuba.

M-19 claimed success in bringing the world's attention to their allegations of torture and infringement of human rights by the Colombian military. The government won accolades for its painstaking negotiations and for avoiding the use of force to free the hostages.

In March 1981 the government reported that its armed forces had killed 19 guerrillas and captured 74 near the Ecuadorean border, virtually wiping out the M-19 command. However, eight months later a major guerrilla offensive against government forces in the southwestern jungle region caused serious concern among officials in Bogotá.

A three-year development plan, made public ir May 1980, calls for investment of $22 billion in transportation, communication, hydroelectric and water-supply facilities. The annnual rate of inflation increased to about 30 percent, but gross national product climbed some 5 percent at constant prices. Coffee exports resulted in record earnings.

The government, meanwhile, was trying to stop another kind of export—illicit drugs. Soldiers swarmed over the Guajira Peninsula, a major point for shipping marijuana to the United States, in late 1978 and in 1979, and the government reported the seizure and burning of more than 100,000 tons of marijuana.

**HISTORY:** Colombia was inhabited perhaps as early as 5000 B.C. by Indian tribes of whom little is known. Prominent among pre-Colombian cultures was that of the highland Chibchas, a sedentary agricultural people located in the eastern chain of the Andes, in the center of the country. European colonization began about five years after Spanish explorers came to Colombia in 1499. With the founding of Bogotá in 1538, Colombia became the nucleus of New Granada, a vast territory that included parts of Panama, Venezuela, and Ecuador. The struggle for Colombian independence was, as elsewhere in Latin America, precipitated by Napoleon's invasion of Spain in the early 19th century

**1810:** Revolutionary leaders stage uprising in Bogotá

**1819:** By defeating Spanish royalist forces, Simón Bolívar secures independence of the new republic of Greater Colombia, which includes the former territory of New Granada

**1830:** Greater Colombia breaks up and New Granada (now Colombia and Panama) becomes a separate state

**1863:** New Granada becomes a federal republic, the United States of Colombia

**1899:** Civil war breaks out between liberal and conservative elements and results in more than 100,000 deaths and virtual economic ruin for the country

**1903:** Panama proclaims its independence from Colombia

**1948-53:** Assassination of left-wing liberal leader Jorge Gaitán in 1948 sets off a major revolt, ultimately costing 200,000 lives and leeading to the declaration of a state of siege. President Laureano Gómez, an archconservative, takes power in 1950 but is ousted in a coup d'état led by the chief of the armed forces, General Gustavo Rojas Pinilla

**1957:** Rojas, in turn, is ousted by a military junta

**1970:** Departmental and municipal elections result in overwhelming defeat for Rojas and victory for Conservative party

**1973:** Agrarian reform bill is passed to reduce amount of land held by any person and to expropriate poorly farmed estates

**1974:** Alfonso López Michelsen elected in landslide Liberal victory

**1977:** Protests against high prices and continued martial law rule erupt in violence; 13 die, 4,000 arrested

**1978:** Julio César Turbay Ayala wins presidency

**1980:** Diplomats of 16 countries are held hostage for two months by M-19 guerrillas who seize Dominican Republic embassy Feb. 27

**1981:** Leftists kidnap and kill Chester Bitterman, American linguist and lay missionary, claiming he served the U.S. Central Intelligence Agency

**1982:** Seven M-19 terrorists hijack domestic jetliner; govern- ment rejects their political demands, but allows them to fly to an unknown destination upon release of 128 hostages. Liberal party is victorious in congressional and local elections, but a Conservative, Belisario Betancur Cuartas, becomes president

## COMOROS

**Area:** 719 sq. mi. **Population:** 356,000 (1980 census—excl. Mayotte)

**Official Name:** Federal and Islamic Republic of the Comoros **Capital:** Moroni **Nationality:** Comoran **Languages:** Arabic, French, Comoran, a Swahili dialect **Religion:** Moslem, some Christians **Flag:** A green field with a white crescent in the center, set at an angle and encompassing four five-pointed stars in a line **Anthem:** N.A. **Currency:** CFA Franc (305 per U.S. $1)

**Location:** The Comoros (12°S., 44°E.) lie in the Mozambique Channel of the Indian Ocean 300 miles northwest of Madagascar. There are three main islands: Njazidja (Grand Comoro), Nzwani (Anjouan), and Mwali (Mohéli), and a number of minor ones. The Republic claims nearby Mayotte as part of its territory **Features:** The islands are of volcanic origin and Karthala (elevation 8,399 ft.) on Njazidja is still active. The climate is tropical with a hot rainy season from November to April, becoming more temperate the rest of the year **Chief Rivers:** There are no large rivers

**Head of State:** President Ahmed Abdallah, born 1919, elected October 1978, following the coup of May 1978 **Head of Government:** Prime Minister Ali Mroudjae, appointed Feb. 8, 1982 **Effective Date of Constitution:** 1978 **Legislative Body:** Federal Assembly (unicameral) of 38 members **Local Government:** The 3 islands are organized into 7 regions

**Ethnic Composition:** The people are largely descendants of Moslem settlers with strains from Africa and Madagascar; there is a small European colony **Population Distribution:** 10% urban **Density:** 495 inhabitants per sq. mi.

**Largest City:** (1974 est.) Moroni 12,000

**Per Capita Income:** $153 (1976 est.) **Gross Domestic Product (GDP):** $51 million (1976) **Economic Statistics:** A wide variety of crops flourish in the rich volcanic soil: rice, cassava, ambrevade (a pea-family plant), sweet potatoes, citrus fruits, and some European vegetables. The chief commercial crops are vanilla, perfume plants, and copra. Fishing and stock raising are important. In 1976, 40% of GDP came from agriculture, 34% from industry **Minerals and Mining:** There are practically no mineral resources **Labor Force:** 184,000 (1976) with 87% in agriculture **Foreign Trade:** Exports chiefly vanilla, ilang-ilang essence for perfumes, copra, cloves and sisal totaled $12 million in 1979. Imports, primarily rice, vegetables, mineral products, textiles, metals and automobiles, totaled $17 million **Principal Trade Partners:** France, Madagascar, Kenya, Italy, West Germany, Tanzania, United States

**Vital Statistics:** Birthrate, 46.6 per 1,000 of pop. (1975); death rate, 21.7 **Life Expectancy:** 49 years **Health Statistics:** 458 inhabitants per hospital bed; 13,810 per physician (1973) **Infant Mortality:** 51.7 per 1,000 births **Illiteracy:** 42% **Primary and Secondary School Enrollment:** 47,629 (1977) **Enrollment in Higher Education:** 320 overseas (1976) **GNP Expended on Education:** 8.7% (1971)

**Transportation:** Paved roads total 183 mi. **Motor Vehicles:** 298 (1975) **Passenger Cars:** 263 **Railway Mileage:** None **Ports:** Mutsamudu, Moroni, Fomboni, Bambao **Major Airlines:** Air Comores provides domestic service **Communications: Radio Transmitters:** 3 (1976) **Receivers:** 36,000 (1976) **Television:** None **Telephones:** 2,000 (1978) **Newspapers:** None

**Weights and Measures:** Metric system **Travel Requirements:** N.A.

After 133 years as, successively, a French colony attached to Madagascar and a French Overseas Territory, three of the four Comoro Islands unilaterally declared independence on July 6, 1975. Still French territory but claimed by the Republic of the Comoros is the fourth island, Mayotte. Ahmed Abdallah was elected president of the new nation. These actions followed a vote in favor of independence in a referendum of December 1974.

In 1975, Ahmed Abdallah was overthrown in a bloodless coup led by Ali Soilih who was selected as president on January 2, 1976. The new nation has been vexed with the problem of the status of the largely Christian island of Mayotte. In 1976, the inhabitants of Mayotte voted to remain within the French Republic and not to join with the other largely Moslem Comoro Islands in independence. An April 12 referendum showed a preference for departmental status within France.

President Ali Soilih was overthrown on May 13, 1978, in a coup led by a French-born mercenary, Bob Denard, and Said Atthoumani, Interior Minister in the former Ahmed Abdallah government of 1975. The new government, headed by Ahmed Abdallah and Mohammed Ahmed, announced the release of political detainees and the restoration of rights and religious freedom. Mohammed Ahmed resigned in October 1978, leaving Ahmed Abdallah in sole command.

**HISTORY:** The original settlers of the Comoros came from mainland Africa. The first detailed knowledge of the area is undoubtedly due to Arab sailors, although the Phoenicians probably visited the islands much earlier. Two Arab invasions swept over the Comoros, the last coming from the Persian Gulf in the 15th century. In the 16th century the islands were visited by Portuguese, Dutch, French and Malagasy navigators

**1843:** French seize Mayotte

**1886:** Anjouan, Grand Comoro and Mohéli come under French protection

**1912:** The islands join administratively with Madagascar

**1946:** The Comoros become partially autonomous and receive the status of an Overseas Territory

**1961:** The islands receive complete internal autonomy

**1975:** Independence is declared. Comoros is admitted to UN. Government of Ahmed Abdallah overthrown by Ali Soilih

**1976:** Mayotte votes to remain French

**1978:** Ali Soilih overthrown in coup. Voters approve new constitution in referendum. Ahmed Abdallah elected president

**1979:** UN General Assembly reaffirms Comoran sovereignty over Mayotte

**1980:** An increasing number of human-rights violations is reported

**1981:** Amnesty is granted in May to 152 political prisoners held following a coup attempt earlier in year and to others imprisoned since 1978

## CONGO

**Area:** 132,046 sq. mi. **Population:** 1,459,000 (1978 est.)

**Official Name:** People's Republic of the Congo **Capital:** Brazzaville **Nationality:** Congolese **Languages:** French is the official language; Lingala and Kikongo are the principal spoken languages **Religion:** 49% animist, 49% Christian (mainly Roman Catholic), and 1% Moslem **Flag:** A red field; in the upper left corner is a yellow 5-pointed star above crossed yellow hammer and hoe, surrounded by green palm branches **Anthem:** The Internationale **Currency:** CFA Franc (305 per U.S. $1)

**Location:** West-central Africa. The Congo is bordered on the north by Cameroon and the Central African Republic, on the east and south by Zaire, on the southwest by the Angolan exclave of Cabinda and the Atlantic Ocean, and on the west by Gabon and Cameroon **Features:** The country consists of a coastal plain, savanna, highlands, and a plateau. Roughly half the land area is covered by dense equatorial forest, and a quarter of the country covered by marshes **Chief Rivers:** Congo, Ubangi, Sangha, Kouilou-Niari

**Head of State and Government:** President: Col. Denis Sassou-Nguesso, born 1941, elected July 1979. He is assisted by a Prime Minister, Col. Louis-Sylvain Goma, born 1941, appointed 1975 by the central committee of the Congolese Workers' party (PCT) **Effective Date of Present Constitution:** 1979 **Legislative Body:** Power is in the hands of the sole political party, the Congolese Workers' party (PCT). A National People's Assembly was elected in 1979 **Local Government:** 9 regions and a capital district, under appointed commissioners

**Ethnic Composition:** The 15 groups and 75 tribes are predominantly Bantu; major ones include the Bakongo, Bateke, M'Boshi, and Sangha. Pygmies number about 5,000. There are about 8,500 Europeans, mostly French **Population Distribution:** 40% urban (1976) **Density:** 11 inhabitants per sq. mi.

**Largest Cities:** (1974 census) Brazzaville 298,967, Pointe-Noire 141,700

**Per Capita Income:** $594 (1980) **Gross Domestic Product (GDP):** $919 million (1980) **Economic Statistics:** In 1978 about 19% of GDP was from agriculture (peanuts, palm kernels, coffee, cocoa, bananas, sugarcane, rice, corn, manioc, and sweet potatoes), forestry, and fishing; 10% from industry (forest products, sugar refining, palm and peanut oil, brewing, flour milling) **Minerals and Mining:** Crude petroleum is the major exploited mineral resource. There are high-grade iron-ore reserves, and some zinc, gold, copper, lead, and natural gas are produced. Potash production ended in 1977 **Labor Force:** 600,000, with 80% engaged in subsistence agriculture **Foreign Trade:** Exports, chiefly petroleum, wood, sugar, tobacco, and industrial diamonds, totaled $844 million in 1980. Imports, mainly machinery, electrical equipment, vehicles, textiles, clothing, foods, and chemicals, totaled $571 million **Principal Trade Partners:** France, West Germany, U.S., Italy

**Vital Statistics:** Birthrate, 44.6 per 1,000 of pop. (1980); death rate, 19 **Life Expectancy:** 48 years **Health Statistics:** 201 inhabitants per hospital bed (1976); 6,338 per physician (1975) **Infant Mortality:** 180 per 1,000 births **Illiteracy:** 80% **Primary and Secondary School Enrollment:** 421,211 (1975) **Enrollment in Higher Education:** 3,249 **GNP Expended on Education:** 8.2% (1975)

**Transportation:** Surfaced roads total 345 miles **Motor Vehicles:** 33,000 (1976) **Passenger Cars:** 20,000 **Railway Mileage:** 500 **Ports:** Pointe-Noire **Major Airlines:** Air Congo and Lina Congo operate internal services **Communications: Radio Transmitters:** 12 (1976) **Receivers:** 88,000 (1977) **Television Transmitters:** 1 **Receivers:** 3,300 (1976) **Telephones:** 13,000 (1978) **Newspapers:** 1 daily (1976), 1 copy per 1,000 inhabitants (1974)

**Weights and Measures:** Metric system **Travel Requirements:** Passport; visa. Contact Congo UN Mission in New York City

Since gaining independence from France in 1960, Congo has swung sharply from right to left politically and moved ahead very slowly economically.

Despite much leftist rhetoric, Congo's Marxist-Leninist "orientation" remains confusing—perhaps more expedient than orthodox. China and the Soviet Union appear to wield considerable influence over the government and speculation about which of them is in the ascendancy is a popular pastime in Brazzaville.

But it is capitalistic France that continues to be Congo's chief trading partner and source of economic and financial aid. Private French companies control most of the country's commerce and small industry.

President Marien Ngouabi, who came to power in 1968 and set up the ruling Congolese Workers' party (PCT), was assassinated March 18, 1977. Gen. Joachim Yhombi-Opango, who succeeded him, was ousted early in 1979 and replaced by Col. Denis Sassou-Nguesso in a leftist reaction against alleged bourgeois tendencies of the former regime. The new president, in response to a Paris report, acknowledged that more than a thousand Congolese children had been sent to Cuba for training.

Because of the unsettled situation in their country, hundreds of Zairians have sought asylum in the Congo. In 1980 the Brazzaville government denied that it was sheltering rebels planning to invade Zaire. Indeed, it deported many Zairians who were living illegally in the Congo.

**HISTORY:** When the Portuguese explorer Diego Cão arrived off the mouth of the Congo River in 1482, he found two long-established Bantu empires. To the north lay the Kingdom of Loango and its vassal states, and to the south, the great Mani-Congo stretching into Angola. Four centuries later, Count Pierre Savorgnan de Brazza (for whom Brazzaville is named) established French control over the area north of the river. In 1885, the Congress of Berlin recognized French claims to the region, later renamed Middle Congo

**1910:** Middle Congo becomes part of French Equatorial Africa

**1958:** The Congo becomes an autonomous member of French Community

**1960:** Full independence is proclaimed Aug. 15, and Fulbert Youlou becomes first president of the republic

**1963:** Youlou is overthrown in a revolt and succeeded by Alphonse Massamba-Débat who founds (in 1964) a Marxist-Leninist party. Chinese mission takes over direction of the economy

**1965:** Following arrests of American diplomats, United States closes Brazzaville embassy

**1968:** Capt. Marien Ngouabi, popular northern army officer, leads coup that ousts Massamba-Débat

**1970:** Ngouabi proclaims a people's republic, the first in Africa

**1972:** Production in offshore oil fields begins

**1977:** Ngouabi assassinated March 18. Emile Cardinal Biayenda murdered; Massamba-Débat executed for his role in assassination plot. Col. Joachim Yhombi-Opango, named president April 13 by military junta, abolishes national assembly. U.S. reopens its embassy

**1978:** Attempted coup to overthrow President Yhombi-Opango fails

**1979:** Col. Denis Sassou-Nguesso named president by PCT in February, following ouster of Yhombi-Opango who is accused of treason. New constitution approved

**1981:** Visiting Moscow, President Sassou-Nguesso signs treaty of cooperation and friendship with Soviet Union

## COSTA RICA

**Area:** 19,652 sq. mi. **Population:** 2,271,000 (1981 est.)

**Official Name:** Republic of Costa Rica **Capital:** San José **Nationality:** Costa Rican **Languages:** Spanish is the official and predominant language; a Jamaican dialect of English is spoken by many of the country's Negroes, descendants of Jamaican workers who emigrated to Costa Rica in the 19th century **Religion:** Overwhelmingly Roman Catholic **Flag:** A blue stripe at top and bottom, separated by two white stripes from a broad center red stripe bearing the national coat of arms on the lefthand side **Anthem:** National Anthem, beginning "Noble country, thy beautiful banner" **Currency:** Colón (36 per U.S. $1)

**Location:** Central America. Costa Rica is bordered on the north by Nicaragua, on the east by the Caribbean Sea, on the southeast by Panama, and on the west by the Pacific Ocean **Features:** About two-thirds of the country is covered by forests. There is a fairly wide coastal plain on the eastern side and a narrower plain on the Pacific coast. A volcanic mountain system composed of 3 ranges crosses the country lengthwise **Chief Rivers:** Río Grande, San Carlos

**Head of State and of Government:** President: Luis Alberto Monge Alvarez, born 1925, elected 1982 **Effective Date of Present Constitution:** November 1949 **Legislative Body:** Legislative Assembly (unicameral), consisting of 57 members elected by popular vote for 4 years **Local Government:** 7 provinces, each with a governor appointed by the president

**Ethnic Composition:** The population is predominantly of European (mainly Spanish) descent, with a large mestizo (mixed European and Indian) minority. Negroes of Jamaican origin number about 2% of the population **Population Distribution:** 41% urban **Density:** 115 inhabitants per sq. mi.

**Largest Cities:** (1973 census) San José 215,441, Alajuela 33,122, Limón 29,621, Puntarenas 26,331, Heredia 22,700, Cartago 21,753

**Per Capita Income:** $1,684 (1980) **Gross National Product (GNP):** $3.7 billion (1980) **Economic Statistics:** In 1979 about 22% of GNP came from agriculture (coffee, bananas, cocoa, sugarcane, rice, beans, and livestock), forestry, and fishing; 20% from industry (food and beverages, textiles, fertilizers, shoes, furniture) **Minerals and Mining:** Gold and manganese are mined. Bauxite is to be exploited **Labor Force:** 740,000 (1979); 34% in agriculture, 36% in industry and commerce, 25% in services and government **Foreign Trade:** Exports, chiefly coffee, bananas, meat, sugar, cocoa, and fertilizers, totaled $925 million in 1979. Imports, mainly manufactures, machinery and transport equipment, chemicals, foodstuffs, and petroleum, totaled $1.4 billion **Principal Trade Partners:** United States, West Germany, Nicaragua, El Salvador, Guatemala, Japan

**Vital Statistics:** Birthrate, 29.2 per 1,000 of pop. (1979); death rate, 4.2 **Life Expectancy:** 68 years **Health Statistics:** 288 inhabitants per hospital bed; 1,524 per physician (1975) **Infant Mortality:** 24.2 per 1,000 births **Illiteracy:** 10% **Primary and Secondary School Enrollment:** 481,994 (1976) **Enrollment in Higher Education:** 38,629 (1977) **GNP Expended on Education:** 5.2% (1974)

**Transportation:** Paved roads total 1,200 mi. **Motor Vehicles:** 122,700 (1977) **Passenger Cars:** 73,400 **Rail- way Mileage:** 661 **Ports:** Limón, Puntarenas, Golfito **Major Airlines:** LACSA (Costa Rican Airlines) operates domestic and international flights **Communications: Radio Transmitters:** 55 **Receivers:** 254,774 (1979) **Television Transmitters:** 15 **Receivers:** 155,000 (1976) **Telephones:** 175,000 (1978) **Newspapers:** 6 dailies, 104 copies per 1,000 inhabitants (1976)

**Weights and Measures:** Metric system **Travel Requirements:** Passport and visa not required if tourist card obtained prior to departure (valid 30 days, $2.00 fee) **International Dialing Code:** 506

For more than a hundred years Costa Rica has been considered to be a model of democratic government and of economic and social progress in Central America. Except for the overthrow of the elected president in 1917-1919 and a six-week civil war in 1948, this country has enjoyed a stable republican form of government in which presidential power is held in check by a strong Legislative Assembly. Elections are held every four years under the exclusive authority of a jealously independent electoral board. Suffrage is universal and voting is compulsory. A president may not succeed himself. Although there are extremes of wealth and poverty, distribution is generally more equitable than elsewhere in Central America.

Costa Rica's fortunes began to go downhill after the 1978 election of Rodrigo Carazo Odio, head of a coalition Unity party, to the presidency. Carazo failed to cope successfully with his country's practice of consuming more than it produces. While the world price for Costa Rica's chief export, coffee, was dropping, the costs of imports, especially oil, were rising. By 1982 the inflation rate had reached 65%, unemployment was running about 15%, the value of the colón had fallen, and the government was unable to make payments of either principal or interest on its $29-billion foreign debt. President Carazo could not reach any agreement with the International Monetary Fund on a stabilization program which would enable Costa Rica to renegotiate its debt.

Costa Rica's political stability has also been severely strained. President Carazo came in for strong criticism from some quarters for allowing Sandinista guerrillas to attack from bases in Costa Rica and establish a left-wing regime in Nicaragua in 1979. Increased terrorist activities within this country since 1980 have been attributed to both Salvadorean leftists and to Costa Rican radicals caught up in the Central American revolutionary fever. The small Civil Guard (there is no regular army) is poorly prepared to deal with major violence.

Against this background, Luis Alberto Monge Alvarez, a former union organizer, was elected president in 1982. His National Liberation party also won a clear majority in the Legislative Assembly. Monge was pledged to deal quickly and forcefully with his country's economic crisis and to remain neutral in the conflicts among the Central American nations.

The economy of Costa Rica is largely agrarian. Coffee and bananas alone account for more than 60 percent of export revenue. Manufactures are limited almost entirely to food, clothing and other products for domestic consumption. A vast hydroelectric project in Guanacaste province is expected to double the nation's electrical capacity by 1984 and reduce dependence on imported oil.

**HISTORY:** Prior to Costa Rica's discovery in 1502 by the Spanish, the country was inhabited by the Guaymi Indians. During the Spanish colonial period, Costa Rica was largely ignored by the mother country because of the paucity of minerals, and administered as part of the captaincy general of Guatemala

**1821:** Costa Rica obtains independence from Spain, and along with the rest of Central America is annexed to Mexico

**1823:** Costa Rica and the other Central American countries secede from Mexico and establish the Central American Federation

**1838:** Costa Rica becomes an independent republic

**1856-57:** William Walker, an American adventurer, attempts to conquer Costa Rica but is defeated by Central American alliance

**1870-72:** Tomás Guardia heads a military dictatorship

**1917:** Federico Tinoco overthrows elected president; is deposed in 1919 by popular revolt and democratic government is restored

**1948:** Assembly annuls election of Otilio Ulate as president. José Figuéres leads revolt and turns over presidency to Ulate in 1949. Costa Rica joins Central American Common Market

**1963:** The volcano Irazú erupts, destroying productive land

**1968:** The volcano Arenal erupts, bringing new devastation

**1970:** José Figuéres wins presidential election

**1974:** Daniel Oduber Quirós is elected president

**1978:** Rodrigo Carazo Odio is elected president

**1979:** Sandinista rebels use Costa Rica as base for operations to seize power in Nicaragua

**1981:** Terrorist bombings disrupt peace in Costa Rica. Government, unable to pay on foreign loans, faces bankruptcy
**1982:** Luis Monge faces severe problems as newly elected president

## CUBA

**Area:** 42,827 sq. mi. **Population:** 9,706,369 (1981 census)

**Official Name:** Republic of Cuba **Capital:** Havana **Nationality:** Cuban **Languages:** Spanish is the official and universal language **Religion:** Predominantly Roman Catholic before Castro **Flag:** Three horizontal blue stripes separated by two white stripes, with an equilateral red triangle at the left containing a 5-pointed white star **Anthem:** Hymn of Bayamo **Currency:** Cuban peso (0.82 per U.S. $1)

**Location:** Northern rim of the Caribbean Sea. The largest and most westerly island of the West Indies, Cuba lies at the entrance of the Gulf of Mexico and some 90 miles south of Florida **Features:** About three-fifths of the country consists of flat to gently rolling terrain with many wide and fertile valleys and plains. The rest is mountainous or hilly **Chief Rivers:** Cauto, Sagua la Grande, Zaza, Caonao, San Pedro, Toa

**Political Leader, Head of State and of Government:** President Fidel Castro Ruz, born 1927, First Secretary of the Central Committee of the Cuban Communist party, and president of the councils of state and of ministers, seized power in 1959 **Effective Date of Present Constitution:** December 1976 **Legislative Body:** National Assembly of People's Power (unicameral), with 481 deputies elected for 5-year terms. Power lies in the Communist party Politburo **Local Government:** 14 provinces, including Havana city and the special municipality of Isla de la Juventud (Isle of Pines), with locally elected assemblies

**Ethnic Composition:** 51% mulatto (mixed European and black), 37% European ancestry, 11% black, 1% Chinese **Population Distribution:** 69% urban (1981) **Density:** 227 inhabitants per sq. mi.

**Largest Cities:** (1981 census) Havana 1,924,886, Santiago de Cuba 345,289, Camagüey 245,235, Holguín 186,013, Santa Clara 171,914, Guantánamo 167,405, Cienfuegos 102,426

**Per Capita Income:** $1,407 (1980) **Gross National Product (GNP):** $14 billion (1980) **Economic Statistics:** 10% of GNP is derived from agriculture (sugar, tobacco, cattle, coffee); 41% from industry (mainly sugar refining, cigarettes and cigars, rum, and textiles); and 33% from trade and finance (1974) **Minerals and Mining:** Cuba has the world's largest deposit of nickel; reserves of iron ore, manganese, cobalt, copper, chromite, salt, petroleum, gold, silver **Labor Force:** 2,700,000 (1976), with 39% in transportation and services, 33% in agriculture, and 26% in industry and construction **Foreign Trade:** Exports, chiefly sugar, nickel, tobacco, shrimp, lobster, and beef, were $4.7 billion (1979). Imports, mainly petroleum, equipment and machinery, and food, totaled $5 billion **Principal Trade Partners:** Soviet bloc, Japan, Spain, Canada, West Germany

**Vital Statistics:** Birthrate, 14.7 per 1,000 of pop. (1979); death rate, 5.6 **Life Expectancy:** 72 years **Health Statistics:** 242 inhabitants per hospital bed; 1,121 per physician (1976) **Infant Mortality:** 19.3 per 1,000 births (1976) **Illiteracy:** 3.1% **Primary and Secondary School Enrollment:** 2,463,545 (1976) **Enrollment in Higher Education:** 82,688 (1975) **GNP Expended on Education:** 9.9% (1974)

**Transportation:** Paved roads total 5,470 mi. **Motor Vehicles:** 120,000 (1976) **Passenger Cars:** 80,000 **Railway Mileage:** 9,100 **Ports:** Havana, Matanzas, Nuevitas, Cienfuegos, Santiago de Cuba **Major Airlines:** Cubana de Aviación, the government-owned airline, operates domestic and international flights **Communications: Radio Transmitters:** 119 (1976) **Receivers:** 1,895,000 (1977) **Television Transmitters:** 19 **Receivers:** 650,000 (1976) **Telephones:** 321,000 (1977) **Newspapers:** 16 dailies (1976), 107 per 1,000 inhabitants

**Weights and Measures:** Metric system **Travel Requirements:** Passport, visa; tourist visa, $6.00 fee, apply to Czechoslovak Embassy, Washington, D.C. 20009

Cuba, largest of the West Indies and the only Communist-controlled country in the Western Hemisphere, lies only 90 miles south of Key West, Florida. Cuba's capital, Havana, is less than an hour's flight southwest from Miami. The country's largest city and principal port, Havana, was originally important as a well-situated way station between Spain and her colonies in the Western Hemisphere. Eventually, settlers moved inland, devoting themselves mainly to growing sugarcane and tobacco.

Despite the physical proximity of Cuba to the U.S. and the potential trade and other ties, the relationship between the two countries has never developed quite as one might expect. Cuba was the last Latin American nation to gain independence from Spain. The United States actually opposed the first attempt to free Cuba begun by Simón Bolívar. A native-based liberation movement starting in 1868 sputtered out after 10 years of fighting. It was not until 1895 that a revolution led by José Martí successfully challenged Spain. The revolutionaries also won strong sentiments of support in the U.S. After the mysterious sinking of the *Maine*, the U.S. declared war on Spain.

When a freely elected Cuban government took office in 1902, it found it had little to sell except land. Many foreign investors, chiefly Americans, stepped forward and purchased enormous areas and began to rebuild the sugar industry. For years after, Cuba was locked into a one-crop agricultural economy with American ownership of the land, mines and other resources. Income was, and still is, almost totally dependent on the world price of sugar. American interests were protected by the Platt Amendment that allowed U.S. to intervene in Cuban affairs, as it did in 1906-1909 and 1912.

Fulgencio Batista, a former army sergeant, dominated the political scene either directly or indirectly from 1934 to 1944 and from 1952 to 1959.

President Batista's regime became repressive and increasingly unpopular, and on July 26, 1953, an armed opposition group led by a young lawyer, Fidel Castro, attacked the Moncada army barracks at Santiago de Cuba. The attack failed and many off those not killed were imprisoned, including Castro. He was released by President Batista under an amnesty in May 1955 and went into exile in Mexico, where he formed his "26th of July Movement." Castro's forces eventually numbering several thousand finally succeeded in forcing Batista to flee the country.

The Castro regime's early promises of agrarian reform to benefit the peasants resulted in state ownership of most of the land and in the organization of state farms. Cuba's business and industrial sectors were nationalized and placed under the direction of the state, which has also effectively abolished all opposition political activity.

A major element of Cuba's foreign policy under Castro has been the "exporting" of revolutionary techniques. To this end, Cuba has supported guerrilla movements in various countries in the Western Hemisphere and elsewhere—notably Africa—by providing weapons, financing, propaganda and, in some cases, advisory personnel. In Cuba itself, on *Isla de la Juventud* (Isle of Youth), formerly the Isle of Pines, thousands of African and Latin American adolescents have received standard Cuban education, including Marxist ideology.

A nod toward normalizing U.S.-Cuban relations was made in 1975 by U.S. Secretary of State Henry Kissinger. But the nod became a "no" when Cuba dispatched troops to help Russian-backed forces in Angola's civil war. After Jimmy Carter became president, he first tested the water with some qualified public overtures toward Cuba, and then on March 9, 1977, announced an end to travel restrictions in Cuba. The two countries soon negotiated fishing and maritime rights agreements.

Still, the United States kept a wary eye on Soviet military gifts to Cuba— MiG-23 jet planes in 1978, a non-nuclear submarine in 1979. In August 1979 the Carter Administration affirmed reports that the Soviet Union had a combat brigade of 2,500 to 3,000 men stationed in Cuba. Moscow insisted that Soviet military personnel were there only for training and advisory purposes.

Cuba's economic plight has steadily worsened, so much so that in a December 1979 speech Castro admitted that his country is "sailing on a sea of difficulties." World sugar prices had plunged, and the cane harvest was curbed by a fungus. A blue mold almost totally wiped out the 1979-80 tobacco crop. Many farm workers were becoming slack on the job and production records were being falsified, a government spokesman noted. Shortages of food and other necessities were growing and rationing was strictly enforced. To keep the economy going at all, Cuba had to depend on a subsidy of $8-$10 million a day from the Soviet Union, with which a $45 billion trade agreement for 1981-85 has been signed. Trade pacts were also made with East Germany and Japan in 1980, and in 1981 an accord was reached with Mexico for that country's assistance in oil and natural gas exploration on Cuba's undersea shelf.

In April 1980 more than 10,000 Cubans crashed their way into the Peruvian embassy compound in Havana, seeking safe exit to other countries. Castro eventually acceded, and some 120,000 men, women and children took advantage of the opportunity to escape oppression in their homeland. The vast majority fled to Florida in a flotilla of small boats. A few refugees, dissatisfied with their treatment in the United States, started a wave of airplane hijackings to get back to Havana; some were thwarted by Castro's decision to return them to the United States.

In 1982 a U.S. joint congressional committee released an opinion that the 20-year-long trade embargo against Cuba had forced that nation deep into economic dependence on the Soviet bloc. The study praised Cuban progress in health and education, but found that Castro's "highly inefficient political and economic management system is perpetuating serious problems."

**HISTORY:** Following the discovery of Cuba by Columbus in 1492, the island remained under Spanish rule until almost the end of the 19th century. A revolt against Spain broke out in 1895 and evoked strong sympathy in the United States. After the brief Spanish-American War of 1898, Cuba became an independent republic, though under U.S. protection. With the abrogation of the Platt Amendment in 1934, the U.S. gave up the right to intervene in Cuban affairs, but retained its right to the naval base at Guantánamo

**1934-59:** Fulgencio Batista y Zaldívar, an army sergeant, overthrows regime and becomes dominant figure in Cuban politics. After ruling through puppet presidents, Batista proclaims new constitution in 1940 and is elected president for four-year term. In 1952 he returns to power through an army coup but his regime is increasingly threatened by rebel uprisings led by Fidel Castro, who finally forces Batista to flee Jan 1, 1959

**1960:** Castro begins to transform Cuba into socialist state modeled on Soviet pattern and installs Communists in leading government posts. Most U.S.-owned property is nationalized without compensation; United States rescinds Cuban sugar quota

**1961:** United States severs diplomatic relations with Havana. Castro turns increasingly to Soviet Union for aid and protection, receiving supplies of arms and oil. Cuban exiles in United States, trained and equipped by Central Intelligence Agency, land invasion force at Bay of Pigs in abortive attempt to overthrow Castro

**1962:** Organization of American States excludes Cuba from membership. Installation of Soviet missiles in Cuba leads to U.S. naval blockade and demand for removal of missiles

**1971:** Cuba signs economic pact with the Soviet Union

**1975:** OAS passes resolution to lift the 11 years of formal diplomatic and economic isolation of Cuba

**1976:** A new constitution is approved by referendum

**1978:** U.S.-Cuba thaw is stalled, prrincipally on issues of U.S. economic blockade against Cuba, $1.8 billion in claims against Cuba by American companies and individuals, and continued Cuban presence in Africa

**1979:** As host to the sixth summit conference of Third World nations in the Non-Aligned movement, Castro defends use of Cuban troops to fight for "just causes" in Africa and elsewhere

**1980:** Cuba loses bid for membership on UN Security Council

**1981:** An attempt by 29 Cubans to get safely out of the country by seizing the Ecuadorean embassy fails. Government takes steps to improve economic ties with Western nations and to attract luxury tourist trade. Castro charges that U.S. is responsible for outbursts of dengue fever and other plagues in Cuba in recent years. Reacting to Cuban intervention in the internal affairs of other countries, several Latin American governments break ties with Cuba

**1982:** United States accuses Cuba of supporting efforts to overthrow government of El Salvador by supplying military aid to leftist guerrillas through Nicaragua. Communist Cuba supports cause of rightist regime in Argentina against Britain in Falkland Islands war

## CYPRUS

**Area:** 3,572 sq. mi. (including the 99 sq. mi. British-leased Sovereign Base Area) **Population:** 637,000 (1981 est.)

**Official Name:** Republic of Cyprus **Capital:** Nicosia **Nationality:** Cypriot **Languages:** Greek and Turkish are the official languages. English is widely understood **Religion:** 77% Greek Orthodox, 18% Moslem, 5% Maronite, Armenian and Apostolic Christians **Flag:** An outline map of Cyprus in gold above crossed green olive branches on a white field **Anthem:** None established **Currency:** Cypriot pound (0.47 per U.S. $1)

**Location:** Middle East. The third-largest island in the Mediterranean, Cyprus lies 44 miles south of Turkey, 60 miles west of Syria, and 260 miles east of Rhodes, the nearest part of Greece **Features:** The Troodos Mountains in the southwest and the Kyrenia range along the northern coast dominate the island. The central plain, or Mesaoria, lies between the two mountain ranges **Chief River:** Pedieos (Pedias)

**Head of State and of Government:** President: Spyros Kyprianou, born 1932, succeeded August 1977, elected for full 5-year term 1978 **Effective Date of Present Constitution:** 1960 **Legislative Body:** House of Representatives (unicameral), consisting of 35 Greek Cypriot members, elected for 5 years. Turkish Cypriots declared their independence and established in February 1975 the Turkish Federated State of Cyprus, with a president (Rauf R. Denkhtash elected in 1976), premier (Mustafa Cagatay, appointed 1978), and a 40-member unicameral Constituent Assembly; a referendum in 1975 approved a constitution **Local Government:** 6 districts

**Ethnic Composition:** About 77% of the population is of Greek descent, 18% of Turkish origin, and the rest composed of Armênians, Maronites, and other minorities **Population Distribution:** 42% urban (1974) **Density:** 178 inhabitants per sq. mi.

**Largest Cities:** (1973 census) Nicosia 116,125; (1972 estimates) Limassol 61,400, Famagusta 44,200, Larnaca 21,800, Paphos 12,100, Kyrenia 5,200

**Per Capita Income:** $2,509 (1980) **Gross National Product (GNP):** $1.6 billion (1980) **Economic Statistics:** About 21% of GNP was derived from agriculture and 19% from manufacturing and mining. Tourism is important **Minerals and Mining:** Copper is the most important mineral, but the mines are becoming depleted; asbestos is becoming increasingly important. Other minerals are iron pyrites, chromite, umber, and yellow ocher **Labor Force:** 202,700 (1977, Greek area only), with 26% in industry, 23% in agriculture, forestry and fishing, 15% employed overseas or in military, 5% in government **Foreign Trade**—*Republic of Cyprus area (Greek):* Exports, chiefly fruits and vegetables, wine, cement and clothing, totaled $422 million in 1979. Imports, mainly machinery, manufactures, fuel and food, totaled $1 billion *Turkish area:* Exports, chiefly fruits and vegetables and pyrites, totaled $40 million in 1979. Imports, chiefly food, fuels and machinery, totaled $108 million **Principal Trade Partners**—*Republic of Cyprus area (Greek):* Britain, Saudi Arabia, West Germany, France, Japan, Greece, Syria, U.S., Lebanon, Kuwait *Turkish area:* Turkey, Britain, West Germany, France, Italy

**Vital Statistics:** Birthrate, 21.7 per 1,000 of pop. (1980); death rate, 9.1 **Life Expectancy:** 71 years **Health Statistics:** 185 inhabitants per hospital bed; 1,276 per physician (Greek area-1977) **Infant Mortality:** 17.2 per 1,000 births **Illiteracy:** 11% **Primary and Secondary School Enrollment:** (Greek area) 104,524 (1977) **Enrollment in Higher Education:** 782 (1976) **GNP Expended on Education:** 4.1% (1976)

**Transportation:** Paved roads total 2,800 mi. **Motor Vehicles:** 96,400 (1978) **Passenger Cars:** 77,700 **Railway Mileage:** None **Ports:** Famagusta, Limassol, Larnaca, Karavostassi **Major Airlines:** Cyprus Airways (government owned) operates domestic and international flights; there is also a Turkish-Cypriot airline **Communications: Radio Transmitters:** 6 **Receivers:** 212,000 (1977) **Television Transmitters:** 26 **Licenses:** 57,000 (1976) **Telephones:** 92,000 (1978) **Newspapers:** 13 dailies (1976), 107 copies per 1,000 inhabitants (1970)

**Weights and Measures:** Both British standards and the metric system are used along with local units **Travel Requirements:** Passport, no visa **International Dialing Code:** 357

The picturesque island of Aphrodite, Cyprus has been an independent but strife-torn nation since 1960. Previously, its strategic location had attracted many foreign conquerors, including the

Egyptians, Phoenicians, Assyrians, Persians, Romans, Greeks, Turks and British. Today Cyprus is divided into two separate states and its future as a single nation is in doubt.

The island is the homeland of two antagonistic peoples—some half-million ethnic Greeks and slightly more than 120,000 ethnic Turks. The Greek Cypriots have traditionally favored *enosis* (union) with Greece, while the Turkish Cypriots want partition or cantonization of the country. In any case, virtually all Cypriots regard themselves as Greeks or Turks, Christians or Moslems first and as Cypriots second.

More than half the total area of Cyprus is cultivated, a noteworthy accomplishment in the largely arid Middle East. Mineral resources maintain a modest industrial complex. Light manufacturing is growing in the Greek area.

The constitution, in effect after independence in 1960, required that the president be a Greek Cypriot and the vice-president a Turkish Cypriot. Archbishop Makarios III, head of the Greek Orthodox Church on Cyprus became president. The Greek and Turkish communities lived under a form of de facto segregation.

Civil war between the two communities erupted in 1963, and terroristic campaigns became a part of Cypriot life. In 1964, the United Nations sent a peace-keeping force to minimize clashes. Turkish Cypriot leaders withdrew from active participation in the government of Cyprus. In 1967 war between Greece and Turkey over Cyprus was narrowly averted, mainly through the mediation of the United States. Turkey had threatened to invade the island but Greece finally agreed to remove nearly all of the 8,000 troops it had there.

The Cypriot national guard which was dominated by officers from Greece continued to press for union with Greece. In 1971 the EOKA B, a guerrilla movement favoring ties to Greece and led by Gen. George Grivas, stepped up its terrorist activities, which tended to undermine the government of President Makarios, who began his third five-year term in February 1973. (His second term had been extended.)

On July 15, 1974, Greek officers of the Cypriot national guard led a coup which overthrew President Makarios and replaced him with an EOKA B terrorist, Nikos Sampson. Turkey responded by invading Cyprus on July 20, and quickly conquered the northern two-fifths of the island. Most of the Greek Cypriots in the conquered territory fled south, and most of the Turkish Cypriots elsewhere moved north. Sampson's government collapsed.

Amid fears of a wider conflict, the UN ordered a cease-fire. Fighting continued sporadically but order was restored with Glafkos Clerides, president of the Cyprus House of Representatives, as interim president. By the time international pressure effected a real cease-fire on August 16, 200,000 Greek Cypriots were refugees. Makarios returned to power in December 1974.

In February 1975 a Turkish-Cypriot Federated State of Cyprus was created in the occupied area without the approval of Makarios, and in June a Turkish Cypriot referendum established a constitution for the state. Talks to establish a unified form of government continue, but accord at times seems distant. In August 1980, the two communities reopened negotiations under UN sponsorship on steps which might lead to the eventual restoration of a unified government for the entire island. In February 1982, Andreas Papandreou became the first Greek premier to visit Cyprus and was warmly welcomed by Greek Cypriots. He endorsed the UN negotiations and declared that the key problem was Turkey's continued occupation of northern Cyprus.

**HISTORY:** Cyprus, which derives its name from "kypros," the Greek word for copper, was settled first by the Greeks c. 1500 B.C. and passed to the Romans in 58 B.C. Later a part of the Byzantine Empire, the island slumbered until 1191, when Richard I of England conquered Cyprus and it became a base for the Crusaders. In the 16th century, the island was conquered by Turkey. Administration was transferred to Britain in 1878 and in 1928 the island became a Crown Colony

**1946:** Greece demands union *(enosis)* with Cyprus
**1956:** Archbishop Makarios, spiritual and political leader of the Greek Cypriots, is deported by British
**1959:** Greek-Turkish conferences in Zurich and London reach agreement on independence for Cyprus. Archbishop Makarios returns and is elected president
**1960:** Independence is officially proclaimed
**1963:** Violence between Greeks and Turks erupts in Nicosia
**1964:** Turks withdraw from active participation in government. Threat of war between Greece and Turkey over Cyprus brings United Nations peace-keeping force to island
**1968:** Makarios announces restoration of freedom of movement for Turkish Cypriots, ending blockade of Turkish sectors
**1973:** Struggle for *enosis* erupts into widespread violence
**1974:** Cypriot National Guard ousts President Makarios. Turkish forces invade Cyprus and gain control of 40 percent of the island. Two-way migration makes occupied territory predominantly Turkish, rest of island predominantly Greek. Makarios returns and resumes the presidency
**1975:** Turkish Cypriots proclaim their own state in northern Cyprus
**1976:** Turkish Cypriots elect Rauf Denktash to serve as president of the Turkish Cypriot Zone
**1977:** Turkish and Greek Cypriot leaders begin talks. Makarios dies. Spyros Kyprianou succeeds him
**1978:** Deadlock in talks between Cypriot leaders continues
**1980:** Talks resume under UN sponsorship but are soon deadlocked

## CZECHOSLOVAKIA

**Area:** 49,373 sq. mi. **Population:** 15,314,000 (1981 est.)

**Official Name:** Czechoslovak Socialist Republic **Capital:** Prague **Nationality:** Czechoslovak **Languages:** Czech and Slovak are the official and principal languages; Hungarian and German are minority languages **Religion:** About 77% of the population is Roman Catholic; 8% are members of the Czechoslovak Church; and 8% are Protestants. All churches are under close government control **Flag:** A blue triangle on the hoist with its apex toward the center; the rest of the flag consists of a white band on top and a red band on the bottom **Anthem:** Where Is My Home? **Currency:** Koruna (11.9 per U.S. $1)

**Location:** Central Europe. Landlocked Czechoslovakia is bordered on the north by Poland, on the east by the USSR, on the south by Hungary and Austria, on the west by West Germany, and on the northwest by East Germany **Features:** Bohemia, Moravia, and Slovakia are the country's principal regions. Bohemia, in the west, is a plateau surrounded by mountains; Moravia, in the central region, is somewhat hillier; and Slovakia, in the east, is partly mountainous and partly lowland **Chief Rivers:** Labe, Vltava, Danube, Morava, Váh, Nitra, Hron, Ohre, Hornád

**Political Leader and Head of State:** President Gustav Husák, born 1913, elected 1975, reelected 1980; general secretary of the Central Committee of the Communist Party **Head of Government:** Premier Lubomir Strougal, born 1924, took office 1970 **Effective Date of Present Constitution:** 1960; the constitution was amended in 1969 to provide for Czech and Slovak local automomy within a federal state, and again in 1971 and 1975 **Legislative Body:** Federal Assembly (bicameral), consisting of 2 equal chambers, the Chamber of the People and the Chamber of the Nations. The Chamber of the People has 200 members. The Chamber of the Nations consists of 75 representatives from the Czech Republic and 75 from the Slovak Republic. Both houses are elected for 5 years. The Federal Assembly is subordinate to the Central Committee of the Presidium of the Communist Party **Local Government:** The two republics have separate premiers and national councils, subordinate to the Federal Assembly. They are divided into 10 regions and 2 independent cities

**Ethnic Composition:** Czechs make up about 65% of the population and Slovaks 30%; Hungarians, Germans, Poles, Ukrainians, and Gypsies make up the rest **Population Distribution:** 67% urban (1974) **Density:** 310 inhabitants per sq. mi.

**Largest Cities:** (1981 est.) Prague 1,182,294, Bratislava 381,165, Brno 371,376, Ostrava 322,110, Kosice 203,109, Plzen 170,957

**Per Capita Income:** $5,542 (1980) **Gross National Product (GNP):** $85 billion (1980) **Economic Statistics:** About 45% of GNP comes from industry (iron and steel, glass, leather products, brewing, and textiles); 12% from agriculture (grains, sugar beets, hops, fruits and vegetables); 8% from construction; 9% from transport and communications; 9% from trade; 5% from housing; 11% from government and other services **Minerals and Mining:** Coal, antimony, magnesite, lignite and uranium **Labor Force:** 7.6 million with about 39% in industry and 14% in agriculture **Foreign Trade:** Exports, chiefly machinery, motor vehicles, iron and steel, and chemicals, totaled $13.9 billion in 1979. Imports, mainly machinery, industrial raw materials, food, fuel, and manufactured goods, totaled $14.4 billion **Principal Trade Partners:** USSR, East Germany, Poland, Hungary, Romania, West Germany, Britain, Bulgaria, Switzerland, Austria, Yugoslavia

**Vital Statistics:** Birthrate, 16.2 per 1,000 of pop. (1980); death rate, 12.1 **Life Expectancy:** 70 years **Health Statistics:** 81 inhabitants per hospital bed; 395 per physician (1977) **Infant Mortality:** 16.6 per 1,000 births (1977) **Illiteracy:** Negligible **Primary and Secondary School Enrollment:** 2,210,915 (1976) **Enrollment in Higher Education:** 155,059 (1975) **GNP Expended on Education:** 4.5% (1976)

**Transportation:** Paved roads total 37,350 mi. **Motor Vehicles:** 2,290,700 (1978) **Passenger Cars:** 1,982,200 **Railway Mileage:** 8,228 **Ports:** None **Major Airlines:** Czechoslovak Airlines operates domestic and international services **Communications: Radio Transmitters:** 89 **Licenses:** 3,721,000 (1977) **Television Transmitters:** 788 **Licenses:** 3,793,000 (1976) **Telephones:** 2,981,000 (1978) **Newspapers:** 29 dailies, 296 copies per 1,000 inhabitants (1977)

**Weights and Measures:** Metric system **Travel Requirements:** Passport, visa, 2 pictures, $10 fee

---

The problem of Czechoslovakia today is trying to mold a socialist state of Marxist-Leninist traditions as determined by its Russian guardians while satisfying a native desire for the freedom and openness of a Western democracy.

The Communist party seized power in 1948, and established one of the world's least free societies. In the 1960s, with a new constitution, a cautious liberalizing movement emerged. A flowering of Czechoslovak artistry in films, the theater and other arts began. When the economy stagnated, Slovak Communists found a chance to replace hard-liner Antonin Novotny with Alexander Dubcek as first secretary of the Communist Party in January 1968.

Under Dubcek the trend toward freedom accelerated. Press censorship was reduced and grievances were aired, thus adding to the pressure for reforms while at the same time arousing the fears of Soviet leaders. The radical experiment to establish "socialism with a human face" ended abruptly on August 20, 1968. Armored units of the Warsaw Pact countries, led by Soviet tanks, entered Czechoslovakia at night to ensure the restoration of a more orthodox brand of Communism.

The dramatic incursion was characterized by its initiators as necessary to thwart a "threatened counterrevolution" by "imperialist forces." It was seen by Western observers—and most Czechs—as a final desperate move by Leonid I. Brezhnev, the Soviet Communist party chief, to curtail Dubcek's essay in socialist democracy.

Dubcek was forced in succeeding days to sign a protocol in Moscow accepting the military "assistance." He was formally replaced in April 1969 by Gustav Husák, who has since moved resolutely to restore the former system of state control in Czechoslovakia.

The aftermath of Dubcek's "Prague Spring" has been characterized by a reversal of his reforms; a broad purge of liberal economists, writers, educators and artists; and a "cleansing" of party ranks as well as the removal of the former leader himself from public life.

Dubcek's error had been to move too quickly, too prominently, and certainly too radically to shed the restrictions and repressions of the earlier Stalinist period of postwar Communist rule.

The new Czech party chief, Husák, has spent the intervening years walking a line between hard-liners in the party, who want to carry the anti-Dubcek purges beyond the stages of ousters and restrictions to arrests and trials, and the many Czechs—revisionists, in party terminology—who watch now with sullen hostility to the withering of a brief, bright flowering of intellectual freedom.

As politically adroit as Dubcek was unsophisticated, Husák removed 400,000 members from the Czech Communist party—one-fifth of the national membership—but only a few have been tried for "anti-State" activities. Many leading educators, commentators, economists, and other leaders who supported Dubcek left the country.

In recent years a slight easing can be detected. Husák has given a second chance to lesser participants in the reform movement and hard-liners were unable to dominate the Communist party congresses in 1975 and 1982. But the government has harassed dissidents who spread the ideas of the 1968 "Prague Spring." Dissident attacks on Husak's "normalization" have been leaked to the West, where they have hindered Czech officials seeking trade contacts. In 1981 the Czech government took a hard line against the successful reform movement in neighboring Poland, apparently fearing that the Polish ideas might spread to Czechoslovakia.

**HISTORY:** In the 6th and 7th centuries, Slavic migrants absorbed Celtic, Germanic, and other cultures. The Czechs, in Bohemia and Moravia, and the Slovaks, in Slovakia, were united in the Great Moravian Empire in the ninth century, a period that also saw the introduction of Christianity. After the empire's collapse in the 10th century, the Slovaks were incorporated into the Kingdom of Hungary and the Czechs established the Kingdom of Bohemia. The 14th century, with its Hussite Revolution, marked the beginning of religious wars in the Czech lands that were to continue through the Reformation and Counter-Reformation. During the decline of the Kingdom of Bohemia, the Czechs came under foreign dynasties, ending up, along with the Slovaks, in the Austro-Hungarian Empire

**1918:** Following the defeat of Austria-Hungary in World War I, Czechoslovakia, incorporating the Czech lands and Slovakia, is proclaimed an independent republic with nationalist leader Thomas Masaryk its first president

**1935:** Masaryk dies. Eduard Beneš elected president

**1938:** Britain, France, Germany, and Italy, without having invited Czechoslovakia to the negotiating table, sign the Munich Pact, a capitulation to German demands for the Sudetenland, the border region of Bohemia inhabited by a large German minority. President Eduard Beneš resigns and goes into exile

**1939-46:** German troops occupy Czechoslovakia during World War II. The country is liberated by Soviet and U.S. forces. Beneš returns and resumes presidency

**1948:** Communists seize power; Beneš resigns; Foreign Minister Jan Masaryk, son of Thomas Masaryk, plunges to death from a window. Though officially termed a suicide, he is believed to have been murdered by the Communists

**1955:** Czechoslovakia joins the Warsaw Pact, the Soviet-bloc military organization

**1968:** Alexander Dubcek, a progressive, becomes first secretary of the Czechoslovak Communist party, replacing Antonin Novotny. The Soviet Union, alarmed by liberalization measures in Czechoslovakia, invades the country

**1969:** Gustav Husák replaces Dubcek as leader of the Czechoslovak Communist party and rescinds liberalization; Dubcek is ousted from ruling Presidium in purge of party progressives

**1970:** Dubcek is expelled from the Communist party

**1973:** First direct consular agreement between Communist Czechoslovakia and the United States is signed

**1974:** U.S. and Czechoslovakia reach preliminary agreement on settlement of postwar financial counterclaims

**1975:** Husák is elected president by Federal Assembly

**1977:** Czech dissidents publish manifesto (Charter 77) protesting the suppression of human rights; detention of signers follows

**1978:** Subdued public protests and destruction of statue mark 10th anniversary of invasion

**1981:** 16th Communist party congress sets moderate economic goals for five-year plan (1981-85); calls for austerity measures

---

## DENMARK

**Area:** 16,633 sq. mi. **Population:** 5,123,989 (1981 est.)

**Official Name:** Kingdom of Denmark **Capital:** Copenhagen **Nationality:** Danish **Languages:** Danish is the official and universal language **Religion:** About 97% of the people belong to the established Lutheran Church **Flag:** A white cross on a red field **Anthem:** There is a Lovely Land **Currency:** Danish krone (7.9 per U.S. $1)

**Location:** Northwest Europe. Denmark is bordered on the north by the Skagerrak; on the east by the Kattegat, Öresund, and the Baltic Sea; on the south by West Germany; and on the west by the North

Sea **Features:** Low-lying elevation, with flat or rolling landscape **Chief Rivers:** Stora, Skjern, Varde, Gudena

**Head of State:** Queen Margrethe II, born 1940, ascended the throne 1972 **Head of Government:** Premier Poul Schlüter, appointed 1982 **Effective Date of Present Constitution:** 1953 **Legislative Body:** Parliament (unicameral *Folketing*), with 179 members, including 2 each from Greenland and the Faeroe Islands, elected on the basis of proportional representation for 4 years **Local Government:** 14 counties and two urban communes, with elected councils

**Ethnic Composition:** Except for foreign "guest workers" the population is almost entirely Scandinavian **Population Distribution:** 83% urban **Density:** 308 inhabitants per sq. mi.

**Largest Cities** (M.A. = Metropolitan Area) (1976 est.): Copenhagen 699,300 (M.A. 1,327,940), Aarhus 246,111, Odense 167,911, Aalborg 154,605

**Per Capita Income:** $9,868 (1980) **Gross Domestic Product (GDP):** $50.7 billion (1980) **Economic Statistics:** About 35% of GDP (1978) comes from manufacturing (food processing, machinery, chemicals), crafts, building and construction; 8% from agriculture (dairy and poultry farming, cattle raising, hog breeding, grain and root crops), forestry and fisheries **Minerals and Mining:** Oil and gas produced from North Sea wells **Labor Force:** 2,625,223 (1979); 25% in manufacturing, 15% in trade, 9% in agriculture, 8% in construction **Foreign Trade:** Exports, chiefly machinery and equipment, textiles and agricultural commodities, totaled $17.4 billion in 1979. Imports, mainly machinery and fittings, fuels, chemicals, iron and steel, totaled $19.3 billion **Principal Trade Partners:** Sweden, West Germany, Britain, United States, Norway

**Vital Statistics:** Birthrate, 11.2 per 1,000 of pop. (1980); death rate, 10.9 **Life Expectancy:** 74 years **Health Statistics:** 115 inhabitants per hospital bed; 512 per physician (1976) **Infant Mortality:** 8.8 per 1,000 (1977) **Illiteracy:** Negligible **Primary and Secondary School Enrollment:** 854,442 (1976) **Enrollment in Higher Education:** 110,271 (1975) **GNP Expended on Education:** 8.3% (1975)

**Transportation:** Roads total 40,000 mi. **Motor Vehicles:** 1,393,900 (1978) **Passenger Cars:** 1,115,400 **Railway Mileage:** 1,609 **Ports:** Copenhagen, Aalborg, Aarhus, Esbjerg **Major Airlines:** Scandinavian Airlines System (SAS) operates domestic and international services. Danair operates domestic routes **Communications: Radio Transmitters:** 44 **Licenses:** 1,851,000 (1976) **Television Transmitters:** 34 **Licenses:** 1,637,000 (1976) **Telephones:** 2,907,000 (1978) **Newspapers:** 49 dailies, 362 copies per 1,000 inhabitants (1977)

**Weights and Measures:** Metric system **Travel Requirements:** Passport, no visa for 3 months **International Dialing Code:** 45

---

Denmark, located strategically at the mouth of the Baltic Sea, consists of the Jutland Peninsula (projecting north from West Germany) and about 500 islands, of which 100 are inhabited. It is one of the smallest countries in the world if only its low-lying islands and the Jutland Peninsula are considered. However, the kingdom also embraces the Faeroe Islands and the island of Greenland, both of which now enjoy great autonomy.

Occupied during World War II by the Nazis, Denmark did not return in the postwar era to the policy of neutrality that it had followed through World War I. Instead it became a charter member of the North Atlantic Treaty Organization in 1949 and joined with the West Germans in forming a joint Baltic command within the alliance in 1961. But the Danes, like the Norwegians, have limited their NATO membership by declaring that neither foreign troops nor nuclear weapons may be stationed on their territory in peacetime.

Small-scale production of oil from wells on the Danish share of the North Sea continental shelf began in 1972, and surface mining of iron ore began in Greenland on a limited scale in 1973. But so far Denmark's natural resources remain largely limited to its rich farmland, and the nation relies heavily upon imports.

Through membership in the British-led European Free Trade Association (EFTA), Denmark and its neighbors—Norway, Sweden and Finland—created what amounted to a Nordic common market in 1960. Most of this was retained when Denmark, along with Britain and Ireland, opted out of EFTA to join the European Communities (European Community, European Coal and Steel Community and European Atomic Energy Community) on January 1, 1973.

The political process is firmly democratic. But no election since 1945 has given any party a majority in the *Folketing*. The Social Democratic party is the largest and usually leads the governing coalition, but decision-making is slow and marked by compromise. Efforts to reduce unemployment and to promote needed exports also require the help of unions and businesses, which are reluctant to help unstable coalitions and which resent the country's high taxes. A two-year austerity program, involving strict wage controls, took effect in 1977 after strikes thwarted it for eight months.

**HISTORY:** During the Viking age the Danes figured importantly in the Norse raids on Western Europe. Denmark became at once an Atlantic and a Baltic power and warred with the English, with German princes, and with Norwegian and Swedish kings. Denmark's period of expansion lasted until about 1600 and was followed by a losing struggle against Swedish and German rivals

**1643-60:** Wars with Sweden determine eastern borders

**1815:** Denmark, having sided with France in the Napoleonic Wars, is among the losers and is forced by Sweden to cede Norway

**1864:** War with Prussia and Austria ends with the loss of Schleswig-Holstein, a third of Denmark's territory, to Prussia

**1914-18:** Denmark remains neutral in World War I

**1920:** Denmark's present southern border is established as northern Schleswig is recovered in a plebiscite

**1940-45:** Nazi troops invade Denmark and occupy country until its liberation by British forces in May 1945

**1949:** Denmark joins in forming NATO

**1960:** Denmark joins European Free Trade Association

**1968:** Social Democrats, Denmark's largest party, are ousted in general elections after 15 years in office

**1972:** King Frederik IX dies; is succeeded on the throne by Queen Margrethe II, Denmark's first reigning queen in six centuries

**1973:** Denmark joins the EC

**1978:** Social Democratic Prime Minister Anker Joergensen forms minority coalition with Liberals and others

**1979:** Greenland is granted autonomy. Social Democrats increase plurality in parliament; Joergensen forms new coalition

**1981:** Joergensen alters his cabinet slightly after indecisive elections

**1982:** Joergensen resigns. Conservative Poul Schlüter becomes premier

---

## DJIBOUTI

**Area:** 8,880 sq. mi. **Population:** 250,000 (1978 est.)

**Official Name:** Republic of Djibouti **Capital:** Djibouti **Nationality:** Djibouti **Languages:** French is the official language; Somali (Issa) and Afar are spoken by their communities; Arabic **Religion:** 94% Moslem, 6% Christian **Flag:** Horizontal stripes of light blue over green, with a red star on a white triangle at the hoist **Anthem:** N.A. **Currency:** Djibouti franc (178 per U.S. $1)

**Location:** Northeastern Africa, around the Gulf of Tadjoura at the western end of the Gulf of Aden, near the southern entrance to the Red Sea. Bordered on the north, west and southwest by Ethiopia, and on the southeast by Somalia **Features:** An arid rocky coastal plain (with salt and freshwater pans) fringed by foothills of the Ethiopian ranges, and an interior plateau in the north and west **Chief Rivers:** None

**Head of State:** President Hassan Gouled Aptidon, born 1916, assumed office June 1977, reelected June 1981 **Head of Government:** Premier Barkat Gourad Hamadou, appointed September 1978 **Effective Date of Present Constitution:** A constitution was approved by the Assembly in 1981 **Legislative Body:** Parliament (unicameral Assembly), with 65 members (33 Issas, 30 Afars, 2 Arabs) elected for 5 years **Local Government:** 5 districts

**Ethnic Composition:** Somalis (chiefly Issas), Afars (including seasonal nomads), French, Arabs **Population Distribution:** c. 65% urban **Density:** 28 inhabitants per sq. mi.

**Largest City:** (1977 est.) Djibouti 130,000

**Per Capita Income:** $1,727 (1978 est.) **Gross National Product (GNP):** $190 million (1978 est.) **Economic Statistics:** Derivation from GNP not available. Nomadic herding (goats, cattle, sheep, camels, donkeys) is the chief occupation in the hinterland. In the capital, shipbuilding, repair and servicing, construction, and the production of liquid gas and foodstuffs (bottling) are the chief activities **Minerals and Mining:** No production other than salt panning **Labor Force:** N.A. **Foreign Trade:** Exports (transit from Ethiopia), chiefly hides and skins, sugar, and Ethiopian coffee, totaled $5 million in 1976. Imports, chiefly machinery, fuels, steel products, chemicals, foods, and grain, totaled $72 million **Principal Trade Partners:** France, Ethiopia, Japan

**Vital Statistics:** Birthrate, 42 per 1,000 of pop. (1970); death rate, 7.6 **Life Expectancy:** N.A. **Health Statistics:** 107 inhabitants per hospital bed; 1,964 per physician (1976) **Infant Mortality:** N.A. **Illiteracy:** 95% **Primary and Secondary School Enrollment:** 11,758 (1975) **Enrollment in Higher Education:** N.A. **GNP Expended on Education:** 4.9% (1971)

**Transportation:** Surfaced roads total 162 mi. **Motor Vehicles:** 15,100 (1977) **Passenger Cars:** 11,800 **Railway Mileage:** 60 **Port:** Djibouti **Major Airlines:** Air Djibouti, which also flies to Ethiopia, Yemen, Southern Yemen and Somalia, provides domestic service **Communications: Radio Transmitters:** 3 (1976) **Receivers:** 15,000 (1976) **Television Transmitters:** 1 **Receivers:** 3,500 (1976) **Telephones:** 4,000 (1978) **Newspapers:** 1 weekly, 34 copies per 1,000 inhabitants (1975)

**Weights and Measures:** Metric system **Travel Requirements:** Passport, visa; contact French Embassy or Consulate for requirements

---

On June 27, 1977, the last remnant of France's once-vast empire on the African continent achieved independence as the Republic of Djibouti.

During its first 83 years of existence, the dependency was known as French Somaliland, but in 1967 this small coastal area was renamed the French Territory of Afars and Issas, in recognition of the two major ethnic groups comprising the population. The Republic of Djibouti takes its name from its capital city, a Red Sea port with a majority of the nation's population.

Economic prospects for the Republic of Djibouti are not auspicious, as the barren tract, smaller in area than New Hampshire, lacks resources. The sole economic reason for the existence of the Republic is the commercial activity at the port of Djibouti, which is the terminus of the 486-mile railway from Addis Ababa, Ethiopia. The line carries half of Ethiopia's exports along its single track, and Djibouti is the transshipment point to the outer world for this trade. Out beyond the urban environment of the capital, the meager population subsists through nomadic herding.

The indigenous population is divided between the Afars, or Danakils, and the Issas, a branch of the Somali ethnic family. Though the two groups had disagreed in the past about the timing of independence, a majority of voters approved an independence proposal on May 8, 1977. France, by agreement, continues to maintain a military force in Djibouti.

In March 1978, Ethiopian forces, aided by 1,000 Soviet advisors, and 11,000 Cuban troops, ended the eight-month Ogaden war by driving the Somalis from the region. Although Kenya and Ethiopia in late 1980 urged Somalia to renounce its territorial claims to parts of Djibouti and of their own countries, the Somalian government has refused. Meanwhile, thousands of Somali refugees have flooded Djibouti, straining the economy. A two-year drought ended on March 18, 1981, when more rain fell than in all of 1980 and left some 100,000 people homeless.

**HISTORY:** French interest in the area began in the 1840s, culminating in the signing of friendship treaties with the local sultans. The purchase of the anchorage at Obock signaled the beginning of French occupation. The opening of the Suez Canal in 1869 and growing Anglo-French competition for territorial spoils in Africa caused France to expand its toehold to include all of the shores of the Gulf of Tadjoura

**1884-85:** The protectorate of French Somaliland is established

**1896:** The administrative capital is moved from Obock to Djibouti

**1897-1917:** The Franco-Ethiopian railway is built from Djibouti to Addis Ababa

**1958:** French Somaliland becomes an Overseas Territory of the French community

**1967:** In a referendum on independence, 60 percent of the voters choose to continue the ties with France. The area is renamed the French Territory of Afars and Issas

**1977:** Following a majority vote for independence, the independent Republic of Djibouti is proclaimed. Premier Ahmed Dini resigns after renewal of tensions between Afars and Issas

**1978:** Abdallay Mohamed Kamil appointed premier in February. In September, he is followed in office by Barkat Gourad Hamadou

---

## DOMINICA

**Area:** 291 sq. mi. **Population:** 74,089 (1980 census)

**Official Name:** Commonwealth of Dominica **Capital:** Roseau **Nationality:** Dominican **Languages:** English is the official language and is everywhere understood, but a patois, based on French and containing many African elements, is widely spoken **Religion:** Mainly Roman Catholic; some Anglicans and Methodists **Flag:** A dark green field quartered by three equal vertical and horizontal stripes of yellow, white and black. In the center a large red disk bears a parrot surrounded by a circle of ten five-pointed stars **Anthem:** Isle of Beauty, Isle of Splendour **Currency:** Dominican dollar (2.7 per U.S. $1)

**Location:** The island, located in the Windward Islands of the West Indies, lies between the French islands of Guadeloupe to the north and Martinique to the south. It is 20 miles long and 16 miles wide with a thickly forested mountainous terrain

**Head of State:** President Aurelius Marie, born 1903, appointed 1980 **Head of Government:** Prime Minister: Mary Eugenia Charles, born 1919, appointed July 1980 **Effective Date of Present Constitution:** November 3, 1978 **Legislative Body:** House of Assembly (unicameral) with 21 elected representatives and 9 appointed senators **Local Government:** 2 town councils and 25 village councils

**Ethnic Composition:** Nearly all of the population is of African or mixed African-European origin. There is a small Carib Indian community **Density:** 255 inhabitants per sq. mi.

**Largest Cities:** (1976 est.) Roseau 16,800, Portsmouth 3,500

**Per Capita Income:** $430 (1979) **Gross National Product (GNP):** $34 million (1979) **Economic Statistics:** The economy is primarily agricultural, with bananas dominant. Citrus fruit and coconut production are also important. Industry and tourism are to be developed **Minerals and Mining:** None **Labor Force:** 22,000 (1977), with 40% in agriculture **Foreign Trade:** Exports, chiefly bananas, grapefruit, lime juice, essential oils and coconuts, totaled $8 million in 1979. Imports, chiefly foods, machinery and consumer goods, totaled $24 million **Principal Trade Partners:** Britain, United States, Canada, Caribbean nations

**Vital Statistics:** Birthrate, 21.4 per 1,000 of pop. (1978); death rate, 5.3 **Life Expectancy:** N.A. **Health Statistics:** 234 inhabitants per hospital bed (1973): 5,385 per physician (1973) **Infant Mortality:** 19.6 per 1,000 births **Illiteracy:** 5% **Primary and Secondary School Enrollment:** 24,106 (1976) **Enrollment in Higher Education:** N.A. **GNP Expended on Education:** N.A.

**Transportation:** Surfaced (paved) roads total 300 mi. **Motor Vehicles:** 4,000 (1975) **Passenger Cars:** N.A. **Railway Mileage:** None **Port:** Roseau **Major Airlines:** LIAT, Air Martinique and Air Guadeloupe provide service to neighboring islands **Communications: Radio Transmitters:** 2 **Receivers:** N.A. **Television Transmitters:** 1 **Receivers:** N.A. **Telephones:** 4,000 (1978) **Newspapers:** 2 weeklies

**Weights and Measures:** British and metric systems **Travel Requirements:** Passport and visa not required of tourist with onward/return ticket and citizenship identification **Direct Dialing Code:** 809

---

The northernmost of the Windward Islands, Dominica has a pleasant climate and a great natural beauty that make it a haven for the sightseer, but its sparse, rocky soil makes life difficult for its predominantly black population, one of the poorest in the Caribbean.

One of the country's most urgent priorities since gaining independence in 1978 is the balanced development of the island's economy. Unemployment is chronic, over 20 percent, and agriculture is the mainstay of most islanders, with one crop—bananas—representing almost 80 percent of exports. Yet barely one third of the arable land is cultivated, mainly because of the mountainous and heavily wooded terrain. Foreign aid has become increasingly important, with Britain being Dominica's chief benefactor since independence.

Since achieving nationhood, Dominica has tottered on the brink of civil turmoil, with islanders divided betweeen two political factions; the social-democratic Dominica Labor party (DLP), which had pressed for independence by termination of the association with the United Kingdom, and the more conservative Dominica Freedom party (DFP), which had opposed independence except by referendum.

On May 29, 1979, amid charges of governmental corruption, police fired on a crowd of 15,000 demonstrators in Roseau, sparking a general strike and the resignation of DLP Prime Minister Patrick R. John. In July 1980 elections, the DFP won a landslide victory and its leader, Mary Eugenia Charles, became the first woman prime minister of a Caribbean nation. Charles launched an economic program that included business incentives but achieved negligible results. With unemployment above 30 percent in 1982, she became one of the area's strongest supporters of a projected U.S.-sponsored Caribbean development plan.

In March 1981, an anti-government plot involving high-ranking military officers was aborted. And, in a bizarre incident a month later, 10 American and Canadian mercenaries were arrested by U.S. authorities near New Orleans as they were about to set sail for Dominica to spearhead another coup attempt, financed by American right-wing extremist groups. Reports of conspiracies against the regime brought repeated impositions of a state of emergency throughout the year. In 1982, former Prime Minister John was put on trial for alleged misdeeds while in office.

**HISTORY:** The warlike Carib Indians are thought to have migrated north from South America to the West Indies in the 1300s, capturing the islands from the more peaceful Arawaks. Columbus first sighted the island on a Sunday in 1493 (by tradition) and named it Dominica after the Latin for that day of the week. Permanent European occupation did not occur until the mid-eighteenth century, when the French established settlements along the coast. Since that time the island has changed hands three times: captured by the British in 1759, retaken by the French in 1778, and restored to Britain by the Treaty of Paris in 1783. With the abolition of the slave trade in 1834, restricted local government developed under British colonial administration

**1871:** Dominica and other British islands to the north are formed into a federation of the Leeward Islands

**1940:** Dominica transferred to jurisdiction of Windward Islands group, under same government as Grenada, St. Vincent and St. Lucia

**1958:** Dominica joins Federation of the West Indies; remains member until its dissolution in 1962

**1960:** Windward Islands Group dissolved; direct rule by Britain reestablished

**1967:** Dominica becomes self-governing member of the West Indies Associated States within British Commonwealth

**1970:** DLP led by Premier Edward O. LeBlanc wins first general election under Associated status

**1974:** Legislature approves emergency powers to combat "Dread" Black Power terrorist movement; Dominica joins Caribbean Community and Common Market (CARICOM)

**1975:** DLP under Patrick R. John, who succeeds LeBlanc, retains power in March 24 elections against opposition DFP

**1978:** Dominica becomes fully independent November 3

**1979:** Antigovernment demonstrations in Roseau May 29 fired on by police, sparking general strike that forces Prime Minister John to resign. Hurricane David makes 65,000 homeless

**1980:** DFP wins landslide election victory. Its leader, Mary Eugenia Charles, becomes prime minister

**1981:** Three coup attempts fail; rightist mercenaries who planned to lead a revolt in Dominica arrested in U.S.

**1982:** Economy worsens. Charles supports U.S. aid plan

## DOMINICAN REPUBLIC

**Area:** 18,816 sq. mi. **Population:** 5,647,977 (1981 census)

**Official Name:** Dominican Republic **Capital:** Santo Domingo **Nationality:** Dominican **Languages:** Spanish is the official and universal language **Religion:** About 95% of the people are Roman Catholic, the state religion **Flag:** Four rectangular sections divided by a white cross bearing the national coat of arms in the center; the upper left and lower right sections are dark blue and the other two sections are red **Anthem:** National Anthem, beginning "Brave men of Quisqueya" **Currency:** Dominican peso (1 per U.S. $1)

**Location:** West Indies, occupying the eastern two-thirds of the Island of Hispaniola. The Dominican Republic is bounded on the north by the Atlantic Ocean; on the east by the Mona Passage, which separates the country from Puerto Rico; on the south by the Caribbean Sea; and on the west by Haiti **Features:** The country is crossed by four east-west mountain ranges, the principal one being the Cordillera Central, which runs across the middle of the country. In the upper central part of the country lies the Cibao valley, often known as the nation's "food basket" **Chief Rivers:** Yaque del Norte, Jaina, Ozama, Yaque del Sur

**Head of State and of Government:** President Salvador Jorge Blanco, born 1926, took office Aug. 16, 1982 **Effective Date of Present Constitution:** November 28, 1966 **Legislative Body:** National Congress (bicameral), consisting of a 27-member Senate and a 91-member Chamber of Deputies, with members of both houses elected every 4 years by popular vote **Local Government:** 26 provinces and 1 national district, each headed by a governor appointed by the president

**Ethnic Composition:** 73% mulatto, 16% of European (chiefly Spanish) origin, 11% Negro **Population Distribution:** 50% urban **Density:** 300 inhabitants per sq. mi.

**Largest Cities:** (1970 census—Metropolitan Areas) Santo Domingo 802,619, Santiago 173,975, San Cristóbal 69,875, La Vega 64,370

**Per Capita Income:** $1,066 (1980) **Gross National Product (GNP):** $6.1 billion (1980) **Economic Statistics:** In 1977 about 21% of GNP came from agriculture (sugar, coffee, cocoa, rice, cotton, tobacco, bananas); 35% from trade and services; 19% from manufacturing (sugar refining, processing of other food products, beverages, tobacco, chemicals) **Minerals and Mining:** Bauxite, nickel, gold, silver and some iron ore are exploited. Oil has been discovered **Labor Force:** 1.5 million (1979), with 55% in agriculture **Foreign Trade:** Exports, chiefly sugar, coffee, chocolate, tobacco, bauxite, gold, silver and nickel, totaled $963 million in 1980. Imports, mainly wheat, petroleum, automobiles, tractors, and pharmaceutical products, totaled $1.4 billion **Principal Trade Partners:** United States, Netherlands, West Germany, Venezuela, Japan, Morocco, Spain, Switzerland

**Vital Statistics:** Birthrate, 36.7 per 1,000 of pop. (1980); death rate, 9.1 **Life Expectancy:** 61 years **Health Statistics:** 351 inhabitants per hospital bed; 1,866 per physician (1973) **Infant Mortality:** 37.2 per 1,000 births **Illiteracy:** 33% **Primary and Secondary School Enrollment:** 984,039 (1973) **Enrollment in Higher Education:** 41,352 (1974) **GNP Expended on Education:** 2.6% (1973)

**Transportation:** Paved roads total 3,500 mi. **Motor Vehicles:** 136,800 (1978) **Passenger Cars:** 90,600 **Railway Mileage:** 1,000 **Ports:** Santo Domingo, Haina, Barahona, Puerto Plata, La Romana, San Pedro de Macorís **Major Airlines:** Dominicana, the national airline, provides internal and international services **Communications: Radio Transmitters:** 134 **Receivers:** 200,000 (1976) **Television Transmitters:** 7 **Receivers:** 160,000 (1976) **Telephones:** 160,000 (1979) **Newspapers:** 10 dailies, 42 copies per 1,000 inhabitants (1975)

**Weights and Measures:** Metric system **Travel Requirements:** Passport, visa, tourist card valid for 60 days, $5.00 fee **Direct Dialing Code:** 809

With the possible exception of Cuba, the Dominican Republic has been the most disrupted Latin American country of this century. Its proximity—physically, historically, and economically—to the United States has produced two armed interventions ordered by Washington since 1916. In the years between 1930 and 1961, the country, which occupies the eastern two-thirds of the island of Hispaniola, lived under the oppression of Generalissimo Rafael Leonidas Trujillo Molina.

Since 1966 the Dominican Republic has enjoyed a measure of stability, thanks to improved economic planning and agrarian reform. With massive assistance from the United States and from international lending agencies, the country continues to be one of the most dynamic and stable nations in Latin America.

In May 1978, after 12 years in office, President Joaquín Balaguer was defeated in his bid for a fourth straight four-year term by Antonio Guzmán of the opposition Dominican Revolutionary party (a centrist movement despite its misleadingly radical name). Balaguer's generals attempted to halt the ballot count, but were defeated by pressure from U.S. and other American nations' leaders.

In his first state-of-the-nation speech, made in 1979, President Guzmán announced that agricultural development would be stressed in an effort to overcome a stagnant economy. And in its first venture into the Eurodollar market, the Dominican Republic signed a $185-million loan agreement with a group of international bankers. However, the economy worsened. Sugar production declined as a result of hurricanes, heavy rain, cane rust and labor problems. Taxes and the prices of electricity and gasoline were raised. Guzmán's own party turned against him and nominated Jorge Blanco, a 55-year-old liberal running on a platform of social progress and fiscal austerity, to be its candidate for president in 1982. Blanco was elected by a substantial majority.

**HISTORY:** The eastern part of the island of Hispaniola was known in pre-Columbian times as Quisqueya and was first settled by Carib and Arawak Indians. The island was discovered by Columbus in 1492 and soon became the springboard for Spanish conquest of the Caribbean. The western third of Hispaniola (Haiti) was ceded to France in 1697, and in 1795 France acquired the eastern part, known as Santo Domingo. The French were expelled from the eastern region in 1809 and in 1814 it reverted to Spain

**1821:** Dominicans proclaim their independence and attempt to unite with the Republic of Gran Colombia, founded by Bolívar

**1822:** Dominicans are conquered by Haiti and the whole island of Hispaniola falls under oppressive Haitian rule

**1844:** Dominicans revolt against Haiti and regain independence; a republic is established under Pedro Santana

**1861-69:** Widespread revolts and continued attacks from Haiti lead Santana to place country under Spanish rule, but popular opposition forces Spain to withdraw (1865). Opposition leader Buenaventura Báez, who succeeds Santana, negotiates treaty calling for annexation of country to the United States; U.S. Senate, however, refuses to ratify it

**1905-24:** United States takes over administration of Dominican customs to forestall intervention by foreign powers seeking to collect their debts; following mounting disorders, the republic is brought under U.S. military rule from 1916 until 1924

**1930-61:** Republic is ruled by dictator Rafael Leonidas Trujillo Molina, who is assassinated in 1961

**1962-63:** Juan Bosch, a leader of the democratic left, is elected president in republic's first free elections since 1924; after only seven months in office Bosch is overthrown by the military

**1965:** Civilian triumvirate installed by leaders of the 1963 coup is overthrown, precipitating civil war between left-wing forces seeking to restore Bosch and right-wing and military elements; U.S. troops intervene against pro-Bosch forces but fail to halt civil war, which ends after mediation by the OAS

**1966:** Joaquín Balaguer defeats Bosch for the presidency

**1970:** Balaguer is reelected president in a disputed election

**1974-75:** Balaguer is reelected to third consecutive term. Antigovernment violence and political uncertainty plague the country

**1976:** King Juan Carlos and Queen Sofía of Spain visit, the first ruling Spanish monarchs ever to set foot in Latin America

**1978:** Antonio Guzmán is elected president

**1979:** Two hurricanes leave 1,300 dead, 500 missing and 100,000 homeless. Rosario Dominica gold mines are nationalized

**1980:** Diplomats are held hostage for two months in Dominican embassy in Bogotá, Colombia. Gulf and Western Industries agrees to undertake economic aid and social development of republic's sugarcane region in settlement of dispute with Santo Domingo government

**1982:** Jorge Blanco, candidate of the Dominican Revolutionary party, wins May 16 election for president; but before he takes office, President Guzmán dies of a self-inflicted bullet wound and is succeeded in the interim by Vice President Jacobo Majluta Azar

## ECUADOR

**Area:** 109,483 sq. mi. **Population:** 8,644,000 (1981 est.)

**Official Name:** Republic of Ecuador **Capital:** Quito **Nationality:** Ecuadorean **Languages:** Spanish, the official language, is spoken by about 93% of the population, and Quechua by 7% **Religion:** Overwhelmingly Roman Catholic **Flag:** Half the width of the flag is yellow and the remaining half consists of blue and red bands; in the center is the national coat of arms **Anthem:** Hail, O Fatherland **Currency:** Sucre (33 per U.S. $1)

**Location:** South America. Crossed by the Equator, from which the country gets its name, Ecuador is bordered on the north by Colombia, on the east and south by Peru, and on the west by the Pacific Ocean. The Galápagos Islands, some 600 miles west of the mainland, are part of the national territory **Features:** About a fourth of the country consists of a coastal plain, and another fourth of the Sierra, or highlands, lying between two chains of the Andes Mountains. The Oriente, or eastern jungle, covers the remaining half of the country **Chief Rivers:** Guayas, Esmeraldas

**Head of State and of Government:** President Osvaldo Hurtado Larrea, born 1939, assumed office on death of President Roldós on May 24, 1981 **Effective Date of Present Constitution:** August 10, 1979 **Legislative Body:** Congress (unicameral) with 12 national and 57 provincial deputies **Local Government:** 20 provinces, each headed by an appointed governor

**Ethnic Composition:** 55% mestizo (mixed Indian and Spanish), 25% Indian, 10% European (chiefly Spanish), 10% African **Population Distribution:** 43% urban **Density:** 79 inhabitants per sq. mi.

**Largest Cities:** (1978 est.) Guayaquil 1,022,010, Quito 742,858, Cuenca 128,788, (1974 census) Ambato 77,052, Machala 68,379

**Per Capita Income:** $1,052 (1980) **Gross National Product (GNP):** $8.4 billion (1980) **Economic Statistics:** In 1980 about 17% of GNP was derived from agriculture (bananas, coffee, cocoa, rice, sugar, cotton, grains, fruits and vegetables), forestry, and fishing; 17% from manufacturing (textiles, food processing, cement); and 16.6% from petroleum **Minerals and Mining:** Petroleum is the primary mineral product. There are large deposits of calcium carbonate and copper; small quantities of gold are mined **Labor Force:** 2,600,000, of which 52% is employed in agriculture **Foreign Trade:** Exports, chiefly bananas, petroleum, coffee, cocoa, sugar and fish products, totaled $2.8 billion in 1981. Imports, mainly machinery, transportation equipment, chemicals, and paper products, totaled $1.9 billion **Principal Trade Partners:** United States, West Germany, Japan, Panama, Italy, Colombia, Chile

**Vital Statistics:** Birthrate, 41.6 per 1,000 of pop. (1980); death rate, 10.4 **Life Expectancy:** 62 years **Health Statistics:** 495 inhabitants per hospital bed; 1,622 per physician (1977) **Infant Mortality:** 70.9 per 1,000 births **Illiteracy:** 16% **Primary and Secondary School Enrollment:** 1,709,717 (1976) **Enrollment in Higher Education:** 170,173 **GNP Expended on Education:** 3.3% (1971)

**Transportation:** Paved roads total 2,050 mi. **Motor Vehicles:** 128,500 (1975) **Passenger Cars:** 51,300 **Railway Mileage:** 697 **Ports:** Guayaquil, Puerto Bolívar, Manta, Bahía de Caráquez, Salinas, Esmeraldas **Major Airlines:** Ecuatoriana de Aviación operates internal and international flights **Communications: Radio Transmitters:** 193 **Receivers:** 1,700,000 (1970) **Television Transmitters:** 17 **Receivers:** 300,000 (1976) **Telephones:** 240,000 (1978) **Newspapers:** 37 dailies, 46 copies per 1,000 inhabitants (1977)

**Weights and Measures:** Metric system **Travel Requirements:** Passport, migratory control card, valid for 90 days, no fee **International Dialing Code:** 593

Despite incredibly rich mineral and agricultural resources, Ecuador remains one of the least developed countries in South America—the result of sharp racial, geographic, and political differences.

One quarter of Ecuador's population is Indian—people held in low esteem by those of mixed blood, African heritage, and the small ruling élite of European background. Although many of the Indians retain their languages and customs, they have been stripped of the rest of their culture by four centuries of European domination.

Aside from the Indians in the Andean highlands and the Amazonian tribes in the east, most of the rest of Ecuador's people live along the western littoral that borders the Pacific Ocean. Mainly of mixed African/Indian/European background, the coastal people have a tropical culture that differs markedly from the highlanders.

In a further division, Ecuador is dominated by the mutual dislike of two "city-states"—Quito, the capital, and Guayaquil, the industrial port.

Some 9,300 feet above sea level in the Andes, long considered the most beautiful city in South America and certainly the cleanest, Quito is a conservative, gracious administrative center. Its residents look with distaste on the boisterous, tropical people of Guayaquil, who, for their part, resent their tax payments to the capital. Despite their industry and commercial aggressiveness, they say, the appalling slums of their city reflect the indifference of Quito.

Since petroleum exports started in 1972, there has been a spurt in overall economic development.

The oil, which is pumped out of the Amazon jungles by Texaco and by the government oil company, CEPE, is Ecuador's No. 1 export. Intensive exploration in 1980 raised reserves to over three billion barrels. The country is now accustomed to trade and balance-of-payment surpluses, and its inflation rate—running at 20% in 1982—is moderate by South American standards.

In 1978 and 1979 the country held its first free national elections since the military seized power in 1972. First, in a referendum on Jan. 15, 1978, the voters chose a new constitution over a revision of the 1945 constitution. Then, on July 16, Jaime Roldós Aguilera, a law professor and a member of the Concentration of Popular Forces (CFP), led the first-round balloting for president. The military, wary because Roldós was a protégé of populist leader Assad Bucaram, delayed the final election for six months, but Roldós won handily in a two-party contest on April 29, 1979. A struggle developed between Roldós and his former chief, Bucaram, the CFP leader in congress. However, Roldós had popular support, and his candidate, Raúl Baca Carbo, was elected leader of congress in August 1980.

President Roldós, his wife and three military leaders were killed in an airplane crash May 24, 1981. Vice President Osvaldo Hurtado Larrea assumed the presidency.

**HISTORY:** Ecuador was ruled by the Incas until their empire fell to the Spanish conquistadors in 1533. Spanish rule, which lasted until the early 19th century, was marked by ruthless exploitation of the native Indians and bloody rivalry among the Spaniards

**1822:** Ecuador is freed from Spanish rule after Spanish forces are defeated at Battle of Pichincha; country becomes part of Greater Colombia, a confederation consisting of the present territories of Ecuador, Colombia, Panama, and Venezuela, constituted under the leadership of Simón Bolívar

**1830-45:** Federation is dissolved in 1830; Republic of Ecuador is proclaimed, with Juan José Flores as first president; his conservative dictatorial rule arouses liberal opposition

**1861-75:** Gabriel García Morena rules as virtual dictator; he consolidates country after years of domestic strife and carries out major economic and social reforms, but his strong conservatism results in bitter strife that culminates in his assassination

**1895-1912:** Liberals dominate Ecuador's politics; separation of church and state is clearly defined, and basic personal freedoms are established

**1913-44:** Liberals continue to dominate political scene, but rival factions, supported by military juntas, bring about rapid changes in government

**1948-52:** Galo Plazo Lasso becomes president; his regime is marked by unprecedented political freedom

**1961:** President José María Velasco Ibarra is forced into exile; Vice-President Julio Arosemena Monroy succeeds as president

**1963:** Arosemena is ousted in military coup; a four-man military junta, headed by R. Adm. Ramon Castro Jijon, takes over. Junta dissolves Congress, decrees martial law, suspends the constitution, and bans Communist party

**1968-69:** In the first election held in seven years, Velasco Ibarra is elected president for fifth time as Ecuador experiences widespread economic and social unrest. Within eight months after taking offfice, president loses support of Liberal party

**1970:** President Velasco assumes dictatorial powers

**1971:** U.S. imposes financial sanctions on Ecuador following seizure of U.S. tuna boats

**1972:** Brig. Gen. Guillermo Rodriguez Lara replaces Velasco Ibarra in bloodless military coup. Lara declares a "nationalist, military, and revolutionary government"

**1975:** Seizure of American fishing boats continues. Gen. Raúl González Alvear leads unsuccessful revolt against Lara

**1976:** President Lara is overthrown in a bloodless coup led by armed forces commanders, who form a military junta

**1977:** Ecuadorean government buys the local assets of Gulf Oil Corp. of the U.S., giving the government a 62.5 percent share in Ecuador's petroleum operations

**1979:** Jaime Roldós Aguilera, popular young advocate of civil rights, wins pressidency under new constitution

**1981:** Ecuador fails in attempt to establish a military base in region of Peru it claims. President Roldós dies in airplane crash; Vice President Osvaldo Hurtado Larrea assumes his office. Declining prices of oil and coffee damage economy

## EGYPT

**Area:** 386,659 sq. mi. **Population:** 42,930,000 (1981 est.)

**Official Name:** Arab Republic of Egypt **Capital:** Cairo **Nationality:** Egyptian **Languages:** Arabic is the official and national language **Religion:** About 90% of the population is Sunni Moslem and Islam is the state religion; about 7% belongs to the Coptic Church (perhaps as high as 18%) **Flag:** Red, white, and black horizontal stripes with a golden hawk and Arabic inscription on the white stripe **Anthem:** National Anthem, beginning "The Time Has Come to Reach for Our Arms" **Currency:** Egyptian pound (0.70 per U.S. $1)

**Location:** Northeast Africa. Egypt is bordered on the north by the Mediterranean Sea; on the east by Israel and the Red Sea; on the south by the Sudan; and on the west by Libya **Features:** About 95% of the country is desert, with only the Nile Valley and delta, and a few oases, under cultivation **Chief River:** Nile

**Head of State:** President Mohammed Hosni Mubarak, born 1928, sworn in Oct. 14, 1981 **Head of Government:** Dr. Ahmad Fuad Mohieddin, appointed Jan. 2, 1982 **Effective Date of Present Constitution:** 1971 **Legislative Body:** People's Assembly (unicameral), consisting of 392 members **Local Government:** 26 governorates headed by governors appointed by the president

**Ethnic Composition:** The homogeneous population is mainly Hamitic **Population Distribution:** 44% urban **Density:** 111 inhabitants per sq. mi.; inhabitable areas 3,000

**Largest Cities:** (1976 census) Cairo 5,084,463, Alexandria 2,318,655, Giza 1,246,713, El Mahalla el Kubra 292,853

**Per Capita Income:** $573 (1980) **Gross National Product (GNP):** $24 billion (1980) **Economic Statistics:** 30% of GNP comes from agriculture (cotton, wheat, corn, rice); 22% from industry (food processing, textiles, petroleum and petroleum products, iron and steel manufactures, chemicals) and mining; 25% from services; 19% from trade and finance **Minerals and Mining:** Petroleum is the chief mineral resource; others are phosphate, iron ore, tin, uranium, manganese, and limestone **Labor Force:** 13,400,000, of which 44% is in agriculture, and 13% in industry **Foreign Trade:** Exports, chiefly cotton and cotton goods, rice, crude oil, and oil products, totaled $3.9 billion in 1980. Imports, mainly wheat, petroleum, industrial machinery, vehicle parts, and edible oils, totaled $7.6 billion **Principal Trade Partners:** EC countries, United States, Japan, USSR

**Vital Statistics:** Birthrate, 41 per 1,000 of pop. (1979); death rate, 11 **Life Expectancy:** 54 years **Health Statistics:** 479 inhabitants per hospital bed (1976); 1,516 per physician (1973) **Infant Mortality:** 73.5 per 1,000 births **Illiteracy:** 56% **Primary and Secondary School Enrollment:** 6,228,827 (1975) **Enrollment in Higher Education:** 455,097 **GNP Expended on Education:** 5.4% (1976)

**Transportation:** Paved roads total 7,640 mi. **Motor Vehicles:** 415,000 (1978) **Passenger Cars:** 330,100 **Railway Mileage:** 3,000 **Ports:** Alexandria, Port Said, Suez, Mersa Matruh, Safaga **Major Airlines:** Egypt Air operates internal and international services **Communications: Radio Transmitters:** 25 (1976) **Receivers:** 5,250,000 (1976) **Television Transmitters:** 28 (1977) **Receivers:** 1,300,000 (1977) **Telephones:** 473,000 (1977) **Newspapers:** 10 dailies, 79 copies per 1,000 inhabitants (1976)

**Weights and Measures:** Metric system is official but various local units are also used **Travel Requirements:** Passport, visa good for stay up to 1 month, $2.80 contribution to Abu Simbel fund

For Egypt, recent years have brought one pressing challenge after another: relentless economic problems, fateful decisions on war or peace with Israel, friendship with the United States at the expense of Soviet-Egyptian amity, and conspiracies against President Anwar el-Sadat that resulted in his assassination in 1981.

Added to these challenges are the realities of Egypt's difficulties as the most populous country in the Arab world and the second most populous on the African continent, with 99 percent of its people compressed into 3.5 percent of its area. Egypt's economic problems are extensive and resistant to ready solutions. There are few natural resources, limited cultivable land and investment funds; in addition, bureaucracies are swollen with unproductive workers. Unemployment and inflation are rising, and illiteracy is 56%.

President Sadat, a leading figure in the 1952 revolution led by Gamal Abdel Nasser, succeeded him in 1970 and emerged as an unexpectedly strong leader. He won support by curbing arbitrary police procedures, calling for a society based on "the sovereignty of law," and outlining a program for accelerated economic development.

Sadat's principal accomplishment was the 1979 peace treaty with Israel which provided for its withdrawal from Sinai within three years; in April 1982, Israel completed the return to Egypt of the Sinai territory, including oil fields and Mt. Sinai itself. The treaty binds Egypt to sell oil to Israel, and this and other trade, along with increased U.S. aid and reduced military needs, have helped Egypt economically. Although other Arab nations have tried to isolate Egypt, Sadat got overwhelming domestic support for the treaty. The negotiations had begun in 1977 when Sadat visited Israel and Israeli Prime Minister Menachem Begin returned the visit. After this dramatic opening, Palestinian terrorist acts against Israel and disagreement on the future of Palestinian territory slowed the negotiations, but U.S. President Jimmy Carter played a crucial role in helping to conclude the treaty.

The murder of President Sadat by fanatic Muslim fundamentalists on Oct. 6, 1981, while he was watching a military parade in Cairo, stunned Egyptians and shocked the world. Hosni Mubarak, vice president and Sadat's closest adviser, immediately succeeded him as president. He pledged to continue Sadat's policies and to carry out the terms of the peace treaty with Israel. On Oct. 10, the slain leader's funeral drew the largest assemblage of world leaders to Cairo since Nasser's death. They included Begin of Israel and three former U.S. presidents—Nixon, Ford, and Carter—all of whom had encouraged President Sadat to make peace with Israel.

In the aftermath of the tragedy, the Egyptian government arrested 230 members of a "terrorist religious group" (24 were later tried and five were executed). In February 1982, Mubarak met with President Reagan in Washington, D.C., and promised to seek a just solution to the "Palestinian problem." He also called on other Arab states to join the Israeli-Egyptian search for peace.

**HISTORY:** The history of Egypt dates back about 5,000 years. The country was united into a single kingdom about 3200 B.C. and was ruled by a succession of dynasties down to the time of Alexander the Great, who conquered Egypt in 332 B.C. Less than three centuries later, the country was under Roman rule. In 616, Egypt was conquered by the Persians before being invaded by the Arabs, who introduced Islam

**1517:** Egypt becomes part of the Ottoman Empire

**1798:** Napoleon conquers Egypt

**1801-5:** British and Turkish troops drive out the French; Mohammed Ali, an Albanian soldier, is appointed Egyptian pasha

**1869:** The Suez Canal is completed

**1914:** Egypt becomes a British protectorate

**1936:** Britain agrees to withdraw eventually from all of Egypt, except the Suez Canal Zone

**1940-42:** British forces use Egypt as a base to fight Italy and Germany in World War II

**1948-49:** Egypt plays major role in war between Arab states and the newly established state of Israel, but suffers humiliating defeats; war ends with an armistice

**1952:** King Farouk is deposed in army coup

**1953-54:** A republic is proclaimed, with Gen. Mohammed Naguib as president; Naguib is forced out of office and replaced by Col. Gamal Abdel Nasser

**1956:** Nasser nationalizes Suez Canal. Israel, barred from the canal, invades the Gaza Strip and the Sinai peninsula; England and France attack Egypt. Forces of all three invading countries are forced to withdraw under pressure from the United States, the USSR and the United Nations

**1958:** Egypt and Syria form the United Arab Republic (U.A.R.)

**1961:** Syrian army revolts and proclaims Syria's withdrawal from U.A.R.

**1962:** Egypt sends troops to Yemen to aid a republican revolution

**1967:** In the Six-Day War with Israel, Egypt loses the entire Sinai peninsula and the Gaza Strip, which are occupied by Israeli armies; Egypt withdraws its troops from Yemen

**1968:** Widespread student riots break out in protest against Nasser regime, which is accused of police-state rule. Egyptian and Israeli troops engage in repeated artillery duels along Suez Canal

**1970:** Egypt agrees to U.S.-sponsored truce with Israel as step toward peace talks; talks are stalled after Israel charges truce is being violated by the installation of Soviet-built missiles in the Suez Canal zone. Nasser dies of heart attack and is succeeded by Vice-President Anwar el-Sadat

**1971:** Sadat allows cease-fire with Israel to lapse but defers warfare. Conspiracy against Sadat erupts; six cabinet members, Vice-President Aly Sabry, and dozens of others are arrested. New constitution approved by national referendum

**1972:** Dr. Aziz Sidky replaces Dr. Mahmoud Fawzi as premier. President Sadat orders the departure of all Soviet military advisors (about 10,000)

**1973:** Sadat forces Sidky to resign, assumes premiership; Egypt launches attack across the Suez Canal, beginning fourth Arab-Israeli War. The Arabs attack on Yom Kippur, the holiest day of the year for Jews. It takes several days for the Israelis to mobilize, but they soon outmaneuver the Arab armies. Iraq, Tunisia, Morocco, and other Arab countries send troops to aid Egypt and Syria. Egypt and Israel negotiate ceasefire

**1974:** President Sadat changes the date of Egypt's national holiday from July 23 to October 6 to commemorate the onset of the Yom Kippur War; Sadat relinquishes the office of premier and appoints Abdul Aziz Hegazy in his place

**1975:** Premier Hegazy resigns and is replaced by Mamdouh Salem. The Suez Canal, closed since 1967, reopens. With the assistance of U.S. Secretary of State Kissinger, Egypt and Israel agree on removal of troops in the Sinai Peninsula

**1976:** Egyptian parliament approves of President Sadat's proposal to end 15-year Treaty of Friendship and Cooperation with the USSR. Sadat is elected to a second six-year term

**1977:** Egyptian and Libyan forces clash along desert border. President Sadat launches peace initiative; he and Israeli Premier Begin trade historic visits

**1978:** Peace talks bog down as Israeli troops enter southern Lebanon following Palestinian terror raid in Israel. Diplomatic relations with Cyprus severed after Cypriot troops kill 15 Egyptian commandos who were storming jet at Larnaca Airport in which Palestinian terrorists held 16 hostages. Egypt to get 50 F-5E fighter-bombers from the U.S. National referendum gives Sadat mandate to carry out proposals for curtailing political dissent

**1979:** Egypt and Israel sign peace treaty, calling for phased Israeli withdrawal from Sinai within three years. Arab states suspend Egypt from several Arab organizations. Referendum in Egypt approves treaty. Sadat dissolves parliament; his National Democratic party wins overwhelming victory in June election

**1980:** Two thirds of Sinai territory is returned to Egypt as Israel completes 2nd phase of withdrawal; countries exchange ambassadors; negotiations continue on Palestinian issue. Sadat assumes premiership; voters approve constitutional amendment permitting Sadat more than two 6-year terms as president

**1981:** Sadat assassinated (Oct. 6) in Cairo by Muslim religious fanatics. Hosni Mubarak becomes president (Oct. 7), is confirmed overwhelmingly in national referendum (Oct. 13), assumes office of premier (Oct. 15); pledges to continue Sadat's policies and to carry out terms of Egyptian-Israeli peace treaty

**1982:** Dr. Fuad Mohieddin named premier. Remaining Sinai territory is turned over to Egypt by Israel on April 25. Of 24 persons tried for participating in Sadat's assassination, five are executed, 17 get prison terms, 2 acquitted

## EL SALVADOR

**Area:** 8,260 sq. mi. **Population:** 4,748,000 (1980 est.)

**Official Name:** Republic of El Salvador **Capital:** San Salvador **Nationality:** Salvadorean **Languages:** Spanish is the official and predominant language; a small number of Indians still speak Nahuatl **Religion:** Overwhelmingly Roman Catholic **Flag:** Blue, white, and blue horizontal stripes, with the national coat of arms centered on the white stripe **Anthem:** National Anthem, beginning "We proudly hail thee, motherland" **Currency:** Salvadorean colón (2.5 per U.S. $1)

**Location:** Central America. El Salvador is bordered on the north, northeast, and east by Honduras, on the south and southwest by the Pacific Ocean, and on the west and northwest by Guatemala **Features:** Mountain ranges running east to west divide the country into a narrow Pacific coastal belt on the south; a subtropical central region of valleys and plateaus, where most of the population lives; and a mountainous northern region **Chief Rivers:** Lempa, Grande de San Miguel

**Head of State and of Government:** Provisional President: Alvaro Alfredo Magaña Borjo, born 1925, sworn in May 2, 1982 **Effective Date of Present Constitution:** 1962. The Constituent Assembly is to prepare a new constitution **Legislative Body:** Constituent Assembly of 60 members **Local Government:** 14 departments, each headed by an appointed governor

**Ethnic Composition:** 89% mestizo (of mixed European—mainly Spanish—and Indian descent); the rest consists of small minorities of European and of Indian ancestry **Population Distribution:** 40% urban **Density:** 575 inhabitants per sq. mi.

**Largest Cities:** (1973 est.) San Salvador 368,000; (1971 census) Santa Ana 96,306, San Miguel 59,304

**Per Capita Income:** $599 (1980) **Gross National Product (GNP):** $2.9 billion (1980) **Economic Statistics:** In 1978 about 15% of GNP was from agriculture (coffee, cotton, sugar, rice, livestock); and 15% from industry (food processing, textiles, shoes, chemicals) **Minerals and Mining:** Substantial deposits of quartz, diatomaceous earth, kaolin, gypsum, limestone, and pumice **Labor Force:** 1,500,000 with 57% in agriculture and 14% in industry **Foreign Trade:** Exports, chiefly coffee, cotton, shrimp, sugar, cottonseed cakes, and cotton fabric, totaled $1 billion in 1980. Imports, mainly transport equipment, chemical products, fuels and lubricants, raw materials, industrial machinery, and consumer goods, totaled $1 billion **Principal Trade Partners:** United States, Latin America, Japan, EC countries

**Vital Statistics:** Birthrate, 39.2 per 1,000 of pop. (1979); death rate, 7.4 **Life Expectancy:** 58 years **Health Statistics:** 603 inhabitants per hospital bed; 3,685 per physician (1977) **Infant Mortality:** 53 per 1,000 births **Illiteracy:** 38% **Primary and Secondary School Enrollment:** 887,872 (1977) **Enrollment in Higher Education:** 28,281 **GNP Expended on Education:** 3.3% (1975)

**Transportation:** Paved roads total 930 mi. **Motor Vehicles:** 60,100 (1974) **Passenger Cars:** 41,000 **Railway Mileage:** 400 **Ports:** La Unión (Cutuco), Acajutla, La Libertad **Major Airlines:** TACA operates internal and international flights **Communications: Radio Transmitters:** 71 **Receivers:** 1,400,000 (1976) **Television Transmitters:** 5 **Receivers:** 136,000 (1976) **Telephones:** 78,000 (1978) **Newspapers:** 12 dailies, 51 copies per 1,000 inhabitants (1974)

**Weights and Measures:** Metric system **Travel Requirements:** Proof of citizenship for issuance of tourist card on arrival **International Dialing Code:** 503

---

The pressure of too many people for its land area has led to constant political unrest within El Salvador and to suspicion of expansionism among its neighbors. In July 1969 a fight which started during a soccer match with Honduras led to a four-day war over alleged discrimination against Salvadorean immigrants in Honduras.

After the disputed election of Gen. Carlos Humberto Romero as president in 1977, a wave of bombings, kidnappings and murders ensued. On Oct. 15, 1979, Romero was deposed by two army colonels who formed a ruling junta with three moderate civilians. In a move to keep the nation's predominantly poor peasants from joining the leftist-led revolutionary forces, the junta initiated a program in 1980 to split up the larger sharecropped plantations owned by the few hundred richest families. By 1981 more than 200,000 sharecropper families owned the land they tilled. This "land to the tiller" reform was seen by the right-wing oligarchy as a leftist move to give political powers to the peasants. In 1981 the head of the agricultural reform program and two American advisers were shot to death.

José Napoleón Duarte, the moderate Christian Democratic party leader, was named to the presidency by the junta on Dec. 13, 1980. U.S. aid, including military advisers, was increased in an effort to offset the materiel and advisory assistance which Cuba and Soviet bloc nations were presumed to be giving to the Salvadorean rebel forces, largely through Nicaragua. Meanwhile, reports of hundreds of slayings and other atrocities by government troops, police, right-wing death squads, and leftist guerrillas as well, persisted. The land reform program appeared to become bogged down by inept bureaucracy and the counteroffensive of wealthy landowners.

In the election held March 28, 1982, an unexpectedly high turnout of voters gave Duarte's followers 40 percent of the seats in the Constituent Assembly which was to determine El Salvador's future course. However, five right-wing partiees, including the National Republican Alliance (ARENA), headed by young, charismatic Roberto d'Aubuisson, received a majority. The assembly elected d'Aubuisson as its leader, but chose a moderate, Alvaro Alfredo Magaña, to be provisional president.

**HISTORY:** El Salvador was the home of the Pipil Indians before the arrival of Pedro de Alvarado, who conquered the country for Spain in the 1520s. Until its independence in the 19th century, El Salvador was administered as part of the captaincy general of Guatemala

**1821:** El Salvador and the other Central American countries gain independence from Spain and are annexed to Mexico

**1823:** El Salvador joins the Central American Confederation; declares independence in 1841; proclaims a republic in 1856

**1931-44:** Gen. Maximiliano Hernández Martínez is dictator

**1945-61:** Governments rise and fall in numerous coups d'état

**1962:** Lt. Col. Julio Adalberto Rivera is elected president; introduces income tax and many reforms

**1967:** Col. Fidel Sánchez Hernández is elected president

**1969:** El Salvador wages 4-day "soccer war" with Honduras

**1977:** Gen. Carlos Humberto Romero wins the presidency amid charges of fraud; violent unrest grips country

**1979:** Two colonels oust Romero, form a governing junta

**1980:** Archbishop Oscar Romero, outspoken champion of peace and civil rights, assassinated; José Napoleón Duarte sworn in as president

**1981:** Commission appointed to prepare for election in 1982. France and Mexico announce support for Salvadorean rebels; U.S. backs Duarte regime with arms and economic aid. UN commission reports "a consistent pattern of gross violations" of human rights in El Salvador

**1982:** Over 1,000 Salvadorean soldiers are sent to U.S. for training. Reports persist of slayings of civilians in outlying villages by both government and rebel forces. Christian Democrats win 40% of seats in Constituent Assembly in March 28 election, but rightist parties carry 59% of vote. Assembly chooses a moderate, Alvaro Magaña, as provisional president. Assembly suspends land-reform law; thousands of peasant families are reported evicted from their farms

---

## EQUATORIAL GUINEA

**Area:** 10,831 sq. mi. **Population:** 346,000 (1978 est.)

**Official Name:** Republic of Equatorial Guinea **Capital:** Malabo **Nationality:** Equatorial Guinean **Languages:** Spanish is the official language. On the mainland Fang is spoken, while the principal local language on Bioko island is Bubi **Religion:** About 80% of the population is Roman Catholic, the rest chiefly animists, with a small number of Moslems **Flag:** Green, white, and red horizontal stripes, with a blue triangle joining them at the staff side; in the center is the national coat of arms **Anthem:** National Anthem, beginning "Let's walk through the jungle of our immense happiness" **Currency:** ekuele (159 per U.S. $1)

**Location:** West Africa. Equatorial Guinea consists of 2 areas: the mainland—Río Muni (Mbini), bordered by Cameroon on the north, Gabon on the east and south, and the Atlantic Ocean on the west; and Bioko (Fernando Po), consisting of the main island of that name, Pagalu, and other small islands **Features:** There are 2 large volcanic formations on the main island, separated by a valley which crosses the island from east to west at its narrowest point. Río Muni consists of a coastal plain, and a series of valleys separated by low hills and spurs of the Crystal Mountains **Chief Rivers:** Benito, Muni, Campo

**Head of State and of Government:** President: Lt. Col. Teodoro Obiang Nguema Mbasogo, born 1942, took office Oct. 1979. He is head of the Supreme Military Council **Effective Date of Present Constitution:** A new constitution is being drafted **Legislative Body:** Power is in the hands of the Supreme Military Council **Local Government:** 7 provinces

**Ethnic Composition:** On Bioko the aboriginal Bubis are the major ethnic group; others include the descendants of liberated slaves. In Río Muni the main tribes are the Fang, Kombe, and Bujeba **Population Distribution:** 15% urban **Density:** 40 inhabitants per sq. mi.

**Largest Cities:** (1973 est.) Malabo 60,000, Bata 30,000

**Per Capita Income:** $312 (1978) **Gross National Product (GNP):** $100 million (1978) **Economic Statistics:** Production is predominantly agricultural, although forestry and fishing are also important. High-grade cocoa, coffee, bananas, and palm oil are the main crops. There is little industry **Minerals and Mining:** Geological surveys have raised hopes for the eventual discovery of petroleum;

uranium deposits have been found and there are indications of iron ore **Labor Force:** More than 95% of the working population is engaged in agriculture **Foreign Trade:** Exports, chiefly cocoa, wood, and coffee, totaled $21 million in 1980. Imports, principally foodstuffs, building materials, petroleum products, textiles, motor vehicles, and pharmaceutical products, totaled $12 million in 1976 **Principal Trade Partner:** Spain

**Vital Statistics:** Birthrate, 42.3 per 1,000 of pop. (1980); death rate 19.4 **Life Expectancy:** 43.5 years **Health Statistics:** 95 inhabitants per hospital bed (1977); 62,000 per physician (1975) **Infant Mortality:** 53.2 per 1,000 births **Illiteracy:** 80% **Primary and Secondary School Enrollment:** 40,500 (1975) **Enrollment in Higher Education:** N.A. **GNP Expended on Education:** N.A.

**Transportation:** Surfaced roads total 200 mi. **Motor Vehicles:** about 1,000 **Passenger Cars:** N.A. **Railway Mileage:** None **Ports:** Malabo, Bata **Major Airlines:** Iberia Airlines provides an international service **Communications: Radio Transmitters:** 2 **Receivers:** 80,000 (1976) **Television:** None **Telephones:** 2,000 **Newspapers:** 1 daily, 3 copies per 1,000 inhabitants

**Weights and Measures:** Metric system **Travel Requirements:** Passport, visa

One of the smallest of Africa's nations, Equatorial Guinea gained independence from Spain in 1968. For 11 years the country experienced repressive rule by President Masie Nguema Biyogo Negue Ndong, along with economic deterioration.

While severing all ties with Spain and taking a sharply anti-Western stance, President Masie welcomed new links with the Soviet Union, Communist China and North Korea.

The island people of Bioko, until recently more prosperous, include the native Bubis; Fernandinos, descendants of freed African slaves; Nigerians, who have been contract laborers on cocoa plantations; and a number of Europeans. The poorer, majority mainland people, the Fangs, looked to independence and the leadership of President Masie, a Fang, to improve their lot, a hope as yet unmaterialized.

Europeans, mainly Spanish and Portuguese, who ran the high-quality cocoa plantations, coffee and lumber production, and other businesses, numbered 7,000 in 1968. But with increasing physical terrorism by government and a youth movement, the *Juventud*, only a few hundred Europeans remain in the country. Thousands of citizens were reportedly killed by the Masie regime, and more thousands fled to other countries.

President Masie was overthrown in a bloodless coup on August 3, 1979, and executed following a public trial. Masie was replaced by a Supreme Military Council led by his nephew, Lt. Col. Teodoro Nguema Mbasogo. Relations were resumed late in 1979 with Spain, which agreed to provide military, economic and technical aid. Despite this and additional help from France and the United States, hopes for economic development remained slim. The government is seeking to establish its territorial waters so it can arrange search concessions with foreign oil companies.

**HISTORY:** Equatorial Guinea's island province of Fernando Po was discovered in the late 15th century by the Portuguese explorer Fernão do Po. It was ceded to Spain, along with mainland trading rights, in 1778. In the early 19th century, the island port of Santa Isabel was leased for a time to the British, who made it a naval base and refuge for freed slaves. Not until the 20th century did Spain actively begin developing the colony, known as Spanish Guinea

**1958-60:** Spain makes colony a Spanish province, grants inhabitants Spanish citizenship and representation in *Cortés*

**1963-64:** Colony is renamed Equatorial Guinea; limited self-government is instituted

**1968:** After numerous appeals to United Nations and long negotiations, Equatorial Guinea becomes an independent republic

**1969:** President Masie assumes dictatorial powers, purges opposition leaders

**1979:** Lt. Col. Teodoro Mbasogo deposes Masie in coup

**1980:** Soviet fishing fleet ordered to withdraw when treaty ends

**1981:** Pres. Mbasogo, acting on his promise to demilitarize his government, appoints a civilian minister of agriculture

**1982:** Pope John Paul II, during February visit, praises native Catholics for keeping faith through years of Masie persecution

## ETHIOPIA

**Area:** 471,776 sq. mi. **Population:** 31,065,000 (1980 est.)

**Official Name:** Ethiopia **Capital:** Addis Ababa **Nationality:** Ethiopian **Languages:** Amharic is the official and predominant language; English is frequently used. Arabic is spoken by about one-third of the population; other spoken languages are Gallinya, Tigrinya, Ge'ez, and Italian **Religion:** About 40% of the population belongs to the established Ethiopian Orthodox (Coptic Christian) Church; 40% is Moslem and the rest animist **Flag:** Green, yellow, and red horizontal stripes **Anthem:** National Anthem, beginning "Let Ethiopia be joyous!" **Currency:** Birr (2.07 per U.S. $1)

**Location:** Eastern Africa. Ethiopia is bordered on the north by the Sudan and the Red Sea, on the east by Djibouti and Somalia, on the south by Kenya, and on the west by the Sudan **Features:** The center of the country consists of a high, partly mountainous plateau cut by numerous rivers and split diagonally by the Rift Valley. The terrain gradually slopes to lowlands in the west and to a plains region in the southeast **Chief Rivers:** Shibeli, Abbai (Blue Nile), Ganale Dorya, Awash, Omo

**Head of State and of Government:** Lt. Col. Mengistu Haile-Mariam, born 1937, named chairman of the Provisional Military Administrative Council (*Dergue*) in 1977 **Effective Date of Present Constitution:** 1955 (suspended) **Legislative Body:** The bicameral National Assembly was dissolved in 1974. All decisions are made by the *Dergue* **Local Government:** 14 provinces

**Ethnic Composition:** The Amharas and the Tigreans are of Semitic origin and make up 37% of the population; the Gallas, a Hamitic peoplle, account for 40%. There are also numerous mixed, Negroid, and other groups, including the Falashas, or so-called "Black Jews," Sidamas, Somalis, and Yemenite Arabs, as well as some 30,000 Europeans, chiefly Italians **Population Distribution:** 14% urban **Density:** 66 inhabitants per sq. mi.

**Largest Cities:** (1978 est.) Addis Ababa 1,196,300, Asmara 393,800; (1975 est.) Dire Dawa 80,890, Dessye 57,420, Harar 56,360

**Per Capita Income:** $118 (1980) **Gross National Product (GNP):** $3.8 billion (1980) **Economic Statistics:** About 52% of GNP comes from agriculture (coffee, cotton, corn, sugar, wheat, sorghum, oilseeds, pulses) and livestock raising; 5% from industry (textiles, food processing, building materials, printing, leather, chemicals) **Minerals and Mining:** Limited output of gold, platinum, salt, iron, and manganese ore. Deposits of potash, copper, nickel, and asbestos have been discovered **Labor Force:** 11,300,000 (1971), with some 86% engaged in subsistence agriculture **Foreign Trade:** Exports, chiefly coffee, hides and skins, oilseeds, and pulses, totaled $417 million in 1980. Imports, mainly machinery and transport equipment, textiles, yarns and fabrics, foodstuffs, building materials, and petroleum products, totaled $751 million **Principal Trade Partners:** United States, Yugoslavia, West Germany, Saudi Arabia, Italy, Japan, Britain, Djibouti

**Vital Statistics:** Birthrate, 49.9 per 1,000 of pop. (1980); death rate, 24.9 **Life Expectancy:** 38 years **Health Statistics:** 3,314 inhabitants per hospital bed; 93,966 per physician (1976) **Infant Mortality:** 84.2 per 1,000 births **Illiteracy:** 94% **Primary and Secondary School Enrollmeent:** 1,150,194 (1974) **Enrollment in Higher Education:** 6,474 **GNP Expended on Education:** 2.3% (1975)

**Transportation:** Paved roads total about 2,000 mi. **Motor Vehicles:** 65,600 (1976) **Passenger Cars:** 52,500 **Railway Mileage:** 680 **Ports:** Massawa, Assab; a substantial portion of Ethiopia's trade moves through Djibouti **Major Airlines:** Ethiopian Airlines, the government line, operates domestic and international services **Communications: Radio Transmitters:** 8 (1976) **Receivers:** 210,000 (1976) **Television Transmitters:** 8 (1975) **Receivers:** 21,000 (1976) **Telephones:** 80,000 (1978) **Newspapers:** 2 dailies, 1 copy per 1,000 inhabitants (1977)

**Weights and Measures:** Metric system is official but traditional units are also used **Travel Requirements:** Passport, visa; check with Ethiopian embassy or consulates for requirements

The 44-year reign of Emperor Haile Selassie ended September 12, 1974, when a group of army officers completed a process which months before had begun to strip the emperor of most of his powers. This Provisional Military Administrative Council (PMAC) or *Dergue* removed him and installed his son, Asfa Wossen, 57, as a figurehead king. And in

March 1975 a proclamation ended the monarchy, annulling the Crown Prince's appointment.

Since he became emperor in 1930, the Lion of Judah had promoted economic innovation and political reform, but progress was slow. Strong resistance came from farmers, aristocratic landowners and the Coptic Church, which owns about a third of all land in a country where agriculture is a livelihood for 86 percent of the population.

Civilian rioting and strikes protesting soaring prices, unemployment, and the government's mismanagement of relief efforts dealing with the country's drought and famine undermined Selassie's power. What finally led to his downfall was the cover-up of the 1973 famine, which caused the deaths of over 100,000 peasants.

In February 1974 an army mutiny forced Selassie's cabinet to resign. Selassie sought to maintain control of the country by naming a new premier, Endalkachew Makonnen, installing a new cabinet, and raising army wages. Meanwhile, Ethiopia remained under military control.

In March, Selassie agreed to call a constitutional convention that could lead to a replacement of his absolute monarchy by a more democratic form of government. Finally, in September, came the coup which ousted him. He died in 1975.

A turning point for the ruling PMAC came in November 1974 when its members voted to execute 60 Ethiopians, including their chairman, Lt. Gen. Aman Michael Andom. These executions solidified the powers off Maj. Mengistu Haile-Mariam, the First Deputy Chairman, and Lt. Col. Atnafu Abate, the Second Deputy Chairman, while the chairman of the Military Council, Brig. Gen. Teferi Bante, remained a figurehead. In February 1977 Bante and six other members of the *Dergue* were killed in a shootout.

With Lt. Col. Mengistu now in control of one of the most brutal and arbitrary regimes in power today, Ethiopia's secretive council has turned into a one-man dictatorship. Among the problems Mengistu faces are the implementation of the land reform program ending 2,000 years of feudalism, domestic dissidence (especially that of the Ethiopian People's Revolutionary party) and the consolidation of the "Socialist revolution."

Under his rule the government is taking a harder and more violent path in dealing with its enemies, both in and outside the country. Among the regime's enemies in arms were three different forces of Eritrean guerrillas fighting for the past 18 years for independence of the northernmost province, containing Ethiopia's entire 540-mile Red Sea coastline; a right-wing army of exiles loyal to the era of Haile Selassie that had made gains in the provinces of Gojjam and Gondar; Somali irrendentists along the Somali frontier; and guerrillas in Tigre province.

In March 1978 Ethiopian forces, aided by some 16,000 Cuban troops and 1,500 Soviet military advisors, captured the last major towns in the Ogaden region after an eight-month campaign. An estimated one million Somalis had fled to Somalia by early 1980, but at least 20,000 guerrillas continued the fight and claimed to control 70 percent of the countryside. Ethiopia launched two full-scale offensives, again with Cuban and Soviet help, against Eritrean rebels in 1978 and 1979; but with limited success.

The Ethiopian Orthodox Christian church, a dominant force under Haile Selassie, is struggling against government attempts to control or crush it. In March 1979, Mengistu launched a full-scale crackdown on the country's 12 million Christians, forcing some to register with the government and others to renounce their faith. Some reportedly were executed for refusing to cooperate.

U.S. military assistance to Somalia continued to strain American-Ethiopian relations in 1982. In January the U.S. government revoked its policy of granting blanket protection to Ethiopians against deportation from the United States.

**HISTORY:** Long isolated from outside influences, Ethiopia developed a culture still suggestive of biblical times. Among its proudest traditions is that of the descent of Ethiopian emperors from King Solomon and the Queen of Sheba, who according to legend was the Ethiopian Queen Makeda of Aksum. Christianity was introduced by Coptic missionaries in the 4th century A.D. Over the centuries, repeated incursions by Arabs and constant feuding by feudal lords disrupted the empire, and it was not until the reign of Menelik II (1889-1913) that it was consolidated. In 1896, Menelik defeated an invading Italian army, but the invaders later took over Eritrea

**1916:** Menelik's grandson, Lij Yasu, suspected of Moslem leanings, is deposed; Menelik's daughter, Judith, is installed as empress, with her cousin, Ras Tafari Makonnen, as regent and heir

**1930-31:** Following death of the empress in 1930, Ras Tafari becomes emperor, taking the name Haile Selassie, meaning "Power of the Trinity"; he proclaims the first constitution

**1935-36:** Italians occupy Ethiopia; emperor flees the country and appeals vainly to the League of Nations for protection

**1941:** Following Italian defeat in World War II East African campaign, Haile Selassie, with Ethiopian and British forces, returns in triumph to Addis Ababa

**1942:** Emperor begins modernization and reforms

**1952:** United Nations approves federation of Eritrea, former Italian colony, with Ethiopia

**1955:** Revised constitution provides for popularly elected Chamber of Deputies and first elections are held

**1960:** Military coup involving crown prince is crushed

**1974:** Army mutiny and general strikes cause Selassie to appoint new cabinet and premier and promise reforms; Haile Selassie's rule ended. Lt. Gen. Aman Michael Andom is appointed premier and chairman of the military government (Sept.). Andom shot to death. Brig. Gen. Teferi Bante emerges as figurehead controlled by Maj. Mengistu Haile-Mariam and Lt. Col. Atnafu Abate

**1975:** Fighting erupts between Eritrean rebels and government troops in Asmara, provincial capital of Eritrea. Selassie dies

**1977:** Bante is killed. Mengistu becomes chief of state and commander in chief of armed forces

**1978** Eight-month Ogaden War ends as Cuban- and Soviet-aided Ethiopian forces drive Somalis from region. Ethiopia launches major offensive against Eritrean rebels, again with Cuban and Soviet help. A million-and-a-half Ethiopians are reportedly starving in nation's worst famine since 1973. In November Ethiopia and the Soviet Union sign a 20-year friendship pact

**1979:** Ethiopia abandons second full-scale offensive in Eritrea

**1980:** Government moves Ethiopians into Eritrea to displace Eritrean civilians; rebels hold Nakfa and countryside

**1981:** Ethiopia signs treaty of friendship with leftist regimes in Libya and Southern Yemen

## FIJI

**Area:** 7,055 sq. mi. **Population:** 634,000 (1980 est.)

**Official Name:** Fiji **Capital:** Suva **Languages:** English is the official language; Fijian, Hindi **Religion:** Almost all indigenous Fijians are Christians, mainly Methodist. The Indian population is mostly Hindu **Flag:** A light blue field with the Union Jack in the upper left and the shield of the Fiji coat of arms in the fly **Anthem:** God Bless Fiji **Currency:** Fijian dollar (0.92 per U.S. $1)

**Location:** Southwest Pacific. Fiji consists of about 320 islands, grouped around the Koro Sea, about 1,100 miles north of New Zealand. The largest of the islands, Viti Levu (18°S., 178°E.), constitutes more than half the land area and is the seat of the capital. The island of Rotuma, about 240 miles north of Vanua Levu, is part of the Fijian group **Features:** The larger islands are of volcanic origin, mountainous, and surrounded by coral reefs. The windward sides of the islands are covered with dense tropical forests; the leeward sides contain grassy plains **Chief Rivers:** Rewa, Dreketi, Sigatoka, Navua, Mba

**Head of State:** Queen Elizabeth II, represented by a governor-general, Ratu Sir George Cakobau, born 1912, took office 1973 **Head of Government:** Prime Minister: Ratu Sir Kamisese Mara, born 1920, appointed chief minister in 1967, assumed the office of prime minister in 1970, reappointed in 1977 and 1982 **Effective Date of Present Constitution:** October 1970 **Legislative Body:** Parliament (bicameral), consisting of the Senate and the House of Representatives. The Senate has 22 members, appointed for 6 years. The House of Representatives has 52 members elected on a communal basis for 5 years **Local Government:** 4 administrative divisions, each headed by a government-appointed commissioner; 10 urban areas have elected councils

**Ethnic Composition:** 50% of the population is descended from Indian laborers who came to Fiji in the late 19th century; the indigenous Fijians, who number 45%, are Melanesians, but with a connsiderable admixture of Polynesian blood. 2% are Europeans and part Europeans, 2% Rotumans and other Pacific islanders, and 1% Chinese **Population Distribution:** 37% urban **Density:** 90 inhabitants per sq. mi.

**Largest Cities:** (1979 est.) Suva 66,018, Lautoka 26,595, Nadi 7,099, Vatukoula 6,807, Ba 6,529, Nausori 6,610, Labasa 5,062

**Per Capita Income:** $1,547 (1980) **Gross National Product (GNP):** $973 million (1980) **Economic Statistics:** In 1973 about 27% of GNP was from agriculture (sugar, coconuts, rice, bananas, ginger); 16% from industry (sugar milling, coconut oil) and mining; and 41% from trade and services **Minerals and Mining:** Gold is mined and exported, although production has declined in recent years **Labor Force:** 176,000 (1979), with about 44% in agriculture, 16% in industry **Foreign Trade:** Exports, chiefly sugar, coconut oil, fish, gold, molasses, and lumber, totaled $258 million in 1979. Imports, mainly machinery, fuels, clothing, cotton fabrics, and food, totaled $471 million **Principal Trade Partners:** Australia, Japan, Britain, New Zealand, United States, Canada, Singapore

**Vital Statistics:** Birthrate, 29.8 per 1,000 of pop. (1979); death rate, 3.8 **Life Expectancy:** 70 years **Health Statistics:** 381 inhabitants per hospital bed; 2,308 per physician (1977) **Infant Mortality:** 9.9 per 1,000 births (1977) **Illiteracy:** 15% **Primary and Secondary School Enrollment:** 162,5633 (1980) **Enrollment in Higher Education:** 1,810 (1975) **GNP Expended on Education:** 5.1% (1976)

**Transportation:** All-weather roads total 746 mi. **Motor Vehicles:** 43,037 (1979) **Passenger Cars:** 19,087 **Railway Mileage:** 400 miles of narrow-gauge track **Ports:** Suva, Lautoka, Levuka **Major Airlines:** Fiji Air operates domestic services **Communications: Radio Transmitters:** 12 **Receivers:** 300,000 (1976) **Television:** None **Telephones:** 35,000 (1978) **Newspapers:** 2 dailies, 66 copies per 1,000 inhabitants (1976)

**Weights and Measures:** Metric system **Travel Requirements:** Passport and onward/return ticket required. Visa issued on arrival for 4 months stay **International Dialing Code:** 679

---

In 1874, when Fiji was the haunt of cannibals, its chiefs ceded the islands to Queen Victoria. Ninety-six years to the dayy later, on October 10, 1970, Britain granted Fiji independence. With independence, domestic problems have risen to the surface, such as differences between mainly urban-dwelling Indians, who make up half of the population, and the indigenous Melanesians, who number about a tenth less than the Indians, but who own over 80 percent of the land.

Political equanimity is kept by an arrangement in which each group elects an equal number of members of government, the balance of power being held by representatives of the minority of voters who are neither Indian nor Melanesian.

Since 1975, political harmony has been threatened because of the formation of splinter groups from both major parties. This imbalance was exemplified in the 1976 elections in which Prime Minister Sir Kamisese Mara resigned after his ruling Alliance party suffered defeat in the general election. The defeat meant political turmoil for Fijians, with no party able to gain an overall majority in the House of Representatives. As a result of this impasse, the governor-general reappointed Mara prime minister. A measure of stability was regained in September 1977 when the Alliance party, led by Mara, won by a landslide in the general elections. The victory was seen as vindicating Mara's determination to preserve Fiji's multiracial society. In the July 1982 elections, however, the Alliance party won by a narrower margin.

Today, Fiji is more than a tourist haven. In education, Fiji draws islanders to its University of the South Pacific, its medical school, and even its Protestant theological school. It is a leading voice of the South Pacific in the United Nations. In commerce, Fiji is a transshipment point for trade to the Pacific islands. Exports include sugar, coconut products, and gold.

**HISTORY:** Vanua Levu, Taveuni and some smaller islands in the northeast of the Fiji archipelago were discovered by the Dutch navigator Tasman in 1643. Other islands in the group were discovered in the following century by Captain James Cook and other British explorers, but it was not until 1804 that the first European settlement was established, at Levuka. Missionaries soon followed and succeeded in abolishing cannibalism and in converting Cakobau, the most influential of the native chiefs, to Christianity

**1874:** Britain annexes the islands at the request of the tribal chiefs

**1879:** Importation begins of indentured Indian laborers for work on the sugar plantations

**1900:** Plan by European settlers for federation with New Zealand is rejected

**1904:** Europeans win elective representation in a 10-man Legislative Council, whose one Indian member and two Fijian members are nominated by governor

**1929:** Indians win right to elective representation in council

**1963:** Legislative Council is reconstituted, giving Fijians elective representation

**1965:** New constitution is introduced, providing for greater self-government

**1970:** Fiji wins independence and joins the UN

**1972:** First general elections since independence are held

**1977:** Alliance party wins by landslide in general elections

**1978:** Fiji contributes 500-man contingent to the United Nations Interim Forcee in Lebanon (UNIFIL) peacekeeping force

**1979:** Cyclone Meli devastates part of Fiji archipelago ((March 27); 52 are killed, thousands left homeless. Fiji provides 1,300-man contingent for peacekeeping force in Zimbabwe-Rhodesia

**1980:** Fiji obtains apology from China for holding missile tests in Pacific without prior consultation

**1981:** Government decision to delay introduction of $20-billion television system becomes a major issue

**1982:** Alliance party wins narrow election victory

## FINLAND

**Area:** 130,128 sq. mi. **Population:** 4,807,000 (1981 est.)

**Official Name:** Republic of Finland **Capital:** Helsinki **Nationality:** Finnish **Languages:** Finnish, the dominant tongue, and Swedish, spoken by 6% of the population, are both official languages. Lappish is spoken by a small minority **Religion:** More than 92% of the population belongs to the established Evangelical Lutheran Church; less than 8% belongs to the Orthodox Church of Finland and the so-called free churches **Flag:** An extended blue cross on a white field with the national coat of arms centered on the cross **Anthem:** Our Land **Currency:** Markka (4.5 per U.S. $1)

**Location:** Northern Europe. Finland is bordered by Norway on the north, by the USSR on the east, by the Gulf of Finland and the Baltic Sea on the south, and by the Gulf of Bothnia and Sweden on the west. A third of Finland's total length lies north of the Arctic Circle **Features:** Finland is a land of 60,000 lakes, nearly all of them in the southern half of the country. About 70% of the land area is covered with forests; swamps, many of them wooded, cover about 30%. The generally low-lying coastal belt rises slightly to a forested plateau. The far north is marked by low, mountainous terrain **Chief Rivers:** Kemijoki, Oulujoki, Muoniojoki-Torniojoki

**Head of State:** President Mauno Koivisto, born 1923, sworn in Jan. 27, 1982 **Head of Government:** Premier Kalevi Sorsa, born 1930, appointed Feb. 17, 1982 **Effective Date of Present Constitution:** 1919 **Legislative Body:** Parliament (unicameral *Edhuskunta*), consisting of 200 members elected by direct universal suffrage for 4-year terms **Local Government:** 12 provinces, (including autonomous Ahvenanmaa—the Aland Islands), each headed by a governor. Urban and rural communes have elected councils

**Ethnic Composition:** Finnish-speaking Finns make up 94% of the population and Swedish-speaking Finns 6%. Lapps number 2,240 **Population Distribution:** 60% urban **Density:** 37 inhabitants per sq. mi.

**Largest Cities:** (1976 est.) Helsinki 493,324, Tampere 166,179, Turku 164,520, Espoo 123,954, Vantaa 122,301

**Per Capita Income:** $7,004 (1980) **Gross Domestic Product (GDP):** $33.4 billion (1980) **Economic Statistics:** 31% of GDP comes from industry (metals, engineering, foodstuffs, paper and paper products, furniture, textiles, chemicals); 10% from agriculture (oats, barley, wheat, rye), fishing and forestry; 14% from commerce and finance **Minerals and Mining:** Copper, nickel, iron, zinc, vanadium, silver and lead are mined in substantial quantities **Labor Force:** 2.2 million (1977), with 14% in agriculture and forestry, 34% in industry and construction, and 38% in trade and services **Foreign Trade:** Exports, chiefly paper products, machinery, transport equipment, chemicals, textiles, dairy products totaled $11.1 billion in 1979. Imports, mainly raw materials for industry, fuels and lubricants, machinery, automobiles, aircraft, foodstuffs, and textiles, totaled

$11.3 billion **Principal Trade Partners:** USSR, Sweden, West Germany, Britain, United States, Saudi Arabia

**Vital Statistics:** Birthrate, 13.1 per 1,000 of pop. (1980); death rate, 9.4 **Life Expectancy:** 72 years **Health Statistics:** 65 inhabitants per hospital bed; 703 per physician (1975) **Infant Mortality:** 7.7 per 1,000 births (1977) **Illiteracy:** Negligible **Primary and Secondary School Enrollment:** 869,894 (1976) **Enrollment in Higher Education:** 77,206 (1975) **GNP Expended on Education:** 7.1% (1976)

**Transportation:** Paved roads total 21,356 mi. **Motor Vehicles:** 1,263,200 (1978) **Passenger Cars:** 1,115,300 **Railway Mileage:** 3,794 **Ports:** Helsinki, Turku, Naantali, Hamina, Hanko, Kemi, Oulu, Pori, Kotka, Sköldvik **Major Airlines:** Finnair operates domestic and international flights **Communications: Radio Transmitters:** 15 **Licenses:** 2,199,575 (1976) **Television Transmitters:** 83 **Licenses:** 1,779,469 (1976) **Telephones:** 2,127,000 (1978) **Newspapers:** 60 dailies, 465 copies per 1,000 inhabitants (1977)

**Weights and Meeasures:** Metric system **Travel Requirements:** Passport; no visa for 3 months **International Dialing Code:** 358

---

With a self-assurance that has grown over the last decade, neutral Finland, which borders the Soviet Union, has been playing a role in international affairs unthinkable a decade ago.

It has served a two-year term (1969-70) on the UN Security Council, where small powers, in taking their turn in the chair, find themselves presiding at times over big-power disputes. Ministers of 35 nations, including the United States and Canada, met in Helsinki in June 1973 to lay groundwork for a European détente. The Conference on Security and Cooperation in Europe (CSCE), held in August 1975 in Helsinki, dealt with the inviolability of frontiers, economic cooperation, and freer movement of people and ideas. The conference was regarded by Finland as an assurance of its independence from the Soviet Union.

To the Finns, these actions are among a series of initiatives that would have been out of the question at the beginning of the 1960s, a period of uneasy relations with the neighboring Soviets.

At the time, a major Finnish political organization, the Social Democratic party, was being kept out of government to avoid repercussions in Moscow. But the Social Democrats returned to cabinet posts in 1966 and were part of the coalition government that achieved the signing of the Free Trade Agreement with the European Community.

Urho Kekkonen served as president for 25 years because of his skill in handling Finland's sensitive foreign policy—especially its delicate relations with the Soviet Union—but he resigned in 1981 due to poor health. He was succeeded as president by Mauno Koivisto, who had been premier of a centrist coalition government since 1979. Koivisto was elected president by the electoral college on Jan. 26, 1982. He formed a new coalition from the same four parties which had formed the previous government. Kalevi Sorsa, chairman of the Social Democratic party, was appointed premier. Finland's foreign policy of neutrality and friendly relations with the USSR was supported by all political parties and was expected to continue.

**HISTORY:** The earliest known inhabitants of Finland were the Lapps. By the 8th century A.D., however, they had been pushed northward by the Finns, coming from the south and southeast. In the 12th century Finland was Christianized by the Swedes and in the 16th century became a grand duchy under the Swedish crown. Russia acquired the province of Vyborg in 1721 and was ceded the rest of the duchy in 1809. Although Finland enjoyed considerable autonomy under Russian rule, Finnish nationalism developed into a powerful movement

**1899-1906:** Tsar Nicholas II begins strong Russification program, evoking stiff Finnish resistance. Russian governor-general is assassinated and a general strike breaks out. Finns win concessions, set up a unicameral diet and introduce universal suffrage

**1917-20:** Following the Bolshevik seizure of power in the Russian Revolution, Finnish diet proclaims Finland's independence. Civil war breaks out between Russian sympathizers (Reds) and Finnish nationalists (Whites), led by Marshal Carl Gustav Mannerheim and aided by German troops. Whites are victorious and after a brief regency under Mannerheim a republic is set up. The Soviet Union recognizes Finland

**1939-40:** Soviet Union, which has been given a free hand in Finland under Moscow's nonagression pact with Nazi Germany, demands demilitarization of Finnish fortifications on Karelian Isthmus north of Leningrad, use of a naval base in Finland, and the cession of islands in Gulf of Finland. Finns refuse to bow to demands and Soviet troops attack. Despite strong resistance by Finnish troops, led by Mannerheim, Finland is defeated and is forced to cede one-tenth of its territory to USSR

**1941-45:** Finland is caught up in war between the Soviet Union and Nazi Germany, the Finns fighting what they regard as the Continuation War against the Russians and not as allies of Germany. Full-scale Soviet offensive results in Finnish defeat in 1944. Armistice terms oblige Finns to expel German troops; resulting warfare leads to further devastation of Finland

**1947:** Under peace treatty signed in Paris, Finland cedes more territory to USSR and agrees to pay heavy indemnity

**1955-61:** Finland joins Nordic Council, and becomes associate member of European Free Trade Association; continues policy of neutrality and cooperation with Soviet Union

**1973:** Finland signs Free Trade Agreement with the EC. President Kekkonen's term extended by four years

**1976:** Finland hit by first police strike in postwar Europe

**1977:** Kalevi Sorsa succeeds Martti Miettunen as premier

**1978:** President Kekkonen reelected to fifth straight term

**1979:** Mauno Koivisto succeeds Sorsa as premier

**1981:** President Kekkonen resigns for reasons of health

**1982:** Koivisto is elected president; Sorsa is named premier

## FRANCE

**Area:** 210,038 sq. mi. **Population:** 53,963,000 (1981 est.)

**Official Name:** French Republic **Capital:** Paris **Nationality:** French **Languages:** French is the official and predominant language. Other languages spoken include Breton (akin to Welsh) in Brittany; a German dialect in Alsace and Lorraine; Flemish in northeastern France; Spanish, Catalan, and Basque in the southwest; and Italian in the southeast and on the island of Corsica **Religion:** Chiefly Roman Catholic, 4% Moslem (mostly immigrants from North Africa), 2% Protestant, 1% Jewish **Flag:** A tricolor of blue, white, and red vertical stripes **Anthem:** La Marseillaise **Currency:** Franc (6.1 per U.S. $1)

**Location:** Western Europe. France is bounded on the north by the English Channel and the Strait of Dover; on the northeast by the North Sea, Belgium and Luxembourg; on the east by Germany, Switzerland, and Italy; on the southeast by the Mediterranean Sea; on the south by Andorra and Spain; and on the west by the Atlantic Ocean **Features:** About two thirds of the country consists of flat or gently rolling terrain, and the remaining third is mountainous. A broad plain covers most of northern and western France, from the Belgian border in the northeast to Bayonne in the southwest. The lowland plains area is bounded on the south by the Pyrenees; on the southeast by the mountainous Massif Central; and on the east by the Alps, Jura, and Vosges mountains **Chief Rivers:** Seine, Loire, Garonne, Rhône, Rhine

**Head of State:** President François Mitterrand, born 1916, elected 1981 for 7 years **Head of Government:** Premier Pierre Mauroy, born 1928, appointed 1981 **Effective Date of Present Constitution:** 1958 **Legislative Body:** Parliament (bicameral), with a National Assembly and the Senate. The National Assembly, elected by direct universal suffrage for 5 years, is composed of 491 deputies. The Senate is composed of 315 members, elected indirectly for 9 years by an electoral college made up of National Assembly members, the General Departmental Councils, and the delegates of the Municipal Councils. The National Assembly can be dissolved by the president with the advice of the premier **Local Government:** Metropolitan France is divided into 96 departments, each headed by a prefect appointed by the central government and each under the authority of an elected General Council. The departments are divided into cantons and communes, with each commune electing its own municipal council and designated mayor. There are also 21 economic regions

**Ethnic Composition:** The French are a mixture of the 3 basic European stocks: Nordic, Alpine, and Mediterranean. The largest foreign-born groups are North Africans, Italians, Portuguese, Spaniards, Czechoslovaks, Poles, and Yugoslavs **Population Distribution:** 73% urban **Density:** 257 inhabitants per sq. mi.

**Largest Cities:** (1975 census) Paris 2,291,554 (Metropolitan Area 9,878,524), Marseille 901,421, Lyon 454,265, Toulouse 371,143, Nice 331,002, Nantes 252,537, Strasbourg 251,520, Bordeaux 220,830, Saint-Étienne 218,289, LeHavre 216,917, Rennes 194,094, Toulon 180,508, Reims 177,320, Lille 171,010, Grenoble 165,431, Brest 163,940

**Per Capita Income:** $9,479 (1980) **Gross Domestic Product (GDP):** $508 billion (1980) **Economic Statistics:** About 38% of GDP comes from industry (metalworking, machinery, chemicals, transport equipment, food and beverages, textiles, clothing) and construction; 57% from trade and servicés; 5% from agriculture and fishing (wheat, barley, potatoes, beet sugar, apples, wine, fish, beef cattle, and pigs) **Minerals and Mining:** The country is an important producer of iron ore, potash, bauxite, coal, natural gas, sulphur, and building raw materials. It also has deposits of zinc, lead, pyrites, phosphates, and uranium **Labor Force:** 20.5 million, with 47% in trade and services, 38% in manufacturing and construction, 10% in agriculture, fishing, and forestry **Foreign Trade:** Exports, chiefly machinery, chemicals, textiles, automobiles, steel, grain, and aircraft, totaled $111 billion in 1980. Imports, mainly machinery, foodstuffs, petroleum, chemicals, steel, nonferrous metals, and transportation equipment, totaled $135 billion **Principal Trade Partners:** West Germany, Belgium, Luxembourg, Italy, United States, Switzerland, Britain, Netherlands, Algeria, Japan, Saudi Arabia, USSR

**Vital Statistics:** Birthrate, 14.8 per 1,000 of pop. (1980); death rate, 10.1 **Life Expectancy:** 72 years **Health Statistics:** 97 inhabitants per hospital bed, 613 per physician (1976) **Infant Mortality:** 10 per 1,000 births **Illiteracy:** Negligible **Primary and Secondary School Enrollment:** 9,511,719 (1976) **Enrollment in Higher Education:** 1,038,576 (1975) **GNP Expended on Education:** 5.8% (1976)

**Transportation:** Surfaced roads total 520,000 mi. **Motor Vehicles:** 19,918,000 (1978) **Passenger Cars:** 17,400,000 **Railway Mileage:** 26,380 **Ports:** Marseille, Le Havre, Dunkirk, Nantes, St-Nazaire, Rouen, Bordeaux, Brest, Nice **Major Airlines:** Air France and UTA operate international flights; Air-Inter operates domestic flights **Communications: Radio Transmitters:** 363 **Licenses:** 26,000,000 (1976) **Television Transmitters:** 3,001 (1974) **Licenses:** 14,197,000 (1975) **Telephones:** 19,870,000 (1978) **Newspapers:** 96 dailies, 205 copies per 1,000 inhabitants (1977)

**Weights and Measures:** Metric system **Travel Requirements:** Passport; no visa for 3 months **International Dialing Code:** 33

---

For a country with a reputation for being ungovernable, France has moved and is continuing to move through a difficult period of transition, politically, economically, and socially, with an uncharacteristic amount of smoothness.

That there is some unrest and dissatisfaction is attested to by strikes, demonstrations, manifestations of violence, and angry meetings. But these fits of temper surge up and die down quickly, and the appearance of crisis they create is quickly dissipated.

Despite some dire predictions, France has moved out of the Gaullist era into more prosaic leadership with the institutions that General de Gaulle had bequeathed intact. A people that history books describe as undisciplined and individualistic appear to accept strong executive power as a fact of political life, particularly when it concentrates as it now does on domestic problems and eschews to a large extent the kind of global diplomacy practiced by de Gaulle.

The main goal of de Gaulle's successor, Georges Pompidou, was to eliminate France's industrial backwardness and move her into the forefront of advanced technical nations. The rich, varied soil of France that produces the food and wines that have contributed to the French art of living have also produced a powerful, conservative rural society that over the centuries has dominated the country.

The shift to an urban, industrialized society is one of the great central facts of contemporary France. As people move from farm to city and enter into radically different ways of life and work, tensions are created. They are aggravated by the failure of the cities to accommodate ever increasing populations with adequate housing and transport. More and more, once sleepy provincial centers are starting to take on the bustle, noise, and discomfort of Paris.

More than just the rural population is in transition. Shopkeepers and artisans who flourished in a slow-moving, small-scale economy are finding themselves squeezed out of the market by the demand for more efficient and cheaper ways of making and distributing goods and services. Workers in small inefficient plants or in traditional industries that are dying out are finding themselves having to adjust to new lines of work in new places. Students and educational authorities are trying to make their schools relevant to a new kind of society that places a premium on technical proficiency and accords declining prestige to the contemplative man of letters.

All these are long-range problems that are more or less painful to resolve and create tensions that sometimes may cause explosions. In May 1968, students and workers exploded together, bringing the government of General de Gaulle and the whole regime into peril. Although de Gaulle weathered the storm, it was the beginning of the end for him; the following year he was defeated in a referendum and was forced into lonely and somewhat bitter retirement. When he died in November 1970, there was a great national and international outpouring of sentiment for him.

The events of May 1968 left a decided impact. The franc was no longer sacrosanct and monetary policies henceforth were more closely coordinated with those of France's European partners. The upheaval has led to a style of government that places great importance on discussion and participation in decisions. At the same time, the memory of the 1968 disorders made most Frenchmen very law-and-order conscious. How to protect civil liberties while putting down the disorders that continue to crop up has become a major subject of debate.

Another great theme of debate is how to loosen the power of one of the most highly centralized countries in the world without destroying national unity. The move is on to satisfy municipal and regional desires for more of a say over personal futures, but the habit of deciding everything in Paris is deep-rooted and hard to change.

Abroad, France, no longer a colonial power, has paid the greatest attention to the movement toward western European unity. Under Pompidou, European unity, long blocked by his predecessor's refusal to accept Britain as a European partner, began again to show movement. The successful negotiation with Britain for entry into the Common Market was due largely to Pompidou.

In April 1974 Pompidou died at the age of 62. On May 19, Finance Minister Valéry Giscard d'Estaing was elected president by a narrow margin. During his seven-year term as president, Giscard d'Estaing displayed an informal style and a willingness to attack France's problems. In foreign affairs, he pursued independent policies which often conflicted with those of the United States. Domestically, his administration at first kept the annual inflation rate under 10 percent, reduced unemployment, and cut France's international payments deficit. In March 1978, his center-right coalition won a formidable 291-to-200 majority of seats in the National Assembly.

In the second round of presidential elections on May 10, 1981, Giscard lost to the candidate of the united Left, François Mitterrand, whose Socialist party won a majority of the assembly's seats in the June 1981 elections. Mitterrand appointed Pierre Mauroy, a moderate leader of his own Socialist party, as premier. The new cabinet included four Communists; this was the first time that the Communist party had participated in a French government since 1947.

President Mitterrand moved at once to put into effect his socialist program by enacting a plan for governmental decentralization and the nationalization of five major industrial companies and 36 important banks. His new government raised the minimum wage by 10 percent and family allowances by 25 percent. Because the value of the French franc fell after Mitterrand's election, the government devalued the franc by an average 3 percent in October 1981.

**HISTORY:** The land of France was inhabited in ancient times by the Gauls, who, by 51 B.C., had been subdued by the Romans. The Latin language predominated by the 5th century A.D., when Roman power collapsed, and the Franks from Germany made the land part of a large domain. Charlemagne ruled from 768 to 814 and extended the domain, but it was divided in 838—"Francia," with its Latin-based language, going to Charles the Bald. The kings lost power to local nobles in the 10th century, but recovered it slowly in later centuries

**1337:** The Hundred Years War breaks out, actually a series of short wars and truces between France and England, whose kings lay claim to the French throne

**1429-53:** Joan of Arc successfully leads French armies in lifting the siege of Orléans but is burned at the stake in 1431 after falling into English hands; English are finally driven out

**1643-1715:** Louis XIV gains military and political primacy for France in continental Europe, creates a great overseas empire, and establishes an absolute monarchy with a highly centralized government; his reign marks the golden age of French culture

**1789-94:** The French Revolution sweeps away Old Regime. A National Convention is formed, the monarchy abolished, Louis XVI executed, and a republic proclaimed. The Reign of Terror sets in, leading to arrest and execution of a huge number of royalists and members of minority political blocs. France's neighbors form an alliance to suppress the Revolution

**1799-1804:** Napoleon Bonaparte becomes first consul under the Consulate, a tripartite executive body; he restores domestic stability and defeats Austrian-British coalition

**1804-14:** Napoleon proclaims himself emperor, leads French armies in a series of unequaled victories against the other powers of Europe. His attempt to conquer Russia, however, results in a decisive defeat for France and the formation of an armed European coalition which forces his abdication

**1815:** Napoleon escapes from exile on Elba, rallies a French army, and is decisively defeated at Waterloo

**1848:** Revolution overthrows Bourbon monarchy, restored after Napoleon; the Second Republic is formed

**1852:** Louis Napoleon, Bonaparte's nephew, engineers coup d'état and overthrows republic; as Napoleon III, he establishes the Second Empire

**1870-71:** France defeated in Franco-Prussian War; Second Empire collapses and the Third Republic is formed

**1914-18:** France plays a major role in World War I against the Austro-German coalition. Nation shares in Allied victory but its economy is devastated by the war

**1939:** France joins Britain in declaring war on Germany following Nazi invasion of Poland

**1940:** France suffers ignominious defeat by Germany. Marshal Henri Pétain forms government at Vichy and sues for peace; Germans occupy half of France. Gen. Charles de Gaulle escapes to London, forms a wartime government and the Free French army

**1944:** Paris is liberated by Allied armies. De Gaulle's provisional exile government is officially recognized by the Allies

**1945-46:** De Gaulle is unanimously elected provisional president of the Fourth Republic but resigns after leftists withdraw support

**1958-61:** De Gaulle is recalled to power as the Fourth Republic is threatened with collapse because of the Algerian conflict. He engineers a new constitution vesting strong powers in the executive and establishing the Fifth Republic; despite considerable opposition, he negotiates Algerian independence

**1966:** De Gaulle withdraws French forces from NATO

**1968:** Student-worker uprisings paralyze France and threaten to topple Gaullist regime, but de Gaulle weathers the storm; his Gaullist party wins smashing victory in parliamentary election

**1969:** President de Gaulle resigns after the defeat of a referendum for constitutional reform; Gaullist candidate Georges Pompidou is elected president; he devalues the franc

**1970:** President Pompidou initiates broad reforms designed to benefit blue-collar workers

**1974:** Pompidou dies; Giscard d'Estaing is elected president. Laws on voting age of 18 and legalized abortion are passed

**1975:** Giscard d'Estaing visits Algeria; first such trip by French head of state since Algerian independence

**1976:** Political parties of the left win a majority in nationwide local elections in March. Premier Jacques Chirac resigns, reconstitutes Gaullist party into the Assembly for the Republic. Raymond Barre, nonpartisan technocrat, becomes premier

**1977:** Socialists and Communists gain in municipal elections; Chirac elected mayor of Paris

**1978:** Center-right candidates win large majority in legislative elections, repulsing strong leftist challenge. France reportedly explodes neutron bomb at South Pacific test base

**1981:** Socialist Party leader François Mitterrand elected president, defeating Giscard; in parliamentary elections, Socialists gain absolute majority. Pierre Mauroy is named premier

## GABON

**Area:** 103,346 sq. mi. **Population:** 649,000 (1981 est.)

**Official Name:** Gabonese Republic **Capital:** Libreville **Nationality:** Gabonese **Languages:** French is the official language; Fang is spoken in the north and a variety of Bantu tongues in the rest of the country **Religion:** About 55% of the population is Christian, mainly Roman Catholic; there are about 3,000 Moslems and the rest are animists **Flag:** Green, yellow, and blue horizontal stripes **Anthem:** Harmony **Currency:** CFA Franc (305 per U.S. $1)

**Location:** West-central Africa. Gabon is bordered on the north by Equatorial Guinea and by Cameroon, on the east and south by the Congo, and on the west by the Atlantic Ocean **Features:** About 85% of the entire country is covered by dense equatorial rain forest. The coastal plain is deeply indented in the north, while inland there are plateaus and mountains through which rivers have carved deep valleys and channels **Chief Rivers:** Ogooué, Ngounié, Abanga

**Head of State and of Government:** President: El Hadj Omar (Albert-Bernard) Bongo, born 1934, succeeded 1967, reelected 1979. He is assisted a prime minister, Léon Mébiame, appointed 1975 **Effective Date of Present Constitution:** 1961 **Legislative Body:** National Assembly (unicameral), consisting of 93 members **Local Government:** 9 regions divided into 36 prefectures, and 8 urban communes, with appointed officials

**Ethnic Composition:** Almost all Gabonese are of Bantu origin. The Fang are the largest of the country's tribes, followed by the Eshira, Bapounou, Bateke, and Okandé **Population Distribution:** 32% urban **Density:** 6.3 inhabitants per sq. mi.

**Largest Cities:** (1973 est.) Libreville 57,000, Port-Gentil 35,000, Franceville 5,000

**Per Capita Income:** $4,186 (1980) **Gross National Product (GNP):** $2.5 billion (1980) **Economic Statistics:** In 1973 about 18% of GNP was from agriculture (cocoa, coffee, palm oil, rice, cassava, bananas, yams, corn, and peanuts) and forestry; 14% from manufacturing and construction (largely timber and mineral processing); 30% from mining; 22% from trade and services **Minerals and Mining:** Very rich deposits of manganese and iron ore; uranium and gold are also produced; there are known deposits of lead, zinc, phosphate, and diamonds. Rich offshore oil and natural gas deposits are being worked **Labor Force:** About 280,000, of which 58% are engaged in agriculture **Foreign Trade:** Exports, wood, petroleum, uranium, manganese and coffee, totaled $2.2 billion in 1979. Imports, chiefly machinery, foods, transportation equipment, metal products, tobacco, refined petroleum products, and industrial chemicals, totaled $202 million **Principal Trade Partners:** France, United States, West Germany, Netherlands, Britain, Japan, Argentina, Brazil

**Vital Statistics:** Birthrate, 32.7 per 1,000 of pop. (1980); death rate, 21.5 **Life Expectancy:** 44 years **Health Statistics:** 132 inhabitants per hospital bed; 2,560 per physician (1977) **Infant Mortality:** 229 per 1,000 births **Illiteracy:** 70% **Primary and Secondary School Enrollment:** 153,858 (1976) **Enrollment in Higher Education:** 1,014 (1975) **GNP Expended on Education:** 4.5% (1976)

**Transportation:** Paved roads total 400 mi. **Motor Vehicles:** 17,400 (1974) **Passenger Cars:** 10,100 **Railway Mileage:** 184 miles; the 400-mile Transgabon line is under construction **Ports:** Libreville, Port-Gentil **Major Airlines:** Air Gabon provides international and domestic services **Communications: Radio Transmitters:** 13 **Receivers:** 93,000 (1976) **Television Transmitters:** 8 **Receivers:** 8,500 (1976) **Telephones:** 11,000 (1976) **Newspapers:** 1 daily (1976), 1 copy per 1,000 inhabitants (1975)

**Weights and Measures:** Metric system **Travel Requirements:** Passport, visa, $10 fee

As the smallest territory of French Equatorial Africa, jungle-matted Gabon was noted chiefly as a source of tropical hardwoods and as the unhealthy land where for 53 years the famous medical missionary, the late Dr. Albert Schweitzer, operated a hospital at Lambaréné.

Most of Gabon is still a humid tangle of trees and creepers, but the increasing number of roads slicing through the jungle attest to the dramatic change that has made the country potentially one of the richest in Africa.

Not long after gaining independence from France in 1960, Gabon was found to possess some of the world's largest deposits of manganese, iron ore, and uranium.

Development of these resources is proceeding impressively, and the airline passenger approaching Libreville, the capital and chief port, may see evidence of new wealth also in the offshore oil rigs glinting above the gray Atlantic.

While tropical woods, particularly those from which the best plywood is made, are still a major export, the rising production of minerals has given Gabon a continuing trade surplus and the highest per capita annual income in black Africa.

Meanwhile, on the economic scene, because of the attractions of newfound mineral wealth, French participation in Gabon's development has grown even greater than it was in the colonial period. In February 1974 the two nations agreed that a detachment of French troops would remain in Gabon, which was to stay within the French zone.

Frenchmen run the new enterprises, the schools, banks, shops, and most businesses, and six French advisors serve in the President's office. President Bongo is actively seeking trade ties and investment from the United States, Britain, and West Germany in an effort to reduce French domination.

By 1976, relations with France had grown increasingly cool, with verbal attacks by President Bongo against "savage capitalism" and "exploitation" of Gabon's natural resources, becoming more frequent. However, Gabon still participates in the annual French-African summit. In 1980, joint Franco-Gabonese military maneuvers were held, and Bongo paid an official visit to France.

**HISTORY:** In the 15th century, Portuguese voyagers became the first Europeans to explore the coastal area of Gabon. However, because of dense jungles and impenetrable highlands the country remained relatively undisturbed by Europeans until the mid-19th century, when the French began making treaties with coastal chieftains and penetrating the interior. In 1890 Gabon formally became part of the French Congo and in 1910 was made a separate colony as part of French Equatorial Africa

**1913:** Dr. Albert Schweitzer, Alsatian-born physician, theologian, and musicologist, establishes medical mission at Lambaréné

**1958-59:** Republic of Gabon is established as autonomous member of the French Community; Léon M'Ba, leader of Gabonese Democratic party, becomes premier of provisional government

**1960:** Republic proclaims full independence

**1961-63:** Two main parties agree on joint list of candidates for election, in which M'Ba becomes president; factional disputes disrupt coalition and new elections are called

**1964:** When election decrees bar opposition candidates, Gabonese Army overthrows M'Ba government, but it is promptly restored by French military intervention

**1967:** President M'Ba dies and is succeeded by Vice-President Albert-Bernard Bongo

**1968:** President Bongo declares Gabon a one-party state and forms new Gabonese Democratic party open to all citizens

**1971:** A new $500-million four-year plan is begun to further develop timber and mineral resources

**1973:** Bongo is elected to a seven-year term as president

**1975:** Léon Mébiame is named premier. Treaty is signed with EC. Gabon is admitted to full membership in OPEC

**1976:** Gabon becomes world's largest exporter of manganese

**1979:** President Bongo is reelected to a third term

**1980:** Bongo's party wins overwhelmingly in legislative elections

**1981:** Gabon joins three other African OPEC member states in refusing to lower oil prices in face of world glut

**1982:** Pope John Paul II visits Gabon during his African tour

## THE GAMBIA

**Area:** 4,127 sq. mi. **Population:** 601,000 (1980 est.)

**Official Name:** Republic of The Gambia **Capital:** Banjul **Nationality:** Gambian **Languages:** English is the official language; Malinke and Wolof are the main spoken languages **Religion:** Approximately 85% of the population is Moslem; about 14% Christian; and the rest animist **Flag:** Red, blue, and green horizontal stripes, with the center blue stripe edged in white **Anthem:** For the Gambia, Our Homeland **Currency:** Dalasi (2.2 per U.S. $1)

**Location:** West Africa. The Gambia is a narrow strip 7-20 miles wide on either side of the Gambia River, extending eastward 200 miles from the Atlantic, and surrounded by Senegal on the land sides **Features:** Coastal mangrove swamps and salt water flats graduate to sand hills and inland plateaus **Chief River:** Gambia

**Head of State and of Government:** President: Alhaji Sir Dawda Kairaba Jawara, born 1924; prime minister since 1962, he became president in April 1970, and was reelected in 1977 and 1982. He is vice president of the Confederation of Senegambia **Effective Date of Present Constitution:** 1970 **Legislative Body:** House of Representatives (unicameral); 35 members elected by universal suffrage for a 5-year term, and 8 special members **Local Government:** Banjul, and 6 administrative divisions

**Ethnic Composition:** The principal groups are the Mandingo (38%), Fula (16%), Wolof (14%), Jola (9%), and Serahuli (8%) **Population Distribution:** 16% urban **Density:** 146 inhabitants per sq. mi.

**Largest Cities:** (1978 est.) Banjul 45,604; (1973 census) Sarrekunda 16,637

**Per Capita Income:** $257 (1980) **Gross National Product (GNP):** $155 million (1980) **Economic Statistics:** 58% of GNP is from agriculture (chiefly peanuts), 26% from trade and services **Minerals and Mining:** No known resources of value apart from laterite and stone **Labor Force:** 165,000, about 85% being engaged in agriculture **Foreign Trade:** Exports, mainly peanuts, fish and palm kernels, totaled $32 million (1980). Imports, chiefly food, textiles and clothing, oil, machine and transport equipment, totaled $163 million **Principal Trade Partners:** Britain, Switzerland, France

**Vital Statistics:** Birthrate, 47.5 per 1,000 of pop. (1980); death rate, 23 **Life Expectancy:** 33 years **Health Statistics:** 771 inhabitants per hospital bed; 13,500 per physician (1976) **Infant Mortality:** 82.6 per 1,000 births **Illiteracy:** 90% **Primary and Secondary School Enrollment:** 32,969 (1976) **Enrollment in Higher Education:** 947 (1971) **GNP Expended on Education:** 4.4% (1976)

**Transportation:** Paved roads total 197 mi. **Motor Vehicles:** 6,092 (1973) **Passenger Cars:** 3,000 **Railway Mileage:** None **Port:** Banjul **Major Airlines:** Gambia Airways provides service **Communications: Radio Stations:** 4 **Receivers:** 61,000 (1976) **Television:** None **Telephones:** 3,000 (1977) **Newspapers:** 1 newspaper published 3 times a week

**Weights and Measures:** British Imperial system is used; transfer to metric system started in 1976 **Travel Requirements:** Passport, entry/transit visa $8.00, 2 photos

The Gambia, Africa's smallest country, has been gaining increasing self-reliance through the unlikely combination of peanut production, Scandinavian tourists, and careful fiscal management. Attention has been focused on The Gambia because of the 1976 bestseller by Alex Haley, *Roots*, which tells the story of his ancestors from tribal life there to slavery in America.

Formerly Britain's oldest African colony, The Gambia became independent in 1965 and proclaimed itself a republic in 1970. It added "The" to its official name to avoid confusion with Zambia, another African country.

Except for a short Atlantic coast, the country is enclosed within Senegal. A sandy strip of land, it stretches some 200 miles in length along either side of the Gambia River and varies in width from seven to 30 miles. The broad mouth of the Gambia River is one of West Africa's finest harbors and the site of the capital, Banjul. Mandingoes, a handsome, friendly people, form the main element of the population.

Peanuts, planted on most of the available land, account for 95 percent of exports, but, in recent years, tourism has become a welcome and fast-growing addition to the economy, luring 25,000 Scandinavians a year. Old hotels have been enlarged and new ones built to meet growing demand. With tourist organizations in other countries now showwing interest in The Gambia, prospects are bright for a continuance of the boom and creation of more jobs and revenue. With Soviet, Chinese and British aid, The Gambia is beginning fishery development and irrigation projects.

An attempted coup in 1981 was promptly put down through intervention of troops from neighboring Senegal requested by Jawara. The Gambia, on Feb. 1, 1982, formed a confederation with Senegal called "Senegambia." Each nation retained its identity for the time being. This raised a question: Was The Gambia to become merely a province of French-speaking Senegal?

**HISTORY:** Along with neighboring Senegal, The Gambia was inhabited in past ages by peoples associated with the great empires of Ghana, Mali, and Songhay. Reached by Portuguese navigators in the 15th century, in 1588 the territory became, through purchase, the first British colony in Africa. After prolonged struggle, the British and French fixed the borders of Senegal and Gambia; in 1888 the latter became a crown colony

**1965:** The Gambia becomes a fully independent member of the British Commonwealth; a referendum to make the country a republic fails to receive necessary two-thirds majority

**1966:** Elections give Prime Minister Sir Dawda Jawara's People's Progressive party an increased majority

**1967-69:** Britain loans The Gambia over $10 million

**1970:** The Gambia becomes a republic

**1980:** Economy is hurt by drought and by rising prices of imported oil. Libya-backed coup attempt is forestalled

**1981:** Leftist coup is crushed with aid of Senegalese troops

**1982:** The Gambia forms a confederation with Senegal. Jawara is reelected president of The Gambia

## EAST GERMANY

**Area:** 41,768 sq. mi. **Population:** 16,736,000 (1981 est.)

**Official Name:** German Democratic Republic **Capital:** East Berlin **Nationality:** German **Languages:** German is the official and universal language **Religion:** 47% Protestant, 7% Roman Catholic, 45% no affiliation. Although the constitution provides for religious freedom, all churches are closely regulated by the state **Flag:** Black, red, and gold horizontal stripes, with the national emblem in the center **Anthem:** Arisen from the Ruins **Currency:** GDR mark (2.4 per U.S. $1)

**Location:** North-central Europe. East Germany is bordered on the north by the Baltic Sea, on the east by Poland, on the southeast by Czechoslovakia, and on the southwest and west by the Federal Republic of Germany **Features:** In the north are the lakes and low hills typical of the Baltic Sea country; the center is partly mountainous and in addition consists of a sandy arid section and a fertile plain. The heavily forested southern region consists of the Mittelgebirge, and the extension of the North German lowlands **Chief Rivers:** Elbe, Oder, Saale, Havel, Spree, Neisse

**Political Leader and Head of State:** Erich Honecker, born 1912, secretary general of the Central Committee of the Socialist Unity Party, since 1971, and chairman of the State Council, since 1976 **Head of Government:** Willi Stoph, born 1914, appointed October 1976 chairman of the Council of Ministers (premier) **Effective Date of Present Constitution:** 1968, amended 1974 **Legislative Body:** *Volkskammer* (unicameral) consisting of 500 members, elected by universal suffrage for 5-year terms; final decisions are made by the party's Politburo **Local Government:** 15 administrative districts named after their respective chief towns. All urban and rural divisions have locally elected bodies

**Ethnic Composition:** The population is ethnically homogeneous. The only minority is a Slavic group called the Sorbs which makes up about 0.2% of the population **Population Distribution:** 76% urban **Density:** 401 inhabitants per sq. mi.

**Largest Cities:** (1980 est.) East Berlin 1,145,743, Leipzig 563,388, Dresden 516,284, Karl-Marx-Stadt (Chemnitz) 316,937, Magdeburg 288,725, Halle 232,217, Rostock 230,280, Erfurt 210,687, Potsdam 129,648, Gera 124,246, Zwickau 122,592

**Per Capita Income:** $5,945 (1980) **Gross National Product (GNP):** $99.6 billion (1980) **Economic Statistics:** About 62% of GNP comes from industry, and 9% from agriculture. The chief industries are iron and steel, chemicals, fertilizers, machinery, transport equipment, synthetic rubber and fibers, drugs, plastics, and vehicles. The chief crops are barley, oats, potatoes, rye, sugar beets, and wheat **Minerals and Mining:** The arbitrary division of Germany left the East with few natural resources. Its only major resources are lignite, potash and uranium **Labor Force:** 8,900,000, with 39% in industry, 21% in services; 10% in commerce, 9% in agriculture **Foreign Trade:** Exports, chiefly machinery, railway rolling stock, chemicals, fertilizers and pesticides, fuel oil, construction materials, ships, motor vehicles, clothing and textiles, were estimated at $17.3 billion in 1979. Imports, mainly mineral ores, coal, rolled steel, fertilizer, tires, crude oil, wood, cotton and wool, paper pulp, foodstuffs, forage and feeds, and raw skins, were estimated at $19.2 billion **Principal Trade Partners:** USSR, Czechoslovakia, Poland, Hungary, France, Britain, West Germany, Bulgaria, Netherlands, Sweden

**Vital Statistics:** Birthrate, 14.6 per 1,000 of pop. (1980); death rate, 14.2 **Life Expectancy:** 72 years **Health Statistics:** 94 inhabitants per hospital bed; 528 per physician (1977) **Infant Mortality:** 12.1 per 1,000 births **Illiteracy:** Negligible **Primary and Secondary School Enrollment:** 3,014,086 (1976) **Enrollment in Higher Education:** 386,000 (1975) **GNP Expended on Education:** 5.6% (1974)

**Transportation:** Surfaced roads total 29,538 mi., with 1,000 mi. of superhighways **Motor Vehicles:** 2,991,000 (1978) **Passenger Cars:** 2,392,300 **Railway Mileage:** 8,823 **Ports:** Rostock, Wismar, Stralsund, Sassnitz **Major Airlines:** Interflug operates domestic and international services **Communications: Radio Transmitters:** 82 **Licenses:** 6,409,200 (1980) **Television Transmitters:** 461 **Licenses:** 5,730,900 (1980) **Telephones:** 2,956,000 (1978) **Newspapers:** 39 dailies, 496 copies per 1,000 inhabitants (1977)

**Weights and Measures:** Metric system **Travel Requirements:** Passport; visa obtainable at border or at East German embassy; visa entitlement certificate **International Dialing Code:** 37

The German Democratic Republic is mainly the work of one man, Walter Ulbricht, a ruthless and fanatical leader. Without his dedication and his seemingly tireless efforts from 1945 to 1971, his ruling Communist party and state apparatus, East Germany would undoubtedly have remained in a kind of Central European limbo.

Throughout the 1960s his prestige and power increased dramatically. In this period East Germany grew to be the 10th largest industrial power in the world and the country with the best living standard in the Communist world. Working to his advantage was the desire for security and comfort of the East Germans and their willingness to persevere under adverse conditions.

A major threat to Ulbricht's rule was posed by the reform program of the new Czechoslovak Communist leadership in 1968. The reform aims proclaimed in Prague by Alexander Dubcek were viewed in East Berlin as an elemental danger to the more or less orthodox, militant Marxism/Leninism practiced by the Ulbricht team. The East German leader recommended suppression; his advice was followed by the Soviet leaders who ordered the August 21, 1968, invasion of Czechoslovakia. Ulbricht was at his zenith in the wake of this move, and it seemed, for a while, that he was setting the tone of Russian foreign policy in Central Europe until his dismissal in 1971 as First Party Secretary for bypassing the Central Committee, overemphasizing large-scale development projects and obstructing Soviet aims for an accommodation with West Germany.

Ulbricht's successor, Erich Honecker, negotiated agreements of recognition with West Germany in 1974. When workers in neighboring Poland challenged their Communist rulers in 1980-81, Honecker at first echoed Ulbricht's view that democratic unions endangered Communist rule, and East Germany took part in Warsaw Pact military exercises in Poland during early 1981. But at the East German Communist Party Congress in April; Honecker softened his hard-line attitude by supporting the Polish government's actions in dealing with the crisis. Honecker undoubtedly feared that the Polish liberalization might spread to East Germany. He supported Poland's imposition of martial law in December 1981 and its subsequent harsh suppression of the Solidarity labor movement.

**HISTORY:** The Germans made their first major appearance in recorded history when they came into contact with the Romans in the 1st century B.C. By the 5th century A.D. various Germanic tribes had overrun the Roman Empire. After the division of Charlemagne's possessions in 843, the kingdom of the Eastern Franks emerged as the nucleus of Germany, but for most of Germany's history political unification was to prove beyond reach. In 1517 Martin Luther precipitated the Protestant Reformation and Germany was torn by religious strife until the end of the Thirty Years' War (1618-48). In the 18th century Prussia began to emerge as an important power and in the next century successfully challenged Austria for domination of Germany

**1815:** Congress of Vienna perpetuates the political divisions of Germany and provides for a German Confederation

**1862:** Bismarck becomes chancellor of Prussia; his goal is to create a unified Germany dominated by Prussia and excluding Austria

**1866:** Prussia is victorious in the Austro-Prussian War

**1870-71:** Prussia defeats France in the Franco-Prussian War, enabling Bismarck to achieve his goal of a unified Germany under Prussia; in 1871 William I of Prussia is proclaimed German Emperor
**1914-19:** Germany is ranged against Allied Powers in World War I and suffers crushing defeat; German Empire collapses and newly formed Weimar Republic is forced to accept harsh terms of Versailles Treaty
**1933-36:** Hitler is appointed chancellor in 1933 and assumes dictatorial powers; Germany is transformed into a brutal police state; anti-Semitism becomes official policy, culminating eventually in the extermination of six million European Jews; intensive rearmament begins
**1938:** Hitler annexes Austria and later takes over the Sudetenland from Czechoslovakia
**1939-45:** Hitler seizes the rest of Czechoslovakia in March 1939; six months later Nazi forces invade Poland, triggering World War II; Nazi forces overrun Western Europe and in 1941 invade the Soviet Union; by 1945, however, Germany is totally defeated, its cities in ruins, and its territory under U.S., Soviet, British, and French occupation; Hitler commits suicide
**1945-48:** East Germany and part of Berlin come under Soviet occupation and are brought under the control of the Communist-dominated Socialist Unity party. A separate East German state is established under Soviet auspices as a result of the failure of the USSR and the Western occupying powers to agree on a uniform policy for all of Germany
**1948-49:** Soviet opposition to the plans of the three other Allies for Germany's future results in breakdown of joint Four Power rule; Russians attempt to blockade Berlin, whereupon Western Allies mount gigantic airlift to bring food to West Berliners; in October 1949, following the creation of the Federal Republic of Germany, Russians set up the German Democratic Republic
**1953:** Anti-Communist revolt in East Germany is crushed by Soviet forces
**1955:** USSR signs treaty declaring East Germany a sovereign state
**1961:** Wall is erected around non-Soviet sectors of Berlin to prevent flight of East Germans to the west via West Berlin
**1968:** East German leader Walter Ulbricht meets with other East European leaders and calls for concerted action to halt liberalization in Czechoslovakia; within months, East German troops join in Soviet-led invasion of Czechoslovakia
**1971:** Ulbricht resigns as head of Socialist Unity party, is succeeded by Erich Honecker of the party's Central Committee
**1972:** Traffic Treaty is signed with West Germany, providing for access to West Berlin
**1973:** East and West Germany ratify a treaty calling for closer relations. Later in the year, both join the UN. Ulbricht dies
**1974:** U.S. establishes diplomatic relations with East Germany in September. The two Germanys exchange representatives
**1978:** Agreement reached with West Germany on construction of new highway to West Berlin and other transit matters
**1979:** Soviets begin token withdrawal of 20,000 troops
**1981:** Honecker reelected secretary-general at 10th Communist party congress; new five-year plan (1981-86) posits moderate production increases

## WEST GERMANY

**Area:** 95,704 sq. mi. **Population:** 61,703,000 (1981 est.)

**Official Name:** Federal Republic of Germany **Capital:** Bonn **Nationality:** German **Languages:** German is the official and universal language **Religion:** 49% Protestant, 45% Roman Catholic **Flag:** Black, red, and gold horizontal stripes **Anthem:** The official national anthem consists of the third verse of the old Deutschlandlied, beginning "Unity and Justice and Freedom" **Currency:** Deutsche Mark (2.3 per U.S. $1)

**Location:** North-central Europe. West Germany is bordered by Denmark and the North Sea on the north, by East Germany and Czechoslovakia on the east, by Austria and Switzerland on the south, and by France, Luxembourg, Belgium, and the Netherlands on the west **Features:** The country is generally flat in the north and hilly in the central and western areas, rising to more than 4,000 feet in the Black Forest and to more than twice that height in the Bavarian Alps **Chief Rivers:** Rhine, Danube, Ems, Weser, Elbe, Main, Mosel, Neckar, Isar

**Head of State:** President Karl Carstens, born 1914, elected 1979 for 5 years **Head of Government:** Chancellor Helmut Schmidt, born 1918, appointed 1974, elected 1976 **Effective Date of Present Constitution:** May 23, 1949 **Legislative Body:** Parliament (bicameral), consisting of the *Bundestag* and *Bundesrat*. The *Bundestag* has 497 elected members and 22 nonvoting members representing West Berlin, chosen for a term of 4 years. The *Bundesrat* has 41 members appointed by the state governments and 4 consultative members appointed by the West Berlin Senate **Local Government:** 10 states (*Länder*), each with its own legislative and ministerial government. West Berlin, though not legally a component state of West Germany, is closely integrated into the government's political and administrative system

**Ethnic Composition:** With the exception of a small Danish population in Schleswig-Holstein, the population is German **Population Distribution:** 86% urban **Density:** 645 inhabitants per sq. mi.

**Largest Cities:** (1980 est.) Berlin (West) 1,896,230, Hamburg 1,645,095, Munich 1,298,941, Cologne 976,694, Essen 647,643, Frankfurt-am-Main 629,375, Dortmund 608,297, Düsseldorf 590,479, Stuttgart 580,648, Duisburg 558,089

**Per Capita Income:** $10,509 (1980) **Gross Domestic Product (GDP):** $642 billion (1980) **Economic Statistics:** About 54.6% of GDP is derived from manufacturing (food industry, chemicals, iron and steel, electrical engineering, machinery); 18.5% is from trade, transportation and communications; 13.5% is from agriculture (rye, wheat, oats, barley, potatoes), forestry and fishing **Minerals and Mining:** Coal is the most important mineral resource. There are also substantial deposits of iron ore (mostly low grade), lead and zinc, potash, salt, fluorspar, barites, pyrites, graphites, and basalt. Some natural gas is produced **Labor Force:** 27 million, with 37% in services, 36% in industry, and 6% in agriculture **Foreign Trade:** Exports, chiefly mechanical engineering products, motor vehicles, chemicals, electrical engineering products, and iron and steel, totaled $172 billion in 1979. Imports, mainly foodstuffs, crude oil, nonferrous metals and semifinished products, chemical products, iron and steel, textiles, totaled $160 billion **Principal Trade Partners:** United States, Canada, France, Netherlands, Great Britain, Belgium, Italy, Japan, Switzerland, Austria, Sweden

**Vital Statistics:** Birthrate, 10 per 1,000 of pop. (1980); death rate, 11.5 **Life Expectancy:** 71 years **Health Statistics:** 85 inhabitants per hospital bed, 490 per physician (1977) **Infant Mortality:** 13.5 per 1,000 births **Illiteracy:** Negligible **Primary and Secondary School Enrollment:** 10,262 047 (1976) **Enrollment in Higher Education:** 836,002 (1975) **GNP Expended on Education:** 5.2% (1975)

**Transportation:** Surfaced roads total 104,487 mi., with 4,200 mi. of superhighways **Motor Vehicles:** 22,601,100 (1978) **Passenger Cars:** 21,212,000 **Railway Mileage:** 19,876 **Ports:** Hamburg, Wilhelmshaven, Bremen, Kiel, Emden, Lübeck **Major Airlines:** Lufthansa operates domestic and international services **Communications: Radio Transmitters:** 385 **Licenses:** 20,909,000 (1975) **Television Transmitters:** 1,153 **Licenses:** 19,226,000 (1975) **Telephones:** 24,743,000 (1978) **Newspapers:** 412 dailies, 423 copies per 1,000 inhabitants (1977)

**Weights and Measures:** Metric system **Travel Requirements:** Passport, no visa for 90 days **International Dialing Code:** 49

The Federal Republic of Germany was created in 1949 in the British, French, and U.S. occupation zones of Germany, as a vehicle for solving the German problem. Located in the center of Europe and in the center of big-power politics, Germany was divided for centuries; in eight decades as a unified nation, it twice frightened the world. At first resentful of their division into two after 1949, the Germans gradually became accustomed to it.

The Christian Democratic Union/Christian Social Union (CDU/CSU) has been the largest party in every West German *Bundestag*, but has had a majority in only one. Konrad Adenauer, CDU/CSU Chancellor from 1949 to 1963, aligned West Germany with NATO, and presided over an "economic miracle" in which the country recovered from the ravages of war and absorbed millions of ethnic German immigrants from East Germany and Eastern Europe. The free-enterprise policies of Adenauer's Minister of Economics, Ludwig Erhard, were credited with the country's surprising growth, but West Germany was aided by having inherited most of prewar Germany's iron ore, coal, and hydropower, and—after 1958—by membership in the European Community.

The Social Democratic party of Germany (SPD) has been the second-largest in every *Bundestag*; the Free Democratic party (FDP) has held the balance of power between the CDU/CSU and the SPD since 1961. The FDP went into coalition with the CDU/CSU in 1961, forced the aging Adenauer to retire in favor of Ludwig Erhard in 1963, and brought down Erhard by withdrawing from the coalition in 1966. Kurt Kiesinger then became leader of the CDU/CSU, formed a "grand coalition" with the SPD, and served as chancellor until 1969.

Originally a socialist party, the SPD has become a party of moderate reform within capitalism. Willy Brandt, former Mayor of West Berlin, was its leader in 1969, when it took power in coalition with the FDP. He concentrated on foreign policy, and shocked many Germans by abandoning talk of reunification and by recognizing the East German regime. He also improved relations with other Communist countries and worked to strengthen and expand the EC. Forced to resign because of an espionage scandal in 1974, he was succeeded by Helmut Schmidt, also a Social Democrat. Two successive SPD chancellors have done little to modify their predecesors' free-enterprise policies, and West Germany has remained an economic giant. Growth is slower than in the heady years of the economic miracle, but inflation and unemployment are lower than elsewhere. Prosperity has not eliminated discontent. Terrorist activity has been severe, especially in 1977. In 1978, a controversial new law increased the authority of the police.

Chancellor Schmidt denounced Poland's imposition of martial law in December 1981 but rejected the harsh economic sanctions demanded by the United States against the USSR. He supported NATO's future deployment of new missiles in Europe but urged that the U.S. first try to negotiate arms reductions with the USSR.

**HISTORY:** The history of West Germany is bound up with that of Germany as a whole until the years immediately following World War II (See East Germany *for pre-WW II chronology*)

**1948-49:** Western Allies mount massive airlift to Berlin, thwarting Soviet attempt to blockade city; West German constituent assembly adopts provisional constitution for the Federal Republic of Germany; Konrad Adenauer is elected chancellor; East Germany, under Soviet occupation, is set up as a Communist state named the German Democratic Republic

**1961:** East German government erects Berlin Wall in effort to halt flight of East Germans to the west via West Berlin

**1963:** Adenauer retires and is succeeded by Ludwig Erhard

**1966:** Kurt Kiesinger becomes chancellor

**1968:** Country is rocked by student demonstrations following attempted slaying of left-wing student leader in West Berlin

**1969:** Willy Brandt becomes chancellor

**1970:** A nonaggression treaty, recognizing present European borders, is signed with Soviet Union

**1972:** Nonaggression pact with Soviet Union and Poland ratified. U.S., USSR, Britain, and France sign Final Quadripartite Protocol in Berlin, putting into effect earlier agreements on civilian travel in and around Berlin

**1974:** Chancellor Willy Brandt resigns over a spy scandal involving a member of his staff. Helmut Schmidt succeeds him. Legal age of majority is lowered from 21 to 18. Two German states recognize each other

**1975:** Economy is slowed by inflation and high unemployment

**1976:** Treaty with Poland to allow ethnic Germans to emigrate is ratified. Ruling coalition of Social Democrats and Free Democrats wins close victory in nationwide parliamentary elections

**1978:** Controversial anti-terrorist laws enacted

**1979:** Karl Carstens is elected president by the Federal Convention (the *Bundestag* plus members of the *Länder* parliaments)

**1980:** Signs agreement with East Germany to improve road, rail, and canal links between the two countries

## GHANA

**Area:** 92,099 sq. mi. **Population:** 11,450,000 (1980 est.)

**Official Name:** Republic of Ghana **Capital:** Accra **Nationality:** Ghanaian **Languages:** English is the official and commercial language; of some 50 tribal languages and dialects spoken, the chief ones are Twi, Fanti, Ga, Ewe, Hausa, Dagbani, and Akan **Religion:** About 43% Christian, 12% Moslem, and the rest animist **Flag:** Red, gold, and green horizontal stripes, with a 5-pointed black star centered on the gold stripe **Anthem:** National Anthem, beginning "Lift high the flag of Ghana" **Currency:** Cedi (2.75 per U.S. $1)

**Location:** West Africa. Ghana is bordered on the north by Upper Volta, on the east by Togo, on the south by the Gulf of Guinea, and on the west by the Ivory Coast **Features:** Half of Ghana is less than 500 feet above sea level. The coastline is largely a low sandy shore, backed by plains and intersected by rivers. Northward is a belt of tropical rain forest, broken by densely forested hills and rivers. The far north is a region covered by savanna and grassland plains **Chief Rivers:** Volta, Pra, Tano

**Head of State and of Government:** Chairman, Provisional National Defense Council: Flt. Lt. Jerry Rawlings, born 1947, took power Dec. 31, 1981 **Effective Date of Present Constitution:** 1979 (suspended Jan. 2, 1982) **Legislative Body:** National Parliament with 140 members has been dissolved **Local Government:** 9 regions divided into districts

**Ethnic Composition:** Ghanaians are chiefly of black Sudanese stock, the principal groups being the Akan, living mostly along the coast, and the Ashanti, in the forest areas immediately to the north; the Guans, living on the plains of the Volta River; the Ga- and Ewe-speaking peoples of the south and southeast; and the Moshi-Dagomba-speaking tribes of the north **Population Distribution:** 31% urban **Density:** 124 inhabitants per sq. mi.

**Largest Cities (M.A. = Metropolitan Area):** (1970 census) Accra 564,194 (M.A. 738,498); Kumasi 260,286 (M.A. 345,117); Sekondi-Takoradi 91,874 (M.A. 160,868); Tema 60,767

**Per Capita Income:** $501 (1980) **Gross National Product (GNP):** $6 billion (1980) **Economic Statistics:** In 1979 about 42% of GNP was from agriculture (cocoa, of which Ghana is the world's leading producer, livestock, fish) and timber; 20% from manufacturing and mining; and 38% from trade and services. Industry consists of aluminum smelting and the processing of cocoa, kola nuts, coffee, coconuts, oil palms, and rubber **Minerals and Mining:** Gold is the most important mineral exploited, followed by diamonds. There are large reserves of manganese and bauxite; other minerals include low-grade deposits of iron ore, and deposits of beryl, ilmenite, nickel, graphite, and chromite **Labor Force:** 3.4 million, of which 57% is employed in agriculture, forestry, and fishing, 15.5% in industry and mining, and 27.5% in trade and services **Foreign Trade:** Exports, chiefly cocoa, cocoa butter, manganese, gold, diamonds, timber and aluminum, totaled $1.4 billion in 1980. Imports, mainly machinery and transport equipment, cereals, alumina, petroleum, and textiles, totaled $1.3 billion **Principal Trade Partners:** Britain, United States, West Germany, USSR, Nigeria

**Vital Statistics:** Birthrate, 48.4 per 1,000 of pop. (1980); death rate, 17.2 **Life Expectancy:** 52 years **Health Statistics:** 660 inhabitants per hospital bed; 9,925 per physician (1977) **Infant Mortality:** 59 per 1,000 births **Illiteracy:** 70% **Primary and Secondary School Enrollment:** 1,790,270 (1976) **Enrollment in Higher Education:** 9,079 (1975) **GNP Expended on Education:** 4.2% (1976)

**Transportation:** Paved roads total 3,780 mi. **Motor Vehicles:** 121,700 (1977) **Passenger Cars:** 72,400 **Railway Mileage:** 600 **Ports:** Tema, Takoradi **Major Airlines:** Ghana Airways operates internal and international services **Communications: Radio Transmitters:** 16 **Receivers:** 10,080,000 (1976) **Television Transmitters:** 4 **Receivers:** 35,000 (1976) **Telephones:** 65,000 (1978) **Newspapers:** 4 dailies, 42 copies per 1,000 inhabitants (1976)

**Weights and Measures:** Metric system **Travel Requirements:** Passport, visa, valid up to 14 days, $4.35 fee, 3 photos

The first of Britain's African possessions to gain freedom in the postwar decolonization era, Ghana has gone from a democratic parliamentary system, through dictatorship, rule by a military junta, a return to democracy, back to alternate short periods of military and civilian government.

During this time, the country also experienced overly ambitious industrialization and near bankruptcy as a result of the extravagances of Kwame Nkrumah, its first leader. Nkrumah was deposed in 1966, and died in exile in 1972.

Ghana, however, possesses a potentially strong economy; major resources range through cocoa, timber, manganese, gold, and electric power. Her people are capable and progressive.

As the Gold Coast, the country had moved steadily toward self-government prior to independence in 1957 and with its new name of Ghana—that of an ancient African empire—was otherwise well prepared for complete sovereignty.

Ghana has many educators, lawyers, doctors, economists, and a well-trained civil service. Development programs are concentrating on diversification of agriculture, an increase of arable land, and the improvement of rural communities. The prime objective is to reduce Ghana's dependency on cocoa exports by increasing exports and self-sufficiency in other products.

From 1966 until 1970, and again beginning with a coup in 1972, Ghana was ruled by military leaders. In 1977 students and professionals rose up in an "intellectuals" revolt, accusing the military government of repression, corruption and fiscal mismanagement. Gen. Ignatius Kutu Acheampong, head of state since 1972, resigned on July 5, 1978, and was succeeded by Lt. Gen. Fred W. K. Akuffo. On Jan. 1, 1979, following a declared state of emergency brought on by workers' and civil servants' strikes, the government legalized political activity for the first time in seven years.

On June 4, 1979, Akuffo's government was overthrown in a coup staged by junior army officers. Flight Lieut. Jerry Rawlings took control. Akuffo and two other former heads-of-state were executed in spite of an appeal for mercy from UN Secretary-General Kurt Waldheim.

Hilla Limann, conservative leader of the People's National party, wwas victorious in a run-off following the 1979 elections and took office as president on Sept. 24. Although his party had a slim majority in parliament, Limann found it difficult to get support for his programs. He was deposed Dec. 31, 1981, by Rawlings who seized the reigns of government for a second time and proceeded to rule by decree.

Progress has been slow in dealing with Ghana's economic problems—lagging production, shortage of staple foods, depressed prices for cocoa and rising costs of imported petroleum products. Transportation has been particularly hard hit by an airline strike in 1980 and by a shortage of replacement parts for the railroad and motor vehicles.

**HISTORY:** Ghana was dominated by independent black kingdoms in precolonial times. Following the arrival of the Portuguese in the 15th century, the coastal region soon became known as the Gold Coast because of the rich trade in gold. The gold trade later gave way to the slave trade, which was eventually abolished by the British in the 19th century. In 1874, Britain established the colony of the Gold Coast and in 1901 annexed the neighboring Ashanti kingdom. In the same year a region to the north, known as the Northern Territories, became a British protectorate

**1922:** Part of neighboring Togoland, a former German colony, is mandated to Britain by League of Nations and administered as part of the Gold Coast

**1942-48:** Africans are admitted into the government of the Gold Coast, but native agitation for independence mounts under the leadership of United Gold Coast Convention party; party leaders Joseph B. Danquah and Kwame Nkrumah are imprisoned

**1949:** Nkrumah, following his release, breaks with Danquah and forms his own party, the Convention People's party, and leads campaign of civil disobedience against the British

**1951-52:** Britain grants new constitution and elections are held; Nkrumah becomes prime minister

**1957:** The state of Ghana, comprising the Gold Coast and British Togoland, obtains independence, becoming the first black African colony to do so. Joins the UN

**1960:** Ghana becomes a republic within the British Commonwealth; Nkrumah becomes both chief of state and head of government, and is given the power to rule without parliament whenever he deems it necessary

**1962-64:** Nkrumah establishes one-party rule; several attempts on his life lead to arrests of numerous leaders in his own Convention People's party and of opposition leader Joseph Danquah, who dies in prison

**1966:** Nkrumah is deposed by a military coup; a National Liberation Council, headed by Lt. Gen. Joseph A. Ankrah, is set up to rule the country

**1969:** Ankrah resigns after admitting he received money for political purposes and is succeeded by Gen. Akwasi Afrifa. Civilian government is restored under new constitution

**1970:** Three-man presidential commission hheaded by Afrifa is dissolved; former Chief Justice Edward Akufo-Addo is elected president by electoral college

**1972:** Col. Ignatius Kutu Acheampong leads military coup and assumes power as head of state; offices of president and prime minister abolished and constitution withdrawn. Kwame Nkrumah dies and his body is returned from Guinea for burial in Ghana

**1978:** Acheampong is replaced by Lt. Gen. Fred W.K. Akuffo

**1979:** Akuffo is overthrown and is replaced by an Armed Forces Revolutionary Council, headed by Flight Lieut. Jerry Rawlings. Hilla Limann is elected president

**1980:** Ghana objects to activities of Libya's Embassy staff and breaks relations with Tripoli

**1981:** Barroom brawl leads to deaths of hundreds in fighting between Nanumba and Konkomba tribes in and around Wulensi; violence leaves 20,000 homeless. Rawlings seizes power again

**1982:** Rawlings suspends constitution, bars political parties, and sets up "people's tribunals" to mete out "revolutionary justice." Ghana resumes relations with Libya

## GREECE

**Area:** 50,944 sq. mi. **Population:** 9,706,687 (1981 census)

**Official Name:** Hellenic Republic **Capital:** Athens **Nationality:** Greek **Languages:** Modern Greek **Religion:** 97% of the population belongs to the Greek Orthodox Church; 2% are Moslems **Flag:** Nine equal horizontal stripes of blue and white with a white cross on a blue field in the upper left corner **Anthem:** Hymn of Liberty **Currency:** Drachma (63.3 per U.S. $1)

**Location:** Southeast Europe, occupying the southern part of the Balkan peninsula and more than 3,000 offshore islands. The Greek mainland is bordered on the north by Bulgaria, Yugoslavia, and Albania; on the east by Turkey and the Aegean Sea; on the south by the Mediterranean Sea; and on the west by the Ionian Sea **Features:** The country is predominantly mountainous, with much of the land dry and rocky **Chief Rivers:** Aliakmon, Peneus, Vardar, Achelous, Nestos, Alpheus, Struma

**Head of State:** President Constantine Karamanlis, born 1907, elected May 1980 **Head of Government:** Premier Andreas Papandreou, born 1919, sworn in Oct. 21, 1981 **Effective Date of Present Constitution:** June 1975 **Legislative Body:** Parliament (unicameral), consisting of 300 deputies **Local Government:** 51 prefectures, each headed by an appointed prefect and the autonomous Mt. Athos district

**Ethnic Composition:** About 98% of the population is Greek. Minorities include Turks (1%), Slavs, Vlachs, Albanians and Bulgarians **Population Distribution:** 65% urban **Density:** 191 inhabitants per sq. mi.

**Largest Cities** : (1980 census) Athens 885,136 (Greater Athens 3,016,457), Salonika 402,403, Patras 140,878, Larisa 103,263, Iraklion 101,668

**Per Capita Income:** $3,089 (1980) **Gross Domestic Product (GDP):** $29.3 billion (1980) **Economic Statistics:** Agriculture accounted for about 14% of the GDP in 1980 (the principal crops are wheat, tobacco, currants, grapes, olives, citrus fruits, and cotton); the industrial sector contributed about 32% (major industries include textiles; aluminum, nickel and chemical refineries; food processing; mining); services accounted for 52% **Minerals and Mining:** Lignite, bauxite, iron ore, petroleum, chromite, barite and magnesite are exploited **Labor Force:** 3,100,000 (1980), with 41% in services, 30% in industry, and 29% in agriculture **Foreign Trade:** Exports, mainly tobacco, currants, cotton, unprocessed aluminum, iron, nickel, and citrus fruits, totaled $4.1 billion (1980). Imports, chiefly machinery, iron and steel, crude oil, meat, passenger cars and trucks, totaled $11.9 billion **Principal Trade Partners:** West Germany, Italy, United States, France, Japan, Saudi Arabia, Britain, Netherlands

**Vital Statistics:** Birthrate, 15.9 per 1,000 of pop. (1979); death rate, 8.7 **Life Expectancy:** 73 years **Health Statistics:** 157 inhabitants per hospital bed; 453 per physician (1977) **Infant Mortality:** 18.7 per 1,000 births (1977) **Illiteracy:** 8% **Primary and Secondary School Enrollment:** 1,615,286 (1975) **Enrollment in Higher Education:** 111,435 (1975) **GNP Expended on Education:** 1.8% (1974)

**Transportation:** Paved roads total 10,000 mi. **Motor Vehicles:** 1,070,200 (1978) **Passenger Cars:** 744,700 **Railway Mileage:** 1,580 mi. **Ports:** Piraeus, Salonika, Iraklion, Patras, Eleusis, Volos **Major Airlines:** Olympic Airways operates domestic and international services **Communications: Radio Transmitters:** 55 **Receivers:** 2,750,000 (1976) **Television Transmitters:** 120 **Receivers:** 1,165,000 (1976) **Telephones:** 2,487,000 (1978) **Newspapers:** 112 dailies (1976), 107 copies per 1,000 inhabitants (1975)

**Weights and Measures:** Metric system **Travel Reequirements:** Passport, no visa for 3 months **International Dialing Code:** 30

The Hellenes (Greeks) inhabit a mountainous peninsula and its neighboring rocky islands. Agriculture is difficult—and so is administration. Trade and navigation—fostered by excellent harbors—have been vital for thousands of years. Individualism and loyalty to locality are strong.

The ancient Greeks had no national unity, but they were leaders in art, literature, and philosophy; and some of their city-states were the world's first democracies.

Conquered by Macedonia, then by Rome, then by the Ottoman Empire, Greece achieved independence and unity in struggles against the last in the 19th and 20th centuries. Disputes with Turkey concerning land and—more recently—territorial waters are still troublesome. Political stability within Greece has been rare.

Greece was occupied by Germany in World War II and needed considerable assistance from the United States to quell a Commmunist guerrilla movement in the war's aftermath. Greece entered NATO, despite the misgivings of many Greeks about U.S. influence, and Turkish membership, in the alliance. Later, the troubles in Cyprus aggravated ill-feelings toward Turkey.

Governed by short-lived coalition governments from 1946 until 1952, Greece achieved stability under Premier Alexander Papagos in 1952. He died in 1955, and Constantine Karamanlis succeeded him, serving until 1963, when he went into exile after a squabble with King Paul. George Papandreou formed a stable government in 1964, but anti-NATO elements in his past worried many. King Constantine II fired him in 1965, and political unrest followed until the army seized power in 1967.

Col. George Papadopoulous emerged as strong man and premier. He abolished the monarchy and made himself president in 1973, only to be deposed by military colleagues. Gen. Demetrios Ioannides ran the government from behind the scenes until 1974, when he sponsored the ill-fated coup against President Makarios of Cyprus. His fellow-officers deposed him and invited Constantine Karamanlis to resume the premiership.

Karamanlis held an election, which his own New Democracy party won handily. He withdrew Greece from NATO's military wing in 1974 to protest the Turkish invasion of Cyprus. In 1979 he brought Greece into the European Community (EC) as its tenth member, effective Jan. 1, 1981. Karamanlis was elected president of Greece in 1980 and pledged to represent the whole nation by removing himself from party politics.

In parliamentary elections on Oct. 18, 1981, Andreas Papandreou, son of the former premier, and his Panhellenic Socialist Movement (PASOK) won a large majority. Although he had lived in exile in the United States and was married to an American, Papandreou was generally regarded as being anti-American because he advocated the end of U.S. control over four military bases in Greece. After succeeding George Rallis as premier, he declared that he would set a timetable for U.S. military withdrawal and would hold a referendum to determine whether Greece would remain in the EC. In late February 1982, he became the first Greek premier to visit Cyprus, where he was warmly welcomed by the Greek community.

**HISTORY:** Ancient Greece, a small land fragmented into frequently warring city-states, attained its golden age in the Athens of the 5th century B.C. In the following century it fell to the forces of Philip of Macedon, whose son, Alexander the Great, spread Hellenistic civilization widely. In the 2nd century B.C., Greece became a territory of the Roman Empire and eventually was incorporated into the Byzantine Empire. Turkish conquests, completed in the 15th century, made Greece part of the Ottoman Empire

**1821-30:** Greeks wage war of independence against Turks, who gain help of Egypt; following intervention by Britain, France, and Russia, Greece wins autonomy and finally independence

**1832-63:** European powers choose Prince Otto of Bavaria to be king of a fully independent Greece; he is deposed in 1862. The following year a Danish prince is chosen as monarch, becoming King George I of the Hellenes

**1912-22:** Greece takes part in the Balkan Wars of 1912-13 and increases its territory. Outbreak of World War I leads to split between pro-Allied government and neutralist King Constantine I; king abdicates in 1917; Greece joins Allied side and gains additional territory in the postwar settlements; Greece invades Asia Minor and is defeated by Turks

**1923:** Hostility to dynasty forces George II to leave Greece

**1924-35:** Greece is proclaimed a republic; after more than a decade of political strife, a plebiscite restores the monarchy

**1936-41:** John Metaxas becomes premier and institutes a dictatorship that lasts through Italy's World War II invasion of Greece, begun in 1940, and continues up to his death in 1941

**1941-50:** Germany invades in 1941 and Greece is occupied by Axis forces. With the expulsion of the last of the German troops in 1944, rivalry between Greek Communist and royalist guerrillas erupts into civil war.. Under the Truman Doctrine, announced in 1947, the United States sends advisers to the Greek Army and provides $300 million in economic and military aid; Communist forces are finally defeated in 1950

**1967:** Military junta seizes power. King Constantine II and the royal family flee to Rome after an abortive countercoup; Col. George Papadopoulos becomes premier

**1973:** Papadopoulos decrees end to monarchy, appoints himself head of new "Hellenic Republic." He is toppled by a bloodless coup. Gen. Phaedon Gizikis becomes president with Dimitrios Ioannides as military dictator; elections are postponed

**1974:** Ioannides sponsors coup in Cyprus. Turkish army invades Cyprus. Military junta leaders turn government over to civilians, ending seven years of military rule. Former Premier Constantine Karamanlis returns from self-imposed exile in Paris and is sworn in as premier by President Gizikis. Britain, Turkey, and Greece, meeting in Geneva, impose new cease-fire on Cyprus. Soon after, when Geneva peace talks break down, Turkish forces resume their advance on Cyprus. Greece withdraws its armed forces from NATO. First free elections in more than a decade result in decisive victory for Premier Karamanlis. In national referendum voters reject monarchy in favor of a republic

**1975:** Parliament adopts a new constitution and elects Konstantinos Tsatsos as president. Trial of the principal organizers of the 1967 coup results in their death sentences being commuted by cabinet to life imprisonment

**1978:** Greek leaders deplore U.S. ending its arms embargo against Turkey. New law makes terrorism a capital offense

**1980:** Karamanlis becomes president; George John Rallis is selected as premier. Greece rejoins NATO's military wing

**1981:** Greece becomes full member of European Community (it had previously been an associate member). Andreas Papandreou succeeds Rallis as premier after his PASOK party wins 170 of the 300 parliamentary seats. Queen Frederika, 68, mother of deposed King Constantine II, dies in Madrid on Feb. 6

## GRENADA

**Area:** 133 sq. mi. **Population:** 103,103 (1981 est.)

**Official Name:** Grenada **Capital:** St. George's **Nationality:** Grenadian **Languages:** English, with a rarely used Franco-African patois **Religion:** Roman Catholicism, Protestantism **Flag:** A diagonally divided field, yellow at top and bottom and green at sides, with red border on all sides, bearing along top and bottom three yellow stars each; in center a yellow star on a red disk; in hoist a green triangle with a nutmeg with yellow shell and brown fruit **Anthem:** Hail Grenada **Currency:** East Caribbean dollar (2.70 per U.S. $1)

**Location:** The southernmost of the Windward Islands in the West Indies. Includes the southern Grenadines, the largest of which is Carriacou **Features:** Volcanic in origin, the islands are chiefly mountainous **Chief Rivers:** There are no large rivers

**Head of State:** Queen Elizabeth II, represented by a governor-general, Sir Paul Scoon, born 1935, appointed 1978 **Head of Government:** Prime Minister Maurice Bishop, born 1944, seized power in 1979 **Effective Date of Present Constitution:** 1967, suspended 1979 **Legislative Body:** Rule is by a People's Revolutionary Government (PRG) **Local Government:** 6 parishes and one dependency (Carriacou)

**Ethnic Composition:** Largely of mixed descent, with strains of white settlers, Africans brought in as slaves, and Carib Indians **Population Distribution:** N.A. **Density:** 775 inhabitants per sq. mi.

**Largest City:** (1981 est.) St. George's 6,463

**Per Capita Income:** $660 (1979 est.) **Gross Domestic Product (GDP):** $71 million (1979 est.) **Economic Statistics:** The economy is agricultural (32% of GDP), with sugar, coconuts, nutmeg, cocoa, and bananas the chief exports. Yams, rice, breadfruit, and corn are grown for food. Tourism is important **Minerals and Mining:** Offshore exploration for gas and oil in progress **Labor Force:** 36,000, of which 40% are employed in agriculture, forestry and fishing **Foreign Trade:** Exports, chiefly cocoa, nutmeg and bananas, totaled $22 million (1979). Imports totaled $45 million **Principal Trade Partners:** Britain, West Germany, United States, Canada, Caribbean countries, Netherlands

**Vital Statistics:** Birthrate, 24.5 per 1,000 of pop. (1979); death rate, 6.8 **Life Expectancy:** 63 years **Health Statistics:** 144 inhabitants per hospital bed; 4,000 per physician (1974) **Infant Mortality:** 15.4 per 1,000 births **Illiteracy:** 2% **Education Statistics:** 71 primary and secondary schools with a combined enrollment of 34,863 (1971) **Enrollment in Higher Education:** c. 100 (1974) **GNP Expended on Education:** 9.4% (1975)

**Transportation:** Surfaced roads total 375 mi. **Motor Vehicles:** 3,900 (1971) **Passenger Cars:** 3,800 **Railway Mileage:** None **Ports:** St. George's, Grenville, Hillsborough **Major Airlines:** LIAT **Communications: Radio Transmitters:** 4 **Receivers:** 22,000 (1976) **Television:** None **Telephones:** 5,000 (1978) **Newspapers:** 1 daily (1976)

**Weights and Measures:** Metric system **Travel Requirements:** Passport **Direct Dialing Code:** 809

---

Formerly a dependency of the United Kingdom and later a member of the British-controlled Federation of the West Indies, Grenada became an internally self-governing state on March 3, 1967. The United Kingdom retained responsibility for defense and external affairs. On February 7, 1974, Grenada became independent within the British Commonwealth of Nations, with a parliamentary system of government based on Great Britain's.

Grenada, known as the "Isle of Spice," is famous for its nutmeg, cocoa and cinnamon. Tourism, traditionally a mainstay of the economy, has suffered due to political unrest. Rioting against the regime of Prime Minister Eric Gairy in 1973 and 1974 was answered with secret-police terrorism and the exodus of many Grenadians. Gairy was reelected by a narrow margin in 1976.

In a coup marked by the killing of two policemen, Maurice Bishop, a London-educated lawyer, and the socialistic New Jewel Movement seized the government on March 13, 1979. Bishop then became prime minister, and a 14-member People's Revolutionary Government took office. The constitution was suspended, but Grenada remained within the British Commonwealth. Bishop invited Cuban instructors to train his new People's Revolutionary Army and made a deal for Cuban workers to build a jet airport near St. George's. In 1981, some 300 islanders (more than one of every 350) were reportedly being held as political prisoners. Land reform had been launched, with state farms created out of some of Grenada's private holdings, and cooperative farms had been established.

In 1982, Bishop described his government as committed to a "mixed economy with a dominant state sector." Cut off from U.S. economic aid, Grenada was receiving development funds from several other sources, including the OPEC natiions.

**HISTORY:** The original inhabitants of the islands were Arawak Indians who were expelled by the warlike Caribs shortly before the visit of Columbus in 1498. An abortive English settlement in 1609 was followed by French settlement and control from 1650 to 1762. Britain controlled the islands for over 200 years, except for five years of French rule (1779-83) during the American Revolution

**1833:** Slavery is abolished
**1967:** Grenada assumes Associated State status
**1974:** Independence is attained. Grenada is admitted to UN
**1979:** The New Jewel (for Joint Endeavor for Welfare, Education and Liberation) Movement seizes the government, and Maurice Bishop becomes prime minister. Grenada joins the "non-aligned" nations in a summit meeting in Cuba
**1980:** Bombing assassination attempt against the life of Bishop fails
**1982:** $70-million airport completed with Cuban aid

---

## GUATEMALA

**Area:** 42,042 sq. mi. **Population:** 6,043,559 (1981 census)

**Official Name:** Republic of Guatemala **Capital:** Guatemala **Nationality:** Guatemalan **Languages:** Spanish is the official and predominant language; 18 varieties of the Maya-Quiché Indian dialects are spoken in the countryside **Religion:** Largely Roman Catholic, some Protestants **Flag:** Blue, white, and blue vertical bands, with the national coat of arms in the center **Anthem:** National Anthem, beginning "Blessed Guatemala" **Currency:** Quetzal (1 per U.S. $1)

**Location:** Central America. Guatemala is bordered on the north by Mexico, on the east by Belize and the Caribbean, on the southeast by Honduras and El Salvador, on the southwest by the Pacific Ocean, and on the west by Mexico **Features:** The central highland region constitutes about one-fifth of the country's land surface. The Pacific plain is a narrow belt between mountains and ocean, while the Caribbean lowlands consist of fertile river valleys. The northern part of the country is dominated by the lowland forest of Petén **Chief Rivers:** Motagua, Usumacinta, Polochic, Samalá

**Head of State and of Government:** President: Brig. Gen. José Efrain Rios Montt, born 1926, took power as leader of 3-man junta in coup of March 23, 1982, assumed sole power on June 9 **Effective Date of Present Constitution:** 1966 (suspended March 24, 1982) **Legislative Body:** National Congress (unicameral), consisting of 61 deputies elected for 4 years (dissolved March 24, 1982) **Local Government:** 22 departments, administered by governors appointed by the president, and a central district, the capital city

**Ethnic Composition:** Pure-blooded descendants of the Maya Indians make up almost 50% of the population; the rest is largely of mixed Spanish and Indian descent **Population Distribution:** 36% urban **Density:** 144 inhabitants per sq. mi.

**Largest Cities:** (1981 census) Guatemala 749,784, Mixco 199,650, Esquintla 73,688, Quezaltenango 72,745

**Per Capita Income:** $1,067 (1980) **Gross National Product (GNP):** $7.5 billion (1980) **Economic Statistics:** In 1979 about 26% of GNP came from agriculture (coffee, cotton, sugar cane, bananas, corn, beans, rice, wheat); 16% is derived from industry (foodstuffs, tobacco, textiles, furniture, paper and paper products, leather goods, chemical products, tires, machinery and metal products) **Minerals and Mining:** Zinc, silver, lead, nickel, petroleum and limestone are exploited **Labor Force:** 1,895,168 (1975), of which 58% is employed in agriculture, 24% in trade and services and 18% in industry **Foreign Trade:** Exports, chiefly coffee, bananas, cotton, sugar and meat, totaled $1.5 billion in 1980. Imports, mainly industrial machinery, textiles, chemicals and pharmaceutical products, and construction materials, totaled $1.5 billion **Principal Trade Partners:** United States, Central American countries, West Germany, Japan, Venezuela

**Vital Statistics:** Birthrate, 42.1 per 1,000 of pop. (1979); death rate, 10.3 **Life Expectancy:** 57 years **Health Statistics:** 457 inhabitants per hospital bed; 4,338 per physician (1973) **Infant Mortality:** 70.2 per 1,000 births **Illiteracy:** 54% **Primary and Secondary School Enrollment:** 749,450 (1975) **Enrollment in Higher Education:** 25,978 (1976) **GNP Expended on Education:** 1.7% (1976)

**Transportation:** Paved roads total 1,700 mi. **Motor Vehicles:** 134,400 (1978) **Passenger Cars:** 90,500 **Railway Mileage:** 588 **Ports:** Pto. Barrios, Sto. Tomás de Castilla, San José, Champerico **Major Airlines:** AVIATECA operates domestic and international services **Communications: Radio Transmitters:** 104 **Receivers:** 265,000 (1976) **Television Transmitters:** 12 **Receivers:** 120,000 **Telephones:** 71,000 (1977) **Newspapers:** 9 dailies (1976), 39 copies per 1,000 inhabitants (1972)

**Weights and Measures:** Metric system and local units **Travel Requirements:** Proof of citizenship; tourist card good for stay up to 6 months but usable only within 6 months of issue; $1 fee **International Dialing Code:** 502

---

Assassinations and kidnappings by extremists of both the left and right continue to plague Guatemala, the largest and potentially the wealthiest of the Central American republics.

In effect, there are two Guatemalas—one Spanish and one Indian. The Indians, concentrated in the picturesque central highlands, speak little Spanish and cling to peasant ways that originated with their Mayan ancestors well before the Spanish conquest. Constituting almost half the population, they account for the low economic and social standards of the country as a whole. They have been caught in the middle of the conflict, and some have been joining guerrilla groups.

The educational deficit alone is staggering. Illiteracy still hovers at over 50 percent, and about half the children of school age get little or no schooling despite some progress in school construction. The problem is complicated by the necessity of teaching in Indian languages before transferring to Spanish, and by the government's failure to provide funds.

Guatemala's wealth has traditionally been land-based. Coffee and cotton, the major products, are picked by the Indian population at low wages. Production of tires, clothing, foodstuffs, and pharmaceuticals has helped to diversify the economy although many of the industries are little more than assembly operations employing few workers. Oil reserves were discovered in 1976, and in 1980 Petromaya began to export modest amounts.

Since 1978 Guatemala has been virtually in a state of civil war between left-wing guerrillas and the government's military and security forces abetted by right-wing "death squads." In February 1981 Amnesty International reported nearly 5,000 persons killed and 615 missing since 1978. Victims included many trade union and community leaders, teachers, students, clergymen, social workers and political opponents of the government.

**HISTORY:** The Mayas, one of the most advanced of the Indian tribes, flourished in Guatemala for centuries before the arrival of the Spanish conquistadors. In the 12th century, however, Mayan civilization began to decline and its downfall was completed by the Spanish conquest in the 16th century. Under Spanish rule Guatemala was the seat of a captaincy general

**1821:** Guatemala is granted independence from Spain and with the other Central American countries is annexed to Mexico

**1823-1825:** Central American nations secede from Mexico and establish United Provinces of Central America

**1839-1944:** Guatemala becomes an independent republic and for more than a century is governed by the military

**1951-57:** Col. Jacobo Arbenz Guzmán, a leftist-leaning president, institutes social and agrarian reforms and expropriates holdings of foreign plantation owners, including United Fruit Co. Communist influence in Arbenz regime leads to strained relations with United States. With U.S. support, Col. Carlos Castillo Armas overthrows Arbenz in 1954 and returns expropriated land; Castillo Armas is assassinated in 1957

**1958-63:** Country is thrown into political turmoil and ruled by military juntas. State of siege is declared in 1963 to deal with growing terrorism and sabotage by extremists of right and left

**1965-68:** A new constitution takes effect in 1965; free elections are held the following year and Julio César Méndez Montenegro, candidate of moderately leftist Revolutionary party, becomes president. He suspends constitutional guarantees in January 1968 following terrorist slayings of two U.S. military officials. In August, U.S. Ambassador John Mein is killed

**1970:** Carlos Arana Osorio, leading a right-wing coalition, wins presidential election. Terrorists kidnap several foreign diplomats, kill West German Ambassador. State of siege imposed

**1974:** Alleged vote fraud installs Gen. Kjell Laugerud García as president; violence ensues

**1975:** Britain agrees to resume talks with Guatemala on future of Belize (British Honduras). Guatemala has claimed sovereignty over the British dependency for more than 100 years

**1976:** Severe damage and 22,500 deaths caused by earthquakes

**1978:** Gen. Romeo Lucas García, government-backed moderate conservative, is elected president in runoff vote in Congress

**1980:** Indian peasants seize Spanish embassy in Guatemala City to protest government strong-arm measures; police storm building and 39 persons die in ensuing fire

**1981:** Guatemala signs treaty with Britain in March settling century-long Belize dispute, but subsequent problems lead to a break in consular ties with U.K. on Sept. 7

**1982:** Claiming fraud in March 2 elections, a 3-man military junta seizes power; three months later Brig. Gen. José Efrain Ríos forces his two colleagues out and proclaims himself president. Four main rebel forces unite under banner of Guatemalan National Revolutionary Unity

## GUINEA

**Area:** 94,925 sq. mi. **Population:** 5,275,000 (1979 est.)

**Official Name:** People's Revolutionary Republic of Guinea **Capital:** Conakry **Nationality:** Guinean **Languages:** French is the official language; the languages of 8 ethnic groups are recognized as national languages. The two main languages are Peul (Fulani) and Mandé **Religion:** About 75% Moslem, 24% animist, less than 1% Christian **Flag:** Red, yellow, and green vertical stripes **Anthem:** Liberty **Currency:** Syli (21.2 per U.S. $1)

**Location:** West Africa. Guinea is bordered by Senegal and Mali on the north, the Ivory Coast on the east, Liberia and Sierra Leone on the south, the Atlantic Ocean on the west, and Guinea-Bissau on the northwest **Features:** The country consists of a low-lying coastal area, a pastoral plateau, a forest region along the Liberian border, and a dry area in the north **Chief Rivers:** Niger, Bafing, Konkouré, Koliba, Milo

**Head of State:** President Ahmed Sékou Touré, born 1922; in power since 1958, reelected 1975 for 7 years; he is secretary-general of the country's only party **Head of Government:** Premier: Dr. Lansana Béavogui, born 1923, took office April 1972 **Effective Date of Present Constitution:** November 12, 1958 **Legislative Body:** National Assembly (unicameral), consisting of 210 members elected for 5 years. All members belong to the Democratic party of Guinea **Local Government:** 35 administrative regions

**Ethnic Composition:** Of about 18 tribes in the country the most important are the Peuls (Fulani), Malinké (Mandingo), and Soussou **Population Distribution:** 9% urban **Density:** 56 inhabitants per sq. mi.

**Largest City:** (1973 est.) Conakry 198,000

**Per Capita Income:** $196 (1980) **Gross National Product (GNP):** $1 billion (1980) **Economic Statistics:** About 40% of GNP is from agriculture (coffee, palm products, corn, millet, pineapples, bananas, rice, cassava), forestry, and fishing; 20% from mining, less tha 4% from manufacturing (textiles, truck assembly, sawmilling, canning, paints, soap, cigarettes, plastics, furniture) **Minerals and Mining:** Bauxite and iron ore deposits are among the richest in the world; other minerals are diamonds and gold **Labor Force:** About 85% of the working population is engaged in plantation and subsistence agriculture. About 134,000 are wage earners, mostly in public service **Foreign Trade:** Exports, chiefly alumina, pineapples, coffee, palm kernels, and bananas, totaled $421 million in 1980. Imports, cotton textiles, rice, vehicles, cement, machinery, petroleum products, and sugar, totaled $375 million **Principal Trade Partners:** United States, France, West Germany, Spain, USSR, Britain

**Vital Statistics:** Birthrate, 46.1 per 1,000 of pop. (1980); death rate, 20.7 **Life Expectancy:** 41 years **Health Statistics:** 588 inhabitants per hospital bed; 15,467 per physician (1977) **Infant Mortality:** 216 per 1,000 births **Illiteracy:** 90% **Education Statistics:** 2,287 primary and secondary schools, with combined enrollment of 241,033 (1971) **Enrollment in Higher Education:** 2,874 (1972) **GNP Expended on Education:** 5.9% (1972)

**Transportation:** Paved roads total 3,000 mi. **Motor Vehicles:** 21,000 (1972) **Passenger Cars:** 10,200 **Railway Mileage:** 500 **Ports:** Conakry, Kassa, Benty, Kamsar **Major Airlines:** Air Guinée provides internal and international services **Communications: Radio Transmitters:** 6 **Receivers:** 120,000 (1976) **Television Transmitters:** 1 **Telephones:** 10,000 (1977) **Newspapers:** 1 daily, 2 copies per 1,000 inhabitants (1976)

**Weights and Measures:** Metric system **Travel Requirements:** Business visas only, check Guinea Embassy, Washington, D.C.

Committed by its militant leader, Ahmed Sékou Touré, in 1958 to "poverty in freedom rather than riches in slavery," Guinea has followed a tortuous course that has assured poverty but little freedom.

In 1958 Guinea was the only French colony to vote *non* to General de Gaulle's proposed community of semiautonomous nations still closely linked to France. Although, for France's former colonies, the community was to be a step toward eventual sovereignty, accompanied by aid and trade, Guinea opted for independence.

Hostility between France and Guinea persisted for the next two decades and ended officially only with a state visit by French President Valéry Giscard d'Estaing in December 1978.

Until recently, Guinea's huge mineral resources and great hydroelectric potential had been neglected. In addition to iron ore, gold, and diamonds, Guinea possesses bauxite deposits estimated to be a third of the world's total. An international consortium of aluminum companies, in which the Guinean government holds 49 percent interest, is now operating a big bauxite mining complex at Boké in northern Guinea. Production at more than nine million tons a year is expected to earn Guinea $500 million over a 20-year period.

In late 1970, Touré's long rule was shaken by the landing at Conakry of a small, seaborne guerrilla force, which Touré charged was an invasion by Portuguese mercenaries and Guinean renegades, backed by Portugal and launched from neighboring Portuguese Guinea. Denied by Portugal, the charge was supported by a UN commission.

**HISTORY:** Guinea possesses a rich ethnic and cultural heritage derived from the empires of Ghana, Malí, and Songhai, which ranged from the western Sudan to the West African coast between the 10th and 15th centuries. In the 15th century, the Portuguese, followed by the Dutch, English, and French, opened the country to European contacts and trade. Following the establishment of a protectorate by France in 1849, French penetration inland met with strong resistance from Fulani and Malinké chieftains. Resistance was finally crushed with the defeat in 1898 of the popular hero and chieftain Samory Touré, from whom President Sékou Touré is said to be descended

**1958:** Guinea, the only French West African territory to vote against membership in the French Community, becomes an independent republic; Sékou Touré, an acknowledged Marxist although rejecting Marxism as inapplicable to Africa, becomes president and his Democratic party of Guinea becomes the only political party; France abruptly withdraws all aid

**1959-61:** Guinea turns to the Soviet bloc and Communist China for assistance, and promotes African unity by forming short-lived union with Ghana and Mali

**1965:** Guinea suspends relations with France after charging that France encouraged a plot to overthrow Touré government

**1970:** Dispute with Portugal develops over charges of rebel infiltration from Guinea to Portuguese Guinea. Post of prime minister is created and the government is reorganized. Dr. Louis Lansana Béavogui becomes prime minister

**1975:** Relations restored with France. Touré elected for third term

**1976:** Discovery of a series of assassination plots on the life of President Touré announced by his administration

**1978:** Guinea and Senegal restore diplomatic relations; French President Giscard d'Estaing visits

**1979:** In move to improve human-rights situation, several hundred political prisoners are freed. Touré visits United States

**1980:** Touré escapes assassination attempt May 14. Dispute arises with neighboring Guinea-Bissau over boundaries of possibly oil-bearing ocean floor

**1981:** Guinea pledges troops to peacekeeping force in Chad

**1982:** Touré leads Islamic mediation mission to Iran and Iraq. In Washington, he urges increased U.S. investment

## GUINEA-BISSAU

**Area:** 13,948 sq. mi. **Population:** 777,214 (1979 census)

**Official Name:** Republic of Guinea-Bissau **Capital:** Bissau **Nationality:** Guinean **Languages:** Portuguese and Crioulo, a creole lingua franca **Religion:** 66% animist, 30% Moslem, 4% Christian **Flag:** A black star on a red vertical stripe at the hoist and equal horizontal stripes in the fly of gold over light green **Anthem:** Long Live the Glorious Country **Currency:** Guinea-Bissau escudo (37.8 per U.S. $1)

**Location:** On the west coast of Africa, bounded by the Atlantic Ocean on the west, Senegal on the north, and Guinea on the east and south **Features:** A low-lying coastal plain with savanna, swamps, and rain forest. Large sections are frequently covered by tidal waters. There are 18 main offshore islands, including the Bijagós Archipelago **Chief Rivers:** Cacheu, Mansoa, Geba, Grande de Buba, Corubal

**Head of State and Goverment:** President of the Council of the Revolution, Gen. João Bernardo Vieira, born 1939, assumed power in coup of Nov. 14, 1980. He is assisted by a prime minister, Victor Saúde Maria **Effective Date of Constitution:** New constitution pending **Legislative Body:** All power resides with the 9-member Council of the Revolution **Local Government:** 12 administrative regions

**Ethnic Composition:** Except for small groups of Portuguese and mulattos the people are mostly indigenous (Balanta, Fulani, Mandyako, Malinké, and Pepel) **Population Distribution:** N.A. **Density:** 56 inhabitants per sq. mi.

**Largest Cities:** (1979 census) Bissau 109,486

**Per Capita Income:** $175 (1979) **Gross Domestic Product (GDP):** $174 million (1979) **Economic Statistics:** Agriculture probably accounts for well over 50% of the GDP. About 70% of the agricultural production is consumed locally **Minerals and Mining:** No commercial mining exists. There are potentially large deposits of bauxite **Labor Force:** 410,000; 94% are employed in agriculture **Foreign Trade:** Exports, chiefly peanuts, coconuts, frozen shrimp and fish, wood, totaled $19 million in 1980. Imports, chiefly textiles, vehicles, rice, consumer goods, fuel totaled approximately $80 million **Principal Trade Partners:** Portugal, France, Angola, USSR

**Vital Statistics:** Birthrate, 40.8 per 1,000 of pop. (1980); death rate 23.2 **Life Expectancy:** 35 years **Health Statistics:** 481 inhabitants per hospital bed; 6,750 per physician (1977) **Infant Mortality:** 47.1 per 1,000 births **Illiteracy:** 88% **Primary and Secondary School Enrollment:** 86,756 (1976) **Enrollment in Higher Education:** N.A. **GNP Expended on Education:** 1.2% (1972)

**Transportation:** Paved roads total 265 mi. **Motor Vehicles:** 5,124 **Passenger Cars:** 3,268 **Railway Mileage:** None **Ports:** Bissau, Bolama **Major Airlines:** TAP **Communications: Radio Transmitters:** 2 **Licenses:** 11,000 (1976) **Television:** None **Telephones:** 3,000 (1973) **Newspapers:** 1 daily, 11 copies per 1,000 inhabitants (1976)

**Weights and Measures:** Metric system **Travel Requirements:** Passport, visa

Poor, diseased and subject to forced labor, Africans of Portuguese Guinea developed a national liberation movement in the early 1960s. By 1970 rebels claimed control of two-thirds of the country. The movement was led by the African Party for the Independence of Guinea and Cape Verde (PAIGC), whose basic tenet of doctrine was the "unity" of Guinea-Bissau and Cape Verde Islands, and was headed by Amilcar and Luis Cabral. The PAIGC proclaimed independence in 1973, but Portugal rejected the claim. However, the 1974 coup in Portugal ultimately resulted in an agreement granting independence for Guinea-Bissau on September 24 of that year, making Guinea-Bissau the first Portuguese African territory to achieve independence. Luis de Almeida Cabral became president, Amilcar Cabral having been killed in 1973.

Guinea-Bissau is currently struggling with all the problems that face developing nations, especially in the areas of education, health care, road development and electrification.

**HISTORY:** The Portuguese, sailing for Prince Henry the Navigator, reached the area in 1446. Slave trading was important in the 17th and 18th centuries

**1879:** Portuguese Guinea is separated from the administrative control of the Cape Verde Islands

**1962:** Revolt against Portuguese rule begins

**1974:** Portuguese Guinea attains independence as Guinea-Bissau

**1978:** Premier Francisco Mendes dies in auto crash

**1980:** Dispute with Guinea arises over limits of possible offshore oilfields. Cabral government is overthrown Nov. 14 in coup led by Premier Vieira, who opposes union with Cape Verde

**1981:** PAIGC unity with Guinea-Bissau is ended by Cape Verde

## GUYANA

**Area:** 83,000 sq. mi. **Population:** 820,000 (1978 est.)

**Official Name:** Cooperative Republic of Guyana **Capital:** Georgetown **Nationality:** Guyanese **Languages:** English is dominant; Hindi, Urdu and American Indian languages are spoken **Religion:** About 57% Christian (chiefly Anglican), 33% Hindu, 9% Moslem **Flag:** A green field with a black-edged red triangular pennant superimposed on a white-edged yellow triangular pennant **Anthem:** Dear land of Guayana **Currency:** Guyana dollar (3 per U.S. $1)

**Location:** Northeast coast of South America. Guyana is bordered on the north by the Atlantic Ocean, on the east by Suriname, on the south and southwest by Brazil, and on the northwest by Venezuela **Features:** The country is divided into a low-lying coastal region, a heavily forested interior, and a region of mountains and savannas in the south and west **Chief Rivers:** Essequibo, Courantyne, Berbice, Mazaruni, Cuyuni, Demerara

**Head of State and Government:** Executive President Forbes Burnham, born 1923, took office Oct. 6, 1980. He is assisted by a prime minister, Ptolemy Alexander Reid, who is also First Vice President **Effective Date of Present Constitution:** Oct. 6, 1980 **Legislative Body:** National Assembly (unicameral), consisting of 53 members elected by proportional representation for 5 years and 12 members elected by local councils **Local Government:** 10 regions

**Ethnic Composition:** About 51% of the population is of East Indian descent; 43% African and African mixed; 6% indigenous Amerindians, and small groups of Portuguese and Chinese **Population Distribution:** 30% urban **Density:** 9.9 inhabitants per sq. mi.

**Largest Cities** (M.A. = Metropolitan Area): (1976 est.) Georgetown 72,049 (M.A. 187,056);(1971 est.) Linden 23,956; New Amsterdam 17,782; Corriverton 10,502; Rosehall 5,018

**Per Capita Income:** $756 (1980) **Gross National Product (GNP):** $635 million (1980) **Economic Statistics:** In 1973 about 20% of GNP came from agriculture (sugar, rice, corn, coconuts, coffee); 12% from manufacturing (cigarettes, matches, margarine, edible oils, beverages, sugar milling, aluminum smelting, wood and pulp); 18% from mining; and 22% from trade and services **Minerals and Mining:** Bauxite is the principal mineral. Diamonds and gold are also mined **Labor Force:** 242,000 (1975), with 31% in industry and mining and 29% in agriculture **Foreign Trade:** Exports, chiefly bauxite and aluminum, sugar, rice, timber, shrimp, gold, and diamonds, totaled $291 million in 1979. Imports, mainly foodstuffs, manufactured goods, machinery, petroleum products, beverages, and tobacco, totaled $318 million **Principal Trade Partners:** Britain, United States, Commonwealth Caribbean countries, Canada, Japan

**Vital Statistics:** Birthrate 28.3 per 1,000 of pop. (1978); death rate, 7.3 **Life Expectancy:** 67 years **Health Statistics:** 207 inhabitants per hospital bed; 3,249 per physician (1975) **Infant Mortality:** 45.9 per 1,000 births **Illiteracy:** 9% **Primary and Secondary School Enrollment:** 213,679 (1976) **Enrollment in Higher Education:** 2,307 (1973) **GNP Expended on Education:** 7.0% (1976)

**Transportation:** Paved roads total 480 mi. **Motor Vehicles:** 43,100 (1977) **Passenger Cars:** 28,400 **Railway Mileage:** 68 **Port:** Georgetown **Major Airlines:** Guyana Airways operates domestic and international flights **Communications: Radio Transmitters:** 7 **Receivers:** 275,000 (1976) **Television:** None **Telephones:** 27,000 (1977) **Newspapers:** 2 dailies, 63 copies per 1,000 inhabitants (1976)

**Weights and Measures:** British standards. The metric system is being introduced **Travel Requirements:** Passport; no visa for 30 days; onward ticket **International Dialing Code:** 592

---

Aptly termed the "land of the waters" by the indigenous Amerindians, Guyana, along most of its coastline, is below sea level. The land along the Atlantic, where most people of the South American country live, is made habitable by the 300-year-old seawalls and drainage system built by the Dutch.

Until the early 19th century, under the British, various colonization plans failed before the lucrative sugar industry was introduced. The British imported African slaves, indentured Portuguese and East Indians, and Chinese. These waves of immigration have determined Guyana's racial composition and the experience of slavery and indentured servitude has molded the country's political and social life.

Guyana has unresolved boundary disputes with two of its neighbors, Venezuela and Suriname. Venezuela claims the mineral-rich area west of the Essequibo River, more than half the size of Guyana as now constituted. In 1982, it refused to renew a 12-year agreement to settle the claim peacefully and was reported by Guyana to have twice sent troops across the present border.

Gaining independence from Britain in 1966, Guyana set out on an autonomous line of development as a "cooperative republic" in 1970. In the words of its prime minister, Forbes Burnham, it planned to "pursue relentlessly the policy of owning and controlling our natural resources." Burnham soon established a Marxist government.

In early 1975, Guyana nationalized the important bauxite mining industry. By mid-1976, after sugar production had also been nationalized, some 80 percent of the nation's goods and services were in government hands. Succeeding years saw a steady economic deterioration. By 1982, despite a 1981 currency devaluation, the three main pillars of Guyana's economy—bauxite, sugar, and rice production—were near collapse, and even basic consumer necessities were in short supply.

In the meantime, Burnham's government became increasingly authoritarian. By 1979, it was estimated that as much as one sixth of the national budget was devoted to the maintenance of the military forces and paramilitary organizations.

Toward the end of 1980, Burnham promulgated a new constitution which concentrated power in the office of the president, to which post he was then elected by the parliament. In December parliamentary elections, denounced by the opposition as fraudulent, his People's National Congress party (PNC) captured 41 of 53 seats, defeating another leftist faction, the People's Progressive party (PPP), led by Burnham's long-time political rival, former Prime Minister Cheddi B. Jagan.

A mass-murder suicide on an appalling scale at Jonestown, a community set up in the jungle by the San Francisco-based People's Temple, turned world attention to Guyana in November 1978. The bizarre tragedy began with the murders of U.S. Representative Leo J. Ryan of California, who had flown to Guyana to investigate reports that cult members were being held against their will, and four members of his party. The five were killed at the Port Kaituma airport on November 18, just after visiting Jonestown and getting word that 20 Temple members wanted to defect. After news of the murders was radioed to Jonestown, the Rev. Jim Jones, self-proclaimed messiah, led the whole community in a previously rehearsed suicide plan. It was carried out mainly by mixing a flavored drink with cyanide, but there was also some gunfire. The U.S. military removed 913 bodies of Temple members by air to Dover (Del.) Air Force Base. As many as 26 Guyanese children may have been among the victims. Nearly all of the other dead, including Jones, were from the U.S.

**HISTORY:** Little is known of the history of Guyana before the arrival of Europeans. When European explorers came to Guyana in the late 1500s and early 1600s, they found Arawak, Carib, and Warrau Indians living in the area. In the late 17th century the country was settled by the Dutch and in the following century alternated between Dutch and British rule. By 1815, British rule was firmly established

**1831:** Three colonies of Berbice, Essequibo, and Demerara are united into the colony of British Guiana

**1837:** Slaves are emancipated

**1928:** British Guiana gains limited representative government

**1953-57:** A new constitution is adopted providing for a bicameral legislature and ministerial responsibility. Elections are held, People's Progressive party (PPP), led by Cheddi Jagan and generally supported by East Indians, captures 18 of the 24 elective seats. Six months after the election, the British suspend the constitution, charging Communist subversion of the British Guiana government; interim regime takes over

**1961:** Colony is granted full internal self-government, a new constitution is introduced; the PPP wins 20 of the 35 seats in the Legislative Assembly, Jagan is named prime minister

**1962-64:** Rivalry between PPP and People's National Congress (PNC), supported by the Negroes, leads to violence

**1964:** Two parties, PNC and the United Force, form a coalition government, with PNC leader Forbes Burnham as prime minister. Communal rioting re-erupts, a state of emergency is declared, and British troops are brought in to restore order

**1966:** Guyana becomes an independent state within the British Commonwealth and joins the UN

**1968:** Burnham's PNC wins general election

**1970:** Guyana is proclaimed a republic

**1973:** Guyana, Barbados, Jamaica, and Trinidad-Tobago establish the Caribbean Community and Common Market (CARICOM)

**1978:** More than 900 die in murder-suicide tragedy of the People's Temple cult in Jonestown

**1980:** New constitution adopted, vesting executive power in the president; Burnham assumes presidency. Amid charges of fraud, PNC overwhelms PPP in general election

**1982:** Economic crisis becomes severe; balance of payments deficit reported at over one-third of annual GNP

---

## HAITI

---

**Area:** 10,683 sq. mi. **Population:** 5,104,000 (1981 est.)

**Official Name:** Republic of Haiti **Capital:** Port-au-Prince **Nationality:** Haitian **Languages:** French is the official language but is spoken by only about 10% of the population; Creole, a mixture of 17th century French, African dialects, and English, Spanish, and Indian words, is spoken by 90% **Religion:** Most of the population professes Roman Catholicism, the state religion; 10% are Protestant; voodoo is widely practiced, especially in the rural areas **Flag:** Black and red vertical halves with the national coat-of-arms in the center **Anthem:** Song of Dessalines **Currency:** Gourde (5 per U.S. $1)

**Location:** West Indies, occupying the western third of the island of Hispaniola in the Caribbean Sea. Haiti's only land border is with the Dominican Republic, on the east **Features:** About two-thirds of the country is mountainous terrain unsuitable for cultivation **Chief Rivers:** Artibonite, Guayamouc

**Head of State and of Government:** President Jean-Claude Duvalier, born 1951; elected president in February 1971, he assumed the title "President for Life" on the death of his father, François Duvalier, in

April 1971 **Effective Date of Present Constitution:** June 1964, amended in 1971 **Legislative Body:** Legislative Chamber (unicameral), consisting of 58 deputies, elected for 6 years but with little power **Local Government:** 5 departments, each headed by an appointed prefect

**Ethnic Composition:** 95% of the population is of African descent, 5% are mulatto or of European descent **Population Distribution:** 25% urban **Density:** 478 inhabitants per sq. mi.

**Largest Cities:** (1978 est.) Port-au-Prince 493,932, (1971 census) Cap-Haïtien 46,217, Pétionville 35,257, Gonaives 29,261

**Per Capita Income:** $258 (1980) **Gross National Product (GNP):** $1.5 billion (1980) **Economic Statistics:** 44.7% of GNP comes from agriculture (coffee, sugar, sisal, cotton); 37% from services, of which 21.8% is derived from tourism; 14.4% from manufacturing (processing of coffee, sugarcane, sisal, and edible oils; textiles, soap, cement); 3.9% from mining **Minerals and Mining:** Bauxite and copper are mined; deposits of gold, silver, antimony, tin, sulphur, coal, nickel, and gypsum are undeveloped **Labor Force:** 3,004,544 (1975), with 80% self-employed in agriculture **Foreign Trade:** Exports, mainly coffee, sugar, bauxite, essential oils, baseballs and softballs, sisal, shellfish, and fruits, totaled $184 million in 1980. Imports, mainly wheat, fish, fats and oils, paper, cotton fabrics, vehicles, petroleum, machinery, electrical equipment, and raw materials, totaled $233 million **Principal Trade Partners:** United States, EC countries, Japan, Curaçâo, Canada

**Vital Statistics:** Birthrate, 41.8 per 1,000 of pop. (1980); death rate, 15.7 **Life Expectancy:** 45 years **Health Statistics:** 1,219 inhabitants per hospital bed (1976); 8,505 per physician (1973) **Infant Mortality:** 200 per 1,000 births **Illiteracy:** 77% **Primary and Secondary School Enrollment:** 566,499 (1976) **Enrollment in Higher Education:** 3,309 **GNP Expended on Education:** 0.9% (1976)

**Transportation:** Paved roads total 400 mi. **Motor Vehicles:** 26,500 (1977) **Passenger Cars:** 22,700 **Railway Mileage:** 50 **Ports:** Port-au-Prince, Miragoâne, Les Cayes **Major Airlines:** Haiti Air Inter operates internal services **Communications: Radio Transmitters:** 37 **Receivers:** 95,000 (1976) **Television Transmitters:** 1 **Receivers:** 14,000 (1976) **Telephones:** 18,000 (1976) **Newspapers:** 6 dailies, 20 copies per 1,000 inhabitants (1976)

**Weights and Measures:** Metric system **Travel Requirements:** Tourist card, valid 90 days, $4 **International Dialing Code:** 509

---

Fourteen years of implacable dictatorship, with little economic or social progress for compensation, ended for Haiti in 1971 with the death of Dr. François Duvalier at the age of 64. Under the harsh rule of his police state, the country had become an anachronism in the Western Hemisphere after having been in the vanguard to win freedom from foreign rule.

Haiti's politics and economy are primitive. The country is nominally a republic with a president, but Dr. Duvalier—"Papa Doc"—was all-powerful. For most of Haiti's independent life, the country was dominated by a cultured and literate, generally mulatto, minority.

Illiteracy persists at 77 percent, and most people lead subsistence lives on little plots of land amid luxuriant and colorful vegetation set against stark, eroded mountains. Roman Catholicism is the dominant religion, but it is mixed with voodoo, a religion of fetish and incantation rooted in the Haitians' African past. Manifestations of Duvalier rule include a force called the *Tontons Macoute*, or Bogeymen, a bulwark of the regime feared for its arbitrary dealings with ordinary people.

All in all, Papa Doc left a staggering legacy to his successor as "President for Life," his son Jean-Claude. When "Baby Doc" assumed power in April 1971, at the age of 19, there were few who assumed he could last long. But so far he has been successful in walking a political tightrope between the "old dinosaurs" of his father's era, who seek to hold the status quo, and the younger technocrats and businessmen who, while not desiring a dramatic change in the form of government, do seek a modernization of Haitian life. The young Duvalier has also had to contend with the political power wielded by his mother, Simone Duvalier.

Duvalier has acted in some instances to ease repression in an apparent attempt to gain favor with other countries. Nevertheless, in 1980 he revised his cabinet to strengthen his rule. In November of the same year 200 human-rights activists, journalists and other opponents of the regime were arrested; 9 were allowed to go into exile in the United States. Thousands of Haitian refugees have entered the United States illegally in recent years. Duvalier asserted that he supports human rights and democracy, but on his own terms.

He has acted to ease repression somewhat, in an apparent attempt to gain favor with other nations which have been critical of Haiti's bleak human rights record. The government said that it released the last political prisoners in 1977, and it invited the Red Cross and the Inter-American Commission on Human Rights to inspect its jails. On the other hand, there are reliable reports that conditions are improved solely for such visits and that inhumane conditions prevail again soon afterward.

The country has few resources with which to solve its staggering economic and social problems and has been characterized as an "environmental disaster." The destruction of the forests for charcoal has triggered massive soil erosion, reducing the amount of arable land. Exports remain largely confined to primary products such as sugar, coffee, essential oils, sisal, and some minerals. Over 150 U.S. companies now have plants in Haiti, and Haitian-controlled companies assemble imported U.S. components. Another major resource is tourism.

**HISTORY:** Haiti was largely ignored by Spain following the discovery of the island of Hispaniola by Columbus in 1492. While most Spanish colonists settled on the eastern part of the island, Haiti became a base for English and French pirates and was eventually ceded to France in the late 17th century. French colonists began to settle in the area, developing a plantation economy based on sugar and worked by black slaves. Following the outbreak of the French Revolution, the slaves rebelled and murdered most of their former masters

**1793:** A French army sent to crush the rebellion is defeated by guerrilla bands led by Toussaint L'Ouverture, a former slave

**1801-03:** Toussaint occupies the entire island of Hispaniola, abolishes slavery, and introduces a constitution: his rule ends when he is captured by a French force sent by Napoleon

**1804-11:** Jean Jacques Dessalines, another black general, continues the struggle against the French and defeats their army; he assumes title of emperor but is soon assassinated; nation becomes split into a northern kingdom ruled by Henri Christophe, a black, and a southern republic governed by a mulatto, Alexandre Pétion

**1820-44:** Haiti is reunited by Jean Pierre Boyer, who also brings Santo Domingo, in the eastern part of the island, under Haitian control; Boyer overthrown; nation regains independence

**1849-59:** Haiti is ruled by a former president and self-declared emperor, Faustin Élie Soulouque, a black; he is dethroned in a revolution led by a mulatto, Nicholas Fabre Geffrard

**1905-34:** United States takes Haiti's customs into receivership in 1905; in 1915, United States takes full control of country; occupation, which lasts for 19 years, results in many material improvements but arouses hostility throughout Latin America

**1957-64:** François Duvalier, a black middle-class physician, is elected president; with the help of a secret police force known as Tontons Macoute, he establishes dictatorship; in 1964 Duvalier has himself declared president for life

**1968:** Haitian exiles attempt to invade the country but fail

**1969:** The Organization of American States charges Duvalier government with terrorism

**1970:** Haitian Coast Guard vessels shell presidential palace in abortive coup

**1971:** François Duvalier dies after 14-year rule; his son, Jean-Claude, succeeds him

**1977:** Severe drought brings hundreds of thousands to brink of starvation and causes major shortages of electricity

**1980:** Boatloads of Haitians flee from oppressive economic and social conditions in their homeland

**1981:** Exodus of refugees increases; 33 drown off Florida coast when their rickety boat capsizes

**1982:** Government troops battle rebels on isle of Tortuga

## HONDURAS

**Area:** 43,277 sq. mi. **Population:** 3,691,000 (1980 est.)

**Official Name:** Republic of Honduras **Capital:** Tegucigalpa **Nationality:** Honduran **Languages:** Spanish is the official and predominant language; English is spoken along the north coast and on the Bay Islands **Religion:** Overwhelmingly Roman Catholic **Flag:** Two blue horizontal stripes separated by a white stripe bearing a cluster of five blue stars **Anthem:** National Anthem, beginning "Thy flag is a heavenly light" **Currency:** Lempira (2 per U.S. $1)

**Location:** Central America. Honduras is bordered on the north by the Caribbean Sea; on the southeast by Nicaragua; on the southwest by El Salvador and the Pacific Ocean; and on the west by Guatemala **Features:** Except for the Caribbean and Pacific coastal plains, the country is generally mountainous **Chief Rivers:** Guayape, Patuca, Aguán, Ulúa

**Head of State and of Government:** President: Dr. Roberto Suazo Córdova, born 1927, took office Jan. 27, 1982 **Effective Date of Present Constitution:** 1965, revised 1981 **Legislative Body:** Congress (unicameral) of 78 members **Local Government:** 18 departments, each with a governor appointed by the president

**Ethnic Composition:** About 90% of the population is mestizo (of mixed European and Indian origin); Indians, Negroes, and Caucasians constitute small minorities **Population Distribution:** 31% urban **Density:** 85 inhabitants per sq. mi.

**Largest Cities:** (1976 est.) Tegucigalpa 316,500, San Pedro Sula 213,600, Choluteca 51,700, La Ceiba 49,900

**Per Capita Income:** $540 (1980) **Gross National Product (GNP):** $2 billion (1980) **Economic Statistics:** About 32% of GNP comes from agriculture (bananas, coffee, lumber, corn, meat, cotton), forestry and fishing; about 17% from industry (light consumer goods; processing of sugar, fruit juices, vegetable oils; meat packing); and 14% from trade **Minerals and Mining:** Gold, silver, lead, zinc, cadmium, mercury, and lime are extracted; other minerals are antimony, iron, copper, tin, coal, limestone, marble, and pitchblende. Petroleum exploration is under way **Labor Force:** 816,000 (1976), with some 66% in agriculture, 17% in trade and services, 8% in manufacturing and mining **Foreign Trade:** Exports, chiefly bananas, coffee, lumber, silver, meat, shellfish, cotton and tobacco, totaled $843 million in 1979. Imports, mainly transportation equipment, machinery, chemicals, fertilizer, petroleum products, and consumer durables, totaled $1 billion **Principal Trade Partners:** United States, West Germany, Japan, Venezuela, Nicaragua, Guatemala

**Vital Statistics:** Birthrate, 47 per 1,000 of pop. (1980); death rate, 11.8 **Life Expectancy:** 56 years **Health Statistics:** 714 inhabitants per hospital bed; 3,297 per physician (1977) **Infant Mortality:** 26.9 per 1,000 births (1976) **Illiteracy:** 43% **Primary and Secondary School Enrollment:** 546,096 (1976) **Enrollment in Higher Education:** 15,499 **GNP Expended on Education:** 3.2% (1974)

**Transportation:** Paved roads total 1,060 mi. **Motor Vehicles:** 50,700 (1976) **Passenger Cars:** 20,500 **Railway Mileage:** 350 **Ports:** Puerto Cortés, Tela, La Ceiba, Amapala, Trujillo **Major Airlines:** SAHSA and TAN operate domestic and international services **Communications: Radio Transmitters:** 121 **Receivers:** 161,000 (1976) **Television Transmitters:** 5 **Receivers:** 48,000 (1976) **Telephones:** 19,000 (1976) **Newspapers:** 8 dailies (1976), 44 copies per 1,000 inhabitants

**Weights and Measures:** Metric system, but local units are also used **Travel Requirements:** Passport, visa, no fee **International Dialing Code:** 504

The weak link in the Central American Common Market, Honduras is the archetype of a Central American banana republic, with a slow economic growth rate and about two thirds of the population involved in agriculture. It is a small country, constantly struggling to keep up with its neighbors and always falling further behind; its politics have frequently been subject to military intervention; its economy is tied to the whims and fortunes of the big foreign banana exporters.

Economically, Honduras seems to have little hope of catching up to its neighbors. Reduced earnings from coffee exports have compelled cutbacks in public spending and imports. In 1982 Honduras joined with Costa Rica and El Salvador in setting up the Central American Democratic Community (CDC) to promote economic development as well as democracy amd security against external aggression in the region.

In foreign affairs, Honduras' principal problem has been its relations with neighboring El Salvador and Nicaragua. Rioting at a soccer match between the teams of Honduras and El Salvador in 1969 led to a war which lasted only four days when the OAS intervened. In October 1980 the two countries finally signed a treaty ending the state of war and setting up procedures for settling their boundary dispute. However, there is evidence that Cuba has been using Honduras as a staging area for Salvadoran guerrillas attacking the government of their homeland. In 1981 Nicaragua charged that Honduran army support for anti-Sandinista guerrilla forces operating from Honduras caused a series of clashes which continued into 1982.

In January 1978 President Juan Melgar announced he would convene a Constitutional Assembly to "reform" the constitution. In August he was overthrown by a three-member military junta, headed by Gen. Policarpo Paz García, which promised free elections. Late in 1981 Roberto Suazo Córdova, a 53-year-old country doctor, was elected president, and his right-of-center Liberal party won an absolute majority in the congress. On Jan. 27, 1982, Suazo Córdova assumed office, ending a decade of military rule in his country.

**HISTORY:** Honduras was a center of Mayan civilization centuries before the arrival of Columbus in 1502. Following attempts by rival Spanish factions in Central America to gain control of it, Honduras was made part of the captaincy general of Guatemala

**1821:** Honduras declares independence from Spain and, along with the other Central American countries, is annexed to Mexico

**1825:** Honduras joins Central American Federation

**1838:** Honduras becomes an independent republic in 1838

**1933-49:** Tiburcio Carias Andino rules as dictator

**1957-63:** Ramón Villeda Morales, elected president, is overthrown in a military coup led by Oswaldo López Arellano

**1965:** Honduras returns to democratic rule when Constituent Assembly elects López president and adopts a new constitution

**1971:** Honduras holds first direct election of a president since 1932; National party candidate Ramón Ernesto Cruz wins

**1972:** Bloodless coup puts Gen. López Arellano back in power

**1974:** Hurricane Fifi strikes, killing about 9,000

**1975:** Pres. López Arellano overthrown in bloodless coup; Juan Alberto Melgar Castro, Commander in Chief of armed forces, becomes president

**1978:** Melgar overthrown by three-member military junta

**1980:** Liberal party gains plurality in Constituent Assembly which names Gen. Paz Garcí, the junta head, as provisional president

**1981:** Border clashes with Nicaragua erupt. Government struggles to maintain payments on $1.4-billion foreign debt and cope with underemployment of 75% of the work force. Dr. Roberto Suazo Córdova and his Liberal party win elections

**1982:** Suazo Córdova assumes office. U.S. increases military aid to help Honduras withstand pressure from Nicaragua. Four leftist gunmen hijack airliner in Tegucigalpa, but are allowed to escape to Cuba after releasing their hostages. UN High Commissioner for Refugees assumes direct control of program to deal with approximately 25,000 refugees from political violence in neighboring countries

## HUNGARY

**Area:** 35,919 sq. mi. **Population:** 10,709,536 (1980 census)

**Official Name:** Hungarian People's Republic **Capital:** Budapest **Nationality:** Hungarian **Languages:** Hungarian (Magyar) is the official and universal language **Religion:** 68% Roman Catholic, 20% Calvinist, 5% Lutheran, 7% other (Unitarian, Jewish, etc.) **Flag:** Red, white, and green horizontal stripes **Anthem:** God bless the Hungarians **Currency:** Forint (35 per U.S. $1)

**Location:** East-central Europe. Landlocked Hungary is bordered on the north by Czechoslovakia, on the northeast by the USSR, on the east by Romania, on the south by Yugoslavia, and on the west by Austria **Features:** Most of the country is a flat plain, with the exception of low mountain ranges in the north-central and northeastern portions and to the north and south of Lake Balaton in the west **Chief Rivers:** Danube, Tisza, Drava, Rába

**Political Leader:** First Secretary of the Hungarian Socialist Workers' (Communist) party: János Kádár, born 1912, took over in 1956 **Head of State:** The Presidential Council is collectively the head of state, usually represented by its president, Pál Losonczi, born 1919, appointed 1967 **Head of Government:** Premier György Lázár, born 1924, appointed 1975 **Effective Date of Present Constitution:** 1949, amended 1972 **Legislative Body:** National Assembly (unicameral) consisting of 352 members elected for 5 years **Local Government:** 19 counties (each divided into districts with locally elected councils); 4 autonomous cities and the capital, all with county status

**Ethnic Composition:** Hungarians (Magyars) make up 97% of the population; minority groups include Germans, Slovaks, Gypsies, Serbs, Croats, and Romanians **Population Distribution:** 46% urban **Density:** 298 inhabitants per sq. mi.

**Largest Cities:** (1980 census) Budapest 2,060,170, Miskolc 206,727, Debrecen 192,484, Szeged 171,342, Pécs 168,788, Gyor 123,618

**Per Capita Income:** $3,665 (1980) **Gross National Product (GNP):** $39 billion (1980) **Economic Statistics:** About 38.5% of GNP is derived from industry (mining, chemical refining, metallurgy, food processing); 18.6% from agriculture (corn, wheat, sugar beets, vegetables, wine grapes); 12% from trade; 11% from services **Minerals and Mining:** Coal, bauxite, iron ore, and lignite are mined **Labor Force:** 5,230,000 (1979), of which 33% is employed in industry and construction, and 20% in agriculture **Foreign Trade:** Exports, chiefly transport equipment, medicine, machinery and shoes, totaled $11 billion in 1979. Imports, mainly crude oil, raw cotton, passenger cars, trucks, and rolled steel, totaled $12 billion **Principal Trade Partners:** USSR, W. Germany, E. Germany, Czechoslovakia, Poland, Italy, Austria

**Vital Statistics:** Birthrate, 13.9 per 1,000 of pop. (1980); death rate, 13.6 **Life Expectancy:** 70 years **Health Statistics:** 114 inhabitants per hospital bed; 434 per physician (1977) **Infant Mortality:** 23.1 per 1,000 births **Illiteracy:** 2% **Primary and Secondary School Enrollment:** 1,438,785 (1976) **Enrollment in Higher Education:** 107,555 (1975) **GNP Expended on Education:** 4.6% (1976)

**Transportation:** Surfaced roads total 15,107 mi. **Motor Vehicles:** 1,076,800 (1978) **Passenger Cars:** 839,100 **Railway Mileage:** 5,293 **Ports:** None **Major Airlines:** Malev, the state-owned airline, operates domestic and international services **Communications: Radio Transmitters:** 45 **Licenses:** 2,538,000 (1975) **Television Transmitters:** 22 **Licenses:** 2,495,000 (1976) **Telephones:** 1,143,000 (1978) **Newspapers:** 27 dailies, 243 copies per 1,000 inhabitants (1977)

**Weights and Measures:** Metric system **Travel Requirements:** Passport, visa valid for 30 days, fee $6, 2 photos

---

"Socialism with gaiety" is the way a top Hungarian has described his country's political formula to an American audience. The slogan is not far from the Czechoslovakian idea of "Socialism with a human face"—a concept that brought the violent downfall of Alexander Dubcek and his reformist government in 1968. However, the implementation of the formula in Hungary is so cautious, moderate, and delicate that no analogy with Czechoslovakia is appropriate.

In the midst of ideological regimentation, the breakdown of which brought Warsaw Pact troops into Prague, there is gaiety in Hungary. Political cabarets in Budapest pull few punches in criticizing bureaucratic ineptness and stuffiness. A television forum in which listeners quiz political leaders on their performance and promises brings sharp questions out into public discussion. Music, dancing, and plentiful good food add esthetic grace notes to the sense of gradual political progress.

The country is no longer traumatized by the uprising that Russian tanks crushed in 1956 and that caused some 200,000 Hungarians to flee to the West. The regime of János Kádár, imposed to fight the liberal ideas of the 1956 revolt, has proved far more progressive than was first thought possible. A surprising degree of dissent is allowed, though there are definite if generally unexpressed limits. Hungary remains, after all, a Communist state, basically faithful to the party line.

Thus, when it was necessary for someone to attack Romania for flirting with Communist China, a Hungarian editor was detailed to fire the first critical salvo. Similarly, the economic liberalization has been only partially mirrored in an effort to develop local political autonomy in small towns and not reflected at all in the repressive policies toward the Catholic Church.

What has emerged in Hungary, however, is a consumer-oriented economy that is the envy of all its neighbors. Hungarians have refined their New Economic Model since its introduction in 1968 to boost exports and imports.

The economy, however, is not without its problems. The high degree of centralization in Budapest sometimes results in mismanagement and inefficiencies, and in return for supplying oil needs in excess of rigid, outdated quotas, the Soviet Union requires agricultural surpluses that might otherwise earn valuable hard currency in the West. In April 1978, the regime adopted a two-year program of phasing out most price controls, subsidies for consumer goods, and heavy producer taxes. In 1979, Kádár called for greater productivity to increase workers' incomes and to combat inflation. But Hungary's industrial growth slowed to a standstill in 1980, while agricultural production increased only slightly.

**HISTORY:** The Magyars migrated from beyond the Urals about the end of the 9th century A.D., conquered most of present-day Hungary, and established a dynasty that lasted more than four centuries. Pre-Magyar inhabitants had included Celts, Germans, Huns, Slavs, and Avars. In the last years of the 10th century, the Magyars embraced Christianity and made alliances with the Holy Roman Empire. Following a disastrous defeat by the Turks in 1526, a faction of Hungarian nobles elected Ferdinand I of Austria as king of Hungary, laying the foundations of Hapsburg rule

**1686:** Budapest is liberated from the Turks, who cede most of Hungary proper and Transylvania to Austria

**1713:** Hungarian Diet accepts Pragmatic Sanction aimed at guaranteeing the integrity of the Hapsburg possessions, thereby binding Hungary to Austria

**1848-49:** Hungarian revolt against Austrian rule is suppressed by Austrian and Russian armies

**1867:** Austro-Hungarian monarchy is established, giving Hungary nearly equal status with Austria

**1918-19:** Monarchy collapses in the aftermath of World War I defeat. A Hungarian republic is proclaimed but is soon supplanted by a Communist regime headed by Bela Kun; Romanian troops invade Hungary and help to suppress leftist government

**1920:** Under Treaty of Trianon, Hungary is deprived of three-fourths of its territory and over one-third of its population; country becomes a kingdom without a king, under the regency of Admiral Nicholas Horthy

**1938-40:** Aided by Italy and Germany, Hungary recovers lands lost to Czechoslovakia and Romania. In 1940 Hungary joins Axis powers and enters World War II

**1944:** Soviet troops occupy Hungary; a provisional government is set up and declares war against Germany

**1947:** Communists win 22 percent of vote in general elections

**1948-49:** Hungarian Communists seize power with Soviet support; in 1949 Hungary is proclaimed a People's Republic

**1955:** Hungary joins the UN

**1956:** Popular anti-Communist uprising breaks out in Budapest and spreads to rest of the country; a new coalition government under Imre Nagy declares Hungary neutral and withdraws country from Warsaw Pact; János Kádár sets up counter-government and calls for Soviet support; Soviet troops and tanks suppress revolution, causing nearly 200,000 Hungarians to flee the country

**1958:** Imre Nagy and some of his ministers are executed. János Kádár resigns as premier and is succeeded by Ferenc Münnich

**1961:** Kádár resumes premiership

**1965:** Gyula Kallai becomes premier; Kádár remains First Secretary of ruling Hungarian Socialist Workers' party

**1967:** Hungary signs a new 20-year friendship and mutual assistance pact with Soviet Union, replacing one signed in 1948. Jeno Fock succeeds Gyula Kallai as premier

**1968:** Hungarian troops march with Soviet troops when Soviets invade Czechoslovakia

**1971:** Government holds first general elections in which voters could choose between nonofficial and official candidates. Newcomers unseat eight incumbents in parliament

**1975:** György Lázár becomes premier

**1978:** Crown of St. Stephen, 1,000-year-old traditional symbol of Hungary's nationhood, is returned by U.S. after having been held in protective custody since the end of World War II. Government announces measures to phase out most subsidies for consumer goods and end heavy producer taxes

**1979:** 12th Communist Party Congress reduces Politburo to 13 members, including young associates of Kádár

## ICELAND

**Area:** 39,768 sq. mi. **Population:** 228,000 (1980 est.)

**Official Name:** Republic of Iceland **Capital:** Reykjavík **Nationality:** Icelandic **Languages:** Icelandic is the official and universal language **Religion:** 97% of the population belongs to the state church, the Evangelical Lutheran Church **Flag:** A red cross edged in white on a field of blue **Anthem:** Our Country's God **Currency:** Króna (10.4 per U.S. $1)

**Location:** North Atlantic. A large island extending about 300 miles from east to west and about 190 miles from north to south, Iceland is the westernmost state of Europe, lying 600 miles west of Norway. The Arctic Circle runs through the small island of Grímsey off Iceland's northern coast **Features:** Almost three fourths of the country's land area, which is of recent volcanic origin, consists of glaciers, lakes, a mountainous lava desert, and other wasteland, with the remainder used for cultivation or grazing. Most of the inhabited areas are on the coast, particularly, in the southwest **Chief Rivers:** Thjórsá, Jökulsa, Ölfusá-Hvítá, Skjálfandafljót

**Head of State:** President: Mrs. Vigdís Finnbogadóttir, born 1930, elected June 1980 **Head of Government:** Premier Gunnar Thoroddsen, born 1910, appointed February 1980 **Effective Date of Present Constitution:** 1874, amended 1903 and 1944 **Legislative Body:** Parliament (*Althing*), composed of 60 members elected for 4 years. After elections it becomes bicameral, dividing itself into 2 chambers with equal powers, one of 20 members and the other of 40 members. The 2 houses often meet together **Local Government:** 23 counties, each with a council, and 14 urban municipalities

**Ethnic Composition:** The population is homogeneous **Population Distribution:** 87% urban **Density:** 5.7 inhabitants per sq. mi.

**Largest Cities:** (1980 est.) Reykjavík 83,766, Kópavogur 13,819, Akureyri 13,420, Hafnarfjördhur 12,205

**Per Capita Income:** $7,018 (1980) **Gross Domestic Product (GDP):** $1.6 billion (1980) **Economic Statistics:** About 18% of GDP comes from fishing and fish processing; 17% from industry other than fish processing (manufacture of electric motors, fertilizer, chemicals, cement, clothing, furniture, books); and 5% from agriculture (sheep raising, dairy products, hay, potatoes) **Minerals and Mining:** Diatomite, peat, lignite, perlite; hydroelectric power **Labor Force:** 100,000 (1978), of which 31% is employed in fishing, fish processing, and other industries; and 9% in agriculture **Foreign Trade:** Exports, chiefly fish and fish products (about 75% of the total), aluminum ingots, and agricultural products, totaled $929 million in 1980. Imports, mainly machinery, textiles, petroleum products, metals and metal products, ships, and food grains, totaled $1 billion **Principal Trade Partners:** United States, West Germany, Britain, USSR, Norway, Sweden, Netherlands, Nigeria

**Vital Statistics:** Birthrate, 20.4 per 1,000 of pop. (1980); death rate, 6.6 **Life Expectancy:** 76 years **Health Statistics:** 58 inhabitants per hospital bed; 550 per physician (1974) **Infant Mortality:** 5.4 per 1,000 births **Illiteracy:** Negligible **Primary and Secondary School Enrollment:** 52,271 (1975) **Enrollment in Higher Education:** 2,970 (1975) **GNP Expended on Education:** 4.2% (1975)

**Transportation:** Paved roads total 120 miles; there are over 6,000 miles of gravel road **Motor Vehicles:** 84,200 (1978) **Passenger Cars:** 75,700 **Railway Mileage:** None **Ports:** Reykjavík, Akureyri **Major Airlines:** Icelandair operates domestic and international services **Communications: Radio Transmitters:** 26 **Licenses:** 64,000 (1976) **Television Transmitters:** 80 **Licenses:** 53,000 (1976) **Telephones:** 100,000 (1978) **Newspapers:** 6 dailies, 554 copies per 1,000 inhabitants (1977)

**Weights and Measures:** Metric system **Travel Requirements:** Passport, no visa for 3 months

Out in the North Atlantic, closer to Greenland than to Western Europe, lies the rugged, largely desolate island of volcanic origin called Iceland, with 228,000 fiercely individualistic inhabitants who have a tradition of preserving their heritage. Their language, for example, has remained virtually unchanged since the 12th century.

Although Iceland has no armed forces, it joined in the cold-war days of 1949 in forming the North Atlantic Treaty Organization. As its contribution, it granted NATO the right to maintain a base, manned by Americans, at Keflavík, 30 miles outside of Reykjavík, the capital. A leftist coalition formed in 1971 announced plans to phase out the installation, but in 1974 a coalition of the former governing and opposition parties agreed to allow the base to remain.

The government extended the fishing limits in 1972 from 12 miles offshore to 50, and in 1975 from 50 to 200 miles. With fish and fish products accounting for 18 percent of the country's gross domestic product and 75 percent of its total exports, the moves were a logical progression of a conservation drive begun in 1958 when Iceland extended its fishing limits from four miles to 12.

Foreign reaction to these extensions has been far more serious than in 1958. In 1973 and 1975-76, Britain, which gets 45 percent of its fish from the waters off Iceland, sent heavily armed frigates into the disputed waters, touching off a "cod war" between the two countries, with shots being fired, boats rammed and nets cut.

In 1976 the two countries reached a diplomatic settlement and British ships were removed. In conjunction with this agreement, important tariff concessions by the European Community (EC) for fish products became effective for Iceland. The EC's adoption of a common 200-mile fishing limit imposed new problems, as it excludes Icelandic vessels from rich waters to which they had previously had access.

Parliamentary elections were called December 1979 after the Social Democrats withdrew from the coalition government. A political crisis ensued when no party won a sizable plurality in the new parliament. After the major parties failed to form a new government, Gunnar Thoroddsen deserted his own conservative Independence party and formed a new coalition government with the People's Alliance and Progressive party in February 1980. To control spiraling inflation, the Thoroddsen government froze prices as of Jan. 1, 1981. At the same time, it announced currency reforms making one new krona equal to 100 old kronas.

Vigdís Finnbogadóttir, manager of the Reykjavík Theater Company, became the world's first popularly elected female head of state by winning the June 1980 presidential election.

**HISTORY:** The first permanent settler of Iceland was Ingolfur Arnason of Norway, who arrived with his family around 870. Others of Norwegian origin followed, some bringing with them Irish and Scottish wives and slaves. In 930 a commonwealth was established and a general assembly, the Althing, instituted. Christianity was introduced in the year 1000. Iceland came under the Norwegian crown in the 13th century, but in 1380 both Iceland and Norway passed under the Danish crown. The former was destined to remain linked to Denmark until the 20th century

**1918:** Iceland is declared a sovereign state in union with Denmark

**1940-41:** British troops occupy Iceland following Germany's World War II occupation of Denmark; U.S. forces take over Iceland's defense in 1941

**1944:** Icelanders vote to terminate union with Denmark; Iceland is proclaimed a republic

**1949:** Iceland joins in forming NATO

**1958-61:** Fishing limits are extended from four miles to 12; so-called "cod war" begins, with Britain challenging the Icelandic pronouncement by sending in trawlers backed by warships; in 1961 Britain finally agrees to the 12-mile limit

**1970:** Iceland becomes member of European Free Trade Association. Premier Bjarni Benediktsson perishes in fire; Justice Minister Johann Hafstein is designated his successor

**1971:** Government defeated in elections. Hafstein resigns. New left-wing coalition government announces it will close the American-manned NATO base at Keflavík

**1972-73:** Fishing limits are extended from 12 miles to 50, touching off new "cod war" with Britain; West Germany joins Britain in protesting extension

**1973:** Iceland signs agreement with Britain giving limited fishing rights within the new zone

**1974:** Iceland signs agreement with U.S. allowing U.S. to maintain NATO base at Keflavík

**1975:** Fishing limits extended from 50 to 200 miles

**1976:** British and Icelandic foreign ministers sign an interim pact to end the "cod war" between the two countries and restore diplomatic relations which had been severed. British frigates, sent into fishing zone in November '75 to protect British trawlers from harassment by Icelandic patrol boats, withdraw. Dr. Kristján Eldjárn is unopposed for third four-year term as president

**1978:** Strike by government workers temporarily isolates nation by cutting international flights, mail and telephone links
**1980:** New center-left coalition govenment is formed under Premier Gunnar Thoroddsen. Vigdís Finnbogadóttir is elected president

## INDIA

**Area:** 1,269,339 sq. mi. **Population:** 683,810,051 (1980 census)

**Official Name:** Republic of India **Capital:** New Delhi **Nationality:** Indian **Languages:** Hindi is the official language; English is an associate language. In addition to Hindi, the constitution recognizes 14 national languages, although as many as 1,652 languages and dialects are spoken in the country. Hindi, however, is spoken by 38% of the population. Telugu 9%, Bengali 8%, Marathi 8%, Tamil 7%, Urdu 6%, Gujarati 5%, Kanarese 4%, Punjabi 3%, Oriya 3%, Malayalam 3% **Religion:** 84% Hindu, 10% Moslem, 3% Christian, 2% Sikh, 1% Buddhist, Jain and others **Flag:** Saffron, white, and green horizontal stripes, with the 24-spoke Wheel of Asoka (chakra) in blue on the white stripe **Anthem:** Morning Song of India **Currency:** Rupee (9.3 per U.S. $1)

**Location:** Southern Asia, occupying most of the Indian sub-continent. India is bordered on the north by Afghanistan, China, Nepal, and Bhutan; on the east by Bangladesh, Burma, and the Bay of Bengal; on the south by the Indian Ocean's Gulf of Mannar and Palk Strait, which separate India from Sri Lanka; on the west by the Arabian Sea; and on the northwest by Pakistan **Features:** The country consists of three major topographical areas: the Himalaya mountains extending along the whole of the northern border; the Indo-Gangetic Plain, a fertile and heavily populated region; and the southern peninsula, including the Deccan Plateau, which is of moderate elevation and less densely populated **Chief Rivers:** Ganges, Brahmaputra, Godavari, Kistna (Krishna), Narbada, Mahanadi

**Head of State:** President: Zail Singh, born 1916, sworn in July 25, 1982 **Head of Government:** Prime Minister: Mrs. Indira Gandhi, born 1917, appointed Jan. 1980. She held the same office from 1966 to 1977 **Effective Date of Present Constitution:** 1950 **Legislative Body:** Parliament (bicameral), consisting of the *Lok Sabha* (House of the People) and the *Rajya Sabha* (Council of States). The *Lok Sabha* has 544 members, elected by universal suffrage for 6 years. The *Rajya Sabha* has 244 members, up to 12 of whom are appointed by the president and the rest elected for 6 year terms by the state and territorial legislatures **Local Government:** 22 states and 9 union territories, each with an appointed governor and with its own elected legislature

**Ethnic Composition:** Two major strains predominate: the Indo-Aryan (72%) in the north and the Dravidian (25%) in the south. There is also an aboriginal population in the central part, and some Mongoloid peoples in the north **Population Distribution:** 24% urban **Density:** 539 inhabitants per sq. mi.

**Largest Cities:** (1981 census) Calcutta 9,165,650, Bombay 8,227,332, Delhi, 5,713,581, Madras 4,276,635, Bangalore 2,913,537, Hyderabad 2,528,198, Ahmadabad 2,515,195, Kanpur 1,688,242, Poona 1,685,300, Nagpur 1,297,977, Lucknow 1,006,538, Jaipur 1,004,669

**Per Capita Income:** $202 (1980) **Gross National Product (GNP):** $137 billion (1980) **Economic Statistics:** About 43% of GNP comes from agriculture (rice, wheat, tea, jute, pulses, cotton, sugar, peanuts); 23% from mining and manufacturing (iron and steel, textiles, chemicals, cement, industrial machinery and equipment); 16% from commerce, transportation, and communications **Minerals and Mining:** Coal and iron are the country's main mineral assets; mica, manganese, natural gas, and bauxite are also abundant. Iron ore reserves are estimated at about one fourth of the world's total; oil supplies half of the nation's refinery requirements **Labor Force:** 273 million, of which 72% is engaged in agriculture, and 10% in industry **Foreign Trade:** Exports, chiefly cotton and jute textiles, tea, sugar, coffee, metallic ores, and iron and steel manufactures, totaled $9 billion in 1980. Imports, mainly petroleum, food grains, nonelectrical machinery and fertilizer, totaled $13.6 billion **Principal Trade Partners:** United States, Japan, Britain, USSR, Iran, West Germany

**Vital Statistics:** Birthrate, 36 per 1,000 of pop. (1980); death rate, 14.8 **Life Expectancy:** 54 years **Health Statistics:** 1,465 inhabitants per hospital bed; 3,586 per physician (1978) **Infant Mortality:** 130 per 1,000 births **Illiteracy:** 64% **Primary and Secondary School Enrollment:** 93,310,864 (1976) **Enrollment in Higher Education:** 3,198,550 **GNP Expended on Education:** 2.7% (1975)

**Transportation:** Surfaced roads totaled about 370,000 mi. **Motor Vehicles:** 1,596,100 (1978) **Passenger Cars:** 846,300 **Railway Mileage:** 38,614 **Ports:** Calcutta, Bombay, Madras, Mormugao, Cochin, Kandla, Visakhapatnam, Paradeep, Mangalore, Tuticorin **Major Airlines:** Indian Airlines Corporation is the domestic carrier and Air India the inter- national line **Communications: Radio Transmitters:** 157 **Licenses:** 14,848,000 (1976) **Television Trans- mitters:** 18 **Licenses:** 280,000 (1976) **Telephones:** 2,096,000 (1977) **Newspapers:** 929 dailies (1977), 16 copies per 1,000 inhabitants (1975)

**Weights and Measures:** Metric system and local units are used **Travel Requirements:** Passport, no visa required for stay up to 30 days

Successive invasions and a long period of subjugation under alien rule have made India what it is today—a land of diverse, often conflicting cultures, religions, and people that is held in unity by a complicated yet resilient political system. The British, who were the masters of the subcontinent for a century and a half, brought its disparate regions under one administration. To overcome the myriad languages and dialects, they made English the communication medium of the elite, the tiny minority that still dominates the government, industry, education, and art.

Indian leaders, as fruit of their long fight for freedom, inherited a truncated land after the carving out of Pakistan as a homeland for Moslems; they have been struggling with the overwhelming problems of the subcontinent ever since.

The country's successive five-year plans, while laying the foundation for a prosperous industrial nation at some future date, have not so far produced any substantial improvement in the average Indian's quality of life. All the benefits of the large development expenses over the last 25 years have been neutralized by a runaway population increase—now almost 2.5 percent a year—that has pushed more and more people below the poverty line. Unemployment has risen sharply. Pressure is increasing on living space, schools, and hospitals. Despite recent record food crops and a rise in industrial output, the population increase, on which only a marginal dent has been made by a costly birth-control program, has resulted in deteriorating living conditions for most Indians.

The social structure, ever in conflict, throws up many obstacles to progress. The Hindus, who make up 84 percent of the population, are divided into countless subcastes. The downtrodden untouchables, who constitute one seventh of the population, have begun asserting their rights. Clashes with upper-caste Hindus have become frequent and often violent.

The Moslem minority, 10 percent of the population, has remained suspect in the eyes of the majority ever since the creation of Pakistan. They live in constant insecurity and threat from militant Hindus. Bloody riots between Hindus and Moslems erupt periodically. The smaller minorities, the Sikhs, Buddhists, Jains, Parsis, and Christians, live in relative security, but the chances of their assimilation into the Hindu-dominated national life are remote.

In 1975 India went through the most important political crisis in its years as a republic when in April the government declared a state of emergency, arrested political leaders opposed to Prime Minister Indira Gandhi, began press censorship and suspended protection of fundamental rights. This repressive action was precipitated by Gandhi's conviction on charges of corrupt practices in the 1971 general election.

In July 1975 Mrs. Gandhi's power was restored when new laws approved by parliament permitted her to rule by proclamation, barred the courts from reviewing her actions and changed the election law retroactively to remove any criminal offenses. In December Gandhi's Congress party delayed general elections, due in March 1976, and extended the state of emergency for six months.

In January 1977 Mrs. Gandhi announced the elections that had been postponed would be held in

March; press censorship was subsequently lifted. In what was hailed as a victory for Indian democracy, Morarji R. Desai, 81, and his Janata party defeated Mrs. Gandhi and her 30-year-old son, Sanjay, in the election. It was the first defeat suffered by the ruling Congress party in the 30 years of India's independence. The new government immediately revoked the emergency rule legislation and released the political prisoners who had been jailed without charges. And since Desai himself was one of the thousands of political prisoners detained during Mrs. Gandhi's 19-month "emergency rule" period, it came as no surprise when the new government launched a series of civil and criminal investigations into her alleged abuses of power.

In February 1978, a month after leaving the Congress party to form a splinter group, Mrs. Gandhi reemerged as a major force in Indian politics when her Congress-I (for Indira) party entered a series of state elections and won decisively in two. Her comeback may have contributed to a split in the ruling Janata party in April. In November, Gandhi herself won a parliamentary seat.

However, Mrs. Gandhi found herself fighting for political survival a month later when the *Lok Sabha*, the lower house of parliament, expelled her on charges of contempt of the house and breach of privilege for her actions while prime minister. In addition, the government set up special courts that would keep her tied up in litigation. In February 1979 her son, Sanjay, was convicted of the theft and burning of a film (during the "emergency rule" period) that ridiculed his mother's conduct in office.

Desai meanwhile grappled with an increase in crime, caste violence, chronic power shortages, labor unrest, and soaring inflation. Food grain production was a bright spot, rising high enough to meet all of the country's needs. In general, however, Desai's government turned India away from large-scale industrialism and toward a "cottage industry" system.

On July 15, 1979, Prime Minister Desai resigned following growing defections from and splits within his Janata party. He was succeeded by Chaudhury Charan Singh, who himself resigned on August 20 when Mrs. Gandhi withdrew support, leading to new elections in early 1980.

Mrs. Gandhi regained the premiership as the Congress-I party swept to a huge victory in those elections, winning 351 seats out of 542 in the lower house. Her son Sanjay also won a seat, and the Supreme Court subsequently acquitted him in the film case. Widely regarded as his mother's most likely political heir, Sanjay was at the peak of his career when he died in a plane crash in June 1980.

Endeavoring to reestablish strong central rule and resume India's industrialization, Indira Gandhi used her new power to considerable effect. Her party took control of nearly all of the 22 state governments by mid-1980, steadily increasing its membership in the *Lok Sabha*.

Even so, India's problems multiplied. Crime increased alarmingly, as did ethnic violence, particularly against immigrants from Bangladesh in the northeast. In 1981, the decennial census revealed that the population was growing far more rapidly than had been supposed, and the prime minister resumed the vigorous promotion of birth control, a policy whose unpopularity had contributed to her defeat in 1977. In foreign policy, Mrs. Gandhi condemned both the Soviet occupation of Afghanistan and U.S. plans to increase aid to Pakistan for military and nuclear development.

Congress-I successes at the polls continued into 1982, owing much to the hopelessly splintered nature of its opposition. Mrs. Gandhi remained the only figure with a national following, and her personality and leadership had become the major issue in Indian politics, the more so because of her apparent effort to groom another son, Rajiv, as the heir to her political power.

**HISTORY:** The Indus Valley was the site of a flourishing civilization from the 3rd millennium to about 1500 B.C., when the region was conquered by the Aryans who, over the next 2,000 years, developed a Brahmanic civilization and introduced a caste system. In 327-325 B.C., Alexander the Great invaded northwest India, only to be driven out, and in the following century most of the subcontinent was united under Asoka the Great, who established Buddhism as the state religion. After his death, however, Buddhism declined in India as Hinduism experienced a resurgence

**4th cent.:** Hindu kingdoms are established

**8th cent.:** Islam is introduced into Sind by Arab invaders

**1498-1510:** European contact with India, begun with the arrival of Portuguese explorer Vasco da Gama, is followed by Portuguese conquest of Goa and spurs rivalry among European powers for trade with subcontinent

**1526-1707:** India is ruled by Mogul dynasty; a large Moslem population grows up and a new culture evolves, developing a characteristic Indo-Islamic style in art and architecture, as evidenced by the Taj Mahal

**1746-63:** India is turned into a battleground for the forces of France and Britain as each tries to carve out colonial domains; with the 1763 Treaty of Paris, British supremacy is assured

**1857-58:** Sepoy Rebellion by native soldiers in the employ of British East India Company is brutally suppressed; company is dissolved and India is placed under the direct rule of the British Crown

**1919:** Mohandas K. Gandhi, later known as the Mahatma or "great-souled," organizes the first of many passive resistance campaigns against British rule; he is imprisoned

**1942-45:** Indian National Congress, largely Hindu-supported, splits with Moslem League, which favors creation of Pakistan as a separate Moslem state, over support for Britain during World War II; Congress is outlawed, while League, which supports Britain, gains strength

**1947:** Subcontinent is partitioned into the independent nations of India and Pakistan; Jawaharlal Nehru becomes India's first prime minister; bloody riots break out between Hindus and Moslems and millions flee in crisscross migration to new states; India and Pakistan fight over Kashmir

**1948:** Gandhi is assassinated by Hindu fanatic who blames him for partition; Kashmir fighting ends with UN cease-fire

**1950:** India becomes republic within Commonwealth of Nations

**1954:** India signs nonaggression pact with Communist China

**1956:** Constitutional amendment redrawing state boundaries along linguistic lines put into effect

**1962:** Chinese Communist troops occupy Ladakh region of Kashmir

**1964:** Nehru dies and is succeeded by Lal Bahadur Shastri

**1965-66:** India and Pakistan fight three-week war in 1965 over Kashmir; hostilities end in a truce, followed by accord signed in 1966 at Tashkent, in the Soviet Union. Indian Prime Minister Lal Bahadur Shastri dies at Tashkent and is succeeded by Mrs. Indira Gandhi, daughter of the former prime minister, Jawaharlal Nehru

**1969:** Death of President Zakir Husain touches off power struggle in governing Congress party as Mrs. Gandhi and old guard party bosses clash over choice of successor; party splits following election of V.V. Giri, the candidate backed by Mrs. Gandhi, as president; bulk of party members remain with her New Congress party but she loses majority strength in parliament, forcing her to rely on Communists and independents for crucial votes

**1970:** Supreme Court rules bank nationalization law unconstitutional; prime minister counters court's action by issuing new ordinance nationalizing the banks. Mrs. Gandhi dissolves lower house of parliament and orders new elections

**1971:** Mrs. Gandhi's party is landslide victor in the elections held in March, winning two-thirds of the parliamentary seats. Civil war breaks out in Pakistan. Millions of East Pakistani refugees flee to India. India supports East Pakistan in fight against West Pakistan, and latter is soon defeated. East Pakistan becomes Bangladesh

**1972:** At Simla Conference India and Pakistan agree to observe "lines of control" in Kashmir

**1973:** At Delhi Conference India and Pakistan agree to repatriation of 93,000 Pakistani POWs held since their 1971 war

**1974:** World Health Organization estimates 30,000 have died in northern India in worst smallpox epidemic of the century. Sikkim becomes an associated state of India. Worst famine since 1943 in West Bengal, Assam, and Bihar

**1975:** Prime Minister Gandhi is convicted on charges of illegal activities in connection with her election. She suspends civil liberties and orders arrest of hundreds of political opponents. Gandhi's powers restored by parliament and Supreme Court

**1976:** Suspension of civil liberties continues throughout the year. India and Pakistan formally establish diplomatic ties

**1977:** Morarji R. Desai elected prime minister. President Fakhruddin Ali Ahmed dies; he is succeeded by Neelam Sanjiva Reddy. Government launches probes into alleged abuses of power by Mrs. Gandhi during her "emergency rule" period

**1978:** High-level talks between India and Pakistan begin; disputed state of Kashmir tops agenda. Mrs. Gandhi's newly formed Congress-I party wins two important state elections. Elected to parliament, she is expelled; special courts are set up to try her for actions taken when prime minister

**1979:** The Soviet Union and India sign agreements covering trade and technological and scientific cooperation for 10 to 15 years, calling for Indian rice to be traded for Soviet oil. Desai government curtails some large-scale industry and encourages "cottage industries" to help rural poor. Desai resigns in June. His successor, Chaudhury Charan Singh, resigns in August

**1980:** Indira Gandhi's Congress-I party wins by landslide in January elections, and she becomes prime minister for second time. Student movement to expel illegal immigrants (Bangladeshi) in Assam State spreads through northeast India and leads to shutting of colleges and reduced oil production. Congress-I party wins eight of nine state elections in May. Mrs. Gandhi's son, Sanjay, dies in crash of his light plane in June 1980.

**1981:** U.S. plan to increase aid to Pakistan for military and nuclear development denounced by Prime Minister Gandhi. Census reveals that, if current trend continues, India's population will double by the year 2000. In worst railroad disaster, June 6, an overcrowded train plunges off bridge in Bihar; 1,000 die

**1982:** Labor unrest escalates in Calcutta and Bombay; mass arrests occur in January. Gandhi initiatives lead to talks with China and Pakistan about long-standing disputes. Congress-I wins three of four state elections (May). Sikh leader Zail Singh is sworn in as president. Mrs. Gandhi visits the United States

## INDONESIA

**Area:** 788,430 sq. mi. **Population:** 147,490,298 (1980 census)

**Official Name:** Republic of Indonesia **Capital:** Jakarta **Nationality:** Indonesian **Languages:** Bahasa Indonesia, a form of Malay developed as a product of Indonesia's nationalist movement, is the official language; English is the second language and is compulsory in secondary schools **Religion:** 90% Moslem, 5% Christian, 3% Hindu (Bali has retained its Buddhist/Hindu heritage) **Flag:** A red horizontal stripe above a white stripe **Anthem:** Great Indonesia **Currency:** Rupiah (652 per U.S. $1)

**Location:** Southeast Asia, in the Malay archipelago. Indonesia consists of six large and 13,662 lesser islands, which form an arc between Asia and Australia. The principal group of islands is the Greater Sunda Islands, which include Java, Bali, Sumatra, Borneo (Kalimantan), and Celebes (Sulawesi). The country shares land borders with Malaysia, Brunei, and Papua New Guinea **Features:** The large islands have a central mountain range rising from fairly extensive lowlands and coastal plains. Many islands throughout the archipelago are dotted with volcanoes, both active and dormant **Chief Rivers:** Kapuas, Digul, Barito, Mahakam, Kajan, Hari, Mamberamo, Idenburg

**Head of State and of Government:** President: Gen. Suharto (Soeharto), born 1921, reelected 1978 **Effective Date of Present Constitution:** 1945 **Legislative Body:** Peoples' Consultative Assembly, consisting of 924 members, within it a 464-member (364 elected and 100 nominated by the president) House of Representatives (Parliament) **Local Government:** 27 provinces, each with an appointed governor and an elected legislature

**Ethnic Composition:** Malayans and Papuans constitute the main ethnic groups, each with numerous subdivisions. Chinese make up the largest nonindigenous group **Population Distribution:** 18% urban **Density:** 187 inhabitants per sq. mi.

**Largest Cities:** (1980 census) Jakarta 6,503,449, Surabaya 2,027,913, Bandung 1,462,637, Medan 1,378,955, Semarang 1,026,671, Palembang 787,187, Ujung Pandang 709,038, Malang 511,780

**Per Capita Income:** $417 (1980) **Gross National Product (GNP):** $63.1 billion (1980) **Economic Statistics:** About 30% of GNP comes from agriculture (rubber, copra, tea, coffee, tobacco, sugar, palm oil, rice); 10% from manufacturing (chiefly processing of agricultural and mineral products and light manufactures), forestry and fishing; and 60% from mining and petroleum **Minerals and Mining:** The country is one of the world's leading producers of tin and is the leading oil producer in the Far East. Other minerals are bauxite, nickel, copper, natural gas, and coal **Labor Force:** 55,000,000, of which some 64% is in agriculture and 7% in industry **Foreign Trade:** Exports, chiefly petroleum and petroleum products (65%), tin ore, copper, nickel, copra, coffee, and tobacco, totaled $23 billion in 1980. Imports, mainly textiles, machinery, transportation equipment, rice, fertilizer, and chemicals, totaled $15 billion **Principal Trade Partners:** Japan, United States, Singapore, West Germany, Taiwan, Netherlands

**Vital Statistics:** Birthrate, 35.9 per 1,000 of pop. (1980); death rate, 12.5 **Life Expectancy:** 48 years **Health Statistics:** 1,670 inhabitants per hospital bed; 15,427 per physician (1976) **Infant Mortality:** 125 per 1,000 births **Illiteracy:** 36% **Primary and Secondary School Enrollment:** 22,613,072 (1976) **Enrollment in Higher Education:** 278,200 (1975) **GNP Expended on Education:** 1.4% (1976)

**Transportation:** Paved roads total c. 16,500 mi. **Motor Vehicles:** 928,200 (1978) **Passenger Cars:** 535,600 **Railway Mileage:** 4,874 **Ports:** Jakarta, Surabaya, Semarang, Palembang, Belawan, Dumai, Balikpapan, Samarinda **Major Airlines:** Garuda Airways and Merapti Nusantara operate domestic and international services **Communications: Radio Transmitters:** 190 **Licenses:** 5,100,000 (1976) **Television Transmitters:** 29 **Licenses:** 325,000 (1976) **Telephones:** 347,000 (1977) **Newspapers:** 178 dailies (1976), 10 copies per 1,000 inhabitants

**Weights and Measures:** Metric system **Travel Requirements:** Passport, tourist visa (to 30 days, $3.00 fee), 2 photos **International Dialing Code:** 62

Indonesia, with 13,662 tropical islands (992 of them inhabited), strung like a necklace along the equator, is one of the world's most beautiful nations. It is green and fertile, but until recently political upheavals guaranteed its backward, impoverished status among nations.

Ruled by Dutch colonialists for about 300 years, Indonesia declared its independence on August 17, 1945, following Japanese occupation during World War II. Four years of fighting and negotiation followed and its sovereignty was recognized in 1949.

The colonial economic and administrative machinery decayed under President Sukarno, who concentrated on building a national identity and pride among a conglomeration of races and religions scattered throughout the islands. He also sought to cast Indonesia in the role of leader of the "third world" while slowly moving closer to Communist China for support.

It was the gradual growth of the ideology of Communism that eventually led to Sukarno's downfall and plunged Indonesia not only into political and economic chaos but also into one of the worst bloodbaths in history.

On the night of September 30, 1965, the Communists and other leftists attempted a coup that was put down by anti-Communist military units under General Suharto. In an ensuing purge of Communists, more than 300,000 Indonesians were slaughtered. Political prisoners were held for years, but the government, pressured by Amnesty International and others, released many thousands annually for several years, beginning in 1977.

President Sukarno was gradually eased out of power and General Suharto became president, running the country under the tight rein of the military. The Communist party was banned.

President Suharto found Indonesia in financial ruin and deeply in debt to other nations for money Sukarno had borrowed to spend on military equipment and prestige projects such as public buildings and monuments. Under the new regime capital was lured into the country with tempting interest rates and guarantees.

Indonesia faces enormous problems, and tremendous overcrowding of the island of Java, where 90 million people live, tops the list. Efforts to move people to underpopulated outer island regions have largely failed. Despite development of roads, electrification, hospitals and schools, much of the outer island area still remains a wilderness.

However, a vast natural treasure of oil, minerals and forests is beginning to be harvested, to the benefit of both Indonesia and the foreign investors who have poured in the money and technical skills to exploit it. Currently, Indonesia is East Asia's main oil exporter and a member of the Organization of Petroleum Exporting Countries (OPEC). Its estimated foreign trade surplus of $13 billion in

1980 was due mainly to its $21 billion in oil and gas exports.

After a parliamentary election in 1977, President Suharto was unanimously reelected by the Congress to a third five-year term in March 1978, and a new cabinet with more military members was installed. A five-year plan was announced for 1979-83, stressing development of small-scale industries and non-petroleum exports to ease the nation's massive and persistent unemployment. In 1980, after he was publicly castigated in a petition signed by 50 prominent political figures, Suharto moved to restrict the rights of his most strident opponents, particularly the Moslem Unitary Development party, representing conservative Islamic elements, and various activist student groups. In 1982 elections, denounced as fraudulent by the opposition, Suharto's ruling Golkar party greatly increased its legislative majority.

Ideological, political, and economic factors all contributed to Indonesia's growing hostility toward Vietnam as the decade of the 1980's began. In June 1981, a major Indonesian military airfield was opened in the Natuna Islands in the South China Sea, dominating an oil-rich area claimed by both nations.

**HISTORY:** The complex racial mixture found in Indonesia today is the result of two waves of invasions from Asia and the Pacific. Early in the Christian era the country came under the influence of Indian civilization and of Hinduism and Buddhism. In the 16th century, however, both of these were replaced by Islam as the dominant religion. In the 17th century, the Dutch emerged as the dominant power in Indonesia, maintaining their rule almost uninterruptedly until World War II, when the islands were occupied by Japan

**1945-49:** Nationalist leaders Sukarno and Mohammad Hatta proclaim Indonesia an independent republic following Japanese defeat in World War II. Attempts to reestablish Dutch rule evoke nationalist resistance; agreement is finally reached for creation of the United States of Indonesia, linked to Netherlands

**1950-54:** United States of Indonesia is dissolved; Republic of Indonesia is proclaimed, with Sukarno as president. Netherlands-Indonesian Union is dissolved

**1959-60:** Sukarno combines premiership with office of president and adopts authoritarian system of "guided democracy"; following disagreement with Hatta, who resigns as vice-president, Sukarno dissolves parliament and bans political parties

**1962:** Dutch withdraw from West Irian, on island of New Guinea, under agreement with United Nations, on condition that territory's people be permitted to decide their own political future

**1965-66:** Indonesia withdraws from UN; Sukarno adopts policy of collaboration with Communist China, which the Indonesian Communist party (PKI) supports in Sino-Soviet split. An attempted Communist coup is suppressed by army and is followed by anti-Communist riots in which more than 300,000 Indonesians are killed; General Suharto emerges as new strong man

**1967-68:** Sukarno is stripped of power and Suharto named acting president. Abandonment of pro-Peking stance is followed by riots directed against Indonesia's economically important Chinese minority; Suharto is formally elected president by People's Consultative Congress

**1969:** Government quells uprising by Papuan natives in West Irian; despite widespread native opposition, Indonesia annexes territory with the approval of tribal leaders

**1971:** July parliamentary elections are first to be held since 1955. The government party wins a majority of House seats

**1973:** Suharto reelected to second five-year term

**1975-76:** Portuguese Timor is incorporated into Indonesia, becoming its 27th province

**1977:** Ruling Golkar party wins elections. Government releases 10,000 political prisoners

**1978:** Weeks of student protests precede presidential election; hundreds arrested, some campuses occupied; Suharto is reelected to third five-year term by Indonesian Congress. Government says it freed another 10,000 political prisoners

**1979:** A volcanic eruption on Mount Sinila, in central Java, kills 175 persons and injures 1,000. Food and medicine are rushed to the province of East Timor, where more than 100,000 persons suffer from famine and disease

**1980:** Suharto restricts right of criticism in press

**1981:** In nation's worst maritime disaster, as many as 580 perish when an inter-island passenger ship catches fire and sinks in Java Sea on Jan. 27

**1982:** In May legislative elections, Suharto's party wins overwhelming majority; fraud is charged

## IRAN

**Area:** 636,293 sq. mi. **Population:** 37,447,000 (1980 est.)

**Official Name:** Islamic Republic of Iran **Capital:** Tehran **Nationality:** Iranian **Languages:** Persian, or Farsi, an Aryan language of the Indo-European group and written Arabic characters, is the official and dominant language. Kurdish, various forms of Turkic, and Arabic are among the other languages spoken **Religion:** About 98% of the population is Moslem, with 90% belonging to the Shi'a sect of Islam and the rest to the Sunni sect. Minority religious groups include Jews, the persecuted Baha'is, Zoroastrians, and Christian Armenians and Assyrians **Flag:** Three unequal horizontal stripes of green, white and red with the red stylized word "Allah" in the center of the white stripe. The words "Allahu Akbar" are written eleven times in Kufic script on the inside edges of the green and red stripes **Anthem:** N.A. **Currency:** Iranian rial (82.9 per U.S. $1)

**Location:** Southwest Asia. Iran is bordered on the north by the USSR and the Caspian Sea, on the east by Afghanistan and Pakistan, on the south by the Persian Gulf, and on the west by Iraq and Turkey **Features:** The country is largely a semiarid plateau, with high mountain ranges and much barren desert. The Caspian coastal region is semitropical and fertile; the area around the Persian Gulf is extremely hot and dry **Chief Rivers:** Karun, Safid, Karkheh, Zayandeh, Dez

**Religious Leader:** Ayatollah Ruhollah Khomeini, born 1900?, is the *faghi* (religious leader) for life, according to the new constitution. The executive, legislative and judicial branches of the government are under the authority of the *faghi* **Head of State:** President Ali Khamenei, born 1939, sworn in Oct. 13, 1981 **Head of Government:** Prime Minister Mir Hussein Musavi- Khamenei, born 1942, confirmed Oct. 29, 1981 **Effective Date of Present Constitution:** December 3, 1979 (approved by electorate in special referendum) **Legislative Body:** *Majlis* or Parliament (unicameral), consisting of 270 members popularly elected for a four-year term **Local Government:** 23 provinces

**Ethnic Composition:** Iranians (Persians) make up about 60% of the population. In addition, there are approximately 5 million Azerbaijanis, over 4 million Kurds, 2 million Arabs, 1 million Turkomans, 1 million Baluchis, 500,000 Qashqais, and smaller numbers of Lurs and Bakhtiaris **Population Distribution:** 49% urban **Density:** 59 inhabitants per sq. mi.

**Largest Cities:** (1976 census) Tehran 4,496,159, Isfahan 671,825, Meshed 670,180, Tabriz 598,576, Shiraz 416,408, Ahwaz 329,006, Abadan 296,081, Kermanshah 290,861

**Per Capita Income:** $1,128 (1980) **Gross National Product (GNP):** $43.7 billion (1980) **Economic Statistics:** About 25% of GNP comes from agriculture (wheat, cotton, barley, rice, fresh and dried fruits and vegetables, pulses, oilseeds, sugar beets), forestry, and fishing; 27% from oil; 17% from industry (textiles, food processing, building materials, rubber tires and mining); 5% from construction; and 21% from trade and services **Minerals and Mining:** Oil (Iran has 10% of the world's known oil resources), iron ore, chromite, natural gas, copper, lead, zinc, coal, gypsum, gold, manganese, and salt **Labor Force:** 12,000,000 (1979) of which 33% is engaged in agriculture and 21% in industry **Foreign Trade:** Exports, mainly oil, carpets, cotton, and fruits, totaled $19.8 billion in 1979. Imports, chiefly machinery, iron and steel, chemicals and drugs, totaled $8.7 billion **Principal Trade Partners:** Japan, West Germany, Britain, Italy, Spain, France, Netherlands

**Vital Statistics:** Birthrate, 45.1 per 1,000 of pop. (1980); death rate, 11.5 **Life Expectancy:** 54 years **Health Statistics:** 650 inhabitants per hospital bed; 2,696 per physician (1975) **Infant Mortality:** 108 per 1,000 births (1977) **Illiteracy:** 63% **Primary and Secondary School Enrollment:** 7,125,466 (1976) **Enrollment in Higher Education:** 154,215 **GNP Expended on Education:** 5.4% (1976)

**Transportation:** Paved roads total 11,620 mi. (1976) **Motor Vehicles:** 1,136,700 (1977) **Passenger Cars:** 932,700 **Railway Mileage:** 3,700 **Ports:** Khorramshahr, Bandar Khomeini (Bandar Shahpur), Bushire, Bandar Abbas, Kharg, Abadan, Enzeli **Major Airlines:** Iran National Airlines operates internal and international services **Communications: Radio Transmitters:** 76 **Receivers:** 6,500,000 (1976) **Television Transmitters:** 157 **Receivers:** 1,720,000 (1976) **Telephones:** 829,000 (1977) **Newspapers:** 23 dailies (1976), 15 copies per 1,000 inhabitants (1974)

**Weights and Measures:** Metric system **Travel Requirements:** The U.S. government has banned all travel to Iran by American citizens, except for newsmen **International Dialing Code:** 98

Iran's revolution of 1979, a popular uprising of civilians, overthrew Shah Mohammed Reza Pahlavi and opened the way for creation of the Islamic

Republic of Iran. Shock waves surged through the world with the exit of the Shah, long regarded as an ally of the U.S., a strong opponent of the spread of communism in the Middle East, and a key figure in assuring the flow of petroleum so vital to the Western world. Terrorism intensified the turmoil later, on Nov. 4, 1979, when young militants seized the U.S. embassy compound in Tehran and vowed to hold the American diplomatic personnel as hostages until the Shah was returned to Iran for trial. A 79-year-old religious leader, Ruhollah Khomeini, successor to the Shah in power, gave his blessing to the capture, and more than 14 months passed before the captives were released.

Iran is a country about two and one-half times larger than Texas. Prone to earthquakes, the country has arable portions that are divided from one another by mountain ranges and deserts. Its most important ethnic group are the Farsi (Persians, whence the traditional name of the country—Persia), but over a third of the population are of other ethnic groups, most of them Indo-European, as are the Farsi. Its oil industry, founded in 1908, is the backbone of the national economy. The wells, although they are beginning to run out, still have enormous potential.

Seat of ancient empires, Iran was conquered by Moslem Arabs in the 7th century A.D. Over centuries, most Iranians became Moslems, but kept their Indo-European languages. In the 15th century, Iran adhered to the Shi'a movement, turning away from Arab leadership.

Shah Reza Pahlavi, an army colonel, who seized power in a military coup in 1921, was favorable to the army and to the promotion of Western ways. Britain and the USSR ousted him in 1941 because he looked to Nazi Germany as a counterweight to British and Soviet influence.

His son and successor, Mohammed Reza Pahlavi, ruled as a figurehead until 1953, when, with the help of the army and Western governments, he ousted Prime Minister Mossadegh. The Shah was identified with foreign influence, and he became more and more dictatorial. The Shah launched a "revolution from the throne" in 1961, and carried out plans to modernize the country, improve public health, and raise the status of women and the poor. Moreover, he offended the mullahs by disregarding their interpretations of the Koran and by seizing mosque property. SAVAK, his secret police, dealt harshly with so-called enemies of progress. Wealth increasingly concentrated in the cities, and city ways became offensive to country people.

When Britain withdrew its soldiers from the Persian Gulf region in 1970, the Shah gave military assistance to neighboring countries. U.S. strategists considered his army crucial to the stability of the region. The army supported him, and the United States gave him aid. The mosques became the centers of opposition to the Shah. In 1978, riots broke out in the name of Khomeini, an exiled mullah who bore the holy title *Ayatollah*.

In 1979, the Shah left Iran, after appointing Shahpur Bakhtiar, a Mossadegh partisan, prime minister. Khomeini, still in exile, mocked the government and appointed a Council of the Islamic Revolution. He returned to Iran and designated his backer, Mehdi Bazargan, as prime minister. Violent demonstrations followed. The army at first supported Bakhtiar, but later became neutral, and the Bakhtiar government collapsed.

Khomeini, Bazargan, and the Council of the Islamic Revolution became power centers—not always in cooperation with each other. Mullahs and *ad hoc* militia units took most of the local authority. But the new order ran into multiple troubles. The Kurds, who had joined in overthrowing the Shah, pursued guerrilla tactics against the Islamic regime. Also opposing it were such ethnic minorities as the Azerbaijanis and the Baluchis and, at various times, certain elements within Iran's badly splintered Marxist movement.

Sixteen days after the embassy seizure, the militants released five white women and eight black men—although all had been denounced initially as "spies." Still held were 50 in the embassy and three in the Foreign Ministry. When Bazargan and his government resigned in protest, Khomeini strengthened the role of the clergy by making the Revolutionary Council the government.

In January 1980, after the adoption of a new constitution, Abolhassan Bani-Sadr, an economist and a critic of the hostage seizure, was elected president, but in parliamentary voting in March and May, the fundamentalist Islamic Republican party, led by the Ayatollah Mohammad Beheshti, won control of the legislature and installed a Moslem "hard-liner," Mohammad Ali Rajai, as prime minister. An unequal power struggle between Bani-Sadr and the fundamentalists continued until June 22, 1981, when Iran's supreme authority, the reclusive Ayatollah Khomeini, stripped the president of his office. Bani-Sadr went into exile in Paris following an order for his arrest. Ayatollah Beheshti was killed on June 28 with 71 others when a bomb exploded at a meeting of the fundamentalist group. In the election of July 24, Prime Minister Ali Mohammad Ali Rajai was elected to the presidency. On August 30, Rajai and newly-appointed Prime Minister Bahonar were killed in a bomb explosion. Ali Khamenei became president on October 13.

In the hostage crisis, the U.S. had retaliated in November 1979 by cutting off oil imports from Iran and freezing Iranian assets in U.S. banks. On April 24, 1980, an attempt by American airborne force to rescue the hostages was halted, before combat, when three helicopters developed mechanical troubles on an Iranian salt desert. Despite the death of the Shah in Cairo in July, negotiations dragged on until January 1981, when, due in part to mediation by Algeria, agreement was reached. The U.S. released frozen Iranian assets, and the 52 remaining hostages left Iran on January 20, the day that U.S. President Carter left office.

Skirmishes between Iran and Iraq over a disputed boundary alignment escalated into a full-scale war in late September 1980. Iraqi troops drove deep into western Iran, damaging oil refineries and capturing the important oil port of Khorramshahr. Iranian planes struck at the Iraqi capital, Baghdad, and other cities. The war, exacerbated by ideological bitterness, dragged on until early 1982, when a major Iranian drive recaptured most of the lost territory. In late June, Iraq withdrew its troops, and, in July, Iranian forces invaded Iraq in the vicinity of Basra.

By 1982, Iranian oil production, disrupted by civil strife and the Iraqi war, had rebounded, but the general economy had yet to recover from the effects of the revolution. Consumer goods, including food, were being rationed and inflation remained high. As guerrilla resistance and terrorism continued, divisions were occurring among the ruling fundamentalists, some of whom even turned against Khomeini in reaction to apparently growing government ties with the USSR.

**HISTORY:** An agricultural civilization existed in Iran as far back as 4000 B.C. The Aryans arrived about 2000 B.C. and split into two main groups, the Medes and the Persians. About 550 B.C., Cyrus the Great founded the Persian Empire, which later fell to successive invaders. The Arabs conquered the country and introduced Islam in the 7th century A.D.; they were in turn replaced by the Turks and Mongols. Internal order was restored by the Safavid dynasty, which ruled from 1499 to 1736

**1736-47:** Nadir Shah establishes Afshar dynasty; he invades India in 1738 and brings back great riches; a despotic ruler, he is assassinated in 1747

**1794:** Aga Mohammad Khan established Kajar dynasty

**19th cent.:** Iran loses vast territories to Afghanistan and Russia

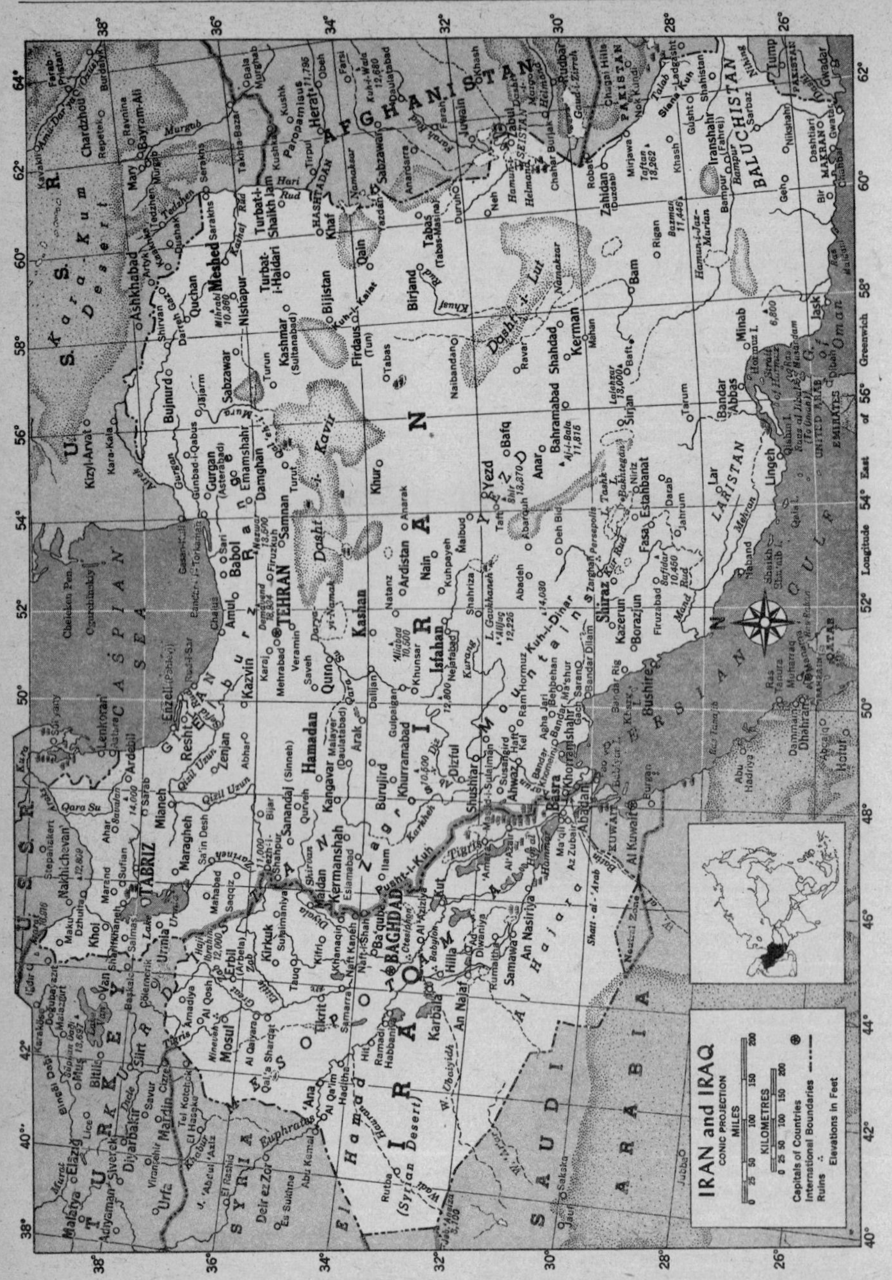
IRAN and IRAQ
CONIC PROJECTION
MILES
0 25 50 100 150 200
KILOMETRES
0 25 50 100 150 200
Capitals of Countries
International Boundaries
Ruins
Elevations in Feet

**1901:** Discovery of oil intensifies the rivalry between Britain and Russia over Iran
**1907:** Britain and Russia divide Iran into spheres of influence
**1921-25:** Reza Khan, an army officer, stages coup d'état, overthrows Kajar dynasty, and establishes military dictatorship; he is elected shah and founds Pahlavi dynasty
**1941:** British and Soviet forces occupy Iran to counter German threat; Reza Shah abdicates and is succeeded by his son, Mohammad Reza Pahlavi
**1946:** Soviet troops are withdrawn from Iran
**1951-53:** Premier Mossadegh, a militant nationalist, forces parliament to nationalize oil industry, which collapses after Britain imposes a blockade. Shah, who opposes Mossadegh, flees the country but returns after Mossadegh is ousted
**1961-62:** Shah launches "revolution from the throne," calling for the end of serfdom, for land distribution, and electoral reform; he personally distributes crown land to peasants
**1963:** Women gain vote
**1971:** U.S. and Britain underwrite a $1-billion defense program for Iran as prelude to British withdrawal from the Persian Gulf
**1972:** Earthquake leaves over 5,000 dead
**1975:** Shah dissolves two-party system
**1978:** Ultraconservative Moslems, leftist extremists riot
**1979:** Shah appoints Shahpur Bakhtiar, former Mossadegh partisan, prime minister, and leaves country. Exiled Ayatollah Ruhollah Khomeini condemns government and returns to Iran, designating Mehdi Bazargan as prime minister. Mass uprising sweeps out Bakhtiar government. Ethnic minorities revolt against government for local autonomy. Bazargan government holds referendum which results in 98% majority for "Islamic republic." Young militants seize the U.S. embassy compound, vowing to hold the hostages until the Shah is returned to Iran for trial. The U.S. freezes an estimated $12 billion in Iranian assets. New constitution is approved in a special referendum
**1980:** Abolhassan Bani-Sadr is elected president, a position subservient to a *faghi* (religious leader), the leading theologian of Iran, Khomeini. U.S. puts embargo on American exports to Iran (April). Eight U.S. soldiers die in collision of plane and helicopter on Iranian desert on April 24 after U.S. military mission to rescue hostages is aborted due to aircraft malfunctions. Clergy-dominated Islamic Republican party wins control of the *Majlis* (parliament) in May voting; Mohammad Ali Rajai becomes premier. One of 53 U.S. hostages released for medical reasons. Shah dies in Egypt on July 27. Iraq invades Iran (Sept. 22)
**1981:** Hostage crisis resolved with help of Algerian mediators; Iranian assets in U.S. unfrozen; 52 hostages flown out of Iran on U.S. Inauguration Day, Jan. 20. Over 3,000 die in June 11 earthquake in Kerman province. Bani-Sadr is ousted as president on June 22. Ayatollah Mohammad Beheshti and 71 other anti-Bani-Sadr politicians are killed in June 28 bomb explosion. Premier Rajai is elected president, July 24. Rajai and newly appointed Premier Bahonar die in bomb blast, Aug. 30. Ali Khamenei becomes president, Oct. 13. Mir Hussein Musavi-Khamenei named premier, Oct. 29; dissident extremists are reported to have killed over 1,000 government officials in six months
**1982:** After nearly two years of sporadic warfare, Iran mounts a major offensive against Iraq, recapturing the oil port Khorramshahr (June). Iranian forces invade Iraq (July)

## IRAQ

**Area:** 172,476 sq. mi. **Population:** 12,767,000 (1979 est.)

**Official Name:** Republic of Iraq **Capital:** Baghdad **Nationality:** Iraqi **Languages:** Arabic is the official and dominant language; Kurdish is spoken in the northeast **Religion:** About 90% of the population is Moslem, almost evenly divided between the Shi'a sect and the Sunni sect; about 8% is Christian **Flag:** Red, white, and black horizontal stripes, with three five-pointed green stars on the white stripe **Anthem:** Anthem of the Republic, no words **Currency:** Iraqi dinar (0.29 per U.S. $1)

**Location:** Southwest Asia. Iraq is bordered on the north by Turkey, on the east by Iran, on the southeast by Kuwait and the Persian Gulf, on the southwest by Saudi Arabia, and on the west by Jordan and Syria **Features:** The country consists of a mountain region in the northeast, a rugged and sparsely wooded area with some good pastures; the vast Syrian Desert, contiguous with the Arabian desert; and a fertile lowland region between the mountains and the desert, watered by the Euphrates and Tigris rivers **Chief Rivers:** Tigris, Euphrates

**Head of State and of Government:** President: Gen. Saddam Hussein, born 1937, took office on July 16, 1979. He is chairman of the Revolutionary Command Council **Effective Date of Present Constitution:** A provisional constitution was issued in 1968; a National Charter was drafted in 1971 as a basis for a permanent constitution **Legislative Body:** National Assembly (unicameral) of 250 members **Local Government:** 18 provinces, each headed by a governor

**Ethnic Composition:** Arabs constitute about 71% of the population; Kurds constitute an estimated 18% **Population Distribution:** 64% urban **Density:** 74 inhabitants per sq. mi.

**Largest Cities:** (1970 estimates) Baghdad 1,028,083, Mosul 333,177, Basra 286,955

**Per Capita Income:** $2,666 (1980) **Gross National Product (GNP):** $35.6 billion (1980) **Economic Statistics:** In 1976, 8% of GNP was from agriculture (dates, wheat, barley, rice, cotton, wool, hides, and skins); 16% from industry, excluding the petroleum industry (foodstuffs, water and power services, bricks and cement, beverages, cigarettes and textiles); 26% from trade and services; and 50% from oil industry **Minerals and Mining:** Petroleum, sulphur, phosphate, natural gas, and salt are exploited **Labor Force:** 3,200,000, of which 53% is employed in agriculture, 17% in industry, 11% in services **Foreign Trade:** Exports, chiefly petroleum (98% of total), agricultural products, livestock, and cement, totaled $22 billion in 1979. Imports, mainly industrial machinery, iron and steel, automobiles, tea, sugar, clothing, and pharmaceutical products, totaled $11 billion **Principal Trade Partners:** EC countries, USSR, Japan, UAE, Brazil, United States, Lebanon, Kuwait, Yugoslavia

**Vital Statistics:** Birthrate, 47.2 per 1,000 of pop. (1980); death rate, 13 **Life Expectancy:** 62 years **Health Statistics:** 496 inhabitants per hospital bed; 2,250 per physician (1977) **Infant Mortality:** 30.6 per 1,000 births **Illiteracy:** 49% **Primary and Secondary School Enrollment:** 2,552,347 (1976) **Enrollment in Higher Education:** 86,111 (1975) **GNP Expended on Education:** 4.3% (1976)

**Transportation:** Paved roads total 4,000 mi. **Motor Vehicles:** 256,200 (1978) **Passenger Cars:** 170,100 **Railway Mileage:** 1,462 **Ports:** Basra, Umm Qasr, Fao, Az Zubair **Major Airlines:** Iraqi Airways operates domestic and international services **Communications: Radio Transmitters:** 26 **Receivers:** 1,252,000 (1975) **Television Transmitters:** 7 **Receivers:** 425,000 (1976) **Telephones:** 320,000 (1977) **Newspapers:** 7 dailies (1976), 22 copies per 1,000 inhabitants (1974)

**Weights and Measures:** Metric system **Travel Requirements:** Passport, visa, valid 3 months, 1 photo **International Dialing Code:** 964

Iraq, the site of the ancient Sumerian, Babylonian, and other civilizations, was among the first Arab countries to free itself from Western European domination, joining the League of Nations in 1932, at the termination of British-mandate rule.

In 1958, after the monarchy was overthrown in a bloody military coup, Iraq became a republic. Ten years later, in the fourth coup in a decade, Maj. Gen. Ahmed Hassan al-Bakr came to power as the head of a military junta. Thirteen days later, he deposed his two partners in the junta and proclaimed himself president. But his ill health resulted in the rise to prominence of Saddam Hussein, Deputy Chairman of the Revolutionary Command Council. On July 16, 1979, Bakr resigned and Saddam Hussein became president.

It is generally accepted that the country is ruled today by the inner core of the Ba'ath party, an ultranationalistic, left-wing, Pan-Arab group, a rival faction of which controls Syria. The Iraqi inner core consists of young intellectual zealots, who rarely appear in public, leaving such functions to the president. The ruling Ba'ath party controls the Revolutionary Command Council, which is the nation's highest authority.

Although the Iraqi authorities have tended to isolate themselves even from the rest of the Arab world, there have been some recent indications that they are beginning to make an effort to enhance their reputation abroad.

The mainstay of Iraq's economy is oil. The revenue it receives through its petroleum exports pays for the bulk of the national expenditure. The oil revenues have been handled sensibly by Iraqi officials and not squandered on prestige projects as in other Middle Eastern lands. There has been a gradual improvement in living standards.

The militant Kurdish minority in the north has long been a problem to Iraqi officials. The Kurds, a nomadic non-Arab people, have traditionally been hostile to rule from Baghdad, and in recent years they engaged the Iraqi army in guerrilla warfare.

Closely related to the issue of the Kurds, who have ethnic ties to the Persians, is Iraq's conflict with Iran over navigation rights in the Shatt al Arab, the estuary formed by the confluence of the Tigris and Euphrates that forms part of a mutual border. In 1975 Iran and Iraq signed a reconciliation agreement, with Iraq abandoning its claim to the estuary and with Iran ending its support of the Kurdish rebellion, which shortly collapsed. On Sept. 17, 1980, Iraq cancelled the 1975 agreement about the estuary, and Iraqi armed forces invaded Iran's oil-rich Khuzistan province on September 23, heavily damaging the major oil refinery at Abadan. Iranian planes bombed the Iraqi refineries at Mosul and Basra, as well as numerous other targets.

After the initial Iraqi thrust, the war settled down to a stalemate. Hussein's hope for a quick victory faded as Iran rejected all peace proposals and the war dragged on well into its second year in 1982. Time seemed to favor Iran as the invaded nation slowly united against the Iraqi aggressors. In September 1981, Iraqi forces were forced to give up their siege of Abadan, and an Iranian counteroffensive pushed Iraqi troops back to within 10 miles of the border by April 1982. In May, Iraqi territory became the target of Iranian helicopters for the first time. On May 24, Iraq quit the key port of Khorramshahr on the Shatt al Arab waterway, and its forces completely withdrew from Iran in June. Iranian forces invaded Iraqi territory near Basra in July.

The war had caused extreme economic difficulties for Hussein's regime. Iraq's important oil exports had fallen well below that before the war. The conflict also had contributed markedly to the general political instability of the Middle East, and other Arab leaders were openly calling for Hussein's downfall.

**HISTORY:** About 3000 B.C. the Sumerians, already long established in the region, founded city-states in southern Mesopotamia. Among the civilizations that flourished there later were the Akkadian, Babylonian, and Assyrian. After about 500 B.C., Persia, and later Macedonia, dominated the area. In the 7th century A.D., Mesopotamia was overrun by the Arabs, who established their capital at Baghdad. Mongol invasions followed in the 12th and 15th centuries, and in the 16th century the region fell to the Ottoman Turks, under whose rule it remained until World War I

**1920:** Iraq is made a British mandate under the League of Nations

**1932:** An independent Iraq is admitted to the League

**1941:** A pro-Axis government, briefly in power, collapses under British military attack

**1948-49:** Iraq sends its forces into Palestine during Arab/Israeli War. The war ends with an armistice

**1958:** Army coup led by Brig. Gen. Abdul Karim Kassem overthrows monarchy and proclaims a republic; King Faisal and Crown Prince Abdul Illah, the king's uncle, are slain

**1961:** Civil war flares as Kurdish tribesmen rebel

**1963:** A Ba'athist military coup, headed by Col. Abdul Salem Aref, ousts regime of Kassem, who is executed

**1964:** Cease-fire is arranged between army and Kurdish rebels, but fighting soon resumes

**1966:** Abdul Salem Aref is killed in helicopter crash; he is succeeded by his brother Abdul Rahman Aref

**1967:** Following Arab defeat in Six-Day War with Israel, Aref forms a new government under Lt. Gen. Tahir Yahya

**1968:** Bloodless coup overthrows Aref and Yahya; Revolutionary Command Council takes control under Gen. Hassan al-Bakr

**1969:** Iraq executes about 40 Iraqis, many of them Jews, convicted of spying for Israel, the United States, and Iran

**1970:** Periodic war with Kurds is ended by granting of a degree of autonomy. Dispute with Iran over Persian Gulf area grows

**1971:** Iraq, in support of Palestinian militants, closes its border with Jordan. U.S. Embassy properties in Iraq are seized

**1973:** Coup attempt led by Col. Nazem Kazzar, Iraqi security chief, fails; Kazzar and 35 followers are executed

**1974:** Kurds declare war on Iraq

**1975:** Agreement is made with Iran, which had supported Kurds. Iraqi troops complete the takeover of former Kurdish strongholds

**1977:** President Bakr's power base is widened as Revolutionary Command Council is increased from 5 to 22 members

**1979:** Iraq helps to settle dispute between North Yemen and South Yemen. Bakr resigns on July 16, turning the presidency over to Saddam Hussein

**1980:** Iraq cancels 1975 agreement ceding Shatt al Arab estuary to Iran; Iraqi forces drive deep into Iran's Khuzistan province and Iraqi planes bomb Abadan oil refinery; Iran bombs Iraqi refineries at Mosul and Basra; war develops into stalemate

**1981:** Hussein objects to peace plan proposed by other Moslem nations; sporadic fighting continues in Khuzistan. Israeli warplanes destroy French-built nuclear reactor near Baghdad

**1982:** Iraqi forces retreat before Iranian counteroffensive, surrendering Khorramshahr port and withdraw from Iran. Iranian troops invade Iraq near Basra

## IRELAND

**Area:** 27,136 sq. mi. **Population:** 3,440,427 (1981 census)

**Official Name:** Ireland **Capital:** Dublin **Nationality:** Irish **Languages:** Irish (Gaelic) and English are the official languages; English, however, is the language in common use **Religion:** About 94% of the population is Roman Catholic, about 5% Protestant Episcopal **Flag:** Green, white, and orange vertical stripes **Anthem:** The Soldier's Song **Currency:** Irish Pound (0.68 per U.S. $1)

**Location:** The republic of Ireland is situated on the second largest of the British Isles, occupying all of the island of Ireland with the exception of Northern Ireland (part of the United Kingdom) with which the republic has its only land border. It is bounded on the east by the Irishh Sea, on the southeast by St. George's Channel, and on the west by the Atlantic Ocean **Features:** The country is shaped like a basin, with high coasts sloping inland to low-lying plains **Chief Rivers:** Shannon, Liffey, Suir, Boyne, Blackwater, Erne, Barrow

**Head of State:** President: Dr. Patrick John Hillery, born 1923, inaugurated 1976 **Head of Government:** Prime Minister Charles James Haughey, born 1925, appointed March 1982 **Effective Date of Present Constitution:** December 29, 1937 **Legislative Body:** Parliament (bicameral *Oireachtas*) consisting of the Senate *(Seaned)* and the House of Representatives *(Dáil)*. The Senate is composed of 60 members, of whom 11 are nominated by the prime minister, 6 elected by the National University of Ireland and the University of Dublin, and 43 from 5 panels of candidates established on a vocational basis. The *Dáil* has 166 elected members. The maximum term of office is 5 years in both houses **Local Government:** 26 administrative counties and 4 county boroughs, each with popularly elected councils

**Ethnic Composition:** The population is mainly Irish, with an Anglo-Irish minority **Population Distribution:** 52% urban **Density:** 127 inhabitants per sq. mi.

**Largest Cities:** (1981 census) Dublin 525,360, Cork 136,269, Limerick 60,721, Waterford 38,457, Galway 37,714

**Per Capita Income:** $3,770 (1980) **Gross Domestic Product (GDP):** $12.4 billion (1980) **Economic Statistics:** In 1980 about 12% of GDP came from agriculture (cattle, dairy products, barley, wheat, oats, potatoes, sugar beets); 40% from industry (food processing, metal and engineering products, beverages, tobacco, textiles, chemicals, clothing, and footwear) **Minerals and Mining:** Rich deposits of lead, zinc, copper, iron ore, natural gas, and silver. Offshore oil resources are being investigated **Labor Force:** 1,133,000 (1978), of which 26% is employed in agriculture and fishing, 19% in industry **Foreign Trade:** Exports, chiefly meat, livestock, textiles, machinery and transportation equipment, dairy products, and metal ores, totaled $8.5 billion in 1980. Imports, mainly machinery and transportation equipment, chemicals, grains and other foodstuffs, textiles, metals and metal products, and petroleum, totaled $11.2 billion **Principal Trade Partners:** Britain, United States, West Germany, France, Netherlands, Japan, Italy

**Vital Statistics:** Birthrate, 21.9 per 1,000 of pop. (1980); death rate, 9.7 **Life Expectancy:** 72 years **Health Statistics:** 95 inhabitants per hospital bed; 831 per physician (1976) **Infant Mortality:** 11.2 per 1,000 births **Illiteracy:** Negligible **Primary and Secondary School Enrollment:** 547,824 (1977) **Enrollment in Higher Education:** 34,615 (1976) **GNP Expended on Education:** 6.2% (1976)

**Transportation:** Surfaced roads total 54,324 mi. **Motor Vehicles:** 707,600 (1978) **Passenger Cars:** 642,900 **Railway Mileage:** 1,334 **Ports:** Dublin, Cork, Limerick, Waterford, Rosslare, New Ross **Major Airlines:** Aer Lingus operates domestic and international services **Communications: Radio Transmitters:** 14 **Licenses:** 949,000 (1976) **Television Transmitters:** 28 **Receivers:** 655,000 (1976) **Telephones:** 554,000 (1978) **Newspapers:** 7 dailies, 220 copies per 1,000 inhabitants (1977)

**Weights and Measures:** British standards and the metric system are used **Travel Requirements:** Passport, no visa for 90 days **International Dialing Code:** 353

After 30 years of something of an economic miracle in which Ireland turned from an agrarian to an industrial society, a little of the power has gone out of Ireland's boom. A period of relatively slow growth, high inflation and unemployment, and problems with its balance of payments has confronted the government with warnings of trouble. Even so, Ireland has come a long way.

Over a half a century ago, when the 26 counties constituting the republic became an independent state, the economy was unbalanced and in indifferent shape. More than 90 percent of exports were agricultural and went to one market—Britain. Beyond a few established businesses—breweries, distilleries, and bakeries—there was no industry. As a result, the drain upon the nation's young through emigration—first to the United States, and later to Britain—was excessive.

Ireland has been greatly aided by foreigners—both as tourists and as developers. Canadians were given mining rights and their exploration and development have shown that Ireland has rich deposits of zinc, lead, copper, and silver. Additionally, Germans helped harness the Shannon River and gave Ireland its first big hydroelectric generators. Beet sugar production was begun, and for many years Ireland has been self-sufficient in sugar supplies. And promising reserves of oil and gas have recently been discovered off the Irish coast in the Irish Sea. In 1977 foreign investment in Ireland amounted to $1 billion.

Ireland, although committed to upholding the rights of private property and private enterprise, has governmental industries. The national transport company, the airline, the sugar company, the tourist board, the peat board, the radio and television service, and the electricity supply board are all owned by the state and administered by semi-governmental bodies. In January 1973, Ireland's economic prospects were brightened somewhat by its entry into the European Common Market.

Economic progress, however, has not erased the age-old "Irish Question," which again came to the fore with the 1969 outbreak of violence between Catholics and Protestants in Northern Ireland. Sporadic street violence has continued since that time. A series of bombings and bank and post-office raids, coupled with the 1976 assassination of British ambassador Christopher Ewart-Biggs by I.R.A. members, unleashed a chain of events which disrupted the government. An Emergency Powers Bill and a Criminal Law Bill, giving police broad powers in dealing with extremist groups was passed; President Cearbhall O'Dálaigh resigned over the laws and was succeeded as president by Patrick J. Hillery.

Following the June 1981 elections, Garret FitzGerald served as prime minister of a Fine Gael-Labour coalition government until January 1982, when he lost a parliamentary vote on his austerity budget. New elections held February 18 failed to give any party a working majority, but Charles Haughey succeeded in forming a new Fianna Fáil government by obtaining the support of two independents and three Workers party members.

**HISTORY:** Celtic tribes from Gaul or Iberian Galicia conquered Ireland about the 4th century B.C. and established a Gaelic civilization. By the 3rd century A.D., five Gaelic kingdoms had been established and gradually became Christianized. Until the 8th century arrival of the Vikings, Ireland remained free from foreign invasion, escaping even the Roman conquest that befell neighboring Britain. In the end, however, beginning with the 12th-century Anglo-Norman conquest, that neighbor was to prove the most troublesome invader of all

**1542:** Henry VIII of England assumes the title of King of Ireland

**1649:** Oliver Cromwell confiscates nine-tenths of Irish land and distributes it among English Protestant settlers

**1801:** United Kingdom of Great Britain and Ireland is formed

**1846-54:** About one million Irish die of starvation as a result of famine, brought on by recurring potato blight; more than 1.5 million Irish emigrate, mostly to the United States

**1916-20:** Easter Rebellion against British rule breaks out in 1916 under leadership of Sinn Fein, a nationalist movement; rebellion is crushed and its leaders executed

**1921-22:** Irish Free State is set up as a British dominion; six northern counties of Ulster remain in United Kingdom. Sinn Fein splits into conservative and republican groups, the latter headed by Eamon de Valera and opposed to division of Ireland; civil war breaks out but conservative elements prevail

**1931:** Equality with Britain is affirmed by Statute of Westminster

**1932:** De Valera becomes prime minister

**1937:** New Constitution makes British monarch ceremonial head of Ireland for external purposes only

**1939-45:** Ireland remains neutral during World War II, but many Irish volunteer for service with British forces

**1949:** Ireland declares itself a republic, withdraws from British Commonwealth, and maintains jurisdictional claims over Northern Ireland

**1951-59:** De Valera becomes prime minister, following victory by Fianna Fáil in parliamentary elections; De Valera resigns his post as prime minister to take over presidency

**1966:** De Valera is reelected president for seven-year term; Jack Lynch becomes prime minister

**1969:** Lynch's Fianna Fáil party wins overall majority in parliament in general elections; government sends troops to northern border as Catholics battle Protestants in Ulster

**1973:** Erskine Childers succeeds De Valera as president. Liam Cosgrave is elected prime minister

**1974:** Cearbhall O'Dálaigh becomes fifth president on death of Childers

**1975:** Severe drought conditions imperil crops

**1976:** British ambassador to Ireland, Christopher Ewart-Biggs, is killed in Dublin by a land mine explosion. O'Dálaigh resigns presidency; Dr. Patrick J. Hillery becomes president

**1977:** Jack Lynch's Fianna Fáil Party wins election, making him new prime minister

**1979:** Prime Minister Lynch resigns and Charles Haughey becomes prime minister. Pope John Paul II visits Ireland

**1981:** Garret FitzGerald becomes prime minister following *Dáil* elections

**1982:** FitzGerald resigns; Haughey returns as prime minister, following inconclusive elections on Feb. 18

## ISRAEL

**Area:** 7,847 sq. mi. **Population:** 3,954,000 (1981 est.)

**Official Name:** State of Israel **Capital:** Jerusalem; Tel Aviv is the diplomatic capital **Nationality:** Israeli **Languages:** Hebrew is the official and dominant language; Arabic is spoken by about 15% of the population; English is the most commonly used foreign language **Religion:** Judaism is the predominant religion; the Arab minority is largely Moslem and the Christian Arabs chiefly Greek Catholic and Greek Orthodox **Flag:** A white field with a blue six-pointed Star of David bordered above and below by blue horizontal stripes **Anthem:** The Hope **Currency:** Shekel (20.5 per U.S. $1)

**Location:** Middle East, at the eastern end of the Mediterranean. Israel is bordered on the north by Lebanon, on the east by Syria and Jordan, on the south by Egypt, and on the west by the Mediterranean Sea **Features:** The Negev Desert in the south constitutes about 50% of the country. The rest of the country consists of a narrow coastal plain in the center and a hilly region to the north **Chief Rivers:** Jordan, Kishon

**Head of State:** President Yitzhak Navon, born in 1921, elected by parliament in 1978 for a 5-year term **Head of Government:** Prime Minister Menachem Begin, born 1913, assumed office June 1977 **Effective Date of Present Constitution:** There is no written constitution; the structure of government is defined by fundamental laws **Legislative Body:** Parliament (unicameral *Knesset*) consisting of 120 members elected by universal suffrage for 4 years **Local Government:** 6 districts, headed by appointed commissioners

**Ethnic Composition:** Jews constitute about 85% of the population, with the rest mainly Arabs **Population Distribution:** 87% urban **Density:** 504 inhabitants per sq. mi.

**Largest Cities:** (1977 est.) Jerusalem 376,000, Tel Aviv 343,300, Haifa 227,800, Bat Yam 124,100, Holon 121,200

**Per Capita Income:** $5,052 (1980) **Gross National Product (GNP):** $19 billion (1980) **Economic Statistics:** 7% of GNP comes from agriculture (citrus fruits, eggs, vegetables); 29% from manufacturing (food processing, metals and machinery, textiles, chemicals, and petroleum products), mining, and quarrying; 20% from commerce and finance; 19% from services **Minerals and Mining:** Potash, phosphate, bromine, phosphate rock, copper, iron, ceramic clays and glass sand, and gypsum are exploited **Labor Force:** 1,252,000, of which 24% is employed in industry, 36% in services, 12% in commerce, 6% in agriculture **Foreign Trade:** Exports, chiefly polished diamonds, citrus fruits, textiles, clothes, food products, chemicals, fertilizers, and mining products, totaled $4.7 billion in 1979. Imports, chiefly rough diamonds, machinery, transport equipment, nonmetallic mineral manufactures, food and live animals, raw materials, and chemicals, totaled $8 billion **Principal Trade Partners:** United States, Britain, West Germany, Netherlands, Belgium, France, Switzerland, Hong Kong, Japan, Italy

**Vital Statistics:** Birthrate, 24.1 per 1,000 of pop. (1980); death rate, 6.7 **Life Expectancy:** 72 years **Health Statistics:** 180 inhabitants per hospital bed; 351 per physician (1976) **Infant Mortality:** 14.1 per 1,000 births **Illiteracy:** 10% **Primary and Secondary School Enrollment:** 705,488 (1975) **Enrollment in Higher Education:** 75,338 (1974) **GNP Expended on Education:** 6.8% (1975)

**Transportation:** Paved roads total 3,350 mi. **Motor Vehicles:** 438,000 (1978) **Passenger Cars:** 327,000 **Railway Mileage:** 476 **Ports:** Haifa, Ashdod, Eilat **Major Airlines:** El Al Israel Airlines, the government airline, handles foreign travel, while Arkia, its subsidiary, handles domestic travel **Communications: Radio Transmitters:** 39 **Receivers:** 655,000 (1976) **Television Transmitters:** 48 **Receivers:** 475,000 (1976) **Telephones:** 993,000 (1978) **Newspapers:** 27 dailies (1977), 231 copies per 1,000 inhabitants (1976)

**Weights and Measures:** Metric system **Travel Requirements:** Passport, no visa for 3 months **International Dialing Code:** 972

---

The proclamation of Israel as a nation in 1947 established after an absence of many centuries a Hebrew state in a land regarded by Jews as their homeland. The ancient kingdoms of Israel and Judah had been conquered repeatedly through several centuries, and the Jews had scattered through many lands. Following the Moslem conquest of the 7th century A.D., Arab culture had become predominant. The 19th-century Zionist movement for restoration of the Jewish homeland promoted Jewish migration to the land—then the Ottoman province of Palestine. Palestine was occupied during World War I by Britain, which governed it as a mandate of the League of Nations from 1919 to 1946, and of the United Nations from 1946 to 1948. Jewish immigration continued, especially after the Nazi persecutions; by 1947, the Jews were in the majority in much of Palestine.

The UN moved to divide Palestine into an Arab and a Jewish state, over the objections of the Palestine Arabs, who rejected the proposal to organize a state. Israel declared its independence on May 14, 1948, and was attacked by five Arab nations. An uneasy truce in 1949 gave Israel almost 50 percent more territory than originally granted; Jordan (then Transjordan) annexed the rest.

Arab-Israeli hostilities continued to seethe under the surface until they erupted in war on October 29, 1956, when Israel staged a "preemptive attack" on Egypt's Sinai during the Suez Canal crisis. A UN cease-fire ended the fighting on November 6 and Israel withdrew its forces.

During the Six Day War of 1967, Israel made large-scale territorial gains in the Gaza Strip, Sinai Peninsula, Old Jerusalem, the Golan Heights, and Jordan's West Bank. The memory of these gains set the stage for the war of 1973-74, when Egyptian, Syrian, and Iraqi forces attacked on October 6. The Arab forces first made large gains, but these were considerably reduced by the time a truce ended the fighting on November 7.

Despite the truce, sporadic fighting continued between Israel and Syrian troops, until U.S. Secretary of State Henry Kissinger arranged a cease-fire on May 31, 1974.

Border agreements with Syria and Egypt which included UN buffer zones were a stabilizing factor in those areas, but in November 1974 there was increased Israeli concern for the future of the West Bank of the Jordan River when the UN General Assembly voted that Palestinians should be entitled to return to their land and property, and granted the Palestine Liberation Organization (PLO) permanent observer status.

In 1975 Kissinger completed negotiations for a second Egyptian-Israeli disengagement agreement setting out details of the new military position in the Sinai Peninsula and the extent of Israeli withdrawal to the eastern entrances of the Giddi and Mitla passes and from the Abu Rudays and Ras Sudar oil fields, which had been supplying 55 percent of Israel's oil needs. By February 1976 the final phase of the troop disengagement agreement was implemented. Meanwhile, many Israelis had settled in the occupied territory, claiming that all of the historic homeland as their land.

In 1977, the Labor Alignment, which had been the largest bloc in every previous legislature, suffered scandal and internal discord. The Likud party won the ensuing election and with two religious groups formed a coalition government more favorable to private enterprise and to Jewish religious tradition. Menachem Begin became prime minister.

Despite Begin's reputation as a hard-liner, President Anwar el-Sadat of Egypt visited Israel in 1977 as an initiative to peace. Begin returned the visit, and negotiations for peace opened. Despite disagreement over Jewish settlements Israel had established in the occupied territory, Begin and Sadat, with the help of U.S. President Jimmy Carter's diplomacy, signed a peace treaty in March 1979. Israel agreed to withdraw from occupied Sinai within three years, and from the oil fields there within a year, and agreed to take steps toward Palestinian self-government. On April 25, 1982, Israel turned back the remainder of the Sinai to Egypt, ending its 15-year occupation of the desert area and fulfilling a chief provision of the treaty. This left unresolved the issue of self-rule for Palestinians living in the West Bank and Gaza Strip. Israel continued to establish settlements on the West Bank despite Egypt's protests and continued Arab terrorism. Violent demonstrations by Palestinians occurred in May.

On the day of the Israeli withdrawal, Begin declared that Israel would make no further territorial concessions. Israelis were uncertain about future provisions of the peace treaty, especially after President Sadat's assassination.

Israeli-Arab relations were exacerbated in April 1981 when Israeli jets shot down two Syrian military helicopters in Lebanon. Syria responded by deploying Soviet-made missiles in that country, and Israeli aircraft bombed PLO bases there through July. In retaliation, Palestinian gunners fired rockets at northern Israeli towns. On July 17, Israeli jets struck at PLO headquarters in Beirut, killing 300 persons and wounding 800 others.

The Israeli bombing of a nearly-completed Iraqi nuclear reactor station near Baghdad on June 7 also resulted in increased Arab-Israeli tensions, and in a UN Security Council condemnation of Israel. The official Israeli announcement of the air attack stated that the real purpose of the nuclear facility was to produce atomic bombs for use against Israel.

The Israeli ambassador to Britain, Shlomo Argov, was wounded by terrorists in London on June 3, 1982. The PLO denied responsibility for the attack but Israeli officials rejected the disclaimer. As a result, Israeli forces invaded southern Lebanon on June 6, destroyed PLO bases within a 25-mile zone north of the Israeli border, captured Tyre and Sidon, and bombed Beirut. Syrian missile sites in Lebanon's Bekaa Valley were destroyed, although the two nations refrained from launching an all-out war. By June 14 Israeli forces had encircled West Beirut, trapping the PLO command and 7,000 guerrillas. After a prolonged and bloody siege, the PLO and Israel agreed to a U.S. plan for the evacuation of the PLO fighters from Beirut to various Arab countries. The first evacuees left the city on August 22.

**HISTORY:** In biblical times Israel (then Canaan and later Palestine) was the home of scattered Hebrew tribes. By about 1000 B.C. a Hebrew kingdom was firmly established at Jerusalem, under King David. After the reign of Solomon, the kingdom split into two states, Israel and Judah, which were respectively destroyed by Assyria and Babylonia. Palestine later fell to the Greeks and finally to the Romans. In the 7th century, the region was conquered by the Moslems. Later, it was an Ottoman province. During World War I, it came under British control. Modern Israel marks the culmination of the Zionist movement for the reconstitution of a Jewish state

**1947:** United Nations adopts Palestine partition plan to divide Palestine into two states, one Jewish and one Arab

**1948:** Israel is proclaimed a nation and British withdraw from Palestine. Armies of surrounding Arab states attack Israel

**1949:** Fighting ends with Israel in possession of almost 50 percent more territory than originally granted. Armistice agreements, but no peace treaties, are signed with Arab countries

**1956:** Israeli forces invade Egypt and occupy Sinai Peninsula and Gaza Strip

**1957:** Under American and Soviet pressure, Israel completes withdrawal to old borders. United States guarantees Israeli passage into Red Sea through previously blockaded Strait of Tiran

**1964:** Palestine Liberation Organization is formed

**1967:** Egyptians reimpose blockade. Israel attacks in Sinai and then into Jordan and Syria. At end of Six-Day War, Israelis occupy all of Sinai Peninsula, Gaza, and east bank of Suez Canal, the Gaza Strip, all of west bank of Jordan, and Golan Heights of Syria

**1969:** Prime Minister Levi Eshkol dies and is succeeded by Mrs. Golda Meir of the Israel Labor party. Arab guerrilla activity continues; Labor Alignment is returned to power

**1972:** Terrorist activity by PLO guerrillas and sympathizers increases, extending to a random massacre at Lod Airport and the kidnapping and death of Israeli athletes at the Olympic games in Munich. Israel carries out retaliatory raids on guerrilla settlements in Lebanon

**1973:** David Ben-Gurion, first prime minister and principal founder of the state of Israel, dies

**1973-74:** Fourth Arab-Israeli war breaks out when Egyptian, Syrian, and Iraqi forces launch surprise attack on October 6, 1973, Yom Kippur, the holiest day of the year for Jews. In January, Israel and Egypt agree on disengagement of forces. Fighting with Syria continues through May 1974

**1975:** Sporadic raids and bombing incidents, are carried out chiefly by the PLO, followed by Israeli reprisals on PLO camps in Syria; tension makes settlement of Arab-Israeli differences difficult

**1976:** Israeli airborne commandos rescue 103 hostages held at Uganda's Entebbe Airport by pro-Palestinian hijackers of an Air France airliner

**1977:** Israeli troops cross into Southern Lebanon and fight with Palestinians in the first direct clash between the two sides in more than two years. Likud party is victorious in general elections; Menachem Begin becomes prime minister. Begin confers with President Carter in Washington. Austerity moves, defense spending cuts, and Israeli pound devaluation are announced. President Sadat's Mideast "peace initiative" spurs round of talks

**1978:** PLO terror attack, worst in Israel's history, leaves 37 dead and 82 wounded; Israeli forces retaliate by invading southern Lebanon and occupy area for three months

**1979:** Peace treaty with Egypt signed. Treaty requires Israel to withdraw from Egypt within three years, from remaining oil fields within one year; and requires Egypt to sell oil to Israel

**1980:** Israeli forces complete withdrawal from Sinai oil fields; government opens borders to Egypt and exchanges ambassadors. Israeli-Egyptian talks on Palestinian autonomy are suspended. A Knesset bill reaffirms *all* of Jerusalem as the Israeli capital

**1981:** Relations with Syria worsen after Syrian forces in Lebanon deploy anti-aircraft missiles. Israeli aircraft destroy Iraqi nuclear reactor near Baghdad. Lebanon-based PLO units fire rockets at Israeli towns. Israeli planes bomb Palestinian targets, including PLO headquarters in Beirut, killing 300 and wounding 800, mostly Lebanese civilians. Cease-fire truce arranged on July 24. Israel annexes the Golan Heights on Dec. 14

**1982:** Israel completes its evacuation of the Sinai in compliance with terms of Israeli-Egyptian peace treaty. Wounding of Israeli ambassador to Britain in London by Arab terrorists results in Israeli invasion of southern Lebanon (June 6). PLO leaders and armed guerrillas come under siege in West Beirut. First group of 7,000 PLO fighters are evacuated from city on Aug. 22, following U.S. arranged agreement with PLO and Israel

## ITALY

**Area:** 116,303 sq. mi. **Population:** 57,197,000 (1981 est.)

**Official Name:** Italian Republic **Capital:** Rome **Nationality:** Italian **Languages:** Italian is the official and predominant language; German, French, Friulian, Slovene, Ladin, Albanian, and Greek are spoken by minorities **Religion:** Roman Catholicism is the religion of about 99% of the population **Flag:** Green, white, and red vertical stripes **Anthem:** Hymn of Mameli **Currency:** Italian lira (1,296 per U.S. $1)

**Location:** Southern Europe. Italy has common land frontiers in the west with France, and in the north with Switzerland, Austria, and Yugoslavia. Its boot-shaped peninsular coastline is bordered by three branches of the Mediterranean: the Tyrrhenian Sea on the west, the Ionian Sea on the south, and the Adriatic Sea on the east. Major offshore islands are Sicily and Sardinia **Features:** The country is rugged and mountainous, except for the Po Valley area in the north, the heel of "the boot" in the south, and small coastal areas **Chief Rivers:** Po, Tiber, Arno, Adige

**Head of State:** President Alessandro Pertini, born 1896, elected in 1978 by Electoral Assembly (Parliament plus 58 regional representatives) **Head of Government:** Premier Giovanni Spadolini, born 1925, appointed 1981 **Effective date of Present Constitution:** January 1, 1948 **Legislative Body:** Parliament (bicameral), consisting of the Senate and the Chamber of Deputies. The Senate is composed of 322 members elected for 5 years. The Chamber of Deputies has 630 members elected for 5 years **Local Government:** 94 provinces, each headed by a prefect appointed by the central government. These are grouped into 20 regions, with limited governing powers

**Ethnic Composition:** The population is virtually homogeneous, with small minority groups of Germans, Friulians, Slovenes, Albanians, Ladins and French **Population Distribution:** 48% urban **Density:** 492 inhabitants per sq. mi.

**Largest Cities:** (1977 est.) Rome 2,897,505, Milan 1,706,268, Naples 1,225,227, Turin 1,181,567, Genoa 795,027, Palermo 679,493, Bologna 481,120, Florence 464,020

**Per Capita Income:** $5,300 (1980) **Gross Domestic Product (GDP):** $303 billion (1980) **Economic Statistics:** 43% of GDP comes from industry (automobiles, oil refining, textiles, machinery, chemicals, food processing); and 7% from agriculture (wheat, rice, grapes, olives, fruits and vegetables) **Minerals and Mining:** Italy is a leading producer of mercury, but is poor in most other minerals. Iron ore, petroleum, natural gas, lignite, pyrites, and sulphur are produced in small quantities **Labor Force:** 20.1 million, with some 43% in industry and 15% in agriculture **Foreign Trade:** Exports, chiefly industrial machinery, office machines, motor vehicles, textiles, and footwear, totaled $78 billion in 1980. Imports, mainly crude oil, minerals, machinery, iron and steel, totaled $100 billion **Principal Trade Partners:** EC and EFTA countries, Latin America, United States, Libya, Saudi Arabia, Iraq, USSR

**Vital Statistics:** Birthrate, 11.2 per 1,000 of pop. (1980); death rate, 9.7 **Life Expectancy:** 73 years **Health Statistics:** 97 inhabitants per hospital bed; 502 per physician (1973) **Infant Mortality:** 14.3 per 1,000 births **Illiteracy:** 2% **Primary and Secondary School Enrollment:** 9,799,953 (1976) **Enrollment in Higher Education:** 976,712 **GNP Expended on Education:** 5.0% (1975)

**Transportation:** Surfaced roads total 179,241 mi., including 3,600 mi. of superhighways **Motor Vehicles:** 17,607,300 (1977) **Passenger Cars:** 16,371,200 **Railway Mileage:** 12,624 **Ports:** Genoa, Augusta, Venice, Naples, Trieste, Taranto, La Spezia **Major Airlines:** Alitalia, a government airline, conducts international flights while Aermediterranea and ATI are domestic **Communications: Radio Transmitters:** 1,962 **Licenses:** 13,024,000 (1976) **Television Transmitters:** 1,199 **Licenses:** 12,377,000 (1976) **Telephones:** 17,088,000 (1978) **Newspapers:** 72 dailies, 97 copies per 1,000 inhabitants (1977)

**Weights and Measures:** Metric system **Travel Requirements:** Passport, no visa for 3 months **International Dialing Code:** 39

Italy—one of the younger of Europe's nation-states, home of one of its oldest civilizations—is a society undergoing profound political, economic, and cultural transformations.

Unified politically only a century ago, Italians still seek a common sense of nationhood that will bridge their vast regional differences and rivalries. The Brenner Pass, in the Alps, and Cape Correnti, on the southern tip of Sicily, lie 750 miles apart, but the distance between them is far greater in terms of the environment, culture, traditions, and temperaments of their peoples.

The northerner is the heir to the Renaissance and *risorgimento*: vigorous, forward-looking, in the mainstream of European life, living in a temperate climate on land endowed with the lion's share of Italy's slender resources.

The southerner, on the other hand, has been less favored both by nature and by history. His land is poor, his climate marked by extremes, his political and cultural tradition still rooted in the aftermath of a feudalism that long resisted the liberating winds of the Renaissance, the French Revolution, and 19th-century liberalism.

The task of molding and governing a postwar republican Italy that will reconcile these vastly divergent interests and enlist equally the loyalties of the Milan industrialist, Roman aristocrat or shopkeeper, and Calabrian peasant has fallen on shifting coalitions of the democratic parties of the center and moderate left.

Until June 1981, the Christian Democratic party had been the largest in every parliament—and had supplied every premier—since 1946. But it never had a majority, and had to negotiate agreements for coalition with other parties. Italy's 40th government since World War II, a four-party coalition formed by Christian Democratic President Arnaldo Forlani in October 1980, fell in May 1981 because of a scandal. Public revelations about *Propaganda Due*, a secretive Masonic lodge which may have been involved in criminal activities, disclosed that its 953 members included 3 cabinet ministers, 43 members of Parliament, and 38 generals and admirals. The cabinet members involved were forced to resign, bringing down the Forlani government. On June 28, Giovanni Spadolini, leader of the Republican party, became premier.

Italy has been troubled by acts of political terrorism, the most spectacular being the kidnap and murder of former Premier Aldo Moro in 1978, and the bombing of the Bologna railroad station in August 1980, which killed 81 people. Another terrorist kidnapping occurred Dec. 17, 1981, when U.S. Brig. Gen. James L. Dozier was kidnapped by a Red Brigade. But brilliant work and a lightning raid by Italian police on a Red Brigade hideout in Padua rescued him unharmed on Jan. 28, 1982. Five of his kidnappers were arrested on the spot, and 17 convicted terrorists in all were sentenced to prison terms for the crime. In 1981 there were fewer than 1,000 terrorist incidents in Italy—the lowest number since 1976.

**HISTORY:** About 500 B.C. Rome began its rise to power, supplanting the earlier Etruscan civilization. The Roman Empire fell in the 5th century A.D. and thereafter the Italian peninsula was largely politically fragmented until modern times. After the great cultural and intellectual flowering of the Renaissance, which reached its height in the late 15th century, much of Italy, divided into kingdoms, principalities, duchies, city-republics, and the Papal States, fell increasingly under foreign sway

**1815:** Following collapse of Napoleonic Empire, former states of Italian peninsula are reconstituted—some under Austrian rule

**1848-49:** Movement for the unification of Italy, known as the *risorgimento*, leads to revolts, but these are suppressed after initial successes

**1859:** Kingdom of Sardinia, aided by France, defeats Austrians at Solferino

**1860-70:** The Italian unification movement, whose most notable figures were Giuseppe Garibaldi, Giuseppe Mazzini, and Camillo di Cavour, moves ahead as various Italian states vote for union with Sardinia; following conquest of Kingdom of Two Sicilies by Garibaldi, that kingdom also votes for union with Sardinia, and in 1861 the Kingdom of Italy is proclaimed under Victor Emmanuel II. With the seizure of the papal possessions, Italian unification is completed by 1870

**1915-18:** Italy engages in World War I on side of Allies after initially declaring neutrality; country suffers heavy losses

**1922:** Benito Mussolini comes to power in wake of severe depression and establishes a fascist dictatorship

**1935-36:** Italy conquers Ethiopia

**1940-43:** Italy enters World War II as ally of Nazi Germany; Italian defeats in Greece and North Africa, and the Allied invasion of Sicily, help topple Mussolini's regime. New government is set up and an armistice signed with the Allies

**1945:** Mussolini is executed by Italian partisans

**1946:** Italy becomes a republic after voters decide by plebiscite to abolish the monarchy

**1947:** Peace treaty is ratified; Italy loses Fiume, Zara, Pula, and Istria to Yugoslavia and the Dodecanese Islands to Greece; its African colonies are placed under UN supervision

**1949:** Italy becomes a founding member of NATO

**1966:** Floods in northern and central Italy destroy or damage many art treasures, especially in Florence

**1974:** Premier Aldo Moro forms Christian-Democratic/Republican minority government

**1975:** Voting age is lowered to 18. The 1954 partition of Trieste territory becomes official

**1976:** Death toll from earthquake in Friuli reaches 1,200. Aldo Moro's government falls and new elections held. Italian Communist party makes major gains but Christian Democrats retain slight edge. Giulio Andreotti is sworn in as premier

**1977:** Italy and Yugoslavia ratify agreement ending World War II border dispute over area south of Trieste, with Italy ceding territory to Yugoslavia. Public protest and extremist violence erupts over Italy's economic crisis

**1978:** Government resigns as wave of violence continues; Communists withdraw tacit support and demand cabinet seats in emergency coalition. President Giovanni Leone reappoints Premier Andreotti to form new government, nation's 40th since World War II. Red Brigades kidnap former Premier Aldo Moro on same day Andreotti presents new government to parliament; Communists given direct role (short of cabinet-level) for first time since 1947. Red Brigades demand release of 13 leftist prisoners for Moro's life; government refuses to negotiate, as huge manhunt is mounted; government decree enhances power of police; Moro found dead; public reaction against Red Brigades noted. Abortion is legalized. President Leone resigns in face of corruption charges and is replaced by Alessandro Pertini. Trial of Red Brigades members ends (29 are sentenced up to 15 years in prison; 16 are acquitted)

**1979:** Communists withdraw from coalition after their demand for cabinet seats is rebuffed. Andreotti resigns; parliament is dissolved; Communists lose seats in elections for new parliament

**1980:** Christian Democrat leader Arnaldo Forlani forms new four-party coalition government. Bombing of Bologna railroad station by right-wing terrorists kills 81 people

**1981:** Forlani government falls after scandal involves three cabinet members; Republican party leader, Giovanni Spadolini, forms new coalition government

**1982:** Spadolini government survives Socialist attempt to bring it down

## IVORY COAST

**Area:** 127,520 sq. mi. **Population:** 7,920,000 (1979 est.)

**Official Name:** Republic of the Ivory Coast **Capital:** Abidjan **Nationality:** Ivorian **Languages:** French is the official and commercial language, but the most common African language is Dioula **Religion:** 66% animist, 22% Moslem, 12% Roman Catholic **Flag:** Orange, white, and green vertical stripes **Anthem:** L'Abidjanaise, beginning "Greetings, O land of hope" **Currency:** CFA Franc (305 per U.S. $1)

**Location:** West Africa. Ivory Coast is bordered on the north by Mali and Upper Volta, on the east by Ghana, on the south by the Gulf of Guinea, and on the west by Liberia and Guinea **Features:** From the coast, a rain forest extends over about 40% of the country. The remainder is wooded and grassy savanna, with a mountainous area in the northwest **Chief Rivers:** Bandama, Sassandra, Komoé, Nzi, Cavally

**Head of State and of Government:** President Félix Houphouët-Boigny, born 1905, reelected October 1980 for fifth 5-year term **Effective Date of Present Constitution:** 1960 **Legislative Body:** National Assembly (unicameral), consisting of 147 members elected for 5 years. All members belong to the Democratic Party of the Ivory Coast, the nation's only party **Local Government:** 24 administrative departments, each headed by an elected council, and 2 autonomous municipalities

**Ethnic Composition:** About 60 groups, the largest being the Mande (26%), Akan (25%), Krou (18%), Sénoufo (13%), Lagoon people (7%) **Population Distribution:** 32% urban **Density:** 62 inhabitants per sq. mi.

**Largest Cities:** (1977 est.—Metropolitan Area) Abidjan 950,000; (1974 est.) Bouaké 140,000

**Per Capita Income:** $932 (1980) **Gross National Product (GNP):** $7.5 billion (1980) **Economic Statistics:** In 1979 about 25% of GNP came from agriculture (coffee, palm oil, cocoa, cotton, bananas, pineapples, rice, coconuts, sugar, rubber, yams, cassava, corn, millet, sorghum, livestock, tropical woods), and 20% from industry (tuna-packing, oil refining, sawmilling, agricultural processing, textiles, clothing, auto, truck and bus assembly) **Minerals and Mining:** Offshore oil production is growing. Small quantities of diamonds and manganese have been produced and exploitation of natural gas, iron ore, oil, nickel and gold is under way **Labor Force:** 2,600,000 (1970), with 78% in agriculture and 14% in industry and trade **Foreign Trade:** Exports, chiefly coffee, wood, cocoa, palm oil, cotton, bananas, and pineapples, totaled $2.8 billion in 1979. Imports, mainly machinery, transport equipment, electrical equipment, and petroleum products, totaled $2.2 billion **Principal Trade Partners:** France, Netherlands, West Germany, Italy, Japan, United States, Spain, Britain

**Vital Statistics:** Birthrate, 47.6 per 1,000 of pop. (1980); death rate, 18.3 **Life Expectancy:** 44 years **Health Statistics:** 589 inhabitants per hospital bed; 15,234 per physician (1975) **Infant Mortality:** 138 per 1,000 births **Illiteracy:** 75% **Primary and Secondary School Enrollment:** 792,189 (1975) **Enrollment in Higher Education:** 8,701 (1976) **GNP Expended on Education:** 7.4% (1975)

**Transportation:** Surfaced roads total 1,500 mi. **Motor Vehicles:** 179,200 (1978) **Passenger Cars:** 112,000 **Railway Mileage:** 408 **Ports:** Abidjan, Sassandra, San Pedro **Major Airlines:** State-owned Air Ivoire is the domestic carrier; Air Afrique, a multinational airline, provides the main regional service **Communications: Radio Transmitters:** 26 **Receivers:** 600,000 (1976) **Television Transmitters:** 10 **Receivers:** 257,000 (1976) **Telephones:** 67,000 (1977) **Newspapers:** 3 dailies, 13 copies per 1,000 inhabitants (1976)

**Weights and Measures:** Metric system **Travel Requirements:** Passport; visa; onward ticket **International Dialing Code:** 225

---

The Ivory Coast, the richest and most economically self-sufficient state in former French West Africa, lies on the south side of the African bulge and is slightly larger than New Mexico. The southern boundary is a 340-mile coastline on the Gulf of Guinea, characterized by heavy surf and a lack of natural harbors. Early European voyagers were discouraged by this coastline and the dense tropical forest, as well as by the scant gold to be found.

Shortly after the former French colony became independent in 1960, officials of the International Monetary Fund advised Ivorian leaders to coordinate fiscal and development planning, encourage competitive private enterprise, and create a favorable investment climate—advice Ivorians followed with huge success.

Ivorian President Félix Houphouët-Boigny, who continues to head the government, set up incentives for foreign investors. Himself an experienced administrator in French government service, he brought in top French economic planners to minutely map development.

Helped by high earnings from coffee and cocoa, the Ivory Coast concentrated initially on diversifying agriculture. Systematically, large new plantations of rubber, palm oil, pineapples, sugarcane, rice, and cotton were established. Offshore petroleum deposits are being exploited that will make Ivory Coast self-sufficient for fuel. In 1980, recognizing that its dense tropical forests are being depleted, Ivory Coast began a reforestation project with World Bank assistance.

Since 1960 the Ivorián gross national product has grown by more than 11 percent a year, and the per capita income is among the highest in black Africa. Projects are under way to spread the prosperity of Abidjan, the capital, to other parts of the country. The new port of San Pedro, designed to open up the little-developed southwestern area, has been completed and iron-ore deposits in the northwest are being readied for development.

Although the French still maintain a strong economic position, they have had to share it with increasing numbers of German, Dutch, British, American, Italian, and Israeli enterprises.

Despite the impressive progress, along with increases of public housing, education, and health facilities, there remains an urgent need for raising rural living standards and creating employment.

**HISTORY:** Although evidence of a neolithic culture has been found in the Ivory Coast, little is known of the country's past before the first contacts by Portuguese and French in the 16th century. The Baoulés and the Agnis, both related to the Ashantis of Ghana, did not arrive until the 18th century, and most of the other tribal groups have their main centers in neighboring countries. The French began to establish control over the area in the 19th century and succeeded in colonizing it after much local resistance

**1893:** Ivory Coast is organized as a French protectorate

**1898:** Anti-French resistance collapses with the defeat of Almamy Samory, the Malinké warrior chief

**1946-57:** Félix Houphouët-Boigny founds African Democratic Rally, the first all-African political party; he is elected to the French National Assembly and wins far-reaching freedoms for France's African territories

**1947:** Upper Volta is detached from the Ivory Coast

**1958:** Ivory Coast becomes an autonomous republic within the French Community

**1960:** Ivory Coast achieves full independence; Houphouët-Boigny is elected president

**1963:** More than 80 persons, including government ministers and Guinean nationals, are convicted of plotting to stage a coup and assassinate the president

**1967:** Ivory Coast and Guinea exchange prisoners in effort to smooth relations

**1970:** President Houphouët-Boigny is elected to third term

**1974:** Proposals for dialogue between black African nations and South Africa lead to talks between South African Premier John Vorster and President Houphouët-Boigny

**1975:** President Houphouët-Boigny reelected without opposition

**1980:** Houphouët-Boigny is reelected without opposition for a fifth five-year term. Oil begins to flow from offshore wells

**1981:** International Monetary Fund grants $626 million in loans to Ivory Coast to aid stabilization. Death by suffocation of 46 Ghanians in overcrowded Abidjan jail again strains relations with Ghana. Ivory Coast decries decision of International Cocoa Organization to lower cocoa prices

**1982:** Freedom House reports gain in civil rights in Ivory Coast

## JAMAICA

**Area:** 4,244 sq. mi. **Population:** 2,184,000 (1980 est.)

**Official Name:** Jamaica **Capital:** Kingston **Nationality:** Jamaican **Languages:** English is the official and dominant language; a Jamaican Creole, a mixture of archaic English and African, is also used **Religion:** 75% Protestant, 5% Roman Catholic, 20% other religions or no affiliation **Flag:** A gold diagonal cross, or saltire, divides the flag into four triangles; the top and bottom triangles are green and the remaining two are black **Anthem:** National Anthem, beginning "Eternal Father bless our land" **Currency:** Jamaican dollar (1.78 per U.S. $1)

**Location:** West Indies. The island of Jamaica lies in the Caribbean Sea, about 90 miles south of Cuba and 100 miles west of Haiti **Features:** Mountains cover about 80% of the island; lowlands stretch across the western end and a narrow plain covers the south **Chief Rivers:** Black, Minho, Cobre

**Head of State:** Queen Elizabeth II, represented by a governor-general, Florizel Glasspole, born 1909, appointed 1973 **Head of Government:** Prime Minister Edward Philip George Seaga, born 1930, appointed Nov. 1, 1980 **Effective Date of Present Constitution:** 1962 **Legislative Body:** Parliament (bicameral), consisting of the Senate and the House of Representatives. The Senate is composed of 21 members, 13 of whom are appointed by the governorgeneral on the advice of the prime minister and the rest on the advice of the leader of the opposition. The 60-member House of Representatives is elected for 5-year terms **Local Government:** 14 parishes, 12 of which are administered by elected councils. Kingston and St. Andrew are jointly governed by a corporation

**Ethnic Composition:** About 95% of the population is of African and mixed descent; other racial and nationality groups are Chinese, East Indian, Syrian, and European **Population Distribution:** 37% urban **Density:** 515 inhabitants per sq. mi.

**Largest Cities:** (1975 est.) Kingston 600,000 (metro area), Montego Bay 50,000, Spanish Town 50,000, May Pen 26,074 (1970)

**Per Capita Income:** $1,602 (1980) **Gross National Product (GNP):** $3.6 billion (1980) **Economic Statistics:** About 15% of GNP comes from manufacturing (sugar processing, rum, beer, clothing, furniture); 14% from wholesale and retail trade; 11% from agriculture (sugar, bananas, cocoa, coffee, citrus fruits, copra), forestry and fishing; 11% from construction; and 10% from mining and refining **Minerals and Mining:** Jamaica is one of the world's largest producers of bauxite; other minerals of commercial significance are gypsum, silica, marble, and limestone **Labor Force:** 730,000 (1980), with 36% in agriculture, 15% in industry and commerce, 33% in services, and 16% in government **Foreign Trade:** Exports, chiefly bauxite, alumina, sugar, rum, citrus fruit, cocoa, and bananas, totaled $960 million in 1981. Imports, mainly fuel, foodstuffs, manufactured goods, machinery and transportation equipment, totaled $1.5 billion **Principal Trade Partners:** United States, Britain, Canada, Venezuela, Caribbean countries, Norway

**Vital Statistics:** Birthrate, 27 per 1,000 of pop. (1979); death rate, 5.9 **Life Expectancy:** 69 years **Health Statistics:** 257 inhabitants per hospital bed; 3,509 per physician (1974) **Infant Mortality:** 16.2 per 1,000 births (1976) **Illiteracy:** 5% **Primary and Secondary School Enrollment:** 593,366 **Enrollment in Higher Education:** 9,039 **GNP Expended on Education:** 6.9% (1976)

**Transportation:** Paved roads total about 4,700 mi. **Motor Vehicles:** 151,591 (1974) **Passenger Cars:** 109,628 **Railway Mileage:** 205 **Ports:** Kingston, Portland Bight **Major Airlines:** Air Jamaica operates international service; Trans-Jamaican Air Service provides domestic flights **Communications: Radio Transmitters:** 25 **Receivers:** 555,000 (1976) **Television Transmitters:** 13 **Receivers:** 111,000 (1976) **Telephones:** 111,000 (1977) **Newspapers:** 3 dailies, 49 copies per 1,000 inhabitants (1977)

**Weights and Measures:** Metric and British standards are used **Travel Requirements:** Proof of U.S. citizenship; return ticket **Direct Dialing Code:** 809

---

Like other Caribbean countries, Jamaica is trying to deal with an economy and a society in difficult transition. From slave days, Jamaica's mountains and lush fields, under British ownership, produced sugar, coffee, bananas, and spices. While these are still important (the sugar industry remaining the single largest employer), the island has striven for better balance, promoting its attractions as a vacation resort, developing light manufacturing industries, and exploiting its deposits of bauxite, now Jamaica's principal export.

Disaffection with agriculture—particularly with the sugar industry, an activity associated with slave exploitation—has caused an influx into Kingston in search of industrial and service jobs. Industry and tourism have not kept pace with the demand,, and the result has been a jobless rate often exceeding 30 percent and heavy emigration to the U.S. and Britain.

Prime Minister Michael Manley won a huge mandate for his program of democratic socialism in 1976, after which the government purchased eight of the island's 12 sugar estates and acquired several other businesses. But the economy went into a steep decline. Bauxite, sugar, cement and banana production fell dramatically and, by 1980, neither private banks nor the International Monetary Fund were willing to make further loans in the absence of austerity measures that Manley remained unwilling to adopt. Serious international payments problems developed as Jamaica's oil import costs came to rival its total export sales.

In the elections of October 1980, which were preceded by a summer of violence in which scores died, the economic crisis proved decisive and Manley's party was defeated by that of Edward P.G. Seaga.

Quickly adopting more moderate, pragmatic policies, Prime Minister Seaga managed to restore some confidence, securing IMF and other loans and foreign investments in excess of $2 billion. Unemployment remained high and bauxite mining depressed in 1982, but the economy was benefiting somewhat from U.S. President Reagan's determination to bolster Jamaica's industries and make the island a showcase of nonsocialist progress.

**HISTORY:** Jamaica was inhabited by Arawak Indians when Columbus discovered the island in 1494. It was settled by the Spaniards early in the 16th century and remained under Spanish rule until 1655, when it was captured by the English. By the 18th century most of the Arawaks haad died off, but a huge population of black slaves grew up around the island's sugar plantations. With the abolition of slavery in 1833, the plantation economy suffered a severe blow, resulting in long-lasting poverty and social unrest

**1865-66:** Uprising by blacks leads to imposition of martial law; British parliament establishes a crown colony government

**1944:** Britain grants the island a new constitution based on adult suffrage and a wide measure of self-government

**1953:** Island is granted full internal autonomy

**1958-62:** Jamaica joins West Indies Federation in 1958 along with nine other British possessions in the Caribbean; three years later, however, the island withdraws. In August 1962, Jamaica wins full independence, with Sir Alexander Bustamente, the island's labor leader, as prime minister

**1967:** Hugh Shearer becomes prime minister following sudden death of Sir Donald Sangster, leader of Jamaica Labor party

**1968:** Jamaica joins Caribbean Free Trade Association

**1972:** Jamaica Labor party is defeated in general election by People's National party; Michael Manley becomes prime minister

**1974:** Legislature enacts a harsh law, providing for secret trials, to reduce a rash of murders and other violence

**1975:** Jamaica signs treaty with EC and reaches agreements with foreign companies mining bauxite on the island whereby the government would purchase controlling shares of stock

**1976:** Martial law is declared in Kingston because of violence among warring extremist factions of Prime Minister Manley's People's National party (PNP) and the opposition Jamaica Labor party (JLP). PNP wins overwhelming victory

**1978:** Government launches five-year economic program based on land reform

**1979:** Tourism drops after seven die in gasoline-price riots

**1980:** Foreign-exchange shortage develops in wake of economic slowdown and refusal of banks to extend further credit. Many killed in pre-election violence. A moderate, Edward Seaga, becomes prime minister after JLP outpolls PNP in October. At least 144 elderly women die in nursing home fire in Kingston

**1981:** Nearly $1 billion in loans pledged by banks and International Monetary Fund to help the island's economy. U.S. agrees to buy 1.6 billion tons of Jamaican bauxite

**1982:** Ronald Reagan becomes first incumbent U.S. president to visit Jamaica (April)

---

## JAPAN

**Area:** 145,730 sq. mi. **Population:** 117,057,485 (1980 census)

**Official Name:** Japan **Capital:** Tokyo **Nationality:** Japanese **Languages:** Japanese is the official and universal language **Religion:** Buddhism and Shintoism are the chief religions; virtually all Japanese practice one or the other and most subscribe to both **Flag:** A red sun on a white field **Anthem:** The Reign of Our Emperor **Currency:** Yen (242 per U.S. $1)

**Location:** Japan is an archipelago forming a 2,360-mile-long arc off the east coast of Asia, between the Sea of Japan and the Pacific Ocean proper. It consists of four main islands: Hokkaido, Honshu, Shikoku, and Kyushu, and more than 3,000 smaller islands **Features:** 72% of the country is covered by hills and mountains, many of them active or dormant volcanoes. Because of the country's unstable geological position beside the Pacific deeps, numerous earthquakes are felt throughout the islands **Chief Rivers:** Tone, Shinano, Ishikari, Kitakami

**Head of State:** Emperor Hirohito, born 1901, ascended the throne 1926 **Head of Government:** Prime Minister Zenko Suzuki, born 1911, appointed Aug. 1980 **Effective Date of Present Constitution:** May 3, 1947 **Legislative Body:** Parliament, or Diet (bicameral), consisting of the House of Representatives and the House of Councillors. The House of Representatives has 511 members elected for 4 years. The House of Councillors has 252 members elected for 6 years **Local Government:** 43 prefectures, each with an elected governor and local assembly, 2 urban prefectures, 1 metropolitan prefecture, and 1 territory

**Ethnic Composition:** The Japanese are a Mongoloid people, closely related to the other groups of east Asia, although there is evidence of admixture with Malayan and Caucasoid strains. Over 700,000 Koreans constitute the only important minority group; about 15,000 Ainu in Hokkaido, physically similar to Caucasians, are rapidly being assimilated **Population Distribution:** 76% urban **Density:** 803 inhabitants per sq. mi.

**Largest Cities:** (1980 census) Tokyo 8,349,209, Yokohama 2,773,822, Osaka 2,648,158, Nagoya 2,087,884, Kyoto 1,472,993, Sapporo 1,401,758, Kobe 1,367,392, Fukuoka 1,088,617, Kitakyushu 1,065,084, Kawasaki 1,040,698

**Per Capita Income:** $8,426 (1980) **Gross Domestic Product (GDP):** $986 billion (1980) **Economic Statistics:** 36.8% of GDP comes from industry (transportation equipment, electrical machinery, iron and steel, ships, chemicals), 8.1% from agriculture (rice, vegetables, fruit, wheat, barley, fish, and potatoes), 23.1% from trade, 11.1% from services **Minerals and Mining:** Coal is plentiful, but only about 25% can be used for industrial purposes. There are small amounts of zinc, limestone, lead, and sulphur **Labor Force:** 55,300,000 (1979) with 34% employed in industry, 11% in agriculture, and 48% in trade and services **Foreign Trade:** Exports, chiefly iron and steel, textiles, electronic equipment, motor vehicles, ships, totaled $101 billion in 1979. Imports, chiefly mineral fuels, metal ores and scrap, machinery and equipment, and foodstuffs, totaled $94 billion **Principal Trade Partners:** United States, Australia, Canada, Iran, South Korea, West Germany, Kuwait, Britain, Saudi Arabia, Indonesia, China

**Vital Statistics:** Birthrate, 13.7 per 1,000 of pop. (1980); death rate, 6.2 **Life Expectancy:** 75 years **Health Statistics:** 94 inhabitants per hospital bed; 845 per physician (1976) **Infant Mortality:** 7.4 per 1,000 births **Illiteracy:** Negligible **Primary and Secondary School Enrollment:** 20,069,305 pupils (1977) **Enrollment in Higher Education:** 2,354,841 **GNP Expended on Education:** 5.5% (1975)

**Transportation:** Paved roads total 243,212 mi. **Motor Vehicles:** 33,508,000 (1978) **Passenger Cars:** 21,280,000 **Railway Mileage:** 17,966 mi. **Ports:** Yokohama, Kobe, Tokyo, Nagoya, Osaka, Chiba, Kawasaki, Hakodate **Major Airlines:** Japan Air Lines, partly government owned and partly privately financed, operates international and domestic flights **Communications: Radio Transmitters:** 976 **Receivers:** 59,650,000 (1976) **Television Transmitters:** 6,117 **Receivers:** 26,545,000 (1975) **Telephones:** 48,646,000 (1978) **Newspapers:** 177 dailies, 546 copies per 1,000 inhabitants (1977)

**Weights and Measures:** Metric system **Travel Requirements:** Passport, visa, valid 60 days **International Dialing Code:** 81

---

Japan, having soared from crushing defeat in World War II to a position among the world's leading industrial nations, is today building for itself an international role commensurate with its economic power, while attempting at the same time to resolve the great social problems caused by swift industrialization.

Crowded into a small island territory off the Asian mainland and isolated from the world by their own choice for centuries prior to 1854, the Japanese created a distinctive society and culture. There has been a large measure of modernization and Westernization, but traditional customs, social practices, and business procedures still are deep-rooted.

Close government/business ties and encouragement for export industries enabled Japan to build a huge international trade throughout the 1970s, while curbs on imports and foreign investments continued to afford protection for domestic industry. Eventually, the trade gap between Japan and the U.S. widened so greatly that relations between the two countries became acrimonious. As protectionist sentiment rose in the U.S., the Japanese voluntarily cut down on their shipments of TV sets and automobiles, removed some restraints on importing foreign goods, and sent buying missions to the U.S. In 1980, the U.S. lifted quotas on imports of Japanese color TV sets and, in 1981, Japan agreed to further limit auto exports, forestalling threatened protective action by the U.S. Congress.

Exports to the U.S. continued to increase, however, rising by 20 percent in 1981 alone, and causing additional strains. In 1982, several top executives of major Japanese companies were indicted in the U.S. on such charges as attempted theft of computer secrets and illegal price fixing in the American steel and computer markets. Meanwhile, pressure from the U.S. and Western Europe was forcing Japan to further lower tariff barriers against imports from the West.

Despite such friction, the Japanese in the early 1980s were maintaining the highest economic growth rate among the industrialized nations (projected at nearly 4 percent in 1982), as well as low rates of inflation (4.5%) and unemployment (2.5%). They had gone far beyond their earlier role as traders, having become worldwide investors, producing Japanese goods in many other nations, including the U.S.

The Ministry of International Trade and Industry (MITI) provides a cohesive business-government approach—sometimes called "Japan Inc."—that has proved effective in economic expansion. The approach includes official subsidy and direction, such as "administrative guidances" in concentrating computer research efforts.

With only one brief interruption, Japan has been ruled by conservatives during the postwar years under the "no-war" 1946 constitution, which was imposed by American occupation authorities. The constitution provided the framework for democratic development and made the emperor, who had served as the nationalistic symbol for prewar militarism, a largely ceremonial chief of state.

Support for the ruling Liberal Democratic party (LDP), which derived much of its strength in rural areas, has gradually declined as a result of the migration, within two decades, of more than one-third of Japan's population from the countryside to the cities. The 1976 Lockheed scandal, involving LDP members accused of accepting bribes from the U.S.-based Lockheed Aircraft Corporation in exchange for lucrative sales contracts, also damaged the party's standing. The 1979 McDonnell Douglas and Grumman scandal, also arising from aircraft sales, again turned the spotlight on the activities of the trading companies and Japanese politicians. The LDP entered the 1980 elections fearing that it would win with such small margins that it would have to share power in a coalition. Instead, it won handily—thanks, in part, to a sympathy vote when Prime Minister Masayoshi Ohira died during the campaign. In July, Zenko Suzuki was chosen prime minister.

Pollution of air and water have reached near-crisis proportions in Japan. Other problems include a fragmented, inefficient agricultural sector, a critical housing shortage, and overburdened transport systems.

In recent years American troops and bases in Japan have been substantially reduced and, though still sheltered under the American nuclear umbrella, Japan has assumed a larger role in its own military defense. Dependent on Mideast oil for much of its energy, it has also been building nuclear power plants. Both of these developments have aroused much opposition in the only nation ever to have been a victim of nuclear bombing. Massive demonstrations against the government occurred in 1981 in response to accidents in a nuclear plant and the revelation that U.S. naval vessels bearing nuclear weapons had regularly put in at Japanese ports. Even larger demonstrations, opposing nuclear arms, occurred in May 1982.

Although in 1972 Japan restored diplomatic ties with China, the peace treaty was not ratified until October 1978, because special care had to be exercised to avoid offending another giant neighbor and traditional enemy, the USSR.

**HISTORY:** Legend attributes the founding of the Japanese empire to Jimmu, a lineal descendant of the sun goddess and ancestor of the present imperial dynasty, in 660 B.C. Reliable records of Japanese history, however, date back only to about 400 A.D. From the 6th to 8th century, Japan came under the strong cultural influence of China and Buddhism was introduced. The development of a feudal system weakened the already diminished power of the emperors, who were to remain in obscurity for 700 years

**1192:** Yoritomo, leader of the feudal family of Minamato, takes the title of shogun (military governor) and sets up dictatorship

**1542:** First European contact is established with the arrival of Portuguese sailors

**1637:** Tokugawa shogunate bans all intercourse with the outside world, with the exception of Dutch traders in Nagasaki

**1854:** Commodore Matthew C. Perry, a U.S. naval officer, forces the opening of Japanese trade with the West

**1867-68:** Shogunate collapses and power is restored to Emperor Mutsuhito; Meiji Restoration, so called after emperor's reign name, is followed by formation of a pro-Western government which proceeds to modernize Japan

**1894-95:** Japan defeats China in Sino-Japanese War and annexes Formosa, the Pescadores, and Liaotung peninsula

**1904-05:** Russian power is smashed by Japanese in Russo-Japanese War

**1910:** Japan annexes Korea

**1931:** Japan seizes Manchuria from China and sets up puppet state of Manchukuo
**1937:** Japan invades China's northern provinces; Chinese resistance leads to full-scale though undeclared war
**1940:** Japan signs military alliance with Germany and Italy
**1941-45:** Surprise Japanese attack on Pearl Harbor in December 1941 triggers U.S. entry into World War II; successive Japanese victories give Japan control over vast territories stretching from India to the Aleutians; in late 1942, however, tide begins to turn and Japan loses ground to Allies; with the dropping of U.S. atomic bombs on Hiroshima and Nagasaki, Japan is forced to surrender and is occupied by U.S. forces
**1946-47:** The occupation, under direction of General Douglas MacArthur, initiates series of reforms aimed at democratization and demilitarization of Japan; a new constitution is adopted and emperor publicly disclaims his divinity
**1954:** Japan and United States sign military assistance pact
**1960:** Antigovernment riots and protests against military pacts force cancellation of visit by U.S. President Eisenhower
**1964:** Eisaku Sato becomes prime minister
**1969:** Japan steps up demand for the return of Okinawa, occupied by U.S. forces since World War II
**1971:** Agreement is reached on reversion of Okinawa from U.S. to Japanese rule; Emperor Hirohito becomes first reigning monarch to leave Japan, visiting seven countries in Europe
**1972:** Okinawa is returned to Japan; Japan opens diplomatic relations with China. Eisaku Sato resigns as prime minister and is succeeded by Kakuei Tanaka
**1974:** Tanaka resigns as a result of accusations that he used his political office to amass a personal fortune. Takeo Miki becomes prime minister
**1975:** Emperor Hirohito visits the U.S.
**1976:** Revelations emerge concerning $12.6 million in alleged payoffs by Lockheed Aircraft Corp. (U.S.) to secure Japanese aircraft contracts. Tanaka is arrested. Miki resigns after his party (LDP) suffers setback in elections. LDP leader, Takeo Fukuda, is elected prime minister by House of Representatives
**1977:** Prime Minister Fukuda shuffles cabinet in effort to better deal with Japan's mounting trade surplus and strained economic relations with industrial nations
**1978:** New Tokyo International Airport opens under heavy guard as protesters try to disrupt flights. Earthquake near Tokyo is worst in 14 years; 21 died, 350 injured. On October 23, four decades after Japan invaded China, the two countries exchange ratifications of a peace treaty. Masayoshi Ohira defeats Fukuda in a party election and becomes prime minister on Dec. 7
**1979:** Ohira visits U.S. President Carter and they jointly pledge to seek "over the next several years a more harmonious pattern of international trade and payments." The LDP wins a September election but lacks a majority until independents lend support.
**1980:** Japan and the U.S. sign an agreement for joint research on high-risk, high-technology problems. A no-confidence vote topples the Ohira government in May. Ohira dies on June 12—10 days before the next parliamentary elections, in which he is a candidate—but the LDP wins by strong majorities and Zenko Suzuki becomes prime minister
**1981:** Pope visits Japan in February. U.S. submarine accidentally sinks Japanese freighter in East China Sea in April. Suzuki visits U.S. in May, gives President Reagan a pledge that Japan will reduce exports of autos to the U.S. Cabinet reorganized in December to cope with excessive trade surplus
**1982:** Visit by French President Mitterrand in April is followed by Japanese tariff reductions on European and U.S. imports. Large increase in military budget is announced. More than 300 die in July floods following the heaviest rains in 25 years in the Nagasaki area

## JORDAN

**Area:** 34,990 sq. mi. (excluding West Bank) **Population:** 2,152,273 (1979 census)

**Official Name:** Hashemite Kingdom of Jordan **Capital:** Amman **Nationality:** Jordanian **Languages:** Arabic is the official and universal language **Religion:** 95% Sunni Moslem, 5% Christian **Flag:** Horizontal black, white, and green stripes, with a seven-pointed white star on a red triangle at the staff **Anthem:** The Royal Salute **Currency:** Jordanian dinar (0.35 per U.S. $1)

**Location:** Southwest Asia. Jordan is bordered by Syria on the north, Iraq on the northeast, Saudi Arabia on the east and south, and Israel on the west **Features:** About four fifths of the country consists of desert. The Jordan River valley divides the land into the small, rocky West Bank (controlled by Israel) and the large East Bank, the latter forming a dry plateau that slopes to flat terrain in the northeast **Chief Rivers:** Jordan, Yarmuk

**Head of State:** King Hussein Ibn Talal, born 1935, proclaimed king 1952 **Head of Government:** Prime Minister Mudar Badran, born 1934, appointed 1980 **Effective Date of Present Constitution:** 1952, amended 1974 and 1976 **Legislative Body:** National Assembly (bicameral) consists of a 60-seat House of Representatives (dissolved by the King in 1976) and a Senate of 30 members, appointed by the King. A National Consultative Council, with advisory functions, was established in 1978 **Local Government:** 8 governorates, each headed by an appointed governor; 3 are in the Israeli-occupied West Bank

**Ethnic Composition:** Virtually 100% Arab **Population Distribution:** 42% urban **Density:** 61.5 inhabitants per sq. mi.

**Largest Cities:** (1979 census) Amman 648,587, Zarqa 215,687, Irbid 112,864

**Per Capita Income:** $1,112 (1980) **Gross National Product (GNP):** $2.6 billion (1980) **Economic Statistics:** About 10% of GNP comes from agriculture (wheat, citrus fruits, olives, grapes, melons, vegetables, barley), 25% from industry (phosphate mining, cement, beverages, tobacco, soap, oil refining, tanning, vegetable oils), and 65% from trade and services **Minerals and Mining:** Exploited minerals include phosphates, potash, copper, and marble; manganese, iron, sulphur and oil deposits also exist **Labor Force:** 638,000, with 20% in agriculture, 20% in industry, and 60% in trade and services **Foreign Trade:** Exports, chiefly fruits and vegetables, phosphates, cement, and marble, totaled $410 million in 1979. Imports, mainly foodstuffs, machinery, vehicles, petroleum, and textiles, totaled $2 billion **Principal Trade Partners:** EC countries, United States, Lebanon, Iraq, Kuwait, Saudi Arabia, Japan, Syria, Romania

**Vital Statistics:** Birthrate, 50 per 1,000 of pop. (1979); death rate, 12 **Life Expectancy:** 57 years **Health Statistics:** 1,182 inhabitants per hospital bed; 2,686 per physician (1977) **Infant Mortality:** 21.6 per 1,000 births **Illiteracy:** 38% **Primary and Secondary School Enrollment:** 588,101 (1976) **Enrollment in Higher Education:** 9,302 **GNP Expended on Education:** 3.5% (1976)

**Transportation:** Paved roads total 3,440 mi. **Motor Vehicles:** 78,000 (1977) **Passenger Cars:** 57,000 **Railway Mileage:** 500 **Port:** Aqaba **Major Airlines:** Royal Jordanian Airlines (ALIA) operates international services **Communications: Radio Transmitters:** 8 **Receivers:** 531,000 (1976) **Television Transmitters:** 3 **Receivers:** 125,000 (1976) **Telephones:** 53,000 (1977) **Newspapers:** 5 dailies, 29 copies per 1,000 inhabitants (1977)

**Weights and Measures:** Metric system **Travel Requirements:** Passport, visa valid for 4 years for multiple entry, no fee

---

The Hashemite Kingdom of Jordan is a largely uninhabited desert, about the size of Indiana. In 1921, after centuries of Turkish rule, the area now comprising Jordan and Israel was awarded to the United Kingdom by the League of Nations as the Mandates for Palestine and Transjordan. In 1922, Britain divided the administration of the Mandate and established Abdullah, grandfather of the present King Hussein, as ruler of a semi-autonomous Amirate of Transjordan in the area east of the Jordan River. The western portion (Palestine) remained under the administration of a British High Commissioner.

Britain granted the eastern territory full independence in 1946, with Abdullah as king. When Arab Palestinians and Jews fought each other and the British for the control of Palestine, Britain asked the UN to help settle the conflict. The UN suggested that Palestine be divided into two states, one Jewish and one Arab.

In the fighting which broke out upon the proclamation of Israeli statehood in 1948, the Transjordan Arab Legion occupied most of the West Bank territories allotted to the Arab Palestinians in the United Nations partition plan, including East Jerusalem, and the Jews established the state of Israel, in large measure on the land given to them in the UN plan. Transjordan became the Hashemite Kingdom of Jordan in 1949.

The present ruler, Hussein Ibn Talal, became king in 1952. In 1967, during the Six-Day War, Israel occupied the West Bank territories.

The problems of the Middle East—particularly, resolution of Arab-Israeli issues—dominate Jordan's foreign policy. The current Mideast peace negotiations, with respect to Jordan, revolve around the ultimate disposition of the Israeli-occupied West Bank and Arab Jerusalem and the issue of the roles for Jordan and the Palestinian Liberation Organization (PLO) in the negotiations. Within Jordan, there is friction between the Palestinian refugees and the Bedouins—the principal ethnic group of unoccupied Jordan.

Following the decision of the Rabat summit conference of Arab heads of state in October 1974 to recognize the PLO's right to represent all Palestinians, King Hussein gave the PLO and its leader, Yasir Arafat, the responsibility for the West Bank. Hussein's foreign policy—long pro-Western—has become increasingly favorable to Arab aspirations—largely because of increasing foreign aid from Arab oil states to his resource-poor kingdom. In 1980, Hussein refused again to commit Jordan to joining the peace negotiations under the Israeli-Egyptian 1979 peace treaty.

Reports that the United States might sell sophisticated missiles and fighter planes to Jordan—a possibility that alarmed Israel—were denied in February 1982 by President Reagan, who said that the U.S. ban on such arms sales continued.

**HISTORY:** The present territory of Jordan was the biblical home of the Moabites, the Ammonites, the Edomites, and some Hebrew tribes. It was conquered in 64 B.C. by Rome, in the 7th century A.D. by Moslem Arabs (from whom it derrived its now-prevailing language and religion), in the 16th century by the Ottoman Empire, and in 1916 by Britain

**1916:** Sykes-Picot Agreement between France and Britain divides Ottoman holdings, with Transjordan (the present East Bank) in British sphere of influence

**1921:** British recognize Abdullah as ruler of Transjordan and Hashemite dynasty is founded

**1928:** Britain recognizes Transjordan as independent but retains suzerainty in the form of military and financial control

**1946:** Kingdom of Transjordan is proclaimed

**1948:** British mandate ends, fighting breaks out with new state of Israel

**1949:** Transjordan and Israel sign armistice, with Transjordan in control of West Bank and part of Jerusalem. Transjordan adopts name of Hashemite Kingdom of Jordan

**1950:** Arab Palestine (West Bank) is formally annexed by Jordan

**1951:** King Abdullah is assassinated in Jerusalem. His son, Talal, becomes king

**1952:** Talal is declared insane and ousted; his son, Hussein, becomes king

**1967:** King Hussein and President Nasser of Egypt sign mutual defense pact. Jordan is drawn into Six-Day War with Israel, which occupies all of Jerusalem and all of West Bank

**1968-69:** Israel attacks Arab guerrilla bases on East Bank

**1970:** Guerrillas hijack four Western airliners to Jordan and hold crews and passengers hostage; all are later released. Civil war breaks out between guerrillas and Jordanian forces

**1971:** Jordanian army's July offensive virtually eliminates all guerrilla bases. Syria severs relations with Jordan. Prime Minister Wasfi Al Tal is assassinated in Cairo

**1973:** Jordan joins in war against Israel

**1974:** Arab leaders at a summit conference recognize the Palestine Liberation Organization as the sole representative of the Palestinian people; King Hussein concurs

**1975:** Syria and Jordan establish a joint military command

**1976:** Syria and Jordan co-ordinate their foreign diplomatic representation in countries where either one maintains a mission. King Hussein reconvenes parliament, with representatives of the West Bank in attendance, after having dissolved it in 1974 to decrease Palestinian participation in Jordanian politics. Prime Minister Zaid al-Rifai resigns and King Hussein asks Mudar Badran, chief of the cabinet, to form a new government

**1977:** Queen Alia is killed in helicopter crash

**1978:** King Hussein marries Elizabeth Halaby, 26-year-old American and proclaims her Jordan's new queen

**1980:** Hussein visits Washington, D.C., for talks with President Carter; refuses to join Israeli-Egyptian peace negotiations

**1981:** Jordan cuts ties with Iran after supporting Iraq in its war with Iran

## KENYA

**Area:** 224,960 sq. mi. **Population:** 15,322,000 (1979 census) **Official Name:** Republic of Kenya **Capital:** Nairobi **Nationality:** Kenyan **Languages:** Swahili and English are used officially; of more than 30 languages, Kikuyu and Luo are the most used **Religion:** 59% are Christian, 38% animist, 3% Moslem **Flag:** Horizontal stripes of black, red, and green, with the center red stripe bordered in white; a shield with black and white markings, and crossed spears behind, appears in the center of the flag **Anthem:** National Anthem, beginning "O, God of all Creation" **Currency:** Kenya shilling (10.6 per U.S. $1)

**Location:** East Africa. Kenya is bordered on the north by Sudan and Ethiopia, on the east by Somalia and the Indian Ocean, on the south by Tanzania, and on the west by Uganda **Features:** The Great Rift Valley in the center and west is girded by rugged plateaus and mountains. To the east are dry bush land and a marshy coastal plain. In the north the land turns to scrub and desert. Kenya has numerous lakes, including a portion of Lake Victoria **Chief Rivers:** Tana, Athi-Galana, Suam-Turkwel, Keiro

**Head of State and of Government:** President Daniel arap Moi, born 1924, took office in 1978, elected 1979 **Effective Date of Present Constitution:** 1963, revised 1969 **Legislative Body:** National Assembly (unicameral), consisting of 158 members elected for up to 5 years and 12 members nominated by the president **Local Government:** 7 provinces and the Nairobi area

**Ethnic Composition:** Of the African population 20% are Kikuyu, 14% Luo, 14% Luhya, 11% Kamba, 7% Kisii, and 5% Meru. About 2% of the population is non-African (Asian, European, Arab) **Population Distribution:** 10% urban **Density:** 68 inhabitants per sq. mi.

**Largest Cities:** (1979 census) Nairobi 827,775, (1978 est.) Mombasa 391,000, (1976 est.) Nakuru 66,000, Kisumu 46,000

**Per Capita Income:** $288 (1980) **Gross National Product (GNP):** $4.6 billion (1980) **Economic Statistics:** About 20% of GNP comes from manufacturing (chiefly agricultural processing, oil refining, and small-scale consumer goods), mining and quarrying; 18% from trade, transportation and communications; 27% from services and about 31% from agriculture (coffee, tea, pyrethrum, sisal, livestock, meat and dairy products, wool, hides, corn, wheat, millet, and cassava), forestry, and fishing **Minerals and Mining:** Small quantities of soda ash, fluorspar, limestone, salt, copper, gold, lead, zinc, and silver are produced **Labor Force:** 5,400,000 (1971), 86% in aggriculture and 13% in industry **Foreign Trade:** Exports, chiefly coffee, tea, sisal, pyrethrum extract and flowers, meat and meat preparations, totaled $1.3 billion in 1980. Imports, mainly machinery, transport equipment, manufactured goods, lubricants, and chemicals, totaled $2.2 billion **Principal Trade Partners:** EC countries, United States, Japan, Saudi Arabia, Iran, Zambia, India, Sweden, Uganda

**Vital Statistics:** Birthrate, 50.8 per 1,000 of pop. (1980); death rate, 12.4 **Life Expectancy:** 52 years **Health Statistics:** 773 inhabitants per hospital bed; 16,292 per physician (1973) **Infant Mortality:** 51.4 per 1,000 births **Illiteracy:** 65% **Primary and Secondary School Enrollment:** 3,183,673 (1976) **Enrollment in Higher Education:** 11,351 (1974) **GNP Expended on Education:** 5.7% (1974)

**Transportation:** Paved roads total 3,300 mi. **Motor Vehicles:** 198,000 (1977) **Passenger Cars:** 114,100 **Railway Mileage:** 1,500 **Port:** Mombasaa **Major Airlines:** Kenya Airways operates domestic and international services **Communications: Radio Transmitters:** 16 **Receivers:** 514,000 (1976) **Television Transmitters:** 5 **Receivers:** 50,000 (1976) **Telephones:** 156,000 (1978) **Newspapers:** 3 dailies, 111 copies per 1,000 inhabitants (1976)

**Weights and Measures:** Metric system **Travel Requirements:** Passport, visa, valid 6 months, $3.35 fee **International Dialing Code:** 254

Kenya is one of Africa's best-known countries; the land of the safari, gameparks, and the lure of the green hills Ernest Hemingway made famous. Tourism has grown spectacularly, with annual earnings rivaling those from coffee export.

The Asian population is being rapidly reduced under a phased program of canceling government permits for Asians to carry on businesses. The influence of Europeans has also declined greatly.

Kenya has made considerable progress in industry and in agriculture, particularly in the success of African farmers settled on the former large British holdings in the old "White Highlands." But these gains have been offset by high population growth, unemployment, and drought. A slump in world demand and prices for coffee and tea produced a severe trade deficit in 1978 that has continued. Kenya is energy-poor, and 60 percent of its foreign exchange goes for oil. Wood is a major fuel.

However, hydroelectric power is being developed on the Tana River.

In leading the former British colony to independence in 1963, President Jomo Kenyatta stressed the need for unity with the slogan of *Harambee*! (Swahili for "Let us all pull together"). Kenyatta, affectionately known as *Mzee* ("the Old One"), was able to hold Kenya together, but not without strain. The Kenyatta government's strength was tested in 1975 when a wave of political unrest was touched off by the murder of Josiah Kariuki, a popular member of parliament and critic of Kenyatta. An investigation committee implicated police officials and top aides of Kenyatta.

Although all Assembly members belong to Kenya's only party, the Kenya African National Union (KANU), dissident members formed an opposition group, which resulted in a KANU leadership decree that any Assembly member not following the party position would be expelled.

In August 1978, Kenyatta died peacefully in his sleep. Daniel arap Moi, 54, became president.

**HISTORY:** Kenya's coast was a familiar area to mariners of past eras, including Phoenicians, Egyptians, and Greeks. Arab coastal colonies were established as early as the 8th century and in the 15th century Portuguese joined in the thriving spice and slave trade. Britain gained a foothold in the 19th century and in 1895 established a protectorate over the area, then known as British East Africa. With the influx of British and South African settlers, Kenya continued to be dominated by the white population

**1944:** Africans win token political representation with the appointment of the first black member of the Legislative Council

**1952-59:** Mau Mau rebellion, led by secret terrorist organization comprising mainly Kikuyu tribesmen, results in brutal slayings of whites and Africans serving whites, and equally brutal retaliation by white community; Africans are granted larger, but still minority, representation in Legislative Council

**1960-61:** Britain agrees to new elections for Legislative Council, in which Africans win majority

**1961-62:** Jomo Kenyatta, imprisoned as alleged Mau Mau leader, is released; he enters Legislative Council as leader of the Kenya African National Union (KANU), backed largely by the Kikuyu and Luo tribes, and forces cooperation with the governing Kenya African Democratic Union (KADU), which is chiefly supported by the smaller tribal units

**1963:** Kenyatta leads KANU to overwhelming election victory; Kenya gains independence, with Kenyatta as prime minister

**1964:** Kenya becomes a republic within the British Commonwealth, under the presidency of Kenyatta; KADU voluntarily dissolves itself and Kenya becomes a one-party state

**1966:** Vice-President Oginga Odinga, an early Kenyatta follower and Luo tribal leader, resigns, charging KANU government with being "capitalistic"; he forms new opposition party, the Kenya People's Union

**1969:** Economics Minister Tom Mboya, a Luo, is slain by a Kikuyu; slaying sparks antigovernment demonstrations and arrest of Oginga Odinga. KPU party is dissolved

**1971:** Opposition leader Oginga Odinga is released from detention

**1974:** Kenyatta orders all unauthorized noncitizen traders to leave. Swahili declared official language. Severe drought affects 70 percent of country

**1977:** Tanzania closes 500-mile border with Kenya indefinitely. This action follows Kenya's withdrawal from participation in East African Airways, which forced the airline to close. Government bans all game hunting in an effort to save wildlife from extinction

**1978:** Kenyatta dies. Daniel arap Moi becomes president

**1979:** Kenya launches 5-year development plan to eliminate poverty, disease and illiteracy, and to reduce unemployment. Moi retains office in November elections

**1980:** Thousands of Ugandans in exile are forcibly repatriated. The United States is given port rights in Mombasa

**1981:** A Kenyan is convicted for the 1980 murder of Joy Adamson, Austrian-born author of *Born Free*. Shilling is devalued 15%

**1982:** Moi accuses Asian community of ruining country's economy. KANU expels Odinga for criticizing party policies and resolves to change constitution to create a one-party state. Forces loyal to the government crush attempted coup by air force units (Aug. 1)

## KIRIBATI

**Area:** 264 sq. mi. **Population:** 56,213 (1978 census)

**Official Name:** Republic of Kiribati **Capital:** Bairiki, on Tarawa **Nationality:** Kiribati **Languages:** I-Kiribati (Gilbertese) and English **Religion:** Evenly divided between Protestant and Roman Catholic **Flag:** Bottom half consists of six wavy, horizontal white stripes over navy blue; top half is red with a flying yellow frigate bird over a yellow sun, displaying nine straight and eight wavy yellow rays **Anthem:** Stand Up Kiribati **Currency:** Australian dollar (0.94 per U.S. $1)

**Location:** The island nation extends widely over the western Pacific, from 5°N to 11°S and 169°E to 150°W, and is scattered over two million sq. mi. of ocean. It includes 33 islands and atolls in the Gilbert, Phoenix and Line groups, plus Banaba (Ocean Island). All but Banaba have coral-ringed lagoons circling the tops of submerged mountains

**Head of State and of Government:** President Ieremia Tabai, born 1950, assumed office July 12, 1979, reelected May 4, 1982. **Effective Date of Present Constitution:** July 12, 1979 **Legislative Body:** a unicameral House of Assembly *(Maneaba ni Maungatabu)* of 35 elected members, one nominated representative of Banaba and the attorney general **Local Government:** 23 election districts

**Ethnic Composition:** Predominantly Micronesian with some Polynesians, mixed Micronesian-Polynesian, and Europeans **Population Distribution:** 30 % urban **Density:** 213 inhabitants per sq. mi.

**Largest City:** Bairiki 1,300

**Per Capita Income:** $630 (1979) **Gross Domestic Product (GDP):** $36 million (1979) **Economic Statistics:** The economy is based largely on the export of copra. The brine shrimp industry on Christmas Island grows shrimps and shrimp eggs for fish farms throughout the world. There is a soft drink factory, a biscuit factory and a boatbuilding concern **Minerals and Mining:** Phosphate mining on Banaba (Ocean Island) has ceased **Labor Force:** 15,921 (1973) **Foreign Trade:** Exports, chiefly phosphate rock and copra, totaled $21.2 million in 1978. Imports totaled $18.4 million **Principal Trade Partners:** Britain, Australia

**Vital Statistics:** Birthrate, 35 per 1,000 of pop. (1978); death rate, 14 **Life Expectancy:** 52 years **Health Statistics:** 201 inhabitants per hospital bed; 2,308 per physician (1977) **Infant Mortality:** 87 per 1,000 births (1978) **Illiteracy:** under 10% **Primary and Secondary School Enrollment:** 14,511 (1977) **Enrollment in Higher Education:** N.A. **GNP Expended on Education:** N.A.

**Transportation:** Motorable roads total 300 mi. **Motor Vehicles:** N.A. **Passenger Cars:** N.A. **Railway Mileage:** None **Ports:** Tarawa, Canton Island **Major Airlines:** Air Tunguru provides domestic and some international service **Communications: Radio Transmitters:** 1 **Receivers:** 8,200 (1975) **Television Transmitters:** None **Telephones:** 866 **Newspapers:** 4 non-dailies, 89 copies per 1,000 inhabitants (1974)

**Weights and Measures:** British and metric **Travel Requirements:** not available

In November 1943, U.S. Marines landed on Tarawa, the central island in the far-flung Gilbert chain, and fought one of the bloodiest battles of the Second World War, defeating Japanese garrison of 5,000. Although time seemed to have forgotten these peaceful islands since, the realities of the modern world have caught up to this newly independent nation—one of the world's poorest—of 33 coral atolls stretched across two million square miles of the South Pacific, at the crossroads of the equator and the international date line.

Independence came to the former Gilbert Islands on July 12, 1979, after 87 years of British rule. One of the most pressing problems facing Kiribati (pronounced "Kiribass") is economic; 99 percent of its annual income was derived from phosphate mining controlled by a joint Australian-New Zealand authority on Banaba. The phosphate deposit was exhausted in 1979, but machinery was maintained pending a redevelopment survey. Diversification is thus the main priority facing the new government on Tarawa. Agriculture is limited by poor soil, although the export of copra—derived from the native coconut palms—has been a source of revenue. There are plans to develop local industries—mainly fruit canning and handicrafts—as well as to exploit the potentially rich fishing grounds within Kiribati's 200-mile offshore boundaries. British pledges of aid and unrestricted access to Australian and New Zealand markets hold some promise for future economic development.

Although fourteen of the islands in the Phoenix and Line groups have long been claimed by both Britain and the United States—including Kanton (Canton), Enderbury and Christmas Islands—the U.S. has agreed to relinquish Canton and Enderbury in 1980, and will cede the rest to Kiribati by treaty in the near future.

But the birth pangs of the new nation have caused other political problems the new government must face. The former residents of Banaba (Ocean Island), who were relocated following World War II after mining had despoiled their island, have fought for 10 years to reassert their claims to their traditional homes, and continue to oppose being part of an independent Kiribati. Kiribati, while assuring the islanders of their continued rights on Banaba, has refused so far to agree to Banaban demands for separation.

**HISTORY:** The main wave of Micronesian settlement of the area is thought to have originated from Samoa around the thirteenth century. Although Spanish navigators are credited with sighting some of the islands in 1537 and 1606, true European discovery of the area came only much later, with the first white settlement dating from the 1830s. Missionaries visited the islands in 1857, and by the 1860s a flourishing trade in coconut oil and copra had been established. Between 1850 and 1875 the islands were raided by "blackbirders" for slave labor in South America, Fiji, Tahiti, Hawaii and Australia. To stamp out this activity, the British established the High Commmission for the Western Pacific over the area in 1877

**1888-89:** Britain annexes Christmas, Fanning and Washington Islands

**1892:** Britain establishes protectorate over Gilberts and neighboring Ellice Islands

**1915:** Protectorate reorganized as Gilbert and Ellice Islands Colony, extended to include Ocean Island (Banaba) and the Northern Line Islands by 1919

**1937:** Phoenix Islands incorporated into the colony

**1939:** Britain and U.S. sign treaty providing for joint control of Kanton (Canton) and Enderbury

**1941-45:** Japanese seize Tarawa and Ocean Island (Banaba) from British at outset of World War II. U.S. forces land on Tarawa November 1943, defeating Japanese occupation force. Australian forces liberate Ocean Island (Banaba) in 1945

**1945-47:** Banabans, dispersed during conflict, are resettled on Rabi, in Fiji Islands

**1972:** Gilbert and Ellice Islands, removed from jurisdiction of Western Pacific Commission, are placed under a British governor

**1975:** Ellice Islands separate from Gilberts, becoming Tuvalu (independent in 1978)

**1978:** London conference, Nov.21-Dec. 7, sets constitutional framework for independence; Banaba representatives bolt meeting after Gilbertese officials reject demands for separation

**1979:** Gilberts become independent nation of Kiribati, July 12. Phosphate on Banaba runs out, mining stops

**1980:** Kiribati is host to a forum which draws up South Pacific Regional Trade and Cooperation Agreement

**1981:** Prices for copra, mainstay of rural economy, fall

## NORTH KOREA

**Area:** 46,540 sq. mi. **Population:** 17,892,000 (1980 est.)

**Official Name:** Democratic People's Republic of Korea **Capital:** Pyongyang **Nationality:** Korean **Languages:** Korean is the official and universal language **Religion:** The traditional religions are Buddhism, Confucianism, Shamanism, and Ch'ondokyo, which combines elements of Buddhism and Christianity; the practice of religion has been discouraged by the government **Flag:** A broad center red stripe bordered on top and bottom by a thin white stripe and a broader blue stripe: left of center is a white disc containing a five-pointed red star **Anthem:** National Anthem, beginning "Morning sun, shine over the rivers and mountains" **Currency:** Won (1.79 per U.S. $1)

**Location:** North Korea occupies the northern portion of a peninsula in northeast Asia projecting southeast from Manchuria. It is bordered on the north by China, on the extreme northeast by the USSR, on the east by the Sea of Japan, on the south by South Korea, and on the west by the Yellow Sea and Korea Bay **Features:** A land of mountains, North Korea contains thousands of peaks, leaving less than one fifth of the total area as cultivable **Chief Rivers:** Tumen, Yalu, Ch'ongch'on, Taedong, Yesong

**Head of State and Political Leader:** President: Marshal Kim Il Sung, born 1912, elected 1972, reelected 1977. The premier is Li Jong Ok, appointed 1977 **Effective Date of Present Constitution:** 1972 **Legislative Body:** Supreme People's Assembly (unicameral), consisting of 579 members elected by universal suffrage for 4 years. Power is in the hands of the Central People's Committee of the Korean Workers' (Communist) party **Local Government:** 9 provinces

**Ethnic Composition:** North Koreans, like the South Koreans, are believed to be of Tungusic stock, ethnically related to the Mongols with some Chinese mixture. There are no ethnic minorities **Population Distribution:** 38.1% urban **Density:** 384 inhabitants per sq. mi.

**Largest Cities:** (1972 est.) Pyongyang 1,500,000, Hamhung 484,000, Chongjin 306,000, Sinuiju 300,000, Wonsan 275,000

**Per Capita Income:** $824 (1980) **Gross National Product (GNP):** $15.9 billion (1980) **Economic Statistics:** About 70% of GNP comes from industry and mining (coal, iron ore, steel, machinery, textiles); 15% from agriculture (rice, corn, barley, wheat, cotton) **Minerals and Mining:** Large deposits of coal, iron ore, lead, zinc, molybdenum, gold, graphite, and tungsten **Labor Force:** 6.1 million, with 48% in agriculture **Foreign Trade:** Exports, mainly ferrous and nonferrous metals, minerals, chemicals, fuel and oil, machinery and equipment, totaled $1.3 billion in 1979. Imports, chiefly machinery and equipment, fuels, chemicals, and textiles, totaled $1.3 billion **Principal Trade Partners:** USSR, China and other Communist countries, Japan

**Vital Statistics:** Birthrate, 32.7 per 1,000 of pop. (1980); death rate, 8.3 **Life Expectancy:** 61 years **Health Statistics:** 333 inhabitants per hospital bed; 909 per physician **Infant Mortality:** N.A. **Illiteracy:** 10% **Primary School Enrollment:** 2,561,674 (1976) **Enrollment in Higher Education:** 214,000 (1973)

**Transportation:** Total road mileage is c. 12,600 **Motor Vehicles:** 60,000 (1971) **Railway Mileage:** 2,950 **Ports:** Chongjin, Hamhung, Nampo, Wonsan, Unggi **Major Airlines:** Civil Aviation Administration operates both international and domestic flights **Communications: Radio Transmitters:** 19 **Receivers:** 800,000 (1971) **Television Transmitters:** 1 **Receivers:** 50,000 (1973) **Telephones:** N.A. **Newspapers:** 11 dailies (1976)

**Weights and Measures:** Metric system **Travel Requirements:** N.A.

---

To the West, North Korea is one of the most isolated and least-known Communist countries. Contacts even between North and South Koreans are almost nonexistent since North and South are still in a technical state of war; the demilitarized zone across the peninsula, set up by the armistice in 1953, is probably the world's most tightly closed border.

The division of Korea along the 38th parallel at the end of World War II left the North with almost all the country's mineral resources and a major share of the industries developed by the Japanese in the former colony. The three-year Korean War devastated much of the industry, but planning, regimentation, and utilization of a trained labor force brought great production increases by the 1960s.

The highly authoritarian, military-dominated government of Marshal Kim Il Sung has sought to steer an independent course between the Soviet Union and China, while remaining antagonistic toward United States "imperialism" and what it calls the "puppet" South Korean regime.

Premier Kim, previously a guerrilla against the Japanese, arrived in Pyongyang with Soviet troops in October 1945 as a leader in the émigré forces trained by the Russians to take over in Korea. He established his dominance as premier when the Democratic People's Republic of Korea was set up in September 1948.

North Korea's military forces were strengthened rapidly as Soviet troops were withdrawn, and in June 1950 a North Korean military attack came close to seizing the entire peninsula before United Nations forces, led by American troops, gained the initiative.

The end of the war was followed by collectivization of agriculture; industry in the North had already been nationalized. Economic progress has been notable, educational facilities have been expanded, and extreme poverty has been sharply reduced. But life is highly regimented, consumer goods are scarce, the vast housing projects are drab, travel is tightly controlled, and freedom of expression is restricted. According to some reports, about 100,000 North Koreans were still detained in camps for ideological reasons in 1982.

In a June 1973 dispatch, Kim was quoted as saying: "We hold that the North and the South should not enter the United Nations separately but as one state under a confederation." Since that time, he has reiterated his wish for a unified Korea under Communist rule.

Tension between the two countries increased after the finding in November 1974 of tunnels under the demilitarized zone emerging into South Korea. The victories of the Communists in South Vietnam and Cambodia and a visit to China by Kim, allegedly to seek Chinese support for military pressure on South Korea, had a negative effect on relations between the two Koreas. A new era was in prospect after the 1977 announcement by the U.S. that it planned the gradual withdrawal of its ground forces from the demilitarized zone.

When South Korea proposed, on Jan. 19, 1979, that fresh talks be held in an effort to prevent war and to unify the two countries, North Korea answered, only six days later, that a "new start" would be a good idea. Delegations began talks almost at once, but quickly bogged down in procedural disputes, as they did again in early 1980, when they met at the behest of UN Secretary General Kurt Waldheim. In 1981 and 1982, with U.S. plans to reduce troop levels apparently abandoned, South Korean requests for talks were rejected.

In October 1980, Kim Il Sung's son, Kim Jong Il, was named the second ranking member of the powerful Communist party Secretariat. By 1982, promotion of the younger Kim's associates had made him his father's likeliest political heir.

**HISTORY:** Korean history goes back into a legendary past, with one of the earliest legends centering around Kitze, or Kija, a scholar credited with the introduction of Chinese culture into the Korean peninsula in the 12th century B.C. Chinese influence remained strong until well after the emergence of separate Korean kingdoms in the early centuries of the Christian era, and it was with Chinese help that one of these, the kingdom of Silla, conquered its rivals in the 7th century A.D. and unified the peninsula. In the 10th century Silla fell to the Koryo dynasty of Kaesong, under whose rule Confucianism gradually replaced Buddhism as the dominant religion

**1231-60:** Mongols occupy Korea

**1392:** Yi Sung-ke, a Korean general, seizes Korean throne

**1592:** Yi dynasty, aided by China, repels invasion by Japanese

**1637:** Korea is made a vassal of Manchu China, beginning a period of isolation from the rest of the world and giving Korea the name of "hermit kingdom"

**1876-82:** Korean ports are opened to Japanese, U.S. and European trade after Japan compels Korea to agree to commercial treaty

**1894-1905:** Japanese victories in Sino-Japanese and Russo-Japanese wars end in complete control of Korea by Japan

**1910:** Japan formally annexes Korea

**1919:** Nationalist leader Syngman Rhee sets up Korean government-in-exile in Shanghai

**1945:** Soviet and U.S. forces occupy Korea after Japan's defeat in World War II; they establish the 38th parallel as the dividing line between their occupation zones, with the Russians in the north and the Americans in the south

**1948:** Division of the peninsula is formalized with the establishment of the two separate regimes of North Korea and South Korea; Democratic People's Republic of North Korea is set up in 1948 under Premier Kim Il Sung, a Moscow-trained military man; Soviet forces evacuate North Korea

**1950-53:** North Korea invades South Korea in 1950; in response to UN request, the U.S. and 15 other member nations send troops to aid South Korea; after initial retreats, UN forces stage counteroffensive and drive North Koreans deep into North Korea; in October 1950 Chinese Communists join North Koreans in successful counterattack; fighting continues until a cease-fire is reached in 1953, leaving Korea divided as before

**1954-61:** Kim Il Sung pushes ambitious program of industrialization; North Korea is economically integrated with Soviet Union and Communist China; military aid treaties are signed with both

**1968:** North Korea seizes U.S. intelligence ship *Pueblo*, charging vessel violated North Korean territorial waters; crew is released after 11 months when U.S. signs a statement, which it labels false, admitting the *Pueblo's* intrusion

**1970:** Kim government proposes a federated Korea, conditional upon U.S. withdrawal from the south

**1976:** North Korean soldiers kill two U.S. Army officers at Panmunjom

**1977:** Travel restrictions for U.S. citizens to North Korea are lifted

**1978:** Working-level talks between North and South Korea break down. Communist Chinese Premier Hua visits, describes North Korea as "sole legitimate sovereign Korean state" and calls for complete withdrawal of U.S. forces from Korea. North Korea denounces "slow" pace of U.S. troop pullout, calls for direct talks with U.S. on reunification of Korea

**1979:** In response to a South Korean suggestion, North Korea enters into unification talks, which soon collapse. Table tennis players from 70 contries participate in world tournament in Pyongyang. Kim Il Sung, now president, denounces U.S. report that Korea's army is the world's fifth largest. UN Secretary General Kurt Waldheim visits both Koreas

**1980:** North and south Korean delegations meet again at Waldheim's request, but fail to make progress. President Kim's son, Kim Jong Il, is given number two post in party Secretariat

**1981:** President Kim rejects repeated bids by South Korea's new leader, Chun Doo Hwan, for a face-to-face meeting

**1982:** Hundreds of thousands celebrate president's 70th birthday in largest rally ever held in Pyongyang (April)

## SOUTH KOREA

**Area:** 38,175 sq. mi. **Population:** 37,448,836 (1980 census)

**Official Name:** Republic of Korea **Capital:** Seoul **Nationality:** Korean **Languages:** Korean is the official and universal language **Religion:** The traditional religions are Buddhism, Confucianism, Shamanism, and Ch'ondokyo, which combines elements of Buddhism and Christianity. However, accurate figures of the numbers of their adherents are not available. There are at least 4 million Christians, chiefly Protestant **Flag:** A divided circle of red (top) and blue (bottom) centered on a white field. A black bar design appears in each corner of the flag **Anthem:** National Anthem, beginning "Until the Eastern Sea is drained" **Currency:** Won (733 per U.S. $1)

**Location:** South Korea occupies the southern portion of a peninsula in northeast Asia projecting southeast from Manchuria. It is bounded on the north by North Korea, on the east by the Sea of Japan, on the south by the Korea Strait, and on the west by the Yellow Sea **Features:** The country is largely mountainous, with the limited arable land in the lowlands and river valleys of the south and southwest **Chief Rivers:** Somjin, Kum, Naktong, Han, Pukhan

**Head of State and of Government:** President Chun Doo Hwan, born 1931, elected by the National Conference for Unification Aug. 27, 1980, and sworn in for 7 years under new constitution, March 3, 1981, following election of Feb. 25. He is assisted by a Prime Minister, Kim Sang Hyup, appointed June 1982 **Effective Date of Present Constitution:** Oct. 27, 1980 **Legislative Body:** National Assembly (unicameral), consisting of 276 members partly elected for 4 years **Local Government:** 9 provinces and 2 specially administered cities

**Ethnic Composition:** The Korean population is one of the most homogeneous in the world. The primary stock is believed to be Tungusic, related to the Mongols with some Chinese mixture **Population Distribution:** 60% urban **Density:** 981 inhabitants per sq. mi.

**Largest Cities:** (1980 census) Seoul 8,366,756, Pusan 3,160,276, Taegu 1,607,458, Inchon 1,084,730, Kwangju 727,627, Taejon 651,642

**Per Capita Income:** $1,067 (1980) **Gross National Product (GNP):** $42 billion (1980) **Economic Statistics:** 59% of GNP comes from manufacturing (textiles, chemicals, electronic equipment, machinery, shipbuilding, motor vehicles, clothing, food processing, clay, glass and stone products) and mining; 17% from agriculture (rice, barley, soybeans, potatoes, wheat, millet, livestock raising), forestry and fishing **Minerals and Mining:** South Korea has less than 30% of the peninsula's estimated reserves of gold, silver, tungsten, molybdenum, and graphite, and about 10% of its coal and iron ore. It produces anthracite coal, tungsten, iron ore, lead, amorphous graphite, fluorite, kaolite, and talc **Labor Force:** 14.2 million (1979), with 36% in agriculture and forestry; 24% in manufacturing and mining **Foreign Trade:** Exports, chiefly clothing and textiles, plywood, ships, iron and steel products, cars, marine products, raw silk, and electronic products, totaled $17 billion in 1980. Imports, mainly fuel, nonelectric machinery, transportation equipment, food grains, electric machinery, textiles yarns and fabrics, totaled $22 billion **Principal Trade Partners:** United States, Japan, Saudi Arabia, Kuwait, West Germany, Britain

**Vital Statistics:** Birthrate, 26.4 per 1,000 of pop. (1980); death rate 8.2 **Life Expectancy:** 68 years **Health Statistics:** 1,406 inhabitants per hospital bed; 905 per physician (1976) **Infant Mortality:** 37 per

1,000 births **Illiteracy:** 6.8% **Primary and Secondary School Enrollment:** 9,060,787 (1977) **Enrollment in Higher Education:** 325,460 (1976) **GNP Expended on Education:** 4.1% (1974)

**Transportation:** Paved roads total 8,400 mi. **Motor Vehicles:** 225,400 (1977) **Passenger Cars:** 125,600 **Railway Mileage:** 3,594 **Ports:** Pusan, Inchon, Pohang, Masan, Mokpo, Gunsan, Mukho **Major Airlines:** Korean Airlines operates domestic and international services **Communications: Radio Transmitters:** 118 **Receivers:** 12,300,000 (1978) **Television Transmitters:** 59 **Receivers:** 5,135,496 (1978) **Telephones:** 2,387,000 (1978) **Newspapers:** 44 dailies, 197 copies per 1,000 inhabitants (1977)

**Weights and Measures:** Metric system and old Korean units are used **Travel Requirements:** Passport, tourist visa valid for initial period of 2 months, no fee; 1 photo; affidavit of support **International Dialing Code:** 82

---

The Korean peninsula has often been described as a dagger pointed from the Asian heartland toward Japan, and its strategic position made it several times a battleground for more powerful neighbors. Long a "hermit kingdom" with a strong indigenous culture, Korea was annexed by the Japanese in 1910. Until the end of World War II it was ruled by a repressive colonial regime and exploited for its mineral resources, living space, and markets.

Considerable dislocation occurred when the primarily agricultural and densely populated South was separated from the industrial North in 1945 and put under United States occupation. After unsuccessful attempts to arrange nationwide elections under United Nations supervision, voting was held in 1948 in the South only and the government of the Republic of Korea was established under the presidency of Syngman Rhee.

The Korean War caused more than 800,000 military and civilian casualties in South Korea and approximately $3 billion worth of property damage. For a decade thereafter the huge U.S. aid effort, coupled with international assistance, was directed toward providing food and shelter, repairing war damage, and laying the groundwork for eventual economic development. During the 1970s, the South Korean economy flourished, and the nation became an important industrial power. By the early 1980s, however, the price of this rapid expansion was being felt in an inflation ranging from 10 to 35 percent a year, a slump in exports (which had come to account for about 30 percent of the economy), and a great increase in the cost of servicing a huge foreign debt.

President Rhee won reelection in 1952 and 1956, but as he grew more despotic and ruthless, police repression and official corruption aroused wide protests. Finally, rigging of elections in 1960 set off student demonstrations that overthrew Dr. Rhee. The subsequent government of Dr. John M. Chang proved ineffective and a military coup in May 1961 brought to power a junta led by Park Chung Hee, then a major general. General Park retired from the army, won the presidency in a national election in 1963, and was reelected in 1967 and 1972. In 1978 his presidency was extended for six years; no other name was on the ballot as the electoral college, the National Conference for Unification, elected him, 2,577 to 0. At the time of voting, all opposition leaders were under house arrest in Seoul.

Threatened by North Korean military power, Park maintained close ties with the U.S. to ensure military assistance, but relations became frayed, especially after the banning of all political dissent from 1975 on. In 1979, in the wake of nationwide student unrest, Park and six of his bodyguards were slain by Kim Jae Kyu, chief of the Korean Central Intelligence Agency, and several aides. Kim and four accomplices were hanged in 1980.

Park's prime minister, Choi Kyu Hah, became president in December 1979, but real power soon passed to Chun Doo Hwan, a paratroop general who was put in charge of "special security" and succeeded, by May 1980, in supressing a series of insurrections. Taking over the presidency in August, Chun promulgated a new constitution which established a less powerful legislature and an electoral-college system for the indirect selection of a president. In early 1981, a pro-Chun electoral college and National Assembly were elected, and Chun was confirmed as president.

Somewhat relaxing security measures, Chun obtained increased U.S. economic and military aid and announced a five-year (1982-86) development plan to cope with a stagnating economy. The costly persistence of high-level corruption was illustrated in May 1982 with the revelation of a multimillion-dollar loan swindle involving bank presidents and relatives of the president.

**HISTORY:** The history of South Korea is bound up with that of Korea as a whole up until 1948 when the government of the Republic of Korea was established under the presidency of Syngman Rhee

**1950-53:** Korean War, brought on by North Korea's invasion of South Korea, rages for three years as U.S. troops and forces of 15 other nations, responding to a request for help by the United Nations, try to repel the inued division of the peninsula at the 38th parallel

**1960:** Rhee is elected for fourth term as president but is accused of rigging the elections; after widespread rioting he is forced from office and goes into exile

**1961:** South Korean armed forces overthrow government; Gen. Park Chung Hee takes power

**1963-67:** Park is elected president in 1963 and is reelected in 1967 amid charges by his opponents that elections were rigged

**1969:** South Korean voters approve a constitutional amendment that allows president to seek a third consecutive term

**1970:** United States agrees to bolster South Korean army after announcing U.S. troop cuts in South Korea

**1972:** Following secret talks, governments of North and South Korea announce agreement in principle on unification. Park institutes constitutional changes that increase his power

**1973:** Opposition leader Kim DaeJung is kidnapped in Japan, resulting in widespread demonstrations. Brought back to Korea, he is placed under house arrest and later released

**1975:** Assassination attempt on President Park fails but wife is victim. North Korea rejects a South Korean proposal to renew talks on unification

**1978:** Economy continues on uptrend. Strained relations between South Korea and U.S. worsen over planned pullout of American ground forces (as withdrawal begins). Influence-buying scandal comes to light, involving South Korean businessman Tongsun Park, U.S. Congressmen, and others. Park, unopposed, is reelected for another six-year presidential term

**1979:** Park asks North Korea for talks "any time, any place" to reunify the countries; delegations meet but bog down on procedural questions. U.S. President Carter visits Seoul in June, prompting government's release of many political dissidents. President Park and his chief bodyguard are killed on October 26 by Kim Jae Kyu, director of the Korean Central Intelligence Agency. Premier Choi Kyu Hah is elected president in December

**1980:** Student protests against martial law start in Seoul in May and spread to other cities. Rebel students seize Kwangju and hold it for 10 days, until paratroopers win back the city on May 27. A paratroop officer, Lt. Gen. Chun Doo Hwan, as top security chief, takes charge of government and is elected president in August. His proposed new constitution is approved by more than 90 percent of voters in October. Economy slows as inflation tops 25 percent. U.S. troop withdrawals suspended

**1981:** Martial law, in force since October 1979, is ended in January, and Chun commutes death sentence against opposition leader Kim Dae Jung before flying to U.S. to meet President Ronald Reagan. Electoral college, chosen in February, names Chun to full presidential term. His newly created Democratic Justice party sweeps Assembly elections in March. Chun renews Park's call for meeting of North and South Korean presidents

**1982:** U.S. Vice President Bush affirms higher level of American support during April visit to Seoul. Chun drops 11 of 22 cabinet members after high banking and government officials are implicated (May) in a vast loan swindle involving hundreds of millions of dollars

## KUWAIT

**Area:** 7,780 sq. mi. **Population:** 1,355,827 (1980 census)

**Official Name:** State of Kuwait **Capital:** Kuwait **Nationality:** Kuwaiti **Languages:** Arabic is the official and universal language; English is widely spoken **Religion:** About 95% Moslem, chiefly of the Sunni sect **Flag:** Green, white, and red horizontal stripes with a black trapezoid at the staff **Anthem:** National Anthem (no words) **Currency:** Kuwaiti dinar (0.29 per U.S. $1)

**Location:** Northeast corner of the Arabian Peninsula. Kuwait is bordered on the north and west by Iraq, on the east by the Persian Gulf, and on the south by Saudi Arabia **Features:** The country is mainly flat desert, with a few oases **Chief Rivers:** There are no rivers

**Head of State and of Government:** Emir: Sheikh Jabir al-Ahmad al-Jabir as-Sabah, born 1928, acceded 1977. The emir is assisted by a council of ministers headed by a prime minister, Sheikh Saad al-Abdullah al-Salim as-Sabah, appointed 1978 **Effective Date of Present Constitution:** 1962 **Legislative Body:** National Assembly (unicameral), with 50 elected members **Local Government:** 3 governorates

**Ethnic Composition:** The population is about 85% Arab but only 48% are native-born. Non-Kuwaitis include Palestinians, Iraqis, Iranians, Egyptians, Indians, and Pakistanis **Population Distribution:** 99% urban **Density:** 174 inhabitants per sq. mi.

**Largest City:** (1980 census) Kuwait 181,774

**Per Capita Income:** $12,920 (1980) **Gross National Product (GNP):** $18 billion (1980) **Economic Statistics:** The economy is based almost entirely on oil, which accounts for about 70% of GNP. About 15% comes from trade and services; the remainder from nonoil industries (chemical fertilizers, building materials, fishing) **Minerals and Mining:** Kuwait possesses nearly one fifth of the world's oil reserves. Large amounts of natural gas are produced from the oil fields **Labor Force:** 360,000, with 70% held by non-Kuwaitis. 40% of the labor force is employed by the government, 34% are in industry (less than 5% in the heavily automated oil industry), and 1% in agriculture **Foreign Trade:** Exports, 96% crude oil and petroleum products, totaled $17.6 billion in 1979. Imports, chiefly foodstuffs, building materials, automobiles, industrial equipment and electrical products, totaled $5.7 billion **Principal Trade Partners:** Japan, United States, Britain, West Germany, Italy, Korea, Netherlands, Saudi Arabia

**Vital Statistics:** Birthrate, 41.5 per 1,000 of pop. (1977); death rate, 4.8 **Life Expectancy:** 69 years **Health Statistics:** 257 inhabitants per hospital bed; 784 per physician (1977) **Infant Mortality:** 39.1 per 1,000 births **Illiteracy:** 20% **Primary and Secondary School Enrollment:** 215,451 (1976) **Enrollment in Higher Education:** 9,934 **GNP Expended on Education:** 2.8% (1976)

**Transportation:** Paved roads total 1,400 mi. **Motor Vehicles:** 380,900 (1977) **Passenger Cars:** 285,800 **Railway Mileage:** None **Ports:** Mina al-Ahmadi, Shuwaikh, Shuaibah, Mina Abdullah **Major Airlines:** Kuwait Airways, government owned, operates international flights **Communications: Radio Transmitters:** 16 **Receivers:** 502,000 (1976) **Television Transmitters:** 7 **Receivers:** 375,000 (1978) **Telephones:** 170,000 (1978) **Newspapers:** 7 dailies, 159 copies per 1,000 inhabitants (1977)

**Weights and Measures:** Metric system **Travel Requirements:** Passport, transit visa, valid 2 days, $1.00; entry visa, valid 1 month, 1 entry, $4.00, 2 photos **International Dialing Code:** 965

---

Tiny, torrid Kuwait, an opulent strip of desert at the northwestern end of the Persian Gulf, enjoys one of the world's highest standards of living. In 1980 it ranked second among all nations in per capita gross national product with $12,920 GNP per person.

Since 1967 Kuwait has helped to subsidize the national economies of Egypt and of Jordan, both of which were defeated in the war with Israel. It must import all of its food but exports enough oil to pay for the people's basic needs.

As a capitalistic welfare state, where poverty is virtually unknown, it provides lavish public services that include: free universal medical service, free education through the university level (including free food and clothing for students), free telephone service, subsidized housing for which only token rentals are paid, and subsidies for those wishing to start business enterprises.

Kuwait has a higher proportion of the latest American cars than any country outside the United States, and the cars are driven over wide, well-surfaced roads. It has more than twice as many air-conditioning units as people, and there is said to be a millionaire for every 230 citizens.

As late as the 1940s, before large-scale oil exports began, Kuwait was little more than a feudal wilderness. It was a primitive, forbidding land, where the temperature would often reach 125 degrees in the shade.

Abd Allah al-Salim as-Sabah, who was emir when the oil boom began, developed the growth program. Following his death in 1965, his policies were continued by his successor, Sheikh Sabah al-Salim as-Sabah. On December 31, 1977, Sheikh Sabah died and his cousin, Sheikh Jabir al-Ahmad al-Jabir as-Sabah, became emir.

The Kuwaitis themselves are a minority of the population of their own country, and they make up only 30 percent of the work force. Of those Kuwaitis who are employed, 70 percent are on the government payroll. Non-Kuwaitis (mainly Palestinians, Saudis, Egyptians, Iraqis, Pakistanis, Indians, and Americans), share in the welfare services, but do not own property or vote.

Kuwaiti society generally consists of five layers, with the members of the ruling family at the top, followed by the old Kuwaiti merchant families. Then come the former Bedouins now living in luxurious urban surroundings, the Arabs from other countries who have been granted Kuwaiti citizenship, and, last, the foreigners.

Many foreigners feel unappreciated by the Kuwaitis, and members of a large Palestinian underground have tried to force the government to take a stronger position than it has against Israel. The activities of this underground were cited by the government in explaining its decision to dissolve the National Assembly in 1976. The assembly was reconvened in 1981 after pro-government conservatives won a majority of its 50 seats.

A British protectorate from 1897 to 1961, Kuwait received informal military protection from the Shah of Iran after 1970. After the Shah fell in 1979, Britain's Queen Elizabeth and Foreign Secretary David Owen visited Kuwait to indicate continuing commitment.

Despite the connection with Britain, Kuwait is very much involved in the Arab bloc. It sent soldiers to fight in the Yom Kippur War against Israel in 1973. The Kuwaiti government joined other Arab states in breaking relations with Cairo after Egypt made peace with Israel in 1979. Kuwait avoided involvement in the 1980-82 war between neighboring Iraq and Iran, although there were four minor Iranian attacks on its oil facilities.

**HISTORY:** Kuwait was settled by Arab tribes in the early 18th century. The present dynasty was established in 1756 by Sheikh Sabah Abdul Rahim. Nominally an Ottoman province, Kuwait asked for British protection in 1897, when the ruling sheikh feared that the Turks wanted to make their authority effective

**1899:** In return for British protection, Kuwait undertakes not to cede or lease any of its territory without Britain's approval

**1914-22:** Britain declares Kuwait independent of Turkey and under British protection. British troops help repel invasion by Saudi Arabia; Saudis and Kuwait set up neutral zone in which they share sovereignty

**1934:** Kuwait's ruler grants a concession to Kuwait Oil Company, a joint American-British enterprise, to drill for oil

**1961:** Britain recognizes Kuwait as an independent state and pledges protection against foreign aggression; Iraq claims Kuwait as a province: British troops prevent Iraqi invasion

**1967:** During Arab-Israeli war, Kuwait declares support for the Arab cause and contributes large subsidies to Egypt and Jordan

**1969:** Government shows increasing alarm over growing Soviet inroads in Persian Gulf area; proposal for the formation of a federation of nine neighboring sheikhdoms raises fear that many will succumb to revolutionary movements

**1973:** Kuwait's forces fight along Suez Canal during Yom Kippur War. Along with other oil-producing nations, Kuwait announces huge increase in oil prices

**1975:** Government announces it intends to acquire 100 percent ownership of domestic oil operations

**1980:** Kuwait reduces oil output to 1.5 million bbls. daily

**1981:** National Assembly reconvenes after 5-year hiatus; pro-government candidates win majority of seats

## LAOS

**Area:** 91,428 sq. mi. **Population:** 3,721,000 (1980 est.)

**Official Name:** Lao People's Democratic Republic **Capital:** Vientiane **Nationality:** Laotian **Languages:** Lao, a tonal language of the Thai group, is the official and dominant language; French serves as the second language **Religion:** Theravada Buddhism is the official and predominant religion (90%); the country's mountain tribes are principally animist **Flag:** Two narrow red bands either side of a wide blue band, with a white disc in the middle **Anthem:** N.A. **Currency:** Kip (10 per U.S. $1)

**Location:** Southeast Asia. Landlocked Laos is bordered on the north by China, on the east by Vietnam, on the south by Cambodia, on the west by Thailand, and on the northwest by Burma **Features:** Northern Laos is laced with jungle-covered mountains and plateaus cut by narrow valleys. Lower Laos is marked by arid limestone terraces, sparsely forested and descending westward to the Mekong River Valley **Chief Rivers:** Mekong, Nam Hou

**Head of State:** President Souphanouvong, born 1902, named in 1975 **Head of Government:** Premier: Kaysone Phoumvihan, born 1920, appointed 1975; he is also secretary general of the party **Effective Date of Present Constitution:** none, at present **Legislative Body:** An appointed 45-member People's Supreme Assembly. The government is actually controlled by the Central Committee of the Lao People's Revolutionary (Communist) Party under its secretary general **Local Government:** 13 provinces

**Ethnic Composition:** More than half of the people are ethnic Lao, descendants of the Thai, a people who migrated from southwestern China in the 13th century. Mountain tribes of Sino-Tibetan and Thai strains are found in the north; many of these tribes, as well as others of Malay background, inhabit central and south Laos **Population Distribution:** 15% urban **Density:** 41 inhabitants per sq. mi.

**Largest Cities:** (1970 est.) Vientiane 150,000, Savannakhet 39,000, Pakse 37,200, Luang Prabang 25,000, Khammouane 13,000

**Per Capita Income:** $97 (1980) **Gross National Product (GNP):** $338 million (1980) **Economic Statistics:** Components of GNP are not available. The economy of the country, the least developed of the nations of the Indochinese peninsula, is 85% agricultural. Major crops are rice, corn, cofffee, cotton, tea, and tobacco. Industry is limited to light consumer goods, with some cottage and family-type production. Lumber, cigarettes, alcohol, and cement are produced in small plants **Minerals and Mining:** Tin is the major mineral resource; surveys indicate deposits of iron ore, potash, gold, copper, and manganese **Labor Force:** About 90% of the population is engaged in agriculture **Foreign Trade:** Exports, chiefly wood, tin, coffee, and resins, totaled $15 million in 1979. Imports, mainly foods, petroleum products, and transportation equipment, totaled $80 million **Principal Trade Partners:** Thailand, Japan, Malaysia, Singapore, Vietnam

**Vital Statistics:** Birthrate, 44.1 per 1,000 of pop. (1980); death rate, 20.3 **Life Expectancy:** 35 years **Health Statistics:** 401 inhabitants per hospital bed (1975); 21,667 per physiciann (1976) **Infant Mortality:** N.A. **Illiteracy:** 72% **Primary and Secondary School Enrollment:** 346,649 (1976) **Enrollment in Higher Education:** 828 (1974) **GNP Expended on Education:** N.A.

**Transportation:** Paved roads total about 800 mi. **Motor Vehicles:** 16,600 (1974) **Passenger Cars:** 14,100 **Railway Mileage:** None **Ports:** None **Major Airlines:** Air Lao operates domestic and international flights **Communications: Radio Transmitters:** 4 **Licenses:** 200,000 (1976) **Television:** None **Telephones:** 7,000 (1977) **Newspapers:** 3 dailies (1976)

**Weights and Measures:** Metric system **Travel Requirements:** Passport, visa; check Laotian embassy for requirements

The old Kingdom of Laos, which formed part of French Indochina, was little known to the outside world until the Vietnam War made its strategic location significant. The largest segment of French Indochina, it was also the most remote and the least developed. French rule did little to turn the ethnic groups into a united Laotian nation.

Most oof the people live in the western quarter of the nation, where they practice subsistence agriculture. Widely scattered hill tribes inhabit the rest of the country, which is mountainous and jungle-covered. Laos lacks modern industrial facilities and technological resources. The country has few significant exports.

The development of Laos has been impeded both by warfare and by the country's physical features. The absence of a network of roads makes communication between the Mekong Valley towns and the rest of the country difficult. The North Vietnamese supply trails into South Vietnam ran through Laos, and these had been the target of intense bombing by U.S. planes. The land war itself spilled over from Vietnam into Laos in 1971, when the South Vietnamese launched a drive into eastern Laos with the stated intention of cutting off the Ho Chi Minh Trail.

The fighting was not confined to the southeast. A civil war was waged, with varying intensity, elsewhere in the country, with the United States supporting the Laotian government forces and the North Vietnamese helping the pro-Communist Pathet Lao.

On February 21, 1973, the war officially ended, as the Pathet Lao and the government signed a cease-fire agreement. By the end of July, a political settlement was reached, whereby the two Laotian parties agreed on the sharing of ministries, the creation of two deputy premierships, and the formation of a political consultative council. On the military side, the parties agreed to the neutralization of the two capitals, Vientiane and Luang Prabang, and the division of the country into two zones.

In April 1974, a third coalition government of neutralists, rightists and pro-Communist Pathet Lao was established and in May and June Thai and U.S. forces withdrew, ending their 10 years of military involvement.

By December of 1975, as an indirect result of the South Vietnamese collapse, a relatively low-key Pathet Lao takeover of Laos was completed with the abolition of both the 600-year-old monarchy and the coalition government and the establishment of a People's Democratic Republic. Prince Souphanouvong, titular leader of the Pathet Lao, was named president and Kaysone Phoumvihan, head of the Marxist-Leninist Laos People's party, was appointed premier.

The tide of refugees flowing out of Vietnamese-dominated Laos has drained the country of most of its professional and commercial elite. The refugees are estimated variously at 130,000 to 250,000, imposing a heavy burden on neighboring Thailand. An additional 40,000 Laotians, many of them officials or military officers of earlier governments, are possibly being detained in "political re-education" centers. In the early 1980s, the economy was in further trouble due to a 1980 Thai ban on trade with Laos, Thailand having been a major source of industrial goods and food.

In 1982, the United States officially charged that Soviet-supplied chemical weapons (fungal poisons producing "yellow rain") had been used repeatedly against insurgents since 1976.

**HISTORY:** The Lao began moving south from China in the 13th century, gradually settling in the territory of the Khmer Empire. After centuries of warfare among the small feudal states of the region, the ruler of Luang Prabang state united most of what is now Laos and Northheast Thailand in the Kingdom of Lan Xang (Kingdom of the Million Elephants). The kingdom split into 2 states in 1707; after constant quarreling they were overrun by neighboring armies. By the early 1800s the Thai had won ascendancy and retained this hold until the French moved in and established a protectorate in 1893

**1945-46:** Japanese invade Lao region of French Indochina. French return and reestablish control

**1949:** Laos becomes independent state within French Union

**1950:** Pathet Lao, a Communist nationalist movement, is founded by Prince Souphanouvong

**1953:** Government battles Pathet Lao and Viet Minh, Vietnamese Communist forces

**1954:** Under terms of Geneva Conference agreement ending Indochina war, Laos becomes fully independent and Pathet Lao is permitted to occupy country's two northern provinces

**1960:** Neutralist-Pathet Lao coalition breaks down. Tug-of-war between Moscow-backed neutralists, American-backed rightists, and Pathet Lao erupts. Rightist Gen. Phoumi Nosavan drives neutralists from Vientiane; Premier Souvanna Phouma, the neutralist leader, flees to Cambodia
**1962:** U.S. troops move into northeast Thailand to discourage Pathet Lao drive on Vientiane. Three factions reach accord on coalition, and second Geneva Conference agrees on Laotian neutrality. Prince Souvanna Phouma returns as premier
**1963:** Pathet Lao abandons its role in the government as neutralist and leftist forces renew fighting
**1965:** Right-wing faction seizes government, banishing Gen. Phoumi Nosavan and reinstating Souvanna Phouma as premier. Neutralist-led government agrees to U.S. flights over Laos and to bombing of Ho Chi Minh Trail
**1967:** The premier, Prince Souvanna Phouma, states that Laos has been invaded by more than 40,000 North Vietnamese troops
**1969:** U.S. planes bomb Ho Chi Minh Trail and other North Vietnamese infiltration routes through Laos
**1971:** South Vietnamese troops supported by U.S. planes and artillery invade Laos in a drive against North Vietnamese supply lines; invasion ends after the retreat of South Vietnamese
**1973:** War in Laos ends as government, Pathet Lao sign cease-fire in February and agree on political settlement in July
**1974:** King Savang Vatthana dissolves Vientiane government and installs new coalition cabinet under Prince Souvanna Phouma, who remains premier
**1975:** National Assembly is dissolved by Pathet Lao. Prince Souphanouvong becomes president
**1977:** Rebels mount attacks against government throughout Laos. Vietnam and Laos sign a 25-year agreement for military and economic cooperation
**1978:** Laos faces flood and drought-caused food shortages and likelihood of famine in many areas. Rebel attacks continue; government is helped by Vietnamese troops
**1979:** Vietnam-Cambodia pact calls for close political and military cooperation between those nations and Laos, which then contributes several thousand troops to the Vietnamese operations in Cambodia
**1980:** Thailand officially bans trade with Laos
**1981:** U.S. Central Intelligence Agency sponsors an expeditionary force of Laotian mercenaries which fails to discover evidence that U.S. military personnel "missing in action" during the Vietnam War are being detained in Laotian prison camps
**1982:** Anti-Communist guerrillas partly destroy Soviet Culture Center in Vientiane in May

## LEBANON

**Area:** 4,015 sq. mi. **Population:** 3,012,000 (1978 est.)

**Official Name:** Republic of Lebanon **Capital:** Beirut **Nationality:** Lebanese **Languages:** Arabic is the official and dominant language; French and English are also widely used **Religion:** 62% Moslem (Sunni and Shi'ite) and 37% Christian (Maronite, Greek Orthodox, Armenian, Greek and Roman Catholic). There are also about 90,000 Druzes and 7,000 Jews **Flag:** A broad white horizontal stripe between narrower red stripes; in the center is a green cedar tree with a brown trunk **Anthem:** National Anthem, beginning "All of us" **Currency:** Lebanese pound (4.9 per U.S. $1)

**Location:** Southwest Asia. Lebanon is bordered on the north and east by Syria, on the south by Israel, and on the west by the Mediterranean Sea **Features:** The country consists of a narrow costal plain behind which are the high Lebanese Mountains. Farther east are the fertile Bekaa Valley and finally the Anti-Lebanon Mountains extending to the Syrian frontier **Chief Rivers:** Litani, Hasbani

**Head of State:** President Amin Gemayel, born 1942, took office Sept. 23, 1982. By convention, the president is a Maronite **Head of Government:** Premier Shafiq Wazzan, appointed Oct. 22, 1980. By convention, the premier is a Sunni Moslem **Effective Date of Present Constitution:** 1926 **Legislative Body:** Parliament (unicameral National Assembly), consisting of 99 members elected for 4 years. By convention, the speaker is a Shi'ite Moslem **Local Government:** 5 provinces

**Ethnic Composition:** 93% Arab, 6% Armenian, and 1% others **Population Distribution:** 60% urban **Density:** 750 inhabitants per sq. mi.

**Largest Cities:** (1972 est.) Beirut 1,000,000, Tripoli 200,000

**Per Capita Income:** $462 (1980) **Gross National Product (GNP):** $1.4 billion (1980) **Economic Statistics:** In 1973 about 55% of GNP came from trade and services; 9% from agriculture (citrus fruits, vegetables, tobacco, livestock production); 21% from industry (food processing, textiles, cement, oil refining) **Minerals and Mining:** Small amounts of bitumen, iron ore, lime, and salt **Labor Force:** 1,000,000, with about 49% in agriculture; and 11% in industry **Foreign Trade:** Exports, chiefly fruits, vegetables, and textiles, totaled $705 million in 1979. Imports, mainly aircraft, motor vehicles, cigarettes, household appliances, wheat and corn, totaled $2.2 billion **Principal Trade Partners:** Saudi Arabia, Kuwait, Jordan, United States, West Germany, France, Britain

**Vital Statistics:** Birthrate, 32.7 per 1,000 of pop. (1980); death rate, 8.4 **Life Expectancy:** 63 years **Health Statistics:** 260 inhabitants per hospital bed; 1,330 per physician (1973) **Infant Mortality:** 82 per 1,000 births **Illiteracy:** 14% **Primary and Secondary School Enrollment:** 672,434 (1972) **Enrollment in Higher Education:** 44,296 (1971) **GNP Expended on Education:** 3.0% (1973)

**Transportation:** Paved roads total 3,775 mi. **Motor Vehicles:** 243,600 (1974) **Passenger Cars:** 220,200 **Railway Mileage:** 250 **Ports:** Beirut, Tripoli, Sidon **Major Airlines:** Middle East Airlines operates international services **Communications: Radio Transmitters:** 10 **Receivers:** 1,600,000 (1976) **Television Transmitters:** 8 **Receivers:** 425,000 (1976) **Telephones:** 222,000 (1975) **Newspapers:** 33 dailies (1976), 92 copies per 1,000 inhabitants

**Weights and Measures:** Metric system **Travel Requirements:** Passport, 6-month visa valid for 2 entries, $20 fee

Lebanon is situated on the eastern shore of the Mediterranean and has an area slightly smaller than that of Connecticut. Its chief topographic features are a narrow coastal plain behind which are the Lebanese Mountains, then the fertile Bekaa Valley, and finally the Anti-Lebanon Mountains extending to the Syrian border. An estimated 64 percent of the land is desert, waste, or urban; 27 percent farmland; and nine percent forest.

Traditionally a part of Greater Syria, which in turn was a sector of the Ottoman Empire, Lebanon became a separate entity after World War I to satisfy its Christian inhabitants. It was administered by France from 1920 to 1941, when it was declared independent by the Free French. With few natural resources besides a good location, Lebanon became a center of commerce and banking. For a time, general prosperity and a desire to keep peace discouraged challenges to the privileged position of the Christians. Uneasy political stability prevailed. So did laissez-faire capitalism and personal freedom; the government governed as little as possible to avoid offending anybody.

In the 1970s, however, Palestinian guerrillas established bases in Lebanon and began raids on Israel, prompting Israeli retaliation. Bitter disputes resulted between the Moslems, who tended to sympathize with the Palestinian cause, and the Christians, who had less sympathy for it. Open war broke out in the spring of 1975, with armed Christian bands on one side, Palestinians and Lebanese Moslem and Druse bands on the other. Israel armed the Christians, but their opponents came close to winning, and Syria sent in army units to protect the Christians and deny Israel a pretext for intervening. But the Syrians actually became a disturbing element and clashed with the Christians.

The worst fighting ended in 1976, but Lebanon remained functionally divided along communal lines and unable to repair the damage of the war or to return to its former commercial and banking activities. Most of the soldiers in its army had joined the warring bands. The legislature elected Elias Sarkis, a Christian respected by Moslems, as president. However, in August 1982 the same body, minus many of its Moslem members, elected Bashir Gemayel, the leader of the rightist Christian militia, to replace him. Gemayel was killed in a bomb explosion in Beirut on September 14 before he could take office. His brother, Amin Gemayel, was elected president on September 21.

In 1978, Israel occupied much of southern Lebanon but shortly withdrew to permit a UN peacekeeping force to establish a buffer zone there. The Palestine Liberation Organization (PLO) established its headquarters in Beirut and armed strongholds in southern Lebanon from which it launched punitive raids against Israel. In turn, Israeli forces struck back at PLO bases.

In July 1981, Israeli warplanes bombed PLO headquarters in Beirut and PLO gunners fired rockets at northern Israeli towns. A cease-fire was agreed to July 24, but sporadic bombardments continued. On June 6, 1982, Israeli forces invaded southern Lebanon, destroyed PLO bases within a 25-mile zone north of the Israeli border, captured Tyre and Sidon, and bombed Beirut. They clashed with Syrian troops in the central Bekaa Valley and destroyed Syrian missile sites, although both nations refrained from starting an all-out war. A cease-fire was proclaimed June 12, but fighting continued as the Israelis drove to the southern suburbs of Beirut, trapping the top PLO leaders and some 7,000 guerrillas in the western part of the city. The Lebanese government formed a ruling Council of National Salvation to try to arrange for the mutual withdrawal of Israeli, Syrian, and PLO forces. Through the efforts of special U.S. envoy Philip Habib, a withdrawal agreement was reached, and the first contingent of PLO guerrillas left Beirut on August 22. Following the withdrawal of the guerrillas, Israeli troops entered West Beirut. On September 18-19, a contingent of Christian militiamen slaughtered an estimated 600 Palestinian civilians remaining in refugee camps. Following the massacre, American, French and Italian troops landed in Beirut to replace withdrawing Israeli forces.

**HISTORY:** In ancient times, Hittite and Aramaean kingdoms occupied the area. The Lebanese coast later became the base for the sea-trading Phoenicians, but their cities soon fell prey to the Assyrians, Persians, and Greeks. Along with neighboring Syria, Lebanon was then brought under Roman rule and afterwards became part of the Byzantine Empire. Even after the spread of Islam by the Arabs, who invaded Lebanon in the 7th century, the country long remained largely Christian

**1516-17:** Lebanon and Syria are absorbed into the Ottoman Empire, but Lebanon retains considerable autonomy

**1841-64:** Massacres of Maronite Christians by Druzes cause European governments to force Ottoman sultans to agree to a pro-Christian government for the area and to the establishment of autonomous province of Mount Lebanon

**1918:** Anglo-French force occupies Lebanon following collapse of Ottoman Empire in World War I

**1920:** Lebanon, along with Syria, becomes a French mandate

**1941-45:** Lebanon, under Free French occupation, is declared independent in 1941; however, French retain actual control of country until 1945

**1958:** Opposition to pro-Western policies of President Camille Chamoun erupts in rebellion; at Chamoun's request, U.S. troops are ordered to Lebanon by President Eisenhower; troops are withdrawn after formation of new Lebanese government

**1968:** Israeli commandos raid Beirut airport, destroying 13 civil aircraft; Israel claims raid was in retaliation for an earlier attack on Israeli airliner in Athens, carried out by two Arab terrorists from Beirut; Lebanon disclaims responsibility for commandos operating against Israel from Lebanese territory

**1970:** Suleiman Franjieh is elected president by legislature; Saeb Salaam succeeds Rashid Karami as premier

**1972:** Israel raids guerrilla bases in Lebanon in retaliation for the killing of Israeli athletes at the Munich Olympics

**1973:** Israeli commando raid on Beirut in which three guerrilla leaders are slain forces resignation of Premier Saeb Salaam and sparks two weeks of fighting in Beirut between guerrillas and Lebanese army; new Premier Takieddin Solh negotiates uneasy truce, but guerrilla activity and Israeli reprisals continue before and after Arab-Israeli war in October

**1975-76:** Some 60,000 die in 19-month civil war between Christians and Moslems; army disintegrates; economy nears collapse. Syria invades; Arab summit arranges cease-fire and establishes Arab League peacekeeping forces—consisting mostly of Syrians who are already there. Elias Sarkis becomes president; he appoints Selim al-Hoss premier

**1978:** Israelis, avenging a PLO terror raid, invade southern Lebanon, attacking PLO bases there; about 200,000 Lebanese and 65,000 Palestinian refugees flee to the north; most return as Israelis pull out three months later. UN peacekeeping forces form buffer zone between Israelis and PLO guerrillas. Conflict develops in southern border zone between central government and Israeli-backed Christian militia units

**1980:** Israeli forces occupy Lebanon's southern border region for five days, in retaliation for Palestinian terrorist raid. Takieddin Solh succeeds al-Hoss as premier for a short time, and is followed by Shafiq Wazzan in office

**1981:** Syria installs missiles in Lebanon and shoots down Israeli jets; heavy fighting between Syrian troops and Christian forces. Israeli aircraft attack PLO bases and Palestinians fire rockets at northern Israeli towns. Israeli airplane raid on PLO headquarters in Beirut kills 300 and wounds 800, mostly Lebanese civilians. Cease-fire truce agreed to by Israel and PLO on July 24

**1982:** Israeli forces invade southern Lebanon, destroy PLO strongholds, clash with Syrian troops, and drive north 50 miles to Beirut; an estimated 10,000 persons, mostly civilians, are killed, and about 600,000 people are made homeless by the heavy bombardment; cease-fire of June 12 fails to stop fighting. President Sarkis forms seven-member Council of National Salvation to try to bring about peace. PLO army and command are trapped and besieged in West Beirut. Following acceptance of U.S. withdrawal plan, first PLO group leaves city on Aug. 22. Lebanese legislature elects Bashir Gemayel president (Aug. 23), but he is killed in a bomb explosion (Sept. 14) before taking office. He is succeeded by his brother, Amin, on Sept. 23. Israeli troops enter West Beirut. Christian militiamen kill estimated 600 civilians in refugee camps (Sept. 18-19). American, French and Italian troops land in Beirut to replace withdrawing Israeli forces.

## LESOTHO

**Area:** 11,720 sq. mi. **Population:** 1,339,000 (1980 est.)

**Official Name:** Kingdom of Lesotho **Capital:** Maseru **Nationality:** Basotho **Languages:** Sesotho, the language of the Sotho people, and English are the official languages **Religion:** About 70% Christian, chiefly Roman Catholic, the rest being mostly animist **Flag:** Green and red vertical stripes to the left of a blue field bearing a white conical Sotho hat **Anthem:** National Anthem, beginning "Lesotho, the country of our fathers" **Currency:** Loti (1.05 per U.S. $1)

**Location:** An enclave within the east-central part of the Republic of South Africa, Lesotho is bordered on the west and north by the Orange Free State Province, on the east by the Province of Natal, and on the south by Cape Province and Transkei **Features:** About a fourth of the western sector is lowland terrain; the rest of the country is mountainous **Chief Rivers:** Orange, Caledon

**Head of State:** King Moshoeshoe II, born 1938; formerly Paramount Chief, he became king in 1966 **Head of Government:** Prime Minister, Dr. Leabua Jonathan, born 1914, appointed 1965; he also acts as defense and internal security minister **Effective Date of Present Constitution:** 1966, suspended 1970 **Legislative Body:** Parliament (bicameral), suspended 1970. An interim National Assembly with limited powers was formed in 1973, the members being nominated by the government **Local Government:** 10 districts, with appointed administrators

**Ethnic Composition:** The population is almost entirely Bantu, with 85% Sotho and 15% Nguni. There are less than 1% South Africans, Asians and mixed **Population Distribution:** 6% urban **Density:** 114 inhabitants per sq. mi.

**Largest City:** (1978 est.) Maseru 71,500

**Per Capita Income:** $251 (1980) **Gross National Product (GNP):** $336 million (1980) **Economic Statistics:** About 36% of GNP came from agriculture (corn, sorghum, wheat, beans, peas, livestock); 15% from industry (printing, carpet weaving, brewing, candlemaking, tire retreading) and mining **Minerals and Mining:** Few known mineral deposits except for diamonds **Labor Force:** 87% of population engaged in subsistence agriculturee. 150,000 to 200,000 work six months to many years as wage earners in South Africa **Foreign Trade:** Exports, mainly diamonds, wool, mohair, and livestock, totaled $36 million in 1979. Imports, chiefly foodstuffs, textiles, clothing, transportation equipment, and chemicals, totaled $311 million **Principal Trade Partner:** South Africa

**Vital Statistics:** Birthrate, 39 per 1,000 of pop. (1975); death rate, 19.7 **Life Expectancy:** 50 years **Health Statistics:** 488 inhabitants per hospital bed; 18,657 per physician (1977) **Infant Mortality:** 111 per 1,000 births **Illiteracy:** 41% **Primary and Secondary School Enrollment:** 239,943 (1976) **Enrollment in Higher Education:** 577 (1974) **GNP Expended on Education:** 3.7% (1973)

**Transportation:** Improved roads total 625 mi. **Motor Vehicles:** 9,200 (1977) **Passenger Cars:** 3,000 **Railway Mileage:** One mile of track links Maseru with South Africa **Ports:** None **Major Airlines:** Government-owned Lesotho Airways operates domestic and international services **Communications: Radio Transmitters:** 3 **Licenses:** 23,000 (1976) **Television:** None **Telephones:** 4,000 (1974) **Newspapers:** Several weeklies

**Weights and Measures:** Metric system **Travel Requirements:** Passport, visa valid for 20 days

An enclave in the southeastern area of South Africa, Lesotho, the former British protectorate of Basutoland, is an island of black African nationalism in a sea of apartheid. The small mountainous kingdom is the remnant of a larger realm, the refuge to which the Basotho were driven by tribal wars and Boer incursions.

In 1818, Moshesh I, a tribal chief from the north, succeeded in uniting the Basotho people. He ruled from about 1820 to 1870 and consolidated various tribes that had been scattered earlier by Zulu and Matabele warriors. During his reign, a series of wars with the Orange Free State (1856-68) resulted in the loss of a large area to the Free State, now known as the "Conquered Territory." Moshesh appealed to the British for help, and in 1868 the country was annexed by Britain.

For a considerable time thereafter the energies of the British administrators were absorbed largely in the task of settling intertribal disputes and in maintaining the position of the Paramount Chief as a symbol of national unity. From 1884 to 1959 legislative and executive authority was vested in a British High Commissioner.

Badly eroded and subject to droughts, the country produces mohair, wool, and hides from livestock. There are only about 1,000 square miles of cultivable land and many food supplies must be imported. Although there has been an increase of revenue under a revised customs union with South Africa, much of Lesotho's income is derived from the wages of Basotho men who work as contract laborers in South African gold and coal mines. Unemployment is a major problem within Lesotho itself.

There has been some development of light induustry, tourism, and an increase of diamond mining, but Lesotho has little prospect of ending its economic dependence on South Africa. To a large extent, Lesotho is little more than one of the *bantustans*, or separate African homelands, that have been created in South Africa itself.

With the attainment of political independence in 1966, the traditional ruler, King Moshoeshoe II, tried to reassert royal authority, but after being forced into exile by the prime minister, Chief Leabua Jonathan, agreed to accept a titular, symbolic position and was allowed to return.

Although professing to abhor apartheid, Chief Jonathan has advocated what he calls a realistic "bread-and-butter good-neighbor policy." But despite extreme poverty, Lesotho has achieved considerable progress in education—it has one of the highest literacy rates in Africa—and many Basotho, who are well educated and highly politicized, resent South Africa's racist regime.

When in early 1970, Jonathan appeared to have lost the country's first national elections, he declared the results invalid, jailed his leading opponents, and seized control. Although threatened with withdrawal of British aid, the plump, disarmingly jolly Jonathan ruled by decree until 1973, when a National Assembly with limited powers was formed.

Chief Jonathan has successfully suppressed several outbreaks of rebellion, including one in 1974 in which 20 rebels were killed in a plot allegedly hatched by the opposition Congress party.

**HISTORY:** Decimated by Zulu and Matabele raids in the early 19th century, the Basotho were later fused into a new nation in the mountains of Basutoland (Lesotho) by Moshesh (Moshoeshoe) I. The king soon had to contend with Boers in the neighboring Orange Free State and sought the protection of the British Cape Colony. Annexation by the colony in 1868, however, led to more fighting, and in 1884 Basutoland again was made a British protectorate. In 1909 a British act of Parliament, establishing the Union of South Africa, stipulated that Basutoland, as well as Bechuanaland (Botswana) and Swaziland, would not be transferred to their more powerful neighbor without prior consent of the inhabitants

**1910:** A consultative Basutoland Council, made up of Basotho chiefs and leaders, is established by the British

**1959-60:** A constitution is promulgated and a more representative legislative body, the Basutoland National Council, is set up

**1961:** South Africa's apartheid policies cause Britain to reaffirm that Basutoland will not be handed over to South African rule

**1966:** Basutoland gains independence as Lesotho

**1967:** Held under house arrest after attempting to assert absolute authority, King Moshoeshoe II accedes to Prime Minister Leabua Jonathan's demands that he reign as constitutional monarch

**1970:** Jonathan seizes control and suspends constitution, following disputed election

**1975:** Miners recruited from Lesotho strike gold mine in South Africa to protest a Lesotho law requiring miners to remit 60 percent of their pay and deposit it in Lesotho banks

**1979:** Bombings attributed to outlawed Congress party cause great damage and loss of life; Jonathan converts paramilitary police unit into regular army to suppress violence

**1980:** Guerrilla activity in support of exiled Congress party leader Ntsu Mokheele increases. Jonathan charges collusion between Lesotho Liberation Army and South Africa; imposes strict security at border posts

**1981:** Liberation Army claims responsibility for bombings of electrical facilities and other installations. Lesotho and South Africa agree on a joint scheme for supplying water to South Africa and hydroelectric power to Lesotho. Jonathan declares readiness to hold elections if Congress party will halt acts of violence

## LIBERIA

**Area:** 43,000 sq. mi. **Population:** 1,873,000 (1980 est.)

**Official Name:** Republic of Liberia **Capital:** Monrovia **Nationality:** Liberian **Languages:** English, the official and commerical language, is spoken by about 20% of the population; some 28 African dialects are also spoken **Religion:** 75% animist, 10% Christian, 15% Moslem **Flag:** Eleven red and white horizontal stripes, with a five-pointed white star on a blue field in the upper left corner **Anthem:** National Anthem, beginning "All hail, Liberia, hail!" **Currency:** U.S. (Liberian) dollar

**Location:** West Africa. Liberia is bordered on the northeast by Guinea, on the east by the Ivory Coast, on the south and west by the Atlantic Ocean, and on the north by Sierra Leone **Features:** The country is flat, with the exception of some hills in the region of Monrovia, the Bomi Hills, and the Guinea Highlands. About 40% of the country is covered by tropical woodlands **Chief Rivers:** Mano, Lofa, St. Paul, St. John, Cestos

**Head of State and of Government:** Gen. Samuel Kanyon Doe, born 1951, took power following the coup of April 12, 1980. He is Chairman of the People's Redemption Council, the highest body of the new government **Effective Date of Present Constitution:** 1847; suspended Apr. 1980 **Legislative Body:** Executive and legislative power is held by the 22-member People's Redemption Council **Local Government:** 9 counties, headed by appointed superintendents

**Ethnic Composition:** About 95% of the population is made up of indigenous Africans belonging to about 16 tribal groups. About 5% of the population are Americo-Liberian descendants of 19th century emancipated black American slaves **Population Distribution:** 28% urban **Density:** 44 inhabitants per sq. mi.

**Largest Cities:** (1976 est.) Monrovia 204,000, Harbel 60,000, Buchanan 25,000, Yekepa 16,000, Harper 14,000

**Per Capita Income:** $526 (1980) **Gross National Product (GNP):** $972 million (1980) **Economic Statistics:** About 33% of GNP comes from mining; 17% from agriculture (rubber, casava, rice, bananas, plantains), forestry, and fishing; and 11% from wholesale and retail trade **Minerals and Mining:** Liberia is a major producer of high-grade iron ore. Diamonds are of importance, and there are unexploited reserves of manganese, gold, columbite, tantalite, and bauxite **Labor Force:** 510,000, with 72% in agriculture, and only 31% in the monetary economy, chiefly on rubber plantations, in government, construction, and mining **Foreign Trade:** Exports, chiefly iron ore, rubber, timber, and diamonds, totaled $600 million in 1980. Imports, mainly manufactured goods, machinery, transportation equipment, fuel, and food, totaled $534 million **Principal Trade Partners:** United States, West Germany, Belgium, Italy

**Vital Statistics:** Birthrate, 49.8 per 1,000 of pop. (1971); death rate, 20.9 **Life Expectancy:** 46 years **Health Statistics:** 652 inhabitants per hospital bed; 9,235 per physician (1975) **Infant Mortality:** 159.2 per 1,000 births **Illiteracy:** 76% **Primary and Secondary School Enrollment:** 191,972 (1975) **Enrollment in Higher Education:** 2,404 (1975) **GNP Expended on Education:** 2.4% (1975)

**Transportation:** Paved roads total 500 mi. **Motor Vehicles:** 16,000 (1978) **Passenger Cars:** 9,600 **Railway Mileage:** 310 **Ports:** Monrovia, Buchanan, Greenville, Harper **Major Airlines:** Air Liberia operates internal services **Communications: Radio Transmitters:** 19 **Receivers:** 265,000 (1976) **Television Transmitters:** 4 **Re-**

**ceivers:** 18,800 (1974) **Telephones:** 8,000 (1977) **Newspapers:** 3 dailies (1976), 8 copies per 1,000 inhabitants

**Weights and Measures:** U.S. standards are used **Travel Requirements:** Passport, visa valid for 90 days, $2 fee, 3 pictures **International Dialing Code:** 231

A green, rainy land settled in the 1820s by freed slaves from the United States, Liberia is Africa's oldest independent republic. As more and more blacks were being liberated early in the 19th century, some Americans became uneasy about their numbers. In 1816 the American Colonization Society was chartered by Congress to promote a "back-to-Africa" movement. The society purchased land from African chiefs in a region that had been largely depopulated by the slave trade, and the first group of an eventual 15,000 settlers established their colony at the present site of Monrovia.

Although it was a neglected stepchild, Liberia modeled its constitution, institutions and flag after those of the United States. It established itself as a sovereign nation in 1847, a status which the United States did not recognize until 1862, long after European powers had done so.

Lacking money and technology, as well as outside interest, the early Liberians were unable to progress beyond a simple rural economy. Contemporary Liberians often say, "We missed out on the benefits of colonialism." However, in the 1920s the Firestone Tire and Rubber Company started to develop a rubber industry which today employs about half of Liberia's wage earners. During World War II, American money and manpower poured in to give the country the big Robertsfield Airport, a new seaport at Monrovia, and the first network of modern roads. There followed the iron-ore boom of the 1950s with huge investments by foreign mining companies.

The making of Liberia into a modern country, with a viable economy and position of leadership in African affairs, has been almost entirely the work of the late William V.S. Tubman, Liberia's president from 1944 until his death in 1971. He spurred economic development through industry and iron-ore mining at a time when Liberia seemed to be lagging behind newer African nations.

Tubman was succeeded as president in 1971 by Vice-President William R. Tolbert, Jr., son of a former South Carolina slave who had prospered as a farmer in Liberia. Tolbert launched a program of widespread reform, but dissatisfaction increased with his autocratic rule and with continued control of the government and economy by the 5% minority of descendants of American slaves.

Tolbert's unpopular repressive measures led to his downfall. On April 12, 1980, he was killed in a coup of non-commissioned officers led by 28-year-old Master Sgt. Samuel K. Doe. Twenty-seven of Tolbert's aides were summarily executed. Liberia was left governed by a poorly educated, inexperienced and insecure regime.

**HISTORY:** Before being colonized early in the 19th century by freed black slaves from the United States, Liberia was known as the Grain Coast for its production of grains of melegueta pepper. The indigenous peoples, among them Kru, Gola, Mandingo, and Vai, are believed to derive from ancient black nations of sub-Saharan regions farther north. During the several centuries of the slave trade, the country was steadily drained of population

**1816:** American Colonization Society is founded to send freed slaves to Western Africa

**1822:** First group of settlers arrives from United States and establishes colony on Providence Island, at present site of Monrovia, purchased by American Colonization Society

**1824:** Name "Liberia" is adopted and chief settlement is named Monrovia in honor of U.S. President James Monroe

**1847:** Joseph Jenkins Roberts, governor of the Liberian Commonwealth, a Virginia-born freeman of part-black ancestry, proclaims Republic of Liberia and becomes first president

**1850-1920:** Territory is lost to neighboring British, French colonies; economy and finances deteriorate, but government rejects proposal for international receivership

**1923-26:** Firestone Tire and Rubber Company assists government financially and begins development of rubber

**1943:** True Whig party candidate William V.S. Tubman becomes president; begins programs of social unification to speed assimilation of indigenous population into the rest of the community, and policy of "open door" for foreign investment

**1955:** Opposition Reformation and Independent True Whig parties are charged with plot to overthrow government by force and are banned; True Whig party becomes dominant

**1971:** Tubman dies and is succeeded by Vice-President Tolbert

**1979:** Police and army fire on demonstrators against food-price increases in April, killing 74

**1980:** Tolbert is killed in coup April 12 by enlisted men of army; Master Sgt. Samuel K. Doe becomes head of state

**1981:** Doe is commissioned Commander in Chief of the armed forces. He announces austerity measures to meet U.S. and International Monetary Fund requirements for increased financial aid; rice subsidies are ended. The deputy leader and four members of the military government are executed following failure of their plot to overthrow Doe

## LIBYA

**Area:** 679,358 sq. mi. **Population:** 3,096,000 (1981 est.)

**Official Name:** Socialist People's Libyan Arab Jamahiriya **Capital:** Tripoli **Nationality:** Libyan **Languages:** Arabic is the official and dominant language; English and Italian are also used **Religion:** 97% Sunni Moslem **Flag:** A plain green field **Anthem:** Almighty God **Currency:** Libyan dinar (0.25 per U.S. $1)

**Location:** North Africa. Libya is bordered on the north by the Mediterranean Sea, on the east by Egypt, on the southeast by the Sudan, on the south by Chad and Niger, on the west by Algeria, and on the northwest by Tunisia **Features:** About 90% of the terrain consists of barren, rock-strewn plains and deserts, with three elevated regions in the northwest, northeast and extreme south **Chief Rivers:** There are no permanent rivers

**Head of State:** Colonel Muammar Qaddafi, born 1942; seized power in 1969; elected Revolutionary Leader (Head of State) in 1977. He also is defense minister **Head of Government:** Muhammad al-Zarruq Rajab is Secretary General of the General Secretariat of the General People's Congress, appointed 1981. Jadallah Azzuz al Talhi is chairman of the General People's Committee, appointed 1979 **Effective Date of Present Constitution:** The political structure is guided by the principles announced at the General People's Congress in March 1977 **Legislative Body:** General People's Congress (unicameral) **Local Government:** 10 governorates, closely controlled by the central government

**Ethnic Composition:** The population is chiefly a racial mixture of Arabs and Berbers **Population Distribution:** 30% urban **Density:** 4.5 inhabitants per sq. mi.

**Largest Cities:** (1973 census) Tripoli 281,497, Benghazi 131,970, Zawia 52,327, Misurata 45,146, Sabratha 30,817, Tarhuna 23,338

**Per Capita Income:** $7,357 (1980) **Gross National Product (GNP):** $22 billion (1980) **Economic Statistics:** In 1975 about 52% of GNP came from oil, 3% from agriculture (wheat, barley, tomatoes, dates, citrus fruits, olives, livestock); and 13% from manufacturing (food processing, textiles, soaps, detergents, paper bags and wrapping paper) **Minerals and Mining:** Libya is one of the worldd's largest oil producers. Other minerals are gypsum, natural gas, marble, iron ore, and potassium **Labor Force:** 900,000 (1977) of which 350,000 are resident foreigners **Foreign Trade:** Exports, consisting almost exclusively of crude oil, totaled $15 billion in 1979. Imports, mainly oil drilling equipment and machinery, iron and steel pipes, tubes, and fittings, manufactured goods, and food products, totaled $7.9 billion **Princiipal Trade Partners:** West Germany, Britain, Italy, United States, France, Japan

**Vital Statistics:** Birthrate, 47.4 per 1,000 of pop. (1980); death rate, 12.8 **Life Expectancy:** 53 years **Health Statistics:** 205 inhabitants per hospital bed; 899 per physician (1977) **Infant Mortality:** 44.5 per 1,000 births **Illiteracy:** 50% **Primary and Secondary School Enrollment:** 790,569 (19766) **Enrollment in Higher Education:** 11,997 **GNP Expended on Education:** 5.2% (1975)

**Transportation:** Paved roads total 4,800 mi. **Motor Vehicles:** 394,400 (1975) **Passenger Cars:** 263,,100 **Railway Mileage:** none **Ports:** Tripoli, Benghazi, El Brega, Ras Lanuf, Zueitina, Syrte, El Hariga, Derna, Tobruk **Major Airlines:** Libyan Arab Airways operates domestic and international services **Communications: Radio Transmitters:** 15 **Licenses:** 110,000 (1976) **Television Transmitters:** 2 **Licenses:** 10,000 (1975) **Telephones:** 45,000 (1975) **Newspapers:** 2 dailies, 26 copies per 1,000 inhabitants (1976)

**Weights and Measures:** Metric system **Travel Requirements:** Passport (with Arabic translation), visa valid for 3 months; $7.25 fee, 2 pictures **International Dialing Code:** 218

---

Consisting mostly of arid desert, the land that is now Libya was a bone of contention among empires for thousands of years. Its most influential conquerors were the Moslem Arabs of the seventh century A.D.; they gave Libya the language and the religion that now prevail. Its most recent conqueror was Italy. After losing World War II, Italy was forced to grant independence to Libya in 1951. Idris, a Moslem chieftain, became king. But, with no natural resources except a location that was strategic in the Cold War, Libya was heavily dependent on the United States, which gave considerable assistance in return for the use of Wheelus Air Force Base.

With the discovery of oil in 1959, Libya, with less than 3 million people, became potentially a power in its own right. King Idris used the oil revenue to build schools, hospitals, highways, and low-cost housing.

But Libya did not achieve its real international potential until after the overthrow of King Idris by the army in 1969. A Revolutionary Command Council of military officers, headed by Col. Muammar Qaddafi, took control of the nation. Desert-born, with little understanding of the non-Moslem world, Qaddafi made Libya a bastion of strict Moslem traditionalism. He outlawed liquor, imposed a strict dress code for women, and made amputation the standard penalty for theft. A bitter enemy of big powers, he closed Wheelus Air Force Base, published manifestos condemning both the U.S. and USSR, and helped Malta to force the closing of British bases. A strident foe of Israel, he joined other Arab militant leaders in denouncing Egypt for making a separate peace with Israel in 1979. On December 2, a mob in Tripoli attacked and damaged the U.S. embassy. The United States closed the embassy in May 1980.

Qaddafi moved in 1980 to silence his opponents and warned Libyan exiles to return or "be liquidated." After four anti-Qaddafi exiles were killed in London and Rome, the United States, in May, expelled four Libyan diplomats charged with threatening Libyan students in America. A year later, the U.S. closed the Libyan mission in Washington, D.C., saying Qaddafi's "support for international terrorism" was unacceptable. Relations between the two countries worsened in August 1981 when U.S. Navy jets shot down two attacking Libyan fighter planes over the Gulf of Sidra. On March 10, 1982, the U.S. embargoed imports of oil from Libya, shortly after reports that Libyan "hit-men" had been sent to assassinate high U.S. officials. Qaddafi angrily denied the reports.

**HISTORY:** In ancient times, Libya was successively ruled by Carthage, Rome, and the Vandals. The Arabs conquered the country in the 7th century A.D. In the Middle Ages, Egypt and Tunisia vied for control of the country, and in the early 16th century Spain and the Knights of Malta replaced the African rivals in dominating Libya. The Ottoman Empire seized control in 1551, although Libya's local pashas continued to enjoy autonomy

**1830:** Turks reassert control over Libya

**1911-33:** Italy occupies Libya following Turco-Italian War (1911-12) and engages in long series of wars of pacification against the Sanusi, a Moslem religious brotherhood

**1943-49:** Libya is conquered by Allied forces in World War II; Tripolitania and Cyrenaica are placed under British administration and the Fezzan under French administration

**1951:** Kingdom of Libya gains formal independence, with Idris I, leader of the Sanusi brotherhood, as the country's first king

**1954:** United States is granted military air base in Libya

**1959:** Oil is discovered in Tripolitania and Cyrenaica

**1967:** Libya charges United States with helping Israel in Six-Day War, calls on U.S. to liquidate Wheelus Air Force Base

**1969:** Monarchy is overthrown by a military junta composed of young nationalist army officers. Colonel Qaddafi, their leader, becomes prime minister in 1970

**1970:** Junta takes over Wheelus Air Force Base, buys Mirage jets from France, and renegotiates contracts with Western oil companies to gain greater share of oil revenues

**1973:** Qaddafi introduces the "cultural revolution," an attempt to govern Libya according to the tenets of Islam. Establishes "people's committees" to carry out the revolution

**1974:** Qaddafi relinquishes political and administrative functions; announces he will concentrate on ideology and organization. Premier Abdul Salam Jalloud assumes Qaddafi's former duties

**1975:** Creation of 618-member General National Congress is decreed to implement theories of Colonel Qaddafi

**1976:** Relations with Egypt deteriorate when Libyan soldiers are arrested in Cairo in connection with a plot to kidnap Maj. Omar Meheishi, a dissident member of the Revolutionary Command Council who fled Libya in 1975 after an attempted coup against Colonel Qaddafi. In retaliation Egyptians are expelled from Libya

**1977:** Libyan and Egyptian troops and aircraft battle along border

**1979:** Libya secretly sends soldiers to Uganda to defend government of President Idi Amin Dada against Tanzanian attack; grants asylum to Amin. Tripoli mob damages U.S. embassy

**1980:** Qaddafi orders Libyan exiles to return to Libya; four of his political opponents are murdered in Europe; U.S. closes embassy in Tripoli. In Washington it is revealed that Billy Carter acted as an agent for Libya and received a loan from the Libyan government. Qaddafi and Syrian President Assad sign merger agreement proclaiming Libya and Syria a single state (unimplemented as of July 1981). Libyan troops invade Chad

**1981:** Qaddafi announces a "merger" of Chad with Libya. U.S. expels Libyan mission from Washington because of Libya's support for international terrorists. Libyan planes shot down by U.S. jets over Gulf of Sidra (Aug. 19)

**1982:** U.S. government imposes embargo on Libya's oil exports to the United States, valued at about $2 billion per year

---

## LIECHTENSTEIN

**Area:** 61 sq. mi. **Population:** 25,220 (1980 census)

**Official Name:** Principality of Liechtenstein **Capital:** Vaduz **Nationality:** Liechtensteiner **Languages:** German is the official language; Alemannic, a dialect, is spoken by most **Religion:** Roman Catholicism is the official religion and claims about 82% of the population. Protestants constitute 7% **Flag:** Blue and red horizontal stripes, with a golden crown near the staff end of the blue stripe **Anthem:** National Anthem, beginning "Above on the German Rhine" **Currency:** Swiss franc (2 per U.S. $1)

**Location:** Western Europe. Liechtenstein, situated in the Rhine River Valley, is bordered by Austria on the east and by Switzerland on the south and west **Features:** One third of the area is level land bordering the right bank of the Rhine, and an upland and mountainous area occupies the remainder **Chief Rivers:** Rhine, Samina

**Head of State:** Prince Franz Josef II, born 1906, ascended the throne 1938 **Head of Government:** Prime Minister: Hans Brunhart, born 1945, chairman of the 5-man Collegial Board, appointed April 1978 **Effective Date of Present Constitution:** 1921 **Legislative Body:** Parliament (unicameral *Landtag*), consisting of 15 members, elected for 4 years by male suffrage **Local Government:** 11 communes, with limited powers of self-government

**Ethnic Composition:** The population is of Germanic descent; one third is alien, mostly Swiss, Italian, Austrian and German **Population Distribution:** Predominantly rural **Density:** 413 inhabitants per sq. mi.

**Largest Towns:** (1980 census) Vaduz 4,614, Schaan 4,552

**Per Capita Income:** $11,330 (1979) **Gross National Product (GNP):** $340 million (1979) **Economic Statistics:** Some 40% of the land is used for raising crops (corn and other cereals, potatoes, garden produce, fruits), but the main source of income from land use is raising beef and dairy cattle. Industry is mainly devoted to the small-scale production of precision manufactures (calculating machines, optical lenses, hiigh vacuum pumps), false teeth and textiles. Between 20,000 and 30,000 foreign firms maintain nominal headquarters in Vaduz, because of liberal tax incentives. Tourism and the sale of stamps are also important sources of income **Minerals and Mining:** Except for some quarrying, there is no mining **Labor Force:** 11,600 (5,320 foreign workers) with 54% in industry, trade and construction, 42% in services and 4% in agriculture, forestry and hunting **Foreign Trade:** Exports are chiefly special machinery and tools, artificial teeth, textiles, chemicals, and food. Liechtenstein has a customs union with Switzerland and there are no records of foreign trade totals **Principal Trade Partners:** EFTA and Common Market countries

**Vital Statistics:** Birthrate, 14.3 per 1,000 of pop. (1979); death rate, 6.7 **Life Expectancy:** 65 years **Health Statistics:** Hospital facilities exist in nearby Switzerland; 1,633 inhabitants per physician (1971) **Infant Mortality:** 6.5 per 1,000 births **Illiteracy:** Negligible **Primary and Secondary School Enrollment:** 4,445 pupils (1972) **Enrollment in Higher Education:** 243 **GNP Expended on Education:** N.A.

**Transportation:** Good paved roads serve the principality **Motor Vehicles:** 11,000 (1976) **Passenger Cars:** 10,000 **Railway Mileage:** 11.5 **Ports:** None **Major Airlines:** None **Communications:** Served by Switzerland **Radio Stations:** None **Licenses:** 5,000 (1976) **Television Stations:** None **Licenses:** 4,500 (1976) **Telephones:** 17,000 (1977) **Newspapers:** 2 dailies, 527 copies per 1,000 inhabitants (1976)

**Weights and Measures:** Metric system **Travel Requirements:** Passport, no visa for 3 months **International Dialing Code:** 41

---

Since 1923 the tiny principality of Liechtenstein, wedged between Austria and Switzerland, has had a customs union with Switzerland, and that country also provides Liechtenstein's currency, administers its postal, telegraph, and telephone services, and handles Liechtenstein's international affairs. In World War II, Liechtenstein, like Switzerland, was a neutral.

Though bucolic, with lush green valleys and houses with red-tile roofs, the state has mainly an industrial economy. Only four percent of the population is engaged in agricultural pursuits.

Liechtenstein has become industrialized in the last quarter of a century; it contains Europe's biggest producer of false teeth and dental supplies, and is noted for such precision products as thin optic coatings and electronic microscopy. The industrialization has brought an influx of Swiss, Austrian, and German workers.

The principality is a tax haven for corporations and holding companies. Additional sources of income are tourism and the sale of postage stamps. Though Liechtenstein has neither a broadcasting station nor an airport, it is the repository of art valued at somewhere near $150 million, the holdings of Liechtenstein's monarch.

In 1978, Liechtenstein joined the Council of Europe, although other nations represented in the Council objected to the principality's voting laws; alone in Europe, Liechtenstein does not allow women to vote for members of its national legislature. Women may vote in local elections in Vaduz.

**HISTORY:** The principality of Liechtenstein was created in 1719 as a fief of the Holy Roman Empire by uniting the barony of Schellenberg and the county of Vaduz, both of which had been purchased from the counts of Hohenem by the Austrian family of Liechtenstein. During the Napoleonic Wars, the principality was invaded by the French. In 1815, after Napoleon's downfall, Liechtenstein joined the newly formed Germanic Confederation

**1866:** Germanic Confederation is dissolved after Prussia's victory over Austria in the Seven Weeks' War, thus ending Liechtenstein's ties to other German states

**1868:** Liechtenstein, which had furnished Austria with 80 soldiers during the war with Prussia, disbands its military force and adopts policy of permanent neutrality

**1919-24:** Switzerland assumes control of Liechtenstein's external affairs and forms customs union with principality

**1938:** Prince Franz I is succeeded by his great-nephew, who, as Franz Josef II, becomes the first ruler to make Liechtenstein his permanent home

**1945-65:** Having avoided involvement in World War II, Liechtenstein enjoys rapid economic growth, developing into a center of tourism, trade, and small-scale manufacturing

**1970:** Traditional minority Patriotic Union wins one-vote majority in *Landtag*, ending 42-year leadership of coalition government by Progressive Citizens party

**1973:** Electorate again denies women the franchise

**1974:** Progressive Citizens party regains majority in parliament

**1978:** Hans Brunhart of Fatherland Union party is appointed prime minister

**1982:** Fatherland Union party wins 53 percent of the popular vote in February general elections, in which 95 percent of the all-male electorate participates; Brunhart remains premier

## LUXEMBOURG

**Area:** 999 sq. mi. **Population:** 363,661 (1979 est.)

**Official Name:** Grand Duchy of Luxembourg **Capital:** Luxembourg **Nationality:** Luxembourgian **Languages:** French is the official language. German is used in local newspapers. Letzeburgisch is everyday language **Religion:** 97% Roman Catholic; 3% Protestant and Jewish **Flag:** A tricolor of red, white, and blue horizontal stripes **Anthem:** Our Homeland **Currency:** Luxembourg franc (44 per U.S. $1)

**Location:** Western Europe. Landlocked Luxembourg is bordered on the north and west by Belgium, on the east by the Federal Republic of Germany, and on the south by France **Features:** The northern part of the country contains the rugged uplands of the Ardennes plateau, while the south consists of undulating terrain with broad valleys **Chief Rivers:** Alzette, Sûre, Moselle, Our

**Head of State:** Grand Duke Jean, born 1921, ascended the throne 1964 **Head of Government:** Premier Pierre Werner, born 1913, appointed 1979 **Effective Date of Present Constitution:** 1868 **Legislative Body:** Parliament (bicameral), consisting of a Chamber of Deputies of 59 members, elected for 5 years, and a Council of State of 21 members appointed by the Grand Duke **Local Government:** 12 cantons grouped into 3 districts

**Ethnic Composition:** Luxembourgers are ethnically a mixture of French and German. Throughout the 20th century, a considerable number of immigrants from Italy and other Mediterranean countries have settled in Luxembourg **Population Distribution:** 68% urban **Density:** 364 inhabitants per sq. mi.

**Largest Cities:** (1979 est.) Luxembourg 79,596, Esch/Alzette 25,538, Differdange 16,898, Dudelange 14,120

**Per Capita Income:** $8,972 (1980) **Gross Domestic Product (GDP):** $3.2 billion (1980) **Economic Statistics:** About 41% of GDP comes from industry (steel, chemicals, auto parts, rubber, synthetic fibers), 3% from agriculture (livestock, dairy products, wine) **Minerals and Mining:** Vast deposits of iron ore are mined; slate is also quarried in commercial quantities **Labor Force:** 147,300 (33% aliens) of which 48% is in services, 46% in industry, 6% in agriculture (grapes, livestock) **Foreign Trade:** Exports, chiefly steel, chemical products, plastic fibers, rubber and textiles, totaled $2.9 billion in 1979. Imports, mainly coal and iron ore, machinery, transportation equipment, and food, totaled $3.1 billion **Principal Trade Partners:** EC countries

**Vital Statistics:** Birthrate, 11.6 per 1,000 of pop. (1980); death rate, 11.5 **Life Expectancy:** 73 years **Health Statistics:** 103 inhabitants per hospital bed; 900 per physician (1977) **Infant Mortality:** 11.5 per 1,000 births (1977) **Illiteracy:** 2% **Primary and Secondary School Enrollment:** 53,423 (1976) **Enrollment in Higher Education:** 446 **GNP Expended on Education:** 5.2% (1973)

**Transportation:** Surfaced roads total 3,085 mi. **Motor Vehicles:** 164,400 (1978) **Passenger Cars:** 153,100 **Railway Mileage:** 168 **Ports:** None **Major Airlines:** LUXAIR operates regular services to Western Europe; Icelandair maintains a regular service to the United States **Communications: Radio Transmitters:** 7 **Licenses:** 205,000 (1976) **Television Transmitters:** 4 **Licenses:** 105,000 (1976) **Telephones:** 192,000 (1978) **Newspapers:** 7 dailies (1976), 560 copies per 1,000 inhabitants (1975)

**Weights and Measures:** Metric system **Travel Requirements:** Passport, no visa for less than 3 months **International Dialing Code:** 352

---

The Grand Duchy of Luxembourg, covering an area of 999 square miles, and with a population of over 360,000, is the equal of Sweden in the production of iron and steel. Centered at Esch-sur-Alzette, Luxembourg's iron and steel industry uses iron ore mined in the area for about half of its needs and imports the remainder, as well as coal. The duchy's steel mills, among the largest and oldest in Europe, were hard hit by the worldwide reduced demand for steel in the 1980s. But Luxembourg has many other manufacturing industries, of which the principal ones are chemicals and automotive parts. American capital was the source of much of this diversification, with investments coming also from Luxembourg's Common Market partners.

Agriculture is of the small-scale, mixed-farming type, and livestock breeding is important. Among Luxembourg's exports are dairy products, pigs, and roses, and its vineyards in the Moselle Valley produce fine white wines. Trilingual Luxembourgers, speaking their own patois plus French and German, call the southern part of the grand duchy *Bon Pays* or *Gutland*—in English, the "Good Land"—because of its agricultural qualities.

Most industry is concentrated in the extreme south, and, all-in-all, Luxembourg offers the tourist picturesque scenery, good food and drink, an excellent road system, and, for the hiker, extensive paths between old villages.

On the darker side is the fact that the duchy has twice been overrun in this century by German troops, with liberation coming both times with the arrival of American forces. At Hamm, outside Luxembourg City, more than 5,000 American soldiers, including General George S. Patton, Jr., lie buried.

Since the war Luxembourg has abandoned neutrality. In 1949 it became a charter member of the North Atlantic Treaty Organization and has since been one of the leading promoters of closer European cooperation. It was a pioneer in the kind of economic cooperation now exemplified by the European Community, having formed, in 1921, a customs union with Belgium; the union became *Benelux* when the Netherlands joined in 1948.

**HISTORY:** The county of Luxembourg, including the present Belgian province of Luxembourg, emerged in the 10th century and rose to prominence in 1308, when its ruler was elected Holy Roman Emperor. Raised to a duchy in 1354, Luxembourg passed to the Hapsburgs in 1482. During the next three centuries, the duchy's history was bound up with the southern Netherlands, which passed from Spanish to Austrian rule in 1714. France occupied the duchy during the French Revolutionary Wars and formally annexed it in 1797

**1815:** Congress of Vienna makes Luxembourg a grand duchy, in personal union with the Kingdom of the Netherlands

**1839:** Belgium, having won its independence from the Netherlands, annexes the present Belgian province of Luxembourg; it constituted the major part of the grand duchy

**1867:** Luxembourg is declared an independent, neutral state in personal union with the Netherlands by the Treaty of London

**1890:** William III of the Netherlands dies and is succeeded on the Dutch throne by his daughter Wilhelmina; however, Luxembourg passes to Duke Adolf of Nassau, who becomes grand duke

**1914-18:** Luxembourg, its neutrality violated by Germany, is occupied by German forces during World War I

**1940:** German forces invade grand duchy in World War II; ducal family and cabinet flee to London

**1944:** Luxembourg is liberated by Allied forces

**1949:** Grand duchy formally abandons its perpetual neutrality and joins North Atlantic Treaty Organization

**1964:** Grand Duchess Charlotte abdicates in favor of son Jean

**1968-69:** Christian Socialist/Socialist coalition government of Premier Pierre Werner falls in October 1968 after government refuses to agree to demands by Socialist trade union leaders for higher wages and greater welfare benefits; following new elections, Werner forms a new government of Christian Socialists and Socialists and is reappointed premier in 1969

**1972:** Voting age is lowered from 21 to 18

**1974:** Premier Werner's government falls, ending 55 years of unbroken control by Christian Socialists. Democrat Gaston Thorn becomes premier, leading a coalition of socialists and liberals

**1979:** Christian Democrats regain control of parliament following new elections; Pierre Werner replaces Thorn as premier and forms Christian Democrat-Liberal coalition

## MADAGASCAR

**Area:** 226,657 sq. mi. **Population:** 8,742,000 (1980 est.)

**Official Name:** Democratic Republic of Madagascar **Capital:** Antananarivo **Nationality:** Malagasy **Languages:** Malagasy and French are the official languages; Hova and other dialects are also widely spoken **Religion:** About 55% animist, 40% Christian, and 5% Moslem **Flag:** A white vertical band at the staff and 2 horizontal bands, the upper red, the lower green **Anthem:** O, Our Beloved Fatherland **Currency:** Malagasy franc (310 per U.S. $1)

**Location:** Indian Ocean. The 4th-largest island in the world—after Greenland, New Guinea, and Borneo—Madagascar is situated some 250 miles off the east coast of Africa, from which it is separated by the Mozambique Channel **Feeatures:** The terrain consists of a central belt of eroded highlands extending from the northeast to the southwest, sloping steeply eastward to a narrow, swampy coast and passing gradually to more extensive lowlands in the west. An inland plateau rises to 9,450 feet **Chief Rivers:** Mangoro, Ikopa, Onilahy, Tsiribihina, Mangoky, Sofia

**Head of State and of Government:** President: Cmdr. Didier Ratsiraka, born 1936, assumed power in a coup in June 1975 as head of Supreme Revolutionary Council, and elected president in December 1975; he is aided by a cabinet headed by the premier, Desire Rakotoarijaona, appointed August 1977 **Effective Date of Present Constitution:** 1975 **Legislative Body:** National Popular Assembly (unicameral) consisting of 137 members, elected for five years **Local Government:** 6 provinces

**Ethnic Composition:** The population is of Malayan-Indonesian origin, with an admixture of Arab and African strains; of 18 major groups, the most numerous are the Merina (Hova), Betsileo, Betsimisaraka, Sakalava and Tsimihety **Population Distribution:** 16% urban **Density:** 39 inhabitants per sq. mi.

**Largest Cities:** (1975 census) Antananarivo 451,808, Toamasina (Tamatave) 77,395, Fianarantsoa 68,054, Majunga 65,864, Toliary (Tuléar) 45,676, Antsiranana (Diégo-Suarez) 40,443

**Per Capita Income:** $321 (1980) **Gross National Product (GNP):** $2.8 billion (1980) **Economic Statistics:** In 1978 about 40% of the GNP came from agriculture (rice, coffee, tobacco, cloves, cocoa, vanilla, livestock), 17% from industry (including oil refining) and mining **Minerals and Mining:** Graphite, mica, gold, and industrial beryl are mined, but are not extensive. Offshore oil deposits are to be exploited **Labor Force:** 4.4 million, of which 88% is in agriculture **Foreign Trade:** Exports, chiefly coffee, vanilla, sugar, rice, cloves, and raffia, totaled $$339 million in 1980. Imports, mainly transportation machinery, crude oil, textiles, chemicals, pharmaceuticals, machinery, and electrical appliances, totaled $603 million **Principal Trade Partners:** France, United States, West Germany, Japan, Italy, United Arab Emirates

**Vital Statistics:** Birthrate, 46 per 1,000 of pop. (1980); death rate, 25 **Life Expectancy:** 466 years **Health Statistics:** 405 inhabitants per hospital bed; 10,306 per physician (1977) **Infant Mortality:** 53.2 per 1,000 births (1972) **Illiteracy:** 47% **Primary and Secondary School Enrollment:** 1,264,849 (1975) **Enrollment in Higher Education:** 8,385 (1975) **GNP Expended on Education:** 3.1% (1975)

**Transportation:** Paved roads total 2,800 mi. **Motor Vehicles:** 109,700 (1977) **Passenger Cars:** 57,400 **Railway Mileage:** 549 **Ports:** Toamasina (Tamatave), Majunga, Nossi-Be, Antsiranana (Diégo-Suarez), Toliary (Tuléar) **Major Airlines:** Air Madagascar operates domestic and international services **Communications: Radio Transmitters:** 19 **Receivers:** 609,000 (1975) **Television Transmitters:** 4 **Receivers:** 8,000 (1976) **Telephones:** 29,000 (1977) **Newspapers:** 12 dailies (1977), 9 copies per 1,000 inhabitants (1974)

**Weights and Measures:** Metric system **Travel Requirements:** Passport, visa valid for stay up to 1 month, $7.15 fee, 4 photos

Madagascar, known as the Malagasy Republic until 1976, is "the land at the end of the earth," a blend of Shangri-la and Lost World. Although near Africa—250 miles off the continent's southeast coast—Madagascar and its people, the Malagasy, appear to be more a part of southeast Asia. The island was settled, according to folklore, more than 2,000 years ago by people who drifted across the Indian Ocean from the Malay-Indonesia area. Their descendants speak a language considered to be of Malayan-Polynesian origin and, while some show admixtures of African and Arab settlers, most have an Indochinese physique.

While unknown to much of the world, Madagascar was prized as a naval base in the contest of the British and French imperialisms. Triumph by the French brought an overthrow of the Malagasy monarchy, but not submission.

Despite their placid appearance, the Malagasy rose in a bloody and unsuccessful revolt against French rule in 1947. When, in 1960, the island became a fully sovereign republic under President Philibert Tsiranana, the Malagasy regarded the event as a return to self-rule rather than a granting of independence by a colonial power.

With self-rule, Madagascar has faced problems of resolving internal conflicts, mainly between the traditionally dominant Merina, or plateau people, and the *côtiers*, or coastal peoples. President Tsiranana was a *côtier* and former professor who sought to promote both national unity and the development of a sluggish agricultural economy.

Tsiranana favored continued close ties with France and, despite Madagascar's membership in the Organization of African Unity and his own condemmnation of apartheid, he welcomed investment and economic aid from South Africa.

A major change in Madagascar's political life came in 1972 when President Tsiranana was removed from office. Student riots had begun to plague his administration, and a formal referendum was held which transferred power to a new military government headed by Premier Gabriel Ramanantsoa, a moderate leftist.

In February 1975, Ramanantsoa turned over full power to Col. Richard Ratsimandrava after 112 days of political crisis. After six days, Ratsimandrava was assassinated by paramilitary policemen.

The National Military Guidance Coommittee governed the country until June 15 when it invested Cmdr. Didier Ratsiraka as head of state and dissolved itself. In a referendum, Ratsiraka's presidency and a new constitution were approved by 95 percent of the voters. The nation was to be known henceforth as the Democratic Republic of Madagascar. The military, in control since 1972, has sought to nationalize important segments of the economy which is overwhelmingly agricultural, largely of the subsistence type. Rice is the main crop. New development efforts have been concentrated in mining and light manufacturing.

**HISTORY:** Despite Madagascar's proximity to Africa, Malagasy tradition and language support the bbelief that the first waves of migration came from the Sunda Islands (present-day Indonesia), starting a century or two before the Christian era. About A.D. 900, Arab settlers and Africans, brought by slave traders, were added to the population. Beginning in the 16th century, Portuguese, French, and English contested with rival Malagasy kingdoms for dominance of the island

**1885-1905:** France invades Madagascar and establishes a limited protectorate. Local resistance continues for many years

**1942-43:** British occupy Vichy-ruled Madagascar to prevent seizure by Japanese; Free French take over

**1947:** Armed revolt by Malagasy nationalists breaks out in opposition to "French Union" self-rule, lasts nearly a year before French suppress it; death toll is put as high as 80,000

**1958:** After reforms in 1956 paving way for independence, Madagascar votes "yes" in referendum creating Malagasy Republic within the French Community

**1959:** Philibert Tsiranana is elected first president of the republic

**1960:** Madagascar is proclaimed a sovereign, independent nation

**1965:** President Tsiranana is reelected by smashing majority

**1972:** Executive powers are transferred to Gen. Ramanantsoa as premier of a military government

**1975:** Ramanantsoa turns over power to Col. Richard Ratsimandrava, who is assassinated after six days. A military committee invests Cmdr. Didier Ratsiraka as head of state. Nation renamed Democratic Republic of Madagascar

**1980:** Oil is discovered. Madagascar arranges for major arms purchases from Soviet Union and signs cultural cooperation agreement with Cuba

**1981:** Militants of opposition Monima party riot following arrest of Monja Joana, their leader. Joana subsequently rejoins the ruling National Front for the Defense of the Revolution (FNDR) and is appointed to the Supreme Revolutionary Council. Economy suffers severely from effects of high oil prices, drought and reduced world markets for coffee, cloves and vanilla. International Monetary Fund grants special drawing rights worth $132 million to Madagascar for period ending June 1982

## MALAWI

**Area:** 45,747 sq. mi. **Population:** 6,123,000 (1981 est.)

**Official Name:** Republic of Malawi **Capital:** Lilongwe **Nationality:** Malawian **Languages:** English is the official language and Chichewa is the national language. Among the other various Bantu languages are Nyanja, Tumbuka, Yao, Tonga, and Ngoni **Religion:** About 35% of the people are Christians, 12% Moslems, and the rest animists **Flag:** 3 horizontal stripes of black, red, and green with a red rising sun on the black stripe **Anthem:** National Anthem, beginning "O God, bless our land of Malawi" **Currency:** Malawian kwacha (1.08 per U.S. $1)

**Location:** East Africa. Landlocked Malawi is bordered on the north and northeast by Tanzania, on the southeast and southwest by Mozambique, and on the northwest by Zambia **Features:** The Great Rift Valley traverses the country from north to south, its deep trough containing the 360-mile-long Lake Nyasa (Malawi). West of the valley, the land rises to form high plateaus between 3,000 and 4,000 feet above sea level, while in the north the Nyika uplands rise to 8,500 feet. South of Lake Nyasa are the Shire Highlands, which rise to steep mountains ranging up to 10,000 feet **Chief Rivers:** Shire, Bua, Rukuru

**Head of State and of Government:** President: Dr. Hastings Kamuzu Banda, born 1906, elected by National Assembly in 1966, made president for life by constitutional amendment in November 1970; he also holds 5 cabinet posts **Effective Date of Present Constitution:** July 1966 **Legislative Body:** National Assembly (unicameral); 87 members for 5-year terms **Local Government:** 3 regions, divided into 24 districts. Each region has an appointed regional miinister

**Ethnic Composition:** The people are almost all descended from Bantu tribes that arrived between the 16th and 19th centuries. They include the Chewa and the Nyanja, descendants of the Maravi, who emigrated from present-day Zaire; the Yao; the Tumbuka; the Lonwe; and the Sena **Population Distribution:** 10% urban **Density:** 134 inhabitants per sq. mi.

**Largest Cities:** (1977 census) Blantyre 222,153, Lilongwe 102,924, Zomba 21,000

**Per Capita Income:** $202 (1980) **Gross Domestic Product (GDP):** $1.2 billion (1980) **Economic Statistics:** In 1977, 47% of the GDP was derived from agriculture (tea, tung nuts and oil, sugarcane, tobacco), and 12% from industry (beverages, textiles, tobacco products) **Minerals and Mining:** Production is limited to quarrying constructional stone and limestone; however there are unexploited deposits of bauxite and coal **Labor Force:** 1,500,000, with 85% in subsistence agricullture **Foreign Trade:** Exports, chiefly tobacco, tea, sugar, peanuts, corn, and cotton, totaled $233 million in 1979. Imports, mainly textiles, motor vehicles, petroleum products, medical and pharmaceutical goods, and food products, totaled $314 million **Principal Trade Partners:** Britain, South Africa, Netherlands, United States, Japan,, West Germany

**Vital Statistics:** Birthrate, 48.5 per 1,000 of pop. (1977); death rate, 25.1 **Life Expectancy:** 45 years **Health Statistics:** 576 inhabitants per hospital bed; 48,462 per physician (1977) **Infant Mortality:** 130 per 1,000 births **Illiteracy:** 78% **Primary and Secondary School Enrollment:** 680,089 (1976) **Enrollment in Higher Education:** 1,148 (1975) **GNP Expended on Education:** 2.0% (1975)

**Transportation:** Paved roads total 1,474 mi. **Motor Vehicles:** 26,900 (1978) **Passenger Cars:** 13,500 **Railway Mileage:** 420 **Ports:** None **Major Airlines:** Air Malawi, Ltd. operates domestic and international services **Communications: Radio Transmitters:** 13 **Receivers:** 130,000 (1976) **Television:** None **Telephones:** 27,000 (1978) **Newspapers:** 2 dailies, 3 copies per 1,000 inhabitants (1977)

**Weights and Measures:** Metric system **Travel Requirements:** Passport, no visa required for stay up to 1 year

Malawi is among Africa's most picturesque yet poorest countries. It is distinguished also in being one of the few independent black African countries to establish official relations with South Africa and in having a despotic president, Dr. H. Kamuzu Banda, who banned the miniskirt, set rules on the length of men's shorts, and, in 1978, banned foreign journalists from the country indefinitely for what he considered unfair, false reporting of recent elections.

Soaring mountains and the long inland sea of Lake Nyasa have won the country the title of "Switzerland of Africa." But the resemblance ends with the scenery. Malawi's economy has been gaining with increased production of tea and tobacco and industrial investment from South Africa, but with a dense population and a very low per capita income, the country is still far from economic takeoff.

Dr. Banda, an associate and admirer of Ghana's erstwhile ruler, Kwame Nkrumah, has been president of Malawi since the former British protectoratee became independent in 1964. In 1970 he had himself made president for life.

While maintaining that he is as much opposed to South Africa's racial policies as any black African leader, Dr. Banda has cited Malawi's need and landlocked position in southern Africa as necessitating close economic ties with her white-ruled neighbor. "I would do business with the Devil himself to help Malawian development," he has said. Employment of more than 20,000 Malawian workers in South Africa brings in needed foreign exchange.

Tourism has become an important business for Malawi. Many hotels, however, have recently reported a drop in bookings as a result of Dr. Banda's rulings about dress, which were aimed at tourists.

Pressures for "Africanization" of property and jobs have been aimed at European landowners and Asian traders. As many as 200,000 Asians have had their businesses "Africanized."

The building of a new capital at Lilongwe, a pet project of Dr. Banda's, was aided by South African loans. Most of the $60-million cost of the new capital is being underwritten by South Africa.

In addition to increasing industry, plans are progressing for bauxite mining and construction of a large aluminum plant. Dr. Banda has said that Malawi either will become economically viable in the next 5 to 10 years or will cease to exist as a truly independent state.

**HISTORY:** Little is known about the history of Malawi, formerly Nyasaland, prior to the arrival of the Scottish missionary and explorer David Livingstone in 1859. His revulsion at the Arab slave trade moved him to promote establishment of Scottish missions and business groups to develop legitimate commerce as a substitute for the trade in human beings. Britain, in fighting the slave trade and also seeking to prevent encroachment by the Portuguese and Germans, gradually gained control of Nyasaland and set up a protectorate in 1891

**1953:** Nyasaland, despite strong Nyasa opposition, is joined to new Central African Federation, including also Northern and Southern Rhodesia

**1959:** Dr. Hastings Kamuzu Banda, leader of Nyasaland African Congress, and more than 1,000 of his followers, are imprisoned, charged with plotting massacre of white officials; after they were absolved they set up Malawi Congress party

**1960-61:** Britain grants Nyasaland constitution assuring African majority in Legislative Council; Malawi party wins overwhelming victory in council election

**1963:** Nyasaland secedes from Central African Federation, which is dissolved; Banda becomes prime minister under new constitution

**1964-65:** Nyasaland becomes independent Malawi

**1966:** Malawi becomes a republic within British Commonwealth, with Banda as president

**1969:** Malawi, at meeting of East and Central African States, refuses to join in manifesto criticizing white-dominated governments of Rhodesia and South Africa

**1970:** Prime Minister John Vorster of South Africa makes official visit to Malawi, the first such visit by a South African leader to a black African state. President Banda returns visit in 1971

**1975:** New capital established at Lilongwe

**1980:** Import controls attempt to offset rising oil prices

**1981:** Constitutional amendment gives president power to name as many members of Parliament as he wishes

**1982:** In wake of falling world prices for its export products, Malawi devalues the kwacha 15%

## MALAYSIA

**Area:** 128,308 sq. mi. **Population:** 13,435,588 (1980 census)

**Official Name:** Malaysia **Capital:** Kuala Lumpur **Nationality:** Malaysian **Languages:** Malay (Bahasa Malaysia) is the official language; English, Tamil, and a variety of native, Chinese, and Indian dialects are also spoken **Religion:** Chiefly Moslem, and Islam is the state religion; in Sabah and Sarawak there are many animists. Most of the Chinese follow Buddhism, Confucianism, and Taoism. Of the Indian community, about 70% are Hindu, 20% Moslem, 5% Christian, and 2% Sikh **Flag:** Fourteen red and white stripes with blue field in upper left corner containing crescent and star in yellow **Anthem:** Our Country **Currency:** ringgit (2.3 per U.S. $1)

**Location:** Southeast Asia. Malaysia consists of West Malaysia (Malaya), and East Malaysia (Sabah and Sarawak). West Malaysia, on the Malay Peninsula, is bordered on the east by the South China Sea, on the south by the Strait of Johore, on the west by the Strait of Malacca and the Andaman Sea, and on the north by Thailand. Sarawak and Sabah, on the northwestern coast of the island of Borneo, are bordered by Brunei, and by the Indonesian province of Kalimantan on the southeast; on the west, north, and east are the South China, Sulu, and Celebes seas **Features:** Some 80% of the total land area of the country is forested. The Malay Peninsula consists of a spinal mountain range running roughly north and south and flanked by coastal plains. In Sabah and Sarawak, coastal plains rise to mountainous interiors **Chief Rivers:** Perak and Pahang in Malaya; Rajang in Sarawak, Kinabatangan in Sabah

**Head of State:** Paramount Ruler: Tuanku Haji Ahmad Shah Al-Mustain Billah Ibni Al-Marhum Sultan Abu Bakar Ri'ayatuddin Al-Mu'adzam Shah, shah of Pahang, born 1930, elected 1979 by the Conference of Rulers for a 5-year term **Head of Government:** Prime Minister: Dr. Mahathir bin Mohamad, took office July 16, 1981 **Effective Date of Present Constitution:** 1957 **Legislative Body:** Parliament (bicameral), consisting of a Senate (Dewan Negara) and a House of Representatives (Dewan Rakyat). The Senate is composed of 58 members, 32 appointed by the Paramount Ruler and 26 elected by state assemblies, for 6-year terms. The House of Representatives consists of 154 members, 114 from West Malaysia, 24 from Sarawak, and 16 from Sabah, all elected for a 5-year term **Local Government:** 13 states, headed by titular rulers and governors. Effective power is in the hands of the chief ministers, selected from the state assemblies

**Ethnic Composition:** Malayans constitute about 45% of the population, Chinese 36%, non-Malay indigenous peoples 8%, and Indians and Pakistanis 9.1% **Population Distribution:** 29% urban **Density:** 105 inhabitants per sq. mi.

**Largest Cities:** (1980 census) Kuala Lumpur 937,875; (1970 census) George Town (Penang) 269,247, Ipoh 247,969

**Per Capita Income:** $1,355 (1980) **Gross National Product (GNP):** $19 billion (1980) **Economic Statistics:** In 1978, 30% of GNP was derived from agriculture (rubber, timber, rice, palm oil, coconut oil, fruits, sago, tea, and pepper); 16% from manufacturing (oil and sugar refining, steel plants, fertilizers, and many smaller import-substitute industries); and 6% from mining (tin, oil, iron) **Minerals and Mining:** Tin, oil and iron ore are the chief minerals. Petroleum from offshore wells is of growing importance in Sarawak and Sabah **Labor Force:** About 4,800,000 (1978 est.), with approximately 50% engaged in agriculture and fishing, and 14% in industry **Foreign Trade:** Exports, chiefly rubber, tin, petroleum, palm oil and forest products, totaled $11 billion in 1979. Imports, mainly foodstuffs, industrial machinery, transportation equipment, metals, electrical equipment, and petroleum products, totaled $7.9 billion **Principal Trade Partners:** Britain, Singapore, Japan, United States, Australia, China, West Germany, Thailand

**Vital Statistics:** Birthrate, 34.6 per 1,000 of pop. (1980); death rate, 8.7 **Life Expectancy:** 68 years **Health Statistics:** 347 inhabitants per hospital bed; 8,319 per physician (1974) **Infant Mortality:** 29.4 per 1,000 births **Illiteracy:** 39% **Primary and Secondary School Enrollment:** 2,462,682 (1977) **Enrollment in Higher Education:** 39,658 **GNP Expended on Education:** 5.1% (1971)

**Transportation:** Paved roads total 10,480 mi. **Motor Vehicles:** 869,400 (1978) **Passenger Cars:** 657,300 **Railway Mileage:** 1,132 **Ports:** Pinang, Port Dickson, Klang, Malacca, Kuching, Miri, Sandakan, Tawau, Kota Kinabalu **Major Airlines:** Malaysian Airline System operates international and domestic flights **Communications: Radio Transmitters:** 89 **Receivers:** 1,450,000 (1976) **Television Transmitters:** 338 **Receivers:** 555,000 (1976) **Telephones:** 434,000 (1978) **Newspapers:** 37 dailies (1976), 87 copies per 1,000 inhabitants (1975)

**Weights and Measures:** Metric system **Travel Requirements:** Passport, no visa for 3 months **International Dialing Code:** 60

For more than a century Malaya, with its rich deposits of tin and its ideal climate for growing rubber trees, has been prosperous and sought after. With the addition in 1963 of Sarawak and Sabah, the former British colonies on the island of Borneo, the Federation of Malaysia now contains one of the largest undeveloped areas in Asia.

The long center spine of Malaya and vast sections of Sarawak and Sabah are covered solidly with towering rain forests and low mountain ranges. Only the coastal areas and the occasional valleys are open and settled. Malaya, economically balanced and commercially progressive, continues to clear new tracts of jungle land for planting for rubber and coconut palm oil. But the efforts to enlarge the slender bands of modern development in Sarawak and Sabah have barely crept along since British colonial rule over these remote territories ended.

Although Malaysia enjoys a healthy balance of trade and its people have the highest per capita income in Southeast Asia after Singapore's, the economy suffers from overspecialization. Two commodities, rubber and tin, account for an important part of the export trade. Both are vulnerable to price swings in world markets. In addition, synthetic rubber has been gaining favor while readily exploitable tin reserves are dwindling. On the plus side the new oil fields in Sabah are now producing; they now account for almost a fifth of Malaysia's exports. The Malaysian Industrial Development Authority, using the "hard sell", attracted during the 1970s some 600 multinational corporations, establishing Malaysia as a production center in electronics and other new industries, but by the early 1980s, the government was moving to establish, through stock purchase, the maximum possible degree of Malaysian control of these companies.

Malaysia, which was actively anti-Communist, has since 1970 modified her foreign policy in favor of peaceful coexistence. In 1974, Prime Minister Abdul Razak visited Peking and established full diplomatic relations with Communist China.

The level of living in Malaysia's cities and small towns is the highest in Southeast Asia and there are no pressures on the land from the population. Malaya has been notably successful in completing a series of five-year development plans. Similar,, though less ambitious, plans have been prepared for East Malaysia. The British, whose business firms reaped impressive profits from Malaya, left behind in that region an excellent civil service, comparatively good medical facilities, and a soundly administered school system that has been markedly successful in the cities and towns where ethnic Chinese and Indians are concentrated.

But amid the prosperity of Malaysia there runs a continuing struggle between the Moslem Malays, who consider themselves the indigenous owners of Malaya, and the ethnic Chinese. The Chinese own 90 percent of the federation's commercial outlets, occupy the majority of the positions in medical, legal, and engineering circles, and possess an energy and drive that the graceful, deliberate, and highly religious Malays do not admire. Since Malaya first became independent in 1957 there has been a subsurface fear among the Malays that the ethnic Chinese may take control by winning a majority in the elected parliament.

The Malays, who now dominate the government, are also in conflict with the native groups in Sarawak and Sabah, with whom they are neither religiously nor culturally allied.

The bloody race riots of 1969 led to a 21-month suspension of parliament and rule by decree. Though parliament reconvened in February 1971, full democracy did not return. A constitutional amendment to outlaw discussion of sensitive issues likely to inflame race hatred was adopted. The 48-member National Unity Council became the sole body permitted to question the government's racial and linguistic policies.

A heavy tide of refugees from Vietnam, known as the "boat people" because of their arrival from across the South China Sea, caused political turbulence in Malaysia in 1978 and 1979. They were mostly Chinese and therefore were viewed by the Malays as a threat to the country's delicate political and social balance. The government had about 70,000 such refugees in makeshift camps in 1979, a number that gradually shrank thereafter as they were resettled in the U.S. and other countries. By 1982, the government was adopting restrictive measures to deal with new social pressures created by a massive influx of Indonesian unskilled laborers into developing areas of Malaysia.

**HISTORY:** By the beginning of the 13th century the coasts of Malaya, Sarawak, and Sabah, which now are joined in the Federation of Malaysia, were dotted with small trading ports where the natives, most of them of ethnic Malay stock, fished and produced spices. The lure of this spice trade brought the Portuguese, Dutch, and British merchant adventurers. As their trade grew, they found it profitable to take control of the ports to protect their enterprises from the natives and from the other European merchants. In 1511 the Portuguese occupied Malacca, on the west coast of Malaya, and in 1592 the British East India Company appeared at Penang

**1867:** British establish the Straits Settlements—Penang, Malacca, Singapore—as a crown colony

**1888:** British declare North Borneo (Sabah), Sarawak, and Brunei British protectorates

**1941:** Japanese invade Malaya in World War II, eventually driving the British and Dutch from the East Indies

**1946:** After Japanese surrender, British form Union of Malaya by uniting Penang and Malacca with the nine Malay states; Singapore, Sabah, and Sarawak become crown colonies

**1948:** Union of Malaya is succeeded by Federation of Malaya; Communist insurrection by ethnic Chinese breaks out, and government declares state of emergency

**1957:** Malaya becomes independent and member of British Commonwealth

**1960:** Emergency is ended with defeat of Communist guerrillas

**1962-63:** Britain and Malaya agree on formation of new Federation of Malaysia that is to include Malaya, Sarawak, Sabah, the tiny Sultanate of Brunei, and Singapore. Brunei decides at last minute to remain outside federation; Malaysia is officially created and joins Commonwealth

**1965:** After months of dispute over status of ethnic Chinese and Malays, stimulated by Malay fear of Chinese dominance, Singapore secedes from federation

**1966:** After three years of sporadic guerrilla war and threats of invasion from Indonesia, which had opposed the creation of the federation, Malaysia and Indonesia agree to peace

**1969:** Tension and rioting between Chinese and Malays in capital leads to suspension of the constitution and formation of a state-of-emergency ruling council

**1970:** Prime Minister Abdul Rahman, the founder and leader of Malaysia, resigns and is succeeded by Abdul Razak

**1971:** State of emergency, in effect for 21 months, is ended on February 19 and parliamentary government restored

**1974:** Prime Minister Razak's National Front Coalition wins an overwhelming election victory

**1975:** Prosperity of early 1970s ends and government faces an ailing economy, student unrest and guerrilla war by the Communists

**1976:** Razak dies on January 14, Deputy Prime Minister Datuk Hussein bin Onn takes office. Government tightens security measures in drive on Communist insurgents. Ethnic Chinese professionals flee to avoid racial discrimination

**1978:** Hussein calls early elections and wins large majority. Number of refugee "boat people" who crossed South China Sea from Vietnam passes 50,000 mark by year's end

**1979:** On Jan. 5, Prime Minister Hussein announces that the government will accept no more refugees. On March 3, a Vietnamese boat is turned back by naval gunfire; eventually it capsizes and 104 persons drown. Tens of thousands of Philippine Moslems flee to the state of Sabah (northeastern Borneo). The elected figurehead king, Sultan Yahya Petra, dies; Sultan Ahmad Shah, shah of Pahang, is elected for a five-year term

**1980:** Peasants riot against government in the state of Kedah

**1981:** Prime Minister Hussein retires, is succeeded by his lieutenant, Mahathir bin Mohamad. Government begins campaign to control growing immigration of Indonesian workers

**1982:** Mahathir urges joint Southeast Asian move against oil multinationals. Mahathir's 11-party National Front coalition wins landslide victory in April elections

## MALDIVES

**Area:** 115 sq. mi. **Population:** 157,000 (1981 est.)

**Official Name:** Republic of Maldives **Capital:** Male **Nationality:** Maldivian **Languages:** Divehi, a dialect of Sinhalese, is the official and universal language; Arabic and English are also spoken **Religion:** Virtually all Maldivians are Sunni Moslems and Islam is the state religion **Flag:** A green rectangle with a white crescent superimposed on a red field **Anthem:** National Anthem **Currency:** Maldivian rupee (7.05 per U.S. $1)

**Location:** Indian Ocean. The Maldive Islands are a 500-mile-long archipelago of some 2,000 coral islands, 400 miles southwest of Sri Lanka. Male, the capital, is located at 4° 10' N., 73°30'W. **Features:** The Maldives rest on a submarine ridge, believed to be of volcanic origin. They are grouped into 19 atolls, or rings of coral islands, each ring encircling a lagoon. Most of the islands are covered with coconut palms **Chief Rivers:** None

**Head of State and of Government:** President: Maumoon Abdul Gayoom, born 1939, elected in 1978 **Effective Date of Present Constitution:** 1964, amended 1968, 1970, 1972, 1975 **Legislative**

**Body:** Majlis (unicameral), 48 members, of whom 8 are appointed by the president and 40 are popularly elected for a 5-year term **Local Government:** Each of the 19 atolls has an elected committee with a head man *(Verin)* appointed by the government

**Ethnic Composition:** The people are of mixed Indian, Sinhalese, and Arabic descent **Population Distribution:** 12% urban **Density:** 1,365 inhabitants per sq. mi. (215 islands are inhabited)

**Largest City:** (1978 census) Male 29,555

**Per Capita Income:** $190 (1978) **Gross National Product (GNP):** $27 million (1978) **Economic Statistics:** The economy has a narrow base, being almost totally dependent on fisheries for its export earnings. Fishing is the basic industry, the catch consisting mainly of bonito and tuna. Cooked and smoked, they are known as Maldive fish and are used as a condiment. The second-largest commercial industry is copra and coconut oil production. A cottage industry based on coir yarn weaving provides work for many of the women in the islands. Tourism is growing **Minerals and Mining:** There are no mineral resources **Labor Force:** 80% of the work force is engaged in fishing **Foreign Trade:** Exports, chiefly fish, coconuts, copra, coir, cowrie shell, tortoise shell, and local handicraft products, totaled $4.6 million in 1979. Imports, mainly rice, flour, kerosene, oil, sugar, textiles, and drugs, totaled $22 million **Principal Trade Partners:** Japan, Sri Lanka, Singapore, Britain

**Vital Statistics:** Birthrate, 44.4 per 1,000 of pop. (1979); death rate, 13.9 **Health Statistics:** 3,500 inhabitants per hospital bed; 15,555 per physician (1977) **Infant Mortality:** 120 per 1,000 births **Illiteracy:** very high **Primary and Secondary School Enrollment:** 3,549 (1977) **GNP Expended on Education:** 3% (1970)

**Transportation:** N.A. **Motor Vehicles:** 97 (1969) **Passenger Cars:** 20 (1969) **Railway Mileage:** None **Port:** Male **Major Airlines:** Maldive International Airlines connects Male with India and Sri Lanka **Communications: Radio Transmitters:** 9 **Licenses:** 3,500 (1976) **Television Transmitters:** 1 **Telephones:** 227 (1969) **Newspapers:** 1 daily (1977), 182 copies per 1,000 inhabitants

**Weights and Measures:** Local units are used **Travel Requirements:** Passport, no visa required

---

The 2,000 islands that comprise the Maldives in the Indian Ocean consist of atolls, none of which are more than 20 feet in elevation. The islands are mostly protected by reefs, which have been the scene of numerous shipwrecks. The total land area is a third that of New York City. The 157,000 Maldivians inhabit only 215 of the islands.

Coconut palms cover the larger islands, on which breadfruit, figs, millet, and edible nuts are grown. Widespread in the hot and humid Maldive climate, malaria has been fought by the World Health Organization.

The Maldivian people live at a more or less subsistence level, and their basic economy is of the one-crop type—what is known as "Maldive fish." This is bonito, caught in local waters, cut up, boiled, smoked, and dried until it resembles hardwood. It is considered a delicacy in Sri Lanka and India, where it is whittled into fragments, cooked with onions and spices, and served as a condiment.

The staple foods of the Maldives are fish and rice. The rice has to be imported along with a host of other necessities, such as salt, sugar, kerosene, oil, and textiles.

There is no income tax, and the bulk of internal revenue is derived from customs duties, the rental of uninhabited islands, the licensing of boats and vehicles, and sale of postage stamps. Tourism is booming, reaching a total of 30,000 visitors annually, most of them West Germans traveling in tour groups that promise sun-and-swim vacations at soft, white beaches.

According to native legend, it was a Sinhalese prince who was the first sultan, having stayed on to rule after becoming becalmed in the Maldives with his royal bride. The country, with one brief exception in 1953, was a sultanate for eight centuries before adopting a republican form of government in 1968.

The role of the Maldives in international affairs has thus far been a limited one, but in 1974 the Maldives and India issued a joint communiqué expressing "full support for the concept of the Indian Ocean as a zone of peace, free from great power rivalries, tensions and military escalations." To stay clear of big-power involvement, the Maldives declined, in 1977, a Soviet offer to move into the Gan Island air base—the site of an 8,700-foot runway—that the British had abandoned two years earlier. But in 1980 a new Maldivian regime signed a cultural agreement with the USSR. Whatever the Soviet's intentions, the Maldives government appeared bent on widening contacts with the outside world, as evidenced by its opening of diplomatic relations with Saudi Arabia in 1981. India and Japan aid the fishing industry through canneries and boat-bulding in the Maldives.

**HISTORY:** Sighted and described by Ibn Batuta in the 14th century, the Maldive Islands were occupied by the Portuguese from 1518 until the 17th century, when they came under the protection of the Dutch, then in control of Ceylon. The Maldives retained a similar status under the British, who expelled the Dutch from Ceylon during the occupation of the Netherlands by French Revolutionary forces

**1887:** British protection of the Maldives is formally recorded in an exchange of letters between the sultan and the governor of Ceylon

**1948:** After Ceylon achieves full independence, new agreement provides that British will control Maldivian foreign affairs but not interfere internally

**1953:** Sultanate is abolished and Maldives become a republic; efforts at reform by the new president arouse opposition from conservative elements; National Assembly votes to restore the sultanate

**1957:** An agreement allowing Britain to reactivate an air base on Gan Island stirs wide opposition

**1960:** Government makes "free gift" to Britain of Gan Island until 1986 in return for British help in quelling a rebellion in the three southernmost atolls

**1965:** Maldives achieve full independence

**1968:** Republican form of government is adopted; Ibrahim Nasir is elected president

**1975:** Premier Ahmed Zaki deposed for attempted coup and exiled in March. British withdraw from base on Gan

**1977:** USSR proposal to use the old air base is declined

**1978:** President Nasir goes nto exile under unclear circumstances. He is succeeded by Maumoon Abdul Gayoom

**1979:** About 20 officials of the Nasir government are tried and sentenced. The usual punishment is banishment to a remote island for three or four years

**1981:** Diplomatic ties with Saudi Arabia are established

---

## MALI

**Area:** 464,873 sq. mi. **Population:** 7,160,000 (1981 est.)

**Official Name:** Republic of Mali **Capital:** Bamako **Nationality:** Malian **Languages:** French is the official language and is the language of instruction in the nation's schools. The chief native languages are Bambara, Malinké, and Dyula **Religion:** About 90% Moslem, 9% animist, 1% Christian **Flag:** 3 vertical stripes of green, yellow, and red **Anthem:** National Anthem, beginning "At thy call, O Mali" **Currency:** Mali franc (611 per U.S. $1)

**Location:** West Africa. Landlocked Mali is bordered on the north by Algeria, on the east by Niger, on the south by Upper Volta, Ivory Coast, and Guinea, and on the west by Senegal and Mauritania **Features:** The country is mainly flat and dry, varying from the desolate Sahara in the north to pasture and croplands in the center and savanna scrub land in the south. The flatness of the landscape is broken in places by striking sandstone mountains and plateaus **Chief Rivers:** Niger, Senegal

**Head of State and of Government:** President: Gen. Moussa Traoré, born 1936; seized power in 1968, elected June 1979 **Effective Date of Present Constitution:** Approved by referendum June 2, 1974, effective June 1979 **Legislative Body:** National Assembly (unicameral) of 82 members, elected for 4-year terms **Local Government:** 7 regions, each headed by an appointed governor

**Ethnic Composition:** Of some 23 ethnic groups, about 50% are Mandé, 17% Peul (Fulani), 12% Voltaic, 6% Songhai, and 5% Tuareg and Moor **Population Distribution:** 17% urban **Density:** 15 inhabitants per sq. mi.

**Largest Cities:** (1976 census) Bamako 404,022, Ségou 64,890, Mopti 53,885, Sikasso 47,030, Kayes 44,736, Gao 30,714

**Per Capita Income:** $99 (1980) **Gross Domestic Product (GDP):** $657 million (1980) **Economic Statistics:** About 37% of GDP is from agriculture (millet, sorghum, rice, cotton), livestock-raising, and fishing; 16% is derived from industry (textiles, cement, fruit processing) **Minerals and Mining:** Unexploited deposits of bauxite, uranium, oil, copper, manganese, and iron. Phosphates, salt and a small amount of gold are mined **Labor Force:** 3,100,000 with about 80% engaged in agriculture and livestock-raising **Foreign Trade:** Exports, mainly cotton, livestock, peanuts, and fish, totaled $184 million in 1980. Imports, chiefly vehicles and parts, cotton cloth, iron and steel, and petroleum products, totaled $432 million **Principal Trade Partners:** France, West Germany, Ivory Coast, Senegal, Britain, China, USSR, United States

**Vital Statistics:** Birthrate, 49.1 per 1,000 of pop. (1980); death rate, 22.1 **Life Expectancy:** 42 years **Health Statistics:** 1,743 inhabitants per hospital bed; 24,094 per physician (1977) **Infant Mortality:** 120 per 1,000 births **Illiteracy:** 90% **Primary and Secondary School Enrollment:** 307,858 (1975) **Enrollment in Higher Education:** 2,936 **GNP Expended on Education:** 4.7% (1975)

**Transportation:** Paved roads total 1,050 mi. **Motor Vehicles:** 24,200 (1976) **Passenger Cars:** 15,000 **Railway Mileage:** 401 **Ports:** None **Major Airlines:** Air Mali operates both domestic and international services **Communications: Radio Transmitters:** 9 **Receivers:** 82,000 (1976) **Television:** None **Telephones:** 5,000 (19711) **Newspapers:** 2 dailies (1976), 0.5 copies per 1,000 inhabitants (1972)

**Weights and Measures:** Metric system **Travel Requirements:** Passport, visa valid 1 week, $8 fee, 2 photos

---

Once the center of a succession of mighty African empires, present-day Mali lives in the shadow of past glories. The old empires gained power and wealth from conquest and the caravan trade in slaves, gold, and salt. But with the decay of this trade and the imposition of French colonial rule, the country reverted to a meager agricultural and pastoral economy.

Now independent, modern Mali, while hoping for the discovery of oil or other minerals, struggles to improve a limited production of cotton, livestock, and food crops.

Mali's most famous city—the fabled Timbuktu—is a symbol of lost prosperity and also of the efforts to regain some of that prosperity. This golden city of the 14th-century Songhai empire, built at the edge of the Sahara on the bend of the Niger, is today a dusty town of 20,000 inhabitants. Malian officials have discovered that the old lure of Timbuktu has lost none of its appeal for tourists.

The majority of Malians, on the other hand, are more concerned with regaining a healthy economy and restoration of traditional freedom of enterprise.

Under former President Modibo Keita, Mali was set "irreversibly" on a path of socialism mainly of the Maoist variety. Large numbers of Communist Chinese were brought in to manage the economy, state enterprises were created and a program of farm collectivization started.

Keita acquired all power and even began wearing Mao tunics in place of the traditional boubou. The people were increasingly terrorized by the president's private militia, which also became a threat to the regular army.

Under the new government, the Military Committee of National Liberation, headed by Lt. Moussa Traoré, farm collectivization was abolished and a start made, with French help, on converting state enterprises into mixed-economy enterprises. While ties were retained with China and Russia the government adopted incentives for private foreign investment.

The ending of farm collectives has brought a marked increase in crop production, and in Bamako and other cities, private business and availability of goods have increased substantially. An American company is exploring for oil and a West German company for uranium. Financial aid has come also from France, the United States, and West Germany, as well as from the Soviet Union and East European countries.

Ten years of military government ended in June 1979 with elections under the new constitution. President Traoré, the only presidential candidate, retained the office for another five years. All 82 elected members of the National Assembly belonged to the only political party, the Democratic Union of the Malian People.

**HISTORY:** Modern Mali was a major part of past Sudanic empires—Ghana, Malinké (Mali), and Songhai—that flourished from the 8th through the 16th century. Ancient Mali reached its zenith about 1325 with the conquest of Gao and Timbuktu, the fabulous Saharan center of trade and learning. Following destruction of the Songhai empire by Moroccan invaders, the country came under the shifting rule of local chieftains. Two of these, Al-Haji Umar, a Tukulor, and Samory Touré, the Mandingo warrior hero and slave trader, waged fierce resistance against the incursions of French forces during the 19th century. With the defeat of Samory in 1898, French control was effectively extended over the country, which became known as French Sudan

**1946:** Sudanese Territorial Assembly is established with limited internal authority

**1957:** Territorial Assembly is given increased powers

**1958:** Sudan votes in constitutional referendum to become autonomous republic within the French Community

**1959:** Sudan and Senegal form union as the Federation of Mali

**1960:** Federation collapses as result of political and economic differences; Sudan proclaims itself the independent Republic of Mali with Modibo Keita as president

**1968:** Army officers overthrow Keita government in bloodless coup; set up military junta with Lt. Moussa Traoré as president

**1969-74:** Severe drought and famine take heavy toll in human life and livestock; refugees flock to the cities

**1974:** Referrendum approves the new constitution calling for elections of president and National Assembly by universal suffrage

**1978:** Malian defense minister, foreign minister and two others are accused of treason. They are convicted in 1979

**1979:** Traoré, the only candidate, is reelected to presidency in June; civilians outnumber military in new government

**1980:** Student violence, strikes, drought and bad management of public enterprises disrupt Mali's economy and political stability

**1981:** U.S. Agency for International Development reports that $13 million in aid to Mali had been spent on an unsuccessful livestock project. Three persons are sentenced to death for attempted coup in 1980. Mali is readmitted to West African Monetary Union

---

## MALTA

**Area:** 122 sq. mi. **Population:** 366,000 (1981 est.)

**Official Name:** Republic of Malta **Capital:** Valletta **Nationality:** Maltese **Languages:** Maltese, a Semitic tongue, and English are the official languages. Maltese is the principal spoken language but Italian is also widely spoken **Religion:** Roman Catholicism is the official religion and about 98% of the population is Catholic **Flag:** Two vertical stripes of white and red with a George Cross edged in red in the upper left corner **Anthem:** To This Sweet Land **Currency:** Maltese pound (0.40 per U.S. $1)

**Location:** Mediterranean Sea, about 58 miles south of Sicily and 180 miles from the coast of North Africa. Malta is comprised of 2 main islands, Malta and Gozo, and several smaller ones **Features:** The country consists of a series of low hills, with terraced fields on the slopes **Chief Rivers:** The country has no rivers

**Head of State:** President Agatha Barabara, born 1922, elected February 1982 **Head of Government:** Prime Minister Dominic Mintoff, born 1916, appointed June 1971 **Effective Date of Present Constitution:** 1964, revised 1974 **Legislative Body:** House of Representatives (unicameral), consisting of 65 members elected for 5-year terms **Local Government:** There is no formally organized local government

**Ethnic Composition:** Chiefly of Carthaginian and Phoenician stock, later mixed with Arabs, Italians, and British **Population Distribution:** 94% urban **Density:** 3,000 inhabitants per sq. mi.

**Largest Cities:** (1979 est.) Sliema 20,095, Valletta 14,042

**Per Capita Income:** $2,786 (1980) **Gross National Product (GNP):** $981 million (1980) **Economic Statistics:** Tourism, ship repair and light manufacturing are the bases of the economy **Minerals and Mining:** There are no mineral resources except for salt and stone **Labor Force:** 119,554 (1977) of which 26% is employed in industry, 6% in agriculture and fishing, and most of the rest in trade and services **Foreign Trade:** Exports, chiefly textiles, potatoes, flowers and seed, totaled $425 million in 1979. Imports, mainly machinery, chemicals, meat, mineral fuels and lubricants, and motor vehicles, totaled $759 million **Principal Trade Partners:** Britain, EC countries, Libya

**Vital Statistics:** Birthrate, 15.4 per 1,000 of pop. (1980); death rate, 9.1 **Life Expectancy:** 71 years **Health Statistics:** 96 inhabitants per hospital bed; 864 per physician (1975) **Infant Mortality:** 15.5 per 1,000 births **Illiteracy:** 17% **Primary and Secondary School Enrollment:** 61,148 (1976) **Enrollment in Higher Education:** 2,158 **GNP Expended on Education:** 4% (1976)

**Transportation:** Surfaced roads total 760 mi. **Motor Vehicles:** 73,200 (1977) **Passenger Cars:** 60,700 **Railway Mileage:** None **Ports:** Valletta **Major Airlines:** Air Malta operates flights to Europe and Africa **Communications: Radio Transmitters:** 3 **Licenses:** 63,000 (1976) **Television Transmitters:** 1 **Licenses:** 63,000 (1976) **Telephones:** 73,000 (1978) **Newspapers:** 5 dailies (1977)

**Weights and Measures:** Metric and English standards are used **Travel Requirements:** Passport, visa for stay exceeding 3 months

---

Over the centuries, the islands of Malta have been occupied by powers that sought control of the Mediterranean. And while under such occupations, the strategically placed islands have suffered much from attackers: in 1565, held by the Knights Hospitalers, a Turkish siege was defied; in World War II, Malta, as the "unsinkable aircraft carrier," withstood merciless Axis aerial bombardment, earning Britain's George Cross for heroism.

Independent from Britain since 1964, a republic since 1974, Malta has asserted some control over its own destiny. In 1971, Dominic Mintoff returned to power as Labor party prime minister following the defeat of the coalition of Giorgio Borg Olivier, the pro-Catholic prime minister. Mintoff took a neutral position between the Soviet and Western blocs. He forced Britain to renegotiate its lease on Maltese military facilities providing for increased rent to be paid to Malta and fixed an expiration date of April 1, 1979. Britain withdrew on schedule, and Malta was free of foreign soldiers for the first time in centuries.

Mintoff promoted light industry, notably textiles and plastics, and cultivated relations with the Arab states. Libya especially has been a good customer for the new industries—and a good provider of foreign aid. Malta's dispute with Libya over offshore oil rights was referred in 1982 to the World Court for settlement.

**HISTORY:** The strategic importance of Malta was recognized as far back as the time of the Phoenicians, whose occupation of the island was followed by invasions by the Greeks, Carthaginians, Romans, Byzantines, and Arabs. Malta was seized by the Normans in 1091. In 1530 it was given by Holy Roman Emperor Charles V to the Knights Hospitalers, who became known as the Knights of Malta and who in 1565 successfully withstood a siege by the Turks. The Knights continued to hold the island until 1798, when it was surrendered to Napoleon

**1800:** The French are ousted from the island by Britain, with the aid of a revolt by the Maltese
**1814:** Treaty of Paris confirms British possession
**1921:** Malta is granted limited self-government
**1939-45:** Malta sustains heavy bombing by Germans and Italians during World War II; entire population is awarded the George Cross in 1942
**1964:** Malta becomes independent
**1969:** Last British warships leave Malta
**1972:** Malta signs new financial and defense agreements with Britain and NATO, replacing the 1964 agreements
**1974:** Malta becomes a republic. Sir Anthony Mamo sworn in as first president
**1976:** Dr. Anton Buttigieg is elected president
**1977:** China promises continued economic and technical aid
**1979:** British lease of military bases ends; last British soldiers leave
**1980:** Giorgio Borg Olivier, former prime minister (1966-71), dies
**1982:** Agatha Barabara is elected Malta's first woman president

---

## MAURITANIA

**Area:** 397,954 sq. mi. **Population:** 1,544,000 (1978 est.)

**Official Name:** Islamic Republic of Mauritania **Capital:** Nouakchott **Nationality:** Mauritanian **Languages:** Arabic is the language most spoken, and with French is the official one; Wolof and Tukolor are also spoken in the South **Religion:** The population is almost entirely Moslem, and Islam is the state religion **Flag:** A gold star and crescent centered on a green field **Anthem:** National Anthem (no words) **Currency:** Ouguiya (50.9 per U.S. $1)

**Location:** West Africa. Mauritania is bordered on the north by Morocco, Algeria and the contested Western Sahara area, on the east and southeast by Mali, on the southwest by Senegal, and on the west by the Atlantic Ocean **Features:** The country on the whole is fairly flat. The Sahara zone in the north consists of shifting dunes and gravel plains, while the south is more fertile and suitable for cultivation **Chief River:** Senegal

**Head of State and of Government:** President: Lt. Col. Mohamed Khouna Ould Haidalla, born 1940, assumed presidency on Jan. 4, 1980. He is chairman of the Military Committee for National Salvation. The MCNS is assisted by a prime minister, Col. Maaouya Ould Sidi Ahmed Taya, appointed 1981 **Effective Date of Present Constitution:** 1961, suspended 1978. A new constitution has been prepared and is to be submitted to popular vote **Legislative Body:** Mauritania is now governed by a Military Committee for National Salvation **Local Government:** 12 regions and one district (Nouakchott)

**Ethnic Composition:** Divided into three groups: 40% Arab-Berber-Negroid, 30% Arab-Berber (Moors), 30% Negroid **Population Distribution:** 23% urban, **Density:** 3.9 inhabitants per sq. mi.

**Largest Cities:** (1976 census) Nouakchott 134,986, Nouadhibou 21,961, Kaédi 20,848, Zouérate 17,474, Rosso 16,466

**Per Capita Income:** $308 (1980) **Gross Domestic Product (GDP):** $462 million (1980) **Economic Statistics:** About 22% of the GDP is derived from agriculture (livestock, millet, corn, rice, sweet potatoes, peanuts, beans, gum arabic); 21% from industry, mining, and fish processing **Minerals and Mining:** Mauritania is second only to Liberia in West African iron-ore production. There are large deposits of gypsum **Labor Force:** 420,00 (1975), of which 90% is in agriculture **Foreign Trade:** Exports, chiefly iron ore, livestock, fish, dates, and gum arabic, totaled $238 million in 1980. Imports, mainly machinery, vehicles, electrical equipment, petroleum products, cement, tires, and tea, totaled $324 million **Principal Trade Partners:** France, Italy, Britain, West Germany, Senegal, Japan, Spain, United States

**Vital Statistics:** Birthrate, 50.2 per 1,000 of pop. (1980); death rate, 22.3 **Life Expectancy:** 42 years **Health Statistics:** 2,328 inhabitants per hospital bed; 15,172 per physician (1975) **Infant Mortality:** 187 per 1,000 births **Illiteracy:** 83% **Primary and Secondary School Enrollment:** 83,029 (1977) **Enrollment in Higher Education:** c. 1,000 study abroad **GNP Expended on Education:** 4.3% (1972)

**Transportation:** Paved roads total 370 mi. **Motor Vehicles:** 11,800 (1974) **Passenger Cars:** 4,400 (1972) **Railway Mileage:** 450 **Ports:** Nouadhibou, Nouakchott **Major Airlines:** Air-Mauritanie operates domestic and international services **Communications: Radio Transmitters:** 5 **Receivers:** 95,000 (1976) **Television Transmitters:** 1 **Telephones:** 1,300 est. (1969) **Newspapers:** 1 daily, 0.2 per 1,000 inhabitants (1972)

**Weights and Measures:** Metric system **Travel Requirements:** Passport, visa valid for 3 months, $10 fee, 3 photos

---

Mauritania is a borderland between Moorish/Arab North Africa and black West Africa. Although cast in the mold of a modern state and with membership in the Organization of African Unity, the former West African territory continues to be divided by racial distinctions dating from the medieval migrations of light-skinned Arabs and Berbers, who forced the darker-skinned natives into the southern region and enslaved many of them. French rule, established by 1920, favored the blacks, who were more inclined than the Arabs to take advantage of European education.

President Moktar Ould Daddah, the country's leader from 1960 to 1978, steered an enlightened and adroit course racially and politically. While promoting more education for the Moorish/Arab majority, President Moktar sought to gain foreign aid from both Western and Eastern sources. In July 1978 the president was overthrown in a bloodless coup led by military officers. Col. Mustapha Ould Salek was named president. In June 1979 Salek resigned and was succeeded by Col. Ahmed Louly. Louly, in turn, was replaced by Lt. Col. Haidalla in 1980.

Although France continues to provide most of the country's aid and development funds, Communist China recently has played a major role in such projects as rice-growing, irrigation, and cement manufacture and in drilling numerous wells to tap ground water.

Mauritania's main source of wealth has been rich deposits of iron ore, which have been developed since independence by French interests. These have provided substantial earnings that have made it possible for the government to embark on the improvement of social services and of agriculture, on which more than 80 percent of Mauritanians depend.

Meanwhile, in addition to French and Chinese aid, Mauritanian development is being aided by countries such as the United States, Yugoslavia, and Spain.

Mauritanian gains in territory from the southern part of former Spanish Sahara were offset by the disruption to the nation's economy caused by raids of the *Polisario Front*, a Saharan liberation guerrilla group based in Algeria. But, after the seizure of power by the army in 1978, the *Polisario* proclaimed a unilateral cease-fire. The military government informally decided to respect the truce, and fighting fell to a sporadic level. On August 5, 1979, Mauritania signed a peace agreement with the *Polisario* under which it renounced all claim to its portion of the contested Western Sahara area. Morocco promptly occupied the region. Mauritania then resumed diplomatic relations with Algeria, ending a three-year break.

**HISTORY:** Mauritania's original inhabitants, a Sudanic black people, were enslaved or driven southward by the 11th-century Berber invasion that destroyed the empire of Ghana to the east. The Berbers in turn were conquered in the 16th century by Arab invaders, the Beni Hassan. Trade with Europeans, opened by the Portuguese in the 15th century, attracted the Dutch, English, and French. Throughout the 19th century, the French gradually extended control over the country, and established a protectorate in 1903. Mauritania was made a French colony in 1920

**1946-56:** Internal self-rule gradually increases along with Mauritanian representation in French parliament and Assembly of the French Union

**1958:** In referendum, Mauritania votes to become autonomous republic within new French Community

**1960:** Mauritania wins full independence, with Moktar Ould Daddah continuing as prime minister

**1961:** With adoption of presidential system, Daddah, the only candidate, is elected president; new People's party becomes the sole political organization

**1963-66:** Completion of iron-ore mining project by French-led consortium and development of extensive copper deposits give strong boost to nation's economy

**1973-74:** Drought causes widespread famine

**1975:** Agreement is signed among Spain, Morocco and Mauritania providing for withdrawal of the Spanish presence from Western Sahara. Daddah is reelected president

**1976:** Morocco and Mauritania partition Western Sahara, giving Mauritania the southern third. The proclamation of an independent republic by the *Polisario Front*, the Saharan liberation movement, is ignored. *Polisario* guerrillas raid Nouakchott

**1977:** *Polisario* units raid iron-mining center at Zouérate

**1978:** Group of Western and Arab banks lends Mauritania $360 million for exploitation of iron ore mines. President Moktar Ould Daddah is overthrown in a bloodless coup by military officers, led by Col. Mustapha Ould Salek, who becomes president. *Polisario* proclaims cease-fire

**1979:** Premier Ahmed Oul Boucif and 10 other Mauritanian delegates to the Economic Community of West African States die in air crash. He is succeeded by Lt. Col. Mohamed Khouna Ould Haidalla. President Salek resigns. Lt. Col. Mohamed Mahmoud Ould Ahmed Louly is chosen by the MCNS to replace him

**1980:** President Louly resigns; Prime Minister Haidalla becomes president

**1981:** Attempted military coup, backed by Morocco, fails as rebel leaders are killed or captured by government soldiers

## MAURITIUS

**Area:** 790 sq. mi. **Population:** 971,000 (1981 est.)

**Official Name:** Mauritius **Capital:** Port Louis **Nationality:** Mauritian **Languages:** English is the official language, but a Creole patois, basically French, is spoken by 52% of the people; Chinese, Hindi, Urdu, and French are also spoken **Religion:** About 51% Hindu, 33% Christian (chiefly Roman Catholic), and 16% Moslem **Flag:** Four horizontal stripes of red, blue, yellow, and green **Anthem:** Motherland **Currency:** Mauritian rupee (10.7 per U.S. $1)

**Location:** Indian Ocean. Mauritius (20°S.,57°30'E.) lies about 500 miles east of Madagascar. Dependencies include Rodrigues and distant smaller islands **Features:** The island is volcanic in origin and almost entirely surrounded by coral reefs. The land rises to a central plateau, surrounded by mountains believed to be the rim of an ancient volcano **Chief Rivers:** Grand, Rempart, Poste

**Head of State:** Queen Elizabeth II, represented by a governor-generaal, Sir Dayendranath Burrenchobay, born 1919, took office 1978 **Head of Government:** Prime Minister Aneerood Jugnauth, appointed June 1982 **Effective Date of Present Constitution:** 1968 **Legislative Body:** Parliament (unicameral Legislative Assembly), 70 members with 5-year terms, 62 of whom are elected **Local Government:** 9 administrative districts, with local councils

**Ethnic Composiition:** Indo-Mauritians (67%), Creoles (28%), Sino-Mauritians (3%), and Franco-Mauritians (2%) **Population Distribution:** 43% urban **Density:** 1,229 inhabitants per sq. mi.

**Largest Cities:** (1978 est.) Port Louis 142,853; (1975 est.) Beau Bassin/Rose Hill 81,353, Curepipe 53,068, Quatre Bornes 52,134

**Per Capita Income:** $904 (1980) **Gross National Product (GNP):** $859 million (1980) **Economic Statistics:** 22% of the GNP comes from agriculture (sugar, tea, ginger, tobacco, vegetables, bananas, peanuts) and 17% from industry (sugar processing, rum, beer) and construction **Minerals and Mining:** There are no known mineral deposits **Labor Force:** 175,000, with 50% in agriculture and 6% in industry **Foreign Trade:** Exports, sugar and sugar products, tea, clothing, and molasses, totaled $474 million in 1980. Imports, chiefly foodstuffs, manufactured goods, machinery and transportation equipment, fuel, chemicals and fertilizers, totaled $622 million **Principal Trade Partners:** Britain, France, South Africa, Japan, Bahrain, United States, West Germany, Belgium

**Vital Statistics:** Birthrate, 26.9 per 1,000 of pop. (1980); death rate, 7.2 **Life Expectancy:** 67 years **Health Statistics:** 273 inhabitants per hospital bed; 2,340 per physician (1977) **Infant Mortality:** 32.9 per 1,000 births **Illiteracy:** 39% **Primary and Secondary School Enrollment:** 208,272 (1976) **Enrollment in Higher Education:** 1,096 (1975) **GNP Expended on Education:** 4.5% (1976)

**Transportation:** Paved roads total 1,020 mi. **Motor Vehicles:** 39,600 (1978) **Passenger Cars:** 25,400 **Railway Mileage:** None **Ports:** Port Louis **Major Airlines:** Air Mauritius provides international service **Communications: Radio Transmitters:** 3 **Licenses:** 200,000 (1976) **Television Transmitters:** 4 **Licenses:** 41,000 (1976) **Telephones:** 32,000 (1978) **Newspapers:** 10 dailies, 94 copies per 1,000 inhabitants (1977)

**Weights and Measures:** Metric system **Travel Requirements:** Passport, visa, no charge except postage

Encircled by coral reefs and the blue-green Indian Ocean, Mauritius looks like the perfect model of a placid tropical island. The former British crown colony, lying nearly 1,500 miles east of southern Africa—its closest proximity to any continent—is renowned as the source of rare postage stamps and as the last refuge of the extinct dodo bird.

The remote volcanic island is also a microcosm of the present-day problems of less-developed countries: overpopulation, racial conflict, and dependence on a single crop, sugar. With no solutions in sight, it seems only a matter of time before the combined pressures of these problems bring an eruption. Indeed, a ban on 12 unions was imposed by the government in 1971 and only lifted in 1974, following lengthy negotiations between dockworkers and government officials.

Within the island's 790 square miles, there are, in addition to a large Indian-Hindu majority, major groups of Africans, Europeans (mainly French), and Creoles (an Afro-French mixture), and a small element of Chinese. Violent racial rioting and also labor unrest accompanied Mauritius' independence in 1968. Despite efforts of the coalition government of former Prime Minister Sir Seewoosagur Ramgoolam to promote harmony, rivalries have remained intense.

Since elimination of malaria recently, the island's population is growing by 1.5 percent a year and birth control is opposed equally by Hindu, Catholic, and Moslem groups.

MEXICO
CONIC PROJECTION
SCALE OF MILES
SCALE OF KILOMETERS
National Capitals ..... State Capitals .....
© Copyright HAMMOND INCORPORATED, Maplewood, N. J.
States Indicated by Numbers:
1 Tlaxcala 6 Querétaro
2 Morelos 7 Guanajuato
3 Distrito Federal 8 Aguascalientes
4 México 9 Nayarit
5 Hidalgo 10 Colima
Longitude West 102° of Greenwich
GULF OF MEXICO
PACIFIC OCEAN
UNITED STATES
MEXICO CITY
Guadalajara
Monterrey
Veracruz Llave
Tampico
Mérida
Bay of Campeche
Campeche Bank
Tropic of Cancer
Gulf of Tehuantepec
GUATEMALA
BELIZE
HONDURAS

Some 90 percent of cultivated land is planted with sugarcane, but production is often drastically reduced by cyclones. It has been a rule of thumb on Mauritius that one ton sugar exports is needed for each inhabitant. Production has not kept pace as the population approaches one million. Faced with depressed sugar prices, Mauritius has merged some of the largest estates to raise cattle for beef and milk.

In 1982 the Labour party, which had ruled Mauritius ever since it had become independent, was swept out of office in elections. The Mauritius Militant Movement and its smaller ally, the Social Democratic party, won all but two of the elective seats in Parliament. Paul Bérenger, 37-year-old driving force in the MMM, promised a program of "socialism with a Mauritian face." The movement was pledged to taking Mauritius out of the Commonwealth of Nations, to nonalignment, and to obtaining sovereignty over the distant British island of Diego Garcia in the Indian Ocean where the United States maintains a military base.

**HISTORY:** Originally uninhabited, Mauritius was first settled and named by the Dutch in the 17th century. The island was abandoned early in the 18th century, after which it was claimed by the French, who renamed it Ile-de-France and laid the foundations of a slave-owning plantation economy based on sugar. In 1814, the island was ceded to Britain and reverted to its original name. Slavery was abolished in 1834, and the planters began importing indentured Indians. Although they soon came to form a majority, the Indians long remained politically powerless because of a restricted franchise based on property qualifications

**1948:** Franchise is broadened by new constitution; in new elections, Indians win majority in legislative council, overthrowing dominance of Franco-Mauritians but causing other minority groups to fear Indian domination

**1961:** Constitutional conference in London paves way toward full self-government, but talks are marred by disputes between Hindu-dominated majority Labour party and minority parties

**1967:** Mauritius becomes self-governing; Labour party leader Seewoosagur Ramgoolam is appointed prime minister; island is wracked by racial and labor unrest

**1968:** Mauritius wins independence amid Creole-Moslem rioting

**1970:** Government begins drafting plans for crop diversification, light industry, and tourism

**1975:** Cyclone Gervaise leaves 90,000 homeless and destroys 30 percent of sugar harvest

**1979:** General strike in support of sugar workers paralyzes economy. Cyclone Claudette makes 4,000 homeless

**1981:** Britain proposes to set up a $7.25 million trust fund for Diego Garcia islanders if Mauritius will provide land for their resettlement

**1982:** Socialist coalition overwhelms Labour party in national elections. Aneerood Jugnauth is appointed prime minister

## MEXICO

**Area:** 761,600 sq. mi. **Population:** 67,395,826 (1980 census)

**Official Name:** United Mexican States **Capital:** Mexico City **Nationality:** Mexican **Languages:** Spanish is the official and predominant language; 7% speak only Indian dialects **Religion:** 97% Roman Catholic; there are some 600,000 Protestants and 100,000 Jews **Flag:** Green, white, and red vertical stripes with the national emblem in the center **Anthem:** National Anthem, beginning "Mexicans, to the call of war" **Currency:** Mexican peso (115 per U.S. $1)

**Location:** North America. Mexico is bordered on the north by the United States, on the east by the Gulf of Mexico, on the south by Belize and Guatemala, and on the west by the Pacific Ocean **Features:** The country consists of a large central plateau, flanked by the eastern and western coastal ranges of the Sierra Madre. From a low desert plain in the north, the plateau rises to 8,000 feet near Mexico City **Chief Rivers:** Rio Bravo (Rio Grande), Lerma, Santiago, Usumacinta, Grijalva, Balsas, Pánuco

**Head of State and of Government:** President Miguel de la Madrid Hurtado, took office Dec. 1, 1982 **Effective Date of Present Constitution:** 1917 **Legislative Body:** Congress (bicameral), consisting of the Senate and the Chamber of Deputies. The Senate is composed of 64 members elected for 6-year terms. The Chamber of Deputies has 400 members elected for 3 years **Local Government:** 31 states, 1 federal district. Each state has its own governor and popularly elected legislature

**Ethnic Composition:** About 60% of the population are mestizos of mixed Indian and Spanish descent. 30% are pure Indian, while 9% are of Spanish or other European ancestry **Population Distribution:** 65% urban **Density:** 88 inhabitants per sq. mi.

**Largest Cities:** (1978 est.) Mexico City (Metropolitan Area)13,993,866, Guadalajara 1,813,131, Monterrey 1,054,029, Puebla 677,959, Ciudad Juárez 597,096, León 589,950, Tijuana 534,993, Acapulco 421,088, Chihuahua 369,545, Mexicali 338,423

**Per Capita Income:** $2,045 (1980) **Gross National Product (GNP):** $138 billion (1980) **Economic Statistics:** In 1977 about 12% of GNP came from agriculture (farming, livestock), forestry, and fishing, 37% from industry (cars, machinery, construction, petrochemicals, steel, cement) and mining (including oil) **Minerals and Mining:** Mexico is the world's largest producer of silver and a major producer of oil, gas, gold, sulfur, lead, and zinc. Coal, tin, antimony, mercury, copper, and iron are also mined **Labor Force:** 20 million (1980), 42% in agriculture and 18% in industry **Foreign Trade:** Exports, chiefly petroleum, gas, cotton, sugar, fruits, vegetables, coffee, sulfur, and shrimp, totaled $15.3 billion in 1980. Imports, mainly industrial machinery, motor vehicles and parts, chemicals, communications and transportation equipment, and electric power equipment, totaled $18.5 billion **Principal Trade Partners:** United States, West Germany, Britain, Japan, France, Spain, Canada

**Vital Statistics:** Birthrate, 41.7 per 1,000 of pop. (1980); death rate, 6 **Life Expectancy:** 65 years **Health Statistics:** 863 inhabitants per hospital bed; 1,385 per physician (1972) **Infant Mortality:** 44.1 per 1,000 births **Illiteracy:** 17% **Primary and Secondary School Enrollment:** 15,389,642 (1976) **Enrollment in Higher Education:** 539,372 (1976) **GNP Expended on Education:** 4.3% (1976)

**Transportation:** Paved roads total 42,727 mi. **Motor Vehicles:** 4,157,600 (1978) **Passenger Cars:** 3,021,100 **Railway Mileage:** 15,600 **Ports:** Veracruz, Tampico, Coatzacoalcos, Guaymas, Salina Cruz, Mazatián, Manzanillo **Major Airlines:** Aeroméxico, the government-owned line and Mexicana, a privately owned line, operate both international and domestic flights **Communications: Radio Transmitters:** 846 **Receivers:** 17,514,000 (1974) **Television Transmitters:** 150 **Receivers:** 4,885,000 **Telephones:** 4,140,000 (1978) **Newspapers:** 352 dailies (1977), 116 copies per 1,000 inhabitants (1975)

**Weights and Measures:** Metric system **Travel Requirements:** Tourist card, valid for stay up to 6 months; no charge **Direct Dialing Code:** Mexico City 905; Northwest Mexico 903

Mexico experienced the world's first social and political revolution of the 20th century, but to this day it still suffers seriously from economic underdevelopment. The bloody struggle that began in 1910 and cost over a million lives gave Mexico stable institutions and a strong constitution, yet most of the revolution's high-sounding principles have yet to be implemented. Glittering long-term hopes for economic advancement were raised, however, with major oil discoveries in 1972 and afterward.

Today this third-largest of Latin American republics, and the most populous Spanish-speaking country in the world, enjoys a large measure of political solidity, under a system of government that falls somewhere between dictatorship and democracy. But the benefits of an economic "miracle" have reached only a small part of Mexico's 67 million inhabitants, and the country's large peasant population is only marginally better off now than in 1910. The unemployed and underemployed exceed 50 percent of the work force. This extremely high rate has swelled the number of Mexicans crossing the border to the U.S. illegally to seek work.

In politics, as in other fields, the contrasts between theory and practice in Mexico are vast. Under the republican form of government, contending parties are permitted, and six of them participated in the 1979 elections. In reality, however, Mexican politics is dominated by one amorphous party—the Revolutionary Institutional party (PRI)—which has provided every president since its creation in 1929.

During his six-year term, the president is an immensely powerful figure, but it is the party that reflects a wide spectrum of national opinion and eventually dictates the limits within which he can move. All significant support for and opposition to a president's policies come from within the ruling party. However, because the constitution forbids immediate reelection for members of the Senate and Chamber of Deputies, many talented politicians are attracted to the bureaucracy instead. Congress traditionally has been regarded as little more than a rubber stamp that ratifies executive decisions.

Although the PRI is technically structured around the three pillars of the peasant, worker, and popular movements, business interests have gained increasing control over the party and government in the past 20 years, giving weight to the saying that "in Mexico business is government and government is business." The economic boom that gave political strength to the business sector also spawned a host of conservative politicians.

The Roman Catholic Church has carried little political weight in Mexico, unlike most Latin American countries, since the revolution, although most people are nominally Catholic and there was a tremendous outburst of enthusiasm when Pope John Paul II visited the country in 1979. The constitution defends religious freedom, and in practice there is considerable tolerance of different creeds.

Mexico's economy, which had been growing at a remarkable average of 6.5 percent annually for the past 20 years, reversed that trend beginning in 1973 with an accelerating inflation rate. In an effort to stimulate exports, investments, and job creation, the government devalued the peso in 1976 for the first time in 22 years. Despite further devaluations in early 1982, the economy continued to grow thanks to oil export revenue. However, in August a decline in oil prices and production, and reduced demand for other Mexican products brought on a financial crisis involving Mexico's huge foreign debt.

Despite a fundamental agrarian reform following the revolution, which gave most peasants their own small plots of land and established a system of farm cooperatives, the shortage of irrigation, credit, and marketing facilities has kept most peasants living at subsistence level.

Mexico's considerable social and economic problems are made more acute by the country's population growth rate, presently close to 3 percent per year. Improved health facilities have brought down the death rate dramatically since World War II, but successive governments have strongly opposed an official family planning program.

In foreign policy, Mexico has long followed a policy of nonintervention, which led it to maintain diplomatic relations with Cuba when all other members of the Organization of American States broke their ties in 1964.

Because of proximity and close economic ties, the United States has considerable influence in Mexican politics. This reality sometimes leads Mexico to take strongly nationalist stands, although differences between the countries are usually settled amicably.

Mexico has been in the oil business since the beginning of the century when foreign companies began to produce "black gold" there. By 1918 Mexico was second only to the United States in output. After the government nationalized the petroleum industry in 1938, production declined, then recovered slowly. In 1972, before new discoveries of oil in the Reforma area of Chiapas and Tabasco, Mexico's known petroleum reserves were put at 2.5 billion barrels. Since then, with new findings of oil and natural gas in the Gulf and Pacific coastal regions and offshore in the Gulf of Campeche, proven reserves have grown by leaps and bounds. In 1981 they were put at nearly 72 billion barrels. Moreover, potential reserves were estimated to exceed those of Saudi Arabia.

By reason of its oil wealth and large labor pool, Mexico was being acclaimed by economists at the outset of the 1980s as one of a handful of less-developed countries likely to gain rapidly in economic power and worldwide political influence. Whether or not the Mexican foreign debt crisis of August 1982 will change this prediction remains to be seen.

**HISTORY:** Before the Spanish conquest of Mexico in 1519, Indian civilizations had flourished there for centuries, with that of the Mayas dating as far back as about 1500 B.C. With the conquest of the Aztecs by Hernán Cortéz, Indian culture was modified and the Indians themselves reduced to peonage on the land and in the mines. Corruption in the Spanish administration helped fan growing discontent among the Creoles, Mexican-born descendants of the Spaniards, leaving the country ripe for the revolutionary ideals spread by the French Revolution

**1810:** Miguel Hidalgo y Costilla, a Creole priest, begins the fight for independence; armies spring up under various leaders

**1821:** Mexico is granted independence; anarchy, corruption, and political rivalry are rife

**1836:** Texas, under domination of U.S. settlers, secedes from Mexico and declares its independence

**1846-48:** Annexation of Texas by the United States in 1845 brings on Mexican War; Mexico, defeated, signs Treaty of Guadalupe Hidalgo ceding vast block of territory to the United States

**1857-61:** Benito Juárez, reform-minded minister of justice and later president, introduces liberal constitution transferring power from Creoles to mestizos and secularizing church lands; conservative opposition leads to War of the Reform (1858-61), which ends in victory for liberals

**1864-67:** France establishes puppet empire under Austrian-born Emperor Maximilian; Juárez leads popular resistance; empire collapses

**1876-1909:** Porfirio Díaz leads successful revolt and establishes ruthless dictatorship; he reforms Mexico's finances, but despite nation's growing prosperity vast numbers of people are reduced to virtual slavery when their communal lands are apportioned to large estate owners; almost three-quarters of Mexico's mineral resources become by purchase the property of foreign interests

**1910-17:** Francisco I. Madero organizes rebellion and forces Díaz to resign; Mexico is thrown into ferment of revolt culminating in rise of leaders such as Venustiano Carranza, Francisco (Pancho) Villa, and Emiliano Zapata. Villa breaks with Carranza, who has U.S. support, and Villa's irregulars raid New Mexico (1916); U.S. Gen. John J. Pershing leads punitive expedition into Mexico in pursuit of Villa. Carranza frames liberal constitution of 1917 nationalizing mineral resources and restoring lands to Indians

**1934-40:** President Lázaro Cárdenas undertakes extensive land reform and expropriates foreign-owned companies

**1968:** Army and police clash with students protesting alleged government repression and violation of constitutional rights

**1970:** Luis Echeverría Alvarez is elected president

**1973:** Mexican terrorists kidnap diplomatically and politically prominent people and ransom them for the release of political prisoners and for money to support their cause

**1974:** Mexico signs agreement for commercial co-operation with European Community, the first Latin American nation to do so

**1976:** José López Portillo is elected president

**1977:** U.S. and Mexico sign first formal trade agreement since 1942

**1978:** Government continues campaign of spraying marijuana fields with toxic chemical known as "paraquat"

**1979::** On June 3, a flaming gusher erupts at offshore Ixtoc I well, creating oil slick in Gulf of Mexico which fouls fishing grounds and beaches as far north as Texas. Agreement is reached to sell natural gas to U.S. at price above U.S. domestic price

**1980:** Government introduces a 10% value added tax (VAT) to increase revenues. Mexican ban on fishing within 200 miles of coast by American boats leads to "tuna war." López Portillo visits France, West Germany, Sweden and Canada to negotiate oil deals, joint investments in Mexican enterprises and exchange of scientific and technical knowledge. Natural gas begins to flow into U.S. at an initial rate of 300,000 cu. ft. per day. Ixtoc I well is at last fully capped after worst spill in history. Mexico and Venezuela reach accord on plan to meet oil needs of Caribbean and Central American countries. Severe drought forces Mexico to import 9 million metric tons of food

**1981:** Mexico moves to modernize its armed forces, especially in the air, in a bid to strengthen its power in the Caribbean basin. Although disapproving of repression, López Portillo backs Sandinist regime in Nicaragua and stays neutral toward government in Guatemala; however, he criticizes U.S. support for El Salvador's civilian-military junta. Significant quantities of natural gas are struck in the Gulf of California. A reduction in Mexico's price for oil in the face of a world oversupply, provokes a political storm which leads to resignation of the head of Petróleos Mexicanos. Investment in Mexico by foreign companies, attracted by oil boom, increases. López Portillo calls for an end to gift-taking, bribery, embezzlement and other corrupt practices of some public officials. Country's proven oil reserves reach 72 billion barrels, moving Mexico up to fourth rank in world. Leaders of 8 industrial powers and 14 developing nations, meeting in Cancún, agree to move toward "global negotiations" to aid poorer countries

**1982:** Confederation of Mexican Workers threatens general strike if its demand for an emergency pay rise to make up loss of purchasing power due to 30% inflation is not met. A cutback in public spending, devaluation of the peso, and wage and price controls are among measures taken to stabilize the economy. López Portillo fosters peace initiatives to reduce tensions between U.S. and leftist forces in Caribbean region. Oil output reaches 2.7 million barrels per day, but public sector's foreign debt rises above $50 billion as lower world prices for petroleum result in lower earnings abroad. The nominee of Mexico's ruling party, Miguel de la Madrid Hurtado, a Harvard-educated lawyer and minister of Planning and Budget, wins election as president. Economic crisis grows as threat of default on massive foreign debt develops

## MONACO

**Area:** 0.708 sq. mi. (453 acres) **Population:** 26,000 (1979 est.)

**Official Name:** Principality of Monaco **Capital:** Monaco **Nationality:** Monacan or Monégasque **Languages:** French is the official language; the principal spoken languages are French, Monégasque, English and Italian **Religion:** 95% Roman Catholic, the official religion **Flag:** Red over white horizontal stripes **Anthem:** Monacan Hymn, beginning "Principality of Monaco, my fatherland" **Currency:** Freench franc (6.1 per U.S. $1)

**Location:** A coastal enclave within the Alpes-Maritimes department of southeastern France, bordering the Mediterranean Sea **Features:** The principality consists of 3 main areas: La Condamine, the business district around the port; Monte Carlo, the site of the famous casino, which is at a higher elevation; and Monaco, the capital, known also as the Rock because of its situation on a high promontory extending into the sea **Chief Rivers:** There are no rivers

**Head of State:** Prince Rainier III, born 1923, succeeded to the throne in 1949 **Head of Government:** Minister of State Jean Herly (by law a French citizen), appointed 1981. He is assisted by a 3-man Council of Government **Effective Date of Present Constitution:** 1911, revised December 1962 **Legislative Body:** National Council (unicameral), consisting of 18 members elected for 5 years **Local Government:** 1 commune (with 4 quarters), under a mayor and a 15-member elected council

**Ethnic Composition:** The native Monacans are a minority (19%); 58% are French, and 17% Italian **Population Distribution:** 100% urban

**Largest Cities:** (1968 census) La Condamine 11,438, Monte Carlo 9,948; (1972 est.) Monaco 1,685

**Per Capita Income:** N.A. **Gross National Product (GNP):** N.A. **Economic Statistics:** About 55% of the income is derived from tourism, 30% from local industry, and 4% from the casino. The substantial part of the tourist revenue is derived from the government controlled Société Anonyme des Bains de Mer, which operates the gambling casino at Monte Carlo as well as hotels and motion picture theaters. Many foreign companies have established their headquarters in Monaco because of the low taxation **Minerals and Mining:** There are no minerals **Labor Force:** Most of the working population is employed by SBM; and some are employed by the small handicraft industry and by service establishments **Foreign Trade:** N.A. **Principal Trade Partner:** France

**Vital Statistics:** Birthrate, 20.6 per 1,000 of pop. (1980); death rate, 21.1 **Life Expectancy:** 75 years **Health Statistics:** 80 inhabitants per hospital bed; 500 per physician (1977) **Infant Mortality:** N.A. **Illiteracy:** Negligible **Primary and Secondary School Enrollment:** 4,227 (1973) **Enrollment in Higher Education:** N.A. **GNP Expended on Education:** N.A.

**Transportation:** City streets **Motor Vehicles:** N.A. **Passenger Cars:** N.A. **Railway Mileage:** 0.6 **Port:** La Condamine **Major Airlines:** None **Communications: Radio Transmitters:** 5 **Receivers:** 7,500 (1976) **Television Transmitters:** 3 **Receivers:** 16,000 (1976) **Telephones:** 29,000 (1978) **Newspapers:** 1 daily, 420 copies per 1,000 inhabitants (1977)

**Weights and Measures:** Metric system **Travel Requirements:** Passport, no visa for 3 months **International Dialing Code:** 33

Monaco has been a principality of three towns covering an area about half the size of New York's Central Park, but Monaco is growing and expanding into the sea. A land-filling program added more than 20 percent to Monaco's area, to a total of 453 acres, or about 0.7 square miles.

Still, the microscopic principality is a state, the second smallest independent state in the world, after the Vatican City. Crammed into its small size are Riviera weather, scenery to match, the gambling paradise of Monte Carlo's casino, a reigning Prince Rainier who married a movie-queen wife (Grace Kelly), the world-famous Oceanographic Museum (under the direction of France's Jacques Cousteau), and the daily changing of the Caribinier Guard at Palace Square.

Of course, as a long-time vacation resort, Monaco is filled with noted hotels. To keep pace with modernization of the principality, existing hotels are being modernized and new ones built, all with government help.

Monaco has a customs union and interchangeable currency with France, whose consent, by a treaty of 1918, is required for accession to the throne of the principality. The birth of Princess Grace's son in 1958 assured a male ruler to follow Prince Rainier.

Without this royal line, Monaco would come under French protection, making the Monégasques, now free of income taxes, subject to French levies. Tax freedom for Monaco-based companies was curtailed by a 1963 fiscal convention with France, under which concerns in Monaco doing more than 25 percent of their business elsewhere must pay taxes. The convention also applies French income taxes to French citizens who moved to Monaco after mid-October 1957.

**HISTORY:** Monaco was occupied by the Phoenicians from the 10th to the 5th century B.C. and then by the Greeks. During the early Christian era it was dominated by Rome until occupied by the barbarians and Saracens. In 1191, the Genoese took possession of Monaco; the Grimaldi family took control in 1297. The male line died out in 1731, but the French Goyon-Matignon family, which succeeded by marriage, assumed the name Grimaldi, still used by the ruling prince

**1793:** Monaco is annexed to France

**1815:** Monaco is placed under the protection of the Kingdom of Sardinia

**1861:** Monaco becomes a French protectorate

**1918:** Principality signs treaty with France, stipulating that succession to the throne of Monaco must be French approved

**1949:** Prince Rainier III succeeds his father, Prince Louis II, as ruler

**1956:** Prince Rainier marries American movie star, Grace Kelly

**1963:** "Tax war" with France ends in signing of new fiscal convention under which Monégasques and others remain free of direct taxation, but French citizens who had taken up residence in Monaco after October 13, 1957, have to pay income taxes, and companies doing more than a quarter of their business outside Monaco are made subject to a levy

**1967:** Prince Rainier wrests control of Société des Bains de Mer (SBM) from Greek shipping magnate Aristotle Onassis, principal stockholder and director of the company, which through its control of the Monte Carlo casino and the principality's hotels, was accused of impeding Monaco's tourist development

**1978:** Princess Caroline, daughter of Prince Rainier and Princess Grace, marries Philippe Junot, French investment banker. They divorce in 1980

**1982:** Princess Grace dies on Sept. 14, following an auto accident

## MONGOLIA

**Area:** 606,163 sq. mi. **Population:** 1,685,400 (1981 est.)

**Official Name:** Mongolian People's Republic **Capital:** Ulaanbaatar **Nationality:** Mongol **Languages:** Khalkha Mongolian, one of the large dialect groups of the Mongolian branch of the Altaic language family, is the official and dominant spoken language (90%). About 7% of the population speak Turkic languages **Religion:** Lamaistic Buddhism is the predominant religion (95%), but religious activity is discouraged by the Communist regime; Moslem 4% **Flag:** Vertical stripes of red, blue, and red with a yellow star and traditional symbols on the left **Anthem:** Our Free Revolutionary Land **Currency:** Tughrik (3.15 per U.S. $1)

**Location:** North Central Asia. Landlocked Mongolia is bordered on the north by the USSR, and on the east, south, and west by China **Features:** The country is essentially a huge steppe plateau with an average elevation of 4,000 feet. It is fringed by forested mountains in the north, while the south includes much of the Gobi Desert **Chief Rivers:** Selenge, Kerulen, Orhon, Dzavhan

**Political Leader, Head of State and of Government:** Yumjaagiyn Tsedenbal, born 1916; first secretary of the Mongolian People's Revolutionary (Communist) party since 1958; chairman of the presidium of the Hural since June 1974. He is assisted by Jambyn Batmonh, chairman of the Council of Ministers since 1974 **Effective Date of Present Constitution:** July 1960 **Legislative Body:** People's Great Hural (unicameral), 370 members elected for a 5-year term by universal suffrage; actual power lies with the Politburo of the Party's Central Committee **Local Government:** 18 provinces and 3 independent cities

**Ethnic Composition:** Khalkha Mongols make up about 76% of the population, Oirat Mongols and Buryat Mongols 13%, and Kazakhs, a Turkic-speaking people about 2%. Russians, Chinese, Khotan Turks, and Tuvinians form smaller minorities **Population Distribution:** 46% urban **Density:** 2.8 inhabitants per sq. mi.

**Largest Cities:** (1980 est.) Ulaanbaatar 418,700, Darhan 53,500, Erdenet 36,600, Sübaatar 35,000, Choybalsan 31,000

**Per Capita Income:** $782 (1980) **Gross National Product (GNP):** $1.3 billion (1980) **Economic Statistics:** In 1976, 25% of GNP was derived from industry, related to the processing of livestock products, 21% was from animal husbandry (sheep, goats, camels, cattle, and horses) and some field crops. Coal, copper, and molybdenum are the chief mining industries **Minerals and Mining:** Coal, copper, fluorspar and molybdenum **Labor Force:** Most work in state farms and collectives. Agriculture employs 55%, industry 11%, and services 10% **Foreign Trade:** Exports are chiefly cattle, coal, copper, molybdenum, wool, raw hides, and butter and meat products. Imports are mainly consumer goods, machinery, equipment, and industrial raw materials **Principal Trade Partners:** USSR (85%), Czechoslovakia, East Germany, Hungary, Poland, Romania

**Vital Statistics:** Birthrate, 37.1 per 1,000 of pop. (1980); death rate, 8.3 **Life Expectancy:** 64 years **Health Statistics:** 94 inhabitants per hospital bed; 493 per physician (1977) **Infant Mortality:** N.A. **Illiteracy:** 5% **Primary and Secondary School Enrollment:** 341,500 (1976) **Enrollment in Higher Education:** 9,861 (1975) **GNP Expended on Education:** N.A.

**Transportation:** Surfaced roads total 992 mi. **Motor Vehicles:** 24,000 **Passenger Cars:** N.A. **Railway Mileage:** 940 **Ports:** None **Major Airlines:** Air Mongol flies internally and to the Soviet Union **Communications: Radio Transmitters:** 90 **Receivers:** 124,000 (1976) **Television Stations:** 1 **Receivers:** 33,800 (1976) **Telephones:** 38,000 (1976) **Newspapers:** 1 daily, 75 copies per 1,000 inhabitants (1976)

**Weights and Measures:** Metric system **Travel Requirements:** Passport, visa (obtainable in London, Paris, or Moscow)

---

One of the most thinly populated countries in the world, Mongolia is three times as large as France, but most of its territory is desert and semiarid rangeland. Mongolia's importance in international politics is less a matter of its size than of its position: wedged directly between Communist China and the Soviet Union, and long a cause for friction between them.

All of Mongolia was considered part of China for centuries. A Mongol movement to gain independence at the turn of the century, supported by the tsarist Russian government, resulted in "autonomy" for Outer Mongolia. However, in 1919, after the tsarist government itself was overthrown by the 1917 revolution, the Chinese sent troops into Mongolia and canceled its autonomy. The Chinese troops were expelled in the early 1920s by White Russian forces, which in turn were defeated by the Soviet Red Army. Outer Mongolia was then established as the second socialist state in the world and the first Soviet satellite.

Lavish Soviet aid has enabled Mongolia to make impressive economic advances. The economy still relies heavily on its livestock base—the country's most important resource—but collective farms for stockbreeding have been established and there are a few nomadic herdsmen left. Industrial production has increased sharply.

The help given by the Soviet Union has not gone unnoticed in China. In a 1973 speech before the UN General Assembly, Chinese Deputy Foreign Minister Chiao Kuan-hua challenged the Soviet Union to remove its troops from Mongolia. China's problem is that there are more Mongols in China—in Inner Mongolia—than there are in the Mongolian Republic, and fears that Mongol nationalism might result in efforts to detach further segments of Chinese territory are apparently real. Possibly to guard against a Mongol nationalist movement in China, Peking in 1970 assigned large segments of Inner Mongolia to neighboring provinces, since rescinded.

In 1968 and 1969 there were small flare-ups along the 2,500-mile Chinese/Mongolian border, and the Mongols charged that the Chinese had sought to subvert their government and install a pro-Peking regime.

A nation of pivotal importance, Mongolia seems to have no alternative but to try to maneuver between Moscow and Peking while striving to maintain its independence.

**HISTORY:** The Mongols, loosely organized nomadic tribes living in Mongolia, China, and Siberia, were united in the 13th century under the leadership of Genghis Khan, who established a far-flung Eurasian empire. After his death, the empire was divided and eventually disintegrated, and a cleavage developed between the southern, or inner, Mongols, ruled by the Chinese, and the northern, or outer, Mongols. In 1691 the northern Mongols accepted Chinese authority and remained under their rule until the 20th century

**1911:** Mongol princes proclaim Outer Mongolia an independent monarchy following the overthrow of China's Manchu dynasty; the throne is given to Bogdo Gegen, the Living Buddha of Urga

**1915:** Outer Mongolia signs treaty with republican China and tsarist Russia accepting autonomous status under Chinese authority; Russia gains control over Mongolia's foreign affairs

**1919-21:** Attempts by China to reassert sovereignty over Outer Mongolia following the Russian Revolution are defeated; Russian forces expel Chinese, and Outer Mongolia again proclaims its independence

**1924:** Mongolian People's Republic is proclaimed following the death of the Living Buddha; Communist rule is inaugurated with Soviet help

**1950:** Communist China and USSR sign treaty guaranteeing Mongolia's independence

**1962:** Mongolia and Communist China sign treaty fixing their 2,500-mile border. Premier Yumjaagiyn Tsedenbal backs Soviet policy on peaceful coexistence, challenged by Peking

**1963:** Mongolia establishes diplomatic relations with Britain in the first such pact with a Western power. Mongolia asks Communist China to withdraw laborers sent by Peking to work on Mongolian construction projects

**1964:** Pro-Peking sympathizers are purged from ruling party

**1966-67:** Relations between Mongolia and Communist China become strained. Soviet troops are stationed on Mongolia border

**1969:** Soviet and Communist Chinese troops clash at the Ussuri River, and tension rises on the Chinese-Mongolian frontier

**1970:** Soviet-Mongolian five-year economic plan drafted. Border troubles with Communist China continue

**1976:** Tsendenbal reelected first secretary for the fifth time

**1978:** The government introduces restrictions to stop the flow of rural people to the cities

**1981:** Severe two-year drought eases; Soviet aid mitigates effect of heavy livestock losses. Mongolian astronaut is member of two-man team in Soviet space launch

**1982:** Mongolian and Chinese officials discuss border problems in six-week conference (the first such meeting) at Ulaanbaatar

## MOROCCO

**Area:** 172,413 sq. mi. **Population:** 20,646,000 (1981 est.)

**Official Name:** Kingdom of Morocco **Capital:** Rabat **Nationality:** Moroccan **Languages:** Arabic, the official language, is spoken by about 65%; Berber dialects are spoken by about 35%. French is also widely used **Religion:** 98.7% are Sunni Moslems (Islam is the state religion), 1.1% are Christians, and 0.2% are Jews **Flag:** A red field with a green 5-pointed star in the center **Anthem:** National Anthem (no words) **Currency:** Moroccan dirham (5.8 per U.S. $1)

**Location:** Northwest Africa. Morocco is bordered on the north by the Mediterranean Sea, on the east by Algeria, on the south, with the contested Western Sahara area interposed, by Mauritania, and on the west by the Atlantic Ocean **Features:** The center is occupied by the dry, rocky Atlas Mountains, which slope downward to narrow fertile coastal plains along the Mediterranean and the Atlantic. The south is occupied by the Sahara **Chief Rivers:** Oum-er-Rbia, Dra, Moulouya, Sous, Sebou

**Head of State:** King Hassan II, born 1929, ascended the throne 1961 **Head of Government:** Prime Minister Maati Bouabid, appointed March 1979 **Effective Date of Present Constitution:** March 1972 **Legislative Body:** Parliament (unicameral Chamber of Representatives), with 264 members elected for 4 years **Local Government:** 36 provinces and 2 urban prefectures, headed by governors

**Ethnic Composition:** The majority of Moroccans are of Arab descent; about 35% are of Berber origin **Population Distribution:** 41% urban **Density:** 120 inhabitants per sq. mi.

**Largest Cities:** (1979 est.) Casablanca 2,220,600, Rabat 768,500, Fez 524,000, Marrakech 499,400, Meknès 449,900, Oujda 429,800, Kénitra 415,500, Tetuan 342,700, Tangier 280,000, Safi 232,400, Agadir 215,900

**Per Capita Income:** $605 (1980) **Gross National Product (GNP):** $12.7 billion (1980) **Economic Statistics:** 22% of the GNP is derived from agriculture (wheat, barley, fruits, corn, sugar, livestock), forestry and fishing; 21% from commerce; 16% from transportation and services; 12% from industry (food processing and canning, sugar refining, milling, tobacco production); and 4% from mining **Minerals and Mining:** Leading minerals are phosphates, iron ore, shale oil, natural gas, coal, manganese, fluorite, cobalt, lead, zinc, copper **Labor Force:** 4.5 million in 1977, with 51% in agriculture, 20% in industry, and 29% in services **Foreign Trade:** Exports, chiefly vegetables, citrus fruit, phosphates, wine, and canned fish, totaled $2.5 billion in 1981. Imports, mainly wheat, sugar, fuel, industrial machinery and equipment, cotton and synthetic textile yarn, iron and steel products, totaled $4.4 billion **Principal Trade Partners:** EC countries, United States, USSR, Spain

**Vital Statistics:** Birthrate, 45.4 per 1,000 of pop. (1980); death rate, 13.6 **Life Expectancy:** 55 years **Health Statistics:** 771 inhabitants per hospital bed; 11,143 per physician (1976) **Infant Mortality:** 149 per 1,000 births **Illiteracy:** 79% **Primary and Secondary School Enrollment:** 2,196,800 (1976) **Enrollment in Higher Education:** 45,322 (1975) **GNP Expended on Education:** 6% (1976)

**Transportation:** Paved roads total 15,300 mi. **Motor Vehicles:** 573,300 (1978) **Passenger Cars:** 394,100 **Railway Mileage:** 1,105 **Ports:** Casablanca, Safi, Kénitra, Mohammedia, Agadir, Essaouira **Major Airlines:** Royal Air Maroc operates both domestically and internationally **Communications: Radio Transmitters:** 33 **Receivers:** 1,500,000 (1976) **Television Transmitters:** 27 **Receivers:** 522,000 (1976) **Telephones:** 216,000 (1978) **Newspapers:** 10 dailies (1976); 21 copies per 1,000 inhabitants (1975)

**Weights and Measures:** Metric system **Travel Requirements:** Passport, no visa for 3 months

---

Geographically, Morocco is the westernmost Arab country, the only one with a border on the Atlantic coast of North Africa. It stands almost as close to the United States as to the eastern end of the Arab world, and at one point—the Strait of Gibraltar—it is literally within sight of Europe.

Politically, too, Morocco shows Western tendencies. Although nominally a member of the Arab League, it remains outside the main thrust of Arab politics, commerce, and culture. In recent years, it has made great efforts to cultivate the friendship of the United States and Western Europe, with which it seems to have closer interests than with the militant Arab countries to its east.

Since independence from France in 1956, Morocco has been a monarchy with a liberal-sounding constitution, but King Hassan II has been as absolute as any ruler in the world.

Dissolving the National Assembly in 1965, the king instituted a "state of exception" that gave him virtually unlimited power. In 1970, by national referendum, a new constitution provided a modified form of parliamentary government; the 1972 constitution further limited the king's powers to challenge legislative decisions. He retains the power to declare a state of emergency.

The nation's chief problems are its rapidly expanding population—the growth rate is three percent a year—and the inability of its economy to keep pace. Since independence, investment has been mostly in agriculture, dams, and irrigation projects.

Although there has been some economic progress, considerably more is still needed. It is estimated that 40 percent of the youth between 20 and 30 are unemployed. Unemployment has forced workers to emigrate to western Europe to find jobs. The money they have returned to their families in Morocco has provided a valuable addition to the Moroccan balance of payments. Tourism has increased greatly in recent years.

A Marxist party exists in the country, but most Moroccan intellectuals, like their Algerian neighbors, have their own ideas about socialism and are not particularly attracted by either the Soviet or Chinese brand. The main support for the king—who is also the country's religious leader—comes from the rural areas.

By Arab-world standards, Morocco has a large middle class, imbued with both Arab and French culture, whose high standard of living coexists with the feudal rural society. In addition, it has the largest remaining French community—numbering some 100,000—in North Africa. The coexistence of the Arab and French cultures, however, adds to the frustration of many young intellectuals, who are increasingly demanding the Arabization of their country.

In March 1973 King Hassan reacted to steadily mounting pressures for an economic shake-up by decreeing the nationalization of farmlands in foreign hands and the elimination of foreign ownership of businesses.

In 1974 opposition to Spain's plans to grant self-rule to the Spanish Sahara, which Morocco claimed, united all Moroccan political elements behind the monarchy for the first time since the early 1960s. By November 1975 Spain agreed to partition Spanish Sahara. Despite Algeria's opposition to the partition, the northern two-thirds, including rich phosphate deposits at Bu Craa, went to Morocco and the southern third to Mauritania, and in December Moroccan officials proclaimed the annexation of Western Sahara as Moroccan troops marched into its capital.

Because Morocco did not recognize the proclamation of the *Polisario Front*, the Saharan liberation movement, and Algeria did, Morocco cut its ties with Algeria. The *Polisario* guerrillas observed a tacit cease-fire with Mauritania, which in 1979 gave up its claim to the southern portion of Western Sahara, which Morocco then occupied. In June 1981, King Hassan offered to hold a "controlled referendum" in the Western Sahara. Pending a solution of the dispute, U.S. military aid to Morocco was made conditional in 1980. In March 1981, however, the new administration of President Ronald Reagan announced that the U.S. would sell army tanks to Morocco unconditionally.

The country's worst riots since independence took place in Casablanca in June 1981, when massive protests against the government's food price increases turned violent. Estimates of the death toll ranged from 60 to 600. Among the 2,000 persons arrested were labor leaders who had called a general strike which had led to the riots.

**HISTORY:** In ancient times, Morocco was part of the empire of Carthage. Under the Romans it was formed into the province of Mauritania and later experienced successive invasions until conquered by the Arabs c. A.D. 683. Morocco became an independent kingdom in 788, but by the 10th century had broken up into several tribal states. The country was ultimately united under the Almoravids, a Berber Moslem dynasty that established a kingdom stretching from Senegal to Spain

**15th cent.:** Portugal and Spain capture all Moroccan ports

**17th cent.:** Morocco recaptures many European strongholds

**1906:** Algeciras Conference grants France special privileges in Morocco

**1912:** Morocco becomes a protectorate; under a French-Spanish agreement the country is divided administratively into French

Morocco, Spanish Morocco, and a Southern Protectorate of Morocco, administered as part of the Spanish Sahara, and the international zone of Tangier

**1953:** Faced with growing movement for independence, French depose Sultan Sidi Mohammed ben Youssef and exile him to Madagascar

**1955:** French permit sultan to return

**1956-57:** Morocco gains freedom in 1956; Tangier is restored. In 1957 Sidi Mohammed ben Youssef becomes King Mohammed V

**1961-62:** King Mohammed dies and is succeeded by his son, Hassan II. In 1962 a draft constitution presented by Hassan is approved by referendum

**1965:** Hassan declares state of emergency and assumes executive and legislative power

**1970:** New constitution is adopted ending king's absolutist rule

**1971:** Hassan survives attempted coup by rebellious army officers and cadets; king charges Libya with inciting the rebellion

**1972:** Hassan survives second attempted coup within 13 months. Defense Minister Oufkir, who had exercised wide civil and military powers after the 1971 attempt, found dead after leading counterattack on rebels. He is charged by Hassan with organizing the attempted takeover

**1974:** Massive deposit of oil shale discovered in Middle Atlas Mountains. King Hassan presses Spain to return Spanish Sahara territory to Morocco

**1975:** Some 200,000 unarmed Moroccans who moved over the border in the "Green March" into Spanish Sahara "to regain the Sahara peacefully," are called back by Hassan

**1976:** Morocco and Mauritania divide the disputed Western Sahara. Relations are severed with Algeria because of Algeria's support of *Polisario* guerrillas

**1977:** Moroccan troops are sent to Zaire to help repel invaders of Shaba province

**1978:** Moroccan government sends troops to Shaba province in Zaire following invasion there by Katangan rebels. Railway workers and civil servants strike for higher pay

**1979:** Maati Bouabid succeeds Ahmed Osman as premier. Morocco occupies southern third of Western Sahara, after Mauritania renounces claim to area

**1981:** U.S. resumes unconditional aid to Morocco after holding up tank shipments because of dispute over Western Sahara. Hassan offers to hold "controlled referendum" in area. Riots occur in Casablanca as the result of price increases in the cost of basic foods

## MOZAMBIQUE

**Area:** 303,769 sq. mi. **Population:** 12,130,000 (1980 census)

**Official Name:** People's Republic of Mozambique **Capital:** Maputo **Nationality:** Mozambican **Languages:** Bantu languages; Portuguese is the official language **Religion:** 66% animist, 22% Christian, 11% Moslem **Flag:** Four diagonal wedges of green, red, black and yellow separated by narrow white wedges, the national emblem of a white cogwheel with red star, white book, black silhouettes of hoe and rifle is at the upper left **Anthem:** Beginning "Viva viva Frelimo" **Currency:** Metical (35 per U.S. $1)

**Location:** On the east coast of Africa, bounded by the Mozambique Channel on the east, Swaziland on the south, South Africa on the south and west, Zimbabwe on the west, Zambia and Malawi on the northwest, and Tanzania on the north **Features:** Lowlands along the 1,700-mile-long coast rise to an 8,000-ft. plateau, with mountains to the north. The northern coastal plain is hot and humid, but is cooler to the south and inland **Chief Rivers:** Ruvuma, Lurio, Zambezi, Save, Limpopo

**Head of State and of Government:** President Samora Moisés Machel, born 1933, installed June 1975. He is head of the Frelimo party **Effective Date of Present Constitution:** 1975 **Legislative Body:** People's Assembly of 210 members **Local Government:** 10 provinces

**Ethnic Composition:** The people are mostly of Bantu stock, with a minority (perhaps 10,000) Europeans (mostly Portuguese) **Population Distribution:** 8% urban **Density:** 40 inhabitants per sq. mi.

**Largest Cities:** (1980 census) Maputo 755,300; (1970 census) Beira 46,293, Nampula 23,072, Quelimane 10,522

**Per Capita Income:** $255 (1980) **Gross National Product (GNP):** $2.6 billion (1980) **Economic Statistics:** Agriculture (cotton, cashew nuts, sugar, tea, copra, sisal) accounts for 45% of GNP; industry (textiles, processed food, beverages, refined oil, cigarettes, cement) for 15% **Minerals and Mining:** Copper, coal, beryl, columbite, fluorite, bauxite and tantalite **Labor Force:** 600,000 wage earners, with 80% of the population in subsistence agriculture **Foreign Trade:** Exports, chiefly cashew nuts, cotton and cotton products, sugar, copra, sisal fiber, tea and vegetable oils, amounted to $448 million in 1980. Imports, chiefly machinery, transportation equipment, metals and metal products, petroleum and wheat, reached $618 million **Principal Trade Partners:** South Africa, Britain, Portugal, West Germany, United States

**Vital Statistics:** Birthrate, 44.8 per 1,000 of pop. (1980); death rate, 19 **Life Expectancy:** 44 years **Health Statistics:** 772 inhabitants per hospital bed; 16,392 per physician (1972) **Infant Mortality:** 92.5 per 1,000 births **Illiteracy:** 80% **Primary and Secondary School Enrollment:** 632,647 (1972) **Enrollment in Higher Education:** 906 (1976) **GNP Expended on Education:** 1.1% (1972)

**Transportation:** Paved roads total 2,686 mi. **Motor Vehicles:** 110,800 (1972) **Passenger Cars:** 89,300 **Railway Mileage:** 2,135 miles **Ports:** Maputo, Beira, Nacala, Pemba, Quelimane **Major Airlines:** LAM provides domestic and international service **Communications: Radio Transmitters:** 45 **Licenses:** 225,000 (1976) **Television Transmitters:** None **Telephones:** 49,000 (1978) **Newspapers:** 2 dailies, 4 copies per 1,000 inhabitants (1976)

**Weights and Measures:** Metric system **Travel Requirements:** Apply to Permanent Mission of the People's Republic of Mozambique, New York 10017

Portuguese rule left an inheritance of poverty and disease for much of Mozambique's population. Forced labor was widespread, political rights and education limited. Ten years of pre-independence guerrilla war, the flight of skilled whites and the imposition of doctrinaire socialism have also taken their toll.

Nationalist forces aiming at independence began guerrilla warfare in 1964, starting in the north. The chief rebel movement was the Front for the Liberation of Mozambique (FRELIMO) which had been working for independence since 1962.

Clashes between the Portuguese army and insurgents increased in early 1974. In September after the military overthrew the home government in Portugal, FRELIMO and the Portuguese High Commissioner signed an agreement under which Mozambique would be ruled by a joint transitional government until full independence.

On June 25, 1975, Mozambique achieved full independence after 500 years of colonial rule, becoming the 45th African state to do so. Samora Moisés Machel, the first president, pledged to transform the country into the "first truly Marxist state in Africa." FRELIMO became the country's sole political party in the new state and the nucleus for the new People's Republic of Mozambique government. Since then the government has been establishing its authority and Marxist-oriented philosophy at all levels of society and planning a post-colonial economy. Among the goals of the FRELIMO program is the eradication of tribalism, regionalism, and racism.

At first Mozambique's future looked relatively bright in comparison to Portugal's other African territories, but most of the 220,000 whites fled, leaving the country almost without skilled and professional workers. All land was nationalized and food production declined by 75 percent in some areas while production of major cash crops was off by half. Many factories have been abandoned and the government now offers incentives for Portuguese managers to stay on. The major income remaining is foreign exchange earned by Mozambique miners in South Africa.

In March 1976 Machel closed the border with Rhodesia (now Zimbabwe) and increased efforts to train guerrillas and help them infiltrate the white-ruled nation. The border closing was costly as it shut off Mozambique's major source of food.

**HISTORY:** Bantu peoples entered Mozambique after 1000 A.D. from Central Africa. Arab traders touched on the coast prior to the coming of the Portuguese under Vasco da Gama in 1498. The Portuguese developed trading posts and a thriving slave trade during the following centuries. Mozambique's colonial boundaries were fixed by the end of the 19th century

**1951:** Portugal establishes Mozambique as an Overseas Province

**1964:** Independence forces begin guerrilla warfare
**1974:** FRELIMO (Mozambique Liberation Front) and Portugal agree to joint rule prior to independence
**1975:** Mozambique achieves independence
**1976:** Mozambique closes border with Rhodesia and declares a state of war. Intermittent border clashes occur
**1977:** Border clashes continue. Black refugees from Rhodesia fill camps in Mozambique
**1978:** Virtually all foreign and local banks are nationalized
**1979:** National Resistance Movement, based in Zimbabwe-Rhodesia, commits acts of sabotage aimed at overthrow of Machel. Mozambique rejects Soviet request for naval base
**1980:** Though still committed to Marxism, Machel seeks economic aid from capitalist West; announces plan to encourage private enterprise and promises incentives for former white businessmen who return to Mozambique. New currency, the metical, replaces the escudo
**1981:** Resistance Movement targets power supplies, rail communications and FRELIMO attempts to organize peasants into collectives. Mozambique joins Soviet-led Council for Mutual Economic Assistance (COMECON)
**1982:** Government troops launch major offensive to clear main rail link to Zimbabwe

## NAMIBIA

*(See Territories and Dependencies section)*

## NAURU

**Area:** 7.7 sq. mi. **Population:** 7,100 (1978 est.)

**Official Name:** Republic of Nauru **Capital:** Yaren (district) **Nationality:** Nauruan **Languages:** Nauruan and English **Religion:** Christian, mainly Protestant **Flag:** A blue field halved by a horizontal gold bar, with a white star at the lower left **Anthem:** N.A. **Currency:** Australian dollar (0.94 per U.S. $1)

**Location:** Central Pacific, 0°30'S.,166°55'E. The island of Nauru lies just south of the equator, about 1,300 miles northeast of Australia **Features:** The island is completely surrounded by a coral reef. A narrow, fertile coastal strip lying between a sandy beach and coral cliffs is the most populated part of the island. The interior consists of a barren plateau containing extensive phosphate deposits, Nauru's major economic resource **Chief Rivers:** No rivers

**Head of State and of Government:** President Hammer De Robure, born 1922, took office in 1978 **Effective Date of Present Constitution:** 1968 **Legislative Body:** Parliament (unicameral Legislative Assembly), consisting of 18 members elected by universal suffrage for 3 years **Local Government:** The island is divided into 14 districts

**Ethnic Composition:** The Nauruans (58% of population) are believed to be a mixture of Polynesian, Micronesian, and Melanesian, with Polynesian predominating. Other Pacific Islanders constitute 26%, Chinese 8%, and Europeans 8% **Population Distribution:** Virtually the entire population is concentrated in settlements along the coast **Density:** 922 inhabitants per sq. mi.

**Per Capita Income:** $21,400 (1977) **Gross National Product (GNP):** $155 million (1977) **Economic Statistics:** Nauru's economy is built around the phosphate industry, which enables the islanders to enjoy one of the highest per capita incomes in the world. Although some food products are grown on the island, the inhabitants are largely dependent on imports of food supplies and all manufactured goods **Labor Force:** Nauruans, as a rule, do not engage in manual labor, and the phosphate industry is largely dependent on outside labor. About 60% of Nauruans are employed in the civil service **Foreign Trade:** Exports, consisting entirely of phosphates, totaled $75 million in 1979. Imports, chiefly food, water, consumer goods, machinery and fuel, totaled $12 million **Principal Trade Partners:** Australia, New Zealand, Britain, Japan, South Korea

**Vital Statistics:** Birthrate, 19.8 per 1,000 of pop. (1976); death rate, 8.3 **Life Expectancy:** 53 years **Health Statistics:** 34 inhabitants per hospital bed; 700 per physician (1971) **Infant Mortality:** 19 per 1,000 births **Illiteracy:** Negligible **Primary and Secondary School Enrollment:** 1,973 (1975) **Enrollment in Higher Education:** 92 studying abroad (1975) **GNP Expended on Education:** 2.8% (1970)

**Transportation:** Paved roads total 13 mi. **Motor Vehicles:** Over 1,000 **Railway Mileage:** A three-mile railway links the phosphate workings with the coast **Ports:** None. Barges transport cargo to offshore ships **Major Airlines:** Air Nauru operates flights to Pacific and Asian cities **Communications: Radio Transmitters:** 1 **Receivers:** 3,600 (1976) **Television:** None **Telephones:** 1,500 **Newspapers:** 1 fortnightly

**Weights and Measures:** British standards are used **Travel Requirements:** Visas obtainable from honorary consul general in San Francisco

The barren central plateau of Nauru, the tiny Pacific island, which is the smallest independent republic in the world, consists of large phosphate deposits, the result of centuries of bird droppings, that provide Nauru with a good source of income: the phosphate, much prized as fertilizer, is the island's main natural resource and only export.

This unique export helps to give the people of Nauru one of the highest per capita incomes in the world, as well as shops filled with luxury goods, free medical care, good housing, good schools, no taxes, and jobs for all.

Only 12 miles in circumference and three-and-a-half-miles wide, Nauru was named Pleasant Island by the captain of a British whaling ship who discovered it in 1798. Early contacts with Europeans brought guns and disease, and a consequent ravaging of the population. The people of Nauru now are more concerned with depletion of the phosphate deposits. Totaling 45 million tons, the deposits are expected to be exhausted in the 1990s.

Intense debate over the nation's course once the phosphate has been depleted led to a rare period of political instability. In April 1978 President Dowiyogo, reelected the preceding November, resigned; his plan to raise a $22-million development loan overseas had been opposed by parliament. He was succeeded by Lagumot Harris, who himself resigned a month later after a money bill of his met a similar fate. Harris was succeeded by Hammer de Roburt, the man who led Nauru to independence in 1968.

**HISTORY:** Nauru, discovered by a British whaling team in 1798, was long known as Pleasant Island. In 1888 it was annexed by Germany and henceforth known by its native name. Phosphate was discovered on the island in the late 1890s and exploitation begun in 1901. With the outbreak of World War I, Australian forces occupied the island. After the war, Nauru was administered by Australia under a League of Nations mandate, which also named Britain and New Zealand as cotrustees
**1942-45:** Nauru is occupied by Japanese forces; 1,200 islanders are deported to Truk as forced labor
**1947:** Island is placed under United Nations Trusteeship, with Australia acting as administrator on behalf of the Australian, New Zealand, and British governments
**1964:** In anticipation of the exhaustion of Nauru's phosphate deposits, expected in about 30 years, Australia proposes that inhabitants be resettled on Curtis Island, off the Queensland coast; islanders reject proposal, choosing to remain on Nauru
**1968:** Nauru becomes independent republic; islanders reject proposals that Australia handle their defense and external affairs. Hammer De Roburt is elected president
**1970:** Nauru assumes management of its phosphate industry
**1976:** Bernard Dowiyogo is elected president
**1977-78:** Debate over nation's future leads to period of instability. President Dowiyogo resigns; Lagumot Harris succeeds him. Harris resigns; Hammer de Roburt succeeds Harris
**1980:** Pres. Hammer de Roburt, unopposed, is reelected
**1981:** While recognizing that only income from phosphate deposits keeps republic's airline running at a loss, government subsidizes it to relieve island's isolation

## NEPAL

**Area:** 54,663 sq. mi. **Population:** 14,179,301 (1981 census)

**Official Name:** Kingdom of Nepal **Capittal:** Kathmandu **Nationality:** Nepalese **Languages:** Nepali, the official language, is the first language of roughly 50% of the population and is spoken by another 30%; Tibeto-Burman languages (chiefly Newari), Indo-Aryan dialects, and English are also spoken **Religion:** Hinduism, the official religion, is the dominant faith (90%); Mahayana Buddhism is the dominant religion in the sparsely inhabited north, and both faiths are followed by many people of the central region **Flag:** Two red right-angled triangles bordered in blue at the hoist; the upper with a white moon crescent, the lower with a white sun **Anthem:** National Anthem, beginning "May glory crown our illustrious sovereign" **Currency:** Nepalese rupee (13.2 per UU.S. $1)

**Location:** Central Asia. Landlocked Nepal is bordered on thee north by China (Tibet), and on the east, south and west by India **Features:** The country is mountainous, with dense swampy jungles. Across the south lies the 20-mile-wide Terai, a region of plain and swamp.

Most of the country, a band across the center, is broken by sharp mountain ranges and traversed by high, fertile valleys. Along the northern border lies the high Himalaya, with 8 of the world's 12 highest peaks, including Mount Everest, whose 29,028-ft. elevation is the highest in the world **Chief Rivers:** Kali, Karnali, Gandak, Kosi

**Head of State:** King Birendra Bir Bikram Shah Dev, born 1945, acceded to the throne January 1972 **Head of Government:** Prime Minister: Surya Bahadur Thapa, born 1928, appointed June 1979 **Effective Date of Present Constitution:** December 1962 **Legislative Body:** Parliament (unicameral National *Panchayat*), with 140 members, of which 112 are directly elected and 28 are nominated by the king. The king has absolute veto power over parliamentary bills **Local Government:** 14 zones, each headed by an appointed commissioner, and 75 districts, each with a district assembly and 11-member executive committee known as the district *panchayat*. The latter, in turn, form a zonal assembly

**Ethnic Composition:** The Nepalese are descendants of 3 major migrations from India and Tibet. In addition to the Brahmans and Chetris whose ancestors came from India, the numerous tribes, called castes, include the Gurungs and Magars in the west; Tamangs and Newars in the center; Bhotias in the north; Rais, Limbus, and Sherpas in the east; and Tharus in the south **Population Distribution:** 4% urban **Density:** 259 inhabitants per sq. mi.

**Largest Cities:** (1971 census) Kathmandu 150,402, Lalitpur 59,049, Biratnagar 45,100, Bhaktapur 40,112

**Per Capita Income:** $121 (1980) **Gross National Product (GNP):** $1.8 billion (1980) **Economic Statistics:** In 1973 about 65% of GNP was from agriculture (paddy rice, maize, wheat, millet, jute) and forestry; 12% from mining and manufacturing (jute, textiles, yarns, cigarettes, vegetable oil crushing); and 17.3% from trade and services **Minerals and Mining:** Coal and mica are mined. There are unexploited deposits of iron ore, copper, lead, zinc, cobalt, nickel, and talc **Labor Force:** 4,852,524 (1971), 94% of which is in agriculture and 2% in industry **Foreign Trade:** Exports, chiefly rice, jute and jute products, ghee, oilseeds, timber, and herbs, totaled $51 million in 1979. Imports, mainly textiles, foodstuffs, petroleum products, machinery and equipment, vehicles and parts, totaled $159 million **Principal Trade Partners:** India, Japan, United States

**Vital Statistics:** Birthrate, 43.2 per 1,000 of pop. (1980); death rate, 20.6 **Life Expectancy:** 40 years **Health Statistics:** 6,204 inhabitants per hospital bed; 36,450 per physician (1974) **Infant Mortality:** 152 per 1,000 births **Illiteracy:** 80% **Primary and Secondary School Enrollment:** 1,031,797 (1977) **Enrollment in Higher Education:** 23,504 **GNP Expended on Education:** 1.5% (1975)

**Transportation:** Paved roads total 1,088 mi. **Motor Vehicles:** 12,646 (1970) **Passenger Cars:** 7,281 **Railway Mileage:** 40 **Ports:** None **Major Airlines:** Royal Nepal Airlines operates domestic and international services **Communications: Radio Transmitters:** 7 **Receivers:** 150,000 (1976) **Television:** None **Telephones:** 9,000 (1977) **Newspapers:** 29 dailies (1976), 3 copies per 1,000 inhabitants (1974)

**Weights and Measures:** Metric system and local standards **Travel Requirements:** Passport, visa valid for 30-day stay, $10 fee, 1 photo

---

Beguiled by the slightly touristic, but not untrue, face that Nepal presents to the outside world, mountaineers, tourists, and hippies have flocked there and found what they sought: a peaceful Himalayan kingdom, backward but pleasant, a land of green valleys and towering mountains (including the world's highest, 29,028-ft. Mt. Everest, shared with Tibet), all presided over by the world's only Hindu king, thought by his people to be an incarnation of the god Vishnu.

The other side of Nepal's character is harsher, revealing a primitive, divided, stratified society unsettled by its leaders' drive for modernization and by bitter political feuding. A 1982 United Nations report charged that the nation was failing to produce or import enough food to meet its citizens' basic caloric requirements.

Caught between two powerful and jealous neighbors, China and India, Nepal lately has halted India's interference in its internal affairs and established close ties with China

Rising taxes, high prices, and shortages have contributed to recent unrest. In 1979, what began as student demands for academic changes turned into a broad call for parliamentary democracy joined by peasants, laborers, and the middle class. About 20 persons died in riots in several towns. In national elections in May 1980, voters settled the issue by casting 54% of their ballots for a streamlined version of the existing system of indirect representation, called *panchayat*, in which King Birenda retained virtually absolute power. Having failed to restore the system of political parties that existed before 1960, pro-democratic forces boycotted the 1981 elections.

**HISTORY:** Nepal, the world's only Hindu kingdom, has a long historical continuity, although little is known about the country before the 15th century. The modern kingdom of Nepal was established in the 18th century by the ruler of Gurkha, a small principality west of Kathmandu. His descendants introduced Hinduism as the state religion and established most of the present boundaries

**1790-93:** Gurkhas invade Tibet. A large Chinese army forces the Gurkhas to come to terms. Seeking assistance against the Chinese, the Gurkhas sign treaty with the British in India

**1814-16:** Series of frontier incidents leads to war between the British and Nepal. Nepal surrenders much of its territory and permits a British residency to be set up at Kathmandu

**1846:** Jung Bahadur Rana seizes the government and reduces the king to a figurehead

**1951:** An end is made to more than a century of rule by a succession of hereditary prime ministers from a noble family, the Ranas, during which the royal family played little part in governing. King Tribhuvana assumes power with Indian help, promises elections to a constituent assembly to formulate new constitution

**1955:** King Tribhuvana dies and is succeeded by Crown Prince Mahendra. Nepal joins UN

**1959:** King Mahendra declares Nepal a constitutional monarchy. In the country's first election, the Nepali Congress party wins an absolute majority

**1960:** King Mahendra dismisses the cabinet, dissolves parliament, bans political parties, and assumes powers of government; many political leaders are arrested

**1962:** New constitution is promulgated, introducing *panchayat* system of government from the village to the national level

**1963:** King Mahendra forms an advisory state council

**1972:** King Mahendra dies and is succeeded by his son, Crown Prince Birendra Bir Bikram Shah Dev

**1974:** Nepal and China sign trade pact

**1975:** King Birendra, who received part of his education at Harvard, is formally crowned. Prime Minister Nagendra Prasad Rijal is replaced by Dr. Tulsi Giri. Heavily armed Khampa refugees from Tibet are driven from the Himalayan passes by Nepalese troops

**1977:** Prime Minister Tulsi Giri resigns; Kirti Nidhi Bista, who has held the post three times in eight years, succeeds him

**1978:** King Birendra slightly eases his stern control of Nepalese life

**1979:** Students, joined by other dissidents, stage violent demonstrations to demand that the monarchy be liberalized. B.P. Koirala, former prime minister who leads efforts for constitutional reform, is charged with sedition. Prime Minister Bista resigns; Surya Bahadur Thapa is appointed in his place

**1980:** Voters reject a parliamentary democracy and instead approve a modified version of partyless government, leaving King Birenda almost unlimited power. Earthquake kills thousands

**1981:** China's Premier Zhao Ziyang visits Nepal

---

## THE NETHERLANDS

**Area:** 15,892 sq. mi. **Population:** 14,275,000 (1981 est.)

**Official Name:** Kingdom of the Netherlands **Capital:** Amsterdam, but the seat of government is at The Hague **Nationality:** Netherlands or Dutch **Languages:** Hollands, or Dutch, is the official and predominant language; Frisian is spoken in the northern province of Friesland **Religion:** About 40.4% Roman Catholic, 32.9% Protestant, and 23.6% no religion **Flag:** Red, white, and blue horizontal stripes **Anthem:** Wilhelmus van Nassouwen (William of Nassau) **Currency:** Guilder (florin) (2.6 per U.S. $1)

**Location:** Northwest Europe. The Netherlands is bounded on the west and north by the North Sea, on the east by West Germany, and on the south by Belgium **Features:** The country is low and flat except for some hills in the southeast. About one-third of the land area is below sea level, and more than one-fifth reclaimed from the sea and protected by dikes **Chief Rivers:** Maas, IJssel, Waal, Lek

**Head of State:** Queen Beatrix, born 1938, invested April 30, 1980 **Head of Government:** Premier Andries A.M. van Agt, born 1931, appointed 1977 **Effective Date of Present Constitution:** 1814; frequently revised **Legislative Body:** The States General (bicameral), consisting of the First Chamber, or upper house, and the Second Chamber, or lower house. The First Chamber consists of 75 members chosen by the 11 provincial legislatures for 6 years. The Second Chamber has 150 members elected directly for 4 years **Local Government:** 11 provinces, with elected provincial executive councils and appointed commissioners, and the IJsselmeer polders

**Ethnic Composition:** 99% Dutch, 1% Indonesian and Surinamese **Population Distribution:** 88% urban **Density:** 898 inhabitants per sq. mi.

**Largest Cities:** (1981 est.) Amsterdam 712,294, Rotterdam 576,330, The Hague 456,726, Utrecht 236,211, Eindhoven 195,669, Groningen 162,952, Haarlem 157,556, Tilburg 153,114

**Per Capita Income:** $7,048 (1980) **Gross Domestic Product (GDP):** $99 billion (1980) **Economic Statistics:** About 42.3% of GDP comes from industry (capital and consumer goods, food processing, chemicals, textiles), mining, construction, and utilities; 17.8% from commerce, banking, and finance; 6.5% from agriculture; and the rest from other activities **Minerals and Mining:** Large reserves of natural gas are exploited along with some salt, and crude oil **Labor Force:** 4,800,000 (1978), of which 35% is employed in industry, 7% in agriculture, 58% in services **Foreign Trade:** Exports, mainly meats, flower bulbs, petroleum products, natural gas, chemicals, textiles, machinery, and electrical equipment, totaled $68 billion in 1981. Imports, chiefly grains, petroleum, chemicals, textiles, iron and steel products, machinery and electrical equipment, and motor vehicles, totaled $66 billion **Principal Trade Partners:** EC countries, United States, Saudi Arabia

**Vital Statistics:** Birthrate, 12.8 per 1,000 of pop. (1980); death rate, 8.1 **Life Expectancy:** 75 years **Health Statistics:** 99 inhabitants per hospital bed; 583 per physician (1977) **Infant Mortality:** 8.7 per 1,000 births **Illiteracy:** Negligible **Primary and Secondary School Enrollment:** 2,779,065 (1976) **Enrollment in Higher Education:** 288,026 (1975) **GNP Expended on Education:** 8.7% (1975)

**Transportation:** Surfaced roads total 53,470 mi. **Motor Vehicles:** 4,345,000 (1978) **Passenger Cars:** 4,020,000 **Railway Mileage:** 1,760 **Ports:** Rotterdam, Amsterdam, IJmuiden, Terneuzen, Vlissingen, Delfzijl **Major Airlines:** K.L.M. (Royal Dutch Airlines) operates domestic and international flights **Communications: Radio Transmitters:** 16 **Licenses:** 3,997,000 (1976) **Television Transmitters:** 21 **Licenses:** 3,774,000 (1976) **Telephones:** 6,341,000 (1978) **Newspapers:** 67 dailies (1976), 311 copiees per 1,000 inhabitants (1973)

**Weights and Measures:** Metric System **Travel Requirements:** Passport, no visa up to 90 days **International Dialing Code:** 31

---

The Netherlands is just that, as much of the country lies below sea level. To a large extent it is man-made and is still being made. In 1932 a barrier dam closed the North Sea mouth of the Zuyder Zee, creating a vast freshwater lake, the IJsselmeer, out of which the hard-working Dutch have been carving habitable tracts, which by 1980 had increased the Netherlands' arable land by a tenth. Spurred by a destructive storm in 1953, the country began to erect dams to create lakes and keep the sea out of southern estuaries.

This age-old battle against the depredations of the sea and the Rhine, Maas, and Scheldt rivers mirrors the centuries-old struggle of the Dutch against encroachment by man, from the conquest by Julius Caesar's legions in 55 B.C. to German occupation in World War II.

Aside from enlarging the country and bringing it freedom, the unity of purpose in the Netherlands' struggles has produced a people able to get along harmoniously and tolerant of other cultures, as shown in the integration of more than 300,000 nonwhite colonials from the former far-flung overseas empire. However, seizures of hostages by South Moluccan terrorists has led to a deterioration in relations between the Moluccans and the Dutch. The South Moluccans had emigrated to the Netherlands in the late 1940s when their islands became part of Indonesia.

Binding the loyalty of its citizens to the state is the four-centuries-old House of Orange, now headed by Queen Beatrix, who succeeded her mother, Juliana, when she abdicated on her 71st birthday, April 30, 1980. Though political parties are organized on religious and ideological principles, recent cabinets have been coalitions. A constitutional democracy, the Netherlands reflects rule by Burgundian kings five centuries ago, Dutch republicanism, and modern liberalism.

Ultimate power lies with parliament, which presides over jammed cities that blend charming old architecture with the new, and a countryside filled with canals, broad rivers, and tidy farms, few of which are larger than 50 acres. In fact, though the Netherlands is popularly believed to be an agricultural land, national income depends more on commerce and industry than on farming.

**HISTORY:** At the time of the conquest of the Lowland areas by Julius Caesar in 55 B.C., the region was settled by Celtic and Germanic tribes. The dominant tribes were the Saxons and Frisians. In the 3rd century A.D. the West Franks (Salic Franks) invaded the Low Countries and gradually conquered the region. Following the breakup of Charlemagne's empire in the 9th century, the Lowlands were parceled up into numerous duchies and counties. In the 16th century, the area passed to Charles V of the House of Hapsburg and then to his son, Philip II of Spain

**1568-81:** Dutch wage war of independence against Spain under leadership of William the Silent, Prince of Orange, who unites the seven northern provinces; Spanish garrisons are expelled and United Provinces declare their independence

**17th cent.:** Treaty of Westphalia (1648), ending the Thirty Years War, recognizes independence of United Provinces. Meanwhile, Dutch build vast overseas empire and by 1700 the Netherlands is the world's leading maritime and commercial power

**18th cent.:** Dutch power begins to decline after 1715. In 1794, French revolutionary forces invade Netherlands; the following year French set up the Batavian Republic

**1815:** Congress of Vienna establishes Kingdom of Netherlands composed of Belgium and Holland

**1830:** Belgium revolts and gains independence

**1914-39:** Netherlands pursues policy of neutrality

**1940-45:** During World War II German forces overrun the Netherlands and subject country to ruthless occupation

**1948:** Queen Wilhelmina abdicates and is succeeded by her daughter, Juliana

**1949:** Netherlands grants Indonesia independence after four years of bitter strife

**1954:** The colonies of Surinam and Netherlands Antilles are incorporated into the Kingdom of the Netherlands

**1957:** Netherlands joins Common Market (EC)

**1962-63:** Netherlands turns western New Guinea (West Irian) over to the United Nations, which places it under Indonesian jurisdiction pending a referendum

**1975:** Independence is granted to Surinam (now Suriname) after 300 years of Dutch rule

**1976:** South Moluccan terrorists, who in support of the independence of South Molucca from Indonesia had in December 1975 hijacked a train and laid siege to the Indonesian consulate, are convicted and sentenced

**1977:** Prime Minister den Uyl's Labor party captures a plurality in parliament in May elections. South Moluccan terrorists hold 100 children hostage in a school and 50 others hostage in a train in an effort to force the Dutch government to help them in their independence struggle. The siege is ended by a Dutch military team staging a raid in which six terrorists and two hostages are killed. Christian Democrat Andreas van Agt becomes prime minister of new center-right coalition government

**1978:** In Assen, South Moluccan terrorists seize hostages for fourth time since 1975, in attempt to force granting of various demands; the three captors kill one of the 72 hostages, though one is killed in crossfire; terrorists arrested

**1979:** Parliament rejects U.S. proposal to deploy medium-range nuclear missiles in Europe

**1980:** Queen Juliana abdicates in favor of her daughter, Beatrix

**1982:** Prime Minister van Agt's center-right coalition loses Labor party support because of its austerity budget but he stays in office as head of a new two-party coalition

---

## NEW ZEALAND

**Area:** 103,736 sq. mi. **Population:** 3,175,737 (1981 census)

**Official Name:** New Zealand **Capital:** Wellington **Nationality:** New Zealand **Languages:** English is the official and predominant language; Maori, a Malayo-Polynesian language, is also spoken, but for the Maoris English is the first language **Religion:** 29% Anglican, 18% Presbyterian, 15% Roman Catholic, 38% other denominations or non-affiliated **Flag:** A blue field, with the British Union Jack in the upper left and the four stars of the Southern Cross in red edged in white on the right **Anthem:** God Save the Queen; National Song: God Defend New Zealand **Currency:** New Zealand dollar (1.3 per U.S. $1)

**Location:** South Pacific, about 1,200 miles southeast of Australia. New Zealand consists of two principal islands, North Island and South Island, separated by Cook Strait; Stewart Island lies off the southern tip of South Island; the Chatham Islands are about 400 miles east of South Island **Features:** North Island contains 72% of the country's population. The northern part of the island has rolling hills and low mountains; the southern half rises from fertile coastal plains to volcanic mountain peaks in the center. South Island is narrow and contains 28% of the population. The Southern Alps extend the entire length of the island and include New Zealand's highest peak, Mount Cook, with an elevation of 12,349 feet. Stewart Island is covered with rugged, forested peaks that rise more than 3,000 feet **Chief Rivers:** Waikato, Clutha, Taieri, Clarence, Oreti, Rangitikei, Wanganui, Waitaki, Mataura

**Head of State:** Queen Elizabeth II, represented by a governor-general, Sir David Beattie, appointed Oct. 1980 **Head of Government:** Prime Minister Robert D. Muldoon, born 1921, appointed 1975 **Effective Date of Present Constitution:** No written constitution **Legislative Body:** Parliament (unicameral House of Representatives), with 92 members elected by universal suffrage for 3 years **Local Government:** 239 local authority areas

**Ethnic Composition:** About 87% of the population is of European descent; Maoris number 9% **Population Distribution:** 83% urban **Density:** 31 inhabitants per sq. mi.

**Largest Cities (Urban Areas):** (1976 census) Auckland 766,183, Wellington 319,615, Christchurch 289,392, Dunedin 107,814, Hamilton 97,599, Lower Hutt Valley 94,502, Palmerston North 66,621, Porirua Basin 54,543

**Per Capita Income:** $6,227 (1980) **Gross Domestic Product (GDP):** $19.5 billion (1980) **Economic Statistics:** Agriculture, forestry and fishing account for 14.2% of the GDP, industry and mining 34.8%, and services 51.2%. The chief industries are food processing (meat and dairy products), transport equipment, textiles, cement, oil refining, and fertilizers. Wool, meat, and dairy products form the bulk of agricultural output **Minerals and Mining:** Iron sands, natural gas, coal, gold, and industrial minerals such as aggregate, limestone, pumice, serpentine, clays, and bentonite **Labor Force:** 1,300,000, of which 35% is engaged in industry and 11% in agriculture **Foreign Trade:** Exports, chiefly meat, dairy products, and wool, amounted to $5.9 billion in 1981. Imports, mainly machinery and related equipment, fuel, and industrial raw materials, totaled $5.5 billion **Principal Trade Partners:** Britain, Australia, United States, Japan, Canada, West Germany

**Vital Statistics:** Birthrate, 16.9 per 1,000 of pop. (1979); death rate, 8.2 **Life Expectancy:** 72 years **Health Statistics:** 97 inhabitants per hospital bed; 731 per physician (1977) **Infant Mortality:** 12.6 per 1,000 births (1976) **Illiteracy:** Negligible **Primary and Secondary School Enrollment:** 755,303 (1976) **Enrollment in Higher Education:** 74,929 **GNP Expended on Education:** 5.5% (1976)

**Transportation:** Paved roads total 29,000 mi. **Motor Vehicles:** 1,481,400 (1978) **Passenger Cars:** 1,236,400 **Railway Mileage:** 2,987 **Ports:** Auckland, Wellington, Lyttelton, Whangarei, Tauranga, Dunedin, Napier, Nelson **Major Airlines:** Air New Zealand operates domestic and international services **Communications: Radio Transmitters:** 63 **Receivers:** 2,715,000 (1976) **Television Transmitters:** 144 **Receivers:** 813,000 (1976) **Telephones:** 1,715,000 (1978) **Newspapers:** 39 dailies (1976), 376 copies per 1,000 inhabitants (1975)

**Weights and Measures:** Metric system **Travel Requirements:** Passport, no visa for 30 days, onward ticket **International Dialing Code:** 64

---

Blessed with an equable climate that lets grass grow green the year around, New Zealand is renowned for butter, race horses, and lush scenery. The New Zealand dairy industry is said to be the most efficient anywhere, and the export of dairy products is the largest in the world despite the country's small size and population.

The reorganization of overseas markets for pastoral products resulting from the formation of the European Community (Common Market), particularly the prospective phasing out of special trading advantages in Britain for New Zealand butter and cheese, accelerated the postwar trend toward economic diversification. Many dairy farmers have turned successfully to raising meat animals, especially sheep, with government encouragement. In recent years New Zealand has been developing rich new outlets for its farm products in Asia and the Middle East.

Geothermal wells, hydropower, natural gas, and coal abound, and the diverse economy includes the production of steel, aluminum, and varied forest products. New Zealand is deficient in oil but, in the early 1980s, was planning to use natural gas from its Maui field near New Plymouth to produce gasoline through a new conversion process.

With the appearance of new independent states in the South Pacific, New Zealand began providing needed guidancce and assistance to the fledgling nations. The first conference of the island heads of government, attended also by high-ranking representatives of Australia and New Zealand, was held in Wellington in August 1971 at the joint request of all the new states—Fiji, Western Samoa, Tonga, Nauru, and the Cook Islands, a self-governing dependency of New Zealand.

The island peoples are attracted to New Zealand by a variety of factors, including the high quality of education available to islanders and the easy interracial relationships. (Nine percent of the New Zealand population are Maoris, a branch of the Polynesian race; Auckland is said to be the biggest Polynesian city in the world, with more than 70,000 Maoris, Cook Islanders, Samoans, Tongans and others in the population.)

Like their Australian neighbors, the New Zealanders are overwhelmingly of British stock. Many of the hardworking pioneer white settlers came from Scotland, some to escape religious conflicts.

With a small population heavily endowed with skills, New Zealand enjoys one of the highest standards of living in the world, only recently threatened by high rates of inflation and unemployment. Government welfare programs provide "womb-to-tomb" security.

The New Zealanders have shared with the Australians a growing consciousness since World War II of belonging to the Pacific and Asian region. New Zealand has joined with Australia and Britain in a five-power pact for the defense of Singapore and Malaysia, and is a partner in the ANZUS (Australia, New Zealand, United States) Treaty of Mutual Security, the keystone of national defense.

The year 1975 saw the replacement of Wallace Rowling's Labour government by Robert Muldoon and the National party after a period of economic uncertainty. Returned to power in 1978, Muldoon weathered an ouster move within his own party in 1980 and, in November 1981, his government barely survived the general elections, amid charges that his pump-priming, pro-business policies had stimulated inflation without stemming a rise in unemployment. In mid-1982, with annual economic growth at less than 2 percent and the inflation rate above the 15 percent level, Muldoon announced a one-year freeze on most wages and prices.

**HISTORY:** The first European to discover New Zealand was the Dutch explorer Abel Tasman, who sighted the islands in 1642 but was prevented from landing by hostile Maori natives. The British explorer Captain James Cook visited the islands in 1769, and by the end of the century British whalinng settlements were established along the coast. It was not until the 19th century, however, that large-scale British immigration began

**1840:** By the Treaty of Waitangi, Maoris surrender sovereignty to Britain in exchange for guarantees that they would be allowed to remain in possession of their lands; British New Zealand Company begins first organized attempt to colonize islands with British settlers

**1845-48:** Maoris, angered by Britain's failure to honor land guarantees, rebel against British rule until uprisings are suppressed by military force

**1860-70:** Maori Wars against Britain are resumed; Maoris are again defeated by superior British force after 10 years of fighting; immigrant population continues to rise, spurred by discovery of gold in 1861

**1907:** New Zealand wins dominion status

**1914-18:** New Zealand fights on Allied side in World War I

**1939-45:** New Zealand fights on Allied side again in World War II

**1945:** New Zealand becomes a founding member of the UN

**1951:** United States, New Zealand, and Australia sign ANZUS treaty binding three nations in mutual defense alliance
**1960:** National party defeats ruling Labour party in general election; Keith J. Holyoake becomes prime minister
**1972:** Labour party wins; Norman E. Kirk is new prime minister
**1974:** Wallace Rowling succeeds after Kirk's death
**1975:** Rowling is defeated by Robert Muldoon of National party
**1978:** Muldoon reelected with reduced majority
**1979:** A sightseeing flight over the South Pole costs 257 lives when an Airr New Zealand DC-10 hits a mountain
**1980:** To reduce the country's dependence on imported oil, the government and Mobil Oil Co. plan a $500-million plant to convert natural gas into methanol and then into gasoline. Attempt by members of his own party to oust Muldoon fails. Inflation rate for year soars to 25 percent
**1981:** Muldoon retains paper-thin majority in November election
**1982:** U.S. Vice-President Bush, during a May visit, reaffirms U.S. support for ANZUS treaty. Trade pact with Australia looks to a possible future two-nation common market. Broadd wage-price freeze is imposed in June

## NICARAGUA

**Area:** 50,193 sq. mi. **Population:** 2,732,000 (1980 est.)

**Official Name:** Republic of Nicaragua **Capital:** Managua **Nationality:** Nicaraguan **Languages:** Spanish is the official and universal language; some English is spoken on the east coast **Religion:** 95% Roman Catholic **Flag:** Horizontal stripes of blue, white, bblue with the national coat of arms in the center **Anthem:** Hail Nicaragua **Currency:** Córdoba (10.05 per U.S. $1)

**Location:** Central America. Nicaragua, the largest of the Central American republics, is bounded on the north by Honduras, on the east by the Caribbean Sea, on the south by Costa Rica, and on the west by the Pacific Ocean **Features:** The western part of the country consists of a coastal plain, gradually rising toward rugged mountains. Beyond these mountains lies the interior, a sparsely populated wilderness of timbered plains and rolling hills cut by rivers. The eastern coastal plain extends about 50 miles inland and is partly swampland **Chief Rivers:** Grande de Matagalpa, Escondido, Coco, San Juan

**Head of State and of Government:** The country is governed by a 3-member junta: Daniel Ortega Saavedra (Junta Coordinator), Sergio Ramírez Mercado, and Rafael Cordoba Rivas **Effective Date of Present Constitution:** April 1974, abbrogated 1979 **Legislative Body:** A 47-member Council of State acts as a legislative body **Local Government:** 16 departments

**Ethnic Composition:** 70% of the population is mestizo (of mixed European and Indian ancestry), 17% of European ancestry, 9% Negro, and 4% Indian **Population Distribution:** 49% urban **Density:** 54 inhabitants per sq. mi.

**Largest Cities:** (1976 est.) Managua 437,666, León 73,757, Granada 50,094, Masaya 40,907, Chinandega 38,646

**Per Capita Income:** $939 (1980) **Gross National Product (GNP):** $2.3 billion (1980) **Economic Statistics:** In 1973 about 40% of GNP came from trade and services, 26% from agriiculture (cotton, coffee, cattle), forestry and fishing; 10% from industry (chemicals, insecticides, food processing, textiles), and mining **Minerals and Mining:** Copper, gold, silver, tungsten, gypsum, and precious stones **Labor Force:** 728,419 (1977), of which 43% is in agriculture, 15% in manufacturing and 13% in commerce **Foreign Trade:** Exports, mainly cotton, cottonseed, coffee, meat, gold, sesame, and wood, totaled $567 million in 1979. Imports, mainly machinery, transportation equipment, manufacturing products, chemical products, and raw materials forr industry, totaled $371 million **Principal Trade Partners:** Central American countries, United States, Japan, West Germany

**Vital Statistics:** Birthrate, 46.6 per 1,000 of pop. (1980); death rate, 12.2 **Life Expectanncy:** 54 years **Health Statistics:** 474 inhabitants per hospital bed; 1,592 per physician (1976) **Infant Mortality:** 101.7 per 1,000 births (1980) **Illiteracy:** 43% **Primary and Secondary School Enrollment:** 741,477 (1975) **Enrollment in Higher Education:** 17,184 **GNP Expended on Education:** 2.5% (1974)

**Transportation:** Paved roads total 975 mi. **Motor Vehicles:** 70,300 (1977) **Passenger Cars:** 46,400 **Railway Mileage:** 235 **Ports:** Corinto, San Juan del Sur **Major Airlines:** Lineas Aéreas de Nicaragua (LANICA) operates domestic and international flights **Communications: Radio Transmitters:** 74 **Receivers:** 126,000 (1974) **Television Transmitters:** 2 **Receivers:** 90,000 (1976) **Telephones:** 43,000 (1977) **Newspapers:** 6 dailies, 51 copies per 1,000 inhabitants (1976)

**Weights and Measures:** Metric system **Travel Requirements:** Passport, visa, check embassy or consulate for requirements **International Dialing Code:** 505

A civil war that cost an estimated 30,000 lives brought an end in 1979 to the Somoza family's political and economic rule of Nicaragua after more than four decades. President Gen. Anastasio ("Tacho") Somoza Debayle, who had made a Managua bunker his home and command post for almost two years, fled by helicopter and airplane to the United States on July 17. In August he went into exile in Paraguay, where he was assassinated on Sept. 16, 1980. The Sandinist National Liberation Front (FSLN), winner over the National Guard that the Somozas had headed since 1933, named a five-member junta as the provisional government.

On the victory day, July 19, cheering Managua crowds toppled the statue of Tacho Somoza's father, Gen. Anastasio Somoza García, founder of the family dynasty. The elder Somoza had taken command of the National Guard in 1933, just after the U.S. Marines ended intermittent intervention that had begun in 1912. It was allegedly Somoza's guardsmen who, in 1934, assassinated Gen. Augusto César Sandino, the revolutionary hero from whom the Sandinists took their name. The elder Somoza seized the presidency on Jan. 1, 1937, and held virtually complete control of Nicaragua—the largest country in Central America—until his assassination in 1956. A son, Luis, president of the senate, was named president immediately; Luis' brother, Anastasio, a West Point graduate, became president in a 1967 election in which charges of fraud and intimidation arose.

The assassination of Pedro Joaquín Chamorro, publisher of *La Prensa* and a longtime critic of Somoza, in downtown Managua in January 1978 was widely attributed to the Somoza regime. Massive unrest and violence followed, culminating in the seizure of the National Palace by the FSLN seven months later. That action won release of 58 political prisoners and safe conduct out of the country. But the National Guard largely succeeded in putting the lid back on the violence until the Sandinists launched a successful revolution from the Costa Rican border on May 29, 1979.

The junta that took over the reins of government in 1979, and also the 15-member cabinet which it appointed, included conservative businessmen and other non-Sandinisists. The United States recognized the new regime and sent badly needed food aid. In 1980, the new government began to lean more and more to the left. Banks and the mining industry were nationalized, and the government assumed control of coffee, cotton and seafood exports. It also imposed severe austerity measures as part of its reconstruction program. It has inherited the large foreign debt contracted by the Somoza regime, and is faced with heavy unemployment and inflation.

Originally, the Sandinist junta disclaimed helping the leftist guerrillas who have been trying to seize power in El Salvador. Gradually, however, evidence came forth that, under pressure from Cuba, Nicaragua was becoming a staging area and supply base for the Salvadoran rebels. In April 1981 the United States suspended all aid to Nicaragua. With this aid cut off, Nicaragua looked elsewhere and obtained moral and material help from Mexico, Libya, France and the Soviet bloc. Nicaragua also looked to western European and Arab countries for assistance.

**HISTORY:** Various Indian tribes inhabited Nicaragua before the arrival of the Spanish conquistador Gil González de Ávila in 1552. During the Spanish colonial period, Nicaragua was administered as part of the captaincy general of Guatemala
**1821:** Nicaragua wins independence from Spain and along with the other countries of Central America becomes annexed to Mexico
**1825-38:** Nicaragua secedes from Mexico and joins Central American Federation. In 1838 the federation is dissolved, and Nicaragua becomes an independent republic
**1856-57:** U.S. soldier of fortune William Walker seizes presidency but is ousted by alliance of Central American states

**1912-33:** Prolonged political turmoil between Liberals and Conservatives leads Provisional President Adolfo Díaz to ask for intervention of U.S. Marines to maintain order. In 1916 the Bryan-Chamorro Treaty is ratified, giving United States an option on route for a canal, but Liberals continue guerrilla warfare in protest against American intervention. U.S. Marines, withdrawn in 1925, again occupy country from 1926 to 1933

**1934:** Gen. Augusto César Sandino, who had defied efforts of U.S. Marines to catch him and who later had won concessions from the government, is assassinated, apparently by members of Gen. Anastasio Somoza's National Guard

**1936-57:** General Somoza seizes power; until his death by an assassin's bullet in 1956 he rules country as virtual private estate. His son, Luis, finishes his father's term and is reelected

**1967:** Anastasio Somoza Debayle, brother of Luis and head of armed forces, is elected president

**1972:** Earthquakes destroy much of Managua, killing an estimated 10,000 and leaving half the city's population homeless

**1974:** Somoza is reelected for second presidential term, after resigning in 1972 because of election provisions but retaining full power in the interim as commander of the armed forces

**1978:** Leftist guerrillas gain broad support in efforts to oust Somoza and capture several towns. However, in heavy fighting, the National Guard recaptures the places

**1979:** On May 29, Sandinist rebels launch a five-pronged attack from Costa Rican border. Somoza flees the country and a military junta takes power

**1980:** Junta puts off elections until 1985, claiming need for 5-year reconstruction period

**1981:** Junta membership is reduced to three—two Sandinists and one Conservative. Nicaraguan exiles are reported to be training in U.S. for action against the Sandinist regime. Nicaragua closes border after series of clashes with Honduran troops; accuses Honduras of aiding anti-Sandinist rebels. Government declares state of economic emergency; slashes spending, raises import taxes and bans strikes for one year. Junta Coordinator Daniel Ortega Saavedra, addressing UN, warns that developing nations will be forced to default on their foreign debts unless realistic solutions are found for their economic problems

**1982:** U.S. spy plane photos purport to show massive military buildup in Nicaragua with Soviet and Cuban assistance; Managua claims buildup is "exclusively defensive." Ortega proclaims a state of siege after anti-Sandinists dynamite two bridges near Honduran border. Nicaragua and U.S. agree to hold talks in effort to reduce tensions. Honduras and Nicaragua exchange accusations over alleged border violations. Soviet Union signs pact granting Nicaragua $169 million in technical aid and credits

## NIGER

**Area:** 489,189 sq. mi. **Population:** 5,098,427 (1977 census)

**Official Name:** Republic of Niger **Capital:** Niamey **Nationality:** Nigerien **Languages:** French is the official language; the principal African languages are Fulani, Tamashek, Djerma, Songhai, and Hausa, used primarily in trade **Religion:** The population is predominantly Moslem **Flag:** Horizontal stripes of orange, white, and green with an orange disc in the center **Anthem:** La Nigérienne **Currency:** CFA Franc (305 per U.S. $1)

**Location:** West-central Africa. Landlocked Niger is bordered on the north by Algeria and Libya, on the east by Chad, on the south by Nigeria and Benin, on the southwest by Upper Volta, and on the west by Mali **Features:** Four fifths of the country (north) is arid desert, and the remainder (south) is mostly savanna **Chief River:** Niger

**Head of State and of Government:** President of the Supreme Military Council: Lt. Col. Seyni Kountché, born 1931, assumed power in 1974 **Effective Date of Present Constitution:** 1960, suspended 1974 **Legislative Body:** All powers are in the hands of the Council **Local Government:** 7 departments under appointed prefects, divided into 32 districts

**Ethnic Composition:** Hausa make up almost 50% of the population and Djerma-Songhai 23%, the rest are nomadic and seminomadic Peuls, or Fulani (15%), Tuaregs (12%), Toubous, and others **Population Distribution:** 8% urban **Density:** 10 inhabitants per sq. mi.

**Largest Cities:** (1977 census) Niamey 225,314, Zinder 58,436, Maradi 45,852, Tahoua 31,265

**Per Capita Income:** $145 (1980) **Gross National Product (GNP):** $795 million (1980) **Economic Statistics:** 60% of GNP is derived from agriculture (peanuts, cotton, cowpeas, tobacco, millet, sorghum, beans, rice, livestock), and 7% from manufacturing (textiles, peanut oil, oxygen-acetylene) and mining **Minerals and Mining:** Niger's uranium deposits are mined in the Arlit and Akouta regions. Two more are to open in the future. Tin, coal, and phosphates are also mined **Labor Force:** 1,900,000 (1970), with about 90% in agriculture and stockraising **Foreign Trade:** Exports, mainly peanuts, uranium and livestock, totaled $458 million in 1980. Imports, chiefly fuels, machinery, motor vehicles and parts, food and clothing, totaled $526 million **Principal Trade Partners:** France, West Germany, Ivory Coast, United States, Britain, Libya

**Vital Statistics:** Birthrate, 51.4 per 1,000 of pop. (1980); death rate, 22.4 **Life Expectancy:** 39 years **Health Statistics:** 1,200 inhabitants per hospital bed; 42,632 per physician (1977) **Infant Mortality:** 200 per 1,000 births **Illiteracy:** 94% **Primary and Secondary School Enrollment:** 177,613 (1976) **Enrollment in Higher Education:** 541 (1975) **GNP Expended on Education:** 3.2% (1976)

**Transportation:** Paved roads total 1,176 mi. **Motor Vehicles:** 26,400 (1978) **Passenger Cars:** 12,600 **Railway Mileage:** None **Ports:** None **Major Airlines:** Air-Niger operates domestic flights **Communications: Radio Transmitters:** 14 **Receivers:** 150,000 (1971) **Television Transmitters:** 1 **Receivers:** N.A. **Telepphones:** 8,000 (1978) **Newspapers::** 1 daily, 1 copy per 1,000 inhabitants (1977)

**Weights and Measures:** Metric system **Travel Requirements:** Passport, visa valid for 7 days, $2.10 fee; for stay up to 3 months, $8.30 fee; 2 photos, onward ticket or guarantee from a bank

Niger has been called "a land where the harvest is won with the soul's scythe." For most of this neglected hinterland of former French West Africa is rocky desert, broken by bleak mountains. The productive southern area, watered in part by the Niger River, is semiarid and subject to droughts and floods.

While rich uranium deposits are being developed in the northern desert area and there is hope for discovery of oil and exploitation of other minerals, Niger still must depend on cattle and on limited export and food crops, chiefly peanuts, cotton, and grains. A hostile climate and need for irrigation are obstacles to increased production.

Lack of transportation is Niger's most serious problem. The landlocked country has no railroad and the rapids-strewn Niger River, a potentially low-cost route to the seacoast, has yet to be made navigable. The nearest seaport, Cotonou, in Benin, is 600 miles from Niamey, Niger's capital, and it is often noted that it takes more than two gallons of gasoline to import a single gallon.

Internal roads and links to neighboring countries, however, are gradually being built with French, American, World Bank, and United Nations aid. Canada, through new ties with French-speaking African countries, has recently become a major aid source for Niger.

A $60-million uranium project at Arlit, which began production in 1971, is a joint Nigerien/French/German/Italian undertaking. A second uranium project, organized in 1974 under a company started by the Nigerien government, the French Atomic Energy Commission, and a Japanese company, is developing deposits in the Akouta district. Additional uranium deposits were discovered in 1979 and 1980.

Like the other nations of the West African Sahel, Niger suffered greatly during the drought and famine of 1968-74. In 1973 cattle were dying; in 1974 people were dying. An estimated two million were starving in the Tuareg tribe alone. By October 1974, the drought ended, but massive international relief efforts were required to prevent starvation.

Hamani Diori, Niger's president from the time the country gained independence from France in 1960 until 1974, sought to promote national development and to unify Niger's traditionally hostile nomadic and settled farming peoples. He emphasized government stability; gradual improvement of agriculture, health, and education; and economic aid from numerous sources.

However, in 1974 when Diori was unable to stop his people's starvation resulting from the drought in the Sahel, he was overthrown by Lt. Col. Seyni

Kountché who formed a 12-member military government with himself as president. Kountché dissolved the National Assembly, suspended the constitution and banned all political groups.

**HISTORY:** The region around Niger was probably known to Egyptians before the beginning of recorded history. Through the next 1,000 years it was a battleground for Arabs; Berbers; Toubous; the Ghana, Mali, Songhai, and Bornu empires; the Hausa states; and the Djermas, Fulanis, and Tuaregs. The first European explorers arrived in the late 18th century and were soon followed by French forces pushing forward still another empire

**1901-22:** French build chain of forts, crush Tuareg resistance, and establish colony of Niger

**1946:** French set up local advisory assembly, grant people of Niger French citizenship

**1958:** Niger becomes an autonomous republic within the French Community

**1960:** Complete independence is declared and Niger joins the UN

**1968-74:** Drought and famine strike the Sahel

**1974:** Army Chief of Staff Lt. Col. Seyni Kountché ousts Diori, and declares himself head of state. Drought ends

**1979:** Rich uranium deposits discovered near Agadez in the Sahara

**1980:** Kountché frees former President Hamani Diori from custody. Drop in uranium price hurts Niger's economy

**1981:** Kountché assumes portfolio of interior minister in addition to that of defense which he already held

**1982:** Niger resumes diplomatic relations with Libya which had been suspended during latter's occupation of Chad

## NIGERIA

**Area:** 379,628 sq. mi. **Population:** 84,500,000 (1978 est.)

**Official Name:** Federal Republic of Nigeria **Capital:** Lagos **Nationality:** Nigerian **Languages:** English is the official and business language. Among the 250 African languages and dialects, the most widely spoken are Hausa, Yoruba, Ibo, and Edo. Sizable minorities speak Fulani, Kanuri, Ijaw, Ibibio, and Tiv **Religion:** Northern Nigeria is largely Moslem, while the south and west have been strongly influenced by Christianity. About 47% of the population are Moslem, 34% Christian and 19% animist **Flag:** Vertical stripes of green, white, green **Anthem:** National Anthem, beginning "Nigeria, we hail thee" **Currency:** Naira (0.68 per U.S. $1)

**Location:** West Africa. Nigeria is bounded on the northwest and north by Niger, on the northeast by Lake Chad, on the east by Cameroon, on the south by the Gulf of Guinea, and on the west by Benin **Features:** The coastal area consists of a belt of mangrove swamps intersected by delta branches of the Niger and innumerable smaller rivers and creeks. Inland, a belt of tropical rain forest extends up to 100 miles over gradually rising country. The country then rises to a plateau, which reaches an elevation of over 6,000 feet in the east. In the north, the savanna approaches the southern part of the Sahara **Chief Rivers:** Niger, Benue, Sokoto, Yobe, Gana, Kaduna, Cross, Gongola, Ogun

**Head of State and of Government:** President Alhaji Shehu Shagari, born 1925, elected Aug. 1979, took office Oct. 1 **Effective Date of Present Constitution:** 1979 **Legislative Body:** National Assembly (bicameral) consisting of a Senate and a House of Representatives. The Senate is composed of 95 members with each of the 19 states sending 5 members. The House of Representatives has 449 members. Both branches are directly elected and their maximum terms are 4 years **Local Government:** 19 states and a federal capital territory

**Ethnic Composition:** Of the country's 250 tribal groups, the dominant ones are the Yoruba (15%) in the west, the Ibo (16%) in the east, and the Hausa (19%) and Fulani (10%) in the north. Other large groups are the Edo (900,000) in the west, the Ibibio (about 1 million) and the Ijaw (900,000) in the east, annd the Kanuri (2.9 million), Nupe (500,000), and Tiv (1.5 million) in the north **Population Distribution:** 23% urban **Density:** 223 inhabitants per sq. mi.

**Largest Cities:** (1975 est.) Lagos 1,060,848, Ibadan 847,000, Ogbomosho 432,000, Kano 399,000, Oshogbo 282,000, Ilorin 282,000, Abeokuta 253,000, Port Harcourt 242,000

**Per Capita Income:** $704 (1980) **Gross Domestic Product (GDP):** $54 billion (1980) **Economic Statistics:** More than 33% of GDP comes from oil and mining, an estimated 23% from agriculture (cocoa, peanuts, African oil palm products, rubber and cotton), and 10% from manufacturing (mainly food processing, oil refining, cotton textiles and cement) **Minerals and Mining:** Nigeria is sub-Saharan Africa's largest oil producer; other minerals are tin, coal, and limestone. Large natural gas deposits are being developed **Labor Force:** 30 million of which 64% are in agriculture, forestry and fishing, and 10% in industry **Foreign Trade:** Exports, crude petroleum (95%), cocoa, peanuts, palm nuts, rubber, tin and raw cotton, totaled $25 billion in 1980. Imports, chiefly machinery, transport equipment, industrial raw materials, manufactured goods, chemicals and food, amounted to $16 billion **Principal Trade Partners:** Britain, United States, West Germany, Japan, Netherlands, France

**Vital Statistics:** Birthrate, 49.8 per 1,000 of pop. (1980); death rate, 17.8 **Life Expectancy:** 50 years **Health Statistics:** 1,248 inhabitants per hospital bed; 14,344 per physician (1976) **Infant Mortality:** 150 per 1,000 births **Illiteracy:** 65% **Primary and Secondary School Enrollment:** 5,458,160 (1973) **Enrollment in Higher Education:** 32,971 (1975) **GDP Expended on Education:** 2.6% (1975)

**Transportation:** Paved roads total 15,650 mi. **Motor Vehicles:** 255,000 (1975) **Passenger Cars:** 150,000 **Railway Mileage:** 2,178 **Ports:** Lagos, Port Harcourt, Bonny, Burutu **Major Airlines:** Nigeria Airways operates international and domestic services **Communications: Radio Transmitters:** 111 **Licenses:** 5,100,000 (1976) **Television Transmitters:** 10 **Licenses:** 121,000 (1976) **Telephones:** 128,000 (1977) **Newspapers:** 19 dailies (1976), 9 copies per 1,000 inhabitants (1974)

**Weights and Measures:** Metric system **Travel Requirements:** Passport, visa valid 3 months from date of issue, $2.30 fee **International Dialing Code:** 234

Nigeria, a country of extraordinary potential—oil, agricultural diversity, talented political leaders, a population that embraces fully a fifth of the black people in Africa——is also a country with extraordinary problems of instability. One of the underlying reasons for that instability is the nation's great ethnic diversity.

Nigeria's major tribal divisions consist of the seminomadic Hausa-Fulani of the north, the urbanized Yorubas in the west, and in the east, the industrious Ibos. Under British rulle, the three regions, together with Lagos, the administrative center, were amallgamated into one vast colonial possession.

As Britain prepared Nigeria for self-government after World War II, it was recognized that the country could achieve its great economic potential only if it remained intact. Nigerian leaders and British authorities were confident, however, that old animosities could be submerged. In 1960 Britain granted full independence and in 1963 Nigeria became a republic.

The largely Moslem north dominated the new government. Distrust soon fanned tribal rivalries into open conflict after incidents of corruption, nepotism, and rigged elections. Ibos grew increasingly resentful as they saw excessive shares of the oil revenues from their region go to northern projects.

Early in 1966, a coup led by young Ibo army officers was accompanied by the murder of many Northern and Western officials, including Prime Minister Sir Abubakar Tafawa Balewa. Gen. Johnson Aguiyi-Ironsi, an Ibo who promised a government free of corruption and tribalism, was installed as president.

However, in a countercoup led by northern officers in July 1966, Ironsi was murdered. He was replaced by Lt. Col. (later Maj. Gen.) Yakubu Gowon, who, as a Christian and member of a minor tribe, was regarded as a neutralist in the tribal conflicts.

Late in 1966 thousands of Ibos working in the north were massacred. Thousands more fled back to their homeland and Gowon's efforts for new political cooperation were frustrated by Ibo fear and distrust. Ibo leader Lt. Col. Odumegwu Ojukwu unsuccessfully sought autonomy for the Eastern Region, then, in May 1967, proclaimed a Republic of Biafra.

In the ensuing conflict Biafran forces were at first victorious, but with growing federal strength, the rebel state was graduallly reduced to a small area. As the war dragged on, starvation ravaged the East—a densely populated, food-deficient region. Despite relief efforts by many groups, Biafran resistance collapsed in January 1970, and Ojukwu fled to the Ivory Coast. The struggle took an estimated one million lives. In the years since there has been a gradual reintegration of Ibos into the national economy.

The Biafra trouble was scarcely over when prolonged drought desiccated the Sahel region in northern Nigeria. Cattle died by the thousands, farm lands suffered and fishing industry on Lake Chad collapsed as the lake shrank in size. The area is recovering, but many problems remain.

In October 1974 General Gowon announced that a previously scheduled return to civilian government (1976) had been canceled because of dispute over the 1973 census and the violent sectional political ambitions that were emerging. This announcement led to student demonstrations. Labor unrest increased over pay demands.

On July 29, 1975, Gowon was deposed in a bloodless coup; Brig. Gen. Murtala Rufai Mohammed was named head of state. In February 1976 Brig. Gen. Mohammed was assassinated by a group of "young revolutionaries" who later failed to gain control of the government. The nation's ruling Supreme Military Council named Lt. Gen. Olusegun Obasanjo as head of state.

A total of 37 persons were executed for their alleged involvement in the abortive coup and assassination. Nigeria's request that Great Britain extradite former Head of State Gowon, so that he could defend himself against accusations of involvement in the attempted coup, was denied.

Political activity, banned since 1966, was restored in September 1978. Four parties sprang up to compete for the right to form the long-promised civilian government. In August 1979 Alhaji Shehu Shagari was declared the winner of the election balloting for president, held under Nigeria's new constitution. The military surrendered control to a civilian government on Oct. 1.

The Nigerian economy under British rule was mainly agricultural. Cocoa, palm oil, peanuts, rubber and cotton were cultivated for export; subsistence farming on small plots satisfied much of the colony's food needs. After oil was discovered in 1958 it came to account for more than 90 percent of the nation's foreign-exchange earnings. Nigeria became, and still is, black Africa's wealthiest nation. However, the world glut of oil developing in the early 1980s has reduced income from this source. Meanwhile, drought, civil war and the migration of millions of farmers to the cities and oilfields have resulted in insufficient food output for a population growing at a rate of 3.5 percent a year. In 1981 the government launched its Green Revolution, a five-year, $13.5-billion program to achieve self-sufficiency in food crops by 1985.

Nigeria has pushed for closer trading ties with its West African neighbors. The government is also seeking greater "Nigerianization" of foreign-owned-and-run enterprises to give Nigerians a greater share of the wealth. Although militant on anti-colonial issues involving the white-ruled nations of Africa, Nigeria maintains a moderate foreign policy.

**HISTORY:** Nigeria's earliest known culture, Nok, flourished around 700-200 B.C. During the 12th century, Nigeria's next great culture grew up around Ife, a sacred Yoruba city. In medieval times, northern Nigeria had contact with the large kingdoms of the western Sudan and by the end of the 14th century A.D. Islam was firmly established in the north. Between the 15th and 17th centuries, the Portuguese and British engaged in commerce and slave trading

**1861-1914:** British annex Lagos (1861); gradually establish administrative control over Nigeria

**1947-54:** Successive steps are taken to allow participation in the government by Africans in preparation for self-government

**1960:** Nigeria becomes an independent federal state within the British Commonwealth

**1963:** Nigeria becomes a federal republic within the Commonwealth

**1966:** Government is ousted by a military coup and a military government is established under Gen. Johnson Aguiyi-Ironsi (an Ibo from the Eastern Region); Ironsi is murdered when another military coup is staged by anti-Ibo elements in the army; a federal military government is set up under Lt. Col. (later Maj. Gen.) Yakubu Gowon. Thousands of Ibos are massacred and more than a million are driven from the north

**1967:** Military government announces the creation of 12 ethnically based states to replace the previous four regions. The Eastern Region, under the leadership of Lt. Col. Odumegwu Ojukwu, secedes from the Federation of Nigeria and proclaims itself the independent Republic of Biafra. Federal troops invade Biafra

**1968-69:** Mass starvation threatens millions in Biafra as a result of the federal government's blockade of the region

**1970:** Surrender of Biafran forces brings end to 30-month civil war; federal government chief, Gen. Yakubu Gowon, pledges protection and political rights to former Biafrans

**1972:** Many small foreign-owned businesses are "Nigerianized"

**1975:** General Gowon is deposed in a bloodless coup. Brig. Gen. Murtala Rufai Mohammed is named head of state

**1976:** Mohammed assassinated in unsuccessful coup. Lt. Gen. Olusegun Obasanjo is named head of state. Nigeria discards British Parliament as a model for its upcoming 1979 civilian government and looks instead to presidential system of the U.S.

**1978:** Twelve-year-old ban on political activity lifted

**1979:** Alhaji Shehu Shagari is elected president under new constitution. Daily oil output reaches 2.5 million barrels

**1980:** Many die in Kano as fanatical Islamic sect clashes with "corrupted" believers

**1981:** After five Nigerian soldiers are killed in border clash, Cameroon makes reparations to resolve dispute. Trade deficit rises to nearly $1 billion

**1982:** Plot of disgruntled businessmen and hired soldiers to overthrow government is uncovered. Decline of 30 percent in oil revenues forces imposition of import restrictions

## NORWAY

**Area:** 125,053 sq. mi. **Population:** 4,100,000 (1981 est.)

**Official Name:** Kingdom of Norway **Capital:** Oslo **Nationality:** Norwegian **Languages:** Norwegian is the official and predominant language; Lappish and Finnish are spoken in the north **Religion:** The state church, the Evangelical Lutheran Church, includes 94% of the population **Flag:** An extended white bordered blue cross on a red field **Anthem:** Yes, We Love This Land of Ours **Currency:** Norwegian krone (6 per U.S. $1)

**Location:** Northern Europe, occupying the smaller, western part of the Scandinavian peninsula. Norway has common land frontiers in the east with Sweden, Finland, and the Soviet Union. It is bounded on the north by the Arctic Ocean, on the west by the Norwegian Sea, and on the south by the Skagerrak, an arm of the North Sea **Features:** The country has a 2,125-mile coastline, deeply indented by numerous fjords. From the coast, the land rises to high plateaus and mountain ranges, the highest of which, Glittertind, reaches 8,110 feet. The highlands are cut by fertile valleys and rapid rivers and are dotted with lakes. Forests cover roughly one-fourth of the country, which also has numerous glaciers. Jostedalsbreen, in the southwest, is the largest ice field in Europe **Chief Rivers:** Glomma, Lagen

**Head of State:** King Olav V, born 1903, acceded to the throne in 1957 **Head of Government:** Premier Kare Willoch, born 1928, appointed Oct. 14, 1981 **Effective Date of Present Constitution:** 1814 **Legislative Body:** *Storting* (bicameral parliament) consisting of 155 members elected by universal suffrage for a 4-year term. When assembled, parliament divides itself by election into 2 chambers, one of 39 members, the other of 116. Bills are introduced in the larger chamber and, when passed, are sent to the smaller one. If the chambers disagree, a joint session is held in which the fate of the bill is decided by a two-thirds majority **Local Government:** 19 counties and the city county of Oslo, each with a council and a governor

**Ethnic Composition:** Norwegians are mainly of Nordic origin; there has been some mixture with the Finns and Lapps, especially in the north, where some 20,000 Lapps still live **Population Distribution:** 44% urban **Density:** 33 inhabitants per sq. mi.

**Largest Cities:** (1980 est.) Oslo 452,023, Bergen 207,799, Trondheim 134,976, Stavanger 90,687, Kristiansand 60,938

**Per Capita Income:** $9,887 (1980) **Gross Domestic Product (GDP):** $40 billion (1980) **Economic Statistics:** 6% of GDP comes from agriculture (dairy farming, beef, pork, eggs and poultry), including animal husbandry, forestry, fishing and whaling; 20% from industry (transport equipment, shipbuilding, metal products, food manufactures, chemicals and chemical products, printing and publishing, paper and ppaper products, electrical and other machinery, nonmetallic mineral products); 19% from trade and finance **Minerals and Mining:** Offshore oil and natural gas, limestone, pyrites, ilmenite, iron ore, coal, molybdenite, copper, zinc, lead **Labor Force:** 1,870,000, of which 32% is employed in services, 21% in industry, and 7% in agriculture **Foreign Trade:** Exports, chiefly petroleum, ships, nonferrous metals, paper and paperboard, paper pulp, iron and steel, totaled $13.5 billion in 1979. Imports, mainly industrial machinery, petroleum and petroleum products, iron and steel, and textiles, amounted to $13.7 billion **Principal Trade Partners:** Britain, West Germany, Sweden, Denmark, United States, Japan, Netherlands, France

**Vital Statistics:** Birthrate, 12.5 per 1,000 of pop. (1980); death rate, 10 **Life Expectancy:** 75 years **Health Statistics:** 67 inhabitants per hospital bed; 541 per physician (1977) **Infant Mortality:** 8.8 per 1,000 births **Illiteracy:** Negligible **Primary and Secondary School Enrollment:** 726,011 (1976) **Enrollment in Higher Education:** 66,628 **GNP Expended on Education:** 7.7% (1976)

**Transportation:** Paved roads total 22,976 mi. **Motor Vehicles:** 1,302,200 (1978) **Passenger Cars:** 1,145,900 **Railway Mileage:** 2,645 **Ports:** Oslo, Narvik, Bergen, Stavanger, Tonsberg, Porsgrunn, Trondheim, Tromso **Major Airlines:** Scandinavian Airlines System (SAS), a consortium owned by the governments of Norway, Denmark, and Sweden, operates domestic and international services **Communications: Radio Transmitters:** 461 **Radio Licenses:** 1,288,000 (1976) **Television Transmitters:** 870 **Licenses:** 1,087,000 (1976) **Telephones:** 1,636,000 (1978) **Newspapers:** 82 dailies, 430 copies per 1,000 inhabitants (1977)

**Weights and Measures:** Metric system **Travel Requirements:** Passport, no visa for 3 months **International Dialing Code:** 47

---

Lying atop Western Europe with nearly half its 1,100-mile length north of the Arctic Circle, Norway—a rugged land of mountains, forests, glaciers, and a coastline deeply cut by fjords—is the most sparsely populated country on the Continent. It has, however, one of the highest living standards in Europe and, like the other Nordic lands, a far-reaching social welfare system.

Norway helped to form NATO in 1949, following its experience during World War II as a country invaded and occupied by the Germans. In doing so, it departed from the strict neutrality that it had observed since 1814, when it was forced during brief hostilities to enter with Sweden into a dual monarchy. Like Denmark, Norway, which, with Denmark, Sweden, and Finland, is a member of the Nordic Council, limits its membership in NATO by stipulating that neither foreign troops nor nuclear weapons may be stationed on its soil. The only Western European country that shares a frontier with the Soviet Union, Norway has a small garrison guarding that border, which is 122 miles long, in the far northeast.

The Norwegians were charter members of the British-led European Free Trade Association, organized in 1960, and for a time sought entry to the European Community (the Common Market). But in a national referendum held September 24-25, 1972, the Norwegian electorate decisively rejected such entry. However, the government negotiated a free trade agreement with the EC to gain advantages for Norway's major exports, particularly fish, aluminum, paper, and steel.

Rich in hydroelectric power, Norway has developed into an industrial nation that produces more than a fifth of its gross national product through manufacturing. All but about nine percent of Norwegian enterprises are privately owned. Small and medium-size plants predominate, with about 70 percent employing fewer than 10 persons.

Along with its promise of considerable riches, the 1968 discovery of huge oil and gas deposits on the continental shelf of the North Sea has brought Norway some major economic problems as well. After borrowing heavily to finance development, the government has found reserves to be smaller than first thought, and production costs higher. In April 1977 a spectacular oil well blowout cost $111 million in lost revenues and has delayed development of the Statfjord fields, where the nation expects to get most of its future oil. In March 1980, a tragic accident claimed the lives of 123 workers when a floating platform at Norway's Ekofisk offshore oil field capsized during a storm. Output of oil and natural gas amounted to only about two thirds of the projected 25 million tons in 1977, while the nation's balance of payments showed a record $5.3 billion deficit. As a result, the government devalued the krone by eight percent, froze prices and tightened credit. Further austerity measures are likely.

**HISTORY:** The history of Norway before the age of the Vikings is indistinct from that of the rest of Scandinavia. Norse Vikings emerge as an identifiable group in the 8th century, when the Anglo-Saxon Chronicle records their arrival in Britain. Norway itself, split into kingdoms and earldoms, was united in the 11th century and reached its peak in the 13th century, holding sway over Iceland and Greenland. Briefly united with Sweden in 1319, Norway formally joined with Denmark and Sweden in the Union of Kalmar in 1397, which lasted until the end of the Napoleonic Wars, although Sweden seceded in the 16th century

**1814:** Denmark, having sided with France in the Napoleonic Wars, is among the losers and is forced to cede Norway to Sweden. The Norwegians react by adopting a constitution of their own and choose a Danish prince to be king of Norway, but a Swedish army forces Norway to agree to a dual monarchy with Sweden

**1905:** Union with Sweden is dissolved and Norway becomes independent. Prince Charles of Denmark is elected king of Norway and ascends throne as Haakon VII

**1914-18:** Norway remains neutral during World War I, but its merchant fleet suffers heavy losses

**1940-45:** Nazi Germany attacks Norway and quickly occupies most of country despite strong Norwegian resistance. King Haakon and his cabinet leave the country and set up a government in exile in London. In occupied Norway, meanwhile, a puppet government is established under Norwegian Nazi leader Vidkun Quisling; despite his attempts to promote collaboration with Germans, the Norwegians continue to defy invaders. Norway is liberated in May 1945

**1945:** Norway becomes founding member of the UN. Trygve Lie elected first UN Secretary-General

**1957:** King Haakon dies and is succeeded by son, Olav V

**1965:** Labor party, which has been dominant for 30 years, is swept out of office in general elections; Per Borten, leader of Center party, forms non-socialist coalition government, which remains in power till 1971

**1968:** Huge oil and gas deposits are discovered in Norwegian sector of North Sea

**1972:** Voting in a national referendum, the Norwegian electorate rejects entry to the European Community (Common Market), toppling Labor government of Premier Bratteli, in power since 1971 and a strong advocate of EC entry; Lars Korvald of the Christian People's party forms a minority coalition government

**1973:** In general elections the Labor party obtains 35.29 percent of popular vote as the largest single group and returns to power with a minority government headed by Premier Trygve Bratteli

**1975:** The *Storting* (parliament) passes a tax law providing for a large surtax on North Sea oil production by oil companies, which will bring the government $1 billion a year

**1976:** Odvar Nordli becomes premier

**1978:** Further austerity measures proposed as Norway's foreign debt nears $19 billion. Work proceeds on nation's third major oil find, the Statfjord field (discovered in 1974)

**1980:** Floating platform at Ekofisk oil field collapses, killing 123 workers, most of whom are Norwegians

**1981:** Gro Harlem Brundtland becomes Norway's first woman premier, succeeding Nordli as head of Labor government. Labor party's nine-year rule ends with Conservatives' election victory in October; Kare Willoch becomes new premier

---

## OMAN

**Area:** 120,000 sq. mi. **Population:** 891,000 (1980 est.)

**Official Name:** Sultanate of Oman **Capital:** Muscat **Nationality:** Omani **Languages:** Arabic is the official and predominant language; Hindi, Baluchi, English, Farsi, and Urdu are spoken by the minorities **Religion:** 50% are Ibadi Moslems and about 25% Sunni Moslems. Islam is the official religion **Flag:** Horizontal white, red, and green bands, with a vertical red band at the hoist, a white symbol of crossed swords in the upper left **Anthem:** National Anthem, beginning "God save our sultan" **Currency:** Omani rial (0.35 per U.S. $1)

**Location:** Southeast Arabia. Bounded on the north and northwest by the Gulf of Oman and the United Arab Emirates, on the east and south by the Arabian Sea, and on the west by Southern Yemen and Saudi Arabia **Features:** The coastline extends for about 1,000 miles, with fertile coastal plain (the Batina), a range of barren hills, and a plateau and desert area with an average height of 1,000 feet. Also included are the detached tip of the Musandam Peninsula, and offshore the Kuria Muria and Masira islands **Chief Rivers:** There are no permanent rivers

**Head of State and of Government:** Sultan Qabus ibn Said al Bu Said, born 1940, seized power in July 1970. The sultan is an absolute monarch and also premier. There is a 45-member advisory council **Constitution and Legislative Body:** None; legislation is by decree **Local Government:** 37 regions, one province and the capital area, ruled by appointed governors

**Ethnic Composition:** The population is almost evenly divided between those of South and North Arabian stock. Minorities of Iranians, Indo-Pakistanis (about 90,000), and East Africans **Population Distribution:** 10% urban **Density:** 7.4 inhabitants per sq. mi.

**Largest Cities:** (1974 estimate) Matrah 20,000, Salala 10,000, Nizwa 10,000, Muscat 7,000

**Per Capita Income:** $3,800 (1980) **Gross National Product (GNP):** $3.4 billion (1980) **Economic Statistics:** About 74% from industry (oil providing 70% of the total GNP, fishing, date-drying) and 2% of GNP is derived from agriculture (dates, bananas, onions, limes, tobacco, oranges, coconuts, melons, grapes, wheat, livestock) **Minerals and Mining:** Oil is the country's chief mineral resource, and there are deposits of natural gas, asbestos, marble, chrome and copper **Labor Force:** 250,000 of which 36% are non-Omani **Foreign Trade:** Exports, oil (95%), dates, fish, and limes, totaled $2.3 billion in 1979. Imports, chiefly foods, machinery, manufactured goods, materials, and clothing, totaled $1.4 billion **Principal Trade Partners:** India, Pakistan, Australia, UAE, Britain, Japan, United States, West Germany

**Vital Statistics:** Birthrate, 48.9 per 1,000 of pop. (1980); death rate, 18.6 **Life Expectancy:** 48 years **Health Statistics:** 658 inhabitants per hospital bed; 1,975 per physician (1976) **Infant Mortality:** 145 per 1,000 births **Illiteracy:** 75% **Primary and Secondary School Enrollment:** 85,937 (1979) **GNP Expended on Education:** 7.4% (1975)

**Transportation:** Paved roads total 1,094 mi. **Motor Vehicles:** 13,200 (1978) **Passenger Cars:** 7,700 **Railway Mileage:** None **Ports:** Muscat (Port Qabus), Matrah, Mina al Fahal, Rasyut **Major Airlines:** Gulf Air provides international service **Communications: Radio Transmitters:** 6 **Receivers:** 1,000 **Television Transmitters:** 2 **Receivers:** 55,000 **Telephones:** 13,000 (1977) **Newspapers:** 1 daily

**Weights and Measures:** Metric system **Travel Requirements:** Passport; business visa, $9.00 fee, valid 3 months, 2 photos, letter from applicant's company and from sponsor in Oman

---

In 1970, Sultan Qabus ibn Said al Bu Said changed the name of Muscat and Oman to simply Oman, but he has not been able to change the fact that Oman is, in a sense, several countries. He belongs to the dynasty of the port city of Muscat, the dynasty which survived the long-standing rivalry among port cities and foreign conquerors for control of the coast. And whoever has controlled the coast has also tried to control the nomads of the desert interior—part of which is traditionally known as Oman. Despite Sultan Qabus's attempt to give a single name to his dominion, Oman is more a dynastic conglomeration than a nation. It has no definite boundaries; control of the interior is weak; and the port cities have little loyalty to the dynasty, and less to an entity called "Oman."

For over a century, the dynasty has relied on British assistance, and many of the high-ranking officers in the army are on loan from Britian. During most of the 1970s, Sultan Qabus could also borrow entire army units from the shah of Iran. The shah's overthrow in 1979 increased Oman's strategic importance in the Middle East to the West. In 1980, Oman agreed to allow the United States to use some ports and air bases in return for U.S. military and economic aid, estimated at $100 million in 1980-81.

Sultan Qabus, who had been educated in Britain, came to power in 1970 by overthrowing his father, Said ibn Taimur, who had been sultan since 1932. The older man had tried to keep his domain together by fear and by preventing change; he had forbidden nomads to enter the cities and city people to enter the interior, outlawed the cultivation of new land, and required his personal approval to build a new house or to repair an old one. While wishing to become the constitutional monarch of a democratic country, Sultan Qabus has indicated that Oman is not yet ready for democracy.

Long an exporter of dates and camels, Muscat and Oman began to export oil in 1967. Although not a member of OPEC, Oman has followed its lead in raising oil prices.

An open revolt against the government which began in Dhofar in 1969 was put down by Sultan Qabus with the assistance of Iraq, Jordan, Iran, and Britain by 1975. However, in 1979 he risked isolation from the Arab world by endorsing the peace treaty between Egypt and Israel. In 1982 Oman was one of six Persian Gulf countries to form a regional defense force, in response to the Iran-Iraq war and the Soviet invasion of Afghanistan.

**HISTORY:** Muscat and Oman was converted to Islam in the 7th century, during the lifetime of Mohammed. In 1508, the Porttuguese conquered the the coastal region. In the 17th century, they were driven out by the Turks, who were themselves expelled in 1741 by Ahmed Ibn Said of Yemen, founder of the present ruling family. In the early 19th century, Muscat and Oman was the most powerful state in Arabia, controlling Zanzibar, much of the Persian coast, and part of present-day West Pakistan, but during this period Muscat lost control of Oman—the interior region

**1856-61:** Rival heirs dispute succession to throne on death of Said ibn Sultan in 1856; dispute is settled through British mediation under an arrangement in 18661 calling for separation of Zanzibar from Muscat

**1913-20:** Tribes in interior of Oman rebel against sultan of Muscat, who controls only the cities of Muscat and Matrah, and elect Imam spiritual head of country; Imam is murdered in 1920, and sultan signs treaty with his successor calling for internal tribal autonomy and mutual nonaggression

**1951:** Traditional association with Britain is confirmed by new treaty of friendship, commerce, and navigation

**1954-57:** Imam dies in 1954; his successor breaks 1920 treaty and is driven from his capital; Muscat regains control of Oman

**1958:** Port of Gwadar in Baluchistan is sold to Pakistan

**1965-66:** UN General Assembly adopts resolution in 1965 calling for elimination of British presence in Muscat and Oman

**1969:** Leftist rebels in Dhofar province engage in guerrilla warfare in effort to overthrow sultan

**1970:** Sultan Said ibn Taimur is overthrown by son, Qabus ibn Said, who promises to establish modern government, end country's isolation, and use oil revenues for the good of the people

**1975:** Victory over rebels in Dhofar province is declared by sultan

**1977:** Britain closes its military base on the Omani island of Masira

**1980:** Oman and United States sign agreement to permit U.S. access to country's ports and airfields in exchange for American miilitary and economic aid

---

## PAKISTAN

**Area:** 342,750 sq. mi. **Population:** 83,782,000 (1981 census)

**Official Name:** Islamic Republic of Pakistan **Capital:** Islamabad **Nationality:** Pakistani **Languages:** Urdu (spoken by only 9%) is the official language, but English is also widely used in government and commerce; Punjabi (65%), Sindhi (11%), Pushtu, Brahui, and Baluchi are regional languages **Religion:** Islam is the state religion and is practiced by 97% of the population; the rest are Hindus, Christians, Buddhists, or of no religious affiliation **Flag:** Green with a white vertical stripe at the hoist and a white crescent and a 5-pointed star in the center **Anthem:** National Anthem, beginning "Blessed be the sacred land" **Currency:** Pakistani rupee (11.7 per U.S. $1)

**Location:** South Asia. It extends c. 1,000 miles from the sea north to the mountain wall of the Hindu Kush and the towering peaks of the Karakoram. It adjoins Iran and Afghanistan on the west and northwest, China on the northeast, India on the east, and the Arabian Sea on the south **Features:** A barren plain stretches along the foothills of the mountains; in the center is the fertile Indus plain **Chief Rivers:** Indus, Sutlej, Chenab, Ravi

**Head of State and of Government:** President: Gen. Mohammad Zia-ul-Haq, born 1924, assumed office in 1978. He is also Chief Martial

Law Administrator, an office he has occupied since the coup of July 1977 **Effective Date of Present Constitution:** 1973, temporarily suspended in 1977, parts restored in 1981 **Legislative Body:** Rule is by President Zia and a council of military chiefs. The establishment of a 350-member advisory council was announced by President Zia on Dec. 24, 1981 **Local Government:** 4 provinces and a federal capital territory plus tribal areas

**Ethnic Composition:** The population of Pakistan is made up chiefly of Punjabi, Sindhi, Pushtan (Pathan), and Baluchi. Several small tribes live in the mountainous areas **Population Distribution:** 28% urban **Density:** 244 inhabitants per sq. mi.

**Largest Cities:** (1981 census) Karachi 5,103,000, Lahore 2,922,000, Faisalabad 1,092,000, Rawalpindi 806,000, Hyderabad 795,000, Multan 730,000, Gujranwala 597,000, Peshawar 555,000, Sialkot 296,000, Sargodha 294,000, Quetta 285,000, Islamabad 201,000

**Per Capita Income:** $239 (1980) **Gross National Product (GNP):** $21 billion (1980) **Economic Statistics:** In 1977 about 33% of GNP came from agriculture (wheat, cotton, rice); 16% from manufacturing (textiles, food processing, chemicals, cement, paper, metal manufacturing) and mining; 15% from trade; and 6% from construction **Minerals and Mining:** There are large reserves of natural gas, coal, copper, and some crude oil **Labor Force:** 24 million, with 55% in agriculture and 12% in industry **Foreign Trade:** Exports, chiefly cotton, cotton products, leather goods, rugs, fish and rice, amounted to $2.6 billion in 1980. Imports, mainly machinery, transportation equipment, iron and steel, animal and vegetable oils and fats, petroleum and products, chemicals, tea and food grains, amounted to $5.5 billion **Principal Trade Partners:** United States, Japan, Kuwait, Britain, Hong Kong, West Germany, Saudi Arabia, China

**Vital Statistics:** Birthrate, 40.5 per 1,000 of pop. (1976); death rate, 12 **Life Expectancy:** 51 years **Health Statistics:** 1,903 inhabitants per hospital bed; 4,049 per physician (1973) **Infant Mortality:** 115 per 1,000 births (1970) **Illiteracy:** 76% **Primary and Secondary School Enrollment:** 7,325,303 (1975) **Enrollment in Higher Education:** 114,913 (1974) **GNP Expended on Education:** 2.1% (1976)

**Transportation:** Surfaced roads total 16,000 mi. **Motor Vehicles:** 459,600 (1977) **Passenger Cars:** 340,500 **Railway Mileage:** 5,475 **Ports:** Karachi, Port Qasim **Major Airlines:** Pakistan International Airlines, operates domestic and international services **Communications: Radio Transmitters:** 28 **Licenses:** 1,200,000 (1976) **Television Transmitters:** 16 **Receivers:** 350,000 (1976) **Telephones:** 259,000 (1976) **Newspapers:** 108 dailies (1977), 18 copies per 1,000 inhabitants

**Weights and Measures:** Metric system **Travel Requirements:** Passport, visa not required for stay up to 30 days

---

Throughout its relatively short history, Pakistan has been shot through with powerfully divisive forces. When the Indian subcontinent was granted independence from Britain in 1947, it was decided that a national homeland for Moslems should be created as a nation separate from predominantly Hindu India. For centuries there had been periodic bloodbaths resulting from communal rioting between Hindus and Moslems, and an independent Pakistan was seen as the solution.

Unfortunately, Indian Moslems were concentrated in two widely separated parts. The first consisted of all or part of four provinces now known as Pakistan, which borders Afghanistan, Iran, India, and China. The second and more populous part was carved from the old state of Bengal and is now Bangladesh, bordering India and Burma.

The gulf between the two wings of Pakistan was reflected in and intensified by the 1970 election, the first since independence. Of the 313 seats that were to be filled in the new National Assembly, 167 were won by the Awami League—a Bengali nationalist party, all the strength of which was in Bangladesh. The runner-up was the Pakistan People's party with 88 seats, all for West Pakistan. There was no major national party to bridge the two wings, and virtually the only cement holding them together was a common religion.

On March 1, 1971, at the urging of the Pakistan People's party, Gen. Yahya Khan announced that the convening of the National Assembly would be postponed pending further discussions of major constitutional issues. Leaders of the Awami League claimed they were being cheated.

Widespread rioting in Bangladesh ensued, and strikes crippled the cities. Bengali extremists murdered substantial numbers of non-Bengalis.

On March 25, President Yahya Khan ordered the national army into Bangladesh to crush the separatist movement. The East Bengal Regiment of the army promptly defected to join Bangladesh armed forces, and key bridges, railroads, and communications were blown up or damaged.

An occupation army remained in Bangladesh and had to contend with hostility from the province, sniping and sabotage from Bangladesh guerrillas, and a vast economic drain on the nation as a whole. Millions of refugees fled and hundreds of civilians were killed in the conflict.

In the ensuing months tension between India and Pakistan increased, and on December 4 Indian troops entered the Bengali province. On December 16 the Pakistani armed forces there surrendered to the Indian and Bangladesh command.

This defeat, and the secession of Bangladesh, for which the Pakistani public had been unprepared, led to the resignation of President Yahya Khan and the succession of Zulfikar Ali Bhutto, leader of the People's party, as the first civilian president. Bhutto negotiated the release of 90,000 prisoners and, as a spellbinding orator, set out to restore national pride. He put in train a series of reforms in education, politics, and social life and announced that the state would assume control, but not ownership, of ten basic industries.

In July 1977, following four months of political violence in which at least 350 people were killed, the Pakistani army seized power in a bloodless coup. The Army Chief of Staff, Gen. Mohammad Zia-ul-Haq, then became chief martial law administrator and the nation's de facto ruler.

In March 1978, Bhutto, the most popular civilian politician in Pakistan's history, was convicted of a 1974 political murder and sentenced to hang. Denying his guilt, he appealed to the nation's Supreme Court, but lost, 4-3. Despite clemency pleas from many world leaders, he was hanged in April 1979. Later that year, Zia postponed scheduled national elections, placed opposition leaders under detention for several months, silenced newspaper criticism, and virtually banned political activity.

The U.S. cut off economic aid in 1979 after accusing Pakistan of secret efforts to build nuclear weapons by importing various pieces and materials from Europe and the U.S. After the USSR invasion of Afghanistan put 80,000 Soviet troops at Pakistan's border, the U.S., in early 1980, offered a modest aid package that Zia scornfully refused, but in 1981, a more militantly anti-Soviet U.S. administration negotiated a six-year, $3.2-billion military and economic aid plan which included a provision for the sale to Pakistan of American F-16 fighter planes, which Zia had eagerly sought.

Despite bilateral talks with Indian representatives in 1981 and 1982, relations with India remained strained over the disputed status of the Indian-administered province of Kashmir and mutual suspicions about armament plans.

The year 1982 brought a minor relaxation of press censorship but continued arrests of political dissenters and increasing unrest. Meanwhile, the presence of over two million Afghan refugees was seriously draining Pakistan's economy.

**HISTORY:** In the 8th century Moslems from Arabia introduced Islam to the lower reaches of what is now Pakistan. Two centuries later, Moslem warriors swept from the northwest down through the Khyber Pass and conquered the upper reaches of Pakistan, converting millions of the inhabitants to Islam. Moslem power and culture on the Indian subcontinent reached their zenith under the Mogul empire (1526-1857). Despite cultural interchange with the Hindus, the Moslem cummunity continued to maintain its distinct identity under British rule, which lasted until the middle of the 20th century

**1906-40:** The Moslem League is founded as a separate political organization. Led by Mohammad Ali Jinnah, it demands the establishment of a Moslem state in India

**1947:** Pakistan is set up as a separate British dominion, with Jinnah as governor-general and Liaqat Ali Khan as prime minister. Establishment of the new state is followed by widespread communal strife between Moslems and Hindus, costing more than a million lives and uprooting millions of Hindus and Moslems

**1948-49:** Pakistan and India are involved in an undeclared war over the state of Jammu and Kashmir (a state whose predominantly Moslem population is ruled by a Hindu prince who signs Kashmir over to India). A cease-fire is arranged, and the state partitioned by a temporary demarcation line

**1951-56:** Liaqat Ali Khan is assassinated (1951), ushering in a period of political instability and tension between East and West Pakistan. A new constitution is adopted, and Pakistan becomes a republic within the British Commonwealth with Gen. Iskander Mirza as president

**1958-62:** Following continued turmoil in both parts of the country, Mirza abrogates the constitution, dismisses the cabinet, and hands over power to the army under Gen. Ayub Khan. Ayub takes over the presidency, dismisses the prime minister, and rules by decree. The new president proclaims new constitution

**1965:** Ayub Khan is elected president. Pakistan and India fight a brief war over the Rann of Kutch and Kashmir

**1969:** Ayub resigns in the face of widespread political unrest. Martial law is proclaimed under Gen. Agha Mohammad Yahya Khan, who takes over as president

**1970:** Yahya Khan proclaims Pakistan an Islamic federal state

**1971:** Civil war breaks out between Bengali and federal forces and Bengalis are defeated; in December brief war between India and Pakistan results in defeat of Pakistan and the secession of the Bengali province, now Bangladesh. Yahya Khan resigns and Zulfikar Ali Bhutto becomes president

**1972:** Pakistan and India sign Simla agreement to stabilize relations

**1973:** New constitution is adopted. Fazal Elahi Chaudhry is elected president by the National Assembly. Former President Bhutto becomes prime minister with no loss of power

**1974:** Civil rights restored. Pakistan recognizes Bangladesh

**1975:** Assassination of Provincial Minister Sherpao leads to opposition Awami party being declared illegal. U.S. lifts 10-year ban on sale of arms to Pakistan

**1976:** India and Pakistan agree to resume diplomatic relations

**1977:** Pakistani army under Gen. Mohammad Zia-ul-Haq seizes power in a bloodless coup, ending the Bhutto regime. Elections, promised for October, are canceled; political activity is banned; martial-law rule is extended indefinitely

**1978:** Bhutto is convicted of a 1974 murder and sentenced to die; denying charge, he appeals to Supreme Court, which later rules against him. General Zia assumes the presidency

**1979:** On April 4, Bhutto, still declaring his innocence, is hanged. Days of rioting follow. U.S. cuts off economic aid, contending that Pakistan is secretly trying to build nuclear weapons with equipment and materials purchased abroad. On Oct. 16, Zia indefinitely postpones national elections scheduled for Nov. 17. He dissolves all political parties, detains opposition leaders, expands jurisdiction of military courts, shuts down critical newspapers. On Nov. 21, a mob, inflamed by false reports from Iran, sets fire to U.S. embassy in Islamabad; Pakistani army rescues embassy personnel after unexplained six-hour delay

**1980:** Soviet invasion of Afghanistan sends hoards of Afghans across border, where they are held in Pakistani internment camps. Offered $400 million over two years by the U.S. to improve defenses against the Soviets, Zia scoffs at it

**1981:** In March, Zia releases 54 prisoners, capitulating to skyjackers who commandeered a Pakistani airliner carrying more than 100 passengers and flew it to Syria. New Reagan Administration in U.S. offers a $3.2-billion, 6-year economic and military aid package. Relations with India worsen; border clashes occur

**1982:** Zia rules out early elections as martial law remains in force. Pakistan reports to UN that it will not develop nuclear weapons. Burdened by more than 2 million Afghan refugees, Pakistan enters into talks at Geneva with the Soviet-supported government of Afghanistan in an effort to end the fighting in that country

## PANAMA

**Area:** 29,762 sq. mi. **Population:** 1,830,175 (1980 census)

**Official Name:** Republic of Panama **Capital:** Panama **Nationality:** Panamanian **Languages:** Spanish is the official and predominant language; English is widely used in the capital and Colón **Religion:** 93% Roman Catholic, 6% Protestant **Flag:** Divided into 4 rectangles: the lower left is blue; the upper right red; the upper left white with a blue star in the center; the lower right white with a red star in the middle **Anthem:** Istmeño Hymn **Currency:** Balboa (1 per U.S. $1)

**Location:** Latin America, occupying the southern end of the Isthmus of Panama, which forms the land connection between the North and South American continents. Panama is bounded on the north by the Caribbean Sea, on the east by Colombia, on the south by the Gulf of Panama and the Pacific Ocean, and on the west by Costa Rica **Features:** The country is largely mountainous and hilly, with 2 mountain ranges forming the backbone of the isthmus. Lowlands lie along both coastlines; the Atlantic side and eastern Panama are covered almost entirely by tropical rain forests. The Panama Canal bisects the country **Chief Rivers:** Tuira, Bayano, Santa María, Chepo, Indio

**Head of State and of Government:** President Ricardo de la Espriella, sworn in July 30, 1982 **Effective Date of Present Constitution:** October 11, 1972 **Legislative Body:** A National Assembly of Community Representatives, with 505 members elected for 6 years; a 56-member National Legislative Council performs legislative functions when the Assembly is not in session **Local Government:** 9 provinces, each headed by an appointed governor, and one intendency

**Ethnic Composition:** The population is 70% mestizo, 14% Antilleans (immigrants from the West Indies and their descendants), 10% white and 6% Indian **Population Distribution:** 51% urban **Density:** 61 inhabitants per sq. mi.

**Largest Cities:** (1980 census) Panama 388,638, San Miguelito 157,063, Colón 59,832, David 50,621

**Per Capita Income:** $1,680 (1980) **Gross National Product (GNP):** $3.2 billion (1980) **Economic Statistics:** In 1973 about 18% came from agriculture (rice, sugar, and bananas); 18% from trade; and 16% from industry (food processing, textiles, clothing, shoes, cement, pharmaceuticals, oil refining, sugar refining) **Minerals and Mining:** There are many minerals that remain unexploited because of poor quality; however, major copper and molybdenum deposits are to be exploited **Labor Force:** 543,000 (1978), of which 45% was engaged in services and commerce, 29% in agriculture, 10% in manufacturing, and 4% in canal activities **Foreign Trade:** Exports, chiefly bananas, shrimp, sugar and petroleum derivatives, totaled $410 million in 1980. Imports, mainly machinery, vehicles and parts, petroleum and food totaled $1.3 billion **Principal Trade Partners:** United States, Saudi Arabia, Ecuador, Venezuela

**Vital Statistics:** Birthrate, 26.8 per 1,000 of pop. (1980); death rate, 5.9 **Life Expectancy:** 70 years **Health Statistics:** 259 inhabitants per hospital bed; 1,262 per physician (1977) **Infant Mortality:** 21.3 per 1,000 births **Illiteracy:** 15% **Primary and Secondary School Enrollment:** 502,932 (1977) **Enrollment in Higher Education:** 32,063 (1976) **GNP Expended on Education:** 4.9% (1976)

**Transportation:** Paved roads total 1,700 mi. **Motor Vehicles:** 92,800 (1977) **Passenger Cars:** 71,000 **Railway Mileage:** 225 **Ports:** Colón, Cristobal, Balboa, Bocas del Toro, Puerto Armuelles, Chiriquí Grande **Major Airlines:** Air Panama and Compania Panameña de Aviación operate international and domestic services **Communications: Radio Transmitters:** 97 **Receivers:** 270,000 (1976) **Television Transmitters:** 13 **Receivers:** 186,000 (1976) **Telephones:** 155,000 (1977) **Newspapers:** 6 dailies, 79 copies per 1,000 inhabitants (1976)

**Weights and Measures:** Metric system **Travel Requirements:** Passport, visa or 30-day tourist card obtainable from airline, $2 fee **International Dialing Code:** 507

Panama, the narrow serpentine isthmus connecting North and South America, is a largely mountainous country, bisected by a 51-mile-long Panama Canal. Since Nov. 1, 1979, Panama has been building up its financial and commercial status through possession of the land, dry docks, ports, and railroads of the former Canal Zone. (The waterway itself is scheduled to be controlled until Dec. 31, 1999, by the U.S.-operated Canal Commission, in which Panama is a junior partner.) As the home of 85 international banks, and well situated for the distribution or transshipment of goods, Panama is rapidly becoming the business center of Central America.

Within the country, access roads are sparse, a handicap that the government, with outside help, has been trying to remedy. The eastern half of the country, down to the Colombian border, consists largely of impenetrable jungle inhabited by a few primitive Indian tribes.

On June 16, 1978, in Panama City, President Carter and Panamanian head of state Brig. Gen. Omar Torrijos Herrera took part in ceremonies formally concluding the two new Panama Canal treaties, thus bringing to fruition 13 years of often difficult negotiations. Basically, one treaty covers control of the canal while the other establishes its future neutrality. Under the accords, Panama will obtain full control of the canal in the year 2000, the U.S. will pay Panama $10 million annually in toll revenues (plus added amounts dependent on traffic), and the U.S. has the right to intervene unilaterally in Panama if the canal's operation is ever threatened after the year 2000.

In the final phase of the canal talks, both leaders absorbed considerable criticism from countrymen who felt too much was being given to the other nation. Carter narrowly averted a serious political setback in April 1978 when the U.S. Senate ratified, with but one vote to spare, the second of the two treaties. In order to gain ratification, the Administration accepted reservations favorable to the U.S. but politically embarrassing for Torrijos, who nonetheless accepted them.

The Panama Canal dominates life in the central region, and it has played an overriding role in the nation's politics. Its transfer to Panamanian control, however, has failed to bring about the economic revival the people anticipated. Unemployment and inflation have increased, and strikes and riots have been recurring.

In 1979 facilities were opened on the Pacific coast for transferring Alaskan oil from supertankers to smaller craft to go through the canal for reloading on big ships at the other end.

**HISTORY:** Little is known about the Indians inhabiting Panama before the arrival of the Spanish explorer Rodrigo de Bastidas in 1502. The region soon fell under the control of Balboa, who in 1513 made his famous crossing of the isthmus and discovered the Pacific. Under Spanish occupation the isthmus became the route by which Inca treasures were shipped to Spain. But Panama was to lose most of its importancce in the carrying trade with the collapse of the Spanish Empire

**1821:** Panama breaks away from Spain and becomes part of Colombia

**1848-49:** California gold rush enhances importance of Panama as westward-bound U.S. settlers use isthmus as bridge between Atlantic and Pacific; crossings stimulate interest in a canal

**1881-89:** French company headed by Ferdinand de Lesseps begins work on a canal in 1881; disease among workers and financial problems drive company into bankruptcy within the decade

**1903:** Panamanians revolt when Colombian senate refuses to ratify Hay-Herrán Treaty granting United States right to build a canal across Panamanian isthmus; United States prevents Colombia from quelling rebellion and Panamanians declare their independence; new republic grants United States exclusive control of a canal zone in perpetuity and permits United States to intervene to protect Panamanian independence

**1914:** Panama Canal is opened

**1939:** Canal treaty is amended, eliminating U.S. right to intervene in Panamanian affairs

**1964:** Riots break out in Canal Zone as Panamanians protest U.S. failure to abide by agreement calling for simultaneous display of Panamanian and American flags

**1967:** United States and Panama negotiate new treaties under which United States would give up sovereignty over canal to U.S.-Panamanian authority and provide military defense for canal, and under which construction of a new canal might be undertaken; treaties, however, remain unratified

**1968:** National Assembly impeaches President Marco Aurelio Robles for having violated constitution by backing government candidate in presidential election; Assembly's decision is voided by Supreme Court. Following a dispute over the outcome of the election, opposition candidate Arnulfo Arias is declared president but is overthrown on October 1, 11 days after taking office, in coup led by National Guard; National Assembly is dissolved and constitutional guarantees suspended; Col. José M. Pinilla is sworn in as provisional president

**1969:** Brig. Gen. Omar Torrijos Herrera, one of the principal leaders of the 1968 coup, emerges as nation's strong man

**1972:** Torrijos acquires full civil and military powers

**1975:** Government moves toward nationalization of banana industry. U.S. and Panama sign a preliminary agreement to end U.S. jurisdiction over the Panama Canal and Zone

**1977:** President Carter and General Torrijos sign two new Panama Canal treaties in Washington, providing for transfer of canal to Panama by the year 2000 and establishing its future neutrality

**1978:** U.S. Senate barely ratifies second of two treaties; last-minute reservations favorable to U.S. prove a political embarrassment to Torrijos but he finally accepts them; Carter visits Panama for formal conclusion of pacts. Aristides Royo, a lawyer and former education minister who helped negotiate the canal treaties, is elected president by the National Assembly. Torrijos continues as commander of National Guard

**1979:** Canal Zone is transferred to Panama on Oct. 1

**1980:** Deposed Shah of Iran goes to Cairo Mar. 23 after 14 weeks of asylum in Panama

**1981:** Petroterminal de Panama awards a contract for constructing a 78-mile pipeline across western Panama; it would save time and cost of shipping Alaskan oil to Gulf and Atlantic ports. Gen. Torrijos is killed in plane crash July 31

**1982:** Power struggle between military leaders and civilian President Aristides Royo follows death of Torrijos. Pres. Royo, citing health problems, resigns July 30. Ricardo de la Espriella succeeds him. Gen. Ruben Dario Paredes, commander of National Guard, emerges as Panama's strongman

## PAPUA NEW GUINEA

**Area:** 183,540 sq. mi. **Population:** 3,006,799 (1980 census)

**Official Name:** Papua New Guinea **Capital:** Port Moresby **Nationality:** Papua New Guinean **Languages:** Melanesian Pidgin and Hiri (Police) Motu serrve as linguas franca, but are not universal; English is the official language; about 750 localized Papuan languages are spoken **Religion:** About 1,400,000 profess Christianity, with half a million Roman Catholics and the rest Protestants; the rest practice animistic forms of worship **Flag:** Divided diagonally from upper left to lower right; the upper section is red with a gold bird of paradise, and the lower section is black with the five principal stars of the Southern Cross in white **Anthem:** O Arise All You Sons **Currency:** Kina (0.72 per U.S. $1)

**Location:** Southwest Pacific. About 100 miles northeast of Australia, it occupies the eastern half of the island of New Guinea and is bordered on the west by Indonesia. 15% of the area is on islands to the north and east: the Bismarck Archipelago, the northwestern Solomons, and the smaller Trobriand, Woodlark, D'Entrecasteaux and Louisiade groups **Features:** A high mountain ridge bisecting the New Guinea portion rises to about 15,000 feet, graduating north and south to broad upland valleys, plains, and along much of the coast vast swamps. The larger islands are mountainous, some with active volcanoes **Chief Rivers:** Fly, Sepik, Markham, Ramu

**Head of State:** Queen Elizabeth II, represented by a governor-general, Sir Tore Lokoloko, born 1930, appointed March 1977 **Head of Government:** Prime Minister Michael Somare, born 1936, appointed Aug. 2, 1982; he is assisted by a National Executive Council **Effective Date of Present Constitution:** 1975 **Legislative Body:** Parliament (unicameral), with 109 members elected for 5 years **Local Government:** 19 provinces and a national capital district

**Ethnic Composition:** The indigenous population is composed of two major groups, Papuans in the interior and on the south coast of New Guinea, and Melanesians on the north and east coastal areas, and on the islands; minorities include Chinese, Europeans, and Polynesians **Population Distribution:** 13% urban **Density:** 16 inhabitants per sq. mi.

**Largest Cities:** (1980 census) Port Moresby 122,761, Lae 61,682, Madang 21,332, Wewak 19,554, Goroka 18,797

**Per Capita Income:** $676 (1980) **Gross National Product (GNP):** $2.1 billion (1980) **Economic Statistics:** About 39% of GNP is derived from manufacturing (meat packing, lumbering, fish and tobacco processing, light industries) and mining and 22% from agriculture (coffee, cocoa, rubber, copra, tea, palm products, timber, livestock) and fishing **Minerals and Mining:** Copper, gold, and silver are exploited, and a search for oil and gas has been started **Labor Force:** 352,500, with 53% in agriculture, 20% in government, 17% in industry and commerce, and 10% in services **Foreign Trade:** Exports, chiefly copper, copra, palm oil, coffee, cocoa, rubber, tea, plywood, tuna, and gold, totaled $960 million in 1979. Imports, mainly foods, machinery, and manufactured goods, chemicals, and petroleum products, totaled $936 million **Principal Trade Partners:** Australia, Japan, United States, West Germany, Singapore

**Vital Statistics:** Birthrate, 41.1 per 1,000 of pop. (1980); death rate, 15.8 **Life Expectancy:** 49 years **Health Statistics:** 169 inhabitants per hospital bed; 14,550 per physician (1977) **Infant Mortality:** 10.2 per 1,000 births **Illiteracy:** 67% **Primary and Secondary School Enrollment:** 295,503 (1977) **Enrollment in Higher Education:** 9,667 **GNP Expended on Education:** 6.8% (1971)

**Transportation:** Paved roads total 400 mi. **Motor Vehicles:** 38,500 (1977) **Passenger Cars:** 17,200 **Railway Mileage:** None **Ports:** Kieta, Rabaul, Lae, Port Moresby, Madang **Major Airlines:** Air Niugini maintains domestic and international services; domestic flights are handled by Talair **Communications: Radio Transmitters:** 26 **Receivers:** 100,000 (1974) **Television:** None **Telephones:** 42,000 (1978) **Newspapers:** 1 daily, 9 copies per 1,000 inhabitants (1977)

**Weights and Measures:** Metric system **Travel Requirements:** Passport, visa not required if arriving via Port Moresby airport **International Dialing Code:** 675

---

Papua New Guinea is one of the more recent additions to the world family of nations. The people of this Pacific island country until recent years lived in a near-Stone Age culture. For many of the dark-skinned Melanesian and Papuan indigenous population, the modern world of the 20th century did not exist until the area became the battleground for opposing Japanese and Allied forces.

The native population, one of the most heterogeneous in the Pacific, includes, besides Melanesians and Papuans, a number of Chinese, Australian and Polynesian peoples. These ethnic groups are divided by language, custom and tradition. The land itself is divisive, with physical isolation, difficult terrain and heavy vegetation reinforcing the pattern of diversity. Contact with the outside world was a hit-or-miss proposition for the long colonial period. Today for many of its people the main way of life is still subsistence farming based on taro, yams and bananas.

Commercial agriculture is largely in the hands of foreign investors who have developed plantations for coffee, copra, rubber and tea. Timber is a more recent cash crop that is being developed and has a great potential. Recently, copper from the mines of Bougainville has become the chief export.

Despite the great potential for self-sufficiency, Papua New Guinea is dependent on food imports. With a growing urban population and a poor road network, rice and other staples have to be imported. It also continues to rely heavily on Australia and New Zealand for financial aid.

Since independence, continuing border problems with the neighboring Indonesian province of Irian Jaya (West New Guinea) due to an off-and-on guerrilla war waged by separatists of the Free West Papua Movement has strained relations between the two nations. Refugees that crossed the border to flee the fighting—and reported Indonesian reprisals—have added to the economic burden on Port Moresby. In 1978, the government cracked down on the guerrillas' highland sanctuaries, and in October captured West Papuan leader Jacob Prai. Indonesia and Papua New Guinea began talks in 1979 to set permanent boundaries in the western highlands area—one of the most rugged and inaccessible in the world.

**HISTORY:** Little is known about the prehistory of Papua New Guinea but it is now established that man was in the New Guinea highlands at least by 8000 B.C. and perhaps as early as 50,000 B.C. The area was settled by Asian peoples by way of Indonesia. The first Europeans to sight New Guinea were probably Portuguese and Spanish navigators in the early 16th century

**1828:** Dutch take possession of West New Guinea; occasional contact is made with eastern regions

**1870s:** German firm begins to develop copra trade to meet European demand for coconut oil

**1884:** The British establish protectorate over southern littoral (Papua) after concern in Australia over German encroachment

**1906:** British New Guinea turned over to Australia

**1914:** Australian troops occupy German New Guinea

**1920:** Australia assumes League of Nations mandate over Territory of New Guinea

**1941:** Japanese invade New Guinea

**1942-43:** American and Australian forces halt Japanese advance on Port Moresby and regain control of New Guinea and adjacent islands in a series of hard-fought campaigns

**1947:** Australian rule is reconfirmed by United Nations

**1949:** Australian territory of Papua and UN trust territory of New Guinea joined under single international trusteeship

**1950-60:** Native local government councils are established

**1964:** House of Assembly replaces Legislative Council

**1973:** Self-government established in December with Michael Somare as Chief Minister. Australia retains control of defense and foreign relations

**1975:** Full independence is achieved on September 16

**1976:** Agreement is reached with Bougainville secessionist leaders after eruption of violence

**1977:** Prime Minister Michael Somare's Pangu Parti coalition is returned to power in general elections for parliament

**1978:** Government, proclaiming 200-mile offshore economic zone, takes control of coastal fishing and seabed resources. Papua New Guinea and Australia sign (Dec. 18) treaty settling 6-year boundary dispute with Queensland over Torres Strait

**1980:** Somare loses vote of confidence in March and is succeeded by Sir Julius Chan as prime minister

**1981:** Depressed commodity prices and reduced copper production weaken economy. Chan visits Indonesia and Australia to maintain good relations

**1982:** Michael Somare returns to power as prime minister following the electoral victory of his Pangu Parti

---

## PARAGUAY

---

**Area:** 157,047 sq. mi. **Population:** 3,268,000 (1981 est.)

**Official Name:** Republic of Paraguay **Capital:** Asunción **Nationality:** Paraguayan **Languages:** Spanish, the official language spoken by 75%, and Guaraní, spoken by 90%, are the national languages **Religion:** Roman Catholicism is the state religion and embraces about 97% of the population; there are Mennonite colonies in the Chaco **Flag:** Horizontal stripes of red, white, and blue; the national coat of arms in the center of the obverse and the treasury seal in the center of the reverse **Anthem:** National Anthem, beginning "Once the land of America" **Currency:** Guaraní (126 per U.S. $1)

**Location:** Southern South America. Landlocked Paraguay is bordered on the northeast and east by Brazil, on the south by Argentina, and on the west and north by Bolivia **Features:** The country is divided by the Paraguay River into 2 disparate regions. The eastern part consists of rolling terrain, with wooded hills, tropical forests, and fertile grasslands. To the west is the Chaco, a low plain covered with marshes and dense scrub forests **Chief Rivers:** Paraguay, Pilcomayo, Paraná, Verde

**Head of State and of Government:** President: Gen. Alfredo Stroessner, born 1912, originally elected in 1954; in 1978 reelected to sixth term of office **Effective Date of Present Constitution:** 1967 **Legislative Body:** Congress (bicameral), consisting of the Senate and the Chamber of Deputies. The Senate is composed of 30 members and the Chamber of Deputies has 60 members, with members of both houses elected for 5 years. Two thirds of the seats in each house are allocated to the majority party and the remaining third proportionately divided among the minority parties **Local Government:** 19 departments, each headed by a governor appointed by the president, and a federal district

**Ethnic Composition:** About 95% of the population is of mixed Spanish and Indian (Guaraní) descent. Italians, Germans, and Japanese constitute small minorities **Population Distribution:** 40% urban **Density:** 21 inhabitants per sq. mi.

**Largest Cities:** (1972 census) Asunción 392,753, Fernando de la Mora 36,834, Lambaré 31,656, Encarnación 23,343, Pedro Juan Caballero 21,033

**Per Capita Income:** $1,028 (1980) **Gross National Product (GNP):** $3.3 billion (1980) **Economic Statistics:** 39% of the GNP comes from agriculture (livestock, lumber, bananas, rice, coconuts, cocoa); 20% from manufacturing (meat packing, refining of quebracho and cotton, sugar, wood, vegetable oils); and 41% from services **Minerals and Mining:** No important deposits of minerals exist, but hydroelectric potential is immense and is coming on line **Labor Force:** 1 million, with 49% in agriculture, 28% in industry and commerce, 19% in services and 4% in government **Foreign Trade:** Exports, chiefly cotton, soybeans, meat products, quebracho extract, vegetable oils, and essential oils, totaled $305 million in 1979. Imports, mainly foodstuffs, machinery and motors, transportation equipment, nonferrous metals and manufactures, and iron and its products, totaled $432 million **Principal Trade Partners:** United States, Argentina, EC countries, Brazil, Switzerland, Japan

**Vital Statistics:** Birthrate, 39 per 1,000 of pop. (1980); death rate, 8 **Life Expectancy:** 62 years **Health Statistics:** 694 inhabitants per hospital bed; 2,196 per physician (1976) **Infant Mortality:** 38.6 per 1,000 births **Illiteracy:** 20% **Primary and Secondary School Enrollment:** 527,668 (1975) **Enrollment in Higher Education:** 12,212 (1973) **GNP Expended on Education:** 1.4% (1974)

**Transportation:** Paved roads total 680 mi. **Motor Vehicles:** 30,000 (1971) **Passenger Cars:** 16,000 **Railway Mileage:** 296 **Ports:** Asunción and Concepción on the Paraguay River **Major Airlines:** Lineas Aéreas Paraguayas (LAP) provides international and domestic service **Communications: Radio Transmitters:** 36 **Receivers:** 180,000 (1976) **Television Transmitters:** 3 **Receivers:** 55,000 (1976) **Telephones:** 48,000 (1978) **Newspapers:** 4 dailies, 39 copies per 1,000 inhabitants (1976)

**Weights and Measures:** Metric system **Travel Requirements:** Passport, no visa for 3 months **International Dialing Code:** 595

---

Wars have shaped Paraguay's progress to an uncommon degree; the most disastrous was the War against the Triple Alliance—Uruguay, Argentina, and Brazil—in which hundreds of thousands of Paraguayans were killed. The six-year conflict ended in 1870. In the Chaco War, which was fought from 1932 to 1935 in the desert lands with Bolivia, Paraguay lost additional men.

World War II brought a period of prosperity, as the prices of beef, hides, and quebracho wood extract (used in tanning leather) rose sharply. But the war had a more lasting effect on Paraguay's economy. The universal shortages of imported goods and the introduction of cargo aircraft in South America combined to produce a still-flourishing, highly lucrative contraband trade.

The last major civil war was in 1947, in which Gen. Alfredo Stroessner rose to power. He assumed command in 1954 and has been president since then, making Paraguay Latin America's most durable dictatorship. Until recently, political dissidents suffered repression in anonymity because Paraguay is a small country out of the spotlight of world attention. Domingo Laino, a leader of the Authentic Radical Liberal party, was arrested in 1976 upon his return home after denouncing Paraguayan human rights' practices before the Organization of American States. Reports of curtailed rights persisted, and in 1979 the Inter-American Association for Democracy and Freedom asserted that the Stroessner government retains power by use of torture. Alcibiades González Valle, head of the Newswriters' Union, was imprisoned in June 1980 for his article deploring the denial of due process to a man held in jail for seven years without formal charges.

The employment picture has brightened as work progresses on three gigantic hydroelectric projects on the Paraná River—Itaipú in collaboration with Brazil, and Yacyreta and Corpus in concert with Argentina. For several years Paraguay's real GNP growth has been the highest in Latin America. Per capita income has doubled and redoubled since the mid 1970s.

**HISTORY:** The several Indian tribes that inhabited eastern Paraguay before the advent of Europeans were known collectively as Guaraní because of their common language. While not as advanced as the Incas or the Mayas, the Guaraní were farmers and lived in large thatched houses, thus presenting a strong contrast to the nomadic tribes of the Chaco and the Amazon Valley. With the coming of the Spaniards in the 16th century, Paraguay at first dominated the La Plata region but by the 18th century was reduced to an outpost of the viceroyalty, which had become centered on Buenos Aires

**1811-13:** Paraguay gains its independence from Spain and rejects the leadership of Buenos Aires

**1865-70:** Paraguay is disastrously defeated in a war against Argentina, Brazil, and Uruguay, losing 55,000 square miles of territory and more than half its population

**1932-35:** Unsettled boundary dispute leads to Chaco War between Paraguay and Bolivia; Paraguay wins but is economically ruined

**1940-48:** President Higinio Morínigo, leader of the Colorado party, establishes a period of dictatorial stability, but civil war breaks out when rival forces rise against him. Rebels are defeated, but the Colorados split into two rival groups; the group opposing Morínigo forces him to leave the country

**1954:** Gen. Alfredo Stroessner engineers a successful coup and is elected president without opposition

**1958:** Stroessner, unopposed, is reelected to the presidency for five years; all 60 congressmen elected are members of his party

**1959-60:** Government troops crush rebel uprisings

**1964:** A "colonels' plot," allegedly organized by exiled officers in Argentina to overthrow Stroessner's government, is crushed

**1967:** A new constitution is adopted providing for redistribution of congressional seats

**1968:** Stroessner is reelected for his fourth term of office; for the first time since 1954, opposition parties are permitted to take part in elections, but Stroessner's Colorado party wins majority in both chambers

**1973:** General Stroessner is reelected with 84 percent of the popular vote. Paraguay and Brazil agree to construct a huge hydroelectric complex on the Paraná River

**1974:** Reports of new antigovernment plots lead to stricter controls and political imprisonments

**1975:** U.S. oil companies continue explorations in Chaco region under pacts criticized as unfavorable to Paraguayan interests

**1977:** Three Communist Party leaders and 11 other political prisoners, jailed since General Stroessner's takeover in 1954, are released, in apparent response to U.S. pressure

**1978:** Stroessner is reelected to sixth term

**1980:** Exiled Nicaraguan dictator Anastasio Somoza is assassinated in Asunción Sept. 17; Paraguay breaks relations with Sandinist government, holding it responsible

**1981:** Amnesty International charges that human rights situation in Paraguay has deteriorated, contradicting report of U.S. State Department. *Acuerdo Nacional*, a coalition of opposition parties in Paraguay, denounces increasing violations of human rights

---

## PERU

**Area:** 496,222 sq. mi. **Population:** 17,031,221 (1981 census)

**Official Name:** Republic of Peru **Capital:** Lima **Nationality:** Peruvian **Languages:** Spanish and Quechua arre official languages, many Indians speaking only the latter or Aymara **Religion:** More than 90% of the population is Roman Catholic **Flag:** Vertical bands of red, white, and red with the national coat of arms in the center **Anthem:** National Anthem, beginning "We are free, let us always be so" **Currency:** Sol (643 per U.S. $1)

**Location:** West coast of South America. Peru is bordered on the north by Ecuador and Colombia, on the east by Brazil and Bolivia, on the south by Chile, and on the west by the Pacific Ocean **Features:** The country is divided into a narrow coastal desert; the high sierra, the zone of the great Andean cordilleras; and the eastern lowlands (montaña), with uncharted hills, forests, and tropical jungles **Chief Rivers:** Amazon, Ucayali-Apurímac, Marañón-Huallaga

**Head of State and of Government:** President Fernando Belaúnde Terry, born 1912, elected May 1980, took office July 1980. He is assisted by a cabinet headed by Prime Minister Manuel Ulloa Elías **Effective Date of Present Constitution:** July 28, 1980 **Legislative Body:** Congress (bicameral), consisting of a Senate of 60 members elected on a regional basis for 5 years plus the former presidents of constitutional govenments as life senators, and a Chamber of Deputies of 180 members elected for 5 years **Local Government:** 24 departments and the constitutional province of Callao

**Ethnic Composition:** 46% Indian, 38% mestizo, 15% white **Population Distribution:** 63% urban **Density:** 34 inhabitants per sq. mi.

**Largest Cities:** (1972 census) (M.A. = Metropolitan Area) Lima 2,981,292 (M.A. 4,000,000), Arequipa 304,653, Callao 296,220, Chimbote 159,045, Chiclayo 148,932

**Per Capita Income:** $1,200 (1980) **Gross National Product (GNP):** $21 billion (1980) **Economic Statistics:** 24% of the GNP is derived from manufacturing (textiles, foodstuffs, iron and steel, ships, metal products and chemicals, automobile assembly) and 12% from agriculture (cotton, sugar, rice, coffee), fisheries, and forestry **Minerals and Mining:** Copper, silver, lead, zinc, iron, petroleum, natural gas, bismuth, molybdenum, gold, and tungsten **Labor Force:** 5.3 million (1978), with 42% engaged in agriculture, 20% in services, and 13% in industry **Foreign Trade:** Exports, mainly copper, fishmeal, silver, iron, petroleum, sugar, cotton, and coffee, totaled $3.5 billion in 1979. Imports, chiefly capital goods, industrial raw materials, and intermediate goods, totaled $2.1 billion **Principal Trade Partners:** United States, Japan, West Germany, Britain, Ecuador, Argentina, Chile, Netherlands

**Vital Statistics:** Birthrate, 39.7 per 1,000 of pop. (1980); death rate, 12.2 **Life Expectancy:** 58 years **Health Statistics:** 547 inhabitants per hospital bed; 1,556 per physician (1977) **Infant Mortality:** 170.3 per 1,000 births **Illiteracy:** 28% **Primary and Secondary School Enrollment:** 3,988,753 (1977) **Enrollment in Higher Education:** 233,420 (1977) **GNP Expended on Education:** 3.6% (1976)

**Transportation:** Paved roads total 3,350 mi. **Motor Vehicles:** 466,600 (1977) **Passenger Cars:** 300,400 **Railway Mileage:** 1,335 **Ports:** Callao, Talara, Chimbotee, Matarani, Ilo, Paita, Pisco **Major Airlines:** Compañía de Aviación Faucett and Aeroperú fly internationally and domestically **Communications: Radio Transmitters:** 189 **Receivers:** 2,068,000 (1976) **Television Transmitters:** 63 **Receivers:** 600,000 (1976) **Telephones:** 420,000 (1978) **Newspapers:** 30 dailies, 51 copies per 1,000 inhabitants (1977)

**Weights and Measures:** Metric system **Travel Requirements:** Passport; visa not required for tourist stay up to 90 days **International Dialing Code:** 51

---

Peru's economy and social structure were long controlled by a few rich families and foreign mining interests. The aristocrats have always been reluctant to see to the business of government themselves, and consequently the army and, occasionally, popular governments have filled the gap. Racial strains between the major groups—Indian, mestizo, and white—have further complicated politics.

Inflation and crippling political infighting led, on October 3, 1968, to a coup by a military junta, which named Gen. Juan Velasco Alvarado as president. Despite broad social and economic reforms—including land reform and redistributions, a half share in business profits for the workers in Peruvian companies, and nationalization of large industries and public utilities—no protest was heard when Velasco was deposed by Gen. Francisco Morales Bermúdez in August 1975. By that time a faltering economy with rampant unemployment and a rise in the cost of living had offset any benefits gained from the socioeconomic changes.

Morales' government suffered from internal unrest, however, when it imposed an unpopular austerity program in its efforts to cope with an immense foreign debt. Its rule was marked by repression of extremist political publications and expulsions of leftist military officers and labor leaders. Nevertheless, a Constituent Assembly elected in 1978 drew up a new constitution in the following year. Fernando Belaúnde Terry, Peru's last civilian president, was reelected to that office in the May 1980 elections and embarked on a course to revive the economy.

**HISTORY:** At the time of the Spanish Conquest, Peru was the heartland of the great Inca Empire extending from northern Ecuador to central Chile. In 1532 the empire, which had recently undergone a civil war, fell to Spaniards led by Francisco Pizarro. In the colonial era the Indians of Peru were reduced to a serfdom from which the majority still have not fully emerged. In 1824 Spain's colonial rule came to an end with the defeat of Spanish forces by the revolutionary armies led by José de San Martín and Simón Bolívar

**1863-79:** Attempts by Spain to regain its former colonies lead to an intermittent war of small naval engagements; in a treaty signed in 1879 Spain finally recognizes the independence of Peru

**1879-84:** Peru and Bolivia fight unsuccessful War of the Pacific with Chile; Peru is forced to cede the nitrate province of Tarapacá to Chile and to allow Chilean occupation of Tacna and Arica

**1924:** Víctor Raúl Haya de la Torre founds APRA (Alianza Popular Revolucionaria Americana), dedicated to radical economic and social reforms to improve the lot of the lower classes, especially the Indians, and nationalization of foreign enterprises

**1929:** A controversy over Tacna and Arica dating back to the War of the Pacific is resolved through U.S. mediation; Arica is awarded to Chile and Tacna is returned to Peru

**1945-48:** APRA, though barred from putting up candidates, helps elect José Luis Bustamante to the presidency; he is deposed by a military junta led by General Manuel Odría

**1956:** Ex-President Manuel Prado is elected president with APRA support and legalizes the party

**1962:** Haya de la Torre wins slim plurality in disputed presidential elections; attempts to form a coalition government fail and army seizes power

**1963-68:** Military junta permits new elections and Fernando Belaúnde Terry, a moderate, becomes president; his government confronts rising opposition from legislature and a deteriorating economy; in 1968 Belaúnde is overthrown by a military junta headed by Gen. Juan Velasco Alvarado, which nationalizes U.S.-owned oil property

**1970:** An earthquake hits northern Peru, killing 50,000

**1971:** Government takes over U.S. copper concession

**1972:** Government seizes U.S. potash and phosphate concessions

**1974:** Major newspapers are expropriated and transferred to community guilds by the military regime

**1975:** Government action against striking civil employees results in widespread rioting in Lima, where hundreds are arrested as army quells demonstrations. Velasco overthrown by Morales

**1976:** Government declares a state of emergency after students and workers riot to protest a new set of austerity measures and call for a return to elected civilian government. Entire cabinet resigns after Prime Minister Fernandez Maldonado quits following an army crisis. Morales replaces resigning leftists with moderates. Huge foreign debt is accumulated

**1977:** Trans-Andean oil pipeline begins operation. Peru, in grave cash squeeze, is told by international banking community to enact austerity measures as condition for further credit

**1978:** Peru's foreign debt nears $7 billion; inflation rate reaches 80 percent; unemployment and recession deepen. APRA wins largest bloc of Constituent Assembly seats in Peru's first nationwide election since 1963

**1979:** New constitution is signed by APRA founder Haya de la Torre shortly before his death

**1980:** Fernando Belaúnde Terry is elected president and takes office after 12 years of military rule

**1981:** Ecuadorean troops are ousted from zone 8 mi. inside Peru in the Cordillera del Condor. General strike and acts of terrorism follow rise in prices of fuel and food. Pres. Belaúnde uses new executive powers to proclaim long prison sentences for convicted terrorists. Opposition leaders and churchmen accuse police of torturing political prisoners. Inflation declines to around 50 percent

**1982:** Javier Pérez de Cuéllar, noted Peruvian diplomat, becomes new Secretary-General of the United Nations in January. Sudden flooding of Chontayacu River wipes out 16 settlements and takes heavy toll of lives. U.S. returns art objects and pre-Columbian artifacts worth $1.3 million which had been smuggled out of Peru. Large force of guerrillas frees 230 inmates of Ayacucho prison

## PHILIPPINES

**Area:** 115,707 sq. mi. **Population:** 47,914,017 (1980 census)

**Official Name:** Republic of the Philippines **Capital:** Manila **Nationality:** Filipino **Languages:** Pilipino (the national language based on Tagalog), English and Spanish are the official languages; almost 90 Philippine languages and dialects are spoken **Religion:** 83% Roman Catholic, 9% Protestant, 5% Moslem, and the rest of other or no affiliation **Flag:** Top half blue, bottom, red, with a white triangle at the hoist containing a gold star in each corner and a golden sun in the center **Anthem:** National Anthem *(Pambansang Awit)*, beginning "Land of the morning, child of the sun returning" **Currency:** Philippine peso (piso) (8.43 per U.S. $1)

**Location:** Southeast Asia. The Philippines is an archipelago of 7,107 islands stretching about 1,100 miles along the southeastern rim of Asia, with the northern islands about 330 miles from China and the southwestern tip about 30 miles from Malaysia **Features:** 11 islands account for 94% of the total land area and population. Most of the larger islands are mountainous, and are also characterized by extensive coastal plains, wide valleys, volcanoes, mineral and hot springs **Chief Rivers:** Cagayan, Agno, Pampanga, Agusan, Cotabato

**Head of State and of Government:** President Ferdinand E. Marcos, born 1917, elected 1965, reelected 1981. He is assisted by a prime minister, César Virata, born 1930, appointed April 1981 **Effective Date of Present Constitution:** 1973 **Legislative Body:** Interim National Assembly of 190 members **Local Government:** 13 regions, comprised of 73 provinces

**Ethnic Composition:** The dominant racial stock of the Philippines is Malay, with an admixture of Indonesian and Chinese strains. Chinese, Americans, and Spaniards constitute the largest alien minorities **Population Distribution:** 32% urban **Density:** 414 inhabitants per sq. mi.

**Largest Cities:** (1980 census) Manila 1,626,249, Quezon City 1,165,990, Davao 611,311, Cebu 489,208, Caloocan 471,289, Zamboanga 344,275

**Per Capita Income:** $589 (1980) **Gross National Product (GNP):** $29 billion (1980) **Economic Statistics:** 39% of the GNP is derived from services, 29% from agriculture (including rice cultivation, sugar, copra, abaca, logs, coconuts); 24% from industry (mining, textiles, and other durable items manufacture) **Minerals and Mining:** There are deposits of iron ore, copper, gold, manganese, chromite, nickel, zinc, coal, and molybdenum. Oil production is beginning **Labor Force:** 17,500,000, with 47% in agriculture, forestry, and fishing; about 12% are in industry **Foreign Trade:** Exports, mainly copra, logs and lumber, sugar, coconut oil, copper concentrates, abaca, and canned pineapple, totaled $5.9 billion in 1980. Imports, chiefly nonelectrical machinery, transportation equipment, mineral fuel and lubricants, base metals, cereals, electric machinery, and textiles, totaled $7.2 billion **Principal Trade Partners:** United States, Japan, EEC, Saudi Arabia

**Vital Statistics:** Birthrate, 39.2 per 1,000 of pop. (1980); death rate, 9 **Life Expectancy:** 62 years **Health Statistics:** 639 inhabitants per hospital bed (1973); 2,793 per physician (1977) **Infant Mortality:** 56.8 per 1,000 births **Illiteracy:** 12% **Primary and Secondary School Enrollment:** 10,210,725 (1976) **Enrollment in Higher Education:** 764,725 **GNP Expended on Education:** 1.4% (1976)

**Transportation:** Paved roads total 12,500 mi. **Motor Vehicles:** 833,800 (1978) **Passenger Cars:** 464,000 **Railway Mileage:** 1,200 **Ports:** Cebu, Manila, Zamboanga, Iloilo, Davao, Batangas **Major Airlines:** Philippine Air Lines operates domestic and international flights **Communications: Radio Transmitters:** 266 **Receivers:** 1,875,000 (1976) **Television Transmitters:** 24 **Receivers:** 800,000 (1976) **Telephones:** 600,000 (1978) **Newspapers:** 17 dailies (1976), 18 copies per 1,000 inhabitants (1975)

**Weights and Measures:** Metric system **Travel Requirements:** Passport, no visa for 21 days, onward ticket **International Dialing Code:** 63

The Philippines, an island nation of plentiful resources, has been unable thus far to realize its rich potential for development. Independence, gained in 1946, has failed to produce effective democratic government. A high rate of population growth has eaten up much of the slow increase in gross national product, while the gap between the ruling rich and the restless poor remains wide.

Among the bright spots have been the dramatic advance in food production and the modest growth of industry, particularly electronics companies, which swarmed to Manila in 1978 and 1979. Aided by new agricultural technology, the Philippines progressed from being a major rice importer to self-sufficiency in that staple. Yet malnutrition remains widespread. With a half million Filipinos entering the labor market each year, unemployment is high (over 15 percent in 1982) and as many as 300,000 workers annually take jobs overseas.

Three hundred years of Spanish rule made the Filipinos, a people of basic Malayan stock, the only Roman Catholic nation in Asia, and left a deep Latin imprint. The subsequent 48-year administration of the extensive archipelago by the United States helped impose a Western educational and political structure, but surging nationalism has recently led the people to try to cast off their long dependence on the United States.

Philippine elections have never been free of violence and corruption, and Ferdinand E. Marcos' decisive victory in the November 1969 race was accompanied by widespread charges of fraud, vote-buying, and intimidation, as well as by huge spending. Marcos, assaulted by a mob in 1970 as he was leaving the Congress building, blamed Communism for the climate of violence, while acknowledging that the discontent could be resolved only by creating more jobs, removing social inequities, reforming the machinery of government and developing a constructive nationalism.

In September 1972, Marcos tightened his grip on the reins of power by imposing martial law. In January 1973, he proclaimed the ratification of a new constitution changing the Philippines from a presidential to a parliamentary form of government. Yet he also extended martial law.

Miffed by U.S. criticism of reported human rights violations, Marcos called a national election for April 1978 (the first in six years) to choose members of an interim parliament that was to legislate until martial law was lifted and a regular parliament formed. (Before permitting the vote, Marcos guaranteed himself a seat in the new assembly, along with the offices of president and prime minister.)

Marcos' strategy, however, backfired badly, as his brief cautious relaxation of restrictions on political activity just prior to the election led to an outburst of antigovernment sentiment, punctuated by public demonstrations against his authoritarian rule. (His main rival, former Senator Benigno Aquino, had to campaign from prison, where he faced a death sentence on a questionable murder conviction.) Though the election results—widely considered fraudulent—showed Aquino to have done poorly, massive anti-Marcos rallies and the arrests of hundreds of protesting workers, students and nuns, demonstrated the existence of widespread opposition to the president. Among the more persistent charges against the regime was that it condoned and fostered corruption in the military. The Marcos government also had to deal with a long-standing Moslem insurrection in the southern Philippines and continuing guerrilla activity in Luzon and the central islands by the Communist New Peoples' Army.

In a new move to consolidate his power, Marcos lifted martial law in January 1981 and, in April, mounted a plebiscite by which he won approval of another constitutional change—the introduction of a six-year presidential term, with no limit on the number of terms that a president might serve. Marcos was elected to the office again in June in a contest boycotted by major opposition leaders on grounds that his control of the nation's election machinery made an effective campaign against him impossible.

**HISTORY:** For centuries after the birth of Christ the Philippine archipelago was an area of trade and settlement for Southeast Asian people of Malay stock. The area came into the sphere of European influence when it was discovered in 1521 by Magellan. By 1571 the Spanish had assumed control over the Philippines (named for Philip II of Spain) and for next 300 years ruled the islands as a colony

**1898:** Control of Philippines is ceded to the United States following Spanish-American War

**1899:** Guerrilla war breaks out against the Americans, ending with complete pacification of islands by 1905

**1934:** United States passes Philippine independence law providing for a 10-year period for final transfer of sovereignty

**1941:** Japanese attack Philippines without warning

**1945:** All of Philippines are freed of Japanese troops

**1946:** On July 4 the Republic of the Philippines is proclaimed. Independence is followed by widespread unrest and violence by Communist-led Huk guerrillas

**1947:** Under a 99-year treaty (amended, 1959), Philippines grants U.S. use of 23 strategically vital military bases

**1954:** Huk rebellion is largely put down

**1970:** Leftist students stage antigovernment demonstrations; Manila is crippled by general strike

**1971:** Urban disturbances and guerrilla violence continue. President Marcos accuses Communists of inciting rebellion

**1972:** Marcos imposes martial law

**1973:** New constitution goes into effect. Marcos assumes indefinite rule; extends martial law; wins endorsement in referendum

**1977:** Voters reject a plan calling for a provisional government in the southwestern portion of the Philippines. Talks are deadlocked over the demands of the Moro National Liberation Front for control of the proposed autonomous region

**1978:** With an eye on U.S. and world opinion, Marcos briefly lifts ban (imposed in 1972) on political activity, prior to election of "interim" national assembly. Election results, allegedly fraudulent, show big win for Marcos' New Society Movement. Propaganda value is mitigated by demonstrations and mass arrests

**1979:** The total of Moslems fleeing the southern Philippines for Sabah, a nearby Malaysian state, passes the 100,000 mark. A treaty gives the U.S. "unhampered use" of Clark Air Force Base and the Subic Bay naval facility, over which the Filipino flag is raised for the first time

machinery made an effective campaign against him impossible.

**HISTORY:** For centuries after the birth of Christ the Philippine archipelago was an area of trade and settlement for Southeast Asian people of Malay stock. The area came into the sphere of European influence when it was discovered in 1521 by Magellan. By 1571 the Spanish had assumed control over the Philippines (named for Philip II of Spain) and for next 300 years ruled the islands as a colony

**1898:** Control of Philippines is ceded to the United States following Spanish-American War

**1899:** Guerrilla war breaks out against the Americans, ending with complete pacification of islands by 1905

**1934:** United States passes Philippine independence law providing for a 10-year period for final transfer of sovereignty

**1941:** Japanese attack Philippines without warning

**1945:** All of Philippines are freed of Japanese troops

**1946:** On July 4 the Republic of the Philippines is proclaimed. Independence is followed by widespread unrest and violence by Communist-led Huk guerrillas

**1947:** Under a 99-year treaty (amended, 1959), Philippines grants U.S. use of 23 strategically vital military bases

**1954:** Huk rebellion is largely put down

**1970:** Leftist students stage antigovernment demonstrations; Manila is crippled by general strike

**1971:** Urban disturbances and guerrilla violence continue. President Marcos accuses Communists of inciting rebellion

**1972:** Marcos imposes martial law

**1973:** New constitution goes into effect. Marcos assumes indefinite rule; extends martial law; receives endorsement by electorate, voting in national referendum. Conflict triggered by Moslem insurgency grows

**1977:** Voters reject a plan calling for a provisional government in the southwestern portion of the Philippines. Talks are deadlocked over the demands of the Moro National Liberation Front for control of the proposed autonomous region

**1978:** With an eye on U.S. and world opinion, Marcos briefly lifts ban (imposed in 1972) on political activity, prior to election of "interim" national assembly. Election results, allegedly fraudulent, show big win for Marcos' New Society Movement. Propaganda value is mitigated by demonstrations and mass arrests

**1979:** The total of Moslems fleeing the southern Philippines for Sabah, a nearby Malaysian state, passes the 100,000 mark. A treaty gives the U.S. "unhampered use" of Clark Air Force Base and the Subic Bay naval facility, over which the Filipino flag is raised for the first time; the U.S. agrees to give $500 million in military and economic aid over five years

**1981:** Martial law lifted in January. Pope John Paul II visits Manila in February. In April plebiscite, Marcos gains approval of change to a six-year presidential term, wins the office in June in an election boycotted by the political opposition. U.S. Vice-President Bush, in Manila, promises greater U.S. support

**1982:** President's son-in-law kidnapped and returned under circumstances that are never fully explained. First nationwide local elections in 10 years are held. All 14 members of the Supreme Court resign in scandal involving chief justice. Noncommunist opposition leaders form anti-Marcos coalition

## POLAND

**Area:** 120,725 sq. mi. **Population:** 36,062,000 (1981 est.)

**Official Name:** Polish People's Republic **Capital:** Warsaw **Nationality:** Polish **Languages:** Polish is the official and universal language **Religion:** About 95% of the population is Roman Catholic; the rest are Eastern Orthodox, Protestant, Jewish, and of other or no affiliation **Flag:** Horizontal bands of white over red **Anthem:** National Anthem, beginning "Poland still is ours forever" **Currency:** Zloty (80 per U.S. $1)

**Location:** Eastern Europe. Poland is bounded on the north by the Baltic Sea, on the east by the Soviet Union, on the south by Czechoslovakia, and on the west by East Germany **Features:** The country consists mainly of lowlands, except the mountains on its southern border **Chief Rivers:** Vistula, Oder, Bug, Warta, Narew, San

**Political Leader:** First Secretary of the Central Committee of the United Workers' Party: Wojciech Jaruzelski, born 1923, elected Oct. 18, 1981 **Head of State:** Chairman of the Council of State: Henryk Jablonski, born 1909, elected 1972, reelected 1976 and 1980 **Head of Government:** Chairman of the Council of Ministers (Premier): Wojciech Jaruzelski, born 1923, appointed Feb. 9, 1981 **Effective Date of Present Constitution:** July 1952 **Legislative Body:** Parliament (unicameral Sejm), with 460 members elected for 4 years. The Sejm is virtually a rubber stamp for the endorsement of party programs **Local Government:** 49 provinces and 3 city provinces, each with a local people's council

**Ethnic Composition:** The population is virtually homogeneous (98% Polish), with Ukrainians and Byelorussians constituting tiny minorities **Population Distribution:** 58% urban **Density:** 299 inhabitants per sq. mi.

**Largest Cities:** (1979 est.) Warsaw 1,572,200, Lodz 832,400, Cracow 704,900, Wroclaw 608,400, Poznan 544,000, Gdańsk 448,200, Szczecin 387,800, Katowice 352,500

**Per Capita Income:** $3,513 (1980) **Gross National Product (GNP):** $125 billion (1980) **Economic Statistics:** 65.9% of the GNP is derived from industry (mining, steel, ships, machine manufacture, chemicals, power production, and foodstuffs); 9.1% is derived from commerce, and 8.9% from agriculture (wheat, rye, potatoes, oats, barley, sugar beets) **Minerals and Mining:** There are large deposits of coal, lignite, sulphur, copper ore, salt, vanadium, titanium, natural gas and zinc **Labor Force:** 19,300,000, with 31% in agriculture and forestry, 25% in industry **Foreign Trade:** Exports, chiefly copper, sulphur, coal, ships, textiles, steel, cement, chemicals, and foodstuffs, totaled $16.8 billion (1979). Imports, mainly oil, iron ore, fertilizers, wheat, and leather footwear, totaled $18.1 billion **Principal Trade Partners:** USSR, East Germany, Czechoslovakia, West Germany, Britain, United States, Iran, Italy, France, Romania, Austria

**Vital Statistics:** Birthrate, 19.5 per 1,000 of pop. (1980); death rate, 9.8 **Life Expectancy:** 71 years **Health Statistics:** 131 inhabitants per hospital bed; 605 per physician (1977) **Infant Mortality:** 21.2 per 1,000 births **Illiteracy:** negligible **Primary and Secondary School Enrollment:** 5,627,132 (1976) **Enrollment in Higher Education:** 575,499 (1975) **GNP Expended on Education:** 6% (1976)

**Transportation:** Paved roads total 40,000 mi. **Motor Vehicles:** 2,441,000 (1978) **Passenger Cars:** 1,835,400 **Railway Mileage:** 16,683 **Ports:** Gdańsk, Gdynia, Szczecin **Major Airlines:** Polish Airlines LOT operates both domestically and internationally **Communications: Radio Transmitters:** 51 **Licenses:** 8,230,000 (1976) **Television Transmitters:** 69 **Licenses:** 6,822,000 (1976) **Telephones:** 3,095,000 (1978) **Newspapers:** 44 dailies, 240 copies per 1,000 inhabitants (1977)

**Weights and Measures:** Metric system **Travel Requirements:** Passport, visa (2 photos, $10 fee) for 90 days

Four times in Poland's postwar history workers' revolts have set the nation on new economic and political courses. The first was in 1956, when factory employees in Poznan took to the streets to demand food. A political convulsion followed, bringing Wladyslaw Gomulka to power as first secretary of the Polish United Workers (Communist) party and ending much of the repression of the Stalinist period. Fourteen years later, in December 1970, port workers in Gdańsk marched in protest and set in motion the riots that led to Gomulka's downfall. His replacement, Edward Gierek, charted new policies in an effort to repair the errors of Gomulka's autocratic rule and improve the living conditions of the average Polish citizen. The June 1976 riots over food-price increases were a warning to Gierek's regime of what had happened twice before. The fourth great upheaval occurred in July and August 1980, when thousands of workers went on strike in Gdańsk and other Baltic cities. The strike caused a major shakeup in the government.

Gierek, with his premier, Piotr Jaroszewicz, a trained economist, recharted Poland's five-year economic plan for 1971-75, emphasizing consumer industries and raising wages significantly. Following the 1976 riots, a system of compulsory deliveries for farmers was replaced by long-term contract deliveries, and planning has been even more consumer-oriented. Gierek also opened the state-controlled press to a limited measure of meaningful debate. Poland has expanded business and political relations with the West.

Gierek sought to resume normal relations with the Roman Catholic Church. In 1979, the Polish-born Pope John Paul II visited Poland on the 900th anniversary of the murder of Saint Stanislaw, whose festival the government had refused to allow him to attend, and praised the saint as an opponent of oppressive government. Bishop Jozef Glemp succeeded the late Cardinal Wyszynski as primate of Poland on July 6, 1981.

The national crisis of 1980 began with wildcat strikes by workers protesting meat price hikes in Gdańsk which soon spread throughout the country. A new Communist government, formed by Stanislaw Kania in September, recognized the Solidarity workers' union of about 10 million members, headed by Lech Walesa, a strike leader in Gdańsk. In May 1981 the government reluctantly recognized the independent farmers' union, Rural Solidarity. But it failed to grant the two unions' main economic demands, and sporadic strikes continued. Although Kania assured the special Communist party congress in July that democratic reforms would continue, he was unable to curb Solidarity's demands for free elections and basic economic changes. He was replaced in October as party chief by Premier Wojciech Jaruzelski, a Communist general.

The Jaruzelski government used military force to prevent strikes protesting food shortages, and its harsh repressive actions apparently kept the USSR from intervening militarily in Poland. When negotiations among party, union, and church leaders broke down, Jaruzelski declared martial law on December 13 and arrested at least 5,000 Solidarity members, including Walesa. Polish soldiers broke up strikes at mines, factories, and shipyards. Strict government censorship made it difficult to estimate the number of workers who were killed, but some observers reported that hundreds had died. At the end of 1981, there were reports of passive resistance and industrial sabotage by some workers.

Martial law continued in 1982 despite Western protests and the imposition of economic sanctions against Poland and the USSR by the United States. Poland was unable to pay interest owed on its estimated $27-billion debt to the West, and creditor nations rescheduled Poland's debt payments. Polish Catholic leaders tried to reconcile party and union leaders, but to no avail. In early May, workers in Warsaw and nine other cities marched to protest martial law and clashed with security police. Although much social unrest continued, Poland remained a Communist state.

**HISTORY:** The recorded history of Poland dates from the 10th century, when Slavic tribes in the region united and their conversion to Christianity began. The medieval era was one of incessant wars, culminating in the defeat of the Teutonic Knights by Poland and Lithuania, united under the Jagiello dynasty. After the last Jagiello king died in 1572, Polish power began a gradual decline as a result of internal weaknesses and external conflicts. Beginning in 1772, and despite the national uprising of 1794 led by Thaddeus Kosciusko, successive partitions eliminated Poland as a sovereign state, a condition that persisted until the close of World War I

**1918-21:** Independent Polish republic is proclaimed; Versailles Treaty gives Poland access to Baltic Sea through Polish Corridor, free city of Danzig is set up; attempts by Allies to award Poland's eastern provinces to Russia lead to war between the 2 countries in 1920; Poles, aided by French, defeat Russians and win most of territorial claims in 1921 Treaty of Riga

**1926-35:** General Joseph Pilsudski, former chief of state, governs as virtual dictator after overthrowing democratic government; at his death in 1935, he is succeeded by Edward Smigly-Rydz

**1939-45:** Germany and Soviet Union, allied in nonaggression pact, invade Poland in September 1939, and the country is once again partitioned; all Poland comes under Nazi rule after Germany attacks USSR in 1941; about six million Poles, half of them Jews, are exterminated by Nazis, and 2.5 million more are deported to Germany as slave labor; Soviet troops reenter Poland in 1944; in August, Poles stage Warsaw uprising, which is crushed by Germans while Soviet forces remain inactive outside city; Germans are expelled in 1945

**1947:** Soviet-dominated government claims huge majority in the officially controlled elections of 1947; Communist regime proceeds to Sovietize country

**1956:** Workers and students in Poznan stage mass demonstration against Communist rule and Soviet control; Wladyslaw Gomulka becomes leader of the Polish United Workers' (Commmunist) party; Stefan Cardinal Wyszynski, under arrest since 1953, is released

**1968:** Poland joins Soviet Union and other Warsaw Pact members in invasion of Czechoslovakia. At home a campaign against "Zionists" and "revisionists" is waged

**1970:** Agreement is reached with West Germany on diplomatic relations, including acceptance of Oder-Neisse line as border between Germany and Poland. Economic unrest leads to ouster of Gomulka, who is succeeded by Edward Gierek

**1973:** Rapprochement with the Vatican

**1974:** Land reform law reorganizes small farms into larger units in exchange for increased social benefits

**1975:** Gierek is named first secretary for a second five-year term

**1976:** Workers stage violent demonstrations and strikes to protest proposed drastic increases in food prices

**1979:** Polish-born Pope John Paul II draws huge crowds during visit to Poland

**1980:** Edward Babiuch replaces Piotr Jaroszewicz as premier. At 8th Communist Party Congress, Gierek admits economy is in bad shape, says economic recovery in 1980s will be slow. Workers in Gdańsk and other cities protest meat price hikes with work stoppages. Strike spreads until 800,000 workers are on strike. Józef Pińkowski supplants Babiuch as premier; other party leaders dismissed in major change. Government gives in to the strikers' demand for independent trade unions. Gierek resigns; he is succeeded by Stanislaw Kania as party leader

**1981:** Wojciech Jaruzelski succeeds Pińkowski as premier and Kania as party leader; his government refuses to meet Solidarity's demands for free elections and drastic economic reforms, imposes martial law Dec. 13, crushes wildcat strikes, and arrests union leaders

**1982:** Solidarity workers protest martial law with unauthorized marches on May Day (May 1); demonstrations are broken up by security police

## PORTUGAL

**Area:** 35,549 sq. mi. **Population:** 9,784,200 (1981 census)

**Official Name:** Portuguese Republic **Capital:** Lisbon **Nationality:** Portuguese **Languages:** Portuguese is the official and universal language **Religion:** 97% Roman Catholic **Flag:** Green and red vertical stripes, the red covering two-thirds of the flag; at the dividing line is the national coat of arms encircled in gold **Anthem:** The Portuguese **Currency:** Escudo (71.7 per U.S. $1)

**Location:** Western Europe, occupying the western portion of the Iberian peninsula. Portugal is bounded on the north and east by Spain and on the south and west by the Atlantic Ocean **Features:** The Tagus River divides the country into 2 distinct regions, the north being mountainous and the south consisting of rolling plains **Chief Rivers:** Tagus, Douro, Guadiana, Sado, Mondego

**Head of State:** President: Gen. António dos Santos Ramalho Eanes, born 1935, elected 1976, reelected 1980 **Head of Government:** Premier Francisco Pinto Balsemão, born 1937, took office Jan. 10, 1981 **Effective Date of Present Constitution:** April 1976 **Legislative Body:** Parliament (unicameral Assembly), with 250 members elected for 4 years. An all-military Revolutionary Council reviews Assembly laws as to their constitutionality **Local Government:** 22 districts (including locally autonomous Madeira and the Azores), each with an appointed governor and district assembly

**Ethnic Composition:** The people are a homogeneous mixture of ethnic strains, including Celtic, Arab, Berber, Roman, Germanic, and Iberian **Population Distribution:** 37% urban **Density:** 275 inhabitants per sq. mi.

**Largest Cities:** (1981 census) Lisbon 817,637, Oporto 330,199, Amadora 93,663, Setúbal 76,812, Coimbra 71,782, Barreiro 64,817

**Per Capita Income:** $2,009 (1980) **Gross Domestic Product (GDP):** $20 billion (1980) **Economic Statistics:** 43% of the GDP is derived from mining, manufacturing, and construction (electronics, textiles, wines, cork, food processing, ship-building, and ship repair); 18% from agriculture (grains, fruits, vegetables, wines); 14% from commerce and finance; and 25% from services **Minerals and Mining:** Wolfram, cassiterite, beryl, copper pyrites, and iron ore **Labor Force:** 4.1 million (1979), with 35% in industry, 34% in services, and 31% in agriculture **Foreign Trade:** Exports, chiefly cork, sardines, wines, textiles, minerals, machinery, and diamonds, totaled $3.4 billion in 1979. Imports, mainly machinery and industrial equipment, petroleum products, optical instruments, cotton, steel, wheat, and corn, amounted to $6.5 billion **Principal Trade Partners:** West Germany, United States, Britain, France, Italy, Spain, Sweden, Iraq

**Vital Statistics:** Birthrate, 16.3 per 1,000 of pop. (1979); death rate, 9.4 **Life Expectancy:** 70 years **Health Statistics:** 189 inhabitants per hospital bed; 817 per physician (1975) **Infant Mortality:** 26 per 1,000 births **Illiteracy:** 29% **Primary and Secondary School Enrollment:** 1,676,378 (1975) **Enrollment in Higher Education:** 79,702 **GNP Expended on Education:** 3.7% (1975)

**Transportation:** Paved roads total 24,800 mi. **Motor Vehicles:** 1,530,000 (1978) **Passenger Cars:** 1,161,400 **Railway Mileage:** 2,214 **Ports:** Lisbon, Leixões, Setúbal, Funchal, Douro **Major Airlines:** Transportes Aéreos Portugueses (TAP) flies internationally **Communications: Radio Transmitters:** 103 **Licenses:** 1,525,000 (1976) **Television Transmitters:** 42 **Licenses:** 723,000 (1976) **Telephones:** 1,175,000 (1977) **Newspapers:** 28 dailies, 54 copies per 1,000 inhabitants (1977)

**Weights and Measures:** Metric system **Travel Requirements:** Passport, no visa for 60 days **International Dialing Code:** 351

---

Portugal is the poorest country in Western Europe. Most of its people still make their living from the soil, but there is a bitter division between the hilly north, with its small independent farmers, and the more level south, where landless peasants lived for centuries in fear of the owners of huge estates. Portugal's experiment in democratic socialism, which began in 1976, has been complicated by the nation's relative lack of experience with democracy. António de Oliveira Salazar, who was premier from 1932 to 1968, governed as a harsh dictator, and his successor, Marcello Caetano, made few meaningful changes. After Portugal's African territories had revolted against Portuguese rule in the 1960s, Caetano was overthrown in 1974 by the Armed Forces Movement (MFA), a coalition of soldiers who were tired of the struggle in Africa and sympathetic to socialism. The MFA government granted independence to the African territories.

The new constitution of 1976 is distinctly socialist and is democratic in all its essentials, although it reserves some power for the military-dominated Revolutionary Council. Gen. António dos Santos Ramalho Eanes was elected president; the National Assembly became an effective legislature. Most restrictions on freedom of expression ended, and peace returned to the country.

The weak economy and continued arguments over the return to private ownership of farms illegally seized in 1974 have troubled the fledgling democracy. The Socialist coalition government of Premier Mário Soares collapsed in 1978, and the cabinet of technocrats headed by Carlos Mota Pinto that replaced it fell the next year.

In the elections of Dec. 2, 1979, the moderate Democratic Alliance won 45 percent of the popular vote and formed a new government with Francisco Sá Carneiro as premier. He managed to curb government spending and to reduce inflation slightly, and his coalition made impressive gains in parliamentary elections on Oct. 55, 1980, at the expense of the Communists. But Sá Carneiro died in a plane crash on December 4; he was succeeded as premier by Francisco Pinto Balsemão on Jan. 9, 1981. In October, Balsemão formed a new cabinet with broader political support—the eighth government since Portugal adopted its democratic system.

One of the Balsemão government's problems was how to deal with the leftist CGTP union confederation, which called for a general strike to demand the ouster of the Democratic Alliance coalition. The strike disrupted some industrial activity but was only partially successful. The government denounced the labor shutdown as part of a Communist plot to overthrow Portuguese democracy.

**HISTORY:** Lusitania, the western part of the Iberian peninsula, was conquered by Julius Caesar and Augustus. The Visigoths gained control over most of the region in the 5th century A.D. and maintained their rule until the coming of the Moors three centuries later. Portugal was established as an independent state by 1185 and was consolidated after the final expulsion of the Moors in 1249. Its independence, however, remained threatened by Castile until 1385, when the Castilians were defeated in battle

**15th cent.:** Prince Henry the Navigator captures Ceuta, on northwest African coast, in 1415; under his aegis, Portuguese navigators undertake series of voyages that result in rediscovery of Madeira Islands and penetration of Africa; Vasco da Gama becomes first European to sail to India (1497-99)

**1500-20:** Pedro Cabral reaches coast of Brazil in 1500 and claims land for Portugal

**1580-1640:** Philip II of Spain seizes Portuguese throne, beginning Portugal's 60-year period of "Spanish Captivity"; Portuguese revolt against Spanish rule and regain independence under John of Braganza, who becomes king

**1807:** Napoleon's forces march on Portugal

**1822:** Brazil declares its independence

**1910:** Manuel II is deposed; Portugal is declared a republic

**1932:** António de Oliveira Salazar, former finance minister, becomes premier after a long period of civil unrest and political instability; he institutes dictatorial rule

**1961:** India annexes Portuguese enclave of Goa; Portuguese crush insurrection in Angola, in southwest Africa

**1968:** Marcello Caetano becomes premier

**1974:** Liberal reforms initiated following bloodless coup which toppled Caetano and installed António de Spínola as president. He is succeeded later the same year by Francisco da Costa Gomes. Violent clashes occur between revolutionary and rightist forces

**1975:** In April, the first free elections in almost half a century give an Assembly majority to moderates and centrists. Azevedo repplaces Gonçalves as premier

**1976:** New constitution is enacted. António dos Santos Ramalho Eanes is elected president and appoints Mário Soares premier

**1977-78:** International Monetary Fund issues stringent conditions as price to Portugal for $750-million loan; ensuing austerity measures lead to collapse of government. Soares forms new government of Socialists and conservatives, which also collapses; President Eanes dismisses him. Carlos Alberto Mota Pinto becomes premier in government of technocrats

**1979:** Mota Pinto submits government's resignation; Democratic Alliance wins plurality in parliamentary elections

**1980:** New cabinet is headed by Premier Francisco Sá Carneiro, who is killed in plane crash in December. President Eanes is reelected to a second four-year term

**1981:** Francisco Pinta Balsemão becomes premier (Jan. 9); he forms a new coalition government with broader political support

---

## QATAR

**Area:** 4,247 sq. mi. **Population:** 250,000 (1979 est.)

**Official Name:** State of Qatar **Capital:** Doha **Nationality:** Qatari **Language:** Arabic is the official and dominant language; English is spoken by some **Religion:** 98% of Qataris are Sunni Moslems of the Wahabi sect **Flag:** Maroon with white serrated border near the hoist **Anthem:** National Anthem (no words) **Currency:** Qatari riyal (3.64 per U.S. $1)

**Location:** Southwest Asia. Qatar forms a 100-mile long peninsula stretching north into the Persian Gulf. It borders Saudi Arabia and the United Arab Emirates on the south **Features:** A low, hot, dry plain, consisting of nearly flat limestone with loose sand and gravel on top **Rivers:** None

**Head of State and of Government:** Emir: Khalifa ibn Hamad al-Thani, born 1932, assumed power in 1972. He is advised by an appointed Council of Ministers which he heads as prime minister **Effective Date of Present Constitution:** 1970 **Legislative Body:** A 30-member advisory council

**Ethnic Composition:** Arabs (38%), Pakistanis (29%), Iranians (15%). The population is almost 80% non-native **Population Distribution:** 71% urban **Density:** 59 inhabitants per sq. mi.

**Largest Cities:** Doha 150,000, (1979 est.); Umm Said 5,500

**Per Capita Income:** $31,838 (1980) **Gross National Product (GNP):** $5.5 billion (1980) **Economic Statistics:** Qatar's national income derives almost wholly from oil recovery; the chemical, steel and cement industries are growing **Minerals and Mining:** Oil is the chief resource; natural gas deposits are being developed; limestone and clay are also mined **Labor Force:** 100,000 (90% non-Qatari) with about 70% in industry, service and commerce, 20% in government and 10% in agriculture **Foreign Trade:** Exports, primarily oil, some fertilizer, chemicals, and steel bars, totaled $6.2 billion in 1980. Imports, chiefly consumer goods and industrial equipment, totaled $1.5 billion **Principal Trade Partners:** EC countries, United States, Japan, Thailand

**Vital Statistics:** Birthrate, 48.8 per 1,000 of pop. (1980); death rate, 18.3 **Life Expectancy:** 47 years **Health Statistics:** 96 inhabitants per hospital bed; 938 per physician (1974) **Infant Mortality:** 42 per 1,000 births **Illiteracy:** 75% **Primary and Secondary School Enrollment:** 38,000 (1980) **Enrollment in Higher Education:** 910 **GNP Expended on Education:** 2.0% (1975)

**Transportation:** Paved roads total 275 mi. **Motor Vehicles:** N.A. **Railway Mileage:** None **Ports:** Doha, Umm Said **Major Airlines:** Gulf Air serves Doha **Communications: Radio Transmitters:** 4 **Receivers:** 40,000 (1976) **Television Transmitters:** 3 **Receivers:** 30,000 (1976) **Telephones:** 29,400 (1978) **Newspapers:** 2 dailies

**Weights and Measures:** Metric system **Travel Requirements:** Passport, visa, valid 6 months, 2 photos

Oil production, begun shortly after World War II and now valued at roughly $5.8 billion a year, is the country's economic base. With oil proceeds, roads have been built, a sea-distilled water supply established, an educational program instituted, and free medical services introduced. Steps toward diversification have included the exploitation of the Gulf's fishery potential, the production of cement from local raw materials, encouragement of investment in domestic projects, investigation of the mechanics of natural gas recovery, transportation, marketing and usage, and the introduction of domestic refining. Qatar has developed a steel and petrochemical industry.

After Britain declared it would withdraw its military forces from the Persian Gulf area by the end of 1971, Qatar declared its independence on September 1, 1971. The ruler of Qatar, Emir Ahmad ibn Ali ben Abdullah al-Thani, was deposed in a bloodless coup by his cousin, Emir Khalifa ibn Hamad al-Thani, on February 22, 1972.

Qatar is a member of the Organization of Petroleum Exporting Countries (OPEC), and the government has gone along with the organization's anti-Israeli policies. Qatar severed diplomatic relations with Egypt in 1979 in concert with other Arab countries after the Egyptian-Israeli peace treaty was signed. It has increased oil prices periodically to the OPEC base price of $34 per barrel of crude oil as of October 1981.

**HISTORY:** For a long time Qatar was under Persian rule, and paid a bounty to the governor of Bushire for the right to fish for pearls. In the 19th century it became independent of Persia under Thani, the founder of the al-Thani dynasty

**1871-1913:** Qatar is occupied by Ottoman Turks
**1916:** Qatar comes under British protection
**1971:** Qatar declares its independence
**1973:** Qatar announces embargo on oil to U.S.
**1977:** Government completes nationalization of all oil operations
**1979:** Qatar cuts diplomatic ties with Egypt after Egyptian-Israeli peace treaty

## ROMANIA

**Area:** 91,699 sq. mi. **Population:** 22,201,000 (1980 est.)

**Official Name:** Socialist Republic of Romania **Capital:** Bucharest **Nationality:** Romanian **Languages:** Romanian is the official and dominant language. Hungarian, German, Ukrainian, and Yiddish are minority languages **Religion:** About 80% of the population nominally belongs to the Romanian Orthodox Church, and about 9% to the Roman Catholic CCurch. The rest are mainly Protestant, Jewish, and Moslem **Flag:** Blue, yellow, and red vertical stripes with the national coat of arms in the center **Anthem:** The Tricolored Song **Currency:** Leu (15 per U.S. $1)

**Location:** Southeastern Europe. Romania is bounded on the northeast by the Soviet Union, on the east by the Black Sea, on the south by Bulgaria, on the southwest by Yugoslavia, and on the west by Hungary **Features:** The Carpathian Mountains and Transylvanian Alps form a semi-circle through the center of the country, separating the plains in the east and south from the Transylvanian plateau in the northwest **Chief Rivers:** Danube, Prut, Siret, Olt, Ialomita, Jiu, Mures

**Political Leader and Head of State:** President Nicolae Ceausescu, born 1918, elected 1974, reelected 1975; since 1965, Secretary-General of the Central Committee of the Romanian Communist Party, and since 1967 president of the State Council, the primary legislative body **Head of Government:** Prime Minister Constantin Dascalescu, appointed May 1982 **Effective Date of Present Constitution:** August 1965 **Legislative Body:** Grand National Assembly (unicameral), consisting of 369 members elected for 5 years; it actually performs little legislative work **Local Government:** 40 counties with people's councils elected for 5 years, and Bucharest municipality

**Ethnic Composition:** 88% of the population is of Romanian stock, tracing its ancestry back to the Latin settlers of the Roman Empire. Hungarians (8%) are the leading ethnic minority, with smaller numbers of Germans, Ukrainians, Serbo-Croats, Jews, and Turks **Population Distribution:** 49% urban **Density:** 242 inhabitants per sq. mi.

**Largest Cities:** (1979 est.) Bucharest 1,832,015, Brasov 299,172, Timisoara 281,320, Constanta 279,308, Cluj 274,095, Iasi 262,493, Galati 252,884, Craiova 220,893

**Per Capita Income:** $4,017 (1980) **Gross National Product (GNP):** $89 billion (1980) **Economic Statistics:** In 1978 industry accounted for 57% of the national income, while agriculture accounted for 15% **Minerals and Mining:** Large deposits of petroleum, natural gas, copper, lead, zinc, bauxite, manganese, bismuth, mercury, silver, iron ore, and coal **Labor Force:** 12 million (1979) with 36% in agriculture and 26% in industry **Foreign Trade:** Exports, mainly oilfield equipment, farm and other machinery, furniture and textiles totaled $11 billion in 1979. Imports, chiefly machinery and equipment, iron ores, coke, fuel, and electric motors, totaled $10 billion **Principal Trade Partners:** West Germany, USSR, Czechoslovakia, Italy, Britain, France, East Germany, Poland, China, United States, Iran, Libya

**Vital Statistics:** Birthrate, 18.6 per 1,000 of pop. (1979); death rate, 9.9 **Life Expectancy:** 70 years **Health Statistics:** 109 inhabitants per hospital bed; 738 per physician (1977) **Infant Mortality:** 31.6 per 1,000 births **Illiteracy:** negligible **Primary and Secondary School Enrollment:** 4,110,930 (1975) **Enrollment in Higher Education:** 381,321 (1976) **GNP Expended on Education:** N.A.

**Transportation:** Paved roads total 17,680 mi. **Motor Vehicles:** 45,100 (1970) **Railway Mileage:** 6,910 **Ports:** Constanta, Galati, Braila **Major Airlines:** Tarom flies internationally and domestically **Communications: Radio Transmitters:** 76 **Licenses:** 3,104,000 (1976) **Television Transmitters:** 194 **Licenses:** 2,963,000 (1976) **Telephones:** 11,196,000 (1975) **Newspapers:** 34 dailies, 171 copies per 1,000 inhabitants (1977)

**Weights and Measures:** Metric system **Travel Requirements:** Passport, visa, valid 60 days **International Dialing Code:** 40

For centuries a rural, backward country, Romania has the largest oil fields (now declining) of any country in Eastern Europe. Building on oil wealth, the Romanians have invested in modern chemical, steel, machinery, and related industries. Close economic ties have been fostered with Western Europe as well as with the Soviet bloc.

Although it remains a member of the Warsaw Pact alliance and of the Communist Council for Mutual Economic Assistance, Romania has successfully asserted its right to conduct its own foreign affairs. Alone among the Eastern European countries, Romania was outspoken in criticizing the Russian invasion of Afghanistan in 1979.

Not wanting to be merely a supplier of raw materials and agricultural products to the more developed Communist countries, Romania has persistently refused to subordinate its desire for rapid economic development to Soviet plans for complete integration of Eastern European and Soviet economies. The nation's industrial production increased by about 8.5% in 1980—the largest gain among Eastern European countries. But Romania's trade debt to the West totaled more than $10 billion in 1982, mainly because of a decline in exports and a rise in the cost of imports.

The heart of Romanian tactics aimed at resisting Moscow's pressure is a balancing act. Its essence is the matching of moves that irritate Moscow with moves that are pleasing. For instance, President Nicolae Ceausescu was the first East European leader to establish (1967) diplomatic relations with

West Germany and the first leader of a Communist country in a quarter century to be visited by a U.S. president (Nixon in 1969).

More recently, this balancing act has become noticeable in Ceausescu's handling of political dissidents. In 1978 the government freed a group of political dissidents as part of an amnesty program in celebration of Romania's 100th anniversary of independence from Turkey. However, Ceausescu continues to keep a tight rein on the dissidents.

Ceausescu in 1974 strengthened his position as undisputed leader by naming himself president, installing a colorless loyalist, Manea Manescu, as premier, and abolishing the nine-member Communist party presidium. He replaced it with a 23-member Executive Committee loyal to himself. In May 1982, Ceausescu replaced Ilie Verdet, premier since 1979, with Constantin Dascalescu, and removed other high-ranking officials, reportedly because of the country's deteriorating economy. Romania has had trouble servicing its growing foreign debt, which totaled $14 billion in 1982.

**HISTORY:** Ancient Dacia, comprising most of present-day Romania, was part of the Roman Empire until the 3rd century A.D. After the Romans legions withdrew, the region was overrun by Goths, Huns, Avars, Slavs, and Mongols. The withdrawal of the Mongols in the 13th century was followed by the establishment of the principalities of Walachia and Moldavia, which soon fell under Turkish rule. Both were to remain in the Ottoman Empire until well into the 19th century

**1828-29:** Walachia and Moldavia are occupied by Russia in Russo-Turkish War; although technically remaining part of the Ottoman Empire, they actually become Russian protectorates

**1859-66:** Alexander John Cuza is elected prince of Walachia and Moldavia, which are officially united as Romania in 1861; 5 years later, Cuza is deposed and is succeeded by Carol I of the house of Hohenzollern-Sigmaringen

**1878:** Congress of Berlin grants Romania full independence

**1916-19:** Romania fights on Allied side in World War I; overrun by Austro-German forces, it is forced to accept a harsh peace treaty, which is later annulled by the Allied victory; Romania seizes Bessarabia from Russia, Bukovina from Austria, and Transylvania from Hungary

**1938:** King Carol II establishes Fascist dictatorship

**1940-45:** Under German pressure, Romania returns territories taken from Russia and Hungary; King Carol is overthrown by Marshal Ion Antonescu, aided by Iron Guard, a militaristic Fascist group; in 1941, Romania enters World War II on Axis side; following the invasion of Soviet troops in 1944, Antonescu is overthrown and Romania switches to Allied side; a Communist-led government is set up in 1945

**1964:** Showing increasing independence of the Soviet Union, Romanian Communist party asserts the right of each Communist party to form its own political program without interference

**1968:** Romania supports liberalization program in Czechoslovakia and refuses to join in invasion of Czechoslovakia by Soviet and other Warsaw Pact forces

**1974:** Communist Party Central Committee approves constitutional change establishing the office of President, which is assumed by Ceausescu. Manea Manescu becomes premier

**1975:** U.S. Congress passes resolution granting Romania most-favored-nation trade status

**1977:** Earthquake kills at least 1,500. Ceausescu asks for eight more years of austerity and sacrifice to raise Romania to ranks of developed nations

**1979:** Ilie Verdet becomes premier

**1982:** Constantin Dascalescu replaces Verdet as premier

## RWANDA

**Area:** 10,169 sq. mi. **Population:** 5,046,000 (1980 est.)

**Official Name:** Republic of Rwanda **Capital:** Kigali **Nationality:** Rwandan **Languages:** Kinyarwanda (the national language) and French are the official languages; Kiswahili is spoken in the commercial centers **Religion:** 60% of the population is Christian, chiefly Roman Catholic; the rest are animist and Moslem **Flag:** Vertical stripes of red, yellow, and green with a black "R" in the center **Anthem:** Our Rwanda **Currency:** Rwanda franc (92.8 per U.S. $1)

**Location:** Central Africa. Landlocked Rwanda is bordered on the north by Uganda, on the east by Tanzania, on the south by Burundi, and on the west by Zaire **Features:** Known as the "Land of a Thousand Hills," the country consists largely of grassy uplands and hills, which roll down southeastward from the chain of volcanoes in the northwest **Chief Rivers:** Kagera, Nyabarongo, Akanyaru

**Head of State and Government:** President: Maj. Gen. Juvénal Habyarimana, born 1937, seized power in a coup July 1973 **Effective Date of Present Constitution:** Dec. 17, 1978 **Legislative Body:** National Development Council (unicameral) of 64 members **Local Government:** 10 prefectures, administered by appointed prefects

**Ethnic Composition:** 89% Hutu, a Bantu farming people; 10% Tutsi, a pastoral people of Hamitic origin; 1% Twa pygmies **Population Distribution:** 4% urban **Density:** 496 inhabitants per sq. mi.

**Largest Cities:** (1978 census) Kigali 117,749, Butare 21,691

**Per Capita Income:** $195 (1980) **Gross Domestic Product (GDP):** $997 million (1980) **Economic Statistics:** 60% of the GDP is derived from agriculture (bananas, coffee, pyrethrum, tea, cotton, manioc, corn, spices, sweet potatoes); 18% from mining (cassiterite, columbo-tantalite, wolfram, amblygonite, beryl); 16% from commerce; and 6% from construction and manufacturing **Minerals and Mining:** Cassiterite is the most abundant mineral, although columbo-tantalite, wolfram, amblygonite, and beryl are also mined. There are unexploited deposits of bismuth, phosphates, monazite, magnatite, and natural gas **Labor Force:** 1,940,000 (1970), with 95% engaged in small handicrafts or agriculture, and less than 5% in industry. Wage earners numbered 70,000 in 1973 **Foreign Trade:** Exports, mainly Arabica coffee, cassiterite, tea, and wolfram, totaled $129 million in 1980. Imports, chiefly textiles, iron, petroleum, and vehicles, totaled $203 million **Principal Trade Partners:** Belgium, France, United States, Britain, Japan, Kenya, Iran, West Germany

**Vital Statistics:** Birthrate, 50 per 1,000 of pop. (1975); death rate, 23.6 **Life Expectancy:** 46 years **Health Statistics:** 610 inhabitants per hospital bed; 36,417 per physician (1977) **Infant Mortality:** 132.9 per 1,000 births **Illiteracy:** 75% **Primary and Secondary School Enrollment:** 446,720 (1976) **Enrollment in Higher Education:** 1,108 (1975) **GNP Expended on Education:** 2.6% (1976)

**Transportation:** Paved roads total 200 mi. **Motor Vehicles:** 11,300 (1975) **Passenger Cars:** 6,500 **Railway Mileage:** None **Ports:** None **Major Airlines:** Air Rwanda operates international flights **Communications: Radio Transmitters:** 4 **Receivers:** 70,000 (1976) **Television:** None **Telephones:** 5,000 (1978) **Newspapers:** 1 daily, 0.1 copies per 1,000 inhabitants (1977)

**Weights and Measures:** Metric system **Travel Requirements:** Passport, visa for stay up to 3 months, $10 fee, 4 photos

Rwanda, formerly part of the Belgian UN trust territory of Ruanda-Urundi, is Africa's most densely populated country. Over five million people live in an area slightly smaller than the state of Maryland. Small and landlocked, it lies atop the mountainous western slope of the Great Rift Valley known as "the Roof of Africa." Through centuries of migratory settlement and population increase, the clearing of land for food production, together with overgrazing of cattle, has made Rwanda one of tropical Africa's most eroded areas. Its people contend with drought as well as poor soil in raising their crops of beans, bananas, sorghum, cassava, corn, and potatoes.

Despite erosion, Rwanda possesses scenic grandeur and great touristic potential, especially around Lake Kivu, considered by many the most beautiful of African lakes. However, the serene-looking highlands have known dark tragedy. In 1959-60, the Hutu people, the short stocky peasants who made up 85 percent of the population, rose up in bloody revolt against the Tutsi (or Watusi), the tall aristocratic people who kept the Hutu in feudal bondage for centuries. Thousands of Tutsi were killed or fled into neighboring countries. Neither willing nor able to stem the tide of Hutu unrest, the Belgian administration gave support to the Hutu on the eve of independence. In 1961 the Tutsi king, Mwami Kigeri V, was deposed and a republic declared, causing more than 160,000 Tutsi to flee to Burundi. Many returned later but in 1963-64 an armed invasion by Tutsi refugees set off another massacre of the tall people and put an apparent end to their minority caste domination.

Since independence, the government has concentrated on food production and the building of internal roads and road links into neighboring coastal countries. More than a fourth of national expenditures are for education and there has been some progress in light industry, but the major problems—population pressures, malnutrition, and poverty—remain largely unsolved.

In July 1973 Rwanda's manifold problems were compounded further as the government of President Grégoire Kayibanda was overthrown in a bloodless military coup, after months of tribal unrest between the governing Hutu majority and the Tutsi minority. The leader of the coup, Maj. Gen. Juvénal Habyarimana assumed the presidency.

**HISTORY:** Rwanda, along with neighboring Burundi, originally was inhabited by the pygmy Twa people, and later occupied by Bantu Hutus from the Congo basin. By the 15th century, the Tutsi, or Watusi, a tall, cattle-keeping people believed to have originated in Ethiopia, had arrived in both countries and imposed a feudal overlordship on the more numerous Hutus. European explorers reached the area in the 19th century, and in 1885 the region was taken over by Germany. It was made a Belgian League of Nations mandate after World War I and remained under Belgian control after World War II. With the growth of African nationalism, Hutu leaders in Rwanda began seeking emancipation from Tutsi domination

**1959:** Bloody Hutu revolt overthrows Tutsi monarchy; Tutsis suffer heavy casualties and 120,000 of them flee to Burundi and other neighboring countries

**1960:** Leaders of Hutu Emancipation Movement (PARMEHUTU) establish provisional government

**1961:** Belgium recognizes PARMEHUTU regime, but United Nations, hoping to preserve ethnic-economic union of Rwanda and Burundi, rules it unlawful and orders elections; PARMEHUTU scores overwhelming victory

**1962:** UN resolution grants Rwanda full independence

**1963:** Abortive Tutsi invasion from Burundi results in massacre of 12,000 Tutsi in Rwanda and renewed Tutsi exodus

**1970:** Rwanda signs friendship pact with Belgium; work is begun on road link to Kampala, Uganda

**1973:** President Grégoire Kayibanda overthrown in bloodless military coup; Maj. Gen. Juvénal Habyarimana takes over

**1974:** Death sentences of ex-President Kayibanda and seven other government officials commuted to life imprisonment

**1976:** Ugandan oil blockade brings economic hardship

**1978:** Habyarimana is elected to a 5-year term as president

**1980:** France gives Rwanda 14.6 million francs for food development program and for modernization of Rehenger hospital

**1981:** Its already dense population augmented by thousands of refugees from neighboring lands, Rwanda continues to fall short of self-sufficiency in food production

## SAINT LUCIA

**Area:** 238 sq. mi. **Population:** 115,783 (1980 census)

**Official Name:** Saint Lucia **Capital:** Castries **Nationality:** Saint Lucian **Languages:** English is the official language; a French patois containing many African elements is widely spoken **Religion:** Chiefly Roman Catholic (90%) with several Protestant churches represented **Flag:** A blue field containing a white-bordered black triangle covered at the bottom by a yellow triangle **Anthem:** Sons and Daughters of Saint Lucia **Currency:** East Caribbean dollar ($2.70 per U.S. $1)

**Location:** St. Lucia, the second largest of the Windward Islands, lies south of Martinique and northeast of St. Vincent in the Eastern Caribbean **Features:** The island is of volcanic origin and mountainous, with magnificent scenery; there is a good harbor at Castries. The climate is tropical and humid, with heavy rainfall in the summer

**Head of State:** Queen Elizabeth II through Acting Governor-General Boswell Williams, took office 1980 **Head of Government:** Prime Minister John Compton, appointed 1982 **Effective Date of Present Constitution:** Feb. 22, 1979 **Legislative Body:** Parliament (bicameral) consisting of a House of Assembly with 17 elected members and a Senate of 11 members, of whom 6 are appointed on the advice of the prime minister, 3 by the Opposition, and two by the governor-general. The Parliament has a five-year term **Local Government:** 16 parishes

**Ethnic Composition:** 90% of the population is of African descent, 6% is of mixed ancestry, 3% of East Indian and 1% of European **Population Distribution:** N.A. **Density:** 486 inhabitants per sq. mi.

**Largest City:** (1980 census) Castries 42,770

**Per Capita Income:** $690 (1979) **Gross Domestic Product (GDP):** $83 million (1979) **Economic Statistics:** The economy is primarily agricultural, with tourism and industry gaining in importance. The chief crops are bananas, coconuts, cocoa, citrus fruits, sugar, spices; there is some timber production and commercial fishing. Industrial development is increasing rapidly. An oil refining and transshipment facility and an industrial free port zone are under construction **Labor Force:** 45,000 (1979), with 40% engaged in agriculture **Foreign Trade:** Exports, including bananas and a growing amount of manufactured goods, totaled $66 million in 1979. Imports, including manufactured goods, machinery, food, fuel and clothing, totaled $105 million **Prinicipal Trade Partners:** Britain, Commonwealth and CARICOM countries, United States

**Vital Statistics:** Birthrate, 31.5 per 1,000 of pop. (1979); death rate, 7.2 **Life Expectancy:** 68 years **Health Statistics:** 202 inhabitants per hospital bed; 2,750 per physician (1977) **Infant Mortality:** 33 per 1,000 births **Illiteracy:** 15% **Primary and Secondary School Enrollment:** 25,386 (1976) **Enrollment in Higher Education:** N.A. **GDP Expended on Education:** N.A.

**Transportation:** Paved roads total 280 mi. **Motor Vehicles:** 7,500 (1978) **Passenger Cars:** 4,900 **Railway Mileage:** None **Port:** Castries **Major Airlines:** St. Lucia Airways and major international airlines **Communications: Radio Transmitters:** 2 **Receivers:** 82,000 (1975) **Television Transmitters:** 1 **Receivers:** 1,700 (1974) **Telephones:** 7,000 (1978) **Newspapers:** 1 daily, 36 copies per 1,000 inhabitants (1976)

**Weights and Measures:** Metric and British systems are used **Travel Requirements:** Proof of U.S. citizenship and return ticket **Direct Dialing Code:** 809

A former British possession in the Windward Islands, Saint Lucia is an island nation characterized by its African heritage, French accent, British political system and all the social and economic burdens attendant on many newly independent mini-states. Independence was attained on February 22, 1979.

Traditionally tied to agriculture for its livelihood, the island had embarked on the path of new industrial and commercial development. The largest single project is a combined oil transshipment terminal and free trade zone being developed by American oil interests. The manufacturing sector has been expanded, accounting for nearly half of the island's exports. The island's even climate and great beauty has made tourism a major industry, especially since the construction of a modern jetport near Castries in 1975. Traditional cash crops (bananas, cocoa, coconuts) have been bolstered under a development plan supported by the World Bank and the International Monetary Fund.

Yet, although St. Lucia's future appears bright in comparison with some of its neighbors, it shares many of their problems. Dependence on imports of finished goods has been largely responsible for continuing balance of payments deficits, and unemployment (25% or more) is a major problem.

A landslide victory for the opposition Labor party in the Jully 2, 1979, elections turned Prime Minister John Compton and his United Workers party out of power after 15 years. A moderate, Compton had sought close cooperation with the Caribbean Economic Community (CARICOM). Former judge Allan Louisy became the new prime minister but was unable to cope with St. Lucia's virulent brand of confrontation politics, which featured constant disruptive strikes by civil servants and others, as well as bitter infighting between some half-dozen charismatic political leaders. Winston Cenac, who took over as prime minister early in 1981, resigned in January 1982 in the wake of a series of crippling strikes, setting the stage for May elections that returned Compton and his party to power.

**HISTORY:** Little is known of the island's early history, but successive waves of Amerindian migration are thought to have populated the island in the 1300s. By the time of the first European landing, in the 16th century, the island was inhabited by the war-like Caribs. Initially a Spanish possession, the first attempts at settlement were made by the English, in 1605 and 1638-40; both succumbed to the Caribs. Subsequent French settlement proved more successful. Britain and France fought for control of the island over the next 150 years, with the last British occupation—in June, 1803—finally accepted by France in the Treaty of Paris in 1814. A plantation economy flourished, based on slavery; by 1834, when slavery was abolished in all British possessions, the island's African population numbered over 13,000

**1838:** St. Lucia, administered as a separate colony, is merged with the government of the Windward Islands

**1958:** St. Lucia joins Federation of the West Indies; remains member until its dissolution is 1962

**1959:** St. Lucia separated from Windward group, becomes dependency under direct British administration

**1962-65:** Discussions ensue between St. Lucia and other smaller British territories on federation with Barbados, without success

**1967:** St. Lucia becomes self-governing member of the West Indies Associated States May 3

**1974:** Elections return United Workers party government to power; Prime Minister John G.N. Compton promises full independence

**1977:** July 24-27 constitutional conference in London agrees on framework for independence

**1979:** Independence attained Feb. 22; Labour party boycotts ceremony, as striking teachers and civil servants threaten the new nation's stability. Labour party scores upset victory over Compton's UWP in July. Allan Louisy becomes prime minister

**1980:** Banana industry devastated by Hurricane Allen, Aug. 4

**1981:** Louisy resigns; Attorney General Winston Cenac becomes Labour party prime minister in April

**1982:** Strikes force Cenac's resignation. Compton becomes prime minister again when UWP sweeps May elections

## SAINT VINCENT AND THE GRENADINES

**Area:** 150 sq. mi. **Population:** 124,000 (1980 est.)

**Official Name:** Saint Vincent and the Grenadines **Capital:** Kingstown **Nationality:** Saint Vincentian **Languages:** English, with some French patois spoken **Religion:** Methodist, Anglican and Roman Catholic **Flag:** Five unequal vertical stripes of blue, white, yellow, white and green with a breadfruit leaf, scroll, sprig of cotton and coat of arms centered on the yellow stripe **Anthem:** National Anthem, beginning "St. Vincent! Land So Beautiful" **Currency:** East Caribbean dollar (2.70 per U.S. $1)

**Location:** Eastern Caribbean. The islands are situated south of St. Lucia and north of Carriacou Island, a part of Grenada **Features:** The island of St. Vincent, 18 miles long and 11 miles wide, is volcanic in origin with a mountain ridge running its length and rising in the north to Soufrière volcano. The climate is tropical with heavy summer rains. The Grenadines portion consists of the islands of Bequia, Canouan, Mayreau, Mustique, Prince, Palm, Petite St. Vincent and Union, among others

**Head of State:** Queen Elizabeth II, represented by a governor-general, Sir Sydney Douglas Gun-Munro, born 1916, took office 1979 **Head of Government:** Prime Minister Robert Milton Cato, born 1915, appointed Dec. 1979 **Effective Date of Present Constitution:** Oct. 27, 1979 **Legislative Body:** House of Assembly (unicameral) with 13 elected representatives and 6 senators (4 appointed on the advice of the prime minister and 2 on the advice of the opposition leader). The normal term is 5 years **Local Government:** 5 parishes plus the Grenadines

**Ethnic Composition:** Mainly of African or mixed origin **Population Distribution:** N.A. **Density:** 827 inhabitants per sq. mi.

**Largest City:** (1978 est.) Kingstown 25,000

**Per Capita Income:** $380 (1979) **Gross National Product (GNP):** $43 million (1979) **Economic Statistics:** About 20% of GNP is from agriculture (bananas, arrowroot, coconuts, nutmeg, mace, sugar, vegetables). St. Vincent is the world's largest producer of arrowroot. 9% of GNP is from industry (agricultural and food processing, furniture, clothing, sugar refining, flour). Tourism is important **Minerals and Mining:** None **Labor Force:** 61,000 (1979) **Foreign Trade:** Exports, chiefly bananas, arrowroot, copra and mace, totaled $15 million in 1979. Imports, mainly fuel, fertilizer, transportation equipment and textiles, totaled $50 million **Principal Trade Partners:** Britain, Trinidad and Tobago, Barbados, Canada, United States

**Vital Statistics:** Birthrate, 35 per 1,000 of pop. (1979); death rate, 7.1 **Life Expectancy:** N.A. **Health Statistics:** 170 inhabitants per hospital bed (1972) **Infant Mortality:** 38 per 1,000 births **Illiteracy:** 5% **Primary and Secondary School Enrollment:** 26,938 (1975)

**Enrollment in Higher Education:** N.A. **GNP Expended on Education:** N.A.

**Transportation:** Paved roads total 185 mi. **Motor Vehicles:** 4,900 (1978) **Passenger Cars:** 3,900 **Railway Mileage:** None **Port:** Kingstown **Major Airlines:** LIAT and Caribbean Airways provide service **Communications: Radio Transmitters:** 1 **Receivers:** N.A. **Television Transmitters:** None **Telephones:** 5,000 (1978) **Newspapers:** 1 weekly

**Weights and Measures:** British system **Travel Requirements:** N.A. **Direct Dialing Code:** 809

On October 27, 1979, Saint Vincent and its dependent islands, the Grenadines, gained independence after 10 years as a British Associated State. But along with its newly independent neighbors in the Caribbean, St. Vincent faces acute social and economic growing pains in the 1980's.

Dependent on tourism and agriculture for their livelihood, the residents of this tiny nation in the Lesser Antilles average an annual per capita income of $380. Unemployment is estimated at 20 percent of the labor force, and the annual growth rate in the population is 2%, which threatens to put an even greater strain on the country's resources.

Despite these inherent problems, the island prospered in the 1970s, with gross domestic product growing 14 percent between 1976 and 1978. Its favorable climate encouraged good harvests and a booming tourist industry, matched by a modest growth in the manufacturing sector aided by government investment. But the eruption of the long-dormant volcano, Soufrière, on April 13, 1979, proved a heavy blow to the island's fragile economy. Although no one was injured—unlike the last major eruption in 1902, in which 2,000 died—the volcano spewed clouds of ash and smoke over the northern half of St. Vincent, forcing evacuation of 20,000 residents. The eruption gravely damaged the banana crop, which received another devastating blow from Hurricane Allen on Aug. 4, 1980.

General elections held December 5 of 1979 saw Milton Cato and his moderately socialist Saint Vincent Labour party returned to power. The SVLP won 11 of the 13 seats in the House of Assembly, with the others going to the centrist New Democrats; the conservative People's Political party failed to gain a seat. A brief rebellion by would-be secessionists on Union and Palm islands on Dec. 7 was quelled by police on the following day, although a state of emergency imposed when the revolt began was not lifted until May 1980.

By 1981, the government had launched a campaign to diversify the economy and, in that year, sugar production was revived, but the island was also experiencing severe labor troubles. Sporadic strikes in 1981 and 1982 interrupted water delivery, police work, and other services. Proposed legislation that would have given government greater power to impose "public order" had to be diluted in the face of a threat of a general strike by workers in both the public and private sectors.

**HISTORY:** The earliest known inhabitants of the island were the Arawak Indians, soon supplanted by the warlike Caribs, who migrated from South America to people most of the Lesser Antilles from 1300 to 1600. Christopher Columbus was the first European to see the island, landing there on January 22, 1498 (Saint Vincent Day). Claimed by the British since 1627, a dispute ensued with France for control of the island, ending only with its formal ceding to Britain in the Treaty of Versailles in 1783. After an abortive uprising by the Caribs in 1795-96, most of the native population was deported to the island of Rattan in the Bay of Honduras, with the island thereafter peopled mainly by African slaves and their descendants

**1833:** St. Vincent is included in the Government of the Windward Islands, remaining a part of that colony until its dissolution in 1960, when it becomes a separately administered territory

**1902:** Volcano of Soufrière erupts, killing over 2,000 people

**1958:** St. Vincent participates in Federation of West Indies until its dissolution in 1962

**1962-65:** St. Vincent joins in discussions on federation of the Windward Island territories—including Grenada and St. Lucia—with Barbados; talks prove fruitless
**1969:** St. Vincent becomes an internally self-governing Associated State, with Britain controlling defense and foreign relations
**1974:** Milton Cato and St. Vincent Labour party swept into power in Dec. 9 elections, with support of Ebenezer Joshua's People's Progressive party; Cato becomes chief minister
**1978:** Constitutional talks are held in London Sept. 18-21
**1979:** Soufrière erupts April 13; 20,000 inhabitants are evacuated, crops destroyed and tourism disrupted. St. Vincent and the Grenadines gain their independence from Britain Oct. 27. Dec. 5 general elections to the House of Assembly result in victory for Milton Cato and the SVLP, which wins 11 of 13 seats
**1980:** Hurricane Allen causes extensive damage Aug. 4
**1981:** Widespread strikes disrupt the economy. The sugar industry is revived, after a 20-year hiatus, with the opening of a grinding plant bought from Trinidad and Tobago
**1982:** Cato joins leaders of several other developing West Indian states in criticism of proposed U.S. Caribbean aid plan

## SAN MARINO

**Area:** 23.4 sq. mi. **Population:** 21,000 (1978 est.)

**Official Name:** Most Serene Republic of San Marino **Capital:** San Marino **Nationality:** Sanmarinese **Language:** Italian is the official and universal language **Religion:** Roman Catholicism **Flag:** Horizontal bands of white and blue with the national coat of arms in the center **Anthem:** National Anthem, beginning "Honor to you, O ancient Republic" **Currency:** Italian lira (1,296 per U.S. $1)

**Location:** Landlocked San Marino is situated in the Apennines, southwest of Rimini, Italy **Features:** The town of San Marino is situated on the slopes of Mount Titano, and much of the republic is coextensive with the mountain, which has three pinnacles **Chief Rivers:** San Marino, Fumicello

**Head of State and of Government:** 2 Captains Regent, elected by the Council for six-month terms, assisted by a Congress of State (cabinet) **Effective Date of Present Constitution:** October 1600 **Legislative Body:** Great and General Council (unicameral), with 60 members elected every 5 years **Local Government:** 9 parishes (*castelli*), headed by Captains of the Castle and elected committees

**Ethnic Composition:** The Sanmarinese are of Italian origin. A small number of aliens reside in the republic **Population Distribution:** 74% urban **Density:** 897 inhabitants per sq. mi.

**Largest Town:** (1977 census) San Marino 4,628

**Per Capita Income:** N.A. **Gross National Product (GNP):** N.A. **Economic Statistics:** The principal occupations are farming, manufacturing, and animal husbandry. Main agricultural products are wheat, cheese and wine, while chief industrial goods are textiles, cement, paper, leather, and furs. Tourism and the sale of postage stamps are major sources of income **Minerals and Mining:** Building stones are quarried for export **Labor Force:** 4,300 mostly employed in the agricultural sector. The rest work for manufacturing and service industries **Foreign Trade:** Exports consist of wine, woolens, furniture, ceramics, and postage stamps. Manufactured goods of all kinds make up the main imports. Because of a customs union with Italy, no record is kept of foreign payment transactions

**Vital Statistics:** Birthrate, 13.6 per 1,000 of pop. (1978); death rate, 7.5 **Life Expectancy:** 72 years **Health Statistics:** Public health institutions include a hospital, a dispensary, and a laboratory of hygiene; 750 inhabitants per physician **Infant Mortality:** 10.8 per 1,000 births **Illiteracy:** Negligible **Primary and Secondary School Enrollment:** 2,884 (1976) **Enrollment in Higher Education:** N.A. **GNP Expended on Education:** N.A.

**Transportation:** Streets and roads total more than 60 miles **Motor Vehicles:** 9,584 **Passenger Cars:** 4,724 **Railway Mileage:** 20 miles of electric funicular railway **Ports:** None **Communications: Radio Transmitters:** No radio or TV transmitters **Radio Licenses:** 6,000 (1976) **Television Licenses:** 4,000 (1976) **Telephones:** 6,000 (1977) **Newspapers:** No dailies, but an edition of *Il Resto Del Carlino* of Bologna gives special attention to San Marino news; there are 3 fortnightlies

**Weights and Measures:** Metric system **Travel Requirements:** Passport, no visa **International Dialing Code:** 39

The Apennine slopes shelter a tiny country with a legendary beginning and an existence almost as fabled. Its founder is said to be Marinus, a Christian stonecutter from Dalmatia seeking refuge from persecution in the fourth century. The republic, named San Marino after the canonized Saint Marinus, is the world's smallest and oldest, having remained independent for some 1,600 years. It lived on after the collapse of the Roman Empire and survived such upheavals as an interdiction by the pope in the Middle Ages, occupation by troops of Giulio Cardinal Alberoni in 1739-40, the conquests of Napoleon, and the unification of Italy in the late 19th century.

San Marino's knack for survival carried it through the Mussolini era and World War II. In 1943 it rid itself of the Fascistlike regime of the Mussolini period, and from 1945 to the autumn of 1957 was ruled by a coalition of Communists and left-wing Socialists. After the defection of six members of the ruling group, an anti-Communist coalition gained control and went on to win subsequent elections. In 1973 that coalition resigned over economic policy disputes. The Christian Democrats formed a new coalition cabinet with Socialists and a splinter party. A coalition of Christian Democrats and Socialists governed from 1976 to 1977; in 1978, a coalition of Communists and Socialists formed a government. No major changes in government policy were made.

San Marino, situated on three-peaked Mount Titano, derives approximately 80 percent of its gross national product from tourism and the sale of postage stamps to collectors. The tourists, numbering about 3 million annually, are afforded a magnificent view of Rimini and the Adriatic Sea from three old fortresses and may visit stately buildings, churches, and museums.

**HISTORY:** According to tradition, San Marino was founded in the 4th century A.D. by Marinus, a Christian stonecutter from Dalmatia who was later canonized. Reputedly the world's oldest republic, it is the last of the Italian peninsula's once-numerous city-states
**1631:** Pope Urban VIII recognizes the independent status of San Marino
**1739-40:** San Marino is occupied by a military force under a papal legate, Giulio Cardinal Alberoni, who attempts to establish sovereignty over republic; occupation is terminated by Pope Clement II
**1862:** San Marino and Italy form a customs union
**1939-44:** San Marino, although officially neutral in World War II, is occupied by the German army and is the scene of heavy fighting during Allied advance into northern Italy
**1945:** Communist and left-wing Socialist coalition wins majority of seats in elections for the Grand Council
**1957:** Defection of six Council members leads to fall of coalition; anti-Communist councillors form new government
**1973:** Coalition government resigns; new cabinet is formed with Socialists and Christian Democrats; women are given expanded legal rights
**1974:** General elections are held and coalition of Christian Democrats and Socialists remains in power. New cabinet is formed. Three women win seats in the Council
**1975:** Socialists withdraw from the two-party coalition, leaving the Christian Democrats without an absolute parliamentary majority
**1976:** New coalition of Socialists and Christian Democrats is formed
**1977:** Socialist-Christian Democrat coalition collapses; Communists fail to form new government
**1978:** Communists form new government after Christian Democrats, winners of a plurality in May elections, fail to do so
**1981:** First woman Captain-Regent, Maria Lea Pedini, takes office

## SAO TOME and PRINCIPE

**Area:** 372 sq. mi. **Population:** 83,000 (1978 est.)

**Official Name:** Democratic Republic of São Tomé and Príncipe **Capital:** São Tomé **Nationality:** São Tomean **Languages:** Portuguese is the main language, and a local creole is also spoken **Religion:** Roman Catholicism is the predominant religion **Flag:** Three equal horizontal stripes of green, yellow and green with a red triangle at the hoist and two black stars on the yellow stripe **Anthem:** Total Independence **Currency:** Dobra (38.9 per U.S. $1)

**Location:** These two islands are in the Gulf of Guinea, about 125 miles off the west coast of Africa **Features:** Hilly, wooded interiors and flat coastal plains **Chief Rivers:** Grande, Abade

**Head of State and of Government:** President Manuel Pinto da Costa, elected 1975 **Effective Date of Constitution:** 1975 **Legislative Body:** Popular Assembly (unicameral), with members elected for 4 years. Control is in the hands of the MLSTP party, headed by the president **Local Government:** 2 island provinces

**Ethnic Composition:** The native population is mostly African, with some Portuguese admixture **Population Distribution:** N.A. **Density:** 223 inhabitants per sq. mi.

**Largest Cities:** (1970 census) São Tomé 7,681; Santo António 1,618

**Per Capita Income:** $421 (1980) **Gross Domestic Product (GDP):** $35 million (1980) **Economic Statistics:** Most of the population is engaged in the growing of plantation agricultural products and fishing **Minerals and Mining:** None **Labor Force:** 40,000, with 62% in agriculture (coffee, cocoa, coconuts, bananas), 7% in industry (beverages, copra, palm oil and fish processing) and commerce **Foreign Trade:** Exports, mostly palm products, coffee, cocoa and fruit, totaled $15 million (1978). Imports totaled $10 million **Principal Trade Partners:** Portugal, Netherlands

**Vital Statistics:** Birthrate, 41.9 per 1,000 of pop. (1978); death rate, 9.6 **Life Expectancy:** N.A. **Health Statistics:** 160 inhabitants per hospital bed; 1,905 per physician (1977) **Infant Mortality:** 49.7 per 1,000 births **Illiteracy:** 90% **Primary and Secondary School Enrollment:** 17,329 (1976) **Enrollment in Higher Education:** N.A. **GDP Expended on Education:** 2.2% (1972)

**Transportation:** All roads total 179 mi. **Motor Vehicles:** 2,000 (1973) **Passenger Cars:** 1,600 **Railway Mileage:** None **Ports:** São Tomé (on São Tomé) and Santo António (on Príncipe) **Major Airlines:** Transportes Aereos de São Tomé **Communications: Radio Transmitters:** 4 **Licenses:** 20,000 (1976) **Television:** None **Telephones:** 900 **Newspapers:** 2 weeklies

**Weights and Measures:** Metric system **Travel Requirements:** Passport, visa

---

One of Africa's smallest countries, São Tomé and Príncipe is part of an extinct volcanic mountain range. The islands' economy is based on cocoa, with copra and coffee also important. A steep drop in the world price of cocoa has greatly affected the country's financial outlook. The crops are grown on company-owned plantations worked by labor imported from Mozambique and Angola. This temporary labor force outnumbers the permanent population, which largely refuses to work on the plantations, where conditions have been much criticized. Most of the 1,000 white settlers, who ran the plantations, and the Cape Verdeans, who served as foremen, left the islands after independence was declared. Malnutrition is a major health problem.

São Tomé and Príncipe, which lie 150 miles west of Gabon in the Gulf of Guinea, became independent on July 12, 1975, after 500 years of Portuguese rule, the fourth and smallest of Portugal's African territories to emerge from colonial status. Manuel Pinto da Costa was proclaimed first president.

**HISTORY:** São Tomé and Príncipe were discovered in 1471 by the Portuguese, who began to settle convicts and exiled Jews on the islands and to establish sugar plantations using African slaves

**1951:** The islands are designated a Portuguese Overseas Province

**1975:** São Tomé and Príncipe becomes independent

**1979:** Prime Minister Miguel Trovoada, accused of attempting a coup, is arrested

**1980:** President Pinto da Costa assumes duties of the prime minister; looks to Cuba and other socialist countries for aid

**1981:** Trovoada released from prison. EEC provides aid to country's fishing industry. OPEC gives $1 million to support balance of payments. Cocoa production regains pre-independence level

## SAUDI ARABIA

**Area:** 829,995 sq. mi. **Population:** 8,960,000 (1980 est.)

**Official Name:** Kingdom of Saudi Arabia **Capital:** Riyadh (Jidda serves as the administrative center, and Taif is the summer capital) **Nationality:** Saudi Arabian **Languages:** Arabic is the official and universal language **Religion:** The overwhelming majority of the population is Sunni Moslem, and Islam is the state religion **Flag:** Green, with a white sword below the Arabic inscription "There is no god but God, and Mohammed is His Prophet" **Anthem:** Royal Anthem of Saudi Arabia, a short instrumental selection **Currency:** Saudi riyal (3.43 per U.S. $1)

**Location:** Arabian peninsula in Southwest Asia, Saudi Arabia is bounded on the north by Jordan, Iraq, and Kuwait; on the east by the Persian Gulf, Qatar, the United Arab Emirates, and Oman; on the south by Yemen and Southern Yemen, and on the west by the Red Sea **Features:** Nine-tenths of the country is covered by a barren plateau, including the Rub al-Khali and Al-Nafud desert regions. In the west, the Hejaz mountains border the narrow coastal plain along the Red Sea; to the east of the central plateau is the low-lying coastal region along the Persian Gulf **Chief Rivers:** There are no permanent rivers

**Head of State and of Government:** King Fahd ibn Abdul-Aziz Al Saud, born 1923, succeeded to the throne June 13, 1982. He named himself premier and his half-brother, Crown Prince Abdullah ibn Abdul-Aziz Al Saud, first deputy premier **Effective Date of Present Constitution:** None. Authority is based on Islamic law (Shari'a) and on Bedouin tradition **Legislative Body:** None. The appointed Council of Ministers performs some legislative functions **Local Government:** 18 provinces, 6 major and 12 minor, each with an appointed governor

**Ethnic Composition:** The population is largely homogeneous, descended from indigenous Arab tribes, with some admixture of Africans, Turks, Iranians, Indians, and Indonesians. At present about 30% are expatriates **Population Distribution:** 28% urban **Density:** 10.8 inhabitants per sq. mi.

**Largest Cities:** (1974 census) Riyadh 666,840, Jidda 561,104, Mecca 366,801, Taif 204,857, Medina 198,186, Dammam 127,844

**Per Capita Income:** $12,521 (1980) **Gross National Product (GNP):** $84 billion (1980) **Economic Statistics:** 62% of GNP is derived from industry, (oil refining, electrical goods, fertilizers, cement, iron and steel) and mining (80% in oil); 15% from trade and services; and 4% from agriculture (dates, grain, vegetables, livestock) **Minerals and Mining:** Saudi Arabia is the world's third-largest producer of oil. Other abundant minerals are natural gas, gypsum, copper, salt, manganese, silver, gold, sulphur, and lead **Labor Force:** About 2.7 million (one-half foreign), with 44% in commerce, services and government, 28% in agriculture, 21% in construction, 4% in industry and 3% in oil **Foreign Trade:** Exports, 99% petroleum and petroleum products, totaled $58 billion in 1979. Imports, principally motor vehicles, cereals, and power generating machinery, totaled $28 billion **Principal Trade Partners:** United States, West Germany, Japan, Italy, Netherlands

**Vital Statistics:** Birthrate, 48.8 per 1,000 of pop. (1980); death rate, 18.3 **Life Expectancy:** 45 years **Health Statistics:** 647 inhabitants per hospital bed; 1,641 per physician (1977) **Infant Mortality:** over 110 per 1,000 births **Illiteracy:** 70% **Primary and Secondary School Enrollment:** 908,905 (1975) **Enrollment in Higher Education:** 26,437 (1975) **GNP Expended on Education:** 10% (1977)

**Transportation:** Paved roads total 11,800 mi. **Motor Vehicles:** 319,900 (1978) **Passenger Cars:** 152,500 **Railway Mileage:** 357 **Ports:** Jidda, Dammam, Yenbo, Ras Tanura, Jubail **Major Airlines:** Saudia operates both domestic and international flights **Communications: Radio Transmitters:** 31 **Receivers:** 260,000 (1976) **Television Transmitters:** 12 **Receivers:** 130,000 (1976) **Telephones:** 185,000 (1977) **Newspapers:** 12 dailies (1976), 11 copies per 1,000 inhabitants (1974)

**Weights and Measures:** Metric system **Travel Requirements:** Passport, transit visa valid 72 hours, no charge, onward ticket. No tourist visas issued **International Dialing Code:** 966

---

The world's 587 million adherents of Islam regard Saudi Arabia with a special reverence because it contains Mecca, the holiest of holy sites. The birthplace of the Prophet Mohammed, Mecca is the direction to which these Moslems turn as they bow in prayer five times each day. It is the destination of some half million people a year from all parts of the world who follow the Koranic exhortation of making the pilgrimage, or *Haj*, during one's lifetime. Closed to non-Moslems, the city contains the Great Mosque, or *Haram*, and the *Kaaba*, with its sacred Black Stone.

The ruler of Saudi Arabia is considered the custodian of the holy sites and the chief defender of Islam. In addition, the present ruler, King Fahd, is the secular head of one of the world's leading oil-exporting countries and, consequently, one of its richest men, although his realm consists mostly of vast expanses of trackless desert. The combination of these functions has long given the Saudi king a strong voice in the Arab world.

Saudi Arabia has been also a country in which the deep Arab tradition of hospitality conflicts with an equally strong xenophobic tendency. It is a country where distrust of Western "imperialism" and American support for Zionism is often overshadowed by dependence on American technology and a fear of Communism.

The assassination of King Faisal by a nephew in 1975 caused reverberations throughout the Middle East. Faisal's brother, Crown Prince Khalid, succeeded him as king and named himself premier and Crown Prince Fahd first deputy premier. The new leaders were less concerned with fierce anti-Communism and were slightly more moderate on the Arab-Israel dispute.

Saudi Arabia has used its tremendous financial power to exert diplomatic pressure and has assumed a major role as a mediator in Middle Eastern affairs. Saudi Arabia has exercised a moderating influence on other Arab nations in raising oil prices in recent years.

The Saudi position in regard to the United States is ambivalent. On the one hand, the government maintains close ties with Washington as the leader of the non-Communist world and admires American know-how; but Saudi Arabia does not hesitate to pressure the United States to stop supporting Israel. In practice, the chief link between Saudi Arabia and the United States is their oil relationship. Saudi Arabia has the largest known oil reserves in the world (180 billion barrels), and the United States has been the world's leading consumer, by far, of Saudi Arabian oil, now being produced at the rate of about 9.2-million barrels a day. Soon after oil was discovered in the Saudi deserts in the 1930s, King Ibn Saud, the kingdom's founder, granted primary exploitation rights to the Standard Oil Company of California. The concession was subsequently transferred to the Arabian American Oil Company, known as Aramco, a conglomerate of several oil companies. Still 40 percent owned by four American oil companies, Aramco is the world's largest oil-producing company.

Aside from Islam, Aramco is perhaps the dominant force in Saudi Arabia. The Saudis have made some attempts to diversify the economy by encouraging agricultural and industrial development, but even the new projects involve Aramco because the company is often the final contractor. It has become almost an administrative arm of the Saudi government; it builds and runs schools and housing, constructs and maintains roads, and manages other important projects.

Before his assassination, King Faisal drafted a far-reaching and comprehensive plan calling for $142 billion in investment and affecting all areas of development. Cities are being transformed with modern buildings; new highway systems are complete, even with rush-hour traffic jams; and two major new industrial centers are being built at Jubail in the midst of Saudi Arabia's Gulf Coast oil fields and at Yanbu, the Red Sea port for Medina. A $15-20 billion gas-gathering system—a project larger than the trans-Alaska pipeline—is being built by an Arabian-American company. Other projects are giant desalination plants and a new airport the size of Manhattan Island to serve Jidda.

Although much of Saudi Arabia's oil revenue goes either to these projects or to the armed forces, some of it is now being spent for social welfare. Free medical service has been made available to all citizens, and elementary, secondary, and higher education is also free, although not compulsory. By contrast, the religious tenets of Islam, which form the common law of the land, are enforced with fundamentalist zeal.

On November 20, 1979, the Grand Mosque in Mecca, which is Islam's holiest shrine, was seized by a band of some 500 Islamic militants, whose leader claimed to be the *Mahdi*, or messiah of the Shiite Moslems. Saudi soldiers retook the mosque by December 4, but some 300 militants and 60 soldiers were killed. Another 63 raiders were executed in early 1980. The Saudi government unofficially declared that the seizure had been led by religious fanatics.

Saudi Arabia has armed itself with costly, sophisticated weapons, including five AWACS electronic surveillance aircraft sold by the U.S. in 1981 despite Israel's objections. The Saudis continued to give financial aid to Iraq for its 1980-82 war against Iran, and it also helped the PLO in Lebanon to withstand a massive Israeli invasion of the country in June 1982.

King Khalid, who had been in poor health since he ascended the throne in 1975, died of a heart attack on June 13, 1982. He was succeeded by a half-brother, Crown Prince Fahd, who reportedly was more of an activist and less a traditionalist than the late ruler.

**HISTORY:** Arabia has been inhabited for thousands of years by nomadic Semitic tribes. Followers of Mohammed, who was born in Mecca in the 6th century A.D., conquered most of the area between Persia on the east and Spain on the west, but Arabia itself declined in importance. As a political unit, Saudi Arabia is of relatively recent origin, dating from the 18th century, when tthe Saud family, adherents of the puritanical Wahabi movement, gained control over most of the Arabian peninsula

**19th cent.:** Wahabi movement is crushed (1811) by Egyptian expedition led by Mohammed Ali; movement revives temporarily, only to be defeated by Rashid dynasty, which gains control of central Arabia and expels Saud family

**1902-32:** Ibn Saud, the exiled Wahabi leader, conquers the Nejd, Hasa, and Hejaz regions and forms the kingdom of Saudi Arabia

**1936:** Oil is discovered near the Persian Gulf

**1953:** Ibn Saud dies and is succeeded by his eldest son, Saud

**1962:** Saud sends aid to royalist troops in Yemen after pro-Nasser rebels depose Imam. Relations with Egypt are cut

**1964:** Saud is deposed and succeeded by Crown Prince Faisal, who introduces sweeping government reorganization and abolishes slavery. Relations with Egypt are restored

**1967-68:** Saudi Arabian troops are sent to Jordan during six-day Arab-Israeli war but take no part in fighting. King Faisal halts aid to Yemeni royalists in return for withdrawal of Egyptian troops; however, aid is temporarily resumed to counteract support for republicans by Soviet Union, Syria, and Southern Yemen

**1969:** Hundreds are arrested as government prevents coup d'état

**1970:** Resumption of ties to Yemen is marked by financial aid from Saudi Arabia

**1973:** The Yom Kippur War prompts King Faisal to cut exports of oil to the U.S. by 10 percent in order to compel the U.S. to demand a cease-fire and Israeli withdrawal from Arab territory

**1975:** King Faisal is assassinated by his nephew, Prince Faisal ibn Musad Abdel Aziz, 31; his brother, Crown Prince Khalid ibn Abdul-Aziz al Saud, 62, succeeds him

**1976:** Saudis hold down OPEC price increases to 5 percent

**1978:** Saudi Arabia buys 60 F-15 jet fighter-planes from U.S.

**1979:** Moslem militants seize and hold Grand Mosque in Mecca for two weeks before Saudi soldiers retake the holy shrine

**1981:** Saudi Arabia buys five AWACS surveillance aircraft from U.S.

**1982:** King Khalid, 69, dies; Crown Prince Fahd, 59, becomes king

## SENEGAL

**Area:** 76,124 sq. mi. **Population:** 5,703,000 (1980 est.)

**Official Name:** Republic of Senegal **Capital:** Dakar **Nationality:** Senegalese **Languages:** French is the official language; among the spoken African languages, Wolof is used by nearly 50%, and Peul (Fulani), Mende, Diola and Mandingo are other main languages **Religion:** More than 75% of the population are Moslems; about 5% are Christians, and the rest animists **Flag:** Vertical stripes of green, yellow, and red with a green star in the center **Anthem:** National Anthem, beginning "Pluck your koras, strike the balafons" **Currency:** CFA Franc (305 per U.S. $1)

**Location:** West Africa. Senegal is bounded on the north by Mauritania, on the east by Mali, on the south by Guinea and Guinea-Bissau, and on the west by the Atlantic Ocean. The nation of The Gambia is an enclave within Senegal **Features:** The country is a transitional zone between the Sahara and the equatorial jungle with semidesert in the north, and open savanna in the center and south **Chief Rivers:** Senegal, Saloum, Gambia, Casamance

**Head of State:** President Abdou Diouf, born 1935, took office Jan. 1, 1981. He is also president of the Confederation of Senegambia **Head of Government:** Premier Habib Thiam, born 1933, appointed Jan. 2, 1981 **Effective Date of Present Constitution:** March 3, 1963 **Legislative Body:** National Assembly (unicameral), consisting of 100 members elected for 5 years **Local Government:** 8 regions, each headed by an appointed governor

**Ethnic Composition:** The largest ethnic group, the Wolof, makes up about 36% of the population. Other important groups are the Peul (Fulani), with 17.5%; the Serere, with 16.5%; the Tukulor, with 9%; Diola, with 9%; and the Mandingo, with 6.5%. A non-African population of 50,000, largely French, is concentrated in Dakar **Population Distribution:** 32% urban **Density:** 75 inhabitants per sq. mi..

**Largest Cities:** (1976 census) Dakar 798,792, Thiès 117,353, Kaolack 106,899, St-Louis 88,404, Ziguinchor 72,726, Rufisque 66,995, Diourrbel 50,618, Mbour 37,663, Louga 35,063

**Per Capita Income:** $321 (1980) **Gross National Product (GNP):** $1.8 billion (1980) **Economic Statistics:** In 1978 about 38% of GNP was derived from trade and finance; 30% from agriculture and fishing (peanuts, accounting for about half of total production; fish; millet; sorghum; rice; cassava; potatoes; livestock); 20% from manufacturing (peanut oil mills, cement, food processing, textiles, leather, shoes, chemicals, and phosphate mining) **Minerals and Mining:** Calcium and aluminum phosphates, limestone, titanium, salt, and ilmenite are being worked **Labor Force:** Of 1,732,000, 70% are engaged in agriculture **Foreign Trade:** Exports, chiefly peanuts, phosphates, and canned fish, totaled $421 million in 1980. Imports, mainly food, textiles, machinery, chemical and petroleum products, totaled $1.1 billion **Principal Trade Partners:** France, United States, Britain, Netherlands, Mali, Ivory Coast

**Vital Statistics:** Birthrate, 47.6 per 1,000 of pop. (1975); death rate, 22.1 **Life Expectancy:** 44 years **Health Statistics:** 853 inhabitants per hospital bed; 17,066 per physician (1976) **Infant Mortality:** 62.7 per 1,000 births **Illiteracy:** 90% **Primary and Secondary School Enrollment:** 373,534 (1975) **Enrollment in Higher Education:** 8,213 (1975) **GNP Expended on Education:** 3.0% (1976)

**Transportation:** Paved roads total 1,840 mi. **Motor Vehicles:** 69,800 (1974) **Passenger Cars:** 44,800 **Railway Mileage:** 642 **Ports:** Dakar, Kaolack, Ziguinchor, Saint-Louis **Major Airlines:** Air Senegal **Communications: Radio Transmitters:** 17 **Receivers:** 290,000 (1976) **Television Transmitters:** 2 **Receivers:** 35,000 (1974) **Telephones:** 42,000 (1977) **Newspapers:** 1 daily, 5 copies per 1,000 inhabitants (1976)

**Weights and Measures:** Metric system **Travel Requirements:** Passport, visa, valid 3 months, 2 photos, $4.75 fee **International Dialing Code:** 221

---

Ever since it gained independence, discouraging economic reverses have beset Senegal, the former administrative and commmercial center of the defunct French West African empire. In colonial times, the French federation, with a population of 20 million, was the market for industry and business based on the great port of Dakar, the Senegalese capital.

With the grant of independence to French African possessions, Senegal was forced to rely on its own meager resources and limited aid. The country has experienced increasing economic difficulty. Peanuts, introoduced by the French more than a century ago, are the main cash crop. In the past they have accounted for nearly 80 percent of exports and provided the main income for more than 90 percent of Senegalese. But with the end of French subsidies, lower prices and droughts, production has fallen sharply. Despite government appeals, growing numbers of farmers have stopped planting peanuts.

American and other foreign assistance is gradually increasing production of rice, millet, sorghum, sugar, and livestock, but the effort is offset by the rapid fall in export earnings, rising debt, the cost of imported oil, and tightened budgets.

Compounding these problems have been the continuing severe drought and famine plaguing not just Senegal but other countries of the sub-Sahara. An estimated 100,000 people died in 1973 and millions more were starving in the sub-Sahara region. Relief efforts were hampered by poor transportation and communications facilities.

President Léopold Senghor, Senegal's leader before and for two decades since independence, showed considerable skill in maintaining stability despite his many problems. A longtime Francophile and also a poet of note, Senghor in 1974 renegotiated all of the accords reached with France in 1960. Terms of the revised accords included partial withdrawal of French troops and the transfer of a military base at Dakar to Senegal. Relations with Arab countries have become closer, although in 1980 Senegal broke off relations with Libya, accusing that Arab country of interfering in Senegal's affairs. In 1973 relations with Israel were ended, and in 1976 Senegal sponsored a UN Commission on Human Rights resolution accusing Israel of war crimes in the occupied Arab territories.

In the 1970s the aging Senghor brought younger men and union leaders into his government. His choice as new premier was Abdou Diouf, an industrious and capable administrator. When Senghor retired on Dec. 31, 1980, Diouf succeeded him on the following day.

Diouf came into office Jan. 1, 1981, advocating a moderate program for legitimizing all political parties, recognizing human rights, and dealing with very rapid population growth through a campaign of family planning.

**HISTORY:** Senegal was largely dominated by the Moslem Tukuler tribe until 1893, when the Tukuler dynasty was overthrown by the French. European settlement, however, had begun as early as the 15th century, when the Portuguese settled along the Senegalese coastline. The French established a foothold in the area in the 17th century and by the 19th century Senegal was the center of French West Africa. In 1946, along with other parts of French West Africa, Senegal became part of the French Union

**1958:** Senegal becomes an autonomous republic within the French Community. Léopold-Sédar Senghor elected president

**1959-60:** Senegal is joined with the Sudanese Republic in the short-lived Mali Federation, which is dissolved after strong political differences develop between the two states

**1963:** Senghor, unopposed, is reelected president

**1964:** All opposition parties except one small one are banned

**1968:** Senghor is reelected and an unopposed list of 80 candidates of his party, the Senegalese Progressive Union, is elected to National Assembly. Widespread strikes by students and workers break out in protest against government austerity measures

**1969:** Senghor declares state of emerrgency to deal with unrest

**1970:** Constitution revised; Abdou Diouf is chosen to be premier

**1973:** Severe drought affects crop production

**1974:** New political party, Senegalese Democratic party, formed

**1976:** At a conference of the Organizaation of African Unity and the Arab League in Dakar, President Senghor calls for a union of the two groups and for the establishment of an Arab-African arbitration and conciliation court

**1978:** Senghor is reelected in first multiparty election in 12 years. Senegal secures $26-million loan from International Monetary Fund to offset economic effects of droought

**1979:** Work begins on $550-million three-nation Senegal River irrigation and hydroelectric project

**1980:** Led by the Parti Démocratique Sénégalaise, 1,000 members of opposition parties demonstrate in Dakar. Senegal breaks relations with Libya June 28. President Senghor retires Dec. 31

**1981:** Abdou Diouf is sworn in as president Jan. 1 to complete Senghor's 5-year term which expires in 1983. National Assembly lifts restrictions on formation of political parrties and unanimously approves pact to join The Gambia in Senegambia confederation

**1982:** Senegambia confederation comes into being

---

## SEYCHELLES

**Area:** 171 sq. mi. **Population:** 63,000 (1980 est.)

**Official Name:** Republic of Seychelles **Capital:** Victoria **Nationality:** Seychellois **Languages:** Creole is spoken by 94% of the population; English and French are official **Religion:** 90% Roman Catholic, 8%

Anglican **Flag:** A field of red over green separated by a wavy white band **Anthem:** National Anthem, beginning "Seychellois both staunch and true" **Currency:** Seychellois rupee (6.4 per U.S. $1)

**Location:** Indian Ocean. The republic lies about 1,000 miles east of Kenya, just south of the Equator **Features:** An archipelago of about 90 islands, it is divided almost equally between a Granitic Group and a Coralline Group. Mahé (4°45'S.,55°30'E.), the mountainous main island, comprises just over half of the total area, and contains most of the population **Chief Rivers:** None

**Head of State and of Government:** President France Albert René, born 1935, assumed office in coup in June 1977, elected 1979 **Effective Date of Present Constitution:** March 26, 1979 **Legislative Body:** National Assembly (unicameral) consists of 25 members. The Seychelles People's Progressive Front is the only party **Local Government:** 8 districts, one including all outlying island groups

**Ethnic Composition:** Most are descendants of 18th century French settlers and their African slaves, with a later mixture of other Europeans and Asians; there is a small minority of Indians and Chinese **Population Distribution:** 26% urban **Density:** 368 inhabitants per sq. mi.

**Largest City:** (1977 census) Victoria 15,559

**Per Capita Income:** $1,030 (1979) **Gross Domestic Product (GDP):** $86 million (1979) **Economic Statistics:** Plantation agriculture (coconuts, vanilla, cinnamon, patchouli, fibers) and fishing at a subsistence level provide 14% of GDP. Tourism (16%) is the chief income-making industry, and there is light manufacturing and the processing of coconuts and vanilla (15%) **Minerals and Mining:** None. Guano deposits; some offshore oil prospecting **Labor Force:** 25,000, of which 19% are employed in mining and construction, 19% in agricIture, 14% in public administration and social services, and 11% in restaurants and hotels **Foreign Trade:** Exports, chiefly light manufactures, copra, coconut oil, cinnamon bark, dried fish, vanilla oil, and patchouli, totaled $6.2 million (1980). Imports, mainly foods, manufactured goods, textiles, machinery, and petroleum products, totaled $93 million **Principal Trade Partners:** Britain, India, Pakistan, France, Mauritius, Kenya, South Africa, Bahrain, Japan, United States

**Vital Statistics:** Birthrate, 27.6 per 1,000 of pop. (1979); death rate, 7 **Life Expectancy:** 66 years **Health Statistics:** 200 inhabitants per hospital bed; 2,857 per physician (1975) **Infant Mortality:** 26.6 per 1,000 births **Illiteracy:** 40% **Primary and Secondary School Enrollment:** 12,986 (1976) **Enrollment in Higher Education:** 142 (1976) **GDP Expended on Education:** 6.2% (1972)

**Transportation:** Paved roads total 90 mi. **Motor Vehicles:** 5,300 (1978) **Passenger Cars:** 4,100 **Railway Mileage:** None **Port:** Victoria **Major Airlines:** Air Mahé operates domestic flights **Communications: Radio Transmitters:** 5 **Receivers:** 17,000 (1976) **Television:** None **Telephones:** 5,000 (1978) **Newspapers:** 1 daily, 65 copies per 1,000 inhabitants (1977)

**Weights and Measures:** British system is used. Metric system is being introduced **Travel Requirements:** Passport, no visa, onward ticket

---

This 90-island archipelago is a beautiful tropical paradise largely isolated from the rest of the world. The climate is equable and healthful, although quite humid, since the islands are small and subject to marine influences. High winds are rarely encountered.. The fortunate natural environment led an early visitor to declare seriously that the Seychelles were the original Garden of Eden.

Although the new republic is promoting agriculture, its principal hopes lie in tourism. The opening of the islands' first commercial airport in 1971 has increased the number of tourists attracted by the beautiful beaches, impressive scenery and fine climate. The government has made considerable effort to assure that the expansion of tourism neither disrupts the islands' cultural life nor spoils the natural beauty. Hotels and condominiums are well spaced so not to "wall off" the beaches. Whale-watching is promoted as a tourist attraction.

Under the stimulus of development and tourism, the Seychelles has virtually obtained full employment for its work force. But even paradise must pay a price, and in the Seychelles, like elsewhere, progress has brought inflation.

Under the nation's first president, James Mancham, the Seychelles remained neutral in foreign affairs, with a pro-Western outlook. The only intrusion of big-power presence is the hosting of an American satellite tracking station on Mahé.

In 1977 Mancham was overthrown by leftist rebels thought to have been supplied with Chinese and Soviet weapons from Tanzania. Mancham's ouster was attributed to his playboy lifestyle, his frequent absences from the country, and his proposal to postpone the 1979 elections. Former Prime Minister France Albert René subsequently became president and vowed some form of socialism for the country, as well as an emphasis on housing, agriculture, fishing and tourism.

**HISTORY:** Although the islands appeared on Portuguese charts as early as 1505 and may have been visited by Arabs much earlier, the Seychelles remained unclaimed and uninhabited until 1742. In that year the French governor of Mauritius, Mahé de Labourdonnais, sent an expedition to the islands. However, the full settlement of the archipelago did not take place until 1794. As a result of French defeat in the Napoleonic Wars, the Seychelles passed to the British in 1814 and became a dependency of Mauritius

**1903:** The Seychelles become a separate crown colony

**1970:** Limited internal self-government is granted

**1976:** Independence is proclaimed on June 29

**1977:** President Mancham overthrown in leftist coup. Former Prime Minister France Albert René assumes presidency

**1979:** René reelected to 5-year term under new one-party constitution. Attempted coup in November fails

**1981:** Airborne mercenaries from South Africa, including Seychelles exiles, land at Victoria but are foiled in attempt to overthrow René and "restore democracy"; most escape to Durban aboard a hijacked plane

**1982:** Seven mercenaries captured in Seychelles are charged with treason. Army units stage mutiny against officers, but loyal troops crush rebellion

---

## SIERRA LEONE

**Area:** 27,925 sq. mi. **Population:** 3,474,000 (1980 est.)

**Official Name:** Republic of Sierra Leone **Capital:** Freetown **Nationality:** Sierra Leonean **Languages:** English is the official language. Mende and Temne are widely spoken, but the most commonly spoken language is Krio, a form of pidgin English **Religion:** 70% are animists, 25% Moslems, and 5% Christians **Flag:** Horizontal stripes of green, white, and blue **Anthem:** National Anthem, beginning "High we exalt thee, realm of the free" **Currency:** Leone (1.21 per U.S. $1)

**Location:** West Africa. Sierra Leone is bounded on the north and east by Guinea, on the southeast by Liberia, and on the west by the Atlantic Ocean **Features:** The country consists of a coastal plain of mangrove swamps that gradually gives way to wooded hills and upland plateaus in the interior, with mountains near the eastern border **Chief Rivers:** Rokel, Sewa, Moa, Jong, Little and Great Scarcies, Sherbro

**Head of State and of Government:** President Siaka P. Stevens, born 1905, elected April 1971, reelected 1976 for 5 years, sworn in for 7-year term in 1978 under new constitution **Effective Date of Present Constitution:** 1978 **Legislative Body:** Parliament (unicameral House of Representatives), with 104 members; 85 are elected by universal suffrage, 112 indirectly elected paramount chiefs, and 7 appointed by the president, all for 5 years. The All-People's Congress is the sole officially recognized party **Local Government:** 3 provinces governed by a minister with cabinet rank, and the Western (Freetown) area, under a council

**Ethnic Composition:** 18 tribal groups, with the Mende and Temne each making up about 30% of the population; others include the Limba, Loko, Kono, Sherbro, Vai, Gallina, Susu, Kissi, Mandingo, and Peul (Fulani). Less than 2% are Creoles, descendants of freed slaves, mostly from the Americas **Population Distribution:** 18% urban **Density:** 124 inhabitants per sq. mi.

**Largest Cities:** (1974 census) Freetown 274,000, Bo 42,216

**Per Capita Income:** $248 (1980) **Gross National Product (GNP):** $851 million (1980) **Economic Statistics:** 31% of the GNP is derived from agriculture (palm kernels, cocoa, coffee, rice, piassava, ginger, cola nuts); 26% from trade and services; 19% from extractive industries (diamonds, rutile, bauxite); and 6% from manufacturing (soap, flour, mineral water, furniture) **Minerals and Mining:** Chiefly diamonds, iron ore, bauxite and the world's largest deposits of rutile **Labor Force:** 1.5 million, with 80% engaged in agriculture **Foreign Trade:** Exports, diamonds, palm kernels, bauxite, rutile, coffee, and cocoa, totaled $271 million in 1980. Imports, chiefly manufactured goods, fuel, machinery and transportation equipment, and food, totaled $393 million **Principal Trade Partners:** Britain, Japan, United States, EC countries, China, Nigeria

**Vital Statistics:** Birthrate, 45.5 per 1,000 of pop. (1980); death rate, 19.2 **Life Expectancy:** 46 years **Health Statistics:** 927 inhabitants per hospital bed; 17,114 per physician (1972) **Infant Mortality:** 136.3 per 1,000 births **Illiteracy:** 90% **Primary and Secondary School Enrollment:** 256,388 (1975) **Enrollment in Higher Education:** 1,642 **GNP Expended on Education:** 3.1% (1976)

**Transportation:** Paved roads total 760 mi. **Motor Vehicles:** 25,200 (1976) **Passenger Cars:** 18,900 **Railway Mileage:** 52 **Ports:** Freetown, Bonthe, Pepel **Major Airlines:** Sierra Leone Airways operates domestic flights **Communications: Radio Transmitters:** 3 **Receivers:** 62,000 (1975) **Television Transmitters:** 2 **Receivers:** 8,500 **Telephones:** 15,000 (1976) **Newspapers:** 2 dailies (1976), 10 copies per 1,000 inhabitants (1975)

**Weights and Measures:** Metric system **Travel Requirements:** Passport, visa valid for 1 month, $6.50 fee, 3 photos

---

One of the oldest and most progressive of Britain's former West African colonies, Sierra Leone got off to a favorable start on independence in 1961 with stable government and promising economic development. But since then the small nation, which depends mainly on the production of diamonds, bauxite, coffee and cocoa, has experienced increasingly violent political upheaval.

In addition to the tendency of some officials to seek personal fortunes at public expense, Sierra Leone has been plagued by coups, states of emergency and, in March 1971, an attempted assassination of the country's present leader, President Siaka Stevens. In the process, economic improvements—particularly in agriculture—have been repeatedly disrupted and new development programs delayed.

Serious trouble began with elections in 1967. Then opposition leader, Stevens appeared to have won by a narrow margin over the bumptious Sir Albert Margai, whose government had been marked by corruption. But almost as soon as Stevens had been sworn in as prime minister, a group of army officers ousted him in a coup. The junta said it had acted to prevent a civil war between the Mende, the largest tribal group, and the rival Temne, a main source of Stevens' strength.

Rule by the military group proved unpopular, and in 1968 it was ousted by a counter-coup led by noncommissioned officers and police. This group promptly restored Stevens to the premiership and the country settled down to legally elected government. Two years later, however, opposition to Stevens' party resumed, with clashes that led to the declaration of a state of emergency.

Then in March 1971 Brig. Gen. John Bangura, the army commander, led an attempted coup and assassination plot. The coup fizzled when other army officers arrested Bangura and proclaimed their loyalty to the Stevens government. Another state of emergency was declared and, under a new mutual defense pact by Stevens and Guinean President Sékou Touré, 200 Guinean troops were flown into Freetown to bolster local troops. Bangura and three followers were executed.

On April 19, 1971, Stevens proclaimed a republic and two days later he was sworn in as president. His power was reconfirmed by elections in 1973 and 1976. In 1978 Stevens pushed through legislation introducing a new constitution which extended the presidential term of office to seven years, abolished the office of prime minister and made the All-People's Congress the only legal party.

On the economic scene, Sierra Leone has taken strides toward the development of the production of bauxite, which amounted to over 700,000 metric tons in 1978. Another resource, rutile, a mineral used in paint manufacture, is being developed under a U.S. investment agreement. Sierra Leone's deposits are among the world's largest.

**HISTORY:** Sierra Leone was originally divided into numerous kingdoms or chiefdoms. The Portuguese explorer Pedro da Cintra visited the coastal area in 1460 and named the mountainous peninsula at the mouth of the Rokel River Serra Lyoa (Lion Mountain), later corrupted to Sierra Leone. Until the 18th century, the region was an important source of slaves. In 1787, a group of abolitionists founded Freetown to resettle freed slaves from Britain, and in 1808 the settlement became a crown colony. In 1896, the interior was made a British protectorate

**1924:** New constitution is introduced permitting nomination of protectorate chiefs to legislative council but fails to satisfy nationalist aspirations

**1943:** Africans are admitted to the executive council

**1951:** New constitution is introduced, providing a framework for decolonization

**1957-58:** Elected House of Representatives replaces legislative council; Dr. Milton Margai, whose Sierra Leone People's party wins a majority of seats, becomes prime minister

**1961:** Sierra Leone becomes an independent Commonwealth state

**1964:** Prime Minister Milton Margai dies; his brother, Finance Minister Albert Margai, is asked by governor-general to form new government

**1967:** Siaka Stevens, leader of the opposition All People's Congress, is appointed prime minister after hotly contested election but is ousted by army chief; group of young army officers stage bloodless coup and a National Reformation Council composed of army and police officers is set up; constitution is suspended

**1968:** Military coup is staged by noncommissioned officers and police; House of Representatives is reconvened and asks Stevens to resume premiership

**1969:** Sierra Leone People's party loses strength in House of Representatives following by-elections; party leaders charge that losses were due to government intimidation of voters

**1971:** An attempted coup led by Brig. Gen. John Bangura, the army commander, is crushed; Prime Minister Stevens calls in troops from Guinea to help suppress dissident elements. Sierra Leone is declared a republic

**1973:** A plot to overthrow the government is uncovered. Sierra Leone increases its military capacity. The All People's Congress wins election, taking 84 of 97 parliamentary seats

**1976:** President Stevens is elected for second five-year term

**1977:** APC wins elections decisively amid charges of vote fraud

**1978:** New constitution increases presidential term to seven years and makes APC sole recognized party

**1979:** Rising prices and shortage of rice cause discontent

**1980:** Agreement is reached with a European mining company to revive iron mines abandoned in 1975. Strong effort is launched to improve agricultural production

**1981:** Pres. Stevens, on visit to London, obtains pledge of U.K. aid worth $6 million. World Bank lends $12 million for agricultural projects. General strike forces government to reduce and control price of rice

---

## SINGAPORE

**Area:** 233 sq. mi. **Population:** 2,413,945 (1980 census)

**Official Name:** Republic of Singapore **Capital:** Singapore **Nationality:** Singaporean **Languages:** Malay, the national language, and English, Chinese, and Tamil are all official languages **Religion:** The majority of the ethnic Chinese are Buddhists, Taoists, or Confucianists; the Malays and Pakistanis are Moslems; and the Indians mainly Hindus. The Europeans and Eurasians are almost all Christians **Flag:** Horizontal stripes of red and white with a white crescent and 5 white stars in the upper left-hand corner **Anthem:** Forward Singapore **Currency:** Singapore dollar (2.10 per U.S. $1)

**Location:** Southeast Asia. The island of Singapore lies south of the Malay peninsula, separated by the Strait of Johore. A three-quarter-milelong causeway connects the island with Malaysia; 54 small islets lie offshore **Features:** Except for a central plateau, most of the island is low lying and originally consisted of swamp and jungle. Downtown Singapore occupies land that for the most part was reclaimed from the sea **Chief Rivers:** Sungei Seletar, Singapore

**Head of State:** President C.V. Devan Nair, born 1923, sworn in Oct. 24, 1981 **Head of Government:** Prime Minister Lee Kuan Yew, born 1923, appointed 1965 **Effective Date of Present Constitution:** 1959 (pre-independence) **Legislative Body:** Parliament (unicameral), consisting of 75 members elected by adult suffrage for 5 years

**Ethnic Composition:** About 77% of the population is ethnically Chinese, 15% Malays, and 6% Indians and Pakistanis. The rest are largely Europeans and Eurasians **Population Distribution:** 100% urban **Density:** 10,360 inhabitants per sq. mi.

**Largest City:** (1980 census) Singapore 2,413,945

**Per Capita Income:** $4,580 (1980) **Gross National Product (GNP):** $11 billion (1980) **Economic Statistics:** In 1973 about 56% of GNP came from trade and services (including banks, financial institutions, transportation and communications); 21% from manufacturing; and 3% from agriculture and fishing **Minerals and Mining:** None **Labor Force:** 1,083,000, with 52% in industry and commerce **Foreign Trade:** Exports, mainly crude rubber, petroleum products, electrical machinery, electronics, textiles, timber, tin, and coffee, totaled $10 billion in 1980. Imports, chiefly rubber, petroleum products, machinery, vehicles, and woven fabrics other than cotton, totaled $24 billion **Principal Trade Partners:** Malaysia, United States, Japan, Saudi Arabia, Britain, China, Hong Kong, Australia, West Germany

**Vital Statistics:** Birthrate, 17.3 per 1,000 of pop. (1980); death rate, 5.2 **Life Expectancy:** 69 years **Health Statistics:** 269 inhabitants per hospital bed; 1,847 per physician (1977) **Infant Mortality:** 11.7 per 1,000 births **Illiteracy:** 16% **Primary and Secondary School Enrollment:** 506,008 (1976) **Enrollment in Higher Education:** 22,607 (1975) **GNP Expended on Education:** 2.7% (1976)

**Transportation:** Paved roads total 1,286 mi. **Motor Vehicles:** 207,900 (1978) **Passenger Cars:** 146,400 **Railway Mileage:** 24 **Port:** Singapore **Major Airlines:** Singapore Airlines operates international flights **Communications: Radio Transmitters:** 20 **Licenses:** 356,000 (1976) **Television Transmitters:** 2 **Licenses:** 294,000 **Telephones:** 475,000 (1978) **Newspapers:** 12 dailies (1976), 201 copies per 1,000 inhabitants (1974)

**Weights and Measures:** Metric system; British, Chinese, and local standards are used **Travel Requirements:** Passport, no visa **International Dialing Code:** 65

---

Since 1819, when Singapore was created out of a mangrove swamp by Sir Stamford Raffles, the visionary agent of the British East India Company, it has served as East Asia's major transshipping point, as the wholesaler for other countries' products, as the bastion of the British Empire, and, more recently, as the area's leading processor of other countries' raw materials.

Blessed with one of the few natural harbors in the region, Singapore grew to become the largest port in Southeast Asia and the fourth largest in the world. Through this port have flowed rubber and tin from Malaysia and Indonesia to the markets of Europe and the United States.

The expanding rubber and tin industries early this century spurred immigration, mainly from southern China. In fact, up to 1957, Singapore's population consisted predominantly of noncitizen aliens. Today, Singapore is the only nation in the world with a population made up primarily of overseas Chinese, although immigration has now been slowed to a minimum. Malays, Indians, and Pakistanis are the other dominant ethnic groups.

Singapore has continued to thrive and maintains the highest per capita income in Southeast Asia, as welll as virtually full employment. The Jurong area, a sprawling section of the island devoted to industrial development, today pulses with the processing of many types of raw materials and the manufacturing of finished goods. By the early 1980s, it was clear that Singapore was veering toward capital-intensive industry and away from labor-intensive industry with large and inexpensive work forces. In 1982, certain classes of foreign laborers with temporary work permits were ordered to leave Singapore by the end of 1984, and the regime announced that it planned to build a wholly local labor force by 1990. Government economists foresaw a continuing diversification into computers, medical equipment, optical equipment, and machine tools, and were predicting an 8 percent real growth rate through the decade of the 1980s.

Business travel and tourism have increased sharply, raising the number of Singapore's visitors from less than one million in 1973 to nearly three million in 1980. July 1, 1981, saw the opening of what was to be, at its completion in 1984, Asia's largest airport. Situated about 20 miles from downtown Singapore, the facility was designed to handle up to 10 million passengers per year.

Since 1959, when Singapore was granted internal self-government, the People's Action party, headed by Lee Kuan Yew, has controlled the island's affairs. In recent years the government has been accused of authoritarianism and repression. In 1974 drastic penalties were decreed for armed robbers, gun runners, and traffickers in illegal immigrants. The Internal Security Act provides for detention without trial for those accused of pro-Communist activities. In 1977 a new campaign was begun to repress dissent—a series of arrests of prominent critics of government policies, who subsequently were pressured into signing confessions and appearing on television to recant.

In 1975 Foreign Minister S. Rajaratnam responded to Peking's more moderate attitude by leading Singapore's first goodwill mission to China where he met with the late Premier Zhou Enlai. In 1976 Prime Minister Lee was one of the last foreign officials to be allowed to meet with Chairman Mao Zedong. With a population that is overwhelmingly of Chinese ancestry, many of whom retain warm feelings for their ancestral land, Singapore cannot afford to antagonize Peking, but neither does it want to be a Chinese satellite.

**HISTORY:** For centuries the island of Singapore was little more than a mangrove swamp occupied by Malay fishermen who owed allegiance to the Sultan of Johore. In 1819, Sir Stamford Raffles of the British East India Company, who saw in Singapore potential for a great trading port, founded a trading post on the island

**1824:** Sultan of Johore cedes Singapore to the British East India Company

**1826:** Singapore becomes part of the British Straits Settlements

**1942:** Supposedly impregnable fortress of Singapore is captured by the Japanese in World War II

**1946:** Singapore becomes a separate British crown colony

**1959:** Singapore becomes a self-governing colony

**1963:** Federation of Malaysia is formed and Singapore joins Malaya, Sarawak, and Sabah in new nation

**1965:** Singapore withdraws from Malaysia federation

**1971:** Singapore, Malaysia, Britain, Australia, and New Zealand sign accord on joint defense of Singapore and Malaysia

**1976:** Prime Minister Lee's ruling People's Action party, in its fifth straight election victory, wins all 69 seats in parliament

**1978:** Amnesty International alleges serious human rights violations in Singapore, including detention without trial of at least 70

**1979:** As one of five countries making up the Association of Southeast Asian Nations (ASEAN), Singapore joins in a decision June 30 to accept no more Vietnamese refugees

**1980:** PAP candidates again win all parliamentary seats in December

**1981:** Changi Airport, Asia's largest, opens in July

**1982:** Citing a need for "national unity," the regime muzzles press criticism, forcing sale or shutdown of some journals

---

## SOLOMON ISLANDS

**Area:** 11,500 sq. mi. **Population:** 221,000 (1979 est.)

**Official Name:** Solomon Islands **Capital:** Honiara **Nationality:** Solomon Islander **Language:** English is the official language; Melanesian Pidgin is the universal lingua franca. A variety of Melanesian tongues are spoken throughout most of the islands. On Vella Lavella, Savo and the Russell Islands the dominant languages are of the Papuan family. Polynesian languages, closely related to Maori, are spoken on the outlying islands of Ontong Java, Rennell and Tikopia **Religion:** 33% Anglican, 17% Roman Catholic, 17% South Sea Evangelical Church. The remainder of the inhabitants are members of the United Church and the Christian Fellowship Church, except for 5%, who are animists **Flag:** A blue triangle with five white stars in the upper left and a plain green triangle in the lower right separated by a diagonal yellow stripe **Anthem:** God Save Our Solomons **Currency:** Solomon Islands dollar (0.9 per U.S. $1)

**Location:** Southwest Pacific Ocean. About 1000 miles northeast of Australia, the islands form a scattered archipelago stretching 900 miles in a southeasterly direction from Papua New Guinea. The six major islands are Choiseul, New Georgia, Santa Isabel, Guadalcanal, Malaita and San Cristobal **Features:** The large islands have a mountainous spine which on one side drops steeply to sea level and on the other drops through a series of foothills to the coast. The highest peaks are found on Guadalcanal, which possesses the only extensive coastal plains in the Solomons. The weather varies from warm to hot and is humid, with annual rainfall exceeding 100 inches **Chief Rivers:** There are many short rivers on the larger islands

**Head of State:** Queen Elizabeth II, represented by a governor-general, Baddeley Devesi, born 1941, sworn in July 1978 **Head of Government:** Prime Minister Solomon Mamaloni, sworn in Aug. 1981 **Effective Date of Present Constitution:** July 1978 **Legislative Body:** National Parliament (unicameral) consisting of 38 members elected for 4 years **Local Government:** At present 4 districts; provinces are to be established

**Ethnic Composition:** Melanesians 93%, Polynesians 4%, Gilbertese 1%, European stock 1% **Population Distribution:** 9% urban **Density:** 19 inhabitants per sq. mi.

**Largest City:** (1981 local census) Honiara 21,334

**Per Capita Income:** $440 (1978) **Gross Domestic Product (GDP):** $94 million (1978) **Economic Statistics:** Copra and rice are the only important cash crops. Fisheries contribute to the economy, and the timber industry is being developed **Minerals and Mining:** Copper, bauxite and nickel deposits are being developed **Labor Force:** 18,500 (1978), with 32% in agriculture, 18% in industry and commerce, and 32% in services **Foreign Trade:** Exports, chiefly fish, timber, palm oil, and copra, amounted to $69 million in 1979. Imports, mainly machinery, transport equipment, food and fuels totaled $58 million **Principal Trade Partners:** Australia, Japan, Britain, Netherlands

**Vital Statistics:** Birthrate, 41 per 1,000 of pop. (1970); death rate, 11 **Life Expectancy:** 57 years **Health Statistics:** 120 inhabitants per hospital bed; 6,666 per physician (1977) **Infant Mortality:** 52 per 1,000 births **Illiteracy:** 40% **Primary and Secondary School Enrollment:** 29,243 (1976) **Enrollment in Higher Education:** 160 (1976) **GDP Expended on Education:** 3.7% (1972)

**Transportation:** All weather roads total 800 miles **Motor Vehicles:** 1,796 (1972) **Passenger Cars:** 727 **Railway Mileage:** None **Ports:** Honiara, Gizo, Yandina **Major Airlines:** Solomon Islands Airways operates domestic and international flights **Communications: Radio Transmitters:** 3 **Radio Receivers:** 11,000 (1976) **Television Transmitters:** None **Television Receivers:** None **Telephones:** 1,726 **Newspapers:** 2 weeklies

**Weights and Measures:** Imperial weights and measures are still in use, but the metric system has been adopted as the future standard **Travel Requirements:** Passport, no visa

For a short period during World II the Solomon Islands were a focus of world attention as Japan and the United States engaged in land, air and sea battles for the control of the South Pacific. Guadalcanal, New Georgia, "the Slot," and Iron Bottom Sound—scenes of major clashes in 1942 and 1943—are all within the confines of the newly independent Solomon Islands.

Following hostilities, the islands returned to the peaceful obscurity of being a remote Britissh protectorate unbothered by the tides of history. However, the worldwide retreat of colonialism during the 1960s resulted in a growing interest in eventual independence for the Solomons on the part of both the British and the islanders. Finally, on July 7, 1978, the Duke of Gloucester, representing Queen Elizabeth II, handed over power to the government of the new nation.

The most pressing problem facing the Solomon Islands is the maintenance of unity among the diverse and geographically separated peoples of the island chain. The commercially developed western islands have demanded more autonomy, and the non-Melanesian minority fears the neglect of its needs by the central government.

One of the main objectives of the government is to diversify the economy. In the past, production has been limited to copra planting, timber cutting and fishing. It is hoped that plans for the introduction of beef cattle and the growing of rice and oil palm will be implemented. Another source of future economic growth would be the successful exploitation of the islands' mineral ores.

**HISTORY:** Ancestors of the present Melanesian inhabitants entered the area from the Malay Archipelago some time between 1000 and 500 B.C. Polynesians came to the islands much later, from Uvea in the Wallis group, northeast of Fiji. The Spaniards reached Santa Isabel in the Solomons in 1568. During the 19th-century missionaries and coconut traders made contact with the Solomon Islanders, and many of the inhabitants were recruited, sometimes forcibly, for labor in Fiji, Australia and New Caledonia

**1893-98:** Britain establishes a protectorate over the Solomons

**1899:** Germany transfers Santa Isabel, Choiseul, the Shortlands and Ontong Java to Britain

**1942-43:** Japanese invade the Solomons. American counteroffensive recaptures Guadalcanal; fighting continues on the islands until Allied forces move on to Bougainville

**1946-52:** Opposition to British rule is carried on by "Marching Rule" movement, a nativist cargo-cult

**1960:** Legislative Council established

**1976:** The Solomons become a self-governing dependency

**1978:** Full independence is achieved on July 7

**1979:** Government opens talks with Papua New Guinea on boundary dispute in North Solomons island group

**1980:** Two-thirds of legislators lose seats in first general election, but Prime Minister Peter Kenilorea retains his post

**1981:** Kenilorea is defeated and replaced by Solomon Mamaloni, leader of the People's Alliance party, by a parliamentary vote of 20 to 17. IMF gives Solomon Islands drawing rights worth $1.9 million to support economic program

## SOMALIA

**Area:** 246,200 **Population:** 4,637,000 (1980 est.)

**Official Name:** Somali Democratic Republic **Capital:** Mogadishu **Nationality:** Somali **Languages:** Somali is the official language; Arabic, English, and Italian are still used extensively **Religion:** 99% are Sunni Moslems and Islam is the state religion **Flag:** Blue field with a 5-pointed white star in the center **Anthem:** Long Live Somalia **Currency:** Somali shilling (Somalo) (6.295 per U.S. $1)

**Location:** East Africa. Somalia is bounded on the north by the Gulf of Aden and Djibouti, on the southeast by the Indian Ocean, and on the west by Kenya and Ethiopia **Features:** Much of the country is arid or semiarid. The northern region is mountainous; the southern part is mostly desert, but with a large fertile area crossed by two large rivers flowing from Ethiopia **Chief Rivers:** Juba, Shebelli

**Head of State and of Government:** President: Maj. Gen. Mohamed Siad Barré, born 1919. He is secretary general of the Somali Revolutionary Socialist party (SRSP), assumed power in 1969, elected 1980 **Effective Date of Present Constitution:** Sept. 23, 1979 **Legislative Body:** People's Assembly (unicameral) of 171 members, elected for 5 years. The SRSP is the only legal party **Local Government:** 15 regions

**Ethnic Composition:** The Hamitic population is mainly Somali. Other sizable ethnic groups include some 35,000 Arabs, 1,000 Indians and Pakistanis, and about 2,000 Italians **Population Distribution:** 9% urban **Density:** 19 inhabitants per sq. mi.

**Largest City:** (1975 census) Mogadishu 371,000

**Per Capita Income:** $111 (1980) **Gross National Product (GNP):** $393 million (1980) **Economic Statistics:** Industry accounts for only about 8% of the GNP with the rest from livestock (cattle, camels, sheep, goats), the mainstay of the Somali economy; banana and sorghum growing; wild animal hides such as Somali leopard skins; spices, fishing, and some minerals **Minerals and Mining:** Commercial production is confined to salt, charcoal, limestone, and meerschaum; uranium, iron ore and certain rare earths are currently being explored **Labor Force:** 1,100,000 (1970). Livestock prooduction employs about 70% of the total; and agriculture 20% **Foreign Trade:** Exports, chiefly livestock, bananas, hides, meat and tuna, totaled $148 million in 1980. Imports, mainly manufactured goods, fuel, cereals, food preparations, transportation equipment, and chemicals, totaled $547 million **Principal Trade Partners:** Italy, Britain, United States, Saudi Arabia, USSR

**Vital Statistics:** Birthrate, 48.3 per 1,000 of pop. (1980); death rate, 20.4 **Life Expectancy:** 41 years **Health Statistics:** 569 inhabitants per hospital bed; 15,544 per physician (1972) **Infant Mortality:** 177 per 1,000 births **Illiteracy:** 90% **Primary and Secondary School Enrollment:** 241,419 (1976) **Enrollment in Higher Education:** 2,100 (1976) **GNP Expended on Education:** 4.8% (1976)

**Transportation:** Paved roads total 1,340 mi. **Motor Vehicles:** 16,000 (1972) **Passenger Cars:** 8,000 **Railway Mileage:** None

**Ports:** Mogadishu, Berbera, Merka, Kismayu **Major Airlines:** Somali Airlines operates domestically and internationally **Communications: Radio Transmitters:** 5 **Receivers:** 69,000 (1976) **Television:** None **Telephones:** 6,000 (1971) **Newspapers:** 1 daily (1976), 1 copy per 1,000 inhabitants (1973)

**Weights and Measures:** Metric system **Travel Requirements:** Passport, visa valid 3 months, $14 fee, 4 photos, onward ticket

Major power changes in the strategically located Horn of Africa have spotlighted Somalia, an arid East African country at the juncture of the Indian Ocean and the Gulf of Aden, as a link important to both the Middle East and Africa. A union of the former Italian and British Somalilands, Somalia became independent in 1960, but efforts at transforming its seminomadic society into a modern state have made scarcely any headway.

Somalis, a lean, handsome, fiercely proud people, have an oral history going back 2,000 years. Because of disputes among scholars, the Somali language had no written form until, in 1972, President Siad announced a system would be developed using the Roman alphabet.

Western and Communist aid has added some modern facilities—an American-built seaport and a Russian-built slaughterhouse—but the Somali economy remains largely a low-yield herding/farming system.

The current regime of Major General Mohamed Siad Barré, who overthrew the government of Premier Mohammed Ibrahim Egal in 1969, until recently had been marked by close ties with the Soviet Union and vociferous anti-Westernism. In exchange for military aid, Somalia provided the Soviets with a missile storage base. Angered by the Soviet buildup in Ethiopia, Somalia's arch-foe, Siad Barré expelled the Soviets from Somalia in mid-1977, and the Somali army invaded Ogaden, an area of Ethiopia claimed by Somalia, to help the Somali rebels operating in the region. But the Ethiopian forces, aided by some 11,000 Cuban troops and 1,000 Soviet military advisors, drove the Somali troops from Ogaden by early 1978. Ethiopia has stated that there can be no lasting peace in the area until Somalia renounces its territorial claims on Ogaden, Djibouti and northern Kenya, and pays for damages caused in the war. Meanwhile, two "western Somali" liberation groups continue to fight on, guerrilla-style.

As a result of the eight-month Ogaden War, Somalia was burdened by the influx of about 1,300,000 refugees who fled from the region. Most of the food supplied to the refugees has been provided by the U.S. In August 1980, Somalia agreed to give the U.S. access to military ports and airfields in the country in return for military aid. In March 1982, Siad Barré visited the U.S. and received military and economic assistance estimated at $95 million for fiscal year 1983.

**HISTORY:** Although arid and desolate in many areas, Somalia was known as the Land of Punt (God's Land) in ancient Egyptian writings. It was reputedly the source of the biblical frankincense and myrrh, and was probably also the breeding ground of the locusts that invaded Egypt in the time of Joseph. Over the centuries the Somalis, a blend of Asian and African peoples, formed a confederation of closely knit clans in which Arab trading enclaves and sultanates evolved. Later, the nation was divided into British and Italian possessions, and, with union of these in 1960, it began a new era as the Somali Republic

**19th cent.:** British and Italians, through treaties with sultans and mutual agreements, divide country, with British occupying northwestern portion, Italians, the east and south

**1901-20:** Mohammed bin Abdallah Hasan, the "Mad Mullah," wages holy war against British

**1936:** Italian Somaliland is merged with Eritrea and Ethiopia as "Italian East Africa," following Ethiopian defeat in Italo-Ethiopian War of 1935-36

**1940-41:** Italians occupy British Somaliland during World War II; they are ousted by British, who take over Italian Somaliland

**1947-50:** Italy renounces colonial rights and is given 10-year UN trusteeship to prepare former possession for independence

**1960:** British and Italian Somaliland are united as Somali Republic

**1961-64:** Droughts and floods deplete crops, livestock; food shipments by United States and other countries avert famine

**1969:** President Abdirashid Ali Shermarke is slain by an assassin; army, with police backing, seizes power

**1975:** 120,000 Somali nomads are airlifted by Soviet planes from drought-stricken areas of north to southern regions

**1977:** Kenya and Somalia pledge maintenance of peace along border, following Kenya's charge of a Somali invasion

**1978:** Eight-month Ogaden war ends in March as Cuban-and Soviet-aided Ethiopian forces drive Somalis from region. Somalia reports that army officers "influenced by foreign powers" attempted coup which failed; thwarted rebels are said to have killed 20 people and injured 34. Ethiopian jets bomb Somali towns and villages while Somali guerrillas recapture major military base in southern part of Ogaden region

**1979:** New constitution adopted

**1980:** People's Assembly, meeting for first time in ten years, reconfirms Siad Barré as president for new six-year term. Somalia gets food from U.S. and other countries for Ogaden refugees. U.S. and Somalia sign agreement granting U.S. use of Somali naval and air bases in exchange for arms aid

**1981:** Somalia cuts ties with Libya after it signs friendship treaty with Ethiopia. Somali press agency reports invasion from Ethiopia. President declares state of emergency

## SOUTH AFRICA

**Area:** 472,359 sq. mi. (inc. Bophuthatswana, Ciskei, Transkei, and Venda) **Population:** 23,771,970 (1980 census) (excluding Bophuthatswana, Transkei, and Venda, but including Ciskei)

**Official Name:** Republic of South Africa **Capitals:** Cape Town (legislative), Pretoria (administrative), and Bloemfontein (judicial) **Nationality:** South African **Languages:** English and Afrikaans are the official languages. Of the white population, 63% speak Afrikaans and 37% speak English. In the *Bantustans*, the individual African languages are official. Indians, who constitute the bulk of the Asian minority, speak Tamil, Hindi, Gujarati, and Telugu **Religion:** Most of the population is Christian, chiefly Protestant. About 50% of the Africans in the *Bantustans* are animists. Most of the Asians are Hindus and Moslems **Flag:** Horizontal stripes of orange, white, and blue with small replicas of the Union Jack, the Boer flag of the Orange Free State, and old Transvaal Vierkleur banner in the center **Anthem:** Die Stem (The Voice of South Africa) **Currency:** Rand (1.08 per U.S. $1)

**Location:** Southern tip of the African continent, between the South Atlantic Ocean on the west and the Indian Ocean on the east. South Africa is landbound on the north and northeast by Namibia, Botswana, Zimbabwe, Swaziland, and Mozambique. Independent Lesotho lies entirely within the borders of South Africa. Walvis Bay, on the Namibian coast, is an exclave of the Cape Province **Features:** On the west, south, and east is a narrow coastal belt of lowlands extending into an extensive interior plateau **Chief Rivers:** Orange, Limpopo

**Head of State:** President Marais Viljoen, born 1915, elected 1979 **Head of Government:** Prime Minister Pieter W. Botha, born 1916, appointed 1978 **Effective Date of Present Constitution:** May 1961 **Legislative Body:** House of Assembly (unicameral) with 165 members elected by white voters, 8 additional members chosen by the House and 4 others nominated by the President **Local Government:** 4 provinces, each with an appointed administrator and an elected provincial council. Ten self-governing *Bantustans* have been created since 1963, four of which, Transkei, Bophuthatswana, Venda, and Ciskei, have been granted independence

**Ethnic Composition: (excl. "independent Bantustans"):** Blacks (Bantus) constitute 67% of the population, whites (largely of Dutch and British descent) 19%, coloureds (mixed Bushmen,Hottentot and white descent) 11%, and Asians 3% **Population Distribution:** 48% urban

**Largest Cities:** (1970 census) (M.A. = Metropolitan Area) Johannesburg 654,232 (M.A. 1,417,818), Cape Town 697,514 (M.A. 833,731), Durban 736,852 (M.A. 975,494), Soweto 602,043, Pretoria 545,450 (M.A. 573,283), Port Elizabeth 392,231 (M.A. 413,961), Germiston 221,972 (M.A. 293,257)

**Per Capita Income:** $1,690 (1980) **Gross National Product (GNP):** $48 billion (1980) **Economic Statistics:** About 27% of GNP is derived from manufacturing (textiles, iron and steel, chemicals, fertilizer, automobile assembly, metalworking, electrical and nonelectrical machinery and equipment, mining machinery); 21% from mining (gold, platinum, coal, diamonds, antimony, iron ore, copper, uranium, manganese, chrome, asbestos); 8% from agriculture (sugar, tobaccco, wool, corn, fruit, dairy products, wheat, fish) **Minerals and Mining:** Extensive mineral deposits, including gold, platinum, coal, diamonds, vanadium, antimony, iron ore, copper, uranium, manganese, chrome, asbestos **Labor Force:** 9,532,000 (1976), with 22.8% in industry, 23.4% in services, and 9.6% in agriculture **Foreign Trade:** Exports, chiefly diamonds, wool, fruit, copper, iron and steel, and gold, amounted to $26 billion in 1979 (excluding gold bullion). Imports, mainly industrial machinery and equipment, transportation equipment, and precision instruments, totaled $9 billion **Principal Trade Partners:** Britain, West Germany, Japan, United States, Switzerland

**Vital Statistics:** Birthrate, 37.9 per 1,000 of pop. (1980); death rate, 10.3 **Life Expectancy:** 52 years **Health Statistics:** 152 inhabitants per hospital bed; 2,016 per physician (1973) **Infant Mortality:** 59 per 1,000 births **Illiteracy:** Negligible (white); 50% (others) **Primary and Secondary School Enrollment:** 4,653,452 (1972) **Enrollment in Higher Education:** 98,577 **GNP Expended on Education:** N.A.

**Transportation:** Paved roads total 50,000 mi. **Motor Vehicles:** 2,984,700 (1977) **Passenger Cars:** 2,163,500 **Railway Mileage:** 13,950 **Ports:** Durban, East London, Port Elizabeth, Cape Town, Richards Bay, Saldanha Bay **Major Airlinees:** South African Airways, the government-owned airline, operates international and domestic flights **Communications: Radio Transmitters:** 177 **Radio Receivers:** 2,500,000 (1976) **Television Transmitters:** 34 **Licenses:** 719,000 (1977) **Telephones:** 2,320,000 (1978) **Newspapers:** 24 dailies, 66 copies per 1,000 inhabitants (1976)

**Weights and Measures:** Metric system **Travel Requirements:** Passport, visa valid for 1 year **International Dialing Code:** 27

## BOPHUTHATSWANA

**Area:** 15,570 sq. mi. **Population:** 1,328,637 (1980 census) **Density:** 85 inhabitants per sq. mi. **Official Name:** Republic of Bophuthatswana **Capital:** Mmabatho **Flag:** An orange diagonal stripe across a blue field with a white disk bearing a black leopard head in the upper hoist **Head of State and of Government:** President and Prime Minister: Chief Lucas Mangope, born 1923, elected December 1977 **Legislative Body:** Legislative Assembly (unicameral), with 99 members of which 48 are elected, 48 appointed by the 12 regional authorities, and 3 appointed by the president **Largest Cities:** (1980 census) Mabopane 48,596, Garankuwa 48,253, Temba 22,784

## CISKEI

**Area:** c. 3,400 sq. mi. **Population:** 635,631 (1980 census) **Density:** 187 inhabitants per sq. mi. **Official Name:** Republic of Ciskei **Capittal:** Bisho **Flag:** Three diagonal stripes of blue, white and blue with a stylized crane in black and white in the center **Head of State and of Government:** President: Chief Lennox L. Sebe, took office Dec. 4, 1981 **Legislative Body:** National Assembly (unicameral), of 50 elected members and 37 hereditary chiefs **Largest Centers:** (1970 census) Zwelitsha 22,131, Alice 4,647, Keiskamahoek 2,858

## TRANSKEI

**Area:** 16,910 sq. mi. **Population:** 2,000,000 **Density:** 118 inhabitants per sq. mi. **Official Name:** Republic of Transkei **Capital:** Umtata **Flag:** Ochre, white, and green horizontal stripes **Head of State:** President: Kaiser Daliwonga Matanzima, born 1915, took office 1979 **Head of Government:** Prime Minister: George Matanzima, born 1919, appointed 1979 **Legislative Body:** National Assembly (unicameral), with 150 members, composed of 75 elected, 70 nominated chiefs, and 5 paramount chiefs, all serving 5-year terms **Largest Cities:** (1974 est.) Umtata 28,100, Butterworth (Gcuma) 24,000

## VENDA

**Area:** 2,510 sq. mi. **Population:** 449,000 **Density:** 179 inhabitants per sq. mi. **Official Name:** Republic of Venda **Capital:** Thohoyandou **Flag:** Three equal horizontal stripes of green, yellow and brown with a vertical blue stripe at the hoist. A brown "V" is centered on the yellow stripe **Head of State and of Government:** Chief Patrick R. Mphephu, took office Sept. 1979 **Legislative Body:** National Assembly (unicameral), with 84 members of which 42 are elected and 42 are chiefs or their nominees **Largest Centers:** Thohoyandou, Sibasa, Makwarela

South Africa is a land of great physical beauty and harsh social contrasts. Its rugged coastlines, steep escarpments, sweeping plateaus, and magnificent mountains afford unparalleled vistas. The setting of Cape Town, the country's oldest city, is among the most beautiful in the world. The modern skyscrapers of Johannesburg tower above the rolling countryside of the plateau *highveld*. The 19th century buildings that dominate the center of the administrative capital, Pretoria, form reminders of the period of conflict between Boer and Briton and the emergence of the Union of South Africa, predecessor of the present Republic.

Contrasted against the wealthy suburbs, modern highways, beach resorts and golf courses lie the bleak, much poorer African townships that house the urban labor reservoirs, the crowded workers' quarters near the mines, the traditional but often deteriorated African villages in the Bantu homelands. Rich South Africa is white South Africa; poorer South Africa tends to be the domain of the black, colored, and to a lesser extent the Asian communities. All *nationwide* statistics relating to the Republic should be considered in this context.

Although racial segregation as a way of life had characterized South Africa for many decades, a turning point came in 1948 when D. F. Malan's National party defeated the United party led by J. C. Smuts. Apartheid now became official state policy, and even the slightest trend toward racial integration was reversed. Public facilities became rigorously segregated, the major universities were restricted to whites, and numerous other steps were taken to eliminate racial contact in daily life. More significantly, however, the Nationalist government also embarked on a program of racial-territorial separation for the country as a whole, with the ultimate aim of the creation of a set of autonomous African states within South Africa's borders. Initially these areas were called *Bantustans*, and the first such territory to be awarded a degree of self-government was the Transkei in 1963. Transkei was declared to be an independent "homeland" in 1976. Three more such black homelands have since been granted independence, Bophuthatswana in 1977, Venda in 1979 and Ciskei in 1981. The homeland plan involves land exchanges, population movements, and numerous hardships for many of the people affected. Other nations have withheld recognition of the independence of these homelands which receive most of their income from South Africa.

South Africa's policies of separate development have been the target of sharp criticism throughout the world, and especially in black Africa. Demands have been voiced for boycotts on trade, business, and sports contests with the Republic. In South Africa itself, leaders of the African Homelands also have begun to put pressure on the government for greater sovereignty than the *Bantustan* plan had first envisaged, and for better conditions for Africans still residing and working in "white" South Africa. The response has been comparatively slight. Some concessions have been made in areas of job opportunity for blacks, equalization of salaries, acceptance of some interracial sports events and in ending discrimination in the use of restrooms and elevators. However, the legacy of apartheid and the straightjacket of separate development continue to dominate life in the Republic.

In 1979 a major political scandal rocked Pretoria, forcing John Vorster to resign the ceremonial post of president. An official investigation alleged that Vorster, while prime minister, had approved, and later tried to cover up, a propaganda program under which some $90 million in secret funds were funneled to friendly politicians and other leaders in Europe and the U.S. Pieter W. Botha, who became prime minister in 1978, was absolved of complicity and attempted to set his government on a reform course of relaxation in apartheid rules and more skilled jobs for blacks. Marais Viljoen, former president of the senate, became the republic's president in June 1979.

**HISTORY:** When European settlers first arrived, there were several distinct native groups occupying different parts of the territory, including the Bushmen, nomadic hunters of the western desert uppland country, and the Hottentots, a pastoral people who occupied the southern and eastern coastal areas. At the same time, Bantu people were moving toward the Cape of Good Hope, having already occupied territories in the north and east

**1488:** Portuguese led by Bartholomew Diaz arrive at Cape

**1652:** First Dutch settlers establish Cape Colony

**1814:** Britain gains formal possession of the Cape Colony as a result of the Napoleonic Wars. Dutch begin eastward movement

**1835-36:** In a migration known as the Great Trek, the Boers (descendants of the Dutch settlers) leave Cape Colony for the north in protest against British rule

**1899-1902:** Boer War breaks out with Britain. By the Treaty of Vereeniging, the Boers acknowledge British sovereignty over Transvaal and the Orange Free State

**1910:** Union of South Africa is constituted under the terms of the South Africa Act passed by the British Parliament

**1926-47:** Ruling whites initiate separatist policies

**1948:** Afrikaner National Party, led by D. F. Malan, defeats J. C. Smuts' governing United Party and apartheid is introduced as official state policy

**1959:** Promotion of Bantu Self-Government Act is passed, providing for eight self-governing African states

**1960:** Seventy-two blacks are killed in protest demonstration against forced carrying of identity passes in Sharpeville

**1961:** South Africa becomes a republic and formally withdraws from British Commonwealth

**1963:** The first partially self-governing *Bantustan* (Bantu "homeland"), the Transkei, is established

**1966:** Prime Minister Hendrik Verwoerd is assassinated and is succeeded by Balthazar J. Vorster

**1969:** UN Security Council condemns South Africa for its refusal to permit the UN to take control of South-West Africa

**1971:** World Court rules that South Africa's administration of South-West Africa is illegal

**1976:** Forced use of Afrikaans language in black schools precipitates rioting in Soweto, leaving 380 dead. Transkei homeland granted independence in October

**1977:** Black political activist Stephen Biko dies under suspicious circumstances while in police custody. UN Security Council unanimously orders worldwide mandatory embargo on arms supplies to South Africa because of its racial policies. Bophuthatswana granted independence

**1978:** Transkei breaks diplomatic relations with South Africa. South African forces enter Angola in "limited military operation" against guerrillas of SWAPO (South-West African People's Organization); action is condemned by UN Security Council. Prime Minister Vorster resigns and is named president. Pieter W. Botha is appointed prime minister

**1979:** Vorster resigns amid scandal, is succeeded by Marais Viljoen. Botha, exonerated, shuffles cabinet, removes hard-line minister of justice, proposes new approach to race relations. His program to provide more skilled jobs for blacks prompts wildcat strike by mine workers. Venda is granted independence

**1980:** Wave of unrest occurs in Cape Town area and elsewhere over inadequacy of nonwhite education. Blacks in Soweto riot against rent increases. Except in mining, black workers are increasingly accepted in skilled occupations and to membership in trade unions. Ciskei votes overwhelmingly in favor of independent homeland status. Parliament is enlarged by 12 seats of which 11 go to the ruling National party

**1981:** An advisory President's Council of handpicked whites, coloureds and Asiatics—but excluding blacks—is inaugurated, replacing the Senate dissolved in 1980. UN General Assembly votes 114-0 for sanctions against South Africa for its failure to settle the Namibian question; sanctions are later vetoed in Security Council. South African troops repeatedly invade Angola in effort to wipe out SWAPO guerrilla forces. National party wins heavily in parliamentary elections open only to whites. Ciskei is granted independent homeland status

**1982:** Forty-two mercenaries involved in unsuccessful 1981 coup attempt in Seychelles are convicted on air piracy charges in Supreme Court, but government is absolved of complicity in the affair. South Africa engages in dialogue with Angolan leaders on future status of Namibia. Dr. Neil Aggett, white leader of a large nonwhite food workers union, held under terrorism act, is found hanged in jail. Rand drops below parity with U.S. dollar; budget deficit widens as world price of gold falls. Strike of thousands of black mine workers, seeking bargaining rights comparable to those of white workers, cripples gold mining industry. Government plan to give voting rights and representation in Parliament to coloureds and Asiatics, but not to blacks, draws heavy criticism from both left and right. Right-wing Conservative party splits off from National party over racial policies. Botha meets with Zambian President Kaunda. Transfer of Kangwane black homeland is discussed with Swaziland, but South African Supreme Court blocks action

## SPAIN

**Area:** 195,988 sq. mi. **Population:** 37,682,355 (1981 census)

**Official Name:** Spanish State **Capital:** Madrid **Nationality:** Spanish **Languages:** Spanish is the official and predominant language; Catalan, Galician, Valencian, and Basque are regional languages recognized for legal purposes **Religion:** The population is overwhelmingly Roman Catholic **Flag:** Horizontal stripes of red **Anthem:** Royal March **Currency:** Peseta (105 per U.S. $1)

**Location:** Southwest Europe, occupying most of the Iberian peninsula. Spain is bounded on the north by the Bay of Biscay, on the northeast by France and Andorra, on the east and south by the Mediterranean Sea, and on the west by Portugal and the Atlantic Ocean **Features:** Most of the country consists of a high plateau divided by mountains and broad depressions. The landmass rises sharply from the sea, leaving a narrow coastal plain except in the Andalusian lowlands in the south **Chief Rivers:** Ebro, Guadalquivir, Duero, Tajo, Guadiana, Miño

**Head of State:** King Juan Carlos I (de Borbón), born 1938, proclaimed king in 1975 **Head of Government:** Premier Leopoldo Calvo Sotelo y Bustelo, born 1926, sworn in Feb. 26, 1981 **Effective Date of Present Constitution:** December 29, 1978 **Legislative Body:** *Cortes* (bicameral), with an elected 350-member Chamber of Deputies, and a Senate with 208 members, all for 4 years **Local Government:** 50 provinces, each headed by an appointed governor and a provincial council, and the 2 African presidios of Ceuta and Melilla. Catalonia, Galicia, Andalusia, and the Basque country have received regional autonomy

**Ethnic Composition:** The Castilians of central Spain, the Basques in the north, the Catalans in the northeast, the Galicians in the northwest, the Valencians in the east, and the Andalusians in the south represent separate cultural groups **Population Distribution:** 64% urban **Density:** 192 inhabitants per sq. mi.

**Largest Cities:** (1975 est.) Madrid 3,520,320, Barcelona 1,809,722, Valencia 713,026, Seville 588,784, Saragossa 542,317, Bilbao 457,655, Málaga 402,978

**Per Capita Income:** $3,022 (1980) **Gross Domestic Product (GDP):** $115 billion (1980) **Economic Statistics:** About 52% of GDP is derived from trade and services; 35% from mining, manufacturing, construction, energy; and 8% from agriculture (cereals, fruits, vegetables, olive oil). Tourism is of great importance **Minerals and Mining:** Coal, iron, mercury, pyrites, zinc, copper and potash are produced **Labor Force:** 13,300,000 (1978), with 40% in services, 36% in industry and construction, and 20% in agriculture **Foreign Trade:** Exports, mainly footwear, citrus fruit, textiles and clothing, steel products, transportation equipment, machinery, chemicals, and furniture, totaled $21 billion in 1980. Imports, chiefly feed grains, machinery, transportation and electrical equipment, fuels, metals, chemicals, and tobacco, totaled $34 billion **Principal Trade Partners:** United States, West Germany, France, Britain, Saudi Arabia, Iran, Italy

**Vital Statistics:** Birthrate, 15.1 per 1,000 of pop. (1980); death rate, 7.7 **Life Expectancy:** 72 years **Health Statistics:** 185 inhabitants per hospital bed; 647 per physician (1975) **Infant Mortality:** 11.1 per 1,000 births **Illiteracy:** 3% **Primary and Secondary School Enrollment:** 6,812,755 (1976) **Enrollment in Higher Education:** 540,238 (1975) **GNP Expended on Education:** 1.7% (1974)

**Transportation:** Surfaced roads total 86,665 mi. **Motor Vehicles:** 7,761,900 (1978) **Passenger Cars:** 6,530,400 **Railway Mileage:**

10,824 **Ports:** Barcelona, Bilbao, Valencia, Cartagena, Sta. Cruz de Tenerife, Gijón, Huelva, Algeciras, Cádiz, Vigo **Major Airlines:** Iberia operates domestic and international flights, Aviaco operates domestic flights **Communications: Radio Transmitters:** 442 **Receivers:** 9,300,000 (1976) **Television Transmitters:** 791 **Receivers:** 6,640,000 (1976) **Telephones:** 10,311,000 (1978) **Newspapers:** 143 dailies, 128 copies per 1,000 inhabitants (1977)

**Weights and Measures:** Metric system **Travel Requirements:** Passport, no visa for 6 months **International Dialing Code:** 34

---

Since the death of the dictatorial head of state, Francisco Franco, on November 20, 1975, Spain has moved steadily toward democracy. Two days after the passing of *El Caudillo*, the 500-year-old monarchy was restored with the proclamation of Juan Carlos de Borbón as king of Spain.

The first free election in 41 years, the pardoning of more than half of the country's 1,600 political prisoners, the granting of the right of assembly, a loosening of press controls and legalization of the Communist party have all occurred since the new monarch promised "profound improvements" at his swearing-in ceremony on November 22, 1975. A new bicameral parliament was instituted in place of the appointed parliament left by Franco.

However, the problem of the "nations within the Spanish nation" still remains; Basque and Catalan separatism and Galician and Valencian regionalism present difficulties. Some concessions have been made to the aspirations to cultural freedom of the non-Castilian peoples, but many more will be required before the ethnic sensibilities of these ethnic groups will be satisfied.

In its economic life, Spain has progressed far from the devastation left by the 1936-1939 civil war. A good part of the prosperity results from the popularity of Spain as a tourist haven for other Europeans and for North Americans. The beauty of the Iberian seaside, plus its easy accessibility from Western Europe and relative inexpensiveness, have turned sleepy fishing villages into thriving vacation resorts.

Burgeoning industry, flourishing foreign trade and an ever-increasing middle class are all signs pointing to the fact that Spain has become a prosperous, 20th-century nation. Though there are still wide areas of poverty, the better life is noticeable in the cities—such as Madrid, Barcelona and Seville—and the wealthier provinces—such as Castile and Catalonia. The deteriorating economy resulted in a high unemployment rate of 12 percent and an inflation rate of 14.5 percent in 1981.

A new constitution adopted in 1978 limited the king to an essentially ceremonial role, guaranteed human rights, and provided for the establishment of autonomous regions. As of early 1982, Catalonia, Galicia, Andalusia and the Basque country have received autonomy. King Juan Carlos' firm actions foiled a military coup led by three right-wing generals on Feb. 23-24, 1981, when rebel civil guards seized Parliament and held the legislators captive for 18 hours. The king went on television to denounce the rebellion and ordered all military commanders to obey their top leaders; when they did, the rebellion collapsed and the rebels surrendered.

---

**HISTORY:** About 1000 B.C. the Iberian peninsula was invaded by Celtic tribes from the north, and two centuries later Phoenicians and Greeks began to establish colonies along the Spanish coast. The Carthaginians conquered most of the peninsula in the 3rd century B.C., but were forced out by the Romans, during whose rule political unity was established and Christianity introduced. Early in the 5th century, Spain was overrun by the Germanic Vandals and Visigoths. After forcing the Vandals to emigrate to Africa, the Visigoths were themselves conquered by the Moors

**711-18:** Roderick, the last of the Visigothic kings, is defeated in battle by the Moors, who gain control over virtually the entire peninsula. Asturias, the only remnant of Visigothic Spain, becomes the focus of the Christian reconquest

**1492:** King Ferdinand of Aragon and his wife, Queen Isabella of Castile, complete the reconquest of Spain by capturing Granada, the last remaining Moorish stronghold. The Catholic rulers order the expulsion of the Jews. Columbus wins the monarchs' support for his voyages and discovers America, where a vast Spanish empire is soon to be established

**1588:** Defeat of the Spanish Armada by England hastens the demise of Spanish power

**1808-14:** Napoleon's armies invade Spain and his brother Joseph is placed on the Spanish throne. The French are finally driven out by Spanish resistance fighters and British troops led by Wellington. Wars of independence break out in Spanish America, leading to the disruption of the empire

**1898:** Spanish-American War destroys remaining empire

**1931-36:** Alfonso XIII is deposed and a republic established. Economic and political unrest culminate in an army revolt against the republic, under the leadership of General Francisco Franco. The revolt precipitates the Spanish Civil War

**1936-39:** The war rages for two and a half years, with the Loyalists (Republicans), aided by the Soviet Union and foreign volunteers, gradually defeated by Franco's forces, aided by Nazi Germany and Fascist Italy. The Loyalist government flees to France, and Franco sets up a dictatorship, with the Fascist Falange as the only legal party

**1942-47:** Franco reestablishes the *Cortes* but on Fascist lines without genuine popular representation. The Law of Succession is promulgated, declaring Spain a kingdom and setting up a regency council, with Franco as head of state

**1966-68:** A new constitution curbing the political power of the National Movement and its political organ, the Falange, is approved by referendum. The position of president of government (premier) is created. However, dissatisfaction with the regime makes itself felt in strikes and university unrest, which lead to severe police repression

**1969:** Franco designates Prince Juan Carlos de Borbón y Borbón to be chief of state and king upon Franco's death or incapacitation

**1970-71:** Military court sentences six Basque separatists to death; Franco commutes sentences following world outcry

**1973:** Spain establishes full diplomatic relations with East Germany and Communist China; Premier Carrero Blanco is assassinated; Carlos Arias Navarro becomes premier

**1975:** U.S. use of Spanish bases is renewed. Franco dies. Prince Juan Carlos becomes head of state as King Juan Carlos I

**1976:** Spain withdraws from Western Sahara, last remnant of this once-vast colonial empire. Carlos Arias Navarro resigns premiership. He is replaced by Adolfo Suárez González

**1977:** Communist party is legalized and declared eligible for participation in national elections. Premier Suárez' Democratic Center Union emerges victorious in first free elections in 41 years. Government devalues peseta by 22 percent as economy continues slump. Catalonians and Basques granted self-rule

**1978:** Basques legally celebrate their national day for first time since civil war. Communist party, holding its ninth congress (first since 1932), drops "Leninist" label despite strong Soviet advice against doing so. Suárez government suffers setback as Senate by-elections show victory for opposition Socialists and big surge by Communists. Government grants provisional autonomy to Balearic Islands and two other regions. New constitution limits king's role and contains detailed bill of rights

**1979:** Democratic Center Union wins plurality in new elections; Suárez is reappointed premier

**1980:** Basque country, Galicia, and Catalonia become autonomous regions

**1981:** Suárez resigns as premier; Leopoldo Calvo Sotelo replaces him. Attempted military coup by a few rebellious army officers fails when most military commanders remain loyal to king. Andalusia becomes an autonomous region

**1982:** Spain becomes 16th member of NATO

---

## SRI LANKA

**Area:** 25,332 sq. mi. **Population:** 14,850,001 (1981 census)

**Official Name:** Democratic Socialist Republic of Sri Lanka **Capital:** Colombo **Nationality:** Sri Lankan **Languages:** Sinhala is the official language; both Sinhala and Tamil are national languages. English is used widely **Religion:** 69% Hinayana Buddhist, 15% Hindu, 8% Moslem, 7% Christian (mainly Roman Catholic) **Flag:** Narrow green and orange vertical stripes on the left side, with a yellow lion carrying a sword in one upraised paw against a red background occupying the rest of the flag. The entire flag is bordered in yellow, with a vertical yellow band separating the orange and green stripes from the red background of the rest of the flag **Anthem:** Hail, Hail, Motherland **Currency:** Sri Lanka rupee (20.7 per U.S. $1)

**Location:** Island in the Indian Ocean, off the southeastern tip of India. Sri Lanka is bounded on the north by the Palk Strait, on the east by the Bay of Bengal, on the south by the Indian Ocean, and on the west by the Gulf of Mannar **Features:** A low-lying plain makes up the northern half of the island and continues around the southern coast. The south-central part is mountainous **Chief Rivers:** Mahaweli, Ganga, Kelani, Walawe, Kalu, Gal

**Head of State and of Government:** President Junius Richard Jayewardene, born 1906, sworn in 1978 for a 6-year term. He is assisted by a prime minister, Ranasinghe Premadasa, born 1924, appointed 1978 **Effective Date of Present Constitution:** September 7, 1978 **Legislative Body:** Parliament (unicameral), with 196 members for 6-year terms **Local Government:** 24 districts, each headed by a governor

**Ethnic Composition:** 74% are Sinhalese. 13% are "Sri Lanka Tamils," citizens whose ancestors have lived in Sri Lanka for many generations and who have full voting rights. The 6% "Indian Tamils" came from south India in the 19th century **Population Distribution:** 22% urban **Density:** 586 inhabitants per sq. mi.

**Largest Cities:** (1974 est.) Colombo 592,000, Dehiwala-Mount Lavinia 162,000, Jaffna 114,000, Moratuwa 100,000; (1971 census) Kandy 93,602, Kotte 93,042, Galle 72,720

**Per Capita Income:** $324 (1980) **Gross National Product (GNP):** $4.8 billion (1980) **Economic Statistics:** In 1973 about 34% of GNP was from agriculture (tea, rice, rubber, pineapples, coconuts), forestry, and fishing; 33% from trade and services; and 13% from industry (foodstuffs, tobacco products, chemicals, garments, leather and footwear, cement, paper and paperboard, tires and tubes, metal products) and mining **Minerals and Mining:** Graphite mining is the principal mineral industry; there are also gemstones, mineral sands and limestone **Labor Force:** 4 million, with 53% in agriculture, and 15% in industry **Foreign Trade:** Exports, chiefly tea, rubber, gems, graphite, and coconut products, totaled $1 billion in 1979. Imports, mainly rice and other food products, textiles, machinery and transport equipment and petroleum, totaled $1.4 billion **Principal Trade Partners:** Britain, China, United States, Japan, India, West Germany, Pakistan, Saudi Arabia

**Vital Statistics:** Birthrate, 28.7 per 1,000 of pop. (1979); death rate, 6.6 **Life Expectancy:** 68 years **Health Statistics:** 334 inhabitants per hospital bed; 4,007 per physician (1976) **Infant Mortality:** 37.1 per 1,000 births **Illiteracy:** 18% **Primary and Secondary School Enrollment:** 2,462,141 (1977) **Enrollment in Higher Education:** 14,568 (1974) **GNP Expended on Education:** 3.1% (1976)

**Transportation:** Paved roads total 15,000 miles **Motor Vehicles:** 160,500 (1978) **Passenger Cars:** 103,800 **Railway Mileage:** 1,016 **Ports:** Colombo, Trincomalee, Galle **Major Airlines:** Air Lanka operates domestic and international services **Communications:** **Radio Transmitters:** 29 **Receivers:** 800,000 (1976) **Television Transmitters:** 1 **Telephones:** 74,000 (1978) **Newspapers:** 22 dailies (1977), 42 copies per 1,000 inhabitants (1971)

**Weights and Measures:** Metric system **Travel Requirements:** Passport, no visa for 30 days, onward ticket **International Dialing Code:** 94

---

Isolated from global and regional rivalries at independence in 1948, Sri Lanka, formerly known as Ceylon, was without an enemy and appeared to be assured of peace and prosperity. But parliamentary democracy has been a forum for radical communal nationalism that has divided the Sinhalese Buddhist majority and the large Tamil minority and often brought the country near civil war. A program to settle the "Indian Tamils" question through the naturalization of some and the repatriation of others to India failed to quell their drive for separate statehood, causing a limited state of emergency to be imposed in 1981-82.

In April 1971 ultraleftist students plunged the country into a full-scale guerrilla war before they faded into the jungled countryside. The movement was believed to have been born in 1964 when youth wings of the various Communist party factions split from adult leaders, accusing them of being both corrupt and irrelevant to the needs of Sri Lanka's peasantry. The revolutionary movement had an obvious attraction to the many students who were the sons of peasants and who had taken advantage of free college education only to find no jobs available upon graduation. The 1971 uprising led to the declaration of a state of emergency that did not end until February 1977.

Mrs. Sirimavo Bandaranaike, the prime minister from 1960-65 and again from 1970-77, was defeated in the general elections of 1977 by Junius Jayewardene's United National party. Nepotism, abuses of power, and corruption, in addition to the poor economic situation, were the major issues in the campaign. In 1976 there had been severe student and labor unrest.

Under the Jayewardene government, Sri Lanka made a dramatically swift turn away from socialism and toward capitalism. The tea plantations, for instance, had been allowed to run down after being seized by the government in the early 1970s; under Jayewardene, private managers were put in charge of money-losing state corporations, particularly in efforts to boost the major exports—tea, rubber, and coconut. Foreign investment increased sharply, aided by tax holidays and other incentives, as well as what Sri Lankans said was worker productivity second only to Singapore in Asian industry. The price of the new policies was an escalation of inflation, particularly affecting food, consumer goods, and some services previously subsidized by the government. Among the benefits were increased U.S. economic aid and growing income from tourism. In the early 1980s, a newly united labor movement was providing the principal political opposition.

**HISTORY:** The earliest inhabitants of Sri Lanka (formerly Ceylon) have left few traces. The Sinhalese, who form the bulk of the present population, came to the island from northern India in the 6th century B.C. They founded their capital at Anuradhapura, which became a major religious center following the conversion of Sri Lanka to Buddhism in the 3rd century B.C. Invasions from south India, notably by the Tamils, forced the Sinhalese into the southwest of the island. In the 12th century A.D., Arab traders appeared in Ceylon. The island's coastal areas were occupied by the Portuguese in the 16th century. By the middle of the 17th century, their possessions had been taken over by the Dutch

**1795:** The Dutch possessions are taken over by Britain

**1802:** The Crown Colony of Ceylon is established

**1815:** All of the island of Ceylon is brought under British rule

**1948:** Sri Lanka becomes independent, with dominion status in the British Commonwealth

**1956-59:** S.W.R.D. Bandaranaike becomes prime minister, heading a leftist coalition. His term is marked by bloody riots between Sinhalese and Tamils, and ends with his assassination

**1960-65:** New elections bring another leftist coalition to power, with Mrs. Sirimavo Bandaranaike, wife of the slain leader, as the world's first woman prime minister. Her government adopts a neutralist policy and nationalizes a number of Western oil companies. A dispute with the United States and Britain results

**1965-66:** Elections result in the victory of the pro-Western United National party, led by Dudley Senanayake. His government agrees to compensation for the expropriated oil companies, and the United States agrees to resume economic aid to Sri Lanka, cut off at the time the companies were nationalized

**1968:** Sri Lanka becomes first of the developing nations to achieve the goal of a 5 percent rise in per capita income

**1970:** Mrs. Bandaranaike returns to power

**1971:** Revolutionary students, seeking to replace the government with one more militantly socialist, lead an uprising that results in the death of thousands of rebels and civilians

**1972:** Ceylon becomes a republic within the Commonwealth and is renamed Sri Lanka under a new constitution; William Gopallawa is appointed the republic's first president by Mrs. Bandaranaike; National Assembly approves land reform plan

**1977:** Sirimavo Bandaranaike's Freedom party is defeated in general elections; Junius Richard Jayewardene becomes prime minister following his United National party's victory. Sri Lanka amends constitution to give nation French-style presidential governing system which dilutes power of elected assembly, reduces prime minister and cabinet to figureheads and concentrates power in hands of a president popularly elected every six years

**1978:** Prime Minister Jayewardene is sworn in as president

**1979:** Foreign investment, encouraged by President Jayewardene's politics, rises to an annual rate of $40 million, 13 times greater than in the last year of the previous government. Tamil extremist group stages a series of killings

**1980:** Trade unions combine to oppose presidential policies. A general strike in July is effectively suppressed by government. Mrs. Bandaranaike is expelled from parliament for "abuses of power" before 1977

**1981:** Steep increase in U.S. aid is projected. Emergency rule imposed in north after Tamil separatist unrest

**1982:** Emergency rule discontinued in January but restored in July. Foreign investment continues to rise, as inflation remains high

## SUDAN

**Area:** 967,494 sq. mi. **Population:** 18,681,000 (1980 est.)

**Official Name:** Democratic Republic of the Sudan **Capital:** Khartoum **Nationality:** Sudanese **Languages:** Arabic, the official language is the native tongue of about 51% of the population; the Negroes of southern Sudan speak about 32 different languages, with English the chief commercial language **Religion:** The religion of the 5 northern regions is Islam, whose adherents include about 70% of the population; most of the southern tribes are animist (25%). There are also some small Christian communities (5%) **Flag:** Horizontal stripes of red, white, and black, with a green triangle at the hoist **Anthem:** Soldiers of God **Currency:** Sudanese pound (0.9 per U.S. $1)

**Location:** Northeast Africa. Sudan, the largest country in Africa is bounded on the north by Egypt, on the east by the Red Sea and Ethiopia, on the south by Kenya, Uganda, and Zaire, and on the west by the Central African Republic, Chad, and Libya **Features:** An immense plateau sprawls over 3 distinct natural regions, ranging from the Libyan and Sahara deserts and plateaus in the north to grassy plains in the center to a great swamp and tropical savanna in the south **Chief Rivers:** Nile (the Blue Nile and White Nile join at Khartoum)

**Head of State and of Government:** President: Gen. Jaafar Muhammad al-Nimeiry, born 1930, seized power in 1969, became the first elected president in 1971 and was reelected in 1977. He is also prime minister (since 1977) **Effective Date of Present Constitution:** 1973 **Legislative Body:** People's Assembly (unicameral), with 151 members (68 popularly elected) belonging to the Sudanese Socialist Union party **Local Government:** 6 regions, each with a president and a regional People's Assembly

**Ethnic Composition:** The population of the 5 northern regions is comprised mainly of Moslem Arabs and Nubians, who together constitute more than two thirds of the population; in the south are Nilotic, Sudanic and black tribes **Population Distribution:** 20% urban **Density:** 19 inhabitants per sq. mi.

**Largest Cities:** (1975 est.) Khartoum 321,666, Omdurman 305,308, Khartoum North 161,278, Port Sudan 123,000

**Per Capita Income:** $346 (1980) **Gross National Product (GNP):** $6.5 billion (1980) **Economic Statistics:** In 1978, 40% of GNP was from agriculture (long-staple cotton, peanuts, sugarcane, gum arabic, livestock), and 24% from industry (food and vegetable oil processing) **Minerals and Mining:** Small-scale production off iron ore, chromite, manganese ore, petroleum, slate, gold, and gypsum; deposits of asbestos, slate and tin exist **Labor Force:** 8.6 million (1979), with 85% in agriculture **Foreign Trade:** Exports, mainly cotton, gum arabic, sesame, peanuts, oil cake and meal, and sheep and goats, totaled $725 million in 1980. Imports, chiefly cotton textiles, motor vehicles and parts, electrical and nonelectrical machinery, base metals and manufactures, chemicals and petroleum products, totaled $1.6 billion **Principal Trade Partners:** Britain, Saudi Arabia, India, Japan, France, China, West Germany, Italy, United States, Egypt

**Vital Statistics:** Birthrate, 45.8 per 1,000 of pop. (1980); death rate, 18.4 **Life Expectancy:** 50 years **Health Statistics:** 1,001 inhabitants per hospital bed; 8,719 per physician (1977) **Infant Mortality:** 93.6 per 1,000 births **Illiteracy:** 85% **Primary and Secondary School Enrollment:** 1,544,553 (1976) **Enrollment in Higher Education:** 21,342 (1975) **GNP Expended on Education:** 5.5% (1974)

**Transportation:** Paved roads total 375 mi. **Motor Vehicles:** 50,400 (1972) **Passenger Cars:** 29,200 **Railway Mileage:** 3,400 **Ports:** Port Sudan, Suakin **Major Airlines:** Sudan Airways operates domestically and internationally **Communications: Radio Transmitters:** 9 **Licenses:** 1,300,000 (1973) **Television Transmitters:** 2 **Receivers:** 100,000 (1975) **Telephones:** 62,000 (1977) **Newspapers:** 4 dailies (1976), 8 copies per 1,000 inhabitants (1975)

**Weights and Measures:** Metric system **Travel Requirements:** Passport, visa valid 3 months, $15.63 fee, 3 photos

The Sudan is Africa's largest country, almost one-third the size of the continental United States, but only a small part of its area, ranging from barren desert to tropical rain forest, is productive. Forty percent of the potentially arable land in the Arab world lies within its boundaries, but only 10 percent of this is under cultivation. Long-staple cotton, the chief export, is grown mainly in the irrigated triangle of land known as the Gezira Plain. This fertile area, just below the confluence of the White and Blue Niles at Khartoum, the capital, and other irrigated areas are a major source also of food and fodder crops.

Crops are raised also in the central rainlands, but production is uncertain because of droughts. Waters of the White Nile backing up into northern Sudan behind Egypt's Aswan Dam will eventually fill the need for additional irrigation.

Of all the African nations only Benin has had a greater number of coups and countercoups. Only Nigeria and Zaire have fought civil wars as cruel as the 17-year conflict, during which 500,000 died, between the Sudan's majority-status Arabs in the north and the minority Christian and pagan blacks in the south. Maj. Gen. Jaafar al-Nimeiry, who himself had seized power in a coup in May 1969, negotiated an end to the war in 1972 by granting regional autonomy to the south.

Nimeiry has survived numerous assassination attempts and two coups that were uncovered before they were begun. Three that were attempted did not succeed, including the revolt led by dissident army elements in July 1976. In this most recent attempt the rebels were defeated by loyal soldiers after having managed to travel 1,000 miles across the desert undetected. Accusing Libya of being behind the uprising, the Sudanese government severed diplomatic relations with the Libyans.

In foreign affairs, the Sudan is a member of the UN, the Arab League, and the Organization of African Unity. The nation participated on the Arab side in the Yom Kippur War. Relations with the U.S. had been troubled by the Arab-Israeli Warr, but in 1981 the Sudan offered air and naval facilities to the U.S., which in turn tripled the amount of its military aid for the Sudan to about $100 million in fiscal year 1982. During March the Sudan and Egypt resumed diplomatic ties after a year's disruption, mainly because of their mutual fear of Libya's recent hostility towards both countries.

In 1979, the Sudan was one of only three Arab states to endorse Egypt's peace treaty with Israel.

**HISTORY:** Nubia, the northern half of Sudan, was colonized by Egypt centuries before the Christian era. In the 6th century A.D., the Nubians embraced Coptic Christianity, but in the 15th century were converted to Islam by conquering Arabs. Although the Arabs extended their conquests to the south, it was not until 1821 that all of Sudan was unified by Egypt

**1881-85:** Sudanese, led by the Mahdi, a Moslem religious fanatic, revolt against Egyptian rule and win control over most of Sudan

**1898-99:** Anglo-Egyptian army defeats Mahdi's followers; Sudan is proclaimed an Anglo-Egyptian condominium under a governor-general; however, Britain dominates the administration

**1924:** Egyptian troops mutiny in the Sudan; the British governor-general is murdered; the British expel the Egyptians from the Sudan and assume its rule

**1936:** Status of Sudan is affirmed by Anglo-Egyptian treaty

**1948:** In Sudan's first elections, Independence Front, favoring an independent republic, wins large majority over National Front, which favors union with Egypt

**1953:** Britain and Egypt conclude an agreement providing for Sudanese self-government

**1956:** Sudan is proclaimed an independent republic

**1958:** Gen. Ibrahim Abboud seizes power in military coup, dissolves parliament, nullifies constitution, and promises reforms

**1964-65:** Abboud resigns following popular rioting against his regime and a civilian government is set up; elections are held for a constituent assembly to draft new constitution; Mohammed Ahmed Mahgoub becomes prime minister of a coalition govern-

ment; black Sudanese rebels in southern provinces launch widespread attacks against government forces
**1968:** Constituent assembly is dissolved and new elections are held; new assembly elects a supreme council, with Ismail al-Azhari as president
**1969:** A military coup led by Col. (now Gen.) Jaafar al-Nimeiry overthrows supreme council, annuls provisional constitution, and establishes revolutionary council
**1971:** Nimeiry is briefly toppled by Communist-backed rebel officers but regains power in countercoup and is elected president
**1973:** Sudan adopts a new constitution. Oil discovered in Red Sea
**1976:** Diplomatic relations with Libya are severed following Libyan support of an abortive coup against Nimeiry
**1977:** U.S. agrees to sell 12 F-5 jet fighters to Sudan
**1978:** Government and opposition announce reconciliation, formally ending nine years of intermittent conflict
**1980:** Nation is reorganized into six regions

## SURINAME

**Area:** 60,239 sq. mi. **Population:** 352,041 (1980 census)

**Official Name:** Republic of Suriname **Capital:** Paramaribo **Nationality:** Surinamese **Languages:** Dutch is the official language; English is also widely used. The majority speak a Creole lingua franca called Sranang Tongo, or Taki Taki **Religion:** 26% Hindu, 26% Moslem, 24% Protestant, and 23% Roman Catholic **Flag:** A wide horizontal red band with a centered golden yellow star, separated by narrow white stripes from green stripes top and bottom **Anthem:** Elevating Our Glorious Land **Currency:** Suriname guilder (florin) (1.785 per U.S. $1)

**Location:** Northeast coast of South America. It is bordered on the north by the Atlantic Ocean, on the east by French Guiana, on the south by Brazil, and on the west by Guyana **Features:** The three chief zones are the coastal belt (partly protected by dikes), the central zones of forests and savannas, and the southern hill zone, comprising 75% of the area, and rising to over 4,000 feet **Chief Rivers:** Suriname, Saramacca, Coppename, Nickerie, Tapanahoni, Marowijne (Maroni), Corantijn (Courantyne)

**Head of State and of Government:** Effective power resides with the National Military Council, whose leading figure is Col. Daysi Bouterse. The Council installed Lachmipersad F. Ramdat-Misier as acting president of Suriname in Feb. 1982, and in March designated Henry N. Neyhorst as prime minister **Effective Date of Present Constitution:** An interim constitution became in force on March 25, 1982 **Legislative Body:** Parliament was abolished in 1980 **Local Government:** 9 districts, under appointed commissioners

**Ethnic Composition:** 37% Hindustanis (descendants of Indian laborers), 31% Creoles (of African descent), 17% Javanese, 11% Bush Negroes (descendants of escaped African slaves), 3% Amerindians (of Carib and Arawak stock), and minorities of 7,000 Chinese and 7,000 Europeans (chiefly Dutch) and Lebanese. More than 100,000 Surinamese Hindustani are currently living in the Netherlands **Population Distribution:** N.A. **Density:** 5.8 inhabitants per sq. mi.

**Largest Cities:** (1980 census) Paramaribo 67,718; (1964 census) Nieuw-Nickerie 7,400, Meerzorg 5,000, Marienburg 3,500, Moengo 2,100

**Per Capita Income:** $1,874 (1980) **Gross National Product (GNP):** $763 million (1980) **Economic Statistics:** About 36% of the GNP is derived from the bauxite industry. Most of the balance comes from agriculture (rice, coffee, sugar, citrus fruits, coconuts, corn, cocoa, tobacco), fishing and shrimping, and lumbering. Industry, other than the processing of alumina and aluminum from bauxite, is confined to sawmilling, rice and sugar milling, and the production of rum and cement **Minerals and Mining:** Suriname is a major source of bauxite; gold is also mined commercially **Labor Force:** 118,000; in 1974, 29% of the workers were engaged in agriculture and 15% in industry **Foreign Trade:** Exports, more than 80% of which was bauxite ore, alumina and aluminum, the rest being citrus fruits, bananas, shrimp, rice, and plywood, totaled $440 million in 1979. Imports, mainly machinery, manufactured goods, textiles, vehicles, petroleum products, iron and steel, and foods, totaled $420 million **Principal Trade Partners:** United States, Netherlands, Norway, Venezuela, Japan, Trinidad and Tobago

**Vital Statistics:** Birthrate, 28 per 1,000 of pop. (1980); death rate, 7.9 **Life Expectancy:** 66 years **Health Statistics:** 184 inhabitants per hospital bed; 1,856 per physician (1975) **Infant Mortality:** 30.4 per 1,000 births **Illiteracy:** 16% **Primary and Secondary School Enrollment:** 120,224 (1976) **Enrollment in Higher Education:** 2,138 **GNP Expended on Education:** 4.7%

**Transportation:** Paved roads total about 300 mi. **Motor Vehicles:** 51,800 (1978) **Passenger Cars:** 38,200 **Railway Mileage:** 100 **Ports:** Paramaribo, Nieuw-Nickerie, Albina **Major Airlines:** Suriname Airways handles domestic and international flights **Communications:** **Radio Transmitters:** 7 **Receivers:** 112,000 (1976) **Television Transmitters:** 6 **Receivers:** 38,000 (1976) **Telephones:** 20,000 (1978) **Newspapers:** 7 dailies, 74 copies per 1,000 inhabitants (1977)

**Weights and Measures:** Metric system **Travel Requirements:** Passport, no visa, onward ticket **International Dialing Code:** 597

On attaining independence in 1975, Suriname immediately faced a major problem stemming from its multiracial composition—37 percent Hindustani, 31 percentt Creole of African descent, 17 percent Javanese, 11 percent Bush Negro. Owing to Hindustani fears of the Creole-dominated government, over 100,000 Surinamers emigrated to the Netherlands prior to independence, thus stripping the emerging nation of a third of its human resources. The emigrants were predominantly well-educated middle-and upper-class entrepreneurs, managers and technicians. The Surinamese government has appealed for the émigrés to return home to help in the development of the resource-rich former colony. To assist in this development the Netherlands has promised to grant Suriname $1.5 billion in aid over the next decade. It has been suggested that the Dutch generosity is based on a desire to improve economic conditions in Suriname enough so that the refugees will return to their tropical homeland and leave poor-paying jobs and welfare rolls in Amsterdam. Another problem is the migration from the countryside to the city, with the result that Suriname may have to import food rather than export it.

Suriname is rich in minerals, forests and potential water power. The country's bauxite deposits are believed to be among the richest in the world. The mining, processing, and exporting of this resource (and since 1965 of alumina and aluminum) constitute the backbone of the economy. Sites of the two major deposits—Moengo and Paranam—are accessible to navigable rivers emptying into the Atlantic. Food processing and lumbering account for other important industries. Alcoa, at a cost of $150 million, has built a dam for the production of hydroelectric energy on the Suriname River.

A government headed by Premier Henck Arron took power in the 1973 elections, when the National Party Coalition, composed mostly of Creoles, unseated the United Reformed Party, led by Jaggernath Lachmon and composed mainly of Hindustanis and Javanese. The Arron government was toppled in February 1980 by a sergeants' coup that appeared to be outside party lines. Henk Chin A Sen was chosen to head a civilian government supervised by a four-man Military Council led by Lieut. Col. Daysi Bouterse. In February 1982, the Council deposed Chin and, in March, after surviving an attempted coup, installed an economist, Henry Neyhorst, as prime minister and minister of finance.

**HISTORY:** Christopher Columbus sighted the coast of the area in 1498, but the first successful settlement was not established until 1651 by the British. The colony prospered on a plantation economy based on slave labor imported from Africa. Notable among the emigrants from other New World colonies were Jews from Brazil, who in 1665 erected the first synagogue in the Western Hemisphere. The Netherlands acquired Suriname from Britain in exchange for Dutch rights in Nieuw Amsterdam (Manhattan Island, New York). In the 18th and early 19th centuries the colony, as a result of wars and treaties, was shuffled among England, France and the Netherlands
**1815:** Netherlands finally regains Suriname at Vienna Congress
**1863:** Slavery is abolished. Importation of Hindustani, Javanese and Chinese contract laborers follows
**1954:** Suriname is granted internal autonomy
**1973:** Creole-dominated National Party Coalition (NPK) wins elections. NPK leader Henck Arron becomes premier

**1975:** Suriname gains independence
**1978:** National Party Coalition reelected by landslide
**1980:** The army is denied the right to form a labor union. On February 25, a sergeants' coup, staged at the cost of six lives and the burning of a police station, ousts the Arron government. Henk Chin A Sen becomes head of a military-supervised civilian government. In May, 300 mercenaries, led by a former Surinamese soldier, invade Suriname from French Guiana, but all are captured and their leader executed
**1981:** Second attempt to overthrow the military government fails in April. Harsh security measures are introduced
**1982:** Third coup attempt fails in March, after Chin was forced to resign. Military junta makes Henry Neyhorst premier

## SWAZILAND

**Area:** 6,705 sq. mi. **Population:** 566,000 (1981 est.)

**Official Name:** Kingdom of Swaziland **Capital:** Mbabane **Nationality:** Swazi **Languages:** The official languages are English and si-Swati **Religion:** About 43% are animists, with about 500 Moslems; the rest of the population is Christian **Flag:** Horizontal stripes of blue, yellow, red, yellow, and blue with a traditional Swazi shield, spears and staff in black and white in the center **Anthem:** National Anthem, beginning "O God, Bestower of the blessings of the Swazi" **Currency:** Lilangeni (1.08 per U.S. $1)

**Location:** Southern Africa. Swaziland is almost entirely surrounded by South Africa, except for a 70-mile-long border with Mozambique on the east **Features:** The country consists of three well-defined regions known locally as the high, middle, and low velds, all roughly of equal breadth. The humid *highveld* in the west is mountainous; a plateau lies in the center, and to the east is a subtropical low plain **Chief Rivers:** Komati, Umbuluzi, Great Usutu, Mkonda

**Head of State:** As of Sept. 6, 1982, a successor had not been chosen following the death of King Sobhuza II on Aug. 21 **Head of Government:** Prime Minister: Prince Mabandla Dlamini, appointed Nov. 1979 **Effective Date of Present Constitution:** October 13, 1978 **Legislative Body:** Parliament, or *Liblandla*, (bicameral) consists of a 20-member Senate, and a 50-member House of Assembly; 10 of each are appointed by the king, the rest are chosen by an electoral college. There are no political parties, and the function of parliament is restricted to advising the king and debating proposals **Local Government:** 4 districts

**Ethnic Composition:** The African population is predominantly Swazi, with a Zulu minority; both belong to the Bantu group. About 2% are white **Population Distribution:** 8% urban **Density:** 84 inhabitants per sq. mi.

**Largest Cities:** (1976 census) Manzini 28,837, Mbabane 23,109

**Per Capita Income:** $558 (1980) **Gross National Product (GNP):** $306 million (1980) **Economic Statistics:** The main activity is subsistence agriculture (maize and such commercial crops as sugar, timber, citrus fruits, cotton, rice, and pineapples), which accounts for about 29% of GNP. Mining and manufacturing (machinery, beverages, chemicals, apparel, metal products, processed agricultural products) contribute about 37% of GNP **Minerals and Mining:** Deposits of iron ore (now depleted), asbestos, and coal are exploited; kaolin, barites, gold, and pyrophyllite are exploited on a smaller scale **Labor Force:** 120,000 (1978), with 60,000 engaged in subsistence agriculture and 18,114 employed in South African mines **Foreign Trade:** Exports, chiefly iron ore, sugar, wood pulp and other forest products, and asbestos, totaled $362 million in 1980. Imports, mainly manufactured goods, machinery and transport equipment, fuel, food and beverages, and tobacco, totaled $350 million **Principal Trade Partners:** South Africa, Britain, Japan

**Vital Statistics:** Birthrate, 46.9 per 1,000 of pop. (1980); death rate, 19 **Life Expectancy:** 46 years **Health Statistics:** 294 inhabitants per hospital bed; 10,000 per physician (1976) **Infant Mortality:** N.A. **Illiteracy:** 40% **Primary and Secondary School Enrollment:** 111,071 (1976) **Enrollment in Higher Education:** 1,150 (1976) **GNP Expended on Education:** 5% (1975)

**Transportation:** Paved roads total 241 mi. **Motor Vehicles:** 18,800 (1978) **Passenger Cars:** 10,900 **Railway Mileage:** 192 **Ports:** None **Major Airlines:** Royal Swazi National Airways operates international flights **Communications: Radio Transmitters:** 9 **Receivers:** 60,000 (1976) **Television Transmitters:** 1 **Telephones:** 10,000 (1978) **Newspapers:** 1 daily, 10 copies per 1,000 inhabitants (1976)

**Weights and Measures:** Metric system **Travel Requirements:** Passport, no visa

The smallest of three former British protectorates in southern Africa to attain independence, Swaziland is the home of a gentle Bantu people. For the Swazis, British protection was not merely a colonialist device. It saved them from Zulu and Boer invasions and was also the shield against absorption into South Africa's apartheid system when the black African nation of Swaziland became independent in 1968.

Along with the other former protectorates, Botswana and Lesotho, Swaziland is geographically and economically linked to South Africa, but all three nations have asserted a determination to preserve political independence. Although all are members of the South African Customs and Monetary Area, in 1974 Swaziland issued its own currency, and political and economic tensions with South Africa have increased.

Despite its small size and landlocked situation between South Africa's *highveld* and the Mozambique border, Swaziland possesses exceptional potential for economic independence. In addition to major resources of iron ore, asbestos, and coal, the country produces sugar, rice, tobacco, cotton, citrus fruits, and other crops. It also has a wood-pulp industry based on a rapidly growing forest of pine and eucalyptus. Rice production has been increased with the help of Nationalist China.

Most of the country's industries are still owned by British and South African interests, but Swazis are buying back foreign-owned property, especially farmland. In order to lessen economic dependence on South Africa, in 1980 Swaziland reached an understanding with Mozambique for cooperation, including use of Mozambique's port of Maputo. Operation of the gambling casino of the Royal Swazi Hotel, near Mbabane, is an attraction for tourists and a major source of revenue.

In 1973 King Sobhuza discarded Swaziland's five-year-old coonstitution and, in 1977, replaced the nation's parliamentary system with an assembly of tribal leaders. The electoral process was restored in October 1978, under a new constitution, as Swazis voted for members of an electoral college, which in turn, was to name 40 members of the 50-man National Assembly and 10 of the nation's 20 senators. The remaining legislators were to be appointed by King Sobhuza.

King Sobhuza died on August 21, 1982, at the age of 83.

**HISTORY:** The Swazis settled in present-day Swaziland in 1820 after being expelled by the Zulus from the land north of the Pongola River. Continued harassment by the Zulus led them to seek aid from the British, who succeeded in establishing friendly relations between the two tribes. The country's independence was guaranteed by the British and Transvaal governments in 1881 and 1884, and was followed by the establishment in 1890 of a provisional government representative of the Swazi and the two guarantors
**1902-7:** The Transvaal's rights in Swaziland pass to Britain following the Boer War; after a period of administration by the British governor of the Transvaal, Swaziland becomes a high commission territory ruled by a British commissioner
**1921:** Sobhuza II becomes Ngwenyama, head of the Swazi nation, after 20-year regency of his mother
**1949:** Opposition to South Africa's apartheid policy causes Britain to reject request that Swaziland, along with Basutoland (now Lesotho) and Bechuanaland (now Botswana), be transferred to South African control
**1967:** Swaziland wins self-government under a new constitution with Sobhuza as king
**1968:** Swaziland becomes independent state and a UN member
**1969:** Swaziland, disappointed by aid offered by Britain, moves to expand trade with African neighbors to boost national revenue
**1973:** Sobhuza repeals constitution; assumes supreme power
**1976:** Colonel Maphevu Dlamini becomes prime minister
**1977:** King Sobhuza abolishes the parliamentary system and replaces it with an assembly based on tribal leadership
**1978:** Voters create electoral college under new constitution. New railroad to South African coast completed
**1979:** Prime Minister Dlamini dies and is replaced by Prince Mabandla Dlamini
**1980:** Economy suffers from drought and inflation

**1981:** Diamond jubilee of King Sobhuza II is celebrated. Coal exports replace those of iron ore which ceased in 1980. Major hydroelectric project in Ezulwini valley is announced—to be financed in part by World Bank and African Development Bank

**1982:** Swaziland and South Africa negotiate transfer of bordering black homeland to the Swazis. South African Supreme Court later blocks plan. King Sobhuza dies on Aug. 21

## SWEDEN

**Area:** 173,665 sq. mi. **Population:** 8,323,033 (1981 est.)

**Official Name:** Kingdom of Sweden **Capital:** Stockholm **Nationality:** Swedish **Languages:** Swedish, the official language, is spoken by the vast majority; in the north there are Lapp-and Finnish-speaking minorities **Religion:** About 94% of the population is Lutheran, the state religion **Flag:** An extended yellow cross on a field of blue **Anthem:** Thou Ancient, Thou Freeborn **Currency:** Swedish Krona (5.9 per U.S. $1)

**Location:** Northern Europe, occupying the eastern part of the Scandinavian Peninsula. It is bordered on the northeast by Finland, on the east and south by the Gulf of Bothnia and the Baltic Sea, on the southwest by the Öresund, Kattegat, and Skagerrak, and on the west by Norway **Features:** The land is gently rolling in the south and mountainous in the north. About half the country is wooded, and lakes cover some 9% of the area **Chief Rivers:** Göta-Klar, Lule, Ume, Angerman, Dal

**Head of State:** King Carrl XVI Gustaf, born 1946, succeeded 1973 **Head of Government:** Prime Minister Thorbjörn Fälldin, born 1926, assumed office Oct. 12, 1979 **Effective Date of Present Constitution:** January 1975 **Legislative Body:** Parliament (unicameral). The *Riksdag* consists of 349 members elected for 3-year terms **Local Government:** 24 counties, with appointed governors and elected councils

**Ethnic Composition:** The population is largely homogeneous, with a Lapp minority of 17,000. There are 425,000 immigrants, mainly from other Nordic countries, Greece, Yugoslavia, and Turkey **Population Distribution:** 83% urban **Density:** 48 inhabitants per sq. mi.

**Largest Cities:** (M.A. = Metropolitan Area) (1978 est.) Stockholm 653,929 (M.A. 1,380,426), Göteborg 436,985 (M.A. 693,971), Malmö 236,716 (M.A. 453,928), Uppsala 143,386, Norrköping 120,251, Västeras 117,599, Orebro 116,817

**Per Capita Income:** $11,111 (1980) **Gross Domestic Product (GDP):** $92 billion (1980) **Economic Statistics:** About 59% of the GDP is derived from trade and services; 36% from manufacturing, construction and mining and 5% from agriculture (chiefly oats, wheat, rye, barley, potatoes, and dairy produce) **Minerals and Mining:** High grade iron ore is the primary mineral but there are also smaller deposits of gold, silver, lead, copper, zinc, pyrites, tungsten, manganese, granite, quartz, and marble **Labor Force:** 4.2 million (1978), with 37% in mining, manufacturing and construction; 31% in public service; 22% in trade and transportation; 6% in agriculture **Foreign Trade:** Exports, chiefly lumber, pulp and paper, ships, iron ore, machinery, and base metals totaled $27.5 billion in 1979. Imports, mainly machinery, chemicals and fuel products, and base metals, totaled $28.6 billion **Principal Trade Partners:** EC countries, United States, Canada, Norway, Finland, USSR, Saudi Arabia

**Vital Statistics:** Birthrate, 11.7 per 1,000 of pop. (1980); death rate, 11 **Life Expectancy:** 74 years **Health Statistics:** 67 inhabitants per hospital bed; 561 per physician (1976) **Infant Mortality:** 6.7 per 1,000 births **Illiteracy:** Negligible **Primary and Secondary School Enrollment:** 1,229,611 (1976) **Enrollment in Higher Education:** 162,640, (1975) **GNP Expended on Education:** 7.7% (1976)

**Transportation:** Surfaced roads total 17,514 mi. (1973) **Motor Vehicles:** 3,019,000 (1978) **Passenger Cars:** 2,856,000 **Railway Mileage:** 7,538 **Ports:** Göteborg, Stockholm, Malmö, Helsingborg, Trelleborg, Gävle, Luleå, Sundsvall, Norrköping **Major Airlines:** Scandinavian Airlines System (SAS), owned jointly by Sweden, Norway and Denmark, operates internationally; AB Linjeflyg, the Swedish affiliate of SAS, operates domestically **Communications: Radio Transmitters:** 104 **Licenses:** 3,203,000 (1976) **Television Transmitters:** 358 **Licenses:** 2,988,000 (1976) **Telephones:** 6,160,000 (1978) **Newspapers:** 112 dailies, 528 copies per 1,000 inhabitants (1977)

**Weights and Measures:** Metric system **Travel Requirements:** Passport, no visa for 3 months **International Dialing Code:** 46

Once upon a time Sweden was world-renowned for its idyllic stability; for life without hunger, war, or other material distress; for an overall reasonableness in settling its affairs. Intruding on the Swedish idyll in the last few years, however, have been such extraordinary developments as strikes by workers in defiance of union leaders now considered part of the Establishment, a new militance among organized salaried employees in the face of heavy taxes and an increasingly steep cost of living. However, Swedish unemployment is still among the world's lowest, and Swedish per capita income is among the highest.

Although Sweden is often described abroad as a socialist state, it is not so in the Marxist sense. According to Swedish authorities, theirs is a pragmatic socialism dedicated to assuring material security for all and establishing state-owned enterprises only in areas that private enterprise cannot or will not enter. Roughly 90 percent of Swedish industry is privately owned. A little more than 5 percent is in public hands, and the remaining enterprises are cooperatives.

The high cost of social welfare, for which roughly one third of the budget is earmarked, is met from the high taxes and from contributions to compulsory insurance plans. Among the principal features of the social welfare state are a national health insurance, a pension system, free prenatal care and child delivery, annual allowances to the mother until a child reaches 16, free tuition at Swedish universities, home-furnishing loans for newlyweds, and rent rebates for large families.

Under a national policy of full employment, the state operates a job service, moves unemployed persons to areas where work is available and offers retraining to those who lose jobs through automation or disability. Despite recent labor troubles, Sweden's union-management relations, compared with those of most other highly industrialized countries, have on the whole been placid since the 1930s. In general, labor's demands have been tempered by the need to compete in world markets; exports account for roughly one fourth of the GNP.

Figuring largely in Sweden's economic and social achievements is its policy of neutrality, under which it has managed to avoid war for close to 160 years. But Sweden's neutrality, the Swedes insist, is an avoidance of alliances, not a neutrality of opinion. This policy, they say, is not abridged by strong stands taken on conflicts far from their shores, notably denunciations by government ministers of U.S. involvement in Vietnam and the military takeover in Chile.

The welfare programs were developed by the Social Democratic party, which dominated Swedish politics from 1936 until 1976. A majority of voters, reacting to high taxes and an unimaginative bureaucracy, then voted into power a coalition of three nonsocialist parties, with Thorbjörn Fälldin as prime minister. The coalition broke down in 1978 and was replaced by a minority Liberal government under Ola Ullsten. In the 1979 parliamentary elections, the Social Democrats failed by only one seat of regaining power as the three nonsocialist parties won 175 seats in the *Riksdag*. Fälldin again became prime minister.

Sweden's first nationwide strike in 70 years involved nearly one million workers for ten days in May 1980, before the unions agreed to a 6.8 percent wage increase.

After Conservatives withdrew from the three-party governing coalition in 1981, due to disagreements over a tax package, Prime Minister Fälldin formed a minority government of Liberals and Centrists. The new government survived a vote of confidence because the Conservatives merely abstained and did not vote against it.

**HISTORY:** The earliest known reference to the Swedes is by the Roman historian Tacitus, who wrote in A.D. 98 that the Suiones (of the Lake Mälaren area) had a mighty fleet and a host of warriors, and were ruled by an absolute king. By the 6th century they had conquered their southern neighbors, the Götar, and merged with them. During the Viking period (9th—12th centuries), Swedes extended their influence across Russia to the Black Sea and joined with Danes and Norwegians in raids and voyages to Western Europe and the British Isles

**829:** Christianity is introduced by a Frankish monk, St. Anskar

**1150-60:** Erik IX stamps out paganism among the Swedes and undertakes a crusade against the Finnish heathens, adding Finland to the Kingdom of Sweden

**1319:** Sweden and Norway are united under Norway's Magnus VII

**1397:** Denmark, Sweden, and Norway are united under Denmark's Queen Margrethe to combat the superiority of the German mercantile organization, the Hanse

**1523-60:** Gustav Eriksson, elected king as Gustavus I, establishes Vasa dynasty, ends the union with Denmark and Norway, cuts ties to the Roman Catholic Church, and establishes a Lutheran state church

**1611-32:** Gustavus II establishes Sweden as a great European power, expanding the kingdom in wars with Russia and Poland and in the Thirty Years War against the Hapsburgs

**1648:** Peace of Westphalia gives Sweden German territory and makes Swedish kings princes of the Holy Roman Empire

**1700-21:** Charles XII launches a brilliant defensive campaign against Russia, Poland, and Denmark in the Northern War, but a series of victories is followed by a disastrous invasion of Russia, capped by the capitulation of the Swedish Army at Poltava (1709). After further defeats, Sweden declines as a major European power, having been forced to give up most of its continental conquests and possessions

**1805-09:** Sweden joins the Allies against Napoleon, loses its German Territories to France and Finland to Russia. Gustavus IV is overthrown; constitutional monarchy is established

**1813-14:** Entering its last major war, Sweden again joins the Allies against Napoleon, with Swedish forces led by the former French Marshal Jean Bernadotte, the chosen successor to the Swedish throne. He compels Denmark to cede Norway to Sweden

**1818:** Bernadotte ascends throne as Charles XIV; he steers Sweden toward a policy of neutrality

**1905:** Union with Norway is terminated peacefully

**1917:** Parliamentary form of government is established

**1920:** Sweden's first Social Democratic government is formed

**1959:** Sweden joins European Free Trade Association

**1973:** Carl XVI Gustaf succeeds to the throne upon the death of his grandfather, Gustaf VI Adolf

**1975:** A new constitution comes into effect which restricts the function of the king to a ceremonial role and approves the unicameral parliament in effect since 1971

**1976:** King Carl XVI Gustaf marries Sylvia Sommerlath. Swedish parliament adopts a law giving employees of certain companies the right to place two worker-delegates on the board of directors. Nonsocialist bloc (Center, Liberal and Moderate Unity parties) wins election; Thorbjörn Fälldin becomes prime minister

**1977:** Swedish cradle-to-grave "welfare state" palls as economy continues slumping badly, with many once-profitable exports reaching uncompetitive price levels due to high labor costs and sated world markets. Three of nation's largest shipbuilders are nationalized and merged. Three devaluations of krona improve its monetary position; investments, GNP decline

**1978:** *Riksdag* abrogates *Salic Law*, thus allowing female succession to the throne; second parliamentary vote needed to make this part of constitution. Liberal and Moderate Unity parties reject plans of Fälldin's Center party to stop building nuclear power plants. Fälldin resigns. Ola Ullsten becomes prime minister in minority Liberal government

**1979:** Nonsocialist bloc wins parliamentary elections by one seat over Social Democrats; Fälldin again becomes prime minister

**1981:** Fälldin forms two-party minority government after Conservatives withdraw from his government coalition

## SWITZERLAND

**Area:** 15,943 sq. mi. **Population:** 6,365,960 (1980 census)

**Official Name:** Swiss Confederation **Capital:** Bern **Nationality:** Swiss **Languages:** German (65%), French (18%), Italian (12%), and Romansch, a Romance language spoken in eastern Switzerland (1%) are official languages. Many Swiss speak more than one language **Religion:** About 48% Protestant, 49% Roman Catholic, 0.3% Jewish **Flag:** A square red field with a white cross in the center **Anthem:** Swiss Psalm **Currency:** Swiss franc (2 per U.S. $1)

**Location:** Central Europe. Switzerland is bounded on the north by Germany, on the east by Austria and Liechtenstein, on the south by Italy, and on the west by France **Features:** About 60% of the country is covered by the great Alpine mountain chain running through the south. The Jura Mountains in the west make up about 10% of the land. The rest is a plateau between the two mountain ranges **Chief Rivers:** Rhine, Rhône, Aare, Inn

**Head of State and of Government:** Executive authority is vested in the Federal Council, composed of 7 councilors elected for 4 years by the Federal Assembly; each year a president and vice-president are elected. The council, whose members head the 7 federal departments, is the directing power in the nation. President (for 1982): Fritz Honegger **Effective Date of Present Constitution:** 1848, amended 1874 **Legislative Body:** Federal Assembly (bicameral), consisting of the Council of States, with 46 members and either 3 or 4 year terms, and the National Council, with 200 members elected directly for 4 years **Local Government:** 26 cantons, with elected unicameral legislatures, divided into communes

**Ethnic Composition:** Traditionally 4 ethnic groups: German, French, Italian, and Romansch, with 932,743 resident foreigners (1978) **Population Distribution:** 55% urban **Density:** 399 inhabitants per sq. mi.

**Largest Cities:** (M.A. = Metropolitan Area) (1980 census) Zürich 369,522 (M.A. 706,220), Basel 182,143 (M.A. 364,813), Geneva 156,505 (M.A. 335,401), Bern 145,254 (M.A. 286,903), Lausanne 127,349 (M.A. 226,145)

**Per Capita Income:** $10,245 (1980) **Gross Domestic Product (GDP):** $65 billion (1980) **Economic Statistics:** 47% of GDP is derived from industry (machinery, chemicals, watches); 46% from commerce and services; and 7% from agriculture (dairy products, grains, fruit and vegetables, and wine-growing) **Minerals and Mining:** None; rich in forests and waterpower **Labor Force:** 2,800,000. About 21% are foreigners. Of the total, some 48% are in trade and services, 44% in industry, and 8% in agriculture and forestry **Foreign Trade:** Exports, chiefly machinery, watches, chemicals, and textiles, totaled $27 billion in 1979. Imports, mainly chemicals, crude oil, clothing, machines, and motor vehicles, totaled $29 billion **Principal Trade Partners:** West Germany, France, United States, Italy, Britain, Austria

**Vital Statistics:** Birthrate, 11.6 per 1,000 of pop. (1980); death rate, 9.3 **Life Expectancy:** 75 years **Health Statistics:** 87 inhabitants per hospital bed; 498 per physician (1977) **Infant Mortality:** 8.5 per 1,000 births **Illiteracy:** Negligible **Primary and Secondary School Enrollment:** 946,048 (1977) **Enrollment in Higher Education:** 64,720 (1975) **GNP Expended on Education:** 5.2% (1976)

**Transportation:** Paved roads total 38,600 mi. **Motor Vehicles:** 2,342,900 (1978) **Passenger Cars:** 1,932,800 **Railway Mileage:** 3,168 **Ports:** None **Major Airlines:** Swissair operates domestic and international flights **Communications: Radio Transmitters:** 215 **Licenses:** 2,108,000 (1976) **Television Transmitters:** 583 **Licenses:** 1,809,000 (1976) **Telephones:** 4,292,000 (1978) **Newspapers:** 91 dailies, 414 copies per 1,000 inhabitants (1977)

**Weights and Measures:** Metric system **Travel Requirements:** Passport, no visa for 3 months **International Dailing Code:** 41

If pacifists want proof of their contentions, they can point to Switzerland, the country that has not sent its troops into foreign wars since 1815. Switzerland has low unemployment amid growing joblessness in much of the rest of the world, and it ranks among the world's wealthiest countries. But, like other countries, it has been plagued by growing inflation rates during the past few years, and federal budgets recently ceased to be balanced.

The Swiss guard their neutrality with a modern army. Switzerland's neutrality was guaranteed by the Congress of Vienna in 1815; dedication to neutrality has even kept Switzerland out of the United Nations. However, Switzerland is a member of several special agencies of the UN and has a permanent observer at the UN. A member of the Council of Europe, Switzerland in 1972 was one of five members of the European Free Trade Association that signed a free-trade agreement with the EEC.

In part, the Swiss have been able to remain neutral because of the rugged Alps, which cover half the country and are uninviting as a battleground. At the same time, the country, which lacks actual mineral resources, has in its terrain and geographical location features that act as natural resources, and which are in fact the bases of the country's prosperity.

Snow-clad Alpine peaks from whose rushing streams hydroelectric power has been widely developed also constitute a winter vacation mecca, and the central European location of their country has enabled the hardworking Swiss to make it a center for trade, shipping, freight-forwarding, banking, and insurance. And more than a third of Swiss exports consists of machinery, precision instruments, and watches.

The Swiss spirit of tolerance is more recent than the policy of neutrality; religious disputes produced a civil war as late as 1847—a revolt of Catholic rural cantons against the increasing influence of the Protestant cities over the federal government. But division along ethnic lines of French-, German-, and Italian-speaking peoples has been avoided by giving the cantons much power and keeping the federal government tightly reined. Taxes, for example, cannot be increased without a constitutional amendment, which requires a national referendum.

Hard-fought issues are usually absent, because Switzerland has been governed for decades by a coalition of major parties. One of the hardest-fought issues was resolved when the male electorate voted in 1971 to enfranchise Swiss women in federal elections, ending Swiss political backwardness and reversing a decision of 12 years before. The national trend of reaching decisions by consensus has produced a well-ordered country where even strikes are almost unknown, and there are no drastic extremes of wealth and poverty.

In 1979, after long discussion, the French-speaking communes of the Canton of Bern were organized into a new canton—Jura.

The staid Swiss were startled by the sudden rioting of 8,000 young people in Zurich in May 1980. They were protesting the city's refusal to provide an "alternative culture" center for youths. After the city government supplied a site for the center but then closed it down because of problems, about 4,000 demonstrators rioted again in March 1981.

**HISTORY:** The Helvetii, a Celtic tribe, were the first known inhabitants of Switzerland. The land was conquered by the Romans in 58 B.C. and remained a Roman province for approximately 300 years. In the 5th century, it was overrun by the Alemanni and the Burgundii, and then passed to the Franks. After being split between Swabia and Transjurane Burgundy in the 9th century, it was united under the Holy Roman Empire in 1033

**1291:** Forest cantons of Schwyz, Uri, and Unterwalden form defensive league in face of growing encroachments by House of Hapsburg

**1315:** League defeats Austrian armies at Morgarten Pass

**1386-88:** Joined by five other cantons, the league decisively defeats Austrians, insuring existence of the confederation

**1499:** Swiss gain virtual independence from Holy Roman Emperor Maximilian I

**1519:** Ulrich Zwingli, vicar of Zurich Cathedral, attacks practices of Roman Catholic Church; his lectures on New Testament mark beginning of Protestant Reformation in Switzerland

**1541:** John Calvin introduces Protestantism into Geneva and establishes a theocratic state

**1648:** Switzerland's formal independence is recognized in the Peace of Westphalia, which ended the Thirty Years War

**1798-1803:** French Revolution results in creation of Helvetic Republic, which is governed as a French appendage

**1815:** Perpetual neutrality is guaranteed by Vienna Congress

**1914-18:** Swiss remain neutral in World War I

**1939-45:** Swiss maintain neutrality during World War II

**1959:** Women's suffrage, in federal elections, although advocated by federal council and assembly, is rejected in referendum

**1971:** Constitutional amendment gives Swiss women the vote in federal elections and the right to hold federal office

**1974:** A plebiscite in the French-speaking Jura region of the largely German-speaking canton of Bern results in a narrow majority favoring a separate Jura canton

**1978:** Acting to stem rise of Swiss franc and protect its export industry and tourism business, government decides to ban further foreign capital investment

**1979:** Canton of Jura established

**1981:** Voters approve constitutional amendment guaranteeing equal rights to women

**1982:** Government proposes to Assembly to approve membership in UN; national referendum would be necessary if Assembly approved

## SYRIA

**Area:** 71,722 sq. mi. **Population:** 9,314,000 (1981 est.)

**Official Name:** Syrian Arab Republic **Capital:** Damascus **Nationality:** Syrian **Languages:** Arabic is the official and predominant language; French and English are also used, and Armenian and Kurdish are spoken by minorities **Religion:** 74% Sunni Moslem, 16% other Moslem, and 10% Christian **Flag:** Three equal horizontal stripes of red, white and black with two five-pointed green stars symmetrically aligned on the white stripe **Anthem:** National Anthem, beginning "Defenders of the homeland, salute" **Currency:** Syrian pound (3.925 per U.S. $1)

**Location:** Southwest Asia. Syria is bounded on the north by Turkey, on the east by Iraq, on the south by Jordan and Israel, and on the west by Lebanon and the Mediterranean Sea **Features:** The country consists of a narrow coastal plain, east of which is a highland region that is continued to the south by the Lebanon and Anti-Lebanon Mountains. Fertile plains form the central region, with the Syrian Desert to the southeast. North of the desert region lies the fertile Euphrates River Valley **Chief Rivers:** Euphrates, Orontes

**Head of State and of Government:** President: Lt. Gen. Hafez al-Assad, born 1928, elected 1971, reelected in 1978 for 7 years. He is assisted by Prime Minister Abdul Rauf al-Kasm, appointed Jan. 1980 **Effective Date of Present Constitution:** 1973 **Legislative Body:** People's Council (unicameral), consisting of 195 elected members **Local Government:** 13 provinces and the municipality of Damascus

**Ethnic Composition:** 90% are Arabs; minorities include Circassians, Armenians, Turks, and Kurds **Population Distribution:** 47% urban **Density:** 130 inhabitants per sq. mi.

**Largest Cities:** (1978 est.) Damascus 1,142,000, Aleppo 878,000, Homs 306,000, Latakia 204,000, Hama 180,000

**Per Capita Income:** $988 (1980) **Gross National Product (GNP):** $8.6 billion (1980) **Economic Statistics:** 36% of the GNP is derived from services; 26% from industry (petroleum refining, textiles, cement, glass, apparel, soap, food processing); 19% from commerce; and 18% from agriculture (wheat, barley, cotton) **Minerals and Mining:** Oil, natural gas, phosphates, asphalt, gypsum and rock salt **Labor Force:** 1.8 million; 32% engaged in agriculture and 26% in industry **Foreign Trade:** Exports, chiefly petroleum (70% of total) and raw cotton, totaled $1.7 billion in 1979. Imports, mainly textiles, machinery, petroleum products, vehicles, and foodstuffs, totaled $3.6 billion **Principal Trade Partners:** EC countries, USSR, Arab countries, United States, Romania

**Vital Statistics:** Birthrate, 45.2 per 1,000 of pop. (1980); death rate, 12.9 **Life Expectancy:** 57 years **Health Statistics:** 956 inhabitants per hospital bed; 2,529 per physician (1977) **Infant Mortality:** 12.6 per 1,000 births **Illiteracy:** 47% **Primary and Secondary School Enrollment:** 1,828,339 (1976) **Enrollment in Higher Education:** 73,660 **GNP Expended on Education:** 5.8% (1975)

**Transportation:** Paved roads total 7,484 mi. **Motor Vehicles:** 146,800 (1978) **Passenger Cars:** 65,400 **Railway Mileage:** 958 **Ports:** Latakia, Baniyas, Tartus **Major Airlines:** Syrian Arab Airlines operates domestically and internationally **Communications: Radio Transmitters:** 14 **Receivers:** 2,500,000 (1972) **Television Transmitters:** 21 **Receivers:** 230,000 (1976) **Telephones:** 212,000 (1978) **Newspapers:** 7 dailies (1976), 9 copies per 1,000 inhabitants

**Weights and Measures:** Metric system and local units are used **Travel Requirements:** Passport; visa valid 6 months, $8.21 fee, 3 photos

Once the center of one of the most ancient civilizations on earth, Syria today seeks a leadership role in the Arab world. As an ardent champion of the Palestinian Liberation Organization, Syria has trained and armed guerrillas at bases within the country.

Syria merged with Egypt in 1958, but seceded in 1961. In the 1970s, it established a joint command and diplomatic coordination with Jordan. In 1979, President Hafez al-Assad of Syria and President Ahmed Hassan al-Bakr of Iraq formed a joint political command. They also agreed to merge their two Ba'ath socialist countries, but took no immediate steps to implement the agreement. Relations between Syria and Iraq have been marred by squabbles about ideological points and national goals. Each expelled the other's diplomats in August 1980.

President Assad is a military man who took power in a coup in 1970 and has brought stablility to Syria. Assad's Ba'ath (Socialist) party is predominant. The press and radio are directly controlled by the state.

Before World War I, Syria was part of the Ottoman Empire and loosely included all of what is now Lebanon, Israel, and Jordan, as well as Syria itself. Even today some people speak wistfully of a "Greater Syria." Between the two world wars, the country was under French mandate; it became independent in 1946.

The Syrian people are considered among the most sophisticated in the Arab world, because for centuries the country has been a passageway between the Mediterranean world and the Far East.

In recent years Syria has aligned itself closely with the Soviet Union. Its armed forces are equipped by Moscow, and there are believed to be upward of 1,000 Soviet military and civilian advisors in the country. However, Syrian intervention in Lebanon has placed a strain on Soviet relations because Russia has been a supporter of the Palestinians in Lebanon and the use of Soviet weapons by Syria against them has embarrassed Moscow. President Assad tried to patch up the differences in his spring 1977 trip to Moscow. In spite of the Soviet presence, the left-wing military rulers have outlawed the Syrian Communist party.

Israeli soldiers have occupied the Golan Heights, a part of southwestern Syria since 1967. A demilitarized zone, patroled by a multinational force under United Nations command, has been established between the Israeli and Syrian forces. The Israeli-occupied area is of strategic importance, and Israel formally annexed it on December 14, 1981.

Since 1975 Syria has been concerned with the civil war in Lebanon, and Syrian troops and tanks have intervened against Palestinian-led forces when it appeared they might install a radical state and incite war with Israel. Beginning in 1978, Syrian-dominated peace-keeping forces have battled Lebanese troops and right-wing militia in and around Beirut. After Israeli jet aircraft had shot down Syrian helicopters in 1981, Syria moved Soviet-made missiles into Lebanon and fired on Israeli warplanes. In June 1982, Israeli forces invaded southern Lebanon to crush PLO strongholds and destroyed 17 of the 19 Syrian missile batteries in the Bekaa Valley. Syrian MIG fighter planes in turn attacked the Israeli bombers, and Syrian troops exchanged fire with the invaders. Syrian losses in Soviet-made aircraft and tanks were heavy.

Although a cease-fire was agreed to by both nations on June 11, Syrian troops in Beirut joined Palestinian guerrillas to fight the Israeli invaders. On June 20, Syria rejected Israel's demand that it withdraw its forces from Beirut, and fighting continued intermittently despite subsequent cease-fires. By June 25, Israeli forces had split the Syrian troops in Beirut and along the Beirut-Damascus highway from the main Syrian army in the Bekaa Valley. But the Syrians trapped in west Beirut continued to resist, as diplomatic efforts were made to end the fighting and to expel all foreign forces from Lebanon. A withdrawal plan was agreed to by all parties on August 18.

**HISTORY:** Ancient Syria was the home of Amorites, Aramaeans, Phoenicians, and Hebrews. After a succession of invaders that included Assyrians, Babylonians, Egyptians, Hittites, and Persians, the country was unified under Alexander the Great in 331 B.C. It later fell under Roman rule, becoming part of the Byzantine Empire when the Roman Empire was divided between East and West. In the 7th century, the country was conquered by the Arabs and became the center of a vast Islamic domain

**11th cent:** Seljuk Turks invade Syria from Asia Minor

**12th cent:** Crusaders gain control over Syrian coastal areas (1189-92) and fight the Moslems led by Saladin

**1516-1918:** Syria is conquered by the Ottoman Empire, remains largely stagnant during four centuries of Turkish rule

**1920:** Syria is made a French mandate

**1941-46:** Free French and British forces occupy Syria during World War II; French proclaim an independent Syrian republic but complete independence is not achieved until 1944. All foreign troops are withdrawn in 1946

**1958-61:** Egypt and Syria form United Arab Republic under presidency of Egypt's President Nasser; attempts to integrate the two economies, nationalization of Syrian industry, and domination of Syrian army posts by Egyptian officers cause widespread discontent, culminating in military coup and restoration of Syrian independence

**1963-66:** Series of military coups results in succession of governments, although left-wing Ba'ath party continues to dominate political scene. In 1966, a new coup leads to installation of Nureddin al-Attassi as president

**1967:** Syria shares in Arab defeat in Six-Day War with Israel, whose forces occupy Golan Heights in southwestern Syria

**1968-71:** Struggle between factions of Ba'ath party led by President Attassi and those of Gen. Hafez al-Assad ends with Assad's seizing power in 1970 and being elected president in 1971

**1971:** Syria breaks off relations with Jordan after border clash

**1973:** Syria settles her differences with Jordan, joins other Arab nations in a full-scale war against Israel and adopts a new constitution

**1975:** King Hussein of Jordan and President Assad announce that their countries will establish a Permanent Joint High Commission to coordinate political, economic, and cultural policies

**1976:** Syria sends troops into Lebanon during the civil war there

**1977:** Syria rejects Egyptian proposals for preliminary meeting to prepare for Geneva Middle-East peace talks involving Israel; it takes part in so-called "refusal summit" with Iraq, Algeria, Libya, Southern Yemen and the PLO; events constitute virtual rupture between Syria and Egypt

**1978:** Syrians and Lebanese Christians battle in Beirut area in heaviest fighting there since Lebanese civil war. Assad, first Syrian president to serve full seven-year term since nation gained independence in 1946, runs unopposed and is reelected; Mohammad Ali al-Halabi appointed prime minister

**1979:** Syrian and Israeli warplanes clash in Lebanese air space. Military Moslem Brotherhood attacks Alawite miniority in Aleppo

**1980:** President Hassad purges 14 members of Ba'ath Socialist party from cabinet, including Premier Halabi; forms new 37-member cabinet with Abdul Rauf al-Kasm as premier. Syria and Iraq expel each other's diplomats. Assad and Libyan leader Qaddafi sign merger agreement proclaiming Syria and Libya a single state (not implemented)

**1981:** Syrian forces in Lebanon employ "defensive" missiles to shoot down Israeli jet aircraft; Israel threatens to remove them by force. Israel formally annexes Golan Heights area

**1982:** Uprising of Moslem Brotherhood forces in Hama is crushed by government troops; large part of city is destroyed and thousands are killed (February). Israeli forces invading southern Lebanon destroy Syrian anti-aircraft missiles June 9; Syrian fighter planes attack Israeli warplanes; Syrian troops in West Beirut trapped by Israelis; Syria rejects (June 20) Israeli demand that it withdraw its forces from Beirut. Withdrawal plan for all forces trapped in Beirut is agreed to on Aug. 18

## TANZANIA

**Area:** 363,708 sq. mi. **Population:** 17,982,000 (1979 est.)

**Official Name:** United Republic of Tanzania **Capital:** Dar es Salaam (future capital by 1990—Dodoma) **Nationality:** Tanzanian **Languages:** English and Swahili, the national language, are official languages. Some 120 dialects, mostly Bantu, are also spoken **Religion:** 35% Moslem, 35% Christian, and the rest animist **Flag:** A green triangle in the upper left and a blue one in the lower right, separated by a diagonal black band edged in yellow **Anthem:** National Anthem, set to new words of hymn "God Bless Africa" **Currency:** Tanzanian shilling (9.43 per U.S. $1)

**Location:** East Africa, comprising the former republics of Tanganyika and Zanzibar. Mainland Tanzania (Tanganyika) is bounded on the north by Lake Victoria, Kenya and Uganda, on the east by the Indian Ocean, on the south by Mozambique, Malawi, and Zambia, and on the west by Rwanda, Burundi, and Zaire. The island of Zanzibar lies some 20 miles to the east of Tanganyika's coastline, in the Indian Ocean **Features:** Tanganyika consists of a low-lying eastern coastal area, a high plateau in the west-central region, and scattered mountainous zones. Zanzibar is a low-lying island of coral limestone **Chief Rivers:** Pangani, Wami, Rufiji, Malagarasi, Ruvuma

**Head of State and of Government:** President Julius Kambarage Nyerere, born 1922, took office 1962 (Tanganyika), reelected 1980, head of the Revolutionary Party. He is assisted by the first vice-president (chairman of thee Zanzibar Revolutionary Council), Sheikh Aboud Jumbe, born 1920, and by a prime minister, Cleopa David Msuya, appointed 1980 **Effective Date of Present Constitution:** April 1977 **Legislative Body:** National Assembly (unicameral), with 239 members, of whom 111 are elected for 5 years and the rest appointed **Local Government:** 25 regions, including 20 on the mainland and 5 in Zanzibar, each administered by an appointed commissioner

**Ethnic Composition:** About 99% of the population are Africans who belong to some 130 different tribes, mostly Bantu. Only the Sukuma numbers over a million members. European, Arab, and Indo-Pakistani minorities total about 150,000 **Population Distribution:** 13% urban **Density:** 49 inhabitants per sq. mi.

**Largest Cities:** (1978 census) Dar es Salaam 757,346, Zanzibar 110,669, Mwanza 110,611, Tanga 103,409, Mbeya 76,606

**Per Capita Income:** $197 (1980) **Gross National Product (GNP):** $3.5 billion (1980) **Economic Statistics:** In 1977, 51% of GNP was from agriculture (sisal, cotton, coffee, oilseeds, nuts, tea, tobacco, sugar, livestock; Zanzibar is the world's largest producer of cloves); 12% from trade and services; and 9% from manufacturing and mining **Minerals and Mining:** Diamonds and gold are the most important minerals being exploited, in addition to salt, mica sheets, gem stones and tin concentrates. Coal and iron deposits are to be exploited **Labor Force:** 5,600,000 (1970), with 90% enngaged in subsistence agriculture. The monetary-sector employment in 1979: 538,000 workers **Foreign Trade:** Exports, chiefly cotton, coffee, diamonds, sisal, petroleum products, cloves, and cashew nuts, totaled $578 million in 1980. Imports, mainly machinery and transportation equipment, manufactured goods, fuel, and textiles, totaled $1.4 billion **Principal Trade Partners:** Britain, Italy, Saudi Arabia, Iran, West Germany, France, Japan, India, United States

**Vital Statistics:** Birthrate, 47 per 1,000 of pop. (1967); death rate, 22 **Life Expectancy:** 51 years **Health Statistics:** 619 inhabitants per hospital bed; 18,480 per physician (1975) **Infant Mortality:** 160 per 1,000 births **Illiteracy:** 34% **Primary and Secondary School Enrollment:** 2,024,179 (1976) **Enrollment in Higher Education:** 3,064 **GNP Expended on Education:** 4.4% (1976)

**Transportation:** Paved roads total 2,228 mi. **Motor Vehicles:** 90,000 (1977) **Passenger Cars:** 43,600 **Railway Mileage:** 2,788 **Ports:** Dar es Salaam, Tanga, Mtwara, Lindi **Major Airlines:** Air Tanzania flies domestically and internationally **Communications:** **Radio Transmitters:** 118 **Receivers:** 300,000 (1976) **Television Transmiitters:** 1 **Receivers:** 4,000 (1970) **Telephones:** 82,000 (1978) **Newspapers:** 2 dailies, 8 copies per 1,000 inhabitants (1977)

**Weights and Measures:** Metric system **Travel Requirements:** Passport, visa, $3.15 fee, 1 photo, onward ticket

---

Tanzania, a union of Tanganyika and Zanzibar, is the site of some of the oldest and newest forms of human society. Its link to man's past was established in 1959 at Olduvai Gorge in the northern part of what was then Tanganyika. There Mary Leakey, the British-born anthropologist, unearthed one of the oldest human fossils ever found, the skull of *Homo zinjanthropus*. Its age was estimated to be more than 1.5 million years.

Now, over a decade after independence from Britain, Tanzania is the testing ground for a form of African Socialism—*ujamaa*—as conceived by President Julius K. Nyerere. *Ujamaa*, which means familyhood in Swahili, refers to kibbutz-like rural developments whose members join in communal farming and general improvement on a basis of "love, sharing, and work." On a broader scale, it means a joint effort by which all Tanzanians may gain an equal share of the nation's resources. In 1973 the ruling party, the Tanganyika African National Union (TANU), decided that all peasants had to join *ujamaa* villages, making the movement no longer voluntary.

The Nyerere government has progressively nationalized private business, banks, and privately owned buildings and homes. The economy depends largely on agriculture—coffee, tea, cotton, sisal and other crops—and between rising population and the vagaries of African weather, there has been little gain on a per-capita share basis.

The government, while striving for self-reliance, has not scorned foreign aid. U.S. funds are providing new highways, but the main new project is the Tanzam Railway, which was built with money, equipment, and labor provided by Communist China, and was handed over to Tanzania and Zambia by China in July 1976 after six years of construction. Although Tanzania had seemed to favor the Chinese, Soviet President Podgorny's 1977 visit to Tanzania was warmly received because of the Zimbabwe nationalist cause, which was actively supported by both countries.

In November 1978 Tanzanian forces invaded neighboring Uganda after Idi Amin had occupied more than 700 square miles of Tanzanian soil. Within five months Tanzanians and Ugandan rebels captured Kampala and drove the Ugandan dictator into exile. The war cost Tanzania more than $500 million, crippling its internal economy. The last Tanzanian troops were withdrawn by mid-1981, leaving only a police force of 1,000.

**HISTORY:** Archaeological discoveries indicate that man inhabited Tanzania more than one million yeaars ago. However, little is known about the early history of the area. Zanzibar, colonized by the Arabs in the 8th century, controlled the East African coastal region until the early 16th century, when both the island and the coast came under Portuguese rule. Arab rule was reestablished in the 17th century by the sultans of Muscat, under whom a large trade in ivory and slaves was established

**1861:** Zanzibar, under British pressure, is separated from control of Sultan of Muscat and becomes an independent sultanate

**1885:** Germany establishes a protectorate over the mainland region, which becomes known as German East Africa

**1920:** As a result of Germany's defeat in World War I, German East Africa is mandated to Britain; territory's name is changed to Tanganyika and German settlers are expelled

**1946:** Tanganyika becomes a trust territory

**1961:** Tanganyika wins independence; Julius K. Nyerere, head of Tanganyika African National Union (TANU) party, becomes prime minister

**1962:** Tanganyika becomes independent republic within Commonwealth; Nyerere is named as republic's first president

**1963:** Zanzibar achieves independence within the Commonwealth

**1964:** Afro-Shirazi party, representing the African majority in Zanzibar, overthrows Arab minority government and forces sultan to flee; Zanzibar becomes a republic, with Sheik Abeid Amani Karume as president. Tanganyika and Zanzibar agree to form United Republic of Tanzania, with Nyerere as president and Karume as first vice-president

**1965-69:** Tanzania becomes one-party state, with TANU constituting the one party in Tanganyika and the Afro-Shirazi party in Zanzibar, and both sharing power on national level. In 1967 government announces plans for socialist development and embarks on widespread nationalization in industry and agriculture

**1971:** Refusal of Tanzania to recognize Uganda government of General Idi Amin leads to bitter dispute and border clashes

**1972:** Sheik Abeid Amani Karume, Chairman of the Revolutionary Council which governed Zanzibar, assassinated. General Amin charges Tanzania with invading Uganda and threatens retaliation

**1975:** Kenya reopens Tanzanian border saying that outbreak of cholera was under control. Nyerere is elected to a fourth term

**1976:** Tanzam Railway is completed

**1977:** Tanzania closes its border with Kenya after Kenya withdraws from jointly-operated East African Airways in order to form separate Kenya Airlines. The Tanganyika African National Union and the Afro-Shirazi party of Zanzibar merge into one party called the Revolutionary party, headed by President Nyerere

**1978:** Government takes steps to combat cholera epidemic, which it reports has killed more than 400 persons. War with Uganda erupts as Idi Amin's troops occupy 710 square miles of northwestern Tanzania before being driven back

**1980:** Zanzibar elects its own National Assembly under a separate constitution. Nyerere, unopposed, is reelected president of Tanzania, but more than half of the members of the National Assembly lose seats in response to government failure to solve nation's economic problems

**1981:** Nyerere begins year of "struggle against economic saboteurs" by firing two top officers of state-run Tanzania Investment Bank. Last of 10,000 Tanzanian troops leave Uganda in June

**1982:** Four gunmen, demanding ouster of Nyerere, hijack an Air Tanzania jet; surrender after forcing flight to England

## THAILAND

**Area:** 198,455 sq. mi. **Population:** 47,173,000 (1980 est.)

**Official Name:** Kingdom of Thailand **Capital:** Bangkok **Nationality:** Thai **Languages:** Thai is the official language and is spoken by most of the population; minority languages are Chinese, Malay, Khmer, and Lao **Religion:** Hinayana Buddhism is the religion of 95.5% of the population; Islam (4%), Confucianism and Christianity are minority religions **Flag:** Horizontal stripes of red, white, blue (double width), white, red **Anthem:** National Anthem, beginning "Thailand is the place for all Thais" **Currency:** Baht (23 per U.S. $1)

**Location:** Southeast Asia. Thailand is bounded on the north and east by Laos, on the east by Cambodia, on the south by Malaysia, and on the west and north by Burma. It extends down the Malay Peninsula between the Andaman Sea and the Gulf of Thailand **Features:** The core of the country is the central plain, with flat alluvial lands watered by a network of canals and irrigation projects. The north consists of parallel north-south mountain ranges and narrow, fertile valleys, while the region east of the central plain, the Khorat Plateau, is relatively barren. North-south mountain ranges also dominate peninsular Thailand **Chief Rivers:** Chao Phraya, Mekong, Nan, Ping, Mun, Pa Sak, Mae Klong

**Head of State:** King Bhumibol Adulyadej (Phumiphol Aduldet), born 1927, succeeded 1946 **Head of Government:** Prime Minister: Gen. Prem Tinsulanonda, born 1920, appointed March 1980 **Effective Date of Present Constitution:** December 1978 **Legislative Body:** Parliament (bicameral), consisting of 225-member Senate, appointed on the recommendation of the prime minister, and a popularly elected 301-member House of Representatives **Local Government:** 71 provinces; under appointed governors

**Ethnic Composition:** 75% Thai, 14% Chinese, 11% minorities (Malays, northern hill tribes, Khmer, Lao) **Population Distribution:** 13% urban **Density:** 238 inhabitants per sq. mi.

**Largest Cities:** (1975 est.) Bangkok 4,178,000; (1970 census) Thonburi 628,015, Chiengmai 83,729, Nakhon Ratchasima 66,071

**Per Capita Income:** $601 (1980) **Gross National Product (GNP):** $28.5 billion (1980) **Economic Statistics:** 33% of 1974 GNP was derived from industry (mining and quarrying, manufacturing, construction, transportation and communications); 28% from agriculture; 25% from commerce and finance (wholesale and retail trade, banking, insurance, real estate, ownership of dwellings); 10% from services **Minerals and Mining:** Major offshore natural gas fields are being exploited. Sizable tin, tungsten and lignite deposits. Other minerals are manganese, molybdenum, antimony and gem stones **Labor Force:** 16,243,000 (1975); 67% agriculture and forestry, 10% industry **Foreign Trade:** Exports, chiefly tapioca, rubber, rice, maize, tin, sugar, brought in $5.3 billion in 1979. Imports, mainly machinery, spare parts, fuel, iron, steel, automobiles, electrical equipment, totaled $7.2 billion **Principal Trade Partners:** United States, Japan, Malaysia, Hong Kong, Singapore, West Germany, Britain, Netherlands, Saudi Arabia

**Vital Statistics:** Birthrate, 37.5 per 1,000 of pop. (1980); death rate, 9.2 **Life Expectancy:** 61 years **Health Statistics:** 823 inhabitants per hospital bed (1976); 8,246 per physician (1976) **Infant Mortality:** 16.6 per 1,000 births **Illiteracy:** 18% **Primary and Secondary School Enrollment:** 8,069,829 (1976) **Enrollment in Higher Education:** 130,965 (1975) **GNP Expended on Education:** 4.1% (1976)

**Transportation:** Paved roads total 12,150 mi. (1975) **Motor Vehicles:** 567,800 (1976) **Passenger Cars:** 270,900 **Railway Mileage:** 2,380 **Ports:** Bangkok, Sattahip **Major Airlines:** Thai Airways, domestic and international (gov't owned) **Communications: Radio Transmitters:** 217 **Receivers:** 5,500,000 (1976) **Television Transmitters:** 48 **Receivers:** 761,000 (1976) **Telephones:** 409,000 (1978) **Newspapers:** 23 dailies (1977), 24 copies per 1,000 inhabitants (1975)

**Weights and Measures:** Metric system **Travel Requirements:** Passport, no visa for 15 days **International Dialing Code:** 66

One of the largest countries in Southeast Asia, Thailand is favored with superb rice land, vast stands of teak, and a guaranteed rainfall that insures agricultural abundance. Thailand is the only Southeast Asian nation that has never been colonized: the word *thai* itself means free, and the Thai people are proud of this heritage.

For generations they have successfully resisted pressure not only of China to the north but also of Cambodia to the east. The Thais, the vast majority of whom are Buddhists, have lived for centuries under the cohesive influence of their line of kings.

A constitutional monarchy replaced the absolute rule of the kings in 1932, but parliamentary democracy was placed in abeyance in 1958, when a military junta seized control of the government in a bloodless coup. Since that time, a series of successful coups has occurred—the most recent being a bloodless coup in October 1977 led by Defense Minister Sa-ngad Chaloryu, a former admiral who said he was deposing Premier Thanin Kraivchien's civilian government because it was taking too long to restore democracy.

Thailand's military commander, Gen. Kriangsak Chamanan, was named to replace Thanin as premier. Kriangsak stayed in power as a result of the elections of April 1979. None of the 36 political groupings won a majority in the 301-seat lower house; he appointed all 225 senators as called for by the constitution, and then the members of the two houses, meeting jointly, reelected him premier. But his government fell on February 19, 1980.

He was succeeded, on March 3, by Gen. Prem Tinsulanonda, whose government was beset by internal divisions that required frequent reshuffling of the cabinet. Prem did, however, survive the so-called "April Fool coup" of April 1981, when a dissident general's attempt to oust him was thwarted, largely because of the extraordinary intervention of the king, who is traditionally "above" partisanship.

Thailand continues to be beset by insurgent activities in the south, north and northeastern provinces, involving groups as diverse as the Thai Communists, Muslim separatists, and rebellious mountain people. In early 1982, it staged a major military operation against the independent Shan tribesmen of the "Golden Triangle" area in the north, a prime world source of opium.

Thailand's largely agricultural economy maintained a real growth rate of over five percent in the early 1980s. Tapioca, shipped to Europe as animal feed, became the nation's top agricultural money-earner in 1978, surpassing rice. Rubber and tin remain important, and light industry is growing.

An influx of Indochinese refugees into Thailand's "rice bowl" threatens to overwhelm the country's economy. Once Cambodia had been a buffer against Vietnam, but the Vietnamese takeover of that nation put Cambodia on the front lines in 1979. An initial wave of 80,000 Cambodians crossed the border into Thailand to escape hunger and death; the Thais at first responded by forcibly returning 45,000 of them. But then Thailand gave international officials assurance that it would let refugees stay in camps "for a short and specified period" while other countries arranged resettlement. Occasionally in later years it revived the threat to refuse entry to further refugees, but in 1982, with more than 300,000 refugees draining its economy, it was still allowing Cambodians and Laotians to cross its northeastern border and giving asylum to the "boat people" that continued to trickle out of Vietnam.

**HISTORY:** In the 11th century the Thai people, living in Yunnan Province of what is now China, began moving southward under pressure from the expanding Chinese. They settled in the valleys of the Chao Phraya and Mekong Rivers and formed political states, many of which were under the rule of King Rama Kamhaeng. In the 15th century they were united with other Thais around Chiang Mai, in the northeast, and with the northern Malays in the south. By the 18th century trade had been established with Europe and Thailand began to consolidate as a nation

**1833:** Trade agreement is signed with the United States

**1917:** Siam (as Thailand was then called) declares war on Germany and sends expeditionary force to Europe

**1932:** Coup d'état by army officers establishes constitutional government to replace absolute monarchy

**1941:** Japanese troops enter Thailand, which is forced to sign alliance

**1946:** King Ananda Mahidol is found shot to death and is succeeded on throne by his younger brother, Bhumibol Adulyadej

**1947:** Coup by military officers forces change in government
**1957-58:** In another bloodless coup, government is replaced by a short-lived military junta. This is followed by another shift of power when Field Marshal Sarit Thanarat seizes control
**1962:** U.S. military unit is sent to northeast Thailand as Lao Communists threaten to sweep to Mekong River
**1963:** Sarit dies and is replaced by Marshal Thanom Kittikachorn
**1971:** On November 17, Thanom's government takes absolute power
**1973:** U.S. congressional order ends U.S. bombing flights from Thai bases. Antigovernment protests organized by students result in violence. Thanom's government resigns and university rector Sanya Thammasak is named premier
**1974:** Exiled former premier Thanom Kittikachorn returns and is expelled. Agreement reached for U.S. to withdraw two of its six remaining air bases by the end of 1974. Air America, funded by CIA, ceases operations in Thailand
**1975:** Kukrit Pramoj becomes premier
**1976:** Seni Pramoj becomes premier. All operations are ended at U.S. installations and military personnel are withdrawn
**1977:** Thai and Cambodian troops fight along the border. Thai military leadership takes power under Gen. Kriangsak Chamanan; 23-member Revolutionary Council is established; new government proclaims interim constitution promising elections by 1979; parliament is dissolved; King appoints 360-member national legislature with heavy military representation
**1978:** Amnesty International, estimating there are possibly up to 1,000 political prisoners in Thailand, calls for their release. Thailand and Cambodia agree to try to end bloody border fighting and to exchange ambassadors
**1979:** Some 80,000 refugees flee to Thailand in the wake of Vietnam's invasion of Cambodia and its establishment of a client regime there. Some 45,000 are forced back across the border. By midyear, Thailand agrees to let Cambodians enter UN transit camps, pending resettlement abroad
**1980:** Kriangsak, facing a no-confidence vote over economic policies, quits as premier; Gen. Prem Tinsulanonda, formerly defense minister and army chief, succeeds him. Vietnamese troops attack Cambodian refugees in two camps inside Thailand for two days in June to show displeasure over shipping of some armed Cambodian refugees back to their own country. Flow of refugees into Cambodia rises
**1981:** Attempted coup, led by a general, fails in April when the king departs from tradition of political neutrality to openly support Premier Prem; the conspirators are later pardoned. Some 250,000 Cambodians remain in Thai border encampments
**1982:** In a bloody February attack, Thai troops capture stronghold of chief warlord in opium-producing "Golden Triangle," at Burmese border. Washington stiffens rules on acceptance of Indochinese immigrants; Thais had urged such a change, hoping to discourage flow of refugees into Thailand camps

## TOGO

**Area:** 21,853 sq. mi. **Population:** 2,472,000 (1979 est.)

**Official Name:** Togolese Republic **Capital:** Lomé **Nationality:** Togolese **Languages:** French is the official language; the dominant indigenous languages are Ewe, Twi, and Hausa. In all, more than 44 different languages are spoken **Religion:** 60% animist, 20% Christian (mostly Roman Catholics), 20% Moslem **Flag:** Five alternating horizontal stripes of green (3) and yellow (2), with a white star on a red square in the upper left **Anthem:** National Anthem, beginning "Hail to thee, land of our forefathers" **Currency:** CFA Franc (305 per U.S. $1)

**Location:** West Africa. Togo is bounded on the north by Upper Volta, on the east by Benin, on the south by the Gulf of Guinea, and on the west by Ghana **Features:** The country is cut in two from the northeast to the southwest by the Chaine du Togo hills. To the north is a large savanna, with a plain in the east and south **Chief Rivers:** Oti, Mono, Haho, Anié

**Head of State and of Government:** President: General Gnassingbé Eyadéma, born 1937, seized power in 1967, elected 1979 **Effective Date of Present Constitution:** Dec. 30, 1979 **Legislative Body:** National Assembly (unicameral), with 67 members elected for 5 years. The Assembly of the Togolese People (RPT) is the only party **Local Government:** 5 regions, headed by appointed inspectors

**Ethnic Composition:** Of the nation's 18 major ethnic groups, the dominant ones are the Ewe and Mina in the south and the Kabyé in the north **Population Distribution:** 15% urban **Density:** 113 inhabitants per sq. mi.

**Largest Cities:** (1974 est.) Lomé 214,200, Sokodé 31,800

**Per Capita Income:** $322 (1980) **Gross Domestic Product (GDP):** $837 million (1980) **Economic Statistics:** In 1973, 44% of GDP was from agriculture (coffee, cocoa, cotton, peanuts, yams, cassava, corn, millet, sorghum, rice); 20% from trade and services; 18% from mining (phosphates) and manufacturing (food processing, cement, a brewery, textile mills) **Minerals and Mining:** Phosphates are abundant; there are iron ore and limestone deposits **Labor Force:** 730,000, with 78% in agriculture and 22% in industry. There are 30,000 wage earners **Foreign Trade:** Exports, mainly phosphates, cocoa, coffee, peanuts, palm nuts, and cotton, totaled $354 million in 1980. Imports, chiefly cotton textiles, machinery, motor vehicles, tobacco, and petroleum products, totaled $542 million **Principal Trade Partners:** France, Japan, Britain, West Germany, United States, Netherlands, Yugoslavia

**Vital Statistics:** Birthrate, 48.8 per 1,000 of pop. (1980); death rate, 19 **Life Expectancy:** 40 years **Health Statistics:** 684 inhabitants per hospital bed; 23,500 per physician (1977) **Infant Mortality:** 127 per 1,000 births **Illiteracy:** 84% **Primary and Secondary School Enrollment:** 476,755 (1976) **Enrollment in Higher Education:** 2,353 (1975) **GNP Expended on Education:** 6.7% (1976)

**Transportation:** Paved roads total 764 mi. **Motor Vehicles:** 20,000 (1974) **Passenger Cars:** 13,000 **Railway Mileage:** 274 **Ports:** Lomé, Kpémé **Major Airlines:** Air Afrique maintains international services **Communications: Radio Transmitters:** 6 **Receivers:** 52,000 (1976) **Television Transmitters:** 3 **Telephones:** 10,000 (1978) **Newspapers:** 1 daily, 3 copies per 1,000 inhabitants (1976)

**Weights and Measures:** Metric system **Travel Requirements:** Passport; visa not required for stay up to 3 months

One of West Africa's smallest countries, Togo has had a disproportionate amount of trouble since it attained independence from France in 1960. The country's first president, Sylvanus Olympio, was assassinated. He was succeeded by his brother-in-law, the late Nicolas Grunitzky, the son of a Polish father and a Togolese mother.

The Grunitzky government became increasingly insecure, and on January 13, 1967 Grunitzky was ousted by then Lt. Col. Étienne Eyadéma (now Gen. Gnassingbé Eyadéma). Eyadéma admitted that he was responsible for the killing of President Olympio in the 1963 coup.

Eyadéma has maintained firm control over the country. With political stability, the nation's economy—based on phosphates, cocoa, and coffee—has shown steady progress. The government also hopes to exploit the country's large limestone deposits. Largely because of improving economic conditions, an attempted coup in August 1970 was taken with relative calm by the Togolese. Nevertheless, President Eyadéma charged that a French mining company had plotted to kill him by causing the crash of an airplane in which he was a passenger in 1974. Two weeks earlier, Eyadéma had announced a 15 percent increase in the government's controlling interest in the mining company. Shortly after making the charges, the Eyadéma government took over the mining facilities.

Liberal trade policies have strengthened an otherwise feeble Togolese economy. Following independence, Togo was the only former French African colony not to give preferential tariff treatment to French goods. As a result, imports from all countries enter Togo at the same relatively low rates. Togo's famous marketing women have consequently benefited from the lower prices generated by the competition in imports.

Although officially nonaligned, Togo has sought closer identification with the Third World, but maintains close ties with Western nations. France remains Togo's principal trading partner.

**HISTORY:** The Ewes, who now constitute the population of southern Togo, moved into the region from the Niger River Valley between the 12th and 14th centuries. Portuguese explorers and traders visited the coast of Togo in the 15th and 16th centuries. During the next two centuries, the coastal region was a major raiding ground for European traders in search of slaves, gaining Togo the name "Coast of Slaves." In 1884, Germany set up a small protectorate on the coast and later expanded inland
**1914:** Togoland is occupied by the French in the east and by the British in the west after the outbreak of World War I

**1922:** League of Nations confirms a French mandate in eastern Togoland and a British mandate in western Togoland
**1946:** United Nations changes the mandates to trusteeships
**1956:** British Togoland votes to join the Gold Coast; as the result of a plebiscite among the French-ruled Togolese, French Togoland is made an autonomous republic within the French Union, but the UN Trusteeship Council rejects this procedure
**1958:** In a UN-supervised election, the Committee for Togolese Unity party (CTU), wins control of Togo's legislature; its leader, Sylvanus Olympio, becomes premier
**1960:** French Togoland becomes the independent Republic of Togo, with Sylvanus Olympio as president
**1963:** Olympio, a southerner, is assassinated by a group of northern noncommissioned army officers; Nicolas Grunitzky, leader of the Togolese Party for Progress, is named president
**1967:** Army chief of staff Lt. Col. Étienne Eyadéma overthrows the Grunitzky government, names himself president, and institutes direct military rule; the constitution is suspended, the National Assembly dissolved, and all political activity prohibited
**1969:** After carefully staged demonstrations demanding that he remain as president, Eyadéma announces he has "acceded to the popular will"
**1970-77:** Government thwarts three plots to overthrow Eyadéma
**1979:** Regime convicts 13 of conspiracies, including two sons of Sylvanus Olympio living in exile. Eyadéma is reelected to another seven-year term under new constitution which creates a parliament to replace the one he dissolved in 1967
**1980:** Eyadéma celebrates proclamation of Third Togolese Republic Jan. 13 by freeing 34 political prisoners and 200 criminals. Forty of his opponents briefly occupy embassy in Paris
**1981:** IMF issues special drawing rights worth $58 million to support Togolese stabilization program for 1981-82

## TONGA

**Area:** 270 sq. mi. **Population:** 97,000 (1980 est.)

**Official Name:** Kingdom of Tonga **Capital:** Nuku'alofa **Nationality:** Tongan **Languages:** Tongan and English **Religion:** Christian, with 60% belonging to sects of the Wesleyan (Methodist) faith, and 20% to the Latter Day Saints (Mormons) **Flag:** A red field with a white rectangle in the upper left containing a red cross **Anthem:** National Anthem, beginning "O Almighty God above" **Currency:** Pa'anga (0.88 per U.S. $1)

**Location:** Southwest Pacific Ocean. An archipelago of 150 islands (45 inhabited), covering 100,000 sq. mi. of sea (24°-15°S., 173°-180°W.), about 400 miles east of Fiji **Features:** There are 3 principal groups. Divided by a north-south line, the eastern chain (including the main island of Tongatapu) is low-lying coralline. The western chain (Ha'apai and Vava'u groups) is volcanic

**Head of State and of Government:** King Taufa'ahau Tupou IV, born 1918, crowned in 1967. He is also president of the appointed Privy Council (cabinet) which includes the prime minister, Prince Fatafehi Tu'ipelehake, born 1922, appointed 1965 **Effective Date of Present Constitution:** 1875, revised 1970 **Legislative Body:** Parliament (unicameral Legislative Assembly), consisting of the cabinet ministers, 7 nobles elected by the 33 hereditary nobles, 7 elected by adult suffrage for 3 years, and the ex-officio governors of Ha'apai and Vava'u **Local Government:** 3 island districts, under appointed governors

**Ethnic Composition:** The Tongans are Polynesians, and make up 98% of the population, which also includes small groups of other Pacific islanders, Europeans and mixed **Population Distribution:** 60% is on Tongatapu **Density:** 359 inhabitants per sq. mi.

**Largest Cities:** (1976 census) Nuku'alofa 18,356

**Per Capita Income:** $370 (1976) **Gross National Product (GNP):** $34 million (1976) **Economic Statistics:** The economy is based on agriculture, (sweet potatoes, yams, taro, tapioca, cassava, corn, coconuts, bananas, vanilla, pineapples, melons, fish, citrus fruits, livestock) and manufacturing (coconut and agricultural processing and canning, coir, tobacco, handicrafts, plastic products) **Minerals and Mining:** None **Labor Force:** 9,300 in agriculture, 9,000 in services and government, 400 in industry and commerce (1976) **Foreign Trade:** Exports, chiefly copra, vanilla and bananas, totaled $5.6 million in 1978. Imports, mainly food, fuels and textiles, totaled $12.4 million **Principal Trade Partners:** Australia, New Zealand, Britain, Japan, Fiji, Netherlands

**Vital Statistics:** Birthrate, 13 per 1,000 of pop. (1976); death rate, 1.9 **Life Expectancy:** 56 years **Health Statistics:** 281 inhabitants per hospital bed; 3,000 per physician (1977) **Infant Mortality:** 20.5 per 1,000 births **Illiteracy:** Negligible **Primary and Secondary School Enrollment:** 30,825 (1976) **Enrollment in Higher Education:** 15 (1976), with 116 studying abroad (1974) **GNP Expended on Education:** 4.4% (1973)

**Transportation:** Surfaced roads total 121 mi. **Motor Vehicles:** 1,700 (1978) **Passenger Cars:** 800 **Railway Mileage:** None **Ports:** Nuku'alofa, Neiafu, Pangai **Major Airlines:** Air Pacific and Polynesian Airlines operate international services; South Pacific Islands Airways operates domestically **Communications: Radio Transmitters:** 1 **Receivers:** 15,000 (1976) **Television:** None **Telephones:** 1,090 (1974) **Newspapers:** 1 weekly, 49 copies per 1,000 inhabitants (1974)

**Weights and Measures:** Metric system **Travel Requirements:** Passport, no visa for 30 days, onward ticket

Though comprising 150 coral and volcanic islands, the Pacific kingdom of Tonga is considered to be one of the world's tiniest countries. For 70 years, it was a British protectorate, becoming an independent nation in the British Commonwealth in 1970. With independence, Tonga has moved to broaden the base of its economy, which has been based on the export of copra, bananas and coconuts.

There are two long-range hopes for broadening the economy. One is oil, the existence of which was discovered through seepage into water wells. An agreement with an international consortium provides that the country will get half the profits from possible oil production.

The other hope is to make Tonga a vacation paradise, with the kingdom looking for further economic development stemming from earnings from planned tourist hotels. Present air service to Tonga is only by small regional airlines that fly from Samoa and Fiji. The drive to independence from Britain was spurred by reported British reluctance to encourage the building of a jetport. In 1976 the Soviets agreed to upgrade the airport and Tonga's dockyard in return for the establishment of fisheries. Japan also expressed interest in Tonga through the signing of an agreement on hotel and fisheries development.

However, King Taufa'ahau Tupou IV has cautioned his countrymen, who wear *ta'ovalas*, or woven mats, around their waists, against basing their future on income from tourism, warning that "if too much tourism happens, we will become like Hawaii, where there are no more Hawaiians."

**HISTORY:** Tonga was at one time ruled by a line of sacred kings, one of whom eventually divested himself of his executive powers and delegated them to a temporal king. The system of dual kingship had become firmly established by the 17th century, when the first European contact was made by Dutch navigators. The peaceful conditions on the islands so impressed the 18th-century explorer Captain James Cook that he christened one of them the Friendly Island, a name later applied to the whole group. Within a few years of his departure, however, the islands were rent by civil war
**1845-93:** Taufa'ahau, a leading chief, rules over Tonga as King George Tupou I after suppressing civil war. He makes treaties with France, Germany, the United States and Britain, all of which recognize his sovereignty, and introduces parliamentary government and a system under which every male taxpayer is entitled to eight and one-quarter acres of suitable farmland
**1900:** Tonga becomes a British protectorate
**1918-65:** Reign of Queen Salote, granddaughter of George Tupou I, sees the elimination of illiteracy and of Tonga's national debt
**1970:** Tonga gains independence from Britain
**1978:** Tonga's Bank of the South Pacific declared bankrupt after its president Jack Meier flees, defaulting on $600,000 contract to develop airport to handle jumbo jets
**1979:** Libya gives Tonga a $3-million loan to finish airport
**1980:** Tonga's economy suffers from drop in copra prices, but gains from new trade pact with Australia and New Zealand
**1981:** Legislative Assembly elections show conservative trend
**1982:** Worst cyclone in islands' history kills dozens, leaves thousands homeless, destroys food crops in many areas

## TRINIDAD AND TOBAGO

**Area:** 1,980 sq. mi. **Population:** 1,067,108 (1980 census)

**Official Name:** Republic of Trinidad and Tobago **Capital:** Port-of-Spain **Nationality:** Trinidadian, Tobagonian **Languages:** English is the official and predominant language; Hindi and other Indian languages are also spoken by a small minority **Religion:** About 49% Christian, chiefly Roman Catholic and Anglican; 23% Hindu; 6% Moslem **Flag:** Red with a black diagonal stripe bordered in white running from upper left to lower right **Anthem:** National Anthem, beginning "Forged from the love of liberty" **Currency:** Trinidad/Tobago dollar (2.4 per U.S. $1)

**Location:** West Indies. Trinidad and Tobago are the most southerly of the Lesser Antilles. They lie 7 miles northeast of the Venezuelan coast and are separated from each other by a 19-mile channel **Features:** Three relatively low mountain ranges cross Trinidad from east to west. The land between the northern and central ranges is flat and well watered; south of the central range it is undulating. On Tobago, a main ridge of volcanic origin runs down the center of the island **Chief Rivers:** Ortoire, Caroni, Oropuche

**Head of State:** President Ellis Emmanuel Innocent Clarke, born 1917, elected by Parliament 1976 **Head of Government:** Prime Minister: George M. Chambers, born 1929, appointed March 1981 **Effective Date of Present Constitution:** August 1976 **Legislative Body:** Parliament (bicameral), consisting of a Senate with 31 appointed members, and a House of Representatives with 36 members elected for 5 years **Local Government:** 8 counties, governed by elected councils. Tobago has an elected House of Assembly

**Ethnic Composition:** 43% of Trinidad's population is black, 40% East Indian, 14% of mixed ancestry, 2% Chinese, and 1% European. Tobago's population is largely black **Population Distribution:** 49% urban **Density:** 539 inhabitants per sq. mi.

**Largest Cities:** (1980 census) Port-of-Spain 67,978, San Fernando 33,490, Arima 11,390

**Per Capita Income:** $3,763 (1980) **Gross National Product (GNP):** $4.2 billion (1980) **Economic Statistics:** Trinidad is a major producer of crude oil and is also a major supplier of natural asphalt. Chief crops are sugar, fruits, bananas, coconuts, cocoa, and rice. Industries are oil refining and the manufacture of sugar, chemicals, fertilizers, molasses, rum, fruit juices, and cotton textiles. Tourism is important **Minerals and Mining:** Petroleum, lignite, asphalt, coal, gypsum, iron, clay, and natural gas **Labor Force:** 395,800 (1978), with 50% in manufacturing and construction, 19% in commerce and transportation and 13% in agriculture **Foreign Trade:** Exports, mainly mineral fuels, lubricants and related products, sugar, chemicals, fertilizers, cocoa, fruits and vegetables, and coffee, totaled $4 billion in 1980. Imports, chiefly petroleum for refining, machinery and transportation equipment, foodstuffs, manufactured goods by material, and chemicals, totaled $3.2 billion **Principal Trade Partners:** United States, Britain, Saudi Arabia, Indonesia, Caribbean countries, Canada, Japan, Netherlands

**Vital Statistics:** Birthrate, 25.1 per 1,000 of pop. (1979); death rate, 6.5 **Life Expectancy:** 66 years **Health Statistics:** 224 inhabitants per hospital bed; 1,964 per physician (1975) **Infant Mortality:** 26.4 per 1,000 births **Illiteracy:** 5% **Primary and Secondary School Enrollment:** 183,238 (1975) **Enrollment in Higher Education:** 2,962 (1974) **GNP Expended on Education:** 4.1% (1973)

**Transportation:** Paved roads total 2,480 mi. **Motor Vehicles:** 168,800 (1978) **Passenger Cars:** 131,500 **Railway Mileage:** None **Ports:** Port-of-Spain, Pte-à-Pierre, Point Lisas **Major Airlines:** British West Indian Airways (BWIA) operates internationally **Communications: Radio Transmitters:** 4 **Receivers:** 270,000 (1976) **Television Transmitters:** 3 **Receivers:** 110,000 (1976) **Telephones:** 75,000 (1977) **Newspapers:** 3 dailies (1976), 92 copies per 1,000 inhabitants (1975)

**Weights and Measures:** British standards are used; the metric system is being introduced **Travel Requirements:** Passport; visa not required for stay up to 2 months

---

Trinidad's petroleum-fed industry has long been the most advanced in the former British West Indies. The island is a major oil transshipment center and, although gradual depletion of its own offshore oil deposits is reducing its importance as a petroleum exporter, it has virtually unlimited reserves of natural gas.

The economic problems are those of any developing country—lack of investment capital, shortage of jobs and lack of skilled personnel to fill those that are available, a small market for the products of light industry, and lack of administrative and technical capability below the top echelons of business and government. However, the democratic legislative and judicial structure inherited from the British has given the nation stability.

Trinidad's main problem is the lack of jobs, with the unemployment rate hovering around 15 percent and mainly affecting the islands' blacks—43 percent of the population. A development program with large investment incentives for foreign capital and high import duties to protect local products have kept joblessness from rising much higher, and a family planning program has substantially reduced the rate of population growth—once the highest in the Caribbean area.

These policies were the work of the island's long-dominant political party, the People's National Movement (PNM), created and led by one of the West Indies' most impressive statesmen, Eric Eustace Williams, Trinidad's first prime minister, who served from 1962 until his death in March 1981. Those policies were only slightly modified by his successor, George M. Chambers, after the PNM swept the elections of late 1981. Continuing problems included the racial orientation of the nation's politics (with the PNM regarded as the "party of the blacks") and the growth of separatist sentiment on the smaller island of Tobago—linked to Trinidad for nearly a century.

**HISTORY:** Trinidad and Tobago were discovered by Columbus in 1498 but were long ignored by the Spaniards because of the lack of precious metals in the islands. Spanish colonists began to establish plantations on Trinidad in the 17th century, importing African slaves to work them. The British captured the island in 1797 and in 1802 it was formally ceded to Britain. Tobago changed hands repeatedly during the 17th and 18th centuries, and in 1814 passed under the British crown

**1834:** Slavery is abolished in Trinidad

**1845:** Trinidad begins to import contract workers from India to replace the former slaves

**1889:** Trinidad and Tobago are amalgamated into a single colony

**1958:** Trinidad and Tobago joins the West Indies Federation

**1962:** Federation is dissolved; Trinidad and Tobago becomes independent

**1970:** Government restores order after island is rocked by black power demonstrations and mutiny in armed forces

**1971:** Elections result in complete victory for the People's National Movement under Prime Minister Dr. Eric Williams

**1975:** Strikes paralyze oil and sugar industries, causing worst government crisis since black power unrest in 1970

**1976:** Trinidad and Tobago becomes a republic, ending a 179-year link with the British monarchy. Governor General Sir Ellis Clarke becomes the first president. People's National Movement retains majority in Parliament following the general elections

**1978:** The nation's reserves of dry natural gas are put at 12 trillion cu. ft., and drilling continues

**1980:** Tobago gets its first island legislature since independence; voters there give a majority of seats to the secessionist Democratic Action Congress party

**1981:** Prime Minister Eric Williams dies on March 29. His successor, George M. Chambers, leads PNM to sweeping victory in parliamentary elections in November

**1982:** Chambers trims heavy industry subsidies as oil production slows and annual food-import bill nears $1 billion

---

## TUNISIA

**Area:** 63,170 sq. mi. **Population:** 6,392,000 (1980 est.)

**Official Name:** Republic of Tunisia **Capital:** Tunis **Nationality:** Tunisian **Languages:** Arabic is the official language, but French is widely used **Religion:** 99% are Moslems; and Islam is the official religion **Flag:** A red field with a white disc containing a red crescent and star in the center **Anthem:** National Anthem, beginning "Immortal and precious the blood we have shed" **Currency:** Tunisian dinar (0.56 per U.S. $1)

**Location:** North Africa. Tunisia is bounded on the north and east by the Mediterranean Sea, on the south by Libya, and on the west by Algeria **Features:** The country consists of a wooded and fertile region in the north, a central region comprising the coastal plains, and a southern region bordering the Sahara **Chief River:** Medjerda

**Head of State and of Government:** President Habib Bourguiba, born 1903, named president for life in 1975. He is assisted by a premier, Mohamed Mzali, appointed 1980 **Effective Date of Present Constitution:** 1959 **Legislative Body:** National Assembly (unicameral), consisting of 136 members elected by universal suffrage for 5 years **Local Government:** 21 governorates

**Ethnic Composition:** The population is largely Arab, with a Berber minority; Europeans number about 50,000 **Population Distribution:** 49% urban **Density:** 101 inhabitants per sq. mi.

**Largest Cities:** (1975 census—Metropolitan Areas) Tunis 873,515, Sfax 256,739, Bizerte 109,879, Sousse 102,097, Kairouan 67,589

**Per Capita Income:** $1,207 (1980) **Gross National Product (GNP):** $7.8 billion (1980) **Economic Statistics:** 30% of the GNP is derived from services; 28% from industry including mining; 23% from commerce and finance; 19% from agriculture **Minerals and Mining:** There are large phosphate deposits and smaller amounts of oil, natural gas, lead, zinc **Labor Force:** 1,581,700, with 35% in agriculture, 22% in industry and commerce, and 11% in services **Foreign Trade:** Exports, chiefly petroleum, phosphates, olive oil, wine, and textiles, totaled $2.3 billion in 1980. Imports, mainly foodstuffs, industrial raw materials, machinery and equipment, and transportation equipment, totaled $2.8 billion **Principal Trade Partners:** EC countries, United States, Saudi Arabia

**Vital Statistics:** Birthrate, 35 per 1,000 of pop. (1980); death rate, 11.5 **Life Expectancy:** 58 years **Health Statistics:** 428 inhabitants per hospital bed; 4,675 per physician (1976) **Infant Mortality:** 52.1 per 1,000 births **Illiteracy:** 38% **Primary and Secondary School Enrollment:** 1,222,776 (1977) **Enrollment in Higher Education:** 23,137 (1976) **GNP Expended on Education:** 4.9% (1975)

**Transportation:** Paved roads total 6,663 mi. **Motor Vehicles:** 169,600 (1975) **Passenger Cars:** 102,600 **Railway Mileage:** 1,256 **Ports:** Tunis, Sousse, Sfax, Bizerte, Skhirra **Major Airlines:** Tunis Air, a government-owned line, operates domestically and internationally **Communications: Radio Transmitters:** 12 **Receivers:** 280,000 (1975) **Television Transmitters:** 11 **Receivers:** 208,000 (1976) **Telephones:** 158,000 (1978) **Newspapers:** 5 dailies (1977), 33 copies per 1,0000 inhabitants (1975)

**Weights and Measures:** Metric system **Travel Requirements:** Passport, no visa for 4 months **International Dialing Code:** 216

Wedged in between Algeria and Libya—two larger and more militant neighbors—Tunisia has traditionally been one of the most stable and moderate Arab countries.

No Arab country has been more closely identified with one individual than Tunisia with Habib Bourguiba, its only president since the establishment of the republic in 1957. Bourguiba has long been one of the most magnetic and controversial figures in the Arab world. A professed "pragmatic idealist," he has befriended both the West and the Soviet Union and has not hesitated to quarrel publicly over the Arab struggle against Israel. His dovish views on that subject havve infuriated many Arab leaders. However, Tunisia gained some prestige in the Arab world after the 1970 Jordanian civil war, which was mediated by an inter-Arab conciliation mission headed by Bourguiba's personal envoy. Moreover, Tunisia has condemned the peace treaty between Egypt and Israel.

The only Arab President outside of Lebanon without a military background, Bourguiba is a French-educated lawyer. He brought to Tunisia a benevolent despotism that has been comparatively free of corruption, and he has permitted relative individual freedom.

As part of a program to modernize the country, special attention was placed on the status of women, who enjoy few rights in much of the Arab world. Polygamy was outlawed; the marriageable age for girls was raised from 15 to 17; and divorce was made a matter of court discretion, rather than that of the husband.

The increase in Tunisia's literacy rate in the last decade was among the most rapid in the world, although some 38 percent of the population has had no schooling. In fact, Tunisia is turning out more educated people than the economy can absorb and they have trouble in finding suitable jobs.

Economically, Tunisia is a significant producer of phosphates, oil, textiles and olives. The government has actively promoted foreign investment in all of these areas, although France remains Tunisia's principal trade partner. Since a 1976 trade agreement with the European Community, the first such pact signed with an Arab country, it is expected that large-scale innvestment will increase greatly.

Relations have deteriorated between Tunisia and neighboring Libya since a failed merger attempt in 1974, attributed to Tunisia's more moderate Arab-Israeli stance. A further erosion of relations occurred after a 1976 assassination plot against Bourguiba by Libyan commandos was uncovered. Subsequently, Tunisian workers were expelled from Libya, and diplomats were withdrawn from both countries. Relations have been restored.

Tunisia today is a nation poised, not always peacefully, on the brink of change. Many Tunisians contend that although a single party system was tolerable during the early years of nationhood, the time has come for full freedom of political expression. They are also concerned that a struggle for power could destroy Tunisian stability. In January 1978, Tunisia was rocked by an outbreak of antigovernment violence when a general strike by the nation's powerful labor unions escalated into a direct challenge to Bourguiba's leadership. Rioting in Tunis and other cities left at least 100 dead and about 450 injured. The government blamed the disorders on "extremists" who were supported by Libya's leftist leaders. In 1980 an attack on Gafsa by Tunisian expatriated workers resulted in 41 deaths, and the Tunisian government again held Libya responsible for the attack.

Although the Communists and other political groups were allowed to participate in the November 1981 parliamentary elections, the ruling Destour Socialist party won all assembly seats.

**HISTORY:** Tunisia was settled by seafaring Phoenicians as far back as the 12th century B.C. In the 6th century B.C. the city of Carthage was founded near modern Tunis and became the center of a powerful city-state that lasted until 146 B.C., when it was destroyed by Rome. A new city of Carthage, built by Julius Caesar, was conquered by the Vandals in the 55th century A.D. and was later recovered for the Byzantine Empire. The Arabs conquered the region in the 7th century and during the Middle Ages transformed it into a major center of Arab power

**1574:** Turks add Tunisia to Ottoman Empire, but under its Turkish governors (beys) country enjoys virtual independence

**1705:** Hussein dynasty of hereditary beys is established

**1881:** Tunisia becomes a French protectorate

**1934:** Habib Bourguiba founds Neo-Destour (New Constitution) Party, which becomes spearhead of independence movement

**1942-43:** Tunisia becomes the site of World War II campaigns

**1956:** Tunisia wins independence

**1957:** Bey Sidi Lamine is deposed; Tunisia is proclaimed a republic; Bourguiba is elected as president

**1963:** France evacuates naval base at Bizerte

**1968:** Tunisia, at meeting of Arab League in Cairo, accuses Egypt of having provoked Six-Day War with Israel in 1967 and calls for Arab recognition of Israel; charges provoke uproar and Tunisian delegation walks out of meeting

**1973:** Tunisia sends token force to aid Arabs in Yom Kippur War

**1974:** Merger is proposed between Libya and Tunisia to form single nation, but the plan fails to materialize

**1975:** Bourguiba is named president for life

**1977:** Tunisian police arrest alleged Libyan agents suspected of plotting to assassinate Premier Hédi Nouira

**1978:** At least 100 die as general strike leads to worst antigovernment violence since nation gained independence

**1980:** Tunisia blames Libya for attack on Gafsa by Tunisia expatriated workers. Mohamed Mzali succeeds ailing Nouira as premier

**1981:** First multiparty legislative elections in November result in ruling Destour Socialist party candidates winning all the seats

## TURKEY

**Area:** 300,946 sq. mi. **Population:** 45,217,556 (1980 census)

**Official Name:** Republic of Turkey **Capital:** Ankara **Nationality:** Turkish **Languages:** Turkish is the official language and is spoken by 90% of the population; Kurdish (7%) and Arabic are spoken by the leading minorities **Religion:** 98% Sunni Moslem; the rest are Christians and Jews **Flag:** A white star and crescent on a red field **Anthem:** March of Independence **Currency:** Turkish lira (153 per U.S. $1)

**Location:** Asia Minor and Southeast Europe. Asiatic Turkey (Asia Minor) occupies 97% of the total area. Turkey is bounded on the north by the Black Sea, on the northeast by the USSR, on the east by

Iran, on the south by Iraq, Syria, and the Mediterranean Sea, on the west by the Aegean Sea, and on the northwest by Greece and Bulgaria **Features:** European Turkey (Eastern Thrace) is separated from Asia Minor by the Dardanelles, the Sea of Marmara, and the Bosporus. The European part consists of rolling agricultural land. Asiatic Turkey has fertile coastal strips and is occupied in the center by the semiarid Anatolian plateau, surrounded by hills and mountains **Chief Rivers:** Kizilirmak, Yesilirmak, Seyhan, Menderes, Tigris (Dicle), Euphrates (Firat), Sakarya

**Head of State:** Following the coup of Sept. 12, 1980, the country is governed by a five-man National Security Council headed by Gen. Kenan Evren, born 1918, assisted by a prime minister, Adm. Bulent Ulusu **Effective Date of Present Constitution:** The draft of a new constitution was published on July 17, 1982. Under its terms the president would have great power. The new constitution must be approved by the voters in a national referendum before it can become effective **Legislative Body:** Following the 1980 coup, the National Security Council assumed all legislative functions. The proposed constitution provides for a 408-member national assembly **Local Government:** 67 provinces, under governors

**Ethnic Composition:** Turks constitute 90% of the population; ethnic minorities include 7% Kurds and small groups of Greeks, Armenians, and Jews **Population Distribution:** 45% urban **Density:** 150 inhabitants per sq. mi.

**Largest Cities:** (1980 census) Istanbul 2,853,539, Ankara 2,203,729, Izmir 753,749, Adana 568,513, Bursa 466,178, Gaziantep 371,000, Konya 325,850, Eskisehir 309,335

**Per Capita Income:** $865 (1980) **Gross Domestic Product (GDP):** $39.5 billion (1980) **Economic Statistics:** About 27% of the GDP is derived from agriculture (cereals, tobacco, grapes, fruits, and cotton) and animal husbandry and 21% from industry (steel, iron, sugar and cotton refining, tires, textiles, fertilizers) **Minerals and Mining:** Exploited minerals include copper, chrome (about 8% of the world's production), boracite, mercury, iron, manganese, coal, oil, natural gas **Labor Force:** 17,000,000 (1979), with 60% in agriculture, and 15% in industry **Foreign Trade:** Exports, mainly tobacco, cotton, hazelnuts, raisins, chrome, and citrus fruits, totaled $2.3 billion in 1979. Imports, chiefly machinery and transportation equipment, petroleum products, iron, steel and related products, fertilizers, and plastics, totaled $5.1 billion **Principal Trade Partners:** West Germany, France, Iraq, United States, Britain, Switzerland, Italy, U.S.S.R.

**Vital Statistics:** Birthrate, 39.6 per 1,000 of pop. (1967); death rate, 14.6 **Life Expectancy:** 57 years **Health Statistics:** 506 inhabitants per hospital bed; 1,772 per physician (1977) **Infant Mortality:** 145 per 1,000 births **Illiteracy:** 38% **Primary and Secondary School Enrollment:** 5,689,506 (1974) **Enrollment in Higher Education:** 322,965 (1975) **GNP Expended on Education:** 4.6% (1976)

**Transportation:** Paved roads total 13,000 mi. **Motor Vehicles:** 702,300 (1976) **Passenger Cars:** 471,500 **Railway Mileage:** 5,700 **Ports:** Istanbul, Izmir, Mersin, Samsun, Iskenderun, Izmit, Trabzon **Major Airlines:** Turkish Airlines, government owned, operates domestically and internationally **Communications: Radio Transmitters:** 26 **Licenses:** 4,228,000 (1976) **Television Transmitters:** 38 **Receivers:** 1,769,000 (1976) **Telephones:** 1,379,000 (1977) **Newspapers:** 493 dailies (1977)

**Weights and Measures:** Metric system **Travel Requirements:** Passport, no visa for 3 months **International Dialing Code:** 90

---

Modern Turkey is the product of its first president, Mustafa Kemal, later surnamed Kemal Atatürk, or Father of the Turks. He was a dictator who believed that he had to be ruthless in bringing his country into the 20th century. Before his death in 1938, Atatürk cut as many ties with the past as possible. He had the Turkish alphabet transcribed from Arabic to Latin characters, outlawed the wearing in public of the traditional fez for men and the veil for women, and secularized the theocratic Moslem state of the former sultans. Islam is still a strong force among Turks, however; more people from Turkey make the holy pilgrimage to Mecca than from any other Moslem country.

Turkey is still plagued by a wide disparity between life in its more affluent cities and its backward rural areas in Asia Minor. There has been a rapid migration to the cities, causing crowding and a demand for goods and services on the part of the peasant who will wait no longer for the benefits of modernization to reach him.

The country's economy is still largely based on agriculture, but the government has been pushing industrial expansion at a rapid pace, causing a strain resulting in high inflation, a foreign exchange crisis marked by declining foreign reserves, and a huge balance-of-payments deficit.

Turkey's principal concern in foreign policy—other than the presence of the Soviet Union as a neighbor—is a recurring conflict with Greece over the nearby island republic of Cyprus. Turkey has maintained troops on the island since 1974 to protect the Turkish Cypriot community. Despite strong U.S. pressure Turkey's occupation of the northern part of the island continues.

In parliamentary by-elections of October 1979, public discontent with the worsening economy and with escalating street violence led to formation of a new government headed by Suleyman Demirel, leader of the conservative Justice party. But increasing terrorism by both rightist and leftist extremists continued to threaten Turkey's fragile democracy. The violent incidents included the murders of a U.S. soldier and three Americans working in Turkey by a left-wing terrorist group in an Istanbul suburb in December 1979. In July 1980, such prominent Turks as a former premier, Nihat Erim, and a labor leader, Kemal Turkler, were assassinated. It was estimated that more than 5,000 persons had been killed by the end of 1980.

Amid public demands that the army take over the country in the crisis, as it had done during past national emergencies, Turkish military leaders seized power in a bloodless coup on Sept. 12, 1980. The new government was headed by a five-man National Security Council, chaired by Gen. Kenan Evren. It immediately abolished the constitution and arrested thousands of suspected terrorists, of whom eight had been executed by mid-1981.

The military council assumed unlimited powers and banned activities of all political parties. Bulent Ecevit resigned as leader of the Republican People's party to protest the ban. Both Ecevit and Demirel were arrested by the council for making political statements in disregard of a government prohibition. Ecevit served two months' imprisonment for the violation before he was released Feb. 1, 1982, but similar charges against Demirel were dropped. Although martial law continued, the military government announced that a referendum on the country's new constitution would be held in late 1982, and that general elections to the national assembly were set for 1984.

**HISTORY:** Asiatic Turkey is one of the oldest inhabited regions on Earth and for centuries served as a battleground for foreign conquerors. It was the site of the ancient states of Hatti, Urartu, Phrygia, Troy, Lydia, and Armenia. In the 7th century B.C., the Greeks founded the city of Byzantium on the site of present-day Istanbul. It was captured by the Romans in A.D. 196 and later rebuilt as Constantinople by the Christian Emperor Constantine. The Ottoman Empire was founded in 1299 by Turkish tribes from Central Asia on the remnants of the Byzantine and the Seljuk Turkish empires in Asia Minor. With its collapse in 1918, modern Turkey was born. The Turks had absorbed most of the major ethnic groups; the major exception were the Armenians, who were virtually exterminated by Ottoman attacks in the early 20th century

**1920-23:** Allied powers strip Ottoman Empire of its vast possessions, reducing it to a small state; Sultan Mohammed VI accepts Allied terms, but Turkish nationalists rally under Mustafa Kemal, later known as Kemal Atatürk, and organize resistance. Sultan is deposed and Turkey is declared a republic, with Atatürk as president

**1924-38:** A constitution is promulgated, providing for parliamentary government, but Atatürk rules as virtual dictator. He introduces sweeping reforms to westernize Turkey, which undergoes an unparalleled revolutionary transformation

**1950-59:** Celal Bayar, leader of the Democratic party, becomes president, with Adnan Menderes as premier. Turkey joins NATO in 1952. In 1955, Turkey and Iraq sign a mutual defense agreement, the Baghdad Pact. Marshall Plan aid leads to expansion of Turkish economy, but rapid industrialization results in economic crisis, forcing government to adopt restrictive measures to deal with discontent. Menderes is returned to office in 1957 elections; political controls tightened

**1960:** Army junta, led by General Cemal Gursel, stages coup, bans Democratic party, and puts Menderes, Bayar, and hundreds of other Democratic party members on trial for having violated the constitution. Most receive long prison sentences, but Menderes and several others are hanged

**1961-62:** A new constitution providing for a bicameral legislature and a strong executive is approved by referendum. Gursel is elected president and Ismet Inonu becomes premier. An attempted coup by army elements is crushed and many officers purged. Government amnesties most of imprisoned supporters of Menderes but keeps Bayar and a number of others in jail

**1964:** Relations between Turkey and Greece, long embroiled in dispute over Cyprus, become further strained as heavy fighting breaks out between Greek and Turkish Cypriots

**1965:** Suleyman Demirel, leader of Justice party, becomes premier following general elections

**1966:** Gursel falls ill; national assembly chooses General Cevdet Sunay, army chief of staff, to succeed him

**1971:** Following prolonged political and economic unrest, armed forces commanders demand resignation of Demirel government; Nihat Erim is named premier

**1973:** Bulent Ecevit elected premier. Retired Admiral Fahri Korutürk elected president

**1974:** Cypriot National Guard, under Greek officers, overthrows Cyprus President Archbishop Makarios. Turkish troops invade Cyprus and fight Greek Cypriots. Cease-fire arranged by UN representatives. Ecevit's coalition government collapses; interim government formed

**1975:** Citing "lack of progress" in Cyprus peace negotiations, U.S. Congress votes to cut off all military aid to Turkey. Turkey responds by seizing all American installations except the NATO base at Adana. Former Prime Minister Suleyman Demirel forms new coalition government

**1977:** Ecevit's Republican People's party wins close to a majority of parliamentary seats in the general elections. Ecevit resigns the premiership 10 days later after his center-left government loses its first vote of confidence in parliament. Prime Minister Suleyman Demirel forms new government but his coalition soon dissolves. Economy continues serious decline

**1978:** Ecevit named premier. U.S. Congress votes to allow President Carter to end embargo on arms sales to Turkey and provide substantial military aid. U.S. military bases reopen

**1979:** Ecevit's party loses local by-elections; Demirel forms new coalition government. Martial law extends to 19 provinces

**1980:** Political violence escalates, prominent leaders are assassinated. Military leaders, headed by Gen. Kenan Evren, seize power on Sept. 12 and assume unlimited powers; new cabinet appointed with Bülent Ulusu as premier

**1981:** Terrorism is reduced drastically under martial law, but violent acts continue sporadically; Gen. Evren announces that a new constitution restoring democratic rule will be prepared by a constituent assembly (scheduled to meet in 1982)

**1982:** Armenian separatists attack Ankara Airport Aug. 7, demanding release of 85 terrorists held in West; one gunman and 6 others killed and 69 people wounded before authorities capture remaining two terrorists

## TUVALU

**Area:** 19.78 sq. mi. **Population:** 7,349 (1979 census)

**Official Name:** Tuvalu **Capital:** Funafuti **Nationality:** Tuvaluan **Languages:** Tuvaluan and English **Religion:** Christian, mostly Protestant **Flag:** A light blue field with the Union Jack in the upper left corner and nine yellow five-pointed stars in the right half **Anthem:** N.A. **Currency:** Australian dollar (0.94 per U.S. $1)

**Location:** Tuvalu is comprised of nine low-lying coral atolls, eight of which are inhabited; the islands form a chain approximately 360 miles long in the southwest Pacific Ocean (5°30′-11°S., 176°-180°E.). Tuvalu's nearest neighbors are Fiji and Kiribati **Features:** The islands have a tropical climate and are mostly covered with coconut palms

**Head of State:** Queen Elizabeth II through a governor-general, Sir Fiatau Penitala Teo, born 1911, took office 1978 **Head of Government:** Prime Minister: Dr. Tomasi Puapua, took office Sept. 1981 **Effective Date of Present Constitution:** October 1, 1978 **Legislative Body:** Unicameral Parliament, consisting of 12 members elected by universal suffrage for four years **Local Government:** Island councils for the eight inhabited islands

**Ethnic Composition:** Almost entirely Polynesian **Population Distribution:** Non-urban **Density:** 751 inhabitants per sq. mi.

**Largest center:** (1979 census) Funafuti 2,120

**Per Capita Income:** $180 (1975) **Gross National Product (GNP):** 1.2 million (1975) **Economic Statistics:** A large part of personal income in Tuvalu is derived from cash remittances from Tuvaluan men working as seamen and in the phosphate industries of Nauru and Banaba (Ocean Island) in Kiribati. Other income is derived from copra, the chief cash crop, the sale of postage stamps and coins, and handicrafts. Fishing is on a subsistence basis. Other agricultural crops are pulaka (taro), pandanus fruit, bananas and pawpaws **Minerals and Mining:** None **Labor Force:** N.A. **Foreign Trade:** Exports of copra totaled $67,000 in 1977. Copra exports usually average 120 tons per year. Imports, chiefly food and fuel, totaled $1.4 million **Principal Trade Partners:** Australia, Britain

**Vital Statistics:** Birthrate, 23.7 per 1,000 of pop. (1979); death rate, 15 **Life Expectancy:** 58 years **Health Statistics:** 42 inhabitants per hospital bed (1978) **Infant Mortality:** 42 per 1,000 births **Illiteracy:** Over 50% **Primary and Secondary School Enrollment:** 1,788 (1976) **GNP Expended on Education:** N.A.

**Transportation:** Gravel roads total 5 mi. **Motor Vehicles:** About 12 cars on Funafuti **Railway Mileage:** None **Port:** Funafuti **Major Airlines:** Air Pacific provides service to Fiji and Kiribati. See Bee Air operates domestic inter-island service with one 5-passenger seaplane **Communications: Radio Transmitters:** 1 **Receivers:** 4,000 **Television:** None **Telephones:** 300 **Newspapers:** 1 fortnightly

**Weights and Measures:** N.A. **Travel Requirements:** N.A.

On October 1, 1978, the nine atolls of the Ellice Islands (Tuvalu's name before 1975) became the independent nation of Tuvalu (Polynesian for "cluster of eight islands," after the eight inhabited atolls). The main post-independence aim of Tuvalu's people is for greater economic self-sufficiency. This goal, however, is not readily forthcoming. The climate makes these "paradise islands" beautiful to see; but the thin, alkaline soil makes them ill-suited for agriculture. The islands are dotted with coconut palms, and copra is the main export. Handicrafts and subsistence fishing are the chief occupations. The chief source of revenue is from remittances from overseas Tuvaluans, working as seamen or as phosphate workers on nearby Nauru and Banaba (Ocean Island). With the end of phosphate production on Banaba in 1980, the economic impact of returning workers has exacerbated an already serious situation.

Future development will probably center on the potentially rich fishing grounds to be found in Tuvalu's lagoons and ocean waters. The South Pacific Commission plans to open a tuna canning plant, and fisheries and other industrial projects may be forthcoming. Foreign aid will also be important in further development. Great Britain has been the islands' chief benefactor and has built up the new nation's administrative infrastructure, but independence is expected to attract aid and possible investment from Australia, New Zealand, the United States and Japan.

**HISTORY:** Tuvaluans consider Samoa as their ancestral home, with which they share a common Polynesian language and culture. Fishermen are thought to have drifted westward from the central Pacific and populated the islands, which were periodically raided by Micronesians from Tonga and the Gilberts. The Spaniard Mendaña is thought to have sighted Nui in 1568 and Niulakita in 1595. Permanent contact with Westerners came in the late 18th and early 19th centuries; the first European settlers were from the London Missionary Society, who arrived in 1865 and soon converted the islanders to Protestantism. During the "blackbirders" slave trade from 1850 to 1875, the islands' population was reduced from 20,000 to about 3,000

**1856:** Guano Act of U.S. Congress establishes American claims to Funafuti, Nukefetau, Nukulaelae and Niulakita atolls

**1877:** Britain establishes the High Commission for the Western Pacific to stamp out "blackbird" raiders

**1892:** Britain proclaims a protectorate over Ellice Islands and neighboring Gilberts

**1915:** Protectorate reorganized as Gilbert and Ellice Islands Colony

**1973:** Britain appoints commissioner to study growing Polynesian demands for autonomy of the Ellice Islands

**1974:** August-September referendum, observed by UN, shows overwhelming support for separation from Gilbert Islands

**1975:** The islands are established as a separate dependency under British administration under the name *Tuvalu*

**1978:** Independence is declared October 1

**1979:** Prime Minister Toalipi Lauti signs Friendship Treaty with the United States; pact recognizes U.S. renunciation of claims over disputed islands and provides for continued consultations on security and marine reserves

**1980:** Tuvalu reaches agreements with Japan and South Korea on fisheries in nearby seas. Chinese tests of intercontinental ballistic missiles near Tuvalu are protested. Tuvalu signs agreement for better access to Australian and New Zealand markets. Overseas press reports indicate that, in 1978, Lauti handed over $640,000 in government funds to a California businessman for investment in west Texas real estate

**1981:** Criticized for financial policies, Lauti is narrowly defeated in parliamentary leadership ballot. Dr. Tomasi Puapua replaces him

## UGANDA

**Area:** 91,076 sq. mi. **Population:** 12,630,076 (1980 census)

**Official Name:** Republic of Uganda **Capital:** Kampala **Nationality:** Ugandan **Languages:** English is the official language and Swahili is widely used; of the many local languages the most important is Luganda **Religion:** About half the population is Christian, 10% Moslem, and the rest animists **Flag:** 6 alternate horizontal stripes of black, yellow, and red, with the national emblem, a crested crane, in a white circle in the center **Anthem:** National Anthem, beginning "O Uganda! May God uphold thee" **Currency:** Ugandan shilling (85.75 per U.S. $1)

**Location:** East Africa. Landlocked Uganda is bordered on the north by Sudan, on the east by Kenya, on the south by Tanzania, Lake Victoria, and Rwanda, and on the west by Zaire **Features:** Most of the country consists of a plateau about 4,000 feet above sea level. About 18% of the total area consists of swamps and open water, including Lakes Victoria, George, Albert (Mobutu Sese Seko), Edward, and Kyoga. Thick forest covers parts of the south; the north is largely savanna with some semidesert areas in the northeast **Chief Rivers:** Victoria Nile, Albert Nile, Katonga

**Head of State and of Government:** President Milton Obote, born 1925, sworn in on Dec. 15, 1980. He is assisted by Prime Minister Erifasi Otema Allimadi, appointed Dec. 18, 1980 **Effective Date of Present Constitution:** 1967 **Legislative Body:** National Assembly (unicameral) of 126 elected members and 10 members appointed by the army **Local Government:** 10 provinces, divided into 33 districts

**Ethnic Composition:** About 98% of the population is African. The largest tribes include the Baganda (over 1,000,000), Iteso, Banyankore, and Basoga. Asians, mainly of Indian extraction, now number fewer than 500, and Europeans less than 3,500. There are 3,000 Arabs **Population Distribution:** 7% urban **Density:** 139 inhabitants per sq. mi.

**Largest Cities:** (1980 census) Kampala 478,895, Jinja 45,060, Mbale 28,039, Entebbe 20,472

**Per Capita Income:** $256 (1980) **Gross National Product (GNP):** $3.5 billion (1980) **Economic Statistics:** 52.7% of the GNP is derived from agriculture (coffee, cotton, tea, tobacco, sugar); 18.7% from commerce and finance; 15.7% from services; and 12.9% from industry (the manufacture of food products and textiles, cigarettes, brewing, enamel hollow ware, cement, wooden boxes, and soap) **Minerals and Mining:** There are substantial deposits of copper and smaller amounts of cobalt, limestone, tin, beryl and wolfram **Labor Force:** 4,500,000 (1979), with 250,000 in paid labor **Foreign Trade:** Exports, mainly coffee, copper, cotton, tea and feeds, totaled $522 million in 1980. Imports, chiefly machinery and transportation equipment, cotton and synthetic fabrics and petroleum products, totaled $451 million **Principal Trade Partners:** Britain, Kenya, United States, West Germany, Japan, Italy, Spain, India, Turkey

**Vital Statistics:** Birthrate, 44.7 per 1,000 of pop. (1980); death rate, 14.4 **Life Expectancy:** 53 years **Health Statistics:** 636 inhabitants per hospital bed; 24,700 per physician (1975) **Infant Mortality:** 160 per 1,000 births **Illiteracy:** 60% **Primary and Secondary School Enrollment:** 1,103,906 (1976) **Enrollment in Higher Education:** 5,474 (1975) **GNP Expended on Education:** 3.0% (1975)

**Transportation:** Paved roads total 1,200 mi. **Motor Vehicles:** 35,900 (1975) **Passenger Cars:** 27,000 **Railway Mileage:** 756 **Ports:** None **Major Airlines:** Uganda Airlines operates both domestically and internationally **Communications: Radio Transmitters:** 12 **Receivers:** 250,000 (1976) **Television Transmitters:** 9 **Licenses:** 71,000 (1976) **Telephones:** 49,000 (1977) **Newspaperss:** 2 dailies, 3 copies per 1,000 inhabitants (1976)

**Weights and Measures:** Metric system **Travel Requirements:** Passport, visa, $3.15 fee, 1 photo

From the lushly green shores of Lake Victoria to the snow-capped Mountains of the Moon on its western border, Uganda's natural beauty is the fulfillment of a tourist's dream. Until recently elephant herds, great flocks of birds and other wildlife, vivid flowers, neat tea plantations, and farmlands rich in coffee and cotton delighted the visitor and gave support to the country's claim to being "the pearl of East Africa."

But Uganda changed drastically under the harsh regime of Field Marshal Idi Amin Dada. The eight-year reign of terror claimed the lives of possibly as many as 300,000 Ugandans. An estimated 250,000 fled to neighboring Kenya, and many more lived in exile in Britain.

Hopes were bright at the outset of Ugandan independence from British rule in 1962, with Milton Obote, leader of the Uganda People's Congress (UPC), as prime minister. The country became a republic in 1963 and elected as president Mutesa II, the revered *Kabaka* (king) of Buganda, largest of the four old kingdoms. In 1966, Obote, a rival Lango tribesman, forced the *Kabaka* into exile. Under a new constitution adopted in 1967, the kingdoms were abolished; Obote became president.

But in January 1971, Obote was ousted in a coup led by the Ugandan army commander, Maj. Gen. Idi Amin. Amin then declared himself president for life, abolished parliament and purged the judiciary and the civil service. During the next eight years he forced some 50,000 Asians to leave the country and had several thousand Acholi and Lango tribesmen killed. Many other persons died in the purge directed mainly at Christians. As a result of the regime's inefficiency and lavish spending, Uganda's economy deteriorated badly.

Amin committed a fatal mistake in October 1978 when he sent troops into Tanzania and occupied more than 700 square miles of foreign soil. Tanzania quickly counterattacked, carried the war into Uganda the next month, and in April 1979 captured Kampala, whose residents greeted the invaders as liberators. Amin eluded capture and gained asylum in Libya.

Virtually the entire world welcomed Amin's ouster, but Uganda was left in a state of upheaval. Yussufu Lule, the man chosen to succeed Amin, lasted barely two months before political wrangling forced his resignation. He was replaced by Godfrey Binaisa, a longtime defender of human rights. In May 1980 a six-man military commission headed by Paulo Muwanga displaced Binaisa and held power until national elections were held in December. Despite charges of fraud and opposition from the Buganda whose king, the *Kabaka*, Obote had forced into exile, the Uganda People's Congress won 68 of the 126 elected seats in Parliament and Milton Obote became president for a 5-year term.

With many probleems, including famine and violence in the drought-stricken northwest region and uncontrolled rampaging by ill-disciplined soldiers, the withdrawal of the last Tanzanian peacekeeping forces in June 1981 left Obote's hold on Uganda shakier than ever.

**HISTORY:** Until the latter part of the 19th century, Uganda experienced a series of migrations extending over hundreds of years. As a result, a number of major chiefdoms grew up, the most powerful of which were the chiefdom of Bunyoro-Kitara and the rival state of Buganda. Britain established a protectorate over Buganda in 1894 and subsequently extended the protectorate to the rest of Uganda. However, the stubborn independence of Buganda's rulers, which continued well into the 20th century, hampered the development of national unity

**1953:** Kabaka (king) Mutesa II of Buganda is deposed and exiled to London when he refuses to help put down riots by local chiefs

**1955:** British restore Mutesa but stipulate he is to reign as constitutional monarch and that Buganda will participate in the central government of Uganda

UNION OF SOVIET SOCIALIST REPUBLICS
(European Part)
CONIC PROJECTION
MILES
0 50 100 200 300
KILOMETRES
0 100 200 300
National Capitals
Capitals of Union Republics
International boundaries
Union Republic boundaries
Canals
ARCTIC OCEAN
KARA SEA
Novaya Zemlya
BALTIC SEA
BLACK SEA
CASPIAN SEA
Sea of Azov
White Sea
FINLAND
SWEDEN
NORWAY
POLAND
ROMANIA
BULGARIA
TURKEY
IRAN
RUSSIAN SOVIET FEDERATED SOCIALIST REPUBLIC
ESTONIAN S.S.R.
LATVIAN S.S.R.
LITHUANIAN S.S.R.
WHITE RUSSIAN S.S.R.
UKRAINIAN S.S.R.
MOLDAVIAN S.S.R.
GEORGIAN S.S.R.
ARMENIAN S.S.R.
AZERBAIDZHAN S.S.R.
MOSCOW
LENINGRAD
Kiev
Minsk
Tallinn
Riga
Vilna
Kishinev
Tbilisi
Erivan
Baku
Helsinki
Stockholm
Bucharest
Ankara
Istanbul
Archangel (Arkhangel'sk)
Murmansk
Gor'kiy
Kazan'
Kuybyshev
Saratov
Volgograd (Stalingrad)
Rostov
Khar'kov
Odessa
Sverdlovsk
Chelyabinsk
Perm' (Molotov)
Ufa
Orenburg (Chkalov)
Astrakhan'
Caucasus Mts.
Ural Mts.
Longitude East of Greenwich
The government of the United States does not recognize the incorporation of Estonia, Latvia and Lithuania into the Soviet Union.
Post-war territorial changes shown on this map do not necessarily represent the final status of such boundaries. Only after the signing of peace treaties can changes be considered official and definite.

**1962:** Uganda gains independence with a federal constitution that gives Buganda large measure of autonomy; Milton Obote becomes prime minister
**1963:** Post of governor-general is abolished; Mutesa is elected president by parliament
**1966:** Obote removes Mutesa, suspends constitution, abolishes federal system, and assumes full powers of government
**1967:** Uganda adopts republican constitution with a presidential form of government headed by Obote; traditional kingdoms are abolished
**1971:** Obote is ousted in coup led by Maj. Gen. Idi Amin, who assumes presidency; refusal of Tanzania to recognize his government results in minor warfare between the two countries
**1972:** Amin orders the expulsion of the estimated 50,000 Asians in Uganda holding British passports
**1973:** U.S. severs ties with Uganda after repeated threats against U.S. Embassy officials and detention of Peace Corps volunteers
**1976:** Israeli commandos rescue skyjacked hostages being held at Entebbe airport, crippling Amin's Soviet-equipped air force
**1977:** Anglican Archbishop Janani Luwum and two of Amin's cabinet ministers are arrested and murdered; the government claims the three were killed in an automobile accident after attempting to escape. Thirty-three Commonwealth nations, including 13 African nations, condemn Amin's regime for its repression. Thirteen die in new anti-Christian purge; many arrested
**1978:** Ugandan forces invade Tanzania; general war ensues
**1979:** Ugandan rebels join Tanzanian forces in advance on Kampala, which falls on April 12 amid wild rejoicing and looting. Amin flees. Yussufu Lule becomes provisional president; he is replaced in June by Godfrey Binaisa
**1980:** Military Commission ousts Binaisa, May 11. Uganda People's Congress wins majority of seats in Dec. 9-10 elections; Milton Obote is inaugurated president Dec. 15 for 5-year term
**1981:** Tanzania withdraws last of its occupation force. Thousand civilians die in continued fighting between government forces and guerrillas; 120,000 flee to Zaire and elsewhere
**1982:** Exiled leaders Lule and Binaisa, in London, announce united front against Obote. In heaviest fighting since fall of Amin, guerrillas assault army barracks in Kampala, but are driven off. Several thousand suspected guerrillas are arrested and held. Red Cross is ordered out of Uganda

## UNION OF SOVIET SOCIALIST REPUBLICS (SOVIET UNION)

**Area:** 8,649,490 sq. mi. **Population:** 268,800,000 (1982 est.) **Population of Union Republics:** (1979 census) Russian S.F.S.R. 137,551,000, Ukraine 49,755,000, Uzbek 15,391,000, Kazakh 14,681,000, Byelorussia 9,560,000, Azerbaidzhan 6,028,000, Georgia 5,015,000, Moldavia 3,947,000, Tadzhik 3,801,000, Kirgiz 3,529,000, Lithuania 3,398,000, Armenia 3,031,000, Turkmen 2,759,000, Latvia 2,521,000, Estonia 1,466,000

**Official Name:** Union of Soviet Socialist Republics **Capital:** Moscow **Nationality:** Soviet **Languages:** Russian, the official language, is the native tongue of about 60% of the population and is spoken as a second language by less than half of the rest; other languages are Ukrainian, Byelorussian, Lithuanian, Latvian, Estonian, Moldavian, Yiddish, Georgian, Armenian, Uzbek, Tatar, Kazakh, Azerbaijani, and over 100 other languages and dialects **Religion:** Atheism, officially propagated by the government, is followed by about 70% of the population; there are also 18% Russian Orthodox, 9% Moslems, and small groups of Roman Catholics, Protestants, Jews, and Buddhists **Flag:** Red field with a golden hammer and sickle (representing the industrial and farm workers) under a golden star in the upper left corner **Anthem:** Hymn of the Soviet Union **Currency:** Ruble (0.71 per U.S. $1)

**Location:** Northern Eurasia, from the Baltic Sea to the Pacific, with the Arctic Ocean on the north. The largest country in the world, the USSR is bordered on the northwest by Norway and Finland; on the west by Poland, Czechoslovakia, Hungary, and Romania; on the south by Turkey, Iran, and Afghanistan, and on the southeast by China, Mongolia, and North Korea **Features:** In the west, from the Pripet Marshes near the Polish frontier to the Ural Mountains, the land consists of a broad plain broken by occasional low hills and crossed by numerous rivers. Between the Black and Caspian seas lie the Caucasus Mountains. East of the Ural Mountains, which mark the traditional division between European and Asiatic Russia, are the Aral Sea, vast Siberian lowlands, steppes, and deserts of Central Asia. Beyond are the vast Siberian highlands and mountain ranges of the Soviet Far East. The highest ranges lie along the Chinese and Mongolian borders **Chief Rivers:** In Europe, the Dnieper, Dniester, Don, Volga; in Asia, the Ob, Yenisey, Lena, Amur, Kolyma, Amu Darya, Syr Darya

**Political Leader and Head of State:** Chairman of the Presidium of the Supreme Soviet (President) and General Secretary of the Central Committee of the Communist Party: Marshal Leonid Ilyich Brezhnev, born 1906, appointed general secretary in 1964 and president in 1977 **Head of Government:** Chairman of the Council of Ministers (Premier): Nikolai Aleksandrovich Tikhonov, born 1905, appointed 1980 **Effective Date of Present Constitution:** 1977 **Legislative Body:** Supreme Soviet (bicameral), consisting of the Soviet (Council) of the Union and the Soviet of Nationalities. The Soviet of the Union has 767 members elected on the basis of population; the Soviet of Nationalities has 750 elected on the basis of territorial units. Elections are called for every 5 years. Formal power is vested in the Presidium of the Supreme Soviet, which also appoints the Council of Ministers. Under Communist party direction, the council supervises all of the work of the government **Local Government:** 15 republics, each with its own Supreme Soviet and Council of Ministers, the latter headed by a premier. Ethnic divisions within the republics include 20 autonomous republics, 8 autonomous regions, and 10 national districts

**Ethnic Composition:** Russians constitute 53% of the population, Ukrainians 17%, Byelorussians 4%, Uzbeks 4%, and more than 150 other nationalities **Population Distribution:** 62% urban **Density:** 31 inhabitants per sq. mi.

**Largest Cities:** (1979 census) Moscow 8,011,000, Leningrad 4,588,000, Kiev 2,144,000, Tashkent 1,780,000, Baku 1,550,000, Khar'kov 1,444,000, Gor'kiy 1,344,000, Novosibirsk 1,312,000, Minsk 1,276,000, Kuybyshev 1,216,000, Sverdlovsk 1,211,000, Dnepropetrovsk 1,066,000, Tbilisi 1,066,000, Odessa 1,046,000

**Per Capita Income:** $4,820 (1980) **Gross National Product (GNP):** $1,281 billion (1980) **Economic Statistics:** 77.5% of the GNP is derived from industry (main industries include oil, steel, electricity, cement, pig iron, foodstuffs, textiles, and other heavy industry); 16.5% from agriculture (2 million square miles of arable land provide wheat, rye, corn, oats, potatoes, sugarbeets, linseed, sunflower seed, cotton, and flax; main livestock are cattle, sheep, and pigs) **Minerals and Mining:** Vast deposits of coal, iron, petroleum, natural gas, copper, nickel, bauxite, zinc, lead, gold, manganese, platinum, and tin **Labor Force:** 125,900,000 (1980), of which 29% were in industry, 21% in services, 20% in agriculture, and 2% in government **Foreign Trade:** Exports, mainly machinery, iron and steel, crude oil, natural gas, foodstuffs, lumber and paper products, and textiles, amounted to $76.5 billion in 1980. Imports, chiefly machinery, foodstuffs, and consumer goods, totaled $68.5 billion **Principal Trade Partners:** East Germany, Czechoslovakia, Poland, Hungary, Bulgaria, Romania, Cuba, Japan, West Germany, Finland, United States, Italy, France, Yugoslavia, Britain, India

**Vital Statistics:** Birthrate, 18.3 per 1,000 of pop. (1980); death rate, 10.4 **Life Expectancy:** 70 years **Health Statistics:** 82 inhabitants per hospital bed; 299 per physician (1976) **Infant Mortality:** 27.7 per 1,000 births **Illiteracy:** Negligible **Primary and Secondary School Enrollment:** 45,283,000 (1976) **Enrollment in Higher Education:** 4,853,958 **GNP Expended on Education:** 7.5% (1976)

**Transportation:** Paved roads total 230,000 mi. **Motor Vehicles:** 4,950,000 (1967) **Passenger Cars:** 1,100,000 **Railway Mileage:** 87,680 **Ports:** Main terminal ports on the Volga-Don system are Astrakhan, Rostov, Moscow, Perm; main transfer ports: Volgograd, Saratov, Kuybyshev, Kazan, Gorky, Yaroslavl; seaports: Leningrad, Odessa, Kaliningrad, Murmansk, Archangel, Riga, Vladivostok, Nakhodka **Major Airlines:** Aeroflot operates all international and domestic flights **Communications: Radio Transmitters:** 3,034 **Receivers:** 122,477,000 (1975) **Television Transmitters:** 1,749 **Receivers:** 55,181,000 (1975) **Telephones:** 20,943,000 (1978) **Newspapers:** 686 dailies, 396 copies per 1,000 inhabitants (1977)

**Weights and Measures:** Metric system **Travel Requirements:** Passport, visa, valid 3 months, 3 photos. Make arrangements through travel agency that has a contract with Intourist

---

The Soviet Union, the world's largest country and one of the leading superpowers, has in recent years been experiencing alternating success and setbacks. Its policy of détente, the peaceful co-existence with non-Communist nations, has raised more ideological dilemmas than its original supporters could have imagined.

Leonid Brezhnev, General Secretary of the Communist party, the only political body in the Soviet Union, has now been in power longer than any of his predecessors since Stalin. Brezhnev's active role in the 25th Congress of the Communist Party of the Soviet Union dispelled rumors of possible illness or lack of support in the Soviet power structure. The Congress, which met in February-March 1976, endorsed the leadership of Secretary Brezhnev. In June 1977 Brezhnev was elected Chairman of the Presidium of the USSR and thus became the first leader in Soviet history to hold both the chief party and state posts.

In the five-year plan for 1976-80 the party leaders had to lower their targets for economic growth. In effect this was an admission of failure of the previous five-year plan to reach anticipated goals. For the new 1981-85 plan, heavy industry continued to receive strong emmphasis at the expense of consumer goods. There again was a retrenchment in the expansion of agriculture. Recent harvest failures have plagued Soviet planners hoping to achieve self-sufficiency in food needs.

Foreign trade, once a small part of the Russian economy, is now of great importance. Commerce with the West has reached an unprecedented level. Trade with the United States was over $2.8 billion in 1978 compared to $200 million in 1971, although it fell to $1.9 billion in 1980 because of U.S. grain restrictions. Purchases of much needed wheat in the United States and Canada have had substantial impact on world prices. Other Western nations, Japan, Britain, West Germany, have become involved with the USSR in trade pacts and long-range projects that require large investments in plant technology and resource development.

The USSR continued to build up its armed forces in the 1980s and to seek influence in the Middle East and Africa. It has transported Cuban soldiers to help pro-Soviet governments in Angola, Ethiopia, and Southern Yemen defeat domestic and foreign enemies. Enmity between China and the USSR continues to divide the Communist world, but the Soviets have maintained the solidarity of most East European Communist nations.

In late December 1979, the Soviet Army invaded Afghanistan to shore up its tottering Communist puppet regime. This was the first time the Soviets had used military force against a neutral country. Brezhnev declared the invasion was directed against "aggressive external forces of reaction" which were threatening Afghanistan, but the military move outraged the West and alarmed neutral countries. The U.S. government banned sales of grain and of high technology systems to the USSR, halted its efforts to have SALT II (strategic arms limitation treaty) ratified by the Senate, and boycotted the 1980 Summer Olympic Games in Moscow. The USSR poured an estimated 90,000 soldiers into Afghanistan, but Soviet forces met with stiff opposition from Afghan guerrillas that continued into 1982.

Soviet leaders denounced the workers' revolt in Poland in mid-1980 and approved the Polish government's imposition of martial law in December 1981.

Although President Reagan resumed U.S. grain sales to the USSR in 1981, the Soviets accused the United States of reviving the Cold War and protested the U.S. ban (Dec. 1981) on exports of equipment to help build a West European-Siberian gas pipeline. In 1982, Brezhnev announced that the USSR would stop deploying new nuclear missiles in Europe and would not be the first nation to use nuclear weapons. Although the U.S. denounced this as propaganda ploys, a Soviet delegation met in Geneva on June 29 with U.S. negotiators to begin strategic arms reduction talks (START).

**HISTORY:** About the 5th century A.D. the Russian steppes began to be peopled by the Slavs. By the 9th century, despite repeated invasions by other tribes, the Slavs constituted the majority of Russia's inhabitants

**862-79:** Rurik, a Scandinavian chieftain, establishes the first Russian city-state, at Novgorod. His successor, Oleg, expands his territory in 879 and makes Kiev his capital

**1237-40:** Mongol (Tatar) hordes overrun Russia, initiating two centuries of the "Tatar Yoke"

**1547:** Ivan IV (the Terrible), Prince of Moscow, is crowned tsar

**1712:** Peter the Great transfers capital from Moscow to St. Petersburg (now Leningrad)

**1812:** Napoleon invades Russia and occupies Moscow. Returning westward, he loses almost his entire army in the Russian snows

**1861:** Alexander II liberates the serfs

**1914:** Russia enters World War I

**1917:** Military setbacks lead to overthrow of Tsar Nicholas II. Succeeding Provisional Government is ousted by Bolsheviks, led by Lenin, who ends war by surrendering much territory

**1922:** Four Communist-ruled states—all formerly parts of Tsar's domain—form Union of Soviet Socialist Republics

**1924-38:** Lenin dies (1924) After a power struggle with Leon Trotsky, Stalin emerges as dictator. He institutes the forcible collectivization of agriculture, liquidating more than five million peasant families. In a great purge of his opponents, thousands of leading officials are executed

**1941-45:** Germany invades the USSR. After years of bitter warfare on Soviet soil, the Nazi armies are crushed. USSR regains most land surrendered in 1917 and dominates Eastern Europe

**1953-56:** Stalin dies (1953), causing another Kremlin power struggle. Nikita Khrushchev assumes leadership, denounces Stalin's "personality cult," and begins "de-Stalinization." Soviet forces invade Hungary and suppress anti-Communist revolution

**1957:** USSR launches world's first artificial satellite (Sputnik)

**1961:** Sino-Soviet split emerges over Khrushchev's policies of de-Stalinization and "peaceful coexistence" with the West

**1962:** USSR secretly installs missiles in Cuba; withdraws them after U.S. Navy quarantines island

**1968:** Soviet troops invade Czechoslovakia in move to halt liberalization of country's Communist regime

**1974:** Novelist Alexander Solzhenitsyn is arrested and deported for his criticisms of Soviet political repression

**1976:** Leadership of Brezhnev is reaffirmed at 25th Communist Party Congress. New five-year plan calls for lowered economic goals

**1979:** Brezhnev and U.S. President Jimmy Carter sign treaty to limit strategic arms (SALT II). Soviet army invades Afghanistan to save tottering Communist regime

**1980:** Estimated 90,000 Soviet troops meet bitter resistance by Afghan rebels. UN condemns Soviet invasion; U.S. halts grain sales to USSR and refuses to ratify SALT treaty to protest Soviet military move; 1980 Olympic Games held in Moscow despite boycott by U.S. and some other Western nations. Kosygin resigns as premier due to ill health (he dies Dec. 18); Nikolai A. Tikhonov is appointed premier

**1981:** U.S. lifts boycott on Soviet grain sales but bans exports of equipment for West European-Siberian gas pipeline

**1982:** Brezhnev declares USSR would not be first nation to use nuclear weapons

## UNITED ARAB EMIRATES

**Area:** 32,278 sq. mi. **Population:** 1,040,275 (1980 census)

**Official Name:** United Arab Emirates **Capital:** Abu Dhabi **Nationality:** Emirian **Languages:** Arabic is the official language; English is widely used **Religion:** 90% Sunni Moslem **Flag:** Equal green, white, and black horizontal stripes, with a red vertical stripe at the hoist **Anthem:** The National Anthem **Currency:** UAE Dirham (3.7 per U.S. $1)

**Location:** Southwest Asia on the Persian Gulf. The federation of seven emirates is bounded by Oman, Saudi Arabia, Qatar, and the Persian Gulf **Features:** A flat, barren island-dotted coastal plain gives way to extensive sand dunes in the interior. At the eastern end are the western Hajar Mountains

**Head of State:** President: Sheikh Zaid ibn Sultan al-Nahayan of Abu Dhabi, born 1918, elected 1971, reelected 1976 and 1981, assisted by a Vice President, Sheikh Rashid ibn Said al-Maktum of Dubai, born 1914, elected 1971, and a Supreme Council of the 7 rulers **Head of Government:** Premier: Sheikh Rashid ibn Said al-Maktum of Dubai, appointed 1979 **Effective Date of Present Constitution:** 1971 interim constitution **Legislative Body:** Federal National Council (unicameral), of 40 members in proportion to emirate population, appointed by the seven rulers **Local Government:** Each of the seven emirates (Abu Dhabi, Ajman, Dubai, Fujairah, Ras al-Khaimah, Sharjah, Umm al-Qaiwain) is self-governing, under a sheikh

**Ethnic Composition:** Arabs (42%), Iranians, Pakistanis, and Indians (50%); only about 25% are native-born **Population Distribution:** 90% urban **Density:** 32 inhabitants per sq. mi.

**Largest Cities:** (1979 est.) Abu Dhabi 347,000; (1972 est.) Dubai 60,000, Sharjah 25,000, Ras al-Khaimah 10,000, Ajman 4,000

**Per Capita Income:** $10,600 (1980) **Gross National Product (GNP):** $9.6 billion (1980) **Economic Statistics:** Oil production in 1978 was

1.8 million barrels per day, with Abu Dhabi producing 80%. Aside from the area's rich oil and natural gas deposits, the economy includes herding, date growing, fishing, aluminum smelting, and trading **Minerals and Mining:** There are rich oil and natural gas deposits, notably in Abu Dhabi, and copper, gypsum, and limestone exist **Labor Force:** 490,000 (1978), of which 87% is foreign **Foreign Trade:** Exports, 95% oil, totaled $14 billion in 1979. Imports, chiefly machinery, foods, and consumer goods, totaled $6.5 billion **Principal Trade Partners:** EC countries, United States, Japan, India

**Vital Statistics:** Birthrate, 50 per 1,000 of pop. (1974); death rate, 18 **Life Expectancy:** 60 years **Health Statistics:** 342 inhabitants per hospital bed; 677 per physician (1977) **Infant Mortality:** 65 per 1,000 births **Illiteracy:** 44% **Primary and Secondary School Enrollment:** 95,800 (1980) **Enrollment in Higher Education:** 3,000 (1980) **GNP Expended on Education:** 9.1% (1976)

**Transportation:** Paved roads total 500 mi. **Motor Vehicles:** 15,000 (1978) **Railway Mileage:** None **Ports:** Dubai, Jebel Ali, Abu Dhabi, Ruwais **Major Airlines:** Gulf Air **Communications: Radio Transmitters:** 15 **Receivers:** 55,000 (1976) **Television Transmitters:** 9 **Receivers:** 26,065 **Telephones:** 165,000 (1978) **Newspapers:** 3 dailies, 8 copies per 1,000 inhabitants (1977)

**Weights and Measures:** Metric, British and local standards **Travel Requirements:** Passport, visa, valid 3 months, $2.75 fee, 3 photos, 1 month stay, sponsorship required **International Dialing Code:** 971

---

The United Arab Emirates consists of seven emirates on the eastern Arabian Peninsula, extending from the southern base of the Qatar Peninsula to Fujairah on the Gulf of Oman. From west to east, they are Abu Dhabi, Dubai, Sharjah, Ajman, Umm al-Qaiwain, Ras al-Khaimah, and Fujairah. Before independence, the area was sometimes referred to as Trucial Oman, the Trucial Coast, or the Trucial Sheikdoms. Boundaries are vague and in many places disputed. The sheikdoms are largely desert, hot and dry.

The main economic link among the emirates is the desire to share in the vast oil wealth of one of them, Abu Dhabi, at least until reserves are found in their own areas, as has happened in Dubai.

British influence in the area was formalized by treaty with the principal sheiks of the coast as early as 1820. The Exclusive Agreement of 1892 provided for British control of foreign agreements and affairs. The agreement terminated, however, following the withdrawal of British troops. Independence was declared on December 2, 1971. The pending withdrawal, coupled with the possibility of border claims by Iran and Saudi Arabia, had led to a proposal for federation with Qatar and Bahrain. But in August 1971, Bahrain announced it would go it alone and Qatar followed suit.

On January 26, 1982, the United Arab Emirates joined five other Persian Gulf states to form a regional defense force, apparently in response to the Iranian revolution and the Iran-Iraq war.

**HISTORY:** European and Arab pirates roamed the Trucial Coast area from the 17th to the 19th centuries, hence the former label "Pirate Coast." Successful British expeditions against the pirates led to further campaigns against their headquarters at Ras al-Khaimah and other harbors along the southwest coast in 1819. In 1820 the sheiks signed a General Treaty of Peace with Britain

**1853:** Coastal sheiks sign treaty with the United Kingdom agreeing to a "perpetual maritime truce"

**1892:** UK and the Trucial States establish closer bonds in another treaty, similar to those entered into by the British and other Persian Gulf principalities

**1955:** UK effectively intervenes on the side of Abu Dhabi in the latter's dispute with Saudi Arabia over the Buraimi Oasis, resulting in control of the Oasis being shared between Abu Dhabi and the Sultanate of Oman

**1958-60:** Vast oil reserves are discovered in Abu Dhabi

**1971:** British protective treaty with the Trucial Sheikdoms ends. They become fully independent as the United Arab Emirates. Oil is discovered in Dubai

**1975:** UAE joins OPEC as its third largest contributor

**1976:** Supreme Defense Council unites the UAE's armed forces. Dubai officials announce plans for a $765-million port, a new airport and an oil refinery at Jebel Ali

**1978:** Dubai pulls forces from federal army and puts them on alert in dispute with Abu Dhabi

**1982:** UAE joins new Persian Gulf defense force of six nations

---

## UNITED KINGDOM

**Area:** 94,399 sq. mi. **Population:** 55,618,791 (1981 census); England 46,220,955, Wales 2,790,462, Scotland 5,117,146, Northern Ireland 1,490,228

**Official Name:** United Kingdom of Great Britain and Northern Ireland **Capital:** London **Nationality:** British **Languages:** English is the official and predominant language; Gaelic is spoken in parts of Scotland, while Welsh is the first language in western Wales and enjoys equal validity with English as an official language in Wales **Religion:** Although the Church of England and the Church of Scotland are established churches, there is complete religious freedom. About half the population belongs to the Church of England (Protestant Episcopal) and to its nonestablished branches in Scotland, Wales, and Northern Ireland. The Church of Scotland (Presbyterian) has about 1.3 million members. The other major Christian denominations are Roman Catholic (6 million); Methodist (900,000); Baptist (300,000); and Congregationalist (200,000). There are several hundred thousand Moslems, 410,000 Jews, and several thousand Buddhists **Flag:** Known as the Union Jack, the flag is a superimposition of the red cross of St. George of England, the white cross of St. Andrew of Scotland, and the red cross of St. Patrick of Ireland, all on a blue background **Anthem:** God Save the Queen **Currency:** Pound sterling (0.56 per U.S. $1)

**Location:** Off the northwest coast of Europe. The island of Great Britain, containing England, Scotland, and Wales, is bordered by the Atlantic Ocean on the north and west, and is separated from the European continent by the North Sea, the Strait of Dover, and the English Channel on the east and south. The Irish Sea and the North Channel separate Great Britain from Ireland, the northern area of which constitutes Northern Ireland, bordered on the south by the Republic of Ireland **Features:** England is divided into hill districts in the north, west, and southwest, and the undulating downs and low-lying plains in the east and southeast. In the extreme north, the Cheviot Hills, running from east to west, separate England from Scotland. The Pennine Chain extends southward from the Cheviots into the Midlands, a plains region with low, rolling hills and valleys. Scotland has three natural topographic divisions: the Southern Uplands; the Central Lowlands; and the Northern Highlands, which contain the highest point in the British Isles. Wales is generally mountainous. Northern Ireland contains many plateaus and hills **Chief Rivers:** Severn, Thames, Trent, Aire, Great Ouse, Wye, Tay, Nene, Clyde, Spey, Tweed, Tyne

**Head of State:** Queen Elizabeth II, born 1926, ascended the throne 1952 **Head of Government:** Prime Minister Margaret Thatcher, born 1925, appointed May 4, 1979 **Effective Date of Present Constitution:** The British Constitution is formed partly by statute, partly by common law, and partly by "traditional rights" known as conventions. The rules of the constitution have never been codified, and can be adapted to changing conditions at any time by Act of Parliament or by the general acceptance of a new convention **Legislative Body:** Parliament (bicameral), consisting of the House of Lords and the House of Commons. The House of Commons, which is the ultimate authority for lawmaking, consists of 635 members elected by universal suffrage for a maximum term of 5 years. The House of Lords, which also functions as the highest court in the land, consists of some 1,200 members, including hereditary and life peers and peeresses, law lords appointed for life to carry out the judicial duties of the house, and the 2 archbishops and 24 senior bishops of the Church of England. The House of Lords has the power to delay, but not prevent, legislation **Local Government:** England is divided into 39 counties, 6 metropolitan counties, Greater London, and the Isles of Scilly; Wales is divided into 8 counties. Scotland is divided into 9 regions and 3 island areas. Northern Ireland is divided into 26 districts. Each local authority division throughout the United Kingdom is administered by its own elected council. In Northern Ireland the shape of the new institutions which will replace the former parliament had not been completely decided, although a 78-seat assembly and an executive or provincial cabinet which shares power between Roman Catholics and Protestants had been formed. A Constitutional Convention begun in 1975 was dissolved in 1976, having failed to agree on a system of government. Direct rule, first initiated in 1974, was therefore renewed. The House of Commons passed into law a bill providing for a new plan of local government on July 23, 1982. Northern Ireland continues to be represented in the U.K. House of Commons

**Ethnic Composition:** The contemporary Briton is descended from varied racial stocks that settled in the British Isles before the 12th century. Under the Normans, descendants of Scandinavian Vikings, pre-Celtic, Celtic, Roman, Anglo-Saxon, and Norse influences were blended into the Briton. The population includes some 1.9 million immigrant Pakistanis, Indians, West Indians and their British-born children **Population Distribution:** 76% urban **Density:** 592 inhabitants per sq. mi.

**Largest Cities:** (1981 census) London 6,696,008, Birmingham 1,006,908, Glasgow 763,162, Leeds 704,974, Sheffield 536,770, Liverpool 510,306, Bradford 457,677, Manchester 449,168, Edinburgh 436,271, Bristol 387,977, Belfast 297,862

**Per Capita Income:** $5,340 (1980) **Gross Domestic Product (GDP):** $298 billion (1980) **Economic Statistics:** About 32% of the GDP comes from manufacturing (iron and steel, engineering [vehicles and aircraft], textiles, chemicals, food products, and consumer goods); 12% from mining and quarrying (petroleum, natural gas, coal, iron ore, limestone, tin, gravel), construction, and public utilities; 9% from transportation and communications; 42% from trade and services; and 3% from agriculture **Minerals and Mining:** There are significant amounts of coal, small deposits of iron, limestone, tin, gravel and oilshale. There are large quantities of natural gas and oil in the North Sea **Labor Force:** 26.1 million (1977), with 28% in manufacturing and 2% in agriculture **Foreign Trade:** Exports, mainly manufactured goods including engineering products, motor vehicles, nonelectric and electric machinery, petroleum and nonmetallic mineral manufactures, totaled $111 billion in 1979. Imports, chiefly petroleum and petroleum products, machinery, nonferrous metals, meat and meat preparations, fruit and vegetables, amounted to $116 billion **Principal Trade Partners:** United States, West Germany, South Africa, Ireland, Canada, France, Netherlands, Switzerland

**Vital Statistics:** Birthrate, 13.5 per 1,000 of pop. (1980); death rate, 11.8 **Life Expectancy:** 73 years **Health Statistics:** 117 inhabitants per hospital bed; 761 per physician (1974) **Infant Mortality:** 11.8 per 1,000 births **Illiteracy:** Negligible **Primary and Secondary School Enrollment:** 10,801,957 (1974) **Enrollment in Higher Education:** 703,645 **GNP Expended on Education:** 6.2% (1974)

**Transportation:** Paved roads total 208,151 mi. **Motor Vehicles:** 16,499,900 (1978) **Passenger Cars:** 14,658,800 **Railway Mileage:** 11,467 **Ports:** London, Liverpool, Glasgow, Southampton, Belfast, Cardiff, Milford Haven, Manchester, Bristol, Hull, Swansea, Edinbugh, Newcastle **Major Airlines:** British Airways flies both domestically and internationally. There are many other independent air transport operations **Communications: Radio Transmitters:** 386 **Receivers:** 39,500,000 (1976) **Television Transmitters:** 596 **Licenses:** 17,729,000 (1976) **Telephones:** 23,182,000 (1978) **Newspapers:** 111 dailies, 410 copies per 1,000 inhabitants (1977)

**Weights and Measures:** Metric system **Travel Requirements:** Passport, no visa **International Dialing Code:** 44

---

The basic problem for Great Britain has been that ever since losing an empire it has been unable to find a new role. When Britain dismantled the Empire, beginning in 1947, it also lost its captive markets and sources of supply. Britain was forced to compete in a changed world market with the disadvantages of aging industrial plants, war-depleted natural resources and an agricultural base that produced only half of the nation's food needs. In the postwar rebuilding, it did not do as well as its competitors, especially West Germany, France and Japan. Even the traditional British luxury goods—autos, liquor, and clothing, faced strong competition.

In economic terms Britain has suffered from slow growth, poor foreign trade results, low investment, weak currency, high inflation—in sum, a sluggish economy. No government has been able to arrest this decline. Entry into the Common Market in 1973 was supposed to revitalize the economy. It has not. Europe sells more to Britain than it buys. Trade balances improved only slightly.

But the economic picture is not all grim. The trickle of North Sea oil which began to flow from the British sector in 1974 has now grown to half a million barrels a day. By 1980 Britain was practically self-sufficient in oil and also able to earn enough in exports to put the country in the black for the first time since before World War II.

The Labour party, which has promoted social programs and nationalization of industry, controlled the government under Prime Ministers Harold Wilson and James Callaghan from 1974 to 1979, when it fell over the issue of Scottish autonomy. The Conservatives won the parliamentary elections in May and installed Margaret Roberts Thatcher as the country's first woman prime minister. She promised to set Britain on a different economic course by trying to establish a market-oriented, capital-owning economy that would free private business from extreme government regulation. But the economy worsened due to high rates of unemployment and inflation.

The violent troubles in Northern Ireland, where some 14,000 troops are stationed, have resisted solution ever since the rioting between Protestant and Catholic communities broke out in Belfast and Londonderry in 1969. Sporadic acts of violence by Irish Republican Army guerrillas continued to occur there and in Britain into the 1980s.

In 1982 Britain rushed to save a remnant of its fading empire by defending the Falkland Islands, a British crown colony situated some 250 miles off Argentina in the South Atlantic. Argentina, which had long claimed the 149-year-old British dependency, with about 1,800 British citizens, seized the islands on April 2. Prime Minister Thatcher immediately dispatched a 65-ship task force to establish a naval blockade around the islands. After efforts by the U.S. and the United Nations to resolve the dispute failed, the U.S. sided with Britain by imposing limited sanctions against Argentina.

This unlikely war became a grim reality in early May when Harrier jets from the task force bombed the Stanley airfield and a British submarine sank Argentina's only cruiser, with a loss of at least 321 crewmen. Argentine warplanes in turn sank the British destroyer *Sheffield*, with a loss of 20 men, and disabled five other ships. On May 21, British troops established a beachhead on East Falkland, captured Port San Carlos and Darwin, poured 8,000 troops ashore, and advanced eastward 50 miles to surround Stanley. The inexperienced, badly out-fought Argentines surrendered to the superior British force on June 14. Argentina admitted to losses of 613 dead and missing; the number of British dead was 252. The last of 11,845 Argentine soldiers taken prisoner were returned to Argentina in July.

Despite the war's casualties and high cost, the British public applauded Mrs. Thatcher's firm actions in the crisis, and her popularity soared. Britons also were buoyed by the birth of a son, William Arthur Philip Louis, to Prince Charles and Princess Diana on June 21, 1982.

**HISTORY:** The first known settlers of Britain were the Celts, who invaded the island from northern Europe before the 6th century B.C. A brief invasion by Julius Caesar in 55 B.C. paved the way for a long Roman occupation that began in the 1st century A.D. and lasted until the early 5th century. As the Roman army withdrew, waves of Anglo-Saxons and Jutes invaded Britain, forcing the Celts to retreat westward and into Brittany. The newcomers gradually established kingdoms of their own but were in turn invaded by the Danes, one of whom, Canute, became king of a united England in 1016

**1066:** William the Conqueror leads Norman army in the last successful invasion of England

**1215:** King John signs Magna Carta; the most important document of the British constitution, it establishes supremacy of law over the king and lays the foundation for parliamentary government

**1337-1453:** Hundred Years War rages as English kings seek to enforce claims to French territory; England is ultimately defeated and ceases to be a continental power

**1455-85:** Houses of York and Lancaster contend for English throne in Wars of the Roses, which end in victory for Henry Tudor, the Lancastrian claimant, and establishment of Tudor dynasty

**1534:** Breach with Rome, precipitated by pope's refusal to grant Henry VIII a divorce, is completed by Act of Supremacy declaring king head of the Church of England

**1558-1603:** Reign of Elizabeth I sees the rise of England as a leading European power, strengthened by the defeat of the Spanish Armada in 1588, and the flowering of the Renaissance in English literature; queen is succeeded by James VI of Scotland who, as James I of England, rules over both kingdoms
**1642-49:** Civil war rends England as Charles I and parliament struggle for power; war ends in defeat and execution of the king and establishment of a commonwealth dominated by Oliver Cromwell
**1660:** Monarchy is restored under Charles II
**18th cent.:** Britain undergoes marked transformation with development of parliamentary government and beginning of the Industrial Revolution; overseas, a huge empire is gained in Canada and India and another lost with the American Revolution, followed by war with Napoleonic France
**1815:** Duke of Wellington's army defeats Napoleon at Waterloo
**1832:** Enactment of Reform Bill extends franchise to middle class
**1837-1901:** Reign of Queen Victoria witnesses Britain's rise to world leadership in commerce and industry; reign closes with Britain industrially outstripped by United States and Germany, and fighting Boer War in South Africa
**1902:** Boers are defeated and accept British sovereignty
**1914-18:** Britain plays leading role in World War I, sharing in Allied victory over Germany but drained of wealth
**1921:** Southern Ireland is separated from United Kingdom
**1924:** Ramsay MacDonald forms Britain's first Labour Cabinet
**1939-45:** Britain again fights Germany in World War II; standing virtually alone after fall of France in 1940, British, under leadership of Winston Churchill, withstand intensive German bombing and defeat Luftwaffe in Battle of Britain; war ends with Britain again victorious but economically weakened; Labour party, under Clement Attlee, is swept into power
**1956:** Britain, under Conservative government of Anthony Eden, joins France and Israel in invasion of Egypt following nationalization of Suez Canal
**1964:** Labour party, led by Harold Wilson, is returned to power
**1969:** Troops are rushed to Northern Ireland after bloody riots break out between Protestants and Roman Catholics
**1970:** Wilson is defeated by Conservative leader Edward Heath
**1971:** Common Market approves Britain's bid for admission
**1973:** Participation in Common Market (EC) begins
**1974:** Wilson again becomes prime minister, negotiates "social compact" with unions for labor peace
**1976:** Wilson resigns. He is succeeded by James Callaghan
**1979:** Unions call winter-time strikes despite social compact. Ambiguous results of autonomy referendum in Scotland lead to a parliamentary vote of no confidence in Callaghan. Conservatives win majority in new House; their leader, Margaret Thatcher, becomes Britain's first woman prime minister
**1981:** David Owen and 11 other dissident Labour MP's form new Social Democratic party to oppose what they called Labour's leftward drift. Hunger strikes by IRA prisoners in Belfast result in ten deaths by mid-August and sporadic rioting in Northern Ireland. Rioting by youths in 30 British towns and cities, protesting police authority and lack of jobs. Charles, Prince of Wales, weds Lady Diana Spencer in London's St. Paul's Cathedral
**1982:** Britain sends 65-ship naval task force to regain Falkland Islands after Argentina invades the crown colony April 2; sets up naval blockade but loses a destroyer; Harrier jets bombard Stanley airfield; British troops invade East Falkland May 21 and advance to Stanley; Argentine garrison of 11,845 soldiers surrenders June 14; British casualties include 252 dead

## UNITED STATES

**Area:** 3,623,420 sq. mi. **Population:** 226,547,346 (1980 census), 229,304,000 (1981 est.)

**Official Name:** United States of America **Capital:** Washington, D.C. **Nationality:** American or United States **Languages:** English is the official and predominant language. According to the 1980 census, the most frequently reported mother tongues other than English were Spanish (7.7 million persons), German (5.1 million), Italian (4.1 million), Polish (2.5 million), French (2.4 million) and Yiddish (1.2 million) **Religion:** About two-thirds of the population is Protestant, one-fourth Roman Catholic, 3% Jewish, and the rest of other or no affiliation **Flag:** Popularly known as the "Stars and Stripes" or "Old Glory," the flag consists of 13 horizontal, alternate red and white stripes, and a union of 50 five-pointed white stars arranged in alternate rows of 6 and of 5 on a blue field in the upper left corner **Anthem:** The Star-Spangled Banner

**Location:** The United States proper (excluding Hawaii and Alaska) stretches across North America from the Atlantic Ocean on the east to the Pacific Ocean on the west, from Canada on the north to Mexico and the Gulf of Mexico on the south **Features:** The United States proper (excluding Hawaii and Alaska) consists of the Atlantic coastal plain, the Appalachian highlands, a vast interior plains region, the Rocky Mountains belt, the intermontane basin and plateaus west of the Rockies, and the mountains and valleys of the Pacific borderland. Another division, part of the Laurentian Plain of Canada, dips into the United States in the Great Lakes region. Alaska's main physical divisions are the Pacific mountain system, the Central Plateau, the Arctic mountain system, and the Arctic Slope. Hawaii consists of a 1,610-mile-long chain of 122 islands, which represent mountain peaks of volcanic origin largely submerged in the Pacific **Chief Rivers:** Mississippi, Missouri, Rio Grande, Yukon, Arkansas, Colorado, Ohio-Allegheny, Red, Columbia, Snake, Pecos, Canadian

**Head of State and of Government:** President Ronald W. Reagan, born 1911, took office 1981 **Effective Date of Constitution:** March 4, 1789 **Legislative Body:** Congress (bicameral), consisting of the Senate and the House of Representatives. The Senate consists of 100 members—2 from each state—chosen by popular vote for a 6-year term; a third of its membership is renewed every 2 years. The House of Representatives has 435 members elected by popular vote every 2 years; each state is entitled to at least one Representative, with the total number determined periodically according to population **Local Government:** 50 states, each with a popularly elected governor and legislature. Below the state level, local self-government is usually conducted through municipalities, townships, and counties

**Ethnic Composition:** The nation's ethnic diversity is chiefly due to large-scale immigration, most of which took place before 1920. Whites comprise about 83.2% of the population, Blacks 11.7%, and other races the remaining 5.1% **Population Distribution:** 74% urban **Density:** 62.5 inhabitants per sq. mi.

**Largest Cities:** (1980 Census; M.A. = Metropolitan Area) New York 7,071,639 (M.A. 9,119,737), Chicago 3,005,072 (M.A. 7,102,328), Los Angeles 2,966,763 (M.A. 7,477,657), Philadelphia 1,688,210 (M.A. 4,716,818), Houston 1,595,138 (M.A. 2,905,350), Detroit 1,203,339 (M.A. 4,352,762), Dallas 904,078 (M.A. 2,974,878), San Diego 875,538 (M.A. 1,861,846), Phoenix 789,704 (M.A. 1,508,030), Baltimore 786,775 (M.A. 2,174,023), San Antonio 786,023 (M.A. 1,071,954), Indianapolis 700,807 (M.A. 1,166,929), San Francisco 678,974 (M.A. 3,252,721)

**Per Capita Income:** $11,596 (1980) **Gross National Product (GNP):** $2,626.5 billion (1980) **Economic Statistics:** About 23% of the GNP is derived from manufacturing; 16% from wholesale and retail trade; 15% from finance, insurance, and real estate; 13% from services; 12% from government and government enterprises; 3% from agriculture, forestry, and fisheries; 5% from construction; 6% from transportation and communications; 3% from electric, gas, and sanitary services; and 4% from mining **Minerals and Mining:** The United States produces a great variety of minerals and consumes more than any other nation in the world. It is the world's leading producer of copper, lead, natural gas, and molybdenum. Though no longer the leading producer, the United States ranks among the top group in petroleum, coal, iron ore, zinc, sulfur, vanadium, cadmium, uranium, phosphate rock, bauxite, gypsum, aluminum, nitrates, magnesium, potash, titanium, tungsten, feldspar and barite. The nation is also rich in waterpower **Labor Force:** 110,812,000 (1981) **Foreign Trade:** Exports, chiefly machinery and transport equipment, food and live animals, crude materials (soybeans, textile fibers, coal, ores and metal scrap), chemicals and other manufactured goods (metals and manufactures, scientific instruments, textiles, rubber, and paper) totaled $233.7 billion in 1981. Imports, mainly machinery and transport equipment, other manufactured goods (metals and manufactures, textiles, iron and steel-mill products, and nonferrous base metals), food and live animals, crude materials, and mineral fuels, totaled $261.3 billion **Principal Trade Partners:** Canada, Japan, Britain, West Germany, Saudi Arabia, Netherlands, Mexico, Nigeria, Italy, France, Venezuela, Brazil, Belgium, China, South Korea, Libya, Algeria

**Vital Statistics:** Birthrate, 16.2 per 1,000 of pop. (1980); death rate, 8.9 **Life Expectancy:** 74 years **Health Statistics:** 130 inhabitants per hospital bed; 621 per physician (1976) **Infant Mortality:** 12.5 per 1,000 births (1980) **Illiteracy:** Negligible **Primary and Secondary School Enrollment:** 45,300,000 (1980) **Enrollment in Higher Education:** 10,200,000 **GNP Expended on Education:** 6.9% (1980)

**Transportation:** Surfaced roads total 3,918,000 mi. (1979) **Motor Vehicles:** 159,029,000 (1980) **Passenger Cars:** 123,467,000 **Railway Mileage:** 163,000 (1979) **Ports:** New York, Philadelphia, Portland, Baltimore, Boston, Houston, Norfolk, Tampa, San Francisco, New Orleans, Los Angeles, Corpus Christi, Baton Rouge, Beaumont **Major Airlines:** Major international and domestic carriers are American Airlines, Eastern Airlines, Trans World Airlines, Pan American World Airways, Continental Air Lines, Delta Airlines, Northwest Orient Airlines, and United Air Lines **Communications: Radio Transmitters:** 8,359 (1977) **Receivers:** 450,000,000 (1979)

**Television Transmitters:** 972 (1977) **Receivers:** 140,000,000 (1979) **Telephones:** 175,535,000 (1979) **Newspapers:** 1,745 dailies (1980)

**Weights and Measuures:** Avoirdupois units of weight and linear measures. Metric system gradually being introduced

---

For articles and statistics on the separate states, see *The Fifty States;* for important national events, see *'81/'82 Month-By-Month Chronology*

---

## UPPER VOLTA

**Area:** 105,869 sq. mi. **Population:** 6,908,000 (1980 est.)

**Official Name:** Republic of Upper Volta **Capital:** Ouagadougou **Nationality:** Upper Voltan **Languages:** The official language is French. Mossi is the main African language, others being Samo, Gourounsi, and Lobi, which belong to the Niger-Congo family of languages **Religion:** The majority of the population are animists. There are over 1 million Moslems, 130,000 Roman Catholics, and 9,000 Protestants **Flag:** Horizontal stripes of black, white, and red **Anthem:** The Volta **Currency:** CFA Franc (305 per U.S. $1)

**Location:** West Africa. Landlocked Upper Volta is bordered on the west and north by Mali, on the east by Niger, and on the south by Benin, Togo, Ghana, and Ivory Coast **Features:** The country consists for the most part of a vast plateau, slightly inclined toward the south and notched by valleys and formed by the three main rivers, with some savanna and semidesert **Chief Rivers:** Black, White, and Red Voltas, and their main tributaries

**Head of State and of Government:** Col. Sayé Zerbo, born 1932, president of the Military Committee of Reform for National Progress, which took power following the coup of Nov. 25, 1980. He is also premier **Effective Date of Present Constitution:** 1977, suspended 1980 **Legislative Body:** Power resides with the Military Committee of Reform for National Progress **Local Government:** 10 departments

**Ethnic Composition:** The two main ethnic groups are the Voltaic people and the Mande (Mandingos). Among the Voltaic, 65% are Mossi and 15% Bobo; the Samo are the most numerous of the Mande group **Population Distribution:** 11% urban **Density:** 65 inhabitants per sq. mi.

**Largest Cities:** (1975 census) Ouagadougou 172,661, Bobo-Dioulasso 115,063, Koudougou 36,838, Ouahigouya 25,690, Banfora 12,358

**Per Capita Income** $144 (1980) **Gross National Product (GNP):** $980 million (1980) **Economic Statistics:** In 1976 about 67% of GNP was from agriculture (sorghum, millet, cotton, sesame, maize, rice, livestock products, peanuts); 6% from industry (textiles, bicycle assembly, maintenance and repairing of vehicles) **Minerals and Mining:** Manganese deposits are to be exploited; deposits of phosphates, copper, gold, bauxite, and limestone exist **Labor Force:** 2,700,000 in 1976, with 87% engaged in subsistence agriculture **Foreign Trade:** Exports, chiefly livestock, cotton, and peanuts, totaled $80 million in 1980. Imports, mainly textiles, petroleum products, motor vehicles and parts, fruits and vegetables, and machinery, totaled $349 million **Principal Trade Partners:** EEC countries, Ivory Coast, Japan, United States

**Vital Statistics:** Birthrate, 47.8 per 1,000 of pop. (1980); death rate, 22.1 **Life Expectancy:** 42 years **Health Statistics:** 1,762 inhabitants per hospital bed; 65,204 per physician (1977) **Infant Mortality:** 182 per 1,000 births **Illiteracy:** 90% **Primary and Secondary School Enrollment:** 167,330 (1976) **Enrollment in Higher Education:** 1,067 (1975) **GNP Expended on Education:** 2.9% (1973)

**Transportation:** Paved roads total 535 mi. **Motor Vehicles:** 24,200 (1978) **Passenger Cars:** 11,800 **Railway Mileage:** 341 **Ports:** None **Major Airlines:** Air Afrique provides international services; Air Volta flies domestically **Communications: Radio Transmitters:** 9 **Receivers:** 105,000 (1976) **Television Transmitters:** 1 **Receivers:** 6,000 (1974) **Telephones:** 8,000 (1978) **Newspapers:** 1 daily, 0.2 copies per 1,000 inhabitants (1976)

**Weights and Measures:** Metric system **Travel Requirements:** Passport, visa valid for 3 months, $2 fee, 2 photos

---

Upper Volta's name derives simply from the fact that its central region is watered by the upper tributaries of the Volta River, which flows southward through Ghana. Most of the country is a plateau where woodland and pasture contrast with a dry northern area seared by the desert wind.

Once the center of the ancient Mossi empire that provided a shield against Moslem conquest of the coastal regions, Upper Volta today is a land of hardworking farmers and cattle-raisers. Poor soil and variable rains, however, make the task of raising food and export crops, chiefly peanuts and cotton, a recurrent struggle. The nation's landlocked situation adds a further handicap.

Since independence from France in 1960, the country has faced the familiar trials of new African nations. Its first president, Maurice Yaméogo, proved an inept financial administrator. In 1966, with the country in virtual bankruptcy, his government was ousted by a military regime headed by army chief Lt. Col. Sangoulé Lamizana.

Elections were held in 1970, establishing a civilian parliament, but in 1974 Lamizana created a new cabinet composed largely of military officers. In 1976 another change occurred, when after two months of strife between the government and the unions, President Lamizana dismissed the military government and formed a new, largely civilian government. In May 1978, Lamizana was elected to the office he had assumed. However, he was deposed in a military coup in November 1980.

Meanwhile Upper Volta has received new aid from France, the Common Market, and the World Bank for further improvement of agriculture and transportation. At the same time, an even greater boost for the country's development is expected from the manganese deposits at Tambao.

Offsetting these pluses in the early 1970s was the long siege of severe drought and famine that plagued Upper Volta and five other nations of the sub-Sahara (Chad, Mali, Mauritania, Niger, and Senegal); at least 150,000 persons were estimated to have died of starvation. Steps were taken in 1977 to deal with this problem through the adoption of a regional agricultural development program aimed at creating food self-sufficiency within 20 years. Nevertheless, drought continued to plague Upper Volta's cattle and cash crop industries.

**HISTORY:** Upper Volta occupies the site of the former Mossi empire and its early history is mostly that of the Mossi people. According to legend, they entered the region as a warrior group between the 11th and 13th centuries and established three independent kingdoms, the most powerful of which was Ouagadougou. Between the 14th and 19th centuries, the Mossi engaged in recurrent wars with the neighboring empires of Mali and Songhai, and after severe defeats their power declined

**1896:** French subjugate territory and establish a protectorate

**1904:** Present-day Upper Volta is incorporated into a French colony called Upper Senegal and Niger

**1919:** Upper Volta is established as a separate French colony

**1932:** Upper Volta is divided among the colonies of French Sudan, Niger, and the Ivory Coast; is reunited in 1947

**1958:** Upper Volta becomes a self-governing state, called the Voltaic Republic, within the French Community

**1959:** Republic's name is changed to Upper Volta; in a general election, the pro-French African Democratic Rally wins a majority of seats in the national assembly and party's leader Maurice Yaméogo is elected premier

**1960:** Upper Volta becomes an independent republic; with Maurice Yaméogo as president

**1966:** Army chief of staff Lt. Col. Sangoulé Lamizana seizes control of the government, dismisses President Yaméogo and declares himself chief of state

**1970-71:** Elections and adoption of a new constitution mark return to constitutional rule the following year

**1974:** Lamizana suspends constitution, abolishes office of prime minister, and dissolves legislature

**1976:** President Lamizana dismisses military government and forms a new, largely civilian cabinet

**1977:** Government lifts three-and-one-half-year ban on political parties. Upper Voltans vote in favor of draft constitution aimed at restoring civilian rule after twelve years of military rule

**1978:** Military rule ends as Lamizana is elected president

**1979:** National Assembly institutes a three-party system

**1980:** A Military Committee of Recovery for National Progress, headed by Col. Sayé Zerbo, comes to power in a bloodless coup in November

**1981:** Zerbo becomes premier. Military Committee announces program for a controlled, planned economy including land reform

## URUGUAY

**Area:** 68,536 sq. mi. **Population:** 2,927,000 (1981 est.)

**Official Name:** Oriental Republic of Uruguay **Capital:** Montevideo **Nationality:** Uruguayan **Languages:** Spanish is the official and universal language **Religion:** 66% Roman Catholic, 2% Protestant, 2% Jewish, 30% other **Flag:** Four blue stripes and 5 white stripes, with a golden sun on a white field in the upper left corner **Anthem:** National Anthem, beginning "Easterners our country or death" **Currency:** Uruguayan peso (12 per U.S. $1)

**Location:** Southeast coast of South America. Uruguay is bounded on the north and northeast by Brazil, on the east by the Atlantic Ocean, on the south by the Rio de la Plata estuary, and on the west by Argentina **Features:** The country consists of rolling, grassy plains and low hills. There are scattered forest areas along the banks of the numerous streams, which provide natural irrigation for the soil **Chief Rivers:** Uruguay, Negro, Rio de la Plata, Cuareim, Yaguarón

**Head of State and of Government:** President: Gen. Gregorio Alvarez, born 1925, took office Sept. 1, 1981, for 3½-year term **Effective Date of Present Constitution:** 1967, partially suspended 1973 **Legislative Body:** Congress dissolved 1973; a 25-member Council of State governs at present **Local Government:** 19 departments

**Ethnic Composition:** About 85% of the population is of European origin, mainly Spanish and Italian, with 10% mestizo, and 5% mulatto or black **Population Distribution:** 83% urban **Density:** 43 inhabitants per sq. mi.

**Largest Cities:** (1975 census) Montevideo 1,173,254, Salto 72,948, Paysandu 62,412, Las Piedras 53,983

**Per Capita Income:** $1,704 (1980) **Gross National Product (GNP):** $5 billion (1980) **Economic Statistics:** In 1979, 29% of GNP from manufacturing (meat packing, shoes, leather, textiles, construction and building materials, beverages, chemicals); 15% of GNP was from agriculture (livestock products, beef, wool, wheat, corn, rice) **Minerals and Mining:** Marble, building stone, gravel, and iron ore **Labor Force:** 1,174,376 (1975), with 34% in industry; 8% in agriculture; 40% in trade and services; 5% in construction; and 6% in transportation and communications **Foreign Trade:** Exports, chiefly wool, meat, and hides, totaled $788 million in 1979. Imports, mainly raw materials, fuels and lubricants, machinery and parts, automotive vehicles and parts, construction materials, and foodstuffs, totaled $1.2 billion **Principal Trade Partners:** Brazil, United States, West Germany, Iraq, Nigeria, Argentina, Netherlands

**Vital Statistics:** Birthrate, 18.6 per 1,000 of pop. (1980); death rate, 10.6 **Life Expectancy:** 71 years **Health Statistics:** 235 inhabitants per hospital bed; 700 per physician (1976) **Infant Mortality:** 37.4 per 1,000 births **Illiteracy:** 6% **Primary and Secondary School Enrollment:** 453,781 (1977) **Enrollment in Higher Education:** 32,627 (1975) **GNP Expended on Education:** 3.6% (1970)

**Transportation:** Paved roads total 4,100 mi. **Motor Vehicles:** 231,300 (1976) **Passenger Cars:** 127,100 **Railway Mileage:** 1,736 **Ports:** Montevideo **Major Airlines:** Primeras Lineas Uruguayas de Navegación Aérea (PLUNA) operates domestically and internationally **Communications: Radio Transmitters:** 105 **Receivers:** 1,600,000 (1976) **Television Transmitters:** 27 **Receivers:** 355,000 (1976) **Telephones:** 270,000 (1978) **Newspapers:** 26 dailies (1977), 140 copies per 1,000 inhabitants (1974)

**Weights and Measures:** Metric system **Travel Requirements:** Passport, no visa for 3 months

The Oriental Republic of Uruguay takes its name from the fact that it is situated on the east bank of the Uruguay River. Uruguay, the second smallest country in South America, is characterized by a high literacy rate and a large urban middle class.

Economic reverses and political repression have seriously affected Uruguayans in the last decade. Although politically stable since 1903, Uruguay began to experience problems in the late 1960s with student riots, general strikes, and the rise of urban terrorism. A series of repressive government measures followed, then a 1973 coup against the presidency of Juan Bordaberry. The military group responsible for the coup retained Bordaberry as president and began tightening its already firm grip on the country. Stability was not enhanced by Bordaberry's government, and dissidents were eliminated through a campaign of arrests, torture and murder. By 1976 the military had ousted Bordaberry in a peaceful putsch because he planned to set up a corporate state structure with the participation of the armed forces written into law. The military preferred a gradual return to representative democracy. Bordaberry was replaced by Aparicio Méndez, who was named president by the conservative Council of the Nation.

Things were not always so sorrowful for Uruguay. Not long ago it could boast one of the highest per capita incomes in the hemisphere and a widely desired currency. The country was envied for its advanced laws, six-hour work day, retirement of workers at age 50 or 55, and incredibly rich soil. But the utopian social system, based on a growing population, became overburdened and began to fall behind in its payments. A 1963 census showed that the population had not grown, that, in fact, well-educated Uruguayans had been leaving for other lands in large numbers.

The economy has been marked by high inflation and, until recently, a high balance of payments deficit. In an effort to deal with the situation, the government has issued a series of mini-devaluations of the peso.

The political situation looked no brighter under Méndez. Upon taking office he immediately issued a decree suspending the political rights of the leaders of existing parties for 15 years. It has been reported that Uruguay, with a population of less than three million, has the highest proportion of political prisoners to total population. In 1978, the regime conceded that 2,511 persons accused of "crimes against state security" had served jail sentences and been released in the preceding six years. In May 1981 human rights leaders asserted that more than 1,200 political prisoners were still being held.

**HISTORY:** The eastern side of the Uruguay and La Plata rivers was occupied by warlike and seminomadic Indians, the Charrúa, until late in the colonial period when Europeans began to settle the area. The first settlers were the Spanish, who established a colony at Soriano in 1624. They were followed by the Portuguese, who were driven out in the 18th century by the Spanish, under whom Uruguay became part of a viceroyalty centered in Argentina. During the Napoleonic Wars, Uruguay was briefly occupied by the British, and the spread of revolutionary ideas during this period soon swept the country into the general Latin American fight for independence

**1810-14:** A war of independence, led by José Gervasio Artigas, begins; Uruguay, with aid from Argentina, ends Spanish rule

**1820-28:** Uruguay is occupied by Brazil. In 1825, a group of patriots known as the Thirty-Three Immortals declare Uruguay an independent republic; country throws off Brazilian rule and, in 1828, Uruguay is established as an independent buffer state between Brazil and Argentina

**1865-70:** Argentina, Brazil, and Uruguay unite in a victorious war against Paraguay

**1911-15:** President José Batlle y Ordóñez introduces wide range of social and economic reforms

**1919-51:** Fearful of the development of a dictatorship, nation adopts new constitution restricting president's power and vesting broad powers in Council of Administration; resulting conflict leads to restoration of strong executive powers to president in 1934. In 1951, office of president is abolished and executive power vested in nine-member
**nal council**

**1958:** The conservative Blancos (National party) win general elections, displacing liberal Colorado party which had governed for more than 90 years

**1966:** Presidential form of government is restored in referendum; Colorados regain majority in general elections

**1967-68:** President Oscar D. Gestido dies and is succeeded by Vice-President Jorge Pacheco Areco; general strikes aand student riots become widespread

**1969:** Pacheco decrees a limited state of siege in June following a new wave of disabling strikes

**1971:** Juan M. Bordaberry is elected president

**1973:** President Bordaberry's military-dominated civilian government suspends constitutional rule, replaces congress with a council of state, and curbs opposition press

**1976:** Bordaberry is ousted. Aparicio Méndez is named president

**1977:** U.S. moves to reduce aid to Uruguay because of human rights violations; Uruguay then rejects aid linked to human rights, claiming it is an internal matter
**1978:** OAS panel charges Uruguay with wholesale violations of human rights
**1979:** Elimination of duties on imported fertilizers and farm machinery leads to increased productivity of farmlands and herds
**1980:** Nov. 30 plebiscite overwhelmingly rejects draft constitution which would give armed forces a permanent share of power
**1981** Gen. Gregorio Alvarez, retired commander in chief of army, is named president by Council of the Nation. Political and military leaders wrangle over new constitution and plans for general elections in 1984
**1982:** Nation falls into deep economic recession. Livestock industry debt reaches over $1 billion due to overextension and drop in world beef prices

## VANUATU

**Area:** 5,700 sq. mi. **Population:** 123,000 (1981 est.)

**Official Name:** Republic of Vanuatu **Capital:** Vila **Nationality:** Vanuatuan **Languages:** Bislama, a pidgin dialect, is the national language. English, French and Bislama are official languages. There are many Melanesian languages throughout the islands **Religion:** Mostly Christian (Presbyterian, Roman Catholic, Anglican); some animists **Flag:** Two equal horizontal stripes of red over green with a black triangle at the hoist containing two crossed yellow mele leaves surrounded by a yellow hog tusk. The triangle is framed on two sides by borders of yellow and black which extend into a triple horizontal stripe of black-yellow-black running to the fly end of the flag **Anthem:** National Anthem, beginning "Yumi yumi yumi I glad blong talem se" **Currency:** Vatu ((100 per U.S. $1)

**Location:** The Y-shaped chain of islands, located in the southwestern Pacific between 13°08′ and 20°12′S., and 166°33′ and 169°49′E., are 600 miles west of Fiji and 250 miles northeast of New Caledonia **Features:** The main islands are Espiritu Santo (the largest), Malekula, Epi, Pentecost and Efate. They are of coral and volcanic origin with active volcanoes on Ambryn, Lopevi and Tanna. Most islands are covered with dense forests

**Head of State:** President Ati George Sokomanu, born 1938, elected June 1980 **Head of Government:** Prime Minister: Father Walter Lini, born 1943, appointed July 1980 **Effective Date of Present Constitution:** July 1980 **Legislative Body:** Representative Assembly (unicameral) with 39 members **Local Government:** 4 regions

**Ethnic Composition:** The population is 92% indigenous Melanesian. There are 5,000 French, 460 British and 1,500 Commonwealth citizens **Population Distribution:** 23% urban **Density:** 22 inhabitants per sq. mi.

**Largest Cities:** (1979 census) Vila 14,797, Luganville 4,935

**Per Capita Income:** N.A. **Gross National Product (GNP):** N.A. **Economic Statistics:** Copra is the principal product, and cocoa and coffee are also grown. Yams, taro, manioc and bananas are produced for local consumption and there are a large number of cattle. Fishing is important, and tourism is growing **Minerals and Mining:** Manganese deposits are exploited **Labor Force:** The native population is mainly engaged in peasant farming **Foreign Trade:** Exports, chiefly copra, fish, prepared meats, and manganese, totaled $32 million in 1977. Imports, chiefly food, fuel, textiles and machinery, totaled $40 million **Principal Trade Partners:** Australia, France, United States, Japan

**Vital Statistics:** Birthrate, 45 per 1,000 of pop. (1966); death rate, 20 **Life Expectancy:** N.A. **Health Statistics:** 102 inhabitants per hospital bed; 3,571 per physician (1977) **Infant Mortality:** N.A. **Illiteracy:** 85% **Primary and Secondary School Enrollment:** 23,840 (1977) **Enrollment in Higher Education:** N.A. **GNP Expended on Higher Education:** N.A.

**Transportation:** Surfaced roads total 160 mi. **Motor Vehicles:** 3,400 (1974) **Passenger Cars:** 2,600 **Railway Mileage:** None **Ports:** Vila, Luganville **Major Airlines:** Air Melanesiae provides domestic service **Communications: Radio Transmitters:** 4 **Receivers:** 15,000 (1976) **Television:** None **Telephones:** 2,400 **Newspapers:** 2 (fortnightly)

**Weights and Measures:** Metric system **Travel Requirements:** Passport; visa not required for stay up to 30 days

A South-Sea islands paradise in so many ways—its main island of Espiritu Santo was the locale for James Michener's *Tales of the South Pacific*—the island nation of Vanuatu faced independence beset by internal divisions and outright rebellion that threatened to tear it apart at the seams.

This small Pacific archipelago situated west of the international date line—formerly known as the New Hebrides, and ruled since 1906 as a joint British-French Condominium—gained its independence July 30, 1980. Though its tropical climate makes it a potential haven for tourism, Vanuatu remains one of the more primitive and underdeveloped areas in the Pacific, with an economy dependent on subsistence agriculture and many tribal Melanesians still practicing various "cargo cult" religions.

In December 1978, a majority coalition government was formed to draft a new constitution and prepare the islands for independence. Father Gerard Lemyang—a French-educated Roman Catholic priest and moderate political leader—became chief minister and formed a Government of National Unity (GNU), with the pro-independence Vanuaaku Party (VP) sharing half the cabinet posts, and its leader, Rev. Walter Lini—an Anglican priest and nationalist spokesman—becoming deputy chief minister.

The constitution adopted in September 1979 provided for elections prior to independence, which was set for May-July 1980. It guaranteed French language rights, established a council of tribal chiefs to preserve Melanesian customs, and set up regional assemblies for Santo and Tanna, in an attempt to mollify separatist sentiment there.

The VP won the November 14 elections to the Representative Assembly, beating the New Hebrides Federal party—a coalition including Lemyang, the Santo-based Na-Griamel separatists and pro-French groups—by two-to-one, with Lini becoming chief minister. The VP also won a majority in the two regional assemblies on Santo and Tanna, causing outbreaks of violence from separatist gangs claiming election fraud.

But on May 25 of 1980, Jimmy (Moli) Stevens and several hundred followers armed with bows and arrows—and backed up by 50 or more French-speaking planters armed with shotguns—stormed government offices in Luganville, took the British District Commiissioner hostage, and declared Santo the independent nation of Vemarana. Stevens, a mixed-race plantation owner and hereditary tribal chief who founded the Na-Griamel movement in the 1960s, was seeking autonomy for Santo under French tutelage, and was supported by many French-speaking residents who feared the VP would nationalize their big plantations following independence.

The insurrection died down when a joint 300-man Anglo-French military force arrived to restore order July 24, after clashes between insurgents and local police resulted in one rebel killed. But these troops were withdrawn soon after independence was declared, as rebel violence increased. Now prime minister of an independent state, Lini called on the United Nations for aid in maintaining Vanuatu's territorial integrity. Support came from other independent Pacific states, with Papua New Guinea sending 400 troops to replace the Anglo-French peacekeeping force. Authorities later arrested some 40 rebels on Santo August 19, including several French citizens. By the end of the month all resistance was crushed.

**HISTORY:** Little is known of the pre-history of the archipelago, though Melanesian settlement is thought to pre-date 400 B.C. The Spanish explorer de Quiros was the first European to sight the islands (1606). The islands were later visited by Bougainville in 1768 and by Captain Cook—who discovered, charted and named most of the southern islands—in 1774. Missionaries came to the islands in the 1820s, and were followed by settlers from Britain and France. The islands suffered during the 1860s from raids by "blackbirders" recruiting forced labor to work in Australia and Fiji
**1887:** Disputes between French and English-speaking settlers over control of the islands—and their possible annexation by either

Australia or French New Caledonia—lead Britain and France to set up Joint Naval Commission to protect their subjects

**1902:** Resident Commissioners representing Britain and France are appointed to administer islands

**1906:** Anglo-French Condominium is established, with dual administration for British and French citizens, the terms of which are set officially in the Anglo-French Protocol of 1914

**1940-45:** French residency in Vila is one of first overseas departments to support Gen. de Gaulle's Free French government against Vichy. Islands become a major base for the Allied offensive in the South Pacific. John Frum "cargo cult" develops as anti-colonial movement among tribal people on Tanna Island; but near-rebellion is avoided with jailing of main leaders

**1957:** Advisory Council, partly elected and partly appointed by the Resident Commissioners, is established

**1974:** Nationalist agitation wins elected Representative Assembly, replacing Advisory Council

**1975:** August municipal elections in Vila and Luganville are won by pro-French and autonomist parties, but pro-independence Nationalist party wins majority in the Representative Assembly. Jimmy (Moli) Stevens, leader of the Na-Griamel movement on Santo, calls for unilateral independence for that island, demanding British withdrawal from the New Hebrides

**1977:** Pro-French "moderates" win uncontested Assembly elections in November; pro-independence Vanuaaku party, led by Rev. Walter Lini, boycotts elections and later forms "People's Provisional Government." George Kalsakau of Natatok party becomes chief minister

**1978:** French Secretary of State for Overseas Departments and Territories Paul Dijoud calls for coaliton goverrnment to end political crisis and move toward independence. Gerard Lemyang becomes chief minister and forms Government of National Unity

**1979:** New constitution is adopted, mandating pre-independence elections and regional legislatures for Espiritu Santo and Tanna. VP wins Nov. 14 elections, gaining 26 seats in the Assembly, with New Hebrides Federal party winning the other 13; Lini becomes chief minister. Violence flares as VP also wins majority in Santo and Tanna assemblies, but order is soon restored

**1980:** Stevens stages revolt on Espiritu Santo May 25, proclaiming the island independent state of Vemarana; rebellion is joined by separatists on Tanna, but Anglo-French military force temporarily restores order July 24. Ati George Sokomanu is chosen president by electoral college. New Hebrides becomes the independent nation of Vanuatu July 30; Walter Lini becomes nation's first prime minister. Secession continues as Lini calls for UN aid; Papua New Guinea sends strong detachment Aug. 18 to replace Anglo-French force. All resistance is crushed. Stevens is sentenced to 14 years in prison; 110 French citizens are deported

**1981:** Government workers stage 4-day strike. Relations with France are strained and France refuses to supply aid. Vanuatu's mobile police force is trained by Papua New Guinea

## VATICAN CITY

**Area:** 0.17 sq. mi. (108.7 acres) **Population:** 733 (1982 est.)

**Official Name:** State of the Vatican City **Nationality:** The Papacy has a citizenship of its own, which is granted to those residing in the Vatican because of their work or rank **Languages:** Italian is the official language of the state; Latin is the official language of the Holy See, the administrative and legislative body for the Roman Catholic Church, and is used for most papal encyclicals and other formal pronouncements **Flag:** Yellow and white vertical bands, with the crossed keys of St. Peter under the triple papal tiara on the white band **Anthem:** Pontifical March (no words) **Currency:** Italian lira (1,296 per U.S. $1)

**Location:** Located in Rome, Vatican City is roughly a triangular area lying near the west bank of the Tiber River and to the west of Castel Sant' Angelo. On the west and south it is bounded by the Leonine Wall. The Vatican area comprises St. Peter's Square; St. Peter's Basilica, the largest Christian church in the world; a quadrangular area north of the square, containing the museums, library, and administrative buildings, and Belvedere Park; the Vatican Palace; and the Papal Gardens. Outside the Vatican City itself, extraterritoriality (but not sovereignty) is exercised over 12 churches and palaces in and near Rome, including St. John Lateran, St. Mary Major, and St. Paul Without the Walls Basilicas, and the papal villa at Castel Gandolfo

**Government:** Vatican City is the center of the worldwide organization of the Roman Catholic Church and the seat of the Pope, who is the absolute sovereign of the tiny state. The Supreme Pontiff is John Paul II (Karol Wojtyla), born 1920, elected Pope on October 16, 1978. He is assisted as temporal ruler by the Pontifical Commission, consisting of the cardinals, and the Administration of the Patrimony of the Apostolic See. Both of these organizations are presided over by a secretary of state (premier), at present held by Agostino Cardinal Casaroli, born 1914, appointed 1979. Religious affairs are governed under the Pope's direction by a number of ecclesiastical bodies collectively known as the Roman Curia. The Pope rules from his election until death, at which time a successor is chosen by the College of Cardinals

**Ethnic Composition:** While the citizenry of the Vatican includes cardinals and other clergymen from all over the world, most of the inhabitants are Italian. The 75 members of the Swiss Guard are a notable exception

**Economic Statistics:** Vatican City does not engage in the economically productive activity common to other states. It is almost entirely dependent for income on the receipt of charitable contributions, the sale of Vatican stamps and tourist mementos, fees for admission to Vatican museums, and the sale of Vatican publications

**Illiteracy:** None **Enrollment in Higher Education:** 7,758 (1975)

**Transportation:** Vatican City is easily reached by the public transportation system of Rome. It has its own railroad station **Communications:** State controlled Radio Vatican. There is no television **Newspapers:** 1 daily, the semiofficial *l'Osservatore Romano*

**Weights and Measures:** Metric system **International Dialing Code:** 39

---

For a long time after the unification of Italy in 1870, which stripped the popes of most of their temporal possessions, the status of the Vatican, the chief papal residence, was uncertain. Then, by the 1929 Lateran Treaty with Italy, the independent enclave of Vatican City came into being. In the treaty, the pontificate formally renounced all claims to the former Papal States.

Vatican City stands on the spot where Caligula constructed a circus and Nero had gardens. The ruler of Vatican City, the Pope, bears the title of Bishop of Rome, Vicar of Jesus Christ, Successor of the Prince of Apostles, Supreme Pontiff of the Universal Church, Patriarch of the West, Archbishop and Metropolitan of the Roman Province, and Sovereign of the State of the Vatican City. Currently he is Pope John Paul II. His .17-square-mile realm includes St. Peter's basilica, the largest church in Christendom; St. Peter's square, a roughly circular plaza set off by Bernini's colonnade; and the pontifical palaces, or the Vatican proper, with magnificent chapels, museums, archives, a library, and a new hall for mass papal audiences.

Among the chapels are the Sistine, the ceiling and one wall of which are decorated with paintings by Michelangelo. The museums, galleries, and various interiors contain works by such masters as Raphael, Leonardo da Vinci, Fra Angelico, Titian, and Correggio, priceless sculpture that includes the Apollo Belvedere and Laocoön, and Egyptian, Etruscan, and other collections. The library, with its enormous wealth of books and manuscripts, is one of the world's great research institutions, and the archives house original material on such matters as the trial of Galileo and the request for annulment of the marriage of Henry VIII to Catherine of Aragon. Among other things, Vatican City also has gardens, courts, and quiet streets; its own daily newspaper and postal, telegraph, and broadcasting facilities; its own "armed forces," the colorfully garbed Swiss Guards; and its own railroad station, used almost exclusively as a freight terminal. Outside its confines but nonetheless enjoying extraterritoriality are a number of churches, palaces, and other structures in Rome and the papal villa at nearby Castel Gandolfo.

Vatican City is administered by a commission of cardinals, and a papal decree of 1968 established a body of 21 lay experts to advise them. A simultaneous decree reorganized the papal court, renaming it the papal household, abolishing hereditary offices, and putting an end to various picturesque anachronisms.

**HISTORY:** The State of the Vatican City and other places over which the Vatican retains control are the remnants of the old Papal States. For almost 1,000 years the papacy held vast temporal possessions, including large areas of Italy, and, until the French Revolution, parts of southern France. During the unification of the Italian peninsula in the 19th century, virtually all these possessions were absorbed by the House of Savoy, leaving only Rome and surrounding territory, protected by a French garrison, still under papal control

**1870:** French garrison withdraws and Rome is annexed by the Kingdom of Italy; Pope Pius IX refuses to recognize the loss of temporal power and initiates what becomes more than a half-century of self-imposed "imprisonment" of Popes

**1929:** Lateran Treaty is signed, by which Italy recognizes the sovereignty and independence of the new Vatican City state

**1947:** Italian Republic reaffirms Italy's adherence to Lateran Treaty

**1962:** Pope John XXIII convenes Second Vatican Council to promote Christian unity

**1963:** Archbishop Giovanni Montini of Milan is elected pope on death of John XXIII and reigns as Paul VI

**1965:** Pope Paul VI makes a historic journey to speak before the UN in New York "for the cause of peace in the world"

**1978:** Pope Paul VI dies on August 6 at age 80; Albino Cardinal Luciani, Patriarch of Venice, is elected new pontiff, John Paul I, but he dies on September 28. Karol Cardinal Wojtyla, Archbishop of Krakow, Poland, succeeds as Pope John Pául II

**1979:** Pope John Paul II visits Mexico, Poland, Ireland, and U.S.

**1980:** The Pope visits Africa, France and Brazil

**1981:** Pope John Paul II is shot by a deranged Turkish terrorist May 13, but recovers from abdominal wounds and resumes duties

**1982:** John Paul II visits Africa, Portugal, Britain, and Argentina

## VENEZUELA

**Area:** 352,143 sq. mi. **Population:** 13,913,000 (1980 est.)

**Official Name:** Republic of Venezuela **Capital:** Caracas **Nationality:** Venezuelan **Languages:** Spanish is the official and universal language **Religion:** 96% Roman Catholic **Flag:** Horizontal stripes of yellow, blue, and red with an arc of 7 white stars in the center and the national coat of arms in the upper left **Anthem:** National Anthem, beginning "Glory to the brave people" **Currency:** Bolívar (4.3 per U.S. $1)

**Location:** North coast of South America. Venezuela is bounded on the north by the Caribbean Sea, on the east by Guyana, on the south by Brazil, and on the west by Colombia **Features:** The main regions are the Andes Mountains and outliers in the northwest; the northern coastal zone, the plains, or llanos, stretching from the mountains south and east to the Orinoco River; and the Guayana Highlands south and east of the Orinoco, consisting of high plateaus and rolling plains **Chief Rivers:** Orinoco, Caroní, Caura, Apure

**Head of State and of Government:** President Luis Herrera Campins, born 1925, inaugurated, March 1979 for 5 years **Effective Date of Present Constitution:** January 1961 **Legislative Body:** Congress (bicameral), consisting of the Senate, with 47 members and the 199-man Chamber of Deputies, both elected by adult suffrage for 5-year terms **Local Government:** 20 states, 2 federal territories, a federal district, and the 72 islands of the federal dependencies. The governors of each are appointed by the president, and each, except the dependencies, has its own elected legislature

**Ethnic Composition:** About 70% of the population is mestizo (of mixed Indian and European ancestry), 17% of European (mainly Spanish) origin, 7% black, 1% Indian, and the rest mulattos off mixed Indian and black ancestry **Population Distribution:** 76% urban **Density:** 40 inhabitants per sq. mi.

**Largest Cities:** (1977 est.) Caracas 2,664,225, Maracaibo 818,000, Valencia 455,000, Barquisimeto 444,000, Maracay 311,000, Barcelona 250,000, San Cristóbal 249,000

**Per Capita Income:** $3,398 (1980) **Gross National Product (GNP):** $51 billion (1980) **Economic Statistics:** 45% of GNP is derived from industry (including oil refining, textiles, building materials, clothing, shoes, food, steel, and chemicals), and 20% from agriculture **Minerals and Mining:** There are large deposits of oil, natural gas, bauxite, iron ore, salt, and smaller amounts of coal, gold, and diamonds **Labor Force:** 4.1 million (1977); 35% were in services, 15% in industry, and 10% in agriculture **Foreign Trade:** Exports, chiefly petroleum (95%) and products, and iron ore, totaled about $19 billion in 1980. Imports, mainly vehicles, iron and steel, wheat, mining and construction equipment, machinery and chemicals, totaled $11 billion **Principal Trade Partners:** United States, Canada, West Germany, Japan, Britain, Netherlands Antilles, Spain

**Vital Statistics:** Birthrate, 36.1 per 1,000 of pop. (1980); death rate, 6.5 **Life Expectancy:** 67 years **Health Statistics:** 429 inhabitants per hospital bed; 875 per physician (1977) **Infant Mortality:** 33.1 per 1,000 births **Illiteracy:** 13% **Primary and Secondary School Enrollment:** 2,835,284 (1976) **Enrollment in Higher Education:** 247,518 **GNP Expended on Education:** 7% (1976)

**Transportation:** Paved roads total 14,800 mi. **Motor Vehicles:** 1,684,700 (1977) **Passenger Cars:** 1,186,700 **Railway Mileage:** 232 **Ports:** La Guaira, Maracaibo, Puerto Cabello, Puerto La Cruz, Puerto Ordaz **Major Airlines:** VIASA, a government-owned airline, flies internationally; Avensa, privately owned, and LAV, government owned, fly domestically **Communications: Radio Transmitters:** 210 **Receivers:** 5,034,000 (1976) **Television Transmitters:** 48 **Receivers:** 1,431,000 (1976) **Telephones:** 847,000 (1977) **Newspapers:** 54 dailies, 178 copies per 1,000 inhabitants (1977)

**Weights and Measures:** Metric system **Travel Requirements:** Passport; tourist card valid 60 days, visa valid 60 days **International Dialing Code:** 58

Venezuela's prosperity has been based for years on petroleum, and this richest, most dynamic and most "American" country in Latin America is one of the world's largest petroleum exporters. In 1975-76 Venezuela nationalized the huge holdings of foreign petroleum and iron-ore mining companies, but did so peacefully, and the firms have been compensated. A government holding company, PETROVEN, controls and regulates the industry. In view of the world oversupply of oil, production was cut one third in the early 1980s in the collective OPEC effort to bolster prices. The United States is the largest customer for Venezuelan oil, most of which is produced for export. No major new fields have been discovered since 1958.

The government has been pumping its revenue into construction and industrial development. Rapid industrialization has created an urban people, alleviating the problem of land hunger, but decreasing agricultural production. Severe food shortages began to develop in 1977.

Venezuela has shown willingness to share part of its oil income with poorer nations of the Caribbean region. However, the reward for this generosity includes suspicion that Venezuela has imperialistic motives and is acting in "Yanqui" interests.

Venezuela's political stability—its last dictatorship was overthrown in 1958—was further demonstrated in 1978 when a new president was elected in what was basically a two-party race. Luis Herrera Campins, the candidate of the Social Christians, the "out" party, defeated Luis Piñerúa Ordaz, of the Democratic Action party. In a six-party contest, the two top parties polled 85% of the vote. In his inaugural speech in 1979, Herrera declared he had inherited "a mortgaged country." He promiseed to halt runaway public spending, and corruption, and give private business more flexibility in its operations.

Basic industries, such as steel and power, are owned and subsidized by the state. Venezuela's best hope for an industrial base to take the place of oil's proved reserves, which will last only through the year 2000, lies in Guayana, a region containing natural reserves of iron ore, sufficient for 75 years of production at current levels, and the hydroelectric potential of the Caroní River. Enough bauxite has been found to make the aluminum industry self-sufficient. The nation's oil riches are being used in a $12-billion industrialization program, in which the U.S. accounts for slightly more than half the foreign participation. However, a Spanish-Canadian group received the contracts for a national railroad grid, and the French for the $250-million Caracas subway.

**HISTORY:** Prior to the Spanish conquest in the 16th century, Venezuela was inhabited by 2 dominant Indian tribes—tthe Arawaks, who lived in agricultural communities, and the warlike Caribs. Charles I of Spain granted the Welsers, a German banking firm, the right to explore and colonize Venezuela but rescinded the right in 1546, after which the colony reverted to the Spanish crown

**1811:** Venezuela, under the leadership of Francisco de Miranda, declares its independence from Spain, but royalist forces maintain control

**1812-21:** Simón Bolívar leads a bloody war of independence against Spain, sets up Greater Colombia, encompassing the present territories of Venezuela, Colombia, Panama, and Ecuador, and is named president

**1830-1900:** Venezuela breaks away from Greater Colombia and becomes an independent republic; during the remainder of the century the nation is wracked by internal strife as dictator succeeds dictator. In 1895, Venezuela loses territory to British Guiana after a heated boundary dispute with Britain

**1908-35:** Gen. Juan Vicente Gómez becomes dictator; a tyrannical ruler, he succeeds in lifting the country to solvency by allotting oil concessions to foreign companies

**1937-38:** Gen. Eleázar López Contreras, Gómez' successor as president, exiles opposition political and labor leaders, declaring a moratorium on political and labor activities; he inaugurates a broad program of social and economic development

**1945:** A revolution breaks out and a liberal government headed by President Rómulo Betancourt takes power; he declares universal suffrage, and institutes social reforms

**1947-48:** A new constitution is adopted, providing for election of the president by direct popular vote. Rómulo Gallegos, of the Democratic Action party, is elected president but is ousted in 1948 by a military junta led by Colonels Marcos Pérez Jiménez and Carlos Delgado Chalbaud

**1953-59:** Pérez Jiménez takes power; he is overthrown in 1958 during a revolt supported by liberal elements of the armed forces. After brief interim government by a civilian-military junta, Betancourt is elected president

**1962:** Venezuela adopts new constitution limiting president to five-year term. Communists launch terrorist campaign to oust Betancourt because of his support for U.S. blockade of Cuba

**1963-67:** Raúl Leoni, leader of the liberal Democratic Action party, is elected president on a platform pledging economic and social reform; he suspends constitutional guarantees in drive against Castro-supported terrorists

**1968:** Rafael Caldera, the Social Christian candidate, is elected president; Democratic Action party retains control of Congress

**1970:** Venezuela and Guyana declare 12-year moratorium on border dispute

**1973:** Caldera government quadruples petroleum reference prices. Venezuela joins the Andean Pact, formed by Bolivia, Chile, Colombia, Ecuador and Peru. Carlos Andrés Pérez of Democratic Action party is elected president

**1976:** Oil industry is nationalized

**1977:** President Pérez announces a series of austerity measures aimed at controlling inflation and cutting government spending

**1978:** Presidents Pérez and Carter sign agreements on maritime boundaries between Venezuela and U.S. and curbing flow of illicit drugs. Luis Herrera Campins of Social Christian party wins presidential election on Dec. 6

**1979:** Herrera is inaugurated on March 12. A U.S. businessman, William F. Niehous, is freed after being held prisoner 41 months by guerrillas. Foreign debt rises from $7.4 to $12.2 billion

**1980:** Venezuela reaches agreement with Mexico on plan to supply oil and loans to nine countries of the Caribbean region. Aid to Bolivia is cut off following a military coup there. Relations with Cuba are strained by acquittal of four men accused of bombing a Cuban passenger plane in 1976

**1981:** PETROVEN cuts price of its best grade of residual oil by $7 per barrel. Leftists hijack three planes to Havana

**1982:** Pres. Herrera assails intervention by United States in Central American affairs. Venezuela renews claim to mineral-rich region of Guyana west of Essequibo River

## VIETNAM

**Area:** 128,405 sq. mi. **Population:** 52,741,766 (1979 census)

**Official Name:** Socialist Republic of Vietnam **Capital:** Hanoi **Nationality:** Vietnamese **Languages:** Vietnamese, spoken by the majority, is the official language; minorities speak Chinese, French, Khmer, Cham, and Montagnard (mountain tribal) languages **Religion:** The majority of the people nominally practice Buddhism and animism, although many combine these with elements of Taoism, Confucianism, and Christianity. However, organized religious activities have been discouraged in the North **Flag:** A yellow five-pointed star centered on a red field **Anthem:** Tien Quan Ca (Hymn of the Marching Army) **Currency:** Dong (2.09 per U.S. $1)

**Location:** Southeast Asia, occupying the eastern part of the Indochinese peninsula. It is bordered by China on the north, by the South China Sea on the east and south, and by Laos and Cambodia on the west **Features:** The jungle-covered hills in the north and northwest rise southeastward into the Annamese Cordillera and its outlying plateaus. East of the mountains are fertile coastal lowlands, with the deltas of the Mekong and Red rivers being the largest and most densely populated **Chief Rivers:** Red, Black, Lo, Ca, Mekong, Ba, Dong Nai

**Political Leader:** Le Duan, Secretary General of the Communist Party, born 1908, appointed 1960 **Head of State:** Truong Chinh, appointed July 4, 1981, is chairman of the Council of State, a collective presidency **Head of Government:** Premier Pham Van Dong, born 1906, elected 1976 **Effective Date of Present Constitution:** Dec. 1980 **Legislative Body:** National Assembly (unicameral), with 496 members. The chief executive and legislative organ of government is the Communist party's 15-man Politburo, the core of the 152-member Central Committee headed by Le Duan **Local Government:** 36 provinces, 3 city provinces, and one special area

**Ethnic Composition:** Vietnamese constitute about 90% of the population; Montagnards of both Malayo-Polynesian and Mon-Khmer ethnic groups make up about 8%, and the rest include Chinese, Khmer, and Cham minorities **Population Distribution:** 19% urban **Density:** 411 inhabitants per sq. mi.

**Largest Cities:** (1979 census) Ho Chi Minh City (Saigon) 3,419,978, Hanoi 2,570,905, Haiphong 1,279,067

**Per Capita Income:** $113 (1980) **Gross National Product (GNP):** $6 billion (1980) **Economic Statistics:** Basically agricultural (rice, sugarcane, tea, maize, manioc, coffee, fish, rubber), rice, the staple food, still has to be imported. Light industry is confined to food processing, textiles, glass, paper, machinery, cement and, in the North, steel **Minerals and Mining:** Coal, iron ore, apatite, phosphates, chromite, tin, salt, granite, and limestone **Labor Force:** About 15 million with 70% in agriculture and 8% in industry **Foreign Trade:** Exports ($300 million, 1978) consist mainly of coal, rubber, ores, wood, tea, spices, and coffee. Imports ($900 million, 1978) include rice, heavy machinery, transportation equipment, vehicles, chemicals, and fuels **Principal Trade Partners:** USSR, Eastern Europe, Japan

**Vital Statistics:** Birthrate, 40.9 per 1,000 of pop. (1980); death rate, 17.6 **Life Expectancy:** 52 years **Health Statistics:** About 284 per hospital bed; 5,441 per physician (1977) **Infant Mortality:** N.A. **Illiteracy:** About 25% **Primary and Secondary School Enrollment:** 10,923,436 (1976) **Enrollment in Higher Education:** 100,027 **GNP Expended on Education:** N.A.

**Transportation:** Paved roads total 3,400 mi. **Motor Vehicles:** N.A. **Railway Mileage:** 1,718 **Ports:** Ho Chi Minh City, Haiphong, Da Nang, Qui Nhon, Cam Ranh, Ben Thuy, Hong Gai, Nha Trang **Major Airlines:** Air Vietnam **Communications: Radio Transmitters:** 43 **Receivers:** North—1,000,000 (1974); South—1,550,000 (1973) **Television Transmitters:** 7 **Receivers:** North—N.A.; South—500,000 **Telephones:** North—N.A.; South—46,509 **Newspapers:** 5 dailies, 5 copies per 1,000 inhabitants (1977)

**Weights and Measures:** Metric system **Travel Requirements:** Traveler should consult U.S. Department of State

A unified Vietnam, from the China border to the Gulf of Siam, came into being on July 2, 1976. The formal reunification after 22 years of division came 16 months after the collapse and surrender of the South Vietnamese government in Saigon to its North Vietnaamese conquerors. After 30 years of struggle against foreign powers and the regimes they fostered, revolutionary forces of Vietnam realized the goal of the late Ho Chi Minh. The Communists, with more than a little help from their friends, had all of Vietnam under one flag and one government. In the years since the fall of the Saigon Government the problems of peace have proved as hard to solve as those of war.

The split into North Vietnam and South Vietnam that marked the end of French presence and the beginnings of American involvement occurred in 1954. As a colonial war ended, a period of insurgency and war began. It was to last over two decades and leave a legacy of bomb craters, street rubble, bullet-pocked buildings, abandoned rice fields and patches of defoliated forest—in addition to the thousands of lost, maimed and dislocated Vietnamese people.

The long war that could not be won came to a close for U.S. troops in 1973. A peace accord that could not be enforced lasted only 20 months after the American withdrawal. The end to the tragic war came with unbelievable swiftness in April of 1975 as the Communist forces swept the coastal cities and took Saigon almost unopposed. The cost to the United States for its misadventure in Indochina was 57,000 lives and $150 billion.

For Vietnam, the process of rebuilding a shattered economy and restructuring society in the South left little time for looks backward. In the South a provisional government took over from the military and began the task of dealing with three million unemployed urban residents and reshaping the economy to fit a different ideology.

To achieve self-sufficiency in food the new unified government resettled millions of refugees from the cities into rural areas so they could resume food production. It is said that nearly 700,000 were moved from Saigon to work abandoned rice fields or develop new agricultural areas, and the population of Da Nang was reduced by half. For many, life in the "new economic zones" is tough, with former clerks, unaccustomed to manual labor, trying to coax crops from marginal lands.

The transfer of people also involves Northerners. Tens of thousands of civil servants, teachers and tax collectors have been moved to the South to provide a dependable cadre at lower echelons. Plans call for the eventual movement of millions from densely populated rural places in the North to the more agriculturally productive South.

Vietnam found itself involved in two wars in 1979, piling up further troubles for its wrecked economy and internal tumult—the latter attested to by an outflow of hundreds of thousands of refugees, largely ethnic Chinese. Vietnam invaded Cambodia in late 1978 and, on January 7, 1979, captured the capital city, Phnom Penh, and set up a puppet government, forcing the troops of the China-backed Pol Pot regime to retreat into remote rural areas. There, together with other rebellious groups, they fought on, tying down more than 200,000 Vietnamese soldiers until some of these were called back in 1981-82.

Meanwhile, on February 17, 1979, The Chinese invaded northern Vietnam, fought for four weeks, and, after advancing no more than 20 miles, withdrew, claiming victory in what they called a punitive invasion brought about by earlier Vietnamese border incursions. (China later admitted the loss of 20,000 killed and wounded.) Thereafter, Vietnam felt impelled to maintain some 40 divisions at the China border despite its costly troop commitments in Cambodia and in Laos, where it was supporting another weak Communist regime.

As emnity toward the Chinese (traditional enemies of the Vietnamese people) increased, ties became closer with the USSR, with which a 25-year treaty of friendship had been signed in 1978. But heavy Soviet aid—estimated at about $3 million a day in 1981, failed to halt deterioration of the Vietnamese economy, and there were indications in 1981 and 1982 of possible major reductions in that assistance. By 1982, runaway inflation, chronic food shortages, lagging industrial development, and uncontrollable black markets in Saigon (now called Ho Chi Minh City) and other areas led the Vietnam regime to make major alterations in government leadership and to admit, belatedly, that policy mistakes and mismanagement of the centrally directed economy were in large measure responsible for the crisis.

**HISTORY:** The Vietnamese are believed to have originated in North China, from where they were slowly driven southward by the Han Chinese. By the 3rd century B.C., the Vietnamese had become settled in the Red River Delta in northern Vietnam. China annexed the region in the 2nd century B.C. and ruled it until 938 A.D., when independence was reestablished by Ngo Quyen. The new state gradually expanded, occupying much of Cambodia and southern Vietnam

**1858:** French and Spanish forces intervene in Vietnam's southern region of Cochin China to halt persecution of native Catholics

**1862-67:** Vietnam is forced to yield Cochin China to the French

**1884:** France establishes a protectorate over Annam, in central Vietnam, and over Tonkin, in the north

**1887:** Cambodia, Cochin China, Annam, and Tonkin are incorporated into the Indo-Chinese Union

**1940-45:** Vietnam is occupied by Japanese forces during World War II; with defeat impending, Japan grants Vietnam independence under a puppet government headed by Bao Dai, emperor of Annam; following Japan's surrender to the Allies, Communist Viet Minh guerrillas, under leadership of Ho Chi Minh, set up Democratic Republic of Vietnam

**1946-54:** Viet Minh wages war against the French for eight years, culminating in the defeat of French forces at Dien Bien Phu; armistice is signed under a series of agreements concluded at Geneva, providing for the partition of Vietnam along the 17th parallel, with the north going to the government of Ho Chi Minh and the south placed under the control of Saigon. The agreements provided for the joining of North and South Vietnam into one country by holding elections in 1956. These were never held

**NORTH VIETNAM**

**1955:** Ho Chi Minh visits Communist China and USSR and signs aid agreements with both

**1956:** Peasant revolts break out in opposition to government's land collectivization program, but are crushed by troops

**1959:** North Vietnam, working through Viet Cong guerrillas, instigates campaign of terror and subversion in South Vietnam in attempt to annex state and unify Vietnam under Communist rule

**1964-65:** U.S. planes bomb North Vietnamese military targets following attacks on U.S. warships in Gulf of Tonkin in 1964; sustained U.S. air attacks are begun in 1965 to stem flow of equipment and North Vietnamese troops into the south

**1968:** United States orders halt to all bombing north of 20th parallel; move leads to an agreement between Hanoi and Washington to open peace talks in Paris

**1969:** Ho Chi Minh dies

**1971:** North Vietnamese troops drive South Vietnamese forces from Laos after the latter fail to cut Ho Chi Minh Trail

**1973:** Peace agreement signed in Paris officially ends Vietnam War, though fighting continues on a diminished scale

**1974-75:** Fighting escalates as both North and South repeatedly violate the cease-fire agreement. A stepped-up Communist offensive in early 1975 results in the abandonment by Saigon forces of the Central Highlands. The last resistance from the Saigon government ends on April 30 as Viet Cong and North Vietnamese troops enter Saigon

**SOUTH VIETNAM**

**1955:** Bao Dai is deposed and a republic established under the presidency of former Prime Minister Ngo Dinh Diem; a U.S. military advisory group is set up in South Vietnam

**1959-63:** South Vietnamese Communist guerrillas, known as Viet Cong, wage war against Diem government; harsh security measures introduced by Saigon regime incur wide resentment; Buddhist monks immolate themselves to protest what they charge is persecution by Diem. After violent demonstrations the government is overthrown and Diem is murdered

**1965:** New military regime is formed, with Gen. Nguyen Van Thieu as chief of state and Air Vice Marshal Nguyen Cao Ky as premier; U.S. planes begin systematic bombing of North Vietnam, while in the south U.S. troop strength mounts to 200,000 men

**1967:** In South Vietnam's first national elections, Nguyen Van Thieu becomes president and Nguyen Cao Ky vice-president

**1968:** President Johnson announces a halt of U.S. bombings over most of North Vietnam; peace talks between United States and North Vietnam open in Paris

**1970:** South Vietnamese and U.S. troops invade Cambodia in drive against Viet Cong and North Vietnamese forces; Saigon troops continue operations after U.S. withdrawal

**1971:** South Viietnamese forces attempting to cut Ho Chi Minh Trail in Laos are driven out by North Vietnamese. Enemy steps up attacks in South Vietnam on eve of elections. Thieu runs unopposed for president and is reelected

**1973:** Paris peace agreement formally ends Vietnam War in January, but fighting continues on reduced level. The first prisoner exchanges worked out at the conference table begin

**1974:** Fighting intensifies in the central highlands near the Cambodian border; the Saigon government suspends its participation with the Viet Cong in Paris reconciliation talks

**1975:** North Vietnamese and Viet Cong forces step up their offensive in the South, seizing major cities. President Ford orders U.S. naval ships to help evacuate refugees. President Thieu resigns but the Viet Cong refuse to negotiate with the new South Vietnamese leadership. Communist troops enter and occupy Saigon. War ends as the South Vietnamese government unconditionally surrenders to the Viet Cong on April 29, 1975. Provisional Revolutionary Government takes control on June 6

**UNIFIED VIETNAM**

**1976:** First countrywide assembly elections are held April 25. North and South are officially reunited July 2

**1977:** Security Council approves Vietnam membership in the UN. Border fighting flares up between Vietnam and Cambodia. Vietnamese face serious food problem, with rice shortage estimated at 18% of need. Talks with U.S. on establishing relations recess without progress as U.S. is slow to make aid commitment

**1978:** Government introduces new national currency, cracks down on black-marketeers. Vietnamese-Cambodian border war intensifies. Refugees reportedly leaving Vietnam at highest rate since end of war in 1975. President Carter approves interim refugee policy permitting admission of Vietnamese "boat people" refused asylum elsewhere. In July, Vietnam is admitted to Soviet bloc's economic and trade group; in November, Vietnam and the Soviet Union sign a 25-year friendship treaty. China blames Vietnam in incident at their border, ends Vietnam aid. Vietnam inducts 350,000 into armed forces. Worst floods in 35 years destroy large part of rice crop. In December, Vietnamese troops advance into Cambodia

**1979:** Vietnamese troops, together with Cambodian rebels, capture Phnom Penh on Jan. 7. But the deposed Cambodian premier, Pol Pot, escapes, and some 130,000 Vietnamese are tied down in Cambodia fighting guerrillas. On Feb. 7, China invades Vietnam with 100,000 troops that penetrate 15 or 20 miles in four weeks. Chinese depart, with both sides claiming victory. By midyear, the number of ethnic Chinese fleeing Vietnam is estimated at 300,000 in a 12-month span

**1980:** More than 200,000 Vietnamese soldiers remain in Cambodia, and 50,000 are still stationed in Laos. At home, at least 20,000 former Vietnamese bureaucrats, military and professional men, and others are confined to "re-education camps." Vietnamese troops stage two-day June attack on refugee camps in Thailand. Mid-year monsoon rains make three million homeless. A new constitution is announced

**1981:** Exodus of "boat people" increases again early in the year. China reports sporadic Vietnamese forays across its border. Vietnam's removal of 24,000 troops from Cambodia is reported as Soviet aid to both Cambodia and Vietnam is reduced

**1982:** Vietnam's leadership is shaken up as Party Secretary Le Duan admits that "party mistakes" are partly to blame for worsening economy; war hero Vo Nguyen Giap dropped from Politburo. In June, Vietnam offers to release prisoners in political detention camps if the U.S. will accept them

## WESTERN SAMOA

**Area:** 1,133 sq. mi. **Population:** 158,130 (1981 census)

**Official Name:** Independent State of Western Samoa **Capital:** Apia **Nationality:** Western Samoan **Languages:** Samoan, the predominant Polynesian language, and English are official **Religion:** The population is almost entirely Christian, with 50% Congregationalist, 20% Methodist, and 20% Roman Catholic **Flag:** A red field with a blue rectangle in the upper left corner bearing 5 white stars representing the Southern Cross **Anthem:** The Flag of Freedom **Currency:** Tala (0.93 per U.S. $1)

**Location:** South Pacific, forming part of an island group lying midway between Honolulu and Sydney, Australia. Western Samoa (14°S., 172°W.) consists of the islands of Savai'i and Upolu and seven smaller islands of which only Manono and Apolima are inhabited **Features:** The islands are formed mainly of volcanic rock, with coral reefs surrounding much of the coasts. Rugged mountain ranges form the core of the two main islands, and there are many dormant volcanoes and lava fields **Chief Rivers:** There are no large rivers

**Head of State:** Chief Malietoa Tanumafili II, born 1913, appointed in 1962; future holders of the office will be elected by the Legislative Assembly for 5-year terms **Head of Government:** Prime Minister Va'ai Kolone, appointed April 13, 1982 **Effective Date of Present Constitution:** January 1962 **Legislative Body:** Legislative Assembly (unicameral), consisting of 47 members, 45 of whom are Samoans elected by family chiefs (*matai*), and 2 are elected by universal suffrage, all for 3-year terms **Local Government:** 24 legislative districts (*faipule*), grouped into 12 political districts. Local government is carried out by the village councils (*fono*)

**Ethnic Composition:** Samoans, who form the second-largest branch of the Polynesian race, constitute 88% of the population. Euronesians (of mixed Polynesian and European ancestry) make up 10%, and the rest consists of Europeans (700) and other Pacific Islanders **Population Distribution:** 22% urban **Density:** 140 inhabitants per sq. mi.

**Largest City:** (1981 census) Apia 33,100

**Per Capita Income:** $450 (1978) **Gross National Product (GNP):** $70 million (1978) **Economic Statistics:** There are no detailed GNP statistics available; however, industries include handicrafts, foods, fruit processing, clothing, soap, and furniture; and agricultural products include taro, timber, fish, coconuts, cocoa, bananas, and pineapples **Minerals and Mining:** None **Labor Force:** 38,200, with 90% in agriculture and fishing **Foreign Trade:** Exports, mainly copra, cocoa, bananas, timber, and taro, totaled $11 million in 1978. Imports, chiefly clothing and textiles, flour, canned fish and meat, motor vehicles, tobacco, sugar, and timber totaled $53 million **Principal Trade Partners:** New Zealand, Australia, Britain, West Germany, United States, Japan

**Vital Statistics:** Birthrate, 16.4 per 1,000 of pop. (1980); death rate, 3.1 **Life Expectancy:** 67 years **Health Statistics:** 214 inhabitants per hospital bed; 2,884 per physician (1977) **Infant Mortality:** 13.7 per 1,000 births **Illiteracy:** 2% **Primary and Secondary School Enrollment:** 51,025 (1977) **Enrollment in Higher Education:** 180 **GNP Expended on Education:** 3% (1977)

**Transportation:** Paved roads total 230 mi. **Motor Vehicles:** 3,500 (1978) **Passenger Cars:** 1,400 **Railway Mileage:** None **Ports:** Apia, Asau **Major Airlines:** Polynesian Airlines operates international and domestic flights **Communications: Radio Transmitters:** 4 **Receivers:** 50,000 (1973) **Television Transmitters:** None; received from American Samoa **Receivers:** 1,800 **Telephones:** 4,000 (1977) **Newspapers:** 2 several times a week, 103 copies per 1,000 inhabitants

**Weights and Measures:** British standards are used **Travel Requirements:** Passport, no visa for stay up to 30 days

Western Samoa became, on January 1, 1962, the first fully independent Polynesian state. Until then, the country, along with Eastern Samoa, had been under foreign control or tutelage since the turn of the century. In 1899 the Samoan islands were apportioned between Germany, which got Western Samoa as a protectorate, and the United States, which obtained, and still holds, the eastern part as American Samoa. Western Samoa was held from 1914 to 1962 by New Zealand, which, after ousting the Germans in World War I, obtained a League of Nations mandate and then a UN trusteeship. Although independent, Western Samoa still has New Zealand handling its foreign relations.

Western Samoa is a nation in transition, struggling to preserve its traditional ways while grappling with a backward economy. The most striking of those ways, perhaps, is the social system, based on *aigas*, or extended family groups, which are headed by *matais*, or chiefs. The *matais* direct the use of *aiga* assets. Supported by most Western Samoans, the system is a conservative force that many observers feel hampers the country, but the government, now headed by younger men, points to the possibility of change.

Western Samoa's economy is predominantly agricultural but efforts are underway to develop its fishing industry and increase tourism.

**HISTORY:** Archaeological evidence indicates that Samoa may have been settled as far back as 1000 B.C., but little is known with certainty of its early history. The first Europeans to visit Samoa were the Dutch in 1722. Throughout the 19th century, the islands became pawns in a struggle for control by the United States, Germany, and Britain. After a brief attempt at tripartite control of Samoa, a treaty was signed in 1899 assigning Eastern Samoa to the United States and Western Samoa to Germany

**1914-20:** New Zealand occupies Western Samoa following outbreak of World War I and is later awarded mandate over islands by League of Nations

**1927-36:** Samoans and European settlers wage campaign of civil disobedience in opposition to the administration; campaign develops into movement for independence

**1946:** Western Samoa becomes United Nations trusteeship under continued supervision of New Zealand

**1962:** Western Samoa becomes independent, with Chiefs Tupua Tamasese Meaole and Malietoa Tanumafili II as joint heads of state. Tupua Tamasese Meaole dies in 1963

**1970:** Tamasese Lealofi IV is named prime minister as head of reform-minded government of younger men

**1973:** Fiame Mata'afa Mulinuu is elected prime minister

**1975:** Treaty is signed with EC. Mata'afa dies and is replaced by Tamasese Lealofi IV

**1976:** Taisi Tupuola Efi becomes prime minister

**1979:** Tupuola Efi barely retains post in 24-23 vote of the parliament; criticized for seeking too rapid a rate of economic growth

**1980:** Government tightens controls on imports and overseas payments to offset loss of foreign exchange. Visiting Japanese mission is greeted by public demonstrations against dumping of nuclear wastes in the Pacific

**1981:** Government faces serious economic problems with exports coming to a virtual standstill. Proposal to give all adults the right to vote is defeated in the assembly

**1982:** Va'ai Kolone becomes prime minister when his Human Rights party wins slim victory in assembly

## YEMEN (YEMEN ARAB REPUBLIC)

**Area:** 77,220 sq. mi. **Population:** 6,456,189 (1981 census)

**Official Name:** Yemen Arab Republic **Capital:** San'a **Nationality:** Yemeni **Languages:** Arabic is the official and universal language **Religion:** Islam is the state religion, with the population almost equally divided between the Zaidi Shi'ite and Shafai Sunnite sects **Flag:** Horizontal stripes of red, white, and black with a green star in the center **Anthem:** National Anthem, beginning "Peace to the land" **Currency:** Yemeni rial (4.56 per U.S. $1)

**Location:** Southwest Arabia. Yemen is bounded on the north and east by Saudi Arabia, on the south by Southern Yemen, and on the west by the Red Sea **Features:** The country consists of a semidesert coastal plain (the Tihama) along the Red Sea and a mountainous area in the interior which receives abundant rainfall **Chief Rivers:** There are no permanent rivers

**Head of State:** President: Col. Ali Abdullah Saleh, born 1942, elected July 1978 **Head of Government:** Premier Abdel Karim Iryani, appointed Oct. 15, 1980 **Effective Date of Present Constitution:** 1971, suspended 1974 **Legislative Body:** Constituent People's Assembly of 159 members **Local Government:** 11 governorates

**Ethnic Composition:** The population is predominantly Arab. 10% are Afro-Arabs, residing in the Tihama **Population Distribution:** 11% urban **Density:** 84 inhabitants per sq. mi.

**Largest Cities:** (1975 census) San'a 134,588, Hodeida 80,314, Ta'izz 78,642, Dhamar 19,467, Ibb 19,066, Al Beida 5,975

**Per Capita Income:** $580 (1980) **Gross National Prooduct (GNP):** $3 billion (1980) **Economic Statistics:** About 35% of GNP comes from agriculture (cotton, Mocha coffee, livestock, cereals, vegetables, fruit). There is some light industry (textiles, food products) **Minerals and Mining:** The only industrial minning enterprise is the extraction of salt. There are traces of copper, coal, sulfur, gypsum and quartz **Labor Force:** 800,000; 70% of the population is engaged in agriculture and animal husbandry, and 13% in trade. Many work abroad **Foreign Trade:** Exports, mainly cotton, coffee, hides and skins, salt, and qat, totaled $12 million in 1980. Imports, chiefly textiles, machinery, fuels, foods, totaled $1.9 billion **Principal Trade Partners:** Southern Yemen, Saudi Arabia, Australia, EC countries, India, Japan

**Vital Statistics:** Birthrate, 48.3 per 1,000 of pop. (1980); death rate, 25.4 **Life Expectancy:** 47 years **Health Statistics:** 1,957 inhabitants per hospital bed (1977); 13,835 per physician (1977) **Infant Mortality:** N.A. **Illiteracy:** 85% **Primary and Secondary School Enrollment:** 279,541 (1975) **Enrollment in Higher Education:** 2,408 **GNP Expended on Education:** 0.6% (1974)

**Transportation:** Paved roads total 300 mi. **Motor Vehicles:** 44,500 (1975) **Passenger Cars:** 14,000 **Railway Mileage:** None **Ports:** Hodeida, Mocha **Major Airlines:** Yemen Airways, government owned, operates domestic and international flights **Communications: Radio Transmitters:** 6 **Receivers:** 90,000 (1976) **Television Transmitters:** 2 **Receivers:** N.A. **Telephones:** 5,000 (1975) **Newspapers:** 6 dailies, 10 copies per 1,000 inhabitants (1970)

**Weights and Measures:** Local units are used **Travel Requirements:** Passport, visa valid 3 months, $2 fee

Yemen is a land whose interior contains gauntly beautiful mountains and green, cultivated fields—a rarity in the Arabian peninsula—and whose crucially important location between the Gulf of Aden and the Red Sea, athwart the Arabian oil route to the West, has brought it a disproportionate degree of world attention.

Yemen remains a country that is difficult to govern, where tribal loyalties are stronger than national considerations. Those tendencies have been aggravated by a civil war (1962-1969), and by memories of ancient times when Yemen and Southern Yemen had common ties. The civil war began in 1962 as a revolt against Mohammed al-Badr, heir to a dynasty of Imams (religious rulers) who had become arbitrary and capricious. The rebels established a republic with Egyptian backing; the Imam continued resistance from the hills, with an army of tribesmen and mercenaries supported by Saudi Arabia. Egypt sent almost a third of its army to help the republic. Egypt and Saudi Arabia agreed to end their intervention in 1967, and the Imam's forces were defeated by those of the republic in 1969. But the republic was, and remained, unstable, plagued by coups and counter-coups.

In a 48-hour period in Juune 1978, the Presidents of both Yemen and Southern Yemen were killed. The violence began in Sa'na just as Yemen's President Ahmed Hussein al-Ghashmi, a close ally of Saudi Arabia, was about to consider Southern Yemen's proposals for a merger of the Yemens. Yemen, blaming Soviet-backed Southern Yemen for the killing, severed their relations. Two days later, Southern Yemen President Salem Rubaye Ali, a moderate Marxist, lost a power struggle with the ultraleftist general secretary of the country's National Liberation Front party, Abdul Fattah Ismail, whom Western and Arab observers suspect may have been behind Ghashmi's murder. Ghashmi was succeed by Ali Abdullah Saleh, and tensions with Southern Yemen continued to build. Southern Yemeni soldiers—with Soviet, Cuban, and East German help—invaded Yemen in February 1979. Saudi Arabia and the United States rushed arms to Yemen, and U.S. ships showed the flag in nearby waters. In March, the League of Arab States arranged a cease-fire; and a special force, under the League's command, was established to patrol the border. President Saleh and President Ismail met in Kuwait and drew up a plan to merge their two countries, but Ismail's resignation as president of South Yemen in early 1980 left the plan in abeyance.

**HISTORY:** Yemen formed part of what was known as Arabia Felix in classical times and was the site of a series of rich mercantile kingdoms. One of these was Sheba, or Saba, which flourished from about 750 to 115 B.C. The Sabaeans were superseded by the Himyarites, under whom Judaism and Christianity took root. Himyarite rule was ended in 525 by an invading force of Christian Ethiopians, who in turn were driven out by the Persians in 575

**7th cent.:** Islam is introduced

**9th cent.:** Yemen comes under the control of the Rassite dynasty, religious leaders, called imams, of the Zaydi sect, who lay the foundations of a theocratic political structure lasting to 1962

**1517-1918:** Ottoman Empire exercises nominal sovereignty

**1948:** Imam Yahya is assassinated; his son, Crown Prince Ahmad, defeats forces of new government and succeeds as imam

**1958:** Yemen and United Arab Republic (union of Egypt and Syria) form confederation called United Arab States

**1961:** Following Syria's withdrawal from UAR, President Nasser dissolves the association with Yemen, denouncing Imam Ahmad as a reactionary

**1962:** Ahmad dies and is succeeded by Crown Prince Mohammad al-Badr, who favors a neutralist foreign policy; he is overthrown by pro-Nasser army officers who proclaim a republic under the leadership of Col. Abdullah al-Salal; civil war breaks out between republican and royalist forces, who win the respective backing of Egypt and Saudi Arabia

**1963:** Egypt sends 40,000 troops to Yemen to assist republicans

**1967:** Egypt withdraws troops from Yemen; riots in San'a force al-Salal to form new government free of Egyptian influence; he is deposed, however, while on a visit to Moscow and a new republican government is set up; royalist forces move on San'a

**1968:** Republicans, aided by Soviet-built aircraft, regain initiative; royalists retreat, reorganize their forces and in an effort to widen their political base fill top posts with officials not related to the Imam, who is deprived of all political power

**1969:** Republican government asserts that civil war has ended; Lt. Gen. Hassan al-Amri resigns as prime minister; a new cabinet is formed and Abdullah al-Karshumi becomes prime minister

**1970:** Amicable settlement is reached between republicans and royalists; Moshen al-Aini is named premier

**1972:** Yemen and Southern Yemen end hostilities after series of border clashes; they agree to future merger. Aini is replaced by Abdullah al-Hagri

**1973:** Border clashes resume between the two Yemens

**1974:** Hagri is replaced by Hassan Makki. Army ousts government in bloodless coup and establishes military junta headed by Col. Ibrahim al-Hamdi. Aini forms new government

**1975:** Premier Aini is replaced by Abd al-Aziz Ad al-Ghani

**1977:** Col. Ibrahim al-Hamdi is assassinated; new military rulers

impose martial law, as Maj. Ahmed Hussein al-Ghashmi assumes leadership of government
**1978:** Constituent assembly formally elects Ghashmi president. Ghashmi is assassinated; Yemen blames Southern Yemen, severs relations. Ghashmi's murder is factor in overthrow two days later of Southern Yemen's President Rubaye Ali by colleagues in pro-Soviet National Front. Constituent People's Assembly elects Col. Ali Abdullah Saleh president
**1979:** Southern Yemen invades Yemen, which gets aid from United States and Saudi Arabia. Cease-fire agreement places Yemen-Southern Yemen border under patrol commanded by League of Arab States. Presidents Saleh and Ismail agree to merger plan
**1982:** Draft constitution is announced for a unified state with Southern Yemen

## SOUTHERN YEMEN

**Area:** 111,101 sq. mi. **Population:** 2,030,000 (1981 est.)

**Official Name:** People's Democratic Republic of Yemen **Capital:** Aden **Nationality:** Southern Yemenite or Yemeni **Languages:** Arabic is the official language; Mahri is spoken in the east, and English is also widely understood **Religion:** 98% of the population are Sunni Moslems of the Shafai sect **Flag:** Horizontal stripes of red, white, and black with a red star on a blue triangle at the hoist **Anthem:** National Anthem (no words) **Currency:** Yemeni dinar (0.35 per U.S. $1)

**Location:** Southern part of the Arabian peninsula. Southern Yemen is bounded on the north by Saudi Arabia, on the east by Oman, on the south by the Gulf of Aden, and on the northwest by Yemen **Features:** A narrow, sandy plain along the coast gives way to mountainous terrain, interspersed with deep valleys. The land retains its mountainous character until it reaches the interior sands. Offshore islands include Socotra, Perim, and Kamaran **Chief Rivers:** There are no permanent rivers

**Head of State and of Government:** Chairman of the Presidium of the Supreme People's Council (President) and Prime Minister: Ali Nasir Mohammed al-Hasani, born 1938, appointed prime minister 1971, became head of state April 1980 **Effective Date of Present Constitution:** December 1, 1970 **Legislative Body:** Supreme People's Council (unicameral) of 111 elected members **Local Government:** 6 governorates under appointed governors

**Ethnic Composition:** The population is mainly Arab; Indians, Pakistanis, and Somalis constitute small minorities **Population Distribution:** 33% urban **Density:** 18 inhabitants per sq. mi.

**Largest Cities:** (1977 est.) Aden 285,373; (1972 est.) Mukalla 45,000, Seiyun 20,000

**Per Capita Income:** $420 (1980) **Gross National Product (GNP):** $803 million (1980) **Economic Statistics:** The subsistence economy is based on agriculture (sorghum, millet, wheat) and fishing, though some cotton is grown for export. Aden, a leading oil bunkering port, is slowly recovering with the reopening of the Suez Canal. There is an oil refinery, and somee light industry **Minerals and Mining:** Salt **Labor Force:** 395,568 (1977), with 62% in subsistence agriculture, and 18% in industry, with 72% of the latter in oil refining **Foreign Trade:** Exports, mainly petroleum products, raw cotton, hides and skins, and fuel oil, totaled $42 million in 1978. Imports, chiefly rice, wheat flour, tea, machinery, textiles, and petroleum products, totaled $312 million **Principal Trade Partners:** Kuwait, Britain, Japan, Yemen, India, Iraq

**Vital Statistics:** Birthrate, 47.5 per 1,000 of pop. (1980); death rate, 20.8 **Life Expectancy:** 45 years **Health Statistics:** 648 inhabitants per hospital bed; 7,940 per physician (1978) **Infant Mortality:** 79.9 per 1,000 births **Illiteracy:** 72% **Primary and Secondary School Enrollment:** 236,162 (1974) **Enrollment in Higher Education:** 934 **GNP Expended on Education:** 3.9% (1976)

**Transportation:** Paved roads total 200 mi. **Motor Vehicles:** 22,400 (1976) **Passenger Cars:** 11,900 **Railway Mileage:** None **Port:** Aden **Major Airlines:** Democratic Yemen Airlines, government owned **Communications: Radio Transmitters:** 5 **Receivers:** 100,000 (1976) **Television Transmitters:** 5 **Receivers:** 32,000 (1976) **Telephones:** 10,000 (1973) **Newspapers:** 4 dailies (1976), 1 copy per 1,000 inhabitants (1973)

**Weights and Measures:** British standards are generally used in Aden; local measures are used in the rest of tthe country **Travel Requirements:** Traveler should consult U.S. Department of State for travel information

One of the poorest member of the Arab League, Southern Yemen comprises the former colony of Aden, at the southwestern corneer of the Arabian peninsula, and a forbidding hinterland with poorly defined borders. Under British rule, the country was known as "Aden," and later as the "Federation of South Arabia." It declared independence in 1967 as "People's Republic of Southern Yemen." In 1970, the official name was changed to the "People's Democratic Republic of Yemen." Hopes for union with the neighboring "Yemen Arab Republic" exist in both states, but each wants union on its own terms.

With its oppressively hot climate and barren terrain, Southern Yemen has few natural resources and little industry, and relied heavily on foreign aid for its 1974-79 five-year development plan. About 62 percent of the population is engaged in primitive agriculture.

The departure of the British in 1967 and the closing of their naval base at Aden has further scarred the country's economy. Aden, once a flourishing port, now gripped by poverty, has not experienced the revitalization which was expected after the reopening of the Suez Canal in 1975.

In a two-day period in June 1978, as Yemen and Southern Yemen were about to work out details of a proposed merger, both Yemeni presidents were killed—the first in an unsolved assassination plot and the latter before a firing squad following a military coup led by Abdul Fattah Ismail, staunchly pro-Soviet general secretary of the country's National Liberation Front party. Assisted by the Soviet Union, East Germany, and Cuba, Southern Yemen invaded the Yemen Arab Republic in February 1979. Saudi Arabia and the United States supplied arms to the YAR. In March, both countries agreed to a resolution of the League of Arab States, under which their armies withdrew from the border, and soldiers under the League's command were stationed between them. The two Yemens agreed on a plan to merge their countries. But Ismail resigned as president in April 1980 and was replaced by the premier, Ali Nasir Mohammed, who reportedly opposed unification.

**HISTORY:** Southern Yemen formed part oof the Minaean, Sabaean, and Himyarite kingdoms that flourished between 1200 B.C. and thee 6th century A.D. The Himyarites were conquered in 525 by Christian Ethiopians, who were driven out by the Persians in 575. Islam was introduced in the 7th century and by the 9th century the highland regions of Southern Yemen had fallen under the rule of the Islamic religious leaders, or imams, of Yemen. The coastal area recognized the primacy of the Baghdad Caliphate and later fell under Egyptian and Turkish rule
**19th cent.:** Britain gains control of Aden and concludes treaties with southern Yemeni sheikhs to protect them from overland attack from Turkey
**1914:** Anglo-Turkish convention establishes demarcation line separating British-controlled Southern Yemeen from Turkish-occupied Yemen
**1959:** Six of the states of Southern Yemen form Federation of Arab Emirates of the South, later renamed Federation of South Arabia
**1963-66:** Aden joins federation; revolt, led by National Liberation Front (NLF), breaks out against British rule; Britain promises to grant southern Yemen independence by 1968 but NLF refuses to negotiate; joined by other groups, it forms Front for the Liberation of Occupied South Yemen (FLOSY) but soon breaks away from new group
**1967:** NLF defeats FLOSY. Britain withdraws from Southern Yemen
**1969:** Qahtan al-Shaabi, Southern Yemen's first president, resigns and is replaced by a five-man Presidential Council
**1970:** Al-Shaabi is ousted from NLF
**1971:** Ali Nasir Mohammed al-Hassani is appointed prime minister, succeeding Mohammed Ali Haithem
**1972:** Southern Yemen and Yemen sign truce after brief border fighting; agreement provides for future merger
**1973:** Border clashes resume between the two Yemens
**1974:** U.S. charges Soviet military buildup in Red Sea-Indian Ocean area involves use of Aden as submarine base
**1975:** Perim Island, which controls southern entrance to Red Sea, is leased to Egypt, as agent for the Arab League, in return for financial aid. Discussion on unity with Yemen is revived
**1976:** A cease-fire between Southern Yemen and Oman, where Southern Yemen had supported left-wing rebel forces, comes into force
**1978:** Yemen blames Southern Yemen for assassination of Yemen president; two days later ultraleftist Abdul Fattah Ismail ousts President Salem Rubaye Ali, who is immediately tried and shot;

five-man council headed by Prime Minister al-Hassani takes over government. Ismail is elected president

**1979:** Southern Yemen invades Yemen, withdraws after both sides agree to station between them a multinational patrol under command of League of Arab States. President Ismail and President Ali Abdullah Saleh of Yemen agree on merger plan

**1980:** Ismail resigns; succeeded by Ali Nasir Mohammed

## YUGOSLAVIA

**Area:** 98,766 sq. mi. **Population:** 22,599,000 (1981 est.)

**Official Name:** Socialist Federal Republic of Yugoslavia **Capital:** Belgrade **Nationality:** Yugoslavia is officially made up of 6 "nations": Serbs, Croats, Slovenes, Macedonians, Montenegrins and Moslems. "Moslem" does not mean religion but nationality. Officially there exists no Yugoslav nation **Languages:** All "national" languages are official, with Serbo-Croatian serving as a lingua franca **Religion:** About 34% of the population belong to the Orthodox Church; 24% are Roman Catholics and 8% Moslems; 34% are of other or no affiliation **Flag:** Horizontal stripes of blue, white, and red with a red star edged in gold in the center **Anthem:** Fellow Slavs **Currency:** Yugoslav dinar (46 per U.S. $1)

**Location:** Southeast Europe. Yugoslavia, on the Balkan Peninsula, is bounded on the north by Austria and Hungary, on the east by Romania and Bulgaria, on the south by Greece and Albania, and on the west by the Adriatic Sea and Italy **Features:** The northern and eastern part consists of lowland hills and plains, with a few mountain ranges. The remaining two-thirds of the country is mountainous, culminating in the Dinaric Alps **Chief Rivers:** Danube, including its tributaries (Drava, Sava, Morava, Tisza), and Vardar

**Head of State:** President Petar Stambolić, born 1912, succeeded to leadership of the 8-man collective presidency on May 14, 1982, for one-year term **Political Leader:** Dusan Dragosavac, selected Oct. 29, 1981, for a one-year term as President of the Presidium of the Central Committee of the League of Communists of Yugoslavia **Head of Government:** Premier: Milka Planinc, born 1924, appointed president of 29-member Federal Executive Council on May 16, 1982 **Effective Date of Present Constitution:** February 1974 **Legislative Body:** Federal Assembly (bicameral), with a Federal Council of 220 proportionately elected delegates, and a Council of Republics and Provinces with 88 delegates **Local Government:** 6 republics and 2 autonomous provinces (within Serbia), each with its own locally elected executive council and assembly

**Ethnic Composition:** Serbs (40%), Croats (22%), Slovenes (8%), Bosnian Moslems (8%), Macedonians (6%), Albanians (6%), Montenegrins (2%), Hungarians (2%), Turks (1%) **Population Distribution:** 39% urban **Density:** 229 inhabitants per sq. mi.

**Largest Cities:** (Metropolitan Areas) (1976 est.) Belgrade 1,319,000; (1974 est.) Zagreb 700,000, Skopje 440,000, Sarajevo 400,000, Ljubljana 300,000; (1971 census) Novi Sad 216,358

**Per Capita Income:** $3,232 (1980) **Gross National Product (GNP):** $72 billion (1980) **Economic Statistics:** About 37% of the GNP is derived from mining and manufacturing (metals, woodworking, chemicals, textiles, food processing); 12% from agriculture (corn, wheat, fruits including wine grapes, sugar beets, tobacco, livestock, timber). Tourism is also an important source of revenue **Minerals and Mining:** Coal, copper, iron ore, lead, zinc, petroleum, bauxite, natural gas **Labor Force:** 8,900,000 (1979), with 32% in agriculture and 24% in industry **Foreign Trade:** Exports, chiefly fresh meat, ships, machinery, clothing, and hardwood, totaled $6.8 billion in 1979. Imports, mainly machinery and transport equipment, iron and steel, fuel raw materials, and chemicals, totaled $14 billion **Principal Trade Partners:** USSR, West Germany, Italy, United States, France, Poland, Iraq

**Vital Statistics:** Birthrate, 17 per 1,000 of pop. (1980); death rate, 9 **Life Expectancy:** 68 years **Health Statistics:** 166 inhabitants per hospital bed; 768 per physician (1977) **Infant Mortality:** 32.8 per 1,000 births **Illiteracy:** 15% **Primary and Secondary School Enrollment:** 3,772,937 (1976) **Enrollment in Higher Education:** 394,992 (1975) **GNP Expended on Education:** 5.4% (1976)

**Transportation:** Paved roads total 31,023 mi. **Motor Vehicles:** 2,114,000 (1978) **Passenger Cars:** 1,857,100 **Railway Mileage:** 6,190 **Ports:** Rijeka, Split, Dubrovnik, Kotor; on the Danube River: Novi Sad, Belgrade **Major Airlines:** Yugoslav Airlines operates domestically and internationally **Communications: Radio Transmitters:** 656 **Licenses:** 4,526,000 (1976) **Television Transmitters:** 430 **Licenses:** 3,463,000 (1976) **Telephones:** 1,556,000 (1977) **Newspapers:** 26 dailies, 96 copies per 1,000 inhabitants (1977)

**Weights and Measures:** Metric system **Travel Requirements:** Passport, visa valid up to 1 year, no fee **International Dialing Code:** 38

A perennial subject of debate among orthodox Communists has been whether Yugoslavia is really Communist. The Yugoslavs insist they are. Others insist that they are not and that Yugoslavia's brand of political ideology is more Titoism than Communism. The question is now being asked after President Josip Broz Tito died in 1980: Can Titoism survive without Tito?

The Communist party of Yugoslavia was renamed the League of Communists of Yugoslavia in 1952. It has remained the dominant political force. But some scope for political activity is provided by the less disciplined Socialist Alliance of Working People of Yugoslavia, to which all League members and about half of the other adults belong. There are few state or collective farms; agriculture is dominated by private small holdings. Most businesses are managed by councils elected by the workers, and workers have been known to strike against their own councils. The worker-managed businesses compete vigorously against each other, and they are allowed to advertise. Individuals may own businesses with no more than five employees, and occupational licensure is almost unknown. More than half of Yugoslavia's trade is with non-Communist countries, and many Yugoslavs work in Western Europe, entering and leaving Yugoslavia across an open frontier. The press is not strictly controlled, and foreign publications are available to those who can read them.

The political system features a parliament with genuine independent power and a decentralization of authority among the nationality sub-republics. Yugoslavia is made up of many different peoples—notably the Serbs, Croats, Slovenes, and Macedonians—and their rivalry has not been diminished by the attempt to give each group a sense of political and cultural independence.

In 1974, Marshal Tito had himself proclaimed president for life and confirmed plans for Communist collective leadership of Yugoslavia after his death. In January 1980, Tito fell ill and had his leg amputated due to poor blood circulation. He grew steadily worse and died on May 4, at the age of 87. His funeral in Belgrade was attended by the heads of state or delegates from 115 nations.

As Tito lay dying, leadership of the Yugoslav presidency and Communist party began to rotate among the leaders of the country's six republics and two autonomous provinces. The goal was to avert ethnic rivalries for power while preserving Yugoslavia's independence and structure of a workers' state.

After 1948, when Yugoslavia was expelled from the world Communist movement, Marshal Tito moved closer to and received much aid from the West. Although Yugoslavia was reconciled with the Soviet Union in 1955, Tito exercised independence in Yugoslav foreign policy by leading a bloc of nonaligned nations.

Ethnic Albanian demonstrators demanding a republic in Kosovo autonomous province caused serious riots there in March-April 1981, in which many persons were killed or injured. The federal government cracked down hard on the rioters and jailed or fined about 1,700 Albanian protestors.

**HISTORY:** In ancient times, what is now Yugoslavia was inhabited chiefly by Illyrian peoples who came under Roman rule in the 1st century B.C. In the 6th century A.D., Slavic immigrants settled in the country; their languages and cultures gradually became dominant. Most of the Yugoslav (Southern Slav) peoples were conquered by the Ottoman Empire in the 14th and 15th centuries. The House of Hapsburg pushed back the Turkish tide, and, by 1878, ruled Croatia, Slovenia, and Bosnia-Hercegovina. Montenegro had maintained a precarious independence, and Serbia had become independent in the 19th century, and had assumed the leadership of the movement for a Pan-Slav state

**1914-15:** Serbia and Montenegro are overrun by Central Powers in World War I, precipitated by assassination of Archduke Francis Ferdinand at Sarajevo, in Bosnia, by a Serbian nationalist

**1918:** Kingdom of Serbs, Croats, and Slovenes is proclaimed under the rule of King Peter I of Serbia
**1929:** Alexander I, Peter's successor, establishes dictatorship following moves toward separatism by Croatia; country's name is changed to Yugoslavia
**1934:** Alexander is assassinated in Marseilles by Croat terrorist; his son succeeds as Peter II under the regency of Prince Paul, Alexander's cousin
**1941:** Yugoslavia signs Berlin-Rome-Tokyo Pact; Prince Paul and his pro-German government are ousted in bloodless coup; new government signs nonaggression pact with USSR; Germany and Italy, joined by Hungary and Bulgaria, invade Yugoslavia, which collapses a week later
**1943:** Civil war breaks out between Chetniks, a Serbian resistance force headed by Draja Mikhailovich, and Communist partisans led by Josip Broz Tito
**1944:** Tito's forces expel Germans
**1945:** Monarchy is abolished and the People's Republic of Yugoslavia is proclaimed under Tito's leadership
**1946:** Tito launches vigorous program of socialization; political opposition is crushed and Mikhailovich executed; Roman Catholic Church comes under government attack, culminating in arrest and imprisonment of Archbishop Aloysius Stepinac
**1948:** Yugoslavia is expelled from Cominform after Tito resists Soviet attempts to control his regime; Tito begins to develop "national communism" and turns to West for aid
**1960:** Yugoslavia moves toward closer relations with Moscow
**1968:** Soviet-led invasion of Czechoslovakia draws warning from Yugoslav Communists that Yugoslavia will defend its independence
**1972:** Tito introduces presidency of Yugoslavia, a collective body designed to rule the country after he dies
**1973:** Tito purges Serbian and Slovenian Communist party leaders accused of "liberalism;" new constitution calls for collective presidency of Yugoslavia
**1976:** Tito attends European Communist party meeting, ending Yugoslav boycott of such Communist conferences since 1957
**1977:** U.S. agrees to expand military ties with Yugoslavia. Government frees dissident author Mihajlo Mihajlov in amnesty affecting 723 prisoners
**1978:** Tito visits U.S. China's Hua Guofeng visits Yugoslavia
**1980:** Tito dies at the age of 87 after long illness. Collective presidency is to rotate annually among Communist leaders of the republics and autonomous provinces
**1981:** Albanian nationalist students demanding autonomy for Kosovo province clash with police at Pristina University, which then is closed by authorities; riots result in some 1,700 arrests of ethnic Albanians

## ZAIRE

**Area:** 918,962 sq. mi. **Population:** 27,483,000 (1980 est.)

**Official Name:** Republic of Zaire **Capital:** Kinshasa **Nationality:** Zairian **Languages:** French is the official and only common language; about 700 languages and dialects are spoken, the four serving as linguas franca being Lingala, Kingwana, Kikongo, and Tshiluba **Religion:** About 50% Christian (75% Roman Catholic); most of the remaining population practices traditional religions, especially animism **Flag:** A green field with yellow disc, in which a brown hand holds a red and brown torch **Anthem:** Song of Independence **Currency:** Zaire (5.63 per U.S. $1)

**Location:** South-central Africa. The Republic of Zaire is bordered on the west and north by the Congo, the Central African Republic, and Sudan; on the east by Uganda, Rwanda, Burundi, and Tanzania; and on the south by Angola and Zambia. Its only outlet to the ocean is a narrow strip of land on the north bank of the Congo (Zaire) estuary on the Atlantic **Features:** The huge Congo Basin, a low-lying, basin-shaped plateau sloping toward the west, is covered by tropical rain forest. Surrounding it are mountainous terraces on the west, plateaus merging into savannas to the south and southeast, and dense grasslands toward the northwest. High mountains lie to the east **Chief Rivers:** The Congo (Zaire) and its many tributaries, including the Ubangi, Aruwimi, Lindi, Lualaba, Lomami, Lomela, Momboyo, Kasai, Kwango, and Kwilu

**Head of State and of Government:** President: Lt. Gen. Mobutu Sese Seko, born 1930; seized power in a coup in 1965, reelected 1977 for a second seven-year term. He is assisted by the first state commissioner (premier), N'Singa Udjuu, appointed Apr. 1981 **Effective Date of Present Constitution:** Feb. 1978 **Legislative Body:** National Legislative Council (unicameral), with 268 members, elected for 5 years. Actual power resides with the president, as head of the Political Bureau of the Popular Revolutionary Movement (MPR) **Local Government:** 8 regions and Kinshasa

**Ethnic Composition:** There are some 200 tribal groups, which can be divided into 3 main categories: the Negroes (Bantu [80%], Sudanese, and Nilotics); the Hamites; and the Pygmies **Population Distribution:** 30% urban **Density:** 30 inhabitants per sq. mi.

**Largest Cities:** (1980 est.) Kinshasa 2,159,000; (1974 est.) Kananga 601,239, Lubumbashi 403,623, Mbuji-Mayi 336,654, Kisangani 310,705, Bukavu 181,774, Kikwit 150,253, Matadi 143,598

**Per Capita Income:** $142 (1980) **Gross National Product (GNP):** $4.1 billion (1980) **Economic Statistics:** About 17% of GNP comes from industry (food processing, consumer durables, and construction materials); 15% from public administration; 15% from commerce and transportation; 15% from subsistence production; 13% from agriculture (coffee, rubber, and palm oil); 7% from mining **Minerals and Mining:** The country is the world's largest producer of industrial diamonds and cobalt; copper provides one-half of export earnings. Other important minerals include bauxite, gold, cassiterite, manganese, oil, and zinc **Labor Force:** 8.3 million, with about 75% in agriculture **Foreign Trade:** Exports, chiefly copper, cobalt, zinc, diamonds, coffee, palm oil and rubber totaled $2.6 billion in 1980. Imports, mainly machinery, transportation equipment, textiles, fuel, and foodstuffs, totaled $1.8 billion **Principal Trade Partners:** Belgium, United States, Italy, France, West Germany, Britain, Japan

**Vital Statistics:** Birthrate, 46.2 per 1,000 of pop. (1980); death rate, 18.7 **Life Expectancy:** 46 years **Health Statistics:** 352 inhabitants per hospital bed; 16,106 per physician (1978) **Infant Mortality:** 104 per 1,000 births **Illiteracy:** 69% **Primary and Secondary School Enrollment:** 3,875,143 (1974) **Enrollment in Higher Education:** 21,021 (1974) **GNP Expended on Education:** 4.2% (1970)

**Transportation:** Paved roads total about 1,650 mi. **Motor Vehicles:** 161,200 (1974) **Passenger Cars:** 84,800 **Railway Mileage:** 3,593 (1970) **Ports:** Matadi, Banana, Boma **Major Airlines:** Air Zaire provides domestic and international services **Communications: Radio Transmitters:** 22 **Receivers:** 2,448,000 (1974) **Television Transmitters:** 3 **Receivers:** 7,000 (1976) **Telephones:** 26,000 (1978) **Newspapers:** 6 dailies (1976), 9 copies per 1,000 inhabitants (1974)

**Weights and Measures:** Metric system **Travel Requirements:** Passport; visa valid 1 to 3 months, $20 fee, 3 photos

Torn by bloody strife through more than half of its first decade of independence, Zaire's early name of Congo had been almost a synonym for disorder. For 85 years the big African country—its area equal to that of the United States east of the Mississippi—was the possession of Belgium. While Belgian administration checked tribal enmities, colonial monopolies reaped the wealth of ivory, gold, copper, and other minerals. Plantations used labor under conditions little different from slavery.

Although the colonial regime grew less harsh in the 20th century, with missionary schools and better economic treatment for Zairians (Congolese), Belgium administrators did little to prepare for self-government.

In 1960, spurred by rebellion in Zaire and the wave of decolonization elsewhere in Africa, the Belgian government reluctantly acceded to the independence demands of Zaire leaders headed by Joseph Kasavubu and Patrice Lumumba. The calm, conservative Kasavubu, who became the first president, and other leaders favored a loose federation, while the passionate, radical Lumumba, who became premier, wanted a strong central government. And with the formal grant of independence on June 30, 1960, the issue remained basically unresolved.

Peaceful independence lasted only five days. On July 5 the army mutinied, public authority broke down and on July 10 Belgian troops intervened to protect Belgian nationals caught in a wave of terror. On July 11 Moise Tshombe, governor of Katanga, declared his mineral-rich province an independent country.

With a UN force backing up the national army, there began the long struggle to quell the Katangan secession. The Katangan forces, with a hard core of white mercenaries—*les affreux* ("the frightful ones")—put up a stiff resistance and it was not until mid-1963 that Tshombe was defeated and forced into exile.

Meanwhile, breakaway governments arose in South Kasai and in Kivu Province. Following a quarrel between Kasavubu and Lumumba, the national army commander, Col. Joseph D. Mobutu, a tough, Israeli-trained paratrooper, took over the government on September 5, 1960 and expelled Soviet and Communist-bloc diplomats and technicians.

The following November, the deposed Lumumba was captured while trying to flee to Kivu Province. Lumumba was taken to Katanga and assassinated in February 1961, becoming a martyr for third-world radicals. That same month Mobutu returned the reins of government to Kasavubu and four groups then contended for power. The country was not unified until 1963.

In 1964 when Zaire seemed to be pulling itself together, Kasavubu, in a gesture of national reconciliation, recalled Tshombe from exile and made him premier. There followed renewed rebellion by former Lumumba followers. The rebels, however, were soon defeated in an attack by Belgian paratroopers brought in by U.S. planes.

But neither Tshombe nor his successor could end the country's malaise of disunity. (Tshombe went into exile and died in Algeria in 1969.) Mobutu, now a general, seized power in November 1965. He reduced provincial authority and began building a strong central government to unify the country's hundred tribes. In a campaign for "African authenticity," in 1971 he changed the name of his country to Zaire.

Mobutu Sese Seko—as the president renamed himself—proved to be an effective salesman in promoting foreign investment to develop his nation's industries. However, by 1975, his mismanaged fiscal policies had resulted in an economic crisis which has persisted: an extremely high rate of inflation, unemployment of more than half of the urban work force, a declining standard of living, and a foreign debt approaching $5 billion.

An important factor in Zaire's economic dislocation is the concentration of most of its mineral wealth in the southern province of Shaba (formerly Katanga). From there the most practical route for shipment abroad is the railroad through Angola to the Atlantic port of Benguela. Mobutu at first backed the guerrilla forces opposed to the Popular Movement for the Liberation of Angola, but after the Movement's victory in 1976 he threw his support to this regime which was backed by Cuba and the Soviet Union. Zaire was then dealt a double blow. The Angolan guerrillas sabotaged the Benguela railroad and have kept it closed. Moreover, the leftist government of Angola has aided Katangan rebels in two invasions of Shaba.

**HISTORY:** Pygmy tribes are believed to be among the earliest inhabitants of Zaire. Bantus from eastern Africa and Nilotes from the Nile region later entered the area. The Bantus established several kingdoms, including Bahuba, Baluba, and the Congo. When Portuguese explorers arrived at the mouth of the Zaire (Congo) River in the 15th century, the kingdom of the Congo included what is now Zaire and Angola

**1879-84:** Henry Stanley explores Zaire on behalf of Belgian king

**1885:** Leopold II sets up the Congo Free State and becomes its absolute monarch

**1908:** Congo Free State becomes Belgian Congo

**1960:** Colony is granted independence; within a week Congolese Army mutinies and Belgian troops intervene to protect Belgian nationals. Premier Moise Tshombe of Katanga, the Congo's richest region, proclaims his province an independent country; Albert Kalonji proclaims the independence of part of Kasai Province. At the request of the central government, UN troops are sent to the Congo to maintain order. Intense rivalry breaks out between Joseph Kasavubu, the head of state, and his premier, Patrice Lumumba; Col. Joseph Mobutu, commander of the Congo Army, seizes control of the government

**1961:** Mobutu returns reins of government to Kasavubu. Lumumba is killed under mysterious circumstances and his death plunges the Congo into further strife

**1962-63:** Heavy fighting takes place between UN troops and Katanga forces; secession of Katanga is ended

**1964:** Tshombe, who had gone into exile, is invited to return and is sworn in as Congo's new premier

**1965:** Tshombe is dismissed and goes into exile. Mobutu again stages military coup and overthrows Kasavubu government

**1967:** Mobutu announces new constitution providing for a federal system of government, with strong president and unicameral legislature. Central government takes over assets of Union Minière, the rich Belgian copper mining company in Katanga

**1969:** Kasavubu dies in March; Tshombe, captive in Algeria, in June

**1970:** Mobutu elected president for a new 7-year term

**1971:** The name of the republic is changed to Zaire

**1973:** Many foreign-owned firms are nationalized

**1974-75:** World price of copper falls, earnings are cut

**1976:** Angolan war disrupts export of Zaire copper. Mobutu establishes relations with Agostinho Neto's victorious Marxist government in Angola after backing losing pro-Western faction

**1977:** Shaba Province invaded by former Katangan soldiers; Moroccan troops, and French, Belgian and U.S. aid end threat. Mobutu wins new seven-year term as president

**1978:** About 4,000 Angolan-based Katangan rebels capture towns in Shaba; France and Belgium drop in paratroopers to rout rebels

**1979:** A $150-million conditional credit from International Monetary Fund improves recovery effort. Mpinga Kasenda is removed as prime minister on corruption charges and replaced by Boboliko Lokonga. Drought causes severe food shortages. Mobutu seeks to improve relations with neighbor states and Soviet bloc while keeping friendship with West

**1980:** Widespread discontent results from country's continuing economic problems. Consultation group of 9 industrial powers, IMF, World Bank and EEC decides in May to recommend more aid for Zaire. Nguza Karl-I-Bond named premier

**1981:** N'Singa Udjuu, a planter and cattleman from the central Bandundu region, succeeds Nguza as premier in April. Zaire announces intent to market its diamonds independently of De Beers Consolidated Mines Ltd., which controls about 85% of the world supply of uncut diamonds

**1982:** IMF freezes $806 million in undrawn 1982 loans to Zaire for failure to meet belt-tightening requirements. Mobutu, reacting to inference by U.S. officials that he embezzled aid money, renounces all U.S. help. Zaire renews diplomatic relations with Israel; Saudis cut ties in protest

## ZAMBIA

**Area:** 290,586 sq. mi. **Population:** 5,679,808 (1980 census)

**Official Name:** Republic of Zambia **Capital:** Lusaka **Nationality:** Zambian **Languages:** The official language is English. Some 70 different Bantu languages and dialects are spoken, but 5 main languages are recognized for educational and administrative purposes: Nyanja, Bemba, Lozi, Luvale, and Tonga **Religion:** Most of the African population follow traditional religions. Christians number about 900,000, and the small Asian community practices Islam and Hinduism **Flag:** A green field with a swatch in the lower right corner of red, black, and orange vertical stripes topped by an orange flying eagle **Anthem:** National Anthem, beginning "Stand and sing of Zambia, proud and free" **Currency:** Zambian kwacha (0.9 per U.S. $1)

**Location:** South-central Africa. Landlocked Zambia is bordered on the north by Zaire, on the east by Tanzania and Malawi, on the southeast by Mozambique, on the south by Zimbabwe, Botswana, and Namibia, and on the west by Angola **Features:** Most of the land mass is a high plateau lying between 3,500 and 4,000 feet above sea level. In the northeast the Muchinga Mountains exceed 7,000 feet in height. Elevations below 2,000 feet are encountered in the valleys of the major river systems. There are 3 large natural lakes: Bangweulu, Mweru, and Tanganyika, all in the northeast **Chief Rivers:** Zambezi, Luangwa, Chambeshi, Kafue, Luapula

**Political Leader and Head of State:** President: Dr. Kenneth David Kaunda, born 1924, head of the United National Independence party, reelected 1978 **Head of Government:** Prime Minister Nalumino Mundia, appointed Feb. 1981 **Effective Date of Present Constitution:** Aug. 1973 **Legislative Body:** National Assembly (unicameral), consisting of 125 members elected for 5 years, and 10 appointed members **Local Government:** 9 provinces, each administered by a cabinet member

**Ethnic Composition:** Over 98% of the population are Africans belonging chiefly to various Bantu-speaking tribes. There are approximately 40,000 Europeans and Asians **Population Distribution:** 43% urban **Density:** 20 inhabitants per sq. mi.

**Largest Cities:** (1980 census) Lusaka 538,469, Kitwe 314,794, Ndola 282,439, Mufulira 149,778, Chingola 145,869, Kabwe 143,635, Luanshya 132,164, Livingstone 71,987

**Per Capita Income:** $455 (1980) **Gross National Product (GNP):** $2.7 billion (1980) **Economic Statistics:** Quarrying and mining account for 50% of the GNP. Agriculture (tobacco, corn, peanuts, cotton) accounts for 11%; indigenous manufacturing (food processing, textile, furniture and construction materials) for 8% **Minerals and Mining:** Zambia is a ranking producer of copper; cobalt, lead, zinc, and unexploited deposits of iron are also abundant **Labor Force:** 402,000 wage earners (1977); 23% in government, 15% in mining, 10% in manufacturing, 9% in agriculture, 9% in commerce and 6% in transportation **Foreign Trade:** Exports, mainly refined copper, lead, zinc, cobalt, and unmanufactured tobacco, totaled $1.5 billion in 1980. Imports, chiefly machinery and transportation equipment, petroleum products, manufactured articles, chemicals, and food totaled $927 million **Principal Trade Partners:** Britain, Japan, West Germany, United States, South Africa, China

**Vital Statistics:** Birthrate, 49.2 per 1,000 of pop. (1980); death rate, 17.2 **Life Expectancy:** 47 years **Health Statistics:** 273 inhabitants per hospital bed (1978); 8,159 per physician (1971) **Infant Mortality:** 160 per 1,000 births **Illiteracy:** 53% **Primary and Secondary School Enrollment:** 945,441 (1975) **Enrollment in Higher Education:** 8,403 (1975) **GNP Expended on Education:** 6.7% (1976)

**Transportation:** Paved roads total 3,410 mi. **Motor Vehicles:** 171,900 (1976) **Passenger Cars:** 93,500 **Railway Mileage:** 1,360 **Ports:** None **Major Airlines:** Zambia Airways operates domestically and internationally **Communications: Radio Transmitters:** 5 **Receivers:** 110,000 (1976) **Television Transmitters:** 4 **Receivers:** 25,000 (1976) **Telephones:** 57,000 (1978) **Newspapers:** 2 dailies, 20 copies per 1,000 inhabitants (1976)

**Weights and Measures:** Metric system **Travel Requirements:** Passport; visa, valid 6 months, $3.50 fee

---

The land above the Zambezi River, Zambia was called a "rich pauper" when, as the former British protectorate of Northern Rhodesia, it adopted a new name and became independent in 1964. The designation was based on the fact that while the country produced great wealth in copper, most Zambians gained barely enough to eat from their meager agricultural economy. Since then President Kenneth D. Kaunda has taken forceful measures to end the paradox. By 1975 Zambia assumed full control of its copper industry.

The government has faced a costly adjustment in trade and transportation in line with black Africa's boycott of Rhodesia (now Zimbabwe). Zambian copper, which formerly had gone out through Rhodesia, was rerouted through Tanzania. The Tanzam railroad, built to link Zambian copper mines with Indian Ocean ports, was completed in 1976.

Kaunda has committed Zambia to a form of socialism which he calls "humanism," designed to satisfy all Zambians' requirements through even distribution of the nation's wealth.

In December 1972 a bill went into effect making the governing United National Independence party (UNIP) Zambia's only legal political party. At the same time, President Kaunda ordered UNIP officials owning businesses to convert them into producers' cooperatives or relinquish their managing directorships.

After Kaunda allowed Patriotic Front guerrilla fighters from Rhodesia to establish bases in Zambia, those bases became subject to repeated air and ground attacks. Many Zambian civilians were killed, Lusaka's new rail link to Indian Ocean ports was broken, and the country's economy suffered severely. Since the struggle in Zimbabwe ended in 1979, efforts to revive the Zambian economy have been handicapped by continuing low prices for copper, chronic strikes by the miners, and general social unrest. In a bid to make peace with the unions, Kaunda in 1981 had expelled union officials readmitted to UNIP, and he appointed Nalumino Mundia, a man experienced in labor relations, as prime minister.

**HISTORY:** The history of the territory constituting present-day Zambia before the coming of the white man is sparse. The first European to penetrate into the region was the Scottish missionary David Livingstone, who made extensive explorations of the area between 1851 and 1873. In 1891, the British South Africa Co., which was developing the local copper resources, took over administration of the territory, naming it Northern Rhodesia

**1924:** British South Africa Co. is relieved of the administration of Northern Rhodesia

**1930-44:** Discovery of large copper deposits brings rush of Europeans to Northern Rhodesia

**1953-63:** Northern Rhodesia is part of the Federation of Rhodesia and Nyasaland

**1964:** Northern Rhodesia becomes independent republic of Zambia; Kenneth Kaunda, leader of the ruling United National Independence party, becomes the nation's first president

**1967:** Zambia accepts offer by Communist China to finance 1,000-mile railroad linking Lusaka with Dar es Salaam

**1968:** Kaunda is reelected president

**1969:** Kaunda announces measures for government takeover of country's $1.2-billion copper industry from foreign owners

**1973:** New constitution is enacted to coincide with new one-party system of government. Kaunda is reelected for third term

**1976:** Angolan MPLA government recognized and Rhodesian guerrillas aided; Tanzam Railway is completed

**1978:** Rhodesia raids guerrilla camps in Zambia. Kaunda is reelected president without opposition

**1980:** Leaders of 9 nations meet in Lusaka to develop a regional economic plan aimed at less dependence on white-ruled South Africa. Government nationalizes petroleum supplies held by 5 international companies and launches a 10-year plan to increase food production. Industrial strikes are banned. China promises aid to repair railroad damaged in Zimbabwe struggle. Kaunda announces failure of an attempt in October to overthrow him; claims South Africa supported plot

**1981:** Government obtains a $944-million loan from IMF to aid Zambia's economic development. Zambia expels 2 U.S. diplomats, charging that they are C.I.A. agents. Mine union leaders are detained as result of two major strikes within 6 months

**1982:** Pres. Kaunda holds "frank" and "useful" talks with South African Prime Minister Botha

## ZIMBABWE

**Area:** 150,803 sq. mi. **Population:** 7,600,000 (1981 est.)

**Official Name:** Republic of Zimbabwe **Capital:** Harare (Salisbury) **Nationality:** Zimbabwean **Languages:** English, the official language, is spoken by the white population and a great number of Africans; the chief Bantu languages are Shona and Ndebele **Religion:** Over 50% practice a combination of animism and Christianity. There are also 25% Christians (mainly Anglicans) and some Moslems **Flag:** 7 equal horizontal stripes of green, yellow, red, black, red, yellow and green separated by a narrow black border from a white triangle at the hoist. The triangle contains a representation of the Great Zimbabwe bird superimposed on a red five-pointed star **Anthem:** Rise, O Voices of Zimbabwe **Currency:** Zimbabwe dollar (1.30 per U.S. $1)

**Location:** South-Central Africa. Landlocked Zimbabwe is bordered on the north by Zambia, on the east by Mozambique, on the south by the Republic of South Africa, and on the west by Botswana **Features:** Most of the country is a high, rolling plateau between 3,000 and 5,000 feet above sea level. The land is largely South African veld, or grassland, with scattered shrubs or trees **Chief Rivers:** Zambezi, Limpopo, Sabi, Gwaai, Shangani

**Head of State:** President: Rev. Canaan Banana, born 1936, took office April 18, 1980, for 6-year term **Head of Government:** Prime Minister Robert Gabriel Mugabe, born 1924, sworn in April 18, 1980 **Effective Date of Present Constitution:** April 18, 1980 **Legislative Body:** Parliament (bicameral), consists of (1) a House of Assembly with 100 members elected for 5 years from 80 black voters' roll constituencies and 20 white roll constituencies, (2) a 40-member Senate for 5 years consisting of 14 Senators elected by the 80 black members of the Assembly, 10 Senators chosen by the 20 white members of the Assembly, 10 Senators elected by traditional chiefs, and 6 appointed by the President **Local Government:** 8 provinces under appointed commissioners

**Ethnic Composition:** 77% are Shona, 19% Ndebele, 3% are of European descent (chiefly British), less than 1% are coloreds (persons of mixed race) and Asians **Population Distribution:** 20% urban **Density:** 50 inhabitants per sq. mi.

**Largest Cities:** (1980 est.) Harare (Salisbury) 654,000, Bulawayo 373,000, Gweru (Gwelo) 72,000, Mutare (Umtali) 64,000, Kwekwe (Que Que) 52,000, Hwange (Wankie) 33,000, Kadoma (Gatooma) 33,000

**Per Capita Income:** $509 (1980) **Gross National Product (GNP):** $3.8 billion (1980) **Economic Statistics:** In 1979 about 25% from manufacturing (metals and metal products, food processing, textiles, clothing and footwear, beverages, tobacco, chemicals); 12% from agriculture and forestry (Oriental tobacco, stock-raising, maize, groundnuts, cotton); 9% from transport and communications; and 8% from mining **Minerals and Mining:** There are deposits of asbestos, chrome ore, coal, copper, gold, iron ore, limestone, lithium, nickel, phosphate rock, and tin **Labor Force:**

991,600 (1978) **Foreign Trade:** Exports, mainly tobacco, asbestos, copper, apparel, meats, chrome, and sugar; totaled $1.4 billion in 1980. Imports, chiefly machinery and transportation equipment, textiles, petroleum products, iron and steel products, fertilizers, and foodstuffs, totaled $1.3 billion **Principal Trade Partners:** South Africa, United States, EC countries, Japan, Malawi, Zambia

**Vital Statistics:** Birthrate, 47.3 per 1,000 of pop. (1980); death rate, 13.6 **Life Expectancy:** 52 years **Health Statistics:** 374 inhabitants per hospital bed; 5,700 per physician (1973) **Infant Mortality:** 122 per 1,000 births **Illiteracy:** 60% **Primary and Secondary School Enrollment:** 963,671 (1976) **Enrollment in Higher Education:** 1,076 (1972) **GNP Expended on Education:** 3.6% (1973)

**Transportation:** Paved roads total 5,007 mi. **Motor Vehicles:** 250,000 (1974) **Passenger Cars:** 180,000 **Railway Mileage:** 2,133 **Ports:** None **Major Airlines:** Air Zimbabwe operates domestic and international flights **Communications: Radio Transmitters:** 22 **Receivers:** 255,000 (1976) **Television Transmitters:** 5 **Receivers:** 72,000 (1976) **Telephones:** 197,000 (1977) **Newspapers:** 2 dailies, 12 copies per 1,000 inhabitants (1976)

**Weights and Measures:** Metric system **Travel Requirements:** Passport; onward/return ticket

---

At midnight April 17, 1980, with Britain's Prince Charles presiding and representatives of a hundred other countries looking on, the Union Jack was lowered for the last time in Salisbury and the striped flag of Zimbabwe went up in its place. The last but one (South Africa) of white-dominated, black-majority states of Africa had been recognized by the world as an independent country. Robert Mugabe, whose Zimbabwe African National Union party had won in free elections, was installed as prime minister. Soldiers of the former Rhodesian army, black and white, paraded side by side with guerrillas against whom they had so recently fought.

Lord Soames, the British governor who had ruled the country since the 1979 cease-fire, said, "This has been nothing less than a series of miracles." As it indeed had been. When, in 1964, Britain granted independence to Northern Rhodesia (now Zambia) and Nyasaland (Malawi), it denied such status to Southern Rhodesia until a government representative of the black majority as well as the whites was assured. A year later, Ian Smith, the white prime minister, unilaterally declared Rhodesia to be independent. Britain said the government was illegal, and the United Nations refused to recognize it.

With Smith's proclamation of a State of Rhodesia in March 1970, following a referendum the previous year in which white Rhodesians formally renounced their last British tie, loyalty to the Crown, there was an eventual withdrawal of all diplomatic missions except that of South Africa.

Despite diplomatic isolation, a total British trade blockade, UN economic sanctions, and its landlocked position in southern Africa, Rhodesia did manage to survive as an economic outcast.

Inspired by successful moves to black rule in the countries surrounding Rhodesia on three sides, nationalists organized the Patriotic Front to try to topple the Smith government by means of guerrilla warfare. Leading the estimated 12,000 guerrillas were Joshua Nkomo, patriarchal figure of Zimbabwe nationalism and Soviet-backed leader of the wing based in Zambia, and Robert Mugabe, whose Chinese-trained forces operated from bases in Mozambique and Tanzania.

Smith steadfastly refused to support equal voting rights as a step toward black rule. He relented only when escalating guerrilla warfare left him no alternative and not before safeguards had been built into an agreement to protect white interests. Finally, he gave in to a plan worked out with moderate black leaders for a black-majority government in which the white minority would retain much of the power. In May 1979, the name of the country was changed to Zimbabwe Rhodesia. Methodist Bishop Abel Muzorewa, who became the country's first black prime minister, faced insurmountable problems, notably the opposition of Patriotic Front leaders who regarded him as a puppet of white Rhodesians.

Bowing to the pressures, Muzorewa agreed late in 1979 to step down pending supervised elections in which all factions, including those of the Patriotic Front, could be represented. An uneasy truce with the guerrilla forces followed as Lord Soames became the interim governor. But after many threatened boycotts, the elections were held Feb. 27-29, 1980. The Zimbabwe African National Union (ZANU) won 57 of the 80 seats allotted to blacks in a 100-member House of Assembly, and Robert Mugabe, the revolutionary most feared by the white Rhodesians, became prime minister. "There is a place for everybody in this country," he said, seeking to reassure the whites and also the blacks who had supported Nkomo and Muzorewa.

Mugabe included two prominent whites in his broad-based cabinet and offered the presidency to his rival, Nkomo, who refused the figurehead post but accepted appointment as Minister of Home Affairs. Mugabe also encouraged white civil servants to remain, promising them security in their positions and prospects for promotion.

Since the coming of independence, some whites, and blacks as well, have been murdered. There have been several armed clashes between members of the rival independence factions. Whites have left the country at an average rate of over 1,200 per month. However, the bloodbath, wholesale exodus of whites, confiscation of property and near-anarchy predicted for Zimbabwe by many pundits have failed to materialize. The change from white rule to black has been remarkably peaceful. Some of Mugabe's followers complain that he is moving too slowly toward socialism and black supremacy.

**HISTORY:** The remains of Stone Age culture dating back 500,000 years have been found in Zimbabwe and it is thought that the Bushmen, who still survive, mostly in the Kalahari Desert of Botswana, are the last descendants of these original inhabitants. The first Bantu are thought to have reached Zimbabwe between the 5th and 10th centuries A.D., though southward migrations continued long after. The first Europeans to visit the region were 16th-century Portuguese explorers

**1889-97:** Cecil Rhodes forms the British South Africa Company; assisted by British troops, the company conquers the Mashona and Matabele; European colonists follow

**1923:** Southern Rhodesia becomes a self-governing colony within the British Commonwealth

**1953:** Britain establishes the Federation of Rhodesia and Nyasaland, linking Northern Rhodesia (now Zambia), Southern Rhodesia, and Nyasaland (now Malawi); the Federation remains dominated by the European settlers

**1964:** Federation of Rhodesia and Nyasaland is dissolved. Britain grants the two northern territories independence under African majority rule, but refuses independence to Southern Rhodesia unless representative government is assured.

**1965:** Prime Minister Ian Smith unilaterally declares Rhodesia's independence from Britain and promulgates a new constitution. Britain declares the Smith government an illegal, rebel regime

**1966:** UN Security Council calls on all member states to break off economic relations with Rhodesia; only Portugal and South Africa refuse to impose an embargo

**1968:** Smith government executes five black Africans convicted of murder, despite commutation of death sentences by Queen Elizabeth; act is viewed as most serious act of defiance against Britain by break-away Rhodesian regime

**1969:** Government publishes proposed constitution designed to perpetuate white minority rule. In a referendum in which 81,583 whites as against 6,634 blacks are eligible to vote, the Smith regime wins a mandate to place the proposed constitution before the Legislative Assembly and to proclaim Rhodesia a republic and cut formal remaining ties to British Crown

**1970:** Rhodesia proclaims a republic, severing ties with Britain; neither Britain nor the United Nations grant recognition

**1974:** Government suppression of black nationalists resumed as terrorism against white minority continues

**1975:** New 90-mile railway link with South Africa is opened

**1978:** On March 3, Prime Minister Smith and three moderate nationalist leaders agree on plan for black-majority rule; while containing many guarantees for whites. Guerrilla leaders denounce pact as "sellout." Bush war turns bloodier

**1979:** Blacks, voting in national elections for first time, elect Bishop Abel Muzorewa as first black prime minister. Zimbabwe Rhodesia is born May 31. Guerrilla war continues until Muzorewa agrees to turn over rule to a British governor pending all-party elections in 1980

**1980:** Robert Mugabe's Zimbabwe African National Union is victorious in elections; Canaan Banana, a Methodist minister, is chosen as president. Britain turns over reins of government of the new Republic of Zimbabwe to Mugabe, as prime minister, April 17. Major Western powers offer assistance

**1981:** Nkomo accepts a ministry without portfolio related to defense and public-service affairs. Zimbabwe establishes diplomatic relations with Soviet Union, but requires latter to cut its long-held ties with Nkomo faction. Conference of 31 nations and 26 international agencies pledges $1.8 billion in aid to Zimbabwe. Government puts restrictions on political gatherings and on household goods that white emigrants can take with them

**1982:** Nkomo ousted from cabinet amid charges of treason. Nine members of all-white Republican Front party in parliament become independents, further weakening Ian Smith's strength in that body. Capital is renamed Harare after 19th-century tribal chief; other non-African names are changed (see **Largest Cities**). Nkomo supporters kidnap six tourists. Mugabe proposes one-party rule after 1985 elections

## TERRITORIES AND DEPENDENCIES

**Anguilla**—*Status*: British Dependency. *Population*: 6,600 (1977 est.). *Area*: 35 sq. mi. *Capital*: The Valley (760).

The island of Anguilla lies in the northern part of the Leeward group of the Lesser Antilles, in the eastern Caribbean. Anguilla is approximately 65 miles N.N.W. of St. Christopher and 9 miles from its neighbor, St. Martin.

Anguilla is a flat, coralline island with its highest point at 213 feet above sea level. The island is covered with low scrub and fringed with white coral-sand beaches. Apart from sheep and goats, Anguilla's main product is salt. The majority of the population are African or of mixed descent, with a small white minority.

Anguilla unilaterally seceded from the associated state of St. Christopher-Nevis-Anguilla when it was formed in 1967. Britain took control of the island in 1969 after landing an "invasion" force, and in 1971 began direct administration of the island. On February 10, 1976, Anguilla was established as a self-governing British dependency with a new constitution, but it remained a legal part of the associated state. The charter created a seven-member Legislative Assembly and a chief minister, and gave the Britishh Commissioner authority over defense, police and civil service, and foreign affairs. On December 16, 1980, Anguilla received full legal separation from St. Christopher-Nevis. The chief minister, Ronald Webster, was reelected in 1981. British engineers have installed a telephone system and improved the roads. In the early 1980s, more hotels were built to support a bid for additional tourist business.

**Ashmore and Cartier Islands**—*Status*: Australian External Territory. *Populationt*: Uninhabited. *Area*: 1.9 sq. mi.

These islands lie in the Indian Ocean, about 300 miles north of Broome in northwestern Australia (12°S.,123°E.). They are administered by the Northern Territory.

**Australian Antarctic Territory**—*Status*: External Territory of Australia. *Population*: Uninhhabited. *Area*: 2,362,875 sq. mi. (of which 29,251 sq. mi. are ice shelf).

Australia claims all Antarctic islands and territories south of 60°S and between 45° and 160°E, except for French-claimed Adélie Land. (The United States does not recognize any Antarctic claims south of 60°S.)

**Bermuda**—*Status*: British Colony. *Population*: 67,761 (1980 census). *Area*: 21 sq. mi. *Capital*: Hamilton (1,624).

The colony is in the western Atlantic (32°20′N.,64°40′W.), less than 600 miles east of Cape Hatteras, North Carolina. There are some 150 small islands, about 20 of which are inhabited. The main islands are close together, connected by bridges, and collectively called Bermuda. The islands are rocky, with lush vegetation. The climate, moderated by the Gulf Stream, is warm and pleasant. About two-thirds of the people are African or of mixed descent, the rest mostly British in origin. They are predominantly Protestant.

Tourism, largely from the United States, accounts for 55 percent of the economy. Also important is the provision of goods to British and American servicemen stationed on the islands. Almost all food is imported.

In 1968 a new constitution put most executive powers in the hands of the premier, who is the head of the majority party in the elected House of Assembly of the bicameral legislature (the oldest among British possessions). The Crown-appointed governor retains direct responsibility for external affairs, defense and internal security.

On March 10, 1973, the governor, Sir Richard Sharples, and his aide-de-camp were assassinated. The execution of their two convicted assassins, both black, in 1977 sparked rioting, with great property loss and lasting damage to tourism. The industry was disrupted again in early 1981 by a 26-day strike that shut down hotel operations and other services. It was attributed in part to frustration over Bermuda's high cost of living and the continuing political domination of the conservative United Bermuda party.

**Bouvet Island (Bouvetöya)**—*Status*: Norwegian Dependency. *Population*: Uninhabited. *Area*: 23 sq. mi.

Situated between the extreme tip of South Africa and the Antarctic coast, Bouvet is in the South Atlantic Ocean at 54°26′S and 3°24′E. It is volcanic in origin and almost completely ice-covered. There are fur seals and seals of other varieties, penguins, and petrels.

**British Antarctic Territory**—*Status*: British Colony. *Population*: Uninhabited, except for personnel at scientific statiions. *Area*: 600,000 sq. mi. *Administrative Center*: Stanley, Falkland Islands.

The territory, created in 1962, extends below 60°S. from 20° to 80°W. and includes the South Orkney Islands, the South Shetland Islands, and the Antarctic Peninsula. Argentina claims the area and occupied one of the South Shetlands in 1976, resulting in a British protest.

**British Indian Ocean Territory**—*Status*: British Colony. *Population*: Unknown since removal of original inhabitants in 1971. *Area*: 29 sq. mi. (land). *Administration Center*: London (U.K.).

The territory, made a separate colony in 1965, includes only the Chagos Archipelago at 7°20′S and 72°25′E, formerly a dependency of Mauritius; Diego Garcia (11 sq. mi.) is the largest island. The climate is tropical, with heavy rainfall.

The territory is administered from London by a commissioner. Diego Garcia is the site of a major U.S. air and naval base. Mauritius has reinstated its claim to Diego Garcia.

**British Virgin Islands**—*Status*: British Crown Colony. *Population*: 11,000 (1980 est.). *Area*: 59 sq. mi. *Capital*: Road Town (2,200) on Tortola.

These are in the eastern Caribbean, east of the U.S. Virgin Islands. They include 36 islands, 16 of which are inhabited, plus numerous rocks and *cays*. Tortola, Virgin Gorda, Anegada, and Jost Van Dyke are the largest islands. The climate is subtropical and pleasant; rainfall is light. Almost all the people are of African descent.

Tourism is the mainstay of the economy. Cattle raising, farming, and fishing are important. There is a developing financial sector.

The colony is governed by a Crown-appointed governor assisted by an appointed executive council and a chief minister. There is a partly elected legislative council.

**Brunei**—*Status*: British Protected State. *Population*: 191,765 (1981 census). *Area*: 2,226 sq. mi. *Capital*: Bandar Seri Begawan, formerly Brunei Town (63,868).

This sultanate is on the north coast of Borneo, being two enclaves within the Malaysian state of Sarawak, washed by the South China Sea. The climate is tropical and humid, the rainfall heavy. The population is more than half Malay and is largely Moslem. Chinese are the second-largest element, and there are Dayak groups.

Oil and natural gas are the major factors in Brunei's economy, making it Southeast Asia's richest state in per capita income. Rice production is being expanded.

Britain is responsible for Brunei's defense and foreign relations. A Crown-appointed high commissioner conducts relations between the two states. There is a council of ministers, presided over by the sultan. In 1967, after 17 years of rule, the Sultan, unwilling to bow to British demands for more representative government, abdicated and was succeeded by his son. In 1970, the new ruler dissolved the partly elected legislative council in favor of an entirely appointive body. Under a 1971 agreement with Britain, Brunei is fully self-governing in internal affairs. In 1979 it was announced in London that Brunei is to become independent on January 1, 1984.

**Cayman Islands**—*Status*: British Crown Colony. *Population*: 16,677 (1979 census). *Area*: 100 sq. mi. *Capital*: George Town (7,617) on Grand Cayman.

Consisting mainly of three islands—Grand Cayman, Little Cayman, and Cayman Brac—this colony is in the Caribbean about 175 miles west of Jamaica. Grand Cayman is flat and rockbound, protected by coral reefs. The climate is tropical, hot and humid. About one-half of the people are of mixed Negro-white descent, about a third of European, and the rest of African ancestry.

Seafaring, commerce, and banking are the principal occupations. Tourism is important. Scuba divers are attracted to the Caymans—considered one of the world's best diving destinations—by the clear waters, wrecks, reefs, and caves.

There is a Crown-appointed governor, a partly elected legislative assembly and an executive council.

**Ceuta and Melilla**—*Status*: Under Spanish sovereignty. *Population*: Ceuta, 67,187; Melilla, 65,271 (1970 census). *Area*: Ceuta, 7.5 sq. mi.; Melilla, 4.8 sq. mi.

These two enclaves are on the Mediterranean coast of Morocco. Ceuta is opposite Gibraltar; Melilla, some 200 miles farther east, is on a rocky promontory. A good deal of fish are caught and exported from both towns. Ceuta, with a splendid climate, is increasingly visited by tourists. In 1975 Morocco laid formal claim.

**Channel Islands**—*Status*: British Crown Bailiwicks. *Population*: 129,000 (1981 est.). *Area*: 74 sq. mi.

These islands lie 80 miles south of the English coast, off the northwest coast of France. They consist of Jersey, Guernsey, and the latter's dependencies of Alderney, Brechou, Sark, Herm, Jethou, and Lihou. Ecrehou Rocks and Les Minquiers are dependencies of Jersey. The land is low and undulating and the climate mild with about 40 inches of annual rainfall. The people are mainly of Norman descent, with some of Breton ancestry. French is the official language of Jersey, English of Guernsey; in some country districts of Jersey and Guernsey and throughout Sark, a Norman-French dialect is spoken. English, however, is commonly used throughout the islands.

The main occupations are agriculture, dairying, and tourism. Agriculture is highly specialized, with Guernsey being noted for its hothouse tomatoes and cut flowers, Jersey for new potatoes and open-grown tomatoes. The farms of Jersey and Guernsey are, typically, tiny fields, the result of centuries of subdivision among heirs.

The Crown appoints the chief executives of Jersey and Guernsey, both of whom have the titles of lieutenant-governor and commander-in-chief. Jersey's partly elected legislature is called the States of Jersey, and St. Helier is the administrative center. The legislative body of Guernsey, partially elected, is the States of Deliberation. St. Peter Port is Guernsey's administrative center. Alderney and Sark have local legislative bodies subordinate to that of Guernsey. St. Anne is the administrative center of Alderney, Creux that of Sark. The head of Sark is *Le Seigneur de Sercq*.

**Chilean Antarctica**—*Status*: Chilean Dependency. *Population*: No permanent inhabitants. *Area*: 482,502 sq. mi.

Chile claims the Antarctic (or O'Higgins) Peninsula in the Antarctic, lying between 59° and 67°W. Parts of the area are also claimed by Great Britain and Argentina.

**Christmas Island**—*Status*: Australian External Territory. *Population*: 3,184 (1980). *Area*: 52 sq. mi. *Administrative Center*: Flying Fish Cove (1,300).

The island is in the Indian Ocean (10°30'S.,105°40'E.) some 1,630 miles northwest of Perth, Australia, and 225 miles south of Java. It is hilly and rather barren. A national park was established in 1980. The climate is warm and dry. Over half the people are Chinese, with some Malayans and fewer Europeans.

Phosphate extraction, undertaken by the governments of Australia and New Zealand, is the island's only economic activity. Most of the deposits are expected to be exhausted at the end of this century.

**Clipperton Island**—*Status*: French Dependency. *Population*: Uninhabited. *Area*: 2 sq. mi.

This atoll is in the eastern Pacific (10°17'N.,109°13'W.), 700 miles southwest of Mexico. Formerly part of French Polynesia, it was placed in 1979 under the direct control of the French government in Paris.

**Cocos (Keeling) Islands**—*Status*: Australian External Territory. *Population*: 555 (1981). *Area*: 5.4 sq. mi. *Administrative Center*: West Island (193).

The territory, two separate atolls with 27 small coral islands, is in the Indian Ocean about 1,725 miles northwest of Perth, Australia, at 12°05'S and 96°53'E. The principal islands are West, Home, Direction, South, and Horsburgh. The climate is pleasant, with moderate rainfall. Three-quarters of the people are Cocos Islanders living on Home Island; the rest are of European descent, most of whom live on West Island, and Asians. Coconuts are the principal product.

Though the islands were placed under Australian authority in 1955, it was not until July 1978 that the Australian government purchased the Cocos from their owner, John Clunies Ross. His family had been granted title to the islands in 1886.

**Cook Islands**—*Status*: New Zealand Dependency. *Population*: 17,695 (1981 census). *Area*: 91 sq. mi. *Administrative Center*: Avarua (4,429) on Rarotonga.

Situated in the South Pacific some 2,000 miles northeast of New Zealand, between 8° and 23°S and 156° and 167°W, the islands are in two groups—the Northern, with seven islands or atolls, and the Lower or Southern Group, with eight. The Northern islands are low and barren; the Lower ones, which are more elevated and fertile, support the greater part of the population. The climate is warm and humid. The people are Polynesian Christians, similar in language and traditions to the New Zealand Maori.

The economy is basically agricultural, with citrus fruits and juices, copra, and tomatoes, among other produce, being exported. Manufactured wearing apparel is also exported. The sale of postage stamps to collectors throughout the world is an important source of revenue.

The Cooks attained internal self-government in 1965, with New Zealand responsible for external affairs and defense. There is a prime minister and cabinet, and an elected legislative assembly.

**Coral Sea Islands Territory**—*Status*: Australian External Territory. *Population*: 3 (1979 est.). *Area*: 8.5 sq. mi.

These islands, spread over 400,000 square miles, are situated east of Queensland, Australia, between the Great Barrier Reef and the 157°10'E meridian. One of the islands in the Willis Group has a meteorological station. The land consists mainly of scattered reefs and sand cays, many little more than sandbanks.

The Coral Sea Islands became an Australian External Territory in 1969, after having been acquired by acts of sovereignty over a number of years. The Australian Minister for Home Affairs is responsible for matters affecting the Territory.

**Easter Island**—*Status*: Chilean Dependency. *Population*: 1,931 (1982 census). *Area*: 63 sq. mi. *Settlement*: Hanga Roa (900).

Easter Island (*Rapa Nui* in Polynesian) lies in the Pacific Ocean some 2,300 miles west of Chile at 27°08'S. and 109°23'W. It is volcanic in origin, rising sharply from the sea. The climate is subtropical: warm, somewhat humid, and there is moderate rainfall. The island has no streams or lakes, and rainwater collects in the extinct volcanoes. The people, who are believed to be Polynesian in origin, speak Spanish. Easter Island is noted for its monolithic, stylized heads carved of volcanic rock.

Sheep raising is the most important activity. Despite the scarcity of fresh water, certain crops, including corn, wheat, taro, and tropical fruits, are grown. The island is administered as part of metropolitan Chile.

**Faeroe Islands**—*Status*: Integral part of the Danish Kingdom. *Population*: 44,000 (1981 est.). *Area*: 540 sq. mi. *Capital*: Tórshavn (11,618) on Streymoy.

These islands are in the Atlantic Ocean, north of Scotland, between 61°26' and 62°24'N and 6°15' and 7°41'W. Among the larger of the 18 islands (17 are inhabited) are Streymoy, Eysturoy and Vágar. They contain many lakes and peat bogs. The climate is mild, rainy, and foggy. The economy is based on fishing and sheep raising. Root vegetables, potatoes, and barley are grown. Norse-descended, the inhabitants speak an old Norse dialect; Danish, however, is the official language. Most of the people are Lutherans.

A self-governing community within the Danish kingdom with a Crown commissioner, the Faeroes have their own elected parliament *(Lögting)* which chooses an administrative body *(Landsstyri)*. The Faeroes send two representatives to the Danish parliament.

**Falkland Islands**—*Status*: British Crown Colony. *Population*: 1,812 (1980 census). *Area*: 6,198 sq. mi. *Capital*: Stanley (1,079) on East Falkland.

Located in the South Atlantic some 500 miles northeast of Cape Horn, this group's major islands are East Falkland and West Falkland (4,618 sq. mi.), South Georgia (1,450 sq. mi.), and South Sandwich Islands (130 sq. mi.). East and West Falkland, which contain most of the population, consist largely of hilly moorland. The climate is cool and rainy, with persistently strong winds. The people are mostly of British origin. Sheep farming is the main occupation, wool the main export. Offshore oil deposits are believed to exist.

British settlers first occupied the Falklands from 1765 until 1774 when, according to Argentine historians, Britain ceded the islands to Spain. On gaining its independence from Spain, the Argentines claimed what they called *Las Islas Malvinas* and sent colonists in 1831. These people were ejected by a British expedition in 1833. The islands were then settled by Britons, whose descendents have repeatedly affirmed their intention to remain British. Argentina has never relinquished its claim to the territory. Exasperated by the failure of negotiations to regain sovereignty, Argentina seized the Falklands and South Georgia April 2, 1982. Britain countered by sending an expeditionary force and, after a short but bitter air, sea and land struggle, compelled the last Argentine garrison to surrender June 14. Argentina admitted to 613 casualities; British deaths numbered 252.

The colony is administered by a Crown-appointed governor, assisted by partly elected councils.

**French Guiana**—*Status*: French Overseas Department. *Population*: 67,000 (1981 est.). *Area*: 35,135 sq. mi. *Capital*: Cayenne (29,405).

Situated on the northeast coast of South America, French Guiana is bounded by the Atlantic Ocean on the north, by Brazil on the east and south, and by Suriname on the west. Its coastline is 200 miles long, and Devil's Island (no longer used as a prison) is among its offshore islands. Extending almost 250 miles into the continent, French Guiana is divided into a low, swampy coastal area that ranges from 10 to 30 miles in width, and a plateau forming a series of low, steep hills inland. Most of the country is covered by rain forest. The climate is tropical, tempered by trade winds, and there is heavy rainfall from December to July. Ninety percent of the people live in the coastal areas; these are mostly a Negro-white mixture. In the interior are small groups of Indians (Carib, Arawak, Tupi-Guaraní) and descendants of escaped African slaves.

Forestry, including wood-veneer production, is a major element in the economy. Gold is mined, and bauxite and tantalite deposits are to be exploited. Arable land is scarce and limited to the coastal areas, where manioc, yams, sugarcane, and bananas are grown. The main source of income is French investment and contributions toward operating expenses and welfare. France's space center at Kourou is the site of an 11-nation European satellite-launching project.

Guiana (in French, *Guyane*) is administered by a Paris-appointed prefect, assisted by an elected general council. It elects a deputy and a senator to the French Parliament.

**French Polynesia**—*Status*: French Overseas Territory. *Population*: 150,000 (1981 est.). *Area*: 1,544 sq. mi. *Capital*: Papeete (51,987) on Tahiti.

These widely scattered islands in the south central Pacific lie between 7° and 27°S. and 134° and 155°W. The territory includes island groups totaling 118 islands and atolls. The Society Islands (named after the Royal Society by their British discoverers) are the most important group and include Tahiti and Moorea; they contain about 70 percent of the Territory's population. Other groups are the Marquesas Islands, the Tuamotu Archipelago, the Gambier Islands, and the Tubuai or Austral Islands. All of these except the Tuamotus are volcanic in origin and mountainous, with fast-flowing streams, and are often circled by coral reefs and lagoons. The climate is hot and humid, tempered by steady winds. The people are predominantly Polynesians, with some Asians and a smaller number of Europeans, principally French. More than 60 percent of the people are Protestants.

The economy is based on agriculture. The main crops are copra, vanilla, and coffee. All common tropical plants and most European vegetables are grown. There has been extensive building in the islands to provide facilities for French nuclear tests, the first of which was held in 1966 on Mururoa Atoll, 800 miles southeast of Tahiti. In August 1968 the French exploded their first H-bomb nearby, at Fangataufa Atoll. In 1971 and 1973, French nuclear test activity in the Mururoa Atoll area met with worldwide protest. French nuclear testing has since continued. Vocal adherents of autonomy increased their representation in the assembly in 1976, and again in 1977.

The Territory is administered by a Paris-appointed high commissioner, aided by a government council, with an elected territorial assembly, and elects two deputies and a senator to the French Parliament.

**French Southern and Antarctic Territories**—*Status*: French Overseas Territory. *Population*: 183 (1975). *Area*: 202,916 sq. mi. *Administrative Center:* Port-aux-Français (94) on Kerguélen.

These territories comprise a number of islands in the far southern Indian Ocean and Adélie Land on the Antarctic continent. The latter, with an area of 200,000 sq. mi., lies between 136° and 142°E. The Kerguélen Islands are between 48° and 50°S. and 68° and 70°E. The principal island, Kerguélen, has an area of 2,510 sq. mi. and is mostly mountainous. The Crozet Islands at 46°S. and between 50° and 52°E. are also mountainous, cold, windy, and inhospitable. Saint Paul Island is at 38°S. and 77°E. and its center is occupied by a large crater with volcanic hot springs. Amsterdam Island is at 37°S. and 70°E., and maintains a hospital.

The Territory, on which various research stations have been established, is under the authority of a high administrator assisted by a conssultative council in Paris.

**Gibraltar**—*Status*: British Colony. *Population*: 29,648 (1981 census). *Area*: 2.28 sq. mi. *Administrative Center:* Gibraltar.

Gibraltar is a tiny peninsula jutting into the western Mediterranean from Spain. It rises from a sandy plain to the 1,400-foot Rock, a cave-riddled, fortified limestone mass. The climate is temperate. The people are mostly of Genoese, Portuguese and Maltese descent. The language of the home is generally Spanish, with English the language of instruction in school. Most of the civilian population are Roman Catholics.

The colony has no natural resources other than its strategic position at the mouth of the Mediterranean, and is dependent on its naval and military bases, transshipments, dockyards, and tourist traffic.

Gibraltar is administered by a governor (also the commander of the fortress) appointed by the Crown, with the advice of the Gibraltar Council, the elected members of which compose a council of ministers presided over by a chief minister. There is also a partly elected House of Assembly.

Gibraltar was ceded in 1713 to Great Britain by Spain in the Treaty of Utrecht. Since 1964, Spain has been seeking its return, applying such pressures as the restriction of transit to and from the mainland. In 1967, the people of Gibraltar voted overwhelmingly to retain the British connection. At the end of 1968, the UN General Assembly's Trusteeship Committee called on Britain to surrender control to Spain. Talks have been held between Britain and Spain on the Gibraltar question since 1972.

**Greenland (Kalâtdlit-Nunât)**—*Status*: Semiautonomous state of the Danish Kingdom. *Population*: 49,773 (1980 est.). *Area*: 840,000 sq. mi. *Capital*: Nûk (Godthab) (9,561).

Greenland, the largest island in the world, lies northeast of Canada between the Arctic Ocean on the north and the Atlantic Ocean on the south. Its ice-free areas—the coastal strips plus the coastal islands—cover 132,000 sq. mi. The rest of Greenland is sheathed in ice at places 11,000 feet thick. The climate is arctic, with considerable variation in temperature betweeen localities. The population, predominantly Eskimo, with some Europeans, lives mostly on the west coast. Danish and Greenlandic are the official languages. The principal occupations are fishing, sheep raising and hunting.

Home rule was established on May 1, 1979, with Denmark retaining control of defense and foreign affairs. A prime minister, the leader of the majority party in the 21-member parliament *(Landsting)* and four secretaries preside over the government *(Landsstyre)*. Greenland sends two elected members to the Danish Parliament. In 1982, Greenland's voters elected to withdraw from the European Economic Community.

**Guadeloupe**—*Status*: French Overseas Department. *Population*: 318,000 (1980 est.). *Area*: 687 sq. mi. *Capital*: Basse-Terre (16,000) on the island of that name.

Guadeloupe lies in the Leeward Islands of the West Indies. In addition to Guadeloupe proper (584 sq. mi.), which a narrow channel divides into two islands, Basse-Terre and Grande-Terre, there are the nearby dependencies of Marie-Galante, La Désirade, Îles des Saintes, and Îsle de la Petite Terre. About 135 miles to the northwest are the dependencies of Saint Barthélemy and the French portion of Saint Martin.

Basse-Terre has a 4,000-foot active volcano, La Soufrière. Grande-Terre is low and encircled by coral reefs; it has the largest town in the department, Point-à-Pitre, twice the size of the capital. The climate is tropical, moderated by trade winds. Basse-Terre's mountains receive heavy rainfall, which feeds numerous streams. The people are blacks and, especially on the dependencies, descendants of Normans and Bretons who settled there in the 17th century, or a racial mixture.

The main crops are sugar and bananas, with cotton, sisal, coffee, vegetables and tropical fruits also grown. Fishing and rum production are significant activities.

Guadeloupe is administered by a Paris-appointed prefect and an elected general council; it elects three deputies and two senators to the French Parliament.

There were serious riots in Guadeloupe in 1967, reportedly sparked by an organization advocating independence. Although support for secession seems slight, another "liberation" group became active in 1980, staging a series of bombings, including some in the city of Paris, in 1981.

**Heard and McDonald Islands**—*Status*: Australian External Territory. *Population*: Uninhabited. *Area*: 113 sq. mi.

These islands lie in the south Indian Ocean, 2,575 miles southwest of Perth, Australia, at 53°S.,73°E. Heard Island is mountainous, the McDonald Islands, small and rocky.

**Hong Kong**—*Status*: British Colony. *Population*: 4,9986,560 (1981 census). *Area*: 403 sq. mi. *Capital*: Victoria on the island of Hong Kong (1,183,621).

The colony is on the southern coast of China about 80 miles southeast of Canton, and surrounded by the Chinese province of Guangdong. It includes Hong Kong proper, an island of about 30 sq. mi., many other islands, and Kowloon and the New Territories on the mainland. The New Territories (370 sq. mi., including a number of small islands) are held under a 99-year lease from China, which expires in 1997. Most of the area is either swampy or rocky andd hilly. The climate is subtropical, with hot, humid summers and heavy rainfall, but can be chilly January to April.

The population density of Hong Kong is very high, as more than 80 percent of the people live in the urban area. An overwhelming number of them are Chinese, including more than a million refugees. (English and Chinese are both official languages.)

Hong Kong is a major center for shipping, banking, commerce and industry, situated as it is at a crossroad of world trade. Light industries, particularly machinery, textiles and clothing, are important. Tourism is important and growing. Agriculture and fishing are intensively practiced, but much food must be imported, mostly from China. A large part of the water supply must also be brought in from China. A tunnel now links Hong Kong Island with the mainland.

Hong Kong is administered by a Crown-appointed governor, advised by executive and legislative councils. Communist China officially claims Hong Kong.

**Isle of Man**—*Status*: British Crown Fiefdom. *Population*: 66,000 (1981 est.). *Area*: 227 sq. mi. *Capital*: Douglas (20,262).

Situated in the Irish Sea, the Isle of Man is about 35 miles from Northern Ireland and the northwest coast of England. The central mass consists of treeless hills, extending in the north and south to low-lying farmland. The climate is pleasant, with mild winters and cool summers. Methodists predominate, but there are Roman Catholics and Anglicans.

By far the most important factor in the economy is the tourist trade. The major export is kippered herring, processed from fish landed by a Scottish fleet. Oats are the main crop, and there is sheep raising and dairying.

The Isle is administered under its own laws (Acts of Parliament do not apply unless they specifically so note). The ruling body is the Court of Tynwald, composed of the Crown-appointed governor, a legislative council, and the elected House of Keys.

**Jan Mayen**—*Status*: Norwegian Dependency. *Population*: Uninhabited. *Area*: 143 sq. mi.

This island 300 miles north-northeast of Iceland at 71°N.,8°30′W. is bleak and desolate. The Norwegian government operates radio, meteorological, and navigational stations and an airstrip. Norway and Iceland settled their dispute over the offshore area around Jan Mayen in 1981.

**Juan Fernández**—*Status*: Chilean Dependency. *Population*: 540. *Area*: 70 sq. mi. (the two main islands). *Administrative Center:* Juan Bautista, on Robinson Crusoe Island.

This island group is in the Pacific some 360 miles west of Chile. Volcanic in origin, rugged and wooded, it was discovered in 1572 by Juan Fernández, a Spanish explorer. The two main islands, about 100 miles apart from east to west, are Robinson Crusoe (33°45′S.,79°W.) and Alejandro Selkirk (33°45′S.,80°45′W.). Lobster fishing is the main occupation.

Daniel Defoe's *Robinson Crusoe* is generally acknowledged to have been inspired by Alexander Selkirk's stay on Robinson Crusoe Island (1704-09).

**Macau**—*Status*: Portuguese Administered Territory *Population*: 271,000 (1978 est.). *Area*: 6.2 sq. mi. *Capital*: Macau (226,880).

Macau or Macao (*Ao-men* in Chinese) is situated on a small peninsula of the south coast of China. It lies at the mouth of the Pearl River and 40 miles west of Hong Kong; the territory also includes two small islands. Macau proper is entirely urban, the islands forested. The climate is hot and humid, but sea breezes make the temperatures tolerable. Only one percent of the population is Portuguese, the rest is Chinese.

Macau is almost completely dependent on imported food, mostly from China. Fishing, commerce, and, in recent years, light industry—textiles, clothing and electronics—are important. There is a brisk tourist trade, some attracted by Macau's gambling houses.

The territory is administered by a Lisbon-appointed governor, a council, which serves as a cabinet, and a partially elected 18-member legislative assembly. China still officially claims dominion over Macau, although the Peking government has not pressed the issue.

**Martinique**—*Status*: French Overseas Department. *Population*: 308,000 (1981 est.). *Area*: 425 sq. mi. *Capital*: Fort-de-France (98,561).

This island is in the West Indies some 130 miles south of Guadeloupe. It is largely mountainous, and its two highest peaks are active volcanoes. In 1902, Mount Pelée erupted and destroyed the city of St-Pierre. The climate is tropical, tempered by the trade winds. The people are descendants of blacks, Europeans, and Carib Indians.

Martinique's economy is agricultural, with sugarcane, pineapples and bananas being the principal crops. Rum is distilled, and there is livestock raising and fishing. Tourism is increasing. The economy is heavily dependent on direct and indirect French subsidies, and substantial emigration to France has not solved the island's stubborn unemployment problem. Efforts have been made for some time to broaden and diversify Martinique's economic base. Yet demand for Martinique's major export crops is leveling off at a time when the number of young persons coming into the labor market is increasing as a result of a high birthrate since the 1940s. Martinique's international airport is its principal transport link with the world, but the island is also visited by numerous oceangoing vessels and cruise

Administration is in the hands of a Paris-appointed prefect with the aid of an elected general council. Martinique elects three deputies and two senators to the French Parliament.

Strike violence in 1980 was blamed on Cuba; France flew in 225 elite police to assist in putting it down. Later France and Cuba concluded an economic agreement, and Cuba's Castro denied that he had intervened in Martinique. In 1980 and 1981 there were terrorist acts by separatists in Fort-de-France.

**Mayotte**—*Status*: French Territorial Collectivity. *Population*: 47,300 (1978 census). *Area*: 144 sq. mi. *Capital*: Dzaoudzi.

The easternmost of the Comoro Islands in the Indian Ocean (13°S.,45°E.), Mayotte is a volcanic island surrounded by coral reefs and islets, with a tropical climate. The population is of African, Arab, and Malagasy origin, and the majority are Moslems. French, Arabic, and Swahili are spoken. Most of the people are engaged in the production of such agricultural products as vanilla, sisal, sugarcane, essential oils, and rum.

An Arab dynasty from Shiraz reigned from the 16th century to 1843, when a French colony was established. It was attached first to Réunion and later to Madagascar as a part of the Comoro Islands territory. When a future Comoro Islands referendum was first announced in 1974, Mayotte was the only island to vote against it, and after the unilateral declaration of independence in 1975, Mayotte refused to be considered a part of the new republic. In 1976 an island referendum resulted in 99.41 percent voting to remain French, and two months later the status as a French Territorial Collectivity was approved. The island sends one deputy to the French Parliament.

**Montserrat**—*Status*: British Crown Colony. *Population*: 12,073 (1980 census). *Area*: 40 sq. mi. *Capital*: Plymouth (1,623).

Situated in the Leeward Islands of the West Indies, Montserrat is 260 miles southeast of Puerto Rico and north of Guadeloupe. In 1493, on his second voyage, Christopher Columbus reached the island and gave it its present name, after the mountaintop monastery in Spain. It has elevations of more than 3,000 feet, and the climate is tropical and humid. The people are mostly of Negro-white descent. English is the formal language and everywhere understood, but a patois is commonly spoken. As a result of an Irish settlement in the 1630s, many people on the island speak with a brogue.

The island is agricultural; cattle, fruit and vegetables being the main exports. Cotton and bananas are also exported and yams, rice, breadfruit, and corn are raised for food. Tourism is of increasing economic importance.

There is a Crown-appointed governor, an executive council and a partly elected legislative council. In 1967, Montserrat elected to remain a British colony.

**Namibia**—*Status*: In dispute; administered by South Africa. *Population*: 1,000,000 (1979 est.). *Area*: 317,827 sq. mi. *Capital*: Windhoek (61,369).

Namibia (formerly South-West Africa) is bounded by Angola on the north, by Zambia on the northeast, by Botswana on the east, by South Africa on the east and south, and by the Atlantic Ocean on the west. The Namib Desert, stretching for 1,000 miles along the coast, is uninhabited except for three towns, including the South African enclave of Walvis Bay (434 sq. mi.), and the diamond workings at the mouth of the Orange River in the south. The Kalahari Desert of sand and limestone is on the east. The Caprivi Strip, 20 to 60 miles wide and some 300 miles long, extends from the northeast corner of the country and separates Botswana from Angola. The greater part of the country consists of a plateau, averaging 3,600 feet, with scattered mountains. The climate is generally hot and dry. There are only a few rivers and water must generally be obtained from boreholes. The people are largely African of various tribal groups, including Ovambo, Damara, Herero, Nama, and Bushmen. Whites are a minority of about 11 percent, mostly of South African and German descent. There is a smaller number of mixed descent, including the Rehoboth Bastards, of Nama-white ancestry. In general, the whites live in the Police Zone in the south, the native population in homelands in the north. Official languages are Afrikaans and English, but German is widely used, as are tribal languages.

Parts of the nonwhite population follow the traditional animist religions, although many Africans have been converted to Christianity. Missionary activity, which began in thee 1800s, encompasses several denominations, including Lutheran, Roman Catholic, Methodist, Anglican, and Dutch Reformed.

Diamonds are Namibia's most valuable economic product, and copper, zinc, lead, uranium, cadmium, and manganese are also mined. Sheep, cattle, and goats are raised, and the production of karakul sheep pelts is increasingly important. The annual haul of fish is over a quarter of a million tons.

South-West Africa had been mandated to South African administration by the League of Nations. When the UN Trusteeship System was established in 1945, South Africa refused to place South-West Africa under it (it was the only such case), claiming that the UN was not the legal successor to the League. In 1966 the UN General Assembly declared that the mandate was terminated; in 1967 it established a council to administer the area until independence; and in 1968 it proclaimed that the area be renamed Namibia. South Africa, however, declaring that the removal of the mandate was an "illegal act" because the UN charter makes no provision for such a move, announced its intention to continue administration, and has done so even after a 1971 ruling against its position by the International Court of Justice.

In January 1976, the UN Security Council voted to invoke mandatory sanctions against South Africa if it failed to accept a UN-supervised election leading to independence. In August the South African government announced plans for a multiracial Namibian government to bring about independence by December 31, 1978. Inasmuch as the South African proposal did not mention a specific date for elections, both the UN and the powerful guerrilla group, the South-West Africa People's Organization (SWAPO) rejected the plan. At a conference in the Turnhalle in Windhoek in August 1976, South Africa announced that it intended to set up an interim government. Sanctions against South Africa for not withdrawing were vetoed in the UN. In 1977 the United States, Britain, France, Canada and West Germany began diplomatic efforts to arrive at an independence plan acceptable to both South Africa and SWAPO. South Africa agreed to the Western plan in April, but SWAPO withheld its consent after a South African raid on its bases in Angola. Further efforts were made by the Western powers, and SWAPO's agreement was secured in July with the help of five black-ruled "front-line" states. Under the plan, all South African troops would be withdrawn except for 1,500 men who would be restricted to camps near the Angolan border. A United Nations force of 5,000 men would be sent into the territory to insure a free election, after which the territory would become independent. In the period leading up to the election, the territory would be administered jointly by a South African administrator and a UN representative. A dispute has arisen between South Africa and SWAPO over the Walvis Bay enclave, the future status of which was not determined in the Western powers' plan.

In a South African-sponsored election in Namibia in 1978, the Democratic Turnhalle Alliance won 41 seats in a 50-member constituent assembly. SWAPO did not vote, and the UN Security Council declared the election null and void. In May 1980, South Africa announced its willingness to cooperate in implementing the 1977 peace plan, but demanded assurances that the UN would not favor SWAPO. Efforts of the five Western powers to find a solution to the Namibian problem continued well into 1982. Some progress toward a settlement was reported, but without the all-important involvement of South Africa, which has insisted on withdrawal of all Cuban military personnel from Angola as a prerequisite for acceptance.

**Netherlands Antilles**—*Status*: Autonomous Part of the Kingdom of the Netherlands. *Population*: 246,000 (1978 est.). *Area*: 390 sq. mi. *Capital*: Willemstad (95,000) on Curaçao.

The Netherlands Antilles, in the Caribbean, consists of two groups of three islands each: Curaçao, Aruba, and Bonaire, 15 to 38 miles off the northern coast of Venezuela; and Saba, St. Eustatius, and St. Maarten, which shares an island with the French St. Martin, more than 500 miles to the northeast. Curaçao and Aruba are by far the most populous and important. On these two islands, Dutch, English, Spanish, and Papiamento (a mixture of the three) are spoken.

The Leewards are semiarid and flat; the Windwards are mountainous, with enough rainfall for flourishing vegetation. The climate is warm and humid. The people are largely blacks, or Carib Indians, or either of these mixed with white strains. Dutch is the official language, and English is current in the Windwards. Papiamento is common. Catholicism predominates on the Leeward Islands, Protestantism on the Windward.

Curaçao and Aruba owe their prosperity to oil refineries, which process crude oil from Venezuela. The refineries also stimulate other industries and commerce on the two islands. After oil refining, tourism is their most important economic factor. On Curaçao and Aruba little farming is possible because the land is so rocky. Most food is imported. On the other islands, small-scale agriculture and fishing are pursued.

In an effort to lessen dependence on the petroleum industry, the government has been attempting to attract new industries by offering tax holidays and customs exceptions to firms locating there and by creating free zones on Curaçao and Aruba.

Fully autonomous in internal affairs, the Netherlands Antilles are constitutionally equal with the Netherlands. There is a governor, who represents the sovereign, and a council of ministers—headed by a prime minister—which is responsible to an elected legislature *(Staten)*. Aruba, Curaçao, Bonaire, and the Windward group each have autonomy in local affairs.

In 1974, Juancho Evertsz, premier of the Netherlands Antilles, met with the Dutch premier at The Hague to discuss the future status of the islands. It was decided that they would wait at least until 1980 to achieve independent status (since postponed into the mid-1980s). In 1977, Aruba held its own referendum, with 57 percent voting for separate independence. In 1981, the Dutch government agreed on independence for Aruba. In 1979, a strike by police and firemen led the government of Premier Silvios Rosendal to resign. The New Antilles Movement, a coalition of trade unions, won the subsequent elections, both in the local council in Curaçao and throughout the islands, and its head, Dom Martina, became the premier.

**New Caledonia**—*Status*: French Overseas Territory. *Population*: 143,000 (1981 est.). *Area*: 7,335 sq. mi. *Capital*: Nouméa (74,335).

This group of about 25 islands in the South Pacific is situated about 750 miles east of Australia. The territory takes its name from the main island, New Caledonia or Grande-Terre (22°S.,166°E.), which is 6,530 square miles in area and mountainous. The territory includes the dependencies of Île des Pins, Loyalty Islands, Île Huon, Îles Belep, Îles Chesterfield, and Île Walpole. The British explorer, James Cook, was the first European to visit New Caledonia (1774). Other Europeans followed. In 1853, France took over control and, eleven years later, turned it into a prison colony. The climate is mildly tropical, tempered by the trade winds. About half the people are Australo-Melanesian indigenes. Most of the rest are of French descent or are Polynesians.

Agriculture and mining are the basic economic activities. Coffee and copra are the commercial crops, while root plants, wheat, corn, fruits, and vegetables are also grown, but food must be imported. Nickel is mined on a large scale, and iron and chrome are also exploited.

Administration is in the hands of a Paris-appointed High Commissioner. In 1979 a new Territorial Assembly of 36 elected members was established. In July 1982, anti-independence rioters disrupted the Assembly and attacked members. Two deputies and a senator are elected to the French Parliament.

**Niue**—*Status*: New Zealand Self-governing Territory. *Population*: 3,578 (1979 census). *Area*: 100 sq. mi. *Administrative Center:* Alofi (960).

Niue is in the South Pacific some 1,340 miles northeast of New Zealand (19°S.,170°W.); although geographically associated with the Cook Islands, its distance and cultural differences have led to separate administration. Niue is a coral island with fertile but sparse soil and a hot climate. The people are of Polynesian stock, speaking Samoan.

There is a prime minister and cabinet, and an elected island assembly. Niue became self-governing in 1974.

**Norfolk Island**—*Status*: Australian External Territory. *Population*: 2,180 (1979 est.). *Area*: 13.3 sq. mi. *Administrative Center:* Kingston.

The island lies in the South Pacific 930 miles northeast of Sydney, Australia (29°S.,168°E.). Many of its inhabitants are descendants of H.M.S. *Bounty* mutineeers, who were moved here in 1856 when they became too numerous for Pitcairn Island. Fruits and bean seed are grown and tourism is important. There is an Australian-appointed administrator and an elected Legislative Assembly.

**Peter I Island**—*Status*: Norwegian Dependency. *Population*: Uninhabited. *Area*: 96 sq. mi.

An Antarctic island, it is southwest of the South Shetland Islands, at 68°47′S and 90°35′W. It is of volcanic origin and almost entirely ice-covered.

**Pitcairn Islands**—*Status*: British Coloony. *Population*: 54 (1981 est.). *Area*: 18 sq. mi. *Administrative Center:* Adamstown.

The colony is in the South Pacific, 4,000 miles southwest of the Panama Canal and 3,200 miles northeast of New Zealand. There are four islands: Pitcairn (1.75 sq. mi.), Henderson, Ducie, and Oeno, of which only Pitcairn (25°05′S.,130°05′W.) is inhabited. The climate is warm throughout the year. The people are descendants of H.M.S. *Bounty* mutineers and Polynesian women from Tahiti. The inhabitants were resettled on Norfolk Island in 1856 when their numbers grew too large for Pitcairn, but several families of them returned soon after.

Subsistence agriculture and fishing are the main occupations. Some fruits, vegetables, and handicrafts are sold to passing ships.

The colony is administered by the British High Commissioner in New Zealand with the assistance of a partly elected island council, presided over by an island magistrate.

**Queen Maud Land**—*Status*: Norwegian Dependency. *Population*: Uninhabited.

The portion of Antarctica between 20°W and 45°E, it is claimed by Norway.

**Réunion**—*Status*: French Overseas Department. *Population*: 503,000 (1981 est.). *Area*: 969 sq. mi. *Capital*: Saint-Denis (103,513).

An island in the Indian Ocean (21°S.,55°30′E.), it is about 400 miles east of Madagascar. Réunion is of volcanic origin and mountainous, the highest peak—Piton des Neiges—rising to more than 10,000 feet. One of its volcanoes is still active. There are many torrential rivers. The climate is essentially tropical, but varies greatly with altitude and exposure to the trade winds. Rainfall is heavy, and there are severe tropical storms. The people are of Malabar Indian, African, Malay, Vietnamese, Chinese, and French descent; the last make up about 20 percent of the population. Ninety-four percent of the population is Roman Catholic.

The cultivation of sugarcane is the main economic activity. Essential oils from geranium and vetiver plants are also important. Corn, potatoes and beans are grown for consumption, but food must be imported.

Réunion is administered by a Paris-appointed prefect and an elected general council; the island elects three deputies and two senators to the French Parliament.

**Ross Dependency**—*Status*: New Zealand Territory. *Population*: No permanent inhabitants. *Area*: 290,000 sq. mi. (of which 130,000 sq. mi. are ice shelf).

New Zealand claims that portion of AAntarctica south of 60°S between 160°E and 150°W.

There are research and exploration activities in the area, and whaling in its territorial waters.

**Saint Christopher-Nevis**—*Status*: British Associated State. *Population*: 44,404 (1980 census). *Area*: 120 sq. mi. *Capital*: Basseterre (14,725) on St. Christopher.

In the Leeward Islands of the West Indies, it includes St. Christopher (commonly called St. Kitts; 68 sq. mi.), Nevis (50 sq. mi.), and Sombrero (2 sq. mi.). The climate of the islands is tropical and humid. The people are largely of mixed black-white descent. English is the formal language, but a patois is commonly spoken.

Sugar, molasses, and cotton are the chief exports. Yams, rice, breadfruit, and corn are grown for food. Tourism is increasingly important.

There is a Crown-appointed governor, a prime minister, and a partially elected house of assembly. In 1975 separatist delegates from Nevis won their assembly seats. Although Anguilla became a self-governing British colony in 1976, the rupture was formally approved only after a five-year delay. In talks in London in late 1979, it was decided that St. Kitts-Nevis should move to full independence within one year, but, due to local political factionalism, independence was still pending in 1982. A post-independence referendum was to determine whether Nevis wants to stay within the state.

**Saint Helena**—*Status*: British Colony. *Population*: 6,400 (1977 est.). *Area*: 162 sq. mi. *Capital*: Jamestown (1,601).

The island of Saint Helena (47 sq. mi.) is in the southeastern Atlantic about 1,200 miles from Africa, at 16°S. and 5°21′W. Its dependencies—Tristan da Cunha (38 sq. mi.) and Ascension (34 sq. mi.)—are about 1,500 miles south-southwest and 750 miles northwest, respectively. Near Tristan da Cunha are the uninhabited islands of Gough, Nightingale, and Inaccessible. St. Helena is rocky, with a pleasant climate due to the trade winds. It was the place of Napoleon's exile from 1815 until his death in 1821. Tristan da Cunha suffered a volcanic eruption in 1961, and the tiny population of 248 was resettled in England. They suffered from respiratory diseases in that climate, however, and returned to their island in 1963 (1981 pop.—323). Ascension Island (1981 pop.—1,024) acquired notoriety in 1982 as a staging base for the British expeditionary force sent against the Argentines who had seized and occupied the Falkland Islands. The people of the colony are of mixed origin, and their language is English.

St. Helena grows flax, fodder, and vegetables. Potatoes are the staple subsistence crop on Tristan da Cunha. Ascension is an important cable and missile tracking station.

The colony is administered by a Crown-appointed governor, assisted by an executive council and a partly elected legislative council.

**Saint Kitts-Nevis:** *See* Saint Christopher-Nevis.

**Saint Pierre and Miquelon**—*Status*: French Overseas Department. *Population*: 5,900 (1977 est.). *Area*: 93.5 sq. mi. *Capital*: Saint Pierre (5,232) on St. Pierre.

This archipelago lies some 15 miles south of Newfoundland in the North Atlantic. There are three main islands, Saint Pierre, Miquelon, and Langlade, the latter two connected by a low isthmus. Although volcanic in origin, the islands are low-lying. The climate is cool to cold, with seasons of strong winds and heavy fogs; there is a good deal of rain and snow. The people are mostly descendants of Breton, Norman, and Basque settlers.

The chief occupation is cod fishing, together with fish freezing and fish meal production.

The department is administered by a Paris-appointed prefect. There is an elected general council. A deputy and a senator are elected to the French Parliament.

**Sala y Gómez Island**—*Status*: Chilean Dependency. *Population*: Uninhabited. *Area*: .05 sq. mi.

In the Pacific Ocean at 26°28′S.,105°28′W., some 2,100 miles west of Chile and 250 miles east of Easter Island, Sala y Gómez, an arid island of volcanic origin, is administered by Valparaíso Province.

**San Ambrosio Island and San Felix Island**—*Status*: Chilean Dependencies. *Population*: Uninhabited. *Area*: 1.29 sq. mi.

These two small islands—some 12 miles apart—are in the Pacific Ocean at 26°20′S.,80°W., about 600 miles west of Chile. They were discovered by the Spanish navigator, Juan Fernández, in 1574, and are administered by Atacama Province.

**Svalbard**—*Status*: Norwegian Dependency. *Population*: 3,431 (1975 est.). *Area*: 23,957 sq. mi. *Administrative Center:* Longyearbyen.

Svalbard is the name of an island territory in the Arctic Ocean between 74° and 81°N and 10° and 35°E. By far the most important of these islands is the Spitsbergen group, the largest of which are Spitsbergen, North East Land, Edge Island, and Barents Island. The islands are bleak and rugged, largely covered with ice running to the sea in glaciers. The climate is moderated, however, by winds from the Atlantic, and the Gulf Stream keeps open water for six months of the year. About two-thirds of the people are Russians who live in mining camps, the rest are Norwegians. Coal is the principal product.

**Tokelau**—*Status*: New Zealand Territory. *Population*: 1,625 (1977 est.). *Area*: 3.95 sq. mi. *Administrative Center:* Fenuafala (649) on Fakaofo.

These islands are in the South Pacific at 9°S.,172°W., 2,100 miles northeast of New Zealand, 300 miles north of Samoa. Geographically the group consists of four atolls—Atafu, Nukunono, Fakaofo, and Swains—but the last belongs to American Samoa. The people are of Polynesian origin. Their language, now dying, resembles Samoan, the official language.

Subsistence farming and copra production for export are the main occupations. Revenue is also derived from the sale of postage stamps.

The islands are administrated by the New Zealand Minister for Foreign Affairs.

**Turks and Caicos Islands**—*Status*: British Colony. *Population*: 7,436 (1980 census). *Area*: 166 sq. mi. *Capital*: Cockburn Town (2,287), on Grand Turk.

Geographically part of the Bahamas, of which they form the southeastern groups, the Turks and Caicos lie in the Atlantic Ocean some 575 miles southeast of Florida. Of the 30 or so small islands, only six are inhabited, among them Grand Turk, Grand Caicos, and Salt Cay. The climate is hot, dry, and subject to hurricanes. The people are almost all of African descent.

Fishing and salt production are economic staples.

The administration of the islands is under a Crown-appointed governor and a partly elected state legislature.

**Wallis and Futuna**—*Status*: French Overseas Territory. *Population*: 9,192 (1976 census). *Area*: 106 sq. mi. *Capital*: Mata Utu (566) on Wallis.

These small island groups are in the South Pacific, Wallis (13°18′S.,176°10′W.) and its surrounding uninhabited islands being about 250 miles west of Samoa, while Futuna (14°19′S.,178°05′W.) and the uninhabited Alofi island are 120 miles to the southwest. The islands are of volcanic origin. The climate is tropical, mitigated by sea breezes, with seasonal hurricanes. The people are mostly Polynesians. The principal crop is copra.

The territory is administered by a Paris-appointed administrator. A territorial assembly is elected, as are a deputy and a senator to the French Parliament.

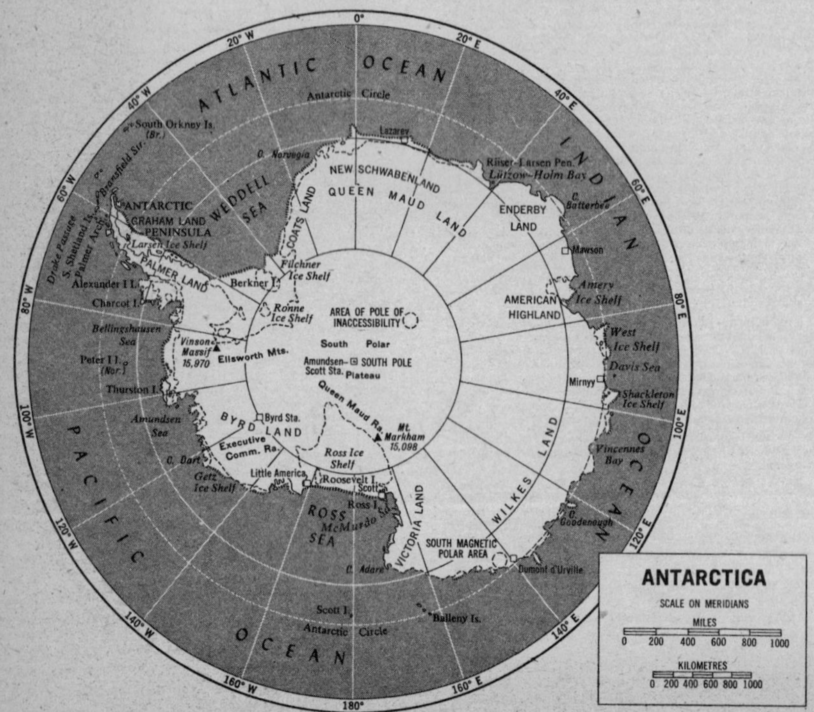

# DIPLOMATIC AFFAIRS

## ROSTER OF THE UNITED NATIONS: 1982 (157 Members as of September 16)

| Member Nation | Date of Admission | |
|---|---|---|
| Afghanistan | 19 Nov. | 1946 |
| Albania | 14 Dec. | 1955 |
| Algeria | 8 Oct. | 1962 |
| Angola | 1 Dec. | 1976 |
| Antigua and Barbuda | 11 Nov. | 1981 |
| Argentina | 24 Oct. | 1945 |
| Australia | 1 Nov. | 1945 |
| Austria | 14 Dec. | 1955 |
| Bahamas | 18 Sept. | 1973 |
| Bahrain | 21 Sept. | 1971 |
| Bangladesh | 17 Sept. | 1974 |
| Barbados | 9 Dec. | 1966 |
| Belgium | 27 Dec. | 1945 |
| Belize | 25 Sept. | 1981 |
| Benin | 20 Sept. | 1960 |
| Bhutan | 21 Sept. | 1971 |
| Bolivia | 14 Nov. | 1945 |
| Botswana | 17 Oct. | 1966 |
| Brazil | 24 Oct. | 1945 |
| Bulgaria | 14 Dec. | 1955 |
| Burma | 19 Apr. | 1948 |
| Burundi | 18 Sept. | 1962 |
| Byelorussian SSR | 24 Oct. | 1945 |
| Cambodia (Kampuchea) | 14 Dec. | 1955 |
| Cameroon | 20 Sept. | 1960 |
| Canada | 9 Nov. | 1945 |
| Cape Verde | 16 Sept. | 1975 |
| Central African Republic | 20 Sept. | 1960 |
| Chad | 20 Sept. | 1960 |
| Chile | 24 Oct. | 1945 |
| China | 24 Oct. | 1945 |
| Colombia | 5 Nov. | 1945 |
| Comoros | 12 Nov. | 1975 |
| Congo | 20 Sept. | 1960 |
| Costa Rica | 2 Nov. | 1945 |
| Cuba | 24 Oct. | 1945 |
| Cyprus | 20 Sept. | 1960 |
| Czechoslovakia | 24 Oct. | 1945 |
| Denmark | 24 Oct. | 1945 |
| Djibouti | 20 Sept. | 1977 |
| Dominica | 18 Dec. | 1978 |
| Dominican Republic | 24 Oct. | 1945 |
| Ecuador | 21 Dec. | 1945 |
| Egypt | 24 Oct. | 1945 |
| El Salvador | 24 Oct. | 1945 |
| Equatorial Guinea | 12 Nov. | 1968 |
| Ethiopia | 13 Nov. | 1945 |
| Fiji | 13 Oct. | 1970 |
| Finland | 14 Dec. | 1955 |
| France | 24 Oct. | 1945 |
| Gabon | 20 Sept. | 1960 |
| Gambia | 21 Sept. | 1965 |
| Germany (Dem. Rep.) | 18 Sept. | 1973 |
| Germany (Fed. Rep.) | 18 Sept. | 1973 |
| Ghana | 8 Mar. | 1957 |
| Greece | 25 Oct. | 1945 |
| Grenada | 17 Sept. | 1974 |
| Guatemala | 21 Nov. | 1945 |
| Guinea | 12 Dec. | 1958 |
| Guinea-Bissau | 17 Sept. | 1974 |
| Guyana | 20 Sept. | 1966 |
| Haiti | 24 Oct. | 1945 |
| Honduras | 17 Dec. | 1945 |
| Hungary | 14 Dec. | 1955 |
| Iceland | 19 Nov. | 1946 |
| India | 30 Oct. | 1945 |
| Indonesia | 28 Sept. | 1950 |
| Iran | 24 Oct. | 1945 |
| Iraq | 21 Dec. | 1945 |
| Ireland | 14 Dec. | 1955 |
| Israel | 11 May | 1949 |
| Italy | 14 Dec. | 1955 |
| Ivory Coast | 20 Sept. | 1960 |
| Jamaica | 18 Sept. | 1962 |
| Japan | 18 Dec. | 1956 |
| Jordan | 14 Dec. | 1955 |
| Kenya | 16 Dec. | 1963 |
| Kuwait | 14 May | 1963 |
| Laos | 14 Dec. | 1955 |
| Lebanon | 24 Oct. | 1945 |
| Lesotho | 17 Oct. | 1966 |
| Liberia | 2 Nov. | 1945 |
| Libya | 14 Dec. | 1955 |
| Luxembourg | 24 Oct. | 1945 |
| Madagascar | 20 Sept. | 1960 |
| Malawi | 1 Dec. | 1964 |
| Malaysia | 17 Sept. | 1957 |
| Maldives | 21 Sept. | 1965 |
| Mali | 28 Sept. | 1960 |
| Malta | 1 Dec. | 1964 |
| Mauritania | 27 Oct. | 1961 |
| Mauritius | 24 Apr. | 1968 |
| Mexico | 7 Nov. | 1945 |
| Mongolia | 27 Oct. | 1961 |
| Morocco | 12 Nov. | 1956 |
| Mozambique | 16 Sept. | 1975 |
| Nepal | 14 Dec. | 1955 |
| Netherlands | 10 Dec. | 1945 |
| New Zealand | 24 Oct. | 1945 |
| Nicaragua | 24 Oct. | 1945 |
| Niger | 20 Sept. | 1960 |
| Nigeria | 7 Oct. | 1960 |
| Norway | 27 Nov. | 1945 |
| Oman | 7 Oct. | 1971 |
| Pakistan | 30 Sept. | 1947 |
| Panama | 13 Nov. | 1945 |
| Papua New Guinea | 10 Oct. | 1975 |
| Paraguay | 24 Oct. | 1945 |
| Peru | 31 Oct. | 1945 |
| Philippines | 24 Oct. | 1945 |
| Poland | 24 Oct. | 1945 |
| Portugal | 14 Dec. | 1955 |
| Qatar | 21 Sept. | 1971 |
| Romania | 14 Dec. | 1955 |
| Rwanda | 18 Sept. | 1962 |
| Saint Lucia | 18 Sept. | 1979 |
| Saint Vincent and The Grenadines | 16 Sept. | 1980 |
| São Tomé and Príncipe | 16 Sept. | 1965 |
| Saudi Arabia | 24 Oct. | 1945 |
| Senegal | 28 Sept. | 1960 |
| Seychelles | 21 Sept. | 1976 |
| Sierra Leone | 27 Sept. | 1961 |
| Singapore | 21 Sept. | 1965 |
| Solomon Islands | 19 Sept. | 1978 |
| Somalia | 20 Sept. | 1960 |
| South Africa | 7 Nov. | 1945 |
| Spain | 14 Dec. | 1955 |
| Sri Lanka | 14 Dec. | 1955 |
| Sudan | 12 Nov. | 1956 |
| Suriname | 4 Dec. | 1975 |
| Swaziland | 24 Sept. | 1968 |
| Sweden | 19 Nov. | 1946 |
| Syria | 24 Oct. | 1945 |
| Tanzania | 14 Dec. | 1961 |
| Thailand | 16 Dec. | 1946 |
| Togo | 20 Sept. | 1960 |
| Trinidad and Tobago | 18 Sept. | 1962 |
| Tunisia | 12 Nov. | 1956 |
| Turkey | 24 Oct. | 1945 |
| Uganda | 25 Oct. | 1962 |
| Ukrainian SSR | 24 Oct. | 1945 |
| USSR | 24 Oct. | 1945 |
| United Arab Emirates | 9 Dec. | 1971 |
| United Kingdom | 24 Oct. | 1945 |
| United States | 24 Oct. | 1945 |
| Upper Volta | 20 Sept. | 1960 |
| Uruguay | 18 Dec. | 1945 |
| Vanuatu | 15 Sept. | 1981 |
| Venezuela | 15 Nov. | 1945 |
| Vietnam | 20 Sept. | 1977 |
| Western Samoa | 15 Dec. | 1976 |
| Yemen | 30 Sept. | 1947 |
| Yemen (Southern Yemen) | 14 Dec. | 1967 |
| Yugoslavia | 24 Oct. | 1945 |
| Zaïre | 20 Sept. | 1960 |
| Zambia | 1 Dec. | 1964 |
| Zimbabwe | 25 Aug. | 1980 |

## PRINCIPAL ORGANS OF THE UNITED NATIONS

There are six principal organs of the UN: the General Assembly, the Security Council, the Economic and Social Council, the Trusteeship Council, the International Court of Justice, and the Secretariat. The official languages in all these organs, other than the International Court of Justice, are Chinese, English, French, Russian, and Spanish. Working languages are English and French, with the addition of Russian, Spanish and Chinese in the General Assembly and the Security Council and Spanish in the Economic and Social Council. Arabic is an official and working language in the General Assembly. The official languages in the International Court of Justice are English and French.

### General Assembly

The UN's main deliberative body, the General Assembly, consists of all member states, each of which has one vote. Any question may be discussed that is within the scope of the UN Charter or relates to the functions of any organ provided for in the Charter, as well as any questions on international peace and security that are brought up by a member, by the Security Council, or by a nonmember, if that state accepts in advance obligations of pacific settlement. The General Assembly may make recommendations to member states or to the Security Council with one exception: it may not make recommendations on any dispute under consideration by the Security Council unless the Council so requests.

Regular sessions of the Assembly convene once a year, commencing on the third Tuesday in September. There is provision for special and emergency special sessions. Voting is by simple majority of those present and voting, except on questions adjudged important, when a two-thirds majority is required. The Assembly controls the finances of the UN; it also elects the 10 nonpermanent members of the Security Council, all the members of the Economic and Social Council, and—with, but independently of, the Security Council—the International Court of Justice. On Security Council recommendations, the Secretary-General is appointed by the General Assembly.

The Assembly elects its president and 17 vice-presidents for each session and adopts its own rules of procedure. It distributes most agenda items among its seven main committees (see list below). There is also a General Committee that organizes the work of each session, a Credentials Committee, an Advisory Committee on Administrative and Budgetary Questions, and a Committee on Contributions, which recommends the scale of members' payments to the UN. They may establish ad hoc and subsidiary bodies such as the Conference on Trade and Development (UNCTAD).

**General Assembly Main Committee Chairmen, 36th Session:**

**First Committee (Political and Security)**—Ygnac Golob (Yugoslavia)

**Special Political Committee**—Nathan Irumba (Uganda)

**Second Committee (Economic and Financial)**—Leandro I. Verceles (Philippines)

**Third Committee (Social, Humanitarian and Cultural)**—Declan O'Donovan (Ireland)

**Fourth Committee (Decolonization)**—Jasim Yousif Jamal (Qatar)

**Fifth Committee (Administrative and Budgetary)**—Abdel Rahman Abdalla (Sudan)

**Sixth Committee (Legal)**—Juan José Calle y Calle (Peru)

### Assembly Actions of the 36th Session:

The opening session of the UN General Assembly took place on September 15, 1981. Ismat Kittani of Iraq was elected president of the Assembly. UN membership increased to 157 during the fall of 1981 when the General Assembly, acting on recommendations of the Security Council, admitted Vanuatu, former Territory of the New Hebrides (Sept. 15); Belize, former British Honduras (Sept. 25); and Antigua & Barbuda, a former British colony (Nov. 11).

MIDDLE EAST—On Feb. 5, 1982, the Assembly adopted a sweeping resolution condemning Israel for its annexation of the Golan Heights in December 1981. A later resolution condemning Israel's actions on settlements in the West Bank was passed in April 1982 but without a proposed clause that threatened Israel with expulsion from the UN.

SOUTHERN AFRICA—The Assembly voted twice in late 1981 for sanctions against South Africa for its failure to settle the war in Namibia.

OTHER MATTERS—The General Assembly approved on Dec. 19, 1981, the Security Council selection of Secretary-General Pérez de Cuéllar. *See p. 716 for biography.* A special session on disarmament was convened at the UN General Assembly on June 7, 1982, and ended July 10 without adopting any comprehensive program.

### Security Council

There are 15 members on the Security Council, five of them permanent—The People's Republic of China, France, the USSR, the United Kingdom, and the United States—and 10 elected by the General Assembly for two-year terms and ineligible for immediate reelection. As of August 1982 the ten nonpermanent members were: Guyana, Ireland, Japan, Jordan, Panama, Poland, Spain, Togo, Uganda and Zaire.

The Council bears primary responsibility under the UN Charter for the maintenance of international peace and security. It may investigate any situation bearing the seeds of international friction. These may be brought to its attention by any UN member, by any nonmember accepting in advance the obligations of pacific settlement, by the General Assembly, or by the Secretary-General.

Having determined the existence of a threat to peace, the Council may make recommendations, or may call on members to take such measures as economic sanctions or other steps short of armed force. Should these be inadequate, the Council may take military action against an aggressor; all members agree under the charter to make available to the Council, in accordance with agreements to be negotiated, armed forces necessary for maintaining international peace. The Council also has responsibility for plans to regulate armaments.

On matters other than procedural, Council decisions need an affirmative vote of nine, including all permanent members (hence the veto; abstentions do not in practice constitute a veto). On procedural matters, an affirmative vote of any nine members suffices. A UN member not on the Council may take part in Council discussion when it is considered that its interests are especially affected. The Council presidency is held by members in monthly rotation in English alphabetical order. There is a *Committee of Experts* to advise the Council on procedural and technical matters, a *Committee on Admission of New Members*, and a *Military Staff Committee*, which is composed of the chiefs of staff of the permanent members or their representatives, to advise on military matters.

**Security Council Actions Fall 1981—Fall 1982:**

MIDDLE EAST—Disputes involving Israel, Lebanon and Syria figured prominently in Security Council proceedings over the last year. When Israel annexed the Golan Heights in late 1981, sanctions against Israel had the support of most Council members, but they were vetoed by the United States. Early in 1982 the Council extended the placement of UN peacekeeping forces in southern Lebanon. These same forces were subsequently brushed aside in the Israeli assault against PLO installations in Lebanon. On June 26, 1982, the Council unanimously demanded that Israel withdraw its forces from Lebanon. Despite heated debate on the violations of territorial integrity and demands for a permanent cease-fire, the Council seemed unable to influence the war in

Lebanon or the sporadic war between Iran and Iraq.

FALKLAND ISLANDS—When Argentina seized the British-held Falkland Islands, the Security Council passed a resolution on April 3, 1982, calling for the withdrawal of Argentine forces. The Council asked Secretary-General Pérez to mediate in the dispute.

AFRICA—The controversy over Western Sahara figured in the UN agenda, as did border clashes between Libya and Sudan, but these problems were overshadowed by larger conflicts elsewhere. The peace plan for Namibia offered by Western "contact" nations in October 1981 has gained some acceptance by the participants.

OTHER MATTERS—After 16 ballots of voting the Security Council chose Javier Pérez de Cuéllar of Peru on December 11, 1981, to be Secretary-General.

### Economic and Social Council

The council makes studies and recommendations to the General Assembly on international social, economic, cultural, educational, health, and related matters. It negotiates agreements with the specialized agencies, defining their relationship with the UN, and coordinates their activities by means of consultation and recommendation.

It is composed of 54 members, 18 of whom are elected each year by the General Assembly to a three-year term. Each member has one vote, and a simple majority rules. The council works through committees, commissions, and various other subsidiary bodies. Its functional commissions include: the *Statistical Commission*, the *Population Commission*, the *Commission for Social Development*, the *Commission on Human Rights*, the *Commission on the Status of Women*, the *Commission on Narcotic Drugs* and the *Commission on Transnational Corporations*. There are also regional commissions for Europe, Asia and the Far East, Latin America, and Africa. There are a number of other related bodies, including the executive board of the children's fund (UNICEF) and the International Narcotics Control Board.

*For list of members, see page 717: Membership of Principal United Nations Organizations.*

### Trusteeship Council

The council bears prime responsibility for supervision of territories placed under the UN Trusteeship System. It consists of member states administering trust territories and permanent members of the Security Council not administering territories. The present administering state is the United States (Trust Territory of the Pacific Islands). The nonadministering members are the People's Republic of China, France, the United Kingdom, and the USSR.

Voting is by simple majority. The Trusteeship Council meets once a year, usually in June.

**Recent Developments:** The timetable for the UN-sponsored plebiscite on near autonomy for the Marshall Islands ran into diplomatic trouble in February 1982 over U.S. military rights in islands in the Pacific Trust Territory.

### International Court of Justice

The principal judicial organ of the UN functions in accordance with its statute, which is an integral part of the UN Charter and is based on the Statute of the Permanent Court of International Justice of the League of Nations. The court is open to all UN members, plus nonmembers who become party to the statute (at present Switzerland, Liechtenstein, and San Marino), as well as other states fulfilling certain conditions. It is not open to private individuals. The court has jurisdiction over all cases that the parties refer to it and over all matters specifically provided for in the charter or in treaties or conventions in force, including treaties that refer to the Permanent Court of International Justice. In the event of a dispute as to whether the court has jurisdiction, it decides the issue itself.

The court is composed of 15 judges of different nationalities, who are elected independently by the General Assembly and the Security Council (election in the latter does not permit the veto). Terms are for nine years. All questions are decided by a majority of judges present, nine constituting a quorum. In case of a tie, the president of the court (elected by the court for a three-year term) casts the deciding vote. The court sits at The Hague, Netherlands.

### Secretariat

The UN's administrative spine is composed of the Secretary-General, who is appointed by the General Assembly on the recommendation of the Security Council, and "such staff as the organization may require." As chief administrative officer, the Secretary-General acts in his capacity at all meetings of the General Assembly, the Security Council, the Economic and Social Council, and the Trusteeship Council. He makes an annual report to the General Assembly and appoints the Secretariat staff. The Secretary-General is also empowered to bring before the Security Council any matter that in his opinion threatens the maintenance of international peace.

The structure of the Secretariat includes the Offices of the Secretary-General (the Executive Office of the Secretary-General, the Director-General for Development and International Economic Co-operation, the Offices of the Under-Secretaries for Special Political Affairs, the Office for Special Political Questions, the Office of Legal Affairs, the Office of the Controller, and the Department of Administration and Management), the Department of Political and Security Council Affairs, the Department of Economic and Social Affairs, the Department of Trusteeship and Non-Self-Governing Territories, the Department of Public Information, the Department of Conference Services, the Office of General Services, and the UN Office in Geneva. There are also separate staffs serving subsidiary organs established by the General Assembly or the Economic and Social Council, including: the children's fund (UNICEF), the development program (UNDP), the office of the high commissioner for refugees (UNHCR), the relief and works agency for Palestine refugees (UNRWA), the institute for training and research (UNITAR), the industrial development organization (UNIDO) and trade and development (UNCTAD).

## SPECIALIZED AGENCIES AND OTHER BODIES OF THE UNITED NATIONS

Specialized agencies are intergovernmental organizations linked to the UN by special agreement, working in partnership with it in social, scientific, and technical fields. The specialized agencies proper report annually to the Economic and Social Council. Although usually listed with them, the IAEA and GATT agencies are not, strictly speaking, specialized agencies. The former is an intergovernmental agency "established under the aegis of the UN" and reports to the General Assembly and, as appropriate, to the Security Council and the Economic and Social Council. The latter cooperates with the UN at the secretariat and intergovernmental levels.

**Food and Agriculture Organization of the United Nations** (FAO) *Function:* To help countries increase food production and improve distribution, to coordinate the Freedom from Hunger Campaign, and to help administer the World Food Program. *Members:* 152 countries. *Headquarters:* Rome. *Chief Officer:* Director-General Edouard Saouma (Lebanon).

**General Agreement of Tariffs and Trade** (GATT) *Function:* To establish and administer the code for orderly conduct of international trade; to assist governments to reduce customs tariffs and abolish other trade barriers; and to operate, jointly with the UN Conference on Trade and Development, the International Trade Center providing export promotion assistance for developing countries. (GATT rules govern an estimated 80 percent of international trade.) *Members:* 85 participating nations. *Headquarters:* Geneva. *Chief Officer:* Director-General Arthur Dunkel (Switzerland). *Recent Developments:* The annual report of GATT for 1981 indicated that world trade dropped 1% to $2 trillion, the first decline since 1958.

**International Atomic Energy Agency** (IAEA) *Function:* To promote the use of nuclear energy for peaceful purposes; to assist in nuclear research, development, and applications; and to apply safeguards against diversion of nuclear materials to military use. *Members:* 111 countries. *Headquarters:* Vienna. *Chief Officer:* Director-General Hans Blix (Sweden).

**International Bank for Reconstruction and Development** (World Bank; IBRD) *Function:* To further members' economic development by loans (all loans made to or guaranteed by government) and technical advice. *Members:* 142 countries. *Headquarters:* Washington, DC *Chief Officer:* President Alden W. Clausen (United States). *Recent Developments:* The World Bank reduced by 40% the volume of low-interest loans it would make in 1982 due to cuts in contributions. On July 2, 1982, the World Bank announced a decision to borrow at floating rates in short-term markets and to lend at a rate that would change every six months.

**International Civil Aviation Organization** (ICAO) *Function:* To promote safety of international civil aviation, to provide statistical and economic information for governments and airlines, to work to reduce the red tape of customs formalities, and to help developing countries benefit from air transport. *Members:* 150 countries. *Headquarters:* Montreal. *Chief Officer:* Secretary-General Yves Lambert (France).

**International Development Association** (IDA) *Function:* To further economic development of members by providing finance on terms bearing less heavily on balance of payments than conventional loans. (Its credits have been for 50-year terms, interest free.) *Members:* 129 countries. *Headquarters:* Washington, DC (IDA is an affiliate of IBRD and has the same officers and staff.)

**International Finance Corporation** (IFC) *Function:* To assist less developed member countries by providing risk capital, without government guarantee, for the growth of productive private enterprise. *Members:* 121 countries. *Headquarters:* Washington, DC *Chief Officer:* Alden W. Clausen (United States). (IFC is an affiliate of IBRD.)

**International Fund for Agricultural Development** (IFAD) *Function:* To grant loans to promote agricultural improvement in developing countries. *Members:* 133 countries. *Headquarters:* Rome. *President:* Abdelmuhsin al-Sudeary (Saudi Arabia).

**International Labour Organization** (ILO) *Function:* To bring together government, labor, and management on pressing international labor and manpower problems; to provide governments with technical assistance, and to develop world labor standards. *Members:* 147 countries. *Headquarters:* Geneva. *Chief Officer:* Director-General Francis Blanchard (France). *Recent Developments:* The U.S. rejoined the ILO on February 18, 1980. It had withdrawn its membership in 1977 in protest that the agency had become politicized.

**International Maritime Organization** (IMO) *Function:* To promote cooperation on technical matters affecting shipping, to encourage the highest standards of maritime safety and efficient navigation, to convene international conferences on shipping, and to draft international maritime conventions. *Members:* 122 countries plus one associate. *Headquarters:* London. *Chief Officer:* Secretary-General C.P. Srivastava (India). *Recent Developments:* The conference on the Law of the Sea completed its seven-year effort on a comprehensive treaty governing the use and exploitation of the seas. The treaty was adopted in the General Assembly, 130 in favor, 4 against (including U.S.) and 17 abstentions. The treaty calls for a system of exploitation of mineral deposits of the sea bed which will benefit private companies who do the mining and the world community, chiefly have-not nations. It gives maritime countries exclusive mineral, oil and fishing rights out to 200 miles, reaffirms right of free passage on the high seas and in world straits, and calls for a uniform 12-mile territorial limit. The U.S. announced that it would not sign the treaty.

**International Monetary Fund** (IMF) *Function:* To promote international monetary cooperation and stabilization of currencies, to facilitate expansion of international trade, and to help members meet temporary difficulties in foreign payments. *Members:* 143 countries. *Headquarters:* Washington, DC *Chief Officer:* Managing Director Jacques de Larosière (France). *Recent Developments:* The IMF cut off $4.9 billion in undrawn portions of loans to 15 financially troubled countries in April 1982.

The loans were frozen because the borrowing countries had not met IMF belt-tightening requirements. Romania was the largest borrower to be forced to renegotiate its loan with $1.06 billion in jeopardy.

**International Telecommunications Union** (ITU) *Function:* To promote international cooperation in radio, telegraph, telephone, and space radio communications; to be instrumental in allocating radio frequencies, and to work to establish the lowest possible charges for telecommunications. *Members:* 157 countries. *Headquarters:* Geneva. *Chief Officer:* Secretary-General Mohammed Mili (Tunisia).

**United Nations Children's Fund** (UNICEF) *Function:* Established in 1946 to carry out post-war relief in Europe but now mainly concerned with the welfare of children in developing countries. *Headquarters:* New York. *Chief Officer:* Executive Director James P. Grant (United States). *Recent Developments:* Relief to the starving children in Africa and Southeast Asia was of prime concern.

**United Nations Development Programme** (UNDP) *Function:* To help developing countries increase the wealth-producing capabilities of their natural and human resources by providing experts or training of the local people. *Headquarters:* New York. *Chief Officer:* Administrator F. Bradford Morse (United States).

**United Nations Educational, Scientific and Cultural Organization** (UNESCO) *Function:* To broaden the base of education in the world, to bring the benefits of science to all countries, and to encourage cultural exchange and appreciation. *Members:* 155 countries. *Headquarters:* Paris. *Chief Officer:* Director-General Amadou M'Bow (Senegal). *Recent Developments:* A recent UNESCO resolution calling for a "new order" in world information continues to be controversial. Western nations view mention of overseeing journalistic conduct as potential curbs on the freedom of the press. Third World countries view "new order" as a way of reducing wholly negative coverage by the Western press and as a chance to promote "developmental strategies."

**United Nations Environment Programme** (UNEP) *Function:* Established in 1972 to provide machinery for international cooperation in matters relating to the human environment. *Members:* 58 countries on the Governing Council. *Headquarters:* Nairobi. *Chief Officer:* Executive Director Mostafa K. Tolba (Egypt).

**United Nations Fund for Population Activities** (UNFPA) *Function:* Created in 1967 to promote population programs and in extending systematic and sustained population assistance to developing countries and help them in dealing with their population problems. *Headquarters:* New York. *Chief Officer:* Rafael M. Salas (Philippines).

**United Nations High Commissioner for Refugees** (UNHCR) *Function:* Set up in 1950, the office of the High Commissioner on Refugees aims chiefly to provide international protection for refugees and seek permanent solution to their problems through voluntary repatriation, migration to other countries or local integration. UNHCR also undertakes special humanitarian tasks. *Headquarters:* Geneva. *High Commissioner:* Poul Hartling (Denmark). *Recent Developments:* The work of UNHCR continues to be dominated by massive relief operations in Southeast Asia, Pakistan and the Horn of Africa. The exodus of refugees from Haiti and El Salvador grew considerably in 1981. In Europe 137,000 Poles have fled to Western Europe since the December 1981 political crackdown.

**United Nations Industrial Development Organization** (UNIDO) *Function:* To encourage and extend assistance to developing countries for development, expansion and modernization of industry; to achieve full utilization of locally available natural and human resources; to provide a forum for consultation and negotiations among developing countries and between developing and industrialized countries. Administers UN Industrial Development Fund. *Headquarters:* Vienna. *Chief Officer:* Executive Director Dr. Abd-El Rahman Khane (Algeria). *Recent Developments:* Operates as an executing agency of the UN Development Programme (UNDP) until final ratification of autonomous specialized agency status.

**Universal Postal Union** (UPU) *Function:* To assure the organization and improvement of the various postal services and to promote, in the sphere, the development of international cooperation. *Members:* 164. *Headquarters:* Bern. *Chief Officer:* Director-General Mohamed I. Sobhi (Egypt).

**World Health Organization** (WHO) *Function:* To direct and coordinate international health work, to help governments in public health programs, to set international drug and vaccine standards, and to promote medical research. *Members:* 157 countries. *Headquarters:* Geneva. *Chief Officer:* Director-General Dr. Halfdan Mahler (Denmark). *Recent Developments:* On Jan. 27, 1982, WHO stripped the World Medical Association of its consultative status after 34 years of close cooperation because of its admission of doctors from South Africa.

**World Intellectual Property Organization** (WIPO) *Function:* To promote and protect intellectual property, such as trademarks, industrial designs, literary and artistic works, throughout the world through new international treaties and harmonization of national legislation. *Members:* 97. *Headquarters:* Geneva. *Chief Officer:* Director-General Arpad Bogsch (United States).

**World Meteorological Organization** (WMO) *Function:* To promote international meteorological cooperation, especially in the establishment of a worldwide network of meteorological stations and rapid exchange of weather data, to promote standardization and publication of observations, and to further meteorological applications. *Members:* 154. *Headquarters:* Geneva. *Secretary-General:* Aksel Wiin-Nielson (Denmark).

## UN SECRETARIES-GENERAL

**Lie, Trygve Halvdan** (1896-1968), Secretary-General from 1946 to 1953. Born in Oslo, Norway, the son of a carpenter, Lie earned a law degree from Oslo University in 1919 and later served as legal adviser to the Norwegian Trade Unions Federation. From 1935 to 1946 he held various Cabinet ministries, including justice, commerce, and foreign affairs. In the last capacity, he led the Norwegian delegation to the 1945 UN conference in San Francisco, where he helped draft the Security-Council provisions of the Charter.

The rugged Norwegian was elected the first Secretary-General of the UN as a compromise candidate acceptable to both East and West. He immediately asserted himself and established the independence of the Secretary-General's office.

His strong stand on East-West issues alienated, at different times, both the United States and the Soviet Union. By endorsing UN membership for Communist China, he angered the Americans; his stand, however, against North Korean aggression so infuriated the Russians that they refused to deal with him during the remainder of his term.

**Hammarskjöld, Dag Hjalmar Agne Carl** (1905-1961), Secretary-General from 1953 to 1961. He was born in Jonkoping, Sweden, of an aristocratic family; his father, an eminent jurist, was Sweden's Prime Minister during World War I. Hammarskjöld earned a law degree from Uppsala University in 1930 and a Ph.D. in political economy from the University of Stockholm in 1934.

In 1949 he entered the foreign ministry, where he established his reputation as an international monetary expert. He became vice-chairman of Sweden's UN delegation in 1952 and was its chairman the following year, when he was elected Secretary-General. Hammarskjöld greatly extended the scope and influence of his office. His personal missions in the cause of peace began with his visit to Peking in 1955 to secure the release of captured American fliers and ended with his 1961 Congo mission on which he died in a plane crash near Ndola, Northern Rhodesia.

He created the international peace-keeping force sent to the Middle East after the 1956 Suez crisis. Hammarskjöld's most controversial action was his insistence, against strong Soviet opposition, on maintaining the UN peace force in the Congo. All these efforts won him the Nobel Peace Prize, awarded posthumously in 1961. Publicly, the bachelor Hammarskjöld was a cool, realistic diplomat, but his diary, published as *Markings* in 1964, revealed a profoundly mystical man.

**U Thant** (1909-1974), Secretary-General from 1961 to 1971. Born in Pantanaw, Burma, the son of a prosperous landowner, Thant graduated from the National High School in Pantanaw and attended University College in Rangoon. He taught English and modern history at his old high school where in 1931 he became headmaster. For many years he was also an active writer on politics.

He became a member of the Burmese UN delegation in 1952 and its chairman five years later. In 1959 he was chosen vice-president of the General Assembly. After Hammarskjöld's death in 1961, Thant, known as a moderate and neutralist, was elected acting Secretary-General, and a year later he was unanimously elected to office for a full term. Thant was widely praised for his role in calming international tensions during the 1962 Cuban missile crisis, for his part in healing the secessionist Katanga breach in the Congo, and for his handling of the 1964 UN financial crisis.

On the other hand, he was criticized for precipitous speed in complying with Cairo's request in 1967 that the UN emergency force be withdrawn from the Sinai peninsula. It was also remarked that while he was an outspoken critic of American policy in Vietnam, he was less critical of the 1968 Soviet invasion of Czechoslovakia.

**Waldheim, Kurt** (1918- ), Secretary-General from 1972 to 1981. Born in Lower Austria, the son of a teacher, Waldheim earned a law degree from the University of Vienna in 1944 and entered the Austrian foreign service the next year. He was Austria's permanent observer to the United Nations from 1955 to 1956 and headed his country's delegation when Austria was admitted to the UN in 1958. Besides years of service as a UN delegate, Waldheim held other high-ranking foreign service posts and served as foreign minister from 1968 to 1970. In April 1971 he ran unsucessfully for president of Austria.

After election as Secretary-General, Waldheim used his considerable skills as a diplomat in the classic mold rather than as an "activist." In difficult Middle East negotiations, the tireless Waldheim met often with opposed national leaders and used his office to keep peace talks alive. He was reelected for a second term in 1976, but in 1981 his bid for an unprecedented third term was opposed by China. After five weeks of deadlocked ballots, Waldheim withdrew his name.

**Pérez de Cuéllar, Javier** (1920- ), Secretary-General since January 1982. The son of a business family from Lima, Peru, Pérez, graduated from Catholic University of Lima and entered the foreign service in 1944. A lawyer and the author of two law texts, Pérez brought impressive diplomatic credentials to his arduous job. He had served as ambassador to Moscow before becoming head of his country's UN delegation in 1971. He won the confidence of both Turks and Greeks as special UN representative to strife-torn Cyprus. Pérez became UN Under Secretary-General for Political Affairs in 1980 and a year later was made Waldheim's troubleshooter in the Afghanistan crisis. On becoming Secretary-General, Pérez called his new job "one of the most difficult in the world"—prophetic words in light of subsequent flare-ups of old wars in the Middle East and the start of a new war in the Falkland Islands.

## UNITED STATES REPRESENTATIVES AND DELEGATES TO THE UNITED NATIONS: 37th Session

(As of September 24, 1982)

**Jeane J. Kirkpatrick** (Ambassador Extraordinary and Plenipotentiary)—Permanent United States Representative to the United Nations and Chairman of the Delegation to the General Assembly*

**Kenneth L. Adelman** (Ambassador)—Deputy U.S. Representative to the United Nations and Vice-Chairman of the U.S. Delegation

**J. Bennett Johnson** (Senator, Louisiana)—U.S. Representative to the General Assembly

**Robert W. Kasten, Jr.** (Senator, Wisconsin)—U.S. Representative to the General Assembly

**John D. Lodge**—U.S. Representative to the General Assembly

**Gordon C. Luce**—Alternate Representative to the General Assembly

**Herman Padilla**—Alternate Representative to the General Assembly

**Jose S. Sorzano** (Ambassador)—Representative to the Economic and Social Council

**Charles M. Lichtenstein** (Ambassador)—Alternate Representative for Special Political Affairs

**William C. Sherman** (Ambassador)—Deputy Representative to the Security Council

**Michael Novak**—Representative to the Commission on Human Rights of the Economic and Social Council

**Nancy C. Reynolds**—Representative to the Commission on the Status of Women of the Economic and Social Council

*The Secretary of State, George P. Shultz, serves as *ex officio* Chairman when present at a session.

## MEMBERSHIP OF PRINCIPAL UNITED NATIONS ORGANS

### SECURITY COUNCIL

Fifteen members: the 5 permanent members and 10 members are elected for two-year terms by the General Assembly.

| | | | | | |
|---|---|---|---|---|---|
| Permanent members: | China | France | USSR | United Kingdom | United States |
| Elected members: | | | | | |
| *Until December 1982:* | Ireland | Japan | Panama | Spain | Uganda |
| *Until December 1983:* | Guyana | Jordan | Poland | Togo | Zaire |

### ECONOMIC AND SOCIAL COUNCIL

54 members: elected for 3-year terms by the General Assembly.

| | | | | | |
|---|---|---|---|---|---|
| Argentina | Burundi | Fiji | Kenya | Norway | Swaziland |
| Australia | Byelorussian SSR | France | Liberia | Pakistan | Thailand |
| Austria | Cameroon | Germany (Fed. Rep.) | Libya | Peru | Tunisia |
| Bahamas | Canada | Greece | Malawi | Poland | USSR |
| Bangladesh | Chile | India | Mali | Portugal | United Kingdom |
| Belgium | China | Iraq | Mexico | Qatar | United States |
| Benin | Colombia | Italy | Nepal | Romania | Venezuela |
| Brazil | Denmark | Japan | Nicaragua | Saint Lucia | Yugoslavia |
| Bulgaria | Ethiopia | Jordan | Negeria | Sudan | Zaire |

### TRUSTEESHIP COUNCIL

5 members: one (*) an administering state, and four nonadministering permanent members of the Security Council.

| | | | | |
|---|---|---|---|---|
| China | France | USSR | United Kingdom | United States* |

### INTERNATIONAL COURT OF JUSTICE

15 members, elected by the General Assembly for 9-year terms that end on 5 February of the year indicated. Judges are listed in order of precedence.

*President:* Taslim Olwale Elias (Nigeria, 1985)
*Vice President:* José Sette Câmara (Brazil, 1988)
Manfred Lachs (Poland, 1985)
Platon D. Morozov (USSR, 1988)
Nagendra Singh (India, 1991)
José María Ruda (Argentina, 1991)
Hermann Mosler (Germany, Fed. Rep., 1985)
Shigeru Oda (Japan, 1985)
Abdallah Fikri El-Khani (Syria, 1985)
Roberto Ago (Italy, 1988)
Stephen M. Schwebel (US, 1988)
Robert Y. Jennings (UK, 1991)
Guy Ladreit de Lacharrière (France, 1991)
Kéba Mbaye (Senegal, 1991)
Mohammed Bedjaoui (Algeria, 1988)

## HEADS OF MISSIONS TO THE UNITED NATIONS (as of September 21, 1982)

| Country | Permanent Representative |
|---|---|
| Afghanistan | Mohammad Farid Zarif |
| Albania | Abdi Baleta |
| Algeria | Abdelouahab Abada |
| Angola | Elisio de Figueiredo |
| Antigua & Barbuda | Lloydston Jacobs |
| Argentina | Carlos M. Muñiz |
| Australia | Richard A. Woolcott |
| Austria | Karl Fischer |
| Bahamas | Davidson L. Hepburn |
| Bahrain | Hussein R. Al-Sabbagh |
| Bangladesh | Khwaja Wasiuddin |
| Barbados | Harley S.L. Moseley |
| Belgium | Edmonde Dever |
| Benin | Thomas Setondji Boya |
| Bhutan | Om Pradhan |
| Bolivia | Fernand Ortiz Sanz |
| Botswana | Legwaila Joseph Legwaila |
| Brazil | Sérgio Corrêa da Costa |
| Bulgaria | Boris Tsvetkov |
| Burma | Saw Hlaing |
| Burundi | Melchior Bwakira |
| Byelorussian SSR | Anatoly Nikitich Sheldov |
| Cambodia (Kampuchea) | M. Thiounn Prasith |
| Cameroon | Ferdinand Léopold Oyono |
| Canada | Gérard Pelletier |
| Cape Verde | Amaro Alexandre da Luz |
| Central African Republic | Simon Pierre Kibanda |
| Chad | Ramadane Barma |
| Chile | Manuel Trucco |
| China | Ling Qing |
| Colombia | Carlos Sanz de Santamaria |
| Comoros | vacant |
| Congo | Nicolas Mondjo |
| Costa Rica | Fernando Zumbado-Jimenez |
| Cuba | Raúl Roa-Kouri |
| Cyprus | Constantine Moushoutas |
| Czechoslovakia | Stanislav Suja |
| Denmark | Wilhelm Ulrichsen |
| Djibouti | Saleh Haji Farah Dirir |
| Dominica | Franklin A. Baron |
| Dom. Rep. | Enriquillo A. Del Rosario |
| Ecuador | Miguel A. Albornoz |
| Egypt | Ahmed Esmat Abdel Meguid |
| El Salvador | Mauricio Rosales-Rivera |
| Equatorial Guinea | Florencio Maye Ela |
| Ethiopia | Mohamed Hamid Ibrahim |
| Fiji | Filipe Nagera Bole |
| Finland | Ilkka Olavi Pastinen |
| France | Luc de la Barre de Nanteuil |
| Gabon | Jean Davin |
| Gambia | Ousman Ahmadou Sallah |
| Germany (Dem. Rep.) | Harry Ott |
| Germany (Fed. Rep.) | Guenter van Well |
| Ghana | James Victor Gbeho |
| Greece | Mihalis Dountas |
| Grenada | Caldwell Taylor |
| Guatemala | Juan Carlos Delpree-Crespo |
| Guinea | Djebel Coumbassa |
| Guinea-Bissau | Inacio Semedo |
| Guyana | Noel G. Sinclair |
| Haiti | Fritz Cinéas |
| Honduras | Enrique Ortez Colindres |
| Hungary | Pál Rácz |
| Iceland | Hördur Helgasun |
| India | Natarajan Krishnan |
| Indonesia | Alex Alataz |
| Iran | Said Rajaie-Khorassani |
| Iraq | Salah Omar Al-Ali |
| Ireland | Noel Dorr |
| Israel | Yehuda Z. Blum |
| Italy | Umberto La Rocca |
| Ivory Coast | Amara Essy |
| Jamaica | Egerton Richardson |
| Japan | Masahiro Nisibori |
| Jordan | Hazem Nuseibeh |
| Kenya | Wafula Wabuge |
| Kuwait | Mohammad A. Abulhassan |
| Laos | Soubanh Srithirath |
| Lebanon | Fakhri Saghiyyah |
| Lesotho | Tseliso Thamae |
| Liberia | Abeodu Bowen Jones |
| Libya | Ali A. Treiki |
| Luxembourg | Paul Peters |
| Madagascar | Blaise Rabetafika |
| Malawi | N. T. Mizere |
| Malaysia | Tan Sri Zainal Abidin |
| Maldives | Ahmed Zaki |
| Mali | Seydou Traore |
| Malta | Victor J. Gauci |
| Mauritania | Mohamed Said Ould Hamody |
| Mauritius | Shree Kreshn Ramlogun |
| Mexico | Porfirio Muñoz Ledo |
| Mongolia | Tsogtyn Narkhllu |
| Morocco | Mehdi Mrani Zentar |
| Mozambique | José Carlos Lobo |
| Nepal | Uddhav Deo Bhatt |
| Netherlands | Hugo Scheltema |
| New Zealand | Harold Huyton Francis |
| Nicaragua | Javier Chamorro Mora |
| Niger | Idé Oumarou |
| Nigeria | Alhaji Y. Maitama-Sule |
| Norway | Tom Eric Vraalsen |
| Oman | Mahmoud Aboul-Nasr |
| Pakistan | S. Shah Nawaz |
| Panama | Carlos Ozores Typaldos |
| Papua New Guinea | Kubulan Los |
| Paraguay | Luis Gonzales Arias |
| Peru | Juan José Calle y Calle |
| Philippines | Luis Moreno Salcedo |
| Poland | Jerzy M. Nowak |
| Portugal | Rui E. Barbosa de Medina |
| Qatar | Jasim Yousif Jamal |
| Romania | Teodor Marinescu |
| Rwanda | Juvénal Renzaho |
| Saint Lucia | Barry B.L. Auguste |
| Saint Vincent & The Grenadines | Joel G. Toney |
| São Tomé & Príncipe | Adriano Cassandra |
| Saudi Arabia | Gaafar M. Allagany |
| Senegal | Massamba Sarré |
| Seychelles | Giovinella Gonthier |
| Sierra Leone | Abdul G. Koroma |
| Singapore | T.T.B. Koh |
| Solomon Islands | vacant |
| Somalia | Ahmed Mohamed Adan |
| South Africa | David W. Steward |
| Spain | Don Jaime de Piniés |
| Sri Lanka | Ignatius Benedict Fonseka |
| Sudan | Abdel-Rahman Abdalla |
| Suriname | Inderdew Sewrajsing |
| Swaziland | Norman M. Malinga |
| Sweden | Anders I. Thunborg |
| Syria | Dia-Allah El-Fattal |
| Tanzania | Paul Milyango Rupia |
| Thailand | Birabhongse Kasemsri |
| Togo | Atsu-Koffi Amega |
| Trinidad & Tobago | Frank Owen Abdulah |
| Tunisia | Taïeb Slim |
| Turkey | A. Coşkun Kirca |
| Uganda | Olara Otunnu |
| Ukrainian SSR | Vladimir Alekseyevich Kravets |
| USSR | Oleg Aleksandrovich Troyanovsky |
| United Arab Emirates | Fahim Sultan Al-Qasimi |
| United Kingdom | John Thompson |
| United States | Jeane J. Kirkpatrick |
| Upper Volta | Michel Kafando |
| Uruguay | Juan Carlos Blanco |
| Venezuela | Alberto Martini Urdaneta |
| Vietnam | Hoang Bich Son |
| Western Samoa | Maiva Iulai Toma |
| Yemen | Mohamed Abdulaziz Sallam |
| Yemen (Southern) | Abdalla Saleh Al-Ashtal |
| Yugoslavia | Miljan Komatina |
| Zaire | Kamanda wa Kamanda |
| Zambia | Paul J.F. Lusaka |
| Zimbabwe | Elleck Mashingaidze |

## UN GENERAL ASSEMBLY PRESIDENTS

| Session | Year | President |
|---|---|---|
| 1st | 1946 | Paul Henri Spaak |
| 2nd | 1947 | Oswaldo Aranha |
| 3rd | 1948-49 | Herbert V. Evatt |
| 4th | 1949 | Carlos P. Romulo |
| 5th | 1950-51 | Nasrollah Entezam |
| 6th | 1951-52 | Luís Padilla Nervo |
| 7th | 1952-53 | Lester B. Pearson |
| 8th | 1953-54 | Mrs. Vijaya Lakshmi Pandit |
| 9th | 1954 | Eelco N. van Kleffends |
| 10th | 1955 | José Maza |
| 11th | 1956-57 | Prince Wan Waithayakon |
| 12th | 1957 | Sir Leslie Munro |
| 13th | 1958-59 | Charles Malik |
| 14th | 1959 | Victor Andrés Belaúnde |
| 15th | 1960-61 | Frederick H. Boland |
| 16th | 1961-62 | Mongi Slim |
| 17th | 1962 | Muhammad Zafrulla Khan |
| 18th | 1963 | Carlos Sosa Rodriguez |
| 19th | 1964-65 | Alex Quaison-Sackey |
| 20th | 1965 | Amintore Fanfani |
| 21st | 1966 | Abdul Rahman Pazhwak |
| 22nd | 1967-68 | Corneliu Manescu |
| 23rd | 1968 | Emilio Arenales |
| 24th | 1969 | Miss Angie Brooks |
| 25th | 1970 | Edvard Isak Hambro |
| 26th | 1971 | Adam Malik |
| 27th | 1972 | Stanislaw Trepczynski |
| 28th | 1973 | Leopoldo Benites |
| 29th | 1974 | Abdelaziz Bouteflika |
| 30th | 1975 | Gaston Thorn |
| 31st | 1976 | Hamilton Shirley Amerasinghe |
| 32nd | 1977 | Lazar Mojsov |
| 33rd | 1978 | Indalecio Lievano Aguirre |
| 34th | 1979 | Salim Ahmed Salim |
| 35th | 1980 | Rudiger von Wechmar |
| 36th | 1981 | Ismat Kittani |
| 37th | 1982 | Imre Hollai |

## REPRESENTATIVE INTERNATIONAL ORGANIZATIONS

**Afro-Mauritian Common Organization** (OCAM) *Formed:* 1965 *Members:* 9 African countries *Headquarters:* Bangui, Central African Republic *Secretary-General:* M. Amri Sued (Rwanda) *Purpose:* To promote economic, technical, and cultural development of member French-speaking states within the framework of the OAU.

**Andean Group** *Formed:* 1969 *Members:* Bolivia, Colombia, Ecuador, Peru and Venezuela *Headquarters:* Lima, Peru *Director-Secretary:* Alberto Zelado Castedo *Purpose:* Regional association with the aim of closer economic and political cooperation among member countries. Venezuela joined in 1973. The Andean Reserve Fund (1977) and Andean Development Corporation (1968) are funding and planning arms for the Andean Group. *Recent Developments:* Members of the Group agreed in April of 1982 to increase trade with Argentina to help offset the economic boycott imposed by the European Community during the Falkland Islands crisis.

**ANZUS Council** *Formed:* 1951 *Members:* Australia, New Zealand, and the United States *Headquarters:* Canberra, Australia *Purpose:* This loose military alliance is pledged to respond to aggression against any of its members. *Recent Developments:* On the 30th anniversary of the ANZUS pact in May 1982, Vice-President Bush made a Pacific tour and assured the two U.S. partners of the continued U.S. interest in maintaining strong ties. At the annual ANZUS conference held on June 22, 1982, the U.S. delegate stressed the need for cooperation on security in the Pacific and opposed restraints on visits of U.S. nuclear-armed vessels to Australian ports.

**Arab League (AL)** *Formed:* 1945 *Members:* Algeria, Bahrain, Djibouti, Egypt, Iraq, Jordan, Kuwait, Lebanon, Libya, Mauritania, Morocco, Oman, Qatar, Saudi Arabia, Somalia, Sudan, Syria, Tunisia, United Arab Emirates, Yemen, Southern Yemen, and the PLO government. *Headquarters:* Tunis *Secretary-General:* Chedli Klibi (Tunisia) *Purpose:* To strengthen member ties and further promote Arab aspirations. *Recent Developments:* Egypt was suspended from the organization in 1979 after signing a peace treaty with Israel. Hints of reconciliation of the Arab world with Egypt appeared during early 1982.

**Association of Southeast Asian Nations** (ASEAN) *Formed:* 1967 *Members:* Indonesia, Malaysia, the Philippines, Singapore and Thailand *Headquarters:* Jakarta, Indonesia *Secretary-General:* Narcisco G. Reyes (Philippines) *Purpose:* To promote economic progress and political stability in Southeast Asia; it seeks to lower trade tariffs for intraregional trade, encourage exchange programs and sharing of scientific knowledge. *Recent Developments:* In a UN report of March 1982 ASEAN nations showed recent significant economic growth. Singapore showed the largest gains in income level. Rural poverty and other problems continue to exist, however.

**Benelux Economic Union** *Formed:* 1958 *Members:* Belgium, Luxembourg, and the Netherlands *Headquarters:* Brussels *Secretary-General:* Egbert Kruijtbosch (Netherlands) *Purpose:* To achieve complete economic union of its members (as a subdivision of the EC).

**Caribbean Community and Common Market** (CARICOM) *Formed:* 1973 *Members:* Antigua & Barbuda, Barbados, Belize, Dominica, Grenada, Guyana, Jamaica, Montserrat, St. Christopher-Nevis, St. Lucia, St. Vincent & the Grenadines, and Trinidad & Tobago *Headquarters:* Georgetown, Guyana *Secretary-General:* Kurleigh D. King (Barbados) *Purpose:* To promote unity in the Caribbean through economic integration, a common external tariff and coordination of development plans.

**Central African Economic and Customs Union** (UDEAC) *Formed:* 1966 *Members:* Cameroon, Central African Republic, Congo, Gabon; Chad has had observer status since 1975 *Headquarters:* Bangui, Central African Republic *Secretary-General:* Vincent Efon (Cameroon) *Purpose:* To promote the gradual establishment of a Central African Common Market and see to the general improvement of living standards of the peoples of member states.

**Central American Common Market** (CACM) *Formed:* 1960 *Members:* Costa Rica, El Salvador, Guatemala, Honduras and Nicaragua. (Honduras withdrew from active membership in 1970) *Headquarters:* Guatemala City, Guatemala *Secretary-General:* Raúl Sierra Franco *Purpose:* To establish a free trade area and a customs union with joint planning for social and economic development of the region.

**Colombo Plan for Cooperative Development in Asia and the Pacific** *Formed:* 1950 *Members:* 26 countries *Headquarters:* Colombo, Sri Lanka *President:* Thomas Abraham (India) *Purpose:* To aid developing countries through bilateral member agreements for the provision of capital, technical experts and training, and equipment.

**Commonwealth, The** (formerly British Commonwealth) *Formed:* 1931 *Members:* 47 countries *Headquarters:* London *Secretary-General:* Shridath Ramphal (Guyana) *Purpose:* A voluntary association of independent states and their dependencies who meet and consult on a regular basis to foster Commonwealth links and achieve a more equitable world society. All Commonwealth countries accept Queen Elizabeth II as the symbolic head of the association.

**Council for Mutual Economic Assistance** (COMECON) *Formed:* 1949 *Members:* Bulgaria, Cuba, Czechoslovakia, East Germany, Hungary, Mongolia, Poland, Romania, the Soviet Union and Vietnam; Associate Member: Yugoslavia *Headquarters:* Moscow *Secretary:* N.V. Faddeyev (Soviet Union) *Purpose:* To coordinate and integrate members' economies, under USSR leadership. *Recent Developments:* According to a 1981 Western study COMECON nations, other than USSR, have experienced an economic growth rate of about 1%. In contrast the Soviet economic growth is estimated at 2 to 3%. Poland, which has declined economically, is in debt for $4 billion to COMECON plus an additional $25.5-billion debt to the West as of Jan. 1982.

**Council of Europe** *Formed:* 1949 *Members:* 21 countries, mostly in Western Europe but also includes Greece and Turkey *Headquarters:* Strasbourg, France *Secretary-General:* Franz Karasek (Austria) *Purpose:* To protect human rights, bring European countries closer together, and voice the views of the European public on the main political and economic questions of the day.

**Eastern European Mutual Assistance Treaty** (Warsaw Pact) *Formed:* 1955 *Members:* Bulgaria, Czechoslovakia, East Germany, Hungary, Poland, Romania, and the Soviet Union *Headquarters:* Moscow *Supreme Military Commander:* Marshal Viktor G. Kulikov (Soviet Union) *Purpose:* This major European military alliance is the Soviet bloc's equivalent of the North Atlantic Treaty Organization, and its forces, like NATO's, are composed of military elements from member countries. *Recent Developments:* In February 1982 the USSR offered a reduction of nuclear arms based in Warsaw Pact countries of East Europe if NATO made similar reductions.

**Economic Community of West African States** (ECOWAS) *Formed:* 1975 *Members:* 16 West African states *Headquarters:* Lagos, Nigeria *Executive Secretary:* Aboubacar Diaby-Quattara (Ivory Coast) *Purpose:* Promoting trade, cooperation and self-reliance in West Africa.

**European Communities** (EC, sometimes called the Common Market) Includes the European Economic Community (EEC, formed 1958), the European Coal and Steel Community (ECSC, formed 1952) and the European Atomic Energy Community (Euratom, formed 1958). The merger of the three European Communities, each legally separate but sharing a common membership and a common institutional organization, became effective July 1, 1967. *Members:* Belgium, Denmark, France, Greece, Ireland, Italy, Luxembourg, the Netherlands, United Kingdom and West Germany. Greece was admitted as a member effective Jan. 1, 1981. Portugal and Spain have applied for membership. *Purposes:* To abolish all internal tariffs and other trade barriers and to align external tariffs, so that there can be free movement of goods, persons, services and capital within the EC. To maintain a common market for coal, iron ore and steel; to abolish discriminatory pricing systems and transport rates among members, while safeguarding continuity of employment. To promote the common development of nuclear energy for peaceful purposes. *Principal organs:* The Council of Ministers (ministers from each member state), the Commission (13 members appointed by member governments), the European Parliament (434 members elected by direct universal suffrage by citizens of member states), and the Court of Justice (9 appointed judges). *President of the Commission:* Gaston Thorn (Luxembourg) *President of the Parliament:* Pieter Dankert (Netherlands) *President of the Court:* J. Mertens de Wilmars *Recent Developments:* Trade sanctions against Argentina were imposed by EC during the Falkland Islands conflict. UK opposition to its high budgetary contribution and to proposed increases in farm prices was resolved by granting Britain an $850-million rebate. On June 29, EC leaders criticized U.S. sanctions on sales of equipment for the Soviet gas pipeline.

**European Free Trade Association** (EFTA) *Formed:* 1960 *Members:* Austria, Iceland, Norway, Portugal, Sweden, and Switzerland; Associate Member: Finland *Headquarters:* Geneva *Secretary-General:* Per Kleppe (Norway) *Purpose:* To maintain the elimination of internal tariffs on industrial goods (achieved at the end of 1966) and negotiate bilateral agreements on agricultural products. *Recent Developments:* Once called the Outer Seven, EFTA has aimed at a lesser degree of economic integration than the European Community. Despite the loss in 1973 of two charter members, Denmark and the United Kingdom, EFTA has continued to be a fruitful economic association.

**International Committee of the Red Cross** (ICRC) *Formed:* 1863 *Members:* 25 Swiss citizens *Headquarters:* Geneva *President:* Alexandre Hay (Switzerland) *Purpose:* To organize care for the victims of war and enforce the various Conventions on wartime practices. The ICRC constitutes, with the League of Red Cross Societies, the International Red Cross. The League of Red Cross Societies, founded in 1929, has member societies in 126 countries.

**International Criminal Police Organization** (Interpol) *Formed:* 1956 *Members:* Official police bodies in 130 countries *Headquarters:* Paris (St. Cloud) *Secretary-General:* A. Bossard (France) *Purpose:* To ensure maximum cooperation between police authorities, with the strict exclusion of political, military, religious, and racial matters. As successor to the International Criminal Police Commission, established in 1923, Interpol acts as a clearinghouse for information on international criminal activities.

**International Energy Agency** (IEA) *Formed:* 1974 *Members:* 21 countries including most Western European nations with Greece and Turkey plus the U.S., Canada and Japan *Headquarters:* Paris *Chief Officer:* Chairman Hiromichi Miyazaki (Japan) *Purpose:* To develop cooperation among major oil importing nations and to strengthen the security and stability of world energy markets.

**Latin American Integration Association** (ALADI) *Formed:* 1980 *Members:* Argentina, Bolivia, Brazil, Chile, Colombia, Ecuador, Mexico, Paraguay, Peru, Uruguay, and Venezuela *Headquarters:* Montevideo, Uruguay *Secretary-General:* Julio César Schuff *Purpose:* To establish bilateral trading agreements which would take into account the different stages of development of members and to work for the establishment of a full common market, although without a definite timetable. ALADI was established to replace the Latin American Free Trade Association (LAFTA). ALADI is scheduled to begin operating fully in 1983.

**Nordic Council** *Formed:* 1953 *Members:* Denmark, Finland, Iceland, Norway, and Sweden *Headquarters:* Stockholm *Secretary of the Presidium:* Gudmund Saxrud (Norway) *Purpose:* To arrange cooperation among members in cultural, legal, social, and economic matters.

**North Atlantic Treaty Organization** (NATO) *Formed:* 1949 *Members:* Belgium, Canada, Denmark, France, West Germany, Great Britian, Greece, Iceland, Italy, Luxembourg, the Netherlands, Norway, Portugal, Spain, Turkey, and the United States *Headquarters:* Brussels *Secretary-General:* Dr. Joseph Luns (Netherlands) *Supreme Commander:* Gen. Bernard Rogers (U.S.) *Purpose:* This major Western military alliance, with prime responsibility for opposing Communist forces in Europe, is composed of elements from the armed forces of member nations. *Recent Developments:* NATO has committed itself to a modernization of its nuclear forces. Greece rejoined NATO's integrated military structure in 1980. Spain formally became a member of NATO on May 30, 1982. Members of NATO meeting at Bonn in June 1982 agreed on the need to improve "defense readiness and military capabilities." At the same time they endorsed efforts to "achieve a genuine détente" and a negotiated reduction in nuclear arms. This last point appeared to be a response to growing opposition to deployment of new nuclear weapons.

**Organization for Economic Cooperation and Development** (OECD) *Formed:* 1961 *Members:* 24 countries, mostly in Western Europe, but also U.S., Australia, New Zealand and Japan *Headquarters:* Paris *Secretary-General:* Emile van Lennep (Netherlands) *Purpose:* To achieve economic growth and full employment and to further world economic development. As successor to the Organization for European Economic Cooperation (OEEC) that was established in 1948 to oversee Marshall Plan reconstruction, OECD has a broadened scope, having established an extensive aid program to developing countries.

**Organization of African Unity** (OAU) *Formed:* 1963 *Members:* All 50 independent African countries, except the white-dominated states and territories of the south. *Headquarters:* Addis Ababa, Ethiopia Secretary-General: Edem Kodjo (Togo) *Purpose:* To promote African solidarity, coordinate policies, defend member sovereignty, and eliminate colonialism in Africa. *Recent Developments:* The OAU announced in early 1982 that it would withdraw its peacekeeping forces in Chad and urged an end to the fighting there. On February 22, 1982, the OAU decided to admit as a member the Polisario Front, a guerrilla group that has been fighting Morocco for control of Western Sahara. The decision seriously split the OAU organization. The issue was still unresolved at mid-year and the August 1982 meeting was canceled.

**Organization of American States** (OAS) *Formed:* 1948 *Members:* 28 American countries *Headquarters:* Washington, D.C. *Secretary-General:* Alejandro Orfila (Argentina) *Purpose:* To promote the solidarity and defend the sovereignty of members and provide through the Pan American Union—the OAS central organ and secretariat—social, political, economic, and technical services. *Recent Developments:* The U.S. unveiled its Caribbean Basin plan to the OAS on Feb. 24, 1982. Reaction to the broad plan of investment incentives and improved security was mixed. On April 28, 1982, the OAS approved a resolution that supported Argentine claims to sovereignty over the Falkland Islands.

**Organization of Petroleum Exporting Countries** (OPEC) *Formed:* 1960 *Members:* Algeria, Ecuador, Gabon, Indonesia, Iran, Iraq, Kuwait, Libya, Nigeria, Qatar, Saudi Arabia, United Arab Emirates and Venezuela *Headquarters:* Vienna *Secretary-General:* Ali Ahmad Attiga (Libya) *Purpose:* To coordinate policies and establish prices regarding petroleum exported to consumer nations. *Recent Developments:* Due to falling demand, total OPEC oil output slumped to 16% in 1981 and revenues generally declined along with oil prices. OPEC ministers meeting in July 1982 failed to achieve common price and marketing policies.

**West African Economic Community** (CEAO) *Formed:* 1973 *Members:* Ivory Coast, Mali, Mauritania, Niger, Senegal and Upper Volta (Observers: Benin and Togo) *Headquarters:* Ouagadougou, Upper Volta *Secretary-General:* Moussa N'gom (Senegal) *Purpose:* To establish an economic and customs union for West African states.

## U.S. CONTRIBUTIONS TO INTERNATIONAL ORGANIZATIONS

SOURCE: U.S. Department of State

**FISCAL YEAR 1981 (In Millions of Dollars)**

| Organization | Estimated Amount |
|---|---|
| **United Nations and Specialized Agencies:** | |
| United Nations | $109.70 |
| Food and Agricultural Organization | 25.45 |
| International Atomic Energy Agency | 17.28 |
| International Civil Aviation Organizations | 3.51 |
| International Labor Union | 23.63 |
| International Telecommunications Union | 3.28 |
| UNESCO | 32.62 |
| World Health Organization | 41.15 |
| World Meteorological Organization | 3.53 |
| Others (9 programs, less than $1 million) | 2.72 |
| **United Nations Peacekeeping Forces:** | |
| UN Disengagement Observer Force (UNDOF/UNIFIL) | 50.00 |
| United Nations Force in Cyprus | 9.00 |
| Multinational Forces & Observers | 10.00 |
| **Inter-American Organizations** | |
| Organization of American States | 36.73 |
| Inter-American Institute for Cooperation on Agriculture | 8.72 |
| Pan American Health Organization | 23.98 |
| Inter-American Tropical Tuna Commission | 2.03 |
| Others (4 programs, less than $1 million) | 0.44 |
| **Regional Organizations:** | |
| NATO Civilian Headquarters | 12.92 |
| Organization for Economic Cooperation and Development | 18.19 |
| Others (3 programs, less than $1 million) | 0.99 |
| **Other International Organizations:** | |
| Customs Cooperation Council | 1.69 |
| General Agreement on Tariffs and Trade | 2.16 |
| International Institute for Cotton | 2.28 |
| Others (32 programs, less than $1 million) | 5.13 |
| **Special Voluntary Programs:** | |
| Consultative Group on International Agricultural Research | 35.00 |
| Intergovernmental Committee for Migration—Special Voluntary | 5.00 |
| International Atomic Energy Agency—Technical Assistance Fund | 12.37[1] |
| Organization of American States—Special Development Assistance Fund | 6.00 |
| Organization of American States—Special Multilateral Fund (Education and Science) | 6.50 |
| Organization of American States—Special Projects Fund | 2.60 |
| Pan American Health Organization—Special Voluntary Program | 3.16 |
| United Nations Capital Development Fund | 2.00 |
| United Nations Children Fund | 35.95 |
| United Nations Decade for Women | 1.00 |
| United Nations Development Program | 125.80 |
| United Nations Educational and Training Program for South Africa | 1.00 |
| United Nations Environment Fund | 9.98[2] |
| UN/FAO World Food Program | 153.49 |
| United Nations Fund for Drug Abuse Control | 2.15 |
| United Nations Fund for Population Activities | 32.00 |
| UN High Commissioner for Refugees—Regular Programs | 105.50 |
| Special Programs | 33.25 |
| United Nations Relief and Works Agency | 62.00 |
| West African Rice Development Association | 2.00 |
| World Health Organization—Special Programs | 9.40 |
| World Meteorological Organization—Voluntary Cooperation Program | 2.24 |
| Others (10 programs, less than $1 million) | 3.04 |
| Total U.S. Contributions | $1,098.51 |

[1]Includes cash, commodities and services and $5.1 million for Safeguards Program. [2]Includes cash, commodities and services.

## U.S. FOREIGN ECONOMIC ASSISTANCE

SOURCE: Program Data Services Division, Bureau for Program and Policy Coordination, Agency for International Development

The table below gives total U.S. foreign economic aid under the Foreign Assistance Act of 1961 and related precedent legislation—loans and grants—since 1946 and foreign aid data for fiscal year 1981. Included also is other foreign economic assistance provided by the U.S. (contributions to multilateral development banks, Food for Peace, Peace Corps, and International Narcotics Control).

The Agency for International Development (AID) has been the administering agency for foreign economic assistance under the Foreign Assistance Act since November 4, 1961. Agencies dealing with economic assistance programs prior to that date have been, successively: the Economic Cooperation Administration (Apr. 3, 1948-Oct. 31, 1951); the Mutual Security Agency (Nov. 1, 1951-July 31, 1953); the Foreign Operations Administration (Aug. 1, 1953-June 30, 1955); the International Cooperation Administration (July 1, 1955-Nov. 3, 1961); and the Development Loan Fund (Aug. 14, 1957-Nov. 3, 1961).

The latter two agencies operated concurrently fo. approximately four years until their functions were combined under the provisions of the Foreign Assistance Act of 1961.

| Region and Country | Total 1946-1981 (Millions) | Fiscal Year 1981 (Millions) |
|---|---|---|
| **GRAND TOTAL** | **$148,872.0** | **$7,305.0** |
| **Near East and South Asia** | **41,360.6** | **2,757.4** |
| Afghanistan | 536.9 | — |
| Bahrain | 2.4 | — |
| Bangladesh | 1,615.1 | 152.1 |
| Bhutan | 1.1 | 0.3 |
| Cyprus | 163.3 | 14.0 |
| Egypt | 7,476.5 | 1,130.4 |
| Greece | 1,910.2 | — |
| India | 10,397.2 | 275.1 |
| Iran | 765.6 | — |
| Iraq | 45.5 | — |
| Israel | 6,350.0 | 764.0 |
| Jordan | 1,432.7 | 10.5 |
| Lebanon | 188.3 | 4.0 |
| Nepal | 278.4 | 19.8 |
| Oman | 8.4 | 0.7 |
| Pakistan | 5,047.7 | 76.8 |
| Saudi Arabia | 31.8 | — |
| Sri Lanka | 575.5 | 70.8 |
| Syria | 587.9 | 1.9 |
| Turkey | 3,187.5 | 201.0 |
| Yemen, People's Democratic Rep. | 4.5 | — |
| Yemen Arab Republic | 143.5 | 20.7 |
| Central Treaty Organization | 39.6 | — |
| Regional | 571.2 | 15.1 |
| **Latin America** | **12,950.7** | **610.9** |
| Argentina | 199.2 | — |
| Bahamas | 0.3 | — |
| Barbados | 3.6 | 0.4 |
| Belize | 11.2 | 1.0 |
| Bolivia | 819.8 | 12.8 |
| Brazil | 2,427.3 | 1.1 |
| Chile | 1,183.7 | 12.1 |
| Colombia | 1,367.8 | 5.7 |
| Costa Rica | 280.9 | 15.3 |
| Cuba | 4.0 | — |
| Dominican Republic | 684.2 | 38.5 |
| Ecuador | 338.3 | 18.5 |
| El Salvador | 381.4 | 114.0 |
| Guatemala | 464.9 | 19.0 |
| Guyana | 128.1 | 1.3 |
| Haiti | 307.6 | 34.6 |
| Honduras | 360.8 | 36.4 |
| Jamaica | 264.5 | 73.5 |
| Mexico | 336.9 | 9.8 |
| Nicaragua | 397.8 | 59.9 |
| Panama | 435.2 | 10.6 |
| Paraguay | 187.6 | 6.2 |
| Peru | 741.0 | 80.2 |
| Suriname | 5.8 | — |
| Trinidad & Tobago | 40.9 | — |
| Uruguay | 159.5 | 0.1 |
| Venezuela | 201.2 | 0.1 |
| Other West Indies— Eastern Caribbean Regional | 211.7 | 29.5 |
| Regional Office Central America & Panama-ROCAP | 308.6 | 10.6 |
| Regional | 697.3 | 20.1 |
| **East Asia** | **27,427.1** | **326.1** |
| Burma | 115.9 | 7.6 |
| Cambodia | 903.5 | 14.1 |
| China | 2.2 | 1.7 |
| Hong Kong | 43.8 | — |
| Indochina[a] | 825.6 | — |
| Indonesia | 2,889.3 | 130.0 |
| Japan | 2,711.1 | — |
| Korea, South | 6,019.6 | 27.6 |
| Laos | 902.6 | — |
| Malaysia | 89.9 | 1.7 |
| Philippines | 2,199.8 | 97.6 |
| Ryukyu Islands (U.S.) | 413.7 | — |
| Singapore | 2.8 | — |
| Taiwan | 2,206.9 | — |
| Thailand | 772.8 | 30.8 |
| Vietnam | 6,945.5 | — |
| Regional | 370.9 | 14.4 |
| **Africa** | **9,120.9** | **922.4** |
| Algeria | 203.3 | — |
| Angola | 12.7 | 3.8 |
| Benin | 55.9 | 7.5 |
| Botswana | $ 136.2 | $ 17.6 |
| Burundi | 30.9 | 6.1 |
| Cameroon | 93.8 | 12.6 |
| Cape Verde | 44.0 | 6.6 |
| Central African Republic | 17.5 | 1.8 |
| Chad | 65.2 | — |
| Comoros | 0.7 | 0.4 |
| Congo, People's Republic of | 12.7 | 2.3 |
| Djibouti, Democratic Republic of | 10.0 | 5.3 |
| Entente States | 38.3 | — |
| Ethiopia | 392.5 | 5.0 |
| Gabon | 13.2 | 1.2 |
| Gambia, The | 30.4 | 7.7 |
| Ghana | 415.4 | 25.8 |
| Guinea | 171.6 | 10.5 |
| Guinea-Bissau | 22.4 | 7.4 |
| Ivory Coast | 47.5 | 1.3 |
| Kenya | 333.8 | 48.8 |
| Lesotho | 103.8 | 24.9 |
| Liberia | 363.8 | 55.1 |
| Libya | 212.5 | — |
| Madagascar | 30.4 | 9.0 |
| Malawi | 73.8 | 9.5 |
| Mali, Republic of | 161.4 | 15.9 |
| Mauritania | 76.9 | 15.8 |
| Mauritius | 27.7 | 4.1 |
| Morocco | 1,061.6 | 55.8 |
| Mozambique | 70.6 | 8.7 |
| Niger | 136.6 | 17.5 |
| Nigeria | 406.5 | — |
| Rwanda | 37.1 | 7.4 |
| São Tomé and Príncipe | 2.3 | 1.8 |
| Senegal | 172.9 | 35.5 |
| Seychelles | 4.3 | 1.2 |
| Sierra Leone | 91.3 | 9.4 |
| Somali Republic | 256.6 | 57.0 |
| South Africa | 1.3 | — |
| Sudan | 357.6 | 109.4 |
| Swaziland | 55.1 | 11.5 |
| Tanzania | 308.8 | 37.2 |
| Togo | 59.7 | 10.0 |
| Tunisia | 933.2 | 39.8 |
| Uganda | 62.5 | 9.0 |
| Upper Volta | 169.4 | 30.7 |
| Zaire | 668.3 | 28.6 |
| Zambia | 213.1 | 30.6 |
| Zimbabwe | 57.7 | 27.8 |
| Portuguese Territories | 3.4 | — |
| Central & West Africa Regional | 136.6 | 22.2 |
| East Africa Regional | 33.3 | — |
| Southern Africa Regional | 108.0 | 17.0 |
| Regional | 514.0 | 47.3 |
| **Europe** | **28,621.3** | **84.6** |
| Albania | 20.4 | — |
| Austria | 1,135.2 | — |
| Belgium-Luxembourg | 592.3 | — |
| Czechoslovakia | 193.0 | — |
| Denmark | 281.9 | — |
| Finland | 56.8 | — |
| France | 3,918.1 | — |
| Germany, East | 0.8 | — |
| Germany, West | 4,041.1 | — |
| West Berlin | 131.9 | — |
| Hungary | 32.7 | — |
| Iceland | 82.2 | — |
| Ireland | 146.5 | — |
| Italy | 3,343.5 | 4.7 |
| Malta | 83.9 | — |
| Netherlands | 1,027.6 | — |
| Norway | 301.8 | — |
| Poland | 586.9 | 47.6 |
| Portugal | 865.0 | 25.0 |
| Romania | 22.4 | — |
| Spain | 1,062.0 | 7.3 |
| Sweden | 109.0 | — |
| United Kingdom | 7,672.1 | — |
| USSR | 186.4 | — |
| Yugoslavia | 2,109.1 | — |
| Regional | 619.0 | — |
| **Oceania and other** | **896.3** | **10.2** |
| **Canada** | **17.5** | **—** |
| **Interregional** | **28,487.3** | **2,594.0** |

— = No economic assistance. [a]Prior to division into Vietnam, Cambodia, and Laos in 1955.

## SELECTED FOREIGN EMBASSIES AND AMBASSADORS

SOURCE: Department of State (as of Sept. 21, 1982)

**Afghanistan:** 2341 Wyoming Ave. NW, 20008
Chargé: Salem M. Spartak

**Algeria:** 2118 Kalorama Rd. NW, 20008
Amb: Layachi Yaker

**Argentina:** 1600 New Hampshire Ave. NW, 20009
Amb: Lucio Garcia del Solar

**Australia:** 1601 Massachusetts Ave. NW, 20036
Amb: Sir Robert C. Cotton

**Austria:** 2343 Massachusetts Ave. NW, 20008
Amb: Dr. Thomas Klestil

**Bahamas:** Suite 865, 600 New Hampshire Ave. NW, 20037
Amb: Reginald L. Wood

**Bahrain:** 3502 International Dr. NW, 20008
Amb: Abdulaziz A. Buali

**Bangladesh:** 3421 Massachusetts Ave. NW, 20007
Amb: Humayun Rasheed Choudhury

**Belgium:** 3330 Garfield St. NW, 20008
Amb: J. Raoul Schoumaker

**Bolivia:** 3014 Massachusetts Ave. NW, 20008
Amb: Julio Sanjines-Goitia

**Brazil:** 3006 Massachusetts Ave. NW, 20008
Amb: Antonio F.A. da Silveira

**Bulgaria:** 1621 22nd St. NW, 20008
Amb: Stoyan I. Zhulev

**Burma:** 2300 S St. NW, 20008
Amb: U Kyee Myint

**Cameroon:** 2349 Massachusetts Ave. NW, 20008
Amb: Paul Pondi

**Canada:** 1746 Massachusetts Ave. NW, 20036
Amb: Allan E. Gotlieb

**Chad:** 2002 R St. NW, 20009
Chargé: Mohamet Ali Adum

**Chile:** 1732 Massachusetts Ave. NW, 20036
Amb: Enrique Valenzuela

**China (P.R.C.):** 2300 Connecticut Ave. NW, 20008
Amb: Chai Zemin

**Colombia:** 2118 Leroy Pl. NW, 20008
Amb: Fernando Gaviria

**Congo:** 4891 Colorado Ave. NW, 20011
Amb: Nicolas Mondjo

**Costa Rica:** 2112 S St. NW, 20008
Amb: Fernando Soto-Harrison

**Cyprus:** 2211 R St. NW, 20008
Amb: Andrew J. Jacovides

**Czechoslovakia:** 3900 Linnean Ave. NW, 20008
Amb: Jaroslav Zantovsky

**Denmark:** 3200 Whitehaven St. NW, 20008
Amb: Otto R. Borch

**Dominican Republic:** 1715 22nd St. NW, 20008
Amb: Carlos Despradel

**Ecuador:** 2535 15th St. NW, 20009
Amb: Ricardo Crespo-Zaldumbide

**Egypt:** 2310 Decatur Pl. NW, 20008
Amb: Dr. Ashraf A. Ghorbal

**El Salvador:** 2308 California St. NW, 20008
Amb: Ernesto Rivas-Gallont

**Ethiopia:** 2134 Kalorama Rd. NW, 20008
Chargé: Tesfaye Demeke

**Fiji:** 1140 19th St. NW, 20036
Amb: Filipe N. Bole

**Finland:** 3216 New Mexico Ave. NW, 20016
Amb: Jaakko Iloniemi

**France:** 2535 Belmont Rd. NW, 20008
Amb: Bernard Vernier-Palliez

**Gabon:** 2034 20th St. NW, 20009
Amb: Hubert Ondias-Souna

**German Democratic Rep.:** 1717 Massachusetts Ave. NW, 20036
Amb: Dr. Horst Grunert

**Germany (Federal Rep.):** 4645 Reservoir Rd. NW, 20007
Amb: Peter Hermes

**Ghana:** 2460 16th St. NW, 20009
Chargé: Ebenezer Akuete

**Greece:** 2221 Massachusetts Ave. NW, 20008
Amb: Nicolas A. Karandreas

**Guatemala:** 2220 R St. NW, 20008
Amb: Jorge Luis Zelaya

**Guinea:** 2112 Leroy Pl. NW, 20008
Amb: Mamadi Lamine Conde

**Guyana:** 2490 Tracy Pl. NW, 20008
Amb: Dr. Cedric H. Grant

**Haiti:** 2311 Massachusetts Ave. NW, 20008
Amb: Georges N. Leger

**Honduras:** Suite 100, 4301 Connecticut Ave. NW, 20008
Amb: Juan Agurcia Ewing

**Hungary:** 3910 Shoemaker St. NW, 20008
Amb: Janos Petran

**Iceland:** 2022 Connecticut Ave. NW, 20008
Amb: Hans G. Andersen

**India:** 2107 Massachusetts Ave. NW, 20008
Amb: K. R. Narayanan

**Indonesia:** 2020 Massachusetts Ave. NW, 20036
Amb: A. Hasnan Habib

**Ireland:** 2234 Massachusetts Ave. NW, 20008
Amb: Tadhg F. O'Sullivan

**Israel:** 3514 International Dr. NW, 20008
Amb: Moshe Arens

**Italy:** 1601 Fuller St. NW, 20009
Amb: Rinaldo Petrignani

**Ivory Coast:** 2424 Massachusetts Ave. NW, 20008
Amb: Rene Amany

**Jamaica:** Suite 355, 1850 K St. NW, 20006
Amb: Keith Johnson

**Japan:** 2520 Massachusetts Ave. NW, 20008
Amb: Yoshio Okawara

**Jordan:** 2319 Wyoming Ave. NW, 20008
Amb: Abdul Hadi Majali

**Kenya:** 2249 R St. NW, 20008
Amb: John P. Mbogua

**Korea:** 2370 Massachusetts Ave. NW, 20008
Amb: Byong Hion Lew

**Kuwait:** 2940 Tilden St. NW, 20008
Amb: Shaikh Saud Nasir Al-Sabah

**Laos:** 2222 S St. NW, 20008
Chargé: Bounkeut Sangsomsak

**Lebanon:** 2560 28th St. NW, 20008
Amb: Khalil Itani

**Liberia:** 5201 16th St. NW, 20011
Amb: Dr. Joseph S. Guannu

**Luxembourg:** 2200 Massachusetts Ave. NW, 20008
Amb: Adrien Meisch

**Malawi:** Bristol House, 1400 20th St. NW, 20036
Amb: Nelson T. Mizere

**Malaysia:** 2401 Massachusetts Ave. NW, 20008
Amb: Zain Azraai

**Mali:** 2130 R St. NW, 20008
Amb: Maki Koreissi Aguibou Tall

**Malta:** 2017 Connecticut Ave. NW, 20008
Amb: Leslie Agius

**Mauritania:** 2129 Leroy Pl. NW, 20008
Amb: Abdellah Ould Daddah

**Mexico:** 2829 16th St. NW, 20009
Amb: Bernardo Sepulveda

**Morocco:** 1601 21st St. NW, 20009
Amb: Ali Bengelloun

**Nepal:** 2131 Leroy Pl. NW, 20008
Amb.: Bekh Bahadur Thapa

**Netherlands:** 4200 Linnean Ave. NW, 20008
Amb: Dr. Jan Hendrik Lubbers

**New Zealand:** 37 Observatory Cir. NW, 20008
Amb: Lancelot Adams-Schneider

**Nicaragua:** 1627 New Hampshire Ave. NW, 20009
Amb: F. Fiallos Navarro

**Niger:** 2204 R St. NW, 20008
Amb: Andre Wright

**Nigeria:** 2201 M St. NW, 20037
Amb: Chief Abudu Yesufu Eke

**Norway:** 2720 34th St. NW, 20008
Amb: Knut Hedemann

**Oman:** 2342 Massachusetts Ave. NW, 20008
Amb: Sadek Jawad Sulaiman

**Pakistan:** 2315 Massachusetts Ave. NW, 20008
Amb: Lt. Gen. Ejaz Azim

**Panama:** 28622 McGill Terr. NW, 20008
Amb: Aquilino Boyd

**Papua New Guinea:** 1140 19th St. NW, 20036
Amb: Kubulan Los

**Paraguay:** 2400 Massachusetts Ave. NW, 20008
Amb: Mario López Escobar

**Peru:** 1700 Massachusetts Ave. NW, 20036
Amb: Fernando Schwalb

**Philippines:** 1617 Massachusetts Ave. NW, 20036
Amb: Benjamin Romualdez

**Poland:** 2640 16th St. NW, 20009
Chargé: Zdzislaw Ludwiczak

**Portugal:** 2125 Kalorama Rd. NW, 20008
Amb: Leonardo Mathias

**Qatar:** 600 New Hampshire Ave. NW, 20037
Amb: Abdelkader Braik Al-Ameri

**Romania:** 1607 23rd St. NW, 20008
Amb: Mircea Malitza

**Saudi Arabia:** 1520 18th St. NW, 20036
Amb: Sheikh Faisal Alhegelan

**Senegal:** 2112 Wyoming Ave. NW, 20008
Amb: Abdourahmane Dia

**Sierra Leone:** 1701 19th St. NW, 20009
Amb: Dauda S. Kamara

**Singapore:** 1824 R St. NW, 20009
Amb: Punch Coomaraswamy

**Somalia:** 600 New Hampshire Ave. NW, 20037
Amb: Mohamud Haji Nur

**South Africa:** 3051 Massachusetts Ave. NW, 20008
Amb: Bernardus G. Fourie

**Spain:** 2700 15th St. NW, 20009
Amb: Nuno Aquirre de Carcer

**Sri Lanka:** 2148 Wyoming Ave. NW, 20008
Amb: Ernest Corea

**Sudan:** 2210 Massachusetts Ave. NW, 20008
Amb: Omer Salih Eissa

**Suriname:** 2600 Virginia Ave. NW, 20037
Amb: Henricus A.F. Heidweiller

**Sweden:** Suite 1200, 600 New Hampshire Ave. NW, 20037
Amb: Count Wilhelm Wachtmeister

**Switzerland:** 2900 Cathedral Ave. NW, 20008
Amb: Anton Hegner

**Syria:** 2215 Wyoming Ave. NW, 20008
Amb: Dr. Rafic Jouejati

**Tanzania:** 2139 R St. NW, 20008
Amb: Paul Bomani

**Thailand:** 2300 Kalorama Rd. NW, 20008
Amb: Prok Amaranand

**Togo:** 2208 Massachusetts Ave. NW, 20008
Amb: Yao Grunitzky

**Trinidad and Tobago:** 1708 Massachusetts Ave. NW, 20036
Amb: Victor C. McIntyre

**Tunisia:** 2408 Massachusetts Ave. NW, 20008
Amb: Habib Ben Yahia

**Turkey:** 1606 23rd St. NW, 20008
Amb: Dr. Sukru Elekdag

**Union of Soviet Socialist Republics:** 1125 16th St. NW, 20036
Amb: Anatoliy F. Dobrynin

**United Arab Emirates:** 600 New Hampshire Ave. NW, 20037
Amb: Ahmed S. Al-Mokarrab

**United Kingdom:** 3100 Massachusetts Ave. NW, 20008
Amb: Sir Oliver Wright

**Upper Volta:** 2340 Massachusetts Ave. NW, 20008
Amb: Tiemoko M. Garango

**Uruguay:** 1918 F St. NW, 20006
Amb: Aleandro Vegh-Villegaz

**Venezuela:** 2445 Massachusetts Ave. NW, 20008
Amb: Marcial Perez-Chiriboga

**Yemen:** 600 New Hampshire Ave. NW, 20037
Amb: Mohamad A. Al-Eryani

**Yugoslavia:** 2410 California St. NW, 20008
Amb: Budimir Loncar

**Zaire:** 1800 New Hampshire Ave. NW, 20009
Amb: Kasongo Mutuale

**Zambia:** 2419 Massachusetts Ave. NW, 20008
Amb: Putteho M. Ngonda

**Zimbabwe:** 2852 McGill Ter. NW, 20008
Amb: Edmund O.Z. Chipamaunga

## AMERICAN DIPLOMATS ABROAD

SOURCE: U.S. Department of State (as of Sept. 28, 1982)

*Chargé d'Affaires.

| Country | Chief of Mission |
|---|---|
| Afghanistan | Charles F. Dunbar, Jr.* |
| Algeria | Michael H. Newlin |
| Antigua & Barbuda | Milan D. Bish |
| Argentina | Harry W. Shlaudeman |
| Australia | Robert D. Nesen |
| Austria | Sol Polansky* |
| Bahamas | Andrew F. Antippas* |
| Bahrain | Peter A. Sutherland |
| Bangladesh | Jane A. Coon |
| Barbados | Milan D. Bish |
| Belgium | Charles H. Price II |
| Belize | Malcolm R. Barnebey* |
| Benin | Charles H. Twining* |
| Bolivia | Edwin G. Corr |
| Botswana | Theodore Maino |
| Brazil | Langhorne A. Motley |
| Bulgaria | Robert L. Barry |
| Burma | Patricia M. Byrne |
| Burundi | Frances D. Cook |
| Cameroon | Hume A. Horan |
| Canada | Paul H. Robinson, Jr. |
| Cape Verde | Peter de Vos |
| Central African Republic | Arthur H. Woodruff |
| Chile | James D. Theberge |
| China (People's Rep.) | Arthur W. Hummel, Jr. |
| Colombia | Thomas D. Boyatt |
| Comoros | Fernando E. Rondon |
| Congo | Kenneth L. Brown |
| Costa Rica | Francis J. McNeil |
| Cyprus | Raymond C. Ewing |
| Czechoslovakia | Jack F. Matlock, Jr. |
| Denmark | John L. Loeb, Jr. |
| Djibouti | Gene Schmiel* |
| Dominica | Milan D. Bish |
| Dominican Republic | Robert Anderson |
| Ecuador | John J. Youle* |
| Egypt | Alfred L. Atherton, Jr. |
| El Salvador | Deane R. Hinton |
| Equatorial Guinea | Alan M. Hardy |
| Ethiopia | David Korn* |
| Fiji | Fred J. Eckert |
| Finland | Keith F. Nyborg |
| France | Evan G. Galbraith |
| Gabon | Francis T. McNamara |
| The Gambia | Sharon E. Ahmad |
| German Democratic Rep. | Rozanne L. Ridgway |
| Germany, Fed. Rep. of | Arthur F. Burns |
| Ghana | Thomas W. M. Smith |
| Greece | Monteagle Sterns |
| Guatemala | Frederic L. Chapin |
| Guinea | Allen C. Davis |
| Guinea-Bissau | Peter de Vos |
| Guyana | Gerald E. Thomas |
| Haiti | Ernest H. Preeg |
| Honduras | John D. Negroponte |
| Hungary | Harry E. Bergold, Jr. |
| Iceland | Marshall Brement |
| India | Harry G. Barnes |
| Indonesia | John C. Monjo* |
| Ireland | Peter H. Dailey |
| Israel | Samuel W. Lewis |
| Italy | Maxwell M. Rabb |
| Ivory Coast | Nancy V. Rawls |
| Jamaica | William Hewitt |
| Japan | Michael J. Mansfield |
| Jordan | Richard N. Viets |
| Kenya | William C. Harrop |
| Kiribati | Fred J. Eckert |
| Korea | Richard L. Walker |
| Kuwait | Francois M. Dickman |
| Laos | William W. Thomas, Jr.* |
| Lebanon | Robert S. Dillon |
| Lesotho | Keith L. Brown |
| Liberia | William L. Swing |
| Luxembourg | John E. Dolibois |
| Madagascar | Fernando E. Rondon |
| Malawi | John A. Burroughs, Jr. |
| Malaysia | Ronald D. Palmer |
| Maldives | John H. Reed |
| Mali | Parker W. Borg |
| Malta | James M. Rentschler |
| Mauritania | Edward P. Brynn* |
| Mauritius | Robert C. F. Gordon |
| Mexico | John A. Gavin |
| Morocco | Joseph V. Reed, Jr. |
| Mozambique | William H. Twaddell* |
| Nauru | Robert D. Nesen |
| Nepal | Carleton S. Coon |
| Netherlands | William J. Dyess |
| New Zealand | H. Monroe Browne |
| Nicaragua | Anthony C.E. Quainton |
| Niger | William R. Casey, Jr. |
| Nigeria | Thomas R. Pickering |
| Norway | Mark E. Austad |
| Oman | John R. Countryman |
| Pakistan | Ronald I. Spiers |
| Panama | Everett E. Briggs |
| Papua New Guinea | M. Virginia Schafer |
| Paraguay | Arthur H. Davis, Jr. |
| Peru | Frank V. Ortiz, Jr. |
| Philippines | Michael H. Armacost |
| Poland | Francis J. Meehan |
| Portugal | Henry A. Holmes |
| Qatar | Charles E. Marthinsen |
| Romania | David B. Funderburk |
| Rwanda | John Blane |
| Saint Lucia | Milan D. Bish |
| St. Vin. & Grens. | Milan D. Bish |
| São Tomé & Príncipe | Francis T. McNamara |
| Saudi Arabia | Richard W. Murphy |
| Senegal | Charles W. Bray III |
| Seychelles | David J. Fischer |
| Sierra Leone | Theresa A. Healy |
| Singapore | Harry E. T. Thayer |
| Solomon Isls. | M. Virginia Schafer |
| Somalia | Robert B. Oakley |
| South Africa | Herman W. Nickel |
| Spain | Terence A. Todman |
| Sri Lanka | John H. Reed |
| Sudan | C. William Kontos |
| Suriname | Robert W. Duemling |
| Swaziland | Robert H. Phinny |
| Sweden | Franklin S. Forsberg |
| Switzerland | Faith R. Whittlesey |
| Syria | Robert P. Paganelli |
| Tanzania | David C. Miller, Jr. |
| Thailand | John G. Dean |
| Togo | Howard K. Walker |
| Tonga | Fred J. Eckert |
| Trinidad and Tobago | Melvin H. Evans |
| Tunisia | Walter L. Cutler |
| Turkey | Robert Strausz-Hupé |
| Tuvalu | Fred J. Eckert |
| Uganda | Gorden R. Beyer |
| U.S.S.R. | Arthur A. Hartman |
| United Arab Emirates | George Q. Lumsden, Jr. |
| United Kingdom | John J. Louis, Jr. |
| Upper Volta | Julius W. Walker, Jr. |
| Uruguay | Thomas Aranda, Jr. |
| Venezuela | George W. Landau |
| Western Samoa | H. Monroe Browne |
| Yemen | David E. Zweifel |
| Yugoslavia | David Anderson |
| Zaire | Peter D. Constable |
| Zambia | Nicholas Platt |
| Zimbabwe | Robert V. Keeley |

**SPECIAL MISSIONS:**

| | Chief of Mission |
|---|---|
| United Nations | Jeane J. Kirkpatrick |
| U.N. (European Office) | Geoffrey Swaebe |
| U.N.E.S.C.O. | Jean B.S. Gerard |
| O.A.S. | J. William Middendorf II |
| N.A.T.O. | W. Tapley Bennett, Jr. |
| O.E.C.D. | Abraham Katz |
| I.A.E.A. | Richard T. Kennedy |
| U.S.E.C. | George S. Vest |
| I.C.A.O. | John E. Downs |
| Ambassadors at Large | Daniel J. Terra<br>Vernon A. Walters<br>Howard E. Douglas |

## BRITISH PRIME MINISTERS

| Monarch and Prime Minister | Party | Served |
|---|---|---|
| **George I, 1714–27** | | |
| Robert Walpole | Whig | 1721–1727 |
| **George II, 1727–60** | | |
| Robert Walpole, Earl of Orford | Whig | 1727–1742 |
| Spencer Compton, Earl of Wilmington | Whig | 1742–1743 |
| Henry Pelham | Whig | 1743–1754 |
| Thomas Pelham-Holles,[1] Duke of Newcastle | Whig | 1754–1756 |
| William Cavendish, Duke of Devonshire | Whig | 1756–1757 |
| Thomas Pelham-Holles, Duke of Newcastle | Whig | 1757–1760 |
| **George III, 1760–1820** | | |
| Thomas Pelham-Holles, Duke of Newcastle | Whig | 1760–1762 |
| John Stuart, Earl of Bute | Tory | 1762–1763 |
| George Grenville | Whig | 1763–1765 |
| Charles Watson-Wentworth, Marquis of Rockingham | Whig | 1765–1766 |
| William Pitt, Earl of Chatham | Coalition | 1766–1767 |
| Augustus Henry Fitzroy, Duke of Grafton | Whig | 1767–1770 |
| Frederick North, Lord North | Tory | 1770–1782 |
| Charles Watson-Wentworth, Marquis of Rockingham | Whig | 1782 |
| William Petty, Earl of Shelburne | Whig | 1782–1783 |
| William Henry Cavendish Bentinck, Duke of Portland | Coalition | 1783 |
| William Pitt (the Younger) | Tory | 1783–1801 |
| Henry Addington | Tory | 1801–1804 |
| William Pitt (the Younger) | Tory | 1804–1806 |
| William Wyndham Grenville,[2] Lord Grenville | Whig | 1806–1807 |
| William Henry Cavendish Bentinck, Duke of Portland | Tory | 1807–1809 |
| Spencer Perceval (assassinated) | Tory | 1809–1812 |
| Robert Banks Jenkinson, Earl of Liverpool | Tory | 1812–1820 |
| **George IV, 1820–30** | | |
| Robert Banks Jenkinson, Earl of Liverpool | Tory | 1820–1827 |
| George Canning | Tory | 1827 |
| Frederick John Robinson, Viscount Goderich | Tory | 1827–1828 |
| Arthur Wellesley, Duke of Wellington | Tory | 1828–1830 |
| **William IV, 1830–37** | | |
| Charles Grey, Earl Grey | Whig | 1830–1834 |
| William Lamb, Viscount Melbourne | Whig | 1834 |
| Sir Robert Peel | Tory | 1834–1835 |
| William Lamb, Viscount Melbourne | Whig | 1835–1837 |
| **Victoria, 1837–1901** | | |
| William Lamb, Viscount Melbourne | Whig | 1837–1841 |
| Sir Robert Peel | Tory | 1841–1846 |
| John Russell,[3] Lord Russell | Whig | 1846–1852 |
| Edward George Geoffrey Smith Stanley, Earl of Derby | Tory | 1852 |
| George Hamilton Gordon, Earl of Aberdeen | Peelite[4] | 1852–1855 |
| **Victoria, 1837–1901** | | |
| Henry John Temple, Viscount Palmerston | Liberal | 1855–1858 |
| Edward George Geoffrey Smith Stanley, Earl of Derby | Tory | 1858–1859 |
| Henry John Temple, Viscount Palmerston | Liberal | 1859–1865 |
| John Russell, Earl Russell | Liberal | 1865–1866 |
| Edward George Geoffrey Smith Stanley, Earl of Derby | Conservative | 1866–1868 |
| Benjamin Disraeli | Conservative | 1868 |
| William Ewart Gladstone | Liberal | 1868–1874 |
| Benjamin Disraeli, Earl of Beaconsfield | Conservative | 1874–1880 |
| William Ewart Gladstone | Liberal | 1880–1885 |
| Robert Arthur Talbot Gascoyne-Cecil, Marquis of Salisbury | Conservative | 1885–1886 |
| William Ewart Gladstone | Liberal | 1886 |
| Robert Arthur Talbot Gascoyne-Cecil, Marquis of Salisbury | Conservative | 1886–1892 |
| William Ewart Gladstone | Liberal | 1892–1894 |
| Archibald Philip Primrose, Earl of Rosebery | Liberal | 1894–1895 |
| Robert Arthur Talbot Gascoyne-Cecil, Marquis of Salisbury | Conservative | 1895–1901 |
| **Edward VII, 1901–1910** | | |
| Robert Arthur Talbot Gascoyne-Cecil, Marquis of Salisbury | Conservative | 1901–1902 |
| Arthur James Balfour | Conservative | 1902–1905 |
| Sir Henry Campbell-Bannerman | Liberal | 1905–1908 |
| Herbert Henry Asquith | Liberal | 1908–1910 |
| **George V, 1910–36** | | |
| Herbert Henry Asquith | Liberal | 1910–1915 |
| Herbert Henry Asquith | Coalition | 1915–1916 |
| David Lloyd George | Coalition | 1916–1922 |
| Andrew Bonar Law | Conservative | 1922–1923 |
| Stanley Baldwin | Conservative | 1923–1924 |
| James Ramsay MacDonald | Labour | 1924 |
| Stanley Baldwin | Conservative | 1924–1929 |
| James Ramsay MacDonald | Labour | 1929–1931 |
| James Ramsay MacDonald | Coalition | 1931–1935 |
| Stanley Baldwin | Coalition | 1935–1936 |
| **Edward VIII, 1936** (abdicated) | | |
| **George VI, 1936–52** | | |
| Stanley Baldwin, Earl Baldwin of Bewdley | Coalition | 1936–1937 |
| (Arthur) Neville Chamberlain | Coalition | 1937–1940 |
| Winston Leonard Spencer Churchill | Coalition | 1940–1945 |
| Winston Leonard Spencer Churchill | Conservative | 1945 |
| Clement Richard Attlee | Labour | 1945–1951 |
| Winston Leonard Spencer Churchill | Conservative | 1951–1952 |
| **Elizabeth II, 1952–** | | |
| Sir Winston Leonard Spencer Churchill | Conservative | 1952–1955 |
| Sir (Robert) Anthony Eden | Conservative | 1955–1957 |
| (Maurice) Harold Macmillan | Conservative | 1957–1963 |
| Sir Alec Douglas-Home | Conservative | 1963–1964 |
| (James) Harold Wilson | Labour | 1964–1970 |
| Edward Heath | Conservative | 1970–1974 |
| Harold Wilson | Labour | 1974–1976 |
| James Callaghan | Labour | 1976–1979 |
| Margaret Thatcher | Conservative | 1979– |

[1] Brother of Henry Pelham. [2] Son of George Grenville. [3] Lord Russell, later Earl Russell, sat in the House of Commons in his first ministry and in the House of Lords in his second. [4] On the sudden death of Sir Robert Peel in 1850, the Earl of Aberdeen became the leader of the Peelites, a coalition that supported the corn law and public reform policies of Sir Robert Peel.

## THE COMMONWEALTH (September 1, 1982)

Formed in 1931, the Commonwealth is now a free association of 47 sovereign states and their dependencies.

| State (date of entry) | Location | Administrative Center | Area (sq. mi.) | Population |
|---|---|---|---|---|
| UNITED KINGDOM* (12/31/31) | Europe | London | 94,399 | 55,618,791 |
| Brunei | Borneo | Bandar Seri Begawan | 2,226 | 191,765 |
| Dependencies | | | | |
| Anguilla | West Indies | The Valley | 35 | 6,600 |
| Bermuda | Atlantic Ocean | Hamilton | 21 | 67,761 |
| British Antarctic Terr. | Antarctica | Stanley, Falkland Islands | 600,000 | uninhabited |
| British Indian Ocean Terr. | Indian Ocean | London, U.K. | 29 | unknown |
| British Virgin Islands | West Indies | Road Town | 59 | 11,000 |
| Cayman Islands | West Indies | George Town | 100 | 16,677 |
| Falkland Islands | Atlantic Ocean | Stanley | 6,198 | 1,812 |
| Gibraltar | Europe | Gibraltar | 2.28 | 29,648 |
| Hong Kong | Asia | Victoria | 403 | 4,986,560 |
| Montserrat | West Indies | Plymouth | 40 | 12,073 |
| Pitcairn Islands | Oceania | Adamstown | 18 | 54 |
| St. Helena | Atlantic Ocean | Jamestown | 162 | 6,400 |
| Turks and Caicos Islands | West Indies | Cockburn Town (on Grand Turk) | 166 | 7,436 |
| West Indies Associated State | | | | |
| St. Christopher-Nevis | West Indies | Basseterre | 120 | 44,404 |
| AUSTRALIA (12/31/31) | Oceania | Canberra | 2,967,909 | 14,574,488 |
| Dependencies | | | | |
| Ashmore & Cartier Islands | Indian Ocean | — | 1.9 | uninhabited |
| Australian Antarctic Terr | Antarctica | — | 2,362,875 | uninhabited |
| Christmas Island | Indian Ocean | Flying Fish Cove | 52 | 3,184 |
| Cocos Islands | Indian Ocean | West Island | 5.4 | 555 |
| Coral Sea Islands | Oceania | — | 8.5 | 3 |
| Heard and McDonald Islands | Indian Ocean | — | 113 | uninhabited |
| Norfolk Island | Oceania | Kingston | 13.3 | 2,180 |
| NEW ZEALAND (12/31/31) | Oceania | Wellington | 103,736 | 3,175,737 |
| Dependencies | | | | |
| Cook Islands | Oceania | Avarua | 91 | 17,695 |
| Niue | Oceania | Alofi | 100 | 3,578 |
| Ross Dependency | Antarctica | — | 290,000 | uninhabited |
| Tokelau Islands | Oceania | Fenuafala | 3.95 | 1,625 |
| ANTIGUA AND BARBUDA (11/1/81) | West Indies | St. John's | 171 | 76,213 |
| BAHAMAS (7/10/73) | Atlantic Ocean | Nassau | 5,382 | 223,455 |
| BANGLADESH (4/18/72) | Asia | Dacca | 55,126 | 87,052,024 |
| BARBADOS (11/30/66) | West Indies | Bridgetown | 166 | 249,000 |
| BELIZE (9/21/81) | Central America | Belmopan | 8,867 | 144,857 |
| BOTSWANA (9/30/66) | Africa | Gaborone | 224,764 | 936,600 |
| CANADA (12/31/31) | North America | Ottawa | 3,831,012 | 24,343,181 |
| CYPRUS (3/13/61) | Mediterranean | Nicosia | 3,572 | 637,000 |
| DOMINICA (11/3/78) | West Indies | Roseau | 291 | 74,089 |
| FIJI (10/10/70) | Oceania | Suva | 7,055 | 634,000 |
| GAMBIA, THE (2/18/65) | Africa | Banjul | 4,127 | 601,000 |
| GHANA (3/6/57) | Africa | Accra | 92,099 | 11,450,000 |
| GRENADA (2/7/74) | West Indies | St. George's | 133 | 103,103 |
| GUYANA (5/26/66) | South America | Georgetown | 83,000 | 820,000 |
| INDIA (8/15/47) | Asia | New Delhi | 1,269,339 | 683,810,051 |
| JAMAICA (8/6/62) | West Indies | Kingston | 4,244 | 2,184,000 |
| KENYA (12/12/63) | Africa | Nairobi | 224,960 | 15,322,000 |
| KIRIBATI (7/12/79) | Oceania | Bairiki (on Tarawa) | 264 | 56,213 |
| LESOTHO (10/4/66) | Africa | Maseru | 11,720 | 1,339,000 |
| MALAWI (7/6/64) | Africa | Lilongwe | 45,747 | 6,123,000 |
| MALAYSIA (9/16/63) | Asia | Kuala Lumpur | 128,308 | 13,435,588 |
| MALDIVES (7/9/81)‡ | Indian Ocean | Male | 115 | 157,000 |
| MALTA (9/21/64) | Mediterranean | Valletta | 122 | 366,000 |
| MAURITIUS (3/12/68) | Indian Ocean | Port Louis | 790 | 971,000 |
| NAURU (1/31/68)‡ | Oceania | Yaren district | 7.7 | 7,100 |
| NIGERIA (10/1/60) | Africa | Lagos | 379,628 | 84,500,000 |
| PAPUA NEW GUINEA (9/16/75) | Oceania | Port Moresby | 183,540 | 3,006,799 |
| SAINT LUCIA (2/22/79) | West Indies | Castries | 238 | 115,783 |
| SAINT VINCENT AND THE GRENADINES (10/27/79)‡ | West Indies | Kingstown | 150 | 124,000 |
| SEYCHELLES (6/28/76) | Indian Ocean | Victoria | 171 | 63,000 |
| SIERRA LEONE (4/27/61) | Africa | Freetown | 27,295 | 3,474,000 |
| SINGAPORE (10/16/65) | Asia | Singapore | 233 | 2,413,945 |
| SOLOMON ISLANDS (7/7/78) | Oceania | Honiara | 11,500 | 221,000 |
| SRI LANKA (2/4/48) | Asia | Colombo | 25,332 | 14,850,001 |
| SWAZILAND (9/6/68) | Africa | Mbabane | 6,705 | 566,000 |
| TANZANIA (4/26/64) | Africa | Dar es Salaam | 363,708 | 17,982,000 |
| TONGA (6/4/70) | Oceania | Nuku'alofa | 270 | 97,000 |
| TRINIDAD AND TOBAGO (8/31/62) | West Indies | Port-of-Spain | 1,980 | 1,067,108 |
| TUVALU (10/1/78)‡ | Oceania | Fongafale | 9.78 | 7,349 |
| UGANDA (10/9/62) | Africa | Kampala | 91,076 | 12,630,076 |
| VANUATU (7/30/80) | Oceania | Vila | 5,700 | 123,000 |
| WESTERN SAMOA (8/28/70) | South Pacific | Apia | 1,133 | 158,130 |
| ZAMBIA (10/24/64) | Africa | Lusaka | 290,586 | 5,679,808 |
| ZIMBABWE (4/18/80) | Africa | Harare | 150,803 | 7,600,000 |

*As crown fiefdoms, the Isle of Man (227 sq. mi.; 66,000 pop.) and the Channel Islands (74 sq. mi.; 129,000 pop.) are included in the Commonwealth.
‡Special member

## WORLD COMMUNIST PARTY STRENGTH

SOURCE: Richard F. Staar (ed.), *1982 Yearbook on International Communist Affairs*. Hoover Institution Press, Stanford, CA 94305 © 1982

| Country or Area | Communist Party Membership | Percent of vote; seats in legislature | Status | Sino-Soviet Dispute |
|---|---|---|---|---|
| Afghanistan | 50,000 | No elections scheduled | In power | Pro-Soviet |
| Albania | 122,600 | 99.9 (1978); all 250 seats | In power | Independent |
| Algeria | 450 | — | Proscribed | Pro-Soviet |
| Argentina | 80,000 | — | Proscribed | Pro-Soviet |
| Australia | 2,500 | — (1980); no seats | Legal | Split (2) |
| Austria | 25,000 | 0.96 (1979); no seats | Legal | Pro-Soviet |
| Bangladesh | 2,500 | — (1979); 1 of 300 seats | Legal | Pro-Soviet |
| Belgium | 10,000 | 2.3 (1981); 2 of 212 seats | Legal | Independent |
| Berlin, West | 7,000 | 0.7 (1981); no seats | Legal | Pro-Soviet |
| Bolivia | 500 | — | Proscribed | Pro-Soviet |
| Brazil | 6,000 | — | Proscribed | Pro-Soviet |
| Bulgaria | 825,000 | 99.9 (1976); 272 of 400 seats | In power | Pro-Soviet |
| Burma | 3,000 | — (1981) | Proscribed | Pro-Chinese |
| Cambodia | 5,000 | 99.0 (1981); all 117 seats | In power | Pro-Soviet |
| Canada | 5,000 | 0.18 (1980); no seats | Legal | Split (2) |
| Chile | 20,000 | — | Proscribed | Pro-Soviet |
| China | 39,000,000 | — (1981); all 3,202 seats | In power | — |
| Colombia | 12,000 | 1.9 (1978); 3 of 311 seats | Legal | Pro-Soviet |
| Costa Rica | 3,200 | 2.7 (1978); 3 of 57 seats | Legal | Pro-Soviet |
| Cuba | 434,000 | — (1981); all 499 seats | In power | Pro-Soviet |
| Cyprus | 12,000 | 32.8 (1981); 12 of 35 Greek Cypriot seats | Legal | Pro-Soviet |
| Czechoslovakia | 1,538,179 | 99.9 (1981); all 350 seats | In power | Pro-Soviet |
| Denmark | 9,000 | 1.1 (1981); no seats | Legal | Pro-Soviet |
| Dominican Republic | 4,500 | — | Proscribed | Split (12) |
| Ecuador | 1,000 | 3.2 (1979); 1 of 69 seats | Legal | Split (2) |
| Egypt | 500 | — | Proscribed | Pro-Soviet |
| El Salvador | 800 | — (1976) | Proscribed | Pro-Soviet |
| Finland | 47,000 | 17.9 (1979); 35 of 200 seats | Legal | Independent |
| France | 700,000 | 16.2 (1981); 44 of 491 seats | Legal | Pro-Soviet |
| Germany, East | 2,172,110 | 99.9 (1981); all 500 seats | In power | Pro-Soviet |
| Germany, West | 48,856 | 0.2 (1980); no seats | Legal | Pro-Soviet |
| Greece | 33,300 | 10.9 (1981); 13 of 300 seats | Legal | Pro-Soviet |
| Guadeloupe | 3,000 | 38.6 (1981); 1 of 36 seats | Legal | Pro-Soviet |
| Guatemala | 750 | — | Proscribed | Pro-Soviet |
| Guyana | Unknown | 20.4 (1980); 10 of 65 seats | Legal | Pro-Soviet |
| Haiti | 350 | — | Proscribed | Pro-Soviet |
| Honduras | 1,500 | — | Proscribed | Pro-Soviet |
| Hong Kong | 2,000 | City council | Legal | Pro-Chinese |
| Hungary | 812,000 | 99.3 (1980); all 352 seats | In power | Pro-Soviet |
| Iceland | 2,200 | 19.7 (1979); 11 of 60 seats | Legal | Isolationist |
| India | 250,000 | 8.8 (1980); 47 of 525 seats | Legal | Split (2) |
| Indonesia | 250 | — | Proscribed | Split (2) |
| Iran | 1,500 | — (1980); no seats | Legal | Pro-Soviet |
| Iraq | 2,000 | — (1980); no seats | Legal | Pro-Soviet |
| Ireland | 500 | — (1981); no seats | Legal | Pro-Soviet |
| Israel | 1,500 | 3.4 (1981); 4 of 120 seats | Legal | Pro-Soviet |
| Italy | 1,715,890 | 30.4 (1979); 201 of 630 seats | Legal | Independent |
| Jamaica | Unknown | — (1980); no seats | Legal | Pro-Soviet |
| Japan | 440,000 | 10.4 (1980); 29 of 511 seats | Legal | Independent |
| Jordan | 500 | — | Proscribed | Pro-Soviet |
| Korea, North | 2,000,000 | 100.0 (1977); all 579 seats | In power | Neutral |
| Laos | 15,000 | No legislature | In power | Pro-Soviet |
| Lebanon | 2,500 | — (1972); no seats | Legal | Pro-Soviet |
| Lesotho | Negligible | — | Proscribed | Pro-Soviet |
| Luxembourg | 600 | 5.0 (1979); 2 of 59 seats | Legal | Pro-Soviet |
| Malaysia | 3,200 | — | Proscribed | Pro-Chinese |
| Malta | 150 | — (1981); no seats | Legal | Pro-Soviet |
| Martinique | 1,000 | 6.4 (1981); no seats | Legal | Pro-Soviet |
| Mexico | 112,000 | 5.4 (1979); 19 of 400 seats | Legal | Independent |
| Mongolia | 76,000 | 99.9 (1977); all 354 seats | In power | Pro-Soviet |
| Morocco | 2,750 | — (1977); 1 of 264 seats | Legal | Pro-Soviet |
| Nepal | 1,500 | — (1981); no seats | Legal | Pro-Soviet |
| Netherlands | 13,000 | 2.1 (1981); 3 of 150 seats | Legal | Independent |
| New Zealand | 300 | 0.5 (1981); no seats | Legal | Split (2) |
| Nicaragua | 250 | — | Legal | Pro-Soviet |
| Nigeria | Unknown | — | Proscribed | Pro-Soviet |
| Norway | 2,500 | 4.9 (1981); 4 of 155 seats | Legal | Pro-Soviet |
| Pakistan | Few hundred | — | Proscribed | Pro-Soviet |
| Panama | 550 | — (1980); no seats | Legal | Pro-Soviet |
| Paraguay | 3,500 | — | Proscribed | Pro-Soviet |
| Peru | 3,200 | 2.8 (1980); 2 of 60 seats | Legal | Pro-Soviet |
| Philippines | 3,200 | — | Proscribed | Split (2) |
| Poland | 2,734,000 | 99.5 (1980); all 460 seats | In power | Pro-Soviet |
| Portugal | 187,000 | 16.7 (1980); 41 of 250 seats | Legal | Pro-Soviet |
| Puerto Rico | 125 | 0.3 (1980); no seats | Legal | Pro-Soviet |

| Country or Area | Communist Party Membership | Percent of vote; seats in legislature | Status | Sino-Soviet Dispute |
|---|---|---|---|---|
| Réunion | 2,000 | —(1981); none | Legal | Pro-Soviet |
| Romania | 3,004,336 | 98.5 (1980); all 369 seats | In power | Independent |
| San Marino | 300 | 25.0 (1978); 16 of 60 seats | Legal | Independent |
| Saudi Arabia | Negligible | — | Proscribed | Pro-Soviet |
| Senegal | 1,000 | 0.32 (1978); no seats | Legal | Pro-Soviet |
| South Africa | Unknown | — | Proscribed | Pro-Soviet |
| Spain | 140,000 | 10.6 (1979); 23 of 350 seats | Legal | Independent |
| Sri Lanka | 6,000 | —(1981); 1 of 168 seats | Legal | Pro-Soviet |
| Sudan | 1,500 | — | Proscribed | Pro-Soviet |
| Sweden | 18,000 | 5.6 (1979); 23 of 349 seats | Legal | Independent |
| Switzerland | 5,000 | 1.5 (1979); 3 of 200 seats | Legal | Pro-Soviet |
| Syria | 5,000 | 3.0 (1981); no seats | Legal | Pro-Soviet |
| Thailand | 1,000 | — | Proscribed | Pro-Chinese |
| Tunisia | 100 | 2.1 (1981); no seats | Legal | Pro-Soviet |
| Turkey | Negligible | — | Proscribed | Pro-Soviet |
| USSR | 17,480,000 | 99.9 (1979); all 1,500 seats CPSU-approved | In power | — |
| United Kingdom | 18,500 | 0.05 (1979); no seats | Legal | Independent |
| United States | 11,000 | 0.01 (1980); no seats | Legal | Pro-Soviet |
| Uruguay | 7,500 | — | Proscribed | Pro-Soviet |
| Venezuela | 4,500 | 9.0 (1978); 22 of 195 seats | Legal | Pro-Soviet |
| Vietnam | 1,480,000 | 97.9 (1981); all 538 seats | In power | Pro-Soviet |
| Yugoslavia | 2,199,444 | —(1978); all 308 seats | In power | Independent |

## SOVIET LEADERS: 1982 SOURCE: U.S. Department of State

**Brezhnev, Leonid I.**
General Secretary, Soviet Communist party; b. 1906

### POLITBURO
FULL MEMBERS

**Brezhnev, Leonid I.**
Chairman of the Presidium of the Supreme Soviet (President of the Soviet Union)

**Kirilenko, Andrei P.**
A secretary, Soviet Communist party (party affairs, industry); b. 1906

**Pelshe, Arvid Y.**
Chairman, Party Control Commission; b. 1899

**Grishin, Viktor V.**
First Secretary, Moscow city party organization; b. 1914

**Kunayev, Dinmukhamed A.**
First Secretary, Kazakhstan Communist party; b. 1912

**Shcherbitsky, Vladimir V.**
First Secretary, Ukrainian Communist party; b. 1918

**Andropov, Yuriy V.**
KGB chief; b. 1914

**Gromyko, Andrei A.**
Minister of Foreign Affairs; b. 1909

**Romanov, Grigory V.**
First Secretary, Leningrad Oblast Party Committee; b. 1923

**Ustinov, Dmitry F.**
Minister of Defense; b. 1908

**Chernenko, Konstantin U.**
Head, General Department, Soviet Communist party Central Committee; b. 1911

**Tikhonov, Nikolai A.**
Premier; b. 1905

**Gorbachev, Mikhail S.**
Secretary of CPSU Central Committee (agriculture); b. 1931

CANDIDATE MEMBERS

**Demichev, Pyotr N.**
Minister of Culture; b. 1918

**Solomentsev, Mikhail S.**
Chairman of RSFSR Council of Ministers; b. 1913

**Rashidov, Sharaf R.**
First Secretary, Uzbek Communist Party; b. 1917

**Ponomaryov, Boris N.**
A secretary (relations with non-ruling parties); b. 1905

**Aliyev, Geidar A.**
First Secretary, Azerbaidzhan Communist party; b. 1923

**Kuznetsov, Vasily V.**
First Deputy Chairman, Presidium of the USSR Supreme Soviet; b. 1901

**Shevardnadze, Eduard A.**
Georgian Republic First Secretary; b. 1928

**Dolgikh, Vladimir I.**
A secretary (heavy industry); b. 1924

**Kiselev, Tikon Y.**
First Secretary, Byelorussian Communist Party; b. 1917

### COMMUNIST PARTY SECRETARIAT

**Brezhnev, Leonid I.; Kirilenko, Andrei P.; Chernenko, Konstantin U.; Gorbachev, M.S.; Andropov, Y.V.; Dolgikh, V.I.**

**Ponomaryov, B. N.**
(candidate member of Politburo)

**Rusakov, Konstantin V.**
A secretary (relations with ruling Communist parties); b. 1909

**Kapitonov, Ivan V.**
Head, Organizational Party Work Department, Soviet Communist Party Central Committee; b. 1915

**Zimyanin, Mikhail V.**
A secretary (culture, propaganda); b. 1914

## RULERS OF CHINA: 1982 SOURCE: Donald W. Klein, Department of Political Science, Tufts University

**POLITBURO—FULL MEMBERS (as of Sept. 30, 1982)**

*Hu Yaobang (General Secretary), b. 1915
*Ye Jiangying, b. 1898
*Deng Xiaoping, b. 1904
*Zhao Ziyang, b. 1919
*Li Xiannian, b. 1907
*Chen Yun, b. c. 1900
Deng Yingchao (Mrs. Zhou Enlai), b. 1903
Fang Yi, b. 1916
Hu Qiaomu, b. 1912
Li Desheng, b. 1912
Liao Chengzhi, b. 1908
Ni Zhifu
Nie Rongzhen, b. 1899
Peng Zhen, b. 1915
Song Renqiong, b. 1909
Ulanhu, b. 1906
Wan Li, b. 1916
Wang Zhen, b. 1909
Wei Quoqing, b. c. 1914
Xi Zhongxun, b. 1913
Xu Xiangqian, b. 1902
Yang Dezhi, b. 1910
Yang Shangkun, b. 1907
Yu Qiuli, b. 1914
Zhang Tingfa

**SECRETARIAT OF THE CHINESE COMMUNIST PARTY CENTRAL COMMITTEE (as of Sept. 30, 1982)**
Chen Pixian, b. 1916
Deng Liqun, b. 1915
Gu Mu, b. 1914
Hu Qili, b. 1929
Wan Li
Xi Chongxun
Yang Yong, b. 1912
Yao Yilin, b. 1917
Yu Qiuli

**CENTRAL ADVISORY COMMISSION (of the Chinese Communist party)**
Deng Xiaoping (Chairman)
Bo Yibo (V.C.)
Li Weihan (V.C.)
Tan Zhenlin (V.C.)
Xu Shiyou (V.C.)
157 members

**CENTRAL COMMISSION FOR DISCIPLINE INSPECTION**
Chen Yun (Secretary)

**MILITARY AFFAIRS COMMITTEE (of the Chinese Communist party)**
Deng Xiaoping (Chairman)
Nie Rongzhen (V.C.)
Xu Xiangqian (V.C.)
Yang Shangkun (Permanent V.C.)
Ye Jiangying (V.C.)

**STATE COUNCIL (of the Government)**
Zhao Ziyang (Premier)
Wan Li (V.P.)
Yao Yilin (V.P.)

*Also member of Politburo Standing Committee.

# MILITARY AFFAIRS

## U.S. WARS AND CASUALTIES

SOURCE: U.S. Department of Defense

Data prior to World War I are based, in many cases, on incomplete records. Casualty data are confined to dead and wounded personnel and therefore exclude personnel captured or missing in action who were subsequently returned to military control.

| War | Branch of Service† | Number Serving | CASUALTIES Battle Deaths | Other Deaths | Not Mortal Wounds |
|---|---|---|---|---|---|
| Revolutionary War (1775–1783) | Total | 184,000–250,000 (estimated) | 4,435 | — | 6,188 |
| | Army | | 4,044 | — | 6,004 |
| | Navy | — | 342 | — | 114 |
| | Marines | — | 49 | — | 70 |
| War of 1812 (1812–1815) | Total | 286,730 | 2,260 | — | 4,505 |
| | Army | — | 1,950 | — | 4,000 |
| | Navy | — | 265 | — | 439 |
| | Marines | — | 45 | — | 66 |
| Mexican War (1846–1848) | Total | 78,718 | 1,733 | 11,550 | 4,152 |
| | Army | — | 1,721 | — | 4,102 |
| | Navy | — | 1 | — | 3 |
| | Marines | — | 11 | — | 47 |
| Civil War (Union Forces only)* (1861–1865) | Total | 2,213,363 | 140,414 | 224,097 | 281,881 |
| | Army | 2,128,948 | 138,154 | 221,374 | 280,040 |
| | Navy | 84,415 | 2,112 | 2,411 | 1,710 |
| | Marines | | 148 | 312 | 131 |
| Spanish-American War (1898) | Total | 306,760 | 385 | 2,061 | 1,662 |
| | Army | 280,564 | 369 | 2,061 | 1,594 |
| | Navy | 22,875 | 10 | 0 | 47 |
| | Marines | 3,321 | 6 | 0 | 21 |
| World War I (6 April 1917–11 November 1918) | Total | 4,734,991 | 53,402 | 63,114 | 204,002 |
| | Army | 4,057,101 | 50,510 | 55,868 | 193,663 |
| | Navy | 599,051 | 431 | 6,856 | 819 |
| | Marines | 78,839 | 2,461 | 390 | 9,520 |
| World War II (7 December 1941–31 December 1946)†† | Total | 16,112,566 | 291,557 | 113,842 | 670,846 |
| | Army | 11,260,000 | 234,874 | 83,400 | 565,861 |
| | Navy | 4,183,466 | 36,950 | 25,664 | 37,778 |
| | Marines | 669,100 | 19,733 | 4,778 | 67,207 |
| Korean War (25 June 1950–27 July 1953) | Total | 5,720,000 | 33,629 | 20,617 | 103,284 |
| | Army | 2,834,000 | 27,704 | 9,429 | 77,596 |
| | Navy | 1,177,000 | 458 | 4,043 | 1,576 |
| | Marines | 424,000 | 4,267 | 1,261 | 23,744 |
| | Air Force | 1,285,000 | 1,200 | 5,884 | 368 |
| Vietnam War (1961—7 May 1975) | Total | 3,300,000 | 47,752 | 10,390 | 303,706 |

* Authoritative statistics for the Confederate Forces are not available. Estimates of the number who served range from 600,000 to 1,500,000. Based upon incomplete information, 133,821 Confederates died (74,524 in battle and 59,297 otherwise). In addition, an estimated 26,000–31,000 Confederate personnel died in Union prisons. † U.S. Coast Guard data are excluded. †† World War II hostilities declared terminated on December 31, 1946, by Presidential Proclamation.

## U.S. VETERANS

SOURCE: Veterans Administration

| Veterans in civil life, end of month— | |
|---|---|
| Total, September 1981 | 30,083,000 |
| War Veterans—Total | 25,789,000 |
| Vietnam Era—Total | 9,087,000 |
| And service in Korean Conflict | 550,000 |
| No service in Korean Conflict | 8,537,000 |
| Korean Conflict—Total (includes line 4) | 5,781,000 |
| And service in WW II | 1,148,000 |
| No service in WW II | 4,633,000 |
| World War II (includes line 7) | 12,170,000 |
| World War I | 449,000 |
| Spanish-American War | 86 |
| Service between Korean Conflict (Jan. 31, 1955) and Vietnam (Aug. 5, 1964) | 3,040,000 |

## U.S. DEFENSE EXPENDITURES

SOURCE: U.S. Office of Management and Budget

| Fiscal Year | National defense[1] $ Billion | GNP $ Billion | Defense as % of GNP |
|---|---|---|---|
| 1960 | 45.2 | 497.3 | 9.1 |
| 1961 | 46.6 | 508.3 | 9.2 |
| 1962 | 50.4 | 546.9 | 9.2 |
| 1963 | 51.5 | 576.3 | 8.9 |
| 1964 | 52.7 | 616.2 | 8.6 |
| 1965 | 48.6 | 657.1 | 7.4 |
| 1966 | 55.9 | 721.1 | 7.8 |
| 1967 | 69.1 | 774.4 | 8.9 |
| 1968 | 79.4 | 829.9 | 9.6 |
| 1969 | 79.4 | 903.7 | 8.8 |
| 1970 | 78.6 | 959.0 | 8.2 |
| 1971 | 75.8 | 1,019.3 | 7.4 |
| 1972 | 76.6 | 1,110.5 | 6.9 |
| 1973 | 74.5 | 1,237.5 | 6.0 |
| 1974 | 77.8 | 1,359.2 | 5.7 |
| 1975 | 85.6 | 1,457.3 | 5.9 |
| 1976 | 89.4 | 1,640.1 | 5.5 |
| 1977 | 97.5 | 1,864.1 | 5.2 |
| 1978 | 105.2 | 2,083.8 | 5.0 |
| 1979 | 117.7 | 2,353.3 | 5.0 |
| 1980 | 135.9 | 2,567.5 | 5.3 |
| 1981 | 159.8 | 2,926.0 | 5.5 |
| 1982 est.[2] | 187.7 | 3,090.0 | 6.1 |
| 1983 est.[2] | 221.5 | 3,436.0 | 6.4 |

[1] Includes budget outlays for military activities of the Department of Defense, military assistance, atomic energy defense activities, and defense-related activities of civilian agencies. [2] Based on estimates of the 1983 Budget of the Mid-Session Review in July 1982.

## NATIONAL GUARD 1981

SOURCE: National Guard Bureau, U.S. Departments of the Army and the Air Force

| State or Territory | Units* | Personnel* | State or Territory | Units* | Personnel* | State or Territory | Units* | Personnel* | State or Territory | Units* | Personnel* |
|---|---|---|---|---|---|---|---|---|---|---|---|
| TOTAL | 4,324 | 464,049 | Idaho | 36 | 3,631 | Missouri | 106 | 10,679 | Puerto Rico | 77 | 10,689 |
| Alabama | 182 | 22,141 | Illinois | 113 | 11,833 | Montana | 29 | 3,256 | Rhode Island | 47 | 4,429 |
| Alaska | 44 | 3,087 | Indiana | 123 | 14,294 | Nebraska | 45 | 5,229 | South Carolina | 108 | 12,646 |
| Arizona | 57 | 6,429 | Iowa | 79 | 7,719 | Nevada | 24 | 1,978 | South Dakota | 45 | 4,728 |
| Arkansas | 95 | 11,158 | Kansas | 78 | 7,131 | New Hampshire | 37 | 2,930 | Tennessee | 140 | 16,024 |
| California | 217 | 21,441 | Kentucky | 64 | 7,751 | New Jersey | 136 | 14,392 | Texas | 180 | 19,783 |
| Colorado | 49 | 4,489 | Louisiana | 85 | 9,362 | New Mexico | 46 | 4,764 | Utah | 56 | 5,585 |
| Connecticut | 56 | 6,832 | Maine | 39 | 4,592 | New York | 228 | 22,173 | Vermont | 39 | 3,679 |
| Delaware | 30 | 2,938 | Maryland | 76 | 7,893 | North Carolina | 108 | 12,923 | Virginia | 80 | 7,951 |
| Dist. of Columbia | 32 | 3,629 | Massachusetts | 132 | 14,385 | North Dakota | 34 | 4,582 | Virgin Islands | 21 | 697 |
| Florida | 90 | 10,767 | Michigan | 115 | 13,069 | Ohio | 161 | 18,997 | Washington | 77 | 7,210 |
| Georgia | 109 | 13,738 | Minnesota | 106 | 10,336 | Oklahoma | 102 | 9,537 | West Virginia | 55 | 5,203 |
| Hawaii | 54 | 5,284 | Mississippi | 121 | 14,253 | Oregon | 74 | 8,117 | Wisconsin | 94 | 10,244 |
| | | | | | | Pennsylvania | 184 | 20,253 | Wyoming | 35 | 2,417 |

* Army National Guard and Air National Guard.

## U.S. MILITARY PAY SCALES BY GRADE: PER MONTH (Oct.) 1981

Years of Service

| Pay Grade | 2 years or less | Over 2 | Over 3 | Over 4 | Over 6 | Over 8 | Over 10 | Over 12 | Over 14 | Over 16 | Over 18 | Over 20 | Over 22 | Over 26 |
|---|---|---|---|---|---|---|---|---|---|---|---|---|---|---|
| **Commissioned Officers[1]** | | | | | | | | | | | | | | |
| O–10[2] | $4,506.60 | $4,665.30 | $4,665.30 | $4,665.30 | $4,665.30 | $4,844.10 | $4,844.10 | $5,215.20 | $5,215.20 | $5,588.10 | $5,588.10 | $5,961.90 | $5,961.90 | $6,333.90 |
| O–9 | 3,994.20 | 4,098.90 | 4,186.20 | 4,186.20 | 4,186.20 | 4,292.70 | 4,292.70 | 4,471.20 | 4,471.20 | 4,844.10 | 4,844.10 | 5,215.20 | 5,215.20 | 5,588.10 |
| O–8 | 3,617.70 | 3,726.00 | 3,814.50 | 3,814.50 | 3,814.50 | 4,098.90 | 4,098.90 | 4,292.70 | 4,292.70 | 4,471.20 | 4,665.30 | 4,844.10 | 5,038.20 | 5,038.20 |
| O–7 | 3,006.00 | 3,210.60 | 3,210.60 | 3,210.60 | 3,354.30 | 3,354.30 | 3,549.00 | 3,549.00 | 3,726.00 | 4,098.90 | 4,380.60 | 4,380.60 | 4,380.60 | 4,380.60 |
| O–6 | 2,228.10 | 2,448.30 | 2,608.20 | 2,608.20 | 2,608.20 | 2,608.20 | 2,608.20 | 2,608.20 | 2,696.70 | 3,123.60 | 3,283.20 | 3,354.30 | 3,549.00 | 3,849.00 |
| O–5 | 1,782.00 | 2,092.80 | 2,237.10 | 2,237.10 | 2,237.10 | 2,237.10 | 2,305.20 | 2,428.80 | 2,591.40 | 2,785.50 | 2,945.40 | 3,034.20 | 3,140.40 | 3,140.40 |
| O–4 | 1,502.10 | 1,828.80 | 1,951.20 | 1,951.20 | 1,986.90 | 2,075.10 | 2,216.40 | 2,341.20 | 2,448.30 | 2,555.40 | 2,626.20 | 2,626.20 | 2,626.20 | 2,626.20 |
| O–3[3] | 1,395.90 | 1,560.60 | 1,668.30 | 1,845.90 | 1,934.10 | 2,004.00 | 2,111.70 | 2,216.40 | 2,271.00 | 2,271.00 | 2,271.00 | 2,271.00 | 2,271.00 | 2,271.00 |
| O–2[3] | 1,217.10 | 1,329.30 | 1,596.90 | 1,650.60 | 1,685.10 | 1,685.10 | 1,685.10 | 1,685.10 | 1,685.10 | 1,685.10 | 1,685.10 | 1,685.10 | 1,685.10 | 1,685.10 |
| O–1[3] | 1,056.60 | 1,099.80 | 1,329.30 | 1,329.30 | 1,329.30 | 1,329.30 | 1,329.30 | 1,329.30 | 1,329.30 | 1,329.30 | 1,329.30 | 1,329.30 | 1,329.30 | 1,329.30 |
| **Commissioned Officers with over 4 years active service as enlisted members or warrant officers** | | | | | | | | | | | | | | |
| O–3 | 0. | 0. | 0. | 1,845.90 | 1,934.10 | 2,004.00 | 2,111.70 | 2,216.40 | 2,305.20 | 2,305.20 | 2,305.20 | 2,305.20 | 2,305.20 | 2,305.20 |
| O–2 | 0. | 0. | 0. | 1,650.60 | 1,685.10 | 1,738.50 | 1,828.80 | 1,899.00 | 1,951.20 | 1,951.20 | 1,951.20 | 1,951.20 | 1,951.20 | 1,951.20 |
| O–1 | 0. | 0. | 0. | 1,329.30 | 1,419.90 | 1,472.40 | 1,525.50 | 1,578.60 | 1,650.60 | 1,650.60 | 1,650.60 | 1,650.60 | 1,650.60 | 1,650.60 |
| **Warrant Officers** | | | | | | | | | | | | | | |
| W–4 | 1,422.00 | 1,525.50 | 1,525.00 | 1,560.00 | 1,631.40 | 1,703.40 | 1,774.80 | 1,899.00 | 1,986.90 | 2,057.10 | 2,111.70 | 2,186.40 | 2,253.60 | 2,428.80 |
| W–3 | 1,292.70 | 1,402.20 | 1,402.20 | 1,419.90 | 1,436.70 | 1,541.70 | 1,631.40 | 1,685.10 | 1,738.50 | 1,790.70 | 1,845.90 | 1,917.30 | 1,986.90 | 2,057.10 |
| W–2 | 1,132.20 | 1,224.60 | 1,224.60 | 1,260.30 | 1,329.30 | 1,402.20 | 1,455.00 | 1,508.40 | 1,560.60 | 1,615.20 | 1,668.30 | 1,721.10 | 1,790.70 | 1,790.70 |
| W–1 | 943.20 | 1,081.50 | 1,081.50 | 1,171.80 | 1,224.60 | 1,277.40 | 1,329.30 | 1,384.20 | 1,436.70 | 1,489.50 | 1,541.70 | 1,596.90 | 1,596.90 | 1,596.90 |
| **Enlisted Members** | | | | | | | | | | | | | | |
| E–9[4] | 0. | 0. | 0. | 0. | 0. | 0. | 1,653.90 | 1,691.40 | 1,729.80 | 1,769.70 | 1,809.00 | 1,844.10 | 1,941.30 | 2,136.00 |
| E–8 | 0. | 0. | 0. | 0. | 0. | 1,387.50 | 1,426.50 | 1,464.30 | 1,542.00 | 1,542.00 | 1,577.70 | 1,616.40 | 1,711.50 | 1,902.30 |
| E–7 | 968.70 | 1,045.50 | 1,084.50 | 1,122.00 | 1,160.70 | 1,197.30 | 1,236.00 | 1,274.10 | 1,331.70 | 1,369.50 | 1,408.20 | 1,426.50 | 1,522.20 | 1,711.50 |
| E–6 | 833.10 | 908.40 | 946.50 | 986.40 | 1,023.00 | 1,060.50 | 1,099.20 | 1,155.90 | 1,192.20 | 1,230.60 | 1,249.20 | 1,249.20 | 1,249.20 | 1,249.20 |
| E–5 | 731.40 | 796.20 | 834.60 | 870.90 | 927.90 | 965.70 | 1,004.40 | 1,041.30 | 1,060.50 | 1,060.50 | 1,060.50 | 1,060.50 | 1,060.50 | 1,060.50 |
| E–4 | 682.20 | 720.30 | 762.30 | 821.70 | 854.40 | 854.40 | 854.40 | 854.40 | 854.40 | 854.40 | 854.40 | 854.40 | 854.40 | 854.40 |
| E–3 | 642.60 | 677.70 | 705.00 | 732.90 | 732.90 | 732.90 | 732.90 | 732.90 | 732.90 | 732.90 | 732.90 | 732.90 | 732.90 | 732.90 |
| E–2 | 618.30 | 618.30 | 618.30 | 618.30 | 618.30 | 618.30 | 618.30 | 618.30 | 618.30 | 618.30 | 618.30 | 618.30 | 618.30 | 618.30 |
| E–1 | 551.40 | 551.40 | 551.40 | 551.40 | 551.40 | 551.40 | 551.40 | 551.40 | 551.40 | 551.40 | 551.40 | 551.40 | 551.40 | 551.40 |

[1]Basic pay is limited to the rate of basic pay payable for Level V of the Executive Schedule. [2] While serving as Chairman of the Joint Chiefs of Staff of the Army, Chief of Naval Operations, Chief of Staff of the Air Force, or Commandant of the Marine Corps, basic pay for this grade is $5,473.80 regardless of cumulative years of service. [3]Does not apply to commissioned officers who have been credited with over 4 years' active service as enlisted members.

[4]Highest Enlisted Rank, while serving as Sergeant Major of the Army, Master Chief Petty Officer of the Navy, Chief Master Sergeant of the Air Force, or Sergeant Major of the Marine Corps, basic pay for this grade is $2,589.00 regardless of cumulative years of service.

## U.S. MILITARY PAY GRADES

SOURCE: U.S. Department of Defense

### COMMISSIONED OFFICERS

| Pay Grade | Army | Navy | Marines | Air Force |
|---|---|---|---|---|
| O–1 | Second Lieutenant | Ensign | Second Lieutenant | Second Lieutenant |
| O–2 | First Lieutenant | Lieutenant Junior Grade | First Lieutenant | First Lieutenant |
| O–3 | Captain | Lieutenant | Captain | Captain |
| O–4 | Major | Lieutenant Commander | Major | Major |
| O–5 | Lieutenant Colonel | Commander | Lieutenant Colonel | Lieutenant Colonel |
| O–6 | Colonel | Captain | Colonel | Colonel |
| O–7 | Brigadier General | Commodore Admiral | Brigadier General | Brigadier General |
| O–8 | Major General | Rear Admiral | Major General | Major General |
| O–9 | Lieutenant General | Vice Admiral | Lieutenant General | Lieutenant General |
| O–10 | General | Admiral | General | General |

### WARRANT OFFICERS (All Services)

| | | | |
|---|---|---|---|
| W–1 | Warrant Officer | W–3 | Chief Warrant Officer |
| W–2 | Chief Warrant Officer | W–4 | Chief Warrant Officer |

### ENLISTED PERSONNEL

| Pay Grade | Army | Navy | Marines | Air Force |
|---|---|---|---|---|
| E–1 | Private | Seaman Recruit | Private | Airman Basic |
| E–2 | Private | Seaman Apprentice | Private First Class | Airman |
| E–3 | Private First Class | Seaman | Lance Corporal | Airman First Class |
| E–4 | Corporal<br>Specialist 4 | Petty Officer, Third Class | Corporal | Sergeant<br>Senior Airman |
| E–5 | Sergeant<br>Specialist 5 | Petty Officer, Second Class | Sergeant | Staff Sergeant |
| E–6 | Staff Sergeant<br>Specialist 6 | Petty Officer, First Class | Staff Sergeant | Technical Sergeant |
| E–7 | Sergeant First Class<br>Specialist 7<br>Platoon Sergeant | Chief Petty Officer | Gunnery Sergeant | Master Sergeant |
| E–8 | First Sergeant<br>Master Sergeant | Senior Chief Petty Officer | First Sergeant<br>Master Sergeant | Senior Master Sergeant |
| E–9 | Command Sergeant Major<br>Sergeant Major | Master Chief Petty Officer | Sergeant Major<br>Master Gunnery Sergeant | Chief Master Sergeant |

## AMERICAN MILITARY CEMETERIES ON FOREIGN SOIL

SOURCE: The American Battle Monuments Commission

The American Battle Monuments Commission, an agency of the U.S. Government, is responsible to the people of the United States for the construction and permanent maintenance of military cemeteries and memorials on foreign soil, as well as for certain memorials on American soil. Monuments are located in Audenarde, Belgium; Bellicourt (Aisne), France; Brest (Finistère), France; Cantigny (Somme), France; Chateau-Thierry (Aisne), France; Gibraltar; Kemmel, Ypres, Belgium; Montfaucon (Meuse), France; Sommepy (Marne), France; Tours (Indre-et-Loire), France; Montsec, Thiaucourt (Meurthe and Moselle), France; and Pointe du Hoc (Calvados), France.

| Cemetery | Location | Size (acres) | Burials Known | Burials Unknown | Missing Commemorated |
|---|---|---|---|---|---|
| Aisne-Marne | Belleau (Aisne), France | 282.5 | 2,039 | 249 | 1,060 |
| Ardennes | Neupre (Neuville-en-Condroz), Belgium | 90.5 | 4,536 | 790 | 462 |
| Brittany | St. James (Manche), France | 27.5 | 4,313 | 97 | 497 |
| Brookwood | Surrey, England | 4.5 | 427 | 41 | 563 |
| Cambridge | Cambridge, England | 30.5 | 3,787 | 24 | 5,126 |
| Corozal | Panama City, Panama | 16 | 4,848 | 000 | 000 |
| Epinal | Epinal (Vosges), France | 46 | 5,186 | 69 | 424 |
| Flanders Field | Waregem, Belgium | 6 | 347 | 21 | 43 |
| Florence | Florence, Italy | 70 | 4,189 | 213 | 1,409 |
| Henri-Chapelle | Henri-Chapelle, Belgium | 57 | 7,895 | 94 | 450 |
| Lorraine | St. Avold (Moselle), France | 114 | 10,338 | 151 | 444 |
| Luxembourg | Luxembourg City, Luxembourg | 50.6 | 4,975 | 101 | 370 |
| Manila | Fort Bonifacio, Philippines | 152 | 13,462 | 3,744 | 36,280 |
| Meuse-Argonne | Romagne (Meuse), France | 130.6 | 13,760 | 486 | 954 |
| Mexico City | Mexico City, Mexico | 1 | 813 | 750 | 000 |
| Netherlands | Margraten, Holland | 65.5 | 8,195 | 106 | 1,722 |
| Normandy | Colleville/St. Laurent (Calvados), France | 172.3 | 9,079 | 307 | 1,557 |
| North Africa | Carthage, Tunisia | 27 | 2,601 | 240 | 3,724 |
| Oise-Aisne | Fere-en-Tardenois (Aisne), France | 36.5 | 5,415 | 597 | 241 |
| Rhone | Draguignan (Var), France | 12 | 799 | 62 | 293 |
| St. Mihiel | Thiaucourt (M. et M.), France | 40.3 | 4,036 | 117 | 284 |
| Sicily-Rome | Nettuno, Italy | 75 | 7,372 | 490 | 3,094 |
| Somme | Bony (Aisne), France | 14.3 | 1,707 | 137 | 333 |
| Suresnes | Suresnes (Seine), France | 7.5 | 1,535 | 30 | 974 |

## THE JOINT CHIEFS OF STAFF

Source: Office of the Assistant Secretary of Defense

| Chairman | From | | To | |
|---|---|---|---|---|
| Gen. Omar N. Bradley, USA | Aug. | 16, 1949 | Aug. | 14, 1953 |
| Adm. Arthur W. Radford, USN | Aug. | 15, 1953 | Aug. | 14, 1957 |
| Gen. Nathan F. Twining, USAF | Aug. | 15, 1957 | Sept. | 30, 1960 |
| Gen. Lyman L. Lemnitzer, USA | Oct. | 1, 1960 | Sept. | 30, 1962 |
| Gen. Maxwell D. Taylor, USA | Oct. | 1, 1962 | July | 3, 1964 |
| Gen. Earle G. Wheeler, USA | July | 3, 1964 | July | 2, 1970 |
| Adm. Thomas H. Moorer, USN | July | 2, 1970 | June | 30, 1974 |
| Gen. George S. Brown, USAF | July | 1, 1974 | June | 30, 1978 |
| Gen. David C. Jones, USAF | July | 1, 1978 | June | 30, 1982 |
| Gen. John W. Vassey | July | 1, 1982 | To Date | |
| **Chief of Staff, U.S. Army** | | | | |
| Gen. of the Army Dwight D. Eisenhower | Nov. | 19, 1945 | Feb. | 7, 1948 |
| Gen. Omar N. Bradley | Feb. | 17, 1948 | Aug. | 15, 1949 |
| Gen. J. Lawton Collins | Aug. | 16, 1949 | Aug. | 14, 1953 |
| Gen. Matthew B. Ridgway | Aug. | 15, 1953 | June | 30, 1955 |
| Gen. Maxwell D. Taylor | June | 30, 1955 | June | 30, 1959 |
| Gen. Lyman L. Lemnitzer | July | 1, 1959 | Sept. | 30, 1960 |
| Gen. George H. Decker | Sept. | 30, 1960 | Sept. | 30, 1962 |
| Gen. Earle G. Wheeler | Oct. | 1, 1962 | July | 3, 1964 |
| Gen. Harold K. Johnson | July | 3, 1964 | July | 3, 1968 |
| Gen. William C. Westmoreland | July | 3, 1968 | July | 1, 1972 |
| Gen. Creighton W. Abrams | Oct. | 16, 1972 | Sept. | 1974 |
| Gen. Fred C. Weyand | Oct. | 7, 1974 | Oct. | 1, 1976 |
| Gen. Bernard W. Rogers | Oct. | 1, 1976 | July | 1, 1979 |
| Gen. Edward C. Meyer | July | 1, 1979 | To Date | |
| **Chief of Naval Operations** | | | | |
| Fleet Adm. Chester W. Nimitz | Dec. | 5, 1945 | Dec. | 15, 1947 |
| Adm. Louis E. Denfeld | Dec. | 15, 1947 | Nov. | 2, 1949 |
| Adm. Forrest P. Sherman | Nov. | 2, 1949 | July | 22, 1951 |

| Chief of Naval Operations (Cont.) | From | | To | |
|---|---|---|---|---|
| Adm. William M. Fechteler | Aug. | 16, 1951 | Aug. | 17, 1953 |
| Adm. Robert B. Carney | Aug. | 17, 1953 | Aug. | 16, 1955 |
| Adm. Arleigh A. Burke | Aug. | 17, 1955 | Aug. | 1, 1961 |
| Adm. George W. Anderson | Aug. | 1, 1961 | July | 31, 1963 |
| Adm. David L. McDonald | Aug. | 1, 1963 | July | 31, 1967 |
| Adm. Thomas H. Moorer | Aug. | 1, 1967 | July | 1, 1970 |
| Adm. Elmo R. Zumwalt | July | 1, 1970 | June | 30, 1974 |
| Adm. James L. Holloway 3rd | July | 1, 1974 | June | 30, 1978 |
| Adm. Thomas C. Hayward | July | 1, 1978 | June | 30, 1982 |
| Adm. James D. Watkins | July | 1, 1982 | To Date | |
| **Chief of Staff, U.S. Air Force** | | | | |
| Gen. Carl Spaatz | Sept. | 26, 1947 | April | 29, 1948 |
| Gen. Hoyt S. Vandenberg | April | 30, 1948 | June | 29, 1953 |
| Gen. Nathan F. Twining | June | 30, 1953 | June | 30, 1957 |
| Gen. Thomas D. White | July | 1, 1957 | June | 30, 1961 |
| Gen. Curtis E. LeMay | June | 30, 1961 | Jan. | 31, 1965 |
| Gen. John P. McConnell | Feb. | 1, 1965 | Aug. | 1, 1969 |
| Gen. John D. Ryan | Aug. | 1, 1969 | July | 31, 1973 |
| Gen. George S. Brown | Aug. | 1, 1973 | June | 30, 1974 |
| Gen. David C. Jones | July | 1, 1974 | June | 30, 1978 |
| Gen. Lew Allen | July | 1, 1978 | June | 30, 1982 |
| Gen. Charles A. Gabriel | July | 1, 1982 | To Date | |
| **Commandant, U.S. Marine Corps** | | | | |
| Gen. Lemuel C. Shepherd | Dec. | 21, 1951 | Dec. | 31, 1955 |
| Gen. Randolph McC. Pate | Jan. | 1, 1956 | Dec. | 31, 1959 |
| Gen. David M. Shoup | Jan. | 1, 1960 | Dec. | 31, 1963 |
| Gen. Wallace M. Greene, Jr. | Jan. | 1, 1964 | Dec. | 31, 1967 |
| Gen. Leonard F. Chapman, Jr. | Jan. | 1, 1968 | Dec. | 31, 1971 |
| Gen. Robert E. Cushman, Jr. | Jan. | 1, 1972 | July | 1, 1975 |
| Gen. Louis H. Wilson | July | 1, 1975 | July | 1, 1979 |
| Gen. Robert H. Barrow | July | 1, 1979 | To Date | |

## U.S. CASUALTIES IN VIETNAM

Source: U.S. Department of Defense

47,752 U.S. military personnel were killed during the period 1961-1976 (June). Hospitalized wounded totaled 153,329. Casualties were highest during 1968, the year of the Tet offensive, with 14,589 killed and 46,796 wounded. Total casualties: 360,706.

## TOTAL COST ESTIMATES OF AMERICAN WARS, BY RANK

Source: James L. Clayton, University of Utah. (Data in millions of dollars)

| | Original Incremental Cost[1] | | SERVICE-CONNECTED VETERANS' BENEFITS | | INTEREST PAYMENTS ON WAR LOANS | |
|---|---|---|---|---|---|---|
| | Constant Dollars (1860) | Current dollars | Cost to Oct. 1, 1980[2] | Total Cost Under Present Programs | Total Cost to 1981[3] | Estimated Current Cost (1981)[4] |
| World War II | 195,000 | 360,000 | 61,187 | UKN | 200,000 | 621,200 |
| Vietnam Conflict | 32,600 | 140,600 | 11,103 | UKN | UKN | 151,700 |
| Korean Conflict | 17,600 | 50,000 | 9,951 | UKN | 0 | 60,000 |
| World War I | 17,600 | 32,700 | 13,615 | UKN | 11,000 | 57,300 |
| Civil War (Union) | 2,300 | 2,300 | 3,289 | 3,300 | 1,200 | 6,200 |
| Civil War (Confederacy) | 1,000 | 1,000 | 0 | UKN | UKN | UKN |
| Spanish-American War | 340 | 270 | 2,104 | 2,500 | 60 | 2,400 |
| American Revolution | 140-200 | 100-140 | 28 | 28 | 20 | 170 |
| War of 1812 | 50 | 87 | 20 | 20 | 14 | 120 |
| Mexican War | 90 | 82 | 26 | 26 | 10 | 120 |

1 Figures are rounded and taken from Claudia D. Goldin, *Encyclopedia of American Economic History*, p. 938. 2 For World War I and later wars, benefits are actual service-connected figures from 1980 Annual Report of the Veterans Admin. For earlier wars, service-connected veterans' benefits are estimated at 40% of total, the approximate ratio of service-connected to total benefits since World War I. 3 Interest payments are a very rough approximation based on the percentage of the original costs of each war financed by money creation and debt, the difference betweeen the level of public debt at the beginning of the war and at its end, and the approximate time required to pay off the war debts. 4 Figures are rounded. UKN = Unknown.

# VETERANS BENEFITS

SOURCE: Veterans Administration

**Benefits:** In order to qualify for most benefits, veterans must have been separated from the Armed Forces under conditions other than dishonorable.

**Compensation for Service-Connected Disability:** Veterans disabled by injury or disease incurred or aggravated during active service in the line of duty may be entitled to monthly payments ranging from $58, for a 10 percent disability, to $1,016 for total disability. Loss of, or loss of use of, certain limbs and organs entitles the disabled veteran to additional compensation, up to a maximum monthly payment of $3,223. Certain veterans who are at least 30 percent disabled are entitled to additional allowances for dependents.

**Pension:** Wartime veterans, including those of Mexican Border Service, World Wars I and II, the Korean conflict, and the Vietnam era who served 90 days or more, or—if less than 90 days—were discharged for a service-connected disability, and who are permanently and totally disabled for reasons not traceable to service, may be eligible for pension benefits. A veteran 65 years of age or older is considered totally and permanently disabled. Pension payment amounts depend upon other income. Veterans with dependents may be entitled to higher amounts.

**Medical Care:** Complete care in VA hospitals, and in some cases private hospitals, is authorized under a priority system for otherwise qualified veterans who require treatment of service-connected disabilities, have compensable disabilities but require treatment of nonservice-connected disabilities, and/or have no service-connected disabilities but require medical treatment (subject to financial need and availability of facilities). Other benefits authorized when certain conditions are met include domiciliary care; outpatient medical and dental treatment in VA field stations or, in some cases, by approved private physicians; fitting and training with prosthetic appliances; medical examinations; aid for the blind; and vocational rehabilitation.

**Educational Assistance—G.I. Bill:** Veterans who served on active duty for more than 180 continuous days, any part of which occurred after Jan. 31, 1955, but before Jan. 1, 1977, and who (a) were released under conditions other than dishonorable, (b) were discharged for a service-connected disability or (c) continue on active duty are eligible for educational assistance for a period of 1.5 months for each month served, up to 45 months. The full 45-month entitlement is earned after 18 months' service.

War orphans and surviving spouses are eligible for similar education benefits, and education benefits are also available to spouses and children of veterans who are permanently and totally disabled as the result of military service.

Educational institutions may include approved public and private secondary schools, junior or senior colleges, and vocational, scientific, or correspondence schools. Farm cooperative, on-the-job, and flight training are included. Eligibility ends ten years after release from active duty, but not later than Dec. 31, 1989.

Basic monthly payments to veterans enrolled in school courses: full time, no dependents, $342; one dependent, $407; two dependents, $464; and $29 for each additional.

A veteran who must complete elementary or high school training to qualify for higher education may receive this training without a charge against his basic entitlement.

**Contributory Plan:** Those who initially entered the service on or after Jan. 1, 1977, may participate by contributing $25 to $100 a month from their military pay, with a maximum contribution of $2,700. The VA then matches contributions at the rate of $2 for every $1 made by the participant. Payments from the fund may be received for school or training purposes for the number of months they contributed, or for 36 months, whichever is less.

**Home Loans:** The VA is authorized to guarantee home loans made to eligible veterans by private lenders. Such loans may be for the purpose of purchasing a conventionally constructed home or mobile home (with or without a lot), refinancing an existing home mortgage, purchasing a condominium unit, or buying a farm home. Loans may also be guaranteed for home improvement purposes, including the installation of a solar heating and/or cooling system or other weatherization improvements.

Eligibility requirements vary based on the period of service. For World War II, Korean Conflict and Vietnam veterans, active duty of at least 90 days' duration (unless discharged earlier for service-connected disability) and a discharge or separation under other than dishonorable conditions are required. Post-World War II, Post-Korean and Post-Vietnam veterans must have 181 days of active duty (unless discharged earlier for service-connected disability) and a discharge or separation under other than dishonorable conditions.

Service personnel who have served at least 181 continuous days in active duty status, though not discharged, are eligible while their service continues without a break.

Unmarried surviving spouses of veterans, including service personnel, who served during a period which occurred between September 16, 1940 and the present and who died as a result of service-connected disabilities are eligible for home loan purposes. Spouses of service personnel on active duty who are officially listed as missing in action or prisoners of war and have been in such status for more than 90 days are also eligible for home loan benefits. Spouses of POWs/MIAs are, however, limited to one loan.

Loan guaranty benefits are available to all eligible veterans and service personnel until used.

The VA may guarantee the lender against loss for up to 60 percent of the loan amount or $27,500, whichever is less, on all types of home loans, except for mobile home loans, for which the maximum guaranty is 50 percent of the loan amount, or $20,000, whichever is less.

There are no established loan maximums. However, no loan may exceed the property value established by VA.

Veterans who used their entitlement before October 1, 1978, may have additional entitlement available for GI home loan purposes. Veterans' maximum home loan entitlement was raised from $4,000 to $7,500 in 1950, to $12,500 in 1968, to $17,500 in 1974, to $25,000 in 1978, and to $27,500 in 1980. The amount of such additional entitlement is the difference between $25,000 and the amount used on prior home loans.

Certain veterans may meet the requirements for having used GI entitlement restored. A veteran may qualify for restoration if VA has been relieved of liability on the GI loan which normally is accomplished by the loan being paid in full and if the property has been disposed of; or if an immediate veteran-transferee agrees to substitute his or her entitlement for that of the original veteran-borrower and meets all other requirements for substitution of entitlement.

**Insurance:** Members of the uniformed services including Ready Reservists, Army and Air National Guards, ROTC members, Reservists eligible for assignment to Retired Reserves who have not received their first increment of retired pay or reached their 61st birthday, whichever is earlier; and the full-time duty cadet or midshipman at a service academy are eligible for Servicemen's Group Life Insurance. Maximum coverage is for $35,000 and premiums are deducted from service pay, except Retired Reservists, who must pay direct. Coverage continues for 120 days after discharge, within which period veterans can apply for automatic conversion of SGLI to a non-renewable 5-year term policy under Veterans Group Life Insurance which may be converted at the end of the 5-year period to an individual policy with a commercial company. For a member totally disabled the 120-day period is extended to one year or to the end of total disability, whichever is earlier.

**Dependency and Indemnity Compensation (DIC):** Payments are authorized for widows, widowers, unmarried children under 18, helpless children, children between 18 and 23 who are attending an approved school, and certain parents of a serviceman or veteran who died on or after January 1, 1957, from a disease or injury incurred or aggravated in the line of duty while on active duty, active or inactive duty for training, or from a disability otherwise compensable under VA-administered laws.

**Employment Preference and Reemployment Rights:** Veterans are entitled to certain preference over nonveterans in obtaining federal civil service jobs, in referral to training programs and job openings by state employment offices, and in restoration to a former job in private employment or with the federal government. The Department of Labor has jurisdiction over veteran employment.

**Burial:** A payment of up to $300 is authorized for the person incurring burial expenses for a veteran who was entitled to receive disability compensation or pension. Up to $1,100 will be payable when death is due to service-connected causes.

Burial is allowed in a national cemetery (except Arlington, Va.) for veterans whose last period of service terminated honorably, and for reservists who die while performing active-duty training. The benefit applies to the deceased person's spouse, minor children, and certain unmarried adult children. Effective August 1, 1973, an interment allowance not exceeding $150, in addition to the $300 basic burial allowance, is payable when burial is in other than a national cemetery.

## U.S. MILITARY AID: PROGRAM DELIVERIES: FISCAL YEARS 1950-1981

SOURCE: Department of Defense (figures in thousands of dollars)

| | 1950-81 |
|---|---|
| **Worldwide** | **$58,304,235** |
| Argentina | 184,197 |
| Australia | 2,003,153 |
| Austria | 156,792 |
| Bahrain | 2,501 |
| Belgium | 895,163 |
| Bolivia | 2,028 |
| Brazil | 269,932 |
| Brunei | 10 |
| Burma | 4,198 |
| Cameroon | 4,648 |
| Canada | 1,493,800 |
| Chile | 177,274 |
| China (Taiwan) | 1,591,321 |
| Colombia | 42,178 |
| Costa Rica | 1,472 |
| Cuba | 4,510 |
| Denmark | 596,379 |
| Dominican Republic | 2,287 |
| Ecuador | 51,899 |
| Egypt | 659,952 |
| El Salvador | 6,282 |
| Ethiopia | 87,086 |
| Fiji | 168 |
| Finland | 24 |
| France | 390,623 |
| Gabon | 2,239 |
| Germany, West | 6,765,853 |
| Ghana | 395 |
| Greece | 1,501,498 |
| Guatemala | 30,279 |
| Haiti | 1,300 |
| Honduras | 11,438 |
| Iceland | 538 |
| India | 76,327 |
| Indochina | 8,542 |
| Indonesia | 212,044 |
| Iran | 10,536,407 |
| Iraq | 13,152 |
| Ireland | 713 |
| Israel | 7,303,878 |
| Italy | 781,358 |
| Jamaica | 157 |
| Japan | 873,717 |
| Jordan | 848,502 |
| Kenya | 90,173 |
| Korea, South | 1,828,964 |
| Kuwait | 592,549 |
| Lebanon | 58,020 |
| Liberia | 4,326 |
| Libya | 28,250 |
| Luxembourg | 3,236 |
| Malaysia | 94,440 |
| Mali | 154 |
| Mexico | 22,374 |
| Morocco | 506,172 |
| Nepal | 73 |
| Netherlands | 1,047,088 |
| New Zealand | 141,722 |
| Nicaragua | 5,226 |
| Niger | 8 |
| Nigeria | 39,117 |
| Norway | 773,347 |
| Oman | 27,087 |
| Pakistan | 402,702 |
| Panama | 5,096 |
| Paraguay | 779 |
| Peru | 158,385 |
| Philippines | 157,218 |
| Portugal | 19,847 |
| Qatar | 104 |
| Saudi Arabia | 7,173,508 |
| Senegal | 6 |
| Singapore | 202,276 |
| Somalia | 3 |
| South Africa | 3,148 |
| Spain | 851,841 |
| Sri Lanka | 4 |
| Sudan | 85,742 |
| Suriname | 1 |
| Sweden | 83,020 |
| Switzerland | 642,582 |
| Syria | 1 |
| Thailand | 735,496 |
| Trinidad & Tobago | 99 |
| Tunisia | 85,168 |
| Turkey | 795,399 |
| United Arab Emirates | 4,927 |
| United Kingdom | 2,798,458 |
| Uruguay | 18,997 |
| Venezuela | 249,106 |
| Vietnam | 1,167 |
| Yemen | 244,453 |
| Yugoslavia | 14,941 |
| Zaire | 65,597 |
| International Organizations | 645,623 |

## NUCLEAR ARMAMENTS: UNITED STATES AND SOVIET UNION

SOURCE: International Institute for Strategic Studies, London

**United States**

| | Type[a] | Max. range (miles)[b] | Estimated Warhead yield[c] | Number deployed July 82 |
|---|---|---|---|---|
| **LAND-BASED MISSILES** | | | | |
| ICBM | Titan II | 9,000 | 9 MT | 52 |
| | Minuteman II | 7,000 | 1-2 MT | 450 |
| | Minuteman III | 8,000 | 3 × 165 KT | 250 |
| | | [f] | 3 × 335 KT | 300 |
| SRBM | Pershing | 450 | KT-range | 108[g] |
| | Lance | 70 | KT-range | 36[g] |
| **SEA-LAUNCHED MISSILES** | | | | |
| SLBM | Poseidon C3 | 2,860 | 10 × 50 KT | 304 |
| | Trident C4 | 4,600 | 8 × 100 KT | 216 |
| **AIR-LAUNCHED MISSILES** | | | | |
| ALCM | SRAM | 35-100 | KT range | 1,250 |

**Soviet Union**

| | Type[a] [d] | Max. range (miles)[b] | Estimated Warhead yield[c] | Number deployed July 82 |
|---|---|---|---|---|
| **LAND-BASED MISSILES** | | | | |
| ICBM | SS-11 Sego | 6,500 | 1 MT[e] | 570 |
| | SS-13 Savage | 6,200 | KT range | 60 |
| | SS-17 | 6,200 | 4 × 750 KT | 150 |
| | SS-18 | 5,700+ | 20 MT[e] | 308 |
| | SS-19 | 6,300+ | 5 MT[e] | 310 |
| M/IRBM | SS-4 Sandal | 1,200 | 1 MT | 275 |
| | SS-5 Skean | 2,500 | 1 MT | 16 |
| | SS-20 | 3-4,500 | 50 KT-1.5 MT | 315 |
| SRBM | SS-1b Scud A | 90 | KT range } | 450 |
| | SS-1c Scud B | 100-190 | KT range } | |
| | FROG 7 | 45 | KT range | 482 |
| | SS-12 Scaleboard | 300-550 | KT range | 70 |
| | SS-21 | 75 | [f] | 10[h] |
| | SS-22 | 600 | KT range | 100[h] |
| | SS-23 | 220 | [f] | 10[h] |
| GLCM | SS-C-1b Sepal | 280 | KT range | 100[h] |
| **SEA-LAUNCHED MISSILES** | | | | |
| SLBM | SS-N-5 Serb | 870 | 1 MT | 57 |
| | SS-N-6 Sawfly | 1,500+ | 1 MT[e] | 400 |
| | SS-N-8 | 4,800+ | 1 MT | 292 |
| | SS-NX-17 | 2,400 | 1 MT[e] | 12 |
| | SS-N-18 | 4,000+ | KT range | 208 |
| | SS-NX-20 | 5,000 | [f] | 20 |
| SLCM | SS-N-3 Shaddock | 280 | KT range | 356 |
| | SS-N-7 Siren | 30 | KT range | 154 |
| | SS-N-9 | 175 | KT range | 136 |
| | SS-N-12 Sandbox | 340-620 | KT range | 32 |
| | SS-N-14 Silex | 35 | KT range | 292 |
| | SS-N-19 | 280 | [f] | 44 |
| **AIR-LAUNCHED MISSILES** | | | | |
| ALCM | AS-2 Kipper | 125 | KT range | [f] |
| | AS-3 Kangaroo | 400 | MT range | 70[h] |
| | AS-4 Kitchen | 190 | KT range | 180[h] |
| | AS-6 Kingfish | 160 | KT range | 65[h] |

### HISTORICAL CHANGES FOR STRENGTH, 1972-1982 (MID-YEARS)

| | | 1972 | 1973 | 1974 | 1975 | 1976 | 1977 | 1978 | 1979 | 1980 | 1981 | 1982 |
|---|---|---|---|---|---|---|---|---|---|---|---|---|
| USA | ICBM | 1,054 | 1,054 | 1,054 | 1,054 | 1,054 | 1,054 | 1,054 | 1,054 | 1,054 | 1,052 | 1,052 |
| | SLBM | 656 | 656 | 656 | 656 | 656 | 656 | 656 | 656 | 656 | 576 | 520 |
| | Long-range bombers[i] | 390 | 397 | 397 | 397 | 387 | 373 | 366 | 365 | 338 | 316 | 316 |
| USSR | ICBM | 1,527 | 1,575 | 1,618 | 1,527 | 1,477 | 1,350 | 1,400 | 1,398 | 1,398 | 1,398 | 1,398 |
| | SLBM | 500 | 628 | 720 | 784 | 845 | 909 | 1,028 | 1,028 | 1,028 | 989 | 989 |
| | Long-range bombers | 140 | 140 | 140 | 135 | 135 | 135 | 135 | 156 | 156 | 150 | 150 |

[a] ICBM = inter-continental ballistic missile (range over 4,000 miles); M/IRBM = medium/intermediate-range ballistic missile (500-4,000 miles); SRBM = short-range ballistic missile (under 500 miles); LRCM = long-range cruise missile (over 350 miles); SLBM = submarine-launched ballistic missile; SLCM = submarine-launched cruise missile; ALCM = air-launched cruise missile; GLCM = ground launched cruise missile. [b] Operational range depends upon payload carried; figures are given in statute miles. [c] MT = megaton = millions tons of TNT equivalent (MT range = 1 MT or over); KT = kiloton = thousands tons of TNT equivalent (KT range = less than 1 MT); 3 ×, 10 × = 3 warheads, 10 warheads. [d] Numerical designation of Soviet missiles are of U.S. origin; names are of NATO origin. [e] Also exists in multiple warhead mode with lesser yield per warhead. [f] Information not available. [g] Figures for systems in Europe only. [h] Estimate. [i] Reserves not included.

## WARPLANES: UNITED STATES AND THE SOVIET UNION

**United States**

| AIRCRAFT | Type | Max. range (statute miles) | Max. speed (Mach no.) | Max. weapons load (lb.) | Number deployed (July 1982) |
|---|---|---|---|---|---|
| Long-range bombers | B-52 D | 6,000 | 0.95 | 60,000 | 75 |
| | B-52 G | 7,500 | 0.95 | 70,000 | 151 |
| | B-52 H | 10,000 | 0.95 | 70,000 | 90 |
| Medium-range bombers | FB-111A | 2,900 | 2.5 | 37,500 | 60 |
| Strike aircraft (incl. short-range bombers): land-based | F-4 C/D/E | 1,400 | 2.4 | 16,000 | 198 |
| | F-111 E/F | 2,900 | 2.2-2.5 | 28,000 | 156 |
| | F-16 | 2,300 | 2.0+ | 20,000 | 48 |
| Strike aircraft: carrier-based | A-6 E | 2,000 | 0.9 | 18,000 | 60[k] |
| | A-7 E | 1,750 | 0.9 | 20,000 | 144[k] |

**Soviet Union**

| Type | Max. range (statute miles) | Max. speed (Mach no.) | Max. weapons load (lb.) | Number deployed (July 1982) |
|---|---|---|---|---|
| Tu-95 Bear | 8,000 | 0.78 | 40,000 | 105 |
| Mya-4 Bison | 7,000 | 0.87 | 20,000 | 45[k] |
| Tu-22M/-26 Backfire | 5,000 | 2.5 | 17,500 | 180 |
| Tu-16 Badger | 3,000 | 0.8 | 20,000 | 580 |
| Tu-22 Blinder | 2,500 | 1.5 | 12,000 | 165 |
| Su-7 Fitter A | 850 | 1.7 | 5,500 | 150 |
| MiG-21 Fishbed | 700 | 2.2 | 2,000 | 100 |
| MiG-27 Flogger D | 900 | 1.7 | 7,500 | 550 |
| Su-19/-24 Fencer | 2,500 | 2.3 | 8,000 | 550 |
| Su-17/-20 Fitter C/D | 1,100 | 1.6 | 11,000 | 650 |
| (no carrier-based strike aircraft) | | | | |

## WARPLANES: NATO AND WARSAW PACT COUNTRIES

**NATO** (excluding U.S.)

| AIRCRAFT[a] | Type[c] | Operated by[d] | Max. range[e] (statute miles) | Max. speed (Mach no.)[f] | Max. weapons load (lb) | No. deployed (July 1982) |
|---|---|---|---|---|---|---|
| Medium-range bombers | Vulcan B2[b] | BR | 4,000 | 0.95 | 21,000 | 48 |
| Strike aircraft: land-based | F-104 | h | 1,500 | 2.2 | 4,000 | 290[j] |
| | F-4 | BR, GE, GR | 1,400 | 2.4 | 16,000 | 172[j] |
| | F-16 | BE | 2,300 | 2.0+ | 20,000 | 20 |
| | Buccaneer | BR | 2,300 | 0.95 | 12,000 | 50[j] |
| | Mirage IV A | FR | 2,000 | 2.2 | 16,000 | 34[j] |
| | Mirage III E | FR | 1,500 | 1.8 | 19,000 | 30[j] |
| | Jaguar | BR FR | 1,000 | 1.4 | 10,000 | 117[j] |
| carrier-based | Super Etendard | FR | 900 | 1.0 | 16,000 | 36[j] |

**Warsaw Pact** (excluding U.S.S.R.)

| Type[g] | Operated by[d] | Max. range[e] (statute miles) | Max. speed (Mach no.)[f] | Max. weapons load (lb) | No. deployed (July 1982) |
|---|---|---|---|---|---|
| Su-7 Fitter A[i] | CZ, PO | 900 | 1.7 | 5,500 | 115 |
| Su-20 Fitter C[i] | PO | 1,100 | 1.6 | 4,000 | 35 |

[a] All aircraft listed are dual-capable and many would be more likely to carry conventional than nuclear weapons. [b] To be replaced by Tornado. [c] Vulcan and Buccaneer are of British origin; F-104, F-16 and F-4 are of American origin; Mirage is of French origin; Jaguar is Anglo-French. [d] BR = Britain, FR = France, CZ = Czechoslovakia; HU = Hungary, PO = Poland, GE = West Germany, GR = Greece, BE = Belgium. [e] Theoretical maximum range, with internal fuel only, at optimum altitude and speed. Ranges for strike aircraft assume no weapons load. Especially in the case of strike aircraft, therefore, range falls sharply for flights at lower altitudes, at higher speed or with full weapons load (e.g. combat radius of F-104, at operational height and speed, with typical weapons load, is approximately 420 miles). [f] Mach 1 (M = 1.0) = speed of sound. [g] Warsaw Pact aircraft of Soviet origin; names (e.g. Fitter) of NATO origin. [h] The dual-capable F-104 is operated by Belgium, West Germany, Greece, Italy, the Netherlands and Turkey. The warheads for all of these aircraft are held in American custody. [i] Nuclear warheads for these dual-capable aircraft are held in Soviet custody. [j] Uncertain as to how many of these nuclear-capable aircraft actually have a nuclear role. [k] Estimate.

## ACTIVE U.S. MILITARY FORCES

Source: U.S. Office of Management and Budget

| Description | Actual Sept. 30 1981 | Estimated Sept. 30 1982 | Estimated Sept. 30 1983 |
|---|---|---|---|
| **Military personnel (in thousands):** | | | |
| End strength: | | | |
| Army | 781 | 784 | 784 |
| Navy | 540 | 553 | 569 |
| Marine Corps | 191 | 192 | 195 |
| Air Force | 570 | 581 | 600 |
| Total, Department of Defense | 2,082 | 2,110 | 2,148 |
| Average strength: | | | |
| Army | 775 | 783 | 782 |
| Navy | 536 | 544 | 558 |
| Marine Corps | 188 | 190 | 194 |
| Air Force | 564 | 577 | 592 |
| Total, Department of Defense | 2,064 | 2,094 | 2,125 |
| General purpose forces: | | | |
| Land forces: | | | |
| Army divisions | 16 | 16 | 16 |
| Marine Corps divisions | 3 | 3 | 3 |
| Tactical air forces: | | | |
| Air Force wings | 26 | 26 | 26 |
| Navy attack wings | 12 | 12 | 13 |
| Marine Corps wings | 3 | 3 | 3 |
| Naval forces: | | | |
| Attack and multipurpose carriers | 12 | 13 | 13 |
| Nuclear attack submarines | 81[1] | 90[1] | 93[1] |
| Other warships | 196 | 207 | 219 |
| Amphibious assault ships | 59 | 59 | 60 |

[1] Includes ex-Polaris ships operating as attack submarines.

## BLACKS IN U.S. ARMED FORCES

SOURCE: U.S. Department of Defense (as of December 1981)

| | Officers | | Enlisted | | TOTAL | |
|---|---|---|---|---|---|---|
| ARMY | 8,163 | (8.0%) | 224,576 | (33.1%) | 232,739 | (29.9%) |
| NAVY | 1,826 | (2.8%) | 57,267 | (12.1%) | 59,093 | (11.0%) |
| AIR FORCE | 4,924 | (4.9%) | 78,123 | (16.6%) | 83,047 | (14.5%) |
| MARINE CORPS | 739 | (4.0%) | 37,436 | (21.7%) | 38,175 | (20.0%) |
| TOTAL | 15,652 | (5.5%) | 397,402 | (22.2%) | 413,054 | (19.9%) |

## THE MILITARY-INDUSTRIAL COMPLEX

SOURCE: U.S. Department of Defense

Companies doing more than $250,000,000 worth of business with the Department of Defense during the 1981 fiscal year, in thousands of dollars.

| Rank | Company Name | 1981 Contracts | % of Total |
|---|---|---|---|
| 1. | McDonnell Douglass Corp. | $4,409,474 | 4.53 |
| 2. | United Technologies Corp. | 3,775,591 | 3.88 |
| 3. | General Dynamics Corp. | 3,402,481 | 3.49 |
| 4. | General Electric Co. | 2,954,734 | 3.03 |
| 5. | Boeing Co. | 2,682,732 | 2.75 |
| 6. | Lockheed Corp. | 2,656,574 | 2.73 |
| 7. | Hughes Aircraft Co. | 2,552,412 | 2.62 |
| 8. | Raytheon Co. | 1,825,945 | 1.87 |
| 9. | Grumman Corp. | 1,710,366 | 1.76 |
| 10. | Chrysler Corp. | 1,414,367 | 1.45 |
| 11. | Litton Industries, Inc. | 1,384,936 | 1.42 |
| 12. | Martin Marietta Corp. | 1,286,994 | 1.32 |
| 13. | Philbro Corp. | 1,223,067 | 1.26 |
| 14. | Exxon Corp. | 1,152,237 | 1.18 |
| 15. | Tenneco Inc. | 1,151,321 | 1.18 |
| 16. | Rockwell International Corp. | 1,125,967 | 1.16 |
| 17. | Westinghouse Electric Corp. | 1,124,748 | 1.15 |
| 18. | FMC Corp. | 1,052,488 | 1.08 |
| 19. | Standard Oil Co. of Calif. | 971,790 | 1.00 |
| 20. | Sperry Corp. | 928,144 | 0.95 |
| 21. | RCA Corp. | 876,826 | 0.90 |
| 22. | Honeywell Inc. | 838,212 | 0.86 |
| 23. | IBM Co. | 804,578 | 0.83 |
| 24. | American Tel. & Tel. Co. | 694,701 | 0.71 |
| 25. | Texas Instruments Inc. | 625,080 | 0.64 |
| 26. | Northrop Corp. | 623,014 | 0.64 |
| 27. | General Motors Corp. | 621,618 | 0.64 |
| 28. | Coastal Corp. | 616,426 | 0.63 |
| 29. | Motor Oil Hellas | 583,470 | 0.60 |
| 30. | Singer Co. | 564,537 | 0.58 |
| 31. | LTV Corp. | $548,396 | 0.56 |
| 32. | Atlantic Richfield Co. | 547,383 | 0.56 |
| 33. | Ford Motor Co. | 543,644 | 0.56 |
| 34. | TRW Inc. | 516,575 | 0.53 |
| 35. | Teledyne Inc. | 498,552 | 0.51 |
| 36. | Guam Oil & Refining Co. Inc. | 496,477 | 0.51 |
| 37. | AVCO Corp. | 492,739 | 0.51 |
| 38. | Textron Inc. | 478,987 | 0.49 |
| 39. | Todd Shipyards Corp. | 472,151 | 0.48 |
| 40. | Bendix Corp. | 458,285 | 0.47 |
| 41. | Fairchild Industries, Inc. | 457,662 | 0.47 |
| 42. | Amerada Hess Corp. | 448,182 | 0.46 |
| 43. | General Tel. & Tel. Corp. | 426,295 | 0.44 |
| 44. | Vinnell Corp. | 409,591 | 0.42 |
| 45. | North American Philips Corp. | 406,649 | 0.42 |
| 46. | Mobil Corp. | 385,616 | 0.40 |
| 47. | Congoleum Corp. | 382,985 | 0.39 |
| 48. | International Tel. & Tel. Corp. | 379,896 | 0.39 |
| 49. | R.J. Reynolds Industries Inc. | 379,852 | 0.39 |
| 50. | Texaco Inc. | 379,683 | 0.39 |
| 51. | Goodyear Tire & Rubber Co. | 341,608 | 0.35 |
| 52. | American Motors Corp. | 326,728 | 0.34 |
| 53. | Al Huseini | 323,890 | 0.33 |
| 54. | General Tire & Rubber Co. | 321,822 | 0.33 |
| 55. | Hercules, Inc. | 281,123 | 0.29 |
| 56. | AGIP SPA | 278,594 | 0.29 |
| 57. | E Systems, Inc. | 275,001 | 0.28 |
| 58. | Harris Corp. | 263,789 | 0.27 |

## ARMED FORCES OF THE WORLD: 1979

SOURCE: U.S. Arms Control and Disarmament Agency (in thousands)

| Country | Active-duty Military Personnel |
|---|---|
| Afghanistan | 40 |
| Albania | 53 |
| Algeria | 89 |
| Angola | 47 |
| Argentina | 155 |
| Australia | 71 |
| Austria | 40 |
| Bangladesh | 72 |
| Belgium | 88 |
| Bolivia | 20 |
| Brazil | 450 |
| Bulgaria | 164 |
| Burma | 174 |
| Burundi | 8 |
| Cambodia | N.A. |
| Cameroon | 11 |
| Canada | 80 |
| Chad | N.A. |
| Chile | 111 |
| China, People's Rep. | 4,500 |
| China, Rep. of | 475 |
| Colombia | 60 |
| Congo | 16 |
| Cuba | 210 |
| Cyprus | 15 |
| Czechoslovakia | 211 |
| Denmark | 34 |
| Dominican Republic | 19 |
| Ecuador | 35 |
| Egypt | 395 |
| El Salvador | 10.5 |
| Equatorial Guinea | 2 |
| Ethiopia | 250 |
| Finland | 36 |
| France | 522 |
| German Dem. Rep. | 228 |
| Germany, Fed. Rep. | 470 |
| Ghana | 15 |
| Greece | 182 |
| Guatemala | 14 |
| Guinea | 18 |
| Guinea-Bissau | 6 |
| Guyana | 7 |
| Haiti | 7 |
| Honduras | 13.5 |
| Hungary | 110 |
| India | 1,104 |
| Indonesia | 242 |
| Iran | 415 |
| Iraq | 212 |
| Ireland | 14 |
| Israel | 165 |
| Italy | 366 |
| Ivory Coast | 6 |
| Japan | 241 |
| Jordan | 67 |
| Kenya | 13 |
| Korea, Dem. People's Rep. | 678 |
| Korea, Rep. of | 600 |
| Kuwait | 11 |
| Laos | 55 |
| Liberia | 7 |
| Libya | 53 |
| Madagascar | 20 |
| Malawi | 5 |
| Malaysia | 66 |
| Mali | 5 |
| Malta | 6 |
| Mauritania | 7.5 |
| Mexico | 145 |
| Mongolia | 36 |
| Morocco | 98 |
| Mozambique | 24 |
| Nepal | 22 |
| Netherlands | 101 |
| New Zealand | 12.7 |
| Nicaragua | N.A. |
| Nigeria | 164 |
| Norway | 36 |
| Oman | 19 |
| Pakistan | 439 |
| Panama | 8 |
| Paraguay | 15 |
| Peru | 125 |
| Philippines | 113 |
| Poland | 425 |
| Portugal | 64 |
| Qatar | 5 |
| Romania | 218 |
| Saudi Arabia | 50 |
| Senegal | 8 |
| Singapore | 60 |
| Somalia | 54 |
| South Africa | 70 |
| Spain | 349 |
| Sri Lanka | 15 |
| Sudan | 65 |
| Sweden | 68 |
| Switzerland | 23 |
| Syria | 250 |
| Tanzania | 53 |
| Thailand | 230 |
| Togo | 4 |
| Tunisia | 24 |
| Turkey | 583 |
| Uganda | 6 |
| USSR | 4,800 |
| United Arab Emirates | 25 |
| United Kingdom | 320 |
| UNITED STATES | 2,024 |
| Upper Volta | 4 |
| Uruguay | 28 |
| Venezuela | 55 |
| Vietnam | 750 |
| Yemen Arab Rep. | 36 |
| Yemen, P.D.R. | 20 |
| Yugoslavia | 260 |
| Zaire | 23 |
| Zambia | 20 |
| Zimbabwe | 22 |

# EDUCATION: FACTS/FIGURES

## EXPENDITURES FOR PUBLIC ELEMENTARY AND SECONDARY SCHOOL EDUCATION

SOURCE: National Center for Education Statistics

| School year | Total | Total per pupil |
|---|---|---|
| 1929/1930 | $ 2,316,790,000 | $108 |
| 1939/1940 | 2,344,049,000 | 106 |
| 1949/1950 | 5,837,643,000 | 259 |
| 1953/1954 | 9,092,449,000 | 351 |
| 1955/1956 | 10,955,047,000 | 388 |
| 1957/1958 | 13,569,163,000 | 449 |
| 1959/1960 | 15,613,255,000 | 472 |
| 1961/1962 | 18,373,339,000 | 530 |
| 1963/1964 | $21,324,993,000 | $ 559 |
| 1965/1966 | 26,248,026,000 | 654 |
| 1967/1968 | 32,977,182,000 | 786 |
| 1969/1970 | 40,683,428,000 | 955 |
| 1971/1972 | 48,050,283,000 | 1,128 |
| 1973/1974 | 56,970,355,000 | 1,364 |
| 1975/1976 | 70,600,573,000 | 1,697 |
| 1977/1978 | 80,844,366,000 | 2,002 |
| 1979/1980[1] | 95,961,561,000 | 2,494 |
| 1980/1981[2] | 103,100,000,000 | 2,710 |

[1] Preliminary Date. [2]Estimated.

## HIGH SCHOOL GRADUATES

SOURCE: National Center for Education Statistics

| School year | Population 17 years old | High school graduates: Total | Boys | Girls |
|---|---|---|---|---|
| 1889/1890 | 1,259,177 | **43,731** | 18,549 | 25,182 |
| 1899/1900 | 1,489,146 | **94,883** | 38,075 | 56,808 |
| 1909/1910 | 1,786,240 | **156,429** | 63,676 | 92,753 |
| 1919/1920 | 1,855,173 | **311,266** | 123,684 | 187,582 |
| 1929/1930 | 2,295,822 | **666,904** | 300,376 | 366,528 |
| 1939/1940 | 2,403,074 | **1,221,475** | 578,718 | 642,757 |
| 1949/1950 | 2,034,450 | **1,199,700** | 570,700 | 629,000 |
| 1951/1952 | 2,040,800 | **1,196,500** | 569,200 | 627,300 |
| 1953/1954 | 2,128,600 | **1,276,100** | 612,500 | 663,600 |
| 1955/1956 | 2,270,000 | **1,414,800** | 679,500 | 735,300 |
| 1957/1958 | 2,324,000 | **1,505,900** | 725,500 | 780,400 |
| 1959/1960 | 2,862,005 | **1,864,000** | 898,000 | 966,000 |
| 1961/1962 | 2,768,000 | **1,925,000** | 941,000 | 984,000 |
| 1963/1964 | 3,001,000 | **2,290,000** | 1,121,000 | 1,169,000 |
| 1965/1966 | 3,515,000 | **2,632,000** | 1,308,000 | 1,324,000 |
| 1966/1967 | 3,518,000 | **2,679,000** | 1,331,000 | 1,348,000 |
| 1967/1968 | 3,521,000 | **2,702,000** | 1,341,000 | 1,361,000 |
| 1968/1969 | 3,622,000 | **2,839,000** | 1,408,000 | 1,431,000 |
| 1969/1970 | 3,825,343 | **2,896,000** | 1,433,000 | 1,463,000 |
| 1970/1971 | 3,859,000 | **3,036,000** | 1,506,000 | 1,530,000 |
| 1971/1972 | 3,957,000 | **3,006,000** | 1,490,000 | 1,516,000 |
| 1972/1973 | 4,024,000 | **3,037,000** | 1,501,000 | 1,536,000 |
| 1973/1974 | 4,096,000 | **3,080,000** | 1,515,000 | 1,565,000 |
| 1974/1975 | 4,210,000 | **3,140,000** | 1,541,000 | 1,599,000 |
| 1975/1976 | 4,215,000 | **3,155,000** | 1,554,000 | 1,601,000 |
| 1976/1977 | 4,206,000 | **3,161,000** | 1,550,000 | 1,611,000 |
| 1977/1978 | 4,208,000 | **3,147,000** | 1,541,000 | 1,606,000 |
| 1978/1979 | 4,238,000 | **3,134,000** | 1,532,000 | 1,602,000 |
| 1979/1980 | 4,162,000 | **3,063,000** | 1,502,000 | 1,561,000 |
| 1980/1981[1] | 4,100,000 | **3,021,000** | 1,480,000 | 1,541,000 |

[1] Estimated.

## COLLEGE AND UNIVERSITY GRADUATES

SOURCE: National Center for Education Statistics

| School year | Degrees conferred: All degrees | Bachelor's and First Professional | Master's | Doctor's |
|---|---|---|---|---|
| 1869/1870 | **9,372** | 9,371 | 0 | 1 |
| 1889/1890 | **16,703** | 15,539 | 1,015 | 149 |
| 1899/1900 | **29,375** | 27,410 | 1,583 | 382 |
| 1909/1910 | **39,755** | 37,199 | 2,113 | 443 |
| 1919/1920 | **53,516** | 48,622 | 4,279 | 615 |
| 1929/1930 | **139,752** | 122,484 | 14,969 | 2,299 |
| 1939/1940 | **216,521** | 186,500 | 26,731 | 3,290 |
| 1949/1950 | **496,661** | 432,058 | 58,183 | 6,420 |
| 1953/1954 | **356,608** | 290,825 | 56,788 | 8,995 |
| 1955/1956 | **376,973** | 308,812 | 59,258 | 8,903 |
| 1957/1958 | **436,979** | 362,554 | 65,487 | 8,938 |
| 1959/1960 | **476,704** | 392,440 | 74,435 | 9,829 |
| 1961/1962 | **514,323** | 417,846 | 84,855 | 11,622 |
| 1963/1964 | **614,194** | 498,654 | 101,050 | 14,490 |
| 1965/1966 | **709,832** | 551,040 | 140,555 | 18,237 |
| 1966/1967 | **768,871** | 590,548 | 157,706 | 20,617 |
| 1967/1968 | **866,548** | 666,710 | 176,749 | 23,089 |
| 1968/1969 | **984,129** | 764,185 | 193,756 | 26,188 |
| 1969/1970 | **1,065,391** | 827,234 | 208,291 | 29,866 |
| 1970/1971 | **1,140,292** | 877,676 | 230,509 | 32,107 |
| 1971/1972 | **1,215,680** | 930,684 | 251,633 | 33,363 |
| 1972/1973 | **1,270,528** | 972,380 | 263,371 | 34,777 |
| 1973/1974 | **1,310,441** | 999,592 | 277,033 | 33,816 |
| 1974/1975 | **1,305,382** | 978,849 | 292,450 | 34,083 |
| 1975/1976 | **1,334,230** | 988,395 | 311,771 | 34,064 |
| 1976/1977 | **1,334,304** | 983,908 | 317,164 | 33,232 |
| 1977/1978 | **1,331,536** | 987,785 | 311,620 | 32,131 |
| 1978/1979 | **1,324,047** | 990,238 | 301,079 | 32,730 |
| 1979/1980 | **1,330,297** | 999,601 | 298,081 | 32,615 |
| 1980/1981[1] | **1,334,600** | 1,003,700 | 298,000 | 32,900 |

[1] Estimated.

## EDUCATION AND INCOME

SOURCE: U.S. Bureau of the Census (based on 1980 data)

| Income Levels | Percent of Male Income Recipients* | School Years Completed** |
|---|---|---|
| $1 to $1,999 or less | 3.2 | 12.1 |
| $2,000 to $2,999 | 2.5 | 9.2 |
| $3,000 to $3,999 | 3.4 | 9.2 |
| $4,000 to $4,999 | 3.7 | 10.4 |
| $5,000 to $5,999 | 3.5 | 11.2 |
| $6,000 to $6,999 | 3.4 | 11.6 |
| $7,000 to $8,499 | 5.6 | 12.0 |
| $8,500 to $9,999 | 4.8 | 12.2 |
| $10,000 to $12,499 | 10.3 | 12.4 |
| $12,500 to $14,999 | 7.6 | 12.5 |
| $15,000 to $17,499 | 9.0 | 12.7 |
| $17,500 to $19,999 | 7.4 | 12.8 |
| $20,000 to $24,999 | 13.7 | 12.9 |
| $25,000 to $29,999 | 8.8 | 13.0 |
| $30,000 to $34,999 | 4.8 | 14.3 |
| $35,000 to $49,999 | 5.3 | 16.2 |
| $50,000 to $74,999 | 2.2 | 16.6 |
| $75,000 and over | 0.9 | 16.9 |

* Males 25 years old and over. ** Median

## ELEMENTARY AND SECONDARY SCHOOLS

SOURCE: National Center for Education Statistics

In the school year 1980–81, there were approximately 16,000 public school systems in the United States that included about 62,000 public elementary schools and 24,500 public secondary schools. As the accompanying table indicates, the number of school districts and public elementary schools has been declining, with a more rapid drop in the number of districts. However, since WWII, the number of pupils per school has risen substantially. In addition to the public schools, there are about 16,800 nonpublic elementary schools and 5,600 nonpublic secondary schools in the country.

| School Year | Districts | PUBLIC SCHOOLS Elementary | PUBLIC SCHOOLS Secondary | NONPUBLIC SCHOOLS* Elementary | NONPUBLIC SCHOOLS* Secondary |
|---|---|---|---|---|---|
| 1945–46 | 101,382 | 160,227 | 24,314 | 9,863 | 3,294 |
| 1949–50 | 83,718 | 128,225 | 24,542 | 10,375 | 3,331 |
| 1955–56 | 54,859 | 104,427 | 26,046 | 12,372 | 3,887 |
| 1959–60 | 40,520 | 91,853 | 25,784 | 13,574 | 4,061 |
| 1965–66 | 26,983 | 73,216 | 26,597 | 15,340 | 4,606 |
| 1970–71 | 17,995 | 65,800 | 25,352 | 14,372 | 3,770 |
| 1972–73 | 16,960 | 64,945 | 25,922 | NA | NA |
| 1973–74 | 16,730 | 65,070 | 25,906 | NA | NA |
| 1974–75 | 16,570 | 63,619[1] | 25,697[1] | NA | NA |
| 1975–76 | 16,376 | 63,242[1] | 25,330[1] | NA | NA |
| 1976–77 | 16,271 | 62,644[1] | 25,378[1] | 16,385 | 5,904 |
| 1978–79 | 16,014 | 61,982[1] | 24,504[1] | 16,097 | 5,766 |
| 1980–81 | 15,912 | NA | NA | 16,771 | 5,607 |

* Data for most years are partly estimated.
[1] Excludes schools not reported by level, such as special education schools for the handicapped.
NA = Not available.

## EDUCATION AND INCOME

SOURCE: U.S. Bureau of the Census

MEDIAN INCOME OF FULL-TIME YEAR-ROUND WORKERS, 25 YEARS OLD AND OVER, BY EDUCATIONAL ATTAINMENT

| | | Median Income, 1980 Male | Median Income, 1980 Female |
|---|---|---|---|
| Elementary: | Total | $13,117 | $ 8,216 |
| | Less than 8 years | 11,753 | 7,742 |
| | 8 years | 14,674 | 8,857 |
| High school: | Total | 18,669 | 11,252 |
| | 1 to 3 years | 16,101 | 9,676 |
| | 4 years | 19,469 | 11,537 |
| College: | 1 or more years | 23,454 | 14,831 |
| | 5 or more years | 27,690 | 18,100 |

MEDIAN INCOME OF MEN 25 YEARS OLD AND OVER, BY EDUCATIONAL ATTAINMENT

| | | Median Income, 1980 Black | White | All Races |
|---|---|---|---|---|
| Elementary: | Total | $ 4,994 | $ 7,906 | $ 7,444 |
| | Less than 8 years | 4,686 | 7,004 | 6,381 |
| | 8 years | 6,623 | 8,948 | 8,732 |
| High school: | Total | 10,986 | 15,505 | 14,958 |
| | 1 to 3 years | 9,172 | 12,053 | 11,536 |
| | 4 years | 12,074 | 16,622 | 16,211 |
| College: | 1 or more years | 14,735 | 21,189 | 20,806 |
| | 5 or more years | 20,741 | 25,368 | 25,234 |

## U.S. PUBLIC LIBRARIES—1978 (with over one million volumes)

U.S. Department of Health, Education, and Welfare, National Center for Education Statistics.

| Library | Number of Volumes* |
|---|---|
| New York Public Library | 8,275,240 |
| Chicago Public Library | 6,214,748 |
| Los Angeles Public Library | 5,236,538 |
| Boston Public Library | 4,236,364 |
| Cleveland Public Library | 3,535,967 |
| Queens Borough Public Library (N.Y.) | 3,506,309 |
| Brooklyn Public Library | 3,452,709 |
| Cincinnati-Hamilton County Public Library | 3,318,683 |
| Free Library of Philadelphia | 3,040,254 |
| Buffalo & Erie County Library System | 3,010,577 |
| Providence (R.I.) Library | 2,861,937 |
| Detroit Public Library | 2,405,694 |
| Enoch Pratt Free Library (Baltimore) | 2,375,721 |
| Milwaukee Public Library | 2,353,672 |
| Carnegie Library of Pittsburgh | 2,039,904 |
| Houston Public Library | 1,974,451 |
| Public Library of Washington, D.C. | 1,930,341 |
| Dallas Public Library | 1,816,019 |
| Cuyahoga County Public Library (Ohio) | 1,804,431 |
| Denver Public Library | 1,709,563 |
| San Francisco Public Library | 1,642,683 |
| Public Library of Fort Wayne & Allen County (Ind.) | 1,512,285 |
| Seattle Public Library | 1,493,712 |
| Minneapolis Public Library | 1,454,462 |
| Miami-Dade County Library | 1,426,519 |
| St. Louis County Library | 1,419,587 |
| Public Library of Newark | 1,385,496 |
| St. Louis Public Library | 1,364,175 |
| Memphis & Shelby County Library | 1,358,026 |
| Montgomery County Library (Md.) | 1,313,061 |
| Dayton & Montgomery County Pub. Lib. (Ohio) | 1,302,269 |
| Indianapolis-Mario County Library | 1,285,152 |
| Toledo-Lucas County Library | 1,255,038 |
| Baltimore County Public Library | 1,220,679 |
| Library Association of Portland | 1,191,870 |
| Kansas City Public Library | 1,186,484 |
| Fairfax County Library (Va.) | 1,180,190 |
| Prince Georges County Library (Md.) | 1,169,173 |
| Columbus Public Library | 1,164,423 |
| King County Library (Wash.) | 1,127,393 |
| Phoenix Public Library | 1,088,095 |
| Mid-Continent Public Library (Mo.) | 1,077,405 |
| Atlanta Public Library | 1,033,507 |
| Orange County Public Library (Calif.) | 1,029,148 |
| Louisville Free Public Library | 1,013,217 |
| Hennepin County Library (Minn.) | 1,011,029 |
| Birmingham-Jefferson County Library | 1,001,615 |

* Book stock and serials

# INDEX OF U.S. COLLEGES AND UNIVERSITIES: 1981-82

SOURCE: Peterson's Guides, Inc.

This list includes all institutionally accredited four-year colleges and universities in the United States and U.S. territories that grant baccalaureate degrees.

**Institutions are listed in standard letter-by-letter alphabetical order. For example, University of Michigan will be found under U, not M; Marshall University comes before Mars Hill College.**

The explanation of the data in each column is as follows. Column 1: **Est** shows the founding date of the institution. Column 2: **Type/Control** shows the student body makeup (C = coed, M = primarily men, W = primarily women) and institutional control (Ind = independent nonprofit, Ind-R = independent-religious, Prop = proprietary, i.e., profit-making, Pub = public). Column 3: **UG Enroll** shows undergraduate enrollment as of fall 1981. Column 4: **State Res** shows the percentage of state residents in the fall 1981 undergraduate enrollment. Column 5: **Grad** indicates with a G each institution that offers graduate-level degree programs. Column 6: **Fac Size** shows the total number of faculty members teaching undergraduate and graduate courses as of fall 1981. Column 7: **Cmps** shows the campus setting (M = metropolitan area with population over 500,000; C = city, 50,000 to 500,000; T = small town, under 50,000; R = rural). Column 8: **ROTC** shows which ROTC program(s) are offered on campus (A = Army, N = Navy, AF = Air Force). Column 9: **Tuition & Fees** shows full-time tuition and mandatory fees per academic year for all students at private colleges or for in-state students at public colleges; a dagger (†) indicates that the figure is a comprehensive fee including tuition, fees, and room and board; an x indicates that college housing is not available.

An asterisk appears where no information is available.

| Name and Location | Est | Type/ Control | UG Enroll | State Res | Grad | Fac Size | Cmps | ROTC | Tuition & Fees |
|---|---|---|---|---|---|---|---|---|---|
| **Abilene Christian University,** Abilene, TX 79699 | 1906 | C/Ind-R | 4,058 | 65% | G | 238 | C | | $2820 |
| **Academy of Art College,** San Francisco, CA 94102 | 1929 | C/Prop | * | 80% | G | 105 | M | | 1360x |
| **Academy of the New Church,** Bryn Athyn, PA 19009 | 1876 | C/Ind-R | 158 | 41% | | 39 | T | | 1437 |
| **Adams State College,** Alamosa, CO 81102 | 1921 | C/Pub | 1,655 | 87% | G | 100 | T | | 880 |
| **Adelphi University,** Garden City, NY 11530 | 1896 | C/Ind | 6,655 | 87% | G | 800 | T | | 5030 |
| **Adrian College,** Adrian, MI 49221 | 1859 | C/Ind-R | 1,100 | 82% | | 98 | T | | 4974 |
| **Agnes Scott College,** Decatur, GA 30030 | 1889 | W/Ind | 559 | 53% | | 82 | T | | 5175 |
| **Alabama A&M University,** Normal, AL 35762 | 1875 | C/Pub | 3,465 | 85% | G | 500 | C | A | 620 |
| **Alabama Christian College,** Montgomery, AL 36193 | 1942 | C/Ind-R | 1,703 | 69% | | 93 | C | | 2310 |
| **Alabama State University,** Montgomery, AL 36195 | 1874 | C/Pub | 3,678 | 88% | G | 237 | C | AF | 600 |
| **Alaska Bible College,** Glennallen, AK 99588 | 1966 | C/Ind-R | 42 | 81% | | 11 | R | | 1160 |
| **Alaska Pacific University,** Anchorage, AK 99504 | 1957 | C/Ind-R | 208 | 75% | G | 39 | C | | 3210 |
| **Albany College of Pharmacy of Union University,** Albany, NY 12208 | 1881 | C/Ind | 558 | 98% | | 37 | C | | 2857x |
| **Albany State College,** Albany, GA 31705 | 1903 | C/Pub | 1,764 | 90% | G | 127 | C | A | 891 |
| **Albertus Magnus College,** New Haven, CT 06511 | 1925 | W/Ind-R | 552 | 81% | | 58 | C | | 4830 |
| **Albion College,** Albion, MI 49224 | 1835 | C/Ind-R | 1,916 | 85% | | 133 | T | | 5546 |
| **Albright College,** Reading, PA 19603 | 1856 | C/Ind-R | 1,421 | 60% | | 125 | C | | 5735 |
| **Alcorn State University,** Lorman, MS 39096 | 1871 | C/Pub | 2,250 | 92% | G | 162 | R | A | 2232 |
| **Alderson-Broaddus College,** Philippi, WV 26416 | 1871 | C/Ind-R | 794 | 44% | | 74 | R | | 3990 |
| **Alfred University,** Alfred, NY 14802 | 1836 | C/Ind | 2,082 | 75% | G | 176 | R | | 6450 |
| **Alice Lloyd College,** Pippa Passes, KY 41844 | 1923 | C/Ind | 395 | 93% | | 22 | R | | 2040 |
| **Allegheny College,** Meadville, PA 16335 | 1815 | C/Ind-R | 1,900 | 50% | G | 153 | T | | 5835 |
| **Allentown College of St Francis de Sales,** Center Valley, PA 18034 | 1962 | C/Ind-R | 850 | 70% | | 58 | R | | 4090 |
| **Allen University,** Columbia, SC 29204 | 1870 | C/Ind-R | 287 | * | | 41 | C | | 2510 |
| **Alliance College,** Cambridge Springs, PA 16403 | 1912 | C/Ind | 261 | 53% | | 35 | R | | 3060 |
| **Alma College,** Alma, MI 48801 | 1886 | C/Ind-R | 1,178 | 74% | | 99 | T | | 5629 |
| **Alvernia College,** Reading, PA 19607 | 1958 | C/Ind-R | 750 | 60% | | 80 | C | | 2300 |
| **Alverno College,** Milwaukee, WI 53215 | 1936 | W/Ind-R | 1,372 | 94% | | 102 | M | | 3850 |
| **Amber University,** Garland, TX 75041 | 1971 | C/Ind | 460 | 80% | G | 40 | C | | 1800x |
| **American Baptist College of ABTS,** Nashville, TN 37207 | 1924 | C/Ind-R | 161 | 20% | | 16 | M | | 1014 |
| **American Christian Theological Seminary,** Anaheim, CA 92806 | 1973 | M/Ind-R | 70 | 60% | G | 26 | M | | 2775x |
| **American College of Puerto Rico,** Bayamon, PR 00619 | 1963 | C/Ind | 2,406 | 100% | | 78 | C | | 1300x |
| **American International College,** Springfield, MA 01109 | 1885 | C/Ind | 1,597 | 64% | G | 123 | C | | 4380 |
| **American Technological University,** Killeen, TX 76540 | 1973 | C/Ind | 380 | * | G | 38 | T | | 1580 |
| **American University,** Washington, DC 20016 | 1893 | C/Ind-R | 5,465 | 9% | G | 1,173 | M | | 6270 |
| **Amherst College,** Amherst, MA 01002 | 1821 | C/Ind | 1,561 | 18% | | 174 | T | | 8255 |
| **Anderson College,** Anderson, IN 46012 | 1917 | C/Ind-R | 1,872 | 40% | G | 110 | C | | 3840 |
| **Andrews University,** Berrien Springs, MI 49104 | 1874 | C/Ind-R | 1,963 | 42% | G | 252 | T | | 4976 |
| **Angelo State University,** San Angelo, TX 76909 | 1928 | C/Pub | 5,308 | 96% | G | 201 | C | AF | 412 |
| **Anna Maria College,** Paxton, MA 01612 | 1946 | C/Ind-R | 550 | 75% | G | 61 | T | | 4290 |
| **Antillian College,** Mayaguez, PR 00708 | 1957 | C/Ind-R | 818 | 69% | | 55 | C | | 1948 |
| **Antioch College,** Yellow Springs, OH 45387 | 1852 | C/Ind | 705 | 24% | | 75 | T | | 6320 |
| **Antioch University Philadelphia,** Philadelphia, PA 19108 | 1852 | C/Ind | 447 | 65% | G | 84 | M | | 3200x |
| **Antioch University West,** San Francisco, CA 94118 | 1852 | C/Ind | 432 | 90% | G | 170 | M | | 4650x |
| **Appalachian Bible College,** Bradley, WV 25818 | 1950 | C/Ind-R | 212 | 40% | | 16 | T | | 2119 |
| **Appalachian State University,** Boone, NC 28608 | 1899 | C/Pub | 8,532 | 92% | G | 587 | T | A | 733 |
| **Aquinas College,** Grand Rapids, MI 49506 | 1886 | C/Ind-R | 2,491 | 89% | G | 122 | M | | 4498 |
| **Arizona College of the Bible,** Phoenix, AZ 85021 | 1971 | C/Ind-R | 111 | 80% | | 13 | M | | 1800 |
| **Arizona State University,** Tempe, AZ 85287 | 1885 | C/Pub | 28,200 | 66% | G | 1,687 | C | A,AF | 710 |
| **Arkansas Baptist College,** Little Rock, AR 72202 | 1884 | C/Ind-R | 270 | * | | * | * | | 2700 |
| **Arkansas College,** Batesville, AR 72501 | 1872 | C/Ind-R | 514 | 75% | | 57 | T | | 3300 |
| **Arkansas State University,** State University, AR 72467 | 1909 | C/Pub | 6,803 | 90% | G | 339 | T | A | 720 |
| **Arkansas Tech University,** Russellville, AR 72801 | 1909 | C/Pub | 3,120 | 85% | G | 150 | T | A | 735 |
| **Arlington Baptist College,** Arlington, TX 76012 | 1939 | C/Ind-R | 467 | 50% | | 24 | C | | 1850 |
| **Armstrong College,** Berkeley, CA 94704 | 1918 | C/Ind | 149 | 40% | G | 48 | M | | 2178x |
| **Armstrong State College,** Savannah, GA 31406 | 1935 | C/Pub | 2,854 | 95% | G | 160 | C | A,N | 660x |
| **Art Center College of Design,** Pasadena, CA 91103 | 1930 | C/Ind | 1,199 | 50% | G | 175 | C | | 3920x |
| **Asbury College,** Wilmore, KY 40390 | 1890 | C/Ind | 1,204 | 12% | | 110 | T | | 3215 |
| **Ashland College,** Ashland, OH 44805 | 1878 | C/Ind-R | 1,860 | 80% | G | 157 | T | | 5336 |
| **Assumption College,** Worcester, MA 01609 | 1904 | C/Ind-R | 1,535 | 50% | G | 148 | C | | 4930 |
| **Athens State College,** Athens, AL 35611 | 1822 | C/Pub | 1,003 | 90% | | 71 | T | | 1080 |
| **Atlanta Christian College,** East Point, GA 30344 | 1937 | C/Ind-R | 186 | 65% | | 23 | T | | 1409 |
| **Atlanta College of Art,** Atlanta, GA 30309 | 1928 | C/Ind | 267 | 40% | | 37 | M | | 3850 |
| **Atlantic Christian College,** Wilson, NC 27893 | 1902 | C/Ind-R | 1,564 | 82% | | 111 | T | | 2994 |
| **Atlantic Union College,** South Lancaster, MA 01561 | 1882 | C/Ind-R | 609 | 40% | | 98 | T | | 5170 |

| Name and Location | Est | Type/ Control | UG Enroll | State Res | Grad | Fac Size | Cmps | ROTC | Tuition & Fees |
|---|---|---|---|---|---|---|---|---|---|
| **Auburn University,** Auburn, AL 36849 | 1856 | C/Pub | 17,009 | 65% | G | 1,091 | T | A,N,AF | $990 |
| **Auburn University at Montgomery,** Montgomery, AL 36193 | 1967 | C/Pub | 3,970 | 100% | G | 350 | C | | 795 |
| **Augsburg College,** Minneapolis, MN 55454 | 1869 | C/Ind-R | 1,575 | 88% | | 140 | M | | 4820 |
| **Augusta College,** Augusta, GA 30910 | 1925 | C/Pub | 3,514 | 90% | G | 165 | C | A | 636x |
| **Augustana College,** Rock Island, IL 61201 | 1860 | C/Ind-R | 2,232 | 80% | G | 153 | C | | 4743 |
| **Augustana College,** Sioux Falls, SD 57197 | 1860 | C/Ind-R | 2,042 | 55% | G | 188 | C | | 4751 |
| **Aurora College,** Aurora, IL 60506 | 1893 | C/Ind-R | 1,270 | 90% | G | 89 | C | | 3975 |
| **Austin College,** Sherman, TX 75090 | 1849 | C/Ind-R | 1,118 | 90% | G | 107 | T | | 4035 |
| **Austin Peay State University,** Clarksville, TN 37040 | 1927 | C/Pub | 4,813 | 88% | G | 257 | T | A | 777 |
| **Averett College,** Danville, VA 24541 | 1859 | C/Ind-R | 1,005 | 70% | G | 54 | T | | 5450† |
| **Avila College,** Kansas City, MO 64145 | 1916 | C/Ind-R | 1,937 | 41% | G | 199 | M | | 3500 |
| **Azusa Pacific University,** Azusa, CA 91702 | 1899 | C/Ind-R | 1,278 | 75% | G | 128 | T | | 4300 |
| **Babson College,** Babson Park, MA 02157 | 1919 | C/Ind | 1,383 | 75% | G | 117 | T | | 6364 |
| **Baker University,** Baldwin City, KS 66006 | 1858 | C/Ind-R | 861 | 64% | G | 84 | R | | 3370 |
| **Baldwin-Wallace College,** Berea, OH 44017 | 1845 | C/Ind-R | 3,064 | 80% | G | 169 | T | | 5181 |
| **Ball State University,** Muncie, IN 47306 | 1918 | C/Pub | 16,099 | 93% | G | 1,220 | C | A | 1275 |
| **Baltimore Hebrew College,** Baltimore, MD 21215 | 1919 | C/Ind-R | 1,150 | 96% | G | 17 | M | | 1080x |
| **Baptist Bible College,** Springfield, MO 65802 | 1950 | C/Ind-R | 1,538 | 1% | | 58 | C | | 1080 |
| **Baptist Bible College of Pennsylvania,** Clarks Summit, PA 18411 | 1932 | C/Ind-R | 804 | 39% | | 42 | T | | 3152 |
| **Baptist Bible Institute,** Graceville, FL 32440 | 1943 | C/Ind-R | 364 | 45% | | 20 | T | | 956 |
| **Baptist College at Charleston,** Charleston, SC 29411 | 1965 | C/Ind-R | 2,280 | 90% | | 100 | C | AF | * |
| **Barat College,** Lake Forest, IL 60045 | 1858 | W/Ind-R | 702 | 88% | | 82 | T | | 4800 |
| **Barber-Scotia College,** Concord, NC 28025 | 1867 | C/Ind-R | 435 | 61% | | 38 | T | | 2423 |
| **Bard College,** Annandale-on-Hudson, NY 12504 | 1860 | C/Ind | 802 | 43% | G | 95 | R | | 8962 |
| **Barnard College,** New York, NY 10027 | 1889 | W/Ind | 2,500 | 45% | | 235 | M | | 8142 |
| **Barrington College,** Barrington, RI 02806 | 1900 | C/Ind-R | 416 | 26% | | 45 | T | | 5085 |
| **Barry University,** Miami, FL 33161 | 1940 | C/Ind-R | 1,690 | 79% | G | 171 | M | | 4465 |
| **Bartlesville Wesleyan College,** Bartlesville, OK 74003 | 1909 | C/Ind-R | 821 | 59% | | 59 | T | | 2960 |
| **Bates College,** Lewiston, ME 04240 | 1864 | C/Ind | 1,430 | 14% | | 136 | C | | 8100 |
| **Bayamón Central University,** Bayamón, PR 00619 | 1970 | C/Ind | 1,600 | 100% | | 78 | * | | *x |
| **Baylor College of Dentistry,** Dallas, TX 75246 | 1905 | C/Ind | 70 | 85% | G | 229 | M | | 2546x |
| **Baylor University,** Waco, TX 76798 | 1845 | C/Ind-R | 9,188 | 77% | G | 502 | C | AF | 2844 |
| **Beacon College,** Washington, DC 20009 | 1970 | C/Ind | 40 | * | G | 160 | M | | 1600x |
| **Beaver College,** Glenside, PA 19038 | 1853 | C/Ind | 1,328 | 69% | G | 152 | T | | 5520 |
| **Belhaven College,** Jackson, MS 39202 | 1883 | C/Ind-R | 1,021 | 84% | | 73 | C | | 3100 |
| **Bellarmine College,** Louisville, KY 40205 | 1950 | C/Ind-R | 2,211 | 78% | G | 103 | M | | 3350 |
| **Bellevue College,** Bellevue, NE 68005 | 1966 | C/Ind | 2,685 | 80% | | 90 | T | | 1320x |
| **Belmont Abbey College,** Belmont, NC 28012 | 1876 | C/Ind-R | 777 | 37% | | 57 | R | | 3030 |
| **Belmont College,** Nashville, TN 37203 | 1951 | C/Ind-R | 1,793 | 66% | | 158 | M | | 2515 |
| **Beloit College,** Beloit, WI 53511 | 1846 | C/Ind-R | 1,071 | 17% | G | 120 | T | | 6586 |
| **Bemidji State University,** Bemidji, MN 56601 | 1919 | C/Pub | 4,573 | 94% | G | 247 | R | A | 904 |
| **Benedict College,** Columbia, SC 29204 | 1870 | C/Ind-R | 1,281 | 90% | | 111 | C | A | 2719 |
| **Benedictine College,** Atchison, KS 66002 | 1971 | C/Ind-R | 1,046 | 45% | | 94 | T | | 3717 |
| **Benjamin Franklin University,** Washington, DC 20036 | 1907 | C/Ind | 600 | 46% | G | 44 | M | | 2700x |
| **Bennett College,** Greensboro, NC 27420 | 1873 | W/Ind-R | 645 | 46% | | 62 | C | | 2800 |
| **Bennington College,** Bennington, VT 05201 | 1932 | C/Ind | 632 | 1% | G | 80 | R | | 9620 |
| **Bentley College,** Waltham, MA 02254 | 1917 | C/Ind | 3,776 | 60% | G | 295 | C | | 5100 |
| **Berea College,** Berea, KY 40404 | 1855 | C/Ind | 1,587 | 37% | | 127 | T | | 118 |
| **Berklee College of Music,** Boston, MA 02215 | 1945 | C/Ind | 2,627 | 19% | | 204 | M | | 3510 |
| **Berkshire Christian College,** Lenox, MA 01240 | 1897 | C/Ind-R | 140 | 33% | | 21 | T | | 2825 |
| **Bernard M Baruch College**—See City U of NY, Bernard M Baruch College | | | | | | | | | |
| **Berry College,** Mount Berry, GA 30149 | 1902 | C/Ind | 1,466 | 75% | G | 98 | T | A | 3480 |
| **Bethany Bible College,** Santa Cruz, CA 95066 | 1919 | C/Ind-R | * | * | | * | R | | 2972 |
| **Bethany College,** Lindsborg, KS 67456 | 1881 | C/Ind-R | 785 | 67% | | 82 | T | | 3155 |
| **Bethany College,** Bethany, WV 26032 | 1840 | C/Ind-R | 862 | 16% | | 80 | R | | 5650 |
| **Bethany Nazarene College,** Bethany, OK 73008 | 1899 | C/Ind-R | 1,239 | 30% | G | 85 | T | | 2432 |
| **Bethel College,** Mishawaka, IN 46544 | 1947 | C/Ind-R | 437 | 97% | | 37 | T | | 3325 |
| **Bethel College,** North Newton, KS 67117 | 1887 | C/Ind-R | 641 | 59% | | 94 | T | | 3520 |
| **Bethel College,** St Paul, MN 55112 | 1871 | C/Ind-R | 2,186 | 59% | | 207 | M | | 4550 |
| **Bethel College,** McKenzie, TN 38201 | 1842 | C/Ind-R | 424 | 72% | | 39 | T | | 1980 |
| **Bethune-Cookman College,** Daytona Beach, FL 32015 | 1923 | C/Ind-R | 1,674 | 81% | | 110 | C | | 3492 |
| **Big Sky Bible College,** Lewistown, MT 59457 | 1952 | C/Ind-R | 133 | 52% | | 15 | R | | 766 |
| **Biola University,** La Mirada, CA 90639 | 1908 | C/Ind-R | 2,288 | 73% | G | 253 | T | | 4082 |
| **Birmingham-Southern College,** Birmingham, AL 35254 | 1856 | C/Ind-R | 1,534 | 75% | | 90 | M | A,AF | 3900 |
| **Biscayne College,** Miami, FL 33054 | 1962 | C/Ind-R | 2,750 | 65% | G | 150 | M | | 3600 |
| **Bishop College,** Dallas, TX 75241 | 1881 | C/Ind-R | 926 | 38% | | 61 | M | A | * |
| **Blackburn College,** Carlinville, IL 62626 | 1837 | C/Ind-R | 531 | 85% | | 50 | T | | 3320 |
| **Black Hills State College,** Spearfish, SD 57783 | 1883 | C/Pub | 2,173 | 91% | G | 109 | T | A | 1060 |
| **Bloomfield College,** Bloomfield, NJ 07003 | 1868 | C/Ind-R | 1,898 | 99% | | 141 | T | | 4470 |
| **Bloomsburg State College,** Bloomsburg, PA 17815 | 1839 | C/Pub | 5,758 | 94% | G | 327 | T | | 1602 |
| **Bluefield College,** Bluefield, VA 24605 | 1922 | C/Ind-R | 387 | 80% | | 29 | T | | 1990 |
| **Bluefield State College,** Bluefield, WV 24701 | 1895 | C/Pub | 2,276 | 8% | | 100 | T | | 480x |
| **Blue Mountain College,** Blue Mountain, MS 38610 | 1873 | C/Ind-R | 356 | 85% | | 32 | T | | 2130 |
| **Bluffton College,** Bluffton, OH 45817 | 1899 | C/Ind-R | 660 | 85% | | 56 | T | | 4320 |
| **Boise State University,** Boise, ID 83725 | 1932 | C/Pub | 9,180 | 96% | G | 457 | C | A | 688 |
| **Boricua College,** New York, NY 10032 | 1974 | C/Ind | 904 | 100% | | 106 | M | | 3500x |
| **Borromeo College of Ohio,** Wickliffe, OH 44092 | 1953 | M/Ind-R | 93 | 71% | | 26 | T | | 3000 |
| **Boston College,** Chestnut Hill, MA 02167 | 1863 | C/Ind-R | 10,647 | 51% | G | 691 | C | AF | 6150 |
| **Boston Conservatory of Music,** Boston, MA 02215 | 1867 | C/Ind | 481 | 40% | G | 93 | M | | 4410 |
| **Boston University,** Boston, MA 02215 | 1839 | C/Ind | 13,090 | 25% | G | 2,543 | M | A,N,AF | 7275 |
| **Bowdoin College,** Brunswick, ME 04011 | 1794 | C/Ind | 1,373 | 11% | | 115 | T | | 7865 |
| **Bowie State College,** Bowie, MD 20715 | 1865 | C/Pub | 1,900 | 85% | G | 159 | T | A | 1260 |

| Name and Location | Est | Type/ Control | UG Enroll | State Res | Grad | Fac Size | Cmps | ROTC | Tuition & Fees |
|---|---|---|---|---|---|---|---|---|---|
| **Bowling Green State University,** Bowling Green, OH 43403 | 1910 | C/Pub | 15,106 | 94% | G | 787 | T | A,AF | $1473 |
| **Bradford College,** Bradford, MA 01830 | 1803 | C/Ind | 386 | 29% | | 44 | T | | 5800 |
| **Bradley University,** Peoria, IL 61625 | 1897 | C/Ind | 5,183 | 78% | G | 377 | C | A | 4600 |
| **Brandeis University,** Waltham, MA 02254 | 1948 | C/Ind | 2,787 | 22% | G | 459 | C | | 7830 |
| **Brenau College,** Gainesville, GA 30501 | 1878 | W/Ind | 796 | 75% | G | 78 | T | | 2976 |
| **Brescia College,** Owensboro, KY 42301 | 1950 | C/Ind-R | 890 | 85% | | 73 | C | | 2700 |
| **Briar Cliff College,** Sioux City, IA 51104 | 1930 | C/Ind-R | 1,342 | 93% | | 78 | C | | 3450 |
| **Bridgeport Engineering Institute,** Bridgeport, CT 06606 | 1924 | C/Ind | 900 | 95% | | 80 | C | | 1600x |
| **Bridgewater College,** Bridgewater, VA 22812 | 1880 | C/Ind-R | 914 | 71% | | 78 | T | | 4080 |
| **Bridgewater State College,** Bridgewater, MA 02324 | 1840 | C/Pub | 4,466 | 95% | G | 258 | T | | 1095 |
| **Brigham Young University,** Provo, UT 84602 | 1875 | C/Ind-R | 24,566 | 27% | G | 1,315 | C | A,AF | 1220 |
| **Brigham Young University—Hawaii Campus,** Laie, Oahu, HI 96762 | 1955 | C/Ind-R | 1,945 | 27% | | 98 | T | | 1150 |
| **Bristol College,** Bristol, TN 37620 | 1895 | C/Prop | 235 | 100% | | 12 | C | | 1830x |
| **Brooklyn College**—See City U of NY, Brooklyn College | | | | | | | | | |
| **Brooks Institute,** Santa Barbara, CA 93108 | 1945 | C/Ind | 800 | 35% | G | 32 | C | | 4650x |
| **Brown University,** Providence, RI 02912 | 1764 | C/Ind | 5,467 | 7% | G | 494 | C | | 8427 |
| **Bryan College,** Dayton, TN 37321 | 1930 | C/Ind-R | 628 | 12% | | 49 | T | | 2800 |
| **Bryant College,** Smithfield, RI 02917 | 1863 | C/Ind | 2,945 | 24% | G | 145 | T | A | 3750 |
| **Bryn Mawr College,** Bryn Mawr, PA 19010 | 1885 | W/Ind | 1,146 | 12% | G | 216 | T | | 7725 |
| **Bucknell University,** Lewisburg, PA 17837 | 1846 | C/Ind | 3,186 | 34% | G | 253 | T | A | 7425 |
| **Buena Vista College,** Storm Lake, IA 50588 | 1891 | C/Ind-R | 952 | 94% | | 70 | T | | 4910 |
| **Burlington College,** Burlington, VT 05401 | 1972 | C/Ind | 146 | 87% | | 38 | T | | 3466x |
| **Butler University,** Indianapolis, IN 46208 | 1855 | C/Ind | 2,595 | 81% | G | 245 | M | | 4452 |
| **Cabrini College,** Radnor, PA 19087 | 1957 | C/Ind-R | 717 | 68% | | 60 | T | | 4170 |
| **Caldwell College,** Caldwell, NJ 07006 | 1939 | W/Ind-R | 766 | 85% | | 78 | T | | 3553 |
| **California Baptist College,** Riverside, CA 92504 | 1950 | C/Ind-R | 656 | 74% | G | 62 | C | | 2975 |
| **California College of Arts and Crafts,** Oakland, CA 94618 | 1907 | C/Ind | 958 | 64% | G | 153 | M | | 4810 |
| **California College of Podiatric Medicine,** San Francisco, CA 94115 | 1914 | C/Ind | 395 | 40% | G | 68 | M | | 8365x |
| **California Institute of Technology,** Pasadena, CA 91125 | 1891 | C/Ind | 860 | 40% | G | 339 | C | | 7560 |
| **California Institute of the Arts,** Valencia, CA 91355 | 1961 | C/Ind | 575 | 54% | G | 139 | T | | 5603 |
| **California Lutheran College,** Thousand Oaks, CA 91360 | 1959 | C/Ind-R | 1,434 | 84% | G | 266 | T | A | 4510 |
| **California Maritime Academy,** Vallejo, CA 94590 | 1929 | M/Pub | 500 | 70% | | 30 | C | | 1192 |
| **California Polytechnic State U, San Luis Obispo,** San Luis Obispo, CA 93407 | 1901 | C/Pub | 15,502 | 99% | G | 949 | T | A | 375 |
| **California State College,** California, PA 15419 | 1852 | C/Pub | 3,908 | 94% | G | 305 | T | A | 1622 |
| **California State College, Bakersfield,** Bakersfield, CA 93309 | 1970 | C/Pub | 2,393 | 87% | G | 205 | R | | 350 |
| **California State College, San Bernardino,** San Bernardino, CA 92407 | 1962 | C/Pub | 3,398 | 93% | G | 272 | C | AF | 300 |
| **California State College, Stanislaus,** Turlock, CA 95380 | 1957 | C/Pub | 2,875 | 93% | G | 227 | T | | 374 |
| **California State Polytechnic U, Pomona,** Pomona, CA 91768 | 1938 | C/Pub | 14,615 | 85% | G | 992 | C | A | 322 |
| **California State University, Chico,** Chico, CA 95929 | 1887 | C/Pub | 11,390 | 97% | G | 704 | T | A | 500 |
| **California State University, Dominguez Hills,** Carson, CA 90747 | 1960 | C/Pub | 5,813 | 95% | G | 447 | C | | 330 |
| **California State University, Fresno,** Fresno, CA 93740 | 1911 | C/Pub | 13,180 | 93% | G | 921 | C | A,AF | 550 |
| **California State University, Fullerton,** Fullerton, CA 92634 | 1957 | C/Pub | 18,445 | 92% | G | 1,324 | C | | 261x |
| **California State University, Hayward,** Hayward, CA 94542 | 1957 | C/Pub | 8,417 | 94% | G | 615 | C | | 345x |
| **California State University, Long Beach,** Long Beach, CA 90840 | 1949 | C/Pub | 23,822 | 90% | G | 1,700 | M | AF | 298 |
| **California State University, Los Angeles,** Los Angeles, CA 90032 | 1947 | C/Pub | 15,180 | 95% | G | 1,200 | M | | 330x |
| **California State University, Northridge,** Northridge, CA 91330 | 1958 | C/Pub | 22,451 | 98% | G | 1,500 | M | | 500 |
| **California State University, Sacramento,** Sacramento, CA 95819 | 1947 | C/Pub | 17,498 | 95% | G | 1,163 | M | A,AF | 314 |
| **Calumet College,** Whiting, IN 46394 | 1951 | C/Ind-R | 1,316 | 79% | | 83 | T | | 2010x |
| **Calvary Bible College,** Kansas City, MO 64147 | 1932 | C/Ind-R | 496 | 33% | G | 38 | M | | 2200 |
| **Calvin College,** Grand Rapids, MI 49506 | 1876 | C/Ind-R | 3,921 | 57% | G | 240 | M | | 3950 |
| **Camden College of Arts and Sciences**—See Rutgers U, Camden College of Arts and Sciences | | | | | | | | | |
| **Cameron University,** Lawton, OK 73505 | 1927 | C/Pub | 4,606 | 99% | | 178 | C | A | 447 |
| **Campbellsville College,** Campbellsville, KY 42718 | 1906 | C/Ind-R | 712 | 76% | | 60 | T | | 2640 |
| **Campbell University,** Buies Creek, NC 27506 | 1887 | C/Ind-R | 1,953 | 75% | G | 120 | T | | 3433 |
| **Canisius College,** Buffalo, NY 14208 | 1870 | C/Ind | 2,729 | 98% | G | 260 | M | A | 4160 |
| **Capital University,** Columbus, OH 43209 | 1850 | C/Ind-R | 1,642 | 87% | G | 192 | M | | 5350 |
| **Capitol Institute of Technology,** Kensington, MD 20795 | 1964 | C/Ind | 800 | 65% | | 34 | T | | 2628x |
| **Cardinal Glennon College,** St Louis, MO 63119 | 1898 | M/Ind-R | 94 | 89% | | 29 | M | | 1650 |
| **Cardinal Newman College,** St Louis, MO 63121 | 1976 | C/Ind-R | 93 | 97% | | 24 | M | | 3980 |
| **Cardinal Stritch College,** Milwaukee, WI 53217 | 1937 | C/Ind-R | 737 | 65% | G | 116 | M | A | 3600 |
| **Caribbean University College,** Bayamon, PR 00619 | 1969 | C/Ind | 1,851 | 100% | | 119 | C | | 1425x |
| **Carleton College,** Northfield, MN 55057 | 1866 | C/Ind | 1,850 | 28% | | 168 | T | | 6951 |
| **Carlow College,** Pittsburgh, PA 15213 | 1929 | W/Ind-R | 924 | 94% | | 102 | M | | 4790 |
| **Carnegie-Mellon University,** Pittsburgh, PA 15213 | 1900 | C/Ind | 4,098 | 40% | G | 552 | M | A,AF | 6350 |
| **Carroll College,** Waukesha, WI 53186 | 1846 | C/Ind-R | 1,150 | 77% | | 106 | C | | 5660 |
| **Carroll College of Montana,** Helena, MT 59625 | 1909 | C/Ind-R | 1,358 | 70% | | 111 | T | | 2878 |
| **Carson-Newman College,** Jefferson City, TN 37760 | 1851 | C/Ind-R | 1,737 | 56% | | 111 | T | A | 3004 |
| **Carthage College,** Kenosha, WI 53141 | 1847 | C/Ind-R | 1,435 | 45% | G | 99 | C | | 4651 |
| **Case Western Reserve University,** Cleveland, OH 44106 | 1826 | C/Ind | 3,446 | 52% | G | 1,465 | M | | 6200 |
| **Castleton State College,** Castleton, VT 05735 | 1787 | C/Pub | 1,930 | 63% | G | 118 | R | | 1560 |
| **Catawba College,** Salisbury, NC 28144 | 1851 | C/Ind-R | 907 | 55% | | 64 | T | A | 3760 |
| **Cathedral College of the Immaculate Conception,** Douglaston, NY 11362 | 1914 | M/Ind-R | 111 | 98% | | 31 | M | | 3300 |
| **Catholic University of America,** Washington, DC 20064 | 1887 | C/Ind-R | 2,798 | * | G | 622 | M | | 5745 |
| **Catholic University of Puerto Rico,** Ponce, PR 00732 | 1948 | C/Ind-R | 11,181 | 99% | G | 377 | C | | 1700 |
| **Cedar Crest College,** Allentown, PA 18104 | 1867 | W/Ind-R | 1,132 | 65% | | 128 | C | | 5100 |
| **Cedarville College,** Cedarville, OH 45314 | 1887 | C/Ind-R | 1,657 | 40% | | 105 | R | | 3207 |
| **Centenary College,** Hackettstown, NJ 07840 | 1867 | W/Ind | 700 | 60% | | 67 | T | | 4195 |
| **Centenary College of Louisiana,** Shreveport, LA 71104 | 1825 | C/Ind-R | 986 | 71% | G | 108 | C | A | 3160 |
| **Ctr for Creative Studies—Coll of Art & Design,** Detroit, MI 48202 | 1926 | C/Ind | 835 | 92% | | 124 | M | | 4321x |

| Name and Location | Est | Type/ Control | UG Enroll | State Res | Grad | Fac Size | Cmps | ROTC | Tuition & Fees |
|---|---|---|---|---|---|---|---|---|---|
| **Central Baptist College,** Conway, AR 72032 | 1952 | C/Ind-R | 271 | 60% | G | 21 | T | | $720 |
| **Central Bible College,** Springfield, MO 65802 | 1922 | C/Ind-R | 1,107 | 14% | | 60 | C | | 1530 |
| **Central Christian College of the Bible,** Moberly, MO 65270 | 1957 | C/Ind-R | 119 | 61% | | 13 | T | | 1128 |
| **Central Connecticut State College,** New Britain, CT 06050 | 1849 | C/Pub | 10,175 | 96% | G | 643 | C | | 951 |
| **Central Florida Bible College,** Orlando, FL 32806 | 1976 | C/Ind-R | 125 | * | | 9 | M | | 1866 |
| **Central Methodist College,** Fayette, MO 65248 | 1854 | C/Ind-R | 681 | 88% | | 62 | R | | 3840 |
| **Central Michigan University,** Mount Pleasant, MI 48859 | 1892 | C/Pub | 14,973 | 98% | G | 740 | T | A | 1337 |
| **Central Missouri State University,** Warrensburg, MO 64093 | 1871 | C/Pub | 8,628 | 95% | G | 540 | T | A | 630 |
| **Central New England College,** Worcester, MA 01610 | 1905 | C/Ind | 1,600 | 75% | | 130 | C | | 2550x |
| **Central State University,** Wilberforce, OH 45384 | 1887 | C/Pub | 2,581 | 75% | | 154 | R | A | 1300 |
| **Central State University,** Edmond, OK 73034 | 1890 | C/Pub | 8,804 | 94% | G | 430 | T | A | 450 |
| **Central University of Iowa,** Pella, IA 50219 | 1853 | C/Ind-R | 1,536 | 68% | | 93 | T | | 4722 |
| **Central Washington University,** Ellensburg, WA 98926 | 1891 | C/Pub | 6,215 | 96% | G | 335 | T | A,AF | 942 |
| **Central Wesleyan College,** Central, SC 29630 | 1906 | C/Ind-R | 431 | 60% | | 30 | T | | 3520 |
| **Centre College of Kentucky,** Danville, KY 40422 | 1819 | C/Ind-R | 700 | 70% | | 70 | T | | 5375 |
| **Chadron State College,** Chadron, NE 69337 | 1911 | C/Pub | 1,537 | 85% | G | 104 | T | | 784 |
| **Chaminade University of Honolulu,** Honolulu, HI 96816 | 1955 | C/Ind-R | 956 | 25% | G | 177 | M | A,AF | 2980 |
| **Chapman College,** Orange, CA 92666 | 1861 | C/Ind-R | 1,190 | 65% | G | 167 | C | | 5570 |
| **Charter Oak College,** Hartford, CT 06115 | 1973 | C/Pub | 1,200 | 95% | | * | * | | *x |
| **Chatham College,** Pittsburgh, PA 15232 | 1869 | W/Ind | 625 | 43% | | 81 | M | | 5512 |
| **Chestnut Hill College,** Philadelphia, PA 19118 | 1924 | W/Ind-R | 770 | 52% | G | 100 | M | | 3100 |
| **Cheyney State College,** Cheyney, PA 19319 | 1837 | C/Pub | 2,182 | 73% | G | 179 | R | | 1380 |
| **Chicago State University,** Chicago, IL 60628 | 1867 | C/Pub | 5,470 | 99% | G | 395 | M | | 872x |
| **Christ College Irvine,** Irvine, CA 92715 | 1972 | C/Ind-R | 212 | 80% | | 33 | C | | 3225 |
| **Christian Brothers College,** Memphis, TN 38104 | 1871 | C/Ind-R | 1,473 | 79% | | 127 | M | | 3390 |
| **Christian Heritage College,** El Cajon, CA 92021 | 1970 | C/Ind-R | 384 | 70% | | 58 | C | | 2980 |
| **Christian University College of the Americas,** San Juan, PR 00936 | * | C/Ind-R | * | * | | * | * | | * |
| **Christopher Newport College,** Newport News, VA 23606 | 1961 | C/Pub | 4,098 | 90% | | 201 | C | A | 1295x |
| **Cincinnati Bible College,** Cincinnati, OH 45204 | 1924 | C/Ind-R | 612 | 50% | | 39 | M | | 1962 |
| **Circleville Bible College,** Circleville, OH 43113 | 1948 | C/Ind-R | 251 | 65% | | 23 | T | | * |
| **The Citadel,** Charleston, SC 29409 | 1842 | M/Pub | 2,425 | 65% | G | 151 | C | A,N,AF | 2700 |
| **City College**—See City U of NY, City College | | | | | | | | | |
| **City College,** Seattle, WA 98104 | 1973 | C/Ind | 1,256 | * | G | 150 | M | | 1600x |
| **City U of NY, Bernard M Baruch College,** New York, NY 10010 | 1968 | C/Pub | 12,600 | 95% | G | 800 | M | | 976x |
| **City U of NY, Brooklyn College,** Brooklyn, NY 11210 | 1930 | C/Pub | 14,651 | 98% | G | 1,318 | M | | 1152x |
| **City U of NY, City College,** New York, NY 10031 | 1847 | C/Pub | 10,639 | 96% | G | 828 | M | | 991x |
| **City U of NY, College of Staten Island,** Staten Island, NY 10301 | 1955 | C/Pub | 10,000 | 99% | G | 379 | M | | 978x |
| **City U of NY, Herbert H Lehman College,** Bronx, NY 10468 | 1931 | C/Pub | 8,550 | 98% | G | 820 | M | | 976x |
| **City U of NY, Hunter College,** New York, NY 10021 | 1870 | C/Pub | 14,448 | 93% | G | 1,234 | M | | 925 |
| **City U of NY, John Jay Coll of Crim Justice,** New York, NY 10019 | 1964 | C/Pub | 5,386 | 97% | G | 385 | M | | 990x |
| **City U of NY, Medgar Evers College,** Brooklyn, NY 11225 | 1969 | C/Pub | 2,693 | 97% | | 323 | M | | 976x |
| **City U of NY, Queens College,** Flushing, NY 11367 | 1937 | C/Pub | 15,367 | 99% | G | 1,400 | M | | 1203x |
| **City U of NY, York College,** Jamaica, NY 11451 | 1967 | C/Pub | 4,000 | 95% | | 200 | M | | 980x |
| **Claflin College,** Orangeburg, SC 29115 | 1869 | C/Ind-R | 650 | 88% | | 65 | T | A | 2778 |
| **Claremont McKenna College,** Claremont, CA 91711 | 1946 | C/Ind | 821 | 60% | | 99 | T | A | 7090 |
| **Clarion State College,** Clarion, PA 16214 | 1867 | C/Pub | 5,000 | 85% | G | 360 | T | A | 1400 |
| **Clark College,** Atlanta, GA 30314 | 1869 | C/Ind-R | 2,086 | 60% | | 145 | M | | 3315 |
| **Clarke College,** Dubuque, IA 52001 | 1843 | W/Ind-R | 823 | 75% | G | 72 | C | | 4150 |
| **Clarkson College,** Potsdam, NY 13676 | 1896 | C/Ind | 3,530 | 80% | G | 231 | T | A,AF | 6120 |
| **Clark University,** Worcester, MA 01610 | 1887 | C/Ind | 2,050 | 25% | G | 175 | C | | 7176 |
| **Clearwater Christian College,** Clearwater, FL 33519 | 1966 | C/Ind-R | 198 | 96% | | 24 | C | | 1818 |
| **Cleary College,** Ypsilanti, MI 48197 | 1883 | C/Ind | 735 | 99% | | 50 | T | | 2475x |
| **Clemson University,** Clemson, SC 29631 | 1889 | C/Pub | 9,870 | 76% | G | 1,005 | T | A,AF | 1210 |
| **Cleveland College of Jewish Studies,** Beachwood, OH 44122 | 1963 | C/Ind | 80 | * | G | 16 | M | | 660x |
| **Cleveland Institute of Art,** Cleveland, OH 44106 | 1882 | C/Ind | 516 | 74% | | 112 | M | | 4000 |
| **Cleveland Institute of Music,** Cleveland, OH 44106 | 1920 | C/Ind | 142 | 25% | G | 152 | M | | 6101 |
| **Cleveland State University,** Cleveland, OH 44115 | 1964 | C/Pub | 14,176 | 98% | G | 710 | M | A | 1377 |
| **Clinch Valley College of the U of Virginia,** Wise, VA 24293 | 1954 | C/Pub | 895 | 91% | | 66 | T | | 964 |
| **Coe College,** Cedar Rapids, IA 52402 | 1851 | C/Ind-R | 1,249 | 55% | | 123 | C | | 5370 |
| **Cogswell College,** San Francisco, CA 94108 | 1887 | C/Ind | 512 | 100% | | 61 | M | | 2700x |
| **Coker College,** Hartsville, SC 29550 | 1908 | C/Ind | 269 | 88% | | 45 | T | | 3930 |
| **Colby College,** Waterville, ME 04901 | 1813 | C/Ind | 1,675 | 13% | | 151 | T | | 7650 |
| **Colby-Sawyer College,** New London, NH 03257 | 1837 | W/Ind | 650 | 14% | | 69 | T | | 6370 |
| **Colegio Universitario del Turabo,** Caguas, PR 00626 | 1972 | C/Ind | 5,310 | * | G | 190 | C | | 1324x |
| **Colegio Universitario Metropolitano,** Cupey, PR 00928 | 1980 | C/Ind | * | * | | * | * | | * |
| **Coleman College,** La Mesa, CA 92041 | 1963 | C/Ind | 644 | * | | 41 | M | | 5100x |
| **Colgate University,** Hamilton, NY 13346 | 1819 | C/Ind | 2,600 | 50% | G | 206 | T | | 7490 |
| **College for Human Services,** New York, NY 10014 | 1964 | C/Ind | 100 | 100% | | 18 | M | | *x |
| **College Misericordia,** Dallas, PA 18612 | 1924 | C/Ind-R | 1,176 | 70% | G | 72 | T | | 3565 |
| **College of Charleston,** Charleston, SC 29424 | 1770 | C/Pub | 4,614 | 93% | G | 222 | C | | 1120 |
| **College of Great Falls,** Great Falls, MT 59405 | 1932 | C/Ind-R | 1,094 | 80% | G | 82 | C | | 3000 |
| **College of Idaho,** Caldwell, ID 83605 | 1891 | C/Ind-R | 535 | 64% | G | 74 | T | | 4753 |
| **College of Insurance,** New York, NY 10038 | 1962 | C/Ind | 1,787 | 45% | G | 255 | M | | 4100x |
| **College of Mount St Joseph on the Ohio,** Mount St Joseph, OH 45051 | 1920 | W/Ind-R | 1,749 | 88% | G | 122 | M | | 3776 |
| **College of Mount Saint Vincent,** Riverdale, NY 10471 | 1847 | W/Ind | 1,150 | 85% | | 99 | M | | 4410 |
| **College of New Rochelle,** New Rochelle, NY 10801 | 1904 | W/Ind | 1,305 | 80% | G | 197 | C | | 4110 |
| **College of New Rochelle, New Resources Division,** New Rochelle, NY 10801 | 1973 | C/Ind | 3,499 | 98% | | 300 | C | | 2290x |
| **College of Notre Dame,** Belmont, CA 94002 | 1868 | C/Ind-R | 829 | 67% | G | 141 | T | | 4700 |
| **College of Notre Dame of Maryland,** Baltimore, MD 21210 | 1896 | W/Ind-R | 510 | 75% | | 71 | M | | 3800 |
| **College of Our Lady of the Elms,** Chicopee, MA 01013 | 1928 | W/Ind-R | 530 | 85% | | 75 | C | | 4100 |
| **College of Saint Benedict,** Saint Joseph, MN 56374 | 1913 | W/Ind-R | 1,750 | 88% | | 137 | R | | 4465 |
| **College of St Catherine,** St Paul, MN 55105 | 1905 | W/Ind-R | 2,093 | 75% | | 214 | M | | 4520 |

| Name and Location | Est | Type/ Control | UG Enroll | State Res | Grad | Fac Size | Cmps | ROTC | Tuition & Fees |
|---|---|---|---|---|---|---|---|---|---|
| **College of Saint Elizabeth,** Convent Station, NJ 07961 | 1899 | W/Ind-R | 610 | 85% | | 92 | T | | $4000 |
| **College of St Francis,** Joliet, IL 60435 | 1925 | C/Ind-R | 800 | 90% | G | 90 | C | | 3620 |
| **College of St Joseph the Provider,** Rutland, VT 05701 | 1954 | C/Ind-R | 290 | 66% | G | 44 | R | | 3815 |
| **College of Saint Mary,** Omaha, NE 68124 | 1923 | W/Ind-R | 897 | 82% | | 97 | M | | 4101 |
| **College of Saint Rose,** Albany, NY 12203 | 1920 | C/Ind | 1,794 | 95% | G | 188 | C | | 3990 |
| **College of St Scholastica,** Duluth, MN 55811 | 1906 | C/Ind-R | 907 | 68% | G | 124 | C | | 4320 |
| **College of Saint Teresa,** Winona, MN 55987 | 1907 | W/Ind-R | 620 | 97% | | 80 | T | | 4500 |
| **College of Saint Thomas,** St Paul, MN 55105 | 1885 | C/Ind-R | 3,688 | 89% | G | 295 | M | AF | 3600 |
| **College of Santa Fe,** Santa Fe, NM 87501 | 1947 | C/Ind-R | 993 | 53% | | 90 | C | | 2730 |
| **College of Staten Island**—See City U of NY, College of Staten Island | | | | | | | | | |
| **College of the Atlantic,** Bar Harbor, ME 04609 | 1969 | C/Ind | 180 | 15% | | 26 | T | | 4850 |
| **College of the Holy Cross,** Worcester, MA 01610 | 1843 | C/Ind-R | 2,494 | 47% | | 217 | C | N,AF | 6340 |
| **College of the Ozarks,** Clarksville, AR 72830 | 1834 | C/Ind-R | 543 | 57% | | 40 | T | A | * |
| **College of the Southwest,** Hobbs, NM 88240 | 1956 | C/Ind | 208 | 87% | | 34 | T | | 1195 |
| **College of the Virgin Islands, St Thomas,** St Thomas, VI 00801 | 1962 | C/Pub | 1,984 | 63% | G | 108 | * | | * |
| **College of William and Mary,** Williamsburg, VA 23185 | 1693 | C/Pub | 4,609 | 70% | G | 481 | T | A | 1574 |
| **College of Wooster,** Wooster, OH 44691 | 1866 | C/Ind-R | 1,797 | 38% | | 170 | T | | 6705 |
| **Colorado College,** Colorado Springs, CO 80903 | 1874 | C/Ind | 1,906 | 37% | G | 175 | C | | 6400 |
| **Colorado School of Mines,** Golden, CO 80401 | 1874 | C/Pub | 2,299 | 70% | G | 205 | T | A | 2048 |
| **Colorado State University,** Fort Collins, CO 80523 | 1870 | C/Pub | 15,600 | 81% | G | 1,158 | C | A,AF | 1091 |
| **Colorado Technical College,** Colorado Springs, CO 80907 | 1965 | C/Prop | 585 | 83% | | 65 | C | | 2645x |
| **Columbia Bible College,** Columbia, SC 29203 | 1923 | C/Ind-R | 532 | 30% | G | 49 | C | | 2475 |
| **Columbia Christian College,** Portland, OR 97220 | 1956 | C/Ind-R | 273 | 39% | | 33 | M | | 2877 |
| **Columbia College,** Los Angeles, CA 90038 | 1952 | C/Ind | 315 | 20% | | 86 | M | | 2726x |
| **Columbia College,** Chicago, IL 60605 | 1890 | C/Ind | 3,912 | 95% | G | 373 | M | | 3015x |
| **Columbia College,** Columbia, MO 65216 | 1851 | C/Ind | 771 | 51% | | 65 | T | | 4115 |
| **Columbia College,** New York, NY 10027 | 1754 | M/Ind | 2,800 | 40% | | 560 | M | | 7894 |
| **Columbia College,** Columbia, SC 29203 | 1854 | W/Ind-R | 1,020 | 90% | G | 76 | C | | 3700 |
| **Columbia Union College,** Takoma Park, MD 20912 | 1904 | C/Ind-R | 805 | 85% | | 86 | M | | 4414 |
| **Columbia University, Barnard College**—See Barnard College | | | | | | | | | |
| **Columbia University, Columbia College**—See Columbia College (NY) | | | | | | | | | |
| **Columbia U, School of Engineering & Applied Sci,** New York, NY 10027 | 1754 | C/Ind | 1,166 | * | G | 143 | M | | 7992 |
| **Columbia U, School of General Studies,** New York, NY 10027 | 1947 | C/Ind | 1,650 | 85% | | 420 | M | | 7288x |
| **Columbia U, School of Nursing,** New York, NY 10032 | 1935 | W/Ind | 234 | 52% | G | 62 | M | | 7700 |
| **Columbus College,** Columbus, GA 31993 | 1958 | C/Pub | 3,982 | 86% | G | 215 | C | A | 733x |
| **Columbus College of Art and Design,** Columbus, OH 43215 | 1879 | C/Ind | 800 | 80% | | 69 | M | | 3960 |
| **Combs College of Music,** Philadelphia, PA 19119 | 1885 | C/Ind | 91 | 70% | G | 38 | M | | * |
| **Conception Seminary College,** Conception, MO 64433 | 1886 | M/Ind-R | 91 | 48% | | 27 | R | | 2140 |
| **Concord College,** Athens, WV 24712 | 1872 | C/Pub | 2,362 | 80% | | 117 | T | | 452 |
| **Concordia College,** River Forest, IL 60305 | 1864 | C/Ind-R | 1,089 | 45% | G | 114 | M | | 3021 |
| **Concordia College,** Ann Arbor, MI 48105 | 1963 | C/Ind-R | 560 | 50% | | 52 | T | | * |
| **Concordia College,** Moorhead, MN 56560 | 1891 | C/Ind-R | 2,586 | 64% | | 186 | C | A,AF | 4805 |
| **Concordia College,** St Paul, MN 55104 | 1893 | C/Ind-R | 716 | 58% | | 65 | M | | 3450 |
| **Concordia College,** Bronxville, NY 10708 | 1881 | C/Ind-R | 404 | 68% | | 56 | T | | 3385 |
| **Concordia College,** Portland, OR 97211 | 1905 | C/Ind-R | 274 | 40% | | 44 | M | | 3640 |
| **Concordia College,** Milwaukee, WI 53208 | 1881 | C/Ind-R | 621 | 90% | | 51 | M | | 3350 |
| **Concordia Lutheran College,** Austin, TX 78705 | 1926 | C/Ind-R | 428 | 85% | | 32 | C | | 2200 |
| **Concordia Teachers College,** Seward, NE 68434 | 1894 | C/Ind-R | 1,061 | 25% | G | 90 | T | A | 3293 |
| **Connecticut College,** New London, CT 06320 | 1911 | C/Ind | 1,637 | 33% | G | 204 | C | | 8000 |
| **Conservatory of Music of Puerto Rico,** San Juan, PR 00936 | 1959 | C/Pub | 268 | * | | 45 | M | | 255x |
| **Consortium of the California State University,** Long Beach, CA 90802 | 1973 | C/Pub | 620 | * | G | * | * | | *x |
| **Converse College,** Spartanburg, SC 29301 | 1889 | W/Ind | 745 | 44% | G | 85 | C | | 4570 |
| **Cook College**—See Rutgers University, Cook College | | | | | | | | | |
| **Cooper Institute,** Knoxville, TN 37917 | 1948 | C/Prop | 100 | 98% | | 10 | C | | 1782x |
| **Cooper Union for the Advancement of Sci & Art,** New York, NY 10003 | 1859 | C/Ind | 884 | 76% | G | 162 | M | | 300x |
| **Coppin State College,** Baltimore, MD 21216 | 1900 | C/Pub | 2,211 | 97% | G | 141 | M | | 1135x |
| **Corcoran School of Art,** Washington, DC 20006 | 1890 | C/Ind | 262 | 9% | | 65 | M | | 3980x |
| **Cornell College,** Mount Vernon, IA 52314 | 1853 | C/Ind-R | 907 | 26% | | 104 | T | | 5616 |
| **Cornell University,** Ithaca, NY 14853 | 1865 | C/Ind | 12,282 | 54% | G | 1,848 | T | A,N,AF | 8050 |
| **Cornish Institute,** Seattle, WA 98102 | 1914 | C/Ind | 525 | 84% | | 91 | M | | 3850x |
| **Corpus Christi State University,** Corpus Christi, TX 78412 | 1973 | C/Pub | 1,474 | 99% | G | 151 | C | A | 328 |
| **Covenant College,** Lookout Mountain, GA 37350 | 1955 | C/Ind-R | 529 | 15% | | 38 | T | | 4070 |
| **Creighton University,** Omaha, NE 68178 | 1878 | C/Ind-R | 3,788 | 39% | G | 964 | M | A | 4070 |
| **Criswell Bible College,** Dallas, TX 75201 | 1971 | C/Ind-R | * | * | G | * | * | | * |
| **Culver-Stockton College,** Canton, MO 63435 | 1853 | C/Ind | 602 | 56% | | 46 | T | | 3700 |
| **Cumberland College,** Williamsburg, KY 40769 | 1889 | C/Ind-R | 2,033 | 74% | G | 115 | T | A | 2380 |
| **Cumberland College of Tennessee,** Lebanon, TN 37087 | 1842 | C/Ind | 501 | 66% | | 27 | T | | 2247 |
| **Curry College,** Milton, MA 02116 | 1879 | C/Ind | 831 | 58% | | 89 | T | | 5985 |
| **C W Post Center of Long Island University,** Greenvale, NY 11548 | 1954 | C/Ind | 7,836 | 91% | G | 880 | T | | 4590 |
| **Daemen College,** Amherst, NY 14226 | 1947 | C/Ind | 1,317 | 95% | | 120 | C | | 4275 |
| **Dakota State College,** Madison, SD 57042 | 1881 | C/Pub | 1,107 | 91% | | 71 | R | | 1021 |
| **Dakota Wesleyan University,** Mitchell, SD 57301 | 1885 | C/Ind-R | 600 | 92% | | 54 | T | | 3200 |
| **Dallas Baptist College,** Dallas, TX 75211 | 1965 | C/Ind-R | * | * | | * | * | | * |
| **Dallas Bible College,** Dallas, TX 75228 | 1941 | C/Ind | * | * | | * | * | | * |
| **Dallas Christian College,** Dallas, TX 75234 | 1950 | C/Ind-R | 148 | 67% | | 17 | M | | 1594 |
| **Dana College,** Blair, NE 68008 | 1884 | C/Ind-R | 595 | 40% | | 48 | T | | 4100 |
| **Daniel Webster College,** Nashua, NH 03063 | 1965 | C/Ind | 500 | 25% | | 30 | C | AF | 4650 |
| **Dartmouth College,** Hanover, NH 03755 | 1769 | C/Ind | 3,523 | 6% | G | 671 | T | | 8190 |
| **David Lipscomb College,** Nashville, TN 37203 | 1891 | C/Ind-R | 2,375 | 54% | | 140 | C | | 2598 |
| **Davidson College,** Davidson, NC 28036 | 1837 | C/Ind-R | 1,356 | 30% | | 107 | T | A | 5580 |

| Name and Location | Est | Type/ Control | UG Enroll | State Res | Grad | Fac Size | Cmps | ROTC | Tuition & Fees |
|---|---|---|---|---|---|---|---|---|---|
| **Davis and Elkins College,** Elkins, WV 26241 | 1904 | C/Ind-R | 1,075 | 25% | | 72 | T | | $4415 |
| **Defiance College,** Defiance, OH 43512 | 1850 | C/Ind-R | 750 | 82% | | 70 | T | | 4130 |
| **Delaware State College,** Dover, DE 19901 | 1891 | C/Pub | 2,037 | 62% | G | 144 | T | | 1300 |
| **Delaware Valley Coll of Science & Agriculture,** Doylestown, PA 18901 | 1896 | C/Ind | 1,394 | 65% | | 89 | R | | 3890 |
| **De Lourdes College,** Des Plaines, IL 60016 | 1927 | W/Ind-R | 93 | 100% | | 25 | C | | 1650x |
| **Delta State University,** Cleveland, MS 38733 | 1925 | C/Pub | 2,490 | 97% | G | 167 | T | A | 770 |
| **Denison University,** Granville, OH 43023 | 1831 | C/Ind | 2,129 | 26% | | 205 | T | | 6670 |
| **Denver Baptist Bible College,** Broomfield, CO 80020 | 1952 | C/Ind-R | 110 | 37% | G | 18 | T | | 2390 |
| **DePaul University,** Chicago, IL 60604 | 1898 | C/Ind-R | 8,000 | 95% | G | 628 | M | A | 4290 |
| **DePauw University,** Greencastle, IN 46135 | 1837 | C/Ind-R | 2,380 | 48% | G | 200 | T | A | 6250 |
| **Detroit Coll of Business,** Dearborn, MI 48126 | 1962 | C/Ind | 2,789 | 100% | | 177 | M | | 2541x |
| **Detroit Coll of Business, Flint Cmps,** Flint, MI 48504 | 1973 | C/Ind | * | * | | * | * | | * |
| **Detroit Coll of Business, Grand Rapids Cmps,** Grand Rapids, MI 49503 | 1978 | C/Ind | 130 | 95% | | 13 | C | | 2928x |
| **DeVry Institute of Technology,** Phoenix, AZ 85016 | 1967 | C/Prop | 3,779 | 33% | | 202 | M | | 3025x |
| **DeVry Institute of Technology,** Atlanta, GA 30341 | 1969 | C/Prop | 2,080 | 41% | | 110 | M | | 3025x |
| **DeVry Institute of Technology,** Chicago, IL 60618 | 1931 | C/Prop | 5,128 | 92% | | 178 | M | | 3025x |
| **DeVry Institute of Technology,** Irving, TX 75062 | 1969 | C/Prop | 1,587 | 65% | | 62 | C | | 3025x |
| **Dickinson College,** Carlisle, PA 17013 | 1773 | C/Ind-R | 1,734 | 45% | | 122 | T | A | 6715 |
| **Dickinson State College,** Dickinson, ND 58601 | 1918 | C/Pub | 1,093 | 90% | | 90 | T | | 708 |
| **Dillard University,** New Orleans, LA 70122 | 1869 | C/Ind-R | 1,208 | 60% | | 90 | M | A,AF | 2600 |
| **Divine Word College,** Epworth, IA 52045 | 1912 | M/Ind-R | 91 | 84% | | 23 | R | | 3000 |
| **Doane College,** Crete, NE 68333 | 1872 | C/Ind-R | 633 | 83% | | 55 | T | A | 4100 |
| **Dr Martin Luther College,** New Ulm, MN 56073 | 1884 | C/Ind-R | 774 | 17% | | 72 | T | | 1620 |
| **Dominican College of Blauvelt,** Orangeburg, NY 10962 | 1952 | C/Ind | 1,602 | 74% | | 69 | R | A | 3160x |
| **Dominican College of San Rafael,** San Rafael, CA 94901 | 1890 | C/Ind-R | 527 | 81% | G | 102 | T | | 4508 |
| **Dominican School of Philosophy and Theology,** Berkeley, CA 94709 | 1932 | C/Ind-R | 20 | 50% | G | 22 | M | | 1810x |
| **Don Bosco College,** Newton, NJ 07860 | 1928 | M/Ind-R | 83 | 30% | | 21 | R | | 3360 |
| **Dordt College,** Sioux Center, IA 51250 | 1955 | C/Ind-R | 1,096 | 20% | | 75 | R | | 3850 |
| **Douglass College**—See Rutgers University, Douglass College | | | | | | | | | |
| **Dowling College,** Oakdale, NY 11769 | 1959 | C/Ind | 1,500 | 98% | G | 197 | T | | 4620 |
| **Drake University,** Des Moines, IA 50311 | 1881 | C/Ind | 4,801 | 40% | G | 340 | C | A | 5230 |
| **Drew University,** Madison, NJ 07940 | 1866 | C/Ind | 1,578 | 59% | G | 187 | T | | 6650 |
| **Drexel University,** Philadelphia, PA 19104 | 1891 | C/Ind | 7,251 | 65% | G | 303 | M | A | 4720 |
| **Drury College,** Springfield, MO 65802 | 1873 | C/Ind | 1,112 | 82% | G | 104 | C | | 3670 |
| **Duke University,** Durham, NC 27706 | 1838 | C/Ind | 5,868 | 12% | G | 1,256 | C | N,AF | 6450 |
| **Duquesne University,** Pittsburgh, PA 15282 | 1878 | C/Ind-R | 4,576 | 80% | G | 494 | M | A | 4175 |
| **Dyke College,** Cleveland, OH 44114 | 1848 | C/Ind | 1,435 | 98% | | 65 | M | | *x |
| **D'Youville College,** Buffalo, NY 14201 | 1908 | C/Ind | 1,528 | 98% | | 102 | M | | 4000 |
| **Earlham College,** Richmond, IN 47374 | 1847 | C/Ind-R | 1,118 | 28% | G | 96 | T | | 6520 |
| **East Carolina University,** Greenville, NC 27834 | 1907 | C/Pub | 11,127 | 88% | G | 783 | T | AF | 1038 |
| **East Central Oklahoma State University,** Ada, OK 74820 | 1909 | C/Pub | 3,288 | 91% | G | 198 | T | A | 486 |
| **East Coast Bible College,** Charlotte, NC 28214 | 1976 | C/Ind-R | 217 | 66% | | 15 | C | | 1600 |
| **Eastern College,** St Davids, PA 19087 | 1932 | C/Ind-R | 724 | 60% | G | 74 | T | | 4800 |
| **Eastern Connecticut State College,** Willimantic, CT 06226 | 1889 | C/Pub | 2,984 | 95% | G | 212 | T | | 992 |
| **Eastern Illinois University,** Charleston, IL 61920 | 1895 | C/Pub | 9,103 | 98% | G | 542 | T | A | 957 |
| **Eastern Kentucky University,** Richmond, KY 40475 | 1906 | C/Pub | 11,736 | 84% | G | 704 | T | A | 749 |
| **Eastern Mennonite College,** Harrisonburg, VA 22801 | 1917 | C/Ind-R | 979 | 28% | G | 106 | T | | 4137 |
| **Eastern Michigan University,** Ypsilanti, MI 48197 | 1849 | C/Pub | 14,499 | 95% | G | 862 | T | A | 1226 |
| **Eastern Montana College,** Billings, MT 59101 | 1927 | C/Pub | 3,474 | 95% | G | 218 | C | A | 624 |
| **Eastern Nazarene College,** Quincy, MA 02170 | 1918 | C/Ind-R | 819 | 34% | G | 66 | C | | 3326 |
| **Eastern New Mexico University,** Portales, NM 88130 | 1934 | C/Pub | 3,029 | 85% | G | 172 | T | A | 714 |
| **Eastern Oregon State College,** La Grande, OR 97850 | 1929 | C/Pub | 1,631 | 83% | G | 194 | R | A | 1335 |
| **Eastern Washington University,** Cheney, WA 99004 | 1882 | C/Pub | 6,717 | 95% | G | 390 | T | A | 942 |
| **East Stroudsburg State College,** East Stroudsburg, PA 18301 | 1891 | C/Pub | 3,600 | 81% | G | 271 | T | A | 1454 |
| **East Tennessee State University,** Johnson City, TN 37614 | 1911 | C/Pub | 7,924 | 86% | G | 404 | T | A | 714 |
| **East Texas Baptist College,** Marshall, TX 75670 | 1912 | C/Ind-R | 936 | 87% | | 90 | T | | 2250 |
| **East Texas State University,** Commerce, TX 75428 | 1889 | C/Pub | 5,151 | 95% | G | 363 | T | AF | 900 |
| **East Texas State University at Texarkana,** Texarkana, TX 75501 | 1971 | C/Pub | 560 | 76% | G | 55 | R | | 300x |
| **Eckerd College,** St Petersburg, FL 33733 | 1958 | C/Ind-R | 1,094 | 38% | | 85 | M | A | 5595 |
| **Edgecliff College**—See Xavier University | | | | | | | | | |
| **Edgewood College,** Madison, WI 53711 | 1927 | C/Ind-R | 741 | 75% | | 79 | C | | 3450 |
| **Edinboro State College,** Edinboro, PA 16444 | 1857 | C/Pub | 5,202 | 92% | G | 360 | T | A | 1400 |
| **Edward Waters College,** Jacksonville, FL 32209 | 1866 | C/Ind-R | 832 | 90% | | 43 | * | | * |
| **Electronic Data Processing College of PR,** Hato Rey, PR 00918 | 1968 | C/Prop | 1,842 | 99% | | 61 | M | | 1382x |
| **Elizabeth City State University,** Elizabeth City, NC 27909 | 1891 | C/Pub | 1,600 | 90% | | 114 | T | | * |
| **Elizabethtown College,** Elizabethtown, PA 17022 | 1899 | C/Ind-R | 1,387 | 68% | | 128 | T | | 4875 |
| **Elmhurst College,** Elmhurst, IL 60126 | 1871 | C/Ind-R | 3,625 | 96% | | 140 | C | | 4340 |
| **Elmira College,** Elmira, NY 14901 | 1855 | C/Ind | 2,653 | 59% | G | 170 | T | | 5450 |
| **Elon College,** Elon College, NC 27244 | 1889 | C/Ind-R | 2,580 | 60% | | 140 | T | A | 2740 |
| **Embry-Riddle Aeronautical University,** Daytona Beach, FL 32014 | 1926 | C/Ind | 5,109 | 5% | G | 310 | C | A,AF | 2915 |
| **Embry-Riddle Aeronautical U, Intl Campus,** Bunnell, FL 32010 | 1926 | C/Ind | 3,659 | 1% | G | 334 | * | | 1320x |
| **Embry-Riddle Aeronautical U, Prescott Campus,** Prescott, AZ 86302 | 1978 | C/Ind | 853 | 2% | | 93 | T | AF | 2915 |
| **Emerson College,** Boston, MA 02116 | 1880 | C/Ind | 1,700 | 45% | G | 152 | M | | 5890 |
| **Emmanuel College,** Boston, MA 02115 | 1919 | W/Ind-R | 972 | 74% | G | 105 | M | | 5080 |
| **Emory and Henry College,** Emory, VA 24327 | 1836 | C/Ind-R | 792 | 80% | | 62 | R | | 3306 |
| **Emory University,** Atlanta, GA 30322 | 1836 | C/Ind-R | 3,085 | 21% | G | 1,305 | M | | 6270 |
| **Emporia State University,** Emporia, KS 66801 | 1863 | C/Pub | 4,463 | 83% | G | 275 | T | A | 730 |
| **Erskine College,** Due West, SC 29639 | 1839 | C/Ind-R | 653 | 65% | G | 60 | R | A | 4300 |
| **Eugene Bible College,** Eugene, OR 97405 | 1925 | C/Ind | * | * | | * | * | | * |
| **Eureka College,** Eureka, IL 61530 | 1855 | C/Ind-R | 435 | 85% | | 37 | T | | 3950 |
| **Evangel College,** Springfield, MO 65802 | 1955 | C/Ind-R | 1,886 | 22% | | 119 | C | A | 2447 |

| Name and Location | Est | Type/ Control | UG Enroll | State Res | Grad | Fac Size | Cmps | ROTC | Tuition & Fees |
|---|---|---|---|---|---|---|---|---|---|
| **Evergreen State College,** Olympia, WA 98505 | 1967 | C/Pub | 2,698 | 80% | G | 159 | C | | $942 |
| **Fairfield University,** Fairfield, CT 06430 | 1942 | C/Ind-R | 2,831 | 46% | G | 296 | C | | 5145 |
| **Fairleigh Dickinson U, Florham-Madison Cmps,** Madison, NJ 07940 | 1958 | C/Ind | 3,308 | 85% | G | 283 | T | A | 4806 |
| **Fairleigh Dickinson U, Rutherford Cmps,** Rutherford, NJ 07070 | 1942 | C/Ind | 2,515 | 85% | G | 310 | T | | 4806 |
| **Fairleigh Dickinson U, Teaneck-Hackensack Cmps,** Teaneck, NJ 07666 | 1954 | C/Ind | 5,437 | 85% | G | 787 | C | | 4806 |
| **Fairmont State College,** Fairmont, WV 26554 | 1865 | C/Pub | 5,165 | 94% | | 312 | T | A,AF | 450 |
| **Faith Baptist Bible College,** Ankeny, IA 50021 | 1921 | C/Ind-R | 452 | 45% | | 27 | T | | 2520 |
| **Fashion Institute of Technology,** New York, NY 10001 | 1944 | C/Pub | 3,607 | 80% | | 611 | M | | 575 |
| **Fayetteville State University,** Fayetteville, NC 28301 | 1877 | C/Pub | 2,314 | 85% | G | 207 | C | AF | 934 |
| **Felician College,** Lodi, NJ 07644 | 1942 | W/Ind-R | 675 | 97% | | 74 | T | | 3410x |
| **Ferris State College,** Big Rapids, MI 49307 | 1884 | C/Pub | 11,261 | 96% | | 647 | T | | 1464 |
| **Ferrum College,** Ferrum, VA 24088 | 1913 | C/Ind-R | 1,615 | 85% | | 104 | R | A | 3440 |
| **Findlay College,** Findlay, OH 45840 | 1882 | C/Ind-R | 1,288 | 80% | | 78 | T | | 4380 |
| **Fisk University,** Nashville, TN 37203 | 1866 | C/Ind-R | 844 | 12% | G | 88 | C | | 5250 |
| **Fitchburg State College,** Fitchburg, MA 01420 | 1894 | C/Pub | 5,501 | 98% | G | 316 | T | A | 1006 |
| **Flagler College,** St Augustine, FL 32084 | 1968 | C/Ind | 850 | 48% | | 74 | T | A | 2700 |
| **Flaming Rainbow University,** Stilwell, OK 74960 | 1971 | W/Ind | 278 | 98% | | 25 | R | | 950x |
| **Florida A&M University,** Tallahassee, FL 32307 | 1887 | C/Pub | 4,795 | 88% | G | 327 | C | A,N,AF | 810 |
| **Florida Atlantic University,** Boca Raton, FL 33431 | 1961 | C/Pub | 5,221 | 88% | G | 317 | C | | 900 |
| **Florida Institute of Technology,** Melbourne, FL 32901 | 1958 | C/Ind | 3,675 | 20% | G | 466 | C | A | 3825 |
| **Florida Inst of Technology, Sch of Applied Tech,** Jensen Beach, FL 33457 | 1972 | C/Ind | 775 | 48% | | 52 | T | A | 3845 |
| **Florida International University,** Miami, FL 33199 | 1965 | C/Pub | 7,354 | 87% | G | 346 | M | | 699x |
| **Florida Memorial College,** Miami, FL 33054 | 1879 | C/Ind-R | 794 | 59% | | 94 | M | A | 2125 |
| **Florida Southern College,** Lakeland, FL 33802 | 1885 | C/Ind-R | 1,822 | 70% | | 135 | T | A | 3360 |
| **Florida State University,** Tallahassee, FL 32306 | 1857 | C/Pub | 18,089 | 90% | G | 1,489 | C | A,AF | 840 |
| **Fontbonne College,** St Louis, MO 63105 | 1917 | C/Ind-R | 839 | 86% | G | 115 | M | | 4100 |
| **Fordham University,** Bronx, NY 10458 | 1841 | C/Ind-R | 4,700 | 86% | G | 930 | M | A | 4950 |
| **Fordham University at Lincoln Center,** New York, NY 10023 | 1841 | C/Ind-R | 3,500 | 90% | G | 898 | M | A | 4448 |
| **Fort Hays State University,** Hays, KS 67601 | 1902 | C/Pub | 4,189 | 93% | G | 271 | T | A | 795 |
| **Fort Lauderdale College,** Ft Lauderdale, FL 33301 | 1940 | C/Ind | 1,134 | 85% | | 40 | C | | 1823x |
| **Fort Lewis College,** Durango, CO 81301 | 1911 | C/Pub | 3,400 | 70% | | 143 | T | | 724 |
| **Fort Valley State College,** Fort Valley, GA 31030 | 1895 | C/Pub | 1,715 | 84% | G | 142 | T | A | 855 |
| **Fort Wayne Bible College,** Fort Wayne, IN 46807 | 1904 | C/Ind-R | 450 | 50% | | 56 | C | | 3188 |
| **Framingham State College,** Framingham, MA 01701 | 1839 | C/Pub | 3,145 | 97% | G | 170 | C | | 1125 |
| **Francis Marion College,** Florence, SC 29501 | 1970 | C/Pub | 2,441 | 98% | G | 138 | R | A | 805 |
| **Franklin and Marshall College,** Lancaster, PA 17604 | 1787 | C/Ind | 2,057 | 32% | | 134 | C | | 6550 |
| **Franklin College of Indiana,** Franklin, IN 46131 | 1834 | C/Ind-R | 556 | 90% | | 62 | T | | 4790 |
| **Franklin Pierce College,** Rindge, NH 03461 | 1962 | C/Ind | 941 | 12% | | 75 | R | | 5500 |
| **Franklin University,** Columbus, OH 43215 | 1902 | C/Ind | 4,966 | 100% | | 215 | M | A | 2160x |
| **Freed-Hardeman College,** Henderson, TN 38340 | 1869 | C/Ind-R | 1,281 | 39% | | 102 | T | | 2700 |
| **Free Will Baptist Bible College,** Nashville, TN 37205 | 1942 | C/Ind-R | 587 | 15% | | 32 | C | | 1764 |
| **Fresno Pacific College,** Fresno, CA 93702 | 1944 | C/Ind-R | 393 | 84% | G | 63 | C | | 3890 |
| **Friends Bible College,** Haviland, KS 67059 | 1917 | C/Ind-R | 151 | 53% | | 18 | R | | 4292 |
| **Friends University,** Wichita, KS 67213 | 1898 | C/Ind-R | 891 | 75% | | 69 | C | | 3635 |
| **Frostburg State College,** Frostburg, MD 21532 | 1898 | C/Pub | 3,200 | 87% | G | 185 | T | A | 1231 |
| **Furman University,** Greenville, SC 29613 | 1826 | C/Ind-R | 2,840 | 46% | G | 157 | C | A | 4256 |
| **Gallaudet College,** Washington, DC 20002 | 1856 | C/Ind | 1,224 | * | G | 244 | M | | 1275 |
| **Gannon University,** Erie, PA 16541 | 1944 | C/Ind-R | 2,700 | 89% | G | 237 | C | A | 3450 |
| **Gardner-Webb College,** Boiling Springs, NC 28017 | 1905 | C/Ind-R | 1,542 | 10% | G | 88 | T | | 3260 |
| **Geneva College,** Beaver Falls, PA 15010 | 1848 | C/Ind-R | 1,406 | 64% | | 99 | T | | 4220 |
| **George Fox College,** Newberg, OR 97132 | 1891 | C/Ind-R | 743 | 71% | | 78 | T | | 4950 |
| **George Mason University,** Fairfax, VA 22030 | 1957 | C/Pub | 10,538 | 91% | G | 782 | T | A | 1192 |
| **Georgetown College,** Georgetown, KY 40324 | 1829 | C/Ind-R | 1,059 | 72% | G | 85 | T | A | 3306 |
| **Georgetown University,** Washington, DC 20057 | 1789 | C/Ind-R | 5,430 | * | G | 1,434 | M | A | 6830 |
| **George Washington University,** Washington, DC 20052 | 1821 | C/Ind | 6,500 | 5% | G | 1,144 | M | | 5010 |
| **George Williams College,** Downers Grove, IL 60515 | 1890 | C/Ind | 636 | 90% | G | 109 | T | | 4680 |
| **Georgia College,** Milledgeville, GA 31061 | 1889 | C/Pub | 2,815 | 95% | G | 179 | T | | 687 |
| **Georgia Institute of Technology,** Atlanta, GA 30332 | 1885 | C/Pub | 9,161 | 53% | G | 572 | M | A,N,AF | 1793 |
| **Georgian Court College,** Lakewood, NJ 08701 | 1908 | W/Ind-R | 993 | 98% | G | 110 | T | | 3265 |
| **Georgia Southern College,** Statesboro, GA 30460 | 1906 | C/Pub | 5,729 | 91% | G | 350 | T | A | 855 |
| **Georgia Southwestern College,** Americus, GA 31709 | 1906 | C/Pub | 1,909 | 97% | G | 112 | T | A | 708 |
| **Georgia State University,** Atlanta, GA 30303 | 1913 | C/Pub | 14,276 | 93% | G | 994 | M | A | 915x |
| **Gettysburg College,** Gettysburg, PA 17325 | 1832 | C/Ind-R | 1,935 | 30% | | 153 | T | A | 6000 |
| **Glassboro State College,** Glassboro, NJ 08028 | 1923 | C/Pub | 9,800 | 97% | G | 534 | T | | 1384 |
| **Glenville State College,** Glenville, WV 26351 | 1872 | C/Pub | 1,998 | 94% | | 96 | T | | 464 |
| **GMI Engineering and Management Institute,** Flint, MI 48502 | 1919 | C/Ind | 2,389 | 42% | | 148 | C | | 1864 |
| **Goddard College,** Plainfield, VT 05667 | 1938 | C/Ind | 105 | 21% | G | 53 | R | | 7700 |
| **Golden Gate University,** San Francisco, CA 94105 | 1901 | C/Ind | 2,634 | * | G | 915 | M | | 3140x |
| **Goldey Beacom College,** Wilmington, DE 19808 | 1886 | C/Ind | 1,802 | 56% | | 85 | C | | 2700 |
| **Gonzaga University,** Spokane, WA 99258 | 1887 | C/Ind-R | 2,123 | 55% | G | 281 | C | A | 4700 |
| **Gordon College,** Wenham, MA 01984 | 1889 | C/Ind-R | 1,100 | 42% | | 69 | T | | 5247 |
| **Goshen College,** Goshen, IN 46526 | 1894 | C/Ind-R | 1,208 | 32% | | 107 | T | | 4165 |
| **Goucher College,** Towson, MD 21204 | 1885 | W/Ind | 1,010 | 30% | G | 136 | T | | 6275 |
| **Governors State University,** Park Forest South, IL 60466 | 1969 | C/Pub | 1,521 | 98% | G | 323 | T | | 852x |
| **Grace Bible College,** Grand Rapids, MI 49509 | 1945 | C/Ind-R | 157 | 25% | | 21 | C | | 1700 |
| **Grace College,** Winona Lake, IN 46590 | 1948 | C/Ind-R | 931 | 99% | | 44 | T | | 3520 |
| **Grace College of the Bible,** Omaha, NE 68108 | 1943 | C/Ind-R | 417 | 43% | | 33 | C | | 2480 |
| **Graceland College,** Lamoni, IA 50140 | 1895 | C/Ind | 1,302 | 24% | | 100 | T | | 4090 |
| **Grambling State University,** Grambling, LA 71245 | 1901 | C/Pub | 3,570 | 79% | G | 200 | T | A,AF | 744 |
| **Grand Canyon College,** Phoenix, AZ 85017 | 1949 | C/Ind-R | 1,227 | 81% | | 93 | M | | 2397 |
| **Grand Rapids Baptist College and Seminary,** Grand Rapids, MI 49505 | 1941 | C/Ind-R | 855 | 47% | G | 76 | C | A | 3160 |
| **Grand Valley State Colleges,** Allendale, MI 49401 | 1960 | C/Pub | 6,000 | 97% | G | 234 | R | | 1380 |

| Name and Location | Est | Type/ Control | UG Enroll | State Res | Grad | Fac Size | Cmps | ROTC | Tuition & Fees |
|---|---|---|---|---|---|---|---|---|---|
| **Grand View College,** Des Moines, IA 50316 | 1896 | C/Ind-R | 1,296 | 91% | | 84 | C | | $3390 |
| **Grantham College of Engineering,** Los Angeles, CA 90034 | 1951 | C/Prop | 800 | * | | 5 | * | | * |
| **Gratz College,** Philadelphia, PA 19141 | 1895 | C/Ind-R | 220 | 95% | G | 17 | M | | 525x |
| **Great Lakes Bible College,** Lansing, MI 48901 | 1949 | C/Ind-R | 178 | 61% | | 18 | C | | 1845 |
| **Green Mountain College,** Poultney, VT 05764 | 1834 | C/Ind | 409 | 10% | | 47 | T | | 5255 |
| **Greensboro College,** Greensboro, NC 27420 | 1838 | C/Ind-R | 682 | 60% | | 50 | C | | 3410 |
| **Greenville College,** Greenville, IL 62246 | 1892 | C/Ind-R | 835 | 62% | | 63 | T | | 4290 |
| **Griffin College,** Seattle, WA 98121 | 1909 | C/Prop | 412 | * | | 32 | M | | 3000x |
| **Griffin College, Bellevue Branch,** Bellevue, WA 98004 | 1909 | C/Prop | 250 | * | | * | * | | * |
| **Grinnell College,** Grinnell, IA 50112 | 1846 | C/Ind | 1,259 | 12% | | 117 | T | | 6710 |
| **Grove City College,** Grove City, PA 16127 | 1876 | C/Ind-R | 2,256 | 72% | | 121 | T | AF | 2620 |
| **Guilford College,** Greensboro, NC 27410 | 1837 | C/Ind-R | 1,115 | 45% | | 93 | M | | 4420 |
| **Gulf-Coast Bible College,** Houston, TX 77008 | 1953 | C/Ind-R | 341 | 98% | | 21 | M | | 2532 |
| **Gustavus Adolphus College,** St Peter, MN 56082 | 1862 | C/Ind-R | 2,302 | 70% | | 255 | T | | 5350 |
| **Gwynedd-Mercy College,** Gwynedd Valley, PA 19437 | 1948 | W/Ind-R | 1,573 | 90% | | 126 | T | A | 3450 |
| **Hahnemann Medical College,** Philadelphia, PA 19102 | 1848 | C/Ind | 710 | 90% | G | 350 | M | | * |
| **Hamilton College,** Clinton, NY 13323 | 1812 | C/Ind | 1,647 | 50% | | 146 | R | | 7950 |
| **Hamline University,** St Paul, MN 55104 | 1854 | C/Ind-R | 1,298 | 80% | G | 170 | M | | 5530 |
| **Hampden-Sydney College,** Hampden-Sydney, VA 23943 | 1776 | M/Ind-R | 750 | 65% | | 62 | R | | 5875 |
| **Hampshire College,** Amherst, MA 01002 | 1965 | C/Ind | 1,200 | 11% | | 101 | R | | 8538 |
| **Hampton Institute,** Hampton, VA 23668 | 1868 | C/Ind | 2,878 | 39% | G | 238 | C | A | 2935 |
| **Hannibal-LaGrange College,** Hannibal, MO 63401 | 1858 | C/Ind-R | 450 | 60% | | 44 | T | | 2613 |
| **Hanover College,** Hanover, IN 47243 | 1827 | C/Ind-R | 1,000 | 50% | | 73 | R | | 3600 |
| **Harding University,** Searcy, AR 72143 | 1924 | C/Ind-R | 3,024 | 30% | G | 168 | T | | 2831 |
| **Hardin-Simmons University,** Abilene, TX 79698 | 1891 | C/Ind-R | 1,802 | 86% | G | 122 | C | A | 2760 |
| **Harris-Stowe State College,** St Louis, MO 63103 | 1857 | C/Pub | 1,242 | 100% | | 66 | M | | 558x |
| **Hartwick College,** Oneonta, NY 13820 | 1928 | C/Ind | 1,452 | 52% | | 118 | T | | 6425 |
| **Harvard and Radcliffe Colleges,** Cambridge, MA 02138 | 1636 | C/Ind | 6,496 | 21% | | 730 | C | | 8820 |
| **Harvey Mudd College,** Claremont, CA 91711 | 1955 | C/Ind | 500 | 60% | G | 65 | T | A | 7250 |
| **Hastings College,** Hastings, NE 68901 | 1882 | C/Ind-R | 798 | 83% | | 67 | T | | 3820 |
| **Haverford College,** Haverford, PA 19041 | 1833 | C/Ind | 1,060 | 19% | | 97 | T | | 8080 |
| **Hawaii Loa College,** Kaneohe, HI 96744 | 1963 | C/Ind-R | 325 | 35% | | 33 | T | | 3320 |
| **Hawaii Pacific College,** Honolulu, HI 96813 | 1966 | C/Ind | 1,765 | 70% | | 110 | M | | 2680x |
| **Hawthorne College,** Antrim, NH 03440 | 1962 | C/Ind | 375 | 5% | | 50 | R | AF | 4655 |
| **Hebrew College,** Brookline, MA 02146 | 1921 | C/Ind | 112 | 90% | G | 7 | C | | 960x |
| **Hebrew Union College–Jewish Inst of Religion,** Los Angeles, CA 90007 | 1954 | C/Ind-R | * | * | G | 38 | M | | *x |
| **Hebrew Union College–Jewish Inst of Religion,** New York, NY 10012 | 1922 | C/Ind-R | * | * | G | * | * | | * |
| **Heidelberg College,** Tiffin, OH 44883 | 1850 | C/Ind-R | 761 | 75% | | 72 | T | | 5620 |
| **Hellenic College,** Brookline, MA 02146 | 1937 | C/Ind-R | 159 | 15% | | 43 | C | | 3095 |
| **Henderson State University,** Arkadelphia, AR 71923 | 1890 | C/Pub | 2,611 | 95% | G | 180 | T | A | 760 |
| **Hendrix College,** Conway, AR 72032 | 1876 | C/Ind-R | 1,017 | 85% | | 66 | T | | 3260 |
| **Herbert H Lehman College**—See City U of NY, Herbert H Lehman College | | | | | | | | | |
| **Heritage College,** Toppenish, WA 98948 | 1907 | C/Ind-R | 312 | 100% | G | 40 | R | | 2280x |
| **High Point College,** High Point, NC 27262 | 1924 | C/Ind-R | 1,385 | 62% | | 61 | C | A | 3330 |
| **Hillsdale College,** Hillsdale, MI 49242 | 1844 | C/Ind | 1,025 | 48% | | 73 | T | | 5370 |
| **Hiram College,** Hiram, OH 44234 | 1850 | C/Ind-R | 1,150 | 66% | | 80 | R | | 6075 |
| **Hobart College,** Geneva, NY 14456 | 1822 | M/Ind-R | 1,050 | 50% | | 126 | T | | 7200 |
| **Hofstra University,** Hempstead, NY 11550 | 1935 | C/Ind | 7,173 | 80% | G | 660 | C | A | 4350 |
| **Hollins College,** Hollins College, VA 24020 | 1842 | W/Ind | 875 | 31% | G | 86 | C | | 6325 |
| **Holy Apostles College,** Cromwell, CT 06416 | 1956 | C/Ind-R | * | * | G | * | * | | * |
| **Holy Family College,** Fremont, CA 94538 | 1946 | C/Ind-R | * | * | | * | * | | * |
| **Holy Family College,** Philadelphia, PA 19114 | 1954 | W/Ind-R | 1,338 | 99% | | 125 | M | | 3300x |
| **Holy Names College,** Oakland, CA 94619 | 1868 | C/Ind-R | 539 | 7% | G | 101 | M | | 4570 |
| **Holy Redeemer College,** Waterford, WI 53185 | 1968 | M/Ind-R | 76 | 20% | | 21 | R | | 2250 |
| **Hood College,** Frederick, MD 21701 | 1893 | W/Ind | 1,125 | 55% | G | 154 | T | | 5585 |
| **Hope College,** Holland, MI 49423 | 1851 | C/Ind-R | 2,458 | 73% | | 185 | T | | 5010 |
| **Houghton College,** Houghton, NY 14744 | 1883 | C/Ind-R | 1,240 | 66% | | 93 | R | | 4207 |
| **Houston Baptist University,** Houston, TX 77074 | 1960 | C/Ind-R | 2,219 | 88% | G | 136 | M | | 2400 |
| **Howard Payne University,** Brownwood, TX 76801 | 1889 | C/Ind-R | 1,172 | 88% | | 87 | T | A | 2300 |
| **Howard University,** Washington, DC 20059 | 1867 | C/Ind | 7,698 | 31% | G | 1,911 | M | A,AF | 2250 |
| **Humboldt State University,** Arcata, CA 95521 | 1913 | C/Pub | 6,432 | 98% | G | 485 | T | | 350 |
| **Hunter College**—See City U of NY, Hunter College | | | | | | | | | |
| **Huntingdon College,** Montgomery, AL 36106 | 1854 | C/Ind-R | 503 | 70% | | 51 | C | | 2700 |
| **Huntington College,** Huntington, IN 46750 | 1897 | C/Ind-R | 456 | 80% | G | 60 | T | | 4085 |
| **Huron College,** Huron, SD 57350 | 1883 | C/Ind-R | 321 | 79% | | 41 | T | | 3485 |
| **Husson College,** Bangor, ME 04401 | 1898 | C/Ind | 812 | 65% | G | 35 | T | | 3825 |
| **Huston-Tillotson College,** Austin, TX 78702 | 1875 | C/Ind-R | 692 | * | | 50 | C | | * |
| **Idaho State University,** Pocatello, ID 83209 | 1901 | C/Pub | 4,695 | 95% | G | 505 | T | A | 680 |
| **Illinois Benedictine College,** Lisle, IL 60532 | 1887 | C/Ind-R | 1,941 | 98% | G | 114 | T | | 3910 |
| **Illinois College,** Jacksonville, IL 62650 | 1829 | C/Ind-R | 800 | 88% | | 60 | T | | 3075 |
| **Illinois College of Optometry,** Chicago, IL 60616 | 1872 | C/Ind | * | * | G | * | * | | * |
| **Illinois Institute of Technology,** Chicago, IL 60616 | 1892 | C/Ind | 4,075 | 80% | G | 535 | M | N,AF | 5700 |
| **Illinois State University,** Normal, IL 61761 | 1857 | C/Pub | 17,392 | 98% | G | 1,112 | C | A | 1079 |
| **Illinois Wesleyan University,** Bloomington, IL 61701 | 1850 | C/Ind-R | 1,675 | 94% | | 159 | C | | 5347 |
| **Immaculata College,** Immaculata, PA 19345 | 1920 | W/Ind-R | 1,567 | 90% | | 101 | T | | 3070 |
| **Incarnate Word College,** San Antonio, TX 78209 | 1881 | C/Ind-R | 1,203 | 90% | G | 126 | M | | 3236 |
| **Indiana Central University,** Indianapolis, IN 46227 | 1902 | C/Ind-R | 3,088 | 96% | G | 189 | M | | 4100 |
| **Indiana Institute of Technology,** Fort Wayne, IN 46803 | 1930 | C/Ind | 850 | 30% | | 44 | C | A | 3527 |
| **Indiana State University,** Terre Haute, IN 47809 | 1865 | C/Pub | 10,493 | 80% | G | 673 | C | A | 1318 |
| **Indiana State University Evansville,** Evansville, IN 47712 | 1965 | C/Pub | 3,586 | 95% | | 186 | C | | 1121x |
| **Indiana University at Kokomo,** Kokomo, IN 46902 | 1945 | C/Pub | 1,803 | 98% | | 145 | T | | 1136x |

| Name and Location | Est | Type/ Control | UG Enroll | State Res | Grad | Fac Size | Cmps | ROTC | Tuition & Fees |
|---|---|---|---|---|---|---|---|---|---|
| **Indiana University at South Bend,** South Bend, IN 46634 | 1922 | C/Pub | 4,611 | 96% | G | 330 | C | | $1124x |
| **Indiana University Bloomington,** Bloomington, IN 47405 | 1820 | C/Pub | 23,888 | 74% | G | 1,637 | T | | 1317 |
| **Indiana University Northwest,** Gary, IN 46408 | 1959 | C/Pub | 3,989 | 99% | G | 309 | C | | 981x |
| **Indiana University of Pennsylvania,** Indiana, PA 15705 | 1875 | C/Pub | 11,458 | 96% | G | 686 | T | A | 1545 |
| **Indiana U–Purdue U at Fort Wayne,** Fort Wayne, IN 46805 | 1917 | C/Pub | 9,245 | 97% | G | 580 | C | A | 1095x |
| **Indiana U–Purdue U at Indianapolis,** Indianapolis, IN 46202 | 1969 | C/Pub | 16,581 | 94% | G | 2,150 | M | A | 1038 |
| **Indiana University Southeast,** New Albany, IN 47150 | 1941 | C/Pub | 3,709 | 98% | G | 198 | T | A,AF | 1137x |
| **Inter American U of PR, Arecibo Regional Coll,** Arecibo, PR 00612 | 1957 | C/Ind | 3,517 | * | | 156 | C | | 1443x |
| **Inter American U of PR, Metro Campus,** Hato Rey, PR 00919 | 1960 | C/Ind | 11,346 | * | G | 571 | C | | 1550x |
| **Inter American U of PR, San Germán Campus,** San Germán, PR 00753 | 1912 | C/Ind | * | * | G | * | * | | * |
| **International Inst of the Americas of World U,** Hato Rey, PR 00917 | 1965 | C/Ind | * | 96% | G | 279 | M | | 1577x |
| **Iona College,** New Rochelle, NY 10801 | 1940 | C/Ind | 3,896 | 90% | G | 291 | C | | 4280 |
| **Iowa State University,** Ames, IA 50011 | 1858 | C/Pub | 20,801 | 77% | G | 2,024 | T | A,N,AF | 1040 |
| **Iowa Wesleyan College,** Mount Pleasant, IA 52641 | 1842 | C/Ind-R | 620 | 72% | | 55 | T | | 4625 |
| **Ithaca College,** Ithaca, NY 14850 | 1892 | C/Ind | 4,720 | 48% | G | 419 | T | | 5526 |
| **Jackson College**—See Tufts University | | | | | | | | | |
| **Jackson State University,** Jackson, MS 39217 | 1877 | C/Pub | 6,136 | 98% | G | 408 | C | A | 832 |
| **Jacksonville State University,** Jacksonville, AL 36265 | 1883 | C/Pub | 5,887 | 80% | G | 348 | T | A | 700 |
| **Jacksonville University,** Jacksonville, FL 32211 | 1934 | C/Ind | 2,253 | 55% | G | 150 | M | N | 4145 |
| **James Madison University,** Harrisonburg, VA 22807 | 1908 | C/Pub | 7,861 | 80% | G | 533 | T | A | 1506 |
| **Jamestown College,** Jamestown, ND 58401 | 1883 | C/Ind-R | 637 | 60% | | 63 | T | | 4300 |
| **Jarvis Christian College,** Hawkins, TX 75765 | 1912 | C/Ind-R | 622 | * | | 55 | R | | * |
| **Jersey City State College,** Jersey City, NJ 07305 | 1927 | C/Pub | 7,700 | 95% | G | 469 | C | A | 1020 |
| **Jewish Theological Seminary of America,** New York, NY 10027 | 1886 | C/Ind | 101 | 26% | G | 108 | M | | 3070 |
| **John Brown University,** Siloam Springs, AR 72761 | 1919 | C/Ind | 742 | 25% | | 51 | R | | 2500 |
| **John Carroll University,** University Heights, OH 44118 | 1886 | C/Ind-R | 3,251 | 60% | G | 285 | T | A | 3968 |
| **John F Kennedy University,** Orinda, CA 94563 | 1964 | C/Ind | 194 | 100% | G | 224 | C | | 2400x |
| **John Jay College of Criminal Justice**—See City U of NY, John Jay Coll of Crim Justice | | | | | | | | | |
| **Johns Hopkins University,** Baltimore, MD 21218 | 1876 | C/Ind | 2,245 | 23% | G | 332 | M | A | 6920 |
| **Johnson and Wales College,** Providence, RI 02903 | 1914 | C/Ind | 3,478 | 20% | | 104 | M | | 3945 |
| **Johnson Bible College,** Knoxville, TN 37920 | 1893 | C/Ind-R | 398 | 17% | | 28 | M | | 1440 |
| **Johnson C Smith University,** Charlotte, NC 28216 | 1867 | C/Ind-R | 1,310 | 41% | | 113 | C | A,AF | 2700 |
| **Johnson State College,** Johnson, VT 05656 | 1828 | C/Pub | 845 | 66% | G | 80 | R | | 1438 |
| **John Wesley College,** High Point, NC 27260 | 1932 | C/Ind-R | 79 | 70% | | 11 | C | | 1574x |
| **Jones College,** Jacksonville, FL 32211 | 1918 | C/Ind | 1,364 | 90% | | 53 | M | | 1440x |
| **Judson Baptist College,** The Dalles, OR 97058 | 1956 | C/Ind-R | 306 | 76% | | 30 | T | | 3600 |
| **Judson College,** Marion, AL 36756 | 1838 | W/Ind-R | 355 | 85% | | 37 | R | | 2165 |
| **Judson College,** Elgin, IL 60120 | 1963 | C/Ind-R | 426 | 60% | | 50 | C | | 4836 |
| **Juilliard School,** New York, NY 10023 | 1905 | C/Ind | 1,007 | 40% | G | 220 | M | | 4600x |
| **Juniata College,** Huntingdon, PA 16652 | 1876 | C/Ind | 1,307 | 76% | | 94 | T | | 5361 |
| **Kalamazoo College,** Kalamazoo, MI 49007 | 1833 | C/Ind-R | 1,367 | 75% | | 102 | C | | 6492 |
| **Kansas City Art Institute,** Kansas City, MO 64111 | 1885 | C/Ind | 518 | 32% | | 51 | M | | 5700 |
| **Kansas Newman College,** Wichita, KS 67213 | 1933 | C/Ind-R | 717 | 91% | | 72 | C | | 3379 |
| **Kansas State University,** Manhattan, KS 66506 | 1863 | C/Pub | 15,106 | 85% | G | 3,000 | T | A,AF | 898 |
| **Kansas Wesleyan,** Salina, KS 67401 | 1886 | C/Ind-R | 450 | 76% | | 46 | T | | 3278 |
| **Kean College of New Jersey,** Union, NJ 07083 | 1855 | C/Pub | 11,293 | 96% | G | 716 | C | | 976 |
| **Kearney State College,** Kearney, NE 68847 | 1903 | C/Pub | 5,845 | 98% | G | * | T | A | 805 |
| **Keene State College,** Keene, NH 03431 | 1909 | C/Pub | 2,750 | 65% | G | 179 | T | A | 1273 |
| **Kendall College,** Evanston, IL 60201 | 1934 | C/Ind-R | 416 | 97% | | 34 | C | | 3710 |
| **Kendall School of Design,** Grand Rapids, MI 49503 | 1928 | C/Ind | 505 | 94% | | 51 | C | | 3345x |
| **Kennesaw College,** Marietta, GA 30061 | 1966 | C/Pub | 4,202 | 95% | | 151 | T | A | 613x |
| **Kent State University,** Kent, OH 44242 | 1910 | C/Pub | 15,770 | 92% | G | 780 | T | A,AF | 1494 |
| **Kentucky Christian College,** Grayson, KY 41143 | 1919 | C/Ind-R | 456 | 23% | | 27 | R | | 1757 |
| **Kentucky State University,** Frankfort, KY 40601 | 1886 | C/Pub | 2,253 | 83% | G | 137 | T | A | 750 |
| **Kentucky Wesleyan College,** Owensboro, KY 42301 | 1858 | C/Ind-R | 925 | 82% | | 73 | C | | 3400 |
| **Kenyon College,** Gambier, OH 43022 | 1824 | C/Ind | 1,443 | 28% | | 120 | R | | 7090 |
| **Keuka College,** Keuka Park, NY 14478 | 1890 | W/Ind | 524 | 86% | | 63 | R | | 4960 |
| **King College,** Bristol, TN 37620 | 1867 | C/Ind-R | 332 | 34% | | 46 | T | | 3440 |
| **King's College,** Briarcliff Manor, NY 10510 | 1938 | C/Ind | 787 | 47% | | 56 | T | | 4600 |
| **King's College,** Wilkes-Barre, PA 18711 | 1946 | C/Ind-R | 1,779 | 63% | | 103 | C | | 4100 |
| **Knox College,** Galesburg, IL 61401 | 1837 | C/Ind | 982 | 70% | | 86 | T | A | 6435 |
| **Knoxville College,** Knoxville, TN 37921 | 1875 | C/Ind-R | 699 | * | | 52 | C | A,AF | * |
| **Kutztown State College,** Kutztown, PA 19530 | 1866 | C/Pub | 4,728 | 80% | G | 303 | T | A | 1532 |
| **Lafayette College,** Easton, PA 18042 | 1826 | C/Ind-R | 2,043 | 26% | | 173 | T | A | 7025 |
| **LaGrange College,** LaGrange, GA 30240 | 1831 | C/Ind-R | 943 | 89% | G | 70 | T | A | 2415 |
| **Lake Erie College,** Painesville, OH 44077 | 1859 | W/Ind | 375 | 50% | G | 90 | T | | 5280 |
| **Lake Forest College,** Lake Forest, IL 60045 | 1857 | C/Ind | 1,091 | 41% | | 93 | T | | 6745 |
| **Lakeland College,** Sheboygan, WI 53081 | 1862 | C/Ind-R | 476 | 80% | | 40 | R | | 4455 |
| **Lake Superior State College,** Sault Ste Marie, MI 49783 | 1946 | C/Pub | 2,309 | 85% | G | 136 | T | A | 1320 |
| **Lamar University,** Beaumont, TX 77710 | 1923 | C/Pub | 13,283 | 95% | G | 625 | C | A | 730 |
| **Lambuth College,** Jackson, TN 38301 | 1843 | C/Ind-R | 740 | 84% | | 61 | T | | 3270 |
| **Lancaster Bible College,** Lancaster, PA 17601 | 1933 | C/Ind-R | 412 | 82% | | 23 | C | | 3200 |
| **Lander College,** Greenwood, SC 29646 | 1872 | C/Pub | 1,825 | 96% | G | 110 | T | A | 1170 |
| **Lane College,** Jackson, TN 38301 | 1882 | C/Ind-R | 673 | 58% | | 47 | * | | * |
| **Langston University,** Langston, OK 73050 | 1897 | C/Pub | 1,322 | 33% | | 168 | R | | 500 |
| **Laredo State University,** Laredo, TX 78040 | 1969 | C/Pub | 409 | 93% | G | 48 | C | | 285x |
| **La Roche College,** Pittsburgh, PA 15237 | 1963 | C/Ind-R | 1,442 | 97% | G | 109 | M | | 3170 |
| **La Salle College,** Philadelphia, PA 19141 | 1863 | C/Ind-R | 6,318 | 80% | G | 289 | M | A | 4150 |
| **Lawrence Institute of Technology,** Southfield, MI 48075 | 1932 | C/Ind | 5,307 | 90% | | 278 | C | | 1890 |
| **Lawrence University,** Appleton, WI 54912 | 1847 | C/Ind | 1,135 | 43% | | 110 | C | | 6675 |
| **Lebanon Valley College,** Annville, PA 17003 | 1866 | C/Ind-R | 938 | 60% | | 90 | T | | 4790 |

| Name and Location | Est | Type/ Control | UG Enroll | State Res | Grad | Fac Size | Cmps | ROTC | Tuition & Fees |
|---|---|---|---|---|---|---|---|---|---|
| **Lee College,** Cleveland, TN 37311 | 1918 | C/Ind-R | 1,330 | 30% | | 70 | T | | $2266 |
| **Lehigh University,** Bethlehem, PA 18015 | 1865 | C/Ind | 4,400 | 43% | G | 397 | C | A,AF | 7200 |
| **Le Moyne College,** Syracuse, NY 13214 | 1946 | C/Ind-R | 1,850 | 80% | | 136 | C | | 4360 |
| **LeMoyne-Owen College,** Memphis, TN 38126 | 1870 | C/Ind-R | 1,049 | 95% | | 77 | M | | 3450x |
| **Lenoir-Rhyne College,** Hickory, NC 28601 | 1891 | C/Ind-R | 1,375 | 70% | G | 117 | T | | 4130 |
| **Lesley College,** Cambridge, MA 02238 | 1909 | W/Ind | 740 | 58% | G | 334 | C | | 5440 |
| **LeTourneau College,** Longview, TX 75601 | 1946 | M/Ind-R | 1,047 | 15% | | 57 | C | | 3536 |
| **Lewis and Clark College,** Portland, OR 97219 | 1867 | C/Ind-R | 1,896 | 35% | G | 165 | M | | 6444 |
| **Lewis-Clark State College,** Lewiston, ID 83501 | 1894 | C/Pub | 1,951 | 90% | | 100 | T | A | 640 |
| **Lewis University,** Romeoville, IL 60441 | 1930 | C/Ind-R | 2,367 | 99% | G | 126 | T | | 4580 |
| **Liberty Baptist College,** Lynchburg, VA 24506 | 1971 | C/Ind-R | 3,341 | 14% | | 168 | C | | 2270 |
| **LIFE Bible College,** Los Angeles, CA 90026 | 1925 | C/Ind-R | 430 | 74% | | 26 | M | | 1980 |
| **Limestone College,** Gaffney, SC 29340 | 1845 | C/Ind | 1,515 | 85% | | 77 | T | | 3940 |
| **Lincoln Christian College,** Lincoln, IL 62656 | 1944 | C/Ind-R | 448 | 70% | G | 48 | T | | 2560 |
| **Lincoln Memorial University,** Harrogate, TN 37752 | 1897 | C/Ind | -1,278 | 60% | | 53 | R | A | 2430 |
| **Lincoln University,** San Francisco, CA 94118 | 1919 | C/Ind | * | * | G | * | * | | * |
| **Lincoln University,** Jefferson City, MO 65101 | 1866 | C/Pub | 2,658 | 66% | G | 189 | T | A | 565 |
| **Lincoln University,** Lincoln University, PA 19352 | 1854 | C/Pub | 1,062 | 60% | G | 88 | R | | 1770 |
| **Lindenwood Colleges,** St Charles, MO 63301 | 1827 | C/Ind | 1,448 | 85% | G | 171 | T | | 4600 |
| **Linfield College,** McMinnville, OR 97128 | 1849 | C/Ind-R | 1,252 | 46% | G | 112 | T | | 5120 |
| **Livingston College**—See Rutgers University, Livingston College | | | | | | | | | |
| **Livingstone College,** Salisbury, NC 28144 | 1879 | C/Ind-R | 879 | 58% | | 77 | * | | * |
| **Livingston University,** Livingston, AL 35470 | 1835 | C/Pub | 1,109 | 82% | G | 73 | T | | 888 |
| **Lock Haven State College,** Lock Haven, PA 17745 | 1870 | C/Pub | 2,531 | 81% | | 170 | T | A | 1522 |
| **Loma Linda University, La Sierra Campus,** Riverside, CA 92515 | 1915 | C/Ind-R | 2,163 | 60% | G | 190 | R | | 5220 |
| **Loma Linda University, Loma Linda Campus,** Loma Linda, CA 92350 | 1905 | C/Ind-R | 952 | 73% | G | * | T | | * |
| **Long Island University, Brooklyn Center,** Brooklyn, NY 11201 | 1926 | C/Ind | 4,938 | 90% | G | 406 | M | | 4318 |
| **Long Island University, C W Post Center**—See C W Post Center of Long Island University | | | | | | | | | |
| **Long Island University, Southampton College,** Southampton, NY 11968 | 1963 | C/Ind | 1,266 | 70% | G | 123 | R | | 5300 |
| **Longwood College,** Farmville, VA 23901 | 1839 | C/Pub | 2,350 | 92% | G | 158 | T | A | 880 |
| **Loras College,** Dubuque, IA 52001 | 1839 | C/Ind-R | 1,810 | 62% | G | 125 | C | | 4180 |
| **Loretto Heights College,** Denver, CO 80236 | 1918 | C/Ind | 850 | 70% | | 106 | M | | 4945 |
| **Los Angeles Baptist College,** Newhall, CA 91322 | 1927 | C/Ind-R | 349 | 75% | | 50 | T | | 3600 |
| **Louise Salinger Academy of Fashion,** San Francisco, CA 94105 | 1939 | C/Ind | 69 | 90% | | 5 | M | | 3392x |
| **Louisiana College,** Pineville, LA 71360 | 1906 | C/Ind-R | 1,294 | 80% | | 93 | T | A | 1700 |
| **Louisiana State University and A&M College,** Baton Rouge, LA 70803 | 1860 | C/Pub | 24,050 | 87% | G | 1,369 | C | A,AF | 790 |
| **Louisiana State University in Shreveport,** Shreveport, LA 71115 | 1965 | C/Pub | 3,731 | 98% | G | 155 | C | A | 580x |
| **Louisiana Tech University,** Ruston, LA 71272 | 1894 | C/Pub | 9,352 | 85% | G | 431 | T | AF | 651 |
| **Lourdes College,** Sylvania, OH 43560 | 1958 | C/Ind-R | 608 | 83% | | 38 | T | | 1700x |
| **Loyola College,** Baltimore, MD 21210 | 1852 | C/Ind-R | 2,500 | 75% | G | 316 | M | A | 4025 |
| **Loyola Marymount University,** Los Angeles, CA 90045 | 1911 | C/Ind-R | 3,716 | 88% | G | 318 | M | AF | 5149 |
| **Loyola University, New Orleans,** New Orleans, LA 70118 | 1912 | C/Ind-R | 3,064 | 75% | G | 303 | M | A | 3725 |
| **Loyola University of Chicago,** Chicago, IL 60611 | 1870 | C/Ind-R | 8,783 | 95% | G | 994 | M | A | 4170 |
| **Lubbock Christian College,** Lubbock, TX 79407 | 1957 | C/Ind-R | 1,128 | 66% | | 97 | C | | 2600 |
| **Lutheran Bible Institute of Seattle,** Issaquah, WA 98027 | 1944 | C/Ind-R | 260 | 50% | | 18 | R | | 2500 |
| **Luther College,** Decorah, IA 52101 | 1861 | C/Ind-R | 2,110 | 48% | | 155 | T | | 5225 |
| **Lycoming College,** Williamsport, PA 17701 | 1812 | C/Ind-R | 1,159 | 60% | | 75 | T | | 4980 |
| **Lynchburg College,** Lynchburg, VA 24501 | 1903 | C/Ind-R | 1,826 | 55% | G | 158 | C | | 4050 |
| **Lyndon State College,** Lyndonville, VT 05851 | 1911 | C/Pub | 1,023 | 57% | G | 81 | R | | 1609 |
| **Macalester College,** St Paul, MN 55105 | 1874 | C/Ind-R | 1,730 | 35% | | 149 | M | | 6280 |
| **MacMurray College,** Jacksonville, IL 62650 | 1846 | C/Ind-R | 686 | 92% | | 71 | T | | 4470 |
| **Madonna College,** Livonia, MI 48150 | 1947 | C/Ind-R | 3,385 | 98% | | 165 | C | | 1958 |
| **Maharishi International University,** Fairfield, IA 52556 | 1971 | C/Ind | 451 | 11% | G | 75 | T | | 4449 |
| **Maine Maritime Academy,** Castine, ME 04421 | 1941 | M/Pub | 645 | 70% | | 60 | T | N | 2515 |
| **Mallinckrodt College,** Wilmette, IL 60091 | 1918 | W/Ind-R | 269 | 96% | | 43 | T | | 2160x |
| **Malone College,** Canton, OH 44709 | 1892 | C/Ind-R | 780 | 51% | | 60 | C | | 4306 |
| **Manchester College,** North Manchester, IN 46962 | 1889 | C/Ind-R | 1,147 | 80% | G | 98 | T | | 4250 |
| **Manhattan Christian College,** Manhattan, KS 66502 | 1927 | C/Ind-R | 275 | 70% | | 21 | T | | 1625 |
| **Manhattan College,** Riverdale, NY 10471 | 1853 | C/Ind | 4,113 | 82% | G | 359 | M | AF | 4200 |
| **Manhattan School of Music,** New York, NY 10027 | 1917 | C/Ind | 427 | 55% | G | 158 | M | | 4600x |
| **Manhattanville College,** Purchase, NY 10577 | 1841 | C/Ind | 948 | 50% | G | 124 | T | | 6440 |
| **Mankato State University,** Mankato, MN 56001 | 1867 | C/Pub | 9,500 | 88% | G | 557 | T | A | 1000 |
| **Mannes College of Music,** New York, NY 10021 | 1916 | C/Ind | 169 | 78% | G | 110 | M | | 4575x |
| **Mansfield State College,** Mansfield, PA 16933 | 1857 | C/Pub | 2,501 | 81% | G | 205 | R | | 1525 |
| **Marian College,** Indianapolis, IN 46222 | 1851 | C/Ind-R | 900 | 86% | | 77 | M | | 3200 |
| **Marian College of Fond du Lac,** Fond du Lac, WI 54935 | 1936 | W/Ind-R | 563 | 87% | | 65 | T | A | 3170 |
| **Marietta College,** Marietta, OH 45750 | 1835 | C/Ind | 1,521 | 45% | G | 94 | T | | 5900 |
| **Marion College,** Marion, IN 46952 | 1920 | C/Ind-R | 1,054 | 67% | G | 87 | T | | 3960 |
| **Marist College,** Poughkeepsie, NY 12601 | 1949 | C/Ind | 1,850 | 80% | G | 120 | T | | 4430 |
| **Marlboro College,** Marlboro, VT 05344 | 1947 | C/Ind | 232 | 19% | | 35 | R | | 6780 |
| **Marquette University,** Milwaukee, WI 53233 | 1881 | C/Ind-R | 9,226 | 43% | G | 908 | M | A,N | 4476 |
| **Marshall University,** Huntington, WV 25701 | 1837 | C/Pub | 8,948 | 85% | G | 514 | C | A | 650 |
| **Mars Hill College,** Mars Hill, NC 28754 | 1856 | C/Ind-R | 1,958 | 71% | | 120 | T | | 3450 |
| **Martin Center College,** Indianapolis, IN 46205 | 1977 | C/Ind | 75 | 95% | | 41 | M | | 2250x |
| **Mary Baldwin College,** Staunton, VA 24401 | 1842 | W/Ind-R | 773 | 48% | | 72 | T | | 4730 |
| **Mary College,** Bismarck, ND 58501 | 1959 | C/Ind-R | 880 | 92% | | 76 | R | | 2840 |
| **Marycrest College,** Davenport, IA 52804 | 1939 | C/Ind-R | 1,052 | 54% | G | 106 | C | | 4200 |
| **Marygrove College,** Detroit, MI 48221 | 1910 | C/Ind-R | 968 | 98% | G | 56 | M | | 3781 |
| **Maryland Institute College of Art,** Baltimore, MD 21217 | 1826 | C/Ind | 836 | 55% | G | 90 | M | | 4850 |
| **Marylhurst College for Lifelong Learning,** Marylhurst, OR 97036 | 1893 | C/Ind | 644 | 94% | | 98 | T | | 3825x |
| **Marymount College,** Tarrytown, NY 10591 | 1919 | W/Ind | 1,269 | 55% | | 144 | T | | 4895 |

| Name and Location | Est | Type/ Control | UG Enroll | State Res | Grad | Fac Size | Cmps | ROTC | Tuition & Fees |
|---|---|---|---|---|---|---|---|---|---|
| **Marymount College of Kansas,** Salina, KS 67401 | 1922 | C/Ind-R | 865 | 87% | | 70 | T | | $3225 |
| **Marymount College of Virginia,** Arlington, VA 22207 | 1950 | W/Ind | 1,175 | 34% | G | 100 | M | | 4200 |
| **Marymount Manhattan College,** New York, NY 10021 | 1937 | W/Ind | 2,333 | 94% | | 156 | M | | 4070 |
| **Maryville College,** Maryville, TN 37801 | 1819 | C/Ind-R | 603 | 35% | | 60 | T | | 4000 |
| **Maryville College–Saint Louis,** St Louis, MO 63141 | 1872 | C/Ind | 1,616 | 85% | G | 122 | M | | 4220 |
| **Mary Washington College,** Fredericksburg, VA 22401 | 1908 | C/Pub | 2,460 | 76% | G | 169 | T | | 1048 |
| **Marywood College,** Scranton, PA 18509 | 1915 | W/Ind-R | 2,100 | 55% | G | 190 | C | | 2630 |
| **Mason Gross School of the Arts**—See Rutgers U, Mason Gross School of the Arts | | | | | | | | | |
| **Massachusetts College of Art,** Boston, MA 02215 | 1873 | C/Pub | 1,050 | 85% | G | 100 | M | | 1095x |
| **Mass Coll of Pharm & Allied Health Sciences,** Boston, MA 02115 | 1823 | C/Ind | 1,004 | 55% | G | 150 | M | | 4755 |
| **Mass Coll Pharm/Allied Health Sci–Hampden Cmps,** Springfield, MA 01119 | 1823 | C/Ind | 80 | 75% | | 24 | C | | 7771 |
| **Massachusetts Institute of Technology,** Cambridge, MA 02139 | 1861 | C/Ind | 4,577 | 19% | G | 1,700 | M | A,N,AF | 8700 |
| **Massachusetts Maritime Academy,** Buzzards Bay, MA 02532 | 1891 | M/Pub | 850 | 85% | | 55 | T | | 1128 |
| **Mayville State College,** Mayville, ND 58257 | 1889 | C/Pub | 675 | 85% | | 52 | R | | 705 |
| **McKendree College,** Lebanon, IL 62254 | 1828 | C/Ind-R | 695 | 81% | | 83 | T | | 3470 |
| **McMurry College,** Abilene, TX 79697 | 1923 | C/Ind-R | 1,548 | 89% | | 124 | C | | 2750 |
| **McNeese State University,** Lake Charles, LA 70609 | 1939 | C/Pub | 5,461 | 94% | G | 302 | C | A | 555 |
| **McPherson College,** McPherson, KS 67460 | 1897 | C/Ind-R | 466 | 56% | | 43 | T | | 3490 |
| **Medaille College,** Buffalo, NY 14214 | 1875 | C/Ind | 775 | 99% | | 72 | M | | 3060x |
| **Medgar Evers College**—See City U of NY, Medgar Evers College | | | | | | | | | |
| **Medical College of Georgia,** Augusta, GA 30912 | 1828 | C/Pub | 865 | 89% | G | 679 | C | | 1014 |
| **Medical University of South Carolina,** Charleston, SC 29425 | 1824 | C/Pub | * | * | G | * | * | | * |
| **Memphis Academy of Arts,** Memphis, TN 38112 | 1936 | C/Ind | 217 | 62% | | 27 | M | | 2800x |
| **Memphis State University,** Memphis, TN 38152 | 1912 | C/Pub | 15,170 | 92% | G | 936 | M | A,AF | 732 |
| **Menlo College,** Atherton, CA 94025 | 1927 | C/Ind | 641 | 78% | | 68 | T | | 5970 |
| **Mercer University,** Macon, GA 31207 | 1833 | C/Ind-R | 2,231 | 73% | G | 184 | C | A | 4119 |
| **Mercer University in Atlanta,** Atlanta, GA 30341 | 1968 | C/Ind-R | 1,313 | 95% | G | 78 | M | | 2970x |
| **Mercy College,** Dobbs Ferry, NY 10522 | 1951 | C/Ind | 10,500 | 92% | | 600 | T | AF | 2850x |
| **Mercy College of Detroit,** Detroit, MI 48219 | 1941 | C/Ind-R | 2,468 | 95% | G | 215 | M | | * |
| **Mercyhurst College,** Erie, PA 16546 | 1926 | C/Ind-R | 1,452 | 75% | G | 103 | C | | 4350 |
| **Meredith College,** Raleigh, NC 27611 | 1891 | W/Ind-R | 1,486 | 85% | | 124 | C | | 3050 |
| **Merrimack College,** North Andover, MA 01845 | 1947 | C/Ind-R | 2,196 | 74% | | 141 | T | | 4950 |
| **Mesa College,** Grand Junction, CO 81501 | 1925 | C/Pub | 4,621 | 95% | | 155 | T | A | 705 |
| **Messiah College,** Grantham, PA 17027 | 1909 | C/Ind-R | 1,467 | 60% | | 108 | T | | 4050 |
| **Methodist College,** Fayetteville, NC 28301 | 1956 | C/Ind-R | 759 | 70% | | 50 | C | A | 3280 |
| **Metropolitan State College,** Denver, CO 80204 | 1965 | C/Pub | 15,436 | 95% | | 670 | M | A | 793x |
| **Metropolitan State University,** St Paul, MN 55101 | 1971 | C/Pub | 2,742 | 99% | | 372 | M | | 798x |
| **Miami Christian College,** Miami, FL 33167 | 1949 | C/Ind | 256 | 77% | | 17 | M | | 2750 |
| **Miami University,** Oxford, OH 45056 | 1809 | C/Pub | 13,703 | 78% | G | 800 | T | N,AF | 2000 |
| **Michigan Christian College,** Rochester, MI 48063 | 1959 | C/Ind-R | 323 | 67% | | 29 | T | | 2485 |
| **Michigan State University,** East Lansing, MI 48824 | 1855 | C/Pub | 34,357 | 91% | G | 2,621 | T | A,AF | 1502 |
| **Michigan Technological University,** Houghton, MI 49931 | 1885 | C/Pub | 7,471 | 86% | G | 448 | T | A,AF | 1512 |
| **Mid-America Nazarene College,** Olathe, KS 66061 | 1966 | C/Ind-R | 1,378 | 46% | | 87 | T | | 2515 |
| **Middlebury College,** Middlebury, VT 05753 | 1800 | C/Ind | 1,900 | 8% | G | 171 | R | | 10,800† |
| **Middle Tennessee State University,** Murfreesboro, TN 37132 | 1911 | C/Pub | 9,491 | 95% | G | 496 | T | A | 760 |
| **Midland Lutheran College,** Fremont, NE 68025 | 1883 | C/Ind-R | 851 | 70% | | 65 | T | | 3850 |
| **Mid-South Bible College,** Memphis, TN 38112 | 1941 | C/Ind | * | * | | * | * | | * |
| **Midwest Christian College,** Oklahoma City, OK 73111 | 1945 | C/Ind-R | 105 | 76% | | 17 | M | | 1360 |
| **Midwest College of Engineering,** Lombard, IL 60148 | 1967 | C/Ind | 204 | 99% | G | 52 | T | | 4329x |
| **Midwestern State University,** Wichita Falls, TX 76308 | 1922 | C/Pub | 3,945 | 90% | G | 211 | C | A | 461 |
| **Miles College,** Birmingham, AL 35208 | 1905 | C/Ind-R | 800 | 86% | | 80 | M | | 2400 |
| **Millersville State College,** Millersville, PA 17551 | 1854 | C/Pub | 5,695 | 96% | G | 360 | T | A | 1405 |
| **Milligan College,** Milligan College, TN 37682 | 1866 | C/Ind-R | 653 | 36% | | 60 | R | | 3150 |
| **Millikin University,** Decatur, IL 62522 | 1901 | C/Ind-R | 1,500 | 93% | | 132 | C | | 4857 |
| **Millsaps College,** Jackson, MS 39210 | 1890 | C/Ind-R | 1,085 | 74% | G | 80 | C | | 4220 |
| **Mills College,** Oakland, CA 94613 | 1852 | W/Ind | 779 | 52% | G | 141 | C | | 6600 |
| **Milton College,** Milton, WI 53563 | 1844 | C/Ind | 225 | 71% | | 32 | R | A | 4030 |
| **Milwaukee School of Engineering,** Milwaukee, WI 53201 | 1903 | M/Ind | 1,413 | 75% | G | 68 | M | | 4605 |
| **Minneapolis College of Art and Design,** Minneapolis, MN 55404 | 1886 | C/Ind | 527 | 62% | | 63 | M | | 4070 |
| **Minnesota Bible College,** Rochester, MN 55901 | 1913 | C/Ind-R | 102 | 64% | | 14 | C | | 1800 |
| **Minot State College,** Minot, ND 58701 | 1913 | C/Pub | 2,480 | 92% | G | 138 | T | | 681 |
| **Mississippi College,** Clinton, MS 39058 | 1826 | C/Ind-R | 1,794 | 90% | G | 155 | T | | 2460 |
| **Mississippi State University,** Mississippi State, MS 39762 | 1878 | C/Pub | 9,934 | 86% | G | 821 | T | A,AF | 1186 |
| **Mississippi University for Women,** Columbus, MS 39701 | 1884 | W/Pub | 1,756 | 80% | G | 182 | T | AF | 800 |
| **Mississippi Valley State University,** Itta Bena, MS 38941 | 1946 | C/Pub | 2,377 | 90% | G | 179 | T | A,AF | 935 |
| **Missouri Baptist College,** St Louis, MO 63141 | 1968 | C/Ind-R | 438 | 90% | | 37 | M | | 2600 |
| **Missouri Institute of Technology,** Kansas City, MO 64114 | 1931 | C/Prop | 2,029 | 44% | | 63 | M | | 3025x |
| **Missouri Southern State College,** Joplin, MO 64801 | 1937 | C/Pub | 4,330 | 95% | | 206 | T | A | 610 |
| **Missouri Valley College,** Marshall, MO 65340 | 1889 | C/Ind-R | 482 | 73% | | 44 | T | | 3400 |
| **Missouri Western State College,** St Joseph, MO 64507 | 1915 | C/Pub | 4,276 | 93% | | 178 | C | A | 780 |
| **Mobile College,** Mobile, AL 36613 | 1961 | C/Ind-R | 1,002 | 92% | | 68 | C | A | 2442 |
| **Molloy College,** Rockville Centre, NY 11570 | 1955 | C/Ind-R | 1,540 | 100% | | 183 | T | | 3700x |
| **Monmouth College,** Monmouth, IL 61462 | 1853 | C/Ind-R | 700 | 86% | | 72 | T | A | 5335 |
| **Monmouth College,** West Long Branch, NJ 07764 | 1933 | C/Ind | 3,150 | 90% | G | 221 | T | A | 5182 |
| **Montana Coll of Mineral Science and Technology,** Butte, MT 59701 | 1893 | C/Pub | 1,854 | 80% | G | 105 | T | | 616 |
| **Montana State University,** Bozeman, MT 59717 | 1893 | C/Pub | 9,963 | 83% | G | 681 | T | A,AF | 956 |
| **Montclair State College,** Upper Montclair, NJ 07043 | 1908 | C/Pub | 11,000 | 95% | G | 779 | T | | 1280 |
| **Monterey Institute of International Studies,** Monterey, CA 93940 | 1955 | C/Ind | 78 | 61% | G | 65 | C | | 5525x |
| **Moody Bible Institute,** Chicago, IL 60610 | 1886 | C/Ind-R | 1,349 | 25% | | 94 | M | | 300 |
| **Moore College of Art,** Philadelphia, PA 19103 | 1844 | W/Ind | 447 | 56% | | 84 | M | | 4375 |
| **Moorhead State University,** Moorhead, MN 56560 | 1887 | C/Pub | 7,508 | 61% | G | 365 | C | | 998 |

| Name and Location | Est | Type/ Control | UG Enroll | State Res | Grad | Fac Size | Cmps | ROTC | Tuition & Fees |
|---|---|---|---|---|---|---|---|---|---|
| **Moravian College,** Bethlehem, PA 18018 | 1742 | C/Ind | 1,372 | 56% | | 118 | C | | $5660 |
| **Morehead State University,** Morehead, KY 40351 | 1922 | C/Pub | 5,110 | 79% | G | 387 | T | A | 714 |
| **Morehouse College,** Atlanta, GA 30314 | 1867 | M/Ind | 1,841 | 30% | | 141 | M | A | 3256 |
| **Morgan State University,** Baltimore, MD 21239 | 1867 | C/Pub | 4,546 | 63% | G | 436 | M | A | 1216 |
| **Morningside College,** Sioux City, IA 51106 | 1894 | C/Ind-R | 1,443 | 78% | G | 94 | C | | 4680 |
| **Morris Brown College,** Atlanta, GA 30314 | 1881 | C/Ind-R | 1,526 | 60% | | 104 | M | | 3170 |
| **Morris College,** Sumter, SC 29150 | 1908 | C/Ind-R | 658 | 94% | | 44 | T | | 2402 |
| **Mount Angel Seminary,** St Benedict, OR 97373 | 1887 | M/Ind-R | 41 | 70% | G | 31 | R | | 1825 |
| **Mount Holyoke College,** South Hadley, MA 01075 | 1837 | W/Ind | 1,922 | 23% | G | 212 | T | | 7830 |
| **Mount Marty College,** Yankton, SD 57078 | 1936 | C/Ind-R | 553 | 46% | | 63 | T | | 3925 |
| **Mount Mary College,** Milwaukee, WI 53222 | 1913 | W/Ind-R | 1,125 | 90% | | 120 | M | | 3350 |
| **Mount Mercy College,** Cedar Rapids, IA 52402 | 1928 | C/Ind-R | 1,115 | 90% | | 74 | C | | 3970 |
| **Mount Saint Clare College,** Clinton, IA 52732 | 1928 | C/Ind-R | 379 | 70% | | 38 | T | | 2500 |
| **Mount Saint Mary College,** Newburgh, NY 12550 | 1930 | C/Ind | 1,015 | 80% | | 80 | C | | 3300 |
| **Mount St Mary's College,** Los Angeles, CA 90049 | 1925 | W/Ind-R | 1,008 | 93% | G | 142 | M | | 4560 |
| **Mount Saint Mary's College,** Emmitsburg, MD 21727 | 1808 | C/Ind-R | 1,520 | 42% | G | 83 | R | A | 4300 |
| **Mount Senario College,** Ladysmith, WI 54848 | 1962 | C/Ind | 503 | 85% | | 54 | T | | 3520 |
| **Mount Union College,** Alliance, OH 44601 | 1846 | C/Ind-R | 1,020 | 82% | | 95 | T | | 6045 |
| **Mount Vernon College,** Washington, DC 20007 | 1875 | W/Ind | 486 | 14% | | 60 | M | | 4800 |
| **Mount Vernon Nazarene College,** Mt Vernon, OH 43050 | 1968 | C/Ind-R | 1,062 | 75% | | 65 | T | | 3051 |
| **Muhlenberg College,** Allentown, PA 18104 | 1848 | C/Ind-R | 1,533 | 35% | | 117 | C | | 5975 |
| **Multnomah School of the Bible,** Portland, OR 97220 | 1936 | C/Ind | 597 | 28% | G | 49 | M | | 2990 |
| **Mundelein College,** Chicago, IL 60660 | 1930 | W/Ind-R | 1,354 | 92% | G | 140 | M | | 4155 |
| **Murray State University,** Murray, KY 42071 | 1922 | C/Pub | 6,308 | 80% | G | 381 | T | A | 714 |
| **Muskingum College,** New Concord, OH 43762 | 1837 | C/Ind-R | 1,046 | 70% | | 73 | R | | 5604 |
| **Naropa Institute,** Boulder, CO 80302 | 1974 | C/Ind | 61 | 25% | G | 33 | T | | 3405x |
| **Nasson College,** Springvale, ME 04083 | 1912 | C/Ind | 525 | 16% | | 53 | T | A | 5405 |
| **National College,** Rapid City, SD 57709 | 1941 | C/Ind | 1,077 | 62% | | 76 | C | | 3900 |
| **National College of Chiropractic,** Lombard, IL 60148 | 1906 | C/Ind | 982 | 27% | G | 82 | C | | 3910 |
| **National College of Education,** Evanston, IL 60201 | 1886 | C/Ind | 532 | 65% | G | 118 | C | | 4665 |
| **National College of Education, Urban Campus,** Chicago, IL 60603 | 1886 | C/Ind | 257 | 100% | G | 50 | M | | 4200x |
| **National University,** San Diego, CA 92108 | 1971 | C/Ind | 3,840 | 94% | G | 502 | M | | 4080x |
| **Native American Educational Services, Inc,** Chicago, IL 60640 | 1974 | C/Ind | 57 | 100% | | 13 | M | | 3300x |
| **Nazareth College,** Nazareth, MI 49074 | 1924 | C/Ind-R | 545 | 97% | | 59 | T | | 4790 |
| **Nazareth College of Rochester,** Rochester, NY 14610 | 1924 | C/Ind | 1,558 | 97% | G | 149 | M | | 4250 |
| **Nebraska Wesleyan University,** Lincoln, NE 68504 | 1887 | C/Ind-R | 1,183 | 84% | | 100 | C | | 4138 |
| **Neumann College,** Aston, PA 19014 | 1965 | C/Ind-R | 786 | 83% | | 65 | T | | 3267x |
| **Newark College of Arts and Sciences**—See Rutgers U, Newark College of Arts and Sciences | | | | | | | | | |
| **Newberry College,** Newberry, SC 29108 | 1856 | C/Ind-R | 737 | 75% | | 76 | T | | 4050 |
| **New College of California,** San Francisco, CA 94110 | 1971 | C/Ind | 300 | 40% | G | 27 | M | | 3040x |
| **New College of the University of South Florida**—See University of South Florida, New College | | | | | | | | | |
| **Newcomb College**—See Tulane University, Newcomb College | | | | | | | | | |
| **New England College,** Henniker, NH 03242 | 1946 | C/Ind | 1,249 | 15% | G | 120 | R | | 5990 |
| **New England College of Optometry,** Boston, MA 02115 | 1894 | C/Ind | * | * | G | * | * | | * |
| **New England Conservatory of Music,** Boston, MA 02115 | 1867 | C/Ind | 484 | 33% | G | 165 | M | | 6475 |
| **New Hampshire College,** Manchester, NH 03104 | 1932 | C/Ind | 1,527 | 30% | G | 75 | C | | 5554 |
| **New Jersey Institute of Technology,** Newark, NJ 07102 | 1881 | C/Pub | 4,823 | 95% | G | 372 | C | AF | 1350 |
| **New Mexico Highlands University,** Las Vegas, NM 87701 | 1893 | C/Pub | 1,680 | 85% | G | 115 | T | | 490 |
| **New Mexico Institute of Mining and Technology,** Socorro, NM 87801 | 1889 | C/Pub | 1,141 | 70% | G | 99 | T | | 678 |
| **New Mexico State University,** Las Cruces, NM 88003 | 1888 | C/Pub | 10,950 | 91% | G | 875 | C | A,AF | 798 |
| **Newport College–Salve Regina,** Newport, RI 02840 | 1934 | C/Ind-R | 1,748 | 43% | G | 176 | T | | 4850 |
| **New School for Social Research,** New York, NY 10011 | 1919 | C/Ind | 270 | 60% | G | 730 | M | | 5360 |
| **New School of Music,** Philadelphia, PA 19103 | 1943 | C/Ind | 75 | 45% | | 46 | M | | 4035x |
| **New York Inst of Tech, Commack College Center,** Commack, NY 11725 | 1975 | C/Ind | 366 | 100% | G | 38 | T | | 3241x |
| **New York Inst of Tech, Metropolitan Center,** New York, NY 10023 | 1957 | C/Ind | 2,762 | 51% | G | 172 | M | | 3241x |
| **New York Inst of Tech, Old Westbury Campus,** Old Westbury, NY 11568 | 1957 | C/Ind | 6,462 | 90% | G | 427 | T | AF | 3241 |
| **New York State College of Ceramics**—See Alfred University | | | | | | | | | |
| **New York University,** New York, NY 10003 | 1831 | C/Ind | 13,482 | 80% | G | 5,422 | M | | 6634 |
| **Niagara University,** Niagara University, NY 14109 | 1856 | C/Ind-R | 2,900 | 86% | G | 267 | C | A | 4370 |
| **Nicholls State University,** Thibodaux, LA 70310 | 1948 | C/Pub | 5,824 | 97% | G | 285 | T | A | 632 |
| **Nichols College,** Dudley, MA 01570 | 1815 | C/Ind | 823 | 65% | G | 41 | T | A | 4390 |
| **Norfolk State University,** Norfolk, VA 23504 | 1935 | C/Pub | 7,000 | 80% | G | 322 | C | A | 862 |
| **North Adams State College,** North Adams, MA 01247 | 1894 | C/Pub | 2,409 | 95% | G | 190 | T | | 1100 |
| **North Carolina A&T State University,** Greensboro, NC 27411 | 1891 | C/Pub | 4,910 | 76% | G | 368 | C | A,AF | 819 |
| **North Carolina Central University,** Durham, NC 27707 | 1910 | C/Pub | 3,922 | 90% | G | 329 | C | AF | 685 |
| **North Carolina School of the Arts,** Winston-Salem, NC 27107 | 1963 | C/Pub | 505 | 37% | G | 105 | C | | 956 |
| **North Carolina State University at Raleigh,** Raleigh, NC 27650 | 1862 | C/Pub | 15,337 | 87% | G | 1,352 | C | A,AF | 682 |
| **North Carolina Wesleyan College,** Rocky Mount, NC 27801 | 1956 | C/Ind-R | 1,037 | 82% | | 40 | T | | 3610 |
| **North Central Bible College,** Minneapolis, MN 55404 | 1930 | C/Ind-R | * | * | | * | * | | * |
| **North Central College,** Naperville, IL 60566 | 1861 | C/Ind-R | 1,329 | 95% | | 101 | T | | 4839 |
| **North Dakota State University,** Fargo, ND 58105 | 1890 | C/Pub | 7,912 | 65% | G | 511 | C | A,AF | 732 |
| **Northeastern Bible College,** Essex Fells, NJ 07021 | 1950 | C/Ind-R | 337 | 72% | | 30 | T | | 3360 |
| **Northeastern Illinois University,** Chicago, IL 60625 | 1961 | C/Pub | 7,849 | 99% | G | 454 | M | | 908x |
| **Northeastern Oklahoma State University,** Tahlequah, OK 74464 | 1846 | C/Pub | 4,662 | 96% | G | 220 | T | A | 447 |
| **Northeastern University,** Boston, MA 02115 | 1898 | C/Ind | 18,439 | 70% | G | 2,834 | M | A | 5083 |
| **Northeast Louisiana University,** Monroe, LA 71209 | 1931 | C/Pub | 9,272 | 90% | G | 439 | C | A | 527 |
| **Northeast Missouri State University,** Kirksville, MO 63501 | 1867 | C/Pub | 5,977 | 75% | G | 351 | T | A | 480 |
| **Northern Arizona University,** Flagstaff, AZ 86011 | 1899 | C/Pub | 10,316 | 86% | G | 550 | T | A,AF | 710 |
| **Northern Illinois University,** DeKalb, IL 60115 | 1895 | C/Pub | 18,348 | 96% | G | 1,222 | T | A | 792 |
| **Northern Kentucky University,** Highland Heights, KY 41076 | 1968 | C/Pub | 7,755 | 88% | G | 441 | M | A | 714 |

| Name and Location | Est | Type/ Control | UG Enroll | State Res | Grad | Fac Size | Cmps | ROTC | Tuition & Fees |
|---|---|---|---|---|---|---|---|---|---|
| **Northern Michigan University,** Marquette, MI 49855 | 1899 | C/Pub | 8,133 | 94% | G | 396 | T | A | $1395 |
| **Northern Montana College,** Havre, MT 59501 | 1929 | C/Pub | 1,446 | 96% | G | 113 | T | | 607 |
| **Northern State College,** Aberdeen, SD 57401 | 1901 | C/Pub | 2,575 | 97% | G | 110 | T | A | 960 |
| **North Georgia College,** Dahlonega, GA 30597 | 1873 | C/Pub | 1,686 | 95% | G | 120 | T | A | 699 |
| **Northland College,** Ashland, WI 54806 | 1892 | C/Ind-R | 653 | 35% | | 46 | T | | 4370 |
| **North Park College,** Chicago, IL 60625 | 1891 | C/Ind-R | 1,214 | 60% | | 106 | M | | 4571 |
| **Northrop University,** Inglewood, CA 90306 | 1942 | C/Ind | 1,202 | 25% | G | 43 | M | | 3825 |
| **North Texas State University,** Denton, TX 76203 | 1890 | C/Pub | 12,379 | 83% | G | 1,165 | T | AF | 438 |
| **Northwest Bible College,** Minot, ND 58701 | 1934 | C/Ind-R | 169 | 32% | | 12 | T | | 1895 |
| **Northwest Christian College,** Eugene, OR 97401 | 1934 | C/Ind-R | 255 | 35% | | 23 | C | A | 3346 |
| **Northwest College of the Assemblies of God,** Kirkland, WA 98033 | 1934 | C/Ind-R | 761 | 55% | | 46 | T | | 2310 |
| **Northwestern College,** Orange City, IA 51041 | 1882 | C/Ind-R | 903 | 65% | | 65 | R | | 3895 |
| **Northwestern College,** Roseville, MN 55113 | 1902 | C/Ind-R | 830 | 65% | | 60 | M | | 3900 |
| **Northwestern College,** Watertown, WI 53094 | 1865 | M/Ind-R | * | * | | * | * | | * |
| **Northwestern Oklahoma State University,** Alva, OK 73717 | 1897 | C/Pub | 1,638 | 92% | G | 74 | T | A | 484 |
| **Northwestern State University of Louisiana,** Natchitoches, LA 71457 | 1884 | C/Pub | 4,653 | 95% | G | 225 | T | A | 580 |
| **Northwestern University,** Evanston, IL 60201 | 1851 | C/Ind | 6,824 | 30% | G | 1,704 | C | N | 8085 |
| **Northwestern University, Chicago Campus,** Chicago, IL 60611 | 1858 | C/Ind | 210 | * | G | 50 | M | | * |
| **Northwest Missouri State University,** Maryville, MO 64468 | 1905 | C/Pub | 4,100 | 65% | G | 245 | T | A | 725 |
| **Northwest Nazarene College,** Nampa, ID 83651 | 1913 | C/Ind-R | 1,338 | 31% | G | 85 | T | A | 3480 |
| **Northwood Institute,** Midland, MI 48640 | 1959 | C/Ind | 1,770 | 50% | | 62 | T | | 3720 |
| **Norwich University,** Northfield, VT 05663 | 1819 | M/Ind | 1,429 | 9% | G | 125 | R | A,AF | 8700† |
| **Notre Dame College,** Manchester, NH 03104 | 1950 | W/Ind-R | 575 | 55% | G | 68 | C | | 3300 |
| **Notre Dame College of Ohio,** Cleveland, OH 44121 | 1922 | W/Ind-R | 690 | 90% | | 60 | M | | 3250 |
| **Nova University,** Ft Lauderdale, FL 33314 | 1964 | C/Ind | 1,189 | 98% | G | 403 | T | | 3060 |
| **Nyack College,** Nyack, NY 10960 | 1882 | C/Ind-R | 522 | 48% | G | 55 | T | | 1975 |
| **Oakland City College,** Oakland City, IN 47660 | 1885 | C/Ind-R | 652 | 65% | | 38 | T | | 3400 |
| **Oakland University,** Rochester, MI 48063 | 1957 | C/Pub | 9,610 | 99% | G | 527 | T | | 1281 |
| **Oakwood College,** Huntsville, AL 35806 | 1896 | C/Ind-R | 1,395 | 16% | | 92 | R | | 3753 |
| **Oberlin College,** Oberlin, OH 44074 | 1833 | C/Ind | 2,811 | 16% | G | 215 | T | | 7755 |
| **Oblate College,** Washington, DC 20017 | 1916 | C/Ind-R | * | * | G | * | * | | * |
| **Occidental College,** Los Angeles, CA 90041 | 1887 | C/Ind | 1,631 | 60% | G | 157 | M | | 6825 |
| **Oglethorpe University,** Atlanta, GA 30319 | 1835 | C/Ind | 1,294 | 51% | G | 51 | M | | 3990 |
| **Ohio Dominican College,** Columbus, OH 43219 | 1911 | C/Ind-R | 956 | 82% | | 72 | M | | 3990 |
| **Ohio Institute of Technology,** Columbus, OH 43209 | 1952 | C/Prop | 3,842 | 42% | | 171 | M | | 3025x |
| **Ohio Northern University,** Ada, OH 45810 | 1871 | C/Ind-R | 2,248 | 85% | G | 192 | T | | 4710 |
| **Ohio State University,** Columbus, OH 43210 | 1870 | C/Pub | 40,312 | 88% | G | 3,080 | M | A,N,AF | 1380 |
| **Ohio University,** Athens, OH 45701 | 1804 | C/Pub | 12,286 | 81% | G | 741 | T | A,AF | 1482 |
| **Ohio University–Lancaster,** Lancaster, OH 43130 | 1968 | C/Pub | 1,450 | 97% | | 106 | * | | *x |
| **Ohio U–Portsmouth Resident Credit Center,** Portsmouth, OH 45662 | 1975 | C/Pub | * | * | | * | * | | * |
| **Ohio Wesleyan University,** Delaware, OH 43015 | 1842 | C/Ind-R | 2,236 | 33% | | 185 | T | | 6300 |
| **Oklahoma Baptist University,** Shawnee, OK 74801 | 1910 | C/Ind-R | 1,427 | 69% | | 134 | T | | 2506 |
| **Oklahoma Christian College,** Oklahoma City, OK 73111 | 1950 | C/Ind-R | 1,610 | 44% | | 73 | M | | 2270 |
| **Oklahoma City University,** Oklahoma City, OK 73106 | 1904 | C/Ind-R | 1,496 | 95% | G | 171 | * | | * |
| **Oklahoma Panhandle State University,** Goodwell, OK 73939 | 1909 | C/Pub | 1,202 | 80% | | 60 | R | A | 493 |
| **Oklahoma State University,** Stillwater, OK 74074 | 1890 | C/Pub | 19,337 | 85% | G | 1,115 | T | A,AF | 637 |
| **Old Dominion University,** Norfolk, VA 23508 | 1930 | C/Pub | 11,670 | 86% | G | 824 | C | A,N | 1114 |
| **Olivet College,** Olivet, MI 49076 | 1844 | C/Ind-R | 615 | 96% | | 58 | T | | 5080 |
| **Olivet Nazarene College,** Kankakee, IL 60901 | 1907 | C/Ind-R | 1,987 | 41% | G | 110 | C | | 3340 |
| **Open Bible College,** Des Moines, IA 50321 | 1930 | C/Ind-R | 100 | 51% | | 10 | C | | 2170 |
| **Oral Roberts University,** Tulsa, OK 74171 | 1963 | C/Ind-R | 3,509 | 10% | G | 383 | C | | 3610 |
| **Oregon Health Sciences University,** Portland, OR 97201 | 1974 | C/Pub | * | * | G | * | * | | * |
| **Oregon Institute of Technology,** Klamath Falls, OR 97601 | 1947 | C/Pub | 2,143 | 92% | | 172 | T | A | 1253 |
| **Oregon State University,** Corvallis, OR 97331 | 1868 | C/Pub | 14,700 | 88% | G | 1,150 | T | A,N,AF | 1386 |
| **Orlando College,** Orlando, FL 32810 | 1918 | C/Ind | 1,350 | 90% | | 38 | M | | 1620x |
| **Otis Art Institute of Parsons School of Design,** Los Angeles, CA 90057 | 1917 | C/Ind | 367 | 50% | G | 102 | M | | 4690 |
| **Ottawa University,** Ottawa, KS 66067 | 1865 | C/Ind-R | 455 | 42% | | 49 | T | | 3392 |
| **Otterbein College,** Westerville, OH 43081 | 1847 | C/Ind-R | 1,692 | 85% | | 110 | T | | 5364 |
| **Ouachita Baptist University,** Arkadelphia, AR 71923 | 1885 | C/Ind-R | 1,470 | 81% | G | 102 | T | A | 1131 |
| **Our Lady of Holy Cross College,** New Orleans, LA 70114 | 1916 | C/Ind-R | 816 | 100% | | 93 | M | | 2315x |
| **Our Lady of the Lake University of San Antonio,** San Antonio, TX 78285 | 1911 | C/Ind-R | 1,254 | 90% | G | 130 | M | | 3090 |
| **Pace University,** New York, NY 10038 | 1906 | C/Ind | 6,391 | 91% | G | 670 | M | | 4360x |
| **Pace University, College of White Plains,** White Plains, NY 10603 | 1923 | C/Ind | 1,356 | 85% | | 166 | C | | 4360 |
| **Pace University–Pleasantville/Briarcliff,** Pleasantville, NY 10570 | 1963 | C/Ind | 4,364 | 89% | G | 403 | T | | 4360 |
| **Pacific Christian College,** Fullerton, CA 92631 | 1928 | C/Ind-R | 507 | 83% | G | 42 | C | | 2780 |
| **Pacific Lutheran University,** Tacoma, WA 98447 | 1890 | C/Ind-R | 3,002 | 72% | G | 263 | C | | 5280 |
| **Pacific Northwest College of Art,** Portland, OR 97205 | 1909 | C/Ind | 161 | 60% | | 33 | M | | 3300x |
| **Pacific Oaks College,** Pasadena, CA 91103 | 1945 | C/Ind | 90 | 90% | G | 31 | C | | 3860x |
| **Pacific Union College,** Angwin, CA 94508 | 1882 | C/Ind-R | 1,962 | 81% | G | 123 | R | | 5220 |
| **Pacific University,** Forest Grove, OR 97116 | 1849 | C/Ind | 836 | 35% | G | 105 | T | | 5610 |
| **Paine College,** Augusta, GA 30910 | 1882 | C/Ind-R | 842 | 85% | | 57 | C | | 2960 |
| **Palm Beach Atlantic College,** West Palm Beach, FL 33401 | 1968 | C/Ind-R | 650 | 76% | | 62 | C | | 2350 |
| **Pan American University,** Edinburg, TX 78539 | 1927 | C/Pub | 8,107 | 96% | G | 415 | R | A | 308 |
| **Park College,** Parkville, MO 64152 | 1875 | C/Ind-R | 471 | 50% | | 40 | T | | 3640 |
| **Parks College of Saint Louis University,** Cahokia, IL 62206 | 1927 | C/Ind-R | 1,072 | 92% | | 57 | T | AF | 3280 |
| **Parsons School of Design,** New York, NY 10011 | 1896 | C/Ind | 1,521 | 40% | G | 235 | M | | 5640 |
| **Patten College,** Oakland, CA 94601 | 1944 | C/Ind | 125 | 95% | | 20 | C | | 2198 |
| **Paul Quinn College,** Waco, TX 76704 | 1872 | C/Ind-R | 502 | 73% | | 34 | C | AF | 2080 |
| **Peabody Conservatory of Music,** Baltimore, MD 21201 | 1857 | C/Ind | 199 | 35% | G | 104 | M | | 6050 |

| Name and Location | Est | Type/ Control | UG Enroll | State Res | Grad | Fac Size | Cmps | ROTC | Tuition & Fees |
|---|---|---|---|---|---|---|---|---|---|
| **Pembroke State University,** Pembroke, NC 28372 | 1887 | C/Pub | 2,008 | 97% | G | 130 | R | A,AF | $846 |
| **Pennsylvania College of Optometry,** Philadelphia, PA 19141 | 1919 | C/Ind | * | 42% | G | 63 | M | | 9320 |
| **Penna State U–Behrend College,** Erie, PA 16563 | 1926 | C/Pub | 1,789 | 91% | G | 106 | C | A | 1677 |
| **Penna State U–Capitol Campus,** Middletown, PA 17057 | 1966 | C/Pub | 1,773 | 97% | G | 120 | T | | 1848 |
| **Penna State U–University Park Campus,** University Park, PA 16802 | 1855 | C/Pub | 28,633 | 88% | G | 1,658 | T | A,N,AF | 1848 |
| **Pepperdine University,** Los Angeles, CA 90044 | 1937 | C/Ind-R | 469 | 100% | G | 184 | M | | 6688x |
| **Pepperdine University,** Malibu, CA 90265 | 1937 | C/Ind-R | 2,377 | 60% | G | 235 | T | | 7100 |
| **Peru State College,** Peru, NE 68421 | 1867 | C/Pub | 818 | 75% | | 53 | R | | 861 |
| **Pfeiffer College,** Misenheimer, NC 28109 | 1885 | C/Ind-R | 800 | 77% | | 75 | R | | 3450 |
| **Philadelphia College of Art,** Philadelphia, PA 19102 | 1876 | C/Ind | 1,131 | 57% | G | 170 | M | | 5110 |
| **Philadelphia College of Bible,** Langhorne, PA 19047 | 1913 | C/Ind-R | 574 | 59% | | 40 | T | | 3340 |
| **Philadelphia College of Pharmacy and Science,** Philadelphia, PA 19104 | 1821 | C/Ind | 1,012 | 65% | G | 132 | M | A | 4425 |
| **Philadelphia College of Textiles and Science,** Philadelphia, PA 19144 | 1884 | C/Ind | 1,755 | 80% | G | 122 | M | | 4000 |
| **Philadelphia College of the Performing Arts,** Philadelphia, PA 19102 | 1870 | C/Ind | 346 | 60% | G | 135 | M | | 4565 |
| **Philander Smith College,** Little Rock, AR 72203 | 1877 | C/Ind-R | 637 | 80% | | 61 | C | A | 1600 |
| **Phillips College,** Gulfport, MS 39501 | 1927 | C/Prop | 821 | 95% | | 37 | T | | 2500x |
| **Phillips University,** Enid, OK 73701 | 1906 | C/Ind-R | 947 | 30% | G | 121 | C | | 3144 |
| **Piedmont Bible College,** Winston-Salem, NC 27101 | 1947 | C/Ind-R | 470 | 48% | | 31 | C | | 2120 |
| **Piedmont College,** Demorest, GA 30535 | 1897 | C/Ind-R | 406 | 90% | | 26 | R | A | 1758 |
| **Pikeville College,** Pikeville, KY 41501 | 1889 | C/Ind-R | 620 | 78% | | 64 | T | | 2825 |
| **Pine Manor College,** Chestnut Hill, MA 02167 | 1911 | W/Ind | 540 | 17% | | 57 | M | | 6975 |
| **Pittsburg State University,** Pittsburg, KS 66762 | 1903 | C/Pub | 3,949 | 84% | G | 269 | T | A | 726 |
| **Pitzer College,** Claremont, CA 91711 | 1963 | C/Ind | 770 | 45% | | 72 | T | | 7334 |
| **Plymouth State Coll of the U System of NH,** Plymouth, NH 03264 | 1871 | C/Pub | 2,700 | 70% | G | 150 | T | | 1295 |
| **Point Loma College,** San Diego, CA 92106 | 1902 | C/Ind-R | 1,482 | 89% | G | 123 | M | AF | 3693 |
| **Point Park College,** Pittsburgh, PA 15222 | 1960 | C/Ind | 2,574 | 81% | G | 147 | M | | 4335 |
| **Polytechnic Inst of NY, Brooklyn Campus,** Brooklyn, NY 11201 | 1854 | C/Ind | 2,102 | 87% | G | 347 | M | A,AF | 6310 |
| **Polytechnic Inst of NY, Farmingdale Campus,** Farmingdale, NY 11735 | 1854 | C/Ind | 635 | 97% | G | 347 | T | A | 6310 |
| **Pomona College,** Claremont, CA 91711 | 1887 | C/Ind | 1,376 | 58% | | 165 | T | | 7390 |
| **Pontifical College Josephinum,** Columbus, OH 43085 | 1888 | M/Ind-R | 97 | 50% | G | 45 | M | | 2377 |
| **Portland School of Art,** Portland, ME 04101 | 1882 | C/Ind | 260 | 49% | | 30 | C | | 4320x |
| **Portland State University,** Portland, OR 97207 | 1946 | C/Pub | 11,085 | 89% | G | 675 | M | | 1380x |
| **Post College,** Waterbury, CT 06708 | 1890 | C/Ind | 1,547 | 85% | | 82 | C | | 4000 |
| **Prairie View A&M University,** Prairie View, TX 77445 | 1878 | C/Pub | 3,848 | 83% | G | 305 | T | A,N | 274 |
| **Pratt Institute,** Brooklyn, NY 11205 | 1887 | C/Ind | 3,323 | 58% | G | 536 | M | | 5410 |
| **Presbyterian College,** Clinton, SC 29325 | 1880 | C/Ind-R | 946 | 53% | | 74 | T | A | 4225 |
| **Prescott College,** Prescott, AZ 86301 | 1975 | C/Ind | 88 | 25% | | 17 | T | | 3675x |
| **Princeton University,** Princeton, NJ 08544 | 1756 | C/Ind | 4,559 | 15% | G | 748 | T | A | 8380 |
| **Principia College,** Elsah, IL 62028 | 1910 | C/Ind-R | 848 | 11% | | 82 | R | | 5616 |
| **Providence College,** Providence, RI 02918 | 1917 | C/Ind-R | 3,500 | 34% | G | 235 | C | A | 5317 |
| **Puget Sound College of the Bible,** Edmonds, WA 98020 | 1950 | C/Ind-R | 150 | 41% | | 13 | T | | 2250 |
| **Purdue University,** West Lafayette, IN 47907 | 1869 | C/Pub | 27,612 | 75% | G | 3,100 | T | A,N,AF | 1350 |
| **Purdue University Calumet,** Hammond, IN 46323 | 1951 | C/Pub | 7,039 | 87% | G | 377 | C | | 1194x |
| **Purdue University North Central,** Westville, IN 46391 | 1967 | C/Pub | 2,207 | 98% | | 108 | R | | 1119x |
| **Queens College**—See City U of NY, Queens College | | | | | | | | | |
| **Queens College,** Charlotte, NC 28274 | 1857 | W/Ind-R | 645 | 65% | G | 70 | C | | 4200 |
| **Quincy College,** Quincy, IL 62301 | 1859 | C/Ind-R | 1,940 | 80% | | 87 | C | | 4030 |
| **Quinnipiac College,** Hamden, CT 06518 | 1929 | C/Ind | 2,659 | 66% | G | 335 | T | | 5100 |
| **Radcliffe College**—See Harvard and Radcliffe Colleges | | | | | | | | | |
| **Radford University,** Radford, VA 24142 | 1913 | C/Pub | 5,258 | 90% | G | 290 | R | A | 1254 |
| **Ramapo College of New Jersey,** Mahwah, NJ 07430 | 1969 | C/Pub | 4,530 | 95% | | 195 | T | | 1033 |
| **Randolph-Macon College,** Ashland, VA 23005 | 1830 | C/Ind-R | 913 | 64% | | 84 | T | | 5000 |
| **Randolph-Macon Woman's College,** Lynchburg, VA 24503 | 1891 | W/Ind-R | 762 | 40% | | 83 | C | | 5900 |
| **Reed College,** Portland, OR 97202 | 1911 | C/Ind | 1,153 | 20% | | 124 | M | | 7160 |
| **Reformed Bible College,** Grand Rapids, MI 49506 | 1940 | C/Ind-R | 216 | 50% | | 18 | C | | 2480 |
| **Regis College,** Denver, CO 80221 | 1877 | C/Ind-R | 1,100 | 45% | G | 95 | M | | 5410 |
| **Regis College,** Weston, MA 02193 | 1927 | W/Ind-R | 1,162 | 81% | G | 91 | T | | 4955 |
| **Reno Business College,** Reno, NV 89502 | 1902 | C/Prop | 210 | 70% | | 22 | C | | 2000 |
| **Rensselaer Polytechnic Institute,** Troy, NY 12181 | 1824 | C/Ind | 4,334 | 44% | G | 423 | C | A,N,AF | 7790 |
| **Research College of Nursing,** Kansas City, MO 64132 | 1980 | C/Ind | 226 | 81% | | 46 | M | | 2075 |
| **Rhode Island College,** Providence, RI 02908 | 1854 | C/Pub | 5,618 | 90% | G | 449 | C | A | 938 |
| **Rhode Island School of Design,** Providence, RI 02903 | 1877 | C/Ind | 1,587 | 10% | G | 166 | C | | 6770 |
| **Rice University,** Houston, TX 77251 | 1891 | C/Ind | 2,462 | 60% | G | 401 | M | A,N | 3700 |
| **Rider College,** Lawrenceville, NJ 08648 | 1865 | C/Ind | 4,620 | 78% | G | 293 | T | A | 4035 |
| **Ringling School of Art and Design,** Sarasota, FL 33580 | 1931 | C/Ind | 470 | 44% | | 31 | C | | 3200 |
| **Rio Grande College/Community College,** Rio Grande, OH 45674 | 1876 | C/Ind | 1,273 | 75% | | 72 | R | | 1035 |
| **Ripon College,** Ripon, WI 54971 | 1851 | C/Ind | 942 | 49% | | 70 | T | A | 6110 |
| **Rivier College,** Nashua, NH 03060 | 1933 | W/Ind-R | 713 | 55% | G | 146 | C | | 3500 |
| **Roanoke Bible College,** Elizabeth City, NC 27909 | 1948 | C/Ind-R | * | * | | * | * | | * |
| **Roanoke College,** Salem, VA 24153 | 1842 | C/Ind-R | 1,335 | 58% | | 86 | T | | 4750 |
| **Robert Morris College,** Coraopolis, PA 15108 | 1921 | C/Ind | 5,069 | 92% | G | 223 | T | | 2580 |
| **Roberts Wesleyan College,** Rochester, NY 14624 | 1866 | C/Ind-R | 613 | 75% | | 85 | M | | 4030 |
| **Rochester Institute of Technology,** Rochester, NY 14623 | 1829 | C/Ind | 8,550 | 60% | G | 1,125 | M | A | 5184 |
| **Rockford College,** Rockford, IL 61101 | 1847 | C/Ind | 1,300 | 85% | G | 101 | C | | 4490 |
| **Rockhurst College,** Kansas City, MO 64110 | 1910 | C/Ind-R | 2,544 | 75% | G | 111 | M | | 3950 |
| **Rockmont College,** Denver, CO 80226 | 1914 | C/Ind-R | 290 | 72% | | 36 | M | | 3215 |
| **Rocky Mountain College,** Billings, MT 59102 | 1878 | C/Ind-R | 394 | 61% | | 45 | C | | 3239 |
| **Roger Williams College,** Bristol, RI 02809 | 1948 | C/Ind | 2,547 | 15% | | 276 | T | | 4624 |
| **Rollins College,** Winter Park, FL 32789 | 1885 | C/Ind | 1,360 | 45% | G | 97 | T | | 5936 |
| **Roosevelt University,** Chicago, IL 60605 | 1945 | C/Ind | 4,407 | 90% | G | 474 | M | | 3882 |

| Name and Location | Est | Type/ Control | UG Enroll | State Res | Grad | Fac Size | Cmps | ROTC | Tuition & Fees |
|---|---|---|---|---|---|---|---|---|---|
| **Rosary College,** River Forest, IL 60305 | 1848 | C/Ind-R | 1,000 | 94% | G | 136 | T | | $4350 |
| **Rose-Hulman Institute of Technology,** Terre Haute, IN 47803 | 1874 | M/Ind | 1,238 | 61% | G | 91 | C | A | 4740 |
| **Rosemont College,** Rosemont, PA 19010 | 1921 | W/Ind-R | 650 | 98% | | 87 | T | | 4780 |
| **Rush University,** Chicago, IL 60612 | 1969 | C/Ind | 281 | 87% | G | 211 | M | | 4275 |
| **Russell Sage College,** Troy, NY 12180 | 1916 | W/Ind | 1,400 | 62% | G | 130 | C | | 5400 |
| **Rust College,** Holly Springs, MS 38635 | 1866 | C/Ind-R | 734 | 76% | | 40 | R | A | 3939 |
| **Rutgers U, Camden College of Arts and Sciences,** Camden, NJ 08102 | 1950 | C/Pub | 2,952 | 98% | | 158 | C | | 1330x |
| **Rutgers University, College of Engineering,** New Brunswick, NJ 08903 | 1864 | C/Pub | 2,665 | 88% | | 85 | T | A,AF | 1422 |
| **Rutgers University, College of Nursing,** Newark, NJ 07102 | 1956 | W/Pub | 566 | 98% | | 58 | C | | 1317x |
| **Rutgers University, College of Pharmacy,** New Brunswick, NJ 08903 | 1927 | C/Pub | 772 | 92% | | 26 | T | A,AF | 1422 |
| **Rutgers University, Cook College,** New Brunswick, NJ 08903 | 1921 | C/Pub | 2,816 | 89% | | 119 | T | A,AF | 1415 |
| **Rutgers University, Douglass College,** New Brunswick, NJ 08903 | 1918 | W/Pub | 3,674 | 94% | | 246 | T | A,AF | 1418 |
| **Rutgers University, Livingston College,** New Brunswick, NJ 08903 | 1969 | C/Pub | 3,494 | 89% | | 217 | T | A,AF | 1430 |
| **Rutgers U, Mason Gross School of the Arts,** New Brunswick, NJ 08903 | 1976 | C/Pub | 272 | 94% | G | 15 | T | A,AF | 1422 |
| **Rutgers U, Newark College of Arts and Sciences,** Newark, NJ 07102 | 1946 | C/Pub | 3,795 | 98% | | 230 | C | | 1328x |
| **Rutgers University, Rutgers College,** New Brunswick, NJ 08903 | 1766 | C/Pub | 8,360 | 92% | | 548 | T | A,AF | 1426 |
| **Rutgers U, University College—Camden,** Camden, NJ 08102 | 1934 | C/Pub | 1,076 | 99% | | 40 | C | | 1130x |
| **Rutgers U, University College—Newark,** Newark, NJ 07102 | 1934 | C/Pub | 1,997 | 99% | | 15 | C | | 1130x |
| **Rutgers U, University College—New Brunswick,** New Brunswick, NJ 08903 | 1934 | C/Pub | 3,428 | 99% | | 72 | T | | 1141x |
| **Sacred Heart College,** Belmont, NC 28012 | 1892 | C/Ind-R | 484 | 72% | | 60 | T | | 3270 |
| **Sacred Heart Seminary College,** Detroit, MI 48206 | 1919 | C/Ind-R | 172 | 100% | | 23 | M | | 2600 |
| **Sacred Heart University,** Bridgeport, CT 06606 | 1963 | C/Ind-R | 3,527 | 98% | G | 267 | C | | 3450x |
| **Saginaw Valley State College,** University Center, MI 48710 | 1963 | C/Pub | 3,786 | 99% | G | 215 | T | | 1395 |
| **St Alphonsus College,** Suffield, CT 06078 | 1963 | M/Ind-R | 72 | 99% | | 23 | T | | 2900 |
| **St Ambrose College,** Davenport, IA 52803 | 1882 | C/Ind-R | 1,818 | 70% | G | 126 | C | | 4460 |
| **St Andrews Presbyterian College,** Laurinburg, NC 28352 | 1958 | C/Ind-R | 771 | 62% | | 57 | T | | 4650 |
| **St Anselm College,** Manchester, NH 03102 | 1889 | C/Ind-R | 1,901 | 23% | | 145 | C | | 5050 |
| **Saint Augustine's College,** Raleigh, NC 27611 | 1867 | C/Ind-R | 1,700 | 61% | | 81 | * | A | * |
| **St Bonaventure University,** St Bonaventure, NY 14778 | 1854 | C/Ind-R | 2,339 | 78% | G | 198 | R | A | 4250 |
| **St Charles Borromeo Seminary,** Philadelphia, PA 19151 | 1832 | M/Ind-R | * | * | G | * | * | | * |
| **St Cloud State University,** St Cloud, MN 56301 | 1869 | C/Pub | 10,523 | 97% | G | 594 | C | A | 993 |
| **St Edward's University,** Austin, TX 78704 | 1885 | C/Ind-R | 2,142 | 80% | G | 101 | C | | 3100 |
| **Saint Francis College,** Fort Wayne, IN 46808 | 1890 | C/Ind-R | 803 | 77% | G | 86 | C | A | 3378 |
| **St Francis College,** Brooklyn, NY 11201 | 1858 | C/Ind | 3,356 | 97% | | 203 | M | | 3070x |
| **Saint Francis College,** Loretto, PA 15940 | 1847 | C/Ind-R | 1,390 | 59% | G | 89 | R | | 4150 |
| **St Hyacinth College and Seminary,** Granby, MA 01033 | 1927 | M/Ind-R | 51 | 30% | | 24 | T | | 3000 |
| **St John Fisher College,** Rochester, NY 14618 | 1948 | C/Ind | 1,889 | 97% | | 134 | M | | 4724 |
| **St John's College,** Camarillo, CA 93010 | 1939 | M/Ind-R | 74 | 74% | | 21 | T | | * |
| **St John's College,** Winfield, KS 67156 | 1893 | C/Ind-R | 298 | 45% | | 30 | T | | 2850 |
| **St John's College,** Annapolis, MD 21404 | 1696 | C/Ind | 377 | 10% | | 50 | T | | 9300 |
| **St John's College,** Santa Fe, NM 87501 | 1964 | C/Ind | 315 | 18% | G | 40 | T | | 6700 |
| **Saint John's Seminary,** Brighton, MA 02135 | 1883 | M/Ind-R | 82 | 80% | G | 48 | M | | 2125 |
| **Saint John's University,** Collegeville, MN 56321 | 1857 | M/Ind-R | 1,870 | 74% | G | 184 | R | A | 4415 |
| **St John's University,** Jamaica, NY 11439 | 1870 | C/Ind-R | 13,095 | 97% | G | 945 | M | A | 3390x |
| **St John Vianney College Seminary,** Miami, FL 33165 | 1959 | M/Ind-R | 56 | 60% | | 24 | M | | 1875 |
| **Saint Joseph College,** West Hartford, CT 06117 | 1932 | W/Ind-R | 760 | 83% | G | 139 | C | | 4570 |
| **St Joseph's College,** Mountain View, CA 94042 | 1898 | M/Ind-R | * | * | | * | * | | * |
| **Saint Joseph's College,** Rensselaer, IN 47978 | 1889 | C/Ind-R | 983 | 51% | G | 68 | T | | 4090 |
| **Saint Joseph's College,** North Windham, ME 04062 | 1912 | C/Ind-R | 500 | 50% | | 54 | R | | 3875 |
| **St Joseph's College,** Brooklyn, NY 11205 | 1916 | C/Ind | 1,077 | 98% | | 113 | M | | 3010x |
| **St Joseph's College, Suffolk Campus,** Patchogue, NY 11772 | 1916 | C/Ind | 1,185 | 100% | | 98 | T | | 3020x |
| **Saint Joseph Seminary College,** St Benedict, LA 70457 | 1891 | M/Ind-R | 105 | 74% | | 30 | T | | 1847 |
| **Saint Joseph's University,** Philadelphia, PA 19131 | 1851 | C/Ind-R | 2,300 | 72% | G | 177 | M | AF | 4110 |
| **St Lawrence University,** Canton, NY 13617 | 1856 | C/Ind | 2,318 | 49% | G | 175 | R | A | 6800 |
| **Saint Leo College,** Saint Leo, FL 33574 | 1889 | C/Ind-R | 1,084 | 50% | | 70 | R | A | 3801 |
| **Saint Louis Christian College,** Florissant, MO 63033 | 1956 | C/Ind-R | 172 | 33% | | 19 | C | | 1500 |
| **St Louis College of Pharmacy,** St Louis, MO 63110 | 1864 | C/Ind | 665 | 51% | | 51 | M | | 3740 |
| **Saint Louis University,** St Louis, MO 63103 | 1818 | C/Ind-R | 6,990 | 60% | G | 2,236 | M | AF | 4690 |
| **Saint Martin's College,** Lacey, WA 98503 | 1895 | C/Ind-R | 451 | 74% | G | 60 | T | | 4422 |
| **Saint Mary College,** Leavenworth, KS 66048 | 1923 | C/Ind-R | 842 | 81% | | 86 | T | | 2850 |
| **Saint Mary of the Plains College,** Dodge City, KS 67801 | 1952 | C/Ind-R | 627 | 60% | | 46 | R | | 3110 |
| **Saint Mary-of-the-Woods College,** St Mary-of-the-Woods, IN 47876 | 1840 | W/Ind-R | 690 | 50% | | 77 | T | | 3990 |
| **Saint Mary's College,** Notre Dame, IN 46556 | 1844 | W/Ind-R | 1,802 | 16% | | 168 | T | | 5080 |
| **Saint Mary's College,** Orchard Lake, MI 48033 | 1885 | C/Ind-R | 256 | 85% | | 40 | T | | 2100 |
| **Saint Mary's College,** Winona, MN 55987 | 1912 | C/Ind-R | 1,264 | 35% | G | 95 | T | | 4340 |
| **Saint Mary's College of California,** Moraga, CA 94575 | 1863 | C/Ind-R | 2,119 | 76% | G | 171 | T | | 5130 |
| **St Mary's College of Maryland,** St Mary's City, MD 20686 | 1839 | C/Pub | 1,348 | 94% | | 107 | R | | 1405 |
| **St Mary's Dominican College,** New Orleans, LA 70118 | 1908 | W/Ind-R | 866 | 83% | | 77 | M | | 3890 |
| **St Mary's Seminary and University,** Baltimore, MD 21210 | 1791 | C/Ind-R | * | * | G | * | * | | * |
| **St Mary's Seminary College,** Perryville, MO 63775 | 1818 | M/Ind-R | 80 | * | | 37 | T | | 0† |
| **St Mary's University of San Antonio,** San Antonio, TX 78284 | 1852 | C/Ind-R | 2,195 | 79% | G | 187 | M | A | 3629 |
| **Saint Meinrad College,** St Meinrad, IN 47577 | 1857 | M/Ind-R | 188 | 20% | | 41 | R | | 2500 |
| **Saint Michael's College,** Winooski, VT 05404 | 1904 | C/Ind-R | 1,700 | 15% | G | 101 | T | AF | 5505 |
| **St Norbert College,** De Pere, WI 54115 | 1898 | C/Ind-R | 1,668 | 45% | | 108 | T | A | 4495 |
| **St Olaf College,** Northfield, MN 55057 | 1874 | C/Ind-R | 3,097 | 64% | | 277 | T | | 5335 |
| **St Paul Bible College,** Bible College, MN 55375 | 1916 | C/Ind-R | 654 | 50% | | 42 | R | | 2580 |
| **Saint Paul's College,** Lawrenceville, VA 23868 | 1888 | C/Ind-R | 619 | 73% | | 41 | T | A | 2678 |
| **Saint Peter's College,** Englewood Cliffs, NJ 07632 | 1975 | C/Ind-R | 450 | 99% | | 45 | T | | 3480x |
| **Saint Peter's College,** Jersey City, NJ 07306 | 1872 | C/Ind-R | 2,613 | 95% | G | 315 | C | A | 4047x |
| **St Thomas Aquinas College,** Sparkill, NY 10976 | 1958 | C/Ind | 1,500 | 80% | | 67 | T | | 3000 |

| Name and Location | Est | Type/ Control | UG Enroll | State Res | Grad | Fac Size | Cmps | ROTC | Tuition & Fees |
|---|---|---|---|---|---|---|---|---|---|
| **Saint Vincent College,** Latrobe, PA 15650 | 1846 | M/Ind-R | 812 | 97% | | 77 | R | | $4845 |
| **Saint Xavier College,** Chicago, IL 60655 | 1847 | C/Ind-R | 1,900 | 96% | G | 160 | M | AF | 4080 |
| **Salem College,** Winston-Salem, NC 27108 | 1772 | W/Ind-R | 562 | 53% | | 70 | C | | 4350 |
| **Salem College,** Salem, WV 26426 | 1888 | C/Ind | 1,000 | 25% | G | 92 | R | | 3810 |
| **Salem State College,** Salem, MA 01970 | 1854 | C/Pub | 5,022 | 98% | G | 274 | T | A | 1050 |
| **Salisbury State College,** Salisbury, MD 21801 | 1925 | C/Pub | 3,644 | 86% | G | 243 | T | A | 1196 |
| **Samford University,** Birmingham, AL 35229 | 1841 | C/Ind-R | 2,808 | 67% | G | 244 | M | AF | 2784 |
| **Sam Houston State University,** Huntsville, TX 77341 | 1879 | C/Pub | 9,326 | 96% | G | 372 | T | A | 720 |
| **San Diego State University,** San Diego, CA 92182 | 1897 | C/Pub | 26,132 | 92% | G | 1,935 | M | A,AF | 400 |
| **San Francisco Art Institute,** San Francisco, CA 94133 | 1871 | C/Ind | 573 | 28% | G | 63 | M | | 4820x |
| **San Francisco Conservatory of Music,** San Francisco, CA 94122 | 1917 | C/Ind | 178 | 63% | G | 62 | M | | 5035x |
| **San Francisco State University,** San Francisco, CA 94132 | 1899 | C/Pub | 18,682 | 97% | G | 1,752 | M | AF | 147 |
| **Sangamon State University,** Springfield, IL 62708 | 1969 | C/Pub | 1,804 | 97% | G | 222 | C | | 780 |
| **San Jose Bible College,** San Jose, CA 95108 | 1939 | C/Ind-R | 220 | 70% | | 21 | M | | 2227 |
| **San Jose State University,** San Jose, CA 95192 | 1857 | C/Pub | 19,180 | 97% | G | 1,554 | M | A,AF | 330 |
| **Sarah Lawrence College,** Bronxville, NY 10708 | 1926 | C/Ind | 814 | 48% | G | 130 | T | | 8150 |
| **Savannah College of Art and Design,** Savannah, GA 31401 | 1976 | C/Ind | 384 | 98% | | 42 | C | | 3325 |
| **Savannah State College,** Savannah, GA 31404 | 1890 | C/Pub | 2,140 | 75% | G | 150 | C | A,N | 1008 |
| **School for International Training,** Brattleboro, VT 05301 | 1964 | C/Ind | 55 | 2% | G | 69 | T | | 5776 |
| **Sch for Lifelong Learning of the U System of NH,** Durham, NH 03824 | * | C/Pub | 1,000 | 95% | | 100 | * | | *x |
| **School of the Art Institute of Chicago,** Chicago, IL 60603 | 1866 | C/Ind | 869 | 70% | G | 107 | M | | 4950x |
| **School of the Associated Arts,** St Paul, MN 55102 | 1924 | C/Ind | * | * | | * | * | | * |
| **School of the Ozarks,** Point Lookout, MO 65726 | 1906 | C/Ind | 1,258 | 70% | | 88 | T | | 2460 |
| **School of Visual Arts,** New York, NY 10010 | 1947 | C/Prop | 2,400 | 50% | | 532 | M | | 4310 |
| **Schreiner College,** Kerrville, TX 78028 | 1917 | C/Ind-R | 494 | 88% | | 41 | T | | 2830 |
| **Scripps College,** Claremont, CA 91711 | 1926 | W/Ind | 575 | 60% | | 84 | T | | 7190 |
| **Seattle Pacific University,** Seattle, WA 98119 | 1891 | C/Ind-R | 2,412 | 64% | G | 178 | M | | 4464 |
| **Seattle University,** Seattle, WA 98122 | 1891 | C/Ind-R | 2,989 | 72% | G | 306 | M | A | 4725 |
| **Seaver College**—See Pepperdine University, Malibu | | | | | | | | | |
| **Seminary of St Pius X,** Erlanger, KY 41018 | 1955 | M/Ind-R | 104 | 18% | | 24 | T | | 2870 |
| **Seton Hall University,** South Orange, NJ 07079 | 1856 | C/Ind-R | 6,716 | 90% | G | 496 | T | A | 4296 |
| **Seton Hill College,** Greensburg, PA 15601 | 1882 | W/Ind-R | 970 | 80% | | 97 | T | | 4360 |
| **Shaw College at Detroit,** Detroit, MI 48202 | 1936 | C/Ind | 631 | 99% | | 48 | M | | 3900x |
| **Shaw University,** Raleigh, NC 27611 | 1865 | C/Ind-R | 1,569 | 50% | | 83 | C | | 2570 |
| **Sheldon Jackson College,** Sitka, AK 99835 | 1878 | C/Ind-R | 230 | 70% | | 32 | T | | 3160 |
| **Shenandoah College and Conservatory of Music,** Winchester, VA 22601 | 1875 | C/Ind-R | 875 | 55% | G | 128 | T | | 4190 |
| **Shepherd College,** Shepherdstown, WV 25443 | 1871 | C/Pub | 3,106 | 60% | | 136 | T | | 576 |
| **Shimer College,** Waukegan, IL 60085 | 1853 | C/Ind | 60 | 50% | | 14 | * | | * |
| **Shippensburg State College,** Shippensburg, PA 17257 | 1871 | C/Pub | 4,667 | 93% | G | 265 | T | | 1414 |
| **Shorter College,** Rome, GA 30161 | 1873 | C/Ind-R | 773 | 78% | | 55 | T | | 2700 |
| **Siena College,** Loudonville, NY 12211 | 1938 | C/Ind-R | 3,331 | 95% | | 192 | T | A | 4150 |
| **Siena Heights College,** Adrian, MI 49221 | 1919 | C/Ind-R | 1,422 | 90% | G | 86 | T | | 3330 |
| **Sierra Nevada College,** Incline Village, NV 89450 | 1969 | C/Ind | 200 | 52% | | 38 | T | | 2400x |
| **Silver Lake College,** Manitowoc, WI 54220 | 1869 | C/Ind-R | 400 | 98% | | 49 | T | | 3400 |
| **Simmons College,** Boston, MA 02115 | 1899 | W/Ind | 1,916 | 51% | G | 283 | M | | 6658 |
| **Simon's Rock of Bard College,** Great Barrington, MA 01230 | 1964 | C/Ind | 292 | 8% | | 37 | T | | 7700 |
| **Simpson College,** San Francisco, CA 94134 | 1921 | C/Ind-R | 220 | 60% | G | 30 | M | | 2880 |
| **Simpson College,** Indianola, IA 50125 | 1860 | C/Ind-R | 1,000 | 75% | | 69 | T | | 5035 |
| **Sinte Gleska College,** Rosebud, SD 57570 | 1971 | C/Ind | 306 | 100% | | 110 | R | | 764x |
| **Sioux Falls College,** Sioux Falls, SD 57105 | 1883 | C/Ind-R | 902 | 44% | G | 60 | C | | 3600 |
| **Skidmore College,** Saratoga Springs, NY 12866 | 1922 | C/Ind | 2,161 | 35% | | 197 | T | | 7410 |
| **Slippery Rock State College,** Slippery Rock, PA 16057 | 1889 | C/Pub | 4,964 | 80% | G | 346 | R | A,AF | 1438 |
| **Smith College,** Northampton, MA 01063 | 1871 | W/Ind | 2,650 | 23% | G | 328 | T | | 7750 |
| **Sojourner-Douglass College,** Baltimore, MD 21205 | 1980 | C/Ind | 176 | 99% | | 32 | M | | *x |
| **Sonoma State University,** Rohnert Park, CA 94928 | 1961 | C/Pub | 3,836 | 97% | G | 360 | R | | 432 |
| **Southampton College**—See Long Island University, Southampton College | | | | | | | | | |
| **South Carolina State College,** Orangeburg, SC 29117 | 1896 | C/Pub | 3,581 | 91% | G | 250 | T | A,AF | 750 |
| **South Dakota School of Mines and Technology,** Rapid City, SD 57701 | 1885 | C/Pub | 2,523 | 80% | G | 137 | C | A | 1125 |
| **South Dakota State University,** Brookings, SD 57007 | 1881 | C/Pub | 6,631 | 88% | G | 392 | R | A,AF | 1073 |
| **Southeastern Bible College,** Birmingham, AL 35256 | 1935 | C/Ind | 210 | 50% | G | 24 | M | | 2745 |
| **Southeastern College of the Assemblies of God,** Lakeland, FL 33801 | 1935 | C/Ind-R | 1,208 | 29% | | 50 | C | A | 1700 |
| **Southeastern Louisiana University,** Hammond, LA 70402 | 1925 | C/Pub | 6,771 | 95% | G | 294 | T | A | 634 |
| **Southeastern Massachusetts University,** North Dartmouth, MA 02747 | 1895 | C/Pub | 5,393 | 95% | G | 358 | T | | 1120 |
| **Southeastern Oklahoma State University,** Durant, OK 74701 | 1909 | C/Pub | 3,550 | 81% | G | 195 | T | A | 460 |
| **Southeastern University,** Washington, DC 20024 | 1879 | C/Ind | 1,122 | * | G | 150 | M | | 3105x |
| **Southeast Missouri State University,** Cape Girardeau, MO 63701 | 1873 | C/Pub | 7,934 | 95% | G | 471 | T | AF | 550 |
| **Southern Arkansas University,** Magnolia, AR 71753 | 1909 | C/Pub | 1,937 | 75% | G | 112 | T | A | 730 |
| **Southern Bible College,** Houston, TX 77213 | 1958 | C/Ind-R | 125 | 52% | | 12 | M | | 1770 |
| **Southern California College,** Costa Mesa, CA 92626 | 1920 | C/Ind-R | 777 | 83% | | 63 | C | | 3092 |
| **Southern California College of Optometry,** Fullerton, CA 92631 | 1904 | C/Ind | 29 | 40% | G | 95 | C | | 5990x |
| **Southern College of Optometry,** Memphis, TN 38104 | 1932 | C/Ind | * | * | G | * | * | | * |
| **Southern Connecticut State College,** New Haven, CT 06515 | 1893 | C/Pub | 6,539 | 94% | G | 639 | C | | 900 |
| **Southern Illinois University at Carbondale,** Carbondale, IL 62901 | 1869 | C/Pub | 20,261 | 82% | G | 1,478 | R | A,AF | 1210 |
| **Southern Illinois University at Edwardsville,** Edwardsville, IL 62026 | 1957 | C/Pub | 8,131 | 89% | G | 650 | R | AF | 1068 |
| **Southern Methodist University,** Dallas, TX 75275 | 1911 | C/Ind | 6,170 | 60% | G | 602 | M | | 5650 |
| **Southern Missionary College,** Collegedale, TN 37315 | 1892 | C/Ind-R | 1,854 | 24% | | 130 | T | | 4160 |
| **Southern Oregon State College,** Ashland, OR 97520 | 1926 | C/Pub | 3,934 | 90% | G | 240 | T | | 1254 |
| **Southern Technical Institute,** Marietta, GA 30060 | 1948 | C/Pub | 2,950 | 85% | | 145 | T | A | 660 |
| **Southern University and A&M College,** Baton Rouge, LA 70813 | 1880 | C/Pub | 7,365 | 81% | G | 486 | M | A,N | 538 |
| **Southern University in New Orleans,** New Orleans, LA 70126 | 1959 | C/Pub | 2,700 | 99% | | 111 | M | | *x |

| Name and Location | Est | Type/ Control | UG Enroll | State Res | Grad | Fac Size | Cmps | ROTC | Tuition & Fees |
|---|---|---|---|---|---|---|---|---|---|
| **Southern Utah State College,** Cedar City, UT 84720 | 1897 | C/Pub | 2,106 | 87% | | 114 | T | | $735 |
| **Southern Vermont College,** Bennington, VT 05201 | 1926 | C/Ind | 713 | 33% | | 32 | T | | 3450 |
| **Southwest Baptist University,** Bolivar, MO 65613 | 1878 | C/Ind-R | 1,636 | 75% | | 99 | T | | 3095 |
| **Southwestern Adventist College,** Keene, TX 76059 | 1894 | C/Ind-R | 744 | 59% | | 70 | T | | 4140 |
| **Southwestern Assemblies of God College,** Waxahachie, TX 75165 | 1927 | C/Ind-R | 318 | 44% | | 10 | T | | 1352 |
| **Southwestern at Memphis,** Memphis, TN 38112 | 1848 | C/Ind-R | 10,551 | 49% | | 116 | M | | 5200 |
| **Southwestern Christian College,** Terrell, TX 75160 | 1949 | C/Ind-R | 267 | 22% | | 26 | T | | 1842 |
| **Southwestern College,** Winfield, KS 67156 | 1885 | C/Ind-R | 649 | 74% | | 44 | T | | * |
| **Southwestern College of Christian Ministries,** Bethany, OK 73008 | 1946 | C/Ind-R | 50 | * | | 9 | T | | 1760 |
| **Southwestern Conservative Baptist Bible College,** Phoenix, AZ 85032 | 1960 | C/Ind-R | 203 | 60% | | 20 | M | | 1680 |
| **Southwestern Oklahoma State University,** Weatherford, OK 73096 | 1903 | C/Pub | 4,198 | 88% | G | 225 | T | A | 725 |
| **Southwestern University,** Georgetown, TX 78626 | 1840 | C/Ind-R | 1,000 | 92% | | 80 | T | | 3500 |
| **Southwest Missouri State University,** Springfield, MO 65802 | 1906 | C/Pub | 13,644 | 96% | G | 685 | C | A | 650 |
| **Southwest State University,** Marshall, MN 56258 | 1963 | C/Pub | 2,024 | 79% | | 107 | T | | 1000 |
| **Southwest Texas State University,** San Marcos, TX 78666 | 1899 | C/Pub | 14,202 | 97% | G | 594 | T | A,AF | 286 |
| **Spalding College,** Louisville, KY 40203 | 1920 | C/Ind | 664 | 88% | G | 96 | M | | 2972 |
| **Spelman College,** Atlanta, GA 30314 | 1881 | W/Ind | 1,450 | 29% | | 122 | M | | 3250 |
| **Spertus College of Judaica,** Chicago, IL 60605 | 1925 | C/Ind | 300 | 95% | G | 23 | M | | 2430x |
| **Spring Arbor College,** Spring Arbor, MI 49283 | 1873 | C/Ind-R | 1,037 | 77% | | 76 | R | | 4445 |
| **Springfield College,** Springfield, MA 01109 | 1885 | C/Ind | 2,050 | 36% | G | 175 | C | | 4500 |
| **Spring Garden College,** Chestnut Hill, PA 19118 | 1851 | C/Ind | 1,345 | 70% | | 80 | M | | 3950x |
| **Spring Hill College,** Mobile, AL 36608 | 1830 | C/Ind-R | 1,020 | 42% | | 77 | C | A | 4250 |
| **Stanford University,** Stanford, CA 94305 | 1891 | C/Ind | 6,590 | 48% | G | 1,219 | C | | 8220 |
| **State U of NY at Albany,** Albany, NY 12222 | 1844 | C/Pub | 11,000 | 99% | G | 840 | C | | 1300 |
| **State U of NY at Binghamton,** Binghamton, NY 13901 | 1950 | C/Pub | 8,871 | 96% | G | 719 | C | | 1180 |
| **State U of NY at Buffalo,** Buffalo, NY 14260 | 1846 | C/Pub | 19,293 | 97% | G | 1,917 | M | | 1237 |
| **State U of NY at Stony Brook,** Stony Brook, NY 11794 | 1957 | C/Pub | 10,525 | 95% | G | 1,252 | T | | 1155 |
| **State U of NY College at Brockport,** Brockport, NY 14420 | 1867 | C/Pub | 6,864 | 99% | G | 512 | T | A | 1075 |
| **State U of NY College at Buffalo,** Buffalo, NY 14222 | 1871 | C/Pub | 10,128 | 98% | G | 579 | M | | 1153 |
| **State U of NY College at Cortland,** Cortland, NY 13045 | 1868 | C/Pub | 5,502 | 98% | G | 340 | T | A | 1162 |
| **State U of NY College at Fredonia,** Fredonia, NY 14063 | 1867 | C/Pub | 4,786 | 97% | G | 252 | T | A | 1050 |
| **State U of NY College at Geneseo,** Geneseo, NY 14454 | 1867 | C/Pub | 5,032 | 98% | G | 314 | T | | 1175 |
| **State U of NY College at New Paltz,** New Paltz, NY 12561 | 1885 | C/Pub | 5,665 | 89% | G | 350 | R | | 1192 |
| **State U of NY College at Old Westbury,** Old Westbury, NY 11568 | 1968 | C/Pub | 3,445 | 96% | | 141 | T | | 1110 |
| **State U of NY College at Oneonta,** Oneonta, NY 13820 | 1889 | C/Pub | 5,855 | 98% | G | 375 | T | | 1208 |
| **State U of NY College at Oswego,** Oswego, NY 13126 | 1861 | C/Pub | 6,690 | 95% | G | 390 | T | A | 1170 |
| **State U of NY College at Plattsburgh,** Plattsburgh, NY 12901 | 1889 | C/Pub | 5,497 | 99% | G | 331 | T | | 1155 |
| **State U of NY College at Potsdam,** Potsdam, NY 13676 | 1816 | C/Pub | 4,038 | 98% | G | 291 | T | | 1155 |
| **State U of NY College at Purchase,** Purchase, NY 10577 | 1972 | C/Pub | 2,174 | 85% | | 185 | T | | 1155 |
| **State U of NY Coll of Envir Sci & Forestry,** Syracuse, NY 13210 | 1911 | C/Pub | 1,126 | 90% | G | 125 | M | | 1140 |
| **State U of NY Coll of Technology at Utica/Rome,** Utica, NY 13502 | 1973 | C/Pub | 3,062 | 98% | G | 183 | C | | 1180x |
| **State U of NY Downstate Medical Center,** Brooklyn, NY 11203 | 1858 | C/Pub | 183 | 95% | G | 43 | M | | * |
| **State U of NY, Empire State College,** Saratoga Springs, NY 12866 | 1971 | C/Pub | 4,995 | 97% | | 184 | * | | 1631x |
| **State U of NY Maritime College,** Bronx, NY 10465 | 1874 | C/Pub | 930 | 80% | G | 70 | M | N | 1250 |
| **State U of NY Upstate Medical Center,** Syracuse, NY 13210 | 1950 | C/Pub | 253 | 99% | G | 233 | C | | 1132 |
| **Steed College,** Johnson City, TN 37601 | 1940 | C/Ind | 433 | 90% | | 35 | C | | 1800x |
| **Stephen F Austin State University,** Nacogdoches, TX 75961 | 1923 | C/Pub | 10,000 | 97% | G | 470 | T | A | 374 |
| **Stephens College,** Columbia, MO 65215 | 1833 | W/Ind | 1,241 | 23% | | 122 | T | | 5175 |
| **Sterling College,** Sterling, KS 67579 | 1887 | C/Ind-R | 431 | 45% | | 50 | T | | 3350 |
| **Stern College for Women,** New York, NY 10033 | 1886 | W/Ind | 523 | 34% | | 229 | M | | 5225 |
| **Stetson University,** Deland, FL 32720 | 1883 | C/Ind-R | 1,950 | 60% | G | 138 | T | A | 4385 |
| **Stevens Institute of Technology,** Hoboken, NJ 07030 | 1870 | C/Ind | 1,607 | 55% | G | 230 | T | AF | 6600 |
| **Stillman College,** Tuscaloosa, AL 35403 | 1876 | C/Ind-R | 523 | 65% | | 34 | C | | 2180 |
| **Stockton State College,** Pomona, NJ 08240 | 1971 | C/Pub | 4,831 | 95% | | 213 | R | | 1136 |
| **Stonehill College,** North Easton, MA 02356 | 1948 | C/Ind-R | 1,737 | 60% | | 111 | T | A | 4840 |
| **Strayer College,** Washington, DC 20005 | 1898 | C/Ind | 2,054 | 30% | | 92 | M | | 2976x |
| **Suffolk University,** Boston, MA 02114 | 1906 | C/Ind | 3,375 | 96% | G | 371 | M | A | 3655x |
| **Sul Ross State University,** Alpine, TX 79830 | 1917 | C/Pub | 1,535 | * | G | 86 | T | | 332 |
| **Susquehanna University,** Selinsgrove, PA 17870 | 1858 | C/Ind-R | 1,497 | 45% | | 119 | T | | 5296 |
| **Swarthmore College,** Swarthmore, PA 19081 | 1864 | C/Ind | 1,309 | 25% | | 150 | T | | 7670 |
| **Sweet Briar College,** Sweet Briar, VA 24595 | 1901 | W/Ind | 669 | 20% | | 87 | R | | 6700 |
| **Syracuse University,** Syracuse, NY 13210 | 1870 | C/Ind | 14,281 | 45% | G | 1,202 | C | A,AF | 6394 |
| **Syracuse University, Utica College**—See Utica College of Syracuse University | | | | | | | | | |
| **Tabor College,** Hillsboro, KS 67063 | 1908 | C/Ind-R | 438 | 58% | | 45 | T | | 3320 |
| **Talladega College,** Talladega, AL 35160 | 1867 | C/Ind-R | 643 | 56% | | 58 | T | | 2369 |
| **Tampa College,** Tampa, FL 33607 | 1890 | C/Ind | 1,413 | 90% | | 65 | M | | 1620x |
| **Tarkio College,** Tarkio, MO 64491 | 1883 | C/Ind-R | 537 | 35% | | 35 | R | | 3550 |
| **Tarleton State University,** Stephenville, TX 76402 | 1899 | C/Pub | 3,023 | 74% | G | 156 | T | A | 364 |
| **Taylor University,** Upland, IN 46989 | 1846 | C/Ind-R | 1,591 | 38% | | 99 | R | | 4514 |
| **Temple University,** Philadelphia, PA 19122 | 1884 | C/Pub | 16,968 | 87% | G | 2,706 | M | A | 2616 |
| **Temple University, Ambler Campus,** Ambler, PA 19002 | * | C/Pub | 4,135 | 95% | G | 206 | T | A | 2616 |
| **Tennessee State University,** Nashville, TN 37203 | 1912 | C/Pub | 6,715 | 77% | G | 380 | M | AF | 792 |
| **Tennessee Technological University,** Cookeville, TN 38501 | 1915 | C/Pub | 5,912 | 94% | G | 376 | T | A | 780 |
| **Tennessee Temple University,** Chattanooga, TN 37404 | 1946 | C/Ind | * | 16% | G | 190 | C | | 1990 |
| **Tennessee Wesleyan College,** Athens, TN 37303 | 1857 | C/Ind-R | 533 | 78% | | 38 | T | | 2640 |
| **Texas A&I University,** Kingsville, TX 78363 | 1925 | C/Pub | 4,158 | 91% | G | 218 | T | A | 363 |
| **Texas A&M University,** College Station, TX 77843 | 1876 | C/Pub | 29,306 | 91% | G | 2,074 | C | A,N,AF | 480 |
| **Texas A&M University at Galveston,** Galveston, TX 77553 | 1971 | C/Pub | 580 | * | | 70 | C | | 303 |
| **Texas Christian University,** Fort Worth, TX 76129 | 1873 | C/Ind-R | 4,500 | 70% | G | 504 | M | A,AF | 4390 |
| **Texas College,** Tyler, TX 75702 | 1894 | C/Ind | 476 | 57% | | 40 | * | A | * |
| **Texas Lutheran College,** Seguin, TX 78155 | 1891 | C/Ind-R | 1,043 | 81% | | 75 | T | A | 2800 |

| Name and Location | Est | Type/ Control | UG Enroll | State Res | Grad | Fac Size | Cmps | ROTC | Tuition & Fees |
|---|---|---|---|---|---|---|---|---|---|
| **Texas Southern University,** Houston, TX 77004 | 1947 | C/Pub | 6,677 | 73% | G | 600 | M | | $532 |
| **Texas Tech University,** Lubbock, TX 79409 | 1923 | C/Pub | 19,288 | 85% | G | 1,500 | C | A,AF | 444 |
| **Texas Wesleyan College,** Fort Worth, TX 76105 | 1891 | C/Ind-R | 1,479 | 91% | G | 101 | M | | 3100 |
| **Texas Woman's University,** Denton, TX 76204 | 1901 | W/Pub | 3,938 | 84% | G | 509 | C | A | 408 |
| **Thiel College,** Greenville, PA 16125 | 1866 | C/Ind-R | 921 | 75% | | 82 | T | | 4941 |
| **Thomas A Edison State College,** Trenton, NJ 08625 | 1972 | C/Pub | 3,600 | * | | * | * | | *x |
| **Thomas Aquinas College,** Santa Paula, CA 93060 | 1971 | C/Ind-R | 110 | 33% | | 16 | T | | 4300 |
| **Thomas College,** Waterville, ME 04901 | 1894 | C/Ind | 794 | 75% | G | 45 | T | | 4690 |
| **Thomas Jefferson University,** Philadelphia, PA 19107 | 1870 | C/Ind | 448 | 74% | G | 63 | M | | 5400 |
| **Thomas More College,** Fort Mitchell, KY 41017 | 1921 | C/Ind-R | 1,300 | 70% | | 117 | T | | 3880 |
| **Tiffin University,** Tiffin, OH 44883 | 1888 | C/Ind | 433 | 95% | | 34 | T | | 2440 |
| **Tift College,** Forsyth, GA 31029 | 1849 | W/Ind-R | 400 | 70% | | 43 | T | | 2385 |
| **Toccoa Falls College,** Toccoa Falls, GA 30598 | 1907 | C/Ind-R | 661 | 31% | | 60 | R | | 2560 |
| **Tougaloo College,** Tougaloo, MS 39174 | 1869 | C/Ind | 838 | 73% | | 86 | C | A | 2450 |
| **Touro College,** New York, NY 10001 | 1971 | C/Ind | 1,883 | 81% | G | 253 | M | | 3290 |
| **Towson State University,** Baltimore, MD 21204 | 1866 | C/Pub | 13,782 | 96% | G | 840 | M | | 1205 |
| **Transylvania University,** Lexington, KY 40508 | 1780 | C/Ind-R | 714 | 75% | | 72 | C | | 5300 |
| **Trenton State College,** Trenton, NJ 08625 | 1855 | C/Pub | 7,300 | 97% | G | 500 | T | | 812 |
| **Trevecca Nazarene College,** Nashville, TN 37210 | 1901 | C/Ind-R | 961 | 40% | | 75 | M | | 2760 |
| **Trinity Bible Institute,** Ellendale, ND 58436 | 1948 | C/Ind-R | 350 | 15% | | 24 | T | | 1643 |
| **Trinity Christian College,** Palos Heights, IL 60463 | 1959 | C/Ind | 428 | 73% | | 58 | M | | 3700 |
| **Trinity College,** Hartford, CT 06106 | 1823 | C/Ind | 1,796 | 25% | G | 154 | C | | 7440 |
| **Trinity College,** Washington, DC 20017 | 1897 | W/Ind-R | 650 | 6% | G | 103 | M | | 5485 |
| **Trinity College,** Deerfield, IL 60015 | 1897 | C/Ind-R | 687 | 57% | | 64 | T | | 4300 |
| **Trinity College,** Burlington, VT 05401 | 1925 | W/Ind-R | 830 | 81% | | 64 | C | | 4205 |
| **Trinity University,** San Antonio, TX 78284 | 1869 | C/Ind | 2,583 | 65% | G | 291 | M | A | 4021 |
| **Tri-State University,** Angola, IN 46703 | 1884 | C/Ind | 1,167 | 40% | | 79 | T | | 3981 |
| **Troy State University,** Troy, AL 36082 | 1887 | C/Pub | 6,230 | 90% | G | 419 | T | AF | 840 |
| **Troy State University at Dothan/Fort Rucker,** Dothan, AL 36301 | 1962 | C/Pub | 926 | 100% | G | 71 | * | | *x |
| **Troy State University in Montgomery,** Montgomery, AL 36195 | 1965 | C/Pub | 1,530 | 100% | G | 145 | C | | 840x |
| **Tufts University,** Medford, MA 02155 | 1852 | C/Ind | 4,314 | 30% | G | 527 | C | | 7883 |
| **Tulane University,** New Orleans, LA 70118 | 1834 | C/Ind | 5,375 | 20% | G | 789 | M | A,N | 6550 |
| **Tulane University, Newcomb College,** New Orleans, LA 70118 | 1886 | W/Ind | 1,623 | 26% | | 162 | M | A,N,AF | 6566 |
| **Tusculum College,** Greeneville, TN 37743 | 1794 | C/Ind-R | 308 | 51% | | 36 | T | | 3100 |
| **Tuskegee Institute,** Tuskegee Institute, AL 36088 | 1881 | C/Ind | 3,384 | 31% | G | 344 | T | A,AF | 2750 |
| **Union College,** Barbourville, KY 40906 | 1879 | C/Ind-R | 648 | 81% | G | 70 | T | A | 3425 |
| **Union College,** Lincoln, NE 68506 | 1891 | C/Ind-R | 942 | 23% | | 103 | C | | 4950 |
| **Union College,** Schenectady, NY 12308 | 1795 | C/Ind | 2,025 | 71% | G | 183 | C | | 7399 |
| **Union for Experimenting Colleges and Universities,** Cincinnati, OH 45201 | 1964 | C/Ind | * | * | G | * | * | | * |
| **Union University,** Jackson, TN 38301 | 1825 | C/Ind-R | 1,382 | 85% | | 86 | T | | 2270 |
| **United States Air Force Academy,** USAF Academy, CO 80840 | 1954 | C/Pub | 4,502 | 5% | | 575 | R | | 0† |
| **United States Coast Guard Academy,** New London, CT 06320 | 1876 | C/Pub | 988 | 7% | | 116 | T | | 0† |
| **United States International University,** San Diego, CA 92131 | 1952 | C/Ind | 1,219 | 52% | G | 166 | M | | 4845 |
| **United States Merchant Marine Academy,** Kings Point, NY 11024 | 1943 | C/Pub | 1,100 | 23% | | 80 | T | | 0† |
| **United States Military Academy,** West Point, NY 10996 | 1802 | C/Pub | 4,439 | 12% | | 639 | R | | 0† |
| **United States Naval Academy,** Annapolis, MD 21402 | 1845 | M/Pub | 4,500 | 2% | | 494 | T | | 0† |
| **United Wesleyan College,** Allentown, PA 18103 | 1921 | C/Ind-R | 198 | 53% | | 20 | C | | 2920 |
| **Unity College,** Unity, ME 04988 | 1966 | C/Ind | 317 | 18% | | 24 | R | | 4440 |
| **Universidad Politécnica de Puerto Rico,** San Juan, PR 00918 | 1974 | C/Ind | * | * | | * | * | | * |
| **University of Akron,** Akron, OH 44325 | 1870 | C/Pub | 22,167 | 98% | G | 1,875 | C | A,AF | 1250 |
| **University of Alabama,** University, AL 35486 | 1831 | C/Pub | 13,607 | 80% | G | 944 | C | A,AF | 1084 |
| **University of Alabama in Birmingham,** Birmingham, AL 35294 | 1966 | C/Pub | 11,000 | 94% | G | 1,665 | C | A | 1065 |
| **University of Alabama in Huntsville,** Huntsville, AL 35899 | 1950 | C/Pub | 4,909 | 95% | G | 351 | C | A | 966 |
| **University of Alaska, Anchorage,** Anchorage, AK 99508 | 1969 | C/Pub | 2,187 | 87% | G | 226 | C | | 482x |
| **University of Alaska, Fairbanks,** Fairbanks, AK 99701 | 1917 | C/Pub | 3,798 | 74% | G | 400 | T | A | 572 |
| **University of Alaska, Juneau,** Juneau, AK 99801 | 1972 | C/Pub | 2,321 | 98% | G | 222 | T | | 440 |
| **University of Albuquerque,** Albuquerque, NM 87140 | 1920 | C/Ind-R | 2,000 | 70% | | 148 | C | A | 2925 |
| **University of Arizona,** Tucson, AZ 85721 | 1885 | C/Pub | 27,205 | 81% | G | 1,756 | M | A,AF | 710 |
| **University of Arkansas,** Fayetteville, AR 72701 | 1871 | C/Pub | 12,489 | 84% | G | 843 | T | A,AF | 720 |
| **University of Arkansas at Little Rock,** Little Rock, AR 72204 | 1927 | C/Pub | 8,622 | 96% | G | 517 | C | A | 730x |
| **University of Arkansas at Monticello,** Monticello, AR 71655 | 1909 | C/Pub | 1,938 | 97% | | 107 | T | A | 708 |
| **University of Arkansas at Pine Bluff,** Pine Bluff, AR 71601 | 1873 | C/Pub | 2,909 | 80% | | 199 | C | A | 719 |
| **University of Arkansas for Medical Sciences,** Little Rock, AR 72201 | 1879 | C/Pub | 617 | 95% | G | 409 | C | | 720 |
| **University of Baltimore,** Baltimore, MD 21201 | 1925 | C/Pub | 2,671 | 94% | G | 257 | M | | 1020x |
| **University of Bridgeport,** Bridgeport, CT 06602 | 1927 | C/Ind | 4,715 | 53% | G | 531 | C | A | 5943 |
| **University of California, Berkeley,** Berkeley, CA 94720 | 1868 | C/Pub | 20,977 | 95% | G | 3,626 | C | A,N,AF | 1173 |
| **University of California, Davis,** Davis, CA 95616 | 1906 | C/Pub | 13,751 | 88% | G | 1,249 | T | A | 1185 |
| **University of California, Irvine,** Irvine, CA 92717 | 1960 | C/Pub | 8,485 | 93% | G | 651 | C | | 1214 |
| **University of California, Los Angeles,** Los Angeles, CA 90024 | 1919 | C/Pub | 22,609 | 94% | G | 2,800 | M | A,N,AF | 1169 |
| **University of California, Riverside,** Riverside, CA 92521 | 1954 | C/Pub | 3,291 | 96% | G | 384 | C | | 1180 |
| **University of California, San Diego,** La Jolla, CA 92093 | 1964 | C/Pub | 9,846 | 90% | G | 820 | M | | 1200 |
| **University of California, San Francisco,** San Francisco, CA 94143 | 1873 | C/Pub | 177 | 94% | G | 1,126 | M | | 1255 |
| **University of California, Santa Barbara,** Santa Barbara, CA 93106 | 1891 | C/Pub | 13,545 | 92% | G | 857 | C | A | 1194 |
| **University of California, Santa Cruz,** Santa Cruz, CA 95064 | 1965 | C/Pub | 6,335 | 89% | G | 493 | T | | 1261 |
| **University of Central Arkansas,** Conway, AR 72032 | 1907 | C/Pub | 5,267 | 96% | G | 297 | T | A | 774 |
| **University of Central Florida,** Orlando, FL 32816 | 1963 | C/Pub | 11,775 | 95% | G | 500 | M | A,AF | 786 |
| **University of Charleston,** Charleston, WV 25304 | 1888 | C/Ind | 2,098 | 78% | G | 101 | C | A | 3350 |
| **University of Chicago,** Chicago, IL 60637 | 1890 | C/Ind | 2,850 | 33% | G | 1,040 | M | | 7164 |
| **University of Cincinnati,** Cincinnati, OH 45221 | 1819 | C/Pub | 32,398 | 86% | G | 2,219 | M | A,AF | 1479 |
| **University of Colorado at Boulder,** Boulder, CO 80309 | 1876 | C/Pub | 18,265 | 66% | G | 1,104 | C | A,N,AF | 1226 |
| **University of Colorado at Colorado Springs,** Colorado Springs, CO 80933 | 1965 | C/Pub | 3,732 | 92% | G | 215 | C | A | 837x |

| Name and Location | Est | Type/ Control | UG Enroll | State Res | Grad | Fac Size | Cmps | ROTC | Tuition & Fees |
|---|---|---|---|---|---|---|---|---|---|
| **University of Colorado at Denver,** Denver, CO 80202 | 1912 | C/Pub | 7,850 | 92% | G | 349 | M | A,AF | $706x |
| **University of Colorado Health Sciences Center,** Denver, CO 80262 | 1898 | C/Pub | 332 | * | G | 3,234 | M | | 2149x |
| **University of Connecticut,** Storrs, CT 06268 | 1881 | C/Pub | 15,131 | 90% | G | 1,600 | R | A,AF | 1225 |
| **University of Dallas,** Irving, TX 75061 | 1956 | C/Ind-R | 1,154 | 44% | G | 182 | C | | 3700 |
| **University of Dayton,** Dayton, OH 45469 | 1850 | C/Ind-R | 7,052 | 57% | G | 605 | C | A | 3910 |
| **University of Delaware,** Newark, DE 19711 | 1743 | C/Pub | 13,374 | 53% | G | 910 | T | A,AF | 1330 |
| **University of Denver,** Denver, CO 80208 | 1864 | C/Ind | 4,932 | 43% | G | 487 | M | | 6150 |
| **University of Detroit,** Detroit, MI 48221 | 1877 | C/Ind-R | 3,620 | 85% | G | 461 | M | A | 4790 |
| **University of Dubuque,** Dubuque, IA 52001 | 1852 | C/Ind-R | 1,094 | 63% | G | 77 | C | A | 4265 |
| **University of Evansville,** Evansville, IN 47702 | 1854 | C/Ind-R | 4,305 | 75% | G | 276 | C | | 4287 |
| **University of Florida,** Gainesville, FL 32611 | 1853 | C/Pub | 27,788 | 93% | G | 2,789 | C | A,N,AF | 796 |
| **University of Georgia,** Athens, GA 30602 | 1785 | C/Pub | 19,828 | 86% | G | 1,931 | T | A,AF | 1086 |
| **University of Guam,** Mangilao, GU 96913 | 1952 | C/Pub | 2,312 | 90% | G | 209 | R | A | 480 |
| **University of Hartford,** West Hartford, CT 06117 | 1877 | C/Ind | 6,840 | 55% | G | 739 | C | | 6336 |
| **University of Hawaii at Hilo,** Hilo, HI 96720 | 1970 | C/Pub | 3,467 | 87% | | 249 | T | | 110 |
| **University of Hawaii at Manoa,** Honolulu, HI 96822 | 1907 | C/Pub | 14,889 | 87% | G | 1,615 | M | A,AF | 481 |
| **U of Hawaii–West Oahu College,** Pearl City, HI 96782 | 1976 | C/Pub | 365 | 89% | | 24 | T | | 400x |
| **University of Health Scis/Chicago Med School,** North Chicago, IL 60064 | 1912 | C/Ind | * | * | G | * | * | | * |
| **University of Houston at Clear Lake City,** Houston, TX 77058 | 1971 | C/Pub | 2,465 | 93% | G | 226 | M | | 400x |
| **University of Houston Central Campus,** Houston, TX 77004 | 1927 | C/Pub | 21,665 | 87% | G | 1,863 | M | A,N | 420 |
| **University of Houston Downtown College,** Houston, TX 77002 | 1974 | C/Pub | 5,000 | 87% | | 200 | M | | 420x |
| **University of Houston Victoria Campus,** Victoria, TX 77901 | 1973 | C/Pub | * | * | G | * | * | | * |
| **University of Idaho,** Moscow, ID 83843 | 1889 | C/Pub | 6,691 | 80% | G | 532 | T | A,N | 716 |
| **University of Illinois at Chicago,** Chicago, IL 60680 | 1965 | C/Pub | 16,993 | 84% | G | 1,258 | M | A | 1155x |
| **University of Illinois at the Medical Center,** Chicago, IL 60612 | 1896 | C/Pub | 1,611 | 93% | G | 2,000 | M | | * |
| **University of Illinois at Urbana-Champaign,** Urbana, IL 61801 | 1868 | C/Pub | 26,597 | 97% | G | 2,796 | C | A,N,AF | 1211 |
| **University of Iowa,** Iowa City, IA 52242 | 1847 | C/Pub | 17,650 | 77% | G | 2,016 | T | A,AF | 1040 |
| **University of Judaism,** Los Angeles, CA 90077 | 1947 | C/Ind-R | 108 | 80% | G | 50 | M | | 2400x |
| **University of Kansas,** Lawrence, KS 66045 | 1866 | C/Pub | 17,128 | 73% | G | 1,323 | C | A,N,AF | 918 |
| **U of Kansas Coll of Health Scis and Hospital,** Kansas City, KS 66103 | 1905 | C/Pub | 571 | 80% | G | 749 | M | | 724x |
| **University of Kentucky,** Lexington, KY 40506 | 1865 | C/Pub | 18,310 | 90% | G | 1,842 | C | A,AF | 846 |
| **University of La Verne,** La Verne, CA 91750 | 1891 | C/Ind | 1,210 | 98% | G | 188 | T | | 5158 |
| **University of Louisville,** Louisville, KY 40292 | 1798 | C/Pub | 14,882 | 93% | G | 1,713 | M | AF | 852 |
| **University of Lowell,** Lowell, MA 01854 | 1894 | C/Pub | 7,656 | 93% | G | 842 | C | AF | 1179 |
| **University of Maine at Augusta,** Augusta, ME 04330 | 1965 | C/Pub | 3,420 | 93% | | 238 | T | | 1320x |
| **University of Maine at Farmington,** Farmington, ME 04938 | 1864 | C/Pub | 1,544 | 84% | | 100 | T | | 1265 |
| **University of Maine at Fort Kent,** Fort Kent, ME 04743 | 1878 | C/Pub | 565 | 85% | | 22 | R | | 1350 |
| **University of Maine at Machias,** Machias, ME 04654 | 1909 | C/Pub | 750 | 80% | | 42 | T | | 1395 |
| **University of Maine at Orono,** Orono, ME 04469 | 1865 | C/Pub | 10,618 | 76% | G | 694 | T | A,AF | 1480 |
| **University of Maine at Presque Isle,** Presque Isle, ME 04769 | 1903 | C/Pub | 975 | 88% | | 86 | R | | 1390 |
| **University of Mary Hardin-Baylor,** Belton, TX 76513 | 1845 | C/Ind-R | 1,034 | 81% | | 74 | T | AF | 2400 |
| **University of Maryland at Baltimore,** Baltimore, MD 21201 | 1807 | C/Pub | 1,331 | 93% | G | 1,168 | M | | 957 |
| **University of Maryland at College Park,** College Park, MD 20742 | 1859 | C/Pub | 30,002 | 79% | G | 2,278 | T | AF | 1185 |
| **University of Maryland Baltimore County,** Catonsville, MD 21228 | 1966 | C/Pub | 6,326 | 95% | G | 386 | M | | 1224 |
| **University of Maryland Eastern Shore,** Princess Anne, MD 21853 | 1886 | C/Pub | 1,069 | 70% | G | 89 | R | | 859 |
| **University of Maryland, University College,** College Park, MD 20742 | 1947 | C/Pub | 10,747 | 79% | G | 496 | T | | 1690x |
| **University of Massachusetts at Amherst,** Amherst, MA 01003 | 1863 | C/Pub | 19,043 | 85% | G | 1,465 | T | A,AF | 1750 |
| **University of Massachusetts at Boston,** Boston, MA 02125 | 1965 | C/Pub | 8,250 | 96% | G | 594 | M | | 1257x |
| **University of Miami,** Coral Gables, FL 33124 | 1925 | C/Ind | 10,532 | 45% | G | 1,398 | C | A,AF | 5896 |
| **University of Michigan,** Ann Arbor, MI 48109 | 1817 | C/Pub | 22,314 | 76% | G | 2,465 | C | A,N,AF | 1759 |
| **University of Michigan–Dearborn,** Dearborn, MI 48128 | 1959 | C/Pub | 6,106 | 99% | G | 336 | C | A,N,AF | 664 |
| **University of Michigan–Flint,** Flint, MI 48503 | 1956 | C/Pub | 4,439 | 99% | G | 201 | C | | 1180x |
| **University of Minnesota, Duluth,** Duluth, MN 55812 | 1948 | C/Pub | 7,178 | 85% | G | 426 | C | AF | 1445 |
| **University of Minnesota, Morris,** Morris, MN 56267 | 1959 | C/Pub | 1,662 | 95% | | 132 | T | | 1248 |
| **University of Minnesota, Twin Cities Campus,** Minneapolis, MN 55455 | 1851 | C/Pub | 38,826 | 85% | G | 3,746 | M | A,N,AF | 1515 |
| **University of Mississippi,** University, MS 38677 | 1844 | C/Pub | 7,924 | 74% | G | 574 | T | A,N,AF | 1165 |
| **University of Mississippi Medical Center,** Jackson, MS 39216 | 1955 | C/Pub | 472 | 98% | G | 511 | C | | 1024 |
| **University of Missouri–Columbia,** Columbia, MO 65211 | 1839 | C/Pub | 18,920 | 88% | G | 1,598 | T | A,N,AF | 1068 |
| **University of Missouri–Kansas City,** Kansas City, MO 64110 | 1933 | C/Pub | 6,352 | 88% | G | 1,448 | M | | 1110 |
| **University of Missouri–Rolla,** Rolla, MO 65401 | 1870 | C/Pub | 6,501 | 84% | G | 322 | T | A,AF | 1219 |
| **University of Missouri–St Louis,** St Louis, MO 63121 | 1963 | C/Pub | 10,185 | 97% | G | 449 | M | | 1104x |
| **University of Montana,** Missoula, MT 59812 | 1893 | C/Pub | 7,305 | 72% | G | 447 | C | A | 801 |
| **University of Montevallo,** Montevallo, AL 35115 | 1896 | C/Pub | 2,301 | 90% | G | 175 | T | A | 918 |
| **University of Nebraska at Omaha,** Omaha, NE 68182 | 1908 | C/Pub | 13,431 | 94% | G | 548 | M | AF | 1064x |
| **University of Nebraska–Lincoln,** Lincoln, NE 68588 | 1869 | C/Pub | 19,903 | 92% | G | 1,077 | C | A,N,AF | 1045 |
| **University of Nebraska Medical Center,** Omaha, NE 68105 | 1869 | C/Pub | * | * | G | * | * | | * |
| **University of Nevada, Las Vegas,** Las Vegas, NV 89154 | 1955 | C/Pub | 7,437 | 82% | G | 304 | C | A | 672 |
| **University of Nevada Reno,** Reno, NV 89557 | 1874 | C/Pub | 6,741 | 83% | G | 389 | C | A | 992 |
| **University of New England,** Biddeford, ME 04005 | 1953 | C/Ind | 406 | 32% | G | 41 | T | | 4785 |
| **University of New Hampshire,** Durham, NH 03824 | 1866 | C/Pub | 8,887 | 65% | G | 639 | T | A,AF | 1450 |
| **University of New Haven,** West Haven, CT 06516 | 1920 | C/Ind | 2,442 | 75% | G | 498 | C | | 4520 |
| **University of New Mexico,** Albuquerque, NM 87131 | 1889 | C/Pub | 18,646 | 93% | G | 1,007 | C | N,AF | 768 |
| **University of New Orleans,** New Orleans, LA 70148 | 1958 | C/Pub | 13,069 | 94% | G | 671 | M | A,AF | 624 |
| **University of North Alabama,** Florence, AL 35632 | 1872 | C/Pub | 4,752 | 88% | G | 214 | T | A | 870 |
| **University of North Carolina at Asheville,** Asheville, NC 28814 | 1927 | C/Pub | 2,266 | 83% | | 89 | C | | 628 |
| **University of North Carolina at Chapel Hill,** Chapel Hill, NC 27514 | 1795 | C/Pub | 14,678 | 85% | G | 1,745 | T | N,AF | 701 |
| **University of North Carolina at Charlotte,** Charlotte, NC 28223 | 1946 | C/Pub | 8,423 | 90% | G | 672 | C | A,AF | 648 |
| **University of North Carolina at Greensboro,** Greensboro, NC 27412 | 1891 | C/Pub | 7,324 | 86% | G | 634 | C | | 744 |

| Name and Location | Est | Type/ Control | UG Enroll | State Res | Grad | Fac Size | Cmps | ROTC | Tuition & Fees |
|---|---|---|---|---|---|---|---|---|---|
| **University of North Carolina at Wilmington,** Wilmington, NC 28403 | 1947 | C/Pub | 4,950 | 93% | G | 307 | C | A | $645 |
| **University of North Dakota,** Grand Forks, ND 58202 | 1884 | C/Pub | 8,977 | 80% | G | 650 | R | | 764 |
| **University of Northern Colorado,** Greeley, CO 80639 | 1890 | C/Pub | 8,702 | 85% | G | 650 | T | AF | 1215 |
| **University of Northern Iowa,** Cedar Falls, IA 50614 | 1876 | C/Pub | 9,737 | 97% | G | 669 | T | A | 990 |
| **University of North Florida,** Jacksonville, FL 32216 | 1965 | C/Pub | 4,152 | 99% | G | 175 | M | A | 840x |
| **University of Notre Dame,** Notre Dame, IN 46556 | 1842 | C/Ind-R | 7,000 | 8% | G | 798 | C | A,N,AF | 5950 |
| **University of Oklahoma,** Norman, OK 73019 | 1890 | C/Pub | 16,666 | 81% | G | 826 | C | A,N,AF | 713 |
| **University of Oklahoma Health Sciences Center,** Oklahoma City, OK 73190 | 1890 | C/Pub | 966 | 89% | G | 690 | M | | 600x |
| **University of Oregon,** Eugene, OR 97403 | 1876 | C/Pub | 12,496 | 76% | G | 1,287 | C | A | 1200 |
| **University of Pennsylvania,** Philadelphia, PA 19104 | 1740 | C/Ind | 9,080 | 25% | G | 2,500 | M | A,N | 8000 |
| **University of Phoenix,** Phoenix, AZ 85004 | 1976 | C/Prop | 1,470 | * | G | 242 | M | | 3280x |
| **University of Pittsburgh,** Pittsburgh, PA 15260 | 1787 | C/Pub | 18,976 | 93% | G | 2,630 | M | A,AF | 2318 |
| **University of Pittsburgh at Bradford,** Bradford, PA 16701 | 1963 | C/Pub | 1,100 | 93% | | 54 | T | A,AF | 2250 |
| **University of Pittsburgh at Greensburg,** Greensburg, PA 15601 | 1963 | C/Pub | 1,000 | 99% | | 43 | T | | 1975x |
| **University of Pittsburgh at Johnstown,** Johnstown, PA 15904 | 1927 | C/Pub | 3,100 | 92% | | 161 | T | | 2310 |
| **University of Portland,** Portland, OR 97203 | 1901 | C/Ind-R | 2,233 | 62% | G | 160 | M | AF | 4400 |
| **U of PR, Arecibo Regional Coll,** Arecibo, PR 00612 | 1967 | C/Pub | 2,821 | 100% | | 150 | C | A | 492x |
| **U of PR, Bayamón Tech University Coll,** Bayamón, PR 00619 | * | C/Pub | * | * | | * | * | | * |
| **U of PR, Cayey University Coll,** Cayey, PR 00633 | 1967 | C/Pub | 2,695 | 100% | | 139 | T | A | 450x |
| **U of PR, Humacao University Coll,** Humacao, PR 00661 | 1962 | C/Pub | 3,200 | 100% | | 221 | T | A | 685x |
| **U of PR, Mayaguez,** Mayaguez, PR 00708 | 1911 | C/Pub | 8,553 | 98% | G | 553 | C | A,AF | 450x |
| **U of PR Medical Sciences Cmps,** San Juan, PR 00936 | 1950 | C/Pub | 1,113 | 98% | G | 689 | M | | 450x |
| **U of PR, Río Piedras,** Río Piedras, PR 00931 | 1903 | C/Pub | 18,683 | 99% | G | 1,102 | M | A,AF | 530 |
| **University of Puget Sound,** Tacoma, WA 98416 | 1888 | C/Ind-R | 2,808 | 50% | G | 206 | C | AF | 5480 |
| **University of Redlands,** Redlands, CA 92373 | 1907 | C/Ind | 1,200 | 70% | G | 132 | T | | 6750 |
| **University of Rhode Island,** Kingston, RI 02881 | 1892 | C/Pub | 8,910 | 70% | G | 830 | T | A | 1543 |
| **University of Richmond,** Richmond, VA 23173 | 1830 | C/Ind-R | 2,486 | 30% | G | 329 | C | A | 5525 |
| **University of Rochester,** Rochester, NY 14627 | 1850 | C/Ind | 5,065 | 55% | G | 1,204 | M | N | 7266 |
| **University of St Thomas,** Houston, TX 77006 | 1947 | C/Ind-R | 1,567 | 90% | G | 126 | M | | 2860 |
| **University of San Diego,** San Diego, CA 92110 | 1949 | C/Ind-R | 2,950 | 65% | G | 276 | M | N | 5160 |
| **University of San Francisco,** San Francisco, CA 94117 | 1855 | C/Ind-R | 3,154 | 63% | G | 434 | M | A | 5020 |
| **University of Santa Clara,** Santa Clara, CA 95053 | 1851 | C/Ind-R | 3,621 | 76% | G | 406 | C | A | 5190 |
| **University of Science and Arts of Oklahoma,** Chickasha, OK 73018 | 1908 | C/Pub | * | * | | * | * | | * |
| **University of Scranton,** Scranton, PA 18510 | 1888 | C/Ind-R | 3,761 | 67% | G | 227 | C | A | 3670 |
| **University of South Alabama,** Mobile, AL 36688 | 1963 | C/Pub | 7,517 | 84% | G | 351 | C | A | 1254 |
| **University of South Carolina,** Columbia, SC 29208 | 1801 | C/Pub | 18,245 | 83% | G | 1,241 | C | A,N,AF | 1180 |
| **University of South Carolina at Aiken,** Aiken, SC 29801 | 1961 | C/Pub | 1,800 | 95% | | 126 | * | | *x |
| **University of South Carolina at Spartanburg,** Spartanburg, SC 29303 | 1967 | C/Pub | 2,640 | 95% | | 189 | C | | 850x |
| **U of South Carolina—Coastal Carolina Coll,** Conway, SC 29526 | 1954 | C/Pub | 2,252 | 93% | | 136 | R | A | 850x |
| **University of South Dakota,** Vermillion, SD 57069 | 1862 | C/Pub | 4,794 | 80% | G | 440 | T | A | 1117 |
| **University of South Dakota at Springfield,** Springfield, SD 57062 | 1881 | C/Pub | 764 | 83% | | 64 | T | A | 840 |
| **University of Southern California,** Los Angeles, CA 90089 | 1880 | C/Ind | 14,761 | 71% | G | * | M | A,N,AF | 7000 |
| **University of Southern Colorado,** Pueblo, CO 81001 | 1933 | C/Pub | 4,566 | 88% | G | 254 | C | A | 974 |
| **University of Southern Maine,** Gorham, ME 04038 | 1878 | C/Pub | 7,394 | 89% | G | 326 | T | A | 1385 |
| **University of Southern Mississippi,** Hattiesburg, MS 39401 | 1910 | C/Pub | 8,902 | 89% | G | 644 | C | A,AF | 1047 |
| **University of South Florida,** Tampa, FL 33620 | 1956 | C/Pub | 18,017 | 90% | G | 1,220 | M | A,AF | 796 |
| **University of South Florida, New College,** Sarasota, FL 33580 | 1960 | C/Pub | 450 | 50% | | 48 | T | | 946 |
| **University of Southwestern Louisiana,** Lafayette, LA 70504 | 1898 | C/Pub | 13,128 | 85% | G | 604 | C | AF | 561 |
| **University of Steubenville,** Steubenville, OH 43952 | 1946 | C/Ind-R | 872 | 40% | G | 76 | T | | 4220 |
| **University of Tampa,** Tampa, FL 33606 | 1931 | C/Ind | 1,844 | 25% | G | 142 | M | A | 5036 |
| **University of Tennessee at Chattanooga,** Chattanooga, TN 37402 | 1886 | C/Pub | 6,028 | 88% | G | 396 | C | A | 730 |
| **University of Tennessee at Martin,** Martin, TN 38238 | 1927 | C/Pub | 5,280 | 93% | G | 255 | T | A | 825 |
| **University of Tennessee Ctr for the Health Scis,** Memphis, TN 38163 | 1851 | C/Pub | 620 | 3% | G | 686 | M | | 311 |
| **University of Tennessee, Knoxville,** Knoxville, TN 37996 | 1794 | C/Pub | 22,904 | 91% | G | 1,665 | C | A,AF | 852 |
| **University of Texas at Arlington,** Arlington, TX 76019 | 1895 | C/Pub | 18,241 | 87% | G | 960 | C | A | 440 |
| **University of Texas at Austin,** Austin, TX 78712 | 1883 | C/Pub | 38,111 | 86% | G | 2,100 | C | A,N,AF | 540 |
| **University of Texas at El Paso,** El Paso, TX 79968 | 1913 | C/Pub | 13,675 | 88% | G | 661 | M | A,AF | 396 |
| **University of Texas at San Antonio,** San Antonio, TX 78285 | 1969 | C/Pub | 8,931 | 98% | G | 494 | M | A,AF | 414x |
| **University of Texas at Tyler,** Tyler, TX 75701 | 1972 | C/Pub | 1,370 | 98% | G | 115 | C | | 640x |
| **U of Texas Health Sci Ctr at Dallas,** Dallas, TX 75235 | 1972 | C/Pub | 215 | 85% | G | 258 | C | | 170x |
| **U of Texas Health Sci Ctr at Houston,** Houston, TX 77030 | 1943 | C/Pub | 561 | 90% | G | 792 | M | | 220 |
| **U of Texas Health Sci Ctr at San Antonio,** San Antonio, TX 78284 | 1976 | C/Pub | 414 | 97% | G | 64 | M | | 195x |
| **U of Texas Med Branch at Galveston,** Galveston, TX 77550 | 1891 | C/Pub | 595 | 99% | G | 450 | C | | 120x |
| **University of Texas of the Permian Basin,** Odessa, TX 79762 | 1973 | C/Pub | 893 | 95% | G | 89 | C | | 685 |
| **University of the District of Columbia,** Washington, DC 20008 | 1976 | C/Pub | 13,311 | 91% | G | 905 | M | | 330x |
| **University of the Pacific,** Stockton, CA 95211 | 1851 | C/Ind | 3,687 | 70% | G | 330 | C | | 7615 |
| **University of the Sacred Heart,** Santurce, PR 00914 | 1939 | C/Ind-R | 6,425 | 97% | | 275 | * | | * |
| **University of the South,** Sewanee, TN 37375 | 1858 | C/Ind-R | 1,072 | 21% | G | 116 | R | | 6520 |
| **U of State of NY Regents External Degree Program,** Albany, NY 12230 | 1970 | C/Pub | 20,945 | * | | * | * | | * |
| **University of Toledo,** Toledo, OH 43606 | 1872 | C/Pub | 17,874 | 90% | G | 1,224 | M | A | 1260 |
| **University of Tulsa,** Tulsa, OK 74104 | 1894 | C/Ind | 4,570 | 70% | G | 410 | C | A | 3270 |
| **University of Utah,** Salt Lake City, UT 84112 | 1850 | C/Pub | 19,608 | 88% | G | 1,350 | M | A,N,AF | 960 |
| **University of Vermont,** Burlington, VT 05405 | 1791 | C/Pub | 7,833 | 48% | G | 720 | T | A | 2356 |
| **University of Virginia,** Charlottesville, VA 22903 | 1819 | C/Pub | 11,052 | 64% | G | 1,579 | T | A,N,AF | 1350 |
| **University of Washington,** Seattle, WA 98195 | 1861 | C/Pub | 26,122 | 88% | G | 2,626 | C | A,N,AF | 1176 |
| **University of West Florida,** Pensacola, FL 32504 | 1963 | C/Pub | 4,295 | 97% | G | 342 | R | | 840 |
| **University of West Los Angeles,** Culver City, CA 90230 | 1966 | C/Ind | 231 | 95% | G | 15 | T | | 9085x |
| **University of Wisconsin—Eau Claire,** Eau Claire, WI 54701 | 1916 | C/Pub | 10,414 | 89% | G | 567 | T | | 1040 |
| **University of Wisconsin—Green Bay,** Green Bay, WI 54302 | 1968 | C/Pub | 4,259 | 93% | G | 230 | C | A | 975 |

| Name and Location | Est | Type/ Control | UG Enroll | State Res | Grad | Fac Size | Cmps | ROTC | Tuition & Fees |
|---|---|---|---|---|---|---|---|---|---|
| **University of Wisconsin–La Crosse,** La Crosse, WI 54601 | 1909 | C/Pub | 8,415 | 85% | G | 410 | C | A | $2451 |
| **University of Wisconsin–Madison,** Madison, WI 53706 | 1849 | C/Pub | 28,127 | 82% | G | 2,269 | C | A,N,AF | 1070 |
| **University of Wisconsin–Milwaukee,** Milwaukee, WI 53201 | 1956 | C/Pub | 22,093 | 95% | G | 1,229 | M | A | 1260 |
| **University of Wisconsin–Oshkosh,** Oshkosh, WI 54901 | 1871 | C/Pub | 9,200 | 97% | G | 600 | C | A | 931 |
| **University of Wisconsin–Parkside,** Kenosha, WI 53141 | 1968 | C/Pub | 5,327 | 97% | G | 280 | C | | 990x |
| **University of Wisconsin–Platteville,** Platteville, WI 53818 | 1866 | C/Pub | 4,510 | 89% | G | 244 | T | A | 800 |
| **University of Wisconsin–River Falls,** River Falls, WI 54022 | 1874 | C/Pub | 5,144 | 60% | G | 279 | T | | 1015 |
| **University of Wisconsin–Stevens Point,** Stevens Point, WI 54481 | 1894 | C/Pub | 8,624 | 90% | G | 526 | T | A | 1000 |
| **University of Wisconsin–Stout,** Menomonie, WI 54751 | 1893 | C/Pub | 6,923 | 67% | G | 560 | T | | 964 |
| **University of Wisconsin–Superior,** Superior, WI 54880 | 1893 | C/Pub | 1,840 | 72% | G | 145 | T | AF | 925 |
| **University of Wisconsin–Whitewater,** Whitewater, WI 53190 | 1868 | C/Pub | 8,666 | 93% | G | 553 | T | A | 940 |
| **University of Wyoming,** Laramie, WY 82071 | 1886 | C/Pub | 7,484 | 69% | G | 868 | T | A,AF | 616 |
| **Upper Iowa University,** Fayette, IA 52142 | 1857 | C/Ind | 450 | 70% | | 50 | T | A | 4140 |
| **Upsala College,** East Orange, NJ 07019 | 1893 | C/Ind-R | 1,740 | 85% | G | 128 | C | | 4768 |
| **Urbana College,** Urbana, OH 43078 | 1850 | C/Ind-R | 641 | 95% | | 75 | T | | 1129 |
| **Ursinus College,** Collegeville, PA 19426 | 1869 | C/Ind-R | 1,139 | 63% | | 91 | T | | 5005 |
| **Ursuline College,** Pepper Pike, OH 44124 | 1871 | W/Ind-R | 1,147 | 95% | G | 70 | T | | 3150 |
| **Utah State University,** Logan, UT 84322 | 1888 | C/Pub | 8,742 | 71% | G | 1,250 | T | A,AF | 795 |
| **Utica College of Syracuse University,** Utica, NY 13502 | 1946 | C/Ind | 1,658 | 84% | | 161 | C | | 4800 |
| **Valdosta State College,** Valdosta, GA 31698 | 1906 | C/Pub | 4,024 | 89% | G | 245 | C | AF | 849 |
| **Valley City State College,** Valley City, ND 58072 | 1890 | C/Pub | 1,208 | 93% | | 64 | T | A | 707 |
| **Valley Forge Christian College,** Phoenixville, PA 19460 | 1938 | C/Ind-R | 438 | 28% | | 26 | R | | 2413 |
| **Valparaiso University,** Valparaiso, IN 46383 | 1859 | C/Ind-R | 3,786 | 29% | G | 360 | T | | 4782 |
| **Vanderbilt University,** Nashville, TN 37240 | 1873 | C/Ind | 5,205 | 21% | G | 2,021 | M | A,N | 6230 |
| **VanderCook College of Music,** Chicago, IL 60616 | 1909 | C/Ind | * | 70% | G | 26 | M | | 3800 |
| **Vassar College,** Poughkeepsie, NY 12601 | 1861 | C/Ind | 2,331 | 41% | G | 242 | C | | 7560 |
| **Vennard College,** University Park, IA 52595 | 1910 | C/Ind-R | 171 | 20% | | 19 | T | | 2011 |
| **Vermont College of Norwich University,** Montpelier, VT 05602 | 1834 | C/Ind. | 667 | 50% | G | 55 | T | A,AF | 7650† |
| **Villa Maria College,** Erie, PA 16505 | 1925 | W/Ind-R | 616 | 93% | | 76 | C | A | 3885 |
| **Villanova University,** Villanova, PA 19085 | 1842 | C/Ind-R | 6,200 | 44% | G | 439 | T | N,AF | 5050 |
| **Virginia Commonwealth University,** Richmond, VA 23284 | 1838 | C/Pub | 15,833 | 93% | G | 2,229 | M | | 1298 |
| **Virginia Intermont College,** Bristol, VA 24201 | 1884 | C/Ind-R | 647 | 38% | | 56 | T | | 3365 |
| **Virginia Military Institute,** Lexington, VA 24450 | 1839 | M/Pub | 1,310 | 53% | | 98 | T | A,N,AF | 900 |
| **Virginia Polytechnic Inst & State U,** Blacksburg, VA 24061 | 1872 | C/Pub | 18,214 | 80% | G | 2,005 | T | A,AF | 1281 |
| **Virginia State University,** Petersburg, VA 23803 | 1882 | C/Pub | 4,148 | 77% | G | 264 | C | A | 1303 |
| **Virginia Union University,** Richmond, VA 23220 | 1865 | C/Ind-R | 1,293 | 58% | G | 129 | M | | 2910 |
| **Virginia Wesleyan College,** Norfolk, VA 23502 | 1960 | C/Ind-R | 826 | 79% | | 55 | C | | 4100 |
| **Viterbo College,** La Crosse, WI 54601 | 1890 | C/Ind-R | 1,123 | 80% | | 116 | C | | 3780 |
| **Voorhees College,** Denmark, SC 29042 | 1897 | C/Ind-R | 708 | 81% | | 49 | T | A | 2329 |
| **Wabash College,** Crawfordsville, IN 47933 | 1832 | M/Ind | 780 | 79% | | 77 | T | | 5280 |
| **Wadhams Hall Seminary-College,** Ogdensburg, NY 13669 | 1924 | M/Ind-R | 63 | 83% | | 17 | R | | 2280 |
| **Wagner College,** Staten Island, NY 10301 | 1883 | C/Ind-R | 1,800 | 80% | G | 216 | M | | 4850 |
| **Wake Forest University,** Winston-Salem, NC 27109 | 1834 | C/Ind-R | 3,171 | 47% | G | 246 | C | A | 4700 |
| **Walla Walla College,** College Place, WA 99324 | 1892 | C/Ind-R | 1,800 | 40% | G | 163 | T | | 5169 |
| **Walsh College,** Canton, OH 44720 | 1958 | C/Ind-R | 1,039 | 90% | G | 60 | C | | 3470 |
| **Walsh College of Accountancy & Business Admin,** Troy, MI 48084 | 1922 | C/Ind | 1,500 | 100% | G | 80 | C | | 1900x |
| **Warner Pacific College,** Portland, OR 97215 | 1937 | C/Ind-R | 474 | 49% | G | 49 | M | | 3825 |
| **Warner Southern College,** Lake Wales, FL 33853 | 1968 | C/Ind-R | 310 | 44% | | 37 | R | | 3150 |
| **Warren Wilson College,** Swannanoa, NC 28778 | 1894 | C/Ind-R | * | 30% | G | 75 | R | | 3950 |
| **Wartburg College,** Waverly, IA 50677 | 1852 | C/Ind-R | 1,086 | 65% | | 86 | T | | 4750 |
| **Washburn University of Topeka,** Topeka, KS 66621 | 1865 | C/Pub | 5,445 | 97% | G | 260 | C | AF | 1164 |
| **Washington and Jefferson College,** Washington, PA 15301 | 1781 | C/Ind | 1,077 | 70% | | 97 | T | A | 6110 |
| **Washington and Lee University,** Lexington, VA 24450 | 1749 | M/Ind | 1,320 | 25% | G | 167 | T | A | 5460 |
| **Washington Bible College,** Lanham, MD 20706 | 1938 | C/Ind-R | 499 | 50% | G | 37 | T | | 2664 |
| **Washington College,** Chestertown, MD 21620 | 1782 | C/Ind | 684 | 48% | G | 68 | T | | 4821 |
| **Washington State University,** Pullman, WA 99164 | 1892 | C/Pub | 14,097 | 84% | G | 1,064 | R | A,AF | 1176 |
| **Washington University,** St Louis, MO 63130 | 1853 | C/Ind | 4,561 | 23% | G | 2,447 | M | A,AF | 7179 |
| **Wayland Baptist College,** Plainview, TX 79072 | 1908 | C/Ind-R | 1,268 | 87% | | 67 | T | | * |
| **Waynesburg College,** Waynesburg, PA 15370 | 1849 | C/Ind-R | 871 | 77% | | 73 | T | A | 4760 |
| **Wayne State College,** Wayne, NE 68787 | 1910 | C/Pub | 2,024 | 85% | G | 126 | T | | 821 |
| **Wayne State University,** Detroit, MI 48202 | 1868 | C/Pub | 22,375 | 99% | G | 2,100 | M | | 1670 |
| **Webber College,** Babson Park, FL 33827 | 1927 | C/Ind | 215 | 55% | G | 21 | T | | 3095 |
| **Webb Institute of Naval Architecture,** Glen Cove, NY 11542 | 1889 | M/Ind | 84 | 30% | | 15 | T | | 0 |
| **Weber State College,** Ogden, UT 84408 | 1889 | C/Pub | 10,140 | 93% | G | 476 | C | A | 750 |
| **Webster College,** St Louis, MO 63119 | 1915 | C/Ind | 1,022 | 70% | G | 621 | M | | 3975 |
| **Wellesley College,** Wellesley, MA 02181 | 1875 | W/Ind | 2,220 | 25% | | 295 | T | | 7510 |
| **Wells College,** Aurora, NY 13026 | 1868 | W/Ind | 532 | 40% | | 54 | R | | 6960 |
| **Wentworth Institute of Technology,** Boston, MA 02115 | 1904 | C/Ind | 3,000 | 75% | | 150 | M | | 3990 |
| **Wesleyan College,** Macon, GA 31297 | 1836 | W/Ind-R | 500 | 50% | | 60 | C | | 3730 |
| **Wesleyan University,** Middletown, CT 06457 | 1831 | C/Ind | 2,515 | 20% | G | 269 | T | | 8370 |
| **Wesley College,** Dover, DE 19901 | 1873 | C/Ind-R | 1,345 | 95% | | 77 | T | | 5230 |
| **Wesley College,** Florence, MS 39073 | 1972 | C/Ind-R | * | * | | * | * | | 1250 |
| **Westbrook College,** Portland, ME 04103 | 1831 | C/Ind | 646 | 51% | | 87 | C | | 4960 |
| **West Chester State College,** West Chester, PA 19380 | 1871 | C/Pub | 7,986 | 89% | G | 495 | T | A | 1525 |
| **West Coast Christian College,** Fresno, CA 93710 | 1944 | C/Ind-R | 253 | 50% | | 17 | M | | 1925 |
| **West Coast University,** Los Angeles, CA 90020 | 1909 | C/Ind | 619 | 75% | G | 250 | M | | 4140x |
| **West Coast University, Orange Center,** Orange, CA 92668 | 1909 | C/Ind | 800 | 70% | G | 88 | C | | 3264x |
| **Western Baptist College,** Salem, OR 97302 | 1935 | C/Ind-R | 359 | 37% | | 29 | C | | 3850 |
| **Western Bible College,** Morrison, CO 80465 | 1948 | C/Ind | 184 | 58% | | 20 | R | | 2615 |
| **Western Carolina University,** Cullowhee, NC 28723 | 1889 | C/Pub | 5,431 | 89% | G | 369 | R | A | 673 |
| **Western Connecticut State College,** Danbury, CT 06810 | 1903 | C/Pub | 4,814 | 89% | G | 220 | T | | 931 |
| **Western Illinois University,** Macomb, IL 61455 | 1899 | C/Pub | 11,299 | 97% | G | 700 | T | A | 1082 |
| **Western International University,** Phoenix, AZ 85021 | 1978 | C/Ind | 245 | 98% | G | 50 | M | | 1800x |

| Name and Location | Est | Type/ Control | UG Enroll | State Res | Grad | Fac Size | Cmps | ROTC | Tuition & Fees |
|---|---|---|---|---|---|---|---|---|---|
| **Western Kentucky University,** Bowling Green, KY 42101 | 1906 | C/Pub | 9,157 | 84% | G | 727 | T | A | $714 |
| **Western Maryland College,** Westminster, MD 21157 | 1867 | C/Ind | 1,387 | 70% | G | 137 | T | A | 5200 |
| **Western Michigan University,** Kalamazoo, MI 49008 | 1903 | C/Pub | 16,839 | 90% | G | 1,095 | C | A | 1396 |
| **Western Montana College,** Dillon, MT 59725 | 1893 | C/Pub | 750 | 89% | G | 45 | R | A | 633 |
| **Western New England College,** Springfield, MA 01119 | 1919 | C/Ind | 3,043 | 64% | G | 264 | C | | 4118 |
| **Western New Mexico University,** Silver City, NM 88061 | 1893 | C/Pub | 1,238 | 91% | G | 75 | T | | 559 |
| **Western Oregon State College,** Monmouth, OR 97361 | 1856 | C/Pub | 2,465 | 96% | G | 200 | T | A | 1360 |
| **Western State College of Colorado,** Gunnison, CO 81230 | 1911 | C/Pub | 2,921 | 80% | G | 165 | R | | 809 |
| **Western State U Coll of Law of Orange County,** Fullerton, CA 92631 | 1966 | C/Prop | 334 | 100% | G | 55 | C | | 4390x |
| **Western State U Coll of Law of San Diego,** San Diego, CA 92101 | 1969 | C/Prop | 170 | * | G | 39 | M | | 4390x |
| **Western Washington University,** Bellingham, WA 98225 | 1893 | C/Pub | 9,216 | 94% | G | 512 | T | | 942 |
| **Westfield State College,** Westfield, MA 01085 | 1838 | C/Pub | 2,871 | 97% | G | 180 | T | | 1045 |
| **West Georgia College,** Carrollton, GA 30118 | 1933 | C/Pub | 4,606 | 97% | G | 281 | T | | 750 |
| **West Liberty State College,** West Liberty, WV 26074 | 1837 | C/Pub | 2,639 | 65% | | 162 | R | | 604 |
| **Westmar College,** Le Mars, IA 51031 | 1890 | C/Ind-R | 534 | 75% | | 44 | T | | 4060 |
| **Westminster Choir College,** Princeton, NJ 08540 | 1926 | C/Ind | 349 | 36% | G | 69 | T | | 5550 |
| **Westminster College,** Fulton, MO 65251 | 1851 | C/Ind-R | 675 | 51% | | 57 | T | A | 4400 |
| **Westminster College,** New Wilmington, PA 16142 | 1852 | C/Ind-R | 1,608 | 72% | G | 140 | T | | 4900 |
| **Westminster College,** Salt Lake City, UT 84105 | 1875 | C/Ind | 996 | 80% | G | 98 | M | | 3280 |
| **Westmont College,** Santa Barbara, CA 93108 | 1940 | C/Ind-R | 1,077 | 70% | | 99 | C | A | 5490 |
| **West Texas State University,** Canyon, TX 79016 | 1909 | C/Pub | 5,458 | 93% | G | 359 | T | A | 455 |
| **West Virginia Institute of Technology,** Montgomery, WV 25136 | 1895 | C/Pub | 3,132 | 80% | G | 185 | T | A | 479 |
| **West Virginia State College,** Institute, WV 25112 | 1891 | C/Pub | 4,485 | 91% | | 210 | T | A | 600 |
| **West Virginia University,** Morgantown, WV 26506 | 1867 | C/Pub | 14,668 | 57% | G | 2,237 | T | A,AF | 840 |
| **West Virginia Wesleyan College,** Buckhannon, WV 26201 | 1890 | C/Ind-R | 1,750 | 32% | G | 113 | T | | 3986 |
| **Wheaton College,** Wheaton, IL 60187 | 1860 | C/Ind-R | 2,044 | 25% | G | 150 | T | A | 4780 |
| **Wheaton College,** Norton, MA 02766 | 1834 | W/Ind | 1,218 | 30% | | 130 | T | | 7825 |
| **Wheeling College,** Wheeling, WV 26003 | 1954 | C/Ind-R | 1,031 | 40% | G | 72 | C | | 4350 |
| **Wheelock College,** Boston, MA 02215 | 1888 | W/Ind | 547 | 48% | G | 113 | M | | 5725 |
| **Whitman College,** Walla Walla, WA 99362 | 1859 | C/Ind | 1,110 | 49% | | 90 | T | | 5850 |
| **Whittier College,** Whittier, CA 90608 | 1901 | C/Ind | 1,200 | 62% | G | 105 | C | | 5886 |
| **Whitworth College,** Spokane, WA 99251 | 1890 | C/Ind-R | 1,243 | 52% | G | 144 | C | | 5235 |
| **Wichita State University,** Wichita, KS 67208 | 1895 | C/Pub | 13,564 | 85% | G | 823 | C | A | 930 |
| **Widener University,** Chester, PA 19013 | 1821 | C/Ind | 2,300 | 65% | G | 200 | C | A | 5260 |
| **Wilberforce University,** Wilberforce, OH 45384 | 1856 | C/Ind-R | 1,034 | 33% | | 75 | R | A | 3280 |
| **Wiley College,** Marshall, TX 75670 | 1873 | C/Ind-R | 613 | 52% | | 52 | T | | 2585 |
| **Wilkes College,** Wilkes-Barre, PA 18766 | 1933 | C/Ind | 2,090 | 78% | G | 193 | C | AF | 4650 |
| **Willamette University,** Salem, OR 97301 | 1842 | C/Ind-R | 1,330 | 53% | G | 172 | C | | 5570 |
| **William Carey College,** Hattiesburg, MS 39401 | 1906 | C/Ind-R | 1,269 | 65% | G | 110 | T | | 2280 |
| **William Jewell College,** Liberty, MO 64068 | 1849 | C/Ind-R | 1,410 | 70% | | 128 | T | | 3580 |
| **William Paterson College of New Jersey,** Wayne, NJ 07470 | 1855 | C/Pub | 10,265 | 97% | G | 601 | T | AF | 1065 |
| **William Penn College,** Oskaloosa, IA 52577 | 1873 | C/Ind-R | 463 | 65% | | 52 | T | | 5110 |
| **Williams College,** Williamstown, MA 01267 | 1793 | C/Ind | 1,922 | 15% | G | 203 | T | | 7906 |
| **William Smith College,** Geneva, NY 14456 | 1908 | W/Ind | 750 | 45% | | 163 | T | | 7200 |
| **William Tyndale College,** Farmington Hills, MI 48018 | 1945 | C/Ind-R | 317 | 98% | | 25 | T | | 2396 |
| **William Woods College,** Fulton, MO 65251 | 1870 | W/Ind-R | 1,093 | 30% | | 88 | T | | 4740 |
| **Wilmington College,** New Castle, DE 19720 | 1967 | C/Ind | 683 | 63% | G | 79 | C | | 3190 |
| **Wilmington College of Ohio,** Wilmington, OH 45177 | 1870 | C/Ind-R | 816 | 87% | | 75 | R | | 6705 |
| **Wilson College,** Chambersburg, PA 17201 | 1869 | W/Ind | 237 | 55% | | 43 | T | | 5418 |
| **Wingate College,** Wingate, NC 28174 | 1895 | C/Ind-R | 1,500 | 85% | | 78 | T | | 2600 |
| **Winona State University,** Winona, MN 55987 | 1858 | C/Pub | 4,500 | 75% | G | 240 | T | A | 1010 |
| **Winston-Salem State University,** Winston-Salem, NC 27102 | 1892 | C/Pub | 2,224 | 91% | | 145 | C | A | 700 |
| **Winthrop College,** Rock Hill, SC 29733 | 1886 | C/Pub | 4,079 | 88% | G | 319 | T | | 1248 |
| **Wisconsin Conservatory of Music,** Milwaukee, WI 53202 | 1899 | C/Ind | 130 | 90% | G | 54 | M | | 3480x |
| **Wittenberg University,** Springfield, OH 45501 | 1845 | C/Ind-R | 2,254 | 53% | G | 175 | C | | 6125 |
| **Wofford College,** Spartanburg, SC 29301 | 1854 | C/Ind-R | 1,012 | 73% | | 75 | C | A | 4295 |
| **Woodbury University,** Los Angeles, CA 90017 | 1884 | C/Ind | 1,104 | 90% | G | 87 | M | | 3744x |
| **Worcester Polytechnic Institute,** Worcester, MA 01609 | 1865 | C/Ind | 2,457 | 49% | G | 248 | C | A | 6792 |
| **Worcester State College,** Worcester, MA 01602 | 1874 | C/Pub | 3,078 | 98% | G | 227 | C | | 1027 |
| **World College West,** San Rafael, CA 94912 | 1971 | C/Ind | 60 | 60% | | 33 | R | | 3910 |
| **Wright State University,** Dayton, OH 45435 | 1967 | C/Pub | 11,667 | 95% | G | 872 | M | A,AF | 1278 |
| **Xavier University,** Cincinnati, OH 45207 | 1831 | C/Ind-R | 3,853 | 80% | G | 343 | M | A | 4150 |
| **Xavier University of Louisiana,** New Orleans, LA 70125 | 1925 | C/Ind-R | 1,837 | 80% | G | 180 | M | A | 3000 |
| **Yale University,** New Haven, CT 06520 | 1701 | C/Ind | 5,128 | 11% | G | 1,761 | C | | 8190 |
| **Yankton College,** Yankton, SD 57078 | 1881 | C/Ind-R | 272 | 38% | | 33 | T | A | 4600 |
| **Yeshiva College,** New York, NY 10033 | 1886 | M/Ind | 796 | 54% | | 291 | M | | 5225 |
| **Yeshiva University**—See Stern College for Women and Yeshiva College | | | | | | | | | |
| **York College**—See City U of NY, York College | | | | | | | | | |
| **York College of Pennsylvania,** York, PA 17405 | 1787 | C/Ind | 4,154 | 74% | G | 195 | C | A | 2922 |
| **Youngstown State University,** Youngstown, OH 44555 | 1908 | C/Pub | 14,317 | 91% | G | 761 | C | A | 1245 |

**LARGE U.S. UNIVERSITY LIBRARIES: 1978-79** SOURCE: *Digest of Education Statistics, 1981*

| University | Number of Volumes |
|---|---|
| Harvard University | 9,913,992 |
| Yale University | 7,072,345 |
| University of Illinois (Urbana Campus) | 5,759,666 |
| University of California at Berkeley | 5,439,883 |
| University of Michigan, Ann Arbor | 5,076,602 |
| Columbia University (Main Division) | 4,893,138 |
| Stanford University | 4,577,827 |
| University of Chicago | 4,182,938 |
| University of California, L.A. | 4,109,146 |
| University of Texas at Austin | 3,972,303 |
| University of Minnesota, Minn.-St. Paul | 3,738,168 |
| Cornell University | 3,544,853 |
| University of Wisconsin, Madison | 3,501,402 |
| Ohio State University, Main Campus | 3,315,029 |
| Indiana University at Bloomington | 3,254,702 |
| Princeton University | 3,172,238 |
| University of Pennsylvania | 3,043,428 |
| Duke University | 3,022,916 |
| University of Washington | 2,903,685 |
| New York University | 2,700,201 |
| Northwestern University | 2,505,509 |
| University of N. Carolina at Chapel Hill | 2,315,237 |
| University of Virginia, Main Campus | 2,313,336 |
| University of Iowa | 2,216,970 |
| Johns Hopkins University | 2,214,282 |
| University of Utah | 2,119,959 |
| University of Missouri, Columbia | 2,109,107 |
| University of Florida | 2,079,344 |
| University of Kansas (Main Campus) | 1,958,429 |
| University of So. California | 1,949,756 |

## THE REFERENCE SHELF

This list of reference books constitutes the nucleus of a reference shelf for small private, public, and organizational libraries.

**Acronyms, Initialisms & Abbreviations Dictionary: Vol. 1; Vol. 2: New Acronyms, Initialisms, and Abbreviations, 1979 & 1980; Vol. 3: Reverse Acronyms, Initialisms, and Abbreviations Dictionary,** Ed. Ellen T. Crowley (Gale Research Co., Vol. 1, 7th ed., 1980; Vol. 2, 6th ed., 1979; Vol. 3, 6th ed., 1978).

**American Authors: 1600-1900,** Ed. Stanley J. Kunitz and Howard Haycraft (H. W. Wilson, 1938).

**American Heritage Dictionary of the English Language,** Ed. William Morris (Houghton Mifflin Co., 1976).

**American Men and Women of Science: The Physical and Biological Sciences,** Ed. The Jaques Cattell Press, 14th ed., 7 vols. plus index vol. (R. R. Bowker Co., 1979).

**American Men and Women of Science: The Social and Behavioral Sciences,** Ed. The Jaques Cattell Press, 13th ed., 2 vols. (R. R. Bowker Co., 1978).

**American Negro Reference Book,** Ed. John P. Davis (Prentice-Hall, Inc., 1966).

**American Universities and Colleges,** Ed. W. Todd Furniss, 11th ed. (American Council on Education, 1973).

**The Amy Vanderbilt Complete Book of Etiquette,** rev. & expanded by Letitia Baldridge (Doubleday and Co., Inc., 1978).

**Baby and Child Care,** Benjamin Spock, new rev. ed. (Hawthorn Books, 1976).

**Baker's Biographical Dictionary of Musicians,** Theodore Baker, ed. Nicolas Slonimsky, 6th ed. (Schirmer Books, 1978).

**Biographical Directory of the American Congress,** 1774-1961, U.S. Congress (Government Printing Office, 1961).

**Biographical Encyclopaedia and Who's Who of the American Theatre,** Ed. Walter Rigdon (James H. Heineman Inc., Publishers, 1966).

**Biography Index: A Cumulative Index to Biographical Materials in Books and Magazines,** annual (H. W. Wilson, 1946).

**Black's Law Dictionary,** Henry C. Black, Ed. Joseph R. Nolan & Michael J. Connolly, 5th ed. (West Publishing Co., 1979).

**The Book of the States,** biennial, Ed. Paul Albright (The Council of State Governments, 1936).

**Books in Print,** annual, 4 vols. (R. R. Bowker Co., 1948).

**Careful Writer: A Modern Guide to English Usage,** Theodore M. Bernstein (Atheneum Pubs., 1965).

**Chases' Calendar of Annual Events,** annual, William D. Chase (Apple Tree Press, Inc., 1957; rev. ed., 1980).

**Columbia Encyclopedia,** Ed. William H. Harris and Judith S. Levy, 4th ed. (Columbia University Press, 1975).

**Columbia-Lippincott Gazetteer of the World,** Ed. Leon E. Seltzer (Columbia University Press, 1952).

**Commercial Atlas and Marketing Guide,** annual (Rand McNally & Co., 1870).

**Concise Dictionary of American Biography,** 3rd ed. (Charles Scribner's Sons, 1980).

**Congress and the Nation, vol. 1, 1945-1964; vol. 2, 1965-1968, vol. 3, 1969-1972, vol. 4, 1972-1976** (Congressional Quarterly, Inc., 1965; 1969; 1973; 1977).

**Congressional Directory,** annual (Government Printing Office, 1935).

**Contemporary Authors,** semiannual, Ed. Frances C. Locher & Ann Evory, 96 vols. to date, vol 1-44 rev. ed. (Gale Research Co., 1967).

**Current Biography Yearbook,** annual (H. W. Wilson, 1940).

**Demographic Yearbook,** annual, Ed.United Nations Statistical Office (International Publications Service, 1949).

**Dictionary of American Biography,** Ed. American Council of Learned Societies, 16 vols. and supplements (Charles Scribner's Sons, 1927-80).

**Dictionary of American History,** Michael Martin & Leonard Gelber, Ed. Leo Lieberman, rev. & enlarged ed. (Littlefield, Adams, & Co., 1978).

**Dictionary of Modern English Usage,** Henry W. Fowler, 2nd ed., rev. by Sir Ernest Gowers (Oxford University Press, Inc., 1965).

**Dictionary of Music and Musicians,** George Grove, Ed. Eric Blom, 5th ed., 10 vols. (St. Martin's Press, Inc., 1954; supplement, 1961).

**Dictionary of National Biography,** George Smith, Ed. Leslie Stephen & Sir Sidney Lee, 22 vols. including 1st supplement, 7 supplements total, 7th suppl. Ed. E.T. Williams & Helen M. Palmer (Oxford University Press, Inc.; 22 vols. reprinted, 1938); abridged: **Concise Dictionary of National Biography,** 2 vols. (Oxford University Press, Inc., vol. 1, 1953; vol. 2, 1961).

**Dictionary of Quotations,** Bergen Evans (Delacorte Press, 1968).

**Dictionary of the Social Sciences,** Hugo F. Reading (Routledge & Kegan Paul, LTD, 1977).

**Dictionary of Universal Biography,** Albert M. Hyamson, 2nd rev. ed. (Routledge & Kegan Paul, LTD, 1981).

**Directory of American Scholars,** Ed. The Jaques Cattell Press, 7th ed., 4 vols. (R. R. Bowker, 1978).

**Documents of American History,** Ed. A. Commager, 9th ed., 2 vols. (Prentice-Hall, Inc., 1974).

**Dorland's Illustrated Medical Dictionary,** 25th ed. (W. B. Saunders Co., 1974).

**Editor & Publisher International Yearbook,** annual (Editor & Publisher, 1920).

**Encyclopaedia Britannica,** Latest ed. 1980, 30 vols. (Encyclopaedia Britannica, 1768).

**Encyclopedia Americana,** 30 vols. (Grolier Educational Corporation, 1981).

**Encyclopedia of American Facts and Dates,** Ed. Gorton Carruth et al., 7th rev. ed. (Thomas Y. Crowell Co., 1979).

**Encyclopedia of American History,** Ed. Richard B. Morris & Jeffrey B. Morris, 5th ed. (Harper & Row Publishers, Inc., 1976).

**Encyclopedia of Associations,** Ed. Denise Akey, 15th ed., 3 vols. (Gale Research Co., 1980).

**Encyclopedia of Biological Sciences,** Peter Gray, 2nd ed. (Van Nostrand Reinhold Co., 1970).

**Encyclopedia of Chemistry,** Ed. Clifford A. Hampel and Gessner G. Hawley, 3rd ed. (Van Nostrand Reinhold Co., 1973).

**Encyclopedia of Philosophy,** Ed. Paul Edwards, 4 vols. (The Free Press, 1973).

**Encyclopedia of Physics,** Ed. Robert M. Besancon, 2nd ed. (Van Nostrand Reinhold Co., 1974).

**Encyclopedia of Sports,** Frank G. Menke, 6th rev. ed. (A. S. Barnes & Co., Inc., 1978).

**Encyclopedia of World Art,** 15 vols. (McGraw-Hill Book Co., 1959-68).

**Encyclopedia of World History,** Ed. William L. Langer, 5th ed. (Houghton Mifflin Co., 1972).

**Europa Year Book,** annual 2 vols. (International Publications Service, 1959).

**European Authors, 1000-1900,** Ed. Stanley J. Kunitz and Vineta Colby (H. W. Wilson, 1967).

**Facts about the Presidents,** Joseph N. Kane, 3rd ed. (H. W. Wilson, 1974).

**Facts on File,** annual (Facts on File, Inc., 1940).

**Familiar Quotations,** John Bartlett, 15th ed., rev. and enl. (Citadel Press, 1971).

**Famous First Facts,** Joseph N. Kane, 3rd ed. (H. W. Wilson, 1964).

**Foundation Directory,** biannual, 8th ed. (The Foundation Center, 1981).

**Future: A Guide to Information Sources, The,** (World Future Society, 1977).

**Granger's Index to Poetry,** Edith Granger, Ed. William J. Smith, 6th ed. (Columbia University Press, 1973).

**Guide to Reference Books,** Ed. Eugene P. Sheehy, 9th ed. (American Library Association, 1976; 1st suppl., 1980).

**Guinness Book of World Records,** Ed. Norris McWhirter, rev. ed. (Sterling Publishing, Inc., 1980).

**Hammond Medallion World Atlas** (Hammond Inc., 1982).

**Harper Bible Dictionary,** Madeleine S. and John L. Miller, 8th ed. (Harper & Row Publishers, Inc., 1973).

**Harper Encyclopedia of Science,** Ed. James R. Newman, rev. ed. (Harper & Row Publishers, Inc., 1967).

**Harvard Guide to American History,** Ed. F. Freidel and R.K. Showman, rev. ed., 2 vols. (Harvard University Press, 1974).

**Historical Statistics of the United States: 1790 to 1970, 2 vols.** (University of Alabama Press, vol. 1, 1973; vol. 2, 1976).

**Home Book of Quotations,** Ed. Burton Stevenson, rev. ed. (Dodd, Mead & Co., 1967).

**Home Book of Verse,** Ed. Burton E. Stevenson, 10th ed., 2 vols. (Holt, Rinehart & Winston, 1953).

**International Encyclopedia of the Social Sciences,** Ed. David E. Sills, 17 vols. (Macmillan Publishing Co., Inc., 1968).

**International Who's Who,** annual (International Publications Service, 1935).

**Keesing's Contemporary Archives,** weekly (Keesing's, London, 1931).

**Lincoln Library, see New Lincoln Library Encyclopedia**

**Literary Market Place,** annual (R. R. Bowker Co., 1940)

**McGraw-Hill Encyclopedia of Science and Technology,** McGraw-Hill, 4th ed., 15 vols. (McGraw-Hill Book Co., 1977).

**Macmillan Book of Proverbs,** Ed. Burton Stevenson (Macmillan Publishing Co., Inc., 1965).

**Manual of Style,** Staff of the University of Chicago Press, rev. 12th ed. (University of Chicago Press, 1969).

**Masterpieces of World Literature in Digest Form,** Ed. Frank N. Magill, 4 vols. (Harper & Row Publishers, Inc., 1952-69).

**Monthly Catalog of United States Government Publications,** monthly (Government Printing Office, 1895).

**Municipal Year Book,** Ed. International City Management Association (National Association of Counties, 1980).

**National Geographic Atlas of the World,** Melville B. Grovenor, 5th ed. (National Geographic Society, 1981).

**Negro Almanac,** Harry A. Ploski and Warren Marr, rev. ed. (Bellwether Publishing Co., 1971).

**New Catholic Encyclopedia,** Editorial Staff at Catholic University of America, 17 vols. (Publishers Guild, 1981).

**New Century Cyclopedia of Names,** ed. Clarence L. Barnhart and William D. Halsey, 3 vols. (Prentice-Hall, Inc., 1954).

**New Emily Post's Etiquette,** Emily Post, rev. by Elizabeth L. Post, 12th rev. ed. (Funk & Wagnalls Co., 1975).

**New Encyclopedia of the Opera,** David Ewen (Hill and Wang, Inc., 1971).

**New Lincoln Library Encyclopedia,** Ed by William H. Seibert, 40th ed., 3 vols. (Frontier Press Co., 1980).

**New York Times Index,** semimonthly and cumulated annually (The New York Times, 1851).

**Oxford Classical Dictionary,** Ed. N. G. Hammond and H. H. Scullard, 2nd ed. (Oxford University Press Inc., 1970).

**Oxford Companion to American History,** Thomas H. Johnson (Oxford University Press, Inc., 1966).

**Oxford Companion to American Literature,** James D. Hart, 4th ed. (Oxford University Press, Inc., 1965).

**Oxford Companion to Classical Literature,** Ed. Paul Harvey, 2nd ed. (Oxford University Press, Inc., 1937).

**Oxford Companion to English Literature,** Ed. Paul Harvey and Dorothy Eagle, 4th ed. (Oxford University Press, Inc., 1967).

**Oxford Companion to Film,** Ed. Liz-Anne Bawden (Oxford University Press, Inc., 1976).

**Oxford Companion to the Theatre,** Phyllis Hartnoll, 3rd ed. (Oxford University Press, Inc., 1967)

**Oxford Dictionary of Quotations,** 3rd ed. (Oxford University Press, Inc., 1979).

**Oxford English Dictionary,** Ed. James A. Murray et al., 13 vols. (Oxford University Press, Inc., 1933).

**Peterson's Annual Guides to Graduate and Undergraduate Study,** Ed. Karen C. Hegener, 14th ed., 6 vols. (Peterson's Guides Inc., 1982).

**Political Handbook of the World: 1980,** Ed. Arthur S. Banks, 6th ed. (McGraw-Hill Book Co., 1980).

**Random House Dictionary of the English Language,** Ed. Jess Stein (Random House, Inc., 1966).

**Reader's Adviser,** 12th ed., 3 vols. (R. R. Bowker Co., 1974-1977).

**Reader's Encyclopedia,** Ed. William R. Benét, 2nd ed. (Thomas Y. Crowell Co., 1965).

**Reader's Guide to Periodical Literature,** annual, 39 vols. (H. W. Wilson, 1900-80).

**Roget's International Thesaurus,** Peter M. Roget, 4th ed. (Thomas Y. Crowell Co., 1977).

**Shepherd's Historical Atlas,** William R. Shepherd, 9th rev. ed. (Barnes & Noble Books, 1976).

**Statesman's Year-Book,** annual, Ed. John Paxton (St. Martin's Press, Inc., 1864).

**Statistical Abstract of the United States,** annual (Government Printing Office, 1878).

**Statistical Yearbook,** annual (United Nations, 1949).

**Stedman's Medical Dictionary,** Thomas L. Stedman, 23rd ed. (The William & Wilkins Co., 1976).

**Times Atlas of the World,** comprehensive ed., London Times (Times Books, 1980).

**Times Atlas of World History,** Ed. Geoffrey Barraclough (London Times/Hammond Inc., 1979).

**Timetables of History,** Bernard Grun (Simon & Schuster, Inc., 1979).

**Twentieth Century Authors,** Ed. Stanley J. Kunitz and Howard Haycraft (H. W. Wilson, 1942; 1st supplement, 1955).

**Ulrich's International Periodicals Directory,** 20th ed. (R. R. Bowker Co., 1981).

**United States Government Organization Manual,** annual (Government Printing Office, 1935).

**Universal Jewish Encyclopedia and Readers Guide,** Ed. Isaac Landman, 11 vols. (Ktav Publishing House, Inc., 1944).

**Van Nostrand's International Encyclopedia of Chemical Science** (Van Nostrand Reinhold Co., 1964).

**Van Nostrand's Scientific Encyclopedia,** Ed. Douglas M. Considine, 5th ed. (Van Nostrand Reinhold Co., 1976).

**Webster's New Geographical Dictionary,** Merriam-Webster Editorial Staff, rev. ed. (G. & C. Merriam Co., 1977).

**Webster's Third New International Dictionary of the English Language,** unabridged, Ed. Merriam Co. (G. & C. Merriam Co., 1980).

**What's What: A Visual Glossary of the Physical World,** Ed. David Fisher and Reginald Bragonier, Jr. (Hammond Inc., 1981).

**Who Was Who,** 6 vols. (St. Martin's Press, Inc., 1897-1961).

**Who Was Who in America,** 7 vols. (Marquis Who's Who, Inc., 1897-1976).

**Who Was Who in America,** Historical Volume, 1607-1896 (Marquis Who's Who, Inc., 1963).

**Who's Who,** annual (St. Martin's Press, Inc., 1849).

**Who's Who in America,** biennial (Marquis Who's Who, Inc., 1899).

**Who's Who in American Politics, 1981-1982,** Ed. The Jaques Cattell Press, 8th ed. (R. R. Bowker Co., 1979).

**Who's Who of American Women, 1979-1980,** 11th ed. (Marquis Who's Who, Inc., 1979).

**Worldmark Encyclopedia of the Nations,** Ed. Moshe Y. Sachs, 5th ed., 5 vols. (John Wiley & Sons, Inc., 1976).

**Worldmark Encyclopedia of the States,** Ed. Moshe Y. Sachs (Harper & Row, 1981).

**World of Learning,** annual, 2 vols. (International Publications Service, 1947).

**World Who's Who in Science,** Ed. Allen G. Debus (Marquis Who's Who, Inc., 1968).

**Yearbook of International Organizations,** annual, Ed. Union of International Associations (International Publications Service, 1948).

**Yearbook of the United Nations,** annual (International Publications Service, 1946/47).

## MOST COMMON AMERICAN SURNAMES

SOURCE: U.S. Social Security Administration

This tabulation is based on the surnames that appear most frequently in social security records for the period of 1936 to 1973.

| Rank | Surname | No. of Persons | Rank | Surname | No. of Persons | Rank | Surname | No. of Persons |
|---|---|---|---|---|---|---|---|---|
| 1 | Smith | 2,382,509 | 21 | Walker | 486,498 | 41 | Campbell | 361,958 |
| 2 | Johnson | 1,807,263 | 22 | Robins(on) | 484,991 | 42 | Gonzalex(ez) | 360,994 |
| 3 | Williams(on) | 1,568,939 | 23 | Peters(on) | 479,249 | 43 | Carter | 349,950 |
| 4 | Brown | 1,362,910 | 24 | Hall | 471,479 | 44 | Garcia | 346,175 |
| 5 | Jones | 1,331,205 | 25 | Allen | 458,375 | 45 | Evans | 343,897 |
| 6 | Miller | 1,131,861 | 26 | Young | 455,416 | 46 | Turner | 329,752 |
| 7 | Davis | 1,047,848 | 27 | Morris(on) | 455,179 | 47 | Stewart | 329,581 |
| 8 | Martin(ez), (son) | 1,046,297 | 28 | King | 434,791 | 48 | Collin(s) | 324,680 |
| 9 | Anders(on) | 825,648 | 29 | Wright | 431,157 | 49 | Parker | 322,482 |
| 10 | Wilson | 787,825 | 30 | Nelson | 421-638 | 50 | Edward | 317,197 |
| 11 | Harris(on) | 754,083 | 31 | Rodriguez | 416,178 | 51 | Murphy | 311,337 |
| 12 | Taylor | 696,046 | 32 | Hill | 414,646 | 52 | Cook | 298,396 |
| 13 | Moore | 693,304 | 33 | Baker | 412,676 | 53 | Rogers | 298,288 |
| 14 | Thomas | 688,054 | 34 | Richards(on) | 409,262 | 54 | Griffin, Griffith | 291,862 |
| 15 | White | 636,185 | 35 | Lee | 409,068 | 55 | Christian(son), Christopher | 281,525 |
| 16 | Thompson | 635,426 | 36 | Scott | 408,439 | | | |
| 17 | Jackson | 630,003 | 37 | Green | 406,989 | 56 | Morgan | 273,267 |
| 18 | Clark | 549,107 | 38 | Adams | 406,841 | 57 | Cooper | 269,560 |
| 19 | Robert(s), (son) | 524,688 | 39 | Mitchell | 371,434 | 58 | Reed | 267,589 |
| 20 | Lewis | 495,026 | 40 | Phillips | 362,013 | 59 | Bell | 267,026 |

## MAJOR WORLD LANGUAGES

SOURCE: Kenneth Katzner, author, **The Languages of the World.**

| Language | Speakers* | Chief Location |
|---|---|---|
| Chinese | 900 | China |
| English | 325 | U.S., U.K., Canada, Ireland, Australia, New Zealand |
| Spanish | 225 | Spain, Latin America |
| Russian | 200 | USSR |
| Hindi | 200 | India |
| Bengali | 135 | Bangladesh, India |
| Portuguese | 130 | Portugal, Brazil |
| Arabic | 130 | Middle East, North Africa |
| Japanese | 115 | Japan |
| German | 100 | Germany, Austria, Switzerland |
| Indonesian | 100 | Indonesia |
| French | 75 | France, Belgium, Switzerland, Canada |
| Punjabi | 65 | India (Punjab), Pakistan |
| Italian | 60 | Italy |
| Korean | 55 | Korea |
| Telugu | 50 | India (Andhra Pradesh) |
| Marathi | 45 | India (Maharashtra) |
| Tamil | 45 | India (Tamil Nadu) Sri Lanka |
| Javanese | 45 | Indonesia (Java) |
| Turkish | 40 | Turkey |
| Urdu | 40 | Pakistan, India |
| Vietnamese | 40 | Vietnam |
| Polish | 35 | Poland |
| Ukrainian | 35 | USSR (Ukraine) |
| Thai | 35 | Thailand |
| Persian | 25 | Iran, Afghanistan |
| Gujarati | 25 | India (Gujarat) |
| Kanarese | 25 | India (Karnataka) |
| Malayalam | 25 | India (Kerala) |
| Burmese | 25 | Burma |
| Tagalog | 25 | Philippines |
| Romanian | 20 | Romania |
| Bihari | 20 | India (Bihar) |
| Oriya | 20 | India (Orissa) |
| Hausa | 20 | Nigeria, Niger |
| Serbo-Croatian | 15 | Yugoslavia |
| Pushtu | 15 | Afghanistan, Pakistan |
| Rajasthani | 15 | India (Rajasthan) |
| Swahili | 15 | East Africa |
| Dutch | 13 | Netherlands |
| Sundanese | 13 | Indonesia (Java) |
| Hungarian | 12 | Hungary, Romania |
| Uzbek | 12 | USSR (Uzbekistan) |
| Chuang | 12 | China |
| Visayan | 12 | Philippines |
| Yoruba | 12 | Nigeria |
| Czech | 10 | Czechoslovakia |
| Greek | 10 | Greece |
| Azerbaijani | 10 | USSR (Azerbaijan), Iran |

| Language | Speakers* | Chief Location |
|---|---|---|
| Nepali | 10 | Nepal |
| Sinhalese | 10 | Sri Lanka |
| Fulani | 10 | West Africa |
| Assamese | 9 | India (Assam) |
| Sindhi | 9 | Pakistan, India |
| Amharic | 9 | Ethiopia |
| Swedish | 8 | Sweden |
| Bulgarian | 8 | Bulgaria |
| Madurese | 8 | Indonesia (Java, Madura) |
| Ibo | 8 | Nigeria |
| Galla | 8 | Ethiopia |
| Belorussian | 7 | USSR (Belorussia) |
| Kazakh | 7 | USSR (Kazakhstan) |
| Berber | 7 | Morocco, Algeria |
| Malagasy | 7 | Malagasy Republic |
| Quechua | 7 | Peru, Bolivia |
| Catalan | 6 | Spain, France, Andorra |
| Uighur | 6 | China, USSR |
| Malay | 6 | Malaysia, Singapore |
| Danish | 5 | Denmark |
| Finnish | 5 | Finland |
| Flemish | 5 | Belgium |
| Tatar | 5 | USSR (Tatar ASSR) |
| Kurdish | 5 | Iraq, Iran, Turkey, Syria, USSR |
| Yi (Lolo) | 5 | China |
| Khmer | 5 | Cambodia |
| Somali | 5 | Somalia, Ethiopia |
| Ruanda | 5 | Rwanda, Zaire |
| Zulu | 5 | South Africa |
| Xhosa | 5 | South Africa |
| Yiddish | 4 | U.S., USSR, Israel |
| Norwegian | 4 | Norway |
| Slovak | 4 | Czechoslovakia |
| Armenian | 4 | USSR (Armenia) |
| Mongolian | 4 | Mongolia, China |
| Tibetan | 4 | Tibet |
| Miao | 4 | China |
| Twi | 4 | Ghana |
| Sidamo | 4 | Ethiopia |
| Rundi | 4 | Burundi |
| Shona | 4 | Rhodesia |
| Nyanja | 4 | Malawi, Zambia |
| Sotho | 4 | South Africa, Lesotho |
| Afrikaans | 4 | South Africa |
| Albanian | 3 | Albania |
| Georgian | 3 | USSR (Georgia) |
| Tadzhik | 3 | USSR (Tadzhikistan) |
| Hebrew | 3 | Israel |
| Kashmiri | 3 | Kashmir |
| Santali | 3 | Eastern India |
| Minangkabau | 3 | Indonesia (Sumatra) |
| Ilocano | 3 | Philippines (Luzon) |
| Mossi | 3 | Upper Volta |
| Ganda | 3 | Uganda |
| Luba | 3 | Zaire |
| Kongo | 3 | Zaire, Congo, Angola |
| Mbundu | 3 | Angola |
| Mayan | 3 | Mexico, Guatemala |

| Language | Speakers* | Chief Location |
|---|---|---|
| Lithuanian | 2.5 | USSR (Lithuania) |
| Moldavian | 2.5 | USSR (Moldavia) |
| Turkmen | 2.5 | USSR (Turkmen SSR), Iran |
| Karen | 2.5 | Burma |
| Lao | 2.5 | Laos |
| Buginese | 2.5 | Indonesia (Celebes) |
| Tigrinya | 2.5 | Ethiopia |
| Tswana | 2.5 | South Africa, Botswana |
| Makua | 2.5 | Mozambique |
| Kirgiz | 2 | USSR (Kirgiz SSR) |
| Gilaki | 2 | Iran |
| Bhili | 2 | India |
| Achinese | 2 | Indonesia (Sumatra) |
| Balinese | 2 | Indonesia (Bali) |
| Bikol | 2 | Philippines (Luzon) |
| Kikuyu | 2 | Kenya |
| Malinke | 2 | West Africa |
| Kanuri | 2 | Nigeria |
| Guarani | 2 | Paraguay |
| Slovenian | 1.5 | Yugoslavia |
| Latvian | 1.5 | USSR (Latvia) |
| Chuvash | 1.5 | USSR (Chuvash ASSR) |
| Mazanderani | 1.5 | Iran |
| Baluchi | 1.5 | Pakistan, Iran |
| Gondi | 1.5 | Central India |
| Puyi | 1.5 | China |
| Shan | 1.5 | Burma |
| Batak | 1.5 | Indonesia (Sumatra) |
| Wolof | 1.5 | Senegal |
| Bambara | 1.5 | Mali |
| Ewe | 1.5 | Ghana, Togo |
| Fang | 1.5 | Cameroon, Gabon |
| Dinka | 1.5 | Sudan |
| Lingala | 1.5 | Zaire, Congo |
| Bemba | 1.5 | Zambia |
| Tsonga | 1.5 | Mozambique |
| Aymara | 1.5 | Bolivia, Peru |
| Breton | 1 | France (Brittany) |
| Macedonian | 1 | Yugoslavia |
| Estonian | 1 | USSR (Estonia) |
| Mordvin | 1 | USSR (Mordovian ASSR) |
| Bashkir | 1 | USSR (Bashkir ASSR) |
| Tulu | 1 | India (Karnataka) |
| Kurukh (Oraon) | 1 | Eastern India |
| Tung | 1 | China |
| Yao | 1 | China |
| Mende | 1 | Sierra Leone |
| Fon | 1 | Benin |
| Tiv | 1 | Nigeria |
| Ibibio | 1 | Nigeria |
| Luo | 1 | Kenya |
| Kamba | 1 | Kenya |
| Sukuma | 1 | Tanzania |
| Swazi | 1 | Swaziland, South Africa |
| Nahuatl | 1 | Mexico |

* In millions of speakers.

## LEADING AMERICAN MAGAZINES

SOURCE: Magazine Publishers Association, Inc.

Based on average circulations per issue, 2nd six months of 1981.

| Rank | Magazine* | Circulation | Rank | Magazine* | Circulation |
|---|---|---|---|---|---|
| 1 | Reader's Digest | 17,926,542 | 26 | Field & Stream | 2,023,785 |
| 2 | TV Guide | 17,670,543 | 27 | Southern Living | 1,973,219 |
| 3 | National Geographic | 10,861,186 | 28 | Smithsonian | 1,936,726 |
| 4 | Better Homes & Gardens | 8,059,717 | 29 | Globe | 1,912,684 |
| 5 | Family Circle | 7,427,979 | 30 | V.F.W. Magazine | 1,867,201 |
| 6 | Modern Maturity | 7,309,035 | 31 | Popular Science | 1,803,309 |
| 7 | AARP News Bulletin | 7,107,362 | 32 | Today's Education | 1,649,494 |
| 8 | Woman's Day | 7,004,367 | 33 | Elks Magazine | 1,645,905 |
| 9 | McCall's | 6,266,090 | 34 | Popular Mechanics | 1,611,239 |
| 10 | Ladies Home Journal | 5,527,071 | 35 | Mechanix Illustrated | 1,602,777 |
| 11 | Good Housekeeping | 5,425,790 | 36 | Parents Magazine | 1,568,221 |
| 12 | Playboy | 5,013,941 | 37 | Workbasket | 1,565,992 |
| 13 | National Enquirer | 4,602,524 | 38 | Outdoor Life | 1,535,929 |
| 14 | Redbook | 4,368,523 | 39 | True Story | 1,525,089 |
| 15 | Time | 4,337,988 | 40 | Seventeen | 1,480,236 |
| 16 | Penthouse | 4,051,969 | 41 | Life | 1,461,964 |
| 17 | Star, The | 3,515,530 | 42 | Boys' Life | 1,450,841 |
| 18 | Newsweek | 2,960,073 | 43 | Changing Times | 1,421,176 |
| 19 | Cosmopolitan | 2,848,399 | 44 | Sunset | 1,417,333 |
| 20 | American Legion | 2,587,751 | 45 | Bon Appetit | 1,340,653 |
| 21 | People Weekly | 2,551,642 | 46 | Motorland | 1,314,538 |
| 22 | Prevention | 2,462,023 | 47 | Organic Gardening | 1,314,536 |
| 23 | Sports Illustrated | 2,284,800 | 48 | Ebony | 1,306,549 |
| 24 | U.S. News & World Report | 2,063,366 | 49 | New Woman | 1,306,387 |
| 25 | Glamour | 2,052,115 | 50 | Hustler | 1,238,955 |

*Includes general and farm magazine members of the Audit Bureau of Circulations. Groups and comics not included.

## U.S. ADVERTISING VOLUME

SOURCE: Reprinted with permission from the March 22, 1982 issue of *Advertising Age*. Copyright 1982 by Crain Communications Inc.

| Medium | 1980 Millions | 1980 % of total | 1981 Millions | 1981 % of total | % change |
|---|---|---|---|---|---|
| **Newspapers** | | | | | |
| **Total** | **$15,541** | **28.5** | **$17,420** | **28.4** | **+12.1** |
| National | 2,353 | 4.3 | 2,729 | 4.4 | +16.0 |
| Local | 13,188 | 24.2 | 14,691 | 24.0 | +11.4 |
| **Magazines** | | | | | |
| **Total** | **3,149** | **5.8** | **3,533** | **5.8** | **+12.2** |
| Weeklies | 1,418 | 2.6 | 1,598 | 2.6 | +12.7 |
| Women's | 782 | 1.4 | 853 | 1.4 | + 9.1 |
| Monthlies | 949 | 1.8 | 1,082 | 1.8 | +14.0 |
| **Farm publications** | **130** | **0.2** | **146** | **0.2** | **+12.2** |
| **Television** | | | | | |
| **Total** | **11,366** | **20.9** | **12,650** | **20.6** | **+11.3** |
| Network | 5,130 | 9.4 | 5,575 | 9.1 | + 8.7 |
| Spot | 3,629 | 6.0 | 3,730 | 6.1 | +14.1 |
| Local | 2,967 | 5.5 | 3,345 | 5.4 | +12.7 |
| **Radio** | | | | | |
| **Total** | **3,702** | **6.8** | **4,212** | **6.9** | **+13.8** |
| Network | 183 | 0.4 | 220 | 0.4 | +20.0 |
| Spot | 779 | 1.4 | 896 | 1.5 | +15.0 |
| Local | 2,740 | 5.0 | 3,096 | 5.0 | +13.0 |
| **Direct mail** | **7,596** | **13.9** | **8,781** | **14.3** | **+15.6** |
| **Business publications** | **1,674** | **3.1** | **1,841** | **3.0** | **+10.0** |
| **Outdoor** | | | | | |
| **Total** | **578** | **1.1** | **650** | **1.1** | **+12.5** |
| National | 364 | 0.7 | 419 | 0.7 | +15.0 |
| Local | 214 | 0.4 | 231 | 0.4 | + 8.0 |
| **Miscellaneous** | | | | | |
| **Total** | **10,744** | **19.7** | **12,087** | **19.7** | **+12.5** |
| National | 5,663 | 10.4 | 6,410 | 10.4 | +13.2 |
| Local | 5,081 | 9.3 | 5,677 | 9.3 | +11.7 |
| **Total** | | | | | |
| **National** | **30,290** | **55.6** | **34,280** | **55.9** | **+13.2** |
| **Local** | **24,190** | **44.4** | **27,040** | **44.1** | **+11.8** |
| **U.S. Grand Total** | **54,480** | **100.0** | **61,320** | **100.0** | **+12.6** |

## LARGEST U.S. SUNDAY NEWSPAPERS

SOURCE: Audit Bureau of Circulations

| Newspaper | Circulation* |
|---|---|
| New York **News** | 2,042,830 |
| New York **Times** | 1,524,833 |
| Los Angeles **Times** | 1,317,817 |
| Chicago **Tribune** | 1,107,574 |
| Philadelphia **Inquirer**† | 1,029,410 |
| Washington **Post** | 986,024 |
| Detroit **News** | 825,384 |
| Detroit **Free Press** | 758,706 |
| Boston **Globe** | 751,289 |
| Chicago **Sun-Times** | 700,769 |
| San Francisco **Examiner and Chronicle** | 673,029 |
| Pittsburgh **Press** | 616,373 |
| Newark **Star-Ledger** | 606,044 |
| Long Island **Newsday** | 582,261 |
| Minneapolis **Tribune** | 576,994 |
| Miami **Herald** | 521,091 |
| Milwaukee **Journal** | 516,858 |
| Atlanta **Journal & Const.** | 499,084 |
| Houston **Chronicle** | 481,319 |
| Cleveland **Plain Dealer** | 448,219 |
| St. Louis **Post-Dispatch** | 443,422 |
| Houston **Post** | 440,135 |
| Phoenix **Republic** | 432,397 |
| Portland **Oregonian** | 409,641 |
| Kansas City (Mo.) **Star** | 391,626 |
| Baltimore **Sun** | 382,953 |
| Dallas **News** | 380,981 |
| Des Moines **Register** | 379,124 |
| Indianapolis **Star**‡ | 361,571 |
| Denver **Post** | 356,372 |
| Dallas **Times Herald** | 352,372 |
| Columbus **Dispatch** | 340,484 |
| Seattle **Times** | 339,921 |
| San Diego **Union** | 339,820 |
| Denver **Rocky Mountain News** | 335,665 |
| New Orleans **Times-Picayune/States-Item**‡ | 332,410 |
| Louisville **Courier-Journal** | 324,624 |
| St. Petersburg **Times** | 321,935 |
| Los Angeles **Herald-Examiner** | 303,805 |
| Oklahoma City **Sunday Oklahoman** | 300,358 |
| Cincinnati **Enquirer** | 298,257 |
| Hartford **Courant** | 290,254 |
| Memphis **Commercial Appeal** | 284,377 |
| Omaha **World-Herald** | 276,431 |
| San Jose **Mercury-News** | 276,293 |
| Cleveland **Press**[1] | 275,701 |
| Orange Co. (Calif.) **Register** | 272,369 |
| Buffalo **Courier Express** | 265,449 |
| Fort Worth **Star-Telegram** | 260,710 |
| Tampa **Tribune** | 256,463 |
| Orlando **Sentinel Star** | 249,974 |
| Nashville **Tennessean** | 246,081 |
| St. Paul **Pioneer Press** | 245,622 |
| Sacramento **Bee** | 244,841 |
| Charlotte **Observer** | 241,903 |
| Rochester **Democrat & Chronicle** | 241,545 |
| Providence (R.I.) **Journal** | 238,908 |
| Syracuse **Herald-American** | 234,258 |
| Fort Lauderdale **News & Sun-Sentinel** | 233,560 |

*Averages for 6 months ending March 31, 1982. †Average taken from Feb. 1 through March 31, 1982. ‡Average for 3 months. [1]Ceased publication June 17, 1982.

## LARGEST U.S. DAILIES[1]

SOURCE: Audit Bureau of Circulations

| Newspaper | Circulation* |
|---|---|
| New York **News** | 1,540,218 |
| Los Angeles **Times** | 1,062,707 |
| New York **Times** | 947,682 |
| New York **Post**[2] | 904,476 |
| Chicago **Tribune**[2] | 770,798 |
| Washington **Post** | 769,950 |
| Chicago **Sun-Times** | 663,410 |
| Detroit **News** | 629,392 |
| Detroit **Free Press** | 627,640 |
| Philadelphia **Inquirer**† | 547,547 |
| San Francisco **Chronicle** | 530,672 |
| Long Island **Newsday** | 513,728 |
| Boston **Globe**[2] | 502,868 |
| Miami **Herald** | 435,071 |
| Newark **Star-Ledger** | 415,406 |
| Cleveland **Plain Dealer** | 405,842 |
| Houston **Chronicle**[2] | 393,730 |
| Houston **Post** | 376,879 |
| Baltimore **Sun**[3] | 344,832 |
| Cleveland **Press**[4] | 316,147 |
| Denver **Rocky Mountain News** | 312,873 |
| Milwaukee **Journal** | 308,764 |
| Philadelphia **Daily News**† | 299,380 |
| Kansas City (Mo.) **Times** | 287,441 |
| Phoenix **Republic**‡ | 286,984 |
| Los Angeles **Herald-Examiner** | 285,656 |
| New Orleans **Times-Picayune/States-Item**‡ | 280,655 |
| Dallas **Times Herald**[2] | 267,579 |
| Pittsburgh **Press** | 266,307 |
| Buffalo **Evening News** | 264,222 |
| St. Louis **Globe-Democrat** | 261,329 |
| St. Petersburg **Times** | 259,715 |
| Denver **Post** | 258,376 |
| Seattle **Times**[2] | 256,888 |
| Orange Co. (Calif.) **Register** | 251,647 |
| Kansas City (Mo.) **Star** | 240,529 |
| Minneapolis **Tribune** | 239,332 |
| St. Louis **Post-Dispatch** | 238,099 |
| Portland **Oregonian** | 237,141 |
| Fort Worth **Star-Telegram**[3] | 230,654 |
| Omaha **World-Herald**[3] | 224,380 |
| Indianapolis **Star**‡ | 220,947 |
| Sacramento **Bee** | 219,216 |
| San Diego **Union** | 216,252 |
| Orlando **Sentinel Star**[2] | 215,015 |
| Boston **Herald American** | 211,930 |
| Hartford **Courant** | 208,845 |
| Atlanta **Constitution** | 208,289 |
| Des Moines **Register** | 205,640 |
| Tampa **Tribune** | 202,363 |
| Memphis **Commercial Appeal** | 202,272 |
| Columbus **Dispatch** | 202,220 |
| Oklahoma City **Daily Oklahoman** | 195,180 |
| Cincinnati **Enquirer** | 193,090 |
| Seattle **Post-Intelligencer** | 191,158 |
| Atlanta **Journal** | 184,237 |
| Louisville **Courier-Journal** | 182,843 |
| Pittsburgh **Post-Gazette, Sun-Telegraph** | 181,397 |
| Milwaukee **Sentinel** | 176,680 |
| Charlotte **Observer** | 169,291 |

[1]Does not include Wall Street Journal, 2,002,727 circulation (National Edition). [2]All day editions. [3]Combined morning and evening editions. [4]Ceased publication on June 17, 1982. †Average taken from Feb. 1 through March 31, 1982. ‡Average for 3 months.

## WORLD'S LARGEST DAILY NEWSPAPERS

| Country and Newspaper | Daily Circulation |
|---|---|
| JAPAN | |
| **Yomiurii Shimbun (A.M. P.M. ed.)** | 13,900,000 |
| **Asahi Shimbun (A.M. P.M. ed.)** | 12,015,169 |
| **Mainichi Shimbun (A.M. P.M. ed.)** | 7,300,000 |
| USSR | |
| **Pravda** | 11,500,000 |
| **Izvestia** | c. 9-10,000,000 |
| CHINA | |
| **Cankao Xiaoxi (Reference News)** | c. 9-10,000,000 |
| **Renmin Ribao (People's Daily)** | c. 6-7,000,000 |
| UNITED KINGDOM | |
| **London Daily Sun**[1] | 4,136,927 |
| **London Daily Mirror**[1] | 3,413,785 |
| **London Daily Express**[1] | 2,126,248 |
| UNITED STATES | |
| **New York News** | 1,540,218 |
| **Los Angeles Times** | 1,062,707 |

[1]U.K. Audit Bureau of Circulation, Ltd.

## LEADING TV ADVERTISERS

SOURCE: Television Bureau of Advertising, Inc.

| Company | Total TV Expenditure (1981) |
|---|---|
| Procter & Gamble Co. | $521,116,400 |
| General Foods Corp. | 328,312,700 |
| American Home Products Corp. | 171,765,500 |
| General Mills, Inc. | 169,324,700 |
| General Motors Corp. | 160,808,100 |
| Pepsico, Inc. | 139,272,200 |
| Lever Brothers Co. | 137,992,100 |
| Ford Motor Co. | 136,345,000 |
| American Telephone & Telegraph, Co. | 129,798,800 |
| McDonald's Corp. | 129,379,300 |
| Bristol Myers Co. | 121,450,000 |
| Philip Morris, Inc. | 119,547,300 |
| Coca Cola Co. | 109,109,400 |
| Warner-Lambert Phar. Co. | 106,551,400 |
| Anheuser-Busch Cos., Inc. | 105,145,800 |
| Johnson & Johnson | 101,403,400 |
| Sears, Roebuck & Co. | 99,519,500 |
| Dart & Kraft, Inc. | 97,392,100 |
| Pillsbury Co. | $91,698,500 |
| The Gillette Co. | 84,984,800 |
| Ralston Purina Co. | 84,912,700 |
| Kellogg Co. | 84,440,600 |
| Richardson-Vicks, Inc. | 82,396,400 |
| Chrysler Corp. | 73,855,900 |
| Consolidated Foods Corp. | 72,013,800 |
| Colgate Palmolive Co. | 70,154,100 |
| Nabisco Brands, Inc. | 64,639,000 |
| Sterling Drug, Inc. | 64,382,800 |
| Toyota Mtr. Distr., Inc. | 64,122,900 |
| Warner Comm. Inc. | 63,914,400 |
| Mars, Inc. | 63,381,500 |
| Heublein, Inc. | 63,363,600 |
| Nesfood, Inc. | 62,244,200 |
| Beecham Group, Ltd. | 59,982,200 |
| Chesebrough Ponds, Inc. | 57,485,100 |
| Wm. Wrigley Jr. Co. | 55,834,500 |
| Esmark, Inc. | 55,588,800 |
| The Clorox Co. | 52,904,000 |
| Gulf & Western Industries Inc. | $50,581,900 |
| H.J. Heinz Co. | 49,158,300 |
| Quaker Oats Co. | 48,579,700 |
| Internat'l Telephone & Telegraph Corp. | 48,470,100 |
| Revlon, Inc. | 48,078,700 |
| RCA Corp. | 48,064,200 |
| Norton Simon, Inc. | 47,312,500 |
| Eastman Kodak Co. | 47,201,700 |
| Schering-Plough Corp. | 47,119,500 |
| Union Carbide Corp. | 45,773,500 |
| Mobil Corp. | 44,896,000 |
| Mattel Inc. | 42,023,100 |
| Nissan Motor Corp., USA | 41,607,900 |
| American Cyanamid Co. | 40,447,700 |
| Bayer A.G. | 40,119,400 |
| Squibb Corp. | 39,995,900 |
| Hershey Foods Corp. | 39,817,300 |
| General Electric Co. | 38,873,700 |

# FORMS OF ADDRESS

| Personage | Address | Social Correspondence | Salutation of Informal Letter* | Salutation of Formal Letter* |
|---|---|---|---|---|
| The President | The President<br>The White House | The President<br>and Mrs. Taylor | Dear Mr. President:<br>or (if preferred)<br>My dear<br>Mr. President:[1] | Mr. President:<br>or<br>Sir: |
| The Vice-President | The Vice-President<br>United States Senate | The Vice-President<br>and Mrs. Taylor | Dear<br>Mr. Vice-President:<br>or (if preferred)<br>My dear<br>Mr. Vice-President: | Sir: |
| Chief Justice of the United States | The Chief Justice<br>The Supreme Court | The Chief Justice<br>and Mrs. Taylor | Dear<br>Mr. Chief Justice:<br>or (if preferred)<br>My dear<br>Mr. Chief Justice: | Sir: |
| Associate Justice, Supreme Court | Mr. Justice Taylor<br>The Supreme Court | Mr. Justice Taylor<br>and Mrs. Taylor | Dear Mr. Justice:<br>or (if preferred)<br>My dear Mr. Justice: | Sir: |
| Cabinet Member[2] | The Honorable Stephen Taylor<br>Secretary of the Treasury<br>(or applicable Cabinet-level department) | The Honorable<br>The Secretary of the Treasury<br>and Mrs. Taylor | Dear Mr. Secretary:<br>or (if preferred)<br>My dear Mr. Secretary: | Sir: |
| United States Senator[3] | The Honorable Stephen Taylor<br>United States Senate | The Honorable<br>Stephen Taylor<br>and Mrs. Taylor<br>(Dear Senator and Mrs. Taylor:)<br>or (for a married woman senator)<br>Mr. and Mrs. Stephen Taylor | Dear Senator Taylor:<br>or (if preferred)<br>My dear Senator: | Sir:<br>or<br>Madam: |
| Member, House of Representatives | The Honorable Stephen Taylor<br>House of Representatives | The Honorable<br>Stephen Taylor<br>and Mrs. Taylor<br>or (for a married woman member)<br>Mr. and Mrs. Stephen Taylor | Dear Mr. [Mrs.]<br>Taylor:<br>or (if preferred)<br>My dear Mr. [Mrs.]<br>Taylor: | Sir:<br>or<br>Madam: |
| American Ambassador | The Honorable Stephen Taylor<br>American Ambassador<br>London | The Honorable<br>The American Ambassador[4]<br>and Mrs. Taylor<br>(Dear Mr. Ambassador and Mrs. Taylor:)<br>or (for a married woman ambassador)<br>Mr. and Mrs. Stephen Taylor | Dear Mr. [Madam]<br>Ambassador:<br>or (if preferred)<br>My dear Mr. [Madam]<br>Ambassador: | Sir:<br>or<br>Madam: |
| American Chargé d'Affaires ad interim[5] | Stephen Taylor, Esquire[6]<br>American Chargée d'Affaires<br>ad interim (or other title) | Mr. and Mrs. Stephen Taylor | Dear Mr. Taylor:<br>or (if preferred)<br>My dear Mr. Taylor: | Sir: |
| Foreign Ambassador | His Excellency<br>Dr.[7] Juan Luis Ortega<br>Ambassador of Mexico | His Excellency<br>The Ambassador of Mexico<br>and Mrs. Ortega | Dear. Mr. [Madam]<br>Ambassador:<br>or (if preferred)<br>My dear Mr. [Madam]<br>Ambassador: | Excellency: |
| Secretary-General, United Nations | His Excellency<br>Juan Luis Ortega<br>Secretary-General of the United Nations | The Secretary-General<br>of the United Nations<br>and Mrs. Ortega | Dear Mr. Secretary-<br>General:<br>or (if preferred)<br>My dear Mr.<br>Secretary-General: | Sir: |
| Governor of a State | The Honorable Stephen Taylor<br>Governor of Idaho<br>or<br>His Excellency[8]<br>Stephen Taylor<br>Governor of the Commonwealth of Massachusetts | The Governor of Idaho<br>and Mrs. Taylor | Dear Governor Taylor:<br>or (if preferred)<br>My dear Governor: | Sir: |
| Mayor of a Large City | The Honorable Stephen Taylor<br>Mayor of Baltimore | The Honorable<br>Stephen Taylor<br>and Mrs. Taylor | Dear Mayor Taylor:<br>or<br>Dear Mr. Mayor: | Sir: |
| Mayor of a Town | Stephen Taylor, Esquire<br>Mayor of Newtown | The Mayor of Newtown<br>and Mrs. Taylor | Dear Mr. Taylor: | Sir: |

*"Sincerely" or "Sincerely yours" is the acceptable mode of ending both informal and formal letters to distinguished personages. [1] In the United States, "My dear Mr. President:" or "My dear Mrs. Taylor:" is a more formal salutation than "Dear Mr. President:"; however, in Great Britain, the reverse is true. [2] All but two Cabinet members use the title "Secretary": The Attorney General and the Postmaster General. Their full titles are used (e.g., on envelope: The Attorney General). [3] State senators and representatives are referred to and addressed the same way as U.S. Senators and Representatives. [4] For an American ambassador on home leave, the proper form of social address on an envelope is: "The Honorable Stephen Taylor and Mrs. Taylor," plus home address. [5] "Chargé d'affaires ad interim" is the official title given to the individual who assumes responsibility for an embassy during an ambassador's absence or change of ambassadors. [6] "Esquire" is never used, if the individual is addressed by another title, even "Mr." [7] "His Excellency" is followed by the individual's personal title, if he has one (e.g., Dr., Prince, Baron). [8] "His Excellency" is acceptable for addressing the governors of the four Commonwealths: Massachusetts, Virginia, Kentucky, and Pennsylvania; however, the State Department prefers to address all U.S. governors as "The Honorable."

## U.S. POSTAL INFORMATION AND REGULATIONS*

SOURCE: U.S. Postal Service

**First-Class Mail** includes letters, postal cards, postcards, all matter wholly or partly in writing (except authorized additions to second-, third-, and fourth-class mail), as well as matter closed against inspection. In addition, a service is available (E-COM) which provides delivery of computer-originated mail within 2 days.

| Kind of mail | Rate |
|---|---|
| All first-class mail weighing 12 oz. or less, except postal cards and postcards: | 20¢ 1st oz. & 17¢ each additional oz. |
| Single postal cards and postcards: | 13¢ each |
| Double postal cards and postcards (reply portion of double postcard does not have to bear postage when originally mailed): | 26¢ (13¢ each portion) |
| Business reply mail: | consult postmaster |

**Express Mail:** Next-day guaranteed service between major U.S. cities for any mailable articles up to 70 lbs. Consult postmaster for services and rates.

**Second-Class Mail** includes all newspapers, magazines, and other periodicals marked as second-class mail. In-county bulk rates are 4.1¢ per lb. and 2.1¢ or 2.6¢ per piece. Outside the county, the non-advertising portion is 12.8¢ per lb., and the advertising portion is from 17.1¢ to 38.3¢ per lb.; either portion is 4.4¢ to 7.0¢ per piece. (Postage is total per lb. charge plus total per piece charge.) Special rates are available to nonprofit organizations, publishers, and news agents. For mailings by the public: 19¢ 1st oz. or fraction, 35¢ (total) over 1 oz. to 2 oz., additional 10¢ per oz. to 8 oz., additional 10¢ per 2 oz. over 8 oz.

**Third-Class Mail** is mailable matter that is not sent or required to be mailed as first-class mail, not entered as second-class mail, and weighs less than 16 oz. Merchandise and printed matter are considered third-class mail. Single-piece rate: 20¢ 0 to 1 oz., additional 17¢ per oz. or fraction through 4 oz., additional 14¢ 4 to 6 oz., additional 10¢ per 2 oz. or fraction through 16 oz. Bulk rates reflect the level of presort. Third-class mail must be prepared so that it can be easily examined. For special bulk rates for nonprofit organizations, consult local postmaster. Note: If matter and mailing qualify both for bulk third-class and fourth-class (in everything except weight), and bulk third-class rate is higher, fourth-class rate may apply without adding additional weight.

**Special Fourth-Class Rate.** A single-piece rate of 63¢ up to 1 pound or fraction, and 23¢ for each additional pound or fraction through 7 lbs., 14¢ per lb. thereafter, is provided for the following: bound books with no advertising; 16 mm films; printed music; book mss, magazine articles, and music; sound recordings; and certain other matter. The maximum size is 84" combined length and girth. The identification statement: Special Fourth Class Rate—Books (or other appropriate notation) must be placed conspicuously.

**Fourth-Class (Parcel Post) Mail** includes merchandise, printed matter, mailable live animals, and all other matter not included in first-, second-, or third-class mail. Parcels weighing 1 pound or more are mailable as fourth-class mail. Mail sent within Bulk Mail Center (BMC) or Auxiliary Service Facility (ASF) areas are charged at a lower rate than intra BMC/ASF mail. Size and weight requirements vary for different classes of post office, and surcharges of 50¢ are applied to nonmachinable and overweight mail. Your local post office can advise you on the best methods to mail parcels of all types and sizes and on the rates which will apply. For faster delivery of parcels overlong distances, use first-class zone-rated (priority) mail or express mail.

**Library Rate.** A special library rate applies to certain items that are conspicuously marked Library Rate and show nonprofit associations or organizations in the address or return address. The postage rate is 35¢ for the first pound, 12¢ for each additional pound through 7 pounds, and 7¢ per pound thereafter.

**Priority Mail** (first-class zone-rated) is carried by air and the fastest connecting surface carriers. It is given the most expeditious handling in dispatch and delivery. Priority mail may weigh over 12 oz., but not more than 70 lbs. Rates depend upon the zone of destination as well as weight, with a minimum charge for parcels under 15 lbs. which measure 84" but no more than 100" in length plus girth.

**Size Standards for Domestic Mail.** Min. size: .007" thick; all mail 1/4" or less thick must be rectangular, with min. height 3-1/2", and min. length 5". (Note: Mail more than 1/4" thick can be mailed even if height and length are smaller than specified above.) Mail weighing 1 oz. or less which is first-class or single-piece rate third class is considered nonstandard under the following conditions: exceeds 11½"x6⅛"x¼", or length divided by height does not fall between 1.3 and 2.5 inclusive. Nonstandard mail is subject to a 9¢ surcharge.

### SPECIAL HANDLING

Third- and fourth-class mail only. Special handling fees (fees in addition to postage):

| Weight | Fee |
|---|---|
| 10 lbs. or less | $0.75 |
| More than 10 lbs. | 1.30 |

### SPECIAL DELIVERY

**Special delivery fees** (fees in addition to postage):

| | Weight | | |
|---|---|---|---|
| Class of mail | 2 lbs. and under | 10 lbs. and less, but over 2 lbs. | Over 10 lbs. |
| First class and priority | $2.10 | $2.35 | $3.00 |
| All other classes | 2.35 | 3.00 | 3.40 |

### MONEY ORDERS

| Amount of money order | Amount of fee Domestic |
|---|---|
| $ 0.01 to $ 25 | $0.75 |
| $25.01 to $ 50 | 1.10 |
| $50.01 to $500 | 1.55 |

### INSURANCE

Fees (in addition to postage):

| Liability | Fee |
|---|---|
| $ 0.01 to $ 20 | $0.45 |
| $ 20.01 to $ 50 | 0.85 |
| $ 50.01 to $100 | 1.25 |
| $100.01 to $150 | 1.70 |
| $150.01 to $200 | 2.05 |
| $200.01 to $300 | 3.45 |
| $300.01 to $400 | 4.70 |

Insurance is optional for registered mail.

### C.O.D. MAIL

Consult postmaster for fees and conditions of mailing.

### CERTIFIED MAIL

Fee (in addition to postage) .......... $0.75

### REGISTRY

Registry fees (in addition to postage):

| Declared actual value | For articles without postal insurance coverage | For articles with postal insurance coverage |
|---|---|---|
| $ 0.00 to $ 100 | $3.25 | $3.30 |
| $100.01 to $ 500 | 3.55 | 3.60 |
| $500.01 to $1,000 | 3.85 | 3.90 |

For higher values and their fees, consult local postmaster.

### RESTRICTED DELIVERY

Delivery only to addressee (or person authorized by addressee).
Fee for insured (over $20), certified, registered, or C.O.D. mail... $1.00

### RETURN RECEIPTS

For insured (over $20), certified, registered, or C.O.D. mail.

| Requested at the time of mailing: | |
|---|---|
| Showing to whom and when | $0.60 |
| Showing to whom, when, and address where delivered | 0.70 |
| Requested after mailing: | |
| Showing to whom and when delivered | 3.75 |

## INTERNATIONAL POSTAL CHARGES

### LETTERS AND LETTER PACKAGES:

**Surface Mail:** Canada and Mexico: 20¢ for the first oz. or fraction, add 17¢ per additional oz. or fraction through 12 oz., $2.58 (tot.) over 12 oz. to 1 lb. For every additional ½ lb. add 49¢ and 50¢ in alternate succession. All other countries: 30¢ for the first oz. or fraction, 17¢ per additional oz. or fraction through 8 oz., $2.76 (tot.) over ½ lb. to 1 lb. Over 1 lb. add $1.02 per ½ lb. or fraction through 2 lb. Over 2 lb. add 75¢ per ½ lb. or fraction. **Airmail:** Canada and Mexico: See surface rates. (Mail at these rates is considered first class in U.S. and airmail in Can. and Mex.) Colombia, Venezuela, Central America, and selected islands: 35¢ per ½ oz. through 2 oz., 30¢ per additional ½ oz. through 2 lbs., 30¢ per additional oz. or fraction thereafter. All other countries: 40¢ per ½ oz. through 2 oz., 35¢ per additional ½ oz. through 32 oz., 35¢ per additional oz. over 32 oz. **Aerogrammes:** To all countries, 30¢ each. **Weight Limit:** 4 lbs. to all countries.

### POSTCARDS:

**Surface Mail:** To Canada and Mexico, 13¢; to all other countries, 19¢.
**Airmail:** To Canada and Mexico, 13¢; to all other countries, 28¢.
Note: Single cards acceptable only. Max. size, 6x4¼"; min. size, 5½x3½".

*Certain rates are subject to change in the near future.

## PARCEL POST ZONE RATES*

| Weight | | Zones | | | | | | |
|---|---|---|---|---|---|---|---|---|
| | | 1 & 2 | 3 | 4 | 5 | 6 | 7 | 8 |
| 1 lb. and not exceeding | Local | Up to 150 mi. | 150 to 300 mi. | 300 to 600 mi. | 600 to 1,000 mi. | 1,000 to 1,400 mi. | 1,400 to 1,800 mi. | Over 1,800 mi. |
| 2 | $1.52 | $1.55 | $1.61 | $1.70 | $1.83 | $1.99 | $2.15 | $2.48 |
| 3 | 1.58 | 1.63 | 1.73 | 1.86 | 2.06 | 2.30 | 2.55 | 3.05 |
| 4 | 1.65 | 1.71 | 1.84 | 2.02 | 2.29 | 2.61 | 2.94 | 3.60 |
| 5 | 1.71 | 1.79 | 1.96 | 2.18 | 2.52 | 2.92 | 3.32 | 4.07 |
| 6 | 1.78 | 1.87 | 2.07 | 2.33 | 2.74 | 3.14 | 3.64 | 4.54 |
| 7 | 1.84 | 1.95 | 2.18 | 2.49 | 2.89 | 3.38 | 3.95 | 5.02 |
| 8 | 1.91 | 2.03 | 2.30 | 2.64 | 3.06 | 3.63 | 4.27 | 5.55 |
| 9 | 1.97 | 2.11 | 2.41 | 2.75 | 3.25 | 3.93 | 4.63 | 6.08 |
| 10 | 2.04 | 2.19 | 2.52 | 2.87 | 3.46 | 4.22 | 5.00 | 6.62 |
| 11 | 2.10 | 2.28 | 2.60 | 3.00 | 3.68 | 4.51 | 5.38 | 7.15 |
| 12 | 2.17 | 2.36 | 2.66 | 3.10 | 3.89 | 4.80 | 5.75 | 7.69 |
| 13 | 2.21 | 2.41 | 2.72 | 3.19 | 4.02 | 4.96 | 5.95 | 7.97 |
| 14 | 2.26 | 2.46 | 2.78 | 3.28 | 4.13 | 5.12 | 6.14 | 8.24 |
| 15 | 2.31 | 2.51 | 2.83 | 3.36 | 4.25 | 5.26 | 6.32 | 8.48 |
| 16 | 2.35 | 2.56 | 2.89 | 3.44 | 4.35 | 5.40 | 6.49 | 8.72 |
| 17 | 2.40 | 2.59 | 2.94 | 3.51 | 4.45 | 5.53 | 6.65 | 8.94 |
| 18 | 2.44 | 2.64 | 2.99 | 3.59 | 4.55 | 5.65 | 6.80 | 9.15 |
| 19 | 2.48 | 2.68 | 3.04 | 3.66 | 4.64 | 5.77 | 6.94 | 9.35 |
| 20 | 2.52 | 2.72 | 3.10 | 3.73 | 4.73 | 5.89 | 7.09 | 9.55 |
| 21 | 2.56 | 2.76 | 3.14 | 3.79 | 4.82 | 6.00 | 7.22 | 9.73 |
| 22 | 2.60 | 2.81 | 3.20 | 3.86 | 4.90 | 6.10 | 7.35 | 9.91 |
| 23 | 2.64 | 2.84 | 3.26 | 3.92 | 4.99 | 6.21 | 7.48 | 10.08 |
| 24 | 2.68 | 2.93 | 3.36 | 4.02 | 5.07 | 6.31 | 7.60 | 10.24 |
| 25 | 2.72 | 3.00 | 3.47 | 4.15 | 5.14 | 6.40 | 7.75 | 10.40 |
| 26 | 2.76 | 3.04 | 3.56 | 4.27 | 5.27 | 6.58 | 8.02 | 10.56 |
| 27 | 2.79 | 3.08 | 3.65 | 4.40 | 5.44 | 6.79 | 8.28 | 10.71 |
| 28 | 2.83 | 3.13 | 3.70 | 4.47 | 5.59 | 7.00 | 8.53 | 10.85 |
| 29 | 2.87 | 3.17 | 3.75 | 4.53 | 5.76 | 7.17 | 8.64 | 10.99 |
| 30 | 2.90 | 3.21 | 3.80 | 4.59 | 5.84 | 7.27 | 8.75 | 11.13 |
| 31 | 2.97 | 3.25 | 3.85 | 4.65 | 5.91 | 7.36 | 8.86 | 11.29 |
| 32 | 3.01 | 3.30 | 3.90 | 4.71 | 5.98 | 7.44 | 8.96 | 11.41 |
| 33 | 3.05 | 3.34 | 3.95 | 4.76 | 6.05 | 7.53 | 9.06 | 11.53 |
| 34 | 3.08 | 3.38 | 4.00 | 4.82 | 6.12 | 7.61 | 9.16 | 11.76 |
| 35 | 3.12 | 3.42 | 4.04 | 4.88 | 6.19 | 7.69 | 9.26 | 12.07 |
| 36 | 3.16 | 3.44 | 4.08 | 4.93 | 6.25 | 7.78 | 9.36 | 11.88 |
| 37 | 3.20 | 3.50 | 4.14 | 4.98 | 6.32 | 7.86 | 9.45 | 12.20 |
| 38 | 3.23 | 3.54 | 4.18 | 5.04 | 6.39 | 7.93 | 9.54 | 12.51 |
| 39 | 3.27 | 3.58 | 4.23 | 5.09 | 6.45 | 8.01 | 9.63 | 12.82 |
| 40 | 3.31 | 3.62 | 4.27 | 5.14 | 6.51 | 8.09 | 9.72 | 13.08 |
| 41 | 3.34 | 3.66 | 4.32 | 5.19 | 6.58 | 8.16 | 9.81 | 13.20 |
| 42 | 3.38 | 3.70 | 4.36 | 5.24 | 6.64 | 8.24 | 9.90 | 13.31 |
| 43 | 3.42 | 3.74 | 4.40 | 5.29 | 6.70 | 8.31 | 9.98 | 13.42 |
| 44 | 3.46 | 3.78 | 4.45 | 5.34 | 6.76 | 8.38 | 10.14 | 13.53 |
| 45 | 3.49 | 3.81 | 4.49 | 5.39 | 6.82 | 8.45 | 10.36 | 13.64 |
| 46 | 3.53 | 3.85 | 4.53 | 5.44 | 6.88 | 8.52 | 10.58 | 13.74 |
| 47 | 3.56 | 3.89 | 4.58 | 5.49 | 6.94 | 8.66 | 10.80 | 13.85 |
| 48 | 3.60 | 3.93 | 4.62 | 5.54 | 6.99 | 8.83 | 11.02 | 13.95 |
| 49 | 3.64 | 3.97 | 4.66 | 5.59 | 7.05 | 9.01 | 11.24 | 14.05 |
| 50 | 3.67 | 4.01 | 4.71 | 5.64 | 7.13 | 9.18 | 11.46 | 14.15 |
| 51 | 3.71 | 4.04 | 4.75 | 5.69 | 7.27 | 9.36 | 11.68 | 14.25 |
| 52 | 3.74 | 4.08 | 4.79 | 5.79 | 7.40 | 9.53 | 11.90 | 14.35 |
| 53 | 3.78 | 4.12 | 4.83 | 5.90 | 7.54 | 9.71 | 12.12 | 14.44 |
| 54 | 3.82 | 4.16 | 4.87 | 6.00 | 7.67 | 9.88 | 12.34 | 14.54 |
| 55 | 3.85 | 4.19 | 4.94 | 6.11 | 7.81 | 10.06 | 12.56 | 14.76 |
| 56 | 3.89 | 4.23 | 5.02 | 6.21 | 7.94 | 10.23 | 12.78 | 15.02 |
| 57 | 3.92 | 4.27 | 5.11 | 6.32 | 8.08 | 10.41 | 13.00 | 15.28 |
| 58 | 3.96 | 4.32 | 5.19 | 6.42 | 8.21 | 10.58 | 13.22 | 15.54 |
| 59 | 3.99 | 4.39 | 5.28 | 6.53 | 8.35 | 10.76 | 13.44 | 15.80 |
| 60 | 4.03 | 4.46 | 5.36 | 6.63 | 8.48 | 10.93 | 13.66 | 16.06 |
| 61 | 4.06 | 4.53 | 5.45 | 6.74 | 8.62 | 11.11 | 13.88 | 16.32 |
| 62 | 4.10 | 4.60 | 5.53 | 6.84 | 8.75 | 11.28 | 14.10 | 16.58 |
| 63 | 4.13 | 4.67 | 5.62 | 6.95 | 8.89 | 11.46 | 14.32 | 16.84 |
| 64 | 4.17 | 4.74 | 5.70 | 7.05 | 9.02 | 11.63 | 14.54 | 17.10 |
| 65 | 4.20 | 4.81 | 5.79 | 7.16 | 9.16 | 11.81 | 14.76 | 17.36 |
| 66 | 4.24 | 4.88 | 5.87 | 7.26 | 9.29 | 11.98 | 14.98 | 17.62 |
| 67 | 4.27 | 4.95 | 5.96 | 7.37 | 9.43 | 12.16 | 15.20 | 17.88 |
| 68 | 4.31 | 5.02 | 6.04 | 7.47 | 9.56 | 12.33 | 15.42 | 18.14 |
| 69 | 4.34 | 5.09 | 6.13 | 7.58 | 9.70 | 12.51 | 15.64 | 18.40 |
| 70 | 4.38 | 5.16 | 6.21 | 7.68 | 9.83 | 12.68 | 15.86 | 18.66 |

* Rates shown apply to mail sent between BMC areas only. Consult post office for weight and size limits. Parcels mailed within BMC areas are eligible for a discount from the rates shown in this table. Nonmachinable Surcharge: Parcels mailed to Zip Code destinations outside the BMC area are subject to a surcharge if they are nonmachinable or if they are overweight.

## U.S. TOWNS AND CITIES: ZIP CODES AND 1980 POPULATIONS

The following is a list of larger places in the United States, according to final population counts of the 1980 U.S. Census. The ZIP code listed for each place is the five-digit national coding system that identifies each postal delivery area and is designated to expedite mail delivery. An asterisk indicates that there is more than one ZIP code for the town or city and that the code number applies to general delivery. To determine the exact ZIP code for a particular area within a place marked by an asterisk, consult the National Zip Code Directory or your nearest post office.

| LOCATION | POPULATION | ZIP |
|---|---|---|
| **ALABAMA** | | |
| Albertville | 12,039 | 35950 |
| Alexander City | 13,807 | 35010 |
| Andalusia | 10,415 | 36420 |
| Anniston | 29,523 | 36201* |
| Athens | 14,558 | 35611 |
| Atmore | 8,789 | 36503 |
| Attalla | 7,737 | 35954 |
| Auburn | 28,471 | 36830 |
| Bay Minette | 7,455 | 36507 |
| Bessemer | 31,729 | 35020 |
| Birmingham | 284,413 | 35203* |
| Brewton | 6,680 | 36426 |
| Chickasaw | 7,402 | 36611 |
| Cullman | 13,084 | 35055 |
| Decatur | 42,002 | 35601* |
| Demopolis | 7,678 | 36732 |
| Dothan | 48,750 | 36303* |
| Enterprise | 18,033 | 36330 |
| Eufaula | 12,097 | 36027 |
| Fairfield | 13,242 | 35064 |
| Florence | 37,029 | 35630* |
| Fort Payne | 11,485 | 35967 |
| Gadsden | 47,565 | 35901* |
| Gardendale | 7,928 | 35071 |
| Greenville | 7,807 | 36037 |
| Guntersville | 7,041 | 35976 |
| Hartselle | 8,858 | 35640 |
| Homewood | 21,412 | 35209 |
| Hoover | 19,792 | 35216 |
| Hueytown | 13,478 | 35020 |
| Huntsville | 142,513 | 35804* |
| Jacksonville | 9,735 | 36265 |
| Jasper | 11,894 | 35501 |
| Lanett | 6,897 | 36863 |
| Leeds | 8,638 | 35094 |
| Midfield | 6,203 | 35228 |
| Mobile | 200,452 | 36601* |
| Montgomery | 177,857 | 36104* |
| Mountain Brook | 19,718 | 35223 |
| Muscle Shoals | 8,911 | 35660 |
| Northport | 14,291 | 35476 |
| Opelika | 21,896 | 36801 |
| Opp | 7,204 | 36467 |
| Oxford | 8,939 | 36203 |
| Ozark | 13,188 | 36360 |
| Phenix City | 26,928 | 36867 |
| Prattville | 18,647 | 36067 |
| Prichard | 39,541 | 36610 |
| Russellville | 8,195 | 35653 |
| Saraland | 9,833 | 36571 |
| Scottsboro | 14,758 | 35768 |
| Selma | 26,684 | 36701 |
| Sheffield | 11,903 | 35660 |
| Sylacauga | 12,708 | 35150 |
| Talladega | 19,128 | 35160 |
| Tarrant City | 8,148 | 35217 |
| Troy | 12,945 | 36081 |
| Tuscaloosa | 75,211 | 35401* |
| Tuscumbia | 9,137 | 35674 |
| Tuskegee | 13,327 | 36083 |
| Vestavia Hills | 15,722 | 35216 |
| **ALASKA** | | |
| Anchorage | 174,431 | 99510* |
| Fairbanks | 22,645 | 99701 |
| Juneau | 19,528 | 99801 |
| Ketchikan | 7,198 | 99901 |
| Sitka | 7,803 | 99840 |
| **ARIZONA** | | |
| Apache Junction | 9,935 | 85220 |
| Avondale | 8,168 | 85323 |
| Bisbee | 7,154 | 85603 |
| Casa Grande | 14,971 | 85222 |
| Chandler | 29,673 | 85224 |
| Douglas | 13,058 | 85607 |
| Flagstaff | 34,743 | 86001 |
| Glendale | 97,172 | 85301* |
| Globe | 6,886 | 85501 |
| Kingman | 9,257 | 86401 |
| Lake Havasu City | 15,909 | 86403 |
| Mesa | 152,453 | 85201* |
| Nogales | 15,683 | 85621 |
| Paradise Valley | 11,085 | 85253 |
| Peoria | 12,307 | 85345 |
| Phoenix | 789,704 | 85026* |
| Prescott | 20,055 | 86301 |
| Scottsdale | 88,622 | 85251* |
| Sierra Vista | 24,937 | 85635 |
| Tempe | 106,743 | 85282* |
| Tucson | 330,537 | 85702* |
| Winslow | 7,921 | 86047 |
| Yuma | 42,481 | 85364 |
| **ARKANSAS** | | |
| Arkadelphia | 10,005 | 71923 |
| Batesville | 8,263 | 72501 |
| Benton | 17,717 | 72015 |
| Bentonville | 8,756 | 72712 |
| Blytheville | 23,844 | 72315 |
| Camden | 15,356 | 71701 |
| Conway | 20,375 | 72032 |
| El Dorado | 25,270 | 71730 |
| Fayetteville | 36,608 | 72701 |
| Forrest City | 13,803 | 72335 |
| Fort Smith | 71,626 | 72901* |
| Harrison | 9,567 | 72601* |
| Helena | 9,598 | 72342 |
| Hope | 10,290 | 71801 |
| Hot Springs | 35,781 | 71901 |
| Jacksonville | 27,589 | 72076 |
| Jonesboro | 31,530 | 72401 |
| Little Rock | 158,461 | 72201* |
| Magnolia | 11,909 | 71753 |
| Malvern | 10,163 | 72104 |
| Monticello | 8,259 | 71655 |
| Morrilton | 7,355 | 72110 |
| Newport | 8,339 | 72112 |
| North Little Rock | 64,288 | 72114* |
| Osceola | 8,881 | 72370 |
| Paragould | 15,248 | 72450 |
| Pine Bluff | 56,636 | 71601* |
| Rogers | 17,429 | 72756 |
| Russellville | 14,031 | 72801 |
| Searcy | 13,612 | 72143 |
| Sherwood | 10,406 | 72116 |
| Springdale | 23,458 | 72764 |
| Stuttgart | 10,941 | 72160 |
| Texarkana | 21,459 | 75502 |
| Van Buren | 12,020 | 72956 |
| Warren | 7,646 | 71671 |
| West Helena | 11,367 | 72390 |
| West Memphis | 28,138 | 72301 |
| Wynne | 7,805 | 72396 |
| **CALIFORNIA** | | |
| Alameda | 63,852 | 94501 |
| Albany | 15,130 | 94706 |
| Alhambra | 64,615 | 91802* |
| Altadena | 40,983 | 91001 |
| Anaheim | 219,494 | 92803* |
| Anderson | 7,381 | 96007 |
| Antioch | 42,683 | 94509 |
| Apple Valley | 14,305 | 92307 |
| Aptos | 7,039 | 95003 |
| Arcadia | 45,994 | 91006 |
| Arcata | 12,850 | 95521 |
| Arroyo Grande | 11,290 | 93420 |
| Artesia | 14,301 | 90701 |
| Arvin | 6,863 | 93203 |
| Atascadero | 16,232 | 93422 |
| Atherton | 7,797 | 94025 |
| Atwater | 17,530 | 95301 |
| Auburn | 7,540 | 95603 |
| Azusa | 29,380 | 91702 |
| Bakersfield | 105,735 | 93302* |
| Baldwin Park | 50,554 | 91706 |
| Banning | 14,020 | 92220 |
| Barstow | 17,690 | 92311 |
| Beaumont | 6,818 | 92223 |
| Bell | 25,450 | 90201 |
| Bellflower | 53,441 | 90706 |
| Bell Gardens | 34,117 | 90201 |
| Belmont | 24,505 | 94002 |
| Benicia | 15,376 | 94510 |
| Berkeley | 103,328 | 94701* |
| Beverly Hills | 32,367 | 90213* |
| Bloomington | 18,888 | 92316 |
| Blythe | 6,805 | 92225 |
| Brawley | 14,946 | 92227 |
| Brea | 27,913 | 92621 |
| Broderick | — | 95605 |
| Buena Park | 64,165 | 90622* |
| Burbank | 84,625 | 91505* |
| Burlingame | 26,173 | 94010 |
| Calexico | 14,412 | 92231 |
| Camarillo | 37,797 | 93010 |
| Campbell | 26,910 | 95008 |
| Capitola | 9,095 | 95010 |
| Carlsbad | 35,490 | 92008 |
| Carmichael | 43,108 | 95608 |
| Carpinteria | 10,835 | 93013 |
| Carson | 81,221 | 90745 |
| Castro Valley | 44,011 | 94546 |
| Ceres | 13,281 | 95307 |
| Cerritos | 53,020 | 90701 |
| Chico | 26,603 | 95926 |
| Chino | 40,165 | 91710 |
| Chula Vista | 83,927 | 92010* |
| Citrus Heights | 85,911 | 95610 |
| Claremont | 30,950 | 91711 |
| Clovis | 33,021 | 93612 |
| Coachella | 9,129 | 92236 |
| Coalinga | 6,593 | 93210 |
| Colton | 15,201 | 92324 |
| Commerce | 10,509 | 90040 |
| Compton | 81,286 | 90220* |
| Concord | 103,255 | 94520* |
| Corcoran | 6,454 | 93212 |
| Corona | 37,791 | 91720 |
| Coronado | 18,790 | 92118 |
| Corte Madera | 8,074 | 94925 |
| Costa Mesa | 82,562 | 92626* |
| Covina | 33,751 | 91722* |
| Cucamonga (Rancho Cucamonga) | 55,250 | 91730 |
| Cudahy | 17,984 | 90201 |
| Culver City | 38,139 | 90230 |
| Cupertino | 34,265 | 95014 |
| Cypress | 40,391 | 90630 |
| Daly City | 78,519 | 94015* |
| Davis | 36,640 | 95616 |
| Delano | 16,491 | 93215 |
| Dinuba | 9,907 | 93618 |
| Dixon | 7,541 | 95620 |
| Downey | 82,602 | 90241* |
| Duarte | 16,766 | 91010 |
| Dublin | 13,496 | 94566 |
| El Cajon | 73,892 | 92020* |
| El Centro | 23,996 | 92243 |
| El Cerrito | 22,731 | 94530 |
| El Monte | 79,494 | 91734* |
| El Segundo | 13,752 | 90245 |
| El Toro | 38,153 | 92630 |
| Escondido | 64,355 | 92025* |
| Eureka | 24,153 | 95501 |
| Fairfax | 7,391 | 94930 |
| Fairfield | 58,099 | 94533 |
| Fair Oaks | 22,602 | 95628 |
| Fall Brooks | — | 92028 |
| Fillmore | 9,602 | 93015 |
| Folsom | 11,003 | 95630 |
| Fontana | 37,107 | 92335 |
| Fortuna | 7,591 | 95540 |
| Foster City | 23,287 | 94404 |
| Fountain Valley | 55,080 | 92708 |
| Fremont | 131,945 | 94538 |
| Fresno | 217,289 | 93706 |
| Fullerton | 102,034 | 92631 |
| Gardena | 45,165 | 90247 |
| Garden Grove | 123,307 | 92640 |
| Gilroy | 21,641 | 95020 |
| Glendale | 139,060 | 91209 |
| Glendora | 38,500 | 91740 |

*General Delivery—for all towns so marked there ismore than one zip code.

| LOCATION | POPULATION | ZIP |
|---|---|---|
| Grand Terrace | 8,498 | 92324 |
| Grass Valley | 6,697 | 95945 |
| Grover City | 8,827 | 93433 |
| Half Moon Bay | 7,282 | 94019 |
| Hanford | 20,958 | 93230 |
| Hawaiian Gardens | 10,548 | 90716 |
| Hawthorne | 56,447 | 90250 |
| Hayward | 94,342 | 94544* |
| Healdsburg | 7,217 | 95448 |
| Hemet | 22,454 | 92343 |
| Hermosa Beach | 18,070 | 90254 |
| Highland | 10,908 | 92346 |
| Hillsborough | 10,372 | 94010 |
| Hollister | 11,488 | 95023 |
| Huntington Beach | 170,505 | 92647* |
| Huntington Park | 46,223 | 90255 |
| Imperial Beach | 22,689 | 92032 |
| Indio | 21,611 | 92201 |
| Inglewood | 94,245 | 90306* |
| Irvine | 62,134 | 92713 |
| La Canada Flintridge | 20,153 | 91011 |
| Lafayette | 20,879 | 94549 |
| Laguna Beach | 17,901 | 92652* |
| La Habra | 45,232 | 90631 |
| Lakeside | 23,921 | 92040 |
| Lakewood | 74,654 | 90714* |
| La Mesa | 50,308 | 92041 |
| La Mirada | 40,986 | 90638 |
| Lamont | 9,616 | 93241 |
| Lancaster | 48,027 | 93534 |
| La Palma | 15,663 | 90624 |
| La Puente | 30,882 | 91747* |
| Larkspur | 11,064 | 94939 |
| La Verne | 23,508 | 91750 |
| Lawndale | 23,460 | 90260 |
| Lemon Grove | 20,780 | 92045 |
| Lemoore | 8,832 | 93245 |
| Lindsay | 6,924 | 93243 |
| Live Oak | 11,482 | 95073 |
| Livermore | 48,349 | 94550 |
| Lodi | 35,221 | 95240 |
| Loma Linda | 10,694 | 92354 |
| Lomita | 18,807 | 90717 |
| Lompoc | 26,267 | 93436 |
| Long Beach | 361,334 | 90801* |
| Los Alamitos | 11,529 | 90720 |
| Los Altos | 25,769 | 94022 |
| Los Altos Hills | 7,421 | 94022 |
| Los Angeles | 2,966,763 | 90053* |
| Los Banos | 10,341 | 93635 |
| Los Gatos | 26,906 | 95030 |
| Lynwood | 48,548 | 90262 |
| Madera | 21,732 | 93637 |
| Manhattan Beach | 31,542 | 90266 |
| Manteca | 24,925 | 95336 |
| Marina | 20,647 | 93933 |
| Martinez | 22,582 | 94553 |
| Marysville | 9,898 | 95901 |
| Maywood | 21,810 | 90201 |
| Menlo Park | 26,369 | 94025 |
| Merced | 36,499 | 95340 |
| Millbrae | 20,058 | 94030 |
| Mill Valley | 12,967 | 94941 |
| Milpitas | 37,820 | 95035 |
| Mira Loma | 8,707 | 91752 |
| Modesto | 106,602 | 95350* |
| Monrovia | 30,531 | 91016 |
| Montclair | 22,628 | 91763 |
| Montebello | 52,929 | 90640 |
| Monterey | 27,558 | 93940 |
| Monterey Park | 54,338 | 91754 |
| Moraga | 15,014 | 94556 |
| Morgan Hill | 17,060 | 95037 |
| Morro Bay | 9,064 | 93442 |
| Mountain View | 58,655 | 94042* |
| Napa | 50,879 | 94558 |
| National City | 48,772 | 92050 |
| Newark | 32,126 | 94560 |
| Newport Beach | 62,556 | 92660* |
| Norco | 21,126 | 91760 |
| North Highlands | 37,825 | 95660 |
| Norwalk | 85,286 | 90650 |
| Novato | 43,916 | 94947 |
| Oakdale | 8,474 | 95361 |
| Oakland | 339,337 | 94617* |
| Oceanside | 76,698 | 92054 |
| Ojai | 6,816 | 93023 |
| Olivehurst | 8,929 | 95961 |
| Ontario | 88,820 | 91761* |
| Orange | 91,450 | 92667* |
| Orangevale | 20,585 | 95662 |
| Orinda | 16,825 | 94563 |
| Oroville | 8,683 | 95965 |
| Oxnard | 108,195 | 93030 |
| Pacifica | 36,866 | 94044 |
| Pacific Grove | 15,755 | 93950 |
| Palmdale | 12,277 | 93550 |
| Palm Desert | 11,801 | 92260 |
| Palm Springs | 32,366 | 92262 |
| Palo Alto | 55,225 | 94302* |
| Palos Verdes Estates | 14,376 | 90274 |
| Paradise | 22,571 | 95969 |
| Paramount | 36,407 | 90723 |
| Pasadena | 118,072 | 91109* |
| Paso Robles | 9,163 | 93446 |
| Perris | 6,827 | 92370 |
| Petaluma | 33,834 | 94952 |
| Pico Rivera | 53,387 | 90660 |
| Piedmont | 10,498 | 94611 |
| Pinole | 14,253 | 94564 |
| Pittsburg | 33,034 | 94565 |
| Placentia | 35,041 | 92670 |
| Placerville | 6,739 | 95667 |
| Pleasant Hill | 25,124 | 94523 |
| Pleasanton | 35,160 | 94566 |
| Pomona | 92,742 | 91766* |
| Porterville | 19,707 | 93257 |
| Port Hueneme | 17,803 | 93041 |
| Poway | 32,263 | 92064 |
| Rancho Cordova | 42,881 | 95670 |
| Rancho Cucamonga | 55,250 | 91730 |
| Rancho Mirage | 6,281 | 92270 |
| Rancho Palos Verdes | 36,577 | 90274 |
| Red Bluff | 9,490 | 96080 |
| Redding | 41,995 | 96001 |
| Redlands | 43,619 | 92373 |
| Redondo Beach | 57,102 | 90277* |
| Redwood City | 54,965 | 94063* |
| Reedley | 11,071 | 93654 |
| Rialto | 37,474 | 92376 |
| Richmond | 74,676 | 94802* |
| Ridgecrest | 15,929 | 93555 |
| Rio Linda | 7,359 | 95673 |
| Riverside | 170,591 | 92502* |
| Rocklin | 7,344 | 95677 |
| Rohnert Park | 22,965 | 94928 |
| Rolling Hills Estates | 7,701 | 90274 |
| Rosemead | 42,604 | 91770 |
| Roseville | 24,347 | 95678 |
| Sacramento | 275,741 | 95814* |
| Salinas | 80,479 | 93901* |
| San Anselmo | 12,067 | 94960 |
| San Bernardino | 118,794 | 92403* |
| San Bruno | 35,417 | 94066 |
| San Buenaventura (Ventura) | 74,474 | 93001* |
| San Carlos | 24,710 | 94070 |
| San Clemente | 27,325 | 92672 |
| San Diego | 875,538 | 92101* |
| San Dimas | 24,014 | 91773 |
| San Fernando | 17,731 | 91340* |
| San Francisco | 678,974 | 94101* |
| San Gabriel | 30,072 | 91776* |
| Sanger | 12,542 | 93657 |
| San Jacinto | 7,098 | 92383 |
| San Jose | 629,546 | 95113* |
| San Juan Capistrano | 18,959 | 92691* |
| San Leandro | 63,952 | 94577* |
| San Lorenzo | 20,545 | 94580 |
| San Luis Obispo | 34,252 | 93401 |
| San Marcos | 17,479 | 92069 |
| San Marino | 13,307 | 91108 |
| San Mateo | 77,640 | 94402* |
| San Pablo | 19,750 | 94806 |
| San Rafael | 44,700 | 94902* |
| Santa Ana | 204,023 | 92711* |
| Santa Barbara | 74,414 | 93102* |
| Santa Clara | 87,700 | 95050* |
| Santa Cruz | 41,483 | 95060* |
| Santa Fe Springs | 14,520 | 90670 |
| Santa Maria | 39,685 | 93454 |
| Santa Monica | 88,314 | 90406* |
| Santa Paula | 20,552 | 93060 |
| Santa Rosa | 83,205 | 95402* |
| Santee | 47,080 | 92071 |
| Saratoga | 29,261 | 95070 |
| Sausalito | 7,338 | 94965 |
| Scotts Valley | 6,891 | 95066 |
| Seal Beach | 25,975 | 90740 |
| Seaside | 36,567 | 93955 |
| Selma | 10,942 | 93662 |
| Shafter | 7,010 | 93263 |
| Sierra Madre | 10,837 | 91024 |
| Simi Valley | 77,500 | 93065* |
| Sonoma | 6,054 | 95476 |
| South El Monte | 16,623 | 91733 |
| South Gate | 66,784 | 90280 |
| South Lake Tahoe | 20,681 | 95705 |
| South Pasadena | 22,681 | 91030 |
| South San Francisco | 49,393 | 94080 |
| Spring Valley | 40,191 | 92077* |
| Stanton | 23,723 | 90680 |
| Stockton | 149,779 | 95202* |
| Suisun City | 11,087 | 94585 |
| Sunnymead | 11,554 | 92388 |
| Sunnyvale | 106,618 | 94088* |
| Susanville | 6,520 | 96130 |
| Temple City | 28,972 | 91780 |
| Thousand Oaks | 77,072 | 91360* |
| Tiburon | 6,685 | 94920 |
| Torrance | 129,881 | 90510* |
| Tracy | 18,428 | 95376 |
| Tulare | 22,526 | 93274 |
| Turlock | 26,287 | 95380 |
| Tustin | 32,317 | 92680 |
| Ukiah | 12,035 | 95482 |
| Union City | 39,406 | 94587 |
| Upland | 47,647 | 91786 |
| Vacaville | 43,367 | 95688 |
| Vallejo | 80,303 | 94590 |
| Ventura (San Buenaventura) | 74,393 | 93001* |
| Victorville | 14,220 | 92392 |
| Villa Park | 7,137 | 92667 |
| Visalia | 49,729 | 93277 |
| Vista | 35,834 | 92083 |
| Walnut | 12,478 | 91789 |
| Walnut Creek | 53,643 | 94596* |
| Wasco | 9,613 | 93280 |
| Watsonville | 23,663 | 95076 |
| West Covina | 80,291 | 91793* |
| Westminster | 71,133 | 92683 |
| West Sacramento | 10,875 | 95691 |
| Whittier | 69,717 | 90605* |
| Woodland | 30,235 | 95695 |
| Yorba Linda | 28,254 | 92686 |
| Yuba City | 18,736 | 95991 |
| Yucaipa | 23,345 | 92399 |

**COLORADO**

| LOCATION | POPULATION | ZIP |
|---|---|---|
| Alamosa | 6,830 | 81101 |
| Arvada | 84,576 | 80001* |
| Aurora | 158,588 | 80010* |
| Boulder | 76,685 | 80302* |
| Brighton | 12,773 | 80601 |
| Broomfield | 20,730 | 80020 |
| Canon City | 13,037 | 81212 |
| Colorado Springs | 214,821 | 80901* |
| Commerce City | 16,234 | 80022 |
| Cortez | 7,095 | 81321 |
| Craig | 8,133 | 81625 |
| Denver | 492,365 | 80201* |
| Durango | 11,649 | 81301 |
| Englewood | 30,021 | 80110* |
| Federal Heights | 7,846 | 80221 |
| Fort Collins | 65,092 | 80521 |
| Fort Morgan | 8,768 | 80701 |
| Fountain | 8,324 | 80817 |
| Golden | 12,237 | 80401 |
| Grand Junction | 27,956 | 81501 |
| Greeley | 53,006 | 80631 |
| Gunnison | 5,785 | 81230 |
| Lafayette | 8,985 | 80026 |
| La Junta | 8,338 | 81050 |
| Lakewood | 113,808 | 80215 |
| Lamar | 7,713 | 81052 |
| Littleton | 28,631 | 80120* |
| Longmont | 42,942 | 80501 |
| Loveland | 30,244 | 80537 |
| Montrose | 8,722 | 81401 |
| Northglenn | 29,847 | 80233 |
| Pueblo | 101,686 | 81002* |
| Sterling | 11,385 | 80751 |
| Thornton | 40,343 | 80229 |
| Trinidad | 9,663 | 81082 |
| Westminster | 50,211 | 80030 |
| Wheat Ridge | 30,293 | 80033 |

**CONNECTICUT**

| LOCATION | POPULATION | ZIP |
|---|---|---|
| Ansonia | 19,039 | 06401 |
| Avon | 11,201 | 06001 |
| Berlin | 15,121 | 06037 |
| Bethel | 16,004 | 06801 |
| Bloomfield | 18,608 | 06002 |
| Branford | 23,363 | 06405 |
| Bridgeport | 142,546 | 06601* |
| Bristol | 57,370 | 06010 |
| Brookfield | 12,872 | 06804 |
| Canton | 7,635 | 06019 |
| Cheshire | 21,788 | 06410 |
| Clinton | 11,195 | 06413 |
| Colchester | 7,761 | 06415 |
| Coventry | 8,895 | 06238 |
| Cromwell | 10,265 | 06416 |
| Danbury | 60,470 | 06810 |
| Darien | 18,892 | 06820 |
| Derby | 12,346 | 06418 |
| East Hampton | 8,572 | 06424 |
| East Hartford | 52,563 | 06108 |
| East Haven | 25,028 | 06512 |
| East Lyme | 13,870 | 06333 |
| East Windsor | 8,925 | 06088 |
| Ellington | 9,711 | 06029 |
| Enfield | 42,695 | 06082 |
| Fairfield | 54,849 | 06430 |
| Farmington | 16,407 | 06032 |
| Glastonbury | 24,327 | 06033 |
| Granby | 7,956 | 06035 |
| Greenwich | 59,578 | 06830 |
| Griswold | 8,967 | 06351 |
| Groton | 41,062 | 06340 |
| Guilford | 17,375 | 06437 |
| Hamden | 51,071 | 06514 |
| Hartford | 136,392 | 06101* |
| Killingly | 14,519 | 06241 |
| Ledyard | 13,735 | 06339 |
| Litchfield | 7,605 | 06759 |
| Madison | 14,031 | 06443 |
| Manchester | 49,761 | 06040 |
| Mansfield | 20,634 | 06250 |
| Meriden | 57,118 | 06450 |
| Middletown | 39,040 | 06457 |
| Milford | 49,101 | 06460 |
| Monroe | 14,010 | 06468 |
| Montville | 16,455 | 06353 |
| Naugatuck | 26,456 | 06770 |
| New Britain | 73,840 | 06050* |
| New Canaan | 17,931 | 06840 |
| New Fairfield | 11,260 | 06810 |
| New Haven | 126,109 | 06510* |
| Newington | 28,841 | 06111 |
| New London | 28,842 | 06320 |
| New Milford | 19,420 | 06776 |
| Newtown | 19,107 | 06470 |
| North Branford | 11,554 | 06471 |
| North Haven | 22,080 | 06473 |
| Norwalk | 77,767 | 06856* |
| Norwich | 38,074 | 06360 |
| Old Saybrook | 9,287 | 06475 |
| Orange | 13,237 | 06477 |
| Plainfield | 12,774 | 06374 |
| Plainville | 16,401 | 06062 |
| Plymouth | 10,732 | 06782 |
| Portland | 8,383 | 06480 |
| Prospect | 6,807 | 06712 |
| Putnam | 8,580 | 06260 |
| Redding | 7,272 | 06875 |
| Ridgefield | 20,120 | 06877 |
| Rocky Hill | 14,559 | 06067 |
| Seymour | 13,434 | 06483 |
| Shelton | 31,314 | 06484 |
| Simsbury | 21,161 | 06070 |
| Somers | 8,473 | 06071 |
| Southbury | 14,156 | 06488 |
| Southington | 36,879 | 06489 |
| South Windsor | 17,198 | 06074 |
| Stafford | 9,268 | 06075 |
| Stamford | 102,453 | 06904* |
| Stonington | 16,220 | 06378 |
| Stratford | 50,541 | 06497 |
| Suffield | 9,294 | 06078 |
| Thomaston | 6,276 | 06787 |
| Thompson | 8,141 | 06277 |
| Tolland | 9,694 | 06084 |
| Torrington | 30,987 | 06790 |
| Trumbull | 32,989 | 06611 |
| Vernon | 27,974 | 06066 |
| Wallingford | 37,274 | 06492 |
| Waterbury | 103,266 | 06720* |
| Waterford | 17,843 | 06385 |
| Watertown | 19,489 | 06795 |
| West Hartford | 61,301 | 06107 |
| West Haven | 53,184 | 06516 |
| Weston | 8,284 | 06880 |
| Westport | 25,290 | 06880 |
| Wethersfield | 26,013 | 06109 |
| Willimantic | 14,652 | 06226 |
| Wilton | 15,351 | 06897 |
| Winchester | 10,841 | 06094 |
| Windham | 21,062 | 06280 |
| Windsor | 25,204 | 06095 |
| Windsor Locks | 12,190 | 06096 |
| Winsted | 8,092 | 06098 |
| Wolcott | 13,008 | 06716 |
| Woodbridge | 7,761 | 06515 |

**DELAWARE**

| LOCATION | POPULATION | ZIP |
|---|---|---|
| Dover | 23,507 | 19901 |
| Elsmere | 6,493 | 19804 |
| Milford | 5,366 | 19963 |
| Newark | 25,247 | 19702* |
| Seaford | 5,256 | 19973 |
| Wilmington | 70,195 | 19899* |

**DISTRICT OF COLUMBIA**

| LOCATION | POPULATION | ZIP |
|---|---|---|
| Washington | 638,432 | 20013* |

**FLORIDA**

| LOCATION | POPULATION | ZIP |
|---|---|---|
| Altamonte Springs | 22,028 | 32701 |
| Apopka | 6,019 | 32703 |
| Arcadia | 6,002 | 33821 |
| Atlantic Beach | 7,847 | 32233 |
| Auburndale | 6,501 | 33823 |
| Avon Park | 8,026 | 33825 |
| Bartow | 14,780 | 33830 |
| Belle Glade | 16,535 | 33430 |
| Boca Raton | 49,505 | 33432* |
| Boynton Beach | 35,624 | 33435* |
| Bradenton | 30,170 | 33506* |
| Callaway | 7,154 | 32401 |
| Cape Coral | 32,103 | 33904 |
| Casselberry | 15,247 | 32707 |
| Clearwater | 85,528 | 33515* |
| Cocoa | 16,096 | 32922 |
| Cocoa Beach | 10,926 | 32931 |
| Coconut Creek | 6,288 | 33060 |
| Cooper City | 10,140 | 33328 |
| Coral Gables | 43,241 | 33134 |
| Coral Springs | 37,349 | 33065 |
| Crestview | 7,617 | 32536 |
| Dania | 11,811 | 33004 |
| Davie | 20,877 | 33314 |
| Daytona Beach | 54,176 | 32015* |
| Deerfield Beach | 39,193 | 33441 |
| De Land | 15,354 | 32720 |
| Delray Beach | 34,325 | 33444* |
| Dunedin | 30,203 | 33528 |
| Edgewater | 6,726 | 32032 |
| Eustis | 9,453 | 32726 |
| Fernandina Beach | 7,224 | 32034 |
| Florida City | 6,174 | 33034 |
| Fort Lauderdale | 153,279 | 33310* |
| Fort Myers | 36,638 | 33902* |
| Fort Pierce | 33,802 | 33450* |
| Fort Walton Beach | 20,829 | 32548 |
| Gainesville | 81,371 | 32601* |
| Greenacres City | 8,843 | 33463 |
| Gulfport | 11,180 | 33737 |
| Haines City | 10,799 | 33844 |
| Hallandale | 36,517 | 33009 |
| Hialeah | 145,254 | 33010* |
| Holly Hill | 9,953 | 32017 |
| Hollywood | 121,323 | 33022* |
| Homestead | 20,668 | 33030* |
| Jacksonville | 540,920 | 32201* |
| Jacksonville Bch. | 15,462 | 32250 |
| Jupiter | 9,868 | 33458 |
| Key West | 24,382 | 33040 |
| Kissimmee | 15,487 | 32741 |
| Lake City | 9,257 | 32055 |
| Lakeland | 47,406 | 33802* |
| Lake Park | 6,909 | 33403 |
| Lake Wales | 8,466 | 33853 |
| Lake Worth | 27,048 | 33460* |
| Lantana | 8,048 | 33462 |
| Largo | 58,977 | 33540* |
| Lauderdale Lakes | 25,426 | 33313 |
| Lauderhill | 37,271 | 33313 |
| Leesburg | 13,191 | 32748 |
| Lighthouse Point | 11,488 | 33064 |
| Live Oak | 6,732 | 32060 |
| Longwood | 10,029 | 32750 |
| Lynn Haven | 6,239 | 32444 |
| Maitland | 8,763 | 32751 |
| Margate | 35,900 | 33063 |
| Marianna | 7,006 | 32446 |
| Melbourne | 46,536 | 32901 |
| Miami | 346,865 | 33101* |
| Miami Beach | 96,298 | 33139 |
| Miami Shores | 9,244 | 33153 |
| Miami Springs | 12,350 | 33166 |
| Milton | 7,206 | 32570 |
| Miramar | 32,813 | 33023 |
| Naples | 17,581 | 33940* |
| New Port Richey | 11,196 | 33552* |
| New Smyrna Bch. | 13,557 | 32069 |
| Niceville | 8,543 | 32578 |
| North Lauderdale | 18,653 | 33314 |
| North Miami | 42,566 | 33161 |
| North Miami Bch. | 36,553 | 33160 |
| North Palm Bch. | 11,344 | 33403 |
| Oakland Park | 23,035 | 33334 |
| Ocala | 37,170 | 32670* |
| Ocoee | 7,803 | 32761 |
| Opa Locka | 14,460 | 33054 |
| Orange Park | 8,766 | 32073 |
| Orlando | 128,291 | 32802* |
| Ormond Beach | 21,378 | 32074 |
| Pahokee | 6,346 | 33476 |
| Palatka | 10,175 | 32077 |
| Palm Bay | 18,560 | 32905 |
| Palm Beach | 9,729 | 33480 |
| Palm Beach Gardens | 14,407 | 33403 |
| Palmetto | 8,637 | 33561 |
| Palm Springs | 8,166 | 33460 |
| Panama City | 33,346 | 32401* |
| Pembroke Pines | 35,776 | 33024 |
| Pensacola | 57,619 | 32502* |
| Perry | 8,254 | 32347 |
| Pinellas Park | 32,811 | 33565 |
| Plantation | 48,653 | 33317 |
| Plant City | 17,064 | 33566 |
| Pompano Beach | 52,618 | 33060* |
| Port Charlotte | 25,770 | 33952 |
| Port Orange | 18,756 | 32019 |
| Port St. Lucie | 14,690 | 33452 |
| Punta Gorda | 6,797 | 33950* |
| Quincy | 8,591 | 32351 |
| Riviera Beach | 26,489 | 33404 |
| Rockledge | 11,877 | 32955 |
| Safety Harbor | 6,461 | 33572 |
| St. Augustine | 11,985 | 32084 |
| St. Cloud | 7,840 | 32769 |
| St. Petersburg | 238,647 | 33733* |
| St. Petersburg Bch. | 9,354 | 33736 |
| Sanford | 23,176 | 32771 |
| Sarasota | 48,868 | 33578* |
| Satellite Beach | 9,163 | 32901 |
| Sebring | 8,736 | 33870 |
| South Daytona | 11,252 | 32021 |
| South Miami | 10,944 | 33143 |
| Springfield | 7,220 | 32401 |
| Stuart | 9,467 | 33495 |
| Sunrise | 39,681 | 33313 |
| Sweetwater | 8,251 | 33144 |
| Tallahassee | 81,548 | 32301* |
| Tamarac | 29,376 | 33321 |
| Tampa | 271,523 | 33602* |
| Tarpon Springs | 13,251 | 33589* |
| Temple Terrace | 11,097 | 33617 |
| Titusville | 31,910 | 32780 |
| Treasure Island | 6,316 | 33740 |
| Valparaiso | 6,142 | 32580 |
| Venice | 12,153 | 33595* |
| Vero Beach | 16,176 | 32960 |
| West Palm Beach | 63,305 | 33401* |
| Wilton Manors | 12,742 | 33305 |
| Winter Garden | 6,789 | 32787 |
| Winter Haven | 21,119 | 33880 |
| Winter Park | 22,339 | 32789* |
| Winter Springs | 10,475 | 32708 |

**GEORGIA**

| LOCATION | POPULATION | ZIP |
|---|---|---|
| Albany | 74,550 | 31706* |
| Americus | 16,120 | 31709 |
| Athens | 42,549 | 30601* |

| LOCATION | POPULATION | ZIP |
|---|---|---|
| Atlanta | 425,022 | 30301* |
| Augusta | 47,532 | 30903* |
| Bainbridge | 10,553 | 31717 |
| Brunswick | 17,605 | 31520 |
| Cairo | 8,777 | 31728 |
| Carrollton | 14,078 | 30117 |
| Cartersville | 9,247 | 30120 |
| Cedartown | 8,619 | 30125 |
| Chamblee | 7,137 | 30341 |
| College Park | 24,632 | 30337 |
| Columbus | 169,441 | 31908* |
| Cordele | 11,184 | 31015 |
| Covington | 10,586 | 30209 |
| Dalton | 20,939 | 30720 |
| Decatur | 18,404 | 30030* |
| Doraville | 7,414 | 30340 |
| Douglas | 10,980 | 31533 |
| Dublin | 16,083 | 31021 |
| East Point | 37,486 | 30344 |
| Elberton | 5,686 | 30635 |
| Fitzgerald | 10,187 | 31750 |
| Forest Park | 18,782 | 30050 |
| Fort Valley | 9,000 | 31030 |
| Gainesville | 15,280 | 30501 |
| Griffin | 20,728 | 30223 |
| Hapeville | 6,166 | 30354 |
| Hinesville | 11,309 | 31313 |
| Jesup | 9,418 | 31545 |
| La Grange | 24,204 | 30240 |
| Macon | 116,896 | 31201* |
| Marietta | 30,829 | 30060* |
| Milledgeville | 12,176 | 31061 |
| Monroe | 8,854 | 30655 |
| Moultrie | 15,708 | 31768 |
| Newnan | 11,449 | 30263 |
| Perry | 9,453 | 31069 |
| Rome | 29,654 | 30161 |
| Roswell | 23,337 | 30075* |
| Savannah | 141,390 | 31402* |
| Smyrna | 20,312 | 30080 |
| Statesboro | 14,866 | 30458 |
| Swainsboro | 7,602 | 30401 |
| Thomaston | 9,682 | 30286 |
| Thomasville | 18,463 | 31792 |
| Thomson | 7,001 | 30824 |
| Tifton | 13,749 | 31794 |
| Toccoa | 9,104 | 30577 |
| Valdosta | 37,596 | 31601 |
| Vidalia | 10,393 | 30474 |
| Warner Robins | 39,893 | 31093 |
| Waycross | 19,371 | 31501 |
| Winder | 6,705 | 30680 |
| **GUAM** | | |
| Tamuning | — | 96911 |
| **HAWAII** | | |
| Aiea | 32,879 | 96701 |
| Ewa Beach | 14,369 | 96706 |
| Hilo | 35,269 | 96720 |
| Honolulu | 365,048 | 96820* |
| Kahului | 12,978 | 96732 |
| Kailua | 35,812 | 96734 |
| Kaneohe | 29,919 | 96744 |
| Lahaina | 6,095 | 96761 |
| Lihue | 4,000 | 96766 |
| Mokapu | 11,615 | 96734 |
| Nanakuli | 8,185 | 96792 |
| Pearl City | 42,575 | 96782 |
| Schofield Barracks | 18,851 | 96786 |
| Wahiawa | 16,911 | 96786 |
| Wailuku | 10,260 | 96793 |
| Waipahu | 29,139 | 96797 |
| **IDAHO** | | |
| Blackfoot | 10,065 | 83221 |
| Boise | 102,160 | 83701* |
| Burley | 8,761 | 83318 |
| Caldwell | 17,699 | 83605 |
| Chubbock | 7,052 | 83202 |
| Coeur d'Alene | 20,054 | 83814 |
| Idaho Falls | 39,590 | 83401 |
| Lewiston | 27,986 | 83501 |
| Moscow | 16,513 | 83843 |
| Mountain Home | 7,540 | 83647 |
| Nampa | 25,112 | 83651 |
| Pocatello | 46,340 | 83201 |
| Rexburg | 11,559 | 83440 |
| Twin Falls | 26,209 | 83301 |

| LOCATION | POPULATION | ZIP |
|---|---|---|
| **ILLINOIS** | | |
| Addison | 29,759 | 60101 |
| Alsip | 17,134 | 60658 |
| Alton | 34,171 | 62002 |
| Arlington Hts. | 66,116 | 60004* |
| Aurora | 81,293 | 60504* |
| Barrington | 9,029 | 60010 |
| Bartlett | 13,254 | 60103 |
| Batavia | 12,574 | 60510 |
| Beardstown | 6,338 | 62618 |
| Belleville | 41,580 | 62220* |
| Bellwood | 19,811 | 60104 |
| Belvidere | 15,176 | 61008 |
| Bensenville | 16,124 | 60106 |
| Benton | 7,778 | 62812 |
| Berwyn | 46,849 | 60402 |
| Bethalto | 8,630 | 62010 |
| Bloomingdale | 12,659 | 60108 |
| Bloomington | 44,189 | 61701 |
| Blue Island | 21,855 | 60406 |
| Bolingbrook | 37,261 | 60439 |
| Bourbonnais | 13,280 | 60914 |
| Bradley | 11,008 | 60915 |
| Bridgeview | 14,155 | 60455 |
| Broadview | 8,618 | 60153 |
| Brookfield | 19,395 | 60513 |
| Buffalo Grove | 22,230 | 60090 |
| Burbank | 28,462 | 60459 |
| Cahokia | 18,904 | 62206 |
| Calumet City | 39,697 | 60409 |
| Calumet Park | 8,788 | 60643 |
| Canton | 14,626 | 61520 |
| Carbondale | 26,414 | 62901 |
| Carol Stream | 15,472 | 60187 |
| Carpentersville | 23,272 | 60110 |
| Centralia | 15,126 | 62801 |
| Centreville | 9,747 | 62206 |
| Champaign | 58,133 | 61820 |
| Charleston | 19,355 | 61920 |
| Chicago | 3,005,072 | 60601* |
| Chicago Heights | 37,026 | 60411 |
| Chicago Ridge | 13,473 | 60415 |
| Cicero | 61,232 | 60650 |
| Clarendon Hills | 6,870 | 60514 |
| Clinton | 8,014 | 61727 |
| Collinsville | 19,613 | 62234 |
| Country Club Hills | 14,676 | 60477 |
| Crest Hill | 9,252 | 60431 |
| Crestwood | 10,852 | 60445 |
| Creve Coeur | 6,851 | 61611 |
| Crystal Lake | 18,590 | 60014 |
| Danville | 38,985 | 61832 |
| Darien | 14,536 | 60559 |
| Decatur | 94,081 | 62521* |
| Deerfield | 17,430 | 60015 |
| De Kalb | 33,099 | 60115 |
| Des Plaines | 53,568 | 60016* |
| Dixon | 15,701 | 61021 |
| Dolton | 24,766 | 60419 |
| Downers Grove | 42,572 | 60515 |
| Du Quoin | 6,594 | 62832 |
| East Alton | 7,096 | 62024 |
| East Moline | 20,907 | 61244 |
| East Peoria | 22,385 | 61611 |
| East St. Louis | 55,200 | 62201* |
| Edwardsville | 12,480 | 62025 |
| Effingham | 11,270 | 62401 |
| Elgin | 63,981 | 60120 |
| Elk Grove Village | 28,907 | 60007 |
| Elmhurst | 44,276 | 60126 |
| Elmwood Park | 24,016 | 60635 |
| Evanston | 73,706 | 60204* |
| Evergreen Park | 22,260 | 60642 |
| Fairview Heights | 12,414 | 62208 |
| Flossmoor | 8,423 | 60422 |
| Forest Park | 15,177 | 60130 |
| Franklin Park | 17,507 | 60131 |
| Freeport | 26,266 | 61032 |
| Galesburg | 35,305 | 61401 |
| Geneva | 9,881 | 60134 |
| Glencoe | 9,200 | 60022 |
| Glendale Heights | 23,163 | 60108 |
| Glen Ellyn | 23,717 | 60137 |
| Glenview | 32,060 | 60025 |
| Glenwood | 10,538 | 60425 |
| Granite City | 36,815 | 62040 |
| Hanover Park | 28,719 | 60103 |
| Harrisburg | 10,410 | 62946 |
| Harvey | 35,810 | 60426 |
| Harwood Heights | 8,228 | 60656 |
| Hazel Crest | 13,973 | 60429 |
| Herrin | 10,708 | 62948 |
| Hickory Hills | 13,778 | 60457 |
| Highland Park | 30,611 | 60035 |
| Hillside | 8,279 | 60162 |
| Hinsdale | 16,726 | 60521 |
| Hoffman Estates | 37,272 | 60195 |
| Homewood | 19,724 | 60430 |
| Hoopeston | 6,411 | 60942 |
| Jacksonville | 20,284 | 62650 |
| Jerseyville | 7,506 | 62052 |
| Joliet | 77,956 | 60431* |
| Justice | 10,552 | 60458 |
| Kankakee | 30,141 | 60901 |
| Kewanee | 14,508 | 61443 |
| La Grange | 15,445 | 60525 |
| La Grange Park | 13,359 | 60525 |
| Lake Forest | 15,245 | 60045 |
| Lansing | 29,039 | 60438 |
| La Salle | 10,347 | 61301 |
| Libertyville | 16,520 | 60048 |
| Lincoln | 16,327 | 62656 |
| Lincolnwood | 11,921 | 60645 |
| Lisle | 13,625 | 60532 |
| Litchfield | 7,204 | 62056 |
| Lockport | 9,170 | 60441 |
| Lombard | 36,897 | 60148 |
| Loves Park | 13,192 | 61111 |
| Lyons | 9,925 | 60534 |
| Macomb | 19,863 | 61455 |
| Marion | 14,031 | 62959 |
| Markham | 15,172 | 60426 |
| Matteson | 10,223 | 60443 |
| Mattoon | 19,055 | 61938 |
| Maywood | 27,998 | 60153 |
| McHenry | 10,908 | 60050 |
| Melrose Park | 20,735 | 60160* |
| Mendota | 7,134 | 61342 |
| Metropolis | 7,171 | 62960 |
| Midlothian | 14,274 | 60445 |
| Moline | 46,278 | 61265 |
| Monmouth | 10,706 | 61462 |
| Morris | 8,833 | 60450 |
| Morton | 14,178 | 61550 |
| Morton Grove | 23,747 | 60053 |
| Mount Carmel | 8,908 | 62863 |
| Mount Prospect | 52,634 | 60056 |
| Mount Vernon | 17,193 | 62864 |
| Mundelein | 17,053 | 60060 |
| Murphysboro | 9,866 | 62966 |
| Naperville | 42,601 | 60540 |
| Niles | 30,363 | 60648 |
| Normal | 35,672 | 61761 |
| Norridge | 16,483 | 60656 |
| Northbrook | 30,778 | 60062 |
| North Chicago | 38,774 | 60064 |
| Northlake | 12,166 | 60164 |
| North Riverside | 6,764 | 60546 |
| Oak Forest | 26,096 | 60452 |
| Oak Lawn | 60,590 | 60454* |
| Oak Park | 54,887 | 60303* |
| O'Fallon | 12,241 | 62269 |
| Olney | 9,026 | 62450 |
| Orland Park | 23,045 | 60462 |
| Ottawa | 18,166 | 61350 |
| Palatine | 32,166 | 60067 |
| Palos Heights | 11,096 | 60463 |
| Palos Hills | 16,654 | 60465 |
| Paris | 9,885 | 61944 |
| Park Forest | 26,222 | 60466 |
| Park Ridge | 38,704 | 60068 |
| Pekin | 33,967 | 61554 |
| Peoria | 124,160 | 61601* |
| Peoria Heights | 7,453 | 61614 |
| Peru | 10,886 | 61354 |
| Pontiac | 11,227 | 61764 |
| Princeton | 7,342 | 61356 |
| Prospect Heights | 11,808 | 60070 |
| Quincy | 42,554 | 62301 |
| Rantoul | 20,161 | 61866 |
| Richton Park | 9,403 | 60471 |
| Riverdale | 13,233 | 60627 |
| River Forest | 12,392 | 60305 |
| River Grove | 10,368 | 60171 |
| Riverside | 9,236 | 60546 |
| Robbins | 8,853 | 60472 |
| Robinson | 7,285 | 62454 |
| Rochelle | 8,982 | 61068 |
| Rock Falls | 10,633 | 61071 |
| Rockford | 139,712 | 61125* |
| Rock Island | 46,928 | 61201 |
| Rolling Meadows | 20,167 | 60008 |
| Romeoville | 15,519 | 60441 |

| LOCATION | POPULATION | ZIP |
|---|---|---|
| Roselle | 16,948 | 60172 |
| Round Lake Beach | 12,921 | 60073 |
| St. Charles | 17,492 | 60174 |
| Sauk Village | 10,906 | 60411 |
| Schaumburg | 53,305 | 60194 |
| Schiller Park | 11,458 | 60176 |
| Skokie | 60,278 | 60076* |
| South Holland | 24,977 | 60473 |
| Springfield | 100,054 | 62701* |
| Steger | 9,269 | 60475 |
| Sterling | 16,281 | 61081 |
| Streamwood | 23,456 | 60103 |
| Streator | 14,795 | 61364 |
| Summit | 10,110 | 60501 |
| Sycamore | 9,219 | 60178 |
| Taylorville | 11,386 | 62568 |
| Tinley Park | 26,171 | 60477 |
| Urbana | 35,978 | 61801 |
| Vernon Hills | 9,827 | 60061 |
| Villa Park | 23,185 | 60181 |
| Washington | 10,364 | 61571 |
| Washington Park | 8,223 | 62204 |
| Waukegan | 67,653 | 60085 |
| Westchester | 17,730 | 60153 |
| West Chicago | 12,550 | 60185 |
| Western Springs | 12,876 | 60558 |
| West Frankfort | 9,437 | 62896 |
| Westmont | 16,718 | 60559 |
| Wheaton | 43,043 | 60187 |
| Wheeling | 23,266 | 60090 |
| Wilmette | 28,229 | 60091 |
| Winnetka | 12,772 | 60093 |
| Wood Dale | 11,251 | 60191 |
| Woodridge | 22,561 | 60517 |
| Wood River | 12,446 | 62095 |
| Woodstock | 11,725 | 60098 |
| Worth | 11,592 | 60482 |
| Zion | 17,861 | 60099 |

**INDIANA**

| LOCATION | POPULATION | ZIP |
|---|---|---|
| Anderson | 64,695 | 46011* |
| Auburn | 8,122 | 46706 |
| Bedford | 14,410 | 47421 |
| Beech Grove | 13,196 | 46107 |
| Bloomington | 52,044 | 47401 |
| Bluffton | 8,705 | 46714 |
| Brazil | 7,852 | 47834 |
| Carmel | 18,272 | 46032 |
| Cedar Lake | 8,754 | 46303 |
| Clarksville | 15,164 | 47130 |
| Columbus | 30,614 | 47201 |
| Connersville | 17,023 | 47331 |
| Crawfordsville | 13,325 | 47933 |
| Crown Point | 16,455 | 46307 |
| Decatur | 8,649 | 46733 |
| Dyer | 9,555 | 46311 |
| East Chicago | 39,786 | 46312 |
| Elkhart | 41,305 | 46514 |
| Elwood | 10,867 | 46036 |
| Evansville | 130,496 | 47708* |
| Fort Wayne | 172,028 | 46802* |
| Frankfort | 15,168 | 46041 |
| Franklin | 11,563 | 46131 |
| Gary | 151,953 | 46401* |
| Goshen | 19,665 | 46526 |
| Greencastle | 8,403 | 46135 |
| Greenfield | 11,299 | 46140 |
| Greensburg | 9,254 | 47240 |
| Greenwood | 19,327 | 46142 |
| Griffith | 17,026 | 46319 |
| Hammond | 93,714 | 46320* |
| Hartford City | 7,622 | 47348 |
| Highland | 25,935 | 46322 |
| Hobart | 22,987 | 46342 |
| Huntington | 16,202 | 46750 |
| Indianapolis | 700,807 | 46206* |
| Jasper | 9,097 | 47546 |
| Jeffersonville | 21,220 | 47130 |
| Kendallville | 7,299 | 46755 |
| Kokomo | 47,808 | 46901 |
| Lafayette | 43,011 | 47901* |
| Lake Station | 14,294 | 46405 |
| LaPorte | 21,796 | 46350 |
| Lawrence | 25,591 | 46226 |
| Lebanon | 11,456 | 46052 |
| Logansport | 17,731 | 46947 |
| Madison | 12,472 | 47250 |
| Marion | 35,874 | 46952 |
| Martinsville | 11,311 | 46151 |
| Merrillville | 27,677 | 46410 |
| Michigan City | 36,850 | 46360 |
| Mishawaka | 40,201 | 46544 |
| Mount Vernon | 7,656 | 47620 |
| Muncie | 77,216 | 47302* |
| Munster | 20,671 | 46321 |
| New Albany | 37,103 | 47150 |
| New Castle | 20,056 | 47362 |
| Noblesville | 12,056 | 46060 |
| Peru | 13,764 | 46970 |
| Plainfield | 9,191 | 46168 |
| Plymouth | 7,693 | 46563 |
| Portage | 27,409 | 46368 |
| Portland | 7,074 | 47371 |
| Princeton | 8,976 | 47670 |
| Richmond | 41,349 | 47374 |
| Rushville | 6,113 | 46173 |
| Schererville | 13,209 | 46375 |
| Seymour | 15,050 | 47274 |
| Shelbyville | 14,989 | 46176 |
| South Bend | 109,727 | 46624* |
| Speedway | 12,641 | 46224 |
| Tell City | 8,704 | 47586 |
| Terre Haute | 61,125 | 47808* |
| Valparaiso | 22,247 | 46383 |
| Vincennes | 20,857 | 47591 |
| Wabash | 12,985 | 46992 |
| Warsaw | 10,647 | 46580 |
| Washington | 11,325 | 47501 |
| West Lafayette | 21,247 | 47906 |

**IOWA**

| LOCATION | POPULATION | ZIP |
|---|---|---|
| Ames | 45,775 | 50010 |
| Ankeny | 15,429 | 50021 |
| Atlantic | 7,789 | 50022 |
| Bettendorf | 27,381 | 52722 |
| Boone | 12,602 | 50036 |
| Burlington | 29,529 | 52601 |
| Carroll | 9,705 | 51401 |
| Cedar Falls | 36,322 | 50613 |
| Cedar Rapids | 110,243 | 52401* |
| Centerville | 6,558 | 52544 |
| Charles City | 8,778 | 50616 |
| Cherokee | 7,004 | 51012 |
| Clear Lake | 7,458 | 50428 |
| Clinton | 32,828 | 52732 |
| Coralville | 7,687 | 52241 |
| Council Bluffs | 56,449 | 51501 |
| Creston | 8,429 | 50801 |
| Davenport | 103,264 | 52802* |
| Decorah | 7,991 | 52101 |
| Denison | 6,675 | 51442 |
| Des Moines | 191,003 | 50318* |
| Dubuque | 62,321 | 52001 |
| Estherville | 7,518 | 51334 |
| Fairfield | 9,428 | 52556 |
| Fort Dodge | 29,423 | 50501 |
| Fort Madison | 13,520 | 52627 |
| Grinnell | 8,868 | 50112 |
| Indianola | 10,843 | 50125 |
| Iowa City | 50,508 | 52240 |
| Iowa Falls | 6,174 | 50126 |
| Keokuk | 13,536 | 52632 |
| Knoxville | 8,143 | 50138 |
| Le Mars | 8,276 | 51031 |
| Marion | 19,474 | 52302 |
| Marshalltown | 26,938 | 50158 |
| Mason City | 30,144 | 50401 |
| Mount Pleasant | 7,322 | 52641 |
| Muscatine | 23,467 | 52761 |
| Newton | 15,292 | 50208 |
| Oelwein | 7,564 | 50662 |
| Oskaloosa | 10,989 | 52577 |
| Ottumwa | 27,381 | 52501 |
| Pella | 8,349 | 50219 |
| Perry | 7,053 | 50220 |
| Red Oak | 6,810 | 51566 |
| Sioux City | 82,003 | 51101* |
| Spencer | 11,726 | 51301 |
| Storm Lake | 8,814 | 50588 |
| Urbandale | 17,869 | 50322 |
| Waterloo | 75,985 | 50701* |
| Waverly | 8,444 | 50677 |
| Webster City | 8,572 | 50595 |
| West Des Moines | 21,894 | 50265 |

**KANSAS**

| LOCATION | POPULATION | ZIP |
|---|---|---|
| Abilene | 6,572 | 67410 |
| Arkansas City | 13,201 | 67005 |
| Atchison | 11,407 | 66002 |
| Augusta | 6,968 | 67010 |
| Chanute | 10,506 | 66720 |
| Coffeyville | 15,185 | 67337 |
| Concordia | 6,847 | 66901 |
| Derby | 9,786 | 67037 |
| Dodge City | 18,001 | 67801 |
| El Dorado | 10,510 | 67042 |
| Emporia | 25,287 | 66801 |
| Fort Scott | 8,893 | 66701 |
| Garden City | 18,256 | 67846 |
| Great Bend | 16,608 | 67530 |
| Hays | 16,301 | 67601 |
| Haysville | 8,006 | 67060 |
| Hutchinson | 40,284 | 67501 |
| Independence | 10,598 | 67301 |
| Iola | 6,938 | 66749 |
| Junction City | 19,305 | 66441 |
| Kansas City | 161,148 | 66110* |
| Lawrence | 52,738 | 66044 |
| Leavenworth | 33,656 | 66048 |
| Leawood | 13,360 | 66206 |
| Lenexa | 18,639 | 66215 |
| Liberal | 14,911 | 67901 |
| Manhattan | 32,644 | 66502 |
| McPherson | 11,753 | 67460 |
| Merriam | 10,794 | 66203 |
| Mission | 8,643 | 66205 |
| Newton | 16,332 | 67114 |
| Olathe | 37,258 | 66061 |
| Ottawa | 11,016 | 66067 |
| Overland Park | 81,784 | 66204 |
| Parsons | 12,898 | 67357 |
| Pittsburg | 18,770 | 66762 |
| Prairie Village | 24,657 | 66208 |
| Pratt | 6,885 | 67124 |
| Roeland Park | 7,962 | 66205 |
| Salina | 41,843 | 67401 |
| Shawnee | 29,653 | 66202* |
| Topeka | 115,266 | 66601* |
| Wellington | 8,212 | 67152 |
| Wichita | 279,835 | 67209* |
| Winfield | 10,736 | 67156 |

**KENTUCKY**

| LOCATION | POPULATION | ZIP |
|---|---|---|
| Ashland | 27,064 | 41101 |
| Bellevue | 7,678 | 41073 |
| Berea | 8,226 | 40403 |
| Bowling Green | 40,450 | 42101 |
| Campbellsville | 8,715 | 42718 |
| Corbin | 8,075 | 40701 |
| Covington | 49,563 | 41011* |
| Danville | 12,942 | 40422 |
| Dayton | 6,979 | 41074 |
| Edgewood | 7,230 | 41017 |
| Elizabethtown | 15,380 | 42701 |
| Elsmere | 7,203 | 41018 |
| Erlanger | 14,433 | 41018 |
| Flatwoods | 8,354 | 41139 |
| Florence | 15,586 | 41042 |
| Fort Mitchell | 7,297 | 41017 |
| Fort Thomas | 16,012 | 41075 |
| Frankfort | 25,973 | 40601 |
| Franklin | 7,738 | 42134 |
| Georgetown | 10,972 | 40324 |
| Glasgow | 12,958 | 42141 |
| Harrodsburg | 7,265 | 40330 |
| Henderson | 24,834 | 42420 |
| Hopkinsville | 27,318 | 42240 |
| Independence | 7,998 | 41051 |
| Jeffersontown | 15,795 | 40299 |
| Lebanon | 6,590 | 40033 |
| Lexington | 204,165 | 40507* |
| Louisville | 298,840 | 40202* |
| Madisonville | 16,979 | 42431 |
| Mayfield | 10,705 | 42066 |
| Maysville | 7,983 | 41056 |
| Middlesborough | 12,251 | 40965 |
| Morehead | 7,789 | 40351 |
| Murray | 14,248 | 42071 |
| Newport | 21,587 | 41071* |
| Nicholasville | 10,319 | 40356 |
| Owensboro | 54,450 | 42301 |
| Paducah | 29,315 | 42001 |
| Paris | 7,935 | 40361 |
| Princeton | 7,073 | 42445 |
| Radcliff | 14,519 | 40160 |
| Richmond | 21,705 | 40475 |
| Russellville | 7,520 | 42276 |
| St. Matthews | 13,519 | 40207 |
| Shively | 16,819 | 40216 |
| Somerset | 10,649 | 42501 |
| Versailles | 6,427 | 40383 |
| Winchester | 15,216 | 40391 |

**LOUISIANA**

| LOCATION | POPULATION | ZIP |
|---|---|---|
| Abbeville | 12,391 | 70510 |
| Alexandria | 51,565 | 71301 |
| Baker | 12,865 | 70714 |
| Bastrop | 15,527 | 71220 |
| Baton Rouge | 219,419 | 70821* |
| Bogalusa | 16,976 | 70427 |
| Bossier City | 50,817 | 71111* |
| Cooper Road | — | 71107 |
| Covington | 7,892 | 70433 |
| Crowley | 16,036 | 70526 |
| Denham Springs | 8,563 | 70726 |
| De Ridder | 11,057 | 70634 |
| Donaldsonville | 7,901 | 70346 |
| Eunice | 12,749 | 70535 |
| Franklin | 9,584 | 70538 |
| Gonzales | 7,287 | 70737 |
| Gretna | 20,615 | 70053 |
| Hammond | 15,043 | 70401 |
| Harahan | 11,384 | 70123 |
| Harvey | 22,709 | 70058 |
| Houma | 32,602 | 70360 |
| Jeanerette | 6,511 | 70544 |
| Jennings | 12,401 | 70546 |
| Kenner | 66,382 | 70062 |
| Lafayette | 81,961 | 70501* |
| Lake Charles | 75,226 | 70601* |
| Lake Providence | 6,361 | 71254 |
| Leesville | 9,054 | 71446 |
| Mansfield | 6,485 | 71052 |
| Marrero | 36,548 | 70072 |
| Metairie | 164,160 | 70001* |
| Minden | 15,084 | 71055 |
| Monroe | 57,597 | 71201* |
| Morgan City | 16,114 | 70380 |
| Natchitoches | 16,664 | 71457 |
| New Iberia | 32,766 | 70560 |
| New Orleans | 557,927 | 70140* |
| Oakdale | 7,155 | 71463 |
| Opelousas | 18,903 | 70570 |
| Pineville | 12,034 | 71360 |
| Plaquemine | 7,521 | 70764 |
| Rayne | 9,066 | 70578 |
| Reserve | 7,288 | 70084 |
| Ruston | 20,585 | 71270 |
| St. Martinsville | 7,965 | 70582 |
| Scotlandville | 15,113 | 70807 |
| Shreveport | 205,820 | 71101* |
| Slidell | 26,718 | 70458 |
| Springhill | 6,516 | 71075 |
| Sulphur | 19,709 | 70663 |
| Tallulah | 11,634 | 71282 |
| Thibodaux | 15,810 | 70301 |
| Ville Platte | 9,201 | 70586 |
| West Monroe | 14,993 | 71291 |
| Westwego | 12,663 | 70094 |
| Winnfield | 7,311 | 71483 |
| Zachary | 7,297 | 70791 |

**MAINE**

| LOCATION | POPULATION | ZIP |
|---|---|---|
| Auburn | 23,128 | 04210 |
| Augusta | 21,819 | 04330 |
| Bangor | 31,643 | 04401 |
| Bath | 10,246 | 04530 |
| Biddeford | 19,638 | 04005 |
| Brewer | 9,017 | 04412 |
| Brunswick | 17,366 | 04011 |
| Cape Elizabeth | 7,838 | 04107 |
| Caribou | 9,916 | 04736 |
| Falmouth | 6,853 | 04105 |
| Gardiner | 6,485 | 04345 |
| Gorham | 10,101 | 04038 |
| Houlton | 6,766 | 04730 |
| Kittery | 9,314 | 03904 |
| Lewiston | 40,481 | 04240 |
| Limestone | 8,719 | 04750 |
| Lisbon | 8,769 | 04250 |
| Millinocket | 7,567 | 04462 |
| Old Town | 8,422 | 04468 |
| Orono | 10,578 | 04473 |
| Portland | 61,572 | 04101* |
| Presque Isle | 11,172 | 04769 |
| Rockland | 7,919 | 04841 |
| Rumford | 8,240 | 04276 |
| Saco | 12,921 | 04072 |
| Sanford | 18,020 | 04073 |
| Scarborough | 11,347 | 04074 |
| Skowhegan | 8,098 | 04976 |
| South Portland | 22,712 | 04106 |
| Waterville | 17,779 | 04901 |
| Westbrook | 14,976 | 04092 |
| Windham | 11,282 | 04082 |
| Winslow | 8,057 | 04901 |

**MARYLAND**

| LOCATION | POPULATION | ZIP |
|---|---|---|
| Aberdeen | 11,533 | 21001 |
| Annapolis | 31,740 | 21401* |
| Arbutus | 20,163 | 21227 |
| Aspen Hill | 47,455 | 20906 |
| Baltimore | 786,775 | 21233* |
| Bel Air | 7,814 | 21014 |
| Beltsville | 12,760 | 20705 |
| Bethesda | 62,736 | 20014* |
| Bladensburg | 7,691 | 20710 |
| Bowie | 33,695 | 20715 |
| Brooklyn | — | 21225 |
| Cambridge | 11,703 | 21613 |
| Camp Springs | 16,118 | 20743 |
| Catonsville | 33,208 | 21228 |
| Cheverly | 5,751 | 20785 |
| Chevy Chase | 12,232 | 20815 |
| Chillum | 32,775 | 20783 |
| Colesville | 14,359 | 20904 |
| College Park | 23,614 | 20740 |
| Columbia | 52,518 | 21045 |
| Cumberland | 25,933 | 21502 |
| Defense Heights | — | 20784 |
| District Heights | 6,799 | 20747 |
| Dundalk | 71,293 | 21222 |
| Easton | 7,536 | 21601 |
| Edgewood | 19,455 | 21040 |
| Elkton | 6,468 | 21921 |
| Ellicott City | 21,784 | 21043 |
| Essex | 39,614 | 21221 |
| Ferndale | 14,314 | 21061 |
| Forestville | 16,401 | 20028 |
| Frederick | 28,086 | 21701 |
| Frostburg | 7,715 | 21532 |
| Gaithersburg | 26,424 | 20760 |
| Glen Burnie | 37,263 | 21061 |
| Greenbelt | 17,332 | 20770 |
| Hagerstown | 34,132 | 21740 |
| Havre de Grace | 8,763 | 21078 |
| Hillcrest Heights | 17,021 | 20031 |
| Hyattsville | 12,709 | 20781* |
| Joppatowne | 11,348 | 21085 |
| Kemp Mill | — | 20901 |
| Kentland | 8,596 | 20785 |
| Langley Park | 14,038 | 20787 |
| Lanham-Seabrook | 15,814 | 20801 |
| Lansdowne | — | 21227 |
| Laurel | 12,103 | 20810* |
| Lexington Park | 10,361 | 20653 |
| Linthicum | 7,457 | 21090 |
| Lutherville | — | 21093 |
| Middle River | 26,756 | 21220 |
| Mount Rainier | 7,361 | 20822 |
| New Carrollton | 12,632 | 20784 |
| Overlea | 12,965 | 21206 |
| Owings Mills | 9,526 | 21117 |
| Oxon Hill | 36,267 | 20745 |
| Parkville | 35,159 | 21234 |
| Pikesville | 22,555 | 21208 |
| Pumphrey | 5,666 | 21090 |
| Randallstown | 25,927 | 21133 |
| Randolph | — | 20853 |
| Reisterstown | 19,385 | 21136 |
| Riviera Beach | 8,812 | 21061 |
| Rockville | 43,811 | 20850* |
| Rosedale | 19,956 | 21237 |
| Salisbury | 16,429 | 21801 |
| Seat Pleasant | 5,217 | 20027 |
| Severna Park | 21,253 | 21146 |
| Silver Spring | 72,893 | 20907* |
| Suitland | — | 20746 |
| Takoma Park | 16,231 | 20912 |
| Towson | 51,083 | 21204 |
| Waldorf | 9,782 | 20601 |
| Westminster | 8,808 | 21157 |
| Wheaton | — | 20902 |
| White Oak | 13,700 | 20901 |
| Woodlawn | 5,306 | 21201 |

**MASSACHUSETTS**

| LOCATION | POPULATION | ZIP |
|---|---|---|
| Abington | 13,517 | 02351 |
| Acton | 17,544 | 01720 |
| Acushnet | 8,704 | 02743 |
| Adams | 10,381 | 01220 |
| Agawam | 26,271 | 01001 |
| Amesbury | 13,971 | 01913 |
| Amherst | 33,229 | 01002 |
| Andover | 26,370 | 01810 |
| Arlington | 48,219 | 02174 |
| Ashland | 9,165 | 01721 |
| Athol | 10,634 | 01331 |
| Attleboro | 34,196 | 02703 |
| Auburn | 14,845 | 01501 |
| Ayer | 6,993 | 01432* |
| Barnstable | 30,898 | 02630 |
| Bedford | 13,067 | 01730 |
| Belchertown | 8,339 | 01007 |
| Bellingham | 14,300 | 02019 |
| Belmont | 26,100 | 02178 |
| Beverly | 37,655 | 01915 |
| Billerica | 36,727 | 01821 |
| Blackstone | 6,570 | 01504 |
| Boston | 562,994 | 02109* |
| Bourne | 13,874 | 02532 |
| Braintree | 36,337 | 02184 |
| Bridgewater | 17,202 | 02324 |
| Brockton | 95,172 | 02403* |
| Brookline | 55,062 | 02146 |
| Burlington | 23,486 | 01803 |
| Cambridge | 95,322 | 02138 |
| Canton | 18,182 | 02021 |
| Carver | 6,988 | 02330 |
| Chelmsford | 31,174 | 01824 |
| Chelsea | 25,431 | 02150 |
| Chicopee | 55,112 | 01021* |
| Clinton | 12,771 | 01510 |
| Cohasset | 7,174 | 02025 |
| Concord | 16,293 | 01742 |
| Dalton | 6,797 | 01226 |
| Danvers | 24,100 | 01923 |
| Dartmouth | 23,966 | 02714 |
| Dedham | 25,298 | 02026 |
| Dennis | 12,360 | 02638 |
| Dracut | 21,249 | 01826 |
| Dudley | 8,717 | 01570 |
| Duxbury | 11,807 | 02332 |
| East Bridgewater | 9,945 | 02333 |
| Easthampton | 15,580 | 01027 |
| East Longmeadow | 12,905 | 01028 |
| Easton | 16,623 | 02334 |
| Everett | 37,195 | 02149 |
| Fairhaven | 15,759 | 02719 |
| Fall River | 92,574 | 02722* |
| Falmouth | 23,640 | 02540* |
| Fitchburg | 39,580 | 01420 |
| Foxboro | 14,148 | 02035 |
| Framingham | 65,113 | 01701 |
| Franklin | 18,217 | 02038 |
| Gardner | 17,900 | 01440 |
| Gloucester | 27,768 | 01930 |
| Grafton | 11,238 | 01519 |
| Great Barrington | 7,405 | 01230 |
| Greenfield | 18,436 | 01301 |
| Hamilton | 6,960 | 01936 |
| Hanover | 11,358 | 02339 |
| Hanson | 8,617 | 02341 |
| Harvard | 12,170 | 01451 |
| Harwich | 8,971 | 02645 |
| Haverhill | 46,865 | 01830 |
| Hingham | 20,339 | 02043 |
| Holbrook | 11,140 | 02343 |
| Holden | 13,336 | 01520 |
| Holliston | 12,622 | 01746 |
| Holyoke | 44,678 | 01040 |
| Hudson | 16,408 | 01749 |
| Hull | 9,714 | 02045 |
| Hyannis | 9,118 | 02601 |
| Ipswich | 11,158 | 01938 |
| Lawrence | 63,175 | 01842* |
| Lee | 6,247 | 01238 |
| Leicester | 9,446 | 01524 |
| Lenox | 6,523 | 01240 |
| Leominster | 34,508 | 01453 |
| Lexington | 29,479 | 02173 |
| Lincoln | 7,098 | 01773 |
| Littleton | 6,970 | 01460 |
| Longmeadow | 16,301 | 01106 |
| Lowell | 92,418 | 01853* |
| Ludlow | 18,150 | 01056 |
| Lunenburg | 8,405 | 01462 |
| Lynn | 78,471 | 01901* |
| Lynnfield | 11,267 | 01940 |
| Malden | 53,386 | 02148 |
| Mansfield | 13,453 | 02048 |
| Marblehead | 20,126 | 01945 |
| Marlborough | 30,617 | 01752 |
| Marshfield | 20,916 | 02050 |

| LOCATION | POPULATION | ZIP |
|---|---|---|
| Maynard | 9,590 | 01754 |
| Medfield | 10,220 | 02052 |
| Medford | 58,076 | 02155 |
| Medway | 8,447 | 02053 |
| Melrose | 30,055 | 02176 |
| Methuen | 36,701 | 01844 |
| Middleboro | 16,404 | 02346 |
| Milford | 23,390 | 01757 |
| Millbury | 11,808 | 01527 |
| Millis | 6,908 | 02054 |
| Milton | 25,860 | 02186 |
| Monson | 7,315 | 01057 |
| Montague | 8,011 | 01351 |
| Natick | 29,461 | 01760 |
| Needham | 27,901 | 02192 |
| New Bedford | 98,478 | 02740* |
| Newburyport | 15,900 | 01950 |
| Newton | 83,622 | 02158 |
| North Adams | 18,063 | 01247 |
| Northampton | 29,286 | 01060 |
| North Andover | 20,129 | 01845 |
| North Attleboro | 21,095 | 02760* |
| North Reading | 11,455 | 01864 |
| Norton | 12,690 | 02766 |
| Norwell | 9,182 | 02061 |
| Norwood | 29,711 | 02062 |
| Orange | 6,844 | 01364 |
| Oxford | 11,680 | 01540 |
| Palmer | 11,389 | 01069 |
| Peabody | 45,976 | 01960 |
| Pembroke | 13,487 | 02359 |
| Pepperell | 8,061 | 01463 |
| Pittsfield | 51,974 | 01201 |
| Plymouth | 35,913 | 02360 |
| Quincy | 84,743 | 02169 |
| Randolph | 28,218 | 02368 |
| Raynham | 9,085 | 02767 |
| Reading | 22,678 | 01867 |
| Rehoboth | 7,570 | 02769 |
| Revere | 42,423 | 02151 |
| Rockland | 15,695 | 02370 |
| Rockport | 6,345 | 01966 |
| Salem | 38,220 | 01970 |
| Sandwich | 8,727 | 02563 |
| Saugus | 24,746 | 01906 |
| Scituate | 17,317 | 02066 |
| Seekonk | 12,269 | 02771 |
| Sharon | 13,601 | 02067 |
| Shrewsbury | 22,674 | 01545 |
| Somerset | 18,813 | 02725 |
| Somerville | 77,372 | 02143 |
| Southbridge | 16,665 | 01550 |
| South Hadley | 16,399 | 01075 |
| Southwick | 7,382 | 01077 |
| Spencer | 10,774 | 01562 |
| Springfield | 152,319 | 01101* |
| Stoneham | 21,424 | 02180 |
| Stoughton | 26,710 | 02072 |
| Sudbury | 14,027 | 01776 |
| Swampscott | 13,837 | 01907 |
| Swansea | 15,461 | 02777 |
| Taunton | 45,001 | 02780 |
| Tewksbury | 24,635 | 01876 |
| Townsend | 7,201 | 01469 |
| Uxbridge | 8,374 | 01569 |
| Wakefield | 24,895 | 01880 |
| Walpole | 18,859 | 02081 |
| Waltham | 58,200 | 02154 |
| Ware | 8,953 | 01082 |
| Wareham | 18,457 | 02571 |
| Watertown | 34,384 | 02172 |
| Wayland | 12,170 | 01778 |
| Webster | 14,480 | 01570 |
| Wellesley | 27,209 | 02181 |
| Westboro | 13,619 | 01581 |
| West Bridgewater | 6,359 | 02379 |
| Westfield | 36,465 | 01085 |
| Westford | 13,434 | 01886 |
| Weston | 11,169 | 02193 |
| Westport | 13,763 | 02790 |
| West Springfield | 27,042 | 01089 |
| Westwood | 13,212 | 02090 |
| Weymouth | 55,601 | 02188 |
| Whitman | 13,534 | 02382 |
| Wilbraham | 12,053 | 01095 |
| Williamstown | 8,741 | 01267 |
| Wilmington | 17,471 | 01887 |
| Winchendon | 7,019 | 01475 |
| Winchester | 20,701 | 01890 |
| Winthrop | 19,294 | 02152 |
| Woburn | 36,626 | 01801 |
| Worcester | 161,799 | 01613* |
| Wrentham | 7,580 | 02093 |
| Yarmouth | 18,449 | 02675 |

**MICHIGAN**

| LOCATION | POPULATION | ZIP |
|---|---|---|
| Adrian | 21,186 | 49221 |
| Albion | 11,059 | 49224 |
| Allen Park | 34,196 | 48101 |
| Alma | 9,652 | 48801 |
| Alpena | 12,214 | 49707 |
| Ann Arbor | 107,966 | 48106* |
| Battle Creek | 35,724 | 49016* |
| Bay City | 41,593 | 48706 |
| Benton Harbor | 14,707 | 49022 |
| Berkley | 18,637 | 48072 |
| Beverly Hills | 11,598 | 48010 |
| Big Rapids | 14,361 | 49307 |
| Birmingham | 21,689 | 48012* |
| Burton | 29,976 | 48507 |
| Cadillac | 10,199 | 49601 |
| Center Line | 9,293 | 48015 |
| Charlotte | 8,251 | 48813 |
| Clawson | 15,103 | 48017 |
| Coldwater | 9,461 | 49036 |
| Dearborn | 90,660 | 48120* |
| Dearborn Heights | 67,706 | 48127 |
| Detroit | 1,203,339 | 48226* |
| Dowagiac | 6,307 | 49047 |
| East Detroit | 38,280 | 48021 |
| East Grand Rapids | 10,914 | 49506 |
| East Lansing | 51,392 | 48823 |
| Ecorse | 14,447 | 48229 |
| Escanaba | 14,355 | 49829 |
| Farmington | 11,022 | 48024* |
| Farmington Hills | 58,056 | 48024 |
| Fenton | 8,098 | 48430 |
| Ferndale | 26,227 | 48220 |
| Flat Rock | 6,853 | 48134 |
| Flint | 159,611 | 48502* |
| Flushing | 8,624 | 48433 |
| Fraser | 14,560 | 48026 |
| Garden City | 35,640 | 48135 |
| Grand Blanc | 6,848 | 48439 |
| Grand Haven | 11,763 | 49417 |
| Grand Ledge | 6,920 | 48837 |
| Grand Rapids | 181,843 | 49501* |
| Grandville | 12,412 | 49418 |
| Greenville | 8,019 | 48838 |
| Grosse Pointe | 5,901 | 48236 |
| Grosse Pte. Farms | 10,551 | 48236 |
| Grosse Pte. Pk. | 13,639 | 48236 |
| Grosse Pte. Woods | 18,886 | 48236 |
| Hamtramck | 21,300 | 48212 |
| Harper Woods | 16,361 | 48225 |
| Hastings | 6,418 | 49058 |
| Hazel Park | 20,914 | 48030 |
| Highland Park | 27,909 | 48203 |
| Hillsdale | 7,432 | 49242 |
| Holland | 26,281 | 49423 |
| Houghton | 7,512 | 49931 |
| Howell | 6,976 | 48843 |
| Huntington Woods | 6,937 | 48070 |
| Inkster | 35,190 | 48141 |
| Ionia | 5,920 | 48846 |
| Iron Mountain | 8,341 | 49801 |
| Ironwood | 7,741 | 49938 |
| Ishpeming | 7,538 | 49849 |
| Jackson | 39,739 | 49201* |
| Kalamazoo | 79,722 | 49003* |
| Kentwood | 30,438 | 49508 |
| Lansing | 130,414 | 48924* |
| Lapeer | 6,198 | 48446 |
| Lincoln Park | 45,105 | 48146 |
| Livonia | 104,814 | 48150 |
| Ludington | 8,937 | 49431 |
| Madison Heights | 35,375 | 48071 |
| Manistee | 7,566 | 49660 |
| Marquette | 23,288 | 49855 |
| Marshall | 7,201 | 49068 |
| Melvindale | 12,322 | 48122 |
| Menominee | 10,099 | 49858 |
| Midland | 37,250 | 48640 |
| Monroe | 23,531 | 48161 |
| Mount Clemens | 18,806 | 48043 |
| Mount Pleasant | 23,746 | 48858 |
| Muskegon | 40,823 | 49440* |
| Muskegon Heights | 14,611 | 49444 |
| Niles | 13,115 | 49120 |
| Norton Shores | 22,025 | 49441 |
| Novi | 22,525 | 48050 |
| Oak Park | 31,537 | 48237 |
| Owosso | 16,455 | 48867 |
| Petoskey | 6,097 | 49770 |
| Plymouth | 9,986 | 48170 |
| Pontiac | 76,715 | 48053* |
| Portage | 38,157 | 49081 |
| Port Huron | 33,981 | 48060 |
| River Rouge | 12,912 | 48218 |
| Riverview | 14,569 | 48192 |
| Rochester | 7,203 | 48063 |
| Romulus | 24,857 | 48174 |
| Roseville | 54,311 | 48066 |
| Royal Oak | 70,893 | 48067* |
| Saginaw | 77,508 | 48605* |
| St. Clair Shores | 76,210 | 48080* |
| St. Johns | 7,376 | 48879 |
| St. Joseph | 9,622 | 49085 |
| Saline | 6,483 | 48176 |
| Sault Ste. Marie | 14,448 | 49783 |
| Southfield | 75,568 | 48034* |
| Southgate | 32,058 | 48195 |
| South Haven | 5,943 | 49090 |
| Sterling Heights | 108,999 | 48077 |
| Sturgis | 9,468 | 49091 |
| Taylor | 77,568 | 48180 |
| Tecumseh | 7,320 | 49286 |
| Three Rivers | 7,015 | 49093 |
| Traverse City | 15,516 | 49684 |
| Trenton | 22,762 | 48183 |
| Troy | 67,102 | 48084* |
| Walker | 15,088 | 49504 |
| Warren | 161,134 | 48089* |
| Wayne | 21,159 | 48184 |
| Westland | 84,603 | 48185 |
| Wixom | 6,705 | 48096 |
| Woodhaven | 10,902 | 48183 |
| Wyandotte | 34,006 | 48192 |
| Wyoming | 59,616 | 49509 |
| Ypsilanti | 24,031 | 48197 |

**MINNESOTA**

| LOCATION | POPULATION | ZIP |
|---|---|---|
| Albert Lea | 19,200 | 56007 |
| Alexandria | 7,608 | 56308 |
| Andover | 9,387 | 55303 |
| Anoka | 15,634 | 55303 |
| Apple Valley | 21,818 | 55124 |
| Arden Hills | 8,012 | 55112 |
| Austin | 23,020 | 55912 |
| Bemidji | 10,949 | 56601 |
| Blaine | 28,558 | 55433 |
| Bloomington | 81,831 | 55420 |
| Brainerd | 11,489 | 56401 |
| Brooklyn Center | 31,230 | 55429 |
| Brooklyn Park | 43,332 | 55444 |
| Burnsville | 35,674 | 55337 |
| Champlin | 9,006 | 55316 |
| Chaska | 8,346 | 55318 |
| Cloquet | 11,142 | 55720 |
| Columbia Heights | 20,029 | 55421 |
| Coon Rapids | 35,826 | 55433 |
| Cottage Grove | 18,994 | 55016 |
| Crookston | 8,628 | 56716 |
| Crystal | 25,543 | 55428 |
| Detroit Lakes | 7,106 | 56501 |
| Duluth | 92,811 | 55806* |
| Eagan | 20,700 | 55121 |
| East Grand Forks | 8,537 | 56721 |
| Eden Prairie | 16,263 | 55344 |
| Edina | 46,073 | 55424 |
| Fairmont | 11,506 | 56031 |
| Faribault | 16,241 | 55021 |
| Fergus Falls | 12,519 | 56537 |
| Fridley | 30,228 | 55432 |
| Golden Valley | 22,775 | 55427 |
| Grand Rapids | 7,934 | 55744 |
| Ham Lake | 7,832 | 55304 |
| Hastings | 12,827 | 55033 |
| Hibbing | 21,193 | 55746 |
| Hopkins | 15,336 | 55343 |
| Hutchinson | 9,244 | 55350 |
| Inver Grove Hts. | 17,171 | 55075 |
| Lakeville | 14,790 | 55044 |
| Little Canada | 7,102 | 55110 |
| Little Falls | 7,250 | 56345 |
| Mankato | 28,651 | 56001 |
| Maple Grove | 20,525 | 55369 |
| Maplewood | 26,990 | 55109 |
| Marshall | 11,161 | 56258 |
| Mendota Heights | 7,288 | 55050 |
| Minneapolis | 370,951 | 55401* |
| Minnetonka | 38,683 | 55343 |
| Moorhead | 29,998 | 56560 |
| Mound | 9,280 | 55364 |

| LOCATION | POPULATION | ZIP |
|---|---|---|
| Mounds View | 12,593 | 55112 |
| New Brighton | 23,269 | 55112 |
| New Hope | 23,087 | 55428 |
| New Ulm | 13,755 | 56073 |
| Northfield | 12,562 | 55057 |
| North Mankato | 9,145 | 56001 |
| North St. Paul | 11,921 | 55109 |
| Oakdale | 12,123 | 55109 |
| Orono | 6,845 | 55323 |
| Owatonna | 18,632 | 55060 |
| Plymouth | 31,615 | 55441 |
| Prior Lake | 7,284 | 55372 |
| Ramsey | 10,093 | 55303 |
| Red Wing | 13,736 | 55066 |
| Richfield | 37,851 | 55423 |
| Robbinsdale | 14,422 | 55422 |
| Rochester | 57,890 | 55901 |
| Roseville | 35,820 | 55113 |
| St. Anthony | 7,981 | 55414 |
| St. Cloud | 42,566 | 56301 |
| St. Louis Park | 42,931 | 55426 |
| St. Paul | 270,230 | 55101* |
| St. Peter | 9,056 | 56082 |
| Shakopee | 9,941 | 55379 |
| Shoreview | 17,300 | 55112 |
| South St. Paul | 21,235 | 55075 |
| Spring Lake Pk. | 6,477 | 55432 |
| Stillwater | 12,290 | 55082 |
| Thief River Falls | 9,105 | 56701 |
| Virginia | 11,056 | 55792 |
| Waseca | 8,219 | 56093 |
| West St. Paul | 18,527 | 55118 |
| White Bear Lake | 22,538 | 55110 |
| Willmar | 15,895 | 56201 |
| Winona | 25,075 | 55987 |
| Woodbury | 10,297 | 55125 |
| Worthington | 10,243 | 56187 |

**MISSISSIPPI**

| LOCATION | POPULATION | ZIP |
|---|---|---|
| Aberdeen | 7,184 | 39730 |
| Amory | 7,307 | 38821 |
| Bay St. Louis | 7,891 | 39520 |
| Biloxi | 49,311 | 39530* |
| Brandon | 9,626 | 39042 |
| Brookhaven | 10,800 | 39601 |
| Canton | 11,116 | 39046 |
| Clarksdale | 21,137 | 38614 |
| Cleveland | 14,524 | 38732 |
| Clinton | 14,660 | 39056 |
| Columbia | 7,733 | 39429 |
| Columbus | 27,383 | 39701 |
| Corinth | 13,839 | 38834 |
| Greenville | 40,613 | 38701 |
| Greenwood | 20,115 | 38930 |
| Grenada | 12,641 | 38901 |
| Gulfport | 39,676 | 39501* |
| Hattiesburg | 40,829 | 39401 |
| Holly Springs | 7,285 | 38635 |
| Indianola | 8,221 | 38751 |
| Jackson | 202,895 | 39205* |
| Kosciusko | 7,415 | 39090 |
| Laurel | 21,897 | 39440 |
| Long Beach | 7,967 | 39560 |
| Louisville | 7,323 | 39339 |
| McComb | 12,331 | 39648 |
| Meridian | 46,577 | 39301 |
| Moss Point | 18,998 | 39563 |
| Natchez | 22,015 | 39120 |
| New Albany | 7,072 | 38652 |
| Ocean Springs | 14,504 | 39564 |
| Oxford | 9,882 | 38655 |
| Pascagoula | 29,318 | 39567 |
| Pearl | 18,580 | 39208 |
| Petal | 8,476 | 39465 |
| Picayune | 10,361 | 39466 |
| Starkville | 15,169 | 39759 |
| Tupelo | 23,905 | 38801 |
| Vicksburg | 25,434 | 39180 |
| West Point | 8,811 | 39773 |
| Yazoo City | 12,092 | 39194 |

**MISSOURI**

| LOCATION | POPULATION | ZIP |
|---|---|---|
| Arnold | 19,141 | 63010 |
| Ballwin | 12,656 | 63011 |
| Bellefontaine Neighbors | 12,082 | 63137 |
| Belton | 12,708 | 64012 |
| Berkeley | 15,922 | 63134 |
| Blue Springs | 25,927 | 64015 |
| Boonville | 6,959 | 65233 |
| Brentwood | 8,209 | 63144 |
| Bridgeton | 18,445 | 63044 |
| Cape Girardeau | 34,361 | 63701 |
| Carthage | 11,104 | 64836 |
| Caruthersville | 7,958 | 63830 |
| Chillicothe | 9,089 | 64601 |
| Clayton | 14,273 | 63105 |
| Clinton | 8,366 | 64735 |
| Columbia | 62,061 | 65201 |
| Crestwood | 12,815 | 63126 |
| Creve Coeur | 11,757 | 63141 |
| Des Peres | 8,254 | 63131 |
| Dexter | 7,043 | 63841 |
| Excelsior Springs | 10,424 | 64024 |
| Farmington | 8,270 | 63640 |
| Ferguson | 24,740 | 63135 |
| Festus | 7,574 | 63028 |
| Florissant | 55,372 | 63033* |
| Fulton | 11,046 | 65251 |
| Gladstone | 24,990 | 64118 |
| Grandview | 24,502 | 64030 |
| Hannibal | 18,811 | 63401 |
| Hazelwood | 12,935 | 63042* |
| Independence | 111,806 | 64050* |
| Jackson | 7,827 | 63755 |
| Jefferson City | 33,619 | 65101 |
| Jennings | 17,026 | 63136 |
| Joplin | 39,023 | 64801 |
| Kansas City | 448,159 | 64108* |
| Kennett | 10,145 | 63857 |
| Kirksville | 17,167 | 63501 |
| Kirkwood | 27,987 | 63122 |
| Ladue | 9,376 | 64758 |
| Lebanon | 9,507 | 65536 |
| Lee's Summit | 28,741 | 64063 |
| Liberty | 16,251 | 64068 |
| Maplewood | 10,960 | 63143 |
| Marshall | 12,781 | 65340 |
| Maryville | 9,558 | 64468 |
| Mexico | 12,276 | 65265 |
| Moberly | 13,418 | 65270 |
| Neosho | 9,493 | 64850 |
| Nevada | 9,044 | 64772 |
| O'Fallon | 8,677 | 63366 |
| Olivette | 7,985 | 63124 |
| Overland | 19,620 | 63114 |
| Perryville | 7,343 | 63775 |
| Pine Lawn | 6,662 | 63120 |
| Poplar Bluff | 17,139 | 63901 |
| Raytown | 31,759 | 64133 |
| Richmond Hts. | 11,516 | 63117 |
| Rolla | 13,303 | 65401 |
| St. Ann | 15,523 | 63074 |
| St. Charles | 37,379 | 63301 |
| St. John | 7,854 | 63114 |
| St. Joseph | 76,691 | 64501* |
| St. Louis | 453,085 | 63166* |
| St. Peters | 15,700 | 63376 |
| Sedalia | 20,927 | 65301 |
| Sikeston | 17,431 | 63801 |
| Springfield | 133,116 | 65801* |
| Trenton | 6,811 | 64683 |
| University City | 42,738 | 63130 |
| Warrensburg | 13,807 | 64093 |
| Washington | 9,251 | 63090 |
| Webb City | 7,309 | 64870 |
| Webster Groves | 23,097 | 63119 |
| West Plains | 7,741 | 65775 |

**MONTANA**

| LOCATION | POPULATION | ZIP |
|---|---|---|
| Anaconda | 12,518 | 59711 |
| Billings | 66,842 | 59101* |
| Bozeman | 21,645 | 59715 |
| Butte | 37,205 | 59701 |
| Great Falls | 56,725 | 59401 |
| Havre | 10,891 | 59501 |
| Helena | 23,938 | 59601 |
| Kalispell | 10,648 | 59901 |
| Lewistown | 7,104 | 59457 |
| Livingston | 6,994 | 59047 |
| Miles City | 9,602 | 59301 |
| Missoula | 33,388 | 59801 |

**NEBRASKA**

| LOCATION | POPULATION | ZIP |
|---|---|---|
| Alliance | 9,869 | 69301 |
| Beatrice | 12,891 | 68310 |
| Bellevue | 21,813 | 68005 |
| Columbus | 17,328 | 68601 |
| Fremont | 23,979 | 68025 |
| Gering | 7,760 | 69341 |
| Grand Island | 33,180 | 68801 |
| Hastings | 23,045 | 68901 |
| Kearney | 21,158 | 68847 |
| La Vista | 9,588 | 68046 |
| Lexington | 7,040 | 68850 |
| Lincoln | 171,932 | 68501* |
| McCook | 8,404 | 69001 |
| Nebraska City | 7,127 | 68410 |
| Norfolk | 19,449 | 68701 |
| North Platte | 24,509 | 69101 |
| Omaha | 313,911 | 68101* |
| Scottsbluff | 14,156 | 69361 |
| South Sioux City | 9,339 | 68776 |
| York | 7,723 | 68467 |

**NEVADA**

| LOCATION | POPULATION | ZIP |
|---|---|---|
| Boulder City | 9,590 | 89005 |
| Carson City | 32,022 | 89701 |
| East Las Vegas | 6,449 | 89112 |
| Elko | 8,758 | 89801 |
| Henderson | 24,363 | 89015 |
| Las Vegas | 164,674 | 89114* |
| North Las Vegas | 42,739 | 89030 |
| Paradise | 84,818 | 89119 |
| Reno | 100,756 | 89501* |
| Sparks | 40,780 | 89431 |

**NEW HAMPSHIRE**

| LOCATION | POPULATION | ZIP |
|---|---|---|
| Berlin | 13,084 | 03570 |
| Claremont | 14,557 | 03743 |
| Concord | 30,400 | 03301 |
| Derry | 18,875 | 03038 |
| Dover | 22,377 | 03820 |
| Durham | 10,652 | 03824 |
| Exeter | 11,024 | 03833 |
| Franklin | 7,901 | 03235 |
| Goffstown | 11,315 | 03045 |
| Hampton | 10,493 | 03842 |
| Hanover | 9,119 | 03755 |
| Hudson | 14,022 | 03051 |
| Keene | 21,449 | 03431 |
| Laconia | 15,575 | 03246 |
| Lebanon | 11,134 | 03766 |
| Manchester | 90,936 | 03101* |
| Merrimack | 15,406 | 03054 |
| Milford | 8,685 | 03055 |
| Nashua | 67,865 | 03060 |
| Portsmouth | 26,254 | 03801 |
| Rochester | 21,560 | 03867 |
| Salem | 24,124 | 03079 |
| Somersworth | 10,350 | 03878 |

**NEW JERSEY**

| LOCATION | POPULATION | ZIP |
|---|---|---|
| Aberdeen Twp | 17,235 | 07747 |
| Absecon | 6,859 | 08201 |
| Asbury Park | 17,015 | 07712 |
| Atlantic City | 40,199 | 08401* |
| Audubon | 9,533 | 08106 |
| Barnegat | 8,702 | 08005 |
| Barrington | 7,418 | 08007 |
| Bayonne | 65,047 | 07002 |
| Beachwood | 7,687 | 08722 |
| Belleville | 35,367 | 07109 |
| Bellmawr | 13,721 | 08031 |
| Belmar | 6,771 | 07719 |
| Bergenfield | 25,568 | 07621 |
| Berkeley Hts. | 12,549 | 07922 |
| Bernardsville | 6,715 | 07924 |
| Bloomfield | 47,792 | 07003 |
| Bloomingdale | 7,867 | 07403 |
| Bogota | 8,344 | 07603 |
| Boonton | 8,620 | 07005 |
| Bound Brook | 9,710 | 08805 |
| Brick | 53,629 | 08723 |
| Bridgeton | 18,795 | 08302 |
| Bridgewater | 29,175 | 08807 |
| Brigantine | 8,318 | 08203 |
| Browns Mills | 10,568 | 08015 |
| Burlington | 10,246 | 08016 |
| Butler | 7,616 | 07405 |
| Caldwell | 7,624 | 07006 |
| Camden | 84,910 | 08101* |
| Carteret | 20,598 | 07008 |
| Cedar Grove | 12,600 | 07009 |
| Chatham | 8,537 | 07928 |
| Cherry Hill | 68,785 | 08034* |
| Cinnaminson | 16,072 | 08077 |
| Clark | 16,699 | 07066 |
| Cliffside Park | 21,464 | 07010 |

| LOCATION | POPULATION | ZIP |
|---|---|---|
| Clifton | 74,388 | 07015 |
| Closter | 8,164 | 07624 |
| Collingswood | 15,838 | 08108 |
| Colts Neck | 7,888 | 07722 |
| Cranford | 24,573 | 07016 |
| Cresskill | 7,609 | 07626 |
| Delran | 14,811 | 08075 |
| Denville | 14,380 | 07834 |
| Deptford | 23,473 | 08096 |
| Dover | 14,681 | 07801 |
| Dumont | 18,334 | 07628 |
| Dunellen | 6,593 | 08812 |
| East Brunswick | 37,711 | 08816 |
| East Hanover | 9,319 | 07936 |
| East Orange | 77,690 | 07019* |
| East Rutherford | 7,849 | 07073 |
| Eatontown | 12,703 | 07724 |
| Edgewater Park | 9,273 | 08010 |
| Edison | 70,193 | 08817 |
| Elizabeth | 106,201 | 07207* |
| Elmwood Park | 18,377 | 07407 |
| Emerson | 7,793 | 07630 |
| Englewood | 23,701 | 07631* |
| Evesham Twp. | 21,508 | 08053 |
| Ewing Twp. | 34,842 | 08618 |
| Fairfield | 7,987 | 07006 |
| Fair Lawn | 32,229 | 07410 |
| Fairview | 10,519 | 07022 |
| Fanwood | 7,767 | 07023 |
| Florham Park | 9,359 | 07932 |
| Fort Lee | 32,449 | 07024 |
| Franklin Lakes | 8,769 | 07417 |
| Freehold | 10,020 | 07728 |
| Garfield | 26,803 | 07026 |
| Glassboro | 14,574 | 08028 |
| Glen Ridge | 7,855 | 07028 |
| Glen Rock | 11,497 | 07452 |
| Gloucester City | 13,121 | 08030 |
| Guttenberg | 7,340 | 07093 |
| Hackensack | 36,039 | 07601* |
| Hackettstown | 8,850 | 07840 |
| Haddonfield | 12,337 | 08033 |
| Haddon Heights | 8,361 | 08035 |
| Haledon | 6,607 | 07508 |
| Hamilton Twp. | 82,801 | 08619 |
| Hammonton | 12,298 | 08037 |
| Hanover | 11,846 | 07981 |
| Harrison | 12,242 | 07029 |
| Hasbrouck Hts. | 12,166 | 07604 |
| Hawthorne | 18,200 | 07507 |
| Hazlet | 23,013 | 07730 |
| Highland Park | 13,396 | 08904 |
| Hillsdale | 10,495 | 07642 |
| Hillside Twp. | 21,440 | 07205 |
| Hoboken | 42,460 | 07030 |
| Holmdel | 8,447 | 07733 |
| Hopatcong | 15,531 | 07843 |
| Howell | 25,065 | 07731 |
| Irvington | 61,493 | 07111 |
| Jackson | 25,644 | 08527 |
| Jersey City | 223,532 | 07303* |
| Keansburg | 10,613 | 07734 |
| Kearny | 35,735 | 07032 |
| Kenilworth | 8,221 | 07033 |
| Keyport | 7,413 | 07735 |
| Kinnelon | 7,770 | 07405 |
| Lakewood | 38,464 | 08701 |
| Leonia | 8,027 | 07605 |
| Lincoln Park | 8,806 | 07035 |
| Linden | 37,836 | 07036 |
| Lindenwold | 18,196 | 08021 |
| Little Falls | 11,496 | 07424 |
| Little Ferry | 9,399 | 07643 |
| Livingston | 28,040 | 07039 |
| Lodi | 23,956 | 07644 |
| Long Branch | 29,819 | 07740 |
| Lyndhurst | 20,326 | 07071 |
| Madison | 15,357 | 07940 |
| Mahwah | 12,127 | 07430 |
| Mantua | 9,193 | 08051 |
| Manville | 11,278 | 08835 |
| Maple Shade | 20,525 | 08052 |
| Maplewood | 22,950 | 07040 |
| Margate City | 9,179 | 08402 |
| Marlboro | 17,560 | 07746 |
| Marlton | 9,411 | 08053 |
| Matawan | 8,837 | 07747 |
| Maywood | 9,895 | 07607 |
| Medford | 17,622 | 08055 |
| Metuchen | 13,762 | 08840 |
| Middlesex | 13,480 | 08846 |
| Middletown | 61,615 | 07748 |
| Midland Park | 7,381 | 07432 |
| Millburn Twp. | 19,543 | 07041 |
| Milltown | 7,136 | 08850 |
| Millville | 24,815 | 08332 |
| Montclair | 38,321 | 07042* |
| Montvale | 7,318 | 07645 |
| Montville | 14,290 | 07045 |
| Moorestown | 15,596 | 08057 |
| Morris Twp. | 18,486 | 07961 |
| Morristown | 16,614 | 07960 |
| Mountainside | 7,118 | 07092 |
| Mount Holly | 10,818 | 08060 |
| Mount Laurel | 17,614 | 08054 |
| Mount Olive | 18,748 | 07828 |
| Neptune | 28,366 | 07753 |
| Newark | 329,248 | 07101* |
| New Brunswick | 41,442 | 08901* |
| New Milford | 16,876 | 07646 |
| New Providence | 12,426 | 07974 |
| Newton | 7,748 | 07860 |
| North Arlington | 16,587 | 07032 |
| North Bergen | 47,019 | 07047 |
| North Brunswick | 22,220 | 08902 |
| Northfield | 7,795 | 08225 |
| North Haledon | 8,177 | 07508 |
| North Plainfield | 19,108 | 07060 |
| Nutley | 28,998 | 07110 |
| Oakland | 13,443 | 07436 |
| Ocean City | 13,949 | 08226 |
| Old Bridge | 51,515 | 08857 |
| Oradell | 8,658 | 07649 |
| Orange | 31,136 | 07050* |
| Palisades Park | 13,732 | 07650 |
| Palmyra | 7,085 | 08065 |
| Paramus | 26,474 | 07652 |
| Park Ridge | 8,515 | 07656 |
| Parsippany-Troy Hills | 49,868 | 07054 |
| Passaic | 52,463 | 07055 |
| Paterson | 137,970 | 07510* |
| Paulsboro | 6,944 | 08066 |
| Pennsauken | 33,775 | 08110 |
| Pennsville | 13,848 | 08070 |
| Pequannock | 13,776 | 07440 |
| Perth Amboy | 38,951 | 08861* |
| Phillipsburg | 16,647 | 08865 |
| Pine Hill | 8,684 | 08021 |
| Piscataway | 42,223 | 08854 |
| Pitman | 9,744 | 08071 |
| Plainfield | 45,555 | 07061* |
| Pleasantville | 13,435 | 08232 |
| Point Pleasant | 17,747 | 08742 |
| Pompton Lakes | 10,660 | 07442 |
| Princeton | 12,035 | 08540 |
| Rahway | 26,723 | 07065* |
| Ramsey | 12,899 | 07446 |
| Randolph | 17,828 | 07801 |
| Readington | 10,855 | 08870 |
| Red Bank | 12,031 | 07701 |
| Ridgefield | 10,294 | 07657 |
| Ridgefield Park | 12,738 | 07660 |
| Ridgewood | 25,208 | 07451* |
| Ringwood | 12,625 | 07456 |
| River Edge | 11,111 | 07661 |
| Riverside | 7,941 | 08075 |
| River Vale | 9,489 | 07675 |
| Rockaway | 6,852 | 07866 |
| Roselle | 20,641 | 07203 |
| Roselle Park | 13,377 | 07204 |
| Rumson | 7,623 | 07760 |
| Runnemede | 9,461 | 08078 |
| Rutherford | 19,068 | 07070* |
| Saddle Brook | 14,084 | 07662 |
| Salem | 6,959 | 08079 |
| Sayreville | 29,969 | 08872 |
| Scotch Plains | 20,774 | 07076 |
| Secaucus | 13,719 | 07094 |
| Somers Point | 10,330 | 08244 |
| Somerville | 11,973 | 08876 |
| South Amboy | 8,322 | 08879 |
| South Orange | 15,864 | 07079 |
| South Plainfield | 20,521 | 07080 |
| South River | 14,361 | 08882 |
| Sparta | 13,333 | 07871 |
| Spotswood | 7,840 | 08884 |
| Springfield | 13,955 | 07081 |
| Stratford | 8,005 | 08084 |
| Summit | 21,071 | 07901 |
| Teaneck | 39,007 | 07666 |
| Tenafly | 13,552 | 07670 |
| Tinton Falls | 7,740 | 07724 |
| Toms River | 7,465 | 08753 |
| Totowa | 11,448 | 07512 |
| Trenton | 92,124 | 08650* |
| Union | 50,184 | 07083 |
| Union Beach | 6,354 | 07735 |
| Union City | 55,593 | 07087 |
| Upper Saddle River | 7,958 | 07458 |
| Ventnor City | 11,704 | 08406 |
| Vernon | 16,302 | 07462 |
| Verona | 14,166 | 07044 |
| Vineland | 53,753 | 08360 |
| Waldwick | 10,802 | 07463 |
| Wall | 18,952 | 07719 |
| Wallington | 10,741 | 07057 |
| Wanaque | 10,025 | 07465 |
| Warren | 9,805 | 07060 |
| Wayne | 46,474 | 07470 |
| Weehawken | 13,168 | 07087 |
| West Caldwell | 11,407 | 07006 |
| West Deptford | 18,002 | 08066 |
| Westfield | 30,447 | 07091* |
| West Long Branch | 7,380 | 07764 |
| West Milford | 22,750 | 07480 |
| West New York | 39,194 | 07093 |
| West Orange | 39,510 | 07052 |
| West Paterson | 11,293 | 07424 |
| Westwood | 10,714 | 07675 |
| Willingboro | 39,912 | 08046 |
| Woodbridge | 90,074 | 07095 |
| Woodbury | 10,353 | 08096 |
| Wood-Ridge | 7,929 | 07075 |
| Wyckoff | 15,500 | 07481 |

## NEW MEXICO

| LOCATION | POPULATION | ZIP |
|---|---|---|
| Alamogordo | 24,024 | 88310 |
| Albuquerque | 331,767 | 87101* |
| Artesia | 10,385 | 88210 |
| Carlsbad | 25,496 | 88220 |
| Clovis | 31,194 | 88101 |
| Deming | 9,964 | 88030 |
| Espanola | 6,803 | 87532 |
| Farmington | 31,222 | 87401 |
| Gallup | 18,167 | 87301 |
| Grants | 11,439 | 87020 |
| Hobbs | 29,153 | 88240 |
| Las Cruces | 45,086 | 88001 |
| Las Vegas | 14,322 | 87701 |
| Los Alamos | 11,039 | 87544 |
| Lovington | 9,727 | 88260 |
| Portales | 9,940 | 88130 |
| Raton | 8,225 | 87740 |
| Roswell | 39,676 | 88201 |
| Santa Fe | 48,953 | 87501 |
| Silver City | 9,887 | 88061 |
| Socorro | 7,173 | 87801 |
| Tucumcari | 6,765 | 88401 |

## NEW YORK

| LOCATION | POPULATION | ZIP |
|---|---|---|
| Albany | 101,727 | 12201* |
| Alden Town | 10,093 | 14004 |
| Amherst Town | 108,706 | 14226 |
| Amityville | 9,076 | 11701 |
| Amsterdam | 21,872 | 12010 |
| Auburn | 32,548 | 13021 |
| Babylon | 12,388 | 11702* |
| Baldwin | 31,630 | 11510 |
| Baldwinsville | 6,446 | 13027 |
| Batavia | 16,703 | 14020 |
| Bay Shore | 10,784 | 11706 |
| Bayville | 7,034 | 11709 |
| Beacon | 12,937 | 12508 |
| Bedford Town | 15,137 | 10506 |
| Bellmore | 18,106 | 11710 |
| Bethpage | 16,840 | 11714 |
| Binghamton | 55,860 | 13902* |
| Brentwood | 44,321 | 11717 |
| Briarcliff Manor | 7,115 | 10510 |
| Brighton Town | 35,776 | 14610 |
| Brockport | 9,776 | 14420 |
| Bronx Borough | 1,168,972 | 10401* |
| Bronxville | 6,267 | 10708 |
| Brooklyn Borough | 2,230,936 | 11201* |
| Buffalo | 357,870 | 14240* |
| Camillus Town | 24,333 | 13031 |
| Canandaigua | 10,419 | 14424 |
| Canton | 7,055 | 13617 |
| Carmel Town | 27,948 | 10512 |
| Central Islip | 19,734 | 11722 |
| Cheektowaga Town | 109,442 | 14225 |
| Chili Town | 23,676 | 14428 |

| LOCATION | POPULATION | ZIP |
|---|---|---|
| Cicero Town | 23,689 | 13039 |
| Clarence Town | 18,146 | 14031 |
| Clifton Park Town | 23,989 | 12118 |
| Cohoes | 18,144 | 12047 |
| Colonie | 8,869 | 12201 |
| Colonie Town | 74,593 | 12201 |
| Commack | 34,719 | 11725 |
| Copiague | 20,132 | 11726 |
| Corning | 12,953 | 14830 |
| Cortland | 20,138 | 13045 |
| Croton-on-Hudson | 6,889 | 10520 |
| Deer Park | 30,394 | 11729 |
| Depew | 19,819 | 14043 |
| De Witt Town | 26,868 | 13214 |
| Dix Hills | 26,693 | 11746 |
| Dobbs Ferry | 10,053 | 10522 |
| Dryden Town | 12,156 | 13053 |
| Dunkirk | 15,310 | 14048 |
| East Aurora | 6,803 | 14052 |
| Eastchester Town | 32,648 | 10709 |
| East Greenbush Town | 12,913 | 12061 |
| East Hampton Town | 14,029 | 11937 |
| East Hills | 7,160 | 11576 |
| East Meadow | 39,317 | 11554 |
| East Northport | 20,187 | 11731 |
| East Rochester | 7,596 | 14445 |
| East Rockaway | 10,917 | 11518 |
| Elmira | 35,327 | 14902* |
| Elmont | 27,592 | 11003 |
| Elwood | 11,847 | 11731 |
| Endicott | 14,457 | 13760 |
| Fallsburg Town | 9,862 | 12733 |
| Farmingdale | 7,946 | 11735 |
| Floral Park | 16,805 | 11002* |
| Franklin Square | 29,051 | 11010 |
| Fredonia | 11,126 | 14063 |
| Freeport | 38,272 | 11520 |
| Fulton | 13,312 | 13069 |
| Garden City | 22,927 | 11530 |
| Gates Town | 29,756 | 14624 |
| Geddes Town | 18,528 | 13209 |
| Geneseo | 6,746 | 14454 |
| Geneva | 15,133 | 14456 |
| Glen Cove | 24,618 | 11542 |
| Glens Falls | 15,897 | 12801 |
| Gloversville | 17,836 | 12078 |
| Grand Island Town | 16,770 | 14072 |
| Great Neck | 9,168 | 11022* |
| Greece Town | 81,367 | 14616 |
| Greenburgh Town | 82,881 | 10591 |
| Greenlawn | 13,869 | 11740 |
| Guilderland Town | 26,515 | 12084 |
| Hamburg | 10,582 | 14075 |
| Harrison | 23,046 | 10528 |
| Hartsdale | 10,216 | 10530 |
| Hastings-on-Hudson | 8,573 | 10706 |
| Hauppague | 20,960 | 11788 |
| Haverstraw | 8,800 | 10927 |
| Hempstead | 40,404 | 11551* |
| Henrietta Town | 36,134 | 14467 |
| Herkimer | 8,383 | 13350 |
| Hewlett | 6,986 | 11557 |
| Hicksville | 43,245 | 11802* |
| Hornell | 10,234 | 14843 |
| Horseheads | 7,348 | 14845 |
| Hudson | 7,986 | 12534 |
| Hudson Falls | 7,419 | 12839 |
| Huntington | 21,727 | 11743 |
| Huntington Sta. | 28,769 | 11746 |
| Hyde Park Town | 20,768 | 12538 |
| Ilion | 9,450 | 13357 |
| Inwood | 8,228 | 11696 |
| Irondequoit Town | 57,648 | 14617 |
| Islip | 13,438 | 11751 |
| Ithaca | 28,732 | 14850 |
| Jamestown | 35,775 | 14701 |
| Jericho | 12,739 | 11753 |
| Johnson City | 17,126 | 13790 |
| Johnstown | 19,360 | 12095 |
| Kenmore | 18,474 | 14271 |
| Kingston | 24,481 | 12401 |
| Lackawanna | 22,701 | 14218 |
| Lake Grove | 9,692 | 11755 |
| Lancaster | 13,056 | 14086 |
| Larchmont | 6,308 | 10538 |
| Latham | 11,182 | 12110 |
| Levittown | 57,045 | 11756 |
| Lewiston Town | 16,219 | 14092 |
| Liberty Town | 9,879 | 12754 |
| Lindenhurst | 26,919 | 11757 |
| Lockport | 24,844 | 14094 |
| Long Beach | 34,073 | 11561 |
| Loudonville | 11,480 | 12211 |
| Lynbrook | 20,424 | 11563 |
| Lysander Town | 13,897 | 13094 |
| Malone | 7,668 | 12953 |
| Malverne | 9,262 | 11565 |
| Mamaroneck | 17,616 | 10543 |
| Manhasset | 8,485 | 11030 |
| Manhattan Borough | 1,428,285 | 10001* |
| Manlius | 28,489 | 13104 |
| Massapequa | 24,454 | 11758 |
| Massapequa Pk. | 19,779 | 11762 |
| Massena | 12,851 | 13662 |
| Mattydale | 7,511 | 13211 |
| Medina | 6,392 | 14103 |
| Melville | 8,139 | 11746 |
| Merrick | 24,478 | 11566 |
| Middletown | 21,454 | 10940 |
| Mineola | 20,757 | 11501 |
| Monroe Town | 14,948 | 10950 |
| Monsey | 12,380 | 10952 |
| Montgomery Town | 16,576 | 12549 |
| Monticello | 6,306 | 12701 |
| Mount Kisco | 8,025 | 10549 |
| Mount Vernon | 66,713 | 10551* |
| Nanuet | 12,578 | 10954 |
| Nesconset | 10,706 | 11767 |
| Newark | 10,017 | 14513 |
| Newburgh | 23,438 | 12550 |
| New City | 35,859 | 10956 |
| New Hartford Town | 21,286 | 13413 |
| New Hyde Park | 9,801 | 11040 |
| New Paltz Town | 10,183 | 12561 |
| New Rochelle | 70,794 | 10802* |
| New Windsor Town | 19,534 | 12550 |
| New York City | 7,071,639 | 10001* |
| Niagara Falls | 71,384 | 14302* |
| North Babylon | 19,019 | 11703 |
| North Bellmore | 20,630 | 11710 |
| North Massapequa | 21,385 | 11758 |
| North Merrick | 12,848 | 11566 |
| North New Hyde Pk. | 15,114 | 11040 |
| Northport | 7,651 | 17768 |
| North Syracuse | 7,970 | 13212 |
| North Tarrytown | 7,994 | 10591 |
| North Tonawanda | 35,760 | 14120 |
| Norwich | 8,082 | 13815 |
| Nyack | 6,428 | 10960 |
| Oakdale | 8,090 | 11769 |
| Oceanside | 33,639 | 11572 |
| Ogdensburg | 12,375 | 13669 |
| Old Bethpage | 6,215 | 11804 |
| Olean | 18,207 | 14760 |
| Oneida | 10,810 | 13421 |
| Oneonta | 14,933 | 13820 |
| Orangetown Town | 48,612 | 10960 |
| Ossining | 20,196 | 10562 |
| Oswego | 19,793 | 13126 |
| Oyster Bay | 6,497 | 11771 |
| Patchogue | 11,291 | 11772 |
| Pearl River | 15,893 | 10965 |
| Peekskill | 18,236 | 10566 |
| Pelham | 6,848 | 10803 |
| Penfield Town | 27,201 | 14526 |
| Plainview | 28,037 | 11803 |
| Plattsburgh | 21,057 | 12901 |
| Pleasantville | 6,749 | 10570 |
| Port Chester | 23,565 | 10573 |
| Port Jefferson | 6,731 | 11777 |
| Port Jervis | 8,699 | 12771 |
| Port Washington | 14,521 | 11050 |
| Potsdam | 10,635 | 13676 |
| Poughkeepsie | 29,757 | 12601* |
| Queens Borough | 1,891,325 | 11101* |
| Rensselaer | 9,047 | 12144 |
| Riverhead Town | 20,243 | 11901 |
| Rochester | 241,741 | 14692* |
| Rockville Centre | 25,412 | 11570 |
| Rome | 43,826 | 13440 |
| Ronkonkoma | — | 11779 |
| Roosevelt | 14,109 | 11575 |
| Rosyln Heights | 6,546 | 11577 |
| Rotterdam Town | 29,451 | 12303 |
| Rye | 15,083 | 10580 |
| St. James | 12,122 | 11780 |
| Salamanca | 6,890 | 14779 |
| Salina Town | 37,400 | 13208 |
| Saranac Lake | 5,578 | 12983 |
| Saratoga Springs | 23,906 | 12866 |
| Sayville | 12,013 | 11782 |
| Scarsdale | 17,650 | 10583 |
| Schenectady | 67,972 | 12301* |
| Scotia | 7,280 | 12302 |
| Seaford | 16,117 | 11783 |
| Selden | 17,259 | 11784 |
| Seneca Falls | 7,466 | 13148 |
| Setauket-East Setauket | 10,176 | 11733 |
| Shirley | 18,072 | 11967 |
| Solvay | 7,140 | 13209 |
| South Farmingdale | 16,439 | 11735 |
| Southport | 8,329 | 14901 |
| Spring Valley | 20,537 | 10977 |
| Staten Island Borough | 352,121 | 10301* |
| Stony Brook | 16,155 | 11790 |
| Stony Point Town | 12,838 | 10980 |
| Suffern | 10,794 | 10901 |
| Syosset | 9,818 | 11791 |
| Syracuse | 170,105 | 13201* |
| Tappan | 8,267 | 10983 |
| Tarrytown | 10,648 | 10591 |
| Thornwood | 7,197 | 10594 |
| Tonawanda | 18,693 | 14150 |
| Troy | 56,638 | 12180* |
| Tuckahoe | 6,076 | 10707 |
| Uniondale | 20,016 | 11553 |
| Utica | 75,632 | 13504* |
| Valley Stream | 35,769 | 11580* |
| Vernon Valley | — | 11768 |
| Vestal | — | 13850 |
| Wantagh | 19,817 | 11793 |
| Warwick | 20,976 | 10990 |
| Watertown | 27,861 | 13601 |
| Watervliet | 11,354 | 12189 |
| Webster Town | 28,925 | 14580 |
| West Babylon | 41,699 | 11704 |
| Westbury | 13,871 | 11590 |
| West Haverstraw | 9,181 | 10993 |
| West Hempstead | 18,536 | 11552 |
| West Islip | 29,533 | 11795 |
| West Sayville | 8,185 | 11796 |
| West Seneca Town | 51,210 | 14224 |
| White Plains | 46,999 | 10602* |
| Williston Park | 8,216 | 11596 |
| Woodmere | 17,205 | 11598 |
| Wyandanch | 13,215 | 11798 |
| Yonkers | 195,351 | 10701* |
| Yorktown Heights | 7,696 | 10598 |
| **NORTH CAROLINA** | | |
| Albemarle | 15,110 | 28001 |
| Asheboro | 15,252 | 27203 |
| Asheville | 53,583 | 28801* |
| Boone | 10,191 | 28607 |
| Burlington | 37,266 | 27215 |
| Carrboro | 7,336 | 27510 |
| Cary | 21,763 | 27511 |
| Chapel Hill | 32,421 | 27514 |
| Charlotte | 314,447 | 28202* |
| Clinton | 7,552 | 28328 |
| Concord | 16,942 | 28025 |
| Dunn | 8,962 | 28334 |
| Durham | 100,538 | 27701* |
| Eden | 15,672 | 27288 |
| Elizabeth City | 14,004 | 27909 |
| Fayetteville | 59,507 | 28302* |
| Forest City | 7,688 | 28043 |
| Garner | 10,073 | 27529 |
| Gastonia | 47,333 | 28052 |
| Goldsboro | 31,871 | 27530 |
| Graham | 8,674 | 27253 |
| Greensboro | 155,642 | 27420* |
| Greenville | 35,740 | 27834 |
| Havelock | 17,718 | 28532 |
| Henderson | 13,522 | 27536 |
| Hendersonville | 6,862 | 28739 |
| Hickory | 20,757 | 28601 |
| High Point | 63,380 | 27260* |
| Jacksonville | 18,237 | 28540 |
| Kannapolis | 34,564 | 28081 |
| Kernersville | 6,802 | 27284 |
| Kings Mountain | 9,080 | 28086 |
| Kinston | 25,234 | 28501 |
| Laurinburg | 11,480 | 28352 |
| Lenoir | 13,748 | 28645 |
| Lexington | 15,711 | 27292 |
| Lumberton | 18,241 | 28358 |
| Mint Hill | 7,915 | 28212 |

| LOCATION | POPULATION | ZIP |
|---|---|---|
| Monroe | 12,639 | 28110 |
| Mooresville | 8,575 | 28115 |
| Morganton | 13,763 | 28655 |
| Mount Airy | 6,862 | 27030 |
| New Bern | 14,557 | 28560 |
| Newton | 7,624 | 28658 |
| Oxford | 7,603 | 27565 |
| Raleigh | 150,255 | 27611* |
| Reidsville | 12,492 | 27320 |
| Roanoke Rapids | 14,702 | 27870 |
| Rockingham | 8,300 | 28379 |
| Rocky Mount | 41,283 | 27801 |
| Roxboro | 7,532 | 27573 |
| Salisbury | 22,677 | 28144 |
| Sanford | 14,773 | 27330 |
| Shelby | 15,310 | 28150 |
| Smithfield | 7,288 | 27577 |
| Southern Pines | 8,620 | 28387 |
| Spring Lake | 6,273 | 28390 |
| Statesville | 18,622 | 28677 |
| Tarboro | 8,634 | 27886 |
| Thomasville | 14,144 | 27360 |
| Washington | 8,418 | 27889 |
| Waynesville | 6,765 | 28786 |
| Wilmington | 44,000 | 28402* |
| Wilson | 34,424 | 27893 |
| Winston-Salem | 131,885 | 27102* |
| **NORTH DAKOTA** | | |
| Bismarck | 44,485 | 58501 |
| Devils Lake | 7,442 | 58301 |
| Dickinson | 15,924 | 58601 |
| Fargo | 61,383 | 58102 |
| Grand Forks | 43,765 | 58201 |
| Jamestown | 16,280 | 58401 |
| Mandan | 15,513 | 58554 |
| Minot | 32,843 | 58701 |
| Valley City | 7,774 | 58072 |
| Wahpeton | 9,064 | 58075 |
| West Fargo | 10,099 | 58078 |
| Williston | 13,336 | 58801 |
| **OHIO** | | |
| Akron | 237,177 | 44309* |
| Alliance | 24,315 | 44601 |
| Amherst | 10,638 | 44001 |
| Ashland | 20,326 | 44805 |
| Ashtabula | 23,449 | 44004 |
| Athens | 19,743 | 45701 |
| Aurora | 8,177 | 44202 |
| Austintown | 33,636 | 44515 |
| Avon | 7,241 | 44011 |
| Avon Lake | 13,222 | 44012 |
| Barberton | 29,751 | 44203 |
| Bay Village | 17,846 | 44140 |
| Beachwood | 9,983 | 44122 |
| Beavercreek | 31,589 | 45690 |
| Bedford | 15,056 | 44146 |
| Bedford Heights | 13,214 | 44146 |
| Bellaire | 8,241 | 43906 |
| Bellefontaine | 11,888 | 43311 |
| Bellevue | 8,187 | 44811 |
| Belpre | 7,193 | 45714 |
| Berea | 19,567 | 44017 |
| Bexley | 13,405 | 43209 |
| Blacklick | 11,223 | 43004 |
| Blue Ash | 9,506 | 45242 |
| Bowling Green | 25,728 | 43402 |
| Brecksville | 10,132 | 44141 |
| Broadview Heights | 10,920 | 44141 |
| Brooklyn | 12,342 | 44144 |
| Brook Park | 26,195 | 44142 |
| Brunswick | 28,104 | 44212 |
| Bryan | 7,879 | 43506 |
| Bucyrus | 13,433 | 44820 |
| Cambridge | 13,573 | 43725 |
| Campbell | 11,619 | 44405 |
| Canton | 93,077 | 44711* |
| Celina | 9,137 | 45822 |
| Centerville | 18,886 | 45459 |
| Cheviot | 9,888 | 45211 |
| Chillicothe | 23,420 | 45601 |
| Cincinnati | 385,457 | 45202* |
| Circleville | 11,700 | 43113 |
| Cleveland | 573,822 | 44101* |
| Cleveland Heights | 56,438 | 44118 |
| Columbus | 565,032 | 43215* |
| Conneaut | 13,835 | 44030 |
| Coshocton | 13,405 | 43812 |
| Cuyahoga Falls | 43,890 | 44222* |
| Dayton | 193,444 | 45401* |
| Deer Park | 6,745 | 45236 |
| Defiance | 16,810 | 43512 |
| Delaware | 18,780 | 43015 |
| Delphos | 7,314 | 45833 |
| Dover | 11,782 | 44622 |
| East Cleveland | 36,957 | 44112 |
| Eastlake | 22,104 | 44094 |
| East Liverpool | 16,687 | 43920 |
| Eaton | 6,839 | 45320 |
| Elyria | 57,538 | 44035* |
| Englewood | 11,329 | 45322 |
| Euclid | 59,999 | 44117 |
| Fairborn | 29,702 | 45324 |
| Fairfield | 30,777 | 45014 |
| Fairview Park | 19,311 | 44126 |
| Findlay | 35,594 | 45840 |
| Forest Park | 18,675 | 45405 |
| Fostoria | 15,743 | 44830 |
| Franklin | 10,711 | 45005 |
| Fremont | 17,834 | 43420 |
| Gahanna | 18,001 | 43230 |
| Galion | 12,391 | 44833 |
| Garfield Heights | 34,938 | 44125 |
| Geneva | 6,655 | 44041 |
| Girard | 12,517 | 44420 |
| Grandview Heights | 7,420 | 43212 |
| Greenville | 12,999 | 45331 |
| Grove City | 16,816 | 43123 |
| Hamilton | 63,189 | 45012* |
| Heath | 6,969 | 43055 |
| Hilliard | 8,008 | 43026 |
| Hillsboro | 6,356 | 45133 |
| Hubbard | 9,245 | 44425 |
| Huber Heights | 35,480 | 45424 |
| Huron | 7,123 | 44839 |
| Independence | 6,607 | 44131 |
| Ironton | 14,290 | 45638 |
| Jackson | 6,675 | 45640 |
| Kent | 26,164 | 44240 |
| Kenton | 8,605 | 43326 |
| Kettering | 61,186 | 45429 |
| Lakewood | 61,963 | 44107 |
| Lancaster | 34,953 | 43130 |
| Lebanon | 9,636 | 45036 |
| Lima | 47,381 | 45801* |
| Logan | 6,557 | 43138 |
| London | 6,958 | 43140 |
| Lorain | 75,416 | 44052* |
| Louisville | 7,873 | 44641 |
| Loveland | 9,106 | 45140 |
| Lyndhurst | 18,092 | 44124 |
| Macedonia | 6,571 | 44056 |
| Madeira | 9,341 | 45243 |
| Mansfield | 53,927 | 44901* |
| Maple Heights | 29,735 | 44137 |
| Marietta | 16,467 | 45750 |
| Marion | 37,040 | 43302 |
| Martins Ferry | 9,331 | 43935 |
| Mason | 8,692 | 45040 |
| Massillon | 30,557 | 44646 |
| Maumee | 15,747 | 43537 |
| Mayfield Heights | 21,550 | 44124 |
| Medina | 15,268 | 44256 |
| Mentor | 42,065 | 44060 |
| Mentor-on-the-Lake | 7,919 | 44060 |
| Miamisburg | 15,304 | 45342 |
| Middleburg Hts. | 16,218 | 44017 |
| Middletown | 43,719 | 45042 |
| Mount Healthy | 7,562 | 45231 |
| Mount Vernon | 14,323 | 43050 |
| Napoleon | 8,614 | 43545 |
| Newark | 41,200 | 43055 |
| New Carlisle | 6,498 | 45344 |
| New Philadelphia | 16,883 | 44663 |
| Niles | 23,088 | 44446 |
| North Canton | 14,228 | 44720 |
| North College Hill | 11,114 | 45239 |
| North Olmsted | 36,486 | 44070 |
| Northridge | 5,559 | 45414 |
| North Ridgeville | 21,522 | 44039 |
| North Royalton | 17,671 | 44133 |
| Norton | 12,242 | 44203 |
| Norwalk | 14,358 | 44857 |
| Norwood | 26,342 | 45212 |
| Oakwood | 9,372 | 45873 |
| Oberlin | 8,660 | 44074 |
| Oregon | 18,675 | 43616 |
| Orrville | 7,511 | 44667 |
| Oxford | 17,655 | 45056 |
| Painesville | 16,391 | 44077 |
| Parma | 92,548 | 44129 |
| Parma Heights | 23,112 | 44130 |
| Perrysburg | 10,215 | 43551 |
| Piqua | 20,480 | 45356 |
| Port Clinton | 7,223 | 43452 |
| Portsmouth | 25,943 | 45662 |
| Ravenna | 11,987 | 44266 |
| Reading | 12,843 | 45215 |
| Reynoldsburg | 20,661 | 43068 |
| Richmond Hts. | 10,095 | 44143 |
| Rittman | 6,063 | 44270 |
| Rocky River | 21,084 | 44116 |
| St. Marys | 8,414 | 45885 |
| Salem | 12,869 | 44460 |
| Sandusky | 31,360 | 44870 |
| Seven Hills | 13,650 | 44131 |
| Shaker Heights | 32,487 | 44120 |
| Sharonville | 10,108 | 45241 |
| Sheffield Lake | 10,484 | 44054 |
| Shelby | 9,645 | 44875 |
| Sidney | 17,657 | 45365 |
| Solon | 14,341 | 44139 |
| South Euclid | 25,713 | 44121 |
| Springdale | 10,111 | 45246 |
| Springfield | 72,563 | 45501* |
| Steubenville | 26,400 | 43952 |
| Stow | 25,303 | 44224 |
| Streetsboro | 9,055 | 44240 |
| Strongsville | 28,577 | 44136 |
| Struthers | 13,624 | 44471 |
| Sylvania | 15,527 | 43560 |
| Tallmadge | 15,269 | 44278 |
| Tiffin | 19,549 | 44883 |
| Toledo | 354,635 | 43601* |
| Toronto | 6,934 | 43964 |
| Trenton | 6,401 | 45067 |
| Trotwood | 7,802 | 45426 |
| Troy | 19,086 | 45373 |
| Twinsburg | 7,632 | 44087 |
| University Hts. | 15,401 | 44118 |
| Upper Arlington | 35,648 | 43221 |
| Urbana | 10,762 | 43078 |
| Vandalia | 13,161 | 45377 |
| Van Wert | 11,035 | 45891 |
| Vermilion | 11,012 | 44089 |
| Wadsworth | 15,166 | 44281 |
| Wapakoneta | 8,402 | 45895 |
| Warren | 56,629 | 44482* |
| Warrensville Hts. | 16,565 | 44128 |
| Washington | 12,682 | 43160 |
| West Carrollton | 13,148 | 45449 |
| Westerville | 23,414 | 43081 |
| Westlake | 19,483 | 44145 |
| Whitehall | 21,299 | 43213 |
| Wickliffe | 16,790 | 44092 |
| Willoughby | 19,329 | 44094 |
| Willoughby Hills | 8,612 | 44094 |
| Willowick | 17,834 | 44094 |
| Wilmington | 10,431 | 45177 |
| Wooster | 19,289 | 44691 |
| Worthington | 15,016 | 43085 |
| Wyoming | 8,282 | 45215 |
| Xenia | 24,653 | 45385 |
| Youngstown | 115,436 | 44501* |
| Zanesville | 28,655 | 43701 |
| **OKLAHOMA** | | |
| Ada | 15,902 | 74820 |
| Altus | 23,101 | 73521 |
| Alva | 6,416 | 73717 |
| Anadarko | 6,378 | 73005 |
| Ardmore | 23,689 | 73401 |
| Bartlesville | 34,568 | 74003 |
| Bethany | 22,130 | 73008 |
| Bixby | 6,969 | 74008 |
| Blackwell | 8,400 | 74631 |
| Broken Arrow | 35,761 | 74012 |
| Chickasha | 15,828 | 73018 |
| Choctaw | 7,520 | 73020 |
| Claremore | 12,085 | 74017 |
| Clinton | 8,796 | 73601 |
| Cushing | 7,720 | 74023 |
| Del City | 28,523 | 73115 |
| Duncan | 22,517 | 73533 |
| Durant | 11,972 | 74701 |
| Edmond | 34,637 | 73034 |
| Elk City | 9,579 | 73644 |
| El Reno | 15,486 | 73036 |
| Enid | 50,363 | 73701 |
| Guthrie | 10,312 | 73044 |
| Guymon | 8,492 | 73942 |
| Henryetta | 6,432 | 74437 |

| LOCATION | POPULATION | ZIP |
|---|---|---|
| Hugo | 7,172 | 74743 |
| Idabel | 7,622 | 74745 |
| Lawton | 80,054 | 73501* |
| McAlester | 17,255 | 74501 |
| Miami | 14,237 | 74354 |
| Midwest City | 49,559 | 73110 |
| Moore | 35,063 | 73160 |
| Muskogee | 40,011 | 74401 |
| Mustang | 7,496 | 73064 |
| Norman | 68,020 | 73069* |
| Oklahoma City | 403,136 | 73125* |
| Okmulgee | 16,263 | 74447 |
| Ponca City | 26,238 | 74601 |
| Poteau | 7,089 | 74953 |
| Pryor | 8,483 | 74361 |
| Sallisaw | 6,403 | 74955 |
| Sand Springs | 13,246 | 74063 |
| Sapulpa | 15,853 | 74066 |
| Seminole | 8,590 | 74868 |
| Shawnee | 26,506 | 74801 |
| Stillwater | 38,268 | 74074 |
| Tahlequah | 9,708 | 74464 |
| The Village | 11,049 | 73120 |
| Tulsa | 360,919 | 74101* |
| Vinita | 6,740 | 74301 |
| Warr Acres | 9,940 | 73132 |
| Weatherford | 9,640 | 73096 |
| Woodward | 13,610 | 73801 |
| Yukon | 17,112 | 73099 |

**OREGON**

| LOCATION | POPULATION | ZIP |
|---|---|---|
| Albany | 26,678 | 97321 |
| Ashland | 14,943 | 97520 |
| Astoria | 9,998 | 97103 |
| Baker | 9,471 | 97814 |
| Beaverton | 30,582 | 97005 |
| Bend | 17,263 | 97701 |
| Canby | 7,659 | 97013 |
| Central Point | 6,357 | 97502 |
| Coos Bay | 14,424 | 97420 |
| Corvallis | 40,960 | 97330 |
| Cottage Grove | 7,148 | 97424 |
| Dallas | 8,530 | 97338 |
| Eugene | 105,624 | 97401* |
| Forest Grove | 11,499 | 97116 |
| Gladstone | 9,500 | 97027 |
| Grants Pass | 15,032 | 97526 |
| Gresham | 33,005 | 97030 |
| Hermiston | 9,408 | 97838 |
| Hillsboro | 27,664 | 97123 |
| Klamath Falls | 16,661 | 97601 |
| La Grande | 11,354 | 97850 |
| Lake Oswego | 22,527 | 97034 |
| Lebanon | 10,413 | 97355 |
| McMinnville | 14,080 | 97128 |
| Medford | 39,603 | 97501 |
| Milwaukie | 17,931 | 97222 |
| Newberg | 10,394 | 97132 |
| Newport | 7,519 | 97365 |
| North Bend | 9,779 | 97459 |
| Ontario | 8,814 | 97914 |
| Oregon City | 14,673 | 97045 |
| Pendleton | 14,521 | 97801 |
| Portland | 366,383 | 97208* |
| Redmond | 6,452 | 97756 |
| Roseburg | 16,644 | 97470 |
| St. Helens | 7,064 | 97051 |
| Salem | 89,233 | 97301* |
| Springfield | 41,621 | 97477 |
| Sweet Home | 6,921 | 97386 |
| The Dalles | 10,820 | 97058 |
| Tigard | 14,286 | 97223 |
| Tualatin | 7,483 | 97062 |
| West Linn | 12,956 | 97068 |
| Woodburn | 11,196 | 97071 |

**PENNSYLVANIA**

| LOCATION | POPULATION | ZIP |
|---|---|---|
| Abington Twp. | 59,084 | 19001 |
| Aliquippa | 17,094 | 15001 |
| Allentown | 103,758 | 18105* |
| Altoona | 57,078 | 16603* |
| Ambler | 6,628 | 19002 |
| Ambridge | 9,575 | 15003 |
| Arnold | 6,853 | 15068 |
| Avalon | 6,240 | 15202 |
| Bala-Cynwyd | — | 19004 |
| Baldwin | 24,712 | 15208 |
| Beaver Falls | 12,525 | 15010 |
| Bellefonte | 6,300 | 16823 |
| Bellevue | 10,128 | 15202 |
| Berwick | 11,850 | 18603 |
| Bethel Park | 34,755 | 15102 |
| Bethlehem | 70,419 | 18015* |
| Blakely | 7,438 | 18447 |
| Bloomsburg | 11,717 | 17815 |
| Bradford | 11,211 | 16701 |
| Brentwood | 11,861 | 15227 |
| Bridgeville | 6,154 | 15017 |
| Bristol | 10,867 | 19007 |
| Brookhaven | 7,912 | 19015 |
| Butler | 17,026 | 16001 |
| Camp Hill | 8,422 | 17011 |
| Canonsburg | 10,459 | 15317 |
| Carbondale | 11,255 | 18407 |
| Carlisle | 18,314 | 17013 |
| Carnegie | 10,099 | 15106 |
| Castle Shannon | 10,164 | 15234 |
| Chambersburg | 16,174 | 17201 |
| Chester | 45,794 | 19013* |
| Clairton | 12,188 | 15025 |
| Clarion | 6,198 | 16214 |
| Clearfield | 7,580 | 16830 |
| Clifton Heights | 7,320 | 19018 |
| Coatesville | 10,698 | 19320 |
| Collingdale | 9,539 | 19023 |
| Columbia | 10,466 | 17512 |
| Connellsville | 10,319 | 15425 |
| Conshohocken | 8,475 | 19428 |
| Corapolis | 7,308 | 15108 |
| Corry | 7,149 | 16407 |
| Crafton | 7,623 | 15205 |
| Darby | 11,513 | 19023 |
| Dickson City | 6,699 | 18519 |
| Donora | 7,524 | 15033 |
| Dormont | 11,275 | 15216 |
| Downingtown | 7,650 | 19335 |
| Doylestown | 8,717 | 18901 |
| Du Bois | 9,290 | 15801 |
| Dunmore | 16,781 | 18512 |
| Duquesne | 10,094 | 15110 |
| Easton | 26,027 | 18042 |
| East Stroudsburg | 8,039 | 18301 |
| Economy | 9,538 | 15005 |
| Elizabethtown | 8,233 | 17022 |
| Ellwood City | 9,998 | 16117 |
| Emmaus | 11,001 | 18049 |
| Ephrata | 11,095 | 17522 |
| Erie | 119,123 | 16501* |
| Farrell | 8,645 | 16121 |
| Folcroft | 8,231 | 19032 |
| Forest Hills | 8,198 | 15221 |
| Franklin | 8,146 | 16323 |
| Gettysburg | 7,194 | 17325 |
| Glassport | 6,242 | 15045 |
| Glenolden | 7,633 | 19036 |
| Glenside | — | 19038 |
| Greensburg | 17,558 | 15601 |
| Greenville | 7,730 | 16125 |
| Grove City | 8,162 | 16127 |
| Hanover | 14,890 | 17331 |
| Harrisburg | 53,264 | 17105* |
| Hatboro | 7,579 | 19040 |
| Hazleton | 27,318 | 18201 |
| Hellertown | 6,025 | 18055 |
| Hershey | 13,249 | 17033 |
| Huntingdon | 7,042 | 16652 |
| Indiana | 16,051 | 15701 |
| Jeannette | 13,106 | 15644 |
| Jefferson | 8,643 | 15344 |
| Johnstown | 35,496 | 15901* |
| Kingston | 15,681 | 18704 |
| Lancaster | 54,725 | 17604* |
| Lansdale | 16,526 | 19446 |
| Lansdowne | 11,891 | 19050 |
| Latrobe | 10,799 | 15650 |
| Lebanon | 25,711 | 17042 |
| Lewistown | 9,830 | 17044 |
| Lititz | 7,590 | 17543 |
| Lock Haven | 9,617 | 17745 |
| Lower Burrell | 13,200 | 15068 |
| Mahanoy City | 6,167 | 17948 |
| McKeesport | 31,012 | 15134* |
| McKees Rocks | 8,742 | 15136 |
| Meadville | 15,544 | 16335 |
| Mechanicsburg | 9,487 | 17055 |
| Media | 6,119 | 19063* |
| Middletown | 10,122 | 17057 |
| Millersville | 7,668 | 17551 |
| Milton | 6,730 | 17847 |
| Monaca | 7,661 | 15061 |
| Monessen | 11,928 | 15062 |
| Monroeville | 30,977 | 15146 |
| Morrisville | 9,845 | 19067 |
| Mount Carmel | 8,190 | 17851 |
| Munhall | 14,535 | 15120 |
| Murrysville | 16,036 | 15668 |
| Nanticoke | 13,044 | 18634 |
| New Brighton | 7,364 | 15066 |
| New Castle | 33,621 | 16101* |
| New Cumberland | 8,051 | 17070 |
| New Kensington | 17,660 | 15068 |
| Norristown | 34,684 | 19401* |
| Northampton | 8,240 | 18067 |
| North Braddock | 8,711 | 15104 |
| Norwood | 6,647 | 19074 |
| Oakmont | 7,039 | 15139 |
| Oil City | 13,881 | 16301 |
| Old Forge | 9,304 | 18518 |
| Palmyra | 7,228 | 17078 |
| Philadelphia | 1,688,210 | 19104* |
| Phoenixville | 14,165 | 19460 |
| Pittsburgh | 423,959 | 15230* |
| Pittston | 9,930 | 18640* |
| Pleasant Hills | 9,374 | 15236 |
| Plum | 25,390 | 15239 |
| Plymouth | 7,605 | 18651 |
| Pottstown | 22,729 | 19464 |
| Pottsville | 18,195 | 17901 |
| Prospect Park | 6,593 | 19076 |
| Punxsutawney | 7,479 | 15767 |
| Quakertown | 8,867 | 18951 |
| Reading | 78,686 | 19603* |
| Ridley Park | 7,889 | 19078 |
| Roslyn | — | 19001 |
| St. Marys | 6,417 | 15857 |
| Sayre | 6,951 | 18840 |
| Scranton | 88,117 | 18501* |
| Shamokin | 10,357 | 17872 |
| Sharon | 19,057 | 16146 |
| Sharon Hill | 6,221 | 19079 |
| Shenandoah | 7,589 | 17976 |
| Somerset | 6,474 | 15501 |
| Souderton | 6,657 | 18964 |
| South Williamsport | 6,581 | 17701 |
| State College | 36,130 | 16801 |
| Steelton | 6,484 | 17113 |
| Sunbury | 12,292 | 17801 |
| Swissvale | 11,345 | 15218 |
| Tamaqua | 8,843 | 18252 |
| Tarentum | 6,419 | 15084 |
| Taylor | 7,246 | 18517 |
| Titusville | 6,884 | 16354 |
| Turtle Creek | 6,959 | 15145 |
| Tyrone | 6,346 | 16686 |
| Uniontown | 14,510 | 15401 |
| Vandergrift | 6,823 | 15690 |
| Warren | 12,146 | 16365 |
| Washington | 18,363 | 15301 |
| Waynesboro | 9,726 | 17268 |
| West Chester | 17,435 | 19380 |
| West Mifflin | 26,552 | 15122 |
| Westmont | 6,113 | 15905 |
| West View | 7,648 | 15229 |
| Whitehall | 15,143 | 15234 |
| White Oak | 9,480 | 15131 |
| Wilkes-Barre | 51,551 | 18703* |
| Wilkinsburg | 23,669 | 15221 |
| Williamsport | 33,401 | 17701 |
| Willow Grove | — | 19090 |
| Wilson | 7,564 | 15025 |
| Wyomissing | 6,551 | 19610 |
| Yeadon | 11,727 | 19050 |
| York | 44,619 | 17405* |

**PUERTO RICO**

| LOCATION | POPULATION | ZIP |
|---|---|---|
| Aguadilla | 20,879 | 00603 |
| Aibonito | 9,369 | 00609 |
| Arecibo | 48,586 | 00612 |
| Arroyo | 8,486 | 00615 |
| Bayamón | 184,854 | 00619 |
| Cabo Rojo | 10,254 | 00623 |
| Caguas | 87,218 | 00625 |
| Canovanas | 7,263 | 00629 |
| Carolina | 147,100 | 00630 |
| Cataño | 26,318 | 00632 |
| Cayey | 23,315 | 00633 |
| Coamo | 12,834 | 00640 |
| Comerio | 5,751 | 00642 |
| Dorado | 10,204 | 00646 |
| Fajardo | 26,845 | 00648 |
| Guánica | 9,627 | 00653 |
| Guayama | 21,044 | 00654 |

| LOCATION | POPULATION | ZIP |
|---|---|---|
| Guaynabo | 65,091 | 00657 |
| Gurabo | 7,646 | 00658 |
| Hormigueros | 11,991 | 00660 |
| Humacao | 19,135 | 00661 |
| Isabela | 12,097 | 00662 |
| Juana Díaz | 10,496 | 00665 |
| Juncos | 7,898 | 00666 |
| Levittown | — | 00632 |
| Manatí | 17,254 | 00701 |
| Mayagüez | 82,703 | 00708 |
| Ponce | 161,260 | 00731 |
| Rio Grande | 12,068 | 00745 |
| Sabana Grande | 7,368 | 00747 |
| Salinas | 6,240 | 00751 |
| San Germán | 13,093 | 00753 |
| San Juan | 422,701 | 00936* |
| San Lorenzo | 8,886 | 00754 |
| San Sebastián | 10,792 | 00755 |
| Santa Isabel | 6,965 | 00757 |
| Trujillo Alto | 41,097 | 00760 |
| Utuado | 11,049 | 00761 |
| Vega Alta | 10,584 | 00762 |
| Vega Baja | 18,020 | 00763 |
| Yabucoa | 6,782 | 00767 |
| Yauco | 14,598 | 00768 |

**RHODE ISLAND**

| LOCATION | POPULATION | ZIP |
|---|---|---|
| Barrington | 16,174 | 02806 |
| Bristol | 20,128 | 02809 |
| Burrillville | 13,164 | 02830 |
| Central Falls | 16,995 | 02863 |
| Coventry | 27,065 | 02816 |
| Cranston | 71,992 | 02910 |
| Cumberland | 27,069 | 02864 |
| East Greenwich | 10,211 | 02818 |
| East Providence | 50,980 | 02914 |
| Johnston | 24,907 | 02919 |
| Lincoln | 16,949 | 02865 |
| Middletown | 17,216 | 02840 |
| Narragansett | 12,088 | 02882 |
| Newport | 29,259 | 02840 |
| North Kingstown | 21,938 | 02852 |
| North Providence | 29,188 | 02908 |
| North Smithfield | 9,972 | 02876 |
| Pawtucket | 71,204 | 02860* |
| Portsmouth | 14,257 | 02871 |
| Providence | 156,804 | 02901* |
| Scituate | 8,405 | 02857 |
| Smithfield | 16,886 | 02917 |
| South Kingstown | 20,414 | 02879 |
| Tiverton | 13,526 | 02878 |
| Wakefield-Peacedale | 6,474 | 02880* |
| Warren | 10,640 | 02885 |
| Warwick | 87,123 | 02887* |
| Westerly | 18,580 | 02891 |
| West Warwick | 27,026 | 02893 |
| Woonsocket | 45,914 | 02895 |

**SOUTH CAROLINA**

| LOCATION | POPULATION | ZIP |
|---|---|---|
| Aiken | 14,978 | 29801 |
| Anderson | 27,965 | 29621* |
| Beaufort | 8,634 | 29902 |
| Bennettsville | 8,774 | 29512 |
| Berea | 13,164 | 29611 |
| Camden | 7,462 | 29020 |
| Cayce | 11,701 | 29169 |
| Charleston | 69,510 | 29401* |
| Chester | 6,820 | 29706 |
| Clemson | 8,118 | 29631 |
| Clinton | 8,596 | 29325 |
| Columbia | 101,208 | 29201* |
| Conway | 10,240 | 29526 |
| Darlington | 7,989 | 29532 |
| Dillon | 7,060 | 29536 |
| Easley | 14,264 | 29640 |
| Florence | 29,176 | 29501 |
| Forest Acres | 6,071 | 29206 |
| Gaffney | 13,453 | 29340 |
| Georgetown | 10,144 | 29440 |
| Goose Creek | 17,811 | 29445 |
| Greenville | 58,242 | 29602* |
| Greenwood | 21,613 | 29646 |
| Greer | 10,525 | 29651 |
| Hanahan | 13,224 | 29410 |
| Hartsville | 7,631 | 29550 |
| Lancaster | 9,703 | 29720 |
| Laurens | 10,587 | 29360 |
| Marion | 7,700 | 29571 |
| Mauldin | 8,143 | 29662 |
| Mount Pleasant | 14,209 | 29464 |
| Myrtle Beach | 18,446 | 29577 |
| Newberry | 9,866 | 29108 |
| North Augusta | 13,593 | 29841 |
| North Charleston | 62,534 | 29406 |
| Orangeburg | 14,933 | 29115 |
| Rock Hill | 35,344 | 29730 |
| St. Andrews | 9,908 | 29407 |
| Seneca | 7,436 | 29678 |
| Simpsonville | 9,037 | 29681 |
| Spartanburg | 43,826 | 29301* |
| Summerville | 6,706 | 29483 |
| Sumter | 24,890 | 29150 |
| Taylors | 15,801 | 29687 |
| Union | 10,523 | 29379 |
| Walterboro | 6,209 | 29488 |
| West Columbia | 10,409 | 29169 |
| York | 6,412 | 29745 |

**SOUTH DAKOTA**

| LOCATION | POPULATION | ZIP |
|---|---|---|
| Aberdeen | 25,851 | 57401 |
| Brookings | 14,951 | 57006 |
| Huron | 13,000 | 57350 |
| Madison | 6,210 | 57042 |
| Mitchell | 13,916 | 57301 |
| Pierre | 11,973 | 57501 |
| Rapid City | 46,492 | 57701 |
| Sioux Falls | 81,343 | 57101* |
| Vermillion | 10,136 | 57069 |
| Watertown | 15,649 | 57201 |
| Yankton | 12,011 | 57078 |

**TENNESSEE**

| LOCATION | POPULATION | ZIP |
|---|---|---|
| Alcoa | 6,870 | 37701 |
| Athens | 12,080 | 37303 |
| Bartlett | 17,170 | 38134 |
| Bolivar | 6,597 | 38008 |
| Brentwood | 9,431 | 37027 |
| Bristol | 23,986 | 37620 |
| Brownsville | 9,307 | 38012 |
| Chattanooga | 169,558 | 37401* |
| Clarksville | 54,777 | 37040 |
| Cleveland | 26,415 | 37311 |
| Collierville | 7,839 | 38017 |
| Columbia | 26,571 | 38401 |
| Cookeville | 20,535 | 38501 |
| Crossville | 6,394 | 38555 |
| Dickson | 7,040 | 37055 |
| Dyersburg | 15,856 | 38024 |
| East Ridge | 21,236 | 37412 |
| Elizabethton | 12,431 | 37643 |
| Fayetteville | 7,559 | 37334 |
| Franklin | 12,407 | 37064 |
| Gallatin | 17,191 | 37066 |
| Germantown | 21,482 | 38138 |
| Goodlettsville | 8,327 | 37072 |
| Greeneville | 14,097 | 37743 |
| Harriman | 8,303 | 37748 |
| Hendersonville | 26,561 | 37075 |
| Humboldt | 10,209 | 38343 |
| Jackson | 49,131 | 38301 |
| Johnson City | 39,753 | 37601 |
| Kingsport | 32,027 | 37662* |
| Knoxville | 175,045 | 37901* |
| La Follette | 8,198 | 37766 |
| Lawrenceburg | 10,184 | 38464 |
| Lebanon | 11,872 | 37087 |
| Lewisburg | 8,760 | 37091 |
| McMinnville | 10,683 | 37110 |
| Manchester | 7,250 | 37355 |
| Martin | 8,898 | 38237 |
| Maryville | 17,480 | 37801 |
| Memphis | 646,174 | 38101* |
| Milan | 8,083 | 38358 |
| Millington | 20,236 | 38053 |
| Morristown | 19,683 | 37814 |
| Murfreesboro | 32,845 | 37130 |
| Nashville | 455,651 | 37202* |
| Newport | 7,580 | 37821 |
| Oak Ridge | 27,662 | 37830 |
| Paris | 10,728 | 38242 |
| Pulaski | 7,184 | 38478 |
| Red Bank | 13,299 | 37415 |
| Ripley | 6,366 | 38063 |
| Savannah | 6,992 | 38372 |
| Shelbyville | 13,530 | 37160 |
| Smyrna | 8,839 | 37167 |
| Soddy-Daisy | 8,388 | 37319 |
| Springfield | 10,814 | 37172 |
| Tullahoma | 15,800 | 37388 |
| Union City | 10,436 | 38261 |

**TEXAS**

| LOCATION | POPULATION | ZIP |
|---|---|---|
| Abilene | 98,315 | 79604* |
| Alice | 20,961 | 78332 |
| Allen | 8,314 | 75002 |
| Alvin | 16,515 | 77511 |
| Amarillo | 149,230 | 79105* |
| Andrews | 11,061 | 79714 |
| Angleton | 13,929 | 77515 |
| Aransas Pass | 7,173 | 78336 |
| Arlington | 160,123 | 76010* |
| Athens | 10,197 | 75751 |
| Austin | 345,496 | 78767* |
| Balch Springs | 13,746 | 75180 |
| Bay City | 17,837 | 77414 |
| Baytown | 56,923 | 77520 |
| Beaumont | 118,102 | 77704* |
| Bedford | 20,821 | 76021 |
| Beeville | 14,574 | 78102 |
| Bellaire | 14,950 | 77401 |
| Bellmead | 7,569 | 76704 |
| Belton | 10,660 | 76513 |
| Benbrook | 13,579 | 76126 |
| Big Spring | 24,804 | 79720 |
| Bonham | 7,338 | 75418 |
| Borger | 15,837 | 79007 |
| Breckenridge | 6,921 | 76024 |
| Brenham | 10,966 | 77833 |
| Bridge City | 7,667 | 77611 |
| Brownfield | 10,387 | 79316 |
| Brownsville | 84,997 | 78520* |
| Brownwood | 19,396 | 76801 |
| Bryan | 44,337 | 77801 |
| Burkburnett | 10,668 | 76354 |
| Burleson | 11,734 | 76028 |
| Canyon | 10,724 | 79015 |
| Carrizo Springs | 6,886 | 78834 |
| Carrollton | 40,595 | 75006* |
| Cedar Hill | 6,849 | 75104 |
| Cleburne | 19,218 | 76031 |
| Clute | 9,577 | 77531 |
| College Station | 37,272 | 77840 |
| Colleyville | 6,700 | 76034 |
| Commerce | 8,136 | 75428 |
| Conroe | 18,034 | 77301* |
| Copperas Cove | 19,469 | 76522 |
| Corpus Christi | 231,999 | 78408* |
| Corsicana | 21,712 | 75110 |
| Crockett | 7,405 | 75835 |
| Crystal City | 8,334 | 78839 |
| Cuero | 7,124 | 77954 |
| Dalhart | 6,854 | 79022 |
| Dallas | 904,078 | 75221* |
| Deer Park | 22,648 | 77536 |
| Del Rio | 30,034 | 78840 |
| Denison | 23,884 | 75020 |
| Denton | 48,063 | 76201 |
| De Soto | 15,538 | 75115 |
| Dickinson | 7,505 | 77539 |
| Donna | 9,952 | 78537 |
| Dumas | 12,194 | 79029 |
| Duncanville | 27,781 | 75116 |
| Eagle Pass | 21,407 | 78852 |
| Edinburg | 24,075 | 78539 |
| El Campo | 10,462 | 77437 |
| El Paso | 425,259 | 79940* |
| Ennis | 12,110 | 75119 |
| Euless | 24,002 | 76039 |
| Farmers Branch | 24,863 | 75234 |
| Forest Hill | 11,684 | 76119 |
| Fort Stockton | 8,688 | 79735 |
| Fort Worth | 385,164 | 76101* |
| Freeport | 13,444 | 77541 |
| Gainesville | 14,081 | 76240 |
| Galena Park | 9,879 | 77547 |
| Galveston | 61,902 | 77550* |
| Garland | 138,857 | 75040* |
| Georgetown | 9,468 | 78626 |
| Gonzales | 7,152 | 78629 |
| Graham | 9,170 | 76046 |
| Grand Prairie | 71,462 | 75050* |
| Grapevine | 11,801 | 76051 |
| Greenville | 22,161 | 75401 |
| Groves | 17,090 | 77619 |
| Haltom City | 29,014 | 76117 |
| Harker Heights | 7,345 | 76541 |
| Harlingen | 43,543 | 78550 |
| Henderson | 11,473 | 75652 |
| Hereford | 15,853 | 79045 |
| Highland Park | 8,909 | 75201 |

| LOCATION | POPULATION | ZIP |
|---|---|---|
| Hillsboro | 7,397 | 76645 |
| Houston | 1,595,138 | 77052* |
| Humble | 6,729 | 77338* |
| Huntsville | 23,936 | 77340 |
| Hurst | 31,420 | 76053 |
| Irving | 109,943 | 75061* |
| Jacinto City | 8,953 | 77029 |
| Jacksonville | 12,264 | 75766 |
| Jasper | 6,959 | 75951 |
| Kermit | 8,015 | 79745 |
| Kerrville | 15,276 | 78028 |
| Kilgore | 11,006 | 75662 |
| Killeen | 46,296 | 76541 |
| Kingsville | 28,808 | 78363 |
| Lake Jackson | 19,102 | 77566 |
| La Marque | 15,372 | 77568 |
| Lamesa | 11,790 | 79331 |
| Lancaster | 14,807 | 75146* |
| La Porte | 14,062 | 77571 |
| Laredo | 91,449 | 78040* |
| League City | 16,578 | 77573 |
| Leon Valley | 9,088 | 78201 |
| Levelland | 13,809 | 79336 |
| Lewisville | 24,273 | 75067* |
| Liberty | 7,945 | 77575 |
| Littlefield | 7,409 | 79339 |
| Live Oak | 8,183 | 78201 |
| Lockhart | 7,953 | 78644 |
| Longview | 62,762 | 75601* |
| Lubbock | 173,979 | 79408* |
| Lufkin | 28,562 | 75901 |
| Mansfield | 8,102 | 76063 |
| Marlin | 7,099 | 76661 |
| Marshall | 24,921 | 75670 |
| McAllen | 66,281 | 78501 |
| McKinney | 16,256 | 75069 |
| Mercedes | 11,851 | 78570 |
| Mesquite | 67,053 | 75149* |
| Mexia | 7,094 | 76667 |
| Midland | 70,525 | 79701* |
| Mineral Wells | 14,468 | 76067 |
| Mission | 22,653 | 78572 |
| Missouri City | 24,533 | 77459* |
| Monahans | 8,397 | 79756 |
| Mount Pleasant | 11,003 | 75455 |
| Nacogdoches | 27,149 | 75961 |
| Nederland | 16,855 | 77627 |
| New Braunfels | 22,402 | 78130 |
| North Richland Hills | 30,592 | 76118 |
| Odessa | 90,027 | 79760* |
| Orange | 23,628 | 77630 |
| Palestine | 15,948 | 75801 |
| Pampa | 21,396 | 79065 |
| Paris | 25,498 | 75460 |
| Pasadena | 112,560 | 77501* |
| Pearland | 13,248 | 77581 |
| Pearsall | 7,383 | 78061 |
| Pecos | 12,855 | 79772 |
| Perryton | 7,991 | 79070 |
| Pharr | 21,381 | 78577 |
| Plainview | 22,187 | 79072 |
| Plano | 72,331 | 75074 |
| Port Arthur | 61,251 | 77640 |
| Portland | 12,023 | 78374 |
| Port Lavaca | 10,911 | 77979 |
| Port Neches | 13,944 | 77651 |
| Raymondville | 9,493 | 78580 |
| Richardson | 72,496 | 75080* |
| Richland Hills | 7,977 | 76118 |
| Richmond | 9,692 | 77469 |
| River Oaks | 6,890 | 77019 |
| Robstown | 12,100 | 78380 |
| Rosenberg | 17,995 | 77471 |
| Round Rock | 12,740 | 78664 |
| Rowlett | 7,522 | 75088 |
| San Angelo | 73,240 | 76901* |
| San Antonio | 786,023 | 78205* |
| San Benito | 17,988 | 78586 |
| San Juan | 7,608 | 78589 |
| San Marcos | 23,420 | 78666 |
| Schertz | 7,262 | 78154 |
| Seagoville | 7,304 | 75159 |
| Seguin | 17,854 | 78155 |
| Sherman | 30,413 | 75090 |
| Silsbee | 7,684 | 77656 |
| Slaton | 6,804 | 79364 |
| Snyder | 12,705 | 79549 |
| South Houston | 13,293 | 77587 |
| Stephenville | 11,881 | 76401 |
| Sugar Land | 8,826 | 77478 |
| Sulphur Springs | 12,804 | 75482 |
| Sweetwater | 12,242 | 79556 |
| Taylor | 10,619 | 76574 |
| Temple | 42,354 | 76501 |
| Terrell | 13,269 | 75160 |
| Texarkana | 31,271 | 75501* |
| Texas City | 41,403 | 77590 |
| The Colony | 11,586 | 75067 |
| Tyler | 70,508 | 75701* |
| Universal City | 10,720 | 78148 |
| University Park | 22,254 | 75205 |
| Uvalde | 14,178 | 78801 |
| Vernon | 12,695 | 76384 |
| Victoria | 50,695 | 77901 |
| Vidor | 11,834 | 77662 |
| Waco | 101,261 | 76703* |
| Watauga | 10,284 | 76248 |
| Waxahachie | 14,624 | 75165 |
| Weatherford | 12,049 | 76086 |
| Weslaco | 19,331 | 78596 |
| West University Pl. | 12,010 | 77005 |
| Wharton | 9,033 | 77488 |
| White Settlement | 13,508 | 76108 |
| Wichita Falls | 94,201 | 76307* |
| Woodway | 7,091 | 76710 |

**UTAH**

| LOCATION | POPULATION | ZIP |
|---|---|---|
| American Fork | 12,693 | 84003 |
| Bountiful | 32,877 | 84010 |
| Brigham City | 15,596 | 84302 |
| Cedar City | 10,972 | 84720 |
| Centerville | 8,069 | 84014 |
| Clearfield | 17,982 | 84015 |
| Kaysville | 9,811 | 84037 |
| Layton | 22,862 | 84041 |
| Lehi | 6,848 | 84043 |
| Logan | 26,844 | 84321 |
| Midvale | 10,144 | 84047 |
| Murray | 25,750 | 84107 |
| North Ogden | 9,309 | 84404 |
| Ogden | 64,407 | 84401* |
| Orem | 52,399 | 84057 |
| Payson | 8,246 | 84651 |
| Pleasant Grove | 10,833 | 84062 |
| Price | 9,086 | 84501 |
| Provo | 74,108 | 84601 |
| Riverton | 7,293 | 84065 |
| Roy | 19,694 | 84067 |
| St. George | 11,350 | 84770 |
| Salt Lake City | 163,697 | 84101* |
| Sandy | 52,210 | 84070 |
| South Jordan | 7,492 | 84065 |
| South Ogden | 11,366 | 84403 |
| South Salt Lake | 9,884 | 84115 |
| Spanish Fork | 9,825 | 84660 |
| Springville | 12,101 | 84663 |
| Tooele | 14,335 | 84074 |
| Vernal | 6,600 | 84078 |
| Washington Terr. | 8,212 | 84403 |
| West Jordan | 27,192 | 84084 |

**VERMONT**

| LOCATION | POPULATION | ZIP |
|---|---|---|
| Barre | 7,090 | 05641 |
| Bennington | 15,815 | 05201 |
| Brattleboro | 11,886 | 05301 |
| Burlington | 37,712 | 05401 |
| Colchester | 12,629 | 05446 |
| Essex | 14,392 | 05451 |
| Essex Junction | 7,033 | 05452 |
| Hartford | 7,963 | 05047 |
| Middlebury | 7,574 | 05753 |
| Montpelier | 8,241 | 05602 |
| Rutland | 18,436 | 05701 |
| St. Albans | 7,308 | 05478 |
| St. Johnsbury | 7,938 | 05819 |
| South Burlington | 10,679 | 05401 |
| Springfield | 10,190 | 05156 |
| Winooski | 6,318 | 05404 |

**VIRGINIA**

| LOCATION | POPULATION | ZIP |
|---|---|---|
| Alexandria | 103,217 | 22301* |
| Annandale | 49,524 | 22003 |
| Arlington | 152,599 | 22210* |
| Bailey's Crossroads | 12,564 | 22041 |
| Blacksburg | 30,638 | 24060 |
| Bon Air | 16,224 | 23235 |
| Bristol | 19,042 | 24201 |
| Buena Vista | 6,717 | 24416 |
| Charlottesville | 39,916 | 22906* |
| Chesapeake | 114,486 | 23320* |
| Christianburg | 10,345 | 24073 |
| Colonial Heights | 16,509 | 23834 |
| Covington | 9,063 | 24426 |
| Culpeper | 6,621 | 22701 |
| Danville | 45,642 | 24541 |
| Fairfax | 19,390 | 22030 |
| Falls Church | 9,515 | 22040 |
| Franklin | 7,308 | 23851 |
| Fredericksburg | 15,322 | 22401 |
| Front Royal | 11,126 | 22630 |
| Galax | 6,524 | 24333 |
| Hampton | 122,617 | 23669* |
| Harrisonburg | 19,671 | 22801 |
| Herndon | 11,449 | 22070* |
| Highland Springs | 12,146 | 23075 |
| Hopewell | 23,397 | 23860 |
| Lake Barcroft | 8,725 | 22041 |
| Lakeside | 12,289 | 23228 |
| Leesburg | 8,357 | 22075 |
| Lexington | 7,292 | 24450 |
| Lynchburg | 66,743 | 24506* |
| Manassas | 15,438 | 22110 |
| Manassas Park | 6,524 | 22110 |
| Marion | 7,029 | 24354 |
| Martinsville | 18,149 | 24112 |
| McLean | 35,664 | 22101* |
| Newport News | 144,903 | 23607* |
| Norfolk | 266,979 | 23501* |
| Petersburg | 41,055 | 23803 |
| Poquoson | 8,726 | 23662 |
| Portsmouth | 104,577 | 23705* |
| Pulaski | 10,106 | 24301 |
| Radford | 13,225 | 24141 |
| Richmond | 219,214 | 23232* |
| Roanoke | 100,220 | 24001* |
| Salem | 23,958 | 24153 |
| South Boston | 7,093 | 24592 |
| Springfield | 21,435 | 22150* |
| Staunton | 21,857 | 24401 |
| Suffolk | 47,621 | 23432* |
| Vienna | 15,469 | 22180 |
| Vinton | 8,027 | 24179 |
| Virginia Beach | 262,199 | 23458* |
| Waynesboro | 15,329 | 22980 |
| Williamsburg | 9,870 | 23185 |
| Winchester | 20,217 | 22601 |
| Woodbridge | 24,004 | 22191* |
| Wytheville | 7,135 | 24382 |

**VIRGIN ISLANDS**

| LOCATION | POPULATION | ZIP |
|---|---|---|
| Charlotte Amalie | 11,756 | 00801 |

**WASHINGTON**

| LOCATION | POPULATION | ZIP |
|---|---|---|
| Aberdeen | 18,739 | 98520 |
| Anacortes | 9,013 | 98221 |
| Auburn | 26,417 | 98002 |
| Bellevue | 73,903 | 98009* |
| Bellingham | 45,794 | 98225 |
| Bothell | 7,943 | 98011 |
| Bremerton | 36,208 | 98310 |
| Centralia | 11,555 | 98531 |
| Cheney | 7,630 | 99004 |
| Clarkston | 6,903 | 99403 |
| Des Moines | 7,378 | 98188 |
| Edmonds | 27,679 | 98020 |
| Ellensburg | 11,752 | 98926 |
| Everett | 54,413 | 98201* |
| Hoquiam | 9,719 | 98550 |
| Kelso | 11,129 | 98626 |
| Kennewick | 34,397 | 99336 |
| Kent | 23,152 | 98031 |
| Kirkland | 18,779 | 98033 |
| Lacey | 13,940 | 98503 |
| Longview | 31,052 | 98632 |
| Lynnwood | 22,641 | 98036 |
| Mercer Island | 21,522 | 98040 |
| Moses Lake | 10,629 | 98837 |
| Mountlake Terr. | 16,534 | 98043 |
| Mount Vernon | 13,009 | 98273 |
| Oak Harbor | 12,271 | 98277 |
| Olympia | 27,447 | 98501* |
| Opportunity | 21,241 | 99214 |
| Parkland | 23,355 | 98444 |
| Pasco | 18,425 | 99301 |
| Port Angeles | 17,311 | 98362 |
| Pullman | 23,579 | 99163 |
| Puyallup | 18,251 | 98371 |
| Redmond | 23,318 | 98052 |
| Renton | 30,612 | 98055 |
| Richland | 33,578 | 99352 |

| LOCATION | POPULATION | ZIP |
|---|---|---|
| Seattle | 493,846 | 98101* |
| Shelton | 7,629 | 98584 |
| Spokane | 171,300 | 99210* |
| Sunnyside | 9,225 | 98944 |
| Tacoma | 158,501 | 98402* |
| Toppenish | 6,517 | 98948 |
| Tumwater | 6,705 | 98501 |
| University Place | 20,381 | 98416 |
| Vancouver | 42,834 | 98660* |
| Walla Walla | 25,618 | 99362 |
| Wenatchee | 17,257 | 98801 |
| Yakima | 49,826 | 98901* |
| **WEST VIRGINIA** | | |
| Beckley | 20,492 | 25801 |
| Bluefield | 16,060 | 24701 |
| Bridgeport | 6,604 | 26330 |
| Buckhannon | 6,820 | 26201 |
| Charleston | 63,968 | 25301 |
| Clarksburg | 22,371 | 26301 |
| Dunbar | 9,285 | 25064 |
| Elkins | 8,536 | 26241 |
| Fairmont | 23,863 | 26554 |
| Grafton | 6,845 | 26354 |
| Huntington | 63,684 | 25701* |
| Keyser | 6,569 | 26726 |
| Martinsburg | 13,063 | 25401 |
| Morgantown | 27,605 | 26505 |
| Moundsville | 12,419 | 26041 |
| New Martinsville | 7,109 | 26155 |
| Nitro | 8,074 | 25143 |
| Oak Hill | 7,120 | 25901 |
| Parkersburg | 39,967 | 26101* |
| Princeton | 7,493 | 24740 |
| St. Albans | 12,402 | 25177 |
| South Charleston | 15,968 | 25303 |
| Vienna | 11,618 | 26105 |
| Weirton | 25,371 | 26062 |
| Weston | 6,250 | 26452 |
| Wheeling | 43,070 | 26003 |
| **WISCONSIN** | | |
| Antigo | 8,653 | 54409 |
| Appleton | 58,913 | 54911 |
| Ashland | 9,115 | 54806 |
| Ashwaubenon | 14,486 | 54304 |
| Baraboo | 8,081 | 53913 |
| Beaver Dam | 14,149 | 53916 |
| Beloit | 35,207 | 53511 |
| Brookfield | 34,035 | 53005 |
| Brown Deer | 12,921 | 53209 |
| Burlington | 8,385 | 53105 |
| Cedarburg | 9,005 | 53012 |
| Chippewa Falls | 12,270 | 54729 |
| Cudahy | 19,547 | 53110 |
| De Pere | 14,892 | 54115 |
| Eau Claire | 51,509 | 54701 |
| Elm Grove | 6,735 | 53122 |
| Fond du Lac | 35,863 | 54935 |
| Fort Atkinson | 9,785 | 53538 |
| Fox Point | 7,649 | 53117 |
| Franklin | 16,871 | 53132 |
| Germantown | 10,729 | 53022 |
| Glendale | 13,882 | 53209 |
| Grafton | 8,381 | 53024 |
| Green Bay | 87,899 | 54305* |
| Greendale | 16,928 | 53129 |
| Greenfield | 31,467 | 53220 |
| Hales Corners | 7,110 | 53130 |
| Hartford | 7,046 | 53027 |
| Howard | 8,240 | 54303 |
| Janesville | 51,071 | 53545 |
| Kaukauna | 11,310 | 54130 |
| Kenosha | 77,685 | 53141* |
| La Crosse | 48,347 | 54601 |
| Little Chute | 7,907 | 54140 |
| Madison | 170,616 | 53714* |
| Manitowoc | 32,547 | 54220 |
| Marinette | 11,965 | 54143 |
| Marshfield | 18,290 | 54449 |
| Menasha | 14,728 | 54952 |
| Menomonee Falls | 27,845 | 53051 |
| Menomonie | 12,769 | 54751 |
| Mequon | 16,193 | 53092 |
| Merrill | 9,578 | 54452 |
| Middleton | 11,848 | 53562 |
| Milwaukee | 636,236 | 53201* |
| Monona | 8,809 | 53716 |
| Monroe | 10,027 | 53566 |
| Muskego | 15,277 | 53150 |
| Neenah | 22,432 | 54956 |
| New Berlin | 30,529 | 53151 |
| New London | 6,210 | 54961 |
| Oak Creek | 16,932 | 53154 |
| Oconomowoc | 9,909 | 53066 |
| Onalaska | 9,249 | 54650 |
| Oshkosh | 49,620 | 54901 |
| Platteville | 9,580 | 53818 |
| Portage | 7,896 | 53901 |
| Port Washington | 8,612 | 53074 |
| Racine | 85,725 | 53401* |
| Rhinelander | 7,873 | 54501 |
| Rice Lake | 7,691 | 54868 |
| Ripon | 7,111 | 54971 |
| River Falls | 9,019 | 54022 |
| St. Francis | 10,042 | 53207 |
| Shawano | 7,013 | 54166 |
| Sheboygan | 48,085 | 53081 |
| Shorewood | 14,327 | 53211 |
| South Milwaukee | 21,069 | 53172 |
| Sparta | 6,934 | 54656 |
| Stevens Point | 22,970 | 54481 |
| Stoughton | 7,589 | 53589 |
| Sturgeon Bay | 8,847 | 54235 |
| Sun Prairie | 12,931 | 53590 |
| Superior | 29,571 | 54880 |
| Tomah | 7,204 | 54660 |
| Two Rivers | 13,354 | 54241 |
| Watertown | 18,113 | 53094 |
| Waukesha | 50,365 | 53186 |
| Waupun | 8,132 | 53963 |
| Wausau | 32,426 | 54401 |
| Wauwatosa | 51,308 | 53226 |
| West Allis | 63,982 | 53214 |
| West Bend | 21,484 | 53095 |
| Whitefish Bay | 14,930 | 53217 |
| Whitewater | 11,520 | 53190 |
| Wisconsin Rapids | 17,995 | 54494 |
| **WYOMING** | | |
| Casper | 51,016 | 82601 |
| Cheyenne | 47,283 | 82001* |
| Cody | 6,790 | 82414 |
| Evanston | 6,421 | 82930 |
| Gillette | 12,134 | 82716 |
| Green River | 12,807 | 82935 |
| Lander | 7,867 | 82520 |
| Laramie | 24,410 | 82070 |
| Rawlins | 11,547 | 82301 |
| Riverton | 9,247 | 82501 |
| Rock Springs | 19,458 | 82901 |
| Sheridan | 15,146 | 82801 |
| Worland | 6,391 | 82401 |

## BIRTHSTONES

SOURCE: Jewelry Industry Council

**January** ........ Garnet
**February** ........ Amethyst
**March** ........ Aquamarine, bloodstone
**April** ........ Diamond
**May** ........ Emerald
**June** ........ Pearl, alexandrite, moonstone
**July** ........ Ruby, star ruby
**August** ........ Peridot, sardonyx
**September** ........ Sapphire, star sapphire
**October** ........ Opal, tourmaline
**November** ........ Topaz
**December** ........ Turquoise, zircon

## FLOWERS OF THE MONTH

SOURCE: Society of American Florists, Alexandria, Va. in conjunction with *Red Book* Magazine 1977

**January** ........ Carnation
**February** ........ Violet
**March** ........ Daffodil
**April** ........ Sweet Pea
**May** ........ Lily of the Valley
**June** ........ Rose
**July** ........ Larkspur (Delphinium)
**August** ........ Gladiolus
**September** ........ Aster
**October** ........ Calendula (Pot Marigold)
**November** ........ Chrysanthemum
**December** ........ Narcissus

## WEDDING ANNIVERSARY GIFTS

| Anniversary | Traditional | Modern |
|---|---|---|
| 1 | Paper/Plastics | Clocks |
| 2 | Cotton/Calico/Straw | China |
| 3 | Leather or leatherlike items | Crystal or glass |
| 4 | Fruit/Flowers/Books; also Linen/Silk or synthetic silks | Electrical appliance |
| 5 | Wood/Decorative home | Silverware accessories |
| 6 | Candy or sugar/Iron | Wood |
| 7 | Wool/Copper, brass, or bronze | Desk set/Pen and pencil set |
| 8 | Bronze/Pottery/Rubber; also Electrical appliances | Linens/Lace |
| 9 | Pottery/Willow/China, glass or crystal | Leather |
| 10 | Tin or aluminum | Diamond jewelry |
| 11 | Steel | Fashion jewelry or accessories |
| 12 | Silk or nylon/Linen | Pearl or colored gem |
| 13 | Lace | Textiles/Furs |
| 14 | Ivory/Agate | Gold jewelry |
| 15 | Crystal or glass | Watch |
| 20 | China/Occasional furniture | Platinum |
| 25 | Silver | Silver |
| 30 | Pearl/Personal gifts | Diamond |
| 35 | Coral/Jade | Jade |
| 40 | Ruby/Garnet | Ruby |
| 45 | Sapphire | Sapphire |
| 50 | Gold | Gold |
| 55 | Emerald/Turquoise | Emerald |
| 60 | Diamond/Gold | Diamond/Gold |
| 75 | Diamond/Gold | Diamond/Gold |

# HISTORY: ANCIENT/MODERN

## PRESENT MONARCHS AND DYNASTIES

### AFRICA

*Lesotho*—**Dynasty:** Before independence, the people of Lesotho accepted authority of the "Paramount Chief" of the House of Moshesh. With independence (October 1966), Moshoeshoe II of the Moshesh became head of state. **Monarch:** Moshoeshoe II ascended the throne in October 1966. In "voluntary exile" Feb.-Dec. 1970 **Born:** May 2, 1938 **Married:** Tabitha' Masentle Lerotholi Mojela **Children:** Two sons, one daughter **Heir:** Crown Prince David Letsie (b. 1963) **Religion:** Christian

*Morocco*—**Dynasty:** The Alaouite dynasty (Filali) has ruled Morocco since the 17th century. The country has been ruled by constitutional kings since independence (1956), and in 1957 King Mohammed V changed his title from "His Sherifian Majesty, the Sultan" to "His Majesty, the King of Morocco." **Monarch:** King Hassan II, son of Mohammed V, ascended the throne on March 3, 1961, following the death of his father on February 26, 1961. **Born:** July 9, 1929 **Married:** Lalla Latifa **Children:** Two sons and three daughters **Heir:** Crown Prince Sidi Mohammed (born 1963). **Religion:** Moslem (Sunni)

*Swaziland*—**Dynasty:** Descended from Sobhuza I, the late king succeeded as Ngwenyama (or lion) of the Swazi nation, after a 20-year regency of the Queen Mother, in 1921. The country gained independence on September 6, 1968. **Monarch:** Vacant as of Sept. 14, 1982 following the death of King Sobhuza II on Aug. 21. The late king, who was born in 1899, had approximately 70 wives and over 100 children. **Heir:** By custom, the heir to the throne is not chosen until after the death of the monarch. **Religion:** Christian

### ARABIA

*Bahrain*—**Dynasty:** The Emir of Bahrain, head of the powerful Bedouin Al Khalifa family, is the tenth of his family to rule in Bahrain. Succession is by primogeniture. **Monarch:** Sheikh Isa ibn Salman al Khalifa became ruler on the death of his father in 1961, and the first Emir of Bahrain on August 14, 1971, the date of Bahrain's independence. **Children:** Hamad, others **Heir:** Sheikh Hamad ibn Isa al Khalifa, defense minister, and the Emir's oldest son **Religion:** Moslem (Sunni)

*Jordan*—**Dynasty:** Hashemite cooperation with the British in World War I resulted in Abdullah Ibn Hussein's rule of British mandated Transjordan. By a 1946 treaty with Great Britain, Abdullah became the first king of the independent Hashemite Kingdom of Jordan. Assassinated in 1951, Abdullah was succeeded by his son, Talal, father of the present king. **Monarch:** King Hussein I (ibn Talal) ascended the throne on May 2, 1953, following the deposition of his sickly father, Talal, on August 11, 1952. **Born:** November 14, 1935 **Married:** Princess Dina Abdel Hamid (April 1955; divorced, 1957); Antoinette (Toni) Avril Gardiner (Muna al Hussein) (May 1961; divorced, 1972); Alia Toukan (1972; died 1977); Elizabeth Halaby (Nur al Hussein) (June 1978) **Children:** Five sons (Abdullah, born 1962; Faisal, born 1963; Ali, born 1976; Hamzah, born 1980; Hashem, born 1981) and four daughters (Alia, born 1956; Zein, born 1968; Ayeshia, born 1968; Haya, born 1974). Abir, an adopted daughter, was born in 1972. **Heir:** Prince Hassan, younger brother of the king **Religion:** Moslem (Sunni)

*Kuwait*—**Dynasty:** The Emir of Kuwait is the thirteenth ruler of the Al Sabah royal family. The nominated successor of the Emir must be approved by the National Assembly; succession usually alternates between the two branches of the royal family. **Monarch:** Sheikh Jabir al-Ahmad al-Jabir al-Sabah of the al-Jabir branch became Emir on the death of his cousin on Dec. 31, 1977. **Married:** one wife **Children:** several **Heir:** Crown Prince Sheikh Saad Abdullah as-Sabah **Religion:** Moslem (Sunni)

*Oman*—**Dynasty:** The al Bu Said dynasty dates from 1741 when its founder, Ahmed Ibn Said, expelled the Turks from Muscat and Oman. **Monarch:** Sultan Qabus ibn Said al Bu Said ascended the throne in July 1970 after overthrowing his father, Said bin Taimur (1910-72), who had reigned since 1932. **Born:** November 18, 1940 **Married:** Kamilla (1976; reportedly divorced, 1980) **Heir:** no heir apparent has been designated **Religion:** Moslem (Ibadi)

*Qatar*—**Dynasty:** In the 19th century, the ruling Khalifa family deposed and forced to move to Bahrain, were succeeded by the Al Thani family. The present Emir, Khalifa ibn Hamad al-Thani, is the sixth ruler. In 1972 Khalifa assumed full power. Succession is designated by family consensus. **Monarch:** Sheikh Khalifa ibn Hamad al-Thani, Emir of Qatar, assumed power Feb. 22, 1972. **Born:** 1937 **Children:** Two sons—**Hamad and Abd al Aziz, others Heir:** no heir apparent has been designated **Religion:** Moslem (Wahhabi)

*Saudi Arabia*—**Dynasty:** The kingdoms of Nejd and Hejaz and their dependencies became the Kingdom of Saudi Arabia in 1932, under King Abdul-Aziz Ibn Abdur-Rahman Al-Faisal Al Saud. **Monarch:** King Fahd ibn Abdul-Aziz Al Saud succeeded to the throne on June 13, 1982, at the death of his brother, Khalid. **Born:** 1923 **Married:** yes **Children:** several **Heir:** Prince Abdullah ibn Abdul-Aziz Al Saud, a younger brother **Religion:** Moslem (Wahhabi sect)

### ASIA

*Bhutan*—**Dynasty:** The present hereditary dynasty of Bhutan was founded in 1907 by Ugyen Dorji Wangchuk, a provincial governor, following the abolition of a dual system of government by spiritual and temporal rulers. The present king, installed in July 1972 after the death of his father, Jigme Dorji Wangchuk, is his great-grandson. **Monarch:** King Jigme Singhi Wangchuk (formally crowned on June 2, 1974) **Born:** 1955 **Children:** None **Heir:** To be selected from the royal family by the National Assembly **Religion:** Buddhist (Mahayana)

*Japan*—**Dynasty:** The Meiji Restoration (1867) placed Emperor Mutsuhito and his male descendants in command of a unified Japan. During the postwar American occupation of Japan, the Emperor, a grandson of Mutsuhito, renounced any claims to divinity, becoming a symbolic ruler. **Monarch:** Emperor Hirohito ascended the throne on the death of his father, Yoshihito, on December 25, 1926; he was enthroned on November 10, 1928. **Born:** April 29, 1901 **Married:** Princess Nagako (1924) **Children:** Seven; two sons (Akihito, born 1933; Masahito, born 1935) and three daughters (Kazuko, born 1929; Atsuko, born 1931; Takako, born 1939) survive **Heir:** Crown Prince Akihito **Religion:** Shinto

*Nepal*—**Dynasty:** The Shah family has ruled the kingdom of Nepal since the middle of the 18th century; however, a hereditary prime minister from the Rana family held actual power from 1846 to 1951. The last prime minister resigned in November 1951, and King Tribhuvan assumed full control. **Monarch:** Maharajadhiraja Birendra Bir Bikram Shah Dev succeeded to the throne in January 1972 (crowned in 1975) at the death of his father, Mahendra Bir Bikram Shah Dev **Born:** 1946 **Married:** Aishwarya Rajya Lakshmi Shah Devi **Children:** Two sons, one daughter **Heir:** Crown Prince Dependra Bir Bikram Shah Dev (b. 1971) **Religion:** Hindu

*Thailand*—**Dynasty:** The present ruling family of Thailand began with Rama I in 1782. His great-grandson, Chulalongkorn, King Rama V, was responsible for accelerating the modernization of Thailand; his nephew is the current monarch. **Monarch:** King Bhumibol Adulyadej, or Phumiphol Aduldet (Rama IX) succeeded to the throne after the death of his elder brother, King Ananda Mahidol, on June 9, 1946; he was crowned on May 5, 1950 **Born:** December 5, 1927 **Married:** Princess Sirikit Kittiyakara (1950) **Children:** One son (Prince Vajiralongkorn, born 1952), and three daughters (Ubol Ratana, born 1951; Sirindhorn, born 1955; Chulabhorn, born 1957) **Heir:** Crown Prince Vajiralongkorn **Religion:** Buddhist (Hinayana)

## EUROPE

*Belgium*—**Dynasty:** The ruling family of Belgium is of the Saxe-Coburg-Gotha line. After Belgian separation from the Netherlands (1830), Leopold, prince of Saxe-Coburg-Gotha, was elected hereditary King of the Belgians on June 4, 1831, as King Leopold I; he was enthroned on July 21, 1831. **Monarch:** King Baudouin I (Albert Charles Leopold Axel Marie Gustave) succeeded to the throne on July 17, 1951, on the abdication of his father, Leopold III, on the previous day. **Born:** September 7, 1930 **Married:** Fabiola de Mora y Aragón (1960) **Children:** None **Heir:** Albert, Prince of Liège, brother of the king (born 1934) **Religion:** Roman Catholic

*Denmark*—**Dynasty:** The House of Glücksburg has ruled Denmark since King Frederik VII of the House of Oldenburg died childless in November 1863. By a treaty (1852), King Frederik VII designated as heir Prince Christian X of Schleswig-Holstein-Sonderburg-Glücksburg, who became King Christian IX on Frederik's death. **Monarch:** Queen Margrethe II succeeded to the throne on the death of her father, King Frederik IX, on January 14, 1972. **Born:** April 16, 1940 **Married:** Count Henri de Laborde de Monpezat, now Prince Henrik of Denmark (1967) **Children:** Two sons: Frederik André Henrik Christian, born 1968; Joachim Holger Waldemar Christian, born 1969 **Heir:** Crown Prince Frederik **Religion:** Evangelical Lutheran

*Liechtenstein*—**Dynasty:** The ruling House of Liechtenstein is descended from Huc von Liechtenstein, who became hereditary ruler of the country in January 1719. **Royal Ruler:** Prince Franz Josef II succeeded at the death of his great-uncle, Prince Franz de Paula, on July 25, 1938. **Born:** August 16, 1906 **Married:** Countess Georgine von Wilczek (1943) **Children:** Four sons, one daughter: Prince Johannes Adam Ferdinand Alois Josef Maria Marko d'Aviano Pius (b. 1945), Prince Philipp Erasmus Alois Ferdinand Maria Sebaldus (b. 1946), Prince Nikolaus Ferdinand Maria Josef Raphael (b. 1947), Prince Franz-Josef Wenzel George Maria (b. 1962), and Princess Nora Elisabeth Maria Anunta Josefine Georgine Omnes Sancti (b. 1950) **Heir:** Crown Prince Johannes (Hans) Adam **Religion:** Roman Catholic

*Luxembourg*—**Dynasty:** Made a Grand Duchy in 1815, the country has been ruled by the Nassau family, the elder line of the House of Nassau, since 1890. According to the succession agreement, Adolphe, Duke of Nassau, succeeded at the death of King William III of the Netherlands. The Grand Duchy is today ruled by the great-grandson of Adolphe. **Royal Ruler:** Grand Duke Jean succeeded to the throne on the abdication of his mother, the Grand Duchess Charlotte, on November 12, 1964. **Born:** January 5, 1921 **Married:** Princess Josephine-Charlotte of Belgium, daughter of King Leopold III (1953) **Children:** Three sons and two daughters: Prince Henri Albert Gabriel Félix Marie Guillaume (b. 1955), Prince Jean Félix Marie Guillaume (b. 1957), Prince Guillaume Marie Louis Christian (b. 1963), Princess Marie Astrid Charlotte Leopolding Wilhelmine Ingeborg Antonia Lilane Alberta Elisabeth Anne (b. 1954), and Princess Margaretha Antonia Maria Félicité (b. 1957) **Heir:** Prince Henri **Religion:** Roman Catholic

*Monaco*—**Dynasty:** The House of Grimaldi has controlled the principality of Monaco since 1297. **Royal Ruler:** Prince Rainier III (Louis Henri Maxence Bertrand) succeeded his grandfather, Prince Louis II, at his death on May 9, 1949. **Born:** May 31, 1923 **Married:** Grace Patricia Kelly of Philadelphia (1956; died 1982) **Children:** One son and two daughters: Prince Albert Alexandre Louis Pierre (b. 1958), Princess Caroline Louise Marguerite (b. 1957), and Princess Stéphanie Marie Elisabeth (b. 1965) **Heir:** Prince Albert **Religion:** Roman Catholic

*Netherlands*—**Dynasty:** The Congress of Vienna, which settled the Napoleonic Wars, created the hereditary kingdom of the Netherlands under King William I in March 1815. The present sovereign is the sixth monarch of the dynasty. **Monarch:** Queen Beatrix Wilhelmina Armgard succeeded her mother, Queen Juliana, at the latter's abdication on April 30, 1980; she was invested on April 30, 1980. **Born:** January 31, 1938 **Married:** Prince Claus von Amsberg (1966) **Children:** Three sons: Prince Willem-Alexander Claus George Ferdinand (b. 1967), Johan Frisco Bernhard Christiaan David (b. 1968), Constantijn Christof Frederik Aschwin (b. 1969) **Heir:** Crown Prince Willem-Alexander **Religion:** Dutch Reformed Church

*Norway*—**Dynasty:** Norway was ruled by the kings of Denmark and Sweden from 1319 until its separation (1905), when Prince Carl of Denmark was elected King Haakon VII of an independent Norway. Married to Queen Maud, daughter of Edward VII of England, King Haakon VII was followed by his son, the present ruler. **Monarch:** King Olav V succeeded to the throne on the death of his father, King Haakon VII, on September 21, 1957. **Born:** July 2, 1903 **Married:** Princess Märtha, daughter of Prince Carl of Sweden (1929; d. 1954) **Children:** One son and two daughters: Prince Harald (b. 1937), Princess Ragnhild Alexandra (b. 1930), and Princess Astrid Maud Ingeborg (b. 1932) **Heir:** Crown Prince Harald **Religion:** Evangelical Lutheran

*Spain*—**Dynasty:** The 1947 law of succession recreated the Spanish Kingdom under the tutelage of Generalissimo Franco, who would select a successor from the royal family. The Bourbon dynasty had ruled from 1700-1808, 1814-1869, and again after 1875 until the abdication of Alfonso XIII in April 1931. In 1969 Franco named Juan Carlos, grandson of Alfonso, as heir, and after being approved by the Cortes he was entitled Prince of Spain on July 23, 1969. He was proclaimed king on November 22, 1975, following the death of Franco. **Monarch:** Juan Carlos I de Borbón y Borbón **Born:** January 5, 1938 **Married:** Princess Sofía of Greece (1962) **Children:** One son and two daughters: Prince of Asturias Felipe Juan Pablo Alfonso de Borbón y Sonderburg-Gluckberg (b. 1968), Princess Elena, Princess Cristina **Heir:** Prince Felipe **Religion:** Roman Catholic

*Sweden*—**Dynasty:** Jean-Baptiste-Jules Bernadotte was elected (1810) Prince Royal of Sweden and adopted by childless King Carl XIII. He ascended to the throne of Norway and Sweden in 1818 as King Carl XIV Johan. His descendant King Oscar II renounced the throne of Norway in 1905; however, the House of Bernadotte still reigns over Sweden. **Monarch:** King Carl XVI Gustav, succeeded to the throne on the death of his grandfather, King Gustav VI Adolf on September 16, 1973. King Carl's father died in 1947. **Born:** April 30, 1946 **Married:** Silvia Renate Sommerlath (1976) **Children:** Crown Princess Victoria Ingrid Alice Desiree (b. 1977), Prince Carl Philip Edmund Bertil (b. 1979) **Heir:** Crown Princess Victoria Ingrid Alice Desiree **Religion:** Lutheran

*United Kingdom*—**Dynasty:** The House of Windsor, a branch of the Saxe-Coburg and Brunswick-Lüneburg line, dates from the accession of King George V in 1910. Although of German heritage, George V abandoned the German name Wettin and adopted the surname Windsor during World War I. He was succeeded by his sons Edward VIII (the Duke of Windsor) and George VI, father of the present monarch. **Monarch:** Queen Elizabeth II succeeded her father, George VI, at his death on February 6, 1952. **Born:** April 21, 1926 **Married:** Philip Mountbatten (Duke of Edinburgh, Earl of Merioneth, Baron Greenwich, and Prince of Great Britain), the son of Prince Andrew of Greece and Denmark (1947) **Children:** Three sons and one daughter: Prince Charles Philip Arthur George (Prince of Wales and Duke of Cornwall) (b. 1948), Prince Andrew Albert Christian Edward (b. 1960), Prince Edward Antony Richard Louis (b. 1964), and Princess Anne Elizabeth Alice Louise (b. 1950) **Heir:** Prince Charles **Religion:** Anglican

## OCEANIA

*Tonga*—**Dynasty:** Tonga was unified by Taufa'ahau Tupou (George I) in 1845. The kingdom is currently ruled by his descendants. **Monarch:** King Taufa'ahau Tupou IV succeeded to the throne at the death of his mother, Queen Salote, in December 1965; he was crowned on April 7, 1967 **Born:** July 4, 1918 **Married:** Princess Halaevalu Mata'aho 'Ahome'e (1947) **Children:** four **Heir:** Crown Prince Tupou To'a (Toufa'ahau Manumatuongo Tukuaho) (b. 1948) **Religion:** Christian

## SELECTED PAST RULERS AND DYNASTIES

### BRITISH RULERS

Victorious over his neighbors, Egbert of Wessex (d. 839) consolidated what was to become the first English kingdom. The British monarchy, although altered by Danish (1016) and Norman (1066) conquest, civil wars, and Cromwell's Commonwealth and weakened by constitutional restraints, still prevails.

| Saxons and Danes | Reign Dates |
|---|---|
| Egbert | 802–839 |
| Ethelwulf | 839–858 |
| Ethelbald | 858–860 |
| Ethelbert | 860–c. 866 |
| Ethelred | c. 866–871 |
| Alfred the Great | 871–c. 899 |
| Edward the Elder | c. 899–924 |
| Athelstan | 924–939 |
| Edmund I | 939–946 |
| Edred | 946–955 |
| Edwy | 955–959 |
| Edgar | 959–975 |
| Edward the Martyr | 975–978 |
| Ethelred II | 978–1016 |
| Edmund Ironside | 1016 |
| Canute the Dane | 1016–1035 |
| Harold I | 1035–1040 |
| Hardicanute | 1040–1042 |
| Edward the Confessor | 1042–1066 |
| Harold II | 1066 |
| **Norman** | |
| William I (the Conqueror) | 1066–1087 |
| William II | 1087–1100 |
| Henry I | 1100–1135 |
| Stephen | 1135–1154 |
| **Plantagenet** | |
| Henry II | 1154–1189 |
| Richard I (Lion-Heart) | 1189–1199 |
| John | 1199–1216 |
| Henry III | 1216–1272 |
| Edward I | 1272–1307 |
| Edward II | 1307–1327 |
| Edward III | 1327–1377 |
| Richard II | 1377–1399 |
| **Lancaster** | |
| Henry IV (Bolingbroke) | 1399–1413 |
| Henry V | 1413–1422 |
| Henry VI | 1422–1461<br>1470–1471 |
| **York** | |
| Edward IV | 1461–1470<br>1471–1483 |
| Edward V | 1483 |
| Richard III | 1483–1485 |
| **Tudor** | |
| Henry VII | 1485–1509 |
| Henry VIII | 1509–1547 |
| Edward VI | 1547–1553 |
| Lady Jane Grey (nine days) | 1553 |
| Mary I | 1553–1558 |
| Elizabeth I | 1558–1603 |
| **Stuart** | |
| James I (VI of Scotland) | 1603–1625 |
| Charles I | 1625–1649 |
| **Commonwealth** | |
| Oliver Cromwell | 1653–1658 |
| Richard Cromwell | 1658–1659 |
| Military Rule | 1659–1660 |
| **Stuart Restoration** | |
| Charles II | 1660–1685 |
| James II | 1685–1688 |
| Interregnum | 1688–1689 |
| **Orange** | |
| William III | 1689–1702 |
| and Mary II | 1689–1694 |
| **Stuart** | |
| Anne | 1702–1714 |
| **Hanover** | |
| George I | 1714–1727 |
| George II | 1727–1760 |
| George III | 1760–1820 |
| George IV | 1820–1830 |
| William IV | 1830–1837 |
| Victoria | 1837–1901 |
| **Saxe-Coburg** | |
| Edward VII | 1901–1910 |
| **Windsor** (Wettin until 1917) | |
| George V | 1910–1936 |
| Edward VIII (325 days) | 1936 |
| George VI | 1936–1952 |

### CHINESE DYNASTIES

| | |
|---|---|
| Hsia (legendary) | c. 1994 B.C.–c. 1523 B.C. |
| Shang | c. 1523 B.C.–c. 1027 B.C. |
| Chou | c. 1027 B.C.–256 B.C. |
| Western Chou | c. 1027 B.C.–771 B.C. |
| Eastern Chou | |
| Spring and Autumn Period | 722 B.C.–481 B.C. |
| Warring States Period | 403 B.C.–221 B.C. |
| Chin | 221 B.C.–206 B.C. |
| Western Han | 206 B.C.–9 A.D. |
| Hsin | 9 A.D.–23 A.D. |
| Eastern Han | 25–220 |
| **The Three Kingdoms** | 220–280 |
| Shu | 221–263 |
| Wei | 220–265 |
| Wu | 222–280 |
| Western Tsin | 266–316 |
| Eastern Tsin | 317–420 |
| **Southern and Northern Dynasties** | 420–581 |
| Liu Sung | 420–479 |
| Southern Ch'i | 479–502 |
| Liang | 502–557 |
| Ch'en | 557–589 |
| Northern Wei and four minor dynasties | 386–535 |
| Sui | 589–618 |
| Tang | 618–907 |
| **Five Dynasties** | 907–960 |
| Later Liang | 907–923 |
| Later Tang | 923–936 |
| Later Chin | 936–947 |
| Later Han | 947–951 |
| Later Chou | 951–960 |
| Northern Sung | 960–1127 |
| Liao | 916–1125 |
| Southern Sung | 1127–1279 |
| Chin | 1115–1234 |
| Yuan | 1271–1368 |
| Ming | 1368–1644 |
| Ching (Manchu) | 1644–1911 |

### FRENCH RULERS

After the death (511) of Clovis I, the Merovingian founder of the Frankish monarchy, his kingdom was divided into Austrasia, Neustria, and Burgundy. These kingdoms were frequently at war. Dagobert I was the last active Merovingian ruler, and his descendants, called the idle kings, were completely subject to their mayors of the palace, the Carolingians, who became the actual rulers of France when Pepin the Short deposed (752) the last Merovingian king.

| | |
|---|---|
| **Carolingians** | |
| *Pepin the Short | 751–768 |
| *Charlemagne (with Carloman up to 771) | 768–814 |
| *Louis I the Pious | 814–840 |
| Charles II the Bald | 840–877 |
| Louis II the Stammerer | 877–879 |
| Louis III and Carloman | 879–882 |
| Carloman | 882–884 |
| Charles the Fat, regent | 884–887 |
| Eudes (Capetian family) | 888–898 |
| Charles III the Simple | 893–922 |
| Robert I (Capetian) | 922–923 |
| Raoul of Burgundy | 923–936 |
| Louis IV d'Outremer | 936–954 |
| Lothaire | 954–986 |
| Louis V | 986–987 |
| **Capetians** | |
| Hugh Capet | 987–996 |
| Robert II | 996–1031 |
| Henry I | 1031–1060 |
| Philip I | 1060–1108 |
| Louis VI | 1108–1137 |
| Louis VII | 1137–1180 |
| Philip II (Augustus) | 1180–1223 |
| Louis VIII | 1223–1226 |
| Louis IX (Saint) | 1226–1270 |
| Philip III | 1270–1285 |
| Philip IV | 1285–1314 |
| Louis X | 1314–1316 |
| John I (the Posthumous) | 1316–1317 |
| Philip V | 1317–1321 |
| Charles IV | 1321–1328 |
| **Valois** | |
| Philip VI | 1328–1350 |
| John II | 1350–1364 |
| Charles V | 1364–1380 |
| Charles VI | 1380–1422 |
| Charles VII | 1422–1461 |
| Louis XI | 1461–1483 |
| Charles VIII | 1483–1498 |
| **Valois-Orléans** | |
| Louis XII | 1498–1515 |
| **Valois-Angoulême** | |
| Francis I | 1515–1547 |
| Henry II | 1547–1559 |
| Francis II | 1559–1560 |
| Charles IX | 1560–1574 |
| Henry III | 1574–1589 |
| **Bourbons** | |
| Henry IV | 1589–1610 |
| Louis XIII | 1610–1643 |
| Louis XIV | 1643–1715 |
| Louis XV | 1715–1774 |
| Louis XVI | 1774–1793 |
| Louis XVII (titular) | 1793–1795 |
| **First Republic** | 1792–1804 |
| **First Empire** | |
| Napoleon I (Bonaparte) | 1804–1814 |
| **Bourbon Restoration** | |
| Louis XVIII | 1814–1824 |
| **First Empire** (100 days) | 1815 |
| **Bourbons** | |
| Charles X | 1824–1830 |
| **Bourbon-Orleans** | |
| Louis Philippe | 1830–1848 |
| **Second Republic** | |
| (Louis) Napoleon III | 1848–1851 |
| **Second Empire** | |
| (Louis) Napoleon III | 1852–1870 |

* King of the Franks.

## GERMAN AND PRUSSIAN RULERS

**House of Hohenzollern, Kings of Prussia**

|  |  |
|---|---|
| Frederick I | 1701–1713 |
| Frederick William I | 1713–1740 |
| Frederick II (the Great) | 1740–1786 |
| Frederick William II | 1786–1797 |
| Frederick William III | 1797–1840 |
| Frederick William IV | 1840–1861 |
| William I (German emperor after 1871) | 1861–1888 |
| *Frederick III | 1888 |
| *William II | 1888–1918 |

* King of Prussia and Emperor of Germany.

## ITALIAN RULERS

Guided by Camillo di Cavour, the House of Savoy undertook to liberate and unify the Italian peninsula, a movement known as the **Risorgimento.** Italy became a kingdom in 1861 and a republic in 1946.

**House of Savoy**

|  |  |
|---|---|
| Emmanuel Philibert | 1553–1580 |
| Charles Emmanuel I | 1580–1630 |
| Victor Amadeus I | 1630–1637 |
| Charles Emmanuel II | 1637–1675 |
| Victor Amadeus II | 1675–1730 |
| Charles Emmanuel III | 1730–1773 |
| Victor Amadeus III | 1773–1796 |
| Charles Emmanuel IV | 1796–1802 |
| Victor Emmanuel I | 1802–1821 |
| Charles Felix | 1821–1831 |

**House of Savoy-Carignano**

|  |  |
|---|---|
| Charles Albert | 1831–1849 |

**Kings of Italy**

|  |  |
|---|---|
| Victor Emmanuel II (king after 1861) | 1849–1878 |
| Humbert I | 1878–1900 |
| Victor Emmanuel III | 1900–1946 |
| Humbert II | 1946 |

## ROMAN EMPERORS

Successor to Julius Caesar, Octavian (also known as Augustus), became the first Roman emperor in 27 B.C. His rule began a long period (200 years) of peace, called the **Pax Romana.** Stretching westward to the British Isles and eastward to the Caucasus, the vast Roman Empire was permanently divided into West and East Empires after the death (395) of Theodosius the Great. The Western Roman Empire came to an end in 476, when the German Odoacer deposed Romulus Augustulus. The Eastern Empire, with its capital at Constantinople, was gradually supplanted by the Byzantine Empire.

**Emperor**

| Emperor | |
|---|---|
| Augustus | 27 B.C.–14 A.D. |
| Tiberius | 14–37 |
| Caligula | 37–41 |
| Claudius | 41–54 |
| Nero | 54–68 |
| Galba | 68–69 |
| Otho | 69 |
| Vitellius | 69 |
| Vespasian | 69–79 |
| Titus | 79–81 |
| Domitian | 81–96 |
| Nerva | 96–98 |
| Trajan | 98–117 |
| Hadrian | 117–138 |
| Antoninus Pius | 138–161 |
| Marcus Aurelius | 161–180 |
| Commodus | 180–192 |
| Pertinax | 193 |
| Didius Julianus | 193 |
| Septimius Severus | 193–211 |
| Caracalla | 211–217 |
| Macrinus | 217–218 |
| Elagabalus (Heliogabalus) | 218–222 |
| Alexander Severus | 222–235 |
| Maximinus | 235–238 |
| Gordian I | 238 |
| Gordian II | 238 |
| Pupienus | 238 |
| Balbinus | 238 |
| Gordian III | 238–244 |
| Philip the Arab | 244–249 |
| Decius | 249–251 |
| Hostilianus | 251 |
| Gallus | 251–253 |
| Volusianus | c. 251–253 |
| Valerian | 253–260 |
| Gallienus | 253–268 |
| Claudius II | 268–270 |
| Aurelian | 270–275 |
| Tacitus | 275–276 |
| Florianus | 276 |
| Probus | 276–282 |
| Carus | 282–283 |
| Carinus | 283–285 |
| Numerianus | 283–284 |
| Diocletian | 284–305 |
| Maximian | 286–305 |
| Constantius | 305–306 |
| Galerius | 305–310 |
| Maxentius | 306–312 |
| Constantine I the Great | 306–337 |
| Licinius | 308–324 |
| Constantine II | 337–340 |
| Constans | 337–350 |
| Constantius II | 337–361 |
| Magnentius | 350–353 |
| Julian the Apostate | 361–363 |
| Jovian | 363–364 |
| Valentinian I | 364–375 |
| Valens | 364–378 |
| Gratian | 375–383 |
| Valentinian II | 375–392 |
| Magnus Maximus | 383–388 |
| Eugenius | 392–394 |
| Theodosius I the Great | 379–395 |

**Emperors in the East**

| Emperor | |
|---|---|
| Arcadius | 395–408 |
| Theodosius II | 408–450 |
| Marcian | 450–457 |
| Leo I | 457–474 |
| Leo II | 474 |

**Emperors in the West**

| Emperor | |
|---|---|
| Honorius | 395–423 |
| Constantius III | 421 |
| Valentinian III | 425–455 |
| Petronius Maximus | 455 |
| Avitus | 455–456 |
| Majorian | 457–461 |
| Libius Severus | 461–465 |
| Anthemius | 467–472 |
| Olybrius | 472 |
| Glycerius | 473 |
| Julius Nepos | 474–475 |
| Romulus Augustulus | 475–476 |

## RUSSIAN RULERS

**Grand Dukes of Moscow**

|  |  |
|---|---|
| Ivan I, Prince of Moscow | 1328–1341 |
| Ivan II, Ivanovich | 1353–1359 |
| Dmitry Donskoi | 1359–1389 |
| Vasily I Dmitrievich | 1389–1425 |
| Vasily II | 1425–1462 |
| Ivan III Vasilyevich | 1462–1505 |
| Vasily III Ivanovich | 1505–1533 |
| Ivan IV (the Terrible), tsar of Russia from 1547 | 1533–1584 |
| Fyodor Ivanovich | 1584–1598 |
| Boris Godunov | 1598–1605 |
| Fyodor II | 1605 |
| False Dmitry I | 1605–1606 |
| Vasily Shuisky | 1606–1610 |

| | |
|---|---|
| **Interregnum** | 1610–1613 |

**House of Romanov**

|  |  |
|---|---|
| Tsar Mikhail | 1613–1645 |
| Tsar Alexei Mikhailovich | 1645–1676 |
| Fyodor Alexeyevich | 1676–1682 |
| Peter I, the Great (with Ivan V until 1689) | 1682–1725 |
| Catherine I | 1725–1727 |
| Peter II | 1727–1730 |
| Anna Ivanovna | 1730–1740 |
| Ivan VI | 1740–1741 |
| Elizabeth | 1741–1761 |
| Peter III | 1761–1762 |
| Catherine II (the Great) | 1762–1796 |
| Paul I | 1796–1801 |
| Alexander I | 1801–1825 |
| Nicholas I | 1825–1855 |
| Alexander II | 1855–1881 |
| Alexander III | 1881–1894 |
| Nicholas II | 1894–1917 |

## SPANISH RULERS

Spain was unified by the marriage of Ferdinand of Aragon and Isabella of Castile. Alfonso XIII was exiled in 1931, when Spain became a republic. The country came under the rule of Gen. Francisco Franco in 1939. The grandson of Alfonso XIII was proclaimed king, as Juan Carlos I, on the death of Franco in 1975.

**Houses of Aragon and Castile**

|  |  |
|---|---|
| Ferdinand II of Aragon and Isabella of Castile | 1474–1504 |
| Ferdinand II and Philip I | 1504–1506 |
| Ferdinand II and Charles I | 1506–1516 |

**Spanish Hapsburgs**

|  |  |
|---|---|
| Charles I (V of Holy Roman Empire) | 1516–1556 |
| Philip II | 1556–1598 |
| Philip III | 1598–1621 |
| Philip IV | 1621–1665 |
| Charles II | 1665–1700 |

**Spanish Bourbons**

|  |  |
|---|---|
| Philip V | 1700–1724 |
| Louis I | 1724 |
| Philip V | 1724–1746 |
| Ferdinand VI | 1746–1759 |
| Charles III | 1759–1788 |
| Charles IV | 1788–1808 |

**French King of Spain**

|  |  |
|---|---|
| Joseph Bonaparte | 1808–1813 |

**Bourbon Restoration**

|  |  |
|---|---|
| Ferdinand VII | 1814–1833 |
| Isabella II | 1833–1868 |

| | |
|---|---|
| **Provisional Government** | 1868–1870 |

**House of Savoy**

|  |  |
|---|---|
| Amadeo I | 1870–1873 |

| | |
|---|---|
| **First Spanish Republic** | 1873–1874 |

**Bourbon Restoration**

|  |  |
|---|---|
| Alfonso XII | 1875–1885 |
| Alfonso XIII | 1886–1931 |

## FAMILY HISTORY IS FOR EVERYONE

*Harriet Stryker Rodda, certified genealogist, lecturer and teacher; author of family histories and professional articles, including* How to Climb Your Family Tree.

Everyone in America is descended from immigrant stock, no matter what the ethnic or cultural background. Even the "native American Indians" were immigrants. They just happened to arrive before the European sailors and settlers.

With the Bicentennial celebrations mostly behind us, we are facing the coming of our Tricentennial in the year 2076. By then, each of us could be an ancestor who could be a missing link to our descendants. Far too many people in this country are bemoaning the fact that they cannot complete their connections with their ancestral families because their folks left no records or they neglected to listen when stories were being told.

Families in the United States are the backbone of the nation, although they are not as stereotyped as they once were. No matter what the ethnic or cultural background, the family unit is still the core of our young, 202-year-old America. *Newsweek* declared in May 1978 "there is an underlying stability of family life that often goes unnoticed. Ninety-eight percent of all American children are raised in families, and last year 79 percent of those were living with their parents." These are the children, plus many more, who by 2076 will be asking "Who am I?", "Where did my family come from?", "When did they get here?", "How did they live?", "Why are we as we are?"

These very same questions are being asked today. The answers are not to be found easily for some, because the fore-parents left no private and often few public records of themselves. For the majority, however, most of the facts they need to answer the who, where, when, why and how are available. They can be found and the family history preserved to be passed along for years to come. "But how do I start?" is the first question.

**Start with yourself.** You are to be author of your family history. Your autobiography will not only inform others of the facts and facets of your life, but more importantly will reveal to you the debt you owe your family. It will show you what you would like to know about those earlier members of the family. *Who, when, where, how* and *why* will be your guides as you record yourself and your times. Add pictures to illustrate, and dig out the certificates of your birth, education, honors, marriage or anything else that will add documentation to your record. Even if you never go on to compile a family history, this autobiography may be of inestimable assistance to someone else who will take up the task where you left off.

**Contact all older living members of your family.** With tape recorder or pencil and notebook, get all the information on the family members they can supply. It will amaze you how much they know and how they will have contacts with relatives you have never heard of. Don't overlook the stories or traditions they may relate to you. There is a core of truth in most of them. Try not to antagonize, but tell them of your deep interest in preparing and preserving the family's history. Check their possession of family or Bible records; ask about certificates, passports, naturalization records, pictures, letters, heirloom furniture or other items. You may want some of these, but don't be greedy. Take pictures of whatever you can and copy whatever you find in their records. But leave the original with the owner unless it is freely given to you.

**Record your in-family findings.** How you do this is for you to decide, but make the final record easily understandable by anyone who sees it. It should contain the time and place and from whom you received the statements so that later you won't have to wonder who told you that and where you heard it. For every statement you use in your final record, you should have some documentation to prove it. Birth, marriage, divorce, death and land ownership records are the basic public records that should be found to support your story.

**Visit a good genealogical library** and use their catalogs to determine whether someone in the past has written a family history or genealogy to which your family can relate. Read the local and general histories for a better understanding of where and how your people lived. See the vital records collected for researchers like you: church records, newspaper items, census records, maps, cemetery records, diaries, account books, and many, many more, including the work of genealogists whose notes on your family may have been deposited for safekeeping. Get acquainted with the publications of genealogical societies, especially those that publish genealogical records. Begin to took at some of the books on the shelves with a critical eye. Decide which of their features you like and what you would not want in your final record. Are they readable, interesting in form and format, well documented and illustrated; do they feel good in the hand; does the type of binding let them lie open readily for reading and research? Make note of those that please you so that you can refer to them when you are ready to prepare your final history.

Despite the wealth of recorded information to be found in the form of tax rolls, military records, probate, land, court and census records, not to mention church and cemetery records and the cemeteries themselves, with their informative gravestones, this information is not always easy to obtain. Help is available. Along the way you will have become acquainted with the many "how-to" books written by people who want to share their knowledge with you. You will hear and read of genealogical seminars, lectures and conferences at every level from the local historical society to the large university and the Federal Archives. Take advantage of as much of this as you can, for you will meet a vast number of people who are learning as you are, who are as eager to accomplish as you will be, and who are happy to share their knowledge with you.

Today, family history is recognized for its value in establishing a keen sense of identity. Such simple projects in elementary schools as collecting information about parents and grandparents are known to help children establish as sense of personal worth and dignity. Genealogy is no longer considered a snob hobby. It has come of age. Good hunting! Become an honored ancestor!

# OUTLINE OF WORLD HISTORY

This capsule presentation of the history of the world covers the period from 4000 B.C. through 1981.

## 4000 B.C.—3000 B.C.

EUROPE

**4000 B.C.** Farmers living along **Danube River in villages** designed stone replicas of deities.

NEAR AND MIDDLE EAST

**4000 B.C. Ubadians,** who were settled in southern Mesopotamia, developed towns in the Tigris-Euphrates plain, laying foundation for future civilization of **Ur.** Semitic nomads from Syria and the Arabian peninsula invaded area and intermingled with Urbaidians.

**3500 B.C. Sumerians,** possibly from Asia, settled along the Euphrates and developed a civilization that flourished.

FAR EAST

**4000 B.C.** Farmers lived in villages in northern **China.**

AMERICAS

**4000 B.C. Indians** in North and South America, descendants of people who migrated from Asia over the Bering Strait many centuries earlier, obtained food by hunting and cultivating corn. The remains of extinct animals, such as the mastodon, as well as arrowheads and spear points found in caves at **Folsom** and **Clovis,** New Mexico, attest to the antiquity of Indians in the Americas.

AFRICA

**4000 B.C.** An early Negro civilization thrived in the **Sahara.** The **Tassili rock paintings** in southeast Algeria, which date from about 6000 B.C., portray an organized society of hunters and herders who had horses and cattle.

**c. 3200 B.C.** Upper and Lower **Egypt** were united by the legendary **Menes,** the first Pharaoh, who built his capital at Memphis.

## 3000 B.C.—2000 B.C.

EUROPE

**2700–2000 B.C.** Early **Helladic culture** existed on Greek mainland, and **Cycladic culture** in the Aegean islands; both noted for primitive figurines.

**2500–1200 B.C.** Barbarian **Celts,** who overran western Europe, rode horses, carried iron weapons, and were ruled by **Druids,** a priestly class.

**2500–1100 B.C. Megalithic culture** of western Europe was noted for its huge stone ceremonial constructions, such as **dolmens,** or chamber tombs, and **menhirs,** or monumental stone slabs, sometimes arranged in circles, as at **Stonehenge** in England; remains also exist at **Carnac,** Brittany.

NEAR AND MIDDLE EAST

**c. 3000 B.C. Kish,** near modern Baghdad, became leading Sumerian city in the reign of King Etana.

**c. 2800 B.C. Meskiaggasher** founded dynasty in **Erech,** which began to rival Kish.

**2686–2181 B.C. Old Kingdom of Egypt:** Egyptian art and architecture developed; **great pyramid** for Pharaoh **Khufu,** one of the Seven Wonders of the Ancient World, was completed (c. 2600 B.C.) at Gizeh.

**c. 2650 B.C. Gilgamesh,** hero of Sumerian legends, reigned as king of Erech.

**2500 B.C. King Lugalannemundu** of Adab briefly united Sumerian city-states; following his death, city-states fought each other for 200 years.

**c. 2450 B.C. King Eannatum** made the Sumerian city-state of Lagash supreme.

**c. 2325 B.C. Sargon the Great** ruled over vast empire in Mesopotamia and built capital at Agade in Akkad that had beautiful temples and palace.

**c. 2300 B.C. Ebla** flourishes in Syria.

**2200 B.C. Gutians,** barbarians from Iran, conquered Sumeria and destroyed Agade.

**2133–1786 B.C. Middle Kingdom of Egypt:** Egypt expanded territory southward and engaged in extensive foreign trade.

**2100 B.C. Ur-Nammu** founded last **Sumerian dynasty** and promulgated law code, the oldest in existence.

FAR EAST

**3000–1500 B.C. Indus valley civilization** of northern India: a sophisticated culture thrived and cities of **Harappa** and **Mohenjo-Daro** were built with courtyard houses and modern drainage systems.

**c. 2205–c. 1766 B.C. Hsia dynasty** of China: first historic Chinese dynasty thrived; horses were domesticated and rice and millet were cultivated.

AMERICAS

**2500 B.C. Indians began to make pottery.**

## 2000 B.C.—1500 B.C.

EUROPE

**c. 2000–1700 B.C. Mycenaeans,** Greek-speaking people, settled in **Greece,** established flourishing civilization, and traded with Crete.

**c. 1900–1400 B.C. Stonehenge,** a massive stone complex used for religious purposes, was erected on Salisbury Plain, England.

**c. 1700–c. 1500 B.C. Minoan culture** on Crete reached its zenith; magnificent Minoan palaces built at **Knossos** and **Phaistos** showed evidence of advanced engineering skills.

**c. 1500 B.C. Linear B** script existed in Crete, evidence of Mycenaean influence.

NEAR AND MIDDLE EAST

**2000 B.C. Elamites** destroyed Ur, marking end of Sumerian dominance in Mesopotamia.

**c. 2000–c. 1900 B.C. Abraham,** founder of **Judaism,** is said to have lived.

**2000–1700 B.C. Hebrews** lived as nomadic shepherds in **Canaan.**

**1786–1567 B.C. Egypt** ruled by **Hyksos kings,** who probably came from Canaan, introduced horse-drawn chariots.

**1750–c. 1708 B.C. Hammurabi** ruled Babylonia, brought most of Mesopotamia and Assyria under his control, and introduced his **law code.**

**c. 1600 B.C. Babylonian dynasty** destroyed by **Hittites** from Anatolia and Syria.

**1567–1085 B.C. New Kingdom in Egypt:** Hyksos kings ousted and Egyptian power and civilization reached its height.

FAR EAST

**1523–1027 B.C. Shang dynasty** ruled China, developing a high civilization characterized by specialized classes, writing, a medium of exchange, and ancestor worship.

AMERICAS

**2000 B.C.** By this time, **Indians** had permanent village settlements and were cultivating manioc, squash, maize, and beans and domesticating dogs.

## 1500 B.C.—1000 B.C.

EUROPE

**1400 B.C. Mycenaeans** gained supremacy of the Mediterranean, and Mycenae, in northern Peloponnesus, became major ancient city following collapse of Knossus.

**c. 1200 B.C. Trojan Wars:** Greece conquered Troy in **Asia Minor.**
**Dorian barbarians** from the north began to invade Greece, initiating Dark Ages of Greek history.

**1150–1000 B.C. Greeks** settled on **Ionian coast** of Asia Minor.

NEAR AND MIDDLE EAST

**c. 1500 B.C. Mitanni kingdom of Hurrians** (known as Horites in Old Testament) ruled much of Mesopotamia and Assyria.

**1468 B.C. Battle of Megiddo:** Egyptians, under **Thutmose III,** conquered Syria and part of Mesopotamia.

**1292–1225 B.C. Ramses II** ruled Egypt and completed temples at Karnak, Thebes, Luxor, and Abu-Simbel. Moses led Hebrews out of Egpt.

**1250 B.C. Phoenicians** flourished on coasts of Syria and Lebanon, establishing great city-states of **Tyre** and **Sidon** and beginning to colonize Mediterranean coast.

**c. 1250 B.C. Hebrews** entered **Canaan.**

**1020–1004 B.C. Saul** became the first king of the Hebrews.

FAR EAST

**1500–500 B.C.** Barbarian **Aryans,** Sanskrit-speaking people from central Asia, invaded **India** and destroyed Indus valley civilization; early *Vedas,* sacred Hindu texts, were composed.

**1027–256 B.C. Chou dynasty** of China superseded **Shang** dynasty and represented the Classical Age of China with the *Five Classics,* and teachings of **Confucius, Lao-tze,** and **Mencius.**

AMERICAS

**c. 1250 B.C. Olmecs** began to settle at **San Lorenzo, Mexico,** and developed civilization with widespread influence that was famous for gigantic sculptured heads (sometimes weighing over 20 tons) and austere figurines; ceremonial center was established at **La Venta** (fl. 800–c. 400 B.C.) for jaguar cult; Stele C found at **Tres Zapotes** has date equivalent to 31 B.C. carved in Mayan calendric system.

AFRICA

**1200 B.C.** Negroes in Nigeria developed **Nok culture,** which became advanced civilization, noted for expressive terra-cotta sculpture, but died out c. 200 B.C.

## 1000 B.C.—700 B.C.

EUROPE

**1000 B.C. Teutonic tribes** settled northern Europe.
**Latin tribes** began to settle in Italy.

**900–400 B.C. Etruscan** people, who had probably migrated from Lydia in Asia Minor, established a high civilization in **Italy** and became maritime power.

**850–600 B.C. Homeric Greece:** Greeks established colonies in Italy and along Mediterranean; the *Iliad* and the *Odyssey* were probably composed by Homer, **Hesiod** wrote poetry, and music developed.

**776 B.C. Olympic games** initiated.

**753 B.C.** Traditional date for **founding of Rome** by **Romulus** and **Remus.**

**750 B.C.** Romans seized **Sabine women** at public spectacle, taking them as wives.

**747 B.C.** Rome taken by **Sabines,** who united with Romans as one people.

**736–630 B.C. Sparta** became powerful on Greek mainland.

NEAR AND MIDDLE EAST

**1000–774 B.C. Phoenicians** dominated the seas, perhaps sailing to Cornwall, England, for tin and probably sailing down west coast of Africa.

**910–606 B.C. Assyrian Empire** controlled Mesopotamia.

**774–625 B.C.** Phoenicia came under **Assyrian** rule.

**747–728 B.C. Tiglath-Pilser III,** king of Assyria, subdued Aramaean tribes in Babylonia, conquered Urartu (Armenia), and established control over Syria.

**721–705 B.C. Sargon II,** king of Assyria, completed conquest of **Israel,** exiling most Israelites.

**705–681 B.C. Sennacherib,** king of Assyria, destroyed Babylon and built magnificent palace at **Nineveh.**

AMERICAS

**c. 1000 B.C. Chavin culture** in northern Peru began to flourish; elaborate stone ceremonial center with painted relief sculpture was erected at **Chavin de Huantar** for jaguar cult; and gold ornaments and ceramics were designed; this culture declined after 200 B.C.

AFRICA

**c. 800–586 B.C. Carthage,** founded in North Africa by **Phoenicians,** became a wealthy commercial center.

**c. 750 B.C. Kushites** settled in **Sudan** and developed high civilization, erecting palaces and pyramids; extensive archaeological remains of ironworks at Meroë; Kushites used elephants and traded as far as Rome and India; their last king died in 320 A.D.

## 700 B.C.—500 B.C.

EUROPE

**c. 700 B.C.** Temple to Hera erected at **Olympia.**
**Spartans,** after a series of wars, annexed eastern part of Messenia.
**Celts** began to invade Spain and France.

**c. 660 B.C. Byzantium** founded by **Megara.**

**c. 621 B.C. Draco** codified harsh Athenian **law.**

**600–300 B.C. Teutonic tribes** invaded western Europe: the **Alemanni** settled on the upper Rhine, the **Franks** and **Saxons** between the Weser and the Elbe, and the **Thuringians** south of the Saxons.

**594 B.C. Solon** introduced constitutional and social reforms into **Athens,** establishing limited democracy.

**c. 580 B.C. Thales,** first Western philosopher, flourished.

**566 B.C.** First Roman **census** taken.

**c. 560–510 B.C. Athens** ruled by **tyrants** after Pisistratus seized power.

**560 B.C. Croesus,** wealthy king of **Lydia,** conquered Ionian cities and was defeated (546 B.C.) by Cyrus the Great.

**c. 550 B.C. Temple of Artemis** (Diana) erected at Ephesus.

**c. 534–510 B.C.** Reign of **Tarquinius Superbus,** Etruscan ruler; Etruscan supremacy ended soon after his death.

**509 B.C.** Traditional date for founding of the **Roman Republic.**
The **Temple of Jupiter,** on the Roman Capitol, was dedicated.

NEAR AND MIDDLE EAST

**681–668 B.C. Esarhaddon,** king of **Assyria,** reigned; at its peak Assyrian Empire extended from Iran to Egypt.

**625–539 B.C. Chaldean Empire** of Mesopotamia.

**612 B.C. Nineveh,** Assyrian capital, fell to Medes, Chaldeans, and Scythians.

**606 B.C.** Battle of **Carchemish** ended Assyrian Empire.

**c. 605–562 B.C.** Reign of **Nebuchadnezzar II, king of** Babylonia; **Babylon,** with its hanging gardens (one of Seven Wonders of Ancient World), was greatest city of its time during his reign; massive palaces, **"Tower of Babel,"** and a temple to the god **Marduk** were also constructed.

**586 B.C.** Nebuchadnezzar took **Jerusalem,** destroying the temple of Solomon and carrying inhabitants back to Babylonia.

**c. 550 B.C. Persian Empire,** founded by **Cyrus the Great,** included vast areas of the Near and Middle East; Persian art and architecture flourished, and **Zoroastrian** religion spread.

**538 B.C. Cyrus the Great** conquered Babylon and returned Hebrews to Jerusalem.

**525–404 B.C.** Persians conquered and **ruled Egypt.**

**521–486 B.C. Darius I** (the Great), king of Persia, extended and strengthened the empire, warred with Greece, and unified Persian power in the East.

FAR EAST

**c. 563–483 B.C. Gautama Buddha** preached in **India.**

**c. 551–479 B.C. Confucius** taught in **China.**

AFRICA

**c. 631 B.C.** Greeks founded North African city of **Cyrene,** which became important commercial center.

## 500 B.C.—400 B.C.

EUROPE

**500–449 B.C. Greek-Persian Wars** were fought, caused by commercial rivalry between Athens and Persia; Athens became leading city-state of Greece.

**500 B.C. Classical Greek civilization** (drama, philosophy, and the arts) developed and flourished, declining after 300 B.C.

**498 B.C.** Earliest extant poem of **Pindar** was written.

**490 B.C.** Battle of **Marathon:** 30,000 Persians, who were sent by Darius I, landed at Marathon to march on Athens and were turned back by Athenian infantrymen under **Miltiades.**

**460 B.C.** Athens warred against **Peloponnesian** cities, which were allied with Sparta.

**457–429 B.C. Age of Pericles** or Golden Age of Athens: philosophy, sculpture, and painting flourished; **Parthenon** was built (447–432 B.C.) on the Acropolis.

**c. 451 B.C.** The Twelve Tablets: **Roman law** codified for the first time.

**c. 435 B.C. Phidias** completed his statue of Zeus (one of Seven Wonders of Ancient World) for temple of Olympia.

**431–404 B.C. Peloponnesian War** developed, growing out of Spartan-Athenian rivalry; Athens destroyed (430).

**c. 411** Thucydides wrote *The Peloponnesian War.*

**404–371 B.C. Sparta** was leading Greek power.

NEAR AND MIDDLE EAST

**490 B.C.** First Persian expedition to Greece under Darius I was turned back at **Marathon.**

**480–479 B.C.** Second Persian expedition to Greece under **Xerxes I** was turned back at Plataea.

AMERICAS

c. 500 B.C. **Zapotecs** established ceremonial center at **Monte Albán, Mexico**, which showed **Olmec** influence.

AFRICA

c. 500 B.C. Kingdom of **Axum** in **Ethiopia** came into existence; palaces, temples, and carved stone obelisks were built and trade took place with Near East and India; this kingdom declined c. 700 A.D.

## 400 B.C.—300 B.C.

EUROPE

400–270 B.C. **Rome** conquered Italy, subduing Etruscans, Samnites, and Greek colonists.

399 B.C. **Socrates** was condemned to death and made to drink hemlock.

390 B.C. Rome sacked by **Gauls.**

c. 387 B.C. **Plato** founded his **Academy** in Athens, which is considered the first university of the Western world.

359–336 B.C. **Philip II** of **Macedon** conquered Thrace, Thebes, and Athens, and attempted to unite Greece during his reign; **Demosthenes**, greatest Greek orator, warned Athenians of Macedonian aims.

336–323 B.C. Reign of **Alexander the Great** of **Macedon** (son of Philip II), first of the great European conquerors; Alexander extended empire to include Egypt and the Near East and invaded India.

335 B.C. **Aristotle** founded a school in the Lyceum at Athens known as Peripatetic from his practice of lecturing in a covered portico (*peripatos*).

323 B.C. **Hellenistic Age** began, during which Greek influence spread throughout Mediterranean; this age ended in 31 B.C.

NEAR AND MIDDLE EAST

c. 352 B.C. **Mausoleum** at **Halicarnassus** in Asia Minor (one of Seven Wonders of Ancient World) was erected in memory of Mausolus of Caria.

334–330 B.C. **Alexander the Great** conquered Asia Minor, Phoenicia, Palestine, Egypt, and Persia and founded **Alexandria.**

323 B.C.–30 A.D. **Ptolemies**, a Greek dynasty, ruled **Egypt.**

FAR EAST

327–326 B.C. **Alexander the Great** and his Greek troops entered **India**, withdrawing after troops revolted.

325–298 B.C. Reign of **Chandragupta Maurya**, who founded Maurya dynasty and united **India.**

AFRICA

350 B.C. Meroë, Kushite capital, fell to **Ethiopians** and was abandoned.

## 300 B.C.—200 B.C.

EUROPE

300 B.C. City of **Rome** became a major power in Mediterranean world.

292–280 B.C. **Colossus of Rhodes** (one of Seven Wonders of Ancient World), a bronze statue, probably more than 100 feet tall, of the sun god, Helios, was constructed on promontory overlooking harbor.

282–272 B.C. **Pyrrhus**, king of **Epirus**, fought Romans and caused its ruin.

264–241 B.C. First **Punic War:** Carthage warred against Roman occupation of Sicily.

227 B.C. **Rome** annexed Sardinia and Corsica.

218–201 B.C. Second **Punic War: Hannibal**, the Carthaginian leader, crossed the Alps and invaded Italy; victorious Romans gained Spanish provinces and Carthaginian war fleet.

NEAR AND MIDDLE EAST

300 B.C. **Alexandria**, Egypt, became intellectual center of Hellenistic world until its influence ended in 50 B.C.

c. 280 B.C. Under Ptolemy II, a **lighthouse** (one of Seven Wonders of Ancient World) was constructed on **Pharos**, Alexandria.

250 B.C. **Parthian Empire**, which succeeded Persian Empire, ended in 226 A.D.

FAR EAST

269–232 B.C. **Emperor Asoka the Great** ruled **India**, making Buddhism state religion.

221–207 B.C. **Ch'in dynasty** of China: country was unified for first time, and construction of **Great Wall** was initiated.

202 B.C. **Han dynasty** of China established: during long peaceful rule, Chinese realized great artistic achievements, expanded territory, and introduced **Buddhism;** this dynasty collapsed in 220 A.D.

## 200 B.C.—100 B.C.

EUROPE

192–189 B.C. During **Syrian War** between Rome and Seleucid kingdom, Romans acquired territory in Asia Minor.

c. 150 B.C. **Polybius** completed six books of his *Universal History*, a political analysis of the rise of Rome.

149–146 B.C. Third **Punic War.**

146 B.C. **Macedonia** became a Roman province.

121 B.C. **Rome** conquered southeastern **Gaul**, modern Provence.

NEAR AND MIDDLE EAST

192–189 B.C. **Syrian War** between Rome and Seleucids: **Antiochus III** forced to give up Asia Minor.

167 B.C. Hebrew **Maccabees** revolted against Antiochus IV, king of Syria, who had tried to Hellenize Palestine.

FAR EAST

c. 200 B.C. *Mahabharata*, Sanskrit epic poem, began to be composed and was completed c. 200 A.D.

AFRICA

149–146 B.C. Third **Punic War:** Carthage destroyed by Romans, who established Roman province of Africa.

## 100 B.C.—A.D. 1

EUROPE

73–71 B.C. **Spartacus** led slave revolt in southern Italy; **Pompey** crushed revolt and crucified 6,000 slaves.

63 B.C. **Cicero**, greatest Roman orator, exposed **Catiline's plot** to seize consulship by force.

60–53 B.C. First Triumvirate: **Julius Caesar,** Pompey, and Marcus Licinius Crassus ruled Rome.

58–49 B.C. Gallic Wars: **Caesar's campaigns** brought Gaul under Roman rule.

48 B.C. Caesar met **Cleopatra** in Egypt.

46–44 B.C. **Caesar** ruled Rome, which included Gaul, Italy, part of Illyria, Macedonia, Greece, Asia Minor, Egypt, and part of North Africa.

44 B.C. Caesar stabbed to death in the Senate on **Ides of March.**

43–31 B.C. Second Triumvirate: **Marc Antony,** Lepidus, and **Octavian,** Caesar's grandnephew, ruled Rome.

c. 35 B.C. Roman poets **Vergil** and **Horace** flourished.

31 B.C. **Octavian** defeated **Antony** and **Cleopatra** at **Actium,** assuming title Augustus and becoming **first Roman emperor; Augustus made Egypt a Roman** province.

27 B.C. **Roman Empire** established.

14 B.C. **Pax Romana:** Roman Empire began 200 years of peace, which ended in 192 A.D.

NEAR AND MIDDLE EAST

74–63 B.C. Third **Mithridatic War** between King Mithridates VI of Pontus and Rome, which resulted in further Roman conquests in Near East.

48 B.C. **Cleopatra**, daughter of Ptolemy XI of Egypt, with the aid of **Julius Caesar,** became Queen of Egypt (47–30 B.C.).

37 B.C. **Rome** began to rule **Palestine;** this rule ended in 395 A.D.

36 B.C. Queen Cleopatra married **Marc Antony.**

30 B.C. **Egypt** annexed by Roman Empire, following the suicides of Antony and Cleopatra.

6 or 4 B.C. **Jesus** born in Bethlehem.

AMERICAS

100 B.C. **Paracus** culture, an offshoot of Chavin civilization in **Peru,** flourished.

## A.D. 1—A.D. 100

EUROPE

1 **Christian era** began.

**Gothic kingdom** on the lower Vistula (Poland) developed.

5–40 **Cymbeline** reigned in Britain.

9 **Arminius** defeated Roman commander **Varus** at the Battle of Teutoburg Forest, ending Roman attempts to conquer Germany.

37 **Caligula** made emperor of Rome by army; his cruel regime ended (41) with his assassination.

41–54 **Reign of Roman Emperor Claudius I, who disenfranchised many non-Italians, annexed Mauretania, expelled Jews from Rome, and initiated Roman rule of Britain.**
43 Romans ruled **Britain** until 407.
54–69 Reign of **Emperor Nero,** last of Julio-Claudian line of Roman emperors; he blamed Christians for fire that almost destroyed (64) Rome and rebuilt city magnificently; Roman persecution of Christians was begun, which may have caused death of **St. Peter** and **St. Paul;** Nero committed suicide.
61–62 **Boadicea,** British queen of Iceni (Norfolk), led revolt against Romans at Fort Londinium; defeated, she took poison.
65 **Seneca,** philosopher and adviser to Nero, committed suicide after he was accused of conspiracy.
69–79 Reign of **Emperor Vespasian,** who founded Flavian dynasty and erected the **Colosseum** and **Forum** in Rome.
79 **Mount Vesuvius** erupted, destroying **Pompeii** and Herculaneum.
81–96 Reign of **Emperor Domitian,** son of Vespasian, was characterized by persecution of Christians; Domitian erected **Arch of Titus** to memorialize his brother's conquest of Jerusalem.
96–180 Reign of **"the Five Good Emperors"** of Rome: Nerva, Trajan, Hadrian, Antonius Pius, and Marcus Aurelius; the empire was enlarged and great public works undertaken.
c. 98 **Tacitus,** Roman historian, completed *Germania.*

NEAR AND MIDDLE EAST

c. 28 **St. John the Baptist** began preaching.
c. 30 **Jesus** crucified in Jerusalem.
c. 42–60 **St. Paul,** one of the apostles, conducted missionary work in Asia Minor and Greece and wrote his *Epistles.*
66 **Jews** revolted against Roman rule in Palestine; **Titus** suppressed rebellion and destroyed (70) Jerusalem.

FAR EAST

9 **Emperor Wang Mang** usurped Chinese throne, initiating agrarian reforms.
25 **Han dynasty** held Chinese throne until 220; Buddhism was introduced during reign of **Emperor Ming-ti** (58–76), and cultural ties with India were increased.
60 **Kushan** kings of Grandhara began to rule in West Pakistan, establishing an empire that extended from central Asia to India; a famous school of Buddhist sculpture was organized.

## 100—200

EUROPE

100 For the next 375 years, **Goths, Vandals,** and **Huns** raided Roman Empire.
117 Roman Empire reached its greatest extent after **Emperor Trajan** subdued Dacia (Rumania), Armenia, and Upper Mesopotamia; Trajan's Column was erected in Rome to honor his conquests.
117–138 Reign of **Emperor Hadrian;** he standardized Roman law throughout the empire, and constructed a 73-mile-long wall named after him in Britain.
130 **Pantheon** built at Rome and consecrated as Christian church in 609.
160–180 **Marcus Aurelius,** Stoic philosopher and author of *Meditations,* ruled Roman Empire and was forced to wage numerous wars.
192–284 Roman Empire ruled by army, **"Barracks Emperors."**
196 **Barbarians** overran northern Britain.

NEAR AND MIDDLE EAST

132–135 **Bar Kokba** led Jewish revolt; defeated by Romans, Jews were barred from Jerusalem and further dispersed.

FAR EAST

100 Traditional date for beginning of **Japanese state.**
c. 100 **Funan Empire** established in Cambodia.
**Champa** kingdom founded in South Vietnam and parts of Cambodia.
c. 132 **Indo-Scythians** destroyed last traces of Hellenic rule in northern India.
c. 150 **Kanishka** reigned in India.

AMERICAS

100 **Teotihuacán** civilization, one of America's most splendid early civilizations, developed in central Mexico; Pyramid of the Sun was as tall as 20-story building, Temple of Quetzalcoátl erected to Feather Serpent deity, and agricultural techniques advanced enough to support large urban population around huge **pyramid complex;** influence ceased when city fell c. 700 to **Chichimecs.**

## 200—300

EUROPE

205 **British revolt against Romans was suppressed in 211.**
211–217 Reign of **Emperor Caracalla,** who constructed in Rome Baths named for him.
220–238 **Goths** invaded Balkans, **Asia Minor,** and eastern Roman Empire.
c. 240 **Franks** first appeared in Europe.
c. 252 Franks, Goths, and **Alemanni** broke through borders of Roman Empire.
268 **Goths** sacked Athens, Corinth, and **Sparta.**
270–275 **Emperor Aurelian** consolidated empire by retreating to Danubian borders, recovered **Gaul,** and overthrew Queen **Zenobia** of Palmyra (Syria).
276 **Great wall around Rome** erected against barbarian attacks.
284–305 Reign of **Emperor Diocletian,** who divided empire into western part (Italy and Africa), which was governed from Milan by **Maximian;** Diocletian ruled eastern part (Near and Middle East and Egypt) from Nicomedia (now Izmit, Turkey).

NEAR AND MIDDLE EAST

200–230 **Clement** and **Origen,** Christian theologians, taught in Alexandria.
226–240 **Ardashir I** (or **Artaxerxes**) overthrew Parthian Empire; founded Neo-Persian Empire under **Sassanid dynasty.**
232 Sassanian-Roman War established **Sassanians** as major Eastern power.
c. 242 **Mani,** founder of **Manichaeism,** began to preach in Persia; he was martyred c. 276.
260 Persians under **Shapur I** captured **Roman Emperor Valerian** and Roman territory in Near and Middle East.
268 **Zenobia,** queen of Palmyra, conquered Syria, Mesopotamia, and parts of Egypt; Zenobia was overthrown (273) by **Roman Emperor Aurelian.**

FAR EAST

205–225 Reign of **Fan Shih-man** in Cambodia extended empire to lower Mekong River.
220 **Han dynasty** came to an end; China was **divided** and invaded for next three centuries.
265 **Western Tsin (Ch'in) dynasty** began, uniting China until **White Huns** began to invade in 317.

## 300—400

EUROPE

303 **Diocletian** harshly persecuted **Christians.**
306–337 Reign of **Constantine I, first Christian emperor.**
313 **Edict of Milan** recognized Christianity as a legal religion in Roman Empire.
325 **First ecumenical council,** which was convened by Constantine at **Nicaea,** voted against Arianism.
330 Constantine made **Constantinople** (now **Istanbul**) new capital of Roman Empire.
337 Romans fought series of wars with **Persians,** which ended (363) with loss of parts of Armenia and Mesopotamia.
c. 340 **Monasticism** developed in the West.
341 **Wulfila** began Christianizing Visigoths and resettling them (c. 348) in Balkans.
c. 350 **Huns,** central Asian nomads, began to invade Europe, forcing Goths westward.
360–367 **Picts, Irish,** and **Saxons** invaded **Britain.**
361–363 Reign of **Julian the Apostate,** who tried unsuccessfully to revive paganism.
363 **Emperor Jovian** restored Christianity.
379–395 **Theodosius,** Roman emperor, resettled Goths in empire, many of whom became soldiers.
383–407 Roman legions evacuated **Britain.**
390 **Massacre** of 7,000 following anti-Roman rebellion at **Thessalonica;** Theodosius did public penance before **Bishop Ambrose** of Milan.
395 **Alaric,** former head of Visigothic troops under Theodosius, became **king of Visigoths** and pillaged Balkans and Greece.
**Roman Empire permanently partitioned.**

NEAR AND MIDDLE EAST

310–379 Reign of **Shapur II** of Persia, who recovered Armenia from Romans.

337 **Persians** fought series of wars with **Romans,** securing (363) territory in Armenia and Mesopotamia.

378 Battle of **Adrianople:** Roman defeat left Greece unprotected from barbarians.

381 First Council of Constantinople, **second ecumenical council** convened, formalized Nicene Creed, and outlawed paganism.

387 **Armenia** partitioned between Rome and Persia.

399–420 Reign of **Yazdegerd I** of Persia; Christianity was tolerated initially, but later persecutions were begun in Armenia and Persia.

FAR EAST

c. 300 **Funan (Cambodia)** ruled by an Indian Brahman, who introduced Hindu customs, Indian legal code, and alphabet of central India.

317 **China** was divided into Northern and Southern dynasties; reunited in 590. **Eastern Tsin dynasty** ruled southern China, and capital at Nanking was established.

c. 320–c. 380 Reign of **Chandragupta I,** who established Gupta Empire that ruled India until c. 544; his reign marked the Golden Age of Hindu art and literature.

386 **Northern Wei dynasty** gained control of northern China, ruled until 495.

AMERICAS

300 **Mayan civilization** in southern **Mexico** entered its Classical Age during which its influence spread into **Guatemala** and **Honduras;** Mayans, ruled by priests, had advanced arts and science: calendar, hieroglyphic writing, and major works of stone architecture; this civilization collapsed in 900.

AFRICA

300 Kingdom of **Ghana** developed in western Sudan.

320–350 Christianity introduced into kingdom of **Axum.**

## 400—500

EUROPE

400 Eastern Roman Empire superseded by **Byzantine Empire.**

400–450 Europe overrun by **Goths.**

402 Roman capital moved to **Ravenna.**

408–450 Reign of **Theodosius II,** Byzantine emperor, who systematized (438) Roman laws (*Codex Theodosianus*) and made separation of Eastern and Western sections of empire official.

410 **Alaric** and Visigoths sacked **Rome.**

413–426 **St. Augustine** wrote *The City of God.*

432 **St. Patrick** began missionary work among the **Irish.**

445–453 **Attila,** king of the Huns, ruled from Hungary over Russia, Poland, and Germany, extorting concessions from Theodosius II and ravaging Balkans.

449 **Angles, Saxons,** and **Jutes** began conquest of Britain.

451 Attila, defeated at Châlons in Champagne, then invaded northern Italy, but allegedly was stopped by **Pope Leo I.**

455–475 Rome ruled by series of puppet emperors; **Ricimer,** Suebi general from central Germany, was virtual ruler of western empire until 472.

466–484 Reign of **Euric,** who established kingdom in Spain, bringing Visigothic power to its peak.

476 **Odoacer,** Ostrogoth chieftain, deposed **Romulus Augustulus,** last Roman emperor of the West; Odoacer was recognized as head of western empire by Zeno, Byzantine emperor.

481–511 Reign of **Clovis I,** king of the Franks and founder of **Merovingian dynasty,** who defeated (486) Romans at Soissons, ending Roman rule in Gaul, and was converted (496) to Christianity.

493 **Theodoric the Great,** king of Ostrogoths, seized Ravenna, assassinated Odoacer, and established Ostrogothic kingdom in Italy.

NEAR AND MIDDLE EAST

428 **Persians** began to rule **Armenia;** their control ceased in 633.

491 **Armenian Church** separated from Byzantine and Roman churches.

FAR EAST

420 **Liu Sung dynasty** came to power in southern China and ruled until 479.

c. 450 **Buddhism** established in **Burma.**

465 By this time, **White Huns** had almost destroyed Gupta empire in India.

479 **Chi dynasty** began to rule southern China; its rule ceased in 502.

AFRICA

429 **Vandal** kingdom established in Africa by **Gaiseric,** who took his people out of Spain.

439 Gaiseric made **Carthage** Vandal capital.

476 Gaiseric concluded **treaty** with **Zeno,** who recognized Vandal rule over Roman Africa, Sicily, Sardinia, Corsica, and Balearic Islands.

## 500—600

EUROPE

500 Golden age of **Irish monastic scholarship** began, which died out c. 800.

506 **Alaric II,** king of Visigoths, issued *Lex Romana Visigothorum,* law code.

527–565 Reign of **Justinian,** Byzantine emperor, who was strongly influenced by his wife **Theodora;** Justinian issued *Corpus Juris Civilis* (also known as the **Justinian Code**), a comprehensive code of Roman law; erected public works; and recovered Africa from Vandals and Italy from Ostrogoths.

529 Benedict of Nursia founded Monte Cassino in Subiaco, Italy, first **Benedictine monastery.**

532–537 Cathedral of **Hagia Sophia** erected in Constantinople.

c. 537 Traditional date of **King Arthur's death** at the Battle of Camlan.

c. 560–616 Reign of **Ethelbert,** king of Kent, who received St. Augustine and was converted to Christianity; Ethelbert made Kent supreme in Britain and drew up first code of English laws.

563 **St. Columba,** an Irish missionary to Scotland, founded church and converted king of the Picts.

567 **Frankish kingdom** divided into Austrasia, Neustria, and Burgundy.

568 **Lombards,** ancient German tribe, invaded northern Italy and established a kingdom that lasted over 200 years.

584 **Slavs** in Balkan peninsula overran Greece and began to menace Byzantine Empire.

c. 585 **Avars,** conquering nomads from steppes of central Asia, reached Danube.

590–604 Papacy of **St. Gregory I** (the Great) laid basis for later papal claims to temporal authority and independence and codified church music; the Gregorian chant is named for him.

597 **St. Augustine,** a Roman monk, sent by Pope Gregory to convert English, founded a church at **Canterbury,** becoming (601) first Archbishop of Canterbury.

NEAR AND MIDDLE EAST

c. 500 **Arabs** invaded **Palestine.**

525 **Yemen** conquered by Abyssinians.

531–579 Reign of **Khosru I** (or Chosroes) of Persia marked political and cultural prime of Persia; Khosru fought Byzantines and overthrew Abyssinian control of Yemen.

c. 550 Migration of **Turks** began, which broke up (565) White Hun settlements in Western Turkestan.

570 **Mohammed,** prophet of Islam, born.

590–628 Reign of **Khosru II** of Persia, who conquered Jerusalem, Damascus, and Egypt and restored Persian boundaries to those at time of Darius I.

FAR EAST

c. 550 **Khmers** from Chen-la state to north began to overrun Funan and made **Cambodia** (about equal to Cambodia and Laos) dominant in Southeast Asia until c. 1400.

**Japanese** began to adopt **Chinese culture,** using Chinese script and introducing Buddhism.

590 **Sui dynasty** began to rule China; Great Wall of China was reconstructed as defense against Turks and Mongols, five million people were employed to construct complex water transport system, and **civil service examination** was introduced; this dynasty ended in 618.

## 600—700

EUROPE

610–641 Reign of **Heraclius,** Byzantine emperor, who recovered lands lost to Persia and then lost them to Moslem Arabs at end of his reign.

**613–629** Reign of **Clotair** (Lothair) **II,** Merovingian king, who reunited Frankish realm and appointed **Pepin of Landen** and **Arnulf,** bishop of Metz, (ancestors of the Carolingians) to govern Austrasia.
**617 Northumbria** became dominant kingdom in **Britain.**
**655 Saracens,** Arab Moslems, destroyed Byzantine fleet.
**664** Saracens began series of attacks on **Constantinople.**
**c. 670 Caedmon,** English poet, wrote early English version of *Old Testament.*
**679** First **Bulgarian Empire** founded by **Khan Asparuhk.**
**685–695** First part of reign of **Justinian II,** Byzantine emperor, who was defeated by Arabs at Sevastopol and later deposed and exiled to Crimea.
**687 Pepin of Héristal** became ruler of all Frankish kingdoms, except Aquitaine.

NEAR AND MIDDLE EAST

**c. 610 Mohammed** began his mission as prophet of Islam.
**622** Traditional date of the **Hegira,** Mohammed's flight from Mecca to Medina, that marked beginning of **Moslem Era.**
**630 Moslems** conquered **Mecca,** which became spiritual center of Islam.
**633** Islam began conquests by taking **Syria** and **Iraq.**
**639** Moslems began to conquer **Egypt.**
**640 Persia** taken by **Moslems.**
**651–652** First edition of the *Koran* issued.
**661** Moawiya founded **Omayyad dynasty** (caliphs of Damascus), which held caliphate until 750.

FAR EAST

**c. 606–647** Reign of **King Harsha,** ruler of Kanauj in northern India, which enjoyed **Hindu renaissance** of literature, arts, and theology; Harsha received Chinese pilgrim Hsuan-Tsang.
**618 T'ang dynasty** founded in China, which annexed Korea and led successful campaigns in Mongolia, Nepal, Tibet, and Turkestan; it marked the **Golden Age of medieval China** with notable advances in astronomy and mathematics, first historical encyclopedia (801), and the development of art of printing, painting, and poetry; this dynasty ended in 906.
**664 Saracens** attacked Afghanistan and India.
**670 Silla** kingdom established in **Korea;** Chinese helped Koreans unite peninsula, instituting a period of prosperity and artistic achievement that lasted until 935.

AMERICAS

**600 Tiahuanaco** became a major ceremonial center near Lake Titicaca; Tiahuanacans established first unified empire that included most of **Peru;** their rule ended c. 1000.

AFRICA

**698 Carthage** fell to **Saracens,** ending Byzantine rule in North Africa.

## 700—800

EUROPE

**700–730** *Beowulf,* oldest extant English epic, was composed.
**711 Tarik,** Berber leader of Moslems, invaded Spain, initiating **Moorish rule** in Spain, which lasted until 1492.
**715–741** Reign of **Charles Martel,** son of Pepin of Héristal and grandfather of Charlemagne; as Frankish ruler, he defeated (732) Saracens at battle of Tours, halting their advance into Europe.
**c. 732 St. Bede** (the Venerable Bede) wrote his *Ecclesiastical History of the English Nation.*
**751–768 Pepin the Short,** first Carolingian king of the Franks and son of Charles Martel, defended Rome from Lombards.
**756 Papal states** began when Pepin granted lands around Ravenna to pope.
**Omayyad dynasty** of Córdoba came to power in **Moslem Spain** and was to rule until 1031.
**768–814** Reign of **Charlemagne** (son of Pepin the Short), who subdued Saxony, annexed Lombardy and Bavaria, and was crowned (800) emperor of the West by Pope Leo III at Rome; Charlemagne created Palace School at his capital, Aix-la-Chapelle, which helped preserve classical and early Christian scholarship.

NEAR AND MIDDLE EAST

**749** Caliph Abul Abbas overthrew Omayyads and founded **Abbasid dynasty,** which ruled until 1258.
**762 Baghdad** founded by Caliph Al-Mansur.
**786–809** Reign of **Caliph Harun al-Rashid,** during which Baghdad became major Islamic city; this glorious period is reflected in *The Thousands and One Nights.*

FAR EAST

**712 Moslem Arabs** devastated most of northwestern **India.**
*Kojiki* [= records of ancient matters], sacred book of the **Shinto,** was completed.
**794 Heian period** of Japan began; during this era, Japanese began to develop their own culture and established capital at **Kyoto;** this period ended 1185.

AMERICAS

**700 Chichimec** nomads from northern Mexico invaded **Teotihuacán** civilization.
Mayan temples built at **Tikal,** in jungles of Guatemala.

AFRICA

**700 Moslem Arabs** conquered northern **Africa,** which became base for invasions of Europe.
**Kingdom of Ghana** developed as first of Sudanese empires and became wealthy trading center, extending from Timbuktu to the Atlantic.

## 800—900

EUROPE

**c. 800 Cynewulf,** Old English religious poet, wrote *Fates of the Apostles.*
**802** The **Vikings** raided **British Isles** and by 880 had permanent settlements in Ireland and England.
**803–814** Reign of **Khan Krum,** Bulgarian ruler, who captured Sofia from Byzantines and besieged Constantinople.
**813–820** Reign of **Leo V,** the Armenian, who ruled Byzantium and revived iconoclasm; he defeated Bulgars and concluded 30-year truce.
**827–880 Moslems** invaded Sicily, Palermo, Messina, Rome, and Malta.
**835** Vikings began to raid **Continent.**
**843** Treaty of **Verdun:** the **Carolingian kingdom** was divided into three separate states: the future **France, Italy,** and **Germany** with Charles the Bald, Emperor Lothair, and Louis the German as rulers of the respective territories.
**847–c. 877 John Scotus Erigena** headed court school at Paris for Charles the Bald and wrote translations and original philosophical works.
**c. 850 Feudalism** developed in western Europe.
**858 Photius** became patriarch of Constantinople, and a schism between eastern and western churches developed during his reign.
**860–869 St. Cyril** and **St. Methodius** performed missionary work among Slavs living near Black Sea and later in Moravia; Cyril developed early **Slavic alphabet.**
**862 Rurik,** a Varangian (Viking), settled **Novgorod,** Russia; house of Rurik ruled Grand Duchy of Moscow and later all Russia until 1598.
**865 Boris I,** ruler of Bulgaria, introduced Christianity of the Greek rite.
**871–899** Reign of **Alfred the Great,** king of England, who made a treaty establishing Danish territory in England and began overseeing compilation of *Anglo-Saxon Chronicle.*
**882 Oleg,** Rurik's nephew, made **Kiev** capital of Russia.
**893–927** Reign of **Simeon I** (Tsar of the Bulgars and autocrat of the Greeks), who drove Magyars into Hungary and conquered most of Serbia; Bulgarian Empire flourished during his reign, which is considered the Golden Age of **Church Slavonic literature.**
**c. 895 Árpád,** chief of Magyars, led his people into **Hungary.**
**c. 899** Medical school in **Salerno** had been established, which merged Greek, Jewish, Arabic, and Latin influences.

FAR EAST

**800 Feudalism** developed in **Japan.**
**889** Golden Age of **Khmer** civilization, which ruled modern Cambodia, Laos, Thailand, and South Vietnam, from capital at Angkor; the temple complex constructed at **Angkor Wat** is one of the largest religious centers in the world; this civilization declined after 1434.

AFRICA

800 **Arabs** colonized **Madagascar** and **Zanzibar,** making expeditions into African interior for slaves for the next 200 years.
Rulers of **Kanem** developed kingdom near caravan routes of eastern Sudan.

## 900—1000

EUROPE

900 **Danish kingdom** founded by **Gorm.**
904 **Saracens** sacked Salonika.
906 **Magyars** began invading Germany, and were defeated (955) at Augsburg.
911 **Rollo,** Norse chieftain, received in fief the future duchy of **Normandy** from **King Charles III;** he was baptized (912), and his descendants included William the Conqueror.
912–960 Omayyad rule in **Spain** at its zenith under Abdu-r-Rahman III; **Córdoba** became intellectual center of Europe.
919–936 Reign of **Henry I,** the Fowler, who was considered the founder of **German realm** and recovered Lorraine for Germany.
962 **Holy Roman Empire** founded after Otto I, German king, united Italy and Germany; it lasted until Francis II renounced the imperial title in 1806.
976–1025 Reign of **Basil II** (Bulgar slayer), Byzantine emperor, who annexed Syria and Bulgaria, bringing empire to greatest size since the time of Justinian I.
c. 980–1015 Reign of **Vladimir I** (Saint Vladimir), duke of Kiev, who made Christianity of the Greek rite the Russian religion.
c. 985 **Eric the Red** established a Viking colony in **Greenland.**
987 **Hugh Capet** became king of **France,** beginning of the Capetian line that ruled France until 1328.
992–1025 Reign of **Boleslaus I** (the Brave), founder of the **Polish kingdom,** who brought most of the western Slavs under his rule.
997–1038 Reign of **Stephen I** (Saint Stephen), called the Apostle of Hungary, first king of **Hungary.**

NEAR AND MIDDLE EAST

969 **Fatimite caliph** established in Egypt; Fatimites, who captured Palestine, parts of Syria, and west Arabia, ruled until 1171.
996 **Hakin,** sixth Fatimite caliph, persecutor of Jews and Christians and self-proclaimed (1020) reincarnation of God, a claim still maintained by **Druses** in Syria and Lebanon; Fatimite power declined rapidly after Hakin's assassination in 1021.
999 Sultan **Mahmud of Ghazni** founded Ghaznevid dynasty, which ruled Afghanistan until c. 1155; he annexed Punjab, India; forced conversions to Islam; destroyed Hindu temples; and built a mosque, the **Celestial Bride,** at Ghazni, his capital.

FAR EAST

907 **Khitan Mongols** began to rule northern China, holding sway until 1123. Kingdom of the **Five Dynasties and Ten States** in China: chaos existed in China until 960.
935 **Koryo kingdom** established in **Korea,** in which literature was cultivated and Confucianism replaced Buddhism; this kingdom ended in 1392.
960 **Sung dynasty** established in China; scholarly works were composed, and drama and picaresque novel flourished; gunpowder was used for first time, and trade was carried on with India and Persia; the dynasty ruled until 1279.
986 **Ghaznevids** from Afghanistan began to rule Punjab, remaining there until 1001.

AMERICAS

900 **Toltec** civilization developed in **Mexico;** capital was established (c. 950) at **Tula,** and warrior gods were worshiped; the Toltec Indians conquered most of Mexico, before influence died out c. 1200.

AFRICA

c. 912–1043 **Fatimite dynasty** dominated most of northwestern Africa and the Near East; fleets raided Mediterranean, capturing Malta, Sardinia, Corsica, and Balearics.
c. 990 **Great Zimbabwe** civilization, probably developed by Bantu people, flourished in **Southern Rhodesia;** huge stone buildings were constructed in about the 15th century; this civilization ended c. 1750.

## 1000—1100

EUROPE

1000 **End of the world expected throughout Christendom.**
c. 1000–1010 Early edition of *Chanson de Roland* probably composed, but not transcribed for many years.
1002 **Massacre of St. Brice: Danes** in England were murdered and, in retaliation, raided England regularly until 1014.
1014 **Knut (Canute) II, king of Denmark,** became (1017) king of England and later of **Norway;** his kingdom was divided after his death in 1035.
1019–1054 Reign of **Yaroslav, duke of Kiev;** he drew up **Russian law code,** encouraged learning, erected **Cathedral of Sancta Sophia** and monastery of Lavra, and consolidated power and prestige of Kiev.
1024 **Franconian house** began to rule **Germany;** great imperial age ended in 1125.
1039–1056 **Henry III,** king of Germany and Holy Roman Emperor (1046–1056); with authority over Hungary, Poland, and Bohemia, his empire was at its height.
1040 **Macbeth** became king of Scotland after murdering his predecessor, **Duncan;** Macbeth was killed (1057) by **Malcolm,** who became king until 1093.
Attempts were made to implement **Truce of God** in France, which would have prohibited war during certain seasons and times of the day.
1042–1066 Reign of **Edward the Confessor,** king of England; he began (c. 1050) construction of **Westminster Abbey.**
1054 **Reciprocal excommunication** of Roman and Greek Churches announced; it was **repealed in 1965.**
1063 Construction was begun on **Cathedral at Pisa,** an example of **Romanesque** style of architecture that flourished in 11th and 12th centuries.
1065–1109 **Alfonso VI of Leon,** king of Castile, reconquered Moorish lands, beginning with capture of Toledo in 1085.
1066 **William,** duke of Normandy, defeated Saxons under King Harold at the **Battle of Hastings,** ending Saxon rule in England; known as William I (the Conqueror) of England, he ordered (1086) all landed property surveyed for tax purposes and recorded in **Domesday Book.**
c. 1071 **Saint Mark's Church** in Venice was rebuilt in **Byzantine style.**
c. 1078 The White Tower, later named the **Tower of London,** was constructed.
1081 **The Cid** (Rodrigo Diaz) fought Moors and Spaniards; he founded and ruled Valencia until 1099.
1086 **Almoravides,** Berber Moslems from Morocco, took over control of Islam in Spain.
c. 1088 **University of Bologna** founded.
1093 **St. Anselm,** founder of Scholasticism, became Archbishop of Canterbury.
1095 **First Crusade** proclaimed by Pope Urban II, who urged battle cry to be *Deus vult* [God wills it]; he established (1099) **Latin Kingdom of Jerusalem** in Syria and Palestine that endured until 1291.
1097 Construction began on the **Houses of Parliament.**

NEAR AND MIDDLE EAST

c. 1000 **Avicenna,** Arabian philosopher and physician, wrote *Canon of Medicine.*
1055 **Seljuk Turks** conquered Baghdad.
1063–1072 **Alp Arslan,** ruler of Seljuks, conquered much of Near East and Asia Minor; he defeated Byzantine army at **Manzikert, Armenia.**
1072–1092 Reign of **Malik Shah** (son of Arslan), who was protector of **Omar Khayyam,** Persian poet and author of the *Rubáiyát.*
1096 **The First Crusade** began, and Crusaders captured Nicaea, Antioch, and Jerusalem, where they massacred the Moslems; Crusaders established (1099) **Latin Kingdom of Jerusalem** in Syria and Palestine, which endured until 1291.

FAR EAST

c. 1020 *The Tale of Genji,* said to be the **world's first** novel, written by Lady Murasaki Shikibu in Japan.
1044 **King Anawratha** made Pagan, Burma, the capital of his dynasty; it became known as the "city of a thousand temples."

AMERICAS

c. 1000 **Lief Ericsson** allegedly discovered part of North American coast and called it **Vinland.**

**Chichén Itzá,** ancient Mayan city in north-central Yucatán, became **Toltec** city and was occupied until 1194.

**Mixtec people,** who developed high culture in Oaxaca valley of Mexico, practised picture writing.

AFRICA

c. 1000 **Kano,** city in northern Nigeria, began to flourish; it became leading Moslem sultanate of **Hausa States,** which were vassals of **Bornu** after 1400.

1054 **Almoravides,** Moslem Berber tribes, began Islamic conquest of **West Africa;** they sacked Kumbi, capital of Ghana, in 1076.

## 1100—1200

EUROPE

1100–1135 Reign of **Henry I** of England; he gained control of Normandy; his attempts to have his daughter **Matilda** succeed him caused long civil strife.

1108–1137 Reign of **Louis VI** (the Fat) of France, who battled with Henry I and checked German invasion.

1113–1125 Reign of **Vladimir Monomakh,** grand duke of Kiev; state grew in power during his reign.

1118 Order of **Knights Templar** founded.

1120–1220 **Aristotelian philosophy** introduced into the West, especially through writings of **Averroës,** Spanish-Arabian philosopher, and **Maimonides,** Hebrew scholar.

1122–1152 **Suger,** abbot of Saint-Denis, was leading French statesman under Louis VI and Louis VII.

1128–1185 Reign of **Alfonso I Henriques** of Portugal; **Portugal** received (1144) papal consent to be independent kingdom.

1134–1150 Western facade of **Chartres Cathedral** was built.

c. 1135 **Geoffrey of Monmouth** completed *History of the Kings of Britain,* major source of **Arthurian legends.**

1147 **Second Crusade** preached by St. Bernard of Clairvaux after Turks captured (1144) Edessa; it was led by Conrad III of Germany and Louis VII of France.

c. 1150 **University of Paris** came into being; **Peter Abelard** is usually regarded as its founder.

1152 **Frederick I (Barbarossa),** became king of Germany, and was crowned (1155) Holy Roman Emperor; he acquired land in Italy, Germany, and Poland and was drowned (1190) in Asia Minor during Third Crusade.

**Louis VII** annulled his marriage to **Eleanor of Aquitaine;** Henry (Plantagenet) married Eleanor.

1154–1189 Reign of **Henry II (Plantagenet)** of England; he appointed **Thomas à Becket** his chancellor and centralized royal administration.

1154–1213 Georgian power reached its peak in Russia, a period known as **Golden Age of Georgian literature.**

1159 **John of Salisbury** dedicated *Policraticus,* his treatise on government, to Thomas à Becket.

**Peter Lombard,** bishop of Paris, began his theological text, *Sentences.*

1162 **Becket** became Archbishop of Canterbury; he opposed Henry's restrictions on ecclesiastical jurisdiction, but was formally reconciled after long quarrel in 1170, only to be murdered five months later by Norman knights.

1163–1235 Cathedral of **Notre Dame** constructed in Paris.

c. 1168 **Oxford University** founded.

1176 Construction of **London Bridge** was begun, and completed in 1209.

**Lombard League** of northern Italian states defeated Barbarossa at **Legnano,** representing the first major defeat of feudal cavalry by infantry.

c. 1180 **Chrestien de Troyes** composed the first literary works of Arthurian legend.

1182 **Jews** banished from **France,** but returned in 1189.

c. 1187 *Igor's Campaign,* first notable work of **Russian literature,** was based on true account of Prince Igor's defeat and release by Cumans.

1189–1193 **Third Crusade** led by Barbarossa, Richard I of England, and Philip II of France.

1189–1199 Reign of **Richard I (the Lionhearted),** king of England; returning from Crusades, he was captured by Leopold of Austria; after release two years later, he warred against Philip II.

1190–1199 **Teutonic Knights,** a German military religious order, was founded.

1191 The *Nibelungenlied* first appeared.

NEAR AND MIDDLE EAST

1144 **Zengi,** Turkish conqueror of Syria, seized **Edessa.**

1145–1174 Reign of **Nureddin,** Zengi's son and Sultan of **Syria;** he ousted Crusaders from northern Syria, made (1154) **Damascus** his capital, and conquered (1171) **Egypt.**

1147–1149 **Second Crusade.**

1157 **Seljuk** Empire fell to **Khorezm shah.**

1169–1193 Reign of **Saladin,** sultan of Egypt; he conquered Syria and Aleppo, defeated (1187) Christians at battle of **Hattin** (near Tiberias) and took Jerusalem, and signed treaty with **Richard the Lionhearted** that allowed Christians small strip of land along Jerusalem coast.

FAR EAST

1149 Rulers of **Ghor** took over **Ghazni** in Afghanistan, which became headquarters for campaigns into India; subjugation of Upper India was completed in 1203.

1186 **Kamakura** era began in **Japan,** establishing rule of military warriors; **Yoritomo,** first shogun, set up centralized feudal system; China and Korea were raided; Zen Buddhism was promoted; this era ended in 1333.

c. 1190 **Temujin** consolidated Mongol tribes in central Asia; he assumed (1206) title **Jenghiz Khan** and led Mongol hordes in conquests of eastern Europe and western Asia.

AFRICA

c. 1174 **Almohades,** fierce Berber Moslems, succeeded Almoravides in Morocco and conquered other parts of **North Africa,** ruling area until 1550.

## 1200—1300

EUROPE

1202–1204 **The Fourth Crusade,** was led by Venetian doge, **Enrico Dandolo;** Constantinople was captured and a Latin empire established.

1204 **Philip II** of France took English lands north of the Loire and established **France** as a leading European power.

1209 Franciscan order founded by **Saint Francis of Assisi.**

1211 Construction began on **Rheims Cathedral.**

1215 **Magna Carta,** signed by **King John,** became basis of modern English constitution with its principle that the king is subject to law.

1217–1221 **Fifth Crusade** led by **Pelasius,** papal legate, was directed against Moslems in Egypt and failed.

1218 **Amiens Cathedral** begun.

1223 **Mongols** invaded Russia.

1226–1270 Reign of **Louis IX** (Saint Louis), a period known as **Golden Age of medieval France.**

1226–1283 **Teutonic Knights** subjugated Prussia and achieved commercial power.

1227 Gothic **Cathedral of Toledo,** Spain, began to be constructed.

1228–1229 **Sixth Crusade;** led by Frederick II, it resulted in Sultan of Egypt signing treaty that restored Jerusalem, Nazareth, and Bethlehem to Christians.

c. 1230 **Salamanca University** founded in Spain.

c. 1231 **Cambridge University** founded.

1233 **The Inquisition** was established when Pope Gregory IX gave Dominicans authority to investigate Albigensian heresy in southern France.

1236–1263 Reign of **Alexander Nevsky** in Russia, under whom country was united; he defeated (1242) Teutonic Knights at Lake Peipus, and Mongols named him **Grand Prince of Russia.**

1237–1242 **Batu Khan** led Mongol invasions, taking Moscow and most of Russia, Hungary, and Poland, and invading Germany; his empire was known as the **Golden Horde** because of brillant tents.

1238 **Kingdom of Granada** became last refuge of the **Moors** until their expulsion from Spain in 1492.

1248–1254 **Seventh Crusade;** King Louis IX of France was its leader.

1270 **Eighth Crusade;** Tunis was attacked, and Louis IX died from plague.

1271 **Marco Polo** left Venice for **China** and other parts of the Far East; he returned in 1292 and informed Europeans of Oriental splendors.

1273 **Rudolph I** founded **Hapsburg dynasty,** which ruled Austria until 1918.

**St. Thomas Aquinas** completed *Summa Theologica.*

1272–1307 Reign of **Edward I of England;** he systematized laws and institutions and called (1295) his **"Model Parliament,"** which represented all classes.

1285–1314 Reign of **Philip IV** (the Fair); he made **France** an absolute monarchy and called (1302) the first meeting of the **Estates-General** (clergy, nobility, and townsmen) to rally against Pope Boniface VIII's claims of papal supremacy.

1290 **Jews** were expelled from **England;** they returned c. 1650.

NEAR AND MIDDLE EAST

1202–1204 **Fourth Crusade:** Crusaders took Constantinople, sacked Byzantine territories, and established a **Latin Empire.**

1217–1221 **Fifth Crusade;** Crusaders failed in **Egypt.**

1218–1224 **Mongols** from central Asia conquered Turkestan, Afghanistan, and Persia.

1228–1229 **Sixth Crusade;** Sultan of Egypt signed a treaty with Crusaders allowing free access to Jerusalem.

1245–1253 Mesopotamia and Armenia ravaged by **Mongols.**

1248–1253 **Seventh Crusade;** Crusaders massacred in **Egypt.**

1250 **Mamelukes,** former slave-soldiers, began to rule **Egypt** and checked Mongol advances; their rule ended in 1517.

1258 **Baghdad** fell to **Hulagu Khan,** grandson of Jenghiz, who devastated surrounding lands.

1270 **Eighth Crusade;** Crusaders attacked **Tunis** and were turned back.

1288 **Osman I,** leader of Ottoman Turks, founded **Ottoman dynasty,** which endured until 1918.

FAR EAST

1206 **Delhi Sultanate** began, the first Moslem kingdom of **India;** Sultan Iltutmish (1210–1235) erected famous minaret, **Qutb Minar;** this dynasty ended in 1398.

1220–1227 **Jenghiz Khan** established his capital at **Karakorum** controlling most of Ch'in Empire of northern China; he conquered Turkestan, Afghanistan, Persia, and southern Russia.

1221–1241 **Ogotai Khan,** son of Jenghiz, captured Ghazni, Afghanistan.

1260 **Yüan,** Mongolian dynasty of China, founded by **Kublai Khan,** grandson of Jenghiz; Kublai's attempts to conquer Japan, Southeast Asia, and Indonesia failed; **Marco Polo** and other westerners visited capital at Peiping; during dynasty an advanced postal system and extensive network of roads and canals were created; gunpowder and printing were introduced into Europe from China at this time; this dynasty ended in 1368.

AMERICAS

1200 The **Incas** began to build empire centered at **Cuzco, Peru,** and established central control over local rulers; eventually empire extended from Quito, Ecuador, to Rio Maule, Chile, with population c. seven million people, who were linked by messenger system and common language; Incan civilization was noted for political organization and luxurious cities; stonework in **Machu Picchu,** fortress city in Andes, shows skillful engineering techniques; empire destroyed by **Francisco Pizarro** in 1533.

**Aztecs** entered the valley of Mexico, establishing powerful political and cultural civilization and capital (c. 1325) at **Tenochtitlán** (now **Mexico City**); Aztecs were noted for developed social organization and religion demanding human sacrifice; in 1519 their population numbered about five million; **Hernán Cortés** destroyed empire in 1521.

AFRICA

1200 **Mali Empire** developed in **western Sudan,** absorbing **Ghana** and neighboring lands; King **Mansa Musa's pilgrimage** (1324) to Mecca brought attention to empire's great wealth; **Timbuktu** grew into center of learning and culture; **Songhai** began to control region c. 1500.

## 1300—1400

EUROPE

1300 The **Renaissance** began, signaling end of Middle Ages and beginning of modern Europe; greatest cultural developments in European history occurred during next 300 years.

1305 **"Babylonian Captivity"** began; chaos in Italy forced Pope Clement V to desert (1309) Rome for Avignon, France, which was the papal seat until 1377.

c. 1306 **Giotto** completed Arena Chapel frescoes in Padua.

1321 Death of **Dante** following completion of *Divine Comedy.*

1325–1341 Reign of **Ivan I** (Money Bag), grand prince of Moscow and vassal of Mongols; Russian Orthodox Church became centered in Moscow during his reign.

1326 **Ottoman Turks** began invading eastern Europe.

1327–1377 Reign of **Edward III** of England, during which Parliament divided into two houses, later called **Lords** and **Commons.**

1337 **Hundred Years War,** which began after Edward III claimed French crown, ended in 1453; **English defeated,** but French devastated by famine, plague, and marauders who terrorized countryside.

1341 **Petrarch,** Italian humanist, crowned poet laureate at Rome.

1346–1355 Reign of **Stephen Dushan** over Serbs, Greeks, Bulgars, and Albanians; his rule marked height of Serbian power.

1347–1352 **Black Death,** an epidemic of plague that began (1334) in Constantinople, struck Europe; within 20 years, it killed up to three quarters of population of Europe and Asia.

1353 **Giovanni Boccaccio** completed the *Decameron.*

1358 French army suppressed the *Jacquerie,* a **peasant revolt** protesting war taxation.

1362 William Langland wrote *Piers the Plowman.*

1370 **Hanseatic League,** mercantile association of German towns, signed a treaty with Denmark giving League a virtual trade monopoly in Scandinavia.

1378 **Great Western Schism:** Rome and France began fight for control of papacy that lasted until 1417.

1379 After Parliament imposed poll tax, **Wat Tyler** led **peasant revolt** in England.

1382 **John Wycliffe** directed translation of the **Vulgate Bible** into English.

1386 **Heidelberg University** founded by Rupert I, Elector of Palatinate.

Lithuania and Poland united under Jagiello dynasty; **Golden Age of Polish culture** and power began; this dynasty came to an end in 1572.

1387 **Chaucer** began to compose his *Canterbury Tales.*

1389 Turks defeated Serbs at **Kossovo,** and Serbia became vassal state of Turks.

1391 **Ottoman Turk** began conquering Byzantine lands.

1399 **House of Lancaster** began reign in **England** that lasted until 1461.

NEAR AND MIDDLE EAST

1334 Epidemic of plague, **Black Death,** began in Constantinople, spreading throughout Europe and Asia and causing extremely large number of fatalities.

1354 **Ottoman Turks** expanded their empire and established capital at Adrianople; by end of century, Ottomans controlled most of Balkans and Byzantine possessions in Asia Minor.

1356–1363 **Sultan Hassan mosque** was constructed in Cairo.

1392 **Baghdad** sacked by **Tamerlane,** Mongol conqueror.

FAR EAST

1336 **Ashikaga** family began to dominate **Japan,** holding sway until 1558; Ashikaga period of warfare among feudal nobles was also a time of extraordinary economic and commercial growth.

1350 **Thais** from southern China established kingdom in modern **Thailand.**

1353 **Lao** kingdom of **Lan Xang** (Land of a Million Elephants) established by branch of Thais in **Laos.**

1368 **Ming dynasty** began to rule China after driving out Mongols; empire at its height extended from Burma to Korea; European settlements made at Macao and Canton; finest **Chinese porcelain** dates from this period, which ended in 1644.

**1369–1405** Reign of **Tamerlane** (or Timur), Mongol leader and conqueror of Persia, Mesopotamia, and western India; Tamerlane ravaged Georgia and captured Angora from Ottomans.

**1392 Yi dynasty** began to rule **Korea** and established capital at Seoul; this dynasty ended in 1919.

AFRICA

**1300 Kingdom** of **Ife** flourished in Nigeria; Ife, a holy city noted for its fine **bronze sculpture,** probably died out c. 1500.

**1350 Kingdom of Benin** developed in **Nigeria;** within a century, Benin became famous commercial center and seat of royal court; bronze plaques on king's palace depict civilization of hunters, traders, and warriors; trade was established with Portugal c. 1486; Benin had disintegrated by 1897.

## 1400—1500

EUROPE

**1409 Leipzig University** founded by German émigrés from Prague.

**1415 Henry V** of England defeated French in Battle of **Agincourt,** making England first among European powers.

**1415–1460** Reign of **Prince Henry the Navigator** of Portugal, who promoted explorations along the coast of Africa.

c. **1417 Donatello** completed his statue of *St. George and the Dragon.*

**1419–1436** Hussite religious wars that broke out following martyrdom of **John Huss** were fought in Bohemia.

c. **1427 Thomas à Kempis,** German monk, wrote *The Imitation of Christ.*

**1429 Joan of Arc** liberated Orléans; she was burned at the stake in Rouen in 1431.

**1432 Jan van Eyck** completed his altarpiece with panels portraying the *Annunciation* and *Adoration of the Lamb.*

**1434 Medicis** began their domination of **Florence,** which lasted until 1494 and made Florence center of Italian Renaissance.

**1450 Fra Angelico** completed the *Annunciation.*
**Vatican Library** founded by Pope Nicholas V.

**1453 Constantinople** was lost to Turks, ending 1,000-year-old **Byzantine Empire.**
**Hundred Years War** came to an end, and English territory on Continent was limited to Calais.

**1455–1485 Wars of the Roses:** English Houses of Lancaster and **York** fought for throne.

**1456 John Hunyadi,** Hungarian ruler, defeated Turks at Belgrade, preventing their conquest of Hungary for 70 years.

c. **1456** Printing of **Mazarin Bible** was completed in Mainz, Germany; it is considered earliest book printed from movable type and attributed to **Gutenberg.**

**1458–1490** Reign of **Matthias Corvinus** of Hungary (son of John Hunyadi), who took (1485) Vienna and made **Hungary** most important state of central Europe.

**1461–1483** Reign of **Louis XI,** who made **France** a nation by annexing Burgundy, Provence, Maine, and Anjou.

**1462–1505** Reign of **Ivan III (the Great),** first national sovereign of Russia; he subjugated Novgorod and almost all Russian principalities under Moscow's rule and repudiated "Tartar Yoke"; Ivan also adopted Byzantine court ceremonials and constructed great **Kremlin palaces** and cathedrals in Moscow.

**1463 Turks** and **Venetians** began major war, in which Venetians were defeated (1479) and had to pay Turks for trading privileges.

**1466 Teutonic Knights** ceded Pomerania and West Prussia to Poland.

**1469** King **Ferdinand** of Aragon married Queen **Isabella I** of Castile, initiating unification of Spain.

**1473** The **Sistine Chapel** in the Vatican was built under Pope Sixtus IV.

**1478** Ferdinand and Isabella instituted the **Spanish Inquisition.**

**1481 Botticelli** began his Biblical frescoes in the Sistine Chapel.

**1485 Henry VII** of England founded the **House of Tudor,** increased power of the **Star Chamber,** developed English navy, sponsored explorations to New World, and ended feudalism by outlawing private armies.

**1488 Bartolomeu Dias** was the first European to round the Cape of Good Hope, thus opening sea route to India.

**1490 Verrocchio's equestrian monument** of *condottiere* Colleoni was cast.

**1492** Ferdinand and Isabella conquered Moorish kingdom of **Granada,** expelled **Jews** who refused to accept Catholicism, and financed **Christopher Columbus** on his first voyage to America.

**1494** Treaty of **Tordesillas:** Spain and Portugal divided the New World.
**Italian Wars** among Italian states and Spain began when Charles VIII of France invaded Italy; after 1559 Spain dominated Italy.

**1497 Portugal** expelled **Jews** who refused Catholic conversion.

**1497–1498 John Cabot** explored North American coast south of **Labrador.**

**1497–1499 Vasco da Gama** sailed from Lisbon to **India.**

**1498 Savonarola,** Dominican monk who preached against corruption in Florence, was burned at the stake.
**Leonardo da Vinci,** painter, engineer, and scientist, completed the *Last Supper* in Milan.

**1499 Swiss independence** acknowledged by Emperor Maximilian I.

NEAR AND MIDDLE EAST

**1451–1481** Reign of **Mohammed II,** Ottoman sultan; he completed conquest of Byzantine Empire by taking (1453) **Constantinople** and making it his capital; conquering most of Balkans and several Venetian possessions in Aegean islands, he was stopped (1478) at Belgrade by John Hunyadi and in Albania by Scanderbeg.

FAR EAST

**1412–1443** Reign of **Ahmad Shah,** king of **Gujarat** (India), who founded city of **Ahmedabad;** Gujarat became an independent, prosperous sultanate.

**1495–1530** Reign of **Baber** (or Babar), remote descendant of Tamerlane; Baber founded **Mogul Empire** of India, captured (1504) Kabul and established a kingdom in **Afghanistan,** and conquered most of northern India.

**1498** Portuguese explorer **Vasco da Gama** landed at Calicut, **India.**

AMERICAS

**1492–1504 Christopher Columbus** made four voyages to **America;** landed on Canary Islands, Bahamas, Cuba, Hispaniola, Jamaica, Virgin Islands, Trinidad, and Honduras.

**1497 John Cabot** arrived in North America; explored coast south of **Labrador.**

AFRICA

**1400 Baluba Kingdom** of the **Congo** first emerged and eventually controlled Katanga and Kivu provinces.

**1415** Portuguese began to explore **West Africa,** gradually building up profitable trade.

**1482 Diego Cão,** Portuguese explorer, discovered mouth of **Congo River.**

**1488 Bartolomeu Dias,** Portuguese explorer, rounded **Cape of Good Hope.**

**1491 Vasco da Gama** rounded the Cape and sailed up East African coast en route to Asia.

## 1500—1600

**1502 Cesare Borgia,** son of Pope Alexander VI, completed conquest of neighboring states and added them to the Papal domain.

**1503 Leonardo da Vinci** began painting the *Mona Lisa.*
**Alexander I,** king of Poland and grand duke of Lithuania, ceded left bank of Dnieper to Ivan the Great.

**1508 Michelangelo** began to paint ceiling of **Sistine Chapel.**

**1509 Erasmus,** Dutch humanist, published *The Praise of Folly.*

**1509–1547** Reign of **Henry VIII** of England; his first wife was Katharine of Aragon (m. 1509, div. 1533), mother of Mary I; second wife, **Anne Boleyn** (m. 1533, beheaded 1536), mother of Elizabeth I; third wife, Jane Seymour (m. 1536, d. 1537), mother of Edward VI; fourth wife, **Anne of Cleves** (m. 1540, div. 1540); fifth wife, **Katharine Howard** (m. 1540, beheaded 1542); sixth wife, **Katharine Parr** (m. 1543); Henry waged war against France and Scotland.

1513 **Macchiavelli** wrote *The Prince.*
**Raphael** painted the *Sistine Madonna.*

1515–47 **Francis I** ruled France; he fought Italian Wars and captured Milan at **Battle of Marignano.**

1515 **Henry VIII** appointed **Thomas Wolsey** cardinal and lord chancellor.

1516 **Sir Thomas More**, English statesman, wrote *Utopia.*

1517 **Martin Luther** began **Protestant Reformation** by posting his 95 theses against the sale of indulgences on door of Wittenberg Palace Church.

1518 **Titian** completed his altarpiece *Assumption of the Virgin.*

1519 **Ulrich Zwingli** began Reformation in **Switzerland.**

1519–1522 **Ferdinand Magellan** circumnavigated the globe.

1519–1556 **Charles V**, Holy Roman Emperor, ruled Spanish lands in Europe and America, as well as Hapsburg lands in central Europe; he sacked (1527) Rome and captured Pope Clement VII.

1520 **Luther** was declared a heretic by Pope **Leo X** and formally excommunicated (1521) by **Edict of Worms.**

1523–1560 Reign of **Gustavus I** (Vasa) of Sweden; he ended (1537) trade monopoly of Hanseatic League and promoted Reformation.

1524–1525 **Peasants' War** in Germany: revolt by south German peasants that was inspired by Lutheran religious ideas; however, Luther sided with princes.

1532 **Rabelais** wrote *Gargantua and Pantagruel.*

1533–1584 Reign of **Ivan IV (the Terrible)**, first tsar of Russia; his conflicts with **boyars**, the powerful nobles who controlled regency, resulted in reign of terror; Ivan seized part of Livonia from Poles and concluded peace among Russia, Sweden, and Poland after much warfare.

1534 **St. Ignatius Loyola** founded **Jesuit order**, which became chief force in Roman Catholic Counter-Reformation.
**Act of Supremacy:** English Parliament made Henry VIII head of Church of England, initiating **English Reformation.**

1535 **Sir Thomas More**, former lord chancellor of England, was beheaded for refusing to subscribe to Act of Supremacy.

1536 **Menno Simons**, Dutch religious reformer, began preaching **Anabaptist doctrines.**
**Hans Holbein, the younger,** of Germany became court painter to Henry VIII.

1541–1564 **John Calvin** headed a theocratic state at **Geneva.**

1543 **Nicholas Copernicus** published his **astronomy** discoveries.

1545 **Council of Trent** was convened by Pope Paul III; it made internal reforms in Roman Catholic Church.

1553–1558 Reign of **Mary Tudor (Bloody Mary)** of England, who restored Catholicism and persecuted Protestants; she lost (1558) Calais, last English stronghold on Continent, to the French.

1555 **Peace of Augsburg** signed, which allowed German princes to choose Catholicism or Lutheranism, but not Calvinism, as religion of their states; Lutheranism prevailed in north; Catholicism, in south.

1556–1598 Reign of **Philip II** of Spain, during which Hapsburg power reached its zenith and **Golden Age of Spanish art and literature** was initiated.

1558–1603 Reign of **Elizabeth I** of England, who established (1563) **Church of England** and increased English power; **Elizabethan Age** was marked by great flowering of literature.

1559 **Pope Paul IV** established the **Index of Forbidden Books.**

1559–1567 Reign of **Mary Stuart, Queen of Scots,** who abdicated in favor of her son, James VI (later James I of England); she was imprisoned by Elizabeth I because of her claims to English throne.

1562 French began harsh persecution of **Huguenots,** French Protestants; Catherine de' Medici ordered (1572) **St. Bartholomew's Day Massacre; religious** wars ended in 1598.

1566 **Netherlands**, led by William the Silent of Orange, revolted against Spanish domination and gained independence in 1581.

1571 **Battle of Lepanto:** Ottoman Turks defeated in naval battle with Austrian and Holy League forces, the greatest naval battle since Actium.

1580 **Montaigne** began composing *Essays.*

1582 **Gregorian calendar** introduced.
**Douay** version of New Testament published.

1587 **John Knox**, founder of **Presbyterianism** in Scotland, wrote *History of the Reformation in Scotland.*

1588 **Spanish Armada** defeated by English fleet under **Sir Francis Drake.**

c. 1589 **Christopher Marlowe** produced *Dr. Faustus.*

1589 **Henry IV** founded **House of Bourbon;** this dynasty ruled France until 1792.

1591–1613 **William Shakespeare** composed his plays and poems.

1597–1625 **Francis Bacon** wrote his *Essays.*

1598 **Henry IV** of France issued the **Edict of Nantes,** which granted religious toleration to Huguenots.
**Boris Godunov** became tsar of Russia and ruled until 1605.

NEAR AND MIDDLE EAST

1501 **Safavid dynasty** began rule of Iran that lasted until 1736.

1512–1520 Reign of **Selim I**, Ottoman sultan; he defeated Mamelukes in Syria and Egypt and assumed succession to Moslem Caliphate.

1520–1566 Reign of **Suleiman I (the Magnificent)**, Ottoman sultan; he captured Belgrade, Rhodes, and Hungary during rule, which was marked by greatest flowering of **Turkish literature, art, and architecture.**

1571 **Turks** seized Cyprus and then suffered their first major defeat from Austrian and Holy League forces at **Lepanto**, the greatest naval battle since Actium.

1587–1628 Reign of **Abbas I**, shah of Iran, who erected palace and mosque at Isfahan.

FAR EAST

1510 Portuguese conquered **Goa, India.**

1526 **Mogul Empire** that was to endure until 1857 founded in India by **Baber.**

1549–1552 **St. Francis Xavier** introduced **Christianity** into **Japan.**

1557 Portuguese settled in **Macao** and began trade with China.

1560–1605 Reign of **Akbar the Great** (grandson of Baber), who enlarged domain and founded (1569) city of Fathpur Sikri, noted for Mogul architecture, especially **Jami Masjid** (the Great Mosque); **Akbar** also encouraged Persian arts and received **European** traders.

1568–1582 **Nobunaga**, who ruled Japan as military dictator, destroyed Buddhism as political force.

1571 **Spanish** founded Manila and began to colonize **Philippines.**

1582 **Hideyoshi** became military dictator of Japan; he initiated unification of country and unsuccessfully invaded Korea.

1590 Portuguese landed in Taiwan, calling it **Formosa.**

1595 Dutch began to colonize **East Indies.**

AMERICAS

1500 **Cabral** claimed **Brazil** for Portugal.

1501–1502 **Amerigo Vespucci** explored the coast of Brazil.

1511 Spanish took **Cuba** and **Puerto Rico,** founding San Juan and settling Jamaica.

1513 **Ponce de Leon** discovered **Florida.**
**Balboa** discovered the **Pacific.**

1519 **Hernán Cortés** of Spain landed in **Mexico; Aztecs** thought Cortés was **Quetzalcoatl**, their god who was supposed to appear at that period; Cortés, who met **Montezuma II** and later imprisoned him, captured (1521) Tenochtitlán and began harsh rule of Mexico.

1523–1524 **Alvarado** took **Guatemala** and **Salvador** for Spain.

1524 **Verrazano** explored the New England coast.

1530 Portuguese colonized **Brazil.**

1531–1535 **Francisco Pizarro** subjugated **Inca Empire** of Peru, executing **Atahuallpa** and installing **Manco Capac** as puppet ruler; Spanish founded (1535) **Lima,** which became capital of viceroyalty of **Peru.**

1534–1541 **Jacques Cartier** explored St. Lawrence River, stopping at sites of **Quebec** and **Montreal.**

**1539–1542 De Soto** made an expedition through **Florida** to the **Mississippi.**

**1540–1542 Coronado** explored the **Southwest,** reaching as far as Kansas.

**1551 National University of Mexico** founded.
**University of San Marcos** founded in Lima, Peru.

**1565 St. Augustine,** Florida, oldest permanent settlement in the United States, was founded.
Portuguese settled **Rio de Janeiro.**

**1576–1577 Martin Frobisher** searched for **Northwest** Passage.

**1579 Sir Francis Drake** claimed New Albion (**California**) for England.

**1580 Buenos Aires,** Argentina, founded by Juan de Garay for Spain.

AFRICA

**1503–1507 Leo Africanus,** Spanish Moslem of Morocco, explored **Sudan;** he issued (1526) book describing **Mali** and **Songhai** kingdoms.

**1508 Portuguese** began to colonize **Mozambique.**

**1513 Songhai Empire** conquered **Hausa States.**

**1520 Portuguese** visited **Ethiopian** court.

**1529 Somali war** in Ethiopia began; Moslems tried to conquer Ethiopia but were defeated (1543) when Portuguese aided Somalis.

**1562** Sir John Hawkins of England began **slave trade** between Africa and the Americas.

**1590 Moroccan** invasions destroyed **Songhai Empire.**

## 1600—1700

EUROPE

**1603** James VI of Scotland became **James I** of England, founding **house of Stuart,** which ruled England until 1688.

**1605 Guy Fawkes** executed for **"Gunpowder Plot"** to blow up Parliament.

**1607 Jonson** completed *Volpone.*

**1609 Kepler** published *Astronomia Nova,* laws of orbits of planets.

**1609–1631 Newspapers** were started on the Continent: *Avisa Relation oder Zeitung* (1609) in Germany; the *Nieuwe Tijdingen* (1616), Antwerp; the *Gazette,* later the *Gazette de France* (1631), Paris.

**1609–1610 Douay** version of Old Testament published.

**1611 King James** version of the Bible compiled by leading English scholars.

**1613 Michael Romanov,** tsar of Russia, founded **Romanov dynasty,** which ruled until 1917.

**1614 The Estates General** met for last time until the French Revolution.

**1615 Cervantes** published *Don Quixote.*

**1618 Thirty Years War,** final great religious war, broke out in Prague; this conflict between Catholic and Protestant Europe devastated Germany.

**1624 Cardinal de Richelieu** became chief minister of Louis XIII; he consolidated royal authority, strengthened army, built navy, and founded (1635) **French Academy.**

**1625 Grotius** published *De Jure Belli ac Pacis,* pioneer work in international law.

**1625–1649** Reign of **Charles I** of England, who was involved with conflicts over supremacy of king or parliament and summoned (1640–1641) the **Long Parliament,** which abolished the courts of High Commission and the Star Chamber; Charles was beheaded for treason.

**1628 William Harvey** discovered principle of blood circulation.
**Petition of Right** signed by Charles I; it prohibited arbitrary imprisonment, martial law, forced loans, and billeting of soldiers and sailors.

**1632 Galileo** published his work confirming Copernican theory of astronomy.

**1640 Puritan revolution** in England began; monarchists fought civil war that ended in 1649 against those who wanted republic.

**1643–1715** Reign of **Louis XIV** (the Sun King) of France, during which royal absolutism reached a new peak; Louis allegedly said, *"L'état c'est moi";* French art and culture flourished and **Versailles palace** was constructed.

**1644 Milton** wrote *Areopagitica.*

**1645–1664 Venetian-Turkish** wars caused further decline of Ottoman power.

**1648 Peace of Westphalia,** which ended Thirty Years War, recognized independence of Netherlands and of Swiss cantons and sovereignty of German states.

**1649 King Charles I** beheaded, and England had commonwealth form of government under **Oliver Cromwell** until 1660.

**1651 Hobbes** published *Leviathan.*

**1652 England** began series of wars with **French** and **Dutch** that lasted until 1678 over supremacy of the seas.

**1659** Spanish power in Europe ended with **Peace of Pyrennes.**

**1660 Monarchy** restored by **Charles II** of England; Cavalier Parliament enacted repressive measures against Puritans.

**1665 Great Plague** hit **London;** the following year **fire** virtually destroyed city.

**1675 Sir Christopher Wren** began St. Paul's Cathedral, London.

**1682–1725** Reign of **Peter the Great** of Russia; he tried to "Westernize" Russia and established schools and a newspaper.

**1683** Turkish seige of **Vienna** repulsed.

**1684 Newton** published his theories of motion and gravitation.

**1685 Edict of Nantes** revoked by Louis XIV; Protestants fled abroad.

**1688 "Glorious Revolution"** occurred in England; this bloodless revolution against James II ended when **William of Orange** and **Mary,** his British wife, accepted crown.
**France** began war against Grand Alliance of European powers that resulted in decline of French power.

**1689** William and Mary began to rule England and signed **Bill of Rights,** limiting royal power; their rule ended in 1702.

**1699 Peace of Karlowitz:** Turkey ceded some of her conquered territories to Austria, Poland, and Venice.

NEAR AND MIDDLE EAST

**1638** Turks won back **Baghdad** from Persians.

**1656** Mohammed **Kuprili** became grand vizier to Mohammed IV and helped Ottoman empire regain some former power.

**1699 Peace of Karlowitz:** Turkey ceded Hungary, Croatia, and Slavonia to Austria; Podolia and Ukraine to Poland; and the Peloponnesus to Venice.

FAR EAST

**1600 William Adams,** an Englishman, arrived in **Japan** and imparted some technology to Japanese.
**British East India Company** chartered for trade in India.

**1603 Ieyasu Tokugawa** came to power in Japan, and his dynasty ruled until 1867; it centralized feudalism, encouraged trade, and established capital at **Tokyo; Kabuki** theater was developed.

**1611 British** began to send envoys to Mogul Empire and later established settlements at Surat and factories in **Bengal** and **Madras.**

**1615 Dutch** seized **Moluccas** (Spice Islands) from Portuguese.

**1616 Manchu Tartars** from Manchuria began to invade China.

**1619** Dutch founded **Batavia, Java.**

**1627 Japan** began to exclude foreigners, allowing one Dutch trading post to remain.

**1628–1658** Reign of **Shah Jehan,** ruler of Mogul Empire; he erected **Taj Mahal,** one of the most beautiful buildings in the world.

**1636** Dutch occupied **Ceylon.**

**1641–1662** Dutch controlled **Formosa.**

**1644 Ch'ing dynasty** in China was founded by **Manchus** and ruled until 1912; **Korea** became vassal state known as the **"Hermit Kingdom"** because of its isolation.

**1661–1722** Reign of **K'ang Hsi,** Chinese emperor who consolidated empire and issued edict of toleration after Jesuit missionaries appeared.

**1668 Bombay** became headquarters of East India Company.

**1674 Mahratta State** in west central India founded by Sivaji.

**1675–1708 Guru Govind Singh** ruled **Sikhs** and built up their military power.

AMERICAS

**1607** English founded **Jame town,** tueir first permanent settlement in America; **John Smith** became leader.

**1608** Champlain founded **Quebec.**

Jesuit state in **Paraguay** founded.

**1620 Pilgrims** arrived at **Plymouth,** Massachusetts.

**1630** Massachusetts Bay colony established by **Puritans.**

**1671 Danes** took St. Thomas.

**British** settled Barbados, and Leeward and Windward Islands.

**1673** Jacques **Marquette** and Louis **Joliet** explored the Mississippi.

**1682** After La Salle descended Mississippi River to its mouth, **French** began to rule colonial empire in North America that extended from Quebec to New Orleans.

AFRICA

**1642** French established base on **Madagascar.**

**c. 1650 Slave trade** from **Gold Coast** thrived until early 19th century.

**1652** Dutch founded **Capetown;** Jan van Riebeeck led settlers.

**1680 Germans** began to colonize West Africa.

**1684** English lost **Tangier** to Morocco.

**1687 Arguin,** Guinea, established as Brandenburgian colony.

**c. 1695 Osei Tutu** founded **Ashanti** kingdom in western Africa and established capital at Kumasi; Ashanti, noted for high-quality **gold work,** grew wealthy from slave trade.

OCEANIA

**1601 Australia** began to be visited by Portuguese, Spanish, and Dutch.

**1642 Abel Tasman,** Dutch navigator, discovered **New Zealand** and **Tasmania,** which was named Van Diemen's Land.

**1688** William **Dampier** of England landed on northwest coast of **Australia.**

# 1700—1800

EUROPE

**1700 Great Northern War** began: Russia, Poland, and Denmark fought Sweden for supremacy in the **Baltic;** when war ended in 1721, Russia emerged as a major European power with "window" on the Baltic.

**Philip V** became first Bourbon king of **Spain.**

**1701 Act of Settlement,** which was passed by English parliament, provided that crown would pass to **house of Hanover;** king could not be Roman Catholic.

**Hohenzollerns** came to power in **Prussia and Germany,** ruling until 1918.

War of the **Spanish Succession** began; Treaty of **Utrecht** (1713) separated thrones of France and Spain and marked rise of British and decline of French.

**1705 Moscow University** founded by Peter the Great.

**1707 Great Britain** formed by union of **England** and **Scotland.**

**1711 Joseph Addison** and **Richard Steele** began publishing the *Spectator* in England.

**1713–1740** Reign of **Frederick William I,** king of Prussia, who became known as the soldier king because he strengthened **Prussian army.**

**1714 George I** began the **Hanoverian rule** of England; house of Hanover was succeeded (1840) by house of Wettin when Queen Victoria married.

**1715** The **Age of Enlightenment** began; also known as the **Age of Reason;** Europe experienced a rich period of **philosophy** that died out after 1789.

**Louis XV** began to rule France, but wars and financial policy weakened government.

**1733** War of **Polish Succession** began: Russia and Austria defeated Spain and placed Augustus III on Polish throne two years later.

**1738 John Wesley,** founder of **Methodism,** began preaching in England.

**1740** War of the **Austrian Succession:** a general European war broke out after **Maria Theresa** became Hapsburg ruler; it ended in 1748.

**1740–1786** Reign of **Frederick the Great,** king of Prussia, who expanded territory and made Prussia leading European military power.

**1747 Denis Diderot** and other writers began editing the *Encyclopédie.*

**1748 Montesquieu** published *Spirit of the Laws.*

**c. 1750 Industrial Revolution** had begun in **England;** factory system, economic specialization, and **urbanization** changed social structure during next **century.**

**1755** An earthquake devastated **Lisbon,** killing 30,000.

**1756 Seven Years War** began between **England** and **France** over colonial possessions in America and India; it ended in 1763; France lost **Canada** and India, England became world's major colonial power.

**1758 Voltaire** completed *Candide.*

**1760 George III** began his 60-year reign in England.

**1762 Jean Jacques Rousseau** completed *Social Contract.*

**1762–1796** Reign of **Catherine II (the Great) of Russia,** who promoted education, the arts, and social reforms.

**1768** Major **Russo-Turkish Wars:** Russia and Turkey waged a series of wars for over a century; in **1878** Turkey was finally ousted from Crimea and much of Slavic Europe.

**1769 James Watt,** Scottish inventor, **patented** his **steam engine.**

**1772–1795 Poland** was partitioned **among Russia,** Austria, and Prussia.

**1773–1774 Pugachev** led rebellion of Russian **peasants** and **Cossacks,** causing Catherine II to **institute** tighter control over serfs.

**1774 Louis XVI** and **Marie Antoinette** became king and queen of France.

**1776 Adam Smith** published *The Wealth of Nations.*

**Edward Gibbon** began *The Decline and Fall of the Roman Empire.*

**1785** *The Times* of London was founded by John Walter.

**1789** The **French Revolution** began when Paris mob stormed the **Bastille;** third estate drafted (1791) new constitution; Louis XVI and Marie Antoinette beheaded (1793).

**1790 Edmund Burke** wrote *Reflections on the French Revolution.*

**1791 Thomas Paine** wrote *The Rights of Man,* directed against critics of French Revolution.

**1798 Robert Malthus** published *Essay on the Principle of Population.*

**1799 Napoleon Bonaparte** staged a coup d'état in France; his conquests made France the most powerful country in Europe; Code Napoléon reformed legal system; Napoleon was exiled in **1815.**

NEAR AND MIDDLE EAST

**1736 Nadir Shah** established Afshar dynasty in **Persia;** considered last of the great Asian conquerors, he conquered Afghanistan, sacked Delhi, and defeated Turks.

**1768 Turkey** and **Russia** began a century of wars, causing Turkey to lose Crimea and much of Slavic Europe to Russia.

**1794 Kajar dynasty** of Persia founded by **Aga Mohammed;** it remained in power until 1925.

**1798 Napoleon Bonaparte** attempted to occupy **Egypt** but was driven out (1801) by British and Turkish forces.

FAR EAST

**1735–1796** Reign of **Emperor Ch'ien Lung,** during which Chinese empire reached its greatest territorial extent; Christian missionaries were persecuted.

**1739 Nadir Shah** of Persia sacked Delhi and conquered Punjab.

**1757** Defeat of Nawab of Bengal by **Robert Clive** marked beginning of **British Empire in India.**

**1758 Burma** became an independent state with capital at Rangoon.

**1782 Rama I** founded **Chakri dynasty** in **Thailand** and established capital at Bangkok; this dynasty rules today.

**1786** British East India Company leased the island of Penang in Malaya, first step in British domination of **Malay Peninsula.**

**1798 Ceylon** became British territory.

AMERICAS

**1721** Revolts in **Paraguay** initiated a series of wars in Latin America for **independence from Spain.**

**1754 French** and **Indian Wars** started in North America; British general, **James Wolfe,** defeated (1759) French under Montcalm on the Plains of Abraham, Quebec, Canada, ending the wars; British dominated Canada thereafter.

1775 **American Revolution** began with battle of **Lexington and Concord;** it ended with British surrender at Yorktown in 1781. Peace treaty signed in 1783.
1776 **Declaration of Independence** signed in Philadelphia.
1788 **U.S. Constitution** ratified.
1789 **George Washington** became first U.S. President.
1791 **Canada Act:** Canada was divided into Upper Canada (chiefly English) and Lower Canada (predominantly French).

AFRICA

1787 **British** abolitionists established colony at **Freetown,** which became center for British settlement of **Sierra Leone.**
1795–1796 **Mungo Park,** British explorer, explored Niger River.
1799 By this time Portuguese, French, Spanish, Danes, Dutch, and Swedes all held **trading posts** along West African coast and engaged in **slave trade.**

OCEANIA

1770 **Captain James Cook** claimed Cape York Peninsula, **Australia,** for Great Britain.
1777 Cook visited **Tasmania.**
1788 British established a penal colony in **Sydney, Australia.**

## 1800—1900

EUROPE

1800 **Socialism** developed in Europe in reaction to deplorable industrial conditions.
1801 **United Kingdom** was formed by union of **Great Britain and Ireland.**
1802 John Dalton introduced **atomic theory** into chemistry.
First **factory law** was introduced in England; it pertained to **child labor.**
1804 **Napoleon I** became emperor of France.
1806 **Holy Roman Empire** came to an end when **Francis II** renounced the imperial title.
1812 **Napoleon** invaded **Russia,** a disastrous campaign.
1814–1815 **Congress of Vienna: Metternich** of Austria, **Talleyrand** of France, **Alexander I** of Russia, **Frederick William I** of Prussia, and **Castlereagh** of England tried to restore European balance of power; the congress reestablished monarchies and organized German Confederation, which was dominated by Austria.
1815 **Napoleon I** returned from Elba and was later defeated by British and Prussian armies at **Waterloo.**
1821 **Greeks** began war with **Turkey,** achieving independence in 1830.
1830 **July Revolution** in France forced abdication of King Charles X; Louis Philippe became constitutional monarch.
1831 Russians suppressed **Polish insurrection,** marking beginning of "Russification" of Poland.
1837–1901 Reign of **Queen Victoria** of England, who married (1840) her cousin **Prince Albert** of Saxe-Coburg; English enjoyed era of prosperity due to industrial and colonial expansion.
1838 **Chartist movement** began, marking first attempt of British working classes to attain power.
1845 **Friedrich Engels** wrote *Situation of the Working Classes in England.*
**Potato blight** began in **Ireland,** which resulted by 1851 in death of about one million people from starvation and disease.
1848 **Marx** and **Engels** issued *Communist Manifesto.*
**Revolutions** broke out in France, Germany, Austria, Hungary, Bohemia, and Italy.
1848–1916 Reign of **Francis Joseph,** Emperor of Austria, who became (1867) ruler of **Austro-Hungarian Empire.**
1852–1870 Reign of **Napoleon III,** emperor of the Second French Empire.
1854–1856 **Crimean War:** Britain and France ended Russian domination of southeastern Europe.
1855–1881 Reign of **Alexander II,** tsar of Russia; he attempted to modernize government, emancipated (1861) **serfs,** and ceded (1867) Alaska to the United States; **Russian literature** began its most creative period.
1856 **Bessemer** invented process of converting **iron** into **steel.**
1859 **De Lesseps** began **Suez Canal,** which opened in 1869.
**Darwin** published *Origin of the Species.*
1859–1870 **Risorgimento** in Italy: a nationalist movement led by middle classes and nobility for political unification; its leaders included **Mazzini, Cavour,** and **Giuseppe Garibaldi.**
1861 **Kingdom of Italy** proclaimed, and **Victor Emmanuel II** of Sardinia became king.
**Rumania** formed by unification of Moldavia and Walachia.
1862 **Otto von Bismarck** became premier and chancellor of Germany and created German Empire.
1864 **First International** organized in London under leadership of **Karl Marx.**
1866 First permanent **transatlantic cable** laid by **Cyrus Field:**
**Austro-Prussian War:** Bismarck expelled Austrians from German Confederation; and established North German Confederation; Austria lost Venetia to **Italy.**
**Nobel** invented **dynamite.**
1867 **Marx** published first volume of *Das Kapital.*
**Austro-Hungarian Empire** founded: under pressure from Hungarian nationalists, Francis Joseph created dual monarchy; this empire collapsed in 1918.
1868–1894 British statesmen **Benjamin Disraeli,** an imperialist and Tory leader, and **William Gladstone,** an anti-imperialist and Liberal party leader, vied for control of prime ministry.
1870 Dogma of **papal infallibility** declared by Vatican Council.
**Vladimir Lenin** (V. I. Ulyanov), founder of modern Communism, was born.
1870–1871 **Franco-Prussian War:** Germans, directed by **von Moltke,** invaded and defeated France; French deposed Napoleon III and established **Third Republic of France,** which endured until 1940.
Italy incorporated **Papal States,** completing unification of the country.
1871 **German Empire** proclaimed at Versailles with **William I** as Emperor; north and south Germany became united into single *Reich.*
**Paris Commune** formed when Parisians refused to surrender to new regime; national troops suppressed revolutionaries.
1875 Charles Stewart **Parnell,** Irish nationalist leader, was elected to Parliament and began movement for **Irish independence.**
1878 **Congress of Berlin:** much of Ottoman Empire divided among Russia, Britain, and Austro-Hungarian Empire.
1881 **Alexander II** of Russia assassinated by member of revolutionary group called **People's Will.**
1882 **Triple Alliance** formed by Germany, Austria-Hungary, and Italy.
1885 **Louis Pasteur** used vaccine to prevent rabies in young boy.
1894–1906 **Dreyfus Affair:** Capt. Alfred Dreyfus, French Jewish military officer, was unjustly convicted of treason by a court-martial, sentenced to Devils Island, but eventually exonerated; his case divided France between left and right factions, causing (1905) separation of church and state.
1894–1917 Reign of **Nicholas II,** last tsar of Russia.
1895 **Roentgen** discovered **X rays.**
**Marconi** sent message over **wireless.**
1898 **Zeppelin** invented motor-driven **airship** and made first trial flight two years later.
**The Curies** discovered radium.
1899 First **Peace Conference** at **The Hague** established a permanent court of arbitration.

NEAR AND MIDDLE EAST

1811–1849 Reign of **Mohammed Ali** in **Egypt** extended Egyptian territory to Persian Gulf.
1854–1856 **Crimean War:** Britain and France backed Turkey in war with Russia that forced Russian concessions and guaranteed integrity of Ottoman Empire.
1859–1869 **Suez Canal** was built by **De Lesseps.**
c. 1870 Turkish government permitted European **Jews** to settle in **Palestine.**
1878 **Congress of Berlin: Turks** lost Cyprus to British, part of Asian lands to Russians, and Bosnia-Hercegovina to Austrians.

1888 European powers declared **neutrality of Suez Canal;** free passage was guaranteed to merchant and war vessels.

1892 British took over **Trucial Oman,** a region of eastern Arabia, and denied local sheiks treaty-making powers.

1894–1896 Sultan **Abdu-l-Hamid II** initiated extermination plan against Armenians; persecutions and massacres were resumed in 1915.

1896 **Young Turks,** a new national force, developed in Turkey, leading (1908) revolt against Sultan.

FAR EAST

1819 **Sir T. Stamford Raffles** secured transfer of **Singapore** to British East India Company.

1839–1842 **Opium War:** British provoked war with China and acquired commercial concessions and **Hong Kong.**

1848 **Taiping Rebellion** began in China, further weakening Ch'ing dynasty; with aid of Western powers, it was suppressed in 1865.

1853 **Commodore Perry,** an American, landed in isolationist **Japan;** the following year Japanese agreed to trade with West.

1857–1858 **Sepoy Rebellion,** or Great Mutiny: Indian soldiers revolted against British, representing first serious revolt of Indians against foreign rule.

1868 **Emperor Meiji Mutsuhito** began to rule **Japan;** he modernized country by abolishing feudalism, promoting foreign trade, and initiating industrialization and military conscription; Meiji period ended in 1912.

1887 France joined Vietnam and Cambodia as **Indo-China;** Laos was added to union in 1893.

1888 Britain completed annexation of **Burma,** making it a dependency of India.

1889 Meiji Mutsuhito issued modern **constitution** for **Japan.**

1894–1895 **Sino-Japanese War:** Japan became an imperial power by defeating Chinese in Korea and acquiring Formosa (Taiwan) and the Pescadores.

1898 Spain ceded **Philippines** to the United States.

1899 Western powers forced **Open Door** policy upon **China** by which equal trade rights for all nations were guaranteed.

AMERICAS

1801–1803 **Toussaint L'Ouverture,** martyred Haitian patriot, liberated **Santo Domingo** from the French and governed the island, thwarting Napoleon's colonial ambitions.

1803 United States purchased **Louisiana Territory** from France.

1806 **Henri Christophe,** Haitian revolutionary, elected president of Haitian republic.

1810 **Mexico** began to fight for independence from Spain.

1811 **Paraguay** achieved independence.

1811–1813 **Venezuela,** led by Francisco de Miranda, gained independence.

1812–1814 **War of 1812:** United States and Great Britain fought over neutrality of the seas and impressment of sailors; struggle strengthened American nationalist feelings.

1816 **Argentina** won independence.

1818 **Chile** gained independence under **José de San Martín.**

1818–1823 **Bernardo O'Higgins,** Chilean revolutionist, ruled **Chile.**

1819–1830 **Simón Bolívar,** the Liberator and greatest **Latin American hero,** defeated Spanish forces at Boyacá and was elected President of Greater Colombia (modern Colombia, Venezuela, Ecuador, and Panama).

1821 **Mexicans** achieved independence.

1822 Independence was won in **Brazil** and **Peru.**

1823 **Monroe Doctrine:** President James Monroe declared that the United States would neither interfere in European affairs nor tolerate European interference in American hemisphere.

1825 **Bolivia** became independent, the last Latin American country to win freedom from Spain.

1841 **Act of Union** joined Upper and Lower **Canada.**

1844 **Samuel Morse** transmitted message over **telegraph** from Washington to Baltimore.

1846 The **Mexican war** between United States (and Texas) and Mexico began; **Treaty of Guadalupe Hidalgo** established (1848) Rio Grande as Mexican-U.S. boundary and made New Mexico and California U.S. territory and Texas a possession.

1848 **Gold** discovered in **California.**

1861 **Civil War** (that ended in 1865) began in the United States.

1863 The **Emancipation Proclamation** ended slavery in the rebel states.

1864 **Maximilian,** Austrian archduke, became emperor of **Mexico;** he and his wife Carlotta retained power with aid of French troops; their rule was overthrown (1867) by **Benito Juárez,** an Indian, who became Mexican national hero.

1865 **War of the Triple Alliance** began: Paraguay fought against Argentina, Brazil, and Uruguay; it ended (1870) with devastation of Paraguay.

1867 **British North America Act:** Canada became a confederation.

United States purchased **Alaska** from Russia.

1868 **Cubans** fought **Ten Years War** for independence, being defeated by Spanish in 1878.

1876 **Porfirio Diaz** seized presidency of **Mexico** and ruled ruthlessly; he encouraged foreign capital, made Mexico prosperous but kept peasants in virtual bondage; deposed by **Madero revolution** in 1911.

1879–1884 **War of the Pacific:** Chile fought against Bolivia and Peru, securing territory from both countries; Bolivia lost sea access.

1889 Republic of **Brazil** established.

1895 Cuban poet, **José Martí,** led revolt against Spain.

1898 **Spanish-American War:** after U.S. battleship *Maine* was sunk in Havana harbor, the United States declared war on Spain and by Treaty of Paris (1898) acquired Puerto Rico, Guam, and the Philippines; the war dissolved Spanish control in Latin America.

1899 **Cuba** became an independent republic under U.S. protection.

AFRICA

1806 Britain annexed **Cape Province** in South Africa.

1807 Britain outlawed **slave trade** with France, Spain, and Portugal following suit.

1808 **Sierra Leone** became a British crown colony and administered **Gambia.**

1822 **Liberia** founded as haven for **freed American slaves;** it was declared an independent republic in 1847.

1830 French troops began conquest of Algeria.

1835 **Boers** began to leave Cape Province; the **"Great Trek"** established republics of Transvaal, Natal, and Orange Free State.

1841 **Dr. David Livingstone** began three decades of explorations in central Africa; he discovered (1855) Victoria Falls and his reports created interest in the **"Dark Continent"** and its natural resources.

1843 British annexed **Natal** after short war with Boers; it was made crown colony in 1856.

1848 British annexed **Orange Free State.**

1867–1871 **Diamonds** were discovered in South Africa, inciting diamond rush; **Kimberley** became center of diamond industry.

1874–1889 Henry Morton **Stanley** explored **Congo River.**

1876 **Leopold II,** with Stanley's aid, set up organization to exploit Congo; he founded (1885) **Congo Free State,** ruling as supreme monarch until 1908.

1878 Cetewayo led **Zulu revolt** against British that was defeated (1879) at Ulundi.

1880 **Brazzaville** founded in Congo by **French.**

1881 **Tunis** became French protectorate.

1884–1885 **Germans** proclaimed protectorates over **Tanganyika, Togoland, Cameroons, and South-West Africa.**

1886 **Gold** discovered in **Witwatersrand** in southern Transvaal.

1888 **Cecil Rhodes,** British diamond tycoon, gained monopoly of Kimberley diamond production; Rhodes became (1890) virtual dictator of Cape Province but resigned (1897) and thereafter developed **Rhodesia.**

1889 **Menelik II** of Ethiopia unwittingly signed Treaty of Uccialli that made Ethiopia an Italian protectorate; Italians invaded after he repudiated treaty; Menelik crushed (1896) Italians at **Aduwa.**

**1891** British annexed **Nyasaland** and fought Arab slave traders.

**1896** British, after a series of wars, defeated **Ashanti** kingdom and annexed it in 1901.

**1899–1902** Boer War: British defeated Boers in South Africa and formed (1910) **Union of South Africa.**

OCEANIA

**1803** British took possession of **Tasmania,** establishing a penal colony there.

**1840** Treaty of **Waitangi** guaranteed **Maoris** in New **Zealand** that they would retain their land for surrendering sovereignty to British crown.

## 1900—1981

EUROPE

**1903 Social Democrats held** second party congress in London and split into **Mensheviks** and **Bolsheviks,** the nascent Communist party.

**1904** France and England signed the **Entente Cordiale,** which became (1907) the **Triple Entente** when Russia joined.

**1905 Einstein** formulated theory of **relativity.**

**1906** Britain launched the *Dreadnought,* first large **battleship,** signaling start of world naval buildup.

**1908** Brief Balkan crisis erupted after **Austria** announced annexation of **Bosnia** and **Hercegovina.**

**1910–1936** Reign of **George V, king of Great Britain** and Northern Ireland and emperor of India, was marked by **Home Rule for Ireland (1914)** and World War I.

**1911 Italy** declared war on **Turkey** and acquired Tripoli.

**1912** First **Balkan War** began between Balkan countries and Turkey; a second broke out when Bulgaria attacked Serbia and Greece.

**1913** European nations increased preparations for war.

**1914** Assassination of **Archduke Francis Ferdinand** of Austria in Sarajevo by **Gavrilo Princip,** a member of Serbian terrorist society, sparked **World War I; Triple Entente** of France, Britain, and Russia and their allies Japan, Belgium, Serbia, and Montenegro fought **Central Powers** of Germany, Austria-Hungary, and Turkey; Italy, Portugal, Rumania, and the United States later sided with Triple Entente, which with its allies achieved victory in 1918, when an armistice was signed. At least 10,000,000 died during war.

**1915** Cunard ship *Lusitania* sunk off the coast of Ireland after attack by German submarine; 1,198 were lost.

**1916 President Wilson** submitted his peace proposals to warring nations.

Gregory **Rasputin,** a hedonistic mystic who influenced Russian royal family, was murdered.

**1917 Bolshevik Revolution** broke out in Russia; **Alexander Kerensky,** a Menshevik, headed provisional government but was overthrown by Bolshevik leader, **Vladimir Lenin.**

**Balfour Declaration:** Great Britain announced that Palestine should become home for Jews.

**1918** Treaty of **Brest-Litovsk:** Russians signed peace treaty with Germans, losing Poland, the Ukraine, and border areas inhabited by non-Russians.

**Kaiser Wilhelm** abdicated, and Germans adopted **Weimar Constitution** the following year.

**Austro-Hungarian Empire** ended, and Austria became a republic, while Poland and Hungary proclaimed their independence.

**Czechoslovakia** became independent; Thomas Masaryk served as president and Eduard Beneš as foreign minister.

"Kingdom of the Serbs, Croats, and Slovenes" was proclaimed under the regency of **Peter I** of Serbia; its name was changed to **Yugoslavia** (land of southern Slavs) in 1929.

**Civil War** began in **Russia** between Reds and Whites that was complicated by Allied interventions; by end of war in 1920, Russia had been devastated.

**1919 Treaty of Versailles** ending World War I was negotiated by Woodrow Wilson (United States), Georges Clemenceau (France), David Lloyd George (England), and Vittorio Orlando (Italy).

**1920 League of Nations** was established in **Geneva;** the United States refused to join.

Northern and Southern Ireland separated; Southern Ireland became (1921) **Irish Free State** with dominion status.

**1922** Russia became the **Union of Soviet Socialist Republics,** the first Communist state in the world.

**Benito Mussolini,** founder of Fascism, became premier of **Italy,** gradually creating dictatorship.

Major powers agreed to limit size of navies at **Washington Disarmament Conference.**

**1923 Adolf Hitler,** leader of National Socialist (Nazi) Party, led unsuccessful **"Beer Hall Putsch"** in Munich; during imprisonment he wrote *Mein Kampf.*

**1924** A power struggle began in Russia after Lenin's death; ultimately **Joseph Stalin** was victorious and became dictator.

**1928** Stalin initiated **Five Year Plan** for rapid industrialization and collectivized farms; **peasants** who refused collectivization were either sent to Siberia to perform forced labor or killed; measures caused "liquidation" of more than five million peasants.

**Kellogg-Briand Pact** outlawing war was signed by the United States and 62 other nations in Paris.

**1929 Lateran Treaties** created independent state of **Vatican City** in Rome.

**1930** Worldwide **economic depression** developed, pushing many countries into bankruptcy; this disaster encouraged rise of **extremist movements.**

**1931 British Commonwealth of Nations** established. Spain became a republic.

**1932 Antonio Salazar** became prime minister of **Portugal,** ruling (1936–1968) as dictator.

**1933** The democratic **Weimar Republic** fell in Germany. **Hitler's Nazi party** won majority in *Reichstag* and the government granted him dictatorial powers; Hitler built up war economy and began to rearm Germany; he withdrew from the League of Nations and set up **concentration camps,** where, in the years that followed, over six million people (mainly Jews and Poles) died.

**1935 Nuremberg Laws** deprived Jews of citizenship, barred them from certain professions, and prohibited marriage between Germans and Jews.

**Ethiopia,** in League of Nations, brought charges against Italy; League economic sanctions against Italy did not prevent annexation (1936) of Ethiopia.

**1936 Hitler** repudiated Locarno Pact and sent troops into **Rhineland.**

**Rome-Berlin-Tokyo Axis** formed.

**Spanish Civil War** began: Republicans were backed by Communist Russia, while Nazi Germany and Fascist Italy supported Falangists; liberals from many countries fought to save republic; Falangist forces, headed by **General Francisco Franco,** were victorious by 1939.

Stalin began liquidation of his enemies with series of purge trials that lasted until 1939.

**George VI** became king of England after Edward VIII abdicated.

**1938 Germany** annexed **Austria.**

**Munich Pact:** French and British, led by Neville Chamberlain, appeased Hitler and allowed Germany to occupy **Sudetenland;** Germans took remainder of Czechoslovakia in 1939.

**1939 Germany** signed nonaggression pact with Soviet Union.

Germans invaded **Poland,** beginning **World War II. Russian troops** invaded Poland, which was partitioned between Soviet Union and Germany.

Russians took **Lithuania, Latvia,** and **Estonia.**

Russians invaded **Finland,** defeating her the following year.

**League of Nations** performed its final act by expelling Soviet Union for invading Finland.

World War II broke out and developed into global conflict between **Axis** and **Allies.**

**1940 Marshal Henri Pétain** became head of French government and concluded peace treaty with Germany; Pétain set up government for unoccupied France in Vichy, which collaborated with Germans.

**1940–1945 Winston Churchill** was prime minister of England; his inspiring leadership helped British during dark days of war.

**1941 Germany** and **Italy** declared war on the **United States** on Dec. 11.

**1942 Vidkun Quisling** appointed by Germans to **head** puppet government in **Norway;** he was executed for collaboration in 1945.

1943 Mussolini's regime collapsed; **Marshal Pietro Badoglio** became prime minister, and **Italy** surrendered unconditionally to Allies and declared war on Germany.

**President Roosevelt** and **Prime Minister Churchill** held conferences at Casablanca, Cairo, and Teheran to coordinate war plans.

German defeat by Russian forces at **Stalingrad** (now Volgograd) marked turning point of war on the Eastern front.

1944 **D-Day:** Allied troops, commanded by **General Dwight D. Eisenhower**, invaded Fortress Europa at Normandy, France.

**German generals** staged unsuccessful attempt on Hitler's life.

U.S. and French troops liberated **Paris.**

**General Charles de Gaulle** established provisional government in France.

1945 **Yalta (Crimea) Conference:** Roosevelt, Churchill, and Stalin made postwar plans for German occupation and agreed to form a United Nations.

**Josip Broz Tito,** partisan leader, became head of **Yugoslavia.**

**Mussolini** captured and executed by Italian partisans.

**Hitler** died in Berlin, reportedly a suicide.

**Germany** surrendered unconditionally to Allies; **Allied Control Council** set up to rule Germany and **Berlin,** both of which were divided among four powers. President Truman, Churchill, and Stalin met at **Potsdam, Germany,** to discuss control of Germany.

**Clement Attlee,** Labour party leader, became prime minister of England.

International War Crimes Tribunal began in **Nuremberg;** Nazi military and civilian leaders were tried for war crimes.

1946 **United Nations General Assembly** held its first session, in London; **Trygve Lie** of Norway became first secretary-general, holding office until 1951.

Civil war erupted in **Greece** between Communists and rightist government forces; Bulgaria, Albania, and Yugoslavia aided Communist guerrillas; conflict, which ended in 1949 with royalists retaining power, brought increased Western-Soviet hostility.

1946–1947 **Bulgaria** and **Rumania** proclaimed people's republics.

1947 **Cominform** was established in response to **Marshall Plan** when Communist leaders from nine countries met in Poland; it was dissolved in 1956.

1948 Communists came to power in **Hungary** and **Czechoslovakia;** Czech President Beneš resigned, and Foreign Minister Jan Masaryk was found dead.

**Yugoslavia** withdrew from Cominform, proclaiming its independence of Soviet influence.

**European Recovery Plan** (the Marshall Plan) went into effect; ERP ended in 1951.

**Berlin Blockade:** Soviets barred road and rail travel between Berlin and West Germany; West airlifted supplies until ban was lifted in 1949.

1949 **North Atlantic Treaty Organization** set up by the United States, Canada, and 10 European countries for collective self-defense.

**Soviet Union** exploded **atomic bomb,** ending U.S. monopoly

Germany divided into **West Germany** (Federal Republic of Germany) and **East Germany** (German Democratic Republic).

1952 Reign of **Queen Elizabeth II** of England began.

1953 Joseph Stalin died; **Georgi Malenkov** became Soviet premier; **Nikita S. Khrushchev** elected first secretary of the Soviet Communist party's Central Committee.

**Russians** exploded their first **hydrogen bomb.**

Workers in **East Germany** staged riots that were suppressed by Soviet troops.

1954 **Geneva settlement** divided **Vietnam** into North and South Vietnam and recognized independence of **Cambodia** and **Laos.**

1955 **Warsaw Pact:** mutual defense treaty signed by Soviet Union, Albania, Czechoslovakia, Bulgaria, Hungary, Poland, Rumania, and East Germany.

1956 Premier Khrushchev denounced Stalin at **20th** Communist Party Congress in Moscow, ushering in a period of **de-Stalinization** in Soviet Union and Eastern Europe. **Workers** rioted in **Poznan,** Poland. **Hungarian rebellion** against Communist regime ruthlessly put down by Soviet troops and tanks.

1957 **Common Market:** European Economic **Community** established by Belgium, Netherlands, Luxembourg, West Germany, France, and Italy; its ultimate aim was political union.

**Sputnik:** Soviet Union launched world's first artificial earth satellite, initiating **Space Age.**

1958 **Nuclear test ban** negotiations began in Geneva between Western and Soviet blocs.

**De Gaulle** elected president of France.

Russians provoked **Berlin crisis** that was limited to diplomatic confrontation.

1960 **Cyprus** gained independence **with Archbishop Makarios** as president.

**European Free Trade Association** established by "Outer Seven": Austria, United Kingdom, Denmark, Norway, Portugal, Sweden, and Switzerland; Finland joined in 1961.

**American U-2 plane,** on photoreconnaissance mission, was shot down over Russian territory; United States agreed to suspend flights.

1961 **Berlin Wall:** East Germans erected wall between East and West Berlin, causing war scare.

**Yuri A. Gagarin,** Russian astronaut, was first man to orbit earth.

1963 **Pope John XXIII** died; Giovanni Battista Cardinal Montini elected as **Pope Paul VI.**

The United States, Soviet Union, and Great Britain signed treaty banning **nuclear tests** above ground and under water.

Fighting broke out between **Greek** and **Turkish Cypriots;** UN force is still on island to maintain order.

1964 Soviet Presidium ousted **Khrushchev** and made **Aleksei N. Kosygin** premier and **Leonid I. Brezhnev** first secretary of Communist party.

1966 **De Gaulle** requested **NATO** troop removal from France.

1967 Military staged coup d'état in **Greece,** installing dictatorship and driving **King Constantine II** into exile.

**Britain** devalued the **pound** and instituted austerity program.

1968 **International monetary crises** developed because of faltering British pound and French franc, but both currencies were held.

**Soviet** troops invaded **Czechoslovakia;** President Ludvik Svodoba and Alexander Dubcek allowed to retain posts, but Czechs had to accept Soviet troop occupation for indefinite time.

**Peace talks** opened in Paris between representatives of Hanoi, National Liberation Front, Saigon, and Washington to discuss **Vietnam cease-fire.**

1969 **Charles de Gaulle** resigned as president of France and was replaced by Georges Pompidou.

1970 **West Germany** and **USSR** signed a nonaggression pact.

Conservative leader **Edward Heath** became prime minister in **England.**

Violent food price riots in **Poland** led to Wladyslav Gomulka's resignation. He was replaced by Edward Gierek as the first secretary of the Communist party.

**Charles De Gaulle** died.

1972 **Great Britain, Ireland,** and **Denmark** joined the EEC.

**Arab commandos** disrupt the **XXth Olympic** games at Munich by taking 13 Israeli athletes hostage. The terrorists and hostages were later killed.

Terrorism rocked **Northern Ireland** in continued Protestant-Catholic conflict.

1973 **East and West Germany** established diplomatic relations, formally acknowledging their separation.

**Greece** formally abolished the monarchy.

**Western Europe** was plunged into an energy crisis when the Arabs embargoed oil shipments to Europe, the U.S., and Japan.

1975 **Western Europe experiences severe inflation and unemployment.**
In **Helsinki,** Western and Eastern leaders signed pact at **Conference on Security and Cooperation.**
Francisco Franco dies; **Juan Carlos** is proclaimed Spanish king.

1978 **Pope Paul VI** died; Albino Cardinal Luciani elected as **Pope John Paul I,** but lives only 34 days. Karol Cardinal Wojtyla of Poland elected **Pope John Paul II.**

1980 **Tito** of Yugoslavia **dies.**
**Polish** workers granted right to form unions following nationwide strikes.

1981 Polish government imposes martial law.

MIDDLE EAST

1900 **Ibn Saud** began to conquer Arabia, which became (1932) kingdom of **Saudi Arabia.**

1901 **Persians** discovered **petroleum,** causing increased rivalry in the area between Russia and England.

1914 **British** declared **Egypt** a protectorate, which it remained until 1922.

1915–1918 Turks slaughtered over one million **Armenians.**

1916 British **Colonel T. E. Lawrence (Lawrence of Arabia)** led Arab military campaigns against Turks, hoping for independent Arab states.

1919 **Kemal Ataturk** organized Turkish Nationalist party and began to form army; he was elected (1923) president of newly founded **Turkish republic** and began **"Westernization"** of country, abolishing (1923) caliphate and ruling until 1938.

1920 **Syria** and **Lebanon** became **French** mandates; their independence was recognized when they were admitted to United Nations in 1945.
**Palestine,** including **Jordan,** became **British** mandate; three-way struggle among Jews, Arabs, and British developed, lasting until 1948.

1921 **Reza Shah Pahlavi,** who staged coup d'etat in **Persia,** eventually ruled as dictator; changed (1935) name of country to **Iran;** abdicated in 1941.

1936 **Farouk** became king of Egypt.

1941 **Mohammed Reza Shah Pahlevi** became shah of Iran.

1945 The **Arab League,** an association of Arab states, was formed for economic unity and as opposition to establishment of Jewish state in Palestine.

1946 **Iran** protested to UN Security Council the presence of **Russian troops** in Azerbaijan province; this incident, which ended the following year, was the first crisis of the **Cold War.**
Kingdom of **Jordan** proclaimed.

1948 State of **Israel** achieved independence after bitter struggle; **David Ben-Gurion** first prime minister.

1948–1949 **Arab-Israeli war** ended in defeat of Arab League forces.

1951–1953 **Iran oil** industry nationalized by Prime Minister Mohammed Mossadegh.

1952 **Gamal Abdel Nasser** led army coup against King Farouk; Nasser was elected (1956) president of **Egypt** and promoted Arab unity.

1956 **Suez Crisis:** when Nasser nationalized Suez Canal, Israel, Britain, and France attacked Egypt but withdrew after UN Emergency Task-Force entered conflict.

1958 **United Arab Republic** formed by unification of Egypt and Syria; Syria withdraws in 1961.
**Lebanon** accused U.A.R. of intervention; President Eisenhower dispatched troops to area.
**Iraqi** monarchy overthrown in bloody **coup** led by General Kassem.
**British** paratroopers landed in **Jordan** to prevent pro-Nasser take-over.

1960 U.A.R., with Russian aid, began construction of **a new Aswan Dam.**

1961 **Kuwait** achieved independence.

1962 **Kurdish tribes** in northern **Iraq** rebelled, demanding independent state. Revolt is crushed in 1975.
**Adolf Eichmann,** chief administrator of Nazi program for exterminating Jews, was tried and executed by **Israel.**
**Yemen** monarchy overthrown; civil war broke out between republicans, who were supported by Egyptians, and royalists, backed by Saudi Arabia.

1963 **Federation of South Arabia** formed by union of Aden and Aden Federation; area achieved independence in 1968 as **Southern Yemen.**

1967 **Arab-Israeli war:** six-day conflict broke out after Nasser closed Gulf of Aqaba to Israeli ships; Israelis defeated Arabs; Sinai and Jerusalem occupied.

1968 President Abdul Rahman Arif of Iraq was ousted in **bloodless coup** led by **former premier Ahmed Hassan al-Bakr,** who later assumed **premiership.**

1970 **Nasser died in Cairo;** succeeded by **Anwar Sadat.**
Civil war broke out between **Jordanian army** and **Palestinian guerrilla groups.**

1973 Large-scale fighting once again broke out between Israel and the Arab nations. The war ended in an inconclusive cease-fire.
The **Arabs** embargoed the shipment of oil to the U.S., Europe, and Japan, and boosted prices.

1974 The organization of petroleum exporting countries **(OPEC) ended its oil embargo.**

1975 Civil war raged in **Lebanon** between Christians and Moslems. **Israel** and **Egypt** signed Sinai disengagement pact. **Suez Canal** reopened.

1979 **Israel** and **Egypt** signed peace treaty calling for phased Israeli withdrawal from Sinai. **Islamic Republic of Iran** was proclaimed under the leadership of the Ayatollah **Khomeini** following the departure of the Shah and subsequent revolution. Militants seized U.S. Embassy in **Tehran** and held personnel hostage. Soviet troops occupied **Afghanistan.**

1980 **Iraq** invaded southwestern **Iran.**

1981 **Iran** released U.S. hostages. Sadat is assassinated near Cairo; succeeded by Hosni Mubarak.

FAR EAST

1904–1905 **Russo-Japanese War:** Russia's fleet was destroyed, and Japan's victory gained her recognition as world power.

1907 **Mohandas Gandhi** organized his first campaign of civil disobedience in Africa; he returned (1915) to **India** and supported England during World War I, hoping to attain Indian independence.

1910 Japan annexed **Korea.**

1911 **Chinese Revolution: Sun Yat-sen** forced Manchu emperor to abdicate and served briefly as **president** of Chinese Republic.

1917 **War** developed in China between **Kuomintang,** Sun Yat-sen's party of the Republic, and **"war lords"** of the national government in the North; **Kuomintang** established capital in **Canton.**

1919 **Amritsar Massacre:** hundreds of **Indian nationalists** were fired upon and killed by British.

1921 **Chinese Communist party** founded and became allied (1923) with Kuomintang.

1926 **Chiang Kai-shek** led **Nationalist** army in capture of Hankow, Shanghai, and Nanking; he drove (1927) Chinese Communists from **Shanghai,** initiating long civil war between Kuomintang forces and Communists.

1927 **Mao Tse-tung,** one of the founders of the Chinese Communist party, led peasant uprising in Hunan province.

1931 **Japanese** invaded Manchuria and set up **Manchukuo,** a puppet state.
Mao Tse-tung elected chairman of **Soviet Republic of China.**

1934–1935 Mao Tse-tung led Red Army on **Long March** (6,000 miles) from Kiangsi province north to new headquarters at Yenan.

1937 **Burma** became independent of **India.**
Japanese invaded northern **China** and fought war that continued until 1945.
**Gandhi's long fasts** forced some Indian **states** to grant democratic reforms.

1940 Japanese established puppet government in Nanking and signed military alliance with Germany and Italy.

1941 **Japan** bombed **Pearl Harbor,** captured Singapore, Philippines, and other areas of the Pacific, initiating **World War II** in the Pacific and drawing **United States** into war.

1945 **United States** dropped atomic bombs on **Hiroshima** and Nagasaki; as a result, Japan surrendered, ending World War II.

Korea was divided into Russian and American occupation zones; partition was formalized in 1948 when country became **North Korea** (Democratic People's Republic of Korea) and **South Korea** (Republic of Korea), which were separated by 38th parallel.
**Vietnamese nationalists** began demands for independence from France; war broke out; **Ho Chi Minh**, founder of Communist party in Vietnam, led **Viet Minh** forces.
**Indonesian nationalists** led by **Sukarno** began to fight Dutch for independence.

**1946 Philippines** granted independence by the United States.

**1947 India** and **Pakistan** became separate independent dominions; **Jawaharlal Nehru** became prime minister of Hindu state of India and **Mahomed Ali Jinnah**, governor general of Moslem state of Pakistan; bloody rioting broke out after partition, causing the death of millions of Hindus and Moslems.

**1948 Gandhi** assassinated by Hindu fanatic.
**Communists** began guerrilla warfare in **Malaya** that lasted over a decade.

**1949 Chinese People's Republic** headed by Mao Tse-tung established government at Peking, after defeating Chiang Kai-shek, whose **Nationalist government** was forced to **Taiwan** (Formosa).

**1950** Sukarno elected president of the Republic of **Indonesia.**
**Korean war** broke out when North Koreans invaded South Korea; United Nations force under U.S. command intervened.
**Chinese Communists** invaded **Tibet** and sent troops to aid **North Koreans.**

**1951** Armistice talks began at **Panmunjon** to end Korean war.

**1954** Battle of **Dienbienphu:** Crushing French defeat ended her control in Indo-China; Vietnam divided at 17th parallel, with **Ho Chi Minh** as president of North Vietnam; Cambodia and Laos became independent.

**1955** A U.S. military advisory group took over training of South Vietnamese army.
**Premier Ngo Dinh Diem** became president of South Vietnam.

**1957 Federation of Malaya gained independence.**

**1959** Communist Chinese suppressed uprising in **Tibet. Communist Pathet Lao** forces began civil war in Laos; a temporary cease-fire was secured (1961) in **Geneva. China and India begun a series of border wars.**

**1961 India** forcibly annexed Portuguese Goa, Damão, and Diu.
**United States** sent guerrilla warfare specialists to train **South Vietnamese** soldiers.

**1962** Neutralist government set up in **Laos** under **Prince Souvanna Phouma,** but Pathet Lao continued sporadic fighting in North.

**1963 Federation of Malaysia** created by union of Federation of Malaya, Singapore, Sarawak, and North Borneo; the union suffered infiltration by Indonesian guerrillas until 1966; **Singapore** seceded (1965) and became independent.
**Diem** regime in South Vietnam overthrown; government changed hands frequently until military regime of **Nguyen Cao Ky** took over in 1965.

**1964 China exploded her first atomic bomb.**
**France** recognized Communist China.
**Nehru** died in India and was succeeded by **Lal Bahadur Shastri.**

**1965 United States began bombing North Vietnam.**
After an abortive Communist coup in **Indonesia,** the army slaughtered at least 100,000 Communists; Indonesia withdrew from United Nations.
India and Pakistan fought over **Kashmir.**

**1966 Communist China initiated "cultural revolution"** aimed at ideological conformity of party leaders.
Sukarno forced to yield power to **Suharto,** who outlawed Communist party.
**Indira Gandhi, Nehru's daughter, became prime minister of India after Shastri's death.**

**1967** Communist China exploded first hydrogen bomb.
**South Vietnam: first national election; Nguyen Van Thieu president and Nguyen Cao Ky vice-president.**

**1968 North Korea seized** *Pueblo,* **U.S.** Navy intelligence ship, holding its officers and crew for 11 months.
**Peace talks** for Vietnam cease-fire began in **Paris. President Johnson** ordered halt to bombing of **North Vietnam.**

**1969 Soviet** and **Chinese forces** fought on the Manchurian border over a disputed island in the Ussuri River.

**1970** Prince **Sihanouk** was deposed as chief of state in **Cambodia.** He was replaced by Gen. Lon Nol.
**U.S.** and **South Vietnamese** troops invaded Cambodia.

**1971 Communist China** admitted to **U.N.; Nationalist** Chinese (Taiwan) ousted.
**East Pakistan** became independent state of **Bangladesh** after bloody civil war.

**1972 President Nixon visits Peking and Moscow.**

**1973 U.S.** and **South Vietnamese** signed cease-fire agreement with **North Vietnamese** and **Vietcong.** Fighting continued through Indochina.

**1975** The thirty year **Indochina** war ended with **the** military collapse of **U.S.**-backed **South Vietnam** and **Cambodia.**

**1976** Communist Chinese leade **Mao Tse-tung** dies.

**1978–79 Vietnam** invaded **Cambodia** and drove Pol Pot regime from Phnom Penh.

**1979** U.S. extended dipolmatic representation to the **People's Republic of China** (Communists) and broke relations with **Taiwan.**
**China** invaded **Vietnam;** withdrew after one month.

AMERICAS

**1901 President William McKinley** assassinated by anarchist; **Theodore Roosevelt** became President and held office until 1909.

**1903 Panama,** with U.S. assistance, revolted against Colombia and gained independence.
**Orville** and **Wilbur Wright** made their first **airplane** flight near Kitty Hawk, North Carolina.

**1910 Francisco Madero** led **Mexican Revolution** against President Diaz; after Madero's assassination, **Francisco (Pancho) Villa, Emiliano Zapata,** and **Venustiano Carranza** continued revolution; Mexico's constitution was enacted 1917.

**1914 Panama Canal** opened.

**1916–1924 U.S.** troops occupied **Dominican Republic.**

**1917** United States entered **World War I** on side of Allies.

**1929 Stock Market** crash in the United States initiated the **Great Depression; during height of depression,** 12 million people were unemployed.

**1932–1935 Chaco War: Bolivia** and **Paraguay** fought exhausting war over disputed Chaco plain.

**1933 President Franklin D. Roosevelt** was inaugurated; he enacted **New Deal** legislation aimed at improving social and economic conditions in the U.S.

**1938** Mexico nationalized foreign oil companies.

**1941–1945 United States in World War II:** after Japanese bombed **Pearl Harbor,** December 7, 1941, the United States declared war; Nazi Germany and Fascist Italy declared war on the United States; war was terminated after defeat of German army and surrender of Japanese after atomic bombing of Hiroshima and Nagasaki.

**1942 Enrico Fermi achieved first self-sustaining nuclear** chain reaction.

**1944 Bretton Woods** (New Hampshire) Conference established the **International Bank for Reconstruction** and the **International Monetary Fund.**
**Dumbarton Oaks,** Washington, D.C., Conference: the United States, Great Britain, and Soviet Union laid plans for an **international organization.**

**1945 Roosevelt** died and was succeeded by **Harry S Truman.**
**United Nations Charter** signed at San Francisco.
United States made **first atom bomb** test at Los Alamos, New Mexico, warned Japan of her complete destruction unless she surrendered, and dropped atomic bombs on **Hiroshima** and **Nagasaki.**

**1946 Juan Perón elected president of Argentina;** he established totalitarian regime and an ultranationalistic program that ultimately ruined economy, and was deposed (1955) by miltary coup.
**Churchill** gave **"iron curtain"** speech at Fulton, Missouri, warning of Soviet expansionism.

**1948 Truman** won upset Presidential victory; he initiated overseas military and economic aid to contain Communism and became leader in NATO formation.
**Organization of American States (OAS)** founded for hemispheric unity and mutual defense.

1949 U.S. Senate ratified **NATO treaty, establishing collective self-defense among Western powers.**

**1950 United States in UN Security Council charged North Korea with invading South Korea and initiated military intervention against aggressors with General MacArthur** as UN Commander.

1952 **Fulgencio Batista** seized power in **Cuba.**
United States exploded its first **hydrogen bomb.**

**1954 General Alfredo Stroessner staged coup in Paraguay;** in spite of opposition, he remains in power.
***Brown* v. *Board of Education:* U.S. Supreme Court** outlawed racial segregation in public schools, initiating **civil rights movement.**

1957 **François Duvalier** elected president of **Haiti;** his harsh rule included reign of terror.

1958 **Explorer I:** United States successfully launched her first artificial satellite.

1959 **Fidel Castro** came to power in **Cuba;** he gradually linked country with Soviet bloc and proclaimed (1961) loyalty to Communism.

1960 **John F. Kennedy** elected U.S. President.

1961 United States severed relations with **Cuba.**
**Bay of Pigs:** U.S.-trained Cuban exiles' invasion of Cuba ended disastrously.
Charter of the **Alliance for Progress** signed in Punta del Este, Uruguay; it was aimed at increasing economic and social development in **Latin America** with U.S. aid.

1962 The United States and Soviet Union appeared on the brink of war when **Soviet missiles** were discovered on **Cuba;** President Kennedy forced **Khrushchev** to have them dismantled.
**John H. Glenn** was first American to orbit earth.

**1963 President Kennedy** assassinated in Dallas, Texas, November 22; **Lyndon Baines Johnson** sworn in as President and defeated Barry M. Goldwater in 1964.

**1964 Panamanians staged anti-U.S. riots.**

1965 U.S. marines landed in **Dominican Republic.**
President Johnson signed **Medicare** and **war on poverty** legislation.
Race riots ravaged Los Angeles suburb of Watts.

1966 **Guyana** became independent.

1967 Race riots wasted **Newark, Detroit,** and other cities.

1968 **Frank Borman, William A. Anders,** and **James A. Lovell, Jr.,** were first men to orbit the **moon.**
**Dr. Martin Luther King, Jr.** and **Senator Robert Kennedy** were assassinated in the United States.
**Richard M. Nixon** won U.S. Presidential contest.
Military coup deposed Peruvian President Fernando Belaúnde Terry.
Pierre Elliott **Trudeau** succeeded to Canadian premiership.

1969 U.S. astronaut **Neil A. Armstrong** became first man to walk on the Moon.

1970 U.S. **student protests** against the Viet Nam war resulted in the killing of four students by National Guard at Kent State, Ohio, and of two students by police at Jackson State, Miss.
Trudeau invoked the War Measures Act in Canada after the murder of Quebec Labor Minister Pierre Laporte by the Quebec Liberation Front.
Salvador Allende was elected president of Chile and Luis Echeverria Alvarez of Mexico.

1971 Wage-price freeze enacted by **Nixon** administration.

**1972 Governor Wallace seriously injured in attempted** assassination while campaigning in Maryland.
Watergate burglars apprehended in Democratic National Headquarters; "Watergate" begins.
**Richard M. Nixon reelected president.**

**1973 Spiro T. Agnew resigned from the vice-presidency; Gerald R. Ford named to replace Agnew. "Watergate" dominates American political scene.**
Salvador Allende Gossens, Marxist President of Chile, overthrown and reportedly committed suicide.
Juan Perón returned from exile to become Argentine president.

**1974 Juan Peron died in Buenos Aires; His wife, Vice-President Isabel Peron assumes the presidency.**
**Richard M. Nixon resigned from the presidency; Gerald R. Ford succeeds to the office.**

1975 **Surinam** and **Grenada** attained **independence.** U.S. suffered severe economic **recession.**

1976 **Argentine** military junta deposed **Mrs. Peron.**
**Jose Lopez Portillo** elected to Mexican presidency.
**Jimmy Carter** elected U.S. President.

1979 Somoza regime was toppled in Nicaragua by Sandinista rebels following 18-month civil war. **Canal** Zone was ceded to Panama by the U.S.

1980 **Ronald Reagan elected U.S. President.**

1981 U.S. orbits **Columbia,** world's first space shuttle.

## AFRICA

1906 **Algeçiras Conference** recognized **predominance** of French and Spanish interests in Morocco but also assured protection of German interests.

1908 Belgium annexed Congo Free State, calling it **Belgian Congo.**

1910 **Union of South Africa** formed from former British colonies of Cape of Good Hope and Natal, Orange Free State, and Transvaal.

1911 **Germans** sent gunboat *Panther* to **Morocco** as show of force.

1912 **African partition** among European powers was completed; only Ethiopia and Liberia remained independent.

1914 **World War I** in Africa: British and French troops occupied German colonies of Togoland and the Cameroons.

1920 Former German colonies became **League mandates** under Great Britain (Tanganyika, parts of Togoland and Cameroons), Belgium (Ruanda-Urundi), France (parts of Togoland and Cameroons), and Union of South Africa (South-West Africa).
Most of **Kenya** became British crown colony.
**Abd-el-Krim,** leader of Riff tribes of Morocco, began fight against Spanish and French rule in Africa; early successes followed by his defeat and deportation (1926) by combined Franco-Spanish troops.

1923 **Rhodesia** was divided into Southern and Northern Rhodesia and placed under British rule.

1930 **Emperor Haile Selassie** ascended Ethiopian throne.

1935 Italy invaded Ethiopia, causing Haile Selassie to flee country; **League of Nations** issued economic sanctions to no avail.

1946 India broke diplomatic relations with **Union of South Africa** because of her treatment of Indian minority.

1948 **Apartheid:** D. F. Malan made apartheid in **Union of South Africa** a political issue; the policy was aimed at perpetuating supremacy of white minority.

1951 Rising **African nationalism** achieved first victory with independence of **Libya.**

1952 **Mau Mau,** secret terrorist organization in **Kenya,** began bloody campaign to oust white settlers; British declared emergency that lasted until 1960.

1954 Algerian nationalists formed **National Liberation Front** and began terrorist campaign against French; war ended with Algeria gaining independence in 1962.

1956 **Tunisia** gained independence from France with **Habib Bourguiba** as premier.

1960 Immediately after **Republic of the Congo** achieved independence, civil war broke out; political struggle within central government developed between **Patrice Lumumba,** premier, and **Joseph Kasavubu,** head of state; UN peace-keeping force entered dispute; when Lumumba was seized by army and murdered (1961), **Moise Tshombe** became premier.
**African nationalism** reached peak of success when 16 nations gained freedom and African nations made up one third of UN membership.

**1961** **Dag Hammarskjöld,** UN secretary-general, killed in plane crash on mission to **Congo.**
**Union of South Africa** became a republic; later left British Commonwealth.

**1963** Jomo Kenyatta became Kenya's first premier.

**1964** **Tanzania** formed by unification of Tanganyika and Zanzibar; **Julius K. Nyerere** became first president.
Nyasaland became independent state of **Malawi;** Northern Rhodesia gained independence as **Zambia.**

**1965** **Mohammed Ben Bella,** Algerian premier, overthrown by **Col. Houari Boumédiene.**
**Rhodesia** unilaterally declared independence from Great Britain.
**President Kasavubu** dismissed Tshombe and his government; **General Mobutu,** commander of Congolese National army, seized power.

**1966** Kwame Nkrumah's government in **Ghana** toppled by military coup; **Nkrumah** went into exile.
**United Nations** terminated South Africa's mandate over **South-West Africa** and proclaimed UN administration over country.

**1967** Congolese troops engaged rebel forces in Kisangani and Bukavu. **Tshombe** died (1969) in Algeria.
**Republic of Biafra** proclaimed when eastern province of **Nigeria** seceded; Nigerian government sent troops and blockaded province, causing widespread famine throughout 1968/69.

**1969** **Pope Paul VI** became the first pope to visit Africa when he flew to Kampala, Uganda to attend an African episcopal symposium meeting.
Portugal utilized 40% of her national budget and 120,000 troops to quell rebels in territories of Angola, Mozambique, and Portuguese Guinea.

**1970** Surrender of secessionist **Biafra** on January 12 ended the 31-month civil war in Nigeria.

**1971** Republic of the Congo renamed **Zaire.**

**1973** A drought-induced famine cripples much of western Africa.

**1975** Mozambique, Cape Verde, São Tomé and Príncipe, and Angola gained independence, ending centuries-old Portuguese colonial empire.

**1976** Proponents of black majority rule wage guerrilla war against white regime in **Rhodesia.**

**1977** Ethiopia and Somalia made war over disputed Ogaden region.

**1978** Belgian and French paratroopers repelled Angola-based rebel invasion of Shaba province of **Zaire.**

**1979** Amin regime was overthrown in Uganda following invasion by **Tanzania.**

**1980** Black majority took power in Rhodesia with establishment of **Republic of Zimbabwe.**

### OCEANIA

**1901** Commonwealth of **Australia** formed by unification of Australia and Tasmania.

**1907** New Zealand attained dominion status.

**1959** Hawaii became a U.S. state.

**1962** Western Samoa obtained independence.

**1968** Nauru became an independent republic.

**1970** Fiji and Tonga gained independence.

**1975** Papua New Guinea achieved independence.

**1978** Solomon Islands and Tuvalu gained independence.

**1979** Kiribati became independent.

**1980** Vanuatu gained independence.

### ARCTIC AND ANTARCTICA

**1908–1909** **E. H. Shackleton's** expedition to **Antarctica** failed to reach **South Pole.**

**1909** **Robert E. Peary** discovered **North Pole.**

**1911** **Roald Amundsen** reached **South Pole.**

**1926** **Richard E. Byrd** flew over North Pole.

**1928** **Byrd** established **Little America,** in Antarctica.

**1955–1958** **Edmund Hillary** and **Vivian Fuchs** from Great Britain led overland crossing of **Antarctica.**

**1957–1958** During the **International Geophysical Year,** many nations participated in studies of Antarctica and the Arctic.

**1958** *Nautilus,* U.S. nuclear submarine, was first ship to cross North Pole under ice pack.

**1959–1960** Treaty accepted by 12 nations, including the United States, reserved **Antarctica** for scientific research and recognized no existing national claims to territory in area.

**1967** **Peter J. Barrett** and geologists from New Zealand discovered bone fragment and plant fossils embedded beneath icy surface of **Antarctica** indicating that Antarctica formerly had warmer climate.

**1968–1969** First overland crossing of the **North Pole** by foot and dog sled. **Royal Geographic Society** of Britain's 3,600-mile expedition, encompassing more than 15 months, reached Pole in April 1969.

## SEVEN WONDERS OF THE ANCIENT WORLD

**The Great Pyramid of Khufu** (or Cheops)—the world's largest pyramid located at Gizeh near Cairo. Built of limestone blocks, it originally stood 756 feet square, 482 feet high and covered 13 acres.

**The Hanging Gardens of Bablyon**—luxurious gardens which added to the glamorous atmosphere of Mesopotamia's most important ancient city.

**The Mausoleum at Halicarnassus**—a magnificent sepulcher in Asia Minor constructed of white marble richly decorated with sculpture and erected (c. 352 B.C.) in memory of Mausolus of Caria.

**The Artemision at Ephesus**—great temple built (c. 550 B.C.) as a center of worship for the nature-goddess Artemis.

**The Colossus of Rhodes**—large bronze statue (height about 100 feet) of the sun god Helios situated in the harbor of Rhodes and thought to be built by Chares of Rhodes between 292 and 280 B.C.

**The Olympian Zeus by Phidias**—built for the temple of Olympia (c. 435 B.C.); it consisted of a majestic bearded figure wearing a mantle and seated upon a huge ornamented throne.

**The Pharos at Alexandria**—celebrated lighthouse (estimated height: 200–600 feet) built by Ptolemy II (c. 280 B.C.) on the peninsula of Pharos.

# WORLD BIOGRAPHY

**Abd-el-Krim,** c. 1882-1963, Moroccan Rif leader and national hero.

**Abdullah,** 1882–1951, assassinated first Hashemite king of Jordan.

**Abrams, Creighton W., Jr.,** 1914-1974, American general in Vietnam.

**Abruzzi, Duca degli (Luigi Amedeo),** 1873–1933, Italian explorer of the Arctic (1899–1900).

**Acheson, Dean G.,** 1893-1971, U.S. Secretary of State (1949-52) who helped to establish NATO.

**Adams, Samuel,** 1722–1803, American patriot, signer of Declaration of Independence, and firebrand of Boston Tea Party.

**Addams, Jane,** 1860–1935, American social worker and cofounder of Hull House.

**Adenauer, Konrad,** 1876–1967, German statesman, postwar chancellor, and architect of West German recovery.

**Aga Khan III,** 1877-1957, fabulously wealthy Moslem leader and statesman.

**Agnelli, Giovanni,** 1921– , Italian industrialist and chairman of FIAT.

**Agrippina the Younger,** A.D. c. 16-59, Nero's mother, who contrived his accession to the throne.

**Aguinaldo, Emilio,** c. 1869–1964, Filipino revolutionary against Spain and the United States.

**Akbar,** 1542–1605, greatest Mogul emperor of India.

**Alanbrooke, Viscount (Alan F. Brooke),** 1883-1963, British general, W.W. II chief of imperial general staff.

**Alaric I,** c. 370–410, Visigothic ruler who devastated southern Europe.

**Albert, Prince,** 1819–61, German-born consort of Victoria of England.

**Albuquerque, Afonso de,** 1453–1515, Portuguese admiral and founder of Portuguese empire in the East.

**Alcibiades,** c. 450–404 B.C., Athenian statesman and general in Peloponnesian War.

**Alexander (III) the Great,** 356–323 B.C., king of Macedon, Greek conqueror, and one of the greatest generals of all time.

**Alexius I (Alexius Comnenus),** 1048–1118, emperor who restored Byzantine military and political power.

**Allen, Ethan,** 1738–89, American Revolutionary hero, leader of Green Mountain Boys.

**Allende (Gossens), Salvador,** 1908–73, President of Chile (1970–73); advocated democratic socialism.

**Altgeld, John P.,** 1847–1902, German-born American political leader and social reformer.

**Amin Dada, Idi,** 1925– , Ugandan president (1971–79).

**Amundsen, Roald,** 1872–1928, Norwegian polar explorer, first to reach the South Pole (December 14, 1911).

**Andrada e Silva, José Bonifácio de,** 1763-1838, Brazilian statesman, chief founder of independent Brazil.

**Andrassy, Julius (Count),** 1823–90, Hungarian statesman and first constitutional premier (1867–71).

**Andreotti, Giulio,** 1919– , Italian premier (1972-73, 1976–79).

**Andropov, Yuri V.,** 1914– , head of Soviet secret police, ambassador to Hungary during 1956 uprising.

**Anthony, Susan B.,** 1820–1906, American reformer and suffragette leader.

**Antonescu, Ion,** 1882–1946, Rumanian dictator (1940–44), executed as a war criminal.

**Antony, Mark,** c. 83-80 B.C., Roman politician and soldier who allied himself with Cleopatra and defied Rome.

**Arafat, Yasir,** 1929– , leader of the Palestine Liberation Organization.

**Armstrong, Neil,** 1930– , American astronaut; first person to set foot on the moon (1969).

**Arnold, Benedict,** 1741–1801, American Revolutionary general and traitor.

**Asoka,** ?–232 B.C., first great Indian emperor; spreader of Buddhism.

**al-Assad, Hafez,** 1928– , Syrian president (1971– ).

**Astor, John Jacob,** 1763–1848, American merchant and fur trader, the richest man in America at his death.

**Astor, Lady (Nancy W.),** 1879–1964, American-born British political leader, first woman member of Parliament.

**Astor, William W. (Viscount),** 1848–1919, Anglo-American financier and philanthropist.

**Atahualpa,** d. 1533, Inca (ruling chief) of Peru, executed by Pizarro.

**Ataturk, Kemal (b. Mustafa Kemal),** 1881–1938, father of modern Turkey and president (1923–1938).

**Attila,** d. 453, Hun leader, conqueror of eastern Europe.

**Attucks, Crispus,** c. 1723–70, American Negro patriot killed by British in Boston Massacre.

**Augustus (Octavius),** 63 B.C.–14 A.D., first Roman emperor; he defeated Antony and returned Rome from military dictatorship to constitutional rule.

**Aurangzeb,** 1618–1707, Mogul Indian emperor who brought his empire to its greatest expanse.

**Auriol, Vincent,** 1884–1966, first president (1947–54) of French Fourth Republic.

**Austin, Stephen F.,** 1793–1836, American leader of colonization in Texas.

**Ayub Khan, Mohammad,** 1907-74, Pakistani military leader who became (1958) president and resigned (1969).

**Babar,** c. 1482-1530, founder of Mogul empire in India.

**Babeuf, François N.,** 1760–97, executed French revolutionary, philosophical forerunner of Marx.

**Badoglio, Pietro,** 1871–1956, Italian field marshal in Ethiopia, premier after fall of Mussolini.

**Bakunin, Mikhail,** 1814–76, militant Russian anarchist, expelled from First International by Marxists.

**Balboa, Vasco Núñez de,** c. 1475–1519, beheaded Spanish conquistador, discoverer of Pacific Ocean.

**Bancroft, George,** 1800–91, American statesman and historian, founder of U.S. Naval Academy.

**Banneker, Benjamin,** 1731–1806, American Negro colonial astronomer, mathematician, and inventor.

**Barry, John,** 1745–1803, Irish-born naval commander during the American Revolution; considered to be the "Father of the American Navy."

**Barton, Clara,** 1821–1912, American humanitarian, organizer of the American Red Cross.

**Baruch, Bernard M.,** 1870–1965, American financier and government economic adviser.

**Batista y Zaldívar, Fulgencio,** 1901-73, Cuban dictator (president 1940-44, 1952-59), overthrown by Castro.

**Batu Khan,** d. 1255, Mongol leader of Golden Horde.

**Beaverbrook, Lord (William Maxwell Aitken),** 1879–1964, Canadian-born British statesman and publisher.

**Begin, Menachem,** 1913– , Israeli prime minister.

**Belisarius,** c. 505-565, Byzantine general under Justinian.

**Bellinghausen, Fabian von,** 1778–1852, Russian admiral and discoverer (1819–21) of Antarctica.

**Ben Bella, Ahmed,** 1918– , Algerian revolutionary, elected (1962) premier and deposed (1965) by Boumédienne.

**Beneš, Eduard,** 1884–1948, Czechoslovak president.

**Ben-Gurion, David,** 1886–1973, Israeli statesman, first prime minister (beginning in 1948).

**Benjamin of Tudela,** d. 1173, Jewish traveler and author of an itinerary of his trip (1159–73) to China.

**Bennett, James Gordon, Jr.,** 1841-1918, American publisher who financed Stanley's trip to find Livingstone.

**Bentinck, Lord William C.,** 1774–1839, British statesman, appointed (1833) first governor-general of British India.

**Beria, Lavrenti P.,** 1899–1953, executed Soviet secret police chief under Stalin.

**Bering, Vitus J.,** 1681–1741, Russian-backed Danish discoverer (1728) of Bering Strait.

**Bernadotte, Count (Folke),** 1895–1948, Swedish internationalist, UN mediator in Palestine until assassinated.

**Betancourt, Romulo,** 1908–81, progressive Venezuelan president (1945-48, 1959-64).

**Bevan, Aneurin,** 1897–1960, British political leader, developer of England's socialized medicine system.

**Bevin, Ernest,** 1881–1951, British labor leader and Labour government foreign minister (1945–51).

**Bhave, Acharya Vinoba,** 1895– , foremost Indian advocate of nonviolent (Gandhian) social revolution.

**Bhutto, Zulfikar Ali,** 1928–79, Pakistani president (1971–73) and prime minister (1973–77). Overthrown (1977) and executed in 1979.

**Biddle, Francis B.,** 1886–1968, American jurist, U.S. Attorney General (1941–45).

**Bismarck, Otto von,** 1815–98, German statesman who unified Germany under Prussian leadership.

**Blackstone, Sir William,** 1723–80, English jurist, first professor of English law at Oxford University.

**Bloomer, Amelia J.,** 1818–94, American reformer, devoted to women's rights.

**Blücher, Gebhard L. von,** 1742–1819, Prussian field marshal who helped Wellington defeat Napoleon at Waterloo.

**Blum, Léon,** 1872–1950, French Socialist statesman, Popular Front organizer, and writer.

**Boleyn, Anne,** c. 1507–36, beheaded second wife of Henry VIII of England, mother of Elizabeth I.

**Bolívar, Simón,** 1783–1830, South American revolutionary who liberated much of the continent from Spanish rule.

**Bonaparte, Joseph,** 1768–1844, eldest brother of Napoleon I, ineffective king of Naples and Spain.

**Bonaparte, Napoleon** see **Napoleon Bonaparte.**

**Booth, John Wilkes,** 1838–65, egomaniacal American actor, assassin of Abraham Lincoln.

**Booth, William,** 1829–1912, English religious leader, founder and first general of Salvation Army.

**Borgia, Caesar,** c. 1475–1507, Italian Renaissance ecclesiastic and statesman; brother of Lucretia Borgia.

**Borgia, Lucretia,** 1480–1519, famous figure of Italian Renaissance, daughter of Pope Alexander VI.

**Bormann, Martin L.,** 1900–1945, German Nazi leader.

**Bosch, Juan,** 1909– , progressive Dominican leader.

**Botha, Louis,** 1862–1919, Boer soldier and first prime minister (1910–19) of Union of South Africa.

**Botha, Pieter W.,** 1916– , South African prime minister (1978– ).

**Bougainville, Louis Antoine de,** 1729–1811, French navigator, leader of scientific expeditions in South Pacific.

**Boumédiene, Houari,** 1927–78, Algerian revolutionary, deposed (1965) Ben Bella.

**Bourguiba, Habib,** 1903– , Tunisian independence leader and first premier (subsequently president).

**Braddock, Edward,** 1695–1755, British general in French and Indian Wars.

**Bradley, Omar N.,** 1893–1981, U.S. Army WW II general, later chairman of joint chiefs of staff.

**Braille, Louis C.,** 1809–52, French inventor of Braille system of printing and writing for the blind.

**Brandt, Willy,** 1913– , West German chancellor (1969-74), leader of Social Democratic party.

**Brauchitsch, Walther von,** 1881–1948, German WW II general.

**Brezhnev, Leonid I.,** 1906– , Soviet Communist party leader, successor to Khrushchev; Chairman of the Presidium of the Supreme Soviet (1977– ).

**Brian Boru,** c. 940–1014, Irish king who broke Norse power in Ireland.

**Briand, Aristide,** 1862–1932, French statesman, chief architect of antiwar Kellogg-Briand Pact (1928).

**Brown, John,** 1800–59, hanged American abolitionist whose raid at Harpers Ferry stunned North and South.

**Bryan, William Jennings,** 1860–1925, American political leader, greatest orator of his day.

**Brzezinski, Zbigniew,** 1928– , foreign affairs adviser to President Carter (1977–81).

**Bulganin, Nikolai A.,** 1895-1975, Soviet Communist leader and premier (1955–58).

**Bullitt, William C.**, 1891–1967, American diplomat, first American ambassador to USSR (1933–36).

**Bunche, Ralph J.**, 1904–1971, American Negro government official and UN mediator.

**Bundy, McGeorge**, 1919– , American professor, Presidential adviser, and Ford Foundation head.

**Bunker, Ellsworth**, 1894– , American business executive and diplomat.

**Burghley, William Cecil (Baron)**, 1520–98, English statesman, influential adviser to Elizabeth I for 40 years.

**Burgoyne, John**, 1722–92, British statesman and general in American Revolution.

**Burke, Edmund**, 1729–97, English political writer and statesman, proponent of conservatism.

**Burnside, Ambrose E.**, 1824–81, American Union general.

**Burton, Sir Richard F.**, 1821–90, English writer, orientalist, and discoverer (1858) of Lake Tanganyika.

**Byrd, Richard E.**, 1888–1957, American admiral and polar explorer, first to fly over the North Pole (1926).

**Caesar, Julius**, c. 102–44 B.C., Roman statesman and general who enlarged and pacified Rome's provinces.

**Cagliostro, Alessandro (Giuseppe Balsamo)**, 1743–95, Italian adventurer.

**Callaghan, James**, 1912– , Labour prime minister of Great Britain (1976–79).

**Calles, Plutarco E.**, 1877–1945, Mexican Revolutionary statesman and president (1924–28).

**Calvo Sotelo (y Bustelo), Leopoldo**, 1926– , Spanish premier (1981– ).

**Campesino, El (Valentín Gonzáles)**, c. 1909– , Spanish Republican soldier in the civil war (1936–39).

**Canaris, Wilhelm**, 1887–1945, German WW II admiral and intelligence chief who opposed Hitler.

**Cárdenas, Lázaro**, 1895–1970, Mexican president (1934–40) and revolutionary general.

**Cardigan, Earl of (James T. Brudenell)**, 1797–1868, British Crimean War general who led disastrous cavalry attack at Balaklava, immortalized in Tennyson's "The Charge of the Light Brigade."

**Carnegie, Andrew**, 1835–1919, Scottish-American iron and steel tycoon and philanthropist.

**Carnot, Lazare**, 1753–1823, French revolutionary general.

**Carpini, Giovanni de Piano**, c. 1180–1252, Italian monk who produced a full record of Mongol life from missionary experiences in Central Asia.

**Carranza, Venustiano**, 1859–1920, Mexican revolutionary leader who arranged Zapata's assassination.

**Casanova de Seingalt, Giovanni G.**, 1725–98, Venetian adventurer and author.

**Castelo Branco, Humberto**, 1900–67, Brazilian revolutionary president.

**Castiglione, Baldassare (Conte)**, 1478–1529, Italian Renaissance statesman and author.

**Castlereagh, Robert S. (Viscount)**, 1769–1822, Irish-born British foreign secretary, and organizer of successful coalition against Napoleon I.

**Castro, Fidel**, 1927– , Cuban Communist premier who wrested power from Fulgencio Batista in 1959.

**Catherine de' Medici**, 1519–89, queen of France who helped to plan (1572) French Protestant massacre on Saint Bartholomew's Day.

**Catherine II**, 1729–96, forceful German-born empress and tsarina of Russia, also known as Catherine the Great.

**Cato the Elder (Cato the Censor)**, 234–149 B.C., Roman statesman and moralist.

**Cavell, Edith**, 1865–1915, English nurse executed by Germans during WW I.

**Cavour, Camillo Benso (conte di)**, 1810–61, Italian statesman, leader in unifying Italy under house of Savoy.

**Ceausescu, Nicolae**, 1918– , Romanian head of state.

**Chamberlain, (A.) Neville**, 1869–1940, British prime minister who signed (1938) Munich Pact with Hitler.

**Chang Tso-lin**, 1873–1928, Chinese general, warlord of Manchuria.

**Charcot, Jean B.**, 1867–1936, French neurologist and explorer in the Antarctic.

**Charlemagne**, 742–814, king of the Franks, (768–814) and Emperor of the West (800–814).

**Chase, Salmon P.**, 1808–73, American abolitionist, statesman, and Secretary of the Treasury under Lincoln.

**Cheops (or Khufu)**, fl. c. 2680 B.C., king of Egypt, builder of great pyramid at Gizeh.

**Chiang Kai-shek**, 1887-1975, Chinese Nationalist leader whose government was driven (1950) from mainland China to island of Taiwan.

**Chiang Kai-shek, Madame (Soong Mai-ling)**, 1898?– , politically active wife of the Chinese Nationalist leader.

**Ch'ien Lung (Hung-li)**, 1711–99, fourth emperor of Ching dynasty who greatly extended borders of China.

**Chou En-lai** see **Zhou Enlai.**

**Christophe, Henri**, 1767–1820, Haitian revolutionary and self-proclaimed king (Henri I).

**Churchill, Sir Winston L. S.**, 1874–1965, British prime minister, soldier, author, and war leader.

**Ciano, Galeazzo**, 1903–44, Italian Fascist foreign minister who helped create Rome-Berlin Axis, executed by Mussolini—his father-in-law.

**Cid, El**, d. c. 1099, Spanish national hero, whose real name was Rodrigo (or Ruy) Díaz de Vivar.

**Clarendon, Earl of (Edward Hyde)**, 1609–74, English statesman, historian, and adviser to Charles II.

**Clark, Charles Joseph** 1939– , Conservative prime minister of Canada (1979–80).

**Clay, Henry**, 1777–1852, American statesman, author of Compromise of 1850.

**Clemenceau, Georges**, 1841–1929, French statesman (the "Tiger"), twice premier (1906–09, 1917–20).

**Cleopatra**, 69–30 B.C., Ptolemaic queen of Egypt, one of the great romantic figures of all time.

**Clinton, De Witt**, 1769–1828, American statesman, Presidential nominee (1812), sponsor of Erie Canal.

**Cobden, Richard**, 1804–65, British statesman, advocate (after 1849) of peace and international conferences.

**Coen, Jan P.**, 1587–1629, Dutch colonial governor, founder of Dutch East Indian empire.

**Coke, Sir Edward**, 1552–1634, one of the most eminent English jurists in history.

**Colbert, Jean B.**, 1619–83, French statesman under Louis XIV, successful practitioner of mercantilism.

**Columbus, Christopher**, 1451–1506, Italian-born discoverer of America for Spain (1492).

**Constantine I (the Great)**, ?–337, first Christian Roman emperor (306–337).

**Constantine V (Constantine Copronymus)**, 718–775, iconoclastic Byzantine emperor (741–775).

**Constantine VI**, b. c. 770, Byzantine emperor (780–797), blinded by Irene, his mother and successor.

**Constantine XI (Constantine Palaeologus)**, d. 1453, last Byzantine emperor (1449–53).

**Cook, James (Captain)**, 1728–79, English explorer along coasts of Australia and New Zealand.

**Cooper, Peter**, 1791–1883, American inventor, industrialist, and philanthropist.

**Corday, Charlotte**, 1768–93, aristocratic French Revolution sympathizer who assassinated Jean Paul Marat.

**Cornwallis, Charles (Marquess)**, 1738–1805, English general in American Revolution.

**Cortés, Hernán**, 1485–1547, Spanish conquistador in Mexico who toppled Aztec empire of Montezuma.

**Cossiga, Francesco**, 1928– , Italian premier (1979–80).

**Coty, René**, 1882–1962, last president of French Fourth Republic.

**Cox, James M.**, 1870–1957, American political leader, U.S. Presidential candidate (1920), and journalist.

**Cranmer, Thomas**, 1489–1556, English churchman, adviser to Henry VIII.

**Croesus**, d. c. 547 B.C., king of Lydia; his name has become synonym for wealth.

**Cromwell, Oliver**, 1599–1658, English general and statesman, lord protector of England (1653–58).

**Cuauhtémoc**, d. c. 1525, Aztec emperor executed by Cortés.

**Cunard, Sir Samuel**, 1787–1865, Canadian pioneer of regular transatlantic steam navigation (Cunard Line).

**Curtis, Cyrus H. K.**, 1850–1933, American publisher and philanthropist.

**Curzon, George N. (Marquess)**, 1859–1925, British statesman and viceroy of India.

**Cyrano de Bergerac, Savinien**, 1619–55, French poet and duelist romanticized by Edmond Rostand's drama.

**Cyrus (the Great)**, ?–529 B.C., founder of the ancient Persian Empire.

**Dalai Lama**, 1935– , theocratic ruler of Tibet, ousted (1959) by Chinese invasion of his country.

**Danton, Georges J.**, 1759–94, French statesman and a leading figure of French Revolution.

**Darius I (the Great)**, d. 486 B.C., king of Persia (521–486 B.C.) who consolidated Persian power in the East.

**Darlan, Jean F.**, 1881–1942, assassinated French admiral, vice-premier of Vichy government.

**Darnley, Lord (Henry S.)**, 1545–67, claimant to English throne, second husband of Mary Queen of Scots.

**Davis, Angela**, 1944– , university lecturer and black political activist.

**Davis, Jefferson**, 1808–89, American statesman, president of Southern Confederacy.

**Davitt, Michael**, 1846–1906, Irish revolutionary and land reformer.

**Dayan, Moshe**, 1915–81, Israeli statesman, soldier, and hero of 1967 June War.

**Debs, Eugene V.**, 1855–1926, American Socialist leader, Presidential candidate (1900, 1904, 1908, 1912, 1920).

**De Gasperi, Alcide**, 1881–1954, Italian premier (1945–53), organizer of Christian Democratic party.

**de Gaulle, Charles**, 1890–1970, French general and controversial nationalist president (1959-69).

**Deng Xiaoping**, 1904– , Chinese Communist Politburo member (1977– ). Central Advisory Commission chairman.

**Desai, Morarji**, 1895– , Indian prime minister (1977–79).

**De Soto, Hernando**, c. 1500–42, Spanish conquistador and explorer in what is now United States.

**Dessalines, Jean J.**, c. 1758–1806, emperor of Haiti, born a slave.

**De Valera, Eamon**, 1882-1975, long-time Irish prime minister and president.

**Dewey, George**, 1837–1917, American admiral, hero of battle of Manila.

**Dewey, Thomas E.**, 1902–71, governor of New York (1942–54), Republican Presidential candidate (1944, 1948).

**Dias, Bartolomeu**, d. 1500, Portuguese navigator, first European to round (1488) the Cape of Good Hope.

**Díaz, Porfirio**, 1830–1915, Mexican president (1876–1911), whose ruthless rule fostered revolution.

**Díaz Ordaz, Gustavo**, 1911-79, progressive Mexican president (1964-70) and lawyer.

**Diefenbaker, John G.**, 1895–1979, Conservative prime minister of Canada (1957–63).

**Diem, Ngo Dinh**, 1901–63, assassinated South Vietnamese president.

**Dimitrov, Georgi**, 1882–1949, Bulgarian Communist premier (1946–49), acquitted of Reichstag fire.

**Dirksen, Everett M.**, 1896–1969, U.S. Senator (Ill., first elected 1950) and Republican minority leader.

**Disraeli, Benjamin (Earl of Beaconsfield)**, 1804–81, British prime minister (1868, 1874–80), founder of the Conservative party.

**Dix, Dorothea L.**, 1802–87, American social reformer, champion of specialized treatment for the mentally ill.

**Djilas, Milovan**, 1911– , Yugoslavian political leader and intellectual, frequently imprisoned by Tito.

**Dobrynin, Anatoly F.**, 1919– , Soviet ambassador to U.S.

**Dollfuss, Engelbert**, 1892–1934, Austrian chancellor assassinated by Austrian Nazis.

**Douglas, Stephen A.**, 1813–61, American statesman who opposed (1860) Lincoln for Presidency.

**Douglass, Frederick**, c. 1817–95, American Negro abolitionist leader.

**Drake, Sir Francis**, c. 1540–96, first Englishman to circumnavigate the earth (1577–80).

**Dreyfus, Alfred**, 1859–1935, French soldier whose treason trial (and ultimate exoneration) was a *cause célèbre.*

**Du Barry, Madame (Jeanne B.)**, 1743–93, mistress of Louis XV of France, guillotined during French Revolution.

**Dubcek, Alexander**, 1921– , liberal Czechoslovak Communist party secretary during 1968 Soviet invasion.

**Du Bois, William E. B.**, 1868–1963, American Negro editor, author, exponent of equality for the Negro.

**Duclos, Jacques**, 1896–1975, French Communist leader.

**Dulles, Allen W.**, 1893–1969, U.S. public official, director of CIA (1953–61).

**Dulles, John Foster**, 1888–1959, U.S. Secretary of State (1953–59), strong anti-Communist.

**Duvalier, François**, 1907–71, Haitian dictator.

**Dzerzhinsky, Felix E.**, 1877–1926, Russian Bolshevik politician, organizer of Soviet secret police.

**Earhart, Amelia**, 1898–1937, pioneering American aviatrix who disappeared on a round-the-world flight.

**Eban, Abba**, 1915– , Israeli diplomat and statesman.

**Ebert, Friedrich**, 1871–1925, first president (1919–25) of the German republic.

**Echeverria Alvarez, Luis**, 1922– , President of Mexico (1970–76).

**Eden, Sir Anthony (Earl of Avon)**, 1897–1977, British statesman, Conservative prime minister (1955–57).

**Edinburgh, Duke of (Philip Mountbatten)**, 1921– , consort of Elizabeth II of Great Britain.

**Eichmann, Adolf**, 1906–62, German Nazi official executed by Israel for crimes against the Jewish people and humanity.

**Elizabeth I**, 1533–1603, queen of England during the great age of British expansion and exploration.

**Ellsworth, Lincoln**, 1880–1951, American explorer, the first man to fly over Antarctic (1935).

**Emin Pasha (Eduard Schnitzer)**, 1840–92, German physician, colonial administrator, and explorer of Sudan.

**Emmet, Robert**, 1778–1803, executed Irish patriot.

**Engels, Friedrich**, 1820–95, German Socialist, co-founder with Karl Marx of modern Communism.

**Enver Pasha**, 1881–1922, Turkish general and political leader.

**Erlander, Tage F.**, 1901– , Swedish Social Democratic premier (1946–69).

**Ervin, Samuel J., Jr.**, 1896– , U.S. Senator from North Carolina (1954-1974).

**Eshkol, Levi**, 1895–1969, Israeli prime minister (1963-69)

**Essex, Earl of (Robert Devereux)**, 1567–1601, favorite of Elizabeth I of England who signed his death warrant.

**Fanfani, Amintore**, 1908– , Italian statesman and premier (1958-59, 1960-63).

**Farouk I**, 1920–65, king of Egypt (1936–52), forced to abdicate (1952) by military coup.

**Fawkes, Guy**, 1570–1606, English Roman Catholic conspirator involved in scheme to blow up Parliament.

**Fish, Hamilton**, 1808–93, American statesman, one of the ablest of U.S. Secretaries of State.

**Foch, Ferdinand**, 1851–1929, French marshal, commander (1918) of British, French, and American armies.

**Ford, Henry**, 1863–1947, American industrialist, pioneer automobile manufacturer.

**Forrestal, James V.**, 1892–1949, U.S. Secretary of the Navy (1944–47), first Secretary of Defense (1947–49).

**Fox, Charles J.**, 1749–1806, British statesman, orator, and liberal reformer.

**Francis (Franz) Ferdinand**, 1863–1914, Austrian archduke whose assassination precipitated WW I.

**Franco, Francisco**, 1892–1975, leader of rebel forces in Spanish Civil War (1936–39) and dictator of Spain (1937–75).

**Frank, Anne**, 1929–45, Dutch Jewish girl killed by the Nazis; her diary made her posthumously famous.

**Franklin, Benjamin**, 1706–90, outstanding American statesman, also printer, scientist, and writer.

**Fraser, John Malcolm**, 1930– , Australian prime minister (1975– ).

**Frederick II (the Great)**, 1712–86, king of Prussia (1740–86) and military genius.

**Frederick William**, 1620–88, "Great Elector" of Brandenburg, who laid the base of the state of Prussia.

**Frémont, John C.**, 1813–90, American explorer, soldier, and politician, a controversial figure of history.

**Frobenius, Leo**, 1873-1938, German archaeologist and authority on prehistoric African art and culture.

**Fugger, Jacob (Jacob the Rich)**, 1459–1525, German merchant prince.

**Fukuda, Takeo**, 1905– , Japanese premier (1976–78).

**Fulbright, J. William**, 1905- , U.S. Senator (Ark., 1945-75) chairman of Senate Foreign Relations Committee (1959–75).

**Gage, Thomas**, 1721–87, English general in America whose orders led to battles of Lexington and Concord.

**Gallatin, Albert**, 1761–1849, American statesman and financier.

**Gama, Vasco da**, c. 1469–1524, Portuguese navigator, first European to journey to India by sea (1497–99).

**Gambetta, Léon**, 1838–82, French republican statesman.

**Gamelin, Maurice G.**, 1872–1958, French general, leader of Allied forces at WW II's outbreak.

**Gandhi, Indira**, 1917– , Indian prime minister (1966–77, 1980– ), daughter of Nehru, and first woman ever elected to head the government of a major power.

**Gandhi, Mohandas K.**, 1869–1948, Indian ascetic who advocated nonviolent resistance to secure independence of India from Great Britain.

**Garibaldi, Giuseppe**, 1807–82, Italian patriot and soldier who fought for Italy's unification.

**Garrison, William Lloyd**, 1805–79, American abolitionist and social reformer.

**Garvey, Marcus**, 1887–1940, American Negro nationalist leader.

**Genghis Khan** see **Jenghiz Khan.**

**Giap, Vo Nguyen**, 1912– , North Vietnamese statesman and victor at Dienbienphu in 1954.

**Giscard d'Estaing, Valéry**, 1926– , French president (1974–81).

**Gladstone, William Ewart**, 1809–98, British Liberal prime minister (1868–74, 1880–85, 1886, 1892–94).

**Gneisenau, August (Graf Neithardt von)**, 1760–1831, Prussian field marshal in Napoleonic Wars.

**Godfrey of Bouillon**, c. 1058–1100, crusader, ruler of Jerusalem.

**Godunov, Boris**, c. 1551–1605, Russian tsar, advisor to Ivan the Terrible.

**Goebbels, Paul J.**, 1897–1945, German Nazi propagandist, master of mass psychology.

**Goering, Hermann W.**, 1893–1946, German Nazi leader, early supporter of Hitler, and head of Luftwaffe.

**Goldwater, Barry M.**, 1909– , U.S. Senator (Ariz.), unsuccessful Republican Presidential candidate (1964).

**Gompers, Samuel,** 1850–1924, American labor leader, founder and president of AFL.

**Gomulka, Wladyslaw,** 1905–82, Polish Communist Party leader.

**Gordon, Charles G. (Chinese Gordon),** 1833–85, British soldier and administrator killed by Moslems at Khartoum.

**Gottwald, Klement,** 1896–1953, Czechoslovak Communist leader, who ushered Communism into his country.

**Gowon, Yakubu,** 1934– , Nigerian head of state who opposed the unsuccessful secession of the late 1960s.

**Grasso, Ella T.,** 1919–81, first woman to be elected governor in her own right (Conn. 1974–80).

**Greeley, Horace,** 1811–72, American newspaper publisher and Presidential candidate (1872).

**Grenville, Sir Richard,** c. 1542–91, English naval hero against Spanish.

**Grey, Lady Jane,** 1537–54, queen of England for nine days, succeeded by Mary I.

**Gromyko, Andrei A.,** 1909– , Soviet foreign minister and ambassador.

**Grotius, Hugo,** 1583–1645, Dutch jurist and humanist, considered the founder of international law.

**Guevara, Che (Ernesto),** 1928–67, Argentine-born Cuban guerrilla leader killed in Bolivia.

**Gwyn, Nell (Eleanor),** 1650–87, English actress, mistress of Charles II.

**Haig, Alexander Meigs, Jr.,** 1924– , U.S. Army General; Chief of Staff of the White House (1973–74); Secretary of State (1981–82).

**Haile Selassie,** 1892–1975, emperor of Ethiopia (1930–74).

**Hale, Nathan,** 1755–76, American Revolutionary patriot, hanged by the British without trial as a spy.

**Halsey, William F.,** 1882–1959, American WW II admiral in Pacific.

**Hamilton, Alexander,** 1755–1804, American Federalist statesman, first Secretary of the Treasury.

**Hammurabi,** fl. 1792–1750 B.C., king of Babylonia; his code of laws is one of the greatest of ancient codes.

**Hannibal,** 247–c. 182 B.C., Carthaginian general, great military opponent of Rome (Second Punic War).

**Harriman, W. Averell,** 1891– , American diplomat, U.S. representative (1968) at Vietnam peace talks.

**Harun-al-Rashid,** c. 764–809, famous caliph of Baghdad under whom the Abbasid empire reached its apogee.

**Hastings, Warren,** 1732–1818, controversial first governor-general of British India.

**Hawkins, Sir John,** 1532–95, Elizabethan sea dog, knighted for his actions in defeat of Spanish Armada.

**Hay, John,** 1838–1905, American author and statesman, who formulated the Open Door policy toward China.

**Haya de la Torre, Victor Raúl,** 1895–1979, Peruvian leader, advocate of Latin-American nationalist revolutions.

**Hearst, William Randolph,** 1863–1951, American journalist and publisher, innovator in mass-appeal newspapers.

**Heath, Edward R. G.,** 1916– , British Conservative prime minister (1970–74).

**Henry, Patrick,** 1736–99, American orator and patriot, who worked to have Bill of Rights added to the Constitution.

**Henry the Navigator,** 1394–1460, Portuguese geographer and prince, who was the patron of the great age of Portuguese exploration.

**Herodotus,** c. 484–c. 425 B.C., Greek historian and traveler considered the father of history.

**Herzl, Theodor,** 1860–1904, Hungarian writer, founder of modern Zionism.

**Hess, Rudolf,** 1894– , erratic German Nazi leader, imprisoned (1946) for life as a war criminal.

**Heydrich, Reinhard,** 1904–42, German Nazi police official ("the Hangman") whose assassination by Czech patriots led to Lidice massacre.

**Heyerdahl, Thor,** 1914– , Norwegian explorer-ethnologist, substantiated the diffusionist theory of anthropology with his trans-pacific raft journeys.

**Hidalgo y Costilla, Miguel,** 1753–1811, executed Mexican national hero and priest.

**Hillary, Sir Edmund P.,** 1919– , New Zealand mountain climber; first to reach summit of Mt. Everest (1953).

**Hillel,** fl. 30 B.C.–10 A.D., Jewish scholar; many of Christ's teachings resemble Hillel's sayings.

**Hillman, Sidney,** 1887–1946, Lithuanian-born American labor leader.

**Himmler, Heinrich,** 1900–45, terroristic Nazi chief of SS and Gestapo.

**Hindenburg, Paul von,** 1847–1934, German president (1925–34) who appointed Hitler as chancellor.

**Hitler, Adolf,** 1889–1945, founder of German Nazism and infamous tyrant who precipitated WW II.

**Ho Chi Minh,** c. 1890–1969, Vietnamese Communist leader and national hero; first president of North Vietnam.

**Hoover, J. Edgar,** 1895–1972, American administrator, director of FBI (1924–72).

**Horthy de Nagybanya, Nicholas,** 1868–1957, Hungarian admiral and political leader.

**Houphouët-Boigny, Félix,** 1905– , president of Ivory Coast, leader of former French Africa.

**Houston, Samuel,** 1793–1863, American frontier hero and Texan statesman.

**Howe, Julia Ward,** 1819–1910, American social reformer and writer of "The Battle Hymn of the Republic."

**Howe, Richard (Earl),** 1726–99, admiral and commander (1776–78) of British fleet in American Revolution.

**Howe, William (Viscount),** 1729–1814, English general in American Revolution.

**Hoxha, Enver** 1908– , Albanian Communist leader.

**Hua Guofeng (Kuo-feng),** 1921– , Chinese Communist premier (1976–80) and Politburo chairman (1976–81).

**Hull, Cordell,** 1871–1955, U.S. Secretary of State (1933–44), recipient (1945) Nobel Peace Prize.

**Hunyadi, John,** c. 1385–1456, Hungarian national hero, resistance leader against Turks.

**Hu Yaobang,** 1915– , Chinese Communist Politburo General Secretary (1981– ).

**Ibn Saud,** c. 1880-1953, founder (1932) and first king of Saudi Arabia.

**Ikhnaton,** d. c. 1354 B.C., pharaoh of Egypt who established perhaps the world's first monotheistic religion.

**Iqbal, Mohammad,** 1873–1938, Moslem leader, national hero of Pakistan.

**Irene,** 752–803, repressive Byzantine empress who had her son blinded.

**Isabella I,** 1451–1504, queen of Spain who supported the 1492 New World voyage of Columbus.

**Jabotinsky, Vladimir,** 1880-1940, Russian-born Zionist leader.

**Jackson, Stonewall (Thomas J.),** 1824–63, American Confederate general.

**Jaurès, Jean,** 1859–1914, assassinated French Socialist leader and historian.

**Jenghiz (also Genghis) Khan,** c. 1167–1227, brilliant Mongol conqueror, ruler of a vast Asian empire.

**Jinnah, Mohammad Ali,** 1876–1948, founder and first governor-general of Pakistan (1947–48).

**Joan of Arc,** c. 1412–31, French saint and national heroine, burned at the stake for heresy.

**Joffre, Joseph J. C.,** 1852–1931, French WW I marshal.

**John III (John Sobieski),** 1620-96, king of Poland, champion of Christian Europe against Turks.

**Jones, John Paul,** 1747–92, Scottish-born American naval hero of American Revolution.

**Jordan, Vernon E., Jr.,** 1935– , civil rights leader and executive director of the National Urban League.

**Josephine,** 1763–1814, empress of the French (1804–09), first wife of Napoleon I.

**Juárez, Benito,** 1806–72, Mexican Indian president, revered by Mexicans as great political figure.

**Juin, Alphonse,** 1888–1967, French soldier and marshal.

**Justinian I,** 483–565, Byzantine emperor (527–65) whose accomplishment was codification of Roman law.

**Kadar, Janos,** 1912– , Hungarian Communist premier who sided with Soviets in 1956 Hungarian revolt.

**Kamenev, Lev B.,** 1883–1936, Soviet Communist leader executed during 1936 Moscow purges.

**Karamanlis, Constantine,** 1907– , twice Greek premier, president of Greece (1980– ).

**Kasavubu, Joseph,** c. 1910–69, first president of the Congo.

**Kaunda, Kenneth,** 1924– , Zambian president, proponent of Gandhian principles.

**Kefauver, (C.) Estes,** 1903–63, U.S. Senator (Tenn., 1949–63), supporter of civil rights legislation.

**Kekkonen, Urho K.,** 1900– , Finnish president (1956–81).

**Kennedy, Edward M.,** 1932– , U. S. Senator (Mass., (1962– ), brother of John and Robert Kennedy.

**Kennedy, Robert F.,** 1925–68, assassinated U.S. Senator (N.Y., 1965–68), brother of slain President John F. Kennedy under whom he was U.S. Attorney General.

**Kenyatta, Jomo,** c. 1893–1978, first Kenyan president, an early African nationalist leader.

**Kerensky, Aleksandr F.,** 1881–1970, exiled Russian revolutionary premier (1917), overthrown by Bolsheviks.

**Keynes, John Maynard,** 1883–1946, influential English economist and monetary authority.

**Khomeini, Ayatollah Ruhollah,** 1900– , Moslem religious leader who led Iranian Revolution of 1979.

**Khrushchev, Nikita S.,** 1894–1971, Soviet Communist leader, deposed (1964) as premier.

**Kidd, Captain (William),** c. 1645–1701, British privateer hanged for murder and piracy.

**Kiesinger, Kurt G.**, 1904– , West German chancellor (1966–69), advocate of reconciliation with Eastern Europe.
**Kim Il Sung**, 1912– , first premier of Communist North Korea.
**King, Martin Luther, Jr.**, 1929–68, assassinated American Negro rights leader and Nobel Prize winner.
**King, (W. L.) Mackenzie**, 1874–1950, liberal Canadian prime minister (1921–30, 1935–48).
**Kissinger, Henry A.**, 1923– , chief foreign affairs adviser to President Nixon, and leading authority on international relations and national defense policy. U.S. Secretary of State (1973-77).
**Kitchener, Horatio H. (Earl)**, 1850–1916, British field marshal during the imperial era.
**Kittikachorn, Thanom**, 1911– , Thai premier and minister of defense (1963–73).
**Knox, Henry**, 1750–1806, American patriot and Revolutionary general, U.S. Secretary of War (1785–94).
**Konev, Ivan S., 1897-1973, Soviet WW II field marshal,** commander (1955–60) of Warsaw Pact military forces.
**Konoye, Prince Fumimaro**, 1891–1945, Japanese premier who allied Japan with Axis.
**Koo, (V. K.) Wellington**, 1887– , Chinese statesman elected (1957) to International Court of Justice at The Hague.
**Kornilov, Lavr G.**, 1870–1918, Russian anti-Bolshevik general.
**Kosciusko, Thaddeus**, 1746–1817, Polish general who fought for patriot cause in American Revolution.
**Kossuth, Louis**, 1802–94, exiled Hungarian revolutionary leader.
**Kosygin, Aleksey N.**, 1904–80, Soviet Communist premier, successor to Khrushchev.
**Kropotkin, Prince (Peter)**, 1842–1921, Russian anarchist who championed peasantry but opposed Bolshevism.
**Kruger, S. J. Paulus (Paul Kruger)**, 1825–1904, South African pioneer, soldier, farmer, and statesman.
**Krupp, Alfred**, 1812–87, German armaments magnate known as the "Cannon King."
**Krupp, Alfred (von Bohlen und Halbach)**, 1907–67, German industrialist and imprisoned war criminal.
**Kublai Khan**, c. 1215–94, Mongol emperor, founder of Yüan dynasty in China.
**Kun, Bela**, 1886–c. 1939, Hungarian Communist dictator.
**Kutuzov, Mikhail I.**, 1745–1813, Russian field marshal, victor over Napoleon I.
**Ky, Nguyen Cao**, 1930– , South Vietnamese general and political leader.
**Lafayette, Marquis de**, 1757–1834, French statesman and general who served in American Revolution.
**La Follette, Robert M.**, 1855–1925, U.S. Senator (Wis., 1906–25), Progressive Party Presidential candidate (1924).
**LaFontaine, Sir Louis H.**, 1807–64, distinguished French-Canadian statesman.
**LaGuardia, Fiorello H.**, 1882–1947, U.S. Congressman (1916, 1923–33) and reform mayor of New York City (1934–45), affectionately known as the "Little Flower."
**Laing, Alexander G.**, 1793–1826, Scottish soldier and explorer who was murdered by Arabs near Timbuktu.
**Langton, Stephen**, c. 1155–1228, English archbishop who acted with barons to obtain Magna Carta's signing.
**Largo Caballero, Francisco**, 1869–1946, Spanish Socialist leader and premier (1936–37).
**Laski, Harold J.**, 1893–1950, English political scientist, economist, author, and lecturer.
**Lassalle, Ferdinand**, 1825–64, a founder of German Socialist movement, killed in a duel over a love affair.
**Lattre de Tassigny, Jean de**, 1889–1952, French general who fought in Indo-China.
**Laval, Pierre**, 1883–1945, executed French politician and foreign minister of Vichy government.
**Lawrence, Thomas E. (Lawrence of Arabia)**, 1888–1935, British scholar and Middle East soldier-adventurer.
**Leahy, William D.**, 1875–1959, American diplomat and WW II admiral.
**Leclerc, Jacques P. (comte de Hauteclocque)**, 1902–47, French WW II general who later served in Indo-China.
**Lee, Henry**, 1756–1818, American cavalry leader in the Revolution; known as Light-Horse Harry Lee.
**Lee, Robert E.**, 1807–70, brilliant American Confederate commander in chief.
**Lee Kuan Yew**, 1923– , Singaporean Socialist prime minister.
**Lehman, Herbert H.**, 1878–1963, liberal U.S. Senator (N.Y.), opponent of Senator Joseph R. McCarthy.
**Lemnitzer, Lyman L.**, 1899– , American general, NATO commander (1963-1969).
**Lenin, Vladimir I.**, 1870–1924, Russian revolutionary statesman, founder of Bolshevism and U.S.S.R.
**Leo Africanus**, c. 1465–1550, Moorish traveler in Africa and the Near East.
**Lesseps, Ferdinand (Vicomte de)**, 1805–94, French diplomat and engineer who conceived idea of Suez Canal.
**Lewis, John L.**, 1880–1969, important American labor spokesman, head of UMW and CIO.
**Liaquat Ali Khan**, 1895–1951, assassinated Moslem leader and first prime minister (1947–51) of Pakistan.
**Liebknecht, Karl**, 1871–1919, murdered German Communist leader.
**Lindbergh, Charles A.**, 1902–74, American aviator, who made first solo transatlantic flight.
**Lin Piao**, 1907–1971, Chinese Communist leader and political heir to Mao.
**Litvinov, Maxim M.**, 1876–1951, Soviet statesman, proponent of Soviet cooperation with Western powers.
**Liu Shao-ch'i, c. 1898-1974, Chinese Communist leader** who fell from grace in "cultural revolution" (1966-67).
**Livingston, Edward**, 1764–1836, American jurist and statesman, U.S. Secretary of State under Andrew Jackson.
**Livingston, Robert R.**, 1746–1813, American Revolutionary political leader who negotiated Louisiana Purchase.
**Livingstone, David**, 1813–73, Scottish medical missionary, abolitionist, and African explorer.
**Lodge, Henry Cabot**, 1850–1924, conservative U.S. Senator (Mass., 1893–1924).
**Lodge, Henry Cabot, Jr.**, 1902– , U.S. Senator, ambassador, and Vietnam peace negotiator.
**Long, Huey P.**, 1893–1935, assassinated American political demagogue in Louisiana.
**López Portillo, José**, 1920- , Mexican president (1976-82).
**Low, Sir David**, 1891–1963, British cartoonist, famous for caricatures.
**Lübke, Heinrich**, 1894-1972, West German administrator and president.
**Luce, Henry R.**, 1898–1967, American publisher, founder of Time, Inc.
**Luckner, Felix, Graf von, 1881-1966, German WW I naval** commander, nicknamed "the Sea Devil."
**Lumumba, Patrice E.**, 1925–61, murdered first prime minister (1960) of Republic of the Congo.
**Luthuli, Albert J., 1898-1967, South African Zulu leader** and Nobel Prize winner.
**Luxemburg, Rosa**, c. 1870–1919, Polish-born German Communist leader, murdered while being taken to prison.
**MacArthur, Douglas**, 1880–1964, distinguished American general in WW II, recalled (1951) from Korea for insubordination.
**Maccabee, Judas**, d. c. 161 B.C., Jewish military leader who opposed foreign rule in Judea.
**McCarthy, Eugene J.**, 1916– , U.S. Senator (Minn.) who became nationally prominent for his opposition to American participation in Vietnam war.
**McCarthy, Joseph R.**, 1908–57, U.S. Senator (Wis.) known for his charges of Communism in government.
**McClellan, George B.**, 1826–85, American Union general.
**McCormick, Robert R.**, 1880–1955, American publisher (Chicago *Tribune*), famous for his isolationist views.
**McGill, James**, 1744–1813, Scottish-born Canadian fur trader and university founder.
**Machado, Gerardo**, 1871–1939, repressive Cuban president (1925–33).
**Machiavelli, Niccolò**, 1469–1527, Florentine diplomat and political philosopher, an outstanding Renaissance figure.
**Macmillan, M. Harold**, 1894– , conservative British prime minister (1957–63).
**McNamara, Robert S.**, 1916– , U.S. Secretary of Defense under Presidents Kennedy and Johnson.
**Madero, Francisco I.**, 1873–1913, assassinated Mexican revolutionist and president (1911–13).
**Magellan, Ferdinand**, c. 1480–1521, Portuguese leader of first expedition to circumnavigate the earth (1519-22).
**Magsaysay, Ramón**, 1907–57, president of the Philippines (1953–57) who campaigned against the Huk rebels.
**Mahan, Alfred T.**, 1840–1914, American naval officer and historian.
**Mahdi**, title claimed by **Mohammed Ahmed**, 1844–85, Moslem religious leader in Anglo-Egyptian Sudan.
**Mahmud of Ghazni**, c. 971–1030, Afghan emperor and conqueror.
**Makarios III**, 1913–77, Cypriot Greek Orthodox archbishop, first president (elected 1960) of Cyprus.
**Malan, Daniel F.**, 1874–1959, Afrikaner prime minister of South Africa.
**Malcolm X (b. Malcolm Little)**, 1925–65, assassinated American Negro separatist leader.
**Malenkov, Georgi M.**, 1902– , Soviet Communist successor to Stalin (1953-55), expelled (1964) from party.
**Malinovsky, Rodion Y.**, 1898–1967, Soviet marshal and minister of defense.
**Malraux, André**, 1901–76, French man of letters and political figure, minister of culture under de Gaulle.
**Mannerheim, Baron Carl G. E.**, 1867–1951, Finnish field marshal, later president (1944–46).
**Mansur**, d. 775, Abbasid caliph (754–775), founder of Baghdad.
**Mao Zedong (Tse-tung)**, 1893–1976, founder of Communist China, leader of radical wing of international Communism.

**Marat, Jean Paul,** 1743–93, French revolutionary stabbed to death in his bath by Charlotte Corday.
**Marcos, Ferdinand E.,** 1917– , Filipino president.
**Maria Theresa,** 1717–80, popular Hapsburg empress, queen of Bohemia and Hungary.
**Marie Antoinette,** 1755–93, guillotined queen of France, wife of Louis XVI.
**Marion, Francis ("the Swamp Fox"),** c. 1732–95, American guerrilla leader in the Revolution.
**Marlborough, Duke of (John Churchill),** 1650–1722, English general and statesman.
**Marti, José,** 1853–95, Cuban poet and patriot, leader of Cuban struggle for independence.
**Marx, Karl H.,** 1818–83, German philosopher, proponent of modern Communism, author of *Das Kapital.*
**Masaryk, Jan,** 1886–1948, Czechoslovak statesman whose "suicide" mysteriously followed Communist coup.
**Masaryk, Thomas G.,** 1850–1937, Czechoslovak statesman, founder and president (1918–35) of Czechoslovakia.
**Massey, Vincent,** 1887–1967, Canadian diplomat and governor-general.
**Mata Hari (Margaretha G. Zelle),** 1876–1917, Dutch dancer executed by the French as a WW I German spy.
**Matteotti, Giacomo,** 1885–1924, murdered Italian Socialist leader, opponent of Mussolini.
**Matthias Corvinus,** c. 1443–90, king of Hungary (1458–90) and of Bohemia (1478–90), crusader against Turks.
**Mawson, Sir Douglas,** 1882–1958, English-born Australian geologist who charted Antarctic coast.
**Maximilian,** 1832–67, Austrian archduke and emperor of Mexico (1864–67), executed by the forces of Juarez.
**Mazarin, Jules,** 1602–61, French statesman and Roman Catholic cardinal.
**Mazzini, Giuseppe,** 1805–72, Italian patriot and revolutionary who figured in Italy's unification.
**Mboya, Tom (Thomas J.),** 1930–69, Kenyan political leader, instrumental in securing independence for his country.
**Medici, Cosimo de',** 1389–1464, Florentine merchant prince and first Medici ruler of Florence.
**Medici, Lorenzo de' (Lorenzo the Magnificent),** 1449–92, Florentine statesman, Renaissance patron of the arts.
**Meir, Golda,** 1898–1978, Israeli prime minister (1969–74).
**Mendès-France, Pierre,** 1907– , French premier (1954–55), who opposed Charles de Gaulle's return to power.
**Menelik II,** 1844–1913, emperor of Ethiopia after 1899, who expanded and modernized his country.
**Mengistu Haile Mariam,** 1937?– , Ethiopian head of state.
**Metaxas, John,** 1871–1941, Greek general and dictator.
**Metternich, Clemens W. N. L., Fürst von,** 1773–1859, Austrian foreign minister and arbiter of Europe.
**Mikhailovich, Draja (Dragoliub),** c. 1893–1946, executed Yugoslav soldier, foe of Tito.
**Miki, Takeo,** 1907- , Japanese prime minister (1974-76).
**Mikoyan, Anastas I.,** 1895–1978, Soviet Communist leader.
**Mindszenty, Cardinal (Jozsef),** 1892-1975, Hungarian Roman Catholic prelate who sought asylum in U.S. legation after Hungarian uprising (1956).
**Minuit, Peter,** c. 1580–1638, director general (1626–31) of New Netherland, who purchased Manhattan for $24.
**Mirabeau, Honoré G. R., comte de,** 1749–91, French revolutionary who favored a strong constitutional monarchy.
**Mitchell, Billy (William),** 1879–1936, American general, demoted for criticism of U.S. military leaders.
**Mitterrand, François,** 1916- , French president (1981- ).
**Mobutu Sese Seko,** 1930– , Zairean president who deposed (1960) Patrice Lumumba.
**Mohammad Reza Pahlavi,** 1919–80, shah of Iran (1941–1979).
**Mohammed V,** 1910–61, sultan of Morocco (1927–53), first king (1957–61) of independent Morocco.
**Moi, Daniel arap,** 1924– , Kenyan president (1978– ).
**Molotov, Vyacheslav M.,** 1890– , Soviet Communist leader whose political fortunes waned in post-Stalin era.
**Moltke, Helmuth J. L., Graf von,** 1800–91, Prussian field marshal, victor in Franco-Prussian War.
**Mongkut (Rama IV),** 1804–68, king of Siam, a main character in 1944 book, *Anna and the King of Siam.*
**Monnet, Jean,** 1888–1979, French political economist who conceived idea of the Common Market.
**Montcalm, Louis de (Marquis de Saint-Véran),** 1712–59, French general in French and Indian Wars, killed at Quebec.
**Montezuma,** c. 1480–1520, murdered Aztec emperor who defied Cortés.
**Montgomery, Bernard L. (1st Viscount Montgomery of Alamein),** 1887–1976, British WW II field marshal.
**More, Sir Thomas,** 1478–1535, English author (*Utopia*) and statesman, celebrated as a Roman Catholic martyr.
**Morelos y Pavón, José M.,** 1765–1815, executed Mexican leader in revolution against Spain.
**Morgan, Daniel,** 1736–1802, American Revolutionary general, victor in the Carolina campaign.
**Morgan, Sir Henry,** c. 1635–88, English buccaneer, later acting governor of Jamaica.
**Morgan, J. P. (John Pierpont),** 1837–1913, American banker who built his family's fortunes into a financial colossus.
**Morgenthau, Henry, Jr.,** 1891–1967, U.S. Secretary of the Treasury (1934–45).
**Morris, Gouverneur,** 1752–1816, American Revolutionary statesman who advocated centralized government.
**Morris, Robert,** 1734–1806, "financier of the American Revolution," signer of Declaration of Independence.
**Mossadegh, Mohammed,** 1880–1967, deposed and imprisoned Iranian premier (1951–53) who attempted to nationalize Iran's British-controlled oil industry.
**Mountbatten, Lord Louis,** 1900–79, British WW II admiral who commanded in both the Atlantic and Pacific.
**Mubarak, Hosni,** 1928– , Egyptian president (1981– ).
**Muñoz Marin, Luis,** 1898–1980, long-time governor of Puerto Rico, supporter of its commonwealth status.
**Mussolini, Benito ("Il Duce"),** 1883–1945, Italian dictator 1922–45), founder of Fascism, ally of Adolf Hitler.
**Mutsuhito (Meiji),** 1852–1912, Japanese emperor (1867–1912) during whose reign feudalism came to an end.
**Nadir Shah,** 1688–1747, shah of Iran, perhaps the last great Asiatic conqueror.
**Nagy, Imre,** c. 1895–1958, Hungarian Communist premier (1953–55), executed after the 1956 uprising.
**Nansen, Fridtjof,** 1861–1930, Norwegian arctic explorer, statesman, and Nobel Peace Prize winner (1922).
**Napoleon Bonaparte (Napoleon I),** 1769–1821, Corsican-born emperor of the French (1804–15).
**Napoleon III (Louis Napoleon Bonaparte),** 1808–73, emperor of the French (nephew of Napoleon I).
**Nasser, Gamal Abdel,** 1918–70, Egyptian leader of Arab unification, became (1956) first president of Egypt.
**Nebuchadnezzar,** d. 562 B.C., king of Babylonia and destroyer of Jerusalem (586 B.C.).
**Necker, Jacques,** 1732–1804, Swiss-born French financier and statesman, father of Madame de Staël.
**Negrin, Juan,** 1891–1956, Spanish Socialist premier (1937–39), who fled from his country after the civil war.
**Nehru, Jawaharlal,** 1889–1964, first prime minister of India, guided country during early years of independence.
**Nelson, Lord (Horatio),** 1758–1805, English admiral in Napoleonic Wars, killed during victory at Trafalgar.
**Nenni, Pietro,** 1891–1980, Italian Socialist leader.
**Ne Win,** 1911– , Burmese general and president, leader of 1962 coup against U Nu.
**Newman, Cardinal (John Henry),** 1801–90, English prelate, a founder (1833) of Oxford Movement.
**Ney, Michel,** 1769–1815, executed marshal of France, commander at Waterloo.
**Nightingale, Florence,** 1820–1910, English nurse in Crimean War, founder of modern nursing.
**Nimeiry, Jaafar Muhammad al,** 1930– , Sudanese president (1971– ).
**Nimitz, Chester W.,** 1885–1966, American admiral who headed Pacific naval forces throughout WW II.
**Nkrumah, Kwame,** 1909–1972, former dictatorial prime minister of Ghana, deposed in 1966.
**Nobel, Alfred B.,** 1833–96, Swedish inventor of dynamite who established annual philanthropic prizes.
**Nobile, Umberto,** 1885–1978, Italian aeronautical engineer, arctic explorer, and pilot.
**Norris, George W.,** 1861–1944, U.S. Senator (Neb.).
**Nostradamus (Michel de Nostredame),** 1503-66, French astrologer and physician.
**Novotny, Antonin,** 1904-1975, Czechoslovak leader eight months before 1968 Soviet invasion.
**Nu, U,** 1907– , Burmese Socialist premier (1948–62).
**Nyerere, Julius K.,** 1922– , African statesman in Tanganyika, elected (1962) first president of Tanzania.
**Oates, Titus,** 1649–1705, English fabricator of Popish Plot (1678).
**Obote, Milton,** 1925?– , Ugandan president.
**Obregón, Alvaro,** 1880–1928, assassinated Mexican revolutionary general and president (1920–24).
**Ochs, Adolph S.,** 1858–1935, American publisher of *The New York Times.*
**O'Connell, Daniel (the Liberator),** 1775–1847, Irish political leader whose nationalism affected Ireland's history.
**O'Connor, Thomas P. (Tay Pay),** 1848–1929, Irish journalist and nationalist who aided cause of Irish Home Rule.
**O'Higgins, Bernardo,** 1778-1842, Chilean revolutionary and dictator (1817–23) who died in exile in Peru.
**Ohira, Masayoshi,** 1910–80, Japanese premier (1978–80).
**Ojukwu, C. Odumegwu,** 1933– , leader of Biafra's unsuccessful war of secession in the late 1960s.
**Oppenheimer, J. Robert,** 1904–67, American physicist who led research effort culminating in atom bomb.
**Orlando, Vittorio Emanuele,** 1860–1952, Italian jurist and premier (1917–19), one of the "Big Four" at WW I Paris Peace Conference.
**Osman I,** 1259–1326, founder of Ottoman dynasty who inaugurated a policy of religious toleration.

**Oswald, Lee Harvey,** 1939–63, President John F. Kennedy's assassin; murdered in Dallas jail by Jack Ruby.

**Owen, Robert,** 1771–1858, British social reformer, socialist, and cooperative-movement pioneer.

**Paderewski, Ignace J.,** 1860–1941, Polish statesman, composer, and popular classical pianist.

**Paley, William S.,** 1901– , American radio and television executive.

**Palmer Nathaniel B.,** 1799-1877, American sea captain, ship designer and Antarctic explorer.

**Pandit, Madame (Vijaya L.),** 1900– , Indian diplomat and president of UN General Assembly (1953–54).

**Pankhurst, Emmeline (née Goulden),** 1858-1928, revered English woman suffragist.

**Papadopoulos, George,** 1919- , Greek premier, seized power in April 1967 and was overthrown in Nov. 1973.

**Papandreou, George,** 1888–1968, Greek premier, opponent of King Constantine and military junta.

**Papen, Franz von,** 1879–1969, German chancellor, diplomat under Hitler, acquitted by Nuremberg tribunal.

**Park Chung Hee,** 1917–79, South Korean president (1963–79).

**Park, Mungo,** 1771–1806, Scottish explorer of Niger River and western Africa.

**Parnell, Charles S.,** 1846–91, magnetic Irish nationalist leader, "uncrowned king of Ireland."

**La Pasionaria (Dolores Ibarruri),** 1895- , Spanish revolutionist and a founder of Spain's Communist party.

**Patiño, Simón I.,** 1868–1947, Bolivian tin king, reputed to have been one of world's wealthiest men.

**Patterson, Joseph M.,** 1879–1946, American publisher of first successful U.S. tab'oid, *Daily News*.

**Patton, George S., Jr.,** 1885–1945, brilliant but controversial American WW II general ("Old Blood and Guts").

**Paulus, Friedrich,** 1890-1957, German field marshal who surrendered (1943) to Russians at Stalingrad.

**Peabody, George,** 1852-1938, American banker and philanthropist who fought for Negro education.

**Pearson, Lester B.,** 1897-1972, Liberal prime minister of Canada (1963–68).

**Peary, Robert E.,** 1856–1920, American rear admiral and first man to reach the North Pole (April 6, 1909).

**Peel, Sir Robert,** 1788–1850, British reformist statesman, organizer of London police force.

**Pérez Jiménez, Marcos,** 1914– , Venezuelan dictator and army officer.

**Pericles,** c. 495–429 B.C., democratic Athenian statesman, great patron of the arts.

**Perkins, Frances,** 1882–1965, U.S. Secretary of Labor during New Deal era, first woman cabinet member.

**Perón, Juan D.,** 1895-1974, Argentine general and dictator (President 1946-55; 1973-74).

**Perry, Oliver H.,** 1785–1819, American naval hero (Battle of Lake Erie) in War of 1812.

**Pershing, John J. (Jack),** 1860–1948, American WW I general, AEF commander in chief.

**Pétain, Henri P.,** 1856–1951, French marshal, head of Vichy France (1940–42).

**Peter I (the Great),** 1672–1725, Russian czar (1682–1725), who westernized his country and made it a great power.

**Pham Van Dong,** 1906– , Vietnamese premier, a founder of the Vietminh.

**Philby, Harold St. J. B.,** 1885–1960, British explorer, author and adviser to King Ibn Saud of Saudi Arabia.

**Philip II,** 382–336 B.C., father of Alexander the Great.

**Pilsudski, Joseph,** 1867–1935, Polish general and authoritarian premier (1926–28, 1930–35).

**Pizarro, Francisco,** c. 1476–1541, rapacious Spanish conquistador, conqueror of Peru.

**Podgorny, Nikolai V.,** 1903– , Chairman of the Presidium of the Supreme Soviet (1965–77).

**Poincaré, Raymond,** 1860–1934, French president (1913–20) and advocate of harsh punishment for Germany after WW I.

**Polo, Marco,** c. 1254–c. 1324, Venetian traveler, favorite of Mongol Emperor Kublai Khan, and author of remarkably accurate Asian travelogue.

**Pol Pot,** 1928– , Communist leader in Cambodia whose regime is believed to be responsible for 2 million deaths in Cambodia after April 1975.

**Pompadour, Madame,** 1721–64, French mistress of Louis XV and his confidante until her death.

**Pompey (the Great),** 106–48 B.C., assassinated Roman general and statesman, rival of Caesar.

**Pompidou, Georges J. R.,** 1911–74, French president (1969–1974).

**Potemkin, Grigori A.,** 1739–91, eccentric Russian field marshal, a favorite of Catherine the Great.

**Primo de Rivera, José A.,** 1903–36, Spanish founder of fascist Falange, executed by Loyalists after outbreak of Spanish Civil War.

**Primo de Rivera, Miguel,** 1870–1930, Spanish general and dictator (1923–30), father of José Primo de Rivera.

**Princip, Gavrilo,** 1895–1918, Serbian political agitator and hero, assassin (1914) of Archduke Francis Ferdinand.

**Przhevalsky, Nikolai M.,** 1839–88, Russian geographer and explorer in central Asia and the Russian Far East.

**Pugachev, Emelyan I.,** d. 1775, beheaded Russian leader who posed as Peter III in peasant rebellion (1773–75).

**Pulaski, Casimir,** c. 1748–79, Polish military commander in American Revolution, mortally wounded at Savannah.

**Pulitzer, Joseph,** 1847–1911, Hungarian-born publisher who established annual prizes for American letters.

**Pu Yi, Henry,** 1906–67, last emperor (1908–12) of China, later emperor of Japanese puppet state of Manchukuo.

**el-Qaddafi, Muammar,** 1942– , Libyan head of state since 1969.

**Quezon, Manuel L.,** 1878–1944, first president of Philippines (1935–44), led it to independence.

**Quisling, Vidkun,** 1887–1945, executed Norwegian Fascist leader who helped Germany conquer his country.

**Radek, Karl,** 1885–1939?, Russian Communist leader and journalist, purged by Stalin.

**Raeder, Erich,** 1876–1960, German WW II admiral who disagreed with Hitler on strategy.

**Raffles, Sir Thomas S. B.,** 1781–1826, British East Indian administrator, founder of Singapore.

**Raglan, Lord (Fitzroy J. H. Somerset),** 1788–1855, British general in Napoleonic and Crimean wars.

**Rahman, Tunku Abdul, Prince,** 1903-1973, first prime minister of Malaya (1957-1970).

**Randolph, Edmund,** 1753–1813, first U.S. Attorney General (1789–94), figure at Constitutional Convention (1787).

**Rasmussen, Knud J. V.,** 1879–1933, Danish explorer of Greenland and the Arctic.

**Rasputin, Grigori Y.,** 1872–1916, Russian libertine monk, a notorious influence on Nicholas II's court.

**Rathenau, Walter,** 1867–1922, assassinated German industrialist, idealistic social theorist, and statesman.

**Rayburn, Sam (Samuel T.),** 1882–1961, U.S. Congressman (Tex.), long-time Democratic House speaker.

**Récamier, Madame (Juliette),** 1777–1849, French beauty who presided over a salon of notables.

**Reid, Ogden M.,** 1882–1947, American newspaper publisher.

**Revere, Paul,** 1735–1818, American Revolutionary patriot immortalized by Longfellow's poem.

**Reza Shah Pahlavi,** 1877-1944, shah of Iran (1925-41) who gained independence for his country.

**Rhee, Syngman,** 1875–1965, authoritarian president (1948–60) of Republic of (South) Korea.

**Rhodes, Cecil J.,** 1853–1902, British statesman and business magnate in South Africa who set up Rhodes scholarship; Rhodesia (now Zimbabwe) was named for him.

**Ribbentrop, Joachim von,** 1893–1946, Anglophobic Nazi foreign minister (1938–45).

**Ricci, Matteo,** 1552–1610, Italian missionary and geographer in China, a favorite at the Chinese court.

**Richelieu, Cardinal (Armand J.), duc de,** 1585–1642, French prelate and statesman, founder of French Academy.

**Riis, Jacob A.,** 1849–1914, Danish-American social reformer and journalist.

**Rizal, José,** 1861–96, Filipino patriot, author, poet, physician; his martyrdom inspired anti-Spanish revolt.

**Robert I (Robert the Bruce),** 1274–1329, king of Scotland who freed his country from England's grip.

**Robert Guiscard,** c. 1015–85, Norman conqueror of southern Italy.

**Robespierre, Maximilien M. I.,** 1758–94, guillotined French revolutionary associated with the Reign of Terror.

**Rob Roy (Robert MacGregor),** 1671–1734, Scottish outlaw who figures in Scott's novel *Rob Roy*.

**Rochambeau, Count (Jean B.),** 1725–1807, French marshal in American Revolution.

**Rockefeller, John D.,** 1839–1937, American oil tycoon and philanthropist, a founder of University of Chicago.

**Rockefeller, Nelson A.,** 1908–79, governor of New York (1959–73), Vice-President of U.S. (1974–1977).

**Rodino, Peter W.,** 1909– , chairman of the House Judiciary Committee which considered the impeachment of President Nixon in 1974.

**Rokossovsky, Konstantin,** 1896–1968, Soviet marshal, symbol of Russian influence in Poland (1949–56).

**Rommel, Erwin,** 1891–1944, German field marshal in Africa ("the Desert Fox") and France (1940–44).

**Romulo, Carlos P.,** 1900– , Filipino statesman, president of UN General Assembly (1949).

**Ronne Finn,** 1899–1980, Norwegian-born American explorer and geographer.

**Root, Elihu,** 1845–1937, U.S. Secretary of State (1905–09), an architect of League of Nations; Nobel Peace Prize winner (1912).

**Rosecrans, William S.,** 1818–98, American Union general.
**Ross, James C.,** 1800–62, British rear admiral and polar explorer.
**Rothschild, Guy, Baron de,** 1909– , descendant of the prominent French banking family and head of the Banque Rothschild.
**Rothschild, Meyer A.,** 1743-1812, German founder (in Frankfurt) of international banking house of Rothschild.
**Rundstedt, Karl R. G. von,** 1875–1953, German WW II field marshal and supreme commander in West (1942-45).
**Rusk, (D.) Dean,** 1909– , U.S. Secretary of State under Presidents Kennedy and Johnson.
**Sadat, Anwar,** 1918–81, Egyptian president (1970-81).
**Sage, Russell,** 1816–1906, American tycoon whose widow established (1907) Russell Sage Foundation.
**Saladin,** c. 1137–93, Moslem warrior and sultan of Egypt, major opponent of Crusaders.
**Salazar, Antonio de Oliveira,** 1889–1970, long-time Portuguese dictator (beginning in 1932).
**Salomon, Haym,** 1740–85, American Revolutionary patriot and financier.
**Sandracottus (Greek for Chandragupta),** fl. c. 321–c. 298 B.C., Indian emperor, founder of the Maurya dynasty.
**Sanger, Margaret,** 1879–1966, American founder of the birth-control movement.
**San Martín, José de,** 1778–1850, South American revolutionary, protector of Peru (1821–22).
**Santa Anna, Antonio L. de,** 1794–1876, Mexican general at Alamo and in Mexican War, several times president.
**Santander, Francisco de Paula,** 1792–1840, Colombian revolutionary and political leader.
**Sarnoff, David,** 1891-1971; Russian-born American pioneer in radio and television.
**Savonarola, Girolamo,** 1452–98, executed Florentine religious reformer.
**Saxe, Comte de (Maurice),** 1696–1750, French marshal, one of the greatest generals of his era.
**Scanderbeg (George Castriota),** c. 1404–68, Albanian national hero who led his people against Turks.
**Schacht, Hjalmar H. G.,** 1877–1970, German president of Reichsbank (1923–30, 1933–39), acquitted by Nuremberg tribunal.
**Schlieffen, Alfred, Graf von,** 1833–1913, German field marshal whose battle strategy was reflected in WWI.
**Schliemann, Heinrich,** 1822–90, German archaeologist, discovered ruins of Troy.
**Schmidt, Helmut,** 1918– , West German chancellor since 1974.
**Schuman, Robert,** 1886–1963, French premier (1947–48) who worked to promote a European community.
**Schurz, Carl,** 1829–1906, German-born U.S. Secretary of the Interior (1877–81), newspaper editor, and author.
**Schuschnigg, Kurt von,** 1897–1977, Austrian chancellor (1934–38) imprisoned by Nazis until 1945.
**Scipio Africanus Major,** c. 234–183 B.C., Roman general, victor over Hannibal in Punic Wars.
**Scott, Dred,** c. 1795–1858, American slave and central figure in law case argued (1856–57) before U.S. Supreme Court.
**Scott, Robert F.,** 1868–1912, British naval officer and antarctic explorer.
**Scott, Winfield,** 1786–1866, American army commander (1841–61), and Mexican War hero.
**Scripps, Edward W.,** 1854–1926, American newspaper publisher.
**Senghor, Léopold S.,** 1906– , African statesman and poet, first president of independent Senegal.
**Sennacherib,** d. 681 B.C., king of Assyria (705–681 B.C.) and conqueror who was murdered by his sons.
**Seward, William H.,** 1801–72, U.S. Secretary of State, purchaser (1867) of Alaska ("Seward's folly").
**Sforza, Ludovico,** c. 1451–1508, duke of Milan (1494–99), Renaissance prince, patron of Leonardo da Vinci.
**Shackleton, Sir Ernest H.,** 1874–1922, Irish-born British explorer whose antarctic expedition (1907–09) crossed within 100 miles of the South Pole.
**Shaftesbury, Earl of (Anthony A. Cooper),** 1801–85, leading English social reformer who advocated government action to reduce misery caused by Industrial Revolution.
**Sharett, Moshe,** 1894–1965, Israeli prime minister (1953–55), Ben-Gurion's closest associate in promoting an independent Jewish state.
**Shastri, Shri L. B.,** 1904–66, prime minister of India (1964–66), disciple of Gandhi.
**Shays, Daniel,** c. 1747–1825, American Revolutionary soldier, leader of Shays's Rebellion (1786–87) of financially depressed small farmers in Massachusetts.
**Sheridan, Philip H.,** 1831–88, American Union general, observer with Prussian army in Franco-Prussian War.
**Sherman, William Tecumseh,** 1820–91, American Union general who practiced war of attrition in the South.
**Smith, Ian Douglas,** 1919– , Rhodesian prime minister (1964–79).
**Smith, John,** c. 1580–1631, English adventurer and colonial leader; Pocahontas probably saved his life.
**Smith, Walter Bedell,** 1895–1961, U.S. WW II general, ambassador to USSR (1946–49), CIA head (1950–53).
**Smuts, Jan C.,** 1870–1950, South African prime minister twice, WW II field marshal, and a UN organizer.
**Snorri Sturluson,** 1178–1241, Icelandic chieftain and historian, leading light in medieval Norse literature.
**Somoza, Anastasio,** 1896–1956, assassinated dictator of Nicaragua (1937–47, 1950–56).
**Soong, T. V.,** 1894–1971, Harvard-educated Chinese statesman.
**Sorge, Richard,** 1895–1944, executed German spy for USSR in Japan.
**Souphanouvong, Prince,** 1902– , Laotian politician, leader of leftist Pathet Lao forces. President since 1975.
**Souvanna Phouma, Prince,** 1901– , Laotian neutralist prime minister (1962–75).
**Spaak, Paul Henri,** 1899–1972, Belgian statesman and Socialist leader, first president of UN general assembly (1946), and secretary-general of NATO (1957–61).
**Spartacus,** d. 71 B.C., Thracian gladiator and leader of Italian slave revolt, killed in battle.
**Speke, John H.,** 1827–64, English explorer in Africa and discoverer (1858) of Lake Victoria.
**Springer, Axel C.,** 1912– , powerful German publisher.
**De Staël, Germaine,** 1766–1817, French-Swiss writer and intellectual leader.
**Stalin, Joseph V. (b. J. V. Dzhugashvili),** 1879–1953, Russian Communist dictator.
**Stambuliski, Alexander,** 1879–1923, murdered Bulgarian premier (1919–23) and agrarian reformer.
**Stanley, Sir Henry M.,** 1841–1904, Anglo-American adventurer, journalist, and empire builder, who was commissioned (1871) by the *New York Herald* to find David Livingstone in Africa.
**Stanton, Edwin M.,** 1814–69, U.S. Secretary of War under Presidents Lincoln and Andrew Johnson.
**Stavisky, Serge A.,** 1886–1934, French swindler, chief figure in scandal that rocked France (1934).
**Stefansson, Vilhjalmur,** 1879–1962, Canadian-born Icelandic ethnologist and arctic explorer.
**Stepinac, Cardinal (Aloysius),** 1898–1960, Yugoslav Roman Catholic prelate convicted (1946) by Tito government of Nazi collaboration but released (1951).
**Steuben, Baron von (Friedrich W.),** 1730–94, Prussian general in American Revolution.
**Stevens, Thaddeus,** 1792–1868, U.S. Congressman (Pa., 1849–53, 1859–68) active during Civil War and Reconstruction, devoted to Negro betterment.
**Stevenson, Adlai E.,** 1900–65, eloquent American lawyer, Presidential candidate (1952, 1956), and U.S. ambassador to UN (1961–65).
**Stimson, Henry L.,** 1867–1950, U.S. Secretary of War (1911–13, 1940–45) and Secretary of State (1929–33).
**Stolypin, Piotr A.,** 1862–1911, Russian premier and minister of interior (1906–11).
**Stowe, Harriet Beecher,** 1811–96, American humanitarian whose novel *Uncle Tom's Cabin* was a factor in bringing about the Civil War.
**Strabo,** b. c. 63 B.C., Greek geographer, historian, and traveler.
**Stresemann, Gustav,** 1878–1929, German foreign minister dedicated to regaining world friendship for post-WW I Germany, and sharer of 1926 Nobel Peace Prize.
**Stroessner, Alfredo,** 1912– , repressive Paraguayan general and president.
**Stuart, Charles Edward,** 1720–88, claimant (Bonnie Prince Charlie) to English throne.
**Stuyvesant, Peter,** c. 1610–72, autocratic Dutch director general of New Netherland (beginning 1647).
**Suárez González, Adolfo,** 1932– , Spanish premier (1976-81).
**Sucre, Antonio J. de,** 1795–1830, South American revolutionary and military commander, associate of Bolívar.
**Suharto,** 1921– , Indonesian general and chief executive who overthrew (1965) Sukarno.
**Sukarno,** 1902–70, independence leader and dictatorial first president of republic of Indonesia (1945–66).
**Sukhe-Bator,** 1893–1923, Mongolian political leader who helped set up Mongolian People's Revolutionary party.
**Suleiman I (the Magnificent),** 1494–1566, Ottoman sultan under whom Ottoman Empire reached its height.
**Sulla, Lucius C.,** 138–78 B.C., notorious Roman general and dictator.
**Sully, Maximilien de B., duc de,** 1560–1641, French statesman and closest adviser to Henry IV of France.
**Sun Yat-sen,** 1866–1925, Chinese revolutionary founder of the Chinese republic and of the Kuomintang.
**Suslov, Mikhail A.,** 1902–82, Soviet ideologist.
**Suvarov, Aleksandr V.,** 1729–1800, revered Russian marshal in French Revolutionary Wars (1798–99).

**Svoboda, Ludvík,** 1895–1979, Communist president of Czechoslovakia during 1968 Soviet invasion.
**Taft, Robert A.,** 1889–1953, conservative U.S. Senator who helped write Taft-Hartley Labor Act.
**Talleyrand, Charles M. de,** 1754–1838, French statesman and diplomat.
**Tamerlane,** c. 1336–1405, cruel Mongol conqueror of Asia, subject of a play by Christopher Marlowe.
**Tanaka, Kakuei,** 1918– , self-made businessman and premier of Japan (1972–74).
**Tasman, Abel Janszoon,** c. 1603–59, Dutch explorer who discovered (1642) Tasmania.
**Teng Hsiao-ping** see **Deng Xiaoping.**
**Tetzel, Johann,** c. 1465-1519, German Roman Catholic preacher who was attacked by Martin Luther.
**Thatcher, Margaret,** 1925– , British Conservative prime minister (1979– ).
**Themistocles,** c. 525-c. 460 B.C., Athenian statesman and naval commander.
**Theodora,** d. 548, Byzantine empress, joint ruler with her husband, Justinian I.
**Thiers, Adolphe,** 1797–1877, French statesman, journalist, and historian of the Revolution and Bonaparte.
**Thieu, Nguyen Van,** 1923– , South Vietnamese president (1967–75), instrumental in 1963 overthrow of Diem.
**Thomas, Norman M.,** 1884–1968, American Socialist leader, lecturer, and writer; frequent Socialist Party Presidential candidate after 1928.
**Thomas à Becket, Saint,** c. 1118–70, martyred English archbishop (Canterbury).
**Thomson, Roy H., (1st Baron Thomson of Fleet),** 1894–1976, Canadian-born British publisher.
**Thorez, Maurice,** 1900–64, French Communist leader, vice premier (1946–47).
**Thurmond, (J.) Strom,** 1902– , conservative U.S. Senator (S.C.), States' Rights Presidential candidate (1948).
**Tilden, Samuel J.,** 1814–86, Democratic Presidential candidate (1876 against Rutherford B. Hayes).
**Tirpitz, Alfred von,** 1849–1930, German WW I admiral, advocate of unrestricted submarine warfare.
**Tito, Josip B. (b. Josip Broz),** 1892–1980, unorthodox Yugoslav Communist leader (1945–80).
**Togliatti, Palmiro,** 1893–1964, Italian Communist leader and party founder in his country.
**Togo, Heihachiro, Count,** 1847–1934, Japanese admiral and naval hero of Russo-Japanese War.
**Tojo, Hideki,** 1884–1948, Japanese general and prime minister (1941–44), executed by Allies as a war criminal.
**Torquemada, Tomás de,** 1420–98, severe Spanish Dominican who headed Spanish Inquisition.
**Touré, Sékou,** 1922– , African left-wing political leader, first president of Republic of Guinea.
**Toussaint L'Ouverture, François D.,** c. 1744–1803, Haitian patriot and martyr who thwarted French colonial aims.
**Trotsky, Leon,** 1879–1940, exiled Soviet revolutionary and a principal founder of USSR.
**Trudeau, Pierre E.,** 1919– , French-Canadian Liberal prime minister (1968–79, 1980– ) and lawyer.
**Trujillo Molina, Rafael L.,** 1891–1961, murdered president (1930–38, 1942–60) of Dominican Republic.
**Trung Trac,** fl. 39-43 A.D., Vietnamese national heroine who led a revolt against China.
**Tshombe, Moise K.,** 1919–69, Congolese political leader of Katanga, which he proclaimed (1960) independent.
**Tubman, Harriet,** c. 1820–1913, slave-born American abolitionist and Underground Railroad "conductor."
**Tubman, William V. S.,** 1895–1971, long-time Liberian president.
**Tukhachevsky, Mikhail N.,** 1893–1937, Soviet marshal who helped to modernize and mechanize Red Army.
**Tupac Amaru,** c. 1742–81, Indian national hero of Peru, executed leader of antigovernment rebellion (1780).
**Turner, Nat,** 1800–31, executed American leader of slave rebellion (1831, Southampton Co., Va.).
**Tutankhamen,** fl. c. 1350 B.C., Egyptian pharaoh whose tomb revealed new knowledge of XVIII dynasty life.
**Tweed, Boss (William M.),** 1823–78, American politician and Tammany leader, who defrauded New York City.
**Tyler, Wat,** d. 1381, English leader of great peasant rebellion (1381) over labor conditions.
**Tz'u Hsi,** 1834–1908, dowager empress of China who encouraged Boxer Rebellion (1898–1900).
**Ulbricht, Walter,** 1893–1973, Communist who became (1960) East German head of state.
**Vance, Cyrus R.,** 1917– , American lawyer, government official, and Secretary of State (1977–80).
**Vanderbilt, Commodore (Cornelius),** 1794–1877, American railroad magnate, founder of Vanderbilt University.
**Vargas, Getúlio D.,** 1883–1954, Brazilian statesman and president (1930–45, 1951–54).
**Venizelos, Eleutherios,** 1864–1936, Cretan-born Greek statesman and reformer.
**Verwoerd, Hendrik F.,** 1901–66, assassinated South African prime minister (1958–66), proponent of apartheid.
**Victoria,** 1819–1901, longest reigning English monarch in history (64 years), who ruled during the height of the British Empire's prestige.
**Videla, Jorge Rafael,** 1925– , Argentine general and president (1976–81).
**Villa, Pancho (b. Doroteo Arango),** c. 1877–1923, assassinated Mexican bandit and revolutionary.
**Viola, Roberto Eduardo,** 1924– , Argentine general and president (1981).
**Visconti, Gian C.,** c. 1351–1402, Italian duke of Milan who reformed and centralized the government.
**Vishinsky, Andrei Y.,** 1883–1954, Soviet jurist and diplomat, foreign minister (1949-53) of USSR.
**Volstead, Andrew J.,** 1860–1947, American legislator, author (1919) of Volstead (alcohol prohibition) Act.
**Voroshilov, Kliment Y.,** 1881-1969, Soviet general and statesman, close associate of Stalin.
**Vorster, Balthazar J.,** 1915- , South African prime minister (1966–78) and lawyer.
**Wainwright, Jonathan M.,** 1883–1953, American general who in World War II defended Bataan and Corregidor.
**Waldheim, Kurt,** 1918– , Austrian career diplomat and Secretary General of the United Nations (1972–81).
**Walesa, Lech,** 1943?– , Polish labor leader.
**Wallace, George C.,** 1919– , American conservative politician, third party Presidential candidate (1968).
**Washington, Booker T.,** 1856-1915, Black American educator, organizer (1881) of Tuskegee Institute; author.
**Wavell, Archibald P. (Earl),** 1883–1950, British field marshal and viceroy of India (1943–47).
**Webb, Beatrice (née Potter),** 1858–1943, English Socialist economist; she and her husband, **Sidney J. Webb** (1859–1947), were leading figures in Fabian Society and building British Labour party.
**Webster, Daniel,** 1782–1852, American statesman, a leading political figure, noted orator, and Whig luminary.
**Weizmann, Chaim,** 1874–1952, Russian-born scientist, Zionist leader, and first president of Israel (1948–52).
**Welles, Sumner,** 1892–1961, American diplomat and statesman, specialist in Latin American affairs.
**Westmoreland, William C.,** 1914– , American general in Vietnam.
**White, William A.,** 1868–1944, American author and editor (1895–1944) of Emporia (Kans.) *Gazette.*
**Wilkes, Charles,** 1798–1877, American naval officer and discoverer of area in Antarctic named Wilkes Land.
**William I (the Conqueror),** 1027?–1087, Norman duke and English king (1066–87), conquered England in 1066.
**Willkie, Wendell L.,** 1892–1944, American industrialist and Republican Presidential candidate (1940).
**Wilson, J. Harold,** 1916- , Labour prime minister (1964-1970, 1974–76), of Great Britain.
**Wingate, Orde C.,** 1903–44, British WW II general, who demonstrated effectiveness of guerrilla warfare.
**Wolfe, James,** 1727–59, British victor against French in battle of Quebec (Plains of Abraham).
**Wollstonecraft, Mary,** 1759–97, English feminist whose writings inspired the American women's rights movement.
**Wolsey, Cardinal (Thomas),** c. 1473–1530, English prelate and favorite of Henry VIII.
**Wrangel, Baron Ferdinand von,** 1796–1870, Russian naval officer, arctic explorer, governor of Russian Alaska.
**Wyszynski, Cardinal (Stefan),** 1901–81, Polish prelate often in conflict with Gomulka government.
**Xenophon,** c. 430 B.C.–c. 355 B.C., Greek historian who led retreat of "Ten Thousand" Greek mercenaries from Persia (401 B.C.).
**Yamamoto, Isoroku,** 1884–1943, Japanese admiral who masterminded (1941) attack on Pearl Harbor.
**Yamani, Ahmed Zaki,** 1930– , Saudi Arabian oil minister; leading figure in Arab and OPEC oil activities.
**Yamashita, Tomoyuki,** 1888–1946, Japanese general defeated (1945) by General MacArthur's invasion of Philippines, hanged in Manila as a war criminal.
**Yoshida, Shigeru,** 1878–1967, Japanese Liberal prime minister (1946–54).
**Yüan Shih-kai,** 1859–1916, dictatorial president of China (1912-16) who declared (1916) himself emperor.
**Zaharoff, Sir Basil (b. Basileios Zacharias),** 1850–1936, Turkish-born British financier and munitions manufacturer.
**Zapata, Emiliano,** c. 1879–1919. Mexican revolutionary.
**Zenger, John Peter,** 1697–1746, German-American journalist whose libel trial acquittal furthered press freedom.
**Zhdanov, Andrei A.,** 1896–1948, murdered Soviet Communist leader who fostered extreme nationalism.
**Zhou Enlai,** 1898–1976, Chinese Communist premier and foreign minister (1949–76).
**Zhukov, Georgi K.,** 1896-1974, Soviet marshal who defeated Germans at Stalingrad and occupied Berlin.
**Zinoviev, Grigori E.,** 1883–1936, Russian Communist leader executed by Stalin after the first spectacular purge trial.

## SCIENTISTS AND MATHEMATICIANS

**Ampère, André Marie**, 1775–1836, French physicist, discovered, 1820, the left-hand and right-hand rules of the magnetic field about a current-carrying wire.

***Archimedes**, c. 287–212 B.C., Greek mathematician.

**Aston, Francis William**, 1877–1945, English chemist and physicist, developed, 1919, the mass spectrograph.

**Avogadro, Amedeo**, 1776–1856, Italian physicist, put forth a hypothesis in which equal volumes of all gasses at the same temperature and pressure contain the same number of molecules.

**Becquerel, Antoine Henri**, 1852–1908, French physicist.

**Bernoulli, Daniel**, 1700–82, Dutch-Swiss mathematician, 1738, advanced the kinetic theory of gases and fluids.

**Berzelius, Jons Jakob**, 1779–1848, Swedish chemist, introduced chemical symbols and chemical radical theory.

**Bethe, Hans Albrecht**, 1906– , German-born American physicist, proposed, 1938, the nuclear mechanism by which stars obtain their energy.

***Bohr, Niels**, 1885–1962, Danish physicist.

**Brahe, Tycho**, 1546–1601, Danish astronomer.

**Carnap, Rudolf**, 1891–1970, German-born American philosopher of science, founded logical positivism.

**Cavendish, Henry**, 1731–1810, English chemist and physicist, discovered, 1766, hydrogen; devised, 1798, a gravitational method for weighing the Earth.

**Charles, Jacques Alexandre César**, 1746–1823, French physicist, discovered, 1787, the law governing the expansion and contraction of gases with changes in temperature.

**Cockcroft, John Douglas**, 1897–1967, English nuclear physicist, with E. T. S. Walton, constructed (c. 1932), the first atomic particle accelerator.

**Compton, Arthur Holly**, 1892–1962, American physicist, discovered, 1923, that X-rays scattered by diffraction in crystals have their wavelengths lengthened, the Compton effect; discovered, c. 1930, that cosmic rays consist of particles.

***Copernicus (Mikolaj Kopernik)**, 1473–1543, Polish astronomer.

**Coulomb, Charles Augustin de**, 1736–1806, French engineer and physicist, established the law describing the attraction and repulsion of electric charges.

***Crick, Francis H. C.**, 1916– , English biophysicist.

**Ctesibius**, 2d century B.C., Greek engineer, invented the water clock, force pump, and air as motive force.

**Curie, Marie**, 1867–1934, and **Pierre**, 1859–1906, French chemists, isolated, 1898, the first radioactive element —radium.

***Darwin, Charles**, 1809–1882, English naturalist.

**Davy, Humphry**, 1778–1829, English chemist, established the electrical nature of chemical affinity.

***Descartes, René**, 1596–1650, French mathematician.

**Dewar, James**, 1842–1923, British chemist and physicist, liquified, 1898, and solidified, 1899, hydrogen.

**Dirac, Paul Adrien Maurice**, 1902– , English physicist, in 1920s, unified relativity and quantum theories, and unified wave mechanics and special relativity; proposed, 1930–31, antiparticles.

**Dubos, René**, 1901–82, French microbiologist and environmentalist in America.

**Edison, Thomas Alva**, 1847-1931, prolific American inventor. Discovered "Edison effect."

***Einstein, Albert**, 1879–1955, American physicist (born Germany).

**Euler, Leonhard**, 1707–83, Swiss mathematician and physicist, produced work in astronomy, mechanics, hydrodynamics, and optics; founded higher mathematics.

**Fahrenheit, Gabriel Daniel**, 1686–1736, German physicist, developed temperature scale that bears his name.

***Faraday, Michael**, 1791–1867, English chemist, physicist.

**Fermat, Pierre de**, 1601–65, French mathematician, discovered analytic geometry; founded modern theory of numbers and the calculus of probabilities.

**Fermi, Enrico**, 1901–54, Italian-born American physicist.

**Fischer, Emil**, 1852–1919, German chemist, especially noted for his work on structure of sugars.

**Fourier, Jean Baptiste Joseph**, 1768–1830, French mathematician, discovered, c. 1822, the theorem governing periodic oscillation.

**Franklin, Benjamin**, 1706–90, American statesman and scientist, discovered, 1752, the electrical nature of lightning; proposed the one-fluid theory of electricity.

**Gabor, Dennis**, 1900–79, Hungarian-born British physicist known for the development of holography.

***Galileo Galilei**, 1564–1642, Italian scientist.

***Gauss, Karl F.**, 1777–1855, German mathematician.

**Gay-Lussac, Joseph Louis**, 1778–1850, French chemist, discovered, 1809, the law of combining volumes.

**Gibbs, Josiah Willard**, 1839–1903, American physicist, founded, 1876–78, chemical thermodynamics.

**Grzimek, Bernhard**, 1909– , Polish zoologist and wildlife conservationist.

**Guericke, Otto von**, 1602–86, German physicist and engineer, invented the first vacuum pump and used it, (c. 1650) to demonstrate atmospheric pressure.

**Haber, Fritz**, 1868–1934, German chemist, developed, 1900–1911, a process for "fixing" atmospheric nitrogen in chemical compounds.

**Hall, James**, 1761–1832, British geologist and chemist, founded, c. 1797, experimental geology, geochemistry.

**Halley, Edmund**, 1656–1742, English astronomer, calculated orbits of many comets.

***Heisenberg, Werner Karl**, 1901–1976, German physicist.

**Helmont, Jan Baptista Van**, 1577–1644, Flemish physician and alchemist, initiated quantitative biochemistry.

**Hero of Alexandria**, c. 1st century, Greek engineer, invented principle of the steam engine; extended Archimedes' principle of the lever.

***Hertz, Heinrich**, 1857–94, German physicist.

**Herzberg, Gerhard**, 1904– , Canadian physicist known for his work on electronic structure and molecular geometry.

**Hilbert, David**, 1862–1943, German mathematician, formulated, 1899, the first set of axioms for geometry.

**Hubble, Edwin Powell**, 1889–1953, American astronomer, discovered, 1929, the universal recession of galaxies.

**Humboldt, Friedrich Wilhelm Heinrich Alexander von**, 1769–1859, established, c. 1830–1859, geophysics.

**Janssen (or Jansen), Zacharias**, 1580–c. 1638, Dutch optician, invented, c. 1590, the microscope.

**Jensen, Arthur Robert**, 1923– , educational psychologist. His view is that intelligence is primarily inherited.

**Kamerlingh Onnes, Heike**, 1853–1926, Dutch physicist, established, 1882, cryogenics.

**Kapitza, Peter**, 1894– , Soviet physicist, research contributed to Soviet space achievements.

**Kelvin, Lord (William Thompson)**, 1826–1907, British physicist, made advances in thermodynamics and thermometry.

***Kepler, Johannes**, 1571–1630, German astronomer.

**Khorana, Har Gobind**, 1922– , Indian organic chemist, synthesized functioning gene, 1976.

**Landau, Lev Davidovich**, 1908–68, Russian physicist, developed mathematical theory explaining behavior of superfluid helium at temperatures near absolute zero.

**LaPlace, Pierre Simon**, 1749–1827, French astronomer and mathematician, put forth, 1796, the nebular hypothesis of the origin of the solar system.

***Lavoisier, Antoine**, 1743–94, French chemist.

**Lawrence, Ernest Orlando**, 1901–58, American physicist, constructed, 1930, the first cyclotron.

**Leakey, Louis**, 1903-72, **Mary**, 1913- , and **Richard**, 1944- , Anglo-Kenyan anthropologists, discovered important fossil remains of early hominids.

**Lee, Tsung-Dao**, 1926– , Chinese-born American physicist, with Yang refuted the law of parity.

**Leeuwenhoek, Anton van**, 1632–1723, Dutch microscopist and the father of microbiology.

***Leibniz, Gottfried**, 1646–1716, German mathematician, philosopher.

**Levene, Phoebus Aaron Theodore**, 1869–1940, Russian-born American chemist, discovered, 1909, the nucleic acids RNA and, 20 years later, DNA.

**Lévi-Strauss, Claude**, 1908– , French anthropologist, leader of the structuralist school of ethnology.

**Liebig, Justus von**, 1803–73, German chemist, established, c. 1831, quantitative organic chemical analysis.

**Lowell, Percival**, 1855–1916, American astronomer, 1930, discovered Pluto.

**Mach, Ernst**, 1838–1916, Austrian physicist, psychologist, and philosopher of science, influential in the development of logical positivism.

**Marshak, Robert E.**, 1916– , American nuclear physicist who helped to develop the first atomic bomb.

***Maxwell, James C.**, 1831–79, English physicist.

***Mendel, Gregor Johann**, 1822–84, Austrian founder of genetics.

**Mead, Margaret**, 1901–78, American anthropologist noted for her studies in primitive and contemporary cultures.

---

* See listing in "Landmarks of Science," pp. 338-339.

***Mendeleyev, Dmitri Ivanovich,** 1834–1907, Russian chemist.
**Michelson, Albert Abraham,** 1852–1931, German-born American physicist, developed the interferometer, which measured, 1881 and 1887, the velocity of light and proved the nonexistence of ether in space.
**Mohorovicic, Andrija,** 1857–1936, Croatian geophysicist, discovered, 1909, the ("Moho") discontinuity that marks the bottom of the Earth's crust.
**Mössbauer, Rudolf Ludwig,** 1929– , German-born American physicist, discovered, 1958, the recoilless emission and absorption of gamma rays by atoms in crystals.
***Napier, John,** 1550–1617, Scottish mathematician.
***Newton, Isaac,** 1642–1727, English mathematician.
**Ochoa, Severo,** 1905– , Spanish-born American biochemist, synthesized, 1955, ribonucleic acid (RNA).
**Ostwald, Wilhelm,** 1853-1932, German chemist, was chief founder, beginning in 1887, of physical chemistry.
**Pascal, Blaise,** 1623–62, French scientist, mathematician, and religious philosopher, founded the modern theory of probability and the law of hydrostatic pressure (Pascal's law).
**Pauling, Linus Carl,** 1901– , American chemist, developed, 1939, the theory of the chemical bond.
***Planck, Max,** 1858–1947, German physicist.
**Priestley, Joseph,** 1733–1804, English theologian and scientist, discovered, 1774, oxygen.
**Raman, Chandrasekhara Vankata,** 1888–1970, Indian physicist, discovered, 1928, the change in wavelength and frequency of monochromatic light passing through a transparent medium.
**Riemann, Georg F. B.,** 1826–66, German mathematician, developed non-Euclidian system of geometry representing elliptic space.
***Rutherford, Lord (Ernest),** 1871–1937, British physicist, born in New Zealand.
***Schroedinger, Erwin,** 1887–1961, Austrian physicist.
**Seaborg, Glenn T.,** 1912– , American chemist, led, 1941–c. 1951, the group that discovered the transuranium elements americium, curium, berkelium, californium, einsteinium, fermium, plutonium, mendelevium and nobelium.
**Stanley, Wendell Meredith,** 1904–71, American biochemist, crystallized, 1935, the tobacco mosaic virus, thus demonstrating that matter may have both living and nonliving forms.
**Steno, Nicolaus (Niels Stensen),** 1638–86, Danish anatomist and Catholic prelate, recognized the nature of fossils.
**Szilard, Leo,** 1898–1964, Hungarian-born American physicist, proved, 1939, with Walter Zinn, the possibility of self-sustaining nuclear fission; worked, 1942, with Enrico Fermi, on development of first nuclear reaction.
**Tsvett (or Tswett), Mikhail Semenovich,** 1872–1919, Italian-born Russian botanist, discovered, 1906, chromatography.
**Urey, Harold Clayton,** 1893–1981, American chemist, discovered, 1931, heavy hydrogen (deuterium).
**Volta, Alessandro,** 1745–1827, Italian physicist, invented the first electric cell and electric battery.
**Von Neumann, John,** 1903–57, Hungarian-born American mathematician, was a founder of the mathematical theory of games and contributed to computer theory.
**Walton, Ernest Thomas Sinton,** 1903– , Irish physicist, constructed, 1929, the first atomic particle accelerator.
***Watson, James Dewey,** 1928– , American biochemist.
**Wegener, Alfred Lothar,** 1880–1930, German meteorologist and geophysicist, postulated theory of continental drift.
**Wiener, Norbert,** 1894–1964, American mathematician, contributed to development of computers; founded cybernetics.
**Wigner, Eugene Paul,** 1902– , Hungarian-born American physicist, accomplished pioneering work in nuclear structure.
***Wilkins, Maurice H. F.,** 1916– , British biophysicist.
**Yang, Chen Ning,** 1922– , Chinese-born American physicist. *See* Lee.
**Yukawa, Hideki,** 1907–81, Japanese physicist who predicted the existence of mesons.

## PHILOSOPHERS, THEOLOGIANS, AND RELIGIONISTS

**Abelard, Peter** (1079–1142), French philosopher.
**Abravanel, Isaac** (1437–1508), Jewish theologian.
**Adler, Felix** (1851–1933), German-American Ethical Culture movement founder.
**Alexander of Hales** (d. 1245), English scholastic philosopher.
**Ambrose, Saint** (c. 340–397), bishop of Milan.
**Anaxagoras** (c. 500–c. 428 B.C.), Greek philosopher.
**Anaximander** (c. 611–c. 547 B.C.), Greek philosopher.
**Anaximenes** (6th cent. B.C.), Greek philosopher.
**Anselm, Saint** (c. 1033–1109), Italian founder of scholasticism.
**Anthony, Saint** (c. 251–c. 350), Egyptian father of Christian monasticism.
**Antisthenes** (c. 444 B.C.–after 371 B.C.), Greek philosopher.
**Aristotle** (384–322 B.C.), Greek philosopher.
**Arius** (c. 256–336), Libyan theologian.
**Arminius, Jacobus** (1560–1609), Dutch Reformed theologian.
**Augustine, Saint** (354–430), North African Doctor of the Church.
**Averroës** (1126–98), Spanish-Arabian philosopher.
**Avicenna** (980–1037), Arabian philosopher.
**Ayer, Alfred Jules** (1910– ), British philosopher.
**Baal-Shem-Tov** (1700–60), Jewish founder of modern Hasidism.
**Bacon, Francis** (1561–1626), English philosopher.
**Bacon, Roger** (c. 1214–c. 1294), English philosopher.
**Balthasar, Hans Urs von** (1905– ), German theologian.
**Barth, Karl** (1886–1968), Swiss Protestant theologian.
**Bentham, Jeremy** (1748–1832), English philosopher, founder of utilitarianism.
**Berdyaev, Nicholas** (1874–1948), Russian philosopher.
**Berengar of Tours** (c. 1000–c. 1088), French theologian.
**Bergson, Henri** (1859–1941), French philosopher.
**Berkeley, George** (1685–1753), Anglo-Irish philosopher.
**Bernard of Clairvaux, Saint** (c. 1090–1153), French mystic.
**Bernard of Cluny** (fl. 1150), Anglo-French monk.
**Bernardine of Siena, Saint** (1380–1444), Italian preacher.
**Biddle, John** (1615–62), English founder of Unitarianism.
**Boehme, Jakob** (1575–1624), German religious mystic.
**Boethius** (c. 475–525), Roman philosopher.
**Bonaventure, Saint** (1221–74), Italian scholastic theologian.
**Bonhoeffer, Dietrich** (1906–45), German theologian.
**Brunner, Emil** (1889–1966), Swiss Protestant theologian.
**Bruno, Giordano** (1548–1600), Italian philosopher.
**Buber, Martin** (1878–1965), German-Israeli philosopher.
**Büchner, Ludwig** (1824–99), German philosopher.
**Bultmann, Rudolf** (1884–1976), German existentialist theologian.
**Cabrini, Mother Francesca** (1850–1917), Italian-born American nun and first American saint.
**Calvin, John** (1509–64), French Protestant theologian.
**Carnap, Rudolf** (1891–1970), German-American philosopher.
**Cassirer, Ernst** (1874–1945), German philosopher.
**Comte, Auguste** (1798–1857), French positivist philosopher.
**Cranmer, Thomas** (1489–1556), English churchman.
**Croce, Benedetto** (1866–1952), Italian philosopher.
**Democritus** (c. 460–c. 370 B.C.), Greek philosopher.
**Descartes, René** (1596–1650), French philosopher.
**Dewey, John** (1859–1952), American philosopher.
**Diderot, Denis** (1713–84), French philosopher.
**Diogenes** (c. 412–323 B.C.), Greek Cynic philosopher.
**Duns Scotus, John** (c. 1266–1308), Scottish theologian.
**Eckhart, Meister** (c. 1260–c. 1328), German theologian.
**Edwards, Jonathan** (1703–58), American theologian.
**Emerson, Ralph Waldo** (1803–82), American transcendentalist.
**Empedocles** (c. 495–c. 435 B.C.), Greek philosopher.
**Engels, Friedrich** (1820–95), German social philosopher.
**Enrique Tarancón, Vicente Cardinal** (1907– ), Spanish religious reformer.
**Epictetus** (c. 50–c. 138), Phrygian Stoic philosopher.
**Epicurus** (341–270 B.C.), Greek philosopher.
**Erigena, John Scotus** (c. 810–c. 877), Irish philosopher.
**Fichte, Johann G.** (1762–1814), German philosopher.
**Fox, George** (1624–91), English founder of Society of Friends.
**George, Henry** (1839–97), American economic theorist.
**Ghazali, al** (c. 1058-1111), Islamic philosopher.
**Gilson, Etienne** (1884–1978), French philosopher.
**Gorton, Samuel** (c. 1592–1677), Anglo-American religious founder.
**Graham, Billy** (1918– ), American evangelist.
**Groote, Gerard** (1340–84), Dutch ecclesiastical reformer.
**Guardini, Romano** (1885–1968), Italian-born German Catholic theologian.
**Hegel, Georg W. F.** (1770–1831), German philosopher.
**Heidegger, Martin** (1889–1976), German philosopher.

* See listing in "Landmarks of Science"

**Heraclitus** (c. 535–c. 475 B.C.), Greek philosopher.
**Hobbes, Thomas** (1588–1679), English philosopher.
**Hooker, Richard** (c. 1554–1600), English theologian.
**Hume, David** (1711–76), Scottish philosopher.
**Hus, Jan** (c. 1369–1415), Czech religious reformer.
**Husserl, Edmund** (1859–1938), German philosopher, founder of phenomenology.
**Huxley, Thomas H.** (1825–95), English agnostic philosopher.
**Ignatius of Loyola, Saint** (1491–1556), Spanish founder of the Jesuits.
**James, William** (1842–1910), American philosopher.
**Jansen, Cornelis** (1585–1638), Dutch Roman Catholic theologian.
**Jaspers, Karl** (1883–1969), German philosopher and psychopathologist.
**John of the Cross, Saint** (1542–91), Spanish mystic.
**Kant, Immanuel** (1724–1804), German metaphysical philosopher.
**Kierkegaard, Soren** (1813–55), Danish philosopher.
**Knox, John** (c. 1514-72), Scottish founder of Presbyterianism.
**Küng, Hans** (1928– ), Swiss Roman Catholic theologian.
**Laing, R. D.** (1927– ), Scottish existentialist psychoanalyst, writer, and social critic.
**Law, William** (1686–1761), English churchman and mystic.
**Leibniz, Gottfried W., Baron von** (1646–1716), German philosopher.
**Locke, John** (1632–1704), English philosopher.
**Lombard, Peter** (c. 1100-c. 1160).Italian theologian.
**Lonergan, Bernard J. F.** (1904– ), Canadian theologian and Thomist philosopher.
**Lucretius** (c. 99–c. 55 B.C.), Roman philosopher-poet.
**Luther, Martin** (1483–1546), German Protestant leader.
**Mahesh Yogi, Maharishi** (1911?– ), Hindu guru.
**Maimonides** (1135–1204), Spanish-Jewish philosopher.
**Malthus, Thomas R.** (1766–1834), English economic and social philosopher.
**Marcel, Gabriel** (1889–1973), French philosopher.
**Marcus Aurelius** (121–180), Stoic philosopher.
**Marías, Julián** (1914– ), Spanish philosopher.
**Maritain Jacques** (1882–1973), French Neo-Thomist philosopher.
**Marx, Karl** (1818–83), German social philosopher.
**Mather, Cotton** (1663–1728), American Puritan minister.
**Mather, Increase** (1639–1723), American Puritan minister.
**May, Rollo** (1909– ), American humanistic psychoanalyst-philosopher.
**Melanchthon, Philip** (1497–1560), German theologian.
**Mencius** (c. 371–c. 288 B.C.), Chinese sage.
**Mill, John Stuart** (1806–73), English philosopher and economist.
**Molina, Luis** (1535–1600), Spanish Jesuit theologian.
**Moore, George E.** (1873–1958), English philosopher.
**Murray, John** (1741–1815), English founder of American Universalist denomination.
**Nestorius** (d. c. 451), Byzantine theologian.
**Newman, John Henry, Cardinal** (1801–90), English philosopher.
**Nicholas of Cusa** (c. 1401–46), German humanist.
**Niebuhr, H. Richard** (1894–1962), American theologian.
**Niebuhr, Reinhold** (1892–1971), American theologian.
**Nietzsche, Friedrich W.** (1844–1900), German philosopher.
**Origen** (c. 185–c. 254), Egyptian Christian philosopher.
**Parmenides** (b. c. 514 B.C.), Greek philosopher.
**Pascal, Blaise** (1623–62), French philosopher and mathematician.
**Peirce, Charles S.** (1839–1914), American philosopher.
**Philo** (c. 20 B.C.–A.D. c. 50), Alexandrian Jewish philosopher.
**Plato** (c. 427–c. 347 B.C.), Greek philosopher.
**Plotinus** (c. 205–270), Egyptian Neoplatonist philosopher.
**Protagoras** (c. 480–c. 410 B.C.), Greek Sophist.
**Rapp, George** (1757–1847), German-American Harmony Society founder.
**Rousseau, Jean Jacques** (1712–78), French philosopher.
**Royce, Josiah** (1855–1916), American philosopher.
**Russell, Bertrand** (1872–1970), British philosopher and mathematician.
**Santayana, George** (1863–1952), American philosopher.
**Savonarola, Girolamo** (1452–98), Italian religious reformer.
**Schelling, Friedrich W. J. von** (1775–1854), German philosopher.
**Schopenhauer, Arthur** (1788–1860), German philosopher.
**Schweitzer, Albert** (1875–1965), Alsatian philosopher and theologian.
**Seneca** (c. 3 B.C.–A.D. 65), Roman philosopher.
**Seton, Elizabeth Ann Bayley** (1774–1821), 1st U.S.-born canonized saint.
**Shaftesbury, Anthony Ashley Cooper, 3d earl of** (1671–1713), English philosopher.
**Smith, Adam** (1723–90), Scottish economist and philosopher.
**Socrates** (469–399 B.C.), Greek philosopher.
**Spencer, Herbert** (1820–1903), English philosopher of evolution.
**Spinoza, Baruch** (1632–77), Dutch philosopher.
**Suso, Heinrich** (c. 1295–1366), German mystic.
**Suzuki, Daisetz Teitaro** (1870–1966), Japanese Buddhist scholar.
**Swedenborg, Emanuel** (1688–1772), Swedish theologian and mystic.
**Taylor, Jeremy** (1613–67), English theologian.
**Teilhard de Chardin, Pierre** (1881–1955), French Jesuit scientist-theologian.
**Thales** (c. 636–c. 546 B.C.), Greek philosopher.
**Theresa, Saint** (1515–82), Spanish mystic.
**Thomas Aquinas, Saint** (1225–74), Italian philosopher and Doctor of the Church.
**Tillich, Paul** (1886–1965), German-born American theologian.
**Tyndale, William** (c. 1494–1536), English Bible translator.
**Ussher, James** (1581–1656), Irish prelate and scholar.
**Veblen, Thorstein** (1857–1929), American economic and social philosopher.
**Vico, Giovanni B.** (1668–1744), Italian philosopher and historian.
**Watts, Isaac** (1674–1748), English clergyman and hymn writer.
**Wesley, John** (1703–91), English founder of Methodism.
**Whitehead, Alfred North** (1861–1947), English philosopher and mathematician.
**William of Occam** (d. c. 1349), English philosopher.
**Williams, Roger** (c. 1603–83), Anglo-American clergyman.
**Winebrenner, John** (1797–1860), American founder of Churches of God in North America.
**Wise, Stephen** (1874–1949), American reform rabbi and Zionist leader.
**Wittgenstein, Ludwig** (1889–1951), Austrian philosopher.
**Woodbridge, Frederick J. E.** (1867–1940), American philosopher.
**Wyclif, John** (c. 1328–84), English reformer.
**Zeno of Citium** (c. 334–c. 262 B.C.), Greek philosopher, founder of Stoicism.
**Zoroaster** (628–551 B.C.), Persian prophet.
**Zwingli, Huldreich** (1484–1531), Swiss Protestant reformer.

## NOTABLES OF MEDICINE AND PHYSIOLOGY

**Abulcasis, or Abu Khasim,** fl. 11th century, Arabian physician, author of the *Tasrif* (collection), a detailed account of surgery and medicine of his day.

**Addison, Thomas,** 1793–1860, English physician, discoverer of the malady of the suprarenal cortex, known as Addison's disease.

**Allbutt, Thomas Clifford,** 1836–1925, English physician, invented, 1866, the clinical thermometer.

**Avicenna, or Ibn Sina,** A.D. 980–1037, Arabian physician and philosopher, wrote the *Canon of Medicine,* most famous textbook of medicine until the 17th century.

**Baer, Karl Ernst von,** 1792–1876, Estonian biologist, founded, 1827–37, embryology.

**Banting, Frederick G.,** 1891–1941, Canadian physician, with Charles Best, discovered, 1921, the use of insulin in diabetic therapy.

**Barnard, Christiaan N.,** 1923– , South African surgeon, performed, 1967, first transplant of a human heart.

**Beaumont, William,** 1785–1853, American physician, first to describe, 1822, the process of digestion.

**Behring, Emil Adolf von,** 1854–1917, German bacteriologist noted for work on diphtheria antitoxin.

**Berger, Johannes (Hans),** 1873–1941, German neurologist, invented, 1929, the electroencephalograph.

**Bernard, Claude,** 1813–78, French physiologist, considered founder of experimental medicine.

**Best, Charles Herbert,** 1899–1978, Canadian physiologist, with Frederick Banting discovered, 1921, the use of insulin in diabetic therapy.

**Bichat, Marie François Xavier,** 1771–1802, French physician, founded, 1800, histology, the study of living tissues.

**Blalock, Alfred,** 1899–1964, American surgeon, with Helen B. Taussig introduced, 1944, corrective heart surgery enabling survival of "blue babies."

**Braun, Heinrich Friedrich Wilhelm,** 1862–1934, German surgeon, introduced, 1905, procaine (Novocain) into clinical use.

**Bright, Richard,** 1789–1858, English physician, first to describe, 1827, the kidney disease known as Bright's disease.

**Canano, Giovanni Battista,** 1515–79, Italian anatomist, first to describe, c. 1547, venous valves.

**Carrel, Alexis,** 1873–1944, French-American surgeon, developed methods for transplanting blood vessels; invented, with Charles A. Lindbergh, a mechanical heart.

**Cohn, Ferdinand Julius,** 1828–98, German botanist, founded, c. 1872, science of bacteriology.

**Cooley, Denton A.,** 1920– , American surgeon, pioneer in cardiovascular surgery.

**De Bakey, Michael Ellis,** 1908– , American surgeon, developed artificial heart.

**De Forest, Lee,** 1873–1961, American inventor, invented, 1907, the electrical high-frequency surgical knife.

**Dick, George F.,** 1881–1967, and **Gladys H. Dick,** isolated, 1923, the scarlet fever toxin.

**Domagk, Gerhard,** 1895–1964, German chemist, used, c. 1932, the first sulfa drug (prontosil) in therapy.

**Eberth, Karl Joseph,** 1835–1926, German pathologist, discovered, 1880, the typhoid bacillus.

**Edelman, Gerald M.,** 1929– , American biochemist, deciphered, 1969, the structure of gamma globulin.

**Ehrlich, Paul,** 1854–1915, German bacteriologist and pathologist, developed, 1897, the differential blood count; established, 1892–94, serology and immunology; established, 1909, chemotherapy.

**Eijkman, Christiaan,** 1858–1930, Dutch bacteriologist, proved, 1896, that beriberi is a deficiency disease, thus leading to discovery of the first vitamin.

**Einthoven, Willem,** 1860–1927, Dutch physiologist, invented, 1903, the electrocardiograph.

**Ermengem, Émile P. M. van,** 1851–1932, Belgian bacteriologist, discovered, 1897, the food-poisoning bacillus.

**Fabricius,Hieronymus, or Geronimo Fabrizio,** 1537–1619, Italian anatomist, discovered, 1603, venous valves.

**Fauchard, Pierre,** 1678–1761, French dentist, founder of modern dentistry; described pyorrhea.

**Finlay, Carlos Juan,** 1833–1915, Cuban physician, first to suggest mosquitoes might be carriers of yellow fever.

**Fleming, Alexander,** 1881–1955, Scottish bacteriologist, discovered, 1928, penicillin.

**Fleming, Lady Amalia,** 1909– , British bacteriologist, physician, civil libertarian.

**Flourens, Marie J. P.,** 1794–1867, French physiologist, distinguished the three main parts of the brain.

**Freud, Sigmund,** 1856–1939, Austrian psychiatrist, founded, c. 1895, psychoanalysis.

**Funk, Casimir,** 1884–1967, Polish-American biochemist, discovered, 1912, the first vitamin.

**Gaffky, Georg T. A.,** 1850–1918, German bacteriologist, proved, 1884, that *Bacillus typhosus,* discovered by Eberth, is cause of typhoid fever.

**Galen, Claudius,** c. A.D. 130–c. 200, Greco-Roman physician, systematized medical knowledge of his day; made first scientific dissections.

**Goldberger, Joseph,** 1874–1929, American public health physician, discovered, 1915, the cure for pellagra.

**Golgi, Camillo,** 1844–1926, Italian physician, established, 1870–1909, the science of neuroanatomy.

**Good, Robert,** 1922– , American pediatrician; pioneer in fields of immunology and cancer research.

**Gross, Robert E.,** 1905– , performed, 1938, first surgery for congenital heart disease.

**Hales, Stephen,** 1677–1761, English physiologist and clergyman, first to demonstrate, c. 1705, blood pressure.

**Haller, Albrecht von,** 1708–77, Swiss physiologist and anatomist, established physiology as a branch of science.

**Harvey, William,** 1578–1657, English physician, discovered, 1628, the circulation of the blood.

**Helmholtz, Hermann Ludwig Ferdinand von,** 1821–94, German physicist and physiologist, invented, 1851, the modern type of ophthalmoscope.

**Hench, Philip S.,** 1896–1965, American physician, introduced, 1949, the use of ACTH in the treatment of disease.

**Herophilus,** fl. 300 B.C., Egyptian-Greek physician and anatomist, distinguished sensory and motor nerves.

**Hippocrates of Cos,** c. B.C. 460–c. 370, Greek physician, "Father of Medicine," took medicine from the realm of superstition to that of disciplined observation.

**Holmes, Oliver Wendell,** 1809–94, American physician and author, recognized, 1843, contagious nature of puerperal fever and advocated antiseptic techniques.

**Hunter, John,** 1728–93, Scottish surgeon, raised surgery from a technical treatment mode to a branch of scientific medicine.

**Ivanovski, Dmitri Iosifovich,** 1864–1920, Russian botanist, discovered, 1892, filterable viruses, thus establishing virology.

**Janssen, Zacharias,** fl. late 16th–early 17th cent., Dutch spectacle maker, invented, c. 1590, the microscope.

**Jenner, Edward,** 1749–1823, English physician, introduced, 1796, the technique of vaccination against disease.

**Kitasato, Shibasaburo,** 1852–1931, Japanese bacteriologist, discovered, 1894, the bubonic plague bacillus.

**Klebs, Edwin T. A.,** 1834–1913, German-American bacteriologist, discovered, 1875, pneumococcus, the bacillus causative of lobar pneumonia; discovered, 1883–84, the diphtheria causative bacillus.

**Koch, Robert,** 1843–1910, German bacteriologist, set forth criteria for establishing the etiology of a disease; introduced, 1877, staining of bacteria with aniline dyes; established, 1882, the identity of the tuberculosis causative cholera.

**Laënnec, René T. H.,** 1781–1826, French physician, invented, 1816, the stethoscope.

**Landsteiner, Karl,** 1868–1943, Austrian-American pathologist, established, 1900, the basis for blood grouping; isolated, 1908, the poliomyelitis virus; discovered, 1940, the Rh factor.

**Lister, Joseph,** 1827–1912, English surgeon, introduced, 1865, antisepsis into surgical procedure.

**Löffler, Friedrich A. J.,** 1852–1915, German pathologist, discovered, 1883–84, the diphtheria causative bacillus.

**Long, Crawford Williamson,** 1815–78, American surgeon, introduced, 1842, the use of ether in surgery.

**Magnus-Levy, Adolf,** 1865–1955, German physiologist, developed, 1893, the method for measuring the basal metabolic rate.

**Malpighi, Marcello,** 1628–94, Italian anatomist, discovered, 1661, that capillaries are vein-artery junctions.

**Mesmer, Friedrich (or Franz) Anton,** c. 1733–1815, Austrian physician, introduced, c. 1778, the use of hypnotism.

**Metchnikoff, Élie,** 1845–1916, Russian biologist, introduced theory of phagocytosis, i.e., the defensive nature of blood cells.

**Minot, George Richards,** 1885–1950, American physician, discovered, 1926, the liver extract treatment for anemia.

**Morgan, Thomas Hunt,** 1886–1945, American geneticist, discovered and demonstrated, c. 1907, the role of chromosomes in heredity.

**Nitze, Max,** 1848–1906, German surgeon and urologist, constructed, 1877, first cystoscope, with the aid of an instrument maker named Leiter.

**Paracelsus (Theophrastus Bombastus von Hohenheim),** c. 1493–1541, Swiss chemist, alchemist, and physician, established, 1526, chemotherapy.

**Paré, Ambroise,** 1510 or 1517–90, French surgeon, introduced modern surgery, including the tying-off of arteries to control bleeding.

**Pasteur, Louis,** 1822–95, French chemist and bacteriologist, discovered (1880–1885) methods for inoculation and vaccination against anthrax, rabies, and chicken cholera.

**Perthes, Georg Clemens,** 1869–1927, German surgeon, noted, 1903, effects of X rays on cancerous growths.

**Piaget, Jean,** 1896–1980, Swiss psychologist, explored cognitive growth in the child.

**Plenciz, Marcus Antonius von,** 1705–1786, Viennese physician, published, 1762, the germ theory of disease.

**Pylarino, James, or Giacomo,** 1659–1715, Italian physician, inoculated, 1701, three Turkish children with smallpox exudate in first attempt at immunization.

**Reed, Walter,** 1851–1902, American surgeon, studied the etiology of yellow fever and reported, 1901, that the disease was caused by a filterable virus transmitted by the mosquito.

**Rhazes, or Rasis,** c. A.D. 860–c. 925, Persian physician, first to differentiate, c. 910, measles and smallpox.

**Roentgen, Wilhelm Conrad,** 1845–1923, German physicist, discovered, 1895, X rays.

**Roux, Pierre Paul Émile,** 1853–1933, French physician and bacteriologist, with A. E. J. Yersin, demonstrated, 1888, that the diphtheria bacillus produces a toxin.

**Rush, Benjamin,** c. 1745–1813, American physician, established, 1786, first free dispensary in U.S.

**Sabin, Albert Bruce,** 1906– , Russian-American bacteriologist, 1957, produced an oral vaccine for poliomyelitis.

**Sakel, Manfred J.**, 1900–1957, Austro-American psychiatrist, introduced, 1929, insulin shock treatment.

**Salk, Jonas Edward**, 1914– , American virologist, introduced, 1954, hypodermic vaccine for poliomyelitis.

**Sanctorius**, 1561–1636, Italian physician, described, c. 1626, the first use of the clinical thermometer in the diagnosis of disease.

**Schick, Bela**, 1877–1967, Hungarian-American pediatrician, developed, 1913, a test for determining susceptibility to diphtheria.

**Schleiden, Matthias Jakob**, 1804–1881, German botanist, founded, 1838, cytology.

**Schwann, Theodor**, 1810–1882, German anatomist, founder, 1839, of cell theory as applied to animals.

**Selye, Hans**, 1907– , Canadian endocrinologist, explored stress and disease relationship.

**Semmelweis, Ignaz P.**, 1818–65, Hungarian physician, obstetrician, independently identified, c. 1850, puerperal (childbed) fever as an infectious disease.

**Servetus, Michael**, 1511–1553, Spanish physician and theologian, described, 1546, pulmonary circulation.

**Sherrington, Charles Scott**, 1857–1952, English physiologist, established, 1906–1940, neurophysiology.

**Spallanzani, Lazzaro**, 1729–99, Italian naturalist, performed, 1768, experiments that led to the discrediting of the doctrine of spontaneous generation.

**Steptoe, Patrick C.**, 1913– , British gynecologist, performed laboratory-conceived human birth (1978).

**Swammerdam, Jan**, 1637–80, Dutch naturalist, discovered, 1658, red blood cells.

**Takamine, Jokichi**, 1854–1922, Japanese chemist working in U.S., isolated, 1901, crystalline epinephrine (adrenalin), the first hormone known in pure form.

**Taussig, Helen Brooke**, 1898– , American physician, with Alfred Blalock, introduced, 1944, corrective heart surgery enabling survival of "blue babies."

**Vesalius, Andreas**, 1514–64, Flemish anatomist, published, 1543, first anatomical text based entirely on observation.

**Virchow, Rudolf L. K.**, 1821–1902, German pathologist, founder, c. 1855, of cellular pathology.

**Waksman, Selman Abraham**, 1888–1973, Russian-American bacteriologist, discovered, 1943, streptomycin and its use in tuberculosis therapy.

**Wassermann, August von**, 1866–1925, German bacteriologist, developed, 1906, specific test for syphilis.

**Wells, Horace**, 1815–48, American dentist, first to use, 1844, nitrous oxide as an anesthetic in surgery.

**Wiley, Harvey Washington**, 1844–1930, American chemist, led fight for U.S. Pure Food Law of 1906.

**Wundt, Wilhelm Max**, 1832–1920, German psychologist, established, 1878, the first laboratory for experimental psychology, bringing mind into the realm of science.

**Yersin, Alexandre Émile John**, 1863–1943, French bacteriologist, discovered, 1888, the diphtheria toxin; discovered, 1894, *Pasteurella pestis*, the bubonic plague causative bacillus.

## NOTABLES OF ART AND ARCHITECTURE

**Aalto, Alvar** (1898–1976), Finnish architect and designer.
**Agam, Yaacov** (1928– ), Israel artist.
**Agostino di Duccio** (1418–1498), Florentine sculptor.
**Albers, Josef** (1888–1976), German-American painter.
**Alberti, Leone B.** (1404–72), Italian architect and painter.
**Alma-Tadema, Sir Lawrence** (1836–1912), English painter.
**Angelico, Fra** (c. 1400–55), Florentine painter.
**Antonello da Messina** (c. 1430–79), Italian painter.
**Apelles** (fl. 330 B.C.), Greek painter.
**Apollodorus** (fl. 430–400 B.C.), Athenian painter.
**Archipenko, Alexander** (1887–1964), Ukrainian-American sculptor.
**Arp, Jean** (1887–1966), French sculptor and painter.
**Asplund, Erik Gunnar** (1885–1940), Swedish architect.
**Audubon, John J.** (d. 1851), American artist.
**Avery, Milton** (1893–1965), American painter.
**Bacon, Francis** (1910– ), English painter.
**Baldovinetti, Alessio**, (c. 1425–99), Florentine painter.
**Barlach, Ernst** (1870–1938), German sculptor.
**Barthé, Richmond** (1901– ), American sculptor.
**Bartolomeo, Fra** (1475–1517), Italian painter.
**Baskin, Leonard** (1922– ), American sculptor.
**Baziotes, William** (1912–63), American painter.
**Bearden, Romare** (1914– ), American realistic painter.
**Beardsley, Aubrey** (1872–98), English illustrator.
**Beckmann, Max** (1884–1950), German painter.
**Bellini, Giovanni** (c. 1430–1516), Venetian painter.
**Bellows, George W.** (1882–1925), American painter.
**Benjamin, Asher** (1773–1845), American architect.
**Benton, Thomas Hart** (1889–1975), American painter.
**Berlage, Hendrik P.** (1856–1934), Dutch architect.
**Bernini, Giovanni Lorenzo** (1598–1680), Italian architect.
**Bertola, Harry** (1915–78), American sculptor and designer.
**Beuys, Joseph** (1921– ), German artist.
**Bierstadt, Albert** (1830–1902), American Western painter.
**Bingham, George Caleb** (1811–79), American genre painter.
**Boccioni, Umberto** (1882–1916), Italian futurist painter.
**Böcklin, Arnold** (1827–1901), Swiss painter.
**Bonheur, Rosa** (1822–99), French painter.
**Bonnard, Pierre** (1867–1947), French painter.
**Borromini, Francesco** (1559–1677), Italian architect.
**Bosch, Hieronymus** (c. 1450–1516), Flemish painter.
**Botero, Fernando** (1932– ), Colombian painter.
**Botticelli, Sandro** (c. 1444–1510), Florentine painter.
**Boucher, François** (1703–70), French painter.
**Boudin, Eugène L.** (1824–98), French painter.
**Bouts, Dierick** (c. 1420–75), Dutch painter.
**Brady, Mathew B.** (c. 1823–96), American photographer.
**Bramante, Donato** (1444–1514), Italian architect.
**Brancusi, Constantin** (1876–1957), Rumanian sculptor.
**Braque, Georges** (1882–1963), French painter.
**Breuer, Marcel** (1902–81), Hungarian-born American architect and designer.
**Bronzino, Il** (1503–72), Florentine mannerist painter.
**Brouwer, Adriaen** (c. 1606–38), Flemish painter.
**Breugel Pieter, the elder** (c. 1525–69), Flemish painter.
**Brunelleschi, Filippo** (1377–1446), Florentine architect.
**Bulfinch, Charles** (1763–1844), American architect.
**Burchfield, Charles E.** (1893–1967), American painter.
**Burne-Jones, Sir Edward** (1833–98), English painter.
**Calder, Alexander** (1898–1976), American sculptor.
**Canaletto** (1697–1768), Venetian painter.
**Candela, Felix** (1910– ), Mexican architect.
**Caravaggio, Michelangelo M. da** (1573–1610), Italian painter.
**Carracci, Annibale** (1560–1609), Bolognese painter.
**Carracci, Lodovico** (1555–1619), Bolognese painter.
**Cartier-Bresson, Henri** (1908– ), French photographer.
**Cassatt, Mary** (1845–1926), American painter.
**Castagno, Andrea del** (c. 1423–57), Florentine painter.
**Catlin, George** (1796–1872), American painter.
**Cellini, Benvenuto** (1500–71), Italian sculptor and metalsmith.
**Cézanne, Paul** (1839–1906), French painter.
**Chagall, Marc** (1889– ), Russian painter.
**Chardin, Jean Baptiste** (1699–1779), French painter.
**Chippendale, Thomas** (1718–79), English cabinetmaker.
**Chirico, Giorgio de** (1888–1978), Italian painter.
**Christo** (1935– ), Bulgarian-born American artist.
**Cimabue, Giovanni** (d. c. 1302), Florentine painter.
**Claude Lorrain** (1600–82), French landscape painter.
**Cole, Thomas** (1801–48), English-born American painter.
**Constable, John** (1776–1837), English painter.
**Copley, John Singleton** (1738–1815), American painter.
**Cornelius, Peter von** (1783–1867), German painter.
**Corot, Jean B. C.** (1796–1875), French landscape painter.
**Correggio, Antonio** (1494–1534), Italian painter.
**Costa, Lucio** (1902– ), Brazilian architect.
**Courbet, Gustave** (1819–77), French painter.
**Cox, Kenyon** (1856–1919), American painter and critic.
**Cranach, Lucas, the elder** (1472–1553), German painter.
**Currier, Nathaniel** (1813–88), American printmaker.
**Curry, John S.** (1897–1946), American painter.
**Dali, Salvador** (1904– ), Spanish surrealist painter.
**Daubigny, Charles F.** (1817–78), French landscape painter.
**Daumier, Honoré** (1808–79), French painter.
**David, Gerard** (c. 1460–1523), Flemish painter.
**David, Jacques L.** (1748–1825), French painter.
**Davis, Stuart** (1894–1964), American painter.
**Decamps, Alexandre G.** (1803–60), French painter.
**Degas, Edgar** (1834–1917), French painter and sculptor.
**de Kooning, Willem** (1904– ), Dutch-born American painter.
**Delacroix, Ferdinand V. E.** (1798–1863), French painter.
**Delaunay, Robert** (1885–1941), French painter.
**Della Robbia, Luca** (c. 1400–82), Florentine sculptor.
**Demuth, Charles** (1883–1935), American watercolorist.
**Derain, André** (1880–1954), French painter.
**Dine, Jim** (1935– ), American neosurrealist artist.
**Dix, Otto** (1891–1969), German painter and draughtsman.
**Doesburg, Theo van** (1883–1931), Dutch painter.

**Donatello** (c. 1386–1466), Italian sculptor.
**Dongen, Kees van** (1877–1968), Dutch painter.
**Dou, Gerard** (1613–75), Dutch painter.
**Dubuffet, Jean** (1901– ), French painter.
**Duccio di Buoninsegna** (fl. 1278–1319), Italian painter.
**Duchamp, Marcel** (1887–1968), French painter.
**Dufy, Raoul** (1877–1953), French painter and illustrator.
**Dürer, Albecht** (1471–1528), German painter and engraver.
**Eakins, Thomas** (1844–1916), American painter.
**Eiffel, Alexandre G.** (1832–1923), French engineer.
**Elisofon, Eliot** (1911–73), American photographer.
**Ensor, James** (1860–1949), Belgian painter and etcher.
**Epstein, Sir Jacob** (1880–1959), American-born English sculptor.
**Ernst, Max** (1891–1976), German painter.
**Evergood, Philip** (1901–1973), American painter.
**Eyck, Hubert van** (c. 1370–1426), Flemish painter.
**Eyck, Jan van** (c. 1390–1441), Flemish painter.
**Fabritius, Carel** (1622–54), Dutch painter.
**Feininger, Lyonel** (1871–1956), American painter and illustrator.
**Flagg, Ernest** (1857–1947), American architect.
**Flandrin, Hippolyte J.** (1809–64), French painter.
**Fouquet, Jean** (c. 1420–1480), French painter.
**Fragonard, Jean-Honoré** (1732–1806), French painter.
**Frasconi, Antonio** (1919– ), South American-born woodcut artist in U.S.
**Friesz, Othon** (1879–1949), French painter.
**Fuller, George** (1822–84), American painter.
**Fuller, (Richard) Buckminster** (1895– ), American architect and engineer.
**Fuseli, Henry** (1741–1825), Anglo-Swiss painter and draughtsman.
**Gabo, Naum** (1890–1977), Russian sculptor and architect.
**Gainsborough, Thomas** (1727–88), English painter.
**Gaudí i Cornet, Antonio** (1852–1926), Spanish architect.
**Gauguin, Paul** (1848–1903), French painter.
**Gentile da Fabriano** (c. 1370–1427), Italian painter.
**Gentileschi, Orazio** (c. 1562–1647), Tuscan painter.
**Gérard, François P. S., Baron** (1770–1837), French painter.
**Géricault, Jean Louis A. T.** (1791–1824), French painter.
**Gérôme, Jean Léon** (1824–1904), French painter.
**Ghiberti, Lorenzo** (c. 1378–1455), Florentine sculptor.
**Ghirlandaio, Domenico** (1449–94), Florentine painter.
**Giacometti, Alberto** (1901–66), Swiss sculptor and painter.
**Gilbert, Cass** (1859–1934), American architect.
**Giordano, Luca** (1632–1705), Italian painter.
**Giorgio, Francesco di** (1439–1502), Italian architect, painter, and sculptor.
**Giorgione** (c. 1478–1510), Venetian painter.
**Giotto** (c. 1266–c. 1337), Florentine painter.
**Giovanni di Paulo** (c. 1403–83), Italian painter.
**Glackens, William J.** (1870–1938), American painter.
**Gleizes, Albert L.** (1881–1953), French cubist painter.
**Goes, Hugo van der** (d. 1482), Flemish painter.
**Gogh, Vincent van** (1853–90), Dutch postimpressionist painter.
**Gorky, Arshile** (1904–48), Armenian-born American painter.
**Goya y Lucientes, Francisco José de** (1746–1828), Spanish painter and etcher.
**Goyen, Jan van** (1596–1656), Dutch landscape painter.
**Greco, El** (c. 1541–1614), Cretan painter in Spain.
**Greuze, Jean Baptiste** (1725–1805), French painter.
**Gris, Juan** (1887–1927), Spanish cubist painter.
**Grooms, Red** (1937– ), American painter.
**Gropius, Walter** (1883–1969), German-American architect.
**Gropper, Wiliam** (1897–1977), American painter and cartoonist.
**Grosz, George** (1893–1959), German-American caricaturist and painter.
**Grunewald, Mathias** (c. 1475–1528), German painter.
**Guardi, Francesco** (1712–93), Venetian painter.
**Guston, Philip** (1913–1980), Canadian-born American painter.
**Hals, Franz** (c. 1580–1666), Dutch portrait painter.
**Hartley, Marsden** (1877–1943), American painter.
**Harunobu, Suzuki** (1725–70), Japanese color-print artist.
**Hassam, Childe** (1859–1935), American painter and etcher.
**Hennebique, François** (1842–1921), French architect.
**Henri, Robert** (1865–1929), American painter.
**Hicks, Edward** (1780–1849), American painter.
**Hilliard, Nicholas** (1537–1619), English miniaturist.
**Hobbema, Meindert** (1638–1709), Dutch landscape painter.
**Hockney, David** (1937– ), English painter.
**Hodler, Ferdinand** (1853–1918), Swiss painter.
**Hofmann, Hans** (1880–1966), German-American painter.
**Hogarth, William** (1697–1764), English painter, satirist, and engraver.
**Hokusai, Katsushika** (1760–1849), Japanese wood engraver.
**Holbein, Hans, the younger** (c. 1497–1543), German-Swiss painter.
**Homer, Winslow** (1836–1910), American painter.
**Hooch, Pieter de** (c. 1629–after 1677), Dutch painter.
**Hopper, Edward** (1882–1967), American painter.
**Houdon, Jean A.** (1741–1828), French neoclassic sculptor.
**Indiana, Robert** (1928– ), American pop artist.
**Ingrès, Jean A. D.** (1780–1867), French painter.
**Inman, Henry** (1801–46), American painter.
**Inness, George** (1825–1894), American landscape painter.
**Ives, James Merritt** (1824–95), American printmaker.
**Jackson, William H.** (1843–1942), American artist and pioneer photographer.
**Jacobsen, Arne** (1902–1971), Danish architect.
**Jenney, William Le Baron** (1832–1907), American architect.
**John, Augustus Edwin** (1879–1961), British painter.
**Johns, Jasper** (1930– ), American pop artist.
**Johnson, Philip C.** (1906– ), American architect.
**Jones, Inigo** (1573–1652), English architect.
**Jordaens, Jacob** (1593–1678), Flemish baroque painter.
**Kandinsky, Wassily** (1866–1944), Russian abstract painter.
**Kano Motonobu** (c. 1476–1559), Japanese artist.
**Kaufmann, Angelica** (1741–1807), Swiss painter and etcher.
**Kepes, György** (1906– ), Hungarian-born artist.
**Kirchner, Ernst L.** (1880–1938), German painter and graphic artist.
**Kiyonaga** (1752–1815), Japanese woodcut designer.
**Klee, Paul** (1879–1940), Swiss painter and graphic artist.
**Klimt, Gustav** (1862–1918), Austrian painter.
**Kokoschka, Oskar** (1886–1980), Austrian expressionist painter.
**Kollwitz, Käthe S.** (1867–1945), German graphic artist and sculptor.
**Kuhn, Walt** (1880–1949), American painter.
**Kuniyoshi, Yasuo** (c. 1892–1953), Japanese-born American painter.
**Kupka, Frank** (1871–1957), Czech painter and illustrator.
**Lachaise, Gaston** (1882–1935), French-born American sculptor.
**La Farge, John** (1835–1910), American painter.
**Lancret, Nicolas** (1690–1743), French rococo painter.
**Landseer, Sir Edwin H.** (1802–73), English animal painter.
**La Tour, Georges de** (1593–1652), French painter.
**Lawrence, Jacob** (1917– ), American painter.
**Lawrence, Sir Thomas** (1769–1830), English portrait painter.
**Le Corbusier** (1887–1965), Swiss-born French architect.
**Ledoux, Claude N.** (1736–1806), French architect.
**Léger, Fernand** (1881–1955), French painter.
**Lehmbruck, Wilhelm** (1881–1919), German sculptor.
**L'Enfant, Pierre C.** (1754–1825), French-American architect and engineer.
**Leonardo da Vinci** (1452–1519), Italian painter, sculptor, and architect.
**Lescaze, William** (1896–1969), Swiss-born American architect.
**Leutze, Emanuel** (1816–68), German-American painter.
**Levine, Jack** (1915– ), American painter.
**Lichtenstein, Roy** (1923– ), American pop artist.
**Lipchitz, Jacques** (1891–1973), Lithuanian-born French sculptor.
**Lippi, Fra Filippo** (c. 1406–69), Italian painter.
**Lippo, Filippino** (c. 1457–1504), Italian painter.
**Lippold, Richard** (1915– ), American sculptor and engineer.
**Lochner, Stephan** (d. 1451), German religious painter.
**Lombardo, Pietro** (c. 1435–1515), Venetian architect.
**Lorenzetti, Ambrogio** (d. c. 1348), Sienese painter.
**Lucas van Leyden** (1494–1533), Dutch painter and engraver.
**Luini, Bernardino** (c. 1480–1532), Italian painter.
**Luks, George B.** (1867–1933), American painter.
**Lysippus** (4th cent. B.C.), Greek sculptor.
**Mabuse, Jan de** (c. 1478–c. 1533), Flemish painter.
**Macke, August** (1887–1914), German painter.
**McKim, Charles F.** (1847–1909), American architect.
**Magritte, René** (1898–1967), Belgian surrealist painter.
**Maillol, Aristide** (1861–1944), French sculptor and painter.
**Manet, Edouard** (1832–83), French painter.
**Mansart, François** (1598–1666), French architect.
**Mansart, Jules H.** (1646–1708), French architect.
**Mantegna, Andrea** (1431–1506), Italian painter of the Paduan school.
**Marc, Franz** (1880–1916), German painter.
**Marisol** (1930– ), Venezuelan-American sculptor.

**Marsh, Reginald** (1898–1954), French-born American painter.
**Martini, Simone** (c. 1283–1344), Sienese painter.
**Masaccio** (1401–c. 1428), Florentine painter.
**Massys, Quentin** (c. 1466–1530), Flemish painter.
**Matisse, Henri** (1869–1954), French painter and sculptor.
**Maurer, Alfred H.** (1868–1932), American painter.
**Meissonier, Jean L. E.** (1815–91), French military painter.
**Memling, Hans** (c. 1430–94), German-born Flemish painter.
**Mendelsohn, Eric** (1887–1953), German architect.
**Mestrovic, Ivan** (1883–1962), Yugoslav sculptor.
**Michelangelo Buonarroti** (1475–1564), Italian sculptor, painter, and architect.
**Miës van der Rohe, Ludwig** (1886–1969), German-American architect.
**Millais, Sir John E.** (1829–96), English painter.
**Millet, Jean F.** (1814–75), French painter.
**Miró, Joan** (1893– ), Spanish surrealist painter.
**Modigliani, Amadeo** (1884–1920), Italian painter.
**Mondrian, Piet** (1872–1944), Dutch painter.
**Monet, Claude** (1840–1926), French impressionist painter.
**Moore, Henry** (1898– ), English sculptor.
**Moreau, Gustave** (1826–98), French painter.
**Morisot, Berthe** (1841–95), French impressionist painter.
**Moronobu, Hishikawa** (c. 1618–c. 1694), Japanese painter.
**Morris, William** (1834–96), English artist, printer, and poet.
**Morse, Samuel F. B.** (1791–1872), American artist and inventor.
**Moses, Grandma (Anna Mary R. Moses)** (1860–1961), American primitive painter.
**Motherwell, Robert** (1915– ), American painter.
**Munch, Edvard** (1863–1944), Norwegian painter.
**Murillo, Bartholomé E.** (c. 1617–82), Spanish painter.
**Muybridge, Eadweard** (1830–1904), English photographer.
**Myron** (5th cent. B.C.), Greek sculptor.
**Nash, John** (1752–1835), English architect.
**Nash, Paul** (1889–1946), English painter and wood engraver.
**Neel, Alice** (1900– ), American painter.
**Nervi, Pier Luigi** (1891–1979), Italian architect.
**Neutra, Richard** (1892–1970), American architect.
**Nevelson, Louise** (1900– ), Russian-born American sculptor.
**Nicholson, Ben** (1894–1982), English abstract painter.
**Niemeyer, Oscar** (1907– ), Brazilian architect.
**Noguchi, Isamu** (1904– ), American sculptor.
**Noland, Kenneth** (1924– ), American color-field painter.
**Nolde, Emil** (1867–1956), German expressionist painter.
**O'Keeffe, Georgia** (1887– ), American painter.
**Oldenburg, Claes** (1929– ), Swedish-born American pop artist.
**Olmsted, Frederick L.** (1822–1903), American landscape architect.
**Orley, Bernard van** (c. 1491–1542), Flemish painter.
**Orozco, José C.** (1883–1949), Mexican mural painter.
**Ostade, Adriaen van** (1610–85), Dutch genre painter.
**Palladio, Andrea** (1508–80), Italian architect.
**Parks, Gordon** (1912– ), American photographer.
**Parmigiano** (1503–40), Italian mannerist painter.
**Parrhasius** (fl. c. 400 B.C.), Greek painter.
**Parrish, Maxfield** (1870–1966), American illustrator.
**Patinir, Joachim de** (d. 1524), Flemish landscape and religious painter.
**Paxton, Sir Joseph** (1803–65), English architect.
**Peale, Charles Willson** (1741–1827), American painter.
**Peale, James** (1749–1831), American portrait painter.
**Peale, Raphaelle** (1774–1825), American portrait painter.
**Peale, Rembrandt** (1778–1860), American portrait painter.
**Pearlstein, Philip** (1924– ), American realist painter.
**Pechstein, Max** (1881–1955), German expressionist painter.
**Pei, I(eoh) M(ing)** (1917– ), Chinese-born American architect.
**Perrault, Claude** (1613–88), French architect.
**Perugino** (c. 1445–c. 1523), Umbrian painter.
**Pevsner, Antoine** (1886–1962), Russian sculptor and painter.
**Phidias** (c. 500–c. 432 B.C.), Greek sculptor.
**Phyfe, Duncan** (c. 1768–1854), Scottish-born cabinetmaker.
**Picasso, Pablo** (1881–1973), Spanish painter and sculptor in France.
**Piero della Francesca** (c. 1420–92), Italian painter.
**Piero di Cosimo** (1462–1521), Florentine painter.
**Pinturicchio** (c. 1454–1513), Umbrian painter.
**Piranesi, Giovanni B.** (1720–78), Italian architect.
**Pisanello** (c. 1395–c. 1455), Italian medalist and painter.
**Pisano, Andrea** (c. 1290–c. 1348), Italian sculptor.
**Pisano, Giovanni** (c. 1250–after 1314), Italian architect.
**Pisano, Nicola** (c. 1220–between 1278 and 1287), Italian sculptor.
**Pissarro, Camille** (1830–1903), French impressionist painter.
**Pollaiuolo, Antonio** (c. 1429–98), Florentine goldsmith, painter, sculptor, and engraver.
**Pollock, Jackson** (1912–56), American painter.
**Polyclitus the elder** (fl. c. 450–c. 420 B.C.), Greek sculptor.
**Polygnotus** (fl. c. 460–447 B.C.), Greek painter.
**Poussin, Nicolas** (1594–1665), French painter.
**Praxiteles** (fl. c. 370–c. 330 B.C.), Greek sculptor.
**Prendergast, Maurice B.** (1859–1924), American painter.
**Primaticcio, Francesco** (1504–70), Italian painter.
**Prud'hon, Pierre Paul** (1758–1823), French painter.
**Puvis de Chavannes, Pierre** (1824–98), French mural painter.
**Pyle, Howard** (1853–1911), American painter, illustrator.
**Quercia, Jacopo della** (c. 1374–1438), Italian sculptor.
**Raeburn, Sir Henry** (1756–1823), Scottish portrait painter.
**Raphael Santi** (1483–1520), Italian Renaissançe painter.
**Rauschenberg, Robert** (1925– ), American pop artist.
**Ray, Man** (1890–1976), American painter and photographer.
**Redon, Odilon** (1840–1916), French painter.
**Reinhardt, Ad** (1913–67), American painter.
**Rembrandt Harmenszoon van Rijn** (1606–69), Dutch painter and etcher.
**Remington, Frederic** (1861–1909), American painter and sculptor.
**Renoir, Pierre A.** (1841–1919), French impressionist painter.
**Reynolds, Sir Joshua** (1723–92), English portrait painter.
**Ribera, Jusepe** (c. 1590–1652), Spanish baroque painter.
**Riley, Bridget** (1931– ), English painter.
**Rivera, Diego** (1886–1957), Mexican muralist.
**Rivers, Larry** (1923– ), American pop artist.
**Rodin, Auguste** (1840–1917), French sculptor.
**Romney, George** (1734–1802), English portrait painter.
**Rosa, Salvator** (1615–73), Italian baroque painter.
**Rosenquist, James** (1933– ), American pop artist.
**Roszak, Theodore** (1907–81), American sculptor.
**Rothko, Mark** (1903–70), Russian-born American abstract expressionist painter.
**Rouault, Georges** (1871–1958), French painter.
**Rousseau, Henri** (1844–1910), French primitive painter.
**Rubens, Peter Paul** (1577–1640), Flemish painter.
**Rudolph, Paul** (1918– ), American architect.
**Ruisdael, Jacob van** (c. 1628–82), Dutch painter and etcher.
**Ryder, Albert P.** (1847–1917), American painter.
**Saarinen, Eero** (1910–61), Finnish-American architect.
**Saarinen, Eliel** (1873–1950), Finnish-American architect.
**Saint-Gaudens, Augustus** (1848–1907), Irish-born American sculptor.
**Samaras, Lucas** (1936– ), Greek collage artist.
**Sargent, John Singer** (1856–1925), American painter.
**Sarto, Andrea del** (1486–1531), Florentine painter.
**Sassetta** (c. 1400–1450), Sienese painter.
**Schongauer, Martin** (1430–1491), German engraver and painter.
**Scopas** (fl. 4th cent. B.C.), Greek sculptor.
**Scorel, Jan van** (1495–1562), Dutch painter.
**Segal, George** (1924– ), American sculptor.
**Seurat, Georges** (1859–91), French neoimpressionist painter.
**Shahn, Ben** (1898–1969), American painter and graphic artist.
**Signac, Paul** (1863–1935), French neoimpressionist painter.
**Signorelli, Luca** (c. 1441–1523), Italian painter of the Umbrian school.
**Siqueiros, David A.** (1898–1974), Mexican muralist.
**Sisley, Alfred** (1839–99), French landscape painter.
**Sloan, John** (1871–1951), American painter and etcher.
**Sloane, Eric** (1910– ), American landscape painter.
**Sluter, Claus** (d. 1406), Flemish sculptor.
**Smith, David** (1906–65), American sculptor.
**Soleri, Paolo** (1919– ), Italian architect.
**Soutine, Chaim** (1894–1943), Russian-born French painter.
**Steen, Jan** (1626–79), Dutch genre painter.
**Steichen, Edward** (1879–1973), Luxembourg-born American photographer.
**Stella, Joseph** (1877–1946), Italian-born American painter.
**Stieglitz, Alfred** (1864–1946), American photographer.
**Still, Clyfford** (1904–80), American painter.
**Stone, Edward Durell** (1902–78), American architect.
**Stoss, Veit** (c. 1445–1533), German sculptor.
**Stuart, Gilbert** (1755–1828), American portrait painter.
**Stuart, James** (1713–88), English architect and painter.
**Sullivan, Louis Henry** (1856–1924), American architect.

**Sutherland, Graham** (1903–80), English painter.
**Tamayo, Rufino** (1899– ), Mexican painter.
**Tange, Kenzo** (1913– ), Japanese architect.
**Tanguy, Yves** (1900–55), French surrealist painter.
**Tchelitchew, Pavel** (1898–1957), Russian-American painter.
**Teniers, David, the younger** (1610–90), Flemish genre painter.
**Ter Borch, Gerard** (1617–81), Dutch painter.
**Terbrugghen, Hendrick** (1588–1629), Dutch painter.
**Thoma, Hans** (1839–1924), German painter and lithographer.
**Thorvaldsen, Albert B.** (1770–1844), Danish sculptor.
**Tiepolo, Giovanni B.** (1696–1770), Venetian painter.
**Tiffany, Louis C.** (1848–1933), American artist and decorative designer.
**Tinguely, Jean** (1925– ), Swiss sculptor.
**Tintoretto** (1518–94), Venetian painter.
**Titian** (c. 1490–1576), Venetian painter.
**Toulouse-Lautrec, Henri de** (1864–1901), French painter and lithographer.
**Trumbull, John** (1756–1843), American painter.
**Tura, Cosmé** (c. 1430–95), Italian painter.
**Turner, Joseph M. W.** (1775–1851), English landscape painter.
**Uccello, Paolo** (c. 1396–1475), Florentine painter.
**Utamaro, Kitagawa** (1753–1806), Japanese color-print artist.
**Utrillo, Maurice** (1883–1955), French painter.
**Utzon, Joern** (1918– ), Danish architect.
**Van Dyck, Sir Anthony** (1599–1641), Flemish portrait painter.
**Vasari, Giorgio** (1511–74), Italian architect, painter, and writer.
**Vaux, Calvert** (1824–95), English-born American landscape architect.
**Velázquez, Diego R. de S. y** (1599–1660), Spanish painter.
**Velde, Henri van de** (1863–1957), Belgian designer and architect.
**Vermeer, Jan** (1632–75), Dutch genre and landscape painter.
**Veronese, Paolo** (1528–88), Italian painter.
**Verrocchio, Andrea del** (1435–88), Florentine sculptor.
**Vigée-Lebrun, Elisabeth** (1755–1842), French painter.
**Vignola, Giacomo da** (1507–73), Italian architect.
**Viollet-le-Duc, Eugène E.** (1814–79), French architect.
**Vlaminck, Maurice de** (1876–1958), French painter.
**Vos, Cornelis de** (1584–1651), Flemish painter.
**Vuillard, Edouard** (1868–1940), French painter.
**Warhol, Andy** (1927?– ), American pop artist.
**Watteau, Antoine** (1684–1721), French painter.
**Wedgwood, Josiah** (1730–95), English potter.
**Wesselmann, Tom** (1931– ), American pop artist.
**West, Benjamin** (1738–1820), American historical painter.
**Westermann, H. C.** (1923–81), American pop sculptor.
**Weyden, Roger van der** (c. 1400–64), Flemish painter.
**Whistler, James A. McN.** (1834–1903), American painter and etcher.
**White, Stanford** (c. 1853–1906), American architect.
**Witz, Conrad** (fl. c. 1434–c. 1447), German painter.
**Wood, Grant** (1891–1942), American painter.
**Wren, Sir Christopher** (1632–1723), English architect.
**Wright, Frank Lloyd** (1869–1959), American architect.
**Wyeth, Andrew N.** (1917– ), American painter.
**Wyeth, Newell Convers** (1882–1945), American painter and illustrator.
**Zorach, William** (1887–1966), Lithuanian-born American sculptor.

## NOVELISTS, DRAMATISTS, POETS, AND OTHER WRITERS

**Adams, Henry** (1838–1918), American biographer, historian, and novelist.
**Addison, Joseph** (1672–1719), English essayist and poet.
**Aeschylus** (525–456 B.C.), Athenian tragedian.
**Aesop** (c. 620–c. 560 B.C.), Greek fabulist.
**Agee, James** (1909–55), American essayist and journalist.
**Agnon (b. Czaczkes), Shmuel Y.** (1888–1970), Polish-born Israeli novelist.
**Aiken, Conrad** (1889–1973), American novelist and poet.
**Alarcón, Pedro Antonio de** (1833–91), Spanish novelist.
**Albee, Edward** (1928– ), American dramatist.
**Alcott, Louisa May** (1832–88), American novelist.
**Aldington, Richard** (1892–1962), English poet and novelist.
**Aleichem, Sholom (Solomon Rabinowitz)** (1859–1916), Russian-born Yiddish writer.
**Algren, Nelson** (1909–81), American novelist.
**Amado, Jorge** (1912– ), Brazilian novelist.
**Ambler, Eric** (1909– ), English suspense novelist.
**Amis, Kingsley** (1922– ), English novelist.
**Andersen, Hans Christian** (1805–75), Danish poet and fairy tale writer.
**Anderson, Maxwell** (1888–1959), American dramatist.
**Anderson, Robert** (1917– ), American dramatist.
**Anderson, Sherwood** (1876–1941), American novelist.
**Andreyev, Leonid** (1871–1919), Russian writer.
**Andric, Ivo** (1892–1975), Yugoslav novelist.
**Angelou, Maya** (1928– ), American writer.
**Anouilh, Jean** (1910– ), French dramatist.
**Apollinaire, Guillaume** (1880–1918), French poet.
**Apuleius, Lucius** (fl. 2d cent. A.D.), Latin romance writer.
**Aragon, Louis** (1897– ), French novelist and poet.
**Arden, John** (1930– ), English dramatist.
**Ariosto, Ludovico** (1474–1533), Italian epic and lyric poet.
**Aristophanes** (c. 448–after 388 B.C.), Athenian comic poet.
**Arnold, Matthew** (1822–88), English poet and critic.
**Arrabel (Terán), Fernando** (1932– ), Spanish dramatist.
**Asch, Sholem** (1880–1957), Polish-born Yiddish novelist.
**Auchincloss, Louis** (1917– ), American novelist.
**Auden, W(ystan) H(ugh)** (1907–73), Anglo-American poet.
**Austen, Jane** (1775–1817), English novelist.
**Ayckbourn, Alan** (1939– ), English playwright.
**Azuela, Mariano** (1873–1952), Mexican novelist.
**Bacon, Francis** (1561–1626), English essayist.
**Bagnold, Enid** (1889-1981), English dramatist and novelist.
**Baldwin, James** (1924– ), American novelist and essayist.
**Balzac, Honoré de** (1799–1850), French novelist.
**Barrie, Sir James M.** (1860–1937), British playwright.
**Barth, John** (1930– ), American novelist.
**Baudelaire, Charles** (1821–67), French poet and critic.
**Beaumarchais, Pierre A. C. de** (1732–99), French dramatist.
**Beaumont, Francis** (c. 1584–1616), English dramatist.
**Beauvoir, Simone de** (1908– ), French novelist and essayist.
**Beckett, Samuel** (1906– ), Irish-French dramatist.
**Bede** (c. 673–735 A.D.), Old English historian.
**Beerbohm, Sir Max** (1872–1956), English parodist.
**Behan, Brendan** (1923–64), Irish dramatist.
**Behn, Aphra** (1640–89), English novelist and dramatist.
**Behrman, S. N.** (1893–1973), American playwright.
**Belloc, Hilaire** (1870–1953), British poet, essayist, satirist, and historian.
**Bellow, Saul** (1915– ), Canadian-American novelist.
**Benchley, Robert** (1889–1945), American humorist.
**Benét, Stephen Vincent** (1898–1943), American poet, novelist, and short story writer.
**Bennett, Arnold** (1867–1931), English novelist.
**Bernstein, Carl** (1944– ), American journalist and author.
**Berryman, John** (1914–72), American poet.
**Betjeman, John** (1906– ), English poet.
**Betti, Ugo** (1892–1953), Italian poet and dramatist.
**Bierce, Ambrose** (1842–1914?), American short story writer and journalist.
**Bishop, Elizabeth** (1911–79), American poet.
**Bjornson, Bjornstjerne** (1832–1910), Norwegian novelist.
**Blackmur, R(ichard) P.** (1904–65), American critic and poet.
**Blake, William** (1757–1827), English poet.
**Blasco-Ibáñez, Vicente** (1867–1928), Spanish novelist.
**Boccaccio, Giovanni** (1313–75), Italian poet and storyteller.
**Bodenheim, Maxwell** (1893–1954), American poet.
**Bogan, Louise** (1897–1970), American poet.
**Boileau-Despréaux, Nicolas** (1636–1711), French literary critic and poet.
**Böll, Heinrich** (1917– ), German novelist.
**Bolt, Robert** (1924– ), English dramatist.
**Borges, Jorge Luis** (1899– ), Argentine poet.
**Boswell, James** (1740–95), Scottish biographer and diarist.
**Bowen, Elizabeth** (1899–1973), Anglo-Irish novelist.
**Bowles, Paul** (1910– ), American novelist.
**Boyle, Kay** (1903– ), American novelist.
**Bradbury, Ray** (1920– ), American science fiction writer.
**Braine, John** (1922– ), English novelist.
**Brecht, Bertolt** (1898–1956), German dramatist and poet.
**Breton, André** (1896–1966), French surrealistic writer.
**Bridges, Robert** (1844–1930), English poet.
**Brontë, Charlotte** (1816–55), English novelist.
**Brontë, Emily** (1818–48), English novelist.
**Brooke, Rupert** (1887–1915), English poet.
**Brooks, Van Wyck** (1886–1963), American critic.

**Brophy, Brigid** (1929– ), English novelist and critic.
**Brown, John Mason** (1900–69), American critic and biographer.
**Browne, Sir Thomas** (1605–82), English author and physician.
**Browning, Elizabeth Barrett** (1806–61), English poet.
**Browning, Robert** (1812–89), English poet.
**Bryant, William Cullen** (1794–1878), American poet.
**Buchan, John** (1875–1940), British novelist and historian.
**Bullins, Ed** (1935– ), American dramatist.
**Bunin, Ivan** (1870–1953), Russian novelist.
**Bunyan, John** (1628–88), English allegorist.
**Burgess, Anthony** (1917– ), English novelist and critic.
**Burns, Robert** (1759–96), Scottish poet.
**Burroughs, Edgar Rice** (1875–1950), American novelist.
**Burroughs, William** (1914– ), American novelist.
**Butler, Samuel** (1835–1902), English novelist and essayist.
**Byron, Lord (George Gordon)** (1788–1824), English poet.
**Cabell, James Branch** (1879–1958), American novelist.
**Caedmon** (fl. 670 A.D.), Old English poet.
**Calderón de la Barca, Pedro** (1600–81), Spanish dramatist.
**Calisher, Hortense** (1911– ), American novelist.
**Callimachus** (fl. c. 265 B.C.), Greek poet and critic.
**Camoes, Luis de** (1524?–80), Portuguese poet.
**Camus, Albert** (1913–60), French essayist, novelist, and dramatist.
**Capek, Karel** (1890–1938), Czech playwright.
**Capote, Truman** (1924– ), American novelist.
**Carew, Thomas** (c. 1595–c. 1639), English poet.
**Carlino, Lewis John** (1932– ), American dramatist.
**Carlyle, Thomas** (1795–1881), Anglo-Scottish essayist, critic, translator, and historian.
**Carroll, Lewis (Charles Lutwidge Dodgson)** (1832–98), English novelist.
**Cary, Joyce** (1888–1957), English novelist.
**Cassill, R(onald) V(erlin)** (1919– ), American novelist, short story writer, and essayist.
**Castiglione, Baldassare** (1478–1529), Italian social critic.
**Cather, Willa** (1876–1947), American novelist.
**Catton, Bruce** (1899–1978), American historian.
**Catullus, Caius Valerius** (c. 84 B.C.–c. 54 B.C.), Roman poet.
**Céline, Louis Ferdinand** (1894–1961), French novelist.
**Cervantes Saavedra, Miguel de** (1547–1616), Spanish novelist.
**Chandler, Raymond** (1888–1959), American detective story writer.
**Chateaubriand, François R.** (1768–1848), French novelist.
**Chaucer, Geoffrey** (c. 1340–1400), English poet.
**Chayefsky, Paddy** (1923–81), American dramatist.
**Cheever, John** (1912–82), American novelist and short story writer.
**Chekhov, Anton** (1860–1904), Russian dramatist.
**Chesterton, G(ilbert) K(eith)** (1874–1936), English novelist, poet, biographer, and essayist.
**Christie, Agatha** (1891–1976), English mystery writer.
**Ciardi, John** (1916– ), American poet and critic.
**Cicero, Marcus Tullius** (106–43 B.C.), Roman essayist.
**Claudel, Paul** (1868–1955), French poet and dramatist.
**Cocteau, Jean** (1889?–1963). French novelist and filmmaker.
**Coleridge, Samuel Taylor** (1772–1834), English poet.
**Colette (Sidonie Gabrielle Collette)** (1873–1954), French novelist.
**Collins, Wilkie** (1824–89), English novelist.
**Collins, William** (1721–59), English poet.
**Colum, Padraic** (1881–1972), Irish-American poet, dramatist, and novelist.
**Compton-Burnett, Ivy** (1892–1969), English novelist.
**Congreve, William** (1670–1729), English dramatist.
**Connolly, Cyril** (1903–74), English critic and editor.
**Conrad, Joseph** (1857–1924), Polish-born English novelist.
**Cooper, James Fenimore** (1789–1851), American novelist.
**Corneille, Pierre** (1606–84), French dramatist.
**Coward, Sir Noël** (1899–1973), English dramatist, composer, lyricist, and autobiographer.
**Cowley, Abraham** (1618–67), English poet.
**Cowper, William** (1731–1800), English poet.
**Cozzens, James Gould** (1903–78), American novelist.
**Crabbe, George** (1754–1832), English poet.
**Crane, Hart** (1899–1932), American poet.
**Crane, Stephen** (1871–1900), American novelist.
**Crashaw, Richard** (c. 1612–49), English poet.
**cummings, e. e.** (1894–1962), American poet.
**Cunha, Euclides da** (1866–1909), Brazilian writer.
**Cynewulf** (fl. c. early 9th cent.), Old English poet.
**D'Annunzio, Gabriele** (1863–1938), Italian poet.
**Dante (Alighieri)** (1265–1321), Italian poet.
**Daudet, Alphonse** (1840–97), French novelist, poet, and short story writer.
**Day Lewis, C(ecil)** (1904–72), Anglo-Irish poet.
**Defoe, Daniel** (c. 1660–1731), English novelist.
**Delaney, Shelagh** (1939– ), English dramatist.
**De la Mare, Walter** (1873–1956), English novelist and poet.
**De la Roche, Mazo** (1885–1961), Canadian novelist.
**Demosthenes** (c. 384–322 B.C.), Greek orator.
**De Quincey, Thomas** (1785–1859), English essayist.
**De Vries, Peter** (1910– ), American novelist.
**Dickens, Charles** (1812–70), English novelist.
**Dickey, James** (1923– ), American poet and critic.
**Dickinson, Emily** (1830–86), American poet.
**Diderot, Denis** (1713–84), French encyclopedist, novelist, dramatist, satirist, and critic.
**Didion, Joan** (1934– ), American novelist.
**Dinesen, Isak (Karen Blixen)** (1885–1962), Danish writer.
**Donleavy, J(ames) P(atrick)** (1926– ), American-born, Irish novelist.
**Donne, John** (1572–1631), English poet and essayist.
**Doolittle, Hilda ("H.D.")** (1886–1961), American poet.
**Dos Passos, John** (1896–1970), American novelist.
**Dostoyevsky, Feodor** (1821–81), Russian novelist.
**Doyle, Sir Arthur Conan** (1859–1930), English detective story and romance writer.
**Drabble, Margaret** (1939– ), British writer.
**Dreiser, Theodore** (1871–1945), American novelist.
**Drexler, Rosalyn** (1926– ), American dramatist.
**Dryden, John** (1631–1700), English poet and dramatist.
**Dumas, Alexandre (fils)** (1824–95), French dramatist.
**Dumas, Alexandre (père)** (1802–70), French novelist and dramatist.
**Duras, Marguerite** (1914– ), French novelist.
**Durrell, Lawrence** (1912– ), British novelist and poet.
**Durrenmatt, Friedrich** (1921– ), Swiss dramatist.
**Eberhart, Richard** (1904– ), American poet.
**Ehrenburg, Ilya** (1891–1967), Russian novelist.
**Eliot, George (Mary Ann Evans)** (1819–80), English novelist.
**Eliot, T(homas) S(tearns)** (1888–1965), American-born British poet, dramatist, and critic.
**Ellison, Ralph** (1914– ), American novelist.
**Elytis, Odysseus** (1911– ), Greek poet.
**Emerson, Ralph Waldo** (1803–82), American essayist and poet.
**Erasmus, Desiderius** (c. 1466–1536), Dutch humanist.
**Euripides** (c. 480–406 B.C.), Greek tragic poet.
**Farrell, James T.** (1904–79), American novelist.
**Faulkner, William** (1897–1962), American novelist.
**Feuchtwanger, Lion** (1884–1958), German novelist.
**Fielding, Henry** (1707–54), English novelist.
**FitzGerald, Edward** (1809–83), English translator.
**Fitzgerald, F. Scott** (1896–1940), American novelist.
**Flaubert, Gustave** (1821–80), French novelist.
**Fleming, Ian** (1908–64), English secret agent novelist.
**Fletcher, John** (1579–1625), English dramatist.
**Ford, Ford Madox (Ford Madox Hueffer)** (1873–1939), English poet, novelist, critic, and essayist.
**Ford, John** (1586–c. 1640), English dramatist.
**Forster, E(dward) M(organ)** (1879–1970), English novelist.
**Foster, Paul** (1931– ), American dramatist.
**France, Anatole (Jacques Anatole Thibault)** (1844–1924), French novelist and satirist.
**Friedman, Bruce Jay** (1930– ), American novelist.
**Friel, Brian** (1929– ), Irish dramatist.
**Frisch, Max** (1911– ), Swiss dramatist.
**Froissart, Jean** (c. 1337–1410?), French chronicler.
**Frost, Robert** (1874–1963), American poet.
**Fry, Christopher** (1907– ), English dramatist.
**Fuentes, Carlos** (1928– ), Mexican short story writer.
**Galsworthy, John** (1867–1933), English novelist.
**Garcia Lorca, Federico** (1898–1936), Spanish poet.
**Garcià Márquez, Gabriel José** (1928– ), Colombian writer.
**Gardner, Erle Stanley** (1889–1970), American detective story writer.
**Garland, Hamlin** (1860–1940), American novelist.
**Gaskell, Elizabeth** (1810–65), English novelist and biographer.
**Gay, John** (1685–1732), English playwright and poet.
**Gelber, Jack** (1932– ), American dramatist.
**Genet, Jean** (1910– ), French novelist and dramatist.
**George, Stefan** (1868–1933), German poet.
**Ghelderode, Michel de** (1898–1962), Belgian dramatist.
**Gibbon, Edward** (1737–94), English historian.
**Gide, André** (1869–1951), French novelist.
**Gilroy, Frank D.** (1925– ), American dramatist.

**Ginsberg, Allen** (1926– ), American poet.
**Giraudoux, Jean** (1882–1944), French dramatist.
**Gissing, George** (1857–1903), English novelist.
**Glasgow, Ellen** (1873–1945), American novelist.
**Godwin, William** (1756–1836), English novelist and political philosopher.
**Goethe, Johann Wolfgang von** (1749–1832), German novelist.
**Gogol, Nikolai** (1809–52), Russian novelist.
**Golding, William** (1911– ), English novelist.
**Goldman, James** (1927– ), American dramatist.
**Goldoni, Carlo** (1707–93), Italian dramatist.
**Goldsmith, Oliver** (1730?–74), English essayist and dramatist.
**Goodman, Paul** (1911–1972), American writer and pacifist.
**Gordimer, Nadine** (1923– ), South African novelist.
**Gorey, Edward** (1925– ), American writer and artist.
**Gorki, Maxim (Aleksey Maximovich Pyeshkov)** (1868–1936), Russian novelist, dramatist, and short story writer.
**Grass, Günter** (1927– ), German novelist.
**Graves, Robert** (1895– ), English poet and novelist.
**Gray, Thomas** (1716–71), English poet.
**Greene, Graham** (1904– ), English novelist.
**Gregory, Lady Augusta** (1859–1932), Irish dramatist.
**Grimm, Jakob** (1785–1863), German folklorist.
**Grimm, Wilhelm** (1786–1859), German folklorist.
**Hafiz (Shams-ud-Din-Mohammed)** (d. 1389?), Persian poet.
**Haley, Alex** (1921– ), American historian.
**Hammett, Dashiell** (1894–1961), American novelist.
**Hamsun, Knut** (1859–1952), Norwegian novelist.
**Hansberry, Lorraine** (1930–65), American dramatist.
**Hardy, Thomas** (1840–1928), English novelist.
**Harris, Joel Chandler** (1848–1908), American short story writer.
**Harte, Bret** (1836–1902), American short story writer.
**Hauptmann, Gerhart** (1862–1946), German dramatist, novelist, and poet.
**Hawthorne, Nathaniel** (1804–64), American novelist.
**Hazlitt, William** (1778–1830), English essayist.
**Hecht, Ben** (1894–1964), American writer.
**Heine, Heinrich** (1797–1856), German poet.
**Heller, Joseph** (1923– ), American novelist.
**Hellman, Lillian** (1905– ), American dramatist and author.
**Hemingway, Ernest** (1899–1961), American novelist.
**Henry, O. (William Sydney Porter)** (1862–1910), American short story writer.
**Herbert, George** (1593–1633), English poet.
**Herder, Johann G. von** (1744–1803), German poet.
**Herodotus** (c. 484–c. 425 B.C.), Greek historian.
**Herrick, Robert** (1591–1674), English poet.
**Hersey, John** (1914– ), American novelist and journalist.
**Hesiod** (fl. c. 8th cent. B.C.), Greek poet.
**Hesse, Hermann** (1877–1962), German novelist.
**Heyward, DuBose** (1885–1940), American novelist.
**Heywood, Thomas** (1574?–1641), English dramatist.
**Hochhuth, Rolf** (1931– ), German dramatist.
**Hoffmann, E(rnst) T(heodor) A(madeus)** (1776–1822), German novelist and short story writer.
**Hölderlin, Johann C. F.** (1770–1843), German poet.
**Homer** (before 700 B.C.), Greek epic poet.
**Hopkins, Gerard Manley** (1844–89), English poet.
**Horace** (65 B.C.–8 B.C.), Latin poet.
**Horovitz, Israel** (1939– ), American dramatist.
**Housman, A. E.** (1859–1936), English poet.
**Howard, Sidney** (1891–1939), American dramatist.
**Howe, Irving** (1920– ), American historian and critic.
**Howells, William Dean** (1837–1920), American novelist.
**Hughes, Langston** (1902–67), American poet.
**Hugo, Victor** (1802–85), French novelist.
**Huxley, Aldous** (1894–1963), English novelist and essayist.
**Huxtable, Ada Louise** (1921– ), American journalist and architecture critic.
**Ibsen, Henrik** (1828–1906), Norwegian dramatist.
**Inge, William** (1913–73), American dramatist.
**Ionesco, Eugène** (1912– ), French dramatist.
**Irving, John** (1942– ), American novelist.
**Irving, Washington** (1783–1859), American short story writer, historian, and biographer.
**Isherwood, Christopher** (1904– ), Anglo-American novelist and dramatist.
**Jackson, Shirley** (1919–65), American novelist.
**James, Henry** (1843–1916), American novelist.
**James, P(hyllis) D(orothy)** (1920– ), English mystery writer.
**Jarrell, Randall** (1914–65), American poet and novelist.
**Jeffers, Robinson** (1887–1962), American poet.
**Jellicoe, Ann** (1927– ), English dramatist and director.
**Jewett, Sarah Orne** (1849–1909), American novelist.
**Johnson, Samuel** (1709–84), English critic, essayist, lexicographer, poet, and biographer.
**Jones, James** (1921–77), American novelist.
**Jones, LeRoi (Imamu Baraka)** (1934– ), American dramatist.
**Jonson, Ben** (1572–1637), English dramatist and poet.
**Joyce, James** (1882–1941), Irish novelist.
**Juvenal** (1st–2d cent. A.D.), Roman satirical poet.
**Kafka, Franz** (1883–1924), German novelist.
**Kawabata, Yasunari** (1899–1972) Japanese novelist.
**Kazantzakis, Nikos** (c. 1883–1957), Greek novelist.
**Keats, John** (1795–1821), English poet.
**Keller, Gottfried** (1819–90), Swiss novelist.
**Kempton, J. Murray** (1918– ), American journalist.
**Kennedy, Adrienne** (1932– ), American dramatist.
**Kerouac, Jack** (1922–69), American novelist.
**Kesey, Ken** (1935– ), American novelist.
**Kingsley, Charles** (1819–75), English novelist.
**Kingsley, Sidney** (1906– ), American playwright.
**Kipling, Rudyard** (1865–1936), British poet and novelist.
**Kleist, Heinrich von** (1777–1811), German dramatic poet.
**Knowles, John** (1926– ), American novelist.
**Koestler, Arthur** (1905– ), Hungarian-born English novelist and essayist.
**Kopit, Arthur** (1937– ), American dramatist.
**Kyd, Thomas** (1558–94), English dramatist.
**La Fontaine, Jean de** (1621–95), French fabulist and poet.
**Lagerkvist, Pär** (1891–1974), Swedish novelist.
**Lagerlof, Selma** (1858–1940), Swedish novelist.
**Lamartine, Alphonse** (1790–1869), French poet.
**Lamb, Charles** (1775–1834), English essayist.
**Langland, William** (c. 1332–c. 1440), English poet.
**Lanier, Sidney** (1842–81), American poet.
**Lardner, Ring** (1885–1933), American short story writer.
**La Rochefoucauld, François, duc de** (1613–80), French classical writer, maximist, and epigrammatist.
**Lash, Joseph** (1909– ), American biographer.
**Lawrence, D(avid) H(erbert)** (1885–1930), English novelist.
**Laxness, Halldor** (1902– ), Icelandic novelist.
**Lear, Edward** (1812–88), English humorist.
**Leavis, F(rank) R(aymond)** (1895–1978), English critic.
**Le Carré, John (David J. M. Carnwell)** (1931– ), English spy novelist.
**Lee, Robert E.** (1918– ), American playwright.
**Leopardi, Giacomo** (1798–1837), Italian poet.
**Lermontov, Mikhail Y.** (1814–41), Russian novelist.
**Lessing, Doris** (1919– ), English novelist.
**Lessing, Gotthold E.** (1729–81), German dramatist.
**Lewis, C(live) S(taples)** (1898–1963), Anglo-Irish critic, spiritual writer, and novelist.
**Lewis, Sinclair** (1885–1951), American novelist.
**Lewis, Wyndham** (1886–1957), English novelist.
**Lind, Jakov** (1927– ), Anglo-Austrian novelist.
**Lindsay, Vachel** (1879–1931), American poet.
**Livy** (59 B.C.–17 A.D.), Roman historian.
**London, Jack** (1876–1916), American novelist.
**Longfellow, Henry Wadsworth** (1807–82), American poet.
**Lope de Vega Carpio, Félix** (1562–1635), Spanish poet.
**Lord, Walter** (1917– ), American historical novelist.
**Lovelace, Richard** (1618–57?), English poet.
**Lowell, Amy** (1874–1925), American poet and critic.
**Lowell, James Russell** (1819–91), American poet.
**Lowell, Robert** (1917–77), American poet and translator.
**Lucian** (c. 125–after 180), Greek satirist.
**Lucretius** (c. 99–c. 55 B.C.), Roman poet.
**Macaulay, Thomas Babington** (1800–59), English historian, essayist, and critic.
**McCarthy, Mary** (1912– ), American novelist and literary critic.
**McCullers, Carson** (1917–67), American novelist.
**Machiavelli, Niccolò** (1469–1527), Italian political essayist.
**MacLeish, Archibald** (1892–1982), American poet.
**McNally, Terrence** (1939– ), American dramatist.
**Maeterlinck, Maurice** (1862–1949), Belgian dramatist.
**Mailer, Norman** (1923– ), American novelist and essayist.
**Malamud, Bernard** (1914– ), American novelist.
**Mallarmé, Stéphane** (1842–98), French poet.
**Malory, Sir Thomas** (d. 1471), English Arthurian romance writer.
**Malraux, André** (1901–76), French man of letters.
**Mann, Heinrich** (1871–1950), German novelist.
**Mann, Thomas** (1875–1955), German novelist.
**Mansfield, Katherine** (1888–1923), British short story writer.
**Manzoni, Alessandro** (1785–1873), Italian novelist.

**Marcus, Frank** (1928– ), English dramatist.
**Marlowe, Christopher** (1564–93), English dramatist.
**Marquand, John P.** (1893–1960), American novelist.
**Marsh, Ngaio** (1899–1982), New Zealand detective story writer.
**Martial** (c. 40–c. 104 A.D.), Roman epigrammatic poet.
**Marvell, Andrew** (1621–78), English poet.
**Masefield, John** (1878–1967), English poet.
**Masters, Edgar Lee** (1869–1950), American poet and biographer.
**Maugham, W(illiam) Somerset** (1874–1965), English novelist.
**Maupassant, Guy de** (1850–93), French novelist and short story writer.
**Mauriac, François** (1885–1970), French novelist.
**Maurois, André** (1885–1967), French biographer.
**Melville, Herman** (1819–91), American novelist.
**Menander** (c. 342 B.C.–c. 291 B.C.), Greek dramatist.
**Mencken, H(enry) L(ouis)** (1880–1956), American satirist, editor, critic, and philologist.
**Meredith, George** (1828–1909), English novelist and poet.
**Mérimée, Prosper** (1803–70), French novelist, dramatist, and poet.
**Merrill, James** (1926– ), American poet.
**Michener, James** (1907– ), American novelist.
**Millay, Edna St. Vincent** (1892–1950), American poet.
**Miller, Arthur** (1915– ), American dramatist.
**Miller, Henry** (1891–1980), American novelist.
**Milne, A(lan) A(lexander)** (1882–1956), English poet, dramatist, and children's author.
**Milton, John** (1608–74), English poet.
**Mistral, Frédéric** (1830–1914), French Provençal poet.
**Mistral, Gabriela** (1889–1957), Chilean poet.
**Molière, Jean Baptiste (Jean Baptiste Poquelin)** (1622–73), French dramatist.
**Molnar, Ferenc** (1878–1952), Hungarian dramatist.
**Montaigne, Michel Eyquem de** (1533–92), French essayist.
**Moore, George** (1852–1933), Irish novelist.
**Moore, Marianne** (1887–1972), American poet.
**Moore, Thomas** (1779–1852), Irish poet.
**Moravia, Alberto** (1907– ), Italian novelist.
**More, Sir Thomas** (1478–1535), English humanist.
**Morison, Samuel Eliot** (1887–1976), American historian.
**Morley, Christopher** (1890–1957), American novelist.
**Morris, William** (1834–96), English poet.
**Morris, Wright** (1910– ), American novelist.
**Murdoch, Iris** (1919– ), British novelist.
**Musset, Alfred de** (1810–57), French dramatist and poet.
**Nabokov, Vladimir** (1899–1977), Russian-American novelist.
**Naipaul, V.S.** (1932– ), West Indian novelist.
**Neruda, Pablo** (1904–73), Chilean poet.
**Nerval, Gérard de (Gérard Labrunie)** (1808–55), French poet, translator, and short story writer.
**Nevins, Allan** (1890–1971), American historian.
**Norris, Frank** (1870–1902), American novelist.
**Novalis (Friedrich von Hardenberg)** (1772–1801), German poet.
**Oates, Joyce Carol** (1938– ), American novelist.
**O'Casey, Sean** (1884–1964), Irish dramatist.
**O'Connor, Flannery** (1925–64), American novelist and short story writer.
**O'Connor, Frank (Michael O'Donovan)** (1903–66), Irish short story writer.
**Odets, Clifford** (1906–63), American dramatist.
**O'Faoláin, Seán** (1900– ), Irish novelist.
**O'Flaherty, Liam** (1897– ), Irish novelist.
**O'Hara, John** (1905–70), American novelist.
**Omar Khayyam** (fl. 11th cent.), Persian poet.
**O'Neill, Eugene** (1888–1953), American dramatist.
**Orwell, George (Eric Blair)** (1903–50), British novelist and essayist.
**Osborne, John** (1929– ), English dramatist.
**Ovid** (43 B.C.–18 A.D.), Latin poet.
**Parker, Dorothy** (1893–1967), American poet, short story writer, satirist, and critic.
**Pasternak, Boris** (1890–1960), Russian poet and novelist.
**Pater, Walter** (1839–94), English essayist and critic.
**Paton, Alan** (1903– ), South African novelist.
**Pavese, Cesare** (1908–50), Italian novelist.
**Pepys, Samuel** (1633–1703), English diarist.
**Perelman, S(idney) J(oseph)** (1904–79), American humorist.
**Perse, St. John (Alexis St. Léger)** (1887–1975), French poet.
**Petrarch** (1304–74), Italian poet and humanist.
**Petronius** (d. c. 66 A.D.), Roman satirist.
**Peyrefitte, Roger** (1907– ), French novelist.
**Pindar** (c. 518–438 B.C.), Greek lyric poet.
**Pinero, Sir Arthur Wing** (1855–1934), English dramatist.
**Pinter, Harold** (1930– ), English dramatist.
**Pirandello, Luigi** (1867–1936), Italian dramatist.
**Plath, Sylvia** (1932–63), American poet and novelist.
**Plautus** (c. 254 B.C.–184 B.C.), Roman comic poet.
**Plutarch** (c. 46–c. 120 A.D.), Greek biographer.
**Poe, Edgar Allan** (1809–49), American poet, short story writer, and critic.
**Pope, Alexander** (1688–1744), English poet.
**Porter, Katherine Anne** (1890–1980), American short story writer and novelist.
**Pound, Ezra** (1885–1972), American poet and critic.
**Powell, Anthony** (1905– ), English novelist.
**Priestley, J(ohn) B(oynton)** (1894– ), English novelist, dramatist, and critic.
**Pritchett, V(ictor) S(awdon)** (1900– ), English novelist and critic.
**Proust, Marcel** (1871–1922), French novelist.
**Purdy, James** (1923– ), American novelist.
**Pushkin, Aleksandr** (1799–1837), Russian poet.
**Queneau, Raymond** (1903– ), French novelist.
**Quintilian** (c. 35–95 A.D.), Roman rhetorician.
**Rabe, David** (1940– ), American playwright.
**Rabelais, François** (c. 1490–1553), French satirist.
**Racine, Jean** (1639–99), French dramatist.
**Ransom, John Crowe** (1888–1974), American poet and critic.
**Rattigan, Terence** (1911–77), English dramatist.
**Remarque, Erich Maria** (1897–1970), German-American novelist.
**Reston, James** (1909– ), Scottish-American journalist.
**Rexroth, Kenneth** (1905–82), American poet and critic.
**Rice, Elmer** (1892–1967), American dramatist.
**Richards, I. A.** (1893–1979), British poet and critic.
**Richardson, Jack** (1935– ), American dramatist.
**Richardson, Samuel** (1689–1761), English novelist.
**Richler, Mordecai** (1931– ), Canadian novelist.
**Richter, Conrad** (1890–1968), American novelist.
**Rilke, Rainer Maria** (1875–1920), German poet.
**Rimbaud, Arthur** (1854–91), French poet.
**Robinson, Edwin Arlington** (1869–1935), American poet.
**Roethke, Theodore** (1908–63), American poet.
**Rolland, Romain** (1866–1944), French novelist.
**Rolvaag, O(le) E(dvart)** (1876–1931), Norwegian-American novelist.
**Romains, Jules** (1885–1972), French novelist.
**Ronsard, Pierre de** (c. 1524–85), French poet.
**Rossetti, Christina** (1830–94), English poet.
**Rossetti, Dante G.** (1828–82), English poet and translator.
**Rostand, Edmond** (1868–1918), French dramatist and poet.
**Roth, Phillip** (1933– ), American novelist.
**Ruskin, John** (1819–1900), English critic and essayist.
**Russell, George ("A.E.")** (1867–1935), Irish poet.
**Sachs, Nelly** (1891–1970), German-born Swedish poet.
**Sagan, Françoise** (1935– ), French novelist.
**Sainte-Beuve, Charles A.** (1804–69), French critic.
**Saint-Exupéry, Antoine de** (1900–44), French writer.
**Saki (Hector H. Munro)** (1870–1916), English short story writer.
**Salinger, J(erome) D(avid)** (1919– ), American novelist.
**Sand, George (Amandine A. L. Dupin, baronne Dudevant)** (1804–76), French novelist.
**Sandburg, Carl** (1878–1967), American poet.
**Santayana, George** (1863–1952), American philosopher, poet, and essayist.
**Sappho** (fl. early 6th cent. B.C.), Greek lyric poet.
**Saroyan, William** (1908–81), American novelist, dramatist, and short story writer.
**Sartre, Jean Paul** (1905–80), French philosopher, novelist, and dramatist.
**Sayers, Dorothy L.** (1893–1957), English novelist.
**Schiller, Friedrich von** (1759–1805), German dramatist.
**Schisgal, Murray** (1926– ), American dramatist.
**Schlegel, Friedrich von** (1772–1829), German philosopher, critic, and writer.
**Schnitzler, Arthur** (1862–1931), Austrian dramatist and novelist.
**Schwartz, Delmore** (1913–66), American poet.
**Scott, Sir Walter** (1771–1832), Scottish novelist.
**Seferis, George** (1900–71), Greek poet.
**Seneca, Lucius Annaeus** (c. 3 B.C.–65 A.D.), Roman dramatist and philosopher.
**Shakespeare, William** (1564–1616), English dramatist and poet.
**Shange, Ntozake** (1948– ), American dramatist and poet.
**Shapiro, Karl** (1913– ), American poet, critic, and editor.
**Shaw, George Bernard** (1856–1950), Irish dramatist.

**Shaw, Irwin** (1913– ), American novelist.
**Sheed, Wilfrid** (1930– ), American novelist and critic.
**Shelley, Mary Wollstonecraft** (1797–1851), English novelist.
**Shelley, Percy Bysshe** (1792–1822), English poet.
**Shepard, Sam** (1943– ), American playwright.
**Sheridan, Richard Brinsley,** (1751–1816), Irish-born dramatist.
**Sherwood, Robert E.** (1896–1955), American dramatist.
**Sholokhov, Mikhail** (1905– ), Russian novelist.
**Sidney, Sir Philip** (1554–86), English poet and essayist.
**Sienkiewicz, Henryk** (1846–1916), Polish novelist.
**Sillanpää, Frans E.** (1888–1964), Finnish novelist.
**Silone, Ignazio** (1900–78), Italian novelist.
**Simenon, Georges** (1903– ), Franco-Belgian novelist.
**Simon, Neil** (1927– ), American playwright.
**Sinclair, Upton** (1878–1968), American novelist.
**Singer, Isaac Bashevis** (1904– ), Polish-born Yiddish American novelist and short story writer.
**Sitwell, Dame Edith** (1887–1964), English poet and critic.
**Sitwell, Sir Osbert** (1892–1969), English poet and essayist.
**Sitwell, Sacheverell** (1897– ), English poet and essayist.
**Smollett, Tobias** (1721–71), Scottish-born novelist.
**Snow, C(harles) P(ercy)** (1905–80), English critic and novelist.
**Solzhenitsyn, Aleksandr I.** (1918– ), Russian novelist.
**Sontag, Susan** (1933– ), American critic and novelist.
**Sophocles** (c. 496–406 B.C.), Greek tragic poet.
**Southey, Robert** (1774–1843), English poet.
**Spark, Muriel** (1918– ), Scottish novelist, short story writer, poet, and biographer.
**Spender, Stephen** (1909– ), English poet.
**Spengler, Oswald** (1880–1936), German historian.
**Spenser, Edmund** (1552?–99), English poet.
**Spigelgass, Leonard** (1908– ), American playwright.
**Steegmuller, Francis** (1906– ), American biographer.
**Steele, Sir Richard** (1672–1729), English essayist.
**Stein, Gertrude** (1874–1946), American poet, novelist, critic, and autobiographer.
**Steinbeck, John** (1902–68), American novelist.
**Stendhal (Marie Henri Beyle)** (1783–1842), French novelist.
**Sterne, Laurence** (1713–68), English novelist.
**Stevens, Wallace** (1879–1955), American poet.
**Stevenson, Robert Louis** (1850–94), Scottish novelist.
**Stoker, Bram** (1847–1912), Irish-born novelist.
**Stone, I. F.** (1907– ), American journalist and editor.
**Stoppard, Tom** (1937– ), English dramatist.
**Strindberg, August** (1849–1912), Swedish dramatist.
**Styron, William** (1925– ), American novelist.
**Sudermann, Hermann** (1857–1928), German dramatist.
**Swados, Harvey** (1920–1972), American novelist, short story writer, and essayist.
**Swift, Jonathan** (1667–1745), English satirist, poet, and essayist.
**Swinburne, Algernon Charles** (1837–1909), English poet.
**Symonds, John Addington** (1840–93), English cultural historian, critic, and translator.
**Symons, Arthur** (1865–1945), English poet and critic.
**Synge, John Millington** (1871–1909), Irish dramatist and poet.
**Tacitus** (c. 55–c. 117 A.D.), Roman historian.
**Tagore, Sir Rabindranath** (1861–1941), Indian poet, novelist, and essayist.
**Taine, Hippolyte** (1828–93), French critic and historian.
**Tarkington, Booth** (1869–1946), American novelist.
**Tasso, Torquato** (1544–95), Italian poet.
**Tate, Allen** (1899–1979), American poet and critic.
**Taylor, Samuel** (1912– ), American playwright.
**Teichmann, Howard** (1916– ), American dramatist.
**Tennyson, Alfred** (1809–92), English poet.
**Thackeray, William Makepeace** (1811–63), English novelist.
**Theocritus** (fl. c. 270 B.C.), Greek poet.
**Thomas, Dylan** (1914–53), Anglo-Welsh poet.
**Thompson, Francis** (1859–1907), English poet.
**Thoreau, Henry David** (1817–62), American essayist.
**Thucydides** (c. 460–c. 400 B.C.), Greek historian.
**Thurber, James** (1894–1961), American humorist.
**Tolkien, J(ohn) R(onald) R(euel)** (1892–1973), English novelist and critic.
**Tolstoy, Leo** (1828–1910), Russian novelist.
**Toynbee, Arnold** (1889–1975), English historian.
**Traven, B. (Traven Torsvan)** (1890–1969), American expatriate novelist.
**Trollope, Anthony** (1815–82), English novelist.
**Trumbo, Dalton** (1905–76), American screenwriter.
**Turgenev, Ivan** (1818–83), Russian novelist.
**Tutuola, Amos** (1920– ), Nigerian writer.
**Twain, Mark (Samuel L. Clemens)** (1835–1910), American novelist and humorist.
**Undset, Sigrid** (1882–1949), Norwegian novelist.
**Updike, John** (1932– ), American novelist and poet.
**Valéry, Paul** (1871–1945), French poet and critic.
**van Itallie, Jean-Claude** (1936– ), Belgian-born American dramatist.
**Van Doren, Mark** (1894–1972), American poet and critic.
**Vergil** (70–19 B.C.), Roman poet.
**Verne, Jules** (1828–1905), French novelist.
**Vidal, Gore** (1925– ), American novelist and critic.
**Vigny, Alfred de** (1797–1863), French dramatist.
**Villon, François** (1431–c. 1463), French poet.
**Voltaire, François M. A. de** (1694–1778), French novelist, dramatist, critic, and poet.
**Vonnegut, Kurt, Jr.** (1922– ), American novelist.
**Wain, John** (1925– ), English poet and novelist.
**Waller, Edmund** (1606–87), English poet.
**Walpole, Horace** (1717–97), English man of letters.
**Walton, Izaak** (1593–1683), English essayist.
**Ward, Douglas Turner** (1930– ), American dramatist.
**Warren, Robert Penn** (1905– ), American novelist, poet, and critic.
**Wassermann, Jakob** (1873–1934), Austrian novelist.
**Waugh, Evelyn** (1903–66), English novelist and satirist.
**Webster, John** (c. 1580–c. 1625), English dramatist.
**Webster, Noah** (1758–1843), American lexicographer.
**Weidman, Jerome** (1913– ), American novelist.
**Weiss, Peter** (1916–82), German-born Swedish dramatist.
**Wells, H(erbert) G(eorge)** (1866–1946), English novelist, essayist, and historian.
**Werfel, Franz** (1890–1945), Austrian novelist.
**Wescott, Glenway** (1901– ), American novelist and critic.
**Wesker, Arnold** (1932– ), English novelist.
**West, Nathanael (Nathan Weinstein)** (1903–40), American novelist.
**Wharton, Edith** (1862–1937), American novelist.
**White, E(lwyn) B(rooks)** (1899– ), American essayist.
**White, Patrick** (1912– ), Australian novelist.
**Whitman, Walt** (1819–92), American poet.
**Whittier, John Greenleaf** (1807–92), American poet.
**Wilbur, Richard** (1921– ), American poet.
**Wilde, Oscar** (1854–1900), Irish dramatist.
**Wilder, Thornton** (1897–1975), American novelist and dramatist.
**Williams, Tennessee** (1914– ), American dramatist.
**Williams, William Carlos** (1883–1963), American poet.
**Wilson, Edmund** (1895–1972), American writer and literary critic.
**Wolfe, Thomas** (1900–38), American novelist.
**Woodward, Robert** (1943– ), American journalist.
**Woolf, Virginia** (1882–1941), English novelist.
**Wordsworth, William** (1770–1850), English poet and critic.
**Wright, Richard** (1908–60), American novelist.
**Wyatt, Sir Thomas** (1503–42), English poet.
**Wylie, Elinor** (1885–1928), American poet and novelist.
**Xenophon** (c. 430–c. 355 B.C.), Greek historian.
**Yeats, William Butler** (1865–1939), Irish poet.
**Yevtushenko, Yevgeny** (1933– ), Russian poet.
**Zola, Emile** (1840–1902), French novelist.
**Zweig, Stefan** (1881–1942), Austrian novelist, poet, and biographer.

## NOTABLES OF THE MUSICAL WORLD

**Abbado, Claudio** (1933– ), Italian conductor.
**Addinsell, Richard** (1904–77), English film composer.
**Adler, Kurt** (1905– ), American opera director.
**Ailey, Alvin, Jr.** (1931– ), American choreographer.
**Albanese, Licia** (1913– ), Italian-American soprano.
**Albéniz, Isaac** (1860–1909), Spanish pianist and composer.
**Amara, Lucine** (1927– ), American soprano.
**Amram, David** (1930– ), American composer.
**Anderson, Marian** (1902– ), American contralto.
**Ansermet, Ernest** (1883–1969), Swiss conductor.
**Antheil, George** (1900–59), American composer.
**Antonio** (1921– ), Spanish dancer.
**Arnold, Malcolm** (1921– ), English composer.
**Arpino, Gerald** (1928– ), American choreographer.
**Arrau, Claudio** (1903– ), Chilean pianist.
**Ashton, Sir Frederick** (1906– ), English choreographer.
**Auber, Daniel F. E.** (1782–1871), French operatic composer.

**Auer, Leopold** (1845–1930), Hungarian violinist-teacher.
**Auric, Georges** (1899– ), French composer.
**Babbitt, Milton** (1916– ), American composer.
**Bach, Carl P. E.** (1714–88), German composer.
**Bach, Johann C.** (1735–82), German composer.
**Bach, Johann Sebastian** (1685–1750), German composer.
**Bach, Wilhelm F.** (1710–84), German composer.
**Bachauer, Gina** (1913–76), Greek pianist.
**Bachaus, Wilhelm** (1884–1969), German pianist.
**Badura-Skoda, Paul** (1927– ), Austrian pianist.
**Baker, Janet** (1933– ), British mezzo-soprano.
**Balanchine, George** (1904– ), American choreographer.
**Balfe, Michael** (1808–70), Irish operatic composer.
**Barber, Samuel** (1910–81), American composer.
**Barbirolli, Sir John** (1899–1970), English conductor.
**Barenboim, Daniel** (1942– ), Israeli pianist and conductor.
**Bartók, Béla** (1881–1945), Hungarian composer.
**Baryshnikov, Mikhail** (1948– ), Russian ballet dancer.
**Bastianini, Ettore** (1923–67), Italian operatic baritone.
**Beecham, Sir Thomas** (1879–1961), English conductor.
**Beethoven, Ludwig van** (1770–1827), German composer.
**Bellini, Vincenzo** (1801–35), Italian operatic composer.
**Bennett, Robert Russell** (1894–1981), American composer.
**Berg, Alban** (1885–1935), Austrian composer.
**Berganza, Teresa** (1935– ), Spanish mezzo-soprano.
**Berlin, Irving** (1888– ), American popular composer.
**Berlioz, Hector** (1803–69), French composer.
**Berman, Lazar** (1930– ), Russian pianist.
**Bernstein, Leonard** (1918– ), American composer, conductor, and pianist.
**Bettis, Valerie** (1920–82), American choreographer.
**Biggs, E. Power** (1906–77), English-American organist.
**Bing, Rudolf** (1902– ), Austrian-English operatic manager.
**Bizet, Georges** (1838–75), French composer.
**Björling, Jussi** (1911–60), Swedish tenor.
**Bliss, Sir Arthur** (1891–1975), English composer.
**Blitzstein, Marc** (1905–64), American composer.
**Bloch, Ernest** (1880–1959), Swiss-American composer.
**Boccherini, Luigi** (1743–1805), Italian composer.
**Boehm, Karl** (1894–1981), German conductor.
**Boito, Arrigo** (1842–1918), Italian composer and librettist.
**Bonynge, Richard** (1930– ), Australian conductor.
**Borkh, Inge** (1921– ), German soprano.
**Borodin, Aleksandr** (1833–87), Russian composer.
**Boulanger, Nadia** (1887–1979), French pianist.
**Boulez, Pierre** (1925– ), French composer and conductor.
**Boult, Sir Adrian** (1889– ), English conductor.
**Brahms, Johannes** (1833–97), German composer.
**Brailowsky, Alexander** (1896–1976), Russian pianist.
**Bream, Julian** (1933– ), English guitarist and lutenist.
**Britten, Benjamin** (1913–76), English composer.
**Browning, John** (1933– ), American pianist.
**Bruch, Max** (1838–1920), German composer.
**Bruckner, Anton** (1824–96), Austrian composer.
**Bülow, Hans von** (1830–94), German pianist and conductor.
**Bumbry, Grace** (1937– ), American mezzo-soprano.
**Buxtehude, Dietrich** (1637–1707), Swedish composer.
**Cage, John** (1912– ), American composer.
**Caldwell, Sarah** (1928– ), American opera conductor.
**Callas, Maria** (1923–77), Greek-American soprano.
**Carreras, José** (1946– ), Spanish operatic tenor.
**Caruso, Enrico** (1873–1921), Italian operatic tenor.
**Casadesus, Robert** (1899–72), French pianist.
**Casals, Pablo** (1876–1973), Spanish cellist and conductor.
**Chabrier, Alexis E.** (1841–94), French composer.
**Chaliapin, Feodor** (1873–1938), Russian operatic bass.
**Charpentier, Gustave** (1860–1956), French composer.
**Chausson, Ernest** (1855–99), French composer.
**Chávez, Carlos** (1899–1978), Mexican composer.
**Cherubini, Luigi** (1760–1842), Italian composer.
**Chopin, Frédéric** (1810–49), Polish composer.
**Christoff, Boris** (1919– ), Bulgarian bass.
**Cimarosa, Domenico** (1749–1801), Italian composer.
**Cliburn, Van** (1934– ), American pianist.
**Clifford, John** (1947– ), American dancer.
**Copland, Aaron** (1900– ), American composer.
**Corelli, Arcangelo** (1653–1713), Italian composer.
**Corelli, Franco** (1924– ), Italian dramatic tenor.
**Couperin, François** (1668–1733), French composer.
**Crespin, Régine** (1927– ), French dramatic soprano.
**Creston, Paul** (1906– ), American composer.
**Cunningham, Merce** (1922?– ), American choreographer.
**Curtin, Phyllis** (c. 1930– ), American operatic soprano.
**Dallapiccola, Luigi** (1904–75), Italian pianist and composer.
**D'Amboise, Jacques** (1934– ), American ballet dancer.
**Damrosch, Leopold** (1832–85), German conductor.
**Damrosch, Walter** (1862–1950), German-American conductor and composer.
**Danilova, Alexandra** (1906– ), Russian ballerina.
**Debussy, Claude** (1862–1918), French composer.
**De Lavallade, Carmen** (1931– ), American dancer.
**Délibes, Léo** (1836–91), French composer.
**Delius, Frederick** (1862–1934), English composer.
**Della Casa, Lisa** (1921– ), Swiss lyric soprano.
**Dello Joio, Norman** (1913– ), American composer.
**Del Mar, Norman** (1919– ), English conductor.
**De Mille, Agnes** (1908– ), American choreographer.
**Del Monaco, Mario** (1915– ), Italian dramatic tenor.
**De los Angeles, Victoria** (1923– ), Spanish lyric soprano.
**Diaghilev, Sergei** (1872–1929), Russian ballet impresario.
**Di Stefano, Giuseppe** (1921– ), Italian lyric tenor.
**Dittersdorf, Karl D. von** (1739–99), Austrian composer.
**Dobbs, Mattiwilda** (1925– ), American coloratura soprano.
**Dohnanyi, Ernst von** (1877–1960), Hungarian composer.
**Dolin, Anton** (1904– ), English ballet choreographer.
**Domingo, Placido** (1941– ), Spanish opera tenor.
**Donizetti, Gaetano** (1797–1848), Italian composer.
**Dorati, Antal** (1906– ), Hungarian-American conductor.
**Druckman, Jacob** (1928– ), American composer.
**Dukas, Paul** (1865–1935), French composer.
**Duncan, Isadora** (1878–1927), American dancer.
**Dunham, Katherine** (1910– ), American choreographer.
**Dvorak, Antonin** (1841–1904), Czech composer.
**Eglevsky, André** (1917–77), Russian-born American dancer.
**Elgar, Sir Edward** (1857–1934), English composer.
**Ellington, Duke** (1899–1974), American composer.
**Elman, Mischa** (1891–1967), Russian-American violinist.
**Enesco, Georges** (1881–1955), Rumanian composer.
**Entremont, Philippe** (1934– ), French pianist and conductor.
**Falla, Manuel de** (1876–1946), Spanish composer.
**Farrar, Geraldine** (1882–1967), American operatic soprano.
**Farrell, Eileen** (1920– ), American dramatic soprano.
**Farrell, Suzanne** (1945– ), American ballerina.
**Fauré, Gabriel** (1845–1924), French composer.
**Feuermann, Emanuel** (1902–42), Polish-American cellist.
**Fiedler, Arthur** (1894–1979), American conductor.
**Fischer-Dieskau, Dietrich** (1925– ), German baritone.
**Flagstad, Kirsten** (1895–1962), Norwegian soprano.
**Flotow, Friedrich von** (1812–83), German operatic composer.
**Fokine, Michel** (1880–1942), Russian-American dancer.
**Fonteyn, Dame Margot** (1919– ), English ballerina.
**Foss, Lukas** (1922– ), German-born American composer.
**Foster, Stephen** (1826–64), American song writer.
**Francescatti, Zino** (1905– ), French violinist.
**Franck, César** (1822–90), Belgian-French composer.
**Frescobaldi, Girolamo** (1583–1643), Italian composer.
**Friml, Rudolf** (1879–1972), Czech-American composer.
**Furtwängler, Wilhelm** (1886–1954), German conductor.
**Gades, Antonio** (1936– ), Spanish dancer.
**Galli-Curci, Amelita** (1882–1963), Italian-American soprano.
**Galway, James** (1939– ), Irish flutist.
**Garden, Mary** (1877–1967), Scottish-American soprano.
**Gatti-Casazza, Giulio** (1869–1940), Italian opera manager.
**Gedda, Nicolai** (1925– ), Swedish operatic tenor.
**Gershwin, George** (1898–1937), American composer.
**Gieseking, Walter** (1895–1956), German pianist.
**Gigli, Beniamino** (1890–1957), Italian tenor.
**Gilbert, Sir William S.** (1836–1911), English librettist.
**Gilels, Emil** (1916– ), Russian pianist.
**Ginastera, Alberto** (1916– ), Argentinian composer.
**Glazunov, Aleksandr** (1865–1936), Russian composer.
**Glière, Reinhold** (1875–1956), Russian composer.
**Glinka, Mikhail** (1804–57), Russian composer.
**Gluck, Christoph W. von** (1714–87), German composer.
**Gobbi, Tito** (1915– ), Italian operatic baritone.
**Godowsky, Leopold** (1870–1938), Polish pianist.
**Goldmark, Karl** (1830–1915), Hungarian composer.
**Goldovsky, Boris** (1908– ), Russian-American conductor.
**Golschmann, Vladimir** (1893-1972), French-American conductor.
**Goossens, Sir Eugene** (1893–1962), English conductor.
**Gould, Glenn** (1932–82), Canadian pianist.
**Gould, Morton** (1913– ), American conductor.
**Gounod, Charles** (1818–93), French composer.
**Graham, Martha** (1893?– ), American choreographer.
**Grainger, Percy** (1882–1961), Australian-American pianist and composer.
**Greco, Jose** (1918– ), Italian-born American dancer.
**Gretchaninov, Aleksandr** (1864–1956), Russian composer.
**Grieg, Edvard** (1843–1907), Norwegian composer.
**Grofé, Ferde** (1892–1972), American composer.

**Gueden, Hilde** (1917– ), Austrian operatic lyric soprano.
**Halévy, Jacques** (1799–1862), French operatic composer.
**Hammerstein, Oscar, II** (1895–1960), American lyricist.
**Handel, George Frederick** (1685–1759), German composer.
**Hanson, Howard** (1896–1981), American composer.
**Harris, Roy** (1898–1979), American composer.
**Hart, Lorenz** (1895–1943), American lyricist.
**Haydée, Marcia** (1937– ), Brazilian ballerina.
**Haydn, Franz Joseph** (1732–1809), Austrian composer.
**Heifetz, Jascha** (1901– ), Russian-American violinist.
**Henze, Hans Werner** (1926– ), German composer.
**Herbert, Victor** (1859–1924), Irish-American musician.
**Hess, Dame Myra** (1890–1965), English pianist.
**Hindemith, Paul** (1895–1963), German-American composer.
**Hines, Jerome** (1921– ), American operatic bass.
**Hofmann, Joseph** (1876–1957), Polish-American pianist.
**Holst, Gustav** (1874–1934), English composer.
**Honegger, Arthur** (1892–1955), Swiss-French composer.
**Horne, Marilyn** (1934– ), American mezzo-soprano.
**Horowitz, Vladimir** (1904– ), Russian-American pianist.
**Humperdinck, Engelbert** (1854–1921), German composer.
**Humphrey, Doris** (1895–1958), American choreographer.
**Hurok, Sol** (1888–1974), Russian-American impresario.
**Ibert, Jacques** (1890–1962), French composer.
**Indy, Vincent d'** (1851–1931), French composer.
**Ippolitov-Ivanov, Mikhail** (1859–1935), Russian composer.
**Istomin, Eugene** (1925– ), American pianist.
**Iturbi, José** (1895–1980), Spanish-American pianist.
**Ives, Charles** (1874–1954), American composer.
**Jamison, Judith** (1944– ), American dancer.
**Jeritza, Maria** (1887–1982), Austrian-American soprano.
**Joffrey, Robert** (1930– ), American ballet director.
**Kabalevsky, Dmitri** (1904– ), Russian composer.
**Karajan, Herbert von** (1908– ), Austrian conductor.
**Kempff, Wilhelm** (1895– ), German pianist.
**Kern, Jerome** (1885–1945), American popular composer.
**Khachaturian, Aram** (1903–1978), Russian composer.
**Kidd, Michael** (1919– ), American choreographer.
**Kiepura, Jan** (1902–66), Polish tenor.
**Kipnis, Alexander** (1891–1978), Russian-American bass.
**Kleiber, Erich** (1890–1956), Austrian conductor.
**Klemperer, Otto** (1885–1973), German conductor.
**Kodály, Zoltán** (1882–1967), Hungarian composer.
**Kogan, Leonid** (1924– ), Russian violinist.
**Kondrashin, Kyril** (1914–81), Russian conductor.
**Kostelanetz, André** (1901–80), Russian-American conductor.
**Koussevitzky, Serge** (1874–1951), Russian-American conductor.
**Kreisler, Fritz** (1875–1962), Austrian-American violinst.
**Krips, Josef** (1902–1974), Austrian conductor.
**Kubelik, Rafael** (1914– ), Czech conductor and composer.
**Kunz, Erich** (1909– ), Austrian singer.
**Lalo, Edouard** (1823–92), French composer.
**Lambert, Constant** (1905–51), English composer.
**Landowska, Wanda** (1877–1959), Polish-French harpsichordist and pianist.
**Lehár, Franz** (1870–1948), Hungarian composer.
**Lehmann, Lilli** (1848–1929), German operatic soprano.
**Lehmann, Lotte** (1888–1976), German-American soprano.
**Leinsdorf, Erich** (1912– ), Austrian-American conductor.
**Leoncavallo, Ruggiero** (1858–1919), Italian composer.
**Lerner, Alan Jay** (1918– ), American lyricist.
**Lewis, Henry** (1932– ), American conductor.
**Lhevinne, Joseph** (1874–1944), Russian-American pianist.
**Lhevinne, Rosina** (1880–1976), Russian-American pianist.
**Limón, José** (1908–72), Mexican-American choreographer.
**Lind, Jenny** (1820–87), Swedish soprano.
**Liszt, Franz** (1811–86), Hungarian composer.
**Loewe, Frederick** (1904– ), American composer.
**London, George** (1920– ), Canadian bass baritone.
**Lorengar, Pilar** (1931?– ), Spanish lyric soprano.
**Loring, Eugene** (1910–82), American choreographer.
**Lully, Jean B.** (1632–87), French operatic composer.
**Lympany, Moura** (1916– ), English pianist.
**Ma, Yo-Yo** (1955– ), American cellist.
**Maazel, Lorin** (1930– ), American conductor.
**McBride, Patricia** (1942– ), American ballerina.
**McCormack, John** (1884–1945), Irish-American tenor.
**McCracken, James** (1926– ), American dramatic tenor.
**MacDowell, Edward** (1861–1908), American composer.
**Mahler, Gustav** (1860–1911), Austrian composer.
**Makarova, Natalia** (1940– ), Russian ballerina.
**Markevich, Igor** (1912– ), Russian-Swiss conductor.
**Markova, Dame Alicia** (1910– ), English ballerina.
**Martinelli, Giovanni** (1885–1969), Italian-American tenor.
**Martinon, Jean** (1910–76), French conductor and composer.
**Mascagni, Pietro** (1863–1945), Italian operatic composer.
**Massenet, Jules** (1842–1912), French operatic composer.
**Massine, Léonide** (1896–1979), Russian-American choreographer.
**Mehta, Zubin** (1936– ), Indian conductor.
**Melba, Dame Nellie** (c. 1859–1931), Australian soprano.
**Melchior, Lauritz** (1890–1973), Danish heroic tenor.
**Mendelssohn, Felix** (1809–47), German composer.
**Mengelberg, Josef W.** (1871–1951), Dutch conductor.
**Mennin, Peter** (1923– ), American composer.
**Menotti, Gian-Carlo** (1911– ), Italian-American composer.
**Menuhin, Yehudi** (1916– ), American violinist.
**Merrill, Robert** (1919– ), American operatic baritone.
**Merriman, Nan** (1920– ), American mezzo-soprano.
**Meyerbeer, Giacomo** (1791–1864), German composer.
**Milanov, Zinka** (1906– ), Yugoslavian operatic soprano.
**Milhaud, Darius** (1892–1974), French composer.
**Milstein, Nathan** (1904– ), Russian violinist.
**Mitchell, Arthur** (1934– ), American ballet dancer.
**Mitropoulos, Dimitri** (1896–1960), Greek-American conductor.
**Moffo, Anna** (c. 1935– ), American soprano.
**Moiseiwitsch, Benno** (1890–1963), Russian-English pianist.
**Moiseyev, Igor** (1906– ), Russian choreographer.
**Monteux, Pierre** (1875–1964), French-American conductor.
**Monteverdi, Claudio** (1567–1643), Italian composer.
**Moore, Douglas** (1893–1969), American operatic composer.
**Moore, Grace** (1901–47), American soprano.
**Morini, Erica** (c. 1905– ), Austrian-American violinist.
**Moussorgsky, Modest** (1839–81), Russian composer.
**Mozart, Wolfgang Amadeus** (1756–91), Austrian composer.
**Münch, Charles** (1891–1968), French conductor.
**Münchinger, Karl** (1915– ), German conductor.
**Munsel, Patrice** (1925– ), American operatic soprano.
**Muti, Riccardo** (1941– ), Italian conductor.
**Muzio, Claudia** (1889–1936), Italian operatic soprano.
**Neway, Patricia** (c. 1923– ), American soprano.
**Nicolai, Otto** (1810–49), German composer.
**Nielsen, Carl** (1865–1931), Danish composer.
**Nijinsky, Vaslav** (1890–1950), Russian ballet dancer.
**Nikolais, Alwin** (1912– ), American dancer.
**Nilsson, Birgit** (1918– ), Swedish dramatic soprano.
**Novaes, Guiomar** (1895–1979), Brazilian pianist.
**Nureyev, Rudolf** (1938– ), Russian ballet dancer.
**Offenbach, Jacques** (1819–80), French composer.
**Oistrakh, David** (1908–74), Russian violinist.
**Orff, Carl** (1895–1982), German composer.
**Ormandy, Eugene** (1899– ), Hungarian-born American conductor.
**Ozawa, Seiji** (1935– ), Japanese conductor.
**Paderewski, Ignace J.** (1860–1941), Polish pianist and composer.
**Paganini, Niccolò** (1782–1840), Italian violinist.
**Palestrina, Giovanni P. da** (c. 1525–94), Italian composer.
**Pavarotti, Luciano** (1935– ), Italian opera singer.
**Pavlova, Anna** (c. 1882–1931), Russian ballerina.
**Peerce, Jan** (1904– ), American tenor.
**Pergolesi, Giovanni B.** (1710–36), Italian composer.
**Perlman, Itzhak** (1945– ), Israeli violinist.
**Peters, Roberta** (1930– ), American coloratura soprano.
**Petit, Roland** (1924– ), French choreographer and dancer.
**Piatigorsky, Gregor** (1903–76), Ukrainian-American cellist.
**Pinza, Ezio** (1892–1957), Italian-American basso.
**Piston, Walter** (1894–1976), American composer.
**Pizzetti, Ildebrando** (1880–1968), Italian composer.
**Plisetskaya, Maya** (1925– ), Russian ballerina.
**Pollini, Maurizio** (1942– ), Italian pianist.
**Ponchielli, Amilcare** (1834–86), Italian composer.
**Pons, Lily** (1904–76), French-American coloratura soprano.
**Ponselle, Rosa** (1897–1981), American operatic soprano.
**Porter, Cole** (1893–1964), American composer and lyricist.
**Poulenc, Francis** (1899–1963), French composer.
**Previn, André** (1929– ), German-American conductor.
**Price, Leontyne** (1927– ), American dramatic soprano.
**Primrose, William** (1904–82), Scottish-American violist.
**Prokofiev, Sergei** (1891–1953), Russian composer.
**Puccini, Giacomo** (1858–1924), Italian operatic composer.
**Purcell, Henry** (1659–95), English composer and organist.
**Putnam, Ashley** (1952– ), American coloratura soprano.
**Queler, Eve** (1936– ), American conductor.
**Rabin, Michael** (1936–1972), American violinist.
**Rachmaninoff, Sergei** (1873–1943), Russian composer.
**Ramey, Samuel** (1942– ), American basso.
**Ravel, Maurice** (1875–1937), French composer.
**Reiner, Fritz** (1888–1963), Hungarian-American conductor.
**Reisenberg, Nadia** (1905– ), Russian-American pianist.
**Resnik, Regina** (1924– ), American mezzo-soprano.
**Respighi, Ottorino** (1879–1936), Italian composer.

**Reszke, Edouard de** (1853–1917), Polish bass.
**Reszke, Jan de** (1850–1925), Polish tenor.
**Ricci, Ruggiero** (1918– ), American violinist.
**Richter, Sviatoslav** (1914– ), Russian pianist.
**Rimsky-Korsakov, Nikolai** (1844–1908), Russian composer.
**Robbins, Jerome** (1918– ), American choreographer.
**Robeson, Paul** (1898–1976), American bass.
**Rodgers, Richard** (1902–79), American popular composer.
**Rodzinski, Artur** (1894–1958), Polish-American conductor.
**Romberg, Sigmund** (1887–1951), Hungarian-American operetta composer.
**Rorem, Ned** (1923– ), American composer.
**Rose, Leonard** (1918– ), American cellist.
**Rosenthal, Moriz** (1862–1946), Polish pianist.
**Rossini, Gioacchino** (1792–1868), Italian composer.
**Rostropovitch, Mstislav** (1927– ), Russian cellist.
**Roussel, Albert** (1869–1937), French composer.
**Rózsa, Miklos** (1907– ), Hungarian-American composer.
**Rubinstein, Anton** (1829–94), Russian pianist and composer.
**Rubinstein, Artur** (1886– ), Polish-American pianist.
**Rysanek, Leonie** (1926– ), Austrian dramatic soprano.
**St. Denis, Ruth** (1877?–1968), American dancer.
**Saint-Saëns, Camille** (1835–1921), French composer.
**Sargent, Sir Malcolm** (1895–1967), English conductor.
**Satie, Erik** (1866–1925), French composer.
**Scarlatti, Alessandro** (c. 1660–1725), Italian composer.
**Scarlatti, Domenico** (1685–1757), Italian composer.
**Scherman, Thomas** (1917–79), American conductor.
**Schipa, Tito** (1889–1965), Italian operatic tenor.
**Schippers, Thomas** (1930–77), American conductor.
**Schmidt-Isserstedt, Hans** (1900–1973), German conductor.
**Schnabel, Artur** (1882–1951), Austrian-American pianist.
**Schneider, Alexander** (1908– ), Russian-American violinist.
**Schoenberg, Arnold** (1874–1951), Austrian composer.
**Schubert, Franz** (1797–1828), Austrian composer.
**Schuller, Gunther** (1925– ), American composer.
**Schuman, William** (1910– ), American composer.
**Schumann, Clara** (1819–96), German pianist and composer.
**Schumann, Elisabeth** (1885–1952), German soprano.
**Schumann, Robert** (1810–56), German composer.
**Schumann-Heink, Ernestine** (1861–1936), Austrian-American contralto.
**Schwarzkopf, Elisabeth** (1915– ), German lyric soprano.
**Scotti, Antonio** (1866–1936), Italian operatic baritone.
**Scotto, Renata** (1936– ), Italian soprano.
**Scriabin, Aleksandr** (1872–1915), Russian composer.
**Seefried, Irmgard** (1919– ), German soprano.
**Segovia, Andrés** (1893– ), Spanish guitarist.
**Serkin, Rudolph** (1903– ), Czech-born American pianist.
**Sessions, Roger** (1896– ), American composer.
**Shaw, Robert** (1916– ), American choral conductor.
**Shawn, Ted** (1891–1972), American dancer.
**Shostakovich, Dmitri** (1906–1975), Russian composer.
**Sibelius, Jean** (1865–1957), Finnish composer.
**Siepi, Cesare** (1923– ), Italian operatic bass.
**Sills, Beverly** (1929– ), American coloratura soprano.
**Slezak, Leo** (1873–1946), Czech tenor.
**Smallens, Alexander** (1899–1972), Russian-born American conductor.
**Smetana, Bedřich** (1824–84), Czech composer.
**Solomon** (1902– ), English pianist.
**Solti, Georg** (1912– ), Hungarian conductor.
**Somes, Michael** (1917– ), English ballet dancer.
**Sousa, John Philip** (1854–1932), American bandmaster and composer.
**Sowerby, Leo** (1895–1968), American organist.
**Spivakovsky, Tossy** (1907– ), Russian-American violinist.
**Steber, Eleanor** (1916– ), American operatic soprano.
**Steinberg, William** (1899–1978), German conductor.
**Steiner, Max** (1888?–1971), Austrian-American composer.
**Stern, Isaac** (1920– ), Russian-born American violinist.
**Stevens, Risë** (1913– ), American mezzo-soprano.
**Stich-Randall, Teresa** (c. 1928– ), American soprano.
**Stokowski, Leopold** (1882–1977), English-born American conductor.
**Stratas, Teresa** (1938– ), Canadian soprano.
**Straus, Oscar** (1870–1954), Austrian operetta composer.
**Strauss, Johann** (1804–49), Austrian composer.
**Strauss, Johann, Jr.** (1825–99), Austrian composer.
**Strauss, Richard** (1864–1949), German composer.
**Stravinsky, Igor** (1882–1971), Russian composer.
**Sullivan, Sir Arthur** (1842–1900), English composer.
**Sutherland, Joan** (1926– ), Australian soprano.
**Swarthout, Gladys** (1904–69), American mezzo-soprano.
**Szell, Georg** (1897–1970), Hungarian-born American conductor.
**Szigeti, Joseph** (1892–1973), Hungarian violinist.
**Tagliavini, Ferruccio** (1913– ), Italian lyric tenor.
**Tallchief, Maria** (1925– ), American ballerina.
**Tauber, Richard** (1892–1948), Austrian tenor.
**Taylor, Deems** (1885–1966), American music critic.
**Taylor, Paul** (1930– ), American choreographer.
**Tchaikovsky, Piotr Ilich** (1840–93), Russian composer.
**Tebaldi, Renata** (1922– ), Italian lyric soprano.
**Te Kanawa, Kiri** (1946– ), New Zealand mezzo-soprano.
**Telemann, Georg P.** (1681–1767), German composer.
**Tetley, Glen** (1926– ), American choreographer.
**Tetrazzini, Luisa** (1871–1940), Italian coloratura soprano.
**Tharp, Twyla** (1941– ), American choreographer.
**Thebom, Blanche** (1918– ), American mezzo-soprano.
**Theodorakis, Mikis** (1925– ), Greek composer.
**Thomas, Ambroise** (1811–96), French operatic composer.
**Thomas, John Charles** (1891–1960), American baritone.
**Thomson, Virgil** (1896– ), American composer and critic.
**Tibbett, Lawrence** (1896–1960), American baritone.
**Toscanini, Arturo** (1867–1957), Italian conductor.
**Tourel, Jennie** (1910–73), Canadian operatic soprano.
**Traubel, Helen** (1899–1972), American soprano.
**Troyanos, Tatiana** (1938– ), American mezzo-soprano.
**Tucker, Richard** (c. 1914–75), American dramatic tenor.
**Tudor, Antony** (1909– ), English choreographer.
**Tureck, Rosalyn** (1914– ), American pianist.
**Ulanova, Galina** (1910– ), Russian ballerina.
**Varèse, Edgard** (1885–1965), French-American composer.
**Varnay, Astrid** (1918– ), Swedish dramatic soprano.
**Vaughan Williams, Ralph** (1872–1958), English composer.
**Verdi, Guiseppe** (1813–1901), Italian composer.
**Verrett, Shirley** (c. 1933– ), American mezzo-soprano.
**Vickers, Jon** (1926– ), Canadian operatic tenor.
**Villa-Lobos, Heitor** (1887–1959), Brazilian composer.
**Villella, Edward** (1936– ), American ballet dancer.
**Vishnevskaya, Galina** (1926– ), Russian soprano.
**Vivaldi, Antonio** (c. 1675–1741), Italian composer.
**von Stade, Frederica** (1945– ), American mezzo-soprano.
**Wagner, Richard** (1813–83), German composer.
**Walter, Bruno** (1876–1962), German-American conductor.
**Walton, Sir William** (1902– ), English composer.
**Warren, Leonard** (1911–60), American baritone.
**Watts, André** (1946– ), American pianist.
**Weber, Carl M. von** (1786–1826), German composer.
**Webern, Anton von** (1883–1945), Austrian composer.
**Weidman, Charles** (1901–75), American choreographer.
**Weill, Kurt** (1900–50), German-American composer.
**Weingartner, Felix** (1863–1942), Austrian conductor.
**Weissenberg, Alexis** (1929– ), French pianist.
**Welitsch, Ljuba** (1913– ), Bulgarian soprano.
**Whiteman, Paul** (1890–1967), American jazz conductor.
**Wilde, Patricia** (1928– ), Canadian ballerina.
**Wilder, Alec** (1907–80), American popular composer.
**Williams, John** (1932– ), American composer and conductor.
**Wolf, Hugo** (1860–1903), Austrian composer of lieder.
**Wolf-Ferrari, Ermanno** (1876–1948), German-Italian operatic composer.
**Wunderlich, Fritz** (1930–66), German lyric tenor.
**Wuorinen, Charles** (1938– ), American composer.
**Youmans, Vincent** (1898–1946), American composer.
**Youskevitch, Igor** (1912– ), Russian ballet dancer.
**Zimbalist, Efrem** (1889– ), Russian-American violinist.
**Zukerman, Pinchas** (1948– ), Israeli-American violinist.

## FILM DIRECTORS

### FRANCE

**Allégret, Yves** (1907– ): *The Proud and the Beautiful, Oasis, Germinal.*

**Becker, Jacques** (1906–60): *Casque d'Or, Montparnasse 19, The Hole.*

**Bresson, Robert** (1907– ): *Les Dames du Bois de Boulogne, Pickpocket, The Trial of Joan of Arc.*

**Camus, Marcel** (1912– ): *Black Orpheus, Le Chant du Monde.*

**Carné, Marcel** (1909– ): *Quai des Brumes, Les Enfants du Paradis, Terrain Vague.*

**Cayatte, André** (1909– ): *Avant de Déluge, Le Passage du Rhin, La Vie Conjugale, La Raison d'état.*
**Chabrol, Claude** (1930– ): *Les Cousins, A Double Tour, Landru, Une Partie de plaisir, Violette Nozière.*
**Christian-Jaque** (1904– ): *La Chartreuse de Parme, Fanfan la Tulipe.*
**Clair, René** (1898–1981): *Sous les Toits de Paris, A Nous la Liberté, And Then There Were None.*
**Clément, René** (1913– ): *Forbidden Games, Gervaise, Is Paris Burning?*
**Clouzot, Henri-Georges** (1907–77): *The Wages of Fear, Diabolique, La Vérité.*
**Cocteau, Jean** (1889–1963): *The Blood of a Poet, Beauty and the Beast, Orpheus.*
**De Broca, Philippe** (1933– ):*Cartouche, That Man from Rio, King of Hearts.*
**Delannoy, Jean** (1908– ): *La Symphonie Pastorale, La Princesse de Clèves.*
**Demy, Jacques** (1931– ): *Lola, The Umbrellas of Cherbourg.*
**Duvivier, Julien** (1896–1967): *Poil de Carotte, Un Carnet de Bal, The Little World of Don Camillo.*
**Godard, Jean-Luc** (1930– ): *Breathless, La Chinoise, Weekend.*
**Guitry, Sacha** (1885–1957): *La Poison, Désiré, Assassins et Voleurs.*
**Malle, Louis** (1932– ): *Les Amants; Viva Maria!; Le Voleur; Lacombe, Lucien; Pretty Baby; Atlantic City.*
**Marker, Chris** (1921– ): *Cuba Si!, Joli Mai.*
**Melville, Jean-Pierre** (1917–73): *Les Enfants Terribles, Le Doulos.*
**Ophuls, Max** (1902–57): *La Ronde, Madame De, Lola Montès.*
**Pagnol, Marcel** (1895–1974): *César, Angèle, Topaze.*
**Renoir, Jean** (1894–1979): *The Crime of M. Lange, La Grande Illusion, The Diary of a Chambermaid.*
**Resnais, Alain** (1922– ): *Hiroshima, Mon Amour; Last Year at Marienbad; La Guerre Est Finie; Providence, Mon Oncle d'Amérique.*
**Tati, Jacques** (1908– ): *Jour de Fête, Mr. Hulot's Holiday, Mon Oncle. Traffic.*
**Truffaut, François** (1932– ): *The 400 Blows, Stolen Kisses, Bed and Board, Jules et Jim, The Wild Child, Day for Night, The Story of Adele H., Small Change, Last Metro.*
**Vadim, Roger** (1928– ): *And God Created Woman, Les Liaisons Dangereuses, Barbarella.*
**Varda, Agnes** (1928– ): *Cléo from 5 to 7, Le Bonheur.*
**Vigo, Jean** (1905–34): *Zéro de Conduite, L'Atalante.*

## GERMANY

**Fassbinder, Rainer W.** (1946–82): *Fox and His Friends, Mother Küsters Goes to Heaven, The Marriage of Maria Braun, Berlin-Alexanderplatz, Lili Marleen.*
**Harlan, Veit** (1899–1964): *Kreutzer Sonata, Jew Süss.*
**Herzog, Werner** (1942– ): *Aguirre: the Wrath of God, The Mystery of Kaspar Hauser, Stroszek, Woyzeck.*
**Käutner, Helmut** (1908– ): *The Captain from Kopenick, The Wonderful Years, The Redhead.*
**Murnau, Friedrich W.** (1899–1931): *Nosferatu, Faust, Sunrise.*
**Pabst, Georg W.** (1885–1967): *The Joyless Street, Kameradschaft, The Threepenny Opera.*
**Riefenstahl, Leni** (1902– ): *Triumph of the Will, Olympiad 1936.*

## GREAT BRITAIN

**Anderson, Michael** (1920– ): *The Naked Edge, The Quiller Memorandum.*
**Asquith, Anthony** (1902–68): *The Importance of Being Earnest, The Net, The Yellow Rolls-Royce.*
**Clayton, Jack** (1921– ): *Room at the Top, The Innocents, The Great Gatsby.*
**Cornelius, Henry** (1913–58): *Passport to Pimlico; Genevieve; I Am a Camera.*
**Crichton, Charles** (1910– ): *The Lavender Hill Mob, Battle of the Sexes, The Third Secret.*
**Hamer, Robert** (1911–63): *Kind Hearts and Coronets, The Scapegoat, School for Scoundrels.*
**Lean, David** (1908– ): *Great Expectations, The Bridge on the River Kwai, Lawrence of Arabia, Dr. Zhivago, Ryan's Daughter.*
**Lester, Richard** (1932– ): *A Hard Day's Night, Help!*
**Mackendrick, Alexander** (1912– ): *The Man in the White Suit, The Ladykillers, The Sweet Smell of Success.*
**Olivier, Sir Laurence** (1907– ): *Henry V, Hamlet, Richard III, Othello.*
**Powell, Michael** (1905– ): *One of Our Aircraft Is Missing, The Red Shoes, Tales of Hoffmann.*
**Reed, Sir Carol** (1906–76): *Odd Man Out, The Third Man, Oliver!*
**Reisz, Karel** (1926– ): *Saturday Night and Sunday Morning, Morgan, Isadora, The Gambler, French Lieutenant's Woman.*
**Richardson, Tony** (1928– ): *Look Back in Anger, The Entertainer, A Taste of Honey, Tom Jones.*
**Schlesinger, John** (1926– ): *A Kind of Loving, Billy Liar, Darling, Midnight Cowboy, Sunday, Bloody Sunday.*

## ITALY

**Antonioni, Michelangelo** (1912– ): *L'Avventura, La Notte, Red Desert, Blow-Up, Zabriskie Point.*
**Camerini, Mario** (1895– ): *I Promessi Sposi, Wife for a Night.*
**Comencini, Luigi** (1916– ): *The Mill on the Po; Bread, Love, and Dreams; Mariti in Citta.*
**De Santis, Giuseppe** (1917– ): *Bitter Rice, Rome Eleven O'Clock, Anna.*
**De Sica, Vittorio** (1902–74): *The Bicycle Thief, Umberto D, Two Women.*
**Fellini, Federico** (1920– ): *La Strada, Nights of Cabiria, La Dolce Vita, 8½, Fellini Satyricon, Amarcord.*
**Germi, Pietro** (1914–74): *Divorce, Italian Style; Seduced and Abandoned.*
**Monicelli, Mario** (1915– ): *The Organizer, Casanova 70.*
**Pasolini, Pier Paolo** (1922–75): *Accattone, Mamma Roma, The Gospel According to St. Matthew, Salo.*
**Pontecorvo, Gillo** (1919– ): *Kapo, The Battle of Algiers.*
**Rossellini, Roberto** (1906–77): *Open City, Stromboli, Il Generale Della Rovere, The Rise of Louis XIV.*
**Visconti, Luchino** (1906–76): *Rocco and His Brothers, The Leopard, The Stranger, The Damned, Death in Venice, The Innocent.*
**Wertmuller, Lina** (1929– ): *Swept Away, All Screwed Up, Seven Beauties.*
**Zampa, Luigi** (1905– ): *City on Trial, The Woman of Rome.*
**Zeffirelli, Franco** (1922– ): *The Taming of the Shrew, Romeo and Juliet, The Champ.*

## SWEDEN

**Bergman, Ingmar** (1918– ): *The Seventh Seal, Wild Strawberries, Virgin Spring, Persona, The Passion of Anna, The Magic Flute, Face to Face, Cries and Whispers.*
**Sjöberg, Alf** (1903– ): *Miss Julie, Barabbas, The Judge.*
**Sjöström, Victor** (1879–1960): *He Who Gets Slapped, The Scarlet Letter.*
**Stiller, Mauritz** (1883–1928): *The Story of Gösta Berling, Hotel Imperial, The Street of Sin.*

## UNITED STATES

**Allen, Woody**, (1935– ), *Annie Hall, Interiors, Manhattan.*
**Altman, Robert** (1925– ): *M*A*S*H, Nashville, Buffalo Bill and the Indians, 3 Women, A Wedding, Popeye.*
**Bogdanovich, Peter** (1939– ): *Targets, The Last Picture Show, What's Up Doc? Saint Jack, They All Laughed.*
**Brooks, Richard** (1912– ): *The Brothers Karamazov, Cat on a Hot Tin Roof, In Cold Blood, Looking for Mr. Goodbar.*
**Capra, Frank** (1897– ): *It Happened One Night, You Can't Take It with You, A Hole in the Head.*
**Cassavetes, John** (1929– ): *Shadows, A Child Is Waiting, Faces.*
**Chaplin, Charles** (1889–1977): *The Gold Rush, City Lights, Modern Times, The Great Dictator, Limelight.*
**Coppola, Francis Ford** (1939– ): *The Godfather I & II, The Conversation, Apocalypse Now.*
**Cukor, George** (1899– ): *Dinner at Eight, Camille, The Women, A Star Is Born, My Fair Lady, Rich and Famous.*
**Curtiz, Michael** (1888–1962): *Casablanca, Mildred Pierce.*
**Dassin, Jules** (1911– ): *The Naked City, Rififi, He Who Must Die, Never on Sunday.*
**De Mille, Cecil B.** (1881–1959): *The King of Kings, Samson and Delilah, The Greatest Show on Earth.*
**De Palma, Brian** (1940– ): *Carrie, The Fury, Dressed to Kill, Blow Out.*
**Donen, Stanley** (1924– ): *Seven Brides for Seven Brothers, Funny Face, Charade, Two for the Road.*
**Flaherty, Robert** (1884–1951): *Nanook of the North, Moana, Louisiana Story.*
**Fleming, Victor** (1883–1949): *Captains Courageous, The Wizard of Oz, Gone with the Wind.*

**Ford, John** (1895–1973): *Stagecoach, The Grapes of Wrath, The Quiet Man, Mogambo.*
**Frankenheimer, John** (1930– ): *Birdman of Alcatraz, The Manchurian Candidate, Grand Prix, Black Sunday.*
**Goulding, Edmund** (1891–1959): *Grand Hotel, The Razor's Edge, Nightmare Alley.*
**Griffith, D. W.** (1875–1948): *The Birth of a Nation, Intolerance, Orphans of the Storm.*
**Hawks, Howard** (1896–1977): *Scarface, Twentieth Century, Bringing Up Baby, The Big Sleep.*
**Hitchcock, Alfred** (1899–1980): *The 39 Steps, Strangers on a Train, Rear Window, North by Northwest, Family Plot.*
**Huston, John** (1906– ): *The Maltese Falcon, The Treasure of the Sierra Madre, The African Queen.*
**Kazan, Elia** (1909– ): *A Streetcar Named Desire, Viva Zapata!, On the Waterfront, East of Eden.*
**King, Henry** (1891–1982): *Stella Dallas, State Fair, The Gunfighter.*
**Kramer, Stanley** (1913– ): *Inherit the Wind, Judgment at Nuremberg, Guess Who's Coming to Dinner?*
**Kubrick, Stanley** (1928– ): *Paths of Glory, Lolita, Dr. Strangelove, 2001, Clockwork Orange, Barry Lyndon.*
**Le Roy, Mervyn** (1900– ): *I Am a Fugitive from a Chain Gang, Quo Vadis, Gypsy.*
**Lubitsch, Ernst** (1892–1947): *The Love Parade, Design for Living, Angel, Ninotchka.*
**Lucas, George** (1944– ): *American Graffiti, Star Wars.*
**Lumet, Sidney** (1924– ): *Long Day's Journey into Night, The Pawnbroker, The Seagull, Murder on the Orient Express, Network, Equus, The Wiz, Prince of the City.*
**McCarey, Leo** (1898–1969): *The Awful Truth, Going My Way, An Affair to Remember.*
**Mankiewicz, Joseph L.** (1909– ): *All About Eve, Julius Caesar, Suddenly Last Summer, Cleopatra.*
**Milestone, Lewis** (1895–1980): *All Quiet on the Western Front, Of Mice and Men, A Walk in the Sun.*
**Nichols, Mike** (1931– ): *Who's Afraid of Virginia Woolf?, The Graduate, Catch 22, Carnal Knowledge.*
**Peckinpah, Sam** (1925– ): *The Wild Bunch, Straw Dogs, Junior Bonner.*
**Penn, Arthur** (1922– ): *The Miracle Worker, Mickey One, Bonnie and Clyde, Alice's Restaurant.*
**Perry, Frank** (1930– ): *David and Lisa, Diary of a Mad Housewife, Last Summer, Mommie Dearest.*
**Preminger, Otto** (1906– ): *Laura, The Moon Is Blue, The Man with the Golden Arm, Anatomy of a Murder.*
**Ray, Nicholas** (1911–79): *Knock on Any Door, Rebel without a Cause, Johnny Guitar, In a Lonely Place.*
**Ritt, Martin** (1920– ): *Edge of the City; The Long, Hot Summer; Hud; The Brotherhood; Sounder; The Front, Norma Rae.*
**Rossen, Robert** (1908–66): *Body and Soul, All the King's Men, The Hustler.*
**Scorsese, Martin** (1942– ): *Mean Streets, Alice Doesn't Live Here Anymore, Taxi Driver, New York, New York, The Last Waltz, Raging Bull.*
**Silverstein, Elliot** (1927– ): *Cat Ballou, The Happening, A Man Called Horse.*
**Siodmak, Robert** (1900–73): *The Spiral Staircase, The Dark Mirror, The Killers.*
**Spielberg, Steven** (1947– ): *The Sugarland Express, Jaws, Close Encounters of the Third Kind, 1941, Raiders of the Lost Ark, E.T.*
**Sternberg, Josef von** (1894–1969): *The Blue Angel, Morocco, Shanghai Express.*
**Stevens, George** (1904–75): *A Place in the Sun, Shane, Giant, The Diary of Anne Frank.*
**Stroheim, Erich von** (1885–1957): *Merry Go Round, Greed, The Merry Widow.*
**Sturges, Preston** (1898–1959): *The Great McGinty, Sullivan's Travels, Hail the Conquering Hero.*
**Vidor, King** (1894– ): *The Big Parade, Northwest Passage, Duel in the Sun, War and Peace.*
**Walsh, Raoul** (1892–1980): *Thief of Bagdad, They Drive by Night, The Naked and the Dead.*
**Warhol, Andy** (1927?– ): *Chelsea Girls, Lonesome Cowboys, Blue Movie.*
**Welles, Orson** (1915– ): *Citizen Kane, The Magnificent Ambersons, Touch of Evil, The Trial.*
**Wellman, William** (1896–1975): *Nothing Sacred, The Story of G. I. Joe, The High and the Mighty.*
**Wilder, Billy** (1906– ): *The Lost Weekend, Sunset Boulevard, Stalag 17, Some Like It Hot.*
**Wood, Sam** (1883–1949): *A Night at the Opera; A Day at the Races; Goodbye, Mr. Chips; Our Town.*
**Wyler, William** (1902–81): *Wuthering Heights, Mrs. Miniver, The Best Years of Our Lives, Ben Hur.*
**Zinnemann, Fred** (1907– ): *High Noon, From Here to Eternity, The Nun's Story, A Man for All Seasons.*

## USSR

**Alexandrov, Grigori** (1903– ): *Jazz Comedy, Circus, Volga Volga.*
**Bondarchuk, Sergei** (1922– ): *Destiny of a Man, War and Peace, The Steppe.*
**Chukrai, Grigori** (1921– ): *The Forty-First, Ballad of a Soldier, Clear Sky.*
**Donskoi, Mark** (1897–1981):*The Maxim Gorki Trilogy, The Rainbow.*
**Dovzhenko, Alexander** (1894–1956): *Arsenal, Earth, Life in Blossom.*
**Eisenstein, Sergei** (1898–1948): *Potemkin, Alexander Nevsky, Ivan the Terrible.*
**Gerasimov, Sergei** (1906– ): *Young Guard, And Quiet Flows the Don.*
**Kalatosow, Mikhail** (1903–1973): *The First Echelon, The Cranes Are Flying.*
**Pudovkin, Vsevolod** (1893–1953): *Mother, Storm over Asia, The Deserter.*
**Pyryev, Ivan** (1901–68): *The Wealthy Bride, The Idiot.*
**Romm, Mikhail** (1901–71): *Boule de Suif, Nine Days of One Year.*

## OTHER COUNTRIES

**Buñuel, Luis** (1900– ), Spain: *Evil Eden, Nazarin, Viridiana, Belle de Jour, Las Olvidados, Tristana, The Discrete Charm of the Bourgeoisie.*
**Cacoyannis, Michael** (1922– ), Greece: *Stella, Electra, Zorba the Greek.*
**Cavalcanti, Alberto** (1897– ), Brazil: *Dead of Night, Champagne Charlie, Monster.*
**Costa-Gavras, Henri** (1933– ), Greece: *Z, The Confession, Claire de Femme, Missing.*
**Dreyer, Carl Theodore** (1889–1968), Denmark: *Joan of Arc, Vampyr, Day of Wrath, Gertrud.*
**Fábri, Zoltán** (1917– ), Hungary: *Professor Hannibal, Twenty Hours, Late Season.*
**Ford, Alexander** (1908– ), Poland: *The Young Chopin, Kings of the Teutonic Order.*
**Forman, Milos** (1932– ), Czechoslovakia: *Loves of a Blonde, The Fireman's Ball, One Flew Over the Cuckoo's Nest, Hair, Ragtime.*
**Ivens, Joris** (1898– ), Netherlands: *Zuyderzee, Spanish Earth.*
**Jancso, Miklos** (c. 1922– ), Hungary: *The Round Up, The Red and the White, The Tyrant's Heart.*
**Kadar, Jan** (1918–79), Czechoslovakia: *The Shop on Main Street, The Angel Levine, Adrift, Lies My Father Told Me.*
**Kinugasa, Teinosuke** (1898– ), Japan: *Gate of Hell, The White Heron.*
**Kurosawa, Akira** (1910– ), Japan: *Rashomon, Seven Samurai, Ikiru, The Lower Depths, Kagemushu.*
**Lang, Fritz** (1890–1976), Austria: *Metropolis, M, The 1,000 Eyes of Dr. Mabuse.*
**Lindtberg, Leopold** (1902– ), Switzerland: *The Last Chance, Four in a Jeep, The Village.*
**McLaren, Norman** (1914– ), Canada: *Blinkity-Blank; Dots, Loops.*
**Menzel, Jiri** (1938– ), Czechoslovakia: *Closely Watched Trains, Capricious Summer, Those Wonderful Movie Cranks.*
**Mizoguchi, Kenji** (1898–1956), Japan: *Ugetsu, The Princess Yang, Street of Shame.*
**Nemec, Jan** (1936– ), Czechoslovakia: *Diamonds of the Night, A Report on the Party and the Guests, The Martyrs of Love.*
**Polanski, Roman** (1933– ), Poland: *Knife in the Water, Repulsion, Rosemary's Baby, Chinatown, The Tenant.*
**Ray, Satyajit** (1921– ), India: *The Apu Trilogy, The Music Room, Devi, The Chess Players.*
**Saura, Carlos** (1932– ), Spain: *The Hunt, Cousin Angelica, Cria!*
**Teshigahara, Hiroshi** (1927– ), Japan: *Pitfall, Woman in the Dunes.*
**Torre-Nilsson, Leopoldo** (1924–78), Argentina: *The House of the Angel, The Hand in the Trap, Summer Skin.*
**Wajda, Andrzej** (1926– ), Poland: *Kanal, Ashes and Diamonds, Fury is a Woman, Man of Marble, Man of Iron.*
**Weir, Peter** (1944– ), Australia: *Picnic at Hanging Rock, The Last Wave, Gallipoli.*

# CELEBRITIES: PAST AND PRESENT

The Almanac celebrity list includes well-known personalities of stage, screen, radio, and television, as well as notables of other popular worlds. Entries indicate the celebrity's birthplace.

**Aaron, Hank** Mobile, Ala., 1934
**Abbott, George** Forestville, N.Y. 1887
**Abel, Walter** St. Paul, Minn., 1898
**Abdul-Jabbar, Kareem** New York, 1947
**Ace, Goodman** Kansas City, Mo., 1899-1982
**Acuff, Roy** Maynardsville, Tenn., 1907
**Adams, Don** New York City, 1927
**Adams, Edie** Kingston, Pa., 1929
**Adams, Joey** New York City, 1911
**Adams, Julie** Waterloo, Iowa, 1928
**Addams, Charles** Westfield, N. J., 1912
**Addams, Dawn** Felixstowe, Eng., 1930
**Adjani, Isabelle** Paris, 1956
**Adler, Larry** Baltimore, 1914
**Adler, Luther** New York City, 1903
**Adler, Stella** New York City, 1902
**Alberghetti, Anna Maria** Pesaro, Italy, 1936
**Albert, Eddie** Rock Island, Ill., 1908
**Albert, Edward** Los Angeles, 1951
**Albertson, Jack** Malden, Mass., 1907-81
**Albright, Lola** Akron, O., 1925
**Alda, Alan** New York City, 1936
**Alda, Robert** New York City, 1914
**Alexander, Ben** Goldfield, Nev., 1911-69
**Alexander, Jane** Boston, 1939
**Allen, Fred** Boston, 1894-1956
**Allen, Gracie** San Francisco, 1906-64
**Allen, Mel** Birmingham, Ala., 1913
**Allen, Steve** New York City, 1921
**Allen, Woody** New York City, 1935
**Allison, Fran** La Porte City, Iowa, 1924?
**Allyson, June** New York City, 1923
**Alpert, Herb** Los Angeles, 1935
**Ameche, Don** Kenosha, Wis., 1908
**Ames, Ed** Boston, 1929
**Ames, Leon** Portland, Ind., 1903
**Amory, Cleveland** Nahant, Mass., 1917
**Amsterdam, Morey** Chicago, 1912
**Anderson, Judith** Adelaide, Austral., 1898
**Anderson, Michael, Jr.** London, 1943
**Andersson, Bibi** Stockholm, 1935
**Andersson, Harriet** Stockholm, 1932
**Andress, Ursula**, Berne, Switz., 1936
**Andretti, Mario** Trieste, 1940
**Andrews, Dana** Collins, Miss., 1912
**Andrews, Julie** Walton-on-Thames, Eng., 1935
**Andrews, LaVerne** Minneapolis, 1915–67
**Andrews, Maxine** Minneapolis, 1918
**Andrews, Patty** Minneapolis, 1920
**Angeli, Pier** Sardinia, 1932-71
**Anka, Paul** Ottawa, Can., 1941
**Annabella** La Varenne-St. Hilaire, Fr., 1910
**Ann-Margret** Valsjobyn, Sweden, 1941
**Arbuckle, "Fatty"** Smith Center, Kans., 1887-1933
**Arcaro, Eddie** Newport, Ky., 1916
**Arden, Elizabeth** Ontario, 1891-1966
**Arden, Eve** Mill Valley, Cal., 1912
**Arkin, Alan** New York City, 1934
**Armstrong, Louis** New Orleans, 1900-71
**Arnaz, Desi** Santiago, Cuba, 1917
**Arness, James** Minneapolis, 1923
**Arno, Peter** New York, 1904-68
**Arnold, Eddy** Henderson, Tenn., 1918
**Arnold, Edward** New York, 1890-1956
**Arquette, Cliff** Toledo, O., 1905-74
**Arthur, Beatrice** New York, 1926
**Arthur, Jean** New York City, 1908
**Ashcroft, Peggy** London, 1907
**Ashe, Arthur** Richmond, Va., 1943
**Ashley, Elizabeth** Ocala, Fla., 1940
**Asner, Edward** Kansas City, Kans., 1929
**Astaire, Adele** Omaha, Neb. 1898–1981
**Astaire, Fred** Omaha, Neb., 1899
**Astor, Mary** Quincy, Ill., 1906
**Atkins, Chet** Luttrell, Tenn., 1924
**Attenborough, Richard** Cambridge, Eng., 1923
**Aumont, Jean-Pierre** Paris, 1913
**Austin, Tracy** Redondo Beach, Cal., 1962
**Autry, Gene** Tioga, Tex., 1907
**Avalon, Frankie** Philadelphia, 1940
**Avedon, Richard** New York City, 1923
**Ayres, Lew** Minneapolis, 1908
**Aznavour, Charles** Paris, 1924
**Bacall, Lauren** New York City, 1924
**Baccaloni, Salvatore** Rome, 1900-69
**Bacharach, Burt** Kansas City, Mo., 1929
**Backus, Jim** Cleveland, 1913
**Baer, Max** Omaha, 1909-59
**Baez, Joan** New York City, 1941
**Bailey, Mildred** Washington, 1903-51
**Bailey, Pearl** Newport News, Va., 1918
**Bainter, Fay** Los Angeles, 1893-1963
**Baird, Bil** Grand Island, Neb., 1904
**Baker, Carroll** Johnstown, Pa., 1935
**Baker, Diane** Hollywood, Cal., 1940?
**Baker, Josephine** St. Louis, 1906-75
**Baker, Kenny** Monrovia, Cal., 1912
**Balenciaga, Cristobal** Guetaria, Sp., 1895-1972
**Ball, Lucille** Jamestown, N. Y., 1911
**Ballard, Kaye** Cleveland, 1926
**Balmain, Pierre** St.-Jean-de-Maurienne, Fr., 1914-82
**Balsam, Martin** New York City, 1919
**Bancroft, Anne** New York City, 1931
**Bankhead, Tallulah** Huntsville, Ala., 1903-68
**Bara, Theda** Cincinnati, 1890-1955
**Barber, Red** Columbus, Miss., 1908
**Bardot, Brigitte** Paris, 1934
**Barnes, Binnie** London, 1906
**Barrault, Jean-Louis** Vesinet, Fr., 1910
**Barrie, Wendy** London, 1913–78
**Barry, Gene** New York City, 1921
**Barrymore, Diana** New York, 1922-60
**Barrymore, Ethel** Phila., 1879-1959
**Barrymore, John** Phila., 1882-1942
**Barrymore, John Blyth** Beverly Hills, Cal., 1932
**Barrymore, Lionel** Phila. 1878-1954
**Barthelmess, Richard** New York, 1895-1963
**Bartholomew, Freddie** London, 1924
**Bartok, Eva** Budapest, 1926
**Basehart, Richard** Zanesville, O., 1914
**Basie, Count** Red Bank, N. J., 1904
**Bassey, Shirley** Cardiff, Wales, 1937
**Bates, Alan** Allestree, Eng., 1934
**Baxter, Anne** Michigan City, Ind., 1923
**Baxter, Warner** Columbus, O., 1893-1951
**Bean, Orson** Burlington, Vt., 1928
**Beaton, Cecil** London, 1904-80
**Beatty, Clyde** Bainbridge, O., 1905-65
**Beatty, Warren** Richmond, Va., 1938
**Bechet, Sidney** New Orleans, 1897-1959
**Bee Gees** see **Gibb**
**Beene, Geoffrey** Haynesville, La., 1927
**Beery, Noah** Kansas City, Mo., 1883-1946
**Beery, Noah, Jr.**, New York City, 1916
**Beery, Wallace** Kansas City, Mo., 1886-1949
**Begley, Ed** Hartford, Conn., 1901-70
**Belafonte, Harry** New York City, 1927
**Belasco, David** San Francisco, 1854-1931
**Bel Geddes, Barbara** New York, 1922
**Bellamy, Ralph** Chicago, 1904
**Belmondo, Jean-Paul** Neuilly-sur-Seine, Fr., 1933
**Belushi, John** Chicago, 1949-82
**Benatar, Pat** Brooklyn, 1953
**Benchley, Robert** Worcester, Mass., 1889-1945
**Bendix, William** New York, 1906-64
**Benjamin, Richard** New York City, 1939
**Bennett, Constance** New York, 1914-65
**Bennett, Joan** Palisades, N. J., 1910
**Bennett, Michael** Buffalo, 1943
**Bennett, Richard** Indiana, 1873-1944
**Bennett, Tony** New York City, 1926
**Benny, Jack** Waukegan, Ill. 1894-1974
**Benzell, Mimi** Bridgeport, Conn., 1924-70
**Berg, Gertrude** New York, 1900-66
**Bergen, Candice** Beverly Hills, Cal., 1946
**Bergen, Edgar** Chicago, 1903-78
**Bergen, Polly** Knoxville, Tenn., 1930
**Bergerac, Jacques** Biarritz, Fr., 1927
**Bergman, Ingrid** Stockholm, 1915-82
**Bergner, Elisabeth** Vienna, 1900
**Berkeley, Busby** Los Angeles, 1895-1976
**Berle, Milton** New York City, 1908
**Berlin, Irving** Russia, 1888
**Berman, Pandro S.** Pittsburgh, 1905
**Berman, Shelley** Chicago, 1926
**Bernardi, Herschel** New York City, 1923
**Bernhardt, Sarah** Paris, 1844-1923
**Bernie, Ben** Bayonne, N.J., 1893-1943
**Berra, Yogi** St. Louis, 1925
**Bickford, Charles** Cambridge, Mass., 1889-1967
**Bikel, Theodore** Vienna, 1924
**Birney, David** Washington, 1940
**Bishop, Joey** New York City, 1918
**Bisset, Jacqueline** Weybridge, Eng., 1944
**Black, Karen** Park Ridge, Ill., 1942
**Blackman, Honor** London, 1929
**Blackmer, Sidney** Salisbury, N. C., 1898-1973
**Blaine, Vivian** Newark, N. J., 1924
**Blair, Janet** Altoona, Pa., 1921
**Blair, Linda** Westport, Conn., 1959
**Blake, Eubie** Baltimore, 1883
**Blake, Robert** Nutley, N.J., 1938
**Blakeley, Ronee** Idaho, 1946
**Blass, Bill** Fort Wayne, Ind., 1922
**Blocker, Dan** Bowie Co., Tex., 1929-72
**Blondell, Joan** New York City, 1912-79
**Bloom, Claire** London, 1931
**Blue, Ben** Montreal, 1901-75
**Blyth, Ann** New York City, 1928
**Bogarde, Dirk** London, 1921
**Bogart, Humphrey** New York, 1899-1957
**Boland, Mary** Phila., 1885-1965
**Bolger, Ray** Dorchester, Mass., 1904
**Bombeck, Erma** Dayton, Ohio, 1927
**Bond, Ward** Denver, 1904-60
**Bono, Sonny** Detroit, 1940
**Boone, Pat** Jacksonville, Fla., 1934
**Boone, Richard** Los Angeles, 1917-81
**Booth, Shirley** New York City, 1909
**Borg, Björn** Södertalje, Sweden, 1956
**Borge, Victor** Copenhagen, 1909
**Borgnine, Ernest** Hamden, Conn., 1917
**Bosley, Tom** Chicago, 1927
**Bourke-White, Margaret** New York City, 1906-71
**Bow, Clara** New York, 1905-65
**Bowes, "Major"** San Francisco, 1874-1946
**Bowie, David** Brixton, Eng., 1947
**Bowman, Lee** Cincinnati, 1914-79
**Boyd, Stephen** Belfast, Northern Ireland, 1928-77
**Boyd, William** Cambridge, O., 1898-1972
**Boyer, Charles** Figeac Lot, Fr., 1899–1978
**Bracken, Eddie** New York City, 1920
**Bradshaw, Terry** Shreveport, La., 1948
**Brady, Alice** New York, 1892-1939
**Brady, Scott** New York City, 1924
**Brand, Neville** Kewanee, Ill., 1921
**Brando, Marlon** Omaha, Neb., 1924
**Brasselle, Keefe** Lorain, O., 1923
**Brazzi, Rossano** Bologna, Italy, 1916
**Brel, Jacques** Brussels, 1929-78
**Brennan, Walter** Lynn, Mass., 1894-1974
**Brenner, David** Philadelphia, 1945
**Brent, George** Dublin, 1904-79
**Brewer, Teresa** Toledo, O., 1931
**Brice, Fanny** New York, 1891-1951
**Bridges, Beau** Los Angeles, 1941
**Bridges, Lloyd** San Leandro, Cal., 1913
**Brinkley, David** Wilmington, N. C., 1920
**Brisson, Frederick** Copenhagen, 1917
**Britt, Mai** Lidingo, Swed., 1936
**Brock, Lou** El Dorado, Ark., 1939
**Broderick, Helen** Phila., 1890-1959
**Brokaw, Tom** Webster, S.D., 1940
**Bronson, Charles**, Ehrenfeld, Pa., 1922
**Brooks, Mel** New York City, 1926
**Brothers, Joyce** New York City, 1928

**Broun, Heywood** New York, 1888-1939
**Broun, Heywood Hale** New York, 1918
**Brown, Helen Gurley** Portland, Me., 1922
**Brown, James** Augusta, Ga., 1930?
**Brown, Jim** Manhasset, N. Y., 1936
**Brown, Joe E.** Holgate, O., 1892-1973
**Brown, Vanessa** Vienna, 1928
**Brubeck, Dave** Concord, Cal., 1920
**Bruce, Carol** Great Neck, N. Y., 1919
**Bruce, Nigel** Mexico, 1895-1953
**Bruce, Virginia** Minneapolis, 1909-82
**Bryant, Anita** Barnsdall, Okla., 1940
**Bryant, Paul "Bear"** Moro Bottom, Ark., 1913
**Brynner, Yul** Sakhalin, 1917
**Buchanan, Edgar** Humansville, Mo., 1903-79
**Buchanan, Jack** Scotland, 1891-1957
**Buchholz, Horst** Berlin, 1933
**Buchwald, Art** Mount Vernon, N. Y., 1925
**Buckley, William F.** New York City, 1925
**Bujold, Genevieve** Montreal, 1942
**Burke, Billie** Washington, 1884-1970
**Burnett, Carol** San Antonio, 1935?
**Burns, George** New York City, 1896
**Burr, Raymond** New Westminster, Can., 1917
**Burrows, Abe** New York City, 1910
**Burstyn, Ellen** Detroit, Mich., 1932
**Burton, Richard** Pontrhydyfen, Wales, 1925
**Bushman, Francis X.** Norfolk, 1883-1966
**Butterworth, Charles** South Bend, Ind., 1897-1946
**Buttons, Red** New York City, 1919
**Buzzi, Ruth** Westerly, R. I., 1936
**Byington, Spring,** Colorado Springs, 1893-1971
**Byrd, Charlie** Chuckatuck, Va., 1925
**Caan, James** New York City, 1939
**Caen, Herb** Sacramento, Cal., 1916
**Caesar, Irving** New York City, 1895
**Caesar, Sid** Yonkers, N. Y., 1922
**Cagney, James** New York City, 1904
**Cahn, Sammy** New York City, 1913
**Caine, Michael** London, 1933
**Caldwell, Zoë** Melbourne, Austral., 1933
**Calhern, Louis** New York, 1895-1956
**Calhoun, Rory** Los Angeles, 1923
**Callan, Michael** Philadelphia, 1935
**Calloway, Cab** Rochester, N. Y., 1907
**Cambridge, Godfrey** New York, 1933-76
**Cameron, Rod** Calgary, Can., 1912
**Campbell, Glen** near Delight, Ark., 1938
**Cannon, Dyan** Tacoma, Wash., 1938?
**Canova, Judy** Jacksonville, Fla., 1916
**Cantinflas** Mexico City, 1911
**Cantor, Eddie** New York, 1892-1964
**Cantrell, Lana** Sydney, Austral., 1944
**Capp, Al** New Haven, Conn., 1909-79
**Capucine** Toulon, Fr., 1935?
**Cardin, Pierre** near Venice, 1922
**Cardinale, Claudia** Tunis, 1940
**Carew, Rod** Gatun, C.Z., 1945
**Carey, Macdonald** Sioux City, Iowa, 1913
**Carlin, George** New York City, 1938
**Carlisle, Kitty** New Orleans, 1914
**Carmichael, Hoagy** Bloomington, Ind., 1899-1981
**Carmines, Al** Hampton, Va., 1937
**Carne, Judy** Northampton, Eng., 1939
**Carney, Art** Mt. Vernon, N. Y., 1918
**Carnovsky, Morris** St. Louis, 1897
**Caron, Leslie** Paris, 1931
**Carr, Vikki** El Paso, Tex., 1942
**Carradine, David** Los Angeles, 1936
**Carradine, John** New York City, 1906
**Carrillo, Leo** Los Angeles, 1881-1961
**Carroll, Diahann** New York City, 1935
**Carroll, Leo G.** Weedon, Eng., 1892-1972
**Carroll, Madeleine** West Bromwich, Eng., 1906
**Carroll, Nancy** New York, 1906-65
**Carroll, Pat** Shreveport, La., 1927
**Carson, Jack** Carman, Can., 1910-63
**Carson, Johnny** Corning, Iowa, 1925
**Carter, Billy** Plains, Ga., 1937
**Carter, Jack** New York City, 1923
**Cash, Johnny** Kingsland, Ark., 1932
**Cass, Peggy** Boston, 1925
**Cassavetes, John** New York, 1929
**Cassidy, Shaun** Los Angeles, 1958
**Cassini, Oleg** Paris, 1913
**Castle, Irene** New Rochelle, N.Y., 1893-1969
**Cauthen, Steve** Covington, Ky., 1960
**Cavett, Dick** Gibbon, Neb., 1936
**Cerf, Bennett** New York City, 1898-1971
**Chakiris, George** Norwood, O., 1933
**Chamberlain, Richard** Beverly Hills, Cal., 1935
**Chamberlain, Wilt** Philadelphia, 1936
**Champion, Gower** Geneva, Ill., 1920-80
**Champion, Marge** Hollywood, Cal., 1925
**Chancellor, John** Chicago, 1927
**Chandler, Jeff** New York, 1918-61
**Chanel, "Coco"** Issoire, Fr., 1883-1971
**Chaney, Lon** Colorado Springs, 1883-1930
**Chaney, Lon, Jr.** Oklahoma City, 1915-73
**Channing, Carol** Seattle, 1921
**Chaplin, Charles** London, 1889–1977
**Chaplin, Geraldine** Santa Monica, Cal., 1944
**Chaplin, Sydney** Los Angeles, 1926
**Charisse, Cyd** Amarillo, Tex., 1923
**Charles, Ray** Albany, Ga., 1932
**Chase, Chevy** New York City, 1943
**Chase, Ilka** New York City, 1905–78
**Chatterton, Ruth** New York, 1893-1961
**Cher** El Centro, Cal., 1946
**Chevalier, Maurice** Paris, 1888-1972
**Child, Julia** Pasadena, Cal., 1912
**Christian, Linda** Tampico, Mexico, 1923
**Christie, Julie** Chukua, India, 1941
**Christopher, Jordan** Akron, O., 1941
**Cilento, Diane** Brisbane, Austral., 1933
**Claire, Ina** Washington, D. C., 1895
**Clapton, Eric** Ripley, Eng., 1945
**Clark, Bobby** Springfield, O., 1888-1960
**Clark, Dane** New York City, 1915
**Clark, Dick** Mt. Vernon, N. Y., 1929
**Clark, Fred** Lincoln, Cal., 1914-68
**Clark, Petula** Ewell, Eng., 1932
**Clark, Roy** Meherrin, Va., 1933
**Clayburgh, Jill** New York City, 1944
**Clift, Montgomery** Omaha, 1920-66
**Clooney, Rosemary** Maysville, Ky., 1928
**Cobb, Irvin S.** Paducah, Ky., 1876-1944
**Cobb, Lee J.** New York City, 1911-76
**Coburn, Charles** Macon, Ga., 1877-1961
**Coburn, James** Laurel, Neb., 1928
**Coca, Imogene** Philadelphia, 1908
**Coco, James** New York City, 1929
**Coe, Sebastian** London, 1956
**Cohan, George M.** Providence, R.I., 1878-1942
**Cohen, Myron** Grodno, Poland, 1902
**Colbert, Claudette** Paris, 1905
**Colby, Anita** Washington, D. C., 1914
**Cole, Nat "King"** Montgomery, Ala., 1919-65
**Cole, Natalie** Los Angeles, 1950
**Coleman, Ornette** Fort Worth, Tex., 1930
**Collingwood, Charles** Three Rivers, Mich., 1917
**Collins, Dorothy** Windsor, Can., 1926
**Collins, Joan** London, 1933
**Collins, Judy** Seattle, 1939
**Colman, Ronald** Richmond, Eng., 1891-1959
**Colonna, Jerry** Boston, 1905
**Comaneci, Nadia** Onesti, Romania, 1961
**Comden, Betty** New York City, 1919
**Como, Perry** Canonsburg, Pa., 1913
**Condon, Eddie** Goodland, Ind., 1905-73
**Conklin, Peggy** Dobbs Ferry, N. Y., 1912
**Connelly, Marc** McKeesport, Pa. 1890-1980
**Connery, Sean** Edinburgh, 1930
**Connolly, Walter** Cincinnati, 1887-1940
**Connors, Chuck** New York City, 1921
**Connors, Jimmy** St. Louis, 1952
**Connors, Mike** Fresno, Cal., 1925
**Conrad, William** Louisville, Ky., 1920
**Conried, Hans** Baltimore, 1915-82
**Conte, Richard** New York City 1914-75
**Conway, Tim** Willoughby, Ohio, 1933
**Conway, Tom** Russia, 1904-67
**Coogan, Jackie** Los Angeles, 1914
**Cook, Joe** Chicago, 1890-1959
**Cooke, Alistair** Manchester, Eng., 1908
**Coolidge, Rita** Nashville, 1944
**Cooney, Joan Ganz** Phoenix, 1929
**Cooper, Alice** Detroit, 1948
**Cooper, Gary** Helena, Mont., 1901-61
**Cooper, Gladys** Lewisham, Eng., 1888-1971
**Cooper, Jackie** Los Angeles, 1922
**Coote, Robert** London, 1909
**Corey, Wendell** Dracut, Mass., 1914-68
**Corio, Ann** Hartford, Conn., 1914?
**Cornell, Katharine** Berlin, 1898-1974
**Cosby, Bill** Philadelphia, 1937
**Cosell, Howard** Winston-Salem, N.C., 1920
**Costello, Lou** Paterson, N.J., 1906-59
**Cotten, Joseph** Petersburg, Va., 1905
**Courrèges, André** Pau, Fr., 1923
**Courtenay, Tom** Hull, Eng., 1937
**Cousins, Norman** Union Hill, N. J., 1912
**Cousteau, Jacques Yves** St. André-de-Cubzac, Fr., 1910
**Cox, Wally** Detroit, 1924-73
**Crabbe, Buster** Oakland, Cal., 1909
**Crain, Jeanne** Barstow, Cal., 1925
**Craven, Frank** Boston, 1878-1948
**Crawford, Broderick** Philadelphia, 1911
**Crawford, Joan** San Antonio, 1908-77
**Cregar, Laird** Phila., 1916-44
**Crenna, Richard** Los Angeles, 1927
**Croce, Jim** Philadelphia, Pa., 1943-73
**Cronkite, Walter** St. Joseph, Mo., 1916
**Cronyn, Hume** London, Can., 1911
**Crosby, Bing** Tacoma, Wash., 1904-77
**Crosby, Bob** Spokane, Wash., 1913
**Crosby, David** Los Angeles, 1941
**Crouse, Russel** Findlay, O., 1893-1966
**Csonka, Larry** Stow, O., 1946
**Cugat, Xavier** Barcelona, 1900
**Cukor, George** New York City, 1899
**Cullen, Bill** Pittsburgh, 1920
**Culp, Robert** Berkeley, Cal., 1930
**Cummings, Robert** Joplin, Mo., 1910
**Curtis, Tony** New York City, 1925
**Dahl, Arlene** Minneapolis, 1927
**Dailey, Dan** New York City, 1915-78
**Dale, Jim** Rothwell, Eng., 1935
**Daly, John** Johannesburg, 1914
**Damone, Vic** New York City, 1928
**Dana, Bill** Quincy, Mass., 1924
**Dandridge, Dorothy** Cleveland, 1924-65
**Daniels, Bebe** Dallas, 1901-71
**Daniels, Billy** Jacksonville, Fla., 1914?
**Danner, Blythe** Philadelphia, 1944
**Danton, Ray** New York City, 1931
**Darcel, Denise** Paris, 1925
**Darin, Bobby** New York City, 1936-73
**Darnell, Linda** Dallas, 1921-65
**Darren, James** Philadelphia, 1936
**Darrieux, Danielle** Bordeaux, Fr., 1917
**Darwell, Jane** Palmyra, Mo., 1880-1967
**da Silva, Howard** Cleveland, 1909
**Dauphin, Claude** Corbeil, Fr., 1903-78
**Davenport, Harry** New York 1866-1949
**Davenport, Nigel** Cambridge, Eng., 1928
**Davidson, John** Pittsburgh, Pa., 1941
**Davies, Marion** New York, 1897-1961
**Davis, Bette** Lowell, Mass., 1908
**Davis, Joan** St. Paul, Minn., 1908-61
**Davis, Mac** Lubbock, Tex., 1942
**Davis, Miles** Alton, Ill., 1927
**Davis, Ossie** Cogdell, Ga., 1921
**Davis, Sammy, Jr.** New York City, 1925
**Day, Dennis** New York City, 1917
**Day, Doris** Cincinnati, 1924
**Day, Laraine** Roosevelt, Utah, 1920
**Dean, Dizzy** Lucas, Ark., 1911-74
**Dean, James** Fairmount, Ind., 1931-55
**DeCamp, Rosemary** Prescott, Ariz., 1914
**De Carlo, Yvonne** Vancouver, Can., 1924
**Dee, Frances** Los Angeles, 1907
**Dee, Ruby** Cleveland, 1923?
**Dee, Sandra** Bayonne, N. J., 1942
**De Fore, Don** Cedar Rapids, Iowa, 1916
**De Haven, Gloria** Los Angeles, 1925
**de Havilland, Olivia** Tokyo, 1916
**Dekker, Albert** New York, 1905-68
**De Laurentiis, Dino** Torre Annunziata, Italy, 1919

**Delon, Alain** Scéaux, Fr., 1935
**Del Rio, Dolores** Durango, Mex., 1905
**DeLuise, Dom** Brooklyn, N.Y., 1933
**Demarest, William** St. Paul, 1892
**De Mille, Cecil B.** Ashfield, Mass., 1881-1959
**Dempsey, Jack** Manassa, Colo., 1895-1974
**Deneuve, Catherine** Paris, 1943
**De Niro, Robert** New York City, 1943
**Dennis, Sandy** Hastings, Neb., 1937
**Denny, Reginald** Richmond, Eng., 1891-1967
**Denver, John** Roswell, N.M., 1943
**Derek, Bo** Long Beach, Cal., 1956
**Dern, Bruce** Chicago, 1936
**Desmond, Johnny** Detroit, 1921
**Devine, Andy** Flagstaff, Ariz., 1905-77
**Dewhurst, Colleen** Montreal, 1926
**de Wilde, Brandon** New York, 1942-72
**De Wolfe, Billy** Wollaston, Mass. 1907-74
**Diamond, Neil** Brooklyn, N.Y., 1941
**Diana, Princess of Wales** Sandringham, Eng., 1961
**Dickinson, Angie** Kulm, N.D., 1932
**Dietrich, Marlene** Berlin, 1904
**Dietz, Howard** New York City, 1896
**Diller, Phyllis** Lima, O., 1917
**Dillman, Bradford** San Francisco, 1930
**Di Maggio, Joe** San Francisco, 1914
**Dior, Christian** Granville, Fr., 1905-57
**Disney, Walt** Chicago, 1901-66
**Dixon, Jeane** Medford, Wis., 1918
**Dolly, Jenny** Hungary, 1892-1941
**Dolly, Rosie** Hungary, 1892-1970
**Donahue, Phil** Cleveland, 1935
**Donahue, Troy** New York City, 1937
**Donat, Robert** Manchester, Eng., 1905-59
**Donlevy, Brian** Portadown, Ire., 1899-1972
**Donovan (Leitch)** Glasgow, 1946
**Dors, Diana** Swindon, Eng., 1931
**Dorsey, Jimmy** Mahonoy Plane, Pa., 1904-57
**Dorsey, Tommy** Mahonoy Plane, Pa., 1905-56
**Douglas, Kirk** Amsterdam, N. Y., 1918?
**Douglas, Melvyn** Macon, Ga., 1901-81
**Douglas, Michael** New Brunswick, N.J., 1944
**Douglas, Mike** Chicago, 1925
**Douglas, Paul** Phila., 1907-59
**Downs, Hugh** Akron, O., 1921
**Drake, Alfred** New York City, 1914
**Drake, Betsy** Paris, 1923
**Draper, Paul** Florence, Italy, 1909
**Draper, Ruth** New York, 1884-1956
**Dressler, Marie** Canada, 1869-1933
**Dreyfuss, Richard** New York City, 1947
**Dru, Joanne** Logan, W. Va., 1923
**Duchin, Eddy** Boston, 1909-51
**Duchin, Peter** New York City, 1937
**Duff, Howard** Bremerton, Wash., 1917
**Duke, Doris** New York City, 1912
**Duke, Patty** New York City, 1946
**Dullea, Keir** Cleveland, 1939
**Dunaway, Faye** Tallahassee, Fla., 1941
**Duncan, Sandy** Henderson, Tex., 1946
**Dunn, James** New York, 1906-67
**Dunne, Irene** Louisville, Ky., 1904
**Dunnock, Mildred** Baltimore, 1906
**Durante, Jimmy** New York, 1893-1980
**Durbin, Deanna** Winnipeg, Can., 1922
**Durocher, Leo** West Springfield, Mass., 1906
**Duryea, Dan** White Plains, N.Y., 1907-68
**Duse, Eleanora** Italy, 1858-1924
**Duvall, Robert** San Diego, Cal., 1931
**Dylan, Bob** Duluth, Minn., 1941
**Eagels, Jeanne** Kansas City, Mo., 1894-1929
**Eastwood, Clint** San Francisco, 1933
**Ebsen, Buddy** Orlando, Fla., 1908
**Eddy, Nelson** Providence, R.I., 1901-67
**Eden, Barbara** San Francisco, 1936
**Edwards, Ralph** Merino, Colo., 1913
**Edwards, Vince** New York City, 1928
**Egan, Richard** San Francisco, 1923
**Eggar, Samantha** London, 1940
**Ekberg, Anita** Malmö, Swed., 1931
**Eldridge, Florence** New York City, 1901
**Elliot, Cass** Arlington, Va., 1943?-74
**Elliott, Bob** Boston, 1923
**Elliott, Maxine** Rockland, Me., 1868-1940
**Emerson, Faye** Elizabeth, N. J., 1917
**Erickson, Leif** Alameda, Cal., 1914
**Erving, Julius** Roosevelt, N.Y., 1950
**Erwin, Stuart** Squaw Valley, Cal., 1903-67
**Esposito, Phil** Sault Ste. Marie, Ont., 1942
**Evans, Bergen** Franklin, O., 1904–78
**Evans, Dale** Uvalde, Tex., 1912
**Evans, Madge** New York City, 1909-81
**Evans, Maurice** Dorchester, Eng., 1901
**Evert-Lloyd, Chris** Fort Lauderdale, Fla., 1954
**Ewell, Tom** Owensboro, Ky., 1909
**Fabray, Nanette** San Diego, Cal., 1920
**Fadiman, Clifton** New York City, 1904
**Fairbanks, Douglas** Denver, 1883-1939
**Fairbanks, Douglas, Jr.** New York, 1909
**Faith, Percy** Toronto, 1908-76
**Falk, Peter** New York City, 1927
**Farber, Barry** Baltimore, 1930
**Farrell, Glenda** Enid, Okla., 1904-71
**Farrow, Mia** Los Angeles, 1945
**Faulk, John Henry** Austin, Tex., 1913
**Fawcett, Farrah** Corpus Christi, Tex., 1947
**Fay, Frank** San Francisco, 1897-1961
**Faye, Alice** New York City, 1915
**Feiffer, Jules** New York City, 1929
**Feldman, Marty** London, 1933
**Feldon, Barbara** Pittsburgh, 1939
**Feliciano, José** Larez, P. R., 1945
**Feller, Bob** Van Meter, Iowa, 1918
**Fernandel** Marseilles, 1903-71
**Ferrer, José** Santurce, P. R., 1912
**Ferrer, Mel** Elberon, N. J., 1917
**Field, Betty** Boston, 1918-73
**Field, Sally** Pasadena, Cal., 1946
**Fields, Dorothy** Allenhurst, N. J., 1905
**Fields, Gracie** Rochdale, Eng., 1898-1979
**Fields, Totie** Hartford, Conn., 1931–78
**Fields, W. C.** Phila., 1879-1946
**Finch, Peter** London, 1916-77
**Finney, Albert** Salford, Eng., 1936
**Fischer, Bobby** Chicago, 1943
**Fisher, Carrie** Beverly Hills, 1956
**Fisher, Eddie** Philadelphia, 1928
**Fitzgerald, Barry** Dublin, 1888-1961
**Fitzgerald, Ella** Newport News, Va., 1918
**Fitzgerald, Geraldine** Dublin, 1914
**Flack, Roberta** Black Mountain, N. C., 1940
**Fleming, Rhonda** Los Angeles, 1923
**Fletcher, Louise** Birmingham, Ala., 1934
**Flynn, Errol** Tasmania, 1909-59
**Foch, Nina** Leyden, Neth., 1924
**Fonda, Henry** Grand Island, Neb., 1905-82
**Fonda, Jane** New York City, 1937
**Fonda, Peter** New York City, 1939
**Fontaine, Frank** Haverhill, Mass., 1920–78
**Fontaine, Joan** Tokyo, 1917
**Fontanne, Lynn** Woodford, Eng., 1887?
**Ford, Glenn** Quebec, 1916
**Ford, Tennessee Ernie** Bristol, Tenn., 1919
**Forsythe, John** Penns Grove, N. J., 1918
**Fosse, Bob** Chicago, 1927
**Foster, Jodie** Los Angeles, 1962
**Foxx, Redd** St. Louis, 1922
**Foy, Eddie, Jr.** New Rochelle,N.Y., 1910
**Frampton, Peter** Beckenham, Eng., 1950
**Franciosa, Anthony** New York City, 1928
**Francis, Arlene** Boston, 1908
**Francis, Connie** Newark, N. J., 1938
**Francis, Kay** Oklahoma City, 1905-68
**Franklin, Aretha** Memphis, Tenn., 1942
**Frazier, Walt** Atlanta, 1945
**Freberg, Stan** Pasadena, Cal., 1926
**Freed, Arthur** Charleston, S. C., 1894
**Friedan, Betty** Peoria, Ill., 1921
**Friendly, Fred W.** New York City, 1915
**Fröbe, Gert** Planitz, Ger., 1913
**Froman, Jane** St. Louis, 1908-80
**Frost, David** Tenterden, Eng., 1939
**Funt, Allen** New York City, 1914
**Furness, Betty** New York City, 1916
**Gabel, Martin** Philadelphia, 1912
**Gable, Clark** Cadiz, O., 1901-60
**Gabor, Eva** Budapest, 1926?
**Gabor, Zsa Zsa** Budapest, 1928
**Gallico, Paul** New York City, 1897-1976
**Gam, Rita** Pittsburgh, 1928
**Garagiola, Joe** St. Louis, 1926
**Garbo, Greta** Stockholm, 1906
**Gardiner, Reginald** Wimbledon, Eng., 1903-80
**Gardner, Ava** Smithfield, N. C., 1922
**Garfield, John** New York, 1913-52
**Garfunkel, Arthur** New York City, 1941
**Gargan, William** New York, 1905-79
**Garland, Judy** Grand Rapids, Minn., 1922-69
**Garner, Erroll** Pittsburgh, 1921-77
**Garner, James** Norman, Okla., 1928
**Garner, Peggy Ann** Canton, O., 1932
**Garroway, Dave** Schenectady, N.Y., 1913-82
**Garson, Greer** County Down, Northern Ireland, 1908
**Gassman, Vittorio** Genoa, Italy, 1922
**Gavin, John** Los Angeles, 1928
**Gayle, Crystal** Paintsville, Ky., 1951
**Gaxton, William** San Francisco, 1893-1963
**Gaynor, Janet** Philadelphia, 1906
**Gaynor, Mitzi** Chicago, 1931
**Gazzara, Ben** New York City, 1930
**Geer, Will** Frankfort, Ind., 1902–78
**Gehrig, Lou** New York, 1903-41
**Gentry, Bobbie** Chickasaw Co., Miss., 1944
**George, Gladys** Patten, Me., 1904-54
**George, Grace** New Yo-k, 1879-1961
**Gere, Richard** Philadelphia, 1950
**Gernreich, Rudi** Vienna, 1922
**Gershwin, George** New York, 1898-1937
**Gershwin, Ira** New York City, 1896
**Gerulaitis, Vitas** Brooklyn, 1954
**Getz, Stan** Philadelphia, 1927
**Ghostley, Alice** Eve, Mo., 1926
**Giannini, Giancarlo** La Spezia, Italy, 1942
**Gibb, Andy** Manchester Eng., 1958
**Gibb, Barry** Douglas, I. of Man, 1946
**Gibb, Maurice** Manchester, Eng., 1949
**Gibb, Robin** Manchester, Eng., 1949
**Gibbs, Georgia** Worcester, Mass., 1923?
**Gielgud, John** London, 1904
**Gilbert, Billy** Louisville, Ky., 1894-1971
**Gilbert, John** Logan, Utah, 1895-1936
**Gilford, Jack** New York City, 1913?
**Gillespie, Dizzy** Cheraw, N. C., 1917
**Gingold, Hermione** London, 1897
**Gish, Dorothy** Massillon, O., 1898-1968
**Gish, Lillian** Springfield, O , 1899
**Givenchy, Hubert** Beauvais, Fr., 1927
**Gleason, Jackie** New York City, 1916
**Gleason, James** New York, 1886-1959
**Gobel, George** Chicago, 1920
**Goddard, Paulette** Great Neck, N. Y., 1911
**Godfrey, Arthur** New York City, 1903
**Goldberg, Rube** San Francisco, 1883-1970
**Golden, Harry** New York City, 1902-81
**Goldwyn, Samuel** Warsaw, 1882-1974
**Gonzales, Pancho** Los Angeles, 1928
**Goodman, Benny** Chicago, 1909
**Goodman, Dody** Columbus, O., 1929
**Goodson, Mark** Sacramento, Cal., 1915
**Goolagong, Evonne** Barellan, Australia, 1951
**Gordon, Ruth** Wollaston, Mass., 1896
**Goren, Charles** Philadelphia, 1901
**Goring, Marius** Isle of Wight, 1912
**Gormé, Eydie** New York City, 1932
**Gould, Chester** Pawnee, Okla., 1900
**Gould, Elliott** New York City, 1939
**Goulding, Ray** Lowell, Mass., 1922
**Goulet, Robert** Lawrence, Mass., 1933
**Grable, Betty** St. Louis, 1916-73
**Graham, Sheilah** London, 1905?
**Graham, Virginia** Chicago, 1912
**Grahame, Gloria** Pasadena, Cal., 1925-81
**Granger, Farley** San José, Cal., 1925
**Granger, Stewart** London, 1913

**Grant, Cary** Bristol, Eng., 1904
**Grant, Lee** New York City, 1927
**Gray, Barry** Red Lion, N. J., 1916
**Gray, Dolores** Chicago, 1930
**Grayson, Kathryn** Winston-Salem, N.C., 1923
**Graziano, Rocky** New York City, 1922
**Greco, Buddy** Philadelphia, 1926
**Green, Adolph** New York City, 1915
**Green, Johnny** New York City, 1908
**Green, Martyn** London, 1899-1975
**Greene, Lorne** Ottawa, 1915
**Greene, Richard** Plymouth, Eng., 1918
**Greenstreet, Sydney** Sandwich, Eng., 1879-1954
**Greenwood, Joan** London, 1921
**Greer, Jane** Washington, D. C., 1924
**Gregory, Dick** St. Louis, 1932
**Grey, Joel** Cleveland, 1932
**Griffin, Merv** San Mateo, Cal., 1925
**Griffith, Andy** Mt. Airy, N. C., 1926
**Griffith, Hugh** Anglesey, Wales, 1912-80
**Grimes, Tammy** Lynn, Mass., 1934
**Grizzard, George** Roanoke Rapids, N. C., 1928
**Guardino, Harry** New York City, 1925
**Guidry, Ron** Lafayette, La., 1950
**Guinness, Alec** London, 1914
**Gunn, Moses** St. Louis, 1930?
**Guthrie, Arlo** New York City, 1947
**Guthrie, Tyrone** Tunbridge Wells, Eng., 1900-71
**Guthrie, Woody** Okemah, Okla., 1912-67
**Gwenn, Edmund** London, 1875-1959
**Hackett, Buddy** New York City, 1924
**Hackman, Gene** Danville, Ill., 1931
**Hagen, Uta** Göttingen, Ger., 1919
**Hagman, Larry** Weatherford, Tex., 1931
**Hailey, Arthur** Luton, Eng., 1920
**Hale, Barbara** De Kalb, Ill., 1922
**Haley, Jack** Boston, 1901-79
**Hall, Gus** Virginia, Minn., 1910
**Hall, Juanita** Keyport, N.J., 1901-68
**Hall, Monty** Winnipeg, Canada, 1923
**Halston (Roy Halston Frowick)** Des Moines, 1932
**Hamill, Dorothy** Riverside, Conn., 1956
**Hamilton, George** Memphis, Tenn., 1939
**Hamilton, Margaret** Cleveland, 1902
**Hamlisch, Marvin** New York, 1944
**Hampden, Walter** New York, 1879-1955
**Hampton, Lionel** Louisville, Ky., 1913
**Handy, W. C.** Florence, Ala., 1873-1958
**Harburg, E. Y.** New York, 1896-1981
**Harding, Ann** San Antonio, 1902-81
**Hardwicke, Cedric** Lye, Eng., 1893-1964
**Hardy, Oliver** Atlanta, 1892-1957
**Harlow, Jean** Kansas City, Mo., 1911-37
**Harmon, Tom** Rensselaer, Ind., 1919
**Harper, Valerie** Suffern, N.Y., 1940
**Harrington, Michael** St. Louis, 1928
**Harris, Barbara** Evanston, Ill., 1935
**Harris, Emmylou** Birmingham, 1949
**Harris, Jed** Vienna, 1900-79
**Harris, Julie** Grosse Pointe, Mich., 1925
**Harris, Phil** Linton, Ind., 1906
**Harris, Richard** Limerick, Ireland, 1933
**Harris, Rosemary** Ashby, Eng., 1930
**Harrison, George** Liverpool, Eng., 1943
**Harrison, Noel** London, 1936
**Harrison, Rex** Huyton, Eng., 1908
**Harry, Deborah** Miami, 1946?
**Hartford, Huntington** New York, 1911
**Hartman, David** Pawtucket, R.I., 1935
**Hartmann, Elizabeth** Youngstown, 1941
**Hartman, Paul** San Francisco, 1910-73
**Harvey, Laurence** Yonishkis, Lith., 1928-73
**Hasso, Signë** Stockholm, 1918
**Haver, June** Rock Island, Ill., 1926
**Havoc, June** Vancouver, Can., 1916
**Hawkins, Jack** London, 1910-73
**Hawn, Goldie** Washington, D. C., 1945
**Haworth, Jill** Sussex, Eng., 1945
**Hayakawa, Sessue** Chiba Prov., Japan, 1890-1973
**Hayden, Melissa** Toronto, 1928
**Hayden, Sterling** Montclair, N.J., 1916
**Hayden, Tom** Royal Oak, Mich., 1940
**Hayes, "Gabby"** Wellsville, N.Y., 1885-1969
**Hayes, Helen** Washington, D. C., 1900
**Hayes, Isaac** Covington, Ten., 1942
**Hayes, Peter Lind** San Francisco, 1915
**Haymes, Dick** Argentina, 1918-80
**Hayward, Susan** New York City, 1919-75
**Hayworth, Rita** New York City, 1919
**Head, Edith** San Bernardino, Cal., 1901?-81
**Healy, Mary** New Orleans, 1918
**Hearst, Patty** San Francisco, 1954
**Heatherton, Joey** Rockville Centre, N. Y., 1944
**Heckart, Eileen** Columbus, O., 1919
**Heflin, Van** Waters, Okla., 1919-71
**Hefner, Hugh** Chicago, 1926
**Heiden, Eric** Madison, Wis., 1958
**Hemingway, Margaux**, Portland, Ore., 1955
**Hemmings, David** Surrey, Eng., 1941
**Henderson, Florence** Dale, Ind., 1934
**Henderson, Skitch** Halstad, Minn., 1918
**Hendrix, Jimi** Seattle, 1943-70
**Henie, Sonja** Oslo, 1913-69
**Henning, Doug** Ft. Garry, Can., 1947
**Henreid, Paul** Trieste, 1908
**Henson, Jim** Greenville, Miss., 1936
**Hentoff, Nat** Boston, 1925
**Hepburn, Audrey** Brussels, 1929
**Hepburn, Katharine** Hartford, 1909
**Herman, Woody** Milwaukee, 1913
**Hersholt, Jean** Copenhagen, 1886-1956
**Heston, Charlton** Evanston, Ill., 1923
**Hickman, Darryl** Los Angeles, 1931
**Hickman, Dwayne** Los Angeles, 1934
**Hildegarde** Adell, Wis., 1906
**Hill, Arthur** Melfort, Can., 1922
**Hiller, Wendy** Bramhall, Eng., 1912
**Hines, Earl Fatha** Duquesne, Pa., 1905
**Hingle, Pat** Denver, 1924
**Hirsch, Judd** New York, 1935
**Hirschfeld, Al** St. Louis, 1903
**Hirt, Al** New Orleans, 1922
**Hodiak, John** Pittsburgh, 1914-55
**Hoffman, Dustin** Los Angeles, 1937
**Holbrook, Hal** Cleveland, 1925
**Holden, William** O'Fallon, Ill., 1918-81
**Holder, Geoffrey** Port-of-Spain, 1930
**Holiday, Billie** Baltimore, 1915-59
**Holliday, Judy** New York, 1921-65
**Holloway, Stanley** London, 1890-1982
**Holm, Celeste** New York City, 1919
**Holman, Libby** Cincinnati, 1906-71
**Holmes, Larry** Cuthbert, Ga., 1949
**Holt, Jack** Winchester, Va., 1888-1951
**Homeier, Skip** Chicago, 1930
**Homolka, Oscar** Vienna, 1903–78
**Hope, Bob** Eltham, Eng., 1903
**Hopkins, Anthony** Port Talbot, Wales, 1937
**Hopkins, Miriam** Bainbridge, Ga., 1902-72
**Hopper, Dennis** Dodge City, Kans., 1936
**Hopper, De Wolfe** New York, 1858-1935
**Hopper, Hedda** Hollidaysburg, Pa., 1890-1966
**Horne, Lena** New York City, 1917
**Hornung, Paul** Louisville, Ky., 1935
**Horton, Edward Everett** New York, 1886-1970
**Houdini, Harry** Budapest, 1874-1926
**Howard, Leslie** London, 1893-1943
**Howard, Ron** Duncan, Okla., 1954
**Howard, Trevor** Cliftonville, Eng., 1916
**Howe, Gordie** Floral, Sask., 1928
**Howe, James Wong** China, 1899-1976
**Howes, Sally Ann** London, 1934
**Hudson, Rock** Winnetka, Ill., 1925
**Hughes, Barnard** Bedford Hills, N.Y., 1915
**Hughes, Howard** Houston, Tex., 1905-76
**Hull, Bobby** Pt. Anne, Ont., 1939
**Humperdinck, Engelbert** Madras, 1940
**Hunt, Marsha** Chicago, 1917
**Hunter, Alberta** Memphis, 1895
**Hunter, Jeffrey** New Orleans, 1925-69
**Hunter, Kim** Detroit, 1922
**Hunter, Tab** New York City, 1931
**Huntley, Chet** Cardwell, Mont., 1911-74
**Hurt, John** Chesterfield, Eng., 1940
**Hussey, Ruth** Providence, R. I., 1917
**Huston, Walter** Toronto, 1884-1950
**Hutton, Barbara** New York City, 1912-79
**Hutton, Betty** Battle Creek, Mich., 1921
**Hutton, Lauren** Tampa, Fla., 1948?
**Hyde-White, Wilfrid** Bourton-on-the-water, Eng., 1903
**Ian, Janice** New York City, 1951
**Ireland, John** Victoria, Can., 1916
**Ives, Burl** Hunt City, Ill., 1909
**Jackson, Anne** Millvale, Pa., 1926
**Jackson, Glenda** Birkenhead, Eng., 1940
**Jackson, Gordon** Glasgow, 1923
**Jackson, Jesse** Greenville, N.C., 1941
**Jackson, Kate** Birmingham, Ala., 1949
**Jackson, Mahalia** New Orleans, 1911-72
**Jackson, Michael** Gary, Ind., 1958
**Jackson, Reggie** Philadelphia, 1946
**Jacobi, Derek** Leytonstone, Eng., 1938
**Jacobi, Lou** Toronto, 1913
**Jaffe, Sam** New York City, 1893
**Jagger, Dean** Lima, O., 1903
**Jagger, Mick** Dartford, Eng., 1944
**Jamal, Ahmad** Pittsburgh, 1930
**James, Dennis** Jersey City, N. J., 1917
**James, Harry** Albany, Ga., 1916
**James, Joni** Chicago, 1930
**Janis, Elsie** Columbus, O., 1889-1956
**Jannings, Emil** Switzerland, 1884?-1950
**Janssen, David** Naponee, Neb., 1930-80
**Jeanmaire, Zizi** Paris, 1924
**Jeffreys, Anne** Goldsboro, N. C., 1928
**Jenkins, Allen** New York City, 1900-74
**Jenkins, Gordon** Webster Groves, Mo., 1910
**Jenner, Bruce** Mt. Kisco, N.Y., 1949
**Jennings, Waylon** Littlefield, Tex., 1937
**Jens, Salome** Milwaukee, 1935
**Jessel, George** New York, 1898-1981
**Joel, Billy** New York City, 1949
**John, Elton** Middlesex, Eng., 1947
**Johns, Glynis** Pretoria, South Africa, 1923
**Johnson, Van** Newport, R. I., 1916
**Jolson, Al** Russia, 1880?-1950
**Jones, Allan** Scranton, Pa., 1908
**Jones, Carolyn** Amarillo, Tex., 1933
**Jones, Dean** Morgan Co., Ala., 1936
**Jones, George** Saratoga, Tex., 1931
**Jones, Jack** Hollywood, Cal., 1938
**Jones, James Earl** Tate Co., Miss., 1931
**Jones, Jennifer** Tulsa, Okla., 1919
**Jones, Shirley** Smithton, Pa., 1934
**Jones, "Spike"** Long Beach, Cal., 1911-64
**Jones, Tom** Pontypridd, Wales, 1940
**Jong, Erica** New York City, 1942
**Joplin, Janis** Port Arthur, Tex., 1943-70
**Jory, Victor** Dawson City, Can., 1902-82
**Jourdan, Louis** Marseilles, 1920
**Julia, Raul** San Juan, 1940
**Jurado, Katy** Guadalajara, Mexico, 1927
**Jurgens, Curt** Munich, 1915-82
**Kael, Pauline** Petaluma, Calif., 1919
**Kahn, Madeline** Boston, 1942
**Kaminska, Ida** Odessa, Russ., 1899-1980
**Kanin, Garson** Rochester, N. Y., 1912
**Kaplan, Gabe** New York City, 1946
**Karloff, Boris** London, 1887-1969
**Karpov, Anatoly** Zlatoust, U.S.S.R., 1951
**Karsh, Yousuf** Mardin, Armenia, 1908
**Kasznar, Kurt** Vienna, 1913-79
**Kaye, Danny** New York City, 1913
**Kaye, Sammy** Lakewood, O., 1913
**Kazan, Elia** Constantinople, 1909
**Kazan, Lainie** New York City, 1940
**Keach, Stacy** Savannah, Ga., 1941
**Keaton, Buster** Piqua, Kans., 1895–1966
**Keaton, Diane** Los Angeles, Cal., 1946
**Keel, Howard** Gillespie, Ill., 1919
**Keeler, Ruby** Halifax, Nova Scotia, 1910
**Keeshan, Bob** Lynbrook, N.Y., 1927
**Keith, Brian** Bayonne, N. J., 1921
**Keller, Helen** Tuscumbia, Ala., 1880-1968
**Kellerman, Sally** Long Beach, Cal., 1938
**Kelly, Gene** Pittsburgh, 1912
**Kelly, Grace** Philadelphia, 1929-82
**Kelly, Nancy** Lowell, Mass., 1921
**Kelly, Patsy** Brooklyn, N. Y., 1910-81
**Kennedy, Arthur** Worcester, Mass., 1914
**Kennedy, George** New York City, 1925
**Kenneth, Mr. (Batelle)** Syracuse, 1927

**Kenton, Stan** Wichita, Kans., 1912-79
**Kern, Jerome** New York, 1885-1945
**Kerr, Deborah** Helensburgh, Scot., 1921
**Kerr, Jean** Scranton, Pa., 1923
**Kerr, John** New York City, 1931
**Kibbee, Guy** El Paso, Tex., 1882-1956
**Kilbride, Percy** San Francisco, 1888-1964
**Kiley, Richard** Chicago, 1922
**Kilgallen, Dorothy** Chicago, 1913-65
**Killy, Jean-Claude** St.-Cloud, Fr.,1943
**King, Alan** New York City, 1927
**King, Billie Jean** Long Beach, Cal., 1943
**King, Carole** New York City, 1941
**King, Dennis** Coventry, Eng., 1897-1971
**Kirk, Lisa** Brownsville, Pa., 1925
**Kirsten, Dorothy** Montclair, N.J., 1919
**Kitt, Eartha** North, S.C., 1928
**Klein, Calvin** New York City, 1942
**Klein, Robert** New York City, 1942
**Klemperer, Werner** Cologne, Ger., 1920
**Klugman, Jack** Philadelphia, 1922
**Knievel, Evel** Butte, Mont., 1938
**Knight, Gladys** Atlanta, 1944
**Knotts, Don** Morgantown, W. Va., 1924
**Knox, Alexander** Strathroy, Can., 1907
**Korbut, Olga** Grodno, Russia, 1956
**Korman, Harvey** Chicago, 1927
**Koufax, Sandy** New York City, 1935
**Kovacs, Ernie** Trenton, N.J., 1919-62
**Kramer, Jack** Las Vegas, Nev., 1921
**Kramer, Stanley** New York City, 1913
**Kristofferson, Kris** Brownsville, Tex., 1936
**Krupa, Gene** Chicago, 1909-73
**Kuralt, Charles** Wilmington, N.C., 1934
**Kwan, Nancy** Hong Kong, 1939
**Ladd, Alan** Hot Springs, Ark., 1913-64
**Ladd, Cheryl** Huron, S. Dak., 1951
**Lahr, Bert** New York, 1895-1967
**Laine, Frankie** Chicago, 1913
**Lake, Veronica** Lake Placid, N.Y., 1919-73
**Lamarr, Hedy** Vienna, 1915
**Lamas, Fernando**, Buenos Aires, 1920
**Lamour, Dorothy** New Orleans, 1914
**Lancaster, Burt** New York City, 1913
**Lanchester, Elsa** Lewisham, Eng., 1902
**Landau, Martin** New York City, 1925?
**Landers, Ann** Sioux City, Iowa, 1918
**Landi, Elissa** Venice, 1904-48
**Landis, Carole** Fairchild, Wis., 1919-48
**Landon, Michael** New York City, 1937
**Lane, Abbe** New York City, 1935
**Langdon, Harry** Council Bluffs, Iowa, 1884-1944
**Lange, Hope** Redding Ridge, Conn., 1933
**Langella, Frank** Bayonne, N. J., 1940
**Langford, Frances** Lakeland, Fla., 1914?
**Langtry, Lily** Jersey, Eng., 1852-1929
**Lansbury, Angela** London, 1925
**Lanza, Mario** Philadelphia, 1921-59
**La Rosa, Julius** New York City, 1930
**Lasser, Louise** New York, 1941
**Lauder, Harry** Scotland, 1870-1950
**Laughton, Charles** Scarborough, Eng., 1899-1962
**Laurel, Stan** Ulverson, Eng., 1890-1965
**Laurie, Piper** Detroit, 1932
**Lawford, Peter** London, 1923
**Lawrence, Carol** Melrose Park, Ill., 1934
**Lawrence, Gertrude** London, 1898-1952
**Lawrence, Steve** Brooklyn, 1935
**Lawrence, Vicki** Los Angeles, 1949
**Leachman, Cloris** Des Moines, 1926
**Lear, Norman** New Haven, 1922
**Learned, Michael** Washington, 1939
**Lederer, Francis** Prague, 1906
**Lee, Brenda** Atlanta, 1944
**Lee, Christopher** London, 1922
**Lee, Gypsy Rose** Seattle, 1914-70
**Lee, Peggy** Jamestown, N. D., 1920
**Le Gallienne, Eva** London, 1899
**Legrand, Michel** Paris, 1932
**Lehrer, Tom** New York City, 1928
**Leigh, Janet** Merced, Cal., 1927
**Leigh, Vivien** India, 1913-67
**Leighton, Margaret** Barnt Green, Eng., 1922-76
**Lembeck, Harvey** New York City, 1923-82
**Lemmon, Jack** Boston, 1925
**Lennon, John** Liverpool, Eng., 1940-80
**Lenya, Lotte** Vienna, 1898-1981
**Leonard, Sheldon** New York City, 1907
**Leonard, Sugar Ray** Wilmington, N.C., 1956
**Leslie, Joan** Detroit, 1925
**Letterman, David** Indianapolis, 1947
**Levant, Oscar** Pittsburgh, 1906-72
**Levene, Sam** Russia, 1905-80
**Levenson, Sam** New York City, 1911-80
**Lewis, Jerry** Newark, N. J., 1926
**Lewis, Joe E.** New York City, 1902?-71
**Lewis, Ramsey** Chicago, 1935
**Lewis, Robert Q.** New York City, 1921
**Lewis, Shari** New York City, 1934
**Lewis, Ted** Circleville, O., 1891-1971
**Liberace** West Allis, Wis., 1919
**Lightfoot, Gordon** Orillia, Can., 1938
**Lillie, Beatrice** Toronto, 1898
**Linden, Hal** New York, 1931
**Lindfors, Viveca** Uppsala, Swed., 1920
**Lindsay, Howard** Saratoga, N.Y., 1889-1968
**Lindsay, Margaret** Dubuque, Iowa, 1910-81
**Linkletter, Art** Moose Jaw, Can., 1912
**Lippmann, Walter** New York, 1889-1974
**Lisi, Virna** Ancona, Italy, 1937
**Little, Rich** Ottawa, Can., 1938
**Littlewood, Joan** London, 1916
**Livingstone, Mary** Seattle, 1909
**Lloyd, Harold** Burchard, Neb., 1893-1971
**Lockhart, Gene** London, Can., 1891-1957
**Lockhart, June** New York City, 1925
**Lockwood, Margaret** Karachi, 1916
**Loesser, Frank** New York, 1910-69
**Logan, Ella** Glasgow, 1913-69
**Loggins, Kenny** Everett, Wash., 1948
**Lollobrigida, Gina** Subiaco, Italy, 1928
**Lom, Herbert** Prague, 1917
**Lombard, Carole** Fort Wayne, Ind., 1908-42
**Lombardi, Vince** New York, 1913-70
**Lombardo, Guy** London, Can., 1902–77
**London, Julie** Santa Rosa, Cal., 1926
**Loos, Anita** Sissons, Cal., 1888-1981
**Lopez, Nancy** Torrence, Cal., 1957
**Lopez, Trini** Dallas, 1937
**Lopez, Vincent** New York, 1895-1975
**Lord, Jack** New York City, 1930
**Loren, Sophia** Rome, 1934
**Lorre, Peter** Hungary, 1904-64
**Louis, Joe** near Lafayette, Ala., 1914-81
**Louise, Anita** New York, 1917-70
**Louise, Tina** New York City, 1937
**Lovejoy, Frank** New York, 1912-62
**Lowe, Edmund** San Jose, Cal., 1892-1971
**Loy, Myrna** Helena, Mont., 1905
**Lubitsch, Ernst** Berlin, 1892-1947
**Luce, Clare Boothe** New York City, 1903
**Lugosi, Bela** Lugos, Hung., 1888-1956
**Lukas, Paul** Budapest, 1894-1971
**Lulu** Glasgow, 1948
**Lumet, Sidney** Philadelphia, 1924
**Lund, John** Rochester, N. Y., 1913
**Lundigan, William** Syracuse, 1914-75
**Lunt, Alfred** Milwaukee, 1892-1977
**Lupino, Ida** London, 1918
**Lynde, Paul** Mt. Vernon, O., 1926-82
**Lynley, Carol** New York City, 1942
**Lynn, Diana** Los Angeles, 1926-71
**Lynn, Loretta** Butcher Hollow, Ky., 1935
**Lyon, Sue** Davenport, Iowa, 1946
**Lyons, Leonard** New York City, 1906-76
**MacArthur, James** Los Angeles, 1937
**McCallum, David** Scotland, 1933
**McCambridge, Mercedes** Joliet, Ill., 1918
**McCarey, Leo** Los Angeles, 1898-1969
**McCartney, Paul** Allerton, Eng., 1942
**McClure, Doug** Glendale, Cal., 1938
**McCormick, Myron** Albany, Ind., 1907-62
**McCrea, Joel** Los Angeles, 1905
**McDaniel, Hattie** Wichita, 1895-1952
**MacDonald, Jeanette** Phila., 1906-65
**McDowell, Malcolm** Leeds, Eng., 1943
**McDowell, Roddy** London, 1928
**McEnroe, John** Wiesbaden, Ger., 1959
**McGavin, Darren** San Joaquin Valley, Cal., 1922
**McGraw, Ali** Westchester Co., N. Y., 1939
**McGuire, Dorothy** Omaha, Neb. 1919
**McHugh, Frank** Homestead, Pa. 1898-1981
**McKenna, Siobhan** Belfast, 1922
**MacKenzie, Gisele** Winnipeg, Can., 1927
**McKuen, Rod** Oakland, Calif. 1933
**McLaglen, Victor** Tunbridge Wells, Eng., 1886-1959
**MacLaine, Shirley** Richmond, Va., 1934
**MacLane, Barton** Columbia, S.C., 1902-68
**McLean, Don** New Rochelle, N.Y., 1945
**McLuhan, Marshall** Edmonton, Can., 1911-80
**MacMahon, Aline** McKeesport, Pa., 1899
**McMahon, Ed** Detroit, 1923
**MacMurray, Fred** Kankakee, Ill., 1908
**McNair, Barbara** Chicago, 1937?
**MacNeil, Robert** Montreal, 1931
**McNichol, Kristy** Los Angeles, 1962
**McQueen, Butterfly** Tampa, Fla., 1911
**McQueen, Steve** Indianapolis, 1930-80
**MacRae, Gordon** East Orange, N. J., 1921
**MacRae, Sheila** London, 1923?
**Madison, Guy** Bakersfield, Cal., 1922
**Magnani, Anna** Rome, 1908-73
**Maharis, George** New York City, 1928
**Main, Marjorie** Acton, Ind., 1890-1975
**Mainbocher** Chicago, 1890-1976
**Makeba, Miriam** Prospect Township, South Africa, 1932
**Malbin, Elaine** New York City, 1932
**Malden, Karl** Chicago, 1914
**Malina, Judith** Kiel, Ger., 1926
**Malone, Dorothy** Chicago, 1930
**Mamoulian, Rouben** Tiflis, Russ., 1897
**Manchester, Melissa** New York, 1951
**Mancini, Henry** Cleveland, 1924
**Mandrell, Barbara** Houston, 1948
**Mangano, Silvana** Rome, 1930
**Mangione, Chuck** Rochester, N.Y., 1940
**Manilow, Barry** New York City, 1946
**Mann, Herbie** New York City, 1930
**Mannes, Marya** New York City, 1904
**Mansfield, Jayne** Bryn Mawr, Pa., 1933-67
**Mantle, Mickey** Spavinaw, Okla., 1931
**Mantovani, Annunzio** Venice, 1905-80
**Marceau, Marcel** Strasbourg, Fr., 1923
**March, Fredric** Racine, Wis., 1897-1975
**March, Hal** San Francisco, 1920-70
**Marciano, Rocky** Boston, 1924-69
**Margo** Mexico City, 1920
**Marlowe, Hugh** Philadelphia, 1911-82
**Marsh, Jean** London, 1934
**Marshall, E. G.** Owatonna, Minn., 1910
**Marshall, Herbert** London, 1890-1966
**Marshall, Penny** New York City, 1942
**Martin, Dean** Steubenville, O., 1917
**Martin, Dick** Battle Creek, Mich., 1927
**Martin, Mary** Weatherford, Tex., 1913
**Martin, Steve** Waco, Tex., 1945
**Marvin, Lee** New York City, 1924
**Marx, Chico** New York, 1891-1961
**Marx, Groucho** New York, 1895-1977
**Marx, Harpo** New York, 1893-1964
**Masina, Giulietta** Bologna, Italy, 1925?
**Mason, Jackie** Sheboygan, Wis., 1931
**Mason, James** Huddersfield, Eng., 1909
**Mason, Marsha** St. Louis, 1942
**Mason, Pamela** Westgate, Eng., 1918
**Massey, Raymond** Toronto, 1896
**Mastroianni, Marcello** Fontana Liri, Italy, 1924
**Mathis, Johnny** San Francisco, 1935
**Matthau, Walter** New York City, 1920
**Mature, Victor** Louisville, Ky., 1916
**Mauldin, Bill** Mountain Park, N. M., 1921
**Maxwell, Elsa** Keokuk, Iowa, 1883-1963
**Maxwell, Marilyn** Clarinda, Iowa, 1922-72
**May, Elaine** Philadelphia, 1932
**Mayehoff, Eddie** Baltimore, 1914

**Mayer, Louis B.** Minsk, Russ., 1885-1957
**Mayo, Virginia** St. Louis, 1928
**Mays, Willie** Westfield, Ala., 1931
**Meadows, Audrey** Wuchang, China, 1922?
**Meadows, Jayne** Wuchang, China, 1920?
**Medford, Kay** New York City, 1920-80
**Meek, Donald** Glasgow, 1880-1946
**Meeker, Ralph** Minneapolis, 1920
**Melton, James** Moultrie, Ga., 1904-61
**Mendes, Sergio** Niteroi, Brazil, 1941?
**Menjou, Adolphe** Pittsburgh, 1890-1963
**Menken, Helen** New York, 1902-66
**Mercer, Johnny** Savannah, Ga., 1909-76
**Mercouri, Melina** Athens, 1925
**Meredith, Burgess** Cleveland, 1908
**Merkel, Una** Covington, Ky., 1903
**Merman, Ethel** New York City, 1909
**Merrick, David** St. Louis, 1912
**Merrill, Dina** New York City, 1925
**Merrill, Gary** Hartford, Conn., 1915
**Mesta, Perle** Sturgis, Mich., 1891-1975
**Middleton, Ray** Chicago, 1907
**Midler, Bette** Honolulu, 1945(?)
**Mielziner, Jo** Paris, 1901-76
**Mifune, Toshiro** Tsingtao, China, 1920
**Miles, Sarah** Ingatestone, Eng., 1941
**Miles, Vera** Boise City, Okla., 1929
**Milland, Ray** Neath, Wales, 1908
**Miller, Ann** Chireno, Tex., 1923
**Miller, Glenn** Clarinda, Iowa, 1909-44
**Miller, Marilyn** Findlay, O., 1898-1936
**Miller, Mitch** Rochester, N.Y., 1911
**Miller, Roger** Erick, Okla., 1936
**Millett, Kate** St. Paul, 1934
**Mills, Hayley** London, 1946
**Mills, John** Felixstowe, Eng., 1908
**Mills, Juliet** London, 1941
**Mimieux, Yvette** Los Angeles, 1939
**Mineo, Sal** New York City, 1939-76
**Mingus, Charlie** Nogales, Ariz., 1922-79
**Minnelli, Liza** Los Angeles, 1946
**Minnelli, Vincente** Chicago, 1913
**Minnesota Fats** New York City, 1903?
**Miranda, Carmen** Portugal, 1917-55
**Mitchell, Cameron** Dallastown, Pa., 1918
**Mitchell, Joni** Ft. MacLeod, Can., 1943
**Mitchell, Thomas** Elizabeth, N.J., 1892-1962
**Mitchum, Robert** Bridgeport, Ct., 1917
**Mix, Tom** El Paso, Tex., 1880-1940
**Monk, Thelonius** Rocky Mount, N. C., 1917-82
**Monroe, Marilyn** Los Angeles, 1926–62
**Monroe, Vaughan** Akron, O., 1912-73
**Montalban, Ricardo** Mexico City, 1920
**Montand, Yves** Monsummano, Italy, 1921
**Montgomery, Elizabeth** Hollywood, 1933
**Montgomery, Robert** Beacon, N.Y. 1904-81
**Moore, Constance** Sioux City, Iowa, 1922
**Moore, Dudley** Dagenham, Eng., 1935
**Moore, Garry** Baltimore, 1915
**Moore, Grace** Del Rio, Tenn., 1901-47
**Moore, Mary Tyler** New York City, 1937
**Moore, Melba** New York City, 1945
**Moore, Terry** Los Angeles, 1929
**Moore, Victor** Hammonton, N.J., 1876-1962
**Moorehead, Agnes** Clinton, Mass., 1906-74
**Moreau, Jeanne** Paris, 1928
**Moreno, Rita** Humacao, P. R., 1931
**Morgan, Frank** New York, 1890-1949
**Morgan, Helen** Danville, Ill., 1900-41
**Morgan, Henry** New York City, 1915
**Morgan, Jane** Newton, Mass., 1924
**Morgan, Ralph** New York, 1883-1956
**Mori, Hanae** Shimane, Japan, 1926
**Moriarty, Michael** Detroit, 1941
**Morison, Patricia** New York City, 1915
**Morley, Robert** Somley, Eng., 1908
**Morris, Chester** New York, 1919-70
**Morris, Wayne** Los Angeles, 1914-59
**Morse, Robert** Newton, Mass., 1931
**Morton, "Jelly Roll"** New Orleans, 1885-1941
**Mostel, Zero** New York City, 1915-77
**Mowbray, Alan** London, 1897-1969
**Mudd, Roger** Washington, 1928
**Muhammad Ali (Cassius Clay)** Louisville, Ky., 1942
**Mulhare, Edward** County Cork, Ire., 1928
**Mull, Martin** Chicago, 1943
**Muni, Paul** Lemberg, Pol., 1895-1967
**Murdoch, Rupert** Melbourne, 1931
**Murphy, Audie** Kingston, Tex., 1924-71
**Murray, Anne** Springhill, Can., 1945
**Murray, Arthur** New York City, 1895
**Murray, Don** Hollywood, Cal., 1929
**Murray, Jan** New York City, 1917
**Murray, Kathryn** Jersey City, N. J., 1906
**Murray, Ken** New York City, 1903
**Murray, Mae** Portsmouth, Va., 1885-1965
**Murrow, Edward R.** Greensboro, N.C., 1908-65
**Musial, Stan** Donora, Pa., 1920
**Myerson, Bess** New York City, 1924
**Nabors, Jim** Sylacauga, Ala., 1932?
**Nader, Ralph** Winsted, Conn., 1934
**Nagel, Conrad** Keokuk, Iowa, 1897-1970
**Naish, J. Carrol** New York City, 1900-73
**Naldi, Nita** New York, 1899-1961
**Namath, Joe** Beaver Falls, Pa., 1943
**Nash, Graham** Blackpool, Eng., 1942
**Nash, Ogden** Rye, N.Y., 1902-71
**Natwick, Mildred** Baltimore, 1908
**Nazimova, Alla** Yalta, Russ., 1879-1945
**Neagle, Anna** London, 1904
**Neal, Patricia** Packard, Ky., 1926
**Neff, Hildegarde** Ulm, Ger., 1925
**Nelson, Barry** Oakland, Cal., 1920
**Nelson, Harriet** Des Moines, 1912?
**Nelson, Ozzie** Jersey City, 1907-75
**Nelson, Rick** Teaneck, N.J. 1940
**Nelson, Willie** Abbott, Tex., 1933
**Nero, Peter** New York City, 1934
**Newhart, Bob** Chicago, 1929
**Newley, Anthony** London, 1931
**Newman, Edwin** New York, 1919
**Newman, Paul** Cleveland, 1925
**Newman, Phyllis** Jersey City, N. J., 1935
**Newman, Randy** Los Angeles, 1943
**Newmar, Julie** Los Angeles, 1935
**Newton, Wayne** Roanoke, Va., 1944
**Newton-John, Olivia** Cambridge, Eng., 1948
**Nichols, Mike** Berlin, 1931
**Nicholson, Jack** Neptune, N.J., 1937
**Nicklaus, Jack** Columbus, Ohio 1940
**Nimoy, Leonard** Boston, 1932
**Niven, David** Kirriemuir, Scot., 1910
**Nizer, Louis** London, 1902
**Nolte, Nick** Omaha, 1942
**Normand, Mabel** Boston, 1894-1930
**North, Sheree** Los Angeles, 1933
**Novak, Kim** Chicago, 1933
**Novarro, Ramon** Durango, Mex., 1899-1968
**Novello, Ivor** Cardiff, Wales, 1893-1951
**Nugent, Elliot** Dover, O., 1896-1980
**Nuyen, France** Marseilles, 1939
**Nyad, Diana** New York City, 1949
**Oakie, Jack** Sedalia, Mo., 1903–78
**Oberon, Merle** Hobart, Tasmania, 1911-79
**O'Brian, Hugh** Rochester, N.Y., 1930
**O'Brien, Edmond** New York City, 1915
**O'Brien, Margaret** San Diego, 1937
**O'Brien, Pat** Milwaukee, 1899
**O'Connell, Arthur** New York, 1908-81
**O'Connor, Carroll** New York City, 1924
**O'Connor, Donald** Chicago, 1925
**O'Connor, Una** Belfast, 1881-1959
**O'Day, Anita** Chicago, 1920
**O'Hara, Jill** Warren, Pa., 1947
**O'Hara, Maureen** Milltown, Ire., 1921
**O'Herlihy, Dan** Wexford, Ire., 1919
**O'Keefe, Dennis** Fort Madison, Iowa, 1910-68
**Oland, Warner** Umea, Swed., 1880-1938
**Oliver, Edna May** Malden, Mass., 1883-1942
**Olivier, Laurence** Dorking, Eng., 1907
**Onassis, Aristotle** Smyrna, Turkey, 1906-75
**Onassis, Christina** New York City, 1950
**O'Neal, Patrick** Ocala, Fla., 1927
**O'Neal, Ryan** Los Angeles, 1941
**O'Neal, Tatum** Los Angeles, 1963
**Ono, Yoko** Tokyo, 1933
**Opatoshu, David** New York City, 1918
**Orbach, Jerry** New York City, 1935
**Orbison, Roy** Texas, 1936
**Orlando, Tony** New York City, 1944
**O'Shea, Milo**, Dublin, 1926
**Osmond, Donny**, Ogden, Utah, 1957
**Osmond, Marie** Ogden, Utah, 1959
**O'Sullivan, Maureen** Boyle, Ire., 1911
**O'Toole, Peter** Connemarra, Ire., 1932
**Ouspenskaya, Maria** Russia, 1876-1949
**Owens, Buck** Sherman, Tex., 1929
**Owens, Jesse** Decatur, Ala., 1913-80
**Paar, Jack** Canton, O., 1918
**Pacino, Al** New York City, 1940
**Page, Geraldine** Kirksville, Mo., 1924
**Page, Patti** Claremore, Okla., 1927
**Paige, Janis** Tacoma, Wash., 1922
**Paige, "Satchell"** Mobile, Ala., 1906?-82
**Palance, Jack** Lattimore Mines, Pa., 1920
**Pallette, Eugene** Winfield, Kans., 1889-1943
**Palmer, Arnold** Latrobe, Pa., 1929
**Palmer, Betsy** East Chicago, Ind., 1929
**Palmer, Lilli** Posen, Poland, 1914
**Papas, Irene** Chiliomodion, Gr., 1926
**Papp, Joseph** New York City, 1921
**Parker, Eleanor** Cedarville, O., 1922
**Parker, Fess** Fort Worth, Tex., 1927
**Parker, Suzy** San Antonio, Tex., 1933
**Parks, Bert** Atlanta, 1915
**Parsons, Estelle** Lynn, Mass., 1927
**Parton, Dolly** nr. Sevierville, Tenn., 1946
**Pauley, Jane** Indianapolis, 1950
**Paulsen, Pat** South Bend, Wash., 1930?
**Paxinou, Katina** Piraeus, Gr., 1900
**Payne, John** Roanoke, Va., 1912
**Peale, Norman Vincent** Bowersville, Ohio, 1898
**Pearl, Minnie** Centerville, Tenn., 1912
**Peck, Gregory** La Jolla, Cal., 1916
**Pelé** Três Coracoes, Brazil, 1941
**Pendleton, Nat** Davenport, Iowa, 1899-1967
**Peppard, George** Detroit, 1932
**Perkins, Anthony** New York City, 1932
**Perrine, Valerie** Galveston, Tex., 1943
**Persoff, Nehemiah** Jerusalem, 1920
**Peters, Bernadette** New York City, 1948
**Peters, Jean** Canton, O., 1926
**Peterson, Oscar** Montreal, 1925
**Piaf, Edith** Paris, 1912-63
**Piazza, Ben** Little Rock, Ark., 1934
**Piazza, Marguerite** New Orleans, 1926
**Pickens, Slim** Kingsberg, Cal., 1919
**Pickford, Mary** Toronto, 1893-1979
**Picon, Molly** New York City, 1898
**Pidgeon, Walter** East St. John, Can., 1897
**Pleasance, Donald** Worksop, Eng., 1921
**Pleshette, Suzanne** New York City, 1937
**Plimpton, George** New York City, 1927
**Plowright, Joan** Scunthorpe, Eng., 1929
**Plummer, Christopher** Toronto, 1929
**Poitier, Sidney** Miami, Fla., 1924
**Pollard, Michael J.** Passaic, N. J., 1939
**Ponti, Carlo** Milan, 1913
**Portman, Eric** Halifax, Eng., 1903-69
**Porter, Cole** Peru, Ind., 1893-1964
**Poston, Tom** Columbus, O., 1927
**Powell, Dick** Mountain View, Ark., 1904-63
**Powell, Eleanor** Springfield, Mass., 1912-82
**Powell, Jane** Portland, Ore., 1929
**Powell, William** Pittsburgh, 1892
**Power, Tyrone** Cincinnati, 1913-58
**Powers, Stefanie** Hollywood, Cal., 1942
**Prentiss, Paula** San Antonio, Tex., 1939
**Presley, Elvis** Tupelo, Miss., 1935-77
**Preston, Robert** Newton, Mass., 1918
**Price, Leontyne** Laurel, Miss., 1927
**Price, Vincent** St. Louis, 1911
**Primus, Pearl** Trinidad, B.W.I., 1919
**Prince, Harold** New York City, 1928
**Prinze, Freddie** New York City, 1954-77
**Provine, Dorothy** Deadwood, S. D., 1937
**Prowse, Juliet** Bombay, 1936
**Pryor, Richard** Peoria, Ill., 1940
**Pucci, Emilio** Naples, 1914
**Purdom, Edmund** London, 1926
**Quant, Mary** London, 1934
**Quayle, Anthony** Ainsdale, Eng., 1913

**Quinn, Anthony** Chihuahua, Mex., 1915
**Quintero, José** Panama, 1924
**Radner, Gilda** Detroit, 1946
**Raft, George,** New York, 1895-1980
**Raines, Ella** Snoqualmie Falls, Wash., 1921
**Rains, Claude** London, 1889-1967
**Raitt, Bonnie** Los Angeles, 1950
**Raitt, John** Santa Ana, Cal., 1917
**Rambeau, Marjorie** San Francisco, 1889-1970
**Rand, Sally** Hickory, Mo., 1904?-79
**Randall, Tony** Tulsa, Okla., 1920
**Rathbone, Basil** South Africa, 1892-1967
**Rather, Dan** Wharton, Tex., 1931
**Ratoff, Gregory** Russia, 1893-1961
**Rawls, Lou** Chicago, 1935
**Ray, Aldo** Pen Argyl, Pa., 1926
**Ray, Johnny** Dallas, Ore., 1927
**Raye, Martha** Butte, Mont., 1916
**Raymond, Gene** New York City, 1908
**Reagan, Ronald,** Tampico, Ill., 1911
**Reasoner, Harry** Dakota City, Iowa, 1923
**Reddy, Helen** Melbourne, Australia, 1941
**Redford, Robert** Santa Monica, Cal., 1937
**Redgrave, Lynn** London, 1943
**Redgrave, Michael** Bristol, Eng., 1908
**Redgrave, Vanessa** London, 1937
**Reed, Donna** Iowa, 1921
**Reed, Rex** Fort Worth, 1940?
**Reese, Della** Detroit, 1932
**Reeve, Christopher** New York City, 1952
**Reeves, Steve** Glasgow, Mont., 1926
**Régine** Etterbeck, Belgium, 1929
**Reiner, Carl** New York City, 1922
**Reiner, Rob** Beverly Hills, Calif., 1947
**Reinhardt, Max** Austria, 1873-1943
**Remick, Lee** Quincy, Mass., 1935
**Rennie, Michael** Bradford, Eng., 1909-71
**Reynolds, Burt** Waycross, Ga., 1936
**Reynolds, Debbie** El Paso, Tex., 1932
**Rich, Buddy** New York City, 1917
**Rich, Charlie** Forrest City, Ark., 1932
**Rich, Irene** Buffalo, N. Y., 1897
**Richardson, Ralph** Cheltenham, Eng., 1902
**Rickles, Don** New York City, 1926
**Riddle, Nelson** Hackensack, N. J., 1921
**Rigg, Diana** Doncaster, Eng., 1938
**Ritchard, Cyril** Sydney, 1897-1977
**Ritter, John** Burbank, Cal., 1948
**Ritter, Tex** Murvaul, Tex., 1907-74
**Ritter, Thelma** New York, 1905-69
**Rivera, Chita** Washington, D. C., 1933
**Rivers, Joan** New York City, 1937?
**Roach, Hal** Elmira, N. Y., 1892
**Robards, Jason, Jr.** Chicago, 1922
**Robbins, Harold** New York City, 1916
**Robertson, Cliff** La Jolla, Cal., 1925
**Robertson, Dale** Oklahoma City, 1923
**Robeson, Paul,** Princeton, N.J., 1898-1976
**Robinson, "Bojangles"** Richmond, Va., 1878-1949
**Robinson, Edward G.** Bucharest, 1893-1973
**Robinson, Jackie** Cairo, Ga., 1919-72
**Robinson, Smokey** Detroit, 1940
**Robinson, Sugar Ray** Detroit, 1921
**Robson, Flora** South Shields, Eng., 1902
**Rockwell, Norman** New York, 1894-1978
**Rogers, Buddy** Olathe, Kans., 1904
**Rogers, Ginger** Independence, Mo., 1911
**Rogers, Kenny** Houston, 1939?
**Rogers, Roy** Cincinnati, 1912
**Rogers, Will** Oologah, Okla., 1879-1935
**Roland, Gilbert** Juarez, Mexico, 1905
**Roman, Ruth** Boston, 1924
**Rome, Harold** Hartford, Conn. 1908
**Romero, Cesar** New York City, 1907
**Ronstadt, Linda** Tucson, Ariz., 1946
**Rooney, Mickey** New York City, 1920
**Rooney, Pat** New York, 1880-1962
**Rose, Billy** New York, 1899-1966
**Rose, David** London, 1910
**Rose, Pete** Cincinnati, 1942
**Ross, Diana** Detroit, 1944
**Ross, Katharine** Hollywood, Cal., 1943
**Ross, Lanny** Seattle, 1906
**Roth, Lillian** Boston, 1910-80
**Rowan, Dan** Okla., 1926
**Rowlands, Gena** Cambria, Wis., 1936
**Rozelle, Pete** South Gate, Cal., 1914
**Ruggles, Charles** Los Angeles, 1892-1970
**Rule, Janice** Norwood, O., 1931
**Runyon, Damon** Manhattan, Kans., 1884-1946
**Rush, Barbara** Denver, 1929
**Russell, Jane** Lake Bemidji, Minn., 1921
**Russell, Kurt** Springfield, Mass., 1951
**Russell, Lillian** Clinton, Iowa, 1861-1922
**Russell, Mark** Buffalo, 1932
**Russell, Nipsey** Atlanta, 1924?
**Russell, "Pee Wee"** St. Louis, 1906-69
**Russell, Rosalind** Waterbury, Conn., 1911-76
**Ruth, "Babe"** Baltimore, 1895-1948
**Rutherford, Ann** Toronto, 1924
**Rutherford, Margaret** London, 1892-1972
**Ryan, Peggy** Long Beach, Cal., 1924
**Ryan, Robert** Chicago, 1913-73
**Rydell, Bobby** Philadelphia, 1942
**Sabu** Mysore, India, 1924-63
**Safer, Morley** Toronto, 1931
**Sahl, Mort** Montreal, 1927
**Saint, Eva Marie** Newark, N. J., 1929
**St. John, Jill** Los Angeles, 1940
**Saint Laurent, Yves** Oran, Algeria, 1936
**Saint-Subber, Arnold** Washington, D. C., 1918
**Sainte-Marie, Buffy** Saskatchewan, 1942
**Sakall, "Cuddles"** Budapest, 1884-1955
**Sales, Soupy** Wake Forest, N. C., 1926?
**Sanders, George** St. Petersburg, Russ., 1906-72
**Sanders, Col. Harland** Henryville, Ind., 1890-1980
**Sarnoff, Dorothy** New York City, 1919
**Sarrazin, Michael** Quebec, Can., 1940
**Sassoon, Vidal** London, 1928
**Savalas, Telly** Garden City, N. Y., 1924
**Sayer, Leo** Sussex, Eng., 1948
**Schary, Dore** Newark, N.J., 1905-80
**Scheider, Roy** Orange, N.J., 1935
**Schell, Maria** Vienna, 1926
**Schell, Maximilian** Vienna, 1930
**Schildkraut, Joseph** Vienna, 1895-1964
**Schiff, Dorothy** New York, 1903
**Schneider, Romy** Vienna, 1938-82
**Schulz, Charles** Minneapolis, 1922
**Schwarzenegger, Arnold** Graz, Austria, 1947
**Scofield, Paul** King's Norton, Eng., 1922
**Scott, George C.** Wise, Va., 1927
**Scott, Hazel** Port of Spain, Trin., 1920-81
**Scott, Lisbeth** Scranton, Pa., 1922
**Scott, Martha** Jamesport, Mo., 1914
**Scott, Randolph** Orange Co., Va., 1903
**Scott, Zachary,** Austin, Tex., 1914-65
**Scourby, Alexander** New York City, 1913
**Scruggs, Earl** Flint Hill, N. C., 1924-79
**Searle, Ronald** Cambridge, Eng., 1920
**Seaver, Tom** Fresno, Cal., 1944
**Seberg, Jean** Marshalltown, Iowa, 1938-79
**Sedaka, Neil** Brooklyn, 1939
**Seeger, Pete** New York City, 1919
**Segal, George** New York City, 1934
**Sellers, Peter** Southsea, Eng., 1925-80
**Selznick, David O.** Pittsburgh, 1902-65
**Sennett, Mack** Danville, Can., 1880-1960
**Sevareid, Eric** Velva, N. D., 1912
**Seymour, Dan** Chicago, 1915
**Shankar, Ravi** Benares, India, 1920
**Sharif, Omar** Cairo, 1933
**Shatner, William** Montreal, 1931
**Shaw, Artie** New York City, 1910
**Shaw, Robert** Westhoughton, Eng., 1927–78
**Shawn, Dick** Buffalo, N. Y., 1929?
**Shearer, Moira** Dunfermline, Scot., 1926
**Shearer, Norma** Montreal, 1905
**Shearing, George** London, 1919
**Sheen, Martin** Dayton, Ohio, 1940
**Shepherd, Jean** Chicago, 1923
**Sheridan, Ann** Denton, Tex., 1916?-67
**Sherman, Allan** Chicago, 1924-73
**Shields, Brooke** New York City, 1965
**Shire, Talia** Long Island, N.Y., 1947
**Shoemaker, Willie** El Paso, 1931
**Shore, Dinah** Winchester, Tenn., 1917
**Short, Bobby** Danville, Ill., 1936
**Shrimpton, Jean** High Wycombe, Eng., 1942
**Shriner, Herb** Toledo, O., 1918-70
**Shubert, Lee** Syracuse, N.Y., 1875-1953
**Shumlin, Herman** Atwood, Colo., 1898-1979
**Sidney, Sylvia** New York City, 1910
**Signoret, Simone** Wiesbaden, Ger., 1921
**Silverman, Fred** New York City, 1937
**Silvers, Phil** New York City, 1911
**Sim, Alastair** Edinburgh, 1900-76
**Simmons, Jean** London, 1929
**Simon, Carly,** New York City, 1945
**Simon, Paul** Queens, N.Y., 1941
**Simon, Simone** Marseilles, 1914
**Simpson, O. J.,** San Francisco, 1947
**Sinatra, Frank** Hoboken, N. J., 1915
**Sinatra, Nancy** Jersey City, N. J., 1940
**Sissle, Noble** Indianapolis, 1889-1975
**Skelton, Red** Vincennes, Ind., 1913
**Skinner, Cornelia Otis** Chicago, 1901-79
**Skinner, Otis** Cambridge, Mass., 1858-1943
**Skulnik, Menasha** Warsaw, 1898-1970
**Slezak, Walter** Vienna, 1902
**Slick, Grace** Chicago, 1939
**Smith, Alexis** Penticton, Can., 1921
**Smith, Bessie** Chattanooga, 1894-1937
**Smith, C. Aubrey** London, 1863-1948
**Smith, Howard K.** Ferriday, La., 1914
**Smith, Kate** Greenville, Va., 1909
**Smith, Maggie** Ilford, Eng., 1934
**Smith, Roger** South Gate, Cal., 1932
**Smothers, Dick** New York City, 1938
**Smothers, Tommy** New York City, 1937
**Snodgress, Carrie** Park Ridge, Ill., 1945
**Snowdon, Lord (Antony Armstrong-Jones)** London, 1930
**Snyder, Tom** Milwaukee, 1936
**Somers, Suzanne** San Bruno, Cal., 1946
**Sommer, Elke** Berlin, 1941
**Sondergaard, Gale** Litchfield, Minn., 1907
**Sondheim, Stephen** New York City, 1930
**Sothern, Ann** Valley City, N. D., 1909
**Spacek, Sissy** Quitman, Tex., 1949
**Sparks, Ned** Guelph, Can., 1884-1957
**Spassky, Boris V.** Leningrad, 1937
**Spewack, Bella** Bucharest, 1899
**Spitalney, Phil** Russia, 1890-1970
**Spitz, Mark** Modesto, Calif., 1950
**Spivak, Lawrence E.** New York City, 1900
**Spock, Benjamin** N. Haven, Ct., 1903
**Springsteen, Bruce** Freehold, N. J., 1949
**Stack, Robert** Los Angeles, 1919
**Stafford, Jo** Coalinga, Cal., 1918
**Stallone, Sylvester** New York City, 1946
**Stamp, Terence** London, 1940
**Stang, Arnold** Chelsea, Mass., 1925
**Stanislavsky, Konstantin** Moscow, 1863-1938
**Stanley, Kim** Tularosa, N. M., 1925
**Stanwyck, Barbara** New York City, 1907
**Stapleton, Jean** New York City, 1923
**Stapleton, Maureen** Troy, N. Y., 1925?
**Starr, Ringo** Dingle, Eng., 1940
**Staubach, Roger** Cincinnati, 1942
**Steele, Tommy** London, 1936
**Steiger, Rod** Westhampton, N. Y., 1925
**Stein, Jules C.** South Bend, Ind., 1896-1981
**Steinberg, Saul** Rumania, 1914
**Steinem, Gloria** Toledo, O., 1936
**Stengel, Casey** Kansas City, Mo., 1891-1975
**Sterling, Jan** New York City, 1923
**Sternberg, Josef von** Vienna, 1894-1969
**Stevens, Connie** New York City, 1938
**Stevens, Kaye** Pittsburgh, 1935
**Stevens, Mark** Cleveland, 1922
**Stevens, Stella** Yazoo City, Miss., 1938
**Stevenson, McLean** Bloomington, Ill., 1929
**Stewart, James** Indiana, Pa., 1908
**Stewart, Rod** London, 1945
**Stickney, Dorothy** Dickinson, N. D., 1900
**Stigwood, Robert** Adelaide, Australia, 1934
**Stills, Stephen** Dallas, 1945
**Stockwell, Dean** Hollywood, Cal., 1936

**Stone, Ezra** New Bedford, Mass., 1917
**Stone, Lewis** Worcester, Mass., 1879-1953
**Straight, Beatrice** Long Island, N.Y., 1918
**Strasberg, Lee** Austria-Hungary, 1901-82
**Strasberg, Susan** New York City, 1938
**Streep, Meryl** Summit, N.J., 1949
**Streisand, Barbra** New York City, 1942
**Stritch, Elaine** Detroit, 1925
**Stroheim, Erich von** Vienna, 1885-1957
**Struthers, Sally** Portland, Ore., 1948
**Sturges, Preston** Chicago, 1898-1959
**Styne, Jule** London, 1905
**Sullavan, Margaret** Norfolk, 1911-60
**Sullivan, Barry** New York City, 1912
**Sullivan, Ed** New York City, 1902-74
**Sullivan, Francis L.** London, 1903-56
**Summer, Donna** Boston, 1948
**Susann, Jacqueline** Philadelphia, 1923-74
**Susskind, David** Brookline, Mass., 1920
**Sutherland, Donald** St. John, Can., 1934
**Suzuki, Pat** Cressy, Cal., 1931
**Swanson, Gloria** Chicago, 1899
**Swarthout, Gladys** Deepwater, Mo., 1904-69
**Syms, Sylvia** London, 1934
**Talbot, Lyle** Pittsburgh, 1902
**Talmadge, Norma** Jersey City, N.J., 1897-1957
**Tamblyn, Russ** Los Angeles, 1934
**Tamiroff, Akim** Baku, Russ., 1901-72
**Tandy, Jessica** London, 1909
**Tanguay, Eva** Marbleton, Can., 1878-1947
**Tarkenton, Fran** Richmond, 1940
**Taurog, Norman** Chicago, 1899-1981
**Taylor, Elizabeth** London, 1932
**Taylor, James** Boston, 1948
**Taylor, June** Chicago, 1918
**Taylor, Laurette** New York, 1884-1946
**Taylor, Robert** Filley, Neb., 1911-69
**Taylor, Rod** Sydney, Austral., 1930
**Teagarden, Jack** Vernon, Tex., 1905-64
**Temple, Shirley** Santa Monica, Cal., 1928
**Templeton, Alec** Cardiff, Wales, 1910-63
**Ter-Arutunian, Rouben** Tiflis, Russ., 1920
**Terry, Ellen** Coventry, Eng., 1848-1936
**Terry-Thomas** London, 1911
**Thalberg, Irving** New York, 1899-1939
**Thaxter, Phyllis** Portland, Me., 1921
**Thomas, Danny** Deerfield, Mich., 1914
**Thomas, John Charles** Meyersdale, Pa., 1892-1960
**Thomas, Lowell** Woodington, O., 1892-1981
**Thomas, Marlo** Detroit, 1937
**Thomas, Richard** New York City, 1951
**Thompson, Sada** Des Moines, 1929
**Thorndike, Sybil** Gainsborough, Eng., 1882-1976
**Thorpe, Jim** Prague, Okla., 1888-1953
**Thulin, Ingrid** Sollefta, Sweden, 1929
**Tierney, Gene** New York City, 1920
**Tiffin, Pamela** Oklahoma City, 1942
**Tilden, William** Phila., 1893-1953
**Tillis, Mel** Tampa, 1932
**Tillstrom, Burr** Chicago, 1917
**Tiny Tim (Herbert Khaury)** New York City, 1923?
**Tiomkin, Dmitri** Russia, 1894-1979
**Todd, Ann** Hartford, Eng., 1910
**Todd, Mike** Minneapolis, 1907-58
**Todd, Richard** Dublin, 1919
**Toler, Sidney** Warrensburg, Mo., 1874-1947
**Tomlin, Lily** Detroit, 1936
**Tone, Franchot** Niagara Falls, N.Y., 1905-68
**Toomey, Regis** Pittsburgh, 1902
**Torme, Mel** Chicago, 1925
**Torn, Rip** Temple, Tex., 1931
**Tracy, Spencer** Milwaukee, 1900-67
**Travers, Mary** Louisville, Ky., 1936
**Travolta, John** Englewood, N.J., 1954
**Treacher, Arthur** Brighton, Eng., 1894-1975
**Trevor, Claire** New York City, 1909
**Trigère, Pauline** Paris, 1912
**Truex, Ernest** Kansas City, 1889-1973
**Tryon, Tom** Hartford, Conn., 1926
**Tucker, Forrest** Plainfield, Ind., 1919
**Tucker, Sophie** Russia, 1888-1966
**Tufts, Sonny** Boston, 1911-70
**Tunney, Gene** New York City, 1897-1978
**Turner, Lana** Wallace, Ida., 1921
**Turner, Ted** Cincinnati, 1938
**Turpin, Ben** New Orleans, 1874-1940
**Tushingham, Rita** Liverpool, Eng., 1942
**Twelvetrees, Helen** New York, 1908-58
**Twiggy (Leslie Hornby)** London, 1949
**Uggams, Leslie** New York City, 1943
**Ullmann, Liv** Tokyo, 1939
**Ulric, Lenore** Milwaukee, 1894-1970
**Unitas, John** Pittsburgh, 1933
**Uris, Leon** Baltimore, 1924
**Ustinov, Peter** London, 1921
**Vaccaro, Brenda** New York City, 1939
**Valenti, Jack** Houston, 1921
**Valentino, Rudolf**, Castellaneta, Italy, 1895-1926
**Vallee, Rudy** Island Pond, Vt., 1901
**Valli, Alida** Pola, Italy, 1921
**Valli, Frankie** Newark, N.J., 1937
**Vallone, Raf** Tropea, Italy, 1918
**Van Buren, Abigail** Sioux City, Iowa, 1919
**Vance, Vivian** Cherryvale, Kan., 1911-79
**Van Cleef, Lee** Somerville, N. J., 1925
**Vanderbilt, Alfred G.** London, 1912
**Vanderbilt, Amy** Staten Island, N. Y., 1908-74
**Vanderbilt, Gloria** New York City, 1924
**Van Doren, Mamie** Rowena, S. D., 1933
**Van Dyke, Dick** West Plains, Mo., 1925
**Van Fleet, Jo** Oakland, Cal., 1922
**Van Heusen, Jimmie** Syracuse, N. Y., 1913
**Van Vooren, Monique** Brussels, 1933
**Vaughan, Sarah** Newark, N. J., 1924
**Vaughn, Robert** New York City, 1932
**Veidt, Conrad** Berlin, 1893-1943
**Velez, Lupe** Mexico, 1908-44
**Vera-Ellen** Cincinnati, O., 1926-81
**Verdon, Gwen** Culver City, Cal., 1925
**Vereen, Ben** Miami, 1946
**Vernon, Jackie** New York City, 1928
**Vinton, Bobby** Canonsburg, Pa., 1935
**Vitti, Monica** Rome, 1933
**Voight, Jon** Yonkers, N. Y., 1938
**Von Furstenberg, Betsy** Neiheim-Heusen, Ger., 1932
**Von Fürstenberg, Diane** Brussels, Belg., 1946
**Von Sydow, Max** Lund, Sweden, 1929
**Wagner, Lindsay** Los Angeles, 1949
**Wagner, Robert** Detroit, 1930
**Walker, Clint** Hartford, Ill., 1927
**Walker, Nancy** Philadelphia, 1922
**Walker, Robert** Salt Lake City, 1919-51
**Wallace, DeWitt** St. Paul, Minn., 1889-1981
**Wallace, Irving** Chicago, 1916
**Wallace, Mike** Brookline, Mass., 1918
**Wallach, Eli** New York City, 1915
**Waller, "Fats"** New York, 1904-43
**Wallis, Hal B.** Chicago, 1899
**Walters, Barbara** Boston, 1931
**Wanger, Walter** San Francisco, 1894-1968
**Warden, Jack** Newark, N. J., 1920
**Warfield, William** West Helena, Ark., 1920
**Waring, Fred** Tyrone, Pa., 1900
**Warner, Jack L.** London, Can., 1892–1978
**Warwicke, Dionne** Orange, N. J., 1941
**Washington, Dinah** Tuscaloosa, Ala., 1924-64
**Waters, Ethel** Chester, Pa., 1900-77
**Waters, Muddy** Rolling Fork, Miss., 1915
**Wayne, David** Traverse City, Mich., 1914
**Wayne, John** Winterset, Iowa, 1907-79
**Weaver, Dennis** Joplin, Mo., 1925
**Weaver, Fritz** Pittsburgh, 1926
**Webb, Clifton** Indianapolis, 1891-1966
**Webb, Jack** Santa Monica, Cal., 1920
**Weissmuller, Johnny** Windber, Pa., 1904
**Welch, Raquel** La Jolla, Cal., 1942
**Weld, Tuesday** New York City, 1943
**Welk, Lawrence** Strasburg, N. D., 1903
**Welles, Orson** Kenosha, Wis., 1915
**Werner, Oskar** Vienna, 1922
**West, Adam** Walla Walla, Wash., 1938?
**West, Mae** New York City, 1893-1980
**Wheeler, Bert** Paterson N.J., 1895–1968
**White, Barry** Galveston, 1944
**White, Josh** Greenville, S.C., 1908-69
**White, Pearl** Greenridge, Mo., 1889-1938
**Whiting, Margaret** Detroit, 1924
**Whitmore, James** White Plains, N. Y., 1921
**Whitty, Dame May** Liverpool, 1865-1948
**Widmark, Richard** Sunrise, Minn., 1914
**Wilde, Cornel** New York City, 1918
**Wilder, Gene** Milwaukee, 1935
**Wilding, Michael** Westcliff, Eng., 1912-79
**William, Warren** Aitkin, Minn., 1895-1948
**Williams, Andy** Wall Lake, Iowa, 1930
**Williams, Cindy** Van Nuys, Cal., 1948
**Williams, Emlyn** Glanrafon, Wales, 1905
**Williams, Esther** Inglewood, Cal., 1923
**Williams, Hank** Georgiana, Ala., 1923-53
**Williams, Joe** Cordele, Ga., 1918
**Williams, Paul** Omaha, 1944?
**Williams, Robin** Chicago, 1952
**Williams, Roger** Omaha, Neb., 1926
**Williams, Ted** San Diego, 1918
**Williamson, Nicol** Hamilton, Scot., 1938
**Wills, Chill** Seagoville, Tex., 1903-78
**Willson, Meredith** Mason City, Iowa, 1902
**Wilson, Don** Lincoln, Neb., 1900-82
**Wilson, Earl** Rockford, O., 1907
**Wilson, Flip** Jersey City, N. J., 1933
**Wilson, Julie** Omaha, Neb., 1925
**Wilson, Marie** Anaheim, Cal., 1917-72
**Wilson, Nancy** Chillicothe, O., 1937
**Winchell, Paul** New York City, 1923
**Winchell, Walter** New York, 1897-1972
**Windsor, Duchess of (Wallis Warfield Simpson)** Blue Ridge Summit, Pa., 1896
**Windsor, Duke of** Richmond Park, Eng., 1894-1972
**Winkler, Henry** New York City, 1947
**Winninger, Charles** Athens, Wis., 1884-1969
**Winters, Jonathan** Dayton, O., 1925
**Winters, Shelley** St. Louis, Ill., 1923
**Withers, Jane** Atlanta, 1926
**Wolfit, Donald** Newark-on-Trent, Eng., 1902-68
**Wonder, Stevie** Detroit, 1951
**Wong, Anna May** Los Angeles, 1907-61
**Wood, Natalie** San Francisco, 1938-81
**Wood, Peggy** New York City, 1892–1978
**Woodward, Joanne** Thomasville, Ga., 1930
**Woollcott, Alexander** Phalanx, N.J., 1887-1963
**Woolley, Monty** New York, 1888-1962
**Worth, Irene** Nebraska, 1916
**Wray, Fay** Alberta, Can., 1907
**Wright, Martha** Seattle, 1926
**Wright, Teresa** New York City, 1918
**Wyatt, Jane** Campgaw, N. J., 1912
**Wyman, Jane** St. Joseph, Mo., 1914
**Wynette, Tammy** Tupelo, Miss., 1942
**Wynn, Ed** Philadelphia, 1886-1966
**Wynn, Keenan** New York City, 1916
**Wynter, Dana** London, 1930?
**Yarborough, Glenn** Milwaukee, 1930
**Yarrow, Peter** New York City, 1938
**York, Dick** Fort Wayne, Ind., 1928
**York, Michael** Fulmer, Eng., 1942
**York, Susannah** London, 1942
**Young, Gig** St. Cloud, Minn., 1917-78
**Young, Loretta** Salt Lake City, 1913
**Young, Neil** Toronto, 1945
**Young, Robert** Chicago, 1907
**Young, Roland** London, 1887-1953
**Young, Sheila** Birmingham, Mich., 1950
**Young, Victor** Chicago, 1900-56
**Youngman, Henny** London, 1906?
**Yurka, Blanche** St. Paul, 1887-1974
**Zanuck, Darryl F.** Wahoo, Neb., 1902-79
**Ziegfeld, Florenz** Chicago, 1869-1932
**Zimbalist, Efrem, Jr.** New York, 1913
**Zolotow, Maurice** New York City, 1913
**Zorina, Vera** Berlin, 1917

# ARTS: POPULAR/CLASSICAL

## ALL-TIME MOVIE MONEYMAKERS

SOURCE: *Variety*

The following list includes all feature films that have grossed $23 million or more domestically (U.S. and Canada), as of Jan. 13, 1982. The film title is followed by the name of the director, producer, production company, and release year.

| Film | Gross |
|---|---|
| **Star Wars** (G. Lucas; G. Kurtz; 20th; 1977) | $185,138,000 |
| **The Empire Strikes Back** (I. Kershner; G. Lucas/G. Kurtz; 20th; 1980) | 134,209,000 |
| **Jaws** (S. Spielberg; Zanuck/Brown; Universal; 1975) | 133,435,000 |
| **Grease** (R. Kleiser; R. Stigwood/A. Carr; Par; 1978) | 96,300,000 |
| **Raiders of the Lost Ark** (S. Spielberg; F. Marshall; Par; 1981) | 90,434,000 |
| **The Exorcist** (W. Friedkin; W.P. Blatty; WB; 1973) | 88,500,000 |
| **The Godfather** (F.F. Coppola; A. Ruddy; Par; 1972) | 86,275,000 |
| **Superman** (R. Donner; P. Spengler; WB; 1978) | 82,500,000 |
| **The Sound of Music** (R. Wise; 20th; 1965) | 79,748,000 |
| **The Sting** (G.R. Hill; T. Bill, M. & J. Phillips; Univ; 1973) | 78,963,000 |
| **Close Encounters of the Third Kind** (S. Spielberg; J. & M. Phillips; Col; 1977) | 77,000,000 |
| **Gone With The Wind** (V. Fleming; D. Selznick; MGM-UA; 1939) | 76,700,000 |
| **Saturday Night Fever** (J. Badham; R. Stigwood; Par; 1977) | 74,100,000 |
| **National Lampoon's Animal House** (J. Landis; M. Simmons/I. Reitman; Univ; 1978) | 74,000,000 |
| **Superman II** (R. Lester; P. Spengler; WB; 1981) | 64,000,000 |
| **Kramer vs. Kramer** (R. Benton; S. Jaffe; Col; 1979) | 61,734,000 |
| **Smokey and the Bandit** (H. Needham; M. Engelberg; Univ; 1977) | 61,055,000 |
| **One Flew Over The Cuckoo's Nest** (M. Forman; S. Zaentz/M. Douglas; UA; 1975) | 59,166,036 |
| **Stir Crazy** (S. Poitier; H. Weinstein; Col; 1980) | 58,408,000 |
| **Nine to Five** (C. Higgins; B. Gilbert; 20th; 1980) | 57,850,000 |
| **Star Trek** (R. Wise; G. Roddenberry; Par; 1979) | 56,000,000 |
| **Rocky** (J. Avildsen; Chartoff/Winkler; UA; 1976) | 55,892,428 |
| **American Graffiti** (G. Lucas; F.F. Coppola; Univ; 1973) | 55,886,000 |
| **Jaws II** (J. Szwarc; Zanuck/Brown; Univ; 1978) | 55,608,000 |
| **Every Which Way But Loose** (J. Fargo; R. Daley; WB; 1978) | 51,800,000 |
| **Love Story** (A. Hiller; H. Minsky; Par; 1970) | 50,000,000 |
| **Towering Inferno** (J. Guillermin; I. Allen; 20th; 1975) | 50,000,000 |
| **Heaven Can Wait** (W. Beatty; Par; 1978) | 49,400,000 |
| **The Graduate** (M. Nichols; L. Turman; Avco Embassy; 1968) | 49,078,000 |
| **Doctor Zhivago** (D. Lean; C. Ponti; MGM-UA; 1965) | 46,550,000 |
| **Butch Cassidy and the Sundance Kid** (G.R. Hill; J. Foreman; 20th; 1969) | 46,039,000 |
| **Airport** (G. Seaton; R. Hunter; Univ; 1970) | 45,300,000 |
| **Blazing Saddles** (M. Brooks; M. Hertzberg; WB; 1974) | 45,200,000 |
| **Mary Poppins** (R. Stevenson; W. Disney; BV; 1964) | 45,000,000 |
| **Rocky II** (S. Stallone; UA; 1979) | 43,049,274 |
| **The Ten Commandments** (C.B. DeMille; Par; 1956) | 43,000,000 |
| **The Jerk** (C. Reiner; D. V. Picker/W. E. McEuen; Univ; 1979) | 43,000,000 |
| **The Poseidon Adventure** (R. Neame; I. Allen; 20th; 1972) | 42,000,000 |
| **Goodbye Girl** (H. Ross; R. Stark; MGM-WB; 1977) | 41,700,000 |
| **Airplane** (J. Abrahams/D. Zucker/J. Zucker; H. W. Koch/J. Davidson; Par; 1980) | 40,610,000 |
| **Fiddler on the Roof** (N. Jewison; UA; 1971) | 40,498,669 |
| **Alien** (R. Scott; G. Carroll/D. Giler/W. Hill; 20th; 1979) | 39,847,000 |
| **Stripes** (I. Reitman; D. Goldberg, I. Reitman; Col; 1981) | 39,514,000 |
| **Any Which Way You Can** (B. Van Horn; F. Manes; WB; 1980) | 39,500,000 |
| **Young Frankenstein** (M. Brooks; M. Gruskoff; 20th; 1975) | 38,823,000 |
| **Coal Miner's Daughter** (M. Apted; B. Larson; Univ; 1980) | 38,500,000 |
| **Smokey and the Bandit II** (H. Needham; H. Moonjean; Univ; 1980) | 37,600,000 |
| **Apocalypse Now** (F.F. Coppola; UA; 1979) | 37,268,881 |
| **A Star Is Born** (F. Pierson; J. Peters; WB; 1976) | 37,100,000 |
| **Arthur** (S. Gordon; R. Greenhut; Orion/WB; 1981) | 37,000,000 |
| **King Kong** (J. Guillermin; D. DeLaurentiis; Par; 1976) | 36,915,000 |
| **MASH** (R. Altman; I. Preminger; 20th; 1970) | 36,720,000 |
| **Ben-Hur** (W. Wyler; S. Zimbalist; MGM-UA; 1959) | 36,650,000 |
| **Earthquake** (M. Robson; Univ; 1974) | 36,250,000 |
| **10** (B. Edwards; B. Edwards/T. Adams; Orion; 1979) | 36,000,000 |
| **The Cannonball Run** (H. Needham; A. Ruddy; 20th; 1981) | 35,378,000 |
| **Amityville Horror** (S. Rosenberg; R. Saland/E. Geisinger; AIP/Filmways; 1979) | 35,000,000 |
| **Hooper** (H. Needham; B. Reynolds/L. Gordon; WB; 1978) | 34,900,000 |
| **Private Benjamin** (H. Zieff; N. Meyers/C. Shyer/H. Miller; WB; 1980) | 34,000,000 |
| **Moonraker** (L. Gilbert; A. Broccoli; UA; 1979) | 33,934,074 |
| **Billy Jack** (T. Frank; M. Solti; WB; 1971) | 32,500,000 |
| **The Blues Brothers** (J. Landis; R. K. Weiss; Univ; 1980) | 32,200,000 |
| **The Muppet Movie** (J. Frawley; J. Henson; AFD; 1979) | 32,000,000 |
| **Oh, God!** (C. Reiner; J. Weintraub; WB; 1977) | 31,440,000 |
| **The Deep** (P. Yates; P. Guber; Col; 1977) | 31,300,000 |
| **The Electric Horseman** (S. Pollack; Col; 1979) | 31,116,000 |
| **The Shining** (S. Kubrick; WB; 1980) | 30,800,000 |
| **Godfather, Part II** (F.F. Coppola; Coppola/Frederickson/Roos; Par; 1974) | 30,673,000 |
| **The Deer Hunter** (M. Cimino; B. Spikings/M. Deeley/M. Cimino; Univ; 1978) | 30,425,000 |
| **The Blue Lagoon** (R. Kleiser; Col; 1980) | 30,327,000 |
| **Silver Streak** (A. Hiller; E.K. Milkis/T.L. Miller; 20th; 1976) | 30,018,000 |
| **All The President's Men** (A. Pakula; W. Coblenz; WB; 1976) | 30,000,000 |
| **California Suite** (H. Ross; R. Stark; Col; 1978) | 29,200,000 |
| **The Omen** (R. Donner; H. Bernhard; 20th; 1976) | 28,544,000 |
| **Thunderball** (T. Young; Eon; UA; 1965) | 28,530,000 |
| **Up In Smoke** (L. Adler; Adler/Lombardo; Par; 1978) | 28,300,000 |
| **Patton** (F. Schaffner; F. McCarthy; 20th; 1970) | 28,100,000 |
| **What's Up Doc?** (P. Bogdanovich; WB; 1972) | 28,000,000 |
| **Foul Play** (C. Higgins; Miller/Milkis; Par; 1978) | 27,500,000 |
| **The Jungle Book** (W. Reitherman; W. Disney; BV; 1967) | 27,300,000 |
| **Four Seasons** (A. Alda; M. Bregman; Univ; 1981) | 26,800,000 |
| **Snow White** (animated; W. Disney; RKO/BV; 1937) | 26,750,000 |
| **Funny Girl** (W. Wyler; R. Stark; Col; 1968) | 26,325,000 |
| **The French Connection** (W. Friedkin; P. D'Antoni/Schine-Moore; 20th; 1971) | 26,315,000 |
| **Main Event** (H. Zieff; J. Peters/B. Streisand; WB; 1979) | 26,300,000 |
| **The China Syndrome** (J. Bridges; M. Douglas; Col; 1979) | 26,073,700 |
| **Cleopatra** (J. Mankiewicz; W. Wanger; 20th; 1963) | 26,000,000 |
| **Airport 1975** (J. Smight; W. Frye; Univ; 1974) | 25,805,000 |
| **Guess Who's Coming To Dinner?** (S. Kramer; Col; 1968) | 25,500,000 |
| **For Your Eyes Only** (J. Glen; A. Broccoli; MGM/UA; 1981) | 25,439,479 |
| **Black Hole** (G. Nelson; R. Miller; BV; 1979) | 25,425,000 |
| **Return of the Pink Panther** (B. Edwards; MGM/UA; 1975) | 25,390,617 |
| **The Lady and the Tramp** (animated; W. Disney; BV; 1955) | 25,150,000 |
| **The Way We Were** (S. Pollack; R. Stark; Col; 1973) | 25,000,000 |
| **Revenge of the Pink Panther** (B. Edwards; UA; 1978) | 25,000,000 |
| **The Bad News Bears** (M. Ritchie; S. Jaffe; Par; 1976) | 24,888,000 |
| **Popeye** (R. Altman; R. Evans; Par; 1980) | 24,568,541 |
| **The Spy Who Loved Me** (L. Gilbert; A. Broccoli; UA; 1977) | 24,322,345 |
| **2001: A Space Odyssey** (S. Kubrick; MGM-UA; 1968) | 24,100,000 |
| **Trial of Billy Jack** (F. Laughlin; D. Cramer; T-L/WB; 1974) | 24,000,000 |
| **The Enforcer** (J. Fargo; R. Daley; WB; 1976) | 24,000,000 |
| **Urban Cowboy** (J. Bridges; R. Evans/I. Azoff; Par; 1980) | 23,810,000 |
| **In Search of Noah's Ark** (J.L. Conway; C.E. Sellier, Jr.; Sunn/Taft/Jenser Farley; 1977) | 23,770,000 |
| **1941** (S. Spielberg; B. Feitshans; Univ; 1979) | 23,400,000 |
| **The Love Bug** (R. Stevenson; W. Walsh; BV; 1969) | 23,150,000 |
| **Ordinary People** (R. Redford; R. Schwary; Par; 1980) | 23,123,000 |
| **Around the World in 80 Days** (M. Anderson; M. Todd; UA; 1956) | 23,120,000 |
| **The Longest Yard** (R. Aldrich; A. Ruddy; Par; 1974) | 23,017,000 |

## LONGEST BROADWAY RUNS

SOURCE: *Variety*

| Play | Performances |
|---|---|
| Grease | 3,388 |
| Fiddler on the Roof | 3,242 |
| Life with Father | 3,224 |
| Tobacco Road | 3,182 |
| A Chorus Line* | 2,866 |
| Hello, Dolly! | 2,844 |
| My Fair Lady | 2,717 |
| Oh! Calcutta!* | 2,443 |
| Man of La Mancha | 2,329 |
| Abie's Irish Rose | 2,327 |
| Oklahoma! | 2,212 |
| Annie* | 2,176 |
| Pippin | 1,944 |
| South Pacific | 1,925 |
| Magic Show | 1,920 |
| Gemini | 1,819 |
| Deathtrap | 1,793 |
| Harvey | 1,775 |
| Dancin' | 1,774 |
| Hair | 1,742 |
| The Wiz | 1,661 |
| Born Yesterday | 1,642 |
| Ain't Misbehavin' | 1,604 |
| The Best Little Whorehouse in Texas | 1,584 |
| Mary, Mary | 1,572 |
| The Voice of the Turtle | 1,557 |
| Barefoot in the Park | 1,532 |
| Mame | 1,503 |
| Arsenic and Old Lace | 1,444 |
| Same Time, Next Year | 1,444 |
| The Sound of Music | 1,443 |
| How to Succeed in Business without Really Trying | 1,417 |
| Hellzapoppin | 1,404 |
| The Music Man | 1,375 |
| Funny Girl | 1,348 |
| Mummenschanz | 1,316 |
| Angel Street | 1,295 |
| Lightnin' | 1,291 |
| Promises, Promises | 1,281 |
| The King and I | 1,246 |
| Cactus Flower | 1,234 |
| Sleuth | 1,222 |
| 1776 | 1,217 |
| Equus | 1,209 |
| Guys and Dolls | 1,200 |
| Evita* | 1,167 |
| Cabaret | 1,166 |
| Mister Roberts | 1,157 |
| Sugar Babies* | 1,152 |
| Annie Get Your Gun | 1,147 |
| The Seven Year Itch | 1,141 |
| Butterflies Are Free | 1,128 |
| Pins and Needles | 1,108 |
| Plaza Suite | 1,097 |
| Kiss Me Kate | 1,071 |
| Don't Bother Me I Can't Cope | 1,065 |
| Pajama Game | 1,063 |
| The Teahouse of the August Moon | 1,027 |
| Damn Yankees | 1,019 |
| Never Too Late | 1,007 |
| Any Wednesday | 984 |
| A Funny Thing Happened on the Way to the Forum | 964 |
| The Odd Couple | 964 |
| Kiss and Tell | 962 |
| Anna Lucasta | 957 |
| The Moon is Blue | 924 |
| Bells Are Ringing | 924 |
| Beatlemania | 914 |
| Luv | 902 |
| Can-Can | 895 |
| Carousel | 890 |
| Hats Off to Ice | 890 |
| Fanny | 888 |
| Follow the Girls | 882 |
| The Bat | 878 |
| Camelot | 873 |
| My Sister Eileen | 866 |
| White Cargo | 864 |
| No, No, Nanette | 861 |
| Song of Norway | 860 |
| A Streetcar Named Desire | 855 |
| Comedy in Music | 849 |
| You Can't Take It with You | 837 |
| La Plume de Ma Tante | 835 |

*As of July 14, 1982. Figures reflect consecutive performances.

## MAJOR WORLD DANCE GROUPS

SOURCE: The Dance Collection, Library & Museum of the Performing Arts, Lincoln Center, New York

Dates in parentheses indicate the founding year.

AMSTERDAM: **The Dutch National Ballet** (1961); *Artistic Director:* Rudi van Dantzig.

BOSTON: **Boston Ballet** (1964); *Director:* E. Virginia Williams.

BRUSSELS: **Ballet of the 20th Century** (1960); *Director:* Jorge Donn.

COPENHAGEN: **Royal Danish Ballet** (1771); *Artistic Director:* Henning Kronstam.

FLEMINGTON: **The Australian Ballet** (1962); *Artistic Director:* Marilyn Jones.

GLASGOW: **The Scottish Ballet** (1969); *Artistic Director:* Peter Darrell.

THE HAGUE: **Nederlands Dans Theater** (1959); *Artistic Director:* Jirí Kylián.

HAMBURG: **Hamburg State Opera Ballet** (c. 1959); *Artistic Director:* John Neumeier.

HAVANA: **Ballet Nacional de Cuba** (1948); *Director:* Alicia Alonso.

HOUSTON: **Houston Ballet** (1968); *Artistic Director:* Ben Stevenson.

LENINGRAD: **Kirov Ballet** (1738); *Director:* Oleg Vinogradov.

LONDON:

**Festival Ballet** (1950); *Artistic Director:* John Field.

**Royal Ballet, Covent Garden** (1931); *Director:* Norman Morrice.

**Ballet Rambert** (1926); *Directors:* Dame Marie Rambert, Robert North.

**London Contemporary Dance Theatre** (1967); *Director:* Robert Cohan.

MOSCOW: **Bolshoi Ballet** (c. 1776); *Artistic Director:* Yuri Grigorovich.

NEW YORK CITY:

**Nikolais Dance Theatre** (1948); *Director:* Alwin Nikolais.

**American Ballet Theatre** (1940); *Director:* Mikhail Baryshnikov.

**Alvin Ailey American Dance Theatre** (1958); *Artistic Director:* Alvin Ailey.

**The Joffrey Ballet** (1954); *Artistic Director:* Robert Joffrey.

**The Dance Theatre of Harlem** (1968); *Directors:* Arthur Mitchell and Karel Shook.

**The Feld Ballet** (1974); *Director:* Eliot Feld.

**Martha Graham Dance Company** (1927); *Director:* Martha Graham.

**Merce Cunningham Dance Group** (1952); *Director:* Merce Cunningham.

**New York City Ballet** (1948); *Dance Masters:* George Balanchine, Jerome Robbins, John Taras.

**Paul Taylor Dance Company** (1954); *Director:* Paul Taylor.

**Twyla Tharp Dance Foundation** (1965); *Artistic Director:* Twyla Tharp.

PARIS: **Paris Opera Ballet** (1671); *Director:* Rosella Hightower.

PHILADELPHIA: **Pennsylvania Ballet** (1963); *Director:* Barbara Weisberger; *Artistic Director:* Benjamin Harkarvy.

PITTSBURGH: **Pittsburgh Ballet Theatre** (1970); *Artistic Director:* Patrick Frantz.

SAN FRANCISCO: **San Francisco Ballet** (1933); *Directors:* Lew Christensen and Michael Smuin.

STOCKHOLM: **Royal Swedish Ballet** (1773); *Artistic Director:* Gunilla Roempke.

STUTTGART: **Stuttgart Ballet** (c. 1759); *Artistic Director:* Marcia Haydée.

TORONTO: **National Ballet of Canada** (1951); *Artistic Director:* Alexander Grant.

WASHINGTON (D.C.): **Washington Ballet** (1962); *Artistic Director:* Mary Day.

WINNIPEG: **Royal Winnipeg Ballet** (1938); *Artistic Director:* Arnold Spohr.

## POPULAR DISCOGRAPHY

**Note:** Numeral and hyphen preceding record label indicate multi-disc album, the numeral indicating the number of discs

### STANDARD POP

**Herb Alpert**—Fandango/A&M 3731; **Paul Anka**—Very Best Of/ Ranwood 8203; **Burt Bacharach**—Greatest Hits/A&M 3661; **Tony Bennett**—Tony/Harmony KH 32171; **Glen Campbell**—Wichita Lineman/Capitol SM 103; **Carpenters**—Singles/A&M 3601; **Nat "King" Cole**—Best/Capitol SKAO-2944; **Ray Conniff**—Harmony/ Columbia KC-32553; **Bing Crosby**—Feels Good/London 679; **Christopher Cross**—Warner Bros. 3383; **John Denver**—Greatest Hits/Victor CPL1-0374; **Neil Diamond**—Hot August Night/2-Mobile 024; **José Feliciano**—Fireworks/RCA LSP 4370; **Four Seasons**—2nd Vault of Golden Hits/Philips PHS 600-221; **Tom Jones**—Greatest Hits/ Paramount XPAS 71062; **Peggy Lee**/Arc. Folk. 294; **Henry Mancini**—Pure Gold/RCA AYL1-3667; **Barry Manilow**—Greatest Hits/2-Arista 8601; **Mantovani**—Greatest Hits, Vol. 1/London XPS 906; **Johnny Mathis**—All-Time Greatest Hits/2-Columbia PG 31345; **Mabel Mercer (w. Bobby Short)**—At Town Hall/2-Atlantic S-604; **Olivia Newton-John**—Totally Hot/MCA 3067; **Tony Orlando & Dawn**—Prime Time/Bell 1317; **Donny & Marie Osmond**—Winning Combination/Polydor I-6127; **Pointer Sisters**—That's a Plenty /Blue Thumb 48; **Diana Ross**—To Love Again/Motown 8-951; **Frank Sinatra**—Trilogy/3-Reprise SFS-2300; **Kate Smith**—At Carnegie Hall/Camden CAS-2587; **Barbra Streisand**—Greatest Hits Vol. 2/Columbia HC-45679; **Dionne Warwick**—Dionne/Arista 4230; **Andy Williams**—Solitaire/Columbia KC-32383.

### ROCK 'N' ROLL

**ABBA**—Super Trouper/Atlantic 16023; **Air Supply**—Lost in Love/Arista 4268; **Beach Boys**—Good Vibrations/Reprise 2223; **Beatles**—Rarities/Capitol SHAL-12060; **Bee Gees**—Greatest Hits/2-RSO 4200; **Pat Benatar**—Crimes of Passion/ Chrysalis 1275; **B-52's**—Wild Planet/Warner Bros. 3471; **Blondie**—Autoamerican/Chrysalis 1290; **Boston**—Epic PE 34188; **David Bowie**—Space Oddity/RCA LSP-4813; **Cars**—Candy-O/ Elektra 507; **Cheap Trick**—All Shook Up/Epic FE-36498; **Chicago**—Hot Streets/Columbia FC-35512; **Alice Cooper**—Welcome to My Nightmare/Atlantic SD 18130; **Cream**—Best of/ Atco SD 33-291; **Crosby, Stills, Nash & Young**—Déja Vu/ Atlantic SD 7200; **Doors**—Elektra 74007; **Eagles**—The Long Run/Asylum 5E-508; **Fleetwood Mac**—Tusk/2-Warner Bros. 2HS-3350; **Hall & Oates**—Private Eyes/RCA AFL1-4028; **Jimi Hendrix**—Are You Experienced?/Reprise S-6261; **Jefferson Starship**—Red Octopus/Grunt BFL1-0999; **Jethro Tull**—War Child/Chrysalis 1067; **Billy Joel**—Glass Houses/Columbia FC-36384; **Elton John**—Greatest Hits/MCA 2128; **Carole King**—Pearls/Capitol S00-12073; **Kiss**—Alive/Casablanca NBLP 7020; **John Lennon & Yoko Ono**—Double Fantasy/ Geffen GHS-2001; **Bette Midler**—The Rose/Atlantic 16010; **Steve Miller**—Greatest Hits 1974-78/Capitol S00-11872; **Mothers of Invention**—We're Only in it for the Money/Verve 65045; **Gary Numan**—Telekon/Atco 38-117; **Pink Floyd**—The Wall/2-Columbia PC2-36183; **Police**—Zenyatta Mondatta/ A&M 4831; **Elvis Presley**—Elvis/RCA APL1-0283; **Suzi Quatro**—If You Knew Suzi/RSO 3044; **Queen**—Greatest Hits/ Elektra 564; **Gerry Rafferty**—City to City/U. Artists LA840-H; **Rolling Stones**—Some Girls/Roll. Stones Rec. 39108; **Santana**—Abraxas/Columbia KC-30130; **Sex Pistols**—Never Mind the Bollocks/Warner Bros. K-3147; **Simon & Garfunkel**—Bridge Over Troubled Water/Columbia KCS-9914; **Rick Springfield**—Success Hasn't Spoiled Me/RCA AFL1-4125; **Bruce Springsteen**—The River/2-Columbia PC2-36854; **Rod Stewart**—Greatest Hits/Warner Bros. HS-3373; **T. Rex**/Reprise 6440; **The Who**—Who Are You?/MCA 3050; **Wings**—Greatest/ Capitol S00-11905; **Neil Young & Crazy Horse**—Rust Never Sleeps/Warner Bros. HS 2295.

### FOLK AND FOLK-ROCK

**Hoyt Axton**—Free Sailin'/MCA 2319; **Joan Baez**—Diamonds and Rust/Nautilus 12; **Jackson Browne**—For Everyman/ Asylum 5067; **Leonard Cohen**—Songs of/Columbia CS 9533; **Judy Collins**—Whales & Nightingales/Elektra 75010; **Jim Croce**—Photographs & Memories/ABC 835; **Bob Dylan**—Blonde on Blonde/2-Columbia C2S-841; **Jack Elliott**/Vanguard 79151; **Kinky Friedman**—Sold American/Vanguard 79333; **Bob Gibson**—Funky in the Country/Mountain Railroad 52783; **Steve Goodman**—Somebody Else's Troubles/Buddah 5121; **Arlo Guthrie**—Power of Love/Warner Bros. 3558; **Woody Guthrie**—Dust Bowl Ballads/Folkways 5212; **Tim Hardin**—Memorial Album/Polydor 6333; **Fred Holstein**—Chicago & Other Ports/Philo PH 1030; **Ian & Sylvia**—Best/2-Columbia CG-32516; **Michael Johnson**—Home Free/EMI SW-17057; Bonnie Koloc—Close-Up/Epic PE-34184; **Leo Kottke**—Balance/Chrysalis 1234; **Leadbelly**—Huddie Ledbetter/Fantasy 24715; **Gordon Lightfoot**—Gord's Gold/2-Reprise 2RS 2237; **Melanie**—Candles in the Rain/Buddah BDS-5060; **Joni Mitchell**—Shadows and Light/2-Asylum 704; **Maria Muldaur**—Sweet Harmony/Reprise MS 2235; **Harry Nilsson**—Nilsson Schmilsson/RCA LSP-4515; **Jim Post**—Slow to 20/ Fantasy 9408; **John Prine**—Bruised Orange/Asylum 139; **Linda Ronstadt**—Greatest Hits II/Elektra 516; **Rotary Connection**—Peace/Cadet-Concept LPS 318; **Leon Russell**—Will o' the Wisp/Shelter SR 2138; **Buffy Sainte-Marie**—It's My Way!/ Vanguard VSD 79142; **Cat Stevens**—Foreigner/A&M 4391; **James Taylor**—Mud Slide Slim/Warner Bros. BS-2561.

### RHYTHM AND BLUES, SOUL, GOSPEL

**Big Bill Broonzy**—Blues/Encore 22017; **James Brown**—Jam 1980s/Polydor 6140(6); **Ray Charles**—Genius Sings the Blues/ Atlantic SD 8052; **Sam Cooke**—You Send Me/Camden ACS1 0445; **Bo Diddley**—Greatest/Checker 8034; **Sleepy John Estes**—Broke & Hungry/Delmark 608; **Roberta Flack**—Killing Me Softly/Atlantic 7271; **Aretha Franklin**—With Everything I Feel in Me/Atlantic SD 18116; **B.B. King**—Best/ABC 724; **Gladys Knight & the Pips**—Knight Time/Soul 741; **Curtis Mayfield**—Curtis in Chicago/Curtom 8018; **Mighty Clouds of Joy**—It's Time/Dunwich 50177; **Teddy Pendergrass**—T.P./Phila. Int'l FZ-36745; **Lou Rawls**—Sit Down & Talk to Me/Phila. Int'l JZ-36304; **Otis Redding**—Tell the Truth/Atco SD 33-333; **Smokey Robinson**—Warm Thoughts/Tamla 8-367; **Sly & Family Stone**—Fresh/Epic KE-32134; **Bessie Smith**—Empty Bed Blues/Columbia G 30450; **Sweet Inspirations**—Sweet Sweet Soul/Atlantic SD 8253; **Temptations**—Greatest Hits, Vol. 2/ Gordy 5 954; **Muddy Waters**—King Bee/Blue Sky JZ-37064; **Stevie Wonder**—Hotter Than July/Tamla 8-373.

### JAZZ

**Gene Ammons**—Greatest Hits/Prestige 10084; **George Benson**—Give Me the Night/Qwest-Warner Bros. HS3453; **Earl Bostic**—16 Sweet Tunes of the '50s/Starday 3022; **Dave Brubeck**—Greatest Hits/Columbia PC-9284; **John Coltrane**—Best/Atlantic 1541; **Miles Davis**—Kind of Blue/Columbia PC 8163; **Ella Fitzgerald**—Best/Reprise S 6354; **Erroll Garner**—Misty/Mercury 60662; **Stan Getz (w. Charlie Byrd)**—Jazz Samba/Verve 68432; **Dizzy Gillespie**—Groovin' High/Savoy 12020; **Benny Goodman**—1938 Carnegie Hall Jazz Concert/2-Columbia OSL-160; **Woody Herman**—Woody/Cadet 845; **Earl Hines**—Tea for Two/Black Lion BL-112; **Billie Holiday**—Lady Day/Columbia CL-637; **Scott Joplin**—Ragtime, Vol. 3/Biograph 1010Q; **Roland Kirk**—Gifts & Messages/Mercury S 90939; **Chuck Mangione**—Best of/2-Mercury 8601; **Charles Mingus**—Mingus Dynasty/Columbia CL 1440; **Wes Montgomery**—Best/Verve 68714; **Jelly Roll Morton**—King of New Orleans Jazz/Victor LPM 1649; **Oliver Nelson**—Blues & the Abstract Truth/Impulse A-5; **Charlie Parker**—Complete Savoy Sessions/5-Savoy 5500; **Joe Pass**—Loves Gershwin/Pablo 2312-133; **Oscar Peterson**—Newport Years/Verve 8828; **Django Reinhardt**—Djangology/Victor LPM 2319; **Judy Roberts**—Inner City 1078; **Sonny Rollins (w. Max Roach)**—Freedom Suite/2-Milestone 47007; **Art Tatum**—Essential/ Verve 68433; **Sarah Vaughan**—Golden Hits/Mercury 60645; **Fats Waller**—One Never Knows, Do One?/Victor LPM 1503; **Lester Young**—Mean to Me/2-Verve 2-2538.

### COUNTRY AND WESTERN

**Bill Anderson**—Bill/MCA 320; **Lynn Anderson**—Greatest Hits/ Columbia KC 31641; **Eddy Arnold**—Best, Vol. 3/RCA LSP 4844; **Chet Atkins**—Mr. Atkins, Guitar Picker/Camden CASX 2464(e); **Jimmy Buffett**—Changes in Latitudes, Changes in Attitudes/ABC 990; **Johnny Cash**—Encore/CBS FC-37355; **Charlie Daniels**—Full Moon/Epic FE-36571; **Jimmy Dean**—Favorite Son/Harmony 11270; **Flatt & Scruggs**—Greatest Hits/ Columbia CS 9370; **Crystal Gayle**—Classic Crystal/U. Artists LOO 982; **Merle Haggard**—190Proof/MCA 3089; **Waylon Jennings**—Greatest Hits/RCA AHL 1-3378; **Loretta Lynn**—Greatest Hits, Vol. 2/MCA 420; **Jody Miller**—Country Girl/Epic KE-33349; **Willie Nelson**—Always on My Mind/Columbia FC-37951; **Oak Ridge Boys**—Fancy Free/MCA 5209; **Dolly Parton**—9 to 5 and Odd Jobs/RCA AHL1-3852; **Charley Pride**—Pride of America/Victor APL1-0757; **Kenny Rogers**—Greatest Hits/U. Artists LOO-1072; **Carl Smith**—Country on My Mind/ Columbia CS-9688; **Statler Bros.**—10th Anniversary/Mercury 5027; **Mel Tillis**—M-M-Mel Live/MCA 3208; **Hank Williams**—Greatest Hits/2-MGM S-4755; **Bob Wills**—Anthology/Columbia KG 32416; **Tammy Wynette**—My Man/Epic KE 31717.

# CLASSICAL DISCOGRAPHY

## OPERA

**Beethoven**—Fidelio: Klemperer/3-Angel S-3625; **Bellini**—Norma: Serafin/3-Angel S-3615; **Berg**—Wozzeck: Böhm/2-DGG 2707023; **Bizet**—Carmen: Troyanos, Solti, London Phil./3-London 13115; **Debussy**—Pelléas et Mélisande: Ansermet/London 1379; **Donizetti**—Lucia di Lammermoor: Pritchard/London 25702; **Flotow**—Martha (highlights): Berlin Mun. Op./Angel S-36236; **Gilbert & Sullivan**—Pirates of Penzance: D'Oyly Carte Op. Co./2-London 1277; **Gluck**—Orfeo ed Euridice: Fasano/3-RCA LSC-6169; **Gounod**—Faust: Cluytens/4-Angel S-3622; **Leoncavallo**—Pagliacci: Gobbi/2-Angel S-3618; **Mascagni**—Cavalleria Rusticana: Serafin/3-London 1330; **Massenet**—Manon: Rudel/4-ABC ATS-20007; **Mozart**—Marriage of Figaro: Fricsay/3-DG 2728004; Don Giovanni: Klemperer/4-Angel S-3700; The Magic Flute: Böhm/3-DG2709017; **Moussorgsky**—Boris Godunov: Cluytens/4-Angel S-3633; **Puccini**—La Bohème: Serafin/2-London 1208; Tosca: Karajan/2-London 1284; Madama Butterfly: Serafin/3-Angel S-3604; **Rossini**—The Barber of Seville: Leinsdorf/4-RCA 6143; **R. Strauss**—Der Rosenkavalier: Solti/4-London 1435; **Verdi**—Aida: Leinsdorf/3-RCA LSC-6198; Falstaff: Karajan/3-Angel S-3552; La Forza del Destino: Previtali/3-London 13122; Otello: Karajan/3-London 1324; Rigoletto: Solti/2-Angel S-3718; La Traviata: Kleiber/2-DG 2707103; **Wagner**—Gotterdämmerung: Solti/6-London 1604.

## SYMPHONY

**Beethoven**—Complete Symphonies, 1-9: Karajan/8-DG 2721001; **Berlioz**—Symphonie Fantastique: Munch/RCA LSC-2608; **Bizet**—Symphony No. 1: Ansermet/London 6208; **Brahms**—Complete Symphonies 1-4: Szell/3-Columbia D3S-758; **Bruckner**—No. 4: Klemperer/Angel S-36245; No. 9: Mehta/London 6462; **Copland**—Symphony No. 3: Bernstein/Columbia MS-6954; **Dvořák**—Nos. 7-9: Szell/3-Columbia D3S-814; **Franck**—Symphony in D minor: Monteux/RCA LSC-2514; **Haydn**—Nos. 93-104: Dorati/3-London STS 15319-15324; **Mahler**—No. 1: Tennstedt/Angel S-37508; No. 4: Reiner/RCA 2364; No. 9: Walter/2-Odyssey Y2-30308; **Mendelssohn**—Nos. 4-5: Munch/RCA LSC-2221; **Mozart**—Nos. 25,29: Marriner/Argo ZRG-706; Nos. 32, 35, 38: Boehm/DG 138112; Nos. 40,41: Klemperer/Angel S-36183; **Nielsen**—No. 5: Bernstein/Columbia MS-6414; **Prokofiev**—Classical Symphony, Lt. Kijé and "Three Oranges" Suites: Ormandy/Columbia MS-6545; **Saint-Saëns**—No. 3: Munch/RCA LSC-2341; **Schubert**—Nos. 5,8: Walter/Columbia MS-6218; No. 9: Szell/Angel S-36044; **Schumann**—Complete Symphonies, 1-4: Bernstein/3-Columbia D3S-725; **Sibelius**—No. 5: Bernstein/Columbia MS-6749; **Stravinsky**—Symphony in Three Movements: Ansermet/London MS-6190; **Tchaikovsky**—No. 4: Monteux/RCA 2369; No. 6: Ormandy/Columbia MS-6160; **Vaughan Williams**—No. 5: Barbirolli/Angel S-35952.

## ORCHESTRAL AND CHORAL

**Bach**—Brandenburg Concertos: Marriner/2-Philips 6700045; Cantatas 56 & 169: Saar Ch. Orch./Nonesuch 71142; Suites for Orchestra: Casals/2-Columbia M2S-755; **Bartók**—Concerto for Orchestra: Ormandy/Columbia MS-6626; Hungarian Sketches: Reiner/RCA VICS 1620; Music for Strings, Percussion and Celesta: Boulez/Columbia MS-7206; **Beethoven**—Overtures: Karajan/2-DG 2707046; **Copland**—Appalachian Spring; El Salon Mexico: Bernstein/Columbia MS-6355; Billy the Kid; Rodeo: Bernstein/Columbia MS-6175; **Debussy**—La Mer; Nocturnes: Giulini/Angel S-35977; Images pour Orchestre: Boulez/Columbia MS-7362; **Dvořák**—Slavonic Dances: Szell/Columbia MS-7208; **Elgar**—Enigma Variations; Cockaigne Overture: Barbirolli/Angel S-36120; **Falla**—Three Cornered Hat & La Vida Breve Dances: Reiner/RCA 2230; **Gershwin**—An American in Paris; Rhapsody in Blue: Bernstein/Columbia MS-6091; **Handel**—Concerti Grossi Op. 6: Leppard/Mercury 9124; Water Music and Royal Fireworks Suites: Szell/London 6236; **Hindemith**—Symphonic Metamorphoses of Themes by Weber; Mathis der Maler: Ormandy/Columbia MS-6562; **Kodály**—Háry János Suite; Dances from Galánta: Kertész/London 6417; **Liszt**—A Faust Symphony; Les Preludes: Bernstein/2-Columbia MG-699; **Mendelssohn**—A Midsummer Night's Dream: Klemperer/Angel S-3588l; **Mozart**—Eine Kleine Nachtmusik; Serenade No. 9: Szell/Columbia MS-7273; **Moussorgsky-Ravel**—Pictures at an Exhibition: Ansermet/London 6177; **Orff**—Carmina Burana: Thomas & Cleveland Orch. Chorus & Boys' Choir/Columbia M-33172; **Ravel**—Daphnis et Chloe: Ansermet/London 6456; La Valse; Menuet Antique; Ma Mère l'Oye: Boulez/Columbia M-32838Q; **Respighi**—The Pines of Rome; The Fountains of Rome: Reiner/RCA LSC-2436; **Rimsky-Korsakov**—Scheherazade: Rostropovich/Angel S-37061(Q); **Rossini**—Overtures: Toscanini/Victrola 1274; **Smetana**—Moldau; Bartered Bride Dances: Szell/Odyssey Y-30049; **R. Strauss**—Also Sprach Zarathustra, Don Juan & Till Eulenspiegel: Solti/London 6978; **Stravinsky**—The Firebird: Stokowski/London 21026; Le Sacre du Printemps: Dorati/London LDR 71048; **Tchaikovsky**—The Nutcracker: Ansermet/London 2203; Romeo and Juliet; Francesca da Rimini: Munch/RCA VICS-1197; The Sleeping Beauty: Previn/3-Angel SX 3812(Q).

## SOLOS WITH ORCHESTRA

**Bach**—Clavier Concertos Nos. 1,2: Kirkpatrick/DG ARC 198013; Violin Concertos Nos. 1,2; **Bartók**—Piano Concertos Nos. 2,3: Anda/DG 138111; **Beethoven**—Piano Concertos Nos. 1-5: Ashkenazy/4-London 2404; Violin Concerto: Stern/Columbia MS-6093; **Berg**—Violin Concerto: Grumiaux/Philips 900194; **Berlioz**—Harold in Italy: Menuhin/Angel S-36123; **Brahms**—Piano Concerto No. 2: Dichter/Philips 9500414; Violin Concerto: Heifetz/RCA LSC-1903; Double Concerto: Oistrakh-Rostropovich/Angel S-36032; **Bruch**—Violin Concerto No. I: Stern/Columbia MS-7003; **Chopin**—Piano Concerto Nos. I,2; Andante: Rubinstein/2-RCA VCS-7091; **Dvořák**—Cello Concerto: Starker/Mercury 90303; **Grieg**—Piano Concerto: Rubinstein/RCA LSC-2566; **Lalo**—Symphonie Espagnole; **Liszt**—Piano Concertos Nos. 1,2: Richter/Philips 835474; **Mendelssohn**—Violin Concerto: Francescatti (w. Tchaikovsky—Violin Concerto)/Columbia MS-6758; **Mozart**—Horn Concertos Nos. 1-4; Rondo K.371: Civil/Philips 6500325; Piano Concertos Nos. 25,27: Gulda/DG 2530642; Violin Concertos Nos. 3,4: Francescatti/Columbia MS-6063; **Paganini**—Violin Concertos Nos. I,2: Gitlis/Turn. 34203; **Poulenc**—Organ Concerto: Duruflé (w. Gloria: Carteri)/Angel S-35953; **Rachmaninoff**—Piano Concerto No. 2: Ashkenazy/London 6390; **Saint-Saëns**—Cello Concertos Nos. 1,2, etc.: Walevska/Philips 6500459; **Schumann**—Cello Concerto: Rostropovich/DG 138674; Piano Concerto: Rubinstein/RCA LSC-2997; **Sibelius**—Violin Concerto: Heifetz/RCA LSC 2435; **Tchaikovsky**—Piano Concerto No. I: Cliburn/RCA LSC-2252; **Vivaldi**—The Four Seasons: Virtuosi di Roma/Angel S-35877.

## CHAMBER MUSIC

**Bartók**—Quartets Nos. 1-6: Hungarian Quartet/3-DG 2728011; **Beethoven**—Quartets (complete): Amadeus Quartet/4-DG 2721006; "Archduke" Trio: Stern-Rose-Istomin/Columbia MS-6819; Violin & Piano Sonatas (complete): Francescatti-Casadesus/4-Columbia D4S-724; **Berg**—Lyric Suite: RCA/Juilliard Quartet/RCA 2531; **Brahms**—Quintet Op. 34: Previn, Yale Quartet/Angel S-36928; Trio Op. 40: Tuckwell-Perlman-Ashkenazy/London 6628; Violin Sonatas: Szeryng, Rubinstein/2-RCA LSC-2619/20; **Debussy, Ravel**—Quartets: Juilliard Quartet/Columbia M-30650; **Dvořák**—Quartets Nos. 2,6: Janácek Quartet/London 6394; **Haydn**—Quartets Op. 76, Nos. 2,5: Hungarian Quartet/Turnabout 34012; Quartets Op. 77, Nos. I,2: Amadeus Quartet/DG 138980; **Hindemith**—Kleine Kammermusik: Boston Symphony Players/RCA 3166; **Mendelssohn**—Octet: Laredo, et al/Columbia MS-6848; **Mozart**—Quartets Nos. 14-19: Italiano/3-Philips S-C 71AX301; Piano Quartets: Horszowski, Budapest/Columbia MS-6683; Quintets K. 515,516: Primrose, Griller/Vanguard S-158; Quintet, K. 581, Trio K. 498: De Peyer, Melos Ensemble/Angel S-36241; **Schubert**—Octet: Melos Ensemble/Angel S-36529; Quartets Nos. 12,14: Amadeus Quartet/DG 138048; "Trout" Quintet: Marlboro Players/Vanguard 71145; **Schumann**—Piano Quintet: Serkin, Budapest/2-Columbia M2S-734; **Stravinsky**—L'Histoire du Soldat: Cocteau, Markevitch/Philips 90046.

## SOLO INSTRUMENTAL

**Bach**—Goldberg Variations: Pinnock/DG ARC-2533425; Well-tempered Clavier, Bk. 1: Kirkpatrick/2-DG ARC 2708006; Sonatas and Partitas for Violin: Grumiaux/3-Philips 835198/200; Organ Music: Walcha/DG 198305; **Beethoven**—Piano Sonatas: 8,14,23: Kempff/DG 139300; 17,21: Brendel/Turnabout 34394; 28,31: Serkin/Columbia M 31239; 30,32: Backhaus/London CS-6246; **Chopin**—Ballades: Rubinstein/RCA LSC-2370; Mazurkas: Novaes/Vox 57920; Nocturnes: Rubinstein/RCA LSC-7050; Scherzos: Rubinstein/RCA LSC-2368; Sonatas Nos. 2,3: Rubinstein/RCA 3194; **Debussy**—Piano Music (complete): W. Haas/5-Philips 5-012; **Liszt**—Sonata in B minor; Piano Music: Curzon/London 6371; **Mozart**—Piano Sonatas (complete), Eschenbach/7-DG 2720031; **Rachmaninoff**—Preludes, etc.: Weissenberg—RCA 7069; **Ravel**—Piano Music (complete): Simon/3-Vox SVBX-5473; **Scarlatti**—Sonatas: Kirkpatrick/DG ARC-2533072; **Schubert**—Sonata in A; Wanderer Fantasy: Richter/Angel S-36150; Sonata in D; Impromptus: Curzon/London 6416; Sonata in A, Op. Posth.; Serkin/Columbia MS-6849; **Schumann**—Carnaval; Fantasia, Op. 17: Arrau/Philips 802746.

## LEADING OPERA COMPANIES

SOURCE: Central Opera Service

### WORLD OPERA COMPANIES (exclusive of U.S.)

AMSTERDAM: **Nederlandse Operastichting;** *Manager:* J.H. de Roo
BARCELONA: **Gran Teatro del Liceo;** *General Director:* Juan A. Pamias
BAYREUTH: **Bayreuther Festspiele;** *Director:* Wolfgang Wagner
BELGRADE: **Srpsko Narodno Pozoriste;** *Director:* D. Djurdjevic
BERLIN: **(West) Deutsche Oper;** *Artistic Director:* Götz Friedrich. **(East) Deutsche Staatsoper;** *General Director:* Hans Pischner. **(East) Komische Oper;** *Director:* Harry Kupfer
BRUSSELS: **Théâtre Royal de la Monnaie;** *Director:* Gérard Mortier
BUCHAREST: **Romanian Opera;** *Director:* Petre Codreanu.
BUDAPEST: **Magyar Allami Operahaz & Erkel Theater (Hungarian State Opera);** *Director:* Andras Mihaly
BUENOS AIRES: **Teatro Colon**
CALGARY: **Southern Alberta Opera;** *General Manager:* Brian Hanson
CARACAS: **Opera Metropolitana;** *Manager:* Lorenzo Gonzalez
COLOGNE: **Bühnen der Stadt Köln;** *Director:* Michael Hampe; *Music Director:* John Pritchard
COPENHAGEN: **Det kongelige Teater;** *Manager:* Niels Moeller
DRESDEN: **Staatsoper Dresden;** *Director:* Horst Seeger
DUSSELDORF/DUISBURG: **Deutsche Oper am Rhein;** *Music Director:* Hiroshi Wakasugi
EDINBURGH: **Edinburgh Festival;** *Director:* John Drummond
EDMONTON: **Edmonton Opera Association;** *Artistic Director:* Irving Guttman
FLORENCE: **Teatro Comunale & Maggio Fiorentino;** *Music Director:* Riccardo Muti
FRANKFURT: **Stadtische Buhnen;** *Director:* Michael Gielen
GENEVA: **Grand Theatre de l'Opera;** *General Director:* Hugues Gall
GLASGOW: **Scottish Opera;** *General Director:* John Cox
GLYNDEBOURNE: **Festival Opera;** *Chairman:* George W. Christie
HAMBURG: **Staatsoper;** *Dir. & Chief conductor:* Christoph von Dohnányi
HELSINKI: **Finnish National Opera;** *General Manager:* J. Raiskinen
LEIPZIG: **Staedtische Theater;** *Director Opera:* Karl Kayser
LENINGRAD: **Kirov Opera & Ballet Theatre;** *Director:* Yuri Temirkanov
LONDON: **Royal Opera, Covent Garden;** *General Administrator:* John Tooley; *Music Director:* Colin Davis. **English National Opera Ltd.;** *Managing Director:* Lord Harewood
MARSEILLE: **Opera de Marseille;** *Artistic Director:* M. Karpo
MILAN: **Teatro alla Scala;** *Music Director:* Francisco Siciliani
MONTE CARLO: **L'Opera de Monte-Carlo;** *Director:* Guy Grinda
MOSCOW: **Bolshoi Theatre of the USSR;** *Director:* Giorgy Ivanov
MUNICH: **Bayerische Staatsoper;** *Director:* August Everding. **Theater am Gartnerplatz;** *Director:* Kurt Pscherer
NAPLES: **Teatro San Carlo;** *Acting General Manager:* Elio Boncompagni
OSLO: **Den Norske Opera (The Norwegian Opera);** *Director:* Knut Hendriksen
OTTAWA: **Ottawa Festival Opera;** *General Director:* Donald MacSween
PARIS: **Theatre National de l'Opera;** *Administrator:* Bernard Lefort; *Administrator Designate:* Massimo Bogiankino
PRAGUE: **National Theatre & Smetana Theatre & Tyl Theatre;** *Director:* Jiri Pauer
RIO DE JANEIRO: **Opera Estaveldo Teatro Municipal;** *Director:* Edmundo Barreto Pintos
ROME: **Teatro dell'Opera;** *Gen. Mgr.:* Roman Vlad
SALZBURG: **Salzburg Festival;** *Director:* Dr. Otto Sertl. Easter Festival; *Director:* Herbert von Karajan
SOFIA: **Bulgarian National Opera;** *Director:* Ruslan Raichev
STOCKHOLM: **Kungliga Teatern;** *General Manager:* Folke Abenius
STRASBOURG: **L'Opera du Rhin;** *Artistic Director:* René Terrasson
STUTTGART: **Wurttembergisches Staatstheater;** *Music Director:* Dennis Russell Davies
SYDNEY: **Australian Opera;** *General Manager:* Patrick Veitch
TEL AVIV: **Israel National Opera;** *Director:* Simha Evan Zohar
TORONTO: **Canadian Opera Company;** *General Director:* Lotfi Mansouri
VANCOUVER: **Vancouver Opera Association;** *General Manager:* Hamilton McClymont
VENICE: **Teatro La Fenice;** *General Manager:* Italo Gomez
VERONA: **Arena di Verona;** *Artistic Director:* Luciano Chailly
VIENNA: **Staatsoper;** *Director:* Lorin Maazel. Volksoper; *Director:* Karl Doench
WARSAW: **Teatr Wielki (Grand Theatre Warsaw);** *Artistic Director:* Antoni Wicherek
WINNIPEG: **Manitoba Opera;** *Artistic Director:* Irving Gottman
ZURICH: **Opernhaus Zurich;** *General Manager:* Klaus Helmut Drese

### AMERICAN OPERA COMPANIES

BALTIMORE: **Baltimore Opera Company;** *General Manager:* Jay Holbrook
BOSTON: **Opera Company of Boston;** *Artistic Director:* Sarah Caldwell
CENTRAL CITY: **Central City Opera House Association;** *Artistic Director:* Vacant
CHARLESTON: **Spoleto Festival USA;** *General Manager:* James Kearney
CHARLOTTE: **Charlotte Opera Association;** *General Director:* Richard Marshall
CHICAGO: **Lyric Opera of Chicago;** *General Manager:* Ardis Krainik. **Chicago Opera Theatre;** *Artistic Director:* Alan Stone
CINCINNATI: **Cincinnati Opera Association;** *General Manager:* James de Blasis
CLEVELAND: **Cleveland Opera;** *Artistic Director:* David Bamberger
DALLAS: **Dallas Civic Opera;** *General Manager:* Plato Karayanis
DETROIT: **Michigan Opera Theater;** *General Director:* David Di Chiera
DISTRICT OF COLUMBIA: **Washington Opera, Inc.;** *Executive Director:* Martin Feinstein
FORT WORTH: **Fort Worth Opera Association;** *General Manager:* Rudolf Kruger
GLENS FALLS: **Lake George Opera Company;** *General Director:* Paulette Haupt-Nolen
HARTFORD: **Connecticut Opera Association, Inc.;** *General Manager:* George Osborne
HONOLULU: **Hawaii Opera Theatre;** *General Manager:* Alice Taylor
HOUSTON: **Houston Grand Opera Association;** *General Director:* R. David Gockley
KANSAS CITY (MO.): **Lyric Opera of Kansas City;** *General Manager:* Russell Patterson
LOUISVILLE: **Kentucky Opera Association;** *Artistic Director:* Thomson Smillie
MEMPHIS: **Opera Memphis;** *General Director:* Anne Randolph
MIAMI: **Greater Miami Opera Association;** *General Manager:* Robert Herman
MILWAUKEE: **Florentine Opera Company;** *General Manager:* John Gage. Skylight Opera; *Managing Director:* Colin Cabot
NEW ORLEANS: **New Orleans Opera;** *General Director:* Arthur Cosenza
NEW YORK: **Metropolitan Opera Association;** *General Manager:* Anthony A. Bliss. **New York City Opera;** *General Director:* Beverly Sills
NEWARK: **New Jersey State Opera;** *Artistic Director:* Alfredo Silipigni
NORFOLK: **Virginia Opera Association;** *Artistic Director:* Peter Mark
OMAHA: **Opera/Omaha;** *Artistic Advisor:* Paulette Haupt-Nolen
PHILADELPHIA: **Opera Company of Philadelphia;** *General Manager:* Margaret Everitt
PITTSBURGH: **Pittsburgh Opera Company;** *Manager:* Vincent Artz
PORTLAND (ORE.): **Portland Opera Association;** *Executive Director:* Robert Bailey; *Artistic Director:* Stefan Minde
ST. LOUIS: **Opera Theater of St. Louis;** *General Manager:* Richard Gaddes
ST. PAUL: **Minnesota Opera Company;** *Artistic Director:* H. Wesley Balk
SAN DIEGO: **San Diego Opera Association;** *Artistic Director:* Tito Capobianco
SAN FRANCISCO: **San Francisco Opera Association;** *General Director:* Terence McEwen
SANTA FE: **Santa Fe Opera;** *General Director:* John O. Crosby
SEATTLE: **Seattle Opera Association, Inc.;** *General Director:* Glynn Ross
TUCSON: **Arizona Opera Company;** *General Director:* Vacant
TULSA: **Tulsa Opera Company;** *General Manager:* Edward Purrington

## MAJOR SYMPHONY ORCHESTRAS OF THE UNITED STATES AND CANADA 1982-83 Season

SOURCE: American Symphony Orchestra League

**Atlanta Symphony Orchestra**
1280 Peachtree Street, NE, Atlanta, Georgia 30309
Mus. Dir.: Robert Shaw
Gen. Mgr.: Stephen Sell

**Baltimore Symphony Orchestra**
1313 St. Paul St., Baltimore, MD 21202
Mus. Dir.: Sergiu Comissiona
Gen. Mgr.: Joseph Leavitt

**Boston Symphony Orchestra**
301 Massachusetts Ave.,
Boston, Massachusetts 02115
Mus. Dir.: Seiji Ozawa
Exec. Dir.: Thomas W. Morris

**Buffalo Philharmonic Orchestra**
26 Richmond Avenue, Buffalo, New York 14222
Mus. Dir.: Julius Rudel
Exec. Dirs.: Michael Bielski & Ruth Spero

**Chicago Symphony Orchestra**
220 South Michigan Avenue, Chicago, Illinois 60604
Mus. Dir.: Sir Georg Solti
Exec. V. Pres. & Gen. Mgr.: John S. Edwards

**Cincinnati Symphony Orchestra**
1241 Elm Street, Cincinnati, Ohio 45210
Mus. Dir.: Michael Gielen
Gen. Mgr.: Steven I. Monder
Manager: Judith Arron

**Cleveland Orchestra**
11011 Euclid Avenue, Cleveland, Ohio 44106
Mus. Dir. Designate: Christoph von Dohnanyi
Gen. Mgr.: Kenneth Haas

**Dallas Symphony Orchestra**
P.O. Box 26207, Dallas, Texas 75226
Mus. Dir.: Eduardo Mata
Exec. Dir.: Leonard David Stone

**Denver Symphony Orchestra**
1245 Champa Street, Denver, Colorado 80204
Mus. Dir.: Gaetano Delogu
Exec. Dir.: Carlos Wilson

**Detroit Symphony Orchestra**
20 Auditorium Drive, Detroit, Michigan 48226
Mus. Dir.: (vacant)
Exec. V. Pres.: Oleg Labanov
Gen. Mgr.: Michael Smith

**Houston Symphony Orchestra**
615 Louisiana Street, Houston, TX 77002
Art Adv.: Sergiu Comissiona
Exec. Dir.: Gideon Toeplitz

**Indianapolis Symphony Orchestra**
P.O. Box 88207, Indianapolis, IN 46208
Mus. Dir.: John Nelson
Gen. Mgr.: Fred H. Kumb, Jr.

**Los Angeles Philharmonic Orchestra**
135 N. Grand Ave., Los Angeles, CA 90012
Mus. Dir.: Carlo Maria Giulini
Exec. Dir.: Ernest Fleischmann
Gen. Mgr. Robert Harth

**Milwaukee Symphony Orchestra**
Performing Arts Center
929 North Water St., Milwaukee, WI 53202
Mus. Dir.: Lukas Foss
Exec. Dir.: Robert Caulfield
Gen. Mgr.: Richard Thomas

**Minnesota Orchestra**
1111 Nicollet Mall, Minneapolis, MN 55403
Mus. Dir.: Neville Marriner
President: Richard M. Cisek
Gen. Mgr.: Robert C. Jones

**Montreal Symphony Orchestra**
200 de Maisonneuve Blvd. W.
Montreal, Quebec H2X 1Y9 Canada
Mus. Dir.: Charles Dutoit
Mng. Dir.: Zarin Mehta

**National Symphony Orchestra**
J.F. Kennedy Center for the Performing Arts
Washington, DC 20566
Mus. Dir.: Mstislav Rostropovich
Exec. Dir: Henry Fogel

**New Orleans Philharmonic Symphony Orchestra**
203 Carondelet St., Suite 903
New Orleans, LA 70130
Mus. Dir.: Philippe Entremont
V.P. & Exec. Man.: James D. Hicks

**New York Philharmonic Orchestra**
Avery Fisher Hall
65th St. and Broadway
New York, NY 10023
Mus. Dir.: Zubin Mehta
Mng. Dir.: Albert K. Webster

**Oregon Symphony Orchestra**
813 SW Alder Street
Portland, OR 97025
Mus. Dir.: James DePreist
Gen. Mgr.: John Graham

**Philadelphia Orchestra**
1420 Locust St., Philadelphia, PA 19102
Mus. Dir.: Ricardo Muti

**Pittsburgh Symphony Orchestra**
Heinz Hall for the Performing Arts
600 Penn Avenue, Pittsburgh, PA 15222
Mus. Dir.: André Previn
Mng. Dir.: Marshall W. Turkin

**Rochester Philharmonic Orchestra**
20 Grove Pl., Rochester, NY 14605
Mus. Dir.: David Zinman
Gen. Mgr.: Tony H. Dechario

**Saint Louis Symphony Orchestra**
718 N. Grand Blvd., St. Louis, MO 63103
Mus. Dir.: Leonard Slatkin
Exec. Dir.: David Hyslop
Manager: Joan Briccetti

**Saint Paul Chamber Orchestra**
Landmark Center
75 West Fifth Street
Saint Paul, MN 55102
Mus. Dir.: Pinchas Zukerman
Mng. Dir.: David Richardson

**San Antonio Symphony Orchestra**
109 Lexington Ave., Suite 207
San Antonio, TX 78205
Mus. Dir.: Lawrence Leighton Smith
Mng. Dir.: Nat Greenberg

**San Diego Symphony Orchestra**
P.O. Box 3175, San Diego, CA 92103
Mus. Dir.: David Atherton
Gen. Mgr.: William L. Denton

**San Francisco Symphony Orchestra**
Davies Symphony Hall
San Francisco, CA 94102
Mus. Dir.: Edo de Waart
Exec. Dir.: Peter Pastreich

**Seattle Symphony Orchestra**
305 Harrison St., Seattle, WA 98109
Mus. Dir.: Rainer Miedel
Pres. & Gen. Mgr.: Ralph Guthrie

**Syracuse Symphony Orchestra**
Suite 40, Civic Center, 411 Montgomery St.
Syracuse, NY 13202
Mus. Dir.: Christopher Keene
Gen. Mgr.: Eleanor Shopiro

**Toronto Symphony Orchestra**
215 Victoria St.
Toronto, Ontario M5B 1V1 Canada
Mus. Dir.: Andrew Davis
Mng. Dir.: Walter Homburger

**Utah Symphony Orchestra**
123 West South Temple
Salt Lake City, UT 84101
Mus. Dir.: Varujan Kojian
Exec. Dir.: Herold L. Gregory
Exec. V. Pres.: W. Boyd Christensen

**Vancouver Symphony Orchestra**
873 Beatty St.
Vancouver, B.C. V6B 2M6 Canada
Mus. Dir.: Kazuyoshi Akiyama
Gen. Mgr.: Michael Allerton

## PROFESSIONAL RESIDENT AND REPERTORY THEATRES

SOURCE: Actors' Equity Association. The following resident and repertory groups are member companies of the League of Resident Theatres or use the L.O.R.T. contract.

ABINGDON (VA): **Barter Theatre;** P.O. Box 250, Abingdon, VA 24210

ALBANY (NY): **The League of Theatre Artists;** P.O. Box 2114, Albany, NY 12220

ALLENTOWN (PA): **Pennsylvania Stage Company;** J.I. Rodale Theatre, 837 Linden St., Allentown, Pa 18101

ANCHORAGE (AK): **Alaska Repertory Theatre;** 705 W. 6th Ave., Suite 201, Anchorage, AK 99501

ANNISTON (AL): **Alabama Shakespeare Festival;** P.O. Box 141, Anniston, AL 36202

ARROW ROCK (MO): **The Lyceum Theatre;** Arrow Rock, MO 63520 (Summer)

ATLANTA (GA): **Alliance Theatre Company;** 1280 Peachtree St. N.E., Atlanta, GA 30309

BALTIMORE (MD): **Center Stage;** 700 N. Calvert St., Baltimore, MD 21202

BUFFALO (NY): **Studio Arena Theatre;** 710 Main St., Buffalo, NY 14202

CAMBRIDGE (MA): **American Repertory Theatre Company;** 64 Brattle St., Cambridge, MA 02138

CHAPEL HILL (NC): **Playmakers Repertory Company;** 103 South Bldg., U. of N.C., Chapel Hill, NC 27514

CHICAGO (IL): **Goodman Theatre Company;** 200 S. Columbus Dr., Chicago, IL 60603

CINCINNATI (OH): **Cincinnati Playhouse in the Park;** P.O. Box 6537, Cincinnati, OH 45206

CLEVELAND (OH): **Cleveland Playhouse;** 2040 E. 86th St., Cleveland, OH 44106
**Great Lakes Shakespeare Festival;** P.O. Box 598, Edgewater, Cleveland, OH 44107

COSTA MESA (CA): **South Coast Repertory Theatre;** 655 South Town Center Dr., Costa Mesa, CA 92626

DALLAS (TX): **Theatre 3;** 2800 Routh St., Dallas TX 75201

DAYTON (OH): **The Victory Theatre Assoc.;** 138 North Main St., Dayton, OH 95402

DENVER (CO): **Denver Center for the Performing Arts;** Denver Center Theatre Co., 1050 13th St., Denver, CO 80204

EAST HADDAM (CT): **Goodspeed Opera House;** East Haddam, CT 06423

EVANSTON (IL): **The North Light Repertory Theatre, Inc.;** 2300 Green Bay Rd., Evanston, IL 60201

GAMBIER (OH): **Kenyon Repertory Theatre and Festival, Inc.;** 202 West Brooklyn, Gambier, OH 43022

HARTFORD (CT): **Hartford Stage Company;** 50 Church St., Hartford, CT 06103

HOLLYWOOD (CA): **L.A. Stage Company;** 1642 N. Las Palmas, Hollywood, CA 90028

HORSE CAVE (KY): **Horse Cave Theatre;** P.O. Box 215, Horse Cave, KY 42749 (Summer)

HOUSTON (TX): **Alley Theatre;** 615 Texas Ave., Houston, TX 77002

INDIANAPOLIS (IN): **Indiana Repertory Theatre;** 140 W. Washington St., Indianapolis, IN 46204

KANSAS CITY (MO): **Missouri Repertory Theatre:** U. of Missouri, Kansas City, 5100 Rockhill Rd., Kansas City, MO 64110

KNOXVILLE (TN): **The Clarence Brown Theatre Company;** P.O. Box 8450, Knoxville, TN 37916

LAKE PLACID (NY): **Center for Music, Drama, and Art;** Saranac Ave. at Fawn Ridge, Lake Placid, NY 12946

LENOX (MA): **Shakespeare and Company;** The Mount, Plunkett Street, Lenox, MA 01240 (Summer)

LOS ANGELES (CA): **Mark Taper Forum;** Center Theatre Group, 135 N. Grand Ave., Los Angeles, CA 90012

LOS GATOS (CA): **California's Actors' Theatre;** P.O. Box 1355, Los Gatos, CA 95030

LOUISVILLE (KY): **Actors Theatre of Louisville;** 316-320 W. Main St., Louisville, KY 40202

LOWELL, (MA): **Merrimack Regional Theatre;** P.O. Box 228, Lowell, MA 01853

MADISON (NJ): **New Jersey Shakespeare Festival;** Drew U., Madison, NJ 07940

MIAMI (FL): **Players State Theatre;** Coconut Grove Playhouse, 3500 Main Hwy., Miami, FL 33133

MILWAUKEE (WI): **Milwaukee Repertory Theatre;** Performing Arts Center, 929 N. Water St., Milwaukee, WI 53202

MINNEAPOLIS (MN): **Cricket Theatre;** Hennepin Center for the Arts, 528 Hennepin Avenue, Minneapolis, MN 55403
**The Guthrie Theater;** 725 Vineland Pl., Minneapolis, MN 55403

NEW BRUNSWICK (NJ): **George Street Playhouse;** 414 George St., New Brunswick, NJ 08901

NEW HAVEN (CT): **Long Wharf Theatre;** 222 Sargent Dr., New Haven, CT 06511
**Yale Repertory Theatre;** Yale School of Drama, New Haven, CT 06520

NEW YORK (NY): **The Acting Company;** 420 W. 42nd St., 3rd Fl., New York, NY 10036
**Circle in the Square;** 1633 Broadway, New York, NY 10019
**The Negro Ensemble Company;** 165 W. 46th St., New York, NY 10036
**New York Shakespeare Festival;** (Delacorte and Mobile Theatres), The Public Theatre, 425 Lafayette St., New York, NY 10003 (Summer)
**The Roundabout Theatre Company;** 333 W. 23rd St., New York, NY 10011

NORFOLK (VA): **Virginia Stage Co.;** 142 West York St., Norfolk, VA 23510

PARK FOREST (IL): **Illinois Theatre Center;** 400 Lakewood Blvd., Park Forest, IL 60466

PHILADELPHIA (PA): **The Philadelphia Drama Guild;** 220 S. 16th St., Philadelphia, PA 19102

PITTSBURGH (PA): **Pittsburgh Public Theatre;** Suite 230, One Allegheny Square, Pittsburgh, PA 15212

PORTSMOUTH (NH): **Theatre by the Sea;** P.O. Box 927, Portsmouth, NH 03801

PRINCETON (NJ): **McCarter Theatre Company, Inc.;** 91 University Place, Princeton U., Princeton, NJ 08540

PROVIDENCE (RI): **Trinity Square Repertory Company;** 201 Washington St., Providence, RI 02903

RICHMOND (VA): **Virginia Museum Theatre;** Boulevard & Grove Aves., Richmond, VA 23221

ROCHESTER (MI): **Meadow Brook Theatre;** Oakland U., Rochester, MI 48063

ROCHESTER (NY): **Genesee Valley Arts Foundation (GeVa);** 168 Clinton Ave. South, Rochester, NY 14604

ST. LOUIS (MO): **The Repertory Theatre of St. Louis;** 130 Edgar Rd., St. Louis, MO 63119

ST. PAUL (MN): **Actors Theatre of St. Paul;** 2115 Summit Ave., St. Paul, MN 55105

SAN DIEGO (CA): **Old Globe Theatre;** P.O. Box 2171, San Diego, CA 92112

SAN FRANCISCO (CA): **American Conservatory;** 450 Geary St., San Francisco, CA 94102

SARASOTA (FL): **Asolo Theatre Festival;** P.O. Box Drawer E, Sarasota, FL 33578

SEATTLE (WA): **Seattle Repertory Theatre;** P.O. Box B, Queen Anne Sta., Seattle Center, Seattle, WA 98109
**A Contemporary Theatre;** 100 West Roy St., Seattle, WA 98119
**Intiman Theatre;** Box 4246, Seattle, WA 98119

STAMFORD (CT): **Hartman Theatre Company;** Box 521, Stamford, CT 06901

STRATFORD (CT): **American Shakespeare Theatre;** 1850 Elm Street, Stratford, CT 06497

SYRACUSE (NY): **Syracuse Stage;** University Regent Theatre, 820 E. Genesee St., Syracuse, NY 13210

TARRYTOWN (NY): **The New Globe Theatre;** 13 Main St., Tarrytown, NY 10591

TUCSON (AZ): **Arizona Theatre Co.;** 120 West Broadway, Tucson, AZ 85701

VISALIA (CA): **California Shakespeare Festival;** 417 North Locust St., Box 590, Visalia, CA 93277

WASHINGTON (DC): **Arena Stage;** Sixth and M Sts. S.W., Washington, DC 20024
**Folger Theatre Group;** 201 E. Capitol St. S.E., Washington, DC 20003
**John F. Kennedy Center for the Performing Arts;** 726 Jackson Place N.W., Washington, DC 20566

WATERFORD (CT): **Eugene O'Neill Memorial Theatre Center;** P.O. Box 206, Waterford, CT 06385 (Summer)

WEST SPRINGFIELD (MA): **Stage West;** 1511 Memorial Ave., W. Springfield, MA 01089

## ART MUSEUMS

### WORLD

AMSTERDAM: **Rijksmuseum (1808)**; *Collections:* 16th/17th-century Dutch paintings and drawings by Rembrandt, Hals, Vermeer, and others.
**Stedelijk Museum (1895)**; *Collections:* Impressionist to modern paintings and sculpture, including works of van Gogh, Chagall, and Dubuffet.

ANTWERP: **Koninklijk Museum voor Schone Kunsten (Royal Museum of Fine Arts) (1890)**; *Collections:* Dutch, Flemish, and French old masters, including Van Eyck, Van der Weyden, Memling, Rubens, Rembrandt, and Hals; 19th/20th-century Belgian art.

BERLIN: **National-Galerie (1876)**; *Collections:* European paintings from the 18th century to the present.

BRUSSELS: **Musée des Beaux-Arts (1892)**; *Collections:* Old and new masters, drawings, and sculpture.

BUDAPEST: **Magyar Nemzeti Museum (Hungarian National Museum) (1802)**; *Collections:* Archaeological finds; medieval to contemporary art; coins.
**Szépmüvészéti Museum (Museum of Fine Arts) (1896)**; *Collections:* Egyptian and Greco-Roman antiquities; Hungarian and foreign old masters; sculpture, drawings, and engravings.

CAIRO: **Coptic Museum (1908)**; *Collections:* Art treasures of early Christian culture in Egypt.
**Museum of Islamic Art (1881)**; *Collections:* Islamic painting, sculpture, ceramics, and applied arts (7th to 19th century).

CALCUTTA: **Indian Museum (1814)**; *Collections:* Indian art from prehistoric to Moslem times; Indian and Persian paintings; and Tibetan banners.

DRESDEN: **National Gallery (1846)**; *Collections:* Italian, Dutch, Flemish, and German old and new masters, including Rembrandt, Correggio, Titian, Rubens, Van Dyck, Veronese, and del Sarto.

FLORENCE: **Galleria dell'Accademia (1784)**; *Collections:* The most complete collection of Michelangelo's statues in Florence, as well as paintings by Tuscan masters of the 13th to 16th centuries.
**Galleria degli Uffizi (16th century)**; *Collections:* The world's finest collection of Italian Renaissance painting.

THE HAGUE: **Keninklijk Kabinet van Schilderijen (Mauritshuis) (Royal Picture Gallery) (1820)**; *Collections:* Dutch and German art; excellent Vermeers and Rembrandts.

ISTANBUL: **Museum of the Seraglio of Topkapi (Built mid-15th century)**; *Collections:* Sultans' treasure; Chinese and Japanese porcelain; enamels, embroidery, miniatures, and precious stones.

JERUSALEM: **Museum of Archaeology and Art (1965)**; *Collections:* Works concerning the Bible and Middle Eastern history; features the Billy Rose Art Garden and the Shrine of the Book.

LENINGRAD: **Hermitage (1764)**; *Collections:* More than 2.5 million objets d'art, including gold artifacts from Helleno-Scythian times, jewelry of the tsars, French impressionist paintings, old and new masters.
**State Russian Museum (1898)**; *Collections:* Exhibits numbering 250,000 of Russian art, sculpture, drawings, coins, and medals.

LONDON: **The British Museum (1753)**; *Collections:* Extensive collections spanning art and culture from neolithic age to present, including the Elgin Marbles.
**National Gallery (1857)**; *Collections:* A superb collection from the 12th century to the present.
**Tate Gallery (1897)**; *Collections:* British painting from the 16th century to the present, including works by Blake, Constable, Turner; French impressionists and modern sculpture.
**Victoria and Albert Museum (1852)**; *Collections:* Fine and applied art of all countries, periods, and styles; ceramics, textile, sculpture, woodwork, paintings, prints, and drawings.

MADRID: **El Prado (1819)**; *Collections:* Italian, Flemish, Dutch, and Spanish Renaissance paintings; classical, Renaissance, and baroque sculpture; includes a large collection of Murillo, Goya, El Greco, Rubens, Bosch, Van Dyck, da Vinci, and Tintoretto.

MEXICO CITY: **Museo Nacional de Antropologia (1865)**; *Collections:* Anthropological, ethnological, and archaeological collections relating to Mexico.

MOSCOW: **State Tretyakov Gallery (1856)**; *Collections:* A rich collection of 40,000 Russian icons; Russian and Soviet sculpture, graphics and paintings, dating from the 11th century to the present.

MUNICH: **Alte Pinakothek (1836)**; *Collections:* German, Dutch, Flemish, Italian, Spanish, and French masters.

NEW DELHI: **National Museum of India (1949)**; *Collections:* Indian and Central Asian treasures that date from 3000 B.C. to the present; sculpture, paintings, manuscripts, miniatures, and crafts.

PARIS: **Galerie du Jeu de Paume (1920)**; *Collections:* Including examples by Monet, Cézanne, van Gogh, Renoir, Degas, Pissarro, and Gaugin.
**Musée Guimet**; *Collections:* The finest European collection of oriental painting, sculpture, and applied arts.
**Musée du Louvre (1793)**; *Collections:* Oriental, Egyptian, Roman, and Greek antiquities, medieval, Renaissance, and modern sculpture and painting.
**Musee National d'Art Moderne (1943) (Centre National d'Art et de Culture Georges Pompidou)**; *Collections:* 20th-century paintings and sculpture.
**Musée de l'Orangerie (1853)**; *Collections:* A group of Utrillos, Cézannes, Monets, and others, exhibited in the atmosphere of a collector's apartment.
**Musée Rodin (1916)**; *Collections:* The sculptor's work and collection are displayed in a home and garden.

ROME: **Borghese Art Gallery (c. 1616)**; *Collections:* Classical and baroque sculpture and painting.

ROTTERDAM: **Museum Boymans-van Beuningen (1847)**; *Collections:* European art from the 15th century to the present, including Van Eyck, Breughel the Elder, Hals, Rembrandt, van Ruisdael, Hobbema, Rubens, Titian, Watteau, and Boucher.

SAO PAULO: **Museu de Arte Contemporãnea (1947)**; *Collections:* Nearly 1,700 works by such modern masters as Kandinsky, Léger, and the early cubists.
**Museu de Arte de São Paulo (1947)**; *Collections:* A panoramic view of Western art from gothic times to the present; paintings by Hals, Raphael, Renoir, Toulouse-Lautrec, and Rembrandt are included.

TAIPEI: **National Palace Museum (1925)**; *Collections:* Examples of Chinese art from the Shang to the Ch'ing dynasty that were brought to Taipei from the Mainland during the Communist revolution.

TORONTO: **Royal Ontario Museum at Toronto (1912)**; *Collections:* Art and archaeological objects from the Americas, Africa, Polynesia, ancient Egypt, Rome and Greece; Chinese, Japanese, Islamic, and Indian art; European art from all ages.

VIENNA: **Kunsthistorisches Museum (Museum of Fine Arts) (1891)**; *Collections:* Egyptian, Greek, Etruscan, Roman, and Cyprian antiquities; excellent Breughel collection; French, Dutch, Italian, and German Renaissance and baroque art.

### UNITED STATES

BALTIMORE: **Baltimore Museum of Art (1914)**; *Collections:* Epstein and Jacobs collections of old masters and sculpture; 19th/20th-century French painting, sculpture, graphics; Toulouse-Lautrec posters; contemporary American art; Oriental art and mosaics.
**Walters Art Gallery (1931)**; *Collections:* More than 25,000 objects, of which the Byzantine and medieval examples are noteworthy; classical art of Greece, Rome, Egypt, medieval to 19th-century European art.

BOSTON: **Isabella Steward Gardner Museum (1900)**; *Collections:* American and European painting and sculpture, from classical times to the 20th century.
**Museum of Fine Arts (1870)**; *Collections:* Exceptionally fine collection of prints, Oriental art, decorative arts; Egyptian, Greek, and Roman art; old masters and 19th-century French paintings.

BUFFALO: **Albright-Knox Art Gallery (1862)**; *Collections:* 18th-century English, 19th-century American and French and contemporary American and European paintings; sculpture (3000 B.C. to the present).

CAMBRIDGE: **Harvard University, Fogg Art Museum (1895)**; *Collections:* Oriental and Western art from ancient times to the present; representative collections of painting, sculpture, prints, and drawings, including Italian primitives and Chinese jades and bronzes.

CHICAGO: **Art Institute of Chicago (1879)**; *Collections:* Major periods of Western, Oriental and primitive art.
**University of Chicago, Oriental Institute Museum (1919)**; *Collections:* More than 70,000 objects that represent the art, religion, and daily life of ancient Egypt, Nubia, Assyria, Babylonia, Persia, Palestine, Syria, Anatolia, Libya, and Cyprus.

CINCINNATI: **Cincinnati Art Museum (1881)**; *Collections:* Sculpture, painting, and ceramics of Egypt, Greece, Rome; Near Eastern and Far Eastern art;

**19th/20th-century European and American art; primitive art from Oceania, Africa, and the Americas.**

CLEVELAND: **Cleveland Museum of Art (1913);** *Collections:* Art from many cultures and periods, including old masters and modern paintings, sculpture, prints, drawings, porcelain, metalwork, and furniture.

COLUMBUS: **Columbus Gallery of Fine Arts (1878);** *Collections:* Old masters; modern French and American painting; major collection of the art of George Bellows; South Pacific primitives.

DALLAS: **Dallas Museum of Fine Arts (1903);** *Collections:* Ancient, pre-Columbian, African sculpture, Japanese, European and American art.

DETROIT: **Detroit Institute of Arts (1885);** *Collections:* Art, dating from prehistoric times to the present, including Italian medieval and Renaissance sculpture, 17th-century Dutch paintings, and French-Canadian art.

DISTRICT OF COLUMBIA: **Corcoran Gallery of Art (1859);** *Collections:* American painting, sculpture, and drawing from the 18th century to the present; Dutch, Flemish, French and English painting.

**Hirshhorn Museum and Sculpture Garden (1974);** *Collections:* Modern paintings and sculpture.

**National Gallery of Art (1937);** *Collections:* West European old masters, French impressionists; American primitive paintings; sculpture, prints and drawings; East building contains permanent and changing exhibits.

**Phillips Collection (1918);** *Collections:* Modern art, especially 19th/20th-century American and European works.

**Smithsonian Institution, Freer Gallery of Art (1906);** *Collections:* Near and Far Eastern art and artifacts, 19th/20th-century American art, including the Peacock Room entirely decorated by Whistler.

FORT WORTH: **Amon Carter Museum of Western Art (1961);** *Collections:* Western paintings and sculpture, includes Frederic Remington and Charles Russell.

**Fort Worth Art Museum (1961);** *Collections:* 20th century paintings and sculpture.

**Kimbell Art Museum (1972);** *Collections:* masterpieces from ancient times to cubism.

HARTFORD: **Wadsworth Atheneum (1842);** *Collections:* European and American painting from 1400 to the present, including medieval and Renaissance European tapestries; early South and Central American art.

HOUSTON: **Museum of Fine Arts of Houston (1900);** *Collections:* Paintings, sculpture, and decorative arts covering most periods of history, including Renaissance painting, classical art and sculpture, and American art.

KANSAS CITY (MO.): **William Rockhill Nelson Gallery and Atkins Museum of Fine Arts (1926);** *Collections:* Oriental art, especially Chinese; classical, European, and American painting, sculpture, and decorative arts.

LOS ANGELES: **Los Angeles County Museum of Art (1961);** *Collections:* Major periods of European and American art; Oriental art.

MALIBU (CALIF.): **J. Paul Getty Museum (1953);** *Collections:* Greek and Roman antiquities, old masters paintings, 18th-century French decorative arts.

MERION STATION (PA.): **Barnes Foundation (1922);** *Collections:* European Renaissance and 20th-century American painting; African sculpture and Chinese art.

MINNEAPOLIS: **Minneapolis Institute of Arts (1914);** *Collections:* Oriental and pre-Columbian art; American and European painting and sculpture.

**Walker Art Center (1972);** *Collections:* 20th century art, changing exhibits.

NEWARK: **Newark Museum (1909);** *Collections:* American painting and sculpture from all periods; Oriental art, emphasizing the expression of Tibet.

NEW HAVEN: **Yale Center for British Art (1977);** *Collections:* British paintings, prints and drawings.

NEW ORLEANS: **Isaac Delgado Museum of Art (1910);** *Collections:* Kress Collection of Renaissance painting; Hyams Collection of the Barbizon school; contemporary European and American painting, sculpture, and drawings; Howard Collection of Greek vases.

NEW YORK CITY: **Brooklyn Museum (1893);** *Collections:* Egyptian, Near and Far Eastern art; Renaissance and medieval painting; American painting from all periods and 19th/20th-century European art; primitive art and artifacts from Oceania, Africa, the Far East, and South America.

**Frick Collection (1935);** *Collections:* European painting, sculpture, prints, and drawings from the 14th century to the 1800s; Limoges enamels, French and Chinese porcelains, and period furniture.

**Jewish Museum (1904);** *Collections:* This largest exhibit of Judaica in the Western Hemisphere is housed in the former Felix Warburg mansion.

**Metropolitan Museum of Art (1870);** *Collections:* Comprehensive collections that cover 5,000 years of history and represent the arts of Egypt, Babylonia, Assyria, Greece, Rome, Near and Far East, Europe, pre-Columbian culture, and the United States; primitive art of Africa and Oceania; includes the Cloisters in Fort Tryon Park.

**Museum of Modern Art (1929);** *Collections:* One of the foremost collections of 19th/20th-century American and European painting, sculpture, prints, photographs, posters, and films.

**Pierpont Morgan Library (1924);** *Collections:* Old master drawings, Rembrandt etchings, and manuscripts.

**Solomon R. Guggenheim Museum (1937);** *Collections:* Impressionist to contemporary painting and sculpture, including the world's largest collection of Kandinsky's work; paintings and sculpture by Picasso, Chagall, Klee, Brancusi, and Modigliani.

**Whitney Museum of American Art (1930);** *Collections:* American paintings, sculpture, drawings, and prints; the 20th-century American art housed ranges from realism to abstract expressionism.

PASADENA (CALIF.): **Norton Simon Museum of Art at Pasadena (1974);** *Collections:* European paintings spanning six centuries; modern sculpture garden; Indian and South Asian bronzes and stone figures.

PHILADELPHIA: **Philadelphia Museum of Art (1875);** *Collections:* Dutch, Flemish, French, American, and Italian masters; cubist and postcubist art; Far Eastern and Near Eastern art; Pennsylvania Dutch folk art; tapestries, silver, china, and period rooms.

**University of Pennsylvania, University Museum (1887);** *Collections:* Archaeological finds of Near East, Egypt, the Mediterranean, and the Americas; ethnology of Africa, Oceania, and art of China, pre-1000 A.D.

PITTSBURGH: **Carnegie Institute, Museum of Art (1896);** *Collections:* American and European painting and sculpture, including old masters and impressionists; international collection of modern art.

PORTLAND (ME.): **Portland Museum of Art (1908);** *Collections:* American painting, sculpture and decorative arts.

RALEIGH (N.C.): **North Carolina Museum of Art (1951);** *Collections:* European and American painting, sculpture and decorative arts.

RICHMOND: **Virginia Museum of Fine Arts (1930);** *Collections:* Painting, prints, sculpture from major world cultures; Fabergé jewelry.

SAN ANTONIO: **San Antonio Museum of Art (1981);** *Collections:* Art of the Americas, especially art of American Indians, Spanish colonial, pre-Columbian and Mexican folk art.

SAN FRANCISCO: **California Palace of the Legion of Honor (1924);** *Collections:* European and American painting, sculpture, and decorative arts; Egyptian and Greek antiquities.

**M. H. De Young Memorial Museum (1895);** *Collections:* European and American art from ancient times to 1850; Oriental and South Pacific art; Flemish tapestries; art of pre-Columbian Central, South, and North American Indians.

**San Francisco Museum of Modern Art (1921);** *Collections:* Contemporary painting, sculpture, drawings, prints, photography, and decorative arts from Europe, the United States, and Latin America.

SAN MARINO (CALIF.): **Henry E. Huntington Library and Art Gallery (1919);** *Collections:* Eighteenth-century British portraits and French sculpture; 15th/16th-century Italian and Flemish paintings; 18th/19th-century French and British decorative arts.

SEATTLE: **Seattle Art Museum (1917);** *Collections:* Chinese, Japanese, Indian, and Near Eastern art; Egyptian, Greek, Roman antiquities; European Renaissance painting, sculpture, and porcelain; Northwest Indian and pre-Columbian primitive art.

TOLEDO: **Toledo Museum of Art (1901);** *Collections:* European art from classical times to the 20th century; American painting and decorative arts.

WORCESTER (MASS.): **Worcester Art Museum (1896);** *Collections:* American, European, and Oriental art—ancient through contemporary; painting, sculpture, prints, decorative arts; early American and Italian art.

# THE REVIEWS: 1981/82

## BOOKS

Like much of the news capturing the attention of the country last year, bulletins from the world of books were not encouraging. Christmastime, the year's most generous gift-giving season that brings booksellers the bulk of their annual income, was disappointing. Income from book sales was hard-put simply to keep up with the rise of inflation. Returns, the unsold books retailers ship back to publishers, reached unprecedented levels. Cover prices escalated beyond the reach of many with limited discretionary funds.

Publishing houses themselves fared poorly. A number of them were absorbed by other publishers. Random House, which includes Pantheon and Knopf hardcovers, as well as Ballantine mass market and Vintage trade paperbacks, bought most of the assets of Fawcett's mass market and trade paperback lines. The Putnam Publishing Group (which already comprised the hardcover lines of Putnam and Coward, McCann & Geoghegan, Perigee trade paperbacks, and the Berkley and Jove mass market paperback lines) had acquisitions on its mind in a big way when it picked up the Grosset & Dunlop hardcover company, Ace paperbacks and Playboy books, both hardcover and paperback.

Even many of the books published were of a grim nature. A primary concern of Americans worsened, and enormous numbers of people demonstrated against the proliferation of nuclear weapons. This was a worry that manifested itself in scores of books on the subject, and contributing to the flood were titles such as *The Fate of the Earth* by Jonathan Schell, a nightmarish examination of the destructive potential of 50,000 warheads in the hands of many nations. A paperback original with the macabre title, *Nuclear War: What's in It for You* added further fuel to the fire. The authorship of this was by Ground Zero, a nonpartisan group dedicated to educating the public on the perils of atomic weaponry.

A book on the last international war, *At Dawn We Slept: The Untold Story of Pearl Harbor* by Gordon W. Prange, was published 40 years following the tragedy in Hawaii. Representing nearly four decades of research, it reportedly proved among other things that FDR did not have prior knowledge of the surprise attack that impelled the U.S. into World War II.

True to the traditional resiliency of the human spirit, however, not everything between book covers was gloomy. Garfield, who has grown into one of America's favorite cartoon cats, made his appearance in four different books by Jim Davis, all of which appeared on bestseller lists simultaneously, a first for any author, not to mention any cat. Another runaway success was Bruce Feirstein's satire on manliness, *Real Men Don't Eat Quiche: A Guidebook to All That Is Truly Masculine.* Fran Lebowitz followed her highly popular and very funny *Metropolitan Life* of a couple of years ago with *Social Studies.*

Just like Lebowitz's second try, several other follow-up titles met with considerably less enthusiasm from book buyers than did the original books, among them Judy Mazel's *The Beverly Hills Diet Lifetime Plan,* which was written to capitalize on the astonishing sales record of her first book, *The Beverly Hills Diet,* a controversial means of weight control that advocated a healthy intake of pineapple.

A sweet of another kind was elevated through the wit and drawings of Sandra Boynton in *Chocolate: The Consuming Passion,* a trade paperback that pulled winningly on the heartstrings of chocoholics all across the country. These may have been some of the buyers of a small explosion of books focusing on another controversial discovery, a pill that promised to prevent the body from adding the horrible pounds lurking in bread and pasta. The substance was the starch-blocker, and the FDA didn't approve.

Those who decided that only physical effort could alleviate the burden of excess avoirdupois paid heed to a movie actress whose own body was one of the best proofs of the benefits of exercise. *Jane Fonda's Workout Book,* by Ms. Fonda herself, sold hundreds of thousands of copies.

Jane was not the only Fonda in bookstores. Father Henry provided *Fonda: My Life as Told to Howard Teichman,* but he didn't come close to his daughter's sales pace. Other personalties who chose to reveal untold facts about themselves or their pasts were Patty Hearst (*Every Secret Thing,* which she wrote with Alvin Moscow) and Abigail Van Buren, whose *The Best of Dear Abby* was her first book in 19 years. Not to be outdone, the sister with whom Dear Abby shared no little rivalry in past years, recounted her life story to her daughter, Margo Howard, who then wrote *Eppie: The Story of Ann Landers.*

Other familial connections, these arranged by marriage, were covered at lengths greater than some thought possible with Kitty Kelley's occasionally racy biography called *Elizabeth Taylor: The Last Star,* Paul Ferris' biography of her two-time husband named *Richard Burton* and *Eddie: My Life, My Loves* by Eddie Fisher.

A man who wrote a sometimes shocking book about his experiences in prison became a figure of some notoriety when he was released from prison at the urging of Norman Mailer and others in publishing. Jack Henry Abbott, who gave us *In the Belly of the Beast,* was released from jail, only to stab a young waiter to death shortly thereafter in July 1981. He was captured in September and convicted of manslaughter in January 1982.

Another matter that held the attention of people around the country was the topic of new technologies. One of the best books to crop up was Tracy Kidder's *The Soul of a New Machine,* an account of developing a new computer. Computerized diversions caused yet another spate of books, exemplified in the runaway paperback success called *Mastering Pac-Man* (TM) by Ken Uston.

One of the biggest sales stories of the year, however, was by James G. Nourse, a man who provided *The Simple Solution to Rubik's Cube.* This paperback original caught the public's fever for the devilish six-colored cube and sold well over a million copies in a short matter of time, just a few months.

Time of another sort, that governed by science fiction and fantasy, was particularly popular during 1981 and 1982. *The One Tree: Book Two of the Second Chronicles of Thomas Covenant* by Stephen Donaldson was one of the most popular books of the period, a hardcover book proving that thousands of readers were eager for highly imaginative fare. Even more copies of

SF and fantasy books were sold in paperback, many of them tie-ins with major money-making movies. *E.T.: The Extra-Terrestrial* became the most successful book written by cultish author William Kotzwinkle. It was based on Steven Spielberg's movie. Another Spielberg creation led to *Poltergeist* by James Kahn, and Vonda McIntyre earned a fortune in royalties from *Star Trek II: The Wrath of Khan.*

Another movie tie-in attested to the ongoing allure of T.S. Garp, when Pocket Books printed 1 million additional copies of *The World According to Garp* by John Irving in time for the movie adaptation of the novel, which already had 3.5 million copies in print. Irving had hardcover success with *The Hotel New Hampshire.* Another John, John Updike, received singular accolades with his book, *Rabbit Is Rich,* which won the Pulitzer Prize for fiction, the American Book Award for fiction and the National Book Critics Circle Award for fiction. Not bad for a character first introduced 21 years earlier in *Rabbit, Run* and brought back 10 years ago in *Rabbit Redux.*

Other important fiction of the year were Mary Renault's *Funeral Games, The Dean's December* by Saul Bellow, and John Cheever's last work published in his lifetime, a brief fable called *Oh What a Paradise It Seems.* Novels also brought about a breakthrough in mass-market paperback publishing when the reprint edition of James Clavell's *Noble House* was shipped out with a cover price of $5.95. *The Covenant* by James Michener was also $5.95, although the first printing went for $4.95.

Mention must be made of the novel with the most peculiar name, one that did not help it in the sales department. Dominick Dunne wrote a sequel that was entitled, believe it or not, *Part II of Joyce Haber's The Users: The Winners.* A novel that was received with much more positive critical words was a trade paperback original in this country, *Waiting for the Barbarians* by African writer J.M. Coetzee.

Finally, proof of the ascendancy of trade paperbacks was seen in the simultaneous publication of hardcover and trade paperback editions of novels by a number of authors customarily published initially in hardcover alone. These pioneers whose books were made available in both hardcover and paperback at the same time were Jerzy Kosinski (*Pinball*), Thomas McGuane (*Nobody's Angel*) and Jerome Charyn (*Panna Maria*). Unfortunately, none of these three met with the critical approval that might have propelled them onto bestseller lists as they were breaking new ground.

—**Robert Dahlin**

## SELECTED BESTSELLERS: 1981-82

### FICTION

| Title | Author | Publisher |
|---|---|---|
| *The Parsifal Mosaic* | Robert Ludlum | Random House |
| *An Indecent Obsession* | Colleen McCullough | Harper & Row |
| *The Hotel New Hampshire* | John Irving | Dutton |
| *Spring Moon* | Bette Bao Lord | Harper & Row |
| *North and South* | John Jakes | Harcourt Brace Jovanovich |
| *Cujo* | Stephen King | Viking |
| *The Man from St. Petersburg* | Ken Follett | Morrow |
| *The Prodigal Daughter* | Jeffrey Archer | Simon & Schuster |
| *The One Tree* | Stephen Donaldson | Del Ray |
| *Eden Burning* | Belva Plain | Delacorte Press |
| *Fever* | Robin Cook | Putnam |
| *Twice Shy* | Dick Francis | Putnam |
| *Celebrity* | Thomas Thompson | Doubleday |
| *Thy Brother's Wife* | Andrew Greeley | Warner/Bernard Geis |
| *No Time for Tears* | Cynthia Freeman | Arbor House |
| *Friday* | Robert Heinlein | Holt, Rinehart & Winston |
| *For Special Services* | John Gardner | Coward, McCann & Geoghegan |
| *A Green Desire* | Anton Myrer | Putnam |
| *Marco Polo, If You Can* | William F. Buckley, Jr. | Doubleday |
| *Rabbit Is Rich* | John Updike | Knopf |
| *Dinner at the Homesick Restaurant* | Anne Tyler | Knopf |

### NONFICTION

| Title | Author | Publisher |
|---|---|---|
| *Jane Fonda's Workout Book* | Jane Fonda | Simon & Schuster |
| *A Few Minutes with Andy Rooney* | Andy Rooney | Atheneum |
| *No Bad Dogs* | Barbara Woodhouse | Summit Books |
| *Living, Loving and Learning* | Leo Buscaglia | Charles B. Slack/Holt, Rinehart & Winston |
| *A Light in the Attic* | Shel Silverstein | Harper & Row |
| *America in Search of Itself* | Theodore H. White | Harper & Row |
| *Years of Upheaval* | Henry Kissinger | Little, Brown |
| *When Bad Things Happen to Good People* | Harold S. Kushner | Schocken |
| *The Fate of the Earth* | Jonathan Schell | Knopf |
| *At Dawn We Slept* | Gordon W. Prange | McGraw-Hill |
| *How to Make Love to a Man* | Alexandra Penney | Clarkson N. Potter |
| *Miss Piggy's Guide to Life* | Miss Piggy as told to Henry Beard | Knopf |
| *The Cinderella Complex* | Colette Dowling | Summit Books |
| *Pathfinders* | Gail Sheehy | Morrow |
| *From Bauhaus to Our House* | Tom Wolfe | Farrar, Straus & Giroux |
| *Elvis* | Albert Goldman | McGraw-Hill |
| *The Walk West* | Peter and Barbara Jenkins | Morrow |
| *Witness to Power* | John D. Ehrlichman | Simon & Schuster |
| *I Love New York Diet* | Bess Myerson and Bill Adler | Morrow |
| *Holy Blood, Holy Grail* | Michael Baigent, Richard Leigh and Henry Lincoln | Delacorte Press |
| *The Umpire Strikes Back* | Ron Luciano and Dave Fisher | Bantam Books |
| *The Invisible Bankers* | Andrew Tobias | Linden Press |

## THEATRE

Priestly cassocks and sisterly habits were the favored costumes on- and Off-Broadway this season, with a surfeit of shows on Catholic themes—"Mass Appeal," "Agnes of God," "Do Black Patent Leather Shoes Really Reflect Up?" and, best of all, Christopher Durang's seditious "Sister Mary Ignatius Explains It All for You." It was also a season of long titles and small casts, with many two- and three-character plays, and one play, "Red and Blue," that entirely did away with actors; it starred two lightbulbs.

All of this was contradicted by "The Life and Adventures of Nicholas Nickleby," a monumental gift from London's Royal Shakespeare Company—David Edgar's eight- and one-half-hour distillation of the Dickens novel, presented in two voluminous parts by a masterful ensemble led by directors Trevor Nunn and John Caird. "Nicholas Nickleby" was the theatrical event of the season, perhaps of the decade, and drew a rapturous audience despite the fact that it set a record high by charging $100 a seat.

In other respects, theatergoers paid more for less. Broadway box office receipts rose to $221 million (according to *Variety*), a fact that was directly attributable to a rise in ticket prices, with $40 becoming a standard top for orchestra seats for musicals.

"Nicholas Nickleby" shared dramatic honors with Athol Fugard's " 'Master Harold' . . . and the Boys," a searing, deeply compassionate play about the relationship between a white teenager and a black waiter in South Africa. At season's end, "Nicholas Nickleby" won both the Tony Award and New York Drama Critics Circle prize as Best Play, with "Master Harold" as its strongest challenger. Both works, one a boldly cinematic adaptation of a literary classic, the other a profound contemporary play by a great living playwright, brought distinction to Broadway. "Nicholas Nickleby" boasted the finest complement of actors to be seen on one stage, with a company headed by Roger Rees (a Tony Award winner as Best Actor) in the title role and David Threlfall as his devoted friend. For his superb performance in "Master Harold," Zakes Mokae was named Best Featured Actor.

Both the Pulitzer Prize and the Critics prize for Best American Play went to Charles Fuller for his "A Soldier's Play," a production of the Negro Ensemble Company that perceptively investigated an incident of violence on a black military base during World War II. "Torch Song Trilogy," written by and starring Harvey Fierstein, was a compelling triptych of plays about a homosexual's life.

Among the other worthy plays were Beth Henley's "Crimes of the Heart," last year's Pulitzer Prize-winner, which moved to Broadway; Ronald Harwood's "The Dresser," about an aged English actor and his dresser; Percy Granger's "Eminent Domain," dealing with an idealistic professor on a midwest campus; John Guare's "Gardenia," a sequel to his "Lydie Breeze," a pair of plays about the decline of the American dream; "Geniuses," Jonathan Reynolds's uproarious spoof of movie-mad directors; A. R. Gurney, Jr.'s "The Dining Room," a Cheeverian look at WASP America.

Playwrights Horizon produced both "Geniuses" and "The Dining Room," along with "Sister Mary Ignatius," proving itself to be the outstanding institutional theater in New York this past year. The Ensemble Studio Theater highlighted its marathon of one-act plays with exceptional new work by Mary Gallagher and Romulus Linney. The American Place Theater ended its season on an upbeat with "The Regard of Flight," a hilarious clown show, devised by, and starring Bill Irwin, a Buster Keaton for the Eighties.

There were continuing contributions from Asian-American actors, directors and playwrights, including David Henry Hwang, represented by "The Dance and the Railroad" and "Family Devotions," and Genny Lim with "Paper Angels," about Chinese immigrants to America. Off-Off-Broadway, Ellen Stewart's La Mama celebrated its twentieth anniversary with a grand season of revivals of past successes and of visits from foreign companies, led by Poland's Tadeusz Kantor with "Weilopole Weilopole."

This was the season of the actor, with many paired in performance: James Earl Jones and Christopher Plummer in "Othello" (one of the year's four certified commercial hits; the others were "Crimes of the Heart," "Nicholas Nickleby" and Katharine Hepburn's vehicle, "West Side Waltz"); Paul Rogers and Tom Courtenay in "The Dresser"; Milo O'Shea and Michael O'Keefe in "Mass Appeal." Actresses came in threes: Marybeth Hurt, Mia Dillon and Lizbeth Mackay in "Crimes of the Heart" and Amanda Plummer, Elizabeth Ashley and Geraldine Page in John Pielmeier's "Agnes of God." Among the individual performances of note were Glenn Close as a woman who adopts the role of a man in "The Singular Life of Albert Nobbs"; Bob Dishy as an anguished *New York Times* reporter in Jules Feiffer's "Grownups"; Zoe Caldwell as an anguished "Medea."

This was an especially unsatisfying year for musicals. Two shows—"Nine," an adaptation of Fellini's "8½," directed by Tommy Tune, and "Dreamgirls," a variation on the Supremes, directed by Michael Bennett—were flawed but successful at the box office. At year's end they split awards. "Nine" received a Tony Award as Best Musical. "Dreamgirls" won in other categories, including Best Musical Actor and Actress for Jennifer Holliday and Ben Harney. For the second year in a row, the Critics Circle declined to name a Best Musical.

There were, however, three entertaining small musical shows, "Joseph and the Amazing Technicolor Dreamcoat," an Andrew Lloyd Webber-Tim Rice high school staple before it came to Broadway; "Pump Boys and Dinettes," a country western hoedown; and "Little Shop of Horrors," a weirdly amusing adaptation of a Roger Corman movie about a man-eating plant. The major musical disappointment was "Merrily We Roll Along," the latest collaboration between Stephen Sondheim and Harold Prince. A regrettable early closing was suffered by "The First," about Jackie Robinson entering baseball. "Forbidden Broadway," an impertinent cabaret revue took sharp shots at sacred cows and told Broadway where to get off.

—Mel Gussow

## MUSIC

The 1981-82 season demonstrated once again that the nation's musical appetite remains not only very large but that its palate runs to a wide variety of tastes.

Traditional music provided the backbone of programming for most organizations, notably the major symphony orchestras and the summer music festivals. But there were some adventurous, even bizarre, performances and productions which showed anew that many American music organizations are willing to take the risks necessary to give new or unusual music a hearing.

Among major modernists represented by new works were David Del Tredici, whose "Quaint Events" was especially commissioned and performed for the opening of the Buffalo Philharmonic's Baird Hall, and Charles Wuorinen, whose "Archaeopteryx" for bass trombone and ten players was presented at the 1982 Caramoor Festival in New York State. George Walker's Cello Concerto made a strong impression at its world premiere by Zubin Mehta and the New York Philharmonic with Lorne Munroe as the soloist. Ned Rorem's new 10-movement Double Concerto for piano and cello received a forceful performance from the Cincinnati Symphony led by Jorge Mester. On the opera scene, George Rochberg's "The Confidence Man," after Herman Melville's novel, was ably premiered by the Santa Fe Opera. Rochberg's music was generally praised; less well received was the treatment of Melville's story line, which did not readily lend itself to an operatic format.

Elliot Carter was the featured composer at the annual Venice festival, where his piano concerto, "Symphony for Three Orchestras" and various chamber works were performed. Another veteran composer, Roger Sessions, was awarded a Pulitzer Prize, his second, for his Concerto for Orchestra.

Bordering on the bizarre were plans announced by the New York Lyric Opera Company to mount a "rock" version of Claudio Monteverdi's 340-year-old "L'Incoronazione di Poppea." The opera has been performed twice in the last decade with electronic instruments, jazz and rock singers—first by the Minnesota Opera and later Yale University.

Surely bizarre, however, was a cello performance by Charlotte Moorman at a John Cage concert in New York where she made music while encased, semi-nude, in a blue parachute bag. Miss Moorman's treatment of the music was not actually unprecedented. She had performed a Cage work in similar fashion back in the 1960s.

Of more substantial stuff were the productions of long-neglected operatic works. In Houston, Marilyn Horne headed the cast in a production of Rossini's "La Donna del Lago" after Sir Walter Scott's "Lady of the Lake," and Calvin Simmons conducted a performance by the same company of Shostakovitch's "Lady Macbeth of Mtsensk." Riccardo Zandonai's 1922 opera "Giuletta and Romeo" was given its first U.S. hearing by the San Diego Opera, and the American premiere of Arrigo Boito's 19th-century opera "Nerone" was presented by Eve Queler's Opera Orchestra of New York. The New York City Opera produced Italo Montemezzi's passionate "L'amore dei tre re" last heard on NBC-TV in 1952, and also gave Verdi's early "I Lombarda alla prima Crociata."

Miss Queler's group announced that its upcoming season would offer Donizetti's "i Duca d'Alba," Berlioz's "Benvenuto Cellini," and Richard Strauss's "Guntram," each of which is far removed from the standard repertory. "Resurrection," a 1904 opera by Franco Alfano, was scheduled by the Cincinnati Opera, and Stanislawu Moniuszko's "The Haunted Castle," premiered in 1865 in Warsaw, was to be played by the Michigan Opera Theater.

A notable operatic event during the year was the gala at Washington, D.C.'s Kennedy Center saluting bass-baritone George London, incapacitated by illness for the last several years. The cast included Nicolai Gedda, Marilyn Horne, James McCracken and Joan Sutherland.

Symphony orchestras were beset with the twin problems of an economic recession and Federal funding cutbacks, but continued to perform before substantial audiences. If they are now musical "museums," as Leonard Bernstein once termed them, they are beloved museums which provide a cultural centerpiece for the cities and regions in which they perform. The New York Philharmonic showed off its longevity with a celebration of its 10,000th concert in a performance of Mahler's Symphony No. 2. At one of its summer concerts, an estimated 220,000 persons heard it play "Scheherazade" and the "1812 Overture."

Although orchestras in Miami and Kansas City, Mo., went out of business, a new orchestra emerged in Hagerstown, Md.—The Maryland Symphony, which will have as its music director Barry Tuckwell, the horn virtuoso. There were the usual number of shifts at the top. Lorin Maazel departed the Cleveland Orchestra to take over the Vienna State Opera. He will be succeeded by Christoph von Dohnanyi. The youthful English conductor Simon Battle became principal guest conductor of the Los Angeles Philharmonic together with Michael Tilson Thomas. And in Detroit, Antal Dorati resigned.

Noteworthy recitals were given by Nina Lelchuck, a Soviet emigre whose musical maturity impressed critics, and Adryzij Wasowski, a Pole who displayed a sure command of his instrument. Paul Jacobs premiered Elliot Carter's first piano sonata since 1946, and Phillippe Bianconi, 21 years old, won the fourth Robert Casadesus International Piano Competition held in Cleveland with his performances of Chopin and Ravel.

Anniversaries of major composers provided an opportunity for performances of their works. The Chamber Music Society of Los Angeles combined the 250th anniversary of Josef Haydn's birth with the 100th anniversary of Igor Stravinsky's to present a week-long festival. The New York Philharmonic scheduled a series of Stravinsky's works to be played over a period of several months to honor his substantial contributions to music. And at Carnegie Hall, the 85th birthday of composer Virgil Thomson was celebrated with a concert performance of his "Four Saints in Three Acts," which was introduced by actor-director John Houseman, who directed the original production in Hartford in 1934.

The music world mourned the deaths of arranger-composer Hershy Kay, 62; conductor Karl Boehm, 86; arranger-composer Robert Russell Bennett, 87; clarinetist Reginald Kell, 75; and soprano Maria Jeritza, 94.

**—Henry T. Wallhauser**

## TELEVISION

This is what happened in television in the 1981-82 season: People started watching nonnetwork alternatives in significant numbers. Just about everything else that happened had either a cause or effect relationship with that one fact. The hard data: Network ratings were down four percent. Network share of the audience was down three percent.

It was the continuation of a pattern even the networks admit is likely to continue for at least a decade: steady erosion of network dominance of TV, thanks to ever-multiplying forms of competition. Cable and pay-TV continued to take their share, but new video choices popped up everywhere—low-power television, direct broadcast satellites, video games. The latter claimed $1 billion in sales of home sets, which hardly reflected the command of Pac-Man and his brethren on America's leisure time.

The competitive atmosphere was fueled by a Federal Communications Commission with an aggressive bent toward deregulating the entire broadcast industry. The FCC announced decision after decision which opened the way for innovations such as low-power TV and direct-broadcast satellite transmission of TV signals. It might have been interpreted as open season on the networks had not the commission at the same time had a mind to unfetter the networks of limitations on their activities. The pro-business slant of the Reagan appointees steered the commission toward permitting the networks to go back into the production and syndication business, and even toward permitting the networks to own their own cable systems.

Indeed, the can't-beat-'em, so-'let's-join-'em philosophy exploded at the networks, as all three began forming entangling alliances to assume fortified positions on the new video landscape.

CBS united with 20th Century Fox; NBC with Columbia Pictures. ABC, which seemed to want a piece of every company in the video field, made separate agreements with Westinghouse Broadcasting for a new satellite news channel, Getty Oil for involvement with that company's all-sports cable channel, Cox Broadcasting for its existing cable systems and Sony Corporation for a novel pay-TV arrangement tied to taping on video cassette recorders.

That last idea made sense, given the proliferation of home tape machines (up to two million sold by the beginning of 1982). But a decision by a Federal Appeals Court in California declared home taping illegal because it violated the rights of copyright holders. That reversed an earlier decision which had permitted such taping.

The decision set off a massive lobbying effort in Congress from both sides of the issue. The Hollywood community sought a hefty royalty fee on both VCRs and blank tapes. The machine and tape manufacturers (virtually all of whom are Japanese) asked Congress for a bill to allow private viewers the freedom to tape what they wish. The Supreme Court finally agreed to rule on the issue.

The shift of audiences away from the networks certainly helped independent stations. They enjoyed an outstanding year, winning large audiences through astute counterprogramming.

This came amid a kind of revisionism in the work thinking about cable. The threat was suddenly being downgraded by network statistical analysts, who predicted difficult days ahead for cable channels, the survival of only a fraction of the ever-expanding list of cable offerings (examples: an all-weather channel, an all-health channel, two new all-news channels) and the loss of only 10 percent of network audiences by the time all the erosion was done.

The cable companies disagreed, of course, but conceded that the free ride was ending. New programming forms were desperately needed, especially by the pay-TV channels, all of whom depend almost exclusively on movies for their programming. With the supply of Hollywood movies diminishing every year, these companies talked openly of producing their own movies or even their own TV series. Home Box Office, the biggest of the pay companies, almost signed a deal to continue the run of the outstanding comedy series "Taxi," which was rudely cancelled by ABC. However, NBC stepped in and picked up "Taxi," leaving HBO's entry into the TV series business for another day.

The specialization of cable programming caused drastic reaction by the networks in one area—news. By year's end, the networks had turned into all-night diners, serving up news at every hour. The opportunity for network-affiliated stations to buy a new service of the Cable News Network clearly influenced this outbreak of news. All three networks went for pre-dawn newscasts; CBS went all the way with an all-night service. NBC and ABC initiated late-late news shows.

At the same time, the move to expand the evening news to a full hour was all but abandoned as the networks ran into intractable opposition from their affiliated stations.

Naturally all the news expansion was expensive, and the networks talked openly of financial austerity. That seemed most imperative at NBC, which suffered through another dismal financial year, mostly thanks to abysmal returns for its daytime programming. NBC's status certainly didn't help its corporate owner, RCA, whose profits were down about $250 million since 1980.

CBS and ABC had happier profit statements. But the financial pressure was such that all three networks announced a plan to add seven 30-second commercials a week.

Public television stations would have relished such an opportunity. The financial crunch from cutbacks in Federal funding set in, though Congress did approve some emergency funding over the objection of the Reagan Administration. New funding ideas for PBS were demanded, however, and two major ones emerged. Ten PBS stations took part in an experiment to go commercial—they sold time to sponsors. Another idea would allow stations to open the avenue of corporate sponsorships to companies trucking in tobacco and alcohol.

The TV season itself offered little that was memorable. PBS's "Brideshead Revisited" was easily the leading show. The networks managed only two new shows that could be labeled hits, a score that reflected their cautious mood. The mood was inspired by the troubled financial picture, and perhaps by the campaigns of some religious groups. TV seemed more sanitized than ever, but that didn't satisfy the Coalition for Better Television. They announced a boycott against the sponsors of shows on beleagured NBC.

The boycott was a bigger flop than any of the shows tried during the season. **—Bill Carter**

## FILMS

No rollercoaster ever had as many ups and downs as the 1981-82 film season. A Christmas-that-wasn't was followed by the biggest summer in box office history. Yet, even as Steven Spielberg's *E.T.* reaffirmed Hollywood's ability to reach audiences at all levels of sophistication, the structure of the industry seemed to be imploding, and at least one major bank stopped making motion picture loans.

Exhibitors counting on the Christmas-week surge of spectacles and escapist family entertainment got instead such improbable holiday fare as Richard Dreyfuss dying in *Whose Life Is It Anyway?* or $20,000,000 "art house" films, e.g., the Arthur Penn-Steve Tesich *Four Friends,* an ambitious but obscure epic vision of an immigrant's coming of age, or Herbert Ross' "Brechtian" musical, *Pennies from Heaven,* that, aside from Bernadette Peters' acting and dancing, a variety of 1930s styles, mainly argued that everybody spent the Depression being depressed.

Perfectly tuned to the "Auld Lang Syne" spirit was the family reconciliation theme of *On Golden Pond,* whose appeal amazed distributors resigned to senior citizen patronage at a matinee discount. For an industry geared to the youth market, oldsters were surprisingly prominent, what with new features from 75-year-old Billy Wilder (*Buddy, Buddy*) and 81-year-old George Cukor (*Rich and Famous*), a quartet of stars whose average age was 78 in *Ghost Story,* sundry octogenarians and nonagenarians as "Witnesses" in *Reds.* And James Cagney's voice cut across the decades in *Ragtime,* a considerably simplified version of E. L. Doctorow's tapestry of American life circa 1906.

For some reason, the period of the First World War (give or take a decade) got extensive attention. Australia's *Gallipoli* revived the tradition of *All Quiet on the Western Front* and *Paths of Glory,* recounting a disastrous 1915 invasion. The sometimes magnificent, sometimes turgid *Chariots of Fire* depicted athletic triumphs of the postwar generation in the 1924 Olympics.

*Ragtime* was not a great success; the script's emphasis on the fictional story of black urban revolutionary Coalhouse Walker over the Thaw-White-Nesbit affair was arguably a commercial miscalculation. In any case, it was overshadowed by Warren Beatty's awesomely ambitious *Reds,* a three and one-half hour epic of America's radical bohemian subculture. Unlike Hollywood epics which reduced historical upheavals to backdrops for heavy breathing, *Reds* was actually weakest in its core romance (Warren Beatty as John Reed and Diane Keaton as Louise Bryant) and strongest at the periphery: Jack Nicholson as Eugene O'Neill, Jerzy Kosinsky as Zinoviev, and Oscar-winner Maureen Stapleton as Emma Goldman. *Reds* excellent reviews overcame a lack of adequate publicity and audience resistance to the subject.

Another star/director, Burt Reynolds, racked up a solid commercial success with *Sharkey's Machine,* mainly notable for introducing sultry Rachel Ward, who went on to star in Steve Martin's black-and-white oddity, *Dead Men Don't Wear Plaid*—a pastiche of old clips and 1940s-style Milos Rozsa scoring that came out as a cross between a *Mad* movie parody and an academic essay on the conventions of *film noir.*

The big loser of the Christmas season was David Begelman, as the whole MGM slate went down to defeat, enlarging an already crushing bank debt from the United Artists takeover. The studio was eager to collect insurance losses resulting from the death of Natalie Wood before completion of *Brainstorm.* Lloyd's of London disallowed the claim, citing director Douglas Trumbull's belief that the film could be salvaged. (Natalie Wood's death was the first of a series of sudden deaths in the acting community—William Holden, John Belushi and Vic Morrow). The final straw came with bad previews of *Cannery Row,* a hoped-for "big" picture based on the John Steinbeck book. Attorney Frank Rothman was brought in to supervise Begelman, who was formally replaced as chairman of MGM/UA in July, coincident with the publication of a book, reviving his check-forging scandal.

At 20th Century-Fox they were waiting for oilman Marvin Davis to drop the other shoe. The company's new owner plans to sell the valuable site adjacent to Century City and move operations to the small CBS Studio Center (formerly the Republic lot). Although Fox made money on the distribution of the crude youth-market picture, *Porky's,* the internally generated product (and one of the first projects initiated by Sherry Lansing) performed poorly.

The acquisition of Columbia Pictures by Coca Cola provided comedians with opportunities, though the disappointing returns on Columbia's *Annie* were no joke to theatres who accepted backbreaking terms requiring a $6.00 admission price. CBS Films curtailed an ambitious schedule; Filmways was acquired by Orion; feisty Embassy, known for exploitation pictures, was sold to a group including Norman Lear. Zoetrope's studio was put up for sale, a casualty of Francis Ford Coppola's *One from the Heart,* a dazzling exercise in directorial virtuosity with such a naive plot that it baffled audiences and critics at a Radio City premiere staged in defiance of Paramount, which had dropped plans to release the film.

The Best-Picture Oscar went to *Chariots of Fire.* Warren Beatty won as Best Director in an unusual split. Katharine Hepburn won a fourth Oscar, while a valedictory for Henry Fonda (who died in August) was a foregone conclusion, as was recognition for John Gielgud's performance for the ages in *Arthur.*

Hollywood's real priorities were illustrated by remakes of *Cat People* and *The Thing,* distinguished in their originals by subtlety of construction, and in their new versions by stomach-wrenching violence.

Once again the alliance of special effects and sentiment saved the industry. *Star Trek: The Wrath of Khan,* with a great lunatic performance by Ricardo Montalban, ignored horrified "trekkies" and killed off Mr. Spock. Above all, it was Steven Spielberg's *E.T.* that caught the sea change in public taste. With its echoes of *Bambi, Mary Poppins,* and a Jiminy Cricket-like alien, Spielberg out-Disneyed Disney.

Disney itself offered the computer-animated *Tron,* aimed at video game-addled adolescents. The video game influence could also be seen in the climax of *Firefox,* a Clint Eastwood Cold War fantasy that future historians will bracket with *Conan the Barbarian* as key reflections of the Reagan era.

**—Stephen Handzo**

## NOBEL PRIZE WINNERS

### PHYSIOLOGY AND MEDICINE

| Year | Winner and Life Dates | Nationality | Achievement |
|---|---|---|---|
| 1901 | Emil A. von Behring (1854–1917) | German | Serum therapy; work on diphtheria antitoxin. |
| 1902 | Ronald Ross (1857–1932) | British | Discovery of the life cycle of the malaria parasite. |
| 1903 | Niels R. Finsen (1860–1904) | Danish | Treatment of skin diseases with concentrated light rays, especially **lupus vulgaris** (skin tuberculosis). |
| 1904 | Ivan P. Pavlov (1849–1936) | Russian | Work on the physiology of digestion. |
| 1905 | Robert Koch (1843–1910) | German | Work on tuberculosis; the development of bacteriology. |
| 1906 | Camillo Golgi (c.1843–1926) | Italian | Their study of the nervous system and of cell distribution. |
| | Santiago Ramón y Cajal (1852–1934) | Spanish | |
| 1907 | Charles L. A. Laveran (1845–1922) | French | Study of protozoa-caused disease. |
| 1908 | Paul Ehrlich (1854–1915) | German | Their work on immunology including the introduction of quantitative methods. |
| | Élie Metchnikoff (1845–1916) | Russian | |
| 1909 | E. Theodor Kocher (1841–1917) | Swiss | Work on the physiology, pathology, and surgery of the thyroid gland. |
| 1910 | Albrecht Kossel (1853–1927) | German | Contributions to the knowledge of cell chemistry. |
| 1911 | Allvar Gullstrand (1862–1930) | Swedish | For his work on ocular dioptrics, the refraction of light through the eye. |
| 1912 | Alexis Carrel (1873–1944) | American (b. France) | Development of vascular suture and surgical transplantation of blood vessels and organs. |
| 1913 | Charles R. Richet (1850–1935) | French | Work on anaphylaxis. |
| 1914 | Robert Bárány (1876–1936) | Austrian | Study of physiology and pathology of the inner ear. |
| 1919 | Jules J. P. V. Bordet (1870–1961) | Belgian | Discoveries in the field of immunity. |
| 1920 | S. August Krogh (1874–1949) | Danish | Discovered mechanism regulating blood-capillary action. |
| 1922 | Archibald V. Hill (1886–1977) | English | Discoveries concerning heat produced by muscular activity. |
| | Otto F. Meyerhof (1884–1951) | American (b. Germany) | Establishing the correlation between oxygen and lactic acid in muscle. |
| 1923 | Frederick G. Banting (1891–1941) | Canadian | Their production of insulin and demonstration of its value in combating diabetes. |
| | John J. R. Macleod (1876–1935) | British | |
| 1924 | Willem Einthoven (1860–1927) | Dutch | Invention of the electrocardiograph. |
| 1926 | Johannes A. G. Fibiger (1867–1928) | Danish | Experimental work in cancer. |
| 1927 | Julius Wagner-Jauregg (1857–1940) | Austrian | Discovery of malarial therapy in paralysis. |
| 1928 | Charles J. H. Nicolle (1866–1936) | French | Work on typhus. |
| 1929 | Christiaan Eijkman (1858–1930) | Dutch | Discovering vitamin B. |
| | Frederick G. Hopkins (1861–1947) | English | Discovering vitamin A. |
| 1930 | Karl Landsteiner (1868–1943) | American (b. Austria) | Discovery of human blood groups. |
| 1931 | Otto H. Warburg (1883–1970) | German | Discovery of the character and action mode of the respiratory enzyme. |
| 1932 | Edgar C. Adrian (1889-1977) | English | Studies on the physiology of the nervous system, especially the function of neurons. |
| | Charles S. Sherrington (1857–1952) | English | |
| 1933 | Thomas H. Morgan (1866–1945) | American | Discovering the functions of chromosomes in heredity. |
| 1934 | George R. Minot (1885–1950) | American | Their discoveries that administering liver extract increases activity in the bone-marrow where red cells are formed. |
| | William P. Murphy (1892– ) | American | |
| | George H. Whipple (1878–1976) | American | |
| 1935 | Hans Spemann (1869–1941) | German | Discovery of organizer effect in embryonic development. |
| 1936 | Henry H. Dale (1875–1968) | English | Their discoveries of the chemical transmission of nerve impulses. |
| | Otto Loewi (1873–1961) | American (b. Germany) | |
| 1937 | Albert von Szent-Györgyi (1893– ) | American (b. Hungary) | Metabolic studies; the effects of vitamins A and C. |
| 1938 | Corneille J. F. Heymans (1892–1968) | Belgian | Discovery of the influence of the carotid sinus on respiration rate. |
| 1939 | Gerhard Domagk (1895–1964) | German | Discovering prontosil, the first sulfa drug. |
| 1943 | C. P. Henrik Dam (1895–1976) | Danish | Discovering vitamin K. |
| | Edward A. Doisy (1893– ) | American | Discovery of the chemical nature of vitamin K. |
| 1944 | E. Joseph Erlanger (1874–1965) | American | Work on the highly differentiated functions of single nerve fibers. |
| | Herbert S. Gasser (1888–1963) | American | |
| 1945 | Alexander Fleming (1881–1955) | British | The discovery of penicillin and its curative properties in infections including those of the heart, syphilis, and certain types of pneumonia. |
| | Howard W. Florey (1898–1968) | British (b. Australia) | |
| | Ernst B. Chain (1906–1979) | British (b. Germany) | |
| 1946 | Hermann Joseph Muller (1890–1967) | American | Discovering the influence of X rays in genetics. |
| 1947 | Carl F. Cori (1896– ) | American (b. Czechoslovakia) | Their research on carbohydrate metabolism and enzymes. |
| | Gerty T. Cori (1896–1957) | American (b. Czechoslovakia) | |
| | Bernardo A. Houssay (1887–1971) | Argentine | Discovery of the role of the pituitary hormone in sugar metabolism. |
| 1948 | Paul H. Müller (1899–1965) | Swiss | Discovering the insect-killing properties of DDT. |
| 1949 | Walter R. Hess (1881–1973) | Swiss | Discovered how parts of the brain control body organs. |
| | Antonio de Egas Moniz (1874–1955) | Portuguese | Discovery of the therapeutic value of prefrontal lobotomy in certain psychoses. |
| 1950 | Philip S. Hench (1896–1965) | American | Their research in hormones including the discovery of cortisone and its antidisease effects. |
| | Edward C. Kendall (1886–1972) | American | |
| | Tadeus Reichstein (1897– ) | Swiss (b. Poland) | |
| 1951 | Max Theiler (1899–1972) | American (b. South Africa) | Developing the yellow-fever vaccine. |
| 1952 | Selman A. Waksman (1888–1973) | American (b. Russia) | Work in the discovery of streptomycin and its value in treating tuberculosis. |
| 1953 | Fritz A. Lipmann (1899– ) | American (b. Germany) | Their biochemical studies on cell metabolism, in- |

| Year | Winner and Life Dates | Nationality | Achievement |
|---|---|---|---|
| | Hans A. Krebs (1900–81) | British (b. Germany) | cluding the discovery of coenzyme A. |
| 1954 | John F. Enders (1897– ) | American | Their successful growth of polio viruses in cultures |
| | Thomas H. Weller (1915– ) | American | of tissues and discovery of more effective methods |
| | Frederick C. Robbins (1916– ) | American | of polio detection. |
| 1955 | A. Hugo T. Theorell (1903–82) | Swedish | Discoveries of the nature of oxidation enzymes. |
| 1956 | D. W. Richards (1895–1973) | American | Developing a technique of inserting a catheter |
| | André F. Cournand (1895– ) | American (b. France) | through a vein into the heart to chart its interior |
| | Werner Forssmann (1904–1979) | German | and to diagnose circulatory ailments. |
| 1957 | Daniel Bovet (1907– ) | Italian (b. Switzerland) | Developing muscle-relaxing drugs used in surgery. |
| 1958 | George W. Beadle (1903– ) | American | Discovery that genes transmit hereditary traits. |
| | Edward L. Tatum (1909–1975) | American | |
| | Joshua Lederberg (1925– ) | American | Experiments establishing that sexual recombination of bacteria results in exchange of genetic material. |
| 1959 | Severo Ochoa (1905– ) | American (b. Spain) | Their synthesis of RNA and DNA, organic com- |
| | Arthur Kornberg (1918– ) | American | pounds that carry hereditary characteristics. |
| 1960 | F. Macfarlane Burnet (1899– ) | Australian | Their discovery of acquired immunity, that is, that |
| | Peter B. Medawar (1915– ) | British (b. Brazil) | an animal can be made to accept foreign tissues. |
| 1961 | Georg von Békésy (1899–1972) | American (b. Hungary) | Work on the mechanism of the inner ear. |
| 1962 | Francis H. C. Crick (1916– ) | English | Their determining the molecular structure of deoxy- |
| | Maurice H. F. Wilkins (1916– ) | British | ribonucleic acid (DNA) and its significance for |
| | James D. Watson (1928– ) | American | information transfer in living material. |
| 1963 | Alan L. Hodgkin (1914– ) | English | Their research on nerve cells and on how electrical |
| | Andrew F. Huxley (1917– ) | English | charges pass through nerve membranes by means |
| | John C. Eccles (1903– ) | Australian | of a sodium-potassium exchange. |
| 1964 | Konrad E. Bloch (1912– ) | American (b. Germany) | Their discovery of the mechanism and control of |
| | Feodor Lynen (1911–1979) | German | cholesterol metabolism. |
| 1965 | François Jacob (1920– ) | French | Their discovery of the regulatory processes in body |
| | Andre M. Lwoff (1902– ) | French | cells that contribute to genetic control of enzymes |
| | Jacques L. Monod (1910–1976) | French | and virus synthesis. |
| 1966 | Charles B. Huggins (1901– ) | American (b. Canada) | Discoveries in hormonal treatment of prostate cancer. |
| | Francis P. Rous (1879–1970) | American | Discovery of a cancer virus. |
| 1967 | Haldan K. Hartline (1903– ) | American | Their discoveries pertaining to the eye's primary |
| | George Wald (1906– ) | American | chemical and physiological processes, including |
| | Ragnar A. Granit (1900– ) | Swedish (b. Finland) | work on color reception. |
| 1968 | Robert W. Holley (1922– ) | American | Their discovery of the process by which enzymes, con- |
| | H. Gobind Khorana (c.1922– ) | American (b. India) | sisting of a sequence of amino acids, determine a |
| | Marshall W. Nirenberg (1927– ) | American | cell's function in genetic development. |
| 1969 | Max Delbrück (1906–1981) | American (b. Germany) | Their discoveries concerning the replication mecha- |
| | Alfred D. Hershey (1908– ) | American | nism and the genetic structure of viruses. |
| | Salvador E. Luria (1912– ) | American (b. Italy) | |
| 1970 | Bernard Katz (1911– ) | British (b. Germany) | Their discoveries on the nature of the substances |
| | Ulf von Euler (1905– ) | Swedish | found at the end of nerve fibers. |
| | Julius Axelrod (1912– ) | American | |
| 1971 | Earl W. Sutherland (1915–1974) | American | Discoveries on the action mechanisms of hormones. |
| 1972 | Gerald M. Edelman (1929– ) | American | Research into the chemical structure of antibodies |
| | Rodney R. Porter (1917– ) | English | (Conducted independently). |
| 1973 | Konrad Lorenz (1903– ) | Austrian | Research into ethology. |
| | Nikolaas Tinbergen (1906– ) | English (b. Netherlands) | |
| | Karl von Frisch (1886– ) | German (b. Austria) | |
| 1974 | Albert Claude (1899– ) | American | Research which helped create the science of cell |
| | Christian Rene de Duve (1917– ) | Belgian | biology. |
| | George Emil Palade (1912– ) | American | |
| 1975 | David Baltimore (1938– ) | American | Discoveries concerning the interaction between tumor |
| | Renato Dulbecco (1914– ) | American (b. Italy) | viruses and the genetic material of the cell. |
| | Howard M. Temin (1935– ) | American | |
| 1976 | Baruch S. Blumberg (1925– ) | American | Discoveries concerning new mechanisms for the origin |
| | Daniel C. Gajdusek (1923– ) | American | and dissemination of infectious diseases. |
| 1977 | Rosalyn S. Yalow (1921– ) | American | Developed analytic radioimmunoassay technique utilizing isotopes for diagnostic purposes. |
| | Roger C. L. Guillemin (1924– ) | American (b. France) | Their use of radioimmunoassay in pituitary hormone |
| | Andrew V. Schally (1927– ) | American (b. Poland) | research. |
| 1978 | Werner Arber (1929– ) | Swiss | Discoveries and studies on the restriction enzymes' |
| | Daniel Nathans (1928– ) | American | linkage control of genes on chromosomes. |
| | Hamilton Smith (1931– ) | American | |
| 1979 | Allan MacLeod Cormack (1924– ) | American (b. S. Africa) | Development of the CAT scan, a three dimensional |
| | Godfrey Newbold Hounsfield (1919– ) | British | X-ray diagnostic technique. |
| 1980 | Baruj Benacerraf (1920– ) | American (b. Venezuela) | Research in cell immunology and discovery of HLA |
| | George D. Snell (1903– ) | American | antigens, which help fight disease and cause im- |
| | Jean Dausset (1916– ) | French | mune reactions to organ transplants. |
| 1981 | Roger W. Sperry (1913– ) | American | Their work in brain physiology; mapping the func- |
| | David H. Hubel (1926– ) | American (b. Canada) | tions of the left and right cerebral hemispheres. |
| | Torsten N. Wiesel (1923– ) | Swedish | Discovery of the process by which visual images are transmitted from the retina to the brain. |
| 1982 | Sune Karl Bergstrom (1916– ) | Swedish | For research on prostaglandins, hormone-like sub- |
| | Bengt Ingemar Samuelsson (1934– ) | Swedish | stances that help regulate cellular activity, can |
| | John R. Vance (1927– ) | British | increase or diminish pain, and prevent blood clots in the heart. |
| **CHEMISTRY** | | | |
| 1901 | Jacobus H. van't Hoff (1852–1911) | Dutch | Discovering laws of chemical dynamics and osmotic pressure in solutions. |
| 1902 | Emil H. Fischer (1852–1919) | German | Synthesizing sugars and purines. |
| 1903 | Svante A. Arrhenius (1859–1927) | Swedish | Originating the theory of ionization. |
| 1904 | William Ramsay (1852–1916) | British | Discovering helium, neon, xenon, and krypton. |
| 1905 | Adolf von Baeyer (1835–1917) | German | Research in organic dye stuffs, especially hydroaromatic compounds. |

| Year | Winner and Life Dates | Nationality | Achievement |
|---|---|---|---|
| 1906 | Henri Moissan (1852–1907) | French | Isolation of the element fluorine; development of the electric furnace. |
| 1907 | Eduard Buchner (1860–1917) | German | Discovering cell-free fermentation. |
| 1908 | Ernest Rutherford (1871–1937) | British | Artificial disintegration of elements; chemistry of radioactive elements. |
| 1909 | Wilhelm Ostwald (1853–1932) | German | Work on catalysts, chemical equilibria, and rate of chemical reactions. |
| 1910 | Otto Wallach (1847–1931) | German | Pioneer work in the field of alicyclic compounds. |
| 1911 | Marie S. Curie (1867–1934) | French (b. Poland) | Discovering radium and polonium. |
| 1912 | F. A. Victor Grignard (1871–1935) | French | Discovering the reagent that is named after him. |
| | Paul Sabatier (1854–1941) | French | Process of hydrogenating organic compounds. |
| 1913 | Alfred Werner (1866–1919) | Swiss (b. Germany) | Study of the linkage of atoms in molecules. |
| 1914 | Theodore W. Richards (1868–1928) | American | Determining the atomic weights of many elements. |
| 1915 | Richard M. Willstätter (1872–1942) | German | Research into plant pigments, especially chlorophyll. |
| 1918 | Fritz Haber (1868–1934) | German | Synthesizing ammonia from nitrogen and hydrogen. |
| 1920 | Walther Nernst (1864–1941) | German | Application of thermodynamics to chemistry. |
| 1921 | Frederick Soddy (1877–1956) | British | Research into radioactive substances and isotopes. |
| 1922 | Francis W. Aston (1877–1945) | British | Discovering isotopes by use of the mass spectrograph. |
| 1923 | Fritz Pregl (1869–1930) | Austrian | Invented methods to microanalyze organic substances. |
| 1925 | Richard A. Zsigmondy (1865–1929) | German (b. Austria) | Clarifying the nature of colloid solutions. |
| 1926 | Theodor Svedberg (1884–1971) | Swedish | Work on colloids. |
| 1927 | Heinrich O. Wieland (1877–1957) | German | Studies of bile acids. |
| 1928 | Adolf O. R. Windaus (1876–1959) | German | Work defining a group of sterols (including cholesterol) and their connection to vitamins. |
| 1929 | Sir Arthur Harden (1865–1940) | British | Investigations into the fermentation of sugar and fermentative enzymes. |
| | Hans von Euler-Chelpin (1873–1964) | Swedish (b. Germany) | |
| 1930 | Hans Fischer (1881–1945) | German | Research into the constitution of hemin (coloring matter of blood) and chlorophyll. |
| 1931 | Carl Bosch (1874–1940) | German | Their invention and development of chemical high pressure methods. |
| | Friedrich Bergius (1884–1949) | German | |
| 1932 | Irving Langmuir (1881–1957) | American | Investigations of the fundamental properties of absorbed films and surface chemistry. |
| 1934 | Harold C. Urey (1893–1981) | American | Discovering heavy hydrogen, or "deuterium." |
| 1935 | Frédéric Joliot-Curie (1900–58) | French | Their synthesizing of new radioactive elements, including radioactive nitrogen and phosphorus. |
| | Irène Joliot-Curie (1897–1956) | French | |
| 1936 | Peter J. W. Debye (1884–1966) | American (b. Netherlands) | Studied the structure of molecules, dipole moments, and the diffraction of electrons and X-rays in gases. |
| 1937 | Walter N. Haworth (1883–1950) | British | Research into carbohydrates and vitamin C. |
| | Paul Karrer (1889–1971) | Swiss (b. Russia) | Chemical anlysis of vitamins A and $B_2$. |
| 1938 | Richard Kuhn (1900–67) | Austrian | Work on carotinoids and vitamins. |
| 1939 | Adolf F. J. Butenandt (1903– ) | German | Studied chemistry of sex hormones; determined chemical structure of the female hormone (progestin), and isolated the male hormone (androsterone). |
| | Leopold Ruzicka (1887–1976) | Swiss (b. Yugoslavia) | Work on polymethylenes and higher terpenes. |
| 1943 | Georg von Hevesy (1885–1966) | Hungarian | Using isotopes as tracer elements in chemistry. |
| 1944 | Otto Hahn (1879–1968) | German | Discovery of the fission of heavy atomic nuclei. |
| 1945 | Artturi I. Virtanen (1895–1973) | Finnish | Work on plant synthesis of nitrogen compounds. |
| 1946 | James B. Sumner (1887–1955) | American | Discovering the crystallizability of enzymes. |
| | John H. Northrop (1891– ) | American | Their preparation of enzymes and virus proteins in pure form. |
| | Wendell M. Stanley (1904–1971) | American | |
| 1947 | Robert Robinson (1886–1975) | British | Research on plant substances, especially alkaloids. |
| 1948 | Arne W. K. Tiselius (1902–1971) | Swedish | Devising new methods of separating and detecting colloids and serum proteins. |
| 1949 | William F. Giauque (1895–1982) | American (b. Canada) | Studies of the properties of substances at extremely low temperatures. |
| 1950 | Otto P. H. Diels (1876–1954) | German | Developing a method of synthesizing organic compounds of the diene group. |
| | Kurt Alder (1902–58) | German | |
| 1951 | Edwin M. McMillan (1907– ) | American | Their work in the field of synthetic transuranium elements. |
| | Glenn T. Seaborg (1912– ) | American | |
| 1952 | Archer J. P. Martin (1910– ) | British | Advancing use of paper partition chromatography (method used to separate and identify chemical substances). |
| | Richard L. M. Synge (1914– ) | British | |
| 1953 | Hermann Staudinger (1881–1965) | German | Work in the nature of giant molecules. |
| 1954 | Linus C. Pauling (1901– ) | American | Studies in molecular structure, especially the nature of the bonding of atoms in molecules. |
| 1955 | Vincent du Vigneaud (1901–1978) | American | Work on pituitary hormones and the first synthesis of a polypeptide hormone. |
| 1956 | Cyril N. Hinshelwood (1897–1967) | British | Parallel but independent research into the kinetics of certain chemical reactions. |
| | Nikolai N. Semenov (1896– ) | Russian | |
| 1957 | Alexander R. Todd (1907– ) | British | Studies of the component compounds of nucleic acid. |
| 1958 | Frederick Sanger (1918– ) | British | Isolating and identifying the amino acid components of the insulin molecule. |
| 1959 | Jaroslav Heyrovsky (1890–1967) | Czech | Developing polarography (an electrochemical method of analysis). |
| 1960 | Willard F. Libby (1908–80) | American | Development of the radioactive carbon-14 dating method. |
| 1961 | Melvin Calvin (1911– ) | American | Establishing the chemical reactions that occur during photosynthesis. |
| 1962 | Max F. Perutz (1914– ) | British (b. Austria) | Discovering the molecular structure of hemoglobin and myoglobin. |
| | John C. Kendrew (1917– ) | British | |
| 1963 | Karl Ziegler (1898–1973) | German | Changing simple hydrocarbons into complex molecular substances. |
| | Giulio Natta (1903–1979) | Italian | |
| 1964 | Dorothy C. Hodgkin (1910– ) | British | Discovery of the structure of biochemical substances. |
| 1965 | Robert B. Woodward (1917–79) | American | Development of fundamental techniques for synthesis of complex organic compounds. |

| Year | Winner and Life Dates | Nationality | Achievement |
|---|---|---|---|
| 1966 | Robert S. Mulliken (1896– ) | American | Basic work on chemical bonds and the electronic structure of molecules using the molecular orbital method. |
| 1967 | Manfred Eigen (1927– )<br>Ronald G. W. Norrish (1897–1978)<br>George Porter (1920– ) | German<br>English<br>English | Studies of extremely fast chemical reactions effected by disturbing equilibrium by very short energy pulsations. |
| 1968 | Lars Onsager (1903–76) | American (b. Norway) | Discovery of the reciprocal relations between voltage and temperature, basic for the thermodynamics of irreversible processes, such as in living cells. |
| 1969 | Derek H. R. Barton (1918– )<br>Odd Hassel (1897– ) | British<br>Norwegian | Independent studies of conformation analysis: how certain compounds react when their three-dimensional molecular shape is known. |
| 1970 | Luis F. Leloir (1906– ) | Argentinian (b. France) | Discovery of sugar nucleotides and their role in the biosynthesis of carbohydrates. |
| 1971 | Gerhard Herzberg (1904– ) | Canadian (b. Germany) | Study of electronic structure, geometry of molecules. |
| 1972 | Dr. Christian Boehmer Anfisen (1916– )<br>Dr. Stanford Moore (1913–82)<br>Dr. William Howard Stein (1911–80) | American<br>American<br>American | Research relating to the chemical structure of a complex protein known as ribonuclease. |
| 1973 | Ernst Otto Fischer (1918– )<br>Geoffrey Wilkinson (1921– ) | German<br>British | Research into how organic and metallic atoms can merge. |
| 1974 | Paul J. Flory (1910– ) | American | For his work in macromolecules. |
| 1975 | John W. Cornforth (1917– )<br>Vladimir Prelog (1906– ) | English (b. Australia)<br>Swiss (b. Yugoslavia) | Contributions to stereochemistry—how properties of a chemical compound are affected by the exact arrangement of their atoms in three-dimensional space. |
| 1976 | William N. Lipscomb, Jr. (1920– ) | American | For studies on the structure and bonding mechanisms of "boranes". |
| 1977 | Ilya Prigogine (1917– ) | Belgian (b. Russia) | Explanation of contradictory biological processes whereby increased molecular growth and structural complexity are promoted while energy is dissipated. |
| 1978 | Peter Mitchell (1920– ) | English | Study of energy reception of human cells. |
| 1979 | Herbert C. Brown (1912– )<br>Georg Wittig (1897– ) | American<br>German | Research on the basic molecular structures of boron and phosphorus. |
| 1980 | Paul Berg (1926– )<br>Walter Gilbert (1932– )<br>Frederick Sanger (1918– ) | American<br>American<br>British | Development of methods to map in detail the structure and function of DNA. |
| 1981 | Kenichi Fukui (1918– )<br>Roald Hoffman (1937– ) | Japanese<br>American (b. Poland) | Their application of quantum mechanics to determine the symmetry of subatomic electrons and predict the course of chemical reactions. |
| 1982 | Aaron Klug (1926– ) | British (b. S. Africa) | For his research in determining the structure of important molecular complexes, such as viruses. |
| **PHYSICS** | | | |
| 1901 | Wilhelm C. Roentgen (1845–1923) | German | Discovering X rays. |
| 1902 | Hendrik A. Lorentz (1853–1928)<br>Pieter Zeeman (1865–1943) | Dutch<br>Dutch | Their research into the influence of magnetism upon radiation. |
| 1903 | Antoine H. Becquerel (1852–1908) | French | Discovery of spontaneous radioactivity. |
| | Pierre Curie (1859–1906)<br>Marie S. Curie (1867–1934) | French<br>French (b. Poland) | Their study of the radiation phenomena that were discovered by Becquerel. |
| 1904 | John W. S. Rayleigh (1842–1919) | British | Discovering argon. |
| 1905 | Philipp E. A. Lenard (1862–1947) | German (b. Hungary) | Experiments with cathode rays. |
| 1906 | Joseph J. Thomson (1856–1940) | British | Investigations on how gases conduct electricity. |
| 1907 | Albert A. Michelson (1852–1931) | American (b. Germany) | Developing optical measuring instruments; spectroscopic and meteorological investigations. |
| 1908 | Gabriel Lippmann (1845–1921) | French (b. Luxembourg) | Color photography. |
| 1909 | Guglielmo Marconi (1874–1937)<br>Karl F. Braun (1850–1918) | Italian<br>German | Their separate but parallel development of the wireless telegraph. |
| 1910 | Johannes van der Waals (1837–1923) | Dutch | Work on an equation relating gases and liquids. |
| 1911 | Wilhelm Wien (1864–1928) | German | Discoveries of the laws governing heat radiation. |
| 1912 | Nils G. Dalén (1869–1937) | Swedish | Invention of automatic gas regulators, that turn acetylene buoys, beacons and railway lights on and off. |
| 1913 | Heike Kamerlingh-Onnes (1853–1926) | Dutch | Experiments with the properties of matter at low temperatures, leading to helium liquefaction. |
| 1914 | Max von Laue (1879–1960) | German | Employing crystals to diffract X rays. |
| 1915 | William H. Bragg (1862–1942)<br>Lawrence Bragg (1890–1971) | British<br>British | Their use of X rays to determine the structure of crystals. |
| 1917 | Charles G. Barkla (1877–1944) | British | Discovery of X-ray radiation of elements. |
| 1918 | Max K. E. L. Planck (1858–1947) | German | Formulation of the quantum theory. |
| 1919 | Johannes Stark (1874–1957) | German | Discovery of the splitting of spectral lines in an electrical field. |
| 1920 | Charles E. Guillaume (1861–1938) | French (b. Switzerland) | Discovering anomalies in nickel-steel alloys. |
| 1921 | Albert Einstein (1879–1955) | American (b. Germany) | Contributing to theoretical physics: especially for the discovery of photoelectric-effect law. |
| 1922 | Niels H. D. Bohr (1885–1962) | Danish | Studies of the structure of atoms and their radiation. |
| 1923 | Robert A. Millikan (1868–1953) | American | Work on electrons and the photoelectric effect. |
| 1924 | Karl M. G. Siegbahn (1886–1978) | Swedish | Discoveries in X-ray spectroscopy. |
| 1925 | James Franck (1882–1964)<br>Gustav Hertz (1887–1975) | German<br>German | Their discovery of the laws governing the impact of an electron on an atom. |
| 1926 | Jean B. Perrin (1870–1942) | French | Work on the discontinuous structure of matter; discovery of sedimentation equilibrium. |
| 1927 | Arthur H. Compton (1892–1962) | American | Discovering the Compton effect (the change in wavelength of X rays colliding with electrons). |
| | Charles T. R. Wilson (1869–1959) | British | Discovery of the cloud chamber method of tracking paths of electrically charged particles. |
| 1928 | Owen W. Richardson (1879–1959) | British | Study of electron emission from heated bodies. |
| 1929 | Louis-Victor de Broglie (1892– ) | French | Discovering the wave nature of electrons. |
| 1930 | Chandrasekhara V. Raman (1888–1970) | Indian | Light diffusion research; discovery of Raman effect. |
| 1932 | Werner Heisenberg (1901–1976) | German | Creating a quantum mechanics; new discoveries in the study of hydrogen. |

| Year | Winner and Life Dates | Nationality | Achievement |
|---|---|---|---|
| 1933 | Erwin Schrödinger (1887–1961)<br>Paul A. M. Dirac (1902– ) | Austrian<br>British | For their development of new useful forms of atomic theory. |
| 1935 | James Chadwick (1891–1974) | British | Discovery of the neutron. |
| 1936 | Victor F. Hess (1883–1964)<br>Carl D. Anderson (1905– ) | American (b. Austria)<br>American | Discovering cosmic radiation.<br>Discovery of the positron. |
| 1937 | Clinton J. Davisson (1881–1958)<br>George P. Thomson (1892–1975) | American<br>British | Their discovery of the diffraction of electrons by crystals. |
| 1938 | Enrico Fermi (1901–54) | American (b. Italy) | Work on radioactive elements, including artificial ones produced by neutron bombardment. |
| 1939 | Ernest O. Lawrence (1901–58) | American | Inventing the cyclotron. |
| 1943 | Otto Stern (1888–1969) | American (b. Germany) | Studies related to the magnetic properties of atoms; discovery of the magnetic moment of the proton. |
| 1944 | Isidor Isaac Rabi (1898– ) | American (b. Austrian) | Discovery of resonance method of recording the magnetic properties of atomic nuclei. |
| 1945 | Wolfgang Pauli (1900–58) | American (b. Austrian) | Discovering the exclusion principle governing the quantum state of electrons in an atom. |
| 1946 | Percy Williams Bridgman (1882–1961) | American | Work in the field of high-pressure physics. |
| 1947 | Edward V. Appleton (1892–1965) | British | Investigation of the physics of the upper atmosphere. |
| 1948 | Patrick M. S. Blackett (1897–1974) | British | Improvement of the Wilson cloud chamber method; discoveries in nuclear physics and cosmic rays. |
| 1949 | Hideki Yukawa (1907–1981) | Japanese | Theoretical deductions of the existence of mesons. |
| 1950 | Cecil F. Powell (1903–69) | British | Photographic method of tracking nuclear particles. |
| 1951 | Sir John D. Cockcroft (1897–1967)<br>Ernest T. S. Walton (1903– ) | British<br>Irish | Their pioneer work in transmuting atomic nuclei with artificially accelerated atomic particles. |
| 1952 | Felix Bloch (1905– )<br>Edward M. Purcell (1912– ) | American (b. Switzerland)<br>American | Developed nuclear resonance method for precision measurement of atomic nuclei magnetic fields. |
| 1953 | Frits Zernike (1888–1966) | Dutch | Inventing the phase-contrast microscope. |
| 1954 | Max Born (1882–1970)<br>Walther Bothe (1891–1957) | British (b. Germany)<br>German | Research in quantum mechanics and nuclear physics.<br>Developed the coincidence method for measuring time. |
| 1955 | Willis E. Lamb, Jr. (1913– ) | American | Discoveries concerning the fine structure of the hydrogen spectrum. |
| | Polykarp Kusch (1911– ) | American (b. Germany) | Precise measurement of the electron's electromagnetic properties. |
| 1956 | John Bardeen (1908– )<br>Walter H. Brattain (1902– )<br>William B. Shockley (1910– ) | American<br>American<br>American (b. England) | Their work on developing the transistor, a device which replaced electronic tubes in many applications. |
| 1957 | Tsung-Dao Lee (1926– )<br>Chen Ning Yang (1922– ) | American (b. China)<br>American (b. China) | Their disproving of the law of parity conservation in nuclear physics. |
| 1958 | Pavel A. Cherenkov (1904– )<br>Ilya M. Frank (1908– )<br>Igor Y. Tamm (1895–1971) | Russian<br>Russian<br>Russian | Discovering the Cherenkov effect (radiated electrons accelerate in water to speeds greater than that of light in the same medium). |
| 1959 | Emilio G. Segrè (1905– )<br>Owen Chamberlain (1920– ) | American (b. Italy)<br>American | Discovery of the antiproton, a particle of mass identical to the proton but of opposite charge. |
| 1960 | Donald A. Glaser (1926– ) | American | Inventing the bubble chamber to study subatomic particles. |
| 1961 | Robert Hofstadter (1915– )<br>Rudolf L. Moessbauer (1929– ) | American<br>German | Discoveries on the structure of the subatomic nucleon.<br>The method named for him of producing and measuring recoil-free gamma rays. |
| 1962 | Lev D. Landau (1908–68) | Russian | Pioneering studies on condensed gases. |
| 1963 | Eugene P. Wigner (1902– )<br>Maria Goeppert-Mayer (1906–1972)<br>J. Hans D. Jensen (1907–1973) | American (b. Hungary)<br>American (b. Poland)<br>German | Contributions to nuclear and theoretical physics.<br>Their discoveries regarding atomic nucleus shell structure. |
| 1964 | Charles H. Townes (1915– )<br>Nikolai G. Basov (1922– )<br>Aleksander M. Prokhorov (1916– ) | American<br>Russian<br>Russian | Their fundamental research in quantum electronics that led to development of the maser-laser principle. |
| 1965 | Richard P. Feynman (1918– )<br>Julian S. Schwinger (1918– )<br>Sin-itiro Tomonaga (1906–1979) | American<br>American<br>Japanese | Research in quantum electrodynamics that contributed to the understanding of elementary particles in high-energy physics. |
| 1966 | Alfred Kastler (1902– ) | French | Discovery and development of optical methods for studying Herzian resonances in atoms. |
| 1967 | Hans A. Bethe (1906– ) | American (b. Germany) | Contributions to the theory of nuclear reaction; discoveries concerning the energy production of stars. |
| 1968 | Luis W. Alvarez (1911– ) | American | Contributions to the physics of subatomic particles and techniques for their detection. |
| 1969 | Murray Gell-Mann (1929– ) | American | Major theoretical insights into the interrelationship of elementary particles ("The Eight-fold Way"). |
| 1970 | Louis Néel (1904– )<br>Hannes Alfvén (1908– ) | French<br>Swedish | Discoveries about ferromagnetism and antiferromagnetism; basic work in magneto-hydrodynamics. |
| 1971 | Dennis Gabor (1900–1979) | British (b. Hungary) | Inventor of holography—lenseless, 3-D photography. |
| 1972 | John Bardeen (1908– )<br>Leon Cooper (1930– )<br>John Robert Schrieffer (1931– ) | American<br>American<br>American | Joint development of a theory explaining the phenomenon of superconductivity. |
| 1973 | Leo Esaki (1925– )<br>Ivar Giaever (1929– )<br>Brian D. Josephson (1940– ) | Japanese<br>American<br>British | Research into how electrons tunnel through conductors to become superconductors. |
| 1974 | Sir Martin Ryle (1918– )<br>Anthony Hewish (1924– ) | British<br>British | For their pioneering work in radio astrophysics. |
| 1975 | James Rainwater (1918– )<br>Aage N. Bohr (1922– )<br>Ben R. Mottelson (1926– ) | American<br>Danish<br>Danish (b. U.S.) | Discovery of the connection between collective motion and particle motion in the atomic nucleus and the development of the theory of the structure of the atomic nucleus based on this connection. |
| 1976 | Burton Richter (1931– )<br>Samuel C.C. Ting (1936– ) | American<br>American | For independent discovery of a new subatomic particle, known as "psi" or "J". |

| Year | Winner and Life Dates | Nationality | Achievement |
|---|---|---|---|
| 1977 | John H. Van Vleck (1899–1980) | American | For their contributions to the development of modern electronic solid state circuitry and basic theories of magnetism and conduction. |
| | Philip W. Anderson (1924– ) | American | |
| | Sir Nevill F. Mott (1905– ) | British | |
| 1978 | Pyotr Kapitsa (1894– ) | Russian | Pioneer work in low-temperature physics. |
| | Arno A. Penzias (1933– ) | American (b. Germany) | Discovery of cosmic microwave background radiation, further support for the Big Bang theory. |
| | Robert W. Wilson (1936– ) | American | |
| 1979 | Steven Weinberg (1933– ) | American | Contributions to unified theory that electromagnetism and the "weak force" in subatomic particles are related phenomena. |
| | Sheldon L. Glashow (1933– ) | American | |
| | Abdus Salam (1926– ) | Pakistani | |
| 1980 | James W. Cronin (1931– ) | American | Research into the symmetry of subatomic particles. |
| | Val L. Fitch (1923– ) | American | |
| 1981 | Nicolaas Bloembergen (1920– ) | American (b. Netherlands) | Their respective development of high-intensity laser spectroscopy and high-resolution electron spectroscopy to discover the inherent properties of matter. |
| | Arthur Schawlow (1922– ) | American | |
| | Kai M. Siegbahn (1918– ) | Swedish | |
| 1982 | Kenneth G. Wilson (1936– ) | American | For his analysis of what basic changes occur in matter under the influence of temperature and pressure, such as when a liquid turns to gas. |

## ECONOMIC SCIENCE

| Year | Winner and Life Dates | Nationality | Achievement |
|---|---|---|---|
| 1969 | Ragnar Frisch (1895–1973) | Norwegian | Their development of econometrics: mathematical models in the analysis of economic processes. |
| | Jan Tinbergen (1903– ) | Dutch | |
| 1970 | Paul Anthony Samuelson (1915– ) | American | Deriving new theorems; devising new applications. |
| 1971 | Simon Kuznets (1901– ) | American (b. Russia) | His use of GNP to measure national economic growth. |
| 1972 | Kenneth J. Arrow (1921– ) | American | Contributions to equilibrium theory and welfare theory. |
| | John R. Hicks (1904– ) | English | |
| 1973 | Wassily Leontief (1906– ) | American (b. Russia) | For the development of "input-output" analysis. |
| 1974 | Gunnar Myrdal (1898– ) | Swedish | Work on the theory of money and the interdependence of economic, social, and institutional phenomena. |
| | Friedrich A. von Hayek (1899– ) | British (b. Austria) | |
| 1975 | Leonid V. Kantorovich (1912– ) | Russian | Independent contributions to the theory of optimum allocation of resources. |
| | Tjalling C. Koopmans (1910– ) | American (b. Netherlands) | |
| 1976 | Milton Friedman (1912– ) | American | Achievements in consumption analysis and monetary theory, and his work on stabilization policy. |
| 1977 | Bertil Ohlin (1899–1979) | Swedish | For their contribution to international trade theory. |
| | James Meade (1907– ) | English | |
| 1978 | Herbert Simon (1916– ) | American | Research in the economic decision-making process. |
| 1979 | Sir Arthur Lewis (1915– ) | British (b. West Indies) | For their work on the economic problems of developing nations. |
| | Theodore W. Schultz (1902– ) | American | |
| 1980 | Lawrence R. Klein (1920– ) | American | Using "econometric" models to forecast economic trends. |
| 1981 | James Tobin (1918– ) | American | For his "portfolio selection" theory of balanced investment, explaining how economic subjects act in practice. |
| 1982 | George J. Stigler (1911– ) | American | For his research on the working of industry and the role of government regulation in the economy. |

## LITERATURE

1901 René F. A. Sully-Prudhomme (1839–1907), French
1902 Theodor Mommsen (1817–1903), German
1903 Björnstjerne Björnson (1832–1910), Norwegian
1904 Frédéric Mistral (1830–1914), French
José Echegaray (1832–1916), Spanish
1905 Henryk Sienkiewicz (1846–1916), Polish
1906 Giosuè Carducci (1835–1907), Italian
1907 Rudyard Kipling (1865–1936), British
1908 Rudolf C. Eucken (1846–1926), German
1909 Selma Lagerlöf (1858–1940), Swedish
1910 Paul J. L. Heyse (1830–1914), German
1911 Maurice Maeterlinck (1862–1949), Belgian
1912 Gerhart Hauptmann (1862–1946), German
1913 Rabindranath Tagore (1861–1941), Indian
1915 Romain Rolland (1866–1944), French
1916 Verner von Heidenstam (1859–1940), Swedish
1917 Karl A. Gjellerup (1857–1919), Danish
Henrik Pontoppidan (1857–1943), Danish
1919 Carl F. G. Spitteler (1845–1924), Swiss
1920 Knut Hamsun (1859–1952), Norwegian
1921 Anatole France (1844–1924), French
1922 Jacinto Benavente y Martínez (1866–1954), Spanish
1923 William Butler Yeats (1865–1939), Irish
1924 Wladyslaw S. Reymont (c. 1867–1925), Polish
1925 George Bernard Shaw (1856–1950), British (b. Ireland)
1926 Grazia Deledda (1875–1936), Italian
1927 Henri Bergson (1859–1941), French
1928 Sigrid Undset (1882–1949), Norwegian (b. Denmark)
1929 Thomas Mann (1875–1955), German
1930 Sinclair Lewis (1885–1951), American
1931 Erik A. Karlfeldt (1864–1931), Swedish
1932 John Galsworthy (1867–1933), English
1933 Ivan A. Bunin (1870–1953), Russian
1934 Luigi Pirandello (1867–1936), Italian
1936 Eugene O'Neill (1888–1953), American
1937 Roger Martin du Gard (1881–1958), French
1938 Pearl S. Buck (1892–1973), American
1939 Frans E. Sillanpää (1888–1964), Finnish
1944 Johannes V. Jensen (1873–1950), Danish
1945 Gabriela Mistral (1889–1957), Chilean
1946 Hermann Hesse (1877–1962), Swiss (b. Germany)
1947 André Gide (1869–1951), French
1948 T. S. Eliot (1888–1965), British (b. United States)
1949 William Faulkner (1897–1962), American
1950 Bertrand A. W. Russell (1872–1970), British
1951 Pär F. Lagerkvist (1891–1974), Swedish
1952 François Mauriac (1885–1970), French
1953 Sir Winston Churchill (1874–1965), British
1954 Ernest Hemingway (1899–1961), American
1955 Halldór K. Laxness (1902– ), Icelandic
1956 Juan Ramón Jiménez (1881–1958), Spanish
1957 Albert Camus (1913–60), French
1958 Boris L. Pasternak (1890–1960), Russian
1959 Salvatore Quasimodo (1901–68), Italian
1960 Saint-John Perse (1887–1975), French
1961 Ivo Andrić (1892–1975), Yugoslav
1962 John Steinbeck (1902–68), American
1963 Giorgos Seferis (1900–71), Greek
1964 Jean Paul Sartre (1905–80), French
1965 Mikhail A. Sholokov (1905– ), Russian
1966 Samuel Y. Agnon (1888–1970), Israeli (b. Poland)
Nelly Sachs (1891–1970), Swedish (b. Germany)
1967 Miguel Angel Asturias (1899–1974), Guatemalan
1968 Yasunari Kawabata (1899–1972), Japanese
1969 Samuel Beckett (1906– ), Irish (res. France)
1970 Aleksandr Solzhenitsyn (1918– ), Russian
1971 Pablo Neruda (1904–1973), Chilean
1972 Heinrich Böll (1917– ), German
1973 Patrick White (1912– ), Australian
1974 Eyvind Johnson (1900–76), Swedish
Edmund Martinson (1904–1978), Swedish
1975 Eugenio Montale (1896–1981), Italian
1976 Saul Bellow (1915– ), American
1977 Vicente Aleixandre (1898– ), Spanish
1978 Isaac Bashevis Singer (1904– ), American (b. Poland)
1979 Odysseus Elytis (1911– ), Greek
1980 Czeslaw Milosz (1911– ), American (b. Poland)
1981 Elias Canetti (1905– ), British (b. Bulgaria)
1982 Gabriel García Márquez (1928– ), Colombian

### PEACE

1901 Jean H. Dunant (1828–1910), Swiss
Frédéric Passy (1822–1912), French
1902 Élie Ducommun (1833–1906), Swiss
Charles A. Gobat (1843–1914), Swiss
1903 William R. Cremer (1828–1908), English
1904 Institute of International Law
1905 Bertha von Suttner (1843–1914), Austrian
1906 Theodore Roosevelt (1858–1919), American
1907 Ernesto T. Moneta (1833–1918), Italian
Louis Renault (1843–1918), French
1908 Klas P. Arnoldson (1844–1916), Swedish
1909 August M. F. Beernaert (1829–1912), Belgian
Paul H. Benjamin Estournelles de Constant (1852–1924), French
1910 International Peace Bureau
1911 Tobias M. C. Asser (1838–1913), Dutch
Alfred H. Fried (1864–1921), Austrian
1912 Elihu Root (1845–1937), American
1913 Henri La Fontaine (1854–1943), Belgian
1917 International Red Cross Committee
1919 Woodrow Wilson (1856–1924), American
1920 Léon Bourgeois (1851–1925), French
1921 Hjalmar Branting (1860–1925), Swedish
Christian L. Lange (1869–1938), Norwegian
1922 Fridtjof Nansen (1861–1930), Norwegian
1925 Sir J. Austen Chamberlain (1863–1937), British
Charles G. Dawes (1865–1951), American
1926 Aristide Briand (1862–1932), French
Gustav Stresemann (1878–1929), German
1927 Ferdinand E. Buisson (1841–1932), French
Ludwig Quidde (1858–1941), German
1929 Frank B. Kellogg (1856–1937), American
1930 Nathan Söderblom (1866–1931), Swedish
1931 Jane Addams (1860–1935), American
Nicholas Murray Butler (1862–1947), American
1933 Norman Angell (c. 1872–1967), British
1934 Arthur Henderson (1863–1935), British
1935 Carl von Ossietzky (1889–1938), German
1936 Carlos Saavedra Lamas (1880–1959), Argentine
1937 E. A. R. Cecil (1864–1958), British
1938 Nansen International Office for Refugees
1944 International Red Cross Committee
1945 Cordell Hull (1871–1955), American
1946 John R. Mott (1865–1955), American
Emily Balch (1867–1961), American
1947 Friends Service Council (British)
American Friends Service Committee (American)
1949 Sir John Boyd Orr (1880–1971), British
1950 Ralph J. Bunche (1904–71), American
1951 Léon Jouhaux (1879–1954), French
1952 Albert Schweitzer (1875–1965), Alsatian
1953 George C. Marshall (1880–1959), American
1954 Office of the UN High Commissioner for Refugees
1957 Lester B. Pearson (1897–1972), Canadian
1958 Father Georges H. Pire (1910–69), Belgian
1959 Philip J. Noel-Baker (1889–1982), British
1960 Albert J. Luthuli (1899–1967), South African
1961 Dag Hammarskjöld (1905–61), Swedish
1962 Linus C. Pauling (1901– ), American
1963 International Red Cross Committee
League of Red Cross Societies
1964 Martin Luther King, Jr. (1929–68), American
1965 UNICEF (UN Children's Fund)
1968 René Cassin (1887–1976), French
1969 International Labor Organization
1970 Norman E. Borlaug (1914– ), American
1971 Willy Brandt (1913– ), German
1973 Henry A. Kissinger (1923– ), American
Le Duc Tho (1910– ), Vietnamese
1974 Eisaku Sato (1901–75), Japanese
Sean McBride (1904– ), Irish
1975 Andrei D. Sakharov (1921– ), Russian
1976 Mairead Corrigan (1944– ), Northern Irish
Betty Williams (1943– ), Northern Irish
1977 Amnesty International
1978 Menachem Begin (1913– ), Israeli
Anwar el-Sadat (1918–81), Egyptian
1979 Mother Teresa (1910– ), Indian
1980 Adolfo Pérez Esquivel (1932– ), Argentine
1981 Office of the UN High Commissioner for Refugees
1982 Alfonso Garcia Robles (1911– ), Mexican
Alva Myrdal (1902– ), Swedish

## PULITZER PRIZES

### LOCAL INVESTIGATIVE REPORTING

1953 Edward J. Mowery (*New York World-Telegram & Sun*)
1954 Alvin Scott McCoy (*Kansas City* [Mo.] *Star*)
1955 Roland Kenneth Towery (*Cuero* [Tex.] *Record*)
1956 Arthur Daley (*N.Y. Times*)
1957 Wallace Turner and William Lambert (*Portland Oregonian*)
1958 George Beveridge (*Evening Star*, Washington, D.C.)
1959 John Harold Brislin (*Scranton* [Pa.] *Tribune* and *Scrantonian*)
1960 Miriam Ottenberg (*Evening Star*, Washington, D.C.)
1961 Edgar May (*Buffalo Evening News*)
1962 George Bliss (*Chicago* [Ill.] *Tribune*)
1963 Oscar O'Neal Griffin, Jr. (*Pecos* [Tex.] *Enterprise*)
1964 James V. Magee, Albert V. Gaudiosi, and Frederick A. Meyer (*Philadelphia* [Pa.] *Bulletin*)
1965 Gene Goltz (*Houston Post*)
1966 John A. Frasca (*Tampa* [Fla.] *Tribune*)
1967 Gene Miller (*Miami Herald*)
1968 J. Anthony Lukas (*New York Times*)
1969 Albert L. Delugach
Denny Walsh (*St. Louis Globe-Democrat*)
1970 Harold Eugene Martin ([Montgomery] *Alabama Journal*)
1971 William Hugh Jones (*Chicago* [Ill.] *Tribune*)
1972 Richard Cooper and John Machacek (*Rochester* [N.Y.] *Times Union*)
1973 *The Sun Newspapers*, Omaha, Nebraska
1974 Arthur M. Petacque
Hugh F. Hough (*The Chicago Sun-Times*)
1976 *The Chicago* [Ill.] *Tribune*
1977 Acel Moore and Wendell Rawls, Jr. (*The Philadelphia* [Pa.] *Inquirer*)
1978 Anthony R. Dolan (*Stamford* [Conn.] *Advocate*)
1979 Gilbert M. Gaul and Elliot G. Jaspin (*Pottsville* [Pa.] *Republican*)
1980 Stephen A. Kurkjian, Alexander B. Hawes, Jr., Nils J. Bruzelius, Joan Vennochi and Robert Porterfield (*The Boston Globe*)
1981 Clark Hallas and Robert B. Lowe (*The Arizona Daily Star*, Tucson, Ariz.)
1982 Paul Henderson (*Seattle* [Wash.] *Times*)

### GENERAL LOCAL REPORTING

1953 *Providence* (R.I.) *Journal and Evening Bulletin*
1954 *Vicksburg* (Miss.) *Sunday Post-Herald*
1955 Mrs. Caro Brown (*Alice* [Tex.] *Daily Echo*)
1956 Lee Hills (*Detroit* [Mich.] *Free Press*)
1957 *Salt Lake* (Utah) *Tribune*
1958 *Fargo* (N.D.) *Forum*
1959 Mary Lou Werner (*Evening Star*, Washington, D.C.)
1960 Jack Nelson (*Atlanta* [Ga.] *Constitution*)
1961 Sanche de Gramont (*New York Herald Tribune*)
1962 Robert D. Mullins (*Deseret News*, Salt Lake City, Utah)
1963 Sylvan Fox, Anthony Shannon, and William Longgood (*New York World-Telegram & Sun*)
1964 **Norman C. Miller, Jr.** (*Wall Street Journal*)
1965 Melvin H. Ruder (*Hungry Horse News*, Columbia Falls, Mont.)
1966 *Los Angeles Times* staff
1967 Robert V. Cox (*Chambersburg* [Pa.] *Public Opinion*)
1968 *Detroit* (Mich.) *Free Press*
1969 John Fetterman (*Louisville* [Ky.] *Times and Courier-Journal*)
1970 Thomas Fitzpatrick (*Chicago* [Ill.] *Sun-Times*)
1971 *Akron* [Ohio] *Beacon Journal*
1972 Timothy Leland, Gerald M. O'Neill, Stephen A. Kurjan, and Ann Desantis (*Boston Globe*)
1973 *Chicago Tribune*
1974 William Sherman (*New York Daily News*)
1976 Gene Miller (*Miami Herald*)
1977 Margo Huston (*The Milwaukee* [Wis.] *Journal*)
1978 Richard Whitt (*Louisville* [Ky.] *Courier-Journal*)
1979 *San Diego Evening Tribune*
1980 *Philadelphia* (Pa.) *Inquirer*
1981 *Longview* (Wash.) *Daily News*
1982 *Kansas City* (Mo.) *Star*/ *Kansas City Times*

## NATIONAL REPORTING

1948 Bert Andrews (*New York Herald-Tribune*) Nat S. Finney (*Minneapolis Tribune*)
1949 C. P. Trussel (*New York Times*)
1950 Edwin O. Guthman (*Seattle* [Wash.] *Times*)
1952 Anthony Leviero (*New York Times*)
1953 **Don Whitehead (AP)**
1954 Richard Wilson (Cowles Newspapers)
1955 Anthony Lewis (*Washington* [D.C.] *Daily News*)
1956 Charles L. Bartlett (*Chattanooga Times*)
1957 James Reston (*New York Times*)
1958 **Relman Morin (AP)** Clark Mollenhoff (*Des Moines* [Iowa] *Register & Tribune*)
1959 Howard Van Smith (*Miami* [Fla.] *News*)
1960 Vance Trimble (Scripps-Howard Newspaper Alliance)
1961 Edward R. Cony (*Wall Street Journal*)
1962 Nathan G. Caldwell and Gene S. Graham (*Nashville Tennessean*)
1963 Anthony Lewis (*New York Times*)
1964 **Merriman Smith (UPI)**
1965 Louis M. Kohlmeier (*Wall Street Journal*)
1966 Haynes Johnson (*Evening Star*, Wash., D.C.)
1967 Monroe W. Karmin and Stanley W. Penn (*Wall Street Journal*)
1968 Howard James (*Christian Science Monitor*) Nathan K. Kotz (*Des Moines* [Iowa] *Register*)
1969 Robert Cahn (*Christian Science Monitor*, Boston, Mass.)
1970 William J. Eaton (*Chicago* [Ill.] *Daily News*)
1971 Lucinda Franks and Thomas Powers (UPI)
1972 Jack Anderson (Columnist)
1973 Robert Boyd and Clark Hoyt (Knight Newspapers)
1974 James R. Polk (*Washington Star News*), and Jack White (*Providence Journal-Bulletin*)
1975 **Donald L. Barlett and James B. Steele (*The Philadelphia Inquirer*)**
1976 James Risser (*Des Moines* [Iowa] *Register*)
1977 Walter Mears (AP)
1978 Gaylord Shaw (*Los Angeles* [Calif.] *Times*)
1979 James Risser (*Des Moines* [Iowa] *Register*)
1980 Bette Swenson Orsini and Charles Stafford (*St. Petersburg* [Fla.] *Times*)
1981 John M. Crewdson (*New York Times*)
1982 Rick Atkinson (*Kansas City* [Mo.] *Times*)

## INTERNATIONAL CORRESPONDENCE

1948 Paul W. Ward (*Sun*, Baltimore, Md.)
1949 Price Day (*Sun*, Baltimore, Md.)
1950 Edmund Stevens (*Christian Science Monitor*, Boston, Mass.)
1951 Keyes Beech and Fred Sparks (*Chicago Daily News*); Homer Bigart and Marguerite Higgins (*New York Herald Tribune*); Relman Morin and Don Whitehead (AP)
1952 John M. Hightower (AP)
1953 Austin Wehrwein (*Milwaukee Journal*)
1954 Jim G. Lucas (Scripps-Howard Newspaper Alliance)
1955 Harrison E. Salisbury (*New York Times*)
1956 William Randolph Hearst, Jr., Kingsbury Smith, and Frank Coniff (International News Service)
1957 Russell Jones (UPI)
1958 *New York Times*
1959 Joseph Martin and Philip Santora (New York *Daily News*)
1960 A. M. Rosenthal (*New York Times*)
1961 Lynn Heinzerling (AP)
1962 Walter Lippmann (*New York Herald Tribune Syndicate*)
1963 Hal Hendrix (*Miami News*)
1964 **Malcolm W. Browne (AP)** David Halberstam (*New York Times*)
1965 J. A. Livingston (*Philadelphia Bulletin*)
1966 **Peter Arnett (AP)**
1967 R. John Hughes (*Christian Science Monitor*, Boston, Mass.)
1968 Alfred Friendly (*Washington* [D.C.] *Post*)
1969 William Tuohy (*Los Angeles Times*)
1970 Seymour M. Hersh (free-lance reporter)
1971 Jimmie Lee Hoagland (*Washington* [D.C.] *Post*)
1972 Peter R. Kann (*Wall Street Journal*)
1973 Max Frankel (*New York Times*)
1974 Hedrick Smith (*The New York Times*)
1975 **William Mullen and Ovie Carter (*The Chicago Tribune*)**
1976 Sydney H. Schanberg (*The New York Times*)
1978 Henry Kamm (*The New York Times*)
1979 Richard Ben Cramer (*Philadelphia* [Pa.] *Inquirer*)
1980 Joel Brinkley and Jay Mather (*The Louisville* [Ky.] *Courier-Journal*)
1981 Shirley Christian (*The Miami* [Fla.] *Herald*)
1982 John Darnton (*The New York Times*)

## EDITORIAL WRITING

1917 *New York Tribune*
1918 *Courier-Journal*, Louisville, Ky.
1920 Harvey E. Newbranch (*Evening World-Herald*, Omaha, Nebr.)
1922 Frank M. O'Brien (*New York Herald*)
1923 William Allen White (*Emporia* [Kans.] *Gazette*)
1924 *Boston* (Mass.) *Herald* Special prize: Frank I. Cobb (*World*, New York, N.Y.)
1925 *Charleston* (S.C.) *News and Courier*
1926 Edward M. Kingsbury (*New York Times*)
1927 F. Lauriston Bullard (*Boston* [Mass.] *Herald*)
1928 Grover Cleveland Hall (*Montgomery* [Ala.] *Advertiser*)
1929 Louis Isaac Jaffe (*Norfolk Virginian-Pilot*)
1931 Charles S. Ryckman (*Fremont* [Nebr.] *Tribune*)
1933 *Kansas City* (Mo.) *Star*
1934 E. P. Chase (*Atlantic News Telegraph*)
1936 Felix Morley (*Washington* [D.C.] *Post*); George B. Parker (Scripps-Howard Newspaper Alliance)
1937 John W. Owens (*Sun*, Baltimore, Md.)
1938 W. W. Waymack (*Register and Tribune*, Des Moines, Iowa)
1939 Ronald G. Callvert (*Oregonian*, Portland, Ore.)
1940 Bart Howard (*St. Louis Post-Dispatch*)
1941 Reuben Maury (*Daily News*, N.Y.)
1942 Geoffrey Parsons (*New York Herald Tribune*)
1943 Forrest W. Seymour (*Register and Tribune*, Iowa)
1944 Henry J. Haskell (*Kansas City* [Mo.] *Star*)
1945 George W. Potter (*Providence* [R.I.] *Journal-Bulletin*)
1946 Hodding Carter (*Delta Democrat-Times*, Greenville, Miss.)
1947 William H. Grimes (*Wall Street Journal*)
1948 Virginius Dabney (*Richmond* [Va.] *Times-Dispatch*)
1949 John H. Crider (*Boston Herald*); Herbert Elliston (*Washington* [D.C.] *Post*)
1950 Carl M. Saunders (*Jackson* [Mich.] *Citizen Patriot*)
1951 William Harry Fitzpatrick (*New Orleans* [La.] *States*)
1952 Louis LaCoss (*St. Louis Globe-Democrat*)
1953 Vermont C. Royster (*Wall Street Journal*)
1954 Don Murray (*Boston Herald*)
1955 Royce Howes (*Detroit* [Mich.] *Free Press*)
1956 Lauren K. Soth (*Des Moines* [Iowa] *Register and Tribune*)
1957 Buford Boone (*Tuscaloosa* [Ala.] *News*)
1958 Harry S. Ashmore (*Arkansas Gazette*)
1959 Ralph McGill (*Atlanta* [Ga.] *Constitution*)
1960 Lenoir Chambers (*Norfolk Virginian-Pilot*)
1961 William J. Dorvillier (*San Juan* [P.R.] *Star*)
1962 Thomas M. Storke (*Santa Barbara News-Press*)
1963 Ira B. Harkey, Jr. (*Pascagoula* [Miss.] *Chronicle*)
1964 Hazel Brannon Smith (*Lexington* [Miss.] *Advertiser*)

1965 John R. Harrison (*Gainesville* [Fla.] *Sun*)
1966 Robert Lasch (*St. Louis Post-Dispatch*)
1967 Eugene Patterson (*Atlanta* [Ga.] *Constitution*)
1968 John S. Knight (Knight Newspapers)
1969 Paul Greenberg (*Pine Bluff* [Ark.] *Commercial*)
1970 Philip L. Geyelin (*Washington* [D.C.] *Post*)
1971 Horance G. Davis, Jr. (*Gainesville* [Fla.] *Sun*)
1972 John Strohmeyer (*Bethlehem* [Pa.] *Globe-Times*)
1973 Roger B. Linscott (*Berkshire Eagle* [Pittsfield, Mass.])
1974 F. Gilman Spencer (*Trenton Trentonian*)
1975 John Daniell Maurice (*Charleston Daily Mail*)
1976 Philip P. Kerby (*The Los Angeles* [Calif.] *Times*)
1977 Warren Lerude, Foster Church, Norman F. Cardoza (*The Reno* [Nev.] *Evening Gazette* and *Nevada State Journal*)
1978 Meg Greenfield (*The Washington* [D.C.] *Post*)
1979 Edwin M. Yoder, Jr. (*The Washington* [D.C.] *Star*)
1980 Robert L. Bartley (*The Wall Street Journal*)
1982 Jack Rosenthal (*The New York Times*)

## CARTOONS

1922 Rollin Kirby (*World*, New York, N.Y.)
1924 Jay Norwood Darling (*New York Tribune*)
1925 Rollin Kirby (*World*, New York, N.Y.)
1926 D. R. Fitzpatrick (*St. Louis Post-Dispatch*)
1927 Nelson Harding (*Brooklyn* [N.Y.] *Daily Eagle*)
1928 Nelson Harding (*Brooklyn Daily Eagle*)
1929 Rollin Kirby (*World*, New York, N.Y.)
1930 Charles R. Macauley (*Brooklyn Daily Eagle*)
1931 Edmund Duffy (*Sun*, Baltimore, Md.)
1932 John T. McCutcheon (*Chicago* [Ill.] *Tribune*)
1933 Harold M. Talburt (*Washington* [D.C.] *Daily News*)
1934 Edmund Duffy (*Sun*, Baltimore, Md.)
1935 Ross A. Lewis (*Milwaukee* [Wis.] *Journal*)
1937 Clarence D. Batchelor (New York *Daily News*)
1938 Vaughn Shoemaker (*Chicago* [Ill.] *Daily News*)
1939 Charles G. Werner (*Daily Oklahoman*, Oklahoma City, Okla.)
1940 Edmund Duffy (*Sun*, Baltimore, Md.)
1941 Jacob Burck (*Times*, Chicago, Ill.)
1942 Herbert L. Block (NEA Service)
1943 Jay Norwood Darling (*New York Herald Tribune*)
1944 Clifford K. Berryman (*Evening Star*, Washington, D.C.)
1945 William (Bill) Mauldin (United Features Syndicate)
1946 Bruce Alexander Russell (*Los Angeles* [Calif.] *Times*)
1947 Vaughn Shoemaker (*Chicago* [Ill.] *Daily News*)
1948 Reuben L. (Rube) Goldberg (*Sun*, New York, N.Y.)
1949 Lute Pease (*Newark* [N.J.] *Evening News*)
1950 James T. Berryman (*Evening Star*, Washington, D.C.)
1951 Reginald W. Manning (*Arizona Republic*, Phoenix)
1952 Fred L. Packer (*New York* [N.Y.] *Mirror*)
1953 Edward D. Kuekes (*Cleveland Plain Dealer*)
1954 Herbert L. Block (*Washington* [D.C.] *Post & Times-Herald*)
1955 Daniel R. Fitzpatrick (*St. Louis Post-Dispatch*)
1956 Robert York (*Louisville* [Ky.] *Times*)
1957 Tom Little (*Nashville Tennessean*)
1958 Bruce M. Shanks (*Buffalo Evening News*)
1959 William (Bill) Mauldin (*St. Louis Post-Dispatch*)
1961 Carey Orr (*Chicago* [Ill.] *Tribune*)
1962 Edmund S. Valtman (*Hartford* [Conn.] *Times*)
1963 Frank Miller (*Des Moines* [Iowa] *Register*)
1964 Paul Conrad (*Denver Post*)
1966 Don Wright (*Miami News*)
1967 Patrick B. Oliphant (*Denver* [Colo.] *Post*)
1968 Eugene Gray Payne (*Charlotte* [N.C.] *Observer*)
1969 John Fischetti (*Chicago* [Ill.] *Daily News*)
1970 Thomas F. Darcy (*Newsday*, Garden City, NY)
1971 Paul Conrad (*Los Angeles* [Calif.] *Times*)
1972 Jeffrey K. MacNelly (*Richmond* [Va.] *News Leader*)
1974 Paul Szep (*Boston Globe*)
1975 Garry Trudeau (Universal Press Syndicate)
1976 Tony Auth (*The Philadelphia* [Pa.] *Inquirer*)
1977 Paul Szep (*Boston Globe*)
1978 Jeffrey K. MacNelly (*Richmond* [Va.] *News Leader*)
1979 Herbert L. Block (*The Washington* [D.C.] *Post*)
1980 Don Wright (*Miami News*)
1981 *Mike Peters* (*Dayton* [Ohio] *Daily News*)
1982 Ben Sargent (*Austin* [Tex.] *American-Statesman*)

## PHOTOGRAPHY

1942 Milton Brooks (*Detroit* [Mich.] *News*)
1943 Frank Noel (AP)
1944 Frank Filan (AP)
Earle L. Bunker (*World-Herald*, Omaha, Nebr.)
1945 Joe Rosenthal (AP)
1947 Arnold Hardy*
1948 Frank Cushing (*Boston* [Mass.] *Traveler*)
1949 Nathaniel Fein (*New York Herald Tribune*)
1950 Bill Crouch (*Oakland* [Calif.] *Tribune*)
1951 Max Desfor (AP)
1952 John Robinson and Don Ultang (*Des Moines* [Iowa] *Register and Tribune*)
1953 William M. Gallagher (*Flint* [Mich.] *Journal*)
1954 Mrs. Walter M. Schau*
1955 John L. Gaunt, Jr. (*Los Angeles* [Calif.] *Times*)
1956 *Daily News*, New York, N.Y.
1957 Harry A. Trask (*Boston* [Mass.] *Traveler*)
1958 William C. Beall (*Washington* [D.C.] *Daily News*)
1959 William Seaman (*Minneapolis* [Minn.] *Star*)
1960 Andrew Lopez (UPI)
1961 Yasushi Nagao (*Mainichi Newspapers*, Tokyo, Japan)
1962 Paul Vathis (AP)
1963 Hector Rondon (*La Republica*, Caracas, Venezuela)
1964 Robert H. Jackson (*Dallas* [Tex.] *Times Herald*)
1965 Horst Faas (AP)
1966 Kyoichi Sawada (UPI)
1967 Jack R. Thornell (AP)
1968 Rocco Morabito (*Jacksonville* [Fla.] *Journal*)
Toshio Sakai (UPI)
1969 Edward T. Adams (AP)
Moneta Sleet, Jr. (*Ebony*)
1970 Steve Starr (AP)
Dallas Kinney (*Palm Beach* [Fla.] *Post*)
1971 John Paul Filo (Kent [Ohio] State University student)*
Jack Dykinga (*Chicago* [Ill.] *Sun-Times*)
1972 Horst Fass and Michael Laurent (AP); Dave Kenerly (UPI)
1973 Huynh Cong Ut (AP)
Brian Lanker (*Topeka* [Kans.] *Capital-Journal*)
1974 Slava Veder (AP)
Anthony K. Roberts (AP)
1975 Gerald H. Gay (*The Seattle Times*)
Matthew Lewis (*Washington Post*)
1976 Stanley Forman (*The Boston* [Mass.] *Herald-American*); *Louisville* [Ky.] *Courier-Journal and Times*
1977 Stanley Forman (*Boston Herald-American*); Neal Ulevich (AP); Robin Hood (*Chattanooga News-Free Press*)
1978 J. Ross Baughman (AP)
John W. Blair (free-lance, UPI Indianapolis bureau)
1979 Thomas J. Kelly 3d (*Pottstown* [Pa.] *Mercury*); the photographic staff of *The Boston* (Mass.) *Herald-American*
1980 Erwin H. Nagler (*The Dallas Times Herald*)
1981 Larry C. Price (*Ft. Worth Star Telegram*); Taro M. Yamasaki (*Detroit Free Press*)
1982 Ron Edmonds (AP)
John H. White (*Chicago Sun-Times*)

## MERITORIOUS PUBLIC SERVICE

1918 *New York Times*
1919 *Milwaukee* (Wis.) *Journal*
1921 *Boston* (Mass.) *Post*

* Amateur photographer.

1922 *World*, New York, N.Y.
1923 *Memphis* (Tenn.) *Commercial Appeal*
1924 *World* (New York, N.Y.)
1926 *Enquirer Sun* (Columbus, Ga.)
1927 *Canton* (Ohio) *Daily News*
1928 *Indianapolis* (Ind.) *Times*
1929 *Evening World*, New York
1931 *Atlanta* (Ga.) *Constitution*
1932 *Indianapolis* (Ind.) *News*
1933 *New York World-Telegram*
1934 *Medford* (Ore.) *Mail Tribune*
1935 *Sacramento* (Calif.) *Bee*
1936 *Cedar Rapids* (Iowa) *Gazette*
1937 *St. Louis* (Mo.) *Post-Dispatch*
1938 *Bismarck* (N.D.) *Tribune*
1939 *Miami* (Fla.) *Daily News*
1940 *Waterbury* (Conn.) *Republican and American*
1941 *St. Louis* (Mo.) *Post-Dispatch*
1942 *Los Angeles* (Calif.) *Times*
1943 *World-Herald*, Omaha, Nebr.
1944 *New York Times*
1945 *Detroit* (Mich.) *Free Press*
1946 *Scranton* (Pa.) *Times*
1947 *Sun*, Baltimore, Md.
1948 *St. Louis* (Mo.) *Post-Dispatch*
1949 *Nebraska State Journal*
1950 *Chicago* (Ill.) *Daily News* and *St. Louis Post-Dispatch*
1951 *Miami* (Fla.) *Herald* and *Brooklyn* (N.Y.) *Eagle*
1952 *St. Louis* (Mo.) *Post-Dispatch*
1953 *News Reporter* (Whiteville, N.C.) and *Tabor City* (N.C.) *Tribune*
1954 *Newsday*, Garden City, N.Y.
1955 *Columbus* (Ga.) *Ledger* and *Sunday Ledger-Enquirer*
1956 *Watsonville* (Calif.) *Register-Pajaronian*
1957 *Chicago* (Ill.) *Daily News*
1958 *Arkansas Gazette*, Little Rock
1959 *Utica* (N.Y.) *Observer-Dispatch* and *Utica Daily Press*
1960 *Los Angeles* (Calif.) *Times*
1961 *Amarillo* (Tex.) *Globe-Times*
1962 *Panama City* (Fla.) *News-Herald*
1963 *Chicago* (Ill.) *Daily News*
1964 *St. Petersburg* (Fla.) *Times*
1965 *Hutchinson* (Kans.) *News*
1966 *Boston* (Mass.) *Globe*
1967 *Courier Journal* (Louisville, Ky.) and *Milwaukee* (Wis.) *Journal*
1968 *Riverside* (Calif.) *Press-Enterprise*
1969 *Los Angeles* (Calif.) *Times*
1970 *Newsday*, Garden City, N.Y.
1971 *Winston-Salem* [N.C.] *Journal & Sentinel*
1972 *The New York Times*
1973 *The Washington Post*
1974 *Newsday*, Garden City, N.Y.
1975 *Boston Globe* and *The Xenia* (Ohio) *Daily Gazette*
1976 *The Anchorage Daily News*
1977 *Lufkin* (Tex.) *News*
1978 *Philadelphia* (Pa.) *Inquirer*
1979 *Point Reyes* (Calif.) *Light*
1980 *The Gannett News Service*
1981 *Charlotte* (N.C.) *Observer*
1982 *Detroit* (Mich.) *News*

## FEATURE WRITING

1979 Jon D. Franklin (*The Baltimore* [Md.] *Evening Sun*)
1980 Madeleine Blais (*The Miami* [Fla.] *Herald*)
1981 Teresa Carpenter (*The Village Voice*, New York)
1982 Saul Pett (AP)

## SPECIAL CITATIONS FOR JOURNALISM

1938 Edmonton (Alta.) *Journal*
1941 *New York Times*
1944 Byron Price, Director of the Office of Censorship
1944 William Allen White
1945 The cartographers of the American press
1947 Columbia University and the Graduate School of Journalism
1947 *St. Louis Post-Dispatch*
1948 Dr. Frank Diehl Fackenthal
1951 Cyrus L. Sulzberger of the *New York Times*
1952 Max Kase of the *New York Journal-American*
1952 *Kansas City* (Mo.) *Star*
1953 *New York Times*
1958 Walter Lippmann
1964 Gannett Newspapers, Rochester, N.Y.
1976 Professor John Hohenberg
1978 Richard L. Strout of *The Christian Science Monitor* and *The New Republic*

## BIOGRAPHY OR AUTOBIOGRAPHY

1917 *Julia Ward Howe*, by Laura E. Richards and Maude Howe Elliott, assisted by Florence Howe Hall
1918 *Benjamin Franklin, Self-Revealed*, by William Cabell Bruce
1919 *The Education of Henry Adams*, by Henry Adams
1920 *The Life of John Marshall* by Albert J. Beveridge
1921 *The Americanization of Edward Bok*, by Edward Bok
1922 *A Daughter of the Middle Border*, by Hamlin Garland
1923 *The Life and Letters of Walter H. Page*, by Burton J. Hendrick
1924 *From Immigrant to Inventor*, by Michael Idvorsky Pupin
1925 *Barrett Wendell and His Letters*, by M. A. DeWolfe Howe
1926 *The Life of Sir William Osler*, by Harvey Cushing
1927 *Whitman*, by Emory Holloway
1928 *The American Orchestra and Theodore Thomas*, by Charles Edward Russell
1929 *The Training of an American: The Earlier Life and Letters of Walter H. Page*, by Burton J. Hendrick
1930 *The Raven*, by Marquis James
1931 *Charles W. Eliot*, by Henry James
1932 *Theodore Roosevelt*, by Henry F. Pringle
1933 *Grover Cleveland*, by Allan Nevins
1934 *John Hay*, by Tyler Dennett
1935 *R. E. Lee*, by Douglas S. Freeman
1936 *The Thought and Character of William James*, by Ralph Barton Perry
1937 *Hamilton Fish*, by Allan Nevins
1938 *Pedlar's Progress*, by Odell Shepard, and *Andrew Jackson* (2 volumes), by Marquis James
1939 *Benjamin Franklin*, by Carl Van Doren
1940 *Woodrow Wilson, Life and Letters* (Vols. VII-VIII), by Ray Stannard Baker
1941 *Jonathan Edwards*, by Ola Elizabeth Winslow
1942 *Crusader in Crinoline*, by Forrest Wilson
1943 *Admiral of the Ocean Sea*, by Samuel Eliot Morison
1944 *The American Leonardo: The Life of Samuel F. B. Morse*, by Carleton Mabee
1945 *George Bancroft: Brahmin Rebel*, by Russell Blaine Nye
1946 *Son of the Wilderness*, by Linnie Marsh Wolfe
1947 *The Autobiography of William Allen White*
1948 *Forgotten First Citizen: John Bigelow*, by Margaret Clapp
1949 *Roosevelt and Hopkins*, by Robert E. Sherwood
1950 *John Quincy Adams and the Foundations of American Foreign Policy*, by Samuel Flagg Bemis
1951 *John C. Calhoun: American Portrait*, by Margaret Louise Coit
1952 *Charles Evans Hughes*, by Merlo J. Pusey
1953 *Edmund Pendleton 1721–1803*, by David J. Mays
1954 *The Spirit of St. Louis*, by Charles A. Lindbergh
1955 *The Taft Story*, by William S. White
1956 *Benjamin Henry Latrobe*, by Talbot Faulkner Hamlin
1957 *Profiles in Courage*, by John F. Kennedy
1958 *George Washington* (Vols. I–VI), by Douglas Southall Freeman; Vol. VII, by Mary Wells Ashworth and John Alexander Carroll
1959 *Woodrow Wilson, American Prophet*, by Arthur Walworth
1960 *John Paul Jones*, by Samuel Eliot Morison
1961 *Charles Sumner and the Coming of the Civil War*, by David Donald
1963 *Henry James* (Volumes II and III), by Leon Edel
1964 *John Keats*, by Walter Jackson Bate
1965 *Henry Adams* (3 volumes), by Ernest Samuels
1966 *A Thousand Days*, by Arthur M. Schlesinger, Jr.
1967 *Mr. Clemens and Mark Twain*, by Justin Kaplan
1968 *Memoirs (1925–1950)*, by George F. Kennan
1969 *The Man from New York: John Quinn and His Friends*, by Benjamin Lawrence Reid

**1970** *Huey Long*, by T.H. Williams
**1971** *Robert Frost: The Years of Triumph*, by L. R. Thompson
**1972** *Eleanor and Franklin*, by Joseph P. Lash
**1973** *Luce and His Empire*, by W. A. Swanberg
**1974** *O'Neill, Son and Artist*, by Louis Sheaffer
**1975** *The Power Broker: Robert Moses and the Fall of New York*, by Robert A. Caro
**1976** *Edith Wharton: A Biography*, by R.W.B. Lewis
**1977** *A Prince of Our Disorder*, by John E. Mack
**1978** *Samuel Johnson*, by Walter Jackson Bate
**1979** *Days of Sorrow and Pain: Leo Baeck and the Berlin Jews*, by Leonard Baker
**1980** *The Rise of Theodore Roosevelt*, by Edmund Morris
**1981** *Peter the Great*, by Robert K. Massie
**1982** *Grant: A Biography*, by William S. McFeely

**DRAMA**

**1918** *Why Marry?*, by Jesse Lynch Williams
**1920** *Beyond the Horizon*, by Eugene O'Neill
**1921** *Miss Lulu Bett*, by Zona Gale
**1922** *Anna Christie*, by Eugene O'Neill
**1923** *Icebound*, by Owen Davis
**1924** *Hell-Bent for Heaven*, by Hatcher Hughes
**1925** *They Knew What They Wanted*, by Sidney Howard
**1926** *Craig's Wife*, by G. Kelly
**1927** *In Abraham's Bosom*, by Paul Green
**1928** *Strange Interlude*, by Eugene O'Neill
**1929** *Street Scene*, by Elmer L. Rice
**1930** *The Green Pastures*, by Marc Connelly
**1931** *Alison's House*, by Susan Glaspell
**1932** *Of Thee I Sing*, by George S. Kaufman, Morrie Ryskind, and Ira Gershwin (with music by George Gershwin)
**1933** *Both Your Houses*, by Maxwell Anderson
**1934** *Men in White*, by Sidney Kingsley
**1935** *The Old Maid*, by Zoe Akins
**1936** *Idiot's Delight*, by Robert E. Sherwood
**1937** *You Can't Take It with You*, by Moss Hart and George S. Kaufman
**1938** *Our Town*, by Thornton Wilder
**1939** *Abe Lincoln in Illinois*, by Robert E. Sherwood
**1940** *The Time of Your Life*, by William Saroyan*
**1941** *There Shall Be No Night*, by Robert E. Sherwood
**1943** *The Skin of Our Teeth*, by Thornton Wilder
**1945** *Harvey*, by Mary Chase
**1946** *State of the Union*, by Russel Crouse & Howard Lindsay
**1948** *A Streetcar Named Desire*, by Tennessee Williams
**1949** *Death of a Salesman*, by Arthur Miller
**1950** *South Pacific*, by Richard Rodgers, Oscar Hammerstein II, and Joshua Logan
**1952** *The Shrike*, by Joseph Kramm
**1953** *Picnic*, by William Inge
**1954** *The Teahouse of the August Moon*, by John Patrick
**1955** *Cat on a Hot Tin Roof*, by Tennessee Williams
**1956** *Diary of Anne Frank*, by Albert Hackett and Frances Goodrich
**1957** *Long Day's Journey into Night*, by Eugene O'Neill
**1958** *Look Homeward, Angel*, by Ketti Frings
**1959** *J. B.*, by Archibald MacLeish
**1960** *Fiorello!*, book by Jerome Weidman and George Abbot; music by Jerry Bock; lyrics by Sheldon Harnick.
**1961** *All the Way Home*, by Tad Mosel
**1962** *How to Succeed in Business Without Really Trying*, by F. Loesser and A. Burrows
**1965** *The Subject Was Roses*, by Frank D. Gilroy
**1967** *A Delicate Balance*, by Edward Albee
**1969** *The Great White Hope*, by Howard Sackler
**1970** *No Place to Be Somebody*, by Charles Gordone
**1971** *The Effect of Gamma Rays on Man-in-the-Moon Marigolds*, by Paul Zindel
**1973** *That Championship Season*, by Jason Miller
**1975** *Seascape*, by Edward Albee
**1976** *A Chorus Line*, by Michael Bennett; book by James Kirkwood & Nicholas Dante; music by Marvin Hamlisch; lyrics by Edward Kleban.
**1977** *The Shadow Box*, by Michael Cristofer
**1978** *The Gin Game*, by Donald L. Coburn
**1979** *Buried Child*, by Sam Shepard
**1980** *Talley's Folly*, by Lanford Wilson
**1981** *Crimes of the Heart*, by Beth Henley
**1982** *A Soldier's Play*, by Charles Fuller

**HISTORY**

**1917** *With Americans of Past and Present Days*, by His Excellency J. J. Jusserand, Ambassador of France to the U.S.
**1918** *A History of the Civil War, 1861–1865*, by James Ford Rhodes
**1920** *The War with Mexico* (2 volumes), by Justin H. Smith
**1921** *The Victory at Sea*, by William Sowden Sims, with Burton J. Hendrick
**1922** *The Founding of New England*, by James T. Adams
**1923** *The Supreme Court in United States History*, by Charles Warren
**1924** *The American Revolution—A Constitutional Interpretation*, by Charles Howard McIlwain
**1925** *A History of the American Frontier*, by F. L. Paxson
**1926** *The History of the United States* (Volume VI: *The War for Southern Independence*), by Edward Channing
**1927** *Pinckney's Treaty*, by Samuel Flagg Bemis
**1928** *Main Currents in American Thought*, 2 volumes, by Vernon Louis Parrington
**1929** *The Organization and Administration of the Union Army, 1861–1865*, by Fred Albert Shannon
**1930** *The War of Independence*, by Claude H. Van Tyne
**1931** *The Coming of the War: 1914*, by Bernadotte E. Schmitt
**1932** *My Experiences in the World War*, by John J. Pershing
**1933** *The Significance of Sections in American History*, by Frederick J. Turner
**1934** *The People's Choice*, by Herbert Agar
**1935** *The Colonial Period of American History*, by Charles McLean Andrews
**1936** *The Constitutional History of the United States*, by Andrew C. McLaughlin
**1937** *The Flowering of New England*, by Van Wyck Brooks
**1938** *The Road to Reunion, 1865–1900* by Paul Herman Buck
**1939** *A History of American Magazines* by Frank Luther Mott
**1940** *Abraham Lincoln: The War Years*, by Carl Sandburg
**1941** *The Atlantic Migration, 1607–1860*, by Marcus Lee Hansen
**1942** *Reveille in Washington*, by Margaret Leech
**1943** *Paul Revere and the World He Lived In*, by Esther Forbes
**1944** *The Growth of American Thought*, by Merle Curti
**1945** *Unfinished Business*, by Stephen Bonsal
**1946** *The Age of Jackson*, by Arthur M. Schlesinger, Jr.
**1947** *Scientists Against Time*, by James Phinney Baxter III
**1948** *Across the Wide Missouri*, by Bernard DeVoto
**1949** *The Disruption of American Democracy*, by Roy Franklin Nichols
**1950** *Art and Life in America*, by Oliver W. Larkin
**1951** *The Old Northwest: Pioneer Period, 1815–1840*, by R. Carlyle Buley
**1952** *The Uprooted*, by Oscar Handlin
**1953** *The Era of Good Feelings*, by George Dangerfield
**1954** *A Stillness at Appomattox*, by Bruce Catton
**1955** *Great River: The Rio Grande in North American History*, by Paul Horgan
**1956** *The Age of Reform*, by Richard Hofstadter
**1957** *Russia Leaves the War: Soviet-American Relations, 1917–1920*, by George F. Kennan

* Declined.

1958 *Banks and Politics in America—From the Revolution to the Civil War,* by Bray Hammond
1959 *The Republican Era: 1869–1901,* by Leonard D. White, with Jean Schneider
1960 *In the Days of McKinley,* by Margaret Leech
1961 *Between War and Peace: The Potsdam Conference,* by Herbert Feis
1962 *The Triumphant Empire: Thunder-Clouds Gather in the West 1763-1766,* by Lawrence H. Gipson
1963 *Washington: Village and Capital, 1800–1878,* by Constance McLaughlin Green
1964 *Puritan Village: The Formation of a New England Town,* by Sumner Chilton Powell
1965 *The Greenback Era,* by Irwin Unger
1966 *Life of the Mind in America From the Revolution to the Civil War,* by Perry Miller
1967 *Exploration and Empire,* by William H. Goetzmann
1968 *The Ideological Origins of the American Revolution,* by Bernard Bailyn
1969 *Origins of the Fifth Amendment,* by Leonard W. Levy
1970 *Present at the Creation: My Years in the State Department,* by Dean Acheson
1971 *Roosevelt: The Soldier of Freedom,* by James MacGregor Burns
1972 *Neither Black Nor White,* by Carl M. Degler
1973 *People of Paradox: An Inquiry Concerning the Origin of American Civilization,* by Michael Kammen
1974 *The Americans,* by Daniel J. Boorstin
1975 *Jefferson and His Time,* by Dumas Malone
1976 *Lamy of Santa Fe,* by Paul Horgan
1977 *The Impending Crisis,* by David M. Potter
1978 *The Invisible Hand: The Managerial Revolution in American Business,* by Alfred D. Chandler
1979 *The Dred Scott Case,* by Don E. Fehrenbacher
1980 *Been in the Storm So Long: The Aftermath of Slavery,* by Leon F. Litwack
1981 *American Education: The National Experience 1783-1876,* Lawrence A. Cremin
1982 *Mary Chesnut's Civil War,* edited by C. Vann Woodward

## PRIZES IN LETTERS

### FICTION

1918 *His Family,* by Ernest Poole
1919 *The Magnificent Ambersons,* by Booth Tarkington
1921 *The Age of Innocence,* by Edith Wharton
1922 *Alice Adams,* by Booth Tarkington
1923 *One of Ours,* by Willa Cather
1924 *The Able McLaughlins,* by Margaret Wilson
1925 *So Big,* by Edna Ferber
1926 *Arrowsmith,* by S. Lewis
1927 *Early Autumn,* by Louis Bromfield
1928 *The Bridge of San Luis Rey,* by Thornton Wilder
1929 *Scarlet Sister Mary,* by Julia Peterkin
1930 *Laughing Boy,* by Oliver La-Farge
1931 *Years of Grace,* by Margaret Ayer Barnes
1932 *The Good Earth,* by Pearl S. Buck
1933 *The Store,* by T. S. Stribling
1934 *Lamb in His Bosom,* by Caroline Miller
1935 *Now in November,* by Josephine Winslow Johnson
1936 *Honey in the Horn,* by Harold L. Davis
1937 *Gone With the Wind,* by Margaret Mitchell
1938 *The Late George Apley,* by John Phillips Marquand
1939 *The Yearling,* by Marjorie Kinnan Rawlings
1940 *The Grapes of Wrath,* by John Steinbeck
1942 *In This Our Life,* by Ellen Glasgow
1943 *Dragon's Teeth,* by Upton Sinclair
1944 *Journey in the Dark,* by Martin Flavin
1945 *A Bell for Adano,* by John Hersey
1947 *All the King's Men,* by Robert Penn Warren
1948 *Tales of the South Pacific,* by James A. Michener
1949 *Guard of Honor,* by James Gould Cozzens
1950 *The Way West,* by A. B. Guthrie, Jr.
1951 *The Town,* by Conrad Richter
1952 *The Caine Mutiny,* by Herman Wouk
1953 *The Old Man and the Sea,* by Ernest Hemingway
1955 *A Fable,* by Wm. Faulkner
1956 *Andersonville,* by MacKinlay Kantor
1958 *A Death in the Family,* by James Agee
1959 *The Travels of Jaimie McPheeters,* by Robert Lewis Taylor
1960 *Advise and Consent,* by Allen Drury
1961 *To Kill a Mockingbird,* by Harper Lee
1962 *The Edge of Sadness,* by Edwin O'Connor
1963 *The Reivers,* by William Faulkner
1965 *The Keepers of the House,* by Shirley Ann Grau
1966 *Collected Short Stories,* by Katherine Ann Porter
1967 *The Fixer,* by Bernard Malamud
1968 *The Confessions of Nat Turner,* by William Styron
1969 *House Made of Dawn,* by M. Scott Momaday
1970 *Collected Stories,* by Jean Stafford
1972 *Angel of Repose,* by Wallace Stegner
1973 *The Optimist's Daughter,* by Eudora Welty
1975 *The Killer Angels,* by Michael Shaara
1976 *Humboldt's Gift,* by Saul Bellow
1978 *Elbow Room,* by James Allan McPherson
1979 *The Stories of John Cheever*
1980 *The Executioner's Song,* by Norman Mailer
1981 *A Confederacy of Dunces,* by John Kennedy Toole
1982 *Rabbit Is Rich,* by John Updike

### POETRY

1918 *Love Songs,* by Sara Teasdale
1919 *Old Road to Paradise,* by Margaret Widdemer
1919 *Corn Huskers,* by Carl Sandburg
1922 *Collected Poems,* by Edwin Arlington Robinson
1923 *The Ballad of the Harp-Weaver; A Few Figs from Thistles;* eight sonnets in *American Poetry, 1922, A Miscellany,* by Edna St. Vincent Millay
1924 *New Hampshire: A Poem with Notes and Grace Notes,* by Robert Frost
1925 *The Man Who Died Twice,* by Edwin Arlington Robinson
1926 *What's O'Clock,* by Amy Lowell
1927 *Fiddler's Farewell,* by Leonora Speyer
1928 *Tristram,* by E. A. Robinson
1929 *John Brown's Body,* by Stephen Vincent Benét
1930 *Selected Poems,* by Conrad Aiken
1931 *Collected Poems,* by Robert Frost
1932 *The Flowering Stone,* by George Dillon
1933 *Conquistador,* by Archibald MacLeish
1934 *Collected Verse,* by Robert Hillyer
1935 *Bright Ambush,* by Audrey Wurdemann
1936 *Strange Holiness,* by Robert P. Tristram Coffin
1937 *A Further Range,* by Robert Frost
1938 *Cold Morning Sky,* by Marya Zaturenska
1939 *Selected Poems,* by John Gould Fletcher
1940 *Collected Poems,* by Mark Van Doren
1941 *Sunderland Capture,* by Leonard Bacon
1942 *The Dust Which Is God,* by William Rose Benét
1943 *A Witness Tree,* by Robert Frost
1944 *Western Star,* by Stephen Vincent Benét
1945 *V-Letter and Other Poems,* by Karl Shapiro
1947 *Lord Weary's Castle,* by Robert Lowell
1948 *The Age of Anxiety,* by W. H. Auden
1949 *Terror and Decorum,* by Peter Viereck
1950 *Annie Allen,* by Gwendolyn Brooks
1951 *Complete Poems,* by Carl Sandburg

1952 *Collected Poems,* by Marianne Moore
1953 *Collected Poems 1917–1952,* by Archibald MacLeish
1954 *The Waking, Poem 1933–1953,* by Theodore Roethke
1955 *Collected Poems,* by Wallace Stevens
1956 *Poems–North & South,* by Elizabeth Bishop
1957 *Things of This World,* by Richard Wilbur
1958 *Promises: Poems 1954–56,* by Robert Penn Warren
1959 *Selected Poems 1928–1958,* by Stanley Kunitz
1960 *Heart's Needle,* by W. D. Snodgrass
1961 *Times Three: Selected Verse from Three Decades,* by Phyllis McGinley
1962 *Poems,* by Alan Dugan
1963 *Pictures from Breughel,* by William Carlos Williams
1964 *At the End of the Open Road,* by Louis Simpson
1965 *77 Dream Songs,* by John Berryman
1966 *Selected Poems,* by Richard Eberhart
1967 *Live or Die,* by Anne Sexton
1968 *The Hard Hours,* by A. Hecht
1969 *Of Being Numerous,* by George Oppen
1970 *Untitled Subjects,* by Richard Howard
1971 *The Carrier of Ladders,* by William S. Merwin
1972 *Collected Poems,* by James Wright
1973 *Up Country,* by Maxine Winokur Kumin
1974 *The Dolphin,* by R. Lowell
1975 *Turtle Island,* by G. Snyder
1976 *Self-Portrait in a Convex Mirror,* by John Ashbery
1977 *Divine Comedies,* by James Merrill
1978 *Collected Poems,* by Howard Nemerov
1979 *Now and Then,* by Robert Penn Warren
1980 *Selected Poems,* by Donald Rodney Justice
1981 *The Morning of the Poem,* by James Schuyler
1982 *The Collected Poems,* by Sylvia Plath

## GENERAL NONFICTION

1962 *The Making of the President 1960,* by Theodore H. White
1963 *The Guns of August,* by Barbara W. Tuchman
1964 *Anti-intellectualism in American Life,* by R. Hofstadter
1965 *O Strange New World,* by Howard Mumford Jones
1966 *Wandering Through Winter,* by Edwin Way Teale
1967 *The Problem of Slavery in Western Culture,* by David Brion Davis
1968 *The Story of Civilization* (Volume X), by Will and Ariel Durant
1969 *So Human An Animal,* by Rene Dubos, and *The Armies of the Night,* by Norman Mailer
1970 *Gandhi's Truth,* by Erik H. Erikson
1971 *The Rising Sun,* by John Toland
1972 *Stilwell and the American Experience in China, 1911–1945,* by Barbara Tuchman
1973 *Fire in the Lake: The Vietnamese and the Americans in Vietnam,* by Frances Fitz-Gerald, and *Children of Crisis,* by Dr. Robert Coles
1974 *The Denial of Death,* by Ernest Becker
1975 *Pilgrim at Tinker Creek,* by Annie Dillard
1976 *Why Survive? Being Old in America,* by Robert N. Butler
1977 *Beautiful Swimmers: Watermen, Crabs and the Chesapeake Bay,* by William W. Warner
1978 *The Dragons of Eden,* by Carl Sagan
1979 *On Human Nature,* by Edward O. Wilson
1980 *Godel, Escher, Bach: An Eternal Golden Braid,* by Douglas R. Hofstadter
1981 *Fin-de-Siecle Vienna: Politics and Culture,* by Carl E. Schorske
1982 *The Soul of a New Machine,* by Tracy Kidder

## CRITICISM/COMMENTARY

1970 Ada Louise Huxtable, *The New York Times* and Marquis Childs, *St. Louis Post-Dispatch*
1971 Harold C. Schonberg, *The New York Times* and William A. Caldwell, *The Hackensack* (N.J.) *Record*
1972 Frank Peters, Jr., *St. Louis* (Mo.) *Post Dispatch*
1973 Ronald Powers, *Chicago Sun-Times* and David S. Broder, *Washington Post*
1974 Emily Genauer, *Newday* Edwin A. Roberts, *National Observer*
1975 Mary McGrory, *The Washington Star* and Roger Ebert, *Chicago Sun Times*
1976 Alan M. Kriegsman, *The Washington* [D.C.] *Post* Walter W. (Red) Smith, *The New York Times*
1977 William McPherson, *The Washington Post;* George F. Will, Washington Post Writers Group
1978 Walter Kerr, *The New York Times;* William Safire, *The New York Times*
1979 Paul Gapp, *The Chicago Tribune;* Russell Baker, *The New York Times*
1980 William A. Henry III, *The Boston Globe;* Ellen H. Goodman, *The Boston Globe*
1981 Jonathan Yardley, *The Washington* (D.C.) *Star* Dave Anderson, *The New York Times*
1982 Martin Bernheimer, *The Los Angeles Times* Art Buchwald, Los Angeles Times Syndicate

## SPECIAL CITATIONS

1944 *Oklahoma!,* by Richard Rodgers and Oscar Hammerstein II
1957 Kenneth Roberts for his historical novels, which have helped to create a greater interest in early American history
1960 Garrett Mattingly for *The Armada*
1961 *American Heritage Picture History of the Civil War*
1973 *George Washington,* by James Thomas Flexner
1976 Scott Joplin, for his contributions to American music
1977 Alex Haley for *Roots*
1978 E. B. White for his contributions to *The New Yorker* and his general enrichment of the American language
1982 Milton Babbitt for his life's work as a distinguished American composer

## PRIZES IN MUSIC

1943 William Schuman: *Secular Cantata No. 2, A Free Song*
1944 Howard Hanson: *Symphony No. 4, Opus 34*
1945 Aaron Copland: *Appalachian Spring*
1946 Leo Sowerby: *The Canticle of the Sun*
1947 Charles Ives: *Symph. No. 3*
1948 Walter Piston: *Symph. No. 3*
1949 Virgil Thomson: *Louisiana Story*
1950 Gian-Carlo Menotti: *The Consul*
1951 Douglas S. Moore: *Giants in the Earth*
1952 Gail Kubik: *Symphony Concertante*
1954 Quincy Porter: *Concerto for Two Pianos and Orchestra*
1955 Gian-Carlo Menotti: *The Saint of Bleecker Street*
1956 Ernst Toch: *Symphony No. 3*
1957 Norman Dello Joio: *Meditations on Ecclesiastes*
1958 Samuel Barber: the score of *Vanessa*
1959 John La Montaine: *Concerto for Piano and Orchestra*
1960 Elliott Carter: *Second String Quartet*
1961 Walter Piston: *Symph. No. 7*
1962 Robert Ward: *The Crucible*
1963 Samuel Barber: *Piano Concerto No. 1*
1966 Leslie Bassett: *Variations for Orchestra*
1967 Leon Kirchner: *Quartet No. 3*
1968 George Crumb: *Echoes of Time and the River*
1969 Karel Husa: *String Quartet No. 3*
1970 Charles W. Wuorinen: *Time's Encomium*
1971 Mario Davidovsky: *Synchronisms No. 6 for Piano and Electronic Sound*
1972 Jacob Druckman: *Windows*
1973 Elliot Carter: *String Quartet No. 3*
1974 Donald Martino: *Notturno*
1975 Dominick Argento: *From the Diary of Virginia Wolff*
1976 Ned Rorem: *Air Music*
1977 Richard Wernick: *Visions of Terror and Wonder*
1978 Michael Colgrass: *Déja Vu for Percussion Quartet and Orchestra*
1979 Joseph Schwantner: *Aftertones of Infinity*
1980 David Del Tredici: *In Memory of a Summer Day*
1982 Roger Sessions: *Concerto for Orchestra*

## OTHER PRIZES AND AWARDS

### ACHIEVEMENT

ALL-AMERICA CITIES AWARD PROGRAM (1981-82) for Community Involvement Through Citizen Action, sponsored by the National Municipal League:

Blacksburg, Virginia; Bloomington, Indiana; Cleveland, Ohio; Des Moines, Iowa; Grand Island, Nebraska; Independence, Missouri; Indianapolis, Indiana; Meyersdale, Pennsylvania; Roanoke, Virginia; Valdez, Alaska.

WOMEN OF THE YEAR AWARDS for outstanding achievement by women in their fields, presented by *Ladies' Home Journal* magazine:

Women of the Decade (selected by *Journal* readers from past recipients): Marian Anderson; Joan Ganz Cooney; Betty Ford; Helen Hayes; Katharine Hepburn; Barbara Jordan; Elisabeth Kubler-Ross; Sylvia Porter; Beverly Sills; Barbara Walters; Margaret Mead (Posthumous award).

### PUBLIC SERVICE

AMERICAN JEWISH COMMITTEE (1982):

**Herbert H. Lehman Award in Human Relations:** Joseph Flam

MEDALS OF FREEDOM awarded by the President of the United States, for exceptionally meritorious contributions to national security, world peace, or to cultural or other significant public or private endeavors. The most recent recipients are:

Roger Baldwin, founder of the American Civil Liberties Union
Harold Brown, U.S. Secretary of Defense
Zbigniew Brzezinski, White House national security adviser
Warren M. Christopher, Deputy Secretary of State
Walter Cronkite, CBS Television News anchorman
Kirk Douglas, actor
Philip C. Habib, special presidential envoy to the Middle East*
Margaret Craig McNamara, educator and founder of Reading Is Fundamental
Dr. Karl Menninger, noted psychiatrist
Edmund S. Muskie, U.S. Secretary of State
Esther Peterson, special presidential assistant for consumer affairs
Gerald C. Smith, U.S. Ambassador at Large and former director of the Arms Control and Disarmament Agency
Robert S. Strauss, special U.S. trade envoy and past chairman of the Democratic National Committee
Judge Elbert Parr Tuttle, Justice of the U.S. Court of Appeals for the Fifth District
Earl Warren (dec.), Chief Justice of the U.S. Supreme Court, 1953-1969
Andrew Young, chief U.S. representative to the United Nations

*This award was bestowed September 7, 1982, as the first Medal given during President Reagan's Administration.

TEACHER OF THE YEAR (1982) awarded by the Chief State School Officers, the *Encyclopaedia Britannica*, and *Good Housekeeping* magazine: Bruce Brombacher, Upper Arlington, Ohio

### SCIENCE

NATIONAL ACADEMY OF SCIENCES AWARDS (1982):

**James Murray Luck Prize:** Victor A. McKusick
**N.A.S. Award in Chemical Sciences:** Gilbert Stork
**N.A.S. Award for Initiatives in Research:** Kerry E. Sieh
**N.A.S. Public Welfare Medal:** Paul G. Rogers
**Gilbert Morgan Smith Medal:** Luigi Provasoli
**Mary Clark Thompson Medal:** William A. Berggren
**U.S. Steel Foundation Award in Molecular Biology:** Joan A. Steitz
**Selman A. Waksman Award:** I.C. Gunsalus
**Charles Doolittle Walcott Medal:** Martin F. Glaessner
**G.K. Warren Prize:** John T. Hack
**James Craig Watson Medal:** Stanton J. Peale

NATIONAL MEDAL OF SCIENCE (1981), the highest award for outstanding achievement in science and engineering in the United States:
Philip Handler*, president, National Academy of Sciences, Washington, D.C.

*Deceased as of 12/81.

WESTINGHOUSE SCIENCE TALENT SEARCH (1982): high school student scholarship competition conducted by Science Service, Inc., sponsored by Westinghouse Educational Foundation and the Westinghouse Corporation:

| | |
|---|---|
| **$12,000:** | Reena Beth Gordon, Brooklyn, N.Y. |
| **$10,000:** | Ronald Marc Kantor, Bronx, N.Y. |
| | Ogan Gurel, New York, N.Y. |
| **$7,500:** | Helen Elaine Getto, Chicago, Ill. |
| | Theron Stanford, San Marino, Calif. |
| | Mitchell Tsai, Kent, Ohio |
| **$5,000:** | Niels Phinn Mayer, Corona del Mar, Calif. |
| | Noam David Elkies, New York, N.Y. |
| | Saechin Kim, Long Island City, N.Y. |
| | Lynne Page Snyder, Smithtown, N.Y. |

### JOURNALISM

GEORGE POLK AWARDS (1982) sponsored by Long Island University:

**Foreign Reporting:** John Darnton, *The New York Times*
**National Reporting:** Seymour M. Hersh, Jeff Gerth and Philip Taubman, *The New York Times*
**Television Reporting:** Ted Koppel, ABC News, managing editor and anchorman, "Nightline"
**Television Documentary:** Pierre Salinger, Paris bureau chief, ABC News, for "America Held Hostage: The Secret Negotiations"
**Special Award:** George Seldes, former correspondent for the *Chicago Tribune*, author of 18 books, and editor-publisher of the journalism watchdog newsletter, *In Fact*

NIEMAN FELLOWSHIPS (1982-83) for working Journalists—(Harvard University):
Eric Best; Daniel Brewster, Jr.; Huntly Collins; Callie W. Crossley; Gilbert M. Gaul; Guy Gugliotta; Sonja Hillgren; David J. Himmelstein; Karl Idsvoog; William Marimow; Eli Reed; Charles Sherman

SIGMA DELTA CHI AWARDS (1981) for distinguished service in print and broadcast journalism:

**Newspapers:**
**General Reporting:** David L. Ashenfelter and Sydney P. Freedberg, *The Detroit News*
**Editorial Writing:** Jon T. Senderling, *The Dallas Times-Herald*
**Washington Correspondence:** Jerome Watson, *The Chicago Sun-Times*
**Foreign Correspondence:** Richard Ben Cramer, *The Philadelphia Inquirer*
**News Photography:** Ron Edmonds, The Associated Press
**Editorial Cartoon:** Paul Conrad, *The Los Angeles Times*
**Public Service:** *The Los Angeles Times*

**Magazines:**
**Reporting:** Seymour M. Hersh, *The New York Times Magazine*
**Public Service:** *The National Geographic Magazine*

**Radio:**
**Reporting:** KVET-AM, Austin, Tex.
**Public Service:** WJR-AM, Detroit, Mich.
**Editorializing:** Michal Regunberg, WEEI, Boston, Mass.

**Television:**
**Reporting:** WHAS, Louisville, Ky.
**Public Service:** WNBC, New York, N.Y.
**Editorializing:** Jack Hurley, WHIO, Dayton, Ohio
**Research About Journalism:** Robert W. Desmond

## ARTS

AMERICAN ACADEMY AND INSTITUTE OF ARTS AND LETTERS AWARDS (1982):

**Academy-Institute Gold Medals:** Francis Steegmuller (Biography), William Schuman (Music)

**ACADEMY-INSTITUTE AWARDS:**

**In Literature:** David H. Bradley, Jr., Frederick Buechner, MacDonald Harris, Daryl Hine, Josephine Jacobsen, Donald Keene, Berton Roueché, Robert Stone

**In Art:** Nizette Brennan, Michael David, George McNeil, Alan Motch, Manuel Neri

**In Music:** Douglas Allanbrook, James Tenney, George Walker, Ramon Zupko

**SPECIAL AWARDS:**

**American Academy in Rome Fellowship in Creative Writing:** Mark Helprin

**Arnold W. Brunner Memorial Prize in Architecture:** Helmut Jahn

**Witter Bynner Prize for Poetry:** William Heyen

**Charles Ives Scholarships:** Michael Gandolfi, Peter Golub, Jeffrey Hall, Charles E. Porter, Preston Stahly, Jr., Karen P. Thomas

**Charles Ives Award:** The Charles Ives Society

**Sue Kaufman Prize for First Fiction:** Ted Mooney

**Goddard Lieberson Fellowship:** Stephen Dembski, Paul Dresher

**The Award of Merit Medal for Painting:** Myron Stout

**Richard and Hinda Rosenthal Foundation Awards:** Fiction—Marilynne Robinson; Painting—Terry Winters

**Harold D. Vursell Memorial Award:** Eleanor Perényi

**Marjorie Peabody Waite Award:** Edouard Roditi

**Morton Dauwen Zabel Award:** Howard Bloom

**Award for Distinguished Service to the Arts:** Alfred A. Knopf

### *Art*

NATIONAL ACADEMY OF DESIGN PRIZES (1982):

**Benjamin Altman Prizes:** Landscape—Paul Resika ($1,500); Figure—Leland Bell ($1,500)

**Emil and Dines Carlsen Award:** Nell Blaine ($1,000)

**Andrew Carnegie Prize:** James Gemmill ($1,000)

**Adolph and Clara Obrig Prize:** Herb Steinberg ($600)

**Thomas B. Clarke Prize:** Jack N. Kramer ($500)

**Grumbacher Art Award and Gold Medal:** Herman Rose ($400)

**Saltus Gold Medal:** Jane Piper

**Frank and Annie Shikler Prize:** St. Julian Fishburne ($250)

**Isaac N. Maynard Prize:** Richard Bober ($150)

**Julius Hallgarten Prizes:** Richard Pantell ($400); Phyllis Berman ($300); Richard N. Birkett ($200)

**Certificate of Merit:** Gretna Campbell

**Sculpture Awards:**

**The Artists Fund Prize:** Marilyn Newmark ($400)

**Dessie Greer Prize:** Archimedes Giacomantonio ($100)

**Elizabeth N. Watrous Gold Medal:** George Lundeen

**N.A.D. Gold Medal:** Nina Winkel

**Thomas R. Proctor Prize:** Edward Fenno Hoffman ($500)

**Leila Gardin Sawyer Prize:** Henry DiSpirito ($50)

**Graphic Arts Awards:**

**Cannon Prize:** Robert Conover ($400)

**Ralph Fabri Prize:** Jacob Landau ($200)

**Leo Meissner Prize:** Sidney Hurwitz ($200)

**Anonymous Prize:** Robert Kipniss ($100)

**William H. Leavin Prize:** David Bumbeck ($100)

**Gladys Emerson Cook Prize:** Alan James Robinson ($100)

**Helen M. Loggie Prize:** Jennifer B. French ($50)

**Certificates of Merit:** Steve Yamin, Mike Goscinsky, William T. Livesay

**Watercolor Awards:**

**William A. Paton Prize:** David Millard ($1,000)

**John Pike Memorial Prize:** Chen Chi ($500)

**Adolph and Clara Obrig Prizes:** Ruth Cobb ($450); Murray Wentworth ($300)

**Ellin P. Speyer Prize:** Robert Handville ($400)

**Walter Biggs Memorial Award:** Philip Jamison ($200)

**Certificates of Merit:** John C. Pellew, John C. Bermingham

### *Literature*

AMERICAN BOOKSELLERS ASSOCIATION AWARD (1981):

**Irita Van Doren Book Award:** The New York Times Book Review

BANCROFT PRIZES (1982) presented by Columbia University for books of exceptional merit and distinction in American history (including biography) and diplomacy:

Edward Countryman, *A People in Revolution: The American Revolution and Political Society in New York, 1760-1790*

Mary P. Ryan, *Cradle of the Middle Class: The Family in Oneida County, New York, 1790-1865*

THE BOLLINGEN PRIZE IN POETRY (1979-80) an award of $5,000 given by Yale University Library: Howard Nemerov, May Swenson

THE AMERICAN BOOK AWARDS (1982) sponsored by the Association of American Publishers:

**General Fiction:** *Rabbit Is Rich*, John Updike

**General Nonfiction:** *The Soul of a New Machine*, Tracy Kidder

**Biography/Autobiography:** *Mornings on Horseback*, David McCullough

**History:** *People of the Sacred Mountain: A History of the Northern Cheyenne Chiefs and Warrior Societies*, Father Peter John Powell

**First Novel:** *Dale Loves Sophie to Death*, Dale Foreman Dew

**Poetry:** *Life Supports*, William Bronk

**Children's Books:** *Westmark*, Lloyd Alexander (Fiction); *A Penguin Year*, Susan Bonners (Nonfiction)

**Translation:** *In the Shade of Spring Leaves*, translated from the Japanese by Robert Lyons Danly; *The Ten Thousand Leaves*, translated from the Japanese by Ian Hideo Levy

**National Medal for Literature:** John Cheever

NEWBERY-CALDECOTT MEDALS (1982) presented by the American Library Association for the most distinguished American books in the children's field:

**John Newbery Medal:** *A Visit to William Blake's Inn: Poems for Innocent and Experienced Travelers*, Nancy Willard, author

**Randolph Caldecott Medal:** *Jumanji*, Chris Van Allsburg, illustrator

POETRY SOCIETY OF AMERICA PRIZES (1982):

**Gordon Barber Memorial Award:** Susan Sonde, John Menfi (shared)

**Melville Cane Award:** Gerald Stern, *The Red Coal*

**Gertrude B. Claytor Memorial Award:** Carole Oles

**Gustav Davidson Memorial Award:** Joan Austin Geier

**Mary Carolyn Davies Memorial Award:** Erika Mumford

**Alice Fay di Castagnola Award:** Robert Peters, *Hawkers of Morwenstowe: Eccentric Cornish Vicar (1803-1875)*

**Consuelo Ford Award:** Phyllis Janowitz, Madeline DeFrees (shared)

**Elias Lieberman Student Poetry Award:** Eva Thaddeus

**John Masefield Memorial Award:** Jay Grover-Rogoff, Carolyn Kizer (shared)

**Alfred Kreymborg Memorial Award:** Frances Minturn Howard

**Celia B. Wagner Award:** Katharyn Machan Aal

**Lucille Medwick Memorial Award:** Joan Swift

## Music

GRAMMY AWARDS (1981) given by the National Academy of Recording Arts and Sciences:

**Record of the Year:** "Bette Davis Eyes" (Kim Carnes)

**Album of the Year:** "Double Fantasy" (John Lennon and Yoko Ono)

**Song of the Year:** "Bette Davis Eyes" (Donna Weiss, Jackie DeShannon, songwriters)

**Best New Artist of the Year:** Sheena Easton

**Best Pop Vocal Performance, Female:** "Lena Horne: The Lady and Her Music Live on Broadway" (Lena Horne)

**Pop Vocal Performance, Male:** "Breakin' Away" (Al Jarreau)

**Pop Vocal Performance, Group:** "Boy From New York City" (The Manhattan Transfer)

**Best Pop Instrumental Performance:** "The Theme from Hill Street Blues" (Mike Post, featuring Larry Carlton)

**Best Rock Vocal Performance, Female:** "Fire and Ice" (Pat Benatar)

**Rock Vocal Performance, Male:** "Jessie's Girl" (Rick Springfield)

**Rock Vocal Performance, Group:** "Don't Stand So Close To Me" (The Police)

**Best Rock Instrumental Performance:** "Behind My Camel" (The Police)

**Best Jazz Vocal Performance:** Female—"Digital III at Montreux" (Ella Fitzgerald); Male—"Blue Rondo A La Turk" (Al Jarreau); Group—"Until I Met You" (The Manhattan Transfer)

**Best Jazz Instrumental Performance:** Soloist—"Bye Bye Blackbird" (John Coltrane); Group—"Chick Corea and Gary Burton in Concert, Zurich, October 28, 1979" (Chick Corea and Gary Burton); Big Band—"Walk On The Water" (Jerry Mulligan and his Orchestra)

**Best Rhythm & Blues Vocal Performance:** Female—"Hold On I'm Comin'" (Aretha Franklin); Male—"One Hundred Ways" (James Ingram)

**Best Rhythm & Blues Instrumental Performance:** "All I Need Is You" (David Sanborn)

**Best Rhythm & Blues Song:** "Just the Two of Us" (Bill Withers, William Salter and Ralph McDonald, songwriters)

**Best Gospel Performance, Contemporary or Inspirational:** "Priority" (Imperials)

**Best Country Song:** "9 To 5" (Dolly Parton, songwriter)

**Best Country Vocal Performance:** Female—"9 To 5" (Dolly Parton); Male—"(There's) No Gettin' Over Me" (Ronnie Milsap); Group—"Elvira" (Oak Ridge Boys)

**Best Country Instrumental Performance:** "Country—After All These Years" (Chet Atkins)

**Best Recording for Children:** "Sesame Country" (Dennis Scott, producer; Jim Henson, Muppets creator)

**Best Comedy Recording:** "Rev. Du Rite" (Richard Pryor)

**Best Cast Show Album:** "Lena Horne: The Lady and Her Music Live on Broadway" (Quincy Jones, producer)

**Best Classical Album:** "Mahler, Symphony No. 2 in C Minor" (Sir Georg Solti, conductor, Chicago Symphony Orchestra; James Mallinson, producer)

**Best Opera Recording:** "Janacek: From the House of the Dead" (Sir Charles Mackerras, conductor, The Vienna Philharmonic, Jiri Zahradnicek, Vaclav Zitek, Ivo Zidek, soloists; James Mallinson, producer)

## Television and Radio

EMMY AWARDS (1981-82): major awards presented by the Academy of Television Arts and Sciences:

**Drama Series**

**Actor:** Daniel J. Travanti, "Hill Street Blues"
**Actress:** Michael Learned, "Nurse"
**Supporting actor:** Michael Conrad, "Hill Street Blues"
**Supporting actress:** Nancy Marchand, "Lou Grant"
**Directing:** Harry Harris, "Fame"
**Writing:** Steven Bochco, Anthony Yerkovich, Jeffrey Lewis, Michael Wagner and Michael Kozoll, "Hill Street Blues"
**Best series:** "Hill Street Blues"

**Comedy Series**

**Actor:** Alan Alda, "MASH"
**Actress:** Carol Kane, "Taxi"
**Supporting actor:** Christopher Lloyd, "Taxi"
**Supporting actress:** Loretta Swit, "MASH"
**Directing:** Alan Rafkin, "One Day At a Time"
**Writing:** Ken Estin, "Taxi"
**Best series:** "Barney Miller"

**Limited Series or Specials**

**Actor:** Mickey Rooney, "Bill"
**Actress:** Ingrid Bergman, "A Woman Called Golda"
**Supporting actor:** Laurence Olivier, "Brideshead Revisited"
**Supporting actress:** Penny Fuller, "The Elephant Man"
**Best series:** "Marco Polo"
**Special (Drama):** "A Woman Called Golda"
**Special (Comedy or Variety):** "Night of a Hundred Stars"

### 1981 GEORGE FOSTER PEABODY BROADCASTING AWARDS

**Radio**

WJR Radio, Detroit, Mich: "Newsfile: A Bankrupt Court"; National Radio Theatre, Chicago, Ill.: "The Odyssey of Homer," an eight-part series; Canadian Broadcasting Corporation, Vancouver: "Carl Sandburg at Connemara"; Societe Radio-Canada, Montreal: "Klimbo: Le lion et la souris" ("The Lion and the Mouse"); Timothy and Susan Todd, Middlebury, Vt.: "The Todd's Teddy Bear Picnic"; WQDR-FM, Raleigh, N.C.: "Our Forgotten Warriors: Vietnam Veterans Face the Challenges of the 80s," a 32-part series

**Television**

WLS-TV, Chicago, Ill.: "Eyewitness News," exemplified by "Traffic Court: Justice or Joke?" and "So You Need a Driver's License"; Bill Leonard, CBS-News, New York: for his outstanding role in developing CBS News; John Goldsmith, WDVM-TV, Washington, D.C.: for "Now That We've Got Your Interest," a year-end report; NBC and MTM Enterprises: "Hill Street Blues"; Nebraska Educational Television Network and the Great Amwell Company: "The Private History of a Campaign That Failed," based on a story by Mark Twain; CBS-TV and Alan Landsburg Productions: "Bill," a GE Theatre special, starring Mickey Rooney; Danny Kaye: for performances in "An Evening With Danny Kaye and the New York Philharmonic: Zubin Mehta, Music Director," produced for PBS by Lincoln Center for the Performing Arts, and "Skokie," produced by Titus Productions for CBS; WNET/Thirteen, New York, and PBS: "Dance in America: Nureyev and the Joffrey Ballet/In Tribute to Nijinsky"; KJRH-TV, Tulsa, Okla.: "Project China"; Home Box Office and *Ms. Magazine*: "She's Nobody's Baby: The History of American Women in the 20th Century"*; ABC and T.A.T. Communications: "The Wave," a presentation of ABC Theatre for Young Americans; WSMV, Nashville, Tenn.: for a series of significant documentaries, including "Crime's Children," "Hot Cars, Cold Cash," "Split Second Justice," and "Crime Carousel"; KATU-TV, Portland, Ore.: for "Ready on the Firing Line," "Out of The Ashes," and "To Begin Again...," an outstanding series of documentaries; WGBH, Boston, Mass., and Granada TV, London: "The Red Army," part of the "World" series; Eight Decade Consortium, Seattle, Wash.: "Fed Up With Fear"; ABC News: "Viewpoint," "Nightline," and "America Held Hostage: The Secret Negotiations," representing the outstanding talents of ABC News, with special mention to Ted Koppel; KTEH, San Jose, Calif.: "The Day After Trinity: J. Robert Oppenheimer and the Atomic Bomb," produced by Jon Else

*First Peabody Award to a television production intended for distribution by non-broadcast (i.e., cable) means.

## ACADEMY AWARD WINNERS

| Year | Best Picture | Best Actor | Supporting Actor | Best Actress | Supporting Actress | Best Director |
|---|---|---|---|---|---|---|
| 1981 | "Chariots of Fire" | Henry Fonda "On Golden Pond" | John Gielgud "Arthur" | Katharine Hepburn "On Golden Pond" | Maureen Stapleton "Reds" | Warren Beatty "Reds" |
| 1980 | "Ordinary People" | Robert De Niro "Raging Bull" | Timothy Hutton "Ordinary People" | Sissy Spacek "Coal Miner's Daughter" | Mary Steenburgen "Melvin & Howard" | Robert Redford "Ordinary People" |
| 1979 | "Kramer vs. Kramer" | Dustin Hoffman "Kramer vs. Kramer" | Melvyn Douglas "Being There" | Sally Field "Norma Rae" | Meryl Streep "Kramer vs. Kramer" | Robert Benton "Kramer vs. Kramer" |
| 1978 | "The Deer Hunter" | Jon Voight "Coming Home" | Christopher Walken "The Deer Hunter" | Jane Fonda "Coming Home" | Maggie Smith "California Suite" | Michael Cimino "The Deer Hunter" |
| 1977 | "Annie Hall" | Richard Dreyfuss "The Goodbye Girl" | Jason Robards "Julia" | Diane Keaton "Annie Hall" | Vanessa Redgrave "Julia" | Woody Allen "Annie Hall" |
| 1976 | "Rocky" | Peter Finch "Network" | Jason Robards "All the President's Men" | Faye Dunaway "Network" | Beatrice Straight "Network" | John G. Avildsen "Rocky" |
| 1975 | "One Flew Over the Cuckoo's Nest" | Jack Nicholson "One Flew Over the Cuckoo's Nest" | George Burns "The Sunshine Boys" | Louise Fletcher "One Flew Over the Cuckoo's Nest" | Lee Grant "Shampoo" | Milos Forman "One Flew Over the Cuckoo's Nest" |
| 1974 | "The Godfather, Part II" | Art Carney "Harry and Tonto" | Robert DeNiro "The Godfather, Part II" | Ellyn Burstyn "Alice Doesn't Live Here Anymore" | Ingrid Bergman "Murder on the Orient Express" | Francis Ford Coppola "The Godfather, Part II" |
| 1973 | "The Sting" | Jack Lemmon "Save the Tiger" | John Houseman "The Paper Chase" | Glenda Jackson "A Touch of Class" | Tatum O'Neal "Paper Moon" | George Roy Hill "The Sting" |
| 1972 | "The Godfather" | Marlon Brando "The Godfather" | Joel Grey "Cabaret" | Liza Minnelli "Cabaret" | Eileen Heckart "Butterflies Are Free" | Bob Fosse "Cabaret" |
| 1971 | "The French Connection" | Gene Hackman "The French Connection" | Ben Johnson "The Last Picture Show" | Jane Fonda "Klute" | Cloris Leachman "The Last Picture Show" | William Friedkin "The French Connection" |
| 1970 | "Patton" | George C. Scott "Patton" | John Mills "Ryan's Daughter" | Glenda Jackson "Women in Love" | Helen Hayes "Airport" | Franklin Schaffner "Patton" |
| 1969 | "Midnight Cowboy" | John Wayne "True Grit" | Gig Young "They Shoot Horses, Don't They?" | Maggie Smith "The Prime of Miss Jean Brodie" | Goldie Hawn "Cactus Flower" | John Schlesinger "Midnight Cowboy" |
| 1968 | "Oliver!" | Cliff Robertson "Charly" | Jack Albertson "The Subject Was Roses" | Katharine Hepburn "The Lion in Winter" Barbra Streisand "Funny Girl" | Ruth Gordon "Rosemary's Baby" | Sir Carol Reed "Oliver!" |
| 1967 | "In the Heat of the Night" | Rod Steiger "In the Heat of the Night" | George Kennedy "Cool Hand Luke" | Katharine Hepburn "Guess Who's Coming to Dinner?" | Estelle Parsons "Bonnie and Clyde" | Mike Nichols "The Graduate" |
| 1966 | "A Man for All Seasons" | Paul Scofield "A Man for All Seasons" | Walter Matthau "The Fortune Cookie" | Elizabeth Taylor "Who's Afraid of Virginia Woolf?" | Sandy Dennis "Who's Afraid of Virginia Woolf?" | Fred Zinnemann "A Man for All Seasons" |
| 1965 | "The Sound of Music" | Lee Marvin "Cat Ballou" | Martin Balsam "A Thousand Clowns" | Julie Christie "Darling" | Shelley Winters "A Patch of Blue" | Robert Wise "The Sound of Music" |
| 1964 | "My Fair Lady" | Rex Harrison "My Fair Lady" | Peter Ustinov "Topkapi" | Julie Andrews "Mary Poppins" | Lila Kedrova "Zorba the Greek" | George Cukor "My Fair Lady" |
| 1963 | "Tom Jones" | Sidney Poitier "Lilies of the Field" | Melvyn Douglas "Hud" | Patricia Neal "Hud" | Margaret Rutherford "The V.I.P.s" | Tony Richardson "Tom Jones" |
| 1962 | "Lawrence of Arabia" | Gregory Peck "To Kill a Mockingbird" | Ed Begley "Sweet Bird of Youth" | Anne Bancroft "The Miracle Worker" | Patty Duke "The Miracle Worker" | David Lean "Lawrence of Arabia" |
| 1961 | "West Side Story" | Maximilian Schell "Judgment at Nuremberg" | George Chakiris "West Side Story" | Sophia Loren "Two Women" | Rita Moreno "West Side Story" | Jerome Robbins, Robert Wise "West Side Story" |
| 1960 | "The Apartment" | Burt Lancaster "Elmer Gantry" | Peter Ustinov "Spartacus" | Elizabeth Taylor "Butterfield 8" | Shirley Jones "Elmer Gantry" | Billy Wilder "The Apartment" |
| 1959 | "Ben-Hur" | Charlton Heston "Ben-Hur" | Hugh Griffith "Ben-Hur" | Simone Signoret "Room at the Top" | Shelley Winters "The Diary of Anne Frank" | William Wyler "Ben-Hur" |
| 1958 | "Gigi" | David Niven "Separate Tables" | Burl Ives "The Big Country" | Susan Hayward "I Want to Live" | Wendy Hiller "Separate Tables" | Vincente Minnelli "Gigi" |
| 1957 | "The Bridge on the River Kwai" | Alec Guiness "The Bridge on the River Kwai" | Red Buttons "Sayonara" | Joanne Woodward "The Three Faces of Eve" | Miyoshi Umeki "Sayonara" | David Lean "The Bridge on the River Kwai" |
| 1956 | "Around the World in 80 Days" | Yul Brynner "The King and I" | Anthony Quinn "Lust for Life" | Ingrid Bergman "Anastasia" | Dorothy Malone "Written on the Wind" | George Stevens "Giant" |
| 1955 | "Marty" | Ernest Borgnine "Marty" | Jack Lemmon "Mister Roberts" | Anna Magnani "The Rose Tattoo" | Jo Van Fleet "East of Eden" | Delbert Mann "Marty" |

| Year | Best Picture | Best Actor | Supporting Actor | Best Actress | Supporting Actress | Best Director |
|---|---|---|---|---|---|---|
| 1954 | "On the Waterfront" | Marlon Brando "On the Waterfront" | Edmond O'Brien "The Barefoot Contessa" | Grace Kelly "The Country Girl" | Eva Marie Saint "On the Waterfront" | Elia Kazan "On the Waterfront" |
| 1953 | "From Here to Eternity" | William Holden "Stalag 17" | Frank Sinatra "From Here to Eternity" | Audrey Hepburn "Roman Holiday" | Donna Reed "From Here to Eternity" | Fred Zinnemann "From Here to Eternity" |
| 1952 | "The Greatest Show on Earth" | Gary Cooper "High Noon" | Anthony Quinn "Viva Zapata!" | Shirley Booth "Come Back, Little Sheba" | Gloria Grahame "The Bad and The Beautiful" | John Ford "The Quiet Man" |
| 1951 | "An American in Paris" | Humphrey Bogart "The African Queen" | Karl Malden "A Streetcar Named Desire" | Vivien Leigh "A Streetcar Named Desire" | Kim Hunter "A Streecar Named Desire" | George Stevens "A Place in the Sun" |
| 1950 | "All About Eve" | Jose Ferrer "Cyrano de Bergerac" | George Sanders "All About Eve" | Judy Holliday "Born Yesterday" | Josephine Hull "Harvey" | Joseph L. Mankiewicz "All About Eve" |
| 1949 | "All the King's Men" | Broderick Crawford "All the King's Men" | Dean Jagger "Twelve O'Clock High" | Olivia de Havilland "The Heiress" | Mercedes McCambridge "All the King's Men" | Joseph L. Mankiewicz "A Letter to Three Wives" |
| 1948 | "Hamlet" | Laurence Olivier "Hamlet" | Walter Huston "The Treasure of the Sierra Madre" | Jane Wyman "Johnny Belinda" | Claire Trevor "Key Largo" | John Huston "The Treasure of the Sierra Madre" |
| 1947 | "Gentleman's Agreement" | Ronald Colman "A Double Life" | Edmund Gwenn "Miracle on 34th Street" | Loretta Young "The Farmer's Daughter" | Celeste Holm "Gentleman's Agreement" | Elia Kazan "Gentleman's Agreement" |
| 1946 | "The Best Years of Our Lives" | Fredric March "The Best Years of Our Lives" | Harold Russell "The Best Years of Our Lives" | Olivia de Havilland "To Each His Own" | Anne Baxter "The Razor's Edge" | William Wyler "The Best Years of Our Lives" |
| 1945 | "The Lost Weekend" | Ray Milland "The Lost Weekend" | James Dunn "A Tree Grows in Brooklyn" | Joan Crawford "Mildred Pierce" | Anne Revere "National Velvet" | Billy Wilder "The Lost Weekend" |
| 1944 | "Going My Way" | Bing Crosby "Going My Way" | Barry Fitzgerald "Going My Way" | Ingrid Bergman "Gaslight" | Ethel Barrymore "None But the Lonely Heart" | Leo McCarey "Going My Way" |
| 1943 | "Casablanca" | Paul Lukas "Watch on the Rhine" | Charles Coburn "The More the Merrier" | Jennifer Jones "The Song of Bernadette" | Katina Paxinou "For Whom the Bell Tolls" | Michael Curtiz "Casablanca" |
| 1942 | "Mrs. Miniver" | James Cagney "Yankee Doodle Dandy" | Van Heflin "Johnny Eager" | Greer Garson "Mrs. Miniver" | Teresa Wright "Mrs. Miniver" | William Wyler "Mrs. Miniver" |
| 1941 | "How Green Was My Valley" | Gary Cooper "Sergeant York" | Donald Crisp "How Green Was My Valley" | Joan Fontaine "Suspicion" | Mary Astor "The Great Lie" | John Ford "How Green Was My Valley" |
| 1940 | "Rebecca" | James Stewart "The Philadelphia Story" | Walter Brennan "The Westerner" | Ginger Rogers "Kitty Foyle" | Jane Darwell "The Grapes of Wrath" | John Ford "The Grapes of Wrath" |
| 1939 | "Gone with the Wind" | Robert Donat "Goodbye, Mr. Chips" | Thomas Mitchell "Stagecoach" | Vivien Leigh "Gone with the Wind" | Hattie McDaniel "Gone with the Wind" | Victor Fleming "Gone with the Wind" |
| 1938 | "You Can't Take It with You" | Spencer Tracy "Boys' Town" | Walter Brennan "Kentucky" | Bette Davis "Jezebel" | Fay Bainter "Jezebel" | Frank Capra "You Can't Take It with You" |
| 1937 | "The Life of Emile Zola" | Spencer Tracy "Captains Courageous" | Joseph Schildkraut "The Life of Emile Zola" | Luise Rainer "The Good Earth" | Alice Brady "In Old Chicago" | Leo McCarey "The Awful Truth" |
| 1936 | "The Great Ziegfeld" | Paul Muni "The Story of Louis Pasteur" | Walter Brennan "Come and Get It" | Luise Rainer "The Great Ziegfeld" | Gale Sondergaard "Anthony Adverse" | Frank Capra "Mr. Deeds Goes to Town" |
| 1935 | "Mutiny on the Bounty" | Victor McLaglen "The Informer" | — | Bette Davis "Dangerous" | — | John Ford "The Informer" |
| 1934 | "It Happened One Night" | Clark Gable "It Happened One Night" | — | Claudette Colbert "It Happened One Night" | — | Frank Capra "It Happened One Night" |
| 1932-33 | "Cavalcade" | Charles Laughton "The Private Life of Henry VIII" | — | Katharine Hepburn "Morning Glory" | — | Frank Lloyd "Cavalcade" |
| 1931-32 | "Grand Hotel" | Wallace Beery "The Champ" Fredric March "Dr. Jekyll and Mr. Hyde" | — | Helen Hayes "The Sin of Madelon Claudet" | — | Frank Borzage "Bad Girl" |
| 1930-31 | "Cimarron" | Lionel Barrymore "A Free Soul" | — | Marie Dressler "Min and Bill" | — | Norman Taurog "Skippy" |
| 1929-30 | "All Quiet on the Western Front" | George Arliss "Disraeli" | — | Norma Shearer "The Divorcee" | — | Lewis Milestone "All Quiet on the Western Front" |
| 1928-29 | "Broadway Melody" | Warner Baxter "In Old Arizona" | — | Mary Pickford "Coquette" | — | Frank Lloyd "The Divine Lady" |
| 1927-28 | "Wings" | Emil Jannings "The Last Command" "The Way of All Flesh" | — | Janet Gaynor "Seventh Heaven" "Street Angel" "Sunrise" | — | Frank Borzage "Seventh Heaven" Lewis Milestone "Two Arabian Knights" |

### *Theatre*

ANTOINETTE PERRY (TONY) AWARDS (1981-82) presented by the League of New York Theatres and Producers and sponsored by the American Theatre Wing:

**Best Play:** "The Life and Adventures of Nicholas Nickleby"
**Best Musical:** "Nine"
**Best Book of a Musical:** Tom Eyen, "Dreamgirls"
**Best Score:** Maury Yeston, "Nine"
**Best Actor, Play:** Roger Rees, "Nicholas Nickleby"
**Best Actress, Play:** Zoe Caldwell, "Medea"
**Best Actor, Musical:** Ben Harney, "Dreamgirls"
**Best Actress, Musical:** Jennifer Holliday, "Dreamgirls"
**Best Featured Actor, Play:** Zakes Mokae, " 'Master Harold'...and the Boys"
**Best Featured Actress, Play:** Amanda Plummer, "Agnes of God"
**Best Featured Actor, Musical:** Cleavant Derricks, "Dreamgirls"
**Best Featured Actress, Musical:** Liliane Montevecchi, "Nine"
**Best Director, Play:** Trevor Nunn and John Caird, "Nicholas Nickleby"
**Best Director, Musical:** Tommy Tune, "Nine"
**Best Scenic Designer:** John Napier and Dermot Hayes, "Nicholas Nickleby"
**Best Costume Designer:** William Ivey Long, "Nine"
**Best Lighting Designer:** Tharon Musser, "Dreamgirls"
**Best Choreographer:** Michael Bennett and Michael Peters, "Dreamgirls"
**Revival of a Play or Musical:** "Othello"
**Special Tony Awards:** Tyrone Guthrie Theater, Minneapolis; Actors Fund of America

OBIE (OFF BROADWAY AWARDS) (1981-82):

**Best New American Play:** "Metamorphosis in Miniature"; "Mr. Dead and Mrs. Free" (tie)
**Best Production:** Tadeusz Kantor, "Wielopole, Wielopole"
**Sustained Achievement:** Maria Irene Fornes
**Distinguished Performances:** Kevin Bacon, "Forty Deuce" and "Poor Little Lambs"; James Barbosa, "Soon Jack November"; Ray Dooley, "Peer Gynt"; Christine Estabrook, "Pastorale"; Michael Gross, "No End of Blame"; E. Katherine Kerr, "Cloud 9"; Kenneth McMillan, "Weekends Like Other People"; Kevin O'Connor, "Chucky's Hunch," "Birdbath," and "Crossing the Crab Nebula"; Carole Shelley, "Twelve Dreams"; Josef Sommer, "Lydia Breeze"; Irene Worth, "The Chalk Garden"
**Distinguished Ensemble Performances:** Lisa Banes, Brenda Currin, Elizabeth McGovern, and Beverly May, "My Sister in This House"; Adolph Caesar, Larry Riley, and Denzel Washington, "A Soldier's Play"
**Distinguished Direction:** Tommy Tune, "Cloud Nine"
**Playwrighting:** Robert Auletta, "Stops" and "Virgins"; Caryl Churchill, "Cloud 9"
**Design:** Jim Clayburgh, sustained excellence, set design; Arden Fingerhut, sustained excellence in lighting design
**Special Citations:** La Mama: 20th anniversary celebration; Harvey Fierstein, "Torch Song Trilogy"; Theatre Communications Group

### *Films*

CANNES INTERNATIONAL FILM FESTIVAL (1982):

**Best Film:** "Missing," Constantin Costa-Gavras (Greek); "Yol," Yilmaz Güney (Turkish) (tie)
**Best Actress:** Jadwiga Jankowska-Cieslak, "Another Look"
**Best Actor:** Jack Lemmon, "Missing"

NEW YORK FILM CRITICS CIRCLE AWARD (1981):

**Best Film:** "Reds"
**Best Director:** Sidney Lumet, "Prince of the City"
**Best Actor:** Burt Lancaster, "Atlantic City"
**Best Actress:** Glenda Jackson, "Stevie"
**Best Supporting Actor:** John Gielgud, "Arthur"
**Best Supporting Actress:** Mona Washbourne, "Stevie"
**Best Screenplay:** John Guare, "Atlantic City"
**Best Foreign Film:** "Pixote," by Hector Babenco (Brazil)
**Special Awards:** Krzysztof Zanussi ("Contact," "Camouflage"); Andrzej Wajda ("Man of Marble," "Man of Iron"); Abel Gance ("Napoleon")

## MISS AMERICA

1921 Margaret Gorman, Washington, D.C.
1922-23 Mary Campbell, Columbus, Ohio
1924 Ruth Malcolmson, Philadelphia, Pennsylvania
1925 Fay Lamphier, Oakland, California
1926 Norma Smallwood, Tulsa, Oklahoma
1927 Lois Delaner, Joliet, Illinois
1933 Marion Bergeron, West Haven, Connecticut
1935 Henrietta Leaver, Pittsburgh, Pennsylvania
1936 Rose Coyle, Philadelphia, Pennsylvania
1937 Bette Cooper, Bertrand Island, New Jersey
1938 Marilyn Meseke, Marion, Ohio
1939 Patricia Donnelly, Detroit, Michigan
1940 Frances Marie Burke, Philadelphia, Pennsylvania
1941 Rosemary LaPlanche, Los Angeles, California
1942 Jo-Caroll Dennison, Tyler, Texas
1943 Jean Bartel, Los Angeles, California
1944 Venus Ramey, Washington, D.C.
1945 Bess Myerson, New York City, N.Y.
1946 Marilyn Buferd, Los Angeles, California
1947 Barbara Walker, Memphis, Tennessee
1948 BeBe Shopp, Hopkins, Minnesota
1949 Jacque Mercer, Litchfield, Arizona
1951 Yolande Betbeze, Mobile, Alabama
1952 Coleen Kay Hutchins, Salt Lake City, Utah
1953 Neva Jane Langley, Macon, Georgia
1954 Evelyn Margaret Ay, Ephrata, Pennsylvania
1955 Lee Meriwether, San Francisco, California
1956 Sharon Ritchie, Denver, Colorado
1957 Marian McKnight, Manning, South Carolina
1958 Marilyn Van Derbur, Denver, Colorado
1959 Mary Ann Mobley, Brandon, Mississippi
1960 Lynda Lee Mead, Natchez, Mississippi
1961 Nancy Fleming, Montague, Michigan
1962 Maria Fletcher, Asheville, North Carolina
1963 Jacquelyn Mayer, Sandusky, Ohio
1964 Donna Axum, El Dorado, Arkansas
1965 Vonda Kay Van Dyke, Phoenix, Arizona
1966 Deborah Irene Bryant, Overland Park, Kansas
1967 Jane Anne Jayroe, Laverne, Oklahoma
1968 Debra Dene Barnes, Moran, Kansas
1969 Judith Anne Ford, Belvidere, Illinois
1970 Pamela Anne Eldred, Birmingham, Michigan
1971 Phyllis Ann George, Denton, Texas
1972 Laurie Lea Schaefer, Columbus, Ohio
1973 Terry Anne Meeuwsen, DePere, Wisconsin
1974 Rebecca Ann King, Denver, Colorado
1975 Shirley Cothran, Fort Worth, Texas
1976 Tawney Elaine Godin, Yonkers, N.Y.
1977 Dorothy Kathleen Benham, Edina, Minnesota
1978 Susan Perkins, Columbus, Ohio
1979 Kylene Baker, Galax, Virginia
1980 Cheryl Prewitt, Ackerman, Mississippi
1981 Susan Powell, Elk City, Oklahoma
1982 Elizabeth Ward, Russellville, Arkansas
1983 Debra Sue Maffett, Anaheim, California

# THE DIRECTORY

## SOCIETIES AND ASSOCIATIONS

Information abstracted from listings in the 1983 *Encyclopedia of Associations*, which includes details on more than 16,000 organizations. Used by permission of the publisher, Gale Research Company, Book Tower, Detroit, Michigan 48226

**Academy of Applied Science,** Two White St., Concord, NH 03301; **Membership:** 300
**Academy of Motion Picture Arts and Science,** 8949 Wilshire Blvd., Beverly Hills, CA 90211; **Membership:** 4,413
**Academy of Political Science,** 2852 Broadway, New York, NY 10025; **Membership:** 10,500
**Actors' Equity Association,** 165 W. 46th St., New York, NY 10036; **Membership:** 30,000
**Adult Education Association of the U.S.A.,** 810 18th St., NW, Washington, DC 20006; **Membership:** 3,500
**Aerospace Industries Association of America,** 1725 De Sales St., NW, Washington, DC 20036; **Membership:** 58 companies
**African-American Institute,** 833 United Nations Plaza, New York, NY 10017
**AFS International/Intercultural Programs,** 313 East 43rd St., New York, NY 10017; **Membership:** 100,000
**Air Force Association,** 1750 Pennsylvania Ave., NW, Washington, DC 20006; **Membership:** 170,000
**Alcoholics Anonymous World Services,** P.O. Box 459, Grand Central Station, New York, NY 10163; **Membership:** 1,000,000
**Alternatives to Abortion International,** Hillcrest Hotel, Suite 511, 16th and Madison Sts., Toledo, OH 43699; **Membership:** 100,000
**Amateur Athletic Union of the United States,** 3400 West 86th St., Indianapolis, IN 46268; **Membership:** 60 regional groups
**America-Mideast Educational and Training Services (AMIDEAST),** 1717 Massachusetts Ave., NW, Washington, DC 20036
**American Academy of Arts and Letters,** 633 West 155th St., New York, NY 10032; **Membership:** 250
**American Academy of Arts and Sciences,** Norton's Woods, 136 Irving St., Cambridge, MA 02138; **Membership:** 2,300
**American Academy of Political and Social Sciences,** 3937 Chestnut St., Philadelphia, PA 19104; **Membership:** 10,500
**American Alliance for Health, Physical Education, Recreation and Dance,** 1900 Association Dr., Reston, VA 22091; **Membership:** 50,000
**American Anthropological Association,** 1703 New Hampshire Ave., NW, Washington, DC 20009; **Membership:** 10,000
**American Antiquarian Society,** 185 Salisbury St., Worcester, MA 01609; **Membership:** 375
**American Anti-Vivisection Society,** Noble Plaza, Suite 204, 801 Old York Rd., Jenkintown, PA 19046; **Membership:** 11,000
**American Arbitration Association,** 140 West 51st St., New York, NY 10020
**American Association for the Advancement of Science,** 1515 Massachusetts Ave., NW, Washington, DC 20005; **Membership:** 138,000
**American Association of Advertising Agencies,** 666 Third Ave., 13th Fl., New York, NY 10017; **Membership:** 534
**American Association of Blood Banks,** 1828 L St., NW, Washington, DC 20036; **Membership:** 9,000
**American Association of Community and Junior Colleges,** National Center for Higher Education, 1 Dupont Circle, No. 410, NW, Washington, DC 20036; **Membership:** 1,250
**American Association of Retired Persons,** 1909 K St., NW, Washington, DC 20049; **Membership:** 12,000,000
**American Association of University Professors,** 1 Dupont Circle, NW, Washington, DC 20036; **Membership:** 70,000
**American Association of University Women,** 2401 Virginia Ave., NW, Washington, DC 20037; **Membership:** 190,000
**American Astronomical Society,** % Dr. Peter B. Boyce, 1816 Jefferson Pl., NW, Washington, DC 20036; **Membership:** 3,800
**American Automobile Association,** 8111 Gatehouse Rd., Falls Church, VA 22047; **Membership:** 22,000,000
**American Bankers Association,** 1120 Connecticut Ave., NW, Washington, DC 20036; **Membership:** 13,588 banks and trust companies
**American Bar Association,** 1155 East 60th St., Chicago, IL 60637; **Membership:** 280,003
**American Bible Society,** 1865 Broadway, New York, NY 10023; **Membership:** 510,000
**American Camping Association,** Bradford Woods, Martinsville, IN 46151; **Membership:** 6,000
**American Cancer Society,** 777 Third Ave., New York, NY 10017; **Membership:** 2,500,000 with 58 divisions and 3,000 county units
**American Chemical Society,** 1155 16th St., NW, Washington, DC 20036; **Membership:** 122,000
**American Civil Liberties Union,** 132 W. 43rd St., New York, NY 10036; **Membership:** 250,000
**American Classical League,** Miami University, Oxford, OH 45056; **Membership:** 3,000
**American College of Hospital Administrators,** 840 N Lake Shore Dr., Chicago, IL 60611; **Membership:** 16,000
**American College of Physicians,** 4200 Pine St., Philadelphia, PA 19104; **Membership:** 54,000
**American College of Surgeons,** 55 E. Erie St., Chicago, IL 60611; **Membership:** 45,000
**American Contract Bridge League,** 2200 Democrat Rd., Memphis, TN 38116; **Membership:** 200,000 in 5,000 clubs
**American Council for the Arts,** 507 Seventh Ave., New York, NY 10018
**American Council on Education,** 1 Dupont Circle, NW, Washington, DC 20036; **Membership:** 1,632
**American Council for Judaism,** 307 Fifth Ave., New York, NY 10016; **Membership:** 20,000
**American Council of Learned Societies,** 800 Third Ave., New York, NY 10022; **Membership:** 43 organizations
**American Council of Life Insurance,** 1850 K St., NW, Washington, DC 20006; **Membership:** 530 companies
**American Council on Schools and Colleges,** 4009 Pacific Coast Hwy., #462, Torrance, CA 90505; **Membership:** 201
**American Council on the Teaching of Foreign Languages,** 385 Warburton Ave., Hastings-on-Hudson, NY 10706; **Membership:** 8,000
**American Dental Association,** 211 E. Chicago Ave., Chicago, IL 60611; **Membership:** 137,000 in 488 societies
**American Diabetes Association,** Two Park Ave., New York, NY 10016; **Membership:** 150,000 in 68 state organizations
**American Dietetic Association,** 430 N. Michigan Ave., Chicago, IL 60611; **Membership:** 45,000 in 52 state groups
**American Economic Foundation,** Liberty Village, Three Church St., Flemington, NJ 08822; **Membership:** 5,000
**American Farm Bureau Federation,** 225 Touhy Ave., Park Ridge, IL 60068; **Membership:** 3,297,224
**American Federation of Arts,** 41 E. 65th St., New York, NY 10021; **Membership:** 1,340
**American Federation of Labor and Congress of Industrial Organizations,** 815 16th St., NW, Washington, DC 20006; **Membership:** 13,600,000 in 105 organizations
**American Federation of Teachers,** 11 Dupont Circle, NW, Washington, DC 20036; **Membership:** 580,000
**American Federation of Television and Radio Artists,** 1350 Ave. of the Americas, New York, NY 10019; **Membership:** 40,000 in 38 locals
**American Forestry Association,** 1319 18th St., NW, Washington, DC 20036; **Membership:** 79,000
**American Friends Service Committee,** 1501 Cherry St., Philadelphia, PA 19102; **Membership:** 10 regional groups
**American Geographical Society,** Broadway at 156th St., New York, NY 10032; **Membership:** 1,000
**American Geological Institute,** 5205 Leesburg Pike, Falls Church, VA 22041; **Membership:** 18 societies
**American Geophysical Union,** 2000 Florida Ave., NW, Washington, DC 20009; **Membership:** 14,000
**American Geriatrics Society,** 10 Columbus Circle, New York, NY 10019; **Membership:** 8,000
**American Group Psychotherapy Association,** 1995 Broadway, 14th Floor, New York, NY 10023; **Membership:** 3,000 in 25 societies
**American Heart Association,** 7320 Greenville Ave., Dallas, TX 75231; **Membership:** 120,000 in 55 affiliates and 110 chapters
**American Historical Association,** 400 A St., SE, Washington, DC 20003; **Membership:** 14,500
**American Home Economics Association,** 2010 Massachusetts Ave., NW, Washington, DC 20036; **Membership:** 40,000 in 52 associations
**American Horse Shows Association,** 598 Madison Ave., New York, NY 10022; **Membership:** 19,675
**American Horticultural Society,** Mt. Vernon, VA 22121; **Membership:** 30,000

**American Hospital Association,** 840 N. Lake Shore Dr., Chicago, IL 60611; **Membership:** 38,328

**American Humane Association,** 9725 E. Hampden, Denver, CO 80231; **Membership:** 2,000,000 in 2,000 societies

**American Institute of Aeronautics and Astronautics,** 1290 Ave. of the Americas, New York, NY 10104; **Membership:** 32,336 in 68 sections and 115 student branches

**American Institute of Architects,** 1735 New York Ave., NW, Washington, DC 20006; **Membership:** 37,000

**American Institute of Biological Sciences,** 1401 Wilson Blvd., Arlington, VA 22209; **Membership:** 7,500

**American Institute of Certified Public Accountants,** 1211 Ave. of the Americas, New York, NY 10036; **Membership:** 170,000

**American Institute of Chemical Engineers,** 345 E. 47th St., New York, NY 10017; **Membership:** 53,000

**American Institute of Chemists,** 7315 Wisconsin Ave., NW, Washington, DC 20014; **Membership:** 5,000 in 25 state groups

**American Institute of Nutrition,** 9650 Rockville Pike, Bethesda, MD 20014; **Membership:** 2,000

**American Institute of Physics,** 335 E. 45th St., New York, NY 10017; **Membership:** nine national societies

**American Jewish Committee,** % Institute of Human Relations, 165 E. 56th St., New York, NY 10022; **Membership:** 40,000 in 80 chapters

**American Jewish Congress,** 15 E. 84th St., New York, NY 10028; **Membership:** 50,000 in 300 groups

**American Kennel Club,** 51 Madison Ave., New York, NY 10010; **Membership:** 422

**American Law Institute,** 4025 Chestnut St., Philadelphia, PA 19104; **Membership:** 2,500

**American Legion,** 700 N. Pennsylvania St., Indianapolis, IN 46206; **Membership:** 2,629,105 in 50 state departments

**American Legion Auxiliary,** 777 N. Meridian St., Indianapolis, IN 46204; **Membership:** 1,000,000

**American Library Association,** 50 E. Huron St., Chicago, IL 60611; **Membership:** 37,000

**American Lung Association,** 1740 Broadway, New York, NY 10019; **Membership:** 7,500

**American Management Associations,** 135 W. 50th St., New York, NY 10020; **Membership:** 91,000

**American Mathematical Society,** P.O. Box 6248, Providence, RI 02940; **Membership:** 19,000

**American Medical Association,** 535 N. Dearborn St., Chicago, IL 60610; **Membership:** 282,000

**American National Theatre and Academy,** 246 W. 44th St., New York, NY 10036

**American Newspaper Publishers Association,** 11600 Sunrise Valley Dr., Reston, VA 22091; **Membership:** 1,400 newspapers

**American Numismatic Association,** P.O. Box 2366, Colorado Springs, CO 80901; **Membership:** 37,000 individuals and 1,000 clubs

**American Numismatic Society,** 1814 Broadway betw. 155th and 156th St., New York, NY 10032; **Membership:** 2,065

**American Nurses' Association,** 2420 Pershing Rd., Kansas City, MO 64108; **Membership:** 165,000 in 53 state groups

**American Optometric Association,** 243 N. Lindbergh Blvd., St. Louis, MO 63141; **Membership:** 20,628

**American Ornithologists' Union,** National Museum of Natural History, Smithsonian Institution, Washington, DC 20560; **Membership:** 4,000

**American Osteopathic Association,** 212 E. Ohio St., Chicago, IL 60611; **Membership:** 14,739 in 54 state groups

**American Personnel and Guidance Association,** 2 Skyline Pl., Suite 400, 5203 Leesburg Pike, Falls Church, VA 22041; **Membership:** 39,000

**American Pharmaceutical Association,** 2215 Constitution Ave., NW, Washington, DC 20037; **Membership:** 56,000

**American Philatelic Society,** P.O. Box 800, State College, PA 16801; **Membership:** 51,000

**American Philological Association,** 617 Hamilton Hall, Columbia University, New York, NY 10027; **Membership:** 2,800

**American Philosophical Society,** 104 S. Fifth St., Philadelphia, PA 19106; **Membership:** 600

**American Physical Society,** 335 E. 45th St., New York, NY 10017; **Membership:** 32,663

**American Podiatry Association,** 20 Chevy Chase Circle, NW, Washington, DC 20015; **Membership:** 7,500 in 52 state groups

**American Political Science Association,** 1527 New Hampshire Ave., NW, Washington, DC 20036; **Membership:** 12,000

**American Power Boat Association,** 17640 E. Nine Mile Rd., East Detroit, MI 48021; **Membership:** 6,000 in 300 clubs

**American Psychiatric Association,** 1700 18th St., NW, Washington, DC 20009; **Membership:** 26,000

**American Psychoanalytic Association,** 1 E. 57th St., New York, NY 10022; **Membership:** 2,667

**American Psychological Association,** 1200 17th St., NW, Washington, DC 20036; **Membership:** 50,000

**American Public Health Association,** 1015 15th St., NW, Washington, DC 20005; **Membership:** 30,248

**American Radio Relay League,** 225 Main St., Newington, CT 06111; **Membership:** 169,000 in 2,100 clubs

**American Red Cross,** 17th and D Sts., NW, Washington, DC 20006; **Membership:** 60 divisions and 3,078 chapters

**American Social Health Association,** 260 Sheridan Ave., Suite 307, Palo Alto, CA 94306; **Membership:** 14,000

**American Society for the Prevention of Cruelty to Animals,** 441 E. 92nd St., New York, NY 10028; **Membership:** 15,000

**American Society of Civil Engineers,** 345 E. 47th St., New York, NY 10017; **Membership:** 80,000

**American Society of Composers, Authors, and Publishers,** 1 Lincoln Plaza, New York, NY 10023; **Membership:** 27,000

**American Society of Interior Designers,** 730 Fifth Ave., New York, NY 10019; **Membership:** 13,000 in 46 chapters

**American Society of Mechanical Engineers,** 345 E. 47th St., New York, NY 10017; **Membership:** 103,918 in 176 local groups

**American Society of Newspaper Editors,** Box 551, 1350 Sullivan Trail, Easton, PA 18042; **Membership:** 900

**American Society of Travel Agents,** 711 Fifth Ave., New York, NY 10022; **Membership:** 17,000 worldwide

**American Sociological Association,** 1772 N St., NW, Washington, DC 20036; **Membership:** 14,000

**American Speech-Language-Hearing Association,** 10801 Rockville Pike, Rockville, MD 20852; **Membership:** 35,000

**American Statistical Association,** 806 15th St., NW, Suite 640, Washington, DC 20005; **Membership:** 14,000

**American Thoracic Society,** 1740 Broadway, New York, NY 10019; **Membership:** 8,200

**American Trucking Associations,** 1616 P St., NW, Washington, DC 20036; **Membership:** 51 organizations

**American Veterans Committee,** 1346 Connecticut Ave., NW, Washington, DC 20036; **Membership:** 25,000

**American Veterinary Medical Association,** 930 N. Meacham Rd., Schaumburg, IL 60196; **Membership:** 35,000

**American Youth Hostels,** 1332 I St., NW, Suite 800, Washington, DC 20005; **Membership:** 100,000 in 32 local councils

**Americans for Democratic Action,** 1411 K St., NW, Washington, DC 20005; **Membership:** 65,000 in 20 state groups

**Amnesty International, U.S. Affiliate,** 304 W. 58th St., New York, NY 10019; **Membership:** 12,000

**AMVETS,** 4647 Forbes Blvd., Lanham, MD 20801; **Membership:** 200,000

**Ancient Order of Hibernians in America,** Box 700, Riverdale Station, Bronx, NY 10471; **Membership:** 191,000

**Anti-Defamation League of B'nai B'rith,** 823 United Nations Plaza, New York, NY 10017

**Appalachian Mountain Club,** 5 Joy St., Boston, MA 02108; **Membership:** 25,000

**Archaeological Institute of America,** 53 Park Place, Eighth Fl., New York, NY 10007; **Membership:** 7,500

**Army and Navy Union, U.S.A.,** P.O. Box 537, 1391 Main St., Lakemore, OH 44250; **Membership:** 9,000

**Arthritis Foundation,** 3400 Peachtree Rd., NE, Atlanta, GA 30326; **Membership:** 71 chapters

**Association for the Study of Afro-American Life and History,** 1401 14th St., NW, Washington, DC 20005; **Membership:** 30,000

**Association of American Colleges,** 1818 R St., NW, Washington, DC 20009; **Membership:** 630 institutions

**Association on American Indian Affairs,** 432 Park Ave. S., New York, NY 10016

**Association of American Railroads,** American Railroads Bldg., 1920 L St., NW, Washington, DC 20036; **Membership:** 229

**Association of American Universities,** 1 Dupont Circle, NW, Suite 730, Washington, DC 20036; **Membership:** 50 university presidents

**Association of Chairmen of Departments of Mechanics,** % M.E. Raville, School of Engineering Science and Mechanics, Georgia Inst. of Technology, Atlanta, GA 30332; **Membership:** 98

**Association of Computer Programmers and Analysts,** 11800 Sunrise Valley Dr., Suite 808, Reston, VA 22091; **Membership:** 1,000

**Association of Governing Boards of Universities and Colleges,** 1 Dupont Circle, NW, Suite 400, Washington, DC 20036; **Membership:** 24,000

**Association of Junior Leagues,** 825 Third Ave., New York, NY 10022; **Membership:** 140,000 in 248 leagues

**Audit Bureau of Circulations,** 900 Meacham Rd., Schaumburg, IL 60195; **Membership:** 5,000

**Authors League of America,** 234 W. 44th St., New York, NY 10036; **Membership:** 10,000

**Benevolent and Protective Order of Elks,** 2750 Lake View Ave., Chicago, IL 60614; **Membership:** 1,650,000 in 2,250 lodges

**Big Brothers/Big Sisters of America,** 117 S. 17th St., Suite 1200, Philadelphia, PA 19103; **Membership:** 425 local agencies

**Blue Cross Association,** 676 St. Clair, Chicago, IL 60611; **Membership:** 78 Blue Cross plans

**Blue Shield Association,** 676 St. Clair, Chicago, IL 60611; **Membership:** 74 medical plans

**B'nai B'rith International,** 1640 Rhode Island Ave., NW, Washington, DC 20036; **Membership:** 500,000 in 3,500 groups

**Boys' Clubs of America,** 771 First Ave., New York, NY 10017; **Membership:** 1,000,000

**Boy Scouts of America,** P.O. Box 61030, Dallas/Ft. Worth Airport, Dallas, TX 75261; **Membership:** 4,326,000 scouts and adult leaders

**Brand Names Foundation,** 470 Park Ave., No. 7D, New York, NY 10022; **Membership:** 400

**Brookings Institution,** 1775 Massachusetts Ave., NW, Washington, DC 20036

**Camp Fire, Inc.,** 4601 Madison Ave., Kansas City, MO 64112; **Membership:** 500,000

**CARE (Cooperative for American Relief Everywhere),** 660 First Ave., New York, NY 10016; **Membership:** 28 agencies

**Catholic Daughters of America,** 10 W. 71st St., New York, NY 10023; **Membership:** 170,000 in 48 state groups

**Catholic War Veterans of U.S.A.,** 2 Massachusetts Ave., NW, Washington, DC 20001; **Membership:** 50,000

**CCCO, An Agency for Military and Draft Counseling,** 2208 South St., Philadelphia, PA 19146

**Chamber of Commerce of the United States,** 1615 H St., NW, Washington, DC 20062; **Membership:** 4,000 chambers of commerce and trade associations, 200,000 business firms

**Chautauqua Literary and Scientific Circle,** Chautauqua, NY 14722; **Membership:** 1,100

**Child Welfare League of America,** 67 Irving Pl, New York, NY 10003

**College Entrance Examination Board,** 888 Seventh Ave., New York, NY 10106; **Membership:** 2,692 colleges, universities, secondary schools, school systems and educational associations

**Colonial Dames XVII Century, National Society,** 1300 New Hampshire Ave., NW, Washington, DC 20036; **Membership:** 11,003

**Committee for Economic Development,** 477 Madison Ave., New York, NY 10022; **Membership:** 200 trustees

**Common Cause,** 2030 M St., NW, Washington, DC 20036; **Membership:** 225,000

**The Conference Board,** 845 Third Ave., New York, NY 10022; **Membership:** 4,000 organizations

**Conference on Jewish Material Claims against Germany,** 15 E. 26th St., New York, NY 10010; **Member Organizations:** 22

**CORE (Congress of Racial Equality),** 1916-38 Park Ave., New York, NY 10037

**Cooperative League of the U.S.A.,** 1828 L St., NW, Washington, DC 20036; **Membership:** 160 organizations

**Correspondence Chess League of America,** 4606 Wisteria Ct., Decatur, IL 62526; **Membership:** 1,400

**Council for the Advancement and Support of Education,** 11 Dupont Circle, NW, Washington, DC 20036; **Membership:** 10,500

**Council of Better Business Bureaus,** 1515 Wilson Blvd., Arlington, VA 22209; **Membership:** 1,000 in 167 member bureaus

**Council on Foreign Relations,** 58 E. 68th St., New York, NY 10021; **Membership:** 2,031 in 37 local groups

**Council of Graduate Schools in the United States,** 1 Dupont Circle, NW, Washington, DC 20036; **Membership:** 360

**Council on International Educational Exchange,** 205 E. 42nd St., New York, NY 10017; **Membership:** 168 North American institutions

**Country Music Association,** P.O. Box 22299, 7 Music Circle N., Nashville, TN 37203; **Membership:** 6,000

**Credit Union National Association, Inc.,** P.O. Box 431, Madison, WI 53701; **Membership:** 52 state groups

**Daughters of the American Revolution, National Society,** 1776 D St., NW, Washington, DC 20006; **Membership:** 208,000

**Day Care Council of America,** 1602 17th St., NW, Washington, DC 20036; **Membership:** 5,000

**Democratic National Committee,** 1625 Massachusetts Ave., NW, Washington, DC 20036; **Membership:** 360

**Disabled American Veterans,** 3725 Alexandria Pike, Cold Spring, KY 41076; **Membership:** 700,000

**Dramatists Guild,** 234 W. 44th St., New York, NY 10036

**Ecological Society of America,** Office of the Chief, Illinois Natural History Survey, 607 E. Peabody, Champaign, IL 61820; **Membership:** 6,200

**English-Speaking Union of the United States,** 16 E. 69th St., New York, NY 10021; **Membership:** 30,000

**Entomological Society of America,** 4603 Calvert Rd., College Park, MD 20740; **Membership:** 7,500

**Environmental Action,** 1346 Connecticut Ave., NW, Suite 731, Washington, DC 20036; **Membership:** 23,000

**Epilepsy Foundation of America,** 4351 Garden City Dr., Landover, MD 20781; **Membership:** 161 affiliates in 50 states

**Experiment in International Living,** United States Headquarters, Brattleboro, VT 05301; **Membership:** national offices in over 60 other countries and 7 regional U.S. offices

**Eye-Bank for Sight Restoration,** 210 E. 64th St., New York, NY 10021

**Federation of American Scientists,** 307 Massachusetts Ave., NE, Washington, DC 20002; **Membership:** 5,000

**Fellowship of Reconciliation,** Box 271, Nyack, NY 10960; **Membership:** 29,000 in 66 groups

**Fleet Reserve Association,** 1303 New Hampshire Ave., NW, Washington, DC 20036; **Membership:** 150,000

**Foreign Policy Association,** 205 Lexington Ave., New York, NY 10016

**Foster Parents Plan,** 155 Plan Way, Warwick, RI 02887

**Garden Club of America,** 598 Madison Ave., New York, NY 10022; **Membership:** 14,000

**General Federation of Women's Clubs,** 1734 N St., NW, Washington, DC 20036; **Membership:** 10,000,000 in 46 countries

**General Society of Mayflower Descendants,** 4 Winslow St., Plymouth, MA 02360; **Membership:** 20,000 in 52 state groups

**Gideons International,** 2900 Lebanon Road, Nashville, TN 37214; **Membership:** 70,000 in 130 countries

**Girl Scouts of the U.S.A.,** 830 Third Ave., New York, NY 10022; **Membership:** 2,829,000 in 336 local groups

**Girls Clubs of America,** 205 Lexington Ave., New York, NY 10016; **Membership:** 220,000

**Grand Aerie, Fraternal Order of Eagles,** 2401 W. Wisconsin Ave., Milwaukee, WI 53233; **Membership:** 695,500 in 50 state groups

**Group Health Association of America,** 624 Ninth St., NW, Suite 700, Washington, DC 20001; **Membership:** 1,000

**Guide Dog Foundation for the Blind, Inc.,** 109-19 72nd Ave., Forest Hills, NY 11375

**Hadassah, the Women's Zionist Organization of America,** 50 W. 58th St., New York, NY 10019; **Membership:** 370,000 in 1,600 chapters and groups

**Helicopter Association International,** 1110 Vermont Ave., NW, Suite 430, Washington, DC 20005; **Membership:** 900 firms

**Humane Society of the United States,** 2100 L St., NW, Washington, DC 20037; **Membership:** 40,000

**Imperial Council of the Ancient Arabic Order of Nobles of the Mystic Shrine,** 2900 Rocky Point Dr., Tampa, FL 33607; **Membership:** 1,000,000

**Independent Order of Odd Fellows,** 16 W. Chase St., Baltimore, MD 21201; **Membership:** 653,664

**Indian Rights Association,** 1505 Race St., Philadelphia, PA 19102; **Membership:** 2,500

**Information Industry Association,** 316 Pennsylvania Ave., SE, Suite 400, Washington, DC 20003; **Membership:** 150 companies

**Institute of International Education,** 809 United Nations Plaza, New York, NY 10017

**Innternational Air Transport Association,** 2000 Peel St., Suite 200, Montreal, PQ, Canada H3A 2R4; **Membership:** 111 airlines

**International College of Surgeons,** 1516 Lake Shore Dr., Chicago, IL 60610; **Membership:** 12,000

**International Council of Associations of Surfing,** P.O. Box 2622, Newport Beach, CA 92663; **Membership:** 76 member nations

**International Game Fish Association,** 3000 E. Las Olas Blvd., Fort Lauderdale, FL 33316; **Membership:** 15,000

**International Student Service,** 291 Broadway, New York, NY 10007; **Membership:** 190 local groups

**Italian American War Veterans of the U.S.,** % Ugo Del Gizzo, 201 Norwood Ave., Warwick, RI 02888; **Membership:** 8,500 in 110 posts

**Izaak Walton League of America,** 1800 N. Kent St., Suite 806, Arlington, VA 22209; **Membership:** 50,000

**Jewish War Veterans of the U.S.A.,** 1712 New Hampshire Ave., NW, Washington, DC 20009; **Membership:** 105,000

**Junior Achievement,** 550 Summer St., Stamford, CT 06901; **Membership:** 400,000

**JWB,** 15 E. 26th St., New York, NY 10010; **Membership:** 375 Jewish community centers and YM-YWHAs

**Kiwanis International,** 101 E. Erie St., Chicago, IL 60611; **Membership:** 300,000 in 8,000 clubs

**Knights of Columbus,** Columbus Plaza, New Haven, CT 06507; **Membership:** 1,349,724

**Knights of Pythias,** Pythian Bldg., Rm. 201, 47 N. Grant St., Stockton, CA 95202; **Membership:** 117,417 in 55 domains

**Knights Templar of the U.S.A.,** 14 E. Jackson Blvd., Suite 1700, Chicago, IL 60604; **Membership:** 350,000

**League of Women Voters of the U.S.,** 1730 M St., NW, Washington, DC 20036; **Membership:** 125,000 in 1,350 leagues

**Leukemia Society of America, Inc.,** 800 Second Ave., New York, NY 10017; **Membership:** 52 local groups

**Lions Clubs International,** 300 22nd, Oak Brook, IL 60570; **Membership:** 1,350,000

**Little League Baseball,** Williamsport, PA 17701; **Membership:** 2,500,000

**Loyal Order of Moose,** Mooseheart, IL 60539; **Membership:** 1,767,914 in 4,209 lodges and chapters

**March of Dimes Birth Defects Foundation,** 1275 Mamaroneck Ave., White Plains, NY 10605

**Marine Corps League,** 933 N. Kenmore St., Suite 321, Arlington, VA 22201; **Membership:** 25,000

**Masonic Service Association of the U.S.,** 8120 Fenton St., Silver Spring, MD 20910; **Membership:** 43 grand lodges

**Mensa,** 1701 W. 3d St., Brooklyn, NY 11223; **Membership:** 50,000 in 125 groups

**Mental Health Association,** 1800 N. Kent St., Rosslyn, VA 22209; **Membership:** 850 local, 47 state groups

**Modern Language Association of America,** 62 Fifth Ave., New York, NY 10011; **Membership:** 28,000

**Modern Woodmen of America,** 1701 First Ave., Rock Island, IL 61201; **Membership:** 510,000 in 1,000 local groups

**Motor Vehicle Manufacturers Association of the United States,** 300 New Center Bldg., Detroit, MI 48202; **Membership:** 11 manufacturers

**Muscular Dystrophy Associations of America, Inc.,** 810 Seventh Ave., New York, NY 10019; **Membership:** 28,000 in 203 chapters

**National Academy of Television Arts and Sciences,** 110 W. 57th St., New York, NY 10019; **Membership:** 12,000

**National Aeronautic Association,** 821 15th St., NW, Washington, DC 20005; **Membership:** 160,000

**National Amputation Foundation,** 12-45 150th St., Whitestone, NY 11357; **Membership:** 5,200 veterans

**National Association for Hearing and Speech Action,** 10801 Rockville Pike, Rockville, MD 20852; **Membership:** 2,000

**National Association for Retarded Citizens,** 2501 Ave. J, Arlington, TX 76011; **Membership:** 200,000 in 2,000 local groups

**National Association for Stock Car Auto Racing,** 1801 Volusia Ave., Daytona Beach, FL 32015; **Membership:** 18,000

**National Association for the Advancement of Colored People,** 1790 Broadway, New York, NY 10019; **Membership:** 500,000

**National Association of Broadcasters,** 1771 N St., NW, Washington, DC 20036; **Membership:** 6,337

**National Association of Colored Women's Clubs,** 5808 16th St., NW, Washington, DC 20011; **Membership:** 45,000

**National Association of Intercollegiate Athletics,** 1221 Baltimore, Kansas City, MO 64106; **Membership:** 520 members and 31 groups

**National Association of Manufacturers,** 1776 F St., NW, Washington, DC 20006; **Membership:** 12,000

**National Association of Negro Business and Professional Women's Clubs,** 1806 New Hampshire Ave., NW, Washington, DC 20009; **Membership:** 10,000 in 300 groups

**National Association of Social Workers,** 1425 H St., NW, Washington, DC 20005; **Membership:** 90,000

**National Association of State Universities and Land Grant Colleges,** 1 Dupont Circle, NW, Suite 710, Washington, DC 20036; **Membership:** 140 colleges and universities

**National Association of Theatre Owners,** 1560 Broadway, New York, NY 10036; **Membership:** 8,000

**National Audubon Society,** 950 Third Ave., New York, NY 10022; **Membership:** 450,000 plus 463 affiliated groups

**National Automobile Dealers Association,** 8400 Westpark Dr., McLean, VA 22101; **Membership:** 20,000

**National Board of Review of Motion Pictures,** P.O. Box 589, New York, NY 10021; **Membership:** 5,000

**National Braille Association,** 645A Godwin Ave., Midland Park, NJ 07432; **Membership:** 2,700

**National Campers and Hikers Association, Inc.,** 7172 Transit Rd., Buffalo, NY 14221; **Membership:** 200,000

**National Catholic Educational Association,** 1 Dupont Circle, NW, Suite 350, Washington, DC 20036; **Membership:** 14,000

**National Civil Service League,** 6001 Montrose Rd., Suite 207, Rockville, MD 20852; **Membership:** 3,000

**National Collegiate Athletic Association,** Nall Ave. At 63rd St., PO Box 1906, Shawnee Mission, KS 66222; **Membership:** 905 colleges and allied organizations

**National Conference of Catholic Charities,** 1346 Connecticut Ave., NW, Washington, DC 20036; **Membership:** 4,000

**National Conference of Christians and Jews,** 43 W. 57th St., New York, NY 10019; **Membership:** 80 regional groups

**National Conference on Social Welfare,** 1730 M St., N.W., Suite 911, Washington, DC 20036; **Membership:** 4,500

**National Congress of American Indians,** 202 E. St., N.E., Washington, DC 20002; **Membership:** representing 600,000 Indians

**National Council of Churches of Christ in the U.S.A.,** 475 Riverside Dr., New York, NY 10115; **Membership:** 40,191,346 in 32 denominations

**National Council of Farmer Cooperatives,** 1800 Massachusetts Ave., NW, Washington, DC 20036; **Membership:** 150 cooperative associations

**National Council of Jewish Women,** 15 E. 26th St., New York, NY 10010; **Membership:** 100,000

**National Council of Negro Women,** 1819 H St., NW, Washington, DC 20006; **Membership:** 4,000,000 in 200 local groups within 27 national affiliated organizations

**National Council of State Garden Clubs,** 4401 Magnolia Ave., St. Louis, MO 63110; **Membership:** 365,680

**National Council of Women of the United States,** 777 UN Plaza, New York, NY 10017

**National Council on the Aging,** 600 Maryland Ave., SW, West Wing 100, Washington, DC 20024; **Membership:** 3,800

**National Council on Crime and Delinquency,** Continental Plaza, 411 Hackensack Ave., Hackensack, NJ 07601; **Membership:** 11,000

**National Democratic Club,** 52 E. 41st St., New York, NY 10017; **Membership:** 1,200

**National Easter Seal Society,** 2023 W. Ogden Ave., Chicago, IL 60612

**National Education Association,** 1201 16th St., NW, Washington, DC 20036; **Membership:** 1,600,800; 53 state and 10,000 local affiliated groups

**National Farmers Union (Farmers Educational and Cooperative Union of America),** PO Box 39251, Denver, CO 80251; **Membership:** 300,000 farm families in 3,000 groups

**National Federation of the Blind,** 1800 Johnson St., Baltimore, MD 21230; **Membership:** 50,000

**National Federation of Business and Professional Women's Clubs,** 2012 Massachusetts Ave., NW, Washington, DC 20036; **Membership:** 160,000

**National Federation of Music Clubs,** 1336 N. Delaware St., Indianapolis, IN 46202; **Membership:** 500,000 in 4,500 clubs

**National 4-H Council,** 7100 Connecticut Ave., Chevy Chase, MD 20815

**National Genealogical Society,** 1921 Sunderland Pl., NW, Washington, DC 20036; **Membership:** 6,000

**National Geographic Society,** 17th & M Sts. NW, Washington, DC 20036; **Membership:** 10,700,000

**National Grange,** 1616 H St., NW, Washington, DC 20006; **Membership:** 475,000 in 5,500 groups

**National Hairdressers and Cosmetologists Assoc., Inc.,** 3510 Olive St., St. Louis, MO 63103; **Membership:** 58,000

**National Health Council, Inc.,** 70 W. 40th St., New York, NY 10018; **Membership:** 80 organizations

**National Institute of Social Sciences,** 150 Amsterdam Ave., New York, NY 10023; **Membership:** 600

**National League of Cities,** 1301 Pennsylvania Ave., NW, Washington, DC 20004; **Membership:** 990 municipal governments in 48 states

**National Legal Aid and Defender Association,** 1625 K St., NW, Washington, DC 20006; **Membership:** 2,600 offices and organizations

**National Medical Association,** 1301 Pennsylvania Ave., NW, Suite 310, Washington, DC 20004; **Membership:** 9,500

**National Multiple Sclerosis Society,** 205 E. 42nd St., New York, NY 10017; **Membership:** 450,000 in 142 chapters

**National Municipal League,** 47 E. 68th St., New York, NY 10021; **Membership:** 6,500

**National Newspaper Publishers Association,** 770 National Press Bldg., Washington, DC 20045; **Membership:** 161 publishers

**National Organization for Women (NOW),** Suite 1048, 425 13th St., NW, Washington, DC 20004; **Membership:** 130,000

**National Parks and Conservation Association,** 1701 18th St., NW, Washington, DC 20009; **Membership:** 33,000

**National Press Club,** National Press Bldg., 529 14th St., NW, Room 1386, Washington, DC 20045; **Membership:** 4,734

**National PTA,** 700 N. Rush St., Chicago, IL 60611; **Membership:** 5,893,047

**National Railway Historical Society,** P.O. Box 2051, Philadelphia, PA 19103; **Membership:** 10,000

**National Rifle Association of America,** 1600 Rhode Island Ave., NW, Washington, DC 20036; **Membership:** 2,100,000

**National Safety Council,** 444 N. Michigan Ave., Chicago, IL 60611; **Membership:** 15,000

**National Small Business Association,** 1604 K St., NW, Washington, DC 20036; **Membership:** 50,000

**National Society to Prevent Blindness,** 79 Madison Ave., New York, NY 10016; **Membership:** 355

**National Tax Association-Tax Institute of America,** 21 E. State St., Columbus, OH 43215; **Membership:** 2,100

**National Urban League,** 500 E. 62nd St., New York, NY 10021; **Membership:** 50,000 in 118 local groups

**National Wildlife Federation,** 1412 16th St., NW, Washington, DC 20036; **Membership:** 4,600,000

**National Woman's Christian Temperance Union,** 1730 Chicago Ave., Evanston, IL 60201; **Membership:** 250,000

**Newspaper Guild, The,** 1125 15th St., NW, Washington, DC 20005; **Membership:** 32,000 in 81 locals

**Optimist International,** 4494 Lindell Blvd., St. Louis, MO 63108; **Membership:** 135,000

**Order of AHEPA (American Hellenic Educational Progressive Association),** 1422 K St., NW, Washington, DC 20005; **Membership:** 50,000 in 500 groups

**Order of the Eastern Star, General Grand Chapter,** 1618 New Hampshire Ave., NW, Washington, DC 20009; **Membership:** 2,500,000

**Overseas Press Club of America,** 52 E. 41st St., New York, NY 10017; **Membership:** 1,600

**Parkinson's Disease Foundation,** William Black Medical Research Bldg., Columbia Presbyterian Medical Center, 640 W. 168th St., New York, NY 10032

**P.E.N. American Center,** 47 Fifth Ave., New York, NY 10003

**Photographic Society of America,** 2005 Walnut St., Philadelphia, PA 19103; **Membership:** 18,700

**Planned Parenthood Federation of America,** 810 Seventh Ave., New York, NY 10019; **Membership:** 188 organizations

**Polish Legion of American Veterans, U.S.A.,** 3024 N. Laramie Ave., Chicago, IL 60641; **Membership:** 15,000 in 114 posts

**Public Relations Society of America,** 845 Third Ave., New York, NY 10022; **Membership:** 10,000 executives

**Puppeteers of America,** 2311 Connecticut Ave. N.W., Washington, DC 20008; **Membership:** 2,800 in 34 guilds

**Republican National Committee,** 310 First St., SE, Washington, DC 20003; **Membership:** 162

**Rotary International,** 1600 Ridge Ave., Evanston, IL 60201; **Membership:** 874,000

**Screen Actors Guild,** 7750 Sunset Blvd., Hollywood, CA 90046; **Membership:** 50,000

**Sierra Club,** 530 Bush St., San Francisco, CA 94108; **Membership:** 225,000

**Society for the Advancement of Education,** 1860 Broadway, New York, NY 10023; **Membership:** 3,000

**Society of Automotive Engineers,** 400 Commonwealth Dr., Warrendale, PA 15096; **Membership:** 35,866 in 53 groups

**Society of the Cincinnati,** 2118 Massachusetts Ave., NW, Washington, DC 20008; **Membership:** 2,800 in 14 groups

**Sons of the American Revolution, National Society,** 1000 S. Fourth St., Louisville, KY 40203; **Membership:** 21,477

**Soroptimist International of the Americas, Inc.,** 1616 Walnut St., Philadelphia, PA 19103; **Membership:** 35,000 in 1,130 groups

**Southern Christian Leadership Conference,** 334 Auburn Ave., NE, Atlanta, GA 30312; **Membership:** 80 chapters

**Speech Communication Association,** 5105 E. Backlick Rd., Annandale, VA 22003; **Membership:** 8,750

**Sports Car Club of America,** 6750 S. Emporia St., Englewood, CO 80112; **Membership:** 24,000

**Supreme Council, Ancient Accepted Scottish Rite of Freemasonry, Northern Jurisdiction,** 33 Marrett Rd., Lexington, MA 02173; **Membership:** 502,000 in 112 groups

**Supreme Council 33°, Ancient Accepted Scottish Rite of Freemasonry, Southern Jurisdiction,** 1733 16th St. NW, Washington DC 20009; **Membership:** 660,000

**Transportation Association of America,** 1100 17th St., NW, Washington, DC 20036; **Membership:** 800

**UNICEF,** 331 E. 38th St., New York, NY 10016; **Membership:** 90

**United Cerebral Palsy Associations,** 66 E. 34th St., New York, NY 10016; **Membership:** 277 affiliates

**United Daughters of the Confederacy,** 328 North Blvd., Richmond, VA 23220; **Membership:** 30,000

**United Jewish Appeal, Inc.,** 1290 Ave. of the Americas, New York, NY 10104; **Membership:** 8 regional groups

**United Nations Association of the United States of America,** 300 E. 42nd St., New York, NY 10017; **Membership:** 26,000 in 200 chapters

**United Negro College Fund,** 500 E. 62nd St., New York, NY 10021; **Membership:** 41 private accredited four-year colleges; 2 graduate and professional schools

**USO (United Service Organizations),** 1146 19th St., NW, Washington, DC 20036

**United States Catholic Conference,** 1312 Massachusetts Ave., NW, Washington, DC 20005

**United States Independent Telephone Association,** 1801 K St., NW, Washington, DC 20006; **Membership:** 1,551

**United States Jaycees, The,** 4 W. 21st St., P.O. Box 7, Tulsa, OK 74121; **Membership:** 300,000 in 51 state groups

**United States Olympic Committee,** 1750 E. Boulder St., Colorado Springs, CO 80909; **Membership:** 52

**United States Power Squadrons,** P.O. Box 30423, Raleigh, NC 27622; **Membership:** 60,000

**United States Space Education Association,** 746 Turnpike Rd., Elizabethtown, PA 17022; **Membership:** 400

**United States Student Association,** 1220 G St., SE, Washington, DC 20003; **Membership:** 400 colleges and universities

**United Way of America,** 801 N. Fairfax St., Alexandria, VA 22314; **Membership:** 1,264

**Variety Clubs International,** 58 W. 58th St., Suite 23-C, New York, NY 10019; **Membership:** 11,000 in 44 groups

**Veterans of Foreign Wars of the U.S.A.,** V.F.W. Bldg., Kansas City, MO 64111; **Membership:** 1,950,000 in 10,000 groups; ladies auxiliary numbers 643,000 in 7,000 groups

**Volunteers of America,** 3939 N. Causeway Blvd., Suite 202, Metairie, LA 70002; **Membership:** 44 state groups

**Wilderness Society,** 1901 Pennsylvania Ave., NW, Washington, DC 20006; **Membership:** 50,000

**Wildlife Society, The,** 5410 Grosvenor Ln., Bethesda, MD 20814; **Membership:** 8,000

**Women Strike for Peace,** 145 S. 13th St., Philadelphia, PA 19107

**Women's American ORT (Organization for Rehabilitation through Training),** 1250 Broadway, New York, NY 10001; **Membership:** 145,000 in 1,250 chapters

**Women's International League for Peace and Freedom,** 1213 Race St., Philadelphia, PA 19107; **Membership:** 110 branches

**Workmen's Benefit Fund of the U.S.A.,** Drawer 73, One Old Country Rd., Carle Place, NY 11514; **Membership:** 34,000 in 108 groups

**Workmen's Circle,** 45 E. 33rd St., New York, NY 10016; **Membership:** 60,000 in 310 groups

**World Future Society,** 4916 St. Elmo Ave., Bethesda, MD 20814; **Membership:** 40,000 in 80 groups

**World Population Society,** 1337 Connecticut Ave., NW, Suite 200, Washington, DC 20006; **Membership:** 1,100

**Writers Guild of America, East,** 555 W. 57th St., New York, NY 10019; **Membership:** 2,500

**Writers Guild of America, West,** 8955 Beverly Blvd., Los Angeles, CA 90048; **Membership:** 5,900

**Young Democrats of America,** ℅ Democratic National Committee, 1625 Massachusetts Ave., NW, Washington, DC 20036; **Membership:** 200,000 in 2,000 groups

**Young Men's and Young Women's Hebrew Association,** 1395 Lexington Ave., New York, NY 10028; **Membership:** 9,000

**Young Men's Christian Associations of the U.S.A.,** 101 N. Wacker Dr., Chicago, IL 60606; **Membership:** 10,000,000 in 1,842 associations

**Young Republican National Federation,** 310 First St, SE, Washington, DC 20003; **Membership:** 300,000 in 4,000 groups

**Young Women's Christian Association of the U.S.A.,** 600 Lexington Ave., New York, NY 10022; **Membership:** 2,416,882 in 4,609 local groups

**Zionist Organization of America,** 4 E. 34th St., New York, NY 10016; **Membership:** 150,000 in 600 groups

# RELIGION: FAITHS/FOLLOWERS

## MAJOR WORLD RELIGIONS

### JUDAISM

The religion of the Jewish people is the world's oldest great monotheism and the parent religion of both Christianity and Islam. The name derives from the Latin *Judaeus* and the Hebrew *Yehudhi,* meaning *descendant of Judah,* who was the fourth son of Jacob.

The founder of Judaism was Abraham, who lived about 1500 B.C. and made a covenant with God that he and his descendants, as the Chosen People, would carry the message of one God to the world. The new nation was given structure by Moses, who in the 13th century B.C. led the Israelites out of slavery in Egypt, received the Ten Commandments from God on Mt. Horeb (Sinai), and brought his people to the edge of the land of Canaan, which had been promised to Abraham as part of the covenant.

Once in the Promised Land, the Israelites built a temple, established a priesthood, and began offering sacrifices in accordance with the teachings of Moses—practices that survived the 6th-century Babylonian Exile. But in A.D. 70, when the temple in Jerusalem was destroyed by the Roman army, sacrificial worship was supplanted by study and prayers in synagogues.

Although Judaism has no specific creeds, its sacred writings consist of laws, prophecies, and traditions that reflect 3,500 years of spiritual experience. The principal text is the Torah, or Pentateuch, which consists of the first five books of the Bible. The rest of the Hebrew Bible, known to Christians as the Old Testament, includes the Psalms and writings of the major and minor prophets.

Another authoritative work is the Talmud, a collection of laws that includes the Mishna, a Hebrew compilation of the Oral Law (in Hebrew), and the Gemara, a collection of comments (in Aramaic) on the Mishna by rabbis. There are actually two Talmuds, one that emanated from Palestine in the 5th century and one from Babylonia a century later.

The basis of Judaism is belief in the living God who is transcendent, omnipotent, and just, and who reveals himself to mankind. The faith rests on the words of Deuteronomy 6:4: "Hear, O Israel, the Lord our God, the Lord is One."

For Jews the oneness of God implies the brotherhood of men, and religious knowledge is considered inseparable from the ethical injunction "to do justly, and love mercy, and to walk humbly with thy God." Judaism's elaborate system of laws and rituals, such as dietary regulations, is designed to give sacred meaning to every aspect of daily life.

Jews have an ordained clergy and observe the Sabbath, which runs from sunset Friday to sunset Saturday and is observed with services of prayer and readings in local synagogues. Major festivals include Pesach (Passover, celebrating the Exodus), Shabuoth (Pentecost), Rosh Hashana (New Year), Yom Kippur (Day of Atonement), and Sukkoth (Feast of Tabernacles).

Judaism has generated numerous internal sects and movements, including the Sadducees and Pharisees during the early Christian era. In the 12th century, Maimonides tried to relate Judaism to Western philosophy, especially that of Aristotle. Modern religious movements developed from Moses Mendelssohn, a rationalist of the 18th-century Enlightenment, and Hasidism, which preaches piety and mysticism.

Present-day American Judaism is divided among three major denominations. The Orthodox stresses strict adherence to the Torah. Reform Jews, in the tradition of Mendelssohn, have repudiated legalism and emphasize the compatibility of Judaism with secular liberal values. Conservative Judaism reflects a middle road—acceptance of the Torah but also a willingness to adapt it to modern conditions. In recent years a Reconstructionist movement, which was originated by Mordecai M. Kaplan and developed out of the Conservative wing, has stressed Judaism as an evolving religious civilization.

Since the destruction of their nation in A.D. 70, Jews have dreamed of once again having their own state. The first Zionist Congress was held (1897) in Basle and, in the wake of the Nazi holocaust that took the lives of six million Jews, the State of Israel came into being in 1948. Although the religious significance of the state's existence is not yet clear, the Six-Day War of 1967 nonetheless made many non-Israeli Jews realize how closely they are involved with Israel both in their cultural and religious lives.

#### MOSES (c. 1350–1250 B.C.)

*According to Biblical accounts, the great lawgiver of Jewish monotheism was born probably in Egypt to slave parents, Amram and Jochebed, of the tribe of Levi. Because of an Egyptian law requiring newborn male Hebrew children to be killed, his mother is said to have hid him in a basket among the reeds of the Nile River. Found by one of Pharaoh's daughters, he was raised by her with Jochebed as his nurse.*

*As a young man Moses became interested in the cause of his people and had to flee to Midian after slaying an Egyptian whom he had discovered beating a Hebrew. Finding refuge as a shepherd for Jethro, a local priest, Moses married his daughter Zipporah.*

*While tending sheep one day at Mt. Horeb, Moses had a vision of God in a bush that burned but was not consumed, and he experienced a call to return to Egypt to liberate his people. With the aid of his brother Aaron, he aproached the Pharaoh (probably Ramses II: reigned c. 1292 to 1225 B.C.), who acceded to the Exodus of the Hebrews after a series of 10 plagues, the last of which took the life of his firstborn son. The Pharaoh subsequently changed his mind, pursued the Hebrews, and his army was drowned in the Red Sea, but the Israelites miraculously escaped.*

*Moses led his people across the Sinai desert to Mt. Horeb (Sinai), where he received the Ten Commandments from God in the form of two tablets, which he smashed on the ground when he discovered his Hebrews worshiping a Golden Calf. Later he prepared two new tablets and placed them in the most sacred section of the Tabernacle, a portable sanctuary that was set up according to divine instructions. He also taught the Hebrews a complete legal code, organized a judicial system, and spelled out sacrificial practices.*

*Moses spent 40 years leading his people in the wilderness, never entering the promised land of Canaan—a privilege that went to his chosen successor, Joshua. Moses' great achievement, however, was the development of a system of morality and law applicable to all aspects of daily life.*

### CHRISTIANITY

Christianity developed among first-century Jews out of the conviction that Jesus of Nazareth, who lived from about c. 4 B.C. to A.D. 29, was the long-awaited Hebrew *Messiah*. . . . The name Jesus is Greek for the Hebrew *Joshua*, a name meaning *Savior*, while Christ derives from the Greek *Christos,* meaning *Messiah*, or *Anointed*.

The Christian Bible includes the Hebrew Bible, which is called the Old Testament, and the New Testament, which contains 27 additional books and was formalized by the 4th century. Central are the four Gospels of Matthew, Mark, Luke, and John, which describe the life and teachings of Jesus. Some Christians also accept the 14-book appendix to the Authorized Version of the Old Testament, known as the Apocrypha, as canonical.

The essence of traditional Christian theology is that Jesus was the Son of God who came to save the world, was crucified, resurrected, and will come again to judge mankind. The core of the Christian ethic is the commandment: "Thou shalt love the Lord thy God with all thy heart and thy neighbor as thyself."

A turning point in Christian history occurred at the Council of Jerusalem in A.D. 49 when St. Paul convinced other church leaders to spread the faith to non-Jews. Early Christians endured severe persecution, but in

A.D. 313 Constantine I officially tolerated Christianity in the Roman Empire.

Fundamental theological issues such as the divinity of Jesus Christ were thrashed out at a series of ecumenical councils during the first eight centuries. Doctrinal statements emanated from these councils, such as the Nicene Creed and the teaching of the Trinity, which asserts that God has appeared to man as the Father, the Son, and the Holy Ghost.

In 1054 Christianity was split into a Western or Roman Catholic Church, which acknowledges the pope—the bishop of Rome—as Christ's supreme vicar on earth, and the Eastern Orthodox Churches, which recognize the patriarch of Constantinople as the preeminent ecclesiastical figure. In the 16th century the Roman Catholic Church was further divided by the Protestant Reformation. The ecumenical movement of this century has now shifted momentum toward a quest for unity among Christian churches. An important development was the founding in 1948 of the World Council of Churches, which has more than 220 Protestant and Orthodox churches as members.

### ROMAN CATHOLICISM

Roman Catholicism is the form of Christianity practiced by those who recognize the authority of the pope—the bishop of Rome—as the successor of Peter and vicar of Christ on Earth. The great majority of Catholics follow the Western or Latin Rite, but there are also a number of Eastern or Uniate churches, including the Byzantine and Armenian rites, that exercise a considerable degree of autonomy.

The Roman Catholic Church claims to be the "One Holy, Catholic and Apostolic Church." Although it acknowledges the Old and New Testaments and the Apocrypha, it also asserts that teachings disclosed in only seminal form to the Apostles have subsequently germinated and flowered in the Christian Community and have been formulated by General Councils and/or the pope. Recent examples of articles of faith include the doctrines of papal infallibility (1870) and the Assumption of the Virgin Mary (1950).

The basis of the Church's claim to sanctity is its authority to offer the sacrifice of the Mass, the Eucharist, that reenacts and re-presents Christ's sacrifice in behalf of man's sins. There are six other recognized sacraments: baptism, confirmation, confession and penance, matrimony, ordination, and extreme unction.

The key figure in the church hierarchy is the bishop, who has the power to confirm and ordain. The members of the College of Cardinals serve as the pope's privy councillors and also have the responsibility of electing new popes. The central administrative body of the church is the Curia Romana, which is located in Rome and organized around a varying number of sacred "congregations."

Priests are divided into "secular," or diocesan, clergy and "regular" clergy, who belong to religious orders living under a "rule." Since the 12th century, celibacy has been required of both types of clergy.

Following the 16th-century Protestant Reformation, the Church entered a period of retrenchment that was characterized by sharply defined standards of orthodoxy. Since the First Vatican Council, which ended in 1870, the papacy has been exceptionally strong. The Second Vatican Council (1962–65), however, produced significant changes, and the Church is now undergoing a period of uncertainty and flux that is marked by demands for increased power for laymen and priests and serious questioning of such traditions as clerical celibacy and papal authority.

### EASTERN ORTHODOXY

The term Eastern Orthodox refers to those churches and their offspring that, for a variety of cultural, political, and theological reasons, split with Rome in A.D. 1054. These churches regard themselves as the true heirs of the early Christian Church and define their theological unity by acceptance of the decrees of the first seven ecumenical (general) councils that were held from A.D. 325 to 787.

The Eastern communion is a fellowship of autonomous churches consisting of the ancient patriarchates of Constantinople, Alexandria, Antioch, and Jerusalem, as well as the Orthodox churches of Cyprus, Russia, Rumania, Yugoslavia, Greece, Bulgaria, Georgia, Albania, Finland, and Czechoslovakia. The leader is the Ecumenical Patriarch of Constantinople, who is regarded as "first among equals" but whose direct authority is limited to the affairs of his own church, whose members are for the most part located in Europe and the Americas.

Eastern Orthodox theology is grounded in Greek philosophy rather than Roman law, and its creeds are important more as acts of worship than as standards of belief. Great reverence is shown for the writings of the church fathers, including Saints Basil the Great, Gregory Nazianzen, and John Chrysostom.

In addition to rejecting the authority of the pope, Eastern Orthodoxy disagrees with the Roman Catholic Church by rejecting of the Nicene Creed's *Filioque*, which asserts that the Holy Spirit proceeds "from the Son" as well as from the Father. Orthodoxy also has no indulgences and pays honor to Mary as the mother of God but rejects the Roman dogma of Immaculate Conception. It reveres relics and icons but bans all "graven images," except the crucifix.

Orthodox priests may marry before but not after ordination, although monks must remain celibate and bishops are chosen from among the celibate clergy. The liturgy of Eastern Orthodox churches is sung, and great emphasis is placed on fasting. Eastern Orthodox church structures, which are normally square, feature a solid screen that separates the sanctuaries and the edifices' main bodies. They are often elaborately decorated with gilded icons and other works of art.

The fact that a majority of Orthodox believers now live in Communist-controlled areas has cut into the vitality of Orthodoxy, but nonetheless many of its churches—including the Russian one—are active in the World Council of Churches. Relations with Rome have greatly improved, and Ecumenical Patriarch Athenagoras I has had several dramatic meetings with Pope Paul VI, including one on the Mount of Olives in Jerusalem.

### PROTESTANTISM

In a broad sense *Protestantism* is a generic term for most Western Christian churches that are not Roman Catholic or Eastern Orthodox. In a narrower connotation, it designates those churches and their heirs that came into being after the 16th-century Protestant Reformation.

The Reformation was sparked by Martin Luther, an Augustinian monk who challenged the papal practice of dispensing indulgences; with the support of German princes, he established a separate church. In addition to the Lutheran, there are at least three other Protestant traditions. The Reformed, or Calvinistic, tradition developed in Switzerland and led to the formation of Presbyterian and related churches. Anglicanism, which is represented in the United States by the Episcopal Church and originated in England, was the parent of Methodism. Numerous "free" or "independent" churches have also developed, including the Baptist and others that exercise a congregational system of government.

The fundamental philosophical characteristics of the reformers were the rejection of the authority of Rome, belief in the Bible as the only source of revelation, recognition of the "priesthood of all believers," and the assertion that salvation is the result of faith rather than good works or the dispensations of a church. Protestantism's characteristic individualism led to the development of religious liberty in many areas, but also contributed to denominational fragmentation.

Protestant churches permit ministers to marry, and even those that have bishops tend to concentrate governing powers in lay boards. Liturgies generally emphasize preaching and Bible reading rather than elaborate ritual; however, some traditions—notably the Anglo-Catholic wing of Anglicanism—are highly liturgical.

The modern ecumenical movement has developed out of Protestantism, and, except for fundamentalist churches (and thereby most Baptist churches), the major Protestant denominations tend to be involved in organizations such as the World Council of Churches. Mergers have been common in recent years, and nine major American denominations are in the process of negotiating a merger that would create a single, 25-million-member church.

## JESUS (c. 4 B.C.–A.D. 29)

*The founder of Christianity was born in Bethlehem to Mary, the wife of Joseph, who was a carpenter from Nazareth. Little is known about his early life. According to the Gospels, at the age of about 30 he was baptized by his cousin John the Baptist and began to preach, soon gathering a band of 12 disciples.*

*Jesus, who preached a message of repentance, made repeated attacks on Pharisees and scribes, the rulers of*

*Judaism. He couched his teachings in parables that could be understood by the masses and reinforced his words with extraordinary deeds that included healing the sick, raising the dead, and changing water into wine at the marriage feast of Cana.*

*After three years of preaching, Jesus set out for Jerusalem with his disciples for the celebration of Passover. He created a disturbance by throwing the money changers out of the Temple. Meanwhile, the Roman Governor Pontius Pilate, who was sensitive to Jewish nationalist threats, became alarmed. The authorities induced one of the disciples, Judas Iscariot, to betray Jesus. Following a Last Supper with his followers in which the Eucharist, or Lord's Supper, was symbolically enacted, Jesus was arrested in the Garden of Gethsemane.*

*He was tried for the treasonous charge of calling himself the Messiah and was crucified under a sign reading "Jesus of Nazareth, King of the Jews." The Gospels report, however, that three days later when Mary Magdalene went to the tomb she found it empty. An angel announced that Jesus had been resurrected; according to the Book of Acts, he appeared to his disciples, remained on earth 40 days, and then ascended into heaven.*

*Orthodox Christian theology asserts that Jesus was God made man and the second Person of the Trinity. The calendar of the Christian Church revolves around the events of his life, beginning with Advent—the preparation for his coming—and concluding with his Resurrection, Ascension, and the reception of the Holy Spirit by the church.*

The discovery in 1947 of the Dead Sea Scrolls in a cave above the waters of the northwest Dead Sea in a section known as Qumran provided information about a pacifist and ascetic community generally identified with the Essene Jewish sect.

Some scholars attempted to link Jesus with the "Teacher of Righteousness," an Essene figure who would be "raised up" by God after death. A more general consensus now is that such ties are tenuous and that the scrolls are important primarily for their information about cultural conditions of the early Christian era, especially Palestinian Judaism and the background of John the Baptist.

## ISLAM

Islam is the religion founded by the prophet Mohammed (c. A.D. 570–632) in 622 at Yathrib (now Medina) in Arabia. The Arabic word *Islam* means *submission to God*, and followers call themselves Moslems.

Mohammed was a caravan conductor and Mecca shopkeeper of the Koreish tribe who experienced a prophetic call at the age of 40. After founding his religion, he also acted as a governor, general, and judge. Mohammed is regarded as the "Seal of the Prophets"—the last in a series of messengers from God, consisting of Adam, Noah, Abraham, Moses, and Jesus.

The sacred text of Islam is the Koran (*Quran* in Arabic), which means *reading* and contains the revelations of Mohammed over a period of 20 years; it also deals with manners, religious laws, and morals. It has been supplemented by the Sunna, a collection of Traditions (moral sayings and anecdotes), and both are reinforced by the principle of Ijma, which states the belief that a majority of Moslems cannot agree in error. The Koran, the Sunna, and the Ijma are the three foundations of Islam.

Islam is radically theistic, and the essence of its creed is simply stated: "There is no God but Allah, and Mohammed is the messenger [or prophet] of Allah." Mohammed rejected the trinitarianism of Christianity, but he incorporated a number of Judeo-Christian concepts into his system. For example, the creed states: "I believe in God, his Angels, his Books and his Messengers, the Last Day, the Resurrection from the dead, Predestination by God, Good and Evil, the Judgment, the Balance, Paradise and Hell-fire."

There is no professional priesthood in Islam, and followers are expected to refrain from drinking wine. In addition to acceptance and recital of the creed, there are four duties required of the devout: prayer, fasting during the lunar month of Ramadan, giving alms, and a pilgrimage to the holy city of Mecca—if at all possible.

Moslems pray five times a day—at dawn, noon, midafternoon, dusk, and at night. The prayers, which consist primarily of thanksgiving and praise of Allah, are performed facing Mecca and involve traditional physical postures. The principal public service takes place at midday on Friday, usually in a mosque.

Early disputes over the "caliph," or successor of Mohammed, led to sectarian divisions within Islam. The most important were the Sunnites, Shiites, and Khawarij, who differed over matters of ceremony and law. Other modern movements have included the Babis and the Wahabis.

Islam is a missionary religion, though Moslems do not regard Jews and Christians as pagans and have normally permitted them to keep practicing their faiths after conquests. In centuries past, Moslem armies took over large sections of India and once came within 100 miles of Paris.

The principal areas of Islamic influence today are the Middle East, North Africa, and western Asia, and there are substantial communities in the Philippines, Indonesia, and Malaysia. It is currently increasing rapidly in African countries south of the Sahara.

Considerable theological activity has gone on during this century toward discrediting such Islamic practices as polygamy, slavery, and intolerance, thus making Islam more acceptable under modern conditions.

### MOHAMMED (c. 570–A.D. 632)

*The founder of Islam was born in Mecca in Arabia, the son of a poor merchant from the ruling tribe of Koreish. Both his parents died shortly after his birth, and he was raised by a grandfather and later an uncle. As a youth he was a shepherd and worked as a conductor of trading caravans.*

*Following his marriage at the age of 24 to the wealthy widow Khadija, who was 15 years his senior, Mohammed settled down in Mecca as a prosperous merchant and began devoting himself to the contemplative life. At the age of 40 in the cave of Mount Hira, north of Mecca, he had a vision, in which he was commanded to preach. This revelation and subsequent ones were recorded in the Koran, the sacred book of the Moslems.*

*Mohammed's first converts were his wife and children, and he began to collect other followers slowly and secretly, because of his many enemies. He taught belief in only one God, Allah, and preached heaven and hell and divine judgment.*

*When he began to operate openly, he aroused considerable hostility; some of his followers had to seek sanctuary in Abyssinia because of persecution. In 622 he himself barely escaped assassination and fled to Yathrib, which was later renamed Medina. Moslems regard this flight, the hegira, as the beginning of Islam and the start of their calendar.*

*Mohammed became the absolute ruler of Yathrib, where he founded his model theocratic state. He built the first mosque, changed the direction of prayers from Jerusalem to Mecca, and instituted the fast month of Ramadan and the practice of tithing. Relations with Christians and Jews deteriorated, but eventually he made treaties granting them freedom of worship in return for taxes. He initiated warfare with the Meccans, eventually gaining control of all of Arabia.*

*His private life has been the source of much attention, especially his frequent marriages—often politically inspired—and troubles with his harem. He basically led a simple and unpretentious life, however, and in 632 died in the arms of his last favorite wife, Ayesha.*

## HINDUISM

Known to its followers as *Santana Dharma* (the Eternal Religion), Hinduism is the religion of the majority of Indians today. It has developed gradually over a period of 5,000 years, making it possibly the world's oldest faith.

Hinduism has no ecclesiastical organization, and there are no beliefs or practices universal to all Hindus. It is polytheistic in the extreme, with literally hundreds of thousands of gods and some forms of animal life worshiped. The principal gods are Brahma, the unapproachable creative spirit, and the two popular gods, Siva and Vishnu—both of which have spawned innumerable cults.

Hindus emphasize the divinity of the soul and the harmony of all religions. Life is seen as a series of lives in which a man's position is determined by his *Karma*, or deeds, in previous lives. The social "caste" into which he is born is thus an indication of his spiritual status. The ultimate goal is to be released from the cycle of rebirths in various human and animal forms through absorption by the absolute. Asceticism and the discipline of Yoga are practiced to help achieve this release.

Hinduism has no fixed canon of sacred books. The principal text is the Veda (Vedic word meaning *divine knowledge*), a collection of 1,200 hymns and incantations addressed to various deities, including those of fire and wind. Some of this material is believed to date from the arrival of the Aryans in India c. 1500 B.C. More philosophical works that have also gained wide acceptance include the *Brahamanas*, the *Upanishads*, and the poem "Bhagavad-Gita" (Sanskrit for Song of the Lord).

For the ordinary man, Hinduism involves careful observance of food and marriage rules, pilgrimages to sacred rivers and shrines, participation in festivals, and worship in the temples and shrines that are found in every village. Entry to ultimate truth comes not from the acceptance of certain dogmas but from worship and religious experience.

Over the centuries Hinduism has produced numerous reform movements, including Buddhism and Sikhism. Modern social and cultural conditions are also bringing about modification of the caste system and other changes such as increased social status for women.

## BUDDHISM

Buddhism is the way of life based on the teachings of Siddhartha Gautama, an Indian prince who lived in the sixth century B.C. and came to be known as the Buddha (Sanskrit for *enlightened one*).

Dissatisfied with the formalism of the Hinduism of his day and vowing to find an explanation for evil and human suffering, the prince left his family and wandered as a hermit for six years in search of a truth that would liberate mankind. He found it after seven weeks of meditation under a bo (pipal or sacred fig) tree (the tree of enlightenment) and began preaching and sending missionaries forth to spread his discovery.

The Buddha taught that the path beyond sorrow and suffering was the "middle way" between austerity and sensuality. He spoke of "four noble truths": existence involves suffering, suffering results from craving, craving can be destroyed, and such destruction of desire is obtainable by following the "noble eightfold path." The steps of this path are right views, right desires, right speech, right conduct, right livelihood, right endeavor, right mindfulness, and right meditation.

The Buddha did not speak of God, and his teachings constitute, in the ordinary Western sense, more of a philosophy and system of ethics than a religion. Buddhism affirms the law of Karma, by which a person's actions in life determine his status in future incarnations. The object of the Buddhist life is to achieve Nirvana, a condition of enlightenment and detachment from the world by which the cycle of successive rebirths comes to an end.

The simple life of the Buddha and his followers gave way after his death to the creation of monasteries, shrines, and temples; however, Buddhism eventually split into numerous branches. The two major ones today are Mahayana (greater vehicle) Buddhism, which is practiced in China, Korea, and Japan and has an elaborate theology in which the Buddha is regarded as a divine savior, and Hinayana (lesser vehicle) Buddhism, which is concentrated in Southeast Asia and preserves the earlier monastic traditions. Zen Buddhism, a Japanese variation of Mahayana Buddhism, stresses contemplation, while the Lamaism of Tibet represents a mixture of Buddhism with local demonolatry.

### BUDDHA (c. 563–483 B.C.)

*The founder of Buddhism, known as the Buddha or "Enlightened One," was born into a military caste in Lumbini, near the Himalayas in southern Nepal. Estimates of the precise year range from 624 to 466* B.C.

*His original name was Siddhartha Gautama (or Gotama), and legend holds that his father, a rajah, had been warned at his birth that Siddhartha would become either a universal ruler or a universal teacher. Preferring the former course, the father took pains to prevent him from seeing any unpleasant aspects of life that might influence him to renounce the world.*

*Riding through the royal park one day when he was 29 years old, however, Siddhartha saw human misery for the first time in the form of an old man, a diseased man, a corpse, and a wandering religious mendicant. Resolving to solve the riddle of human suffering, he left his wife and newborn son and spent the next six years as a wandering hermit and ascetic.*

*His austere living failed to bring illumination, and he became an ordinary mendicant. One day he sat under a bo tree in the village of Buddh Gaya in northern India and resolved not to rise until he had found enlightenment. He stayed 49 days, resisting temptations by Mara, the Buddhist devil, and was finally rewarded with the "bliss of emancipation," or Nirvana. Suffering, he concluded, was caused by attachment to the world and could only be eliminated through mental discipline and correct living.*

*Two merchants heard his teachings and became his first lay disciples. Later he preached a sermon to five monks with whom he had shared his ascetic quest, and they were ordained as the first members of the Sangha, the Buddhist monastic order. He returned home briefly and converted his family, thereafter spending the rest of his life teaching among neighboring tribes and organizing monks to spread the message of life lived according to the "middle way" between the extremes of pleasure-seeking and self-mortification.*

*He died at the age of 80 in the lap of Ananda, his favorite disciple, and his last words were said to have been: "Decay is inherent in all component things. Work out your own salvation with diligence."*

## SHINTOISM

The ancestral religion of Japan, Shinto developed out of primitive nature and ancestor worship sometime before the sixth century, when written records first appeared. The term *Shinto* is the Chinese equivalent of *the way of the gods*, and came into use at that time to distinguish it from the Buddhism that was then being imported from the Chinese mainland.

Shinto is essentially a set of customs and rituals rather than an ethical or moral system. Followers participate in festivals and pilgrimages, and great emphasis is placed on ceremonial purity and bodily cleanliness. Many Shintoists are also practicing Buddhists.

The religion has a complex pantheon of *kami*, or deities, the most exalted of whom is the sun-goddess known as Ruler of Heaven. Other objects of veneration include deified emperors, guardian family spirits, national heroes, and the divinities of trees, rivers, villages, and water sources.

Shrines ranging from small wayside god-houses to great national sanctuaries have been constructed and dedicated to these deities. Each Shinto home also has a "god-shelf" on which is placed a miniature wooden shrine holding tablets bearing beloved ancestors' names.

## TAOISM

The chief rival to Confucianism in influencing Chinese philosophy and culture, Taoism actually consists of two movements: a philosophy (Tao Chia) and a religion (Tao Chiao). Both derive from the philosopher Lao-tze, who, according to tradition, lived in the sixth century B.C.

The term *Tao* has been translated as *way*, *road*, and even *being*. The book *Tao-teh-king*, attributed to Lao-tze, states that "the eternal Tao cannot be put into words, nor can the unchanging name be given a definition."

Philosophical Taoism espoused a radical naturalism that urged the acceptance of "all things in their natural state" and deplored passion, unnecessary invention, artificial ceremonies, and government activities such as war and taxation. Virtue was cast in passive and feminine terms. "There is nothing softer and weaker than water, and yet there is nothing better for attacking hard and strong things," was one of its precepts.

Tao Chia declined by the fourth century, partly because of the excessive assimilation of Buddhism, but its spirit of simplicity and harmony has contributed to such Chinese customs as tea drinking.

Religious Taoism originated in the first century under the leadership of Chang Tao-lin, a popular religious leader who healed the sick and founded large numbers of monasteries, nunneries, and temples. His work was continued in the next four centuries by Wei Po-yang and Ko Hung, both philosophers, and by K'ou Ch'ien-chih, who organized elaborate ceremonies and fixed the names of its multifarious deities.

Taoism has been marked by a proliferation of sects and societies. Since a brief period of state patronage during the T'ang dynasty (618–907), it has been a religion of the semiliterate.

### LAO-TZE OR LAO-TZU (b. c. 604 B.C.)

*The reputed founder of Taoism is usually said to have been born in 604* B.C. *in Honan province, China, though confusion about his historical identity and whether there even was such a person has existed since early times. The name means simply "the old philosopher."*

*According to Chinese tradition, he was born as Li Erh, lived as a recluse, and became an archivist in the Chou court. He was said to have met his younger contemporary Confucius in 517 and to have rebuked him for his pride and ambition. When he retired in his old age, Lao-tze supposedly journeyed westward and was never heard from again.*

*Legend says that as he was about to pass out of Honan the gatekeeper asked him to write down his views of the Tao and that in response he created the* Tao-teh-king, *the text of which became the basis of Taoist philosophy and religion.*

*Scholars now date the anthology in the mid-third century. It is a remarkable collection that is thought to have been built on Indian legends, especially those about Buddha; however, the work is Chinese in texture and emphasizes ethics and politics.*

*Living according to Tao (literally* Way *or* Being) *involved submission to natural actions and avoidance of all formality and artificiality. It emphasized the virtues of passivity and harmony in an effort to maintain "the original simplicity of human nature." Modern religious Taoism, however, has become highly institutionalized and marked by numerous gods, the use of magic and superstition, and an emphasis on earthly blessings such as wealth and long life.*

## CONFUCIANISM

More a religious philosophy or ethical system than a religion in the strict sense, Confucianism is known to the Chinese as *Ju Chaio* (teachings of the scholars) and was the dominant force in Chinese thought, education, and government for 2,000 years.

Its founder was Confucius (c. 551–c. 479 B.C.), who was not so much an original thinker as a teacher and compiler of wisdom from the past. His sayings, together with those of Mencius and other disciples, have been collected in the *Wu Ching* (*Five Classics*), and the *Shih Shu* (*Four Books*), the latter of which includes the *Analects*—the sayings of Confucius.

The central concept of Confucian ethics is *jen*, which originally signified benevolence on the part of rulers but was broadened to encompass the supreme virtue of love and goodness: "that by which a man is a man." Confucianism teaches that man is good and possesses free will and that virtue is its own reward.

There are no churches, clergy, or creeds in Confucianism, and its founder was far more interested in making this world more human than in contemplating the supernatural. Nevertheless, he believed in Heaven—although it was often interpreted in naturalistic terms—and encouraged the Chinese custom of ancestor-worship as a sign of gratitude and respect. Temples were built for this purpose and sacrificial rites performed in them.

From A.D. 125 to 1905 Confucianism dominated Chinese education, and members of the mandarin class of civil servants were appointed to government posts on the basis of examinations in the Confucian classics. This system had the effect of permitting many individuals from humble backgrounds to rise to prominence, and it placed a premium on the moral basis of the ruler and ruled. At the same time, its emphasis on book learning at the expense of natural science, for example, proved a liability in modern times.

Confucianism went into a period of decline following the elimination of the examination system (1905) and of the sacrificial rites (1911), but its ideas continued to play a part in the thought of some Chinese leaders, including Sun Yat-sen (1866–1925).

### CONFUCIUS (551–479 B.C.)

*The name of the founder of Confucianism and China's most prominent teacher and philosopher is a Latinized version of the Chinese* K'ung Fu-tse.

*Little reliable data is available about his life, although it is known that he was born in the feudal province of Lu, now Shantung, probably into an impoverished noble family. His father died when he was three, and he was evidently self-educated and as a young man earned his living keeping accounts.*

*Confucius became perhaps the most learned man of his day, but he was at heart a reformer rather than a scholar, a pragmatist rather than an intellectual. He was shocked by the constant warfare that went on between various states and by the suffering that aristocratic rulers brought upon the masses. He dedicated his life to relieving this suffering through governmental reforms, including the reduction of taxes, more humane punishments, and a system of statecraft that was based on mutual moral responsibilities between the ruler and the ruled.*

*His lifelong ambition was to occupy a governmental post from which he could implement his reforms, and for a short period he was apparently administrator of justice in his native province. Clashes with the nobility, however, forced him out of office and into voluntary exile.*

*At the age of 55, Confucius began touring neighboring states speaking to the feudal lords about his ideas. He was received as a scholar, but none of the rulers were willing to put his ideas into practice. He returned home to concentrate on teaching, in which he was successful; some of his students achieved positions of authority that Confucius himself had been unable to reach.*

## ESTIMATED MEMBERSHIP OF THE PRINCIPAL RELIGIONS OF THE WORLD

SOURCE: Reprinted with permission from the 1980 BRITANNICA BOOK OF THE YEAR, copyright 1980, Encyclopaedia Britannica, Inc., Chicago, Ill.

| Religions | No. Amer.[1] | So. Amer. | Europe[2] | Asia[3] | Africa | Oceania[4] | World |
|---|---|---|---|---|---|---|---|
| Total Christian | 235,109,500 | 177,266,000 | 342,630,400 | 95,987,240 | 129,717,000 | 18,063,500 | 998,773,640 |
| Roman Catholic | 132,489,000 | 165,640,000 | 176,087,300 | 55,077,000 | 47,224,500 | 4,395,500 | 580,913,300 |
| Eastern Orthodox | 4,763,000 | 517,000 | 57,035,600 | 2,428,000 | 14,306,000[5] | 414,000 | 79,463,600 |
| Protestant[6] | 97,857,500 | 11,109,000 | 109,507,500 | 38,482,240 | 68,186,500[7] | 13,254,000 | 338,396,740 |
| Jewish | 6,155,340 | 635,800 | 4,061,620 | 3,212,860 | 176,400 | 76,000 | 14,318,020 |
| Muslim[8] | 371,200 | 251,500 | 14,145,000 | 427,266,000 | 145,214,700 | 87,000 | 587,335,400 |
| Zoroastrian | 250 | 2,100 | 7,000 | 254,000 | 650 | — | 264,000 |
| Shinto[9] | 60,000 | 92,000 | — | 57,003,000 | 200 | — | 57,155,200 |
| Taoist | 16,000 | 10,000 | — | 31,261,000 | — | — | 31,287,000 |
| Confucian | 97,100 | 70,150 | — | 157,887,500 | 1,500 | 80,300 | 158,136,550 |
| Buddhist[10] | 171,250 | 192,300 | 192,000 | 254,241,000 | 14,000 | 30,000 | 254,840,550 |
| Hindu[11] | 88,500 | 849,300 | 350,000 | 473,073,000 | 1,079,800 | 499,000 | 475,939,600 |
| Totals | 242,069,140 | 179,369,150 | 361,386,020 | 1,500,185,600 | 276,204,250 | 18,835,800 | 2,578,049,960 |

[1] Includes Central America and the West Indies. [2] Includes the U.S.S.R. and other countries with established Marxist ideology where religious adherence is difficult to estimate. [3] Includes areas in which persons have traditionally enrolled in several religions, as well as China with an official Marxist establishment. [4] Includes Australia and New Zealand as well as islands of the South Pacific. [5] Includes Coptic Christians. [6] Protestant statistics usually count "full members," that is adults, rather than all family members or baptized infants and are therefore not comparable with the statistics of ethnic religions or churches counting all constituents of all ages. [7] Including many new sects and cults among African Christians. [8] The chief base of Islam is still ethnic, although some missionary work is now carried on in Europe and America (viz. "Black Muslims"). In countries where Islam is established, minority religions are frequently persecuted and their statistics are hard to come by. [9] A Japanese ethnic religion, Shinto has declined since the Japanese emperor gave up his claim to divinity (1947). Neither does it survive well outside the homeland. [10] Buddhism has produced several modern renewal movements which have gained adherents in Europe and America and other areas not formerly ethnic-Buddhist. In Asia it has made rapid gains in recent years in some areas, and under persecution it has shown greater staying power than Taoism or Confucionism. It transplants better. [11] Hinduism's strength in India has been enhanced by nationalism, a phenomenon also observable in Islam. Modern Hinduism has also developed renewal movements that have won converts in Europe and America.

# THE POPES

In the list below, the name of each pope is given, with, if known, his family name and birthplace, and the dates of his pontificate. The dates of the early popes are uncertain.

St. Peter (Simon, son of Jona); Bethsaida in Galilee; c.42–c.67
St. Linus; Tuscany; c.67–c.79
St. Anacletus or St. Cletus; Rome; c.79–c.92
St. Clement I (Clement of Rome); c.92–c.101
St. Evaristus; Asia Minor; c.99–c.107
St. Alexander I; Rome; c.107–c.116
St. Sixtus I; Rome; c.116–c.125
St. Telesphorus; Greece; c.125–c.138
St. Hyginus; Greece; 138–142
St. Pius I; Venetia; 142–155
St. Anicetus; Syria; 155–166
St. Soterus or St. Soter; Campania; c.166–c.174
St. Eleutherius or St. Eleuterius; Greece; c.174–c.189
St. Victor I; Africa; c.189–c.199
St. Zephyrinus; Rome; 199–217
St. Callistus I or St. Calixtus I; Rome; c.217–c.222
St. Urban I; Rome; 222–230
St. Pontianus or St. Pontian; Rome; 230–235
St. Anterus; Greece; c.235
St. Fabian; Rome; 236–250
St. Cornelius; Rome; 251–253
St. Lucius I; Rome; 253–254
St. Stephen I; Rome; 254–257
St. Sixtus II; Greece; 257–258
St. Dionysius; 259–268
St. Felix I; Rome; 269–274
St. Eutychian or St. Eutychianus; Tuscany; 275–283
St. Caius or St. Gaius; Dalmatia; 283–296
St. Marcellinus; Rome; 296–304
St. Marcellus I; Rome; 308–309
St. Eusebius; Greece; c.309–c.310
St. Melchiades or Meltiades or Miltiades; Africa; 311–314
St. Sylvester I; Rome; 314–335
St. Marcus or St. Mark; Rome; 10 months, 336
St. Julius I; Rome; 337–352
Liberius; Rome; 352–366
St. Damascus I; Spain; 366–384
St. Siricius; Rome; 384–399
St. Anastasius I; Rome; 399–401
St. Innocent I; Latium; 401–417
St. Zozimus or St. Zosimus; Greece; 417–418
St. Boniface I; Rome; 418–422
St. Celestine I; Campania; 422–432
St. Sixtus III; Rome; 432–440
St. Leo I (the Great); Tuscany; 440–461
St. Hilary or St. Hilarius; Sardinia; 461–468
St. Simplicius; Latium; 468–483
St. Felix II; Rome; 483–492
St. Gelasius I; Africa; 492–496
Anastasius II; Rome; 496–498
St. Symmacus or St. Symmachus; Sardinia; 498–514
St. Hormisdas; Frosinone; 514–523
St. John I; Tuscany; 523–526
St. Felix III; Rome; 526–530
Boniface II; Rome; 530–532
John II; Rome; 533–535
St. Agapitus or St. Agapetus; Rome; 535–536
St. Silverius; Campania; 536–537
Vigilius; Rome; 537–555
Pelagius I; Rome; 556–561
John III; Rome; 561–574
Benedict I; Rome; 575–579
Pelagius II; Rome; 579–590
St. Gregory I (the Great); Rome; 590–604
Sabinianus or Sabinian; Tuscany; 604–606
Boniface III; Rome; 9 months, 607
St. Boniface IV; 608–615
St. Deusdedit I or St. Adeodatus I; Rome; 615–618
Boniface V; Naples; 619–c.625
Honorius I; Campania; 625–638
Severinus; Rome; 4 months, 640
John IV; Dalmatia; 640–642
Theodore I; Greece?; 642–649
St. Martin I; Umbria?; 649–655
St. Eugene I or St. Eugenius I; Rome; 654–657[a]
St. Vitalian; Latium; 657–672
Adeodatus II or Deusdedit II; Rome; 672–676
Donus I; Rome; 676–678
St. Agatho or St. Agathonus; Sicily; 678–681
St. Leo II; Sicily; 682–683
St. Benedict II; Rome; 684–685
John V; Syria; 685–686
Conon; 686–687
St. Sergius I; Palermo; 687–701
John VI; Greece; 701–705
John VII; Greece; 705–707
Sisinnius; Syria; 2 months, 708
Constantine; Syria; 708–715
St. Gregory II; Rome; 715–731
St. Gregory III; Syria; 731–741
St. Zachary or St. Zacharias; Greece; 741–752
Stephen II; Rome; 752–757
St. Paul I; Rome; 757–767
Stephen III; Sicily; 768–772
Adrian I or Hadrian I; Rome; 772–795
St. Leo III; Rome; 795–816
Stephen IV; Rome; 816–817
St. Paschal I or St. Pascal I; Rome; 817–824
Eugene II or Eugenius II; Rome; 824–827
Valentine; Rome; 2 months, 827
Gregory IV; Rome; 827–844
Sergius II; Rome; 844–847
St. Leo IV; Rome; 847–855
Benedict III; 855–858
St. Nicholas I (the Great); Rome; 858–867
Adrian II; Rome; 867–872
John VIII; Rome; 872–882
Marinus I or Martin II; Rome; 882–884
St. Adrian III; Rome; 884–885
Stephen V; Rome; 885–891
Formosus; Rome; 891–896
Boniface VI; Rome; one month, 896
Stephen VI; Rome; 896–897
Romanus; 4 months, 897
Theodore II; Rome; one month, 897
John IX; Tivoli; 898–900
Benedict IV; Rome; 900–903
Leo V; 3 months, 903
Sergius III; Rome; 904–911
Anastasius III; Rome; 911–913
Lando; Rome; 913–914
John X (John of Tossignano); Emilia-Romagna; 914–928
Leo VI; Rome; 8 months, 928
Stephen VII; Rome; 928–931
John XI; 931–c.935
Leo VII; Rome; 936–939
Stephen VIII; Rome; 939–942
Marinus II or Martin III; Rome; 942–946
Agapitus II or Agapetus II; Rome; 946–955
John XII (Octavian); Latium; 955–964[b]
Leo VIII; Rome; 963–965[b]
Benedict V; Rome; 2 months; 964[b]
John XIII; Rome; 965–972
Benedict VI; Rome; 973–974
Benedict VII; Rome; 974–983
John XIV (Peter Canepanova); 983–984
John XV; Rome; 985–996
Gregory V (Bruno of Carinthia); Germany; 996–999
Sylvester II (Gerbert); France; 999–1003
John XVII (John Sicco); Rome; 7 months, 1003
John XVIII (Fasanus); Rome; 1003–09
Sergius IV (Peter Buccaporci); Rome; 1009–12
Benedict VIII (Theophylactus); 1012–24
John XIX (Romanus); Latium; 1024–c.32
Benedict IX (Theophylactus); 1032–44[c]
Sylvester III (John); Rome; 2 months, 1045
Benedict IX; 2 months, 1045
Gregory VI (John Gratian); Rome; 1045–46
Clement II (Suidger, Lord of Morsleben and Hornburg); Germany; 1046–47
Benedict IX; 1047–48
Damascus II (Poppo); Germany; 2 months, 1048
St. Leo IX (Bruno of Egisheim); Germany; 1048–54
Victor II (Gebhard); Germany; 1055–57
Stephen IX (Frederick); France; 1057–58
Nicholas II (Gerard); France; 1058–61
Alexander II (Anselmo da Baggio); Milan; 1061–73
St. Gregory VII (Hildebrand); Tuscany; 1073–85
Victor III (Dauferius; Desiderius); Campania; 1086–87
Urban II (Odo of Châtillon-sur-Marne); France; 1088–99
Paschal II or Pascal II (Rainerius); Latium; 1099–1118
Gelasius II (John of Gaeta); Latium; 1118–19
Callistus II or Calixtus II (Guido of Burgundy); France; 1119–24
Honorius II (Lambert Scannabecchi); Emilia-Romagna; 1124–30
Innocent II (Gregory Papareschi); Rome; 1130–43
Celestine II (Guido of Castellis); Ancona; 1143–44
Lucius II (Gerardo Caccianemici); Bologna; 1144–45
Eugene III (Bernard); Pisa; 1145–53
Anastasius IV (Conrad de Suburra); Rome; 1153–54
Adrian IV (Nicholas Breakspear); England; 1154–59
Alexander III (Roland Bandinelli); Siena; 1159–81
Lucius III (Ubaldus Allucingolus); Lucca; 1181–85
Urban III (Uberto Crivelli); Milan; 1185–87
Gregory VIII (Alberto de Morra); Benevento; 2 months, 1187
Clement III (Paolo Scolari); Rome; 1187–91
Celestine III (Giacinto Bobo); Rome; 1191–98
Innocent III (Lothar of Segni); Latium; 1198–1216
Honorius III (Cencio Savelli); Rome; 1216–27
Gregory IX (Hugo, Count of Segni); Latium; 1227–41

Celestine IV (Goffredo Castiglioni); Milan; 2 months, 1241
Innocent IV (Sinibaldo Fieschi); Genoa; 1243–54
Alexander IV (Rainaldo, Count of Segni); Latium; 1254–61
Urban IV (Jacques Pantaléon); France; 1261–64
Clement IV (Guy Fulcodi); France; 1265–68
Gregory X (Tedaldo Visconti); Emilia-Romagna; 1271–76
Innocent V (Peter of Tarentaise); Savoy; 5 months, 1276
Adrian V (Ottobono Fieschi); Genoa; 2 months, 1276
John XXI (Petrus Juliani or Petrus Hispanus); Portugal; 1276–77
Nicholas III (Giovanni Gaetano Orsini); Rome; 1277–80
Martin IV (Simon de Brie); France; 1281–85
Honorius IV (Jacobus Savelli); Rome; 1285–87
Nicholas IV (Girolamo Masci); Ascoli; 1288–92
St. Celestine V (Peter of Morrone); Abruzzi e Molise; 5 months, 1294
Boniface VIII (Benedetto Gaetani); Latium; 1294–1303
Benedict XI (Niccolo Boccasini); Venetia; 1303–04
Clement V (Bertrand de Got); France; 1305–14
John XXII (Jacques Duèse); France; 1316–34
Benedict XII (Jacques Fournier); France; 1334–42
Clement VI (Pierre Roger); France; 1342–52
Innocent VI (Étienne Aubert); France; 1352–62
Urban V (Guillaume de Grimoard); France; 1362–70
Gregory XI (Pierre Roger de Beaufort); France; 1370–78
Urban VI (Bartolomeo Prignano); Naples; 1378–89
Boniface IX (Pietro Tomacelli); Naples; 1389–1404
Innocent VII (Cosimo de' Migliorati); Abruzzi e Molise; 1404–06
Gregory XII (Angelo Correr); Venice; 1406–15
Martin V (Oddo Colonna); Abruzzi; 1417–31
Eugene IV (Gabriel Condulmaro); Venice; 1431–47
Nicholas V (Tommaso Parentucelli); Liguria; 1447–55
Callistus III or Calixtus III (Alfonso Borgia); Spain; 1455–58
Pius II (Enea Silvio Piccolomini); Siena; 1458–64
Paul II (Pietro Barbo); Venice; 1464–71
Sixtus IV (Francesco Della Rovere); Liguria; 1471–84
Innocent VIII (Giovanni Battista Cibo); Genoa; 1484–92
Alexander VI (Rodrigo Borgia); Spain; 1492–1503
Pius III (Francesco Todeschini Piccolomini); Siena; 2 months, 1503
Julius II (Giuliano Della Rovere); Liguria; 1503–13
Leo X (Giovanni de' Medici); Florence; 1513–21
Adrian VI (Adrian Florensz Dedal); Utrecht; 1522–23
Clement VII (Giulio de' Medici); Florence; 1523–34
Paul III (Alessandro Farnese); Rome; 1534–49
Julius III (Giovanni Maria Ciocchi del Monte); Rome; 1550–55
Marcellus II (Marcello Cervini); Siena; 2 months, 1555
Paul IV (Gian Pietro Carafa); Avellino; 1555–59
Pius IV (Giovanni Angelo de' Medici); Milan; 1559–65
St. Pius V (Antonio Ghislieri); Alessandria; 1556–72
Gregory XIII (Ugo Boncompagni); Bologna; 1572–85
Sixtus V (Felice Peretti); Astoli-Piceno; 1585–90
Urban VII (Giovanni Battista Castagna); Rome; one month, 1590
Gregory XIV (Niccolo Sfondrati); Milan; 1590–91
Innocent IX (Giovanni Antonio Facchinetti); Bologna; 2 months, 1591
Clement VIII (Ippolito Aldobrandini); Pesaro e Urbino, 1592–1605
Leo XI (Alessandro de' Medici); Florence; one month, 1605
Paul V (Camillo Borghese); Rome; 1605–21
Gregory XV (Alessandro Ludovisi); Bologna; 1621–23
Urban VIII (Maffeo Barberini); Florence; 1623–44
Innocent X (Giovanni Battista Pamphili); Rome; 1644–55
Alexander VII (Fabio Chigi); Siena; 1655–67
Clement IX (Giulio Rospigliosi); Tuscany; 1667–69
Clement X (Emilio Altieri); Rome; 1670–76
Innocent XI (Benedetto Odescalchi); Lombardy; 1676–89
Alexander VIII (Pietro Vito Ottoboni); Venice; 1689–91
Innocent XII (Antonio Pignatelli); Bari; 1691–1700
Clement XI (Giovanni Francesco Albani); Pesaro e Urbino; 1700–1721
Innocent XIII (Michelangelo dei Conti); Rome; 1721–24
Benedict XIII (Pietro Francesco Orsini); Bari; 1724–30
Clement XII (Lorenzo Corsini); Florence; 1730–40
Benedict XIV (Prospero Lambertini); Bologna; 1740–58
Clement XIII (Carlo Rezzonico); Venice; 1758–69
Clement XIV (Giovanni Vincenzo Antonio Ganganelli); Emilia-Romagna; 1769–74
Pius VI (Giovanni Angelo Braschi); Emilia-Romagna; 1775–99
Pius VII (Barnaba Chiaramonti); Emilia-Romagna; 1800–23
Leo XII (Annibale Della Genga); Spoleto; 1823–29
Pius VIII (Francesco Saverio Castiglioni); Ancona; 1829–30
Gregory XVI (Bartolomeo Alberto-Mauro-Cappellari); Venetia; 1831–46
Pius IX (Giovanni M. Mastai Ferretti); Ancona; 1846–78
Leo XIII (Gioacchino Pecci); Latium; 1878–1903
St. Pius X (Giuseppe Melchiorre Sarto); Treviso; 1903–14
Benedict XV (Giacomo Della Chiesa); Genoa; 1914–22
Pius XI (Achille Ratti); Milan; 1922–39
Pius XII (Eugenio Pacelli); Rome; 1939–58
John XXIII (Angelo Giuseppe Roncalli); Lombardy; 1958–63
Paul VI (Giovanni Battista Montini); Lombardy; 1963–1978
John Paul I (Albino Luciani), Venetia; 34 days, 1978
John Paul II (Karol Wojtyla); Wadowice, Poland; 1978–

[a] He was elected during the exile of St. Martin I, who had been banished to Crimea for his condemnation of the Monothelite heresy.
[b] There is confusion about the legitimacy of claims to the pontificate by Leo VIII and Benedict V. John XII was deposed on Dec. 4, 963. If his deposition was invalid, Leo was an antipope. If it was valid, Leo was the legitimate pope, and Benedict was an antipope.
[c] If the triple deposition of Benedict IX (in 1044, in 1046, and again in 1048) was illegitimate, Sylvester III, Gregory VI, and Clement II were antipopes.

## CALENDAR OF RELIGIOUS HOLIDAYS: 1982-1983

SOURCE: *Yearbook of American and Canadian Churches 1982*, edited by Constant H. Jacquet, Jr. Copyright © 1982, by the National Council of the Churches of Christ in the U.S.A. Used by permission of the publisher, Abingdon Press.

| | | |
|---|---|---|
| 1st Sunday in Advent | Nov. | 28, 1982 |
| 1st Day of Hanukkah | Dec. | 11 |
| Mawlid al-Nabi (Prophet Muhammad's Birthday) | Dec. | 17 |
| Christmas | Dec. | 25 |
| New Year's Day | Jan. | 1, 1983 |
| The Epiphany (Armenian Christmas) | Jan. | 6 |
| Week of Prayer for Christian Unity | Jan. | 18 to 25 |
| Presentation of Jesus in the Temple | Feb. | 2 |
| Brotherhood Week | Feb. | 20 to 26 |
| Last Sunday after the Epiphany | Feb. | 13 |
| Ash Wednesday* | Feb. | 16 |
| Purim | Feb. | 27 |
| Easter Lent Begins† | Mar. | 21 |
| The Annunciation | Mar. | 25 |
| Holy Week* | Mar. | 27 to Apr. 2 |
| Palm Sunday (Passion Sunday)* | Mar. | 27 |
| 1st Day of Passover | Mar. | 29 |
| Maundy Thursday* | Mar. | 31 |
| Good Friday* | Apr. | 1 |
| Easter* | Apr. | 3 |
| Holy Week† | May | 1 to 7 |
| Palm Sunday† | May | 1 |
| Holy Thursday† | May | 5 |
| Holy (Good) Friday† | May | 6 |
| Easter† | May | 8 |
| Rural Life Sunday | May | 8 |
| Ascension Day* | May | 12 |
| 1st Day of Shavuot | May | 18 |
| Pentecost (Whitsunday)* | May | 22 |
| Trinity Sunday | May | 29 |
| First Day of the Month of Ramadan | Jun. | 12 |
| St. Jean Baptiste Day (Canada) | Jun. | 24 |
| Pentecost† | Jun. | 26 |
| Festival of the End of Ramadan | Jul. | 10 |
| The Transfiguration | Aug. | 6 |
| Feast of the Blessed Virgin Mary | Aug. | 15 |
| 1st Day of Rosh Hashanah | Sep. | 8 |
| Sacrificial Festival, Pilgrimage to Mecca | Sep. | 16 |
| Yom Kippur | Sep. | 17 |
| 1st Day of Sukkot | Sep. | 22 |
| Shemini Atzeret | Sep. | 29 |
| Simhat Torah | Sep. | 30 |
| World Communion Sunday | Oct. | 2 |
| Opening of Muslim liturgical year | Oct. | 8 |
| Thanksgiving Day (Canada) | Oct. | 10 |
| Reformation Sunday | Oct. | 30 |
| Reformation Day | Oct. | 31 |
| All Saints' Day | Nov. | 1 |
| All Souls' Day | Nov. | 2 |
| World Community Day | Nov. | 4 |
| Stewardship Day | Nov. | 13 |
| Bible Sunday | Nov. | 20 |
| Thanksgiving Sunday (U.S.) | Nov. | 20 |
| Thanksgiving Day (U.S.) | Nov. | 24 |
| 1st Sunday in Advent | Nov. | 27 |
| 1st Day of Hanukkah | Dec. | 1 |
| Christmas | Dec. | 25 |

*Western Churches. †Eastern Orthodox Churches.

## COLLEGE OF CARDINALS

SOURCE: 1983 Catholic Almanac. Data as of June 1, 1982.

The cardinals are bishops chosen by the pope to serve as his principal advisers in the central administration of church affairs; those under the age of 80 are electors of the pope. Collectively, they form the Sacred College of Cardinals.

The college evolved gradually during the first 11 centuries from the synods of Roman clergy. The first cardinals, in about the sixth century, were priests of the leading churches of Rome who assisted the Holy See in directing church affairs.

| Name | Office or Dignity | Nationality | Created |
|---|---|---|---|
| Alfrink, Bernard | Former Archbishop of Utrecht | Dutch | 1960 |
| Antonelli, Ferdinando | | Italian | 1973 |
| Aponte Martinez, Luis | Archbishop of San Juan | Puerto Rican | 1973 |
| Aramburu, Juan Carlos | Archbishop of Buenos Aires | Argentinian | 1976 |
| Arns, Paulo Evaristo | Archbishop of Sao Paolo | Brazilian | 1973 |
| Bafile, Corrado | Former Prefect of Sacred Congregation for Causes of Saints | Italian | 1976 |
| Baggio, Sebastiano | Prefect of Sacred Congregation for Bishops | Italian | 1969 |
| Ballestrero, Anastasio, O.C.D. | Archbishop of Turin | Italian | 1979 |
| Baum, William W. | Prefect of the Congregation for Catholic Education | American | 1976 |
| Benelli, Giovanni | Archbishop of Florence | Italian | 1977 |
| Beras Rojas, Octavio Antonio | Former Archbishop of Santo Domingo | Dominican | 1976 |
| Bertoli, Paolo | Chamberlain of Holy Roman Church | Italian | 1969 |
| Brandao Vilela, Avelar | Archbishop of Sao Salvador | Brazilian | 1973 |
| Bueno y Monreal, Jose M. | Former Archbishop of Seville | Spanish | 1958 |
| Caprio, Giuseppe | President of Prefecture of Holy See's Economic Affairs | Italian | 1979 |
| Carberry, John | Former Archbishop of St. Louis | American | 1969 |
| Carpino, Francesco | Referendary of Sacred Congregation of Bishops | Italian | 1967 |
| Carter, Gerald Emmett | Archbishop of Toronto | Canadian | 1979 |
| Casariego, Mario | Archbishop of Guatemala | Guatamalan | 1969 |
| Casaroli, Agostino | Secretary of State | Italian | 1979 |
| Cé, Marco | Patriarch of Venice | Italian | 1979 |
| Ciappi, Mario Luigi | Pro-Theologian of the Pontifical Household | Italian | 1977 |
| Civardi, Ernesto | | Italian | 1979 |
| Colombo, Giovanni | Former Archbishop of Milan | Italian | 1965 |
| Confalonieri, Carlo | Dean of College of Cardinals | Italian | 1958 |
| Cooke, Terence | Archbishop of New York | American | 1969 |
| Cooray, Thomas B. | Former Archbishop of Colombo | Sri Lankan | 1965 |
| Cordeiro, Joseph | Archbishop of Karachi | Pakistani | 1973 |
| Corripio Ahumada, Ernesto | Archbishop of Mexico City & Primate of Mexico | Mexican | 1979 |
| Darmojuwono, Justin | Former Archbishop of Semarang | Indonesian | 1967 |
| De Araujo Sales, Eugenio | Archbishop of Rio de Janeiro | Brazilian | 1969 |
| Dearden, John | Former Archbishop of Detroit | American | 1969 |
| de Furstenberg, Maximilien | | Dutch | 1967 |
| Duval, Leon-Etienne | Archbishop of Algiers | Algerian | 1965 |
| Ekandem, Dominic | Bishop of Ikot Ekpene | Nigerian | 1976 |
| Enrique y Tarancon, Vicente | Archbishop of Madrid | Spanish | 1969 |
| Etchegaray, Roger | Archbishop of Marseilles | French | 1979 |
| Flahiff, George | Former Archbishop of Winnipeg | Canadian | 1969 |
| Florit, Ermenegildo | Former Archbishop of Florence | Italian | 1965 |
| Freeman, James Darcy | Archbishop of Sydney | Australian | 1973 |
| Gantin, Bernardin | President of Pontifical Commission for Justice and Peace | Beninese | 1977 |
| Garrone, Gabriele M. | | French | 1967 |
| Gonzalez Martin, Marcelo | Archbishop of Toledo | Spanish | 1973 |
| Gouyon, Paul | Archbishop of Rennes | French | 1969 |
| Gray, Gordon | Archbishop of St. Andrews and Edinburgh | Scottish | 1969 |
| Guerri, Sergio | | Italian | 1969 |
| Guyot, Jean | Former Archbishop of Toulouse | French | 1973 |
| Hoeffner, Joseph | Archbishop of Cologne | German | 1969 |
| Hume, George Basil, O.S.B. | Archbishop of Westminster | English | 1976 |
| Jubany Arnau, Narcisco | Archbishop of Barcelona | Spanish | 1973 |
| Kim Sou Hwan, Stephan | Archbishop of Seoul | Korean | 1969 |
| Knox, James | President of Pontifical Council for the Family | Australian | 1973 |
| Koenig, Franz | Archbishop of Vienna | Austrian | 1958 |
| Krol, John | Archbishop of Philadelphia | American | 1967 |
| Landazuri Ricketts, Juan, O.F.M. | Archbishop of Lima | Peruvian | 1962 |
| Leger, Paul | Former Archbishop of Montreal | Canadian | 1953 |
| Lekai, Laszlo | Archbishop of Esztergom | Hungarian | 1976 |
| Lorscheider, Aloisio, O.F.M. | Archbishop of Fortaleza | Brazilian | 1976 |
| Macharski, Franciszek | Archbishop of Krakow | Polish | 1979 |
| Malula, Joseph | Archbishop of Kinshasa | Zairean | 1969 |

| Name | Office or Dignity | Nationality | Created |
|---|---|---|---|
| Manning, Timothy | Archbishop of Los Angeles | American | 1973 |
| Marella, Paolo | Sub-Dean of College of Cardinals; Archpriest of Vatican Basilica | Italian | 1959 |
| Marty, François | Former Archbishop of Paris | French | 1969 |
| Maurer, Jose, C.SS.R. | Archbishop of Sucre | Bolivian | 1967 |
| McCann, Owan | Archbishop of Cape Town | South African | 1965 |
| Medeiros, Humberto | Archbishop of Boston | American | 1973 |
| Miranda y Gomez, Miguel | Former Archbishop of Mexico City | Mexican | 1969 |
| Mozzoni, Umberto | President ot Pontifical Commission for Sanctuaries of Pompei, Loreto, and Bari | Italian | 1973 |
| Munoz Duque, Anibal | Archbishop of Bogota | Colombian | 1973 |
| Munoz Vega, Pablo | Archbishop of Quito | Ecuadorian | |
| Nasalli Rocca di Corneliano, Mario | | Italian | 1969 |
| Nsubuga, Emmanuel | Archbishop of Kampala | Ugandan | 1976 |
| O'Boyle, Patrick | Former Archbishop of Washington | American | 1967 |
| Oddi, Silvio | Prefect of the Sacred Congregation for the Clergy | Italian | 1969 |
| O'Fiaich, Tomas | Archbishop of Armagh and Primate of All Ireland | Irish | 1979 |
| Otunga, Maurice | Archbishop of Nairobi | Kenyan | 1973 |
| Palazzini, Pietro | Prefect of Sacred Congregation for Causes of Saints | Italian | 1973 |
| Pappalardo, Salvatore | Archbishop of Palermo | Italian | 1973 |
| Parecattil, Joseph | Archbishop of Ernakulam | Indian | 1969 |
| Parente, Pietro | | Italian | 1967 |
| Paupini, Giuseppe | Major Penitentiary | Italian | 1969 |
| Pellegrino, Michele | Former Archbishop of Turin | Italian | 1967 |
| Philippe, Paul | Former Prefect of Sacred Congregation for Oriental Churches | French | 1973 |
| Picachy, Lawrence Trevor, S.J. | Archbishop of Calcutta | Indian | 1976 |
| Pironio, Eduardo | Prefect of Sacred Congregation for Religious and Secular Institutes | Argentinian | 1976 |
| Poletti, Ugo | Vicar General of Rome | Italian | 1973 |
| Poma, Antonio | Archbishop of Bologna | Italian | 1969 |
| Primatesta, Raul | Archbishop of Cordoba | Argentinian | 1973 |
| Quintero, Jose | Former Archbishop of Caracas | Venezuelan | 1961 |
| Ratzinger, Joseph | Prefect of Sacred Congregation for Doctrine of the Faith | German | 1977 |
| Razafimahatrata, Victor, S.J. | Archbishop of Tananarive | Madagascan | 1976 |
| Renard, Alexandre | Former Archbishop of Lyons | French | 1967 |
| Ribeiro, Antonio | Patriarch of Lisbon | Portuguese | 1973 |
| Righi-Lambertini, Egano | | Italian | 1979 |
| Rosales, Julio | Archbishop of Cebu | Filipino | 1969 |
| Rossi, Agnelo | Prefect of the Sacred Congregation for the Evangelization of Peoples | Brazilian | 1965 |
| Rossi, Opilio | President of Pontifical Council for Laity | Italian | 1976 |
| Roy, Maurice | Former Archbishop of Québec | Canadian | 1965 |
| Rubin, Wladislaw | Prefect of Sacred Congregation for Oriental Churches | Polish | 1979 |
| Rugambwa, Laurean | Archbishop of Dar-es-Salaam | Tanzanian | 1960 |
| Salazar Lopez, Jose | Archbishop of Guadalajara | Mexican | 1973 |
| Samore, Antonio | Librarian and Archivist of Holy Roman Church | Italian | 1967 |
| Satowaki, Joseph Asajiro | Archbishop of Nagasaki | Japanese | 1979 |
| Scherer, Alfredo | Former Archbishop of Porto Alegre | Brazilian | 1969 |
| Schröffer, Joseph | | German | 1976 |
| Sensi, Giuseppe M. | | Italian | 1976 |
| Shehan, Lawrence | Former Archbishop of Baltimore | American | 1965 |
| Sidarouss, Stephanos, C.M. | Coptic Patriarch of Alexandria | Egyptian | 1965 |
| Silva Henriquez, Raul, S.D.B. | Archbishop of Santiago | Chilean | 1962 |
| Sin, Jaime L. | Archbishop of Manila | Filipino | 1976 |
| Siri, Giuseppe | Archbishop of Genoa | Italian | 1953 |
| Slipyj, Josyf | Archbishop of Lwow | Ukrainian | 1965 |
| Suenens, Leo | Former Archbishop of Mechelen-Brussels | Belgian | 1962 |
| Taofinu'u, Pius | Bishop of Samoa and Tokelau | Samoan | 1973 |
| Thiandoum, Hyacinthe | Archbishop of Dakar | Senegalese | 1976 |
| Tomasek, Frantisek | Archbishop of Prague | Czech | 1976 |
| Trinh-Van-Can, Joseph-Marie | Archbishop of Hanoi | Vietnamese | 1979 |
| Ursi, Corrado | Archbishop of Naples | Italian | 1967 |
| Volk, Hermann | Bishop of Mainz | German | 1973 |
| Willebrands, Johannes | Archbishop of Utrecht, President of the Secretariat for the Union of Churches | Dutch | 1969 |
| Zoungrana, Paul | Archbishop of Ouagadougou | Upper Voltese | 1965 |

## U.S. RELIGIOUS BODIES

SOURCE: *Yearbook of American and Canadian Churches 1982*, edited by Constant H. Jacquet, Jr. Copyright © 1982, by the National Council of the Churches of Christ in the U.S.A. Used by permission of the publisher, Abingdon Press.

This directory of American religious denominations includes only those with a membership of 50,000 or more. Membership and other data are for 1980-81 unless otherwise noted.

**African Methodist Episcopal Church** This church began (1787) in Philadelphia when members of St. George's Methodist Episcopal Church withdrew as a protest against color segregation. In 1816 the denomination was started, led by Rev. Richard Allen. Membership: 2,050,000; Gen. Sec., Dr. Richard A. Chappelle, Sr., P.O. Box 183, St. Louis, MO 63166

**African Methodist Episcopal Zion Church** The A.M.E. Zion Church is an independent body, having withdrawn (1796) from the John Street Methodist Church of New York City. Membership: 1,134,176; Gen. Sec.-Aud., Earle E. Johnson, P.O. Box 32843, Charlotte, NC 28232

**American Baptist Association** A fellowship of regular and independent missionary Baptist churches distributed throughout the United States, with their greatest strength in the South. Their national fellowship was formed in 1905. Membership: 1,500,000; Headquarters: 4605 N. State Line Ave., Texarkana, TX 75501

**American Baptist Churches in the U.S.A.** Formerly known as the Northern Baptist Convention, this body of Baptist churches changed the name to American Baptist Convention at the annual meeting in Boston, May 24, 1950. In 1972 the present name was adopted. Membership: 1,271,688 (1978); Headquarters: Valley Forge, PA 19481

**The American Carpatho-Russian Orthodox Greek Catholic Church** This body is a self-governing diocese that is in communion with the Ecumenical Patriarchate of Constantinople. In 1938 the late Patriarch Benjamin I canonized the Diocese in the name of the Orthodox Church of Christ. Membership: 100,000 (1976); Headquarters: Johnstown, PA 15906

**The American Lutheran Church** This body was organized (1960) in Minneapolis. It combined the American Lutheran Church, The Evangelical Lutheran Church, and the United Evangelical Lutheran Church. The union brought together major Lutheran church bodies of different national heritage. In 1963 the Lutheran Free Church merged with The American Lutheran Church. Membership: 2,353,229; National Offices: 422 S. 5th St., Minneapolis, MN 55415

**The Antiochian Orthodox Christian Archdiocese of North America** was formed (1975) as a result of a merger of The Antiochian Orthodox Christian Archdiocese of NY and All N.A. and the Antiochian Orthodox Archdiocese of Toledo, OH and Dependencies in N.A. It is under the jurisdiction of the Patriarch of Antioch. Membership: 152,000 (1977); Headquarters: 358 Mountain Rd., Englewood, NJ 07631

**Apostolic Overcoming Holy Church of God** A black body incorporated (1920) in Alabama. It is evangelistic in purpose and emphasizes sanctification, holiness, and divine healing. Membership: 75,000 (1956); Sec., Mrs. Juanita R. Arrington, 909 Jasper Rd. W., Birmingham, AL 35204

**Armenian Apostolic Church of America** This church was under the jurisdiction of the Etchmiadzin See (now in Soviet Armenia) from 1887 to 1933, when a division occurred over the church's condition in Soviet Armenia. One group remained independent until 1957 when it came under the jurisdiction of the Holy See of Cilicia in Lebanon. Membership: 125,000 (1972); Headquarters: 138 E. 39th St., New York, NY 10016

**Armenian Church of America, Diocese of the (Including Diocese of California)** The American branch of the ancient Armenian Church was established in America in 1889. Diocesan organization is under the jurisdiction of the Holy See of Etchmiadzin, Armenia, USSR. Membership: 450,000 (1979); Diocesan offices: St. Vartan Cathedral, 630 Second Ave., New York, NY 10016

**Assemblies of God** An evangelical missionary fellowship which grew out of the Pentecostal revivals at the turn of this century. Founded (1914) in Hot Springs, Ark., the organization is now composed of self-governing churches which constitute 56 districts including seven foreign language districts. Membership: 1,732,371; Headquarters: 1445 Boonville Ave., Springfield, MO 65802

**Baptist General Conference** This body has operated as a Conference since 1879; its first church was organized in 1852. It has a ministry through 780 churches and five boards of operation. Membership: 133,385; Headquarters: 2002 S. Arlington Heights Rd., Arlington Heights, IL 60005

**Baptist Missionary Association of America** A group of regular Baptist churches organized in associational capacity in Little Rock (1950) as North American Baptist Association (present name adopted 1969). In theology these churches are evangelical, missionary, fundamental, and in the main premillennial. Membership: 224,533; Rec. Sec.: Rev. Ralph Cottrell, P.O. Box 2866, Texarkana, AR 75501

**Buddhist Churches of America** Organized in 1914 as the Buddhist Mission of North America, this body was incorporated in 1942 under the present name and represents the Jodo Shinshu Sect of Buddhism in this country. Membership: 60,000 (1975); Headquarters: 1710 Octavia St., San Francisco, CA 94109

**Bulgarian Eastern Orthodox Church (Diocese of N. & S. America and Australia)** The Holy Synod of the Bulgarian Eastern Orthodox Church established the diocese as an Episcopate (1938), and it was officially incorporated (1947) in New York State. In 1972 the Church was divided into the New York and Akron Dioceses. Membership: 86,000 (1971); Headquarters: NY Diocese, 550 A, West 50th St., New York, NY 10019; Akron Diocese, 1953 Stockbridge Rd., Akron, OH 44313

**The Christian and Missionary Alliance** An evangelical, evangelistic, and missionary movement, organized (1887) by Rev. A.B. Simpson, in New York. It stresses "the deeper Christian life and consecration to the Lord's service." Membership: 189,710; Headquarters: 350 N. Highland Ave., Nyack, NY 10960

**Christian Church (Disciples of Christ)** Started on the American frontier in the early 1800s as a movement to unify Christians, this body drew its major inspiration from Thomas and Alexander Campbell in western Pennsylvania and Barton W. Stone in Kentucky. Developing separately, the "Disciples," under Alexander Campbell and the "Christians," led by Stone, merged (1832) in Lexington, Ky. Membership: 1,177,984; Headquarters: 222 S. Downey Ave., Box 1986, Indianapolis, IN 46206

**Christian Churches and Churches of Christ** The fellowship has its origin in the American movement to "restore the New Testament church in doctrine, ordinances and life" initiated by Thomas and Alexander Campbell, Walter Scott and Barton W. Stone in the early 1800s. Membership: 1,063,254; no general organization.

**The Christian Congregation, Inc.** Original incorporation, March 10, 1887; revised incorporation, October 29, 1898. The New Commandment, John 13:34-35, is the bond of fellowship in creative ethical activism. Membership: 89,379; Gen. Supt.: Rev. Ora W. Eads, 804 W. Hemlock St., LaFollette, TN 37766

**Christian Methodist Episcopal Church** In 1870 the General Conference of the M.E. Church, South, approved the request of its colored membership for the formation of a separate ecclesiastical body, which became the Colored Methodist Episcopal Church. The Christian Methodist Episcopal Church became the official name in 1956. Membership: 786,707; Sec., Rev. N. Charles Thomas, P.O. Box 74, Memphis, TN 38101

**Christian Reformed Church in North America** A group of Dutch Calvinists that dissented (1857) from the Reformed Church in America and was strengthened by later accessions from the same source and by immigration. Doctrines: the Heidelberg Catechism (1563), the Canons of Dort (1618-19), and the Belgic Confession (1561).

Membership: 213,995; Office Address: 2850 Kalamazoo Ave. SE, Grand Rapids, MI 49560

**The Church of Christ, Scientist (Christian Scientists)** The Church of Christ, Scientist was founded in 1879 when Mrs. Mary Baker Eddy and 15 students met and voted to "organize a church designed to commemorate the word and works of our Master, which should reinstate primitive Christianity and its lost element of healing." Membership: not given; Headquarters: Christian Science Church Center, Boston, MA 02115

**The Church of God** This evangelical body was inaugurated by Bishop A.J. Tomlinson, who served (1903-43) as General Overseer, and many groups of the Pentecostal and Holiness Movement stem from it. It is episcopal in administration. Membership: 75,890 (1979); Headquarters: 2504 Arrow Wood Drive SE, Huntsville, AL 35803

**Church of God (Anderson, IN)** This body is one of the largest of the groups that have taken the name "Church of God." It originated about 1880 and emphasizes Christian unity. Membership: 176,429; Exec. Sec.: Paul A. Tanner, Box 2420, Anderson, IN 46018

**Church of God (Cleveland, TN)** America's oldest Pentecostal church began (1886) as an outgrowth of the holiness revival under the name Christian Union. Reorganized (1902) as the Holiness Church, the church adopted (1907) the name Church of God. Its doctrine is fundamental and Pentecostal; it maintains a centralized form of government and a missionary program. Membership: 435,012; Headquarters: Keith St. at 25th NW, Cleveland, TN 37311

**The Church of God in Christ** was founded (1906) in Memphis by Charles Harrison Mason, a former Baptist Minister. It is trinitarian in doctrine.. Membership: 425,000 (1965); Headquarters: 938 Mason St., Memphis, TN 38126

**The Church of God in Christ, International** Organized in 1969 in Kansas City, Mo., by 14 bishops of the Church of God in Christ of Memphis, Tenn. The doctrine is the same, but the separation came because of a disagreement over polity and governmental authority. Membership: 501,000 (1971); Headquarters: 170 Adelphi St., Brooklyn, NY 11025

**The Church of God of Prophecy** Organized (1886) in Monroe Cty., Tenn., and reorganized (1902) at Camp Creek, N.C., this church formally adopted the name Church of God (1907), but since 1952 the name Church of God of Prophecy has been used for secular purposes and in order to avoid confusion with similarly named organizations. Membership: 72,977; Headquarters: Bible Place, Cleveland, TN 37311

**The Church of Jesus Christ of Latter-day Saints (The Mormons)** was organized (1830) at Fayette, N.Y., by Joseph Smith. Its members consider the Bible, Book of Mormon, Doctrine and Covenants, and the Pearl of Great Price to be the word of God. Their belief is summed up in 13 Articles of Faith written by Joseph Smith. Membership: 2,811,000; Headquarters: 50 East North Temple St., Salt Lake City, UT 84150

**Church of the Brethren** German pietists-anabaptists founded (1708) under Alexander Mack, Schwarzenau, Germany, entered the colonies in 1719 and settled at Germantown, Pa. They have no creed other than the New Testament, hold to principles of nonviolence, temperance, and voluntarism, and emphasize religion in life. Membership: 170,839; Headquarters: Church of the Brethren General Offices, 1451 Dundee Ave., Elgin, IL 60120

**Church of the Nazarene** One of the larger holiness bodies, it was organized (1908) in Pilot Point, Tex. It is in general accord with the early doctrines of Methodism and emphasizes entire sanctification as a second definite work of grace. Membership: 484,276; Headquarters: 6401 The Paseo, Kansas City, MO 64131

**Churches of Christ** This body is made up of a large group of churches, formerly reported with the Disciples of Christ but reported separately since the Religious Census (1906). They are strictly congregational and have no organization larger than the local congregation. Membership: 1,240,000

**Community Churches, National Council of** This body is a fellowship of locally autonomous, ecumenically minded, congregationally governed, noncreedal Protestant churches. It is the union (1950) of the all-black Biennial Council of Community Churches, and a council of white churches with the same name as the present body. Membership: 190,000 (1979); National Office: 89 E. Wilson Bridge Rd., Worthington, OH 43085

**Congregational Christian Churches, National Association of** Organized (1955) in Detroit by delegates from Congregational Christian Churches committed to continuing the Congregational way of faith and order in church life. It has no doctrinal requirements. Participation by member churches is voluntary. Membership: 104,000; Headquarters: P.O. Box 1620, Oak Creek, WI 53154

**Conservative Baptist Association of America** Organized (May 17, 1947) at Atlantic City, N.J., the association regards the Old and New Testaments as the divinely inspired Word of God and as infallible and of supreme authority. Each local church is independent and autonomous. Membership: 225,000; Headquarters: 25W560 Geneva Rd., P.O. Box 66, Wheaton, IL 60187

**Coptic Orthodox Church** is part of the ancient Coptic Orthodox Church of Egypt, currently headed by His Holiness Pope Shenouda III. Membership: 100,000; Correspondent: Archpriest Fr. Gabriel Abdelsayed, 427 West Side Ave., Jersey City, NJ 07304

**Cumberland Presbyterian Church** An outgrowth of the Great Revival of 1800, the Cumberland Presbytery was organized on February 4, 1810, in Dickson County, Tenn., by three Presbyterian ministers, Revs. Finis Ewing, Samuel King, and Samuel McAdow. Membership: 96,553; Headquarters: Box 40149, Memphis, TN 38104

**The Episcopal Church** entered the colonies with the earliest settlers (Jamestown, Va., 1607) as the Church of England. It became autonomous and adopted its present name in 1789. It is an integral part of the Anglican Communion. In 1967 the General Convention adopted "The Episcopal Church" as an alternate name for the Protestant Episcopal Church in the U.S.A. Membership: 2,786,004; Headquarters: 815 Second Ave., New York, NY 10017

ACTIVE EPISCOPAL BISHOPS IN THE U.S.

Note: Address: Right Reverend; MB, Missionary Bishop

Headquarters Staff: Presiding Bishop, John M. Allin; Exec. Vice-Pres., Milton L. Wood; Exec. for Mission and Ministry, Elliott Sorge; Suffragan Bishop for the Chaplaincies to Military, Prisons, and Hospitals, Charles L. Burgreen; 815 Second Ave., New York, NY 10017

Alabama: Furman C. Stough, 521 N. 20th St., Birmingham, AL 35203

Alaska: George C. Harris, Box 441, Fairbanks, AK 99707

Albany: Wilbur E. Hogg, 62 S. Swan St., Albany, NY 12210

Arizona: Joseph T. Heistand, 110 W. Roosevelt St., Phoenix, AZ 85003

Arkansas: Herbert Donovan, Jr., 300 W. 17th St., P.O. Box 6120, Little Rock, AR 72206

Atlanta: Bennett J. Sims, 2744 Peachtree Rd. NW, Atlanta, GA 30305

Bethlehem: Lloyd E. Gressle, 826 Delaware Ave., Bethlehem, PA 18015

California: William E. Swing, 1055 Taylor St., San Francisco, CA 94108

Central Florida: William H. Folwell, 324 N. Interlachen Ave., Box 790, Winter Park, FL 32789

Central Gulf Coast: Charles F. Duvall, 3809 Old Shell Rd., P.O. Box 8395, Mobile, AL 36608

Central New York: Ned Cole, Jr., 310 Montgomery St., Syracuse, NY 13203

Central Pennsylvania: Dean T. Stevenson, 221 N. Front St., Harrisburg 17101; P.O. Box W, Harrisburg, PA 17108

Chicago: James W. Montgomery, 65 E. Huron St., Chicago, IL 60611

Colorado: William C. Frey, P.O. Box M, Capitol Hill Sta., Denver, CO 80218

Connecticut: Arthur E. Walmsley, 1335 Asylum Ave., Hartford, CT 06105

Dallas: A. Donald Davies, 1630 Garrett St., Dallas, TX 75206

Delaware: William Hawley Clark, 2020 Tatnall St., Wilmington, DE 19802

East Carolina: Hunley A. Elebash, 305 S. 3rd St., Wilmington, NC 28401
Eastern Oregon: Rustin R. Kimsey, 1336 W. Glacier, Redmond, OR 97756
Easton: Moultrie Moore, Box 1027, Easton, MD 21601
Eau Claire: William C. Wantland, 510 S. Farwell St., Eau Claire, WI 54701
El Camino Real: C. Shannon Mallory, % St. Paul's Church, 1071 Pajaro St., Salinas, CA 93901
Erie: Donald J. Davis, 145 W. 6th St., Erie, PA 16501
Florida: Frank S. Cerveny, 325 Market St., Jacksonville, FL 32202
Fond du Lac: William L. Stevens, Box 149, Fond du Lac, WI 54935
Georgia: G. Paul Reeves, 611 E. Bay St., Savannah, GA 31401
Hawaii: Edmond L. Browning, Queen Emma Square, Honolulu, HI 96813
Idaho: —, Box 936, Boise, ID 83701
Indianapolis: Edward W. Jones, 1100 W. 42nd St., Indianapolis, IN 46208
Iowa: Walter C. Righter, 225 37th St., Des Moines, IA 50312
Kansas: Richard F. Grein, Bethany Pl., Topeka, KS 66612
Kentucky: David B. Reed, 421 S. 2nd St., Louisville, KY 40202
Lexington: Addison Hosea, 530 Sayre Ave., Lexington, KY 40508
Long Island: Robert Campbell Witcher, 36 Cathedral Ave., Garden City, NY 11530
Los Angeles: Robert C. Rusack, 1220 W. 4th St., Los Angeles, CA 90017
Louisiana: James Barrow Brown, P.O. Box 15719, New Orleans, LA 70175
Maine: Frederick B. Wolf, 143 State St., Portland, ME 04101
Maryland: David Leighton, Sr., 105 W. Monument St., Baltimore, MD 21230
Massachusetts: John B. Coburn, 1 Joy St., Boston, MA 02108
Michigan: H. Coleman McGehee, Jr., 4800 Woodward Ave., Detroit, MI 48201
Milwaukee: Charles T. Gaskell, 804 E. Juneau Ave., Milwaukee, WI 53202
Minnesota: Robert M. Anderson, 309 Clifton Ave., Minneapolis, MN 55403
Mississippi: Duncan M. Gray, Jr., P.O. Box 1636, Jackson, MS 39205
Missouri: William Augustus Jones, Jr., 1210 Locust St., St. Louis, MO 63103
Montana: Jackson E. Gilliam, 303 Horsky Block, Helena, MT 59601
Navajoland Area Mission: Frederick W. Putnam, P.O. Box 720, Farmington, NM 47401
Nebraska: James Daniel Warner, 200 N. 62nd St., Omaha, NB 68132
Nevada: Wesley Frensdorff, 2930 W. 7th St., Reno, NV 89503
Newark: John Shelby Spong, 24 Rector St., Newark, NJ 07102
New Hampshire: Philip A. Smith, 63 Green St., Concord, NH 03301
New Jersey: Albert W. Van Duzer, 808 W. State St., Trenton, NJ 08618
New York: Paul Moore, Jr., 1047 Amsterdam Ave., New York, NY 10025
North Carolina: Thomas A. Fraser, Jr., 201 St. Alban's, P.O. Box 17025, Raleigh, NC 27609
North Dakota: Harold A. Hopkins, Jr., 809 8th Ave. S., Fargo, ND 58102
Northern California: John L. Thompson III, 1322 27th St., P.O. Box 161268, Sacramento, CA 95816
Northern Indiana: William C.R. Sheridan, 117 N. Lafayette Blvd., South Bend, IN 46601
Northern Michigan: William Arthur Dimmick, 131 E. Ridge St., Marquette, MI 49855
Northwest Texas: Sam Byron Hulsey, Texas Commerce Bank Bldg., Ste. 506, 1314 Ave. K, P.O. Box 1067, Lubbock, TX 79408
Ohio: John H. Burt, 2230 Euclid Ave., Cleveland, OH 44115
Oklahoma: Gerald N. McAllister, P.O. Box 1098, Oklahoma City, OK 73101
Olympia: Robert H. Cochrane, 1551 Tenth Ave. E., Seattle, WA 98102
Oregon: Matthew P. Bigliardi, 11800 S.W. Military La., Portland 97219; P.O. Box 467, Portland, OR 97034
Panama: Lemuel B. Shirley (MB), Box R, Balboa, Panama
Pennsylvania: Lyman C. Ogilby, 1700 Market St., Ste. 1600, Philadelphia, PA 19103
Pittsburgh: Robert B. Appleyard, 325 Oliver Ave., Pittsburgh, PA 15222
Puerto Rico: Francisco Reus-Froylán (MB), P.O. Box C, Saint Just, PR 00750
Quincy: Donald J. Parsons, 3601 N. North St., Peoria, IL 61604
Rhode Island: George Hunt, 275 N. Main St., Providence, RI 02903
Rio Grande: Richard M. Trelease, Jr., 120 Vassar S.E., Ste. 1-B, P.O. Box 4130, Albuquerque, NM 87106
Rochester: Robert R. Spears, Jr., 935 East Ave., Rochester, NY 14607
San Diego: Robert M. Wolterstorff, St. Paul's Church, 2728 6th Ave., San Diego, CA 92103
San Joaquin: Victor M. Rivera, 4159 E. Dakota, Fresno, CA 93726
South Carolina: Gray Temple, 1020 King St., Drawer 2127, Charleston, SC 29403
South Dakota: Walter H. Jones, 200 W. 18th St., P.O. Box 517, Sioux Falls, SD 57101
Southeast Florida: Calvin O. Schofield, Jr., 525 NE 15th St., Miami, FL 33132
Southern Ohio: William G. Black, 412 Sycamore St., Cincinnati, OH 45202
Southern Virginia: Claude Charles Vaché, 600 Talbot Hill Rd., Norfolk, VA 23505
Southwest Florida: Emerson Paul Hayes, P.O. Box 20899, St. Petersburg, FL 33742
Southwestern Virginia: A. Heath Light, P.O. Box 2068, Roanoke, VA 24009
Spokane: Leigh Allen Wallace, Jr., 245 E. 13th Ave., Spokane, WA 99202
Springfield: —, 821 S. 2nd St., Springfield, IL 62704
Tennessee: William E. Sanders, Box 3807, Knoxville, TN 37917
Texas: Maurice M. Benitez, 520 San Jacinto St., Houston, TX 77002
Upper South Carolina: William A. Beckham, P.O. Box 1789, Columbia, SC 29202
Utah: E. Otis Charles, 231 E. First St. S., Salt Lake City, UT 84111
Vermont: Robert S. Kerr, Rock Point, Burlington, VT 05401
Virgin Islands: Edward M. Turner (MB), P.O. Box 1589, St. Thomas, U.S. VI 00801
Virginia: Robert B. Hall, 110 W. Franklin St., Richmond, VA 23220
Washington: John T. Walker, Mt. St. Alban, Washington, DC 20016
West Missouri: Arthur Vogel, 415 W. 13th St., P.O. Box 23216, Kansas City, MO 64141
West Texas: Scott Field Bailey, P.O. Box 6885, San Antonio, TX 78209
West Virginia: Robert P. Atkinson, 1608 Virginia St. E., Charleston, WV 25311
Western Kansas: John F. Ashby, 142 S. 8th St., P.O. Box 1383, Salina, KS 67401
Western Louisiana: Willis R. Henton, P.O. Box 4046, Alexandria, LA 71301
Western Massachusetts: Alexander D. Stewart, 37 Chestnut St., Springfield, MA 01103
Western Michigan: Charles E. Bennison, 2600 Vincent Ave., Kalamazoo, MI 49001
Western New York: Harold B. Robinson, 1114 Delaware Ave., Buffalo, NY 14209
Western North Carolina: William G. Weinhauer, P.O. Box 368, Black Mountain, NC 28711
Wyoming: Bob Gordon Jones, 104 S. 4th St., Box 1007, Laramie, WY 82070

**The Evangelical Covenant Church of America** This church has its roots in historical Christianity. It emerged in the Protestant Reformation, the Biblical instruction of the Lutheran State Church of Sweden, and the spiritual awakenings of the 19th century. The denomination was organized (1885) in Chicago; prior to 1957 it was named the Evangelical Mission Covenant Church of America. Membership: 77,737; Headquarters: 5101 N. Francisco Ave., Chicago, IL 60625

**The Evangelical Free Church of America** was organized in Boone, Iowa, in the 1880s, as the Swedish Evangelical Free Mission. The Evangelical Free Church Association merged (1950) with this group, and the merged body is known as the Evangelical Free Church of America. Membership: 77,592 (1979); Headquarters: 1515 E. 66th St., Minneapolis, MN 55423

**Evangelical Lutheran Churches, Association of** Organized (1976) in Chicago, the AELC is a church body whose members have joined together to be in mission and ministry. The AELC is divided into four regional synods. Membership: 107,782; Headquarters: 12015 Manchester Rd. Ste. 80LL, St. Louis, MO 63131

**Free Methodist Church of North America** This body grew out of a movement in the Methodist Episcopal Church to return to the original doctrines and life-style of Methodism. It was organized in 1860. Membership: 68,477; Headquarters: 901 College Ave., Winona Lake, IN 46590

**Free Will Baptists** This evangelical group of Arminian Baptists was organized (1727) by Paul Palmer in N.C. Another movement (teaching the same doctrines of free grace, free salvation and free will) was organized (1780) in N.H. Many northern line churches merged with the Northern Baptist Convention but a remnant of these churches reorganized (1916) into the Cooperative General Association of Free Will Baptists. This Association and the General Conference (churches in the southern line) joined together (1935) to form the National Association of Free Will Baptists. Membership: 227,888; National Offices: 1134 Murfreesboro Rd., Nashville, TN 37217

**Friends United Meeting** The Friends United Meeting became the name in 1965 for the Five Years Meeting of Friends, a body founded (1902) to facilitate a united Quaker witness in missions, peace education, and Christian education. Additional programs have since been added. There are now fifteen Yearly Meetings with members within and beyond the U.S. Membership: 60,745; Presiding Clerk, Clifford Winslow, 101 Quaker Hill Dr., Richmond, IN 47374

**Full Gospel Fellowship of Churches and Ministers, International** Founded in 1962, the FGFCMI is a fellowship of locally autonomous churches and ministers. All members believe that the Holy Scriptures are the inspired Word of God. Membership: 59,100; Headquarters: FGFCMI General Conference, 1545 W. Mockingbird Lane, Ste. 1012, Lock Box 209, Dallas, TX 75235

**General Association of Regular Baptist Churches** Founded (1932) in Chicago by a group of churches that had withdrawn from the Northern Baptist Convention (now the American Baptist Churches in the U.S.A.) because of doctrinal differences. It requires all churches to subscribe to the historic New Hampshire Confession of Faith (with a premillennial ending applied to the last article.) Membership: 243,000; Headquarters: 1300 N. Meacham Rd., Schaumburg, IL 60195

**General Baptists (General Association of)** An Arminian group of Baptists first organized (1607) by John Smyth and Thomas Helwys in England, and transplanted to the colonies in 1714. It died out along the Seaboard, but was revived (1823) in the Midwest by Rev. Benoni Stinson. Membership: 74,159; Exec. Sec., Rev. Glen O. Spence, 100 Stinson Dr., Poplar Bluff, MO 63901

**Greek Orthodox Archdiocese of North and South America** is under the jurisdiction of the Ecumenical Patriarchate of Constantinople (Istanbul). Chartered in 1922, it has parishes in the U.S., Canada, and Central and South America. Membership: 1,950,000 (1977); Headquarters: 8-10 E. 79th St., New York, NY 10021

**Independent Fundamental Churches of America** Organized (1930) at Cicero, Ill., by representatives of various independent churches. Membership: 120,446; Headquarters: 1860 Mannheim Rd., P.O. Box 250, Westchester, IL 60153

**International Church of the Foursquare Gospel** An evangelistic missionary body organized (1927) by Aimee Semple McPherson. The parent church is Angelus Temple in Los Angeles (organized 1923), with mission stations and meeting places in 39 foreign countries. Membership: 89,215 (1963); Headquarters: Angelus Temple, 1100 Glendale Blvd., Los Angeles, CA 90026

**Jehovah's Witnesses** It is the belief of Jehovah's Witnesses that they adhere to the oldest religion on earth: the worship of Almighty God revealed in his Bible as Jehovah. All of Jehovah's Witnesses are considered to be ministers of the gospel and have no human leader. Their Yearbook shows them active (1980) in 205 countries. Membership: 565,309; Headquarters: 25 Columbia Heights, Brooklyn, NY 11201

**Jewish Congregations** Jews arrived in the colonies before 1650. The first congregation is recorded (1654) in New York City, the Shearith Israel (Remnant of Israel). Membership of Jewish congregations in the U.S.: 5,920,000

CONGREGATIONAL AND RABBINICAL ORGANIZATIONS

Reconstructionist Federation of Congregations and Fellowships: 432 Park Ave., S., New York, NY 10016; Pres., Herbert Winer; Exec. Dir., Ludwig Nadelman

*Union of American Hebrew Congregations (Reform): 838 Fifth Ave., New York, NY 10021; Pres., Rabbi Alexander M. Schindler

*United Synagogue of America (Conservative): 155 Fifth Ave., New York, NY 10010; Pres., Simon Schwartz; Exec. Vice-Pres., Rabbi Benjamin Z. Kreitman

*Union of Orthodox Jewish Congregations of America: 116 E. 27th St., New York, NY 10016; Pres., Julius Berman; Exec. Vice-Pres., Rabbi Pinchas Stolper

*Central Conference of American Rabbis (Reform): 790 Madison Ave., New York, NY 10021; Pres., Rabbi Jerome R. Malino; Exec. Vice-Pres., Rabbi Joseph B. Glaser

Rabbinical Alliance of America (Orthodox): 156 Fifth Ave., Ste. 807, New York, NY 10010; Pres., Rabbi Abraham B. Hecht

*The Rabbinical Assembly (Conservative): 3080 Broadway, New York, NY 10027; Pres., Rabbi Saul I. Teplitz; Exec. Vice-Pres., Rabbi Wolfe Kelman

*Rabbinical Council of America, Inc. (Orthodox): 1250 Broadway, New York, NY 10001; Pres., Bernard Rosenweig; Exec. Vice-Pres., Rabbi Israel Klavan

Reconstructionist Rabbinical Association: 432 Park Ave., S., New York, NY 10016; Pres., Rabbi Dennis Sasso; Secs., Rabbis Ilene Schneider, Neil Weinberg

Union of Orthodox Rabbis of the United States and Canada: 235 E. Broadway, New York, NY 10002; Pres., Rabbi Moshe Feinstein, Chpsn., Rabbi Symcha Elberg

*Synagogue Council of America: 10 E. 40th St., New York, NY 10016; Pres., Rabbi Walter S. Wurzburger; Exec. Vice-Pres., Rabbi Bernard Mandelbaum

*Synagogue Council of America is the coordinating body of the organizations starred above

**Lutheran Church in America** This body was organized (1962) by consolidation of the American Evangelical Lutheran Church (1872); the Augustana Lutheran Church (1860); the Finnish Lutheran Church (1891); and the United Lutheran Church in America (1918). Membership: 2,923,260; Headquarters: 231 Madison Ave., New York, NY 10016

**The Lutheran Church—Missouri Synod** This body (organized 1847) is the second-largest Lutheran church in America. It holds to an unwavering confessionalism coupled with a strong outreach in ministry. Membership: 2,625,650; Headquarters: 500 N. Broadway, St. Louis, MO 63102

**Mennonite Church** The largest group of the Mennonites who began arriving in the U.S. as early as 1683, settling in Germantown, Pa. They derive their name from Menno Simons, their outstanding leader, b. 1496. Membership: 99,511; General Office: 528 E. Madison St., Lombard, IL 60148

**Moravian Church in America (Unitas Fratrum)** In 1735 Moravian missionaries of the pre-Reformation faith of John Hus came to Georgia, in 1740 to Pennsylvania, and in 1753 to North Carolina. They established the Moravian Church, which is broadly evangelical, liturgical, with an episcopacy as a spiritual office and in form of government "conferential." NORTHERN PROVINCE: Membership: 32,724; Headquarters: 69 W. Church St., P.O. Box 1245, Bethlehem, PA 18018. SOUTHERN PROVINCE: Membership: 21,057; Headquarters: 459 S. Church St., Winston-Salem, NC 27108

**Muslims** Islam claims adherents in the U.S. through immigrants or Americans, mostly black, who converted to Islam. There are Islamic centers in 300 large U.S. cities. All Muslims hold to prayers, fasting, almsgiving, and pilgrimage to Mecca. Membership: over 2,000,000. Information: Mr. Dawud Assad, Pres., The Federation of Islamic Associations in the U.S. and Can., 300 E. 44th St., 2nd Fl., New York, NY 10017

**National Baptist Convention of America (organized 1880)** is the "unincorporated" body of National Baptists. Membership: 2,668,799 (1956); Corr. Sec., Albert E. Chew, 2823 N. Houston, Ft. Worth, TX 76106

**National Baptist Convention, U.S.A., Inc.** The older and parent convention of black Baptists, this body is to be distinguished from the National Baptist Convention of America, usually referred to as the "unincorporated" body. Membership: 5,500,000 (1958); Pres., Rev. J.H. Jackson, 405 E. 31st St., Chicago, IL 60616

**National Primitive Baptist Convention, Inc.** A group of Baptists having associations, state conventions, and a National Convention (organized 1907). Membership: 250,000 (1975); Headquarters: P.O. Box 2355, Tallahassee, FL 32304

**North American Old Roman Catholic Church** A body with the doctrine of the Old Catholics in right and succession of Catholic orders. Knott Missal used for Masses. Pontificale used for all Order Rights. Not under Papal jurisdiction. Membership: 61,263; Presiding Archbishop of the Americas and Canada: Most Rev. John E. Schweikert, 4200 N. Kedvale Ave., Chicago, IL 60641

**Old Order Amish Church** The congregations have no annual conference. They worship in private homes, and adhere to the older forms of worship and attire. This body has bishops, ministers, and deacons. Membership: 80,250; No general organization; Information: Der Neue Amerikanische Calendar, % Raber's Book Store, Baltic, OH 43804

**The Orthodox Church in America** The Russian Orthodox Greek Catholic Church of America entered Alaska in 1792 before its purchase by the United States in 1867. Its canonical status of independence (autocephaly) was granted (1970) by its Mother Church, the Russian Orthodox Church. Membership: 1,000,000 (1978); Sec. to the Metropolitan: Serge Troubetzkoy, P.O. Box 675, Syosset, NY 11791

**Pentecostal Church of God** Organized originally in Chicago as the Pentecostal Assemblies of the U.S.A., the present name was adopted (1922) at a subsequent convention. Membership: 113,000; Headquarters: Messenger Plaza, 211 Main St., Joplin, MO 64801

**Pentecostal Holiness Church, International** This body grew out of the holiness movement (1895-1900) in the South and Middle West. It is premillennial in belief, emphasizes Christian perfection as taught by John Wesley, and believes in the Pentecostal baptism with the Holy Spirit, accompanied by glossolalia. Membership: 86,103 (1977); Headquarters: P.O. Box 12609, Oklahoma City, OK 73157

**Plymouth Brethren (Christian Brethren)** An orthodox and evangelical movement to unite Christians from various denominations which began in the British Isles in the 1820s. In the 1840s the movement divided. The smaller "exclusive" branch stresses the interdependency of congregations. The "open" branch, stressing congregational independence, is greatly involved in evangelism and foreign missions. Membership: 98,000; No general organization.

**Polish National Catholic Church of America** After a long period of dissatisfaction with Roman Catholic administration and ideology, accompanied by a strong desire for religious freedom, this body was organized in 1897. Membership: 282,411 (1960); Headquarters: 529 E. Locust St., Scranton, PA 18505

**Presbyterian Church in America** This body was formed (1973), in Birmingham, Ala., as the result of an act of separation from the Presbyterian Church in the U.S. The PCA, which has no sectional boundaries, is committed to the Reformed Faith as set forth in the Westminster Confession and Catechisms. Membership: 90,991; Stated Clk., Rev. Morton H. Smith, P.O. Box 312, Brevard, NC 28712

**Presbyterian Church in the United States** is a branch of the major American Presbyterian tradition which broke apart during the Civil War. Organized as a separate denomination (1861) in Augusta, Ga., it was constituted as the Presbyterian Church in the U.S. in 1865. Membership: 838,485; Office of the General Assembly: 341 Ponce de Leon Ave. NE, Atlanta, GA 30365

**Primitive Baptists** A large group of Baptists, located mainly in the South, who are opposed to all centralization and to modern missionary societies. Membership: 72,000 (1960); Headquarters: Cayce Publ. Co., S. Second St., Thornton, AR 71766

**Progressive National Baptist Convention, Inc.** This body held its organizational meeting at Cincinnati (1961). The first annual session was held in Philadelphia (1962). Membership: 521,692 (1967); Gen. Sec., Rev. C.J. Malloy, Jr., 601 50th St. NE, Washington, DC 20019

**Reformed Church in America** This body was established (1628) by the earliest Dutch settlers of New York as the Reformed Protestant Dutch Church. It is the oldest Protestant denomination with a continuous ministry in North America. Membership: 345,532; National Office: 475 Riverside Drive, New York, NY 10115

**Reorganized Church of Jesus Christ of Latter Day Saints** was founded (1830) by Joseph Smith, Jr., and reorganized (1860) under the leadership of Joseph Smith III. The Church is established in 35 countries in addition to the U.S. and Canada. Membership: 190,087; Headquarters: The Auditorium, P.O. Box 1059, Independence, MO 64051

**The Roman Catholic Church** The largest single body of Christians in the U.S., the Roman Catholic Church is under the spiritual leadership of His Holiness the Pope. Its establishment in America dates back to the priests who accompanied Columbus on his second voyage to the New World. A settlement, later discontinued, was made at St. Augustine, Fla. The continuous history of this Church in the colonies began (1634) at St. Mary's, in Maryland. Membership: 50,449,842. The following information has been furnished by the editor of *The Official Catholic Directory* for 1982, published by P.J. Kenedy & Sons, P.O. Box 729, New York, NY 10022:

### VISIBLE HEAD OF THE CHURCH

His Holiness the Pope, Bishop of Rome, Vicar of Jesus Christ, Supreme Pontiff of the Catholic Church, Pope John Paul II (Karol Wojtyla, b. 1920, installed 1978). APOSTOLIC DELEGATE IN THE UNITED STATES: Most Rev. Pio Laghi, 3339 Massachusetts Ave. NW, Washington, DC 20008

### BISHOPS AND ARCHBISHOPS

Archdiocese of Anchorage, Alaska–Most Rev. Francis T. Hurley; Diocese of Fairbanks, Alaska–Most Rev. Robert L. Whelan; Diocese of Juneau, Alaska–Most Rev. Michael H. Kenny.

Archdiocese of Atlanta, GA–Most Rev. Thomas A. Donnellan; Diocese of Charlotte, NC–Most Rev. Michael J. Begley; Diocese of Charleston, SC–Most Rev. Ernest L. Unterkoefler; Diocese of Raleigh, NC–Most Rev. F. Joseph Gossman; Diocese of Savannah, GA–Most Rev. Raymond W. Lessard.

Archdiocese of Baltimore, MD–Most Rev. William D. Borders; Diocese of Arlington, VA–Most Rev. Thomas J. Welsh; Diocese of Richmond, VA–Most Rev. Walter F. Sullivan; Diocese of Wheeling-Charleston, WV–Most Rev. Joseph H. Hodges; Diocese of Wilmington, DE–Most Rev. Thomas J. Mardaga.

Archdiocese of Boston, MA–His Eminence Humberto Cardinal S. Medeiros; Diocese of Burlington, VT–Most Rev. John A. Marshall; Diocese of Fall River, MA–Most Rev. Daniel A. Cronin; Diocese of Manchester, NH–Most Rev. Odore J. Gendron; Diocese of Portland, ME–Most Rev. Edward C. O'Leary; Diocese of Springfield, MA–Most Rev. Joseph F. Maguire; Diocese of Worcester, MA–Most Rev. Bernard J. Flanagan.

Archdiocese of Chicago, IL–Most Rev. Joseph L. Bernardin; Diocese of Belleville, IL–Most Rev. John N. Wurm; Diocese of Joliet, IL–Most Rev. Joseph L. Imesch; Diocese of Peoria, IL–Most Rev. Edward W. O'Rourke; Diocese of Rockford, IL–Most Rev. Arthur J. O'Neill; Diocese of Springfield, IL–Most Rev. Joseph A. McNicholas.

Archdiocese of Cincinnati, OH–Vacant; Diocese of Cleveland, OH– Most Rev. Anthony M. Pilla; Diocese of Columbus, OH–Most Rev. Edward J. Herrmann; Diocese of Steubenville, OH–Most Rev. Albert H. Ottenwell; Diocese of Toledo, OH–Most Rev. James R. Hoffman; Diocese of Youngstown, OH–Most Rev. James W. Malone.

Archdiocese of Denver, CO–Most Rev. James V. Casey; Diocese of Cheyenne, WY–Most Rev. Joseph H. Hart; Diocese of Pueblo, CO–Most Rev. Arthur N. Tafoya.

Archdiocese of Detroit, MI–Most Rev. Edmund C. Szoka; Diocese of Gaylord, MI–Most Rev. Robert J. Rose; Diocese of Grand Rapids, MI–Most Rev. Joseph M. Breitenbeck; Diocese of Kalamazoo, MI–Most Rev. Paul V. Donovan; Diocese of Lansing, MI–Most Rev. Kenneth J. Povish; Diocese of Marquette, MI–Most Rev. Mark F. Schmitt; Diocese of Saginaw, MI–Most Rev. Kenneth E. Untener.

Archdiocese of Dubuque, IA–Most Rev. James J. Byrne; Diocese of Davenport, IA–Most Rev. Gerald F. O'Keefe; Diocese of Des Moines, IA–Most Rev. Maurice J. Dingman; Diocese of Sioux City, IA–Most Rev. Frank H. Greteman.

Archdiocese of Hartford, CT–Most Rev. John F. Whealon; Diocese of Bridgeport, CT–Most Rev. Walter W. Curtis; Diocese of Norwich, CT–Most Rev. Daniel P. Reilly; Diocese of Providence, RI–Most Rev. Louis E. Gelineau.

Archdiocese of Indianapolis, IN–Most Rev. Edward T. O'Meara; Diocese of Evansville, IN–Most Rev. Francis R. Shea; Diocese of Fort Wayne-South Bend, IN–Most Rev. William E. McManus; Diocese of Gary, IN–Most Rev. Andrew G. Grutka; Diocese of Lafayette in Indiana, IN–Most Rev. Raymond J. Gallagher.

Archdiocese of Kansas City, KS–Most Rev. Ignatius J. Strecker; Diocese of Dodge City, KS–Most Rev. Eugene J. Gerber; Diocese of Salina, KS–Most Rev. Daniel W. Kucera, O.S.B.; Diocese of Wichita, KS–Most Rev. David M. Maloney.

Archdiocese of Los Angeles, CA–His Eminence Timothy Cardinal Manning; Diocese of Fresno, CA–Most Rev. Joseph J. Madera; Diocese of Monterey, CA–Most Rev. Harry A. Clinch; Diocese of Orange, CA–Most Rev. William R. Johnson; Diocese of San Bernardino, CA–Most Rev. Phillip F. Straling; Diocese of San Diego, CA–Most Rev. Leo T. Maher.

Archdiocese of Louisville, KY–Most Rev. Thomas C. Kelly, O.P.; Diocese of Covington, KY–Most Rev. William A. Hughes; Diocese of Memphis, TN–Most Rev. Carroll T. Dozier; Diocese of Nashville, TN–Most Rev. James D. Niedergeses; Diocese of Owensboro, KY–Most Rev. Henry Soennecker.

Archdiocese of Miami, FL–Most Rev. Edward A. McCarthy; Diocese of Orlando, FL–Most Rev. Thomas J. Grady; Diocese of Pensacola-Tallahassee, FL–Most Rev. Rene H. Gracida; Diocese of St. Augustine, FL–Most Rev. John J. Snyder; Diocese of St. Petersburg, FL–Most Rev. W. Thomas Larkin.

Archdiocese of Milwaukee, WI–Most Rev. Rembert G. Weakland, O.S.B.; Diocese of Green Bay, WI–Most Rev. Aloysius J. Wycislo; Diocese of La Crosse, WI–Most Rev. Frederick W. Freking; Diocese of Madison, WI–Most Rev. Cletus F. O'Donnell; Diocese of Superior, WI–Most Rev. George A. Hammes.

Archdiocese of Mobile, AL–Most Rev. Oscar Lipscomb; Diocese of Birmingham, AL–Most Rev. Joseph G. Vath; Diocese of Biloxi, MS–Most Rev. Joseph Lawson Howse; Diocese of Jackson, MS–Most Rev. Joseph B. Brunini.

Archdiocese of Newark, NJ–Most Rev. Peter L. Gerety; Diocese of Camden, NJ–Most Rev. George H. Guilfoyle; Diocese of Metuchen, NJ–Most Rev. Theodore E. McCarrick; Diocese of Paterson, NJ–Most Rev. Frank J. Rodimer; Diocese of Trenton, NJ–Most Rev. John C. Reiss.

Archdiocese of New Orleans, LA–Most Rev. Philip M. Hannan; Diocese of Alexandria-Shreveport, LA–Most Rev. Lawrence P. Graves; Diocese of Baton Rouge, LA–Most Rev. Joseph V. Sullivan; Diocese of Houma-Thibodaux, LA–Most Rev. Warren L. Boudreaux; Diocese of Lafayette, LA–Most Rev. Gerard L. Frey; Diocese of Lake Charles, LA–Most Rev. Jude Speyrer.

Archdiocese of New York, NY–His Eminence Terence Cardinal Cooke; Diocese of Albany, NY–Most Rev. Howard J. Hubbard; Diocese of Brooklyn, NY–Most Rev. Francis J. Mugavero; Diocese of Buffalo, NY–Most Rev. Edward D. Head; Diocese of Ogdensburg, NY–Most Rev. Stanislaus J. Brzana; Diocese of Rochester, NY–Most Rev. Matthew H. Clark; Diocese of Rockville Centre, NY–Most Rev. John R. McGann; Diocese of Syracuse, NY–Most Rev. Frank J. Harrison; Military Vicariate–His Eminence Terence Cardinal Cooke.

Archdiocese of Oklahoma City, OK–Most Rev. Charles A. Salatka; Diocese of Little Rock, AR–Most Rev. Andrew J. McDonald; Diocese of Tulsa, OK–Most Rev. Eusebius Beltran.

Archdiocese of Omaha, NE–Most Rev. Daniel E. Sheehan; Diocese of Grand Island, NE–Most Rev. Lawrence J. McNamara; Diocese of Lincoln, NE–Most Rev. Glennon P. Flavin.

Archdiocese of Philadelphia, PA–His Eminence John Cardinal Krol; Diocese of Allentown, PA–Most Rev. Joseph McShea; Diocese of Altoona-Johnstown, PA–Most Rev. James J. Hogan; Diocese of Erie, PA–Most Rev. Alfred M. Watson; Diocese of Greensburg, PA–Most Rev. William G. Connare; Diocese of Harrisburg, PA–Most Rev. Joseph T. Daley; Diocese of Pittsburgh, PA–Most Rev. Vincent M. Leonard; Diocese of Scranton, PA–Most Rev. J. Carroll McCormick.

Archdiocese of Portland, OR–Most Rev. Cornelius M. Power; Diocese of Baker, OR–Most Rev. Thomas J. Connolly; Diocese of Boise, ID–Most Rev. Sylvester W. Treinen; Diocese of Great Falls-Billings, MT–Most Rev. Thomas J. Murphy; Diocese of Helena, MT–Most Rev. Elden F. Curtiss.

Archdiocese of St. Louis, MO–Most Rev. John L. May; Diocese of Jefferson City, MO–Most Rev. Michael F. McAuliffe; Diocese of Kansas City-St. Joseph, MO–Most Rev. John J. Sullivan; Diocese of Springfield-Cape Girardeau, MO–Most Rev. Bernard F. Law.

Archdiocese of St. Paul and Minneapolis, MN–Most Rev. John R. Roach; Diocese of Bismarck, ND–Most Rev. Hilary B. Hacker; Diocese of Crookston, MN–Most Rev. Victor H. Balke; Diocese of Duluth, MN–Most Rev. Paul F. Anderson; Diocese of Fargo, ND–Most Rev. Justin A. Driscoll; Diocese of New Ulm, MN–Most Rev. Raymond A. Lucker; Diocese of Rapid City, SD–Most Rev. Harold J. Dimmerling; Diocese of St. Cloud, MN–Most Rev. George H. Speltz; Diocese of Sioux Falls, SD–Most Rev. Paul V. Dudley; Diocese of Winona, MN–Most Rev. Loras J. Watters.

Archdiocese of San Antonio, TX–Most Rev. Patrick F. Flores; Diocese of Amarillo, TX–Most Rev. Leroy T. Matthiesen; Diocese of Austin, TX–Most Rev. Vincent M. Harris; Diocese of Beaumont, TX–Most Rev. Bernard J. Ganter; Diocese of Brownsville, TX–Most Rev. John J. Fitzpatrick; Diocese of Corpus Christi, TX–Most Rev. Thomas J. Drury; Diocese of Dallas, TX–Most Rev. Thomas Tschoepe; Diocese of Fort Worth, TX–Most Rev. Joseph P. Delaney; Diocese of Galveston-Houston, TX–Most Rev. John L. Morkovsky; Diocese of San Angelo, TX–Most Rev. Joseph A. Fiorenza.

Archdiocese of San Francisco, CA–Most Rev. John R. Quinn; Diocese of Agana, Guam–Most Rev. Felixberto C. Flores; Diocese of Honolulu, HI–Vacant; Diocese of Oakland, CA–Most Rev. John S. Cummins; Diocese of Reno-Las Vegas, NV–Most Rev. Norman F. McFarland; Diocese of Sacramento, CA–Most Rev. Francis A. Quinn; Diocese of Salt Lake City, UT–Most Rev. William K. Weigand; Diocese of San Jose, CA–Most Rev. Pierre DuMaine; Diocese of Santa Rosa, CA–Most Rev. Mark J. Hurley; Diocese of Stockton, CA–Most Rev. Roger M. Mahony.

Archdiocese of Santa Fe, NM–Most Rev. Robert F. Sanchez; Diocese of El Paso, TX–Most Rev. Raymond J. Pena; Diocese of Gallup, NM–Most Rev. Jerome J. Hastrich; Diocese of Phoenix, AZ–Most Rev. Thomas J. O'Brien; Diocese of Tucson, AZ–Most Rev. Manuel D. Moreno.

Archdiocese of Seattle, WA–Most Rev. Raymond G. Hunthausen; Diocese of Spokane, WA–Most Rev. Lawrence H. Welsh; Diocese of Yakima, WA–Most Rev. William S. Skylstad.

Archdiocese of Washington, DC–Most Rev. James A. Hickey; Diocese of St. Thomas, Virgin Islands–Most Rev. Edward J. Harper, C.SS.R.

Archeparchy (Ukrainian) of Philadelphia, PA–Most Rev. Stephen Sulyk; Eparchy of St. Nicholas in Chicago, IL–Most Rev. Innocent Lotocky, O.S.B.M.; Diocese of Stamford, CT–Most Rev. Basil H. Losten.

Archdiocese of Pittsburgh, PA–Most Rev. Stephen J. Kocisko; Eparchy of Parma, OH–Most Rev. Emil Mihalik; Eparchy of Passaic, NJ–Most Rev. Michael J. Dudick; Diocese of Van Nuys, CA–Most Rev. Thomas V. Dolinay.

MARONITES

Diocese of St. Maron, Brooklyn, NY–Most Rev. Francis Zayek.

MELKITES

Exarchy of Newton, MA–Most Rev. Joseph Tawil.

**Russian Orthodox Church in the U.S.A., Patriarchal Parishes of the** This group of parishes is under the direct jurisdiction of the Patriarch of Moscow and All Russia. Membership: 51,500 (1975); Headquarters: St. Nicholas Patriarchal Cathedral, 15 E. 97th St., New York, NY 10029

**The Russian Orthodox Church Outside Russia** This body was organized (1920) to unite the missions and parishes of the Russian Orthodox Church outside of Russia. This church emphasizes being true to the old traditions of the Russian Church, but it does not compromise with official church leaders in Moscow. Membership: 55,000 (1955); Headquarters: 75 E. 93rd St., New York, NY 10028

**The Salvation Army** An international Christian religious & charitable organization with a paramilitary government, founded (1865) by General William Booth in England and introduced (1880) into America. Membership: 417,359; National Headquarters: 120-130 W. 14th St., New York, NY 10011

**Serbian Eastern Orthodox Church for the U.S.A. and Canada** was organized (1921) as a diocese of Serbian Orthodox Church; reorganized in 1963. The Patriarchal seat is in Belgrade, Yugoslavia. Membership: 65,000 (1967); Chancery: St. Sava Monastery, P.O. Box 519, Libertyville, IL 60048

**Seventh-day Adventists** This Protestant body developed out of an interdenominational movement that appeared in the early 19th century, stressing the imminence of the Second Advent of Christ. Seventh-day Adventists were formally organized in 1863. They believe in the personal, imminent, and premillennial return of Christ, and in the observance of the seventh day as the Sabbath. Membership: 571,141; Headquarters: 6840 Eastern Ave. NW, Washington, DC 20012

**Southern Baptist Convention** was organized (1845) in Augusta, Ga. Its purpose is "to provide a general organization for Baptists in the United States and its territories for the promotion of Christian missions at home and abroad and any other objects...which it may deem proper and advisable for the furtherance of the Kingdom of God." Membership: 13,600,126; Executive Committee Offices: 460 James Robertson Pkwy., Nashville, TN 37219

**Triumph the Church and Kingdom of God in Christ (International)** The Triumph Church, as this body is more commonly known, was founded in 1902. It was incorporated (1918) in Washington, DC, and currently operates in 31 states and overseas. Membership: 54,307 (1972); Nat. Gen. Rec. Sec., Bishop C.H. Whittaker, 9200 Miles Ave., Cleveland, OH 44105

**Ukrainian Orthodox Church in the U.S.A.** was formally organized in the United States in 1919. Archbishop John Theodorovich arrived from Ukraine in 1924. Membership: 87,745 (1966); Headquarters: South Bound Brook, NJ 08880

**Unitarian Universalist Association** The Unitarian movement arose in Congregationalism in the 18th century and produced (1825) the American Unitarian Association. The philosophy of Universalism originated with the doctrine of universal salvation in the first century, and was brought to America in the 1700s. Universalists were organized in 1793. In 1961 the Unitarian and Universalist bodies were consolidated to become the present noncreedal association. Membership: 139,052 (1979); Pres., Dr. O. Eugene Pickett; Headquarters: 25 Beacon St., Boston, MA 02108

**United Church of Christ** This body results from a union (1957) of the Evangelical and Reformed Church and the Congregational Christian Churches. Membership: 1,736,244; Headquarters: 105 Madison Ave., New York, NY 10016

**The United Free Will Baptist Church** A body that was organized in 1870. Membership: 100,000 (1952); Headquarters: Kinston College, 1000 University St., Kinston, NC 28501

**The United Methodist Church** The church was formed (1968) in Dallas by the union of The Methodist Church and The Evangelical United Brethren Church. The Methodist movement began in 18th-century England under John Wesley. The organized Methodist Church was founded (1784) in Baltimore. Francis Asbury was elected the first bishop in this country. The Evangelical United Brethren Church was formed (1946) with the merger of the Evangelical Church and the Church of the United Brethren in Christ. Membership: 9,584,711; Sec. of Gen. Conference, Dr. John B. Holt, Perkins School of Theology, Southern Methodist University, Dallas, TX 75222

METHODIST BISHOPS IN U.S.

*North Central Jurisdiction:* Central Illinois, Leroy C. Hodapp; Detroit, Edsel A. Ammons; East Ohio, James S. Thomas; Iowa, Wayne K. Clymer; Minnesota, Emerson S. Colaw; North Dakota & South Dakota, Edwin C. Boulton; North Indiana, James Armstrong; Northern Illinois, Jesse R. DeWitt; South Indiana, James Armstrong; Southern Illinois, Leroy C. Hodapp; West Michigan, Edsel A. Ammons; West Ohio, Dwight E. Loder; Wisconsin, Marjorie S. Matthews. *Northeastern Jurisdiction:* Baltimore, D. Frederick Wertz; Central New York, Joseph H. Yeakel; Central Pennsylvania, John B. Warman; Eastern Pennsylvania, F. Herbert Skeete; Maine, George W. Bashore; New Hampshire, George W. Bashore; New York, Roy C. Nichols; Northern New Jersey, Dale White; Northern New York, Joseph H. Yeakel; Peninsula, D. Frederick Wertz; Puerto Rico, F. Herbert Skeete; Southern New England, George W. Bashore; Southern New Jersey, Dale White; Troy, Roy C. Nichols; West Virginia, William B. Grove; Western New York, Joseph H. Yeakel; Western Pennsylvania, James M. Ault; Wyoming, John B. Warman. *South Central:* Central Texas, John W. Russell; Kansas East, B. R. Oliphint; Kansas West, B. R. Oliphint; Little Rock, Kenneth W. Hicks; Louisiana, Kenneth W. Shamblin; Missouri East, W.T. Handy, Jr.; Missouri West, W.T. Handy, Jr.; Nebraska, Monk Bryan; New Mexico, L.W. Schowengerdt; North Arkansas, Kenneth W. Hicks; North Texas, John W. Russell; Northwest Texas, L.W. Schowengerdt; Oklahoma, John W. Hardt; Oklahoma Indian Missionary, John W. Hardt; Rio Grande, Ernest T. Dixon; Southwest Texas, Ernest T. Dixon; Texas, Finis A. Crutchfield. *Southeastern Jurisdiction:* Alabama-West Florida, Frank L. Robertson; Florida, Earl G. Hunt, Jr.; Holston, H. Ellis Finger, Jr.; Kentucky, Paul A. Duffey; Louisville, Paul A. Duffey; Memphis, Edward L. Tullis; Mississippi, C.P. Minnick, Jr.; North Alabama, Frank L. Robertson; North Carolina, William R. Cannon; North Georgia, Joel D. McDavid; North Mississippi, C.P. Minnick, Jr.; Red Bird Missionary (KY), Paul A. Duffey; South Carolina, Roy C. Clark; South Georgia, Joel A. McDavid; Tennessee, Edward L. Tullis; Virginia, Robert M. Blackburn; Western North Carolina, L. Scott Allen. *Western Jurisdiction:* Alaska Missionary, Calvin D. McConnell; California-Nevada, Wilbur W.Y. Choy; Oregon-Idaho, Calvin D. McConnell; Pacific Northwest, Melvin G. Talbert; Pacific and Southwest, Jack M. Tuell; Rocky Mountain, Melvin E. Wheatley, Jr.; Yellowstone, Melvin E. Wheatley, Jr.

**United Pentecostal Church International** The Pentecostal Church, Inc. and Pentecostal Assemblies of Jesus Christ merged (1945) at St. Louis. Membership: 465,000; Headquarters: 8855 Dunn Rd., Hazelwood, MO 63042

**The United Presbyterian Church in the United States of America** was formed (1958) through a merger of the United Presbyterian Church of N.A. and the Presbyterian Church in the U.S.A. The Presbyterian Church in the U.S.A. dated from 1706 in Philadelphia, while the United Presbyterian Church of N.A. was formed in 1858 when the Associate Reformed Presbyterian Church and the Associate Presbyterian Church united. Membership: 2,423,601; Headquarters: Office of the General Assembly, 475 Riverside Dr., Rm. 1201, New York, NY 10115

**The Wesleyan Church** This body originated (1968) through the uniting of the Pilgrim Holiness Church (1897) and The Wesleyan Methodist Church of America (1843). It emphasizes scriptural truth concerning the new birth, the entire sanctification of believers, the personal return of Christ, and worldwide holiness evangelism. Membership: 103,160; Headquarters: P.O. Box 2000, Marion, IN 46952

**Wisconsin Evangelical Lutheran Synod** This body was organized (1850) in Wisconsin and subscribes to the confessional writings of the Lutheran Church. Membership: 407,043; Pres., Rev. Carl H. Mischke, 3512 W. North Ave., Milwaukee, WI 53208

# DISASTERS/CATASTROPHES

## MAJOR DISASTERS

This list encompasses both natural disasters and such "technological" catastrophes as rail and aircraft crashes (50 or more deaths), shipwrecks (200 or more deaths), and mine accidents (50 or more deaths). Some other calamities that resulted in fewer fatalities are also cited because of their recentness and/or significance. The list is worldwide in scope.

| Year | Type of Disaster | Place | Remarks |
|---|---|---|---|
| 64 A.D. | Fire | Rome | Fire destroyed most of Rome; Christians were blamed and executed as arsonists |
| 79 A.D. | Volcanic eruption | Pompeii and Herculaneum, Italy | Mount Vesuvius erupted, destroying both cities; more than 2,000 dead |
| 80 A.D. | Epidemic | Rome | Anthrax killed thousands |
| 250–265 | Epidemic | Roman Empire | Bubonic plague killed thousands |
| 444 | Epidemic | Great Britain | Bubonic plague claimed thousands |
| 526 | Earthquake | Antioch, Syria | Shock results killed 250,000 (?) |
| 542 | Epidemic | Roman Empire | Bubonic plague killed tens of thousands |
| 558 | Epidemic | Europe, Asia, and Africa | Bubonic plague and smallpox pandemic killed millions; 5,000–10,000 died daily in Constantinople |
| 681 | Earthquake | Tosa, Japan | Three-square-mile area submerged |
| 740–744 | Epidemic | Constantinople | Bubonic plague killed 200,000 (?) |
| 772 | Epidemic | Chichester, England | Disease killed 34,000 (?) |
| 856 | Earthquake | Corinth, Greece | Disaster killed 45,000 (?) |
| 869 | Earthquake | Sanriku coast, Japan | Shock followed by tidal wave; thousands killed |
| 954 | Epidemic | Scotland | Bubonic plague killed 40,000 (?) |
| 1038 | Earthquake | Shansi, China | Recorded deaths: 23,000 |
| 1057 | Earthquake | Chihli, China | Earthquake killed 25,000 (?) |
| 1228 | Flood | Friesland, Holland | Killed 100,000 (?) |
| 1290 | Earthquake | Chihli, China | September 27; 100,000 (?) victims |
| 1293 | Earthquake | Kamakura, Japan | May 20; 30,000 (?) lives lost |
| 1340s | Epidemic | Asia and Europe | "The Black Death," bubonic plague pandemic, is said to have killed 25 million |
| 1361 | Earthquake | Kotyi, Japan | Thousands killed by quakes |
| 1382–85 | Epidemic | Ireland | Bubonic plague claimed thousands |
| 1407 | Epidemic | London | Bubonic plague killed 30,000 (?) |
| 1456 | Earthquake | Naples | December 5; 30,000–40,000 killed |
| 1491 | Fire | Dresden | City almost destroyed |
| 1499–1500 | Epidemic | London | Bubonic plague and other scourges killed 30,000 (?) |
| 1528 | Epidemic | Italy | July; typhus killed 21,000 (?) |
| 1531 | Earthquake | Lisbon | January 26; 30,000 (?) killed |
| 1545 | Epidemic | Cuba | Typhus killed 250,000 (?) |
| 1556 | Earthquake | Shensi Province, China | January 24; quake killed more than 800,000, the largest number of fatalities from one earthquake in recorded history |
| 1560 | Epidemic | Brazil | Smallpox killed several million |
| 1603 | Epidemic | London | Bubonic plague killed more than 30,000 |
| 1618 | Epidemic | Naples | Diphtheria fatal for 8,000 (?) |
| 1624 | Fire | Oslo | City destroyed |
| 1625 | Epidemic | London | Bubonic plague claimed 35,000 |
| 1628 | Epidemic | Lyons, France | Typhus killed 60,000 (?) |
| 1631 | Volcanic eruption | southern Italy | Mount Vesuvius erupted, followed by earthquake and tidal wave; more than 4,000 dead |
| 1642 | Flood | China | Fatalities: 300,000 (?) |
| 1665 | Epidemic | London | Bubonic plague killed more than 70,000 |
| 1666 | Fire | London | September 2–6; "The Great Fire" destroyed about 14,000 buildings, leaving 200,000 homeless |
| 1669 | Volcanic eruption | Catania, Italy | Mt. Etna erupted, killing 20,000 (?) |
| 1672 | Epidemic | Lyons, France | Bubonic plague killed 60,000 (?) |
| | Epidemic | Naples | In six months bubonic plague claimed 400,000 (?) |
| 1693 | Earthquake | Catania, Italy | January 11; 60,000 died |
| 1694 | Fire | Warwick, England | Destroyed more than half of city |
| 1703 | Storm | England | November 26–27; "Great Storm" killed 8,000 (?) |
| | Earthquake | Tokyo | December 30; earthquake killed 200,000 (?) |
| 1711 | Epidemic | Germany and Austria | Bubonic plague; more than 500,000 fatalities |
| | Marine | Egg Island, Labrador | August 23; 8 English transports wrecked; 900 (?) deaths |
| 1716 | Earthquake | Algiers | Earthquake killed 20,000 (?) |
| 1720 | Epidemic | Marseilles | Bubonic plague killed 50,000–60,000 |
| 1728 | Fire | Copenhagen | City nearly destroyed |
| 1737 | Cyclone | Calcutta | October 7–11; earthquake followed tornado, killing 300,000 (?) |
| 1741 | Epidemic | Cadiz, Spain | Yellow fever fatal for 10,000 (?) |
| 1752 | Fire | Moscow | Destroyed about 18,000 houses |
| 1755 | Earthquake | Lisbon | November 1; quake, fire, and tidal waves killed 60,000 (?) |
| 1759 | Earthquake | Baalbek, Lebanon | October 30; death toll: 30,000 |
| 1783 | Earthquake | southern Italy and Sicily | February 5–March 28; a series of six quakes claimed 50,000 (?) |
| | Volcanic eruption | Iceland | June 8; Mount Skaptar erupted, killing one fifth of the population |
| 1787 | Flood | eastern India | Storm drove seas 20 miles inland; 10,000 (?) fatalities |
| 1792 | Earthquake | Hizen, Japan | Earthquake killed 15,000 (?) |
| | Epidemic | Egypt | Bubonic plague; 800,000 (?) victims |
| 1793 | Epidemic | Philadelphia | Yellow fever killed 5,000 (?) |
| 1797 | Earthquake | Cuzco, Peru and Quito, Ecuador | February 4; quake killed 40,000 (?) |
| 1800 | Epidemic | Spain | Yellow fever claimed 80,000 (?) |
| 1802 | Epidemic | Santo Domingo | Yellow fever killed 29,000 (?) of Napoleon's soldiers |
| 1810 | Epidemic | Cadiz and Barcelona, Spain | Yellow fever fatal for 25,000 (?) |

| Year | Type of Disaster | Place | Remarks |
|---|---|---|---|
| 1815 | Volcanic eruption | Sumbawa Island, Indonesia | April 5; Tamboro erupted, followed by whirlwinds and tidal waves; 12,000 (?) fatalities |
| 1816–19 | Epidemic | Ireland | Typhus lessened population by one fourth |
| 1822 | Earthquake | Aleppo, Syria | September 5; quake claimed 22,000 (?) victims |
| 1826–37 | Epidemic | continental Europe | Cholera pandemic killed millions; 900,000 (?) died in 1831 alone |
| 1828 | Earthquake | Echigo, Japan | December 28; quake killed 30,000 (?) |
| 1831 | Marine | off Cape May, New Jersey | July 9; immigrant vessel **Lady Sherbrooke** sank; 263 dead |
| 1833 | Marine | North Atlantic | May 11; **Lady of the Lake** struck iceberg; 215 dead |
| 1834 | Fire | London | October 16; Houses of Parliament and part of city burned |
| 1835 | Fire | New York City | December 16; 700 buildings destroyed; damage: $20 million |
| 1840–62 | Epidemic | worldwide | Cholera pandemic claimed millions |
| 1841 | Earthquake | Shinano, Japan | Quake killed 12,000 (?) |
| 1842 | Fire | Hamburg, Germany | May 4–7; much of the city destroyed; damage: $35 million |
| 1845–48 | Famine | Ireland | Potato crop failure; over 750,000 died of starvation and hundreds of thousands left the country |
| 1846 | Fire | Quebec | June 12; theater burned; 200 (?) dead |
| 1847–48 | Epidemic | London | Influenza killed 15,000 (?) |
| 1849 | Fire | St. Louis | May 17; 15 blocks of the city destroyed; damage: $3.5 million |
| 1850 | Marine | off Margate, England | March 29; **Royal Adelaide** wrecked; 400 (?) lost |
| 1851–55 | Epidemic | England | Tuberculosis killed an average of 51,000 a year |
| 1852 | Marine | off South Africa | February 26; British troopship **Birkenhead** wrecked; 454 dead |
| 1853 | Marine | off Scotland | September 29; immigrant ship **Annie Jane** wrecked; 348 dead |
| 1854 | Marine | in the Atlantic between London and Philadelphia | March; **City of Glasgow** vanished; 450 lost |
| | Marine | in the Atlantic near Grand Banks | September 27; U.S.S. **Arctic** sank; 350 (?) dead |
| | Marine | off New Jersey coast | November 13; immigrant ship **New Era** wrecked; over 300 dead |
| 1855 | Mine | Coalfield, Virginia | Coal mine exploded; 55 dead |
| 1856 | Rail | near Philadelphia | July 17; train wrecked; 66 fatalities |
| | Hurricane | Ile Dernière, Louisiana | August 10–11; tropical storm destroyed island, killing over 400 |
| 1857 | Blizzard | U.S. eastern seaboard | January 17–19; this violent storm caused widespread damage |
| | Marine | in the Atlantic between New York and Havana | September 12; **Central America** sank; 400 (?) dead |
| 1858 | Marine | in the Atlantic between Hamburg and New York City | September 13; **Austria** burned; 471 dead |
| 1859 | Marine | off Ireland | April 27; **Pomona** wrecked; 400 (?) lost |
| | Marine | in the Irish Sea | October 25; **Royal Charter** wrecked; 450 (?) dead |
| 1860 | Marine | on Lake Michigan | September 8; excursion steamer **Lady Elgin** and lumbership **Augusta** collided; 300 (?) dead |
| 1863 | Epidemic | England | Scarlet fever killed more than 30,000 |
| | Fire | Santiago, Chile | December 8; Church of Campania burned, killing over 2,000 |
| 1863–75 | Epidemic | worldwide | Cholera pandemic; in 1866 Prussia lost 120,000 (?) and Austria, 110,000 |
| 1864 | Rail | near St. Hilaire, Canada | June 29; train ran through open switch; 90 (?) dead |
| | Rail | near Shohola, Pennsylvania | July 15; two-train collision; 65 dead |
| | Cyclone | Calcutta | October 1; most of city destroyed by storm; 70,000 (?) dead |
| 1865 | Marine | Memphis, Tennessee | April 27; river steamer **Sultana** exploded and sank; 1,400 dead |
| 1866 | Fire | Portland, Maine | July 4; city almost destroyed by fire; damage: $10 million |
| | Fire | Quebec | October 13; about 2,500 buildings destroyed |
| 1867 | Mine | Winterpock, Virginia | April 3; coal mines exploded, killing 69 |
| | Marine | St. Thomas, West Indies | October 29; **Rhone, Wye,** and many small vessels wrecked in storm; 1,000 (?) dead |
| 1868 | Earthquake | Peru and Ecuador | August 13–15; quake killed 25,000 (?); damage: $300 million |
| 1869 | Mine | Plymouth, Pennsylvania | September 6; coal mine fire killed 110 |
| 1870 | Marine | off Finistère, France | September 6; English warship **Captain** foundered; 472 fatalities |
| 1871 | Fire | Chicago | October 8–9; 3.5 sq. miles destroyed and 250 (?) dead from "Mrs. O'Leary's cow kicking over lantern"; damage $200 million |
| | Fire | Michigan and Wisconsin | October 8–14; more than 1 million acres of forest consumed; 1,000 (?) dead, mostly in Peshtigo, Wis. |
| 1872 | Fire | Boston | November 9–11; more than 600 buildings burned; damage: $75 million |
| | Marine | in the Atlantic | About November 25; Nova Scotian **Mary Celeste** abandoned; 10 lost |
| 1873 | Marine | off Nova Scotia | April 1; British steamer **Atlantic** wrecked; 481 dead |
| 1875 | Earthquake | Venezuela and Colombia | May 16; quake killed 16,000 (?) |
| 1876 | Cyclone | Bakarganj, India | October 31; storm and subsequent wave killed 200,000 (?) |
| | Fire | Brooklyn, New York | December 5; Conway's Theater burned; 300 (?) dead |
| | Rail | Ashtabula River, Ohio | December 29; train derailed as iron bridge collapsed; 91 dead |
| 1877 | Fire | St. John, New Brunswick | June 20; this Canadian fire killed 100; damage: $12.5 million |
| 1878 | Epidemic | southern United States | Yellow fever claimed 14,000 (?) |
| | Marine | on the Thames, London | September 3; British **Princess Alice** sank; 700 (?) dead |
| 1881 | Typhoon | China and Indo-China | October 8; violent storm plus tidal wave killed 300,000 (?) |
| | Fire | Vienna | December 8; Ring Theater burned; more than 600 dead |
| 1882 | Cyclone | Bombay | June 5; storm and subsequent tidal wave killed 100,000 (?) |
| | Rail | near Tchery, Russia | July 13; train derailed; more than 150 dead |
| 1883 | Fire | Berdichev, Russia | January 13; theater fire killed more than 150 |
| | Mine | Braidwood, Illinois | February 16; coal mine flooded; 69 drowned |
| | Earthquakes | Ischia, Tyrrhenian Sea | July 28 and August 3; these two quakes killed 2,000 (?) |
| 1883 | Volcanic eruption | Sunda Strait, Indonesia | August 26–28; Krakatoa erupted, destroying two thirds of the island; 36,419 dead and many missing after the greatest eruption of modern times. |
| 1883–94 | Epidemic | worldwide | Cholera pandemic killed millions |
| 1884 | Mine | Crested Butte, Colorado | January 24; coal mine exploded; 59 dead |
| | Tornado | central United States | February 18–19; series of tornadoes destroyed 10,000 (?) buildings and killed 800 (?) |
| | Mine | Pocahontas, Virginia | March 13; coal mine explosion killed 112 |
| 1886 | Blizzard | central United States | January 6–13; Kansas was hardest hit; 70 (?) dead |
| | Earthquake | Charleston, S.C. | August 31; quake caused severe damage and killed 60 |
| 1887 | Flood | Honan, China | Yellow River overflowed; more than 900,000 dead |
| | Fire | Paris | May 25; Opéra Comique burned, killing 200 (?) |

| Year | Type of Disaster | Place | Remarks |
|---|---|---|---|
| | Rail | Chatsworth, Illinois | August 10; train wrecked by collapse of burning bridge; 81 dead |
| | Fire | Exeter, England | September 4; theater burned; 200 (?) dead |
| 1888 | Blizzard | U.S. eastern seaboard | March 11–14; blizzard paralyzed major cities of Northeast, and killed more than 400; damage: several million dollars |
| | Rail | Mud Run, Pennsylvania | October 10; locomotive hit standing train; more than 50 dead |
| 1889 | Flood | Johnstown, Pennsylvania | May 31; this legendary American deluge killed more than 2,000 |
| 1889–90 | Epidemic | worldwide | Influenza pandemic affected about 40 percent of the globe's population |
| 1891 | Mine | Mount Pleasant, Pennsylvania | January 27; coal mine exploded; 109 dead |
| | Marine | off Gibraltar | March 17; British steamer **Utopia** sank; 574 dead |
| | Rail | near Basel, Switzerland | June 14; trains collided; 100 (?) dead |
| | Earthquake | Mino-Owari, Japan | October 28; quake killed 10,000 (?) |
| 1892 | Mine | Krebs, Oklahoma | January 7; coal mine exploded; 100 dead |
| 1893 | Hurricane | southern United States and Caribbean | August 23–30; tropical storm devastated Charleston, S.C., and Savannah, Ga.; 1,000 (?) dead |
| 1894 | Fire | Hinckley, Minnesota | September 1; more than 160,000 acres of forest burned |
| 1895 | Marine | near Gibraltar | March 14; Spanish cruiser **Reina Regenta** foundered; 400 dead |
| | Mine | Red Canyon, Wyoming | March 20; coal mine exploded, killing 60 |
| 1896 | Tornado | St. Louis | May; storm that devastated city killed 306; damage: $13 million |
| | Earthquake | Sanriku coast, Japan | June; quake and tidal wave killed 27,000 (?) |
| | Mine | Pittston, Pennsylvania | June 28; coal mine cave-in; 58 dead |
| | Rail | Atlantic City, New Jersey | July 30; train wrecked; 60 dead |
| 1898 | Marine | Havana | February 15; U.S. battleship **Maine** exploded; more than 260 dead |
| | Marine | near Sable Island, off Nova Scotia | July 4; French **La Bourgogne** and British **Cromartyshire** collided; 560 lost |
| | Marine | in the Atlantic off U.S. coast | November 26; **Portland** wrecked during storm; 200 (?) dead |
| 1898–1908 | Epidemic | China and India | Bubonic plague killed 3 (?) million |
| 1900 | Fire | Hull and Ottawa, Canada | April 26; conflagration damage: $10 million |
| | Mine | Scofield, Utah | May 1; coal mine exploded; 200 dead |
| | Fire | Hoboken, New Jersey | June 30; pier burned and 300 died; damage: over $4.6 million |
| | Hurricane | Texas | August 27–September 15; storm was followed by storm tide that inundated Galveston Island; 6,000 (?) dead |
| 1901 | Fire | Jacksonville, Florida | May 3; damage: $10 million |
| 1902 | Volcanic eruption | Martinique, West Indies | May 8; Mont Pelée erupted, totally destroying the city of St. Pierre and killing more than 30,000 |
| | Mine | Coal Creek, Tennessee | May 19; coal mine exploded, killing 184 |
| | Mine | Johnstown, Pennsylvania | July 10; coal mine exploded; 112 dead |
| | Fire | Birmingham, Alabama | September 20; church burned; 115 dead |
| 1903 | Flood | Heppner, Oregon | Flood destroyed this town and killed more than 250 |
| | Mine | Hanna, Wyoming | June 30; coal mine explosion and fire killed 169 |
| | Rail | Laurel Run, Pennsylvania | December 23; train crashed into fallen timber; 75 (?) dead |
| | Fire | Chicago | December 30; Iroquois Theater burned; 600 (?) victims |
| 1904 | Mine | Cheswick, Pennsylvania | January 25; coal mine exploded; 179 dead |
| | Fire | Baltimore | February 7–8; 75 city blocks burned; damage: $85 million |
| | Fire | Toronto | April 19; damage: $12 million |
| | Marine | New York City | June 15; steamer **General Slocum** burned in East River; more than 1,000 dead |
| | Marine | Rockall Reef, Scotland | June 28; **Norge** wrecked; more than 600 dead |
| | Rail | Eden, Colorado | August 7; train wreck killed 96 |
| | Rail | New Market, Tennessee | September 24; train wrecked; 56 dead |
| 1905 | Mine | Virginia City, Alabama | February 26; coal mine exploded; 112 dead |
| 1906 | Mine | Courrières, France | March 10; explosion fatal for 1,060 |
| | Earthquake | San Francisco | April 18; fire followed famous 'Frisco quake, which together killed 700 (?) and left more than 250,000 homeless; damage: $524 million |
| | Typhoon | Hong Kong | September 19; tropical cyclone claimed 50,000 (?) |
| | Rail | Washington, D.C. | December 30; train wrecked; 53 dead |
| 1907 | Mine | Stuart, West Virginia | January 29; coal mine exploded; 84 dead |
| | Mine | Monongah, West Virginia | December 6; coal mines exploded, killing 361 |
| | Mine | Jacobs Creek, Pennsylvania | December 19; coal mine exploded; 239 dead |
| | Epidemic | India | Bubonic plague killed 1.3 million |
| 1908 | Fire | Boyertown, Pennsylvania | January 13; Rhoades Opera House burned; more than 100 dead |
| | Fire | Collinwood, Ohio | March 4; school burned, killing more than 160 |
| | Mine | Hanna, Wyoming | March 28; coal mine exploded; 59 lost |
| | Fire | Chelsea, Massachusetts | April 12; city destroyed by fire; damage: $17 million |
| | Mine | Marianna, Pennsylvania | November 28; coal mines exploded; 154 killed |
| | Earthquake | southern Italy and Sicily | December 28; quake rendered one million (?) homeless and took lives of 100,000 (?) |
| | Mine | Switchback, West Virginia | December 29; coal mine exploded; 50 dead |
| 1909 | Mine | Switchback, West Virginia | January 12; coal mine exploded; 67 dead |
| | Fire | Acapulco | February 15; Flores Theater burned; 250 (?) dead |
| | Hurricane | Louisiana and Mississippi | September 14–21; this tropical storm killed 350 |
| | Mine | Cherry, Illinois | November 13; coal mine fire killed 259 |
| 1909–18 | Epidemic | China and India | Bubonic plague fatal for 1.5 million (?) |
| 1910 | Mine | Primero, Colorado | January 31; coal mine exploded; 75 dead |
| | Rail | Wellington, Washington | March 1; avalanche swept two trains into canyon; 96 dead |
| | Rail | Green Mountain, Iowa | March 21; train wrecked; 55 dead |
| | Mine | Palos, Alabama | May 5; coal mine exploded; 90 dead |
| | Mine | Starkville, Colorado | October 8; coal mine exploded; 56 dead |
| | Mine | Delagua, Colorado | November 8; coal mine explosion and fire killed 79 |
| 1910–11 | Epidemic | Manchuria | Pneumonic plague killed 60,000 (?) |
| 1911 | Flood | China | Yangtze River overflowed; 100,000 (?) dead |
| | Fire | New York City | March 25; Triangle Shirtwaist Factory holocaust claimed 145 |
| | Mine | Throop, Pennsylvania | April 7; coal mine burned; 72 dead |
| | Mine | Littleton, Alabama | April 8; coal mine exploded; 128 dead |
| | Mine | Briceville, Tennessee | December 9; coal mine explosion killed 84 |
| 1912 | Marine | off Spain | March 5; Spanish **Principe de Asturias** wrecked; 500 dead |
| | Mine | McCurtain, Oklahoma | March 20; coal mine exploded; 73 dead |
| | Mine | Jed, West Virginia | March 26; coal mine exploded; 83 dead |

| Year | Type of Disaster | Place | Remarks |
|---|---|---|---|
| | Marine | in the North Atlantic | April 15; "unsinkable" British **Titanic** struck an iceberg and sank; 1,500 (?) dead |
| | Marine | off Japan | September 28; Japanese **Kichemaru** sank; 1,000 lost |
| 1913 | Tornado | Omaha | March 23; storm fatal for 100 (?); damage: $3.5 million |
| | Flood | Ohio and Indiana | March 25–27; Ohio and Indiana Rivers overflowed; 700 (?) dead |
| | Mine | Finleyville, Pennsylvania | April 23; coal mine exploded; 96 dead |
| | Mine | Dawson, New Mexico | October 22; coal mine exploded, killing 263 |
| 1914 | Mine | Eccles, West Virginia | April 28; coal mines exploded; 183 dead |
| | Marine | St. Lawrence River | May 29; Canadian Pacific **Empress of Ireland** collided with collier and sank; 1,024 dead |
| | Fire | Salem, Massachusetts | June 25–26; conflagration destroyed 1,700 (?) buildings; damage: $14 million |
| | Mine | Royalton, Illinois | October 27; coal mine exploded; 52 dead |
| 1915 | Earthquake | central Italy | January 13; quake killed 30,000 (?) |
| | Mine | Layland, West Virginia | March 2; coal mine exploded; 112 dead |
| | Marine | off coast of Ireland | May 7; **Lusitania** sunk by German submarine; 1,198 dead |
| | Rail | near Gretna, Scotland | May 22; three trains crashed; 227 killed |
| | Marine | Chicago River, Chicago | July 24; excursion boat **Eastland** capsized in port; 800–900 dead |
| | Epidemic | Serbia | Summer; typhus claimed 150,000 (?) |
| | Hurricane | Texas and Louisiana | August 5–25; tropical storm followed by storm tide; 275 (?) dead |
| | Hurricane | Gulf Coast | September 22–October 1; in large area of Louisiana, 90 percent of the buildings were destroyed; more than 250 dead |
| 1916 | Marine | in the Mediterranean | February 26; French cruiser **Provence** sank; 3,100 (?) dead |
| | Fire | Paris, Texas | March 21; fire destroyed 1,440 structures; damage: $11 million |
| | Tornado | Arkansas | June 5; series of twisters claimed 100 (?) |
| | Explosion | Jersey City, New Jersey | July 30; German sabotage (explosion and fire) on Black Tom Island killed 4; damage: more than $14 million |
| | Marine | off China | August 29; **Hsin Yu** sank; 1,000 (?) dead |
| 1917 | Explosion | Chester, Pennsylvania | April 10; munitions-plant blast killed 125 |
| | Mine | Hastings, Colorado | April 27; coal mine exploded; 121 dead |
| | Mine | Clay, Kentucky | August 4; coal mine exploded; 62 dead |
| | Fire | Halifax, Nova Scotia | December 6; S.S. **Mont Blanc** and Belgian relief ship **Imo** collided and exploded, with resulting fire consuming one square mile of the city; more than 1,400 dead |
| | Rail | near Modane, France | December 12; troop train derailed near entrance to Mont Cenis tunnel; 550 (?) dead |
| 1917–19 | Epidemic | worldwide | Influenza pandemic killed 20–30 million |
| 1917–21 | Epidemic | Russia | Typhus killed 2.5–3 million |
| 1918 | Marine | Barbados, West Indies | March 4; U.S.S. **Cyclops** lost at sea; 280 fatalities |
| | Rail | Ivanhoe, Indiana | June 22; two trains collided; 85 dead |
| | Rail | near Nashville, Tennessee | July 9; head-on collision killed 100 (?) |
| | Marine | Tokayama Bay, Japan | July 12; Japanese battleship **Kawachi** exploded; 500 (?) dead |
| | Earthquake | Puerto Rico | October 11; sea wave followed quake; 116 dead |
| | Fire | Minnesota and Wisconsin | October 13–15; death toll: 1,000 (?); damages from the forest fires: $100 million |
| | Rail | Brooklyn, New York | November 1; derailment at Malbone St. tunnel; 100 (?) dead |
| 1919 | Marine | in the Strait of Messina | January 17; French **Chaonia** wrecked; 460 dead |
| | Mine | Wilkes-Barre, Pennsylvania | June 5; coal powder explosion killed 92 |
| | Fire | San Juan, Puerto Rico | June 20; Mayaguez Theater burned, killing 150 |
| | Tornado | Fergus Falls, Minnesota | June 22; storm killed 59; damages: $3.5 million |
| | Hurricane | Florida, Louisiana, and Texas | September 2–15; cyclone killed 287 |
| 1920s | Epidemic | India | Bubonic plague claimed 2 (?) million |
| 1920 | Blizzard | New England | March 5–6; this severe snowstorm considered comparable with "Blizzard of '88" |
| | Earthquake | Kansu, China | December 16; quake destroyed 10 cities and killed 180,000 (?) |
| 1921 | Epidemic | India | Cholera claimed 500,000 (?) |
| | Marine | off Swatow, South China Sea | March 18; **Hong Kong** wrecked on rocks; 1,000 (?) dead |
| | Aircraft | near Hull, England | August 24; British dirigible **ZR–2** broke in two; 62 dead |
| | Explosion | Oppau, Germany | September 21; ammonium nitrate blast killed 600 (?) |
| 1922 | Fire | Smyrna, Asia Minor | September 13; city almost destroyed; hundreds dead; damage: $100 million |
| | Mine | Spangler, Pennsylvania | November 6; coal mine exploded; 77 dead |
| | Mine | Dolomite, Alabama | November 22; coal mine explosion killed 90 |
| 1923 | Mine | Dawson, New Mexico | February 8; coal mine exploded; 120 dead |
| | Mine | Kemmerer, Wyoming | August 14; coal mine exploded; 99 dead |
| | Earthquake | Tokyo and Yokohama | September 1; quake followed by fire destroyed most of both Japanese cities; 200,000 (?) dead |
| | Fire | Berkeley, California | September 17; fire destroyed more than 600 buildings; damage: $12.5 million |
| | Aircraft | in the Mediterranean or Sahara Desert | December 21; French dirigible **Dixmude** disappeared; 50 (?) lost |
| 1924 | Epidemic | India | Cholera death toll: 300,000 (?) |
| | Mine | Castle Gate, Utah | March 8; coal mine exploded; 171 dead |
| 1924 | Mine | Benwood, West Virginia | April 28; coal mine explosion killed 119 |
| | Tornado | Lorain and Sandusky, Ohio | June 28; twister killed 85; damage: $12 million |
| 1925 | Mine | Sullivan, Indiana | February 20; coal mine exploded; 52 dead |
| | Tornado | Missouri, Illinois, and Indiana | March 18; tornado killed 689; damage: $17 million |
| | Mine | Coal Glen, North Carolina | May 27; coal mine exploded; 53 dead |
| | Rail | Hackettstown, New Jersey | June 16; train derailed at highway crossing; 50 dead |
| | Mine | Acemar, Alabama | December 10; coal mine exploded; 53 dead |
| 1926–30 | Epidemic | India | Smallpox claimed 423,000 (?) |
| 1926 | Mine | Wilburton, Oklahoma | January 13; coal mine explosion killed 91 |
| | Hurricane | Florida and Alabama | September 11–22; 243 dead |
| 1927 | Mine | Everettville, West Virginia | April 30; coal mine exploded; 97 dead |
| | Tornado | Arkansas and Missouri | May 9; 92 dead from storm |
| | Tornado | St. Louis | September 29; death toll: 90; damage: $40 million |
| 1928 | Flood | Santa Paula, California | March 13; St. Francis Dam collapsed; 450 dead |
| | Mine | Mather, Pennsylvania | May 19; coal mine explosion killed 195 |

| Year | Type of Disaster | Place | Remarks |
|---|---|---|---|
| | Flood | southern Florida | September 6–20; hurricane caused Lake Okeechobee to overflow; 1,836 lives lost |
| | Marine | off the Virginia Capes | November 12; British steamer **Vestris** sank; 110 (?) dead |
| 1929 | Fire | Cleveland | May 15; hospital burned; 125 suffocations from poisonous fumes |
| | Mine | McAlester, Oklahoma | December 17; coal mine exploded; 61 dead |
| 1930 | Fire | Columbus | April 21; Ohio State Penitentiary burned, killing 317 convicts |
| | Earthquake | Naples | July 23–25; shock results killed 1,883 and injured 10,000 (?) |
| | Hurricane | Dominican Republic | September 3; storm fatalities: 2,000 (?) |
| | Aircraft | Beauvais, France | October 5; British dirigible **R–101** crashed; 47 dead |
| | Mine | Millfield, Ohio | November 5; coal mine exploded; 82 dead |
| 1931 | Flood | Yangtze River, China | July–August; flood waters of Yangtze leave over 2 million homeless and 140,000 dead |
| 1932 | Tornado | southern United States | March 21–22; tornadoes hit five states; at least 362 dead |
| | Mine | Moweaqua, Illinois | December 23; coal mine exploded; 54 dead |
| | Earthquake | Kansu, China | December 26; quake killed 70,000 (?) |
| 1933 | Earthquake | Sanriku coast, Japan | March 3; quake killed more than 2,500 |
| | Earthquake | Long Beach, California | March 10; quake claimed 115 lives; damage: $40 million |
| | Aircraft | New Jersey coast | April 4; U.S. dirigible **Akron II** crashed; 73 dead |
| 1934 | Fire | Hakodate, Japan | March 22; fire destroyed city; 1,500 dead (?) |
| | Marine | off New Jersey | September 8; luxury liner **Morro Castle** burned; 134 dead |
| | Typhoon | Honshu, Japan | September 21; storm killed 4,000 (?); damage: $50 million |
| | Mine | Wrexham, Wales | September 22; coal mine exploded; 265 dead |
| 1935 | Epidemic | Uganda | Bubonic plague killed 2,000 (?) |
| | Earthquake | India and Pakistan | May 31; quake killed more than 50,000 |
| | Hurricane | southern Florida | August 29–September 10; storm killed 408; damage: up to $50 million |
| | Hurricane | Haiti | October 22; storm and flood fatalities: more than 2,000 |
| 1936 | Tornado | southern United States | April 5–6; series of twisters, mostly in Mississippi and Georgia, killed 455; damage: $21 million |
| 1937 | Fire | Antung, Manchuria | February 13; theater burned, killing 658 |
| | Explosion | New London, Texas | March 19; natural gas explosion destroyed school; more than 400 dead |
| | Aircraft | Lakehurst, New Jersey | May 6; German zeppelin **Hindenburg** exploded; 36 dead |
| | Rail | near Patna, India | July 16; Delhi-Calcutta express derailed; 107 dead |
| 1938 | Aircraft | Bogotá, Colombia | July 24; military stunt plane crashed into grandstand, killing 53 |
| | Hurricane | Long Island and lower New England | September 10–22; this storm killed 600; damage: $50–500 million |
| | Rail | near Kishinev, Rumania | December 25; two-train collision killed 100 (?) |
| 1939 | Earthquake | Chile | January 24; quake killed 40,000 (?) |
| | Marine | off New Hampshire | May 23; U.S. submarine **Squalus** sank; 26 dead |
| | Marine | in the Irish Sea | June 1; British submarine **Thetis** sank; 99 lost |
| | Marine | off Indochina | June 15; French submarine **Phenix** sank; 63 dead |
| | Flood | Tientsin, China | July–August; millions rendered homeless and thousands dead |
| | Fire | Langunillas, Venezuela | November 14; oil town built over Lake Maracaibo destroyed |
| | Rail | near Magdeburg, Germany | December 22; two trains collided; 132 dead |
| | Rail | near Freidrichshafen, Germany | December 22; train wrecked; 99 dead |
| | Earthquake | Anatolia, Turkey | December 27; series of shocks and subsequent floods devastated about 60,000 square miles; more than 30,000 dead |
| 1940 | Mine | Bartley, West Virginia | January 10; coal mine exploded; 91 dead |
| | Rail | Osaka, Japan | January 29; two trains collided; 200 (?) dead |
| | Mine | St. Clairsville, Ohio | March 16; coal mine exploded; 72 dead |
| | Mine | Portage, Pennsylvania | July 15; coal mine explosion killed 63 |
| | Blizzard | U.S. Northeast and Midwest | November 11–12; one of the most destructive snowstorms ever caused 144 deaths; damage: $6 million |
| 1941 | Marine | off Maine | June 16; U.S. submarine **O–9** sank in test dive; 33 fatalities |
| 1942 | Marine | New York City | February 9; French liner **Normandie** burned at pier; 1 dead |
| | Tornado | U.S. South and Midwest | March 17; twister killed 111 |
| | Mine | Honkeiko Colliery, Manchuria | April 26; worst mine disaster in history; 1,549 dead |
| | Mine | Osage, West Virginia | May 12; coal mine exploded; 56 dead |
| | Marine | off England | October 2; British **Curacao** rammed and sunk by **Queen Mary**; more than 330 dead |
| | Cyclone | Bengal, India | October 16; storm fatalities: 40,000 (?) |
| | Fire | Boston | November 28; Cocoanut Grove night club burned; 492 dead |
| 1943 | Mine | Red Lodge, Montana | February 27; coal mine exploded; 74 dead |
| | Rail | Philadelphia | September 6; "Congressional Limited" derailed; 80 dead |
| | Rail | near Lumberton, North Carolina | December 16; two trains collided; 72 dead |
| 1944 | Earthquake | San Juan, Argentina | January 15; quake killed 5,000 (?) |
| | Rail | Leon Province, Spain | January 16; train wrecked inside tunnel; 500–800 dead |
| | Rail | near Salerno, Italy | March 2; train stalled in tunnel, suffocating 526 |
| | Mine | Belmont, Ohio | July 5; coal mine fire claimed 66 |
| | Fire | Hartford, Connecticut | July 6; circus "big top" burned, killing 168 |
| | Marine | Port Chicago, California | July 18; two ammunition ships exploded; 322 dead |
| | Aircraft | Freckleton, England | August 23; U.S. bomber crashed into school; more than 70 dead |
| | Hurricane | U.S. eastern seaboard | September 9–16; storm killed 46; damage: $50–500 million |
| | Fire | Cleveland | October 20; liquid gas tanks exploded, setting fire to 50-block area and killing 130; damage: $10 million |
| | Rail | near Ogden, Utah | December 31; sections of "Pacific Limited" collided; 50 dead |
| 1945 | Marine | off Danzig | January 30; German passengership **Wilhelm Gustloff** loaded with refugees and hospital ship **General Steuben** sunk by Soviet submarine; 6,800 lives lost in world's largest marine disaster |
| | Rail | Cazadero, Mexico | February 1; train struck from rear by freight train; 100 (?) dead |
| | Marine | Bari, Italy | April 9; U.S.S. **Liberty** exploded in harbor; 360 dead |
| | Tornado | Oklahoma and Arkansas | April 12; twister killed 102; damage: $4 million |
| | Aircraft | New York City | July 28; U.S. bomber crashed into Empire State Building; 13 dead |
| 1946 | Rail | near Aracaju, Brazil | March 20; train wreck killed 185 |
| | Earthquake | Dutch Harbor, Alaska | April 1; subterranean quake caused tidal waves that hit Hawaiian Islands, Aleutians, and the West Coast; 173 dead in Hawaii alone and damage there $25 million |

| Year | Type of Disaster | Place | Remarks |
|---|---|---|---|
| | Fire | Atlanta | December 7; Winecoff Hotel burned; 119 dead |
| | Aircraft | near Shanghai | December 25; three China Air Transport planes crashed, separately, in fog; at least 71 dead |
| 1947 | Marine | off Athens | January 19; Greek ship **Himera** struck mine and sank; 392 lost |
| | Aircraft | Bogotá, Colombia | February 15; Avianca DC–4 crashed into Mount Tablazo; 53 fatalities |
| | Mine | Centralia, Illinois | March 25; coal mine exploded; 111 dead |
| | Tornado | Texas, Oklahoma, and Kansas | April 9; twister killed 167; damage: $10 million |
| | Explosion | Texas City, Texas | April 16; S.S. **Grandcamp** blew up, destroying most of city and killing 561; damage: $67 million |
| | Aircraft | Leesburg, Virginia | June 13; Pennsylvania Central DC–4 crashed; 50 dead |
| | Explosion | Cadiz, Spain | August 18; dockyard exploded; 147 dead |
| | Epidemic | Egypt | September–December; cholera killed 10,276 |
| | Hurricane | Florida and Gulf coasts | September 4–21; storm fatalities: 51; damage: $50–500 million |
| | Typhoon | Honshu, Japan | September 15–19; storm plus floods killed 2,000 (?) |
| | Aircraft | Bryce Canyon, Utah | October 24; United DC–6 crashed into hillside; 52 dead |
| | Fire | Bar Harbor, Maine | October 25; forest fire on Mount Desert Island burned large part of famous summer resort; damage: $30 million |
| 1948 | Marine | in the Inland Sea, Japan | January 28; freighter **Joo Maru** struck mine and sank; 250 dead |
| | Earthquake | Fukui, Japan | June 28; quake destroyed most of city; more than 5,000 dead |
| | Explosion | Ludwigshafen, Germany | July 28; blast and fire at I. G. Farben chemical works killed more than 200; damage: $6 million |
| | Aircraft | French West Africa | August 1; Air France plane disappeared on flight from Martinique; 53 lost |
| | Explosion | Hong Kong | September 22; chemical warehouse blast and fire killed 135 |
| 1949 | Marine | off southern China | January 27; Chinese **Taiping** and collier collided and sank; more than 600 dead |
| | Fire | Effingham, Illinois | April 5; St. Anthony's Hospital burned; 74 dead |
| | Aircraft | Puerto Rico | June 7; U.S. Strato Freight crashed into water ; 54 dead |
| | Earthquake | Ecuador | August 5; shock razed 50 towns; 100,000 (?) homeless and 6,000 (?) dead; damage: $20 million |
| | Marine | Toronto | September 17; Canadian **Noronic** burned at pier; 130 (?) dead |
| | Rail | Nowy Dwor, Poland | October 22; Danzig-Warsaw express derailed; 200 (?) dead |
| | Cyclone | southeastern India | October 27; storm fatalities: 1,000 (?) |
| | Typhoon | Philippine Islands | October 31–November 2; storm killed 1,000 (?) |
| | Aircraft | Washington, D.C. | November 1; Bolivian fighter plane and Eastern DC–4 collided over airport; 55 dead |
| 1950 | Marine | in the Thames estuary, England | January 12; British submarine **Truculent** rammed by Swedish tanker; more than 60 dead |
| | Aircraft | near Cardiff, Wales | March 12; British Avro Tudor V crashed; 80 dead |
| | Rail | near Tangua, Brazil | April 6; train plunged into Indios River; 108 dead |
| | Rail | near Jasidih, India | May 7; Punjab mail train crash killed 81 |
| | Fire | Rimouski, Quebec | May 7; blaze left 2,000 homeless; damage: $12 million |
| | Trolley | Chicago | May 25; trolley and gas truck collided; 34 dead |
| | Aircraft | in Lake Michigan | June 24; Northwest DC–4 crash claimed 58 |
| | Flood | Anhwei Province, China | August 14; cataclysm inundated more than five million acres, leaving 10 million homeless and killing 500 |
| | Earthquake | Assam, India | August 15; quake killed 1,500 (?) and devastated area of about 30,000 miles |
| | Aircraft | Cairo | August 31; TWA Constellation crashed; 55 dead |
| | Aircraft | Grenoble, France | November 13; Canadian Curtiss-Reid DC–4 crashed; 58 dead |
| | Rail | Richmond Hill, New York | November 22; commuter train rammed by another; 79 dead |
| | Blizzard | U.S. Northeast | November 25; this storm killed 100 (?) |
| 1951 | Tornado | Comoro Islands | January 4; more than 500 victims |
| | Rail | Woodbridge, New Jersey | February 6; commuter train plunged through overpass; 84 dead |
| | Aircraft | in the North Atlantic | March 23; U.S.A.F. plane wreckage found off Ireland; 53 lost |
| | Marine | off Isle of Wight | April 16; British submarine **Affray** sank; 75 dead |
| | Earthquake | Jacuapa, El Salvador | May 6; fatalities numbered more than 1,000 |
| | Mine | Easington, England | May 29; coal mine explosion killed 81 |
| | Rail | Nova Iguaca, Brazil | June 7; train and gasoline truck collided; 54 dead |
| | Aircraft | Colorado | June 30; United DC–6 crashed; 50 dead |
| | Flood | Kansas and Missouri | July 2–19; the most severe floods in American history killed 41 and left 200,000 homeless; damage: $1 billion |
| | Aircraft | near Decoto, California | August 24; United DC–6B crashed; 50 dead |
| | Flood | Manchuria | August 28; deluge caused extensive damage; 5,000 (?) dead or missing |
| | Typhoon | Philippine Islands | December 9–10; fatalities: 724 |
| | Aircraft | Elizabeth, New Jersey | December 16; nonscheduled plane plunged into river after take-off from Newark Airport; 56 dead |
| | Mine | West Frankfort, Illinois | December 21; coal mine exploded; 119 dead |
| 1952 | Rail | near Rio de Janeiro | March 4; two trains crashed; 119 dead |
| | Tornado | Mississippi Valley | March 21–22; twisters killed 229 |
| | Aircraft | Moscow | March 27; two Soviet planes collided over Tula Airport; 70 dead |
| | Aircraft | San Juan, Puerto Rico | April 11; Pan Am DC–4 crashed; 52 dead |
| | Marine | in the Atlantic | April 26; U.S. destroyer-minesweeper **Hobson** and aircraft carrier Wasp collided; **Hobson** sank; 176 dead |
| | Aircraft | northern Brazil | April 29; Pan Am Stratocruiser crashed in jungle; 50 dead |
| | Rail | near Rzepin, Poland | July 9; train wrecked; 160 dead |
| | Earthquake | southern California | July 21; quake killed 14; damage: $60 million |
| | Bus | near Waco, Texas | August 4; two buses collided; 28 dead |
| | Rail | Harrow-Wealdstone, England | October 8; two trains collided with a third; 112 dead |
| | Typhoon | Luzon, Philippine Islands | October 22; this tropical cyclone left 1,000 (?) dead or missing |
| | Aircraft | near Elmendorf A.F.B., Alaska | November 23; U.S.A.F. plane crashed; 52 dead |
| | Aircraft | in Moses Lake, Washington | December 20; after takeoff, U.S.A.F. plane crashed and caught fire; 87 dead |
| 1953 | Marine | off Pusan, South Korea | January 9; South Korean liner sank in heavy seas; 249 dead |
| | Flood | northern Europe | January 31–February 1; floods devastated North Sea coastal areas; more than 2,000 dead |
| | Trolley | Mexico City | February 21; two trolley cars collided; more than 60 dead |
| | Earthquake | eastern Iran | February 22; town of Trud destroyed; 1,000 dead |

| Year | Type of Disaster | Place | Remarks |
|---|---|---|---|
| | Earthquake | northwestern Turkey | March 18; quake killed 1,200 (?) |
| | Tornado | Waco, Texas | May 11; series of twisters killed 114 |
| | Tornado | Michigan and Ohio | June 8; tornado series killed 142 |
| | Tornado | central Massachusetts | June 9; storm killed 92; damage: $52 million |
| | Aircraft | near Tokyo | June 18; U.S.A.F. plane crashed; 129 fatalities |
| | Aircraft | off Wake Island | July 12; nonscheduled plane crashed in Pacific, killing 58 |
| | Marine | near New Caledonia | August 1; French **Monique** vanished in South Pacific; 120 lost |
| | Tornado | Vicksburg, Mississippi | December 5; tornado killed 38; damage: $25 million |
| | Rail | near Waiouru, New Zealand | December 24; Wellington-Auckland express plunged into stream; 155 dead |
| 1954 | Rail | near Karachi, Pakistan | January 21; mail express wrecked; 60 dead |
| | Rail | near Seoul, South Korea | January 31; train wreck killed 56 |
| | Marine | off Quonset Point, Rhode Island | May 26; U.S. aircraft carrier **Bennington** exploded and burned; 103 dead |
| | Flood | Kazvin District, Iran | August 1; flash flood killed 2,000 (?) |
| | Hurricane | U.S. eastern seaboard | August 25–31; Hurricane Carol left 60 dead; damage $500 million |
| | Rail | Negros Island, Philippines | September 2; train wrecked; 55 dead |
| | Earthquake | Orléansville, Algeria | September 9–12; quake killed 1,600 (?) |
| | Marine | in Tsugaru Strait, Japan | September 26; Japanese ferry **Toya Maru** sank; 1,172 dead |
| | Rail | east of Hyderabad, India | September 28; express train plunged from bridge; 137 dead |
| | Hurricane | Haiti, U.S. eastern seaboard and Canada | October 5–18; Hurricane Hazel took 410 lives in Haiti, 95 in U.S. and 80 in Canada; damage: $400 million |
| 1955 | Fire | Yokohama, Japan | February 16–17; home for aged burned, killing 100 (?) |
| | Aircraft | Honolulu | March 22; U.S. Navy plane hit cliff; 66 dead |
| | Rail | near Guadalajara, Mexico | April 3; train plunged into canyon; 300 (?) dead |
| | Tornado | Kansas, Missouri, Oklahoma, and Texas | May 25; series of tornadoes killed 115 |
| | Hurricane | U.S. eastern seaboard | August 7–21; storm and floods, by Hurricane Diane, took 184 lives, caused $1.75 million in damages |
| | Aircraft | near Edelweiler, West Germany | August 11; two U.S.A.F. planes collided in midair; 66 dead |
| | Hurricane | Mexico and West Indies | September 22–28; more than 750 lives lost; extensive damage |
| | Flood | Pakistan and India | October 4; claiming more than 1,700 lives, this deluge devastated about 5.6 million crop acres valued at $63 million |
| | Aircraft | near Laramie, Wyoming | October 6; United DC–4 crashed in mountains; 66 dead |
| 1956 | Aircraft | Malta | February 18; British Lancaster bomber crashed; 50 dead |
| | Aircraft | near Cairo | February 20; Transport Aeriens Intercontinentaux DC–6B crashed; 52 dead |
| | Earthquake | northern Afghanistan | June 10–17; series of shocks caused 2,000 (?) deaths |
| | Aircraft | in the Atlantic, south of New York City | June 20; Venezuelan Super-Constellation crashed; 74 dead |
| | Aircraft | Grand Canyon, Arizona | June 30; TWA Super-Constellation and United DC–7 collided in midair; 128 dead |
| | Marine | off Massachusetts | July 25; Italian **Andrea Doria** and Swedish **Stockholm** collided in fog, sinking the **Doria**; 50 (?) dead or missing |
| | Typhoon | Chekiang, China | August 1; storm and subsequent floods killed more than 2,000 |
| | Explosion | Cali, Colombia | August 7; seven truckloads of dynamite exploded, killing more than 1,200 and destroying town; damage: $40 million |
| | Mine | Marcinelle, Belgium | August 8; coal mine fire claimed 263 |
| | Rail | near Secunderabad, India | September 21; two trains plunged into river as bridge collapsed; 121 dead |
| | Aircraft | in the Atlantic, north of the Azores | October 10; U.S.A.F. plane disappeared; 59 lost |
| | Rail | Marudaiyar River, India | November 23; express train derailed; 143 dead |
| | Aircraft | near Vancouver, Canada | December 9; Trans-Canada North Star crashed; 62 dead |
| 1957 | Fire | Warrenton, Missouri | February 17; home for aged burned; 72 dead |
| | Aircraft | in the Pacific | March 21; U.S.A.F. transport disappeared; 67 lost |
| | Blizzard | Midwest | March 22–25; storm claimed 21 lives; damage: $5–6 million |
| | Tornado | Kansas and Missouri | May 18–21; twister killed 40 (?); damage: over $2 million |
| | Hurricane | Texas to Alabama | June 25–28; Hurricane Audrey killed 390; damage: $50–500 million |
| | Earthquake | Caspian Coast, Iran | July 2; quake killed more than 1,500; left 10,000 homeless |
| | Marine | in the Caspian Sea | July 14; USSR **Eshghabad** ran aground in storm; 270 dead |
| | Aircraft | off Netherlands New Guinea | July 16; KLM Super-Constellation crashed in sea; 57 dead |
| | Aircraft | Quebec | August 11; Maritime Central DC–4 charter crashed; 79 dead |
| | Rail | near Kendal, Jamaica | September 1; train plunged into ravine; 175 (?) dead |
| | Rail | near Montgomery, West Pakistan | September 29; express crashed into standing train; 250 dead |
| | Earthquake | Outer Mongolia | December 2; quake fatal for 1,200 (?) |
| | Rail | near London | December 4; two-train collision killed 92 |
| | Aircraft | near Bolivar, Argentina | December 8; Aerolineas Argentina DC–4 crashed; 62 dead |
| | Earthquake | western Iran | December 13 and 15–17; quake killed 1,392 |
| 1958 | Mine | near Asansoi, India | February 19; coal mine exploded; more than 180 dead |
| | Marine | near Istanbul | March 1; Turkish ferry **Uskudar** sank; 238 dead |
| | Rail | Santa Cruz, Brazil | March 7; two trains collided; 67 dead |
| | Rail | near Rio de Janeiro | May 8; two-train collision killed 128 |
| | Aircraft | Casablanca | May 18; Sabena DC–6B crashed; 65 dead |
| | Aircraft | in the Atlantic, off Ireland | August 14; KLM Super-Constellation crashed; 99 dead |
| | Typhoon | Tokyo | September 21; at least 681 killed |
| | Typhoon | Honshu, Japan | September 27–28; storm killed 679; many missing |
| | Aircraft | Kanash, USSR | October 17; Aeroflot TU–104 crashed; 65 dead |
| | Fire | Chicago | December 1; parochial school burned; 95 dead |
| | Fire | Bogotá, Colombia | December 16; department store conflagration caused 84 deaths |
| 1959 | Aircraft | New York City | February 3; American Electra crashed in the East River; 65 dead |
| | Rail | Java | May 28; train derailed, spilling into ravine and killing 92 |
| | Rail | São Paulo, Brazil | June 5; two trains collided; 60 (?) dead |
| | Aircraft | near Milan | June 26; TWA Super-Constellation exploded in storm; 68 dead |
| | Typhoon | Fukien coast, China | August 20; storm claimed 2,334 lives |
| | Typhoon | Honshu, Japan | September 26–27; tropical cyclone killed more than 4,400 |
| | Hurricane | Jalisco and Colima, Mexico | October 27–28; storm caused mudslides and floods; 1,400 dead |
| | Flood | Frejus, France | December 2; Malpasset Dam collapsed; 412 victims |

| Year | Type of Disaster | Place | Remarks |
|---|---|---|---|
| 1960 | Aircraft | near Wilmington, North Carolina | January 6; National DC–6B "disintegrated" in flight; 34 dead |
| | Aircraft | near Richmond, Virginia | January 18; Capitol Viscount crashed into ravine; 50 dead |
| | Mine | Coalbrook, South Africa | January 21; coal mine cave-in and explosion killed over 400 |
| | Aircraft | near La Paz, Bolivia | February 5; Lloyd Aereo Boliviano DC–4 crashed; 56 dead |
| | Mine | Zwickau, East Germany | February 22; explosion killed 123 |
| | Aircraft | Rio de Janeiro | February 25; U.S. Navy plane and DC–3 collided; 61 dead |
| | Earthquake | Agadir, Morocco | February 29 and March 1; quakes followed by tidal waves destroyed city; 20,000 (?) dead |
| | Aircraft | near Tell City, Indiana | March 17; Northwest Electra exploded in flight; 63 dead |
| | Tornado | Oklahoma and Arkansas | May 5; tornadoes killed 29 |
| | Rail | Leipzig, East Germany | May 15; two trains collided; 59 dead |
| | Earthquake | Chile, Japan, and Hawaii | May 22–29; series of earthquakes, volcanic eruptions, landslides, and tsunami caused widespread devastation; in Chile, more than 2,000 dead and damage: $550 million; in Hawaii, 61 dead and damage: $22 million; in Japan, 138 dead and damage: $50 million |
| | Fire | Guatemala City | July 14; hospital burned; 225 (?) dead |
| | Aircraft | near Dakar, Senegal | August 29; Air France Super-Constellation down at sea; 63 dead |
| | Hurricane | South and northeast U.S. | September 10; Hurricane Donna killed 50 |
| | Aircraft | Agaña, Guam | September 18–19; World DC–6B exploded; 78 dead |
| | Aircraft | Boston | October 4; Eastern Electra crashed into harbor; 62 dead |
| | Cyclone | East Pakistan | October 10 and 31; fatalities from cyclones (6,000) and tidal waves (4,000) |
| | Fire | Amude, Syria | November 13; movie house burned; 152 deaths |
| | Rail | Pardubice, Czechoslovakia | November 14; two trains collided; 110 dead |
| | Aircraft | New York City | December 16; United DC–8 and TWA Super Constellation collided in mid-air over Staten Island, New York; 134 dead |
| | Fire | Brooklyn Navy Yard | December 19; fire swept aircraft carrier; 50 dead |
| 1961 | Aircraft | Berg, Belgium | February 15; Sabena Boeing 707 crashed; 73 dead, including 18 American figure skaters |
| | Aircraft | Nuremberg, West Germany | March 28; Czechoslovak Ilyushin–18 crashed; 52 dead |
| | Marine | in the Persian Gulf | April 8; British ship **Dara** burned; more than 200 dead |
| | Floods | Midwest United States | Early May; floods caused deaths of 25 |
| | Typhoon | East Pakistan | May 9; cyclone plus tidal waves killed 2,000 (?) |
| | Aircraft | Ghadames, Libya | May 10; Air France Starliner crashed; 79 dead |
| | Marine | off Mozambique | July 8; Portuguese **Save** burned and exploded; 227 dead |
| | Mine | Dolna Suce, Czechoslovakia | July 8; coal gas explosion killed 108 |
| | Aircraft | Casablanca | July 12; Czechoslovak Ilyushin–18 crashed; 72 dead |
| | Aircraft | near Chicago | September 1; TWA Constellation crashed in a field; 78 dead |
| | Aircraft | Shannon, Ireland | September 10; Presidential DC–6 charter crashed; 83 dead |
| | Hurricane | Southwest and Midwest United States | September 10–14; Hurricane Carla and associated tornadoes and floods caused deaths of 46 |
| | Aircraft | Rabat, Morocco | September 12; Air France Caravelle crashed, killing 77 |
| | Typhoon | Japan | September 16–17; storm killed 185; extensive damage |
| | Rail | west of Calcutta, India | October 20; express train derailed; more than 50 dead |
| | Hurricane | Belize, British Honduras | October 31; hurricane devastated city, causing 250 (?) deaths and damage: $150 million |
| | Aircraft | near Richmond, Virginia | November 8; charter Constellation crashed in woods; 77 dead |
| | Hurricane | southern Mexico | November 14; hurricane killed at least 330 |
| | Fire | Niteroi, Brazil | December 17; circus tent burned, killing more than 320 |
| | Rail | Catanzaro, Italy | December 23; train fell into gorge; 69 dead |
| 1962 | Rail | Woerden, Netherlands | January 8; two trains collided; 91 dead |
| | Avalanche | Mt. Huscaran, Peru | January 10; Andean avalanche buried more than 3,000 |
| | Mine | Voelklingen, West Germany | February 7; coal mine exploded; 298 dead |
| | Aircraft | New York City | March 1; American 707 plunged into Jamaica Bay; 95 dead |
| | Aircraft | near Douala, Cameroon | March 4; British Caledonian DC–7C crashed in jungle; 111 dead |
| | Hurricane | eastern United States | March 6–7; windstorm and high tides caused 35 deaths |
| | Aircraft | in the western Pacific | March 16; Flying Tiger charter disappeared; 107 lost |
| | Rail | Tokyo | May 3; three trains collided; 163 dead |
| | Rail | Voghera, Italy | May 31; two trains collided; 63 dead |
| | Aircraft | Paris | June 3; Air France Boeing 707 crashed; 130 killed |
| | Aircraft | Guadeloupe, West Indies | June 22; Air France Boeing 707 crashed; 113 dead |
| | Aircraft | Bombay | July 7; Alitalia DC–8 crashed; 94 dead |
| | Rail | Dumraon, India | July 21; two trains collided; 69 dead |
| | Earthquake | northwestern Iran | September 1; quake killed more than 10,000 |
| | Flood | Barcelona | September 27; flash flood killed more than 470 |
| | Hurricane | Pacific coast of United States | October 12–13; near-hurricane winds and floods killed 40 |
| | Cyclone | Thailand | October 27; hurricane toll: 769 dead and 142 missing |
| | Aircraft | Lima, Peru | November 27; Varig Boeing 707 crashed; 97 dead |
| | Aircraft | in the Amazon jungle, Brazil | December 14; Panair Do Brasil Constellation crashed; 50 dead |
| | Flood | northern Europe | December 31; winter-storm floods caused over 300 deaths |
| 1963 | Aircraft | Ankara | February 1; Turkish Air Force plane and Lebanese Viscount collided; 95 dead |
| | Volcanic eruption | Bali | March 18; Mount Agung erupted, forcing 78,000 to flee homes; 1,584 deaths recorded |
| | Marine | in the Atlantic, east of Boston | April 10; **Thresher,** U.S. Navy nuclear submarine, sank; 129 dead in navy's worst peacetime submarine disaster |
| | Cyclone | Bay of Bengal, East Pakistan | May 28–29; cyclones and tidal waves took lives of 12,000 (?) |
| | Aircraft | in the Pacific, off Alaska | June 3; Northwest DC–7 charter crashed; 101 dead |
| | Earthquake | Skopje, Yugoslavia | July 26; quake killed 1,100 (?) |
| | Aircraft | near Bombay | July 28; wreckage found of United Arab Comet; 62 dead |
| | Aircraft | Zurich | September 4: Swissair Caravelle crashed; 80 dead |
| | Hurricane | Caribbean | October 1–9; Hurricane Flora killed 3,500 (?) |
| | Flood | near Belluno, Italy | October 9; landslides and flooding, near Vaiont Dam, resulted in death for more than 2,000 |
| | Fire | Indianapolis, Indiana | October 31; explosion and fire at Coliseum; 74 dead |
| | Rail | near Yokohama | November 9; two Japanese trains hurtled into derailed freight train; at least 162 dead |
| | Mine | Omuta, Japan | November 9; coal mine exploded; 446 dead |
| | Flood | Haiti | November 14–15; deluges and landslides killed 500 (?) |

| Year | Type of Disaster | Place | Remarks |
|---|---|---|---|
| | Fire | near Norwalk, Ohio | November 23; fire at nursing home for aged; 63 dead |
| | Aircraft | Montreal | November 29; Trans-Canada DC–8F crashed; 118 dead |
| | Aircraft | near Elkton, Maryland | December 8; Pan Am Boeing 707 crashed into a field; 81 dead |
| 1964 | Rail | Altamirano, Argentina | February 1; two trains collided; 70 dead |
| | Aircraft | near New Orleans, Louisiana | February 25; Eastern DC–8 crashed into Lake Pontchartrain; 58 dead |
| | Aircraft | near Innsbruck, Austria | February 29; British turboprop crashed, killing 83 |
| | Aircraft | near Lake Tahoe, California | March 1; nonscheduled carrier plane crashed; 85 dead |
| | Earthquake | Alaska | March 27; earthquake was responsible for 114 deaths |
| | Aircraft | Clark A.F.B., Philippines | May 11; U.S. military transport crashed; 75 dead |
| | Floods | northern Montana | June 8–9; floods were responsible for 36 deaths |
| | Aircraft | near Fengyuan, Taiwan | June 20; Chinese Civil Air Patrol plane crashed; 57 dead |
| | Rail | near Oporto, Portugal | July 26; train wreck killed 94 |
| | Bridge | near Caracas, Venezuela | August 23; 50 (?) killed in collapse of bridge over Caroni Falls |
| | Aircraft | near Granada, Spain | October 2; Union Transports Africains DC–6 crashed; 80 dead |
| | Floods | western United States | Late December; floods responsible for 45 deaths |
| 1965 | Aircraft | in the Andes, Chile | February 6; Chilean Airline DC–6B crashed; 87 dead |
| | Aircraft | near New York | February 8; Eastern DC–7B crashed in Atlantic; 84 dead |
| | Earthquake | near Santiago, Chile | March 28; quake killed 400 (?); damage: $200 million |
| | Aircraft | in the Strait of Gibraltar | March 31; Iberia Convair charter crashed; 50 dead |
| | Aircraft | near Damascus | April 10; Royal Jordanian plane crashed; 54 dead |
| | Tornadoes | Midwest United States | April 11; tornadoes killed 272 |
| | Cyclone | Barisal, East Pakistan | May 12; storm killed 12,000 to 20,000; millions homeless |
| | Aircraft | near Cairo | May 20; Pakistan International Boeing 707 crashed; 119 dead |
| | Mine | Bihar State, India | May 28; coal mine accident; more than 400 dead |
| | Mine | Kyushu, Japan | June 1; accident killed 236 |
| | Mine | Kakanj, Yugoslavia | June 7; gas explosion claimed 108 |
| | Aircraft | near El Toro, California | June 25; military plane hit mountain; 84 dead |
| | Aircraft | British Columbia | July 8; Canadian Pacific DC–6B crashed; 52 dead |
| | Explosion | near Searcy, Arkansas | August 9; explosion and fire at missile site killed 53 |
| | Hurricane | Florida and Louisiana | August 27–Sept. 12; Hurricane Betsy killed 75, injured 17,500 |
| | Rail | near Durban, South Africa | October 4; train derailed; 81 dead |
| | Aircraft | near Cincinnati, Ohio | November 8; American Boeing 727 crashed into hill; 58 dead |
| | Marine | in the Caribbean | November 13; Panamanian cruise ship **Yarmouth Castle** caught fire and sank; 89 dead |
| | Rail | near Toungoo, Burma | December 9; two trains collided, killing 76 |
| | Cyclone | Karachi, Pakistan | December 15; cyclone killed 10,000 (?) |
| 1966 | Flood | Rio de Janeiro | January 11–13; deluge and landslides killed more than 300 |
| | Aircraft | in the French Alps | January 24; Air India 707 crashed into Mont Blanc; 117 dead |
| | Marine | near Belawan, Indonesia | February 2; Indonesian oil tanker sank; 89 lost |
| | Aircraft | Tokyo | February 4; Boeing 727 plunged into Tokyo Bay; 133 dead |
| | Tornadoes | Mississippi and Alabama | March 3; tornadoes killed 58 |
| | Aircraft | Honshu, Japan | March 5; BOAC Boeing 707 caught fire and crashed into Mount Fujiyama; 124 dead |
| | Rail | Lumding Junction, India | April 20; train exploded, killing 55 |
| | Aircraft | near Ardmore, Oklahoma | April 22; military charter plane crashed; 83 dead |
| | Rail | Bombay | June 13; two-train collision claimed 60 |
| | Earthquake | eastern Turkey | August 19; quake killed 2,529, rendering 108,000 (?) homeless |
| | Aircraft | Belgrade | August 31; British Airways turboprop crashed; 96 dead |
| | Hurricane | Caribbean and Mexico | September 25–October 1; cyclone fatal for at least 200 |
| | Marine | in the Gulf of Tonkin | October 26; U.S. aircraft carrier **Oriskany** caught fire; 43 lost |
| | Marine | in Kosi River, India | October 26; Indian vessel sank; more than 100 dead |
| | Flood | Arno Valley, Italy | November 3–4; overflow of Arno River, which killed 113, destroyed priceless art treasures in Florence and elsewhere |
| | Aircraft | Bratislava, Czechoslovakia | November 24; TABSO Bulgarian Ilyushin–18 crashed; 82 dead |
| | Marine | in the Sea of Crete | December 8; Greek ferry **Heraklion** sank in storm; 217 dead |
| 1967 | Flood | southern Brazil | January–March; heavy rain floods killed more than 600 |
| | Missile | Cape Kennedy, Florida | January 27; the three-man crew of Apollo 1 die in fire |
| | Fire | Tasmania | February 7–9; forest fire killed 52; damage: $11.2 million |
| | Aircraft | Nicosia, Cyprus | April 20; Swiss Globe Britannia turboprop charter crashed while landing; 126 dead |
| | Tornadoes | northeastern Illinois | April 21; tornadoes killed 55 |
| | Fire | Brussels | May 22; Innovation department store burned; 322 lost their lives |
| | Aircraft | in the French Pyrenees | June 3; British Air Ferry Ltd. DC–6 charter crashed into Mont Canigou; 88 dead |
| | Aircraft | Stockport, England | June 4; British Midland charter DC–4 crashed; 72 dead |
| | Rail | Langenweddingen, East Germany | June 6; train collided with gasoline truck and exploded; 82 dead |
| | Aircraft | near Hendersonville, North Carolina | July 19; Piedmont 727 and private plane collided; 82 dead |
| | Marine | off Vietnam | July 25; U.S. aircraft carrier **Forrestal** crippled by fire; 134 dead |
| | Earthquake | Venezuela | July 30–31; quake, ranging from the Andes to Caribbean, killed 277; damage in Caracas alone: $15 million |
| | Aircraft | southern Turkey | October 12; BEA Comet crashed; 67 dead |
| | Rail | London | November 5; express train derailed; 53 dead |
| | Aircraft | near Cincinnati, Ohio | November 20; TWA Convair 880 crashed near airport; 70 dead |
| | Flood | Lisbon | November 26; fatality toll: 457 |
| 1968 | Marine | in the eastern Mediterranean | January 26; Israeli submarine **Dakar** sank; 69 dead |
| | Marine | in the western Mediterranean | January 27; French submarine **Minerve** went down; 52 lost |
| | Aircraft | Guadeloupe, West Indies | March 5; Air France Boeing 707 crashed; 63 dead |
| | Aircraft | Atlantic Ocean off Wales | March 24; Irish International Viscount crashed; 61 dead |
| | Marine | Wellington Harbor | April 10; New Zealand ferry **Wahine** crashed and sank; 51 dead |
| | Aircraft | Windhoek, South-West Africa | April 20; South African Boeing 707 crashed; 123 dead |
| | Aircraft | near Dawson, Texas | May 3; Braniff Electra crashed; 85 dead |
| | Tornadoes | Midwest United States | May 15; tornadoes killed 71 |
| | Marine | Atlantic Ocean, off Azores | May 27; U.S. nuclear submarine **Scorpion** sank; 99 lost |
| | Flood | Gujarat, India | August 8–14; floods killed 1,000 (?) |
| | Earthquake | northeastern Iran | August 31; quake killed 12,000 (?) |
| | Aircraft | off the French Riviera | September 11; Air France Caravelle crashed; 95 dead |
| | Mine | Mannington, West Virginia | November 20; coal mine exploded and caught fire; 78 dead |
| | Aircraft | off Caracas, Venezuela | December 12; Pan Am Boeing 707 crashed; 51 dead |

| Year | Type of Disaster | Place | Remarks |
|---|---|---|---|
| 1969 | Floods | southern California | January 25–29; floods killed 95 |
| | Aircraft | La Coruba, Venezuela | March 16; VIASA DC-9 crashed near Maracaibo; 154 dead |
| | Aircraft | Aswan Airport, Egypt | March 20; United Arab IL-18 crashed while landing; 91 dead |
| | Mine | Barroteran, Mexico | March 31; gas mine exploded; 156 dead |
| | Cyclone | Dacca, East Pakistan | April 15; storm killed 500 (?) |
| | Marine | in the South China Sea | June 2; U.S. destroyer **Frank E. Evans** sliced in two by the Australian carrier **Melbourne;** 74 assumed dead |
| | Aircraft | near Monterrey, Mexico | June 4; Mexican Airways Boeing 727 crashed; 79 dead |
| | Rail | near Benares, India | June 21; train plunged off tracks into river bed; 75 dead |
| | Rail | Jaipur, India | July 15; freight train rammed standing passenger train; 85 dead |
| | Hurricane | Mississippi and Louisiana | August 17; Hurricane Camille killed 256; $1.5 billion damage |
| | Floods | Virginia | August 23; floods killed 100 (?) |
| | Aircraft | near Indianapolis, Indiana | September 9; small plane and Allegheny DC–9 collided; 83 dead |
| | Aircraft | near Danang | September 20; Air Vietnam DC-4 crashed; 77 dead |
| | Aircraft | near La Paz, Bolivia | September 26; Bolivian DC-6 crashed in the Andes; 74 dead |
| 1970 | Rail | near Buenos Aires | February 4; commuter train struck by express train; 236 killed |
| | Avalanche | Val d'Isère, France | February 10; worst snowslide in French history killed 42 at hostel |
| | Aircraft | in the Caribbean | February 15; Dominican DC–9 crashed, killing 102 |
| | Marine | in the Mediterranean | March 4; French submarine **Eurydice** exploded, sank; 57 dead |
| | Earthquake | Kutahya, Turkey | March 28; quake toll: more than 1,000 |
| | Aircraft | Casablanca, Morocco | April 1; Royal Air Maroc Caravelle jetliner crashed; 61 killed |
| | Explosion | Osaka, Japan | April 8; serial gas-main blasts killed 73; 300 injured |
| | Avalanche | Saint-Gervais, France | April 16; snowslide hit tuberculosis sanatorium, killing 72 |
| | Flood | Oradea, Rumania | May 11–23; 200 (?) killed; more than 225 towns destroyed |
| | Earthquake | northern Peru | May 31; quake plus floods and landslides killed 30,000 (?) |
| | Aircraft | Barcelona | July 4; British charter Comet jet crashed; 112 dead |
| | Aircraft | Toronto | July 5; Air Canada DC-8 crashed; 108 killed |
| | Bus | New Delhi | July 22; 25 buses, 5 taxis, and an army vehicle swept into narrow gorge by floods; 600 dead |
| | Aircraft | near Cuzco, Peru | August 9; Peruvian Electra crashed; 100 dead |
| | Fire | Saint-Laurent-du-Pont, France | November 1; fire in a dance hall killed 146 |
| | Cyclone | East Pakistan, delta region | November 12; storm and floods killed 200,000 (?) |
| | Aircraft | Huntington, West Virginia | November 14; Southern Airways DC-9 carrying the Marshall Univ. football team exploded while landing; 75 killed |
| 1971 | Aircraft | Moscow | January 1; Aeroflot Il-18 crashed during takeoff; 90 killed |
| | Earthquake | Los Angeles area | February 9; quake killed 64, of these, 43 were at V.A. hospital |
| | Tornado | Mississippi and Louisiana | February 21; storm killed 115 |
| | Avalanche | Lima, Peru | February 19; Andean avalanche killed 600 (?) |
| | Earthquake | Bingol, Turkey | May 23; quake killed 800 |
| | Aircraft | Belgrade | May 23; Yugoslav TU-134A crashed at Rijeka Airport; 78 killed |
| | Aircraft | Honshu, Japan | July 30; Japanese airliner and fighter plane collide; 162 dead |
| | Aircraft | Alaska | September 4; Alaska Airlines 727 crashed into a mountain in the Tongass National Forest; all 111 passengers killed |
| | Fire | Seoul, S. Korea | December 25; explosion and fire at hotel; 163 dead |
| 1972 | Flood | Buffalo Creek, W. Virginia | February 26; coal mine waste waters caused a makeshift dam to collapse; 118 dead |
| | Aircraft | United Arab Emirates | March 14; Danish Sterling Airways charter crashed near Dubai; all 112 passengers killed |
| | Poisoning | Iraq | March–April; outbreak of mercury poisoning; over 100 dead |
| | Earthquake | Iran | April 10; 45 villages leveled; over 5,000 dead |
| | Mine | Kellogg, Idaho | May 2; fire in the Sunshine Silver Mine; 91 miners dead |
| | Aircraft | Palermo, Italy | May 6; Alitalia DC-8 struck a mountainside in bad weather; all 115 passengers killed |
| | Fire | Osaka, Japan | May 13; Sennichi department store gutted by flames; 115 killed |
| | Mine | Northwest Rhodesia | June 6; explosion in Wankie Colliery Co. coal mine; 427 dead |
| | Flood | Rapid City, S. Dakota | June 10; flash flooding caused over $120 million damage; 226 dead, 124 missing |
| | Hurricane | Eastern United States | June 10–20; Hurricane Agnes hit Florida, Maryland, Pennsylvania, New York, and Virginia; $1.7 billion damage; 134 dead |
| | Rail | Soissons, France | June 17; falling rocks in a tunnel cause derailment; 107 dead |
| | Aircraft | London | June 18;BEA Trident crashed on takeoff; 118 dead |
| | Flood | Luzon Island, Philippines | June-August; Typhoon Rita and six weeks of rain caused landslides and burst dams; 427 dead |
| | Aircraft | East Berlin | August 14; Interflug Ilyushin-62 crashed on takeoff; 156 dead |
| | Rail | Saltillo, Mexico | October 6; speeding passenger train jumped its tracks; 204 dead |
| | Aircraft | Krasnaya Polyana, USSR | October 14; Aeroflot Ilyushin-62 crashed; 176 dead |
| | Aircraft | Canary Islands | December 3; Spanish charter plane exploded; 155 dead |
| | Earthquake | Managua, Nicaragua | December 23; worst earthquake in Nicaraguan history; leveled 70% of the city; 10,000 dead |
| | Aircraft | near Miami | December 29; Eastern Airlines Tristar jetliner crashed into Everglades; 98 dead |
| 1973 | Aircraft | Kano, Nigeria | January 22; Boeing 707 jet carrying 200 Moslems from a pilgrimage to Mecca crashed in thick fog; 176 dead |
| | Epidemic | Bangladesh | Reported March 1; smallpox swept country, killing at least 1,000 |
| | Flood | Western Tunisia | March 31; week-long rains flooded Mejerda River; 150 dead |
| | Aircraft | Basel, Switzerland | April 10; British charter flight crashed; 104 dead |
| | Marine | Dacca coast | May 5; two riverboats collided; 250 dead |
| | Storms | Indonesian Islands | Reported June 16; spring storms took 1,650 lives |
| | Aircraft | Paris | July 11; Brazilian Boeing 707 crashed in an emergency landing at Orly; 122 dead |
| | Aircraft | Boston | July 31; Delta jetliner crashed in fog; 88 dead |
| | Earthquake | central Mexico | August 28; earthquake and rains killed 527; 200,000 homeless |
| | Fire | Kumamoto, Japan | November 29; fire hit department store which had no fire escape chutes; 101 dead; 84 injured |
| | Marine | Ecuador coast | December 24; overloaded ferryboat capsized, killing 200 |
| 1974 | Aircraft | Pago Pago, Samoa | January 31; Pan Am jet crashed on landing; 92 dead |
| | Fire | Sao Paulo, Brazil | February 1; a faulty air conditioner caused a flash fire to sweep a modern bank, killing 189 people in 25 minutes |
| | Famine | Sahel, West Africa | Reported March 3; 100,000 persons were estimated dead and millions starving due to drought in this sub-Sahara region |

| Year | Type of Disaster | Place | Remarks |
|---|---|---|---|
| | Aircraft | Paris | March 3; Turkish DC-10 crashed on takeoff from Orly; 346 dead |
| | Flood | Tubarão, Brazil | March 29; floodwaters leave over 1,000 dead |
| | Tornado | central and southern U.S. | April 3–4; tornado series in 11-state area; 336 dead |
| | Aircraft | Bali, Indonesia | April 22; Pan Am 707 crashed on landing; 107 dead |
| | Aircraft | Leningrad | April 27; Soviet Ilyushin 18 crashed on takeoff; 108 killed |
| | Flood | Bangladesh | July–August; floods leave 1,500 dead |
| | Rail | Zagreb, Yugoslavia | August 30; express train derailed; 124 dead |
| | Aircraft | Charlotte, North Carolina | September 11; Eastern jet crashed; 88 dead |
| | Hurricane | Honduras | September 18–19; Hurricane Fifi killed 5,000 (?) |
| | Aircraft | near Washington, D.C. | December 1; TWA jet crashed into hill; 92 dead |
| | Aircraft | Sri Lanka | December 4; Jet carrying pilgrims crashed; 191 dead |
| | Earthquake | northern Pakistan | December 28; quake toll about 5,000 |
| 1975 | Aircraft | Saigon, South Vietnam | April 4; U.S. Air Force C–5A transport jet carrying South Vietnamese orphans to U.S. crashed on takeoff; 155 dead |
| | Famine | East Africa | Reported May 25; drought since October 1974 in Ethiopia and Somalia; 40,000 dead |
| | Aircraft | New York | June 24; Eastern Airlines Boeing 727 crashed on landing at Kennedy International Airport; 113 dead |
| | Flood | northern India | July; month-long monsoon rains caused flooding; 300 dead |
| | Marine | near Canton, China | August 3; two ferries collided on Hsi River; 500 (?) drowned |
| | Aircraft | near Agadir, Morocco | August 3; charter Boeing 707 hit mountainside; 188 dead |
| | Aircraft | Damascus, Syria | August 20; Czechoslovak airliner crashed; 126 dead |
| | Flood | eastern India | August-September; monsoon rains cause flooding and spread of cholera; 450 (?) dead |
| | Earthquake | Lice, Turkey | September 6; earthquake leaves 2,312 dead, 3,372 injured |
| | Mine | near Dhanbad, India | December 27; coal mine explosion caused flooding of mine; 372 believed dead |
| 1976 | Aircraft | Saudi Arabia | January 1; Middle East Airlines Boeing 707 crashed; 82 dead |
| | Earthquake | Guatemala | February 4; earthquake toll estimated 22,419 dead, 74,105 injured and 1 million homeless |
| | Aircraft | Erivan, USSR | March 5; Soviet Il-18 crashed; 120 dead |
| | Earthquake | Friuli region of Italy | May 6; earthquake in northeast Italy; more than 1,000 dead |
| | Earthquake | Indonesia | June 26 and July 14; successive quakes, the first on West New Guinea caused mudslides, which left 443 dead, 3,000 missing; the second quake in Bali left 600 dead, 3,400 injured |
| | Earthquake | Tangshan area of China | July 28; two major quakes devastated industrial city of Tangshan; casualities estimated to be about 700,000, the second worst disaster in recorded history |
| | Flood | Big Thompson River, Colo. | July 31; vacationers and campers caught in flash flood in canyon; 138 dead, 5 missing |
| | Earthquake | southern Philippines | August 17; earthquake hit Mindanao and neighboring islands, 8,000 (?) dead or missing and 175,000 homeless |
| | Aircraft | near Zagreb, Yugoslavia | September 10; Yugoslav charter jet DC–10 and British Airlines Trident collided in world's worst midair collision; 176 dead |
| | Aircraft | near Isparta, Turkey | September 19; Turkish Boeing 727 hit mountain; 155 dead |
| | Flood | La Paz, Mexico | October 1; earthen dam broke after heavy rains; 630 dead |
| | Aircraft | Santa Cruz, Bolivia | October 15; Boeing 707 cargo plane crashed in downtown Santa Cruz; 100 dead |
| | Earthquake | Van Province, Turkey | November 24; earthquake; estimated 4,000 dead |
| 1977 | Rail | Granville, Australia | January 18; Sydney-bound commuter train derailed; 82 dead |
| | Earthquake | Bucharest, Romania | March 4; earthquake leaves 1,541 dead, 11,275 injured |
| | Aircraft | Tenerife, Canary Islands | March 27; Pan American 747 and KLM 747 jumbo jets collide on runway; 579 dead in worst disaster in aviation history |
| | Tornado | near Dacca, Bangladesh | April 1; tornado struck Madaripur district; about 900 dead |
| | Aircraft | New Hope, Georgia | April 4; Southern Airways DC–9 landed on highway; 72 dead |
| | Fire | Southgate, Kentucky | May 28; supper club fire; 161 dead, 129 injured |
| | Flood | Johnstown, Pennsylvania | July 19-20; nine-inch rainfall caused flash flood; over 70 dead |
| | Storm | Andhra Pradesh, India | November 19; cyclone caused tidal wave killing 20,000 |
| | Aircraft | Funchal, Madeira | November 19; Portuguese 727 crashed on landing; 130 dead |
| | Aircraft | Johore Strait, Malaysia | December 4; Malaysian 737 exploded after hijacking; 100 dead |
| | Earthquake | Kerman Province, Iran | December 20; earthquake hit rural villages; over 520 dead |
| 1978 | Aircraft | near Bombay, India | January 1; Air India 747 exploded and crashed; 213 dead |
| | Aircraft | near Sofia, Bulgaria | March 16; Bulgarian airliner crashed; 73 dead |
| | Tornado | Orissa, India | April 16; storm killed 400 to 500 in six villages |
| | Construction | St. Marys, West Virginia | April 27; scaffolding on cooling tower collapsed; 51 dead |
| | Explosion | near Tarragona, Spain | July 11; propylene gas truck exploded at tourist camp; 200 dead |
| | Explosion | Beirut, Lebanon | August 13; blast destroyed building, killing 150 to 200 |
| | Fire | Abadan, Iran | August 20; arsonist-set theater fire killed 430 |
| | Earthquake | Tabas, Iran | September 16; major quake; estmated 25,000 dead |
| | Aircraft | San Diego, California | September 25; Pacific Southwest 727 jet and private plane collided; 137 aboard planes and 7 on ground dead |
| | Marine | Bay of Bengal | April 4; fleet of cargo boats lost in storm; 1,000 dead |
| | Mass suicide | Jonestown, Guyana | November 18; mass poisoning and murder in American religious commune; death toll placed at 913 |
| | Aircraft | Leh, India | November 19; Indian Air Force transport crashed; 78 killed |
| | Storm | Sri Lanka and India | November 23; cyclone leveled 500,000 buildings; over 1,500 dead |
| | Aircraft | Colombo, Sri Lanka | November 25; charter DC–8 jet crashed; 183 dead |
| | Aircraft | Tyrrhenian Sea | December 23; Alitalia DC–9 jet ditched at sea; 103 dead |
| 1979 | Earthquake | eastern Iran | January 16; quake killed 199 |
| | Flood | southeast Brazil | early February; over 40 days of heavy rain caused severe flooding; over 600 dead, 350,000 homeless |
| | Volcanic eruption | central Java | February 21; 175 killed, 1,000 others injured by lava flow |
| | Aircraft | near Moscow | March 17; Tupolev 104 crashed after takeoff; 90 dead |
| | Poison | near Sverdlovsk, U.S.S.R. | April–May; anthrax epidemic reported, but experts suspect biological weapon mishap; toll put at more than 1,000 dead |
| | Tornado | Texas and Oklahoma | April 10; twisters struck border area; 60 dead, over 800 injured |
| | Earthquake | Yugoslavia and Albania | April 15; shocks hit coast; over 120 dead; 1,500 injured |
| | Cyclones | southeast India | May 12–13; storms killed over 600 |
| | Aircraft | Chicago | May 25; American Airlines DC–10 crashed; 271 on board and 2 on ground dead in worst U.S. air disaster |

| Year | Type of Disaster | Place | Remarks |
|---|---|---|---|
| | Aircraft | Sumatra, Indonesia | July 11; domestic airliner crashed into mountain; 61 dead |
| | Fire | Saragossa, Spain | July 13; hotel fire; 80 dead |
| | Bus | Lugezi, Tanzania | July 14; overcrowded bus fell into Lake Victoria; 60 dead |
| | Tidal wave | Lomblem, Indonesia | July 17; death toll estimated at 539 |
| | Fire | Tuticorin, India | July 29; movie tent fire; 92 dead |
| | Flood | Morvi, India | August 11; dam collapsed; at least 5,000 dead |
| | Aircraft | over Ukraine | August 11; two Soviet jet liners collide; 173 dead |
| | Rail | Bangkok, Thailand | August 21; trains collided; 51 dead |
| | Hurricane | Caribbean and east coast of U.S. | Aug. 30–Sept. 7; Hurricane David took over 1,100 lives, left 150,000 homeless |
| | Rail | Stalac, Yugoslavia | Sept. 13; freight and passenger train collided; 80 dead |
| | Aircraft | Mexico City | October 31; Western Airlines DC-10 crashed; 75 dead |
| | Marine | near Khulna, Bangladesh | early November; cargo ship and launch collided; 200 dead |
| | Earthquake | northeastern Iran | November 14; quake took 248 lives |
| | Marine | Bo Hai Gulf, China | November 25; oil drilling rig collapsed during storm; 70 dead |
| | Aircraft | Taif, Saudi Arabia | November 26; Boeing 707 jetliner carrying pilgrims from Mecca crashed; 156 dead |
| | Aircraft | Mt. Erebus, Antarctica | November 28; New Zealand DC–10 hit mountain; 257 dead |
| | Earthquake | Colombia-Ecuador border | December 12; quake and tidal waves took 200 lives |
| 1980 | Aircraft | near Tehran, Iran | January 21; Boeing 707 crashed; 128 dead |
| | Structural | Sincelejo, Colombia | January 21; bullring collapsed; 222 dead |
| | Aircraft | near Warsaw | March 14; Polish Ilyushin 62 crashed; 87 dead |
| | Marine | North Sea | March 27; Oil platform collapsed during storm; 123 dead |
| | Aircraft | Florianopolis, Brazil | April 12; Boeing 727 crashed; 54 dead |
| | Aircraft | Canary Islands | April 25; British Boeing 727 crashed; 146 dead |
| | Volcanic eruption | Mt. St. Helens, Washington | May 18; volcano erupted devastating large area; 60 dead |
| | Fire | Kingston, Jamaica | May 20; Fire involving arson, in home for elderly; 157 dead |
| | Aircraft | Tyrrhenian Sea | June 28; Italian DC–9 jet lost; 81 dead |
| | Aircraft | Alma Ata, U.S.S.R. | July 7; Soviet TU–142 jetliner crashed; 163 dead |
| | Hurricane | Gulf of Mexico | August 4–11; Hurricane Allen left 273 dead |
| | Explosion | Bologna, Italy | August 6; bomb exploded in train station; 76 dead |
| | Flood | Uttar Pradesh, India | August 12; monsoon flooding of Ganges; over 600 dead |
| | Riot | Moradabad, India | August 13; riot in mosque caused 86 deaths |
| | Aircraft | Riyadh, Saudi Arabia | August 19; fire aboard Lockheed L–1011 jet liner; 301 dead |
| | Rail | near Torun, Poland | August 19; passenger and freight train collided; 69 dead |
| | Flood | Ibadan, Nigeria | August 31; flooding from rainstorms; 240 dead |
| | Aircraft | near Medina, Saudi Arabia | Sept. 14; Saudi Air Force transport crashed; 89 killed |
| | Earthquake | Al Asnam, Algeria | October 10; earthquake toll over 3,000 dead |
| | Explosion | Ortuella, Spain | October 23; explosion destroyed school; 64 killed |
| | Fire | Las Vegas, Nevada | November 21; hotel five; 84 dead and 500 injured |
| | Earthquake | southern Italy | November 23; quake leaves over 3,000 dead, 200,000 homeless |
| | Fire | near Ankara, Turkey | November 24; engagement party fire; 97 dead |
| 1981 | Marine | Amazon River, Brazil | January 6; steamer capsized; 230 dead |
| | Earthquake | Sichuan, China | January 23; quake leaves 150 dead |
| | Marine | Java Sea, Indonesia | January 27; ferry burns; 430 dead |
| | Aircraft | Leningrad, USSR | February 7; Soviet military transport crashed; 70 reported dead |
| | Fire | Dublin, Ireland | February 14; discotheque fire; 46 dead |
| | Poisoning | Spain | May–August; poisonous cooking oil sold; estimated 200 dead |
| | Rail | Bihar state, India | June 6; train plunges off bridge; 268 dead |
| | Earthquake | Kerman Prov., Iran | June 11; earthquake toll over 1,000 dead |
| | Rail | Georgia, U.S.S.R. | Announced June 28; 2 train collision; 70 dead, 100 injured |
| | Structural | Kansas City, Missouri | July 17; collapse of hotel skywalks; 113 dead |
| | Flood | Sichuan, China | Late July; flooding of Yangtze; 1,300 dead, 1.5 million homeless |
| | Earthquake | Kerman Prov., Iran | July 28; quake toll over 1,500 |
| | Marine | Seram Sea, Indonesia | August 5; overloaded passenger ship sinks; 225 lost at sea |
| | Aircraft | Sanyi, Taiwan | August 22; passenger jetliner exploded and crashed; 110 dead |
| | Mine | Zaluzi, Czechoslovakia | September 3; coal mine explosion; 65 dead |
| | Marine | Obidos, Brazil | September 19; Amazon riverboat sank; over 300 drowned |
| | Avalanche | southern Philippines | October 9; avalanche buried sleeping miners and families; 200 (?) dead |
| | Mine | Yubari, Japan | October 16; coal mine explosion; 93 dead |
| | Storm | Luzon, Philippines | November 25; Typhoon Irma leaves 270 dead |
| | Aircraft | Ajaccio, Corsica | December 1; Yugoslav DC-9 jetliner hits mountain; 178 dead |
| 1982 | Mudslides | Bay area, California | January 3–6; mudslides cause damage of $300 million; 31 dead |
| | Aircraft | Washington, D.C. | January 13; Air Florida 737 jet liner crashed into Potomac after hitting bridge; 74 of 79 aboard aircraft and 4 motorists dead |
| | Aircraft | Krasnoyarsk, USSR | January 23; Aeroflot jet crashed; 150 reported dead |
| | Flood | near Uchiza, Peru | January 23; flood on Chontayacu River; 600 (?) dead |
| | Rail | near Miliana, Algeria | January 27; train derailed, 110 dead |
| | Marine | off Newfoundland | February 15; offshore oil rig sank in storm; 84 dead |
| | Marine | near Rangoon, Burma | March 28, April 11; separate ferry sinkings; 130 and 160 dead |
| | Aircraft | near Guilin, China | April 26; Chinese jet liner crashed into mountain; 112 dead |
| | Flood | Guangdong Province, China | May 12; flooding after heavy rains; 430 (?) dead |
| | Flood | Sumatra, Indonesia | June 3; flash flood after heavy rains; 225 dead |
| | Storm | Orissa, India | June 4; wind and tidal waves ravaged coastal area; 200 dead |
| | Aircraft | northeastern Brazil | June 8; VASP Boeing 727 crashed into mountain; 137 dead |
| | Storm | Nicaragua and Honduras | June 24–29; tropical storm from Pacific caused floods; 226 dead |
| | Aircraft | Moscow, USSR | July 6; Aeroflot Ilyushin-62 crashed; 90 thought dead |
| | Aircraft | New Orleans, Louisiana | July 9; Pan American 727 jet crashed after takeoff in storm; 146 aboard dead along with 8 on the ground |
| | Rail | western Mexico | July 11; passenger train derailed; 120 dead |
| | Flood | Kyushu, Japan | July 24–August 3; monsoon rains caused flooding and mudslides; over 380 dead |
| | Bus | near Beaune, France | July 31; multiple bus and car collision; 44 children and 9 adults dead |
| | Aircraft | Malaga, Spain | September 13; charter DC-10 jet liner crashed and burned on takeoff; 56 (?) dead |
| | Flood | San Salvador and Guatemala | Late September; flood and mudslides after 4 days of torrential rains; over 1,200 dead |

# SPORTS

## CONTENTS:



## THE OLYMPICS

### THE SUMMER OLYMPIC GAMES

| | Sites | Year | Total Events | Total Nations | Total Athletes | | Sites | Year | Total Events | Total Nations | Total Athletes |
|---|---|---|---|---|---|---|---|---|---|---|---|
| I | Athens | 1896 | 42 | 13 | 285 | XV | Helsinki | 1952 | 149 | 69 | 5,867 |
| II | Paris | 1900 | 60 | 20 | 1,066 | XVI | Melbourne | 1956 | 145 | 67 | 3,184 |
| III | St. Louis | 1904 | 67 | 11 | 496 | XVI | Stockholm* | 1956 | 3 | 29 | 154 |
| IV | London | 1908 | 104 | 22 | 2,059 | XVII | Rome | 1960 | 150 | 84 | 5,396 |
| V | Stockholm | 1912 | 106 | 28 | 2,541 | XVIII | Tokyo | 1964 | 163 | 94 | 5,565 |
| VII | Antwerp | 1920 | 154 | 29 | 2,606 | XIX | Mexico City | 1968 | 172 | 109 | 6,082 |
| VIII | Paris | 1924 | 137 | 44 | 3,092 | XX | Munich | 1972 | 194 | 121 | 8,500 |
| IX | Amsterdam | 1928 | 120 | 46 | 3,015 | XXI | Montreal | 1976 | 198 | 87 | 6,512 |
| X | Los Angeles | 1932 | 124 | 37 | 1,408 | XXII | Moscow | 1980 | 203 | 80 | 5,923 |
| XI | Berlin | 1936 | 142 | 49 | 4,069 | XXIII | Los Angeles | 1984 | | | |
| XIV | London | 1948 | 138 | 59 | 4,468 | XXIV | Seoul | 1988 | | | |

* Equestrian Games only.

### 1980 SUMMER OLYMPIC GAMES Moscow, U.S.S.R., July 19–August 3

**Participating Nations**

Afghanistan
Algeria
Andorra
Angola
Australia
Austria
Belgium
Benin
Botswana
Brazil
Bulgaria
Burma
Cameroon
Colombia
Congo
Costa Rica
Cuba
Cyprus
Czechoslovakia
Denmark
Dominican Rep.
Ecuador
Ethiopia
Finland
France
Germany, East
Greece
Guatemala
Guinea
Guyana
Hungary
Iceland
India
Iraq
Ireland
Italy
Jamaica
Jordan
Korea, North
Kuwait
Laos
Lebanon
Lesotho
Libya
Luxembourg
Madagascar
Mali
Malta
Mexico
Mongolia
Mozambique
Nepal
Netherlands
New Zealand
Nicaragua
Nigeria
Peru
Poland
Portugal
Puerto Rico
Romania
San Marino
Senegal
Seychelles
Sierra Leone
Spain
Sri Lanka
Sweden
Switzerland
Syria
Tanzania
Trinidad & Tobago
Uganda
USSR
United Kingdom
Venezuela
Vietnam
Yugoslavia
Zambia
Zimbabwe

**Non-Participating Nations**

Albania
Antigua
Argentina
Bahamas
Bahrain
Bangladesh
Barbados
Belize
Bermuda
Bolivia
Canada
Cayman Is.
Central African Rep.
Chad
Chile
China
China (Taiwan)
Egypt
El Salvador
Fiji
Gabon
Gambia
Germany, West
Ghana
Haiti
Honduras
Hong Kong
Indonesia
Iran
Israel
Ivory Coast
Japan
Kenya
Korea, South
Liberia
Liechtenstein
Malawi
Malaysia
Mauritania
Mauritius
Monaco
Morocco
Neth. Antilles
Nigeria
Norway
Pakistan
Panama
Papua New Guinea
Paraguay
Philippines
Qatar
Saudi Arabia
Singapore
Somalia
Sudan
Suriname
Swaziland
Thailand
Togo
Tunisia
Turkey
United Arab Emirates
United States
Upper Volta
Uruguay
Virgin Islands
Zaire

## 1980 SUMMER OLYMPICS MEDAL TABLE

| | Gold (1st) | Silver (2nd) | Bronze (3rd) | Total |
|---|---|---|---|---|
| USSR | 80 | 69 | 46 | 195 |
| East Germany | 47 | 37 | 43 | 127 |
| Bulgaria | 8 | 16 | 17 | 41 |
| Cuba | 8 | 7 | 5 | 20 |
| Italy | 8 | 3 | 4 | 15 |
| Hungary | 7 | 10 | 15 | 32 |
| Romania | 6 | 6 | 13 | 25 |
| France | 6 | 5 | 3 | 14 |
| Britain | 5 | 7 | 9 | 21 |
| Poland | 3 | 14 | 15 | 32 |
| Sweden | 3 | 3 | 6 | 12 |
| Finland | 3 | 1 | 4 | 8 |
| Czechoslovakia | 2 | 3 | 8 | 13 |
| Yugoslavia | 2 | 3 | 4 | 9 |
| Australia | 2 | 2 | 5 | 9 |
| Denmark | 2 | 1 | 2 | 5 |
| Brazil | 2 | 0 | 2 | 4 |
| Ethiopia | 2 | 0 | 2 | 4 |
| Switzerland | 2 | 0 | 0 | 2 |
| Spain | 1 | 3 | 2 | 6 |
| Austria | 1 | 2 | 1 | 4 |
| Greece | 1 | 0 | 2 | 3 |
| Belgium | 1 | 0 | 0 | 1 |
| India | 1 | 0 | 0 | 1 |
| Zimbabwe | 1 | 0 | 0 | 1 |
| North Korea | 0 | 3 | 2 | 5 |
| Mongolia | 0 | 2 | 2 | 4 |
| Mexico | 0 | 1 | 3 | 4 |
| Netherlands | 0 | 1 | 2 | 3 |
| Jamaica | 0 | 0 | 3 | 3 |
| Tanzania | 0 | 2 | 0 | 2 |
| Ireland | 0 | 1 | 1 | 2 |
| Venezuela | 0 | 1 | 0 | 1 |
| Uganda | 0 | 1 | 0 | 1 |
| Guyana | 0 | 0 | 1 | 1 |
| Lebanon | 0 | 0 | 1 | 1 |

## MEDALISTS AT MOSCOW: 1980

1st (gold), 2nd (silver), 3rd (bronze)

### ARCHERY

**Men**–Tomi Poikolainen, Finland
2. USSR, 3. Italy

**Women**–Keto Losaberidze, USSR
2. USSR, 3. Finland

### BASKETBALL

**Men**–Yugoslavia
2. Italy, 3. USSR

**Women**–USSR
2. Bulgaria, 3. Yugoslavia

### BOXING

**106 lb**–Shamil Sabyrov, USSR
2. Cuba, 3. Bulgaria, N. Korea

**112 lb**–Petar Lessov, Bulgaria
2. USSR, 3. Hungary, Ireland

**119 lb**–Juan Hernandez, Cuba
2. Venezuela, 3. Guyana, Romania

**126 lb**–Rudi Fink, E. Germany
2. Cuba, 3. Poland, USSR

**132 lb**–Angel Herrera, Cuba
2. USSR, 3. E. Germany, Poland

**140 lb**–Patrizio Oliva, Italy
2. USSR, 3. Britain, Cuba

**148 lb**–Andres Aldama, Cuba
2. Uganda, 3. E. Germany, Poland

**157 lb**–Armando Martinez, Cuba
2. USSR, 3. Czechoslovakia, E. Germany

**165 lb**–Jose Gomez, Cuba
2. USSR, 3. Poland, Romania

**179 lb**–Slobodan Kacar, Yugoslavia
2. Poland, 3. Cuba, E. Germany

**Hvywt**–Teofilo Stevenson, Cuba
2. USSR, 3. E. Germany, Hungary

### CANOEING—MEN

**Single Canoe**
**500 m**–Sergei Postrekhin, USSR
2. Bulgaria, 3. E. Germany

**1000 m**–Lubomir Lubenov, Bulgaria
2. USSR, 3. E. Germany

**Double Canoe**
**500 m**–Hungary (Foltan, Vaskuti)
2. Romania, 3. Bulgaria

**1000 m**–Romania (Potzaichin, Simionov)
2. E. Germany, 3. USSR

**Single Kayak**
**500 m**–Vladimir Parfenovich, USSR
2. Australia, 3. Romania

**1000 m**–Rudiger Helm, E. Germany
2. France, 3. Romania

**Double Kayak**
**500 m**–USSR (Parfenovich, Chukhrai)
2. Spain, 3. E. Germany

**1000 m**–USSR (Parfenovich, Chukhrai)
2. Hungary, 3. Spain

**Four-Man Kayak**
**1000 m**–East Germany
2. Romania, 3. Bulgaria

### CANOEING—WOMEN

**Single Kayak**
**500 m**–Birgit Fischer, E. Germany
2. Bulgaria, 3. USSR

**Double Kayak**
**500 m**–E. Germany (Genauss, Bischof)
2. USSR, 3. Hungary

### CYCLING

**100 km Team Road Race**–USSR
2. E. Germany, 3. Czechoslovakia

**4000 m Team Pursuit**–USSR
2. E. Germany, 3. Czechoslovakia

**1000 m Time Trial**–Lothar Thoms, E. Germany, 2. USSR, 3. Jamaica

**Individual Sprint**–Lutz Hesslich, E. Germany, 2. France, 3. USSR

**Individual Pursuit**–Robert Dill-Bundi, Switzerland, 2. France, 3. Denmark

**Individual Road Race**–Sergei Sukhoruchenkov, USSR
2. Poland, 3. USSR

### DIVING

**Springboard**
**Men**–Aleksandr Portnov, USSR
2. Mexico, 3. Italy

**Women**–Irina Kalinina, USSR
2. E. Germany, 3. E. Germany

**Platform**
**Men**–Falk Hoffman, E. Germany
2. USSR, 3. USSR

**Women**–Martina Jaschke, E. Germany
2. USSR, 3. USSR

### EQUESTRIAN

**Three-Day Individual**–Frederico Euro Roman, Italy, 2. USSR, 3. USSR

**Three-Day Team**–USSR
2. Italy, 3. Mexico

**Dressage Individual**–Elisabeth Theurer, Austria, 2. USSR, 3. USSR

**Dressage Team**–USSR
2. Bulgaria, 3. Romania

**Jumping Individual**–Jan Kowalczyk, Poland, 2. USSR, 3. Mexico

**Jumping Team**–USSR
2. Poland, 3. Mexico

### FENCING—MEN

**Individual Foil**–Vladimir Smirnov, USSR, 2. France, 3. USSR

**Team Foil**–France
2. USSR, 3. Poland

**Individual Epee**–Johan Harmenberg, Sweden, 2. Hungary, 3. France

**Team Epee**–France
2. Poland, 3. USSR

**Individual Sabre**–Viktor Krovopuskov, USSR, 2. USSR, 3. Hungary

**Team Sabre**–USSR
2. Italy, 3. Hungary

### FENCING—WOMEN

**Individual Foil**–Pascale Trinquet, France, 2. Hungary, 3. Poland

**Team Foil**–France
2. USSR, 3. Hungary

### FIELD HOCKEY

**Men**–India
2. Spain, 3. USSR

**Women**–Zimbabwe
2. Czechoslovakia, 3. USSR

### GYMNASTICS—MEN

**All-Around**–Aleksandr Ditiatin, USSR
2. USSR, 3. Bulgaria

**Parallel Bars**–Aleksandr Tkachyov, USSR, 2. USSR, 3. E. Germany

**Vault**–Nikolai Andrianov, USSR
2. USSR, 3. E. Germany

**Pommel Horse**–Zoltan Magyar, Hungary
2. USSR, 3. E. Germany

**Rings**–Aleksandr Ditiatin, USSR
2. USSR, 3. Czechoslovakia

**Horizontal Bar**–Stoyan Deltchev, Bulgaria, 2. USSR, 3. USSR

**Floor Exercise**–Roland Bruckner, E. Germany, 2. USSR, 3. USSR

**Team Competition**–USSR
2. E. Germany, 3. Hungary

### GYMNASTICS—WOMEN

**All-Around**–Yelena Davydova, USSR
2. (tie) E. Germany, Romania

**Balance Beam**–Nadia Comaneci, Romanià, 2. USSR, 3. USSR

**Uneven Bars**–Maxi Gnauck, E. Germany
2. Romania, 3. (tie) Romania, E. Germany, USSR

**Vault**–Natalia Shaposhnikova, USSR, 2. E. Germany, 3. Romania

**Floor Exercise**–**(tie)** Nelli Kim, USSR-Nadia Comaneci, Romania, 3. (tie) USSR, E. Germany

**Team Competition**–USSR
2. Romania, 3. E. Germany

### HANDBALL

**Men**–East Germany
2. USSR, 3. Romania

**Women**–USSR
2. Yugoslavia, 3. E. Germany

### JUDO

**132 lb**–Thierry Rey, France
2. Cuba, 3. USSR, Hungary

**143 lb**–Nikolai Solodukhin, USSR
2. Mongolia, 3. Bulgaria, Poland

**157 lb**–Ezio Gamba, Italy
2. Britain, 3. Mongolia, E. Germany

**172 lb**–Shota Khabareli, USSR
2. Cuba, 3. E. Germany, France

**190 lb**–Juerg Roethlisberger, Switzerland
2. Cuba, 3. E. Germany, USSR

**209 lb**–Robert Van De Walle, Belgium
2. USSR, 3. E. Germany, Netherlands

**Over 209 lb**–Angelo Parisi, France
2. Bulgaria, 3. Czechoslovakia, Yugoslavia

**Open Weight**–Dietmar Lorenz, E. Germany
2. France, 3. Hungary, Britain

### MODERN PENTATHLON

**Individual**–Anatoly Starostin, USSR
2. Hungary, 3. USSR

**Team**–USSR
2. Hungary, 3. Sweden

### ROWING—MEN

**Single Sculls**–Pertti Karppinen, Finland, 2. USSR, 3. E. Germany

**Double Sculls**–East Germany (Dreipke-Kroppelein), 2. Yugoslavia, 3. Czechoslovakia

**Pairs w/o Coxswain**–E. Germany (B. Landvoigt-J. Landvoigt)
2. USSR, 3. Britain

**Pairs with Coxswain**–East Germany
2. USSR, 3. Yugoslavia

**Fours w/o Coxswain**–East Germany
2. USSR, 3. Britain

**Fours with Coxswain**–East Germany
2. USSR, 3. Poland

**Quadruple Sculls**–East Germany
2. USSR, 3. Bulgaria

**Eights**–East Germany
2. Britain, 3. USSR

### ROWING—WOMEN

**Single Sculls**–Sanda Toma, Romania
2. USSR, 3. E. Germany

**Double Sculls**–USSR (Khloptseva-Popova), 2. E. Germany, 3. Romania

**Pairs w/o Coxswain**–East Germany (Steindorf-Klier), 2. Poland 3. Bulgaria

**Fours with Coxswain**–East Germany
2. Bulgaria, 3. USSR

**Quadruple Sculls**–East Germany
2. USSR, 3. Bulgaria

**Eights**–East Germany
2. USSR, 3. Romania

### SHOOTING

**Free Pistol**–Aleksandr Melentev, USSR, 2. E. Germany, 3. Bulgaria

**Rapid Fire Pistol**–Corneliu Ion, Romania, 2. E. Germany, 3. Austria

**Rifle, Prone**–Karoly Varga, Hungary
2. E. Germany, 3. Bulgaria

**Rifle, 3-Position**–Viktor Vlasov, USSR
2. E. Germany, 3. Sweden

**Moving Target**–Igor Sokolov, USSR
2. E. Germany, 3. USSR

**Skeetshooting**–Hans Kjeld Rasmussen, Denmark, 2. Sweden, 3. Cuba

**Trapshooting**–Luciano Giovannetti, Italy, 2. USSR, 3. E. Germany

### SOCCER (FOOTBALL)

**Team**–Czechoslovakia
2. E. Germany, 3. USSR

### SWIMMING—MEN

(*Olympic Record)

**100 m Freestyle**–Jorg Woithe, E. Germany 50.40, 2. Sweden, 3. Sweden

**200 m Freestyle**–Sergei Kopliakov, USSR 1:49.81*, 2. USSR, 3. Australia

**400 m Freestyle**–Vladimir Salnikov, USSR 3:51.31*, 2. USSR, 3. USSR

**1500 m. Freestyle**–Vladimir Salnikov, USSR 14:58.27*, 2. USSR, 3. Australia

**100 m Backstroke**–Bengt Baron, Sweden 56.53, 2. USSR, 3. USSR

**200 m Backstroke**–Sandor Wladar, Hungary 2:01.93, 2. Hungary, 3. Australia

**100 m Breaststroke**–Duncan Goodhew, Britain 1:03.34, 2. USSR, 3. Australia

**200 m Breaststroke**–Robertas Zulpa, USSR 2:15.85, 2. Hungary, 3. USSR

**100 m Butterfly**–Par Arvidsson, Sweden 54.92, 2. E. Germany, 3. Spain

**200 m Butterfly**–Sergei Fesenko, USSR 1:59.76, 2. Britain, 3. E. Germany

**400 m Indiv. Medley**–Aleksandr Sidorenko, USSR 4:22.89*, 2. USSR, 3. Hungary

**400 m Medley Relay**–Australia 3:45.70
2. USSR, 3. Britain

**800 m Freestyle Relay**–USSR 7:23.50
2. E. Germany, 3. Brazil

### SWIMMING—WOMEN

(*Olympic Record)

**100 m Freestyle**–Barbara Krause, E. Germany 54.79*, 2. E. Germany, 3. E. Germany

**200 m Freestyle**–Barbara Krause, E. Germany 1:58.33*, 2. E. Germany, 3. E. Germany

**400 m Freestyle**–Ines Diers, E. Germany 4:08.76*, 2. E. Germany, 3. E. Germany

**800 m Freestyle**–Michelle Ford, Australia 8:28.90*, 2. E. Germany, 3. E. Germany

**100 m Backstroke**–Rica Reinisch, E. Germany 1:00.86*, 2. E. Germany 3. E. Germany

**200 m Backstroke**–Rica Reinisch, E. Germany 2:11.77*, 2. E. Germany, 3. E. Germany

**100 m Breaststroke**–Ute Geweniger, E. Germany 1:10.11*, 2. USSR, 3. Denmark

**200 m Breaststroke**–Lina Kachusite, USSR 2:29.54*, 2. USSR, 3. USSR

**100 m Butterfly**–Caren Metschuck, E. Germany 1:00.42, 2. E. Germany, 3. E. Germany

**200 m Butterfly**–Ines Geissler, E. Germany 2:10.44*, 2. E. Germany, 3. Australia

**400 m Indiv. Medley**–Petra Schneider, E. Germany 4:36.29*, 2. Britain, 3. Poland

**400 m Medley Relay**–East Germany 4:06.67*, 2. Britain, 3. USSR

**400 m Freestyle Relay**–East Germany 3:42.71*, 2. Sweden, 3. Netherlands

**TRACK AND FIELD–MEN**
(*Olympic Record)

**100 m Dash**–Allan Wells, Britain 10.25 2. Cuba, 3. Bulgaria

**200 m Dash**–Pietro Mennea, Italy 20.19, 2. Britain, 3. Jamaica

**400 m Dash**–Viktor Markin, USSR 44.60 2. Australia, 3. E. Germany

**800 m Run**–Steve Ovett, Britain 1:45.4, 2. Britain, 3. USSR

**1500 m Run**–Sebastian Coe, Britain 3:38.4, 2. E. Germany, 3. Britain

**5000 m Run**–Miruts Yifter, Ethiopia 13:21.0*, 2. Tanzania, 3. Finland

**10,000 m Run**–Miruts Yifter, Ethiopia 27:42.7, 2. Finland, 3. Ethiopia

**Marathon**–Waldemar Cierpinski, E. Germany 2:11:3, 2. Netherlands, 3. USSR

**110 m Hurdles**–Thomas Munkelt, E. Germany 13.39, 2. Cuba, 3. USSR

**400 m Hurdles**–Volker Beck, E. Germany 48.70, 2. USSR, 3. Britain

**3000 m Steeplechase**–Bronislaw Malinowski, Poland 8:09.7, 2. Tanzania, 3. Ethiopia

**400 m Relay**–USSR 38.26 2. Poland, 3. France

**1600 m Relay**–USSR 3:01.1 2. E. Germany, 3. Italy

**20 km Walk**–Maurizio Damilano, Italy 1:23:35.5*, 2. USSR, 3. E. Germany

**50 km Walk**–Hartwig Gauder, E. Germany 3:49:24.0*, 2. Spain, 3. USSR

**Long Jump**–Lutz Dombrowski, E. Germany 28′ ¼″, 2. E. Germany, 3. USSR

**Triple Jump**–Jaak Uudmae, USSR 56′ 11⅛″, 2. USSR, 3. Brazil

**High Jump**–Gerd Wessig, E. Germany 7′ 8¾″*, 2. Poland, 3. E. Germany

**Pole Vault**–Wladyslaw Kozakiewicz, Poland 18′ 11½″*, 2. (tie) USSR, Poland

**Shot Put**–Vladimir Kiselyov, USSR 70′ ½″*, 2. USSR, 3. E. Germany

**Discus Throw**–Viktor Rashchupkin, USSR 218′ 8″, 2. Czechoslovakia, 3. Cuba

**Javelin Throw**–Dainis Kula, USSR 299′ 2⅜″, 2. USSR, 3. E. Germany

**Hammer Throw**–Yuri Sedykh, USSR 268′ 4½″*, 2. USSR, 3. USSR

**Decathlon**–Daley Thompson, Britain 8,495 pts., 2. USSR, 3. USSR

**TRACK AND FIELD—WOMEN**
(*Olympic Record)

**100 m Dash**–Lyudmila Kondrateva, USSR 11.06, 2. E. Germany, 3. E. Germany

**200 m Dash**–Barbel Wockel, E. Germany 22.03*, 2. USSR, 3. Jamaica

**400 m Dash**–Marita Koch, E. Germany 48.88*, 2. Czechoslovakia, 3. E. Germany

**800 m Run**–Nadezhda Olizarenko, USSR 1:53.5*, 2. USSR, 3. USSR

**1500 m Run**–Tatyana Kazankina, USSR 3:56.6*, 2. E. Germany, 3. USSR

**100 m Hurdles**–Vera Komisova, USSR 12.56*, 2. E. Germany, 3. Poland

**400 m Relay**–East Germany 41.60* 2. USSR, 3. Britain

**1600 m Relay**–USSR 3:20.2 2. E. Germany, 3. Britain

**Long Jump**–Tatiana Kolpakova, USSR 23′ 2″*, 2. E. Germany, 3. USSR

**High Jump**–Sara Simeoni, Italy 6′ 5½″*, 2. Poland, 3. E. Germany

**Shot Put**–Ilona Slupianek, E. Germany 73′ 6¼″*, 2. USSR, 3. E. Germany

**Discus Throw**–Evelin Jahl, E. Germany 229′ 6½″*, 2. Bulgaria, 3. USSR

**Javelin Throw**–Maria Colon, Cuba 224′ 5″*, 2. USSR, 3. E. Germany

**Pentathlon**–Nadezhda Tkachenko, USSR 5083 pts.*, 2. USSR, 3. USSR

**VOLLEYBALL**

**Men**–USSR 2. Bulgaria, 3. Romania

**Women**–USSR 2. E. Germany, 3. Bulgaria

**WATER POLO**

**Team**–USSR 2. Yugoslavia, 3. Hungary

**WEIGHTLIFTING**

**115 lb**–Kanybek Osmanoliev, USSR 2. N. Korea, 3. N. Korea

**123 lb**–Daniel Nunez, Cuba 2. USSR, 3. Poland

**132 lb**–Viktor Mazin, USSR 2. Bulgaria, 3. Poland

**149 lb**–Yanko Roussev, Bulgaria 2. E. Germany, 3. Bulgaria

**165 lb**–Assen Zlatev, Bulgaria 2. USSR, 3. Bulgaria

**182 lb**–Yurik Vardanyan, USSR 2. Bulgaria, 3. Czechoslovakia

**198 lb**–Peter Baczako, Hungary 2. Bulgaria, 3. E. Germany

**220 lb**–Ota Zaremba, Czechoslovakia 2. USSR, 3. Cuba

**242 lb**–Leonid Taranenko, USSR 2. Bulgaria, 3. Hungary

**Over 242 lb**–Sultan Rakhmanov, USSR 2. E. Germany, 3. Poland

**WRESTLING, FREESTYLE**

**106 lb**–Claudio Pollio, Italy 2. N. Korea, 3. USSR

**115 lb**–Anatoly Beloglazov, USSR 2. Poland, 3. Bulgaria

**126 lb**–Sergei Beloglazov, USSR 2. N. Korea, 3. Mongolia

**137 lb**–Magomedgasan Abushev, USSR 2. Bulgaria, 3. Greece

**149 lb**–Saipulla Absaidov, USSR 2. Bulgaria, 3. Yugoslavia

**165 lb**–Valentin Raitchev, Bulgaria 2. Mongolia, 3. Czechoslovakia

**181 lb**–Ismail Abilov, Bulgaria 2. USSR, 3. Hungary

**198 lb**–Sanasar Oganesyan, USSR 2. E. Germany, 3. Poland

**220 lb**–Ilya Mate, USSR 2. Bulgaria, 3. Czechoslovakia

**Over 220 lb**–Soisan Andiev, USSR 2. Hungary, 3. Poland

**WRESTLING, GRECO-ROMAN**

**106 lb**–Zaksylik Ushkempirov, USSR 2. Romania, 3. Hungary

**114 lb**–Vakhtang Blagidze, USSR 2. Hungary, 3. Bulgaria

**125 lb**–Shamil Serikov, USSR 2. Poland, 3. Sweden

**136 lb**–Stilianos Migiakis, Greece 2. Hungary, 3. USSR

**150 lb**–Stefan Rusu, Romania 2. Poland, 3. Sweden

**165 lb**–Ferenc Kocsis, Hungary 2. USSR, 3. Finland

**180 lb**–Gennady Korban, USSR 2. Poland, 3. Bulgaria

**198 lb**–Norbert Nottny, Hungary 2. USSR, 3. Romania

**220 lb**–Gheorghi Raikov, Bulgaria 2. Poland, 3. Romania

**Over 220 lb**–Aleksandr Kolchinsky, USSR 2. Bulgaria, 3. Lebanon

**YACHTING**

**Tornado Class**–Brazil 2. Denmark, 3. Sweden

**470 Class**–Brazil 2. E. Germany, 3. Finland

**Flying Dutchman Class**–Spain 2. Ireland, 3. Hungary

**Soling Class**–Denmark 2. USSR, 3. Greece

**Finn Class**–Finland 2. Austria, 3. USSR

**Star Class**–USSR 2. Austria, 3. Italy

# SUMMER OLYMPIC CHAMPIONS: SWIMMING AND DIVING, TRACK AND FIELD, TEAM SPORTS

NOTE: An asterisk * denotes Olympic record.

## SWIMMING AND DIVING (Men)

| Year Champion and Country | Time |
|---|---|
| **100 Meter Free Style** | **Min./Sec.** |
| 1896—Alfred Hajos, Hungary | 1:22.2 |
| 1904—Zoltan de Halmay, Hungary (100 yds.) | 1:02.8 |
| 1908—Charles Daniels, United States | 1:05.6 |
| 1912—Duke Kahanamoku, United States | 1:03.4 |
| 1920—Duke Kahanamoku, United States | 1:01.4 |
| 1924—John Weissmuller, United States | 59.0 |
| 1928—John Weissmuller, United States | 58.6 |
| 1932—Yasuji Miyazaki, Japan | 58.2 |
| 1936—Ferenc Csik, Hungary | 57.6 |
| 1948—Walter Ris, United States | 57.3 |
| 1952—Clarke Scholes, United States | 57.4 |
| 1956—Jon Hendricks, Australia | 55.4 |
| 1960—John Devitt, Australia | 55.2 |
| 1964—Donald A. Schollander, United States | 53.4 |
| 1968—Michael Wenden, Australia | 52.2 |
| 1972—Mark Spitz, United States | 51.2 |
| 1976—Jim Montgomery, United States | 49.99* |
| **200 Meter Free Style** | |
| 1968—Michael Wenden, Australia | 1:55.2 |
| 1972—Mark Spitz, United States | 1:52.8 |
| 1976—Bruce Furniss, United States | 1:50.29 |
| **400 Meter Free Style** | |
| 1896—Paul Neumann, Austria (500 m.) | 8:12.6 |
| 1904—Charles Daniels, United States (440 yds.) | 6:16.2 |
| 1908—Henry Taylor, Great Britain | 5:36.8 |
| 1912—George Hodgson, Canada | 5:24.4 |
| 1920—Norman Ross, United States | 5:26.8 |
| 1924—John Weissmuller, United States | 5:04.2 |
| 1928—Albert Zorilla, Argentina | 5:01.6 |
| 1932—Clarence Crabbe, United States | 4:48.4 |
| 1936—Jack Medica, United States | 4:44.5 |
| 1948—William Smith, United States | 4:41.0 |
| 1952—Jean Boiteux, France | 4:30.7 |
| 1956—Murray Rose, Australia | 4:27.3 |
| 1960—Murray Rose, Australia | 4:18.3 |
| 1964—Donald A. Schollander, United States | 4:12.2 |
| 1968—Michael Burton, United States | 4:09.0 |
| 1972—Bradford Cooper, Australia | 4:00.3 |
| 1976—Brian Goodell, United States | 3:51.93 |
| **1,500 Meter Free Style** | **Min./Sec.** |
| 1896—Alfred Hajos, Hungary (1,200 m.) | 18:22.2 |
| 1900—John Jarvis, Great Britain (1,000 m.) | 13:40.2 |
| 1904—Emil Rausch, Germany (1,609 m.) | 27:18.2 |
| 1908—Henry Taylor, Great Britain | 22:48.4 |
| 1912—George Hodgson, Canada | 22:00.0 |
| 1920—Norman Ross, United States | 22:23.2 |
| 1924—Andrew Charlton, Australia | 20:06.6 |
| 1928—Arne Borg, Sweden | 19:51.8 |
| 1932—Kusuo Kitamura, Japan | 19:12.4 |
| 1936—Noboru Terada, Japan | 19:13.7 |
| 1948—James P. McLane, United States | 19:18.5 |
| 1952—Ford Konno, United States | 18:30.0 |
| 1956—Murray Rose, Australia | 17:58.9 |
| 1960—John Konrads, Australia | 17:19.6 |
| 1964—Robert Windle, Australia | 17:01.7 |
| 1968—Michael Burton, United States | 16:38.9 |
| 1972—Michael Burton, United States | 15:52.6 |
| 1976—Brian Goodell, United States | 15:02.40 |
| **100 Meter Backstroke** | |
| 1904—Walter Brack, Germany (100 yds.) | 1:16.8 |
| 1908—Arno Bieberstein, Germany | 1:24.6 |
| 1912—Harry Hebner, United States | 1:21.2 |
| 1920—Warren Kealoha, United States | 1:15.2 |
| 1924—Warren Kealoha, United States | 1:13.2 |
| 1928—George Kojac, United States | 1:08.2 |
| 1932—Masaji Kiyokawa, Japan | 1:08.6 |
| 1936—Adolph Kiefer, United States | 1:05.9 |
| 1948—Allen Stack, United States | 1:06.4 |
| 1952—Yoshinobu Oyakawa, United States | 1:05.4 |
| 1956—David Thiele, Australia | 1:02.2 |
| 1960—David Thiele, Australia | 1:01.9 |
| 1964—Not on Program | |
| 1968—Roland Matthes, East Germany | 58.7 |
| 1972—Roland Matthes, East Germany | 56.6 |
| 1976—John Naber, United States | 55.49* |
| **200 Meter Backstroke** | |
| 1900—Ernest Hoppenberg, Germany | 2:47.0 |
| 1964—Jed R. Graef, United States | 2:10.3 |
| 1968—Roland Matthes, East Germany | 2:09.6 |
| 1972—Roland Matthes, East Germany | 2:02.8 |
| 1976—John Naber, United States | 1:59.19* |
| **100 Meter Breaststroke** | |
| 1968—Donald McKenzie, United States | 1:07.7 |
| 1972—Nobutaka Taguchi, Japan | 1:04.9 |
| 1976—John Hencken, United States | 1:03.11* |
| **200 Meter Breaststroke** | |
| 1908—Frederick Holman, Great Britain | 3:09.2 |
| 1912—Walter Bathe, Germany | 3:01.8 |
| 1920—Haken Malmroth, Sweden | 3:04.4 |
| 1924—Robert Skelton, United States | 2:56.6 |
| 1928—Yoshiyuki Tsuruta, Japan | 2:48.8 |
| 1932—Yoshiyuki Tsuruta, Japan | 2:45.4 |
| 1936—Tetsuo Hamuro, Japan | 2:41.5 |
| 1948—Joseph Verdeur, United States | 2:39.3 |
| 1952—John Davies, Australia | 2:34.4 |
| 1956—Masura Furukawa, Japan | 2:34.7 |
| 1960—William Mulliken, United States | 2:37.4 |
| 1964—Ian O'Brien, Australia | 2:27.8 |
| 1968—Felipe Muñoz, Mexico | 2:28.7 |
| 1972—John Hencken, United States | 2:21.5 |
| 1976—David Wilkie, Great Britain | 2:15.11* |
| **100 Meter Butterfly** | |
| 1968—Douglas Russell, United States | 55.9 |
| 1972—Mark Spitz, United States | 54.3* |
| 1976—Matt Vogel, United States | 54.35 |
| **200 Meter Butterfly** | |
| 1956—William Yorzyk, United States | 2:19.3 |
| 1960—Michael Troy, United States | 2:12.8 |
| 1964—Kevin Berry, Australia | 2:06.6 |
| 1968—Carl Robie, United States | 2:08.7 |
| 1972—Mark Spitz, United States | 2:00.7 |
| 1976—Michael Bruner, United States | 1:59.23* |
| **200 Meter Individual Medley** | |
| 1968—Charles Hickcox, United States | 2:12.0 |
| 1972—Gunnar Larsson, Sweden | 2:07.2* |
| **400 Meter Individual Medley** | |
| 1964—Richard W. Roth, United States | 4:45.4 |
| 1968—Charles Hickcox, United States | 4:48.4 |
| 1972—Gunnar Larsson, Sweden | 4:32.0 |
| 1976—Rod Strachan, United States | 4:23.68 |
| **400 Meter Free Style Relay** | |
| 1964—United States | 3:33.2 |
| 1968—United States | 3:31.7 |
| 1972—United States | 3:26.4* |
| **400 Meter Medley Relay** | |
| 1960—United States | 4:05.4 |
| 1964—United States | 3:58.4 |
| 1968—United States | 3:54.9 |
| 1972—United States | 3:48.2 |
| 1976—United States | 3:42.22* |
| **800 Meter Free Style Relay** | |
| 1908—Great Britain | 10:55.6 |
| 1912—Australia | 10:11.2 |
| 1920—United States | 10:04.4 |
| 1924—United States | 9:53.4 |
| 1928—United States | 9:36.2 |
| 1932—Japan | 8:58.2 |
| 1936 Japan | 8:51.5 |
| 1948—United States | 8:31.1 |
| 1952—United States | 8:31.1 |
| 1956—Australia | 8:23.6 |
| 1960—United States | 8:10.2 |
| 1964—United States | 7:52.1 |
| 1968—United States | 7:52.3 |
| 1972—United States | 7:38.8 |
| 1976—United States | 7:23.22* |
| **Springboard Diving** | **Points** |
| 1908—Albert Zurner, Germany | 85.50 |
| 1912—Paul Guenther, Germany | 79.23 |
| 1920—Louis Kuehn, United States | 675.00 |
| 1924—Albert C. White, United States | 696.40 |
| 1928—Pete Desjardins, United States | 185.04 |
| 1932—Michael Galitzen, United States | 161.38 |
| 1936—Richard Degener, United States | 163.57 |
| 1948—Bruce Harlan, United States | 163.64 |
| 1952—David Browning, United States | 205.29 |
| 1956—Robert L. Clotworthy, United States | 159.56 |
| 1960—Gary Tobian, United States | 170.00 |
| 1964—Kenneth R. Sitzberger, United States | 159.90 |
| 1968—Bernard Wrightson, United States | 170.15 |
| 1972—Vladimir Vasin, USSR | 594.09 |
| 1976—Phil Boggs, United States | 619.52 |
| **High Diving** | |
| 1904—Dr. G. E. Sheldon, United States | 12.75 |
| 1908—Hjalmar Johansson, Sweden | 83.75 |

1912—Erik Adlerz, Sweden 73.94
1920—Clarence Pinkston, United States 100.67
1924—Albert C. White, United States 97.46
1928—Pete Desjardins, United States 98.74
1932—Harold Smith, United States 124.80
1936—Marshall Wayne, United States 113.58
1948—Dr. Samuel Lee, United States 130.05
1952—Dr. Samuel Lee, United States 156.28
1956—Joaquin Capilla, Mexico 152.44
1960—Robert Webster, United States 165.56
1964—Robert Webster, United States 148.58
1968—Klaus DiBiasi, Italy 164.18
1972—Klaus DiBiasi, Italy 504.12
1976—Klaus DiBiasi, Italy 600.51

**SWIMMING AND DIVING (Women)**

**100 Meter Free Style** **Min./Sec.**

1912—Fanny Durack, Australia 1:22.2
1920—Ethelda Bleibtrey, United States 1:13.6
1924—Ethel Lackie, United States 1:12.4
1928—Albina Osipowich, United States 1:11.0
1932—Helene Madison, United States 1:06.8
1936—Hendrika Mastenbroek, Netherlands 1:05.9
1948—Greta Andersen, Denmark 1:06.3
1952—Katalin Szoke, Hungary 1:06.8
1956—Dawn Fraser, Australia 1:02.0
1960—Dawn Fraser, Australia 1:01.2
1964—Dawn Fraser, Australia 59.5
1968—Margo Jan Henne, United States 1:00.0
1972—Sandra Neilson, United States 58.6
1976—Kornelia Ender, East Germany 55.65

**200 Meter Free Style**

1968—Deborah Meyer, United States 2:10.5
1972—Shane Gould, Australia 2:03.6
1976—Kornelia Ender, East Germany 1:59.26

**400 Meter Free Style**

1920—Ethelda Bleibtrey, United States (300 m.) 4:34.0
1924—Martha Norelius, United States 6:02.2
1928—Martha Norelius, United States 5:42.4
1932—Helene Madison, United States 5:28.5
1936—Hendrika Mastenbroek, Netherlands 5:26.4
1948—Ann Curtis, United States 5:17.8
1952—Valeria Gyenge, Hungary 5:12.1
1956—Lorraine Crapp, Australia 4:54.6
1960—S. Chris Von Saltza, United States 4:50.6
1964—Virginia Duenkel, United States 4:43.3
1968—Deborah Meyer, United States 4:31.8
1972—Shane Gould, Australia 4:19.0
1976—Petra Thuemer, East Germany 4:09.89

**800 Meter Free Style**

1968—Deborah Meyer, United States 9:24.0
1972—Keena Rothhammer, United States 8:53.7
1976—Petra Thuemer, East Germany 8:37.14

**100 Meter Backstroke**

1924—Sybil Bauer, United States 1:23.2
1928—Marie Braun, Netherlands 1:22.0
1932—Eleanor Holm, United States 1:19.4
1936—Dina Senff, Netherlands 1:18.9
1948—Karen Harup, Denmark 1:14.4
1952—Joan Harrison, South Africa 1:14.3
1956—Judy Grinham, Great Britain 1:12.9
1960—Lynn Burke, United States 1:09.3
1964—Cathy Ferguson, United States 1:07.7
1968—Kaye Hall, United States 1:06.2
1972—Melissa Belote, United States 1:05.8
1976—Ulrike Richter, East Germany 1:01.83

**200 Meter Backstroke**

1968—Lillian (Pokey) Watson, United States 2:24.8
1972—Melissa Belote, United States 2:19.2
1976—Ulrike Richter, East Germany 2:13.43

**100 Meter Butterfly**

1956—Shelley Mann, United States 1:11.0
1960—Carolyn Schuler, United States 1:09.5
1964—Sharon Stouder, United States 1:04.7
1968—Lynn McClements, Australia 1:05.5
1972—Mayumi Aoki, Japan 1:03.3
1976—Kornelia Ender, East Germany 1:00.13*

**200 Meter Butterfly**

1968—Ada Kok, Netherlands 2:24.7
1972—Karen Moe, United States 2:15.6
1976—Andrea Pollack, East Germany 2:11.41

**100 Meter Breaststroke**

1968—Djurdjica Bjedov, Yugoslavia 1:15.8
1972—Cathy Carr, United States 1:13.6
1976—Hannelore Anke, East Germany 1:11.16

**200 Meter Breaststroke**

1924—Lucy Morton, Great Britain 3:33.2
1928—Hilde Schrader, Germany 3:12.6
1932—Clare Dennis, Australia 3:06.3
1936—Hideko Maehata, Japan 3:03.6
1948—Nelly Van Vliet, Netherlands 2:57.2
1952—Eva Szekely, Hungary 2:51.7
1956—Ursula Happe, Germany 2:53.1
1960—Anita Lonsbrough, Great Britain 2:49.5
1964—Galina Prozumenshikova, USSR 2:46.4
1968—Sharon Wichman, United States 2:44.4
1972—Beverly Whitfield, Australia 2:41.7
1976—Marina Koshevaya, USSR 2:33.35

**400 Meter Free Style Relay**

1912—Great Britain 5:52.8
1920—United States 5:11.6
1924—United States 4:58.8
1928—United States 4:47.6
1932—United States 4:38.0
1936—Netherlands 4:36.0
1948—United States 4:29.2
1952—Hungary 4:24.4
1956—Australia 4:17.1
1960—United States 4:08.9
1964—United States 4:03.8
1968—United States 4:02.5
1972—United States 3:55.2
1976—United States 3:44.82

**400 Meter Medley Relay**

1960—United States 4:41.1
1964—United States 4:33.9
1968—United States 4:28.3
1972—United States 4:20.7
1976—East Germany 4:07.95

**200 Meter Individual Medley**

1968—Claudia Kolb, United States 2:24.7
1972—Shane Gould, Australia 2:23.1*

**400 Meter Individual Medley**

1964—Donna de Varona, United States 5:18.7
1968—Claudia Kolb, United States 5:08.5
1972—Gail Neall, Australia 5:03.0
1976—Ulrike Tauber, East Germany 4:42.77

**Springboard Diving** **Points**

1920—Aileen Riggin, United States 539.90
1924—Elizabeth Becker, United States 474.50
1928—Helen Meany, United States 78.62
1932—Georgia Coleman, United States 87.52
1936—Marjorie Gestring, United States 89.27
1948—Victoria Draves, United States 108.74
1952—Patricia McCormick, United States 147.30
1956—Patricia McCormick, United States 142.36
1960—Ingrid Kramer, Germany 155.81
1964—Ingrid Engle-Kramer, Germany 145.00
1968—Sue Gossick, United States 150.77
1972—Micki King, United States 450.03
1976—Jennifer Chandler, United States 506.19

**High Diving**

1912—Greta Johansson, Sweden 39.90
1920—Stefani Fryland-Clausen, Denmark 34.60
1924—Caroline Smith, United States 33.20
1928—Elizabeth Pinkston, United States 31.60
1932—Dorothy Poynton, United States 40.26
1936—Dorothy Poynton Hill, United States 33.93
1948—Victoria Draves, United States 68.87
1952—Patricia McCormick, United States 79.37
1956—Patricia McCormick, United States 84.85
1960—Ingrid Kramer, Germany 91.28
1964—Lesley Bush, United States 99.80
1968—Milena Duchkova, Czechoslovakia 109.59
1972—Ulrika Knape, Sweden 390.00
1976—Yelena Vaitsekhovskaya, USSR 406.49

**TRACK AND FIELD (Men)**

**100 Meter Dash** **Sec.**

1896—Thomas E. Burke, United States 12.0
1900—Francis W. Jarvis, United States 10.8
1904—Archie Hahn, United States 11.0
1908—Reginald E. Walker, South Africa 10.8
1912—Ralph C. Craig, United States 10.8
1920—Charles W. Paddock, United States 10.8
1924—Harold M. Abrahams, Great Britain 10.6
1928—Percy Williams, Canada 10.8
1932—Eddie Tolan, United States 10.3
1936—Jesse Owens, United States 10.3
1948—Harrison Dillard, United States 10.3
1952—Lindy J. Remigino, United States 10.4
1956—Bobby J. Morrow, United States 10.5
1960—Armin Hary, Germany 10.2
1964—Robert L. Hayes, United States 10.0
1968—James Hines, United States 9.9*
1972—Valery Borzov, USSR 10.1
1976—Hasely Crawford, Trinidad & Tobago 10.06

**200 Meter Dash**

| | |
|---|---|
| 1900—John W. B. Tewksbury, United States | 22.2 |
| 1904—Archie Hahn, United States | 21.6 |
| 1908—Robert Kerr, Canada | 22.6 |
| 1912—Ralph C. Craig, United States | 21.7 |
| 1920—Allan Woodring, United States | 22.0 |
| 1924—Jackson V. Scholz, United States | 21.6 |
| 1928—Percy Williams, Canada | 21.8 |
| 1932—Eddie Tolan, United States | 21.2 |
| 1936—Jesse Owens, United States | 20.7 |
| 1948—Melvin Patton, United States | 21.1 |
| 1952—Andrew W. Stanfield, United States | 20.7 |
| 1956—Bobby J. Morrow, United States | 20.6 |
| 1960—Livio Berruti, Italy | 20.5 |
| 1964—Henry Carr, United States | 20.3 |
| 1968—Tommie Smith, United States | 19.8* |
| 1972—Valery Borzov, USSR | 20.0 |
| 1976—Donald Quarrie, Jamaica | 20.23 |

**400 Meter Dash**

| | |
|---|---|
| 1896—Thomas E. Burke, United States | 54.2 |
| 1900—Maxwell W. Long, United States | 49.4 |
| 1904—Harry I. Hillman, United States | 49.2 |
| 1908—Wyndham Halswelle, Great Britain | 50.0 |
| 1912—Charles D. Reidpath, United States | 48.2 |
| 1920—Bevil G. D. Rudd, South Africa | 49.6 |
| 1924—Eric H. Liddel, Great Britain | 47.6 |
| 1928—Ray Barbuti, United States | 47.8 |
| 1932—William A. Carr, United States | 46.2 |
| 1936—Archie Williams, United States | 46.5 |
| 1948—Arthur Wint, Jamaica | 46.2 |
| 1952—George Rhoden, Jamaica | 45.9 |
| 1956—Charles L. Jenkins, United States | 46.7 |
| 1960—Otis Davis, United States | 44.9 |
| 1964—Michael D. Larrabee, United States | 45.1 |
| 1968—Lee Evans, United States | 43.8* |
| 1972—Vince Matthews, United States | 44.7 |
| 1976—Alberto Juantorena, Cuba | 44.26 |

| **800 Meter Run** | **Min./Sec.** |
|---|---|
| 1896—Edwin H. Flack, Australia | 2:11.0 |
| 1900—Alfred E. Tysoe, Great Britain | 2:01.4 |
| 1904—James D. Lightbody, United States | 1:56.0 |
| 1908—Melvin W. Sheppard, United States | 1:52.8 |
| 1912—James E. Meredith, United States | 1:51.9 |
| 1920—Albert G. Hill, Great Britain | 1:53.4 |
| 1924—Douglas G. A. Lowe, Great Britain | 1:52.4 |
| 1928—Douglas G. A. Lowe, Great Britain | 1:51.8 |
| 1932—Thomas Hampson, Great Britain | 1:49.8 |
| 1936—John Woodruff, United States | 1:52.9 |
| 1948—Malvin Whitfield, United States | 1:49.2 |
| 1952—Malvin Whitfield, United States | 1:49.2 |
| 1956—Thomas W. Courtney, United States | 1:47.7 |
| 1960—Peter Snell, New Zealand | 1:46.3 |
| 1964—Peter Snell, New Zealand | 1:45.1 |
| 1968—Ralph Doubell, Australia | 1:44.3 |
| 1972—Dave Wottle, United States | 1:45.9 |
| 1976—Alberto Juantorena, Cuba | 1:43.50* |

**1,500 Meter Run**

| | |
|---|---|
| 1896—Edwin H. Flack, Great Britain | 4:33.2 |
| 1900—Charles Bennett, Great Britain | 4:06.2 |
| 1904—James D. Lightbody, United States | 4:05.4 |
| 1908—Melvin W. Sheppard, United States | 4:03.4 |
| 1912—Arnold N. S. Jackson, Great Britain | 3:56.8 |
| 1920—Albert G. Hill, Great Britain | 4:01.8 |
| 1924—Paavo Nurmi, Finland | 3:53.6 |
| 1928—Harry E. Larva, Finland | 3:53.2 |
| 1932—Luigi Beccali, Italy | 3:51.2 |
| 1936—Jack E. Lovelock, New Zealand | 3:47.8 |
| 1948—Henry Eriksson, Sweden | 3:49.8 |
| 1952—Joseph Barthel, Luxembourg | 3:45.2 |
| 1956—Ronald Delany, Ireland | 3:41.2 |
| 1960—Herbert Elliott, Australia | 3:35.6 |
| 1964—Peter Snell, New Zealand | 3:38.1 |
| 1968—Kipchoge Keino, Kenya | 3:34.9* |
| 1972—Pekka Vasala, Finland | 3:36.3 |
| 1976—John Walker, New Zealand | 3:39.17 |

**5,000 Meter Run**

| | |
|---|---|
| 1912—Hannes Kolehmainen, Finland | 14:36.6 |
| 1920—Joseph Guillemot, France | 14:55.6 |
| 1924—Paavo Nurmi, Finland | 14:31.2 |
| 1928—Willie Ritola, Finland | 14:38.0 |
| 1932—Lauri Lehtinen, Finland | 14.30.0 |
| 1936—Gunnar Hockert, Finland | 14:22.2 |
| 1948—Gaston Reiff, Belgium | 14:17.6 |
| 1952—Emil Zatopek, Czechoslovakia | 14:06.6 |
| 1956—Vladimir Kuts, USSR | 13.39.6 |
| 1960—Murray Halberg, New Zealand | 13:43.4 |
| 1964—Robert K. Schul, United States | 13:48.8 |
| 1968—Mohamed Gammoudi, Tunisia | 14:05.0 |
| 1972—Lasse Viren, Finland | 13:26.4 |
| 1976—Lasse Viren, Finland | 13:24.76 |

**10,000 Meter Run**

| | |
|---|---|
| 1912—Hannes Kolehmainen, Finland | 31:20.8 |
| 1920—Paavo Nurmi, Finland | 31:45.8 |
| 1924—Willie Ritola, Finland | 30:23.2 |
| 1928—Paavo Nurmi, Finland | 30:18.8 |
| 1932—Janusz Kusocinski, Poland | 30:11.4 |
| 1936—Ilmari Salminen, Finland | 30:15.4 |
| 1948—Emil Zatopek, Czechoslovakia | 29:59.6 |
| 1952—Emil Zatopek, Czechoslovakia | 29:17.0 |
| 1956—Vladimir Kuts, USSR | 28:45.6 |
| 1960—Petr Bolotnikov, USSR | 28:32.2 |
| 1964—William Mills, United States | 28:24.4 |
| 1968—Naftali Temu, Kenya | 29:27.4 |
| 1972—Lasse Viren, Finland | 27:38.4* |
| 1976—Lasse Viren, Finland | 27:40.38 |

| **Marathon** | **Hr./Min./Sec.** |
|---|---|
| 1896—Spyros Loues, Greece | 2:58:50.0 |
| 1900—Michel Theato, France | 2:59:45.0 |
| 1904—Thomas J. Hicks, United States | 3:28:53.0 |
| 1908—John J. Hayes, United States | 2:55:18.4 |
| 1912—Kenneth McArthur, South Africa | 2:36:54.8 |
| 1920—Hannes Kolehmainen, Finland | 2:32:35.8 |
| 1924—Albin Stenroos, Finland | 2:41:22.6 |
| 1928—A. B. El Ouafi, France | 2:32:57.0 |
| 1932—Juan Zabala, Argentina | 2:31:36.0 |
| 1936—Kitei Son, Japan | 2:29:19.2 |
| 1948—Delfo Cabrera, Argentina | 2:34:51.6 |
| 1952—Emil Zatopek, Czechoslovakia | 2:23:03.2 |
| 1956—Alain Mimoun, France | 2:25:00.0 |
| 1960—Abebe Bikila, Ethiopia | 2:15:16.2 |
| 1964—Abebe Bikila, Ethiopia | 2:12:11.2 |
| 1968—Mamo Wolde, Ethiopia | 2:20:26.4 |
| 1972—Frank Shorter, United States | 2:12:19.7 |
| 1976—Waldemar Cierpinski, East Germany | 2:09:55.0* |

| **110 Meter Hurdles** | **Sec.** |
|---|---|
| 1896—Thomas P. Curtis, United States | 17.6 |
| 1900—Alvin E. Kraenzlein, United States | 15.4 |
| 1904—Frederick W. Schule, United States | 16.0 |
| 1908—Forrest Smithson, United States | 15.0 |
| 1912—Frederick W. Kelley, United States | 15.1 |
| 1920—Earl J. Thomson, Canada | 14.8 |
| 1924—Daniel C. Kinsey, United States | 15.0 |
| 1928—Sydney Atkinson, South Africa | 14.8 |
| 1932—George Saling, United States | 14.6 |
| 1936—Forrest Towns, United States | 14.2 |
| 1948—William Porter, United States | 13.9 |
| 1952—Harrison Dillard, United States | 13.7 |
| 1956—Lee Q. Calhoun, United States | 13.5 |
| 1960—Lee Q. Calhoun, United States | 13.8 |
| 1964—Hayes W. Jones, United States | 13.6 |
| 1968—Willie Davenport, United States | 13.3 |
| 1972—Rod Milburn, United States | 13.2* |
| 1976—Guy Drut, France | 13.30 |

**400 Meter Hurdles**

| | |
|---|---|
| 1900—John W. B. Tewksbury, United States | 57.6 |
| 1904—Harry L. Hillman, United States | 53.0 |
| 1908—Charles J. Bacon, United States | 55.0 |
| 1920—Frank F. Loomis, United States | 54.0 |
| 1924—F. Morgan Taylor, United States | 52.6 |
| 1928—Lord David Burghley, Great Britain | 53.4 |
| 1932—Robert Tisdall, Ireland | 51.8 |
| 1936—Glenn Hardin, United States | 52.4 |
| 1948—Roy Cochran, United States | 51.1 |
| 1952—Charles Moore, United States | 50.8 |
| 1956—Glenn A. Davis, United States | 50.1 |
| 1960—Glenn A. Davis, United States | 49.3 |
| 1964—Warren (Rex) Cawley, United States | 49.6 |
| 1968—David Hemery, Great Britain | 48.1 |
| 1972—John Akii-Bua, Uganda | 47.8 |
| 1976—Edwin Moses, United States | 47.64* |

| **3,000 Meter Steeplechase** | **Min./Sec.** |
|---|---|
| 1920—Percy Hodge, Great Britain | 10:00.4 |
| 1924—Willie Ritola, Finland | 9:33.6 |
| 1928—Toivo A. Loukola, Finland | 9:21.8 |
| 1932—Volmari Iso-Hollo, Finland (3,460 meters—extra lap by official error) | 10:33.4 |
| 1936—Volmari Iso-Hollo, Finland | 9:03.8 |
| 1948—Thore Sjostrand, Sweden | 9:04.6 |
| 1952—Horace Ashenfelter, United States | 8:45.4 |
| 1956—Chris Brasher, Great Britain | 8:41.2 |
| 1960—Zdzislaw Krzyszkowiak, Poland | 8:34.2 |
| 1964—Gaston Roelants, Belgium | 8:30.8 |
| 1968—Amos Biwott, Kenya | 8:51.0 |
| 1972—Kipchoge Keino, Kenya | 8:23.6 |
| 1976—Anders Gärderud, Sweden | 8:08.20* |

| **20,000 Meter Walk** | **Hr./Min./Sec.** |
|---|---|
| 1956—Leonid Spirine, USSR | 1:31:27.4 |
| 1960—Vladimir Golubnichy, USSR | 1:34:07.2 |
| 1964—Kenneth Matthews, Great Britain | 1:29:34.0 |
| 1968—Vladimir Golubnichy, USSR | 1:33:58.4 |

| | |
|---|---|
| 1972—Peter Frenkel, East Germany | 1:26:42.4 |
| 1976—Daniel Bautista, Mexico | 1:24:40.6 |

**50,000 Meter Walk**

| | |
|---|---|
| 1932—Thomas W. Green, Great Britain | 4:50:10.0 |
| 1936—Harold Whitlock, Great Britain | 4:30:41.4 |
| 1948—John A. Ljunggren, Sweden | 4:41:52.0 |
| 1952—Giuseppe Dordoni, Italy | 4:28:07.8 |
| 1956—Norman Read, New Zealand | 4:30:42.8 |
| 1960—Donald Thompson, Great Britain | 4:25:30.0 |
| 1964—Abdon Pamich, Italy | 4:11:12.4 |
| 1968—Christoph Kohne, East Germany | 4:20:13.6 |
| 1972—Bernd Kannenberg, West Germany | 3:56:11.6 |

| **400 Meter Relay** | **Sec.** |
|---|---|
| 1912—Great Britain | 42.4 |
| 1920—United States | 42.2 |
| 1924—United States | 41.0 |
| 1928—United States | 41.0 |
| 1932—United States | 40.0 |
| 1936—United States | 40.0 |
| 1948—United States | 40.3 |
| 1952—United States | 40.1 |
| 1956—United States | 39.5 |
| 1960—Germany | 39.5 |
| 1964—United States | 39.0 |
| 1968—United States | 38.2 |
| 1972—United States | 38.2* |
| 1976—United States | 38.33 |

| **1,600 Meter Relay** | **Min./Sec.** |
|---|---|
| 1908—United States | 3:29.4 |
| 1912—United States | 3:16.6 |
| 1920—Great Britain | 3:22.2 |
| 1924—United States | 3:16.0 |
| 1928—United States | 3:14.2 |
| 1932—United States | 3:08.2 |
| 1936—Great Britain | 3:09.0 |
| 1948—United States | 3:10.4 |
| 1952—Jamaica | 3:03.9 |
| 1956—United States | 3:04.8 |
| 1960—United States | 3:02.2 |
| 1964—United States | 3:00.7 |
| 1968—United States | 2:56.1* |
| 1972—Kenya | 2:59.8 |
| 1976—United States | 2:58.65 |

| **Pole Vault** | **Height** |
|---|---|
| 1896—William W. Hoyt, United States | 10′ 9¾″ |
| 1900—Irving K. Baxter, United States | 10′ 9 9/10″ |
| 1904—Charles E. Dvorak, United States | 11′ 6″ |
| 1908—Albert C. Gilbert, United States<br>Edward T. Cook, Jr., United States | 12′ 2″ |
| 1912—Harry S. Babcock, United States | 12′ 11½″ |
| 1920—Frank K. Foss, United States | 12′ 5 9/16″ |
| 1924—Lee S. Barnes, United States | 12′ 11½″ |
| 1928—Sabin W. Carr, United States | 13′ 9⅜″ |
| 1932—William Miller, United States | 14′ 1⅞″ |
| 1936—Earle Meadows, United States | 14′ 3¼″ |
| 1948—O. Guinn Smith, United States | 14′ 1¼″ |
| 1952—Robert Richards, United States | 14′ 11¼″ |
| 1956—Robert Richards, United States | 14′ 11½″ |
| 1960—Donald Bragg, United States | 15′ 5⅛″ |
| 1964—Fred M. Hansen, United States | 16′ 8¾″ |
| 1968—Robert Seagren, United States | 17′ 8½″ |
| 1972—Wolfgang Nordwig, East Germany | 18′ ½″ |
| 1976—Tadeusz Slusarki, Poland | 18′ ½″ |

**High Jump**

| | |
|---|---|
| 1896—Ellery Clark, United States | 5′ 11¼″ |
| 1900—Irving K. Baxter, United States | 6′ 2⅘″ |
| 1904—Samuel Jones, United States | 5′ 11″ |
| 1908—Harry Porter, United States | 6′ 3″ |
| 1912—Almer Richards, United States | 6′ 4″ |
| 1920—Richmond Landon, United States | 6′ 4¼″ |
| 1924—Harold Osborn, United States | 6′ 5 15/16″ |
| 1928—Robert W. King, United States | 6′ 4⅜″ |
| 1932—Duncan McNaughton, Canada | 6′ 5⅝″ |
| 1936—Cornelius Johnson, United States | 6′ 7 15/16″ |
| 1948—John Winter, Australia | 6′ 6″ |
| 1952—Walter Davis, United States | 6′ 8¼″ |
| 1956—Charles E. Dumas, United States | 6′ 11¼″ |
| 1960—Robert Shavlakadze, USSR | 7′ 1″ |
| 1964—Valery Brumel, USSR | 7′ 1¾″ |
| 1968—Richard Fosbury, United States | 7′ 4¼″ |
| 1972—Juri Tarmak, USSR | 7′ 3¾″ |
| 1976—Jacek Wszola, Poland | 7′ 4½″ |

| **Long Jump** | **Distance** |
|---|---|
| 1896—Ellery Clark, United States | 20′ 10″ |
| 1900—Alvin Kraenzlein, United States | 23′ 6⅞″ |
| 1904—Myer Prinstein, United States | 24′ 1″ |
| 1908—Francis Irons, United States | 24′ 6½″ |
| 1912—Albert Gutterson, United States | 24′ 11¼″ |
| 1920—William Pettersson, Sweden | 23′ 5½″ |
| 1924—DeHart Hubbard, United States | 24′ 5⅛″ |
| 1928—Edward Hamm, United States | 25′ 4¾″ |
| 1932—Edward Gordon, United States | 25′ ¾″ |
| 1936—Jesse Owens, United States | 26′ 5⅜″ |
| 1948—Willie Steel, United States | 25′ 8″ |
| 1952—Jerome Biffle, United States | 24′ 10″ |
| 1956—Gregory C. Bell, United States | 25′ 8¼″ |
| 1960—Ralph H. Boston, United States | 26′ 7¾″ |
| 1964—Lynn Davies, Great Britain | 26′ 5¾″ |
| 1968—Robert Beamon, United States | 29′ 2½″* |
| 1972—Randy Williams, United States | 27′ ½″ |
| 1976—Arnie Robinson, United States | 27′ 4¾″ |

**Triple Jump**

| | |
|---|---|
| 1896—James B. Connolly, United States | 45′ 0″ |
| 1900—Myer Prinstein, United States | 47′ 4¼″ |
| 1904—Myer Prinstein, United States | 47′ 0″ |
| 1908—Timothy Ahearne, Great Britain | 48′ 11¼″ |
| 1912—Gustaf Lindblom, Sweden | 48′ 5⅛″ |
| 1920—Vilho Tuulos, Finland | 47′ 6⅞″ |
| 1924—Archibald Winter, Australia | 50′ 11⅛″ |
| 1928—Mikio Oda, Japan | 49′ 10 13/16″ |
| 1932—Chuhei Nambu, Japan | 51′ 7″ |
| 1936—Naoto Tajima, Japan | 52′ 5⅞″ |
| 1948—Arne Ahman, Sweden | 50′ 6¼″ |
| 1952—Adhemar Ferreira da Silva, Brazil | 53′ 2½″ |
| 1956—Adhemar Ferreira da Silva, Brazil | 53′ 7½″ |
| 1960—Jozef Schmidt, Poland | 55′ 1¾″ |
| 1964—Jozef Schmidt, Poland | 55′ 3¼″ |
| 1968—Viktor Saneyev, USSR | 57′ ¾″* |
| 1972—Viktor Saneyev, USSR | 56′ 11″ |
| 1976—Viktor Saneyev, USSR | 56′ 8¾″ |

**16-Pound Shot Put**

| | |
|---|---|
| 1896—Robert Garrett, United States | 36′ 9¾″ |
| 1900—Richard Sheldon, United States | 46′ 3⅛″ |
| 1904—Ralph Rose, United States | 48′ 7″ |
| 1908—Ralph Rose, United States | 46′ 7½″ |
| 1912—Patrick McDonald, United States | 50′ 4″ |
| 1920—Ville Porhola, Finland | 48′ 7⅛″ |
| 1924—Clarence Houser, United States | 49′ 2½″ |
| 1928—John Kuck, United States | 52′ 13/16″ |
| 1932—Leo Sexton, United States | 52′ 6 3/16″ |
| 1936—Hans Woellke, Germany | 53′ 1¾″ |
| 1948—Wilbur Thompson, United States | 56′ 2″ |
| 1952—Wm. Parry O'Brien, Jr., United States | 57′ 1½″ |
| 1956—Wm. Parry O'Brien, Jr., United States | 60′ 11″ |
| 1960—William Nieder, United States | 64′ 6¾″ |
| 1964—Dallas C. Long, United States | 66′ 8¼″ |
| 1968—James Randel Matson, United States | 67′ 4¾″ |
| 1972—Wladyslaw Komar, Poland | 69′ 6″ |
| 1976—Udo Beyer, East Germany | 69′ 6.7″ |

**Discus Throw**

| | |
|---|---|
| 1896—Robert Garrett, United States | 95′ 7½″ |
| 1900—Rudolf Bauer, Hungary | 118′ 2 9/10″ |
| 1904—Martin Sheridan, United States | 128′ 10½″ |
| 1908—Martin Sheridan, United States | 134′ 2″ |
| 1912—Armas Taipale, Finland | 145′ 9/16″ |
| 1920—Elmer Niklander, Finland | 146′ 7″ |
| 1924—Clarence Houser, United States | 151′ 5¼″ |
| 1928—Clarence Houser, United States | 155′ 2⅘″ |
| 1932—John Anderson, United States | 162′ 4⅞″ |
| 1936—Kenneth Carpenter, United States | 165′ 7½″ |
| 1948—Adolfo Consolini, Italy | 173′ 2″ |
| 1952—Sim Iness, United States | 180′ 6½″ |
| 1956—Alfred A. Oerter, United States | 184′ 10½″ |
| 1960—Alfred A. Oerter, United States | 194′ 2″ |
| 1964—Alfred A. Oerter, United States | 200′ 1½″ |
| 1968—Alfred A. Oerter, United States | 212′ 6½″ |
| 1972—Ludwick Danek, Czechoslovakia | 211′ 3½″ |
| 1976—Mac Wilkins, United States | 221′ 5.4″* |

**16-Pound Hammer Throw**

| | |
|---|---|
| 1900—John Flanagan, United States | 167′ 4″ |
| 1904—John Flanagan, United States | 168′ 1″ |
| 1908—John Flanagan, United States | 170′ 4¼″ |
| 1912—Matthew McGrath, United States | 179′ 7⅛″ |
| 1920—Patrick Ryan, United States | 173′ 5⅝″ |
| 1924—Frederick Tootell, United States | 174′ 10¼″ |
| 1928—Patrick O'Callaghan, Ireland | 168′ 7½″ |
| 1932—Patrick O'Callaghan, Ireland | 176′ 11⅛″ |
| 1936—Karl Hein, Germany | 185′ 4¼″ |
| 1948—Imre Nemeth, Hungary | 183′ 11½″ |
| 1952—Jozsef Csermak, Hungary | 197′ 11¾″ |
| 1956—Harold V. Connolly, United States | 207′ 3½″ |
| 1960—Vasiliy Rudenkov, USSR | 220′ 1⅝″ |
| 1964—Romuald Klim, USSR | 228′ 9½″ |
| 1968—Gyula Zsivotzky, Hungary | 240′ 8″ |
| 1972—Anatol Bondarchuk, USSR | 247′ 8″ |
| 1976—Yuri Sedykh, USSR | 254′ 4″ |

**Javelin Throw**

| | |
|---|---|
| 1908—Erik Lemming, Sweden | 179′ 10½″ |
| 1912—Erik Lemming, Sweden | 198′ 11¼″ |
| 1920—Jonni Myyra, Finland | 215′ 9¾″ |
| 1924—Jonni Myyra, Finland | 206′ 6¾″ |

1928—Erik Lundquist, Sweden 218′ 6⅛″
1932—Matti Jarvinen, Finland 238′ 7″
1936—Gerhard Stock, Germany 235′ 8 5/16″
1948—Tapio Rautavaara, Finland 228′ 10½″
1952—Cyrus Young, United States 242′ ¾″
1956—Egil Danielson, Norway 281′ 2¼″
1960—Viktor Tsibulenko, USSR 277′ 8⅜″
1964—Pauli Nevala, Finland 271′ 2¼″
1968—Janis Lusis, USSR 295′ 7¼″
1972—Klaus Wolfermann, West Germany 296′ 10″
1976—Miklos Nemeth, Hungary 310′ 4½″*

**Decathlon** — Points

1912—Jim Thorpe, United States 8413.00
Hugo Wieslander, Sweden 7724.49
1920—Helge Lovland, Norway 6804.35
1924—Harold Osborn, United States 7710.77
1928—Paavo Yrjola, Finland 8053.29
1932—James Bausch, United States 8462.23
(Old point system, 1912 through 1932)
1936—Glenn Morris, United States 7900.00
1948—Robert Mathias, United States 7139.00
1952—Robert Mathias, United States 7887.00
1956—Milton G. Campbell, United States 7937.00
1960—Rafer Johnson, United States 8392.00
(Revised point system, 1936 through 1960)
1964—Willi Holdorf, Germany (New point system) 7887.00
1968—William Toomey, United States 8193.00
1972—Nikolai Avilov, USSR 8454.00
1976—Bruce Jenner, United States 8618.00*

**TRACK AND FIELD (Women)**

**100 Meter Dash** — Sec.

1928—Elizabeth Robinson, United States 12.2
1932—Stanislawa Walasiewicz, Poland 11.9
1936—Helen Stephens, United States 11.5
1948—Francina Blankers-Koen, Netherlands 11.9
1952—Marjorie Jackson, Australia 11.5
1956—Betty Cuthbert, Australia 11.5
1960—Wilma Rudolph, United States 11.0
1964—Wyomia Tyus, United States 11.4
1968—Wyomia Tyus, United States 11.0
1972—Renate Stecher, East Germany 11.1
1976—Annegret Richter, West Germany 11.01*

**200 Meter Dash**

1948—Francina Blankers-Koen, Netherlands 24.4
1952—Marjorie Jackson, Australia 23.7
1956—Betty Cuthbert, Australia 23.4
1960—Wilma Rudolph, United States 24.0
1964—Edith McGuire, United States 23.0
1968—Irena Kirszenstein Szewinska, Poland 22.5
1972—Renate Stecher, East Germany 22.4
1976—Baerbel EcKert, East Germany 22.37

**400 Meter Dash**

1964—Betty Cuthbert, Australia 52.0
1968—Colette Besson, France 52.0
1972—Monika Zehrt, East Germany 51.1
1976—Irena Szewinska, Poland 49.29

**800 Meter Run** — Min./Sec.

1928—Linda Radke-Batschauer, Germany 2:16.8
1960—Ljudmila Shevcova-Lysenko, USSR 2:04.3
1964—Ann Packer, Great Britain 2:01.1
1968—Madeline Manning, United States 2:00.9
1972—Hildegard Falck, West Germany 1:58.6
1976—Tatyana Kazankina, USSR 1:54.94

**1,500 Meter Run**

1972—Ludmila Bragina, USSR 4:01.4
1976—Tatyana Kazankina, USSR 4:05.48

**400 Meter Relay** — Sec.

1928—Canada 48.4
1932—United States 47.0
1936—United States 46.9
1948—Netherlands 47.5
1952—United States 45.9
1956—Australia 44.5
1960—United States 44.5
1964—Poland 43.6
1968—United States 42.8
1972—West Germany 42.8
1976—East Germany 42.55

**1,600 Meter Relay** — Min./Sec.

1972—East Germany 3:23.0
1976—East Germany 3:19.23*

**80 Meter Hurdles** — Sec.

1932—Mildred Didrikson, United States 11.7
1936—Trebisonda Valla, Italy 11.7
1948—Francina Blankers-Koen, Netherlands 11.2
1952—Shirley Strickland de la Hunty, Australia 10.9
1956—Shirley Strickland de la Hunty, Australia 10.7
1960—Irina Press, USSR 10.8
1964—Karin Balzer, Germany 10.5
1968—Maureen Caird, Australia 10.3*

**100 Meter Hurdles**

1972—Annelie Erhardt, East Germany 12.6
1976—Johanna Schaller, East Germany 12.77

**High Jump** — Height

1928—Ethel Catherwood, Canada 5′ 3″
1932—Jean Shiley, United States 5′ 5¼″
1936—Ibolya Csak, Hungary 5′ 3″
1948—Alice Coachman, United States 5′ 6⅛″
1952—Esther Brand, South Africa 5′ 5¾″
1956—Mildred McDaniel, United States 5′ 9¼″
1960—Iolanda Balas, Rumania 6′ ¼″
1964—Iolanda Balas, Rumania 6′ 2¾″
1968—Miloslava Rezkova, Czechoslovakia 5′ 11¾″
1972—Ulrika Meyfarth, West Germany 6′ 3½″
1976—Rosemarie Ackermann, East Germany 6′ 4″

**Long Jump** — Distance

1948—Olga Gyarmati, Hungary 18′ 8¼″
1952—Yvette Williams, New Zealand 20′ 5¾″
1956—Elizbieta Krzeskinska, Poland 20′ 9¾″
1960—Vyera Krepkina, USSR 20′ 10¾″
1964—Mary Rand, Great Britain 22′ 2″
1968—Viorica Viscopoleanu, Rumania 22′ 4½″
1972—Heidemarie Rosendahl, West Germany 22′ 3″
1976—Angela Voigt, East Germany 22′ 2½″

**Discus Throw**

1928—Helena Konopacka, Poland 129′ 11⅞″
1932—Lillian Copeland, Unted States 133′ 2″
1936—Gisela Mauermayer, Germany 156′ 3 3/16″
1948—Micheline Ostermeyer, France 137′ 6½″
1952—Nina Romaschkova, USSR 168′ 8½″
1956—Olga Fikotova, Czechoslovakia 176′ 1½″
1960—Nina Ponomareva, USSR 180′ 8¼″
1964—Tamara Press, USSR 187′ 10¾″
1968—Lia Manoliu, Rumania 191′ 2½″
1972—Faina Melnik, USSR 218′ 7″
1976—Evelin Schlaak, East Germany 226′ 4½″

**8-Lb./13-Oz. Shot Put**

1948—Micheline Ostermeyer, France 45′ 1½″
1952—Galina Zybina, USSR 50′ 1½″
1956—Tamara Tishkyevich, USSR 54′ 5″
1960—Tamara Press, USSR 56′ 9¾″
1964—Tamara Press, USSR 59′ 6″
1968—Margitta Gummel, East Germany 64′ 4″
1972—Nadezhda Chizhova, USSR 69′
1976—Ivanka Khristova, Bulgaria 69′ 5″

**Javelin Throw**

1932—Mildred Didrikson, United States 143′ 4″
1936—Tilly Fleischer, Germany 148′ 2¾″
1948—Herma Bauma, Austria 149′ 6″
1952—Dana Zatopekova, Czechoslovakia 165′ 7″
1956—Inessa Janzeme, USSR 176′ 8″
1960—Elvira Ozolina, USSR 183′ 8″
1964—Mihaela Penes, Rumania 198′ 7½″
1968—Angela Nemeth, Hungary 198′ ½″
1972—Ruth Fuchs, East Germany 209′ 7″
1976—Ruth Fuchs, East Germany 216′ 4″

**Pentathlon** — Points

1964—Irina Press, USSR 5,246
1968—Ingrid Becker, West Germany 5,098
1972—Mary Peters, Britain 4,801
1976—Siegrun Siegl, East Germany 4,745

**TEAM SPORTS** (since 1948)

**Basketball–Men**

1948—United States
1952—United States
1956—United States
1960—United States
1964—United States
1968—United States
1972—USSR
1976—United States

**Basketball–Women**

1976—USSR

**Field Hockey**

1948—India
1952—India
1956—India
1960—Pakistan
1964—India
1968—Pakistan
1972—West Germany
1976—New Zealand

**Handball–Men**

1972—Yugoslavia
1976—USSR

**Handball–Women**

1976—USSR

**Soccer (Football)**

1948—Sweden
1952—Hungary
1956—USSR
1960—Yugoslavia
1964—Hungary
1968—Hungary
1972—Poland
1976—East Germany

**Volleyball–Men**

1964—USSR
1968—USSR
1972—Japan
1976—Poland

**Volleyball–Women**

1964—Japan
1968—USSR
1972—USSR
1976—Japan

**Water Polo**

1948—Italy
1952—Hungary
1956—Hungary
1960—Italy
1964—Hungary
1968—Yugoslavia
1972—USSR
1976—Hungary

## THE WINTER OLYMPIC GAMES

| | Sites | Year |
|---|---|---|
| I | Chamonix, France | 1924 |
| II | St. Moritz, Switzerland | 1928 |
| III | Lake Placid, New York | 1932 |
| IV | Garmisch-Partenkirchen, Germany | 1936 |
| V | St. Moritz, Switzerland | 1948 |
| VI | Oslo, Norway | 1952 |
| VII | Cortina, Italy | 1956 |
| VIII | Squaw Valley, California | 1960 |
| IX | Innsbruck, Austria | 1964 |
| X | Grenoble, France | 1968 |
| XI | Sapporo, Japan | 1972 |
| XII | Innsbruck, Austria | 1976 |
| XIII | Lake Placid, New York | 1980 |
| XIV | Sarajevo, Yugoslavia | 1984 |
| XV | Calgary, Alberta | 1988 |

## 1980 WINTER OLYMPICS MEDAL STANDINGS

| | Gold (1st) | Silver (2d) | Bronze (3d) | Total |
|---|---|---|---|---|
| East Germany | 9 | 7 | 7 | 23 |
| U.S.S.R. | 10 | 6 | 6 | 22 |
| U.S.A. | 6 | 4 | 2 | 12 |
| Norway | 1 | 3 | 6 | 10 |
| Finland | 1 | 5 | 3 | 9 |
| Austria | 3 | 2 | 2 | 7 |
| Switzerland | 1 | 1 | 3 | 5 |
| West Germany | 0 | 2 | 3 | 5 |
| Sweden | 3 | 0 | 1 | 4 |
| Liechtenstein | 2 | 2 | 0 | 4 |
| Netherlands | 1 | 2 | 1 | 4 |
| Italy | 0 | 2 | 0 | 2 |
| Canada | 0 | 1 | 1 | 2 |
| United Kingdom | 1 | 0 | 0 | 1 |
| Hungary | 0 | 1 | 0 | 1 |
| Japan | 0 | 1 | 0 | 1 |
| Bulgaria | 0 | 0 | 1 | 1 |
| Czechoslovakia | 0 | 0 | 1 | 1 |
| France | 0 | 0 | 1 | 1 |

## LAKE PLACID MEDALISTS: 1980 ( *Olympic Record, ** World Record)

**ALPINE SKIING (Men)**

**Downhill**
1. Leonhard Stock, Austria
2. Peter Wirnsberger, Austria
3. Steve Podborski, Canada

**Giant Slalom**
1. Ingemar Stenmark, Sweden
2. Andreas Wenzel, Liechtenstein
3. Hans Enn, Austria

**Slalom**
1. Ingemar Stemark, Sweden
2. Phil Mahre, U.S.A.
3. Jacques Luethy, Switzerland

**ALPINE SKIING (Women)**

**Downhill**
1. Annemarie Moser-Proell, Austria
2. Hanni Wenzel, Liechtenstein
3. Marie-Theres Nadig, Switzerland

**Giant Slalom**
1. Hanni Wenzel, Liechtenstein
2. Irene Epple, West Germany
3. Perrine Pelen, France

**Slalom**
1. Hanni Wenzel, Liechtenstein
2. Christa Kinshofer, West Germany
3. Erika Hess, Switzerland

**NORDIC SKIING (Men)**

**15-kilometer cross-country**
1. Thomas Wassberg, Sweden
2. Juha Mieto, Finland
3. Ove Aunli, Norway

**30-kilometer cross-country**
1. Nikolai Zimyatov, U.S.S.R.
2. Vasili Rochev, U.S.S.R.
3. Ivan Lebanov, Bulgaria

**50-kilometer cross-country**
1. Nikolai Zimyatov, U.S.S.R.
2. Juha Mieto, Finland
3. Aleksandr Zavjalov, U.S.S.R.

**4 x 10-kilometer cross-country relay**
1. U.S.S.R. (Rochev, Bazhukov, Beliaev, Zimyatov)
2. Norway
3. Finland

**70-meter jump**
1. Anton Innauer, Austria
2. (tie) Manfred Deckert, East Germany-Hirokazu Yagi, Japan

**90-meter special jump**
1. Jouko Tormanen, Finland
2. Hubert Neuper, Austria
3. Jari Puikkonen, Finland

**Nordic combined (jumping and cross-country)**
1. Ulrich Wehling, East Germany
2. Jouko Karjalainen, Finland
3. Konrad Winkler, East Germany

**NORDIC SKIING (Women)**

**5-kilometer cross-country**
1. Raisa Smetanina, U.S.S.R.
2. Hilkka Riihivuori, Finland
3. Kveta Jeriova, Czechoslovakia

**10-kilometer cross-country**
1. Barbara Petzold, East Germany
2. Hilkka Riihivuori, Finland
3. Helena Takalo, Finland

**4 x 5-kilometer cross-country relay**
1. East Germany (Rostock, Anding, Hesse, Petzold)
2. U.S.S.R.
3. Norway

**BIATHLON**

**10-kilometer individual**
1. Frank Ullrich, East Germany
2. Vladimir Alikin, U.S.S.R.
3. Anatoli Alabyev, U.S.S.R.

**20-kilometer individual**
1. Anatoli Alabyev, U.S.S.R.
2. Frank Ullrich, East Germany
3. Eberhard Rosch, East Germany

**4 x 7.5-kilometer relay**
1. U.S.S.R. (Alikin, Tikhonov, Barnaschov, Alabyev)
2. East Germany
3. West Germany

**HOCKEY**
1. U.S.A.
2. U.S.S.R.
3. Sweden

**BOBSLED**

**Two-man**
1. Switzerland II (Erich Schaerer-Josef Benz)
2. East Germany II
3. East Germany I

**Four-man**
1. East Germany I (Nehmer, Musiol, Germeshausen, Gerhardt)
2. Switzerland I
3. East Germany II

**LUGE**

**Singles (Men)**
1. Bernhard Glass, East Germany
2. Paul Hildgartner, Italy
3. Anton Winkler, East Germany

**Doubles (Men)**
1. Hans Rinn-Norbert Hahn, East Germany
2. Peter Gschnitzer-Karl Brunner, Italy
3. Georg Fluckinger-Karl Schrott, Austria

**Singles (Women)**
1. Vera Zozulya, U.S.S.R.
2. Melitta Sollmann, East Germany
3. Ingrida Amantova, U.S.S.R.

**FIGURE SKATING**

**Men**
1. Robin Cousins, United Kingdom
2. Jan Hoffmann, East Germany
3. Charles Tickner, U.S.A.

**Women**
1. Anett Poetzsch, East Germany
2. Linda Fratianne, U.S.A.
3. Dagmar Lurz, West Germany

**Pairs**
1. Irina Rodnina-Aleksandr Zaitsev, U.S.S.R.
2. Marina Chereskova-Sergei Shakrai, U.S.S.R.
3. Manuela Mager-Uwe Bewersdorf, East Germany

**Ice Dancing**
1. Natalia Linichuk-Gennadi Karponosov, U.S.S.R.
2. Krisztina Regoczy-Andras Sallay, Hungary
3. Irina Moiseeva-Andrei Minenkov, U.S.S.R.

**SPEED SKATING (Men)**

**500-meter**
1. Eric Heiden, U.S.A., 38.03*
2. Evgeni Kulikov, U.S.S.R.
3. Lieuwe DeBoer, Netherlands

**1,000-meter**
1. Eric Heiden, U.S.A., 1:15.18*
2. Gaetan Boucher, Canada
3. (tie) Frode Roenning, Norway–Vladimir Lobanov, U.S.S.R.

**1,500-meter**
1. Eric Heiden, U.S.A., 1:55.44*
2. Kai Arne Stenshjemmet, Norway
3. Terje Andersen, Norway

**5,000-meter**
1. Eric Heiden, U.S.A., 7:2.29*
2. Kai Arne Stenshjemmet, Norway
3. Tom Erik Oxholm, Norway

**10,000-meter**
1. Eric Heiden, U.S.A. 14:28.13**
2. Piet Kleine, Netherlands
3. Tom Erik Oxholm, Norway

**SPEED SKATING (Women)**

**500-meter**
1. Karin Enke, East Germany, 41.78*
2. Leah Poulos Mueller, U.S.A.
3. Natalia Petruseva, U.S.S.R.

**1,000-meter**
1. Natalia Petruseva, U.S.S.R., 24.1*
2. Leah Poulos Mueller, U.S.A.
3. Silvia Albrecht, East Germany

**1,500-meter**
1. Annie Borckink, Netherlands, 2:10.95*
2. Ria Visser, Netherlands
3. Sabine Becker, East Germany

**3,000-meter**
1. Bjoerg Eva Jensen, Norway, 4:32.13*
2. Sabine Becker, East Germany
3. Beth Heiden, U.S.A.

## WINTER OLYMPIC CHAMPIONS

### ALPINE SKIING (Men)

**Downhill**

1948—Henri Oreiller, France
1952—Zeno Colo, Italy
1956—Toni Sailer, Austria
1960—Jean Vuarnet, France
1964—Egon Zimmermann, Austria
1968—Jean Claude Killy, France
1972—Bernhard Russi, Switzerland
1976—Franz Klammer, Austria

**Giant Slalom**

1952—Stein Eriksen, Norway
1956—Toni Sailer, Austria
1960—Roger Staub, Switzerland
1964—Francois Bonlieu, France
1968—Jean Claude Killy, France
1972—Gustavo Thoeni, Italy
1976—Heini Hemmi, Switzerland

**Slalom**

1948—Edi Reinalter, Switzerland
1952—Othmar Schneider, Austria
1956—Toni Sailer, Austria
1960—Ernst Hinterseer, Austria
1964—Josef Stiegler, Austria
1968—Jean Claude Killy, France
1972—Francisco Fernandez Ochoa, Spain
1976—Piero Gros, Italy

### ALPINE SKIING (Women)

**Downhill**

1948—Hedi Schlunegger, Switzerland
1952—Trude Jochum-Beiser, Austria
1956—Madeleine Berthod, Switzerland
1960—Heidi Biebl, Germany
1964—Christl Haas, Austria
1968—Olga Pall, Austria
1972—Marie-Theres Nadig, Switzerland
1976—Rosi Mittermaier, West Germany

**Giant Slalom**

1952—Andrea Mead Lawrence, United States
1956—Ossi Reichert, Germany
1960—Yvonne Ruegg, Switzerland
1964—Marielle Goitschel, France
1968—Nancy Greene, Canada
1972—Marie-Theres Nadig, Switzerland
1976—Kathy Kreiner, Canada

**Slalom**

1948—Gretchen Fraser, United States
1952—Andrea Mead Lawrence, United States
1956—Renee Colliard, Switzerland
1960—Anne Heggtveigt, Canada
1964—Christine Goitschel, France
1968—Marielle Goitschel, France
1972—Barbara Cochran, United States
1976—Rosi Mittermaier, West Germany

### NORDIC SKIING AND JUMPING (Men)

**15-Kilometer Cross-Country**

1924—Thorleif Haug, Norway
1928—Johan Grottumsbraaten, Norway
1932—Sven Utterstrom, Sweden
1936—Erik-August Larsson, Sweden
1948—Martin Lundstrom, Sweden
1952—Hallgeir Brenden, Norway
1956—Hallgeir Brenden, Norway
1960—Hakon Brusveen, Norway
1964—Eero Mantyranta, Finland
1968—Harald Groenningen, Norway
1972—Sven-Ake Lundback, Sweden
1976—Nikolai Bajukov, USSR

**30-Kilometer Cross-Country**

1956—Veikko Hakulinen, Finland
1960—Sixten Jernberg, Sweden
1964—Eero Mantyranta, Finland
1968—Franco Nones, Italy
1972—Vyacheslav Vedenin, USSR
1976—Sergei Saveliev, USSR

**50-Kilometer Cross-Country**

1924—Thorleif Haug, Norway
1928—Per Erik Hedlund, Sweden
1932—Veli Saarinen, Finland
1936—Elis Viklund, Sweden
1948—Nils Karlsson, Sweden
1952—Veikko Hakulinen, Finland
1956—Sixten Jernberg, Sweden
1960—Kalevi Hamalainen, Finland
1964—Sixten Jernberg, Sweden
1968—Ole Ellefsaeter, Norway
1972—Paal Tyldum, Norway
1976—Ivar Formo, Norway

**4 x 10-Kilometer Cross-Country Relay**

1936—Finland
1948—Sweden
1952—Finland
1956—USSR
1960—Finland
1964—Sweden
1968—Norway
1972—USSR
1976—Finland

**70-Meter Special Jump**

1964—Veikko Kankkonen, Finland
1968—Jiri Raska, Czechoslovakia
1972—Yukio Kasaya, Japan
1976—Hans-Georg Aschenbach, East Germany

**90-Meter Special Jump**

1924—Jacob T. Thambs, Norway
1928—Alfred Andersen, Norway
1932—Birger Ruud, Norway
1936—Birger Ruud, Norway
1948—Petter Hugsted, Norway
1952—Arnfinn Bergmann, Norway
1956—Antti Hyvarinen, Finland
1960—Helmut Recknagel, Germany
1964—Toralf Engan, Norway
1968—Vladimir Beloussov, USSR
1972—Wojiech Fortuna, Poland
1976—Karl Schnabl, Austria

**Nordic Combined**

1924—Thorleif Haug, Norway
1928—Johan Grottumsbraaten, Norway
1932—Johan Grottumsbraaten, Norway
1936—Oddbjorn Hagen, Norway
1948—Heikki Hasu, Finland
1952—Simon Slattvik, Norway
1956—Sverre Stenersen, Norway
1960—Georg Thoma, Germany
1964—Tormod Knutsen, Norway
1968—Franz Keller, West Germany
1972—Ulrich Wehling, East Germany
1976—Ulrich Wehling, East Germany

### NORDIC SKIING (Women)

**5-Kilometer Cross-Country**

1964—Claudia Boyarskikh, USSR
1968—Toini Gustafsson, Sweden
1972—Galina Koulacova, USSR
1976—Helena Takalo, Finland

**10-Kilometer Cross-Country**

1952—Lydia Wideman, Finland
1956—Lyubov Kozyreva, USSR
1960—Marija Gusakova, USSR
1964—Claudia Boyarskikh, USSR
1968—Toini Gustafsson, Sweden
1972—Galina Koulacova, USSR
1976—Raisa Smetanina, USSR

**15-Kilometer Relay**

1956—Finland
1960—Sweden
1964—USSR
1968—Norway
1972—USSR
1976 (20 km.)—USSR

### BIATHLON

**20-Kilometer Individual**

1960—Klas Lestander, Sweden
1964—Vladimir Melanin, USSR
1968—Magnar Solberg, Norway
1972—Magnar Solberg, Norway
1976—Nikolai Kruglov, USSR

**40-Kilometer Relay**

1968—USSR
1972—USSR
1976—USSR

### HOCKEY

1920—Canada
1924—Canada
1928—Canada
1932—Canada
1936—Great Britain
1948—Canada
1952—Canada
1956—USSR
1960—United States
1964—USSR
1968—USSR
1972—USSR
1976—USSR

## BOBSLEDDING

### Two-Man

1932—United States
1936—United States
1948—Switzerland
1952—Germany
1956—Italy
1964—Great Britain
1968—Italy
1972—West Germany
1976—East Germany

### Four-Man

1924—Switzerland
1928—United States (5-Man)
1932—United States
1936—Switzerland
1948—United States
1952—Germany
1956—Switzerland
1964—Canada
1968—Italy
1972—Switzerland
1976—East Germany

## LUGE

### Singles (Men)

1964—Thomas Kohler, Germany
1968—Manfred Schmid, Austria
1972—Wolfgang Scheidel, East Germany
1976—Detlef Guenther, East Germany

### Doubles (Men)

1964—Austria
1968—East Germany
1972—Italy, East Germany (tie)
1976—East Germany

### Singles (Women)

1964—Ortrun Enderlein, Germany
1968—Erica Lechner, Italy
1972—Anna M. Muller, East Germany
1976—Margit Schumann, East Germany

## FIGURE SKATING

### Men

1908—Ulrich Salchow, Sweden
1920—Gillis Grafstrom, Sweden
1924—Gillis Grafstrom, Sweden
1928—Gillis Grafstrom, Sweden
1932—Karl Schafer, Austria
1936—Karl Schafer, Austria
1948—Richard Button, United States
1952—Richard Button, United States
1956—Hayes Alan Jenkins, United States
1960—David W. Jenkins, United States
1964—Manfred Schnelldorfer, Germany
1968—Wolfgang Schwartz, Austria
1972—Ondrej Nepela. Czechoslovakia
1976—John Curry, United Kingdom

### Women

1908—Madge Syers, Great Britain
1920—Magda Julin-Mauroy, Sweden
1924—Heima von Szabo-Planck, Austria
1928—Sonja Henie, Norway
1932—Sonja Henie, Norway
1936—Sonja Henie, Norway
1948—Barbara Ann Scott, Canada
1952—Jeanette Altwegg, Great Britain
1956—Tenley Albright, United States
1960—Carol Heiss, United States
1964—Sjoukje Dijkstra, Netherlands
1968—Peggy Fleming, United States
1972—Beatrix Schuba, Austria
1976—Dorothy Hamill, United States

### Pairs

1908—Germany-Anna Hubler, Heinrich Burger
1920—Finland-Ludovika & Walter Jakobsson
1924—Austria-Helene Engelman, Alfred Berger
1928—France-Andree Joly, Pierre Brunet
1932—France-Andree & Pierre Brunet
1936—Germany-Maxie Herber, Ernst Baier
1948—Belgium-Micheline Lannoy, Pierre Baugniet
1952—Germany-Ria & Paul Falk
1956—Austria-Elisabeth Schwartz, Kurt Oppelt
1960—Canada-Barbara Wagner, Robert Paul
1964—USSR-Ludmila Beloussova, Oleg Protopopov
1968—USSR-Ludmila Beloussova, Oleg Protopopov
1972—USSR-Irina Rodnina, Alexei Ulanov
1976—USSR-Irina Rodnina, Aleksandr Zaitsev

### Ice Dancing

1976—USSR-Lyudmila Pakhomova, Aleksandr Gorshkov

## SPEED SKATING (Men)

### 500-Meters

1924—Charles Jewtraw, United States, 44.0
1928—Clas Thunberg, Finland and
Bernt Evensen, Norway (tie), 43.4
1932—John A. Shea, United States, 43.4
1936—Ivar Ballangrud, Norway, 43.4
1948—Finn Helgesen, Norway, 43.1
1952—Ken Henry, United States, 43.2
1956—Yevgeni Grishin, USSR, 40.2
1960—Yevgeni Grishin, USSR, 40.2
1964—Terry McDermott, United States, 40.1
1968—Erhard Keller, West Germany, 40.3
1972—Erhard Keller, West Germany, 39.4
1976—Evgeni Kulikov, USSR, 39.17

### 1,000 Meters

1976—Peter Mueller, United States, 1:19.32

### 1,500-Meters

1924—Clas Thunberg, Finland, 2:20.8
1928—Clas Thunberg, Finland, 2:21.1
1932—John A. Shea, United States, 2:57.5
1936—Charles Mathisen, Norway, 2:19.2
1948—Sverre Farstad, Norway, 2:17.6
1952—Hjalmar Andersen, Norway, 2:20.4
1956—Yevgeni Grishin and Yuri
Mikhailov, USSR (tie), 2:08.6
1960—Roald Aas, Norway and
Yevgeni Grishin, USSR (tie), 2:10.4
1964—Ants Anston, USSR, 2:10.3
1968—Cornelis Verkerk, Netherlands, 2:03.4
1972—Ard Schenk, Netherlands, 2:02.9
1976—Jan Egil Storholt, Norway, 1:59.38

### 5.000-Meters

1924—Clas Thunberg, Finland, 8:39
1928—Ivar Ballangrud, Norway, 8:50.5
1932—Irving Jaffee, United States, 9:40.8
1936—Ivar Ballangrund, Norway, 8:19.6
1948—Reidar Liaklev, Norway, 8:29.4
1952—Hjalmar Andersen, Norway, 8:10.6
1956—Boris Shilkov, USSR, 7:48.7
1960—Viktor Kosichkin, USSR, 7:51.3
1964—Knut Johannesen, Norway, 7:38.4
1968—F. Anton Maier, Norway, 7:22.4*
1972—Ard Schenk, Netherlands, 7:23.6
1976—Sten Stensen, Norway, 7:24.48

### 10,000-Meters

1924—Julien Skutnabb, Finland, 18:04.8
1928—(ice thawed, event cancelled)
1932—Irving Jaffee, United States, 19:13.6
1936—Ivar Ballangrud, Norway, 17:24.3
1948—Ake Seyffarth, Sweden, 17:26.3
1952—Hjalmar Andersen, Norway, 16:45.8
1956—Sigvard Ericsson, Sweden, 16:35
1960—Knut Johannessen, Norway, 15:46.6
1964—Jonny Nilsson, Sweden, 15:50.1
1968—Johnny Hoeglin, Sweden, 15:23.6
1972—Ard Schenk, Netherlands, 15:01.3
1976—Piet Kleine, Netherlands, 14:50.59

## SPEED SKATING (Women)

### 500-Meters

1960—Helga Haase, Germany, 45.9
1964—Lydia Skoblikova, USSR, 45.0
1968—Ludmila Titova, USSR, 46.1
1972—Anne Henning, United States, 43.3
1976—Sheila Young, United States, 42.76

### 1,000-Meters

1960—Klara Guseva, USSR, 1:34.1
1964—Lydia Skoblikova, USSR, 1:33.2
1968—Carolina Geijssen, Netherlands, 1:32.6
1972—Monika Pflug, West Germany, 1:31.4
1976—Tatiana Averina, USSR, 1:28.43

### 1,500-Meters

1960—Lydia Skoblikova, USSR, 2:25.2
1964—Lydia Skoblikova, USSR, 2:22.6
1968—Kaija Mustonen, Finland, 2:22.4
1972—Dianne Holum, United States, 2:20.8
1976—Galina Stepanskaya, USSR, 2:16.58

### 3,000-Meters

1960—Lydia Skoblikova, USSR, 5:14.3
1964—Lydia Skoblikova, USSR, 5:14.9
1968—Johanna Schut, Netherlands, 4:56.2
1972—Stien Kaiser-Baas, Netherlands, 4:52.1
1976—Tatiana Averina, USSR, 4:45.19

## 1982 U.S. NATIONAL SPORTS FESTIVAL CHAMPIONS
Source: U.S. Olympic Committee

### ARCHERY

**Men**–Rick McKinney, Glendale, Ariz.
**Women**–Luanne Ryon, Parker Dam, Calif.

### BASEBALL

**Team**–North

### BASKETBALL

**Men's Team**–South
**MVP**–Ed Pinckney, New York, N.Y.
**Women's Team**–South
**MVP**–Sheila Collins, Colbert, Ga.

### BOXING

**106 lb**–Bryan Jones, Philadelphia, Pa.
**112 lb**–Jesse Benavides, Corpus Christi, Tex.
**119 lb**–Floyd Favors, Capitol Hts., Md.
**125 lb**–Bernard Gray, Boynton Beach, Fla.
**132 lb**–Pernell Whitaker, Norfolk, Va.
**139 lb**–Jerry Page, Columbus, Ohio
**147 lb**–Roman George, Lafayette, La.
**156 lb**–Dennis Milton, Bronx, N.Y.
**165 lb**–Nathan Houser, Detroit, Mich.
**178 lb**–Bennie Heard, Augusta, Ga.
**Heavyweight**–Craig Payne, Livonia, Mich.

### CANOE/KAYAK

CANOE

**500 m**–Rod McLain, Groversville, N.Y.
**1000 m**–Rod McLain
**500 m Doubles**–Tom Smith, Bronx, N.Y. - Bret Young, Hastings-on-Hudson, N.Y.
**1000 m Doubles**–Tom Smith - Bret Young

KAYAK

**500 m**–David Gilman, Berkeley, Calif.
**Women**–Roxanne Barton, Homer, Mich.
**1000 m**–Greg Barton, Homer, Mich.
**500 m Doubles**–William Clark-Stanley, Berkeley, Calif. - David Gilman
**Women**–Lynn Capen, Lansing, Mich. - Roxanne Barton
**1000 m Doubles**–William Clark-Stanley-David Gilman
**1000 m Fours**–East

### CYCLING

**Men's 100 km**–Davis Phinney, Boulder, Colo.
**Women's 50 km**–Rebecca Twigg, Seattle, Wash.
**Kilometer**–Stephen Hegg, Dana Point, Calif.
**Individual Pursuit**–Dave Grylls, San Diego, Calif.
**Sprint**–Mark Gorski, La Jolla, Calif.
**Points**–Leonard Nitz, Flushing, N.Y.

### DIVING

**3-Meter**–Greg Louganis, Mission Viejo, Calif.
**Women**–Megan Neyer, Mission Viejo, Calif.
**Platform**–Greg Louganis
**Women**–Wendy Wyland, Mission Viejo, Calif.

### EQUESTRIAN

**Dressage**–Darcy Drije, Elmhurst, Ill.
**Team**–East
**Jumping**–Daniel Langan, Manlius, N.Y.
**Team**–South

### FENCING

**Epee**–Tim Glass, Houston, Tex.
**Team**–North
**Sabre**–Steve Mormando, Lakewood, N.J.
**Team**–West
**Foil**–Alex Flom, Fairfax, Va.
**Team**–West
**Women's Foil**–Stacy Johnson, San Antonio, Tex.
**Team**–North

### FIELD HOCKEY

**Men's Team**–West
**Women's Team**–North

### FIGURE SKATING

**Men**–Brian Boitano, Sunnyvale, Calif.
**Women**–Vikki deVries, Colorado Sprs., Colo.
**Pairs**–Lea Ann Miller, Wilmington, Del. - William Fauver, Claymont, Del.
**Ice Dancing**–Elisa Spitz, Short Hills, N.J.-Scott Gregory, Wilmington, Del.

### GYMNASTICS–MEN

**All-Around**–Mitch Gaylord, Tempe, Ariz.
**Floor Exercise**–Mitch Gaylord
**Pommel Horse**–Roy Palassou, Santa Clara, Calif.
**Rings**–Matt Arnot, Albuquerque, N.M.
**Vault**–Chris Riegel, Wyomissing, Pa.
**Parallel Bars**–Scott Johnson, Colorado Sprs., Colo.
**Horizontal Bar**–Mitch Gaylord
**Team**–West

### GYMNASTICS–WOMEN

**All-Around**–Kelly Garrison, Altus, Okla.
**Floor Exercise**–Kym Fischler, Center Valley, Pa.
**Beam**–Jessica Armstrong, Allentown, Pa.
**Vault**–Barrie Muzbeck, Novi, Mich.
**Uneven Bars**–Lucy Wener, Memphis, Tenn.
**Team**–South

### ICE HOCKEY

**Team**–North

### JUDO–MEN

**132 lb**–Eddie Liddie, Union City, Ga.
**143 lb**–James Martin, San Gabriel, Calif.
**156 lb**–Steve Seck, Los Angeles, Calif.
**172 lb**–Nicky Yonezuka, Watchung, N.J.
**189 lb**–Robert Berland, Wilmette, Ill.
**209 lb**–Leo White, Colorado Sprs., Colo.
**Over 209 lb**–Brad Moss, Colorado Sprs., Colo.
**Open Div.**–Mitchell Santa Maria, Roselle Park, N.J.

### JUDO–WOMEN

**106 lb**–Janice Zakarzecki, Rockford, Mich.
**114 lb**–Mary Lewis, Albany, N.Y.
**123 lb**–Eve Arnoff, Hartsdale, N.Y.
**134 lb**–Robin Chapman, Rahway, N.J.
**145 lb**–Becky Scott, Kansas City, Mo.
**158 lb**–Maureen Braziel, Brooklyn, N.Y.
**Over 158 lb**–Margaret Castro, New York, N.Y.
**Open Class**–Heidi Bauersachs, Brooklyn, N.Y.

### MODERN PENTATHLON

**Individual**–John Helmick, Long Beach, Calif.
**Team**–North

### RHYTHMIC GYMNASTICS

**All-Around**–Valerie Zimring, Los Angeles, Calif.
**Ribbon**–Lisa Aaronson, Culver City, Calif.
**Rope**–Valerie Zimring
**Hoop**–Valerie Zimring
**Clubs**–Michelle Berube, Rochester, Minn.
**Team**–South

### ROLLER HOCKEY

**Team**–South (Sacramento, Calif.)

### ROLLER SKATING

**Figures**–Tony St. Jacques, Virginia Beach, Va.
**Women**–Anna Conklin, Bakersfield, Calif.
**Singles**–Tim McGuire, Flint, Mich.
**Women**–Kathleen O'Brien DeFelice, Langhorne, Pa.
**Mixed Pairs**–Tina Kneisley, Marion, Ohio-Paul Price, Brighton, Mich.
**Free Dance**–Mark Howard-Cindy Smith, Richmond, Va.
**500 m**–Ken Sutton, Rancho Cucamonga, Calif.
**Women**–Sandy Dulaney, Buena Park, Calif.
**1000 m**–Ken Sutton
**Women**–Sandy Dulaney
**1500 m**–Chris Snyder, Euless, Tex.
**Women**–Sandy Dulaney
**3000 m**–Donnie Van Patter, Little Rock, Ark.
**Women**–Sandy Dulaney
**4000 m Relay**–North
**Women**–East
**4000 m Mixed Relay**–West

### ROWING–MEN

**Single Scull**–Mike Florio, Rye, N.Y.
**Single Scull, Petite**–Glenn Florio, Rye, N.Y.
**Pairs without Coxswain**–Jon Norelius and Dennis Moran, Bellevue, Wash.
**Pairs without Coxswain, Petite**–David Nesbit, Greenbrae, Calif.-Glenn Breeding, Alexandria, Va.
**Four with Coxswain**–North
**Four with Coxswain, Petite**–North
**Eight**–North

### ROWING–WOMEN

**Single Scull**–Elizabeth Hud-Broderick, Philadelphia, Pa.
**Single Scull, Petite**–Kate O'Brien, Corning, N.Y.
**Double Scull**–Jean Harcourt, Durham, N.H.-Sue Montesi, Barrington, R.I.
**Double Scull, Petite**–Laura Emmons and Paige Nilles, Seattle, Wash.
**Pair without Coxswain**–Cathy Ryan, Matawan, N.J.-Lisa Black, Allston, Mass.
**Four with Coxswain**–South
**Eight**–North

### SHOOTING

**Int'l Trap**–Terry Howard, Scott AFB, Ill.
**Int'l Skeet**–Dean Clark, Ft. Benning, Ga.
**Men's Free Rifle**–Ernest Vande Zande, Columbus, Ga.
**Women's Standard Rifle**–Elizabeth McKay, Huntsville, Ala.
**English Match**–Bart McNealy, Morgantown, W. Va.
**Air Rifle**–Ray Slonena, Alexandria, Va.
**Women**–Mary Godlove, Ft. Benning, Ga.
**Air Pistol**–Ken Swanson, Birmingham, Ala.
**Rapid Fire Pistol**–Melvin Makin, Aumsville, Ore.

**Free Pistol**–Ken Swanson
**Women's Standard Pistol**–Lori Kamler, San Francisco, Calif.
**Running Game Target**–Randy Stewart, Columbus, Ga.

## SOCCER

**Team**–East

## SOFTBALL

**Men's Team**–West (Decatur, Ill. ADM)
**Women's Team**–West (Sun City, Ariz. Saints)

## SPEED SKATING

**500 m**–Steve Merrifield, Canoga Park, Calif.
**Women**–Lydia Stephans, Northbrook, Ill.
**1000 m**–Steve Merrifield
**Women**–Lydia Stephans
**1500 m**–Steve Merrifield
**Women**–Lydia Stephans
**Men 5000 m Relay**–West
**Women 3000 m Relay**–South

## SWIMMING–MEN

**100 m Freestyle**–Stuart MacDonald, Mission Viejo, Calif.
**200 m Freestyle**–Geoff Gaberino, Chattanooga, Tenn.
**400 m Freestyle**–Matt Cetlinski, Lake Worth, Fla.
**800 m Freestyle**–Matt Cetlinski
**1500 m Freestyle**–Paul Budd, Memphis, Tenn.
**100 m Butterfly**–Robert Placak, San Rafael, Calif.
**200 m Butterfly**–Dennis Baker, Portland, Ore.
**100 m Breaststroke**–Robert Lager, Mission Viejo, Calif.
**200 m Breaststroke**–Greg Rhodenbaugh, Cincinnati, Ohio
**100 m Backstroke**–Eric Ericson, Wilmington, Del.
**200 m Backstroke**-Rich Hughey, Atlanta, Ga.
**200 m Indiv. Medley**–Roger Von Jouanne, Renton, Wash.
**400 m Indiv. Medley**–Roger Von Jouanne
**400 m Freestyle Relay**–North
**800 m Freestyle Relay**–East
**400 m Medley Relay**–East
**Team**–East

## SWIMMING–WOMEN

**100 m Freestyle**–Heather Strang, E. Lansing, Mich.
**200 m Freestyle**–Stacy Shupe, Cerritos, Calif.
**400 m Freestyle**–Sherri Hanna, Miami, Fla.
**800 m Freestyle**–Michele Richardson, Memphis, Tenn.
**100 m Butterfly**–Laurie Lehner, Ft. Lauderdale, Fla.
**200 m Butterfly**–Terrianne McGuirk, Churchville, Pa.
**100 m Breaststroke**–Jacqueline Komenij, Rohnert Park, Calif.
**200 m Breaststroke**–Susan Rapp, Alexandria, Va.
**100 m Backstroke**–Theresa Andrews, Annapolis, Md.
**200 m Backstroke**–Theresa Andrews
**200 m Indiv. Medley**–Karin Werth, Austin, Tex.
**400 m Indiv. Medley**–Karen La Berge, Doylestown, Pa.
**400 m Freestyle Relay**–West
**800 m Freestyle Relay**–West
**400 m Medley Relay**–East
**Team**–East

## SYNCHRONIZED SWIMMING

**Solo**–Karen Josephson, Bristol, Conn.
**Duet**–Alice and Margarita Smith, Bethesda, Md.
**Figures**–Karen Josephson
**Team**–South

## TABLE TENNIS

**Singles**–Scott Boggan, Merrick, N.Y.
**Women**–Angelita Rosal-Sistrunk, Cardiff-by-the-Sea, Calif.
**Doubles**–Brandon Olson, Hopkins, Minn.-Scott Boggan
**Women**–Thomasina Burke, Phoenix, Ariz.-Alice Green, Great Neck, N.Y.
**Mixed Doubles**–Paul Rapheal, Los Angeles, Calif.-Angelita Rosal-Sistrunk

## TEAM HANDBALL

**Men**–East
**Women**–South

## TENNIS

**Singles**–Mike Velasquez, Albuquerque, N.M.
**Women**–Tracy Becker, Tempe, Ariz.
**Doubles**–Richard Matuszewski, Hopewell Jct., N.Y.-Oliver Sebastian, Dover, Del.
**Women**–Nancy Boggs, Bay Village, Ohio-Tracy Becker
**Mixed Doubles**–Pat Harrison, Shreveport, La.-De Ann Watlington, Baton Rouge, La.

## TRACK AND FIELD–MEN

**100 m Dash**–Calvin Smith, Boulton, Miss.
**200 m Dash**–James Butler, Broken Bow, Okla.
**400 m Dash**–Sunder Nix, Chicago, Ill.
**800 m Run**–James Mays, Hereford, Tex.
**1500 m Run**–Chuck Aragon, Las Lunas, N.M.
**5000 m Run**–Jim Spivey, Wood Dale, Ill.
**10,000 m Run**–Pat Porter, Alamosa, Colo.
**Marathon**–Tom Raunig, Great Falls, Mont.
**3000 m Steeplechase**–Henry Marsh, Bountiful, Utah
**20 km Walk**–(tie) Jim Heiring and Ray Sharp, Colorado Springs, Colo.
**50 km Walk**–Ray Somers, Flemington, N.J.
**110 m Hurdles**–Willie Gault, Knoxville, Tenn.
**400 m Hurdles**–Andre Phillips, Los Angeles, Calif.
**400 m Relay**–South
**1600 m Relay**–South
**High Jump**–Dwight Stones, Irvine, Calif.
**Long Jump**–Carl Lewis, Willingboro, N.J.
**Triple Jump**–Robert Cannon, Lake Charles, La.
**Pole Vault**–Dave Volz, Bloomington, Ind.
**Discuss Throw**–John Powell, San Jose, Calif.
**Hammer Throw**–Dave McKenzie, Fairfield, Calif.
**Javelin Throw**–Brian Crouser, Gresham, Ore.
**Shot Put**–Dean Crouser, Gresham, Ore.
**Decathlon**–Bob Stebbins, Reading, Pa.
**Team**–West

## TRACK AND FIELD–WOMEN

**100 m Dash**–Evelyn Ashford, Hollywood, Calif.
**200 m Dash**–Florence Griffith, Los Angeles, Calif.
**400 m Dash**–Rosalyn Bryant, Inglewood, Calif.
**800 m Run**–Kim Gallagher, Ambler, Pa.
**1500 m Run**–Francie Larrieu-Smith, Lubbock, Tex.
**3000 m Run**–Jan Merrill, New London, Conn.
**Marathon**–Carol Chilcoat, Seattle, Wash.
**100 m Hurdles**–Stephanie Hightower, Columbus, Ohio
**400 m Hurdles**–Edna Brown, Philadelphia, Pa.
**400 m Relay**–West
**1600 m Relay**–East
**High Jump**–Kym Carter, Wichita, Kans.
**Long Jump**–Jodi Anderson, Santa Monica, Calif.
**Discuss Throw**–Leslie Deniz, Gridley, Calif.
**Javelin Throw**–Karin Smith, Venice, Calif.
**Shot Put**–Denise Wood, Knoxville, Tenn.
**Heptathlon**–Patsy Walker, Yelm, Wash.
**Team**–West

## VOLLEYBALL

**Men's Team**–West
**Women's Team**–West

## WATER POLO

**Team**–West

## WEIGHTLIFTING

**52 kg**–Brad Wickersham, Louisville, Ohio
**56 kg**–Brian Miyamoto, Los Angeles, Calif.
**60 kg**–Steve Gambon, Gainesville, Ga.
**67.5 kg**–Michael Jacques, Albany, Ga.
**75 kg**–Cal Schake, Butler, Pa.
**82.5 kg**–Mike Cohen, Savannah, Ga.
**90 kg**–Val Balison, Colorado Sprs., Colo.
**100 kg**–Ken Clark, Pacifica, Calif.
**110 kg**–Guy Carlton, Colorado Springs, Colo.
**Over 110 kg**–Mario Martinez, Salinas, Calif.
**Team**–East

## WRESTLING

### FREESTYLE

**106 lb**–Steve Brown, Troy, Mich.
**115 lb**–Scott Hinckel, Fairfield, Ohio
**123 lb**–Jim Picolo, Springfield, Ohio
**132 lb**–Joe Ghezzi, Wortington, Ohio
**143 lb**–Tony Cook, Perry, Okla.
**154 lb**–Duane Peoples, Allentown, Pa.
**165 lb**–Fred Little, Carson City, Nev.
**178 lb**–John Stafford, Somerdale, N.J.
**192 lb**–Mike Davies, Chardon, Ohio
**Unlimited**–Andy Cope, Indianapolis, Ind.

### GRECO-ROMAN

**106 lb**–Shawn Sheldon, Greenbush, N.Y.
**115 lb**–Jeff Clark, Voorheesville, N.Y.
**123 lb**–Dick Howell, Newark, Del.
**132 lb**–Todd Nicholson, Tillanook, Ore.
**143 lb**–John Placak, Schenectady, N.Y.
**154 lb**–Angelo Cazulina, McAlester, Okla.
**165 lb**–Alan Marwill, Slingersland, N.Y.
**178 lb**–Tony Kourmoulous, Birmingham, Ala.
**192 lb**–Brad Stewart, W. Anchorage, Alaska
**Unlimited**–Dave Koplovitz, Schenectady, N.Y.

## YACHTING

**Laser Class Skipper**–John Kostecki, Novato, Calif.

# BASEBALL

## MAJOR LEAGUE BASEBALL

**Office of the Commissioner:** 75 Rockefeller Plaza, New York City 10019

Prior to 1920, major league baseball was governed by a three-man commission. However, in that year, following the "Black Sox" scandal of the 1919 World Series, the office of baseball commissioner was created. The first commissioner was Kenesaw M. Landis (1921–44); he was succeeded by Albert B. Chandler (1945–51), Ford C. Frick (1951–65), William D. Eckert (1965–69), and the current commissioner, Bowie Kuhn (1969– ).

**NATIONAL LEAGUE:** One Rockefeller Plaza, Suite 1602, New York City 10020. Organized in 1876.

| Eastern Division | Chief Executive | Manager |
|---|---|---|
| Chicago Cubs | Andrew J. McKenna | Lee Elia |
| Montreal Expos | John McHale | Jim Fanning |
| New York Mets | Fred Wilpon | George Bamberger |
| Philadelphia Phillies | Bill Giles | Pat Corrales |
| Pittsburgh Pirates | Daniel Galbreath | Chuck Tanner |
| St. Louis Cardinals | August Busch, Jr. | Whitey Herzog |

| Western Division | Chief Executive | Manager |
|---|---|---|
| Atlanta Braves | Ted Turner | Joe Torre |
| Cincinnati Reds | Richard Wagner | Russ Nixon |
| Houston Astros | Albert Rosen | Bob Lillis |
| Los Angeles Dodgers | Peter O'Malley | Tom Lasorda |
| San Diego Padres | Ballard Smith | Dick Williams |
| San Francisco Giants | Robert Lurie | Frank Robinson |

**AMERICAN LEAGUE:** 280 Park Avenue, New York City 10017. Founded in 1900.

| Eastern Division | Chief Executive | Manager |
|---|---|---|
| Baltimore Orioles | Edward B. Williams | Earl Weaver |
| Boston Red Sox | Jean Yawkey | Ralph Houk |
| Cleveland Indians | Gabe Paul | Dave Garcia |
| Detroit Tigers | John Fetzer | Sparky Anderson |
| Milwaukee Brewers | Allan Selig | Harvey Kuenn |
| New York Yankees | George Steinbrenner | Clyde King |
| Toronto Blue Jays | Pat Gillick | Bobby Cox |

| Western Division | Chief Executive | Manager |
|---|---|---|
| California Angels | Gene Autry | Gene Mauch |
| Chicago White Sox | Edward Einhorn | Tony LaRussa |
| Kansas City Royals | Ewing Kauffman | Dick Howser |
| Minnesota Twins | Calvin Griffith | Billy Gardner |
| Oakland A's | Roy Eisenhardt | Billy Martin |
| Seattle Mariners | Daniel O'Brien | Rene Lachemann |
| Texas Rangers | Eddie Chiles | Darrell Johnson |

## MAJOR LEAGUE RECORDS: 1900–1982

### BATTING

**Highest Batting Average, Lifetime:** .367, Ty Cobb (AL), 1905–1928; .358, Rogers Hornsby (NL), 1915–1937.

**Highest Batting Average, Season:** .424, Rogers Hornsby, St. Louis (NL), 1924; .420, George Sisler, St. Louis (AL), 1922.

**Most Years Led League in Batting:** 12, Ty Cobb, Detroit (AL), 1907–1915, 1917–1919; 8, Honus Wagner, Pittsburgh (NL), 1900, 1903–1904, 1906–1909, 1911.

**Most Years Batting .300 or More:** 23, Ty Cobb, Detroit and Philadelphia (AL), 1906–1928; 17, Honus Wagner, Louisville and Pittsburgh (NL), 1897–1913; 17, Stan Musial, St. Louis (NL), 1942–1944, 1946–1958, 1962.

**Most Hits:** 4,191, Ty Cobb (AL), 1905–1928; 3,869, Pete Rose (NL), 1963–1982.

**Most Hits, Season:** 257, George Sisler, St. Louis (AL), 1920; 254, Lefty O'Doul, Philadelphia (NL), 1929; 254, Bill Terry, New York (NL), 1930.

**Most Consecutive Games Batted Safely:** 56, Joe DiMaggio, New York (AL), 1941; 44, Pete Rose, Cincinnati (NL), 1978

**Most Consecutive Games Played:** 2,130, Lou Gehrig, New York (AL), 1925-39; 1,117, Billy Williams, Chicago (NL), 1963-70.

**Most Runs:** 2,244, Ty Cobb (AL), 1905–1928; 2,174, Babe Ruth, Boston (AL), New York (AL), Boston (NL), 1914–1935.

**Most Runs, Season:** 177, Babe Ruth, New York (AL), 1921; 158, Chuck Klein, Philadelphia (NL), 1930.

**Most Consecutive Years 100 or More Runs:** 13, Lou Gehrig, New York (AL), 1926–1938; 13, Hank Aaron, Milwaukee and Atlanta (NL), 1955–1967.

**Most Runs Batted In, Lifetime:** 2,297, Hank Aaron, 1954–1976; 2,204, Babe Ruth, 1914–1935.

**Most Runs Batted In, Season:** 190, Hack Wilson, Chicago (NL), 1930; 184, Lou Gehrig, New York (AL), 1931.

**Highest Slugging Percentage, Lifetime:** .690, Babe Ruth, Boston and New York (AL), Boston (NL); .634, Ted Williams, Boston (AL).

**Most Home Runs, Lifetime:** 755, Hank Aaron, Milwaukee and Atlanta (NL), Milwaukee (AL), 1954–1976; 714, Babe Ruth, Boston and New York (AL), Boston (NL).

**Most Home Runs, Season:** 61, Roger Maris, New York (AL), 1961, 162-game schedule; 60, Babe Ruth, New York (AL), 1927, 154-game schedule.

**Most Years League Home-Run Leader:** 12, Babe Ruth (AL), 1918–1919, 1920–1921, 1923–1924, 1926–1931; 7, Ralph Kiner, Pittsburgh (NL), 1946–1952.

**Most Years 20 or More Home Runs:** 19, Henry Aaron (NL); 17, Willie Mays (NL); 16, Babe Ruth (AL).

**Most Grand Slam Home Runs, Lifetime:** 23, Lou Gehrig, New York (AL); 18, Willie McCovey, San Francisco, San Diego (NL).

**Most Grand Slam Home Runs, Season:** 5, Ernie Banks, Chicago (NL), 1955; 5, Jim Gentile, Baltimore (AL), 1961.

**Most Bases on Balls, Season:** 170, Babe Ruth, New York (AL), 1923; 162, Ted Williams, Boston (AL), 1947, 1949.

**Fewest Strikeouts, Lifetime (7,000 or More At Bats):** 114, Joe Sewell (AL); 173, Lloyd Waner (NL).

**Most Consecutive Games without Strikeouts:** 98, Nelson Fox, Chicago (AL), 1958; 77, Lloyd Waner (NL), 1941.

**Most Pinch Hits, Lifetime:** 150, Manny Mota (NL).

**Most Stolen Bases, Lifetime:** 938, Lou Brock (NL); 892, Ty Cobb (AL).

**Most Stolen Bases, Season:** 130, Ricky Henderson, Oakland (AL), 1982; 118, Lou Brock, St. Louis (NL), 1974.

### PITCHING

**Most Games Won, Lifetime:** 511, Cy Young (NL–AL); 416, Walter Johnson (AL).

**Most Games Won, Season:** 41, Jack Chesbro, New York (AL), 1904; 39, Ed Walsh, Chicago (AL), 1908.

**Most Years 20-or-More-Game Winner:** 16, Cy Young (NL–AL), 1891–1904, 1907–1908; 13, Christy Mathewson (NL), 1901, 1903–1914; 13, Warren Spahn (NL), 1947, 1949–1951, 1953–1954, 1956–1961, 1963; 12, Walter Johnson (AL), 1910–1919, 1924–1925.

**Most Consecutive Games Won, Lifetime:** 24, Carl Hubbell, New York (NL), 16 in 1936, 8 in 1937; 17, John Allen, Cleveland (AL), 2 in 1936, 15 in 1937; 17, Dave McNally, Baltimore (AL), 2 in 1968, 15 in 1969.

**Most Consecutive Games Won, Season:** 19, Rube Marquard, New York (NL), 1912; 17, ElRoy Face, Pittsburgh (NL), 1959.

**Most Shutout Games, Lifetime:** 113, Walter Johnson (AL); 90, Grover Alexander (NL).

**Most Shutout Games, Season:** 16, Grover Alexander, Philadelphia (NL), 1916; 13, Jack Coombs, Philadelphia (AL), 1910; 13, Bob Gibson, St. Louis, 1968.

**Most Consecutive Shutout Games, Season:** 6, Don Drysdale, Los Angeles (NL), 1968; 5, Harris White, Chicago (AL), 1904.

**Most Consecutive Shutout Innings, Season:** 58, Don Drysdale, Los Angeles (NL), 1968; 56, Walter Johnson, Washington (AL), 1913; 46⅓, Carl Hubbell, New York (NL), 1933.

**Lowest Earned Run Average, Season:** 1.01, Hubert Leonard, Boston (AL), 1914; 1.04, Three Finger Brown, Chicago (NL), 1906.

**Most Consecutive Years Lowest Earned Run Average:** 5, Sandy Koufax, Los Angeles (NL), 1962–1966; 4, Lefty Grove, Philadelphia (AL), 1929–1932.

**Highest Won-Lost Percentage, Lifetime (100 or More Decisions):** .717, Spud Chandler, New York (AL), 1937–1947.

**Highest Won-Lost Percentage, Season (15 or More Decisions):** .947, ElRoy Face, Pittsburgh (NL), 1959.

**Most Strikeouts, Lifetime:** 3,508, Walter Johnson (AL), 1907–27; 3,494, Nolan Ryan (AL-NL), 1966–82.

**Most Strikeouts, Season:** 383, Nolan Ryan, California (AL), 1973; 382, Sandy Koufax, Los Angeles (NL), 1965.

**Most Strikeouts in 9-Inning Game:** 19, Steve Carlton, St. Louis (NL), 1969; 19, Tom Seaver, New York (NL), 1970; 19, Nolan Ryan, California (AL), 1974, 1977.

**Most Games Won, Relief Pitcher, Lifetime:** 123, Hoyt Wilhelm (NL-AL), 1952-70; 119, Lindy McDaniel (NL-AL), 1955-73.

# MAJOR LEAGUE BASEBALL ALL-TIME LEADERS[1]

## BATTING

### SEASONS

| | |
|---|---|
| James McGuire | 26 |
| Eddie Collins | 25 |
| Bobby Wallace | 25 |
| Ty Cobb | 24 |
| Hank Aaron | 23 |
| Brooks Robinson | 23 |
| Rabbit Maranville | 23 |
| Rogers Hornsby | 23 |
| Stan Musial | 22 |
| Tris Speaker, Mel Ott | 22 |
| Babe Ruth | 22 |
| Bill Dahlen | 22 |
| Jimmie Dykes | 22 |
| Cap Anson, Harry Davis | 22 |
| Phil Cavarretta | 22 |
| Carl Yastrzemski | 22 |
| Willie Mays, Al Kaline | 22 |
| Harmon Killebrew | 22 |
| Willie McCovey | 22 |

### GAMES

| | |
|---|---|
| Hank Aaron | 3,298 |
| Carl Yastrzemski | 3,189 |
| Pete Rose | 3,099 |
| Ty Cobb | 3,033 |
| Stan Musial | 3,026 |
| Willie Mays | 2,992 |
| Brooks Robinson | 2,896 |
| Al Kaline | 2,834 |
| Eddie Collins | 2,826 |
| Frank Robinson | 2,808 |
| Tris Speaker | 2,789 |
| Honus Wagner | 2,785 |
| Mel Ott | 2,730 |
| Rusty Staub | 2,715 |
| Rabbit Maranville | 2,670 |
| Lou Brock | 2,616 |
| Luis Aparicio | 2,599 |
| Willie McCovey | 2,588 |
| Paul Waner | 2,549 |

### BATTING AVERAGE

| | |
|---|---|
| Ty Cobb | .367 |
| Rogers Hornsby | .358 |
| Joe Jackson | .356 |
| Ed Delahanty | .346 |
| Willie Keeler | .345 |
| Ted Williams | .344 |
| Tris Speaker | .344 |
| Billy Hamilton | .344 |
| Dan Brouthers | .342 |
| Babe Ruth | .342 |
| Harry Heilmann | .342 |
| Pete Browning | .341 |
| Bill Terry | .341 |
| George Sisler | .340 |
| Lou Gehrig | .340 |
| Jesse Burkett | .340 |
| Nap Lajoie | 339 |

### AT BATS

| | |
|---|---|
| Pete Rose | 12,544 |
| Hank Aaron | 12,364 |
| Carl Yastrzemski | 11,608 |
| Ty Cobb | 11,429 |
| Stan Musial | 10,972 |
| Willie Mays | 10,881 |
| Brooks Robinson | 10,654 |
| Honus Wagner | 10,427 |
| Lou Brock | 10,332 |
| Luis Aparicio | 10,230 |
| Tris Speaker | 10,208 |
| Al Kaline | 10,116 |
| Rabbit Maranville | 10,078 |
| Frank Robinson | 10,006 |
| Eddie Collins | 9,949 |
| Vada Pinson | 9,645 |
| Nap Lajoie | 9,589 |
| Sam Crawford | 9,579 |
| Rusty Staub | 9,488 |

### HITS

| | |
|---|---|
| Ty Cobb | 4,191 |
| Pete Rose | 3,869 |
| Hank Aaron | 3,771 |
| Stan Musial | 3,630 |
| Tris Speaker | 3,515 |
| Honus Wagner | 3,430 |
| Carl Yastrzemski | 3,318 |
| Eddie Collins | 3,311 |
| Willie Mays | 3,283 |
| Nap Lajoie | 3,251 |
| Paul Waner | 3,152 |
| Cap Anson | 3,081 |

### SINGLES

| | |
|---|---|
| Ty Cobb | 3,052 |
| Pete Rose | 2,888 |
| Eddie Collins | 2,641 |
| Willie Keeler | 2,534 |
| Honus Wagner | 2,426 |
| Tris Speaker | 2,383 |
| Nap Lajoie | 2,357 |
| Cap Anson | 2,330 |
| Jesse Burkett | 2,303 |
| Hank Aaron | 2,294 |
| Sam Rice | 2,272 |
| Stan Musial | 2,253 |

### DOUBLES

| | |
|---|---|
| Tris Speaker | 793 |
| Stan Musial | 725 |
| Ty Cobb | 724 |
| Pete Rose | 697 |
| Honus Wagner | 651 |
| Nap Lajoie | 650 |
| Hank Aaron | 624 |
| Carl Yastrzemski | 622 |
| Paul Waner | 603 |
| Charlie Gehringer | 574 |
| Harry Heilmann | 542 |
| Rogers Hornsby | 541 |

### TRIPLES

| | |
|---|---|
| Sam Crawford | 312 |
| Ty Cobb | 297 |
| Honus Wagner | 252 |
| Jake Beckley | 246 |
| Roger Connor | 227 |
| Tris Speaker | 224 |
| Fred Clarke | 219 |
| Dan Brouthers | 212 |
| Paul Waner | 190 |
| Joe Kelley | 189 |
| Bid McPhee | 189 |
| Eddie Collins | 186 |

### HOME RUNS

| | |
|---|---|
| Hank Aaron | 755 |
| Babe Ruth | 714 |
| Willie Mays | 660 |
| Frank Robinson | 586 |
| Harmon Killebrew | 573 |
| Mickey Mantle | 536 |
| Jimmie Foxx | 534 |
| Ted Willams | 521 |
| Willie McCovey | 521 |
| Eddie Mathews | 512 |
| Ernie Banks | 512 |
| Mel Ott | 511 |
| Lou Gehrig | 493 |
| Stan Musial | 475 |
| Willie Stargell | 475 |
| Reggie Jackson | 464 |
| Carl Yastrzemski | 442 |
| Billy Williams | 426 |
| Duke Snider | 407 |
| Al Kaline | 399 |
| Frank Howard | 382 |
| Orlando Cepeda | 379 |
| Norm Cash | 377 |
| Johnny Bench | 375 |
| Rocky Colavito | 374 |
| Gil Hodges | 370 |

### TOTAL BASES

| | |
|---|---|
| Hank Aaron | 6,838 |
| Stan Musial | 6,134 |
| Willie Mays | 6,066 |
| Ty Cobb | 5,863 |
| Babe Ruth | 5,793 |
| Carl Yastrzemski | 5,384 |
| Frank Robinson | 5,373 |
| Pete Rose | 5,292 |
| Tris Speaker | 5,101 |
| Lou Gehrig | 5,059 |
| Mel Ott | 5,041 |
| Jimmie Foxx | 4,956 |

### EXTRA BASE HITS

| | |
|---|---|
| Hank Aaron | 1,477 |
| Stan Musial | 1,377 |
| Babe Ruth | 1,356 |
| Willie Mays | 1,323 |
| Lou Gehrig | 1,190 |
| Frank Robinson | 1,186 |
| Ty Cobb | 1,139 |
| Tris Speaker | 1,132 |
| Carl Yastrzemski | 1,123 |
| Jimmie Foxx | 1,117 |
| Ted Williams | 1,117 |
| Mel Ott | 1,071 |

### RUNS

| | |
|---|---|
| Ty Cobb | 2,244 |
| Babe Ruth | 2,174 |
| Hank Aaron | 2,174 |
| Willie Mays | 2,062 |
| Pete Rose | 1,995 |
| Stan Musial | 1,949 |
| Lou Gehrig | 1,888 |
| Tris Speaker | 1,881 |
| Mel Ott | 1,859 |
| Frank Robinson | 1,829 |
| Eddie Collins | 1,818 |
| Ted Williams | 1,798 |

### STOLEN BASES

| | |
|---|---|
| Lou Brock | 938 |
| Ty Cobb | 892 |
| Eddie Collins | 743 |
| Max Carey | 738 |
| Bert Campaneris | 733 |
| Honus Wagner | 720 |
| Joe Morgan | 663 |
| Maury Wills | 586 |
| Luis Aparicio | 506 |
| Cesar Cedeno | 503 |
| Clyde Milan | 494 |
| Bobby Bonds | 461 |

### RUNS BATTED IN

| | |
|---|---|
| Hank Aaron | 2,297 |
| Babe Ruth | 2,204 |
| Lou Gehrig | 1,990 |
| Ty Cobb | 1,954 |
| Stan Musial | 1,951 |
| Jimmie Foxx | 1,921 |
| Willie Mays | 1,903 |
| Mel Ott | 1,860 |
| Ted Williams | 1,839 |
| Al Simmons | 1,827 |
| Frank Robinson | 1,812 |
| Carl Yastrzemski | 1,788 |

### SAVES (since 1969)

| | |
|---|---|
| Rollie Fingers | 301 |
| Sparky Lyle | 222 |
| Bruce Sutter | 194 |
| Rich Gossage | 184 |
| Tug McGraw | 179 |
| Mike Marshall | 178 |
| Gene Garber | 149 |
| Dave Giusti | 140 |
| Kent Tekulve | 127 |
| Dave La Roche | 126 |
| John Hiller | 119 |
| Clay Carroll | 113 |

## PITCHING

### SEASONS

| | |
|---|---|
| Jim Kaat | 24 |
| Early Wynn, Jack Quinn | 23 |
| Cy Young | 22 |
| Sad Sam Jones | 22 |
| Red Ruffing | 22 |
| Herb Pennock | 22 |
| Hoyt Wilhelm | 21 |
| Walter Johnson | 21 |
| Warren Spahn | 21 |
| Eppa Rixey | 21 |
| Waite Hoyt, Ted Lyons | 21 |
| Gaylord Perry | 21 |

### WINS

| | |
|---|---|
| Cy Young | 511 |
| Walter Johnson | 416 |
| Christy Mathewson | 373 |
| Grover Alexander | 373 |
| Warren Spahn | 363 |
| Pud Galvin | 361 |
| Kid Nichols | 360 |
| Tim Keefe | 343 |
| John Clarkson | 327 |
| Eddie Plank | 327 |
| Mickey Welch | 311 |

### COMPLETE GAMES

| | |
|---|---|
| Cy Young | 751 |
| Pud Galvin | 639 |
| Tim Keefe | 554 |
| Walter Johnson | 531 |
| Kid Nichols | 531 |
| Mickey Welch | 525 |
| John Clarkson | 488 |
| Old Hoss Radbourn | 479 |
| Tony Mullane | 464 |
| Jim McCormick | 462 |
| Gus Weyhing | 448 |

### INNINGS PITCHED

| | |
|---|---|
| Cy Young | 7,377 |
| Pud Galvin | 5,959 |
| Walter Johnson | 5,924 |
| Warren Spahn | 5,246 |
| Grover Alexander | 5,189 |
| Gaylord Perry | 5,165 |
| Kid Nichols | 5,067 |
| Tim Keefe | 5,043 |
| Christy Mathewson | 4,781 |
| Mickey Welch | 4,784 |
| Robin Roberts | 4,689 |

### SHUTOUTS

| | |
|---|---|
| Walter Johnson | 113 |
| Grover Alexander | 90 |
| Christy Mathewson | 83 |
| Cy Young | 77 |
| Eddie Plank | 64 |
| Warren Spahn | 63 |
| Ed Walsh | 58 |
| Three Finger Brown | 58 |
| Pud Galvin | 57 |

### STRIKEOUTS

| | |
|---|---|
| Walter Johnson | 3,508 |
| Nolan Ryan | 3,494 |
| Gaylord Perry | 3,452 |
| Steve Carlton | 3,434 |
| Tom Seaver | 3,137 |
| Bob Gibson | 3,117 |
| Ferguson Jenkins | 3,096 |
| Don Sutton | 2,931 |
| Jim Bunning | 2,855 |

### BASES ON BALLS

| | |
|---|---|
| Nolan Ryan | 1,921 |
| Early Wynn | 1,775 |
| Bob Feller | 1,764 |
| Bobo Newsom | 1,732 |
| Amos Rusie | 1,637 |
| Gus Weyhing | 1,569 |
| Red Ruffing | 1,541 |
| Bump Hadley | 1,442 |
| Warren Spahn | 1,434 |

### EARNED RUN AVERAGE

| | |
|---|---|
| Ed Walsh | 1.82 |
| Addie Joss | 1.88 |
| Three Finger Brown | 2.06 |
| Monte Ward | 2.10 |
| Christy Mathewson | 2.13 |
| Rube Waddell | 2.16 |
| Walter Johnson | 2.17 |
| Orval Overall | 2.24 |
| Tommy Bond | 2.25 |

[1]At start of 1983 season.

## HALL OF FAME

### ELECTED FOR MERITORIOUS SERVICE

**Barrow, Edward,** manager and executive
**Bulkeley, Morgan G.,** first National League president
**Cartwright, Alexander J.,** formulated first baseball rules
**Chadwick, Henry,** first reporter and keeper of records
**Chandler, Albert (Happy),** commissioner
**Comiskey, Charles A.,** player, manager, and executive
**Conlan, Jocko,** National League umpire
**Connolly, Thomas,** American League umpire
**Cummings, William A.,** early pitcher, said to have invented the curve ball
**Evans, William,** American League Umpire
**Frick, Ford C.,** National League president and commissioner
**Giles, Warren G.,** general manager and National League pres.
**Griffith, Clark C.,** player, manager, and executive
**Harridge, William,** American League president
**Harris, Stanley (Bucky),** player, manager, executive
**Hubbard, Robert C. (Cal),** American League umpire
**Huggins, Miller J.,** manager
**Johnson, Byron Bancroft,** first American League president
**Klem, William,** National League umpire
**Landis, Kenesaw M.,** first commissioner of baseball
**Lopez, Alfonso R.,** manager
**Mack, Connie,** manager and executive
**Mac Phail, Larry,** executive
**McCarthy, Joseph,** manager
**McGraw, John J.,** player and manager
**McKechnie, William B.,** manager
**Rickey, W. Branch,** manager and executive
**Robinson, Wilbert,** player and manager
**Spalding, Albert G.,** early pitcher and organizer of the National League
**Stengel, Charles D.,** player and manager
**Weiss, George,** general manager
**Wright, George,** early player
**Wright, Harry,** early player and manager
**Yawkey, Tom,** executive

### PITCHERS

| PITCHERS | Years | Won | Lost |
|---|---|---|---|
| Alexander, Grover Cleveland | 1911–1930 | 373 | 208 |
| Bender, Charles (Chief) | 1903–1925 | 212 | 128 |
| Brown, Mordecai (Three-Finger) | 1903–1916 | 239 | 130 |
| Chesbro, John | 1899–1909 | 199 | 128 |
| Clarkson, John | 1882–1894 | 328 | 175 |
| Coveleski, Stanley | 1912–1928 | 215 | 141 |
| Dean, Jerome (Dizzy) | 1930–1947 | 150 | 83 |
| Faber, Urban (Red) | 1914–1933 | 254 | 212 |
| Feller, Robert | 1936–1956 | 266 | 162 |
| Ford, Edward (Whitey) | 1950–1967 | 236 | 106 |
| Galvin, James (Pud) | 1879–1892 | 361 | 309 |
| Gibson, Robert | 1959–1975 | 251 | 174 |
| Gomez, Vernon (Lefty) | 1930–1943 | 189 | 102 |
| Grimes, Burleigh | 1916–1934 | 270 | 212 |
| Grove, Robert (Lefty) | 1925–1941 | 300 | 141 |
| Haines, Jesse | 1918–1937 | 210 | 158 |
| Hoyt, Waite | 1918–1938 | 237 | 182 |
| Hubbell, Carl | 1928–1943 | 253 | 154 |
| Johnson, Walter (Big Train) | 1907–1927 | 416 | 279 |
| Joss, Adrian (Addie) | 1902–1910 | 160 | 97 |
| Keefe, Timothy | 1880–1893 | 346 | 225 |
| Koufax, Sanford | 1955–1966 | 165 | 87 |
| Lemon, Robert | 1941–1958 | 207 | 128 |
| Lyons, Theodore | 1923–1946 | 260 | 230 |
| Marquard, Richard (Rube) | 1908–1925 | 201 | 177 |
| Mathewson, Christopher | 1900–1916 | 373 | 188 |
| McGinnity, Joseph (Iron Man) | 1899–1908 | 247 | 142 |
| Nichols, Charles (Kid) | 1890–1906 | 360 | 202 |
| Pennock, Herbert | 1912–1934 | 240 | 162 |
| Plank, Edward | 1901–1917 | 325 | 190 |
| Radbourne, Charles (Old Hoss) | 1880–1891 | 308 | 191 |
| Rixey, Eppa | 1912–1933 | 266 | 251 |
| Roberts, Robin | 1948–1966 | 286 | 245 |
| Ruffing, Charles (Red) | 1924–1947 | 273 | 225 |
| Rusie, Amos | 1889–1901 | 246 | 174 |
| Spahn, Warren | 1942–1965 | 363 | 245 |
| Vance, Arthur (Dazzy) | 1915–1935 | 197 | 140 |
| Waddell, George (Rube) | 1897–1910 | 193 | 140 |
| Walsh, Edward (Big Ed) | 1904–1917 | 195 | 126 |
| Welch, Mickey | 1880–1892 | 308 | 209 |
| Wynn, Early | 1939–1963 | 300 | 244 |
| Young, Denton (Cy) | 1890–1911 | 511 | 315 |

### ELECTED FROM NEGRO LEAGUES

Bell, James (Cool Papa)
Charleston, Oscar
Dihigo, Martin
Foster, Andrew (Rube)
Gibson, Joshua
Irvin, Monte
Johnson, William (Judy)
Leonard, Walter (Buck)
Lloyd, John Henry (Pop)
Paige, Leroy (Satchel)

### BATTERS

| BATTERS | Years | Average |
|---|---|---|
| Aaron, Henry (Hank) | 1954–1976 | .305 |
| Anson, Adrian (Cap) | 1876–1897 | .339 |
| Appling, Lucius B. (Luke) | 1930–1950 | .310 |
| Averill, H. Earl | 1929–1941 | .318 |
| Baker, J. Frank (Home Run) | 1908–1922 | .307 |
| Bancroft, Dave | 1915–1930 | .279 |
| Banks, Ernest | 1953–1971 | .274 |
| Beckley, Jake | 1888–1907 | .309 |
| Berra, Lawrence (Yogi) | 1946–1965 | .285 |
| Bottomley, James | 1922–1937 | .310 |
| Boudreau, Louis | 1938–1952 | .295 |
| Bresnahan, Roger | 1897–1915 | .279 |
| Brouthers, Dennis (Dan) | 1879–1904 | .349 |
| Burkett, Jesse | 1890–1905 | .342 |
| Campanella, Roy | 1948–1957 | .276 |
| Carey, Max | 1910–1929 | .285 |
| Chance, Frank | 1898–1914 | .297 |
| Clarke, Fred | 1894–1915 | .315 |
| Clemente, Roberto | 1955–1972 | .317 |
| Cobb, Tyrus | 1905–1928 | .367 |
| Cochrane, Gordon (Mickey) | 1925–1937 | .320 |
| Collins, Edward | 1906–1930 | .333 |
| Collins, James | 1895–1908 | .294 |
| Combs, Earle | 1924–1935 | .325 |
| Connor, Roger | 1880–1897 | .325 |
| Crawford, Samuel (Wahoo) | 1899–1917 | .309 |
| Cronin, Joseph | 1926–1945 | .302 |
| Cuyler, Hazen (Kiki) | 1921–1938 | .321 |
| Delahanty, Edward | 1888–1903 | .346 |
| Dickey, William | 1928–1946 | .313 |
| DiMaggio, Joseph | 1936–1951 | .325 |
| Duffy, Hugh | 1888–1906 | .330 |
| Evers, John | 1902–1929 | .270 |
| Ewing, William (Buck) | 1880–1897 | .311 |
| Flick, Elmer | 1898–1910 | .315 |
| Foxx, James | 1925–1945 | .325 |
| Frisch, Frank | 1919–1937 | .316 |
| Gehrig, Henry (Lou) | 1923–1939 | .340 |
| Gehringer, Charles | 1924–1942 | .320 |
| Goslin, Leon (Goose) | 1921–1938 | .316 |
| Greenberg, Henry | 1930–1947 | .313 |
| Hafey, Charles (Chick) | 1924–1937 | .317 |
| Hamilton, William | 1888–1901 | .344 |
| Hartnett, Charles (Gabby) | 1922–1941 | .297 |
| Heilmann, Harry | 1914–1932 | .342 |
| Herman, William | 1931–1947 | .304 |
| Hooper, Harry | 1909–1925 | .281 |
| Hornsby, Rogers (Rajah) | 1915–1937 | .358 |
| Jackson, Travis | 1922–1936 | .291 |
| Jennings, Hugh | 1891–1918 | .314 |
| Kaline, Al | 1953–1974 | .297 |
| Keeler, William (Wee Willie) | 1892–1910 | .345 |
| Kelley, Joe | 1891–1908 | .321 |
| Kelly, George | 1915–1932 | .297 |
| Kelly, Michael (King) | 1878–1893 | .313 |
| Kiner, Ralph | 1946–1955 | .279 |
| Klein, Charles (Chuck) | 1928–1944 | .320 |
| Lajoie, Napoleon | 1896–1916 | .339 |
| Lindstrom, Fred | 1924–1939 | .311 |
| McCarthy, Thomas | 1884–1896 | .294 |
| Manush, Henry (Heinie) | 1923–1939 | .330 |
| Mantle, Mickey | 1951–1968 | .298 |
| Maranville, Walter (Rabbit) | 1912–1935 | .258 |
| Mathews, Eddie | 1952–1968 | .271 |
| Mays, Willie | 1951–1973 | .302 |
| Medwick, Joseph (Ducky) | 1932–1948 | .324 |
| Mize, Johnny | 1936–1953 | .312 |
| Musial, Stan | 1941–1963 | .331 |
| O'Rourke, James | 1876–1904 | .314 |
| Ott, Melvin | 1926–1947 | .304 |
| Rice, Edgar (Sam) | 1915–1934 | .322 |
| Robinson, Frank | 1956–1976 | .294 |
| Robinson, Jack | 1947–1956 | .311 |
| Roush, Edd | 1913–1931 | .323 |
| Ruth, George (Babe) | 1914–1935 | .342 |
| Schalk, Raymond | 1912–1929 | .253 |
| Sewell, Joseph | 1920–1933 | .312 |
| Simmons, Al | 1924–1944 | .334 |
| Sisler, George | 1915–1930 | .340 |
| Snider, Edwin (Duke) | 1947–1964 | .295 |
| Speaker, Tris | 1907–1928 | .344 |
| Terry, William | 1923–1936 | .341 |
| Thompson, Samuel L. | 1885–1906 | .336 |
| Tinker, Joseph | 1902–1916 | .264 |
| Traynor, Harold (Pie) | 1920–1937 | .320 |
| Wagner, John (Honus) | 1897–1917 | .329 |
| Wallace, Roderick (Bobby) | 1894–1918 | .267 |
| Waner, Lloyd (Little Poison) | 1927–1945 | .316 |
| Waner, Paul (Big Poison) | 1926–1945 | .333 |
| Ward, John Montgomery | 1878–1894 | .283 |
| Wheat, Zachary | 1909–1927 | .317 |
| Williams, Theodore | 1939–1960 | .344 |
| Wilson, Hack | 1923–1934 | .307 |
| Youngs, Ross (Pep) | 1917–1926 | .322 |

## 1982 MAJOR LEAGUE STANDINGS

### NATIONAL LEAGUE

| Eastern Division | W | L | Pct. | GB |
|---|---|---|---|---|
| St. Louis | 92 | 70 | .568 | — |
| Philadelphia | 89 | 73 | .549 | 3 |
| Montreal | 86 | 76 | .531 | 6 |
| Pittsburgh | 84 | 78 | .519 | 8 |
| Chicago | 73 | 89 | .451 | 19 |
| New York | 65 | 97 | .401 | 27 |

| Western Division | W | L | Pct. | GB |
|---|---|---|---|---|
| Atlanta | 89 | 73 | .549 | — |
| Los Angeles | 88 | 74 | .543 | 1 |
| San Francisco | 87 | 75 | .537 | 2 |
| San Diego | 81 | 81 | .500 | 8 |
| Houston | 77 | 85 | .475 | 12 |
| Cincinnati | 61 | 101 | .377 | 28 |

### AMERICAN LEAGUE

| Eastern Division | W | L | Pct. | GB |
|---|---|---|---|---|
| Milwaukee | 95 | 67 | .586 | — |
| Baltimore | 94 | 68 | .580 | 1 |
| Boston | 89 | 73 | .549 | 6 |
| Detroit | 83 | 79 | .512 | 12 |
| New York | 79 | 83 | .488 | 16 |
| Cleveland | 78 | 84 | .481 | 17 |
| Toronto | 78 | 84 | .481 | 17 |

| Western Division | W | L | Pct. | GB |
|---|---|---|---|---|
| California | 93 | 69 | .574 | — |
| Kansas City | 90 | 72 | .556 | 3 |
| Chicago | 87 | 75 | .537 | 6 |
| Seattle | 76 | 86 | .469 | 17 |
| Oakland | 68 | 94 | .420 | 25 |
| Texas | 64 | 98 | .395 | 29 |
| Minnesota | 60 | 102 | .370 | 33 |

## 1982 ALL-STAR GAME Montreal, July 13

| AMERICAN LEAGUE | ab | r | h | bi | NATIONAL LEAGUE | ab | r | h | bi |
|---|---|---|---|---|---|---|---|---|---|
| Henderson, lf | 4 | 1 | 3 | 0 | Raines, lf | 1 | 0 | 0 | 0 |
| Lynn, cf | 2 | 0 | 0 | 0 | Carlton, p | 0 | 0 | 0 | 0 |
| Wilson, cf | 2 | 0 | 0 | 0 | Horner, ph | 1 | 0 | 0 | 0 |
| Hrbek, ph | 1 | 0 | 0 | 0 | Soto, p | 0 | 0 | 0 | 0 |
| Brett, 3b | 2 | 0 | 2 | 0 | Thompson, ph | 1 | 0 | 0 | 0 |
| Bell, 3b | 3 | 0 | 0 | 0 | Valenzuela, p | 0 | 0 | 0 | 0 |
| Jackson, rf | 1 | 0 | 0 | 1 | Minton, p | 0 | 0 | 0 | 0 |
| Winfield, rf | 2 | 0 | 1 | 0 | Howe, p | 0 | 0 | 0 | 0 |
| Cooper, 1b | 2 | 0 | 1 | 0 | Hume, p | 0 | 0 | 0 | 0 |
| Murray, 1b | 1 | 0 | 0 | 0 | Rose, 1b | 1 | 0 | 0 | 1 |
| Yount, ss | 3 | 0 | 0 | 0 | Oliver, 1b | 2 | 1 | 2 | 0 |
| Grich, 2b | 1 | 0 | 0 | 0 | Dawson, cf | 4 | 0 | 1 | 0 |
| Yastr'mski, ph | 1 | 0 | 0 | 0 | Schmidt, 3b | 1 | 0 | 0 | 0 |
| Quisenberry, p | 0 | 0 | 0 | 0 | Knight, 3b | 3 | 0 | 0 | 0 |
| McRae, ph | 0 | 0 | 0 | 0 | Carter, c | 3 | 0 | 1 | 1 |
| Fingers, p | 0 | 0 | 0 | 0 | Pena, c | 1 | 0 | 0 | 0 |
| Fisk, c | 2 | 0 | 0 | 0 | Stearns, c | 0 | 0 | 0 | 0 |
| Parrish, c | 2 | 0 | 1 | 0 | Murphy, rf | 2 | 1 | 0 | 0 |
| Eckersley, p | 1 | 0 | 0 | 0 | Concepcion, ss | 3 | 1 | 1 | 2 |
| Thornton, ph | 1 | 0 | 0 | 0 | O. Smith, ss | 0 | 0 | 0 | 0 |
| Clancy, p | 0 | 0 | 0 | 0 | Trillo, 2b | 2 | 0 | 1 | 0 |
| Bannister, p | 0 | 0 | 0 | 0 | Sax, 2b | 1 | 0 | 1 | 0 |
| White, 2b | 1 | 0 | 0 | 0 | Rogers, p | 0 | 0 | 0 | 0 |
| Oglivie, ph | 1 | 0 | 0 | 0 | Jones, ph | 1 | 1 | 1 | 0 |
| | | | | | Baker, lf | 2 | 0 | 0 | 0 |
| | | | | | L. Smith, lf | 0 | 0 | 0 | 0 |
| Total | 33 | 1 | 8 | 1 | Total | 29 | 4 | 8 | 4 |

| | | | | | | | | | | |
|---|---|---|---|---|---|---|---|---|---|---|
| American League | 1 | 0 | 0 | 0 | 0 | 0 | 0 | 0 | 0 | —1 |
| National League | 0 | 2 | 1 | 0 | 0 | 1 | 0 | 0 | x | —4 |

E—Sax, Henderson, Bell. DP—National 1. LOB American 11, National 4. 2B—Oliver, Parrish. 3B—Jones. HR—Concepion. SB—Raines, Pena, Henderson. SF—Jackson, Rose.

| | IP | H | R | ER | BB | SO |
|---|---|---|---|---|---|---|
| American—Eckersley (L) | 3 | 2 | 3 | 3 | 2 | 1 |
| Clancy | 1 | 0 | 0 | 0 | 0 | 0 |
| Bannister | 1 | 1 | 0 | 0 | 0 | 0 |
| Quisenberry | 2 | 3 | 1 | 1 | 0 | 1 |
| Fingers | 1 | 2 | 0 | 0 | 0 | 0 |
| National—Rogers (W) | 3 | 4 | 1 | 1 | 0 | 2 |
| Carlton | 2 | 1 | 0 | 0 | 2 | 4 |
| Soto | 2 | 3 | 0 | 0 | 0 | 4 |
| Valenzuela | ⅔ | 0 | 0 | 0 | 2 | 0 |
| Minton | ⅔ | 0 | 0 | 0 | 1 | 0 |
| Howe | ⅓ | 0 | 0 | 0 | 0 | 0 |
| Hume (S) | ⅓ | 0 | 0 | 0 | 0 | 0 |

WP—Rogers. Time—2:53. Attendance—59,057.

## 1982 PLAYOFF RESULTS

### NATIONAL LEAGUE

League Championship—St. Louis defeated Atlanta, 7-0, 4-3, 6-2

### AMERICAN LEAGUE

League Championship—Milwaukee defeated California, 3-8, 2-4, 5-3, 9-5, 4-3

## 1982 WORLD SERIES BOX SCORES

### FIRST GAME: Busch Memorial Stadium, October 12

| MILWAUKEE (AL) | ab | r | h | bi | ST. LOUIS (NL) | ab | r | h | bi |
|---|---|---|---|---|---|---|---|---|---|
| Molitor, 3b | 6 | 1 | 5 | 2 | Herr, 2b | 3 | 0 | 0 | 0 |
| Yount, ss | 6 | 1 | 4 | 2 | L. Smith, lf | 4 | 0 | 0 | 0 |
| Cooper, 1b | 4 | 1 | 0 | 0 | Hernandez, 1b | 4 | 0 | 0 | 0 |
| Simmons, c | 5 | 1 | 2 | 1 | Hendrick, rf | 4 | 0 | 0 | 0 |
| Oglivie, lf | 4 | 1 | 0 | 0 | Tenace, dh | 3 | 0 | 0 | 0 |
| Thomas, cf | 4 | 0 | 1 | 1 | Porter, c | 3 | 0 | 2 | 0 |
| Howell, dh | 2 | 0 | 0 | 0 | Green, cf | 3 | 0 | 0 | 0 |
| Money, dh | 2 | 1 | 1 | 1 | Oberkfell, 3b | 3 | 0 | 1 | 0 |
| Moore, rf | 5 | 2 | 2 | 0 | O. Smith, ss | 3 | 0 | 0 | 0 |
| Gantner, 2b | 4 | 2 | 2 | 2 | | | | | |
| Total | 42 | 10 | 17 | 9 | Total | 30 | 0 | 3 | 0 |

| | | | | | | | | | | |
|---|---|---|---|---|---|---|---|---|---|---|
| Milwaukee | 2 | 0 | 0 | 1 | 1 | 2 | 0 | 0 | 4 | —10 |
| St. Louis | 0 | 0 | 0 | 0 | 0 | 0 | 0 | 0 | 0 | — 0 |

E—Hernandez. DP—St. Louis 1. LOB—Milwaukee 10, St. Louis. 4. 2B—Porter, Moore, Yount. 3B—Gantner. HR—Simmons. S—Gantner.

| | IP | H | R | ER | BB | SO |
|---|---|---|---|---|---|---|
| Milwaukee—Caldwell (W, 1-0) | 9 | 3 | 0 | 0 | 1 | 3 |
| St. Louis—Forsch (L, 0-1) | 5⅔ | 10 | 6 | 4 | 1 | 1 |
| Kaat | 1⅓ | 1 | 0 | 0 | 1 | 1 |
| LaPoint | 1⅔ | 3 | 2 | 2 | 1 | 0 |
| Lahti | ⅓ | 3 | 2 | 2 | 0 | 1 |

HBP—Howell (by Forsch). Time—2:30. Attendance—53,723.

### SECOND GAME: Busch Memorial Stadium, October 13

| MILWAUKEE (AL) | ab | r | h | bi | ST. LOUIS (NL) | ab | r | h | bi |
|---|---|---|---|---|---|---|---|---|---|
| Molitor, 3b | 5 | 1 | 2 | 0 | Herr, 2b | 3 | 1 | 1 | 1 |
| Yount, ss | 4 | 1 | 1 | 1 | Oberkfell, 3b | 3 | 1 | 2 | 1 |
| Cooper, 1b | 5 | 0 | 3 | 1 | Tenace, ph | 1 | 0 | 0 | 0 |
| Simmons, c | 3 | 1 | 1 | 1 | Ramsey, 3b | 0 | 0 | 0 | 0 |
| Oglivie, lf | 4 | 0 | 1 | 0 | Hernandez, 1b | 3 | 0 | 0 | 0 |
| Thomas, cf | 3 | 0 | 0 | 0 | Hendrick, rf | 3 | 2 | 0 | 0 |
| Howell, dh | 4 | 1 | 0 | 0 | Porter, c | 4 | 0 | 2 | 2 |
| Gantner, 2b | 3 | 0 | 0 | 0 | L. Smith, lf | 3 | 0 | 0 | 0 |
| | | | | | Iorg, dh | 2 | 0 | 1 | 0 |
| | | | | | Green, ph | 1 | 0 | 0 | 0 |
| | | | | | Braun, ph | 0 | 0 | 0 | 1 |
| | | | | | McGee, cf | 4 | 1 | 0 | 0 |
| | | | | | O. Smith, ss | 4 | 0 | 2 | 0 |
| Total | 35 | 4 | 10 | 4 | Total | 31 | 5 | 8 | 5 |

| | | | | | | | | | | |
|---|---|---|---|---|---|---|---|---|---|---|
| Milwaukee | 0 | 1 | 2 | 0 | 1 | 0 | 0 | 0 | 0 | —4 |
| St. Louis | 0 | 0 | 2 | 0 | 0 | 2 | 0 | 1 | x | —5 |

E—Oglivie. DP—St. Louis 1. LOB—Milwaukee 8, St. Louis 7. 2B—Moore, Herr, Yount, Porter, Cooper. HR—Simmons (2). SB—Molitor, McGee, Oberkfell, O. Smith

| | IP | H | R | ER | BB | SO |
|---|---|---|---|---|---|---|
| Milwaukee—Sutton | 6 | 5 | 4 | 4 | 1 | 3 |
| McClure (L, 0-1) | 1⅓ | 2 | 1 | 1 | 2 | 2 |
| Ladd | ⅔ | 1 | 0 | 0 | 2 | 0 |
| St. Louis—Stuper | 4* | 6 | 4 | 4 | 3 | 3 |
| Kaat | ⅔ | 1 | 0 | 0 | 0 | 0 |
| Bair | 2 | 1 | 0 | 0 | 0 | 3 |
| Sutter (W, 1-0) | 2⅓ | 2 | 0 | 0 | 1 | 1 |

*Pitched to one batter in the fifth.
WP—Stuper. Time—2:54. Attendance—53,723.

### THIRD GAME: County Stadium, October 15

| ST. LOUIS (NL) | ab | r | h | bi |
|---|---|---|---|---|
| Herr, 2b | 5 | 0 | 0 | 0 |
| Oberkfell, 3b | 4 | 0 | 0 | 0 |
| Hernandez, 1b | 4 | 0 | 0 | 0 |
| Hendrick, rf | 2 | 1 | 1 | 0 |
| Porter, c | 4 | 0 | 0 | 0 |
| L. Smith, lf | 4 | 2 | 2 | 0 |
| Green, lf | 0 | 0 | 0 | 0 |
| Iorg, dh | 4 | 1 | 1 | 0 |
| McGee, cf | 3 | 2 | 2 | 4 |
| O. Smith, ss | 3 | 0 | 0 | 1 |
| Total | 33 | 6 | 6 | 5 |

| MILWAUKEE (AL) | ab | r | h | bi |
|---|---|---|---|---|
| Molitor, 3b | 4 | 0 | 0 | 0 |
| Yount, ss | 3 | 1 | 0 | 0 |
| Cooper, 1b | 4 | 1 | 1 | 2 |
| Simmons, c | 4 | 0 | 1 | 0 |
| Oglivie, lf | 4 | 0 | 0 | 0 |
| Thomas, cf | 4 | 0 | 1 | 0 |
| Howell, dh | 2 | 0 | 0 | 0 |
| Money, dh | 1 | 0 | 0 | 0 |
| Moore, rf | 3 | 0 | 0 | 0 |
| Gantner, 2b | 3 | 0 | 2 | 0 |
| Total | 32 | 2 | 5 | 2 |

| | | | | | | | | | | |
|---|---|---|---|---|---|---|---|---|---|---|
| St. Louis | 0 | 0 | 0 | 0 | 3 | 0 | 2 | 0 | 1 | —6 |
| Milwaukee | 0 | 0 | 0 | 0 | 0 | 0 | 0 | 2 | 0 | —2 |

E—Cooper, Gantner, Simmons, Hernandez. DP—St. Louis 1. LOB—St. Louis 4, Milwaukee 6. 2B—Gantner, L. Smith, Iorg. 3B—L. Smith. HR—McGee 2, Cooper.

| | IP | H | R | ER | BB | SO |
|---|---|---|---|---|---|---|
| St. Louis—Andujar (W, 1-0) | 6⅓ | 3 | 0 | 0 | 1 | 3 |
| Kaat | ⅓ | 1 | 0 | 0 | 0 | 1 |
| Bair | 0* | 0 | 0 | 0 | 1 | 0 |
| Sutter (S, 1) | 2⅓ | 1 | 2 | 2 | 1 | 1 |
| Milwaukee—Vuckovich (L, 0-1) | 8⅔ | 6 | 6 | 4 | 3 | 1 |
| McClure | ⅓ | 0 | 0 | 0 | 0 | 0 |

*Pitched to one batter in the seventh.

Time—2:53. Attendance—56,556.

### FOURTH GAME: County Stadium, October 16

| ST. LOUIS (NL) | ab | r | h | bi |
|---|---|---|---|---|
| Herr, 2b | 4 | 0 | 0 | 2 |
| Oberkfell, 3b | 2 | 2 | 1 | 0 |
| Tenace, ph | 1 | 0 | 0 | 0 |
| Hernandez, 1b | 4 | 0 | 0 | 0 |
| Hendrick, rf | 4 | 0 | 1 | 1 |
| Porter, c | 3 | 0 | 1 | 0 |
| L. Smith, lf | 4 | 1 | 1 | 0 |
| Iorg, dh | 4 | 0 | 2 | 1 |
| Green, pr | 0 | 0 | 0 | 0 |
| McGee, cf | 4 | 1 | 1 | 0 |
| O. Smith, ss | 3 | 1 | 1 | 0 |
| Total | 33 | 5 | 8 | 4 |

| MILWAUKEE (AL) | ab | r | h | bi |
|---|---|---|---|---|
| Molitor, 3b | 4 | 1 | 0 | 0 |
| Yount, ss | 4 | 1 | 2 | 2 |
| Cooper, 1b | 4 | 1 | 2 | 1 |
| Simmons, c | 2 | 0 | 0 | 0 |
| Thomas, cf | 4 | 0 | 1 | 2 |
| Oglivie, lf | 3 | 1 | 1 | 0 |
| Money, dh | 4 | 2 | 2 | 0 |
| Moore, rf | 4 | 0 | 1 | 0 |
| Gantner, 2b | 4 | 1 | 1 | 1 |
| Total | 33 | 7 | 10 | 6 |

| | | | | | | | | | | |
|---|---|---|---|---|---|---|---|---|---|---|
| St. Louis | 1 | 3 | 0 | 0 | 0 | 1 | 0 | 0 | 0 | —5 |
| Milwaukee | 0 | 0 | 0 | 0 | 1 | 0 | 6 | 0 | x | —7 |

E—Gantner, Yount, LaPoint. DP—St. Louis 2, Milwaukee 2. LOB—St. Louis 6, Milwaukee 6. 2B—Oberkfell, Money, L. Smith, Iorg, Gantner. 3B—Oglivie. SB—McGee, Oberkfell. SF—Herr.

| | IP | H | R | ER | BB | SO |
|---|---|---|---|---|---|---|
| St. Louis—LaPoint | 6⅔ | 7 | 4 | 1 | 1 | 3 |
| Bair (L, 0-1) | 0* | 1 | 2 | 2 | 1 | 0 |
| Kaat | 0* | 1 | 1 | 1 | 1 | 0 |
| Lahti | 1⅓ | 1 | 0 | 0 | 1 | 0 |
| Milwaukee—Haas | 5⅓ | 7 | 5 | 4 | 2 | 3 |
| Slaton (W, 1-0) | 2 | 1 | 0 | 0 | 2 | 1 |
| McClure (S, 1) | 1⅔ | 0 | 0 | 0 | 0 | 2 |

*Pitched to two batters in the seventh.

WP—Haas, Kaat. Time—3:04. Attendance—56,560.

### FIFTH GAME: County Stadium, October 17

| ST. LOUIS (NL) | ab | r | h | bi |
|---|---|---|---|---|
| L. Smith, dh | 5 | 0 | 2 | 0 |
| Green, lf | 5 | 2 | 2 | 0 |
| Hernandez, 1b | 4 | 1 | 3 | 2 |
| Hendrick, rf | 5 | 0 | 3 | 2 |
| Porter, c | 5 | 0 | 1 | 0 |
| Ramsey, pr | 0 | 0 | 0 | 0 |
| McGee, cf | 5 | 0 | 1 | 0 |
| Oberkfell, 3b | 4 | 0 | 3 | 0 |
| Tenace, ph | 1 | 0 | 0 | 0 |
| Herr, 2b | 4 | 0 | 0 | 0 |
| O. Smith, ss | 3 | 1 | 0 | 0 |
| Total | 41 | 4 | 15 | 4 |

| MILWAUKEE (AL) | ab | r | h | bi |
|---|---|---|---|---|
| Molitor, 3b | 4 | 1 | 1 | 1 |
| Yount, ss | 4 | 2 | 4 | 1 |
| Cooper, 1b | 4 | 0 | 1 | 1 |
| Simmons, c | 3 | 0 | 0 | 1 |
| Oglivie, lf | 4 | 1 | 2 | 0 |
| Thomas, cf | 4 | 0 | 0 | 0 |
| Money, dh | 3 | 1 | 0 | 0 |
| Moore, rf | 4 | 1 | 2 | 1 |
| Gantner, 2b | 4 | 0 | 1 | 1 |
| Total | 34 | 6 | 11 | 6 |

| | | | | | | | | | | |
|---|---|---|---|---|---|---|---|---|---|---|
| St. Louis | 0 | 0 | 1 | 0 | 0 | 0 | 1 | 0 | 2 | —4 |
| Milwaukee | 1 | 0 | 1 | 0 | 1 | 0 | 1 | 2 | x | —6 |

E—Forsch, Gantner, Herr. DP—St. Louis 2, Milwaukee 1. LOB—St. Louis 12, Milwaukee 7. 2B—Hernandez 2, Yount, Moore, Green. 3B—Green. HR—Yount. SB—L. Smith.

| | IP | H | R | ER | BB | SO |
|---|---|---|---|---|---|---|
| St. Louis—Forsch (L, 0-2) | 7 | 8 | 4 | 3 | 2 | 3 |
| Sutter | 1 | 3 | 2 | 2 | 1 | 2 |
| Milwaukee—Caldwell (W, 2-0) | 8⅓ | 14 | 4 | 4 | 2 | 3 |
| McClure (S, 2) | ⅔ | 1 | 0 | 0 | 0 | 1 |

Time—3:02. Attendance—56,562.

### SIXTH GAME: Busch Memorial Stadium, October 19

| MILWAUKEE (AL) | ab | r | h | bi |
|---|---|---|---|---|
| Molitor, 3b | 4 | 0 | 1 | 0 |
| Yount, ss | 4 | 0 | 0 | 0 |
| Cooper, 1b | 4 | 0 | 0 | 0 |
| Simmons, c | 2 | 0 | 0 | 0 |
| Yost, c | 0 | 0 | 0 | 0 |
| Oglivie, lf | 4 | 0 | 1 | 0 |
| Thomas, cf | 3 | 0 | 0 | 0 |
| Edwards, cf | 0 | 0 | 0 | 0 |
| Money, dh | 3 | 0 | 0 | 0 |
| Moore, rf | 3 | 0 | 1 | 0 |
| Gantner, 2b | 3 | 1 | 1 | 0 |
| Total | 30 | 1 | 4 | 0 |

| ST. LOUIS (NL) | ab | r | h | bi |
|---|---|---|---|---|
| L. Smith, lf | 3 | 1 | 1 | 0 |
| Green, lf | 1 | 1 | 0 | 0 |
| Oberkfell, 3b | 5 | 1 | 0 | 0 |
| Hernandez, 1b | 5 | 2 | 2 | 4 |
| Hendrick, rf | 5 | 2 | 2 | 1 |
| Porter, c | 4 | 1 | 1 | 2 |
| Brummer, c | 0 | 0 | 0 | 0 |
| Iorg, dh | 4 | 3 | 3 | 0 |
| McGee, cf | 4 | 1 | 1 | 1 |
| Herr, 2b | 3 | 1 | 2 | 2 |
| O. Smith, ss | 4 | 0 | 0 | 0 |
| Total | 38 | 13 | 12 | 10 |

| | | | | | | | | | | |
|---|---|---|---|---|---|---|---|---|---|---|
| Milwaukee | 0 | 0 | 0 | 0 | 0 | 0 | 0 | 0 | 1 | — 1 |
| St. Louis | 0 | 2 | 0 | 3 | 2 | 6 | 0 | 0 | x | —13 |

E—Yount 2, Gantner 2, Oberkfell. DP—St. Louis 2. LOB—Milwaukee 4, St. Louis 3. 2B—Iorg 2, Herr, Gantner. 3B—Iorg. HR—Porter, Hernandez. SB—L. Smith. S—Herr.

| | IP | H | R | ER | BB | SO |
|---|---|---|---|---|---|---|
| Milwaukee—Sutton (L, 0-1) | 4⅓ | 7 | 7 | 5 | 0 | 2 |
| Slaton | ⅔ | 0 | 0 | 0 | 0 | 0 |
| Medich | 2 | 5 | 6 | 4 | 1 | 0 |
| Bernard | 1 | 0 | 0 | 0 | 0 | 1 |
| St. Louis—Stuper (W, 1-0) | 9 | 4 | 1 | 1 | 2 | 2 |

WP—Medich 2, Stuper. Balk—Sutton. Time—2:21. Attendance—53,723.

### SEVENTH GAME: Busch Memorial Stadium, October 20

| MILWAUKEE (AL) | ab | r | h | bi |
|---|---|---|---|---|
| Molitor, 3b | 4 | 1 | 2 | 0 |
| Yount, ss | 4 | 0 | 1 | 0 |
| Cooper, 1b | 3 | 0 | 1 | 1 |
| Simmons, c | 4 | 0 | 0 | 0 |
| Oglivie, lf | 4 | 1 | 1 | 1 |
| Thomas, cf | 4 | 0 | 0 | 0 |
| Howell, dh | 3 | 0 | 0 | 0 |
| Moore, rf | 3 | 0 | 1 | 0 |
| Gantner, 2b | 3 | 1 | 1 | 0 |
| Total | 32 | 3 | 7 | 2 |

| ST. LOUIS (NL) | ab | r | h | bi |
|---|---|---|---|---|
| L. Smith, lf | 5 | 2 | 3 | 1 |
| Oberkfell, 3b | 3 | 0 | 0 | 0 |
| Tenace, ph | 0 | 0 | 0 | 0 |
| Ramsey, 3b | 1 | 1 | 0 | 0 |
| Hernandez, 1b | 3 | 1 | 2 | 2 |
| Hendrick, rf | 5 | 0 | 2 | 1 |
| Porter, c | 5 | 0 | 1 | 1 |
| Iorg, dh | 3 | 0 | 2 | 0 |
| Green, ph | 0 | 0 | 0 | 0 |
| Braun, dh | 2 | 0 | 1 | 1 |
| McGee, cf | 5 | 1 | 1 | 0 |
| Herr, 2b | 3 | 0 | 1 | 0 |
| O. Smith, ss | 4 | 1 | 2 | 0 |
| Total | 39 | 6 | 15 | 6 |

| | | | | | | | | | | |
|---|---|---|---|---|---|---|---|---|---|---|
| Milwaukee | 0 | 0 | 0 | 0 | 1 | 2 | 0 | 0 | 0 | —3 |
| St. Louis | 0 | 0 | 0 | 1 | 0 | 3 | 0 | 2 | x | —6 |

E—Andujar. LOB—Milwaukee 3, St. Louis 13. 2B—Gantner, L. Smith 2. HR—Oglivie. SF—Cooper.

| | IP | H | R | ER | BB | SO |
|---|---|---|---|---|---|---|
| Milwaukee—Vukovich | 5⅓ | 10 | 3 | 3 | 2 | 3 |
| McClure (L, 0-2) | ⅓ | 2 | 1 | 1 | 1 | 1 |
| Haas | 2 | 1 | 2 | 2 | 1 | 1 |
| Caldwell | ⅓ | 2 | 0 | 0 | 0 | 0 |
| St. Louis—Andujar (W, 2-0) | 7 | 7 | 3 | 2 | 0 | 1 |
| Sutter (S, 2) | 2 | 0 | 0 | 0 | 0 | 2 |

Time—2:50. Attendance—53,723.

# 1982 CLUB AND INDIVIDUAL RECORDS

## NATIONAL LEAGUE

| TEAM BATTING | R | H | HR | Avg. |
|---|---|---|---|---|
| Pittsburgh | 724 | 1,535 | 134 | .273 |
| St. Louis | 685 | 1,439 | 67 | .264 |
| Los Angeles | 691 | 1,487 | 138 | .264 |
| Montreal | 697 | 1,454 | 133 | .262 |
| Philadelphia | 664 | 1,417 | 112 | .260 |
| Chicago | 676 | 1,436 | 102 | .260 |
| San Diego | 675 | 1,435 | 81 | .257 |
| Atlanta | 739 | 1,411 | 146 | .256 |
| San Francisco | 673 | 1,393 | 133 | .253 |
| Cincinnati | 545 | 1,375 | 82 | .251 |
| New York | 609 | 1,361 | 97 | .247 |
| Houston | 569 | 1,342 | 74 | .247 |

| INDIVIDUAL BATTING | H | HR | RBI | Avg. |
|---|---|---|---|---|
| Oliver, Montreal | 204 | 22 | 109 | .331 |
| Madlock, Pittsburgh | 181 | 19 | 95 | .319 |
| Durham, Chicago | 168 | 22 | 90 | .312 |
| L. Smith, St. Louis | 182 | 8 | 69 | .307 |
| Buckner, Chicago | 201 | 15 | 105 | .306 |
| Guerrero, Los Angeles | 175 | 32 | 100 | .304 |
| Dawson, Montreal | 183 | 23 | 83 | .301 |
| Baker, Los Angeles | 171 | 23 | 88 | .300 |
| Hernandez, St. Louis | 173 | 7 | 94 | .299 |
| Pena, Pittsburgh | 147 | 11 | 63 | .296 |

**Runs** — L. Smith (St. L.) 120, Murphy (Atl.) 113, Schmidt (Phila.) 108, Dawson (Mont.), 107
**Hits** — Oliver (Mont.) 204, Buckner (Chi.) 201, Dawson (Mont.) 183, Ray (Pitt.)-L. Smith (St. L.) 182
**Doubles** — Oliver (Mont.) 43, Kennedy (S.D.) 42, Dawson (Mont.) 37, Knight (Hou.) 36
**Triples** — Thon (Hou.) 10, Wilson (N.Y.)-Moreno (Pitt.)-Puhl (Hou.) 9
**Home Runs** — Kingman (N.Y.) 37, Murphy (Atl.) 36, Schmidt (Phila.) 35, Horner (Atl.)-Guerrero (L.A.) 32
**Runs Batted In** — Oliver (Mont.)-Murphy (Atl.) 109, Buckner (Chi.) 105, Hendrick (St. L.) 104
**Stolen Bases** — Raines (Mont.) 78, L. Smith (St. L.) 68, Moreno (Pitt.) 60, Wilson (N.Y.) 58

| TEAM PITCHING | H | BB | SO | ERA |
|---|---|---|---|---|
| Los Angeles | 1,356 | 468 | 932 | 3.26 |
| Montreal | 1,371 | 448 | 936 | 3.31 |
| St. Louis | 1,420 | 502 | 689 | 3.37 |
| Houston | 1,338 | 479 | 899 | 3.42 |
| San Diego | 1,348 | 502 | 765 | 3.52 |
| Philadelphia | 1,395 | 472 | 1,002 | 3.61 |
| San Francisco | 1,507 | 466 | 810 | 3.64 |
| Cincinnati | 1,414 | 570 | 998 | 3.66 |
| Pittsburgh | 1,434 | 521 | 934 | 3.81 |
| Atlanta | 1,484 | 502 | 813 | 3.82 |
| New York | 1,508 | 582 | 759 | 3.88 |
| Chicago | 1,510 | 452 | 764 | 3.92 |

| INDIVIDUAL PITCHING | IP | W | L | ERA |
|---|---|---|---|---|
| Rogers, Montreal | 277 | 19 | 8 | 2.40 |
| Niekro, Houston | 270 | 17 | 12 | 2.47 |
| Andujar, St. Louis | 265 | 15 | 10 | 2.47 |
| Soto, Cincinnati | 275 | 14 | 13 | 2.79 |
| Valenzuela, Los Angeles | 285 | 19 | 13 | 2.87 |
| Calendaria, Pittsburgh | 174 | 12 | 7 | 2.94 |
| Sutton, Houston | 195 | 13 | 8 | 3.00 |
| Carlton, Philadelphia | 295 | 23 | 11 | 3.10 |
| Reuss, Los Angeles | 254 | 18 | 11 | 3.11 |
| Krukow, Philadelphia | 208 | 13 | 11 | 3.12 |

**Innings Pitched** — Carlton (Phila.) 295, Valenzuela (L.A.) 285, Rogers (Mont.) 277, Niekro (Hou.) 270
**Complete Games** — Carlton (Phila.) 19, Valenzuela (L.A.) 18, Niekro (Hou.) 16, Rogers (Mont.) 14
**Wins** — Carlton (Phila.) 23, Rogers (Mont.)-Valenzuela (L.A.) 19, Reuss (L.A.) 18
**Shutouts** — Carlton (Phila.) 6, Andujar (St. L.)-Niekro (Hou.) 5, 3 tied with 4
**Strikeouts** — Carlton (Phila.) 286, Soto (Cinc.) 274, Ryan (Hou.) 245, Valenzuela (L.A.) 199
**Saves** — Sutter (St. L.) 36, Garber (Atl.)-Minton (S.F.) 30, Reardon (Mont.), 26

## AMERICAN LEAGUE

| TEAM BATTING | R | H | HR | Avg. |
|---|---|---|---|---|
| Kansas City | 784 | 1,603 | 132 | .285 |
| Milwaukee | 891 | 1,599 | 216 | .279 |
| Boston | 753 | 1,536 | 136 | .274 |
| California | 814 | 1,518 | 186 | .274 |
| Chicago | 786 | 1,523 | 136 | .273 |
| Detroit | 729 | 1,489 | 177 | .266 |
| Baltimore | 774 | 1,478 | 179 | .266 |
| Cleveland | 683 | 1,458 | 109 | .262 |
| Toronto | 651 | 1,447 | 106 | .262 |
| Minnesota | 657 | 1,427 | 148 | .257 |
| New York | 709 | 1,417 | 161 | .256 |
| Seattle | 651 | 1,431 | 130 | .254 |
| Texas | 590 | 1,354 | 115 | .249 |
| Oakland | 691 | 1,287 | 149 | .236 |

| INDIVIDUAL BATTING | H | HR | RBI | Avg. |
|---|---|---|---|---|
| Wilson, Kansas City | 194 | 3 | 46 | .332 |
| Yount, Milwaukee | 210 | 29 | 114 | .331 |
| Carew, California | 167 | 3 | 44 | .319 |
| Murray, Baltimore | 174 | 32 | 110 | .316 |
| Cooper, Milwaukee | 205 | 32 | 121 | .313 |
| Garcia, Toronto | 185 | 5 | 42 | .310 |
| Rice, Boston | 177 | 24 | 97 | .309 |
| McRae, Kansas City | 189 | 27 | 133 | .308 |
| Harrah, Cleveland | 183 | 25 | 78 | .304 |
| Molitor, Milwaukee | 201 | 19 | 71 | .302 |

**Runs** — Molitor (Milw.) 136, Yount (Milw.) 129, Evans (Bost.) 122, Henderson (Oak.) 119
**Hits** — Yount (Milw.) 210, Cooper (Milw.) 205, Molitor (Milw.) 201, Wilson (K.C.) 194
**Doubles** — Yount (Milw.)-McRae (K.C.) 46, White (K.C.) 45, DeCinces (Calif.) 42
**Triples** — Wilson (K.C.) 15, Herndon (Det.) 13, Yount (Milw.) 12, Mumphrey (N.Y.) 10
**Home Runs** — Thomas (Milw.)-Jackson (Calif.) 39, Winfield (N.Y.) 37, Oglivie (Milw.) 34
**Runs Batted In** — McRae (K.C.) 133, Cooper (Milw.) 121, Thornton (Cleve.) 116, Yount (Milw.) 114
**Stolen Bases** — Henderson (Oak.) 130, Garcia (Tor.) 54, J. Cruz (Seat.) 46, Molitor (Milw.) 41

| TEAM PITCHING | H | BB | SO | ERA |
|---|---|---|---|---|
| Detroit | 1,371 | 554 | 740 | 3.80 |
| California | 1,436 | 482 | 728 | 3.82 |
| Chicago | 1,502 | 460 | 753 | 3.87 |
| Seattle | 1,431 | 547 | 1,002 | 3.88 |
| Toronto | 1,428 | 493 | 776 | 3.95 |
| Milwaukee | 1,514 | 511 | 717 | 3.98 |
| Baltimore | 1,437 | 488 | 719 | 3.99 |
| New York | 1,471 | 491 | 939 | 3.99 |
| Boston | 1,557 | 478 | 816 | 4.03 |
| Kansas City | 1,443 | 471 | 650 | 4.08 |
| Cleveland | 1,433 | 589 | 882 | 4.11 |
| Texas | 1,554 | 483 | 690 | 4.28 |
| Oakland | 1,506 | 648 | 697 | 4.54 |
| Minnesota | 1,484 | 643 | 813 | 4.72 |

| INDIVIDUAL PITCHING | IP | W | L | ERA |
|---|---|---|---|---|
| Sutcliffe, Cleveland | 216 | 14 | 8 | 2.96 |
| Stanley, Boston | 168 | 12 | 7 | 3.10 |
| Palmer, Baltimore | 227 | 15 | 5 | 3.13 |
| Petry, Detroit | 246 | 15 | 9 | 3.22 |
| Stieb, Toronto | 288 | 17 | 14 | 3.25 |
| Vuckovich, Milwaukee | 223 | 18 | 6 | 3.34 |
| Beattie, Seattle | 172 | 8 | 12 | 3.34 |
| Bannister, Seattle | 247 | 12 | 13 | 3.43 |
| Witt, California | 179 | 8 | 6 | 3.51 |
| Hoyt, Chicago | 239 | 19 | 15 | 3.53 |

**Innings Pitched** — Stieb (Tor.) 288, Clancy (Tor.)-Morris (Det.) 266, Caldwell (Milw.) 258
**Complete Games** — Stieb (Tor.) 19, Morris (Det.) 17, Langford (Oak.) 15, Hoyt (Chi.) 14
**Wins** — Hoyt (Chi.) 19, Zahn (Calif.)-Gura (K.C.)-Vuckovich (Milw.) 18
**Shutouts** — Stieb (Tor.) 5, Zahn (Calif.)-Forsch (Calif.) 4, 7 tied with 3
**Strikeouts** — Bannister (Seat.) 209, Barker (Cleve.) 187, Righetti (N.Y.) 163, Guidry (N.Y.) 162
**Saves** — Quisenberry (K.C.) 35, Gossage (N.Y.) 30, Fingers (Mont.) 29, Caudill (Seat.) 26

## ALL-TIME WORLD SERIES RESULTS

| Year | Winner | Won | Lost | Loser |
|---|---|---|---|---|
| 1903 | Boston (AL) | 5 | 3 | Pittsburgh (NL) |
| 1905 | New York (NL) | 4 | 1 | Philadelphia (AL) |
| 1906 | Chicago (AL) | 4 | 2 | Chicago (NL) |
| 1907 | Chicago (NL) | 4 | 0 | Detroit (AL) |
| 1908 | Chicago (NL) | 4 | 1 | Detroit (AL) |
| 1909 | Pittsburgh (NL) | 4 | 3 | Detroit (AL) |
| 1910 | Philadelphia (AL) | 4 | 1 | Chicago (NL) |
| 1911 | Philadelphia (AL) | 4 | 2 | New York (NL) |
| 1912 | Boston (AL) | 4 | 3 | New York (NL) |
| 1913 | Philadelphia (AL) | 4 | 1 | New York (NL) |
| 1914 | Boston (NL) | 4 | 0 | Philadelphia (AL) |
| 1915 | Boston (AL) | 4 | 1 | Philadelphia (NL) |
| 1916 | Boston (AL) | 4 | 1 | Brooklyn (NL) |
| 1917 | Chicago (AL) | 4 | 2 | New York (NL) |
| 1918 | Boston (AL) | 4 | 2 | Chicago (NL) |
| 1919 | Cincinnati (NL) | 5 | 3 | Chicago (AL) |
| 1920 | Cleveland (AL) | 5 | 2 | Brooklyn (NL) |
| 1921 | New York (NL) | 5 | 3 | New York (AL) |
| 1922 | New York (NL) | 4 | 0 | New York (AL) |
| 1923 | New York (AL) | 4 | 2 | New York (NL) |
| 1924 | Washington (AL) | 4 | 3 | New York (NL) |
| 1925 | Pittsburgh (NL) | 4 | 3 | Washington (AL) |
| 1926 | St. Louis (NL) | 4 | 3 | New York (AL) |
| 1927 | New York (AL) | 4 | 0 | Pittsburgh (NL) |
| 1928 | New York (AL) | 4 | 0 | St. Louis (NL) |
| 1929 | Philadelphia (AL) | 4 | 1 | Chicago (NL) |
| 1930 | Philadelphia (AL) | 4 | 2 | St. Louis (NL) |
| 1931 | St. Louis (NL) | 4 | 3 | Philadelphia (AL) |
| 1932 | New York (AL) | 4 | 0 | Chicago (NL) |
| 1933 | New York (NL) | 4 | 1 | Washington (AL) |
| 1934 | St. Louis (NL) | 4 | 3 | Detroit (AL) |
| 1935 | Detroit (AL) | 4 | 2 | Chicago (NL) |
| 1936 | New York (AL) | 4 | 2 | New York (NL) |
| 1937 | New York (AL) | 4 | 1 | New York (NL) |
| 1938 | New York (AL) | 4 | 0 | Chicago (NL) |
| 1939 | New York (AL) | 4 | 0 | Cincinnati (NL) |
| 1940 | Cincinnati (NL) | 4 | 3 | Detroit (AL) |
| 1941 | New York (AL) | 4 | 1 | Brooklyn (NL) |
| 1942 | St. Louis (NL) | 4 | 1 | New York (AL) |
| 1943 | New York (AL) | 4 | 1 | St. Louis (NL) |
| 1944 | St. Louis (NL) | 4 | 2 | St. Louis (AL) |
| 1945 | Detroit (AL) | 4 | 3 | Chicago (NL) |
| 1946 | St. Louis (NL) | 4 | 3 | Boston (AL) |
| 1947 | New York (AL) | 4 | 3 | Brooklyn (NL) |
| 1948 | Cleveland (AL) | 4 | 2 | Boston (NL) |
| 1949 | New York (AL) | 4 | 1 | Brooklyn (NL) |
| 1950 | New York (AL) | 4 | 0 | Philadelphia (NL) |
| 1951 | New York (AL) | 4 | 2 | New York (NL) |
| 1952 | New York (AL) | 4 | 3 | Brooklyn (NL) |
| 1953 | New York (AL) | 4 | 2 | Brooklyn (NL) |
| 1954 | New York (NL) | 4 | 0 | Cleveland (AL) |
| 1955 | Brooklyn (NL) | 4 | 3 | New York (AL) |
| 1956 | New York (AL) | 4 | 3 | Brooklyn (NL) |
| 1957 | Milwaukee (NL) | 4 | 3 | New York (AL) |
| 1958 | New York (AL) | 4 | 3 | Milwaukee (NL) |
| 1959 | Los Angeles (NL) | 4 | 2 | Chicago (AL) |
| 1960 | Pittsburgh (NL) | 4 | 3 | New York (AL) |
| 1961 | New York (AL) | 4 | 1 | Cincinnati (NL) |
| 1962 | New York (AL) | 4 | 3 | San Francisco (NL) |
| 1963 | Los Angeles (NL) | 4 | 0 | New York (AL) |
| 1964 | St. Louis (NL) | 4 | 3 | New York (AL) |
| 1965 | Los Angeles (NL) | 4 | 3 | Minnesota (AL) |
| 1966 | Baltimore (AL) | 4 | 0 | Los Angeles (NL) |
| 1967 | St. Louis (NL) | 4 | 3 | Boston (AL) |
| 1968 | Detroit (AL) | 4 | 3 | St. Louis (NL) |
| 1969 | New York (NL) | 4 | 1 | Baltimore (AL) |
| 1970 | Baltimore (AL) | 4 | 1 | Cincinnati (NL) |
| 1971 | Pittsburgh (NL) | 4 | 3 | Baltimore (AL) |
| 1972 | Oakland (AL) | 4 | 3 | Cincinnati (NL) |
| 1973 | Oakland (AL) | 4 | 3 | New York (NL) |
| 1974 | Oakland (AL) | 4 | 1 | Los Angeles (NL) |
| 1975 | Cincinnati (NL) | 4 | 3 | Boston (AL) |
| 1976 | Cincinnati (NL) | 4 | 0 | New York (AL) |
| 1977 | New York (AL) | 4 | 2 | Los Angeles (NL) |
| 1978 | New York (AL) | 4 | 2 | Los Angeles (NL) |
| 1979 | Pittsburgh (NL) | 4 | 3 | Baltimore (AL) |
| 1980 | Philadelphia (NL) | 4 | 2 | Kansas City (AL) |
| 1981 | Los Angeles (NL) | 4 | 2 | New York (AL) |
| 1982 | St. Louis (NL) | 4 | 3 | Milwaukee (AL) |

## THE ALL-STAR GAMES

| Year | Site | Winner | Score |
|---|---|---|---|
| 1933 | Comiskey Park, Chicago | American | 4-2 |
| 1934 | Polo Grounds, New York | American | 9-7 |
| 1935 | Municipal Stadium, Cleveland | American | 4-1 |
| 1936 | Braves Field, Boston | National | 4-3 |
| 1937 | Griffith Stadium, Washington | American | 8-3 |
| 1938 | Crosley Field, Cincinnati | National | 4-1 |
| 1939 | Yankee Stadium, New York | American | 3-1 |
| 1940 | Sportsman's Park, St. Louis | National | 4-0 |
| 1941 | Briggs Stadium, Detroit | American | 7-5 |
| 1942 | Polo Grounds, New York | American | 3-1 |
| 1943 | Shibe Park, Philadelphia | American | 5-3 |
| 1944 | Forbes Field, Pittsburgh | National | 7-1 |
| 1945 | Not played | — | — |
| 1946 | Fenway Park, Boston | American | 12-0 |
| 1947 | Wrigley Field, Chicago | American | 2-1 |
| 1948 | Sportsman's Park, St. Louis | American | 5-2 |
| 1949 | Ebbets Field, Brooklyn | American | 11-7 |
| 1950 | Comiskey Park, Chicago | National | 4-3 |
| 1951 | Briggs Stadium, Detroit | National | 8-3 |
| 1952 | Shibe Park, Philadelphia | National | 3-2 |
| 1953 | Crosley Field, Cincinnati | National | 5-1 |
| 1954 | Municipal Stadium, Cleveland | American | 11-9 |
| 1955 | Milwaukee County Stadium | National | 6-5 |
| 1956 | Griffith Stadium, Washington | National | 7-3 |
| 1957 | Busch Stadium, St. Louis | American | 6-5 |
| 1958 | Memorial Stadium, Baltimore | American | 4-3 |
| 1959 | Forbes Field, Pittsburgh | National | 5-4 |
| | Memorial Coliseum, L.A. | American | 5-3 |
| 1960 | Municipal Stadium, Kansas City | National | 5-3 |
| | Yankee Stadium, New York | National | 6-0 |
| 1961 | Candlestick Park, San Francisco | National | 5-4 |
| | Fenway Park, Boston | Tie | 1-1 |
| 1962 | D.C. Stadium, Washington | National | 3-1 |
| | Wrigley Field, Chicago | American | 9-4 |
| 1963 | Municipal Stadium, Cleveland | National | 5-3 |
| 1964 | Shea Stadium, New York | National | 7-4 |
| 1965 | Metropolitan Stadium, Bloomington, Minnesota | National | 6-5 |
| 1966 | Busch Stadium, St. Louis | National | 2-1 |
| 1967 | Anaheim Stadium, California | National | 2-1 |
| 1968 | Houston Astrodome | National | 1-0 |
| 1969 | R. F. Kennedy Stadium, Wash. | National | 9-3 |
| 1970 | Riverfront Stadium, Cincinnati | National | 5-4 |
| 1971 | Tiger Stadium, Detroit | American | 6-4 |
| 1972 | Atlanta, Georgia | National | 4-3 |
| 1973 | Kansas City, Missouri | National | 7-1 |
| 1974 | Pittsburgh, Pennsylvania | National | 7-2 |
| 1975 | Milwaukee, Wis. | National | 6-3 |
| 1976 | Veterans Stadium, Philadelphia | National | 7-1 |
| 1977 | Yankee Stadium, New York | National | 7-5 |
| 1978 | San Diego Stadium | National | 7-3 |
| 1979 | Seattle Kingdome | National | 7-6 |
| 1980 | Dodger Stadium, Los Angeles | National | 4-2 |
| 1981 | Municipal Stadium, Cleveland | National | 5-4 |
| 1982 | Olympic Stadium, Montreal | National | 4-1 |

## MODERN FRANCHISE CHANGES IN MAJOR LEAGUES

### NATIONAL LEAGUE

| Year | New Team | How Created |
|---|---|---|
| 1953 | Milwaukee Braves | Formerly, Boston Braves |
| 1958 | Los Angeles Dodgers | Formerly, Brooklyn Dodgers |
| 1958 | San Francisco Giants | Formerly, New York Giants |
| 1962 | New York Mets | Expansion team |
| 1962 | Houston Astros† | Expansion team |
| 1966 | Atlanta Braves | Formerly, Milwaukee Braves |
| 1969 | Montreal Expos | Expansion team |
| 1969 | San Diego Padres | Expansion team |

### AMERICAN LEAGUE

| Year | New Team | How Created |
|---|---|---|
| 1954 | Baltimore Orioles | Formerly, St. Louis Browns |
| 1955 | Kansas City Athletics | Formerly, Philadelphia Athletics |
| 1961 | Minnesota Twins | Formerly, Washington Senators |
| 1961 | Washington Senators* | Expansion team |
| 1961 | Los Angeles Angels | Expansion team |
| 1965 | California Angels | Formerly, Los Angeles Angels |
| 1968 | Oakland Athletics | Formerly, Kansas City Athletics |
| 1969 | Kansas City Royals | Expansion team |
| 1969 | Seattle Pilots | Expansion team |
| 1970 | Milwaukee Brewers | Formerly, Seattle Pilots |
| 1972 | Texas Rangers | Formerly, Washington Senators |
| 1977 | Seattle Mariners | Expansion team |
| 1977 | Toronto Blue Jays | Expansion team |

† Originally Colts, then Colt-45's. * New Washington Senators.

## NATIONAL LEAGUE PENNANT WINNERS

| Year | Club | Won | Lost | Pct. | Manager |
|---|---|---|---|---|---|
| 1901 | Pittsburgh | 90 | 49 | .647 | Fred C. Clarke |
| 1902 | Pittsburgh | 103 | 36 | .741 | Fred C. Clarke |
| 1903 | Pittsburgh | 91 | 49 | .650 | Fred Clarke |
| 1904 | New York | 106 | 47 | .693 | John McGraw |
| 1905 | New York | 105 | 48 | .686 | John McGraw |
| 1906 | Chicago | 116 | 36 | .763 | Frank Chance |
| 1907 | Chicago | 107 | 45 | .704 | Frank Chance |
| 1908 | Chicago | 99 | 55 | .643 | Frank Chance |
| 1909 | Pittsburgh | 110 | 42 | .724 | Fred Clarke |
| 1910 | Chicago | 104 | 50 | .675 | Frank Chance |
| 1911 | New York | 99 | 54 | .647 | John McGraw |
| 1912 | New York | 103 | 48 | .682 | John McGraw |
| 1913 | New York | 101 | 51 | .664 | John McGraw |
| 1914 | Boston | 94 | 59 | .614 | George Stallings |
| 1915 | Philadelphia | 90 | 62 | .592 | Patrick Moran |
| 1916 | Brooklyn | 94 | 60 | .610 | Wilbert Robinson |
| 1917 | New York | 98 | 56 | .636 | John McGraw |
| 1918 | Chicago | 84 | 45 | .651 | Fred Mitchell |
| 1919 | Cincinnati | 96 | 44 | .686 | Patrick Moran |
| 1920 | Brooklyn | 93 | 61 | .604 | Wilbert Robinson |
| 1921 | New York | 94 | 59 | .614 | John McGraw |
| 1922 | New York | 93 | 61 | .604 | John McGraw |
| 1923 | New York | 95 | 58 | .621 | John McGraw |
| 1924 | New York | 93 | 60 | .608 | John McGraw |
| 1925 | Pittsburgh | 95 | 58 | .621 | William McKechnie |
| 1926 | St. Louis | 89 | 65 | .578 | Rogers Hornsby |
| 1927 | Pittsburgh | 94 | 60 | .610 | Owen Bush |
| 1928 | St. Louis | 95 | 59 | .617 | William McKechnie |
| 1929 | Chicago | 98 | 54 | .645 | Joseph McCarthy |
| 1930 | St. Louis | 92 | 62 | .597 | Charles Street |
| 1931 | St. Louis | 101 | 53 | .656 | Charles Street |
| 1932 | Chicago | 90 | 64 | .584 | Charles Grimm |
| 1933 | New York | 91 | 61 | .599 | William Terry |
| 1934 | St. Louis | 95 | 58 | .621 | Frank Frisch |
| 1935 | Chicago | 100 | 54 | .649 | Charles Grimm |
| 1936 | New York | 92 | 62 | .597 | William Terry |
| 1937 | New York | 95 | 57 | .625 | William Terry |
| 1938 | Chicago | 89 | 63 | .586 | Charles Hartnett |
| 1939 | Cincinnati | 97 | 57 | .630 | William McKechnie |
| 1940 | Cincinnati | 100 | 53 | .654 | William McKechnie |
| 1941 | Brooklyn | 100 | 54 | .649 | Leo Durocher |
| 1942 | St. Louis | 106 | 48 | .688 | William Southworth |
| 1943 | St. Louis | 105 | 49 | .682 | William Southworth |
| 1944 | St. Louis | 105 | 49 | .682 | William Southworth |
| 1945 | Chicago | 98 | 56 | .636 | Charles Grimm |
| 1946 | St. Louis | 98 | 58 | .628 | Edwin Dyer |
| 1947 | Brooklyn | 94 | 60 | .610 | Burton Shotton |
| 1948 | Boston | 91 | 62 | .595 | William Southworth |
| 1949 | Brooklyn | 97 | 57 | .630 | Burton Shotton |
| 1950 | Philadelphia | 91 | 63 | .591 | Edwin Sawyer |
| 1951 | New York | 98 | 59 | .624 | Leo Durocher |
| 1952 | Brooklyn | 96 | 57 | .627 | Charles Dressen |
| 1953 | Brooklyn | 105 | 49 | .682 | Charles Dressen |
| 1954 | New York | 97 | 57 | .630 | Leo Durocher |
| 1955 | Brooklyn | 98 | 55 | .641 | Walter Alston |
| 1956 | Brooklyn | 93 | 61 | .604 | Walter Alston |
| 1957 | Milwaukee | 95 | 59 | .617 | Fred Haney |
| 1958 | Milwaukee | 92 | 62 | .597 | Fred Haney |
| 1959 | Los Angeles | 88 | 68 | .564 | Walter Alston |
| 1960 | Pittsburgh | 95 | 59 | .617 | Daniel Murtaugh |
| 1961 | Cincinnati | 93 | 61 | .604 | Fred Hutchinson |
| 1962 | San Francisco | 103 | 62 | .624 | Alvin Dark |
| 1963 | Los Angeles | 99 | 63 | .611 | Walter Alston |
| 1964 | St. Louis | 93 | 69 | .574 | John Keane |
| 1965 | Los Angeles | 97 | 65 | .599 | Walter Alston |
| 1966 | Los Angeles | 95 | 67 | .586 | Walter Alston |
| 1967 | St. Louis | 101 | 60 | .627 | Albert Schoendienst |
| 1968 | St. Louis | 97 | 65 | .599 | Albert Schoendienst |
| 1969 | New York | 100 | 62 | .617 | Gil Hodges |
| 1970 | Cincinnati | 102 | 60 | .630 | Sparky Anderson |
| 1971 | Pittsburgh | 97 | 65 | .599 | Danny Murtaugh |
| 1972 | Cincinnati | 95 | 59 | .617 | Sparky Anderson |
| 1973 | New York | 82 | 79 | .509 | Lawrence Berra |
| 1974 | Los Angeles | 102 | 60 | .630 | Walter Alston |
| 1975 | Cincinnati | 108 | 54 | .667 | Sparky Anderson |
| 1976 | Cincinnati | 102 | 60 | .630 | Sparky Anderson |
| 1977 | Los Angeles | 98 | 64 | .605 | Tom Lasorda |
| 1978 | Los Angeles | 95 | 67 | .586 | Tom Lasorda |
| 1979 | Pittsburgh | 98 | 64 | .605 | Chuck Tanner |
| 1980 | Philadelphia | 91 | 71 | .562 | Dallas Green |
| 1981 | Los Angeles | 63 | 47 | .573 | Tom Lasorda |
| 1982 | St. Louis | 92 | 70 | .568 | Whitey Herzog |

## AMERICAN LEAGUE PENNANT WINNERS

| Year | Club | Won | Lost | Pct. | Manager |
|---|---|---|---|---|---|
| 1901 | Chicago | 83 | 53 | .610 | Clark Griffith |
| 1902 | Philadelphia | 83 | 53 | .610 | Connie Mack |
| 1903 | Boston | 91 | 47 | .659 | James Collins |
| 1904 | Boston | 95 | 59 | .617 | James Collins |
| 1905 | Philadelphia | 92 | 56 | .622 | Connie Mack |
| 1906 | Chicago | 93 | 58 | .616 | Fielder Jones |
| 1907 | Detroit | 92 | 58 | .613 | Hugh Jennings |
| 1908 | Detroit | 90 | 63 | .588 | Hugh Jennings |
| 1909 | Detroit | 98 | 54 | .645 | Hugh Jennings |
| 1910 | Philadelphia | 102 | 48 | .680 | Connie Mack |
| 1911 | Philadelphia | 101 | 50 | .669 | Connie Mack |
| 1912 | Boston | 105 | 47 | .691 | J. Garland Stahl |
| 1913 | Philadelphia | 96 | 57 | .627 | Connie Mack |
| 1914 | Philadelphia | 99 | 53 | .651 | Connie Mack |
| 1915 | Boston | 101 | 50 | .669 | William Carrigan |
| 1916 | Boston | 91 | 63 | .591 | William Carrigan |
| 1917 | Chicago | 100 | 54 | .649 | Clarence Rowland |
| 1918 | Boston | 75 | 51 | .595 | Edward Barrow |
| 1919 | Chicago | 88 | 52 | .629 | William Gleason |
| 1920 | Cleveland | 98 | 56 | .636 | Tris Speaker |
| 1921 | New York | 98 | 55 | .641 | Miller Huggins |
| 1922 | New York | 94 | 60 | .610 | Miller Huggins |
| 1923 | New York | 98 | 54 | .645 | Miller Huggins |
| 1924 | Washington | 92 | 62 | .597 | Stanley Harris |
| 1925 | Washington | 96 | 55 | .636 | Stanley Harris |
| 1926 | New York | 91 | 63 | .591 | Miller Huggins |
| 1927 | New York | 110 | 44 | .714 | Miller Huggins |
| 1928 | New York | 101 | 53 | .656 | Miller Huggins |
| 1929 | Philadelphia | 104 | 46 | .693 | Connie Mack |
| 1930 | Philadelphia | 102 | 52 | .662 | Connie Mack |
| 1931 | Philadelphia | 107 | 45 | .704 | Connie Mack |
| 1932 | New York | 107 | 47 | .695 | Joseph McCarthy |
| 1933 | Washington | 99 | 53 | .651 | Joseph Cronin |
| 1934 | Detroit | 101 | 53 | .656 | Gordon Cochrane |
| 1935 | Detroit | 93 | 58 | .616 | Gordon Cochrane |
| 1936 | New York | 102 | 51 | .667 | Joseph McCarthy |
| 1937 | New York | 102 | 52 | .662 | Joseph McCarthy |
| 1938 | New York | 99 | 53 | .651 | Joseph McCarthy |
| 1939 | New York | 106 | 45 | .702 | Joseph McCarthy |
| 1940 | Detroit | 90 | 64 | .584 | Delmar Baker |
| 1941 | New York | 101 | 53 | .656 | Joseph McCarthy |
| 1942 | New York | 103 | 51 | .669 | Joseph McCarthy |
| 1943 | New York | 98 | 56 | .636 | Joseph McCarthy |
| 1944 | St. Louis | 89 | 65 | .578 | James Sewell |
| 1945 | Detroit | 88 | 65 | .575 | Stephen O'Neill |
| 1946 | Boston | 104 | 50 | .675 | Joseph Cronin |
| 1947 | New York | 97 | 57 | .630 | Stanley Harris |
| 1948 | Cleveland | 97 | 58 | .626 | Louis Boudreau |
| 1949 | New York | 97 | 57 | .630 | Charles Stengel |
| 1950 | New York | 98 | 56 | .636 | Charles Stengel |
| 1951 | New York | 98 | 56 | .636 | Charles Stengel |
| 1952 | New York | 95 | 59 | .617 | Charles Stengel |
| 1953 | New York | 99 | 52 | .656 | Charles Stengel |
| 1954 | Cleveland | 111 | 43 | .721 | Alfonso Lopez |
| 1955 | New York | 96 | 58 | .623 | Charles Stengel |
| 1956 | New York | 97 | 57 | .630 | Charles Stengel |
| 1957 | New York | 98 | 56 | .636 | Charles Stengel |
| 1958 | New York | 92 | 62 | .597 | Charles Stengel |
| 1959 | Chicago | 94 | 60 | .610 | Alfonso Lopez |
| 1960 | New York | 97 | 57 | .630 | Charles Stengel |
| 1961 | New York | 109 | 53 | .673 | Ralph Houk |
| 1962 | New York | 96 | 66 | .593 | Ralph Houk |
| 1963 | New York | 104 | 57 | .646 | Ralph Houk |
| 1964 | New York | 99 | 63 | .611 | Lawrence Berra |
| 1965 | Minnesota | 102 | 60 | .630 | Sabath Mele |
| 1966 | Baltimore | 97 | 63 | .606 | Henry Bauer |
| 1967 | Boston | 92 | 70 | .568 | Richard Williams |
| 1968 | Detroit | 103 | 59 | .636 | Mayo Smith |
| 1969 | Baltimore | 109 | 53 | .673 | Earl Weaver |
| 1970 | Baltimore | 108 | 54 | .667 | Earl Weaver |
| 1971 | Baltimore | 101 | 57 | .639 | Earl Weaver |
| 1972 | Oakland | 93 | 62 | .600 | Dick Williams |
| 1973 | Oakland | 94 | 68 | .580 | Dick Williams |
| 1974 | Oakland | 90 | 72 | .556 | Alvin Dark |
| 1975 | Boston | 95 | 65 | .594 | Darrell Johnson |
| 1976 | New York | 97 | 62 | .610 | Billy Martin |
| 1977 | New York | 100 | 62 | .617 | Billy Martin |
| 1978 | New York | 100 | 63 | .613 | Bob Lemon |
| 1979 | Baltimore | 102 | 57 | .642 | Earl Weaver |
| 1980 | Kansas City | 97 | 65 | .599 | Jim Frey |
| 1981 | New York | 59 | 48 | .551 | Bob Lemon |
| 1982 | Milwaukee | 95 | 67 | .586 | Harvey Kuenn |

## NATIONAL LEAGUE BATTING CHAMPIONS

| Year | Player and Club | Average |
|---|---|---|
| 1901 | Jesse Burkett, St. Louis | .382 |
| 1902 | Clarence Beaumont, Pittsburgh | .357 |
| 1903 | Honus Wagner, Pittsburgh | .355 |
| 1904 | Honus Wagner, Pittsburgh | .349 |
| 1905 | Cy Seymour, Cincinnati | .377 |
| 1906 | Honus Wagner, Pittsburgh | .339 |
| 1907 | Honus Wagner, Pittsburgh | .350 |
| 1908 | Honus Wagner, Pittsburgh | .354 |
| 1909 | Honus Wagner, Pittsburgh | .339 |
| 1910 | Sherwood Magee, Philadelphia | .331 |
| 1911 | Honus Wagner, Pittsburgh | .334 |
| 1912 | Henry Zimmerman, Chicago | .372 |
| 1913 | Jake Daubert, Brooklyn | .350 |
| 1914 | Jake Daubert, Brooklyn | .329 |
| 1915 | Larry Doyle, New York | .320 |
| 1916 | Hal Chase, Cincinnati | .339 |
| 1917 | Edd Roush, Cincinnati | .341 |
| 1918 | Zack Wheat, Brooklyn | .335 |
| 1919 | Edd Roush, Cincinnati | .321 |
| 1920 | Rogers Hornsby, St. Louis | .370 |
| 1921 | Rogers Hornsby, St. Louis | .397 |
| 1922 | Rogers Hornsby, St. Louis | .401 |
| 1923 | Rogers Hornsby, St. Louis | .384 |
| 1924 | Rogers Hornsby, St. Louis | .424 |
| 1925 | Rogers Hornsby, St. Louis | .403 |
| 1926 | Gene Hargrave, Cincinnati | .353 |
| 1927 | Paul Waner, Pittsburgh | .380 |
| 1928 | Rogers Hornsby, Boston | .387 |
| 1929 | Lefty O'Doul, Philadelphia | .398 |
| 1930 | Bill Terry, New York | .401 |
| 1931 | Chick Hafey, St. Louis | .349 |
| 1932 | Lefty O'Doul, Brooklyn | .368 |
| 1933 | Chuck Klein, Philadelphia | .368 |
| 1934 | Paul Waner, Pittsburgh | .362 |
| 1935 | Arky Vaughan, Pittsburgh | .385 |
| 1936 | Paul Waner, Pittsburgh | .373 |
| 1937 | Joe Medwick, St. Louis | .374 |
| 1938 | Ernie Lombardi, Cincinnati | .342 |
| 1939 | Johnny Mize, St. Louis | .349 |
| 1940 | Debs Garms, Pittsburgh | .355 |
| 1941 | Pete Reiser, Brooklyn | .343 |
| 1942 | Ernie Lombardi, Boston | .330 |
| 1943 | Stan Musial, St. Louis | .357 |
| 1944 | Dixie Walker, Brooklyn | .357 |
| 1945 | Phil Cavaretta, Chicago | .355 |
| 1946 | Stan Musial, St. Louis | .365 |
| 1947 | Harry Walker, St. Louis-Philadelphia | .363 |
| 1948 | Stan Musial, St. Louis | .376 |
| 1949 | Jackie Robinson, Brooklyn | .342 |
| 1950 | Stan Musial, St. Louis | .346 |
| 1951 | Stan Musial, St. Louis | .355 |
| 1952 | Stan Musial, St. Louis | .336 |
| 1953 | Carl Furillo, Brooklyn | .344 |
| 1954 | Willie Mays, New York | .345 |
| 1955 | Richie Ashburn, Philadelphia | .338 |
| 1956 | Hank Aaron, Milwaukee | .328 |
| 1957 | Stan Musial, St. Louis | .351 |
| 1958 | Richie Ashburn, Philadelphia | .350 |
| 1959 | Hank Aaron, Milwaukee | .355 |
| 1960 | Dick Groat, Pittsburgh | .325 |
| 1961 | Roberto Clemente, Pittsburgh | .351 |
| 1962 | Tommy Davis, Los Angeles | .346 |
| 1963 | Tommy Davis, Los Angeles | .326 |
| 1964 | Roberto Clemente, Pittsburgh | .339 |
| 1965 | Roberto Clemente, Pittsburgh | .329 |
| 1966 | Matty Alou, Pittsburgh | .342 |
| 1967 | Roberto Clemente, Pittsburgh | .357 |
| 1968 | Pete Rose, Cincinnati | .335 |
| 1969 | Pete Rose, Cincinnati | .348 |
| 1970 | Rico Carty, Atlanta | .366 |
| 1971 | Joe Torre, St. Louis | .363 |
| 1972 | Billy Williams, Chicago | .333 |
| 1973 | Pete Rose, Cincinnati | .338 |
| 1974 | Ralph Garr, Atlanta | .353 |
| 1975 | Bill Madlock, Chicago | .354 |
| 1976 | Bill Madlock, Chicago | .339 |
| 1977 | Dave Parker, Pittsburgh | .338 |
| 1978 | Dave Parker, Pittsburgh | .334 |
| 1979 | Keith Hernandez, St. Louis | .344 |
| 1980 | Bill Buckner, Chicago | .324 |
| 1981 | Bill Madlock, Pittsburgh | .341 |
| 1982 | Al Oliver, Montreal | .331 |

## NATIONAL LEAGUE HOME RUN CHAMPIONS

| Year | Player and Club | Home Runs |
|---|---|---|
| 1901 | Sam Crawford, Cincinnati | 16 |
| 1902 | Tom Leach, Pittsburgh | 6 |
| 1903 | James Sheckard, Brooklyn | 9 |
| 1904 | Harry Lumley, Brooklyn | 9 |
| 1905 | Fred Odwell, Cincinnati | 9 |
| 1906 | Tim Jordan, Brooklyn | 12 |
| 1907 | David Brain, Boston | 10 |
| 1908 | Tim Jordan, Brooklyn | 12 |
| 1909 | John Murray, New York | 7 |
| 1910 | Fred Beck, Boston | 10 |
| | Frank Schulte, Chicago | 10 |
| 1911 | Frank Schulte, Chicago | 21 |
| 1912 | Henry Zimmerman, Chicago | 14 |
| 1913 | Cliff Cravath, Philadelphia | 19 |
| 1914 | Cliff Cravath, Philadelphia | 19 |
| 1915 | Cliff Cravath, Philadelphia | 24 |
| 1916 | Davis Robertson, New York | 12 |
| | Cy Williams, Chicago | 12 |
| 1917 | Davis Robertson, New York | 12 |
| | Gavvy Cravath, Philadelphia | 12 |
| 1918 | Gavvy Cravath, Philadelphia | 8 |
| 1919 | Gavvy Cravath, Philadelphia | 12 |
| 1920 | Cy Williams, Philadelphia | 15 |
| 1921 | George Kelly, New York | 23 |
| 1922 | Rogers Hornsby, St. Louis | 42 |
| 1923 | Cy Williams, Philadelphia | 41 |
| 1924 | Jack Fournier, Brooklyn | 27 |
| 1925 | Rogers Hornsby, St. Louis | 39 |
| 1926 | Hack Wilson, Chicago | 21 |
| 1927 | Hack Wilson, Chicago | 30 |
| | Cy Williams, Philadelphia | 30 |
| 1928 | Hack Wilson, Chicago | 31 |
| | Jim Bottomley, St. Louis | 31 |
| 1929 | Chuck Klein, Philadelphia | 43 |
| 1930 | Hack Wilson, Chicago | 56 |
| 1931 | Chuck Klein, Philadelphia | 31 |
| 1932 | Chuck Klein, Philadelphia | 38 |
| | Mel Ott, New York | 38 |
| 1933 | Chuck Klein, Philadelphia | 28 |
| 1934 | Mel Ott, New York | 35 |
| | Rip Collins, St. Louis | 35 |
| 1935 | Wally Berger, Boston | 34 |
| 1936 | Mel Ott, New York | 33 |
| 1937 | Mel Ott, New York | 31 |
| | Joe Medwick, St. Louis | 31 |
| 1938 | Mel Ott, New York | 36 |
| 1939 | Johnny Mize, St. Louis | 28 |
| 1940 | Johnny Mize, St. Louis | 43 |
| 1941 | Dolph Camilli, Brooklyn | 34 |
| 1942 | Mell Ott, New York | 30 |
| 1943 | Bill Nicholson, Chicago | 29 |
| 1944 | Bill Nicholson, Chicago | 33 |
| 1945 | Tommy Holmes, Boston | 28 |
| 1946 | Ralph Kiner, Pittsburgh | 23 |
| 1947 | Ralph Kiner, Pittsburgh | 51 |
| | Johnny Mize, New York | 51 |
| 1948 | Ralph Kiner, Pittsburgh | 40 |
| | Johnny Mize, New York | 40 |
| 1949 | Ralph Kiner, Pittsburgh | 54 |
| 1950 | Ralph Kiner, Pittsburgh | 47 |
| 1951 | Ralph Kiner, Pittsburgh | 42 |
| 1952 | Ralph Kiner, Pittsburgh | 37 |
| | Hank Sauer, Chicago | 37 |
| 1953 | Eddie Mathews, Milwaukee | 47 |
| 1954 | Ted Kluszewski, Cincinnati | 49 |
| 1955 | Willie Mays, New York | 51 |
| 1956 | Duke Snider, Brooklyn | 43 |
| 1957 | Hank Aaron, Milwaukee | 44 |
| 1958 | Ernie Banks, Chicago | 47 |
| 1959 | Eddie Mathews, Milwaukee | 46 |
| 1960 | Ernie Banks, Chicago | 41 |
| 1961 | Orlando Cepeda, San Francisco | 46 |
| 1962 | Willie Mays, San Francisco | 49 |
| 1963 | Hank Aaron, Milwaukee | 44 |
| | Willie McCovey, San Francisco | 44 |
| 1964 | Willie Mays, San Francisco | 47 |
| 1965 | Willie Mays, San Francisco | 52 |
| 1966 | Hank Aaron, Atlanta | 44 |
| 1967 | Hank Aaron, Atlanta | 39 |
| 1968 | Willie McCovey, San Francisco | 36 |
| 1969 | Willie McCovey, San Francisco | 45 |
| 1970 | Johnny Bench, Cincinnati | 45 |
| 1971 | Willie Stargell, Pittsburgh | 48 |
| 1972 | Johnny Bench, Cincinnati | 40 |
| 1973 | Willie Stargell, Pittsburgh | 44 |
| 1974 | Mike Schmidt, Philadelphia | 36 |

## NATIONAL LEAGUE HOME RUN CHAMPIONS (Cont.)

| Year | Player and Club | Home Runs |
|---|---|---|
| 1975 | Mike Schmidt, Philadelphia | 38 |
| 1976 | Mike Schmidt, Philadelphia | 38 |
| 1977 | George Foster, Cincinnati | 52 |
| 1978 | George Foster, Cincinnati | 40 |
| 1979 | Dave Kingman, Chicago | 48 |
| 1980 | Mike Schmidt, Philadelphia | 48 |
| 1981 | Mike Schmidt, Philadelphia | 31 |
| 1982 | Dave Kingman, New York | 37 |

## NATIONAL LEAGUE RUNS BATTED IN CHAMPIONS

| Year | Player and Club | RBI |
|---|---|---|
| 1920 | Rogers Hornsby, St. Louis | 94 |
| | George Kelly, New York | 94 |
| 1921 | Rogers Hornsby, St. Louis | 126 |
| 1922 | Rogers Hornsby, St. Louis | 152 |
| 1923 | Irish Meusel, New York | 125 |
| 1924 | George Kelly, New York | 136 |
| 1925 | Rogers Hornsby, St. Louis | 143 |
| 1926 | Jim Bottomley, St. Louis | 120 |
| 1927 | Paul Waner, Pittsburgh | 131 |
| 1928 | Jim Bottomley, St. Louis | 136 |
| 1929 | Hack Wilson, Chicago | 159 |
| 1930 | Hack Wilson, Chicago | 190 |
| 1931 | Chuck Klein, Philadelphia | 121 |
| 1932 | Don Hurst, Philadelphia | 143 |
| 1933 | Chuck Klein, Philadelphia | 120 |
| 1934 | Mel Ott, New York | 135 |
| 1935 | Wally Berger, Boston | 130 |
| 1936 | Joe Medwick, St. Louis | 138 |
| 1937 | Joe Medwick, St. Louis | 154 |
| 1938 | Joe Medwick, St. Louis | 122 |
| 1939 | Frank McCormick, Cincinnati | 128 |
| 1940 | Johnny Mize, St. Louis | 137 |
| 1941 | Dolf Camilli, Brooklyn | 120 |
| 1942 | Johnny Mize, New York | 110 |
| 1943 | Bill Nicholson, Chicago | 128 |
| 1944 | Bill Nicholson, Chicago | 122 |
| 1945 | Dixie Walker, Brooklyn | 124 |
| 1946 | Enos Slaughter, St. Louis | 130 |
| 1947 | Johnny Mize, New York | 138 |
| 1948 | Stan Musial, St. Louis | 131 |
| 1949 | Ralph Kiner, Pittsburgh | 127 |
| 1950 | Del Ennis, Philadelphia | 126 |
| 1951 | Monte Irvin, New York | 121 |
| 1952 | Hank Sauer, Chicago | 121 |
| 1953 | Roy Campanella, Brooklyn | 142 |
| 1954 | Ted Kluszewski, Cincinnati | 141 |
| 1955 | Duke Snider, Brooklyn | 136 |
| 1956 | Stan Musial, St. Louis | 109 |
| 1957 | Hank Aaron, Milwaukee | 132 |
| 1958 | Ernie Banks, Chicago | 129 |
| 1959 | Ernie Banks, Chicago | 143 |
| 1960 | Hank Aaron, Milwaukee | 126 |
| 1961 | Orlando Cepeda, San Francisco | 142 |
| 1962 | Tommy Davis, Los Angeles | 153 |
| 1963 | Hank Aaron, Milwaukee | 130 |
| 1964 | Ken Boyer, St. Louis | 119 |
| 1965 | Deron Johnson, Cincinnati | 130 |
| 1966 | Hank Aaron, Atlanta | 127 |
| 1967 | Orlando Cepeda, St. Louis | 111 |
| 1968 | Willie McCovey, San Francisco | 105 |
| 1969 | Willie McCovey, San Francisco | 126 |
| 1970 | Johnny Bench, Cincinnati | 148 |
| 1971 | Joe Torre, St. Louis | 137 |
| 1972 | Johnny Bench, Cincinnati | 125 |
| 1973 | Willie Stargell, Pittsburgh | 119 |
| 1974 | Johnny Bench, Cincinnati | 129 |
| 1975 | Greg Luzinski, Philadelphia | 120 |
| 1976 | George Foster, Cincinnati | 121 |
| 1977 | George Foster, Cincinnati | 149 |
| 1978 | George Foster, Cincinnati | 120 |
| 1979 | Dave Winfield, San Diego | 118 |
| 1980 | Mike Schmidt, Philadelphia | 121 |
| 1981 | Mike Schmidt, Philadelphia | 91 |
| 1982 | Al Oliver, Montreal | 109 |
| | Dale Murphy, Atlanta | 109 |

## AMERICAN LEAGUE BATTING CHAMPIONS

| Year | Player and Club | Average |
|---|---|---|
| 1901 | Nap Lajoie, Phila | .422 |
| 1902 | Ed Delahanty, Wash. | .376 |
| 1903 | Nap Lajoie, Cleve. | .355 |
| 1904 | Nap Lajoie, Cleve. | .381 |
| 1905 | Elmer Flick, Cleve. | .306 |
| 1906 | George Stone, St. Louis | .358 |
| 1907 | Ty Cobb, Det. | .350 |
| 1908 | Ty Cobb, Det. | .324 |
| 1909 | Ty Cobb, Det. | .377 |
| 1910 | Ty Cobb, Detroit | .385 |
| 1911 | Ty Cobb, Detroit | .420 |
| 1912 | Ty Cobb, Detroit | .410 |
| 1913 | Ty Cobb, Detroit | .390 |
| 1914 | Ty Cobb, Detroit | .368 |
| 1915 | Ty Cobb, Detroit | .369 |
| 1916 | Tris Speaker, Cleveland | .386 |
| 1917 | Ty Cobb, Detroit | .383 |
| 1918 | Ty Cobb, Detroit | .382 |
| 1919 | Ty Cobb, Detroit | .384 |
| 1920 | George Sisler, St. Louis | .407 |
| 1921 | Harry Heilmann, Detroit | .394 |
| 1922 | George Sisler, St. Louis | .420 |
| 1923 | Harry Heilmann, Detroit | .403 |
| 1924 | Babe Ruth, New York | .378 |
| 1925 | Harry Heilmann, Detroit | .393 |
| 1926 | Henry Manush, Detroit | .378 |
| 1927 | Harry Heilmann, Detroit | .398 |
| 1928 | Goose Goslin, Washington | .379 |
| 1929 | Lew Fonseca, Cleveland | .369 |
| 1930 | Al Simmons, Philadelphia | .381 |
| 1931 | Al Simmons, Philadelphia | .390 |
| 1932 | Dale Alexander, Detroit-Boston | .367 |
| 1933 | Jimmy Foxx, Philadelphia | .356 |
| 1934 | Lou Gehrig, New York | .363 |
| 1935 | Buddy Myer, Washington | .349 |
| 1936 | Luke Appling, Chicago | .388 |
| 1937 | Charley Gehringer, Detroit | .371 |
| 1938 | Jimmy Foxx, Boston | .349 |
| 1939 | Joe DiMaggio, New York | .381 |
| 1940 | Joe DiMaggio, New York | .352 |
| 1941 | Ted Williams, Boston | .406 |
| 1942 | Ted Williams, Boston | .356 |
| 1943 | Luke Appling, Chicago | .328 |
| 1944 | Lou Boudreau, Cleveland | .327 |
| 1945 | George Sternweiss, New York | .309 |
| 1946 | Mickey Vernon, Washington | .353 |
| 1947 | Ted Williams, Boston | .343 |
| 1948 | Ted Williams, Boston | .369 |
| 1949 | George Kell, Detroit[1] | .343 |
| 1950 | Billy Goodman, Boston | .354 |
| 1951 | Ferris Fain, Philadelphia | .344 |
| 1952 | Ferris Fain, Philadelphia | .327 |
| 1953 | Mickey Vernon, Washington | .337 |
| 1954 | Bobby Avila, Cleveland | .341 |
| 1955 | Al Kaline, Detroit | .340 |
| 1956 | Mickey Mantle, New York | .353 |
| 1957 | Ted Williams, Boston | .388 |
| 1958 | Ted Williams, Boston | .328 |
| 1959 | Harvey Kuenn, Detroit | .353 |
| 1960 | Pete Runnels, Boston | .320 |
| 1961 | Norm Cash, Detroit | .361 |
| 1962 | Pete Runnels, Boston | .326 |
| 1963 | Carl Yastrzemski, Boston | .321 |
| 1964 | Tony Oliva, Minnesota | .323 |
| 1965 | Tony Oliva, Minnesota | .321 |
| 1966 | Frank Robinson, Baltimore | .316 |
| 1967 | Carl Yastrzemski, Boston | .326 |
| 1968 | Carl Yastrzemski, Boston | .301 |
| 1969 | Rod Carew, Minnesota | .332 |
| 1970 | Alex Johnson, California[2] | .329 |
| 1971 | Tony Oliva, Minnesota | .337 |
| 1972 | Rod Carew, Minnesota | .318 |
| 1973 | Rod Carew, Minnesota | .350 |
| 1974 | Rod Carew, Minnesota | .364 |
| 1975 | Rod Carew, Minnesota | .359 |
| 1976 | George Brett, Kansas City | .333 |
| 1977 | Rod Carew, Minnesota | .388 |
| 1978 | Rod Carew, Minnesota | .333 |
| 1979 | Fred Lynn, Boston | .333 |
| 1980 | George Brett, Kansas City | .390 |
| 1981 | Carney Lansford, Boston | .336 |
| 1982 | Willie Wilson, Kansas City | .332 |

[1] Kell .3429; Ted Williams, Boston .3427. [2] Johnson .3289; Carl Yastrzemski, Boston .3286.

## AMERICAN LEAGUE HOME RUN CHAMPIONS

| Year | Player and Club | Home Runs |
|---|---|---|
| 1901 | Nap Lajoie, Philadelphia | 13 |
| 1902 | Ralph Seybold, Philadelphia | 16 |
| 1903 | Buck Freeman, Boston | 13 |
| 1904 | Harry Davis, Philadelphia | 10 |
| 1905 | Harry Davis, Philadelphia | 8 |
| 1906 | Harry Davis, Philadelphia | 12 |
| 1907 | Harry Davis, Philadelphia | 8 |
| 1908 | Sam Crawford, Detroit | 7 |
| 1909 | Ty Cobb, Detroit | 9 |
| 1910 | J. Garland Stahl, Boston | 10 |
| 1911 | Franklin Baker, Philadelphia | 9 |
| 1912 | Franklin Baker, Philadelphia | 10 |
| 1913 | Franklin Baker, Philadelphia | 12 |
| 1914 | Franklin Baker, Philadelphia | 8 |
| | Sam Crawford, Detroit | 8 |
| 1915 | Robert Roth, Chi.-Cleve. | 7 |
| 1916 | Wally Pipp, New York | 12 |
| 1917 | Wally Pipp, New York | 9 |
| 1918 | Clarence Walker, Philadelphia | 11 |
| | Babe Ruth, Boston | 11 |
| 1919 | Babe Ruth, Boston | 29 |
| 1920 | Babe Ruth, New York | 54 |
| 1921 | Babe Ruth, New York | 59 |
| 1922 | Ken Williams, St. Louis | 39 |
| 1923 | Babe Ruth, New York | 41 |
| 1924 | Babe Ruth, New York | 46 |
| 1925 | Bob Meusel, New York | 33 |
| 1926 | Babe Ruth, New York | 47 |
| 1927 | Babe Ruth, New York | 60 |
| 1928 | Babe Ruth, New York | 54 |
| 1929 | Babe Ruth, New York | 46 |
| 1930 | Babe Ruth, New York | 49 |
| 1931 | Babe Ruth, New York | 46 |
| | Lou Gehrig, New York | 46 |
| 1932 | Jimmy Foxx, Philadelphia | 58 |
| 1933 | Jimmy Foxx, Philadelphia | 48 |
| 1934 | Lou Gehrig, New York | 49 |
| 1935 | Jimmy Foxx, Philadelphia | 36 |
| | Hank Greenberg, Detroit | 36 |
| 1936 | Lou Gehrig, New York | 49 |
| 1937 | Joe DiMaggio, New York | 46 |
| 1938 | Hank Greenberg, Detroit | 58 |
| 1939 | Jimmy Foxx, Boston | 35 |
| 1940 | Hank Greenberg, Detroit | 41 |
| 1941 | Ted Williams, Boston | 37 |
| 1942 | Ted Williams, Boston | 36 |
| 1943 | Rudy York, Detroit | 34 |
| 1944 | Nick Etten, New York | 22 |
| 1945 | Vern Stephens, St. Louis | 24 |
| 1946 | Hank Greenberg, Detroit | 44 |
| 1947 | Ted Williams, Boston | 32 |
| 1948 | Joe DiMaggio, New York | 39 |
| 1949 | Ted Williams, Boston | 43 |
| 1950 | Al Rosen, Cleveland | 37 |
| 1951 | Gus Zernial, Chicago-Philadelphia | 33 |
| 1952 | Larry Doby, Cleveland | 32 |
| 1953 | Al Rosen, Cleveland | 43 |
| 1954 | Larry Doby, Cleveland | 32 |
| 1955 | Mickey Mantle, New York | 37 |
| 1956 | Mickey Mantle, New York | 52 |
| 1957 | Roy Sievers, Washington | 42 |
| 1958 | Mickey Mantle, New York | 42 |
| 1959 | Rocky Colavito, Cleveland | 42 |
| | Harmon Killebrew, Washington | 42 |
| 1960 | Mickey Mantle, New York | 40 |
| 1961 | Roger Maris, New York | 61 |
| 1962 | Harmon Killebrew, Minnesota | 48 |
| 1963 | Harmon Killebrew, Minnesota | 45 |
| 1964 | Harmon Killebrew, Minnesota | 49 |
| 1965 | Tony Conigliaro, Boston | 32 |
| 1966 | Frank Robinson, Baltimore | 49 |
| 1967 | Harmon Killebrew, Minnesota | 44 |
| | Carl Yastrzemski, Boston | 44 |
| 1968 | Frank Howard, Washington | 44 |
| 1969 | Harmon Killebrew, Minnesota | 49 |
| 1970 | Frank Howard, Washington | 44 |
| 1971 | Bill Melton, Chicago | 33 |
| 1972 | Dick Allen, Chicago | 37 |
| 1973 | Reggie Jackson, Oakland | 32 |
| 1974 | Dick Allen, Chicago | 32 |
| 1975 | Reggie Jackson, Oakland | 36 |
| | George Scott, Milwaukee | 36 |
| 1976 | Graig Nettles, New York | 32 |
| 1977 | Jim Rice, Boston | 39 |
| 1978 | Jim Rice, Boston | 46 |
| 1979 | Gorman Thomas, Milwaukee | 45 |
| | Ben Oglivie, Milwaukee | 41 |
| 1980 | Reggie Jackson, New York | 41 |
| 1981 | Eddie Murray, Baltimore | 22 |
| | Dwight Evans, Boston | 22 |
| | Bobby Grich, California | 22 |
| | Tony Armas, Oakland | 22 |
| 1982 | Gorman Thomas, Milwaukee | 39 |
| | Reggie Jackson, California | 39 |

## AMERICAN LEAGUE RUNS BATTED IN CHAMPIONS

| Year | Player and Club | RBI |
|---|---|---|
| 1920 | Babe Ruth, New York | 137 |
| 1921 | Babe Ruth, New York | 171 |
| 1922 | Ken Williams, St. Louis | 155 |
| 1923 | Babe Ruth, New York | 131 |
| 1924 | Goose Goslin, Washington | 129 |
| 1925 | Bob Meusel, New York | 138 |
| 1926 | Babe Ruth, New York | 145 |
| 1927 | Lou Gehrig, New York | 175 |
| 1928 | Lou Gehrig, New York | 142 |
| | Babe Ruth, New York | 142 |
| 1929 | Al Simmons, Philadelphia | 157 |
| 1930 | Lou Gehrig, New York | 174 |
| 1931 | Lou Gehrig, New York | 184 |
| 1932 | Jimmie Foxx, Philadelphia | 169 |
| 1933 | Jimmie Foxx, Philadelphia | 163 |
| 1934 | Lou Gehrig, New York | 165 |
| 1935 | Hank Greenberg, Detroit | 170 |
| 1936 | Hal Trosky, Cleveland | 162 |
| 1937 | Hank Greenberg, Detroit | 183 |
| 1938 | Jimmie Foxx, Boston | 175 |
| 1939 | Ted Williams, Boston | 145 |
| 1940 | Hank Greenberg, Detroit | 150 |
| 1941 | Joe DiMaggio, New York | 125 |
| 1942 | Ted Williams, Boston | 137 |
| 1943 | Rudy York, Detroit | 118 |
| 1944 | Vern Stephens, St. Louis | 109 |
| 1945 | Nick Etten, New York | 111 |
| 1946 | Hank Greenberg, Detroit | 127 |
| 1947 | Ted Williams, Boston | 114 |
| 1948 | Joe DiMaggio, New York | 155 |
| 1949 | Ted Williams, Boston | 159 |
| | Vern Stephens, Boston | 159 |
| 1950 | Vern Stephens, Boston | 144 |
| | Walt Dropo, Boston | 144 |
| 1951 | Gus Zernial, Chicago-Phliadelphia | 129 |
| 1952 | Al Rosen, Cleveland | 105 |
| 1953 | Al Rosen, Cleveland | 145 |
| 1954 | Larry Doby, Cleveland | 126 |
| 1955 | Ray Boone, Detroit | 116 |
| | Jackie Jensen, Boston | 116 |
| 1956 | Mickey Mantle, New York | 130 |
| 1957 | Roy Sievers, Washington | 114 |
| 1958 | Jackie Jensen, Boston | 122 |
| 1959 | Jackie Jensen, Boston | 112 |
| 1960 | Roger Maris, New York | 112 |
| 1961 | Roger Maris, New York | 142 |
| 1962 | Harmon Killebrew, Minnesota | 126 |
| 1963 | Dick Stuart, Boston | 118 |
| 1964 | Brooks Robinson, Baltimore | 118 |
| 1965 | Rocky Colavito, Cleveland | 108 |
| 1966 | Frank Robinson, Baltimore | 122 |
| 1967 | Carl Yastrzemski, Boston | 121 |
| 1968 | Ken Harrelson, Boston | 109 |
| 1969 | Harmon Killebrew, Minnesota | 140 |
| 1970 | Frank Howard, Washington | 126 |
| 1971 | Harmon Killebrew, Minnesota | 119 |
| 1972 | Richie Allen, Chicago | 113 |
| 1973 | Reggie Jackson, Oakland | 117 |
| 1974 | Jeff Burroughs, Texas | 118 |
| 1975 | George Scott, Boston | 109 |
| 1976 | Lee May, Baltimore | 109 |
| 1977 | Larry Hisle, Minnesota | 119 |
| 1978 | Jim Rice, Boston | 139 |
| 1979 | Don Baylor, California | 139 |
| 1980 | Cecil Cooper, Milwaukee | 122 |
| 1981 | Eddie Murray, Baltimore | 78 |
| 1982 | Hal McRae, Kansas City | 133 |

## PITCHERS WITH BEST WON-AND-LOST PERCENTAGES

**NATIONAL LEAGUE**

| Year | Pitcher and Club | Won | Lost | Per-cent |
|---|---|---|---|---|
| 1941 | Elmer Riddle, Cincinnati | 19 | 4 | .826 |
| 1942 | Larry French, Brooklyn | 15 | 4 | .789 |
| 1943 | Mort Cooper, St. Louis | 21 | 8 | .724 |
| 1944 | Ted Wilkes, St. Louis | 17 | 4 | .810 |
| 1945 | Harry Brecheen, St. Louis | 15 | 4 | .789 |
| 1946 | Murry Dickson, St. Louis | 15 | 6 | .714 |
| 1947 | Larry Jansen, New York | 21 | 5 | .808 |
| 1948 | Harry Brecheen, St. Louis | 20 | 7 | .741 |
| 1949 | Preacher Roe, Brooklyn | 15 | 6 | .714 |
| 1950 | Sal Maglie, New York | 18 | 4 | .818 |
| 1951 | Preacher Roe, Brooklyn | 22 | 3 | .880 |
| 1952 | Hoyt Wilhelm, New York | 15 | 3 | .833 |
| 1953 | Carl Erskine, Brooklyn | 20 | 6 | .769 |
| 1954 | Johnny Antonelli, New York | 21 | 7 | .750 |
| 1955 | Don Newcombe, Brooklyn | 20 | 5 | .800 |
| 1956 | Don Newcombe, Brooklyn | 27 | 7 | .794 |
| 1957 | Bob Ruhl, Milwaukee | 18 | 7 | .720 |
| 1958 | Warren Spahn, Milwaukee | 22 | 11 | .667 |
| | Lew Burdette, Milwaukee | 20 | 10 | .667 |
| 1959 | El Roy Face, Pittsburgh | 18 | 1 | .947 |
| 1960 | Ernie Broglio, St. Louis | 21 | 9 | .700 |
| 1961 | Johnny Podres, Los Angeles | 18 | 5 | .783 |
| 1962 | Bob Purkey, Cincinnati | 23 | 5 | .821 |
| 1963 | Ron Perranoski, Los Angeles | 16 | 3 | .842 |
| 1964 | Sandy Koufax, Los Angeles | 19 | 5 | .792 |
| 1965 | Sandy Koufax, Los Angeles | 26 | 8 | .765 |
| 1966 | Juan Marichal, San Francisco | 25 | 6 | .806 |
| 1967 | Dick Hughes, St. Louis | 16 | 6 | .727 |
| 1968 | Steve Blass, Pittsburgh | 18 | 6 | .750 |
| 1969 | Tom Seaver, New York | 25 | 7 | .781 |
| 1970 | Bob Gibson, St. Louis | 23 | 7 | .767 |
| 1971 | Tug McGraw, New York | 11 | 4 | .733 |
| 1972 | Steve Carlton, Philadelphia | 27 | 10 | .730 |
| 1973 | Tommy John, Los Angeles | 16 | 7 | .696 |
| 1974 | Tommy John, Los Angeles | 13 | 3 | .813 |
| 1975 | Al Hrabosky, St. Louis | 13 | 3 | .813 |
| 1976 | Steve Carlton, Philadelphia | 20 | 7 | .741 |
| 1977 | John Candelaria, Pittsburgh | 20 | 5 | .800 |
| 1978 | Gaylord Perry, San Diego | 21 | 6 | .778 |
| 1979 | Tom Seaver, Cincinnati | 16 | 6 | .727 |
| 1980 | Jim Bibby, Pittsburgh | 19 | 6 | .760 |
| 1981 | Tom Seaver, Cincinnati | 14 | 2 | .875 |
| 1982 | Phil Niekro, Atlanta | 17 | 4 | .810 |

**AMERICAN LEAGUE**

| Year | Pitcher and Club | Won | Lost | Per-cent |
|---|---|---|---|---|
| 1941 | Lefty Gomez, New York | 15 | 5 | .750 |
| 1942 | Ernie Bonham, New York | 21 | 5 | .808 |
| 1943 | Spud Chandler, New York | 20 | 4 | .833 |
| 1944 | Tex Hughson, Boston | 18 | 5 | .783 |
| 1945 | Hal Newhouser, Detroit | 25 | 9 | .735 |
| 1946 | Dave Ferriss, Boston | 25 | 6 | .806 |
| 1947 | Allie Reynolds, New York | 19 | 8 | .704 |
| 1948 | Jack Kramer, Boston | 18 | 5 | .783 |
| 1949 | Ellis Kinder, Boston | 23 | 6 | .793 |
| 1950 | Vic Raschi, New York | 21 | 8 | .724 |
| 1951 | Bob Feller, Cleveland | 22 | 8 | .733 |
| 1952 | Bobby Shantz, Philadelphia | 24 | 7 | .774 |
| 1953 | Ed Lopat, New York | 16 | 4 | .800 |
| 1954 | Sandy Consuegra, Chicago | 16 | 3 | .842 |
| 1955 | Tommy Byrne, New York | 16 | 5 | .762 |
| 1956 | Whitey Ford, New York | 19 | 6 | .760 |
| 1957 | Dick Donovan, Chicago | 16 | 6 | .727 |
| | Tom Sturdivant, New York | 16 | 6 | .727 |
| 1958 | Bob Turley, New York | 21 | 7 | .750 |
| 1959 | Bob Shaw, Chicago | 18 | 6 | .750 |
| 1960 | Jim Perry, Cleveland | 18 | 10 | .643 |
| 1961 | Whitey Ford, New York | 25 | 4 | .862 |
| 1962 | Ray Herbert, Chicago | 20 | 9 | .690 |
| 1963 | Whitey Ford, New York | 24 | 7 | .774 |
| 1964 | Wally Bunker, Baltimore | 19 | 5 | .792 |
| 1965 | Jim Grant, Minnesota | 21 | 7 | .750 |
| 1966 | Sonny Seibert, Cleveland | 16 | 8 | .667 |
| 1967 | Joel Horlen, Chicago | 19 | 7 | .731 |
| 1968 | Denny McLain, Detroit | 31 | 6 | .836 |
| 1969 | Jim Palmer, Baltimore | 16 | 4 | .800 |
| 1970 | Mike Cuellar, Baltimore | 24 | 8 | .750 |
| 1971 | Dave McNally, Baltimore | 21 | 5 | .807 |
| 1972 | James Hunter, Oakland | 21 | 7 | .750 |
| 1973 | James Hunter, Oakland | 21 | 5 | .808 |
| 1974 | Mike Cuellar, Baltimore | 22 | 10 | .688 |
| 1975 | Roger Moret, Boston | 14 | 3 | .824 |
| 1976 | Wayne Garland, Baltimore | 20 | 7 | .741 |
| 1977 | Paul Splittorff, Kansas City | 16 | 6 | .727 |
| 1978 | Ron Guidry, New York | 25 | 3 | .893 |
| 1979 | Mike Caldwell, Milwaukee | 16 | 6 | .727 |
| 1980 | Steve Stone, Baltimore | 25 | 7 | .781 |
| 1981 | Pete Vuckovich, Milwaukee | 14 | 4 | .778 |
| 1982 | Pete Vuckovich, Milwaukee | 18 | 6 | .750 |
| | Jim Palmer, Baltimore | 15 | 5 | .750 |

## PITCHERS WITH LOWEST-EARNED-RUN AVERAGES

**NATIONAL LEAGUE**

| Year | Pitcher and Club | Innings Pitched | ERA |
|---|---|---|---|
| 1945 | Hank Borowy, Chicago | 122 | 2.14 |
| 1946 | Howie Pollet, St. Louis | 266 | 2.10 |
| 1947 | Warren Spahn, Boston | 290 | 2.33 |
| 1948 | Harry Brecheen, St. Louis | 233 | 2.24 |
| 1949 | Dave Koslo, New York | 212 | 2.50 |
| 1950 | Jim Hearn, St. Louis-New York | 134 | 2.49 |
| 1951 | Chet Nichols, Boston | 156 | 2.88 |
| 1952 | Hoyt Wilhelm, New York | 159 | 2.43 |
| 1953 | Warren Spahn, Milwaukee | 266 | 2.10 |
| 1954 | John Antonelli, New York | 259 | 2.29 |
| 1955 | Bob Friend, Pittsburgh | 200 | 2.84 |
| 1956 | Lew Burdette, Milwaukee | 256 | 2.71 |
| 1957 | John Podres, Brooklyn | 196 | 2.66 |
| 1958 | Stu Miller, San Francisco | 182 | 2.47 |
| 1959 | Sam Jones, San Francisco | 271 | 2.82 |
| 1960 | Mike McCormick, San Francisco | 253 | 2.70 |
| 1961 | Warren Spahn, Milwaukee | 263 | 3.01 |
| 1962 | Sandy Koufax, Los Angeles | 184 | 2.54 |
| 1963 | Sandy Koufax, Los Angeles | 311 | 1.88 |
| 1964 | Sandy Koufax, Los Angeles | 223 | 1.74 |
| 1965 | Sandy Koufax, Los Angeles | 336 | 2.04 |
| 1966 | Sandy Koufax, Los Angeles | 323 | 1.73 |
| 1967 | Phil Niekro, Atlanta | 207 | 1.87 |
| 1968 | Bob Gibson, St. Louis | 305 | 1.12 |
| 1969 | Juan Marichal, San Francisco | 300 | 2.10 |
| 1970 | Tom Seaver, New York | 291 | 2.81 |
| 1971 | Tom Seaver, New York | 286 | 1.76 |
| 1972 | Steve Carlton, Philadelphia | 346 | 1.98 |
| 1973 | Tom Seaver, New York | 290 | 2.08 |
| 1974 | Buzz Capra, Atlanta | 217 | 2.28 |
| 1975 | Randy Jones, San Diego | 288 | 2.24 |
| 1976 | John Denny, St. Louis | 207 | 2.52 |
| 1977 | John Candelaria, Pittsburgh | 231 | 2.34 |
| 1978 | Craig Swan, New York | 207 | 2.43 |
| 1979 | J. Rodney Richard, Houston | 292 | 2.71 |
| 1980 | Don Sutton, Los Angeles | 212 | 2.21 |
| 1981 | Nolan Ryan, Houston | 149 | 1.69 |
| 1982 | Steve Rogers, Montreal | 277 | 2.40 |

**AMERICAN LEAGUE**

| Year | Pitcher and Club | Innings Pitched | ERA |
|---|---|---|---|
| 1945 | Hal Newhouser, Detroit | 313 | 1.81 |
| 1946 | Hal Newhouser, Detroit | 293 | 1.94 |
| 1947 | Spud Chandler, New York | 128 | 2.46 |
| 1948 | Gene Bearden, Cleveland | 230 | 2.43 |
| 1949 | Mel Parnell, Boston | 295 | 2.78 |
| 1950 | Early Wynn, Cleveland | 214 | 3.20 |
| 1951 | Saul Rogovin, Detroit-Chicago | 217 | 2.78 |
| 1952 | Allie Reynolds, New York | 244 | 2.07 |
| 1953 | Eddie Lopat, New York | 178 | 2.43 |
| 1954 | Mike Garcia, Cleveland | 259 | 2.64 |
| 1955 | Billy Pierce, Chicago | 206 | 1.97 |
| 1956 | Whitey Ford, New York | 226 | 2.47 |
| 1957 | Bobby Shantz, New York | 173 | 2.45 |
| 1958 | Whitey Ford, New York | 219 | 2.01 |
| 1959 | Hoyt Wilhelm, Baltimore | 226 | 2.19 |
| 1960 | Frank Baumann, Chicago | 185 | 2.68 |
| 1961 | Dick Donovan, Washington | 169 | 2.40 |
| 1962 | Hank Aguirre, Detroit | 216 | 2.21 |
| 1963 | Gary Peters, Chicago | 243 | 2.33 |
| 1964 | Dean Chance, Los Angeles | 278 | 1.65 |
| 1965 | Sam McDowell, Cleveland | 273 | 2.18 |
| 1966 | Gary Peters, Chicago | 205 | 1.98 |
| 1967 | Joel Horlen, Chicago | 258 | 2.06 |
| 1968 | Luis Tiant, Cleveland | 258 | 1.60 |
| 1969 | Dick Bosman, Washington | 193 | 2.19 |
| 1970 | Diego Segui, Oakland | 162 | 2.56 |
| 1971 | Vida Blue, Oakland | 312 | 1.82 |
| 1972 | Luis Tiant, Boston | 179 | 1.91 |
| 1973 | Jim Palmer, Baltimore | 296 | 2.40 |
| 1974 | James Hunter, Oakland | 318 | 2.49 |
| 1975 | Jim Palmer, Baltimore | 323 | 2.09 |
| 1976 | Mark Fidrych, Detroit | 250 | 2.34 |
| 1977 | Frank Tanana, California | 241 | 2.54 |
| 1978 | Ron Guidry, New York | 274 | 1.74 |
| 1979 | Ron Guidry, New York | 236 | 2.78 |
| 1980 | Rudy May, New York | 175 | 2.47 |
| 1981 | Steve McCatty, Oakland | 185 | 2.33 |
| 1982 | Rick Sutcliffe, Cleveland | 216 | 2.96 |

## MOST NO-HITTERS IN A LIFETIME

5, Nolan Ryan, California (AL), 1973, 1973, 1974, 1975; Houston (NL), 1981
4, Sandy Koufax, Los Angeles (NL), 1962, 1963, 1964, 1965.
3, Cy Young, Boston (NL–AL), 1897, 1904, 1908.
3, Bob Feller, Cleveland (AL), 1940, 1946, 1951.
3, Jim Maloney, Cincinnati (NL), 1965 (2), 1969

## NO-HITTERS OF TEN OR MORE INNINGS

| Year | Pitcher | Clubs Playing | Score |
|---|---|---|---|
| 1884 | Samuel Kimber | Brooklyn–Toledo (AA) | 0–0 |
| 1906 | Harry McIntire | Brooklyn–Pittsburgh (NL) | 0–1 |
| 1908 | George Wiltse | New York–Philadelphia (NL) | 1–0 |
| 1917 | Fred Toney | Cincinnati–Chicago (NL) | 1–0 |
| 1959 | Harvey Haddix | Pittsburgh–Milwaukee (NL)* | 0–1 |
| 1965 | Jim Maloney | Cincinnati–New York (NL) | 0–1 |
| 1965 | Jim Maloney | Cincinnati–Chicago (NL) | 1–0 |

* Perfect game for 12 innings. Lost in 13th.

## PERFECT GAMES

| Year | Pitcher | Clubs Playing | Score |
|---|---|---|---|
| 1880 | John Richmond | Worcester–Cleveland (NL) | 1–0 |
| 1880 | John Ward | Providence–Buffalo (NL) | 5–0 |
| 1904 | Cy Young | Boston–Philadelphia (AL) | 3–0 |
| 1908 | Addie Joss | Cleveland–Chicago (AL) | 1–0 |
| 1917 | Ernie Shore* | Boston–Washington (AL) | 4–0 |
| 1922 | Charles Robertson | Chicago–Detroit (AL) | 2–0 |
| 1956 | Don Larsen† | New York (AL)–Brooklyn (NL) | 2–0 |
| 1964 | Jim Bunning | Philadelphia–New York (NL) | 6–0 |
| 1965 | Sandy Koufax | Los Angeles–Chicago (NL) | 1–0 |
| 1968 | Jim Hunter | Oakland–Minnesota (AL) | 4–0 |
| 1981 | Len Barker | Cleveland–Toronto (AL) | 3–0 |

* Babe Ruth, the starting pitcher, was ejected from the game by the umpire after walking the first batter. Ernie Shore relieved him, the base-runner was thrown out trying to steal second base, and Shore retired the next 26 batters to complete a perfect game. † The only World Series perfect game.

## CY YOUNG AWARD

| Year | Pitcher |
|---|---|
| **BOTH MAJOR LEAGUES** | |
| 1956 | Don Newcombe, Dodgers (NL) |
| 1957 | Warren Spahn, Boston (NL) |
| 1958 | Bob Turley, New York (AL) |
| 1959 | Early Wynn, Chicago (AL) |
| 1960 | Vernon Law, Pittsburgh (NL) |
| 1961 | Whitey Ford, New York (AL) |
| 1962 | Don Drysdale, Los Angeles (NL) |
| 1963 | Sandy Koufax, Los Angeles (NL) |
| 1964 | Dean Chance, Los Angeles (AL) |
| 1965 | Sandy Koufax, Los Angeles (NL) |
| 1966 | Sandy Koufax, Los Angeles (NL) |
| **NATIONAL LEAGUE** | |
| 1967 | Mike McCormick, San Francisco |
| 1968 | Bob Gibson, St. Louis |
| 1969 | Tom Seaver, New York |
| 1970 | Bob Gibson, St. Louis |
| 1971 | Ferguson Jenkins, Chicago |
| 1972 | Steve Carlton, Philadelphia |
| 1973 | Tom Seaver, New York |
| 1974 | Mike Marshall, Los Angeles |
| 1975 | Tom Seaver, New York |
| 1976 | Randy Jones, San Diego |
| 1977 | Steve Carlton, Philadelphia |
| 1978 | Gaylord Perry, San Diego |
| 1979 | Bruce Sutter, Chicago |
| 1980 | Steve Carlton, Philadelphia |
| 1981 | Fernando Valenzuela, Los Angeles |
| **AMERICAN LEAGUE** | |
| 1967 | Jim Lonborg, Boston |
| 1968 | Denny McLain, Detroit |
| 1969 | Denny McLain, Detroit<br>Mike Cuellar, Baltimore |
| 1970 | Jim Perry, Minnesota |
| 1971 | Vida Blue, Oakland |
| 1972 | Gaylord Perry, Cleveland |
| 1973 | Jim Palmer, Baltimore |
| 1974 | James Hunter, Oakland |
| 1975 | Jim Palmer, Baltimore |
| 1976 | Jim Palmer, Baltimore |
| 1977 | Sparky Lyle, New York |
| 1978 | Ron Guidry, New York |
| 1979 | Mike Flanagan, Baltimore |
| 1980 | Steve Stone, Baltimore |
| 1981 | Rollie Fingers, Milwaukee |

## MAJOR LEAGUE NO-HIT GAMES SINCE 1969

| Year | Pitcher | Clubs Playing | Score |
|---|---|---|---|
| 1969 | Bill Stoneman | Montreal–Philadelphia (NL) | 6–0 |
| 1969 | Jim Maloney | Cincinnati–Houston (NL) | 10–0 |
| 1969 | Don Wilson | Houston–Cincinnati (NL) | 4–0 |
| 1969 | Jim Palmer | Baltimore–Oakland (AL) | 8–0 |
| 1969 | Ken Holtzman | Chicago–Atlanta (NL) | 3–0 |
| 1969 | Bob Moose | Pittsburgh–New York (NL) | 4–0 |
| 1970 | Dock Ellis | Pittsburgh–San Diego (NL) | 2–0 |
| 1970 | Clyde Wright | California–Oakland (AL) | 4–0 |
| 1970 | Bill Singer | Los Angeles–Philadelphia (NL) | 5–0 |
| 1970 | Vida Blue | Oakland–Minnesota (AL) | 6–0 |
| 1971 | Ken Holtzman | Chicago–Cincinnati (NL) | 1–0 |
| 1971 | Rick Wise | Philadelphia–Cincinnati (NL) | 4–0 |
| 1971 | Bob Gibson | St. Louis–Pittsburgh (NL) | 11–0 |
| 1972 | Burt Hooton | Chicago–Philadelphia (NL) | 4–0 |
| 1972 | Milt Pappas | Chicago–San Diego (NL) | 8–0 |
| 1972 | Bill Stoneman | Montreal–New York (NL) | 7–0 |
| 1973 | Steve Busby | Kansas City–Detroit (AL) | 3–0 |
| 1973 | Nolan Ryan | California–Kansas City (AL) | 3–0 |
| 1973 | Nolan Ryan | California–Detroit (AL) | 6–0 |
| 1973 | Jim Bibby | Texas–Oakland (AL) | 6–0 |
| 1973 | Phil Niekro | Atlanta–San Diego (NL) | 9–0 |
| 1974 | Steve Busby | Kansas City–Milwaukee (AL) | 2–0 |
| 1974 | Dick Bosman | Cleveland–Oakland (AL) | 4–0 |
| 1974 | Nolan Ryan | California–Minnesota (AL) | 4–0 |
| 1975 | Nolan Ryan | California–Baltimore (AL) | 1–0 |
| 1975 | Ed Halicki | San Francisco–New York (NL) | 6–0 |
| 1975 | Vida Blue, Glenn Abbott, Paul Lindblad, Rollie Fingers | Oakland–California (AL) | 5–0 |
| 1976 | Larry Dierker | Houston–Montreal (NL) | 6–0 |
| 1976 | John Odom, Francisco Barrios | Chicago–California (AL) | 2–1 |
| 1976 | John Candelaria | Pittsburgh-Los Angeles (NL) | 2–0 |
| 1976 | John Montefusco | San Francisco–Atlanta (AL) | 9–0 |
| 1977 | Jim Colborn | Kansas City–Texas (AL) | 6–0 |
| 1977 | Dennis Eckersley | Cleveland–California (AL) | 1–0 |
| 1977 | Bert Blyleven | Texas–California (AL) | 6–0 |
| 1978 | Bob Forsch | St. Louis–Philadelphia (NL) | 5–0 |
| 1978 | Tom Seaver | Cincinnati–St. Louis (NL) | 4–0 |
| 1979 | Ken Forsch | Houston–Atlanta (NL) | 6–0 |
| 1980 | Jerry Reuss | Los Angeles–San Francisco (NL) | 8–0 |
| 1981 | Charlie Lea | Montreal-San Francisco (NL) | 4–0 |
| 1981 | Len Barker | Cleveland–Toronto (AL) | 3–0 |
| 1981 | Nolan Ryan | Houston–Los Angeles (NL) | 5–0 |

## LONGEST GAMES IN THE MAJOR LEAGUES

| Innings | Teams | Date |
|---|---|---|
| 26 | Brooklyn 1, Boston 1, NL | May 1, 1920 |
| 25 | St. Louis 4, New York 3, NL | Sept. 11, 1974 |
| 24 | Philadelphia 4, Boston 1, AL | Sept. 1, 1906 |
| 24 | Detroit 1, Philadelphia 1, AL | July 21, 1945 |
| 24 | Houston 1, New York 0, NL | April 15, 1968 |
| 23 | Brooklyn 2, Boston 2, NL | June 27, 1939 |
| 23 | San Francisco 8, New York 6, NL | May 31, 1964 |

## MOST-VALUABLE-PLAYER AWARD Source: Baseball Writers' Association of America

### NATIONAL LEAGUE

| Year | Player | Club |
|---|---|---|
| 1935 | Gabby Hartnett | Chicago |
| 1936 | Carl Hubbell | New York |
| 1937 | Joe Medwick | St. Louis |
| 1938 | Ernie Lombardi | Cincinnati |
| 1939 | Bucky Walters | Cincinnati |
| 1940 | Frank McCormick | Cincinnati |
| 1941 | Dolph Camilli | Brooklyn |
| 1942 | Mort Cooper | St. Louis |
| 1943 | Stan Musial | St. Louis |
| 1944 | Marty Marion | St. Louis |
| 1945 | Phil Cavarretta | Chicago |
| 1946 | Stan Musial | St. Louis |
| 1947 | Bob Elliott | Boston |
| 1948 | Stan Musial | St. Louis |
| 1949 | Jackie Robinson | Brooklyn |
| 1950 | Jim Konstanty | Philadelphia |
| 1951 | Roy Campanella | Brooklyn |
| 1952 | Hank Sauer | Chicago |
| 1953 | Roy Campanella | Brooklyn |
| 1954 | Willie Mays | New York |
| 1955 | Roy Campanella | Brooklyn |
| 1956 | Don Newcombe | Brooklyn |
| 1957 | Hank Aaron | Milwaukee |
| 1958 | Ernie Banks | Chicago |
| 1959 | Ernie Banks | Chicago |
| 1960 | Dick Groat | Pittsburgh |
| 1961 | Frank Robinson | Cincinnati |
| 1962 | Maury Wills | Los Angeles |
| 1963 | Sandy Koufax | Los Angeles |
| 1964 | Ken Boyer | St. Louis |
| 1965 | Willie Mays | San Francisco |
| 1966 | Roberto Clemente | Pittsburgh |
| 1967 | Orlando Cepeda | St. Louis |
| 1968 | Bob Gibson | St. Louis |
| 1969 | Willie McCovey | San Francisco |
| 1970 | Johnny Bench | Cincinnati |
| 1971 | Joe Torre | St. Louis |
| 1972 | Johnny Bench | Cincinnati |
| 1973 | Pete Rose | Cincinnati |
| 1974 | Steve Garvey | Los Angeles |
| 1975 | Joe Morgan | Cincinnati |
| 1976 | Joe Morgan | Cincinnati |
| 1977 | George Foster | Cincinnati |
| 1978 | Dave Parker | Pittsburgh |
| 1979 | Willie Stargell | Pittsburgh |
| | Keith Hernandez | St. Louis |
| 1980 | Mike Schmidt | Philadelphia |
| 1981 | Mike Schmidt | Philadelphia |

### AMERICAN LEAGUE

| Year | Player | Club |
|---|---|---|
| 1935 | Hank Greenberg | Detroit |
| 1936 | Lou Gehrig | New York |
| 1937 | Charley Gehringer | Detroit |
| 1938 | Jimmy Foxx | Boston |
| 1939 | Joe DiMaggio | New York |
| 1940 | Hank Greenberg | Detroit |
| 1941 | Joe DiMaggio | New York |
| 1942 | Joe Gordon | New York |
| 1943 | Spud Chandler | New York |
| 1944 | Hal Newhouser | Detroit |
| 1945 | Hal Newhouser | Detroit |
| 1946 | Ted Williams | Boston |
| 1947 | Joe DiMaggio | New York |
| 1948 | Lou Boudreau | Cleveland |
| 1949 | Ted Williams | Boston |
| 1950 | Phil Rizzuto | New York |
| 1951 | Yogi Berra | New York |
| 1952 | Bobby Shantz | Philadelphia |
| 1953 | Al Rosen | Cleveland |
| 1954 | Yogi Berra | New York |
| 1955 | Yogi Berra | New York |
| 1956 | Mickey Mantle | New York |
| 1957 | Mickey Mantle | New York |
| 1958 | Jackie Jensen | Boston |
| 1959 | Nelson Fox | Chicago |
| 1960 | Roger Maris | New York |
| 1961 | Roger Maris | New York |
| 1962 | Mickey Mantle | New York |
| 1963 | Elston Howard | New York |
| 1964 | Brooks Robinson | Baltimore |
| 1965 | Zoilo Versalles | Minnesota |
| 1966 | Frank Robinson | Baltimore |
| 1967 | Carl Yastrzemski | Boston |
| 1968 | Denny McLain | Detroit |
| 1969 | Harmon Killebrew | Minnesota |
| 1970 | John (Boog) Powell | Baltimore |
| 1971 | Vida Blue | Oakland |
| 1972 | Dick Allen | Chicago |
| 1973 | Reggie Jackson | Oakland |
| 1974 | Jeff Burroughs | Texas |
| 1975 | Fred Lynn | Boston |
| 1976 | Thurman Munson | New York |
| 1977 | Rod Carew | Minnesota |
| 1978 | Jim Rice | Boston |
| 1979 | Don Baylor | California |
| 1980 | George Brett | Kansas City |
| 1981 | Rollie Fingers | Milwaukee |

## ROOKIE-OF-THE-YEAR AWARD

### NATIONAL LEAGUE

| Year | Player and Position | Club |
|---|---|---|
| 1949 | Don Newcombe, pitcher | Brooklyn |
| 1950 | Sam Jethroe, outfielder | Boston |
| 1951 | Willie Mays, outfielder | New York |
| 1952 | Joe Black, pitcher | Brooklyn |
| 1953 | Jim Gilliam, second baseman | Brooklyn |
| 1954 | Wally Moon, outfielder | St. Louis |
| 1955 | Bill Virdon, outfielder | St. Louis |
| 1956 | Frank Robinson, outfielder | Cincinnati |
| 1957 | Jack Sanford, pitcher | Philadelphia |
| 1958 | Orlando Cepeda, first baseman | San Francisco |
| 1959 | Willie McCovey, first baseman | San Francisco |
| 1960 | Frank Howard, outfielder | Los Angeles |
| 1961 | Billy Williams, outfielder | Chicago |
| 1962 | Ken Hubbs, second baseman | Chicago |
| 1963 | Pete Rose, second baseman | Cincinnati |
| 1964 | Richie Allen, third baseman | Philadelphia |
| 1965 | Jim Lefebvre, second baseman | Los Angeles |
| 1966 | Tommy Helms, third baseman | Cincinnati |
| 1967 | Tom Seaver, pitcher | New York |
| 1968 | Johnny Bench, catcher | Cincinnati |
| 1969 | Ted Sizemore, second baseman | Los Angeles |
| 1970 | Carl Morton, pitcher | Montreal |
| 1971 | Earl Williams, catcher | Atlanta |
| 1972 | Jon Matlack, pitcher | New York |
| 1973 | Gary Mathews, outfielder | San Francisco |
| 1974 | Bake McBride, outfielder | St. Louis |
| 1975 | John Montefusco, pitcher | San Francisco |
| 1976 | Pat Zachry, pitcher | Cincinnati |
| | Butch Metzger, pitcher | San Diego |
| 1977 | Andre Dawson, outfielder | Montreal |
| 1978 | Bob Horner, third baseman | Atlanta |
| 1979 | Rick Sutcliffe, pitcher | Los Angeles |
| 1980 | Steve Howe, pitcher | Los Angeles |
| 1981 | Fernando Valenzuela, pitcher | Los Angeles |

### AMERICAN LEAGUE

| Year | Player and Position | Club |
|---|---|---|
| 1949 | Roy Sievers, outfielder | St. Louis |
| 1950 | Walt Dropo, first baseman | Boston |
| 1951 | Gil McDougald, third baseman | New York |
| 1952 | Harry Byrd, pitcher | Philadelphia |
| 1953 | Harvey Kuenn, shortstop | Detroit |
| 1954 | Bob Grim, pitcher | New York |
| 1955 | Herb Score, pitcher | Cleveland |
| 1956 | Luis Aparicio, shortstop | Chicago |
| 1957 | Tony Kubek, infielder-outfielder | New York |
| 1958 | Albie Pearson, outfielder | Washington |
| 1959 | Bob Allison, outfielder | Washington |
| 1960 | Ron Hansen, shortstop | Baltimore |
| 1961 | Don Schwall, pitcher | Boston |
| 1962 | Tom Tresh, infielder-outfielder | New York |
| 1963 | Gary Peters, pitcher | Chicago |
| 1964 | Tony Oliva, outfielder | Minnesota |
| 1965 | Curt Blefary, outfielder | Baltimore |
| 1966 | Tommie Agee, outfielder | Chicago |
| 1967 | Rod Carew, second baseman | Minnesota |
| 1968 | Stan Bahnsen, pitcher | New York |
| 1969 | Lou Piniella, outfielder | Kansas City |
| 1970 | Thurman Munson, catcher | New York |
| 1971 | Chris Chambliss, infielder | Cleveland |
| 1972 | Carlton Fisk, catcher | Boston |
| 1973 | Al Bumbry, outfielder | Baltimore |
| 1974 | Mike Hargrove, first baseman | Texas |
| 1975 | Fred Lynn, outfielder | Boston |
| 1976 | Mark Fidrych, pitcher | Detroit |
| 1977 | Eddie Murray, first baseman | Baltimore |
| 1978 | Lou Whitaker, second baseman | Detroit |
| 1979 | John Castino, third baseman | Minnesota |
| | Alfredo Griffin, shortstop | Toronto |
| 1980 | Joe Charboneau, outfielder | Cleveland |
| 1981 | Dave Righetti, pitcher | New York |

## ROBERTO CLEMENTE AWARD

Ability, sportsmanship, character, community involvement, humanitarianism, contribution to team and baseball

| | | | | | |
|---|---|---|---|---|---|
| 1971 | Willie Mays, San Francisco | 1975 | Lou Brock, St. Louis | 1979 | Andre Thornton, Cleveland |
| 1972 | Brooks Robinson, Baltimore | 1976 | Pete Rose, Cincinnati | 1980 | Phil Niekro, Atlanta |
| 1973 | Al Kaline, Detroit | 1977 | Rod Carew, Minnesota | 1981 | Steve Garvey, Los Angeles |
| 1974 | Willie Stargell, Pittsburgh | 1978 | Greg Luzinski, Philadelphia | 1982 | Ken Singleton, Baltimore |

## BASEBALL STADIUMS

### AMERICAN LEAGUE

| | | Field Distances | | | Wall Heights | | |
|---|---|---|---|---|---|---|---|
| | Seating | LF | CF | RF | LF | CF | RF |
| Baltimore (Memorial Stadium) | 52,860 | 309′ | 405′ | 309′ | 14′ | 7′ | 14′ |
| Boston (Fenway Park) | 33,538 | 315′ | 390′ | 302′ | 37′ | 17′ | 3–5′ |
| California (Anaheim Stadium) | 67,335 | 333′ | 404′ | 370′ | 8′ | 8′ | 8′ |
| Chicago (Comiskey Park) | 44,492 | 352′ | 445′ | 352′ | 9′ | 17′ | 9′ |
| Cleveland (Municipal Stadium) | 76,713 | 320′ | 400′ | 320′ | 9′ | 8′ | 9′ |
| Detroit (Tiger Stadium) | 52,687 | 340′ | 440′ | 325′ | 9′ | 9′ | 9′ |
| Kansas City (Royals Stadium) | 40,760 | 330′ | 410′ | 330′ | 12′ | 12′ | 12′ |
| Milwaukee (County Stadium) | 54,192 | 320′ | 402′ | 315′ | 10′ | 10′ | 10′ |
| Minnesota (Metrodome) | 54,711 | 344′ | 407′ | 327′ | 7′ | 7′ | 7′ |
| New York (Yankee Stadium) | 57,545 | 312′ | 417′ | 310′ | 8′ | 7′ | 10′ |
| Oakland (Oakland Coliseum) | 50,000 | 330′ | 400′ | 330′ | 8′ | 8′ | 8′ |
| Seattle (Kingdome) | 59,438 | 316′ | 410′ | 316′ | 11½′ | 11½′ | 11½′ |
| Texas (Arlington Stadium) | 41,097 | 330′ | 400′ | 330′ | 11′ | 11′ | 11′ |
| Toronto (Exhibition Stadium) | 43,737 | 330′ | 400′ | 330′ | 12′ | 12′ | 12′ |

### NATIONAL LEAGUE

| | | Field Distances | | | Wall Heights | | |
|---|---|---|---|---|---|---|---|
| | Seating | LF | CF | RF | LF | CF | RF |
| Atlanta (Atlanta Stadium) | 52,194 | 330′ | 402′ | 330′ | 6′ | 6′ | 6′ |
| Chicago (Wrigley Field) | 37,741 | 355′ | 400′ | 353′ | 11½′ | 11½′ | 11½′ |
| Cincinnati (Riverfront Stadium) | 52,392 | 330′ | 404′ | 330′ | 12′ | 12′ | 12′ |
| Houston (Astrodome) | 45,000 | 340′ | 406′ | 340′ | 10′ | 10′ | 10′ |
| Los Angeles (Dodger Stadium) | 56,000 | 330′ | 395′ | 330′ | 8′ | 8′ | 8′ |
| Montreal (Olympic Stadium) | 59,984 | 325′ | 404′ | 325′ | 12′ | 12′ | 12′ |
| New York (Shea Stadium) | 55,300 | 341′ | 410′ | 341′ | 8′ | 8′ | 8′ |
| Philadelphia (Veterans Stadium) | 65,454 | 330′ | 408′ | 330′ | 12′ | 12′ | 12′ |
| Pittsburgh (Three Rivers Stadium) | 54,499 | 335′ | 400′ | 335′ | 10′ | 10′ | 10′ |
| San Diego (San Diego Stadium) | 51,362 | 330′ | 420′ | 330′ | 17′ | 17′ | 17′ |
| San Francisco (Candlestick Park) | 58,000 | 335′ | 410′ | 335′ | 12′ | 12′ | 12′ |
| St. Louis (Busch Memorial Stadium) | 50,222 | 330′ | 414′ | 330′ | 10½′ | 10½′ | 10½′ |

## MINOR LEAGUE BASEBALL AFFILIATIONS: 1982

| American League | Class AAA | Class AA |
|---|---|---|
| Baltimore | Rochester (IL) | Charlotte (SL) |
| Boston | Pawtucket (IL) | Bristol (EL) |
| California | Spokane (PCL) | Holyoke (EL) |
| Chicago | Edmonton (PCL) | Glens Falls (EL) |
| Cleveland | Charleston (IL) | Chattanooga (SL) |
| Detroit | Evansville (AA) | Birmingham (SL) |
| Kansas City | Omaha (AA) | Jacksonville (SL) |
| Milwaukee | Vancouver (PCL) | El Paso (TL) |
| Minnesota | Toledo (IL) | Orlando (SL) |
| New York | Columbus (IL) | Nashville (SL) |
| Oakland | Tacoma (PCL) | West Haven (EL) |
| Seattle | Salt Lake City (PCL) | Lynn (EL) |
| Texas | Denver (AA) | Tulsa (TL) |
| Toronto | Syracuse (IL) | Knoxville (SL) |

| National League | Class AAA | Class AA |
|---|---|---|
| Atlanta | Richmond (IL) | Savannah (SL) |
| Chicago | Iowa (AA) | Midland (TL) |
| Cincinnati | Indianapolis (AA) | Waterbury (EL) |
| Houston | Tucson (PCL) | Columbus (SL) |
| Los Angeles | Albuquerque (PCL) | San Antonio (TL) |
| Montreal | Wichita (AA) | Memphis (SL) |
| New York | Tidewater (IL) | Jackson (TL) |
| Philadelphia | Oklahoma City (AA) | Reading (EL) |
| Pittsburgh | Portland (PCL) | Buffalo (EL) |
| St. Louis | Louisville (AA) | Arkansas (TL) |
| San Diego | Hawaii (PCL) | Amarillo (TL) |
| San Francisco | Phoenix (PCL) | Shreveport (TL) |

(AA) American Association, (IL) International League, (PCL) Pacific Coast League, (EL) Eastern League, (SL) Southern League, (TL) Texas League.

## COLLEGE BASEBALL CHAMPIONS

| | NCAA DIV. I | NCAA DIV. II | NCAA DIV. III | N.A.I.A. | JR. COLLEGES |
|---|---|---|---|---|---|
| 1974 | So. California | Calif.-Irvine | — | Lewis (Ill.) | Ranger (Tex.) |
| 1975 | Texas | Florida Southern | — | Lewis (Ill.) | Meramec (Mo.) |
| 1976 | Arizona | Cal. Poly-Pomona | Stanislaus St. | Lewis (Ill.) | Central Arizona |
| 1977 | Arizona State | Calif.-Riverside | Stanislaus St. | Lipscomb (Tenn.) | Yavapai (Ariz.) |
| 1978 | So. California | Florida Southern | Glassboro St. | Emporia St. | Ranger (Tex.) |
| 1979 | Cal. St.-Fullerton | Valdosta State | Glassboro St. | Lipscomb (Tenn.) | Middle Georgia |
| 1980 | Arizona | Cal. Poly-Pomona | Ithaca | Grand Canyon | Middle Georgia |
| 1981 | Arizona State | Florida Southern | Marietta | Grand Canyon | Miami-Dade |
| 1982 | Miami (Fla.) | Cal.-Riverside | E. Connecticut St. | Grand Canyon | Middle Georgia |

# BASKETBALL

## NATIONAL BASKETBALL ASSOCIATION (NBA)

Olympic Tower, 645 5th Ave., New York City 10022. Commissioner: Lawrence F. O'Brien.

### EASTERN CONFERENCE

| Atlantic Division | Governor | Coach |
|---|---|---|
| Boston Celtics | Harry Mangurian | Bill Fitch |
| New York Knicks | Michael Burke | Hubie Brown |
| New Jersey Nets | Alan Cohen | Larry Brown |
| Philadelphia 76ers | F. Eugene Dixon | Billy Cunningham |
| Washington Bullets | Abe Pollin | Gene Shue |

| Central Division | Governor | Coach |
|---|---|---|
| Atlanta Hawks | Mike Gearon | Kevin Loughery |
| Chicago Bulls | William Wirtz | Paul Westhead |
| Cleveland Cavaliers | Ted Stepien | Bill Musselman |
| Detroit Pistons | William Davidson | Scotty Robertson |
| Indiana Pacers | Sam Nassi | Jack McKinney |
| Milwaukee Bucks | James Fitzgerald | Don Nelson |

### WESTERN CONFERENCE

| Midwest Division | Governor | Coach |
|---|---|---|
| Dallas Mavericks | Donald Carter | Dick Motta |
| Denver Nuggets | Carl Scheer | Donnie Walsh |
| Houston Rockets | Ray Patterson | Del Harris |
| Kansas City Kings | Paul Rosenberg | Cotton Fitzsimmons |
| San Antonio Spurs | Angelo Drossos | Stan Albeck |
| Utah Jazz | Sam Battistone | Frank Leyden |

| Pacific Division | Governor | Coach |
|---|---|---|
| Golden State Warriors | Franklin Mieuli | Al Attles |
| Los Angeles Lakers | Jerry Buss | Pat Riley |
| Phoenix Suns | Richard Bloch | John MacLeod |
| Portland Trail Blazers | Lawrence Weinberg | Jack Ramsay |
| San Diego Clippers | Irving Levin | Paul Silas |
| Seattle SuperSonics | Samuel Schulman | Lenny Wilkens |

## THE NBA CHAMPIONS

| Season | Eastern Conference (W–L) | Western Conference (W–L) | Playoff Champions (W–L) |
|---|---|---|---|
| 1958/59 | Boston Celtics (52–20) | St. Louis Hawks (49–23) | Boston Celtics (4–0) over Minneapolis |
| 1959/60 | Boston Celtics (59–16) | St. Louis Hawks (46–29) | Boston Celtics (4–3) over St. Louis |
| 1960/61 | Boston Celtics (57–22) | St. Louis Hawks (51–28) | Boston Celtics (4–1) over St. Louis |
| 1961/62 | Boston Celtics (60–20) | Los Angeles Lakers (54–26) | Boston Celtics (4–3) over Los Angeles |
| 1962/63 | Boston Celtics (58–22) | Los Angeles Lakers (53–27) | Boston Celtics (4–2) over Los Angeles |
| 1963/64 | Boston Celtics (59–21) | San Francisco Warriors (48–32) | Boston Celtics (4–1) over San Francisco |
| 1964/65 | Boston Celtics (62–18) | Los Angeles Lakers (49–31) | Boston Celtics (4–1) over Los Angeles |
| 1965/66 | Philadelphia 76ers (55–25) | Los Angeles Lakers (45–35) | Boston Celtics (4–3) over Los Angeles |
| 1966/67 | Philadelphia 76ers (68–13) | San Francisco Warriors (44–37) | Philadelphia 76ers (4–2) over San Francisco |
| 1967/68 | Philadelphia 76ers (62–20) | St. Louis Hawks (56–26) | Boston Celtics (4–2) over Los Angeles |
| 1968/69 | Baltimore Bullets (57–25) | Los Angeles Lakers (55–27) | Boston Celtics (4–3) over Los Angeles |
| 1969/70 | New York Knickerbockers (60–22) | Los Angeles Lakers (46–36) | New York Knicks (4–3) over Los Angeles |
| 1970/71 | Baltimore Bullets (42–40) | Milwaukee Bucks (66–16) | Milwaukee Bucks (4–0) over Baltimore |
| 1971/72 | New York Knickerbockers (48–34) | Los Angeles Lakers (69–13) | Los Angeles Lakers (4–1) over New York |
| 1972/73 | New York Knickerbockers (57–25) | Los Angeles Lakers (60–22) | New York (4–1) over Los Angeles |
| 1973/74 | Boston Celtics (56–26) | Milwaukee Bucks (59–23) | Boston (4–3) over Milwaukee |
| 1974/75 | Washington Bullets (60–22) | Golden State Warriors (48–34) | Golden State (4–0) over Washington |
| 1975/76 | Boston Celtics ([illegible]–28) | Phoenix Suns (42–40) | Boston Celtics (4–2) over Phoenix |
| 1976/77 | Philadelphia 76ers (50–32) | Los Angeles Lakers (53–29) | Portland Trail Blazers (4–2) over Phila. |
| 1977/78 | Philadelphia 76ers (55–27) | Portland Trail Blazers (58–24) | Washington Bullets (4–3) over Seattle |
| 1978/79 | Washington Bullets (54–28) | Seattle SuperSonics (52–30) | Seattle (4–1) over Washington |
| 1979/80 | Boston Celtics (61–21) | Los Angeles Lakers (60–22) | Los Angeles (4–2) over Philadelphia |
| 1980/81 | Boston Celtics (62-20) | Phoenix Suns (57-25) | Boston (4-2) over Houston |
| 1981/82 | Boston Celtics (63-19) | Los Angeles Lakers (57-25) | Los Angeles (4-2) over Philadelphia |

### TOP NBA SCORERS

| Season | Player and Team | Points | Game Avg. |
|---|---|---|---|
| 1958/59 | Bob Pettit, St. Louis | 2,105 | 29.2 |
| 1959/60 | Wilt Chamberlain, Philadelphia | 2,707 | 37.6 |
| 1960/61 | Wilt Chamberlain, Philadelphia | 3,033 | 38.4 |
| 1961/62 | Wilt Chamberlain, Philadelphia | 4,029 | 50.4 |
| 1962/63 | Wilt Chamberlain, San Francisco | 3,586 | 44.8 |
| 1963/64 | Wilt Chamberlain, San Francisco | 2,948 | 36.5 |
| 1964/65 | Wilt Chamberlain, Philadelphia | 2,534 | 34.7 |
| 1965/66 | Wilt Chamberlain, Philadelphia | 2,649 | 33.5 |
| 1966/67 | Rick Barry, San Francisco | 2,775 | 35.6 |
| 1967/68 | Dave Bing, Detroit | 2,142 | 27.1 |
| 1968/69 | Elvin Hayes, San Diego | 2,327 | 28.4 |
| 1969/70 | Jerry West, Los Angeles | 2,309 | 31.2 |
| 1970/71 | Lew Alcindor, Milwaukee | 2,596 | 31.7 |
| 1971/72 | Kareem Abdul-Jabbar, Milwaukee | 2,822 | 34.8 |
| 1972/73 | Nate Archibald, Kansas City-Omaha | 2,719 | 34.0 |
| 1973/74 | Bob McAdoo, Buffalo | 2,261 | 30.6 |
| 1974/75 | Bob McAdoo, Buffalo | 2,831 | 34.5 |
| 1975/76 | Bob McAdoo, Buffalo | 2,427 | 31.1 |
| 1976/77 | Pete Maravich, New Orleans | 2,273 | 31.1 |
| 1977/78 | George Gervin, San Antonio | 2,232 | 27.2 |
| 1978/79 | George Gervin, San Antonio | 2,365 | 29.6 |
| 1979/80 | George Gervin, San Antonio | 2,585 | 33.1 |
| 1980/81 | Adrian Dantley, Utah | 2,452 | 30.7 |
| 1981/82 | George Gervin, San Antonio | 2,551 | 32.3 |

### TOP NBA FIELD GOAL PERCENTAGE

| Season | Pct. | Player and Team |
|---|---|---|
| 1958/59 | .490 | Ken Sears, New York |
| 1959/60 | .477 | Ken Sears, New York |
| 1960/61 | .509 | Wilt Chamberlain, Philadelphia |
| 1961/62 | .519 | Walt Bellamy, Chicago |
| 1962/63 | .528 | Wilt Chamberlain, San Francisco |
| 1963/64 | .527 | Jerry Lucas, Cincinnati |
| 1964/65 | .510 | Wilt Chamberlain, Philadelphia |
| 1965/66 | .540 | Wilt Chamberlain, Philadelphia |
| 1966/67 | .683 | Wilt Chamberlain, Philadelphia |
| 1967/68 | .595 | Wilt Chamberlain, Philadelphia |
| 1968/69 | .583 | Wilt Chamberlain, Los Angeles |
| 1969/70 | .559 | Johnny Green, Cincinnati |
| 1970/71 | .587 | Johnny Green, Cincinnati |
| 1971/72 | .649 | Wilt Chamberlain, Los Angeles |
| 1972/73 | .727 | Wilt Chamberlain, Los Angeles |
| 1973/74 | .547 | Bob McAdoo, Buffalo |
| 1974/75 | .539 | Don Nelson, Boston |
| 1975/76 | .561 | Wes Unseld, Washington |
| 1976/77 | .579 | Kareem Abdul-Jabbar, Los Angeles |
| 1977/78 | .578 | Bobby Jones, Denver |
| 1978/79 | .584 | Cedric Maxwell, Boston |
| 1979/80 | .609 | Cedric Maxwell, Boston |
| 1980/81 | .670 | Artis Gilmore, Chicago |
| 1981/82 | .652 | Artis Gilmore, Chicago |

### TOP NBA FREE THROW PERCENTAGE

| Season | Pct. | Player and Team |
|---|---|---|
| 1958/59 | .932 | Bill Sharman, Boston |
| 1959/60 | .892 | Dolph Schayes, Syracuse |
| 1960/61 | .921 | Dolph Schayes, Syracuse |
| 1961/62 | .896 | Bill Sharman, Boston |
| 1962/63 | .881 | Larry Costello, Syracuse |
| 1963/64 | .853 | Oscar Robertson, Cincinnati |
| 1964/65 | .877 | Larry Costello, Philadelphia |
| 1965/66 | .881 | Larry Siegfried, Boston |
| 1966/67 | .903 | Adrian Smith, Cincinnati |
| 1967/68 | .873 | Oscar Robertson, Cincinnati |
| 1968/69 | .864 | Larry Siegfried, Boston |
| 1969/70 | .898 | Flynn Robinson, Milwaukee |
| 1970/71 | .859 | Chet Walker, Chicago |
| 1971/72 | .894 | Jack Marin, Baltimore |
| 1972/73 | .902 | Rick Barry, Golden State |
| 1973/74 | .902 | Ernie DiGregorio, Buffalo |
| 1974/75 | .904 | Rick Barry, Golden State |
| 1975/76 | .923 | Rick Barry, Golden State |
| 1976/77 | .945 | Ernie DiGregorio, Buffalo |
| 1977/78 | .924 | Rick Barry, Golden State |
| 1978/79 | .947 | Rick Barry, Houston |
| 1979/80 | .935 | Rick Barry, Houston |
| 1980/81 | .958 | Calvin Murphy, Houston |
| 1981/82 | .899 | Kyle Macy, Phoenix |

### NBA REBOUND LEADERS

| Season | Rebs. | Player and Team |
|---|---|---|
| 1958/59 | 1612 | Bill Russell, Boston |
| 1959/60 | 1941 | Wilt Chamberlain, Philadelphia |
| 1960/61 | 2149 | Wilt Chamberlain, Philadelphia |
| 1961/62 | 2052 | Wilt Chamberlain, Philadelphia |
| 1962/63 | 1946 | Wilt Chamberlain, San Francisco |
| 1963/64 | 1930 | Bill Russell, Boston |
| 1964/65 | 1878 | Bill Russell, Boston |
| 1965/66 | 1943 | Wilt Chamberlain, Philadelphia |
| 1966/67 | 1957 | Wilt Chamberlain. Philadelphia |
| 1967/68 | 1952 | Wilt Chamberlain, Philadelphia |
| 1968/69 | 1712 | Wilt Chamberlain, Los Angeles |
| 1969/70 | 1386 | Elvin Hayes, San Diego |
| 1970/71 | 1493 | Wilt Chamberlain, Los Angeles |
| 1971/72 | 1572 | Wilt Chamberlain, Los Angeles |
| 1972/73 | 1526 | Wilt Chamberlain, Los Angeles |
| 1973/74 | 1463 | Elvin Hayes, Capital |
| 1974/75 | 1077 | Wes Unseld, Washington |
| 1975/76 | 1383 | Kareem Abdul-Jabbar, Los Angeles |
| 1976/77 | 1090 | Kareem Abdul-Jabbar, Los Angeles |
| 1977/78 | 1288 | Truck Robinson, New Orleans |
| 1978/79 | 1444 | Moses Malone, Houston |
| 1979/80 | 1216 | Swen Nater, San Diego |
| 1980/81 | 1180 | Moses Malone, Houston |
| 1981/82 | 1188 | Moses Malone, Houston |

### NBA ASSIST LEADERS

| Season | Asst. | Player and Team |
|---|---|---|
| 1958/59 | 557 | Bob Cousy, Boston |
| 1959/60 | 715 | Bob Cousy, Boston |
| 1960/61 | 690 | Oscar Robertson, Cincinnati |
| 1961/62 | 899 | Oscar Robertson, Cincinnati |
| 1962/63 | 825 | Guy Rodgers, San Francisco |
| 1963/64 | 868 | Oscar Robertson, Cincinnati |
| 1964/65 | 861 | Oscar Robertson, Cincinnati |
| 1965/66 | 847 | Oscar Robertson, Cincinnati |
| 1966/67 | 908 | Guy Rodgers, Chicago |
| 1967/68 | 702 | Wilt Chamberlain, Philadelphia |
| 1968/69 | 772 | Oscar Robertson, Cincinnati |
| 1969/70 | 683 | Len Wilkens, Seattle |
| 1970/71 | 832 | Norm Van Lier, Cincinnati |
| 1971/72 | 747 | Jerry West, Los Angeles |
| 1972/73 | 910 | Nate Archibald, Kansas City-Omaha |
| 1973/74 | 663 | Ernie DiGregorio, Buffalo |
| 1974/75 | 650 | Kevin Porter, Washington |
| 1975/76 | 661 | Don Watts, Seattle |
| 1976/77 | 685 | Don Buse, Indiana |
| 1977/78 | 837 | Kevin Porter, New Jersey |
| 1978/79 | 1099 | Kevin Porter, Detroit |
| 1979/80 | 832 | Mike Richardson, New York |
| 1980/81 | 734 | Kevin Porter, Washington |
| 1981/82 | 762 | Johnny Moore, San Antonio |

## NBA FINAL STANDINGS: 1981-82

EASTERN CONFERENCE

| ATLANTIC DIVISION | Won | Lost | Pct. | G.B. |
|---|---|---|---|---|
| Boston Celtics | 63 | 19 | .768 | — |
| Philadelphia 76ers | 58 | 24 | .707 | 5 |
| New Jersey Nets | 44 | 38 | .537 | 19 |
| Washington Bullets | 43 | 39 | .524 | 20 |
| New York Knicks | 33 | 49 | .402 | 30 |

| CENTRAL DIVISION | Won | Lost | Pct. | G.B. |
|---|---|---|---|---|
| Milwaukee Bucks | 55 | 27 | .671 | — |
| Atlanta Hawks | 42 | 40 | .512 | 13 |
| Detroit Pistons | 39 | 43 | .476 | 16 |
| Indiana Pacers | 35 | 47 | .427 | 20 |
| Chicago Bulls | 34 | 48 | .415 | 21 |
| Cleveland Cavaliers | 15 | 67 | .183 | 40 |

WESTERN CONFERENCE

| MIDWEST DIVISION | Won | Lost | Pct. | G.B. |
|---|---|---|---|---|
| San Antonio Spurs | 48 | 34 | .585 | — |
| Denver Nuggets | 46 | 36 | .561 | 2 |
| Houston Rockets | 46 | 36 | .561 | 2 |
| Kansas City Kings | 30 | 52 | .366 | 18 |
| Dallas Mavericks | 28 | 54 | .341 | 20 |
| Utah Jazz | 25 | 57 | .305 | 23 |

| PACIFIC DIVISION | Won | Lost | Pct. | G.B. |
|---|---|---|---|---|
| Los Angeles Lakers | 57 | 25 | .695 | — |
| Seattle SuperSonics | 52 | 30 | .634 | 5 |
| Phoenix Suns | 46 | 36 | .561 | 11 |
| Golden State Warriors | 45 | 37 | .549 | 12 |
| Portland Trail Blazers | 42 | 40 | .512 | 15 |
| San Diego Clippers | 17 | 65 | .207 | 40 |

## NBA PLAYOFFS: 1982

EASTERN CONFERENCE

FIRST ROUND: Philadelphia over Atlanta (2-0)
Washington over New Jersey (2-0)
SEMIFINALS: Philadelphia over Milwaukee (4-2)
Boston over Washington (4-1)
FINALS; Philadelphia over Boston (4-3)

WESTERN CONFERENCE

FIRST ROUND: Seattle over Houston (2-1)
Phoenix over Denver (2-1)
SEMIFINALS: San Antonio over Seattle (4-1)
Los Angeles over Phoenix (4-0)
FINALS: Los Angeles over San Antonio (4-0)

CHAMPIONSHIP SERIES — Los Angeles 4 Philadelphia 2

Game 1 — Los Angeles 124, Philadelphia 117
Game 2 — Philadelphia 110, Los Angeles 94
Game 3 — Los Angeles 129, Philadelphia 108
Game 4 — Los Angeles 111, Philadelphia 101
Game 5 — Philadelphia 135, Los Angeles 102
Game 6 — Los Angeles 114, Philadelphia 104

## NBA PLAYOFFS: MOST VALUABLE PLAYERS

1975 — Rick Barry, Golden State
1976 — Jo Jo White, Boston
1977 — Bill Walton, Portland
1978 — Wes Unseld, Washington
1979 — Dennis Johnson, Seattle
1980 — Earvin Johnson, Los Angeles
1981 — Cedric Maxwell, Boston
1982 — Earvin Johnson, Los Angeles

## NBA INDIVIDUAL LEADERS: 1981-82

### SCORING

Minimum: 70 games played or 1400 points

| | Games | FG | FT | Pts. | Avg. |
|---|---|---|---|---|---|
| Gervin, San Ant. | 79 | 993 | 555 | 2551 | 32.3 |
| Malone, Houston | 81 | 945 | 630 | 2520 | 31.1 |
| Dantley, Utah | 81 | 904 | 648 | 2457 | 30.3 |
| English, Denver | 82 | 855 | 372 | 2082 | 25.4 |
| Erving, Phila. | 81 | 780 | 411 | 1974 | 24.4 |
| Abdul-Jabbar, L.A. | 76 | 753 | 312 | 1818 | 23.9 |
| Williams, Seattle | 80 | 773 | 320 | 1875 | 23.4 |
| King, Golden St. | 79 | 740 | 352 | 1833 | 23.2 |
| Free, Golden St. | 78 | 650 | 479 | 1789 | 22.9 |
| Bird, Boston | 77 | 711 | 328 | 1761 | 22.9 |
| Issel, Denver | 81 | 651 | 546 | 1852 | 22.9 |
| Long, Detroit | 69 | 637 | 238 | 1514 | 21.9 |
| Tripucka, Detroit | 82 | 636 | 495 | 1772 | 21.6 |
| Vandeweghe, Denver | 82 | 706 | 347 | 1760 | 21.5 |
| Vincent, Dallas | 81 | 719 | 293 | 1732 | 21.4 |
| Wilkes, L.A. | 82 | 744 | 246 | 1734 | 21.1 |
| Thompson, Portland | 79 | 681 | 280 | 1642 | 20.8 |
| Mitchell, San Ant. | 84 | 753 | 220 | 1726 | 20.5 |
| R. Williams, N.J. | 82 | 639 | 387 | 1674 | 20.4 |
| Parish, Boston | 80 | 669 | 252 | 1590 | 19.9 |

### FIELD GOAL PERCENTAGE

Minimum: 300 FG made

| | FG | Attempted | Pct. |
|---|---|---|---|
| Gilmore, Chicago | 546 | 837 | .652 |
| S. Johnson, Kansas City | 395 | 644 | .613 |
| B. Williams, New Jersey | 513 | 881 | .582 |
| Abdul-Jabbar, Los Angeles | 753 | 1301 | .579 |
| Natt, Portland | 515 | 894 | .576 |

### FREE THROW PERCENTAGE

Minimum: 125 FT made

| | FT | Attempted | Pct. |
|---|---|---|---|
| Macy, Phoenix | 152 | 169 | .899 |
| Criss, San Diego | 141 | 159 | .887 |
| Long, Detroit | 238 | 275 | .865 |
| Gervin, San Antonio | 555 | 642 | .864 |
| Bird, Boston | 328 | 380 | .863 |

### REBOUNDS

Minimum: 70 games or 800 rebounds

| | Games | Total | Avg. |
|---|---|---|---|
| Malone, Houston | 81 | 1188 | 14.7 |
| Sikma, Seattle | 82 | 1038 | 12.7 |
| B. Williams, New Jersey | 82 | 1005 | 12.3 |
| Thompson, Portland | 79 | 921 | 11.7 |
| Lucas, New York | 80 | 908 | 11.3 |

### ASSISTS

Minimum: 70 games or 400 assists

| | Games | Total | Avg. |
|---|---|---|---|
| Moore, San Antonio | 79 | 762 | 9.6 |
| E. Johnson, Los Angeles | 78 | 743 | 9.5 |
| Cheeks, Philadelphia | 79 | 667 | 8.4 |
| Archibald, Boston | 68 | 541 | 8.0 |
| Nixon, Los Angeles | 82 | 652 | 8.0 |

### STEALS

Minimum: 70 games or 125 steals

| | Games | Total | Avg. |
|---|---|---|---|
| E. Johnson, Los Angeles | 78 | 208 | 2.67 |
| Cheeks, Philadelphia | 79 | 209 | 2.65 |
| Richardson, New York | 82 | 213 | 2.60 |
| Buckner, Milwaukee | 70 | 174 | 2.49 |
| R. Williams, New Jersey | 82 | 199 | 2.43 |

### BLOCKED SHOTS

Minimum: 70 games or 100 blocked shots

| | Games | Total | Avg. |
|---|---|---|---|
| Johnson, San Antonio | 75 | 234 | 3.12 |
| Rollins, Atlanta | 79 | 224 | 2.84 |
| Abdul-Jabbar, Los Angeles | 76 | 207 | 2.72 |
| Gilmore, Chicago | 82 | 221 | 2.70 |
| Parish, Boston | 80 | 192 | 2.40 |

## NBA ALL-STAR TEAMS: 1981-82

### First Team

| Player, Club | Position |
|---|---|
| Julius Erving, Philadelphia | F |
| Larry Bird, Boston | F |
| Moses Malone, Houston | C |
| George Gervin, San Antonio | G |
| Gus Williams, Seattle | G |

### Second Team

| Player, Club | Position |
|---|---|
| Alex English, Denver | F |
| Bernard King, Golden State | F |
| Robert Parish, Boston | C |
| Earvin Johnson, Los Angeles | G |
| Sidney Moncrief, Milwaukee | G |

## NBA ALL-ROOKIE TEAM: 1981-82

### First Team

**Player, Club, Votes**

Kelly Tripucka, Detroit (22)
Jay Vincent, Dallas (22)
Isiah Thomas, Detroit (20)
Buck Williams, New Jersey (20)
Jeff Ruland, Washington (11)

### Others Receiving Votes

**Player, Club, Votes**

Tom Chambers, San Diego (10)
Mark Aguirre, Dallas — Frank Johnson, Washington — Elston Turner, Dallas (2)
Rolando Blackman, Dallas — Herb Williams, Indiana — Albert King, New Jersey — Darnell Valentine, Portland (1)

## NBA ROOKIE OF THE YEAR

| Year | Player |
|---|---|
| 1952–53 | Don Meineke, Fort Wayne |
| 1953–54 | Ray Felix, Baltimore |
| 1954–55 | Bob Pettit, Milwaukee |
| 1955–56 | Maurice Stokes, Rochester |
| 1956–57 | Tom Heinsohn, Boston |
| 1957–58 | Woody Sauldsberry, Philadelphia |
| 1958–59 | Elgin Baylor, Minneapolis |
| 1959–60 | Wilt Chamberlain, Philadelphia |
| 1960–61 | Oscar Robertson, Cincinnati |
| 1961–62 | Walt Bellamy, Chicago |
| 1962–63 | Terry Dischinger, Chicago |
| 1963–64 | Jerry Lucas, Cincinnati |
| 1964–65 | Willis Reed, New York |
| 1965–66 | Rick Barry, San Francisco |
| 1966–67 | Dave Bing, Detroit |
| 1967–68 | Earl Monroe, Baltimore |
| 1968–69 | Wes Unseld, Baltimore |
| 1969–70 | Lew Alcindor, Milwaukee |
| 1970–71 | Dave Cowens, Boston, and Geoff Petrie, Portland |
| 1971–72 | Sidney Wicks, Portland |
| 1972–73 | Bob McAdoo, Buffalo |
| 1973–74 | Ernie DiGregorio, Buffalo |
| 1974–75 | Keith Wilkes, Golden State |
| 1975–76 | Alvan Adams, Phoenix |
| 1976–77 | Adrian Dantley, Buffalo |
| 1977–78 | Walter Davis, Phoenix |
| 1978–79 | Phil Ford, Kansas City |
| 1979–80 | Larry Bird, Boston |
| 1980–81 | Darrell Griffith, Utah |
| 1981–82 | Buck Williams, New Jersey |

## NBA COACH OF THE YEAR

| Year | Coach, Team |
|---|---|
| 1963–64 | Alex Hannum, San Francisco |
| 1964–65 | Red Auerbach, Boston |
| 1965–66 | Dolph Schayes, Philadelphia |
| 1966–67 | Johnny Kerr, Chicago |
| 1967–68 | Richie Guerin, St. Louis |
| 1968–69 | Gene Shue, Baltimore |
| 1969–70 | Red Holzman, New York |
| 1970–71 | Dick Motta, Chicago |
| 1971–72 | Bill Sharman, Los Angeles |
| 1972–73 | Tom Heinsohn, Boston |
| 1973–74 | Ray Scott, Detroit |
| 1974–75 | Phil Johnson, Kansas City–Omaha |
| 1975–76 | Bill Fitch, Cleveland |
| 1976–77 | Tom Nissalke, Houston |
| 1977–78 | Hubie Brown, Atlanta |
| 1978–79 | Cotton Fitzsimmons, Kansas City |
| 1979–80 | Bill Fitch, Boston |
| 1980–81 | Jack McKinney, Indiana |
| 1981–82 | Gene Shue, Washington |

## NBA PODOLOFF TROPHY WINNERS (Most Valuable Player)

| Year | Player, Team |
|---|---|
| 1962–63 | Bill Russell, Boston |
| 1963–64 | Oscar Robertson, Cincinnati |
| 1964–65 | Bill Russell, Boston |
| 1965–66 | Wilt Chamberlain, Philadelphia |
| 1966–67 | Wilt Chamberlain, Philadelphia |
| 1967–68 | Wilt Chamberlain, Philadelphia |
| 1968–69 | Wes Unseld, Baltimore |
| 1969–70 | Willis Reed, New York |
| 1970–71 | Lew Alcindor, Milwaukee |
| 1971–72 | Kareem Abdul-Jabbar, Milwaukee |
| 1972–73 | Dave Cowens, Boston |
| 1973–74 | Kareem Abdul-Jabbar, Milwaukee |
| 1974–75 | Bob McAdoo, Buffalo |
| 1975–76 | Kareem Abdul-Jabbar, Los Angeles |
| 1976–77 | Kareem Abdul-Jabbar, Los Angeles |
| 1977–78 | Bill Walton, Portland |
| 1978–79 | Moses Malone, Houston |
| 1979–80 | Kareem Abdul-Jabbar, Los Angeles |
| 1980–81 | Julius Erving, Philadelphia |
| 1981–82 | Moses Malone, Houston |

## 1982 NBA FIRST ROUND COLLEGE DRAFT

| | Team | Player | College |
|---|---|---|---|
| 1. | Los Angeles | James Worthy | North Carolina |
| 2. | San Diego | Terry Cummings | DePaul |
| 3. | Utah | Dominique Wilkins | Georgia |
| 4. | Dallas | Bill Garnett | Wyoming |
| 5. | Kansas City | LaSalle Thompson | Texas |
| 6. | New York | Trent Tucker | Minnesota |
| 7. | Chicago | Quintin Dailey | San Francisco |
| 8. | Indiana | Clark Kellogg | Ohio State |
| 9. | Detroit | Cliff Levingston | Wichita State |
| 10. | Atlanta | Keith Edmonson | Purdue |
| 11. | Portland | Lafayette Lever | Arizona State |
| 12. | Cleveland | John Bagley | Boston College |
| 13. | New Jersey | Eric Floyd | Georgetown |
| 14. | Golden State | Lester Conner | Oregon State |
| 15. | Phoenix | David Thirdkill | Bradley |
| 16. | Houston | Terry Teagle | Baylor |
| 17. | Kansas City | Brook Steppe | Georgia Tech |
| 18. | Detroit | Ricky Pierce | Rice |
| 19. | Denver | Rob Williams | Houston |
| 20. | Milwaukee | Paul Pressey | Tulsa |
| 21. | New Jersey | Eddie Phillips | Alabama |
| 22. | Philadelphia | Mark McNamara | California |
| 23. | Boston | Darren Tillis | Cleveland State |

## BASKETBALL HALL OF FAME Springfield, Massachusetts

| Player | Year Elected |
|---|---|
| Paul Arizin | 1977 |
| Thomas Barlow | 1981 |
| Elgin Baylor | 1976 |
| John Beckman | 1972 |
| Bennie Borgmann | 1961 |
| Joseph Brennan | 1974 |
| Wilt Chamberlain | 1979 |
| Charles (Tarzan) Cooper | 1976 |
| Bob Cousy | 1970 |
| Bob Davies | 1969 |
| Forrest DeBernardi | 1961 |
| H. G. (Dutch) Dehnert | 1968 |
| Paul Endacott | 1971 |
| Harold (Bud) Foster | 1964 |
| Max (Marty) Friedman | 1971 |
| Joe Fulks | 1977 |
| Lauren (Laddie) Gale | 1976 |
| Tom Gola | 1975 |
| Hal Greer | 1982 |
| Robert (Ace) Gruenig | 1963 |
| Cliff Hagan | 1977 |
| Victor Hanson | 1960 |
| Nat Holman | 1964 |
| Chuck Hyatt | 1959 |
| William Johnson | 1976 |
| Edward (Moose) Krause | 1975 |
| Bob Kurland | 1961 |
| Joe Lapchick | 1966 |
| Jerry Lucas | 1980 |
| Hank Luisetti | 1959 |
| Branch McCracken | 1960 |
| Jack McCracken | 1962 |
| Ed Macauley | 1960 |
| Slater Martin | 1982 |
| George Mikan | 1959 |
| Charles (Stretch) Murphy | 1960 |
| H. O. (Pat) Page | 1962 |
| Bob Pettit | 1970 |
| Andy Phillip | 1961 |
| Jim Pollard | 1977 |
| Frank Ramsey | 1982 |
| Willis Reed | 1982 |
| Oscar Robertson | 1980 |
| Col. John Roosma | 1961 |
| John (Honey) Russell | 1964 |
| Bill Russell | 1974 |
| Dolph Schayes | 1972 |
| Ernest Schmidt | 1973 |
| John Schommer | 1959 |
| Barney Sedran | 1962 |
| Bill Sharman | 1975 |
| Christian Steinmetz | 1961 |
| John (Cat) Thompson | 1962 |
| Robert (Fuzzy) Vandivier | 1974 |
| Edward Wachter | 1961 |
| Jerry West | 1980 |
| John Wooden | 1960 |

| Coach | Year Elected |
|---|---|
| A. J. (Red) Auerbach | 1968 |
| Sam Barry | 1979 |
| Ernest Blood | 1960 |
| Howard Cann | 1967 |
| Dr. H. Clifford Carlson | 1959 |
| Ben Carnevale | 1969 |
| Everett Case | 1982 |
| Everett Dean | 1966 |
| Edgar Diddle | 1971 |
| Bruce Drake | 1972 |
| Clarence (Big House) Gaines | 1982 |
| Amory (Slats) Gill | 1967 |
| Ed Hickey | 1979 |
| Howard Hobson | 1965 |
| Hank Iba | 1968 |
| A. F. (Doggie) Julian | 1967 |
| Frank Keaney | 1960 |
| George Keogan | 1961 |
| Ward Lambert | 1960 |
| Harry Litwack | 1975 |
| Ken Loeffler | 1964 |
| A. C. (Dutch) Lonborg | 1972 |
| Arad McCutchan | 1981 |
| John McLendon | 1979 |
| Frank McGuire | 1976 |
| Dr. Walter Meanwell | 1959 |
| Ray Meyer | 1979 |
| Pete Newell | 1979 |
| Adolph Rupp | 1968 |
| Leonard Sachs | 1961 |
| Everett Shelton | 1980 |
| John Wooden | 1972 |

| Referee | Year Elected |
|---|---|
| James Enright | 1979 |
| George Hepbron | 1960 |
| George Hoyt | 1961 |
| Matthew Kennedy | 1959 |
| John Nucatola | 1977 |
| Ernest Quigley | 1961 |
| J. Dallas Shirley | 1980 |
| David Tobey | 1961 |
| David Walsh | 1961 |

| Contributor | Year Elected |
|---|---|
| Dr. Forrest (Phog) Allen | 1959 |
| Clair Bee | 1967 |
| Walter Brown | 1965 |
| John Bunn | 1964 |
| Bob Douglas | 1971 |
| Al Duer | 1982 |
| Harry Fisher | 1973 |
| Edward Gottlieb | 1971 |
| Dr. Luther Gulick | 1959 |
| Les Harrison | 1980 |
| Dr. Ferenc Hepp | 1981 |
| Edward Hickox | 1959 |
| Paul (Tony) Hinkle | 1965 |
| Ned Irish | 1964 |
| William Jones | 1964 |
| Walter Kennedy | 1981 |
| Emil Liston | 1974 |
| Bill Mokray | 1965 |
| Ralph Morgan | 1959 |
| Frank Morgenweck | 1962 |
| Dr. James Naismith | 1959 |
| John O'Brien | 1961 |
| Harold Olsen | 1959 |
| Maurice Podoloff | 1973 |
| H. V. Porter | 1960 |
| William Reid | 1963 |
| Elmer Ripley | 1972 |
| Lynn St. John | 1962 |
| Abe Saperstein | 1970 |
| Arthur Schabinger | 1961 |
| Amos Alonzo Stagg | 1959 |
| Chuck Taylor | 1968 |
| Oswald Tower | 1959 |
| Arthur Trester | 1961 |
| Clifford Wells | 1971 |

## NBA ALL-STAR GAMES

| Year | Result | Site | Year | Result | Site | Year | Result | Site |
|---|---|---|---|---|---|---|---|---|
| 1953 | West 79, East 75 | Ft. Wayne | 1963 | East 115, West 108 | Los Angeles | 1973 | East 104, West 84 | Chicago |
| 1954 | East 98, West 93 | New York | 1964 | East 111, West 107 | Boston | 1974 | West 134, East 123 | Seattle |
| 1955 | East 100, West 91 | New York | 1965 | East 124, West 123 | St. Louis | 1975 | East 108, West 102 | Phoenix |
| 1956 | West 108, East 94 | Rochester | 1966 | East 137, West 94 | Cincinnati | 1976 | East 123, West 109 | Philadelphia |
| 1957 | East 109, West 97 | Boston | 1967 | West 135, East 120 | San Francisco | 1977 | West 125, East 124 | Milwaukee |
| 1958 | East 130, West 118 | St. Louis | 1968 | East 144, West 124 | New York | 1978 | East 133, West 125 | Atlanta |
| 1959 | West 124, East 108 | Detroit | 1969 | East 123, West 112 | Baltimore | 1979 | West 134, East 129 | Detroit |
| 1960 | East 125, West 115 | Philadelphia | 1970 | East 142, West 135 | Philadelphia | 1980 | East 144, West 136 | Washington |
| 1961 | West 153, East 131 | Syracuse | 1971 | West 108, East 107 | San Diego | 1981 | East 123, West 120 | Cleveland |
| 1962 | West 150, East 130 | St. Louis | 1972 | West 112, East 110 | Los Angeles | 1982 | East 120, West 118 | New Jersey |

## ALL-TIME NBA LEADERS

SOURCE: National Basketball Association

At start of 1982/83 season

### Top Scorers

| Player | Years | Games | Points | Avg. |
|---|---|---|---|---|
| Wilt Chamberlain | 14 | 1,045 | 31,419 | 30.1 |
| Kareem Abdul-Jabbar | 13 | 1,011 | 28,088 | 27.8 |
| Oscar Robertson | 14 | 1,040 | 26,710 | 25.7 |
| John Havlicek | 16 | 1,270 | 26,395 | 20.8 |
| Elvin Hayes | 14 | 1,141 | 25,865 | 22.7 |
| Jerry West | 14 | 932 | 25,192 | 27.0 |
| Elgin Baylor | 14 | 846 | 23,149 | 27.4 |
| Hal Greer | 15 | 1,122 | 21,586 | 19.2 |
| Walt Bellamy | 14 | 1,043 | 20,941 | 20.1 |
| Bob Pettit | 11 | 792 | 20,880 | 26.4 |
| Dolph Schayes | 16 | 1,059 | 19,249 | 18.2 |
| Gail Goodrich | 14 | 1,031 | 19,181 | 18.6 |
| Chet Walker | 13 | 1,032 | 18,831 | 18.2 |
| Rick Barry | 10 | 794 | 18,395 | 23.2 |
| Dave Bing | 12 | 901 | 18,327 | 20.3 |
| Lou Hudson | 13 | 890 | 17,940 | 20.2 |
| Bob Lanier | 12 | 848 | 17,853 | 21.1 |
| Len Wilkens | 15 | 1,077 | 17,772 | 16.5 |
| Bailey Howell | 12 | 950 | 17,770 | 18.7 |
| Earl Monroe | 13 | 926 | 17,454 | 18.8 |
| Calvin Murphy | 12 | 938 | 17,133 | 18.3 |
| Bob Cousy | 14 | 924 | 16,960 | 18.4 |
| Paul Arizin | 10 | 713 | 16,266 | 22.8 |
| Bob McAdoo | 10 | 640 | 16,184 | 25.3 |
| Pete Maravich | 10 | 658 | 15,948 | 24.2 |
| Jack Twyman | 11 | 823 | 15,840 | 19.2 |
| Randy Smith | 11 | 896 | 15,599 | 17.4 |
| Walt Frazier | 13 | 825 | 15,581 | 18.9 |
| Bob Dandridge | 13 | 839 | 15,530 | 18.5 |
| Nate Archibald | 11 | 764 | 15,446 | 20.2 |
| Sam Jones | 12 | 871 | 15,411 | 17.7 |
| Dick Barnett | 14 | 971 | 15,358 | 15.8 |
| Dick Van Arsdale | 12 | 921 | 15,079 | 16.4 |
| Richie Guerin | 13 | 848 | 14,676 | 17.3 |
| Bill Russell | 13 | 963 | 14,522 | 15.1 |
| Nate Thurmond | 14 | 964 | 14,437 | 15.0 |
| Jo Jo White | 12 | 837 | 14,399 | 17.2 |
| Spencer Haywood | 11 | 722 | 14,279 | 19.8 |
| Tom Van Arsdale | 12 | 929 | 14,232 | 15.3 |
| Dave DeBusschere | 12 | 875 | 14,053 | 16.1 |

### Most Games Played

| | |
|---|---|
| John Havlicek | 1,270 |
| Paul Silas | 1,254 |
| Elvin Hayes | 1,141 |
| Hal Greer | 1,122 |
| Len Wilkens | 1,077 |
| Dolph Schayes | 1,059 |
| Johnny Green | 1,057 |
| Don Nelson | 1,053 |
| Leroy Ellis | 1,048 |
| Wilt Chamberlain | 1,045 |

### Most Field Goals Made

| | |
|---|---|
| Wilt Chamberlain | 12,681 |
| Kareem Abdul-Jabbar | 11,568 |
| John Havlicek | 10,513 |
| Elvin Hayes | 10,394 |
| Oscar Robertson | 9,508 |
| Jerry West | 9,016 |
| Elgin Baylor | 8,693 |
| Hal Greer | 8,504 |
| Walt Bellamy | 7,914 |
| Gail Goodrich | 7,431 |

### Most Field Goals Attempted

| | |
|---|---|
| John Havlicek | 23,900 |
| Wilt Chamberlain | 23,497 |
| Elvin Hayes | 22,993 |
| Kareem Abdul-Jabbar | 20,741 |
| Elgin Baylor | 20,171 |
| Oscar Robertson | 19,620 |
| Jerry West | 19,032 |
| Hal Greer | 18,811 |
| Bob Pettit | 16,872 |
| Bob Cousy | 16,468 |

### Most Assists

| | |
|---|---|
| Oscar Robertson | 9,887 |
| Len Wilkens | 7,211 |
| Bob Cousy | 6,955 |
| Guy Rodgers | 6,917 |
| Jerry West | 6,238 |
| John Havlicek | 6,114 |
| Nate Archibald | 5,897 |
| Dave Bing | 5,397 |
| Kevin Porter | 5,268 |
| Norm Van Lier | 5,217 |

### Highest Scoring Average (400 Games Minimum)

| Player | G | FG | FTM | Pts. | Avg. |
|---|---|---|---|---|---|
| Wilt Chamberlain | 1,045 | 12,681 | 6,057 | 31,419 | 30.1 |
| George Gervin | 483 | 5,404 | 2,990 | 13,849 | 28.7 |
| Kareem Abdul-Jabbar | 1,011 | 11,568 | 4,952 | 28,088 | 27.8 |
| Elgin Baylor | 846 | 8,693 | 5,763 | 23,149 | 27.4 |
| Jerry West | 932 | 9,016 | 7,160 | 25,192 | 27.0 |
| Bob Pettit | 792 | 7,349 | 6,182 | 20,880 | 26.4 |
| Oscar Robertson | 1,040 | 9,508 | 7,694 | 26,710 | 25.7 |
| Bob McAdoo | 640 | 6,376 | 3,429 | 16,184 | 25.3 |
| Adrian Dantley | 445 | 4,039 | 3,032 | 11,113 | 25.0 |
| Pete Maravich | 658 | 6,187 | 3,564 | 15,948 | 24.2 |

### Most Minutes Played

| | |
|---|---|
| Wilt Chamberlain | 47,859 |
| Elvin Hayes | 46,704 |
| John Havlicek | 46,471 |
| Oscar Robertson | 43,886 |
| Bill Russell | 40,726 |
| Kareem Abdul-Jabbar | 40,567 |
| Hal Greer | 39,789 |
| Walt Bellamy | 38,940 |
| Len Wilkens | 38,064 |
| Jerry West | 36,571 |

### Highest Field Goal Percentage (2,000 FG Minimum)

| Player | FGA | FGM | Pct. |
|---|---|---|---|
| Artis Gilmore | 5,827 | 3,425 | .588 |
| Kareem Abdul-Jabbar | 20,741 | 11,568 | .558 |
| Darryl Dawkins | 3,715 | 2,062 | .555 |
| Bobby Jones | 4,584 | 2,540 | .554 |
| Adrian Dantley | 7,387 | 4,039 | .547 |
| Walter Davis | 5,792 | 3,150 | .544 |
| Swen Nater | 4,255 | 2,302 | .541 |
| Marques Johnson | 5,875 | 3,177 | .541 |
| Wilt Chamberlain | 23,497 | 12,681 | .540 |
| Bernard King | 5,712 | 3,050 | .534 |

### Highest Free Throw Percentage (1,200 FTM Minimum)

| Player | FTA | FTM | Pct. |
|---|---|---|---|
| Rick Barry | 4,243 | 3,818 | .900 |
| Calvin Murphy | 3,714 | 3,307 | .890 |
| Bill Sharman | 3,557 | 3,143 | .884 |
| Mike Newlin | 3,456 | 3,005 | .870 |
| Fred Brown | 2,053 | 1,761 | .858 |
| Larry Siegfried | 1,945 | 1,662 | .854 |
| James Silas | 1,690 | 1,440 | .852 |
| Flynn Robinson | 1,881 | 1,597 | .849 |
| Junior Bridgeman | 1,432 | 1,212 | .846 |
| Rickey Sobers | 1,959 | 1,655 | .845 |

### Most Free Throws Made

| | |
|---|---|
| Oscar Robertson | 7,694 |
| Jerry West | 7,160 |
| Dolph Schayes | 6,979 |
| Bob Pettit | 6,182 |
| Wilt Chamberlain | 6,057 |
| Elgin Baylor | 5,763 |
| Len Wilkens | 5,394 |
| John Havlicek | 5,369 |
| Walt Bellamy | 5,113 |
| Chet Walker | 5,079 |

### Most Free Throws Attempted

| | |
|---|---|
| Wilt Chamberlain | 11,862 |
| Oscar Robertson | 9,185 |
| Jerry West | 8,801 |
| Dolph Schayes | 8,273 |
| Bob Pettit | 8,119 |
| Walt Bellamy | 8,088 |
| Elvin Hayes | 7,580 |
| Elgin Baylor | 7,391 |
| Len Wilkens | 6,973 |
| Kareem Abdul-Jabbar | 6,928 |

### Most Rebounds

| | |
|---|---|
| Wilt Chamberlain | 23,924 |
| Bill Russell | 21,620 |
| Elvin Hayes | 15,403 |
| Nate Thurmond | 14,464 |
| Walt Bellamy | 14,241 |
| Kareem Abdul-Jabbar | 13,826 |
| Wes Unseld | 13,769 |
| Jerry Lucas | 12,942 |
| Bob Pettit | 12,849 |
| Paul Silas | 12,357 |

### Most Personal Fouls

| | |
|---|---|
| Hal Greer | 3,855 |
| Elvin Hayes | 3,838 |
| Dolph Schayes | 3,664 |
| Walt Bellamy | 3,536 |
| Bailey Howell | 3,498 |
| Bill Bridges | 3,375 |
| Len Wilkens | 3,285 |
| John Havlicek | 3,281 |
| Sam Lacey | 3,264 |
| Paul Silas | 3,105 |

## NCAA CONFERENCE CHAMPIONS: 1981-82 (Record of all games shown in parentheses; does not include NCAA and NIT tournaments)

| Conference | Champion | CONFERENCE Won | Lost | Conf. Runner Up | Tournament Winner |
|---|---|---|---|---|---|
| Atlantic Coast | North Carolina (27-2) | 12 | 2 | — | North Carolina |
| | Virginia (29-3) | 12 | 2 | | |
| Big East | Villanova (22-7) | 11 | 3 | Georgetown (26-6) | Georgetown |
| Big Eight | Missouri (26-3) | 12 | 2 | Kansas State (21-7) | Missouri |
| Big Sky | Idaho (24-2) | 13 | 1 | Montana (17-9) | Idaho |
| Big Ten | Minnesota (22-5) | 14 | 4 | Iowa (20-7) | — |
| | | | | Ohio State (21-9) | |
| | | | | Indiana (18-9) | |
| East Coast (East) | Temple (19-7) | 11 | 0 | St. Joseph's (25-4) | St. Joseph's |
| East Coast (West) | West Chester State (13-14) | 8 | 8 | Rider (11-16) | |
| | | | | Lafayette (12-15) | |
| E.C.A.C. Metro South | Fairleigh Dickinson (16-11) | 12 | 3 | Long Island (20-9) | Robert Morris (17-12) |
| E.C.A.C. North | Northeastern (22-6) | 8 | 1 | Canisius (19-8) | Northeastern |
| | | | | Niagara (19-10) | |
| E.C.A.C. South | James Madison (24-5) | 10 | 1 | Richmond (18-10) | Old Dominion (18-11) |
| Eastern Eight | West Virginia (26-3) | 13 | 1 | Rutgers (19-9) | Pittsburgh (20-9) |
| Ivy League | Pennsylvania (17-9) | 12 | 2 | Columbia (16-10) | — |
| | | | | Princeton (13-13) | |
| Metro Atlantic | St. Peter's (20-8) | 9 | 1 | Fordham (18-10) | Iona (24-8) |
| Metro | Memphis State (23-4) | 10 | 2 | Tulane (17-8) | Memphis State |
| Mid-American | Ball State (17-11) | 12 | 4 | Bowling Green (17-11) | Northern Illinois (16-13) |
| Mid-Eastern Athletic | North Carolina A & T (18-8) | 10 | 2 | Howard (17-10) | — |
| Midwestern City | Evansville (23-5) | 10 | 2 | Oral Roberts (18-11) | Evansville |
| | | | | Loyola (Chicago) (17-12) | |
| Missouri Valley | Bradley (21-10) | 13 | 3 | Wichita State (22-6) | Tulsa |
| | | | | Tulsa (24-5) | |
| Ohio Valley | Murray State (20-7) | 13 | 3 | — | Middle Tenn. State (21-7) |
| | Western Kentucky (19-9) | 13 | 3 | | |
| Pacific Coast Athletic | Fresno State (26-2) | 13 | 1 | Calif.-Irvine (22-6) | Fresno State |
| Pacific 10 | Oregon State (23-4) | 16 | 2 | UCLA (21-6) | — |
| Southeastern | Kentucky (22-7) | 13 | 5 | — | Alabama (23-6) |
| | Tennessee (19-9) | 13 | 5 | | |
| Southern | Tenn.-Chattanooga (26-3) | 15 | 1 | Western Carolina (19-9) | Tenn.-Chattanooga |
| Southland | S.W. Louisiana (24-7) | 8 | 2 | Lamar (22-6) | S.W. Louisiana |
| Southwest | Arkansas (23-5) | 12 | 4 | Houston (21-7) | Arkansas |
| Southwestern Athletic | Jackson State (21-9) | 10 | 2 | — | Alcorn State |
| | Alcorn State (22-7) | 10 | 2 | | |
| Sun Belt | Ala.-Birmingham (23-5) | 9 | 1 | Va. Commonwealth (17-11) | Ala.-Birmingham |
| Trans-America Athletic | Ark.-Little Rock (18-8) | 11 | 4 | N.W. Louisiana (19-9) | N.E. Louisiana (19-10) |
| West Coast Athletic | Pepperdine (21-6) | 14 | 0 | San Francisco (25-5) | — |
| Western Athletic | Wyoming (22-6) | 14 | 2 | San Diego State (20-8) | — |

### MAJOR INDEPENDENTS (NCAA DIV. I)

| Team | Won | Lost | Team | Won | Lost | Team | Won | Lost |
|---|---|---|---|---|---|---|---|---|
| DePaul | 26 | 1 | Nevada-Las Vegas | 19 | 9 | So. Mississippi | 15 | 11 |
| Marquette | 21 | 7 | Cleveland State | 17 | 10 | North Texas State | 15 | 12 |
| Dayton | 19 | 8 | S.E. Louisiana | 16 | 11 | Penn State | 15 | 12 |
| New Orleans | 18 | 8 | | | | | | |

## NATIONAL COLLEGE TOURNAMENT CHAMPIONS

### NCAA (Division I)

| Year | Champion | Year | Champion |
|---|---|---|---|
| 1951 | Kentucky | 1967 | UCLA |
| 1952 | Kansas | 1968 | UCLA |
| 1953 | Indiana | 1969 | UCLA |
| 1954 | LaSalle | 1970 | UCLA |
| 1955 | San Francisco | 1971 | UCLA |
| 1956 | San Francisco | 1972 | UCLA |
| 1957 | North Carolina | 1973 | UCLA |
| 1958 | Kentucky | 1974 | N.C. State |
| 1959 | California | 1975 | UCLA |
| 1960 | Ohio State | 1976 | Indiana |
| 1961 | Cincinnati | 1977 | Marquette |
| 1962 | Cincinnati | 1978 | Kentucky |
| 1963 | Loyola (Chicago) | 1979 | Michigan State |
| 1964 | UCLA | 1980 | Louisville |
| 1965 | UCLA | 1981 | Indiana |
| 1966 | Texas Western | 1982 | North Carolina |

### NIT

| Year | Champion | Year | Champion |
|---|---|---|---|
| 1951 | Brigham Young | 1967 | Southern Illinois |
| 1952 | LaSalle | 1968 | Dayton |
| 1953 | Seton Hall | 1969 | Temple |
| 1954 | Holy Cross | 1970 | Marquette |
| 1955 | Duquesne | 1971 | North Carolina |
| 1956 | Louisville | 1972 | Maryland |
| 1957 | Bradley | 1973 | Virginia Tech |
| 1958 | Xavier of Ohio | 1974 | Purdue |
| 1959 | St. John's | 1975 | Princeton |
| 1960 | Bradley | 1976 | Kentucky |
| 1961 | Providence College | 1977 | St. Bonaventure |
| 1962 | Dayton | 1978 | Texas |
| 1963 | Providence College | 1979 | Indiana |
| 1964 | Bradley | 1980 | Virginia |
| 1965 | St. John's | 1981 | Tulsa |
| 1966 | Brigham Young | 1982 | Bradley |

### NCAA (Division II)

| Year | Champion | Year | Champion |
|---|---|---|---|
| 1975 | Old Dominion | 1979 | North Alabama |
| 1976 | Puget Sound | 1980 | Virginia Union |
| 1977 | Tenn.-Chattanooga | 1981 | Florida Southern |
| 1978 | Cheyney St. (Pa.) | 1982 | Dist. of Columbia |

### NCAA (Division III)

| Year | Champion | Year | Champion |
|---|---|---|---|
| 1975 | LeMoyne Owen | 1979 | North Park (Chicago) |
| 1976 | Scranton | 1980 | North Park (Chicago) |
| 1977 | Wittenberg | 1981 | Potsdam St. |
| 1978 | North Park (Chicago) | 1982 | Wabash (Ind.) |

## 1982 NCAA BASKETBALL TOURNAMENT CHAMPIONSHIPS

**REGIONALS:** North Carolina 70, Villanova 60
Houston 99, Boston College 92
Louisville 75, Alabama (Birmingham) 68
Georgetown 69, Oregon State 45

**SEMIFINALS:** North Carolina 68, Houston 63
Georgetown 50, Louisville 46

**CHAMPIONSHIP:** North Carolina 63, Georgetown 62

## 1982 COLLEGE ALL-AMERICA SELECTIONS

Associated Press (AP), United Press (UPI), Sporting News (SN), NBA Coaches (NBA)

| Player | Height | School | Class | Selected by | NBA Draft by |
|---|---|---|---|---|---|
| Ralph Sampson | 7'4" | Virginia | Junior | AP, UPI, SN, NBA | — |
| Terry Cummings | 6'9" | DePaul | Junior | AP, UPI, SN, NBA | San Diego |
| Quintin Dailey | 6'3" | San Francisco | Junior | AP, UPI, SN, NBA | Chicago |
| James Worthy | 6'9" | North Carolina | Junior | UPI, SN, NBA | Los Angeles |
| Eric Floyd | 6'3" | Georgetown | Senior | AP, UPI | New Jersey |
| Kevin Magee | 6'8" | Cal-Irvine | Senior | AP | Phoenix |
| Trent Tucker | 6'5" | Minnesota | Senior | SN | New York |
| Dominique Wilkins | 6'7" | Georgia | Junior | NBA | Utah |

## NCAA DIVISION I BASKETBALL RECORDS

SOURCE: N.C.A.A.

### INDIVIDUAL

**Scoring Average (Career)** : 44.2, Maravich, LSU, 1968–70
**Scoring Average (Season)** : 44.5, Maravich, LSU, 1970
**Scoring (Game)** : 100 points, Selvy, Furman, 1954
**Field Goals Attempted (Season)** : 1168, Maravich, LSU, 1970
**Field Goal Percentage (Season)** : .710, Steve Johnson, Oregon State, 1980
**Free Throws Attempted (Season)** : 444, Selvy, Furman, 1954
**Free Throw Percentage (Season)** : .944, Gibson, Marshall, 1978
**Rebounds (Season)** : 734, Dukes, Seton Hall, 1953
**Rebounds Per Game (Season)** : 25.6, Slack, Marshall, 1955

### TEAM

**Points Per Game (Season)** : 110.5, Nevada-Las Vegas, 1976
**Field Goals Per Game (Season)** : 46.3, Nevada-Las Vegas, 1976
**Field Goal Percentage (Season)** : .572, Missouri, 1980
**Free Throw Percentage (Season)** : .809, Ohio State, 1970
**Least Points Allowed Per Game (Season)** : 32.5, Oklahoma State, 1948

# WOMEN'S BASKETBALL

## 1982 NCAA WOMEN'S BASKETBALL TOURNAMENT CHAMPIONSHIPS

**EAST:** Cheyney State 93, Kansas State 71
**WEST:** Maryland 89, Drake 78
**MIDEAST:** Tennessee 91, Southern California 90
**MIDWEST:** Louisiana Tech 82, Kentucky 60

**SEMIFINALS:** Cheyney State 76, Maryland 66
Louisiana Tech 69, Tennessee 46

**CHAMPIONSHIP:** Louisiana Tech 76, Cheyney State 62

## 1982 AIAW BASKETBALL TOURNAMENT CHAMPIONSHIPS

**REGIONALS:** Villanova 87, Delaware 72
Rutgers 83, Minnesota 75
Texas 73, Wisconsin 61
Wayland Baptist 85, California 70

**SEMIFINALS:** Rutgers 83, Villanova 75
Texas 82, Wayland Baptist 73

**CHAMPIONSHIP:** Rutgers 83, Texas 77

## 1982 WOMEN'S ALL-AMERICA SELECTIONS

Selected by the Women's Basketball Coaches Association

### UNIVERSITY DIVISION

Pam Kelly, Louisiana Tech
Angela Turner, Louisiana Tech
Barbara Kennedy, Clemson
Val Walker, Cheyney State
June Olkowski, Rutgers
Cathy Boswell, Illinois State
Ann Donovan, Old Dominion
Sheila Foster, South Carolina
Latanya Pollard, Long Beach State

### COLLEGE DIVISION

Pam Brisby, Missouri Southern
Sherry Raney, Arkansas Tech
Laura Beuhning, Cal Poly-San Luis Obispo
Holly Stilley, Charleston (S.C.)
Donna Hammond, California-Riverside
Robin Mortensen, St. John's Fisher (N.Y.)
Jackie White, Cal Poly-Pomona
Carol Welch, Cal Poly-Pomona
Alison Fay, Bentley (Mass.)
Kelli Leitch, Southwestern Oklahoma

## OTHER 1982 BASKETBALL CHAMPIONS

**NCAA Women Division II**—Cal Poly-Pomona

**NCAA Women Division III**—Elizabethtown (Pa.)

**N.A.I.A. Tournament:** Men—South Carolina-Spartanburg
Women—Southwestern Oklahoma State

**Junior College:** Men—Midland (Texas)
Women—Moberly (Missouri)

# FOOTBALL

## NATIONAL FOOTBALL LEAGUE 410 Park Avenue, New York City 10022. Commissioner: Pete Rozelle.

### NATIONAL FOOTBALL CONFERENCE (George Halas, Pres.)

| Eastern Division | Chief Executive | Coach |
|---|---|---|
| Dallas Cowboys | Clint W. Murchison, Jr. | Tom Landry |
| New York Giants | Wellington T. Mara | Ray Perkins |
| Philadelphia Eagles | Leonard H. Tose | Dick Vermeil |
| St. Louis Cardinals | William V. Bidwill | Jim Hanifan |
| Washington Redskins | Jack Kent Cooke | Joe Gibbs |
| **Central Division** | | |
| Chicago Bears | George Halas, Sr. | Mike Ditka |
| Detroit Lions | William Clay Ford | Monte Clark |
| Green Bay Packers | Dominic Olejniczak | Bart Starr |
| Minnesota Vikings | Max Winter | Bud Grant |
| Tampa Bay Buccaneers | Hugh Culverhouse | John McKay |
| **Western Division** | | |
| Atlanta Falcons | Rankin M. Smith | Leeman Bennett |
| Los Angeles Rams | Georgia Frontiere | Ray Malavasi |
| New Orleans Saints | John W. Mecom, Jr. | Bum Phillips |
| San Francisco 49ers | Edward J. DeBartolo, Jr. | Bill Walsh |

### AMERICAN FOOTBALL CONFERENCE (Lamar Hunt, Pres.)

| Eastern Division | Chief Executive | Coach |
|---|---|---|
| Baltimore Colts | Robert Irsay | Frank Kush |
| Buffalo Bills | Ralph C. Wilson, Jr. | Chuck Knox |
| Miami Dolphins | Joseph Robbie | Don Shula |
| New England Patriots | William H. Sullivan, Jr. | Ron Meyer |
| New York Jets | Jim Kensil | Walt Michaels |
| **Central Division** | | |
| Cincinnati Bengals | John Sawyer | Forrest Gregg |
| Cleveland Browns | Arthur B. Modell | Sam Rutigliano |
| Houston Oilers | K. S. Adams, Jr. | Ed Biles |
| Pittsburgh Steelers | Art Rooney | Chuck Noll |
| **Western Division** | | |
| Denver Broncos | Edgar F. Kaiser, Jr. | Dan Reeves |
| Kansas City Chiefs | Lamar Hunt | Marv Levy |
| Los Angeles Raiders | Al Davis | Tom Flores |
| San Diego Chargers | Eugene V. Klein | Don Coryell |
| Seattle Seahawks | Elmer Nordstrom | Jack Patera |

## PROFESSIONAL FOOTBALL HALL OF FAME (Canton, Ohio)

MEMBERS

**Herb Adderly,** Defensive Back, Green Bay Packers, 1961–69, Dallas Cowboys, 1970–72.

**Lance Alworth,** Wide Receiver, San Diego Chargers, 1962–70.

**Doug Atkins,** Defensive End, Cleveland Browns, 1953–54; Chicago Bears, 1955–66; New Orleans Saints, 1967–69.

**Morris (Red) Badgro,** End, New York Yankees, New York Giants, Brooklyn Dodgers, 1927, 1930–36.

**Cliff Battles,** Back, 1932, Boston Braves; 1933–36, Boston Redskins; 1937, Washington Redskins.

**Sammy Baugh,** Quarterback, Washington Redskins, 1937–52.

**Chuck Bednarik,** Center and Linebacker, Philadelphia Eagles, 1949–62.

**Bert Bell,** Founder, Philadelphia Eagles, 1933, and Head Coach; Commissioner, National Football League, 1946–59.

**Raymond Berry,** End, Baltimore Colts, 1955–67.

**Charles W. Bidwill,** Founder, Chicago Cardinals, 1933–47

**George Blanda,** Quarterback, Kicker, Chicago Bears, Baltimore Colts, Houston Oilers, Oakland Raiders, 1949–75.

**Jim Brown,** Fullback, Cleveland Browns, 1957–65.

**Paul E. Brown,** Head Coach, Cleveland Browns, 1946–62; Cincinnati Bengals, 1968–75.

**Roosevelt Brown,** Tackle, N.Y. Giants, 1953–65.

**Dick Butkus,** Linebacker, Chicago Bears, 1965–73.

**Tony Canadeo,** Backfield, Green Bay Packers, 1940–52.

**Joe Carr,** Founder, Columbus Panhandles, 1904; Organizer, National Football League, 1920; President of League, 1921–39.

**Guy Chamberlin,** Head Coach, Halfback, End, Canton Bulldogs, Decatur Staleys, Cleveland Bulldogs, Frankford Yellowjackets, Chicago Cardinals, 1918–28.

**Jack Christiansen,** Defensive Back, Detroit Lions, 1951–58.

**Dutch Clark,** Quarterback and Head Coach, Portsmouth (O.) Spartans, Detroit Lions, Cleveland Rams, 1931–42.

**George Connor,** Tackle, Defensive Tackle, Linebacker, Chicago Bears, 1948–55.

**Jimmy Conzelman,** Head Coach, Halfback, Executive, Decatur Staleys, Rock Island Independents, Milwaukee Badgers, Detroit Panthers, Providence Steam Rollers, Chicago Cardinals, 1920–48.

**Willie Davis,** Defensive End, Cleveland Browns, Green Bay Packers, 1956–67.

**Art Donovan,** Tackle, 1950, Baltimore Colts; 1951, New York Yanks; 1952, Dallas Texans; 1953–61, Baltimore Colts.

**Paddy Driscoll,** Halfback and Head Coach, Chicago Cardinals and Chicago Bears, 1919–31, 1941–68.

**Bill Dudley,** Halfback, Pittsburgh Steelers, Detroit Lions, Washington Redskins, 1942, 1945–53.

**Turk Edwards,** Tackle, Washington Redskins, 1932–40.

**Weeb Ewbank,** Head Coach, 1954–62 Baltimore Colts; 1963–73, New York Jets

**Tom Fears,** End, Los Angeles Rams, 1948–56.

**Ray Flaherty,** End and Head Coach, New York Giants, New York Yankees, Boston & Washington Redskins, Chicago Hornets, 1928–49.

**Len Ford,** Defensive End, Los Angeles Dons, Cleveland Browns, Green Bay Packers, 1948–58.

**Daniel J. Fortmann, M.D.,** Guard, Chicago Bears, 1936–46.

**Bill George,** Middle Linebacker, Chicago Bears, 1952–65.

**Frank Gifford,** Halfback, New York Giants, 1952–60, 1962–64.

**Otto Graham,** Quarterback, Cleveland Browns, 1946–55.

**Red Grange,** Halfback, Chicago Bears, New York Yankees, 1925–37.

**Forrest Gregg,** Tackle, 1956, 1958–70, Green Bay Packers; 1971, Dallas Cowboys.

**Lou Groza,** Tackle, Kicker, Cleveland Browns, 1946–67.

**Joe Guyon,** Halfback, Canton Bulldogs, Cleveland Indians, Oorang Indians, Rock Island Independents, Kansas City Cowboys, New York Giants, 1919–27.

**George Halas,** Founder, Head Coach, End, Decatur Staleys (1920) which became the Chicago Bears; retired as Bears' head coach in 1968.

**Ed Healey,** Tackle, Rock Island Independents, Chicago Bears, 1920–27.

**Mel Hein,** Center, New York Giants, 1931–45.

**Pete Henry,** Tackle, Canton Bulldogs, Akron, New York Giants, Pottsville Maroons, Staten Island Stapletons, 1920–30.

**Arnie Herber,** Halfback, Green Bay Packers, New York Giants, 1930–41, 1944–45.

**Bill Hewitt,** End, 1932–36, Chicago Bears; 1936–39, Philadelphia Eagles; 1943, Philadelphia-Pittsburgh.

**Clarke Hinkle,** Fullback, Green Bay Packers, 1932–41.

**Elroy Hirsch,** End, 1946–48, Chicago Rockets (AAFC); 1949–57, Los Angeles Rams; Rams' club executive, 1960–68.

**Cal Hubbard,** Tackle, New York Giants, Green Bay Packers, Pittsburgh Pirates, 1927–36.

**Sam Huff,** Linebacker, New York Giants, 1956–63; Washington Redskins, 1964–67, 69.

**Lamar Hunt,** Founder, American Football League, 1959. Owner, Dallas Texans, 1960–1962, Kansas City Chiefs, 1963 to present.

**Don Hutson,** End, Green Bay Packers, 1935–45.

**Deacon Jones,** Defensive End, Los Angeles Rams, 1961–71, San Diego Chargers, 1972–73, Washington Redskins, 1974.

**Walt Kiesling,** Player-Coach, Duluth Eskimos, Pottsville Maroons, Boston Braves, Chicago Cardinals, Chicago Bears, Green Bay Packers, Pittsburgh Steelers, Philadelphia-Pittsburgh, Chicago-Pittsburgh, 1926–61.

**Frank (Bruiser) Kinard,** Tackle, 1938–43, Brooklyn Dodgers; 1944, Brooklyn Tigers; 1946–47, New York Yankees.

**Curly Lambeau,** Founder, Head Coach, Halfback, Green Bay Packers, 1919–49; also Head Coach of Chicago Cardinals and Washington Redskins, 1950–54.

**Dick Lane,** Defensive Back, Los Angeles Rams, Chicago Cardinals, Detroit Lions, 1952–65.

**Yale Lary,** Defensive Back, Detroit Lions, 1952–53, 1956–64.

**Dante Lavelli,** End, Cleveland Browns, 1946–56.

**Bobby Layne,** Quarterback, Chicago Bears, New York Bulldogs, Detroit Lions, Pittsburgh Steelers, 1948–62.

**Alphonse (Tuffy) Leemans,** Fullback, New York Giants, 1937–43

**Bob Lilly,** Defensive Tackle, Dallas Cowboys, 1961–74.

**Vince Lombardi,** Head Coach, 1959–67, Green Bay Packers; 1969, Washington Redskins.

**Sid Luckman,** Quarterback, Chicago Bears, 1939–50.

**Link Lyman,** Tackle, Canton Bulldogs, Cleveland Bulldogs, Chicago Bears, 1922–34.

**Tim Mara,** Founder, New York Giants, 1925.

**Gino Marchetti,** Defensive End, Dallas Texans, 1952; Baltimore Colts, 1953–1964–1966.

**George P. Marshall,** Founder, Washington Redskins (as Boston Braves) in 1932.

**Ollie Matson,** Halfback, Chicago Cardinals, 1952, 1954–1958, Los Angeles Rams, 1959–1962, Detroit Lions, 1963, Philadelphia Eagles, 1964–1966.

**George McAfee,** Halfback, Chicago Bears, 1940–41, 1945–50.

**Hugh McElhenny,** Halfback, San Francisco 49ers, Minnesota Vikings, New York Giants, Detroit Lions, 1952–64.

**John Blood McNally,** Halfback, Milwaukee Badgers, Duluth Eskimos, Pottsville Maroons, Green Bay Packers, Pittsburgh Steelers, 1925–39.

**Mike Michalske,** Guard, New York Yankees, Green Bay Packers, 1926–37.

**Wayne Millner,** End, 1936, Boston Redskins; 1937–41, 1945 Washington Redskins.

**Ron Mix,** Tackle, Los Angeles-San Diego Chargers, 1960–69, Oakland Raiders, 1971.

**Lenny Moore,** Running Back, Baltimore Colts, 1956–67.

**Marion Motley,** Fullback, 1946–53, Cleveland Browns; 1955, Pittsburgh Steelers.

**George Musso,** Tackle, Guard, Chicago Bears, 1933–44.

**Bronko Nagurski,** Fullback and Tackle, Chicago Bears, 1930–37, 1943.

**Earl (Greasy) Neale,** Head Coach, Philadelphia Eagles, 1941–50.

**Ernie Nevers,** Fullback and Head Coach, Duluth Eskimos, Chicago Cardinals, 1926–31, 1939.

**Ray Nitschke,** Linebacker, Green Bay Packers, 1958–72.

**Leo Nomellini,** Defensive Tackle, San Francisco 49ers, 1950–63.

**Merlin Olsen,** Defensive Tackle, Los Angeles Rams, 1962–76.

**Jim Otto,** Center, Oakland Raiders, 1960–74.

**Steve Owen,** Player-Coach, Kansas City Cowboys, New York Giants, 1924–53.

**Ace Parker,** Quarterback, Brooklyn Dodgers, 1937–1941, Boston Yanks, 1945, New York Yankees (AAFC), 1946.

**Jim Parker,** Tackle, Baltimore Colts, 1957–67.

**Joe Perry,** Fullback, San Francisco 49ers, Baltimore Colts, 1949–63.

**Pete Pihos,** End, Philadelphia Eagles, 1947–55.

**Hugh (Shorty) Ray,** National Football League technical adviser and supervisor of officials, 1938–56.

**Dan Reeves,** Founder, Cleveland Rams, 1941 (moved to Los Angeles in 1946).

**Jim Ringo,** Center, Green Bay Packers, Philadelphia Eagles, 1953–67.

**Andy Robustelli,** Defensive End, 1951–55, Los Angeles Rams; 1956–64, New York Giants.

**Art Rooney,** Founder, Pittsburgh Steelers, 1933.

**Gale Sayers,** Running Back, 1965–1971, Chicago Bears.

**Joe Schmidt,** Linebacker, Detroit Lions, 1953–65.

**Bart Starr,** Quarterback, Green Bay Packers, 1956–71.

**Ernie Stautner,** Defensive End, Pittsburgh Steelers, 1950–63.

**Ken Strong,** Halfback, Staten Island Stapletons, New York Giants, New York Yankees, 1929–37, 1939, 1944–47.

**Joe Stydahar,** Tackle, Chicago Bears, 1936–42, 1945–46. Head Coach of Los Angeles Rams, 1950–51; Head Coach of Chicago Cardinals, 1953–54.

**Jim Taylor,** Fullback, Green Bay Packers, New Orleans Saints, 1958–67.

**Jim Thorpe,** Halfback, Canton Bulldogs, Pine Village (Ind.) A. A., Oorang Indians, Toledo Maroons, Rock Island Independents, New York Giants, 1915–26; President of American Professional Football Association, forerunner of N.F.L., 1920.

**Y. A. Tittle,** Quarterback, 1948–50, Baltimore Colts; 1951–60, San Francisco 49ers; 1961–64, New York Giants.

**George Trafton,** Center, Chicago Bears, 1920–32.

**Charley Trippi,** Halfback-Quarterback, 1947–55, Chicago Cardinals.

**Emlen Tunnell,** Halfback, New York Giants, Green Bay Packers, 1946–61.

**Clyde (Bulldog) Turner,** Center, Chicago Bears, 1940–52.

**Johnny Unitas,** Quarterback, Baltimore Colts, 1956–72, San Diego Chargers, 1973.

**Norm Van Brocklin,** Quarterback, 1949–57, Los Angeles Rams; 1958–60, Philadelphia Eagles.

**Steve Van Buren,** Halfback, Philadelphia Eagles, 1944–51.

**Bob Waterfield,** Quarterback, Cleveland and Los Angeles Rams, 1945–52; Head Coach of Rams, 1960–62.

**Bill Willis,** Guard, 1946–53, Cleveland Browns.

**Larry Wilson,** Defensive Back, St. Louis Cardinals, 1960–72

**Alex Wojciechowicz,** Center and Linebacker, 1938–46, Detroit Lions; 1946–50, Philadelphia Eagles.

## NATIONAL FOOTBALL LEAGUE RECORDS

Source: Elias Sports Bureau and N.F.L.

Through 1981 season; includes all performances in American Football League (1960–69)

**Most Points, Lifetime:** 2,002, George Blanda, Chicago Bears, Baltimore, Houston, Oakland

**Most Points, Season:** 176, Paul Hornung, Green Bay, 1960

**Most Points, Game:** 40, Ernie Nevers, Chicago Cards vs. Chicago Bears, November 28, 1929

**Most Touchdowns, Lifetime:** 126, Jim Brown, Cleveland

**Most Touchdowns, Season:** 23, O. J. Simpson, Buffalo, 1975.

**Most Yards Gained Rushing, Lifetime:** 12,312, Jim Brown, Cleveland, 1957–65

**Most Yards Gained Rushing, Season:** 2,003, O. J. Simpson, Buffalo, 1973

**Most Yards Gained Rushing, Game:** 275, Walter Payton, Chicago vs. Minnesota, Nov. 20, 1977

**Highest Average Gain Rushing, Lifetime:** 5.22, Jim Brown, Cleveland

**Most Touchdowns Rushing, Lifetime:** 106, Jim Brown, Cleveland

**Most Touchdowns Rushing, Season:** 19, Jim Taylor, Green Bay, 1962; Earl Campbell, Houston, 1979; Chuck Muncie, San Diego, 1981

**Most Passes Completed, Lifetime:** 3,686, Fran Tarkenton, Minnesota, New York Giants, Minnesota

**Most Passes Completed, Season:** 360, Dan Fouts, San Diego, 1981

**Most Passes Completed, Game:** 42, Richard Todd, N.Y. Jets, 1980

**Passing Percent (Attempts-Completions), Season:** 70.33, Sammy Baugh, Washington, 1945

**Most Yards Gained Passing, Lifetime:** 47,003, Fran Tarkenton, Minnesota, New York Giants, Minnesota

**Most Yards Gained Passing, Season:** 4,802 Dan Fouts, San Diego, 1981

**Most Yards Gained Passing, Game:** 554, Norm Van Brocklin, Los Angeles, 1951

**Most Touchdown Passes, Lifetime:** 342, Fran Tarkenton, Minnesota, New York Giants, Minnesota

**Receptions, Most Yards Gained, Lifetime:** 11,834, Don Maynard, New York Giants, New York Jets, St. Louis

**Receptions, Most Yards Gained, Season:** 1,746, Charlie Hennigan, Houston, 1961

**Receptions, Most Touchdowns, Lifetime:** 99, Don Hutson, Green Bay

**Receptions, Most Touchdowns, Season:** 17, Don Hutson, Green Bay, 1942; 17, Elroy Hirsch, Los Angeles, 1951; 17, Bill Groman, Houston, 1961

**Most Receptions, Lifetime:** 649, Charley Taylor, Washington

**Interceptions, Most Touchdowns from, Lifetime:** 9, Ken Houston, Washington

**Most Consecutive Points After Touchdown:** 234, Tommy Davis, San Francisco, 1959–65

**Most Field Goals, Lifetime:** 335, George Blanda, Chicago Bears, Baltimore, Houston, Oakland

**Most Field Goals, Season:** 34, Jim Turner, New York Jets, 1968

**Most Field Goals, Game:** 7, Jim Bakken, St. Louis vs. Pittsburgh, September 24, 1967

**Longest Field Goal:** 63 yards, Tom Dempsey, New Orleans vs. Detroit, November 8, 1970

**Most Consecutive Field Goals:** 20, Garo Yepremian, Miami, 1978; New Orleans, 1979

**Longest Punt:** 98, Steve O'Neal, New York Jets, 1969

**Most Punt Returns, Lifetime:** 258, Emlen Tunnell, New York Giants and Green Bay

**Punt Returns, Most Yardage Gained, Lifetime:** 2,714, Rick Upchurch, Denver, 1975–81

**Kickoff Returns, Highest Average Yardage Gained, Season:** 41.06, Travis Williams, Green Bay, 1967

**Most Seasons, Active Player:** 26, George Blanda, Chicago Bears, Baltimore, Houston, Oakland

**Most Games Played, Lifetime:** 340, George Blanda, Chicago Bears, Baltimore, Houston, Oakland

**Most Seasons NFL Champion Team:** 11, Green Bay, 1929-1931, 1936, 1939, 1944, 1961-1962, 1965-1967.

**Team, Most Consecutive Victories, Regular Season:** 17, Chicago Bears, 1933-1934

## NATIONAL FOOTBALL LEAGUE ALL-TIME LEADERS

**Rushing Yardage**

| | |
|---|---|
| 12,312 | Jim Brown |
| 11,236 | O. J. Simpson |
| 10,339 | Franco Harris |
| 9,608 | Walter Payton |
| 8,597 | Jim Taylor |

**Pass Receptions**

| | |
|---|---|
| 649 | Charley Taylor |
| 633 | Don Maynard |
| 631 | Raymond Berry |
| 589 | Fred Biletnikoff |
| 571 | Harold Jackson |

**Points**

| | |
|---|---|
| 2,002 | George Blanda |
| 1,439 | Jim Turner |
| 1,380 | Jim Bakken |
| 1,365 | Fred Cox |
| 1,349 | Lou Groza |

**Interceptions**

| | |
|---|---|
| 81 | Paul Krause |
| 79 | Emlen Tunnell |
| 68 | Night Train Lane |
| 62 | Dick LeBeau |
| 58 | Emmitt Thomas |

# NFL FINAL 1981 STANDINGS

## AMERICAN FOOTBALL CONFERENCE

| EASTERN DIVISION | W | L | T | Pct. | Pts. | OP |
|---|---|---|---|---|---|---|
| Miami | 11 | 4 | 1 | .719 | 345 | 275 |
| *N.Y. Jets | 10 | 5 | 1 | .656 | 355 | 287 |
| *Buffalo | 10 | 6 | 0 | .625 | 311 | 276 |
| Baltimore | 2 | 14 | 0 | .125 | 259 | 533 |
| New England | 2 | 14 | 0 | .125 | 322 | 370 |
| **CENTRAL DIVISION** | | | | | | |
| Cincinnati | 12 | 4 | 0 | .750 | 421 | 304 |
| Pittsburgh | 8 | 8 | 0 | .500 | 356 | 297 |
| Houston | 7 | 9 | 0 | .438 | 281 | 355 |
| Cleveland | 5 | 11 | 0 | .313 | 276 | 375 |
| **WESTERN DIVISION** | | | | | | |
| San Diego | 10 | 6 | 0 | .625 | 478 | 390 |
| Denver | 10 | 6 | 0 | .625 | 321 | 289 |
| Kansas City | 9 | 7 | 0 | .563 | 343 | 290 |
| Oakland | 7 | 9 | 0 | .438 | 273 | 343 |
| Seattle | 6 | 10 | 0 | .375 | 322 | 388 |

*Wild card qualifiers

## NATIONAL FOOTBALL CONFERENCE

| EASTERN DIVISION | W | L | T | Pct. | Pts. | OP |
|---|---|---|---|---|---|---|
| Dallas | 12 | 4 | 0 | .750 | 367 | 277 |
| *Philadelphia | 10 | 6 | 0 | .625 | 368 | 221 |
| *N.Y. Giants | 9 | 7 | 0 | .563 | 295 | 257 |
| Washington | 8 | 8 | 0 | .500 | 347 | 349 |
| St. Louis | 7 | 9 | 0 | .438 | 315 | 408 |
| **CENTRAL DIVISION** | | | | | | |
| Tampa Bay | 9 | 7 | 0 | .563 | 315 | 268 |
| Detroit | 8 | 8 | 0 | .500 | 397 | 322 |
| Green Bay | 8 | 8 | 0 | .500 | 324 | 361 |
| Minnesota | 7 | 9 | 0 | .438 | 325 | 369 |
| Chicago | 6 | 10 | 0 | .375 | 253 | 324 |
| **WESTERN DIVISION** | | | | | | |
| San Francisco | 13 | 3 | 0 | .813 | 357 | 250 |
| Atlanta | 7 | 9 | 0 | .438 | 426 | 355 |
| Los Angeles | 6 | 10 | 0 | .375 | 303 | 351 |
| New Orleans | 4 | 12 | 0 | .250 | 207 | 378 |

**POST-SEASON GAMES**

| | AMERICAN CONFERENCE | NATIONAL CONFERENCE |
|---|---|---|
| WILD CARD TEAMS | Buffalo 31, N.Y. Jets 27 | N.Y. Giants 27, Philadelphia 21 |
| DIVISION PLAYOFFS | San Diego 41, Miami 38 | San Francisco 38, N.Y. Giants 24 |
| | Cincinnati 28, Buffalo 21 | Dallas 38, Tampa Bay 0 |
| CONFERENCE CHAMPIONSHIP | Cincinnati 27, San Diego 7 | San Francisco 28, Dallas 27 |

LEAGUE CHAMPIONSHIP (SUPER BOWL) San Francisco 26, Cincinnati 21

# 1981 INDIVIDUAL LEADERS

| RUSHING-AFC | Att. | Yds. | Avg. | Long | TDs. |
|---|---|---|---|---|---|
| Campbell, Houston | 361 | 1376 | 3.8 | 43 | 10 |
| Muncie, San Diego | 251 | 1144 | 4.6 | 73 | 19 |
| Delaney, Kansas City | 234 | 1121 | 4.8 | 82 | 3 |
| M. Pruitt, Cleveland | 247 | 1103 | 4.5 | 21 | 7 |
| Cribbs, Buffalo | 257 | 1097 | 4.3 | 35 | 3 |

| PASSING-AFC | Att. | Comp. | Yds. | Int. | TDs. |
|---|---|---|---|---|---|
| Anderson, Cincinnati | 479 | 300 | 3754 | 10 | 29 |
| Morton, Denver | 376 | 225 | 3195 | 14 | 21 |
| Fouts, San Diego | 609 | 360 | 4802 | 17 | 33 |
| Bradshaw, Pittsburgh | 370 | 201 | 2892 | 14 | 22 |
| Zorn, Seattle | 397 | 236 | 2788 | 9 | 13 |

| RECEIVING-AFC | No. | Yds. | Avg. | TDs. |
|---|---|---|---|---|
| Winslow, San Diego | 88 | 1075 | 12.2 | 10 |
| Largent, Seattle | 75 | 1224 | 16.3 | 9 |
| Ross, Cincinnati | 71 | 910 | 12.8 | 5 |
| Lewis, Buffalo | 70 | 1244 | 17.8 | 4 |
| Joiner, San Diego | 70 | 1188 | 17.0 | 7 |

| INTERCEPTIONS-AFC | No. | Yds. | Long | TDs. |
|---|---|---|---|---|
| Harris, Seattle | 10 | 155 | 42 | 2 |

| PUNTING-AFC | No. | Yds. | Long | Avg. |
|---|---|---|---|---|
| McInally, Cincinnati | 72 | 3272 | 62 | 45.4 |

| PUNT RETURNS-AFC | No. | Yds. | Avg. | TDs. |
|---|---|---|---|---|
| Brooks, San Diego | 22 | 290 | 13.2 | 0 |

| KICKOFF RETURNS-AFC | No. | Yds. | Avg. | TDs. |
|---|---|---|---|---|
| Roaches, Houston | 28 | 769 | 27.5 | 1 |

| SCORING/KICKING-AFC | XP | FG | Pts. |
|---|---|---|---|
| Breech, Cincinnati | 49-51 | 22-32 | 115 |
| Lowery, Kansas City | 37-38 | 26-35 | 115 |

| RUSHING-NFC | Att. | Yds. | Avg. | Long | TDs. |
|---|---|---|---|---|---|
| Rogers, New Orleans | 378 | 1674 | 4.4 | 79 | 13 |
| Dorsett, Dallas | 342 | 1646 | 4.8 | 75 | 4 |
| Sims, Detroit | 296 | 1437 | 4.9 | 51 | 13 |
| Montgomery, Philadelphia | 286 | 1402 | 4.9 | 41 | 8 |
| Anderson, St. Louis | 328 | 1376 | 4.2 | 28 | 9 |

| PASSING-NFC | Att. | Comp. | Yds. | Int. | TDs. |
|---|---|---|---|---|---|
| Montana, San Francisco | 488 | 311 | 3565 | 12 | 19 |
| D. White, Dallas | 391 | 223 | 3098 | 13 | 22 |
| Bartkowski, Atlanta | 533 | 297 | 3829 | 23 | 30 |
| Dickey, Green Bay | 354 | 204 | 2593 | 15 | 17 |
| Theismann, Washington | 496 | 293 | 3568 | 20 | 19 |

| RECEIVING-NFC | No. | Yds. | Avg. | TDs. |
|---|---|---|---|---|
| Clark, San Francisco | 85 | 1105 | 13.0 | 4 |
| Brown, Minnesota | 83 | 694 | 8.4 | 2 |
| Andrews, Atlanta | 81 | 735 | 9.1 | 2 |
| Senser, Minnesota | 79 | 1004 | 12.7 | 8 |
| Lofton, Green Bay | 71 | 1294 | 18.2 | 8 |

| INTERCEPTIONS-NFC | No. | Yds. | Long | TDs. |
|---|---|---|---|---|
| Walls, Dallas | 11 | 133 | 33 | 0 |

| PUNTING-NFC | No. | Yds. | Long | Avg. |
|---|---|---|---|---|
| Skladany, Detroit | 64 | 2784 | 74 | 43.5 |

| PUNT RETURNS-NFC | No. | Yds. | Avg. | TDs. |
|---|---|---|---|---|
| Irvin, Los Angeles | 46 | 615 | 13.4 | 3 |

| KICKOFF RETURNS-NFC | No. | Yds. | Avg. | TDs. |
|---|---|---|---|---|
| Nelms, Washington | 37 | 1099 | 29.7 | 0 |

| SCORING/KICKING-NFC | XP | FG | Pts. |
|---|---|---|---|
| Murray, Detroit | 46-46 | 25-35 | 121 |
| Septien, Dallas | 40-40 | 27-35 | 121 |

# ALL-PRO SELECTIONS (AP) Associated Press, (UPI) United Press International, (SN) Sporting News

**Offense**

Quarterback —Ken Anderson, Cincinnati (AP, UPI, SN)
Running backs —Tony Dorsett, Dallas (AP, UPI, SN)
—George Rogers, New Orleans (AP, SN)
—Billy Sims, Detroit (UPI)
Wide receivers —Alfred Jenkins, Atlanta (AP, UPI, SN)
—James Lofton, Green Bay (AP, UPI, SN)
Tight end —Kellen Winslow, San Diego (AP, UPI, SN)
Center —Mike Webster, Pittsburgh (AP, UPI, SN)
Guards —John Hannah, New England (AP, UPI, SN)
—Herbert Scott, Dallas (AP, SN)
—Randy Cross, San Francisco (UPI)
Tackles —Anthony Munoz, Cincinnati (AP, UPI, SN)
—Marvin Powell, N.Y. Jets (AP, UPI, SN)

**Specialists**

Punter —Pat McInally, Cincinnati (AP, UPI, SN)
Place kicker —Rafael Septien, Dallas (AP, UPI, SN)
Punt returns —LeRoy Irvin, Los Angeles (AP, UPI, SN)
Kickoff returns —Mike Nelms, Washington (UPI, SN)

**Defense**

Ends —Fred Dean, San Francisco (AP, UPI, SN)
—Joe Klecko, N.Y. Jets (AP, UPI, SN)
Tackles —Randy White, Dallas (AP, UPI, SN)
—Gary Johnson, San Diego (AP, UPI)
—Charlie Johnson, Philadelphia (AP)
—Bob Baumhower, Miami (SN)
Linebackers —Jack Lambert, Pittsburgh (AP, UPI, SN)
—Lawrence Taylor, N.Y. Giants (AP, UPI, SN)
—Bob Swenson, Denver (AP, SN)
—Jerry Robinson, Philadelphia (UPI)
—Randy Gradishar, Miami (SN)
Cornerbacks —Ronny Lott, San Francisco (AP, UPI, SN)
—Mel Blount, Pittsburgh (AP, UPI)
—Lester Hayes, Oakland (SN)
Free safety —Nolan Cromwell, Los Angeles (AP, UPI, SN)
Strong safeties —Gary Fencik, Chicago (AP, SN)
—Gary Barbaro, Kansas City (UPI)

## CHAMPIONSHIP GAMES

### NATIONAL FOOTBALL LEAGUE

1933 Dec. Chicago Bears 23, New York Giants 21
1934 Dec. New York Giants 30, Chicago Bears 13
1935 Dec. Detroit Lions 26, New York Giants 7
1936 Dec. Green Bay Packers 21, Boston Redskins 6
1937 Dec. Washington Redskins 28, Chicago Bears 21
1938 Dec. New York Giants 23, Green Bay Packers 17
1939 Dec. Green Bay Packers 27, New York Giants 0
1940 Dec. Chicago Bears 73, Washington Redskins 0
1941 Dec. Chicago Bears 37, New York Giants 9
1942 Dec. Washington Redskins 14, Chicago Bears 6
1943 Dec. Chicago Bears 41, Washington Redskins 21
1944 Dec. Green Bay Packers 14, New York Giants 7
1945 Dec. Cleveland Rams 15, Washington Redskins 14
1946 Dec. Chicago Bears 24, New York Giants 14
1947 Dec. Chicago Cardinals 28, Philadelphia Eagles 21
1948 Dec. Philadelphia Eagles 7, Chicago Cardinals 0
1949 Dec. Philadelphia Eagles 14, Los Angeles Rams 0
1950 Dec. Cleveland Browns 30, Los Angeles Rams 28
1951 Dec. Los Angeles Rams 24, Cleveland Browns 17
1952 Dec. Detroit Lions 17, Cleveland Browns 7
1953 Dec. Detroit Lions 17, Cleveland Browns 16
1954 Dec. Cleveland Browns 56, Detroit Lions 10
1955 Dec. Cleveland Browns 38, Los Angeles Rams 14
1956 Dec. New York Giants 47, Chicago Bears 7
1957 Dec. Detroit Lions 59, Cleveland Browns 14
1958 Dec. Baltimore Colts 23, New York Giants 17
1959 Dec. Baltimore Colts 31, New York Giants 16
1960 Dec. Philadelphia Eagles 17, Green Bay Packers 13
1961 Dec. Green Bay Packers 37, New York Giants 0
1962 Dec. Green Bay Packers 16, New York Giants 7
1963 Dec. Chicago Bears 14, New York Giants 10
1964 Dec. Cleveland Browns 27, Baltimore Colts 0
1966 Jan. Green Bay Packers 23, Cleveland Browns 12
1967 Jan. Green Bay Packers 34, Dallas Cowboys 27
1967 Dec. Green Bay Packers 21, Dallas Cowboys 17
1968 Dec. Baltimore Colts 34, Cleveland Browns 0
1970 Jan. Minnesota Vikings 27, Cleveland Browns 7

### NATIONAL FOOTBALL CONFERENCE

1971 Jan. Dallas Cowboys 17, San Francisco 49ers 10
1972 Jan. Dallas Cowboys 14, San Francisco 49ers 3
1972 Dec. Washington Redskins 26, Dallas Cowboys 3
1973 Dec. Minnesota Vikings 27, Dallas Cowboys 10
1974 Dec. Minnesota Vikings 14, Los Angeles Rams 10
1976 Jan. Dallas Cowboys 37, Los Angeles Rams 7
1976 Dec. Minnesota Vikings 24, Los Angeles Rams 13
1978 Jan. Dallas Cowboys 23, Minnesota Vikings 6
1979 Jan. Dallas Cowboys 28, Los Angeles Rams 0
1980 Jan. Los Angeles Rams 9, Tampa Bay Buccaneers 0
1981 Jan. Philadelphia Eagles 20, Dallas Cowboys 7
1982 Jan. San Francisco 49ers 28, Dallas Cowboys 27

### AMERICAN FOOTBALL LEAGUE

1961 Jan. Houston Oilers 24, San Diego Chargers 16
1961 Dec. Houston Oilers 10, San Diego Chargers 3
1962 Dec. Dallas Texans 20, Houston Oilers 17
1964 Jan. San Diego Chargers 51, Boston Patriots 10
1964 Dec. Buffalo Bills 20, San Diego Chargers 7
1965 Dec. Buffalo Bills 23, San Diego Chargers 0
1967 Jan. Kansas City Chiefs 31, Buffalo Bills 7
1967 Dec. Oakland Raiders 40, Houston Oilers 7
1968 Dec. New York Jets 27, Oakland Raiders 23
1970 Jan. Kansas City Chiefs 17, Oakland Raiders 7

### AMERICAN FOOTBALL CONFERENCE

1971 Jan. Baltimore Colts 27, Oakland Raiders 17
1972 Jan. Miami Dolphins 21, Baltimore Colts 0
1972 Dec. Miami Dolphins 21, Pittsburgh Steelers 17
1973 Dec. Miami Dolphins 27, Oakland Raiders 10
1974 Dec. Pittsburgh Steelers 24, Oakland Raiders 13
1976 Jan. Pittsburgh Steelers 16, Oakland Raiders 10
1976 Dec. Oakland Raiders 24, Pittsburgh Steelers 7
1978 Jan. Denver Broncos 20, Oakland Raiders 17
1979 Jan. Pittsburgh Steelers 34, Houston Oilers 5
1980 Jan. Pittsburgh Steelers 27, Houston Oilers 13
1981 Jan. Oakland Raiders 34, San Diego Chargers 27
1982 Jan. Cincinnati Bengals 27, San Diego Chargers 7

## SUPER BOWL GAMES

| | | | | | | |
|---|---|---|---|---|---|---|
| **I** | Jan. 15, 1967—Memorial Coliseum, Los Angeles | | | | | |
| | **Green Bay Packers** (NFL) | 7 | 7 | 14 | 7 | 35 |
| | **Kansas City Chiefs** (AFL) | 0 | 10 | 0 | 0 | 10 |
| **II** | Jan. 14, 1968—Orange Bowl, Miami | | | | | |
| | **Green Bay Packers** (NFL) | 3 | 13 | 10 | 7 | 33 |
| | **Oakland Raiders** (AFL) | 0 | 7 | 0 | 7 | 14 |
| **III** | Jan. 12, 1969—Orange Bowl, Miami | | | | | |
| | **New York Jets** (AFL) | 0 | 7 | 6 | 3 | 16 |
| | **Baltimore Colts** (NFL) | 0 | 0 | 0 | 7 | 7 |
| **IV** | Jan. 11, 1970—Tulane Stadium, New Orleans | | | | | |
| | **Kansas City Chiefs** (AFL) | 3 | 13 | 7 | 0 | 23 |
| | **Minnesota Vikings** (NFL) | 0 | 0 | 7 | 0 | 7 |
| **V** | Jan. 17, 1971—Orange Bowl, Miami | | | | | |
| | **Baltimore Colts** (AFC) | 0 | 6 | 0 | 10 | 16 |
| | **Dallas Cowboys** (NFC) | 3 | 10 | 0 | 0 | 13 |
| **VI** | Jan. 16, 1972—Tulane Stadium, New Orleans | | | | | |
| | **Dallas Cowboys** (NFC) | 3 | 7 | 7 | 7 | 24 |
| | **Miami Dolphins** (AFC) | 0 | 3 | 0 | 0 | 3 |
| **VII** | Jan. 14, 1973—Memorial Coliseum, Los Angeles | | | | | |
| | **Miami Dolphins** (AFC) | 7 | 7 | 0 | 0 | 14 |
| | **Washington Redskins** (NFC) | 0 | 0 | 0 | 7 | 7 |
| **VIII** | Jan. 13, 1974—Rice Stadium, Houston | | | | | |
| | **Miami Dolphins** (AFC) | 14 | 3 | 7 | 0 | 24 |
| | **Minnesota Vikings** (NFC) | 0 | 0 | 0 | 7 | 7 |
| **IX** | Jan. 12, 1975—Tulane Stadium, New Orleans | | | | | |
| | **Pittsburgh Steelers** (AFC) | 0 | 2 | 7 | 7 | 16 |
| | **Minnesota Vikings** (NFC) | 0 | 0 | 0 | 6 | 6 |
| **X** | Jan. 18, 1976—Orange Bowl, Miami | | | | | |
| | **Pittsburgh Steelers** (AFC) | 7 | 0 | 0 | 14 | 21 |
| | **Dallas Cowboys** (NFC) | 7 | 3 | 0 | 7 | 17 |
| **XI** | Jan. 9, 1977—Rose Bowl, Pasadena | | | | | |
| | **Oakland Raiders** (AFC) | 0 | 16 | 3 | 13 | 32 |
| | **Minnesota Vikings** (NFC) | 0 | 0 | 7 | 7 | 14 |
| **XII** | Jan. 15, 1978—Superdome, New Orleans | | | | | |
| | **Dallas Cowboys** (NFC) | 10 | 3 | 7 | 7 | 27 |
| | **Denver Broncos** (AFC) | 0 | 0 | 10 | 0 | 10 |
| **XIII** | Jan. 21, 1979—Orange Bowl, Miami | | | | | |
| | **Pittsburgh Steelers** (AFC) | 7 | 14 | 0 | 14 | 35 |
| | **Dallas Cowboys** (NFC) | 7 | 7 | 3 | 14 | 31 |
| **XIV** | Jan. 20, 1980—Rose Bowl, Pasadena | | | | | |
| | **Pittsburgh Steelers** (AFC) | 3 | 7 | 7 | 14 | 31 |
| | **Los Angeles Rams** (NFC) | 7 | 6 | 6 | 0 | 19 |
| **XV** | Jan. 25, 1981—Superdome, New Orleans | | | | | |
| | **Oakland Raiders** (AFC) | 14 | 0 | 10 | 3 | 27 |
| | **Philadelphia Eagles** (NFC) | 0 | 3 | 0 | 7 | 10 |
| **XVI** | Jan. 24, 1982—Silverdome, Pontiac, Michigan | | | | | |
| | **San Francisco 49ers** (NFC) | 7 | 13 | 0 | 6 | 26 |
| | **Cincinnati Bengals** (AFC) | 0 | 0 | 7 | 14 | 21 |

## TEAM DEPARTMENTAL CHAMPIONS

| Total Yards Gained | | Yards Rushing | | Yards Passing | | Points Scored | |
|---|---|---|---|---|---|---|---|
| 1981–San Diego (AFC) | 6,744 | 1981–Detroit (NFC) | 2,795 | 1981–San Diego (AFC) | 4,739 | 1981–San Diego (AFC) | 478 |
| 1980–San Diego (AFC) | 6,410 | 1980–Los Angeles (NFC) | 2,799 | 1980–San Diego (AFC) | 4,531 | 1980–Dallas (NFC) | 454 |
| 1979–Pittsburgh (AFC) | 6,258 | 1979–New York (AFC) | 2,646 | 1979–San Diego (AFC) | 3,915 | 1979–Pittsburgh (AFC) | 416 |
| 1978–New England (AFC) | 5,965 | 1978–New England (AFC) | 3,165 | 1978–San Diego (AFC) | 3,375 | 1978–Dallas (NFC) | 384 |
| 1977–Dallas (NFC) | 4,812 | 1977–Chicago (NFC) | 2,811 | 1977–Buffalo (AFC) | 2,530 | 1977–Oakland (AFC) | 351 |
| 1976–Baltimore (AFC) | 5,236 | 1976–Pittsburgh (AFC) | 2,971 | 1976–Baltimore (AFC) | 2,933 | 1976–Baltimore (AFC) | 417 |
| 1975–Buffalo (AFC) | 5,467 | 1975–Buffalo (AFC) | 2,974 | 1975–Cincinnati (AFC) | 3,241 | 1975–Buffalo (AFC) | 420 |
| 1974–Dallas (NFC) | 4,983 | 1974–Pittsburgh (AFC) | 2,417 | 1974–Washington (NFC) | 2,978 | 1974–Oakland (AFC) | 355 |
| 1973–Los Angeles (NFC) | 4,906 | 1973–Buffalo (AFC) | 3,088 | 1973–Philadelphia (NFC) | 3,236 | 1973–Dallas (AFC) | 388 |
| 1972–Miami (AFC) | 5,036 | 1972–Miami (AFC) | 2,960 | 1972–New York Jets (AFC) | 2,777 | 1972–Miami (AFC) | 385 |
| 1971–Dallas (NFC) | 5,035 | 1971–Miami (AFC) | 2,429 | 1971–San Diego (AFC) | 3,134 | 1971–Dallas (NFC) | 406 |
| 1970–Oakland (AFC) | 4,829 | 1970–Dallas (NFC) | 2,300 | 1970–San Francisco (NFC) | 2,923 | 1970–San Francisco (NFC) | 352 |
| 1969–Dallas (NFL) | 5,122 | 1969–Dallas (NFL) | 2,276 | 1969–Oakland (AFL) | 3,271 | 1969–Minnesota (NFL) | 379 |
| 1968–Oakland (AFL) | 5,696 | 1968–Chicago (NFL) | 2,377 | 1968–San Diego (AFL) | 3,623 | 1968–Oakland (AFL) | 453 |
| 1967–New York (AFL) | 5,152 | 1967–Cleveland (NFL) | 2,139 | 1967–New York (AFL) | 3,845 | 1967–Oakland (AFL) | 468 |
| 1966–Dallas (NFL) | 5,145 | 1966–Kansas City (AFL) | 2,274 | 1966–New York (AFL) | 3,464 | 1966–Kansas City (AFL) | 448 |
| 1965–San Francisco (NFL) | 5,270 | 1965–Cleveland (NFL) | 2,331 | 1965–San Francisco (NFL) | 3,487 | 1965–San Francisco (NFL) | 421 |
| 1964–Buffalo (AFL) | 5,206 | 1964–Green Bay (NFL) | 2,276 | 1964–Houston (AFL) | 3,527 | 1964–Baltimore (NFL) | 428 |
| 1963–San Diego (AFL) | 5,153 | 1963–Cleveland (NFL) | 2,639 | 1963–Baltimore (NFL) | 3,296 | 1963–New York (NFL) | 448 |
| 1962–New York (NFL) | 5,005 | 1962–Buffalo (AFL) | 2,480 | 1962–Denver (AFL) | 3,404 | 1962–Green Bay (NFL) | 415 |
| 1961–Houston (AFL) | 6,288 | 1961–Green Bay (NFL) | 2,350 | 1961–Houston (AFL) | 4,392 | 1961–Houston (AFL) | 513 |
| 1960–Houston (AFL) | 4,936 | 1960–St. Louis (NFL) | 2,356 | 1960–Houston (AFL) | 3,203 | 1960–New York (AFL) | 382 |
| 1959–Baltimore | 4,458 | 1959–Cleveland | 2,149 | 1959–Baltimore | 2,753 | 1959–Baltimore | 374 |
| 1958–Baltimore | 4,539 | 1958–Cleveland | 2,526 | 1958–Pittsburgh | 2,752 | 1958–Baltimore | 381 |
| 1957–Los Angeles | 4,143 | 1957–Los Angeles | 2,142 | 1957–Baltimore | 2,388 | 1957–Los Angeles | 307 |
| 1956–Chicago Bears | 4,537 | 1956–Chicago Bears | 2,468 | 1956–Los Angeles | 2,419 | 1956–Chicago Bears | 363 |
| 1955–Chicago Bears | 4,316 | 1955–Chicago Bears | 2,388 | 1955–Philadelphia | 2,472 | 1955–Cleveland | 349 |
| 1954–Los Angeles | 5,187 | 1954–San Francisco | 2,498 | 1954–Chicago Bears | 3,104 | 1954–Detroit | 337 |
| 1953–Philadelphia | 4,811 | 1953–San Francisco | 2,230 | 1953–Philadelphia | 3,089 | 1953–San Francisco | 372 |
| 1952–Cleveland | 4,352 | 1952–San Francisco | 1,905 | 1952–Cleveland | 2,566 | 1952–Los Angeles | 349 |
| 1951–Los Angeles | 5,506 | 1951–Chicago Bears | 2,408 | 1951–Los Angeles | 3,296 | 1951–Los Angeles | 392 |
| 1950–Los Angeles | 5,420 | 1950–New York Giants | 2,336 | 1950–Los Angeles | 3,709 | 1950–Los Angeles | 466 |
| 1949–Chicago Bears | 4,873 | 1949–Philadelphia | 2,607 | 1949–Chicago Bears | 3,055 | 1949–Philadelphia | 364 |
| 1948–Chicago Cards | 4,705 | 1948–Chicago Cards | 2,560 | 1948–Washington | 2,861 | 1948–Chicago Cards | 395 |
| 1947–Chicago Bears | 5,053 | 1947–Los Angeles | 2,171 | 1947–Washington | 3,336 | 1947–Chicago Bears | 363 |
| 1946–Los Angeles | 3,793 | 1946–Green Bay | 1,765 | 1946–Los Angeles | 2,080 | 1946–Chicago Bears | 289 |
| 1945–Washington | 3,549 | 1945–Cleveland Rams | 1,714 | 1945–Chicago Bears | 1,857 | 1945–Philadelphia | 272 |
| 1944–Chicago Bears | 3,239 | 1944–Philadelphia | 1,661 | 1944–Washington | 2,021 | 1944–Philadelphia | 267 |
| 1943–Chicago Bears | 4,045 | 1943–Phil-Pitt | 1,730 | 1943–Chicago Bears | 2,310 | 1943–Chicago Bears | 303 |
| 1942–Chicago Bears | 3,900 | 1942–Chicago Bears | 1,881 | 1942–Green Bay | 2,407 | 1942–Chicago Bears | 376 |
| 1941–Chicago Bears | 4,265 | 1941–Chicago Bears | 2,263 | 1941–Chicago Bears | 2,002 | 1941–Chicago Bears | 396 |
| 1940–Green Bay | 3,400 | 1940–Chicago Bears | 1,818 | 1940–Washington | 1,887 | 1940–Washington | 245 |
| 1939–Chicago Bears | 3,988 | 1939–Chicago Bears | 2,043 | 1939–Chicago Bears | 1,965 | 1939–Chicago Bears | 298 |
| 1938–Green Bay | 3,037 | 1938–Detroit | 1,893 | 1938–Washington | 1,536 | 1938–Green Bay | 223 |
| 1937–Green Bay | 3,201 | 1937–Detroit | 2,074 | 1937–Green Bay | 1,398 | 1937–Green Bay | 220 |
| 1936–Detroit | 3,703 | 1936–Detroit | 2,885 | 1936–Green Bay | 1,629 | 1936–Green Bay | 248 |
| 1935–Chicago Bears | 3,454 | 1935–Chicago Bears | 2,096 | 1935–Green Bay | 1,449 | 1935–Chicago Bears | 192 |
| 1934–Chicago Bears | 3,750 | 1934–Chicago Bears | 2,847 | 1934–Green Bay | 1,165 | 1934–Chicago Bears | 286 |
| 1933–New York Giants | 2,970 | 1933–Boston Redskins | 2,260 | 1933–New York | 1,348 | 1933–New York Giants | 244 |
| 1932–Chicago Bears | 2,755 | 1932–Chicago Bears | 1,770 | 1932–Chicago Bears | 1,013 | 1932–Green Bay | 152 |

## NATIONAL FOOTBALL LEAGUE STARS: BY YEARS

| PASSERS | Passes | Comp | Yards | Tds | Inter. |
|---|---|---|---|---|---|
| 1981—Ken Anderson, Cincinnati (AFC) | 479 | 300 | 3,754 | 29 | 10 |
| 1980—Brian Sipe, Cleveland (AFC) | 554 | 340 | 4,132 | 30 | 14 |
| 1979—Roger Staubach, Dallas (NFC) | 461 | 267 | 3,586 | 27 | 11 |
| 1978—Roger Staubach, Dallas (NFC) | 413 | 231 | 3,190 | 25 | 16 |
| 1977—Bob Griese, Miami (AFC) | 307 | 180 | 2,252 | 22 | 13 |
| 1976—Ken Stabler, Oakland (AFC) | 291 | 194 | 2,737 | 27 | 17 |
| 1975—Ken Anderson, Cincinnati (AFC) | 377 | 228 | 3,169 | 21 | 11 |
| 1974—Ken Anderson, Cincinnati (AFC) | 328 | 213 | 2,667 | 18 | 10 |
| 1973—Roger Staubach, Dallas Cowboys (NFC) | 286 | 179 | 2,428 | 23 | 15 |
| 1972—Norm Snead, New York Giants (NFC) | 325 | 196 | 2,307 | 17 | 12 |
| 1971—Bob Griese, Miami (AFC) | 263 | 145 | 2,089 | 19 | 9 |
| 1970—John Brodie, San Francisco (NFC) | 378 | 223 | 2,941 | 24 | 10 |
| 1969—C. A. (Sonny) Jurgensen, Wash. (NFL) | 442 | 274 | 3,102 | 22 | 15 |
| 1968—Earl Morrall, Baltimore (NFL) | 317 | 182 | 2,909 | 26 | 17 |
| 1967—C. A. (Sonny) Jurgensen, Wash. (NFL) | 508 | 288 | 3,747 | 31 | 16 |
| 1966—Len Dawson K.C. (AFL) | 284 | 159 | 2,527 | 26 | 10 |
| 1965—John Hadl, San Diego (AFL) | 348 | 174 | 2,798 | 20 | 21 |
| 1964—Len Dawson, Kansas City (AFL) | 354 | 199 | 2,879 | 30 | 18 |

| PASSERS | Passes | Comp | Yards | Tds | Inter. |
|---|---|---|---|---|---|
| 1963—Y. A. Tittle, New York (NFL) | 367 | 221 | 3,145 | 36 | 14 |
| 1962—Len Dawson, Dallas (AFL) | 310 | 189 | 2,759 | 29 | 17 |
| 1961—George Blanda, Houston (AFL) | 362 | 187 | 3,330 | 36 | 22 |
| 1960—Jack Kemp, L.A. (AFL) | 406 | 211 | 3,018 | 20 | 25 |
| 1959—Charles Conerly, N.Y. | 194 | 113 | 1,706 | 14 | 4 |
| 1958—Eddie LeBaron, Wash. | 145 | 79 | 1,365 | 11 | 10 |
| 1957—Tommy O'Connell, Cleveland | 110 | 63 | 1,229 | 9 | 8 |
| 1956—Eddie Brown, Chicago | 168 | 96 | 1,667 | 11 | 12 |
| 1955—Otto Graham, Clev. | 185 | 98 | 1,721 | 15 | 8 |
| 1954—Norman Van Brocklin, L.A. | 260 | 139 | 2,637 | 13 | 21 |
| 1953—Otto Graham, Clev. | 258 | 167 | 2,722 | 11 | 9 |
| 1952—Norman Van Brocklin, L.A. | 205 | 113 | 1,736 | 14 | 17 |
| 1951—Bob Waterfield, L.A. | 176 | 88 | 1,566 | 13 | 10 |
| 1950—Norman Van Brocklin, L.A. | 233 | 127 | 2,061 | 18 | 14 |
| 1949—Sammy Baugh, Wash. | 255 | 145 | 1,903 | 18 | 14 |
| 1948—Tommy Thompson, Phila. | 246 | 141 | 1,965 | 25 | 11 |
| 1947—Sammy Baugh, Wash. | 354 | 210 | 2,938 | 25 | 15 |
| 1946—Bob Waterfield, L.A. | 251 | 127 | 1,747 | 18 | 17 |
| 1945—Sid Luckman, Chicago | 217 | 117 | 1,725 | 14 | 10 |
| 1944—Frank Filchock, Wash. | 147 | 84 | 1,139 | 13 | 9 |
| 1943—Sammy Baugh, Wash. | 239 | 133 | 1,754 | 23 | 19 |
| 1942—Cecil Isbell, Green Bay | 268 | 146 | 2,021 | 24 | 14 |
| 1941—Cecil Isbell, Green Bay | 206 | 117 | 1,479 | 15 | 11 |
| 1940—Sammy Baugh, Wash. | 177 | 111 | 1,367 | 12 | 10 |
| 1939—Parker Hall, Clev.* | 208 | 106 | 1,227 | 9 | 13 |
| 1938—Ed Danowski, N.Y. | 129 | 70 | 848 | 8 | 8 |

* First year in League

| RUSHERS | Yards | Att. | TDs |
|---|---|---|---|
| 1981—George Rogers, New Orleans (NFC)* | 1,674 | 378 | 13 |
| 1980—Earl Campbell, Houston (AFC) | 1,934 | 373 | 13 |
| 1979—Earl Campbell, Houston (AFC) | 1,697 | 368 | 19 |
| 1978—Earl Campbell, Houston (AFC)* | 1,852 | 339 | 14 |
| 1977—Walter Payton, Chicago (NFC) | 1,503 | 290 | 8 |
| 1976—O. J. Simpson, Buffalo (AFC) | 1,450 | 302 | 13 |
| 1975—O. J. Simpson, Buffalo (AFC) | 1,817 | 329 | 16 |
| 1974—Otis Armstrong, Denver (AFC) | 1,407 | 263 | 9 |
| 1973—O. J. Simpson, Buffalo (AFC) | 2,003 | 332 | 12 |
| 1972—O. J. Simpson, Buffalo (AFC) | 1,251 | 292 | 6 |
| 1971—Floyd Little, Denver (AFC) | 1,133 | 284 | 6 |
| 1970—Larry Brown, Washington (NFC) | 1,125 | 237 | 5 |
| 1969—Gale Sayers, Chicago (NFL) | 1,032 | 236 | 8 |
| 1968—Leroy Kelly, Cleveland (NFL) | 1,239 | 248 | 16 |
| 1967—Jim Nance, Boston (AFL) | 1,216 | 269 | 7 |
| 1966—Jim Nance, Boston (AFL) | 1,458 | 299 | 11 |
| 1965—Jim Brown, Cleveland (NFL) | 1,544 | 289 | 17 |
| 1964—Jim Brown, Cleveland (NFL) | 1,446 | 280 | 7 |
| 1963—Jim Brown, Cleveland (NFL) | 1,863 | 291 | 12 |
| 1962—Jim Taylor, Green Bay (NFL) | 1,474 | 272 | 19 |
| 1961—Jim Brown, Cleveland (NFL) | 1,408 | 305 | 8 |
| 1960—Jim Brown, Cleveland (NFL) | 1,257 | 215 | 9 |
| 1959—Jim Brown, Cleveland | 1,329 | 290 | 14 |
| 1958—Jim Brown, Cleveland | 1,527 | 257 | 17 |
| 1957—Jim Brown, Cleveland* | 942 | 202 | 9 |
| 1956—Rick Casares, Chicago Bears | 1,126 | 234 | 12 |
| 1955—Alan Ameche, Baltimore* | 961 | 213 | 9 |
| 1954—Joe Perry, San Francisco | 1,049 | 173 | 8 |
| 1953—Joe Perry, San Francisco | 1,018 | 192 | 10 |
| 1952—Dan Towler, Los Angeles | 894 | 156 | 10 |
| 1951—Eddie Price, New York Giants | 971 | 271 | 7 |
| 1950—Marion Motley, Cleveland* | 810 | 140 | 3 |
| 1949—Steve Van Buren, Philadelphia | 1,146 | 263 | 11 |
| 1948—Steve Van Buren, Philadelphia | 945 | 201 | 10 |
| 1947—Steve Van Buren, Philadelphia | 1,008 | 217 | 13 |
| 1946—Bill Dudley, Pittsburgh | 604 | 146 | 3 |
| 1945—Steve Van Buren, Philadelphia | 832 | 143 | 15 |
| 1944—Bill Paschal, New York | 737 | 196 | 9 |
| 1943—Bill Paschal, New York* | 572 | 147 | 10 |
| 1942—Bill Dudley, Pittsburgh* | 696 | 162 | 5 |
| 1941—Clarence Manders, Brooklyn | 486 | 111 | 6 |
| 1940—Byron White, Detroit | 514 | 146 | 5 |
| 1939—Bill Osmanski, Chicago Bears* | 699 | 121 | 7 |
| 1938—Byron White, Pittsburgh* | 567 | 152 | 4 |

| RECEIVERS | No. | Yards | TDs |
|---|---|---|---|
| 1981—Kellen Winslow, San Diego (AFC) | 88 | 1,075 | 10 |
| 1980—Kellen Winslow, San Diego (AFC) | 89 | 1,290 | 9 |
| 1979—Joe Washington, Baltimore (AFC) | 82 | 750 | 3 |
| 1978—Rickey Young, Minnesota (NFC) | 88 | 704 | 5 |
| 1977—Lydell Mitchell, Baltimore (AFC) | 71 | 620 | 4 |
| 1976—MacArthur Lane, Kansas City (AFC) | 66 | 686 | 1 |
| 1975—Chuck Foreman, Minnesota (NFC) | 73 | 691 | 9 |
| 1974—Lydell Mitchell, Baltimore (AFC) | 72 | 544 | 2 |
| 1973—Harold Carmichael, Philadelphia (NFC) | 67 | 1,116 | 9 |
| 1972—Harold Jackson, Philadelphia (NFC) | 62 | 1,048 | 4 |
| 1971—Fred Biletnikoff, Oakland (AFC) | 61 | 929 | 9 |
| 1970—Dick Gordon, Chicago (NFC) | 71 | 1,026 | 13 |
| 1969—Dan Abramowicz, New Orleans (NFL) | 73 | 1,015 | 7 |
| 1968—Lance Alworth, San Diego (AFL) | 68 | 1,312 | 10 |
| 1967—George Sauer, New York (AFL) | 75 | 1,189 | 6 |
| 1966—Lance Alworth, San Diego (AFL) | 73 | 1,383 | 13 |
| 1965—Dave Parks, San Francisco (NFL) | 80 | 1,344 | 12 |
| 1964—Charley Hennigan, Houston (AFL) | 101 | 1,546 | 8 |
| 1963—Lionel Taylor, Denver (AFL) | 78 | 1,101 | 10 |
| 1962—Bobby Mitchell, Washington (NFL) | 72 | 1,384 | 11 |
| 1961—Lionel Taylor, Denver (AFL) | 100 | 1,176 | 4 |
| 1960—Raymond Berry, Baltimore, (NFL) | 74 | 1,298 | 10 |
| 1959—Raymond Berry, Baltimore | 66 | 959 | 14 |
| 1958—Raymond Berry, Baltimore | 56 | 794 | 9 |
| 1957—Billy Wilson, San Francisco | 52 | 757 | 6 |
| 1956—Billy Wilson, San Francisco | 60 | 889 | 5 |
| 1955—Pete Pihos, Philadelphia | 62 | 864 | 7 |
| 1954—Pete Pihos, Philadelphia | 60 | 872 | 10 |
| 1953—Pete Pihos, Philadelphia | 63 | 1,049 | 10 |
| 1952—Mac Speedie, Cleveland | 62 | 911 | 5 |
| 1951—Elroy Hirsch, Los Angeles | 66 | 1,495 | 17 |
| 1950—Tom Fears, Los Angeles | 84 | 1,116 | 7 |
| 1949—Tom Fears, Los Angeles | 77 | 1,013 | 9 |
| 1948—Tom Fears, Los Angeles* | 51 | 698 | 4 |
| 1947—Jim Keane, Chicago Bears | 64 | 910 | 10 |
| 1946—Jim Benton, Los Angeles | 63 | 981 | 6 |
| 1945—Don Hutson, Green Bay | 47 | 834 | 9 |
| 1944—Don Hutson, Green Bay | 58 | 866 | 9 |
| 1943—Don Hutson, Green Bay | 47 | 776 | 11 |
| 1942—Don Hutson, Green Bay | 74 | 1,211 | 17 |
| 1941—Don Hutson, Green Bay | 58 | 738 | 10 |
| 1940—Don Looney, Philadelphia* | 58 | 707 | 4 |
| 1939—Don Hutson, Green Bay | 34 | 846 | 6 |
| 1938—Gaynell Tinsley, Chi. Cards | 41 | 516 | 1 |

*First year in League

| PUNTERS | Att. | Avg. |
|---|---|---|
| 1981—Pat McInally, Cincinnati (AFC) | 72 | 45.4 |
| 1980—Dave Jennings, New York (NFC) | 94 | 44.8 |
| 1979—Bob Grupp, Kansas City (AFC) | 89 | 43.6 |
| 1978—Pat McInally, Cincinnati (AFC) | 91 | 43.1 |
| 1977—Ray Guy, Oakland (AFC) | 59 | 43.3 |
| 1976—Marv Bateman, Buffalo (AFC) | 86 | 42.8 |
| 1975—Ray Guy, Oakland (AFC) | 68 | 43.8 |
| 1974—Ray Guy, Oakland (AFC) | 74 | 42.2 |
| 1973—Jerrel Wilson, Kansas City (AFC) | 80 | 45.5 |
| 1972—Jerrel Wilson, Kansas City (ACF) | 66 | 44.8 |
| 1971—Dave Lewis, Cincinnati (AFC) | 72 | 44.8 |
| 1970—Dave Lewis, Cincinnati (AFC)* | 79 | 46.2 |
| 1969—David Lee, Baltimore (NFL) | 57 | 45.3 |
| 1968—Jerrel Wilson, Kansas City (AFL) | 63 | 45.1 |
| 1967—Bob Scarpitto, Denver (AFL) | 105 | 44.9 |
| 1966—Bob Scarpitto, Denver (AFL) | 76 | 45.8 |
| 1965—Gary Collins, Cleveland (NFL) | 65 | 46.7 |
| 1964—Bobby Walden, Minnesota (NFL) | 72 | 46.4 |
| 1963—Yale Lary, Detroit (NFL) | 35 | 48.9 |
| 1962—Tommy Davis, San Francisco (NFL) | 48 | 45.6 |
| 1961—Yale Lary, Detroit (NFL) | 52 | 48.4 |
| 1960—Jerry Norton, St. Louis (NFL) | 39 | 45.6 |
| 1959—Yale Lary, Detroit | 45 | 47.1 |
| 1958—Sam Baker, Washington | 48 | 45.4 |
| 1957—Don Chandler, New York | 60 | 44.6 |
| 1956—Norm Van Brocklin, Los Angeles | 48 | 43.1 |
| 1955—Norm Van Brocklin, Los Angeles | 60 | 44.6 |
| 1954—Pat Brady, Pittsburgh | 66 | 43.2 |
| 1953—Pat Brady, Pittsburgh | 80 | 46.9 |
| 1952—Horace Gillom, Cleveland Browns | 61 | 45.7 |
| 1951—Horace Gillom, Cleveland Browns | 73 | 45.5 |
| 1950—Fred Morrison, Chicago Bears* | 57 | 43.3 |
| 1949—Mike Boyda, N.Y. Bulldogs* | 56 | 44.2 |
| 1948—Joe Muha, Philadelphia | 57 | 47.3 |
| 1947—Jack Jacobs, Green Bay | 57 | 43.5 |
| 1946—Roy McKay, Green Bay | 64 | 42.7 |
| 1945—Roy McKay, Green Bay | 44 | 41.2 |
| 1944—Frank Sinkwich, Detroit | 45 | 41.0 |
| 1943—Sammy Baugh, Washington | 50 | 45.9 |
| 1942—Sammy Baugh, Washington | 37 | 48.2 |
| 1941—Sammy Baugh, Washington | 30 | 48.7 |

| TOTAL POINTS | TDs | XP | FG | Points |
|---|---|---|---|---|
| 1981—Ed Murray, Detroit (NFC) | 0 | 46 | 25 | 121 |
| —Rafael Septien, Dallas (NFC) | 0 | 40 | 27 | 121 |
| 1980—John Smith, New England (AFC) | 0 | 51 | 26 | 129 |
| 1979—John Smith, New England (AFC) | 0 | 46 | 23 | 115 |
| 1978—Frank Corral, Los Angeles (NFC) | 0 | 31 | 29 | 118 |
| 1977—Errol Mann, Oakland (AFC) | 0 | 39 | 20 | 99 |
| 1976—Tony Linhart, Baltimore (AFC) | 0 | 49 | 20 | 109 |
| 1975—O. J. Simpson, Buffalo (AFC) | 23 | 0 | 0 | 138 |
| 1974—Chester Marcol, Green Bay (NFC) | 0 | 19 | 25 | 94 |
| 1973—David Ray, Los Angeles (NFC) | 0 | 40 | 30 | 130 |
| 1972—Chester Marcol, Green Bay (NCF)* | 0 | 29 | 33 | 128 |
| 1971—Garo Yepremian, Miami (ACF) | 0 | 33 | 18 | 117 |
| 1970—Fred Cox, Minnesota (NFC) | 0 | 35 | 30 | 125 |
| 1969—Jim Turner, New York (AFL) | 0 | 33 | 32 | 129 |
| 1968—Jim Turner, New York (AFL) | 0 | 43 | 34 | 145 |
| 1967—Jim Bakken, St. Louis (NFL) | 0 | 36 | 27 | 117 |
| 1966—Gino Cappelletti, Boston (AFL) | 6 | 35 | 16 | 119 |
| 1965—Gale Sayers, Chicago (NFL)* | 22 | 0 | 0 | 132 |
| —Gino Capelletti, Boston (AFL) | 9 | 27 | 17 | 132 |
| 1964—Gino Cappelletti, Boston (AFL) | 7 | 36 | 25 | 155 |
| 1963—Gino Cappelletti, Boston (AFL) | 2 | 35 | 22 | 113 |
| 1962—Gene Mingo, Denver (AFL) | 4 | 32 | 27 | 137 |
| 1961—Gino Cappelletti, Boston (AFL) | 8 | 48 | 17 | 147 |
| 1960—Paul Hornung, Green Bay (NFL) | 15 | 41 | 15 | 176 |
| 1959—Paul Hornung, Green Bay | 7 | 31 | 7 | 94 |
| 1958—Jim Brown, Cleveland Browns | 18 | 0 | 0 | 108 |
| 1957—Sam Baker, Washington | 1 | 29 | 14 | 77 |
| —Lou Groza, Cleveland Browns | 0 | 32 | 15 | 77 |
| 1956—Bobby Layne, Detroit | 5 | 33 | 12 | 99 |
| 1955—Doak Walker, Detroit | 7 | 27 | 9 | 96 |
| 1954—Robert Walston, Philadelphia | 11 | 36 | 4 | 114 |
| 1953—Gordon Soltau, San Francisco | 6 | 48 | 10 | 114 |
| 1952—Gordon Soltau, San Francisco | 7 | 34 | 6 | 94 |
| 1951—Elroy Hirsch, Los Angeles | 17 | 0 | 0 | 102 |
| 1950—Doak Walker, Detroit* | 11 | 38 | 8 | 128 |
| 1949—Pat Harder, Chicago Cardinals | 8 | 45 | 3 | 102 |
| —Gene Roberts, New York Giants | 17 | 0 | 0 | 102 |
| 1948—Pat Harder, Chicago Cardinals | 6 | 53 | 7 | 110 |
| 1947—Pat Harder, Chicago Cardinals | 7 | 39 | 7 | 102 |
| 1946—Ted Fritsch, Green Bay | 10 | 13 | 9 | 100 |
| 1945—Steve Van Buren, Philadelphia | 18 | 2 | 0 | 110 |
| 1944—Don Hutson, Green Bay | 9 | 31 | 0 | 85 |
| 1943—Don Hutson, Green Bay | 12 | 36 | 3 | 117 |
| 1942—Don Hutson, Green Bay | 17 | 33 | 1 | 138 |
| 1941—Don Hutson, Green Bay | 17 | 20 | 1 | 95 |
| 1940—Don Hutson, Green Bay | 7 | 15 | 0 | 57 |
| 1939—Andy Farkas, Washington | 11 | 2 | 0 | 68 |
| 1938—Clarke Hinkle, Green Bay | 7 | 7 | 3 | 58 |

## PLAYER OF THE YEAR AWARDS

**National Football Conference**

|  |  |
|---|---|
| 1970 | John Brodie, San Francisco 49ers |
| 1971 | Alan Page, Minnesota Vikings |
| 1972 | Larry Brown, Washington Redskins |
| 1973 | John Hadl, Los Angeles Rams |
| 1974 | Jim Hart, St. Louis Cardinals |
| 1975 | Fran Tarkenton, Minnesota Vikings |
| 1976 | Chuck Foreman, Minnesota Vikings |
| 1977 | Walter Payton, Chicago Bears |
| 1978 | Archie Manning, New Orleans Saints |
| 1979 | Ottis Anderson, St. Louis Cardinals |
| 1980 | Ron Jaworski, Philadelphia Eagles |
| 1981 | Tony Dorsett, Dallas Cowboys |

**American Football Conference**

|  |  |
|---|---|
| 1970 | George Blanda, Oakland Raiders |
| 1971 | Otis Taylor, Kansas City Chiefs |
| 1972 | O.J. Simpson, Buffalo Bills |
| 1973 | O.J. Simpson, Buffalo Bills |
| 1974 | Ken Stabler, Oakland Raiders |
| 1975 | O.J. Simpson, Buffalo Bills |
| 1976 | Bert Jones, Baltimore Colts |
| 1977 | Craig Morton, Denver Broncos |
| 1978 | Earl Campbell, Houston Oilers |
| 1979 | Dan Fouts, San Diego Chargers |
| 1980 | Brian Sipe, Cleveland Browns |
| 1981 | Ken Anderson, Cincinnati Bengals |

## 1982 NATIONAL FOOTBALL LEAGUE DRAFT

First Two Choices of Each Team, Position Played, School and Order of Selection

| | |
|---|---|
| Atlanta | Gerald Riggs, rb, Arizona State (10)<br>Doug Rogers, de, Stanford (37) |
| Baltimore | Johnny Cooks, lb, Mississippi State (2)<br>Art Schlichter, qb, Ohio State (5) |
| Buffalo | Perry Tuttle, wr, Clemson (20)<br>Matt Kofler, qb, San Diego State (49) |
| Chicago | Jim McMahon, qb, Brigham Young (6)<br>Tim Wrightman, te, UCLA (63) |
| Cincinnati | Glen Collins, dt, Mississippi State (27)<br>Emanuel Weaver, dt, South Carolina (55) |
| Cleveland | Chip Banks, lb, USC (4)<br>Keith Baldwin, de, Texas A & M (32) |
| Dallas | Rod Hill, db, Kentucky State (26)<br>Jeff Rohrer, lb, Yale (54) |
| Denver | Gerald Willhite, rb, San Jose State (22)<br>Orlando McDaniel, wr, LSU (51) |
| Detroit | Jimmy Williams, lb, Nebraska (16)<br>Bobby Watkins, db, SW Texas State (43) |
| Green Bay | Ron Hallstrom, t, Iowa (23)<br>Del Rodgers, rb, Utah (72) |
| Houston | Mike Munchak, g, Penn State (9)<br>Oliver Luck, qb, West Virginia (45) |
| Kansas City | Anthony Hancock, wr, Tennessee (12)<br>Calvin Daniels, lb, North Carolina (47) |
| L.A. Raiders (Oakland) | Marcus Allen, rb, USC (11)<br>Jack Squirek, lb, Illinois (36) |
| L.A. Rams | Barry Redden, rb, Richmond (15)<br>Bill Bechtold, c, Oklahoma (68) |
| Miami | Roy Foster, g, USC (25)<br>Mark Duper, wr, NW Louisiana (53) |
| Minnesota | Darrin Nelson, rb, Stanford (8)<br>Terry Tausch, t, Texas (40) |
| New England | Kenneth Sims, de, Texas (1)<br>Lester Williams, dt, Miami (Fla.) (28) |
| New Orleans | Dave Wilson, qb, Illinois (3)<br>Lindsey Scott, wr, Georgia (14) |
| N.Y. Giants | Butch Woolfolk, rb, Michigan (19)<br>Joe Morris, rb, Syracuse (46) |
| N.Y. Jets | Bob Crable, lb, Notre Dame (24)<br>Reggie McElroy, t, W. Texas State (52) |
| Philadelphia | Mike Quick, wr, North Carolina State (21)<br>Lawrence Sampleton, te, Texas (48) |
| Pittsburgh | Walter Abercrombie, rb, Baylor (13)<br>John Meyer, t, Arizona State (44) |
| St. Louis | Luis Sharpe, t, UCLA (17)<br>David Galloway, dt, Florida (39) |
| San Diego | Hollis Hall, db, Clemson (189)<br>Maury Buford, p, Texas Tech (216) |
| San Francisco | William Paris, t, Michigan (30)<br>Newton Williams, rb, Arizona State (140) |
| Seattle | Jeff Bryant, dt, Clemson (7)<br>Bruce Scholtz, lb, Texas (34) • |
| Tampa Bay | Sean Farrell, g, Penn State (18)<br>Booker Reese, de, Bethune-Cookman (33) |
| Washington | Vernon Dean, db, San Diego State (50)<br>Carl Powell, wr, Jackson State (62) |

## NATIONAL FOOTBALL LEAGUE STADIUMS

AMERICAN FOOTBALL CONFERENCE

| Team | Stadium | Capacity |
|---|---|---|
| Baltimore | Memorial Stadium | 60,000 |
| Buffalo | Rich Stadium | 80,000 |
| Cincinnati | Riverfront Stadium | 59,000 |
| Cleveland | Cleveland Stadium | 80,000 |
| Denver | Mile High Stadium | 75,000 |
| Houston | Astrodome | 50,000 |
| Kansas City | Arrowhead Stadium | 78,000 |
| Miami | Orange Bowl | 75,000 |
| New England | Schaefer Stadium (Foxboro, Mass.) | 61,000 |
| N.Y. Jets | Shea Stadium | 60,000 |
| Oakland | Memorial Coliseum | 92,000 |
| Pittsburgh | Three Rivers Stadium | 54,000 |
| San Diego | San Diego Stadium | 52,000 |
| Seattle | Kingdome | 64,000 |

NATIONAL FOOTBALL CONFERENCE

| Team | Stadium | Capacity |
|---|---|---|
| Atlanta | Atlanta-Fulton Co. Stadium | 60,000 |
| Chicago | Soldier Field | 65,000 |
| Dallas | Texas Stadium | 65,000 |
| Detroit | Pontiac Silverdome | 80,000 |
| Green Bay | Lambeau Field | 56,000 |
| | Milwaukee Co. Stadium | 55,000 |
| Los Angeles | Anaheim Stadium | 69,000 |
| Minnesota | Metrodome | 62,000 |
| New Orleans | Louisiana Superdome | 71,000 |
| N.Y. Giants | Giants Stadium (E. Rutherford, N.J.) | 76,000 |
| Philadelphia | Veterans Stadium | 72,000 |
| St. Louis | Busch Memorial Stadium | 51,000 |
| San Francisco | Candlestick Park | 61,000 |
| Tampa Bay | Tampa Stadium | 72,000 |
| Washington | Robert F. Kennedy Stadium | 55,000 |

## 1981 CANADIAN FOOTBALL LEAGUE FINAL STANDINGS

| EASTERN CONFERENCE | W | L | T | PF | PA | Pts. |
|---|---|---|---|---|---|---|
| Hamilton Tiger-Cats | 11 | 4 | 1 | 414 | 335 | 23 |
| Ottawa Rough Riders | 5 | 11 | 0 | 306 | 446 | 10 |
| Montreal Alouettes | 3 | 13 | 0 | 267 | 518 | 6 |
| Toronto Argonauts | 2 | 14 | 0 | 241 | 506 | 4 |

| WESTERN CONFERENCE | W | L | T | PF | PA | Pts. |
|---|---|---|---|---|---|---|
| Edmonton Eskimos | 14 | 1 | 1 | 566 | 277 | 29 |
| Winnipeg Blue Bombers | 11 | 5 | 0 | 517 | 299 | 22 |
| British Columbia Lions | 10 | 6 | 0 | 438 | 377 | 20 |
| Saskatchewan Roughriders | 9 | 7 | 0 | 431 | 371 | 18 |
| Calgary Stampeders | 6 | 10 | 0 | 306 | 367 | 12 |

Conference Semifinals: Ottawa 20–Montreal 16, British Columbia 15– Winnipeg 11
Conference Finals: Ottawa 17–Hamilton 13, Edmonton 22–British Columbia 16
Championship (Grey Cup): Edmonton 26, Ottawa 23

## CANADIAN FOOTBALL LEAGUE CHAMPIONS (GREY CUP)

| Year | Champion | Year | Champion | Year | Champion | Year | Champion |
|---|---|---|---|---|---|---|---|
| 1954 | Edmonton | 1961 | Winnipeg | 1968 | Ottawa | 1975 | Edmonton |
| 1955 | Edmonton | 1962 | Winnipeg | 1969 | Ottawa | 1976 | Ottawa |
| 1956 | Edmonton | 1963 | Hamilton | 1970 | Montreal | 1977 | Montreal |
| 1957 | Hamilton | 1964 | British Columbia | 1971 | Calgary | 1978 | Edmonton |
| 1958 | Winnipeg | 1965 | Hamilton | 1972 | Hamilton | 1979 | Edmonton |
| 1959 | Winnipeg | 1966 | Saskatchewan | 1973 | Ottawa | 1980 | Edmonton |
| 1960 | Ottawa | 1967 | Hamilton | 1974 | Montreal | 1981 | Edmonton |

# COLLEGE FOOTBALL

## RECORD OF THE MAJOR COLLEGE BOWL GAMES

### ROSE BOWL Pasedena, California (January)

| Year | Result |
|---|---|
| 1902 | Michigan 49, Stanford 0 |
| 1916 | Washington State 14, Brown 0 |
| 1917 | Oregon 14, Pennsylvania 0 |
| 1918 | Mare Island Marines 19, Camp Lewis 7 |
| 1919 | Great Lakes 17, Mare Island 0 |
| 1920 | Harvard 7, Oregon 6 |
| 1921 | California 28, Ohio State 0 |
| 1922 | Washington and Jefferson 0, California 0 |
| 1923 | So. California 14, Penn State 3 |
| 1924 | Navy 14, Washington 14 |
| 1925 | Notre Dame 27, Stanford 10 |
| 1926 | Alabama 20, Washington 19 |
| 1927 | Alabama 7, Stanford 7 |
| 1928 | Stanford 7, Pittsburgh 6 |
| 1929 | Georgia Tech 8, California 7 |
| 1930 | So. California 47, Pittsburgh 14 |
| 1931 | Alabama 24, Washington State 0 |
| 1932 | So. California 21, Tulane 12 |
| 1933 | So. California 35, Pittsburgh 0 |
| 1934 | Columbia 7, Stanford 0 |
| 1935 | Alabama 29, Stanford 13 |
| 1936 | Stanford 7, Southern Methodist 0 |
| 1937 | Pittsburgh 21, Washington 0 |
| 1938 | California 13, Alabama 0 |
| 1939 | So. California 7, Duke 3 |
| 1940 | So. California 14, Tennessee 0 |
| 1941 | Stanford 21, Nebraska 13 |
| 1942* | Oregon State 20, Duke 16 |
| 1943 | Georgia 9, UCLA 0 |
| 1944 | So. California 29, Washington 0 |
| 1945 | So. California 25, Tennessee 0 |
| 1946 | Alabama 34, So. California 14 |
| 1947 | Illinois 45, UCLA 14 |
| 1948 | Michigan 49, Southern California 0 |
| 1949 | Northwestern 20, California 14 |
| 1950 | Ohio State 17, California 14 |
| 1951 | Michigan 14, California 6 |
| 1952 | Illinois 40, Stanford 7 |
| 1953 | So. California 7, Wisconsin 0 |
| 1954 | Michigan State 28, UCLA 20 |
| 1955 | Ohio State 20, So. California 7 |
| 1956 | Michigan State 17, UCLA 14 |
| 1957 | Iowa 35, Oregon State 19 |
| 1958 | Ohio State 10, Oregon 7 |
| 1959 | Iowa 38, California 12 |
| 1960 | Washington 44, Wisconsin 8 |
| 1961 | Washington 17, Minnesota 7 |
| 1962 | Minnesota 21, UCLA 3 |
| 1963 | So. California 42, Wisconsin 37 |
| 1964 | Illinois 17, Washington 7 |
| 1965 | Michigan 34, Oregon State 7 |
| 1966 | UCLA 14, Michigan State 12 |
| 1967 | Purdue 14, So. California 13 |
| 1968 | So. California 14, Indiana 3 |
| 1969 | Ohio State 27, Southern California 16 |
| 1970 | So. California 10, Michigan 3 |
| 1971 | Stanford 27, Ohio State 17 |
| 1972 | Stanford 13, Michigan 12 |
| 1973 | So. California 42, Ohio State 17 |
| 1974 | Ohio State 42, So. California 21 |
| 1975 | So. California 18, Ohio State 17 |
| 1976 | UCLA 23, Ohio State 10 |
| 1977 | So. California 14, Michigan 6 |
| 1978 | Washington 27, Michigan 20 |
| 1979 | So. California 17, Michigan 10 |
| 1980 | So. California 17, Ohio State 16 |
| 1981 | Michigan 23, Washington 6 |
| 1982 | Washington 28, Iowa 0 |

* Played at Durham, North Carolina.

### ORANGE BOWL Miami, Florida (January)

| Year | Result |
|---|---|
| 1933 | Miami (Fla.) 7, Manhattan 0 |
| 1934 | Duquesne 33, Miami (Fla.) 7 |
| 1935 | Bucknell 26, Miami (Fla.) 0 |
| 1936 | Catholic Univ. 20, Mississippi 19 |
| 1937 | Duquesne 13, Miss. State 12 |
| 1938 | Auburn 6, Michigan State 0 |
| 1939 | Tennessee 17, Oklahoma 0 |
| 1940 | Georgia Tech 21, Missouri 7 |
| 1941 | Miss. State 14, Georgetown 7 |
| 1942 | Georgia 40, Texas Christian 26 |
| 1943 | Alabama 37, Boston College 21 |
| 1944 | LSU 19, Texas A&M 14 |
| 1945 | Tulsa 26, Georgia Tech 12 |
| 1946 | Miami (Fla.) 13, Holy Cross 6 |
| 1947 | Rice 8, Tennessee 0 |
| 1948 | Georgia Tech 20, Kansas 14 |
| 1949 | Texas 41, Georgia 28 |
| 1950 | Santa Clara 21, Kentucky 13 |
| 1951 | Clemson 15, Miami (Fla.) 14 |
| 1952 | Georgia Tech 17, Baylor 14 |
| 1953 | Alabama 61, Syracuse 6 |
| 1954 | Oklahoma 7, Maryland 0 |
| 1955 | Duke 34, Nebraska 7 |
| 1956 | Oklahoma 20, Maryland 6 |
| 1957 | Colorado 27, Clemson 21 |
| 1958 | Oklahoma 48, Duke 21 |
| 1959 | Oklahoma 21, Syracuse 6 |
| 1960 | Georgia 14, Missouri 0 |
| 1961 | Missouri 21, Navy 14 |
| 1962 | Louisiana State 25, Colorado 7 |
| 1963 | Alabama 17, Oklahoma 0 |
| 1964 | Nebraska 13, Auburn 7 |
| 1965 | Texas 21, Alabama 17 |
| 1966 | Alabama 39, Nebraska 28 |
| 1967 | Florida 27, Georgia Tech 12 |
| 1968 | Oklahoma 26, Tennessee 24 |
| 1969 | Penn State 15, Kansas 14 |
| 1970 | Penn State 10, Missouri 3 |
| 1971 | Nebraska 17, Louisiana State 12 |
| 1972 | Nebraska 38, Alabama 6 |
| 1973 | Nebraska 40, Notre Dame 6 |
| 1974 | Penn State 16, Louisiana State 9 |
| 1975 | Notre Dame 13, Alabama 11 |
| 1976 | Oklahoma 14, Michigan 6 |
| 1977 | Ohio State 27, Colorado 10 |
| 1978 | Arkansas 31, Oklahoma 6 |
| 1979 | Oklahoma 31, Nebraska 24 |
| 1980 | Oklahoma 24, Florida State 7 |
| 1981 | Oklahoma 18, Florida State 17 |
| 1982 | Clemson 22, Nebraska 15 |

### SUGAR BOWL New Orleans, Louisiana (January)

| Year | Result |
|---|---|
| 1935 | Tulane 20, Temple 14 |
| 1936 | TCU 3, Louisiana State 2 |
| 1937 | Santa Clara 21, LSU 14 |
| 1938 | Santa Clara 6, Louisiana State 0 |
| 1939 | TCU 15, Carnegie Tech 7 |
| 1940 | Texas A&M 14, Tulane 13 |
| 1941 | Boston College 19, Tennessee 13 |
| 1942 | Fordham 2, Missouri 0 |
| 1943 | Tennessee 14, Tulsa 7 |
| 1944 | Georgia Tech 20, Tulsa 18 |
| 1945 | Duke 29, Alabama 26 |
| 1946 | Oklahoma A & M 33, St. Mary's (Calif.) 13 |
| 1947 | Georgia 20, North Carolina 10 |
| 1948 | Texas 27, Alabama 7 |
| 1949 | Oklahoma 14, North Carolina 6 |
| 1950 | Oklahoma 35, Louisiana State 0 |
| 1951 | Kentucky 13, Oklahoma 7 |
| 1952 | Maryland 28, Tennessee 13 |
| 1953 | Georgia Tech 24, Mississippi 7 |
| 1954 | Georgia Tech 42, West Va. 19 |
| 1955 | Navy 21, Mississippi 0 |
| 1956 | Georgia Tech 7, Pittsburgh 0 |
| 1957 | Baylor 13, Tennessee 7 |
| 1958 | Mississippi 39, Texas 7 |
| 1959 | Louisiana State 7, Clemson 0 |
| 1960 | Mississippi 21, Louisiana State 0 |
| 1961 | Mississippi 14, Rice 6 |
| 1962 | Alabama 10, Arkansas 3 |
| 1963 | Mississippi 17, Arkansas 13 |
| 1964 | Alabama 12, Mississippi 7 |
| 1965 | Louisiana State 13, Syracuse 10 |
| 1966 | Missouri 20, Florida 18 |
| 1967 | Alabama 34, Nebraska 7 |
| 1968 | Louisiana State 20, Wyoming 13 |
| 1969 | Arkansas 16, Georgia 2 |
| 1970 | Mississippi 27, Arkansas 22 |
| 1971 | Tennessee 34, Air Force 13 |
| 1972 | Oklahoma 40, Auburn 22 |
| 1972 (Dec.) | Oklahoma 14, Penn State 0 |
| 1973 (Dec.) | Notre Dame 24, Alabama 23 |
| 1974 (Dec.) | Nebraska 13, Florida 10 |
| 1975 (Dec.) | Alabama 13, Penn State 6 |
| 1977 | Pittsburgh 27, Georgia 3 |
| 1978 | Alabama 35, Ohio State 6 |
| 1979 | Alabama 14, Penn State 7 |
| 1980 | Alabama 24, Arkansas 9 |
| 1981 | Georgia 17, Notre Dame 10 |
| 1982 | Pittsburgh 24, Georgia 20 |

### COTTON BOWL Dallas, Texas (January)

| Year | Result |
|---|---|
| 1937 | Texas Christian 16, Marquette 6 |
| 1938 | Rice 28, Colorado 14 |
| 1939 | St. Mary's 20, Texas Tech 13 |
| 1940 | Clemson 6, Boston College 3 |
| 1941 | Texas A&M 13, Fordham 12 |
| 1942 | Alabama 29, Texas A&M 21 |
| 1943 | Texas 14, Georgia Tech 7 |
| 1944 | Randolph Field 7, Texas 7 |
| 1945 | Oklahoma A & M 34, TCU 0 |
| 1946 | Texas 40, Missouri 27 |
| 1947 | Louisiana State 0, Arkansas 0 |
| 1948 | So. Methodist 13, Penn St. 13 |
| 1949 | So. Methodist 21, Oregon 13 |
| 1950 | Rice 27, North Carolina 13 |
| 1951 | Tennessee 20, Texas 14 |
| 1952 | Kentucky 20, Texas Christian 7 |
| 1953 | Texas 16, Tennessee 0 |
| 1954 | Rice 28, Alabama 6 |
| 1955 | Georgia Tech 14, Arkansas 6 |
| 1956 | Mississippi 14, TCU 13 |
| 1957 | Texas Christian 28, Syracuse 27 |
| 1958 | Navy 20, Rice 7 |
| 1959 | Air Force 0, Texas Christian 0 |
| 1960 | Syracuse 23, Texas 14 |
| 1961 | Duke 7, Arkansas 6 |
| 1962 | Texas 12, Mississippi 7 |
| 1963 | Louisiana State 13, Texas 0 |
| 1964 | Texas 28, Navy 6 |
| 1965 | Arkansas 10, Nebraska 7 |
| 1966 | Louisiana State 14, Arkansas 7 |
| 1966 | (Dec.) Georgia 24, SMU 9 |
| 1968 | Texas A&M 20, Alabama 16 |
| 1969 | Texas 36, Tennessee 13 |
| 1970 | Texas 21, Notre Dame 17 |
| 1971 | Notre Dame 24, Texas 11 |
| 1972 | Penn State 30, Texas 6 |
| 1973 | Texas 17, Alabama 13 |
| 1974 | Nebraska 19, Texas 3 |
| 1975 | Penn State 41, Baylor 20 |
| 1976 | Arkansas 31, Georgia 10 |
| 1977 | Houston 30, Maryland 21 |
| 1978 | Notre Dame 38, Texas 10 |
| 1979 | Notre Dame 35, Houston 34 |
| 1980 | Houston 17, Nebraska 14 |
| 1981 | Alabama 30, Baylor 2 |
| 1982 | Texas 14, Alabama 12 |

**SUN BOWL** El Paso, Texas (J=January, D=December)

| Year | Result |
|---|---|
| 1936J | H.-Simmons 14, N.M. State 14 |
| 1937J | H.-Simmons 34, Tex. Mines 6 |
| 1938J | West Virginia 7, Texas Tech 6 |
| 1939J | Utah 26, New Mexico 0 |
| 1940J | Catholic U. 0, Arizona St. 0 |
| 1941J | W. Reserve 26, Arizona St. 13 |
| 1942J | Tulsa 6, Texas Tech 0 |
| 1943J | 2nd Air Force 13, H.-Simmons 7 |
| 1944J | Southwestern 7, New Mexico 0 |
| 1945J | Southwestern 35, U. Mexico 0 |
| 1946J | New Mexico 34, Denver 24 |
| 1947J | Cincinnati 18, Virginia Tech 6 |
| 1948J | Miami (Ohio) 13, Texas Tech 12 |
| 1949J | W. Virginia 21, Texas Mines 12 |
| 1950J | Tex. Western 33, Georgetown 20 |
| 1951J | W. Tex. St. 14, Cincinnati 13 |
| 1952J | Texas Tech 25, Col. Pacific 14 |
| 1953J | Col. Pacific 26, Miss. Southern 7 |
| 1954J | Tex. Western 37, Miss. So. 14 |
| 1955J | Tex. Western 47, Florida St. 20 |
| 1956J | Wyoming 21, Texas Tech 14 |
| 1957J | George Wash. 13, Texas W. 0 |
| 1958J | Louisville 34, Drake 20 |
| 1958D | Wyoming 14, H.-Simmons 6 |
| 1959D | N.M. State 28, N. Tex. State 8 |
| 1960D | N.M. State 20, Utah State 13 |
| 1961D | Villanova 17, Wichita 9 |
| 1962D | W. Texas St. 15, Ohio U. 14 |
| 1963D | Oregon 21, SMU 14 |
| 1964D | Georgia 7, Texas Tech 0 |
| 1965D | Texas Western 13, TCU 12 |
| 1966D | Wyoming 28, Florida State 20 |
| 1967D | Texas-El Paso 14, Miss. 7 |
| 1968D | Auburn 34, Arizona 10 |
| 1969D | Nebraska 45, Georgia 6 |
| 1970D | Georgia Tech 17, Texas Tech 9 |
| 1971D | LSU 33, Iowa State 15 |
| 1972D | N. Carolina 32, Texas Tech 28 |
| 1973D | Missouri 34, Auburn 17 |
| 1974D | Miss. State 26, N. Carolina 24 |
| 1975D | Pittsburgh 33, Kansas 19 |
| 1977J | Texas A & M 37, Florida 14 |
| 1977D | Stanford 24, LSU 14 |
| 1978D | Texas 42, Maryland 0 |
| 1979D | Washington 14, Texas 7 |
| 1980D | Nebraska 31, Mississippi St. 17 |
| 1981D | Oklahoma 40, Houston 14 |

**GATOR BOWL** Jacksonville, Florida (J=January, D=December)

| Year | Result |
|---|---|
| 1946J | Wake Forest 26, S. Carolina 14 |
| 1947J | Oklahoma 34, N.C. State 13 |
| 1948J | Maryland 20, Georgia 20 |
| 1949J | Clemson 24, Missouri 23 |
| 1950J | Maryland 20, Missouri 7 |
| 1951J | Wyoming 20, Wash. & Lee 7 |
| 1952J | Miami (Fla.) 14, Clemson 0 |
| 1953J | Florida 14, Tulsa 13 |
| 1954J | Texas Tech 35, Auburn 13 |
| 1954D | Auburn 33, Baylor 13 |
| 1955D | Vanderbilt 25, Auburn 13 |
| 1956D | Georgia Tech 21, Pittsburgh 14 |
| 1957D | Tennessee 3, Texas A & M 0 |
| 1958D | Mississippi 7, Florida 3 |
| 1960J | Arkansas 14, Georgia Tech 7 |
| 1960D | Florida 13, Baylor 12 |
| 1961D | Penn State 30, Georgia Tech 15 |
| 1962D | Florida 17, Penn State 7 |
| 1963D | N. Carolina 35, Air Force 0 |
| 1965J | Florida St. 36, Oklahoma 19 |
| 1965D | Georgia Tech 31, Texas Tech 21 |
| 1966D | Tennessee 18, Syracuse 12 |
| 1967D | Penn State 17, Florida St. 17 |
| 1968D | Missouri 35, Alabama 10 |
| 1969D | Florida 14, Tennessee 13 |
| 1971J | Auburn 35, Mississippi 28 |
| 1971D | Georgia 7, N. Carolina 3 |
| 1972D | Auburn 24, Colorado 3 |
| 1973D | Texas Tech 28, Tennessee 19 |
| 1974D | Auburn 27, Texas 3 |
| 1975D | Maryland 13, Florida 0 |
| 1976D | Notre Dame 20, Penn State 9 |
| 1977D | Pittsburgh 34, Clemson 3 |
| 1978D | Clemson 17, Ohio State 15 |
| 1979D | N. Carolina 17, Michigan 15 |
| 1980D | Pittsburgh 37, South Carolina 9 |
| 1981D | North Carolina 31, Arkansas 27 |

**TANGERINE BOWL** Orlando, Florida (J=January, D=December)

| Year | Result |
|---|---|
| 1947J | Catawba 31, Maryville 6 |
| 1948J | Catawba 7, Marshall 0 |
| 1949J | Murray St. 21, Sul Ross St. 21 |
| 1950J | St. Vincent 7, Emory & Henry 6 |
| 1951J | Mor. Harvey 35, Emory & Henry 14 |
| 1952J | Stetson 35, Arkansas St. 20 |
| 1953J | E. Texas St. 33, Tenn. Tech 0 |
| 1954J | E. Texas St. 7, Arkansas St. 7 |
| 1955J | Nebraska (Omaha) 7, E. Ken. 6 |
| 1956J | Juniata 6, Missouri Valley 6 |
| 1957J | W. Texas St. 20, So. Miss. 13 |
| 1958J | E. Texas St. 10, So. Miss. 9 |
| 1958D | E. Texas St. 26, Missouri Va. 7 |
| 1960J | Middle Tenn. 21, Presbyterian 12 |
| 1960D | Citadel 27, Tennessee Tech 0 |
| 1961D | Lamar 21, Middle Tennessee 14 |
| 1962D | Houston 49, Miami (Ohio) 21 |
| 1963D | W. Kentucky 27, Coast Guard 0 |
| 1964D | E. Carolina 14, Massachusetts 13 |
| 1965D | E. Carolina 31, Maine 0 |
| 1966D | Morgan St. 14, West Chester 6 |
| 1967D | Tenn. (Martin) 25, West Chester 8 |
| 1968D | Richmond 49, Ohio U. 42 |
| 1969D | Toledo 56, Davidson 33 |
| 1970D | Toledo 40, William & Mary 12 |
| 1971D | Toledo 28, Richmond 3 |
| 1972D | Tampa 21, Kent State 18 |
| 1973D | Miami (Ohio) 16, Florida 7 |
| 1974D | Miami (Ohio) 21, Georgia 10 |
| 1975D | Miami (Ohio) 20, S. Carolina 7 |
| 1976D | Okla. State 49, Brigham Young 21 |
| 1977D | Florida St. 40, Texas Tech 17 |
| 1978D | N. Carolina St. 30, Pittsburgh 17 |
| 1979D | LSU 34, Wake Forest 10 |
| 1980D | Florida 35, Maryland 20 |
| 1981D | Missouri 19, So. Mississippi 17 |

**BLUEBONNET BOWL** Houston, Texas (December)

| Year | Result |
|---|---|
| 1959 | Clemson 23, TCU 7 |
| 1960 | Texas 3, Alabama 3 |
| 1961 | Kansas 33, Rice 0 |
| 1962 | Missouri 14, Georgia Tech 10 |
| 1963 | Baylor 14, LSU 7 |
| 1964 | Tulsa 14, Mississippi 7 |
| 1965 | Tennessee 27, Tulsa 6 |
| 1966 | Texas 19, Mississippi 0 |
| 1967 | Colorado 31, Miami (Fla.) 21 |
| 1968 | SMU 28, Oklahoma 27 |
| 1969 | Houston 36, Auburn 7 |
| 1970 | Alabama 24, Oklahoma 24 |
| 1971 | Colorado 29, Houston 17 |
| 1972 | Tennessee 24, LSU 17 |
| 1973 | Houston 47, Tulane 7 |
| 1974 | N.C. State 31, Houston 31 |
| 1975 | Texas 38, Colorado 21 |
| 1976 | Nebraska 27, Texas Tech 24 |
| 1977 | USC 47, Texas A & M 28 |
| 1978 | Stanford 25, Georgia 22 |
| 1979 | Purdue 27, Tennessee 22 |
| 1980 | North Carolina 16, Texas 7 |
| 1981 | Michigan 33, UCLA 14 |

**LIBERTY BOWL** Memphis, Tennessee* (December)

| Year | Result |
|---|---|
| 1959 | Penn State 7, Alabama 0 |
| 1960 | Penn State 41, Oregon 12 |
| 1961 | Syracuse 15, Miami (Fla.) 14 |
| 1962 | Oregon St. 6, Villanova 0 |
| 1963 | Mississippi St. 16, N.C. State 12 |
| 1964 | Utah 32, West Virginia 6 |
| 1965 | Mississippi 13, Auburn 7 |
| 1966 | Miami (Fla.) 14, Virginia Tech 7 |
| 1967 | N.C. State 14, Georgia 7 |
| 1968 | Mississippi 34, Virginia Tech 17 |
| 1969 | Colorado 47, Alabama 33 |
| 1970 | Tulane 17, Colorado 3 |
| 1971 | Tennessee 14, Arkansas 13 |
| 1972 | Georgia Tech 31, Iowa State 30 |
| 1973 | N.C. State 31, Kansas 18 |
| 1974 | Tennessee 7, Maryland 3 |
| 1975 | USC 20, Texas A & M 0 |
| 1976 | Alabama 36, UCLA 6 |
| 1977 | Nebraska 21, N. Carolina 17 |
| 1978 | Missouri 20, LSU 15 |
| 1979 | Penn State 9, Tulane 6 |
| 1980 | Purdue 28, Missouri 25 |
| 1981 | Ohio State 31, Navy 28 |

*Philadelphia 1960-1964, Atlantic City 1965

**PEACH BOWL** Atlanta, Georgia (December)

| Year | Result |
|---|---|
| 1968 | LSU 31, Florida State 27 |
| 1969 | W. Virginia 14, S. Carolina 3 |
| 1970 | Arizona St. 48, N. Carolina 26 |
| 1971 | Mississippi 41, Georgia Tech 18 |
| 1972 | N.C. State 49, W. Virginia 13 |
| 1973 | Georgia 17, Maryland 16 |
| 1974 | Vanderbilt 6, Texas Tech 6 |
| 1975 | W. Virginia 13, N.C. State 10 |
| 1976 | Kentucky 21, N. Carolina 0 |
| 1977 | N.C. State 24, Iowa State 14 |
| 1978 | Purdue 41, Georgia Tech 21 |
| 1979 | Baylor 24, Clemson 18 |
| 1981 (Jan.) | Miami (Fla.) 20, Va. Tech 10 |
| 1981 | West Virginia 26, Florida 6 |

**FIESTA BOWL** Tempe, Arizona (December)

| Year | Result |
|---|---|
| 1971 | Arizona St. 45, Florida St. 38 |
| 1972 | Arizona St. 49, Missouri 35 |
| 1973 | Arizona St. 28, Pittsburgh 7 |
| 1974 | Okla. St. 16, Brigham Young 6 |
| 1975 | Arizona St. 17, Nebraska 14 |
| 1976 | Oklahoma 41, Wyoming 7 |
| 1977 | Penn State 42, Arizona St. 30 |
| 1978 | Arkansas 10, UCLA 10 |
| 1979 | Pittsburgh 16, Arizona 10 |
| 1980 | Penn State 31, Ohio State 19 |
| 1982 (Jan.) | Penn State 26, USC 10 |

## NATIONAL COLLEGE FOOTBALL CHAMPIONS

The college football team selected each year by The Associated Press poll of sportswriters and the United Press International poll of football coaches is unofficially recognized as national champion. Where the polls disagree, both teams are given.

| Year | Champion |
|---|---|
| 1926 | Stanford |
| 1927 | Illinois |
| 1928 | Southern California |
| 1929 | Notre Dame |
| 1930 | Notre Dame |
| 1931 | Southern California |
| 1932 | Michigan |
| 1933 | Michigan |
| 1934 | Minnesota |
| 1935 | Southern Methodist |
| 1936 | Minnesota |
| 1937 | Pittsburgh |
| 1938 | Texas Christian |
| 1939 | Texas A & M |
| 1940 | Minnesota |
| 1941 | Minnesota |
| 1942 | Ohio State |
| 1943 | Notre Dame |
| 1944 | Army |
| 1945 | Army |
| 1946 | Notre Dame |
| 1947 | Notre Dame |
| 1948 | Michigan |
| 1949 | Notre Dame |
| 1950 | Oklahoma |
| 1951 | Tennessee |
| 1952 | Michigan State |
| 1953 | Maryland |
| 1954 | Ohio State-UCLA |
| 1955 | Oklahoma |
| 1956 | Oklahoma |
| 1957 | Auburn-Ohio State |
| 1958 | Louisiana State |
| 1959 | Syracuse |
| 1960 | Minnesota |
| 1961 | Alabama |
| 1962 | Southern California |
| 1963 | Texas |
| 1964 | Alabama |
| 1965 | Alabama-Mich. St. |
| 1966 | Notre Dame |
| 1967 | Southern California |
| 1968 | Ohio State |
| 1969 | Texas |
| 1970 | Texas-Nebraska |
| 1971 | Nebraska |
| 1972 | Southern California |
| 1973 | Notre Dame |
| 1974 | Oklahoma-USC |
| 1975 | Oklahoma |
| 1976 | Pittsburgh |
| 1977 | Notre Dame |
| 1978 | Alabama-USC |
| 1979 | Alabama |
| 1980 | Georgia |
| 1981 | Clemson |

## COLLEGE FOOTBALL CONFERENCE CHAMPIONS

### ATLANTIC COAST

| Year | Champion |
|---|---|
| 1964 | No. Carolina State |
| 1965 | Duke |
| 1966 | Clemson |
| 1967 | Clemson |
| 1968 | No. Carolina State |
| 1969 | South Carolina |
| 1970 | Wake Forest |
| 1971 | North Carolina |
| 1972 | North Carolina |
| 1973 | No. Carolina State |
| 1974 | Maryland |
| 1975 | Maryland |
| 1976 | Maryland |
| 1977 | North Carolina |
| 1978 | Clemson |
| 1979 | No. Carolina State |
| 1980 | North Carolina |
| 1981 | Clemson |

### BIG EIGHT

| Year | Champion |
|---|---|
| 1964 | Nebraska |
| 1965 | Nebraska |
| 1966 | Nebraska |
| 1967 | Oklahoma |
| 1968 | Kansas-Oklahoma |
| 1969 | Missouri-Nebraska |
| 1970 | Nebraska |
| 1971 | Nebraska |
| 1972 | Oklahoma |
| 1973 | Oklahoma |
| 1974 | Oklahoma |
| 1975 | Nebraska-Oklahoma |
| 1976 | Colorado-Oklahoma-Oklahoma State |
| 1977 | Oklahoma |
| 1978 | Nebraska-Oklahoma |
| 1979 | Oklahoma |
| 1980 | Oklahoma |
| 1981 | Nebraska |

### BIG TEN

| Year | Champion |
|---|---|
| 1964 | Michigan |
| 1965 | Michigan State |
| 1966 | Michigan State |
| 1967 | Indiana-Purdue-Minnesota |
| 1968 | Ohio State |
| 1969 | Ohio State-Michigan |
| 1970 | Ohio State |
| 1971 | Michigan |
| 1972 | Ohio State-Michigan |
| 1973 | Michigan-Ohio State |
| 1974 | Michigan-Ohio State |
| 1975 | Ohio State |
| 1976 | Michigan-Ohio State |
| 1977 | Michigan-Ohio State |
| 1978 | Michigan St.-Michigan |
| 1979 | Ohio State |
| 1980 | Michigan |
| 1981 | Iowa-Ohio State |

### IVY LEAGUE

| Year | Champion |
|---|---|
| 1964 | Princeton |
| 1965 | Dartmouth |
| 1966 | Dartmouth-Harvard-Princeton |
| 1967 | Yale |
| 1968 | Yale-Harvard |
| 1969 | Princeton-Yale-Dartmouth |
| 1970 | Dartmouth |
| 1971 | Cornell-Dartmouth |
| 1972 | Dartmouth |
| 1973 | Dartmouth |
| 1974 | Yale-Harvard |
| 1975 | Harvard |
| 1976 | Yale-Brown |
| 1977 | Yale |
| 1978 | Dartmouth |
| 1979 | Yale |
| 1980 | Yale |
| 1981 | Yale-Dartmouth |

### MISSOURI VALLEY

| Year | Champion |
|---|---|
| 1964 | Cincinnati |
| 1965 | Tulsa |
| 1966 | North Texas-Tulsa |
| 1967 | North Texas |
| 1968 | Memphis State |
| 1969 | Memphis State |
| 1970 | Louisville |
| 1971 | North Texas |
| 1972 | Louisville-Drake-West Texas |
| 1973 | North Texas-Tulsa |
| 1974 | Tulsa |
| 1975 | Tulsa |
| 1976 | Tulsa-N. Mexico State |
| 1977 | West Texas State |
| 1978 | New Mexico State |
| 1979 | West Texas State |
| 1980 | Wichita St.-Tulsa |
| 1981 | Drake-Tulsa |

### PACIFIC TEN

| Year | Champion |
|---|---|
| 1964 | Oregon State-Southern California |
| 1965 | UCLA |
| 1966 | Southern California |
| 1967 | Southern California |
| 1968 | Southern California |
| 1969 | Southern California |
| 1970 | Stanford |
| 1971 | Stanford |
| 1972 | Southern California |
| 1973 | Southern California |
| 1974 | Southern California |
| 1975 | UCLA-California |
| 1976 | Southern California |
| 1977 | Washington |
| 1978 | Southern California |
| 1979 | Southern California |
| 1980 | Washington |
| 1981 | Washington |

### SOUTHEASTERN

| Year | Champion |
|---|---|
| 1964 | Alabama |
| 1965 | Alabama |
| 1966 | Georgia-Alabama |
| 1967 | Tennessee |
| 1968 | Georgia |
| 1969 | Tennessee |
| 1970 | Louisiana State |
| 1971 | Alabama |
| 1972 | Alabama |
| 1973 | Alabama |
| 1974 | Alabama |
| 1975 | Alabama |
| 1976 | Georgia |
| 1977 | Alabama |
| 1978 | Alabama |
| 1979 | Alabama |
| 1980 | Georgia |
| 1981 | Georgia-Alabama |

### SOUTHERN

| Year | Champion |
|---|---|
| 1964 | West Virginia |
| 1965 | West Virginia |
| 1966 | William & Mary-East Carolina |
| 1967 | West Virginia |
| 1968 | Richmond |
| 1969 | Richmond-Davidson |
| 1970 | William & Mary |
| 1971 | Richmond |
| 1972 | East Carolina |
| 1973 | East Carolina |
| 1974 | VMI |
| 1975 | Richmond |
| 1976 | East Carolina |
| 1977 | VMI-Tenn.-Chattanooga |
| 1978 | Tenn.-Chattanooga-Furman |
| 1979 | Tenn.-Chattanooga |
| 1980 | Furman |
| 1981 | Furman |

### MID-AMERICAN

| Year | Champion |
|---|---|
| 1964 | Bowling Green |
| 1965 | Miami (Ohio)-Bowling Green |
| 1966 | Miami (Ohio)-Western Michigan |
| 1967 | Toledo-Ohio U. |
| 1968 | Ohio University |
| 1969 | Toledo |
| 1970 | Toledo |
| 1971 | Toledo |
| 1972 | Kent State |
| 1973 | Miami (Ohio) |
| 1974 | Miami (Ohio) |
| 1975 | Miami (Ohio) |
| 1976 | Ball State |
| 1977 | Miami (Ohio) |
| 1978 | Ball State |
| 1979 | Central Michigan |
| 1980 | Central Michigan |
| 1981 | Toledo |

### SOUTHWEST

| Year | Champion |
|---|---|
| 1964 | Arkansas |
| 1965 | Arkansas |
| 1966 | Southern Methodist |
| 1967 | Texas A & M |
| 1968 | Texas-Arkansas |
| 1969 | Texas |
| 1970 | Texas |
| 1971 | Texas |
| 1972 | Texas |
| 1973 | Texas |
| 1974 | Baylor |
| 1975 | Texas-Texas A & M-Arkansas |
| 1976 | Houston-Texas Tech |
| 1977 | Texas |
| 1978 | Houston |
| 1979 | Arkansas |
| 1980 | Baylor |
| 1981 | Southern Methodist |

### WESTERN

| Year | Champion |
|---|---|
| 1964 | N.M.-Utah-Arizona |
| 1965 | Brigham Young |
| 1966 | Wyoming |
| 1967 | Wyoming |
| 1968 | Wyoming |
| 1969 | Arizona State |
| 1970 | Arizona State |
| 1971 | Arizona State |
| 1972 | Arizona State |
| 1973 | Arizona-Ariz. St. |
| 1974 | Brigham Young |
| 1975 | Arizona State |
| 1976 | Wyoming-Brigham Young |
| 1977 | Arizona State-Brigham Young |
| 1978 | Brigham Young |
| 1979 | Brigham Young |
| 1980 | Brigham Young |
| 1981 | Brigham Young |

### PACIFIC COAST

| Year | Champion |
|---|---|
| 1969 | San Diego State |
| 1970 | Long Beach State |
| 1971 | Long Beach State |
| 1972 | San Diego State |
| 1973 | San Diego State |
| 1974 | San Diego State |
| 1975 | San Jose State |
| 1976 | San Jose State |
| 1977 | Fresno State |
| 1978 | Utah State-San Jose State |
| 1979 | Utah State-San Jose State |
| 1980 | Long Beach State |
| 1981 | San Jose State |

## 1981 REGULAR SEASON RECORDS OF MAJOR COLLEGE FOOTBALL TEAMS

| Team | W | L | T | Team | W | L | T | Team | W | L | T |
|---|---|---|---|---|---|---|---|---|---|---|---|
| Air Force | 4 | 7 | 0 | Kansas | 8 | 3 | 0 | Richmond | 3 | 7 | 0 |
| Alabama | 9 | 1 | 1 | Kansas State | 2 | 9 | 0 | Rutgers | 5 | 6 | 0 |
| Arizona | 6 | 5 | 0 | Kentucky | 3 | 8 | 0 | San Diego State | 6 | 5 | 0 |
| Arizona State | 9 | 2 | 0 | Louisiana State | 3 | 7 | 1 | San Jose State | 9 | 2 | 0 |
| Arkansas | 8 | 3 | 0 | Louisville | 4 | 6 | 0 | South Carolina | 6 | 6 | 0 |
| Army | 3 | 7 | 1 | Maryland | 4 | 6 | 1 | Southern California | 9 | 2 | 0 |
| Auburn | 5 | 6 | 0 | Memphis State | 1 | 10 | 0 | Southern Methodist | 10 | 1 | 0 |
| Baylor | 5 | 6 | 0 | Miami (Fla.) | 8 | 2 | 0 | Southern Mississippi | 9 | 1 | 1 |
| Boston College | 5 | 6 | 0 | Michigan | 8 | 3 | 0 | Stanford | 4 | 7 | 0 |
| Brigham Young | 10 | 2 | 0 | Michigan State | 5 | 6 | 0 | Syracuse | 4 | 6 | 1 |
| Brown | 3 | 7 | 0 | Minnesota | 6 | 5 | 0 | Temple | 5 | 5 | 0 |
| California | 2 | 9 | 0 | Mississippi | 4 | 6 | 1 | Tennessee | 7 | 4 | 0 |
| Cincinnati | 6 | 5 | 0 | Mississippi State | 7 | 4 | 0 | Tenn.-Chattanooga | 7 | 3 | 1 |
| Citadel | 7 | 3 | 1 | Missouri | 7 | 4 | 0 | Texas | 8 | 1 | 1 |
| Clemson | 11 | 0 | 0 | Navy | 7 | 3 | 1 | Texas A & M | 6 | 4 | 0 |
| Colgate | 7 | 3 | 0 | Nebraska | 9 | 2 | 0 | Texas Christian | 2 | 7 | 2 |
| Colorado | 3 | 8 | 0 | Nevada-Las Vegas | 6 | 6 | 0 | Texas-El Paso | 1 | 10 | 0 |
| Colorado State | 0 | 12 | 0 | New Mexico | 4 | 7 | 1 | Texas Tech | 1 | 9 | 1 |
| Columbia | 1 | 9 | 0 | New Mexico State | 3 | 8 | 0 | Tulane | 6 | 5 | 0 |
| Cornell | 3 | 7 | 0 | North Carolina | 9 | 2 | 0 | Tulsa | 6 | 5 | 0 |
| Dartmouth | 6 | 4 | 0 | North Carolina State | 4 | 7 | 0 | UCLA | 7 | 3 | 1 |
| Duke | 6 | 5 | 0 | North Texas State | 2 | 9 | 0 | Utah | 8 | 2 | 1 |
| East Carolina | 5 | 6 | 0 | Northwestern | 0 | 11 | 0 | Utah State | 5 | 5 | 1 |
| Florida | 7 | 4 | 0 | Notre Dame | 5 | 6 | 0 | Vanderbilt | 4 | 7 | 0 |
| Florida State | 6 | 5 | 0 | Ohio State | 8 | 3 | 0 | Virginia | 1 | 10 | 0 |
| Furman | 8 | 3 | 0 | Oklahoma | 6 | 4 | 1 | Virginia Military | 6 | 3 | 1 |
| Georgia | 10 | 1 | 0 | Oklahoma State | 7 | 4 | 0 | Virginia Tech | 7 | 4 | 0 |
| Georgia Tech | 1 | 10 | 0 | Oregon | 2 | 9 | 0 | Wake Forest | 4 | 7 | 0 |
| Harvard | 5 | 4 | 1 | Oregon State | 1 | 10 | 0 | Washington | 9 | 2 | 0 |
| Hawaii | 9 | 2 | 0 | Pacific | 5 | 6 | 0 | Washington State | 8 | 2 | 1 |
| Holy Cross | 6 | 5 | 0 | Pennsylvania | 1 | 8 | 0 | West Virginia | 8 | 3 | 0 |
| Houston | 7 | 3 | 1 | Pennsylvania State | 9 | 2 | 0 | Wichita State | 4 | 6 | 1 |
| Illinois | 7 | 4 | 0 | Pittsburgh | 10 | 1 | 0 | William & Mary | 6 | 5 | 0 |
| Indiana | 3 | 8 | 0 | Princeton | 5 | 4 | 1 | Wisconsin | 7 | 4 | 0 |
| Iowa | 8 | 3 | 0 | Purdue | 5 | 6 | 0 | Wyoming | 8 | 3 | 0 |
| Iowa State | 5 | 5 | 1 | Rice | 4 | 7 | 0 | Yale | 9 | 1 | 0 |

## 1981 FINAL COLLEGE FOOTBALL RANKINGS

### ASSOCIATED PRESS

1. Clemson
2. Texas
3. Penn State
4. Pittsburgh
5. Southern Methodist
6. Georgia
7. Alabama
8. Miami (Florida)
9. North Carolina
10. Washington
11. Nebraska
12. Michigan
13. Brigham Young
14. Southern California
15. Ohio State
16. Arizona State
17. West Virginia
18. Iowa
19. Missouri
20. Oklahoma

### UNITED PRESS INTERNATIONAL

1. Clemson
2. Pittsburgh
3. Penn State
4. Texas
5. Georgia
6. Alabama
7. Washington
8. North Carolina
9. Nebraska
10. Michigan
11. Brigham Young
12. Ohio State
13. Southern California
14. Oklahoma
15. Iowa
16. Arkansas
17. Mississippi State
18. West Virginia
19. Southern Mississippi
20. Missouri

## MAJOR COLLEGE FOOTBALL STADIUMS (45,000 or more seats)

| Team (Stadium) Location | Capacity |
|---|---|
| Air Force (Falcon) A.F. Academy, Colo. | 46,600 |
| Alabama (Bryant-Denny) University, Ala. | 59,000 |
| Arizona (Arizona) Tucson, Ariz. | 57,000 |
| Arizona State (Sun Devil) Tempe, Ariz. | 70,300 |
| Auburn (Jordan Hare) Auburn, Ala. | 71,800 |
| Baylor (Baylor) Waco, Tex. | 48,500 |
| California (Memorial) Berkeley, Cal. | 76,700 |
| Clemson (Memorial) Clemson, S.C. | 53,400 |
| Colorado (Folsom Field) Boulder, Colo. | 52,000 |
| Florida (Florida Field) Gainesville, Fla. | 62,800 |
| Florida State (Campbell) Tallahassee, Fla. | 51,000 |
| Georgia (Sanford) Athens, Ga. | 76,000 |
| Georgia Tech (Grant Field) Atlanta, Ga. | 58,100 |
| Hawaii (Aloha) Honolulu, Hawaii | 50,000 |
| Illinois (Memorial) Champaign, Ill. | 71,200 |
| Indiana (Memorial) Bloomington, Ind. | 52,300 |
| Iowa (Kinnick) Iowa City, Iowa | 60,000 |
| Iowa State (Iowa State) Ames, Iowa | 50,000 |
| Jackson State (Miss. Memorial) Jackson, Miss. | 61,000 |
| Kansas (Memorial) Lawrence, Kans. | 51,500 |
| Kentucky (Commonwealth) Lexington, Ky. | 58,000 |
| Long Beach State (Anaheim), Calif. | 69,000 |
| Louisiana State (Tiger) Baton Rouge, La. | 76,000 |
| Maryland (Byrd) College Park, Md. | 45,000 |
| Memphis State (Liberty Bowl) Memphis, Tenn. | 50,100 |
| Michigan (Michigan) Ann Arbor, Mich. | 101,700 |
| Michigan State (Spartan) East Lansing, Mich. | 76,000 |
| Minnesota (Memorial) Minneapolis, Minn. | 56,700 |
| Missouri (Faurot Field) Columbia, Mo. | 75,000 |
| Nebraska (Memorial) Lincoln, Neb. | 73,500 |
| North Carolina (Kenan) Chapel Hill, N.C. | 49,500 |
| North Carolina State (Carter-Finley) Raleigh, N.C. | 45,600 |
| Northwestern (Dyche) Evanston, Ill. | 49,200 |
| Notre Dame (Notre Dame) South Bend, Ind. | 59,000 |
| Ohio State (Ohio) Columbus, Ohio | 83,100 |

| Team (Stadium) Location | Capacity |
|---|---|
| Oklahoma (Owen Field) Norman, Okla. | 74,700 |
| Oklahoma State (Lewis) Stillwater, Okla. | 50,800 |
| Pennsylvania (Franklin Field) Philadelphia, Pa. | 60,500 |
| Pennsylvania State (Beaver) University Park, Pa. | 83,700 |
| Pittsburgh (Pitt) Pittsburgh, Pa. | 56,500 |
| Princeton (Palmer) Princeton, N.J. | 45,700 |
| Purdue (Ross-Ade) West Lafayette, Ind. | 69,200 |
| Rice (Rice) Houston, Tex. | 70,000 |
| San Diego State (San Diego) San Diego, Cal. | 53,000 |
| South Carolina (Williams-Brice) Columbia, S.C. | 54,400 |
| Stanford (Stanford) Stanford, Cal. | 84,800 |
| Tennessee (Neyland) Knoxville, Tenn. | 91,200 |
| Texas (Memorial) Austin, Tex. | 80,000 |
| Texas A & M (Kyle Field) College Station, Tex. | 70,100 |
| Texas Christian (TCU-Amon Carter) Fort Worth, Tex. | 46,000 |
| Texas Tech (Jones) Lubbock, Tex. | 47,000 |
| Virginia Tech (Lane) Blacksburg, Va. | 52,500 |
| Washington (Husky) Seattle, Wash. | 59,800 |
| West Virginia (Mountaineer Field) Morgantown, W.Va. | 50,000 |
| Wisconsin (Camp Randall) Madison, Wis. | 77,200 |
| Yale (Yale Bowl) New Haven, Conn. | 70,800 |

### OTHER STADIUMS USED BY MAJOR COLLEGE TEAMS

| Stadium | Capacity |
|---|---|
| Astrodome, Houston (Houston, Texas Southern) | 50,100 |
| Cotton Bowl, Dallas | 72,000 |
| Gator Bowl, Jacksonville, Fla. | 72,000 |
| Giants, E. Rutherford, N.J. (Rutgers) | 76,500 |
| Legion Field, Birmingham, Ala. (Alabama) | 76,000 |
| Los Angeles Memorial Coliseum (USC, UCLA) | 92,600 |
| Louisiana Superdome, New Orleans (Tulane) | 71,000 |
| Mississippi Memorial, Jackson (Miss., Miss. St.) | 61,000 |
| Orange Bowl, Miami (Miami, Fla.) | 76,100 |
| Texas Stadium, Irving (Southern Methodist) | 65,000 |
| Veterans Stadium, Philadelphia (Temple) | 72,000 |

## THE HEISMAN MEMORIAL TROPHY: Awarded annually to the nation's outstanding college football player.

| Year | Player and College |
|---|---|
| 1946 | Glenn Davis, Army |
| 1947 | John Lujack, Notre Dame |
| 1948 | Doak Walker, Southern Methodist |
| 1949 | Leon Hart, Notre Dame |
| 1950 | Vic Janowicz, Ohio State |
| 1951 | Dick Kazmaier, Princeton |
| 1952 | Billy Vessels, Oklahoma |
| 1953 | John Lattner, Notre Dame |
| 1954 | Alan Ameche, Wisconsin |
| 1955 | Howard Cassady, Ohio State |
| 1956 | Paul Hornung, Notre Dame |
| 1957 | John Crow, Texas A&M |
| 1958 | Pete Dawkins, Army |
| 1959 | Billy Cannon, Louisiana State |
| 1960 | Joe Bellino, Navy |
| 1961 | Ernie Davis, Syracuse |
| 1962 | Terry Baker, Oregon State |
| 1963 | Roger Staubach, Navy |
| 1964 | John Huarte, Notre Dame |
| 1965 | Mike Garrett, Southern California |
| 1966 | Steve Spurrier, Florida |
| 1967 | Gary Beban, UCLA |
| 1968 | O. J. Simpson, USC |
| 1969 | Steve Owens, Oklahoma |
| 1970 | Jim Plunkett, Stanford |
| 1971 | Pat Sullivan, Auburn |
| 1972 | Johnny Rogers, Nebraska |
| 1973 | John Capelletti, Penn State |
| 1974 | Archie Griffin, Ohio State |
| 1975 | Archie Griffin, Ohio State |
| 1976 | Tony Dorsett, Pittsburgh |
| 1977 | Earl Campbell, Texas |
| 1978 | Billy Sims, Oklahoma |
| 1979 | Charles White, USC |
| 1980 | George Rogers, S. Carolina |
| 1981 | Marcus Allen, USC |

## COLLEGE FOOTBALL COACH OF THE YEAR (American Football Coaches Ass'n)

| Year | Coach and College |
|---|---|
| 1946 | Earl H. Blaik, Army |
| 1947 | Fritz Crisler, Michigan |
| 1948 | Bennie Oosterbaan, Michigan |
| 1949 | Bud Wilkinson, Oklahoma |
| 1950 | Charlie Caldwell, Princeton |
| 1951 | Chuck Taylor, Stanford |
| 1952 | Biggie Munn, Michigan State |
| 1953 | Jim Tatum, Maryland |
| 1954 | Red Sanders, UCLA |
| 1955 | Duffy Daugherty, Michigan State |
| 1956 | Bowden Wyatt, Tennessee |
| 1957 | Woody Hayes, Ohio State |
| 1958 | Paul Dietzel, Louisiana State |
| 1959 | Ben Schwartzwalder, Syracuse |
| 1960 | Murray Warmath, Minnesota |
| 1961 | Paul Bryant, Alabama |
| 1962 | John McKay, Southern California |
| 1963 | Darrell Royal, Texas |
| 1964 | Ara Parseghian, Notre Dame |
| 1965 | Tommy Prothro, UCLA |
| 1966 | Tom Cahill, Army |
| 1967 | John Pont, Indiana |
| 1968 | Joe Paterno, Penn State |
| 1969 | Bo Schembechler, Michigan |
| 1970 | Darrell Royal, Texas<br>Charlie McLendon, La. State |
| 1971 | Paul Bryant, Alabama |
| 1972 | John McKay, Southern California |
| 1973 | Paul Bryant, Alabama |
| 1974 | Grant Teaff, Baylor |
| 1975 | Frank Kush, Arizona State |
| 1976 | Johnny Majors, Pittsburgh |
| 1977 | Don James, Washington |
| 1978 | Joe Paterno, Penn State |
| 1979 | Earl Bruce, Ohio State |
| 1980 | Vince Dooley, Georgia |
| 1981 | Danny Ford, Clemson |

## OUTLAND AWARDS: Awarded annually to the nation's leading college football lineman.

| Year | Player, College, Pos. |
|---|---|
| 1946 | George Connor, Notre Dame, T |
| 1947 | Joe Steffy, Army, G |
| 1948 | Bill Fischer, Notre Dame, G |
| 1949 | Ed Bagdon, Michigan St., G |
| 1950 | Bob Gain, Kentucky, T |
| 1951 | Jim Weatherall, Oklahoma, T |
| 1952 | Dick Modzelewski, Maryland, T |
| 1953 | J. D. Roberts, Oklahoma, G. |
| 1954 | Bill Brooks, Arkansas, G |
| 1955 | Calvin Jones, Iowa, G |
| 1956 | Jim Parker, Ohio State, G |
| 1957 | Alex Karras, Iowa, T |
| 1958 | Zeke Smith, Auburn, G |
| 1959 | Mike McGee, Duke, T |
| 1960 | Tom Brown, Minnesota, G |
| 1961 | Merlin Olsen, Utah State, T |
| 1962 | Bobby Bell, Minnesota, T |
| 1963 | Scott Appleton, Texas, T |
| 1964 | Steve DeLong, Tennessee, T |
| 1965 | Tommy Nobis, Texas, G |
| 1966 | Lloyd Phillips, Arkansas, T |
| 1967 | Ron Yary, Southern Cal, T |
| 1968 | Bill Stanfill, Georgia, T |
| 1969 | Mike Reid, Penn State, DT |
| 1970 | Jim Stillwagon, Ohio State, LB |
| 1971 | Larry Jacobson, Nebraska, DT |
| 1972 | Rich Glover, Nebraska, MG |
| 1973 | John Hicks, Ohio State, T |
| 1974 | Randy White, Maryland, DT |
| 1975 | Leroy Selmon, Oklahoma, DT |
| 1976 | Ross Browner, Notre Dame, DT |
| 1977 | Brad Shearer, Texas, DT |
| 1978 | Greg Roberts, Oklahoma, G |
| 1979 | Jim Richter, N. Carolina St., C |
| 1980 | Mark May, Pittsburgh, T |
| 1981 | David Rimington, Nebraska, C |

## 1981 COLLEGE ALL-AMERICA SELECTIONS

### OFFENSIVE TEAM

**Receivers**
Anthony Carter, Michigan (AP) (UPI) (SN) (FW)
Tim Wrightman, UCLA (AP) (UPI)
Julius Dawkins, Pittsburgh (AP)
Perry Tuttle, Clemson (SN)
Pat Beach, Washington State (SN)
Stanley Washington, TCU (FW)

**Linemen**
Sean Farrell, Penn State (AP) (UPI) (SN) (FW)
Terry Tausch, Texas (AP) (UPI) (SN)
Roy Foster, USC (UPI) (SN) (FW)
Ed Muransky, Michigan (AP) (UPI)
Kurt Becker, Michigan (AP)
Luis Sharpe, UCLA (SN)
Terry Crouch, Oklahoma (FW)
Dave Drechsler, North Carolina (FW)

**Centers**
Dave Rimington, Nebraska (AP) (UPI) (FW)
Brad Edelman, Missouri (SN)

**Quarterbacks**
Jim McMahon, Brigham Young (AP) (UPI) (FW)
Dan Marino, Pittsburgh (SN)

**Running backs**
Marcus Allen, USC (AP) (UPI) (SN) (FW)
Herschel Walker, Georgia (AP) (UPI) (SN) (FW)
Curt Warner, Penn State (UPI)
Rich Diana, Yale (FW)

**Placekickers**
Morten Andersen, Michigan St. (UPI) (SN)
Gary Anderson, Syracuse (AP)
Bruce Lahay, Arkansas (FW)

### DEFENSIVE TEAM

**Linemen**
Kenneth Sims, Texas (AP) (UPI) (SN) (FW)
Billy Ray Smith, Arkansas (AP) (UPI) (SN) (FW)
Andre Tippett, Iowa (AP) (UPI) (FW)
Tim Krumrie, Wisconsin (AP) (UPI)
Lester Williams, Miami (Fla.) (UPI) (SN)
Jeff Gaylord, Missouri (AP)
Glen Collins, Mississippi St. (SN)
Steve Clark, Utah (FW)
David Galloway, Florida (FW)

**Linebackers**
Bob Crable, Notre Dame (AP) (UPI) (SN)
Johnie Cooks, Mississippi St. (AP) (SN) (FW)
Sal Sunseri, Pittsburgh (AP) (FW)
Chip Banks, USC (UPI) (SN)
Jeff Davis, Clemson (UPI) (FW)

**Defensive backs**
Mike Richardson, Arizona St. (AP) (SN) (FW)
Tommy Wilcox, Alabama (AP) (UPI)
Terry Kinard, Clemson (AP) (FW)
Fred Marion, Miami (Fla.) (UPI)
Matt Vanden Boom, Wisconsin (UPI)
James Burroughs, Michigan St. (SN)
Rodney Lewis, Nebraska (SN)
John Krimm, Notre Dame (SN)
Johnny Jackson, Air Force (FW)

**Punters**
Reggie Roby, Iowa (AP) (UPI)
Rohn Stark, Florida St. (SN) (FW)

Selections by (AP) Associated Press, (UPI) United Press International, (SN) The Sporting News, (FW) Football Writers Association of America

## NATIONAL CHAMPIONSHIP GAMES

| Year | NCAA Division I-AA |
|---|---|
| 1978 | Florida A&M 35, Massachusetts 28 |
| 1979 | Eastern Kentucky 30, Lehigh 7 |
| 1980 | Boise State 31, Eastern Kentucky 29 |
| 1981 | Idaho State 34, Eastern Kentucky 23 |

| Year | NCAA Division II |
|---|---|
| 1978 | Eastern Illinois 10, Delaware 9 |
| 1979 | Delaware 38, Youngstown State 21 |
| 1980 | Cal Poly-S. L. Obispo 21, Eastern Illinois 13 |
| 1981 | SW Texas St. 42, North Dakota St. 13 |

| Year | NCAA Division III |
|---|---|
| 1978 | Baldwin-Wallace 24, Wittenberg 10 |
| 1979 | Ithaca (N.Y.) 14, Wittenberg 10 |
| 1980 | Dayton 63, Ithaca 0 |
| 1981 | Widener 17, Dayton 10 |

| Year | NAIA Division I |
|---|---|
| 1978 | Angelo State (Tex.) 34, Elon (N.C.) 14 |
| 1979 | Texas A & I 20, Central State Okla. 14 |
| 1980 | Elon (N.C.) 17, Northeastern Oklahoma 10 |
| 1981 | Elon (N.C.) 3, Pittsburg (Kans.) 0 |

| Year | NAIA Division II |
|---|---|
| 1978 | Concordia (Minn.) 7, Findlay (Ohio) 0 |
| 1979 | Findlay (Ohio) 51, Northwestern (Iowa) 6 |
| 1980 | Pacific Lutheran 38, Wilmington (Ohio) 10 |
| 1981 | Austin (Tex.) 24, Concordia (Minn.) 24 |

# HOCKEY

## NATIONAL HOCKEY LEAGUE (NHL)

League Offices: 960 Sun Life Bldg., 1155 Metcalfe St., Montreal, Quebec, H3B 2W2; Suite 1444, 1221 Ave. of the Americas, New York, N.Y. 10020.

President: John A. Ziegler, Jr. Chairman of the Board: William W. Wirtz. Organized in 1917.

### PRINCE OF WALES CONFERENCE

| Adams Division | Pres./Owner | Coach |
|---|---|---|
| Boston Bruins | Paul A. Mooney | Gerry Cheevers |
| Buffalo Sabres | Seymour H. Knox III | Scotty Bowman |
| Hartford Whalers | Howard L. Baldwin | Larry Kish |
| Montreal Canadiens | Morgan McCammon | Bob Berry |
| Quebec Nordiques | Marcel Aubut | Michel Bergeron |
| **Patrick Division** | | |
| New Jersey Devils | John McMullen | Billy MacMillan |
| New York Islanders | John O. Pickett, Jr. | Al Arbour |
| New York Rangers | Jack Krumpe | Herb Brooks |
| Philadelphia Flyers | Edward M. Snider | Bob McCammon |
| Pittsburgh Penguins | Edward J. DeBartolo, Sr. | Ed Johnston |
| Washington Capitals | Abe Pollin | Bryan Murray |

### CLARENCE CAMPBELL CONFERENCE

| Norris Division | Pres./Owner | Coach |
|---|---|---|
| Chicago Black Hawks | William W. Wirtz | Orval Tessier |
| Detroit Red Wings | Michael Ilitch | Nick Polano |
| Minnesota North Stars | George Gund III | Glen Sonmor |
| St. Louis Blues | Emile Francis | Emile Francis |
| Toronto Maple Leafs | Harold E. Ballard | Mike Nykoluk |
| **Smythe Division** | | |
| Calgary Flames | Cliff Fletcher | Bob Johnson |
| Edmonton Oilers | Peter Pocklington | Glen Sather |
| Los Angeles Kings | Jerry Buss | Don Perry |
| Vancouver Canucks | Frank A. Griffiths | Roger Neilson |
| Winnipeg Jets | Michael Gobuty | Tom Watt |

## NATIONAL HOCKEY LEAGUE RECORDS At start of 1982/83 season

Most Goals, Lifetime: **801, Gordie Howe, Detroit Red Wings, Hartford Whalers.**

Most Goals, One Season: **92, Wayne Gretzky, Edmonton Oilers, 1981/82.**

Most Assists, One Season: **120, Wayne Gretzky, Edmonton Oilers, 1981/82.**

Most Points, One Season: **212, Wayne Gretzky, Edmonton Oilers, 1981/82.**

Most Points, One Game: **10, Darryl Sittler, Toronto Maple Leafs, February 7, 1976.**

Most Victories, One Season: **60, Montreal Canadiens, 1976/77.**

Longest Winning Streak: **15 games, N.Y. Islanders, 1981/82.**

Most Goals, One Season: **417, Edmonton Oilers, 1981/82.**

Most Shutouts by a Goaltender: **103, Terry Sawchuk, Detroit, Boston, Toronto, Los Angeles, N.Y. Rangers.**

Most Penalty Minutes, One Season: **472, Dave Schultz, Philadelphia Flyers, 1974/75.**

Most Seasons: **26, Gordie Howe, Detroit Red Wings, 1946/47 through 1970/71, Hartford Whalers, 1979/80.**

Most Games, Including Playoffs, Lifetime: **1,924, Gordie Howe, Detroit Red Wings, Hartford Whalers.**

Most Goals, Including Playoffs, Lifetime: **869, Gordie Howe, Detroit Red Wings, Hartford Whalers.**

Most Assists, Including Playoffs, Lifetime: **1,141, Gordie Howe, Detroit Red Wings, Hartford Whalers.**

Most Points, Including Playoffs, Lifetime: **2,010, Gordie Howe, Detroit Red Wings, Hartford Whalers.**

Most Penalty Minutes, Including Playoffs, Lifetime: **2,706, Dave Schultz, Philadelphia Flyers, Los Angeles Kings, Pittsburgh Penguins, Buffalo Sabres.**

Most Consecutive Games: **914, Garry Unger, Toronto Maple Leafs, Detroit Red Wings, St. Louis Blues, Atlanta Flames, 1967/68–1979/80.**

Most Consecutive Complete Games by Goaltender: **502, Glenn Hall, Detroit Red Wings and Chicago Black Hawks, 1955/56 through 1962/63.**

Most Shutouts by a Goaltender, One Season: **22, George Hainsworth, Montreal Canadiens, 1928/29.**

Longest Shutout Sequence by a Goaltender: **461 Minutes 29 Seconds, Alex Connell, Ottawa Senators, 1927/28.**

Most Goals, One Game: **7, Joe Malone, Quebec Bulldogs, January 31, 1920.**

Most Assists, One Game: **7, Billy Taylor, Detroit Red Wings, March 16, 1947; Wayne Gretzky, Edmonton Oilers, February 15, 1980.**

Most Penalties, One Game: **9, Jim Dorey, Toronto Maple Leafs, October 16, 1968; Dave Schultz, Pittsburgh Penguins, April 6, 1978; Randy Holt, Los Angeles Kings, March 11, 1979; Russ Anderson, Pittsburgh Penguins, January 19, 1980; Kim Clackson, Quebec Nordiques, March 8, 1981.**

Most Penalty Minutes, One Game: **67, Randy Holt, Los Angeles Kings, March 11, 1979.**

Most Goals in One Period: **4, Harvey (Busher) Jackson, Toronto Maple Leafs, November 20, 1934; Max Bentley, Chicago Black Hawks, January 28, 1943; Clint Smith, Chicago Black Hawks, March 4, 1945; Gordon (Red) Berenson, St. Louis Blues, November 7, 1968; Wayne Gretzky, Edmonton Oilers, February 18, 1981.**

Fastest Two Goals: **4 seconds, Nels Stewart, Montreal Maroons, January 3, 1931.**

Fastest Three Goals: **21 seconds, Bill Mosienko, Chicago Black Hawks, March 23, 1952; Grant Mulvey, Chicago Black Hawks, Feb. 3, 1982; Bryan Trottier, N.Y. Islanders, Feb. 13, 1982.**

## NHL CHAMPIONS

| Season | Regular Season | Stanley Cup |
|---|---|---|
| 1954/55 | Detroit Red Wings | Detroit Red Wings |
| 1955/56 | Montreal Canadiens | Montreal Canadiens |
| 1956/57 | Detroit Red Wings | Montreal Canadiens |
| 1957/58 | Montreal Canadiens | Montreal Canadiens |
| 1958/59 | Montreal Canadiens | Montreal Canadiens |
| 1959/60 | Montreal Canadiens | Montreal Canadiens |
| 1960/61 | Montreal Canadiens | Chicago Black Hawks |
| 1961/62 | Montreal Canadiens | Toronto Maple Leafs |
| 1962/63 | Toronto Maple Leafs | Toronto Maple Leafs |
| 1963/64 | Montreal Canadiens | Toronto Maple Leafs |
| 1964/65 | Detroit Red Wings | Montreal Canadiens |
| 1965/66 | Montreal Canadiens | Montreal Canadiens |
| 1966/67 | Chicago Black Hawks | Toronto Maple Leafs |
| 1967/68 | Montreal Canadiens* Philadelphia Flyers† | Montreal Canadiens |
| 1968/69 | Montreal Canadiens* St. Louis Blues† | Montreal Canadiens |
| 1969/70 | Chicago Black Hawks* St. Louis Blues† | Boston Bruins |
| 1970/71 | Boston Bruins* Chicago Black Hawks† | Montreal Canadiens |
| 1971/72 | Boston Bruins* Chicago Black Hawks† | Boston Bruins |
| 1972/73 | Montreal Canadiens* Chicago Black Hawks† | Montreal Canadiens |
| 1973/74 | Boston Bruins* Philadelphia Flyers† | Philadelphia Flyers |
| 1974/75 | Montreal, Buffalo, Philadelphia, Vancouver | Philadelphia Flyers |
| 1975/76 | Montreal, Boston, Philadelphia, Chicago | Montreal Canadiens |
| 1976/77 | Montreal, Boston, Philadelphia, St. Louis | Montreal Canadiens |
| 1977/78 | Montreal, Boston, N.Y. Islanders, Chicago | Montreal Canadiens |
| 1978/79 | Montreal, Boston, N.Y. Islanders, Chicago | Montreal Canadiens |
| 1979/80 | Montreal, Buffalo, Philadelphia, Chicago | New York Islanders |
| 1980/81 | Montreal, Buffalo, N.Y. Islanders, St. Louis | New York Islanders |
| 1981/82 | Montreal, N.Y. Islanders Edmonton, Minnesota | New York Islanders |

* East Division. † West Division.

## NHL FINAL STANDINGS: 1981-82

### WALES CONFERENCE

| PATRICK DIVISION | W | L | T | Pts. | GF | GA |
|---|---|---|---|---|---|---|
| NY Islanders | 56 | 16 | 10 | 118 | 385 | 250 |
| NY Rangers | 39 | 27 | 14 | 92 | 316 | 306 |
| Philadelphia | 38 | 31 | 11 | 87 | 325 | 313 |
| Pittsburgh | 31 | 36 | 13 | 75 | 310 | 337 |
| Washington | 26 | 41 | 13 | 65 | 319 | 338 |
| **ADAMS DIVISION** | | | | | | |
| Montreal | 46 | 17 | 17 | 109 | 360 | 223 |
| Boston | 43 | 27 | 10 | 96 | 323 | 285 |
| Buffalo | 39 | 26 | 15 | 93 | 307 | 273 |
| Quebec | 33 | 31 | 16 | 82 | 356 | 345 |
| Hartford | 21 | 41 | 18 | 60 | 264 | 351 |

### CAMPBELL CONFERENCE

| NORRIS DIVISION | W | L | T | Pts. | GF | GA |
|---|---|---|---|---|---|---|
| Minnesota | 37 | 23 | 20 | 94 | 346 | 288 |
| Winnipeg | 33 | 33 | 14 | 80 | 319 | 332 |
| St. Louis | 32 | 40 | 8 | 72 | 315 | 349 |
| Chicago | 30 | 38 | 12 | 72 | 332 | 363 |
| Toronto | 20 | 44 | 16 | 56 | 298 | 380 |
| Detroit | 21 | 47 | 12 | 54 | 271 | 350 |
| **SMYTHE DIVISION** | | | | | | |
| Edmonton | 48 | 17 | 15 | 111 | 417 | 295 |
| Vancouver | 30 | 33 | 17 | 77 | 290 | 286 |
| Calgary | 29 | 34 | 17 | 75 | 334 | 345 |
| Los Angeles | 24 | 41 | 15 | 63 | 314 | 369 |
| Colorado | 18 | 49 | 13 | 49 | 241 | 362 |

## STANLEY CUP PLAYOFFS: 1982 Top 16 Teams (Total Points) Qualify

**Preliminary Round** (Best-of-five series)

NY Islanders over Pittsburgh: 3-2
NY Rangers over Philadelphia: 3-1
Quebec over Montreal: 3-2
Boston over Buffalo: 3-1
Chicago over Minnesota: 3-1
St. Louis over Winnipeg: 3-1
Los Angeles over Edmonton: 3-2
Vancouver over Calgary: 3-0

**Quarter Finals** (Best-of-seven series)

NY Islanders over NY Rangers: 4-2
Quebec over Boston: 4-3
Chicago over St. Louis: 4-2
Vancouver over Los Angeles: 4-1

**Semi-Finals** (Best-of-seven series)

NY Islanders over Quebec: 4-0
Vancouver over Chicago: 4-1

**Finals** (Best-of-seven series)

1. NY Islanders 6, Vancouver 5
2. NY Islanders 6, Vancouver 4
3. NY Islanders 3, Vancouver 0
4. NY Islanders 3, Vancouver 1
(NY Islanders win series: 4-0)

## STANLEY CUP CHAMPIONS

| Season | Champions | Manager |
|---|---|---|
| 1920-21 | Ottawa Senators | Tommy Gorman |
| 1921-22 | Toronto St. Pats | Charlie Querrie |
| 1922-23 | Ottawa Senators | Tommy Gorman |
| 1923-24 | Montreal Canadiens | Leo Dandurand |
| 1924-25 | Victoria Cougars | Lester Patrick |
| 1925-26 | Montreal Maroons | Eddie Gerard |
| 1926-27 | Ottawa Senators | Dave Gill |
| 1927-28 | New York Rangers | Lester Patrick |
| 1928-29 | Boston Bruins | Art Ross |
| 1929-30 | Montreal Canadiens | Cecil Hart |
| 1930-31 | Montreal Canadiens | Cecil Hart |
| 1931-32 | Toronto Maple Leafs | Conn Smythe |
| 1932-33 | New York Rangers | Lester Patrick |
| 1933-34 | Chicago Black Hawks | Tommy Gorman |
| 1934-35 | Montreal Maroons | Tommy Gorman |
| 1935-36 | Detroit Red Wings | Jack Adams |
| 1936-37 | Detroit Red Wings | Jack Adams |
| 1937-38 | Chicago Black Hawks | Bill Stewart |
| 1938-39 | Boston Bruins | Art Ross |
| 1939-40 | New York Rangers | Lester Patrick |
| 1940-41 | Boston Bruins | Art Ross |
| 1941-42 | Toronto Maple Leafs | Conn Smythe |
| 1942-43 | Detroit Red Wings | Jack Adams |
| 1943-44 | Montreal Canadiens | Tommy Gorman |
| 1944-45 | Toronto Maple Leafs | Conn Smythe |
| 1945-46 | Montreal Canadiens | Tommy Gorman |
| 1946-47 | Toronto Maple Leafs | Conn Smythe |
| 1947-48 | Toronto Maple Leafs | Conn Smythe |
| 1948-49 | Toronto Maple Leafs | Conn Smythe |
| 1949-50 | Detroit Red Wings | Jack Adams |
| 1950-51 | Toronto Maple Leafs | Conn Smythe |
| 1951-52 | Detroit Red Wings | Jack Adams |
| 1952-53 | Montreal Canadiens | Frank Selke |
| 1953-54 | Detroit Red Wings | Jack Adams |
| 1954-55 | Detroit Red Wings | Jack Adams |
| 1955-56 | Montreal Canadiens | Frank Selke |
| 1956-57 | Montreal Canadiens | Frank Selke |
| 1957-58 | Montreal Canadiens | Frank Selke |
| 1958-59 | Montreal Canadiens | Frank Selke |
| 1959-60 | Montreal Canadiens | Frank Selke |
| 1960-61 | Chicago Black Hawks | Tommy Ivan |
| 1961-62 | Toronto Maple Leafs | Punch Imlach |
| 1962-63 | Toronto Maple Leafs | Punch Imlach |
| 1963-64 | Toronto Maple Leafs | Punch Imlach |
| 1964-65 | Montreal Canadiens | Sam Pollock |
| 1965-66 | Montreal Canadiens | Sam Pollock |
| 1966-67 | Toronto Maple Leafs | Punch Imlach |
| 1967-68 | Montreal Canadiens | Sam Pollock |
| 1968-69 | Montreal Canadiens | Sam Pollock |
| 1969-70 | Boston Bruins | Milt Schmidt |
| 1970-71 | Montreal Canadiens | Sam Pollock |
| 1971-72 | Boston Bruins | Milt Schmidt |
| 1972-73 | Montreal Canadiens | Hector Blake |
| 1973-74 | Philadelphia Flyers | Keith Allen |
| 1974-75 | Philadelphia Flyers | Keith Allen |
| 1975-76 | Montreal Canadiens | Sam Pollock |
| 1976-77 | Montreal Canadiens | Sam Pollock |
| 1977-78 | Montreal Canadiens | Sam Pollock |
| 1978-79 | Montreal Canadiens | Irving Grundman |
| 1979-80 | New York Islanders | Bill Torrey |
| 1980-81 | New York Islanders | Bill Torrey |
| 1981-82 | New York Islanders | Bill Torrey |

## NHL SCORING LEADERS

| Season | Player and Team | Points |
|---|---|---|
| 1949-50 | Ted Lindsay, Detroit | 78 |
| 1950-51 | Gordie Howe, Detroit | 86 |
| 1951-52 | Gordie Howe, Detroit | 86 |
| 1952-53 | Gordie Howe, Detroit | 95 |
| 1953-54 | Gordie Howe, Detroit | 81 |
| 1954-55 | Bernie Geoffrion, Montreal | 75 |
| 1955-56 | Jean Beliveau, Montreal | 88 |
| 1956-57 | Gordie Howe, Detroit | 89 |
| 1957-58 | Dickie Moore, Montreal | 84 |
| 1958-59 | Dickie Moore, Montreal | 96 |
| 1959-60 | Bobby Hull, Chicago | 81 |
| 1960-61 | Bernie Geoffrion, Montreal | 95 |
| 1961-62 | Bobby Hull, Chicago | 84 |
| 1962-63 | Gordie Howe, Detroit | 86 |
| 1963-64 | Stan Mikita, Chicago | 89 |
| 1964-65 | Stan Mikita, Chicago | 87 |
| 1965-66 | Bobby Hull, Chicago | 97 |
| 1966-67 | Stan Mikita, Chicago | 97 |
| 1967-68 | Stan Mikita, Chicago | 87 |
| 1968-69 | Phil Esposito, Boston | 126 |
| 1969-70 | Bobby Orr, Boston | 120 |
| 1970-71 | Phil Esposito, Boston | 152 |
| 1971-72 | Phil Esposito, Boston | 133 |
| 1972-73 | Phil Esposito, Boston | 130 |
| 1973-74 | Phil Esposito, Boston | 145 |
| 1974-75 | Bobby Orr, Boston | 135 |
| 1975-76 | Guy Lafleur, Montreal | 125 |
| 1976-77 | Guy Lafleur, Montreal | 136 |
| 1977-78 | Guy Lafleur, Montreal | 132 |
| 1978-79 | Brian Trottier, NY Islanders | 134 |
| 1979-80 | Marcel Dionne, Los Angeles | 137 |
| | Wayne Gretzky, Edmonton | 137 |
| 1980-81 | Wayne Gretzky, Edmonton | 164 |
| 1981-82 | Wayne Gretzky, Edmonton | 212 |

## NHL SCORING LEADERS: 1981/82

| Player | Team | G | A | Pts. |
|---|---|---|---|---|
| Wayne Gretzky | Edmonton | 92 | 120 | 212 |
| Mike Bossy | N.Y. Islanders | 64 | 83 | 147 |
| Peter Stastny | Quebec | 46 | 93 | 139 |
| Dennis Maruk | Washington | 60 | 76 | 136 |
| Bryan Trottier | N.Y. Islanders | 50 | 79 | 129 |
| Denis Savard | Chicago | 32 | 87 | 119 |
| Marcel Dionne | Los Angeles | 50 | 67 | 117 |
| Bobby Smith | Minnesota | 43 | 71 | 114 |
| Dino Ciccarelli | Minnesota | 55 | 51 | 106 |
| Dave Taylor | Los Angeles | 39 | 67 | 106 |
| Glenn Anderson | Edmonton | 38 | 67 | 105 |
| Dale Hawerchuk | Winnipeg | 45 | 58 | 103 |
| Mike Rogers | N.Y. Rangers | 38 | 65 | 103 |
| Neal Broten | Minnesota | 38 | 60 | 98 |
| Real Cloutier | Quebec | 37 | 60 | 97 |
| Rick Middleton | Boston | 51 | 43 | 94 |
| John Tonelli | N.Y. Islanders | 35 | 58 | 93 |
| Barry Pederson | Boston | 44 | 48 | 92 |
| Morris Lukowich | Winnipeg | 43 | 49 | 92 |
| Bernie Federko | St. Louis | 30 | 62 | 92 |
| Kenny Linseman | Philadelphia | 24 | 68 | 92 |

## NHL ALL-TIME SCORING LEADERS

At start of 1982/83 season.

| Player (Team) | Seasons | Games | Goals | Assists | Points | Scoring Percentage |
|---|---|---|---|---|---|---|
| Gordie Howe (Detroit, Hartford) | 26 | 1,767 | 801 | 1,049 | 1,850 | 1.047 |
| Phil Esposito (Chicago, Boston, N.Y. Rangers) | 18 | 1,282 | 717 | 873 | 1,590 | 1.240 |
| Stan Mikita (Chicago) | 22 | 1,394 | 541 | 926 | 1,467 | 1.052 |
| Johnny Bucyk (Detroit, Boston) | 23 | 1,540 | 556 | 813 | 1,369 | .889 |
| Alex Delvecchio (Detroit) | 24 | 1,549 | 456 | 825 | 1,281 | .827 |
| Jean Ratelle (N.Y. Rangers, Boston) | 21 | 1,281 | 491 | 776 | 1,267 | .989 |
| Norm Ullman (Detroit, Toronto) | 20 | 1,410 | 490 | 739 | 1,229 | .872 |
| Jean Beliveau (Montreal) | 20 | 1,125 | 507 | 712 | 1,219 | 1.084 |
| Marcel Dionne (Detroit, Los Angeles) | 11 | 857 | 488 | 692 | 1,180 | 1.377 |
| Bobby Hull (Chicago, Winnipeg, Hartford) | 16 | 1,063 | 610 | 560 | 1,170 | 1.100 |
| Frank Mahovlich (Toronto, Detroit, Montreal) | 18 | 1,181 | 533 | 570 | 1,103 | .934 |
| Guy Lafluer (Montreal) | 11 | 794 | 459 | 636 | 1,095 | 1.379 |
| Bobby Clarke (Philadelphia) | 13 | 991 | 318 | 747 | 1,065 | 1.075 |
| Henri Richard (Montreal) | 12 | 871 | 391 | 610 | 1,001 | 1.149 |
| Rod Gilbert (N.Y. Rangers) | 20 | 1,256 | 358 | 688 | 1,046 | .833 |
| Gilbert Perreault (Buffalo) | 18 | 1,065 | 406 | 615 | 1,021 | .959 |
| Dave Keon (Toronto, Hartford) | 18 | 1,296 | 396 | 590 | 986 | .761 |
| Andy Bathgate (N.Y. Rangers, Toronto, Detroit, Pittsburgh) | 17 | 1,069 | 349 | 624 | 973 | .910 |
| Maurice Richard (Montreal) | 18 | 978 | 544 | 421 | 965 | .987 |
| Darryl Sittler (Toronto, Philadelphia) | 12 | 879 | 403 | 545 | 948 | 1.078 |
| Bobby Orr (Boston, Chicago) | 12 | 657 | 270 | 645 | 915 | 1.393 |
| Yvan Cournoyer (Montreal) | 16 | 968 | 428 | 435 | 863 | .892 |
| Dean Prentice (N.Y. Rangers, Boston, Detroit, Pittsburgh, Minnesota) | 22 | 1,378 | 391 | 469 | 860 | .624 |
| Ted Lindsay (Detroit, Chicago) | 17 | 1,068 | 379 | 472 | 851 | .797 |
| Jacques Lemaire (Montreal) | 12 | 853 | 366 | 469 | 835 | .979 |
| Red Kelly (Detroit, Toronto) | 20 | 1,316 | 281 | 542 | 823 | .625 |
| Bernie Geoffrion (Montreal, N.Y. Rangers) | 16 | 883 | 393 | 429 | 822 | .931 |
| Pit Martin (Detroit, Boston, Chicago, Vancouver) | 17 | 1,101 | 324 | 485 | 809 | .735 |
| Garry Unger (Toronto, Detroit, St. Louis, Atlanta, Los Angeles, Edmonton) | 15 | 1,089 | 411 | 391 | 802 | .736 |
| Ken Hodge (Chicago, Boston, N.Y. Rangers) | 14 | 881 | 328 | 472 | 800 | .908 |
| Wayne Cashman (Boston) | 16 | 962 | 273 | 505 | 778 | .809 |
| Jean Pronovost (Pittsburgh, Atlanta, Washington) | 14 | 998 | 391 | 383 | 774 | .776 |
| Pete Mahovlich (Detroit, Montreal, Pittsburgh) | 16 | 884 | 288 | 486 | 773 | .874 |
| Bill Barber (Philadelphia) | 10 | 774 | 371 | 398 | 769 | .994 |
| Butch Goring (Los Angeles, N.Y. Islanders) | 13 | 893 | 319 | 443 | 762 | .853 |
| Bryan Trottier (N.Y. Islanders) | 7 | 540 | 278 | 482 | 760 | 1.407 |
| Brad Park (N.Y. Rangers, Boston) | 14 | 890 | 185 | 574 | 759 | .853 |
| Murray Oliver (Detroit, Boston, Toronto, Minnesota) | 17 | 1,127 | 274 | 454 | 728 | .646 |
| Bob Nevin (Toronto, N.Y. Rangers, Minnesota, Los Angeles) | 18 | 1,128 | 307 | 419 | 726 | .644 |
| Rick MacLeish (Philadelphia, Hartford, Pittsburgh) | 12 | 786 | 339 | 383 | 722 | .919 |
| George Armstrong (Toronto) | 21 | 1,187 | 296 | 417 | 713 | .601 |
| Vic Hadfield (N.Y. Rangers, Pittsburgh Penguins) | 16 | 1,002 | 323 | 389 | 712 | .711 |

## NATIONAL HOCKEY LEAGUE TROPHY WINNERS

### HART TROPHY For Most Valuable Player

1958/59 Andy Bathgate, New York
1959/60 Gordie Howe, Detroit
1960/61 Bernie Geoffrion, Montreal
1961/62 Jacques Plante, Montreal
1962/63 Gordie Howe, Detroit
1963/64 Jean Beliveau, Montreal
1964/65 Bobby Hull, Chicago
1965/66 Bobby Hull, Chicago
1966/67 Stan Mikita, Chicago
1967/68 Stan Mikita, Chicago
1968/69 Phil Esposito, Boston
1969/70 Bobby Orr, Boston
1970/71 Bobby Orr, Boston
1971/72 Bobby Orr, Boston
1972/73 Bobby Clarke, Philadelphia
1973/74 Phil Esposito, Boston
1974/75 Bobby Clarke, Philadelphia
1975/76 Bobby Clarke, Philadelphia
1976/77 Guy Lafleur, Montreal
1977/78 Guy Lafleur, Montreal
1978/79 Bryan Trottier, N.Y. Islanders
1979/80 Wayne Gretzky, Edmonton
1980/81 Wayne Gretzky, Edmonton
1981/82 Wayne Gretzky, Edmonton

### VEZINA TROPHY For Best Goalie Record

1965/66 Lorne Worsley and Charlie Hodge, Montreal
1966/67 Denis DeJordy and Glenn Hall, Chicago
1967/68 Lorne Worsley and Rogatien Vachon, Montreal
1968/69 Glenn Hall and Jacques Plante, St Louis
1969/70 Tony Esposito, Chicago
1970/71 Ed Giacomin and Gilles Villemure, New York
1971/72 Tony Esposito and Gary Smith, Chicago
1972/73 Ken Dryden, Montreal
1973/74 Bernie Parent, Philadelphia and Tony Esposito, Chicago
1974/75 Bernie Parent, Philadelphia
1975/76 Ken Dryden, Montreal
1976/77 Ken Dryden and Michel Larocque, Montreal
1977/78 Ken Dryden and Michel Larocque, Montreal
1978/79 Ken Dryden and Michel Larocque, Montreal
1979/80 Don Edwards and Bob Sauve, Buffalo
1980/81 R. Sevigny, D. Herron and M. Larocque, Montreal
1981/82 Billy Smith, N.Y. Islanders

WILLIAM JENNINGS TROPHY **For Best Goalie Record**

1981/82 Denis Herron, Rick Wamsley, Montreal

JAMES NORRIS TROPHY **For Best Defenseman**

1956/57 Doug Harvey, Montreal
1957/58 Doug Harvey, Montreal
1958/59 Tom Johnson, Montreal
1959/60 Doug Harvey, Montreal
1960/61 Doug Harvey, Montreal
1961/62 Doug Harvey, New York
1962/63 Pierre Pilote, Chicago
1963/64 Pierre Pilote, Chicago
1964/65 Pierre Pilote, Chicago
1965/66 J. Laperriere, Montreal
1966/67 Harry Howell, New York
1967/68 Bobby Orr, Boston
1968/69 Bobby Orr, Boston
1969/70 Bobby Orr, Boston
1970/71 Bobby Orr, Boston
1971/72 Bobby Orr, Boston
1972/73 Bobby Orr, Boston
1973/74 Bobby Orr, Boston
1974/75 Bobby Orr, Boston
1975/76 Denis Potvin, N.Y. Islanders
1976/77 Larry Robinson, Montreal
1977/78 Denis Potvin, N.Y. Islanders
1978/79 Denis Potvin, N.Y. Islanders
1979/80 Larry Robinson, Montreal
1980/81 Rudy Carlyle, Pittsburgh
1981/82 Doug Wilson, Chicago

FRANK J. SELKE TROPHY **For Best Defensive Forward**

1977/78 Bob Gainey, Montreal
1978/79 Bob Gainey, Montreal
1979/80 Bob Gainey, Montreal
1980/81 Bob Gainey, Montreal
1981/82 Steve Kasper, Boston

CALDER TROPHY **For Best Rookie**

1953/54 Camille Henry, New York
1954/55 Ed Litzenberger, Chicago
1955/56 Glenn Hall, Detroit
1956/57 Larry Regan, Boston
1957/58 Frank Mahovlich, Toronto
1958/59 Ralph Backstrom, Montreal
1959/60 Billy Hay, Chicago
1960/61 Dave Keon, Toronto
1961/62 Bobby Rousseau, Montreal
1962/63 Kent Douglas, Toronto
1963/64 Jacques Laperriere, Montreal
1964/65 Roger Crozier, Detroit
1965/66 Brit Selby, Toronto
1966/67 Bobby Orr, Boston
1967/68 Derek Sanderson, Boston
1968/69 Danny Grant, Minnesota
1969/70 Tony Esposito, Chicago
1970/71 Gil Perreault, Buffalo
1971/72 Ken Dryden, Montreal
1972/73 Steve Vickers, N. Y. Rangers
1973/74 Denis Potvin, N. Y. Islanders
1974/75 Eric Vail, Atlanta
1975/76 Bryan Trottier, N.Y. Islanders
1976/77 Willie Plett, Atlanta
1977/78 Mike Bossy, N. Y. Islanders
1978/79 Bobby Smith, Minnesota
1979/80 Ray Bourque, Boston
1980/81 Peter Stastny, Quebec
1981/82 Dale Hawerchuk, Winnipeg

LADY BYNG TROPHY **For Sportsmanship**

1953/54 Red Kelly, Detroit
1954/55 Sid Smith, Toronto
1955/56 Earl Reibel, Detroit
1956/57 Andy Hebenton, New York
1957/58 Camille Henry, New York
1958/59 Alex Delvecchio, Detroit
1959/60 Don McKenney, Boston
1960/61 Red Kelly, Toronto
1961/62 Dave Keon, Toronto
1962/63 Dave Keon, Toronto
1963/64 Ken Wharram, Chicago
1964/65 Bobby Hull, Chicago
1965/66 Alex Delvecchio, Detroit
1966/67 Stan Mikita, Chicago
1967/68 Stan Mikita, Chicago
1968/69 Alex Delvecchio, Detroit
1969/70 Phil Goyette, St. Louis
1970/71 Johnny Bucyk, Boston
1971/72 Jean Ratelle, New York
1972/73 Gil Perreault, Buffalo
1973/74 John Bucyk, Boston
1974/75 Marcel Dionne, Detroit
1975/76 Jean Ratelle, Boston
1976/77 Marcel Dionne, Los Angeles
1977/78 Butch Goring, Los Angeles
1978/79 Bob MacMillan, Atlanta
1979/80 Wayne Gretzky, Edmonton
1980/81 Rick Kehoe, Pittsburgh
1981/82 Rick Middleton, Boston

CONN SMYTHE TROPHY **For Most Valuable Player in Stanley Cup Playoffs**

1965 Jean Beliveau, Montreal
1966 Roger Crozier, Detroit
1967 Dave Keon, Toronto
1968 Glenn Hall, St. Louis
1969 Serge Savard, Montreal
1970 Bobby Orr, Boston
1971 Ken Dryden, Montreal
1972 Bobby Orr, Boston
1973 Yvan Cournoyer, Montreal
1974 Bernie Parent, Philadelphia
1975 Bernie Parent, Philadelphia
1976 Reggie Leach, Philadelphia
1977 Guy Lafleur, Montreal
1978 Larry Robinson, Montreal
1979 Bob Gainey, Montreal
1980 Bryan Trottier, N.Y. Islanders
1981 Butch Goring, N.Y. Islanders
1982 Mike Bossy, N.Y. Islanders

## 1982 NHL ALL-STARS

Results of voting by members of the Professional Hockey Writers Association

| | FIRST TEAM | | SECOND TEAM |
|---|---|---|---|
| Goal | Billy Smith, N.Y. Islanders | Goal | Grant Fuhr, Edmonton |
| Defense | Doug Wilson, Chicago | Defense | Paul Coffey, Edmonton |
| Defense | Ray Bourque, Boston | Defense | Brian Engblom, Montreal |
| Center | Wayne Gretzky, Edmonton | Center | Bryan Trottier, N.Y. Islanders |
| Right Wing | Mike Bossy, N.Y. Islanders | Right Wing | Rick Middleton, Boston |
| Left Wing | Mark Messier, Edmonton | Left Wing | John Tonelli, N.Y. Islanders |

## NHL ALL-STAR GAME RESULTS

Prior to 1969 the All-Star Game between the chosen team and the holder of the Stanley Cup.

| Year | Score | Location |
|---|---|---|
| 1947 | All-Stars 4, Toronto 3 | Toronto |
| 1948 | All-Stars 3, Toronto 1 | Chicago |
| 1949 | All-Stars 3, Toronto 1 | Toronto |
| 1950 | Detroit 7, All-Stars 1 | Detroit |
| 1951 | 1st Team 2, 2nd Team 2 | Toronto |
| 1952 | 1st Team 1, 2nd Team 1 | Detroit |
| 1953 | All-Stars 3, Montreal 1 | Montreal |
| 1954 | All-Stars 2, Detroit 2 | Detroit |
| 1955 | Detroit 3, All-Stars 1 | Detroit |
| 1956 | All-Stars 1, Montreal 1 | Montreal |
| 1957 | All-Stars 5, Montreal 3 | Montreal |
| 1958 | Montreal 6, All-Stars 3 | Montreal |
| 1959 | Montreal 6, All-Stars 1 | Montreal |
| 1960 | All-Stars 2, Montreal 1 | Montreal |
| 1961 | All-Stars 3, Chicago 1 | Chicago |
| 1962 | Toronto 4, All-Stars 1 | Toronto |
| 1963 | All-Stars 3, Toronto 3 | Toronto |
| 1964 | All-Stars 3, Toronto 2 | Toronto |
| 1965 | All-Stars 5, Montreal 2 | Montreal |
| 1967 | Montreal 3, All-Stars 0 | Montreal |
| 1968 | Toronto 4, All-Stars 3 | Toronto |
| 1969 | East 3, West 3 | Montreal |
| 1970 | East 4, West 1 | St. Louis |
| 1971 | West 2, East 1 | Boston |
| 1972 | East 3, West 2 | Minnesota |
| 1973 | East 5, West 4 | New York |
| 1974 | West 6, East 4 | Chicago |
| 1975 | Prince of Wales 7, Campbell 1 | Montreal |
| 1976 | Wales 7, Campbell 5 | Philadelphia |
| 1977 | Wales 4, Campbell 3 | Vancouver |
| 1978 | Wales 3, Campbell 2 | Buffalo |
| 1979 | no game played | |
| 1980 | Wales 6, Campbell 3 | Detroit |
| 1981 | Campbell 4, Wales 1 | Los Angeles |
| 1982 | Wales 4, Campbell 2 | Washington |

## HOCKEY HALL OF FAME

Source: N.H.L.

**Players**

Sidney Abel
John Adams
C. J. "Syl" Apps
George Armstrong
I. W. "Ace" Bailey
Donald Bain
Hobart Baker
Martin Barry
Andrew Bathgate
Jean Beliveau
Clinton Benedict
Douglas Bentley
Maxwell Bentley
Hector "Toe" Blake
Richard Boon
Emile "Butch" Bouchard
Frank Boucher
George "Buck" Boucher
John Bower
Russell Bowie
Francis Brimsek
H. L. "Punch" Broadbent
W. E. "Turk" Broda
Johnny Bucyk
Billy Burch
Harold Cameron
F. M. "King" Clancy
Aubrey "Dit" Clapper
Sprague Cleghorn
Neil Colville
Charles Conacher
Alex Connell
William Cook
Arthur Coulter
Yvan Cournoyer
William Cowley
S. R. "Rusty" Crawford
John Darragh
A. M. "Scotty" Davidson
Clarence "Hap" Day
Alex Delvecchio
Cyril Denneny
Gordon Drillon
Charles Drinkwater
Thomas Dunderdale
William Durnan
M. A. "Red" Dutton
C. H. "Babe" Dye
Arthur Farrell
Frank Foyston
Frank Frederickson
William Gadsby
Charles Gardiner
Herbert Gardiner
James Gardner
J. A. Bernard Geoffrion
Eddie Gerard
Rod Gilbert
H. L. "Billy" Gilmour
F. X. "Moose" Goheen

**Players**

Ebenezer Goodfellow
Michael Grant
W. "Shorty" Green
Silas Griffis
George Hainsworth
Glenn Hall
Joseph Hall
Douglas Harvey
George Hay
W. M. "Riley" Hern
Bryan Hextall
Harry Holmes
C. Thomas Hooper
G. R. "Red" Horner
M. G. "Tim" Horton
Gordon Howe
Sydney Howe
Harry Howell
J. B. "Bouse" Hutton
Harry Hyland
J. D. "Dick" Irvin
H. "Busher" Jackson
E. "Moose" Johnson
Ivan "Ching" Johnson
Thomas Johnson
Aurel Joliat
G. "Duke" Keats
L. P. "Red" Kelly
T. S. "Teeder" Kennedy
Elmer Lach
E. C. "Newsy" Lalonde
Jean Laviolette
Hugh Lehman
Percy LeSeur
Robert "Ted" Lindsay
Harry Lumley
D. "Mickey" MacKay
Frank Mahovlich
Joseph Malone
Sylvio Mantha
John Marshall
Fred "Steamer" Maxwell
Frank McGee
William McGimsie
George McNamara
Richard Moore
Patrick Moran
Howie Morenz
William Mosienko
Frank Nighbor
E. Reginald Noble
Harry Oliver
Bobby Orr
Lester Patrick
Lynn Patrick
Tommy Phillips
J. A. Pierre Pilote
Didier "Pit" Pitre
J. Jacques Plante
Walter "Babe" Pratt

**Players**

A. Joseph Primeau
J. R. Marcel Pronovost
Harvey Pulford
H. G. "Bill" Quackenbush
Frank Rankin
C. E. "Chuck" Rayner
Kenneth Reardon
Henri Richard
J. H. Maurice Richard
George Richardson
Gordon Roberts
Arthur Ross
Blair Russel
J. D. "Jack" Ruttan
Terrance Sawchuk
Fred Scanlan
Milton Schmidt
D. "Sweeney" Schriner
Earl Seibert
Oliver Seibert
Edward Shore
A. C. "Babe" Siebert
Harold Simpson
Alfred Smith
R. "Hooley" Smith
Thomas Smith
Allan Stanley
R. "Barney" Stanley
John Stewart
Nelson Stewart
Bruce Stuart
Hod Stuart
F. "Cyclone" Taylor
C. R. "Tiny" Thompson
Col. Harry J. Trihey
Norm Ullman
Georges Vezina
John Walker
Martin Walsh
Harry Watson
Ralph "Cooney" Weiland
Harry Westwick
Fred Whitcroft
Gordon Wilson
Lorne "Gump" Worsley
Roy Worters

**Referees**

John Ashley
William Chadwick
Chaucer Elliott
Robert Hewitson
Fred "Mickey" Ion
Michael Rodden
J. Cooper Smeaton
R. A. "Red" Storey
Frank Udvari

**Builders**

Charles Adams

**Builders**

Weston Adams
Thomas "Frank" Ahearn
John "Bunny" Ahearne
Sir Montague Allen
Harold Ballard
John Bickell
George Brown
Walter Brown
Frank Buckland
Jack Butterfield
Frank Calder
Angus Campbell
Clarence Campbell
Joseph Cattarinich
Joseph "Leo" Dandurand
Francis Dilio
George Dudley
James Dunn
Emile Francis
Dr. John Gibson
Thomas Gorman
Charles Hay
James Hendy
Foster Hewitt
William Hewitt
Fred Hume
Thomas Ivan
William Jennings
Gen. John Kilpatrick
George Leader
Robert LeBel
Thomas Lockhart
Paul Loicq
Maj. Frederic McLaughlin
Hon. Hartland Molson
Francis Nelson
Bruce Norris
James Norris, Sr.
James D. Norris
William Northey
John O'Brien
Frank Patrick
Allan Pickard
Samuel Pollock
Sen. Donat Raymond
John Robertson
Claude Robinson
Philip Ross
Frank Selke
Frank Smith
Conn Smythe
Lord Stanley of Preston
Capt. James Sutherland
Anatoli Tarasov
Lloyd Turner
William Tutt
Carl Voss
Fred Waghorne
Arthur Wirtz
William Writz

## NCAA HOCKEY CHAMPIONSHIPS

### DIVISION I

1957 Colorado College 13, Michigan 6
1958 Denver 6, North Dakota 2
1959 North Dakota 4, Michigan State 3
1960 Denver 5, Michigan Tech 3
1961 Denver 12, St. Lawrence 2
1962 Michigan Tech 7, Clarkson 1
1963 North Dakota 6, Denver 5
1964 Michigan 6, Denver 3
1965 Michigan Tech 8, Boston College 2
1966 Michigan State 6, Clarkson 1
1967 Cornell 4, Boston University 1
1968 Denver 4, North Dakota 0
1969 Denver 4, Cornell 3
1970 Cornell 6, Clarkson 4
1971 Boston University 4, Minnesota 2
1972 Boston University 4, Cornell 0
1973 Wisconsin 4, Denver 2
1974 Minnesota 4, Michigan Tech 2
1975 Michigan Tech 6, Minnesota 1
1976 Minnesota 6, Michigan Tech 4
1977 Wisconsin 6, Michigan 5
1978 Boston University 5, Boston College 3
1979 Minnesota 4, North Dakota 3
1980 North Dakota 5, Northern Michigan 2
1981 Wisconsin 6, Minnesota 3
1982 North Dakota 5, Wisconsin 2

### DIVISION II

1978 Merrimack 12, Lake Forest 2
1979 Lowell 6, Mankato State 4
1980 Mankato State 5, Elmira 2
1981 Lowell 5, Plattsburgh State 4
1982 Lowell 6, Plattsburgh State 1

# SOCCER

## NORTH AMERICAN SOCCER LEAGUE 1133 Avenue of the Americas, New York City 10036

### 1982 FINAL STANDINGS

| Eastern Division | Won | Lost | Pts. | Goals For | Goals Ag'st |
|---|---|---|---|---|---|
| New York Cosmos | 23 | 9 | 203 | 73 | 52 |
| Montreal Manic | 19 | 13 | 159 | 60 | 43 |
| Toronto Blizzard | 17 | 15 | 151 | 64 | 47 |
| Chicago Sting | 13 | 19 | 129 | 56 | 67 |
| **Southern Division** | | | | | |
| Ft. Lauderdale Strikers | 18 | 14 | 163 | 64 | 74 |
| Tulsa Roughnecks | 16 | 16 | 151 | 69 | 57 |
| Tampa Bay Rowdies | 12 | 20 | 112 | 47 | 77 |
| Jacksonville Tea Men | 11 | 21 | 105 | 41 | 71 |

| Western Division | Won | Lost | Pts. | Goals For | Goals Ag'st |
|---|---|---|---|---|---|
| Seattle Sounders | 18 | 14 | 166 | 72 | 48 |
| San Diego Sockers | 19 | 13 | 162 | 71 | 54 |
| Vancouver Whitecaps | 20 | 12 | 160 | 58 | 48 |
| Portland Trail Blazers | 14 | 18 | 122 | 49 | 44 |
| San Jose Earthquakes | 13 | 19 | 114 | 47 | 62 |
| Edmonton Drillers | 11 | 21 | 93 | 38 | 65 |

| LEADING SCORERS | Games | Goals | Assists | Pts. |
|---|---|---|---|---|
| Giorgio Chinaglia, New York | 32 | 20 | 15 | 55 |
| Karl-Heinz Granitza, Chicago | 32 | 20 | 9 | 49 |
| Peter Ward, Seattle | 32 | 18 | 13 | 49 |
| Ricardo Alonso, Jacksonville | 30 | 21 | 4 | 46 |
| Laurie Abrahams, Tulsa | 31 | 17 | 10 | 44 |

| LEADING GOALKEEPERS | Games | Saves | Goals Ag'st | Avg. |
|---|---|---|---|---|
| Tino Lettieri, Vancouver | 27 | 129 | 34 | 1.23 |
| Victor Nogueira, Montreal | 19 | 75 | 23 | 1.25 |
| Paul Hammond, Seattle | 32 | 140 | 43 | 1.29 |
| Bill Irwin, Portland | 25 | 121 | 34 | 1.32 |
| Jan Moller, Toronto | 30 | 149 | 42 | 1.39 |

### AWARD WINNERS

**Most Valuable Player** — Peter Ward, Seattle
**Three Star Player of the Year** — Peter Ward, Seattle
**North American Player of the Year** — Mark Peterson, Seattle
**Rookie of the Year** — Pedro DeBrito, Tampa Bay
**Goal of the Year** — Ade Coker, San Diego
**Top Forward** — Giorgio Chinaglia, New York
**Top Midfielder** — Vladislav Bogicevic, New York
**Top Defender** — Frantz Mathieu, Chicago
**Top Goalkeeper** — Hubert Birkenmeier, New York
**Top Scorer** — Giorgio Chinaglia, New York
**Most Valuable Player, Soccer Bowl 1982** — Giorgio Chinaglia, New York
**Coach of the Year** — John Giles, Vancouver

## 1982 NASL PLAYOFFS

**First Round**
New York over Tulsa, 5-0, 0-1, 1-0
Fort Lauderdale over Montreal, 3-2, 0-1, 4-1
San Diego over Vancouver, 5-1, 0-1, 2-1
Seattle over Toronto, 4-2, 1-2, 4-2

**Semifinals**
New York over San Diego, 2-1, 2-1
Seattle over Ft. Lauderdale, 2-1, 3-4, 1-0

**CHAMPIONSHIP GAME (SOCCER BOWL 1982)** — New York 1, Seattle 0

## NASL ALL-STAR TEAMS: 1982

| Position | First Team | Second Team | Honorable Mention |
|---|---|---|---|
| Goalkeeper | Hubert Birkenmeier, New York | Jan van Beveren, Ft. Lauderdale | Jan Moller, Toronto |
| Defender | Frantz Mathieu, Montreal | Barry Wallace, Tulsa | Bruce Wilson, Toronto |
| Defender | Young Jeung Cho, Portland | Jeff Durgan, New York | Mike Connell, Tampa Bay |
| Defender | Peter Nogly, Tampa Bay | Carlos Alberto, New York | John Wile, Vancouver |
| Defender | Andranik Eskandarian, New York | Ray Evans, Seattle | Bob Lenarduzzi, Vancouver |
| Midfielder | Vladislav Bogicevic, New York | Steve Daley, Seattle | Vince Hilaire, San Jose |
| Midfielder | Ace Ntsoelengoe, Toronto | Johan Neeskens, New York | Ray Hudson, Ft. Lauderdale |
| Midfielder | Arno Steffenhagen, Chicago | Teofilo Cubillas, Ft. Lauderdale | Julie Veee, San Diego |
| Forward | Giorgio Chinaglia, New York | Steve Hunt, New York | Branko Segota, Ft. Lauderdale |
| Forward | Peter Ward, Seattle | Karl-Heinz Granitza, Chicago | David Byrne, Toronto |
| Forward | Ricardo Alonso, Jacksonville | Pato Margetic, Chicago | (tie) Laurie Abrahams, Tulsa; Carl Valentine, Vancouver; Godfrey Ingram, San Jose |

## NORTH AMERICAN SOCCER LEAGUE CHAMPIONS: 1968–1982

| | | | | | | | |
|---|---|---|---|---|---|---|---|
| 1968 | Atlanta | 1972 | New York | 1976 | Toronto | 1980 | New York |
| 1969 | Kansas City | 1973 | Philadelphia | 1977 | New York | 1981 | Chicago |
| 1970 | Rochester | 1974 | Los Angeles | 1978 | New York | 1982 | New York |
| 1971 | Dallas | 1975 | Tampa Bay | 1979 | Vancouver | | |

## 1982 WORLD CUP CHAMPIONSHIP (Spain, June 13 — July 11)

**Qualified for First Round:** Algeria, Argentina, Austria, Belgium, Brazil, Cameroon, Chile, Czechoslovakia, El Salvador, England, France, Germany (West), Honduras, Hungary, Italy, Kuwait, New Zealand, Northern Ireland, Peru, Poland, Scotland, Spain, U.S.S.R., Yugoslavia

**Advanced to Second Round:** Argentina, Austria, Belgium, Brazil, England, France, Germany (West), Italy, Northern Ireland, Poland, Spain, U.S.S.R.
**Third Place Game:** Poland 3, France 2
**Championship Game:** Italy 3, Germany (West) 1

## OTHER CHAMPIONSHIPS (1982)

| | |
|---|---|
| American Soccer League | Detroit Express |
| NASL Indoor | San Diego Sockers |
| Major Indoor League | New York Arrows |
| NCAA Division I (1981) | Connecticut |
| NCAA Division II (1981) | Tampa |
| NCAA Division III (1981) | Glassboro State (N.J.) |
| NAIA (1981) | Quincy (Ill.) |
| Junior Colleges (1981) | Florissant Valley C.C. |
| AIAW (1981) | North Carolina |

# GOLF

## TOTAL MONEY-WINNING LEADERS: 1981 Source: PGA

Official Money shall be awarded to individual prize winners in major tournaments and such other events as the Tournament Policy Board may designate, even if part of the tournament is canceled provided; however, that Official Money shall not be awarded, in any team competition or a pro-am tournament (but Official Money will be awarded in a major tournament for individuals even if held concurrently with a pro-am tournament). The scale of Official Money will be determined from time to time by the Tournament Policy Board.

| Rank | Name | Winnings |
|---|---|---|
| 1. | Tom Kite | $375,699 |
| 2. | Ray Floyd | 359,360 |
| 3. | Tom Watson | 347,660 |
| 4. | Bruce Lietzke | 343,446 |
| 5. | Bill Rogers | 315,411 |
| 6. | Jerry Pate | 280,627 |
| 7. | Hale Irwin | 276,499 |
| 8. | Craig Stadler | 218,829 |
| 9. | Curtis Strange | 201,513 |
| 10. | Larry Nelson | 193,342 |
| 11. | Jack Renner | 193,292 |
| 12. | Johnny Miller | 193,167 |
| 13. | David Graham | 188,286 |
| 14. | Bobby Clampett | 184,710 |
| 15. | Jay Haas | 181,894 |
| 16. | Jack Nicklaus | 178,213 |
| 17. | Tom Weiskopf | 177,396 |
| 18. | Gil Morgan | $171,184 |
| 19. | Fuzzy Zoeller | 151,571 |
| 20. | Ben Crenshaw | 151,038 |
| 21. | Keith Fergus | 150,792 |
| 22. | Lon Hinkle | 144,307 |
| 23. | Lee Trevino | 134,801 |
| 24. | John Mahaffey | 128,795 |
| 25. | John Cook | 127,608 |
| 26. | J.C. Snead | 126,175 |
| 27. | Tom Purtzer | 122,812 |
| 28. | Peter Oosterhuis | 115,862 |
| 29. | Ron Streck | 114,895 |
| 30. | Andy North | 111,401 |
| 31. | George Archer | 111,093 |
| 32. | Hubert Green | 110,133 |
| 33. | Jim Simons | 109,210 |
| 34. | Scott Simpson | $108,793 |
| 35. | Andy Bean | 105,755 |
| 36. | Ed Fiori | 105,510 |
| 37. | George Burns | 105,395 |
| 38. | Jim Colbert | 100,847 |
| 39. | Tommy Valentine | 97,323 |
| 40. | Leonard Thompson | 95,517 |
| 41. | Mike Sullivan | 94,844 |
| 42. | Dan Pohl | 94,303 |
| 43. | Calvin Peete | 93,243 |
| 44. | Mike Reid | 93,037 |
| 45. | D.A. Weibring | 92,365 |
| 46. | Mark Hayes | 91,624 |
| 47. | Dan Halldorson | 90,064 |
| 48. | Barry Jaeckel | 87,931 |
| 49. | Bob Murphy | 87,192 |
| 50. | Peter Jacobsen | 85,624 |

## THE BRITISH OPEN

| Year | Winner | Score |
|---|---|---|
| 1868 | Tom Morris, Jr. | 154 |
| 1869 | Tom Morris, Jr. | 157 |
| 1870 | Tom Marris, Jr. | 149 |
| 1871 | No championship played | |
| 1872 | Tom Morris, Jr. | 166 |
| 1873 | Tom Kipp | 179 |
| 1874 | Mungo Park | 159 |
| 1875 | Willie Park | 166 |
| 1876 | Robert Martin | 176 |
| 1877 | Jamie Anderson | 160 |
| 1878 | Jamie Anderson | 157 |
| 1879 | Jamie Anderson | 169 |
| 1880 | Robert Ferguson | 162 |
| 1881 | Robert Ferguson | 170 |
| 1882 | Robert Ferguson | 171 |
| 1883 | *Willie Fernie | 159 |
| 1884 | Jack Simpson | 160 |
| 1885 | Bob Martin | 171 |
| 1886 | David Brown | 157 |
| 1887 | Willie Park, Jr. | 161 |
| 1888 | Jack Burns | 171 |
| 1889 | *Willie Park, Jr. | 155 (158) |
| 1890 | John Ball | 164 |
| 1891 | Hugh Kirkaldy (Championship extended from 36 to 72 holes) | 166 |
| 1892 | Harold H. Hilton | 305 |
| 1893 | William Auchterlonie | 322 |
| 1894 | John H. Taylor | 326 |
| 1895 | John H. Taylor | 322 |
| 1896 | *Harry Vardon | 316 (157) |
| 1897 | Harold H. Hilton | 314 |
| 1898 | Harry Vardon | 307 |
| 1899 | Harry Vardon | 310 |
| 1900 | John H. Taylor | 309 |
| 1901 | James Braid | 309 |
| 1902 | Alexander Herd | 307 |
| 1903 | Harry Vardon | 300 |
| 1904 | Jack White | 296 |
| 1905 | James Braid | 318 |
| 1906 | James Braid | 300 |
| 1907 | Arnaud Massy | 312 |
| 1908 | James Braid | 291 |
| 1909 | John H. Taylor | 295 |
| 1910 | James Braid | 299 |
| 1911 | Harry Vardon | 303 |
| 1912 | Edward (Ted) Ray | 295 |
| 1913 | John H. Taylor | 304 |
| 1914 | Harry Vardon | 306 |
| 1915–1919 | No championships played | |
| 1920 | George Duncan | 303 |
| 1921 | *Jock Hutchison | 296 (150) |
| 1922 | Walter Hagen | 300 |
| 1923 | Arthur G. Havers | 295 |
| 1924 | Walter Hagen | 301 |
| 1925 | James M. Barnes | 300 |
| 1926 | Robert T. Jones, Jr. | 291 |
| 1927 | Robert T. Jones, Jr. | 285 |
| 1928 | Walter Hagen | 292 |
| 1929 | Walter Hagen | 292 |
| 1930 | Robert T. Jones, Jr. | 291 |
| 1931 | Tommy D. Armour | 296 |
| 1932 | Gene Sarazen | 283 |
| 1933 | *Denny Shute | 292 (149) |
| 1934 | Henry Cotton | 283 |
| 1935 | Alfred Perry | 283 |
| 1936 | Alfred Padgham | 287 |
| 1937 | Henry Cotton | 290 |
| 1938 | R. A. Whitcombe | 295 |
| 1939 | Richard Burton | 290 |
| 1940–1945 | No championships played | |
| 1946 | Sam Snead | 290 |
| 1947 | Fred Daly | 293 |
| 1948 | Henry Cotton | 294 |
| 1949 | *Bobby Locke | 283 (135) |
| 1950 | Bobby Locke | 279 |
| 1951 | Max Faulkner | 285 |
| 1952 | Bobby Locke | 287 |
| 1953 | Ben Hogan | 282 |
| 1954 | Peter Thomson | 283 |
| 1955 | Peter Thomson | 281 |
| 1956 | Peter Thomson | 286 |
| 1957 | Bobby Locke | 279 |
| 1958 | Peter Thomson | 278 (139) |
| 1959 | Gary Player | 284 |
| 1960 | Kel Nagle | 278 |
| 1961 | Arnold Palmer | 284 |
| 1962 | Arnold Palmer | 276 |
| 1963 | *Bob Charles | 277 |
| 1964 | Tony Lema | 279 |
| 1965 | Peter Thomson | 285 |
| 1966 | Jack Nicklaus | 282 |
| 1967 | Roberto De Vicenzo | 278 |
| 1968 | Gary Player | 289 |
| 1969 | Tony Jacklin | 280 |
| 1970 | *Jack Nicklaus | 283 (72) |
| 1971 | Lee Trevino | 278 |
| 1972 | Lee Trevino | 278 |
| 1973 | Tom Weiskopf | 276 |
| 1974 | Gary Player | 282 |
| 1975 | *Tom Watson | 279 (71) |
| 1976 | Johnny Miller | 279 |
| 1977 | Tom Watson | 268 |
| 1978 | Jack Nicklaus | 281 |
| 1979 | Severiano Ballesteros | 283 |
| 1980 | Tom Watson | 271 |
| 1981 | Bill Rogers | 276 |
| 1982 | Tom Watson | 284 |

* Winner in playoff, figures in parentheses indicate playoff scores.

## THE MASTERS

| Year | Winner | Score |
|---|---|---|
| 1934 | Horton Smith | 284 |
| 1935 | Gene Sarazen | 282 |
| 1936 | Horton Smith | 285 |
| 1937 | Byron Nelson | 283 |
| 1938 | Henry Picard | 285 |
| 1939 | Ralph Guldahl | 279 |
| 1940 | Jimmy Demaret | 280 |
| 1941 | Craig Wood | 280 |
| 1942 | Byron Nelson* | 280 |
| 1946 | Herman Keiser | 282 |
| 1947 | Jimmy Demaret | 281 |
| 1948 | Claude Harmon | 279 |
| 1949 | Sam Snead | 282 |
| 1950 | Jimmy Demaret | 283 |
| 1951 | Ben Hogan | 280 |
| 1952 | Sam Snead | 286 |
| 1953 | Ben Hogan | 274 |
| 1954 | Sam Snead* | 289 |
| 1955 | Cary Middlecoff | 279 |
| 1956 | Jack Burke | 289 |
| 1957 | Doug Ford | 283 |
| 1958 | Arnold Palmer | 284 |
| 1959 | Art Wall | 284 |
| 1960 | Arnold Palmer | 282 |
| 1961 | Gary Player | 280 |
| 1962 | Arnold Palmer* | 280 |
| 1963 | Jack Nicklaus | 286 |
| 1964 | Arnold Palmer | 276 |
| 1965 | Jack Nicklaus | 271 |
| 1966 | Jack Nicklaus* | 288 |
| 1967 | Gay Brewer | 280 |
| 1968 | Bob Goalby | 277 |
| 1969 | George Archer | 281 |
| 1970 | Billy Casper* | 279 |
| 1971 | Charles Coody | 279 |
| 1972 | Jack Nicklaus | 286 |
| 1973 | Tommy Aaron | 283 |
| 1974 | Gary Player | 278 |
| 1975 | Jack Nicklaus | 276 |
| 1976 | Ray Floyd | 271 |
| 1977 | Tom Watson | 276 |
| 1978 | Gary Player | 277 |
| 1979 | Fuzzy Zoeller* | 280 |
| 1980 | Severiano Ballesteros | 275 |
| 1981 | Tom Watson | 280 |
| 1982 | Craig Stadler | 284 |

* Won in playoff.

## THE UNITED STATES OPEN Source: U. S. Golf Association

| Year | Site | Winner | Score | Year | Site | Winner | Score |
|---|---|---|---|---|---|---|---|
| 1895 | Newport, R.I. | Horace Rawlins | 173 | 1938 | Denver, Colo. | Ralph Guldahl | 284 |
| 1896 | Southampton, N.Y. | James Foulis | 152 | 1939 | W. Conshohocken, Pa. | Byron Nelson | 284* |
| 1897 | Wheaton, Ill. | Joe Lloyd | 162 | 1940 | Cleveland, Ohio | Lawson Little | 287* |
| 1898 | S. Hamilton, Mass. | Fred Herd | 328 | 1941 | Ft. Worth, Texas | Craig Wood | 284 |
| 1899 | Baltimore, Md. | Willie Smith | 315 | 1942–1945 No Competition Held | | | |
| 1900 | Wheaton, Ill. | Harry Vardon | 313 | 1946 | Cleveland, Ohio | Lloyd Mangrum | 284* |
| 1901 | S. Hamilton, Mass. | Willie Anderson | 331* | 1947 | Clayton, Mo. | Lew Worsham | 282* |
| 1902 | Garden City, N.Y. | Lawrence Auchterlonie | 307 | 1948 | Los Angeles, Calif. | Ben Hogan | 276 |
| 1903 | Springfield, N.J. | Willie Anderson | 307* | 1949 | Medinah, Ill. | Cary Middlecoff | 286 |
| 1904 | Golf, Ill. | Willie Anderson | 303 | 1950 | Ardmore, Pa. | Ben Hogan | 287* |
| 1905 | S. Hamilton, Mass. | Willie Anderson | 314 | 1951 | Birmingham, Mich. | Ben Hogan | 287 |
| 1906 | Lake Forest, Ill. | Alex Smith | 295 | 1952 | Dallas, Texas | Julius Boros | 281 |
| 1907 | Philadelphia, Pa. | Alex Ross | 302 | 1953 | Oakmont, Pa. | Ben Hogan | 283 |
| 1908 | S. Hamilton, Mass. | Fred McLeod | 322* | 1954 | Springfield, N.J. | Ed Furgol | 284 |
| 1909 | Englewood, N.J. | George Sargent | 290 | 1955 | San Francisco, Calif. | Jack Fleck | 287* |
| 1910 | St. Martins, Pa. | Alex Smith | 298* | 1956 | Rochester, N.Y. | Cary Middlecoff | 281 |
| 1911 | Wheaton, Ill. | John J. McDermott | 307* | 1957 | Toledo, Ohio | Dick Mayer | 282* |
| 1912 | Buffalo, N.Y. | John J. McDermott | 294 | 1958 | Tulsa, Okla. | Tommy Bolt | 283 |
| 1913 | Brookline, Mass. | Walter Hagen | 290 | 1959 | Mamaroneck, N.Y. | Bill Casper, Jr. | 282 |
| 1914 | Blue Island, Ill. | Francis Ouimet (A) | 304* | 1960 | Englewood, Colo. | Arnold Palmer | 280 |
| 1915 | Springfield, N.J. | Jerome D. Travers (A) | 297 | 1961 | Birmingham, Mich. | Gene Littler | 281 |
| 1916 | Minneapolis, Minn. | Charles Evans, Jr. (A) | 286 | 1962 | Oakmont, Pa. | Jack Nicklaus | 283* |
| 1917–1918 No Competion Held | | | | 1963 | Brookline, Mass. | Julius Boros | 293* |
| 1919 | West Newton, Mass. | Water Hagen | 301* | 1964 | Washington, D.C. | Ken Venturi | 278 |
| 1920 | Toledo, Ohio | Edward Ray | 295 | 1965 | St. Louis, Mo. | Gary Player | 282* |
| 1921 | Chevy Chase, Md. | James M. Barnes | 289 | 1966 | San Francisco, Calif. | Bill Casper, Jr. | 278* |
| 1922 | Glencoe, Ill. | Gene Sarazen | 288 | 1967 | Springfield, N.J. | Jack Nicklaus | 275 |
| 1923 | Inwood, N.Y. | Robert T. Jones, Jr. (A) | 296* | 1968 | Rochester, N.Y. | Lee Trevino | 275 |
| 1924 | Birmingham, Mich. | Cyril Walker | 297 | 1969 | Houston, Texas | Orville Moody | 281 |
| 1925 | Worcester, Mass. | William Macfarlane | 291* | 1970 | Chaska, Minn. | Tony Jacklin | 281 |
| 1926 | Columbus, Ohio | Robert T. Jones, Jr. (A) | 293 | 1971 | Ardmore, Pa. | Lee Trevino | 280* |
| 1927 | Oakmont, Pa. | Tommy Armour | 301* | 1972 | Pebble Beach, Calif. | Jack Nicklaus | 290 |
| 1928 | Mateson, Ill. | Johnny Farrell | 294* | 1973 | Oakmont, Pa. | John Miller | 279 |
| 1929 | Mamaroneck, N.Y. | Robert T. Jones, Jr. (A) | 294* | 1974 | Mamaroneck, N.Y. | Hale Irwin | 287 |
| 1930 | Minneapolis, Minn. | Robert T. Jones, Jr. (A) | 287 | 1975 | Medinah, Ill. | Lou Graham | 287* |
| 1931 | Toledo, Ohio | Billy Burke | 292* | 1976 | Duluth, Ga. | Jerry Pate | 277 |
| 1932 | Flushing, N.Y. | Gene Sarazen | 286 | 1977 | Tulsa, Okla. | Hubert Green | 278 |
| 1933 | Glen View, Ill. | John G. Goodman (A) | 287 | 1978 | Denver, Colo. | Andy North | 285 |
| 1934 | Ardmore, Pa. | Olin Dutra | 293 | 1979 | Toledo, Ohio | Hale Irwin | 284 |
| 1935 | Oakmont, Pa. | Sam Parks, Jr. | 299 | 1980 | Springfield, N.J. | Jack Nicklaus | 272 |
| 1936 | Springfield, N.J. | Tony Manero | 282 | 1981 | Ardmore, Pa. | Dave Graham | 273 |
| 1937 | Birmingham, Mich. | Ralph Guldahl | 281 | 1982 | Pebble Beach, Calif. | Tom Watson | 282 |

(A) Amateur. *Won Playoff

## PGA CHAMPIONSHIP Source: P.G.A.

| Year | Winner | Score | Year | Winner | Score | Year | Winner | Score |
|---|---|---|---|---|---|---|---|---|
| 1916 | James M. Barnes | 1 up | 1939 | Henry Picard | 1 up | 1961 | Jerry Barber | 277* |
| 1917–1918 No Competition Held | | | 1940 | Byron Nelson | 1 up | 1962 | Gary Player | 278 |
| 1919 | James M. Barnes | 6 & 5 | 1941 | Vic Ghezzi | 1 up | 1963 | Jack Nicklaus | 279 |
| 1920 | Jock Hutchison | 1 up | 1942 | Sam Snead | 2 & 1 | 1964 | Bobby Nichols | 271 |
| 1921 | Walter Hagen | 3 & 2 | 1943 | No Competition Held | | 1965 | Dave Marr | 280 |
| 1922 | Gene Sarazen | 4 & 3 | 1944 | Bob Hamilton | 1 up | 1966 | Al Geiberger | 280 |
| 1923 | Gene Sarazen | 1 up | 1945 | Byron Nelson | 4 & 3 | 1967 | Don January | 281* |
| 1924 | Walter Hagen | 2 up | 1946 | Ben Hogan | 6 & 4 | 1968 | Julius Boros | 281 |
| 1925 | Walter Hagen | 6 & 5 | 1947 | Jim Ferrier | 2 & 1 | 1969 | Ray Floyd | 276 |
| 1926 | Walter Hagen | 5 & 3 | 1948 | Ben Hogan | 7 & 6 | 1970 | Dave Stockton | 279 |
| 1927 | Walter Hagen | 1 up | 1949 | Sam Snead | 3 & 2 | 1971 | Jack Nicklaus | 281 |
| 1928 | Leo Diegel | 6 & 5 | 1950 | Chandler Harper | 4 & 3 | 1972 | Gary Player | 281 |
| 1929 | Leo Diegel | 6 & 4 | 1951 | Sam Snead | 7 & 6 | 1973 | Jack Nicklaus | 277 |
| 1930 | Tommy Armour | 1 up | 1952 | Jim Turnesa | 1 up | 1974 | Lee Trevino | 276 |
| 1931 | Tom Creavy | 2 & 1 | 1953 | Walter Burkemo | 2 & 1 | 1975 | Jack Nicklaus | 276 |
| 1932 | Olin Dutra | 4 & 3 | 1954 | Chick Harbert | 4 & 3 | 1976 | Dave Stockton | 281 |
| 1933 | Gene Sarazen | 5 & 4 | 1955 | Doug Ford | 4 & 3 | 1977 | Lanny Wadkins | 282* |
| 1934 | Paul Runyan | 1 up | 1956 | Jack Burke | 3 & 2 | 1978 | John Mahaffey | 276* |
| 1935 | Johnny Revolta | 5 & 4 | 1957 | Lionel Hebert | 2 & 1 | 1979 | Dave Graham | 272* |
| 1936 | Denny Shute | 3 & 2 | 1958 | Dow Finsterwald | 276 | 1980 | Jack Nicklaus | 274 |
| 1937 | Denny Shute | 1 up | 1959 | Bob Rosburg | 277 | 1981 | Larry Nelson | 273 |
| 1938 | Paul Runyan | 8 & 7 | 1960 | Jay Hebert | 281 | 1982 | Ray Floyd | 272 |

*Won Playoff

## THE CANADIAN OPEN

| Year | Winner | Score | Year | Winner | Score | Year | Winner | Score |
|---|---|---|---|---|---|---|---|---|
| 1950 | Jim Ferrier | 271 | 1961 | Jacky Cupit | 270 | 1972 | Gay Brewer | 275 |
| 1951 | Jim Ferrier | 273 | 1962 | Ted Kroll | 278 | 1973 | Tom Weiskopf | 278 |
| 1952 | John Palmer | 263 | 1963 | Doug Ford | 280 | 1974 | Bobby Nichols | 270 |
| 1953 | Dave Douglas | 273 | 1964 | Kel Nagle | 277 | 1975 | Tom Weiskopf | 274* |
| 1954 | Pat Fletcher | 280 | 1965 | Gene Littler | 273 | 1976 | Jerry Pate | 267 |
| 1955 | Arnold Palmer | 265 | 1966 | Don Massengale | 280 | 1977 | Lee Trevino | 280 |
| 1956 | Doug Sanders (A) | 273 | 1967 | Bill Casper | 279* | 1978 | Bruce Lietzke | 283 |
| 1957 | George Bayer | 271 | 1968 | Bob Charles | 274 | 1979 | Lee Trevino | 281 |
| 1958 | Wesley Ellis, Jr. | 267 | 1969 | Tommy Aaron | 275* | 1980 | Bob Gilder | 274 |
| 1959 | Doug Ford | 276 | 1970 | Kermit Zarley | 279 | 1981 | Peter Oosterhuis | 280 |
| 1960 | Art Wall, Jr. | 269 | 1971 | Lee Trevino | 275* | 1982 | Bruce Lietzke | 277 |

(A) Amateur. *Won Playoff

## PROFESSIONAL GOLF'S LEADING MONEY WINNERS, 1935–1981

| Year | Player | Winnings | Year | Player | Winnings | Year | Player | Winnings |
|---|---|---|---|---|---|---|---|---|
| 1935 | Johnny Revolta | $ 9,543 | 1950 | Sam Snead | $ 35,758 | 1966 | Billy Casper | $121,944 |
| 1936 | Horton Smith | 7,682 | 1951 | Lloyd Mangrum | 26,088 | 1967 | Jack Nicklaus | 188,998 |
| 1937 | Harry Cooper | 14,138 | 1952 | Julius Boros | 37,032 | 1968 | Billy Casper | 205,168 |
| 1938 | Sam Snead | 19,534 | 1953 | Lew Worsham | 34,002 | 1969 | Frank Beard | 175,223 |
| 1939 | Henry Picard | 10,303 | 1954 | Bob Toski | 65,819 | 1970 | Lee Trevino | 157,037 |
| 1940 | Ben Hogan | 10,655 | 1955 | Julius Boros | 63,121 | 1971 | Jack Nicklaus | 244,490 |
| 1941 | Ben Hogan | 18,358 | 1956 | Ted Kroll | 72,835 | 1972 | Jack Nicklaus | 320,542 |
| 1942 | Ben Hogan | 13,143 | 1957 | Dick Mayer | 65,835 | 1973 | Jack Nicklaus | 308,362 |
| 1943 | No statistics compiled | | 1958 | Arnold Palmer | 42,607 | 1974 | Johnny Miller | 353,021 |
| 1944 | Byron Nelson | 37,967 | 1959 | Art Wall, Jr. | 52,167 | 1975 | Jack Nicklaus | 298,149 |
| 1945 | Byron Nelson | 63,335 | 1960 | Arnold Palmer | 75,262 | 1976 | Jack Nicklaus | 266,426 |
| 1946 | Ben Hogan | 42,556 | 1961 | Gary Player | 64,540 | 1977 | Tom Watson | 310,653 |
| 1947 | Jimmy Demaret | 27,936 | 1962 | Arnold Palmer | 81,448 | 1978 | Tom Watson | 362,429 |
| 1948 | Ben Hogan | 32,112 | 1963 | Arnold Palmer | 128,230 | 1979 | Tom Watson | 462,636 |
| 1949 | Sam Snead | 31,593 | 1964 | Jack Nicklaus | 113,284 | 1980 | Tom Watson | 530,808 |
| | | | 1965 | **Jack Nicklaus** | **140,752** | 1981 | **Tom Kite** | 375,699 |

## RYDER CUP MATCHES (Professionals)

| Year | Played at | Results |
|---|---|---|
| 1927 | Worcester C.C., Worcester, Mass. | U.S. 9½–Britain 2½ |
| 1929 | Moortown, England | Britain 7 –U.S. 5 |
| 1931 | Scioto C.C., Columbus, Ohio | U.S. 9 –Britain 3 |
| 1933 | Southport & Ainsdale Courses, England | Britain 6½–U.S. 5½ |
| 1935 | Ridgewood C.C., Ridgewood, N.J. | U.S. 9 –Britain 3 |
| 1937 | Southport & Ainsdale Courses, England | U.S. 8 –Britain 4 |
| | Ryder Cup Matches not held during World War II years. | |
| 1947 | Portland Golf Club, Portland, Oregon | U.S. 11 –Britain 1 |
| 1949 | Ganton Golf Course, Scarborough, England | U.S. 7 –Britain 5 |
| 1951 | Pinehurst C.C., Pinehurst, N.C. | U.S. 9½–Britain 2½ |
| 1953 | Wentworth, England | U.S. 6½–Britain 5½ |
| 1955 | Thunderbird Ranch and C.C., Palm Springs, Calif. | U.S. 8 –Britain 4 |
| 1957 | Lindrick Golf Club, Yorkshire, England | Britain 7½–U.S. 4½ |
| 1959 | Eldorado C.C., Palm Desert, Calif. | U.S. 8½–Britain 3½ |
| 1961 | Royal Lytham and St. Anne's Golf Club, St. Anne's-On-The-Sea, England | U.S. 14½–Britain 9½ |
| 1963 | East Lake C.C., Atlanta, Georgia | U.S. 23 –Britain 9 |
| 1965 | Royal Birkdale Golf Club, Southport, England | U.S. 19½–Britain 12½ |
| 1967 | Champions Golf Club, Houston | U.S. 23½–Britain 8½ |
| 1969 | Royal Birkdale Golf Club, Southport, England | U.S. 16–Tie –Britain 16 |
| 1971 | Old Warson Country Club, St. Louis, Mo. | U.S. 18½–Britain 13½ |
| 1973 | Muirfield, Scotland | U.S. 18 –Britain 13 |
| 1975 | Laurel Valley Golf Club, Ligonier, Pa. | U.S. 21 –Britain 11 |
| 1977 | Royal Lytham and St. Annes Golf Club, England | U.S. 12½–Britain 7½ |
| 1979 | Greenbrier Hotel Resort, White Sulphur Sprs., W.Va. | U.S. 17 –Europe 11 |
| 1981 | Walton Heath Golf Club, England | U.S. 18½–Europe 9½ |

## PGA HALL OF FAME Source: P.G.A.

| Member | Year Elected | Member | Year Elected | Member | Year Elected |
|---|---|---|---|---|---|
| Willie Anderson | 1940 | Johnny Farrell | 1961 | Byron Nelson | 1953 |
| Tommy Armour | 1940 | Doug Ford | 1975 | Francis Ouimet | 1940 |
| Jim Barnes | 1940 | Vic Ghezzi | 1965 | Arnold Palmer | 1980 |
| Patty Berg | 1978 | Ralph Guldahl | 1963 | Henry Picard | 1961 |
| Julius Boros | 1974 | Walter Hagen | 1940 | Johnny Revolta | 1963 |
| Mike Brady | 1960 | Chick Harbert | 1968 | Paul Runyan | 1959 |
| Billy Burke | 1966 | Chandler Harper | 1969 | Gene Sarazen | 1940 |
| Jack Burke, Jr. | 1975 | Dutch Harrison | 1962 | Denny Shute | 1957 |
| Harry Cooper | 1959 | Ben Hogan | 1953 | Alex Smith | 1940 |
| Bobby Cruickshank | 1967 | Jock Hutchison, Sr. | 1959 | Horton Smih | 1958 |
| Jimmy Demaret | 1960 | Bobby Jones | 1940 | MacDonald Smith | 1954 |
| Roberto De Vicenzo | 1978 | Lawson Little | 1961 | Sam Snead | 1953 |
| Leo Diegel | 1955 | Lloyd Mangrum | 1964 | Jerry Travers | 1940 |
| Ed Dudley | 1964 | John McDermott | 1940 | Walter Travis | 1940 |
| Olin Dutra | 1962 | Fred McLeod | 1960 | Craig Wood | 1956 |
| Chick Evans | 1940 | Cary Middlecoff | 1974 | Babe Zaharias | 1976 |

## WORLD AMATEUR TEAM CHAMPIONSHIPS Source: U. S. Golf Association

| Year | Men's Champion | Women's Champion | Site |
|---|---|---|---|
| 1958 | Australia | — | St. Andrews, Scotland |
| 1960 | United States | — | Ardmore, Pa. |
| 1962 | United States | — | Kanawa, Japan |
| 1964 | Great Britain & Ireland | — | Rome, Italy |
| | | France | St. Germain, France |
| 1966 | Australia | United States | Mexico City, Mexico |
| 1968 | United States | United States | Melbourne, Australia |
| 1970 | United States | United States | Madrid, Spain |
| 1972 | United States | United States | Buenos Aires, Argentina |
| 1974 | United States | United States | LaRomana, Dominican Rep. |
| 1976 | Great Britain & Ireland | United States | Algarve, Portugal |
| 1978 | United States | Australia | Pacific Harbour, Fiji |
| 1980 | United States | United States | Pinehurst, North Carolina |
| **1982** | United States | United States | Switzerland |

## LPGA TOTAL MONEY WINNERS: 1981

SOURCE: L.P.G.A.

| Rank | Name | Amount | Rank | Name | Amount | Rank | Name | Amount |
|---|---|---|---|---|---|---|---|---|
| 1. | Beth Daniel | $206,977 | 18. | Dot Germain | $62,981 | 34. | Cindy Hill | $43,637 |
| 2. | JoAnne Carner | 206,648 | 19. | Patty Hayes | 59,932 | 35. | Penny Pulz | 42,857 |
| 3. | Pat Bradley | 197,050 | 20. | Cathy Reynolds | 56,971 | 36. | Judy Clark | 42,570 |
| 4. | Donna Caponi | 193,916 | 21. | Carolyn Hill | 53,347 | 37. | Jerilyn Britz | 41,869 |
| 5. | Jan Stephenson | 180,528 | 22. | Betsy King | 51,029 | 38. | Pat Meyers | 41,291 |
| 6. | Nancy Lopez-Melton | 165,679 | 23. | Dale Lundquist | 50,594 | 39. | Julie Stanger Pyne | 41,049 |
| 7. | Amy Alcott | 149,089 | 24. | Marlene Floyd | 50,190 | 40. | Sandra Spuzich | 39,805 |
| 8. | Sally Little | 142,251 | 25. | Debbie Massey | 48,777 | 41. | Vicki Tabor | 38,308 |
| 9. | Hollis Stacy | 138,908 | 26. | Myra Van Hoose | 48,314 | 42. | Cathy Sherk | 38,177 |
| 10. | Kathy Whitworth | 134,937 | 27. | Judy Rankin | 48,198 | 43. | Susie McAllister | 37,907 |
| 11. | Patty Sheehan | 118,463 | 28. | Kyle O'Brien | 48,083 | 44. | Beth Solomon | 34,449 |
| 12. | Jane Blalock | 96,962 | 29. | Janet Coles | 47,539 | 45. | Jo Ann Washam | 33,900 |
| 13. | Sandra Haynie | 94,124 | 30. | Kathy Postlewait | 47,507 | 46. | Shelley Hamlin | 32,798 |
| 14. | Debbie Austin | 72,881 | 31. | Alice Miller | 46,799 | 47. | Martha Hansen | 30,866 |
| 15. | Sandra Post | 71,191 | 32. | Barbara Moxness | 46,253 | 48. | Vicki Fergon | 30,817 |
| 16. | Janet Alex | 66,662 | 33. | Alice Ritzman | 44,664 | 49. | Cathy Morse | 30,587 |
| 17. | Sandra Palmer | 63,596 | | | | 50. | Silvia Bertolaccini | 30,181 |

## LEADING LPGA MONEY WINNERS BY YEAR, 1948–1981

| Year | Player | Amount | Year | Player | Amount | Year | Player | Amount |
|---|---|---|---|---|---|---|---|---|
| 1948 | Babe Zaharias | $ 3,400.00* | 1959 | Betsy Rawls | $26,774.39 | 1970 | Kathy Whitworth | $ 30,235.01 |
| 1949 | Babe Zaharias | 4,650.00* | 1960 | Louise Suggs | 16,892.12 | 1971 | Kathy Whitworth | 41,181.75 |
| 1950 | Babe Zaharias | 14,800.00* | 1961 | Mickey Wright | 22,236.21 | 1972 | Kathy Whitworth | 65,063.99 |
| 1951 | Babe Zaharias | 15,087.00* | 1962 | Mickey Wright | 21,641.99 | 1973 | Kathy Whitworth | 82,864.25 |
| 1952 | Betsy Rawls | 14,505.00 | 1963 | Mickey Wright | 31,269.50 | 1974 | JoAnne Carner | 87,094.04 |
| 1953 | Louise Suggs | 19,816.25 | 1964 | Mickey Wright | 29,800.00 | 1975 | Sandra Palmer | 76,374.51 |
| 1954 | Patty Berg | 16,011.00 | 1965 | Kathy Whitworth | 28,658.00 | 1976 | Judy Rankin | 150,734.28 |
| 1955 | Patty Berg | 16,492.34 | 1966 | Kathy Whitworth | 33,517.50 | 1977 | Judy Rankin | 122,890.44 |
| 1956 | Marlene Hagge | 20,235.50 | 1967 | Kathy Whitworth | 32,937.50 | 1978 | Nancy Lopez | 189,813.83 |
| 1957 | Patty Berg | 16,272.00 | 1968 | Kathy Whitworth | 48,379.50 | 1979 | Nancy Lopez | 197,488.61 |
| 1958 | Beverly Hanson | 12,639.55 | 1969 | Carol Mann | 49,152.50 | 1980 | Beth Daniel | 231,000.42 |
| | | | | | | 1981 | Beth Daniel | 206,977.66 |

* Approximate Figure

## WOMEN'S OPEN CHAMPIONSHIP

SOURCE: U.S. Golf Association

| Year | Site | Winner | Score | Year | Site | Winner | Score |
|---|---|---|---|---|---|---|---|
| 1946 | Spokane, Wash. | Patty Berg | 5 & 4 | 1964 | Chula Vista, Calif. | Mickey Wright | 290* |
| 1947 | Greensboro, N.C. | Betty Jameson | 295* | 1965 | Northfield, N.J. | Carol Mann | 290 |
| 1948 | Northfield, N.J. | Babe Zaharias | 300 | 1966 | Minneapolis, Minn. | Sandra Spuzich | 297 |
| 1949 | Landover, Md. | Louise Suggs | 291 | 1967 | Hot Springs, Va. | Catherine Lacoste (A) | 294 |
| 1950 | Wichita, Kans. | Mildred Zaharias | 291 | 1968 | Fleetwood, Pa. | Susie Berning | 289 |
| 1951 | Atlanta, Ga. | Betsy Rawls | 293 | 1969 | Pensacola, Fla. | Donna Caponi | 294 |
| 1952 | Philadelphia, Pa. | Louise Suggs | 284 | 1970 | Muskogee, Okla. | Donna Caponi | 287 |
| 1953 | Rochester, N.Y. | Betsy Rawls | 302* | 1971 | Erie, Pa. | JoAnne Carner | 288 |
| 1954 | Peabody, Mass. | Babe Zaharias | 291 | 1972 | Mamaroneck, N.Y. | Susie Berning | 299 |
| 1955 | Wichita, Kans. | Fay Crocker | 299 | 1973 | Rochester, N.Y. | Susie Berning | 290 |
| 1956 | Duluth, Minn. | Kathy Cornelius | 302* | 1974 | LaGrange, Ill. | Sandra Haynie | 295 |
| 1957 | Mamaroneck, N.Y. | Betsy Rawls | 299 | 1975 | Northfield, N.J. | Sandra Palmer | 295 |
| 1958 | Bloomfield Hills, Mich. | Mickey Wright | 290 | 1976 | Springfield, Pa. | JoAnne Carner | 292* |
| 1959 | Pittsburg, Pa. | Mickey Wright | 287 | 1977 | Chaska, Minn. | Hollis Stacy | 292 |
| 1960 | Worcester, Mass. | Betsy Rawls | 292 | 1978 | Indianapolis, Ind. | Hollis Stacy | 289 |
| 1961 | Springfield, N.J. | Mickey Wright | 293 | 1979 | Fairfield, Conn. | Jerilyn Britz | 284 |
| 1962 | Myrtle Beach, S.C. | Murle Lindstrom | 301 | 1980 | Nashville, Tenn. | Amy Alcott | 280 |
| 1963 | Cincinnati, Ohio | Mary Mills | 289 | 1981 | LaGrange, Ill. | Pat Bradley | 279 |
| | | | | 1982 | Sacramento, Calif. | Janet Alex | 283 |

(A) Amateur. *Won Playoff

## LPGA CHAMPIONSHIP

SOURCE: L.P.G.A.

| Year | Winner | Score | Year | Winner | Score | Year | Winner | Score |
|---|---|---|---|---|---|---|---|---|
| 1955 | Beverly Hanson | 4 & 3 | 1964 | Mary Mills | 278 | 1973 | Mary Mills | 288 |
| 1956 | Marlene Hagge | 291* | 1965 | Sandra Haynie | 279 | 1974 | Sanda Haynie | 288 |
| 1957 | Louise Suggs | 285 | 1966 | Gloria Ehret | 282 | 1975 | Kathy Whitworth | 288 |
| 1958 | Mickey Wright | 288 | 1967 | Kathy Whitworth | 284 | 1976 | Betty Burfeindt | 287 |
| 1959 | Betsy Rawls | 288 | 1968 | Sandra Post | 294* | 1977 | Chako Higuchi | 279 |
| 1960 | Mickey Wright | 292 | 1969 | Betsy Rawls | 293 | 1978 | Nancy Lopez | 275 |
| 1961 | Mickey Wright | 287 | 1970 | Shirley Englehorn | 285* | 1979 | Donna Caponi Young | 279 |
| 1962 | Judy Kimball | 282 | 1971 | Kathy Whitworth | 288 | 1980 | Sally Little | 285 |
| 1963 | Mickey Wright | 294 | 1972 | Kathy Ahern | 293 | 1981 | Donna Caponi | 280 |
| | | | | | | 1982 | Jan Stephenson | 279 |

*Won Playoff

## LPGA HALL OF FAME

SOURCE: L.P.G.A.

| Member | Year Elected | Member | Year Elected | Member | Year Elected |
|---|---|---|---|---|---|
| Patty Berg | 1951 | Babe Zaharias | 1951 | Kathy Whitworth | 1975 |
| Betty Jameson | 1951 | Betsy Rawls | 1960 | Sandra Haynie | 1977 |
| Louise Suggs | 1951 | Mickey Wright | 1964 | Carol Mann | 1977 |
| | | | | JoAnne Carner | 1982 |

## U.S. AMATEUR CHAMPIONSHIP WINNERS

SOURCE: U. S. Golf Association

1895 Charles B. Macdonald
1896 H. J. Whigham
1897 H. J. Whigham
1898 Findlay S. Douglas
1899 H. M. Harriman
1900 Walter J. Travis
1901 Walter J. Travis
1902 Louis N. James
1903 Walter J. Travis
1904 H. Chandler Egan
1905 H. Chandler Egan
1906 Eben M. Byers
1907 Jerome D. Travers
1908 Jerome D. Travers
1909 Robert A. Gardner
1910 William C. Fownes, Jr.
1911 Harold H. Hilton
1912 Jerome D. Travers
1913 Jerome D. Travers
1914 Francis Ouimet
1915 Robert A. Gardner
1916 Charles Evans, Jr.
1917–1918 No Competition
1919 S. Davidson Herron
1920 Charles Evans, Jr.
1921 Jesse P. Guilford
1922 Jess W. Sweetser
1923 Max R. Marston
1924 Robert T. Jones, Jr.
1924 Robert T. Jones, Jr.
1926 George Von Elm
1927 Robert T. Jones, Jr.
1928 Robert T. Jones, Jr.
1929 Harrison R. Johnston
1930 Robert T. Jones, Jr.
1931 Francis Ouimet
1932 C. Ross Somerville
1933 George T. Dunlap, Jr.
1934 Lawson Little
1935 Lawson Little
1936 John W. Fischer
1937 John Goodman
1938 William P. Turnesa
1939 Marvin H. Ward
1940 Richard D. Chapman
1941 Marvin H. Ward
1942–1945 No Competition
1946 S. E. (Ted) Bishop
1947 R. H. (Skee) Riegel
1948 William P. Turnesa
1949 Charles R. Coe
1950 Sam Urzetta
1951 Billy Maxwell
1952 Jack Westland
1953 Gene Littler
1954 Arnold Palmer
1955 E. Harvie Ward, Jr.
1956 E. Harvie Ward, Jr.
1957 Hillman Robbins, Jr.
1958 Charles R. Coe
1959 Jack Nicklaus
1960 Deane R. Beman
1961 Jack Nicklaus
1962 Labron Harris, Jr.
1963 Deane R. Beman
1964 William C. Campbell
1965 Robert J. Murphy, Jr.
1966 Gary Cowan
1967 Robert B. Dickson
1968 Bruce Fleisher
1969 Steven Melnyk
1970 Lanny Wadkins
1971 Gary Cowan
1972 Marvin Giles
1973 Craig Stadler
1974 Jerome Pate
1975 Fred Ridley
1976 Bill Sander
1977 John Fought
1978 John Cook
1979 Mark O'Meara
1980 Hal Sutton
1981 Nathaniel Crosby
1982 Jay Sigel

## WOMEN'S AMATEUR CHAMPIONSHIP WINNERS

SOURCE: U. S. Golf Association

1951 Dorothy Kirby
1952 Jacqueline Pung
1953 Mary Faulk
1954 Barbara Romack
1955 Patricia Lesser
1956 Marlene Stewart
1957 JoAnne Gunderson
1958 Anne Quast
1959 Barbara McIntire
1960 JoAnne Gunderson
1961 Anne Quast Decker
1962 JoAnne Gunderson
1963 Anne Quast Welts
1964 Barbara McIntire
1965 Jean Ashley
1966 JoAnne Carner
1967 Mary Lou Dill
1968 JoAnne Carner
1969 Catherine Lacoste
1970 Martha Wilkinson
1971 Laura Baugh
1972 Mary Budke
1973 Carol Semple
1974 Cynthia Hill
1975 Beth Daniel
1976 Donna Horton
1977 Beth Daniel
1978 Cathy Sherk
1979 Carolyn Hill
1980 Juli Inkster
1981 Juli Inkster
1982 Juli Inkster

## THE WALKER CUP (Men Amateur Golfers)

SOURCE: U. S. Golf Association

| Year | Results | Site |
|---|---|---|
| 1922 | U.S. 8, Great Britain 4 | Southampton, N.Y. |
| 1923 | U.S. 6, Great Britain 5 | St. Andrews, Scotland |
| 1924 | U.S. 9, Great Britain 3 | Garden City, N.Y. |
| 1926 | U.S. 6, Great Britain 5 | St. Andrews, Scotland |
| 1928 | U.S. 11, Great Britain 1 | Wheaton, Ill. |
| 1930 | U.S. 10, Great Britain 2 | Sandwich, England |
| 1932 | U.S. 8, Great Britain 1 | Brookline, Mass. |
| 1934 | U.S. 9, Great Britain 2 | St. Andrews, Scotland |
| 1936 | U.S. 9, Great Britain 0 | Clementon, N.J. |
| 1938 | Great Britain 7, U.S. 4 | St. Andrews, Scotland |
| 1947 | U.S. 8, Great Britain 4 | St. Andrews, Scotland |
| 1949 | U.S. 10, Great Britain 2 | Mamaroneck, N.Y. |
| 1951 | U.S. 6, Great Britain 3 | Southport, England |
| 1953 | U.S. 9, Great Britain 3 | Marion, Mass. |
| 1955 | U.S. 10, Great Britain 2 | St. Andrews, Scotland |
| 1957 | U.S. 8, Great Britain 3 | Minneapolis, Minn. |
| 1959 | U.S. 9, Great Britain 3 | Muirfield, Scotland |
| 1961 | U.S. 11, Great Britain 1 | Seattle, Wash. |
| 1963 | U.S. 12, Great Britain 8 | Turnberry, Scotland |
| 1965 | U.S. 11, Great Britain 11 | Baltimore, Md. |
| 1967 | U.S. 13, Great Britain 7 | Sandwich, England |
| 1969 | U.S. 10, Great Britain 8 | Milwaukee, Wis. |
| 1971 | Great Britain 13, U.S. 11 | St. Andrews, Scotland |
| 1973 | U.S. 14, Great Britain 10 | Brookline, Mass. |
| 1975 | U.S. 15½, Great Britain 8½ | St. Andrews, Scotland |
| 1977 | U.S. 16, Great Britain 8 | Southampton, N.Y. |
| 1979 | U.S. 15½, Great Britain 8½ | Muirfield, Scotland |
| 1981 | U.S. 15, Great Britain 9 | Pebble Beach, Calif. |

## THE CURTIS CUP (Women Amateur Golfers)

SOURCE: U. S. Golf Association

| Year | Results | Site |
|---|---|---|
| 1934 | U.S. 6½, British Isles 7½ | Chevy Chase, Md. |
| 1936 | U.S. 4½, British Isles 4½ | Gleneagles, Scotland |
| 1938 | U.S. 5½, British Isles 3½ | Manchester, Mass. |
| 1948 | U.S. 6½, British Isles 2½ | Southport, England |
| 1950 | U.S. 7½, British Isles 1½ | Williamsville, N.Y. |
| 1952 | British Isles 5, U.S. 4 | Muirfield, Scotland |
| 1954 | U.S. 6, British Isles 3 | Ardmore, Pa. |
| 1956 | British Isles 5, U.S. 4 | Sandwich Bay, England |
| 1958 | British Isles 4½, U.S. 4½ | West Newton, Mass. |
| 1960 | U.S. 6½, British Isles 2½ | Worksop, England |
| 1962 | U.S. 8, British Isles 1 | Colorado Sprs., Colo. |
| 1964 | U.S. 10½, British Isles 7½ | Porthcawl, South Wales |
| 1966 | U.S. 13, British Isles 5 | Hot Springs, Va. |
| 1968 | U.S. 10½, British Isles 7½ | Newcastle, No. Ireland |
| 1970 | U.S. 11½, British Isles 6½ | West Newton, Mass. |
| 1972 | U.S. 10, British Isles 8 | Western Gailes, Scotland |
| 1974 | U.S. 13, British Isles 5 | San Francisco, Calif. |
| 1976 | U.S. 11½, British Isles 6½ | St. Annes-On-Sea, Eng. |
| 1978 | U.S. 12, British Isles 6 | Rye, N.Y. |
| 1980 | U.S. 13, British Isles 5 | Chepstow, Wales |
| 1982 | U.S. 14½, British Isles 3½ | Denver, Colo. |

## OTHER GOLF CHAMPIONS

| Year | NCAA Team | NCAA Individual | Women's Intercollegiate |
|---|---|---|---|
| 1969 | Houston | Bob Clark, California (L.A.) State | Jane Bastanchury, Arizona State |
| 1970 | Houston | John Mahaffey, Houston | Cathy Gaughan, Arizona State |
| 1971 | Texas | Ben Crenshaw, Texas | Shelley Hamlin, Stanford |
| 1972 | Texas | Ben Crenshaw & Tom Kite, Texas | Ann Laughlin, Miami (Florida) |
| 1973 | Florida | Ben Chrenshaw, Texas | Bonnie Lauer, Michigan State |
| 1974 | Wake Forest | Curtis Strange, Wake Forest | Mary Budke, Oregon State |
| 1975 | Wake Forest | Jay Haas, Wake Forest | Barbara Barrow, San Diego State |
| 1976 | Oklahoma State | Scott Simpson, Southern California | Nancy Lopez, Tulsa |
| 1977 | Houston | Scott Simpson, Southern California | Cathy Morse, Miami (Florida) |
| 1978 | Oklahoma State | David Edwards, Oklahoma State | Deborah Petrizzi, Texas-Austin |
| 1979 | Ohio State | Gary Hallberg, Wake Forest | Kyle O'Brien, Southern Methodist |
| 1980 | Oklahoma State | Jay Don Blake, Utah State | Patty Sheehan, San Jose State |
| 1981 | Brigham Young | Ron Commans, Southern California | Terri Moody, Florida State |
| 1982 | Houston | Billy Ray Brown, Houston | Kathy Baker, Tulsa |

# TENNIS

United States Tennis Association (USTA); 51 East 42nd Street, New York 10017

## USTA NATIONAL CHAMPIONS (U.S. Open since 1968)

### Men's Singles

|  |  |
|---|---|
| 1920 | Bill Tilden (U.S.A.) |
| 1921 | Bill Tilden (U.S.A.) |
| 1922 | Bill Tilden (U.S.A.) |
| 1923 | Bill Tilden (U.S.A.) |
| 1924 | Bill Tilden (U.S.A.) |
| 1925 | Bill Tilden (U.S.A.) |
| 1926 | Rene Lacoste (France) |
| 1927 | Rene Lacoste (France) |
| 1928 | Henri Cochet (France) |
| 1929 | Bill Tilden (U.S.A.) |
| 1930 | John Doeg (U.S.A.) |
| 1931 | Ellsworth Vines (U.S.A.) |
| 1932 | Ellsworth Vines (U.S.A.) |
| 1933 | Fred Perry (England) |
| 1934 | Fred Perry (England) |
| 1935 | Wilmer Allison (U.S.A.) |
| 1936 | Fred Perry (England) |
| 1937 | Don Budge (U.S.A.) |
| 1938 | Don Budge (U.S.A.) |
| 1939 | Bobby Riggs (U.S.A.) |
| 1940 | Don McNeill (U.S.A.) |
| 1941 | Bobby Riggs (U.S.A.) |
| 1942 | Ted Schroeder (U.S.A.) |
| 1943 | Joe Hunt (U.S.A.) |
| 1944 | Frank Parker (U.S.A.) |
| 1945 | Frank Parker (U.S.A.) |
| 1946 | Jack Kramer (U.S.A.) |
| 1947 | Jack Kramer (U.S.A.) |
| 1948 | Pancho Gonzales (U.S.) |
| 1949 | Pancho Gonzalez (U.S.A.) |
| 1950 | Art Larsen (U.S.A.) |
| 1951 | Frank Sedgman (Australia) |
| 1952 | Frank Sedgman (Australia) |
| 1953 | Tony Trabert (U.S.A.) |
| 1954 | Vic Seixas (U.S.A.) |
| 1955 | Tony Trabert (U.S.A.) |
| 1956 | Ken Rosewall (Australia) |
| 1957 | Mal Anderson (Australia) |
| 1958 | Ashley Cooper (Australia) |
| 1959 | Neale Fraser (Australia) |
| 1960 | Neale Fraser (Australia) |
| 1961 | Roy Emerson (Australia) |
| 1962 | Rod Laver (Australia) |
| 1963 | Rafael Osuna (Mexico) |
| 1964 | Roy Emerson (Australia) |
| 1965 | Manuel Santana (Spain) |
| 1966 | Fred Stolle (Australia) |
| 1967 | John Newcombe (Australia) |
| 1968 | Arthur Ashe (U.S.A.) |
| 1969 | Rod Laver (Australia) |
| 1970 | Ken Rosewall (Australia) |
| 1971 | Stan Smith (U.S.A.) |
| 1972 | Ilie Nastase (Romania) |
| 1973 | John Newcombe (Australia) |
| 1974 | Jimmy Connors (U.S.A.) |
| 1975 | Manuel Orantes (Spain) |
| 1976 | Jimmy Connors (U.S.A.) |
| 1977 | Guillermo Vilas (Argentina) |
| 1978 | Jimmy Connors (U.S.A.) |
| 1979 | John McEnroe (U.S.A.) |
| 1980 | John McEnroe (U.S.A.) |
| 1981 | John McEnroe (U.S.A.) |
| 1982 | Jimmy Connors (U.S.A.) |

### Men's Doubles

| | |
|---|---|
| 1926 | Vinnie Richards–R. Norris Williams |
| 1927 | Bill Tilden–Frank Hunter |
| 1928 | George Lott–John Hennessey |
| 1929 | George Lott–John Doeg |
| 1930 | George Lott–John Doeg |
| 1931 | Wilmer Allison–John Van Ryn |
| 1932 | Ellsworth Vines–Keith Gledhill |
| 1933 | George Lott–Lester Stoefen |
| 1934 | George Lott–Lester Stoefen |
| 1935 | Wilmer Allison–John Van Ryn |
| 1936 | Don Budge–Gene Mako |
| 1937 | Gottfried von Cramm–Henner Henkel |
| 1938 | Don Budge–Gene Mako |
| 1939 | Adrian Quist–Jack Bromwich |
| 1940 | Jack Kramer–Ted Schroeder |
| 1941 | Jack Kramer–Ted Schroeder |
| 1942 | Gardnar Mulloy–Bill Talbert |
| 1943 | Jack Kramer–Frank Parker |
| 1944 | Don McNeill–Bob Falkenburg |
| 1945 | Gardnar Mulloy–Bill Talbert |
| 1946 | Gardnar Mulloy–Bill Talbert |
| 1947 | Jack Kramer–Ted Schroeder |
| 1948 | Gardnar Mulloy–Bill Talbert |
| 1949 | Jack Bromwich–William Sidwell |
| 1950 | Jack Bromwich–Frank Sedgman |
| 1951 | Frank Sedgman–Ken McGregor |
| 1952 | Vic Seixas–Mervyn Rose |
| 1953 | Rex Hartwig–Mervyn Rose |
| 1954 | Vic Seixas–Tony Trabert |
| 1955 | Kosei Kamo–Atsushi Miyagi |
| 1956 | Lew Hoad–Ken Rosewall |
| 1957 | Ashley Cooper–Neale Fraser |
| 1958 | Alex Olmedo–Ham Richardson |
| 1959 | Neale Fraser–Roy Emerson |
| 1960 | Neale Fraser–Roy Emerson |
| 1961 | Chuck McKinley–Dennis Ralston |
| 1962 | Rafael Osuna–Antonio Palafox |
| 1963 | Chuck McKinley–Dennis Ralston |
| 1964 | Chuck McKinley–Dennis Ralston |
| 1965 | Roy Emerson–Fred Stolle |
| 1966 | Roy Emerson–Fred Stolle |
| 1967 | John Newcombe–Tony Roche |
| 1968 | Stan Smith–Bob Lutz |
| 1969 | Ken Rosewall–Fred Stolle |
| 1970 | Nikki Pilic–Pierre Barthes |
| 1971 | John Newcombe–Roger Taylor |
| 1972 | Cliff Drysdale–Roger Taylor |
| 1973 | Owen Davidson–John Newcombe |
| 1974 | Bob Lutz–Stan Smith |
| 1975 | Jimmy Connors–Ilie Nastase |
| 1976 | Marty Riessen–Tom Okker |
| 1977 | Bob Hewitt–Frew McMillan |
| 1978 | Stan Smith–Bob Lutz |
| 1979 | John McEnroe–Peter Fleming |
| 1980 | Stan Smith–Bob Lutz |
| 1981 | John McEnroe–Peter Fleming |
| 1982 | Kevin Curren–Steve Denton |

### Women's Singles

|  |  |
|---|---|
| 1920 | Molla Bjurstedt Mallory (U.S.A.) |
| 1921 | Molla Bjurstedt Mallory (U.S.A.) |
| 1922 | Molla Bjurstedt Mallory (U.S.A.) |
| 1923 | Helen Wills (U.S.A.) |
| 1924 | Helen Wills (U.S.A.) |
| 1925 | Helen Wills (U.S.A.) |
| 1926 | Molla Bjurstedt Mallory (U.S.A.) |
| 1927 | Helen Wills (U.S.A.) |
| 1928 | Helen Wills (U.S.A.) |
| 1929 | Helen Wills (U.S.A.) |
| 1930 | Betty Nuthall (England) |
| 1931 | Helen Wills Moody (U.S.A.) |
| 1932 | Helen Hull Jacobs (U.S.A.) |
| 1933 | Helen Hull Jacobs (U.S.A.) |
| 1934 | Helen Hull Jacobs (U.S.A.) |
| 1935 | Helen Hull Jacobs (U.S.A.) |
| 1936 | Alice Marble (U.S.A.) |
| 1937 | Anita Lizana (Chile) |
| 1938 | Alice Marble (U.S.A.) |
| 1939 | Alice Marble (U.S.A.) |
| 1940 | Alice Marble (U.S.A.) |
| 1941 | Sarah Palfrey Cooke (U.S.A.) |
| 1942 | Pauline Betz (U.S.A.) |
| 1943 | Pauline Betz (U.S.A.) |
| 1944 | Pauline Betz (U.S.A.) |
| 1945 | Sarah Palfrey Cooke (U.S.A.) |
| 1946 | Pauline Betz (U.S.A.) |
| 1947 | Louise Brough (U.S.A.) |
| 1948 | Margaret Osborne du Pont (U.S.A.) |
| 1949 | Margaret Osborne du Pont (U.S.A.) |
| 1950 | Margaret Osborne du Pont (U.S.A.) |
| 1951 | Maureen Connolly (U.S.A.) |
| 1952 | Maureen Connolly (U.S.A.) |
| 1953 | Maureen Connolly (U.S.A.) |
| 1954 | Doris Hart (U.S.A.) |
| 1955 | Doris Hart (U.S.A.) |
| 1956 | Shirley Fry (U.S.A.) |
| 1957 | Althea Gibson (U.S.A.) |
| 1958 | Althea Gibson (U.S.A.) |
| 1959 | Maria Bueno (Brazil) |
| 1960 | Darlene Hard (U.S.A.) |
| 1961 | Darlene Hard (U.S.A.) |
| 1962 | Margaret Smith (Australia) |
| 1963 | Maria Bueno (Brazil) |
| 1964 | Maria Bueno (Brazil) |
| 1965 | Margaret Smith (Australia) |
| 1966 | Maria Bueno (Brazil) |
| 1967 | Billie Jean King (U.S.A.) |
| 1968 | Virginia Wade (England) |
| 1969 | Margaret Smith Court (Australia) |
| 1970 | Margaret Court (Australia) |
| 1971 | Billie Jean King (U.S.A.) |
| 1972 | Billie Jean King (U.S.A.) |
| 1973 | Margaret Court (Australia) |
| 1974 | Billie Jean King (U.S.A.) |
| 1975 | Chris Evert (U.S.A.) |
| 1976 | Chris Evert (U.S.A.) |
| 1977 | Chris Evert (U.S.A.) |
| 1978 | Chris Evert (U.S.A.) |
| 1979 | Tracy Austin (U.S.A.) |
| 1980 | Chris Evert Lloyd (U.S.A.) |
| 1981 | Tracy Austin (U.S.A.) |
| 1982 | Chris Evert Lloyd (U.S.A.) |

### Women's Doubles

| | |
|---|---|
| 1926 | Elizabeth Ryan–Eleanor Goss |
| 1927 | Mrs. Kathleen McKane Godfree–Ermyntrude Harvey |
| 1928 | Mrs. Hazel Wightman–Helen Wills |
| 1929 | Mrs. Phoebe Watson–Mrs. L. R. C. Michell |
| 1930 | Betty Nuthall–Sarah Palfrey |
| 1931 | Betty Nuthall–Mrs. Eileen Whittingstall |
| 1932 | Helen Jacobs–Sarah Palfrey |
| 1933 | Betty Nuthall–Freda James |
| 1934 | Helen Jacobs–Sarah Palfrey |
| 1935 | Helen Jacobs–Mrs. Sarah Palfrey Fabyan |
| 1936 | Mrs. Marjorie Van Ryn–Carolin Babcock |
| 1937–40 | Mrs. Sarah Palfrey Fabyan–Alice Marble |
| 1941 | Mrs. Sarah Palfrey Cooke–Margaret Osborne |
| 1942–47 | Louise Brough–Margaret Osborne |
| 1948–50 | Louise Brough–Mrs. Margaret Osborne duPont |
| 1951–54 | Shirley Fry–Doris Hart |
| 1955–57 | Louise Brough–Mrs. Margaret Osborne duPont |
| 1958–59 | Jeanne Arth–Darlene Hard |
| 1960 | Maria Bueno–Darlene Hard |
| 1961 | Darlene Hard–Lesley Turner |
| 1962 | Darlene Hard–Maria Bueno |
| 1963 | Robyn Ebbern–Margaret Smith |
| 1964 | Billie Jean Moffitt–Mrs. Karen Susman |
| 1965 | Carole Graebner–Nancy Richey |
| 1966 | Maria Bueno–Nancy Richey |
| 1967 | Mrs. Billie Jean King–Rosemary Casals |
| 1968 | Maria Bueno–Margaret Smith Court |
| 1969 | Darlene Hard–Françoise Durr |
| 1970 | Margaret Smith Court–Judy Tegart Dalton |
| 1971 | Rosemary Casals–Judy Tegart Dalton |
| 1972 | Françoise Durr–Betty Stove |
| 1973 | Mrs. Margaret Smith Court–Virginia Wade |
| 1974 | Billie Jean King–Rosemary Casals |
| 1975 | Mrs. Margaret Smith Court–Virginia Wade |
| 1976 | Linky Boshoff–Ilana Kloss |
| 1977 | Betty Stove–Martina Navratilova |
| 1978 | Billie Jean King–Martina Navratilova |
| 1979 | Betty Stove–Wendy Turnbull |
| 1980 | Billie Jean King–Martina Navratilova |
| 1981 | Kathy Jordan–Anne Smith |
| 1982 | Rosemary Casals–Wendy Turnbull |

## ALL-ENGLAND CHAMPIONS, WIMBLEDON (Open competition since 1968)

**Men's Singles**

1932 Ellsworth Vines (U.S.A.)
1933 John Crawford (Australia)
1934 Fred Perry (England)
1935 Fred Perry (England)
1936 Fred Perry (England)
1937 Don Budge (U.S.A.)
1938 Don Budge (U.S.A.)
1939 Bobby Riggs (U.S.A.)
1946 Yvon Petra (France)
1947 Jack Kramer (U.S.A.)
1948 Bob Falkenburg (U.S.A.)
1949 Ted Schroeder (U.S.A.)
1950 Budge Patty (U.S.A.)
1951 Dick Savitt (U.S.A.)
1952 Frank Sedgman (Australia)
1953 Vic Seixas (U.S.A.)
1954 Jaroslav Drobny (Egypt)
1955 Tony Trabert (U.S.A.)
1956 Lew Hoad (Australia)
1957 Lew Hoad (Australia)
1958 Ashley Cooper (Australia)
1959 Alex Olmedo (U.S.A.)
1960 Neale Fraser (Australia)
1961 Rod Laver (Australia)
1962 Rod Laver (Australia)
1963 Chuck McKinley (U.S.A.)
1964 Roy Emerson (Australia)
1965 Roy Emerson (Australia)
1966 Manuel Santana (Spain)
1967 John Newcombe (Australia)
1968 Rod Laver (Australia)
1969 Rod Laver (Australia)
1970 John Newcombe (Australia)
1971 John Newcombe (Australia)
1972 Stan Smith (U.S.A.)
1973 Jan Kodes (Czechoslovakia)
1974 Jimmy Connors (U.S.A.)
1975 Arthur Ashe (U.S.A.)
1976 Bjorn Borg (Sweden)
1977 Bjorn Borg (Sweden)
1978 Bjorn Borg (Sweden)
1979 Bjorn Borg (Sweden)
1980 Bjorn Borg (Sweden)
1981 John McEnroe (U.S.A.)
**1982 Jimmy Connors (U.S.A.)**

**Men's Doubles**

1932 Jean Borotra–Jacques Brugnon
1933 Jean Borotra–Jacques Brugnon
1934 George Lott–Lester Stoefen
1935 John Crawford–Adrian Quist
1936 George Hughes–Charles Tuckey
1937 Don Budge–Gene Mako
1938 Don Budge–Gene Mako
1939 Bobby Riggs–Elwood Cooke
1946 Jack Kramer–Tom Brown
1947 Jack Kramer–Bob Falkenburg
1948 Jack Bromwich–Frank Sedgman
1949 Pancho Gonzalez–Frank Parker
1950 Jack Bromwich–Adrian Quist
1951 Ken McGregor–Frank Sedgman
1952 Ken McGregor–Frank Sedgman
1953 Lew Hoad–Ken Rosewall
1954 Rex Hartwig–Mervyn Rose
1955 Rex Hartwig–Lew Hoad
1956 Lew Hoad–Ken Rosewall
1957 Gardnar Mulloy–Budge Patty
1958 Sven Davidson–Ulf Schmidt
1959 Neale Fraser–Roy Emerson
1960 Rafael Osuna–Dennis Ralston
1961 Neale Fraser–Roy Emerson
1962 Fred Stolle–Bob Hewitt
1963 Rafael Osuna–Antonio Palafox
1964 Bob Hewitt–Fred Stolle
1965 John Newcombe–Tony Roche
1966 Ken Fletcher–John Newcombe
1967 Bob Hewitt–Frew McMillan
1968 John Newcombe–Tony Roche
1969 John Newcombe–Tony Roche
1970 John Newcombe–Tony Roche
1971 Rod Laver–Roy Emerson
1972 Bob Hewitt–Frew McMillan
1973 Jim Connors–Ilie Nastase
1974 John Newcombe–Tony Roche
1975 Vitas Gerulatis–Sandy Mayer
1976 Brian Gottfried–Raul Ramirez
1977 Ross Case–Geoff Masters
1978 Bob Hewitt–Frew McMillan
1979 John McEnroe–Peter Fleming
1980 Peter McNamara–Paul McNamee
1981 John McEnroe–Peter Fleming
1982 Peter McNamara–Paul McNamee

**Women's Singles**

1932 Helen Wills Moody (U.S.A.)
1933 Helen Wills Moody (U.S.A.)
1934 Dorothy Round (England)
1935 Helen Wills Moody (U.S.A.)
1936 Helen Hull Jacobs (U.S.A.)
1937 Dorothy Round (England)
1938 Helen Wills Moody (U.S.A.)
1939 Alice Marble (U.S.A.)
1946 Pauline Betz (U.S.A.)
1947 Margaret Osborne (U.S.A.)
1948 Louise Brough (U.S.A.)
1949 Louise Brough (U.S.A.)
1950 Louise Brough (U.S.A.)
1951 Doris Hart (U.S.A.)
1952 Maureen Connolly (U.S.A.)
1953 Maureen Connolly (U.S.A.)
1954 Maureen Connolly (U.S.A.)
1955 Louise Brough (U.S.A.)
1956 Shirley Fry (U.S.A.)
1957 Althea Gibson (U.S.A.)
1958 Althea Gibson (U.S.A.)
1959 Maria Bueno (Brazil)
1960 Maria Bueno (Brazil)
1961 Angela Mortimer (England)
1962 Karen Hantze Susman (U.S.A.)
1963 Margaret Smith (Australia)
1964 Maria Bueno (Brazil)
1965 Margaret Smith (Australia)
1966 Billie Jean King (U.S.A.)
1967 Billie Jean King (U.S.A.)
1968 Billie Jean King (U.S.A.)
1969 Ann Haydon Jones (England)
1970 Margaret S. Court (Australia)
1971 Evonne Goolagong (Australia)
1972 Billie Jean King (U.S.A.)
1973 Billie Jean King (U.S.A.)
1974 Chris Evert (U.S.A.)
1975 Billie Jean King (U.S.A.)
1976 Chris Evert (U.S.A.)
1977 Virginia Wade (England)
1978 Martina Navratilova (U.S.A.)
1979 Martina Navratilova (U.S.A.)
1980 Evonne G. Cawley (Australia)
1981 Chris Evert Lloyd (U.S.A.)
1982 Martina Navratilova (U.S.A.)

**Women's Doubles**

1932 D. Metaxa–J. Sigart
1933 Elizabeth Ryan–Rene Mathieu
1934 Elizabeth Ryan–Rene Mathieu
1935 Kay Stammers–Freda James
1936 Kay Stammers–Freda James
1937 Rene Mathieu–A. M. Yorke
1938 Alice Marble–Sarah Palfrey Fabyan
1939 Alice Marble–Sarah Palfrey Fabyan
1946 Louise Brough–Margaret Osborne
1947 Doris Hart–Patricia Canning Todd
1948 Louise Brough–Margaret Osborne duPont
1949 Louise Brough–Margaret Osborne duPont
1950 Louise Brough–Margaret Osborne duPont
1951 Shirley Fry–Doris Hart
1952 Shirley Fry–Doris Hart
1953 Shirley Fry–Doris Hart
1954 Louise Brough–Margaret Osborne duPont
1955 Angela Mortimer–Anne Shilcock
1956 Angela Buxton–Althea Gibson
1957 Althea Gibson–Darlene Hard
1958 Maria Bueno–Althea Gibson
1959 Jeanne Arth–Darlene Hard
1960 Maria Bueno–Darlene Hard
1961 Karen Hantze–Billie Jean Moffitt
1962 Karen Hantze Susman–Billie Jean Moffitt
1963 Maria Bueno–Darlene Hard
1964 Margaret Smith–Lesley Turner
1965 Maria Bueno–Billie Jean Moffitt
1966 Maria Bueno–Nancy Richey
1967 Billie Jean King–Rosemary Casals
1968 Billie Jean King–Rosemary Casals
1969 Margaret S. Court–Judy Tegart
1970 Billie Jean King–Rosemary Casals
1971 Billie Jean King–Rosemary Casals
1972 Billie Jean King–Betty Stove
1973 Billie Jean King–Rosemary Casals
1974 Peggy Michel–Evonne Goolagong
1975 Kazuko Sawamatsu–Ann Kiyomura
1976 Chris Evert–Martina Navratilova
1977 Helen G. Cawley–Joanne Russell
1978 Wendy Turnbull–Kerry Reid
1979 Billie Jean King–Martina Navratilova
1980 Kathy Jordan–Anne Smith
1981 Martina Navratilova–Pam Shriver
1982 Martina Navratilova–Pam Shriver

## WIGHTMAN CUP

| Year | Result | Year | Result | Year | Result |
|---|---|---|---|---|---|
| 1931 | United States 5, Great Britain 2 | 1952 | United States 7, Great Britain 0 | 1967 | United States 6, Great Britain 1 |
| 1932 | United States 4, Great Britain 3 | 1953 | United States 7, Great Britain 0 | 1968 | Great Britain 4, United States 3 |
| 1933 | United States 4, Great Britain 3 | 1954 | United States 6, Great Britain 0 | 1969 | United States 5, Great Britain 2 |
| 1934 | United States 5, Great Britain 2 | 1955 | United States 6, Great Britain 1 | 1970 | United States 4, Great Britain 3 |
| 1935 | United States 4, Great Britain 3 | 1956 | United States 5, Great Britain 2 | 1971 | United States 4, Great Britain 3 |
| 1936 | United States 4, Great Britain 3 | 1957 | United States 6, Great Britain 1 | 1972 | United States 5, Great Britain 2 |
| 1937 | United States 6, Great Britain 1 | 1958 | Great Britain 4, United States 3 | 1973 | United States 5, Great Britain 2 |
| 1938 | United States 5, Great Britain 2 | 1959 | United States 4, Great Britain 3 | 1974 | Great Britain 6, United States 1 |
| 1939 | United States 5, Great Britain 2 | 1960 | Great Britain 4, United States 3 | 1975 | Great Britain 5, United States 2 |
| 1946 | United Sisters 7, Great Britain 0 | 1961 | United States 6, Great Britain 1 | 1976 | United States 5, Great Britain 2 |
| 1947 | United States 7, Great Britain 0 | 1962 | United States 4, Great Britain 3 | 1977 | United States 7, Great Britain 0 |
| 1948 | United States 6, Great Britain 1 | 1963 | United States 6, Great Britain 1 | 1978 | Great Britain 4, United States 3 |
| 1949 | United States 7, Great Britain 0 | 1964 | United States 5, Great Britain 2 | 1979 | United States 7, Great Britain 0 |
| 1950 | United States 7, Great Britain 0 | 1965 | United States 5, Great Britain 2 | 1980 | United States 5, Great Britain 2 |
| 1951 | United States 6, Great Britain 1 | 1966 | United States 4, Great Britain 3 | 1981 | United States 7, Great Britain 0 |

## DAVIS CUP CHALLENGE ROUND (No matches in 1910, 1915–18, and 1940–45)

| Year | Result |
|---|---|
| 1906 | British Isles 5, United States 0 |
| 1907 | Australasia 3, British Isles 2 |
| 1908 | Australasia 3, United States 2 |
| 1909 | Australasia 5, United States 0 |
| 1911 | Australasia 5, United States 0 |
| 1912 | British Isles 3, Australasia 2 |
| 1913 | United States 3, British Isles 2 |
| 1914 | Australasia 3, United States 2 |
| 1919 | Australasia 4, British Isles 1 |
| 1920 | United States 5, Australasia 0 |
| 1921 | United States 5, Japan 0 |
| 1922 | United States 4, Australasia 1 |
| 1923 | United States 4, Australasia 1 |
| 1924 | United States 5, Australia 0 |
| 1925 | United States 5, France 0 |
| 1926 | United States 4, France 1 |
| 1927 | France 3, United States 2 |
| 1928 | France 4, United States 1 |
| 1929 | France 3, United States 2 |
| 1930 | France 4, United States 1 |
| 1931 | France 3, Great Britain 2 |
| 1932 | France 3, United States 2 |
| 1933 | Great Britain 3, France 2 |
| 1934 | Great Britain 4, United States 1 |
| 1935 | Great Britain 5, United States 0 |
| 1936 | Great Britain 3, Australia 2 |
| 1937 | United States 4, Great Britain 1 |
| 1938 | United States 3, Australia 2 |
| 1939 | Australia 3, United States 2 |
| 1946 | United States 5, Australia 0 |
| 1947 | United States 4, Australia 1 |
| 1948 | United States 5, Australia 0 |
| 1949 | United States 4, Australia 1 |
| 1950 | Australia 4, United States 1 |
| 1951 | Australia 3, United States 2 |
| 1952 | Australia 4, United States 1 |
| 1953 | Australia 3, United States 2 |
| 1954 | United States 3, Australia 2 |
| 1955 | Australia 5, United States 0 |
| 1956 | Australia 5, United States 0 |
| 1957 | Australia 3, United States 2 |
| 1958 | United States 3, Australia 2 |
| 1959 | Australia 3, United States 2 |
| 1960 | Australia 4, Italy 1 |
| 1961 | Australia 5, Italy 0 |
| 1962 | Australia 5, Mexico 0 |
| 1963 | United States 3, Australia 2 |
| 1964 | Australia 3, United States 2 |
| 1965 | Australia 4, Spain 1 |
| 1966 | Australia 4, India 1 |
| 1967 | Australia 4, Spain 1 |
| 1968 | United States 4, Australia 1 |
| 1969 | United States 5, Rumania 0 |
| 1970 | U.S. 5, W. Germany 0 |
| 1971 | United States 3, Rumania 2 |
| 1972 | United States 3, Rumania 2 |
| 1973 | Australia 5, United States 0 |
| 1974 | South Africa defeated India, by default |
| 1975 | Sweden 3, Czechoslovakia 2 |
| 1976 | Italy 4, Chile 1 |
| 1977 | Australia 3, Italy 1 |
| 1978 | U.S. 4, Great Britain 1 |
| 1979 | U.S. 5, Italy 0 |
| 1980 | Czechoslovakia 4, Italy 1 |
| 1981 | U.S. 3, Argentina 1 |

## OTHER FOREIGN CHAMPIONSHIPS (Open competition since 1969)

**Men's Singles**

| Year | AUSTRALIAN | CANADIAN | FRENCH | ITALIAN |
|---|---|---|---|---|
| 1970 | Arthur Ashe | Rod Laver | Jan Kodes | Ilie Nastase |
| 1971 | Ken Rosewall | John Newcombe | Jan Kodes | Rod Laver |
| 1972 | Ken Rosewall | Ilie Nastase | Andres Gimeno | Manuel Orantes |
| 1973 | John Newcombe | Tom Okker | Ilie Nastase | Ilie Nastase |
| 1974 | Jimmy Connors | Guillermo Vilas | Bjorn Borg | Bjorn Borg |
| 1975 | John Newcombe | Manuel Orantes | Bjorn Borg | Raul Ramirez |
| 1976 | Mark Edmondson | Guillermo Vilas | Adriano Panatta | Adriano Panatta |
| 1977 | Roscoe Tanner | Jeff Borowiak | Guillermo Vilas | Vitas Gerulaitis |
| 1978 | Vitas Gerulaitis | Eddie Dibbs | Bjorn Borg | Bjorn Borg |
| 1979 | Guillermo Vilas | Bjorn Borg | Bjorn Borg | Vitas Gerulaitis |
| 1980 | Guillermo Vilas | Ivan Lendl | Bjorn Borg | Guillermo Vilas |
| 1981 | Brian Teacher | Ivan Lendl | Bjorn Borg | Jose-Luis Clerc |
| 1982 | Johan Kriek | Vitas Gerulaitis | Mats Wilander | Andres Gomez |

**Women's Singles**

| Year | AUSTRALIAN | CANADIAN | FRENCH | ITALIAN |
|---|---|---|---|---|
| 1970 | Margaret Smith Court | Margaret Smith Court | Margaret Smith Court | Billie Jean King |
| 1971 | Margaret Smith Court | Françoise Durr | Evonne Goolagong | Virginia Wade |
| 1972 | Virginia Wade | Evonne Goolagong | Billie Jean King | Linda Tuero |
| 1973 | Margaret Court | Evonne Goolagong | Margaret Court | Evonne Goolagong |
| 1974 | Evonne Goolagong | Chris Evert | Chris Evert | Chris Evert |
| 1975 | Evonne Goolagong | Marcie Louie | Chris Evert | Chris Evert |
| 1976 | Evonne Goolagong | Mima Jausovec | Sue Barker | Mima Jausovec |
| 1977 | Kerry Reid | Regina Marsikova | Mima Jausovec | Janet Newberry |
| 1978 | Evonne Goolagong | Regina Marsikova | Virginia Ruzici | Regina Marsikova |
| 1979 | Chris O'Neill | Laura DuPont | Chris Evert Lloyd | Tracy Austin |
| 1980 | Barbara Jordan | Chris Evert Lloyd | Chris Evert Lloyd | Chris Evert Lloyd |
| 1981 | Hana Mandlikova | Tracy Austin | Hana Mandlikova | Chris Evert Lloyd |
| 1982 | Martina Navratilova | Martina Navratilova | Martina Navratilova | Chris Evert Lloyd |

## THE GRAND SLAM OF TENNIS

Winners of the Australian, French, British and United States Championships in the same season.

| Year | Champions | Country | Event |
|---|---|---|---|
| 1938 | Don Budge | United States | Men's Singles |
| 1951 | Frank Sedgman–Ken McGregor | Australia | Men's Doubles |
| 1953 | Maureen Connolly | United States | Women's Singles |
| 1960 | Maria Bueno | Brazil | Women's Doubles* |
| 1962 | Rod Laver | Australia | Men's Singles |
| 1963 | Margaret Smith–Ken Fletcher | Australia | Mixed Doubles |
| 1967 | Owen Davidson | Australia | Mixed Doubles* |
| 1969 | Rod Laver | Australia | Men's Singles |
| 1970 | Margaret Smith Court | Australia | Women's Singles |

*Won in Australia with a different doubles partner.

## COLLEGIATE CHAMPIONS (Division I)

| Year | Man | School | Woman | School |
|---|---|---|---|---|
| 1968 | Stan Smith | Southern California | Emilie Burrer | Trinity |
| 1969 | Joaquin Loyo-Mayo | Southern California | Emilie Burrer | Trinity |
| 1970 | Jeff Borowiak | U.C.L.A. | Laura DuPont | North Carolina |
| 1971 | Jimmy Connors | U.C.L.A. | Pam Richmond | Arizona State |
| 1972 | Dick Stockton | Trinity | Janice Metcalf | Redlands |
| 1973 | Alex Mayer | Stanford | Janice Metcalf | Redlands |
| 1974 | John Whitlinger | Stanford | Carrier Meyer | Marymount |
| 1975 | Bill Martin | U.C.L.A. | Stephanie Tolleson | Trinity |
| 1976 | Bill Scanlon | Trinity | Barbara Hallquist | Southern California |
| 1977 | Matt Mitchell | Stanford | Barbara Hallquist | Southern California |
| 1978 | John McEnroe | Stanford | Jeanne DuVall | U.C.L.A. |
| 1979 | Kevin Curran | Texas | Kathy Jordan | Stanford |
| 1980 | Robert Van't Hof | Southern California | Wendy White | Rollins College |
| 1981 | Tim Mayotte | Stanford | Anna Maria Fernandez | Southern California |
| 1982 | Mike Leach | Michigan | Alycia Moulton | Stanford |

## FEDERATION CUP

Women's International Team Competition

SOURCE: U.S.T.A.

| Year | Final Round Results |
|---|---|
| 1963 | United States, 2, Australia 1 |
| 1964 | Australia 2, United States 1 |
| 1965 | Australia 2, United States 1 |
| 1966 | United States 3, West Germany 0 |
| 1967 | United States 2, Great Britain 0 |
| 1968 | Australia 3, Netherlands 0 |
| 1969 | United States 2, Australia 1 |
| 1970 | Australia 3, West Germany 0 |
| 1971 | Australia 3, Great Britain 0 |
| 1972 | South Africa 2, Great Britain 1 |
| 1973 | Australia 3, South Africa 0 |
| 1974 | Australia 2, United States 1 |
| 1975 | Czechoslovakia 3, Australia 0 |
| 1976 | United States 2, Australia 1 |
| 1977 | United States 2, Australia 1 |
| 1978 | United States 2, Australia 1 |
| 1979 | United States 3, Australia 0 |
| 1980 | United States 3, Australia 0 |
| 1981 | United States 3, Great Britain 0 |
| 1982 | United States 3, West Germany 0 |

## 1982 TOP MONEY WINNERS (to October 6)

**MEN**

| | | |
|---|---|---|
| 1. | Ivan Lendl, Czechoslovakia | $1,399,050 |
| 2. | Jimmy Connors, United States | 533,450 |
| 3. | Jose-Luis Clerc, Argentina | 501,100 |
| 4. | Tomas Smid, Czechoslovakia | 452,817 |
| 5. | Guillermo Vilas, Argentina | 380,150 |
| 6. | John McEnroe, United States | 368,325 |
| 7. | Johan Kriek, South Africa | 254,898 |
| 8. | Vitas Gerulaitis, United States | 242,475 |
| 9. | Wojtek Fibak, Poland | 223,625 |
| | Peter McNamara, Australia | 223,625 |

**WOMEN**

| | | |
|---|---|---|
| 1. | Martina Navratilova, United States | $1,107,905 |
| 2. | Chris Evert Lloyd, United States | 355,658 |
| 3. | Andrea Jaeger, United States | 260,378 |
| 4. | Wendy Turnbull, Australia | 214,171 |
| 5. | Bettina Bunge, West Germany | 195,075 |
| 6. | Barbara Potter, United States | 190,540 |
| 7. | Sylvia Hanika, West Germany | 169,567 |
| 8. | Pam Shriver, United States | 169,456 |
| 9. | Anne Smith, United States | 164,329 |
| 10. | Mima Jausovec, Yugoslavia | 153,159 |

## 1982 COLLEGIATE TENNIS CHAMPIONS

NCAA DIVISION I

Singles — Mike Leach, Michigan
Doubles — Pat Doohan - Pat Serret, Arkansas
Team — UCLA

NCAA DIVISION II

Singles — Ken Flach, Southern Illinois (Edwardsville)
Doubles — Ken Flach - Doug Burke, Southern Illinois (Edwardsville)
Team — Southern Illinois (Edwardsville)

NCAA DIVISION III

Singles — Shaun Miller, Gustavus Adolphus
Doubles — Shaun Miller - Rich Skanse, Gustavus Adolphus
Team — Gustavus Adolphus (Minn.)

NCAA WOMEN DIVISION I

Singles — Alycia Moulton, Stanford
Doubles — Heather Ludloff - Lynn Lewis, UCLA
Team — Stanford

NCAA WOMEN DIVISION II

Singles — Iwona Kuczynska, Bakersfield State
Doubles — Wendi Luhmann - Cindy Woodhouse, Northridge State
Team — Northridge State

NCAA WOMEN DIVISION III

Singles — Becky Donecker, Elizabethtown
Doubles — Jean Marie Sanders - Kathleen McFadden, Occidental
Team — Occidental

NAIA

Men's Singles — Chuck Nunn, SW Texas State
Team — Southwest Texas State
Women's Singles — Tarja Koho, Guilford (N.C.)
Team — Westmont (Calif.)

## JAMES E. SULLIVAN MEMORIAL TROPHY

Sportsmanship — Outstanding Amateur Athlete

| Year | Athlete | Sport |
|---|---|---|
| 1930 | Bobby Jones | Golf |
| 1931 | Bernard Berlinger | Track & Field |
| 1932 | James Bausch | Track & Field |
| 1933 | Glenn Cunningham | Track & Field |
| 1934 | Bill Bonthron | Track & Field |
| 1935 | Lawson Little | Golf |
| 1936 | Glen Morris | Track & Field |
| 1937 | Don Budge | Tennis |
| 1938 | Donald Lash | Track & Field |
| 1939 | Joe Burk | Rowing |
| 1940 | Greg Rice | Track & Field |
| 1941 | Leslie MacMitchell | Track & Field |
| 1942 | Cornelius Warmerdam | Track & Field |
| 1943 | Gilbert Dodds | Track & Field |
| 1944 | Ann Curtis | Swimming |
| 1945 | Doc Blanchard | Football |
| 1946 | Arnold Tucker | Football |
| 1947 | John Kelly, Jr. | Rowing |
| 1948 | Robert Mathias | Track & Field |
| 1949 | Richard Button | Skating |
| 1950 | Fred Wilt | Track & Field |
| 1951 | Bob Richards | Track & Field |
| 1952 | Horace Ashenfelter | Track & Field |
| 1953 | Sammy Lee | Diving |
| 1954 | Mal Whitfield | Track & Field |
| 1955 | Harrison Dillard | Track & Field |
| 1956 | Patricia McCormick | Diving |
| 1957 | Bobby Morrow | Track & Field |
| 1958 | Glenn Davis | Track & Field |
| 1959 | Parry O'Brien | Track & Field |
| 1960 | Rafer Johnson | Track & Field |
| 1961 | Wilma Rudolph Ward | Track & Field |
| 1962 | Jim Beatty | Track & Field |
| 1963 | John Pennel | Track & Field |
| 1964 | Don Schollander | Swimming |
| 1965 | Bill Bradley | Basketball |
| 1966 | Jim Ryun | Track & Field |
| 1967 | Randy Matson | Track & Field |
| 1968 | Debbie Meyer | Swimming |
| 1969 | Bill Toomey | Track & Field |
| 1970 | John Kinsella | Swimming |
| 1971 | Mark Spitz | Swimming |
| 1972 | Frank Shorter | Track & Field |
| 1973 | Bill Walton | Basketball |
| 1974 | Rick Wohlhuter | Track & Field |
| 1975 | Tim Shaw | Swimming |
| 1976 | Bruce Jenner | Track & Field |
| 1977 | John Naber | Swimming |
| 1978 | Tracy Caulkins | Swimming |
| 1979 | Kurt Thomas | Gymnastics |
| 1980 | Eric Heiden | Skating |
| 1981 | Carl Lewis | Track & Field |

# AUTO RACING

## STOCK CARS

SOURCE: The National Association for Stock Car Auto Racing, Inc.

### RESULTS OF 1981 NASCAR WINSTON CUP GRAND NATIONAL SEASON

| EVENT-LOCATION | DATE | FIRST | SECOND |
|---|---|---|---|
| WINSTON WESTERN 500<br>Riverside, Calif. | Jan. 11 | Bobby Allison<br>Chevrolet | Terry Labonte<br>Chevrolet |
| DAYTONA 500<br>Daytona Beach, Fla. | Feb. 15 | Richard Petty<br>Buick | Bobby Allison<br>Pontiac |
| RICHMOND 400<br>Richmond, Va. | Feb. 22 | Darrell Waltrip<br>Buick | Ricky Rudd<br>Oldsmobile |
| CAROLINA 500<br>Rockingham, N.C. | Mar. 1 | Darrell Waltrip<br>Buick | Cale Yarborough<br>Buick |
| COCA-COLA 500<br>Atlanta, Ga. | Mar. 15 | Cale Yarborough<br>Buick | Harry Gant<br>Buick |
| VALLEYDALE 500<br>Bristol, Tenn. | Mar. 29 | Darrell Waltrip<br>Buick | Ricky Rudd<br>Oldsmobile |
| NORTHWESTERN BANK 400<br>North Wilkesboro, N.C. | Apr. 5 | Richard Petty<br>Buick | Bobby Allison<br>Pontiac |
| CRC CHEMICALS REBEL 500<br>Darlington, S.C. | Apr. 12 | Darrell Waltrip<br>Buick | Harry Gant<br>Pontiac |
| VIRGINIA 500<br>Martinsville, Va. | Apr. 26 | Morgan Shepherd<br>Pontiac | Neil Bonnett<br>Ford |
| WINSTON 500<br>Talladega, Ala. | May 3 | Bobby Allison<br>Buick | Buddy Baker<br>Buick |
| MELLING TOOL 420<br>Nashville, Tenn. | May 9 | Benny Parsons<br>Ford | Darrell Waltrip<br>Buick |
| MASON DIXON 500<br>Dover, Del. | May 17 | Jody Ridley<br>Ford | Bobby Allison<br>Buick |
| WORLD 500<br>Charlotte, N.C. | May 24 | Bobby Allison<br>Buick | Harry Gant<br>Chevrolet |
| BUDWEISER NASCAR 400<br>College Station, Tex. | Jun. 7 | Benny Parsons<br>Ford | Dale Earnhardt<br>Pontiac |
| WARNER W. HODGDON 400<br>Riverside, Calif. | Jun. 14 | Darrell Waltrip<br>Buick | Dale Earnhardt<br>Pontiac |
| GABRIEL 400<br>Brooklyn, Mich. | Jun. 21 | Bobby Allison<br>Buick | Harry Gant<br>Pontiac |
| FIRECRACKER 400<br>Daytona Beach, Fla. | Jul. 4 | Cale Yarborough<br>Buick | Harry Gant<br>Buick |
| BUSCH NASHVILLE 420<br>Nashville, Tenn. | Jul. 11 | Darrell Waltrip<br>Buick | Bobby Allison<br>Buick |
| MOUNTAIN DEW 500<br>Pocono, Pa. | Jul. 26 | Darrell Waltrip<br>Buick | Richard Petty<br>Buick |
| TALLADEGA 500<br>Talladega, Ala. | Aug. 2 | Ron Bouchard<br>Buick | Darrell Waltrip<br>Buick |
| CHAMPION SPARK PLUG 400<br>Brooklyn, Mich. | Aug. 16 | Richard Petty<br>Buick | Darrell Waltrip<br>Buick |
| BUSCH VOLUNTEER 500<br>Bristol, Tenn. | Aug. 22 | Darrell Waltrip<br>Buick | Ricky Rudd<br>Chevrolet |
| SOUTHERN 500<br>Darlington, S.C. | Sept. 7 | Neil Bonnett<br>Ford | Darrell Waltrip<br>Buick |
| WRANGLER SANFORSET 400<br>Richmond, Va. | Sept. 13 | Benny Parsons<br>Ford | Harry Gant<br>Pontiac |
| CRC CHEMICALS 500<br>Dover, Del. | Sept. 20 | Neil Bonnett<br>Ford | Darrell Waltrip<br>Buick |
| OLD DOMINION 500<br>Martinsville, Va. | Sept. 27 | Darrell Waltrip<br>Buick | Harry Gant<br>Pontiac |
| HOLLY FARMS 400<br>No. Wilkesboro, N.C. | Oct. 4 | Darrell Waltrip<br>Buick | Bobby Allison<br>Buick |
| NATIONAL 500<br>Charlotte, N.C. | Oct. 11 | Darrell Waltrip<br>Buick | Bobby Allison<br>Chevrolet |
| AMERICAN 500<br>Rockingham, N.C. | Oct. 25 | Darrell Waltrip<br>Buick | Bobby Allison<br>Buick |
| ATLANTA JOURNAL 500<br>Atlanta, Ga. | Nov. 8 | Neil Bonnett<br>Ford | Darrell Waltrip<br>Buick |
| WINSTON WESTERN 500<br>Riverside, Calif. | Nov. 22 | Bobby Allison<br>Buick | Joe Ruttman<br>Buick |

### NASCAR WINSTON CUP GRAND NATIONAL CHAMPIONS

1964—Richard Petty, Randleman, N.C. (Plymouth)
1965—Ned Jarrett, Camden, S.C. (Ford)
1966—David Pearson, Spartanburg, S.C. (Dodge)
1967—Richard Petty, Randleman, N.C. (Plymouth)
1968—David Pearson, Spartanburg, S.C. (Ford)
1969—David Pearson, Spartanburg, S.C. (Ford)
1970—Bobby Isaac, Catawba, N.C. (Dodge)
1971—Richard Petty, Randleman, N.C. (Plymouth)
1972—Richard Petty, Randleman, N.C. (Plymouth-Dodge)
1973—Benny Parsons, Ellerbe, N.C. (Chevrolet)
1974—Richard Petty, Randleman, N.C. (Dodge)
1975—Richard Petty, Randleman, N.C. (Dodge)
1976—Cale Yarborough, Timmonsville, S.C. (Chevrolet)
1977—Cale Yarborough, Timmonsville, S.C. (Chevrolet)
1978—Cale Yarborough, Timmonsville, S.C. (Oldsmobile)
1979—Richard Petty, Randleman, N.C. (Chevrolet)
1980—Dale Earnhardt, Kannapolis, N.C. (Chevrolet)
1981—Darrell Waltrip, Franklin, Tenn. (Buick)

### 1981 NASCAR WINSTON CUP GRAND NATIONAL STANDINGS

| Pos. Driver | Points | Starts | Wins | Top 5 | Top 10 | Money Won |
|---|---|---|---|---|---|---|
| 1. Darrell Waltrip | 4880 | 31 | 12 | 21 | 25 | $693,342 |
| 2. Bobby Allison | 4827 | 31 | 5 | 21 | 26 | 644,311 |
| 3. Harry Gant | 4210 | 31 | 0 | 13 | 18 | 280,047 |
| 4. Terry Labonte | 4052 | 31 | 0 | 8 | 17 | 334,987 |
| 5. Jody Ridley | 4002 | 31 | 1 | 3 | 18 | 257,318 |
| 6. Ricky Rudd | 3988 | 31 | 0 | 14 | 17 | 381,968 |
| 7. Dale Earnhardt | 3975 | 31 | 0 | 9 | 17 | 347,113 |
| 8. Richard Petty | 3880 | 31 | 3 | 12 | 16 | 389,214 |
| 9. Dave Marcis | 3507 | 31 | 0 | 4 | 9 | 162,213 |
| 10. Benny Parsons | 3449 | 31 | 3 | 10 | 12 | 287,949 |
| 11. Buddy Arrington | 3381 | 31 | 0 | 0 | 7 | 133,928 |
| 12. Kyle Petty | 3335 | 31 | 0 | 1 | 10 | 112,289 |
| 13. Morgan Shepherd | 3261 | 29 | 1 | 3 | 10 | 165,329 |
| 14. Jimmy Means | 3142 | 30 | 0 | 0 | 2 | 100,484 |
| 15. Tommy Gale | 3140 | 30 | 0 | 0 | 0 | 105,474 |
| 16. Tim Richmond | 3091 | 29 | 0 | 0 | 6 | 91,305 |

### OTHER NASCAR CHAMPIONS

| | WINSTON WEST GRAND NATIONAL | LATE MODEL SPORTSMAN | MODIFIED |
|---|---|---|---|
| 1969 | Ray Elder, Caruthers, Calif. | Charles (Red) Farmer, Hueytown, Ala. | Carl (Bugs) Stevens, Rehoboth, Mass. |
| 1970 | Ray Elder, Caruthers, Calif. | Charles (Red) Farmer, Hueytown, Ala. | Fred De Sarro, Hope Valley, R.I. |
| 1971 | Ray Elder, Caruthers, Calif. | Charles (Red) Farmer, Hueytown, Ala. | Jerry Cook, Rome, N.Y. |
| 1972 | Ray Elder, Caruthers, Calif. | Jack Ingram, Asheville, N.C. | Jerry Cook, Rome, N.Y. |
| 1973 | Jack McCoy, Modesto, Calif. | Jack Ingram, Asheville, N.C. | Richie Evans, Rome, N.Y. |
| 1974 | Ray Elder, Caruthers, Calif. | Jack Ingram, Asheville, N.C. | Jerry Cook, Rome, N.Y. |
| 1975 | Ray Elder, Caruthers, Calif. | L.D. Ottinger, Newport, Tenn. | Jerry Cook, Rome, N.Y. |
| 1976 | Chuck Brown, Portland, Ore. | L.D. Ottinger, Newport, Tenn. | Jerry Cook, Rome, N.Y. |
| 1977 | Bill Schmitt, Redding, Calif. | Butch Lindley, Greenville, S.C. | Jerry Cook, Rome, N.Y. |
| 1978 | Jim Insolo, Mission Hills, Calif. | Butch Lindley, Greenville, S.C. | Richie Evans, Rome, N.Y. |
| 1979 | Bill Schmitt, Redding, Calif. | Gene Glover, Kingsport, Tenn. | Richie Evans, Rome, N.Y. |
| 1980 | Roy Smith, Victoria, B.C., Canada | Morgan Shepherd, Conover, N.C. | Richie Evans, Rome, N.Y. |
| 1981 | Roy Smith, Victoria, B.C., Canada | Tommy Ellis, Richmond, Va. | Richie Evans, Rome, N.Y. |

## FORMULA 1 GRAND PRIX CHAMPIONS

Source: Sports Car Club of America

| Year | Champion | Car | Country |
|---|---|---|---|
| 1950 | Giuseppe Farina | Alfa Romeo | Italy |
| 1951 | Juan Manuel Fangio | Alfa Romeo | Argentina |
| 1952 | Alberto Ascari | Ferrari | Italy |
| 1953 | Alberto Ascari | Ferrari | Italy |
| 1954 | Juan Manuel Fangio | Mercedes & Maserati | Argentina |
| 1955 | Juan Manuel Fangio | Mercedes | Argentina |
| 1956 | Juan Manuel Fangio | Lancia | Argentina |
| 1957 | Juan Manuel Fangio | Maserati | Argentina |
| 1958 | Mike Hawthorn | Ferrari | Great Britain |
| 1959 | Jack Brabham | Cooper | Australia |
| 1960 | Jack Brabham | Cooper | Australia |
| 1961 | Phil Hill | Ferrari | USA |
| 1962 | Graham Hill | BRM | Great Britain |
| 1963 | Jim Clark | Lotus | Great Britain |
| 1964 | John Surtees | Ferrari | Great Britain |
| 1965 | Jim Clark | Lotus | Great Britain |
| 1966 | Jack Brabham | Brabham | Australia |
| 1967 | Denis Hulme | Brabham | New Zealand |
| 1968 | Graham Hill | Lotus | Great Britain |
| 1969 | Jackie Stewart | Matra | Great Britain |
| 1970 | Jochen Rindt | Lotus | Austria |
| 1971 | Jackie Stewart | Tyrrell | Great Britain |
| 1972 | Emerson Fittipaldi | Lotus | Brazil |
| 1973 | Jackie Stewart | Tyrrell | Great Britain |
| 1974 | Emerson Fittipaldi | McLaren | Brazil |
| 1975 | Niki Lauda | Ferrari | Austria |
| 1976 | James Hunt | McLaren | Great Britain |
| 1977 | Niki Lauda | Ferrari | Austria |
| 1978 | Mario Andretti | Lotus | USA |
| 1979 | Jody Scheckter | Ferrari | South Africa |
| 1980 | Alan Jones | Williams | Australia |
| 1981 | Nelson Piquet | Brabham | Brazil |
| 1982 | Keke Rosberg | Williams | Finland |

## UNITED STATES GRAND PRIX, WATKINS GLEN, N.Y.

Source: Sports Car Club of America

| Year | Winner | Car |
|---|---|---|
| 1959* | Bruce McLaren | Cooper |
| 1960** | Stirling Moss | Lotus |
| 1961 | Ines Ireland | Lotus |
| 1962 | Jim Clark | Lotus |
| 1963 | Graham Hill | BRM |
| 1964 | Graham Hill | BRM |
| 1965 | Graham Hill | BRM |
| 1966 | Jim Clark | Lotus |
| 1967 | Jim Clark | Lotus |
| 1968 | Jackie Stewart | Matra |
| 1969 | Jochen Rindt | Lotus |
| 1970 | Emerson Fittipaldi | Lotus |
| 1971 | Francois Cevert | Tyrrell |
| 1972 | Jackie Stewart | Tyrrell |
| 1973 | Ronnie Peterson | Lotus |
| 1974 | Carlos Reutemann | Brabham |
| 1975 | Niki Lauda | Ferrari |
| 1976 | James Hunt | McLaren |
| 1977 | James Hunt | McLaren |
| 1978 | Carlos Reutemann | Ferrari |
| 1979 | Gilles Villeneuve | Ferrari |
| 1980 | Alan Jones | Williams |
| 1981 | (not scheduled) | |
| 1982*** | John Watson | McLaren |

* Held at Sebring ** Held at Riverside *** Held at Detroit

## UNITED STATES GRAND PRIX WEST, LONG BEACH, CALIF.

Source: Sports Car Club of America

| Year | Winner | Car |
|---|---|---|
| 1976 | Clay Regazzoni | Ferrari |
| 1977 | Mario Andretti | Lotus |
| 1978 | Carlos Reutemann | Ferrari |
| 1979 | Gilles Villeneuve | Ferrari |
| 1980 | Nelson Piquet | Brabham |
| 1981 | Alan Jones | Williams |
| 1982 | Niki Lauda | McLaren |

## SPORTS CAR CLUB OF AMERICA SERIES CHAMPIONS

Source: Sports Car Club of America

**Can-Am Challenge**

| Year | Champion | Car |
|---|---|---|
| 1966 | John Surtees | Lola |
| 1967 | Bruce McLaren | McLaren M6A |
| 1968 | Denis Hulme | McLaren M6A |
| 1969 | Bruce McLaren | McLaren M8B |
| 1970 | Denis Hulme | McLaren M8D |
| 1971 | Peter Revson | McLaren M8F |
| 1972 | George Follmer | Porsche 917/10 |
| 1974 | Mark Donohue | Porsche 917/30 |
| 1973 | Jackie Oliver | Shadow |
| 1975–1976 | (no series) | |
| 1977 | Patrick Tambay | Lola T-333CS |
| 1978 | Alan Jones | Lola T-333CS |
| 1979 | Jacky Ickx | Lola T-333CS |
| 1980 | Patrick Tambay | Lola T530 |
| 1981 | Geoff Brabham | Lola T530/ VDS 001 |

**Rabbit/Bilstein Cup**

| Year | Champion | Car |
|---|---|---|
| 1976 | Paul Hacker | Scirocco |
| 1977 | Bill Deters | Scirocco |
| 1978 | Gary Benson | Rabbit |
| 1979 | Gary Benson | Rabbit |
| 1980 | Gary Benson | Rabbit |
| 1981 | Paul Hacker | Rabbit |

**Trans-Am® Championship**

| Year | Champion | Car |
|---|---|---|
| 1973 | Peter Gregg | Chevrolet |
| 1974 | Peter Gregg | Porsche |
| 1975 | John Greenwood | Chevrolet |
| 1976 | George Follmer | Porsche |
| 1977 | Category I Bob Tullius | Jaguar |
| | Category II Ludwig Heimrath | Porsche |
| 1978 | Category I Bob Tullius | Jaguar |
| | Category II Greg Pickett | Corvette |
| 1979 | Category I Gene Bothello | Corvette |
| | Category II John Paul | Porsche |
| 1980 | John Bauer | Porsche |
| 1981 | Eppie Wietzes | Corvette |

**Robert Bosch/VW Super Vee (Gold Cup)**

| Year | Champion | Car |
|---|---|---|
| 1971 | Bill Scott | Royale |
| 1972 | Bill Scott | Royale |
| 1973 | Bertil Roos | Tui BH3 |
| 1974 | Elliott Forbes-Robinson | Lynn |
| 1975 | Eddie Miller | Lola T-324 |
| 1976 | Tom Bagley | Zink Z-11 |
| 1977 | Bob Lazier | Lola T-324 |
| 1978 | Bill Alsup | Argo |
| 1979 | Geoff Brabham | Ralt RT-1 |
| 1980 | Peter Kuhn | Ralt RT-5 |
| 1981 | Al Unser, Jr. | Ralt RT-5 |

## INDIANAPOLIS 500 Source: Jack C. Fox, The Indianapolis 500 (1967), and other sources

| Year | Winner | Chassis | Engine | Cylinders | Mph | Gross | Second Place |
|---|---|---|---|---|---|---|---|
| 1920 | Gaston Chevrolet | Frontenac | Frontenac | 4 | 88.16 | $ 93,550 | Rene Thomas |
| 1921 | Tommy Milton | Frontenac | Frontenac | 8 | 89.62 | $ 86,650 | Roscoe Sarles |
| 1922 | Jimmy Murphy | Duesenberg | Miller | 8 | 94.48 | $ 70,575 | Harry Hartz |
| 1923 | Tommy Milton | Miller | Miller | 8 | 90.95 | $ 83,425 | Harry Hartz |
| 1924 | L. L. Corum, Joe Boyer | Duesenberg | Duesenberg | 8 | 98.23 | $ 86,850 | Earl Cooper |
| 1925 | Peter DePaolo | Duesenberg | Duesenberg* | 8 | 101.13 | $ 87,750 | Dave Lewis |
| 1926 | Frank Lockhart | Miller | Miller* | 8 | 95.885[1] | $ 88,100 | Harry Hartz |
| 1927 | George Souders | Duesenberg | Duesenberg* | 8 | 97.545 | $ 89,850 | Earl DeVore |
| 1928 | Lou Meyer | Miller | Miller* | 8 | 99.482 | $ 90,750 | Lou Moore |
| 1929 | Ray Keech | Miller | Miller* | 8 | 97.585 | $ 95,150 | Lou Meyer |
| 1930 | Billy Arnold | Summers | Miller† | 8 | 100.448 | $ 97,600 | Shorty Cantlon |
| 1931 | Lou Schneider | Stevens | Miller | 8 | 96.629 | $ 81,800 | Fred Frame |
| 1932 | Fred Frame | Wetteroth | Miller† | 8 | 104.144 | $ 93,900 | Howdy Wilcox 2d |
| 1933 | Lou Meyer | Miller | Miller | 8 | 104.162 | $ 54,450 | Wilbur Shaw |
| 1934 | Bill Cummings | Miller | Miller† | 4 | 104.863 | $ 83,775 | Mauri Rose |
| 1935 | Kelly Petillo | Wetteroth | Offenhauser | 4 | 106.240 | $ 78,575 | Wilbur Shaw |
| 1936 | Lou Meyer | Stevens | Miller | 4 | 109.069 | $ 82,525 | Ted Horn |
| 1937 | Wilbur Shaw | Shaw | Offenhauser | 4 | 113.580 | $ 92,135 | Ralph Hepburn |
| 1938 | Floyd Roberts | Wetteroth | Miller | 4 | 117.200 | $ 91,075 | Wilbur Shaw |
| 1939 | Wilbur Shaw | Maserati | Maserati* | 8 | 115.035 | $ 87,050 | Jimmy Snyder |
| 1940 | Wilbur Shaw | Maserati | Maserati* | 8 | 114.277 | $ 85,525 | Rex Mays |
| 1941 | Floyd Davis, Mauri Rose | Wetteroth | Offenhauser | 4 | 115.117 | $ 90,925 | Rex Mays |
| 1946 | George Robson | Adams | Sparks* | 6 | 114.820 | $115,450 | Jimmy Jackson |
| 1947 | Mauri Rose | Deidt | Offenhauser† | 4 | 116.338 | $137,425 | Bill Holland |
| 1948 | Mauri Rose | Deidt | Offenhauser† | 4 | 119.814 | $171,075 | Bill Holland |
| 1949 | Bill Holland | Deidt | Offenhauser† | 4 | 121.327 | $179,050 | Johnnie Parsons |
| 1950 | Johnnie Parsons | Kurtis Kraft | Offenhauser | 4 | 124.002[2] | $201,135 | Bill Holland |
| 1951 | Lee Wallard | Kurtis Kraft | Offenhauser | 4 | 126.244 | $207,650 | Mike Nazaruk |
| 1952 | Troy Ruttman | Kuzma | Offenhauser | 4 | 128.922 | $230,100 | Jim Rathmann |
| 1953 | Bill Vukovich | Kurtis Kraft 500A | Offenhauser | 4 | 128.740 | $246,300 | Art Cross |
| 1954 | Bill Vukovich | Kurtis Kraft 500A | Offenhauser | 4 | 130.840 | $269,375 | Jimmy Bryan |
| 1955 | Bob Sweikert | Kurtis Kraft 500C | Offenhauser | 4 | 128.209 | $270,400 | Tony Bettenhausen |
| 1956 | Pat Flaherty | Watson | Offenhauser | 4 | 128.490 | $282,052 | Sam Hanks |
| 1957 | Sam Hanks | Epperly | Offenhauser | 4 | 135.601 | $300,252 | Jim Rathmann |
| 1958 | Jimmy Bryan | Epperly | Offenhauser | 4 | 133.791 | $305,217 | George Amick |
| 1959 | Rodger Ward | Watson | Offenhauser | 4 | 135.857 | $338,100 | Jim Rathmann |
| 1960 | Jim Rathmann | Watson | Offenhauser | 4 | 138.767 | $369,150 | Rodger Ward |
| 1961 | A. J. Foyt | Watson | Offenhauser | 4 | 139.130 | $400,000 | Eddie Sachs |
| 1962 | Rodger Ward | Watson | Offenhauser | 4 | 140.293 | $426,152 | Len Sutton |
| 1963 | Parnelli Jones | Watson | Offenhauser | 4 | 143.137 | $494,031 | Jim Clark |
| 1964 | A. J. Foyt | Watson | Offenhauser | 4 | 147.350 | $506,625 | Rodger Ward |
| 1965 | Jim Clark | Lotus | Ford‡ | 8 | 151.388 | $628,399 | Parnelli Jones |
| 1966 | Graham Hill | Lola | Ford‡ | 8 | 144.317 | $691,809 | Jim Clark |
| 1967 | A. J. Foyt | Coyote | Ford‡ | 8 | 151.207 | $737,109 | Al Unser |
| 1968 | Bobby Unser | Eagle | Ford‡** | 8 | 152.882 | $809,627 | Dan Gurney |
| 1969 | Mario Andretti | Hawk | Ford‡** | 8 | 156.867 | $805,127 | Dan Gurney |
| 1970 | Al Unser | P. J. Colt | Ford‡** | 8 | 155.749 | $1,000,002 | Mark Donohue |
| 1971 | Al Unser | P. J. Colt | Ford‡** | 8 | 157.735 | $1,001,604 | Peter Revson |
| 1972 | Mark Donohue | McLaren | Offenhauser | 8 | 162.962 | $1,011,846 | Al Unser |
| 1973 | Gordon Johncock | Eagle | Offenhauser | 4 | 159.014 | $1,006,105 | Billy Vukovich |
| 1974 | Johnny Rutherford | McLaren | Offenhauser | 4 | 158.589 | $1,015,686 | Bobby Unser |
| 1975 | Bobby Unser | Eagle | Offenhauser | 4 | 149.213[3] | $1,001,322 | Johnny Rutherford |
| 1976 | Johnny Rutherford | McLaren | Drake-Offenhauser | 4 | 148.7[4] | $1,038,776 | A. J. Foyt |
| 1977 | A. J. Foyt | Coyote | Foyt | 8 | 161.331 | $1,116,807 | Tom Sneva |
| 1978 | Al Unser | Lola | Cosworth | 8 | 161.363 | $1,145,255 | Tom Sneva |
| 1979 | Rick Mears | Penske | Cosworth | 8 | 155.899 | $1,271,954 | A. J. Foyt |
| 1980 | Johnny Rutherford | Chaparral | Cosworth | 8 | 142.862 | $1,502,425 | Tom Sneva |
| 1981 | Bobby Unser | Penske | Cosworth | 8 | 139.084 | $1,609,375 | Mario Andretti |
| 1982 | Gordon Johncock | Wildcat | Cosworth | 8 | 162.029 | $2,063,470 | Rick Mears |

*Supercharged. **Turbocharged. †Front drive. ‡Rear engine. [1]400 miles. [2]345 miles; all other races at 500 miles. [3]Race stopped at 435 miles due to rain. [4]Race stopped at 255 miles due to rain.

## NATIONAL RACING CHAMPIONS—USAC*

| Year | Champion | Year | Champion | Year | Champion | Year | Champion |
|---|---|---|---|---|---|---|---|
| 1902 | Harry Harkness | 1921 | Thomas Milton | 1940 | Rex Mays | 1963 | A. J. Foyt |
| 1903 | Barney Oldfield | 1922 | James Murphy | 1941 | Rex Mays | 1964 | A. J. Foyt |
| 1904 | George Heath | 1923 | Eddie Hearne | 1946 | Ted Horn | 1965 | Mario Andretti |
| 1905 | Victor Hemery | 1924 | James Murphy | 1947 | Ted Horn | 1966 | Mario Andretti |
| 1906 | Joe Tracy | 1925 | Peter DePaolo | 1948 | Ted Horn | 1967 | A. J. Foyt |
| 1907 | Eddie Bald | 1926 | Harry Hartz | 1949 | Johnnie Parsons | 1968 | Bobby Unser |
| 1908 | Louis Strang | 1927 | Peter DePaolo | 1950 | Henry Banks | 1969 | Mario Andretti |
| 1909 | George Robertson | 1928 | Louis Meyer | 1951 | Tony Bettenhausen | 1970 | Al Unser |
| 1910 | Ray Harroun | 1929 | Louis Meyer | 1952 | Chuck Stevenson | 1971 | Joe Leonard |
| 1911 | Ralph Mulford | 1930 | Billy Arnold | 1953 | Sam Hanks | 1972 | Joe Leonard |
| 1912 | Ralph DePalma | 1931 | Louis Schneider | 1954 | Jimmy Bryan | 1973 | Roger McCluskey |
| 1913 | Earl Cooper | 1932 | Bob Carey | 1955 | Bob Sweikert | 1974 | Bobby Unser |
| 1914 | Ralph DePalma | 1933 | Louis Meyer | 1956 | Jimmy Bryan | 1975 | A. J. Foyt |
| 1915 | Earl Cooper | 1934 | Bill Cummings | 1957 | Jimmy Bryan | 1976 | Gordon Johncock |
| 1916 | Dario Resta | 1935 | Kelly Petillo | 1958 | Tony Bettenhausen | 1977 | Tom Sneva |
| 1917 | Earl Cooper | 1936 | Mauri Rose | 1959 | Rodger Ward | 1978 | Tom Sneva |
| 1918 | Ralph Mulford | 1937 | Wilbur Shaw | 1960 | A. J. Foyt | 1979 | A. J. Foyt |
| 1919 | Howard Wilcox | 1938 | Floyd Roberts | 1961 | A. J. Foyt | 1980 | Johnny Rutherford |
| 1920 | Gaston Chevrolet | 1939 | Wilbur Shaw | 1962 | Rodger Ward | 1981/82 | George Snider |

* USAC (United States Auto Club) founded 1956.

## 1981 USAC DIVISION CHAMPIONS (SOURCE: U.S. Auto Club)

**Gold Crown Series** (1981/82) — George Snider, Bakersfield California
**Stock Car** — Dean Roper, Fair Grove, Missouri
**Silver Crown** — Larry Rice, Brownsburg, Indiana
**Sprint Car** — Sheldon Kinser, Bloomington, Indiana
**Midget Car** — Mel Kenyon, Lebanon, Indiana
**Regional Midget Series** — Mack McClellan, Kokomo, Indiana

## 1981 USAC TOP MONEY WINNERS (SOURCE: U.S. Auto Club)

| | Driver | Amount |
|---|---|---|
| 1. | Bobby Unser, Albuquerque, N.M. | $279,002 |
| 2. | Mario Andretti, Nazareth, Pa. | 118,611 |
| 3. | A. J. Foyt, Houston, Tex. | 100,070 |
| 4. | Geoff Brabham, Sydney, Australia | 93,919 |
| 5. | Vern Schuppan, Whyalla, Australia | 86,915 |
| 6. | Sheldon Kinser, Bloomington, Ind. | $82,125 |
| 7. | Tom Bigelow, Whitewater, Wis. | 80,140 |
| 8. | Rich Vogler, Indianapolis, Ind. | 61,282 |
| 9. | Gordon Johncock, Coldwater, Mich. | 58,867 |
| 10. | Kevin Cogan, Redondo Beach, Calif. | 54,675 |

## USAC NATIONAL CHAMPIONSHIP ALL-TIME RACE WINNERS (1956-1981)

| Driver | Wins | Driver | Wins | Driver | Wins | Driver | Wins |
|---|---|---|---|---|---|---|---|
| A. J. Foyt | 67 | Johnny Rutherford | 20 | Lloyd Ruby | 7 | Danny Ongais | 6 |
| Al Unser | 35 | Gordon Johncock | 19 | Johnny Thomson | 6 | Jud Larson | 5 |
| Mario Andretti | 33 | Eddie Sachs | 8 | Parnelli Jones | 6 | Jim McElreath | 5 |
| Bobby Unser | 27 | Jimmy Bryan | 7 | Don Branson | 6 | Wally Dallenbach | 5 |
| Rodger Ward | 24 | Dan Gurney | 7 | Joe Leonard | 6 | Roger McCluskey | 5 |

## USAC ROOKIE OF THE YEAR

| Year | Rookie | Year | Rookie | Year | Rookie |
|---|---|---|---|---|---|
| 1971 | George Eaton | 1975 | Spike Gehlhausen | 1979 | Tony Bettenhausen, Jr. |
| 1972 | Mike Hiss | 1976 | Rick Mears | 1980 | Bill Alsup |
| 1973 | Tom Sneva | 1977 | Danny Ongais | 1981/82 | Geoff Brabham |
| 1974 | Duane Carter, Jr. | 1978 | Tom Bagley | | |

## 1982 CHAMPIONSHIP AUTO RACING DRIVERS (CART) MONEY WINNERS—INDY SERIES

(to October 10)

| | Driver | Amount |
|---|---|---|
| 1. | Gordon Johncock | $475,384 |
| 2. | Rick Mears | 426,648 |
| 3. | Bobby Rahal | 216,403 |
| 4. | Mario Andretti | 199,235 |
| 5. | Tom Sneva | 188,322 |
| 6. | Pancho Carter | $167,262 |
| 7. | Al Unser, Sr. | 161,772 |
| 8. | Kevin Cogan | 156,092 |
| 9. | Geoff Brabham | 127,923 |
| 10. | Roger Mears | 119,191 |

## 1982 CART WORLD SERIES STANDINGS (to October 10)

| | Driver | Points |
|---|---|---|
| 1. | Rick Mears | 277* |
| 2. | Bobby Rahal | 232** |
| 3. | Gordon Johncock | 186 |
| 4. | Mario Andretti | 174 |
| 5. | Al Unser, Sr. | 125 |
| 6. | Kevin Cogan | 124 |
| 7. | Tom Sneva | 123 |

* Clinched 1st Place. ** Clinched 2nd Place.

## 1982 DAYTONA-LE MANS 24-HOUR ENDURANCE RACES

| | Drivers | Laps | Car | Avg. Speed (Mph) |
|---|---|---|---|---|
| DAYTONA: | 1. John Paul, John Paul, Jr. and Rolf Stommelen (W. Germany) | 719 (2,760.96 mi.) | Porsche | 114.794 |
| | 2. Bob Akin, Derek Bell and Craig Seibert | 708 | Porsche | ...... |
| LE MANS: | 1. Jacky Ickx (Belgium) and Derek Bell (U.K.) | 359 (3,044.15 mi.) | Porsche | 126.839 |
| | 2. Jochen Mass (W. Germany) and Vern Schuppan (Australia) | 356 | Porsche | ...... |

## THE HISTORY OF THE MILE RECORD

| DATE | DRIVER | CAR | AMERICAN TIME | AVG. | WORLD'S TIME | AVG. |
|---|---|---|---|---|---|---|
| 12/18/98 | Chasseloup-Laubat | Jeantaud | | | 57.000 | 39.24 |
| 1/17/99 | Camille Jenatzy | Jamais Contente Jeantzy | | | 54.000 | 41.42 |
| 1/17/99 | Chasseloup-Laubat | Jeantaud | | | 51.500 | 43.69 |
| 1/27/99 | Camille Jenatzy | Jamais Contente Jeantzy | | | 44.800 | 49.40 |
| 3/4/99 | Chasseloup-Laubat | Jeantaud | | | 38.400 | 58.25 |
| 4/29/99 | Camille Jenatzy | Jamais Contente Jeantzy | | | 34.400 | 65.79 |
| 4/13/02 | Serpollet | Serpollet | | | 29.800 | 76.06 |
| 8/5/02 | W. K. Vanderbilt | Mors | | | 29.400 | 76.08 |
| 11/5/02 | H. Fournier | Mors | | | 29.200 | 76.60 |
| 11/17/02 | Augieres | Mors | | | 29.000 | 77.13 |
| 3/17/03 | Rigolly | Gorbron-Brillie | | | 26.800 | 83.46 |
| 11/5/03 | A. Duray | Gobron-Brillie | | | 26.400 | 84.73 |
| 1/12/04 | Henry Ford | Ford "999" | 39.40 | 91.370 | | |
| 1/22/04 | W. K. Vanderbilt | Mercedes | 39.00 | 92.307 | | |
| 3/31/04 | Rigolly | Gobbron-Brillie | | | 23.600 | 94.78 |
| 5/12/04 | De Caters | Mercedes | | | 23.000 | 97.26 |
| 7/21/04 | Rigolly | Gobron-Brillie | | | 21.600 | 103.56 |
| 11/13/04 | Victor Hemery | Darracq | | | 21.400 | 104.53 |
| 12/30/04 | Barras | Darracq | | | 20.400 | 109.65 |
| 1/24/05 | Arthur MacDonald | Napier | 34.40 | 104.65 | | |
| 1/25/05 | H. L. Bowden | Mercedes | 32.80 | 109.75 | | |
| 1/26/06 | Fred Marriott | Stanley (Steam) | 28.20 | 127.659 | | |
| 11/8/09* | Victor Hemery | Benz | | | 17.761 | 125.914* |
| 3/16/10 | Barney Oldfield | Benz | 27.33 | 131.724 | | |
| 4/23/11 | Bob Burman | Benz | 25.40 | 141.732 | | |
| 6/24/14 | L. G. Hornsted | Benz | | | 29.01 | 124.095 |
| 2/12/19 | Ralph DePalma | Packard | 24.02 | 149.875 | | |
| 4/27/20 | Tom Milton | Duesenberg | 23.07 | 156.046 | | |
| 5/17/22 | K. Lee Guinness | Sunbeam | | | 27.87 | 129.171 |
| 6/26/24 | J. G. Parry-Thomas | Leyland-Thomas | | | 27.75 | 129.730 |
| 7/6/24 | Rene Thomas | Delage | | | 25.12 | 143.312 |
| 7/12/24 | E. A. D. Eldridge | Fiat | | | 24.675 | 145.897 |
| 9/25/24 | Capt. M. Campbell | Sunbeam | | | 24.630 | 146.163 |
| 7/21/25 | Capt. M. Campbell | Sunbeam | | | 23.878 | 150.766 |
| 4/27/26 | J. G. Parry-Thomas | Thomas Special | | | 21.419 | 168.075 |
| 4/28/26 | J. G. Parry-Thomas | Thomas Special | | | 21.099 | 170.624 |
| 2/4/27 | Capt. M. Campbell | Napier-Campbell | | | 20.663 | 174.224 |
| 3/29/27 | Maj. H. O. D. Seagrave | Sunbeam | 17.665 | 203.790 | 17.665 | 203.790 |
| 2/19/28 | Capt. M. Campbell | Napier-Campbell | 17.395 | 206.956 | 17.395 | 206.956 |
| 4/22/28 | Ray Keech | White Triplex | 17.345 | 207.552 | 17.345 | 207.552 |
| 3/11/29 | Maj. H. O. D. Seagrave | Irving-Napier | 15.56 | 231.446 | 15.56 | 231.446 |
| 2/5/31 | Sir Malcolm Campbell | Napier-Campbell | 14.65 | 245.086 | 14.65 | 246.086 |
| 2/24/32 | Sir Malcolm Campbell | Napier-Campbell | 14.175 | 253.96 | 14.175 | 253.96 |
| 2/22/33 | Sir Malcolm Campbell | Napier-Campbell | 13.23 | 272.109 | 13.23 | 272.109 |
| 3/7/35 | Sir Malcolm Campbell | Bluebird Special | 13.01 | 276.82 | 13.01 | 276.82 |
| 9/3/35 | Sir Malcolm Campbell | Bluebird Special | 11.96 | 301.13 | 11.96 | 301.13 |
| 11/19/37 | Capt. G. E. T. Eyston | Thunderbolt No. 1 | 11.56 | 311.42 | 11.56 | 311.42 |
| 8/27/38 | Capt. G. E. T. Eyston | Thunderbolt No. 1 | 10.42 | 345.5 | 10.42 | 345.5 |
| 9/15/38 | John Cobb | Railton | 10.28 | 350.2 | 10.28 | 350.2 |
| 9/16/38 | Capt. G. E. T. Eyston | Thunderbolt No. 1 | 10.07 | 357.5 | 10.07 | 357.5 |
| 8/23/39 | John Cobb | Railton | 9.76 | 368.9 | 9.76 | 368.9 |
| 9/16/47 | John Cobb | Railton-Mobil Special | 9.1325 | 394.2 | 9.1325 | 394.2 |
| 8/5/63 | Craig Breedlove | Spirit of America | 8.8355 | 407.45 | 8.8355 | 407.45 |
| 10/2/64 | Tom Green | Wingfoot Express | 8.7125 | 413.20 | 8.7125 | 413.20 |
| 10/5/64 | Art Arfons | Art Arfons Green Monster | 8.2945 | 434.02 | 8.2945 | 434.02 |
| 10/13/64 | Craig Breedlove | Spirit of America | 7.6805 | 468.719 | 7.6805 | 468.719 |
| 10/15/64 | Craig Breedlove | Spirit of America | 6.8405 | 526.277 | 6.8405 | 526.277 |
| 10/27/64 | Art Arfons | Art Arfons Green Monster | 6.7075 | 536.71 | 6.7075 | 536.71 |
| 11/2/65 | Craig Breedlove | Spirit of America–Sonic I | 6.485 | 555.127 | 6.485 | 555.127 |
| 11/7/65 | Art Arfons | Art Arfons Green Monster | 6.244 | 576.553 | 6.244 | 576.553 |
| 11/15/65 | Craig Breedlove | Spirit of America–Sonic I | 5.994 | 600.601 | 5.994 | 600.601 |
| 10/23/70 | Gary Gabelich | Blue Flame | 5.784 | 622.407 | 5.784 | 622.407 |
| 9/9/79** | Stan Barrett | The Budweiser Rocket | 5.637 | 638.637 | 5.637 | 638.637 |

* Records above this point for World's Time were made over the flying kilometer, the recognized distance in the early years.

NOTE: The above records are the average of two runs made in opposite directions within one hour. ** Run made in one direction. Record not officially sanctioned.

# THOROUGHBRED RACING

SOURCE: *American Racing Manual,* 1982 ed. Reproduced with permission of the copyright owner, Daily Racing Form, Inc.

## HIGHEST ANNUAL PAYOFF ODDS

| Date | Winner | Track | Payoff Odds |
|---|---|---|---|
| 1948 Sept. 30 | Buddie Bones | Rockingham Park | 192–1 |
| 1949 Sept. 20 | Luxuriant | Narragansett Park | 282–1 |
| 1950 Oct. 30 | Minnix | Lincoln Downs | 253–1 |
| 1951 Sept. 27 | Royal Marvel | Rockingham Park | 183–1 |
| 1952 Sept. 16 | Rock House | Woodbine Park | 214–1 |
| 1953 Aug. 28 | Can It Yes | Exhibition Park | 253–1 |
| 1954 Nov. 10 | Ruff Mate | Pimlico Race Course | 209–1 |
| 1955 May 27 | Gold Champ | Suffolk Downs | 144–1 |
| 1956 July 24 | Buster Bell | Charles Town | 203–1 |
| 1957 Aug. 27 | Miss Profit | Detroit Race Course | 172–1 |
| 1958 Mar. 22 | Whisk Tru | Bowie Race Course | 231–1 |
| 1959 June 5 | Janie Brown | Thistledown | 168–1 |
| 1960 Nov. 4 | Kamal Bey | Laurel Race Course | 175–1 |
| 1961 Sept. 29 | Djebonita | Bay Meadows | 259–1 |
| 1962 July 20 | Wee Highway | Delaware Park | 170–1 |
| 1963 Sept. 13 | Confiancita | El Comandante | 201–1 |
| 1963 Aug. 12 | Ivalinda | Arlington Park | 190–1 |
| 1964 Dec. 11 | Wilson Hill Doll | Bay Meadows | 279–1 |
| 1965 June 5 | Blunt Edge | Cahokia Downs | 142–1 |
| 1966 Oct. 7 | Dutch Wrackateer | Narragansett Park | 186–1 |
| 1967 May 26 | Mambo Rhythm | Seminole Downs | 214–1 |
| 1968 June 24 | Waverley Steps | Woodbine | 396–1 |
| 1969 Sept. 24 | Judes Song | Latonia | 241–1 |
| 1970 May 7 | Corpus Delicti | Fort Erie | 175–1 |
| 1971 Apr. 1 | Moonlight City | Portland Meadows | 169–1 |
| 1972 Nov. 16 | Norton | Churchill Downs | 190–1 |
| 1973 Sept. 28 | Cedars Crown | Detroit Race Course | 256–1 |
| 1974 Mar. 17 | Campus Bright | Yakima Meadows | 156–1 |
| 1975 Sept. 1 | Second Ticking | Narragansett Park | 147–1 |
| 1976 Sept. 21 | Tiger Red K | Columbus | 188–1 |
| 1977 Mar. 10 | Black Ticket | Fonner Park | 259–1 |
| 1978 Nov. 21 | Golden Rubies | Churchill Downs | 246–1 |
| 1979 Mar. 14 | Young Migrant | Portland Meadows | 228–1 |
| 1980 Nov. 23 | Pogong | Sundland Park | 220–1 |

## STRAIGHT MUTUEL PAYOFFS RECORD

Tabulation based on a $2 straight mutuel ticket

| Horse | Track and Date | Payoff |
|---|---|---|
| Wishing Ring | Latonia, June 17, 1912 | $1,885.50 |
| Augeas | Agua Caliente, February 14, 1933 | 840.00 |
| Muzetta W. | Lexington, May 7, 1910 | 830.70 |
| King Jack | Agua Caliente, January 8, 1933 | 820.00 |
| Trycook | Hagerstown, May 19, 1934 | 810.00 |
| Fincastle | Havana, December 19, 1923 | 702.60 |
| Lt. Wm. J. Murray | Havana, February 11, 1923 | 696.00 |
| Miss Fountain | Havana, February 9, 1930 | 685.60 |
| Playmay | Santa Anita Park, February 4, 1938 | 673.40 |
| Fleetglow | Green Mountain, May 9, 1968 | 658.80 |
| Meadow Money | Lincoln Fields, June 5, 1941 | 652.40 |
| Nanamay | Tanforan, April 14, 1932 | $602.20 |
| Zombro | Charles Town, December 5, 1933 | 590.00 |
| Cadeau | Pimlico, May 7, 1913 | 577.10 |
| Escohigh | Tropical Park, December 29, 1937 | 571.00 |
| Luxuriant | Narragansett Park, September 20, 1949 | 566.80 |
| Welga | Douglas Park, May 29, 1916 | 560.40 |
| Wilson Hill Doll | Bay Meadows, December 11, 1964 | 559.80 |
| Mad Scramble | Bay Meadows, April 22, 1941 | 530.80 |
| Djebonita | Bay Meadows, September 29, 1961 | 520.80 |
| Black Ticket | Fonner Park, March 10, 1977 | 520.50 |
| Cedars Crown | Detroit Race Course, September 28, 1973 | 514.20 |
| Minnix | Lincoln Downs, October 30, 1950 | 508.80 |

## THE TRIPLE CROWN

Only eleven three-year-olds have managed to win the celebrated Triple Crown of American Racing—the Kentucky Derby, the Preakness Stakes, and the Belmont Stakes:

1919—Sir Barton
1930—Gallant Fox
1935—Omaha
1937—War Admiral
1941—Whirlaway
1943—Count Fleet
1946—Assault
1948—Citation
1973—Secretariat
1977—Seattle Slew
1978—Affirmed

The following horses won two of the three great races: Clover-brook (1877), Duke of Magenta (1878), Grenada (1880), Saunterer (1881), Belmar (1895), Man o' War (1920), Pillory (1922), Zev (1923), Twenty Grand (1931), Burgoo King (1932), Bold Venture (1936), Johnstown (1939), Bimelech (1940), Shut Out (1942), Pensive (1944), Capot (1949), Middleground (1950), Native Dancer (1953), Nashua (1955), Needles (1956), Tim Tam (1958), Carry Back (1961), Chateaugay (1963), Northern Dancer (1964), Kauai King (1966), Damascus (1967), Forward Pass (1968), Majestic Prince (1969), Canonero II (1971), Riva Ridge (1972), Little Current (1974), Spectacular Bid (1979), Pleasant Colony (1981).

## LEADING MONEY-WINNING THOROUGHBRED HORSES

| Year | Horse | Age | Starts | 1st | 2d | 3d | Amount Won |
|---|---|---|---|---|---|---|---|
| 1926 | Crusader | 3 | 15 | 9 | 4 | 0 | $166,033 |
| 1927 | Anita Peabody | 2 | 7 | 6 | 0 | 1 | 111,905 |
| 1928 | High Strung | 2 | 6 | 5 | 0 | 0 | 153,590 |
| 1929 | Blue Larkspur | 3 | 6 | 4 | 1 | 0 | 153,450 |
| 1930 | Gallant Fox | 3 | 10 | 9 | 1 | 0 | 308,275 |
| 1931 | Top Flight | 2 | 7 | 7 | 0 | 0 | 219,000 |
| 1932 | Gusto | 3 | 16 | 4 | 3 | 2 | 145,940 |
| 1933 | Singing Wood | 2 | 9 | 3 | 2 | 2 | 88,050 |
| 1934 | Cavalcade | 3 | 7 | 6 | 1 | 0 | 111,235 |
| 1935 | Omaha | 3 | 9 | 6 | 1 | 2 | 142,255 |
| 1936 | Granville | 3 | 11 | 7 | 3 | 0 | 110,295 |
| 1937 | Seabiscuit | 4 | 15 | 11 | 2 | 2 | 168,580 |
| 1938 | Stagehand | 3 | 15 | 8 | 2 | 3 | 189,710 |
| 1939 | Challedon | 3 | 15 | 9 | 2 | 3 | 184,535 |
| 1940 | Bimelech | 3 | 7 | 4 | 2 | 1 | 110,005 |
| 1941 | Whirlaway | 3 | 20 | 13 | 5 | 2 | 272,386 |
| 1942 | Shut Out | 3 | 12 | 8 | 2 | 0 | 238,872 |
| 1943 | Count Fleet | 3 | 6 | 6 | 0 | 0 | 174,055 |
| 1944 | Pavot | 2 | 8 | 8 | 0 | 0 | 179,040 |
| 1945 | Busher | 3 | 13 | 10 | 2 | 1 | 273,735 |
| 1946 | Assault | 3 | 15 | 8 | 2 | 3 | 424,195 |
| 1947 | Armed | 6 | 17 | 11 | 4 | 1 | 376,325 |
| 1948 | Citation | 3 | 20 | 19 | 1 | 0 | 709,470 |
| 1949 | Ponder | 3 | 21 | 9 | 5 | 2 | 321,825 |
| 1950 | Noor | 5 | 12 | 7 | 4 | 1 | 346,940 |
| 1951 | Counterpoint | 3 | 15 | 7 | 2 | 1 | 250,525 |
| 1952 | Crafty Admiral | 4 | 16 | 9 | 4 | 1 | 277,225 |
| 1953 | Native Dancer | 3 | 10 | 9 | 1 | 0 | 513,425 |
| 1954 | Determine | 3 | 15 | 10 | 3 | 2 | $328,700 |
| 1955 | Nashua | 3 | 12 | 10 | 1 | 1 | 752,550 |
| 1956 | Needles | 3 | 8 | 4 | 2 | 0 | 440,850 |
| 1957 | Round Table | 3 | 22 | 15 | 1 | 3 | 600,383 |
| 1958 | Round Table | 4 | 20 | 14 | 4 | 0 | 662,780 |
| 1959 | Sword Dancer | 3 | 13 | 8 | 4 | 0 | 537,004 |
| 1960 | Bally Ache | 3 | 15 | 10 | 3 | 1 | 455,045 |
| 1961 | Carry Back | 3 | 16 | 9 | 1 | 3 | 565,349 |
| 1962 | Never Bend | 2 | 10 | 7 | 1 | 2 | 402,969 |
| 1963 | Candy Spots | 3 | 12 | 7 | 2 | 1 | 604,481 |
| 1964 | Gun Bow | 4 | 16 | 8 | 4 | 2 | 580,100 |
| 1965 | Buckpasser | 2 | 11 | 9 | 1 | 0 | 568,096 |
| 1966 | Buckpasser | 3 | 14 | 13 | 1 | 0 | 669,078 |
| 1967 | Damascus | 3 | 16 | 12 | 3 | 1 | 817,941 |
| 1968 | Forward Pass | 3 | 13 | 7 | 2 | 0 | 546,674 |
| 1969 | Arts and Letters | 3 | 14 | 8 | 5 | 1 | 555,604 |
| 1970 | Personality | 3 | 18 | 8 | 2 | 1 | 444,049 |
| 1971 | Riva Ridge | 2 | 9 | 7 | 0 | 0 | 503,263 |
| 1972 | Droll Role | 4 | 19 | 7 | 3 | 4 | 471,633 |
| 1973 | Secretariat | 3 | 12 | 9 | 2 | 1 | 860,404 |
| 1974 | Chris Evert | 3 | 8 | 5 | 1 | 2 | 551,063 |
| 1975 | Foolish Pleasure | 3 | 11 | 5 | 4 | 1 | 716,278 |
| 1976 | Forego | 6 | 8 | 6 | 1 | 1 | 491,701 |
| 1977 | Seattle Slew | 3 | 7 | 6 | 0 | 0 | 641,370 |
| 1978 | Affirmed | 3 | 11 | 8 | 2 | 0 | 901,541 |
| 1979 | Spectacular Bid | 3 | 12 | 10 | 1 | 1 | 1,279,333 |
| 1980 | Temperence Hill | 3 | 17 | 8 | 3 | 1 | 1,130,452 |
| 1981 | John Henry | 6 | 10 | 8 | 0 | 0 | 1,798,030 |

## THE KENTUCKY DERBY (THREE-YEAR-OLDS) Distance: 1¼ miles (Churchill Downs, Ky.)

| Year | Winner | Jockey | Net to Winner | Time | Second |
|---|---|---|---|---|---|
| 1940 | Gallahadion | C. Bierman | $ 60,150 | 2:05 | Bimelech |
| 1941 | Whirlaway | E. Arcaro | 61,275 | 2:01⅖ | Staretor |
| 1942 | Shut Out | W. D. Wright | 64,225 | 2:04⅖ | Alsab |
| 1943 | Count Fleet | J. Longden | 60,275 | 2:04 | Blue Swords |
| 1944 | Pensive | C McCreary | 64,675 | 2:04⅕ | Broadcloth |
| 1945 | Hoop Jr. | E. Arcaro | 64,850 | 2:07 | Pot o' Luck |
| 1946 | Assault | W. Mehrtens | 96,400 | 2:06⅗ | Spy Song |
| 1947 | Jet Pilot | E. Guerin | 92,160 | 2:06⅗ | Phalanx |
| 1948 | Citation | E. Arcaro | 83,400 | 2:05⅖ | Coaltown |
| 1949 | Ponder | S. Brooks | 91,600 | 2:04⅕ | Capot |
| 1950 | Middleground | W. Boland | 92,650 | 2:01⅗ | Hill Prince |
| 1951 | Count Turf | C. McCreary | 98,050 | 2:02⅗ | Royal Mustang |
| 1952 | Hill Gail | E. Arcaro | 96,300 | 2:01⅗ | Sub Fleet |
| 1953 | Dark Star | H. Moreno | 90,050 | 2:02 | Native Dancer |
| 1954 | Determine | R. York | 102,050 | 2:03 | Hasty Road |
| 1955 | Swaps | W. Shoemaker | 108,400 | 2:01⅘ | Nashua |
| 1956 | Needles | D. Erb | 123,450 | 2:03⅖ | Fabius |
| 1957 | Iron Liege | W. Hartack | 107,950 | 2:02⅕ | Gallant Man |
| 1958 | Tim Tam | I. Valenzuela | 116,400 | 2:05 | Lincoln Road |
| 1959 | Tomy Lee | W. Shoemaker | 119,650 | 2:02⅕ | Sword Dancer |
| 1960 | Venetian Way | W. Hartack | 114,850 | 2:02⅖ | Bally Ache |
| 1961 | Carry Back | J. Sellers | 120,500 | 2:04 | Crozier |
| 1962 | Decidedly | W. Hartack | 119,650 | 2:00⅖ | Roman Line |
| 1963 | Chateaugay | B. Baeza | 108,900 | 2:01⅘ | Never Bend |
| 1964 | Northern Dancer | W. Hartack | 114,300 | 2:00 | Hill Rise |
| 1965 | Lucky Debonair | W. Shoemaker | 112,000 | 2:01⅕ | Dapper Dan |
| 1966 | Kauai King | D. Brumfield | 120,500 | 2:02 | Advocator |
| 1967 | Proud Clarion | R. Ussery | 119,700 | 2:00⅗ | Barbs Delight |
| 1968 | Forward Pass | I. Valenzuela | 122,600 | 2:02⅕ | Francie's Hat |
| 1969 | Majestic Prince | W. Hartack | 113,200 | 2:01⅘ | Arts & Letters |
| 1970 | Dust Commander | M. Manganello | 127,800 | 2:03⅖ | My Dad George |
| 1971 | Canonero II | G. Avila | 145,500 | 2:03⅕ | Jim French |
| 1972 | Riva Ridge | Ron Turcotte | 140,300 | 2:01.8 | No Le Hace |
| 1973 | Secretariat | Ron Turcotte | 155,050 | 1:59⅖ | Sham |
| 1974 | Cannonade | Angel Cordero, Jr. | 274,000 | 2:04 | Hudson County |
| 1975 | Foolish Pleasure | Jacinto Vasquez | 209,600 | 2:02 | Avatar |
| 1976 | Bold Forbes | Angel Cordero, Jr. | 217,700 | 2:01⅗ | Honest Pleasure |
| 1977 | Seattle Slew | Jean Cruguet | 214,700 | 2:02⅕ | Run Dusty Run |
| 1978 | Affirmed | Steve Cauthen | 186,900 | 2:01⅕ | Alydar |
| 1979 | Spectacular Bid | Ron Franklin | 228,650 | 2:02⅖ | General Assembly |
| 1980 | Genuine Risk | Jacinto Vasquez | 250,550 | 2:02 | Rumbo |
| 1981 | Pleasant Colony | Jorge Velasquez | 317,200 | 2:02 | Woodchopper |
| 1982 | Gato Del Sol | Eddie Delahoussaye | 428,850 | 2:02⅖ | Laser Light |

## THE PREAKNESS STAKES (THREE-YEAR-OLDS) Distance 1-3/16 miles (Pimlico, Md.)

| Year | Winner | Jockey | Net to Winner | Time | Second |
|---|---|---|---|---|---|
| 1940 | Bimelech | F. A. Smith | $ 53,230 | 1:58⅗ | Mioland |
| 1941 | Whirlaway | E. Arcaro | 49,365 | 1:58⅘ | King Cole |
| 1942 | Alsab | B. James | 58,175 | 1:57 | tie |
| 1943 | Count Fleet | J. Longden | 43,190 | 1:57⅖ | Blue Swords |
| 1944 | Pensive | C. McCreary | 60,075 | 1:59⅕ | Platter |
| 1945 | Polynesian | W. D. Wright | 66,170 | 1:58⅘ | Hoop Jr. |
| 1946 | Assault | W. Mehrtens | 96,620 | 2:01⅖ | Lord Boswell |
| 1947 | Faultless | D. Dodson | 98,005 | 1:59 | On Trust |
| 1948 | Citation | E. Arcaro | 91,870 | 2:02⅖ | Vulcan's Forge |
| 1949 | Capot | T. Atkinson | 79,985 | 1:56 | Palestinian |
| 1950 | Hill Prince | E. Arcaro | 56,115 | 1:59⅕ | Middleground |
| 1951 | Bold | E. Arcaro | 83,110 | 1:56⅖ | Counterpoint |
| 1952 | Blue Man | C. McCreary | 86,135 | 1:57⅖ | Jampol |
| 1953 | Native Dancer | E. Guerin | 65,200 | 1:57⅘ | Jamie K. |
| 1954 | Hasty Road | J. Adams | 91,600 | 1:57⅖ | Correlation |
| 1955 | Nashua | E. Arcaro | 67,550 | 1:54⅗ | Saratoga |
| 1956 | Fabius | W. Hartack | 84,250 | 1:58⅖ | Needles |
| 1957 | Bold Ruler | E. Arcaro | 65,250 | 1:56⅕ | Iron Liege |
| 1958 | Tim Tam | I. Valenzuela | 97,900 | 1:57⅕ | Lincoln Road |
| 1959 | Royal Orbit | W. Harmatz | 136,200 | 1:57 | Sword Dancer |
| 1960 | Bally Ache | R. Ussery | 121,000 | 1:57⅗ | Victoria Park |
| 1961 | Carry Back | J. Sellers | 126,200 | 1:57⅗ | Globemaster |
| 1962 | Greek Money | J. L. Rotz | 135,800 | 1:56⅕ | Ridan |
| 1963 | Candy Spots | W. Shoemaker | 127,500 | 1:56⅕ | Chateaugay |
| 1964 | Northern Dancer | W. Hartack | 124,200 | 1:56⅘ | The Scoundrel |
| 1965 | Tom Rolfe | R. Turcotte | 128,100 | 1:56⅕ | Dapper Dan |
| 1966 | Kauai King | D. Brumfield | 129,000 | 1:55⅖ | Stupendous |
| 1967 | Damascus | W. Shoemaker | 141,500 | 1:55⅕ | In Reality |
| 1968 | Forward Pass | I. Valenzuela | 142,700 | 1:56⅘ | Out of the Way |
| 1969 | Majestic Prince | W. Hartack | 129,500 | 1:55⅗ | Arts & Letters |
| 1970 | Personality | E. Belmonte | 151,300 | 1:56⅕ | My Dad George |
| 1971 | Canonero II | G. Avila | 137,400 | 1:54 | Eastern Fleet |
| 1972 | Bee Bee Bee | Eldon Nelson | 135,000 | 1:55.4 | No Le Hace |
| 1973 | Secretariat | Ron Turcotte | 129,900 | 1:54⅖ | Sham |
| 1974 | Little Current | Miguel Rivera | 156,500 | 1:54⅗ | Neopolitan Way |
| 1975 | Master Derby | Darrel McHarque | 158,100 | 1:56⅖ | Foolish Pleasure |
| 1976 | Elocutionist | John Lively | 129,700 | 1:55 | Play the Red |
| 1977 | Seattle Slew | Jean Cruguet | 138,600 | 1:54⅖ | Iron Constitution |
| 1978 | Affirmed | Steve Cauthen | 136,200 | 1:54⅖ | Alydar |
| 1979 | Spectacular Bid | Ron Franklin | 165,300 | 1:54⅕ | Golden Act |
| 1980 | Codex | Angel Cordero | 180,600 | 1:54⅕ | Genuine Risk |
| 1981 | Pleasant Colony | Jorge Velasquez | 200,800 | 1:54⅗ | Bold Ego |
| 1982 | Aloma's Ruler | Jack Kaenel | 209,900 | 1:55⅖ | Linkage |

## THE BELMONT STAKES (THREE-YEAR-OLDS) Distance: 1½ miles. (Elmont, N.Y.)

| Year | Winner | Jockey | Net to Winner | Time | Second |
|---|---|---|---|---|---|
| 1940 | Bimelech | F. A. Smith | $35,030 | 2:29⅗ | Your Chance |
| 1941 | Whirlaway | E. Arcaro | 39,770 | 2:31 | Robert Morris |
| 1942 | Shut Out | E. Arcaro | 44,520 | 2:29⅕ | Alsab |
| 1943 | Count Fleet | J. Longden | 35,340 | 2:28⅕ | Fairy Manhurst |
| 1944 | Bounding Home | G. L. Smith | 55,000 | 2:32⅕ | Pensive |
| 1945 | Pavot | E. Arcaro | 52,675 | 2:30⅕ | Wildlife |
| 1946 | Assault | W. Mehrtens | 75,400 | 2:30⅘ | Natchez |
| 1947 | Phalanx | R. Donoso | 78,900 | 2:29⅖ | Tide Rips |
| 1948 | Citation | E. Arcaro | 77,700 | 2:28⅕ | Better Self |
| 1949 | Capot | T. Atkinson | 60,900 | 2:30⅕ | Ponder |
| 1950 | Middleground | W. Boland | 61,350 | 2:28⅗ | Lights Up |
| 1951 | Counterpoint | D. Gorman | 82,000 | 2:29 | Battlefield |
| 1952 | One Count | E. Arcaro | 82,400 | 2:30⅕ | Blue Man |
| 1953 | Native Dancer | E. Guerin | 82,500 | 2:28⅗ | Jamie K. |
| 1954 | High Gun | E. Guerin | 89,000 | 2:30⅘ | Fisherman |
| 1955 | Nashua | E. Arcaro | 83,700 | 2:29 | Blazing Count |
| 1956 | Needles | D. Erb | 83,600 | 2:29⅘ | Career Boy |
| 1957 | Gallant Man | W. Shoemaker | 77,300 | 2:26⅗ | Inside Tract |
| 1958 | Cavan | P. Anderson | 73,440 | 2:30⅕ | Tim Tam |
| 1959 | Sword Dancer | W. Shoemaker | 93,525 | 2:28⅖ | Bagdad |
| 1960 | Celtic Ash | W. Hartack | 96,785 | 2:29⅗ | Venetian Way |
| 1961 | Sherluck | B. Baeza | 104,900 | 2:29⅕ | Globemaster |
| 1962 | Jaipur | W. Shoemaker | 109,550 | 2:28⅘ | Admiral's Voyage |
| 1963 | Chateaugay | B. Baeza | 101,700 | 2:30⅕ | Candy Spots |
| 1964 | Quadrangle | M. Ycaza | 110,850 | 2:28⅖ | Roman Brother |
| 1965 | Hail to All | J. Sellers | 104,150 | 2:28⅖ | Tom Rolfe |
| 1966 | Amberoid | W. Boland | 117,700 | 2:29⅗ | Buffle |
| 1967 | Damascus | W. Shoemaker | 104,950 | 2:28⅘ | Cool Reception |
| 1968 | Stage Door Johnny | H. Gustines | 117,700 | 2:27⅕ | Forward Pass |
| 1969 | Arts and Letters | B. Baeza | 104,050 | 2:28⅘ | Majestic Prince |
| 1970 | High Echelon | J. L. Rotz | 115,000 | 2:34 | Needles n Pens |
| 1971 | Pass Catcher | W. Blum | 97,710 | 2:30⅖ | Jim French |
| 1972 | Riva Ridge | Ron Turcotte | 93,540 | 2:28 | Ruritania |
| 1973 | Secretariat | Ron Turcotte | 90,720 | 2:24 | Twice a Prince |
| 1974 | Little Current | Miguel Rivera | 101,970 | 2:29⅕ | Jolly Johu |
| 1975 | Avatar | W. Shoemaker | 116,160 | 2:28 | Foolish Pleasure |
| 1976 | Bold Forbes | Angel Cordero, Jr. | 117,000 | 2:29 | McKenzie Bridge |
| 1977 | Seattle Slew | Jean Cruguet | 109,080 | 2:29⅗ | Run Dusty Run |
| 1978 | Affirmed | Steve Cauthen | 110,580 | 2:26⅘ | Alydar |
| 1979 | Coastal | Ruben Hernandez | 161,400 | 2:28⅗ | Golden Act |
| 1980 | Temperence Hill | Eddie Maple | 176,220 | 2:29⅘ | Genuine Risk |
| 1981 | Summing | George Martens | 170,580 | 2:29 | Highland Blade |
| 1982 | Conquistador Cielo | Laffit Pincay, Jr. | 159,720 | 2:28⅕ | Gato del Sol |

## WORLD THOROUGHBRED RACING RECORDS

| Distance | Horse, age, weight | Track | Date | Time |
|---|---|---|---|---|
| ¼ mi. | Big Racket, 4, 114 | Hipodromo de las Americas, Mexico City | Feb. 5, 1945 | :20⅘ |
| 2½ f. | Tie Score, 5, 115 | Hipodromo de las Americas, Mexico City | Feb. 5, 1946 | :26⅘ |
| ⅜ mi. | Atoka, 6, 105 | Butte, Mont. | Sept. 7, 1906 | :33½ |
| 3½ f. | Tango King, 6, 116 | Northlands Park, Canada | April 22, 1978 | :38⅘ |
| ½ mi. | Norgor, 9, 118 | Ruidoso Downs, Ruidoso, N.M. | Aug. 14, 1976 | :44¾ |
| 4½ f. | Kathryn's Doll, 2, 111 | Turf Paradise, Phoenix, Ariz. | April 9, 1967 | :50⅖ |
| | Dear Ethel, 2, 114 | Miles Park, Louisville, Ky. | July 4, 1967 | :50⅖ |
| | Scott's Poppy, 2,118 | Turf Paradise, Phoenix, Ariz. | Feb. 22, 1976 | :50⅖ |
| ⅝ mi. | Zip Pocket, 3, 122 | Turf Paradise, Phoenix, Ariz. | April 22, 1967 | :55⅖ |
| 5½ f. | Zip Pocket, 3, 129 | Turf Paradise, Phoenix, Ariz. | Nov. 19, 1967 | 1:01⅗ |
| 5¾ f. | Last Freeby, 4, 116 | Timonium, Md. | July 20, 1974 | 1:07⅕ |
| ¾ mi | Grey Papa, 6, 112 | Longacres, Seattle, Wash. | Sept. 4, 1972 | 1.07⅕ |
| 6½ f. | Best Hitter, 4, 114 | Longacres, Seattle, Wash. | Aug. 24, 1973 | 1:13⅘ |
| ⅞ mi. | Rich Cream, 5, 118 | Hollywood Park, Inglewood, Calif. | May 28, 1980 | 1:19⅖ |
| 1 mi. | Dr. Fager, 4, 134 | Arlington Park, Arlington Heights, Ill. | Aug. 24, 1968 | 1:32⅕ |
| 1 mi. 70 yd. | Aborigine, 6, 119 | Penn National, Pa. | Aug. 20, 1978 | 1:37⅕ |
| 1 1/16 mi. | Told, 4, 123 | Penn National, Pa. | Sept. 14, 1980 | 1:38 |
| 1⅛ mi. | Tentam, 4, 118 | Saratoga, Saratoga Springs, N.Y. | Aug. 10, 1973 | 1:45⅖ |
| | Secretariat, 3, 124 | Belmont Park, Elmont, N.Y. | Sept. 15, 1973 | 1:45⅖ |
| 1 3/16 mi. | Toonerville, 5, 120 | Hialeah Park, Hialeah, Fla. | Feb. 7, 1976 | 1:51⅖ |
| 1¼ mi. | Double Discount, 4, 116 | Santa Anita, Arcadia, Calif. | Oct. 9, 1977 | 1:57⅖ |
| 1 5/16 mi. | Roberto, 3, 122 | York, England | Aug. 15, 1972 | 2:07 |
| 1⅜ mi. | Cougar II, 6, 126 | Hollywood Park, Inglewood, Calif. | April 29, 1972 | 2:11 |
| 1½ mi. | Fiddle Isle, 5, 124 | Santa Anita Park, Arcadia, Calif. | Mar. 21, 1970 | 2:23 |
| | John Henry, 5, 126 | Santa Anita, Arcadia, Calif. | Mar. 16, 1980 | 2:23 |
| 1 9/16 mi. | Lone Wolf, 5, 115 | Keeneland, Lexington, Ky. | Oct. 31, 1961 | 2:37⅗ |
| 1⅝ mi. | Red Reality, 6, 113 | Saratoga, Saratoga Springs, N.Y. | Aug. 23, 1972 | 2:37⅘ |
| | Malwak, 5, 110 | Saratoga, Saratoga Springs, N.Y. | Aug. 22, 1973 | 2:37⅘ |
| 1¾ mi. | Noor, 5, 117 | Santa Anita Park, Arcadia, Calif. | March 4, 1950 | 2:52⅘ |
| 1⅞ mi. | El Moro, 8, 116 | Delaware Park, Wilmington, Del. | July 22, 1963 | 3:11⅘ |
| 2 mi. | Polazel, 3, 142 | Salisbury, England | July 8, 1924 | 3:15 |
| 2 1/16 mi. | Midafternoon, 4, 126 | Jamaica, Jamaica, N.Y. | Nov. 15, 1956 | 3:29⅗ |
| 2⅛ mi. | Ceinturion, 5, 119 | Newbury, England | Sept. 29, 1923 | 3:35 |
| 2 3/16 mi. | Santiago, 5, 112 | Narragansett Park, Pawtucket, R.I. | Sept. 27, 1941 | 3:51⅕ |
| 2¼ mi. | Dakota, 4, 116 | Lingfield, England | May 27, 1927 | 3:37⅗ |
| 2⅜ mi. | Pamroy, 4, 120 | Goodwood Park, Sussex, England | Aug. 1, 1973 | 4:10⅗ |
| 2½ mi. | Miss Grillo, 6, 118 | Pimlico, Baltimore, Md. | Nov. 12, 1948 | 4:14⅗ |
| 2⅝ mi. | Girandole, 4, 126 | Goodwood Park, Sussex, England | July 31, 1975 | 4:38⅘ |
| 2¾ mi. | Shot Put, 4, 126 | Washington Park, Homewood, Ill. | Aug. 14, 1940 | 4:48⅘ |
| 2⅞ mi. | Bosh, 5, 100 | Tijuana, Mexico | Mar. 8, 1925 | 5:23 |
| 3 mi. | Farragut, 5, 113 | Agua Caliente, Mexico | Mar. 9, 1941 | 5:15 |

# HARNESS RACING

Source: The U.S. Trotting Association

## LEADING MONEY-WINNERS

TROTTERS

| Year | Horse | Amount Won |
|---|---|---|
| 1952 | Sharp Note | $101,625 |
| 1953 | Newport Dream | 94,933 |
| 1954 | Katie Key | 84,867 |
| 1955 | Scott Frost | 186,101 |
| 1956 | Scott Frost | 85,851 |
| 1957 | Hoot Song | 114,877 |
| 1958 | Emily's Pride | 118,830 |
| 1959 | Diller Hanover | 149,897 |
| 1960 | Su Mac Lad | 159,662 |
| 1961 | Su Mac Lad | 245,750 |
| 1962 | Duke Rodney | 206,113 |
| 1963 | Speedy Scot | 244,403 |
| 1964 | Speedy Scot | 235,710 |
| 1965 | Dartmouth | 252,348 |
| 1966 | Noble Victory | 210,696 |
| 1967 | Carlisle | 231,243 |
| 1968 | Nevele Pride | 427,440 |
| 1969 | Lindy's Pride | 323,997 |
| 1970 | Fresh Yankee | 359,002 |
| 1971 | Fresh Yankee | 293,950 |
| 1972 | Super Bowl | 436,258 |
| 1973 | Spartan Hanover | 262,023 |
| 1974 | Delmonica Hanover | 252,165 |
| 1975 | Savoir | 351,385 |
| 1976 | Steve Lobell | 357,005 |
| 1977 | Green Speed | 584,405 |
| 1978 | Speedy Somolli | 362,404 |
| 1979 | Chiola Hanover | 553,058 |
| 1980 | Classical Way | 350,410 |
| 1981 | Shiaway St. Pat | 480,095 |

PACERS

| Year | Horse | Amount Won |
|---|---|---|
| 1952 | Good Time | $110,299 |
| 1953 | Keystoner | 59,131 |
| 1954 | Red Sails | 66,615 |
| 1955 | Adios Harry | 98,900 |
| 1956 | Adios Harry | 129,912 |
| 1957 | Torpid | 113,982 |
| 1958 | Belle Acton | 167,887 |
| 1959 | Bye Bye Byrd | 199,933 |
| 1960 | Bye Bye Byrd | 187,612 |
| 1961 | Adios Butler | 180,250 |
| 1962 | Henry T. Adios | 220,302 |
| 1963 | Overtrick | 208,833 |
| 1964 | Race Time | 199,292 |
| 1965 | Bret Hanover | 341,784 |
| 1966 | Bret Hanover | 407,534 |
| 1967 | Romulus Hanover | 277,636 |
| 1968 | Rum Customer | 355,618 |
| 1969 | Overcall | 373,150 |
| 1970 | Most Happy Fella | 387,239 |
| 1971 | Albatross | 558,009 |
| 1972 | Albatross | 459,921 |
| 1973 | Sir Dalrae | 307,354 |
| 1974 | Armbro Omaha | 357,146 |
| 1975 | Silk Stockings | 336,312 |
| 1976 | Keystone Ore | 539,759 |
| 1977 | Governor Skipper | 522,148 |
| 1978 | Abercrombie | 703,260 |
| 1979 | Hot Hitter | 826,542 |
| 1980 | Niatross | 1,414,313 |
| 1981 | McKinzie Almahurst | 936,418 |

## HARNESS HORSE OF THE YEAR

| Year | Horse | Gait |
|---|---|---|
| 1952 | Good Time | pacer |
| 1953 | Hi-Lo's Forbes | pacer |
| 1954 | Stenographer | trotter |
| 1955 | Scott Frost | trotter |
| 1956 | Scott Frost | trotter |
| 1957 | Torpid | pacer |
| 1958 | Emily's Pride | trotter |
| 1959 | Bye Bye Byrd | pacer |
| 1960 | Adios Butler | pacer |
| 1961 | Adios Butler | pacer |
| 1962 | Su Mac Lad | trotter |
| 1963 | Speedy Scot | trotter |
| 1964 | Bret Hanover | pacer |
| 1965 | Bret Hanover | pacer |
| 1966 | Bret Hanover | pacer |
| 1967 | Nevele Pride | trotter |
| 1968 | Nevele Pride | trotter |
| 1969 | Nevele Pride | trotter |
| 1970 | Fresh Yankee | trotter |
| 1971 | Albatross | pacer |
| 1972 | Albatross | pacer |
| 1973 | Sir Dalrae | pacer |
| 1974 | Delmonica Hanover | trotter |
| 1975 | Savoir | trotter |
| 1976 | Keystone Ore | pacer |
| 1977 | Green Speed | trotter |
| 1978 | Abercrombie | pacer |
| 1979 | Niatross | pacer |
| 1980 | Niatross | pacer |
| 1981 | Fan Hanover | pacer |

## THE HAMBLETONIAN (THREE-YEAR-OLD TROTTERS)

| Year | Purse | Winner | Second | Winning Driver | Fastest Heat |
|---|---|---|---|---|---|
| 1952 | $ 87,637 | Sharp Note | Hit Song | Bion Shively | 2:02⅗ |
| 1953 | 117,117 | Helicopter | Morse Hanover | Harry M. Harvey | 2:01⅗(a) |
| 1954 | 106,830 | Newport Dream | Princess Rodney | Adelbert Cameron | 2:02⅘ |
| 1955 | 86,863 | Scott Frost | (1) | Joe O'Brien | 2:00⅗ |
| 1956 | 100,603 | The Intruder | Valiant Rodney | Ned F. Bower | 2:01⅖ |
| 1957 | 111,126 | Hickory Smoke | Hoot Song | John F. Simpson, Sr. | 2:00⅕ |
| 1958 | 106,719 | Emily's Pride | Little Rocky | Flave T. Nipe | 1:59⅘ |
| 1959 | 125,283 | Diller Hanover | Tie Silk | Frank Ervin | 2:01⅕ |
| 1960 | 147,481 | Blaze Hanover | Quick Song | Joe O'Brien | 1:59⅗(b) |
| 1961 | 131,573 | Harlan Dean | Caleb | James W. Arthur | 1:58⅖ |
| 1962 | 116,612 | A. C.'s Viking | Isaac | Sanders Russell | 1:59⅗ |
| 1963 | 115,549 | Speedy Scot | Florlis | Ralph N. Baldwin | 1:57⅗(c) |
| 1964 | 115,281 | Ayres | Big John | John F. Simpson | 1:56⅘(R) |
| 1965 | 122,245 | Egyptian Candor | Armbro Flight | Adelbert Cameron | 2:03⅘(d) |
| 1966 | 122,540 | Kerry Way | Polaris | Frank Ervin | 1:58⅘ |
| 1967 | 122,650 | Speedy Streak | Keystone Pride | Adelbert Cameron | 2:00 |
| 1968 | 116,190 | Nevele Pride | Keystone Spartan | Stanley Dancer | 1:59⅖ |
| 1969 | 124,910 | Lindy's Pride | The Prophet | Howard Beissinger | 1:57⅗ |
| 1970 | 143,630 | Timothy T. | Formal Notice | John F. Simpson, Jr. | 1:58⅖(e) |
| 1971 | 129,770 | Speedy Crown | Savoir | Howard Beissinger | 1:57⅖ |
| 1972 | 119,090 | Super Bowl | Delmonica Hanover | Stanley Dancer | 1:56⅖(R) |
| 1973 | 144,710 | Flirth | Florinda | Ralph Baldwin | 1:57⅕ |
| 1974 | 160,150 | Christopher T. | Nevele Diamond | Wm. Haughton | 1:58⅗ |
| 1975 | 232,192 | Bonefish | Yankee Bambino | Stanley Dancer | 1:59 |
| 1976 | 263,524 | Steve Lobell | Zoot Suit | Wm. Haughton | 1:56⅖(R) |
| 1977 | 284,000 | Green Speed | Texas | Wm. Haughton | 1:55⅗(R) |
| 1978 | 241,000 | Speedy Somolli | Briscoe Hanover | Howard Beissinger | 1:55(R) |
| 1979 | 300,000 | Legend Hanover | Chiola Hanover | George Sholty | 1:56⅕ |
| 1980 | 293,570 | Burgomeister | Devil Hanover | Wm. Haughton | 1:56⅗ |
| 1981 | 419,000 | Shiaway St. Pat | Super Juan | Ray Remmen | 2:02⅕ |
| 1982 | 875,000 | Speed Bowl | Jazz Cosmos | Tom Haughton | 1:56⅘ |

(1) Galophone and Leopold Hanover divided second and third monies. (a) By Morse Hanover. (b) By Quick Song and Hoot Frost. (c) By Floris. (d) By Armbro Flight. (e) By Formal Notice. (R) Record.

## THE KENTUCKY FUTURITY

**(THREE-YEAR-OLD TROTTERS)**

| Year | Winner | Driver |
|---|---|---|
| 1953 | Kimberly Kid | Thomas S. Berry |
| 1954 | Harlan | Delvin Miller |
| 1955 | Scott Frost | Joe O'Brien |
| 1956 | Nimble Colby | Ralph N. Baldwin |
| 1957 | Cassin Hanover | Fred Egan |
| 1958 | Emily's Pride | Flave T. Nipe |
| 1959 | Diller Hanover | Ralph N. Baldwin |
| 1960 | Elaine Rodney | Clint T. Hodgins |
| 1961 | Duke Rodney | Eddie T. Wheeler |
| 1962 | Safe Mission | Joe O'Brien |
| 1963 | Speedy Scot | Ralph N. Baldwin |
| 1964 | Ayres | John F. Simpson, Sr. |
| 1965 | Armbro Flight | Joe O'Brien |
| 1966 | Governor Armbro | Joe O'Brien |
| 1967 | Speed Model | Arthur L. Hult |
| 1968 | Nevele Pride | Stanley F. Dancer |
| 1969 | Lindy's Pride | Howard Beissinger |
| 1970 | Timothy T. | John F. Simpson, Jr. |
| 1971 | Savoir | James Arthur |
| 1972 | Super Bowl | Stanley Dancer |
| 1973 | Arnie Almahurst | Joe O'Brien |
| 1974 | Waymaker | John Simpson, Jr. |
| 1975 | Noble Rogue | William Herman |
| 1976 | Quick Pay | Peter Haughton |
| 1977 | Texas | William Herman |
| 1978 | Doublemint | Peter Haughton |
| 1979 | Classical Way | John Simpson, Jr. |
| 1980 | Final Score | Tom Haughton |
| 1981 | Filet of Sole | John Simpson, Jr. |
| 1982 | Jazz Cosmos | Mickey McNichol |

## LITTLE BROWN JUG

**(THREE-YEAR-OLD PACERS)**

| Year | Winner | Driver |
|---|---|---|
| 1953 | Keystoner | Frank Ervin |
| 1954 | Adios Harry | Morris MacDonald |
| 1955 | Quick Chief | William Haughton |
| 1956 | Noble Adios | John Simpson, Sr. |
| 1957 | Torpid | John Simpson, Sr. |
| 1958 | Shadow Wave | Joe O'Brien |
| 1959 | Adios Butler | Clint Hodgins |
| 1960 | Bullet Hanover | John Simpson, Sr. |
| 1961 | Henry T. Adios | Stanley Dancer |
| 1962 | Lehigh Hanover | Stanley Dancer |
| 1963 | Overtrick | John Patterson, Sr. |
| 1964 | Vicar Hanover | William Haughton |
| 1965 | Bret Hanover | Frank Ervin |
| 1966 | Romeo Hanover | George Sholty |
| 1967 | Best of All | James Hackett |
| 1968 | Rum Customer | William Haughton |
| 1969 | Laverne Hanover | William Haughton |
| 1970 | Most Happy Fella | Stanley Dancer |
| 1971 | Nansemond | Herve Filion |
| 1972 | Strike Out | Keith Waples |
| 1973 | Melvins Woe | Joe O'Brien |
| 1974 | Armbro Omaha | William Haughton |
| 1975 | Seatrain | Ben Webster |
| 1976 | Keystone Ore | Stanley Dancer |
| 1977 | Governor Skipper | John Chapman |
| 1978 | Happy Escort | Bill Popfinger |
| 1979 | Hot Hitter | Herve Filion |
| 1980 | Niatross | Clint Galbraith |
| 1981 | Fan Hanover | Glen Garnsey |
| 1982 | Merger | John Campbell |

## WORLD HARNESS RACING RECORDS

| Age | Record | Horse | Driver | Track | Year |
|---|---|---|---|---|---|
| **TROTTERS: MILE TRACK** | | | | | |
| | 1:54⅘ | Nevele Pride | Stanley Dancer | Indianapolis, Ind. | 1969 |
| All Ages | 1:54⅘ (r) | Lindy's Crown | Howard Beissinger | DuQuoin, Ill. | 1980 |
| 2-year-old | 1:57 (r) | Briscoe Hanover | James Miller | Du Quoin, Ill. | 1977 |
| 3-year-old | 1:55 (r) | Speedy Somolli | Howard Beissinger | DuQuoin, Ill. | 1978 |
| | 1:55 (r) | Florida Pro | George Sholty | DuQuoin, Ill. | 1978 |
| 4-year-old | 1:54⅘ (r) | Lindy's Crown | Howard Beissinger | DuQuoin, Ill. | 1980 |
| **TROTTERS: FIVE-EIGHTHS MILE** | | | | | |
| All Ages | 1:57⅕ (r) | Lindy's Crown | Howard Beissinger | Wilmington, Del. | 1980 |
| 2-year-old | 1:58⅖ (r) | Mr. Drew | Jan Nordin | Wilmington, Del. | 1982 |
| 3-year-old | 1:57⅖ (r) | Arndon | Del Miller | Montreal, Que., Canada | 1982 |
| 4-year-old | 1:57⅕ (r) | Lindy's Crown | Howard Beissinger | Wilmington, Del. | 1980 |
| **TROTTERS: HALF-MILE TRACK** | | | | | |
| All Ages | 1:56⅘ (r) | Nevele Pride | Stanley Dancer | Saratoga Springs, N.Y. | 1969 |
| 2-year-old | 2:00 (r) | Incredible Nevele | Glen Garnsey | Delaware, Ohio | 1981 |
| 3-year-old | 1:58 (r) | Incredible Nevele | Glen Garnsey | Saratoga Springs, N.Y. | 1982 |
| 4-year-old | 1:56⅘ (r) | Nevele Pride | Stanley Dancer | Saratoga Springs, N.Y. | 1969 |
| **PACERS: MILE TRACK** | | | | | |
| All Ages | 1:49⅕ | Niatross | Clint Galbraith | Lexington, Ky. | 1980 |
| 2-year-old | 1:53⅘ (r) | Merger | John Campbell | Lexington, Ky. | 1981 |
| 3-year-old | 1:49⅕ | Niatross | Clint Galbraith | Lexington, Ky. | 1980 |
| 4-year-old | 1:52 | Steady Star | Joe O'Brien | Lexington, Ky. | 1971 |
| **PACERS: FIVE-EIGHTHS MILE** | | | | | |
| All Ages | 1:53⅖ (r) | Storm Damage | Joe O'Brien | Meadow Lands, Pa. | 1980 |
| 2-year-old | 1:56⅕ (r) | French Chef | Stanley Dancer | Columbus, Ohio | 1980 |
| 3-year-old | 1:53⅖ (r) | Storm Damage | Joe O'Brien | Meadow Lands, Pa. | 1980 |
| 4-year-old | 1:54⅖ (r) | Direct Scooter | Warren Cameron | Windsor, Ont. | 1980 |
| **PACERS: HALF-MILE TRACK** | | | | | |
| All Ages | 1:54⅘ (r) | Niatross | Clint Galbraith | Delaware, Ohio | 1980 |
| 2-year-old | 1:56⅕ (r) | Temujin | Clarence Martin | Louisville, Ky. | 1981 |
| 3-year-old | 1:54⅘ (r) | Niatross | Clint Galbraith | Delaware, Ohio | 1980 |
| 4-year-old | 1:55⅕ (r) | Willow Wiper | John Campbell | Freehold, N.J. | 1982 |

(r) Record made in race. Other records were set in time trials.

## HARNESS RACING DOLLAR EARNINGS (through September 9, 1982)

**Pacers, All-Time**

| Rank | Horse | Winnings |
|---|---|---|
| 1. | Niatross | $2,019,213 |
| 2. | Rambling Willie | 1,961,894 |
| 3. | McKinzie Almahurst | 1,496,596 |
| 4. | Fortune Teller | 1,313,175 |
| 5. | Albatross | 1,201,470 |
| 6. | Land Grant | 1,125,919 |
| 7. | Governor Skipper | 1,039,756 |
| 8. | Rum Customer | 1,001,548 |
| 9. | Cardigan Bay | 1,000,837 |
| 10. | Abercrombie | 984,391 |

**Trotters, All-Time**

| Rank | Horse | Winnings |
|---|---|---|
| 1. | Ideal du Gazeau | $2,538,324 |
| 2. | Bellino II | 1,960,945* |
| 3. | Un De Mai | 1,660,627* |
| 4. | Jorky | 1,537,252* |
| 5. | Eleazar | 1,465,454 |
| 6. | Savoir | 1,365,145 |
| 7. | Fresh Yankee | 1,294,252 |
| 8. | Hadol du Vivier | 1,263,121 |
| 9. | Keystone Pioneer | 1,071,927 |
| 10. | Green Speed | 953,013 |

**Drivers, All-Time**

| Rank | Driver | Winnings |
|---|---|---|
| 1. | Herve Filion | $38,391,732 |
| 2. | William Haughton | 34,734,531 |
| 3. | Carmine Abbatiello | 30,466,124 |
| 4. | Del Insko | 25,585,484 |
| 5. | Stanley Dancer | 23,302,536 |
| 6. | William Gilmour | 23,072,310 |
| 7. | John Chapman | 21,359,746 |
| 8. | Ben Webster | 20,204,628 |
| 9. | Joe O'Brien | 19,975,523 |
| 10. | Lucien Fontaine | 18,307,380 |

* Compiled by French authorities.

# BOXING

## AMATEUR BOXING CHAMPIONS

| 1982 NORTH AMERICAN CHAMPIONS | CLASS | 1982 U.S.A. BOXING FEDERATION |
|---|---|---|
| Jorge Gonalez, Cuba | Super Heavyweight (over 201 lbs.) | Tyrone Biggs, Philadelphia, Pa. |
| Willie DeWit, Canada | Heavyweight (201 lbs.) | Elmer Martin, U.S. Navy |
| Keith Vining, Detroit, Mich. | Light Heavyweight (178 lbs.) | Bennie Heard, Augusta, Ga. |
| Michael Grogan, Atlanta, Ga. | Middleweight (165 lbs.) | Michael Grogan, Atlanta, Ga. |
| Louis Howard, St. Louis, Mo. | Light Middleweight (156 lbs.) | Dennis Milton, Bronx, N.Y. |
| Roman George, Lafayette, La. | Welterweight (147 lbs.) | Mark Breland, Brooklyn, N.Y. |
| Bernardo Munoz, Cuba | Light Welterweight (139 lbs.) | Henry Hughes, Cleveland, Ohio |
| Ramon Goire, Cuba | Lightweight (132 lbs.) | Pernell Whitaker, Norfolk, Va. |
| Samuel Fuentes, Puerto Rico | Featherweight (125 lbs.) | Orlando Johnson, Chicago, Ill. |
| Rafael Cardenas, Cuba | Bantamweight (119 lbs.) | Floyd Favors, Capitol Hts., Md. |
| Steve McCrory, Detroit, Mich. | Flyweight (112 lbs.) | Steve McCrory, Detroit, Mich. |
| Rafael Sainz, Cuba | Light Flyweight (106 lbs.) | Mario Lesperance, Vallejo, Calif. |

## PROFESSIONAL BOXING CHAMPIONS To October 15, 1982

| DIVISION | WORLD BOXING ASSOCIATION (WBA) | WORLD BOXING COUNCIL (WBC) |
|---|---|---|
| Heavyweight | Mike Weaver, Los Angeles, Calif. | Larry Holmes, Easton, Pa. |
| Cruiserweight | Ossie Ocasio, Puerto Rico | S. T. Gordon, Los Angeles, Calif. |
| Light Heavyweight | Michael Spinks, Philadelphia, Pa. | Dwight Braxton, Camden, N.J. |
| Middleweight | Marvin Hagler, Brockton, Mass. | Marvin Hagler |
| Jr. Middleweight | Davey Moore, New York, N.Y. | Wilfred Benitez, Puerto Rico |
| Welterweight | Sugar Ray Leonard, Palmer Park, Md. | Sugar Ray Leonard |
| Jr. Welterweight | Aaron Pryor, Cincinnati, Ohio | Leroy Haley, Las Vegas, Nev. |
| Lightweight | Ray Mancini, Youngstown, Ohio | Alexis Arguello, Nicaragua |
| Jr. Lightweight | Sammy Serrano, Puerto Rico | Rafael Limon, Mexico |
| Featherweight | Eusebio Pedroza, Panama | Juan LaPorte, Puerto Rico |
| Jr. Featherweight | Leo Cruz, Dominican Republic | Wilfredo Gomez, Panama |
| Bantamweight | Jeff Chandler, Philadelphia, Pa. | Lupe Pintor, Mexico |
| Jr. Bantamweight | Jiro Watanabe, Japan | Chul Ho-Kim, South Korea |
| Flyweight | Santos Laciar, Argentina | Prudencio Cardona, Colombia |
| Jr. Flyweight | Katsuo Tokashiki, Japan | Hilario Zapata, Panama |

## HEAVYWEIGHT CHAMPIONSHIP FIGHTS IN WHICH TITLE CHANGED HANDS

| Date | Site | Winner Weight (age) | Citizen | Loser Weight (age) | Rounds | Referee |
|---|---|---|---|---|---|---|
| July 8, 1889[a] | Richburg, Miss. | John L. Sullivan, 198 (30) | U.S. | Jake Kilrain, 185 (30) | 75 | John Fitzpatrick |
| Sept. 7, 1892 | New Orleans | James J. Corbett, 178 (26) | U.S. | John L. Sullivan, 212 (33) | 21 | Prof. John Duffy |
| Mar. 17, 1897 | Carson City, Nev. | Bob Fitzsimmons, 167 (34) | England | James J. Corbett, 183 (30) | KO 14 | George Siler |
| June 9, 1899 | Coney Island | [b]James J. Jeffries, 206 (24) | U.S. | Bob Fitzsimmons, 167 (37) | KO 11 | George Siler |
| Feb. 23, 1906 | Los Angeles | [c]Tommy Burns, 180 (24) | Canada | Marvin Hart, 188 (29) | 20 | James J. Jeffries |
| Dec. 26, 1908 | Sydney, Australia | Jack Johnson, 196 (30) | U.S. | Tommy Burns, 176 (27) | KO 14 | Hugh McIntosh |
| April 5, 1915 | Havana, Cuba | Jess Willard, 230 (33) | U.S. | Jack Johnson, 205½ (37) | KO 26 | Jack Welch |
| July 4, 1919 | Toledo | Jack Dempsey, 187 (24) | U.S. | Jess Willard, 245 (37) | KO 3 | Ollie Pecord |
| Sept. 23, 1926 | Philadelphia | [d]Gene Tunney, 189 (28) | U.S. | Jack Dempsey, 190 (31) | 10 | Pop Reilly |
| June 12, 1930 | New York | [h]Max Schmeling, 188 (24) | Germany | Jack Sharkey, 197 (27) | 4 | Jim Crowley |
| June 21, 1932 | Long Island City | Jack Sharkey, 205 (29) | U.S. | Max Schmeling, 188 (26) | 15 | Gunboat Smith |
| June 29, 1933 | Long Island City | Primo Carnera, 260½ (26) | Italy | Jack Sharkey, 201 (30) | KO 6 | Arthur Donovan |
| June 14, 1934 | Long Island City | Max Baer, 209½ (25) | U.S. | Primo Carnera, 263¼ (27) | KO 11 | Arthur Donovan |
| June 13, 1935 | Long Island City | Jim Braddock, 193¾ (29) | U.S. | Max Baer, 209½ (26) | 15 | Jack McAvoy |
| June 22, 1937 | Chicago | Joe Louis, 197¼ (23) | U.S. | Jim Braddock, 197 (31) | KO 8 | Tommy Thomas |
| June 22, 1949 | Chicago | [e]Ezzard Charles, 181¾ (27) | U.S. | Joe Walcott, 195½ (35) | 15 | Davey Miller |
| Sept. 27, 1950 | New York | [f]Ezzard Charles, 184½ (29) | U.S. | Joe Louis, 218 (36) | 15 | Mark Conn |
| July 18, 1951 | Pittsburgh | Joe Walcott, 194 (37) | U.S. | Ezzard Charles, 182 (30) | KO 7 | Buck McTiernan |
| Sept. 23, 1952 | Philadelphia | [g]Rocky Marciano, 184 (29) | U.S. | Joe Walcott, 196 (38) | KO 13 | Charley Daggert |
| Nov. 30, 1956 | Chicago | Floyd Patterson, 182¼ (21) | U.S. | Archie Moore, 187¾ (42) | KO 5 | Frank Sikora |
| June 26, 1959 | New York | Ingemar Johansson, 196 (26) | Sweden | Floyd Patterson, 182 (24) | KO 3 | Ruby Goldstein |
| June 20, 1960 | New York | Floyd Patterson, 190 (25) | U.S. | Ingemar Johansson, 193¾ (27) | KO 5 | Arthur Mercante |
| Sept. 25, 1962 | Chicago | Sonny Liston, 214 (28) | U.S. | Floyd Patterson, 189 (27) | KO 1 | Frank Sikora |
| Feb. 25, 1964 | Miami Beach | Cassius Clay, 210 (22) | U.S. | Sonny Liston, 218 (30) | KO 7 | Barney Felix |
| March 4, 1968 | New York | [i]Joe Frazier, 204½ (24) | U.S. | Buster Mathis, 243½ (23) | KO 11 | Arthur Mercante |
| April 27, 1968 | Oakland, Calif. | [i]Jimmy Ellis, 197 (28) | U.S. | Jerry Quarry, 195 (22) | 15 | Elmer Costa |
| Feb. 16, 1970 | New York | [i]Joe Frazier, 205 (26) | U.S. | Jimmy Ellis, 201 (29) | KO 5 | Tony Perez |
| Jan. 22, 1973 | Kingston, Jamaica | George Foreman, 217½ (25) | U.S. | Joe Frazier, 214 (29) | TKO 2 | Arthur Mercante |
| Oct. 30, 1974 | Zaire, Africa | Muhammad Ali, 216 (32) | U.S. | George Foreman, 220 (25) | KO 8 | Zach Clayton |
| Feb. 15, 1978 | Las Vegas | Leon Spinks, 197½ (24) | U.S. | Muhammad Ali, 224½ (36) | 15 | David Pearl |
| Sept. 15, 1978 | New Orleans | Muhammad Ali, 221 (36) | U.S. | Leon Spinks, 201 (25) | 15 | Locien Joubert |

[a] Last bareknuckle heavyweight title fight. [b] Jim Jeffries retired in March 1905 for lack of opposition. He named Marvin Hart and Jack Root as the leading contenders; they fought on July 3, 1905, and Hart knocked out Root in the 12th round. [c] Burns claimed title after beating Hart. [d] Tunney retired in July 1928. [e] On March 1, 1949, Joe Louis retired; the NBA named Charles champion after he defeated Walcott. [f] Charles became undisputed champion by beating Louis, who had come out of retirement. [g] Marciano retired as champion in April 1956. [h] Won on a foul. [i] Immediately after a Federal Grand Jury had indicted Clay (also known as Muhammad Ali) on May 9, 1967, for refusing to accept induction into the Army, his title was vacated by the World Boxing Association and the New York State Athletic Commission. The WBA then staged an eight-man tournament, won by Ellis, to crown a successor. Frazier eventually earned recognition in New York and several other states and later defeated Ellis.

## BOXING CHAMPIONS

Source: World Boxing Association

### LIGHT HEAVYWEIGHT DIVISION

1903–05 Bob Fitzsimmons
1905–12 "Philadelphia" Jack O'Brien
1912–16 Jack Dillon
1916–20 Battling Levinsky
1920–22 Georges Carpentier
1922–23 Battling Siki
1923–25 Mike McTigue
1925–26 Paul Berlenbach
1926–27 Jack Delaney
1927 Mike McTigue
1927–29 Tommy Loughran
1930 Jimmy Slattery
1930–34 Maxie Rosenbloom
1934–35 Bob Olin
1935–39 John Henry Lewis
1939 Melio Bettina
1939–41 Billy Conn
1941 Anton Christoforidis (NBA)
1941–48 Gus Lesnevich
1948–50 Freddie Mills
1950–52 Joey Maxim
1952–61 Archie Moore
1961–63 Harold Johnson
1963–65 Willie Pastrano
1965–66 Jose Torres
1966–68 Dick Tiger
1968–71 Bob Foster
1971–72 Vicente Rondon
1972–73 Bob Foster
1973–78 Victor Galindez
1978–79 Mike Rossman (WBA)
1979 Victor Galindez (WBA)
1979–80 Marvin Johnson (WBA)
1980–81 Mustafa Muhammad (WBA)
1981– Michael Spinks (WBA)

### MIDDLEWEIGHT DIVISION

1908 Stanley Ketchel, Billy Papke
1908–10 Stanley Ketchel
1913 Frank Klaus
1913–14 George Chip
1914–17 Al McCoy
1917–20 Mike O'Dowd
1920–23 Johnny Wilson
1923–26 Harry Greb
1926 Tiger Flowers
1926–31 Mickey Walker
1931–41 Title in dispute
1941–47 Tony Zale
1947–48 Rocky Graziano
1948 Tony Zale
1948–49 Marcel Cerdan
1949–51 Jake LaMotta
1951 Ray Robinson, Randy Turpin
1951–52 Ray Robinson
1953–55 Bobo Olson
1955–57 Ray Robinson
1957 Gene Fullmer, Ray Robinson
1957–58 Carmen Basilio
1958–60 Ray Robinson
1959–62 Gene Fullmer (NBA)
1960–61 Paul Pender
1961–62 Terry Downes
1962 Paul Pender
1962–63 Dick Tiger
1963–65 Joey Giardello
1965–66 Dick Tiger
1966–67 Emile Griffith
1967 Nino Benvenuti
1967–68 Emile Griffith
1968–70 Nino Benvenuti
1970–77 Carlos Monzon
1977–78 Rodrigo Valdes
1978–79 Hugo Corro
1979–80 Vito Antuofermo
1980 Alan Minter
1980– Marvin Hagler

### WELTERWEIGHT DIVISION

1904–06 Joe Walcott
1906–07 Honey Mollody
1907–15 Mike (Twin) Sullivan
1915–19 Ted Lewis
1919–22 Jack Britton
1922–26 Mickey Walker
1926–27 Pete Latzo
1927–29 Joe Dundee
1929–30 Jackie Fields
1930 Young Jack Thompson
1930–31 Tommy Freeman
1931 Young Jack Thompson
1931–32 Lou Brouillard
1932–33 Jackie Fields
1933 Young Corbett 3d
1933–34 Jimmy McLarnin
1934 Barney Ross
1934–35 Jimmy McLarnin
1935–38 Barney Ross
1938–40 Henry Armstrong
1940–41 Fritzie Zivic
1941–46 Freddie Cochrane
1946 Marty Servo
1946–51 Ray Robinson
1951 Johnny Bratton (NBA)
1951–54 Kid Gavilan
1954–55 Johnny Saxton
1955 Tony DeMarco
1955–56 Carmen Basilio
1956 Johnny Saxton
1956–57 Carmen Basilio
1958 Virgil Akins
1958–60 Don Jordan
1960–61 Benny (Kid) Paret
1961 Emile Griffith
1961–62 Benny (Kid) Paret
1962–63 Emile Griffith
1963 Luis Rodriguez
1963–66 Emile Griffith
1966–69 Curtis Cokes
1969–70 Jose Napoles
1970–71 Billy Backus
1971–72 Jose Napoles
1972–76 Angel Espada
1976–80 Jose Cuevas (WBA)
1980–81 Thomas Hearns (WBA)
1981– Ray Leonard

### LIGHTWEIGHT DIVISION

1901–08 Joe Gans
1908–10 Battling Nelson
1910–12 Ad Wolgast
1912–14 Willie Ritchie
1914–17 Freddie Welsh
1917–25 Benny Leonard
1925 Jimmy Goodrich
1925–26 Rocky Kansas
1926–30 Sammy Mandell
1930 Al Singer
1930–33 Tony Canzoneri
1933–35 Barney Ross
1935–36 Tony Canzoneri
1936–38 Lou Ambers
1938–39 Henry Armstrong
1939–40 Lou Ambers
1940–41 Lew Jenkins
1941–42 Sammy Angott
1943–47 Title holders, according to the N.Y. Commission, were Beau Jack and Bob Montgomery, and according to the NBA, Sammy Angott, Juan Zurita, and Ike Williams.
1947–51 Ike Williams
1951–52 Jimmy Carter
1952 Lauro Salas
1952–54 Jimmy Carter
1954 Paddy DeMarco
1954–55 Jimmy Carter
1955–56 Wallace (Bud) Smith
1956–62 Joe Brown
1962–65 Carlos Ortiz
1965 Ismael Laguna
1965–68 Carlos Ortiz
1968–69 Carlos (Teo) Cruz
1969–70 Mando Ramos
1970 Ismael Laguna
1970–71 Ken Buchanan
1971–72 Mando Ramos
1972–73 Chango Carmona
1973–78 Roberto Duran
1979–80 Ernesto Espana (WBA)
1980–81 Hilmer Kenty (WBA)
1981 Sean O'Grady (WBA)
1981 Claude Noel (WBA)
1981–82 Arturo Frias (WBA)
1982– Ray Mancini (WBA)

### FEATHERWEIGHT DIVISION

1912–23 Johnny Kilbane
1923 Eugene Criqui
1923–25 Johnny Dundee
1926–27 Louis (Kid) Kaplan
1927–28 Benny Bass
1928 Tony Canzoneri
1928–29 Andre Routis
1929–32 Battling Battalino
1932 Tommy Paul (NBA)
1932 Kid Chocolate (NY)
1933–36 Freddie Miller
1936–37 Petey Sarron
1937–38 Henry Armstrong
1938–40 Joey Archibald
1940–41 Harry Jeffra
1941 Joey Archibald
1941–42 Chalky Wright
1942–48 Willie Pep
1948–49 Sandy Saddler
1949–50 Willie Pep
1950–57 Sandy Saddler
1957–59 Kid Bassey
1959–63 Davey Moore
1963–64 Sugar Ramos
1964–67 Vicente Saldivar
1968 Raul Rojas, Sho Saiyo
1969 Johnny Famechon
1969–70 Vicente Saldivar
1970–71 Kuniaki Shibata
1971–72 Clemente Sanchez
1972–74 Ernesto Marcell
1974–77 Alexis Arguello
1977 Rafael Ortega
1977–78 Celio Lastra
1978– Eusebio Pedroza (WBA)

### BANTAMWEIGHT DIVISION

1936 Tony Marino
1936–37 Sixto Escobar
1937–38 Harry Jeffra
1938–40 Sixto Escobar
1940–42 Lou Salica
1942–47 Manuel Ortiz
1947 Harold Dade
1947–50 Manuel Ortiz
1950–52 Vic Toweel
1952–54 Jimmy Carruthers
1954–56 Robert Cohen
1956–57 Mario D'Agata
1957–59 Alphonse Halimi
1959–60 Joe Becerra
1961–65 Eder Jofre
1965–68 Masahiko (Fighting) Harada
1968–69 Lionel Rose
1969–70 Ruben Olivares
1970–71 Chucho Castillo
1971–72 Ruben Olivares
1972–73 Enrique Pinder
1973–74 Arnold Taylor
1974–77 Alfonso Zamora
1977–80 Jorge Lujan (WBA)
1980 Julian Solis (WBA)
1980– Jeff Chandler (WBA)

### FLYWEIGHT DIVISION

1938–43 Peter Kane
1943–48 Jackie Paterson
1948–50 Rinty Monaghan
1950 Terry Allen
1950–52 Dado Marino
1952–54 Yoshio Shirai
1954–60 Pascual Perez
1960–62 Pone Kingpetch
1962–63 Masahiko (Fighting) Harada
1963 Pone Kingpetch
1963–64 Hiroyuki Ebihara
1964–65 Pone Kingpetch
1965–66 Salvatore Burruni
1966 Horacio Accavallo
1966 Walter McGowan
1966–69 Chartchai Choinoi
1969 Hiroyuki Ebihara
1969–70 Bernabe Villacampo
1970 Berkrek Chartvanchai
1970–71 Masao Ohba
1971–72 Bertulio Gonzales
1972–73 Masao Ohba
1973–74 Chatchai Chionoi
1974–75 Erbito Salavarria
1976 Alfonso Lopez
1976–78 Gutty Espadas
1978–79 Betulio Gonzalez (WBA)
1979–80 Luis Ibarra (WBA)
1980 Kim Tae-Shik (WBA)
1980–81 Peter Mathebula (WBA)
1981 Santos Laciar (WBA)
1981 Luis Ibarra (WBA)
1981–82 Juan Herrera (WBA)
1982 Santos Laciar (WBA)

# TRACK AND FIELD

## 1982 NCAA INDOOR CHAMPIONS

**60-Yard Dash—** Rod Richardson, Texas A & M, 6.07
**440-Yard Dash—** Anthony Ketchum, Houston, 47.47
**600-Yard Run—** Eugene Sanders, Miss. Valley, 1:08.51
**880-Yard Run—** David Patrick, Tennessee, 1:49.94
**1,000-Yard Run—** John Stephens, Arkansas, 2:07.37
**One-Mile Run—** Suleiman Nyambui, Texas-El Paso, 4:00.65
**Two-Mile Run—** Suleiman Nyambui, Texas-El Paso, 8:38.91
**Three-Mile Run—** Gabriel Kamau, Texas-El Paso, 13:07.81
**60-Yard Hurdles—** Tony Campbell, USC, 7.14
**One-Mile Relay—** Oklahoma, 3:11.07
**Two-Mile Relay—** Richmond, 7:24.48
**Distance Medley Relay—** Georgetown, 9:45.97
**High Jump—** Leo Williams, Navy, 7′ 5¾″
**Long Jump—** Gilbert Smith, Texas-Arlington, 26′ 1″
**Triple Jump—** Keith Connor, SMU, 55′ 3″
**Pole Vault—** Doug Lytle, Kansas State, 17′ 9¾″
**Weight Throw—** Tore Johnson, Texas-El Paso, 70′ 3¼″
**Shot Put—** Mike Lehmann, Illinois, 67′ 7¾″
**Team—** Texas-El Paso

## 1982 NAIA INDOOR CHAMPIONS

**MEN'S EVENTS**
**60-Yard Dash—** Freddie Johnson, Hampton Inst., 6.18
**440-Yard Dash—** Kevin Jones, Northwood Inst., 48.27
**600-Yard Run—** Eugene Sanders, Miss. Valley, 1:11.66
**880-Yard Run—** Joel Ngetich, Wayland Baptist, 1:52.03
**1,000-Yard Run—** Joel Ngetich, Wayland Baptist, 2:11.02
**One-Mile Run—** Kregg Einspahr, Concordia, 4:06.34
**Two-Mile Run—** Pat Porter, Adams State, 8:51.13
**Three-Mile Run—** Jerrold Wynia, Dordt, 13:57.88
**Two-Mile Walk—** Tom Edwards, Wis.-Parkside, 13:32.71
**60-Yard Hurdles—** Steve Parker, Abilene Christian, 7.19
**One-Mile Relay—** Mississippi Valley, 3:17.22
**Two-Mile Relay—** Doane, 7:48.58
**Distance Medley Relay—** Central State, 10:12.73
**High Jump—** Mark Norman, Northwood Inst., 7′ 2¾″
**Long Jump—** James Palmer, Texas Southern, 23′ 11¾″
**Triple Jump—** Britt Courville, Texas Southern, 52′ 2″
**Pole Vault—** Billy Olson, Abilene Christian, 18′ 10″
**Weight Throw—** Doug Barnett, Azusa Pacific, 65′ 2¾″
**Shot Put—** Doug Barnett, Azusa Pacific, 57′ 6¾″
**Team—** Saginaw Valley

**WOMEN'S EVENTS**
**60-Yard Dash—** Katherine Wallace, Texas Southern, 6.87
**440-Yard Dash—** Loretta Edwards, Prairie View A & M, 57.32
**600-Yard Run—** Easter Gabriel, Prairie View A & M, 1:23.97
**880-Yard Run—** Cathy Schmidt, Saginaw Valley, 2:18.95
**1,000-Yard Run—** Cathy Schmidt, Saginaw Valley, 2:39.83
**One-Mile Run—** Debbie Spino, Wis.-Parkside, 5:11.46
**Two-Mile Run—** Angie Pikschus, Ozarks, 10:40.47
**60-Yard Hurdles—** Linda Weekly, Texas Southern, 7.96
**One-Mile Relay—** Prairie View A & M, 3:47.23
**Two-Mile Relay—** Texas Southern, 9:19.17
**Distance Medley Relay—** Texas Southern, 12:41.01
**High Jump—** Paula Benne, Mid-Amer. Nazarene, 5′ 5″
**Long Jump—** Thomasina Busch, Hampton Inst., 19′ 4¾″
**Shot Put—** Karen Waddell, Prairie View A & M, 47′ 10¼″
**Team—** Texas Southern

## 1982 U.S. INDOOR CHAMPIONS

**MEN'S EVENTS**
**60-Yard Dash—** Ron Brown, Arizona State, 6.14
**440-Yard Dash—** Walter McCoy, Athletic Attic, 48.24
**600-Yard Run—** Fred Sowerby, D.C. International, 1:09.50
**1,000-Yard Run—** Don Paige, Athletic Attic, 2:05.81
**One-Mile Run—** Jim Spivey, Indiana, 3:57.04
**Three-Mile Run—** Paul Cummings, New Balance T.C., 13:00.52
**Two-Mile Walk—** Jim Heiring, Athletic Attic, 12:24.82
**60-Yard Hurdles—** Tonie Campbell, unattached, 7.13
**One-Mile Relay—** Morgan State, 3:13.46
**Two-Mile Relay—** Richmond, 7:28.14
**Sprint Medley Relay—** Athletic Attic, 2:03.98
**High Jump—** Dwight Stones, Pacific Coast Club, 7′ 4½″
**Long Jump—** Carl Lewis, unattached, 28′ ¾″
**Triple Jump—** Keith Connor, SMU, 55′ 11″
**Pole Vault—** Billy Olson, Pacific Coast Club, 18′ 6½″
**Weight Throw—** Ed Kania, Pacific Coast Club, 70′ ½″
**Shot Put—** Jeff Brown, U. of Chicago T.C., 65′ 10½″
**Team—** Athletic Attic

**WOMEN'S EVENTS**
**60-Yard Dash—** Evelyn Ashford, Medalist T.C., 6.54
**220-Yard Dash—** Chandra Cheeseborough, Tenn. St., 23.46
**440-Yard Dash—** Maxine Underwood, Boston Int'l T.C., 54.55
**880-Yard Run—** Leann Warren, Oregon, 2:04.61
**One-Mile Run—** Cathie Twomey, Athletics West, 4:32.92
**Two-Mile Run—** Joan Hansen, Athletics West, 9:37.03
**One-Mile Walk—** Sue Brodock, So. Calif. Road Runners, 7:07.14
**60-Yard Hurdles—** Stephanie Hightower, L.A. Naturite T.C., 7.38
**640-Yard Relay** Tennessee State, 1:09.36
**One-Mile Relay—** Atoms Track Club, 3:40.54
**Sprint Medley Relay—** Tennessee State, 1:44.26
**High Jump—** Coleen Rienstra-Sommer, Wilt's A.C., 6′ 3¼″
**Long Jump—** Veronica Bell, So. Calif. Cheetahs, 21′ 11¾″
**Shot Put—** Marita Walton, Maryland, 55′ 11¾″
**Team—** Tennessee State

## 1982 U.S.A./MOBIL INDOOR GRAND PRIX FINAL STANDINGS

**MEN'S EVENTS**
**60-Yard Dash—** Ron Brown, Arizona State
**440-Yard Dash—** Bert Cameron, Texas-El Paso
**600-Yard Run—** Fred Sowerby, D.C. International
**1,000-Yard Run—** Don Paige, Athletic Attic
**One-Mile Run—** Ray Flynn, New Balance T.C.
**Three-Mile Run—** Doug Padilla, Athletics West
**Two-Mile Walk—** Jim Heiring, Athletic Attic
**60-Yard Hurdles—** Renaldo Nehemiah, Athletic Attic
**High Jump—** Dwight Stones, Pacific Coast Club
**Long Jump—** Carl Lewis, unattached
**Triple Jump—** Willie Banks, Athletics West
**Pole Vault—** Billy Olson, Pacific Coast Club
**Weight Throw—** Ed Kania, Pacific Coast Club
**Shot Put—** Jeff Braun, U. of Chicago T.C.-Dave Laut, Athletics West
**Overall Champion—** Billy Olson, Pacific Coast Club

**WOMEN'S EVENTS**
**60-Yard Dash—** Evelyn Ashford, Medalist T.C.
**220-Yard Dash—** Chandra Cheeseborough, Tenn. St.
**440-Yard Dash—** Gwen Gardner, L.A. Mercurettes
**880-Yard Run—** Leann Warren, Oregon-Delisa Walton, Tennessee
**One-Mile Run—** Mary Decker Tabb, Athletics West
**Two-Mile Run—** Joan Hansen, Athletics West
**One-Mile Walk—** Sue Brodock, So. Calif. Road Runners
**60-Yard Hurdles—** Stephanie Hightower, L.A. Naturite T.C.
**High Jump—** Debbie Brill, Pacific Coast Club
**Long Jump—** Veronica Bell, So. Calif. Cheetahs
**Shot Put—** Marita Walton, Maryland
**Overall Champion—** Mary Decker Tabb, Athletics West

## 1982 NCAA OUTDOOR CHAMPIONS (DIVISION I)

**MEN'S EVENTS**

|  |  |
|---|---|
| **100-Meter Dash—** | Stanley Floyd, Houston, 10.03 |
| **200-Meter Dash—** | James Butler, Oklahoma State, 20.07 |
| **400-Meter Dash—** | Kasheef Hassan, Oregon State, 45.47 |
| **800-Meter Run—** | David Mack, Oregon, 1:48.00 |
| **1,500-Meter Run—** | Jim Spivey, Indiana, 3:45.42 |
| **5,000-Meter Run—** | Suleiman Nyambui, Texas-El Paso, 13:54.09 |
| **10,000-Meter Run—** | Suleiman Nyambui, Texas-El Paso, 29:03.54 |
| **3,000-Meter Steeplechase—** | Richard Tuwei, Washington State, 8:42.73 |
| **110-Meter Hurdles—** | Milan Stewart, USC, 13.53 |
| **400-Meter Hurdles—** | David Patrick, Tennessee, 48.44 |
| **400-Meter Relay—** | Houston, 38.53 |
| **1,600-Meter Relay—** | Mississippi State, 3:03.49 |
| **High Jump—** | Milt Ottey, Texas-El Paso, 7′ 7¼″ |
| **Long Jump—** | Vance Johnson, Arizona, 26′ 11¼″ |
| **Triple Jump—** | Keith Connor, SMU, 57′ 7¾″ |
| **Pole Vault—** | Dave Kenworthy, USC, 17′ 11¾″ |
| **Discus Throw—** | Dean Crouser, Oregon, 207′ 4″ |
| **Hammer Throw—** | Richard Olsen, SMU, 204′ 6″ |
| **Javelin Throw—** | Brian Crouser, Oregon, 274′ 7″ |
| **Shot Put—** | Dean Crouser, Oregon, 68′ 4¼″ |
| **Decathlon—** | Trond Skramstad, Mt. St. Mary's, 7,770 pts. |
| **Team—** | Texas-El Paso |
| **Division II Team—** | Abilene Christian |
| **Division III Team—** | Glassboro State |

**WOMEN'S EVENTS**

|  |  |
|---|---|
| **100-Meter Dash—** | Merlene Ottey, Nebraska, 10.97 |
| **200-Meter Dash—** | Florence Griffith, UCLA, 22.39 |
| **400-Meter Dash—** | Marita Payne, Florida State, 52.01 |
| **800-Meter Run—** | Delisa Walton, Tennessee, 2:05.22 |
| **1,500-Meter Run—** | Leann Warren, Oregon, 4:17.90 |
| **3,000-Meter Run—** | Ceci Hopp, Stanford, 9:28.92 |
| **5,000-Meter Run—** | Kathy Bryant, Tennessee, 16:10.41 |
| **10,000-Meter Run—** | Kim Schnurpfeil, Stanford, 33:36.51 |
| **100-Meter Hurdles—** | Benita Fitzgerald, Tennessee, 13.13 |
| **400-Meter Hurdles—** | Tonja Brown, Florida State, 56.46 |
| **400-Meter Relay—** | Nebraska, 43.72 |
| **1,600-Meter Relay—** | Tennessee, 3:28.55 |
| **High Jump—** | Disa Gisladottir, Alabama, 6′ 1¼″ |
| **Long Jump—** | Jennifer Innis, Los Angeles State, 21′ 9½″ |
| **Discus Throw—** | Meg Ritchie, Arizona, 202′ |
| **Javelin Throw—** | Karen Smith, Calif. Poly.-SLO, 206′ 8″ |
| **Shot Put—** | Meg Ritchie, Arizona, 55′ 5¼″ |
| **Heptathlon—** | Jackie Joyner, UCLA, 6,099 pts. |
| **Team—** | UCLA |
| **Division II Team—** | Calif. Poly.-San Luis Obispo |
| **Division III Team—** | Central (Iowa) |

## 1982 NAIA OUTDOOR CHAMPIONS

**MEN'S EVENTS**

|  |  |
|---|---|
| **100-Meter Dash—** | Innocent Egbinike, Azusa Pacific, 10.32 |
| **200-Meter Dash—** | Darrell Green, Texas A & I, 20.84 |
| **400-Meter Dash—** | Eugene Sanders, Miss. Valley, 46.02 |
| **800-Meter Run—** | Joel Ngetich, Wayland Baptist, 1:47.77 |
| **1,500-Meter Run—** | Mike Duran, Southern Colorado, 3:46.46 |
| **5,000-Meter Run—** | Garry Henry, Pembroke State, 14:13.05 |
| **10,000-Meter Run—** | Garry Henry, Pembroke State, 29:30.76 |
| **Marathon—** | Todd Sperling, Wisconsin-Superior, 2:21:38.53 |
| **3,000-Meter Steeplechase—** | Kregg Einspahr, Concordia, 8:51.74 |
| **10,000-Meter Walk—** | Mel McGinnis, Spring Arbor, 45:09.69 |
| **110-Meter Hurdles—** | Robert Thomas, Prairie View, 13.99 |
| **400-Meter Hurdles—** | Ed Brown, Saginaw Valley, 50.36 |
| **400-Meter Relay—** | Abilene Christian, 40.03 |
| **1,600-Meter Relay—** | Saginaw Valley, 3:11.39 |
| **High Jump—** | Carl Garcia, Prairie View, 7′ 1″ |
| **Long Jump—** | Greg Johnson, Abilene Christian, 24′ 5½″ |
| **Triple Jump—** | David McFadgen, Virginia State, 53′ 1½″ |
| **Pole Vault—** | Billy Olson, Abilene Christian, 18′ 3″ |
| **Discus Throw—** | Roger Axelsson, Point Loma, 183′ 9″ |
| **Hammer Throw—** | Doug Barnett, Azusa Pacific, 225′ 10″ |
| **Javelin Throw—** | Mike Barnett, Azusa Pacific, 255′ 8″ |
| **Shot Put—** | Mike Manders, Hamline, 61′ ¼″ |
| **Decathlon—** | Greg Culp, Arkansas-Monticello, 7,304 pts. |
| **Team—** | Abilene Christian (Texas) |

**WOMEN'S EVENTS**

|  |  |
|---|---|
| **100-Meter Dash—** | Cassandra Graham, Prairie View, 11.82 |
| **200-Meter Dash—** | Cassandra Graham, Prairie View, 24.03 |
| **400-Meter Dash—** | Easter Gabriel, Prairie View, 52.53 |
| **800-Meter Run—** | Denise Day, Midland, 2:12.61 |
| **1,500-Meter Run—** | Debbie Spino, Wisconsin-Parkside, 4:35.47 |
| **3,000-Meter Run—** | Mary Jaqua, Adams State, 10:04.15 |
| **5,000-Meter Run—** | Mary Jaqua, Adams State, 16:56.97 |
| **Marathon—** | Liz Garman, Azusa Pacific, 3:03:00.43 |
| **100-Meter Hurdles—** | Thomasina Busch, Hampton Inst., 14.28 |
| **400-Meter Hurdles—** | Margaret Gamble, Prairie View, 59.30 |
| **400-Meter Relay—** | Prairie View, 45.25 |
| **1,600-Meter Relay—** | Prairie View, 3:37.82 |
| **3,200-Meter Relay—** | Midland, 9:08.67 |
| **Medley Relay—** | Prairie View, 1:39.32 |
| **High Jump—** | Lori Shepard, Taylor, 5′ 6″ |
| **Long Jump—** | Yvonne Taylor, Southern Colorado, 19′ 2¼″ |
| **Discus Throw—** | Lynette Antoine, St. Augustine's, 151′ 7″ |
| **Javelin Throw—** | Carol Woodside, Hampton Inst., 145′ 7″ |
| **Shot Put—** | Karen Waddell, Prairie View, 47′ 1½″ |
| **Team—** | Prairie View (Texas) |

## 1982 U.S. OUTDOOR CHAMPIONS

**MEN'S EVENTS**

|  |  |
|---|---|
| **100-Meter Dash—** | Carl Lewis, Santa Monica T.C., 10.11 |
| **200-Meter Dash—** | Calvin Smith, Athletic Attic, 20.47 |
| **400-Meter Dash—** | Cliff Wiley, unattached, 45.05 |
| **800-Meter Run—** | James Robinson, Inner City A.C., 1:46.12 |
| **1,500-Meter Run—** | Steve Scott, Sub 4 T.C., 3:34.92 |
| **5,000-Meter Run—** | Matt Centrowitz, New York A.C., 13:31.96 |
| **10,000-Meter Run—** | Craig Virgin, Front Runner T.C., 28:33.02 |
| **3,000-Meter Steeplechase—** | Henry Marsh, Athletics West, 8:22.94 |
| **20,000-Meter Walk—** | Jim Heiring, Athletic Attic, 1:30:21.3 |
| **110-Meter Hurdles—** | Willie Gault, Athletic Attic, 13.54 |
| **400-Meter Hurdles—** | David Patrick, Athletics West, 48.57 |
| **High Jump—** | Milt Ottey, Phila. Pioneers, 7′ 5¾″ |
| **Long Jump—** | Carl Lewis, Santa Monica T.C., 27′ 10″ |
| **Triple Jump—** | Robert Cannon, Athletic Attic, 55′ ¾″ |
| **Pole Vault—** | (tie) Dan Ripley-Billy Olson, Pacific Coast Club, 18′ 9¼″ |
| **Discus Throw—** | Louis Delis, Cuba, 225′ 5″ |
| **Hammer Throw—** | David McKenzie, unattached, 235′ 2″ |
| **Javelin Throw—** | Bob Roggy, Athletics West, 289′ 9″ |
| **Shot Put—** | Kevin Akins, unattached, 69′ 9½″ |
| **Decathlon—** | John Crist, Athletics West, 8,087 pts. |

**WOMEN'S EVENTS**

|  |  |
|---|---|
| **100-Meter Dash—** | Evelyn Ashford, Medalist T.C., 10.96 |
| **200-Meter Dash—** | Merlene Ottey, L.A. Naturites, 22.17 |
| **400-Meter Dash—** | Denean Howard, L.A. Naturites, 50.87 |
| **800-Meter Run—** | Delisa Walton, L.A. Naturites, 2:00.91 |
| **1,500-Meter Run—** | Mary Decker Tabb, Athletics West, 4:03.37 |
| **3,000-Meter Run—** | Francie Larrieu Smith, New Balance T.C., 8:58.66 |
| **10,000-Meter Run—** | Kim Schnurpfeil, Stanford T.C., 33:25.88 |
| **5,000-Meter Walk—** | Susan Liers Westerfield, Island T.C., 24:56.6 |
| **100-Meter Hurdles—** | Stephanie Hightower, L.A. Naturites, 12.86 |
| **400-Meter Hurdles—** | Tammy Etienne, Metroplex Striders, 56.55 |
| **400-Meter Relay—** | Wilt's A.C., 43.45 |
| **1,600-Meter Relay—** | L.A. Naturites, 3:28.68 |
| **3,200-Meter Relay—** | Stanford T.C., 8:22.26 |
| **800-Meter Medley Relay—** | Wilt's A.C., 1:36.79 |
| **High Jump—** | Debbie Brill, Pacific Coast Club, 6′ 4¾″ |
| **Long Jump—** | Carol Lewis, Santa Monica T.C., 22′ 4¼″ |
| **Discus Throw—** | Ria Stalman, L.A. Naturites, 203′ 10″ |
| **Javelin Throw—** | Lynda Hughes, Oregon, 202′ 3″ |
| **Shot Put—** | Maria Saria, Cuba, 61′ 8¼″ |
| **Heptathlon—** | Jackie Joyner, Wilt's A.C., 6,041 pts. |

## AMERICAN TRACK AND FIELD RECORDS

| Men's Event | Time/Distance | Name/Site | Date |
|---|---|---|---|
| 100-Meter Dash | 9.95 sec. | Jim Hines, Mexico City | Oct. 1968 |
| 200-Meter Dash | 19.83 sec. | Tommie Smith, Mexico City | Oct. 1968 |
| 400-Meter Dash | 43.86 sec. | Lee Evans, Mexico City | Oct. 1968 |
| 800-Meter Run | 1 min., 43.9 sec. | Rick Wohlhuter, Los Angeles, Calif. | June 1974 |
| 1,000-Meter Run | 2 min., 13.9 sec. | Rick Wohlhuter, Oslo, Norway | July 1974 |
| 1,500-Meter Run | 3 min., 33.1 sec. | Jim Ryun, Los Angeles, Calif. | July 1967 |
| One-Mile Run | 3 min., 47.69 sec. | Steve Scott, Oslo, Norway | July 1982 |
| 2,000-Meter Run | 5 min., 1.4 sec. | Steve Prefontaine, Coos Bay, Ore. | May 1975 |
| 3,000-Meter Run | 7 min., 36.69 sec. | Steve Scott, Ingleheim, W. Germany | Sept. 1981 |
| 5,000-Meter Run | 13 min., 11.93 sec. | Alberto Salazar, Stockholm, Sweden | July 1982 |
| 10,000-Meter Run | 27 min., 25.61 sec. | Alberto Salazar, Oslo, Norway | June 1982 |
| 20,000-Meter Run | 58 min., 37.46 sec. | Herb Lindsay, Manchester, Vt. | Sept. 1981 |
| 25,000-Meter Run | 1 hr., 14 min., 9 sec. | Herb Lindsay, Michigan | May 1981 |
| 30,000-Meter Run | 1 hr., 29 min., 4 sec. | Bill Rodgers, New York, N.Y. | Mar. 1976 |
| Marathon | 2 hr., 8 min., 13 sec. | Alberto Salazar, New York, N.Y. | Oct. 1981 |
| 20-Kilometer Walk | 1 hr., 30 min., 10 sec. | Larry Young, Columbia, Mo. | May 1972 |
| 30-Kilometer Walk | 2 hr., 23 min., 14 sec. | Goetz Klopfer, Seattle, Wash. | Nov. 1970 |
| 50-Kilometer Walk | 4 hr., 13 min., 36 sec. | Bob Kitchen, San Francisco, Calif | Feb. 1972 |
| 110-Meter Hurdles | 12.93 sec. | Renaldo Nehemiah, Zurich, Switz. | Aug. 1981 |
| 400-Meter Hurdles | 47.13 sec. | Edwin Moses, Milan, Italy | July 1980 |
| 3000-Meter Steeplechase | 8 min., 15.68 sec. | Henry Marsh, Eugene, Ore. | June 1980 |
| 4 X 100-Meter Relay | 38.03 sec. | World Cup Team, Dusseldorf, W. Ger. | Sept. 1977 |
| 4 X 200-Meter Relay | 1 min., 20.26 sec. | Southern California, Tempe, Ariz. | May 1978 |
| 4 X 400-Meter Relay | 2 min., 56.16 sec. | Olympic Team, Mexico City | Oct. 1968 |
| 4 X 800-Meter Relay | 7 min., 10.4 sec. | Univ. of Chicago T.C., Durham, N.C. | May 1973 |
| 4 X 1,500-Meter Relay | 14 min., 46.3 sec. | National Team, Bourges, France | June 1979 |
| Sprint Medley Relay (Mile) | 3 min., 13.39 sec. | Oklahoma, Des Moines, Iowa | Apr. 1981 |
| Distance Medley Relay (2½ Mi.) | 9 min., 24.09 sec. | Georgetown, Philadelphia, Pa. | Apr. 1980 |
| High Jump | 2.32 m (7′7¼″) | Del Davis, Provo, Utah | June 1982 |
| Long Jump | 8.90 m (29′2½″) | Bob Beamon, Mexico City | Oct. 1968 |
| Triple Jump | 17.56 m (57′7½″) | Willie Banks, Sacramento, Calif. | June 1981 |
| Pole Vault | 5.74 m (18′10″) | Dave Volz, Nice, France | Aug. 1982 |
| Shot Put | 22.02 m (72′3″) | Brian Oldfield, Modesto, Calif. | May 1981 |
| | | David Laut, Koblenz, W. Germany | Aug. 1982 |
| Discus Throw | 71.19 m (233′7″) | Ben Plucknett, Modesto, Calif. | May 1981 |
| Hammer Throw | 74.34 m (243′11″) | David McKenzie, Durham, N.C. | June 1982 |
| Javelin Throw | 95.78 m (314′3″) | Bob Roggy, Stuttgart, W. Germany | Aug. 1982 |
| Decathlon | 8,617 points | Bruce Jenner, Montreal, Canada | July 1976 |

| Women's Event | Time/Distance | Name/Site | Date |
|---|---|---|---|
| 100-Meter Dash | 10.90 sec. | Evelyn Ashford, Colorado Sprs., Colo. | July 1981 |
| 200-Meter Dash | 21.83 sec. | Evelyn Ashford, Montreal, Canada | Aug. 1979 |
| 400-Meter Dash | 50.62 sec. | Rosalyn Bryant, Montreal, Canada | July 1976 |
| 800-Meter Run | 1 min., 57.90 sec. | Madeline Jackson, College Park, Md. | Aug. 1976 |
| 1,000-Meter Run | 2 min., 37.3 sec. | Madeline Jackson, Montreal, Canada | July 1976 |
| 1,500-Meter Run | 3 min., 59.43 sec. | Mary Decker, Zurich, Switz. | Aug. 1980 |
| 2,000-Meter Run | 5 min., 47.5 sec. | Francie Larrieu, Montreal, Canada | July 1976 |
| One-Mile Run | 4 min., 18.08 sec. | Mary Decker Tabb, Paris, France | July 1982 |
| 3,000-Meter Run | 8 min., 29.71 sec. | Mary Decker Tabb, Oslo, Norway | July 1982 |
| 5,000-Meter Run | 15 min., 8.26 sec. | Mary Decker Tabb, Eugene, Ore. | June 1982 |
| 10,000-Meter Run | 31 min., 35.3 sec. | Mary Decker Tabb, Eugene, Ore. | July 1982 |
| Marathon | 2 hr., 27 min., 51 sec. | Patti Lyons-Catalano, Boston, Mass. | Apr. 1981 |
| 5-Kilometer Walk | 23 min., 19.1 sec. | Sue Brodock, Walnut, Calif. | June 1980 |
| 10-Kilometer Walk | 50 min., 32.6 sec. | Sue Brodock, Walnut, Calif. | June 1979 |
| 100-Meter Hurdles | 12.80 sec. | Stephanie Hightower, K. Marx-Stadt, E. Germany | July 1982 |
| 400-Meter Hurdles | 56.16 sec. | Esther Mahr, Sittard, Neth. | Aug. 1980 |
| 4 X 100-Meter Relay | 42.47 sec. | National Team, K. Marx-Stadt, E. Germany | July 1982 |
| 4 X 200-Meter Relay | 1 min., 32.6 sec. | National Team, Bourges, France | June 1979 |
| 4 X 400-Meter Relay | 3 min., 22.8 sec. | Olympic Team, Montreal, Canada | July 1976 |
| 4 X 800-Meter Relay | 8 min., 19.9 sec. | National Team, Bourges, France | June 1979 |
| 800-Meter Medley Relay | 1 min., 36.79 sec. | Wilt's A.C., Knoxville, Tenn. | June 1982 |
| High Jump | 1.98 m (6′6″) | Coleen Sommer, Durham, N.C. | June 1982 |
| Long Jump | 7.00 m (22′11½″) | Jodi Anderson, Eugene, Ore. | June 1980 |
| Shot Put | 19.09 m (62′7¾″) | Maren Seidler, Walnut, Calif. | June 1979 |
| Discus Throw | 63.22 m (207′5″) | Lorna Griffin, Long Beach, Calif. | May 1980 |
| Javelin Throw | 69.32 m (227′5″) | Kate Schmidt, Fuerth, W. Ger. | Sept. 1977 |
| Pentathlon | 4,708 points | Jane Frederick, Gotzis, Austria | May 1979 |
| Heptathlon | 6,458 points | Jane Frederick, Santa Barbara, Calif. | July 1982 |

## WORLD TRACK AND FIELD RECORDS

| Men's Event | Time/Distance | Name (Country) | Date |
|---|---|---|---|
| 100–Meter Dash | 9.95 sec. | Jim Hines (United States) | Oct. 1968 |
| 200–Meter Dash | 19.83 sec. | Tommie Smith (United States) | Oct. 1968 |
| 400–Meter Dash | 43.86 sec. | Lee Evans (United States) | Oct. 1968 |
| 800–Meter Run | 1 min., 41.72 sec. | Sebastian Coe (United Kingdom) | June 1981 |
| 1,000–Meter Run | 2 min., 12.18 sec. | Sebastian Coe (United Kingdom) | July 1981 |
| 1,500–Meter Run | 3 min., 31.36 sec. | Steve Ovett (United Kingdom) | Aug. 1980 |
| One–Mile Run | 3 min., 47.33 sec. | Sebastian Coe (United Kingdom) | Aug. 1981 |
| 2,000–Meter Run | 4 min., 51.4 sec. | John Walker (New Zealand) | June 1976 |
| 3,000–Meter Run | 7 min., 32.1 sec. | Henry Rono (Kenya) | June 1978 |
| 5,000–Meter Run | 13 min., 00.42 sec. | David Moorcroft (United Kingdom) | July 1982 |
| 10,000–Meter Run | 27 min., 22.4 sec. | Henry Rono (Kenya) | June 1978 |
| 20,000–Meter Run | 57 min., 24.2 sec. | Jos Hermens (Netherlands) | May 1976 |
| 25,000–Meter Run | 1 hr., 13 min., 55.8 sec. | Toshihiko Seko (Japan) | March 1981 |
| 30,000–Meter Run | 1 hr., 29 min., 18.8 sec. | Toshihiko Seko (Japan) | March 1981 |
| Marathon | 2 hr., 8 min., 34 sec. | Derek Clayton (Australia) | May 1969 |
| One–Hour Run | 13 miles, 24 yards | Jos Hermens (Netherlands) | May 1976 |
| 20–Kilometer Walk | 1 hr., 20 min., 7 sec. | Daniel Bautista (Mexico) | Oct. 1979 |
| 30–Kilometer Walk | 1 hr., 49 min., 54 sec. | Raul Gonzalez (Mexico) | May 1978 |
| 50–Kilometer Walk | 3 hr., 52 min., 24 sec. | Raul Gonzalez (Mexico) | May 1978 |
| Two–Hour Walk | 16 miles, 1637 yards | Raul Gonzalez (Mexico) | May 1978 |
| 110–Meter Hurdles | 12.93 sec. | Renaldo Nehemiah (United States) | Aug. 1981 |
| 400–Meter Hurdles | 47.13 sec. | Edwin Moses (United States) | July 1980 |
| 3,000–Meter Steeplechase | 8 min., 5.4 sec. | Henry Rono (Kenya) | April 1978 |
| 4 X 100–Meter Relay | 38.03 sec. | United States | Sept. 1977 |
| 4 X 200–Meter Relay | 1 min., 20.26 sec. | United States | May 1977 |
| 4 X 400–Meter Relay | 2 min., 56.16 sec. | United States | Oct. 1968 |
| 4 X 800–Meter Relay | 7 min., 3.89 sec. | United Kingdom | Sept. 1982 |
| 4 X 1,500–Meter Relay | 14 min., 38.8 sec. | West Germany | Aug. 1977 |
| High Jump | 2.36m (7′8¾″) | Gerd Wessig (East Germany) | Aug. 1980 |
| Long Jump | 8.90m (29′2½″) | Bob Beaman (United States) | Oct. 1968 |
| Triple Jump | 17.89m (58′8¼″) | Joao Oliveira (Brazil) | Oct. 1975 |
| Pole Vault | 5.81m (19′¾″) | Vladimir Polyakov (U.S.S.R.) | June 1981 |
| Shot Put | 22.15m (72′8″) | Udo Beyer (East Germany) | July 1978 |
| Discus Throw | 71.19m (233′7″) | Ben Plucknett (United States) | May 1981 |
| Hammer Throw | 83.97 m (275′6″) | Sergei Litvinov (U.S.S.R.) | June 1982 |
| Javelin Throw | 96.72m (317′4″) | Ferenc Paragi (Hungary) | April 1980 |
| Decathlon | 8,744 points | Daley Thompson (United Kingdom) | Sept. 1982 |

| Women's Event | Time/Distance | Name (Country) | Date |
|---|---|---|---|
| 100–Meter Dash | 10.88 sec. | Marlies Gohr (East Germany) | July 1977, 1982 |
| 200–Meter Dash | 21.71 sec. | Marita Koch (East Germany) | June 1979 |
| 400–Meter Dash | 48.15 sec. | Marita Koch (East Germany) | Sept. 1982 |
| 800–Meter Run | 1 min., 53.42 sec. | Nadezhde Olizarenko (U.S.S.R.) | July 1980 |
| 1,000–Meter Run | 2 min., 30.6 sec. | Tatyana Providokhina (U.S.S.R.) | Aug. 1978 |
| 1,500–Meter Run | 3 min., 52.47 sec. | Tatyana Kazankina (U.S.S.R.) | July 1980 |
| One–Mile Run | 4 min., 17.44 sec. | Maricica Puica (Romania) | Sept. 1982 |
| 2,000–Meter Run | 5 min., 25.5 sec. | Maricica Puica (Romania) | May 1979 |
| 3,000–Meter Run | 8 min., 26.78 sec. | Svetlana Ulmasova (U.S.S.R.) | July 1982 |
| 5,000–Meter Run | 15 min., 8.26 sec. | Mary Decker Tabb (United States) | June 1982 |
| 10,000–Meter Run | 31 min., 35.3 sec. | Mary Decker Tabb (United States) | July 1982 |
| Marathon | 2 hr., 27 min., 33 sec. | Greta Waitz (Norway) | Oct. 1979 |
| 100–Meter Hurdles | 12.36 sec. | Grazyna Rabsztyn (Poland) | June 1980 |
| 400–Meter Hurdles | 54.28 sec | Karin Rossley (East Germany) | May 1980 |
| 4 X 100–Meter Relay | 41.60 sec. | East Germany | Aug. 1980 |
| 4 X 200–Meter Relay | 1 min., 28.15 sec. | East Germany | Aug. 1980 |
| 4 X 400–Meter Relay | 3 min., 19.05 sec. | East Germany | Sept. 1982 |
| 4 X 800–Meter Relay | 7 min., 52.3 sec. | U.S.S.R. | Aug. 1976 |
| 800-Meter Medley Relay | 1 min., 36.79 sec. | United States | June 1982 |
| High Jump | 2.02 m (6′7½″) | Ulrike Meyfart (West Germany) | Sept. 1982 |
| Long Jump | 7.20 m (23′7½″) | Vali Ionescu (Romania) | July 1982 |
| Shot Put | 22.45m (73′8″) | Ilona Slupianek (East Germany) | May 1980 |
| Discus Throw | 71.80m (235′7″) | Maria Vergova-Petkova (Bulgaria) | July 1980 |
| Javelin Throw | 74.19 m (243′5″) | Sofia Sakorafa (Greece) | Sept. 1982 |
| Pentathlon | 5083 points | Nadyezhda Tkachenko (U.S.S.R.) | July 1980 |
| Heptathlon | 6,772 points | Ramona Neubert (West Germany) | June 1982 |

# SWIMMING AND DIVING

## 1982 NCAA CHAMPIONS (Division I)

**MEN**

|  |  |
|---|---|
| 50 yd. Freestyle | Robin Leamy, UCLA |
| 100 yd. Freestyle | Robin Leamy, UCLA |
| 200 yd. Freestyle | Pelle Holmertz, California |
| 500 yd. Freestyle | Andy Astbury, Arizona State |
| 1,650 yd. Freestyle | Arne Borgstrom, Alabama |
| 100 yd. Backstroke | Clay Britt, Texas |
| 200 yd. Backstroke | Rick Carey, Texas |
| 100 yd. Breaststroke | Steve Lundquist, SMU |
| 200 yd. Breaststroke | Steve Lundquist, SMU |
| 100 yd. Butterfly | Matt Gribble, Miami (Fla.) |
| 200 yd. Butterfly | Craig Beardsley, Florida |
| 200 yd. Indiv. Medley | Bill Barrett, UCLA |
| 400 yd. Indiv. Medley | Jeff Float, USC |
| 400 yd. Freestyle Relay | UCLA |
| 800 yd. Freestyle Relay | California |
| 400 yd. Medley Relay | Texas |
| One Meter Dive | Bob Bollinger, Indiana |
| Three Meter Dive | Ron Merriott, Michigan |
| Team | UCLA |
| Division II Team | Northridge State (Calif.) |
| Division III Team | Kenyon (Ohio) |

**WOMEN**

|  |  |
|---|---|
| 50 yd. Freestyle | Diane Johnson, Arizona |
| 100 yd. Freestyle | Amy Caulkins, Florida |
| 200 yd. Freestyle | Marybeth Linzmeir, Stanford |
| 500 yd. Freestyle | Marybeth Linzmeir, Stanford |
| 1,650 yd. Freestyle | Marybeth Linzmeir, Stanford |
| 50 yd. Backstroke | Sue Walsh, North Carolina |
| 100 yd. Backstroke | Sue Walsh, North Carolina |
| 200 yd. Backstroke | Sue Walsh, North Carolina |
| 50 yd. Breaststroke | Kathy Treible, Florida |
| 100 yd. Breaststroke | Kathy Treible, Florida |
| 200 yd. Breaststroke | Kathy Treible, Florida |
| 50 yd. Butterfly | Barb Harris, North Carolina |
| 100 yd. Butterfly | Tracy Caulkins, Florida |
| 200 yd. Butterfly | Tracy Caulkins, Florida |
| 100 yd. Indiv. Medley | Tracy Caulkins, Florida |
| 200 yd. Indiv. Medley | Tracy Caulkins, Florida |
| 400 yd. Indiv. Medley | Tracy Caulkins, Florida |
| 200 yd. Freestyle Relay | Stanford |
| 400 yd. Freestyle Relay | Stanford |
| 800 yd. Freestyle Relay | Stanford |
| 200 yd. Medley Relay | Florida |
| 400 yd. Medley Relay | Florida |
| One Meter Dive | Megan Neyer, Florida |
| Three Meter Dive | Megan Neyer, Florida |
| Team | Florida |
| Division II Team | Northridge State (Calif.) |
| Division III Team | Williams (Mass.) |

## 1982 NAIA CHAMPIONS

**MEN**

|  |  |
|---|---|
| 50 m. Freestyle | Steve Koga, Willamette (Ore.) |
| 100 m. Freestyle | Steve Koga, Willamette (Ore.) |
| 200 m. Freestyle | Dan Sullivan, Drury (Mo.) |
| 400 m. Freestyle | Dan Sullivan, Drury (Mo.) |
| 1,500 m. Freestyle | Russell Dale, Simon Fraser (Can.) |
| 100 m. Backstroke | Sean Allison, Drury (Mo.) |
| 200 m. Backstroke | Bryce Fleming, Simon Fraser (Can.) |
| 100 m. Breaststroke | Ray Markle, Drury (Mo.) |
| 200 m. Breaststroke | Ray Markle, Drury (Mo.) |
| 100 m. Butterfly | Thomas Ullrich, Denver (Colo.) |
| 200 m. Butterfly | Roger Bird, Drury (Mo.) |
| 200 m. Indiv. Medley | Paul Stanford, Denver (Colo.) |
| 400 m. Indiv. Medley | Paul Stanford, Denver (Colo.) |
| 400 m. Freestyle Relay | Denver (Colo.) |
| 800 m. Freestyle Relay | Drury (Mo.) |
| 400 m. Medley Relay | Drury (Mo.) |
| One Meter Dive | Mike Lewis, Drury (Mo.) |
| Three Meter Dive | Mike Lewis, Drury (Mo.) |
| Team | Drury (Missouri) |

**WOMEN**

|  |  |
|---|---|
| 50 m. Freestyle | Celeste Robischon, Central Washington |
| 100 m. Freestyle | Suzanne Melody, Simon Fraser (Can.) |
| 200 m. Freestyle | Suzanne Melody, Simon Fraser (Can.) |
| 400 m. Freestyle | Judy Baker, Simon Fraser (Can.) |
| 1,500 m. Freestyle | Suzanne Melody, Simon Fraser (Can.) |
| 100 m. Backstroke | Karen Workman, Shepherd (W. Va.) |
| 200 m. Backstroke | Suzanne Melody, Simon Fraser (Can.) |
| 100 m. Breaststroke | Michelle Langsford, Ozarks (Mo.) |
| 200 m. Breaststroke | Judy Baker, Simon Fraser (Can.) |
| 100 m. Butterfly | Suzanne Melody, Simon Fraser (Can.) |
| 200 m. Butterfly | Judy Baker, Simon Fraser (Can.) |
| 100 m. Indiv. Medley | Michelle Langsford, Ozarks (Mo.) |
| 200 m. Indiv. Medley | Judy Baker, Simon Fraser (Can.) |
| 400 m. Indiv. Medley | Judy Baker, Simon Fraser (Can.) |
| 200 m. Freestyle Relay | Simon Fraser (Can.) |
| 400 m. Freestyle Relay | Simon Fraser (Can.) |
| 800 m. Freestyle Relay | Simon Fraser (Can.) |
| 200 m. Medley Relay | Shepherd (W. Va.) |
| 400 m. Medley Relay | Simon Fraser (Can.) |
| One Meter Dive | Kendra Langley, Simon Fraser (Can.) |
| Three Meter Dive | Kendra Langley, Simon Fraser (Can.) |
| Team | Simon Fraser (Canada) |

## 1982 U.S. SHORT COURSE CHAMPIONS

**MEN**

|  |  |
|---|---|
| 50 yd. Freestyle | Siong Ang, Houston |
| 100 yd. Freestyle | Rowdy Gaines, War Eagle |
| 200 yd. Freestyle | Rowdy Gaines, War Eagle |
| 500 yd. Freestyle | Jeff Kostoff, Industry Hills |
| 1,000 yd. Freestyle | Jeff Kostoff, Industry Hills |
| 1,650 yd. Freestyle | Jeff Kostoff, Industry Hills |
| 100 yd. Backstroke | Dave Bottom, Walnut Creek |
| 200 yd. Backstroke | Sandor Wladar, Hungary |
| 100 yd. Breaststroke | Steve Lundquist, Mustang |
| 200 yd. Breaststroke | John Moffet, Beach |
| 100 yd. Butterfly | David Cowell, Mid-Ohio Valley Y |
| 200 yd. Butterfly | Craig Beardsley, Florida |
| 200 yd. Indiv. Medley | Roger Von Jouanne, Southern Illinois |
| 400 yd. Indiv. Medley | Ricardo Prado, Mission Viejo |
| 400 yd. Freestyle Relay | Mission Viejo |
| 800 yd. Freestyle Relay | Florida Aquatic |
| 400 yd. Medley Relay | Mission Viejo |

**WOMEN**

|  |  |
|---|---|
| 50 yd. Freestyle | Dara Torres, Tandem |
| 100 yd. Freestyle | Jill Sterkel, Longhorn |
| 200 yd. Freestyle | Cynthia Woodhead, Mission Viejo |
| 500 yd. Freestyle | Tiffany Cohen, Mission Viejo |
| 1,000 yd. Freestyle | Tiffany Cohen, Mission Viejo |
| 1,650 yd. Freestyle | Tiffany Cohen, Mission Viejo |
| 100 yd. Backstroke | Debbie Risen, K.C. Blazers |
| 200 yd. Backstroke | Tracy Caulkins, Nashville |
| 100 yd. Breaststroke | Tracy Caulkins, Nashville |
| 200 yd. Breaststroke | Kim Rhodenbaugh, Cinc. Pepsi Marlins |
| 100 yd. Butterfly | Jill Sterkel, Longhorn |
| 200 yd. Butterfly | Mary T. Meagher, Lakeside |
| 200 yd. Indiv. Medley | Tracy Caulkins, Nashville |
| 400 yd. Indiv. Medley | Tracy Caulkins, Nashville |
| 400 yd. Freestyle Relay | Mission Viejo |
| 800 yd. Freestyle Relay | Mission Viejo |
| 400 yd. Medley Relay | Nashville Aquatic |

## 1982 U.S. LONG COURSE CHAMPIONS

**MEN**

| | |
|---|---|
| 50 m. Freestyle | Peng Siong Ang, San Luis Obispo, Calif. |
| 100 m. Freestyle | Rowdy Gaines, Winter Haven, Fla. |
| 200 m. Freestyle | Rowdy Gaines, Winter Haven, Fla. |
| 400 m. Freestyle | Bruce Hayes, Mission Viejo, Calif. |
| 800 m. Freestyle | Tony Corbisiero, New York, N.Y. |
| 1,500 m. Freestyle | Jeff Kostoff, Upland, Calif. |
| 100 m. Backstroke | Mark Rhodenbaugh, Cincinnati, Ohio |
| 200 m. Backstroke | Steve Barnicoat, Mission Viejo, Calif. |
| 100 m. Breaststroke | Steve Lundquist, Jonesboro, Ga. |
| 200 m. Breaststroke | John Moffet, Costa Mesa, Calif. |
| 100 m. Butterfly | David Cowell, Belpre, Ohio |
| 200 m. Butterfly | Craig Beardsley, Gainesville, Fla. |
| 200 m. Indiv. Medley | Bill Barrett, Mission Viejo, Calif. |
| 400 m. Indiv. Medley | Ricardo Prado, Mission Viejo, Calif. |
| 400 m. Freestyle Relay | Mission Viejo Nadadores |
| 800 m. Freestyle Relay | Mission Viejo Nadadores |
| 400 m. Medley Relay | Mission Viejo Nadadores |

**WOMEN**

| | |
|---|---|
| 50 m. Freestyle | Dara Torres, Beverly Hills, Calif. |
| 100 m. Freestyle | Paige Zemina, Ft. Lauderdale, Fla. |
| 200 m. Freestyle | Sara Linke, Walnut Creek, Calif. |
| 400 m. Freestyle | Tiffany Cohen, Mission Viejo, Calif. |
| 800 m. Freestyle | Marybeth Linzmeier, Mission Viejo, Calif. |
| 1,500 m. Freestyle | Karin LaBerge, Doylestown, Pa. |
| 100 m. Backstroke | Sue Walsh, Hamburg, N.Y. |
| 200 m. Backstroke | Tracy Caulkins, Nashville, Tenn. |
| 100 m. Breaststroke | Kim Rhodenbaugh, Cincinnati, Ohio |
| 200 m. Breaststroke | Beverly Acker, Cocoa Beach, Fla. |
| 100 m. Butterfly | Mary T. Meagher, Louisville, Ky. |
| 200 m. Butterfly | Mary T. Meagher, Louisville, Ky. |
| 200 m. Indiv. Medley | Tracy Caulkins, Nashville, Tenn. |
| 400 m. Indiv. Medley | Tracy Caulkins, Nashville, Tenn. |
| 400 m. Freestyle Relay | Mission Viejo Nadadores |
| 800 m. Freestyle Relay | Mission Viejo Nadadores |
| 400 m. Medley Relay | Cincinnati Pepsi Marlins |

## 1982 U.S. WORLD CHAMPIONSHIP TRIALS

**MEN**

| | |
|---|---|
| 100 m. Freestyle | Chris Cavanaugh, Santa Clara, Calif. |
| 200 m. Freestyle | Rowdy Gaines, Auburn Univ. |
| 400 m. Freestyle | Bruce Hayes, Mission Viejo, Calif. |
| 1,500 m. Freestyle | George DiCarlo, Tucson, Ariz. |
| 100 m. Backstroke | Rick Carey, Larchmont, N.Y. |
| 200 m. Backstroke | Rick Carey, Larchmont, N.Y. |
| 100 m. Breaststroke | Steve Lundquist, Dallas, Texas |
| 200 m. Breaststroke | John Moffet, Costa Mesa, Calif. |
| 100 m. Butterfly | Matt Gribble, Miami, Fla. |
| 200 m. Butterfly | Craig Beardsley, Gainesville, Fla. |
| 200 m. Indiv. Medley | Steve Lundquist, Dallas, Texas |
| 400 m. Indiv. Medley | Bruce Hayes, Mission Viejo, Calif. |

Others qualifying for U.S. Team: Rich Saeger, Kyle Miller, Jeff Float, Sam Worden, Doug Towne, Chris Rives, Jeff Kostoff, Robin Leamy, David McCagg, Tom Jager, Steve Barnicoat, Glenn Mills, Robert Patten, Clay Britt, Bill Barrett

**WOMEN**

| | |
|---|---|
| 100 m. Freestyle | Jill Sterkel, Austin, Texas |
| 200 m. Freestyle | Marybeth Linzmeier, Mission Viejo, Calif. |
| 400 m. Freestyle | Tiffany Cohen, Mission Viejo, Calif. |
| 800 m. Freestyle | Tiffany Cohen, Mission Viejo, Calif. |
| 100 m. Backstroke | Sue Walsh, Univ. of N. Carolina |
| 200 m. Backstroke | Tracy Caulkins, Nashville, Tenn. |
| 100 m. Breaststroke | Kim Rhodenbaugh, Cincinnati, Ohio |
| 200 m. Breaststroke | Jeanne Childs, Honolulu, Hawaii |
| 100 m. Butterfly | Mary T. Meagher, Louisville, Ky. |
| 200 m. Butterfly | Mary T. Meagher, Louisville, Ky. |
| 200 m. Indiv. Medley | Tracy Caulkins, Nashville, Tenn. |
| 400 m. Indiv. Medley | Tracy Caulkins, Nashville, Tenn. |

Others qualifying for U.S. Team: Kathy Treible, Sue Habernig, Julie Williams, Beth Washut, Patty Gavin, Beverly Acker, Libby Kinkead, Melanie Buddemeyer, Polly Winde, Kim Linehan, Sara Linke

## 1982 WORLD SWIMMING CHAMPIONS

**MEN**

| | |
|---|---|
| 100 m. Freestyle | Jorg Woithe, E. Germany |
| 200 m. Freestyle | Michael Gross, W. Germany |
| 400 m. Freestyle | Vladimir Salnikov, U.S.S.R. |
| 1,500 m. Freestyle | Vladimir Salnikov, U.S.S.R. |
| 100 m. Backstroke | Dirk Richter, E. Germany |
| 200 m. Backstroke | Rick Carey, U.S.A. |
| 100 m. Breaststroke | Steve Lundquist, U.S.A. |
| 200 m. Breaststroke | Victor Davis, Canada |
| 100 m. Butterfly | Matt Gribble, U.S.A. |
| 200 m. Butterfly | Michael Gross, W. Germany |
| 200 m. Indiv. Medley | Aleksandr Sidorenko, U.S.S.R. |
| 400 m. Indiv. Medley | Ricardo Prado, Brazil |
| 400 m. Freestyle Relay | United States |
| 800 m. Freestyle Relay | United States |
| 400 m. Medley Relay | United States |

**WOMEN**

| | |
|---|---|
| 100 m. Freestyle | Birgit Meineke, E. Germany |
| 200 m. Freestyle | Annemarie Verstappen, Netherlands |
| 400 m. Freestyle | Carmela Schmidt, E. Germany |
| 800 m. Freestyle | Kim Linehan, U.S.A. |
| 100 m. Backstroke | Kristin Otto, E. Germany |
| 200 m. Backstroke | Cornelia Sirch, E. Germany |
| 100 m. Breaststroke | Ute Geweniger, E. Germany |
| 200 m. Breaststroke | Svetlana Varganova, U.S.S.R. |
| 100 m. Butterfly | Mary T. Meagher, U.S.A. |
| 200 m. Butterfly | Ines Geissler, E. Germany |
| 200 m. Indiv. Medley | Petra Schneider, E. Germany |
| 400 m. Indiv. Medleyform | Petra Schneider, E. Germany |
| 400 m. Freestyle Relay | East Germany |
| 400 m. Medley Relay | East Germany |

## 1982 WORLD DIVING CHAMPIONS

| | |
|---|---|
| **MEN—Springboard** | Greg Louganis, U.S.A. |
| **Platform** | Greg Louganis, U.S.A. |
| **WOMEN—Springboard** | Megan Neyer, U.S.A. |
| **Platform** | Wendy Wyland, U.S.A. |

## 1982 AIAW SYNCHRONIZED SWIMMING CHAMPIONS

Solo Routine.................................. Tracie Ruiz, Arizona

Duet Routine........................ Tracie Ruiz-Candie Costie, Arizona

Trio Routine....................... Karen Callaghan, Sarah Josephson, Karen Josephson, Ohio State

Team.......................................... Ohio State

## 1982 U.S. DIVING CHAMPIONS

| EVENT | INDOOR—MEN | WOMEN | OUTDOOR—MEN | WOMEN |
|---|---|---|---|---|
| One Meter | Ron Merriott | Megan Neyer | Greg Louganis | Megan Neyer |
| Three Meter | Ron Merriott | Megan Neyer | Greg Louganis | Kelly McCormick |
| Ten Meter | Dan Watson | Wendy Wyland | Bruce Kimball | Wendy Wyland |

## WORLD SWIMMING RECORDS (September 1982)

### MEN'S EVENTS

| Event | Time | Name | Country | Date | |
|---|---|---|---|---|---|
| 100 meter freestyle | 49.36 | Rowdy Gaines | United States | April | 1981 |
| 200 meter freestyle | 1:48.93 | Rowdy Gaines | United States | July | 1982 |
| 400 meter freestyle | 3:49.57 | Vladimir Salnikov | USSR | March | 1982 |
| 800 meter freestyle | 7:52.83 | Vladimir Salnikov | USSR | February | 1982 |
| 1500 meter freestyle | 14:56.35 | Vladimir Salnikov | USSR | March | 1982 |
| 400 meter freestyle relay | 3:19.26 | Cavanaugh, Leamy, McCagg, Gaines | United States | August | 1982 |
| 800 meter freestyle relay | 7:20.82 | Furniss, Forrester, Gaines, Hackett | United States | August | 1978 |
| 100 meter breaststroke | 1:02.53 | Steve Lundquist | United States | August | 1982 |
| 200 meter breaststroke | 2:14.77 | Victor Davis | Canada | August | 1982 |
| 100 meter butterfly | 53.81 | William Paulus | United States | April | 1981 |
| 200 meter butterfly | 1:58.01 | Craig Beardsley | United States | August | 1981 |
| 100 meter backstroke | 55.49 | John Naber | United States | July | 1976 |
| 200 meter backstroke | 1:59.19 | John Naber | United States | July | 1976 |
| 200 meter individual medley | 2:02.25 | Alex Baumann | Canada | Oct. | 1982 |
| 400 meter individual medley | 4:19.78 | Ricardo Prado | Brazil | August | 1982 |
| 400 meter medley relay | 3:40.84 | Carey, Lundquist, Gribble, Gaines | United States | August | 1982 |

### WOMEN'S EVENTS

| Event | Time | Name | Country | Date | |
|---|---|---|---|---|---|
| 100 meter freestyle | 54.79 | Barbara Krause | East Germany | July | 1980 |
| 200 meter freestyle | 1:58.23 | Cynthia Woodhead | United States | Sept. | 1979 |
| 400 meter freestyle | 4:06.28 | Tracey Wickham | Australia | August | 1978 |
| 800 meter freestyle | 8:18.77 | Cynthia Woodhead | United States | February | 1980 |
| 1500 meter freestyle | 16:04.49 | Kim Linehan | United States | August | 1979 |
| 400 meter freestyle relay | 3:42.17 | Krause, Metschuck, Diers, Hulsenbeck | East Germany | July | 1980 |
| 100 meter breaststroke | 1:08.60 | Ute Geweniger | East Germany | Sept. | 1981 |
| 200 meter breaststroke | 2:28.36 | Lina Kachushite | USSR | April | 1979 |
| 100 meter butterfly | 57.93 | Mary T. Meagher | United States | August | 1981 |
| 200 meter butterfly | 2:05.96 | Mary T. Meagher | United States | August | 1981 |
| 100 meter backstroke | 1:00.86 | Rica Reinisch | East Germany | July | 1980 |
| 200 meter backstroke | 2:09.91 | Cornelia Sirch | East Germany | August | 1982 |
| 200 meter individual medley | 2:11.73 | Ute Geweniger | East Germany | July | 1981 |
| 400 meter individual medley | 4:36.10 | Petra Schneider | East Germany | August | 1982 |
| 400 meter medley relay | 4:05.88 | Otto, Geweniger, Geissler, Meineke | East Germany | August | 1982 |

## SPORTS FIGURES OF THE CENTURY

Results of a 1980 international poll of twenty leading newspapers of the world.

1. **Pele,** Brazil, soccer
2. **Jesse Owens,** U.S., track and field
3. **Eddy Merckx,** Belgium, cycling
4. **Paavo Nurmi,** Finland, track and field
5. **Bjorn Borg,** Sweden, tennis, and **Mark Spitz,** U.S., swimming
7. **Emil Zatopek,** Czechoslovakia, track and field
8. **Fauto Coppi,** Italy, cycling
9. **Muhammad Ali,** U.S., boxing
10. **Sugar Ray Robinson,** U.S., boxing
11. **Jack Nicklaus,** U.S., golf
12. **Joe Louis,** U.S., boxing
13. **Babe Ruth,** U.S., baseball
14. **Juan Manuel Fangio,** Argentina, auto racing
15. **Jean-Claude Killy,** France, skiing, and **Eric Heiden,** U.S., speed skating
17. **Dawn Fraser,** Australia, swimming, and **Irena Szewinska,** Poland, track and field
19. **Vasily Alexeyev,** USSR, weightlifting, and **Nadia Comaneci,** Romania, gymnastics

# BOWLING

## 1982 LEADING MONEY WINNERS (to Sept. 1)

Source: PBA

| | Bowler | Tournaments | Amount |
|---|---|---|---|
| 1. | Earl Anthony, Dublin, Calif. | 22 | $122,100 |
| 2. | Art Trask, Fresno, Calif. | 28 | 89,430 |
| 3. | Dave Husted, Milwaukie, Ore. | 27 | 88,170 |
| 4. | Mike Durbin, Chagrin Falls, Ohio | 27 | 87,670 |
| 5. | Ted Hannahs, Zanesville, Ohio | 27 | 80,995 |
| 6. | Pete Weber, St. Louis | 26 | 75,935 |
| 7. | Joe Berardi, Brooklyn, N.Y. | 20 | 69,525 |
| 8. | Charlie Tapp, S. St. Paul, Minn. | 24 | 68,855 |
| 9. | Guppy Troup, Jacksonville, Fla. | 20 | 68,145 |
| 10. | Steve Cook, Roseville, Calif. | 25 | 67,040 |
| 11. | Wayne Webb, Indianapolis | 27 | $65,983 |
| 12. | Marshall Holman, Medford, Ore. | 17 | 58,618 |
| 13. | Tom Baker, Buffalo, N.Y. | 26 | 56,185 |
| 14. | Bob Handley, Fairway, Kan. | 27 | 51,605 |
| 15. | Mike Aulby, Indianapolis | 27 | 50,915 |
| 16. | Pete Couture, Windsor Locks, Conn. | 29 | 50,222 |
| 17. | Steve Westberg, Cottage Grove, Ore. | 25 | 47,300 |
| 18. | Gil Sliker, Nashua, N.H. | 25 | 47,030 |
| 19. | Mal Acosta, Hayward, Calif. | 25 | 45,810 |
| 20. | George Pappas, Charlotte, N.C. | 25 | 45,380 |

## PBA TOP-MONEY WINNERS, 1960—1981

| Year | Bowler | Winnings |
|---|---|---|
| 1960 | Don Carter | $22,525 |
| 1961 | Dick Weber | 26,280 |
| 1962 | Don Carter | 49,972 |
| 1963 | Dick Weber | 46,333 |
| 1964 | Bob Strampe | 33,592 |
| 1965 | Dick Weber | 47,675 |
| 1966 | Wayne Zahn | 54,720 |
| 1967 | Dave Davis | 54,165 |
| 1968 | Jim Stefanich | 67,375 |
| 1969 | Billy Hardwick | 64,160 |
| 1970 | Mike McGrath | 52,049 |
| 1971 | John Petraglia | $ 85,065 |
| 1972 | Don Johnson | 56,648 |
| 1973 | Don McCune | 69,000 |
| 1974 | Earl Anthony | 99,585 |
| 1975 | Earl Anthony | 107,585 |
| 1976 | Earl Anthony | 110,883 |
| 1977 | Mark Roth | 105,583 |
| 1978 | Mark Roth | 134,500 |
| 1979 | Mark Roth | 124,517 |
| 1980 | Wayne Webb | 116,700 |
| 1981 | Earl Anthony | 164,735 |

## BOWLING CHAMPIONS

| Year | BPAA U.S. Open (Formerly All-Star) | ABC Masters | PBA National Championship | ABC All-Events |
|---|---|---|---|---|
| 1962 | Dick Weber | Billy Golembiewski | Carmen Salvino | Jack Winters |
| 1963 | Dick Weber | Harry Smith | Billy Hardwick | Tom Hennessey |
| 1964 | Bob Strampe | Billy Welu | Bob Strampe | Billy Hardwick |
| 1965 | Dick Weber | Billy Welu | Dave Davis | Tom Hennessey |
| 1966 | Dick Weber | Bob Strampe | Wayne Zahn | Les Schissler |
| 1967 | Les Schissler | Lou Scalia | Dave Davis | Bob Strampe |
| 1968 | Jim Stefanich | Pete Tountas | Wayne Zahn | Jim Stefanich |
| 1969 | Billy Hardwick | Jim Chestney | Mike McGrath | Larry Lichstein |
| 1970 | Bobby Cooper | Don Glover | Mike McGrath | Bob Strampe |
| 1971 | Mike Lemongello | Jim Godman | Mike Lemongello | Gary Dickinson |
| 1972 | Don Johnson | Bill Beach | John Guenther | Teata Semiz |
| 1973 | Mike McGrath | Dave Soutar | Earl Anthony | Jimmy Mack |
| 1974 | Larry Laub | Paul Colwell | Earl Anthony | Jim Godman |
| 1975 | Steve Neff | Ed Ressler | Earl Anthony | Bobby Meadows |
| 1976 | Paul Moser | Nelson Burton, Jr. | Paul Colwell | Gary Fust |
| 1977 | John Petraglia | Earl Anthony | Tommy Hudson | Dick Ritger |
| 1978 | Nelson Burton, Jr. | Frank Ellenburg | Warren Nelson | Bill Beach |
| 1979 | Joe Berardi | Doug Myers | Mike Aulby | Nelson Burton, Jr. |
| 1980 | Steve Martin | Neil Burton | Johnny Petraglia | Steve Fehr |
| 1981 | Marshall Holman | Randy Lightfoot | Earl Anthony | Rod Toft |
| 1982 | Dave Husted | Joe Berardi | Earl Anthony | Rich Wonders |

## BOWLER OF THE YEAR

Selected by Bowling Writers Associaton of America

| Year | MEN | WOMEN |
|---|---|---|
| 1956 | Bill Lillard, Chicago, Ill. | Anita Cantaline, Detroit, Mich. |
| 1957 | Don Carter, St. Louis, Mo. | Marion Ladewig, Grand Rapids, Mich. |
| 1958 | Don Carter, St. Louis, Mo. | Marion Ladewig, Grand Rapids, Mich. |
| 1959 | Ed Lubanski, Detroit, Mich. | Marion Ladewig, Grand Rapids, Mich. |
| 1960 | Don Carter, St. Louis, Mo. | Sylvia Wene, Philadelphia, Pa. |
| 1961 | Dick Weber, St. Louis, Mo. | Shirley Garms, Palatine, Ill. |
| 1962 | Don Carter, St. Louis, Mo. | Shirley Garms, Palatine, Ill. |
| 1963 | Dick Weber, St. Louis, Mo. | Marion Ladewig, Grand Rapids, Mich. |
| 1964 | Billy Hardwick, San Mateo, Calif. | LaVerne Carter, St. Louis, Mo. |
| 1965 | Dick Weber, St. Louis, Mo. | Betty Kuczynski, Chicago, Ill. |
| 1966 | Wayne Zahn, Atlanta, Ga. | Joy Abel, Chicago, Ill. |
| 1967 | Dave Davis, Phoenix, Ariz. | Mildred Martorella, Rochester, N.Y. |
| 1968 | Jim Stefanich, Joliet, Ill. | Dotty Fothergill, N. Attleboro, Mass. |
| 1969 | Billy Hardwick, Louisville, Ky. | Dotty Fothergill, N. Attleboro, Mass. |
| 1970 | Nelson Burton, Jr., St. Louis, Mo. | Mary Baker, Central Islip, N.Y. |
| 1971 | Don Johnson, Akron, Ohio | Paula Sperber, Miami, Fla. |
| 1972 | Don Johnson, Akron, Ohio | Patty Costello, New Carrollton, Md. |
| 1973 | Don McCune, Munster, Ind. | Judy Soutar, Kansas City, Mo. |
| 1974 | Earl Anthony, Tacoma, Wash. | Betty Morris, Stockton, Calif. |
| 1975 | Earl Anthony, Tacoma, Wash. | Judy Soutar, Kansas City, Mo. |
| 1976 | Earl Anthony, Tacoma, Wash. | Patty Costello, Scranton, Pa. |
| 1977 | Mark Roth, Staten Island, N.Y. | Betty Morris, Stockton, Calif. |
| 1978 | Mark Roth, N. Arlington, N.J. | Donna Adamek, Monrovia, Calif. |
| 1979 | Mark Roth, Little Silver, N.J. | Donna Adamek, Duarte, Calif. |
| 1980 | Wayne Webb, Tucson, Ariz. | Donna Adamek, Duarte, Calif. |
| 1981 | Earl Anthony, Dublin, Calif. | Donna Adamek, Duarte, Calif. |

## 1981 LADIES TOUR MONEY WINNERS

SOURCE: Ladies Professional Bowlers Tour

| | Bowler | Amount |
|---|---|---|
| 1. | Donna Adamek, Duarte, Calif. | $41,270 |
| 2. | Cindy Coburn, Buffalo, N.Y. | 38,200 |
| 3. | Nikki Gianulias, Vallejo, Calif. | 36,835 |
| 4. | Lorrie Nichols, Island Lake, Ill. | 20,120 |
| 5. | Katsuko Sugimoto, Japan | 16,970 |
| 6. | Cindy Mason, La Habra, Calif. | 16,590 |
| 7. | Pat Costello, Dublin, Calif. | 15,210 |
| 8. | Robin Romeo, Beverly Hills, Calif. | 14,875 |
| 9. | Pam Buckner, Reno, Nev. | 14,565 |
| 10. | Aleta Rzepecki, Detroit, Mich. | 13,550 |
| 11. | Patty Costello, Scranton, Pa. | 12,245 |
| 12. | Virginia Norton, South Gate, Calif. | 11,737 |
| 13. | Lisa Rathberger, Palmetto, Fla. | 7,905 |
| 14. | Linda Sherwood, Overland Park, Kans. | 7,732 |
| 15. | Jeanne Maiden, Solon, Ohio | 7,707 |

## 1981 LADIES TOUR POINT STANDINGS

SOURCE: LPBT

| | Bowler | Points |
|---|---|---|
| 1. | Nikki Gianulias | 7,090 |
| 2. | Donna Adamek | 7,060 |
| 3. | Lorrie Nichols | 5,408 |
| 4. | Cindy Coburn | 5,330 |
| 5. | Pat Costello | 5,200 |
| 6. | Robin Romeo | 4,960 |
| 7. | Cindy Mason | 4,932 |
| 8. | Pam Buckner | 4,650 |
| 9. | Lisa Rathberger | 4,070 |
| 10. | Shirley Hintz, Merritt Island, Fla. | 3,930 |
| 11. | Aleta Rzepecki | 3,700 |
| 12. | Patty Costello | 3,280 |
| 13. | Pat Mercatanti, Newtown, Pa. | 3,030 |
| 14. | Jeanne Maiden | 2,807 |
| 15. | Debbie Rainone, South Euclid, Ohio | 2,791 |

## WOMEN'S BOWLING CHAMPIONS

| | U.S. Open (Formerly All-Star) | WIBC Queen's Tournament | WPBA National Championship |
|---|---|---|---|
| 1961 | Phyllis Notaro | Janet Harman | Shirley Garms |
| 1962 | Shirley Garms | Dorothy Wilkinson | Stevie Balogh |
| 1963 | Marion Ladewig | Irene Monterosso | Janet Harman |
| 1964 | LaVerne Carter | D.D. Jacobson | Betty Kuczynski |
| 1965 | Ann Slattery | Betty Kuczynski | Helen Duval |
| 1966 | Joy Abel | Judy Lee | Judy Lee |
| 1967 | Gloria Bouvia | Mildred Martorella | Betty Mivalez |
| 1968 | Dotty Fothergill | Phyllis Massey | Dotty Fothergill |
| 1969 | Dotty Fothergill | Ann Feigel | Dotty Fothergill |
| 1970 | Mary Baker | Mildred Martorella | Bobbe North |
| 1971 | Paula Sperber | Mildred Martorella | Patty Costello |
| 1972 | Lorrie Koch | Dotty Fothergill | Patty Costello |
| 1973 | Mildred Martorella | Dotty Fothergill | Betty Morris |
| 1974 | Pat Costello | Judy Soutar | Pat Costello |
| 1975 | Paula Sperber | Cindy Powell | Pam Rutherford |
| 1976 | Patty Costello | Pam Rutherford | Patty Costello |
| 1977 | Betty Morris | Dana Stewart | Vesma Grinfelds |
| 1978 | Donna Adamek | Loa Boxberger | Toni Gillard |
| 1979 | Diana Silva | Donna Adamek | Cindy Coburn |
| 1980 | Pat Costello | Donna Adamek | Donna Adamek |
| 1981 | Donna Adamek | Katsuko Sugimoto | |
| 1982 | Shinobu Saitoh | Katsuko Sugimoto | |

## 1982 LADIES TOUR MONEY WINNERS

SOURCE: LPBT (to October 1)

| | Bowler | Amount |
|---|---|---|
| 1. | Nikki Gianulias, Vallejo, Calif. | $37,600 |
| 2. | Robin Romeo, Beverly Hills, Calif. | 21,355 |
| 3. | Katsuko Sugimoto, Japan | 20,525 |
| 4. | Donna Adamek, Duarte, Calif. | 19,587 |
| 5. | Cindy Coburn, Buffalo, N.Y. | 13,850 |
| 6. | Dana Miller, Albuquerque, N.M. | 11,200 |
| 7. | Pat Costello, Fremont, Calif. | 10,750 |
| 8. | Shinobu Saitoh, Japan | 10,350 |
| 9. | Tish Johnson, Napa, Calif. | 9,945 |
| 10. | Lisa Rathberger, Palmetto, Fla. | 9,907 |
| 11. | Pam Buckner, Reno, Nev. | 9,575 |
| 12. | Lorrie Nichols, Island Lake, Ill. | 8,930 |
| 13. | Patty Ann, Arlington Heights, Ill. | 8,550 |
| 14. | Jeanne Maiden, Solon, Ohio | 7,987 |
| 15. | Virginia Norton, South Gate, Calif. | 7,725 |

# CHESS

SOURCE: U.S. Chess Federation

## WORLD CHAMPIONSHIPS

| Year | Winner, Country |
|---|---|
| 1886 | Wilhelm Steinitz, Austria |
| 1889 | Wilhelm Steinitz, Austria |
| 1891 | Wilhelm Steinitz, Austria |
| 1892 | Wilhelm Steinitz, Austria |
| 1894 | Emanuel Lasker, Germany |
| 1897 | Emanuel Lasker, Germany |
| 1907 | Emanuel Lasker, Germany |
| 1908 | Emanuel Lasker, Germany |
| 1909 | Emanuel Lasker, Germany |
| 1910* | Emanuel Lasker, Germany |
| 1921 | Jose Capablanca, Cuba |
| 1927 | Alexander Alekhine, France |
| 1929 | Alexander Alekhine, France |
| 1934 | Alexander Alekhine, France |
| 1935 | Max Euwe, Netherlands |
| 1937 | Alexander Alekhine, France |
| 1948 | Mikhail Botvinnik, USSR |
| 1951 | Mikhail Botvinnik, USSR |
| 1954 | Mikhail Botvinnik, USSR |
| 1957 | Vassily Smyslov, USSR |
| 1958 | Mikhail Botvinnik, USSR |
| 1960 | Mikhail Tal, USSR |
| 1961 | Mikhail Botvinnik, USSR |
| 1963 | Tigran Petrosian, USSR |
| 1966 | Tigran Petrosian, USSR |
| 1969 | Boris Spassky, USSR |
| 1972 | Bobby Fischer, US |
| 1975 | Anatoly Karpov, USSR |
| 1978 | Anatoly Karpov, USSR |
| 1981 | Anatoly Karpov, USSR |

* Two championship matches held in 1910. Lasker won both.

## U.S. NATIONAL CHAMPIONSHIPS

**UNOFFICIAL CHAMPIONS**

|  |  |
|---|---|
| 1857-71 | Paul Morphy |
| 1871-76 | George Mackenzie |
| 1876-80 | James Mason |
| 1880-89 | George Mackenzie |
| 1889-90 | S. Lipschutz |
| 1890 | Jackson Showalter |
| 1890-91 | Max Judd |
| 1891 | Jackson Showalter |

**CHAMPIONS**

|  |  |
|---|---|
| 1892 | Jackson Showalter |
| 1892 | S. Lipschutz |
| 1894 | Jackson Showalter |
| 1894 | Albert Hodges |
| 1895 | Jackson Showalter |
| 1896 | Jackson Showalter |
| 1896 | Jackson Showalter |
| 1897 | Harry Pillsbury |
| 1898 | Harry Pillsbury |
| 1909 | Frank Marshall |
| 1923 | Frank Marshall |
| 1936 | Samuel Reshevsky |
| 1938 | Samuel Reshevsky |
| 1940 | Samuel Reshevsky |
| 1941 | Samuel Reshevsky |
| 1942 | Samuel Reshevsky |
| 1944 | Arnold Denker |
| 1946 | Arnold Denker |
| 1946 | Samuel Reshevsky |
| 1948 | Herman Steiner |
| 1951 | Larry Evans |
| 1952 | Larry Evans |
| 1954 | Arthur Bisguier |
| 1958 | Bobby Fischer |
| 1959 | Bobby Fischer |
| 1960 | Bobby Fischer |
| 1961 | Bobby Fischer |
| 1962 | Larry Evans |
| 1963 | Bobby Fischer |
| 1964 | Bobby Fischer |
| 1965 | Bobby Fischer |
| 1966 | Bobby Fischer |
| 1968 | Larry Evans |
| 1969 | Samuel Reshevsky |
| 1972 | Robert Byrne |
| 1973 | Lubomir Kavalek and John Grefe |
| 1974 | Walter Browne |
| 1975 | Walter Browne |
| 1977 | Walter Browne |
| 1978 | Lubomir Kavalek |
| 1980 | Walter Browne<br>Larry Christiansen<br>Larry Evans |
| 1981 | Walter Browne<br>Yasser Seirawan |

## WORLD FRESHWATER FISHING RECORDS

SOURCE: International Game Fish Association (All tackle records, as of September 1, 1982)

| Species | Weight | Where Caught | Date | Angler |
|---|---|---|---|---|
| Bass, Largemouth | 22 lbs. 4 oz. | Montgomery Lake, Ga. | June 2, 1932 | George W. Perry |
| Bass, Redeye | 8 lbs. 3 oz. | Flint River, Ga. | Oct. 23, 1977 | David A. Hubbard |
| Bass, Rock | 3 lbs. | York River, Ontario | Aug. 1, 1974 | Peter Gulgin |
| Bass, Smallmouth | 11 lbs. 15 oz. | Dale Hollow Lake, Ky. | July 9, 1955 | David L. Hayes |
| Bass, Spotted | 8 lbs. 15 oz. | Smith Lake, Ala. | Mar. 18, 1978 | Philip C. Terry, Jr. |
| Bass, Striped | 59 lbs. 12 oz. | Colorado R., Ariz. | May 26, 1977 | Frank W. Smith |
| Bass, White | 5 lbs. 9 oz. | Colorado R., Texas | Mar. 31, 1977 | David S. Cordill |
| Bass, Whiterock | 20 lbs. 6 oz. | Savannah R., Ga. | May 28, 1978 | Danny Wood |
| Bass, Yellow | 2 lbs. 4 oz. | Lake Monroe, Ind. | Mar. 27, 1977 | Donald L. Stalker |
| Bluegill | 4 lbs. 12 oz. | Ketona Lake, Ala. | Apr. 9, 1950 | T. S. Hudson |
| Bowfin | 21 lbs. 8 oz. | Florence, S.C. | Jan. 29, 1980 | Robert L. Harmon |
| Buffalo, Bigmouth | 70 lbs. 5 oz. | Bussey Brake, La. | Apr. 21, 1980 | Delbert Sisk |
| Buffalo, Smallmouth | 51 lbs. | Lawrence, Kansas | May 2, 1979 | Scott Butler |
| Bullhead, Black | 8 lbs. | Lake Waccabuc, N.Y. | Aug. 1, 1951 | Kani Evans |
| Burbot | 18 lbs. 4 oz. | Pickford, Mich. | Jan. 31, 1980 | Thomas Courtemanche |
| Carp | 55 lbs. 5 oz. | Clearwater Lake, Minn. | July 10, 1952 | Frank J. Ledwein |
| Catfish, Blue | 97 lbs. | Missouri River, S.D. | Sept. 16, 1959 | Edward B. Elliott |
| Catfish, Channel | 58 lbs. | Santee-Cooper Res., S.C. | July 7, 1964 | W. B. Whaley |
| Catfish, Flathead | 91 lbs. 4 oz. | Lake Lewisville, Texas | Mar. 28, 1982 | Mike Rogers |
| Catfish, White | 17 lbs. 7 oz. | California | Nov. 15, 1981 | Chuck Idell |
| Char, Arctic | 29 lbs. 11 oz. | Arctic River, N.W.T. | Aug. 21, 1968 | Jeanne P. Branson |
| Crappie, Black | 6 lbs. | Seaplane Canal, La. | Nov. 28, 1969 | Lettie Robertson |
| Crappie, White | 5 lbs. 3 oz. | Enid Dam, Miss. | July 31, 1957 | Fred L. Bright |
| Dolly Varden | 3 lbs. 13 oz. | Unalakleet R., Alaska | Aug. 29, 1980 | Ray Lawson |
| Drum, Freshwater | 54 lbs. 8 oz. | Nickajack Lake, Tenn. | Apr. 20, 1972 | Benny E. Hull |
| Gar, Alligator | 279 lbs. | Rio Grande, Texas | Dec. 2, 1951 | Bill Valverde |
| Gar, Longnose | 50 lbs. 5 oz. | Trinity River, Texas | July 30, 1954 | Townsend Miller |
| Grayling, Arctic | 5 lbs. 15 oz. | Katseyedie R., N.W.T. | Aug. 16, 1967 | Jeanne P. Branson |
| Kokanee | 6 lbs. 9 oz. | Priest L., Idaho | June 9, 1975 | Jerry Verge |
| Muskellunge | 69 lbs. 15 oz. | St. Lawrence R., N.Y. | Sept. 22, 1957 | Arthur Lawton |
| Muskellunge, Tiger | 51 lbs. 3 oz. | Lac Vieux-Desert, Wis./Mich. | July 16, 1919 | John A. Knobla |
| Perch, White | 4 lbs. 12 oz. | Messalonskee Lake, Me. | June 4, 1949 | Mrs. Earl Small |
| Perch, Yellow | 4 lbs. 3 oz. | Bordentown, N.J. | May 1865 | Dr. C. C. Abbot |
| Pickerel, Chain | 9 lbs. 6 oz. | Homerville, Ga. | Feb. 17, 1961 | Baxley McQuaig, Jr. |
| Pike, Northern | 62 lbs. 8 oz. | Reuss-Weiher, Switz. | June 15, 1979 | Jürg Nötzli |
| Redhorse, Silver | 5 lbs. 14 oz. | Shelbyville, Ind. | Oct. 20, 1980 | Ernest Harley, Jr. |
| | | Frankfort, Mich. | May 4, 1980 | Darrell T. Hasler |
| Salmon, Atlantic | 79 lbs. 2 oz. | Tana River, Norway | 1928 | Henrik Henriksen |
| Salmon, Chinook | 93 lbs. | Kelp Bay, Alaska | June 24, 1977 | Howard C. Rider |
| Salmon, Chum | 27 lbs. 3 oz. | Raymond Cove, Alaska | June 11, 1977 | Robert A. Jahnke |
| Salmon, Coho | 31 lbs. | Cowichan Bay, B.C. | Oct. 11, 1947 | Mrs. Lee Hallberg |
| Salmon, Pink | 12 lbs. 9 oz. | Moose/Kenai Rivers, Alaska | Aug. 17, 1974 | Steven Alan Lee |
| Salmon, Sockeye | 7 lbs. 14 oz. | American River, Alaska | July 19, 1981 | Brooke P. Halsey, Jr. |
| Sauger | 8 lbs. 12 oz. | Lake Sakakawea, N.D. | Oct. 6, 1971 | Mike Fischer |
| Shad, American | 9 lbs. 4 oz. | Delaware River, Pa. | Apr. 26, 1979 | J. Edward Whitman |
| | 9 lbs. 4 oz. | Connecticut R., Conn. | Apr. 20, 1981 | Edward W. Cypus |
| Sturgeon | 407 lbs. | Sacramento R., Calif. | May 10, 1979 | Raymond Pittenger |
| Sunfish, Green | 2 lbs. 2 oz. | Stockton Lake, Mo. | June 18, 1971 | Paul M. Dilley |
| Sunfish, Redbreast | 1 lb. 8 oz. | Suwanee R., Fla. | Apr. 30, 1977 | Tommy D. Cason, Jr. |
| Sunfish, Redear | 4 lbs. 8 oz. | Chase City, Va. | June 19, 1970 | Maurice E. Ball |
| Trout, Brook | 14 lbs. 8 oz. | Nipigon River, Ontario | July 1916 | Dr. W. J. Cook |
| Trout, Brown | 35 lbs. 15 oz. | Nahuel Huapi, Arg. | Dec. 16, 1952 | Eugenio Cavaglia |
| Trout, Cutthroat | 41 lbs. | Pyramid Lake, Nev. | Dec. 1925 | John Skimmerhorn |
| Trout, Golden | 11 lbs. | Cook's Lake, Wyo. | Aug. 5, 1948 | Chas. S. Reed |
| Trout, Lake | 65 lbs. | Great Bear Lake, N.W.T. | Aug. 8, 1970 | Larry Daunis |
| Trout, Rainbow | 42 lbs. 2 oz. | Bell Island, Alaska | June 22, 1970 | David R. White |
| Trout, Tiger | 20 lbs. 13 oz. | Lake Michigan, Wis. | Aug. 12, 1978 | Pete M. Friedland |
| Walleye | 25 lbs. | Old Hickory L., Tenn. | Aug. 1, 1960 | Mabry Harper |
| Warmouth | 2 lbs. 2 oz. | Douglas Swamp, S.C. | May 19, 1973 | Willie Singletary |
| Whitefish, Lake | 13 lbs. 15 oz. | Meaford, Ontario | Apr. 19, 1981 | Wayne Caswell |
| Whitefish, Mountain | 5 lbs. | Athabasca R., Alberta | June 3, 1963 | Orville Welch |

## WORLD SALTWATER FISHING RECORDS

SOURCE: International Game Fish Association (All tackle records, as of September 1, 1982)

| Species | Weight | Where Caught | Date | Angler |
|---|---|---|---|---|
| Albacore | 88 lbs. 2 oz. | Morgan Port, Canary Islands | 11/19/77 | Siegfried Dickemann |
| Amberjack (Greater) | 155 lbs. 10 oz. | Challenger Bank, Bermuda | 6/24/81 | Joseph Dawson |
| Barracuda (Great) | 83 lbs. | Lagos, Nigeria | 1/13/52 | K. J. W. Hackett |
| Bass (Black Sea) | 8 lbs. 12 oz. | Oregon Inlet, N.C. | 4/21/79 | Joe W. Mizelle, Sr. |
| Bass (Giant Sea) | 563 lbs. 8 oz. | Anacapa Island, Calif. | 8/20/68 | James D. McAdam, Jr. |
| Bass (Striped) | 76 lbs. | Montauk, N.Y. | 7/17/81 | Robert A. Rocchetta |
| Bluefish | 31 lbs. 12 oz. | Hatteras Inlet, N.C. | 1/30/72 | James M. Hussey |
| Bonefish | 19 lbs. | Zululand, South Africa | 5/26/62 | Brian W. Batchelor |
| Bonito (Atlantic) | 16 lbs. 12 oz. | Puerto Rico, Canary Is. | 12/6/80 | Rolf Fedderies |
| Bonito (Pacific) | 23 lbs. 8 oz. | Victoria, Seychelles | 2/19/75 | Mrs. Anne Cochain |
| Cobia | 110 lbs. 5 oz. | Mombasa, Kenya | 9/8/64 | Eric Tinworth |
| Cod | 98 lbs. 12 oz. | Isles of Shoals, N.H. | 6/8/69 | Alphonse J. Bielevich |
| Dolphin | 87 lbs. | Papagayo Gulf, Costa Rica | 9/25/76 | Manuel Salazar |
| Drum (Black) | 113 lbs. 1 oz. | Lewes, Del. | 9/15/75 | Gerald M. Townsend |
| Drum (Red) | 90 lbs. | Rodanthe, N.C. | 11/7/73 | Elvin Hooper |
| Flounder (Summer) | 22 lbs. 7 oz. | Montauk, N.Y. | 9/15/75 | Charles Nappi |
| Halibut (Atlantic) | 250 lbs. | Gloucester, Mass. | 7/3/81 | Louis P. Sirard |
| Halibut (California) | 42 lbs. | Santa Rosa I., Calif. | 5/24/81 | Jerry Yahiro |
| Jack (Crevalle) | 54 lbs. 7 oz. | Port Michel, Gabon | 1/15/82 | Thomas Gibson, Jr. |
| Jack (Horse-Eye) | 23 lbs. 2 oz. | Cancún, Mexico | 10/2/81 | Norman A. Carpenter |
| Jewfish | 680 lbs. | Fernandina Beach, Fla. | 5/20/61 | Lynn Joyner |

**SALTWATER FISHING RECORDS (Continued)**

| Species | Weight | Where Caught | Date | Angler |
|---|---|---|---|---|
| Kawakawa | 26 lbs. | Merimbula, N.S.W., Australia | 1/26/80 | Wally Elfring |
| Mackerel (King) | 90 lbs. | Key West, Fla. | 2/16/76 | Norton I. Thomton |
| Marlin (Atlantic Blue) | 1282 lbs. | St. Thomas, Virgin Is. | 8/6/77 | Larry Martin |
| Marlin (Black) | 1560 lbs. | Cabo Blanco, Peru | 8/4/53 | Alfred C. Glassell, Jr. |
| Marlin (Pacific Blue) | 1376 lbs. | Kona, Hawaii | 5/31/82 | William de Beaubien |
| Marlin (Striped) | 417 lbs. 8 oz. | Cavalli Is., New Zealand | 1/14/77 | Phillip Bryers |
| Marlin (White) | 181 lbs. 14 oz. | Vitoria, Brazil | 12/8/79 | Evandro Luiz Coser |
| Permit | 51 lbs. 8 oz. | Lake Worth, Fla. | 4/28/78 | William M. Kenney |
| Pollock | 46 lbs. 7 oz. | Brielle, N.J. | 5/26/75 | John Tomes Holton |
| Pompano (African) | 41 lbs. 8 oz. | Fort Lauderdale, Fla. | 2/15/79 | Wayne Sommers |
| Roosterfish | 114 lbs. | LaPaz, Mexico | 6/1/60 | Abe Sackheim |
| Runner (Rainbow) | 33 lbs. 10 oz. | Clarion Island, Mexico | 3/14/76 | Ralph A. Mikkelsen |
| Sailfish (Atlantic) | 128 lbs. 1 oz. | Luanda, Angola | 3/27/74 | Harm Steyn |
| Sailfish (Pacific) | 221 lbs. | Santa Cruz Island, Galapagos Is. | 2/12/47 | C. W. Stewart |
| Seabass (White) | 83 lbs. 12 oz. | San Felipe, Mexico | 3/31/53 | L. C. Baumgardner |
| Seatrout (Spotted) | 16 lbs. | Mason's Beach, Va. | 5/28/77 | William Katko |
| Shark (Blue) | 437 lbs. | Catherine Bay, Australia | 10/2/76 | Peter Hyde |
| Shark (Hammerhead) | 717 lbs. | Jacksonville Beach, Fla. | 7/27/80 | Richard E. Morse |
| Shark (Mako) | 1080 lbs. | Montauk, N.Y. | 8/26/79 | James L. Melanson |
| Shark (Porbeagle) | 465 lbs. | Padstow, Cornwall, England | 7/23/76 | Jorge Potier |
| Shark (Thresher) | 802 lbs. | New Zealand | 2/8/81 | Dianne North |
| Shark (Tiger) | 1780 lbs. | Cherry Grove, S.C. | 6/14/64 | Walter Maxwell |
| Shark (White) | 2664 lbs. | Ceduna, Australia | 4/21/59 | Alfred Dean |
| Skipjack (Black) | 14 lbs. 8 oz. | Cabo San Lucas, Mexico | 5/24/77 | Lorraine Carlton |
| Snapper (Cubera) | 60 lbs. 12 oz. | Miami Beach, Fla. | 2/27/80 | Dr. Richard A. Klein |
| Snook | 53 lbs. 10 oz. | Rio de Parasmina, Costa Rica | 10/18/78 | Gilbert Ponzi |
| Spearfish | 90 lbs. 13 oz. | Madeira, Port. | 6/2/80 | Joseph Larkin |
| Swordfish | 1182 lbs. | Iquique, Chile | 5/7/53 | L. Marron |
| Tanguigue | 99 lbs. | Scottburgh, S. Africa | 3/14/82 | Michael J. Wilkinson |
| Tarpon | 283 lbs. | Lake Maracaibo, Venezuela | 3/19/56 | M. Salazar |
| Tautog | 21 lbs. 6 oz. | Cape May, New Jersey | 6/12/54 | R. N. Sheafer |
| Trevally (Giant) | 116 lbs. | Pago Pago, Amer. Samoa | 2/20/78 | William G. Foster |
| Tuna (Atlantic Bigeye) | 375 lbs. 8 oz. | Ocean City, Md. | 8/26/77 | Cecil Browne |
| Tuna (Blackfin) | 42 lbs. | Bermuda | 6/2/78 | Alan J. Card |
| Tuna (Bluefin) | 1496 lbs. | Aulds Cove, Nova Scotia, Canada | 10/26/79 | Ken Fraser |
| Tuna (Dog-tooth) | 194 lbs. | Korea | 9/27/80 | Kim Chul |
| Tuna (Longtail) | 79 lbs. 2 oz. | Montague I., Australia | 4/12/82 | Jim Simpson |
| Tuna (Pacific Bigeye) | 435 lbs. | Cabo Blanco, Peru | 4/17/57 | Dr. Russel V. A. Lee |
| Tuna (Skipjack) | 41 lbs. 12 oz. | Black River, Mauritius | 3/13/82 | Bruno de Ravel |
| Tuna (Southern Bluefin) | 348 lbs. 5 oz. | New Zealand | 1/16/81 | Rex Wood |
| Tuna (Yellowfin) | 388 lbs. 12 oz. | San Benedicto I., Mexico | 4/1/77 | Curt Wiesenhutter |
| Tunny (Little) | 27 lbs. | Key Largo, Fla. | 4/20/76 | William E. Allison |
| Wahoo | 149 lbs. | Cat Cay, Bahamas | 6/15/62 | John Pirovano |
| Weakfish | 17 lbs. 14 oz. | Rye, N.Y. | 5/31/80 | William N. Herold |
| Yellowtail (California) | 71 lbs. 15 oz. | Alijos Rocks, Mexico | 6/24/79 | Michael Carpenter |
| Yellowtail (Southern) | 111 lbs. | Bay of Islands, New Zealand | 6/11/61 | A. F. Plim |

# WRESTLING

## 1982 NAT'L AAU FREESTYLE CHAMPIONS

105.5 lbs.—Bill Rosado, Sunkist Kids
114.5 lbs.—Bob Weaver, N.Y. Athletic Club
125.5 lbs.—Gene Mills, N.Y. Athletic Club
136.5 lbs.—Lee Roy Smith, Cowboy Wrestling Club
149.5 lbs.—Andy Rein, Wisconsin Wrestling Club
163 lbs.—Lee Kemp, Wisconsin Wrestling Club
180.5 lbs.—Bruce Kinseth, Hawkeye Wrestling Club
198 lbs.—Bill Scherr, Nebraska Olympic Club
220 lbs.—Greg Gibson, U.S. Marines
Heavyweight—Bruce Baumgartner, N.Y. Athletic Club
Outstanding Wrestler—Lee Roy Smith
Team—New York Athletic Club

## 1982 NAT'L AAU GRECO-ROMAN CHAMPIONS

105.5 lbs.—T. J. Jones, U.S. Navy
114.5 lbs.—Mark Fuller, Little C Athletic Club
125.5 lbs.—Dan Mello, U.S. Marines
136.5 lbs.—Frank Famiano, Adirondack 3-Style Club
149.5 lbs.—Doug Yeats, Canada
163 lbs.—John Matthews, Michigan Wrestling Club
180.5 lbs.—Tom Press, Minnesota Wrestling Club
198 lbs.—Steve Fraser, Michigan Wrestling Club
220 lbs.—Greg Gibson, U.S. Marines
Heavyweight—Pete Lee, Grand Rapids, Mich.
Outstanding Wrestler—Dan Mello
Team—U.S. Marine Corps.

## 1982 NCAA CHAMPIONS

DIVISION I
118 lbs.—Barry Davis, Iowa
126 lbs.—Dan Cuestas, Bakersfield State
134 lbs.—C. D. Mock, North Carolina
142 lbs.—Andre Metzger, Oklahoma
150 lbs.—Nate Carr, Iowa State
158 lbs.—Jim Zalesky, Iowa
167 lbs.—Dave Schultz, Oklahoma
177 lbs.—Mark Schultz, Oklahoma
190 lbs.—Pete Bush, Iowa
Heavyweight—Bruce Baumgartner, Indiana State
Team—Iowa
Division II Team—Bakersfield State
Division III Team—Brockport State

## 1982 WORLD CUP FREESTYLE CHAMPIONS

105.5 lbs.—Adam Cuestas, U.S.A.
114.5 lbs.—Joe Gonzales, U.S.A.
125.5 lbs.—Sergey Beloglazov, U.S.S.R.
136.5 lbs.—Viktor Alexeev, U.S.S.R.
149.5 lbs.—Mikhail Kharachura, U.S.S.R.
163 lbs.—Lee Kemp, U.S.A.
180.5 lbs.—Mark Schultz, U.S.A.
198 lbs.—Clark Davis, Canada
220 lbs.—Magomed Magomedov, U.S.S.R.
Heavyweight—Salman Chasimikov, U.S.S.R.
Teams—1. U.S.A., 2. U.S.S.R., 3. Canada, 4. South Korea, 5. Africa

# OTHER SPORTS

## ARCHERY (1982)

**Nat'l Field Archery Champions**

PROFESSIONAL DIVISION

Freestyle—Mike Leiter, Maryland
Women—Martha Lorence, Ohio
Freestyle Limited—Jerry Podratz, Minnesota
Bowhunter Freestyle—Keith Barner, Montana

ADULT DIVISION

Freestyle—Richard Johnson, Massachusetts
Women—Kitty Frazier, West Virginia
Freestyle Limited—Donald Maus, Colorado
Women—Carolyn Griffith, Utah
Barebow—Dennis Cline, Virginia
Women—Gloria Shelley, Connecticut
Bowhunter—Ben Rogers, California
Women—Lura Free, Washington
Bowhunter Freestyle—Jim Kelly, Mississippi
Women—Leiona Roach, Oregon
Bowhunter Freestyle Limited—Charles Langston, Texas
Women—Joyce McClellen, Washington

**Nat'l Target Champions**

Men—Rick McKinney, Glendale, Ariz.
Women—Luann Ryon, Parker Dam, Calif.

## BADMINTON (1982)

**U.S. National Champions**

Men's Singles—Gary Higgins, Manhattan Beach, Calif.
Women's Singles—Cheryl Carton, San Diego, Calif.
Men's Doubles—Don Paup, Vienna, Va.-Bruce Pontow, Chicago, Ill.
Women's Doubles—Judianne Kelly, Costa Mesa, Calif.-Pam Brady, Grand Blanc, Mich.
Mixed Doubles—Pam Brady-Danny Brady, Grand Blanc, Mich.

**World Champions (1980)**

Men's Singles—Rudy Hartono, Indonesia
Women's Singles—Wiharjo Verawaty, Indonesia
Men's Doubles—Ade Chandra-Christian Hadinata, Indonesia
Women's Doubles—Nora Perry-Jane Webster, England

## BIATHLON

**World Cup** (1981)—Frank Ullrich, E. Germany

**U.S. Nat'l Champions (1981)**

(20 km)—Glen Jobe, California
(10 km)—Lyle Nelson, California
(15 km-Women)—Betty Stroock, Wyoming
(10 km-Women)—Betty Stroock

## BILLIARDS (1982)

**World Pocket Champions**

Men—Steve Mizerak, Fords, N.J.
Women—Jean Balukas, New York, N.Y.
BCA All-American Team
Men: Wizards, Colorado Springs, Colo.
Women: Richard's Pigeon Inn, DeWitt, Mich.

## BOBSLEDDING (1982)

World 2-Man—Switzerland
World 4-Man—Switzerland
U.S. 2-Man (1981)-Brent Rushlaw, Bob Burrel
U.S. 4-Man—U.S. Navy (Bill Renton, Steve Clayton, Wayne De Atley, Carl Flanagan)

## CANOEING (1982)

**U.S. Flatwater Champions** — KAYAK

Singles (500m.)—Greg Barton, Homer, Mich.
Women—Cathy Marino-Gregory, Hunt. Beach, Calif.
Singles (1000m.)—Greg Barton
Women's Singles (5000m.)—Theresa Haught, Arlington, Va.
Singles (10,000m.)—Greg Barton
Tandem (500m.)—Brent Turner, Craftsbury, Vt.-Terry White, Peru, Vt.
Women's Tandem—Ann Turner, St. Charles, Ill.-Theresa Haught
Tandem (1000 m.)—Brent Turner-Terry White
Women's Tandem (5000m.)—Ann Turner-Theresa Haught
Tandem (10,000m.)—Brent Turner-Terry White

**U.S. Flatwater Champions** — CANOE

Singles (500m.)—Rob Plankenhorn, Roselle, Ill.
Singles (1000m.)—Blaise Stanek, New York, N.Y.
Singles (10,000m.)—Rob Plankenhorn
Tandem (500m.)—Barry Merritt, Gaithersburg, Md.-Bruce Merritt, Ridge, Md.
Tandem (1000m.)—Barry Merritt-Bruce Merritt
Tandem (10,000m.)—Barry Merritt-Bruce Merritt

**U.S. Slalom Champions**

Kayak—Chris McCormick, Potomac, Md.
Women—Sue Norman
Canoe—David Hearn, Garrett Park, Md.
Tandem Canoe—Mike Garvis, Great Falls, Va.-Steve Garvis, Annandale, Va.

**U.S. Wildwater Champions**

Kayak—Jon Fishburn, Billings, Mont.
Women—Carol Fisher, Hanover, N.H.
Canoe—Jim Underwood, Lake Placid, N.Y.
Tandem Canoe—Mike Hipsher, Bryson City, N.C.-David Jones, Atlanta, Ga.

## CROSS-COUNTRY (1981)

**U.S. National Champions**

Men—Adrian Royle, Reno, Nevada
Women—Julie Brown, L.A. Naturite T.C.

**National Collegiate Champions**

NCAA Div. I—Mathews Motshwarateu, Texas-El Paso
Team—Texas-El Paso
NCAA Div. II—Mark Conover, Humboldt State
Team—Millersville State
NCAA Div. III—Mark Whalley, Principia (Ill.)
Team—North Central (Ill.)
NCAA Women Div. I—Betty Springs, North Carolina State
Team—Virginia
NCAA Women Div. II—Eileen Kramer, Cal Poly-San Luis Obispo
Team—South Dakota State
NCAA Women Div. III—Cynthia Sturm, Westfield State (Mass.)
Team—Central (Iowa)
NAIA Team—Adams State
Women—Adams State

**1982 World Champions**

Men—Mohammed Kedir, Ethiopia
Women—Marcica Puica, Romania

## CYCLING

**1982 World Road Champion (Professional)**

Giuseppe Saronni, Italy

**1982 Tour de France**

Bernard Hinault, France

**1982 Coors International Classic**

Men—Jose Patrocinio Jimenez, Colombia
Women—Connie Carpenter, Boulder, Colo.
Team—Colombia

**1982 World Amateur Champions**

Men—Bernd Drogan, E. Germany
Women—Mandy Jones, United Kingdom

**1982 U.S. Champions**—TIME TRIALS

Men—Andrew Weaver, Florida
Women—Rebecca Twigg, Washington
Team—7-Eleven

**1982 U.S. Champions**—ROAD RACING

Men—Greg Demgen, LaCrosse, Wis.
Women—Sue Novara-Reber, Flint, Mich.

**1982 U.S. Professional Champion**

Shane Sutton, Australia

**1981 World Professional Champions**

Sprint—Koichi Nakano, Japan
Pursuit—Alain Bondue, France
Road—Freddy Maertens, Belgium
Women—Ute Enzenhauer, W. Germany

## DOGS

**Best-in-Show Winners**

1982 Westminister (N.Y.)—Ch. St. Aubrey Dragonora (Pekingese); Ann Snelling, Ontario, Can.
1982 International (Chicago)—Ch. Beaucrest Ruffian (Bouvier des Flandres); Pat and Roy Schiller, Ijamsville, Md.
1982 Golden Gate—Ch. Goodspice for All Seasons (Sealyham Terrier); Carol Ravrer, Danville, Calif.
1981 Boardwalk (Atlantic City)—Ch. Thrumpton's Lord Brady (Norwich Terrier); Ruth Cooper, Glenview, Ill.
1982 Westchester (Tarrytown, N.Y.)—Ch. Salilyn's Private Stock (English Springer Spaniel); Robert Gough and Julia Gasow
1981 Philadelphia—Ch. Thrumpton's Lord Brady (Norwich Terrier)

## FENCING (1982)

**U.S. Champions**

Foil—Michael Marx, Salle Auroil
Team—N.Y. Fencers Club
Epee—Lee Shelley, Orsi Village
Team—U.S. Modern Pentathlon
Sabre—Peter Westbrook, N.Y. Fencers Club
Team—N.Y. Athletic Club
Women's Foil—Jana Angelakis, Tanner City
Team—Tanner City
Women's Epee—Vincent Bradford
Women's Sabre—Marlene Adrian

**NCAA Champions**

Foil—Alexander Flom, George Mason
Epee—Peter Schifrin, San Jose State
Sabre—Neil Hick, Wayne State
Team—Wayne State
Women's Individual—Joy Ellingson, San Jose State
Women's Team—Wayne State

**Nat'l Intercollegiate Fencing Association Champions** — MEN

Foil—Paul Schmidt, Princeton
Team—M.I.T.
Epee—Mike Storm, Pennsylvania
Team—Pennsylvania
Sabre—Kevin McDonald, Yale
Team—Pennsylvania
Overall Team—Pennsylvania

**North American Cup**

Foil—Greg Massialas, U.S.
Epee—Lee Shelley, U.S.
Sabre—Peter Westbrook, U.S.
Women's Foil—Jana Angelakis, U.S.

**World Team Champions**

Foil—U.S.S.R.
Epee—France
Sabre—Hungary
Women's Foil—Italy

## FIELD HOCKEY (1982)

**NCAA Women Champions**

Div. I—Connecticut
Div. II—Pfeiffer (N.C.)
Div. III—Trenton State

**AIAW Champions**

Div. I—Penn State

## GYMNASTICS (1982)

**U.S. Nat'l Champions**—MEN

All-Around—Peter Vidmar, Los Angeles, Calif.
Floor Exercise—Jim Hartung, Lincoln, Neb.
Pommel Horse—Jim Hartung
Rings—Jim Hartung
Vault—Jim Hartung
Parallel Bars—Peter Vidmar
High Bar—Mitch Gaylord, Los Angeles, Calif.

**U.S. Nat'l Champions**—WOMEN

All-Around—Tracee Talavera, Eugene, Ore.
Floor Exercise—Amy Koopman, Minneapolis, Minn.
Vault—Yumi Modre, Eugene, Ore.
Balance Beam—Julianne McNamara, Eugene, Ore.
Uneven Parallel Bars—Marie Roethlisberger, Minneapolis, Minn.

**NCAA Men's Champions**

Division I
All-Around—Peter Vidmar, UCLA

## OTHER SPORTS (Cont.)

Floor Exercise—Steve Elliott and Jim Mikus, Nebraska
Pommel Horse—Peter Vidmar
Rings—Alex Schwartz, UCLA and Jim Hartung, Nebraska
Vault—Randall Wickstrom, California
Parallel Bars—Phil Cahoy, Nebraska
High Bar—Bill Paul, California
Team—Nebraska
Div. II Team—Wisconsin-Oshkosh
**NCAA Women's Champions**
Division I
All-Around—Sue Stednitz, Utah
Floor Exercise—Mary Ayotte Law, Oregon State
Vault—Elaine Alfano, Utah
Balance Beam—Sue Stednitz
Uneven Parallel Bars—Lisa Shirk, Pittsburgh
Team—Utah
Div. II Team—Northridge State
**American Cup**
All-Around—Bart Conner, Oklahoma
Women—(tie) Julianne McNamara, Eugene, Ore.-Zoya Grantcharova, Bulgaria
**NAIA Team—Wisconsin-Oshkosh**
Women—Georgia College
**World Champions (1981)—Overall**
Men—Yuri Korolev, U.S.S.R.
Women—Olga Bicherova, U.S.S.R.

## HANDBALL (1982)

**U.S. Handball Ass'n Champions**
Singles—Naty Alvarado, Hesperia, Calif.
Women—Rosemary Bellini, New York, N.Y.
Doubles—Vern Roberts, Chicago, Ill.-Naty Alvarado
Women—Allison Roberts, Cincinnati, Ohio-Glorian Motal, Houston, Tex.

## HORSE SHOWS (1981)

**National Horse Show Champions**
Working Hunter Champion—Super Flash, Mrs. Sylvester Johnson
Conformation Hunter Champion—Henry the Hawk, Mrs. Stewart McKinney
Grand Hunter Champion—Super Flash
**National Horse Show Equitation Champions**
Saddle Seat (Good Hands)—Janice Christensen, Madison, Conn.
ASPCA Trophy (Maclay)—Laura Tidball, Langley, B.C., Canada
The Nations Cup—U.S. Equestrian Team

## ICE SKATING (1982)

**World Figure Skating Champions**
Men—Scott Hamilton, Denver, Colo.
Women—Elaine Zayak, Paramus, N.J.
Pairs—Sabine Baess-Tassilo Thierbach, E. Germany
Dance—Jayne Torvill-Christopher Dean, Great Britain
**U.S. Figure Skating Champions**
Men—Scott Hamilton, Denver, Colo.
Women—Rosalyn Sumners, Edmonds, Wash.
Pairs—Kitty and Peter Carruthers, Wilmington, Del.
Dance—Judy Blumberg-Michael Seibert, Colorado Springs, Colo.
**World Speed Skating Champions**
Men—Sergei Khlebnikov, USSR
Women—Natalya Petruseva, USSR
Sprint—Hilbert Van Der Duim, Netherlands
Women's Sprint—Karin Busch, E. Germany
**U.S. Speed Skating Champions**
Outdoor—Greg Oly, Minneapolis, Minn.
Women—Lisa Merrifield, Butte, Mont.
Indoor—(tie) Jack Mortell, Evanston, Ill.-Paul Jacobs, Park Ridge, Ill.
Women—Lydia Stephans, Northbrook, Ill.
**North American Speed Skating Champions**
Outdoor—Kevin O'Brien, Pr. Edw. I., Canada
Women—Katie Class, St. Paul, Minn.
Indoor—Louis Baril, Quebec, Canada
Women—Susan Hellingwerf, Quebec, Canada

## JUDO (1982)

**U.S. Nat'l Champions—MEN**
132 Lbs.—Rod Conduriago, San Jose, Calif.
143 Lbs.—James A. Martin, San Gabriel, Calif.
156 Lbs.—Mike Swain, San Jose, Calif.
172 Lbs.—Brett Barron, San Mateo, Calif.
189 Lbs.—Robert Berland, San Jose, Calif.
Under 209 Lbs.—Leo White, Ft. Eustis, Va.
Over 209 Lbs.—Doug E. Nelson, Williamsburg, Ky.
Open Division—Mitch Santa Maria, Roselle Park, N.J.
**U.S. Nat'l Champions—WOMEN**
106 Lbs.—Darlene Anaya, Albuquerque, N.M.
114 Lbs.—Mary Lewis, Albany, N.Y.
123 Lbs.—Geri Bindell, New Milford, N.J.
134 Lbs.—Cindy Sovljanski, Sterling Hts., Mich.
145 Lbs.—Christine Penick, San Jose, Calif.
Under 158 Lbs.—Eileen O'Connell, Bayside, N.Y.
Over 158 Lbs.—Margaret Castro, New York, N.Y.
Open Division—Heidi Bauersachs, Brooklyn, N.Y.

## JUNIOR COLLEGES (1981-82)

**Nat'l J.C. Champions — Men's Div.**
Baseball—Middle Georgia College
Basketball—Midland College
Bowling—Erie C.C.
Cross-Country—Southwestern Michigan College
Decathlon—Conny Silfver, Ricks Coll.
Football—Butler County C.C.
Golf—Scottsdale C.C.
Gymnastics—Long Beach City College
Ice Hockey—Canton Ag. & Tech. College
Lacrosse—Nassau C.C.
Marathon—Mike Peveto, Brevard College
Skiing (Alpine)—(tie) North Country C.C., Champlain College
Skiing (Nordic)—Vermont Technical C.C.
Soccer—Florissant Valley C.C.
Swimming—Indian River C.C.
Tennis—Seminole C.C.
Track & Field (Indoor)—Odessa College
Track & Field (Outdoor)—Odessa College
Wrestling—North Idaho College
**Nat'l J.C. Champions—Women's Div.**
Basketball—Moberly J.C.
Bowling—Erie C.C.
Cross-Country—Golden Valley Lutheran College
Field Hockey—Mitchell College
Golf—Midland College
Gymnastics—Spokane C.C.
Skiing (Alpine)—Champlain College
Skiing (Nordic)—Adirondack C.C.
Softball (Fast Pitch)—Illinois Central C.C.
Swimming—Daytona Beach C.C.
Tennis—Indian River C.C.
Track & Field (Indoor)—Santa Fe C.C.
Track & Field (Outdoor)—E. Oklahoma St. College
Volleyball—Scottsdale C.C.

## KARATE

**1981 Nat'l AAU Champions**
MEN (18-34) KATA
Nov.—Daniel Contino
Int.—Gary Roney
Adv.—Domingo Llanos
MEN (18-34) KUMITE
Nov.—Michael Dodson
Int.—Dann Deere
Adv. Weapons—Glenn Hart
WOMEN (18-34) KATA
Nov.—Cynthia Finger
Int.—Faith Barbera
Adv.—Pamela Glaser
Weapons—Katherine Baxter
WOMEN (18-34) KUMITE
Nov.—Donna Smack
Int.—Linda Yaille
Under 120 lbs.—Gina Schiavone
Over 120 lbs.—Gail Egeland

## LACROSSE (1982)

World Champion—United States
NCAA Div. I—North Carolina
NCAA Div. III—Hobart
NCAA Women—Massachusetts

## LUGE (1981)

**World Champions**
Singles—Sergei Danilin, U.S.S.R.
Women—Melitta Sollman, E. Germany
Doubles—Ulrich and Bernd Hahn, E. Germany
**U.S. Nat'l Champions**
Singles—Frank Masley, Newark, Del.
Women—Donna Burke, Lake Placid, N.Y.
Doubles—Terry Morgan, Saranac Lake, N.Y.-Beau Jamison, Hudson, Ohio

## MARATHON

1982 Boston Marathon—Alberto Salazar, Eugene, Ore.
Women—Charlotte Teske, W. Germany
1982 N.Y. City Marathon—Alberto Salazar, Eugene, Ore.
Women—Grete Waitz, Norway
1982 London Marathon—Hugh Jones, United Kingdom
Women Joyce Smith, United Kingdom
1982 America's Marathon, Chicago—Greg Meyer, Wellesley, Mass.
Women—Nancy Conz, Northampton, Mass.
1982 TAC U.S. Champion—Joel Menges, Birmingham, Mich.
Women—Lorraine Moeller, New Zealand

## MODERN PENTATHLON

World Champion (1982)—Daniele Masala, Italy
U.S. Champion (1981) Michael Burley, Berea, Ohio

## MOTORCYCLING (1982)

**AMA National Champions**
125 cc Motocross—Mark Barnett, Bridgeview, Ill. (Suzuki)
250 cc Motorcross—Donnie Hansen, Canyon Country, Calif. (Honda)
500 cc Motorcross—Darrell Shultz, Trinidad, Calif. (Honda)
Speedway—Shawn Moran
AMA Wrangler Supercross—Donnie Hansen (Honda)
U.S. Road Racing—Formula I (750 cc)—Mike Baldwin, Darien, Conn. (Honda)
Superbike—Eddie Lawson, Upland, Calif. (Kawasaki)
Trans-USA Int'l—Dave Hollis, Oxford, Mich. (Suzuki)
Trans-USA Support—Joe Baker, Kentwood, Mich. (Honda)
Grand National—Ricky Graham

## PADDLEBALL (1981)

**Nat'l Four-Wall Champions**
Singles—Steve Wilson, Flint, Mich.
Women—Caprice Behner, St. Charles, Ill.
Doubles—Andy Kasalo-Andy Mitchell, Kalamazoo, Mich.
Women—Grace Louwsma-Judy Shirley, Ann Arbor, Mich.

## PADDLE TENNIS (1982)

**U.S. National Champions**
Singles—Mark Rifenbark, Los Angeles, Calif.
Doubles—Sol Hauptman-Jeff Fleitman, Brooklyn, N.Y.
Women—Carolyn Dadian, Venice, Calif.
Doubles—Kathy May Paben-Carolyn Dadian, Venice, Calif.
Mixed Doubles—Kathy May Paben-Brian Lee, Venice, Calif.
**U.S. National Beach Champions**
Doubles—Joe Heim, W. Palm Beach, Fla.-Mike Legge, St. Augustine, Fla.
Women—Kim Johns-Mary Ellen Stewart, St. Augustine, Fla.

# OTHER SPORTS (Cont.)

Mixed Doubles—Janet and Ron Sass, St. Augustine, Fla.

## PARACHUTING (1982)

**U.S. Champions**
Men's Accuracy—Cliff Jones
Men's Style—Maurice Fernandez
Men's Overall—Maurice Fernandez
Women's Accuracy—Cheryl Stearns
Women's Style—Cheryl Stearns
Women's Combined—Cheryl Stearns
Four-way Relative Work—Fire
Eight-way Relative Work—Visions
Ten-way Relative Work—Freak Brothers
Canopy Relative Work
4-way Rotation—Considerable Difficulty
4-way Sequential—Po Folks
8-way Speed—Eclipse

## PLATFORM TENNIS (1982)

**U.S. National Champions**
Singles—Doug Russell, New York, N.Y.
Doubles—Steve Baird, Harrison, N.Y.-Rich Maier, Allendale, N.J.
Women—Yvonne Hackenberg, Kalamazoo, Mich.-Hilary Hilton Marold, Glen Ellyn, Ill.
Mixed—Doug Russell-Hilary Hilton Marold

## POLO

**1982 Champions**
America Cup—Aiken
Gold Cup—Boehm-Palm Beach
Bronze Cup—Broad Acres
Delegate's Cup—Pegasus
**1981 Champions**
U.S. Open—Rolex A & K
World Cup—Boehm-Palm Beach
Women's College—Calif.-Davis

## POWERBOATING

**1982 U.S. National Champion**—Chip Hanauer, Seattle, Wash.
**1982 Championship Boat**—Atlas Van Lines
**1981 U.S. Offshore Champion**—Betty Cook, Newport Beach, Calif.
**1981 World Offshore Champion**—Jerry Jacoby

## QUARTER HORSE RACING (1982)

**Race—Winner and Jockey**
All American Futurity—Mr. Master Bug, Jackie Martin
All American Gold Cup—Higheasterjet, W.R. Hunt
Special Effort Futurity—Make Mine Cash, Jerry Nicodemus
All American Derby—Justanold Love, Jerry Nicodemus
Rainbow Derby—Cute Investment, Jimmie Hunt
Kansas Futurity—Chicks Etta Wind, Rudy Bustamante
Rainbow Futurity—Yankee Win, Bruce Pilkinton
Kindergarten Futurity—Sail On Bunny, Gary Sumpter
Dash For Cash Futurity—Sail On Bunny, Gary Sumpter

## RACQUETBALL (1982)

U.S. Champion—Marty Hogan, San Diego
Women's Pro Champion—Lynn Adams

## RODEO (1981)

**World Champions**
All-Around—Jimmie Cooper, Monument, N.M.
Saddle Bronc Riding—Brad Gjermundson, Marshall, N.D.
Bareback Bronc Riding—J.C. Trujillo, Steamboat Springs, Colo.
Bull Riding—Don Gay, Mesquite, Tex.
Steer Wrestling—Byron Walker, Ennis, Tex.
Calf Roping—Roy Cooper, Durant, Okla.
Steer Roping—Arnold Felts, Mutual, Okla.
Team Roping—Walt Woodard, Stockton, Calif.-Doyle Gellerman, Oakdale, Calif.
Women's Barrel Racing—Lynn McKenzie, Shreveport, La.

## ROLLER SKATING (1982)

**World Champions—Artistic**
Singles—Tim McGuire, Flint, Mich.
Women—Kathleen O'Brien Di Felice, Longhorne, Pa.
Dance—Cindy Smith-Mark Howard, Richmond, Va.
Mixed Pairs—Tina Kneisley-Paul Price, Brighton, Mich.
**U.S. Champions—Speed**
Men—Robb Dunn, Farmington Hills, Mich.
Women—Denise McLeod, Livonia, Mich.
**U.S. Champions—Artistic**
Singles—Tim McGuire, Flint, Mich.
Women—Kathleen O'Brien Di Felice, Langhorne, Pa.
Figures—Tony St. Jacques, Virginia Beach, Va.
Women—Debbie Isenhour, Houston, Tex.
Dance—Cindy Smith-Mark Howard, Richmond, Va.
Mixed Pairs—Tina Kneisley-Paul Price, Brighton, Mich.

## ROWING (1982)

**U.S. Men's Elite Champions**
Singles—Pete MacGowan, Ridley Graduate B.C.
Quarter Mile Singles—Jim Dietz, N.Y.A.C.
Doubles—Ridley Graduate B.C.
Pairs without Coxswain—Detroit B.C.
Pairs with Coxswain—Detroit B.C.
4s without Coxswain—Vesper B.C.
4s with Coxswain—Vesper B.C.
Quadruple Sculls—Ridley Graduate B.C.-Burnaby Lake R.C.
8s—Lightweight Camp
**U.S. Women's Elite Champions**
Singles—Judy Geer, Dartmouth R.C.
Singles (Dash)—Ann Marden, 1980 R.C.
Doubles—Dartmouth R.C.
Pairs—Lake Washington "A"
4s—College Boat Club
Quads—Boston/Dartmouth/Calif.-Irvine/ZLAC
8s—College Boat Club
**Intercollegiate Champions**
National—Yale
IRA Varsity—Cornell
IRA Freshman—California
IRA Junior Varsity—Navy
Women—Washington
Eastern Regional Sprint—Yale
San Diego Classic—California
**The Boat Race** (Cambridge-Oxford)—Oxford; series:Cam: 68, Oxf: 59, 1 tie
**Royal Henley Regatta**
Grand Challenge Cup—Leander & London Rowing Club
Thames Cup—Charles R. Rowing Assn.

## RUGBY

**1982 Champions**
Club—Old Blue R.F.C., Oakland, Calif.
College—Univ. of Calif. at Berkeley
Women—Beantown R.F.C., Boston, Mass.
Military—Camp Pendleton Ghost Riders, Calif.
Territorial Union—Pacific Coast R.F.U.

## SHOOTING (1982)

**U.S. National Outdoor Champions**
Men's Pistol—MSG Bonnie Harmon, Columbus, Ga.
Women's Pistol—SP5 Ruby E. Fox, Parker, Ariz.
Smallbore Rifle (Prone)—Presley W. Kendall, Carlisle, Ky.
Smallbore Rifle (Position)—LTC Lones Wigger, Jr., Ft. Benning, Ga.
High Power Rifle—Middleton Tompkins, Long Beach, Calif.
**U.S. National Indoor Champions**
Conv. Rifle—LTC Lones Wigger, Jr.
Women—Karen E. Monez, Weatherford, Tex.
Int'l Rifle—LTC Lones Wigger, Jr.
Women—Karen Monez
Conv. Pistol—MSG Bonnie Harmon
Women—SP5 Ruby E. Fox
Int'l Std. Pistol—Dr. Darius Young, Winterburn, Alta., Canada
Women—Lori Kamler, San Francisco, Calif.
Int'l Free Pistol—Erich Buljung, Ft. Benning, Ga.
Women—SP5 Ruby E. Fox
**NRA Int'l Clay Pigeon Champions**
Men—Michael Coleman, Ackerly, Tex.
Women—Connie Tomsovic, Las Vegas, Nev.
**NRA Int'l Skeet Champions**
Men—Matthew H. Dryke, Sequim, Wash.
Women—Ila Hill, Birmingham, Mich.
**NCAA Rifle**
Smallbore—Kurt Fitz-Randolph, Tennessee Tech
Air Rifle—John Rost, West Virginia
Team—Tennessee Tech

## SKIING

**1981-82 Alpine World Cup Champions**
Overall—Phil Mahre, Yakima, Wash.
Women—Erika Hess, Switzerland
Downhill—Steve Podborski, Canada
Women—Marie Cecile Grosgaudenier, France
Slalom—Phil Mahre
Women—Erika Hess
Giant Slalom—Phil Mahre
Women—Irene Epple, W. Germany
Combined—Phil Mahre
Women—Irene Epple
**1982 Nordic World Cup Champions**
Cross-Country—Bill Koch, Putney, Vt.
Women—Berit Aunli, Norway
Jumping—Armin Kogler, Austria
**1982 World Alpine Champions**
Overall—Michel Vion, France
Women—Erika Hess, Switzerland
Downhill—Harti Weirather, Austria
Women—Gerry Sorenson, Canada
Slalom—Ingemar Stenmark, Sweden
Women—Erika Hess
Giant Slalom—Steve Mahre, Yakima, Wash.
Women—Erika Hess
**1982 U.S. Alpine Champions**
Downhill—Steve Hegg, Olympic Valley, Calif.
Women—Cindy Oak, Orchard Park, N.Y.
Slalom—Francois Jodoin, Quebec, Canada
Women—Tamara McKinney, Squaw Valley, Calif.
**1982 U.S. Nordic Champions**
Combined—Pat Ahern, Breckenridge, Colo.
Jumping—70m-Reed Zuehlke, Eau Claire, Wis., 90m-Jeff Hastings, Norwich, Vt.
Men's Cross-Country
15km.—Bill Koch, Putney, Vt.
30km.—Stan Dunklee, Barton, Vt.
50km.—Tim Caldwell, Putney, Vt.
Women's Cross-Country
5km.—Lynn Galanes, Brattleboro, Vt.
10km.—Lynn Galanes
20km.—Lynn Galanes
**1982 NCAA Champions**
Slalom—Tiger Shaw, Dartmouth
Giant Slalom—Seth Bayer, Colorado
Cross-Country—Egil Nilsen, Colorado
Cross-Country Relay—Colorado
Team—Colorado

## SOFTBALL (1982)

**Amateur Softball Ass'n Champions**
Men's Fast Pitch—Peterbilt Western, Seattle, Wash.
Women—Raybestos Brakettes, Stratford, Conn.
Men's Slow Pitch—Triangle, Minneapolis, Minn.
Women—Stompers, Richmond, Va.
Co-Ed—C.E. Zumstein, Englewood, Ohio
Men's Super Slow Pitch—Jerry's Caterers, Miami, Fla.
Industrial Slow Pitch—Sikorsky Aircraft, Shelton, Conn.

## OTHER SPORTS (Cont.)

Women—Provident Vets, Chattanooga, Tenn.
16" Slow Pitch—Park Avenue Spats, Chicago, Ill.
Men's Class A Fast Pitch—Tee House, Stockton, Calif.
Women—San Diego Astros, California
Men's Class A Slow Pitch—Lawson Auto Parts, Altamonte Sprs., Fla.
Women—Circle K Roadrunners, Phoenix, Ariz.
Men's Class A Industrial Slow Pitch—General Dynamics, Detroit, Mich.
Men's Church Slow Pitch—Grace Methodist Black, Okla. City, Okla.
Women—First Baptist, Tallahassee, Fla.
Modified Fast Pitch—Silvestri's, Staten Island, N.Y.
**NCAA Women** Div. I—UCLA
Div. II—Sam Houston State
Div. III—Eastern Connecticut State
**NAIA**—Missouri Western

## SQUASH RACQUETS (1982)

**U.S. Association Champions**
Men's Singles—John Nimick, Narberth, Pa.
Women's Singles—Alicia McConnell, Brooklyn, N.Y.
Men's Doubles—Lawrence Heath III, Cos Cob, Conn.-John Reese, Cold Spring Harbor, N.Y.
Women's Doubles—Joyce Davenport, King of Prussia, Pa.-Carol Thesieres, Broomall, Pa.
Mixed Doubles—Gail Ramsay, Brooklyn, N.Y.-Bill Ramsay, Bala Cynwyd, Pa.
Intercollegiate—Victor Wagner, Yale
North American Open—Michael Desaulniers, New York, N.Y.
U.S. Pro Singles—Clive Caldwell, Toronto, Canada
World Series—Michael Desaulniers

## TABLE TENNIS

**1981 World Champions**
Singles—Guo Yuehua, China
Women—Tong Ling, China
Doubles—Li Zhenshi-Cai Zhenhua, China
Women—Zhang Deying-Cao Yanhua, China
Mixed Doubles—Xie Saike-Huang Junqun, China
Men's Team—China
Women's Team—P.R. China
**1982 U.S. Open Champions**
Singles—Zoran Kosanovic, Canada
Women—Kayoko Kawahigashi, Japan
Doubles—Danny and Rick Seemiller, Pittsburgh, Pa.
Women—Shin Deuk Hwa-Jung Kyung, Japan
Mixed Doubles—Koichi Kawamura-Tomoko Tamura
Men's Team—Japan
Women's Team—South Korea

## TEAM HANDBALL (1982)

**U.S. Champion**—West Coast All-Stars
**Collegiate**—Army
Women—Army

## VOLLEYBALL (1982)

**U.S. Volleyball Ass'n Champions**
Men's Open—Chuck's Steak House National, Los Angeles, Calif.
Women's Open—Monarch, Honolulu, Hawaii
Men's Senior—Outrigger Canoe Club, Honolulu, Hawaii
Women's Senior—South Bay Spoilers, Hermosa Beach, Calif.
Men's Golden Masters—Outrigger Canoe Club
**NCAA**—UCLA
**NCAA Women** (1981) Div. I—So. California
Div. II—Sacramento State
Div. III—California-San Diego
**NAIA Women**—Hawaii-Hilo (1981)

## WATER POLO (1982)

World Champion—USSR
NCAA Champion (1981)—Stanford
**Nat'l AAU Outdoor Champions**
Men—Industry Hills Aquatic Club (Calif.)
Women—Slippery Rock
**Nat'l AAU Indoor Champions**
Women—Industry Hills Aquatic Club
Men—(1981) N.Y. Athletic Club

## WATER SKIING (1982)

**U.S. Open Champions**
Overall—Carl Roberge, Orlando, Fla.
Women—Cyndi Benzel, Newberry Sprs., Calif.
Slalom—Kris LaPoint, Castro Valley, Calif.
Women—Deena Brush, W. Sacramento, Calif.
Tricks—Cory Pickos, Eagle Lake, Fla.
Women—Cyndi Benzel
Jumping—Sammy Duvall, Orlando, Fla.
Women—Cindy Todd, Pierson, Fla.
**Masters Tournament**
Overall—Sammy Duvall, Orlando, Fla.
Women—Cindy Todd, Pierson, Fla.
Slalom—Bob LaPoint, Castro Valley, Calif.
Women—Cindy Todd
Tricks—Sammy Duvall
Women—Anita Carlman, Sweden
Jumping—Sammy Duvall
Women—Cindy Todd
**World Champions** (1981)
Overall—Sammy Duvall, U.S.A.
Women—Karin Roberge, U.S.A.
Slalom—Andy Mapple, Great Britain
Women—Cindy Todd, U.S.A.
Tricks—Cory Pickos, U.S.A.
Women—Ana Maria Carrasco, Venezuela
Jumping—Mike Hazelwood, Great Britain
Women—Deena Brush, U.S.A.
Team—United States

## WEIGHTLIFTING (1982)

**World Champions**
52 kilos—Leletko, Poland
56 kilos—Kodjahashev, Bulgaria
60 kilos—Sarkisian, U.S.S.R.
67½ kilos—Mandra, Poland
75 kilos—Rusev, Bulgaria
82½ kilos—Zlatev, Bulgaria
90 kilos—Blagoev, Bulgaria
100 kilos—Sots, U.S.S.R.
110 kilos—Arakelov, U.S.S.R.
Over 110 kilos—Pisarenko, U.S.S.R.
**Nat'l Champions—MEN**
52 kilos—Brian Okada, Wailuku, Hawaii
56 kilos—Albert Hood, Los Angeles, Calif.
60 kilos—Phil Sanderson, Billings, Mont.
67½ kilos—Don Abrahamson, San Jose, Calif.
75 kilos—Carl Schake, Butler, Pa.
82½ kilos—Curt White, Colorado Sprs., Colo.
90 kilos—Kevin Winter, San Jose, Calif.
100 kilos—Ken Clark, Pacifica, Calif.
110 kilos—Jeff Michels, Chicago, Ill.
Over 110 kilos—Mario Martinez, San Francisco, Calif.
**Nat'l Champions—WOMEN**
44 kilos—Pamela Bickler
48 kilos—Michelle Evris
52 kilos—Rachael Silverman
56 kilos—Mary Beth Cervenak
60 kilos—Diane Redgate
67½ kilos—Judy Glenney
75 kilos—Karyn Tarter
82½ kilos—Mary Hyden
Over 82½ kilos—Lorna Griffin

## YACHTING

**1982 U.S. Yacht Racing Union Champions**
Mallory Cup—Mark Golison, Long Beach, Calif.
Adams Trophy—Heidi Backus, Vermilion, Ohio
Sears Cup—Ron Rosenberg, Long Beach, Calif.
O'Day Trophy—Tom Lihan, Ft. Lauderdale, Fla.
Prince of Wales Bowl—Dave Perry, Southport, Conn.
Bemis Trophy—Eldon Harvey, New Orleans, La.
Smythe Trophy—Mike Sentovich, Los Alamitos, Calif.
**1982 World Champions**
Etchells 22—Dave Curtis, Marblehead, Mass.
505—Gary Knapp, Syosset, N.Y.
Sunfish—John Kostecki, Novato, Calif.
Finn—Graig Healy, Point Richmond, Calif.
470—Steve Benjamin, Oyster Bay, N.Y.
Star—Carl Buchan, Seattle, Wash.
Tornado—Randy Smyth, Huntington Beach, Calif.
**1982 North American Champions**
Hawk Trophy—HOT FLASH, George and John Uznis, Dearborn, Mich.
Jeffries Trophy—CIAO, Brack Ward, Minneapolis, Minn.
Sopranino Trophy—WILD CARD, Ed Polidor, Rochester, N.Y.
**1980 America's Cup**—US (Freedom; Dennis Conner, skipper) over Australia (Australia; Jim Hardy, skipper) 4-1

## POPULARITY OF DOG BREEDS

Source: American Kennel Club

| 1981 Rank | Breed | 1981 Registrations | 1980 Rank |
|---|---|---|---|
| 1. | Poodles | 93,050 | 1 |
| 2. | Cocker Spaniels | 83,504 | 3 |
| 3. | Doberman Pinschers | 77,387 | 2 |
| 4. | German Shepherd Dogs | 60,976 | 4 |
| 5. | Labrador Retrievers | 58,569 | 5 |
| 6. | Golden Retrievers | 48,473 | 6 |
| 7. | Miniature Schnauzers | 35,912 | 8 |
| 8. | Beagles | 35,655 | 7 |
| 9. | Dachshunds | 33,560 | 9 |
| 10. | Shetland Sheepdogs | 29,481 | 10 |
| 11. | Yorkshire Terriers | 25,698 | 11 |
| 12. | Lhasa Apsos | 25,424 | 12 |
| 13. | English Springer Spaniels | 22,574 | 14 |
| 14. | Collies | 20,843 | 13 |
| 15. | Siberian Huskies | 20,465 | 15 |
| 16. | Shih Tzu | 19,547 | 17 |
| 17. | Chow Chows | 18,511 | 24 |
| 18. | Pekingese | 18,366 | 16 |
| 19. | Pomeranians | 17,926 | 18 |
| 20. | Brittany Spaniels | 17,411 | 20 |
| 21. | Basset Hounds | 17,262 | 19 |
| 22. | Chihuahuas | 16,495 | 21 |
| 23. | Boxers | 15,574 | 23 |
| 24. | Great Danes | 13,311 | 25 |
| 25. | Boston Terriers | 11,681 | 26 |
| 26. | Irish Setters | 10,972 | 22 |
| 27. | German Shorthaired Pointers | 10,542 | 28 |
| 28. | Old English Sheepdogs | 9,697 | 27 |
| 29. | Samoyeds | 8,307 | 29 |
| 30. | Maltese | 7,775 | 31 |

# OBITUARIES

**Abdullah, Mohammad,** 76, sheik known as the Lion of Kashmir who became the chief minister of India's predominantly Moslem Jammu and Kashmir state in 1975 after more than 40 years fighting for Kashmiri independence; in Srinagar, Kashmir, Sept. 8, 1982.
**Ace, Goodman,** 83, comic writer who teamed with his wife, the late Jane Ace, on the "Easy Aces" radio program in the 1930s and '40s; in New York City, March 25, 1982.
**Adair, Frank E.,** 94, surgeon and cancer specialist whose 60-year career included teaching and working for government support for cancer research; in Bedford, N.Y., Dec. 31, 1981.
**Adams, Harriet Stratemeyer,** 89, creator of the Nancy Drew, Bobsey Twins and Hardy Boys novels penned under a variety of pseudonyms, with almost 200 books to her credit; in Pottersville, N.J., March 27, 1982.
**Albertson, Jack,** 74, stage, film and television actor honored with a Tony Award for his performance in "The Subject Was Roses," and with three Emmys, two of which were for his series, "Chico and the Man"; in Hollywood Hills, Calif., Nov. 25, 1981.
**Anders, Glenn,** 92, Broadway actor whose career began in vaudeville and continued on stage and in films to 1960; in Englewood, N.J., Oct. 26, 1981.
**Anderson, Walter S.,** 100, Vice Admiral, former chief of naval intelligence and the oldest living Annapolis graduate; in Washington, D.C., Oct. 24, 1981.
**Ashbrook, John Milan,** 53, U.S. Representative from Ohio's 17th Congressional District, who served 21 years as a staunch conservative Republican and who had been campaigning for a U.S. Senate seat at the time of his death; in Newark, Ohio, April 24, 1982.
**Ashkin, Julius,** 61, leading theoretical and experimental physicist who co-authored a study with Hans Bethe and who worked on development of the first atomic bomb; in Pittsburgh, Pa., June 4, 1982.
**Asther, Nils,** 84, Swedish-born film actor of the 1920s and '30s who played opposite such stars as Greta Garbo and Joan Crawford; near Stockholm, Sweden, Oct. 13, 1981.
**Bader, Douglas,** 72, British fighter pilot who, despite losing both legs in a plane crash in 1931, flew fighter aircraft during World War II, and destroyed at least two dozen enemy planes, a feat for which he was knighted in 1976; in Fulham, Eng., Sept. 5, 1982.
**Bagramyan, Ivan K.,** 84, Soviet army marshal, leader of the Red Army at the Western Front during World War II, and member of the Communist Party Central Committee; in the USSR, Sept. 21, 1982.
**Balmain, Pierre,** 68, French fashion designer famous for his elegant, feminine gowns and subdued suits worn by fashion leaders since the 1950s; in Paris, June 29, 1982.
**Banning, Margaret Culkin,** 90, prolific writer of both fiction and nonfiction, with 40 books and more than 400 short stories to her credit; in Tryon, N.C., Jan. 4, 1982.
**Barlow, Samuel L. M.,** 90, composer of "Mon Ami Pierrot" and other musical works, including a ballet and chamber music pieces; in Wyndmoor, Pa., Sept. 19, 1982.
**Barnes, Djuna,** 90, avant-garde writer whose work, "Nightwood," brought her wide acclaim upon publication in 1937; in New York City, June 18, 1982.
**Barr, Stringfellow,** 84, educator who while president of St. John's College devised a curriculum based on the study of 100 great books; in Alexandria, Va., Feb. 3, 1982.
**Barsky, Arthur,** 83, innovative plastic surgeon credited with treating more than 1,000 children annually during the Vietnam War at his hospital in Saigon; in Le Beausset, France, Feb. 9, 1982.
**Beaumont, Hugh,** 72, Hollywood actor who starred in a series of "Michael Shane" films, but was most widely remembered for his portrayal of Ward Cleaver in the "Leave It to Beaver" television show; in Munich, West Ger., May 14, 1982.
**Belushi, John,** 33, television, film and stage comedic actor who rose to national prominence while a regular of the "Saturday Night Live" television program; in Hollywood, Calif., March 5, 1982.
**Benchley, Nathaniel,** 66, son of author Robert Benchley and a writer of novels, short stories, and children's books; in Boston, Mass., Dec. 13, 1981.
**Benjamin, Adam, Jr.,** 47, three-term Democratic member of the U.S. House of Representatives from the First District of Indiana; found dead in Washington, D.C., Sept. 7, 1982.
**Bergman, Ingrid,** 67, Swedish-born actress who won Academy Awards for her roles in "Gaslight," "Anastasia," and "Murder on the Orient Express," but is probably most widely remembered for her role opposite Humphrey Bogart in "Casablanca"; in London, Eng., Aug. 29, 1982.
**Berlin, Don R.,** 83, aircraft designer whose work while associated with the Curtiss-Wright Corp. during World War II resulted in three major fighter plane designs; in Middletown, Pa., May 17, 1982.
**Bernbach, William,** 71, founder and former chairman of Doyle Dane Bernbach, the advertising agency noted for its creative and soft sell campaigns; in New York City, Oct. 2, 1982.
**Bettis, Valerie,** 62, dancer and choreographer for films, television and many dance organizations; she also appeared in several Broadway shows including "Tiger Lily" for which she received two Donaldson Awards; in New York City, Sept. 26, 1982.
**Bird, Junius Bouton,** 74, former curator of South American archaeology at New York's American Museum of Natural History and an expert on primitive cultures of the Americas; in New York City, April 2, 1982.
**Bishop, Wallace B.,** 76, creator of the "Muggs and Skeeter" comic strip and its artist from 1927 to 1974; in St. Petersburg, Fla., Jan. 15, 1982.

**Blair, William McCormick,** 97, Chicago investment banker and civic leader who served as president of the Art Institute of Chicago and on the boards of various religious, academic and civic institutions in his community; in Chicago, March 29, 1982.

**Bloomingdale, Alfred S.,** 66, developer of the Diners' Club, grandson of the founder of the New York City department store bearing his name, and confidant of Pres. Reagan; in Santa Monica, Calif., Aug. 20, 1982.

**Bolotowsky, Ilya,** 74, Russian-born pioneering artist of the Neo-Plasticist school of nonobjective art and a founder of the American Abstract Artists group; found dead in New York City, Nov. 22, 1981.

**Boyer, Ken,** 51, third base player for the St. Louis Cardinals and winner of the National League's Most Valuable Player Award in 1964; in St. Louis, Mo., Sept. 7, 1982.

**Braestrup, Carl,** 85, American physicist, a leading authority on the effects of radiation, and one-time Surgeon General of the U.S.; in Middletown, Conn., Aug. 8, 1982.

**Bruce, Virginia,** 72, film star of the 1930s and '40s who played opposite many of Hollywood's leading men, including her first husband, John Gilbert; in Hollywood, Calif., Feb. 24, 1982.

**Bugbee, Emma,** 93, newspaper reporter known for her close association with Eleanor Roosevelt; in Warwick, R.I., Oct. 6, 1981.

**Bullard, Dexter M.,** 83, former director of the Chestnut Lodge mental hospital in Rockville, Md., and an innovator in the treatment of schizophrenia; in Rockville, Md., Oct. 5, 1981.

**Buono, Victor,** 43, film and television character actor often cast as a villain and an Academy Award nominee for his role in "Whatever Happened to Baby Jane?" on the screen; in Apple Valley, Calif., Jan. 1, 1982.

**Burnett, W(illiam) R(iley),** 82, screenwriter and novelist whose best-known works include "Little Caesar," "Scarface," and "High Sierra"; in Santa Monica, Calif., April 25, 1982.

**Bushmiller, Ernie,** 76, for more than 50 years the creator and artist of the "Nancy" comic strip; in Stamford, Conn., Aug. 15, 1982.

**Butterfield, Lyman Henry,** 72, historian and former director of the Institute of Early American History and Culture, Williamsburg, Va., and editor of the 20-volume collected writings by the Adams family members; in Cambridge, Mass., April 25, 1982.

**Canham, Erwin D.,** 77, editor of *The Christian Science Monitor* from 1945 to 1964, a period during which the newspaper expanded its international coverage; in Agana, Guam, Jan. 3, 1982.

**Carmichael, Hoagy,** 82, actor and songwriter best remembered for mellow tunes such as "Stardust" and "Lazy River"; in Rancho Mirage, Calif., Dec. 27, 1981.

**Carritt, David,** 55, British art historian and dealer, whose ability to uncover paintings by the Old Masters won him world renown; in London, Eng., Aug. 3, 1982.

**Case, Clifford P.,** 77, liberal Republican member of the U.S. Congress for 34 years from New Jersey who gained national attention in the early 1950s with his opposition to fellow-Republican Sen. Joseph R. McCarthy; in Washington, D.C., March 5, 1982.

**Caton, Edward,** 81, ballet dancer and teacher who numbered Agnes de Mille and Cynthia Gregory among his pupils; in New York City, Oct. 22, 1981.

**Chase, Mary,** 74, playwright best remembered for her long-running classic, "Harvey"; in Denver, Colo., Oct. 20, 1981.

**Cheever, John,** 70, Pulitzer Prize-winning novelist and short-story writer whose fiction presented the often empty lives of the upper-middle class; in Ossining, N.Y., June 18, 1982.

**Chuikov, Vasily I.,** 82, Soviet marshal who successfully led his troops in defending Stalingrad from Nazi invaders during World War II; in the USSR, March 19, 1982.

**Churchill, Sarah,** 67, stage actress and daughter of British Prime Minister Winston Churchill; in London, Eng., Sept. 24, 1982.

**Clancy, William,** 59, liberal Roman Catholic priest, writer, and founder of *Worldview* magazine; in Pittsburgh, Pa., Jan. 6, 1982.

**Clark, Edna McConnell,** 96, heiress to the Avon cosmetics fortune with which she established the foundation bearing her name to aid disadvantaged youth and promote penal reform; in Woods Hole, Mass., April 21, 1982.

**Cody, John Cardinal,** 74, Archbishop of Chicago, in the nation's most populous Roman Catholic diocese, whose traditional rule continued even after the Second Vatican Council advocated the decentralization of Church decision making; in Chicago, April 25, 1982.

**Condliffe, John B.,** 90, economics professor and international monetary expert who participated in the Bretton Woods Conference at which proposed monetary reforms resulted in the establishment of the World Bank and International Monetary Fund; in San Francisco, Calif., Dec. 23, 1981.

**Conley, Eugene,** 73, operatic tenor who performed with the Metropolitan and New York City Opera companies and who, in 1949, became the first tenor from the U.S. to open La Scala's opera season; in Denton, Tex., Dec. 18, 1981.

**Conried, Hans,** 66, American-born actor in stage, film and television roles of continental, accented, often villainous, men; in Burbank, Calif., Jan. 5, 1982.

**Copeland, Jo,** 80(?), fashion designer of finely detailed, sophisticated women's clothing who popularized the two-piece suit worn without a blouse; in New York City, March 20, 1982.

**Coppola, Francesco (Frank "Three Fingers"),** 83, crime figure, considered by some to be one of the last Mafia "godfathers," who was deported from the U.S. in the late 1940s and was alleged to operate in international drug trafficking rings; in Aprilia, Italy, April 26, 1982.

**Corcoran, Thomas G.,** 80, attorney and Pres. Franklin D. Roosevelt's adviser on major New Deal legislation creating the Securities and Exchange Commission among other agencies; in Washington, D.C., Dec. 6, 1981.

**Corner, George Washington,** 91, physician and researcher instrumental in the development of the contraceptive pill; in Huntsville, Ala., Sept. 28, 1981.

**Coslow, Sam,** 79, songwriter-turned-stock market analyst whose discography includes "My Old Flame" and "Cocktails for Two"; in Bronxville, N.Y., April 2, 1982.

**Cox, Allyn,** 86, muralist, who over an almost 30-year period, painted murals in the U.S. Capitol building; in Washington, D.C., Sept. 26, 1982.

**Craig, Charles Frost,** 86, U.S. Army brigadier general for whom Checkpoint Charlie, a gate in the Berlin Wall, was named; in Asheville, N.C., Jan. 23, 1982.

**Crisler, Herbert Orin (Fritz),** 83, football coach and athletic director at the Univ. of Michigan, where he devised the offensive and defensive platoon system on the gridiron; in Ann Arbor, Mich., Aug. 19, 1982.

**Curzon, Clifford,** 75, pianist who favored Romantic music and who was knighted in 1977 as the outstanding pianist of his day; in London, Eng., Sept. 1, 1982.

**Dali, Gala,** 89(?), wife and frequent model of Salvador Dali, the Surrealist painter; in Catalonia Prov., Spain, June 10, 1982.

**Daniels, Jonathan,** 79, press secretary to Pres. Franklin D. Roosevelt and adviser to Pres. Truman, and editor of *The Raleigh* (N.C.) *News and Observer* from 1933 to 1942; in Hilton Head Island, S.C., Nov. 6, 1981.

**Dannay, Frederic,** 76, co-author, with his late cousin, Manfred B. Lee, of the Ellery Queen detective novels; in Larchmont, N.Y., Sept. 3, 1982.

**Dantine, Helmut,** 63, Austrian-born film and stage actor frequently cast as an arrogant Nazi in World War II movies; in Beverly Hills, Calif., May 3, 1982.

**Darrah, Peggy Neppel,** 28, distance runner who set three world records during 1976 and 1977; in Ames, Iowa, Oct. 16, 1981.

**Davis, Loyal,** 86, pioneering and teaching neurosurgeon and stepfather of First Lady Nancy Reagan; in Scottsdale, Ariz., Aug. 19, 1982.

**Dayan, Moshe,** 66, former chief of staff, foreign minister and defense minister of Israel and leader of Israeli forces in the 1967 and 1973 wars; in Tel Aviv, Israel, Oct. 16, 1981.

**de Graff, Robert F.,** 86, founder and one-time president of Pocket Books, a major paperback book publishing firm; in Mill Neck, N.Y., Nov. 1, 1981.

**Demara, Ferdinand Waldo, Jr.,** 60, "The Great Imposter," who, during his life, took on such diverse persona as a Trappist monk and a surgeon; in Anaheim, Calif., June 7, 1982.

**Demarest, Victoria Booth,** 93, granddaughter of William Booth, the founder of the Salvation Army. An author of inspirational books, plays, and music as well as a member of the clergy, she traveled extensively, preaching in four languages; in St. Petersburg, Fla., April 4, 1982.

**de Rochemont, Richard G.,** 78, film maker and producer of the newsreel program, "The March of Time"; in Flemington, N.J., Aug. 4, 1982.

**Devi, Ragini,** 86, American-born dancer credited with promoting classical Indian dances in both the U.S. and in the Asian nation in which they originated; in Englewood, N.J., Jan. 23, 1982.

**Dietrich, Noah,** 92, for 32 years, financial adviser and, later, biographer of industrialist Howard R. Hughes; in Palm Springs, Calif., Feb. 15, 1982.

**Dillard, Hardy Cross,** 79, former dean of the University of Virginia School of Law and a justice on the International Court of Justice (1970-78); in Charlottesville, Va., May 12, 1982.

**Dixon, Robert E.,** 75, retired rear admiral of the U.S. Navy and author of the message, "Scratch one flattop!" after the aircraft under his command sank the first Japanese carrier in World War II; in Virginia Beach, Va., Oct. 21, 1981.

**Dolph, Jack,** 53, sports television producer and commissioner of the American Basketball Assoc. from 1969 to 1972; in Riverside, Conn., Oct. 3, 1981.

**Donon, Joseph,** 94, private chef in the employ of noteworthy U.S. families and the last surviving student of the cooking master Augusté Escoffier; in Newport, R.I., March 19, 1982.

**Dooley, Edwin B.,** 76, former chairman of the New York State Athletic Commission and three-term member of the U.S. House of Representatives; in Boca Raton, Fla., Jan. 25, 1982.

**Dubinsky, David,** 90, president of the International Ladies Garment Workers Union from 1932 to 1966 who secured a 35-hour workweek for union members and fought racketeering in the unions; in New York City, Sept. 17, 1982.

**Dubos, Rene,** 81, bacteriologist-turned-environmentalist and Pulitzer Prize-winning author of "So Human an Animal"; in New York City, Feb. 20, 1982.

**Dukas, Helen,** 85, longtime personal secretary to Albert Einstein and archivist of his papers; in Princeton, N.J., Feb. 10, 1982.

**Dunfey, Catherine A.,** 87, founder of the 27-building hotel chain bearing her name and a leading fund raiser for the Democratic party; in Miami, Fla., March 25, 1982.

**Durant, Ariel,** 83, historian and wife of her co-author in *The Story of Civilization*, an 11-volume acclaimed series on world history; in Hollywood Hills, Calif., Oct. 25, 1981.

**Durant, Will,** 96, historian and author, with his wife Ariel (see above), of the 11-volume *The Story of Civilization*, a volume of which earned him a Pulitzer Prize for History; in Los Angeles, Calif., Nov. 7, 1981.

**Dwan, Allan,** 96, motion picture director credited with more than 1,800 films, including Douglas Fairbanks's "Robin Hood" and Shirley Temple's "Heidi"; in Woodland Hills, Calif., Dec. 21, 1981.

**Eberly, Bob,** 65, singer who rose to prominence during the "Big Band" era while performing with the Dorsey brothers; in Glen Burnie, Md., Nov. 17, 1981.

**Elahi Chaudhry, Fazal,** 78, former U.N. delegate and president of Pakistan (1973-78); in Lahore, Pak., June 1, 1982.

**Eldjarn, Kristjan,** 65, president of Iceland from 1968 to 1980; in Cleveland, Ohio, Sept. 13, 1982.

**Engel, Lehman,** 71, conductor of more than 100 musicals as well as composer and musical director; in New York City, Aug. 29, 1982.

**Enoch, Kurt,** 86, German-born co-founder of New American Library, a leading paperback book publishing house; in Puerto Rico, Feb. 15, 1982.

**Euwe, Max,** 80, world chess champion from 1935 to 1937 and president of the International Chess Federation from 1970 to 1978; in Amsterdam, the Netherlands, Nov. 26, 1981.

**Evans, Luther H.**, 79, Librarian of Congress from 1945 to 1953, director-general of U.N.E.S.C.O. from 1953 to 1958, and participant in international efforts to achieve intellectual freedoms; in San Antonio, Tex., Dec. 23, 1981.

**Fairchild, Louis W.**, 80, publisher of *Women's Wear Daily*, among other periodicals, and one-time head of the publishing firm founded by and named for his father; in Hanover, N.H., Oct. 16, 1981.

**Farber, Edward R.**, 67, inventor of the portable strobe light for use with still cameras; in Delafield, Wis., Jan. 22, 1982.

**Fassbinder, Rainer Werner**, 36, German film maker known for his incisive political and social analyses of postwar Germany; in Munich, West Germany, June 10, 1982.

**Fedorov, Yevgeny**, 71, prominent Soviet geophysicist who served as head of various government agencies including the Hydrometeorological Service and the Institute for Applied Geophysics; in Moscow, USSR, Dec. 30, 1981.

**Fehr, Howard F.**, 80, mathematics education professor instrumental in the development of new math in the 1960s; in New York City, May 6, 1982.

**Feingold, Ben F.**, 81, pediatric allergist responsible for the theory that relates hyperactivity in children to food additives; in San Francisco, Calif., Mar. 23, 1982.

**Feldkamp, Fred**, 67, writer, film producer and editor whose television adaptation of Dwight D. Eisenhower's book, *Crusade in Europe*, won him a Peabody Award; in Bryn Mawr, Pa., Dec. 7, 1981.

**FitzGerald, Neil**, 90, Irish-born stage, television and film actor who received a Drama Critics Circle Award nomination for his performance in "All Over"; in Princeton, N.J., June 15, 1982.

**Florinsky, Michael T.**, 86, economics professor and expert on the USSR and Europe, whose books on Russian history are considered classics; in Switzerland, Oct. 10, 1981.

**Fonda, Henry**, 77, stage and film actor best known for his rôles as the penultimate American hero in such films as "The Grapes of Wrath," "Young Mr. Lincoln," "The Best Man," and "Mister Roberts," among his more than 80 movies; in Los Angeles, Aug. 12, 1982.

**Ford, O'Neil**, 76, architect known for his combining of modern design with Texas pioneer characteristics; in San Antonio, Tex., July 20, 1982.

**Fortas, Abe**, 71, liberal U.S. Supreme Court associate justice (1965-69); in Washington, D.C., April 5, 1982.

**Foster, Harold R.**, 89, artist, illustrator and creator of the Prince Valiant comic strip; in Spring Hill, Fla., July 25, 1982.

**Frazier, Brenda**, 60, socialite whose 1938 debut epitomized the social whirl of the day; in Boston, May 3, 1982.

**Frei Montalva, Eduardo**, 71, Chilean president from 1964 to 1970 and the first Christian Democrat to hold the post of president in a Western Hemisphere country; in Santiago, Chile, Jan. 22, 1982.

**Fuller, Rosalinde**, 90, British actress and singer remembered by Broadway audiences for her portrayal of Ophelia opposite John Barrymore's Hamlet in the 1922 production; in London, Eng., Sept. 15, 1982.

**Fyodorova, Zoya**, 68, film actress in the USSR whose child was fathered by a U.S. naval officer serving in Moscow during World War II, a liaison that resulted in her conviction on charges of espionage; in Moscow, USSR, Dec. 11, 1981.

**Gance, Abel**, 92, pioneering French film maker whose 1927 "Napoleon" has remained a popular classic, in part because of its innovative wide-screen technique; in Paris, France, Nov. 10, 1981.

**Gardner, John**, 49, avant-garde writer of novels and poetry and recipient of the National Book Critics Circle Award for his book, *October Light;* in Susquehanna, Pa., Sept. 14, 1982.

**Garroway, Dave**, 69, radio and television personality best remembered as the first host of the "Today" morning television program; in Swarthmore, Pa., July 21, 1982.

**Gaver, John M.**, 81, Greentree Stables's head horse trainer and a member of the thoroughbred racing hall of fame, under whose supervision numerous thoroughbred champions were raised; in Aiken, S.C., July 11, 1982.

**Gemayel, Bashir**, 34, leader of the Lebanese Christian Phalangist party and president-elect of Lebanon; in Beirut, Leb., Sept. 14, 1982.

**Gershwin, Arthur**, 81, music composer and younger brother of Ira and George Gershwin; in New York City, Nov. 20, 1981.

**Gerstad, John L.**, 57, theatrical director, playwright, actor and producer, best remembered for hs staging of "The Seven-Year Itch"; in New York City, Dec. 1, 1981.

**Ghotbzadeh, Sadegh**, 46, one-time protege of Ayatollah Khomieni and foreign minister of Iran from December 1979, until retiring in September 1980, only to be arrested and sentenced to death for treason; in Iran, Sept. 15, 1982.

**Gikow, Ruth**, 67, Ukrainian-born American painter whose canvases depicted the many moods of individuals; in New York City, April 2, 1982.

**Gimbel, Sophie**, 83, high-fashion designer credited with the introduction of the coulotte while head of the custom department at Saks Fifth Avenue, the store headed by her husband; in New York City, Nov. 28, 1981.

**Glenn, Frank**, 80, past president of the American College of Surgeons who treated the Shah of Iran in 1951 and was consulted in 1979 when the Shah was flown to the U.S. for treatment; in New York City, Jan. 12, 1982.

**Goff, Bruce**, 78, innovative and imaginative architect noted for his use of unusual materials and unique designs; in Tyler, Tex., Aug. 4, 1982.

**Goldman, Nahum**, 87, major force in world Zionism, credited with securing reparation agreements from East and West Germany for victims of Nazism; in Bad Reichenhall, W. Ger., Aug. 29, 1982.

**Gomulka, Wladyslaw**, 77, Polish Communist party leader from 1956 to 1970, a period in which his nation experienced increased economic, religious and cultural freedom; in Poland, Sept. 1, 1982.

**Gorin, Igor**, 72, opera, radio, and television baritone who sang with a number of opera companies during his career; in Tucson, Ariz., March 4, 1982.

**Gould, Glenn**, 50, Canadian pianist renowned for his Bach interpretations; in Toronto, Oct. 4, 1982.

**Grace, Princess of Monaco,** 52, formerly **Grace Kelly,** Academy Award-winning actress whose marriage to Prince Rainier of Monaco in 1956 was termed a "fairytale come true"; in Monte Carlo, Monaco, Sept. 14, 1982.
**Grahame, Gloria,** 55, film actress and Academy Award winner for her role in "The Bad and the Beautiful"; in New York City, Oct. 5, 1981.
**Greer, William Alexander (Sonny),** 78, original drummer with Duke Ellington's Orchestra from 1923 until 1951, and later a free-lance performer with a number of groups; in New York City, March 23, 1982.
**Gregory, Horace,** 83, poet, biographer and essayist whose works gained for him poetry's Bollingen Prize and a membership in the National Academy-Institute of Arts and Letters; in Shelburne Falls, Mass., March 11, 1982.
**Griffin, Marvin,** 74, staunch segregationist governor of Georgia (1954-62) who spoke out against the Supreme Court's ruling against segregated schools; in Tallahassee, Fla., June 13, 1982.
**Grosvenor, Melville Bell,** 80, former president of the National Geographic Society, which was founded by his great-grandfather, and editor (1957-67) of the society's magazine; in Miami, Fla., April 22, 1982.
**Grumman, Leroy R.,** 87, founder and former chairman of Grumman Aerospace Corp., famed for its World War II fighter planes and for the lunar excursion module; in Manhasset, N.Y., Oct. 4, 1982.
**Guion, David Wendell,** 88, popular music composer whose most famous adaptation is "Home on the Range"; in Dallas, Tex., Oct. 17, 1981.
**Hall, Helen,** 90, director of the Henry Street Settlement for more than 30 years and creator of innovative programs to help the poor; in New York City, Aug. 31, 1982.
**Hallstein, Walter,** 80, German diplomat and attorney instrumental in the establishment of the European Economic Community; in Stuttgart, W. Ger., March 29, 1982.
**Hamilton, Pierpont Morgan,** 83, descendant of Secretary of the Treasury Alexander Hamilton and banker J. P. Morgan, and U.S. Air Force major general awarded the Medal of Honor for his gallantry in the North Africa campaign of World War II; in Brentwood, Calif., March 6, 1982.
**Hampton, Hope,** 84, silent film actress and opera singer who was a legendary first-nighter at stage performances of every kind in Manhattan; in New York City, Jan. 23, 1982.
**Handler, Philip,** 64, president of the National Academy of Sciences from 1969 to June 1981, advocate for scientific research and recipient of the National Medal of Science; in Boston, Mass., Dec. 29, 1981.
**Handy, Gen. Thomas T.,** 90, Deputy Chief of Staff under Gen. George C. Marshall and Gen. Dwight D. Eisenhower in World War II and later commander of all U.S. troops in Europe; in San Antonio, Tex., April 14, 1982.
**Harman, Fred,** 79, creator of the "Red Ryder" comic strip and founder of the Cowboy Artists Association; in Phoenix, Ariz., Jan. 2, 1982.
**Harrison, Wallace K.,** 86, innovative architect and planner instrumental in major building projects such as Rockefeller Center, the United Nations complex, and Lincoln Center in New York City, and the Empire State Plaza in Albany, N.Y.; in New York City, Dec. 2, 1981.
**Hays, Brooks,** 83, Democratic U.S. representative from Arkansas, political moderate, and presidential advisor; in Bethesda, Md., Oct. 12, 1981.
**Head, Edith,** 80(?), motion picture costume designer for more than 50 years and recipient of eight Academy Awards; in Hollywood, Calif., Oct. 24, 1981.
**Hemingway, Leicester,** 67, writer of novels and a biography of his brother, Ernest Hemingway; in Miami Beach, Fla., Sept. 13, 1982.
**Henry, Pat,** 58, comedian who often performed on the same bill with Frank Sinatra; in Las Vegas, Nev., Feb. 18, 1982.
**Hicks, Granville,** 80, novelist, critic and columnist who wrote for Marxist publications during the 1930s; in Franklin Park, N.J., June 18, 1982.
**Hillenkoetter, Roscoe H.,** 85, retired vice admiral of the U.S. Navy and director of the Central Intelligence Agency from its establishment in 1947 until 1950; in New York City, June 18, 1982.
**Hinton, Walter,** 92, pioneering airplane pilot who was part of the U.S. Navy crew that flew across the Atlantic in 1919, and the first pilot to fly between New York and Rio de Janeiro, Brazil; in Pompano Beach, Fla., Oct. 28, 1981.
**Hoagland, Hudson,** 82, neuroendocrinology pioneer credited with discoveries into the nature of schizophrenia and the electrical properties of human functions; in Southborough, Mass., March 4, 1982.
**Holden, William,** 63, Academy Award-winning actor whose film credits included "Sunset Boulevard," "Stalag 17," and "Network"; found dead in Santa Monica, Calif., Nov. 16, 1981.
**Holloway, Stanley,** 91, British actor brought to the attention of U.S. audiences by his portrayal of Eliza Doolittle's father in "My Fair Lady" in both the stage and screen versions; in Littlehampton, Eng., Jan. 30, 1982.
**Hopkins, Sam (Lightnin'),** 69, country blues singer and major influence on contemporary rock guitarists; in Houston, Tex., Jan. 30, 1982.
**Horan, James D.,** 67, historian of the Old West as well as Pulitzer Prize-winning newsman and novelist; in New York City, Oct. 12, 1981.
**Horikoshi, Jiro,** 78, Japanese aircraft designer known for his Zero fighter planes used in the 1941 attack on Pearl Harbor; in Tokyo, Japan, Jan. 11, 1982.
**Hsu, Shuhsi,** 89, Taiwanese foreign diplomat and former delegate from Taiwan to the U.N.; in Westfield, N.J., Jan. 14, 1982.
**Hunter, Francis T.,** 87, Davis Cup and Wimbledon tennis player frequently paired in doubles matches with Bill Tilden, and member of the Tennis Hall of Fame; in Palm Beach, Fla., Dec. 2, 1981.
**Hunter, Maj. Gen. Frank O'Driscoll,** 87, ace pilot during World War I and, in World War II, commander general of the Eighth Air Force Fighter Command, which protected Allied forces attempting to take the port of Dieppe, France, from the Nazis; in Savannah, Ga., June 25, 1982.
**Jakobson, Roman,** 85, Russian-born scholar known as the father of modern structural linguistics, who, it is said, was able to read 25 languages and speak six fluently; in Boston, July 18, 1982.

**Jeritza, Maria,** 94, operatic soprano who sang with the Metropolitan Opera from 1921 to 1932 and was referred to as the "golden girl of opera's golden age"; in Orange, N.J., July 10, 1982.
**Jory, Victor,** 79, actor most often cast as a rough-voiced villain on stage and in films; found dead in Santa Monica, Calif., Feb. 12, 1982.
**Jurgens, Curt,** 66, film actor best known for his frequent portrayal of World War II Germans; in Vienna, Austria, June 18, 1982.
**Kaiser, Edgar F.,** 73, industrialist in the aluminum and steel business and founder of the Kaiser Foundation Medical Care Program, the largest private, prepaid medical care plan in the U.S.; in San Francisco, Calif., Dec. 11, 1981.
**Kaufman, Murray (Murray the K),** 60, rock music disk jockey credited with bringing U.S. popularity to the Beatles; in Los Angeles, Calif., Feb. 21, 1982.
**Kay, Hershy,** 62, orchestral arranger and composer for film, stage and television productions, including "On the Town," "A Chorus Line," and "Barnum"; in Danbury, Conn., Dec. 2, 1981.
**Khan, Fazlur R.,** 52, architect with the firm of Skidmore, Owings & Merrill whose innovative "bundled tube" system of construction was first used in the Sears Tower, the world's tallest building; in Saudi Arabia, March 27, 1982.
**Kieran, John F.,** 89, newspaper sportswriter, regular participant on the "Information Please" radio program, and author of works on natural history; in Rockport, Mass., Dec. 10, 1981.
**King, Henry,** 91, director of more than 100 films, including "Tol'able David," "The Song of Bernadette," "Twelve O'Clock High" and "Love Is a Many-Splendored Thing"; in the San Fernando Valley, Calif., June 29, 1982.
**King, Pete,** 68, composer, orchestrator and conductor of music for films such as "South Pacific" and "Camelot"; in Newport Beach, Calif., Sept. 20, 1982.
**Kleinsinger, George,** 68, composer of varied orchestral works such as "Tubby the Tuba" for children and the opera "Archy and Mehitable"; in New York City, July 28, 1982.
**Knott, Walter,** 91, founder of the California amusement complex, Knott's Berry Farm, and promoter of conservative political causes; in Buena Park, Calif., Dec. 3, 1981.
**Kohut, Heinz,** 68, major psychoanalyst who promoted the concept of "self psychology" and the importance of a sense of self; in Chicago, Ill., Oct. 8, 1981.
**Krebs, Hans,** 81, biochemist and winner of the 1953 Nobel Prize in Physiology and Medicine for his discoveries on the processes by which food is converted to energy in the body; in Oxford, Eng., Nov. 22, 1981.
**Lal, Gobind Behari,** 92, Pulitzer Prize-winning journalist whose writings promoted independence for the State of India and scientific research; in San Francisco, Calif., April 1, 1982.
**Lam, Wilfredo,** 80, Cuban-born multi-media artist of Surrealist paintings, graphics and sculpture; in Paris, France, Sept. 11, 1982.
**Lawrenson, Helen,** 74, sophisticated author, critic, and cafe society figure who wrote about the celebrities she knew; in New York City, April 5, 1982.
**Lembeck, Harvey** 58, actor on Broadway and in films and television, who gained prominence in his role as Cpl. Rocco Barbella in Phil Silvers's series, "You'll Never Get Rich"; in Los Angeles, Calif., Jan. 5, 1982.
**Lenya, Lotte,** 83, professional name of Karoline Blaumer, singer and stage and film star who popularized the works of her late husband, composer Kurt Weill; in New York City, Nov. 27, 1981.
**Lindstrom, Fred,** 79, baseball hall of fame member, 13-year veteran of the major leagues, and the youngest player ever in a World Series; in Chicago, Ill., Oct. 4, 1981.
**Lockridge, Richard,** 83, author whose Mr. & Mrs. North detective series—some segments of which were co-authored by his wife, Frances—was adapted for stage, screen and television; in Tryon, N.C., June 19, 1982.
**Loring, Eugene,** 72, dancer-choreographer most remembered for his creation of and starring role in the ballet "Billy the Kid"; in Kingston, N.Y., Aug. 30, 1982.
**Loughran, Tommy,** 79, light-heavyweight boxing champion (1925-29) and member of the Boxing Hall of Fame; in Hollidaysburg, Pa., July 7, 1982.
**Lynd, Helen Merrell,** 85, social philosopher best known for "Middletown" and "Middletown in Transition," sociological studies co-authored with her husband, Robert, and considered classics in the field; in Warren, Ohio, Jan. 30, 1982.
**Lynde, Paul,** 55, stage, movie and television comic actor most recently seen on the television show "Hollywood Squares"; in Los Angeles, Calif., Jan. 9, 1982.
**MacLeish, Archibald,** 89, three-time Pulitzer Prize-winning poet and playwright who served both the U.S. government and U.N. organizations; in Boston, Mass., April 20, 1982.
**Malina, Frank J.,** 69, scientific pioneer who, as co-founder of the Jet Propulsion Laboratory, aided in aerospace technology development; in Paris, France, Nov. 9, 1981.
**Markey, Enid,** 91(?), stage, television, and screen actress whose silent film credits included westerns and the role of Jane in the first Tarzan movie; in Bay Shore, N.Y., Nov. 15, 1981.
**Markey, Lucille Park,** 85, owner of Calumet Farms, famed thoroughbred horse-breeding institution in Lexington, Ky., whose colors were worn by jockeys riding eight Kentucky Derby winners and two Triple Crown victors; in Miami, Fla., July 25, 1982.
**Markham, Dewey (Pigmeat),** 77, vaudeville and television performer most widely remembered for his "Here comes the judge" skits; in New York City, Dec. 13, 1981.
**Marlowe, Hugh,** 71, radio, television, stage and screen actor most recently cast as Jim Matthews in the television daytime serial "Another World"; in New York City, May 2, 1982.
**Marsh, Ngaio,** 82, New Zealand-born author of 32 mystery novels featuring the character Chief Inspector Roderick Alleyn, C.I.D., and a Dame of the British Empire; in Christchurch, N.Z., Feb. 18, 1982.
**Mayer, Albert,** 83, city planner instrumental in the creation of Chandigarh, India, and influential housing designer; in New York City, Oct. 14, 1981.
**Mills, Harry,** 68, member of the Mills Brothers singing group, which recorded 2,246 records since the early 1930s; in Los Angeles, Calif., June 28, 1982.

**Monk, Thelonious,** 64, innovative jazz pianist and composer whose professional career spanned 50 years; in Englewood, N.J., Feb. 17, 1982.

**Moore, Stanford,** 68, Nobel Prize-winning biochemist who researched the chemical structure of the enzyme pancreatic nuclease; in New York City, Aug. 23, 1982.

**More, Kenneth,** 67, British stage, screen and television actor best remembered in the U.S. for his portrayal of Young Jolyon in "The Forsyte Saga" television series; in London, Eng., July 12, 1982.

**Morhouse, L. Judson,** 68, New York State Republican chairman credited with the successful 1958 gubernatorial campaign of Nelson A. Rockefeller; in Ticonderoga, N.Y., March 21, 1982.

**Morrow, Vic,** 51, television and screen actor best known for his role of Sgt. Chip Saunders in the television series "Combat"; near Los Angeles, Calif., July 23, 1982.

**Morton, Thruston B.,** 74, Republican party chairman, member of the U.S. House of Representatives (1947-53) and U.S. Senate (1956-68); in Louisville, Ky., Aug. 14, 1982.

**Namgyal, Palden Thondup,** 58, deposed king of Sikkim, the former Himalayan protectorate and now a state of India; in New York City, Jan. 30, 1982.

**Nashua,** 30, thoroughbred stallion, winner of the 1955 Preakness and Belmont Stakes, and sire to 85 stakes winners; at Spendthrift Farms, Ky., Feb. 3, 1982.

**Nesbitt, Cathleen,** 93, British character actress, cast in her later years as the elegant mother of such personalities as Cary Grant and Rex Harrison, in the latter's role of Henry Higgins in "My Fair Lady"; in London, Eng., Aug. 2, 1982.

**Nicholson, Ben,** 87, abstract artist known for his all-white reliefs made of wood; in London, Eng., Feb. 6, 1982.

**Orff, Carl,** 86, German musical educator and composer best known for his 1937 work "Carmina Burana"; in Munich, W. Ger., March 29, 1982.

**Paige, Leroy "Satchel,"** 75(?), baseball pitching star of the old Negro leagues and a member of the Baseball Hall of Fame, whose career spanned 40 years and who was known for his advice, "Don't look back. Something might be gaining on you"; in Kansas City, Mo., June 8, 1982.

**Parri, Ferruccio,** 91, first post-World War II leader of Italy, founder of Italy's Republican party, and anti-Fascist resistance leader during Mussolini's 20 years in power; in Rome, Italy, Dec. 8, 1981.

**Pepper, Art,** 56, leading jazz alto saxaphonist with Stan Kenton's orchestra for 30 years; in Los Angeles, June 9, 1982.

**Powell, Eleanor,** 69, stage and film tap-dancing actress remembered for her roles in Hollywood musicals during the 1930s and '40s; in Beverly Hills, Calif., Feb. 11, 1982.

**Primrose, William,** 77, Scottish-born violist known for his advocacy on behalf of his chosen musical instrument; in Provo, Utah, May 1, 1982.

**Rambert, Dame Marie,** 94, director of the British ballet troupe bearing her name and an influential figure in 20th-century dance; in England, June 12, 1982.

**Rand, Ayn,** 77, objectivist writer and philosopher best remembered for her books, including *The Fountainhead* and *Atlas Shrugged*, and her editorial work for the journal *The Objectivist;* in New York City, March 6, 1982.

**Reese, Algernon B.,** 85, opthalmologist who pioneered in the treatment of serious eye diseases in children, especially retinoblastoma; in Bedford Hills, N.Y., Oct. 19, 1981.

**Reiser, Pete,** 62, baseball outfielder for the Brooklyn Dodgers and winner of the 1941 National League batting title; in Palm Springs, Calif., Oct. 25, 1981.

**Rexroth, Kenneth,** 76, poet, author, artist, member of the National Institute of Arts and Letters, and a role model for San Francisco's Beat generation of the 1950s; in Montecito, Calif., June 6, 1982.

**Ritola, Willie,** 86, Finnish Olympic distance runner who won five gold medals—four in the 1924 Games and one in the 1928 Olympiad; in Finland, April 24, 1982.

**Roa Garcia, Raul,** 75, foreign minister of Cuba following the assumption to power of Fidel Castro in 1959, and later National Assembly vice president and Council of State member; in Havana, Cuba, July 6, 1982.

**Roosevelt, Nicholas,** 88, relative of Pres. Theodore Roosevelt, conservationist, historian-writer, and U.S. envoy to Hungary; in Monterey, Calif., Feb. 16, 1982.

**Rosen, Samuel,** 84, ear surgeon credited with restoring hearing to countless partly deaf people with his "Rosen stapes" operation; in Peking, China, Nov. 5, 1981.

**Ross, Joe E.,** 67, television comedy actor best remembered for his portrayal of Officer Gunther Toody in the "Car 54, Where Are You?" series; in Burbank, Calif., Aug. 13, 1982.

**Rotmistrov, Pavel A.,** 80, Soviet marshal who served the Red Army since 1919, helping to crush the Kronstadt sailors' mutiny in 1921 and commanding the Fifth Guards Tank Army in the Battle of Kursk in 1943; death announced in Moscow, April 7, 1982.

**Ryan, T. Claude,** 84, aviation pioneer and founder of the aircraft manufacturing firm that built the *Spirit of St. Louis,* the plane flown by Charles A. Lindbergh in the first transatlantic solo flight; in San Diego, Calif., Sept. 11, 1982.

**Sawyer, Joe,** 75, film and television actor who was best remembered for the role of Sgt. Biff O'Hara on the "Rin Tin Tin" television program; in Oregon, April 21, 1982.

**Schneider, Romy,** 43, Austrian-born film actress best known for her roles in "Boccaccio '70" and "Good Neighbor Sam"; in Paris, May 29, 1982.

**Scott, Hazel,** 61, jazz pianist, singer and film actress active in promoting racial harmony; in New York City, Oct. 2, 1981.

**Sears, Henry,** 69, real estate investor and yachtsman credited with reviving the America's Cup yacht race in 1958 after a 21-year absence; in Chestertown, Md., March 23, 1982.

**Seymour, Dan,** 68, radio announcer during the 1930s and 1940s and, later, president and board chairman of the J. Walter Thompson advertising agency; in New York City, July 27, 1982.

**Shaw, Wini,** 72, Broadway and Hollywood actress and singer best known for her renditions of "Lullaby of Broadway" and "The Lady in Red"; in New York City, May 2, 1982.

**Sheed, Frank J.,** 84, lay theologian of the Roman Catholic Church and co-founder of Sheed

& Ward, a major publishing house for theological works; in Jersey City, N.J., Nov. 20, 1981.

**Shehu, Mehmet**, 68, prime minister of Albania since 1954 and frequently mentioned successor to Enver Hoxha, leader of Albania's Communist party; in Albania, Dec. 18, 1981.

**Shimura, Takashi**, 76, Japanese actor often featured in the films of director Akira Kurosawa, including "Ikiru" and "Kagemusha"; in Tokyo, Japan, Feb. 11, 1982.

**Sillman, Leonard**, 72, Broadway producer who introduced many of today's major stars through his 13 "New Faces" revues; in New York City, Jan. 23, 1982.

**Simmons, Calvin**, 32, orchestral conductor and music director of the Oakland, Calif., Symphony; near Lake Placid, N.Y., Aug. 21, 1982.

**Smith, Red**, 76, author and Pulitzer Prize-winning sportswriter for *The New York Times;* in Stamford, Conn., Jan. 15, 1982.

**Sobhuza II**, 83, king of Swaziland since the age of 1 and longest-reigning monarch in the world; near Mbabane, Swaziland, Aug. 31, 1982.

**Solomon, Harry C.**, 92, pioneering psychiatrist who instituted major reforms in the treatment of mentally ill patients, including the early practice of psychoanalysis to treat mental disorders; in Boston, Mass., May 23, 1982.

**Spivak, Charlie**, 77, trumpet player for such leading big bands as those of the Dorsey brothers and Jack Tegarden in the early '40s and a leader of his own dance orchestra; in Greenville, S.C., March 1, 1982.

**Stern, Curt**, 79, geneticist who pioneered work in human heredity; in Sacramento, Calif., Oct. 23, 1981.

**Stoddard, George D.**, 84, educator and administrator for universities and foreign governments attempting to improve their educational systems; in New York City, Dec. 28, 1981.

**Strasberg, Lee**, 80, developer of the Method school of acting in the U.S., trainer of many leading performers, and artistic director of the Actors Studio; in New York City, Feb. 17, 1982.

**Strong, Kenneth**, 81, British major general and chief of Allied intelligence during World War II, knighted in 1952 for his strategic military contributions; in Eastbourne, Eng., Jan. 11, 1982.

**Struss, Karl**, 95, cinematographer for movies starring such personalities as Mary Pickford, Charlie Chaplin, Fredric March and Mae West, and Academy Award winner for his camera work on the 1925 version of "Ben Hur"; in Santa Monica, Calif., Dec. 16, 1981.

**Suslov, Mikhail A.**, 79, chief ideologist of the Communist party in the USSR and a member of the party's Politburo since 1955; in Moscow, USSR, Jan. 25, 1982.

**Tex, Joe**, 47, singer whose soul music recordings span nearly a 30-year career; in Navasota, Tex., Aug. 13, 1982.

**Theorell, Hugo**, 79, Swedish biochemist and recipient of the 1955 Nobel Prize in Medicine for his work on enzyme research; in Sweden, Aug. 15, 1982.

**Thoma, Michael**, 55, television actor featured as the doctor-family friend in the series "Eight is Enough" and a drama teacher in "Fame"; in Los Angeles, Calif., Sept. 3, 1982.

**Thornton, Charles B.**, 68, "Whiz Kid" of modern management systems and a founder of the Litton Industries conglomerate; in Holmby Hills, Calif., Nov. 24, 1981.

**Tjader, Cal**, 56, jazz vibraphonist with Dave Brubeck, George Shearing, as well as his own group; in the Philippines, May 5, 1982.

**Trepper, Leopold**, 77, leader of the "Red Orchestra" spy network in Nazi-controlled Europe during World War II, which provided information for Soviet intelligence, but Trepper was later imprisoned by the Soviet government; in Jerusalem, Israel, Jan. 19, 1982.

**Truman, Bess**, 97, widow of Harry S Truman, 33rd President of the United States. She avoided publicity during her years as First Lady (1945-53), but was a strong helpmate to her husband in those crucial times; in Kansas City, Mo., Oct. 18, 1982.

**Twining, Nathan F.**, 84, U.S. Air Force general, Chairman of the Joint Chiefs of Staff (1957-60), and Allied air commander in Europe and the South Pacific during World War II; at Lackland Air Force Base, Tex., March 29, 1982.

**Tworkov, Jack**, 82, Abstract Expressionist painter, teacher and member of the New York School of artists; in Provincetown, Mass., Sept. 4, 1982.

**von Zell, Harry**, 75, radio and television announcer who performed with such leading entertainers as George Burns and Gracie Allen, Fred Allen, Jack Benny, and Will Rogers; in Calabas, Calif., Nov. 21, 1981.

**Wallenberg, Marcus**, 82, Swedish banker and industrialist, and member of one of his nation's most powerful families, counting Electrolux appliances and Saab-Scania transportation equipment in its empire; in Stockholm, Sweden, Sept. 14, 1982.

**Waner, Lloyd ("Little Poison")**, 76, baseball outfielder and Hall of Fame member who, with his brother, Paul, "Big Poison," played for the Pittsburgh Pirates from 1927 through 1941; in Oklahoma City, Okla., July 22, 1982.

**Weiss, Peter**, 65, noted German-born author most widely remembered for his play, commonly known by its abbreviated title, "Marat/Sade"; in Stockholm, Sweden, May 10, 1982.

**Wertham, Frederic**, 86, psychiatrist who opposed violence portrayed in comic books, films, and television on grounds that such exposure to crime and horror damaged the human psyche; in Kempton, Pa., Nov. 18, 1981.

**Whitney, John Hay**, 77, head of Whitney Communications, philanthropist, investor, sportsman, ambassador to Britain from 1957 to 1961, and descendant of U.S. cabinet members; in Manhasset, N.Y., Feb. 8, 1982.

**Wilson, Don**, 81, radio and television announcer who for 42 years played Jack Benny's foil; in Palm Springs, Calif., April 25, 1982.

**Wood, Natalie**, 43, film star who began her career at the age of 4 and was nominated for three Academy Awards; off Santa Catalina Island, Calif., Nov. 29, 1981.

**Wurf, Jerry**, 62, president since 1964 of the American Federation of State, County, and Municipal Employees, the nation's largest union of public workers; in Washington, D.C., Dec. 10, 1981.

**Zworykin, Vladimir K.**, 92, Russian-born scientist instrumental in the development of television and the electron microscope; in Princeton, N.J., July 29, 1982.

## A

## B

## I

## J

## M

## N

## O

## Q

## T

## U

## V